WHO'S *who* AMONG

Black Americans

ISSN 0362-5753

WHO'S *who* AMONG

6th EDITION

Black Americans

Foreword by the Honorable Damon J. Keith,
Judge of the United States Court of Appeals
for the Sixth Circuit

1990/91

Iris Cloyd, *Editor*

William C. Matney, Jr., *Consulting Editor*

 Gale Research Inc. • DETROIT • NEW YORK • FORT LAUDERDALE • LONDON

STAFF

Consulting Editor: William C. Matney, Jr.

Senior Editor: Deborah Gillan Straub

Editor: Iris Cloyd

Assistant Editor: Shirelle Goss
Editorial Assistant: John Dodt

Production Manager: Mary Beth Trimper
Assistant Production Manager: Evi Seoud

Art Designer: Art Chartow
Graphic Designer: Kathleen A. Mouzakis
Keyliner: C. J. Jonik

Production Supervisor: Laura Bryant
Internal Production Associate: Louise Gagné

Editorial Data Systems Director: Dennis LaBeau
Editorial Data Systems Supervisor: Theresa Rocklin
Program Designers: Robert D. Aitchison and Barry Trute

Copyright © 1990
Gale Research Inc.
835 Penobscot Bldg.
Detroit, MI 48226-4094

ISBN 0-8103-2243-9
ISSN 0362-5753

Printed in the United States of America

Contents

Foreword

Those who stand tall in our presence appear to be of unusual height because, in most cases, they stand on the shoulders of giants who have preceded them.

—John Hope Franklin,
James B. Duke Professor Emeritus of History
at Duke University

This reference work, the sixth edition of *Who's Who Among Black Americans,* contains biographical entries on over 17,000 accomplished Black professionals, each of whom stands upon a legacy of Black success and achievement. In the decades since the civil rights movement, many Black men and women have secured positions providing economic security as well as decision-making authority. In government, business, education, religion, science, journalism, civic affairs, fine arts, law, medicine, civil rights, sports, and entertainment, successful Black professionals have been given golden opportunities to set examples, to meet challenges, and to assume responsibilities.

As Black Americans, we enjoy unique opportunities to serve our community—the Black community that gave us life, nurturing, and love. While serving as role models to our Black youth, we have the opportunity to exhibit the highest standards of private morality. While serving as active participants in the political process, we have the opportunity to demand that our federal, state, and local officials posit a public policy addressing racism, a social disease that continues to cloud America's democratic vision. While serving as volunteers in civil rights organizations, neighborhood groups, schools, and churches, we have the opportunity to give our time, talents, and tithes—to offer spiritual, material, emotional, and intellectual equipment to those Black Americans who have been denied the tools of success. By reinvesting in our community, we can make a difference. Committing our vast resources to the Black community is our duty and privilege. Certainly, our successful life journeys would not have been possible without the sacrifices and investments of those who walked before us.

Indeed, how should we, as Black professionals, measure success? For example, one can be a "success" as an entertainer starring in a highly rated television show, as a managing partner in a large corporate law firm, or as the president of a prestigious private college. Admittedly, achievement in the professions is one mark of success. From my perspective, however, we are not truly "successful" Black professionals unless we use our intellectual and financial resources to serve the community to which we owe so much. When the entertainer endows Black institutions with millions of dollars, he exemplifies "commitment." When the managing partner argues civil rights cases before the Supreme Court *pro bono,* he illustrates "achievement." And when the university president prepares Black youth to compete in the automation age, she personifies "dedication." All individuals who share the fruits of their professional accomplishments with the Black community become shining and true examples of "Black success."

Therefore, as Black professionals, we should not sever the ties with our humble roots. Instead, our achievements should remind us that in the community that gave birth to our success, there are many more entertainers, lawyers, and university

presidents waiting for us to help them reach their goals. We have an obligation to return to the Black community and to use our talents to balance an otherwise unequal scale of opportunity. Dr. Johnnetta Betsch Cole, president of Spelman College, eloquently phrased the question: "How can we call ourselves either educated or leaders if we turn away from the very reality that a third of Black America lives in poverty? We must build sturdy Black bridges into the very communities from which we have come and into those which surround us. For if we do not build those bridges, then we will surely drown in our own selfishness and inaction."

Not long ago, I spoke before the Harvard Black Law Students' Association and responded to their inquiry, "What Is Success? Can We Have It As Blacks Without Serving the Collective Interests of the Black Community?" During the address, I asked how many of those present were attending Harvard because of a trust fund. Not surprisingly, none of the students raised their hands. However, I suggested to them that all of them were there, in fact, because of trusts—perhaps not legal trusts set up by their parents or grandparents through investments in securities, but trusts from the heart established through their families' investments in religious faith and hard work. Certainly, all of the students had overcome substantial obstacles to get into law school, but they had not struggled alone. I reminded them that their endowment fund was the support and encouragement of the Black community—their parents, grandparents, neighbors, ministers, teachers, and the thousands of Blacks who engaged in years of struggle to make it possible for them to attend Harvard Law School.

As successful Black professionals, we are individually and collectively challenged to pay back the debt owed to those who made our success possible. An opportunity for service may come from the leaders of a community-based organization who, even though unable to pay legal fees, require documents to be drafted before they can develop additional affordable housing. The debt may be paid by spending time each week in drug abuse prevention programs and community centers where Black children are guided along the path to success. Evidence of our commitment to a more just society might even come from the generous financial contributions that we make to political, civic, educational, and religious organizations.

However we choose to pay back our debt to the Black community, the debt ought to be paid. Because our community must still travel a great distance, the elder runners must prepare the youth and pass on their batons. Together, we can build upon the positive accomplishments of our collective past. In the spirit of kinship that has brought us thus far, we can become mothers, fathers, employers, and mentors to a new generation of successful Black professionals. With humility and commitment, we can provide the strong shoulders upon which our young leaders might now stand.

* * *

Words cannot express the depth of my gratitude to William C. Matney. As founding editor of *Who's Who Among Black Americans,* Mr. Matney has developed an invaluable reference work recording the lives of accomplished Black Americans. From those Black men and women who have been recognized for their great gifts, much is expected.

The Honorable Damon J. Keith
Judge of the United States Court of Appeals for the Sixth Circuit

Introduction

Now in its sixth edition and published for the first time by Gale Research Inc., *Who's Who Among Black Americans (WWBA)* is your guide to more than 17,000 men and women who have changed today's world and are shaping tomorrow's. The biographical entries you will find on these pages reflect the diversity of African-American achievement by documenting the contributions of leaders in business, education, religion, government, science, technology, journalism, civic affairs, law, medicine, civil rights, sports, fine arts, music, theatre, motion pictures, and television. Together these entries make *Who's Who Among Black Americans* the single most comprehensive publication devoted to recording the dynamic growth of Black accomplishment—your one-stop source for information that will help you stay up to date on the scope of African-American achievement.

Compilation Methods

The selection of *WWBA* listees is based primarily on reference value. In order to identify noteworthy new achievers as well as monitor significant events in the lives of current listees, the editorial staff scans a wide variety of books, magazines, newspapers, and other material on an ongoing basis. For this edition, more than 400 associations, businesses, and individuals were also contacted for their suggestions. Users, current listees, and members of the *WWBA* Advisory Board continue to provide their recommendations as well.

These candidates become eligible for inclusion by virtue of positions held through election or appointment to office, notable career achievements, or outstanding community service. Black persons who are not American citizens are considered eligible if they live or work in the United States and contribute significantly to American life. Such broad coverage makes *Who's Who Among Black Americans* the logical source for you to consult when gathering facts on a distinguished leader or a favorite celebrity, locating a colleague, contacting an expert, recruiting personnel, or launching a fund-raising effort.

Once this identification process is complete, we make every effort to secure information directly from biographees. Potential new listees, for example, receive a questionnaire asking them to furnish the data that forms the basis of an entry. The listee often supplements this data with a resume or perhaps a few articles, and we in turn may cull additional material from *WWBA* files. Those candidates whose achievements merit inclusion proceed through the remaining stages of entry compilation.

In an almost simultaneous process, current listees receive copies of their entries from the most recent edition in which they appeared. They then update their biographies as necessary to reflect new career positions, address changes, or recent awards or achievements. For this inaugural Gale edition of *Who's Who Among Black Americans,* the editors also made a special effort to solicit revisions from the nearly 4,000 people whose entries were dropped from one edition of the directory to the next.

Sometimes potential and current listees decline to furnish biographical data. Recognizing that this does not satisfy your need for comprehensiveness, we have compiled selected entries from a variety of secondary sources to help ensure that the people you want to see in *WWBA* are indeed listed. These entries are marked by an asterisk, indicating that the listees have not personally provided or reviewed the data. But you still benefit from having basic biographical information at your fingertips.

New Features of This Edition

In addition to its more thorough coverage, *Who's Who Among Black Americans* has a different look—inside and out. These new features are designed to make *WWBA* even easier to use:

- **New Type Size.** A slightly larger type size makes entries easier to read.

- **New Boldface Rubrics.** With the addition of boldface rubrics, *WWBA* lends itself to quick and easy scanning for specifics on personal data, educational background, career positions, organizational affiliations, honors and achievements, military service, home address, and business address.

- **New Obituaries Section.** Beginning with this edition, a separate obituary section will include listees whose deaths have been reported since the last edition. This section provides a full entry plus date and place of death, when available. Death dates have been confirmed through contacts with listees' family members or most recent employers or by checking other published obituaries.

    Once a listee has been included in the obituary section, subsequent editions of *WWBA* will not republish the listing. Beginning with the next edition of *Who's Who Among Black Americans,* however, a cumulative index to entries that have appeared in the obituaries section will lead you to the edition in which you can find a particular obituary.

Indexing

This edition of *Who's Who Among Black Americans* features two indexes, one of which—the occupational index—has been substantially improved to meet your need for more specific information. These indexes make quick work of your searches:

- **Geographic Index.** Locate biographees by specific city, state, and country of residence and/or employment. Only those listees who agree to allow their addresses to be printed in the directory will appear in this index.

- **Occupational Index.** We have refined and expanded the terms from 40 to over 150, allowing you to identify listees working in fields ranging from accounting to zoology.

Acknowledgments

The editors wish to thank the Advisory Board members whose names appear at the front of this volume for their advice and encouragement as we compiled the sixth edition of *Who's Who Among Black Americans.*

We would also like to thank the many individuals and organizations who nominated achievers for consideration in this edition.

Suggestions Welcome

Comments and suggestions from users on any aspect of *Who's Who Among Black Americans* are welcome. You are cordially invited to write:

The Editor
Who's Who Among Black Americans
Gale Research Inc.
835 Penobscot Bldg.
Detroit, Michigan 48226-4094

Key to Biographical Information

1 MATNEY, WILLIAM C., JR.
2 Public affairs, communications consultant. **3** PERSONAL: Born Sep 02, 1924, Bluefield, WV, son of William C Matney Sr and Jane A Matney; widowed; children: Alma, Angelique, William III. **4** EDUCATION: Wayne State Univ, 1940-42; Univ of Michigan, BA 1946. **5** CAREER: The Michigan Chronicle, reporter, sports editor, city editor, mng editor 1946-61; Detroit News, reporter, writer, 1962-63; WMAQ-NBC, TV and radio reporter 1963-65; NBC Network Television, correspondent 1966-72; ABC Network News, correspondent 1972-78; Who's Who Among Black Americans, founding editor 1974-88, consulting editor 1988-; US Bureau of Census, public affairs coord 1979-. **6** ORGANIZATIONS: Mem, Big Ten Championship Track Team, 1943; pres, Cotillion Club, 1962-63; mem, NAACP; AFTRA; Alpha Phi Alpha; Natl Acad of Television Arts and Sciences. **7** HONORS/ACHIEVE-MENTS: 1st black exec sec, Michigan State Ath Assn, 1950-61; 1st black reporter, Detroit News, 1960-63; 1st black network news correspondent, NBC News, 1965-70; Natl Achievement Award, Lincoln Univ, 1966; Man of the Year, Intl Pioneers, 1966; Sigma Delta Chi Citation, 1967; Outstanding Achievement Citation (Emmy), Natl Acad of Television Arts and Sciences, 1967; 1st black correspondent permanently assigned to the White House, Washington NBC News, 1970-72; Natl Award, Southern Press Inst, 1976; Hon Dr Jour, Benedict Coll, 1973; Outstanding TV Correspondent, Women in Media, 1977; Outstanding Natl Corres Serv Award, Michigan Minority Business Enterprise Assn, 1977; Natl Advisory Comm, Crisis Magazine, NAACP, 1981-. **8** MILITARY SERVICE: USAAF 1943-45. **9** BUSINESS ADDRESS: US Bureau of the Census, Washington, DC 20233.

1 Name of biographee
2 Occupation
3 Personal data
4 Educational background
5 Career information
6 Organizational affiliations
7 Honors and special achievements
8 Military service
9 Home and/or business address (at listee's discretion)

Biographees are listed alphabetically by surname. In cases where the surnames are identical, biographees are arranged first by surname, then by first and middle names, and finally by suffixes such as Jr., Sr., or II, III, etc. Surnames beginning with a prefix (such as Du, Mac, or Van), however spaced, are listed alphabetically under the first letter of the prefix and are treated as if there were no space. Hyphenated names are treated as if the hyphen were a space; thus, hyphenated surnames beginning with Williams would follow all of the listings for which Williams alone is the surname. Names with apostrophes are treated as if there were no punctuation. Surnames beginning with Saint, Sainte, St., or Ste. appear after names that begin with Sains and are then alphabetized according to the second part of the name.

The various abbreviations used in the entries are explained in the Abbreviations Table, which begins on page xv.

Abbreviations Table

AA	Associate in Arts
AAA	Agricultural Adjustment Administration; anti-aircraft artillery
AAAS	American Association for the Advancement of Science
AAC	Army Air Corps
AAF	Army Air Force
AAHPER	American Association for Health, Physical Education and Recreation (now known as AAHPERD)
AAHPERD	American Alliance for Health, Physical Education, Recreation and Dance
A&I	Agricultural and Industrial
A&M	Agricultural and Mechanical
A&T	Agricultural and Technical
AAONMS	Ancient Arabic Order of the Nobles of the Mystic Shrine
AAS	Associate in Applied Science
AASR	Ancient Accepted Scottish Rite (Masonic)
AB	Alberta (Canada); Bachelor of Arts
AB&C RR	Atlanta, Birmingham and Coast Railroad
ABC	American Broadcasting Company
ABCFM	American Board of Commissioners for Foreign Missions (Congregational Church)
AC	Air Corps
acad	academy; academies; academic
acct	accounting
ACL RR	Atlantic Coast Line Railroad
ACP	American College of Physicians
ACS	American College of Surgeons
adc	aide-de-camp
adj	adjunct; adjutant
adm	admiral
admin	administration; administrative; administrator(s)
adv	advisory; advocate(s)
AE	Agricultural Engineer
AE&P	Ambassador Extraordinary and Plenipotentiary
AEC	Atomic Energy Commission
AEF	American Expeditionary Forces
aeronaut	aeronautic(s); aeronautical
AFB	Air Force Base
AF&AM	Ancient Free and Accepted Masons
AFD	Doctor of Fine Arts
affil	affiliation(s); affiliate(s); affiliated
AFL	American Federation of Labor
AFTRA	American Federation of Television and Radio Artists
agr	agriculture; agricultural
agt	agent(s)
AIA	American Institute of Architects
AID	Agency for International Development
AIEE	American Institute of Electrical Engineers (predecessor organization of IEEE)
AIM	American Institute of Management
AK	Alaska
AL	Alabama
Ala	Alabama
ALA	American Library Association
Alta	Alberta (Canada)
AM	Master of Arts
AMA	American Medical Association
AME	African Methodist Episcopal
Amer	America(n)
ANA	Associate National Academician
anat	anatomy; anatomical
ann	annual
ANTA	American National Theatre and Academy
anthrop	anthropology; anthropological
AP	Associated Press
apptd	appointed
Apr	April
apt	apartment
AR	Arkansas
ARC	American Red Cross
archaeol	archaeology; archaeological
archit	architecture; architectural; architect(s)
Ariz	Arizona
Ark	Arkansas
ArtsD	Doctor of Arts
AS	Air Service; Associate in Science
ASCAP	American Society of Composers, Authors and Publishers
ASCE	American Society of Civil Engineers
ASF	Air Service Force
ASME	American Society of Mechanical Engineers
assn	association
assoc	associate(s); associated
asst	assistant
astron	astronomy; astronomical
astrophys	astrophysics; astrophysical
ATSC	Air Technical Service Command
atty	attorney
Aug	August
AUS	Army of the United States
aux	auxiliary
ave	avenue
awd	award
AZ	Arizona
B	Bachelor (academic degree)
BA	Bachelor of Arts
BAE	Bachelor of Art Education
BAgr	Bachelor of Agriculture
B&A RR	Boston and Albany Railroad

B&M RR	Boston and Maine Railroad
B&O RR	Baltimore and Ohio Railroad
Bapt	Baptist(s)
BArch	Bachelor of Architecture
BAS	Bachelor of Agricultural Science
BASc	Bachelor of Arts and Sciences
BBA	Bachelor of Business Administration
BBC	British Broadcasting Corporation
BC	British Columbia
BCE	Bachelor of Chemical Engineering; Bachelor of Christian Education; Bachelor of Civil Engineering
BChir	Bachelor of Surgery
BCL	Bachelor of Civil Law
BCS	Bachelor of Commercial Science
bd	board
BD	Bachelor of Divinity
BE	Bachelor of Education; Bachelor of Engineering
BEd	Bachelor of Education
BEE	Bachelor of Electrical Engineering
BEF	British Expeditionary Force
BES	Bachelor of Engineering Science
BFA	Bachelor of Fine Arts
bibliog	bibliography; bibliographies; bibliographical
BIE	Bachelor of Industrial Engineering
biog	biography; biographies; biographical
biol	biology; biological
BJ	Bachelor of Journalism
BL	Bachelor of Letters
bldg	building
BLS	Bachelor of Library Science
blvd	boulevard
BMechEng	Bachelor of Mechanical Engineering
BMus	Bachelor of Music
BMusEd	Bachelor of Music Education
bn	battalion
BO	Bachelor of Oratory
bot	botany; botanical
BP	Bachelor of Painting
BPd	Bachelor of Pedagogy
BPE	Bachelor of Physical Education
BPharm	Bachelor of Pharmacy
BPOE	Benevolent and Protective Order of Elks
BPS	Bachelor of Professional Studies
BPy	Bachelor of Pedagogy
br	branch(es)
BRE	Bachelor of Religious Education
BRelEd	Bachelor of Religious Education
brig gen	brigadier general
Brit	Britain; British; Britannica
bro	brother(s)
BS	Bachelor of Science
BSA	Bachelor of Science in Agriculture
BSc	Bachelor of Science
BSC	Bachelor of Christian Science
BSCerE	Bachelor of Science in Ceramic Engineering
BSD	Bachelor of Didactic Science
BSE	Bachelor of Science in Education
BSEE	Bachelor of Science in Electrical Engineering; Bachelor of Science in Elementary Education; Bachelor of Science in Engineering and Economics
BSFS	Bachelor of Science in Forestry Service
BSME	Bachelor of Science in Mechanical Engineering; Bachelor of Science in Mining Engineering; Bachelor of Science in Music Education
BSN	Bachelor of Science in Nursing
BST	Bachelor of Sacred Theology
BT	Bachelor of Teaching; Bachelor of Theology
BTh	Bachelor of Theology
bull	bulletin(s)
bur	bureau(s)
bus	business
BVA	Bachelor of Vocational Agriculture
BWI	British West Indies
C of C	Chamber of Commerce
CA	California
CAA	Civil Aeronautics Administration
CAB	Civil Aeronautics Board
CAC	Coast Artillery Corps
Calif	California
CAm	Central America(n)
Can	Canada
C&EI RR	Chicago and Eastern Illinois Railroad
Capt	Captain
Cath	Catholic(s)
cav	cavalry
CB&Q RR	Chicago, Burlington and Quincy Railroad Company
CBI	China, Burma, India Theater of Operations, U.S. Army (World War II)
CBS	Columbia Broadcasting System
CCC	Commodity Credit Corporation
CCC & St L Ry	Cleveland, Cincinnati, Chicago and St. Louis Railway
CE	civil engineer; Corps of Engineers
CEF	Canadian Expeditionary Force
cert	certificate(s); certified
CGW Ry	Chicago Great Western Railway
ch	church(es)
chap	chapter(s)
ChD	Doctor of Chemistry
ChemE	chemical engineer
chmn	chairman
CIA	Central Intelligence Agency
CI&L Ry	Chicago, Indianapolis and Louisville Railway
CIC	Counter Intelligence Corps
CIO	Congress of Industrial Organizations
clin	clinic(s); clinical
clk	clerk
CLU	chartered life underwriter
CM	Master in Surgery
cnsl	counsel
co	company; county
CO	Colorado
COF	Catholic Order of Foresters

col	colonel	dep	deputy
coll	college(s)	dept	department
Colo	Colorado	dermatol	dermatology; dermatological
comd	command; commanded	desc	descendant(s)
comdg	commanding	devel	development(s); developmental; developed
comdr	commander	DFC	Distinguished Flying Cross
commdt	commandant	DHL	Doctor of Humane Letters
comm	committee(s)	dir	director(s); directed
commd	commissioned	disch	discharge(d)
comml	commercial	dist	district(s)
commn	commission	distrib	distributor(s); distribution; distributing
commr	commissioner	div	division(s); divinity; divorced
commun	communication(s)	DMD	Doctor of Medical Dentistry
comp	computer(s)	DMS	Doctor of Medical Science
condr	conductor	DO	Doctor of Osteopathy
conf	conference(s)	DPA	Defense Production Administration
cong	congress; congressional	DPH	Diploma in Public Health
Congl	Congregational	dr	drive
Conn	Connecticut	Dr	Doctor
consol	consolidated	DR	Daughters of the Revolution
const	constitution; constitutional	DRE	Doctor of Religious Education
constrn	construction	DrPH	Doctor of Public Health; Doctor of Public Hygiene
cont	controller(s); comptroller(s)	DSc	Doctor of Science
contrib	contribution(s); contributor(s); contributed	DSC	Distinguished Service Cross
conv	convention(s)	DSM	Distinguished Service Medal
coord	coordinator(s)	DST	Doctor of Sacred Theology
CORE	Congress of Racial Equality	DTM	Doctor of Tropical Medicine
corp	corporation(s); corporate	DVM	Doctor of Veterinary Medicine
corpl	corporal	DVS	Doctor of Veterinary Surgery
corr	correspondence; correspondent(s); cor-responding	E	east
coun	council(s)	ECA	Economic Cooperation Administration
CPA	certified public accountant	eccles	ecclesiastical
CPCU	chartered property and casualty under-writer	ecol	ecology; ecological
		econ	economy; economic
CPH	certificate of public health	ECOSOC	Economic and Social Council (of the United Nations)
CS	Christian Science	ED	Doctor of Engineering
CSB	Bachelor of Christian Science	EdB	Bachelor of Education
ct	court	EdD	Doctor of Education
CT	Candidate in Theology; Connecticut	edit	edition(s); edited
ctr	center	EdM	Master of Education
CWS	Chemical Warfare Service	educ	education(al); educator(s)
cyclo	cyclopedia	EE	electrical engineer(ing)
D	Doctor (academic degree)	Egyptol	Egyptology; Egyptological
DAgr	Doctor of Agriculture	elec	electricity; electric(al)
DAR	Daughters of the American Revolution	electrochem	electrochemistry; electrochemical
DAV	Disabled American Veterans	electrophys	electrophysics; electrophysical
DC	District of Columbia	EM	engineer of mines
DCL	Doctor of Civil Law	ency	encyclopedia(s)
DCS	Doctor of Commercial Science	eng	engineering
DD	Doctor of Divinity	Eng	England; English
DDS	Doctor of Dental Surgery	engr	engineer
DE	Delaware; Doctor of Engineering	entomol	entomology; entomological
dec	deceased	ethnol	ethnology; ethnological
Dec	December	ETO	European Theater of Operations, U.S. Army (World War II)
def	defense	Evang	Evangelical
del	delegate(s)	exam	examination(s); examining
Del	Delaware	exec	executive(s)
Dem	Democrat(s); Democratic	exhbn	exhibition
DEng	Doctor of Engineering		
denom	denomination(s); denominational		

expdn	expedition	HM	Master of Humanities
expo	exposition(s)	HOLC	Home Owners Loan Corporation
expt	experiment	homeo	homeopathy; homeopathic
exptl	experimental	hon	honorable; honorary
F	fellow	hort	horticulture; horticultural
FA	Field Artillery	hosp	hospital(s)
FAA	Federation Aviation Agency	hwy	highway
FAO	Food and Agriculture Organization (of the United Nations)	hydrog	hydrography; hydrographic
		IA	Iowa
FBI	Federal Bureau of Investigation	IAEA	International Atomic Energy Agency
FCA	Farm Credit Administration	ICA	International Cooperation Administration
FCC	Federal Communications Commission	ICC	Interstate Commerce Commission
FCDA	Federal Civil Defense Administration	ID	Idaho
FDA	Food and Drug Administration	IEEE	Institute of Electrical and Electronics Engineers
FDIA	Federal Deposit Insurance Administration		
FDIC	Federal Deposit Insurance Corporation	IFC	International Finance Corporation
FE	forest engineer	IL	Illinois
Feb	February	Ill	Illinois
fed	federal	illus	illustrator(s); illustrated
fedn	federation	ILO	International Labor Organization
fgn	foreign	IMF	International Monetary Fund
FHA	Federal Housing Administration	IN	Indiana
fin	finance; financial	inc	incorporated
fl	floor	Ind	Indiana
FL	Florida	indep	independent
Fla	Florida	indus	industry; industries; industrial
FOA	Foreign Operations Administration	inf	infantry
found	foundation(s); founder(s); founded	info	information
frat	fraternity	ins	insurance
FRCP	Fellow, Royal College of Physicians (England)	insp	inspector
		inst	institute(s)
FRCS	Fellow, Royal College of Surgeons (England)	instn	institution
		instr	instruction; instructor
FSA	Federal Security Agency	intl	international
ft	fort	intro	introduction
FTC	Federal Tariff Commission; Federal Trade Commission	IOOF	Independent Order of Odd Fellows
		IRE	Institute of Radio Engineers
G-1, G-2, etc.	Division of General Staff	Jan	January
Ga	Georgia	JB	Bachelor of Laws
GA	Georgia	JCB	Bachelor of Canon Law
gastroent	gastroenterology; gastroenterological	JCL	Licentiate in Canon Law
GATT	General Agreement on Tariffs and Trade	JD	Doctor of Jurisprudence; Doctor of Law(s)
GD	graduate in divinity	jg	junior grade
gen	general	jour	journal(s); journalism
geneal	genealogy; genealogical	jr	junior
geod	geodesy; geodetic	JSD	Doctor of Juristic Science
geog	geography; geographic(al)	jud	judicial
geophys	geophysics; geophysical	JUD	doctor of both laws, i.e., canon and civil
GHQ	general headquarters	Jul	July
gov	governor	Jun	June
govt	government	Kan	Kansas
govtl	governmental	KC	Knights of Columbus
grad	graduate(s); graduated	KCCH	Knight Commander of Court of Honor
GT Ry	Grand Trunk Railway System	KP	Knight of Pythias
GU	Guam	KS	Kansas
gynecol	gynecology; gynecological	KT	Knight Templar
hdqrs	headquarters	Ky	Kentucky
HHD	Doctor of Humanities	KY	Kentucky
HHFA	Housing and Home Finance Agency	La	Louisiana
HI	Hawaii	LA	Louisiana
hist	history; historic(al)	lab	laboratory; laboratories

lang	language(s)	**Meth**	Methodist(s)
laryngol	laryngology; laryngological	**metrol**	metrology; metrological
lectr	lecturer	**MF**	Master of Forestry
LHD	Doctor of Humane Letters	**MFA**	Master of Fine Arts
LI	Long Island	**mfg**	manufacturing
lieut	lieutenant	**mfr**	manufacturer
lit	literature; literary	**mgmt**	management
LittB	Bachelor of Letters	**mgr**	manager
LittD	Doctor of Letters	**MHA**	Master of Hospital Administration
LLB	Bachelor of Laws	**MI**	Michigan; Military Intelligence
LLD	Doctor of Laws	**Mich**	Michigan
LLM	Master of Laws	**micros**	microscopy; microscopic(al)
ln	lane	**mil**	military
LOM	Loyal Order of Moose	**mineral**	mineralogy; mineralogical
LRCP	Licentiate, Royal College of Physicians	**Minn**	Minnesota
LRCS	Licentiate, Royal College of Surgeons	**mktg**	marketing
LS	library science	**ML**	Master of Laws
Lt	Lieutenant	**MLitt**	Master of Literature
ltd	limited	**Mlle**	Mademoiselle
Luth	Lutheran(s)	**MLS**	Master of Library Science
M	Master (academic degree)	**Mme**	Madame
MA	Massachusetts; Master of Arts	**MME**	Master of Mechanical Engineering
mag	magazine(s)	**MN**	Minnesota
MAgr	Master of Agriculture	**mng**	managing
maj	major	**Mo**	Missouri
Man	Manitoba	**MO**	Missouri
Mar	March	**Mont**	Montana
MArch	Master of Architecture	**MPd**	Master of Pedagogy
Mass	Massachusetts	**MPE**	Master of Physical Education
math	mathematics; mathematical	**MPH**	Master of Public Health
MB	Bachelor of Medicine; Manitoba	**MPL**	Master of Patent Law
MBA	Master of Business Administration	**MRE**	Master of Religious Education
MBS	Mutual Broadcasting System	**MS**	Master of Science; Mississippi
MC	Medical Corps	**MSc**	Master of Science
MCE	Master of Civil Engineering	**MSF**	Master of Science in Forestry
mcht	merchant	**MST**	Master of Sacred Theology
MCS	Master of Commercial Science	**MSW**	Master of Social Work
Md	Maryland	**mt**	mount
MD	Doctor of Medicine; Maryland	**MT**	Montana
MDi	Master of Didactics	**MTO**	Mediterranean Theater of Operations, U.S. Army (World War II)
MDip	Master of Diplomacy	
MDiv	Master of Divinity	**mus**	museum(s); music(al)
mdse	merchandise	**MusB**	Bachelor of Music
MDV	Doctor of Veterinary Medicine	**MusD**	Doctor of Music
Me	Maine	**MusM**	Master of Music
ME	Maine; Master of Education; Master of Engineering; Mechanical Engineer	**MWA**	Modern Woodmen of America
		mycol	mycology; mycological
mech	mechanical	**N**	north
MECh	Methodist Episcopal Church	**NA**	National Academician; National Army
med	medicine; medical	**NAACP**	National Association for the Advancement of Colored People
MEd	Master of Education	
MedORC	Medical Officers' Reserve Corps	**NACA**	National Advisory Committee for Aeronautics
MedRC	Medical Reserve Corps	
MEE	Master of Electrical Engineering	**NAD**	National Academy of Design
mem	member(s)	**NAm**	North America(n)
meml	memorial	**NAM**	National Association of Manufacturers
merc	mercantile	**NASA**	National Aeronautics and Space Administration
met	metropolitan	
metall	metallurgy; metallurgical	**natl**	national
MetE	metallurgical engineer	**NATO**	North Atlantic Treaty Organization
meteorol	meteorology; meteorological	**NATOUSA**	North African Theater of Operations, U.S. Army (World War II)

nav	navigation	org	organization(s)
NB	New Brunswick	ornithol	ornithology; ornithological
NBC	National Broadcasting Company	OSRD	Office of Scientific Research and Development
NC	North Carolina		
ND	North Dakota	OSS	Office of Strategic Services
NDRC	National Defense Research Committee	osteo	osteopathy; osteopathic
NE	Nebraska; northeast	OT	Old Testament
NEA	National Education Association	OTC	Officers' Training Corps
Neb	Nebraska	otol	otology; otological
neurol	neurology; neurological	otolaryn	otolaryngology; otolaryngological
Nev	Nevada	OTS	Officers' Training School
NF	Newfoundland	OUAM	Order of United American Mechanics
NG	National Guard	OWI	Office of War Information
NH	New Hampshire	Pa	Pennsylvania
NIH	National Institutes of Health	PA	Pennsylvania
NJ	New Jersey	paleontol	paleontology; paleontological
NLRB	National Labor Relations Board	path	pathology; pathologic(al)
NM	New Mexico	PdB	Bachelor of Pedagogy
no	northern	PdD	Doctor of Pedagogy
Nov	November	PdM	Master of Pedagogy
NPA	National Production Authority	PE	Protestant Episcopal
nr	near	PeB	Bachelor of Pediatrics
NRA	National Recovery Administration	PEN	Poets, Playwrights, Essayists, Editors and Novelists (association)
NRC	National Research Council		
NS	Nova Scotia	penol	penology; penological
NSC	National Security Council	pers	personnel
NSF	National Science Foundation	pfc	private first class
NSRB	National Security Resources Board	PHA	Public Housing Administration
NT	New Testament	pharm	pharmacy; pharmacies; pharmacist(s); pharmaceutical(s)
numis	numismatic(s)		
NV	Nevada	PharmD	Doctor of Pharmacy
NW	northwest	PharmM	Master of Pharmacy
NY	New York	PhB	Bachelor of Philosophy
OAS	Organization of American States	PhC	pharmaceutical chemist
OB	Bachelor of Oratory	PhD	Doctor of Philosophy
observ	observatory; observatories	PhG	graduate in pharmacy
obstet	obstetrics; obstetrical	philol	philology; philological
OCDM	Office of Civil and Defense Mobilization	philos	philosophy; philosophical
Oct	October	photog	photography; photograph(ic); photographer(s)
ODM	Office of Defense Mobilization		
OECD	Organization for Economic Cooperation and Development	phys	physical
		Phys and Surg	Physicians and Surgeons (College at Columbia University)
OEEC	Organization for European Economic Co-operation		
		physiol	physiology; physiological
OES	Order of the Eastern Star	PI	Philippine Islands
ofcr	officer	pkg	packaging
offl	official	pkwy	parkway
OH	Ohio	pl	place
OK	Oklahoma	PO	post office
ON	Ontario	polit	politics; political; politician(s)
Ont	Ontario	pomol	pomology; pomological
OPA	Office of Price Administration	PQ	Province of Quebec
oper	operations	PR	Puerto Rico
ophthal	ophthalmology; ophthalmological	prep	preparatory
OPM	Office of Production Management	pres	president
OPS	Office of Price Stabilization	Presb	Presbyterian(s)
OQMG	Office of Quartermaster General	prin	principal(s)
OR	Oregon	pro tem	pro tempore
ORC	Officers' Reserve Corps	proc	proceedings
orch	orchestra(s)	prod	product(s); produced
Ore	Oregon	prodn	production

prof	professor(s)	**Sat Eve Post**	Saturday Evening Post
profl	professional	**sav**	savings
prog	program(s)	**SB**	Bachelor of Science
proj	project(s)	**SC**	South Carolina
propr	proprietor(s)	**SCAP**	Supreme Commander, Allies Pacific
pros atty	prosecuting attorney	**ScB**	Bachelor of Science
prov	province(s)	**ScD**	Doctor of Science
psychol	psychology; psychological	**SCD**	Doctor of Commercial Science
PTA	Parent-Teacher Association	**sch**	school(s)
ptnr	partner	**sci**	science(s); scientific
PTO	Pacific Theater of Operations, U.S. Army (World War II)	**SCV**	Sons of Confederate Veterans
pub	publisher(s); publishing; publication(s); published	**SD**	South Dakota
		SE	southeast
pvt	private	**SEATO**	Southeast Asia Treaty Organization
PWA	Public Works Administration	**sec**	secretary; secretaries
qm	quartermaster	**SEC**	Securities and Exchange Commission
QMC	Quartermaster Corps	**sect**	section(s)
QMORC	Quartermaster Officers' Reserve Corps	**seismol**	seismology; seismological
quar	quarterly	**sem**	seminary; seminaries
Que	Quebec	**Sept**	September
radiol	radiology; radiological	**serv**	service(s)
RAF	Royal Air Force	**sgt**	sergeant
RAM	Royal Arch Mason	**SI**	Staten Island
RC	Reserve Corps; Roman Catholic	**SJ**	Society of Jesus (Jesuit)
RCA	Radio Corporation of America	**SJD**	Doctor of Juristic Science
RCAF	Royal Canadian Air Force	**SM**	Master of Science
rd	road	**so**	southern
RD	rural delivery	**soc**	society; societies
RE	Reformed Episcopal	**sociol**	sociology; sociological
rec	recreation	**SOS**	Service of Supply
ref	reformed	**spl**	special
reg	region(al)	**sq**	square
regt	regiment	**sr**	senior
regtl	regimental	**SR**	Sons of the Revolution
rehab	rehabilitation	**SS**	steamship
rel	relations	**SSS**	Selective Service System
rep	representative(s); republic	**st**	street
Repub	Republican(s)	**St**	Saint
res	reserve	**sta**	station
ret	retired	**stat**	statistics; statistical
rev	review; revised	**STB**	Bachelor of Sacred Theology
Rev	Reverend	**STD**	Doctor of Sacred Theology
RFC	Reconstruction Finance Corporation	**ste**	suite
RFD	rural free delivery	**Ste**	Sainte
rhinol	rhinology; rhinological	**STL**	Lector of Sacred Theology; Licentiate in Sacred Theology
RI	Rhode Island		
RN	registered nurse	**subs**	subsidiary; subsidiaries
ROSC	Reserve Officers' Sanitary Corps	**supt**	superintendent
ROTC	Reserve Officers' Training Corps	**supvr**	supervisor
RP	Reformed Presbyterian	**surg**	surgery; surgical
RR	railroad; rural route	**SW**	southwest
rsch	research	**TB**	tuberculosis
RTC	Reserve Training Corps	**tchr**	teacher(s)
rte	route	**tech**	technical
ry	railway	**technol**	technology; technological
S	south	**Tel & Tel**	telephone and telegraph
SAC	Strategic Air Command	**temp**	temporary
SAm	South America(n)	**Tenn**	Tennessee
sanit	sanitation; sanitary	**territ**	territory
Sask	Saskatchewan	**Tex**	Texas
		TH	Territory of Hawaii

ThD	Doctor of Theology
theol	theology; theological
ThM	Master of Theology
TN	Tennessee
topog	topography; topographical
trans	transaction(s); transferred
transl	translation(s); translator(s); translated
transp	transportation
treas	treasurer(s)
TV	television
TVA	Tennessee Valley Authority
twp	township
TX	Texas
typog	typography; typographic(al)
UAR	United Arab Republic
UAW	International Union, United Automobile, Aerospace, and Agricultural Implement Workers of America (AFL-CIO)
UB	United Brethren in Christ
UDC	United Daughters of the Confederacy
UK	United Kingdom
UN	United Nations
UNESCO	United Nations Educational, Scientific and Cultural Organization
UNICEF	United Nations International Children's Emergency Fund
univ	university; universities
UNRRA	United Nations Relief and Rehabilitation Administration
UP	United Presbyterian
UPI	United Press International
US	United States
USA	United States of America
USAAF	United States Army Air Force
USAC	United States Air Corps
USAF	United States Air Force
USCG	United States Coast Guard
USCGR	United States Coast Guard Reserve
USES	United States Employment Service
USIA	United States Information Agency
USIS	United States Information Service
USMC	United States Marine Corps
USMCR	United States Marine Corps Reserve
USMHS	United States Marine Hospital Service
USN	United States Navy

USNA	United States National Army
USNG	United States National Guard
USNR	United States Naval Reserve
USNRF	United States Naval Reserve Force
USO	United Service Organizations
USOM	United States Operations Mission
USPHS	United States Public Health Service
USS	United States Ship
USSR	Union of Soviet Socialist Republics
USV	United States Volunteers
UT	Utah
Va	Virginia
VA	Veterans Administration; Virginia
vet	veteran; veterinary
VFW	Veterans of Foreign Wars
VI	Virgin Islands
vice pres	vice president(s)
vol	volume(s); volunteer(s)
vs	versus
Vt	Vermont
VT	Vermont
W	west
WA	Washington
WAC	Women's Army Corps
Wash	Washington
WAVES	Women's Reserve, U.S. Naval Reserve
WCTU	Women's Christian Temperance Union
WHO	World Health Organization (of the United Nations)
WI	West Indies; Wisconsin
Wis	Wisconsin
WP RR Co	Western Pacific Railroad Company
WPA	Works Progress Administration
WPB	War Production Board
WSB	Wage Stabilization Board
WV	West Virginia
WVa	West Virginia
WY	Wyoming
Wyo	Wyoming
YMCA	Young Men's Christian Association
YMHA	Young Men's Hebrew Association
YWCA	Young Women's Christian Association
YWHA	Young Women's Hebrew Association
YT	Yukon Territory
zool	zoology; zoological

WHO'S *who* AMONG

Black Americans

BIOGRAPHIES

A

AARON, HENRY L.
Professional athlete. **PERSONAL:** Born Feb 05, 1934, Mobile, AL; married Billye Suber Williams; children: Gail, Hank, Larry, Gary (dec), Dorenda, Ceci. **EDUCATION:** Josephine Allen Inst, attended 1951. **CAREER:** Milwaukee Braves, professional baseball player 1954-65; Atlanta Braves, prof baseball player 1966-76; Milwaukee Brewers, vice pres player devel 1975-76; Atlanta Braves 6 Team Farm System, exec 1976-. **ORGANIZATIONS:** Mem Atlanta Braves Bd Dirs; vice pres & dir Player Develop Club; pres No Greater Love 1974-; natl sports chmn Natl Easter Seal Soc 1974; sponsor Hank Aaron Celebrity Bowling Tourn for Sickle Cell Anemia 1972; natl chmn Friends of Fisk for Athletes; state chmn Wisconsin Easter Seals Soc 1975. **HONORS/ACHIEVEMENTS:** Broke Babe Ruth's home run record April 18, 1974; only Black exec among 26 major league teams; holds 18 major league records; holds 9 natl league records; Rookie of the Yr 18 yrs old; holds major league record for most home runs hit. **BUSINESS ADDRESS:** Team Executive, Atlanta Braves, Inc, PO Box 4064, Atlanta, GA 30302.

ABAJIAN, JAMES DETARR
Author. **PERSONAL:** Born May 30, 1914, Sacramento, CA. **EDUCATION:** Univ of Wisconsin, BS 1938; Univ of Michigan, grad school 1939-41. **CAREER:** Univ of Michigan Library, asst curator rare books 1940-43; State Hist Soc of Wisconsin, asst curator manuscripts 1944; California Hist Soc, library dir 1949-68; Friends San Francisco Publ Libr, dir M L King Jr Coll 1969-71; California Hist Soc, curator Kemble Coll 1974-78; Archdiocese of San Francisco, chief archivist 1978-82; retired. **ORGANIZATIONS:** Mem adv com Afro-Amer Publ Co Chicago 1968-70; Living Webster Dict of Eng Language 1970-71; mem Soc Amer Archivists; San Francisco African Amer Hist & Cultural Soc. **HONORS/ACHIEVEMENTS:** Author, "Blacks & Their Contributions to the American West"; Bibliography & Union List of Library Holdings Through 1970 (Boston 1974); author, Blacks in sel newspapers census 3 vol index to names & subjects 1977; contrib monographs and book reviews to professional journals. **MILITARY SERVICE:** AUS 1943-44.

ABBOTT, GREGORY
Singer. **PERSONAL:** Born in Harlem, NY. **EDUCATION:** Boston Univ, undergrad degree; Univ of CA San Francisco, MA Psych; Stanford Univ, grad work in Lit. **CAREER:** Wall Street, municipal bond researcher; singer. **ORGANIZATIONS:** Boy soprano NY St Patrick's Cathedral. **HONORS/ACHIEVEMENTS:** "Shake You Down" LP no 1 hit on Billboard pop charts. **BUSINESS ADDRESS:** Singer, c/o Columbia Records, 51 W 52nd St, New York, NY 10019.

ABBOTT, LORETTA
Dancer, actress, singer, educator. **CAREER:** Alvin Ailey, George Faison, soloist with dance co; Robert De Cormier Choraie, Clyde Turner Chorale, guest artist; Hofstra Univ, NYACK Acad of Classical Ballet, Amer Univ, Philadanco, College of Staten Island, Sarah Lawrence, Manhattan Comm Coll, guest instructor; TV Appearances, Tony TV Awds, Jerry Lewis MD Telethon, commercials, Studio 32 Video Party; Broadway, Reggae, Porgy & Bess, Amen Corner, Broadway Soul at Lincoln Ctr, Miss Truth; Off Broadway, Stompin' at the Savoy, Reflections, Sweet Saturday Nite (principal dancer); Hot Rags (asst to choreographer/ principal dancer); A Spark of Faith, choreographer; Stravinsky Cantata; To be Young Gifted & Black; Raisin in the Sun; Fiesta Fantastica.

ABDUL, RAOUL
Writer, editor, concert singer. **PERSONAL:** Born Nov 07, 1929, Cleveland, OH; son of Abdul Hamid and Beatrice Shreve Abdul. **EDUCATION:** Attended Acad of Mus & Dramatic Art Vienna, Austria; Harvard Summer Sch, additional studies 1966; Salzburg Mozarteum, Salzburg Austria, diploma 1988. **CAREER:** 3000 Years of Black Poetry, co-editor 1970; Blacks in Classical Music, author 1977; Famous Black Entertainers of Today, author; The Magic of Black Poetry, editor; lieder recitals in Austria, Germany, Holland, Hungary, US & Canada; TV & radio guest appearances; lectr, Kennedy Ctr for the Performing Arts/ Lincoln Ctr for the Performing Arts/Harvard Univ/Atlanta Univ/Univ of CT/Howard Univ/Columbia; faculty, Harlem Sch of Arts; music critic, Amsterdam News. **ORGANIZATIONS:** Founder Coffee Concerts Series in Harlem; bd mem, NY Singing Teachers Assn 1989-. **HONORS/ACHIEVEMENTS:** Recipient Harold Jackman Meml Com Award 1978; received Key to City of Cleveland from Mayor Ralph Perk 1974; recipient Natl Assn of Negro Musicians Distinguished Serv Award 1974, 1978. **HOME ADDRESS:** 360 W 22 St, New York, NY 10011.

ABDUL-HAMID, ISMAIL
Architect. **PERSONAL:** Born Feb 10, 1950, Philadelphia, PA; married Sharifa Beckton; children: Idrisa, Zaid. **EDUCATION:** Pennsylvania State Univ, attended 1967-68; Comm Coll of Philadelphia, attended 1971-72. **CAREER:** Rahenkamp Sachs Wells & Assoc Inc Philadelphia, archit landscape draftsman 1968-72; Architects Workshop, archit intern 1968-75; Redevel Auth of Philadelphia, urban renewal tech/architect 1973-79; Abdul-Hamid Cons,

owner/urban architect 1972-. **ORGANIZATIONS:** Mem Assn of Diving Instr 1977-; pres Hajj-Am Enterprises Inc 1979-; managing partner Amoeba Assoc 1979-; pres Stanton Civic Assn 1978-; mem Germantown Settlement 1979-; co-chmn Coalition of Housing Orgn in Philadelphia 1980-. **BUSINESS ADDRESS:** Abdul-Hamid Consult, Greater Germantown Housing Dev, 48 E Penn St, Philadelphia, PA 19144.

ABDUL-JABBAR, KAREEM (LEW ALCINDOR)
Professional basketball player. **PERSONAL:** Born Apr 16, 1947, New York, NY; children: Habiba, Sultana, Kareem, Amir. **EDUCATION:** UCLA, BA 1969. **CAREER:** Actor, Game of Death, Airplane, The Fish that Saved Pittsburgh, Fletch, Airplane;TV appearances, Mannix, Different Strokes; NBA Milwaukee Bucks, 1969-75; Los Angeles Lakers, 1975-. **ORGANIZATIONS:** Pres Cranberry Records affiliated with MCA. **HONORS/ ACHIEVEMENTS:** MVP of NCAA Tournament 3 consecutive years; MVP 6 times; All Star Team 14 times; Rookie of the Yr 1970; Maurice Podoloff Cup 1971-77; author autobiography "Giant Steps" 1984 w/Peter Krobler; received in 1985 The Jackie Robinson Award for Athletics for career accomplishments as the NBA's Most Valuable Player, for achievements as all-time leading scorer, and for leadership of the world-champion LA Lakers; Sports Illustrated Sportsman of the Year 1985; mem 36th & 37th NBA All- Star Teams. **BUSINESS ADDRESS:** Los Angeles Lakers, PO Box 10, Inglewood, CA 90306.

ABDUL-MALIK, AHMED H.
Musician. **PERSONAL:** Born Jan 30, 1927, Brooklyn, NY; children: Amina, Khadija, Rashida, Halima. **EDUCATION:** New York Univ, BS Music Educ 1969, MA Music Educ 1977. **CAREER:** Bd of Educ New York City High School, music teacher 1969-84; New York Univ Div of Music Educ, prof of music 1970-; Brooklyn Coll Dept of African Studies, adjunct prof of African & Middle Eastern music & jazz 1973-; New York Univ, New York, NY, prof of music, 1973-; Numerous appearances as solo bassist or oudist. **HONORS/ ACHIEVEMENTS:** Major recordings East Meets West RCA Victor LPM 2015; Spellbound Status Subsidiary Prestige New Jazz 8266; Jazz Sahara Riverside 12287, Eastern Moods of Ahmed Abdul-Malik New Jazz 8298; Playboy "Bassist of the Year", recognition as Innovator in the Meshing of Middle Eastern Musicand Jazz; recognition throughout Middle Eastern countries as Oudist & Bassist; United Nations Org of groups of Eastern music specialists and presentation for Upper Volta Delegation to the UN (The Waldorf Astoria) and the Cameroon Delegation (The Plaza), Oud and Bass under sponsorship of US Dept of State; org/supervision of music groups performing/lecturing throughout Europe & So Amer sponsored by Amer Soc for African Culture. **BUSINESS ADDRESS:** Professor of Music, Brooklyn College, Africana Studies, Brooklyn, NY 10003.

ABDUL-MALIK, IBRAHIM
Nutritional consultant, health counselor. **EDUCATION:** CCNY, BS 1952, MA 1954; Harvard Univ, EdD 1971. **CAREER:** Tchr/asst prin/staff developer 1954-65; Bank St Coll, dir Educ Resources Ctr 1965-68; Harlem Sch NYC, prin 1968-69; New York City Urban Educ, dir Devel Div Ctr 1971-72; New York City Bd of Educ, vice chmn Bd of Examiners 1972-74, educational planner 1974-76, science assoc 1976-79; UNESCO, overseas science advisor 1979-81; curriculum spec coll/univ faculty; faculty; educ counsel; admin; researcher; writer; health counselor & practitioner/nutritional consultant. **ORGANIZATIONS:** Bd dir Harlem Neighborhood Assn; 1968-70; mem Comm Serv Soc; Family Life Educ Comm 1966-70; mem Natl Assn for Bilingual Educ; mem Amer Assn of Sch Personnel Admin; Intl Coun on Educ for Teaching; mem Kappa Delta Pi; Phi Delta Kappa. **HONORS/ACHIEVEMENTS:** Recipient Natl Sci Found Fellow. **BUSINESS ADDRESS:** Nutritional Consultant, 131 Livingston St, New York, NY 11201.

ABDUL-RAHMAN, TAHIRA SADIQA
Social service director. **PERSONAL:** Born Dec 15, 1947, Shreveport, LA; married Mustafa Abdul-Rahman; children: Jamilla, Zainab, Naeema, Ibn, Ismail. **EDUCATION:** Howard Univ, BA 1968; Howard Univ Sch of Social Work, MSW 1970. **CAREER:** New Careers Prog, specialty instructor 1970-71; Parent and Child Ctr, supervisor 1971-72; Morgan Univ, assoc prof 1972-74; Assoc for Comm Training Inc,dir homemaker prog 1984-87; The Family Center Assoc for Community Training Inc, dir 1987-. **ORGANIZATIONS:** Pres PTA West Shreveport Elem Sch 1982-84; exec bd mem Dist Parent Teachers Assoc 1984-85; guest columnist The Shreveport Sun 1985-87; vice pres PTA Booker T Washington HS 1986-87; realtor assoc Marak Realtors 1986-; guest speaker Annual Luncheon for the Sr Citizens of the Union Mission Baptist Ch 1987;steering comm YMCA Annual Awareness Banquet 1986; mem Delta Sigma Theta Sor Inc, Political Action Comm Delta Sigma Theta Sor Inc. **HONORS/ACHIEVEMENTS:** Certificate of Appreciation West Shreveport School Annually 1980-87; Honorary Life Mem Louisiana State PTA 1984; Outstanding Leadership Awd West Shreveport School PTA 1984. **BUSINESS ADDRESS:** Dir The Family Center, Assoc for Comm Training Inc, 1116 Pierre Ave, Shreveport, LA 71103.

ABDULLAH, LARRY BURLEY
Dentist. **PERSONAL:** Born Apr 17, 1947, Malvern, AR; married Barbara; children: Zakkiyya, Jeffery, Kerry, Larry II, Najla. **EDUCATION:** Univ of AR, BS 1968; Meharry Dental Coll, DDS 1972. **CAREER:** Private practice, dentist. **ORGANIZATIONS:** Mem Amer Dental Assoc 1974-87, Chicago Dental Soc 1974-87, IL Dental Assoc 1974-87, Acad

1

of General Dentistry 1974-87, Amer Straight Wire Orthodontic Soc 1982-87. **BUSINESS ADDRESS:** Dentist, 7013 S Western Ave, Chicago, IL 60636.

ABDULLAH, TARIQ HUSAM
Physician. **PERSONAL:** Born Oct 23, 1941, Florala, AL; married Khadijah Marie Cole; children: Eric Merrit, Kyle Bernard Nichols, Keith Freeman Nichols. **EDUCATION:** Lane Coll, BS 1962; Emory Univ Med Ctr, Externship 1964; Meharry Med Coll, MD 1967. **CAREER:** Hubbard Hosp, internship 1968; Washington Univ Med Ctr, resident 1968-71; Natl Inst of Health, resident/capt 1971-73; Howard Univ Med Ctr, instructor1973-74; Thrash Med Clinic, dir 1974-82; Akbar Clinic Panama, staff 1983-86; Coston & Laton Clinic, dir 1974-86. **ORGANIZATIONS:** Medical licensures Natl Bd of Medical Examiners States of FL, AL, GA 1968-; hon counsul Republic of Guyana 1978-87; mem AAAS 1985-87. **HONORS/ACHIEVEMENTS:** Alumni Awd Lane College; listed in Who's Who in the South and Southwest, Marquis Who's Who in Amer. **HOME ADDRESS:** PO Box 458, Paxton, FL 32538. **BUSINESS ADDRESS:** Dir, Coston & Laton Memorial Clinic, Rt 2 Box 124, Flowerview Dr, Laurel Hill, FL 32567.

ABE, BENJAMIN OMARA A.
Educator. **PERSONAL:** Born Nov 19, 1943, Gulu, Uganda;married Joan B White; children: Daudi John, Peter Okech. **EDUCATION:** Carleton Coll Northfield MN, BA Soc Anth 1968; Washington State Univ Pullman WA, MA Anth 1970. **CAREER:** TransWorld Trading Corp, pres & chmn bd 1974-75; BAS Assoc Intl, mng gen partner 1975-; N Seattle Comm Coll, dir E-African Study Tour Programme 1978-; prof of anthropology 1970-. **ORGANIZATIONS:** Mem Amer Anthrop Assn. **BUSINESS ADDRESS:** Prof of Anthropology, N Seattle Comm Coll, 9600 College Way, Seattle, WA 98103.

ABEBE, RUBY
Civil rights commissioner. **PERSONAL:** Born Apr 19, 1949, Waterloo, IA; married Assefa Abebe; children: Yeshi Marie, Tsehay, Saba DyAnn. **EDUCATION:** Univ of IA, BA 1972. **CAREER:** Natl Black Republicans, IA state chair 1984; Governor Branstad Black Adv Bd, ad hoc 1985; Retired Senior Volunteer Program, adv bd 1985; IA Civil Rights Commn, commissioner 1986. **HOME ADDRESS:** 637 Independence Ave, Waterloo, IA 50703.

ABEBE, TESHOME
Educational administrator. **PERSONAL:** Married Assegedeth Haile-Mariam; children: Yetnayet; Nitsuh. **EDUCATION:** Illinois State Univ, BA 1974, MA 1976; Northern Illinois Univ, PhD 1980. **CAREER:** Northern Illinois Univ, instr finance 1978-80; Eastern New Mexico Univ, asst prof 1980-83; Univ of Southern Colorado, MBA dir 1983-84; Univ of Southern Colorado, asst dean for bus 1983-86; dean School of Business, Univ of Southern Colorado, 1986-. **ORGANIZATIONS:** Mem Professional Org 1980-; referee Prof Jrnl 1981-. **HONORS/ACHIEVEMENTS:** Publ Professional Jrnls 1980-84; Presidents Awd Eastern New Mexico Univ 1982; Presidents Awd Univ of Southern CO 1983-84. **BUSINESS ADDRESS:** Dean School of Business, Univ of Southern Colorado, 2200 Bonforte Blvd, Pueblo, CO 81001.

ABEL, RENAUL N.
Plant manager. **PERSONAL:** Born Dec 28, 1940, Philadelphia, PA; son of William Abel; married Patricia Fenner, Aug 24, 1964; children: Sean Abel, Damien Abel. **EDUCATION:** Central State Univ, Wilberforce, Ohio, BS, Biology, 1962; Ohio State Univ, Columbus, Ohio, 1972. **CAREER:** Anheuser-Busch Inc, Newark, NJ, Columbus, OH, asst plant mgr, mgr beer packaging and shipping, mgr packaging, mgr warehouse and shipping, asst mgr industrial relations, coord technical serv for operations dept, quality control laboratory supvr, Tampa, FL, beer packaging and shipping mgr, asst plant mgr, plant mgr, 1965-. **ORGANIZATIONS:** Bd mem, Greater Tampa Urban League, Pinellas County Urban League, Boy Scouts of Amer, Gulf Ridge Council, Hillsborough Community Coll Found; mem, Pebble Creek Civic Assn, Master Brewers Assn, Beer & Beverage Packaging Assn, Boys & Girls Clubs of Amer, Greater Tampa Chamber of Commerce; mentor, Hillsborough Community Coll, Minority Affairs. **HONORS/ACHIEVEMENTS:** Outstanding Participant, Greater Tampa Urban League, 1987, 1988; Leadership Award, Boy Scouts of Amer, Gulf Ridge Council, 1988; Support Award, Univ of S Florida Inst on Black Life, 1989. **MILITARY SERVICE:** Air Defense School; AUS, special weapons instructor, first lieutenant; special weapons detatchment commander. **BUSINESS ADDRESS:** Plant Mgr, Anheuser-Busch Inc, 3000 E Busch Blvd, PO Box 9245, Tampa, FL 33674-9245.

ABERCRUMBIE, PAUL ERIC
University administrator, faculty member. **PERSONAL:** Born Jun 14, 1948, Cleveland, OH; son of Margaret Louise Taylor-Nelson; married Claudia Marie Colvard-Abercrumbie, Jun 14, 1987; children: Paul Eric Abercrumbie. **EDUCATION:** Eastern Kentucky Univ, BA, 1970, MA, 1971; Univ of Cincinnati, PHD, 1987. **CAREER:** Princeton City School District, Advisory Specialist, 1971-72; Univ of Cincinnati, Resident counselor, 1972-73; Special Services Counselor, 1973-75; Dir, Minority Programs, 1975-present. **ORGANIZATIONS:** Member, Omega Psi Phi Fraternity Inc; Bd Member, Dr Martin Luther King Jr Coalition; Coach, Athletic Assn; Member, NAACP; Exec Bd Member, Dr Martin Luther King Jr Coalition 1980-; Head Basketball Coach, BON-PAD Athletic Assn, 1979-. **HONORS/ACHIEVEMENTS:** Omicron Delta Kappa Honor Soc, Univ of Cincinnati, 1974; Outstanding Young Men of Amer, US Jaycees, 1978, 1982; Dr Martin Luther King Jr Award of Excellence, Alpha Phi Alpha Fraternity Inc, 1980; Graduate Minority Fellows & Scholars, 1984-85; Community Leaders of the World, Amer Biographical Inst, 1985; Black Educator of the Year, US Peace Corps, 1989; Black Achiever, YMCA, 1989. **BUSINESS ADDRESS:** Office of Minority Programs & Services, Univ of Cincinnati, ML 92, Cincinnati, OH 45221.

ABERNATHY, JAMES R., II
Attorney. **PERSONAL:** Married Claudia Mitchell; children: Kevin, Christopher, Tracey. **EDUCATION:** Howard Univ, BA 1949, JD 1952; Univ of So CA, MPA 1975. **CAREER:** HEW, legal counsel on natl immun liab prog, legal consult black health providers task force on high blood pressure educ & control; NBA-NMA Health Law Comm, chmn; Black Congress on Health & Law; Amer Health Care Plan, atty & gen counsel. **ORGANIZATIONS:** Mem, St Bar of CA, Natl Bar Assn, Charles Houston Bar Assn, Natl Health Lawyers Assn, Natl Conf of Black Lawyers, San Fran Lawyers Club, CA Trial Lawyers Assn, NAACP, Natl Lawyers Guild, Southern Pov Law Ctr, Minority Public Admin, Alpha Phi Alpha Frat; seminars on Health Law 1979-83 Natl Bar Assn Convention; lecturer McGeorge Sch of Law at Univ of So CA; numerous publications including, "Legal Issues Confronting Health Maint Orgs", "Evolution Strikes Blood Banking & Hospitals", "Sickle Cell Anemia, A Legal Conspectus"; mem Southeast Comm Health Comp, Golden St Med Assoc.

ABERNATHY, RALPH DAVID
Clergyman, association executive. **PERSONAL:** Born Mar 11, 1926, Linden, AL; married Juanita Odessa Jones; children: Juandalynn Ralpheda, Donzaleigh Avis, Ralph David III, Kwame Lithuli. **EDUCATION:** Alabama State Univ, BS 1950, grad studies; Allen Univ, Hon LLD 1960; Southhampton Coll, Hon LLD 1969; Morehouse Coll, Hon DD 1971; AL State Univ, Hon LLD 1974. **CAREER:** W Hunter St Baptist Ch, pastor 1961-; Southern Christian Leadership Conf (succeeded late Dr Martin Luther King Jr), pres 1975-. **ORGANIZATIONS:** Together with Dr Martin Luther King Jr led Montgomery, AL, bus boycott 1955-56; founded Montgomery Improvement Assn, direct forerunner of SCLC; led Poor People's Campaign Resurrection City 1968; mem bd dirs, Martin Luther King, Jr, Ctr for Social Change; mem adv comm, Cong of Racial Equality; pres with hon, World Peace Council; chmn, Commn Racism & Apartheid; chmn, Southern Christian Leadership Found; mem, NAACP, Natl Urban League, Natl Coun Christians & Jews, YMCA, Georgia Voters League, Poor People's Union of Amer, Atlanta Baptist Ministers Conf, Natl Comm Black Churchmen, Natl Black Pol Assembly, Anti-Defamation League, Amer Legion, Natl Coun Christians, Baptist World Alliance, Amer Baptist Conv, World Coun of Churches, Amer Indian Movement, Alpha Kappa Mu, Alpha Kappa Delta, Kappa Alpha Psi, Mason, Elks, World Peace Coun, Conf World Religions; extensive travel, both nationally and abroad, as speaker, lecturer, pastor and civil rights leader. **HONORS/ACHIEVEMENTS:** Addressed UN 1971; first of four Most Outstanding Alumni, Alabama State Univ 1974. **BUSINESS ADDRESS:** Pastor, West Hunter St Baptist Ch, 1040 Gordon St SW, Atlanta, GA 30310.

ABERNATHY, RONALD LEE
Educator. **PERSONAL:** Born Dec 13, 1950, Louisville, KY. **EDUCATION:** Morehead State Univ, BA Soc 1972; LA State Univ, MA Admin 1979. **CAREER:** Shawnee HS Louisiana KY, head basketball coach 1972-76; LSU Baton Rouge, asst basketball coach 1976-83, assoc head coach 1983-. **ORGANIZATIONS:** Pres S&R Oilfield Serv Co 1981-; mem NABC 1976-; dir, lead singer Gospel Chorus Gr Salem Baptist Church 1954-76; lead singer Young Adult Choir Shiloh Baptist Church 1976-; bd mem Morehead Rec Commiss 1971-72; big brother prog Family Court Baton Rouge LA 1982; head basketball coach Belgium All-Star Team NamurBelgium 1981; exec dir LA Assoc of Basketball Coaches All-Star Game 1981; asst basketball coach Natl Assoc of Basketball Coaches All-Star Game 1982; memLA Pageant Judges & Entertainers Assoc 1983-. **HONORS/ACHIEVEMENTS:** Teacher of the Year Shawnee HS Louisville KY 1976; Louisville Urban League HS Coach of the Year 1976; Runner-up State of KY HS Coach of the Year 1976; Houston Post Top Ten Asst Coaches in Amer 1980; Who's Who Among Black Amers 1981; Final Four Basketball Team Philadelphia, PA coach 1981; Outstanding Young Menof Amer 1982; elected to Blue Book of Outstanding Blacks in LA 1982; host for Sickle Cell Anemia Telethon 1982; Selected as major host for Sickle Cell Anemia Telethon 1983, major campaign speaker for United Way 1983, one of LA's 10 Best Dressed Men 1983, one of LA's Most Eligible Bachelors 1983, Baton Rouge's Most Fashionable Man 1983; Final Four Basketball Team Dallas, TX coach 1986; 1st black appt to full time coaching position LSU; Sporting Magazine Recruiter of the Year in College Basketball. **BUSINESS ADDRESS:** Assoc Head Basketball Coach, Louisana State Univeristy, LSU Basketball Office, Baton Rouge, LA 70893.

ABNEY, ROBERT
Coordinator. **PERSONAL:** Born Jul 02, 1949, Washington, DC; married Stephanie Early; children: Keisha, Kara. **EDUCATION:** DC Teachers Coll, BS Ed Psychologyt 1972. **CAREER:** First Georgetown Adv DC, vice pres 1981-82; Windstar, Ltd DC, pres 1981-; Washington DC, advertising consultant 1982-; Creative Connection DC, dirmkts adver 1982-83; DC Public Schools, coord home study program 1987-. **ORGANIZATIONS:** Clring house mgr D C Public Lib Comm Info Serv DC 1976-81; chrmn SNEA Human Rel Coun Natl Ed Assn DC 1970-71, consltnt US Dept Comm DC PubSchl Systm 1983-; pres Amidon Ele PTA 1984-86; mem Internation Platform Assn, Internation Who's Who of Intellectuals, Natl Leadersship Conf The Honor Book; bd of dirs Southwest Neighborhood Assembly. **HONORS/ACHIEVEMENTS:** Special Award Jaycee's Vlntr Citation 1969, Headstart Vlntr Citation 1977-84, DC Public Schl 1976-84; award for Artistic Achvmnt 1978. **HOME ADDRESS:** 1001 3rd St SW Apt 615, Washington, DC 20024.

ABRAHAM, GUY EMMANUEL
Physician. **PERSONAL:** Born Apr 12, 1936, Port-au-Prince, Haiti;divorced. **EDUCATION:** Mont St Louis Coll, BA 1955; Montreal Univ, MD 1961; Hotel Dieu Montreal CAN, intern 1960-61. **CAREER:** Sinai Hosp Baltimore, asst resident ob/gyn 1961-62; Jackson Memorial Hosp Miami, resident physician 1962-64; Decaoness Hosp Buffalo, chief resident physician 1964-65; Worcester Found Exptl Biology Shrewsbury, fellow steroid training prog 1965-67; Worcester State Hosp, staff physician 1966-69, planned parenthood attending physician 1968-69; Harbor Genl Hosp, rsch fellow endocrinology rsch unit 1969-71, chief & assoc prof div reproductive biology dept obstetrics & gynecology 1971-. **ORGANIZATIONS:** Consult WHO Contraceptive Rev Br NIH 1972. **BUSINESS ADDRESS:** Harbor General Hosp, 1000 W Carson St, Torrance, CA 90509.

ABRAHAM, SINCLAIR REGINALD
Educator. **PERSONAL:** Born Jun 06, 1951, Orangeburg, SC; son of Theodore Abraham, Sr and Willie Lee Martin Abraham; married Bessie Bowman; children: Sinclair Reginald Jr, Stephanie Lynette. **EDUCATION:** South Carolina State Coll, BS 1973, MS Ed 1977. **CAREER:** Bowman School District, asst principal/coach. **ORGANIZATIONS:** Mem SC Assoc of School Administrators, SC Assoc of Secondary Sch Principals; bd of dirs SC Coaches Assoc of Woman Sport, SC Basketball Assoc, SC Athletic Coaches Assoc, Natl Teachers Educ Assoc; mem Omega Psi Phi Fraternity; trustee bd Hickory Grove Baptist Church. **HONORS/ACHIEVEMENTS:** Four-time State Coach of the Year for the South Carolina Basketball Assn. **HOME ADDRESS:** 1396 Essex Dr, Orangeburg, SC 29115. **BUSINESS ADDRESS:** Asst Principal & Athletic Dir/Coach, Orangeburg School District #2, PO Box 36, Bowman, SC 29115.

ABRAHAMS, ANDREW WORDSWORTH
Physician. **PERSONAL:** Born Oct 08, 1936, Kingston, Jamaica. **EDUCATION:** Columbia Univ, BS 1961; NY Med Coll, MD 1966, resident 1972. **CAREER:** Kings Co Hospital, physician 1973-. **ORGANIZATIONS:** Fndr dir Bedford Stuyvesant Alcoholism Treatment

Ctr 1972; med dir Bur of Alcoholism New York City 1970-72; med consult Comm Health Facilities; bd mem NY State Assn of Cncl on Alcoholism Inc 1975; mem NY State Senate Legislative Adv Comm 1976 New York City affiliate Natl Cncl on Alcoholism 1972; lectr consult Natl Cncl on Alcoholism 1972. **HONORS/ACHIEVEMENTS:** Cert of Appreciation Bedford Alcoholism Treatment Ctr NY State Assn of Alcoholism Cncl; New York City AFL-CIO. **BUSINESS ADDRESS:** Kings Co Hosp, 1121 Bedford Ave, Brooklyn, NY 11216.

ABRAM, JAMES B.
Educator. **PERSONAL:** Born Dec 05, 1937, Tulsa, OK; married Darlene Sheppard; children: James B III, Carmelita. **EDUCATION:** Langston Univ, BS 1959; OK State Univ, MS 1963, PhD 1968. **CAREER:** Ardmore Douglass HS, sci tchr 1959-62; Inst of Biology, sci tchr 1963-66; MD State Coll, asst prof of biology 1966-68, assoc prof of biology 1968-70; Hampton Inst, prof of biology. **ORGANIZATIONS:** Mem Amer Soc of Parasitologists, Helminthological Soc of Washington, AIBS, Sigma Xi, Kappa Delta Pi, Alpha Kappa Mu, Beta Kappa Chi; editor-in-chief BKX Bulletin; Phi Sigma; Ancient & Beneficient Order of Red Red Rose; Eastern Province Polemarch Kappa Alpha Psi; bd deacons First Bapt Ch; mem Amer Men of Sci. **HONORS/ACHIEVEMENTS:** Kappa Man of Yr OK City Alumni Chap 1968; Eastern Province of Kappa Alpha Psi Achievement Awd 1970 1974; Outstanding Tchr of Yr Univ of MD Eastern Shore1969; Outstanding Educators of Amer 1970; Danforth Assoc 1973.

ABRAMS, ROSLYN MARIA
Reporter, host. **PERSONAL:** Born Sep 07, 1948, Lansing, MI. **EDUCATION:** Western MI U, BA 1970; Univ of MI, MA 1971. **CAREER:** KRON-TV; WXIA-TV, rprtr talk show host 1977; WSB Radio, rprtr anchor 1975-77. **ORGANIZATIONS:** Vp Atlanta Press Club; Am Wmn in Radio & TV; chrtr mem Atlanta Assn of Blk Jour. **HONORS/ACHIEVEMENTS:** Delta Sigma Theta Sor flwshp Univ MI Grad Sch 1970-71. **BUSINESS ADDRESS:** KRON TV, 1001 Van Ness Ave, San Francisco, CA 94109.

ABRAMSON, FREDERICK BRUCE
Attorney. **PERSONAL:** Born Feb 11, 1935, New York, NY; son of Fred Abramson and Mary Ella Abramson. **EDUCATION:** Yale Univ, BA 1956; Univ of Chicago Law School, JD 1959. **CAREER:** US Dept of Justice, attorney 1961-66; American Telephone and Telegraph Co Regional Office, attorney 1966-67; US Equal Employment Opportunity Commn, special asst to the chmn 1967-69; Arnold & Porter, associate 1969-73; Rollinson & Schaumberg, partner 1973-77; Sachs Greenebaum & Tayler, partner 1977-. **ORGANIZATIONS:** Court admissions US Supreme Court, US Courts of Appeals for the Second Third Fourth Fifth Sixth Seventh Eighth Ninth Tenth and District of Columbia Circuits, US Dist Courts for the Dist of Columbia and Dist of MD; mem bd dirs Natl Women's Law Center 1980-89; mem bd dirs Washington Area Lawyers' for the Arts 1982-87; mem Washington Council of Lawyers; mem Washington, American, Natl Bar Assocs; mem Natl Conference of Bar Presidents; chmn, bd of governors, Dist of Columbia School of Law 1987-; mem, bd of trustees, Dist of Clumbia Public Defender Serv 1987-. **BUSINESS ADDRESS:** Partner, Sachs, Greenebaum & Tayler, 1140 Connecticut Ave NW, Ste 900, Washington, DC 20036-4301.

ABSTON, NATHANIEL, JR.
Clinical psychologist. **PERSONAL:** Born Jul 18, 1952, Mobile, AL; married Elverna McCants; children: Jamila Aziza, Khalid Amir. **EDUCATION:** Univ of So AL, BA 1975, MS 1978; Univ of So MS, PhD 1984. **CAREER:** Mobile Youth Court, student social worker, 1971-74; Mobile Mental Health Center, counselor 1974-76; Univ of So AL, instructor/prof 1978-; VA Medical Ctr, staff clinical psychologist 1984-. **ORGANIZATIONS:** Officer/mem Alpha Phi Alpha Frat 1974-; mem Amer 1977-, AL 1978-, MS 1981- Psychological Assocs; mem Urban League of Mobile 1984-. **HONORS/ACHIEVEMENTS:** Mem Psi Chi Honorary Psychology Club Univ So AL Chap 1975-; USA Rsch Grant Awd Univ of So AL 1978-79; several scientific publications, presentation 1980-. **BUSINESS ADDRESS:** Staff Psychologist, VA Medical Center, Psych Serv (116B), Gulfport, MS 39501.

ACKER, DANIEL R.
Chemist. **PERSONAL:** Born Feb 28, 1910, Radford, VA; married Louise Broome; children: Carolyn, Daniel Jr, Nannette. **EDUCATION:** WV State Coll, BS; Univ of MI, MA 1942. **CAREER:** Williamson, teacher chemistry & physics 1932-42; Sandusky, analytical rsch chemist, group suprv 1942-44; Union Carbide Corp, rsch chemist, group leader 1944-. **ORGANIZATIONS:** Comm mem Erie Co Affirmative Action 1974, Alpha Kappa Boule Sigma Pi Phi; chmn bd, trustees New Covenant United Church Christ; pres NAACP, Housing OpptyMADE Equal; mem Natl Council YMCA, United Fund Buffalo; pres Minority Faculty & Staff Assoc SUNY Buffalo 1984. **HONORS/ACHIEVEMENTS:** Amer Chem Soc Medgar Evers Civil Rights Awd 1975; Buffalo Urban League Evans-Young Awd for Commitment to Human Dignity & Equal Oppty 1976; Bus & Professional Womens Org Awd for Comm Serv 1976; apptd admin of student affairs Cora P Maloney Coll, State Univ of NY Buffalo; YMCA Gold Key Awd 1972; City Buffalo Good Neighbor Awd; Kappa Alpha Psi No Provicne Achievement Awd; Comm Serv Awd Minority Student Org 1974; WV State Coll Alumnus Awd; Natl Conf of Christians & Jews Brotherhood Awd 1981; Inducted into Alpha Kappa Alpha Sor Black Hall of Fame 1983; So Christian Leadership Conf Comm Awd 1984; Amer Affirm Action Assoc Comm Serv Awd 1984. **BUSINESS ADDRESS:** Research Chemist, Group Leader, Union Carbide Corp, Mass Spectroscopy Lab, 531 E Ferry St, Buffalo, NY 14214.

ACKERMAN, PATRICIA A.
Educator. **PERSONAL:** Born Feb 06, 1944, Cleveland, OH; daughter of Amos A Ackerman and Ruth Glover Ackerman; divorced. **EDUCATION:** Ohio Univ, Athens, OH, BA, Educ, 1966; Cleveland State Univ, OH, MEd, Admin, 1974; Kent State Univ, OH, PhD, Admin, 1983. **CAREER:** Cleveland Bd of Educ, OH, teacher, 1966-72; Beachwood Bd of Educ, OH, teacher, 1972-74; Lima City Schools, OH, dean of girls, 1974-75; Cleveland Heights-Univ Heights Bd of Educ, OH, coord, 1975, high school asst principal, 1975-87, principal Taylor Acad, 1987-. **ORGANIZATIONS:** Pres, Natl Alliance of Black School Educ, 1987-89; mem, Leadership Cleveland, 1988-89. **HONORS/ACHIEVEMENTS:** George A Bowman Fellowship, Kent State Univ, 1981; Commendation, Intl Assn of Business Communicators, 1982; African-Amer Educ of the Year, African Amer Museum, Cleveland, OH, 1988; sr editor, Black Role Model series, Beckham House Publishers, 1989.

ACKORD, MARIE M.
Educator. **PERSONAL:** Born Jan 05, 1939, Bronwood, GA; daughter of Clarence Mallory

and Lula Perry Mallory; married Rondal A Ackord, Sep 14, 1983; children: Monique Patrice. **EDUCATION:** Bethune-Cookman Coll, BS Math 1960; Nova University, Fort Lauderdale FL, MS, 1982. **CAREER:** North Ft Myers High School, Math teacher 1973; Dunbar Middle School, head Math Dept & teacher 1970-73; N Ft Myers High School, Math teacher 1966-70; Dunbar High School, Math teacher 1964-66; Carver High School, Naples FL, spon varsity cheerleader 1976-77; Math Dept, chairperson; Vol Prgram, adv council retired Sr; Ft Myers Comm Relations Commin, commr; School Bd of Lee Co, North Fort Myers Fl, math teacher, 1983-, humna relations specialist, 1980-83. **ORGANIZATIONS:** Mem School Comm Adv Com; NCTM Fl Math Teachers; Lee Co Teachers of Math Delta Sigma Theta Inc; sec Fort Myers Alumnae Chapter Delta Sigma Theta 1975-77; past charter pres vice pres Ft Myers Alumnae Chapter Delta Sigma Theta; Oratorical Chmn Dunbar Heights Opti-mrs Club; advisory bd Dunbar Day Care; com Woman Lee Co De M N High Teacher of Month 1976; Deputy Elections Clerk, Lee County, 1987-. **HONORS/ACHIEVEMENTS:** Nom Lee Co Woman of the Yr 1976-77; Elected Beta Kappa Chi 1960. **HOME ADDRESS:** 1921 SE 8th Street, Cape Coral, FL 33990.

ACKRIDGE, FLORENCE GATEWARD
Director. **PERSONAL:** Born Jun 14, 1939, Philadelphia, PA; married John C Ackridge; children: Anthony, Antoinette, Angelo. **EDUCATION:** Temple Univ, BSW 1977. **CAREER:** Norris Brown & Hall, legal sec 1965-68; Rentex Systems, ofc asst 1968-69; Philadelphia Urban Coalition, sec 1969-71; Rebound Med Group, clerical supr 1971-73; YMCA Youth Leadership Inst, prog coord 1973-74; YMCA. **ORGANIZATIONS:** Vol consult Prisoners Rights Cncl; social worker Walton Village; mem Natl Concl for Black Child Develop; Black Social Workers Alliance; W Oak Lane Comm Group; Black & Non-White YMCA; staff Model Legisl Plan Com Model Judicial Plan Com; vol Christian St YMCA Mem Drive. **HONORS/ACHIEVEMENTS:** Recog Vol Serv to Comm Temple Univ; Trophy Outstanding Serv to Youth in Struggle for Peace. **BUSINESS ADDRESS:** YMCA, 1421 Arch St, Philadelphia, PA 19102.

ACON, JUNE KAY
Publicist, public relations specialist, producer. **PERSONAL:** Born Apr 09, 1948, Philadelphia, PA; children: Rory Edward. **EDUCATION:** San Diego State Univ, MPA 1971; Univ of Southern CA, Broadcast Mgmt 1980; Los Angeles City Coll, TV Production/Media Law 1982. **CAREER:** Caltrans State of CA, dir personnel & public information 1971-75; San Diego City Coll, communication instructor/counselor 1975-80; Human Behavior Inst, dir public relations/media relations 1980-85; June Kay Productions Inc, production coord 1985-87. **ORGANIZATIONS:** Mem Women in Communications, Black Women Network, Univ Women 1977-87; exec bd mem Hollywood/Beverly Hills NAACP 1982-87; mem Acad of TV Arts & Sciences, Black Journalists Assn, Black Public Relations Soc; governing bd County Human Relations Commn; mem City's Advisory Bd on Women, Council on Black Amer Affairs, Natl Academic Advisory Assn, New Coalition for Economic and Social Change, United Way Advisory Bd; productions film for tv, art and community serv; exec bd mem Help Public Serv Foundation; drug and aids prevention program for youths; Sickle Cell Anemia Radio-a-Thon 1986-87; producer host TV talk show "June Acon Show". **HONORS/ACHIEVEMENTS:** Service Award United Negro Coll Fund Telethon 1980-85; Media Relations Jesse Jackson Presidential Campaign 1984; Image Award Outstanding Media Relations & Publicity 1984; Media Award 1984 Olympics; Role Model Women of the Year 1985; Help Public Serv Foundation Award Youth "No Dope" film 1987; PBWA Rose Awards Professional Black Women's Alliance 1989; Certificate of Merit for Distinguished Service to the Community 1989. **BUSINESS ADDRESS:** Producer/Dir Public Relations, June Kay Productions Inc, 8306 Wilshire Blvd Ste 697, Beverly Hills, CA 90211.

ACREY, AUTRY
Educational administrator. **PERSONAL:** Born Mar 20, 1948, Frederick, OK. **EDUCATION:** Jarvis Christian Coll, BSEd 1970; TX Christian Univ, MA 1972; North TX State Univ. **CAREER:** Jarvis Christian College, instructor of history 1973-76, asst dean 1976-79, asst prof 1976-; assoc dean 1981-. **ORGANIZATIONS:** Dir Consortium on Rsch Training 1974-76; mem/sec Mu Rho Lambda chapter of Alpha Phi Alpha 1978; dir East TX Rsch Council 1983-84; dir Cooperative Educ 1981-. **HONORS/ACHIEVEMENTS:** Outstanding teacher Jarvis Christian College 1975; outstanding member Mu Rho Lambda of Alpha Phi Alpha 1979; panel leader 1983, presenter 1983 Black History Celebration. **HOME ADDRESS:** PO Box 351, Hawkins, TX 75765. **BUSINESS ADDRESS:** Associate Dean of Academic Affairs, Jarvis Christian College, Drawer G, PO Box 351, Hawkins, TX 75765.

ADAIR, ALVIS V.
Former college president, educator. **PERSONAL:** Born Jul 19, 1940, Hare Valley, VA; married Deloris; children: Almaz, Poro. **EDUCATION:** VA State Coll, BS 1962, MS 1964; Univ of MI, PhD 1971; Monrovia Coll Liberia W Africa, LLD 1973. **CAREER:** Peace Corps, tchr & comm developer 1965-68; Allen Univ, assessor & dir spl experimental progs 1968-69, asst prof 1971, assoc prof 1972, chmn of social rsch 1973, pres 1977-79; Howard Univ, full prof & asst to dean for rsch develop. **ORGANIZATIONS:** Past bd mem Social Work Abstracts; Hillcrest Children Ctr; DC Commn on Aging; State Planning Comm for White House Conf on Families & Aging 1980-81; co-chairperson Assn of Black Psychologists; trustee of St Paul AME Ch; Assn of Univ Prof, Social Workers, Black Social Workers, Psychologists. **HONORS/ACHIEVEMENTS:** Outstanding Educator of Amer 1974; Outstanding Young Men of Amer 1974; Outstanding Univ Prof 1972 1974; Serv Awd Fed City Coll Chap Black Social Workers 1974; Honorary Paramount Chief of Loma Kpelle Chieftain of W Africa 1968; Hon mem Crossroads Africa 1966; Expert Testimonies House Select Comm on Aging & Fed Trade Commn on TV 1978-80. **BUSINESS ADDRESS:** Full Prof Asst Dean Rsch Devel, HowardUniv, Sch of Social Work, Washington, DC 20059.

ADAIR, ANDREW A.
Chief executive officer, attorney. **PERSONAL:** Born Aug 05, 1933, Chicago, IL; children: Andrew Jr, Suzanne. **EDUCATION:** Morehouse Coll, BS 1965; Univ Toledo Coll of Law, JD 1969. **CAREER:** Natl Urban League, assoc dir field oper 1971-72, assoc dir progs 1973-74, dir Mauy Devel Ctr 1975-79, acting gen cnsel 1978-79; dir cntrl region 1979-. **ORGANIZATIONS:** Legal counsel Ctr for Students Rights Dayton 1969-70; mem IN Bar Assn 1971; mem Fed Bar US Dist Ct 1971; mem Natl Bar Assn 1971; sec natl cncl exec dir Natl Urban League 1971-72; mem Amer Bar Assn 1976; natl advisor & cnsel Natl Cncl of Urban League Guilds 1972-79; bd mem Human Rights Commn Dayton 1969-71; bd mem ACLU Dayton Chap 1969-71; bd mem Council of Econ Educ NY 1975-78. **MILITARY SERVICE:** AUS

corpl 1953-55; Korean Serv Medal. **BUSINESS ADDRESS:** Director, Central Region, Natl Urban League, 36 S Wabash Ave &, Chicago, IL 60603.

ADAIR, CHARLES, JR.
Mayor & educator. **PERSONAL:** Born Apr 01, 1950, Gadsden, AL. **EDUCATION:** Alabama A&M Univ, BS 1977; Univ of Alabama, MA 1980. **CAREER:** Woolco/Woolworth, Birmingham, AL; division mgr 1978; Attalla City School System, teacher 1979-; Town of Ridgeville, mayor. **ORGANIZATIONS:** Councilman Town of Ridgeville, AL 1978-82; member Kappa Alpha Psi Fraternity, Inc 1980-; member board of dir East AL Regional Commission 1982-; member board of dir Etowah County Chapter SCLC 1983-; member board of dir Etowah County Com Serv Assn 1983. **HONORS/ACHIEVEMENTS:** Voice of Democracy Freedom's Foundation Falley Forge 1973. **MILITARY SERVICE:** AUS Specialist Five 1972-75. **HOME ADDRESS:** Route 1 Box 470, Ridgeville, AL 35954. **BUSINESS ADDRESS:** Mayor, Town of Ridgeville, Rt 1 Box 475, Ridgeville Town Hall, Ridgeville, AL 35954.

ADAIR, JAMES E.
Educator. **PERSONAL:** Married Marjorie P Spellen; children: Andrea Denice, Tonja Michelle. **EDUCATION:** Fort Valley State Coll, BS. **CAREER:** Adair's Art Gallery Atlanta, dir 1963-64; Barber-Scotia Coll Concord, art instr 1964-66; Parks Jr HS Atlanta, art instr 1967-69; Morris Brown Coll Atlanta, art lectr 1970-. **HONORS/ACHIEVEMENTS:** Executed murals, Ft Valley State Coll 1962, GA Tchrs Educ Assn Bldg Atlanta 1957; Annual Negro Exhibition 1st Place Awd 1969; presented one man show at Miles Coll Birmingham 1962; Fine Arts Gallery Atlanta 1964 1968. **MILITARY SERVICE:** USNR. **BUSINESS ADDRESS:** Art Lecturer, Morris Brown College, Atlanta, GA 30314.

ADAIR, KENNETH
Editor, legislator. **PERSONAL:** Born Jul 21, 1904, Hot Springs, AR; married Helen Lee Roach. **EDUCATION:** LaSalle Extension Univ Chicago, attended 1936-37. **CAREER:** Pythian Hotel & Bath House, hotel mgr 1965-70; Hot Springs AR, alderman 1972-; The AR Citizen, editor-publisher 1954-. **ORGANIZATIONS:** Mem NAACP 1968-; mem ACORN 5 yrs; mem îWorkshop for Informal Dem 5 yrs; mem Roanoke Bapt Ch 50 yrs; mem Hot Springs C of C 1977. **HONORS/ACHIEVEMENTS:** In Support of the Aging Sr Companion 1975; Valiant Awd Gamma Phi Delta 1976; Untiring Serv to comm Bus & Progressive Club 1977; Awd for Significant Serv Alpha Chi Chap Gamma Phi Delta. **BUSINESS ADDRESS:** Editor & Publisher, The AR Citizen, 515 Pleasant, Hot Springs, AR 71901.

ADAIR, ROBERT A.
Physician. **PERSONAL:** Born Jun 27, 1943, New York, NY; married Ella; children: Kai, Robert A. **EDUCATION:** Univ of PA, BA 1965; Howard Univ Med Sch, MD 1969; Met Hosp, med intern 1970; Dept of Hlth NYC, pub hlth rsdcy 1972; Columbia U, MPH 1972. **CAREER:** Sydenham Hosp NYC, dir of ambul serv 1972-; New York City Dept of Correc, physic 1971; New York City Dept of Hlth, act dist hlth offcr for Cent Harlem 1970-71; WNBC-TV, med consult co-prod 4 TV films 1971-72; Pub Hlth Nurses of New Pub Hlth Sch syst, spl consult & instr 1971-72; E Harlem Alcoh Anony Assn,spl consult 1970; Narcot Addict & Ven Dis Mt Morr Presb Ch, spl consult 1970-72; Morrisania Yth Ctr & box tm, consult physic 1970-72; Bd Educ Harlem Pub Sch, consult 1970-71; Staten Is Comm Coll, adj prof 1970-; Manhattanville Coll, spl hl. **ORGANIZATIONS:** Tght spl hlth course on stud hlth prob Manhattanville Coll 1972; fell Am Pub Hlth Assn 1969; mem NY Co Med Soc; NY State Med Soc; NY StateMed Soc; Nat Med Assn; Blck Am Med & Dent Assn of Stud; Blck Cauc of Hlth Wkrs; Am Med Assn; med adv bd Found for Rsrch & Educ in SickCell Dis; sec adv counc of Pres Med Bd New York City Hlth & Hosp Corp; bd pres med bd Sydenham Hosp; bd dir Physic For Inc; chmn Hlth Com 10 Blck Men; consult Hlth Dept Englewood NY; admis com Bio-Med Prog City Coll of NY 1973-; mem NAACP; Harlem Alli of May Orgn Task Force; Duke Elling Jazz Soc; elder Mt Morris Unit Presb Ch; sub-area hlth plan body of mod cit; fin com Mt Morris Fed Cred Un; bd trust Mary Holmes Coll; bd trust Harl Interf Couns Svc; mem 1st Aid Com Red Cross Assn; adv counc NY Urban League Manhat; bd dir Sherm Terr Corp. **HONORS/ACHIEVEMENTS:** Woodrow Wilson Acad Scholar 1961-65; diplo Nat Med Bd 1970; bd Elig Am Acad of Pub Hlth & Prevent Med 1972; chmn Prevent Med Sect of 1973 Nat Med Conv 1973; auth of sev pub; hon disc 1974. **BUSINESS ADDRESS:** 41 W 96th St, New York, NY 10025.

ADAMO, DAVID TUESDAY
Educator. **PERSONAL:** Born Jan 05, 1949, Irunda-Isanlu, Nigeria;children: Oluwayomi Bamidele. **EDUCATION:** ECWA Tehol Seminary Nigeria, BTh 1977; Southern Methodist Univ Dallas, MTh 1980; Univ of the State of NY, BS 1982; Indiana Christian Univ, RelD 1983; Baylor Univ, PhD 1986. **CAREER:** Titcome Coll Nigeria, instructor 1977-78; Paul Quinn Coll Waco TX, prof 1983-85; Univ of Illorin, prof of religion. **ORGANIZATIONS:** Mem Amer Acad of Religion 1987, Amer Schools of Oriental Rsch 1987, Nigeria Assoc for Biblical Studies 1987, Soc of Biblical Literature 1987. **HONORS/ACHIEVEMENTS:** Publications "The Problem of Translating the Hebrew Old Testament Book Titles into Yoruba Language of Nigeria," The Bible Translator 1984; "Black American Heritage," Texian Press 1985; "The Black Prophet in the Old Testament," Journal of Arabic and Religion 1987.

ADAMS, AFESA M.
Educator. **PERSONAL:** Born Feb 20, 1936, Greenwood, MS; daughter of Eddie Adams and Annie Miller Adams; married Allan Nathaniel, Jul 19, 1975; children: Suzanne Bell-Brown, Steven A Bell, David C Bell. **EDUCATION:** Weber State Coll, BS 1969; Univ of Utah, MS 1973, PhD 1975. **CAREER:** Univ of FL, asst prof of behavioral studies 1974-79, acting chair behavioral studies 1976-78, assoc prof of psychology 1976-80; Univ of Utah, dept of family & consumer studies chairperson 1980-83, assoc vice pres of acad affairs 1984-, assoc prof family & consumer studies, adjunct assoc prof dept of psych. **ORGANIZATIONS:** American Psychological Assoc, Division 8, 9, 27; Nat'l Council on Family Relations; Utah Council on Family Relations; Nat'l Council of Negro Women, Inc; Southeastern Psychological Assoc; Amer Psychological Assoc; Gainesville Women's Health Center, board of directors; State of UT Divison of Children, Youth & Families Day Care, advisory board 1980-83; Governor's Committee for Exec Reorganization 1983-85; Governor's Task Force, to study financial barriers to health care 1983-84, employer sponsored childcare 1984; NAACP education comm 1983; Western States Psych Services, board of dirctors; KUTV Minority Advisory Board 1984-86; United Way, allocation board 1985-86; several publications and papers; NAACP life mem. **HONORS/ACHIEVEMENTS:** Beehive Lodge of the Elks, community service award 1986; Phi Kappa Phi; United Way of the Great Salt Lake Area, award of recognition for community service 1986; Hall of Fame, Granite High School, 1987-88; Civil Rights Worker of the Year, NAACP SL Branch, 1988; Educational Equity Unit, recognition for appearing in and dedication to the film, "Building on a Legacy: Contemporary Pioneering Women," 1988. **BUSINESS ADDRESS:** Assoc VP/Academic Affairs, Univ of Utah, 205 Park Bldg, Salt Lake City, UT 84112.

ADAMS, ALBERT W., JR.
Mortgage company human resources manager. **PERSONAL:** Born Nov 22, 1948, Detroit, MI; son of Albert W Adams, Sr and Goldie I Davis Adams; married Linda; children: Nichole Leahna, Albert III, Melanie Rachel, Kimberly Monet. **EDUCATION:** Harris Tchr Coll St Louis, BA 1970; Harris Tchr Coll, post grad; So IL Univ, MBA 1974. **CAREER:** City of St Louis, recreation supr 1968-70; St Louis Pub Sch, tchr 1970-71; Magdala Found, counselor 1971-77; Seven-Up Co, personnel asst 1971-74, EEO adminstr 1974-77, mgr employment 1977-79, mgr affirmative action 1979-80, mgr indus relations 1981-83, mgr personnel progs & serv 1983-85, manager personnel operations 1985-89; Citicorp Mortgage Inc Sales Division, asst vice pres human resources 1989-. **ORGANIZATIONS:** Corp chmn United Negro Coll Fund 1972; nominated to US Naval Acad 1965; mem ASPA 1971-; St Louis Indus Relations Assn 1971-; trustee San Luis Hills subd 1975-78; comm mem at large St Louis Univ Affirmative Action Comm 1975-77; Mo Advsy Comm for Vocational Placement 1980-83; St Louis EEO Group charter mem 1974-; mem Kappa Alpha Psi; Antioch Baptist Church, St Louis MO; commissioner, St Louis Civil Rights Enforcement Agency, 1988-; mem board of directors, United Way of St Louis, 1989-; mem board of directors, Vanderschmidt School, 1989-. **HONORS/ACHIEVEMENTS:** Recognition for raising funds for United Negro Coll Fund; Jr Achievement Scholarship 1966. **HOME ADDRESS:** 2331 Albion Pl, St Louis, MO 63104.

ADAMS, ALGER LEROY
Editor. **PERSONAL:** Born Aug 01, 1910, Omaha, NE; married Jessie Wells; children: Patricia. **EDUCATION:** Hobart Coll, Geneva, NY, BA (magna cum laude) 1932; NY Sch of Social Work, Columbia U, 1933; Gen Theological Sem NYC, STB 1937; Teachers Coll, Columbia Uni v, MA 1968; Columbia Grad School of Journalism, 1969. **CAREER:** Teamsters Local 445 Dispatch, managing editor, 1960-75; NY Episcopal Diocesan Bulletin, managing editor 1947-62; Ebony, Johnson Publications, Chicago, assoc editor 1968; CB Powell Found NYC, consultant & advisor 1983-; Westchester County Press, editor & publisher emeritus 1950-87. **ORGANIZATIONS:** Bd of dir, Travelers Aid Soc 1975-83, Intl Soc Serv 1980-83; mem Natl Newspaper Publishers Assn, 1950-, Phi Beta Kappa 1932, Kappa Delta Pi 1968 , Natl NAACP 1958, Soc of Professional Journalists, 1983-, Natl Newspaper Publishers Assn, 1950-. **HONORS/ACHIEVEMENTS:** Special recognition, New Rochelle NAACP Award 1980; Key West, FL "Honorary Conk Award" 1982; Honorary Doctorate of Divinity, Hobart Coll Geneva, NY 1983. **HOME ADDRESS:** 61 Pinecrest Dr, Hastings-on-Hudson, NY 10706. **BUSINESS ADDRESS:** Editor & Publisher Emeritus, Westchester County Press, PO Box 173, Hastings-on-Hudson, NY 10706.

ADAMS, ALICE OMEGA
Physician. **PERSONAL:** Born Apr 28, 1951, Washington, DC; children: Sharon, Leslie Wilbanks. **EDUCATION:** Univ of the District of Columbia, BS 1974; Howard Univ Grad Sch, PhD 1979; Howard Univ Coll of Medicine, MD 1984. **CAREER:** Univ of District of Columbia, teaching asst 1972-74; Childrens Hosp Natl Medical Ctr, rsch assoc 1975-77; Howard Univ, grad teaching asst 1976-79, medical student tutor 1978-79; Children's Hospital, medical tech 1977-81; Univ of DC, asst prof 1979-81; Howard Univ, resident physician internal medicine 1984-85, neurology 1985-. **ORGANIZATIONS:** Asst prof & course coord Special Academic Programs Univ of DC. **HONORS/ACHIEVEMENTS:** Outstanding Achievement DC Medical Chirolurgical Soc 1983; Outstanding Achievement Howard Univ Dept of Internal medicine 1984; Outstanding Achievement Alpha Omega Alpha Honor Medical Soc 1984; Outstanding Young Women of Amer 1985. **BUSINESS ADDRESS:** Resident Physician, Howard University Hospital, 2041 Georgia Ave NWCt, Washington, DC 20906.

ADAMS, ANNE CURRIN
Educator. **PERSONAL:** Born Jun 28, 1942, Hackensack, NJ; married Thomas E Adams; children: Tracey Anne. **EDUCATION:** Keuka Coll NY, BA 1964; Rutgers Univ Grad Sch of Social Work, MSW 1970; Rutgers Univ, Doctoral studies. **CAREER:** YWCA, prog dir youth & teen-agers 1964-66; NJ Bureau of Children's Serv, caseworker/activities dir 1966-70; Newark NJ Bd of Educ, sch social worker 1970-72; Newark Coll of Engrg, adminstr asst to EOP dir 1971-72; Rutgers Grad Sch of Social Work, asst prof 1972-. **ORGANIZATIONS:** Adminstrative bd chairperson Christ Ch United Meth 1980-81; alumnae trustee Keuka Coll NY 1979-82; commr Paterson Rent Leveling Bd 1974-75; Book Revoiew Intl Social Welfare Journal 1980. **HONORS/ACHIEVEMENTS:** Article "Field Training for Social Work Students in Maternal & Child Health" 1978; Outstanding Student Awd Rutgers GSSW 1969; Who's Who Amer Univs & Colls Keuka Coll 1964. **BUSINESS ADDRESS:** Assistant Professor, RutgersUniv, George St, Grad Sch of Social Work, New Brunswick, NJ 08903.

ADAMS, ARMENTA ESTELLA (ARMENTA ADAMS HUMMINGS)
Concert pianist. **PERSONAL:** Born Jun 27, 1936, Cleveland, OH; son of Albert Adams and Estella Mitchell Adams; married Gus Lester Hummings, Feb 01, 1973; children: Amadi, Gus Jr, Martin, Marcus. **EDUCATION:** New England Conservatory, Preparatory Div 1941-53; Julliard School of Music, MS 1960; Post Graduate Study, London England 1961-63. **CAREER:** Julliard School Preparatory Div, piano teacher 1967-69; Harlem School of Music, piano teacher 1968-69; Florida A&M Univ, piano faculty 1965-66; Urban Arts Winston-Salem, artist-in-residence 1983-84; Winston-Salem State Univ, instrumental faculty 1984-85; NC A&T Univ, piano faculty 1987-88. **ORGANIZATIONS:** Extensive concert tours throughout the world US State Dept 1963-67. **HONORS/ACHIEVEMENTS:** First prize Musicians Club of NY 1956; John Hay Whitney grant; Martha Baird Rockefeller grant; First prize Natl Assn of Negro Musicians; Special prize Intl Competition Leeds England; grant Intl Inst of Educ; Freida Loewenthal Eising Award; performance at Univ of Maryland International Piano Festival Great Performer Series 1985. **HOME ADDRESS:** 2012 Milford St, Winston-Salem, NC 27107.

ADAMS, BILLIE MORRIS WRIGHT
Pediatrican, pediatric hematologist. **PERSONAL:** Born in Bluefield, WV; married Frank M Adams; children: Frank M Jr. **EDUCATION:** Fisk Univ, BS 1950; IN Univ, MA 1951; Howard Univ, MD 1960. **CAREER:** Cook Co Hosp Hekutoen Inst, rotating intern 1960,

pediatric residency 1961-63, hematology fellowship 1963-65, rsch assoc hematology dept 1965-67; Martin Luther King Ctr, pediatrician 1967-68; Michael Reese Hosp, Mercy Hosp Med Ctr, attending med staff; Pediatric Hematology Clinic Mercy Hosp, pediatric hematologist, acting bureau chief. **ORGANIZATIONS:** Mem Natl Medical Assoc 1962; mem Pediatric Assn SC; mem Amer Acad of Pediatrics 1963; mem Amer Soc of Hematology 1968; mem Chicago Pediatric Soc; med adv Com Planned Parenthood 1972-75; mem Alpha Gamma Pi 1972; mem Cook Co Physicians Assoc 1974-; mem med adv com Chicago Bd of Health's Child & Maternal Com; mem AMA; mem Chicago Inst of Med; mem operational consult Sickle Cell Comprehensive Ctr Univ of IL Coll of Med; clinical asst prof Deptof Pediatrics Univ of IL Coll of Med; mem Chicago Med Assn; IL State & Med Soc; bd dir Midwest Assn; mem Art Inst of Chicago; mem Lyric Opera Guild; mem Ounce of Prevention Bd, Links Inc, Delta Sigma Theta; mem bd South Side Comm Art Ctr; mem Friends Carter G Woodson Library. **HONORS/ACHIEVEMENTS:** Who's Who in Amer Colls & Univs 1950; diplomate Amer Bd of Pediatrics 1964; apptd chairperson State of IL Commn for Sickle Cell Anemia 1972; Alpha GammaPi Honoree 1973; PUSH Woman of the Yr 1975; 1st Congressional Dist Awd in Medicine 1985; United Negro College Fund Star 1986. **BUSINESS ADDRESS:** Pediatric Hematologist Dir, Mercy Hosp Ped Hema Clinic, 2011 E 75th St, Chicago, IL 60649.

ADAMS, CAROL LAURENCE
Professor. **PERSONAL:** Born May 11, 1944, Louisville, KY; divorced; children: Nia Malika Augustine. **EDUCATION:** Fisk Univ, BA 1965; Boston Univ, MA 1966; Union Grad School, PhD 1976. **CAREER:** Northeastern IL Univ Ctr for Inner City Studies, asst dir 1969-78; The Neighborhood Inst, dir of rsch & plng 1978-81; Loyola Univ, dir Afro-Amer studies, assoc prof sociology 1981-. **ORGANIZATIONS:** Mem Natl Assoc of Blacks in Criminal Justice, African Heritage Studies Assoc; Amer Sociological Assoc; bd mem Ebony Talent Creative Arts Found, Assocfor the Advancement of Creative Musicians; bd of dir Cable Access Corp; mem Natl Council on Black Studies, IL Council on Black Studies. **HONORS/ACHIEVEMENTS:** Phi Beta Kappa Fisk Univ 1965; George Edmund Hayes Social Sci Awd Fisk Univ 1965; Community Achievement Awd Hubame Assoc; Leadership in Ed Awd YMCA Metropolitan Chicago; Governors Awd in the Arts; Black Business Awd Black Book Directory; Achievement Awd IL Board of Higher Educ. **HOME ADDRESS:** 6929 S Crandon #3A, Chicago, IL 60649. **BUSINESS ADDRESS:** Assoc Prof Sociology, Loyola University of Chicago, Afro-American Studies, Dir, 6225 N Sheridan Rd, Chicago, IL 60626.

ADAMS, CLARENCE LANCELOT, JR.
Educator, psychologist. **PERSONAL:** Born in New York, NY. **EDUCATION:** Yeshiva Univ NYC, EdD 1973; NY Univ, MA 1952; Long Island Univ, BS 1950. **CAREER:** Private practice, NY State licensed clinical psychotherapist 1958-; Hunter Coll CUNY, psychologist 1961-64; Bureau of Child Guid, New York City Bd of Ed, psychologist 1967-68; SEEK Prog, Hunter College CUNY, psychologist, counselor 1968-70; New York City Bd of Ed, research consultant 1970-73; Bronx C of C, CUNY, assoc prof 1973-; Psychology Dept, Pace Univ, NYC, adjunct prof 1981-. **ORGANIZATIONS:** Consultant, Psychol Proj 145 1976-, AMCRO Inc 1977-; comm for educ & mental health, 100 Black Men 1973-; mem Harlem Cultural Council, Natl Assoc Blacks Concerned in Criminal Justice, Coll Publ Agency Prog Comm, US Civil Serv Comm, NY Psychol Assn, Amer Psychol Assn, NY Soc of Clinical Psychol, Assn of Black Psychol, Amer Ortho Psychol Assn, Amer Assn on Mental Def, Amer Soc Gp Psychol, Soc for Study of Gr Tensions, NEA, Professional Staff Congress; bd mem, sec SAGE 1986. **HONORS/ACHIEVEMENTS:** NY Perm Cert School Psychol, 1968; published A Study of Factors Which Affect Academic Success Among SEEK Students; NY Academic Scholarship, 1946; diplomate, Amer Acad of Behavioral Medicine; Natl Registered Health Provider in Psychol, 1975-. **MILITARY SERVICE:** AUS. **BUSINESS ADDRESS:** Professor, Pace University, 1 Pace Plaza, New York, NY 10038.

ADAMS, CLAUDETTE COLEMAN
Educator, business executive. **PERSONAL:** Born Jan 31, 1952, Chicago, IL; married Dr Edward Francis Adams; children: Christina; Matthew Gregory. **EDUCATION:** Carleton Coll, BA 1974; Northwestern Univ, MAT 1975. **CAREER:** Chicago Public Schools, educator 1974-75; Urbana Public Schools, educator 1975-78; Ridgewood Public Schools, educator 1978-81; AT&T, systems analyst 1982-87. **ORGANIZATIONS:** Bd mem, chairperson of policy com, mem of curriculum & facilities com Franklin Twp Bd of Educ 1982-85; mem coord Tri-State Sounding Bd 1984-86; finmem The Committee of AT&T Black Employees 1984-; mem NAACP 1984-85; voter reg coord NAACP 1983; bds assoc mem Somerset Cty Schools 1982-83; mem Natl Black Womens's Political Caucus 1984-85. **HONORS/ACHIEVEMENTS:** Outstanding Young Women of Amer Recognition 1982.

ADAMS, CURTIS N.
Dentist. **PERSONAL:** Born Mar 28, 1931, Waycross, GA; married Jean; children: Cheryl, Curtis Jr. **EDUCATION:** SC State Coll, BS 1954; Howard Univ, attended 1958, DDS 1962; Provident Hosp, 1963. **CAREER:** Private Practice, Baltimore MD 1963-68; Provident Hosp, staff-oral surg 1963-; Rosewood St Hosp, staff 1964-68; Provident Compreh Neigh Hlth Ctr, dental clinical supr 1968-; Work Incentive Prog, lectr 1970-71; Provident Hosp Compl, lectr 1970-71; Private Practice, dentist 1968-. **ORGANIZATIONS:** Mem Amer Dental Assn, Natl Dental Assn, MD Dental Soc, MD St Dental Assn, Alpha Phi Alpha Frat; mem Chi Delta Mu Frat; NW Civic Forum; Model Cities Policy Steering Bd; Provident Hosp Med Staff; bd dir Hlth & Welfare coun of Ctr MD; bd dir Commun Coll Allied Health Fields; chmn Hlth Task Force 1969-71; treas med staff Provident Hosp 1970-73; treas NW Civic Forum 1971-73; pres elect MD Dental Soc 1971-73; pres MD Dental Soc 1971; chmn med audit Provident Hosp Complex; mem patient care com Provident Hosp; mem utiliz com Provident Hosp; mem med exec com Provident Hosp; orgzng com HarborNat Bank 1973. **BUSINESS ADDRESS:** Adams, Ashford Dental Assoc, 2300 Garrison Blvd, Baltimore, MD 21216.

ADAMS, DAVID, JR.
Business executive. **PERSONAL:** Born Oct 29, 1927, Monroe, LA; married Virginia Lee Parker; children: Ronda O, Onie M Brown. **EDUCATION:** Grambling Coll, BS 1950; NLU, Grad Study 1970, Cert 1971; Morgan State Coll, Cert. **CAREER:** Mineral Springs HS, instr 1950-51; Vet Ed of Ouachita Parish, instr 1951-52; Clark Elem School, instr 1956-67; Reliable Life Ins Co, gen mgr 1967-. **ORGANIZATIONS:** Mem Doric Lodge 1 AF&AM; deacon Macedonia Bapt Church; big brother 1958-64. **HONORS/ACHIEVEMENTS:** 1st black on Mun Police & Fireman Civ Serv Bd apptd by Mayor 3 yrs term 1973. **BUSINESS ADDRESS:** General Manager, Reliable Life Insurance Co, 108 N 23 St, Monroe, LA 71201.

ADAMS, DOLLY DESSELLE
Educational administrator. **PERSONAL:** Born Aug 18, Marksville, LA; married Bishop John Hurst Adams; children: Gaye D, Jann Hurst, Madelyn Rose. **EDUCATION:** Southern Univ, BA 1951; Univ of MI, MA 1953; Baylor Univ, EdD 1979. **CAREER:** Paul Quinn Coll, visiting prof 1973-75; KWTX-TX, producer/host; College Without Walls Prairie View A&M Univ 1973-74; free lance consultant 1975-81; Howard Univ School of Law, visiting lecturer 1981-83; The Links Inc, natl pres. **ORGANIZATIONS:** Vice chmn McLennan Co United Way; consultant White House Conf on Families; bd mem WHMM TV Washington; advisory bd mem African-American Institute NY; organizer & pres Black Women's Consultation Washington; Alpha Kappa Alpha Sor; chair Board of Mgrs YWCA; editor of newsletter Church Women United; consultant & speaker World Federation of Methodist Women; Jack and Jill Clubs of Amer 1980-; supvr Women's Missionary Soc AME Ch 2nd and 10th Districts 1972-80. **HONORS/ACHIEVEMENTS:** College grad magna cum laude; Alpha Kappa Mu Honor Soc; citation of merit Business & Prof Women's Club 1971; Woman of the Year Paul Quinn College 1980; distinguished leadership UNCF 1983; 100 Most Influential Black Amers Ebony Mag 1982-85; distinguished service Africare 1984. **HOME ADDRESS:** 1212 Fountain Dr SW, Atlanta, GA 30314.

ADAMS, DON L.
Investment advisor. **PERSONAL:** Born Nov 27, 1927, Jonesboro, GA; married Mary Wilson; children: Don Jr. **EDUCATION:** Northwestern Univ, attended 1970. **CAREER:** Professional Basketball Player, San Diego-Houston Rockets, Atlanta Hawks, Detroit Pistons, St Louis Spirits, Buffalo Braves. **HONORS/ACHIEVEMENTS:** Twice co-MVP at Northwestern Univ; All-Rookie Team 1971.

ADAMS, EARL LEONARD, III
Orthopedic surgeon. **PERSONAL:** Born Mar 31, 1953, Elizabeth, NJ. **EDUCATION:** Harvard Univ, AB 1975; Howard Univ Coll of Medicine, MD 1980. **CAREER:** CA State Univ, team physician 1983-84. **ORGANIZATIONS:** Chmn bd of dirs Student Natl Medical Assoc 1979-80; pres Assoc of Interns & Residents Oakland CA 1981-82; mem Kappa Alpha Psi Frat. **HONORS/ACHIEVEMENTS:** Resident of the Year Highland General Hosp Oakland CA 1981. **HOME ADDRESS:** 28 Rynda Road, Maplewood, NJ 07040.

ADAMS, EDWARD B.
State external affairs manager. **PERSONAL:** Born Jan 31, 1939, New York, NY; son of Clarence Adams and Erna Adams; married Mary; children: Jennifer, Teddy, Michele. **EDUCATION:** NY Univ, BIE 1959; Brooklyn Polytechnic Inst, grad study; Stanford University, Sloan Fellow, 1974. **CAREER:** IBM Corp CO, buying mgr, indus engrg mgr, plant mgr, dir of site operations, mgr of external pgms. **ORGANIZATIONS:** Past pres Austin Urban League; mem MW St Joseph Grand Lodge AF & AM; mem Sigma Pi Phi; past chmn mem Brackenridge Hospital Bd; chmn trustees Huston-Tillotson Coll; mem bd of dir TX Research League and TX Computer Industry Council; vicechmn govt relations Austin Chamber of Congress. **HONORS/ACHIEVEMENTS:** Stanford Sloan Fellow 1973-74; judge TX Women's Hall of Fame; Whitney Young Award, Austin Area Urban League, 1989. **BUSINESS ADDRESS:** Manager External Programs, IBM, 11400 Burnet Rd, Austin, TX 78758.

ADAMS, ELAINE PARKER
Educational administrator. **PERSONAL:** Born Nov 12, 1940, New Orleans, LA; married A Andrew; children: Albert Jr. **EDUCATION:** Xavier Univ of LA, BA (cum laude) 1961; LA State U, MS 1966; Univ of Southern CA, PhD 1973; Harvard Univ, Management Development Program 1986-. **CAREER:** Orleans Parish School System, Librarian/tchr 1961-68; Grossmont Union HS Dist, dist catalog librarian 1971; Upper St Clair School Dist, librarian 1972-73; Univ of MD, visiting asst prof 1973; Univ So CA Health Sciences Campus, media specialist 1974-75; TX Southern Univ, coord learning resource ctr 1976-80; Getty Oil Co Rsch Ctr, supervisor library service 1980-83; Prairie View A&M Univ, assoc vice pres, acad serv & planning 1983-85, vice pres student affairs 1985-. **ORGANIZATIONS:** Various comm assign Amer Library Assn 1970-, Special Libraries Assn 1981-84; chairperson CA Librarians Black Caucus, So Area 1975; rec sec Natl Coalition of 100 Black Women Houston 1984-86; area rep Youth for Understanding Int Student Exch 1979-82; mem Alpha Kappa Alpha Sor 1967-; pres Xavier Univ Alumni Assn 1989-; various comm assign Natl Assn of Student Personnel Adminis 1986-; inst rep Prairie View A&M Univ Army ROTC Adv Camp 1986; mem Amer Assn for Higher Educ 1987-; Natl Assn of Women Deans, Administrators, and Counselors 1985-. **HONORS/ACHIEVEMENTS:** Coeditor, Media and The Young Adult, Chicago ALA 1981; Fellow, HEA Title II Univ of So CA 1968-71; articles Various Journals in Librarianship & Educ 1970-; contributor Media and the Young Adult Series 1977-84. **HOME ADDRESS:** 10906 Holly Springs Dr, Houston, TX 77042. **BUSINESS ADDRESS:** Vice Pres Student Affairs, Prairie View A&M University, P O Box 337, Prairie View, TX 77446.

ADAMS, EVA W.
Educator. **PERSONAL:** Born Feb 01, 1928, Eutaw, AL; daughter of Mr & Mrs S H Walker; married Willie G Adams. **EDUCATION:** Alabama A&M Univ, BSc 1949; Ohio State Univ, MSc 1955; Pennsylvania State Univ, EdD 1968. **CAREER:** Univ of DE, assoc prof; AL A&M Univ, prof; DE State Coll Dept Home Econ, prof & chmn. **ORGANIZATIONS:** Amer Home Economics Assn, secretary/treasurer of the Coll and Univ Section; Assn of Home Economics Admin, chairperson, North East Home Economics Admin Section; Council of 1890 Home Economics Admin, past pres; Amer Vocational Educ, past pres, Natl Assn for Teacher Educ in Home Economics; Natl Assn for the Advancement of Colored People; Natl Coalition for Black Devel in Home Economics. **HONORS/ACHIEVEMENTS:** Personalities of the South 1971; Outstanding Educators of Amer 1972; Dictionary of Intl Biography 1973; Honorary mem in Future Homemakers of Amer AL 1970; Hon mem in Future Homemakers of Amer DE 1975; Outstanding Achievement by Natl Alumni Normalite Assn 1974 Alabama A & M Univ; Plaque for Outstanding Leadership as President of Delaware Assn for Supervision and Instruction 1986; Plaque for Outstanding Leadership as pres of Delaware Home Economics Assn, 1987; Alumni Achievement Award for Class of 1949, at Commencement, May 1989, by Alabama A & M Univ, Natl Alumni Normalite Assn; mem Alpha Mu Natl Honors Society; mem Omicron Nu Natl Society; mem Phi Lambda Theta Honors Society for Women in Educ; mem Delta Kappa Gamma Natl Teachers Org Professional Org for Women. **BUSINESS ADDRESS:** Chairman, Home Econ Dept, DE State College, Box 759, Dover, DE 19901.

ADAMS, FREDERICK G.
Educator. **PERSONAL:** Born Jul 27, 1931, Columbus, OH; married Olivia P Marshall;

children: Christie Lynn, Keline Marie, Alexis Jean. **EDUCATION:** OH State Univ, BS 1956, DDS 1960; Yale Univ, MPH 1970. **CAREER:** State Dept of Hlth Psychiat Hosp for Emotionally Disturbed Children, therapist 1956-60; General Practice, dentist 1960-69; Univ CT, ombudsman 1969-70, spl asst to pres allied health prof devel 1969-72, dean 1972-74, vice pres student affairs & serv 1974-. **ORGANIZATIONS:** Bd dir CT Bank & Trust Corp 1976; bd dir So New England Tel Co 1977; various offices coms Amer Assn of Comm & Jr Colls; mem Amer Dental Assn; Amer Pub Health Assn; Amer Soc of Allied Health Professions; CT Health League; CT Hosp Assn; CT Inst for Health Manpower Resources; CT Pub Health Assn; CT State Dental Assn; CT Adv Com for the Health Scis Rsch Project; Hartford Dental Soc; corporator Hartford Hosp; adv bd Manchester Comm Coll; Natl Dental Assn; New England Bd Higher Educ State Adv Comm Royal Soc of Health England; S Central Comm Coll Adv Cncl; Amer Assn Allied Health Professions; chmn Statewide Hlth Coord Cncl for CT 1977-; pres Urban League of Greater Hartford 1978-80. **HONORS/ACHIEVEMENTS:** Numerous civic, community affiliations; consultantships, honors, publications & writings in field. **MILITARY SERVICE:** USAF 1951-54. **BUSINESS ADDRESS:** Vice Pres Student Afrs & Serv, Univ of CT, Storrs, CT 06268.

ADAMS, GLEASON R. W.
Financial analyst. **PERSONAL:** Born Aug 04, 1949, Huntsville, AL. **EDUCATION:** Univ of Notre Dame, AB 1971; Yale Univ, M Phil 1975. **CAREER:** NASA/Army Missile Command, translator 1973. **HONORS/ACHIEVEMENTS:** Fulbright Fellowship 1971; Ford Fellow 1971-75; paper delivered New England Modern Language Assn 1979; book translated/published Les Cenelles GK Hall 1979.

ADAMS, GREGORY ALBERT
Assistant district attorney. **PERSONAL:** Born Jun 10, 1958, Atlanta, GA; son of Enoch Q Adams, Sr and Emily E Jackson Adams; married Wanda C Adams, Oct 27, 1984. **EDUCATION:** Georgia State Univ, Atlanta, GA, BS, 1981; Univ of Georgia School of Law, Athens, GA, JD, 1983. **CAREER:** Georgia State Univ, Atlanta, GA, supvr, 1977-81; Inst of Continuing Judicial Educ, Athens, GA, researcher, 1983-84; Dekalb County Solicitor, Decatur, GA, asst solicitor, 1984-87; Dekalb County Dist Atty, Decatur, GA, asst dist atty, 1987-. **ORGANIZATIONS:** Bd mem, Decatur-Dekalb Bar Assn, 1988-89; past pres, 1987-88. mem, 1984-, Dekalb Lawyers Assn; past pres, Scarbrough Square Homeowners Assn, 1986, 1987; parliamentarian, Alpha Phi Alpha Fraternity Inc, 1988-90; vice pres, Dekalb Jaycees, 1989-; mem, Alpha Phi Alpha Fraternity Inc, 1980-, Assn of Trial Lawyers of Amer, 1984-88, State Bar of Georgia, 1984-, Dekalb County NAACP, 1987-. **HONORS/ACHIEVEMENTS:** Outstanding Young Man, 1985; Service Award, Dekalb Branch NAACP, 1988; Merit Award, Dekalb Lawyers Assn, 1988; Legion of Honor, Dekalb-Atlanta Voters Council, 1988; workshop, "From Detection to Treatment," Georgia Council on Child Abuse, 1989; lecturer, 1984-. **HOME ADDRESS:** 2069 Kimber Trail, Stone Mountain, GA 30088.

ADAMS, GREGORY KEITH
Meeting planner. **PERSONAL:** Born Apr 09, 1958, Philadelphia, PA. **EDUCATION:** Rutgers Univ, Economics/Business 1977-81. **CAREER:** Hyatt Hotels Corp, sales mgr 1981-83; Westin Hotels Corp, sales mgr 1983-85; Radisson Corp, asst dir of sales 1985; NAACP, natl conf dir 1985-. **ORGANIZATIONS:** Mem Greater Washington Soc of Assoc Execs, Natl Assoc Exposition Mgrs, Omega Psi Phi Frat, Prince Hall Master Mason; bd mem Natl Coalition of Black Meeting Planners; steering comm Baltimore Black Enterprise Professional Exchange. **BUSINESS ADDRESS:** Natl Conference Dir, NAACP, 4805 Mt Hope Dr, Baltimore, MD 21215.

ADAMS, HARRISON LESLIE **See ADAMS, LESLIE**

ADAMS, HENRIETTA FAULCONER
Business executive. **PERSONAL:** Born Sep 12, 1939, Hallittsville, TX; married Albert III; children: Mark, Blair, Keith, Eric. **EDUCATION:** Univ MN. **CAREER:** Operation De Novo Inc, exec dir present; Operation de Novo, asst to dir 1977; Legal Rights Ctr, ct & comm worker 1970-71; Juvenile Unit Legal Aid Soc of MN, para-legal asst 1968-69; Minn Urban & Coalition of Law & Justice Task Force, 1968-; Comm Health & Welfare-Council Legal Serv to the Poor, 1973-; Hennepin Area Youth Diversion Prgm Central Bd, 1974-; Metro Council Corrections Task Force, 1973-74. **ORGANIZATIONS:** Mem Minn Urban League Guild; Nat Assn of Pre-trial Serv Agys 1974-; 3rd World Com 1977; Criminal Justice Com; mem Nat Assn of Black Criminal Justice1978. **HONORS/ACHIEVEMENTS:** Comm serv award Metro Council. **BUSINESS ADDRESS:** 321 S 3rd St, Minneapolis, MN 55415.

ADAMS, HOWARD GLEN
Educator. **PERSONAL:** Born Mar 28, 1940, Danville, VA; married Eloise Christine Davis; children: Stephanie Glenn. **EDUCATION:** Norfolk State Univ, BS 1964; Virginia State Univ, MS 1970; Syracuse Univ, PhD 1979. **CAREER:** Norfolk City Pulbic Schools, biology/general science teacher 1964-70; Norfolk State Univ, alumni affairs dir 1970-73; vice pres student affairs 1974-77. **ORGANIZATIONS:** Exec dir Natl Consortium GEM 1978-; comm serv bd YMCA 1979-85; bd of trustees Meadville/Lombard Theol Sch 1980-; corp adv bd Natl Assoc for EqualOppor in Higher Educ 1981-; mem Natl Action Cncl for Minorities in Engrg 1982-; consultant Black Collegian Publications 1984-. **HONORS/ACHIEVEMENTS:** Natl Teachers of Science Fellowship 1964-65; Natl Alumni Service Awd Norfolk State Alumni 1974; Torch Bearers Awd Natl Society of Black Engineers 1986. **BUSINESS ADDRESS:** Executive Dir, Natl Consortium for Grad Degr, Box 537, Notre Dame, IN 46556.

ADAMS, JACKIE W., SR.
Engineering artist. **PERSONAL:** Born May 16, 1927, Atlanta, GA; married Bernice Poole; children: Jackie W Jr. **EDUCATION:** Clark Coll, 3 yrs; Morris Brown Coll, 1 yr; Tuskegee Inst AL, 1 yr. **CAREER:** Atlanta Daily World Newspaper, photo engraver 1949-50; Lockheed GA Co, structural assy, illustrator, tech illustrator, engr artist, artist, teacher, photo engraver 1953-. **ORGANIZATIONS:** Mem Atlanta Parks & Rec Chastain Park Atlanta, Natl Conf of Artist, Nantucket Artist Assoc, Creative Artist Guild. **HONORS/ACHIEVEMENTS:** Listed in Who's Who Among Afro-Amer Artists; 1st Prize Painting, 2nd Prize Graphs Atlanta Univ 1963-64; Roswell 2nd Prize Graphics 1971; feature story Pride Mag 1972; Drawing High Mus Atlanta GA Artist Exhibit; Drawing-Movie, "Together for Days". **MILITARY SERVICE:** US Merchant Marine 1945-49. **BUSINESS ADDRESS:** Lockheed GA Co, S Cobb Dr Dept 73-12 Illust, Marietta, GA 30067.

ADAMS, JAMES MALCOLM
Journalist. **PERSONAL:** Born Jan 30, 1954, Pittsburgh, PA; married Barbara Henderson; children: Bryce, Marti. **EDUCATION:** Fisk Univ, Political Sci, Speech & Drama 1975. **CAREER:** WRFN-FM, news dir 1971-75; WSM-TV, studio camera operator 1971-75; KHOU-TV, news reporter 1975-76; WTTG-TV, news anchor 1976-. **ORGANIZATIONS:** Mem Natl Press Club; mem Natl Acad TV Arts & Sci, Natl Assoc of Black Broadcaster. **HONORS/ACHIEVEMENTS:** 32 Emmy Nominations Natl Acad for TV Arts & Sci 1976-86; Communications Excellence for Black Aduiences NY 1985. **BUSINESS ADDRESS:** News Anchor, WTTG-TV Fox Broadcasting, 5151 Wisconsin Ave, NW, Washington, DC 20016.

ADAMS, JEAN TUCKER
Appointed government official. **PERSONAL:** Born in Baltimore, MD; children: Stuart Randall, Scott Hamilton. **EDUCATION:** Coppin State Teachers Coll, BS 1958; Univ of MD, MSW 1972. **CAREER:** Baltimore City, teacher 1958-64; Health & Mental Hygiene Juvenile Serv Admin, asst reg dir 1965-76; Private practice, psychotherapist 1975-; Office of Mayor Baltimore MD, dep dir 1976-80; State House Governors Office, exec asst. **ORGANIZATIONS:** Consult Private Public 1975-; mem Natl Assoc Soc Workers 1975-; legislative adv Exec & Professional Women's Council of MD 1980-; vice pres United Serv Org 1982-; bd mem Sudden Infant Death Syndrome Inst 1983-. **HONORS/ACHIEVEMENTS:** Mayor's Citation Baltimore City 1979; Governor's Citation State of MD 1984; Scroll of Appreciation Wiesbaen Germany Military Comm 1984; Social Worker of the Year Natl Assoc of Soc Workers 1984.

ADAMS, JOHN HURST
Clergyman. **PERSONAL:** Born Nov 27, 1929, Columbia, SC; married Dolly Jacqueline Desselle; children: Gaye Desselle, Jann Hurst, Madelyn Rose. **EDUCATION:** Johnson C Smith Univ, AB 1948; Boston Univ Sch of Theology, STB & STM 1951-52; Attended, Union Theol Sem NYC; Payne Theol Sem, DD 1956; Paul Quinn Coll, HHD 1972; Wilberforce Univ, LLD 1956. **CAREER:** Payne Theol Sem, prof 1952-56; Paul Quinn Coll Waco, pres 1956-62; First AME Ch Seattle, sr pastor 1962-68; Grant AME Ch LA, sr pastor 1968-72; African Meth Epis Ch, 87th bishop 1972-. **ORGANIZATIONS:** Chmn of bd Paul Quinn Coll 1972-; chmn Commn on Higher Educ AME Ch 1976-; dir Amer Income Life Ins Co 1977-; chmn AME Ch Serv & Devel Agency 1978; dir The Fund for Theol Educ 1976-; vice pres Natl Black United Fund 1977-; chmn The Congress of Natl Black Ch 1978-; dir Interdenominational Theol Ctr 1978-. **HONORS/ACHIEVEMENTS:** Man of the Yr B'nai B'rith Northwest 1964; Man of the Yr Urban League (Seattle & Northwest Area) 1965. **BUSINESS ADDRESS:** AME Church, 208 Auburn Ave, NE, Atlanta, GA 30303.

ADAMS, JOHN OSCAR
Attorney, art dealer, lecturer. **PERSONAL:** Born Apr 03, 1937, Chatanooga, TN; son of John M Adams and Queen M Adams. **EDUCATION:** Wayne State Univ, BS 1962; Loyola Univ, JD 1970. **CAREER:** Detroit Publ School, instr 1962-64; Pasadena City Coll, lecturer 1964-65; IBM LA, mgr, sys engr, instr 1964-70; IBM Corp Hdqtr, attny antitrust 1970-72; US Senate Small bus Comm, minor coun 1972-75; City of Los Angeles, dep city attny 1975-76; Wallace & Wallace, special counsel 1975-80; Adams Industries Inc of CA, president, bd chmn 1978-82; attorney at law 1982-; art dealer 1985-. **ORGANIZATIONS:** Mem and bd of dirs Hollywood Chamber of Commerce; bd dirs Holywood Arts Council; bd dirs Options House; bd dirs Hollywood Kiwanis, Stages Theatre; mem Supreme Court, CA, NY, Washington DC Bar Assns; mem Hollywood Kiwanis. **HONORS/ACHIEVEMENTS:** Special Achievement Awd Los Angeles Urban League 1970; Saturday Review Commen Issue 1975; author "Notes of an Afro-Saxon"; Men of Achievement; Future Hope for the US. **MILITARY SERVICE:** USN So Pacific Fleet 1958-62. **BUSINESS ADDRESS:** Sr Partner, Adams & Associates, 6922 Hollywood Blvd #500, Hollywood, CA 90028.

ADAMS, JOSEPH LEE, JR.
Educator. **PERSONAL:** Born Jan 05, 1944, Kansas City, MO; son of Joseph L Adams Sr and Thelma V O'Neal Adams; married Christine Carolyn Manthei; children: Joseph III, Patrick. **EDUCATION:** Univ of MO Kansas City, BA 1970, MA 1971; Washington Univ St Louis, Post Grad 1976-79. **CAREER:** IBM, data ctr suprv 1968-70; Univ of MO Kansas City, teaching asst 1970-71; University City, councilman, 1974-; Meramec Comm Coll, assoc prof to prof history 1971-. **ORGANIZATIONS:** Mem So Hist Assn, Natl League Cities; bd of dir MO Mcpl League, St Louis Cty Mcpl League; mem Episcopalian Church, Creve Coeur Democrats; MO gov comm on Local Govt Coop 1985-; steering comm on transportation commun, Natl League of Cities 1982-; vice chmn, Transportation and Communication Steering Comm 1988. **MILITARY SERVICE:** USAF sgt 1962-66. **BUSINESS ADDRESS:** Professor of History, Meramec Community College, 11333 Big Bend, St Louis, MO 63122.

ADAMS, KATHERINE
Journalist. **PERSONAL:** Born Oct 16, 1952, Pittsburgh, PA; married Herman L Adams Jr. **EDUCATION:** Malone Coll, Communications 1970-72; Kent State Univ, Communications 1972-74; Cleveland State Univ, Communications. **CAREER:** WJKW-TV Storer Broadcasting, desk asst 1974-75, reporter trainee prod asst 1976-77, news anchor woman reporter show host 1977-. **ORGANIZATIONS:** Comm Commn Cleveland Chap NAACP; hostess Focus Black-Pub Serv Prog; mem City of Cleveland Comm Relations Bd; adv bd Salvation Army Hough Multi Purpose Center. **HONORS/ACHIEVEMENTS:** Salute to Black Clevelanders Awd Greater Cleveland Interchurch Cncl 1980. **BUSINESS ADDRESS:** WJKW-TV, 5800 S Marginal Rd, Cleveland, OH 44103.

ADAMS, KATTIE JOHNSON
Educator. **PERSONAL:** Born Sep 08, 1938, Orlando, FL; married Henry Adams; children: Kathie Jenan. **EDUCATION:** Edward Waters Coll, AA 1959; FL A&M Univ, BS 1961. **CAREER:** Orange Co School System, teacher 1962-80; Valencia Comm Coll, internship coord 1983-; Orange Co School Bd, elected official 1980-. **ORGANIZATIONS:** Vice chairperson 1980,81,83, chairperson 1982 Orange County Sch Bd; mem State Comm on Black Educ in FL 1985-; mem dist adv comm We Care HRS & Rollins Coll 1985-; nominating bd Citrus Cncl of Girl Scouts 1986-. **HONORS/ACHIEVEMENTS:** Outstanding Contributions to the Field of Educ Alpha Phi Alpha Frat 1981; Educational Leadership Phi Delta Kappa 1981; Outstanding Leadership in Comm Serv Alpha Kappa Alpha Sor 1982; Faith and Devoted Efforts to the Comm Kappa Frat 1982. **HOME ADDRESS:** 2500 Lauderdale

Court, Orlando, FL 32805. **BUSINESS ADDRESS:** Elected Official, Orange County FL Sch Bd, 434 No Tampa Ave, Orlando, FL 32801.

ADAMS, LEHMAN D.
Dentist. **PERSONAL:** Born Feb 19, 1925, Mansfield, LA; married Gloria Estelle Williams; children: Troy S, Traci L. **EDUCATION:** Wilberforce Univ, BS 1945; IN Univ Sch of Dentistry, DDS 1949; IN Univ, grad study 1951. **CAREER:** Private Practice Indianapolis, dentist. **ORGANIZATIONS:** Mem Natl Dental Assn; Amer Dental Assn, IN Dental Assn, IN Implant Soc, Midwest Soc of Periodontia, Amer Analgesia Soc, Acad of Gen Practice; various other professional organs; pres WECAN Found; chmn life mem Com NAACP; bd dirs Indianapolis Br NAACP; bd dirs Indianapolis Natl Bus League; treas bd dir OIC; Indianapolis C of C; bd dir Summit Lab 1959-72; bd dir Midwest Natl Bank 1975; mem Alpha Phi Alpha, Chi Delta Mu, Omicron Kappa Upsilon (hon); mem elderWitherspoon Presb Ch. **HONORS/ACHIEVEMENTS:** Freedom Awd NAACP Natl Office 1973; Man of the Yr Alpha Phi Alpha 1958.

ADAMS, LESLIE (HARRISON LESLIE ADAMS)
Composer, executive vice president. **PERSONAL:** Born Dec 30, 1932, Cleveland, OH; son of Harrison Leslie Adams Sr and Jessie B Adams. **EDUCATION:** Oberlin Coll, BME 1955; Long Beach State Univ, MA 1967; OH State Univ, PhD 1973. **CAREER:** Univ of KS, assoc prof 1970-79; Yaddo Artist Colony, composer fellow 1980-84, Rockefeller Found 1977; artist in residence, Martha Holden Jennings Found, 1981-83; Cleveland Music School Settlement, resident composer 1982-84; Karamu House, resident composer, 1980-82; Accord Assoc/ Blake Productions, composer in residence & exec vice pres 1980-. **ORGANIZATIONS:** Mem Amer Composers Alliance 1984-, Dramatists Guild 1985-, Phi Kappa Phi 1965-, Phi Kappa Lambda 1972-, Phi Mu Alpha Sinfonia 1973-, Phi Delta Kappa 1974-. **HONORS/ ACHIEVEMENTS:** Natl Endowment for the Arts, Washington, DC 1979; Natl Choral Comp Competition Award, New York City 1974; Rockefeller Foundation Fellowship Award 1979; Yaddo Artists Fellowship Award 1980-84; KC Composers Forum winner choral composition competition Christian Arts Inc 1974; compositions Symphony No 1, A Kiss In Xanadu, Ode to Life, Piano Concerto, Sonata for Violin & Piano, Sonata for Horn & Piano, Sonata for Cello & Piano, five Millay songs, six Afro American songs; The Wider View (songs); The Righteous Man-Cantata to the Memory of Dr ML King, Blake (opera); numerous other works for solo and ensemble vocal & instrumental groups; Black History Archives Comm Award, Western Reserve Historical Society of Greater Cleveland 1989. **HOME ADDRESS:** 9409 Kempton Ave, Cleveland, OH 44108. **BUSINESS ADDRESS:** Executive Vice President, Accord Associates/ Blake Productions, 4500 Lee Road, Suite 244, Cleveland, OH 44128.

ADAMS, LILLIAN LOUISE T.
Educator. **PERSONAL:** Born Aug 08, 1929, Greenwood, SC; married David H Adams; children: Hannah Iula, David Jr, Debra. **EDUCATION:** Fisk Univ, AB 1951; SC State Coll, MEd 1970. **CAREER:** Teacher, Gordon HS 1951-53, Lincoln HS 1955-57, Willow Creek Elem 1957-68, Harllee Elem Sch 1968-. **ORGANIZATIONS:** Mem Florence Co Educ Assn; Assn Classroom Tchr; NEA; mem Cumberland United Meth Ch; bd Ministries; chmn Stewardship Commn. **HONORS/ACHIEVEMENTS:** United Meth Woman saved 4th Grade Student's Life; 1st Black Zone Pres Amer Legion Aux; Tchr Month 1974; Dist Tchr Yr 1975. **BUSINESS ADDRESS:** Teacher, Harllee Elem Sch, 408 E Pine St, Florence, SC 29501.

ADAMS, M. ELIZABETH
Retired educator. **PERSONAL:** Born Mar 12, 1906, Jefferson, TX; daughter of John S Wilkinson and Millie Elizabeth Jones; married William P Adams, Jul 19, 1934 (deceased); children: Amelia, W Patrick. **EDUCATION:** Wiley Coll, BA Math (Cum Laude) 1928; SE State Coll, grad work; attended OK State Univ, OK Univ. **CAREER:** Teacher, Leesville LA 1928-31, Oak Hill TX 1931-33, Jefferson TX 1933-36, Linden TX 1942-44, Texarkana TX 1944-45, DeKalb TX 1945-48, Hallsville TX 1948-49, Haynesville LA 1950-53, Booker T Washington High School 1953-71, Hugo School System OK retired. **ORGANIZATIONS:** Mem LA Teachers Assn 1928-31, TX State Teachers Assn 1932-36 1942-49, OK Educ Assn 1953-71, OK Teachers of Math 1953-71, OK Classroom Teachers 1953-71, Natl Educ Assn 1953-71, OK Retired Teachers Assn 1971-, Amer Assn of Retired Persons 1971-; sec Belles Lettres Club; bd dirs Hugo Child Devel Center; sec PAC Com of Hugo Urban Renewal; mem Hugo Chamber of Commerce; Alpha Kappa Sorority Phi Chapter 1926-36; Choctaw Co Black Heritage Club; RSVP Program; Choctaw Co Youth Serv Center (tutor). **HONORS/ACHIEVEMENTS:** Distinguished Achievement, The Natl Caucus & Center on Black Aged, 1988; Serv to Community, Retired Sr Volunteer Program (15 years), 1989; Service as Volunteer Tutor, Choctaw Co Youth Serv Center, 1989.

ADAMS, MARTIN P.
Associate executive. **PERSONAL:** Born Jan 19, 1956, Chicago, IL. **EDUCATION:** IL State Univ, BS Psych 1978; Univ of IL at Chicago, MSW 1981. **CAREER:** Family Serv of Oak Park & River Forest, client flow mgr 1978-82; Woods Charitable Fund Inc, staff assoc. **ORGANIZATIONS:** Steering committee Chicago Blacks in Philanthropy 1983-; mem Chicago Support Center 1983-; bd mem Donors Forum Emergency Loan Fund 1984-; public responsibility comm Donors Forum of Chicago 1984-; mem Comm Devel Citizens Adv Committee; selection committee Village Mgr Assoc Oak Park; adv bd Center for UrbanEcon Devel Univ of IL Chgo; oper consult Clockwork Intl; mem Oak Park Housing Center. **BUSINESS ADDRESS:** Staff Associate, Woods Charitable Fund Inc, 3 First Natl Plaza, Chicago, IL 60602.

ADAMS, NELSON EDDY
Association executive. **PERSONAL:** Born Aug 11, 1945, Southport, NC; married Yvonne McKenzie; children: Nelson Demond, Marius Anton. **EDUCATION:** Cape Fear Tech Inst, nondestructive testing 1973, rec admin 1972; Convair Sch for Nondestructive Testing, 1974; Southeastern Comm Coll, police sci 1975; Northwestern Univ, super of police personnel 1976. **CAREER:** Brown & Root Const Co, quality control inspector 1974; Brunswick Co Sheriff's Dept, jailer-patrolman-sgt-detective 1974-80; Intl Longshoremans Assn, pres. **ORGANIZATIONS:** Mem & steward Mt Carmel AME Church; mem Pythagoras Lodge No 6 F&AM; mem Southport Lions Club; city alderman Southport Bd of Aldermen 2nd 4 yr term; former advisor NAACP Youth Council 1967-69. **HONORS/ACHIEVEMENTS:** Cert of Appreciation pres elect S Brunswick Middle Sch PTO 1982-83; Cert of Appreciation pres S Brunswick Middle Sch PTO 1984. **HOME ADDRESS:** 303 W 10th St, Southport, NC 28461. **BUSINESS ADDRESS:** President, Intl Longshoremans Assn, PO Box 7, Southport, NC 28461.

ADAMS, OSCAR W., JR.
Attorney. **PERSONAL:** Born Feb 07, 1925, Birmingham, AL; married Willa Ingersoll; children: Oscar W III, Gaile A, Frank T. **EDUCATION:** Talladega Coll, AB 1944; Howard Univ Law School, LLB 1947. **CAREER:** Adams Banker & Clemon Birmingham, attny 27 yrs. **ORGANIZATIONS:** Mem Birmingham Bar Asso, AL Black Lawyers Assoc; pres Freedom Cable TV, Natl Bar Assoc, AL Bar, Bar US 5th Circuit Court Appeasl, US Court Military Appeals, Bar Supreme Court US, Amer Judicature Soc; mem adv comm Supreme Court AL; mem Public Serv Law Firm, Omega Psi Phi, AME Zion Church, NAACP. **HONORS/ACHIEVEMENTS:** Omega Man of the Year 1972. **BUSINESS ADDRESS:** Attorney, Adams, Banker & Clemon, 1600 2121 N B Ave, Birmingham, AL 35203.

ADAMS, PAUL BROWN
Police lieutenant. **PERSONAL:** Born Jul 09, 1929, Roanoke, VA; married Elaine D Frogg; children: Beverly P Adams, Susan A Hughes, Constance A Reid, Paul B Jr. **EDUCATION:** Attended, Bluefield St Coll. **CAREER:** Roanoke City Police Dept, patrolman 1955-64, detective 1964-71, chief homicide investigator 1967-71, lieutenant 1973-. **ORGANIZATIONS:** Vice chmn Natl Conf of Minority Police Officers 1971. **HONORS/ ACHIEVEMENTS:** Black Business League Award for Achievement in Law Enforcement 1971; Good Neighbor Award, Natl Council of Christians & Jews 1972; Natl Council of Christians & Jews Brotherhood Citation 1983; 1st & only black commanding officer in Roanoke City Police Dept. **MILITARY SERVICE:** AUS Corps of Engrs 1950-52. **BUSINESS ADDRESS:** Lieutenant, Roanoke City Police Dept, 309 3rd St SW, Roanoke, VA 24011.

ADAMS, QUINTON DOUGLAS
Salesman. **PERSONAL:** Born Apr 03, 1919, Etowah Co, AL; married Ozella Oliver; children: Gwendolyn Delores, Roderick Douglas. **CAREER:** Adams Cleaners Gadsden AL, owner/oper 1940-66; Gadsden AL, bail bonder 1960-; John Thomas Ford Inc, sales rep. **ORGANIZATIONS:** Governing bd Headstart Inc 1974-; bd mem Quality of Life & Health Ctr 1977-; com mem State Bd of Educ Competency Testing 1978-; master Lodge No 790 Masons 1945-; pres Etowah Co Voters League 1952; chmn Polit Action Com NAACP 1970-. **HONORS/ACHIEVEMENTS:** Gold Star Serv Awd RSVP Retired Sr Vol Prog 1978; Plaque for Serv Recognition 40 yrs of Civil Religious & Polit Serv 1980; Law Commr State of AL 1980; Serv Awd Goodsell United Meth Ch 1980. **BUSINESS ADDRESS:** Sales Rep, John Thomas Ford Inc, 205 Broad St, Gadsden, AL 35901.

ADAMS, RICHARD MELVIN, JR.
Administrator. **PERSONAL:** Born May 13, 1951, Pittsburgh, PA; son of Richard Adams and Marion Adams; married JoAnn Kirk. **EDUCATION:** Bowdoin Coll, AB Govt & Afro-Amer Studies 1973; Univ of Pittsburgh, Grad Sch of Public & Intl Affairs attended 1974. **CAREER:** GMAC, field rep 1974-75; Homewood-Brushton Comm Improvement Assoc, field rep 1975-76; Operation Better Block Inc, comm develop specialist 1976-85; CommColl of Allegheny County, asst to the exec dean. **ORGANIZATIONS:** Vice chair, Primary Care Health Serv Inc 1978-; bd mem Dist I Pittsburgh Public Schools 1985-; regional vice chair Natl Assoc of Neighborhoods 1985-; bd mem Northeast Region Council of Black Amer Affairs 1985-; bd dirs Amer Assoc of Sch Administrators; mem NAACP, Operation PUSH, Transafrica; state chairman, PA Natl Rainbow Coalition, 1986-. **HONORS/ ACHIEVEMENTS:** Named one of Pittsburgh Press 200 Most Influential Pittsburghers 1983; Outstanding Young Men of Amer 1983. **HOME ADDRESS:** 7325 Race St, Pittsburgh, PA 15208. **BUSINESS ADDRESS:** Asst to the Executive Dean, Comm College of Allegheny Co, 1750 Clairton Rd Rt 885, West Mifflin, PA 15122.

ADAMS, ROBERT HUGO
Editor, publisher. **PERSONAL:** Born Dec 06, 1943, Washington, DC; son of Gerald H Adams (deceased) and Ella Mary Hodge Adams (deceased); divorced; children: Tiffany K Adams. **EDUCATION:** Dist of Columbia Teachers Coll, Washington, DC, BS, 1967; Univ of Hawaii, Honolulu, 1971-73. **CAREER:** Xerox Corp, Honolulu, HI, salesman, 1973-74; KGMB Radio & Television, Honolulu, salesman, writer, 1974-75; RH Adams & Assoc, Honolulu, owner, 1975-76; CS Wo Furniture, Honolulu, salesman, 1976-78; Levitts Furniture, Garden City, NY, salesman, 1978-80; New York Amsterdam News, Harlem, NY, acct exec, business editor, 1980-81; Minority Business Review, Hempstead, NY, editor, publisher, 1981-. **ORGANIZATIONS:** Omega Psi Phi Fraternity, 1962-; Assn of Minority Enterprises of New York, 1980-; Natl Minority Business Council, 1981-; Minority Business Enterprise Week Planning Comm, 1984-; Natl Assn of Minority Contractors, 1986-; St George's Episcopal Church, 1986-; New York Region Small Business Admin Advisory Council, 1988-; mentor, Small Business Enterprise Center, State Univ of New York at Old Westbury, 1988-; advisor, New York State Science and Technology Program, 1988-; Procurement Task Force, 100 Black Men of Nassau/Suffolk, 1989-. **HONORS/ACHIEVEMENTS:** Writing Excellence Award, Advertising Club of New York, 1980; Outstanding Journalism Award, Assn of Minority Enterprises of New York, 1983; Regional Minority Advocate of the Year, Minority Business Devel Agency, US Dept of Commerce, 1987; Serv Award, Equal Opportunity Commn of Nassau County, 1988; African Amer Achievement Award, New York Million Dollar Boys Club, 1988; African Amer Award, United New Jersey Minority Business Brain Trust, 1989; began publishing first newspaper dedicated to minority business success, Minority Business Review, 1981; author, "When WBLS Comes to Harlem," article picked up by the New York Times, resulting in funding for the Apollo Theater, 1982; author, articles on White House Conf of Small Business, 1986, articles on African-Americans abused by corporations and agencies, 1988; series of radio interviews, MBR Forum, 1989. **MILITARY SERVICE:** AUS, captain, 1968-72. **BUSINESS ADDRESS:** Editor and Publisher, Minority Business Review, 250 Fulton Ave, Suite 507, Hempstead, NY 11550.

ADAMS, ROBERT THOMAS
Economist. **PERSONAL:** Born Nov 19, 1913, Griffin, GA; son of Robert T Adams and Rosa Lee Adams; married Marguerite. **EDUCATION:** Amer Univ, MA 1958, BSA 1948. **CAREER:** Economist, Bur of Labor Statistics, 1947-67; Office of the Undersec for transp, 1967-69; US Dept Commerce, chief economic analysis unit, asst sec of transportation, US Dept of Transportation, chief transp econ div, Fed Hwy Admin, 1969-74; acting dir, office prog & policy plng FHWA, consultant, econs & transp 1974-81. **ORGANIZATIONS:** Mem, Amer Soc Traffic & Transp, Photog Soc of Amer, USCG Aux 1972. **HONORS/**

ACHIEVEMENTS: Hwy Admin Awd 1974; Group Hon Awd Productivity Div Bur Labor Stat 1967; 2 Star Color Award, PSA. **MILITARY SERVICE:** AUS pfc 1941-42.

ADAMS, RONALD, JR.
Social services. **PERSONAL:** Born Oct 15, 1958, The Bronx, NY. **EDUCATION:** Benjamin Franklin HS, Regents Diploma 1976; Wagner Coll, BA Soc Work & Spec Ed 1980. **CAREER:** Police Athletic League 25th Precint, asst track coord 1973-74; Dunlevy Milbank Day Care Ctr, sr day camp counselor 1974-75; Gramercy Boys Club, head camp unit leader 1977-79; People Care Inc, head suprv 1981-85; Progressive Home Hlth Serv; sr health care mngr 1985-. **ORGANIZATIONS:** Natl governing council Sigma Phi Rho 1978-; volunteer worker March of Dimes 1980-, Spec Olympics 1981-; Boys Club of Amer 1981-. **HONORS/ACHIEVEMENTS:** Spec Serv Awds Black Concern Wagner Coll 1976-80; Sports Letter Awds Track Team 1976-80; Acad Awd Pre-Freshman Summer Session Wagner Coll 1976; Track Team Capt Wanger Coll 1979-80; Service Awd March of Dimes 1984; 1 of 13 founding mems of Sigma Phi Rho Frat; Outstanding Young Men of Amer 1985; Who's Who In Society 1986. **HOME ADDRESS:** 110 East 177th St #2C-#2E, Bronx, NY 10453.

ADAMS, ROSCOE H.
Engineer. **PERSONAL:** Born Aug 24, 1941, St Louis, MO; children: Gregory, Glen. **EDUCATION:** Univ of MO, BSEE 1962. **CAREER:** McDonnel Douglas, elect design engr 1962-67; IBM St Louis, syst engr asst 1967-68, syst engr 1968-71; Med Applications Mktg, reg indust mktg rep 1971-72; St Louis Dist Ed Ctr, instr mgr 1972-73, sr dist mktg rep 1973; IBM St Louis GSD Br, syst engr mgr 1974, mktg mgr Dallas 1977, br mgr 1978-. **ORGANIZATIONS:** Mem IBM Speakers Bur Guest Lecture Series; bd of dirs Tri-Cty Urban League; mem adv comm TSTM; mem priorities com Heart of IL United Way; past pres Kappa Alpha Psi, Armory Sports Ctr; mem Kappa Alpha Psi Leadership Dev League. **HONORS/ACHIEVEMENTS:** Top System Engrg Mgr IBM 1975; Top Basic Syst Engr IBM 1971; Man of the Year for Professionalism Kappa Alpha Psi 1973; IBM Golden Circle 1975; IBM Systems Engrg Symposium 1971; 6 IBM 100% Clubs; author "Goalstorming"; article & publ Adv Mgmt Jrnl 1979. **BUSINESS ADDRESS:** Branch Manager, IBM, 222 N E Monroe Ave, Peoria, IL 61602.

ADAMS, RUSSELL LEE
Educator. **PERSONAL:** Born Aug 13, 1930, Baltimore, MD; married Eleanor P; children: Sabrina, Russell. **EDUCATION:** Morehouse Coll, BA 1952; Univ of Chgo, MA 1954, PhD 1971. **CAREER:** Fed City Coll, assoc prof 1969-71; Howard Univ, assoc prof, chmn 1971-. **ORGANIZATIONS:** Priv consult Afro-Amer Studies Career Prog In-Serv & Dept Montg Cty Bd Ed; consult Univ Pittsburgh Ctr for Deseg 1976-, Wilmington DE Publ School 1977,Newark New Castle-Marshalton McKean School Dist DE, Jackson Publ School 1969-70; lecturer, consult US Info Agency 1977; chmn comm on status of blacks in profession Amer Pol Sci Assoc 1974-77; mem NAACP, Curr Eval Pool Prince Georges Cty Bd Ed 1976-. **HONORS/ACHIEVEMENTS:** Author Great Negroes Past & Present 1963-69,72; Leading Amer Negroes 1965; Perceptual Difficulties Dev Pol Sci Varia Spring 1976; publ Black Studies Mov Assessment Jrnl of Negro Ed 1977. **BUSINESS ADDRESS:** Associate Professor, Chmn, HowardUniv, Box 746, Dept of Afro-Amer Studies, Washington, DC 20001.

ADAMS, SAMUEL CLIFFORD, JR.
Retired foreign service officer. **PERSONAL:** Born Aug 15, 1920, Houston, TX; son of Samuel C Adams and Sarah C Adams; married Evelyn Sheppard Baker. **EDUCATION:** Dept of State Sr Sem for Policy, Post PhD 1965; Syracuse Univ Maxwell Sch00ll, Post-PhD 1958; School of Oriental & African Studies, Post-PhD 1957; Univ of Chicago, PhD 1953; Fisk Univ, BA & MA 1940-47. **CAREER:** Samuel C Adams Jr & Co Intl, pres 1975-; US Dept of State, admin Bur of Africa 1969; US Dept of State, US ambassador 1968; UN Gen Assembly, US Rep 1967; Morocco Mall Nigera Indo China Assoc States, career foreign serv AID 1952-68. **ORGANIZATIONS:** Mem Adv Comm Science, Technol & Devel, Exec Office of Pres 1978, Economic Devel Adv Bd Volta River 1977-78, Subcommittee on Intl Economic Policy Chamber of Commerce US 1977-78, Adv Comm on S Natl Academy of Sci 1979-81; mem bd dir Houston World Trade Assn 1980-81; mem bd trustees Fisk Univ 1978-81; mem bd dir Texas Greehouse Vegetable Growers Assn, TX A&M Univ. **HONORS/ACHIEVEMENTS:** Rockefeller Public Serv Princeton Univ 1971; Cross of the Ouizzan Alouite Dec by King Hassan II Robat, Morocco 1968; Ralph Bunche Award 1972; Distinguished Honor Award US Dept of State AID 1972. **MILITARY SERVICE:** USAAF priv first class 1944-46; received Certificate of Meritorious Serv 1946. **BUSINESS ADDRESS:** Consultant, S C Adams Jr & Co Intl, 3226 N MacGregor Way, Houston, TX 77004.

ADAMS, SAMUEL LEVI, SR.
Educator. **PERSONAL:** Born Jan 25, 1926, Waycross, GA; son of Jos Nathan Adams and Viola Virgil Adams (deceased); married Elenora Willette Grimes; children: Carol W, Bruce L, Samuel L, Jr. **EDUCATION:** WV State Coll, BA 1948; Wayne State Univ, AB 1950; Univ of MN, MA 1954; Univ of WI, Russell Sage Fellow Behavioral Sci Writing 1965-66. **CAREER:** Atlanta Daily World, reporter 1954-56; Des Moines Register, copy editor 1956-57; Gibbs-St Petersburg Jr Coll, dir pub rel 1958-60, half-time teacher 1960-64; St Petersburg Times, reporter 1960-65; So Reg Council Inc, dir res 1965-66; WI St Jour, corr 1966-67; St Petersburg Times, investigative reporter 1967-68; Univ of WI, visiting prof 1968-69; Univ of S FL, asst prof 1969-71; Dem Natl Comm, asst dir Minorities Div & asst press sec 1970-72; Univ of KS, assoc prof journalism 1972-; Hampton Univ, visiting prof journalism 1982-83; Univ of the Virgin Islands, visiting prof of journalism 1985-87. **ORGANIZATIONS:** Founder, dir Continuing Acad Cultural Enrich Prog 1962-64 (programs won natl Lane Bryant Vol Serv Awards); 1st vice pres Greater St Petersburg Council of Churches 63-65; prog dir div & joint sessions San Diego Conv 1974; Assn Educ Journ Head Minorities Div 1974-75; dir Gannett-AEJ Project for Enrichment of Journalism Educ 1975-80; pres & bd chmn Natl Youth Communication Inc 1977-82; dir The Newspaper Fund's Natl Minority Internship Prog 1979-80; KU Tenure Study Task Force; Task Force Univ Outreach; Minority Affairs Adv Bd; AAUP; co-founder and curator, Ida B Wells Award, 1983-; mem of board of directors and educ resource chmn, Jones Holloway-Bryan Foundation, 1986-; consultant for communications, Amnesty International USA, 1988-. **HONORS/ACHIEVEMENTS:** Regional Award Natl Conf Christians & Jews 1962; Pulitzer Prize Award nominee in journalism 1964-65; Lane Bryant Awards semi-finalist outstanding volunteer service 1966; Russell Sage Fellow Univ of WI 1966-67; Hampton Jr Coll Award 1966; Green Eyeshade Sweepstakes Award Sigma Delta Chi Atlanta 1969; state, local &regional awards, journalism; Award for Distinguished Serv to Journalism NC A&T State Univ 1978; Distinguished Visiting Prof Hampton Univ 1981-82; "Blackening in the Media," in NUL's State of Black America, 1985; "Highways to Hope," in St Peter Times and Hohenburg's The New Front Page, 1965. **MILITARY SERVICE:** AUS field artillery survey & chem warfare specialist 1950-52. **BUSINESS ADDRESS:** Associate Professor Journalism, Univ of Kansas, 207-B Stauffer-Flint Hall, Lawrence, KS 66045.

ADAMS, THEODORE ADOLPHUS, JR.
Business executive. **PERSONAL:** Born Sep 09, 1929, Newark, NJ; married Jeanie Perry; children: Karen, Deborah, Christina, Theodore III. **EDUCATION:** AUS Engr School, 1961; AUS Command & Gen Staff Coll, 1962; AUS Mgmt Engrg Training Agency, 1967; Harvard Univ 1977. **CAREER:** Unified Ind Inc, pres 1970-. **ORGANIZATIONS:** Exec dir Natl Assoc of Black Mgrs 1972-74; proj mgr Astro Reliability Corp 1969-72; assoc prof Agr Coll of NC 1957-59; dir Natl Assoc of Black Mfrs 1974-76; bd mem Retired Officers Assoc, Intl Business Serv Inc, Natl Minority Purchasing Council 1972-74; life mem Natl Business League; bd of councilors Fed City Coll, Ripon Soc, ASAE, WA Urban League; mem Amer Platform Assoc, Amer Natl Metric Council, bd mem YMCA of Metro WA 1976, District of Columbia Chamber of Commerce 1977, Legion of Merit AUS 1967, 1968, citation Natl Bus League 1974, Small Business Admin 1976; life mem Natl Business League 1977; mem Republican Senatorial Trust, Republican Congressional Leadership Council, Natl Black Leadership Roundtable; co-chmn Legal Defense & Educ Fund. **HONORS/ACHIEVEMENTS:** Spec Serv Awd Natl Assoc of Black Mfrs 1974,76. **MILITARY SERVICE:** AUS pvt ltd 1947-69; Vietnamese Medal of Honor 1st Class. **BUSINESS ADDRESS:** President, Unified Ind Inc, 6551 Loisdale Court, Ste 400, Springfield, VA 22150.

ADAMS, V. TONI
Business executive. **PERSONAL:** Born Dec 13, 1946, Oakland, CA; married James L Robinson; children: Karla, Doyle, Todd, Vikki. **EDUCATION:** Oxford Univ England, 1976; CA State Univ, MPA 1976; Mills Coll, BA 1968; Golden Gate Univ, DPA. **CAREER:** UC Berkeley, cont ed spec 1968-77; City of Oakland, spec asst to mayor 1977-84; Natl Assoc of Black & Minority Chamber of Commerce, vice pres of tourism. **ORGANIZATIONS:** Grand juror Alameda Cty superior Court 1973-74; mem bd of dir CA Alcoholism Found 1975-77; mem Alameda Cty Juvenile Delinquency Prevention 1976-78; chief fin officer Builders Mutual Suriety Co 1982-83; adv bd mem Displaced Homemakers Ctr 1983-; bd of dir Oakland Convention Ctr Mgt Inc 1983-. **HONORS/ACHIEVEMENTS:** Outstanding Service to Ed Coll Bounders Oakland 1979; Outstanding Young Women of Amer 1981,83. **BUSINESS ADDRESS:** Vice President of Tourism, Natl Assoc of Black & Minor, Chambers of Commerce, 654 13th St, Oakland, CA 94612.

ADAMS, VERNA MAY
Retired educational administrator. **PERSONAL:** Born Jul 01, 1928, Toledo, OH; daughter of John H Shoecraft and Ogrietta Lee Shoecraft; married Fred Andrew; children: Jacqueline O Redd, Fred A Jr, Douglas F, Cynthia V McBride. **EDUCATION:** St Francis Coll Ft Wayne IN, BS 1962, MS Ed 1964; Ball State Univ Muncie IN, EdD, 1979. **CAREER:** Ft Wayne Comm Schools, teacher 1961-67; St Francis Coll Ft Wayne IN, instr, lecturer 1964-74; Ft Wayne Comm Schools, guidance couns, consulting teacher 1966-68, elem cons, teacher 1967-71, elem principal 1971-80, dir title I prog 1980-82; dir, Supplemental Instructional Programs, 1982-89. **ORGANIZATIONS:** Bd of dirs, Fort Wayne Foundation Board of Directors, Fort Wayne Philharmonic Board of Directors, Committee of 24 Civic Group, Turner Chapel AME Trustee Board, The Links, Inc; mem, NAACP; Urban League, Phi Delta Kappa Ft Wayne Chapter. **HONORS/ACHIEVEMENTS:** Woman of the Year Ft Wayne Urban League 1964; Woman of the Year Kappa Alpha Psi Ft Wayne Alumni Chap 1976.

ADAMS, VICTORINE QUILLE
City official. **PERSONAL:** Born Apr 28, Baltimore, MD; married William Adams; children: 1 child. **EDUCATION:** Morgan State Univ, Coppin State Teachers Coll. **CAREER:** Health & Welfare Council of Central MD, vp, treas; Woman Power Inc, exec dir 12 yrs; 4th Dist Baltimore MD, city councilwoman. **ORGANIZATIONS:** Past mem House of Del 4th Dist MD Gen Assembly, Archdiocesan Urban Comm Chmn Mun Works; mem United Fund Campaign 1972, Phi Delta Kappa, Sigma Gamma Phi, Iota Phi Lambda, Com for Hist & Archit Preservation, NAACP, YWCA, YMCA, Unite Negro Women; adv com Cultural Progress for Mayor's Ball Cert. **HONORS/ACHIEVEMENTS:** USAF Defense Team Rubensteen's Success Sch; Afro-Amer Citz Awd Woman Power Inc; Serv Awd Natl Sojourner Truth Awd; Zeta Phi Beta's Woman of the Year; Century Club Awd YMCA; Alumni Awd Howard Univ; OES Awd Naomi Grand Chapt. **BUSINESS ADDRESS:** City Councilwoman, 4th Dist Baltimore, Holiday St City Hall, Room 523, Baltimore, MD 21202.

ADAMS, WILHELMINA F.
Politician. **PERSONAL:** Born Jan 31, 1901, Florida. **EDUCATION:** Attended, Hunter Coll 1927-30, Pratt Inst. **CAREER:** 17th District, dem leader 10 yrs. **ORGANIZATIONS:** Sec Bd of Assessors NYC; comm organizer NY Urban League; state committeewoman chmn mem various offices coms NAACP; Woman's Aux NY Urban League; Nannie Burrough's Philantropic Club; Martin Smith Music Sch; Harlem Fresh Air Fund Inc; Harlem Coop Com; Aeolian Ladies of Charity Inc; Utopia Neighborhood Club Inc; Natl Council of Negro Women Inc; Natl Assn Negro Bus & Professional Women Inc; The City Club of NY; Friends of Liberian Youth Inc; Natl & State Commn Against Discrimination; Intl Council of Women. **HONORS/ACHIEVEMENTS:** Plaque from govt for Outstanding Work in the Community; listed in Community Leaders of Amer; numerous other awds honors special achievements & publs.

ADAMS-DUDLEY, LILLY ANNETTE
Educator, consultant. **PERSONAL:** Born Jun 07, 1950, Lochgelley, WV; daughter of James Alfred Adams Sr and Jerlena Paulanne williams Adams; married Jerry Lee Dudley, Sr; children: Jerry Jr. **EDUCATION:** Canisius College, BA 1972, MA 1976, MS 1984. **CAREER:** Hampton City Schools, english teacher 1972-73; Buffalo Public Schools, english teacher 1974-75; Canisius Coll, language arts specialist 1975-78, asst dir 1978-80, writing lab instr 1982-84, reading & study skills instr 1981-, dir COPE office, consultant on self-esteem devel & multiculturalism in workplace. **ORGANIZATIONS:** Policy bd mem Consortium of the Niagara Frontier 1980-; treas & campus rep AJCU Conf on Minority Affairs 1980-81; Buffalo/Rochester regional rep HEOP Professional Org 1980-; mem Amer Assn of Black Women in Higher Educ, Amer Soc for Training & Develop, Amer Assn of Univ Women, Natl Assn of Female Executives;seminar developer and co-leader Today's Professional Woman, Developing Attitudes for Success; Self-Esteem and Your Success; Professional Black Women and Success; mem American Soc of Professional and Exec Women 1986-. **HONORS/ACHIEVEMENTS:** Martin Luther King Jr Full Academic Scholarship 1968-72; Outstand-

ing Young Woman of America 1979, 80; Canisius Coll Di Gamma Honor Soc 1983; Who's Who AmongHuman Service Profls 1986; workshop given: Managering the Multicultural Workforce 1989. **HOME ADDRESS:** 72 Andover Ave, Buffalo, NY 14215. **BUSINESS ADDRESS:** Dir COPE Office, Canisius College, 2001 Main St, Buffalo, NY 14208.

ADDEI, ARTHELLA HARRIS
Educational administrator. **PERSONAL:** Born Mar 23, 1943, St Louis, MO; daughter of Jessie K Harris and Iona L Harris (deceased); married Kwabena A Addei MD, Nov 28, 1970; children: D'Asante. **EDUCATION:** Harris Teacher Coll St Louis MO, BA; Columbia Univ NYC, MA; CUNY, MS; Long Island Univ, professional diploma educ admin supervision. **CAREER:** New Perspectives WWRL Radio NYC, producer & moderator; Essence Magazine, contributing editor; New York City Public Schools, guidance counselor; Manpower Prog NYC, supv counselor; St Louis Public School, tchr; Comm Sch Dist 19 New York City Public Schools, dist supervisor; NY Public School System, principal Ethan Allen Elem School. **ORGANIZATIONS:** Mem prog chairperson NY State Div for Youth Adv Bd & Youth Serv Action Team; mem Alpha Kappa Alpha Sor; Women's Aux of Nassau Co Med Soc AMA; Amer Personnel & Guidance Assn; comm on non-white concerns; NY State & NY City chapts Personnel & Guidance Assn; mem CSA Council of Supervisors and Administrators, NY City Principals Assoc. **HONORS/ACHIEVEMENTS:** Awd for Service Recognition Westbury Mothers Group of Westbury Long Island 1974; Community Service, Assn for Study of African-American Life & History, 1974; Honorary Education Fraternity, Kappa Delta Pi, 1962. **BUSINESS ADDRESS:** Principal, New York City Board of Education, 970 Vermont St, Brooklyn, NY 11207.

ADDERLEY, HERB ANTHONY
Professional athlete, business executive. **PERSONAL:** Born Jun 08, 1939, Philadelphia, PA; married Bell; children: Toni. **EDUCATION:** MI State Univ, BS 1961. **CAREER:** Green Bay Packers 1961-69, Dallas Cowboys 1970-73, New England Patriots, Rams 1973 retired, professional football player; Giant Step Record Co, vp. **HONORS/ACHIEVEMENTS:** Partic Super Bowl 1967,68,71; All Star Game 1963-67; played in Pro Bowl 1963-67; Inducted into Football Hall of Fame 1980. **MILITARY SERVICE:** AUS 1962-66.

ADDERLEY, NATHANIEL
Musician, composer. **PERSONAL:** Born Nov 25, 1931, Tampa, FL; married Ann; children: Nat, Alison. **EDUCATION:** FL A&M Univ, AB, BS 1951. **CAREER:** Lionel Hampton 1954-55, Julian Adderly 1956-67, 1960-75, JJ Johnson 1957-58, Woody Herman 1959, musician; Sermonnette 1956, Jive Samba 1962, composer; Big Man, The Legend of John Henry, co-composer. **ORGANIZATIONS:** Mem Top of Gate 1976. **MILITARY SERVICE:** AUS 1951-53. **BUSINESS ADDRESS:** 119 W 57th St, New York, NY 10011.

ADDERLY, ALFONSO LEO
Judge. **EDUCATION:** Morehouse Coll, BA 1960; Howard Univ Sch of Law, JD 1964. **CAREER:** Dade Co, teacher 1960-61; Natl Urban League, proj dir voter educ 1964; Law Private Prac, attorney 1965-81; Dade Co Court, co ct judge. **ORGANIZATIONS:** Vice pres NW Miami Jaycees 1969-74; bd of dir S FL Council Boy Scouts 1973-77; bd of dir United Family & Childrens Serv 1976-83; mem FL Bar 1965-; mem District of Columbia Bar 1981-; mem Greater Miami Urban League 1982-; judicial council Natl Bar Assn 1983-; civil rules comm FL Assoc of Co Court Judges 1984-. **HONORS/ACHIEVEMENTS:** Meritorious Public Serv Awd FL Bar 1981; Outstanding Comm Serv Awd Beta Beta Lambda Chap Alpha Phi Alpha Frat 1982; Comm Serv Awd Hialeah & Opa Locka FL 1983; Exemplary Ach Jud Serv FL Chap Natl Bar Assoc 1984.

ADDISON, ADELE
Singer. **PERSONAL:** Born Jul 24, 1925, New York City, NY; married Norman Berger; children: Julius B, Janette. **EDUCATION:** Westminster Choir Coll, BMus, Scholar 1946; Univ of MA, DHV 1963. **CAREER:** Town Hall NYC, recital debut 1952; US, CAN, Soviet Union, recital tours 1963. **HONORS/ACHIEVEMENTS:** Appeared w/New Eng City Ctr Washington Opera Co; orchestral & engagements w/symphonies Boston, Cleveland , NY Philharmonic, Natl, Chgo, Pittsburgh, Indpls, LA, SF; World Premiere performances incl John La Montaigne's Fragments from Song of Songs w/New Haven Symphony 1959, Poulenc's Gloria w/Boston Symphony 1961, Foss' Time Cycle w/NY Philharmonic 1960; faculty artist Aspen Music Festival 1956; sang role of Bess in Goldwyn's Porgy & Bess 1958; soloist opening concert Philharmonic Hall of Lincoln Ctr 1962; spec interest in German Lieder.

ADDISON, CAROLINE ELIZABETH
Director/associate professor. **PERSONAL:** Born Nov 14, 1938, Brooklyn, NY; married Dr Wallace O'Kelly Peace; children: Douglas K, Rock P. **EDUCATION:** Bronx Comm Coll, AAS 1964; Long Island Univ, BSN 1972, MS 1974; New York Univ, MPA 1976; Walden Univ, PhD 1978; Wayne State Univ, EdD 1986. **CAREER:** Passaic County Coll, dir of nursing/allied health prog 1978-80; St Joseph's Coll, dean of faculty 1976-78; VA State Univ, dean/dir nursing 1980-81; Univ of Detroit, dir/chair nursing educ 1981-. **ORGANIZATIONS:** Mem Natl League of Nursing 1964-, Amer Nursing Assoc 1964-, MI Assoc of Colleges of Nursing 1981-; mem MI Holistic Assoc 1983-; mem League of Women Voters 1984-; mem Wellness Network 1986. **HONORS/ACHIEVEMENTS:** "Factors Associate with Educational Success of Black Inner City Nursing Students" Wayne State Univ 1986; "Selected Factors Related to Admission and Retention of Adult Registered Nurses". **HOME ADDRESS:** 29264 Franklin Hills Dr, Southfield, MI 48034-1149. **BUSINESS ADDRESS:** Dir BA&C Nursing & Prof, University of Detroit, School of Education, 4001 W McNichols, Detroit, MI 48221.

ADDISON, TERRY HUNTER, JR.
Educational administrator. **PERSONAL:** Born May 15, 1950, Memphis, TN; son of Terry H Addison Sr and Carsaunder Goosby Addison; married Michele Ann Walker Addison, Mar 09, 1985; children: Terry III, Matthew Kenneth. **EDUCATION:** Univ of Minnesota-Minneapolis, BA (magna cum laude), 1971, MA, 1973. **CAREER:** ABC Prog Carleton Coll, instructor 1972; English Dept Macalester Coll, instructor 1972; Minority Programs Augsburg Coll, dir 1972-73; Minneapolis Urban League St Acad, instructor 1979-81; Macalester Coll, coord minority program 1981-84; Univ of Rhode Island, dir minority student serv 1984-. **ORGANIZATIONS:** Mem, Natl Assn Student Personnel Admin, 1984-; mem, New England Assn Educ Opportunity Program Personnel, 1985-; bd of dir, Cane Day Care Center, United Way Agency, 1985-; mem, Coll Personnel Assn of Rhode Island, 1985-; mem, Natl Educ Assn, 1986; mem, Friends of Kingston Free Library, 1987-; mem, Omega Psi Phi Frat Inc, Urban League, NAACP; mem, Rhode Island Educ Opportunity Assn, 1988-. **HONORS/ACHIEVEMENTS:** Positive Image Award, Minneapolis Urban League, 1984; Henry L Williams Memorial Award, Univ of Minnesota; Awareness Award, 1987, Leadership Award, 1989, USN Recruiting Dist Boston. **MILITARY SERVICE:** USMC, pfc, 1976-77. **BUSINESS ADDRESS:** Dir, Minority Student Serv, Univ of Rhode Island, Office of Student Life, 332 Memorial Union, Kingston, RI 02881.

ADDY, TRALANCE OBUAMA
Medical products company executive. **PERSONAL:** Born Aug 24, 1944, Kumasi, Ghana;son of Matthew Biala Addy (deceased) and Docea L Baddoo Addy (deceased); married Jo Alison Phears, May 26, 1979; children: Mantse, Miishe, Dwetri, Naakai. **EDUCATION:** Swathmore Coll, Swathmore, PA, BA, Chemistry, BS, Mechanical Engineering, 1969; Univ of Massachusetts, Amherst, MA, MSME, PhD, 1974; Harvard Business School, Boston, MA, Advanced Mgmt Program, 1987. **CAREER:** Scott Paper Co, Philadelphia, PA, sr research project engineer, 1973-76, research scientist, 1976-79, program leader, 1979-80; SURGIKOS Inc, Arlington, TX, dir applied research, 1980-85, dir technological venture devel, 1986-88, vice pres research & devel, gen mgr ASP div, 1988-. **ORGANIZATIONS:** Teacher, Upward Bound, 1967-73; mem, Amer Soc of Mechanical Engineers, 1979-Amer Assn for the Advancement of Science, 1983-, Black/Jewish Dialogue of Dallas, 1986-; chmn, co-chmn, SURGIKOS United Way Campaign, 1985-86. **HONORS/ACHIEVEMENTS:** First person to receive two separate bachelor's degrees from Swathmore since1965; Johnson & Johnson Entrepreneurial Achievement Award, 1986; one of 125 alumni to watch, Univ of Massachusetts, Amherst, 1988; mem, Sigma XI; inventor on several patents; author, several publications on nonconventional food resources and production. **BUSINESS ADDRESS:** Vice Pres, Research & Devel, SURGIKOS Inc, Johnson & Johnson, 2500 ArbrookBlvd, Arlington, TX 76014.

ADEGBILE, GIDEON SUNDAY ADEBISI
Physician/educator. **PERSONAL:** Born May 18, 1941, Iree, Nigeria;son of Rev John and Sarah; married Doris Mae Goodman; children: Lisa, Titilayo, Babalola. **EDUCATION:** Virginia Union Univ, BS (cum laude) 1966; Meharry Med Coll, MD 1971. **CAREER:** Good Samaritan Hosp, intern 1971-72; Drexel Hlth Ctr, comm health physician 1972-73; Peg Inc, emergency physician 1972-75; Wright State Univ Sch of Med, clinical instr 1975-79; private practice, physician 1973-; Wright State Univ School of Med, asst clinical prof 1979-85, assoc clinical prof 1985-. **ORGANIZATIONS:** Pres Gem City Med Dental & Pharm Soc 1978-80; chmn of bd Dayton Contemp Dance Co 1978-80; chmn Horizon in Med Prog 1978-; trustee Montgomery County Med Soc 1978; bd mem adv mental health bd Good Samaritan Hosp & Health Center 1979-85; chmn Long Term Care Comm Region II Med Review Corp 1979-81; sec Buckeye Med Assn 1980-82; mem House of Delegate of Natl Med Assn 1980-; chmn Quality Assurance Comm St Elizabeth Med Center 1980-82,84; bd mem Region II Review Corp 1981-84, exec bd mem 1982-84; med dir Christel Manor Nursing Homes; mem AMA; Ohio State & Natl Med Assn; Montgomery County Med Soc; NAACP; Alpha Phi Alpha Frat; Dem Bapt; Miami Valley Racquet Club; bd mem Dayton Area Health Plan 1985-; pres Selectmen 1986-87; sec Montgomery County med Soc 1987; chmn Dept of Family Practice GSH& HC1987-88; chmn Credentials & Accreditation Comm St Eliz Med Center 1987-88; pres Buckeye Med Assoc 1987-. **HONORS/ACHIEVEMENTS:** Cert of Appreciation Christel Manor Nursing Home 1977. **BUSINESS ADDRESS:** Assoc Clinical Professor, Wright StateUniv, School of Medicine, 4001 Free Pike, Dayton, OH 45416.

ADESUYI, SUNDAY ADENIJI
Educator. **PERSONAL:** Born Jun 27, 1948, Igbajo, Oyo, Nigeria;son of Jacob Owolabi Adesuyi and Mary Ojuolape Adesuyi. **EDUCATION:** Howard Univ, Washington, DC, BS (with Honors), 1974, PhD, 1980. **CAREER:** Howard Univ, Chem Dept, Teaching Asst, 1974-75, Teaching Fellow, 1974-78, Instructor, 1978-79; St Paul's Coll, Science & Math Dept, Asst Prof, 1979-83; Med Coll of Virginia, Dept of Pharmacology, Rsch Assoc, 1983-84; St Paul's Coll, Interim Provost, Academic Vice Pres, Acting Pres, 1988. **ORGANIZATIONS:** Reporter, BKX Science Honor Soc, Howard Univ Chapter, 1973-74; Pres, Graduate Student Assoc, 1976-78; Exec Bd Mem, US Student Assoc, 1977-78; Co-Chmn, St Paul's Subcommittee; Howard Univ's Steering Committee on Self-Study, 1977-79; Coordinator, Science & Math Fair, St Paul's Coll, 1980-82; Member, ACS, 1976-; Coordinator, Annual Project, STEP (Service to Elderly People), Lawrenceville, VA 1981-; Founder & Advisor, Xi Rho Chapter, Phi Beta Sigma, 1983-; Advisor, Science & Math Club, St Paul's Coll, 1984-; Faculty Rep to Bd of Trustees, St Paul's Coll, 1985-; Advisor, Inter-Fraternal Council, St Paul's Coll 1986-; Intl Student Assoc, St Paul's Coll, 1986; Member, Presidential Search Committee, St Paul's Coll, 1986; Chmn, Provost Search Committee, St Paul's Coll, 1987; Member, Steering Committee, Self-Study, St Paul's Coll, 1987-; Chmn, Institutional Purpose Committee, Self-Study, St Paul's Coll, 1987-; Chmn, Athletic Committee, St Paul's Coll, 1988-; Faculty Athletic Chair, CIAA, 1988-. **HONORS/ACHIEVEMENTS:** Dean's List, Coll of Liberal Arts, Howard Univ, 1972; Honor Roll, BKX Science Honor Soc, Howard Univ, 1973; Teaching Assistantship, Chemistry Dept, Howard Univ, 1974-75; Teaching Fellow, Chemistry Dept, Howard Univ, 1975-78; Most Outstanding Graduate Student, Graduate Student Assoc, Howard Univ, 1978; Presented Silver Award, Howard Univ Student Assoc, 1978; Appreciation Award, Sophomore class, St Paul's Coll, 1979-80; Student Merit Award, Student Body, St Paul's Coll, 1982, 1983; Most Outstanding Dept Faculty Mem, Science & Math Club, St Paul's COll, 1982; # 1 Supporter Award, Tennis Team, St Paul's Coll, 1982; Appreciation Award, Senior Class, St Paul's Coll, 1983; Presidential Medal for Outstanding Contributions to St Paul's Coll, 1988. **HOME ADDRESS:** PO Box 71, Lawrenceville, VA 23868. **BUSINESS ADDRESS:** Professor & Chairman, St Pauls College, Science & Math Dept, 406 Windsor Ave, Lawrenceville, VA 23868.

ADEYIGA, ADEYINKA A.
Educator. **PERSONAL:** Born Jan 20, 1948, Irolu, Nigeria;son of Alhaji Adeyiga Osinbowale and Alhaja Oladunni Apadiya-Osinbowale; married Abidemi Adibi-Adeyiga, Dec 21, 1975; children: Adeleke, Adebunmi, Adetayo. **EDUCATION:** Tennessee Tech Univ, BS, 1974; Univ of Missouri, MS, 1977; Oklahoma State Univ, PhD, 1980. **CAREER:** Oklahoma State Univ Fluid Properties Research Inc, research asst, 1979-80; EI DuPont DeNemours Co, research engr, 1981-82; Shell Petroleum Devel, reservoir engr, 1982-84; Virginia State Univ, asst prof, 1984-85; Hampton Univ, assoc prof of chem engr, 1985-, head of engrg, 1986-. **ORGANIZATIONS:** Chief consultant, Padson Engineering Co, 1983-84; mem, Engineering Deans Council of HBCU, 1986-; mem, State of Virginia Engineering Dean Council, 1986-; mem, HBCU of ASEE, 1986-; mem, US Dept of Energy Exec Comm HBCU Research 1989-.

HONORS/ACHIEVEMENTS: Vapor-liquid equil co-efficient for acid gas constituents and physical solvents, 1980; equilibrium constants for physical solvents in natural gas, 1980; a manual of chemical engineering labs, 1988; evaluation of on-board hydrogen storage for aircraft, 1989; catalytic gasification of coal chars by non-transition metal catalyst, 1986. **BUSINESS ADDRESS:** Head, Department of Engineering, Hampton University, East Queen St, 318 Olin Engineering Building, Hampton, VA 23668.

ADEYIGA, OLANREWAJU MUNIRU
Physician. **PERSONAL:** Born Sep 30, 1949, Irolu, Nigeria;married Mosekunola Omisakin; children: Adebowale, Oladunni, Adeniyi, Temitope. **EDUCATION:** Southern IL Univ Edwardsville, BA 1973, MSc 1975; Howard Univ Coll of Medicine, MD 1979. **CAREER:** SIP Prog Southern IL Univ, vstg lecturer 1976-77; Howard Univ Hosp, instructor/attending 1985-86; Columbia Hosp for Women, attending 1985-; Washington Hosp Ctr, attending 1985-; Group Health Assoc, physician. **ORGANIZATIONS:** Mem AMA 1976-, ACOG 1986-. **HONORS/ACHIEVEMENTS:** Diplomate Natl Bd of Med Exam 1981, Amer Bd of Ob/Gyn 1986; Fellow Amer Coll of Ob/Gyn 1987. **BUSINESS ADDRESS:** Group Health Assoc, GHA 2121 Pennsylvania Ave, Washington, DC 20010.

ADIELE, N. MOSES
Government official. **PERSONAL:** Born Jun 22, 1951, Umuahia, Nigeria;married Vickie I Eseonu; children: Elizabeth. **EDUCATION:** Georgia Inst of Tech, BSHS 1976; Howard Univ, MD 1980; Johns Hopkins Univ, MPH 1981. **CAREER:** Baltimore City Health Dept, public health clinician 1980-81; Howard Univ, medical house officer 1981-84; Richmond City Health Dept, asst dir of public health 1984-86; Virginia State Health Dept, dist health dir 1986-. **ORGANIZATIONS:** Pres 1981-84, mem bd of dirs 1984-, Assoc of African Physicians in North Amer; active prof mem Amer & Virginia Assoc of Family Physicians 1982-; membd of advisors Intl United Black Fund 1984-. **HONORS/ACHIEVEMENTS:** Outstanding Resident Physician Awd 1982, Who Most Exemplifies a Family Physician Awd 1982 both at Howard Univ Hospital; Mead-Johnson Scientific PresentationAwd 1983; Outstanding Serv Awd Richmond Redevelop and Housing Auth 1984; Outstanding Serv Awd Richmond Area High Blood Pressure Ctr 1985,86. **BUSINESS ADDRESS:** District Health Dir, VA State Health Department, Mecklenburg Co Health Dept, PO Box 370, Boydton, VA 23917.

ADKINS, CECELIA NABRIT
Executive director. **PERSONAL:** Born Sep 03, 1923, Atlanta, GA. **EDUCATION:** Fisk Univ, BS (Summa Cum Laude). **CAREER:** Sunday School Public Bd of the Natl Baptist Convention USA Inc, first woman to serve as chief accountant 1952, chief fiscal agent (first woman) 1965, first woman to become exec dir, 1975-. **ORGANIZATIONS:** First woman mem exec comm Protestant Church Owned Publishers Assn; first woman on bd of dirs Nashville Br Federal Reserve Bank; first woman elected Bd of Trustees Fisk Univ; first black woman apptd Metro-Nashville Bd of Educ; mem YWCA Investment Mgmt Comm and Capital Fund Dr Plng comm; first black mem, pres Travelers Aid Soc of Nashville; mem United Way Bd; mem Educ Comm Nashville C of C, Scholarship Comm for Residents of Nashville Housing Projects; mem Progressive Bapt Church. **HONORS/ACHIEVEMENTS:** Presidential Citation for Exemplary Exp, Natl Assn for Equal Opportunity in Higher Educ, 1979-84; Outstanding Leadership & Serv of the Community, Alpha Kappa Alpha Sor Southeastern Regional Conf 1984; Commr, Nashville Convention Ctr, 1986-87. **BUSINESS ADDRESS:** Executive Dir, Sunday School Publishing Bd, 330 Charlotte Ave, Nashville, TN 37201.

ADKINS, IONA W.
Government official & educational administrator. **PERSONAL:** Born Jul 20, 1925, Charles City Cty, VA; married Malchi Adkins Sr; children: Barry E Sr, Malchi Jr, Byron M Sr, Mona Adkins-Easley. **EDUCATION:** Ruthville HS, Diploma (with honors) 1941. **CAREER:** St John Baptist Church, clerk 1955; Charles City Cty VA, clerk, circuit court 1968-. **ORGANIZATIONS:** Mem exec comm Charles City Branch NAACP 1942-; mem Charles Cty Civic League Inc 1942-, VA Court Clerks Assoc 1970-; mem Charles City Democratic Comm 1974; sec Charles City Fair Comm 1980-; correspondance sec Star of the East Baptist Assoc 25 yrs; mem exec bd VA Assoc of Democratic Elected Officials. **HOME ADDRESS:** Rt 2 Box 1010, Charles City, VA 23030. **BUSINESS ADDRESS:** Clerk Circuit Court, Charles City County, PO Box 86, Charles City, VA 23030.

ADOLPH, GERALD STEPHEN
Management consultant. **PERSONAL:** Born Dec 30, 1953, New York, NY. **EDUCATION:** MIT, BS Chem Engrg 1976, BS Mgmt 1976, MS Chem Engrg 1981; Harvard Business School, MBA 1981. **CAREER:** Polaroid, engr 1976-81; Booz Allen & Hamilton, assoc 1981-83, sr assoc 1983-85, principal 1985-. **ORGANIZATIONS:** Mem Black MBA Assoc; vice chmn 21st Century Political Action Comm; bd of dirs Malcolm-King Coll. **HOME ADDRESS:** 203 West 102nd, New York, NY 10025. **BUSINESS ADDRESS:** Principal, Booz Allen & Hamilton, 101 Parker Ave 21st Fl, New York, NY 10178.

ADOM, EDWIN NII AMALAI
Psychiatrist. **PERSONAL:** Born Jan 12, 1941, Accra, Ghana;married Margaret Odarkor Lamprey; children: Edwin Nii Nortey Jr, Isaac Michael Nii Nortei. **EDUCATION:** Univ of Pennsylvania, BA 1963; Meharry Medical Coll, MD 1968. **CAREER:** Pennsylvania Hosp, internship 1968-69; Thomas Jefferson Univ, residency 1969-72; West Philadelphia Consortium, staff psychiatrist 1972—; Philadelphia Psychiatric Ctr, attending psychiatrist; Univ of Penna Sch of Medicine, faculty 1972—; St of PA, cons psychiatrist for Bur of Visually Handicap & Blindness, 1974—, and Bur of Disability Determination, 1975—; Parents Preparing for Parenthood, Philadelphia PA, cons psychiatrist, 1975-76; The Graduate Hosp, Philadelphia, cons psychiatrist, 1976—; St Joseph Hosp, Philadelphia, cons psychiatrist, 1976-80; Stephen Smith Home for the Aged, Philadelphia, cons psychiatrist, 1976-80; Mercy Douglas Human Services Center, Philadelphia, cons psychiatrist, 1977-79; St Ignatius Home for the Aged, Phildelphia, cons psychiatrist, 1978-85; Philadelphia Psychiatric Center, attending psychiatrist, 1987—; Horizon House Rehabilitation Center, Philadelphia, cons psychiatrist, 1987-89; Hosp of the Univ of PA, cons psychiatrist, 1989—. **ORGANIZATIONS:** Mem APA, NMA, PMS, MSEP; mem Black Psych of Amer, World Federation of Mental Health, Royal Soc of Health. **HONORS/ACHIEVEMENTS:** The nation's first black blind physician and psychiatrist; diplomate Amer Bd of Psych & Neurology 1978; Fellow Royal Soc of Health of England; Citizens Citation Chapel of 4 Chaplins Philadelphia. **HOME ADDRESS:** 2017 Church Rd, Glenside, PA 19038. **BUSINESS ADDRESS:** 255 So 17th St, Ste 1906, Philadelphia, PA 19103.

ADRINE, RONALD BRUCE
Judge. **PERSONAL:** Born Apr 21, 1947, Cleveland, OH; married Michele; children: Tonyia. **EDUCATION:** Wittenberg Univ, 1965-66; Fisk Univ, BA History 1966-69; Cleveland State Univ, JD 1973. **CAREER:** Cuyahoga Cty, asst pros atty 1974-77; Adrine & Adrine, partner 1977-78; US House of Reps, staff counsel 1978-79; Adrine & Adrine, partner 1979-82; Cleveland Municipal Court, judge 1982-. **ORGANIZATIONS:** Trustee Urban League of Greater Cleveland 1972; commiss Cuyahoga Metro Housing Auth 1981; mem Governor's Task Force on Fa Violence 1983, Mayor's Citizen Charter Review Comm 1983. **HONORS/ACHIEVEMENTS:** Man of the Year Omega Psi Phi Frat 4th Dist 1983. **HOME ADDRESS:** 13515 Drexmore Rd, Cleveland, OH 44120. **BUSINESS ADDRESS:** Judge Municipal Court, Justice Center, 1200 Ontario Ave, #15A, Cleveland, OH 44113.

AGEE, ROBERT EDWARD
Physician. **PERSONAL:** Born Nov 07, 1935, Jenks, OK; married Helen Doreis Gillespie; children: Shena Ann, Robert E Jr, Ronald Edwin. **EDUCATION:** Central State Coll, Coll Wilberforce OH, BS 1957; Meharry Med Coll, MD 1961; Hurley Hosp Flint MI, Internship 1961-62; Brooke AMC Ft Sam Houston, Uro/Resd 1964-67; Amer Bd of Urology, Diploma 1975; Amer Coll of Surgeons, Fellowship 1975. **CAREER:** 67th EVAC Hosp Qui Nhon RSVN, chief urology serv 1968, Tuy Hoa, chief urology serv 1968-69; 91st EVAC Hosp Tuy Hoa, chief urology serv 1969-69; Womack Hosp,chief urology serv 1969-73, chief dept of surg 1973; Brooke AMC, asst chief uro serv 1973-77; UCSF, assoc clin prof 1982-; Gov Ser Uro Soc, pres 1983; Surgeon Gen US Army, consult 1984-; Letterman AMC, chief urology serv 1977-. **ORGANIZATIONS:** Mem Amer Fertility soc, Amer Med Assoc, Natl Med Assoc, Assoc of Govt Serv Urologists, Assoc of Military Surgeons of US, So Central Sect of AUA Inc, Amer Urological Assoc, San Antonio Surgical Soc, San Antonio Urological Soc, CW Whittier San Antonio Chap of NMA, Amer Assoc of Clinical Urologists Inc, Amer Coll of Surgeons So TX Chapt, Amer Coll of Surgeons CA 1977, Western Section Amer Urological Assoc 1978, No CA Urological Soc, Assoc ofthe US Army, John Hale Medical Soc of San Fran, AUA Allied Health Professional Comm 1984. **HONORS/ACHIEVEMENTS:** Physician Recognitian Awd Amer Med Assoc 1973-76,76-79; "A" Prefix Awd 1981; num publs incl, "Acute Urinary Rentention in Women, Brief Discussion & Unusual Case Report" 1973, "Surgical Injury to the Ureter" 1976, "Malignant Fibrous Histiocytoma of the Spermatic Cord" 1982, "Allergic Reaction to Protamine, A Late Complication of Elective Vasectomy?" 1983; num presentations incl, Leiomyoma of the Female Urethra, Case Report & Review of the Literature presented at Kimbrough Urological Sem 1978, Designated as Consultant to Urology to the Surgeon Gen 1984, Amer Coll of Surgeons 1984. **MILITARY SERVICE:** AUS 1962-, ROTC 1957-60; Bronze Star Medal 1969; Meritorious Serv Medal 1969-73; Disting Military Student 1957. **BUSINESS ADDRESS:** Chief Urology Serv, Letterman Army Med Center, PO Box 51, Presidio of San Francisco, CA 94129.

AGGREY, KWEGYIR
State government official. **PERSONAL:** Born Jul 11, Salisbury, NC; married Thelma Hunter. **EDUCATION:** Attended, Hampton Inst, Oberlin Coll 1927-29; Otterbein Coll, BA, 1932; Case Western Res Univ, grad study admin/mgmt; attended, Ohio State Univ. **CAREER:** Cuyahoga Co Welfare Dept & Cleveland Div of Relief, caseworker 1934-46; City of Cleveland, health investigator, 1948-52; Cuyahoga Co Aid for Aged, chief casework supr, 1952-55; Aid for the Aged, admin asst, 1955-63, acting chief, 1963; Dept State Welfare, dir, northeast Ohio, 1963-75, acting asst dir, 1975-76; Ohio Dept of Public Welfare, dir, 1976-77. **ORGANIZATIONS:** Mem bd dir OH Welfare Conf 1976-77; pres OH Welfare Conf 1975; mem adv bd Proj Thrive of Columbus OH Urban League; mem Amer Public Welfare Assn; mem NAACP, Alpha Phi Alpha. **MILITARY SERVICE:** AUS 1st lt 1941-46.

AGGREY, O. RUDOLPH
University administrator. **PERSONAL:** Born Jul 24, 1926, Salisbury, NC; son of J E Kwegyir Aggrey (deceased) and Rose Douglass Aggrey (deceased); married Francoise Christiane Fratacci; children: Roxane Rose. **EDUCATION:** Hampton Inst, BS 1946; Syracuse Univ, MS 1948; Harvard Univ, Fellow 1964-65; Livingstone Coll, Hon LLD 1973. **CAREER:** Cleveland Call and Post, news reporter 1948-49; Chicago Defender, correspondent 1948-49; Bennet College, publicity director 1950; Dept of State Lagos, Nigeria, vice consul & information officer 1951-53; USIA, Lille, France, asst public affairs officer 1953-54; USIA, Paris, France, asst cultural office director of cultural center 1954-60; Dept of State, deputy public affairs adviser for African Affairs 1961-64; Voice of Amer, chief of the french branch 1965; Amer Embassy Kinshasa Zaire, firstsec & deputy public affairs 1966-68; US Info Agency, prog mgr motion picture & TV serv 1968-70; Dept of State, dir of The Office of West African Affairs 1970-73; US, ambassador to Senegal & The Gambia 1973-77, ambassador to Romania 1977-81; Georgetown University Dept of State Foreign Affairs Sr Fellow, rsch prof of diplomacy & rsch assoc, Georgetown University 1981-83; Bur of Rsch & Intelligence Dept of State, spl asst 1983-84; intl relations consul 1984-;. **ORGANIZATIONS:** Mem bd dirs Assn Black Amer Ambs 1984-; Washington-Dakar Sister Cities Comm, Assn for Diplomatic Studies; consul Dept of State Natl Geographic 1984-; Howard Univ USAID. **HONORS/ACHIEVEMENTS:** Meritorious & Superior Serv Awds USIA 1950, 1955; Hon mem French Acad of Jazz Paris 1960; Alumni Awd Hampton Inst 1961; Presidential Meritorious Awd US Govt 1984; Syracuse Univ Chancellor's Medal 1984; FL A&M Univ Meritorious Achievement Awd 1985; Distinguished Achievement Award, Dillard Univ 1987. **HOME ADDRESS:** 1257 Delaware Avenue SW, Washington, DC 20024.

AGUIRRE, MARK
Professional athlete. **PERSONAL:** Born Dec 10, 1959, Chicago, IL. **EDUCATION:** De Paul, 1982. **CAREER:** Dallas Mavericks, basketball forward 1981-. **ORGANIZATIONS:** Big brother Big Brothers & Big Sisters. **HONORS/ACHIEVEMENTS:** Placed 11th in NBA MVP; named to The Sporting News second-team all NBA squad; 1st Maverick to partic in the All-Star game as reserve; 5th in NVA free throw attempts; Named NBA Player of the Month; Dallas Pro Athlete of the Year 19th Annual Dallas All Sports Assoc Awds Banquet; been on the cover of The Sporting News, NBA Today, Basketball Digest; Mavericks all-time leading scorer; 6th in NBA scoring in 1982-83; leading Western Conf All-Star Vote Getter; 2 time consensus All-Amer; won the Player of the Year Awd from assorted publs; played in 3 exhibitions against the Olympians; was a starter on the 1980 US Olympic Team. **BUSINESS ADDRESS:** Dallas Mavericks, Reunion Arena, 777 Sports St, Dallas, TX 75207.

AGURS, DONALD STEELE (SIMON FRY)
Journalist. **PERSONAL:** Born Jun 01, 1947, Rock Hill, SC; married Brenda Louise Crenshaw; children: Renda, Chris. **EDUCATION:** Howard Univ, 1965-67,75-77; DC Teachers Coll, 1970-71; Fed City Coll, 1971-72; AUS Inst, 1969-70. **CAREER:** Westinghouse Broad-

casting Co, newsman 1970-71; WHUR-FM, newsman/producer 1972; WSOC Radio & TV, newsman 1973; 236 Housing Proj, admin 1973-75; WGIV, newscaster 1975; WHUR-FM, NBN, White House corr 1975-78; Sheridan Broadcasting Network, White House corr 1978-. **ORGANIZATIONS:** Bd dir Mecklenburg Co Public Access 1974,75; mem AFTRA, Natl Assoc of Black Journalist, WA press Club, Congressional Corr Assoc, White House Corr Assoc, NAACP, PAG 1973,74, Laytonsville Golf Club, Pinetuck Golf Club. **HONORS/ACHIEVEMENTS:** Spec Awd Assoc Press 1972; Birthday Spec WHUR Martin Luther King Jr 1976. **MILITARY SERVICE:** AUS sp4 1967-70. **BUSINESS ADDRESS:** White House Correspondent, Sheridan Broadcasting Network, 1755 S Jefferson Davis Hwy, Arlington, VA 22202.

AHART, THOMAS I.
Consulting firm executive. **PERSONAL:** Born Apr 03, 1938, Detroit, MI; married Menda Britton; children: Pamela M, Thomas. **EDUCATION:** Wayne State Univ, BA 1962. **CAREER:** The Ram Group, pres, 1987-; Dyma Assoc, pres 1978-87; Natl Min Purch Council, exec dir 1977-78; Amer Bankers Assn, dir 1970-77; Ford Motor Co, ind rel adm 1967-70. **ORGANIZATIONS:** Dir, Crispus Attucks Soc, 1989-; chmn, Hughes PTA Human Relations; chmn Bus Invstmnt 1985-; cnslnt US Comm Dept 195-, Export-Import Bank of US 1985, Control Data Corp 1984; mem Omega Psi Phi 1962-. **HONORS/ACHIEVEMENTS:** "Bankers and Urban Affairs," Future of Comm Bnkg Praeger, 1976; "Poems" Rustlings, Reston Publishers, 1975. **HOME ADDRESS:** 1937 Barton Hill Road, Reston, VA 22091. **BUSINESS ADDRESS:** President, The Ram Group, 1629 K St NW, Suite 1100, Washington, DC 20006.

AHMAD, JADWAA
Attorney. **PERSONAL:** Born Jul 23, 1935, Detroit, MI; married Ruth Joyce; children: Jamar H, Jadwaa W, Jamil O. **EDUCATION:** W MI Univ, attended; E MI Univ, BS 1957; Detroit Coll of Law, JD 1970. **CAREER:** City of Detroit, jr chemist 1957-59; Stroh Brewery Co Detroit, chemist 1959-70; Wayne Cty Neighborhood Legal Svcs, attny trainee 1970-71; Gragg & Gardner Detroit, attny 1970-72; Terry Ahmad & Bradfield Detroit, attny 1972-. **ORGANIZATIONS:** Mem Legal Frat Sigma Nu Phi, Kappa Alpha Psi, State Bar of MI, Wolverine Bar Assoc, Natl Bar Assoc, Detroit Bar Assoc, Amer Bar Assoc, Hse Counsel for PEACE Inc 1972-. **HONORS/ACHIEVEMENTS:** NAACP Recip Scholastic Awds in Coll 1954-57; listed in Who's Who in MI 1974. **MILITARY SERVICE:** AUS pvt 1958. **BUSINESS ADDRESS:** Attorney, Terry, Ahmad & Bradfield, 1200 David Stott Bldg, Detroit, MI 48226.

AHMANN, MATHEW HALL
Social action director. **PERSONAL:** Married Margaret Cunningham; children: Elizabeth, Teresa, Timothy, Ruth, Thomas, Katherine. **EDUCATION:** St Johns Univ, BA, 1952; Univ of California, Post Grad, 1953-54. **CAREER:** Chicago Dept Welfare, social worker, 1954-56; Today Mag, bus & circulation mgr, 1956-57; Catholic Interracial Council, Chicago IL, field rep, 1957-59, asst & acting dir, 1959-60; Natl Catholic Conf Interracial Justice, exec dir, 1959-68; Comm on Ch & Soc Archdiocese, San Antonio TX, exec dir, 1969-73; Natl Conf Catholic Charities, assoc dir for govt, rel 1973-. **ORGANIZATIONS:** Org, exec sec natl Conf Religion & Race 1962-63; exec comm Liturgical Conf; natl exec bd Workers Def League; bd govs Ctr Rsch & Ed in Amer Liberties; adv bd Law Students Civil Rights Rsch Counsil; mem Amer Civil Liberties Union; ed The New Negro 1961, Race, Challenge to Religion 1963. **HONORS/ACHIEVEMENTS:** Co-author with Margaret Roach The Church & The Urban Racial Crisis.

AIKEN, WILLIAM
Business executive. **PERSONAL:** Born Mar 11, 1934, New York City, NY; married Dorothy Harris; children: Adrienne, William Jr, Candice, Nicole. **EDUCATION:** Baruch Coll, MBA 1970; City Coll, BBA 1963. **CAREER:** NY State Ins Dept, state ins examiner 1963-67; Arthur Young & Co, sr accountant 1967-72; Aiken & Wilson CPA's 1972-78; New York City Human Resources Admin, asst dep commiss 1978-80. **ORGANIZATIONS:** Mem CPA NY; past pres, chmn of bd Natl Assoc of Black Accountants 1971-73; mem NY State Bd for Publ Accountancy 1974-, Natl Assoc of Black Accountancy, Council of Amer Inst of CPA's 1975-78, Natl Assoc of Black Accountants, NY Soc of CPA's, Accountants Club of Amer, 100 Black Men; former mem, comm on Comm Affairs; comm on Ins Cos & Agencies Accounting; mem NC A&T Univ Cluster Prog, NC Central Univ Bus Adv Council, Natl Bus League Comm for Natl Policy Review; adj prof accountancy Medgar Evers Coll; mem Natl Urban League Black Exec Exchange Prog; com on Minority Recruitment, Amer Inst of CPA's; adv bd Borough of Manhattan Comm Coll; bd dir Natl Assoc of Black Accountants, Westchester Minority Bus Asst Org Inc, mem Ethical-Fieldston Fund, Studio Mus in Harlem. **HONORS/ACHIEVEMENTS:** Author "The Black Experience in Large Publ Accounting Firms" 1971; 1st black to receive appt to NY State Bd for Publ Accountancy 1974; 2nd black in the nation to receive such an appt; Natl Assoc of Black Accountant's Annual Achievement Awd 1975; Achievement Awd Jackson State Chap Natl Assoc of Black Accountants 1972; listed in Who's Who in Amer 1975; Ebony Success Library 1974; Men of Achievement 1976. **MILITARY SERVICE:** USMC sgt 1953-56. **BUSINESS ADDRESS:** Assistant Dep Commissioner, New York City Human Resources, 250 Church St, New York, NY 10013.

AIKENS, CHESTER ALFRONZA
Dentist. **PERSONAL:** Born Feb 08, 1951, Quitman, GA; son of Augustus Davis Aikens, Sr and Lucile Balloon Aikens; married E Jean Johnson Aikens, Aug 04, 1974; children: Chester Alfronza Aikens II, Chae Rashard Aikens. **EDUCATION:** North FL Jr Coll, AA 1970; FL State Univ, BS 1973; Howard Univ, DDS 1977. **CAREER:** UA Army Ft Benning GA, Dentist 1977-79; Marchand & Brown Dental Practice, dentist 1979-80; FL Army Reserve Natl Guard, dentist (major) 1980-; Private Practice, dentist 1980-. **ORGANIZATIONS:** House of delegates Natl Dental Assoc 1980-; pres Jacksonville Chap FL Medical Dental & Pharmaceutical Assoc 1983-85; bd of dirs Joseph E Lee Child Develop Ctr 1983-; dental examiner FL Dept of Professional Regulation 1985-; mem Northwest Council Chamber of Commerce 1985; bd of dirs Jacksonville Urban League 1986-, YMCA John Weldon Johnson Branch 1986-; pres Howard Univ Alumni Assoc Jacksonville Chap 1986-; bd of dirs The Midal Touch Daycare Ctr 1986-; Parliamentarian Natl Dental Assn 1988; telethon chairman Jacksonville UNCF Telethon Campaign 1988, 1989; bd chairman Jacksonville Urban League 1988, 1989; bd mem Metro Board of Dir Jacksonville YMCA 1989. **HONORS/ACHIEVEMENTS:** Polemarch's Award, Kappa Alpha Psi Frat Jacksonville Chapter 1983; President's Achievement Award, Florida Medical Dental & Pharmacist Assn 1986; Community Serv Award, Mother Midway AME Church 1986; Service Award, Jacksonville Urban League 1986; Greek of The Year, Jacksonville Panhellenic Council 1988; Professional Man of The Year, Greater Grant Memorial AME Church 1989; Award of Appreciation, Edward Waters College Alumni Assn 1989; performed the role Rev. Perlie in the production of Perlie 1989. **MILITARY SERVICE:** AUS capt 1977-79; Dedication to Others Award 1977; Florida Army Reserve Natl Guard major 1980-. **HOME ADDRESS:** 4196 Old Mill Cove Trail West, Jacksonville, FL 32211. **BUSINESS ADDRESS:** 531 West Union St, Jacksonville, FL 32202.

AIKENS, WILLIE MAYS
Professional athlete. **PERSONAL:** Born Oct 14, 1954, Seneca, SC. **EDUCATION:** SC State Coll. **CAREER:** Calif Angels, 1979; Kansas City Royals, outfielder/designated hitter 1980-83; Toronto Blue Jays, infielder. **HONORS/ACHIEVEMENTS:** All NAIA hon in baseball; named TOPPS Texas League Player of Yr & Double A Player of Year Natl Sportwriters Assn 1976; Kenny Myers Mem Award MVP in Angels orgn 1976.

AIKINS-AFFUL, NATHANIEL AKUMANYI
Physician. **PERSONAL:** Born Nov 04, 1935, Accra, Ghana;married Josephine Brown; children: Viola, Aimee, Iris. **EDUCATION:** Bates Coll, BA 1962; Howard Univ, MD 1967. **CAREER:** Mercy Hosp, intern 1967-68; Univ of MD, resident 1968-72; Private Practice, physician 1972-. **ORGANIZATIONS:** Mem Amer Assn of Abdominal Surgeons & Gynecologic Laparoscopists; mem MD Observ & Gyn Soc; mem Balts & City Med Soc, Med & Chirungical Faculty of MD; attd physician Provident, Mercy, Bon Secours, S Baltimore Gen & Ch Hosps; mem AMA; NMA Bd Cert Am Bd of Observ & Gyn 1974. **HONORS/ACHIEVEMENTS:** Fellow Amer Coll of Observ & Gyn 1975. **BUSINESS ADDRESS:** 4000 W Northern Pkwy, Baltimore, MD 21215.

AILEY, ALVIN
Artistic director. **PERSONAL:** Born Jan 05, 1931, Rogers, TX. **EDUCATION:** Univ of CA at Los Angeles, 1949-50; Los Angeles City Coll, 1950-51; San Francisco State Coll, 1952-53; Lester Horton Dance Theatre Los Angeles, studied dancing 1949-51,53; Princeton Univ, AFD (Hon); Bard Coll, Adelphi Univ, Cedar Crest Coll with Hanya Holm 1954-55, Martha Graham 1955, Anna Sokolow 1956, Karel Shook 1954-56, Charles Weidman 1957, attended; Hon Degrees, Princeton, Cedar Coll. **CAREER:** Lester Horton Dancers, dancer/artistic dir/choreographer 1951-53; Alvin Ailey Amer Dance Theatre, dancer/artistic dir/choreographer 1958-; freelance choreographer. **ORGANIZATIONS:** Mem Dance Panel of NY State Council on Arts; mem Black Acad Arts & Letters, Advocates for the Arts. **HONORS/ACHIEVEMENTS:** First Prize Intl Dance Festival Paris 1970; Dance Mag Awd 1975; Spingarn Medal 1976; Capezio Awd Capezio Found 1979; A Philip Randolph Freedom Awd & NCCA 1984 Monarch Awd; Distinguished New Yorker Awd Bowery Bank; UN Peace Medal. **BUSINESS ADDRESS:** Artistic Dir, Alvin Ailey Am Dance Theatre, 1515 Broadway 8th Floor, New York, NY 10036.

AIRALL, ANGELA MAUREEN
Educational marketing. **PERSONAL:** Born Nov 08, 1954, Ft Dix, NJ; daughter of Dr Guillermo E Airall and Clara Airall. **EDUCATION:** The Amer Univ, BS 1976; Boston Univ Grad Sch of Communication, MS 1978; Univ of Southern California, MBA 1988. **CAREER:** US Census Bureau, comm serv specialist 1978-79; New Jersey Assoc of Counties, program dir 1979-81; Educ Testing Servs, assoc prog dir 1981-86; Grad Mgmt Admission Council, natl dir of prog devel 1986-; founder/principal, The Success Factor Inc, 1989. **ORGANIZATIONS:** Registered lobbyist NJ State Dept of Secretary 1979-82; mem Alpha Kappa Alpha Sorority Inc 1980-; mem Natl Black MBA Assoc 1983-. **HONORS/ACHIEVEMENTS:** Thesis "Communicating with Blacks in the Marketplace A Challenge to Marketing Management," 1978. **BUSINESS ADDRESS:** Natl Dir of Prog Development, Grad Mgmt Admission Council, 11601 Wilshire Blvd #1060, Los Angeles, CA 90230.

AIRALL, GUILLERMO EVERS
Dentist. **PERSONAL:** Born Apr 17, 1919, Paraiso, Panama;son of Josiah C Airall Sr (deceased) and Rosetta Letitia Christian Airall; married Clara; children: Zoila, Angela, Sheldon. **EDUCATION:** Panama Univ, BS 1946; Howard Univ, DDS 1953. **CAREER:** Public Health Detroit, dentist 1953; AUS, dentist 1953-74; Temple Univ Phila, inst prof 1978-82; Dental Office, private practice 1972-. **ORGANIZATIONS:** Mem admin bd & stewardship bd United Meth Ch 1983-; mem Burlington Chamber of Commerce 1982-; vice pres Boy Scout Germany 1969-71; pres Little League BB Germany 1969-71; pres Lions Club Willingboro NJ 1979-80; vice pres pres elect Chi Delta Mu Fraternity Philadelphia 1984-; chmn, Church and Society 1988, co-chmn 1989, Outreach, St Paul United Methodist Church; vice pres elect Chi Delta Mu Fraternity, Nu Chapter, Philadelphia 1984-85, pres 1986-87; mem Alpha Phi Alpha Fraternity Kappa Iota Lambda Chapter, Willingboro, NJ 1989-. **MILITARY SERVICE:** AUS col 21 yrs; Certificate of Achievement; Certificate of Apprreciation; Natl Defense Serv Med w/Oak Leaf Cluster; Armed Forces Res Medal; Meritorious Unit Emblem. **BUSINESS ADDRESS:** 28 Windsor Ln, Willingboro, NJ 08046.

AIRALL, ZOILA ERLINDA
Educational administrator. **PERSONAL:** Born Jan 21, 1951, Washington. **EDUCATION:** Douglass Coll Rutgers Univ, BA 1973; Columbia Univ Teachers Coll, MA 1974, EdM 1975. **CAREER:** Pemberton Twp HS, guidance counselor 1975-81; Zurbrugg Hosp, mental health therapist 1981; Bethany Coll, dir of counseling 1981-, asst dean 1984-. **ORGANIZATIONS:** Pres/basileus Beta Theta Omega-Alpha Kappa Alpha 1978-; organist Cove United Presbyterian Church 1983-; mem Fellows of Menniger Found 1984. **HONORS/ACHIEVEMENTS:** Grad Fellowship Columbia Univ 1973 & 1974; Keynote Spkr Annual Breakfast Bethany Coll 1984; Outstanding Young Women publication 1984. **BUSINESS ADDRESS:** Dir Counseling/Asst Dean, Bethany College, Bethany, WV 26032.

AKBAR, NA'IM (LUTHER B. WEEMS)
Educator. **PERSONAL:** Born Apr 26, 1944, Tallahassee, FL; son of Luther Weems and Bessie Weems; married Renee V Beach; children: Shaakira, Mutaqee, Tareeq. **EDUCATION:** Univ of Michigan, BA 1965, MS 1969, PhD 1970. **CAREER:** Morehouse Coll, assoc prof & dept head 1970-75; Norfolk State Univ, assoc prof 1977-79; Florida State Univ, visiting prof 1979-81, clinical psychol 1981-85. **ORGANIZATIONS:** Pres Mind Productions & Assoc 1980-85; dir office of Human Devel Amer Muslim Mission 1975-77; assoc editor Journal of Black Psychol 1980-85; bd of dir Natl Assn of Black Psychol 1983-84, Natl Black Child Devel Inst 1978-81; editorial bd, Journal of Black Studies 1981-. **HONORS/ACHIEVEMENTS:** Annual Research Award Assn of Black Psychol 1980; ML King out-

standing Fac Award Florida State Univ 1983; authored Chains & Images of Psychol Slavery 1984, From Miseducation to Educ 1982; guest appearances on Phil Donahue Show, Oprah Winfrey, Geraldo Show, Tony Brown's Journal. **HOME ADDRESS:** 1307 Maude Street, Tallahassee, FL 32310. **BUSINESS ADDRESS:** Professor of Psychology, Florida State University, Dept of Psychology, Tallahassee, FL 32306.

AKIN, EWEN M., JR.
Educator. **PERSONAL:** Born Jun 28, 1930, Chicago, IL; married Doris Lowery; children: Patsy, Helen, Alva. **EDUCATION:** Univ of IL, BS 1951; DePaul Univ, MS 1957; Nova Univ, EdD 1977. **CAREER:** Englewood HS, physics teacher 1958; Wilson Jr Coll, asst prof of physics 1963; DePaul Univ, lectr in physics 1968; Kennedy-King Coll, vice pres acad affairs 1970-73; Malcolm X Coll, City Coll of Chgo, president 1973-76; Kennedy-King Coll, president 1976-. **ORGANIZATIONS:** Mem IL Comm Coll Council of Pres, Am Assn of Acad Admin; bd dir Schwab Rehab Hosp; bd dir Blenwood Sch for Boys; mem Chicago Urban League, Amer Assoc Comm & Jr Colls. **HONORS/ACHIEVEMENTS:** DePaul Univ Alumni Achievement Award 1973; City Coll Chicago Foundation; Evaluator Middle State Assn Coll & Schools; Radio Station WGRT Achievement Award; presenter Amer Council on Educ Admin Fellows Program; Affirmative Action Awd Breadbasket Comml Assoc; Education Awd El Centro De La Causa. **MILITARY SERVICE:** USMC 1951-53. **BUSINESS ADDRESS:** President, Kennedy-King College, 6800 S Wentworth, Chicago, IL 60621.

AKINS, ALLEN CLINTON
Dentist. **PERSONAL:** Born Jun 06, 1919, Lakeland, FL; married Marie; children: Marian, Audrey. **EDUCATION:** Hampton Inst, BA 1941; Howard Univ, 1946-51; Howard Univ Coll Dentistry, 1951. **CAREER:** Burlington Woods Nursing Home, vis dentist; Private Practice, dentist 1955-. **ORGANIZATIONS:** Mem NJ State Dept Hlth; passed VA, FL, NJ, Natl Bd Dentistry; mem So Dental Soc NJ; Am & NJ Natl Dental Assn; Am Acad Oral Med; mem 2nd Bapt Church; supt Ch Sch 10 yrs; mem Burlington City Rotary Club; Big Bros Assn; Burlington City NAACP; Woodlin Lodge #30 of Prince Hall Masons; past presTrenton Chap Hampton Alumni Assn; past pres Zeta Iota Lambda Chap Alpha Phi Alpha Frat; past committeman burlington City 3rd Ward Dem; mem Human Rel Comm Burlington City; Orgn Comm Action Prgm for Burlington co Eagle Scout BSA. **HONORS/ACHIEVEMENTS:** Comm Serv Award NAACP; Man of the Year Award Natl Med Assn S NJ; Man of the Year Zeta Iota Lambda Chptr Alpha Phi Alpha; Testimonial Banquet Citiz Burlington, NJ. **MILITARY SERVICE:** AUSR Col Ret. **BUSINESS ADDRESS:** 113 E Federal St, Burlington, NJ 08016.

AKLILU, TESFAYE
High technology company executive. **PERSONAL:** Born Nov 10, 1944, Addis Ababa, Ethiopia;son of Captain Aklilu Dadi and Trige Reda Foulas; married Negest Retta Aklilu, Mar 01, 1986; children: Wolansa Aklilu. **EDUCATION:** Oklahoma State Univ, Stillwater OK, BS 1969, MS 1970, PhD 1975. **CAREER:** UN Industrial Devel Org, Addis Ababa, Ethiopia, sr consultant, 1972-75; Babson Coll, Wellesley MA, asst prof, 1975-79; GTE, consultant (retained), 1976-78; Digital Equipment Corp, consultant, 1976-79; Xerox Corp, Rochester NY, mgr, 1979-85, Stamford CT, mgr, 1985-88, McLean VA, mgr 1988-. **HONORS/ACHIEVEMENTS:** Author, Office Automation/Office Productivity, the Missing Link, 1981, Automating Your Office, 1982. **HOME ADDRESS:** 172 Bennett Rd, Teaneck, NJ 07666. **BUSINESS ADDRESS:** Mgr, Advanced Technology Devel, Xerox Corp, 7900 Westpark Dr, 4th Fl, McLean, VA 22102.

AKRIDGE, PAUL BAI
Program manager. **PERSONAL:** Born Jul 15, 1952, Chicago, IL; son of Andrew Akridge and Lois M Akridge; married Carrie O Johnson; children: Anike, Akili. **EDUCATION:** Univ of Nairobi, Kenya, attended 1973; DePauw Univ, BA (with honors) 1974; Univ of WI at Madison, MA political science 1974 & public policy admin 1978, PhD political science 1979; The Wharton School Univ of PA, cert in business admin 1983. **CAREER:** City of Madison Wisconsin Public Schools, researcher 1975; Governor's Manpower Council, research analyst 1976-77; Wisconsin Public Service Comm, research asst to chairperson; Univ of MO, asst prof dept of political science & research fellow 1979-82; Washington Univ postdoctoral fellow 1982-83; Edison Electric Inst, Natl Research Council/Ford Foundation postdoctoral fellow, consultant 1982-83; IBM Corp, public affairs specialist 1983-85, senior public affairs specialist 1985-86, program mgr public affairs 1986-88; IBM World Trade Asia Corp, Program Mgr 1988-. **ORGANIZATIONS:** Mem editorial brd Pub Admin Review 1984-87; Am Soc of Public Admin 1976-, World Future Soc 1984, St Louis Comm on Foreign Rel 1981-83; mem bd of dir DePauw Univ Alumni Assn 1980-86; mem bd dir Amer Lung Assn of E Missouri 1981-83; mem Inst of Noetic Sci 1985; mem Concerned Black Men Inc 1985-; mem Amer Soc of Public Admin Natl Capitol Area Chap 1985-87; grad fellowships selections panel behavioral & soc sci chmn Natl Sci found 1986; mem Japan Afro-Amer Friendship Assn 1988-. **HONORS/ACHIEVEMENTS:** Pullman Scholarship 1970-74; rector scholar DePauw Univ 1970-74; grad fellowship Univ of WI 1974-78; grad fellowship The Natl Fellowships Fund 1978-79; faculty fellow NASPAA 1982; postdoctoral fellow Ford Foundation/Natl Research Council 1982-83; Research Papers Invited to Various Conferences. **BUSINESS ADDRESS:** Program Manager, IBM World Trade Asia Corp, Shuwa Kamiyacho Building, 3-13, Toranomon 4-chome, Minato-Ku, Tokyo 105, Japan.

AL-AMIN, JAMIL ABDULLAH (H. RAP BROWN)
Writer, political activist. **PERSONAL:** Born Oct 04, 1943, Baton Rouge, LA; son of Eddie C Brown (deceased) and Thelma Warren Brown (deceased); married Karima; children: C Ali, Kairi. **EDUCATION:** Southern Univ/Baton Rouge Campus, attended. **CAREER:** Dial Press, writer, lecturer; The Community Mosque, Atlanta, GA, Imam (leader). **ORGANIZATIONS:** Chmn Student Non-Violent Coord Comm 1967-. **HONORS/ACHIEVEMENTS:** Author "Die Nigger Die" 1969. **BUSINESS ADDRESS:** Proprietor, The Community Store, 1128 Oak St SW, Atlanta, GA 30310.

AL-HAFEEZ, HUZEMA
Business executive. **PERSONAL:** Born Feb 28, 1931, New York, NY; son of Asa Mose Weir and Rosa May Danielson-Weir; married Clarissa R Mitchell, Mar 01, 1980; children: Rasul, Bismillah, Habib, Wardi, Yuhana, Larry, Don, Mariama, Jacqueline, Nia. **CAREER:** US Justice Dept, comm relations consultant; Lloyd Sealy, asst chief; WWRL, host/comm relations cons; Law & Order, lecturerr/TV host 1972-75; Trinity Mission Ch, boxing instr; NYPD, law enforcer 1959-76; WLIB-TV, host "Our Times"; Al-Hafeez Sec & Investigations Serv State of New york and Commonwealth of Virginia, owner/dir/lic private investigator. **ORGANIZATIONS:** Fdr/past pres Natl Soc of Afro-Amer Policemen 1964; editor & chief "Your Muhammad Speaks"; capt Muhammad's Temple of Islam Inc; mem Natl Assn of Chfs of Police; inspector NY State Athletic Commn; minister Muhammad's Temple of Islam Inc; mem Pastoral Care Comm Interfaith Hosp & St John's Hosp; mem Intl Platform Assn; mem Intl Police Congress. **HONORS/ACHIEVEMENTS:** Father of the Year Awd Kinlock Mission for the Blind 1974; Comm Serv Awd City of NY Council of Churches 1975; Natl Black Police Assn Person of the Year 1982; 6 Medals Excell Police Duty NYPD; Marksman Sharpshooter NYPD; many TV and radio appearances; Ebony Success Library 1000 Successful Blacks; Sojourner Truth Rm Prince George's Meml Libr; Appreciation Awd US Penitentiary Terre Haute IN 1986; Service Awd US Penitentiary at Lewisburg 1986; author "Our Time, Book #1" The Slanderer 1987. **BUSINESS ADDRESS:** Dir, Al-Hafeez Sec & Invest Serv, 549 Nostrand Ave, Brooklyn, NY 11216.

AL-MATEEN, CHERYL SINGLETON
Physician. **PERSONAL:** Born Aug 26, 1959, Washington, DC; daughter of Israel Benjamin Singleton and Carole Waters Singleton; married Kevin Bakeer Al-Mateen. **EDUCATION:** Howard Univ, Coll of Liberal Arts BS 1981, Coll of Medicine MD 1983. **CAREER:** Howard Univ Hospital, transitional medicine internship 1983-84; Hahnemann Univ Hospital, psychiatry residency 1984-87; Hahnemann Univ Hospital, Philadelphia, PA, Child Psychiatry Residency 1987-89. **ORGANIZATIONS:** Vice pres of administration Howard Univ Coll of Medicine Class of '83' 1982-; editor-in-chief Spectrum APA/NIMH Fellowship Newsletter 1986-87. **HONORS/ACHIEVEMENTS:** Service Citation Howard Univ Coll of Medicine Faculty 1983; Outstanding Young Woman of Amer 1983; Amer Psychiatric Assn Natl Inst of Mental Health Fellow Amer Psychiatric Assoc 1985-87. **BUSINESS ADDRESS:** Physician, Department of Psychiatry, Medical College of Virginia, MCV Station, PO Box 710, Richmond, VA 23298.

AL-MATEEN, KEVIN BAKEER
Physician. **PERSONAL:** Born Aug 31, 1958, Pasadena, CA; son of Eddie Johnson Jr and Margaret Strain Johnson; married Cheryl Singleton, Benjamin. **EDUCATION:** Univ of CA Davis, attended 1976-80; Howard Univ Coll of Medicine, MD 1984. **CAREER:** Third World Forum Newspaper, production manager 1978-79; St Christopher's Hospital, pediatric resident; Medical Coll of Virginia Dept of Neonatology, neonatal fellow, currently. **ORGANIZATIONS:** Pres Class of 1984 Howard Univ Coll of Medicine 1983-; judge Sister Clara Muhammad School Science Fair 1985; block captain Philadelphia Clean Block Campaign 1986-. **HONORS/ACHIEVEMENTS:** Malcolm X Scholarship Howard Univ Coll of Medicine 1984; Service Citation Howard Univ Coll of Medicine 1984. **HOME ADDRESS:** 2212 Turtle Hill Lane, Midlothian, VA 23112.

ALAAN, MANSOUR
Government official. **PERSONAL:** Children: 5. **CAREER:** Chesilhurst NJ, mayor, 1975-. **BUSINESS ADDRESS:** Government Official, Burrough of 2nd & Grant Avs, Chesilhurst, NJ 08089.

ALBAM, MANNY
Educator, musician. **PERSONAL:** Born Jun 24, 1922; children: Amy, Evan. **CAREER:** Solid State Records, former music dir; composer, conductor, arranger 1940-; Eastman School of Music Glassboro State Coll, assoc prof 1975-. **ORGANIZATIONS:** Mem Natl Acad Recording Arts & Scis; vice pres NARAS Inst Liaison NY State Council Arts; coord Jazz in the NY State Prison System. **HONORS/ACHIEVEMENTS:** Arranged & composed for Count Basie, Kenton, Woody Herman, Sarah Vaughan, Carmen McRae, Buddy Rich, Stan Getz, Gerry Mulligan, Clark Terry, Chuck Mangione; Grammy nom West Side Story; composed scores for TV & movies incl, "Around the World of Mike Todd", "Four Clowns", "Glory Trail", "Artists USA", "Chicago Picasso"; albums include, "Soul of the City', "Brass on Fire", "Jazz Goes to the Movies,; recorded albums with Coleman Hawkins & O'Donnel Levy. **BUSINESS ADDRESS:** Associate Professor, Eastman School of Music, 1697 Broadway, Room 810, New York, NY 10019.

ALBERT, CHARLES GREGORY
Attorney. **PERSONAL:** Born May 12, 1955, Chicago, IL; son of Eugie Albert and Essie L. **EDUCATION:** Princeton Univ, AB 1976; Harvard Law Sch, JD 1979. **CAREER:** Bell Boyd & Lloyd, assoc 1979-86, partner 1987-. **ORGANIZATIONS:** Dir Better Boys Foundation 1986-, Young Execs In Politics 1986-, Project Skil 1986-. **BUSINESS ADDRESS:** Partner, Bell, Boyd and Lloyd, 3 First Natl Plaza, Chicago, IL 60602.

ALBERT, DONNIE RAY
Singer. **PERSONAL:** Born Jan 10, 1950, New Orleans, LA; son of Junior and Etta Mae; married Gwendolyn Elaine Veal; children: Dimitri Rholas, Domenic Raoul. **EDUCATION:** Louisiana State Univ, BM 1972; Southern Meth Univ, MM 1975. **CAREER:** Richland Jr Coll, instr; Wolf Trap Co, 1974-77; Southern Opera Theater & Memphis Opera Theater, 1975-76; Washington Civic Opera, 1975; Houston Grand Opera, singer 1976-77; Affiliate Artist, 1978-83; Chicago Lyric Opera, 1979; Baltimore Opera Company 1984, 1988; Boston Concert & Opera, 1979; New York City Opera,1979-80; Ft Worth Opera, 1980-81; San Francisco Opera, 1985; Theater der Stadt Heidelberg Bremen & Saarbrucken, 1985-86; Canadian Opera, 1986; Houston Grand Opera, 1986-87; Theater des Westens Berlin, 1988-89; Florentine Opera Co, 1989; many other major orchestras throughout North America. **ORGANIZATIONS:** Mem Am Guild of Musical Artists; Actor's Equity; Am Fedn of TV & Radio Artists. **HONORS/ACHIEVEMENTS:** Grant Natl Opera Inst 1976; Shreveport Sym Award 1973; 1st Place Metro Opera Natl Cncl SW Reg 1975; RCA record "Porgy & Bess" 1976; Inaugural Gala Concert Appearance 1977; Grammy Awd for Best Opera Recording 1977.

ALBRIGHT, ROBERT, JR.
University president. **PERSONAL:** Born Dec 02, 1944; married Linda Diane Pittman; children: Keia Lorriane, Lance Robert. **EDUCATION:** Lincoln Univ, AB 1966; Tufts Univ, MA 1972; Kent State Univ, PhD 1978. **CAREER:** Lincoln Univ, dir 1969-71, vice pres 1972-76; Morton Consortium RR Morton Meml Inst Washington, dir 1977-79; US Dept Ed Washington, spec asst to asst sec 1979-81; Univ NC Charlotte, vchancellor 1981-83; Harvard Univ Summer Inst Cambridge MA, instr 1970-; Johnson C Smith Univ Charlotte, pres 1983-. **ORGANIZATIONS:** Consult US Office Ed Washington 1970-79, PA Dept Ed Harrisburg 1972-79, Rsch Triangle Inst 1982-; editor Student Serv Issues Problems & Oppty Jrnl 1983;

bd dir United Family Serv Charlotte 1982; mem Urban League 1983; bd visitors Univ NC 1983; mem Amer Assoc Higher Ed, Natl Assoc Equal Oppty; vice pres Acad Affairs Admin; mem Natl Assoc Student Personnel Admin; vice pres Natl Assoc Personnel Workers 1975-76; mem Rotary. **HONORS/ACHIEVEMENTS:** Author Motion Guide to Historically Black Colleges 1978; Sec's Cert of Appreciation US Dept of Ed 1981. **BUSINESS ADDRESS:** President, Johnson C Smith University, 100 Beattisford Rd, Charlotte, NC 28216.

ALBRIGHT, WILLIAM DUDLEY, JR.
Human resources executive. **PERSONAL:** Born Dec 01, 1949, Los Angeles, CA; son of William Dudley Albright, Jr and Mattie Pearl Dabner Albright; divorced; children: Anterine Penee Albright. **EDUCATION:** Univ of Redlands, Redlands, CA, BS, Chemistry, 1971; California State Univ Dominguez Hills, CA, MBA, 1975. **CAREER:** Aerospace Corp, El Segundo, CA, personnel head, 1972-78; MITRE Corp, McLean, VA, dir of human resources, 1978-. **ORGANIZATIONS:** Life mem, Alpha Phi Alpha Fraternity Inc, 1968-; bd mem, Graduate Engineering for Minorities Inc, 1981-, Mid-Atlantic Human Resource Assn, 1988-; mem, Black Human Resource Professionals, 1988-; exec comm, Fairfax/Falls Church, VA United Way, 1985-86. **HONORS/ACHIEVEMENTS:** Outstanding Young Man of Amer, US Jaycees, 1985. **BUSINESS ADDRESS:** Dir of Human Resources, MITRE Corp, 7525 Colshire Dr, McLean, VA 22102.

ALCINDOR, LEW See ABDUL-JABBAR, KAREEM

ALDREDGE, JAMES EARL
Government manager. **PERSONAL:** Born May 01, 1939, Gilmer, TX; married Daisy Rae. **EDUCATION:** Fresno City Coll, AA Business 1959; CA State Univ BA Therapeutic Recreation 1964, MPA Publ Admin 1978; USC/Golden Gate Univ, Doctorate Publ Admin1985. **CAREER:** Fresno Cty Econ Opportunities, program coord 1965; City of Fresno, city manager. **ORGANIZATIONS:** Bd mem Fresno Cty United Way, CA State Univ Fresno. **BUSINESS ADDRESS:** City Manager, City of Fresno, 2326 Fresno St, Fresno, CA 93721.

ALDRIDGE, DELORES P.
Educator. **PERSONAL:** Born Jun 08, 1941, Tampa, FL; married Kwame Essuon. **EDUCATION:** Clark Coll, BA Soc Sci 1963; Atlanta Univ, MSW 1966; Univ of Irelant, psychology cert 1967; Purdue Univ, PhD Sociology 1971. **CAREER:** Tampa Urban League, assoc dir 1966; Greater Lafayette comm Cntrs Inc, dir comm devel 1969-70, exec dir 1970-71; Emory Univ, coord Afro-Am & African Studies/asst prof of soc 1971-75; Shaw Univ & Spellman Coll, adj assoc prof of soc 1971-75; Emory Univ, dir of Afro-Am & African Stud/assoc prof of Soc 1975-. **ORGANIZATIONS:** Cons/panelist Natl Sci Found/Natl Endow of the Humanities/HEW 1971-; consult So Reg Counc 1972-78; consult So Assn of Coll & Schs 1973-; consult Cntr for the Study of Black Family Life 1975-; editorial bd Journ of Afro-Am Issues/Journ of Soc & Behavioral Sci/Umoja, Journ of Black Studies 1979-; bd mem Natl Counc of Black Studies 1979-; vice pres Assn of Social & Behavioral Sci 1980. **HONORS/ACHIEVEMENTS:** Recipient of Gold Plaques & Cert; various Pol & Social organizations incl Delta Sigma Theta Sor 1959-79; fellowships/grants NIMH-NDEA-NIE etc 1962-80; many publications on social change and policy women Blacks & educ 1970-. **BUSINESS ADDRESS:** Dir African & Afro-Amer Stds, EmoryUniv, 201 B Candler Library Bldg, Atlanta, GA 30322.

ALEX, GREGORY K.
Minister, director. **PERSONAL:** Born Nov 30, 1948, Seattle, WA; son of Joseph P Alex and Delores Alex. **EDUCATION:** Univ of Washington, BA Special Studies 1971. **CAREER:** HUD Washington DC, urban planner, intern 1971-; HUD Disaster Recreation Operation Wilkes Barre PA, dir Liason Operation 1972-75; Seattle Housing Authority, pres/dir Target Projects Program 1975-78; A & R Imports Inc, pres 1978-. **ORGANIZATIONS:** Dir soc planning bd, mem Urban Planning & Architect Consultant, Seattle WA 1970; mem Amer Soc of Planning Officials; Natl Assn of Planners; Interagency Coastal Zone Mgmt Comm; Natl Urban Intern Training Comm; mem Yale Univ Black Enviornmental Studies Team Curriculum Comm. **HONORS/ACHIEVEMENTS:** Sec Outstanding Achievement Award HUD 1972; Outstanding Achievement Award Univ of WA; Black Athletic Alumni Award 1971. **BUSINESS ADDRESS:** Minister/Director, Matt Talbot Center, 119 Yale North, Seattle, WA 98122.

ALEXANDER, A. MELVIN
Dermatologist. **PERSONAL:** Born Feb 04, 1943, Cleveland, OH; son of A Melvin Alexander and Grace C Alexander; married Leslie Gaillard; children: Hollie C, Allison L. **EDUCATION:** Hillsdale Coll, BS 1964; Howard Univ Coll of Medicine, MD 1968. **CAREER:** US Army Medical Center Okinawa, chief dermatology serv 1972-74; Howard Univ, asst prof 1975-80; Shaw Health Center, dermatology consultant 1977-78; Centers for Dermatology & Dermatologic Surgery, dir 1978-. **ORGANIZATIONS:** Consultant Amer Safety Razor Co 1980-82; chmn dermatology section Natl Medial Assoc 1985-87. **HONORS/ACHIEVEMENTS:** Upjohn Award for Excellence in Research, Howard Univ; contributor "Conn's Textbook of Current Therapy," 1983, 1984; author of several published professional articles. **MILITARY SERVICE:** AUS major 2 yrs. **BUSINESS ADDRESS:** Dir, Alexander Dermatology Center, 11085 Little Patuxent, Suite 102, Columbia, MD 21044.

ALEXANDER, ALMA DUNCAN
Educator. **PERSONAL:** Born May 13, 1939, New Orleans, LA; married Lorrie; children: Sybil. **EDUCATION:** Dillard Univ, BA 1961; IN Univ, MS 1969. **CAREER:** Orleans Parish School Bd, teacher 1968-70; IN Univ, intern counseling & guidance of children & foreign born 1969; Univ New Orleans, conselor 1970-71; TX Southern Univ, administrative asst to dean of students . **ORGANIZATIONS:** Mem Am Inst Parliamentarians; natl pres Eta Phi Beta Sor; exec bd mem Natl Cncl Negro Women; mem Amer Assn Univ Women; mem Natl Assn Women Deans, Cnslrs and Adminstrs. **HONORS/ACHIEVEMENTS:** Citation Dept Common Cncl 1977; Awards from City Miami Beach 1976, NAACP 1977. **BUSINESS ADDRESS:** Admin Asst to Dean of Student, TX SoUniv, PO Box 543, Houston, TX 77004.

ALEXANDER, BENJAMIN HAROLD
Chief executive officer. **PERSONAL:** Born Oct 18, 1921, Roberta, GA; son of Manoah Alexander and Annie Alexander; married Mary E; children: Drew W, Dawn C. **EDUCATION:** Univ of Cincinnati, BA 1943; Bradley Univ, MS 1950; Georgetown Univ, PhD 1957. **CAREER:** Dept of Agriculture, rsch chemist 1945-62; Walter Reed Army Inst Rsch, chief rsch chemist 1962-67; HEW, health sci admin 1967-74; Chicago State Univ, pres 1974-82; Univ of Dist of Columbia, pres 1982-83; Dist of Columbia, pres 1982-83; US Dept of Educ, dep asst sec 1983-84; Drew Dawn Enterprises Inc, pres 1984-. **ORGANIZATIONS:** Mem Amer Chem Soc 1945-; fellow Washington Acad of Sci 1957-; rsch prof Amer Univ 1960-74, 1984-; mem Bradley Univ Bd Trustee 1980-; pres YMCA Trustee Council 1983-; mem Natl Bd Fund for Improvement Post Sec Educ 1985-. **HONORS/ACHIEVEMENTS:** Plaque Best Coll Pres 1978; Hon Doctor of Law 1979; Dr Percy L Julian Awd 1982; Plate of Appreciation 1985. **MILITARY SERVICE:** USA tsgt 1945-47; USAR maj 1947-65; 13 commendations, 12 citations 1945-47. **BUSINESS ADDRESS:** President, Drew Dawn Enterprises, Inc, 30 Kennedy Street, N W, Suite 110, Washington, DC 20011.

ALEXANDER, CHARLES
Professional athlete. **PERSONAL:** Born Jul 28, 1957, Galveston, TX; married Yvette; children: Nicole. **EDUCATION:** LSU, 1975-79. **CAREER:** Cincinnati Bengals, running-back/fullback 1979-. **HONORS/ACHIEVEMENTS:** All-Am at LSU; Only LSU player to ever account for 4000 or more yards in a career. **BUSINESS ADDRESS:** Cincinnati Bengals, 200 Riverfront Stadium, Cincinnati, OH 45202.

ALEXANDER, CLIFFORD L., JR.
Management consultant. **PERSONAL:** Born Sep 21, 1933, New York, NY; married Adele Logan; children: Elizabeth, Mark Clifford. **EDUCATION:** Harvard Univ, AB (Cum Laude) 1955; Yale Univ, LLB 1958; Malcolm X Coll, LLD (hon) 1972; Morgan State Univ, LLD (hon) 1972; Wake Forest Univ, LLD (hon) 1978; Univ MD, LLD (hon) 1980; Atlanta Univ, LLD (hon) 1982. **CAREER:** NY County, asst to dist atty 1959-61; Manhattanville Hamilton Grange (neighborhood consult proj), exec dir 1961-62; HARYOU Inc, exec dir 1962-63; Private Practice, atty New York City 1962-63; Natl Security Cncl, staff mem 1963-64; Pres Johnson, dep special asst 1964-65, assoc special counsel 1965-66, dep special counsel 1966-67; Equal Employment Opportunity Commn, chmn 1967-69; Arnold & Porter, partner 1969-75; Verner, Liipfert, Bernhard, McPherson & Alexander, partner 1975-76; sec army 1977-80; Alexander & Assoc Inc Washington, pres 1981-. **ORGANIZATIONS:** Dir PA Power & Light Co; dir Dreyfus Third Century Fund, Dreyfus Gen Money Market Fund, Dreyfus Common Stock Fund, Dreyfus Govt Sec Fund, Dreyfus Tax Exempt Fund, MCI Corp; adj prof Georgetown Univ; prof Howard Univ; mem Pres's Commn on Income Maint Progs 1967-68; Pres's spl ambassador to the Independence of Swaziland 1968; mem Pres's Commn for Observation Human Rights Yr 1968; bd dirs Mex-Amer Legal Def and Educ Fund; NAACP Legal and Educ Fund; bd overseers Harvard Univ 1969-75; trustee Atlanta Univ; host/co-producer TV prog Cliff Alexander, Black on White 1971-74; mem Amer & DC Bar Assns; dir Equitable Resources, Inc; chairman The Comm for Food & Shelter, Inc. **HONORS/ACHIEVEMENTS:** Named Hon Citizen Kansas City, MO 1965; recip Ames Award Harvard Univ 1955; Frederick Douglass Award 1970; Outstanding Civilian Serv Award Dept Army 1980; Disting Publ Serv Award Dept Def 1981. **MILITARY SERVICE:** AUS 1958-59. **BUSINESS ADDRESS:** President, Alexander & Assoc Inc, 400 C St NE, Washington, DC 20002.

ALEXANDER, CORNELIA (CONNIE)
Government administrator. **PERSONAL:** Born in Winona, MS; married John Alexander, Sr (deceased); children: Margaret Alexander McLaughlin, John, Jr, Leslie B Hardy, Charles, Carl E Hardy, Constance E Hardy Atkins. **EDUCATION:** Vestal Laboratories, Certificate 1969; Youngstown State Univ, Certificate 1977; Independence OH, attend workshop & seminar for elected officials of cities & villages 1986. **CAREER:** Alexander's Garage, office manager 1959-77; Salem City Hospital, laundry manager 1965-80; Mary Kay Cosmetics, beauty consultant 1979-; NCSC Senior Aide Program, senior aide 1982-83; Columbiana County Recorder's Office, deputy recorder 1982-; Salem City Council, 2nd ward city councilman 1984-85, 87-. **ORGANIZATIONS:** Mt Zion AME Church mem 1957-82; mem Salem YWCA 1968-; dir Salem YWCA 1971-75; dem precinct comm 1980-; mem Bus & Professional Women-Lisbon OH 1981-83, Amer Cancer Soc 1982-83, Believer's Christian Fellowship 1982-; Salem YWCA Spec Exec ard 1982-83; Believer's Christian Fellowship 1982-; spec exec nom comm Salem YWCA 1984-85; bd dir Mobile Meals of Salem 1978, 87-91; chmn Fed & State Funding Comm of City Council; served on all 9 council committees (only Democrat); mem Salem Bus & Professional Women Org. **HONORS/ACHIEVEMENTS:** One of three nominees Chosen as Democrat of the Year 1985. **HOME ADDRESS:** 189 W Wilson St, Salem, OH 44460.

ALEXANDER, DAWN CRIKET
Assistant marketing manager. **PERSONAL:** Born Nov 05, 1960, Washington, DC. **EDUCATION:** Oberlin Coll, BA 1982; Harvard Univ JFK Sch of Govt, Certificate 1985; Yale Sch of Mgmt, MPPM 1987. **CAREER:** Morgan-Stanley, systems analyst 1982-84; Drew-Dawn Enterprises, pres 1984-85; Morgan-Stanley, data ctr oper supv 1984-85; DFS Dorland Worldwide, asst acct exec 1986; Pepsi-Cola Co, asst mktg mgr 1987-. **ORGANIZATIONS:** Alumni admissions rep Oberlin Coll 1982-; mem Natl Black MBA Assoc 1986-; dir Drew-Dawn Enterprises 1984-. **HONORS/ACHIEVEMENTS:** Natl Register of Outstanding College Graduates 1982; Outstanding Young Women of Amer 1984,86; Who's Who in Professional & Exec Women 1987. **BUSINESS ADDRESS:** 135 Prospect St, New Haven, CT 06520.

ALEXANDER, DON H.
Business executive. **PERSONAL:** Born Jul 09, 1924, Bremerton, WA; married Verna Alexander; children: Judy Ann. **EDUCATION:** Univ of WA, BA 1962; Amer Inst of Banking, Grad Degree 1965; Pacific Coast Sch of Banking, Honor Student Degree 1973. **CAREER:** Seattle First Natl Bank, mgmt trainee 1962, asst mgr 1965, br mgr 1968, asst vice pres 1971-. **ORGANIZATIONS:** Mem Urban Affairs Com of ABA 1970-72; Minority Lending Comm; Amer Bankers Assn 1972-74; Bankers & Accts Relations Com ABA 1974; assoc mem of Natl Bankers Assn 1971-74; pres/assoc mem Natl Bankers Assn 1977; Urban League; NAACP; pres Central Area Youth Assn 1969-70; mem exec bd United Good Neighbors 1974; mem Natl Business League 1974; Kappa Alpha Psi Frat. **HONORS/ACHIEVEMENTS:** Man of the Year Award Central Area Youth Assn 1971; Spl Recognition for Banking & Comm Contrib 1971 NAACP; Unselfish Serv Award Black Bus Students Univ of WA 1971; Outstanding Businessman & Comm Award United Inner-City Devel Found & Natl Bus League 1974; Author & publisher book "Banking For the Non-Banker" 1974. **MILITARY SERVICE:** USN 1943-46. **BUSINESS ADDRESS:** Assistant Vice President, Seattle First Natl Bank, PO Box 3586, Seattle, WA 98124.

ALEXANDER, DONALD
News correspondent. **PERSONAL:** Born Jul 24, 1937, New York, NY. **EDUCATION:** CCNY, attended 1955-59; Queens Coll Flushing; Tech Pub Inst LA 1956; Bible Sch of Gilead Ithaca 1965. **CAREER:** WCBS NY, WTTG-TV Washington, KYW Phila, WINS NY, WNEW NY, WLIB NY and sev other smaller local stations in metro NY area, staff newscaster/reporter/writer/editor; NBC News NY, news correspondent. **ORGANIZATIONS:** Mem Am Fedn TV, Radio Artists; Writers Guild of Am; Capitol Press Club; natl Assn of Securities Dealers; pres Alpha Omega Organ; Blacks in BroadcastingWash, DC; Intl Direct Marketing Assn; Radio-TV Corresp Assn; Newspaper Rptrs Assn of New York City Volunteer Joint Action in Comm Svc; Big Brothers of NY; Chinese Kung-Fu, Wu Su, Martial Arts Assn. **HONORS/ACHIEVEMENTS:** Recip Excellence in TV Reporting Capitol Press Club 1971; Vol Achievement Award Joint Action in Comm Serv 1970; NY Times Youth Forum TV panelist rep Bronx HS of Sci 1954. **BUSINESS ADDRESS:** Correspondent, NBC News Room 839, 30 Rockefeller Plaza, New York, NY 10020.

ALEXANDER, DREW W.
Physician, educator. **PERSONAL:** Born Dec 21, 1948, Peoria, IL. **EDUCATION:** Earlham Coll, BA 1970; Med Coll of OH, MD 1973; Albert Einstein Coll of Med, Ped Training 1976. **CAREER:** Univ of TX Health Sci Dallas, fellow adolescent med 1976-77; W Dallas Youth Clinic, health team leader 1977-; Univ of TX Health Sci Ctr Dallas, asst prof pediatrics 1977-. **ORGANIZATIONS:** Mem ed comm Soc for Adolescent Med 1976-; asst med dir Dallas Cty Juvenile Detention Clinic 1977-; consult Multidisciplinary Adolescent Health Training Proj 1977-; admissions comm Univ of TX Dallas 1978-; coord Minority Affairs 1979-; big brother Big Brothers & Sisters 1976-; bd mem Child Care Assoc Metro Dallas 1978-. **BUSINESS ADDRESS:** Assistant Professor Pediatrics, Univ of Texas Health Sci Ctr, 5323 Harry Hines Blvd, Dallas, TX 75235.

ALEXANDER, E. CURTIS
Educator. **PERSONAL:** Born Sep 24, 1941, Chesapeake, VA; married Barbara Elaine Johnson; children: Kwame, Sia, Nataki, Ade. **EDUCATION:** Norfolk State Univ, AB 1967; Bank St Coll, MS 1970; Tchrs Coll Columbia Univ, EdM 1972, EdD 1977; Rutgers Univ, Certificate; Univ of Ghana, Certificate. **CAREER:** William Paterson Coll of NJ, prof of educ 1972-75; NC A&T State Univ, prof of educ 1975; Norfolk State Univ, prof of sociology 1975-76; Tidewater CommColl, adj prof history 1975-77; Passaic Co Comm Coll, adj prof educ 1980; Vermont Coll of Norwhich Univ, prof of educ; ECA Assoc, pres. **ORGANIZATIONS:** Consult US Office of Educ 1970-74; consult United Meth Ch New York City 1974-; rsch dir Wooten Assoc New York City 1977-; mem Phi Delta Kappa Honor Soc 1970-; mem Kappa Delta Pi Hon Soc 1972-; advisor Volunteers of Amer 1975-; writer Norfolk Journal & Guide Newspaper; writer Small Press Magazine. **HONORS/ACHIEVEMENTS:** Outstanding Young Men of Amer C of C 1972; Comm Serv Awd Phileman DCC NJ 1974; Comm Serv Awd Tidewater Comm Coll 1977; numerous articles & ten booklets published; Fellow Intl Inst of Comm Svcs; Coolidge Fellow at Andover Newton Theol Sch 1985; selected to Cncl of Elders Mandala Inst 1986; mem Educ Materials Task Force 1987. **MILITARY SERVICE:** USAF A/3c 1960-63. **BUSINESS ADDRESS:** President, ECA Assoc, P O Box 15004, Chesapeake, VA 23320.

ALEXANDER, EDWARD CLEVE
Educator, scientist. **PERSONAL:** Born Nov 20, 1943, Knoxville, TN; son of Robert W Alexander and Gladys Clardy Alexander; married Edwina Carr; children: Everett, Erika, Efrem. **EDUCATION:** Univ of NY City Coll of City, BS 1965; State Univ of NY at Buffalo, PhD 1969. **CAREER:** IA State Univ, post doctoral fellowship 1969-70; Univ of CA at San Diego, ast prof of chem 1970-78; CA State Univ at Los Angeles, lecturer 1978 -82; BOOST Prog San Diego, supervisor dept of math & sci 1982-. **ORGANIZATIONS:** Consultant NIH, Minority Biomed Support Branch 1974-78, IBM, San Jose, CA 1976; mem bd of dir and exec bd San Diego Urban League 1972-76; Amer Chem Soc 1965-. **HONORS/ACHIEVEMENTS:** Published fourteen research papers in field of Phys & Organic Chem. **HOME ADDRESS:** 9777 Genesee Ave, San Diego, CA 92121. **BUSINESS ADDRESS:** Dept Supervisor, Science Dept, Naval Training Center, Boost Program Service School Cmd, NTC, San Diego, CA 92133.

ALEXANDER, ERROL D.
Company president. **PERSONAL:** Born Jul 11, 1941, Sandusky, OH; divorced; children: Kay, Doug. **EDUCATION:** Ohio State Univ, BS 1963; Univ of Mich, MBA 1966. **CAREER:** Bendix Corp, asst proj mgr 1965-70; United Tech Corp, engrg 1968-70; Planned Resource Corp, exec vice pres 1970-71; HCCC Div of Hartford Natl Bank, gen mgr 1970-71; Profiles Rsch & Consult Groups Inc, pres, founder, chmn of bd 1971-. **ORGANIZATIONS:** Adj prof Manchester Comm Coll 1975-80; bd of dir Black Corp Presidents of New England 1976-85, United Way Inc of Gr Hartford 1979-81; pres Urban League 1980; managing dir Bauer Electro Mfg Co 1983-85; dir Task Force for US FAA 1985-86; rsch fellow Univ of Strathclyde 1986-87; post bus grad class chmn Strathclyde Bus School in Scotland 1986; bd dir Catholic Family Serv; mem Tri-Town C of C; Heraldic Coll of Arms. **HONORS/ACHIEVEMENTS:** "How to Be a Corp Expert" Bd Room Mag 1977; "Selecting a Consulting Firm" Black Enteprise Mag 1978; "Devel of FDO Organizations" MOAA Dept of Commerce 1980; "How To Conduct a Perceptional Survey" Manage Mag 1981; conf key note speaker "Delphi Business Forecasting" Univ of NC, "A Profile of Black Executives, Conceptually, Globally and Statistically" Harvard Bus School 1981, 1983; Distinguished Serv Awd, Hartford Area Small Bus Admin 1983. **BUSINESS ADDRESS:** President, Chmn of the Board, Profiles Research & Consult Grp, Profiles Corp Bldg, Vernon, CT 06066.

ALEXANDER, ESTELLA CONWILL
Educator. **PERSONAL:** Born Jan 19, 1949, Louisville, KY; children: Patrice Sales, Dominic. **EDUCATION:** Univ of Louisville, BA 1975, MA 1976; Univ of IA, PhD 1984. **CAREER:** Univ of Iowa, instructor/director of black poetry 1976-79; Grinnell Coll, asst prof 1979-80; KY State Univ, prof of english. **HONORS/ACHIEVEMENTS:** Recording Motion Grace Gospel Recordings 1983; KY Arts Council Grant 1986; Art Grant KY Foundation for Women 1986. **BUSINESS ADDRESS:** Professor of English, Kentucky StateUniv, Frankfort, KY 40601.

ALEXANDER, F. S. JACK
State official. **PERSONAL:** Born Dec 07, 1930, Iola, KS; son of James Floyd Alexander and Agnes Marie Stewart; married Tillie Marie Simon; children: Patricia M, Jack Jr, Stephanie R, Terrell L. **EDUCATION:** Washburn Univ, BA 1954. **CAREER:** Topeka Bd of Educ, stockroom mgr 1948-51; Goodyear Tire & Rubber Co, quality control 1951-; City of Topeka, water commn 1973-85; State of KS Oilfield and Environmental Geology, consultant 1985-86, dept of health & environment 1986-. **ORGANIZATIONS:** On leave ex-com & bd NLC 1975-85; Economic & Comm Devel Comm 1975-85; mem vice pres Topeka United Way Bd 1975-85; pres Topeka Cty Comm 1975-85; trustee St Vail Hospital Bd 1976-85; mem State Water Authority 1981-86; ex comm NAACP; past pres KS League of Municipalities 1983-84. **HONORS/ACHIEVEMENTS:** Public Serv Shawnee County Comm Asst 1972-83; Outstanding Public Official Awd Topeka Comm Devel 1976; Awd USA #501 Dir Assoc 1977; Awd Reg 7 Comm Action 1979. **MILITARY SERVICE:** USN radiomen 2nd class 4 yrs. **HOME ADDRESS:** 2509 Fillmore St, Topeka, KS 66611. **BUSINESS ADDRESS:** Health & Environmental Analyst, State of Kansas, Forbes Field Bldg #740, Topeka, KS 66620-7300.

ALEXANDER, FRITZ W., II
Judge. **PERSONAL:** Born Apr 24, 1926, Apopka, FL; married Beverly J; children: Karen, Kelly Marie, Fritz III. **EDUCATION:** Dartmouth Coll, AB 1947; NY Univ School of Law, LLB; NY Bar 1952; US Supreme Ct & US Circuit Court, Natl Coll of State Judiciary Reno NV, graduate. **CAREER:** Demov Morris Levin & Hammerling, assoc; Thomas B Dyett, attny 1952-58; Dyett Alexander & Dinkins, founding partner 1958-62, 1963-68; Upper Manhattan Dist Off of the City Ren & Rehab Admin, dist dir 1962-63; NY Urban Coalition, chmn lawyers comm 1968-70; Civil Court 5th Munic Dist, judge 1970-77; Appellate Div, assoc justice 1977-84; NY Court of Appeals, assoc judge 1985-. **ORGANIZATIONS:** Mem Amer & Natl Bar Assoc; founding mem, exec comm Judicial Council of the Natl Bar Assoc; vice pres Assoc of the Bar of the City of NY; former mem Committee on Lectures & Continuing Ed & the Centennial Study on Decentralization of Govt in NYC; mem Metro Black Bar Assoc, NY Bar Assoc, Amer Judicature Soc, Adv Comm of the Ctr for Judicial Conduct Org of the Amer Judicature Soc; trsutee NY Univ Law Ctr Found, dir NY Soc for the Prevention of Cruelty toChildren past pres founding mem Dartmouth Coll Black Alumni Assoc; past pres Harlem Lawyers Assoc; founding mem 100 Black Men Inc; former mem, bd of dir Harlem Neighborhhods Assoc Inc; former dir, exec vice pres United Mutual Life Ins Co; former mem Bd of Mgrs & Treas of United Charities; former mem, bd of dir NY City Mission Soc; hon mem The Order of the Coif. **HONORS/ACHIEVEMENTS:** Man of the Year Awd Omicron Chap Omega Psi Phi 1981; Achievement Awd of NY Univ Law School Alumni Assn 1982; Golda Meir Award Jewish Lawyer's Guild 1985;William H Hastie Achievement Award Natl Bar Assn Judicial Cncl 1985; Spec Recogn Award Metro Black Bar Assn 1985; Arthur T Vanderbilt Gold Medal Awd NYU Sch of Law 1985; Hope R Stevens Awd NBA Region II Regional Conf 1985; LLD Pace Univ and Long Island Univ. **MILITARY SERVICE:** USN Reserve 1942-46, 1948-52. **BUSINESS ADDRESS:** Associate Judge, NY Court of Appeals, 20 Eagle St, Albany, NY 12207.

ALEXANDER, HARRY TOUSSAINT
Retired judge. **PERSONAL:** Born Jul 22, 1924, New Orleans, LA; married Beatrice Perkins; children: Agnes, Harry Jr, Beatrice, Louis. **EDUCATION:** Georgetown Univ School of Law, JD 1952; Xavier Univ, BS 1949. **CAREER:** Georgetown Univ, rsch asst Cmdr Langdon P Marvin 1951-52; Office of Price Stabilization, atty adv 1952-53; Private practice, attny 1953; US Attny DC, asst 1953-61, spec attny 1961-64, staff asst criminal div 1964-65; US Dept of Justice, attny 1961-66; Superior Ct DC, assoc judge 1966-76; Howard Univ School of Law, adj prof 1970-. **ORGANIZATIONS:** Mem Judicial Conf DC; comm Abolition of Mandatory Capital Punishment DC 1959-62; mem Prob Connected with Mental Exams of the Accused in Criminal Cases Before Trial 1960-63, Cardoza Comm on Judicial Conf, Amer Bar Assoc; mem 1961-65, recording sec 1955-60, WA Bar Assoc; mem Phi Delta Phi Intl Legal Frat, PAlpha Delta Intl Legal Frat; pres NAACP DC 1977, United Natl Bank of WA 1977, Family & Child Serv of WA 1971, Natl Conf of Christians & Jews 1965-70; vchmn BSA 1966, Interreligious Comm on Race Rels 1963-66, Scouters Intl Rep St Gabriels Cath Church 1963-65; mem, 1st natl vice pres 1960-62 Xavier Univ Alumni Assoc; pres NW Boundary Civic Assoc 1958-60; vice pres Natl Fed of Cath Coll Students LA Reg; mem US Natl Students Assoc; pres, vice pres LA-MS-AR Reg 1947-48,48-49; treas NAACP Youth Council New Orleans LA. **HONORS/ACHIEVEMENTS:** Dr Cruezot Awd; Frederick W Shea Awd; Wm H Hastie Awd Natl Conf of Black Lawyers 1976; Outstanding Comm Serv Awd 1975; Outstanding Serv DC C of C;Cert of Degree Strategic Air Command 1973; Martin Luther King Jr Outstanding Serv Awd Howard Univ School of Law 1977; Harry Toussaint Alexander Day DC Council; publ "Appeals in Fed Jurisdiction" NBA 1960, "Curbing Juvenile Delinquency with Adequate Playground Facilities" 1957, "The Nature of Our Heritage" 1950-51, "The Unconstitutionality of Segregation in Ed" 1950-51, "Due Process Required in Revocation of a Conditional Pardon" 1950-51, "The Antislavery Origins of the Fourteenth Amendment", "Convention Coverage" Assoc Negro Press Inc 1947, Xavier Herald 1946-49;TV appearances The Admin of Juv Criminal Justice; radio appearances The Admin of Criminal Juv Justice. **MILITARY SERVICE:** USN 1943-46.

ALEXANDER, JAMES, JR.
Attorney. **PERSONAL:** Born Oct 07, 1945, Charlotte, NC. **EDUCATION:** Columb Coll Columb U, BA 1967; Case West Res U, JD 1970; Nat Coll of Crim Def Lawy, cert 1974. **CAREER:** Reginal Heber Smith Fellow Cleveland, 1970-72; Hough Area & Devel Corp Cleveland, gen couns 1971-72; Cuyahoga Co, asst co prosec 1972; Tolliver Nimrod & Alexender, atty 1972-75; Hardiman Alexander Buchanan Pittman & Howland Co LPA, atty. **ORGANIZATIONS:** Mem Cleveland Bar Assn, Amer Acad of Trial Layers, Natl Bar Assoc, Cuyahoga Bar Assn, Nat Conf of Blck Lawyers Assn; pres Hough Comm Coun Inc 1972; treas Columbia Univ Clb of Cleve; mem bd of trust Un Torch Svcs; Fedn for Comm Plan Bd; Goodrich Soc Settle Bd; vice pres Legal Aid Soc of Cleve; pres Hough Area Devel Corp. **HONORS/ACHIEVEMENTS:** Recpt 1972 Pres awd; Hough Comm Coun; Martin Luth King awd Case West Res Law Sch 1970; Who's Who in OH 1974. **BUSINESS ADDRESS:** Attorney, Hardiman, Alexander, Buchanan,, Pittman & Howland Co LPA, 1100 Superior Ave, Suite 1404, Cleveland, OH 44114.

ALEXANDER, JAMES BRETT
Staff reporter, journalist. **PERSONAL:** Born Nov 19, 1948, Boston, MA. **EDUCATION:** Northeastern Univ, BA 1971. **CAREER:** NE Univ Div of Instr Commun The Urban Confrontation, producer, dir 1968; The Christian Sci Monitor Boston, staff writer 1968-71; Random House Inc Lang Arts Div, editorial asst 1972-73; Manhattan Comm Coll, dir publs New York City 1973-74; New York Post, staff reporter, journalist. **ORGANIZATIONS:** Mem The Experiment in Intl Living 1969-, The Amer Forum for Intl Study, The Boston Black United Front 1969-70, The Intl Peace Acad 1972-, The Sixth Pan-African Cogn-ress; dir of publ No Amer Reg Ford Found Fellow 1966-69; mem The Experiment in Intl Liv-

ing 1969. **HONORS/ACHIEVEMENTS:** Martin Luther King Fellow Univ of Denver 1971-72. **BUSINESS ADDRESS:** Staff Reporter, Journalist, New York Post, 210 South St, New York, NY 10019.

ALEXANDER, JAMES W.
Business executive, songwriter. **PERSONAL:** Born Jan 21, 1916, Hamilton, MS; children: Loretta, Anthony, Adrienne. **CAREER:** Record producer Sam Cooke, Billy Preston, Mel Carter, Johnny Taylor, Bobby Womack, The Soul Stirrers, Clara Ward, Bro Joe May, The Original Gospel Harmonettes, Simms Twins, Patience Valentine; gospel singer, mgr The Pilgrim Travelers; record mfg SAR/DERBY Records, Kags Music Corp, Malloy Music Corp, Sam Cooke & JW Alexander; songwriter, personal mgr Sam Cooke, Lou Rawls, Little Richard, Billy Preston, Bobby Womack, Willie Hutch; Doheny Gallagher Music Co, pres. **ORGANIZATIONS:** Mem Mothers of Watts, Copyright Conf, NARAS. **HONORS/ACHIEVEMENTS:** Honored by Mothers of Watts contrib to BIARRIA Relief 1968,69; Inspiration to Todays Youth; Gold Record Songwriter "Looking for a Love" 1974.

ALEXANDER, JOHN STANLEY
Association executive. **PERSONAL:** Born Dec 31, 1944, Charlotte, NC; divorced; children: Rave, Richard, Reginia. **EDUCATION:** Johnson C Smith Univ Charlotte NC, BA 1967; Atlanta Univ, MA 1970. **CAREER:** Hickory Job Counseling Svc, dir 1968; Charlotte Youth Prog, dir 1969; Atlanta Univ, instr 1970-71; Voter Ed Proj Inc Atlanta, dir res 1972-78; NatlConf of Black Mayors Inc, proj dir 1978-. **ORGANIZATIONS:** Mem Amer Peace Corps India 1967; consult Interpreters House 1969-76; consult Dallas Legal Serv Found 1977-79; consult AR Delta Proj Inc 1980-; bd of dir PennComm Ctr 1977-, Atlanta Black United Fund Inc 1977-; chmn Atlanta Metro Human Rel Comm; comm mem Atlanta United Way 1976-78. **BUSINESS ADDRESS:** Project Dir, Natl Conf of Black Mayors, 1430 W Peachtree St, Atlanta, GA 30309.

ALEXANDER, JOHN WESLEY, JR.
Educational administrator. **PERSONAL:** Born May 17, 1938, Salem, OH; son of John Wesley and Virgina. **EDUCATION:** Southern CO State Coll, AA 1958; Boston Univ, BS 1961; Bowling Green State Univ, MA 1965; Boston Univ, EdD 1985; California Coast Univ MBA 1985-87, PhD 1987-89. **CAREER:** Model Cities Coll Consortium, acad dean 1969-70; West African Reg Math Prog, math adv 1970-77; Ed Devel Ctr, consult editor 1977-78; CT Mutual Life Ins Co, acturial analyst 1978-81; Wentworth Inst of Tech, dean arts & sci. **ORGANIZATIONS:** Campaign chairperson United Combined Health Appeal CT Mutual Life Ins Co 1981; Chief Statistician The Futures Group 1981-82; prof of math Wentworth Inst of Tech 1982-84; dean, coll of arts & sci Wentworth Inst of Tech 1984-. **HONORS/ACHIEVEMENTS:** CO & Boston Univ, athletic scholarships 1956-60; Fellowship Bowling Green State Univ 1964-65; Assistantship Boston Univ 1977-78; Awd of Excellence CT Mutual Life Ins Co 1981. **HOME ADDRESS:** One Tierney Ave, Hull, MA 02045. **BUSINESS ADDRESS:** Dean of Arts & Sciences, Wentworth Inst of Tech, 550 Huntington Ave, Boston, MA 02115.

ALEXANDER, JOHNNIE WILBERT
Recreation administrator, restaurant owner. **PERSONAL:** Born Nov 05, 1928, Kerens, TX; son of Ambus and Emma; married Edith Marie Hensley; children: Marcus A, Bonita Louise, Douglas Alan, Dana April. **EDUCATION:** Amer River Coll, AA Gen Educ 1971; Sacramento Univ, BA Speech Communications 1977. **CAREER:** Pit Stop Bar-B-Que Restaurant, owner 1972-; Postal Serv North Highlands CA, supvr mail & delivery 1980-; Sacramento Juvenile Hall, career counselor 1980-; North Highlands Park & Recreation Dist, dir 1970-. **ORGANIZATIONS:** Mem Big Bros & Sisters Sacramento 1970-75; pres Disabled Amer Veteran Chapter 93 1972-74; mem N Highlands Chamber of Commerce 1972-; pres N Highlands Comm Council 1977-; elder Church of Christ Roseville CA 1978-. **HONORS/ACHIEVEMENTS:** Achievement Merit Award Toastmasters intl 1968. **MILITARY SERVICE:** USAF t/sgt 1947-67; various awards & commendaton medals. **BUSINESS ADDRESS:** Dir, N Highlands Park & Rec Dist, 6040 Watt Ave N, Highlands, CA 95660.

ALEXANDER, JOSEPH LEE
Physician. **PERSONAL:** Born Oct 29, 1929, Oneonta, AL; married Phyllis L Campbell; children: Arnold Larry. **EDUCATION:** Fisk Univ Nashville, BA 1947-51; Univ of Louisville, MD 1951-55; Harvard Univ, Rsch Fellow Surgery 1967-69; UCLA School of Publ Health, MPH 1977. **CAREER:** US Army Hosp Ft Hood TX, chief gen surgery 1961-62; 5th Surg Hosp Heidelberg Germany, comdg officer 1962-63; 2nd Gen Hosp Landsthul Germany, asst chief gen surgery 1963-64; Kimbrough Army Hosp Ft Meade MD, chief gen surgery serv 1964-66; Walter Reed Gen Hosp Wash DC, chief organ transplant serv 1969-71; Charles Drew Postgrad Med School, chief surgery 1971-76; UCLA School of Med, prof of surgery 1971-; Private practice Los Angeles, physician 1978-; St Vincent Medical Ctr, chief of surgery 1985-86. **ORGANIZATIONS:** Mem Alpha Phi Alpha, Phi Delta Epsilon Med Frat Univ of Loisville; diplomate Natl Bd of Med Examiners; fellow Amer Coll of Surgeons 1956. **HONORS/ACHIEVEMENTS:** Mem Beta Kappa Chi Hon Sci Soc Fisk Univ, Sigma Upsilon Phi Fisk Univ 1951, Alpha Omega Alpha Hon Med Soc Univ of Louisville 1954, Phi Kappa Phi Honor Soc Univ of Louisville 1955; listed in Who's Who in Amer Univ 1951. **MILITARY SERVICE:** AUS col 14 yrs; Cert of Achievement 1964; Commendation Medal 1971. **BUSINESS ADDRESS:** Chief of Surgery, St Vincent Medical Center, 201 S Alvarado St, Ste 711, Los Angeles, CA 90057.

ALEXANDER, JOSEPHINE
Registered nurse. **PERSONAL:** Born in Tuskegee, AL; daughter of P Alexander and Daisy Menefee Alexander. **EDUCATION:** Tuskegee University, Tuskegee, AL, BSN, 1958; University of California, Los Angeles, CA, MN, 1972. **CAREER:** Veterans Administration Medical Center, West Los Angeles, CA, staff nurse, 1958-60, nurse manager, 1960-72, psychiatric clinical specialist, 1972-, primary adult care nurse practitioner, 1977-. **ORGANIZATIONS:** Life member, American Nurses Association; National League of Nursing; member, National Council of Negro Women; historian, 1974-84, first vice president, 1980-84, president, 1985-, Chi Eta Phi. **HONORS/ACHIEVEMENTS:** Outstanding Leadership Award, Chi Eta Pi, Southwest Region, 1987; Outstanding Service Award, Tuskegee University Alumni Association, Los Angeles, Ca, chapter, 1988. **HOME ADDRESS:** 4206 West Adams Blvd, Apartment 2, Los Angeles, CA 90018-2229. **BUSINESS ADDRESS:** Clinical Nurse Specialist/Psychiatry, Veterans Administration Medical Center, Brentwood Division, Wilshire and Sawtelle Blvds, West Los Angeles, CA 90073.

ALEXANDER, JOYCE LONDON
Judge. **EDUCATION:** Howard Univ, BA 1969; New England Law School, JD 1972; Northeastern Univ Law School, honorary doctor of law 1980; New England Law School, honorary doctorof law 1985. **CAREER:** Boston Legal Assistance Project, Reginald Heber Smith community law fellowship 1972-74; Tufts Univ, asst professor 1975-76; MA Board of Higher Education, general counsel 1976-79; WBZ-TV Boston, on-camera legal editor 1978-79; US District Court for MA, judge. **ORGANIZATIONS:** Urban League of Eastern MA, president emeritus 1979-; Nat'l Council of US Magistrates, 1st circuit dir 1984-; MA Black Judges Conference, chairperson 1985-; Nat'l Bar Assoc Judicial Council, chair-elect 1986-87. **BUSINESS ADDRESS:** United States Magistrate, US District Court, District of Massachusetts, 932 JW McCormack POCH, Boston, MA 02109.

ALEXANDER, KELLY MILLER, JR.
Controller. **PERSONAL:** Born Oct 17, 1948, Charlotte, NC; married Veronica Motsepe. **EDUCATION:** Univ of NC, AB Polit Sci 1960, MPA 1973. **CAREER:** NC Personnel Dept, admin intern 1971-72; Charlotte Area Fund, planner 1972-74; Alexander Enterprises, secty/treas 1986; Alexander Funeral Home, controller 1973-. **ORGANIZATIONS:** Exec vice pres US Youth Council 1976-85; consultant Kayo Oil co 1983-85, Bahakel Broadcasting 1985; vice pres Natl NAACP; chmn Natl NAACP Economic Develop Comm. **HONORS/ACHIEVEMENTS:** UNCF Labor Dept Rsch Grant 1977. **BUSINESS ADDRESS:** Controller, Alexander Funeral Home, 112 No Irwin Ave, Charlotte, NC 28202.

ALEXANDER, LENORA COLE
Director. **PERSONAL:** Born Mar 09, 1935, Buffalo, NY; married Theodore M Alexander Sr. **EDUCATION:** State Univ Coll Buffalo NY, BS 1957; State Univ of New York at Buffalo, MEd 1969, PhD 1974. **CAREER:** State Univ of New York, rsch asst 1968-69, asst to vice pres for student life 1969-73; The American Univ, vice pres for student life 1973-77; Univ of the District of Columbia, vice pres for student affairs 1978-81; US Dept of Labor, dir women's bureau 1981-86; George Mason Univ, commonwealth vstg prof ofpublic admin 1986-. **ORGANIZATIONS:** Bd dirs DC Chamber of Commerce 1979-81; US Rep to Working Party on Role of Women in the Econ, Org for Econ Devel & Coop Paris France 1981-86; mem advcomm Women Veterans Affairs US Vet Admin 1983-86; US rep conf Intl Commiss on the Status of Women Cartegena Colombia 1983; conf Vienna Austria 1984; mem US Del to United Nations Decade for Women Conf Nairobi Kenya 1985; bd dirs Jerusalem Intl Forum of Amer Israel Friendship League 1987-. **HONORS/ACHIEVEMENTS:** Salute to an Influential Decision Maker Alpha Kappa Alpha Sor Inc 1982; Special Citation Awd Commission for Women's Affairs Office of Governor Puerto Rico 1982; Salute for Contributions Awd Club Twenty Washington 1983; Disting Amer and Humanitarian Coahoma Jr College 1983; Distinguished Alumnus Awd State Univof NY 1983; Special Proclamation Coahoma Jr Coll 1984; Pauline Weeden Maloney Awd in Natl Trends and Serv The Links Inc Philadelphia 1984; Gratitude for Success Awd Unit Church Usher's League Chicago 1984; Disting Serv Citation Natl Black MBA Assn Inc Washington 1984; Outstanding Women Awd Progressive DC Chaptof Federally Employed Women Washington 1984; Outstanding Political Achievement Awd Natl Assoc of Minority Political Women 1985; Outstanding Career Woman Awd Alpha Phi Alpha 1986; Woman of Achievement Awd Women's City Club of Cleveland 1986. **HOME ADDRESS:** 3020 Brandywine St NW, Washington, DC 20008. **BUSINESS ADDRESS:** Visiting Professor, George MasonUniv, Fairfax, VA 22030.

ALEXANDER, LOUIS G.
Business executive. **PERSONAL:** Born Feb 14, 1910, Houston, TX; widowed; children: Louis G III. **EDUCATION:** Bishop Coll, attended 1927-29; Armour Inst of Tech, attended 1929-33; IL Inst of Tech, attended 1939; Univ of HI, attended 1943. **CAREER:** Reliable Elec Serv Co, 1933-42; Murray's Superior Prods Co, 1945-47; Circuit Engrg Sales & Serv Co, 1947-49; APTI Inc 1948-52; SPEMCO Inc 1952-66; Alexander & Assoc, 1967-68; Amalgamated Trust & Savings Bank, vice pres 1968-. **ORGANIZATIONS:** Mem bd dir Better Boys Found; mem bd dir Hyudr Park Coop Fed Credit Union; mem bd dir Chicago Chap NAACP; mem Omega Psi Phi; Natl Tech Assn; Chicago Cncl of Foreign Relations; Amer Veterans Comm. **HONORS/ACHIEVEMENTS:** Author "The New Amer Crisis" publ in The Race for Space; 1972 Good Guy Awd Lawndale Scholarship Fund. **MILITARY SERVICE:** AUS 1942-45. **BUSINESS ADDRESS:** Louis Alexander & Assoc, PO Box 1086, Chicago, IL 60690.

ALEXANDER, MARGARET WALKER (MARGARET WALKER)
Educator, author, writer. **PERSONAL:** Born Jul 07, 1915, Birmingham, AL; daughter of Sigismund C Walker and Marion Dozier Walker; married Firnist James Alexander, Jun 13, 1943; children: Marion Elizabeth, Firnist James, Sigismund Walker, Margaret Elvira. **EDUCATION:** Northwestern Univ, AB, 1935; Univ of Iowa, MA, 1940, PhD, 1965. **CAREER:** West Virginia State College, Institute WV, English instructor, 1942-43; Natl Concert & Artists Corp, lecturer 1943-48; Livingstone Coll, teacher english 1945-46; Jackson Coll, dir Black studies, professor of English, 1949-; Inst Study History Life & Culture of Black Peoples, dir 1968-. **ORGANIZATIONS:** Mem, Modern Lang Assn; mem, Amer Assn Univ Prof; mem, NEA; mem, Poetry Soc Amer; Natl Council of Teachers of English; mem, Alpha Kappa Alpha. **HONORS/ACHIEVEMENTS:** Author of For My People (poetry), Yale University Press, 1942; author of Jubilee (novel), Houghton, 1966; author of Prophets for a New Day, Broadside Press, 1970; author of How I Wrote Jubilee, Third World Press, 1972; author of Richard Wright: Daemonic Genius, Dodd, 1987; published in magazines; Yale Award for Younger Poets; Rosenwald Fellowship; honorary degrees from Northwestern Univ, Rust College, Dennison Univ, and Morgan Univ. **HOME ADDRESS:** 2205 Guynes St, Jackson, MS 39213. **BUSINESS ADDRESS:** Department of English, Jackson State College, Jackson, MS 39217. *

ALEXANDER, MERVIN FRANKLIN
Executive administrator. **PERSONAL:** Born Jul 29, 1938, Clover, SC; children: Mervin F, Michael F. **EDUCATION:** Benedict Coll, 1958-60; New York City Coll, 1960-62; Rutgers Univ MEd 1976; Riden Coll, MPa 1980-. **CAREER:** Day Care 100, regional admin 1970; Div of Youth & Family Servs, adm of day care oper 1976; Div of Youth & Fam Serv, chief bur of licensing 1977; SpecServ for Children, dir office of dir child care 1978-. **ORGANIZATIONS:** Pres Piscataway Bd of Ed 1979-80; councilman Township of Piscataway 1980-; pres Piscataway Twnshp Council 1985-. **HOME ADDRESS:** 390 Rushmore Ave, Piscataway, NJ 08854.

ALEXANDER, OTIS DOUGLAS (SULE)
Librarian. **PERSONAL:** Born Jun 01, 1949, Norfolk, VA; son of Gilbert Alexander and

Vivian Bell-Alexander. **EDUCATION:** Federal City Coll, Washington, DC, BA Urban Studies 1972; Federal City Coll , Washington, DC MSc, Media Science 1974; Ball State Univ, Muncie, IN, MLS Library Science 1983; Atlanta Univ GA, 1982. **CAREER:** African Heritage Dancers & Drummers Washington DC, professional dancer 1973-76; Dept of Educ of VI St John, itinerant libr 1976-77; Bur of Libr Mus & Archeol Serv Christiansted St Croix US VI, juvenile serv libr 1977-78; Cuttington Univ Coll Liberia W Africa, asst libr & lectr childrens lit 1978-79; Dept of Educ of VI, info spec 1979-83; Bur of Libr & Mus, head librn 1983-; St Dunstan's Episcopal School St Croix VI, literature teacher 1985-. **ORGANIZATIONS:** Mem Amer Libr Assn 1983-; dir St John Ethnic Theatre 1976-77, Children's Theatre on Isl of St Croix 1977-78; dir, performer Cuttington Cultural Troop West Afr 1978-79; artistic dir St Theatre 1986-; Research Representative, Phi Delta Kappa 1988-; Amer Library Assn, 1983-. **HONORS/ACHIEVEMENTS:** Publs, "Librarianship in a Developing Nation" Bur of Libr Mus & Archael Servs, "Media-Children-Reading" Personality & Instrl Strat Thesis 1974; publ book reviews "They Came Before Columbus", "The Red Wind", "Where Did I Come From?", "Sturdy Black Bridges", "When Harlem Was In Vogue"; Awds, Fellowship USDOE 1982-83, Scholarship Atlanta Univ 1982; The Encyclopedia As An Information Source, A Study of the Usefulness & Objectivity of Selected Encyclopedias as Perceived by School & Public Librarians in Muncie IN 1983; "Arthur Homburg Alfonso and his Contributions to Black Culture" in St Croix Avis; Virgin Islands and Caribbean Comm, (joint author), 1988; "Writers in the Comm", 1984. **MILITARY SERVICE:** USMC Reserve, 1968-69. **HOME ADDRESS:** 609 Obendorfer Rd, Norfolk, VA 23523.

ALEXANDER, PAMELA GAYLE
District court judge. **PERSONAL:** Born Sep 25, 1952, Minneapolis, MN; daughter of Robert W Bellesen and Frances L Smith; married Albert G Alexander, Jan 16, 1982; children: April Katherine Alexander. **EDUCATION:** Augsburg Coll, BA 1975-81; Univ of MN School of Law, JD 1977. **CAREER:** Legal Rights Ctr Inc, criminal defense atty 1978-81; Hennepin County Attorney's Office, prosecutor-criminal div 1981-83; State of MN, county court judge 1983-86, district court judge 1986-. **ORGANIZATIONS:** Trust administrator First Bank Minneapolis 1977-78; charter mem former vice pres Minnesota Minority Lawyers Assoc 1977-; trustee Greater Friendship Missionary Bapt Church 1980-; mem Natl Bar Assoc Judicial Counsel 1983-; parliamentarian, treas Mpls/St Paul Links Inc 1985-. **HONORS/ACHIEVEMENTS:** Special Recognition Awd Phi Beta Sigma Frat 1982; Constance B Motley Awd TCBWTC Comm 1982,83; Community Serv Awd Inner City Youth League 1983, Loft Teen Ctr 1983; Disting Serv Awd Hennepin Co Attorney's Office 1983. **BUSINESS ADDRESS:** District Court Judge, State of Minnesota, 951-C Government Center, Minneapolis, MN 55487.

ALEXANDER, PAUL CRAYTON
Physician. **PERSONAL:** Born Aug 05, 1946, Tulsa, OK; children: Vyron. **EDUCATION:** Coll of Pharmacy Howard Univ, BS 1970; Meharry Medical Coll, MD 1974. **CAREER:** Meharry Medical Sch, asst prof of medicine 1978-85; TN Dept of Corrections, medical consultant 1984-; TN State Penitentiary Hosp, med director. **ORGANIZATIONS:** Mem Amer Heart Assoc 1978-; mem House of Delegates Natl Medical Assoc 1980,81,82,83; pres RF Boyd Medical Soc 1983-85; vice pres Middle TN Div Volunteer State Medical Assoc 1985-. **HONORS/ACHIEVEMENTS:** Chief Coord for Hypertension Patient Educ Grant Meharry Medical Coll Ambulatory Serv 1979-80; Outstanding Young Men of Amer; 8 publications including "Innovative Chemotherapy (nifedipine and verapamil) in Hereditary Hypertension," w/WJ Crawford, LE Burgess, MT Scott, JM Stinson Lab Ani Sci 1982. **BUSINESS ADDRESS:** Medical Dir, TN State Penitentiary Hospital, 1900 12th Ave So, Nashville, TN 37203.

ALEXANDER, PRESTON PAUL, JR.
Medical supply company executive. **PERSONAL:** Born Apr 20, 1952, Bronx, NY; son of Preston Alexander, Sr. and Sylvia Alexander; children: Drew Philip, Jason Ross. **EDUCATION:** Fairleigh Dickinson Univ, BA, Psychology, 1973, M, Public Admin, 1980. **CAREER:** Teaneck Volunteer Ambulance Corps, Sunday evening crew chief 1972-; Midlantic Natl Bank/Citizens, internal auditor 1973-74; Fairleigh Dickinson Univ Central Admiss, dir of admission relations 1974-79; Natl Assn of Coll Admission Counselors, vice pres human relations 1978-79; Citibank NA, dir human resources; Co-Owner, Alexanders Surgical Supply Co, 1979-89. **HONORS/ACHIEVEMENTS:** Outstanding/Distinguished Serv Award, Fairleigh Dickinson Univ, 1978. **BUSINESS ADDRESS:** Alexanders Surgical Supply, 288 E 149th St, Bronx, NY 10432.

ALEXANDER, ROBERT I.
Social worker. **PERSONAL:** Born Feb 17, 1913; son of Israel Alexander and Frances Alexander; married J L Black; children: Arthur Harris Jr, Claudette E Douglas, Robert A, John Rodney. **EDUCATION:** St Augustine's Coll, BA 1943; Atlanta Univ, MA 1948. **CAREER:** Buncombe Co NC Welfare Dept, child welfare caseworker 1948-53; Guildord Co NC Welfare Dept, child welfare caseworker 1953-65; A&T Coll Greensboro, soc worker, Project Uplift 1965-66; Meharry Med Coll, chief soc worker, child develop clinic 1966-79. **ORGANIZATIONS:** Ruby Am Bridge Assn 1976-77; coord Preventive Serv Meharry Med Coll Comm 1975-79; candidate 20th Councilman Dist Nashville 1975,79; past scoutmaster & troup committeeman; past prog chmn PTA; past chmn Educ Comm; past pres Nashville Branch NAACP; organizer & past chmn Z Alexander Freedom Fund Ball; past pres, Middle Tennessee Chap, Natl Assn of Soc Work; past area rep, State of Tennessee, Natl Assn of Soc Workers; various comm in connection with Baptist Ch; mem Phi Beta Sigma; past pres Nashville Duplicate Bridge Club; mem Emerald Soc Club; past vice chmn Comm Sch Inc; past mem governance bd, Community Mental Health Ctr, Meharry Med Coll; 19th Dist Representative, Metro Nashville Davidson Co 1979; organized Hadley Senior Center Bridge Club (ABA) Nashville, 1988; general chairman, ABA Spring National Tournament Nashville, 1989. **MILITARY SERVICE:** AUS 1943-46.

ALEXANDER, ROBERT L.
Consultant. **PERSONAL:** Born Jul 29, 1945, Tallahassee, FL. **EDUCATION:** FL A&M Univ, BS 1965, MS 1966; Rutgers Univ, PhD 1970; Attended, AUS Sch Officer Armor Trng, Officer Leadership Reaction. **CAREER:** FL A&M Univ, instr training sch editor in chief 1964-65; Mobil Oil Corp, jr exec 1969; Cleveland, dir & commr of offender rehab 1970-72; The White House,dir criminal justice projects 1972; A Criminal Justice Manual on Drug Abuse, editor/publisher 1973; Hardees of WA Fast Food Franchise, pres/owner; CIA, apptdspl consult & asst 1974-. **ORGANIZATIONS:** Brother of the Masonic Lodge; Reserve Officers Assn; Amer Personnel & Guidance Assn; Amer Correctional Assn; Natl Council for Criminal Delinquency; NatlVocational Assn; Natl Black Correctional Assn; consult to various penal inst throughout the country; consult to Bd of Fundamental Educ; Rubicon Drug Abuse Programs State of VA Health Facilities Resources. **HONORS/ACHIEVEMENTS:** Outstanding Acad Achievement; Who's Who in Amer Colls & Univs; Who's Who in N Amer 1976; Pi Gamma Mu Natl Hon Soc; Most Outstanding Youth Journalist State of FL 1962; Journalists Consult Awd Natl 1963; Natl Mil Stakes Awd; Second Academic AUS Basic Officers Class of 125 Combat Officers 1967; Master Tactician Awd Outstanding Instr of Mil Tactics Ft Benning GA 1968. **MILITARY SERVICE:** AUS capt 1965-69. **BUSINESS ADDRESS:** Special Consul & Asst, The CIA, Washington, DC 20505.

ALEXANDER, ROLAND E.
Musician. **PERSONAL:** Born Sep 25, 1935, Boston, MA; divorced; children: Tarv Alexander, Denise McNickes. **EDUCATION:** Boston Conservatory of Music, BM 1958. **CAREER:** Long Island Univ, music instr 1975; Medgar Evers, music instr 1976; New Muse, music instr, woodwind instr conductor Muse Big Band. **HONORS/ACHIEVEMENTS:** NatlEndowment for the Arts Grants 1970; Father of the Year Sisterhood of Black Singles Mothers 1985. **HOME ADDRESS:** 104 Empire Blvd, Brooklyn, NY 11225.

ALEXANDER, RONALD ALGERNON
Government official. **PERSONAL:** Born Oct 24, 1950, New Orleans, LA; son of Reginald A Alexander and Essie M Alexander; married Angela J; children: Regina Ashley. **EDUCATION:** Nicholls State Univ, attended 1968-71. **CAREER:** Pan Amer World Airways Inc, accountant 1971-78; City of Thibodaux LA, dir mayor's office of fed grants 1978-85; Terrebonne Parish Consolidated Govt, asst dir, community development programs 1985-. **ORGANIZATIONS:** Chmn, bd of commissioners, City of Thibodaux Housing Authority 1985; regional worshipful master, Region I Prince Hall Grand Lodge of Louisiana, 1987-89. **HONORS/ACHIEVEMENTS:** District #4 Master of the Year, Prince Hall Grand Lodge of Louisiana, 1985; Outstanding Community Service Award, NAACP, 1988. **HOME ADDRESS:** 414 E 7th St, Thibodaux, LA 70301.

ALEXANDER, ROOSEVELT MAURICE
Attorney. **PERSONAL:** Born Sep 29, 1941, Chicago, IL; divorced; children: Maurice, Michael, Alicia. **EDUCATION:** Northwestern Univ, BA 1963, JD 1973. **CAREER:** Private Practice, attorney; City of Evanston 5th Ward, alderman. **ORGANIZATIONS:** Former pol action chmn Local NAACP; adv bd Dist 65 Sch Sys title VII Funds; bd of Way Out Drug Abuse Prog; former bd mem locally funded OEO Ctr Neighbors at Work; former co-chmn Evanston Black Caucus; mem IL State Bar Assn. **HONORS/ACHIEVEMENTS:** Man of Yr Awd Evanston Chessmens Club 1970. **BUSINESS ADDRESS:** Alderman Ward 5, City of Evanston, 1625 Simpson St, Evanston, IL 60201.

ALEXANDER, ROSA M.
Business executive. **PERSONAL:** Born Sep 25, 1928, Dunn, NC; married Nathaniel L Alexander; children: Helen M Vaughan, Amos, Thaddeus, Nathaniel, Nathalin. **EDUCATION:** Harnett HS, diploma 1945. **CAREER:** Ford Motor Co, cafeteria mgr 1950-70; Norfolk Naval Air Station, electronics 1974-78; A&B Contract Svcs, pres 1978-. **ORGANIZATIONS:** Treas Amer Business Women Assn 1969; bd mem Tidewater Business & Contractors Assn 1978-; mem Norfolk & Chespeake Chamber of Comm 1984. **HONORS/ACHIEVEMENTS:** Outstanding Achievement Chesapeake Men for Progress 1980; Businessperson of the Yr TABCA 1980; Outstanding Business US Dept of Commerce 1983; Citizen of the Yr Lambda Omega Chap 1984; Notable Achievement Norfolk State Univ 1984. **BUSINESS ADDRESS:** President, A&B Contract Serv, 3001 Lafayette Blvd, Norfolk, VA 23509.

ALEXANDER, SADIE TANNER MOSSELL
Retired attorney. **PERSONAL:** Born Jan 02, 1898, Philadelphia, PA; daughter of Aaron Mossell and Mary Tanner Mossell; married Raymond Pace Alexander (deceased); children: Mary Elizabeth (Brown), Rae Pace (Minter). **EDUCATION:** Univ of Pennsylvania, BS Educ, 1918; MA Economics 1919, PhD 1921, LlB 1927. **CAREER:** Philadel PA, atty 1927-; Philadel Bar, admitt 1927; asst city solic 1928-30, 1934-38. **ORGANIZATIONS:** Appointed Lawyer Commn on Civil Rights; pres Philadelphia Bar Found 1972; mem Natl Adv Cncl Amer Civil Liberties Union; bd dir Grtr Philadelphia Br of Amer Civil Liberties Union; fdng mem Advis Com to Amer Com on Africa; mem Natl Com for Support of Public Schools. **HONORS/ACHIEVEMENTS:** First black woman in the US to receive PhD; first black woman to earn a law degree from Univ of Pennsylvania; first woman to practice law in Commonwealth of Pennsylvania; second woman in law to hold position of asst city solic.

ALEXANDER, SIDNEY H., JR.
Personnel manager. **PERSONAL:** Born Oct 26, 1919, Pueblo, CO; married Ruby R Autry; children: Sidney III, Saundra L, Steven W. **EDUCATION:** Univ of Denver, BA 1949, MSW 1951; Cornell Univ State Sch of Labor & Ind Relations, cert 1966; Kingsborough Comm Coll, cert 1967. **CAREER:** Lectr & field work supr various colls & Univs 1953-; Urban League Affiliates in Lincoln NE, Grand Rapids MI, Wichita KS, New Haven CT, exec dir 1953-65; Anti-Poverty Agencies Nassau Co, Harlem, Brooklyn, dir/coord 1965-69; St Philip's Comm Serv Counc, adminstrv officer 1969-70; Newsweek Inc, mgr personnel serv 1970-. **ORGANIZATIONS:** Consult US Dept of Labor & HEW 1962; mem NY Personnel Mgmt Assn; mem Natl Urban League; mem NAACP; mem natl Cncl of Negro Women; mem Natl Assn ofSoc Workers; mem Omicron Delta Kappa; mem Phi Sigma Iota. **HONORS/ACHIEVEMENTS:** Who's Who Among Students in Amer Univs & Colls; Who's Who in the Midwest; Hon Life Mem KS Congress of Parents & Tchrs. **MILITARY SERVICE:** USAF sgt 1943-45. **BUSINESS ADDRESS:** Manager of Personnel Service, Newsweek Inc, 444 Madison Ave, New York, NY 10022.

ALEXANDER, SILAS
Dentist. **PERSONAL:** Born Sep 11, 1895, Pendleton, SC; married Inez L Walker; children: Silas Ulysses, Carolyn Louise. **EDUCATION:** Morris Coll, BA 1918; Meharry Med Coll, DDS Coll of Dentistry 1923. **CAREER:** Private Practice, dentist. **ORGANIZATIONS:** Mem Ewell Neil Dental Soc 1923-; mem Natl Dental Assn 1925; Buckeye State Med, Dental & Pharmaceutical Soc 1948; Mason St Mark Lodge; mem Alpha Phi Alpha Frat; Amer Legion. **HONORS/ACHIEVEMENTS:** Red Cross Serv Awds. **MILITARY SERVICE:** Vet WW I.

ALEXANDER, THEODORE MARTIN, SR.
Insurance executive/educator. **PERSONAL:** Born Mar 07, 1909, Montgomery, AL; married Lenora; children: Theodore Martin Jr (dec), Alvia Elizabeth, Dorothy Gwendolyn M. **EDUCATION:** Morehouse Coll, BA Bus Admin (with honors) 1971, LLD 1970. **CAREER:** Alexander & Co Gen Ins Agency Atlanta, founder 1931-; Howard Univ, adj prof. **ORGANIZATIONS:** Chmn bd Alexander & Assoc Inc; founder 1949/former exec vice pres Southeastern Fidelity Fire Ins Co Atlanta; pres treas Univ Plaza Apts Inc; sec/dir exec com Mut Fed Savngs & Loan Assn Atlanta 1932-68; partner Met Atlanta Rapid Transit Authority Ins Mgrs; v chmn Atlanta Univ Cntr Corp; fed jurycommr No Dist GA Trustee Atlanta Comm Chest; sec bd trustees Morehouse Coll; bd dirs Butler St YMCA Atlanta 1958; mem Race Rel Comm Intl Comm Del World Council 1961; mem natl bd Citizens Adv Com; chmn Relocation Comm Atlanta Urban Renewal; mem Better Housing Commn; mem Housing Appeal Bd; v chmn Ethics Bd City of Atlanta; mem Natl Citizens' Comm for Community Rel Dept Commerce 1964; mem Adv Comm Met Planning Commn Atlanta; asst treas Atlanta Comm Chest; mem Atlanta Comm Relations; pres Sr Citizens Met Atlanta 1968-69; bd mem Greater Wash Boys Club; candidate Atlanta City Cncl 1957;mem NAACP, Urban League, Alpha Phi Alpha, Delta Sigma Rho; Republican; Baptist; Mason. **BUSINESS ADDRESS:** President, TM Alexander & Co, Inc, PO Box 76677, Atlanta, GA 30358.

ALEXANDER, WALTER GILBERT, II
Dentist. **PERSONAL:** Born Jul 06, 1922, Petersburg, VA. **EDUCATION:** Rutgers Univ, BS Mech Engrg 1943; Howard Univ, DDS 1952. **CAREER:** Douglas Aircraft Co LA, designer 1943; Private Practice S Orange NJ, dentist 1952-. **ORGANIZATIONS:** Mem post-grad dental faculty NJ Coll of Med & Dentistry 1967-; clin asst prof 1969; mem Amer Natl, NJ Dental Assns; Commonwealth, Essex Co Dental Soc; mem Urban League; life mem NAACP; mem NJ St Bd of Dentistry 1972-76; pres NJ St Bd of Dentistry 1976; mem Amer Assn of Dental Examiners; active mem Northeast Regional Bd of Dental Examiners; mem Tau Beta Pi, Omicron Kappa Upsilon; Episcopalian. **BUSINESS ADDRESS:** 555 Center St, South Orange, NJ 07079.

ALEXANDER, WARREN DORNELL
Businessman. **PERSONAL:** Born May 27, 1921, San Antonio, TX; married Mary Catherine Bryant; children: Lawrence, Lynette, Sharon. **EDUCATION:** Omaha Univ, BGE 1958; Iliff Sch of Theology Univ of Denver, postgrad; ordained Meth Min, 1963. **CAREER:** CO Civil Rights Commn, dep dir 1965-74; Metro Denver Urban Coalition, pres 1975-78; Western First Financial Corp, financial consult 1979-. **ORGANIZATIONS:** Pres NE Park Hill Civic Assn 1964-67; orign mem Skyline Urban Renewal Proj 1965-67; bd dir Rocky Mountain Reg Kidney Found 1967-68; pres Inter-AgyOrgn 1966-67; vice pres CO Conf of Soc Workers 1968-69; co-found/1st bd chmn Denver Fair Housing Ctr 1965-66; chmn Commn of Christian Soc Concerns Park Hill United Meth Ch 1968-69; cand Denver Bd of Educ 1971; chmn bd dir Denver Head Start 1972-74; chmn bd dir Denver Owl Club 1975-76; pres Hubert L "Hooks" Jones Chap Tuskegee Airmen 1976-; St of CO Adv Councl for Vocational Educ 1976-78; dir selective serv St of CO 1978-; Kappa Alpha Psi 1974-. **HONORS/ACHIEVEMENTS:** 1st Annual Martin Luther King Jr Award Outstanding Contb in Field of Civic & Human Rights 1977. **MILITARY SERVICE:** USAF Maj 1942-46/1948-64.

ALEXANDER, WILLIAM H.
Judge. **PERSONAL:** Born Dec 10, 1930, Macon, GA; children: Jill Marie. **EDUCATION:** Ft Valley State Coll, BS 19581; Univ of MI, JD 1956; Georgetown Univ, LLM 1961. **CAREER:** GA House of Rep, state rep 1962-75; City Court of Atlanta, judge 1975-76; Criminal Court of Fulton County, judge 1976-77; State Court of Fulton County, judge 1977-July 1985; Judge, Fulton Superior Court 1985- . **ORGANIZATIONS:** Mem Amer Bar Assn, Atlanta Bar Assn, Amer Judicature Soc, Lawyers Club of Atlanta,Gate City Bar Assn, Old War Horse Lawyers Club, Natl Bar Assn. **MILITARY SERVICE:** AUS 1951-53. **HOME ADDRESS:** 4540 Birdie Ln SW, Atlanta, GA 30331. **BUSINESS ADDRESS:** Judge, Fulton Superior Court, 136 Pryor St SW, Atlanta, GA 30303.

ALEXANDER, WILLIAM M., JR.
Business executive. **PERSONAL:** Born Mar 18, 1928, St Louis, MO; married Delia; children: Brian. **EDUCATION:** Univ of IL, BS Mechanical Engineering, 1948. **CAREER:** Northrop Aircraft Corp, Hawthorne, CA, thermodynamicist, 1948-50; Rockwell International, Downey, CA, mgr, sr project engineer, 1955-68; Golden Oak Inc, pres, gen mgr, 1968-79; G/O Furniture Inc, chmn of the bd, 1979-. **ORGANIZATIONS:** Mem, Amer Soc of Mechanical Engineers; vice pres, Epis City Mission Soc. **HONORS/ACHIEVEMENTS:** Special Achievement Award, Natl Urban League, 1948. **MILITARY SERVICE:** AUS, 1953-55. **BUSINESS ADDRESS:** Chmn of the Bd, G/O Furniture Inc, 2392 E 48th St, Los Angeles, CA 90058.

ALEXANDER-WHITING, HARRIETT
Educator. **PERSONAL:** Born Apr 20, 1947, Charlotte, NC; daughter of Mr & Mrs James Alexander, Sr; married Robert W Whiting. **EDUCATION:** Northern IL Univ, BS Educ 1968; Kent State Univ, MA 1970. **CAREER:** Virginia Regional Medical Prog, asst allied health officer 1971-72; Emory Univ, instructor 1972-74; Alabama Inst for the Deaf & Blind, program coord/supervising teacher 1974-80; Gallaudet Univ, speech/lang path & coord of communication unit & lab 1980-84, program supervisor 1985-. **ORGANIZATIONS:** Mem Amer Speech Language and Hearing Assoc 1971-; bd of trustees AL Assoc of Retarded Citizens 1977-79; mem task group Mayor's Comm on Early Childhood 1987; mem Natl Comm on Deafness Amer Speech Language & Hearing Assoc 1987-90. **HONORS/ACHIEVEMENTS:** Natl Accreditation Cncl Site Team 1978; Outstanding Young Women of Amer 1979; mem Natl Task Force on Deaf-Blind US Dept of Educ 1979; mem Natl Comm on Develop Disabilities Amer Speech Language and Hearing Assoc 1980-82; mem Middle States Accreditation Team 1983. **BUSINESS ADDRESS:** Program Supervisor, Gallaudet Univ-KDES, 800 Florida Ave, Washington, DC 20002.

ALEXANDRE, JOURNEL
Physician. **PERSONAL:** Born Jul 14, 1931, Arcahaie, Haiti;children: Cibe, Colette. **EDUCATION:** Lycee Toussaint Louverture, BS 1952; Univ of Mexico, MD 1960. **CAREER:** Physician, St Joseph Hosp, Mercy Cath Med Ctr, Montgomery Hosp, Valley Forge Med Ctr; Scarborough Genl Hosp, internship 1960-61; Mercy Douglass Hosp, resid 1961-65; Montgomery Hosp, 1965-66; Private Practice, physician. **ORGANIZATIONS:** Mem PA & Montgomery Co Med Soc 1967; Intl Coll of Surgeons; fellow Amer Coll of Surgeons 1969; diplomate Amer Bd of Surgery 1968. **BUSINESS ADDRESS:** 731 W Erie Ave, Philadelphia, PA 19140.

ALEXIS, CARLTON PETER
Education administrator. **PERSONAL:** Born Jun 29, 1929, Port of Spain, Trinidad and Tobago;married Ogbonia M; children: Carla, Anthony, Lisa. **EDUCATION:** NY Univ, BA 1953; Howard Univ, MD 1957; Haiti, DHC 1972; Georgetown, DSc 1980. **CAREER:** Walter Reed Army Hosp, intern 1957-58; Bronx VA Hosp, res int med 1961-63; Georgetown Univ Hosp, fellow endocrinology 1963-64; Freedmens Hosp, pres med-dent staff 1968-69; Howard Univ, instr prof med 1964-; Howard Univ, vice pres health affairs 1969-. **ORGANIZATIONS:** Mem Natl Med Assn; Amer Med Assn; Amer Coll Phys; Amer Soc Int med; Assn Acad Hlth Ctr; Med Soc DC; Med Chirurgical soc of DC; chmn GovBd DC Gen Hosp; mem Mayors Task Force on reorg dept of Human Resources DC; mem adv comm to Comm IRS; Mayors Comm on Drug Abuse; mem Ed Bd Jour of Med Edn. **HONORS/ACHIEVEMENTS:** Elected Alpha Omega Alpha; Fellowship Amer Coll of Phys; Outstanding Tchr Howard Univ Coll of Med 1966. **MILITARY SERVICE:** Med Corps 2nd lt to capt 1956-61. **BUSINESS ADDRESS:** Vice President Health Affairs, HowardUniv, 2400 6th St NW, Washington, DC 20059.

ALEXIS, DORIS VIRGINIA
Director. **PERSONAL:** Born Jul 10, 1921, Brooklyn, NY; married Joseph Alexis; children: Neal Howe, Priscilla Rand. **EDUCATION:** Hunter Coll, New York NY, attended, 1946; Univ of California, Los Angeles CA, attended 1960; Univ of California, Davis, Cert of Program Mgmt, 1976. **CAREER:** California Dept of Motor Vehicles, dep dir, 1975-77, first woman and first career dir 1977-. **ORGANIZATIONS:** Bd trustees Sacramento Safety Cncl (chpt of Natl Safety Cncl) 1978-79; bd dir Amer Assn of Motor Vehicle Admin 1979-; bd dir Sacramento Safety Cncl (chpt Natl Safety Cncl) 1979-; pres bd trustees Commonwealth Equity Trust 1979-; mem Women's Forum 1977-; mem bd dir YWCA 1978-; mem NAACP 1978-; mem Urban League 1978-. **HONORS/ACHIEVEMENTS:** Let planning & implementation DVM Child Care Cntr for children of State Employees 1975; Grand Masters Award MW Prince Hall Grand Lodge F and AM; Honoree Coalition of Women in State Svc; 1st CA Official nominated for membership Women's Forum. **BUSINESS ADDRESS:** Dir, CA Dept of Motor Vehicles, 2415 1st Ave, Sacramento, CA 95818.

ALEXIS, MARCUS
Educator. **PERSONAL:** Born Feb 26, 1932, Brooklyn, NY; married Geraldine M. **EDUCATION:** Brooklyn Coll, BA 1953; MI State Univ, MA 1954, PhD 1959; Harvard & MIT, post-doctoral fellow 1961-62. **CAREER:** Macalester Coll, asst prof 1957-60; DePaul Univ, assoc prof 1960-62; Univ of Rochester, prof 1962-70; Univ of CA at Berkeley, vis prof 1969-71; USInterstate Commerce Commn, commr 1979; Northwestern Univ, prof econs & urban affairs 1970-85; Univ of IL at Chicago Coll of Business Admin, dean 1985-. **ORGANIZATIONS:** Pres bd dir Urban League of Rochester 1966-69; mem Natl Bd Amer Mktg Assoc 1968-70; mem chmn Caucus Black Economists 1969-71; com Increasing SupplyMinority Economists Amer Econ Assn 1970-73; natl bd dirs PUSH 1972-73; chmn com Status Minorities Prof Amer Econ Assn 1974-; com Minorities in Sci Natl Rsch Cncl Nat Acads Sci 1975; trustee Macalester Coll 1983-; mem educ policy bd review Black Political Economy 1984-; chair economic policy task force Joint Ctr for Political Studies 1985-; deputy chairman Federal Reserve Bank of Chicago 1986-; trustee Teachers Insurance and Annuity Assoc 1987; Beta Gamma Sigma; Order Artus. **HONORS/ACHIEVEMENTS:** Ford Found Fellow Harvard Univ & MIT 1961-62; Samuel Z Westerfield Disting Achievement Awd Natl Economic Assoc 1979; Outstanding Achievement Awd Univ of MN 1981; Caribbean Amer Intercultural Org Scholar Awd 1981; Minority Trucking/Transportation Develop Cncl President's Awd 1981. **BUSINESS ADDRESS:** Dean, Coll of Business Admin, Univ of IL at Chicago, Coll Bus Admin Mail Code 075, PO Box 4348Rm 2201 UH, Chicago, IL 60680.

ALFONSO, PEDRO
President. **PERSONAL:** Born Jun 28, 1948, Tampa, FL; son of Eugenio Alfonso and Florenola Alfonso. **EDUCATION:** Brevard Jr Coll, Assoc of Arts 1970; Howard Univ, Business Admin 1973. **CAREER:** General Electric Co, consultant 1973-78; Seymore Systems Inc, mktg representative 1971-73; IBM Corp, systms engineer 1968-71; Dynamic Concepts Inc, Washington DC, pres 1978-89. **ORGANIZATIONS:** Bd mem Washington DC Chamber of Commerce 1982-; mem Natl Business League 1982-, Amer Assn of Blacks in Energy 1980-; dinner comm Washington Urban League; treasurer Washington DC Coalition for Drug Treatment; mem NAACP, Leadership Washington 1987-; pres-elect Washington DC Chamber of Commerce 1987-; pres Black President's Round Table Assn 1988-89. **HONORS/ACHIEVEMENTS:** Mayor's appointment Washington DC Citizen's Energy Advsory Comm 1983-; elected Advisory Neighborhood Commissioner 1980-81; Outstanding Entrepeneur of The Year, Natl Black Master of Business Admin Assn 1987; Businessman of The Year Washington DC Chamber of Commerce 1987. **BUSINESS ADDRESS:** President, Dynamic Concepts Inc, 2176 Wisconsin Ave, NW, Washington, DC 20007.

ALFORD, BRENDA
Business executive & association executive. **PERSONAL:** Born Jan 27, 1947, Atlanta, GA; daughter of James Alford and Rosette Alford. **EDUCATION:** TN State Univ, BS 1969; Univ of Pittsburgh, MSW 1975. **CAREER:** City of Houston, prog mgr human resources 1975-78; US Dept Health & Human Svcs, public health advisor 1978-83; RABA Inc, exec vice pres 1981-84; Brasman Health and Business Research, pres 1984-; Amer Assoc of Black Women Entrepreneurs Inc, natl pres, exec dir 1982-89. **ORGANIZATIONS:** Mem Natl Assoc of Social Workers, Amer Public Health Assoc, treas WA Urban League Guild 1980-82; Silver Spring Chamber of Commerce, Federation of Republican Women, Natl Assn of Small Research Companies. **HONORS/ACHIEVEMENTS:** Fellowship Natl Inst Mental Health Fellowship 1973-75; edited "Predicted Kilograms Quantities of Medical & Rsch Needs for Controlled Substances" 1980-81. **BUSINESS ADDRESS:** Natl President, Amer Assn Black Women Entrepreneurs, 814 Thayer Ave, Ste 202, Silver Spring, MD 20910.

ALFORD, HAILE LORRAINE
Attorney, lecturer. **PERSONAL:** Born Jul 02, 1949, Brooklyn, NY; children: Julian Alexander Moore, Kaamilah Michelle Moore. **EDUCATION:** Herbert H Lehman, BA 1971; Rutgers Univ School of Law Camden, JD 1976. **CAREER:** Jr HS, teacher 1971; Wiltwyck School for Boys, teacher 1972-73; Lincoln Univ, adj lecturer 1981-; Hercules Inc, attny 1976-. **ORGANIZATIONS:** Mem ABA Labor Law Sect 1976-, NBA Corp Sect 1976-, PA Bar

Assoc 1976-, DE Bar Assoc 1981-. **BUSINESS ADDRESS:** Attorney, Hercules Inc, Hercules Plaza, Wilmington, DE 19894.

ALFRED, DEWITT C., JR.
Medical educator. **PERSONAL:** Born Oct 12, 1937, Chattanooga, TN; married Leticia Bottoms; children: Leticia, Dewitt C III. **EDUCATION:** Morehouse Coll, BS (Cum Laude) 1956; Howard Univ, MD 1960. **CAREER:** Homer G Phillips Hosp St Louis, internship 1960-61; Wash Univ St Louis, asst res psychiatry 1961-62; USAF Reg Hosp Chanute AFB, med offcr neuro-psychiatry clinic 1967-68; Walter Reed Gen Hosp, chief resident 1966-67; physician. **ORGANIZATIONS:** Mental health admins/dipl Amistrv Legal & Comm Psychiatry Amer Psychiatric Assn 1978; diplomate Am Bd of Psychiatry & Neurology 1970; dir Inpatient Psych & asst chf of psych Malcolm-Grow USAF Area Med Cntr Andrews AFB 1967-68; chmn Dept Mental Hlth USAF Reg Hosp Sheppard AFB TX & REg Consult in Psychiatry USAF Surgeon Gen 1968-71; dir Inpt Psych & Asst supt Psychiatry & Grady Meml Hosp Atlanta, GA 1971-73; staff psychiatrist Emory Univ Clinic & Emory univ Hosp 1971-; Dept of Psychiatry Grady meml Hosp Atlanta 1973-; mem Amer Med Assn; mem Natl Med Assn; fellow Amer Psychiatric Assn 1977; Amer Acad pf Psychiatry & Law; So Psychiatric Assn; past pres Soc USAF Psychiatrists; mem Black Psychiatrists of Amer; trustee GA Psychiatric Assn 1979-82.

ALFRED, RAYFIELD
Firefighter. **PERSONAL:** Born Jul 11, 1939, Ville Plate, LA; married Cynthia A Patterson; children: A LaChelle, Shaun C, Raphael W, Jonathan K. **EDUCATION:** Univ of VA, Certs 1975; Univ of DC, AA 1977, BS 1981; OK State Univ, Certs 1981 & 1983; US Fire Acad, Certs 1983 & 1984. **CAREER:** Univ of DC, asst professor cardiopulmonary resuscitation 1980-81; DC Fire Dept, spec asst 1981, med liaison officer 1983, firefighter 1963-, public info officer. **ORGANIZATIONS:** Instructor/trainer Amer Heart Assoc 1977; advisory neighborhood comm DC Govt 1981-84; advisory subcommittee of facilities, bd of trustees Univ of DC 1982-83; udc professional advisory committee Greater SE Comm Hosp 1983-85; emergency cardiac committee Amer Heart Assn 1983-84. **HONORS/ACHIEVEMENTS:** Cert of Hon Mention DC Fire Dept 1967; Cert of Appreciation DC Dental Soc/Amer Red Cross 1978-83; Cert of Appreciation Amer Heart Assoc 1982-83; Silver Medal for Valor DC Fire Dept 1984. **MILITARY SERVICE:** AUS Sergeant/Sp-5 3 years; Hon Discharge 1958-61. **BUSINESS ADDRESS:** Public Information Officer, DC Fire Dept, 1923 Vermont Ave NW, Washington, DC 20001.

ALI, FATIMA (ANN LOUISE REDMON)
Educational administrator; marriage, family therapist. **PERSONAL:** Born Apr 20, 1925, Indianapolis, IN; daughter of Theophilus A. Adams and Eugenia Adams; married LeRoy Redmon (deceased); children: Lydia Ann. **EDUCATION:** Purdue Univ, BS 1946, MS 1960, Ph D 1970; Univ of Pittsburgh, NDEA Summer Fellow 1964. **CAREER:** Gary IN Public Schools, teacher, counselor, 1948-65; Purdue Univ, asst dir admissions, dir Black Students Affairs 1965-70; Univ of CA Berkeley, assoc coord Afro-Am Studies 1970-71; CA State Univ, Hayward, asst prof of educ psychology 1971-74; Contra Costa County Hosp, clin psych 1971-75; Amer Muslim Mission, natl minister of educ & dir of educ 1974-79; clinical dir Pueblo House 1980-83; Reading Rsch Council Burlingame CA, CEO 1982-; vice pres Davis Research Foundation, 1988-. **ORGANIZATIONS:** Consultant US Dept of Educ 1979, CA State Dept of Public Health 1972-73, CA State Dept of Educ 1972, Contra Costa County CETA Prog 1978, IN St Dept of Public Instr 1978, Jenkins Homes for Disabled Chldrn 1981-82, Oakland, CA Public Lib Adult Literacy Prog 1984; prof educ psy Univ of Santa Barbara, Santa Barbara, CA 1982-; consultant Serene Comm Schools Sacramento, CA 1972-; trustee Benicia, CA Unified School Dist 1973-75; mem Assn for Children With Learning Disabilities, The Common Wealth Club of CA, CA Alliance of Black Educators, Alpha Kappa Alpha Sor, Assn for Humanistic Psychology 1985-; Advisory Council, International Biographical Centre, Cambridge, England, 1988; Deputy Governor and Research Board of Advisors, American Biographical Institute, 1988. **HONORS/ACHIEVEMENTS:** Sabbatical leave Gary IN Public Schools 1959-60; teaching asst Purdue Univ 1959-60; coll student personal internship Purdue Univ 1965-66; NDEA summer fellowship Purdue Univ 1962; EOP summer fellowship Purdue Univ 1966-67; Distinguished Leadership Award, American Biographical Institute, 1987; International Leaders in Achievement Award, International Biographical Centre, Cambridge, England, 1987. **BUSINESS ADDRESS:** Chief Executive Officer, Reading Research Council, 1799 Old Bayshore Hwy, Ste 248, Burlingame, CA 94010.

ALI, KAMAL HASSAN
Educator. **PERSONAL:** Born Sep 03, 1944, Springfield, MA; son of Edwin Harold Marshall, Sr and Stella Abrams Bridges-Marshall; married Ayesha Ali, Apr 01, 1966; children: Ahmed Hassan Ali, Quesiyah Sana'a Ali, Ibrahim Suhnoon Ali. **EDUCATION:** Hunter Coll, New York, NY, 1963-64; New York Univ, 1964-65; Univ of Massachusetts, Amherst, MEd, 1977, EdD, 1981. **CAREER:** Human Resources Admin, New York, NY, sr human resource specialist, 1967-71; Harlem East-Harlem Model Cities, New York, NY, project liason, 1971-74; Univ of Massachusetts, Amherst, graduate research and teaching asst, 1974-78; Vantage Consultants, Hartford, CT, training program developer, 1978-79; Westfield State Coll, MA, dir minority, bilingual vocational teacher educ programs, 1980-81, dir minority affairs, 1981-. **ORGANIZATIONS:** Vice pres, Islamic Soc of Western Massachusetts, 1983-; chmn, bd of dir, 1984-86, chmn New Bldg Comm, 1986-, Dunbar Community Center. **HONORS/ACHIEVEMENTS:** Producer, host, cable television program "Coll Journal," Springfield, MA, 1983-; public speaking on educ, foreign policy, apartheid, 1984-86; author, "Islamic Education in the United States: An Overview of Issues, Problems and Possible Approaches," 1984, "The Shariah and Its Implications to Muslim School Planning," 1986, Amer Journal of Islamic Social Studies. **BUSINESS ADDRESS:** Dir of Minority Affairs, Westfield State Coll, Western Ave, Rm 235 Wilson Hall, Westfield, MA 01086.

ALI, MUHAMMAD (CASSIUS CLAY)
Professional boxer. **PERSONAL:** Born Jan 17, 1942, Louisville, KY; married Veronica Porche; children: Hana, Laila, 3 other children by previous marriage. **CAREER:** Former World Heavyweight Boxing Champion; starred in autobiographical film The Greatest, 1976; appeared in TV movie Freedom Road. **ORGANIZATIONS:** Mem World Community Islam. **HONORS/ACHIEVEMENTS:** Winner of 6 Golden Glove Titles in Kentucky; Natl Golden Gloves Title 1959-60; Olympic Gold Medal Boxing 1960; World Heavyweight Championship 1964-67, 1974-78, 1978-79; author, The Greatest, My Own Story, 1975.

ALI, RASHEEDAH ZIYADAH
Vice president, community services. **PERSONAL:** Born Jul 03, 1950, Springfield, IL; married Rahman Munir Ali; children: Jamillah, Sakinah, Rahman II. **EDUCATION:** Sangamon State Gerontology Seminars, certificates 1976,77,78; United Way, counselors training certificate 1986. **CAREER:** Springfield Fair Housing Coalition, vice pres, pres 1987. **ORGANIZATIONS:** Bd mem Advocates for Health 1986-; adv council mem and bd mem Community Action Agency 1986; volunteer Community Energy Systems 1986, Access to Housing 1986, People for Progress 1986-. **HOME ADDRESS:** 2000 E Lawrence # B, Springfield, IL 62703.

ALI, RASHIED
Musician. **PERSONAL:** Born Jul 01, 1933, Philadelphia, PA; son of Randolph Patterson and Dorothy Mae Christopher; married Patricia Bea Wyatt; children: Akeela, Annik. **EDUCATION:** Wm Penn Business Inst Phila, attended 1953; Granoff Music School, 1954-55; studied with Philly Joe Jones 1953-55, and Joe Jones 1963-64. **CAREER:** Played drums with Len Bailey various local groups rock & roll combos; also worked with Bill Dixon, Paul Bley, Sonny Rollins, Archie Shepp, Marion Brown, Sun Ra, New York City 1963-; joined John Coltrane Combo 1965; special concert performances; recorded with A Shepp, John Coltrane, Jackie McLean, Alice Coltrane; 5 recordings as Leader Survival Records; formed own quintet, The Funkyfreeboppers; Ali's Alley Jazz Club, owner.

ALI, SCHAVI MALI
Educator. **PERSONAL:** Born Apr 30, 1948, Detroit, MI; daughter of William Earl Ross, Sr and Margaret Walton Ross; married Derrick Ali, Apr 19, 1986. **EDUCATION:** Wayne State Univ, Detroit, MI, BA, 1970, MA, 1977; Univ of Michigan, Ann Arbor, MI, PhD, 1989. **CAREER:** Highland Park High School, Highland Park, MI, English, social studies teacher, 1970-71; Roeper City & Country School, Bloomfield Hills, MI, English teacher, 1973-77; Wayne State Univ, English, Afro-Amer Studies teacher, 1978-89; Oakland Community Coll, Farmington Hills, MI, English teacher, 1989-. **ORGANIZATIONS:** Assn for the Study of Afro-Amer Life and History; Natl Council of Black Studies, 1980-; Phi Delta Kappa, 1982-; Amer Business Women's Assn, 1988-; mem, bd dir, Afro-Amer Studio Theater, 1983-89, Cartograph Inc, 1989-; dir, Assn for Human Devel, 1988-; historian and lecturer, Alkebulan Assn, 1989-. **HONORS/ACHIEVEMENTS:** Outstanding Educ, Woodward Ave Presbyterian Church, 1982; Spirit of Detroit, Detroit City Council, 1984; Outstanding Educ, governor James Blanchard, 1984; Outstanding Community Leader, Phi Beta Sigma Fraternity, 1984; Univ Author Recognition Award, Wayne State Univ, 1987, 1988; author, Growing Together, 1971, Lament for the Sixties, 1981, "Struggling and Surviving," Black Literature Forum, 1982, Moments in Time, 1987, "Claude McKay," Dictionary of Literary Biography, 1984. **BUSINESS ADDRESS:** Oakland Community Coll, Orchard Ridge Campus, English Dept, 27055 Orchard Lake Rd, Farmington Hills, MI 48018.

ALLAIN, LEON GREGORY
Architect. **PERSONAL:** Born Nov 17, 1924, New Orleans, LA; son of George Allain and Cecile Warnick Allain; married Gloria Grace Dinvaut, Sep 04, 1952; children: Rene'e, Diane. **EDUCATION:** Univ of MI, BArch 1949. **CAREER:** Parsons, Brinckerhoff, Hall & McDonald, draftsman, 1953-58; Skidmore, Owings & Merrill, draftsman 1956-58; Miller & Allain, Architects, partner 1958-67; Allain & Assoc Inc, Architects, pres 1967-. **ORGANIZATIONS:** Mem, Amer Inst of Architects, 1965-87; Natl Orgn of Minority Architects, 1970-87. **HONORS/ACHIEVEMENTS:** Permanent deacon Roman Catholic Church 1982. **MILITARY SERVICE:** AUS 1st lt.

ALLARD, MARJORIE MARTINE (MARTINE ALLARD)
Actress. **PERSONAL:** Born Aug 24, 1970, Brooklyn, NY. **EDUCATION:** Professional Childrens School, 1985. **CAREER:** The Tap Dance Kid, actress; Theatre Now Inc, actress 1981-85. **HONORS/ACHIEVEMENTS:** Grants Friends of Young Artists 1981-83; Theatre World Awd 1984.

ALLARD, MARTINE See ALLARD, MARJORIE MARTINE

ALLEN, ALEX JAMES, JR.
Judge. **PERSONAL:** Born Dec 08, 1934, Louise, MS; married Nancy Ann Green; children: Alex III, Michael P, Derek J. **EDUCATION:** Wayne State Univ, BA 1964; Detroit Coll of Law, JD 1969. **CAREER:** Total Action Against Poverty Med Div, admin asst 1966-68; Comm on Children & Youth for City of Detroit, asst dir 1968-71; Stone Richardson & Allen PC, atty 1971-82; 36th Dist Court Detroit MI, presiding judge. **ORGANIZATIONS:** Mem Omega Psi Phi, NAACP, Founders Soc Detroit Inst of Arts, State Bd of MI, Amer Judges Assoc, MI Dist Judges Assoc; bd of dir MI Black Judge Assoc. **MILITARY SERVICE:** USAF s/sgt 1954-57. **HOME ADDRESS:** 1943 Hyde Park Drive, Detroit, MI 48207. **BUSINESS ADDRESS:** Presiding Judge, 36th Judicial Dist, 600 Randolph, OCB, Detroit, MI 48226.

ALLEN, ALEXANDER J.
Business executive. **PERSONAL:** Born Apr 30, 1916, Boston, MA; married Elizabeth V Banks; children: Alexander J III, Leslie M, Sydney K. **EDUCATION:** Wilberforce Univ, BS 1937; Yale Univ, BD 1940; Columbia Univ, MSSW 1942; Wilberforce Univ, D Humanities 1972. **CAREER:** Baltimore Urban League, exec dir 1944-50; Pittsburgh Urban League, exec dir 1950-60; Philadelphia Counc for Comm Advancement, assoc & dir 1963; NY Urban League, exec dir 1964-66; Natl Urban League NYC, vice pres for prog 1971-. **ORGANIZATIONS:** Pres SW PA Chap natl Assn of Soc Workers 1957-59; pres Natl Assn of Intergroup Rel Officials 1966-67; trustee Wilberforce Univ 1960-; bd mem RegPlan Assn of NY 1965-. **HONORS/ACHIEVEMENTS:** Fellowship Natl Urban League Columbia Univ Sch of Social Work 1940-42; Ann Tanneyhill Award Natl Urban League 1976. **BUSINESS ADDRESS:** Vice President For Programming, Natl Urban League, 500 E 62nd St, New York, NY 10021.

ALLEN, ANDREW A.
Dental surgeon. **PERSONAL:** Born Jul 30, 1921, Port Allen, LA. **EDUCATION:** St Augustine Coll, BS 1942; Howard Univ, DDS 1945; Guggenheim Dental Clinic, certificate 1946; Med Field Serv Sch, attended 1951; AF Inst Pathology, cert 1952; NY Univ, post grad studies 1972; Harvard Sch of Den Med, post grad studies 1976; UCLA Sch of Dentistry, post grad studies. **CAREER:** Self-Employed, dental surgeon. **ORGANIZATIONS:** Pres Chas A George Dental Soc 1948-49; chmn Prog Com Chas A George Dental Soc 1954-64; Gulf State

Dental Soc 1954-64; treas Gulf State Dental Soc 1971-; mem Natl Dental Assn; Amer Dental Assn; Houston Dist Dental Soc; TX Dental Assn; Acad of Dental Dentistry; mem St Lukes Epis Ch; NAACP; YMCA; mem Intl Coll of Oral Implantologists 1976; Pres Club Howard Univ 1976; Alpha Phi Alpha; Chi Delta Mu. **HONORS/ACHIEVEMENTS:** Awd of Merit Natl Found for Infantile Paralysis 1958; Cert Awd Howard Univ Dental Alumni Assn 1956. **MILITARY SERVICE:** AUS pfc 1943-45; AUS capt Dental Corp 1951-56. **BUSINESS ADDRESS:** 2916 Southmore, Houston, TX 77004.

ALLEN, ANITA FORD
Business executive, former public administrator. **PERSONAL:** Born in Washington, DC; daughter of Leonard G Ford and Jerlean Reynolds Ford; children: George A Ferguson III, Stephen F Ferguson. **EDUCATION:** Howard Univ, BA (Summa Cum Laude); Univ of Chicago, MA (w/honors); Univ of MA, EdD 1976. **CAREER:** Dept of Education, mgr 1964-81; Federal Govt, mgr 30 yrs ending 1981; Several Organizations, mgmt consultant 1982; Robt R Moton Meml Inst, pres; Anita F Allen Assocs, pres 1983-. **ORGANIZATIONS:** Apptd by mayor to mem DC Adv Comm on Educ 1985-; mem Metro Baptist Ch Washington; sec exec comm mem Bapt Home of DC 1978-82; vice pres & Pres Dist of Columbia Bd of Educ 1967-72; life mem Delta Sigma Theta Sor; mem bd of dirs DC League of Women Voters 1987-89. **HONORS/ACHIEVEMENTS:** Distinguished public serv awds and/or hon degrees, Prairie View A&M Univ 1976, AL; Broaddus Coll 1976. **HOME ADDRESS:** 6101 16th St NW, #209, Washington, DC 20011.

ALLEN, ARIS TEE
Physician. **PERSONAL:** Born Dec 27, 1910, Beeville, TX; son of James Allen and Marietta Whitby Allen; married Faye W. Allen MD, Feb 28, 1947; children: Aris T Jr, Lonnie W. **EDUCATION:** Howard Univ, MD, 1944, BA, 1985. **CAREER:** Private practice, physician 1945-82; Maryland State Legislature, delegate, 1966-74, senator, 1978-81; US Dept Health & Human Serv Health Care Financial Admin, dir Health Standards and Quality Bureau, 1981, medical affairs advisor, 1981-1989. **ORGANIZATIONS:** Honorary member, Anne Arundel County Gen Hospital Staff; member, Anne Arundel County Medical Soc, Monumental Medical Soc, Amer Medical Assn, Amer Acad of Family Physicians, Golden Heritage, Senators Past, Anne Arundel County Bd of Educ, Regional Advisory Council of Small Business Admin, Maryland Commn on Ethnic Affairs, Maryland Hospital Regulation Task Force; life member, NAACP; bd of dir, Amer Red Cross, Annapolis Rotary Intl, Salvation Army, Amer Cancer Society; advisory bd, Maryland Seafood Festival; bd of trustees, Mount Moriah AME Church; lay bd of dir, Local Banking Institution; vice pres, Racial Ethnic Native Amer Affairs; ex-officio member, Maryland Commn on Capital City; past member, Bd of Medical Examiners of Maryland, Annexation Charter Commn, Comm of Bicentennial Commn; past bd of dir, Maryland Acad Family Physicians, Citizens Housing and Planning Assn, Parole Day Care Center, Parole Health Center, Anne Arundel County YMCA, Chamber of Commerce of Greater Annapolis, Anne Arundel County Community Coll Bd of Trustees, Boy Scouts of Amer; past pres, Medical Staff Anne Arundel Gen Hospital; past vice pres, Medical-Chirurgical Faculty of the State of Maryland; past vice pres, Acad of Family Practice. **HONORS/ACHIEVEMENTS:** Award for outstanding serv to church and community, city of Annapolis, 1955; outstanding achievement in medicine and civic affairs, Maryland Medical Assn, 1967; Richard Allen award for service to church and state, AME Church, 1969; NAACP Award of Honor, Maryland State Conference Branches, 1969; AH Robbin Award, Medical and Chirurgical Faculty of Maryland, 1970, 1981; resolution for unusual and extraordinary serv, passed by Maryland State Legislature, 1970, 1971; Alpha Phi Alpha Fraternity Award, 1973; Salute to Aris Allen, one week-long activity, 1975; NAACP award, Anne Arundel County Conference Branches, 1976; Award of Merit, Monumental Medical Soc; Intl Humanitarian Award, Frontier, 1977; Paul Harris Fellow, Rotary Intl, 1978; Distinguished Serv Award, Mt Olive AME Church, 1979; Johnson Publishing Co Award, 1980; Wisdom Award of Honor, 1980; Certificate of Appreciation, Anne Arundel County Police Dept, 1980; Alphonse G. Addison Political Award, 1980; Governor's Citation, 1980; Howard Univ Alumni Achievement Award, 1981; member, Presidential Delegation attending the independence ceremony for the country of Belize, 1981; Calvert County Commr Award, 1981; Hon Thomas Rymer Award, 1981; Chesapeake Bay Railroad Museum Found Award, 1981; Hon Larry Young Convocation Citation, 1981; Coord for Combined Federal Campaign, Dept of Health and Human Serv, District of Columbia, 1982; EBO Arts Found Award, Annapolis, MD, 1983. **MILITARY SERVICE:** AUS, second lt, 1939-41; USAF, flight surgeon, lt captain, 1952-54. **HOME ADDRESS:** 1323 Magnolia Ave, Arundel on the Bay, Annapolis, MD 21487.

ALLEN, BENJAMIN P., III
Administrator. **PERSONAL:** Born Feb 27, 1942, Washington, DC; son of Benjamin Allen and Elizabeth Allen; married Francesca M Winslow; children: Nicole, Camille. **EDUCATION:** Howard Univ, BS 1963; Rutgers Univ MBA 1976. **CAREER:** Marine Midland Bank, project officer 1970-78, asst branch manager 1978-80, branch manager 1980-84, operations 1985; corporate manager employee relations 1986-87; asst vice pres, branch manager 1987-88; Riggs Natl Bank, vice pres, private banking officer 1988-;. **ORGANIZATIONS:** Treas Edges Group Inc 1984-88; mem Urban Bankers Coalition 1984-88; Natl Black MBA Assoc 1984-88; vestry mem St Andrews Church 1985; Washington Urban Bankers Assn, 1988-. **HONORS/ACHIEVEMENTS:** Black achiever Harlem Branch YMCA 1974. **MILITARY SERVICE:** USAR-MSC Col; USNA achievement award 1983. **HOME ADDRESS:** 1238 Aspen St, Washington, DC 20012. **BUSINESS ADDRESS:** Vice President Riggs National Bank, 800 17th St NW, 2nd Floor, Washington, DC 22030.

ALLEN, BERNESTINE
International transportation specialist. **PERSONAL:** Born Aug 20, 1944, Soperton, GA. **EDUCATION:** Ft Valley State Coll, BS 1967; Northeastern Univ, MA 1968. **CAREER:** Dept Labor Washington, econ analyst 1967; Gen Elec Co, financial analyst 1968-69; Dept Transportation Washington, economist 1969-71; Airport & Airway Cost Allocation Study, economist asst dir 1971-73; Intl Aviation Policy, economist 1973-75; Dept of Transportation, intl transportation specialist 1975-. **ORGANIZATIONS:** Mem Amer Econ Assn; mem Amer Fedn Govt Employees 1970-72; Natl Econ Assn; Amer Acad Polit & Social Scis; Bus & Professional Women's League; mem DC Assn for Retarded Citizens; mem Delta Sigma Theta Inc pres chap 1966-67 1972-74; bd dirs DST Telecommunications Inc; Outstanding Young Women of Amer 1975 1979; Garfield Home for Sr Citizens; Project Women; Women Ex-Offenders Prog 1973; Natl Council of Negro Women; NAACP; Natl Urban League. **HONORS/ACHIEVEMENTS:** Alpha Kappa Mu Natl Honor Soc 1965; Wall St Journal Scholastic Achievement Awd 1967; Natl Sic Found Grant 1967. **BUSINESS ADDRESS:** Intl Transportation Specialist, Dept of Transportation, OST/P-42, 400-7 St SW, Washington, DC 20590.

ALLEN, BETTIE JEAN
State government official. **PERSONAL:** Born Oct 21, 1926, Springfield, IL; divorced. **EDUCATION:** Grad, Springfield Coll, Lincoln Coll of Law, Univ of IL, Sangamon State Univ. **CAREER:** YWCA in Kenya, vol intl div, 1967-68; Springfield Human Rel Commn, exec dir, 1969-70; entrepreneur, 1970-74; Assoc Gen Contr of Illinois, training dir, 1971-72; State of Illinois, Capitol Devel Bd, coord, 1973-. **ORGANIZATIONS:** Past pres NAACP; Serv Bur for Colored Children; supr Zion Bapt Ch Sch; trustee bd mem YWCA 1954-70; bd mem United Way; mem RR Relocation Auth. **HONORS/ACHIEVEMENTS:** Webster Plaque Awd Springfield NAACP 1957; Achievement Awd Urban League 1964; Affirmative Action Awd 1975; Breadbasket Commercial Achiev Awd 1977. **BUSINESS ADDRESS:** Coordinator, State of IL, CDB 3rd Fl, Wm G Stratton Bldg, Springfield, IL 62706.

ALLEN, BETTY (MRS. R. EDWARD LEE III)
Educator, retired opera and concert singer. **PERSONAL:** Born in Campbell, OH; daughter of James Corr Allen and Cora Catherine Mitchell Allen; married Ritten Edward Lee, III, Oct 17, 1953; children: Juliana Catherine Hogue, Anthony Edward. **EDUCATION:** Wilberforce Univ, Wilberforce OH, attended 1944-46; Hartford School of Music, Hartford CT, certificate 1952; studied voice under Sarah Peck More, Paul Ulanousky, Carolina Segrera Holden, Zinka Milanov. **CAREER:** North Carolina School of the Arts, teacher, faculty mem, 1978-87; Curtis Inst of Music, Philadelphia PA, teacher, faculty mem; Manhattan School of Music, New York City, trustee, teacher, faculty mem; Harlem School of the Arts, New York City, exec dir, chair of voice dept, 1979-. **ORGANIZATIONS:** Mem, NAACP; Hartford Mus Club; Metropolitan Opera Guild; Urban League; Amer Guild Mus; Artists Equity; Amer Museum of Natl History; AFTRA; UN Assn USA; Silvermine Guild Artists; Jeunesses Musicales; Gioventu Musicales; Unitarian Universalist Women's Federation; Student Sanguerein Trondheim; life mem, Natl Negro Musicians Assn; hon mem, Sigma Alpha Iota; mem, Cosmopolitan Club, Women's City Club NY; bd mem, exec comm mem, Carnegie Hall, Natl Found for Advancement in the Arts, Arts and Business Council, Amer Arts Alliance; bd mem, US Comm for UNICEF, Manhattan School of Music; trustee, Chamber Music Soc of Lincoln Center, Children's Storefront, Symphony Orchestra of NYC Housing Authority, InterSchools Orchestras, Theatre Development Fund (NYC); co-chair, Schomburg Commission, Harlem Arts Advocacy Coalition; mem, New York City Advisory Comm for Cultural Affairs, New York City Commn on the Bicentennial of the Constitution. **HONORS/ACHIEVEMENTS:** Marian Anderson Award, 1952-53; Natl Mus League Mgmt Award, 1953; named Best Singer of Season Critics' Circle, Argentina & Chile 1959, Uruguay 1961; Martha Baird Rockefeller Aid to Mus Grantee, 1953, 1958; John Hay Whitney Fellow, 1953-54; Ford Found Concert Soloist Grantee, 1963-64; Hon Doctor of Humane Letters Degree, Wittenberg Univ, Ohio; Hon Doctor of Music Degree, Union Coll, Schenectady NY, 1988; Exceptional Achievement Award, Women's Project and Productions, 1988; Amer Eagle Award, Natl Music Council, 1988; first recipient, ISO Award, InterSchools Orchestras, NYC, 1988; Philadelphia Natl Bank Distinguished Artist of the Year, Settlement Music School, Philadelphia PA, 1989; Laurel Leaf Award, Amer Composers' Alliance, 1989; 15th Anniversary Harlem Week Award, Harlem Week and the Uptown Chamber of Commerce, 1989; has appeared as soloist with world's leading orchestras and renowned conductors, including Bernstein, Casals, Dorati, Leinsdorf, Maazel, Martinon, Munch, Ormandy, Ozawa, Pritchard, Solti, Steinberg, and Stokowski; major performances include the 1952 production of Virgil Thomson's "Four Saints in Three Acts," the ANTA Theatre's 1973 production, and all major productions of it until 1982; appeared as recitalist in England, the Netherlands, Norway, Germany, and Canada; made North Amer opera debut in 1966 with the San Francisco Opera; made Canadian Opera debut 1971, New York City Opera debut 1973, Metropolitan Opera's Mini-MET debut 1974; regularly appears at the Marlboro, Casals, Tanglewood, and other music festivals. **BUSINESS ADDRESS:** Exec Dir, Harlem School of the Arts, 645 St Nicholas Ave, New York, NY 10030.

ALLEN, BLAIR SIDNEY
Educator. **PERSONAL:** Born Aug 07, 1952, Abington, PA; divorced; children: Thageron. **EDUCATION:** PA State Univ, BS Biophysics 1974; Univ of CA at Berkeley, Master Biophysics 1979. **CAREER:** Presbyterian Univ of PA Med Ctr, rsch teacher 1980-81; Harcum Jr Coll, instr of sci. **ORGANIZATIONS:** Pres Rsch Inst Tech Inc 1978-, Oppty Council of Eastern Montgomery Cty 1980-82; mem NAACP Amber Branch 1984-85. **HONORS/ACHIEVEMENTS:** 1st Prize Chem Montgomery & DE Valley Sci Fairs 1970; Scholarship PA Senatorial Scholarship & Grad 1970-74; Grad Fellowshp Minority Fellowship 1974-79; Fellowship Nato Advance Study Inst 1981; Fellowship Faculty Summer Inst 1983. **BUSINESS ADDRESS:** Asst Professor of Science, Harcum Jr Coll, Morris & Montgomery Aves, Bryn Mawr, PA 19010.

ALLEN, BRENDRA FOSTER
Educator. **PERSONAL:** Born Jan 24, 1947, Gloucester, VA; married Robert P Allen; children: Tameka D. **EDUCATION:** VA State Univ, BS 1969; NC State Univ, MS 1976, EdD 1985. **CAREER:** Cornell Univ Coop Extension Service, youth development specialist 1971-72, county 4-H agent 1969; Natl 4-H Foundation Div of Leadership Development, program specialist 1972-75; NC State Univ, School of Educ research asst 1975-76, Div of Student Affairs coord 1976-80, asst dir 1980-83, Office of the Provost coord 1983-85; Agricultural Extension Service program specialist 1985-. **ORGANIZATIONS:** NC State Univ, graduate student's assoc adult education executive board; Natl 4-H Foundation, staff development and training committee, volunteers' forum planning committee; Task Force on Program Development for 4-H volunteers; Natl Teen Leaders' Symposium Planning Committee; American Home Economics Assn; Natl 4-H Assn; Kappa Omicron Phi; Image of NC State Univ Seminars, facilitator 1979-80, task force mem 1978-79; Outstanding Young Women of America, mem 1980; NCSU committe on Recruitment and Retention of Black Students, mem 1982-83; Governor's Conf on Women and the Economy, facilitator 1983; Shaw Univ Seminary Ext Program, teacher 1984-86, Youth Motivation Task Force mem 1985-86; NC Home Economics Ext Program Comm, mem 1983-84; NC 4-H Volunteer Task Force, mem 1986; NC Home Econ Volunteer Task Force, mem 1986; mem, Epsilon Sigma Phi, Natl Honorary Extension Fraternity 1989. **HONORS/ACHIEVEMENTS:** Publications, "Making Incentives Work for You" 1976, "Competencies Needed by 4-H Volunteers for the Effective Use of Incentives - A Needs Asesssment Study" 1976, "Criteria for Selection, Evaluating or Developing Learning Modules" 1976, "Are Your Reading Habits a Liability?" 1977, "Videotapes Help University Students Learn How to Learn" 1981, "Build Up One Another" 1986, "Women, Builders of Communities and Dreams" 1986, "Rural Minority Women As Community Volunteers"

1986; NC Coordinator, Women and Chronic Disease Teleconference, 1988; received Infant Mortality Grant from United Church of Christ, 1989. **HOME ADDRESS:** 2025 Rabbit Run, Raleigh, NC 27603. **BUSINESS ADDRESS:** Leadership Development Spec, NC Agricultural Extension Serv, NCState University, Box 7605, Raleigh, NC 27695.

ALLEN, BROWNING E., JR.
Physician. **PERSONAL:** Born Mar 24, 1925, Raton, NM; married Betty Mae Williams; children: Julie E Grier, Marie E Allen, Browning E III, Emile A. **EDUCATION:** Univ of OR, BS 1947; Meharry Med Coll, MD 1949. **CAREER:** Homer G Phillips Hosp, intern 1949-50; LA Cty Hosp, resd urology 1951-56; Univ of So CA Med School, instr dept urology 1957-60; Permanente Med Group Sacramento, chief dept urology 1965-69; Kaiser Hosp Sacramento, chief dept surg 1966-67; LA Cty USC Med School, asst dir dept urology 1969-70; Private practice, urologist, surgeon 1970-. **ORGANIZATIONS:** Dir ped urology, prof urology, chief LA Cty USC Med School; mem Amer Med Assoc 1956-78, Natl Med Assoc 1957-, Western Sect Amer Urol Assoc 1958, Amer Urol Assoc Inc 1961, Soc for Ped Urol 1969-80; pres LA Urol Soc 1981-, Aesclepiads Premed Hon Frat Univ of OR 1944; mem Alpha Phi Alpha 1945, Kappa Pi Hon Frat Meharry Med Coll 1948, Govs Task Force Veneral Disease Control State of CA 1971-72; exec comm Western Sect AUA 1973-77; bd ofgov Soc for LA Cty Gen to Urinary Surg 1974. **MILITARY SERVICE:** AUS 1st lt 1951-53. **BUSINESS ADDRESS:** Urologist, Surgeon, 1904 N Orange Grove Ave, Pomona, CA 91767.

ALLEN, BYRON
Performer. **PERSONAL:** Born Apr 22, 1961, Detroit, MI. **EDUCATION:** Attending, Univ of So CA. **CAREER:** Appearances on the Johnny Carson Show; comedian "The Comedy Store"; co-host "Real People" NBC-TV. **BUSINESS ADDRESS:** George Schlater Prods NBC, 300 W Alameda, Burbank, CA 91523.

ALLEN, CHARLES CLAYBOURNE
Public administrator-urban planning. **PERSONAL:** Born Sep 21, 1935, Newport News, VA; son of John C Allen and Margaret C Allen; married Sallie; children: Charles II, John IV, Sallie, Monique. **EDUCATION:** Hampton Inst, BS 1958; Columbia Univ, MSUP 1963. **CAREER:** Clarke & Rapuano Inc, urban planner 1963-68; Dept of Devel & Planning Gary, dir 1968-74; The Soul City Coll, vice pres gen manager 1974-75; Wendell Campbell Assoc Inc, sr vice pres 1975-88; deputy dir, Depart of Planning and Devel, Newport News, VA. **ORGANIZATIONS:** Bd mem Amer Planning Assn 1979-; mem Amer Inst of Certified Planners; bd mem Amer Soc of Planning off 1971-73; mem Amer Inst of Planners 1977-78; chmn joint AIP/ASPO Comm for Min Affairs 1973-78; pres Natl Assn of Planners 1976; Kappa Alpha Psi Fraternity 1955; bd mem Interracial Council for Business Opportunity 1987-; mem Lambda Alpha. **HONORS/ACHIEVEMENTS:** Dept Head of Yr City of Gary 1973; Outstanding Govt Award Gary Jaycees 1974; Meritorious Serv Award Gary Chapter Frontiers 1974; City Council Resol Gary City County 1974; Outstanding 20 Yr Alumnus Hampton Inst 1978; Outstanding Person DuPage Co NAACP 1978. **MILITARY SERVICE:** AUS lt 1958-60; USAR capt 1963-66; USANG capt 1966-68. **BUSINESS ADDRESS:** Deputy Director, Planning Division, Department of Planning and Development, 240 Washington Avenue, Newport News, VA 23607.

ALLEN, CHARLES E.
Educator. **PERSONAL:** Born Dec 23, 1931, Cynthiana, KY; son of Isham Allen and Mildred Wilson Allen; married Anna; children: Paula, Pamela, Phillip. **EDUCATION:** Central State Univ, BS 1954; USC, MS 1970. **CAREER:** Los Angeles Unified School Dist, math specialist 1970-85, teacher 1986. **ORGANIZATIONS:** Dir, Natl Council of Teachers of Math 1972-75, Los Angeles Teachers Assn 1960-62, consultant State Dept of Educ in Iowa, Minnesota, New Mexico, California, Nebraska, Oregon, and North Carolina. **HONORS/ACHIEVEMENTS:** Author "Daily Chores Math," "Adventures in Computing I & II," "Supermath," "Consumer Math," "Metric Syst Film Loops"; co-author of "Houghton Mifflin Mathematics" 1988. **MILITARY SERVICE:** Infantry 1st lt 1955-57. **BUSINESS ADDRESS:** Natl Speaker Mathematics, 1557 Farland St, Covina, CA 91724.

ALLEN, CHARLES EDWARD
Real estate investor. **PERSONAL:** Born Feb 22, 1947, Atlanta, GA; son of Charles Edward Allen, Sr and Ruby Lee Collins Allen Hill; married Elizabeth Ann Glover, Jul 06, 1972; children: Charles Phillip, David Kennedy, Rebecca Ann. **EDUCATION:** Morehouse College, Atlanta, GA, BA, 1970; Graduate School of Business, Chicago, IL, MBA, 1972. **CAREER:** First Natl Bank, Chicago Il; Bank of CA, vice pres & manager, 1976-78; First Bank Natl Assn, pres & COO, 1978-80; United Natl Bank, Washington DC, exec vice pres & CAO, 1980-81; First Ind Natl Bank, pres & CEO, 1981-88; MIG Realty Adv, vice pres & reg manager, 1988-. **ORGANIZATIONS:** Corp Dir, First Ind Natl Bank, 1981-; corp dir, AAA Michigan; corp dir, Blu Cross/Blue Shield of Michigan; mem, Detroit Econ Club; past pres, Natl Bankers Assn; mem, Greater Detroit Chamber of Commerce; mem, Detroit Area Boy Scouts; mem, Museum of Afro-American History; trustee, Benedict College. **HONORS/ACHIEVEMENTS:** Black Achiever's Award 1976; Outstanding Young Men of America, YMCA, 1981, Boy Scouts of Amer, 1984, Alpha Theta GPD Sorority, 1981; Citizen of the Year, Hartford Ave Baptist Church, 1982; Mayor's Award of Merit, 1984; America's Best & Brightest Young Men & Women, 1987; During tenure, First Ind Natl Bank was featured as Bank of the Year, Black Enterprise Magazine; profiled in Minority Business Entrepreneur Magazine. **BUSINESS ADDRESS:** President, Graistone Realty Advisors, Inc, 300 River Place, Suite 2050, Detroit, MI 48207.

ALLEN, CLYDE CECIL
Business executive. **PERSONAL:** Born Jan 29, 1943, Youngstown, OH; married Gayle Thigpen; children: Michael Clyde, Brett Donaldo. **EDUCATION:** Kent State Univ, BA Bio 1965; Rutgers Univ, MA Ind Rel 1977. **CAREER:** Schering Corp, sr microbiologist 1965-70, personnel admin 1970-72; Ind Comm Ctr, exec dir 1972-74; Johnson & Johnson, sr personnel admin 1974-75, sr comps admin 1975-76, mgr human resource planning 1976-78; M&M Mars Inc, mgr compensation benefits 1978-80; JE Seagrams Inc, corp mgr EEO 1980-. **ORGANIZATIONS:** EDGES NY NJ 1972-; Amer Comps Assoc 1976-; chairperson US Comm on Civil Rights 1968-; Employer Assoc NJ 1976-; Port Auth Airport Rev Cncl 1972-74; pres Frontiers Intl Inc 1974-; chairperson Plainfield Econ Dev Comm 1975-; fndr dir Youth Leadership Club Inc 1968-; vice chmn Bd dir Union Co OIC 1973-75. **HONORS/ACHIEVEMENTS:** Outstanding Serv Awd Frontiers Intl 1978; Malcolm X Awd YLC Inc 1971; Outstanding Serv Awd Elizabeth YMCA 1970; Lineman of Week Mid-Amer Conf 1964. **BUSINESS ADDRESS:** Corp Manager, Joseph E Seagram & Sons, Inc, 800 E 3rd Avenue, New York, NY 10022.

ALLEN, DEBBIE
Dancer, singer, actress. **PERSONAL:** Born Jan 1953, Houston, TX; married Norman Nixon; children: Vivian Nicole, Norman Ellard Jr. **EDUCATION:** Howard Univ Sch of Fine Arts, BA Speech & Drama (with honors). **CAREER:** Appeared in Broadway shows incl, Purlie; Raisin in the Sun; West Side Story (1980 revival); Ain't Misbehavin'; TV Mini-Series, Roots; Motion Pictures, The Fish That Saved Pittsburgh; Ragtime; Fame; Featured Star of TV Series Fame; Dir of TV Series Fame, Family Ties, Bronx Zoo; now appearing on Broadway. **HONORS/ACHIEVEMENTS:** Appeared on 1984 Academy Awards; received Ebony's Dramatic Awd. **BUSINESS ADDRESS:** c/o William Morris Agency, 1350 Avenue of the Americas, New York, NY 10019.

ALLEN, DEMETRICE MICHEALLE
Television producer. **PERSONAL:** Born Dec 04, 1958, Augusta, GA. **EDUCATION:** Spelman Coll Atlanta, BA 1981. **CAREER:** USDA Food & Nutrition Svcs, prog specialist 1980-82; Buffalo Arts & Music School, music theory & piano 1981-84; United Negro College Fund, project asst 1986-87; WKBW-TV, asst/public affairs dir 1984-. **ORGANIZATIONS:** Mem NAACP Buffalo Chap 1984-, Coalition of 100 black Women Buffalo Chap 1985-, Alpha Kappa Alpha Sor 1985-, Natl Black Media Coalition Buffalo Chap 1985-, Amer Women in Radio & TV 1986-. **HONORS/ACHIEVEMENTS:** Outstanding Young Woman in Amer 1984. **BUSINESS ADDRESS:** Asst to the Public Afrs Dir, WKBW-TV, 7 Broadcast Plaza, Buffalo, NY 14202.

ALLEN, DOZIER T., JR.
Trustee. **PERSONAL:** Born Jan 10, 1931, Gary, IN; married Arlene McKinney; children: 4 children. **EDUCATION:** Los Angeles Jr Coll; Indiana Univ; Valparaiso Univ. **CAREER:** Allen Ent, vice pres, 1957-67; Northwest Indiana Urban League, field rep, 1968-69; Gary City Council, vice pres, 1970; Gary IN, city councilman-at-large, 1968-72; Dozier T Allen, Jr Ent, pres; Double AA Inc, pres; Lake Shore-Birch Inc, pres; MACH Investors Inc, vp; Downtown Deli-Mart, proprietor; Calumet Township, trustee, 1970-. **ORGANIZATIONS:** Founder & chmn bd dir NW IN Sickle Cell Found 1971-73; mem Natl PTA; Natl Roster of Black Elected Officials; Natl Black Caucus of Local Elected Officials; IN Black Caucus; In Township Trustee Assn; NW IN Urban League; Gary Toastmasters Intl; life mem NAACP Gary Br; charter mem Gary Hum Rel Commn; bd mem Gary Marona House Drug Abuse Inc; chmn IN 1st Congr Democratic Dist 1971; pres Lake County Mental Health Board; mem Amer Pub Welfare Assn; contrib mem Democratic Natl Comm; mem IN Township Trustee Assn; mem Lake County Bd of Edn; mem Gary C of C; mem IN Assn of Commerce & Ind; mem Downtown Gary Merchant's Assn; mem Chancellor's Assoc IN Univ; mem Natl Sheriff's Assn; asst chief Lake County Sheriff's Police Res Unit. **HONORS/ACHIEVEMENTS:** Sponsors Award Gary Greens Pop Warners Football League 1974; Boss of Century Award 1974; Recognition for Comm Serv Gary Pub Sch 1974; Mexican Amer Award 1974; Recipient NAACP Ovington Award; Recipient NAACP Humanitarian Award; incl over 150 additional awards.

ALLEN, EDNA ROWERY
Educational administrator. **PERSONAL:** Born Jul 20, 1938, Carrollton, AL; married Robert H Allen; children: Robin, Dawn, Robert Jr. **EDUCATION:** Lincoln Univ, BS, Business Educ, 1960; Univ of IL, MS, Counselor Educ, 1970; Edwardsville IL, postgraduate work, 1974; McMurray Coll, Dr of Humanities, 1983. **CAREER:** Rock Jr HS, teacher 1962-70, counselor 1970-71; Bd of Ed Dist 189 E St Louis, Dr of gifted programs 1971-. **ORGANIZATIONS:** Chmn of social action Delta Sigma Theta Sorority Inc 1971-; bd of dirs Natl Assn of Gifted Children 1973-83; bd of dirs E St Louis Public Library 1974-83; bd of trustees State Comm Coll E St Louis 1975-78; pres St Ann's Sodality of St Patrick's Church 1982-; vice pres Concerned Citizens for the Comm 1984-; chmn of social action Top Ladies of Distinction 1984-; chmn Status of Women Comm, Top Ladies of Distinction; mem Phi Delta Kappa. **HONORS/ACHIEVEMENTS:** "Those Who Excel" IL Office of Education 1978; Service Awd State Comm Coll 1978; Merit Awd ML King Jr HS E St Louis 1979; Recognition Awd Delta Sigma Theta Sor Inc 1984; Honorary Doctorate MacMurray Coll Jacksonville IL 1983. **HOME ADDRESS:** 664 N 33rd St, East St Louis, IL 62205. **BUSINESS ADDRESS:** Dir of Gifted Programs, E St Louis Bd of Educ 189, 1005 State St, East St Louis, IL 62201.

ALLEN, ELBERT E.
Dentist. **PERSONAL:** Born Sep 19, 1921, Shreveport, LA; married Carolyn Sims. **EDUCATION:** Wiley Coll TX, BS 1942; Meharry Med Coll TN, DDS 1945; Acad Gen Dentistry, FAGD 1969. **CAREER:** Private Practice, dentist. **ORGANIZATIONS:** Fndg mem Pelican State Dental Assn 1946; editor NAA Jour Natl Dental Assn 1950-51; assoc mem Chicago Dental Soc; mem NW LA Dental Assn; LA State Dental Assn; Amer Dental Assn; past finance chmn Pioneer Div BSA 10 yrs; fndg mem & past mem bd dirs Mt Moriah Day Care Ctr & Nursery past 10 yrs numerous other orgns & affiliations; pres Supreme Camp of the Amer Woodmen. **HONORS/ACHIEVEMENTS:** Pierre Fuchared Awd for Outstanding Serv to the Country for Military Serv 1952; first black elected to any elective office since reconstruction days; Liberty Bell Awd, Shreveport Bar Assn 1970; Silver Beaver Awd 1972; Notable Amer Awd 1976-77. **MILITARY SERVICE:** AUS Reserve Corps 2nd lt 1941-43; AUS pfc 1943-44; USAF capt 1951-53; USAF Reserve 1953-58. **BUSINESS ADDRESS:** Dentist, Allens' Dental Clinic, 1004 Sprague St, Shreveport, LA 71101.

ALLEN, ESTHER LOUISA
Retired army officer/teacher. **PERSONAL:** Born Jan 20, 1912, Raton, NM; daughter of John Allen and Alice Matilda Woods Allen. **EDUCATION:** KC General Hospital School of Nursing, Diploma 1940; Univ of Colorado School of Nursing, BS 1949; Univ of Washington School of Nursing, MS 1958. **CAREER:** Hubbard Hospital, Meharry Medical College, supervisor operating rooms; San Joaquin County Hosp, Stockton CA, asst supervisor operating rooms 1951-58; Santa Rosa Junior Coll School of Nursing, first and only black instructor 1960-73 (retired). **ORGANIZATIONS:** Mem Retired Officers Assn, Disabled American Veterans, Alpha Kappa Alpha Sor. **HONORS/ACHIEVEMENTS:** Plaque for Outstanding Service to the Cause of Nursing Educ, Alumni of Santa Rosa Jr Coll. **MILITARY SERVICE:** AUS Nurse Corps 2nd lt 26 months; American Defense Medal, American Campaign Medal, World War II Medal.

ALLEN, GEORGE
Educator. **PERSONAL:** Born May 22, 1955, Bay City, TX; married Cathy Hunt; children: Amanda Michele. **EDUCATION:** Attended, Kilgore Coll 1974; Stephen F Austin State Univ, BS 1977, MEd 1979. **CAREER:** Lufkin State School, therapy asst 1977; Lufkin Independent Schools, teacher/coach 1978, asst principal 1979; Youth Opportunity Unlimited, recreation coordinator 1985-86; Stephen F Austin State Univ, asst football coach 1979-86, athletic academic counselor. **ORGANIZATIONS:** Mem Natl Assn of Collegiate Dirs of Athletics; mem Amer Football Coaches Assn; mem TX HS Coaches Assn; mem Natl Assn of Academic Advisors for Athletics. **HONORS/ACHIEVEMENTS:** Mr Black SFA Stephen F Austin St Univ; Merit Awd Council of Black Organizations 1980-81. **BUSINESS ADDRESS:** Athletic Advisor, Stephen F Austin StateUniv, PO Box 13010 SFA Station, Nacogdoches, TX 75962.

ALLEN, GEORGE LOUIS
City official, business executive. **PERSONAL:** Born Nov 26, 1910, New Orleans, LA; married Norma; children: Don, George II, Norma, Arthur. **EDUCATION:** Xavier Univ, AB 1931; Southern Methodist Univ, grad Inst of Ins Marketing. **CAREER:** Tecog Serv Industries, pres; City of Dallas TX, city council 1969-. **ORGANIZATIONS:** Certified public accountant; bd mem TX Accountant; bd dir Dallas Negro C of C; bd dir TX So Univ Dallas Co United Fund; N TX Planning Cncl for Hosps & Related Health Facilities; vice pres bd mem Comm Cncl of Greater Dallas, Cath Charities. **HONORS/ACHIEVEMENTS:** 20 Yr Serv Awd Dallas Big Brothers Inc; Disting Councilman's Awd City of Dallas; numerous other citations & awds. **BUSINESS ADDRESS:** City Council Member, Dallas Co Pct 8 Pl 1, 414 S Thornton Frwy, Dallas, TX 75203.

ALLEN, GEORGE MITCHELL
Business executive. **PERSONAL:** Born Nov 14, 1932, Boston, MA; married E Louise; children: Leslie. **EDUCATION:** Mississippi Univ, Ext Courses; US Army Career Ext Courses. **CAREER:** Special Asst to Gov, 1970-74; Commonwealth of MA, dep commr of vet serv; Intergovernmental Relations, notary public 1972; Dept of Army, fed women's prog mgr, equal employment opportunity officer. **ORGANIZATIONS:** Real estate broker; town rep Stoughton MS; past pres Roxbury Med Tech Found 1971-73; external adv bd for Minorities Educ Advancement; MS Coll of Pharmacy 1972-; natl pres Afro-Amer Vet; mem NAACP; MS Joint Ctr for Polit Studies; vice pres Blacks in Govt AZ Chapt. **MILITARY SERVICE:** AUS sfc e7 20 yrs retired; Army Commendation Medal; many serv medals Japan, Korea, Germany; Certificates of Commendation from Military Serv & Comm Agencies. **BUSINESS ADDRESS:** Equal Employment Opportunity Officer, Dept of Army, US Army Garrison ASH-EE, Fort Huachuca, AZ 85613.

ALLEN, GLADSTONE WESLEY
Physician. **PERSONAL:** Born May 17, 1915, Panama Canal Zone, Panama;married Sylvia Ximinies; children: Resna, Wesley Jr, Cyril, Robert, John, S Katherine, B Clare, Elizabeth. **EDUCATION:** Lincoln Univ, BA 1935; Univ PA Grad School of Med, 1951; Meharry Med Coll, MD 1941; Philadelphia Gen, resd 1951-54. **CAREER:** Gladhaven Nursing Home, admin; Private practice, physician. **ORGANIZATIONS:** Fellow Amer Coll of Admin; charter mem NC State Bd of Exam for Nursing Homes; mem NMA, AAA; exec bd mem NC Br of Amer Cancer Soc; mem Amer Geriatrics Soc, Cumberland Cty State Med Soc; sec, bd of dir United Natl Bank; pres Old N State Med Soc of NC 1963-64; mem Gov Plng Bd of NC for Mental Health Council 1971-74, NC Cumberland Cty Dem Exec Com 1971-75, Grand Dep of Scottish Rite Masonry, Orient of NC; chmn bd of dir Health Med Rsch Found; mem AEAONMS; grand jr warden Prince Hall Grand Lodge NC; charter mem Cape Fear Ind of Fayetteville & Cumberland Cty; apptd Cumberland Cty Rep of Professions on State Employment Commn. **HONORS/ACHIEVEMENTS:** Listed in Who's Who in NC by US Pub Rels Serv 1973; awarded medal & trubutes WR Tolbert; pres Rep of Liberia as Knight Grand Commander of Liberation of Humane Order of African Redemption; apptd Police Surgeon 1980; Gold Medal of Achievement (highest hon) Scottish Rite Masonry; Disting Citizens Awd 1980. **BUSINESS ADDRESS:** 1804 Murchison Rd, Fayetteville, NC 28301.

ALLEN, GLORIA MARIE
Physician. **PERSONAL:** Born in Washington, DC; married William Henry Toles; children: William Henry III, Allen Wooley. **EDUCATION:** Howard Univ, BS 1947; Howard Univ Med Sch, MD 1951. **CAREER:** Harlem Hosp, asst attending phys 1954-56; Jamaica Hosp NY, asst attending phys 1963-; Carter Comm Health Ctr, chief of pediatrics 1974-. **ORGANIZATIONS:** Mem Med Soc of the Co of Queens 1964-; sec Empire State Med Assn 1975-; treas/charter mem Susan S McKinney Smith Med Soc 1976-; bd dirs Queens Urban League 1970-; nom comm YMCA of New York City 1974-75; chmn Merrick YM-YWCA Day Care Ctr 1975-77. **HONORS/ACHIEVEMENTS:** Woman's World Awd Bethel Temple 1958; Sr to Youth Comm Queens YWCA 1973; Community Awd Queens Fresh Air Fund 1978; Commnr Commn on the Status of Women New York City apptd Mayor Koch 1979. **BUSINESS ADDRESS:** Chief of Pediatrics, Carter Comm Health Ctr, 97-04 Staphin Blvd, Jamaica, NY 11435.

ALLEN, HARRIETTE LOUISE
Educator. **PERSONAL:** Born Oct 24, 1943, Savannah, GA; divorced; children: Tracy Marcette, Heather Lenae. **EDUCATION:** Fisk Univ, BA 1964; Univ of WI, MST 1972; George Peabody Coll for Tchrs Vanderbilt Univ, PhD English Educ 1980. **CAREER:** S America Columbia, foreign exchange tchr of english 1964-65; Chicago Bd of Educ, spanish resource consult 1965-68; WI State Univ, asst proj dir tutorialprog 1970-72; Fisk Univ, poet-storyteller 1973-; Univ TN, poet-in-residence 1977-79; TN State Univ, asst prof of comm 1979-; State of TN, ambassador of letters 1979-. **ORGANIZATIONS:** Mem Alpha Kappa Alpha; Natl Theatre Assn; Black Theatre Assn SCETC; Natl Assn for Preservation & Perpetuation of Storytelling; Theta Alpha Phi Hon Forensic Frat; GA Soc of Poets; Natl Soc Pub Poets; Originator of Ballad Folk Theatre Art; star Jubas Jubilee Folktale Traveling Ensemble Co; 1st black storyteller at Natl Storytelling Fest Jonesboro TN. **HONORS/ACHIEVEMENTS:** 1st Black to receive Gov Spotlight Awd; 1st Black poet to be read into the Congressional Record; author "Genesis & Jubas Folk Games"; 1st poet to be pub in Attica Rebirth Newspaper of Attica Prison. **BUSINESS ADDRESS:** Ambassador of Letters, State of TN, #35 Legislative Plz, Nashville, TN 37219.

ALLEN, HERBERT J.
Educator. **PERSONAL:** Born Apr 19, 1922, Jersey City, NJ; divorced; children: Deborah. **EDUCATION:** Univof Cincinnati Teachers Coll, BS 1946; Casewestern Reserve Univ, MSSW 1948; Natl Cincinnati Admin/Mgmt Training Prog, Grad. **CAREER:** Cincinnati Gen Hosp, sr caseworker; Montgomery Cty Child Welfare Bd, suprv 1952-64; Barney Childrens Med Ctr, dir social serv 1964-66; Good Samaritan Hosp, dir soc serv 1966-67; Univ Cincinnati Med Ctr, adj assoc prof, dir soc work 1970-. **ORGANIZATIONS:** Mem Acad of Cert Soc Workers; past pres OH Valley Chap of Natl Assoc of Soc Workers 1972-74; past vice pres OH Council of Chapters of Natl Assoc of SocWorkers; past pres Miami Valley Chap Dayton Natl Assoc of Social Workers 1969; mem, trustee Central Comm Health Bd of Hamilton Cty Inc 1976-77; chmnCommun Action Commiss 1974-77; mem Soc Serv Assoc of Gr Cincinnati; mem, past pres Child Health Assoc; clin instr School of Soc Work OH State Univ; pres Mt Auburn Health Ctr 1975-; mem Manpower Serv Adv Council of City of Cincinnati 1975-; mem Cincinnati Gen Hosp Med Audit Comm 1975; mem Coll of Med Expanded Deans Conf 1977; pres OH Valley Chapt; soc dir Hosp Soc Work Depts. **HONORS/ACHIEVEMENTS:** Cert Outstanding Social Worker of the Year Natl Assoc of Social Workers 1973; Cert Cincinnati Gen Hosp Empl Arts & Crafts Awd Gold Medal 1973; Cert Leadership Training Prog for Soc Workrs in Mental Health Natl Assoc of Social Workers 1974; Cert Rsch Neigh Commun Assoc 1975; Cert of Apprec Mt Auburn Comm Council 1975; Cert of Apprec Lincoln Heights Health Ctr Inc 1975; Cert Admin Mgmt Interns Univ of Cincinnati 1975; Cert Cincinnati Gen Hosp Arts& Crafts Harvest & Merit Awd Gold Medal 1975; Cert Natl Inst of Law Enforcement & Criminal Justice (Rape & its Victims) 1977; nominee Social Worker of the Year 1974; nominee Outstanding Citizen Awd 1976. **MILITARY SERVICE:** AUS t/sgt 1942-45. **BUSINESS ADDRESS:** Adj Assoc Prof, Dir, Univ Cincinnati Med Ctr, 234 Goodman St, ML #743, Cincinnati, OH 45267.

ALLEN, JAMES H.
Auditor, real estate. **PERSONAL:** Born Apr 20, 1934, Farmville, VA; married Angelene Elliott; children: James Jr, Anita, Edward. **EDUCATION:** Johnson C Smith Univ, AB 1960; Rutgers State Univ, MBA 1976. **CAREER:** Progressive Life Ins Co, debit mgr 1960-62; Jet-Heet Creative Mfg, perpetual inventory control clerk 1962-64; Wyssmont Engr Co, asst to ofc mgr 1964-68; Bendix Corp, expeditor 1968-69; State of NJ Div of Taxation, field auditor. **ORGANIZATIONS:** Mem Passaic Cty Bd of Realtors, Amer Soc of Notaries, Fed Govt Accountants Assoc, Natl Assoc of Black Accountants, Natl Assoc of Black MBA's, NatlAssoc of MBA; exec pres Delta Mu Lambda Chap Alpha Phi Alpha; pres Clavary Bapt Church, Fed Credit Union; exec bd mem Paterson Br NAACP; volunteer probation sponsor for Passaic Cty Probation Dept; mem Paterson Financial Aid Corp, Amer Legion Post 268. **HONORS/ACHIEVEMENTS:** Faithful Serv Awd NAACP 1968; Outstanding Alumnus Johnson C Smith Univ Alumni Assoc Reg I 1971; Johnson C Smith Univ Gen Alumni Assoc Dedicated Serv 1973; State of NJ Outstanding Performance Awd 1971.

ALLEN, JAMES TRINTON
Elected official. **PERSONAL:** Born Oct 31, 1924, Michigan, MS; married Magnolia Hudson; children: James Jr, Charles Banks, Sam, Margie Ree Holcomb, Melvin, Helen Ruth Thomas, Meleri Ruth, Auther Wayne. **EDUCATION:** Garman School, 1940. **ORGANIZATIONS:** Mem Masonic #68 1979. **HOME ADDRESS:** Rt 1 Box 244, Lamar, MS 38642.

ALLEN, JOHN HENRY
Engineer. **PERSONAL:** Born Jan 16, 1938, Youngstown, OH; married Shirley; children: Kristine, Eric. **EDUCATION:** CA State Univ LA, BS 1964, MSEE 1969; Pepperdine Univ, MBA 1983. **CAREER:** Packard Bell Electronics, system test tech 1959-61; Lockheed CA Cty, rsch engr 1961-64; Gen Dynamics Pomona Div, dynamics engr 1964-65; Teledyne SystemsCo, mem tech staff 1965-66; Systems Integration & Support Ctrs, asst mgr 1966-79; CA State Coll, asst prof 1969-78; Aerojet Electro Systems Azusa CA Co Data Systems Integration Test, mgr. **ORGANIZATIONS:** Sr mem IEEE, EIT CA; second class radio telephone license patents-disclosures, Doppler Oper Test Sets & Dissimilar Metal Anti-Corrosion Ground Stub. **MILITARY SERVICE:** USN electronics tech 1st class 1955-59. **BUSINESS ADDRESS:** Manager, Aerojet Electro Syst Azusa CA, Data Systems Integration Test, Box 296, Azusa, CA 91702.

ALLEN, LUCIUS OLIVER
Business executive. **PERSONAL:** Born Sep 26, 1947, Kansas City, KS; children: Kahlil, Bakir. **EDUCATION:** UCLA, BS Sociology 1969. **CAREER:** Heavyrope, owner v pres 1984-; Technical Mgmnt Serv, v pres brd of dir 1984-; Sports Time Cable Network, color analyst 1984-. **ORGANIZATIONS:** Pres Lucius Allen Enterprises 1972-. **HOME ADDRESS:** 915 Buckingham Rd, Los Angeles, CA 90016. **BUSINESS ADDRESS:** VP Heavyrope Vice Pres TMS Inc, 11050 Santa Monica Blvd, Los Angeles, CA 90025.

ALLEN, MARCUS
Educator. **PERSONAL:** Born Mar 02, 1924, Pittsburgh, PA; married Mary; children: Diane. **EDUCATION:** Univ of Pittsburgh, BA 1949; Columbia Univ, MA 1951; Univ of Pittsburgh, PhD 1964. **CAREER:** Morgan State Univ, teacher 1955-66; Univ of MO, teacher 1966-. **ORGANIZATIONS:** Chmn Dept of Modern Lang; mem Amer Assoc of Teachers of French, Modern Lang Assoc. **MILITARY SERVICE:** AUS 1942-46. **BUSINESS ADDRESS:** Teacher, Univ of Missouri, 8001 Natural Bridge Road, St Louis, MO 63103.

ALLEN, MARCUS
Professional athlete. **PERSONAL:** Born Mar 26, 1960, San Diego, CA. **EDUCATION:** Attended, Southern CA. **CAREER:** Los Angeles Raiders, player 1982-. **HONORS/ACHIEVEMENTS:** Holds NCAA record for 200 yard rushing games with 11; established 12 NCAA records and tied another; played in Hula Bowl and Olympic Gold Bowl; Walter Camp, Maxwell Club and Football News Awds as Coll Player of the Year; Heisman Trophy winner 1981; set an all time single season rushing record with 2,342 yds; led NFLin scoring as rookie in 1982 with 84 pts in 9 games; Top receiver among AFC backs 3 straight years 1982-84; MVP 1983 Super Bowl; set Super Bowl rushing recordwith 191 yds; highest scoring non-kicker in NFL with 108 pts 1984; mem Pro Bowl team 3 times; named NFL's MVP by Professional Football Writers Assoc and the Associated Press; Player of the Year by The Sporting News and Football News; Offensive Player of Year by UPI; led NFL in rushing with Raider record 1,759 yds during fourth pro season. **BUSINESS ADDRESS:** Los Angeles Raiders, 322 Center St, El Segundo, CA 90245.

ALLEN, MAXINE BOGUES
Educational administrator. **PERSONAL:** Born Jul 31, 1942, Portsmouth, VA; daughter of Raymond A Bogues and Essie M Kemp; married George Stanley Allen; children: Vanya G. **EDUCATION:** Norfolk State Univ, BS 1966; Hampton Univ, MA 1972; Virginia Polytech Inst & State Univ, EdD 1976. **CAREER:** Portsmouth City Schools, head of math dept 1966-74; Norfolk State Univ, prof of math 1976-79, dir inst rsch AA/EEO 1980-86, exec asst to pres dir inst rsch 1986-87; associate vice president for academic affairs 1987-; director, institutional research and planning, 1980-. **ORGANIZATIONS:** Mem Alpha Kappa Alpha Sor 1974-; consultant A&T Univ 1978-79; consultant Inst for Services to Educ 1982; bd of trustees Southeastern Univs Rsch Assoc 1984-; pres Suffolk Chap of The Links Inc 1985-; bd dirs WHRO Educ TV 1986; school bd Suffolk City 1986-. **HONORS/ACHIEVEMENTS:** Math Textbook for Health Science NSU Press 1978; Administrative/Mgmt Grant Title III 1980-90; Presidential Citation, Assn for Equal Opportunity, 1988. **BUSINESS ADDRESS:** Associate Vice President, Academic Affairs, Director, Institutional Research and Planning, Norfolk State University, 410 Wilson Hall, 2401 Corprew Ave, Norfolk, VA 23504.

ALLEN, MILTON B.
Public official, attorney. **PERSONAL:** Born Dec 10, 1917, Baltimore, MD; married Martha; children: David, Peter, Milton Jr. **EDUCATION:** Coppin State Teachers Coll, BA 1938, LLB 1948, JD 1971; Univ of MD, Hon LLD. **CAREER:** Baltimore, defense attny 23 yrs; City of Baltimore MD, states attny 1971-75; Supreme Bench Baltimore, assoc judge 1976. **ORGANIZATIONS:** Mem Natl Bar Assoc, Amer Bar Assoc, Amer Civil Liberties Union, Natl Bar Found, Gov Comm on Law Enforcement. **HONORS/ACHIEVEMENTS:** 1st black elected states attny for any major city in US.

ALLEN, MINNIE LOUISE
Health insurance. **PERSONAL:** Born Jun 28, 1956, Lilesville, NC. **EDUCATION:** Durham Business Coll, AAS 1976; Attended, NC Central Univ, Univ of SC. **CAREER:** Duke Power Co, programmer 1977-78; Blue Cross Blue Shield of SC, programmer systems analyst 1978-86; Blue Cross Blue Shield of TN, systems analyst 1986-. **ORGANIZATIONS:** Program chairperson Amer Business Women Las Mujeres Chap 1984; health fair volunteer NAACP. **HONORS/ACHIEVEMENTS:** Woman of the Year Amer Business Women Assoc 1984. **BUSINESS ADDRESS:** Systems Analyst, Blue Cross Blue Shield of TN, 730 Chestnut St, Chattanooga, TN 37403.

ALLEN, OTTIS EUGENE, JR.
Educational administrator. **PERSONAL:** Born Feb 02, 1953, Fletcher, NC; son of Eugene Allen and Georgia Bradley Allen; married Vanessa R Northcutt; children: Dawn, Ottis III, Eboni. **EDUCATION:** Appalachian State Univ, BA 1975, MA 1976; Univ of SC, additional studies in Ed TV; Spartanburg Methodist Coll, additional studies in Computer Science. **CAREER:** Council on Ministries of the United Methodist Church of SC, field coord 1981; Radio Shack Corp, salesman 1982-; Spartanburg Methodist Coll, dir of audio-visual services. **ORGANIZATIONS:** Mem SC Library Assn 1977-; mem Piedmont Library Assn 1980-; mem Mt Moriah Baptist Church 1980-; chmn of sound comm Mt Moriah Baptist Church 1983-; mem bd of trustees Mt Moriah Baptist Church 1983-; mem United Way Allocation Comm of Spartanburg 1986-; mem, Epsilon Nu Chapter of Omega Psi Phi Fraternity, 1987-. **HOME ADDRESS:** 208 Sheffield Dr, Spartanburg, SC 29301. **BUSINESS ADDRESS:** Dir Audio Visual Services, Spartanburg Methodist College, 1200 Textile Road, Spartanburg, SC 29301.

ALLEN, PERCY, II
Administrator. **PERSONAL:** Born Apr 07, 1941, New Orleans, LA; married Zennia Marie McKnight; children: Merrily Marie, Percy III. **EDUCATION:** Delgado Trade & Tech Inst, 1965; Oakland Univ Rochester MI, BA Econ 1973; Cornel Univ Grad Sch of Bus & Pub Adminstrn, MPA 1975. **CAREER:** Sinai Hosp, asst adminstr; Pkvw Meml Hosp Ft Wayne IN, asst hosp adminstr 1975-; Cornell Univ Ithaca NY, prgm consult 1973-75; Oakland Univ Rochester MI, res hall dir 1972-73; Chrysler Corp Detroit, qlty cntrl supr 1968-70; Gr New Mt Moiah Bapt Ch Detroit, yth dir/fdr & dir smmr camp 1968-73. **ORGANIZATIONS:** Exec com NE IN EmrgcyMed Serv Commn 1977-; mem Emrgcy Med Serv Commn IN Hosp Assn 1978-; mem Counc on Hlth Care Dlvry Sys IN Hosp Assn 1979-; 1st vice pres Ft Wayne Urban Leag 1976-; bd mem Am Cancer Soc 1977-; 1st vice pres Allen Co Oppor Indstrlztn Ctr 1978-; bd mem United Way of Allen Co 1979-. **HONORS/ACHIEVEMENTS:** Outst ldrshp serv Oakland URochester MI 1971-73; in apprctn for serv as fdr & dir of smmr cmpng prgm Mt Moriah Bapt Ch Detroit 1973; Who's Who Among Stdnts in AmUniv & Coll OaklandUniv Rochester MI 1973-74; recog for 1st in empl postn Union Bapt Ch Ft Wayne IN 1976; cert of apprctn Sickle CellFound 1979. **BUSINESS ADDRESS:** Asst Vice President, New York City Hlth & Hosp Corp, 125 Worth St, New York, NY 10013.

ALLEN, PHILIP C.
Internal audit manager. **PERSONAL:** Born Nov 20, 1936, Pittsburgh, PA; son of Elmer C Allen and Vivian A Taylor; children: Lauretta L, Wanda I, Karl C, Phylis D, Michelle, L, Sylvia D, Arthur K, Marlyn L. **EDUCATION:** Univ of Pittsburgh, BBA 1958; retail mgmt school 1960; systems engineering school (IBM) 1962; banking mgmt school Brown Univ 1966; Dale Carnegie training 1967; advanced audit school, Inst of Internal Auditors 1972; Univ of Pittsburgh, MEd 1977. **CAREER:** May Co-Kaufmanns Dept Store, asst buyer 1959-60; IBM Corp, systems engr 1960-65; Dollar Savings Bank, internal auditor 1965-67; PPG Ind, sr EDP auditor 1967-73; Comm Coll of Allegheny Co, admin internal auditor 1973-. **ORGANIZATIONS:** Basileus Omega Psi Phi 1962; treas Bidwell Cultural & Training Ctr 1969; treas Pro-Sports Orgn 1975-; chmn US Bond Dr CCAC 1976; vice pres CCAC Credit Union 1977-; bd mem United Way of Amer 1977-; vice chmn Allegheny YMCA 1978-80; mem NAACP, Amer Mgmt Assn, Inst of Internal Auditors, EDP Auditors Found; pres CCAC Credit Union 1984-; bd mem United Negro Coll Fund. **HONORS/ACHIEVEMENTS:** Distinguished Serv Awd United Way 1977-79; Distinguished Serv Awd YMCA 1978-79; Cert Data Processing Auditor CDPA, EDP Auditors Found 1979; certified information systems auditor CISA 1982. **BUSINESS ADDRESS:** Administrator Internal Auditor, Comm Coll of Allegheny County, 800 Allegheny Ave, Pittsburgh, PA 15233.

ALLEN, RICHARD ANTHONY
Professional baseball player. **PERSONAL:** Born May 08, 1942, Chewton, PA; married Barbara. **CAREER:** Philadelphia Phill, ret base plyr 1975-76; Chicago White Sox, 1972-75; Philadelphia Phillies, farm syst 1960, jnd maj league tm 1963-69; St Louis Card, infldr 1970; L A Dodgers 1971. **HONORS/ACHIEVEMENTS:** Nam rook of yr Nat League 1963; most val plyr Am League Base Writ Assn 1972; base dig plyr of yr 1972; Am League plyr of yr Sprtng News 1972;all-Star tm mem 1972-74.

ALLEN, ROBERT L. (BENJAMIN PETERSON)
Editor. **PERSONAL:** Born May 29, 1942, Atlanta, GA; son of Robert Lee Allen and Sadie Sims Allen; married Pamela Parker, Aug 28, 1965; children: Casey Douglass. **EDUCATION:** Attended Univ of Vienna, 1961-62; Morehouse College, BS, 1963; attended Columbia Univ, 1963-64; New School for Social Research, New York NY, MA, 1967; Univ of California, San Francisco, PhD, 1983. **CAREER:** Guardian Newsweekly NYC, staff reporter 1967-69; San Jose State Coll, asst prof new coll & black studies dept 1969-72; The Black Scholar Mag, editor; Mills College, Oakland CA, began as lecturer, became asst prof of ethnic studies, 1973-. **ORGANIZATIONS:** Pres, Black World Foundation; mem, American Sociological Assn; mem, American Historical and Cultural Society; mem, Association of Black Sociologists; mem, Pacific Sociological Assn; mem, Council for Black Studies; Bay Area Black Journalists. **HONORS/ACHIEVEMENTS:** Author "Black Awakening in Capitalist Amer" Doubleday, 1969, "Reluctant Reformers, The Impact of Racism on Amer Social Reform Movements" Howard Univ Press, 1974; Guggenheim fellowship, 1978; author of The Port Chicago Disaster and Its Aftermath, University of California, San Francisco, 1983; contributor to periodicals. **BUSINESS ADDRESS:** Ethnic Studies Department, Mills College, Oakland, CA 94613. *

ALLEN, SAMUEL WASHINGTON
Poet, retired educator. **PERSONAL:** Born Dec 09, 1917, Columbus, OH; son of Alexander Joseph Allen and Jewett Washington Allen; divorced; children: Marie-Christine. **EDUCATION:** Fisk Univ, AB 1938; Harvard Law Sch, JD 1941; New Sch for Soc Rsch, grad study 1946-47; Sorbonne, 1949-50. **CAREER:** NYC, dep asst dist atty 1946-47; USAF Europe, 1951-55; NYC, claims atty 1956-57; TX So Univ, assoc prof 1958-60; Washington, DC, atty 1961-68; Tuskegee Inst, prof 1968-70; Wesleyan Univ, vis prof 1970-71; Boston Univ, prof 1971-81; professor emeritus, 1981-. **ORGANIZATIONS:** Mem/vp/bd dirs So Educ Found Atlanta 1969-76; mem bd dir Afrikan Heritage Inst Roxbury, MA 1974-78; bd SVB; bd New England Museum of African-American History; board mem, Boston Partners in Educ. **HONORS/ACHIEVEMENTS:** Ellenbeinzahne (poems) 1956; translated Orphee Noir (Jean Paul Satre), 1951;public reading and recording of poetry Libr of Congr Wash, DC 1972; NEA Award Poetry 1979; author pen name Paul Vesey Ivory Tusks & Other Poems 1968; editor Poems from Africa 1973; Paul Vesey's Ledger (poems) 1975; Every Round (poems), 1987. **MILITARY SERVICE:** AUS 1st Lt 1942-46. **HOME ADDRESS:** 145 Cliff Ave, Winthrop, MA 02152.

ALLEN, SANFORD
Violinist. **PERSONAL:** Born Feb 26, 1939, New York City, NY; married Madhur Jaffrey. **EDUCATION:** Julliard School of Music, attended; Mannes Coll of Music, attended. **CAREER:** Livingston Coll of Rutgers Univ, former faculty mem; NY Philharmonic, former violinist; violinist recitals, concerts, solo engagements. **ORGANIZATIONS:** Past adv panel NY Stte Arts Council; recorded Cordero Violin Concerto with Detroit Symphony on Black Composers Series; vchmn, adv comm HS Performing Arts Fed Music Clubs Awd. **HONORS/ACHIEVEMENTS:** Won High Fidelity Mag Koussevitzky Intl Recording Awd 1974.

ALLEN, SHIRLEY JEANNE
Educator. **PERSONAL:** Born Dec 19, 1941, Tyler, TX; daughter of Ralph C Allen and Theressa Carter McDonald; divorced. **EDUCATION:** Talladega Coll, Music 1959-60; Jarvis Christian Coll Hawkins TX, Music 1960-63; Gallaudet Coll Wash DC, BA Eng Lit 1963-66; Howard Univ Wash DC, MA Couns 1969-72; Univ of Rochester, Doctorate in progress; received her BA & MA after becoming deaf in 1962. **CAREER:** Rochester Inst of Tech, asst prof Gen educ 1973-; Gallaudet Coll Wash DC, couns instr 1967-73; US Peace Corp, clssfctn clk 1964-65; Univ S IRS, ed clk; US Post Ofc, dist clk 1966-67. **ORGANIZATIONS:** Mem Nat Assn of Deaf; mem Conf of Am Instr of Deaf; mem Am Assn of Univ Prof; mem Nat Assn of Women Deans-Admin & Couns; mem Natl Black Deaf Advocates. **BUSINESS ADDRESS:** Associate Professor, Rochester Inst of Technology, One Lomb Memorial Drive, PO Box 9887, Rochester, NY 14623.

ALLEN, STANLEY M.
Airline pilot. **PERSONAL:** Born Dec 06, 1941, Washington, DC; married Josita E Hair; children: Khyron Shane, Kesha Lynette. **EDUCATION:** Howard Univ, BA 1965. **CAREER:** Eastern Airlines Inc, airline pilot. **ORGANIZATIONS:** Mem Airline Pilots Assoc; co-capt Howard Univ Football 1964; sr class pres Fairmont Hts HS 1960. **HONORS/ACHIEVEMENTS:** MD State High Hurdles Champion 1960. **MILITARY SERVICE:** USAF capt 1965-70. **BUSINESS ADDRESS:** Airline Pilot, Eastern Airlines Inc, Washington Natl Airport, Washington, DC.

ALLEN, TERRELL ALLISON, III
Association executive. **PERSONAL:** Born Feb 10, 1959, Washington, DC. **EDUCATION:** Howard Univ, BS Elec Engrg 1982; Univ of Pennsylvania, MBA Finance 1987. **CAREER:** Eastman Kodak Co, coop educ student 1978-81; Howard Univ, electronics lab asst 1980-82; Commonwealth Edison Co, general engr 1982-85; Coopers & Lybrand,consultant; Wharton Black MBA Assoc, pres. **ORGANIZATIONS:** Vice pres Phi Beta Sigma Frat Inc Alpha Chap 1981-82; comm chmn Chicago Jr Assoc of Commerce and Industry 1982-85; science club dir Chicago Adopt-A-School Program 1982-85. **HONORS/ACHIEVEMENTS:** Outstanding Young Men of Amer 1984; Leadership Awd/Fellowship Johnson & Johnson Family of Companies 1985; Fellowship Consortium for Grad Study in Mgmt 1985. **BUSINESS ADDRESS:** President, Wharton Black MBA Association, 115 Vance Hall, 3733 Spruce St, Philadelphia, PA 19104.

ALLEN, THOMAS G.
Pastor. **PERSONAL:** Born Jul 28, 1945, Pine Bluff, AR; married Aline. **EDUCATION:** Shorter Coll, AA 1971; Philander Smith Coll, BA 1973; Jackson Theological Seminary, MDiv 1982. **CAREER:** SNCC, former field sec 1962-65; Pinesgrove AME Ch Arkadelphia, pastor 1969-74; St Paul AME Ch Hot Springs, pastor 1974-75; St Paul AME Ch Newport AR, former pastor; Allen Temple AME Church, former pastor; St James AME Ch, pastor. **ORGANIZATIONS:** Pres Pine Bluff Ministerial Assn 1984; mem Pine Bluff Sch Bi-Racial Comm 1984; 33rd Degree Mason United Supreme Council PHA 1981; worshipful master Electric Light Masonic Lodge 45 PHGL 1983; mem Genl Conf Comm AME Ch 1984; social action

consul Central AR Conf AME Ch 1982; mem Urban League, NAACP, Omega Psi Phi. **HONORS/ACHIEVEMENTS:** Hon Title One of Fulton County's Outstanding Citizens 1978; Fellow Amer Biog Inst; Fellow Intl Biog Assn 1978; Most Important Accomplishment Book of Honour 1978; Intl Who's Who of Intellectuals 1978; Cert of Merit United Supreme Council Masons Awd; Personalities of the South 1976-77; Hon Degree DD ShorterColl 1986-. **HOME ADDRESS:** 233 Center St, Camden, AR 71701.

ALLEN, VAN SIZAR
Educator. **PERSONAL:** Born Apr 02, 1926, Edwards, MS; divorced; children: Van S, Nathaniel B. **EDUCATION:** Tougaloo Coll, BA 1950; Univ of MI, MS 1952; Yale Univ, Certificate 1955; Univ of NC, MPH 1962, PhD 1969. **CAREER:** Bennett Coll, assoc prof 1952-68; Guilford Co Anti-Poverty Prog, deputy dir 1966-68; Southern Regional Educ Bd, assoc dir of inst of higher educ opp 1969-71; TACTICS, exec dir 1971-80; Tougaloo Coll, vice pres for acad affrs 1980-85; Paul Quinn Coll, vice pres for acad affairs 1985-87; assistant to the president and dir of State & Federal Relations 1987-; dir of the Central Texas Cancer Network Program 1988-. **ORGANIZATIONS:** Mem Amer Assoc of Univ Profs, Beta Kappa Chi Scientific Soc, Natl Inst of Science, Amer Assoc for the Advancement of Sci; mem John Hay Whitney Oppor Fellow Org, Phi Delta Kappa Natl Educ Frat; mem NC Comm Develop Assoc, Omega Psi Phi Frat, Sigma Pi Phi Frat; mem NAACP, SOPHE; pres Tougaloo Coll Natl Alumni Assoc 1978-80; chmn Tougaloo Coll Natl Alumni Fundraising Campaign 1980-84. **HONORS/ACHIEVEMENTS:** John Hay Whitney Oppor Fellowship Univ of MI 1950; Natl Science Foundation Scholarship Univ of NC 1960; Centennial Awd for Disting Serv to Tougaloo Coll1970; Alumnus of the Year Tougaloo Coll 1977; Presidential Citation/NAFFFOHE/For exemplary experience that honor Alma Mater Washington DC 1979; Meritorious Serv TACTICS Prog 1980; Outstanding Serv Awd Greensboro NC Public Housing Auth 1981; Tougaloo Comm Alumni Club Awd 1984; Outstanding Commitment to Strengthening Black Colls & Univs NAFEO 1987; numerous publications and book reviews. **MILITARY SERVICE:** USN 3rd class petty officer 1944-46; Asiatic Theater Ribbon, Good Conduct Ribbon. **HOME ADDRESS:** 225 Garrison St, Waco, TX 76704.

ALLEN, W. GEORGE
Attorney. **PERSONAL:** Born Mar 03, 1936, Sanford, FL; married Enid Meadows; children: Timothy, Frederick, Amy. **EDUCATION:** FL A&M Univ, BA (Hon) Pol Sci 1954; Univ FL Law School, JD 1962. **CAREER:** FL Human Relations Comm, commiss; Orr & Kaplan Miami, attny 1963; Private practice, attny 1963-. **ORGANIZATIONS:** Commiss FL Ethics Commiss; mem FL FL Adv Commiss, US Civil Rights Comm, Govs prop Rights Study Commun; mem, pres elect 1974-75 Natl Bar Assoc; mem FL Bar Assoc, Broward Cty Bar Assoc, Amer Trial Lawyers Assoc, FL Acad of Trail Lawyers, Broward Crim Defense Assoc, Natl Assoc of Crim Defense Lawyers, NAACP, Alpha Phi Alpha, Elks, YMCA, FL A&M Univ Alumni Assoc, State of FL. **HONORS/ACHIEVEMENTS:** 1st black to finish the Univ of FL; 1st black to work in integrated law firm. **MILITARY SERVICE:** AUS 1st lt spec agent CIC 1958-60. **BUSINESS ADDRESS:** Attorney, 116 SE 6 Ct, Fort Lauderdale, FL 33301.

ALLEN, WALTER R.
Educator. **PERSONAL:** Born Aug 18, 1930, Allendale, SC; married Mary Clay; children: Walter Jr, Jeffrey, Brian. **EDUCATION:** Claflin Coll Orangeburg SC, AB 1951; Oberlin Coll Oberlin OH, BM 1957; W Reserve Univ Cleveland, MA, MM 1960; Univ of GA, EdD 1974. **CAREER:** Shoals HS, asst principal; Univ of GA, Athens GA, asst prof. **ORGANIZATIONS:** Mem Kappa Alpha Psi, Phi Delta Kappa, Kappa Kappa Psi, 32nd Degree Mason, Amer Psych Assoc, Natl Assoc of Musicologists; educator Haile Selassie in Ethiopia; social psychol, musician & admin 100 Percenters Org; mem Hill First Bapt Church, NAACP, Free Lance Musician, Athens Alumni Chap of Kappa Alpha Psi. **HONORS/ACHIEVEMENTS:** Kappa Alpha Psi Achievement Awd; 100 Percenters Awd; Educators Awd; Phi Delta Kappa Awd; Natl Assoc of Musicologists; Kappa Kappa Psi Awd. **MILITARY SERVICE:** AUS 1951-53. **BUSINESS ADDRESS:** Assistant Professor, Univ of Georgia, Cedar Shoals HS, Athens, GA 30605.

ALLEN, WENDELL
Associate executive. **PERSONAL:** Born Aug 21, 1947, Chattanooga, TN; married Jacqueline; children: Kristen, Adrienne, Ian. **EDUCATION:** Fisk Univ, BA, 1970; Case Western Reserve Univ School of Law, 1970-72. **CAREER:** Fisher Body Div, Gen Motors Corp, conf leader, 1972-73; Amer Steel Corp, corp mgr, 1973-75; Paine Webber Jackson & Curtis, stockbroker, 1975-76; 1st Ward, city councilman; Gen Motors Corp, Hydra-Matic Div, coord. **ORGANIZATIONS:** Bd dir Oppty Indust Ctr 1977; sec, bd dir Oppty Indust Ctrs Cleveland 1972-75; Phi Alpha Delta Intl Law Frat Prince Hall F&AM Masons, Alpha Phi Alpha, Kiwanis Intl, Repub Party; bd of dir Ann Arbor Chamber of Commerce 1981-82. **BUSINESS ADDRESS:** Exec Asst to the President, McAuley Health Center, PO Box 992, Ann Arbor, MI 48106.

ALLEN, WILLIAM BARCLAY
Educator. **PERSONAL:** Born Mar 18, 1944, Fernandina Beach, FL; son of Rev James P Allen and Rosa Lee Johnson Allen (deceased); married Susan Ayers Macall; children: Danielle Susan, Bertrand Marc. **EDUCATION:** Pepperdine Coll, BA 1967; Claremont Grad School, MA 1968, PhD 1972. **CAREER:** Univ de Rouen, lecteur 1970-71; The Amer Univ, asst prof 1971-72; Harvey Mudd Coll, asst prof 1972-76, assoc prof 1976-83; St John's Coll Grad Inst, visiting tutor 1977-; Harvey Mudd Coll, prof of govt. **ORGANIZATIONS:** Mem Claremont Rotary 1980-86; mem pres Claremont Unified School Dist Bd 1981-84; bd mem CA Assembly Fellowship Prog 1982-; prog dir Liberty Fund Inc1982-89; chmn CA Scholars for Reagan 1984; mem CA State Adv Commiss of US Civil Rights Commiss 1985-; bd mem LeRoy Boys Home; mem Natl Council for the Humanities, 1984-87; mem Am Pol Sci Assoc, Academie Montesquieu; mem, Chair US Commission on Civil Rights, 1987-. **HONORS/ACHIEVEMENTS:** Fulbright Fellowship 1970-71; Kellogg Natl Fellow WK Kellogg Found 1984-87; Prix Montesquieu Academic France 1986; Pi Sigma Alpha, Sigma Alpha; LID, Pepperdine University, 1988. **MILITARY SERVICE:** USATC 1968, Colonel's Orderly. **BUSINESS ADDRESS:** Professor of Government, Harvey Mudd College, Kingston Hall, Claremont, CA 91711.

ALLEN, WILLIAM DUNCAN
Musician. **PERSONAL:** Born Dec 15, 1906, Portland, OR; son of William Duncan Allen Sr and Lillian Medley Allen. **EDUCATION:** Oberlin Coll, Bachelor of Music 1928; Juilliard School of Music, certificate 1929; Oberlin Coll, master of music 1936; David Mannes School of Music, certificate 1939. **CAREER:** Howard Univ School of Music, instructor Piano 1929-35; Fisk Univ, assistant prof 1936-43; Talladedga Coll, visiting prof of Piano 1980-82. **ORGANIZATIONS:** Pres Golden Gate Branch/Music Tchrs Assn CA 1970-74, Golden Gate Branch/Natl Assn Negro Musicians 1970-74; counselor San Fran Boy's Chorus 1957-62; music dir Jr Bach Fesitval, Berkeley 1956-76; mnstr of music S Berkeley Comm Church 1954-79; ACT-SO NAACP Program; Accompanist "Art of the Spiritual" Concert Carnegie Hall 1987, 1988 & 1989; board mem, Stern Gove Festival Assn, San Francisco; board mem, DeBose Natl Piano Competitions, Southern University, Baton Rouge, Louisiana. **HONORS/ACHIEVEMENTS:** Doctorate of Music Black Theological School for Urban Studies, Berkeley 1978; 11th Annual Afro-Amer Music Workshop Homage Atlanta Univ Center 1982. **HOME ADDRESS:** 3400 Atlas Rd, Hilltop Bayview #4009, Richmond, CA 94806.

ALLEN, WILLIAM HENRY
Dentist, educator. **PERSONAL:** Born Jan 27, 1917, New Orleans, LA; son of William H Allen and Victoria Allen; married Martha Mae Mosley. **EDUCATION:** Tougaloo Coll, AB 1935; Meharry Medical Coll, DDS 1943; Univ of Michigan, Post-graduate 1944. **CAREER:** Meharry Medical Coll, Nashville TN, instructor 1943-44; School of Dentistry, asst prof dental materials, prosthetics & clinical dentistry 1945-47, acting dean 1946-47, dir,dean, dental educ 1949-50, dean 1950-71, prof prosthetics, dir div dental technology 1947-. **ORGANIZATIONS:** Mem Council Natl Bd Dental Examiners; pres Capitol City Dental Soc 1958-59; mem Pan-TN, Amer, TN, Natl Dental Assoc, Amer Assoc Dental Schools; advisory comm Negro Scholarship Program, Amer Fund for Dental Educ; dental training comm Natl Inst Dental Research 1971-; regional med advisory comm, fellow AAAS; hon mem AL State Dental Soc; mem Amer Assoc Cleft Palate Rehabilitation, Amer Assoc Dental Schools, Nashville Dental Soc, Amer Assoc Endodontists, Intl Assoc Dental Research, Kappa Sigma Pi, Kappa Alpha Psi, Omicron Kappa Upsilon, Chi Boul Frat. **HONORS/ACHIEVEMENTS:** Author of articles to professional journals.

ALLEN, WILLIAM OSCAR
Business executive. **PERSONAL:** Born Nov 29, 1923, Tuscaloosa, AL; married Ruth Jordan; children: Gwendolyn, Renee, William III. **EDUCATION:** Tuskegee Inst, BS 1947; Columbia Univ, Cert 1958; NY Univ School of Publ Admin & Health Svc, MPA 1972. **CAREER:** Knickerbocker Hosp, admin asst 1963-68, asst exec dir 1968-70; AC Logan Meml Hosp, exec dir 1970-. **ORGANIZATIONS:** Mem Amer Coll of Hosp Admins, Amer Publ Health Assoc, House of Del, Hosp Assoc of NY State, 100 Black Men. **HONORS/ACHIEVEMENTS:** Comm Serv Awd for Health 1972; Outstanding Achievement Awd Assoc PTA Tuscaloosa AL 1974; Outstanding Achievement Awd Tuscaloosa Womens Club 1974. **BUSINESS ADDRESS:** Executive Dir, AC Logan Memorial Hospital, 70 Convent Ave, New York, NY 10027.

ALLEN, WILLIE B.
Clergyman. **PERSONAL:** Born Jul 12, 1921, Richmond, VA; married Ella Sizer; children: 7 sons, 1 daughter. **EDUCATION:** VA Union Univ, attended; Monrovia Coll & Indus Inst West Africa, Hon Doctor of Humane Letters 1984. **CAREER:** Bethlehem Baptist Church Washington, pastor; Upper Room Baptist Ch Washington, pastor/founder/organizer 1957-. **ORGANIZATIONS:** Mem Progressive Natl Baptist Convention Inc; former pres Baptist Ministers' Conf of Washington & Vicinity; pres Ministers' Youth Advocacy Comm of Metro Police Dept; founder/first pres North East Center for the Amer Red Cross; former pres Ministerial Alliance of Far North East Washington; former mem Mayor's Advisory Comm on Alcoholism; chaplain Greater Southeast Hospital; chief consultant DC Substance Abuse Partnership Program; mem District of Columbia Armory Bd Stadium Advisory Comm 1989-. **HONORS/ACHIEVEMENTS:** Hon Doctor of Divinity VA Seminary and Coll Lynchburg VA 1985. **BUSINESS ADDRESS:** Pastor, Upper Room Baptist Church, 3760 Minnesota Ave NE, Washington, DC 20019.

ALLEN, WINSTON EARLE
Business executive. **PERSONAL:** Born May 28, 1933, New York, NY; children: Vaughn, Julie. **EDUCATION:** NY Univ Washington Square Coll of Arts & Sci, BA 1955; City Coll of NY, MA 1958; Fordham Univ, PhD 1971. **CAREER:** New York City Bd of Educ, teacher of econ 1956-68; Fordham Univ, asst prof 1970-72; George Washington Univ, adj prof mgmt sci dept 1974-75; Creative Investor Serv Inc, pres 1965-; Xerox Corp Educ Planning & Devel, mgr 1972-. **ORGANIZATIONS:** Rschr Proj Threshold 1968; bd mem US Comm for UNICEF 1972-; bd mem Childs Guidance Clinic of Gr Stamford 1978-; mem Phi Delta Kappa Professional Frat. **HONORS/ACHIEVEMENTS:** Fulbright Grant Inst d'Etudes Politques Univ of Paris France 1962; 2000 Men of Achievement; listed in Intl Who's Who in Community Svc. **BUSINESS ADDRESS:** Manager, Xerox Corp, 800 Long Ridge Road, Stamford, CT 06904.

ALLEN-NOBLE, ROSIE ELIZABETH
Educational administrator. **PERSONAL:** Born Jun 22, 1938, Americus, GA; daughter of Ulysses Grant Allen and Velma Douglas; divorced; children: Antoinette Celine. **EDUCATION:** Albany State Coll, BS 1960; Atlanta Univ, MS 1967; Rutgers Univ, MS 1974. **CAREER:** Rutgers Univ, instructor 1970-76; Seton Hall Univ, visiting asst prof 1972-78; Univ of Medicine & Dentistry of NJ, instructor 1972-; Fairleigh Dickinson Univ, asst prof 1974-80; Upsala Coll, dir science enrichment program 1976-; Montclair State Coll, dir health careers program 1979-. **ORGANIZATIONS:** Mem Alpha Kappa Alpha Sorority 1959, Amer Assn of Univ Women 1969-; consultant Univ of Medicine & Dentistry of NJ 1972-; Soroptomist Intl 1974-; bd of dir Gladys Dickerson Health Center 1974; mem NJ Chapter of Albany State Coll Alumni Assn 1974, Natl Assn of Medical Minority Educ 1980; consultant/evaluator Univ of CT 1981-83; consultant Hobart William Smith Coll 1983, Long Island Univ 1984, Omicrom Xi Omega 1984; Wichita State Univ 1984; evaluation comm on Higher Educ Middle State Assoc Evaluation Team 1984; mem Natl Assoc Pre-Professional Advisors 1984, Natl Assn of Medical Minority Educ Inc natl treasurer 1984; consultant Univ of Medicine & Dentistry of NJ-school of Health Related Professions 1986-. **HONORS/ACHIEVEMENTS:** Honor student at all academic levels 1956-; Merit Award for Outstanding Serv, Montclair State Coll 1982; Outstanding Leadership & Serv, Upsala Coll 1982; Natl Science Found Grants; Numerous Fed, State & Private Found Fellowship Grants over the past 20 years; Outstanding Serv Award, Montclair State Coll 1984-85; Merit Award for Outstanding Serv, Montclair State College 1987. **HOME ADDRESS:** 364 Orange Rd 5C, Montclair, NJ 07042. **BUSINESS ADDRESS:** Dir Health Careers Prog, Montclair State College, School of Math & Nat Sciences, Upper Montclair, NJ 07043.

ALLEN-RASHEED, JAMAL RANDY
Judiciary/corrections. **PERSONAL:** Born Dec 15, 1953, Memphis, TN; married Jacquline Carlotte Gipson; children: Randy D. **EDUCATION:** Southern IL Univ Carbondale, BS 1980; Prairie View A&M Univ, MA 1986. **CAREER:** KEWC-AM/FM Radio, disc jockey/reporter 1975-76; WPHD-NBC TV, news asst 1979-80; Black Observer Newspaper, managing editor 1979-80; WLS-ABC Network, productionengr 1980; Lackland Tailspinner Airforce Pub, reporter 1981; Forward Times Newspaper, asst circulation mgr 1982-83; Sam Houston State Univ/Housing, publicrelations dir 1983-84; The Martin Luther King Jr Ctr for Nonviolent Social Change Inc, comm develop asst 1984; TX Dept of Corrections, correctional officer 1984-86. **ORGANIZATIONS:** Mem Alpha Epsilon Rho Hon Radio/TV 1978-80; natl bd of dirs 1978-79, natl dir coll bro 1979-80 Alpha Phi Alpha Frat Inc; mem Sigma Delta Chi Prof Journalist 1979-80; publ relations dir Black Affairs Council SI U-C 1979-80; founder/dir The Martin Luther King Jr Inst for Afro-Amer Studies/Soc Change 1985-86; bd of dirs Hillvale Educ Assoc for Substance Abuse 1986-; mem Blacks in Soc, Blacks in Journalism, Blacks in Criminal Justice, 32 Degree Ancient & Accepted Scottish Rite Masonary Prince Hall Affiliation. **HONORS/ACHIEVEMENTS:** Outstanding Serv to Midwest Region Alpha Phi Alpha 1979; Outstanding Serv on Bd of Dirs Alpha Phi Alpha 1979; Outstanding Serv Black Affairs Council SIU-C1980; Certificate for Training in Nonviolent Social Change The Martin Luther King Jr Ctr for Nonviolent Social Change Inc 1984; Intl Disting Young Leaders1987. **MILITARY SERVICE:** USAF airman 1st class 2 yrs; Basic Training Leadership Awd. **HOME ADDRESS:** 36 West 103rd Place, Chicago, IL 60628.

ALLEYNE, EDWARD D.
Roman Catholic priest. **PERSONAL:** Born Jun 14, 1928, Brooklyn, NY. **EDUCATION:** Catholic Univ of Amer, BA 1956. **CAREER:** Mother of the Savior Seminary, instructor 1960-67; various parishes in Diocese of Camden, assoc pastor 1968-84; St Monica's Church, pastor 1984-. **ORGANIZATIONS:** Dir Parkside Catholic Ctr 1971-75; mem Diocesan Bd of Educ 1969-; mem Diocesan Ecumenical Commn 1971-; mem Diocesan Campaign for Human Devel Com 1971-; mem Diocesan Social Justice Commn 1972-; Camden Region Moderator Diocesan PTA 1971-; Financial coord of Consolidated Catholic Sch in City of Camden 1972-75. **BUSINESS ADDRESS:** Pastor, St Monica's RC Church, 108 N Pennsylvania Ave, Atlantic City, NJ 08401.

ALLEYNE, WINSTON A.
Business executive. **PERSONAL:** Born Jun 07, 1944; married Arlene F Hall; children: Joanna Victoria. **EDUCATION:** Paralegal Inst NY, Certificate 1972-73; Sacred Heart Univ, BS 1984. **CAREER:** JA Wharton Esq Trinidad WI, legal sec 1966-68; Parker Duryee Malone & Carter, paralegal 1972-75; General Host Corp, asst corporate sec 1975-84; Alleyne Assocs Inc d/b/a Everything Yogurt, president. **ORGANIZATIONS:** Mem Amer Soc of Corporate Secretaries 1980-; dir Comm Children & Family Serv 1985-. **BUSINESS ADDRESS:** 330 Bassett St, New Haven, CT 06511-1021.

ALLIGOOD, DOUGLASS LACY
Business executive. **PERSONAL:** Born Feb 15, 1934, St Louis, MO; son of Forest D Alligood and Countess M Murphy Alligood; married Linda A Monaco; children: Donna, Craig, Debra, Douglass Jr. **EDUCATION:** Bradley Univ Peoria, IL, BFA 1956. **CAREER:** Seymour, Leatherwood & Cleveland, Inc, Detroit, staff artist/copy Writer 1956; Radio Station WCHB, Detroit, MI, merch dir 1959-62; Batten, Barton Durstine & Osborn, Inc Detroit, acct exec 1962-64; Batten, Barton, Durstine & Osborn, Inc, NYC, sr acct exec 1964-71; dir, corp adv RCA Corp, New York 1971-83; pres UniWorld Group, Inc New York, NY 1983-84; vice pres, special markets, BBDO Inc 1984-. **ORGANIZATIONS:** Dir Adv Council 1976, Intrnl Film & TV Festival of NY 1983; mem, Amer Assn of Advertising Agencies EOO Committee 1986-; speaker, Advertising Educational Foundation 1985-. **HONORS/ACHIEVEMENTS:** Hon degree humane letters King Memorial Coll 1976-; CEBA Advertising Campaign Awards 1980-82; "Five To Watch Award" Amer Women In Radio & TV, Detroit 1964; A P Phillips Lecturer, Univ of Florida 1989; An Analysis of Hispanic Audience Primetime Network Viewing Preferences 1988; An Analysis of Black Audience Primetime Network Viewing Preferences 1984-89. **MILITARY SERVICE:** USAF capt 1956-59. **BUSINESS ADDRESS:** Vice President Special Mkts, BBDO Inc, 383 Madison Ave, New York, NY 10017.

ALLISON, FERDINAND V., JR.
Chief executive officer. **PERSONAL:** Born Jan 15, 1923, Emporia, VA; son of F V Allison Sr (deceased) and Elizabeth R Allison; married E Lavonia Ingram; children: Karen Michele Allison-Davis, Ferdinand Vincent Allison III. **EDUCATION:** Hampton Inst, BS 1943; NYU, MBA 1952. **CAREER:** Army Air Force, inventory clerk, squadron clerk 1943-46; Hampton Inst, budget clerk 1948-50, invoice auditor 1952-53; Mutual Savings & Loan Assn, dir, pres 1953-. **ORGANIZATIONS:** Dir Natl Bus League; dir & past pres Durham Bus & Professional Chain Inc; dir John Avery Boys Club; mem exec comm, treas Durham Co Comm on Affairs of Black People; life mem NAACP; mem Omega Psi Phi; mem AS Hunter Lodge 825 F&AM; mem Durham Chap Hampton Inst Natl Alumni; mem Durham C of C; trustee White Rock Bapt Ch; mem Rotary Club of Durham; mem Salvation Army; mem Financial Mgr Soc for Savings Inst; mem US League of Savings Assn; mem 1979 Invest & Mortgage Lending Comm of US League of Savings Assn; Found for Better Health of Durham; mem NC Savings & Loan League; dir, exec comm Natl Bus League; bd dir, mem Durham Merchants Assoc; trustee White Rock Baptist Church; mem Rotary Club of Durham; vchmn Amer League of Financial Insts; mem Durham County Hosp Corp. **MILITARY SERVICE:** USAC served 3 years. **BUSINESS ADDRESS:** President, Mutual Savings & Loan Assn, 112 W Parrish St PO Box 3827, Durham, NC 27702.

ALLISON, JAMES M., JR.
Physician. **PERSONAL:** Born Jun 10, 1926, Chicago, IL; children: Sheila, Rosalyn, Carita, James III. **EDUCATION:** Fisk Univ, BA 1949; Meharry Med Coll, MD 1953. **CAREER:** Homer G Phillips Hosp St Louis MO, resd gen surgery 4 yrs; Amer Bd of Surgery, diplomat 1959; Amer Coll Surgeons, fellow 1962; Northwestern Univ, assoc in surgery 1974; Provident Hosp, sr attending surgeon; Columbus Hosp, sr attending surgeon; IL Masonic Hosp, attending surgeon; Private practice, physician. **ORGANIZATIONS:** Past pres Cook Cty Physicians Assoc; mem Chicago Med Soc, IL State Med Soc, Amer Med Assoc; bd dir Washington Park YMCA. **MILITARY SERVICE:** USAF 2nd lt 1945-46.

ALLISON, W. ANTHONY
Physician, surgeon. **PERSONAL:** Born Oct 10, 1926, Durham, NC; son of Willis F Allison and Lydia Hammie Allison; married Dale Muther; children: Patricia, Vivian, Anita. **EDUCATION:** Morgan State Coll Univ Baltimore MD, BS 1951; Univ of Munich Med Univ Munich Germany, MD 1958. **CAREER:** Friedman Hosp Howard Univ Med School, emergency room phys & clin instr 1965-67; Mercy Douglass Hosp Phila, attending phys, surg 1967-73; Philadelphia Gen Hosp, attending phys dept rehab med 1967-75; St Josephs Hosp Phila, attending phys, surg 1973-75; VA Ambulatory Care Clinic, acting chief surg serv 1975-79, physician, surgeon; VA Ambulatory Care Clinic, mgmt & care of veteran patients with musculoskeletal conditions, surgeon 1980-. **ORGANIZATIONS:** Mem PA DE Cty Med Soc 1967-72, AMA 1967-72, Natl Med Assoc 1967-, Amer Coll of Sports Med 1977-, NY Natl Acad of Sci, Assoc for Computing Machinery, Amer Professional Practice Assoc; diplomate, Amer Academy of Pain Management, 1988-; mem, Eastern Pennsylvania Medical Society of the Natl Medication Association 1973-; mem, The Computer Society of the IEEE, 1986-. **HONORS/ACHIEVEMENTS:** Awd improved method of titanium dioxide determination in paint pigments US Quartermaster Gen Testing Lab Philadelphia 1952; improved method of determining iron inpaint pigments US Quartermaster Gen Testing Lab Philadelphia 1953; Honor Mem Chapel of Four Chaplains 1976; Awarded Cert of Appreciation for Outstanding Dedication to the Disabled Amer Veterans by Chap 4 of Camden County NJ 1981; Citation for Appreciation & Coop of Serv Rendered Awd by Disabled Amer Vets of the Philadelphia Liberty Bell Chap 96 & Aux 1984; Citation of Merit in appreciation for outstanding service, Disabled Amer Veterans, Delaware County Chapter No 113, 1987; "A Physician's Approach-Designing in Prolog: A Deductive Database of Patient Statistics of Patients with Musculoskeletal Disorders," proceedings-12th Annual Symposium on Computer Application in Medical Care, 1988; "Patient Visits: A Survey of Veterans with Musculoskeletal Disorders" VA Practicioner Vol 5, 1988. **MILITARY SERVICE:** AUS sgt 1945-46. **BUSINESS ADDRESS:** Surgeon, VA Ambulatory Care Clinic, 1421 Cherry St, Philadelphia, PA 19102.

ALLMAN, MARIAN ISABEL
Physician. **PERSONAL:** Born Feb 18, 1946, Birmingham, AL. **EDUCATION:** Fisk Univ, BA 1966; Meharry Med Coll,; MD 1970. **CAREER:** Hubbard Hosp, intern 1970-71; Homer G Phillips Hosp, resd 1971-74; VA Hosp, staff ophthalmologist 1976-77; VA Hosp, chief ophthalmology sect 1977-. **ORGANIZATIONS:** Mem Assoc for Rsch & Vision in Ophthalmology, Assoc of VA Ophthalmologist, Amer Acad of Ophthalmology & Otolaryngology, Roman-Barnes Soc, Natl Med Assoc, Med Assoc State of AL, Macon Cty Med Soc, Natl Med Assoc, Dexter Ave Bapt Church, Montgomery League of Women Voters, Agnes J Lewis Fed Club, Alpa Kappa Alpha Sor Fellow Univ PA 1974-76; bd of advisers Habitat for Humanity. **HONORS/ACHIEVEMENTS:** Outstanding Young Women of Amer 1976; Physicians Recognition Awd; co-author "Rabbit Corneal Epithelial Cells Grown in Vitro Without Serum" Inves Ophthalmol 1976, "Endothelialization of Filtering Bleb in Iris Nevus Syndrome" Arch Ophthalmol 1976, "Bilateral Optic System Aplasia with Relatively Normal Eyes" Arch Ophthalmol, "Congenital Herpes Simplex Virus Type 2 Bilaterial Endophthalmitis", Trans Amer Ophthalmol Soc, "Orbital Neurilemmoma" Ann Ophthalmol. **BUSINESS ADDRESS:** Chief Ophthalmology Sect, VA Hospital, Dept Opthalmology, VA Hosp, Tuskegee, AL 36083.

ALLSTON, THOMAS GRAY, III (TIM)
Public relations executive. **PERSONAL:** Born Jul 13, 1954, Stoneham, MA; son of Thomas G Allston and Zeola (Germany) Allston. **EDUCATION:** Hampton Inst, BA English 1977. **CAREER:** Burson-Marsteller, asst acct executive 1977-78; Hampton Inst/Univ, asst dir of public relations 1979-85; Hill and Knowlton Inc, account exec 1985-87; Renaissance Comm, vice pres 1987-. **ORGANIZATIONS:** Life mem Alpha Phi Alpha Fraternity Inc 1974-; mem Natl Hampton Alumni Assoc 1977-; mem Public Relations Soc of Amer 1977-, Chicago Assoc of Black Journalists 1986-; mem Shiloh SDA Church 1986-. **HOME ADDRESS:** PO Box 06024, Chicago, IL 60606-0024. **BUSINESS ADDRESS:** Vice President, Research & Development, Renaissance Communications Corporation, 738 N LaSalle St, Third Floor, Chicago, IL 60610.

ALSANDOR, JUDE
Business executive. **PERSONAL:** Born Nov 13, 1938, Opelousas, LA; married Donnelle; children: Gerald, Gerard, Marcia, Gary, Creig, Eric, Jude. **EDUCATION:** Univ of Southwest LA, attended. **CAREER:** Continental Marine Serv, catering business owner 1973-; Jude Aslandor Constr & Real Estate, owner 1970-. **ORGANIZATIONS:** Sec, treas Acadian Home Bldrs Assoc; mem Natl Assoc of Home Bldrs, mem bd trustees Lafayette Gen Hosp, mem bd of trustees Lafayette Housing Auth; mem exec comm Boys Club; mem Atchafalaya Basin Comm, mem Goals Comm for LA; mem bd of dir Jr Achievement; mem Ed Comm Gr Lafayette C of C, Knights of Peter Claver St Pauls, LA State Council on Human Rel, Citizens Adv Comm to City of Lafayette, Natl Fed of Indep Busmen, BAM Club at USL, Sheriffs Adv Comm, Sportmans Club of Lafayette; past-pres St Pauls Booster Club, Lafayette Council on Human Rel; past vice pres Cathedral-Carmel PTA. **HONORS/ACHIEVEMENTS:** Award for Bus Achievement Interracial Council for Bus Achievement 1976; Most Disting Prom Black Citizen Southern Consum Ed Found 1976; Volun LeadershipAwd Dillard-Xavier-United Negro Coll Fund 1976; Awd for Ded Serv of Bd of Dr Gr Lafayette C of C. **BUSINESS ADDRESS:** Jude Aslandor Constr & RE, PO Box 2669, Lafayette, LA 70502.

ALSTON, BETTY BRUNER
Educator. **PERSONAL:** Born Jul 05, 1933, Concord, NC; daughter of Buford Bruner and Ethel Bruner; married Henry Clay Alston; children: Henry Clay Jr, Terry Verice. **EDUCATION:** Barber-Scotia College, BS 1955; A&T State Univ, 1957; Appalachian State Univ, 1969. **CAREER:** PTA/Odell Elem School, secretary 1979; PTSA/Northwest Middle School, secretary 1980; First United Pres Church, 1981; Northwest High School, Booster Club secretary 1982, vice president 1983; Briarwood, school teacher 1983-. **ORGANIZATIONS:** Member North Carolina Association of Educators; elder, organist First United Presbyterian Church; board of directors, Stonewall Jackson School, 1989; mem, Cabarrus County Board of Educ, 1988; second vice pres, Democrat Women's Organization, 1989. **HONORS/ACHIEVEMENTS:** Member Alpha Kappa Alpha; member Cabarrus County School Board; member Northwest HS Board of Directors; Publication-Poem-Teachers' Invitation to Writing 1983; first vice chairperson of the Democratic Party of Cabarrus Co 1985; apptd by Gov Jim Martin to serve on the Cabarrus Co Resource Council of Mt Pleasant Prison Unit 1986; Outstanding Achievement in Educ and Comm Service Omega Psi Phi Frat 1986; Service to the Welfare of the Community West Central Cabarrus Optimist 1986. **HOME ADDRESS:** P O Box 1365, Concord, NC 28025.

ALSTON, CASCO, JR.
Physician, educator. **PERSONAL:** Born Sep 13, 1923, Philadelphia, PA; married Majorie Poysky; children: Christofer, Angela, Gwen. **EDUCATION:** Univ of PA, BA 1936; Howard Med Coll, MD 1942; City Hosp & Western Reserve Univ Med School, resd 1946. **CAREER:** Harlem & Presbyterian Hosp, staff mem 1951; Columbia Univ Coll of P&S, asst clinic prof med 1951-. **ORGANIZATIONS:** Dir of med Sydenhom Hosp 1965-75; dir family med plan NY Med Coll 1960-62; asst prof clinical med NY Univ 1955-65; asst dir Diagnostic Clinic 1951-59; lecturer Western Reserve Univ 1946-48; asst supt med Metro Gen Hosp 1946-48; chmn med bd NY City Employees Retirement System; assoc Amer Mus ofNatural Hist; mem NY Cty med Soc 1977, MY Acad Sci 1964, Amer Heart Assoc 1964, Amer Geriatric Soc 1977; leading role WPA THeatre Prod 1935-38; mem Hedgerow Repertory Theatre 1934-38. **BUSINESS ADDRESS:** Asst Clinic Prof of Medicine, ColumbiaUniv Coll of P&S, 1865 Amsterdam Ave, New York, NY 10031.

ALSTON, DENISE ADELE
Research psychologist. **PERSONAL:** Born Aug 12, 1952, Norton, MA. **EDUCATION:** CA State Univ Los Angeles, BA (w/Honors) 1979; Univ of CA Santa Cruz, PhD 1985. **CAREER:** Univ of CA Santa Cruz, teaching fellow 1984; Joint Ctr for Political Studies, public policy fellow. **ORGANIZATIONS:** Mem Amer Psychological Assoc 1985-. **HONORS/ACHIEVEMENTS:** Natl Sci Foundation Minority Grad Fellowship 1980-83; Ford Foundation Young Scholars Public Policy Fellowship 1985-.

ALSTON, FLOYD WILLIAM
Business executive. **PERSONAL:** Born Oct 23, 1925, Brooklyn, NY; married Marilyn Deloris Baker; children: Craig E F, Marilyn Suzanne. **EDUCATION:** Temple Univ, BS Business Admin 1970; Fels Inst of State and Local Govnmnt Univ of PA. **CAREER:** HOPE Development Corp, pres 1968-73; Philadelphia Housing Authry, housing mgr 1958-68. **ORGANIZATIONS:** Pres Union Benevolent Assoc Fdn 1979-; pres JM Nursing Serv 1980-85, Philadelphia Housing Dvlmnt Corp 1982; past pres Comm Servc Plng Cncl 1982-84; natl vp, acting exec dir Frontiers Intl Inc 1984-, Philadelphia Tribune Charities 1980-83. **HONORS/ACHIEVEMENTS:** Tribune Charities Chrmn Award Philadelphia Tribune Charities 1983; Don Alexander award Natl Bankers Assoc 1978; Prentice-Hall article published "Helping Troubled Employees" 1978. **MILITARY SERVICE:** USMC sgt 1943-46, 1950-51. **BUSINESS ADDRESS:** Vice President, First Pennsylvania Bank, 16th & Market Streets, Philadelphia, PA 19101.

ALSTON, GILBERT C.
Judge. **PERSONAL:** Born Apr 04, 1931, Philadelphia, PA; married Lydia Mary Wold; children: Carl, Anita. **EDUCATION:** UCLA, BA Economics 1959; Univ of S CA, JD Law 1965. **CAREER:** LA Co Dist Atty, deputy dist atty 1965-67; Hauptman & Alston, private prac 1967-71; LA Mun Court, judge 1971-77; Pasadena Mun Court, judge 1977-80; LA Superior Court, judge 1980-. **MILITARY SERVICE:** USAF capt fighter pilot 5 1/2 yrs. **BUSINESS ADDRESS:** Judge Superior Court, Los Angeles Co, 300 E Walnut, Pasadena, CA 91101.

ALSTON, HARRY L.
Associate executive. **PERSONAL:** Born Dec 12, 1914, Winston Salem, WV; children: Harry Jr, Gloria, Douglas B. **EDUCATION:** WV State Coll, BS 1938; Atlanta Univ, MSW 1949. **ORGANIZATIONS:** Mem Winston-Salem Urban League 1948-51; sec 1951-55, dir 1955-58 Indust Relations So Field Div Natl Urban League 1951-55; dir prog dept United Packinghouse Food & Allied Workers AFL-CIO 1958-68; ed rep Amalgamated Meat Cutters AFL-CIO 1968-72; past dir civil rights United Food & Commercial Workers Intl Union 1972-80; retired bd mem Gary Urban League, Coaliton of Black Trade Unionists, NAACP, 1st United Presb Church of Gary, Natl Assoc of Social Workers, Amer Acad of Social Workers, Alpha Phi Alpha. **MILITARY SERVICE:** USCG 1942-46.

ALSTON, JAMES L.
Manager. **PERSONAL:** Born Jan 14, 1947, Bronx, NY; children: Lorraine, Jeanette. **EDUCATION:** Loras Coll Dubuque IA, BA Sociol 1970; CCNY, 1972-73; NY Univ, 1975-76. **CAREER:** Simpson St Devel Assoc Youth Prog, training coord 1970-74; Fox St Relocation Shelter, asst dir 1974-76, dir 1975-76; S Bronx Comm Housing Bronx, dir 1976-80; Sebco Mgmt Co Inc, dir 1980-. **ORGANIZATIONS:** Chmn hsg com Bronx Comm Plng Bd 1971-; bd mem Comm Greening Com 1975-; bd of dirs Natl Assoc of Hsg Mgmt & Owners 1976-79; vchmn Sebco Housing Corp 1971-80; chmn PTA Fin Com St Athanasius 1975-; bd mem Prospect Hosp Adv 1978-. **HONORS/ACHIEVEMENTS:** Cardinal Spellman Youth Awd Archdiocese of NY 1966; John F Kennedy Youth Awd casita Maria/Bronx NY 1974; Cert of Achievement Comm Serv Soc 1976; Spec Cert Awd Comm Plng Bd Bronx Comm Coll 1976. **BUSINESS ADDRESS:** Dir, Sebco Mgmt Co Inc, 953 Southern Blvd, Bronx, NY 10459.

ALSTON, KATHY DIANE
Physician. **PERSONAL:** Born Mar 29, 1958, Staten Island, NY. **EDUCATION:** Univ of VA, BA 1980; Howard Univ Coll of Medicine, MD 1984. **CAREER:** Martin Luther King Genl Hosp, physician. **ORGANIZATIONS:** Mem Assoc of Black Women Physicians 1985-86; dorm council Joint Council of Interns & Residents 1986-87. **HONORS/ACHIEVEMENTS:** Natl Health Serv Corp Scholarship 1980-83. **HOME ADDRESS:** 6709 Hazen Place, McLean, VA 22101. **BUSINESS ADDRESS:** Martin L King Genl Hosp, 12021 So Wilmington Ave, Los Angeles, CA 90059.

ALSTON, ROBERT MILTON, JR.
Social services administrator. **PERSONAL:** Born Mar 20, 1949, New York, NY; married Josette Marie Calloway; children: Robert M III. **EDUCATION:** Adelphi Univ, BSW 1978; Columbia Univ Sch of Bus Admin, Certificate Mgmt/Admin 1979. **CAREER:** A Better Chance Inc, asst regional dir 1972-73; Speedworld Serv for Children, assoc dir 1973-75; NY Urban League Manpower Educ, training dir 1975-77; NY Urban League Manhatton Br, deputy branch dir 1977-78; NY Urban League Stanton Island Br, branch dir 1978-82; Charlotte-Mecklenburg Urban League, pres/ceo. **ORGANIZATIONS:** Mem SI Rep New York City Bd of Ed Chancellors Com/Equal Oppor 1980-82; chair educ comm Alpha Phi Alpha Frat In Beta NV Lambda 1983-84; mem charter Friends of JC Smith Univ 1984-85; mem sub-comm-chair C-M Bd of Educ Task Force Truancy Dropouts 1984; mem C-M Comm Relations Comm 1983-86; mem JC Smith Univ Comm Adv 1983-86; mem Charter C-M Citizen Forum. **HONORS/ACHIEVEMENTS:** Outstanding Young Man of Amer Natl Jaycees 1978; Outstanding Volunteer Awd United Negro Coll Fund natl office 1980; Partner in Educ Awd New York City Bd of Educ1981; Certificate of Recognition Awd NC State Assoc Natl Assn of Black Social Workers 1983. **HOME ADDRESS:** 7018 Heatherford Dr, Charlotte, NC 28226.

ALSTON, TRACEY DANIEL (TRACY ANN DANIEL-ALSTON)
National sales manager. **PERSONAL:** Born Dec 04, 1961, Gary, IN; daughter of Thomas Lee Daniel Jr and Freddia Campkin Daniel; married Marcus Alston, Oct 16, 1987; children: Marquise Danielle. **EDUCATION:** Indiana State Univ, Terre Haute IN, BS Early-Childhood Educ, 1982; Columbia Coll, Chicago IL, BA Radio & Television Communications, 1983. **CAREER:** WBEE Radio, Chicago IL, account exec, 1983-85, natl sales mgr, 1985-87, co-owner, 1987-. **ORGANIZATIONS:** Women in Broadcast, 1987-; founding mem, TAP, 1988-; team captain, Cistic Fibrosis, 1988-. **HONORS/ACHIEVEMENTS:** Chicago's Up & Coming Women, Dollars & Sense, 1988; Chicago Radio Outstanding Women, RAB, 1988.

ALVERANGA, GLANVIN L.
Business executive. **PERSONAL:** Born Feb 20, 1928, New York, NY; married Ramona E Fontany; children: Denise, Glenn. **EDUCATION:** City College of New York, BS, 1958; John Jay Coll of Criminal Justice, New York NY, MA, 1976. **CAREER:** New York City Police Dept, dep insp, 1955-77; New York City Health & Hosp Corp, dir of security corp, 1977-. **ORGANIZATIONS:** Ed consult New York City Bd of Ed 1977; sec NOBLE 1977; mem 100 Black Men 1978-. **MILITARY SERVICE:** AUS corpl 1951-52. **BUSINESS ADDRESS:** Dir of Security Corp, Health & Hosp Corp, 125 Worth St, New York, NY 10013.

AMAKER, NORMAN CAREY
Attorney/educator. **PERSONAL:** Born Jan 15, 1935, New York, NY; son of Carey Amaker and Gladys Corley Amaker; married Mattie Jeannette Owens, Oct 20, 1962; children: Alicia, Alana, Arthur. **EDUCATION:** Amherst Clg, BA (cum laude) 1956; Columbia U, JD 1959. **CAREER:** NAACP Legal Def Fund NYC, atty 1960-68, first asst cnsl 1968-71; Nbrh Legal Serv Prog Wash DC, exec dir 1971-73; Rutgers Univ, prof of law 1973-76; Loyola Univ of Chicago Law Sch, prof of law 1976-. **ORGANIZATIONS:** Gen cnsl Natl Comm Agnst Dscrmntn in hsng 1973; vstng prof Rutgers Law Sch Newark, NJ 1973-76; sch bd mem Dist 202 Evanston Twnshp H S 1980-87, pres pro-tem 1983-84; pres Chicago Forum Chicago 1982-83; bd of gov Soc of Am Law Tchrs 1979-87. **HONORS/ACHIEVEMENTS:** IBPOE of W Awd 1965; BALSA Awd 1973; Civil Liberties & Civil Rghts Oceana 1967; Civil Rights Enfrcmnt and the Reagan Adm, Urban Inst Wash DC 1988. **MILITARY SERVICE:** USAR 1960-66. **BUSINESS ADDRESS:** Professor of Law, Loyola University of Chicago, 1 E Pearson St, 526, Chicago, IL 60611.

AMAN, MOHAMMED M.
Educator, educational administrator. **PERSONAL:** Born Jan 03, 1940, Alexandria, Egypt;son of Mohammed Aman and Fathia Ali al-Maghrabi Aman; married Mary Jo Parker, Sep 15, 1972; children: David. **EDUCATION:** Cairo Univ Egypt, BA (with honors), 1961; Columbia Univ New York NY, MS, 1965; Univ of Pittsburgh, PhD, 1968; New York Univ, postdoctoral studies in Comp Sci, 1970-71. **CAREER:** Univ of Pittsburgh, research asst, 1965-66; Duquesne Univ Pittsburgh, reference librarian, 1966-68; Pratt Inst NY, asst prof; St Johns Univ NY, asst and assoc prof 1969-73, dir and prof 1973-76; Long Island Univ, Greenvale Long Island NY, dean & prof 1976-79; Univ of Wisconsin-Milwaukee, dean and prof, 1979-. **ORGANIZATIONS:** Info mgmt consultant UNIDO 1978-; UNESCO 1982-, USAID 1984-; chmn Intl Relations Comm Amer Lib Assn 1984-85, Assn Lib & Info Sci Ed 1985-86; Amer Soc for Info Science Intl Rel Comm; chair, Intl Issues in Information Special Interest Group; life mem NAACP 1984-; mem Amer Arab Affairs Council 1983-; mem Egyptian Amer Scholars Assn 1971-; bd member, A Wisconsin African Relief Effort (AWARE), 1986-89; bd member, Wisconsin African Historical Society/Museum, 1988-. **HONORS/ACHIEVEMENTS:** Beta Phi Mu Intl Lib & Info Sci Honor Soc, Univ of Pittsburgh; author, contributing consultant Intl Library Review, 1969-, Arab Serials & Periodicals, 1979, Cataloging & Classification of Non-Western Library Material, 1980, Librarian in the Third World, 1976, Developing Computer Based Library Sys 1984, Online Access to Database 1984, Information Services 1986; award of appreciation from the Black Caucus of the Amer Library Assn, 1986; Award of Serv, Assn for Library and Information Science Educ, 1988; UNESCO consultant on the Revival of the Alexandrian Library Project, 1988-; John Awes Humphry/Forest Press Award for Outstanding Contributions to Intl Librarianship, Amer Library Assn, 1989. **BUSINESS ADDRESS:** Dean & Prof, School of Library & Information Science, University of Wisconsin, PO Box 413, Enderis Hall, Milwaukee, WI 53201.

AMARO, RUBEN
Sports manager. **PERSONAL:** Born Jan 07, 1936, Monterrey, Mexico;married Judy; children: David, Ruben Jr. **CAREER:** Philadelphia, shortstop 1960; NY Yankees, shortstop 1966-68; CA Angels, shortstop 1969-72; Philadelphia Phillies, scout 1972, first base coach 1980-81; Chicago Cubs, asst mgr 1982-; Zulia Eagles of Maracaibo, gen mgr 1983-84. **ORGANIZATIONS:** Guided Zulia to Venezuelan League title, Caribbean World Series championship when Zulia defeated defending champion Puerto Rico; hit major league career-high in 1964; led Intl League shortstops in double plays with 84 in 1959. **HONORS/ACHIEVEMENTS:** NL Gold Glove for his shortstop work in 129 games. **BUSINESS ADDRESS:** Chicago Cubs, 1060 W Addison, Chicago, IL 60613.

AMBROSE, ETHEL L.
City official. **PERSONAL:** Born Dec 18, 1930, Perryville, AR; divorced; children: Ethel M Harris, Derek S Brown, Lakeitha Brown. **EDUCATION:** Univ of MI, Licensed Soc Worker 1973; Highland Park Comm Coll, 1975; Southeastern Univ, BS Sociology 1980. **CAREER:** City of Highland Park, spec asst to mayor 1969-76; Detroit Adult Ed, substitute teacher 1978-79; Diversified Health Ctr, social worker 1979-80; Alpha AnnexNursing Ctr, soc worker 1984-. **ORGANIZATIONS:** Mem Citizen of Interest Scholarship Comm 1967-; life mem Highland Park Caucus Club 1973-; bd pres Wayne Metro Comm Serv Agency 1983-84; mem, trustee Highland Park Bd of Ed/Comm Coll 1983-; pres ACCT Minorities Affairs/Central Region 1984-; mem Natl Political Congress of Black Women 1984.

AMBUSH, ROBERT C.
Auto dealer executive. **CAREER:** Ace Golden Oldsmobile, Inc, Port Richey, FL, chief executive. **BUSINESS ADDRESS:** Ace Golden Oldsmobile, 11613 US Hwy 19, Port Richey, FL 34668. *

AMES, DERRICK LEE
Physician. **PERSONAL:** Born Oct 18, 1950, Baltimore, MD. **EDUCATION:** Univ of Notre Dame, BS Biol 1971; Meharry Med Coll, MD 1975. **CAREER:** New Orl Hlth Corp, physic 1978-; Tulane Med Sch, res intnl med 1977-78; Touro Infirm, res intnl med 1975-77. **ORGANIZATIONS:** Dipl Nat Bd of Med 1976; dipl Am Bd of Intnl Med 1980; sr wdrn Prince Hall Mason Odr 1979-80.

AMIJI, HATIM M.
Educator. **PERSONAL:** Born Jun 11, 1939, Zanzibar. **EDUCATION:** London, BA (Hons) 1964; Princeton Univ, MA, PhD. **CAREER:** Univ of MA Dept of History, assoc prof. **ORGANIZATIONS:** Sec gen Zanzibar Youth League 1960; lecturer Trinity Coll Nabingo Uganda 1964; lecturer Princeton Univ 1969-70; rsch assoc Dept of History Univ of Nairobi Kenya 1967-68; lecturer Dept of History & Centre for African Studies Boston Univ 1972; dir African Studies Workshop World Affairs Council Boston 1972; mem Middle Eastern Studies Assoc; fellow E African Acad; mem African Studies Assoc of USA; ed bd Gemini Review; founder mem Pan-African Univ Org. **HONORS/ACHIEVEMENTS:** E African Railways & Harbours Rsch Awd 1963; Rockefeller Found Fellow 1965-67; Princeton Univ Fellow 1969-70; Zanzibar Govt Scholar 1961-64; Superior Merit Awd Univ of MA. **BUSINESS ADDRESS:** Associate Professor, Univ of Massachusetts, Dept of History, Harbor Campus Univ of MA, Boston, MA 02125.

AMIN, KARIMA
Educator. **PERSONAL:** Born Jun 01, 1947, Buffalo, NY; children: Abdur Rahman, Takiyah Nur, Sabriyah. **EDUCATION:** St Univ of NY at Buffalo, BA 1969, MEd 1974. **CAREER:** Buffalo Public Schools, teacher of language arts scndry, 1969-. **ORGANIZATIONS:** Spec apt Natl Cncl of Tchrs of Eng 1982-86; Comm for Prsrvtn of Multicultural Lit in Am bd of dir Afro-Am Hstrcl Asso of Niagara Frontier 1984-86; past treas & sec Taara Zakkiyya Islamic Strhd 1975-; coord Spin-a-Story Tellers of Western NY 1984-. **HONORS/ACHIEVEMENTS:** Wm Wells Brown Awd Afro-Am Hstrcl Asso 1984; tchr of tomarrow awd Buffalo Bd of Ed 1978; co-author Black Lit for H S Stdnts NCTE 1978; Black Edctrs of the Yr Black Edctrs Asso of Wstrn NY 1977; Awd English Speaking Union of Western NY 1986. **HOME ADDRESS:** 207 Herman St, Buffalo, NY 14211. **BUSINESS ADDRESS:** Teacher of Language Arts, Buffalo Public Schools, City Hall, Buffalo, NY 14202.

AMMONS, EDSEL ALBERT
Clergyman. **PERSONAL:** Born Feb 17, 1924, Chicago, IL; married June; children: Marilyn, Edsel Jr, Carol, Kenneth, Carlton, Lila. **EDUCATION:** Roosevelt Univ, BA 1948; Garrett Theol Sem, MDiv 1956; Chicago Theol Sem, DMin 1975. **CAREER:** Chicago & NY, pastor; Urban Ministries Rockford IL, dir 1963-66; Garrett Theol Sem, annual conf, prof 1968-76; United Meth Church, bishop 1976-. **ORGANIZATIONS:** Mem Natl Com Black Chmn; pres W Avalon Com Council 1958-61; vice pres Chatham-Avalon Com Org 1960-61; mem Alpha Phi Alpha; pres United Meth Gen Bd of Discipleship 198—84; pres Helth & Welfare Prog Dept United Meth Gen Bd of Global Ministries; mem bd US Health Corp Riverside Meth Hosp Columbus OH. **MILITARY SERVICE:** World War II 1943-46.

AMMONS, TAMARA NASH
Educator. **PERSONAL:** Born Jun 04, 1957, Cleveland, OH; married Richard Allen Ammons. **EDUCATION:** Wellesley Coll, BA 1979; Harvard Univ Sch of Educ, EdM 1982. **CAREER:** Brown Univ, admission officer 1979-81; Marymount Coll of Virginia, admissions counselor 1982-83; The Amer Univ, program rep 1983-. **ORGANIZATIONS:** Mem Alpha Kappa Alpha Sor Inc 1978-; mem Metro Washington/Amer Assoc of Adults in Continuing Educ 1983-85; mem Natl Univ Continuing Educ Assoc 1983-; mem exec comm Amer Univ Black Coalition 1984-; mem Amer Univ Staff Personnel Review Bd 1986-; volunteer Minority Student/Mentor Program The Washington Ctr 1986-. **HOME ADDRESS:** 1110 Fidler Lane #1002, Silver Spring, MD 20910. **BUSINESS ADDRESS:** Program Representative, The American University, Office of Contract Programs, 4400 Massachusetts Ave NW, Washington, DC 20016.

AMORY, REGINALD L.
Engineer, educator. **PERSONAL:** Born Jul 17, 1936, Peekskill, NY; married Marion Rose Boothe; children: Reginald, Susan. **EDUCATION:** NY Univ, BCE 1960; Clarkson Coll, MCE 1963; Rensselaer Polytechnic Inst, PhD 1967. **CAREER:** Throop & Feiden, engr 1960-61; Abbott, Jerkt & Co, engr 1961-63; RPI, tch asst 1963-64, instr 1965-66; NE Univ, asst prof 1966-68; NC A&T Univ, dean 1968-74; Northeastern Univ, prof 1974-. **ORGANIZATIONS:** Consult GE Co, Natl Sci Found, B&M Tech Serv, US Dept of Energy, Educ Devel Corp, Natl Acad of Engrg, SC Comn on Higher Educ, TN State Univ, Mobil Oil Co, Robert Charles Assoc; mem Amer Soc for Eng Educ; Amer Soc of Civil Engrs; Intl Assoc for Bridge & Structural Engrs; Natl Soc of Prof Engrs; Amer Assn for Advancement of Sci; mem advis panel of Engr Mech Sect Natl Sci Found; chmn Comn of Educ for the Engr Profsn; vice pres exec bd Amer Soc for Engr Educ; mem Proj Bd Amer Soc for Engr Educ; bd of trustees St Augustine's Coll; adv bd Natl Urban League; Sigma Psi Phi. **HONORS/ACHIEVEMENTS:** Excellence Awd NC A&T State Univ 1972; Engr of Distinction Engr Joint Council 1973; Alumni Achievement Awd RPI 1977; Visiting Scholar Univ of Cambridge 1983; Alcoa Found Profshp NE Univ; Natl Sci Honor Soc; Who's Who in Amer; Men of Achievement; Dict of Intl Biography; Personalities of the South; Leaders in Educ; Com Leaders & Noteworthy Americans. **BUSINESS ADDRESS:** Professor, NortheasternUniv, 360 Huntington Ave, Boston, MA 02115.

AMOS, JOSEPH H.
Law enforcement, attorney. **PERSONAL:** Born Feb 19, 1929, Atlanta, GA; married Mary V Talmadge; children: Audrey Dozier, Michael, Kenneth. **EDUCATION:** Woodrow Wilson Coll of Law, JD 1968. **CAREER:** Served with Atlanta Police Dept since 1957; Atlanta Bur of Police Svcs, major. **ORGANIZATIONS:** Mem GA Bar Assn; Natl Bar Assn; Gate City Bar Assn; Amer Bar Assn; bd dir GW Carver Boy's Club; bd dir Police Athl League; mem WC Thomas Masonic Lodge; bd dir Chaplaincy Prog for Atlanta. **HONORS/ACHIEVEMENTS:** Police Dept's Citizen's Award Frontiers Intl 1972; Outstanding Citizen Award Business Women's Assn 1973. **BUSINESS ADDRESS:** Major, City of Atlanta Bur Police Serv, 165 Decatur St SE, Atlanta, GA 30303.

AMOS, KENT B.
Management consulting firm president. **PERSONAL:** Born May 21, 1944, Washington, DC; son of Benjamin F Amos and Gladys C Amos; married Carmen. **EDUCATION:** DE State Coll, BS, 1970. **CAREER:** Xerox Corp, sales mgr 1975-76, area mgr 1976-77, mgr ISG Affirm Action 1977-78, dir corp affirm action, EEO 1978-82; pres, The Triad Group. **ORGANIZATIONS:** Mem Corp Few 1971-79; bus consultant Congressional Black Caucus 1975-79; mem Business Policy Review Comm 1977-79; mem Big Bros 1971-74; mem Inside/Outside 1972-; mem Alpha Kappa Mu Natl Hon Soc 1968-69; also mem of NAACP, Natl Urban League, Natl Council of Negro Women, Delaware State Coll Alumni Assn, Coolidge High School Alumni Assn, and Omega Psi Phi. **HONORS/ACHIEVEMENTS:** Black History Week Awards, WMAL Radio/TV Station, 1974; Merit Awards for Job Performance, Xerox Corp; President's Sales Recognition Award, Xerox Corp; Chair's Award, Congressional Black Caucus, 1979; awards from DC Public Schools Bd of Educ, Natl Assn for Equal Oppportunity in Higher Educ; Legacy Award, Natl Council of Negro Women; Image Award, NAACP; Whitney Young Award, Urban League; Roy Dykes Memorial Award, Xerox Corp; Citizen of the Year, Omega Psi Phi; Man of the Year, Shiloh Baptist Church; Alumnus of the Century, Delaware State Coll; Alumnus of the Year, Calvin Coolidge High School; Alumnus of the Year, Delaware State Coll; scholarship funds created in his name at Calvin Coolidge High School and Delaware State Coll. **MILITARY SERVICE:** AUS, lt, 1964-71; numerous Vietnam Decorations, 1970. **BUSINESS ADDRESS:** Pres, The Triad Group, 1625 K St, NW, #1210, Washington, DC 20006.

AMOS, LARRY C.
Attorney. **PERSONAL:** Born Jul 28, 1935, Atlanta, GA; married Nancy A Saine; children: Kevin, Delaina, Miles. **EDUCATION:** Morehouse Coll, attended 1952-53; Lafayette Coll, BS 1957; IN Univ, MBA 1958, JD 1963. **CAREER:** Ford Motor Co, ind rel rep & labor rel rep 1963-69; Brown & Williamson Tobacco Co, corp atty 1969-. **ORGANIZATIONS:** Mem Lousiville IN, KY, Natl, Amer Bar Assns; adv bd chmn United Negro Coll Fund Local Campaign; bd of dir Sr House Inc. **MILITARY SERVICE:** AUS sp-4 1958-60. **BUSINESS ADDRESS:** Corporate Attorney, Brown & Willaimson Tobacco Co, PO Box 35090, Louisville, KY 40232.

AMOS, ORIS ELIZABETH CARTER
Educator. **PERSONAL:** Born in Martinsville, VA; daughter of Samuel Carter (deceased) and Fannie Carter; married Winsom; children: Patsi. **EDUCATION:** VA State Coll, BA 1951; OH State Univ, MA 1963, PhD 1971. **CAREER:** VA Pub Schools, teacher 1951-55; Columbus OH Pub Sch, teacher 1963-66; OH State Univ, instr 1966-69; Otterbein Coll, asst prof 1971-75; Council for Exceptional Children, pres 1975; Coll of Educ, chmn Human Rel Comm 1975; Wright State Univ, prof of educ 1975-88; educ development consultant, 1988-. **ORGANIZATIONS:** Teachers Adv Comm State of OH 1975; adv Black Students Otterbein Coll 1975; adv bd Miami Valley Reg Res Ctr; adv bd Dayton Area United Cerebral Palsy Professional Serv; adv bd Sinclair Comm Coll Special Educ; Panel of Experts to review proposals St Bd of Educ Columbus, OH 1975; mem Delta Sigma Theta Sorority; Pi Lambda Theta Women's Honorary in Educ; Central Chapel Church Yellow Springs. **HONORS/ACHIEVEMENTS:** Named Outstanding Educator of Yr 1972; Award for Distinguished Comm Serv Delta Sigma Theta Sorority 1972; Special Award Serv to Black Students at Otterbein Coll 1973; Teacher Excellence Award Wright State Univ 1979; Educator of Yr OH Fed Council of Exceptional Children 1982; Coord of Special Educ 1978-87; WSU Trustees Award, 1987; Greene County Hall of Fame for Women, Greene County OH, 1988. **BUSINESS ADDRESS:** Prof Emeritus of Education, Wright State Univ, PO Box 416, Yellow Springs, OH 45387.

AMOS, WALLY
Business owner/president. **PERSONAL:** Born 1937, Tallahasse, FL; married Christine. **CAREER:** Wm Morris Agency, from mail clerk to exec vice pres 1961-, agent Simon & Garfunkle, The Temptations, The Supremes, the late Marvin Gaye, Dionne Warwick, Patti LaBelle; he also managed Franklin Ajaye, Abby Lincoln, Oscar Brown Jr & sev other singers & actresses; Famous Amos Chocolate Chip Cookies, owner/pres. **ORGANIZATIONS:** Mem Literary Vol of Amer. **HONORS/ACHIEVEMENTS:** HS Diploma & Chef's Hat NY Foods Trade HS; straw Panama hat and embroidered Indian pullover shirt corporate symbols added to Business Americana Collection at Smithsonian Inst. **MILITARY SERVICE:** USAF 4 yrs. **BUSINESS ADDRESS:** President, Famous Amos Choc Chip Cookies, 14734 Calvert St, Van Nuys, CA 91411.

AMPY, FRANKLIN R.
Educator/researcher. **PERSONAL:** Born Jun 22, 1936, Dinwiddie, VA; son of Preston Ampy (deceased) and Beatrice Tucker Ampy. **EDUCATION:** Virginia State Coll,Petersburg, VA, BS, 1954-58; Oregon State Univ, Corvallis, OR, MS, PhD 1958-62; Univ of California Post Doctorate 1968-70. **CAREER:** Amer Univ of Beirut, asst prof, Lebanon, 1962-68; Univ of California, Davis CA, post doctorate 1968-70, Educ Oppor Prog, assoc dean 1970-71; Howard Univ, assoc prof zoology, Washington, DC, 1971-, acting chmn zoology 1973-75, 1984-86; Oregon State Univ, Corvallis, OR, Research Asst 1958-62. **ORGANIZATIONS:** Consultant Natl Inst of Health 1981, 1983; treasure Howard Chapter Amer Assoc Univ Prof 1983-84; evaluator VA Talent Search 1980-; mem Project Thirty, Carnegie Found New York City, comm selected to make recommendation on the improvement of secondary teacher training, profs & admins were selected from 30 inst of higher educ. **HONORS/ACHIEVEMENTS:** Geneticist World Poultry Con Kiev Russia 1966; Faculty Fellow NASA/Ames Moffett Fields CA 1976; Fulbright Nominee Natl Council of Scholars 1984-85. **BUSINESS ADDRESS:** Assoc Prof, Department of Zoology, Howard University, 414 College St NW, Washington, DC 20059.

ANDERS, CORRIE MICHAEL
Journalist. **PERSONAL:** Born Aug 26, 1944, Washington, DC; divorced; children: Karen Michele. **CAREER:** United Press Intl Washington Bureau, copy aide dictationist reporter 1963-68; Washington Evening Star News, journalist 1969-. **ORGANIZATIONS:** Mem Washington Press Club. **HONORS/ACHIEVEMENTS:** First John Knight Fellow under auspices of Stanford Professional Journalism Fellowship Prog 1972-73. **BUSINESS ADDRESS:** Journalist, Washington Evening Star News, 225 Virginia Ave SE, Washington, DC 20002.

ANDERS, RICHARD H.
Educator. **PERSONAL:** Born Jul 29, 1925, Arcadia, FL; married Charlotte King; children: Kenneth, Keith, Rosalind. **EDUCATION:** FL A&M Univ, BS 1947; IN Univ, MS 1963. **CAREER:** Dunbar HS Ft Myers, athletic dir coach 1947-48; Richardson HS Lake City, 1948-69; Part time city recreation asst, 1968-; Coord summer recreation 1973-74; Columbia HS,

supr phys educ health 1973-75, intramural dir 1970-. **ORGANIZATIONS:** 1st vice pres Columbia Educ Assn 1974-75; sec Gateway Serv Unit of FL Educ Assn 1974-75; adv bd N Central FL Phys Educ Clinics 1970-; mem CEA ExecBd; pres FL A&M Alumni Gateway Chap Lake City 1974-; Polemarch Gainesville Alumni Chap Kappa Alpha Psi Frat 1968-69 1972-73; keeper records KAW 1973-74;mem Lake City Optimist Club; Emerg Med Training Com (EMT); Columbia Co Planning Bd; mem FHSAA Game Ofcls; Versiteers Soc Club; Masonic Fraternal Order Shiloh 619; chorister New Bethel Bapt Ch. **HONORS/ACHIEVEMENTS:** Football Championships 1947-51-53-59 1963-65; runner up 1955-56 1961-62; Coach of Yr Awd 1963 1966; FL Athletic Coaches Assn Life Mem Awd 1970; FL Interscholastic Coaches Assn Awd 1967; Music Dir Trophy 1974. **BUSINESS ADDRESS:** Intramural Dir, Columbia HS, Lake City, FL 32055.

ANDERSON, ABBIE H.
Educational administrator. **PERSONAL:** Born Jun 03, 1928, Terrell, TX; married Frances R Morgan; children: Donna R, Rosalind T, Abbie H Jr, Michael EC. **EDUCATION:** Tuskegee Inst, BS 1953; Lincoln Univ of MO, MEd 1966. **CAREER:** Brigade exec ofcr; Vietnamese Chf of Reg Forces/Popular Forces, dist sr adv/adv; asst prof military sci; mem gen staff; chief auto weapons sec; marksmanship Unit, co commander; co exec ofcr; rifle platoon leader/weapons & platoon leader; AUS, ret Lt Col sect leader; NY Life Ins Co, ins salesman; Terrell Ind Schl Dist, school bd trustee. **ORGANIZATIONS:** Mem Dallas Assn of Life Underwriters 1971-; pres Amer Heart Assn Kaufman Cnty 1983-85; mem NAACP; treas Tuskegee Alumni Club of Dallas; sch bd mem Terrell Ind Sch Dist; bd mem Rosehill Water Coop; mem Cath Ch; mem Omega Psi Phi Frat; grand knight Father Vincius Council #6887 of the Knights of Columbus; chmn bd Jackson Comm Hosp; bd mem Terrell Comm Hosp. **HONORS/ACHIEVEMENTS:** Rookie of the Year NY Life Ins Co; Recip Bronze Star; Combat Infantryman's Badge; Armed Forces Honor & Medal 1st Class Vietnam; Army Cooupational Medal Germany; Natl Def Medal & First Oak Leaf Cluster; Armed Forces Reserve Medal; Vietnam Serv Medal. **MILITARY SERVICE:** AUS Lt Col served over 24 years; Repub of Vietnam Campaign Medal; Meritorious Serv Medal. **HOME ADDRESS:** Rt 3 Box 336, Terrell, TX 75160. **BUSINESS ADDRESS:** School Board Trustee, Terrell Ind School Dist, 12201 Merit Dr, Dallas, TX 75251.

ANDERSON, AL H., JR.
Company executive. **PERSONAL:** Born May 01, 1942, Winston-Salem, NC; son of Albert H Anderson, Sr and Gladys H Anderson; married Jeanette Anderson, Nov 25, 1971; children: April, Albert III. **EDUCATION:** Morehouse Coll, Atlanta, GA, BS, 1964; Georgia State Univ, Atlanta, GA, 1970; Rutgers Univ, Newark, NJ, 1971. **CAREER:** Allstate Insurance Co, Atlanta, underwriter, 1967-68; C&S Natl Bank, Atlanta, loan officer, 1968-70; Citizens Trust Bank, Atlanta, vice pres, 1970-72; Enterprises Now Inc, Atlanta, exec dir, 1971-73; Anderson Communications, Atlanta, pres, 1973-. **ORGANIZATIONS:** Bd mem, Atlanta Business League, 1972-, Cascade Youth Org, 1985-, Hillside Chapel & Truth Center, 1984-88; pres, Natl Assn of Market Developers-Atlanta Chapter, 1979-81; vice pres, Black Public Relations Soc, 1985-87. **HONORS/ACHIEVEMENTS:** Achievement Award, Amer Health & Beauty Aids Inst, 1987; Pioneer Awardl, Jack the Rapper; Billboard Award, Billboard Magazine, 1988; CEBA Award, World Inst of Black Communications, 1988; author, numerous magazine & newspaper articles, 1968-. **BUSINESS ADDRESS:** Pres, Anderson Communications/Media Serv, 2245 Godby Rd, Suite 2000, Atlanta, GA 30349.

ANDERSON, AMEL
Educational administrator. **PERSONAL:** Born Nov 17, 1936, Hazelhurst, MS; children: Kurt, Debra, Reynaldo, Terrence, Robert. **EDUCATION:** Jackson State Univ, BS 1962; Univ of Houston, MS 1969; Va Polytechnic Inst & State Uiv, EdD 1976. **CAREER:** USAF OH, chemist 1969-71; USAF VA Tech & State Univ, asst prof 1971-75; VA Polytechnic Inst State Univ, rsch asst 1975-76; Univ of MD Div of Agricultural & Life Scis, asst to the provost 1976-. **ORGANIZATIONS:** MD Assn of Non-White Concerns in Personnel & Guidance 1980-81; vol instr Receiving Home for Children Washington DC 1977-79; pres Jackson State Univ Alumni Chap 1978-79; pres PTA Happy Acres Elementary School, 1978-80. **HONORS/ACHIEVEMENTS:** Civitan Jackson MS 1960; Graduated w/Honors Jackson State Univ 1962; NSF Fellow Univ of Houston 1967. **MILITARY SERVICE:** USAF capt 1964-75. **BUSINESS ADDRESS:** Assistant Dean, Univ of MD, College of Life Sciences, 1110 Symons Hall, College Park, MD 20742.

ANDERSON, AMELIA VERONICA
Interior designer. **PERSONAL:** Born Mar 13, 1947, New York, NY; daughter of Howard A Anderson and Bernardine Turbee Grissom. **EDUCATION:** Bernard M Baruch Coll, BBA 1969. **CAREER:** Bloomingdales, dept mgr & personnel rep 1967-74; Essence Magazine, dir sales promotion & merchandising 1974-83; Playboy Enterprises Inc, promotion mgr, Games Magazine, 1983-84, promotion mgr, Playboy Magazine, 1985-87; Mary Gilliatt Interiors Ltd, design asst/office mgr, 1987-88; Anderson-Rooke Designs, partner, 1988-. **ORGANIZATIONS:** Mem Advertising Women of New York; mem, Amer Women Entrepreneurs; mem, bd of mgrs, Inwood House, 1979-89. **HONORS/ACHIEVEMENTS:** CEBA Award of Excellence, 1980; Outstanding Achievements in Communications, BESI Inc, 1982; CEBA Award of Merit, 1983; CEBA Award of Excellence, 1983. **BUSINESS ADDRESS:** Partner, Anderson-Rooke Designs, PO Box 6921, New York, NY 10128.

ANDERSON, ARNETT ARTIS
Orthodontist. **PERSONAL:** Born Apr 01, 1931, Georgia; married Delores C Perry; children: Angela C, Andrea C. **EDUCATION:** Savannah State Coll, BS 1953; Howard Univ, grad sch 1955-57; Howard Univ, DDS 1962; Univ of MI, MS 1965. **CAREER:** Inst of Health, nutrition & endocrinology rsch 1956-58; Howard Univ, cardiovascular rsch part-time 1960-62, pedodontics & instr 1962-63; Children's Orthodontic Clinic Livonia MI, dir 1964-65; Howard Univ Coll of Dentistry, assoc prof 1965-69; Private Practice Washington DC, dentist 1966-. **ORGANIZATIONS:** Orthodontic consult for Comm Group Health found St Elizabeth Hosp Washington DC; mem NE Regional Bd of Dental Examiners; DC Bd of Dental Examiners Sec; mem Amer Assn of Orthodontists; Middle Atlantic Soc of Orthodontists; Amer Coll of Dentists; Amer Assn of Dental Examiners; Natl Dental Assn; Amer Dental Assn; Intl Assn of Dental Rsch; Amer Soc of Dentistry for Children; Robt T Freeman Dental Soc; mem SW Neighborhood Assembly; Alpha Phi Alpha Frat. **HONORS/ACHIEVEMENTS:** Best Thesis Awd Univ of MI Sch of Orthodontics, C Edward Martin Awd 1965; 1st Place Intl competition in Dental Rsch Edward H Hetton Awd 1966; Who's Who in the West & SW; nominated to be included in Outstanding Young Men of Amer; Omicron Kappa Upsilon Natl Hon Dental Soc; Sigma Xi Hon Scientific Soc; Beta Kappa Chi; Alpha Kappa Mu. **MILITARY SERVICE:** AUS. **BUSINESS ADDRESS:** 635 G St SW, Washington, DC 20024.

ANDERSON, AVIS OLIVIA
Educator. **PERSONAL:** Born Aug 27, 1949, Vivian, WV; married Weldon Edward Anderson. **EDUCATION:** Bronx Comm Coll, AAS 1970; Herbert H Lehman Coll, BS 1971; Hunter Coll, MS 1973; New York Univ, PhD 1986. **CAREER:** Bronx Comm Coll, coll lab tech 1971-72; Herbert H Lehman Coll, adjunct instructor 1972-73; LaGuardia Comm Coll, full-time instructor 1973-75, asst/assoc/full professor 1975-. **ORGANIZATIONS:** Mem Morrisania Educ Council 1972-; exec bd mem Business Educ Assoc 1978-; pres Coll Business Educators 1981-82; mem Charismatic Prayer Group 1985-; Conf Coordinator SUNY Office Tech/Secretarial Educators 1986-87; 2nd vice pres Business Educ Assoc 1986-87; past pres Gregg Shorthand Teachers Assoc 1986-87. **HONORS/ACHIEVEMENTS:** Outstanding Administrator Morrisania Educ Council 1980; Service Awd Business Educ Assoc 1987. **BUSINESS ADDRESS:** Professor of Business Educ, LaGuardia Community College, 31-10 Thomson Ave, Long Island City, NY 11101.

ANDERSON, BARBARA JENKINS
Physician, educator. **PERSONAL:** Born Nov 21, 1928, Chicago, IL; daughter of Rev Carlyle F Stewart and Alyce Walker Stewart; married Arthur E Anderson, Sep 30, 1972; children: Kevin C Jenkins, Judith Jenkins Kelly, Sharolyn Jenkins Sanders,Marc J Jenkins, Kayla S Jenkins. **EDUCATION:** Univ of MI, BS 1950; Wayne State Med Sch, MD 1957l. **CAREER:** Wayne Co Hosp, 1966-70; Detroit Genl Hosp, dir of clinical lab; Wayne State Med Sch, assoc prof 1970-, staff pathol 1970-. **ORGANIZATIONS:** Mem Wayne Co Med Soc, MI State Med Soc, AMA, Detroit Med Soc, Wolverine Med Soc, Natl Med Soc, Coll of Amer Pathol; Amer Soc of Clinical Pathol; Amer Assn of Blood Banks; MI Assn of Blood Banks; Amer Cytology Assn; MI Cytology Assn; Amer Women's Med Assn; mem Admissions Com Wayne Med Sch; Minority Recruitment Com Wayne Med Sch; Careers Club for HS Students; elected Alpha Omega Alpha 1956. **HONORS/ACHIEVEMENTS:** Alexander McKenzie Campbell Awd 1957; Alpha Omega Alpha 1957. **BUSINESS ADDRESS:** Assoc Professor Pathology/ Director of Clinical Labs, Wayne State Medical School/Detroit Receiving Hospital, 4201 St Antoine, Third floor 3E, Detroit, MI 48201.

ANDERSON, BARBARA LOUISE
Librarian. **PERSONAL:** Born in San Diego, CA. **EDUCATION:** San Diego State Coll, BS 1954; KS State Tchrs Coll, MS in LS 1955. **CAREER:** LA Public Library, br young adult librarian 1956-59; San Diego Pub Libr, ref young adult librarian 1959-64; Serra Regl Library Systems San Diego, ref proj coord 1969-70; Riverside Pub Library, head of reader serv 1971-74; San Bernardino Co Library, dir 1974-. **ORGANIZATIONS:** Mem Amer, CA Library Assns; mem NAACP; Alpha Delta Chi. **MILITARY SERVICE:** AUS 1964-69. **BUSINESS ADDRESS:** Dir, San Bernardino Co Library, 3581 7 St, Riverside, CA 92501.

ANDERSON, BENJAMIN STRATMAN, JR.
Physician. **PERSONAL:** Born Feb 23, 1936, Dothan, AL; son of Benjamin Sutton and Lula Sutton; married Sandra C Wright; children: Benjamin III, Kevin, Carita. **EDUCATION:** Fisk Univ, BS 1957; Meharry Medical Coll, MD 1962; Amer Bd of Family Practice, diplomate 1975, recertified 1981 and 1987; Amer Acad of Family Physicians, fellow 1979. **CAREER:** Polk General Hosp, staff pres 1969-70, 1978-79, 1988-89; GA State Med Assn, exec bd 1973-85; Polk Co Bd of Health, mem 1980-1988; chmn 1985; GA Bd Human Resources, sec 1972-86; medical director, Brentwood Park Nursing Home, 1988-. **ORGANIZATIONS:** Vice speaker House of Delegates GA Acad Family Physicians 1975-77; health serv dir Project Headstart Tallatoona EOA Inc 1974-79; consultant & preceptor Polk Co Primary Care Project 1981-83; consultant/advisor Polk Emergency Medical Serv 1979-87; life mem Kappa Alpha Psi Frat 1970-; life mem NAACP 1975-; adv council Cedartown City Commission 1970-86; bd dirs of Cedartown Little League 1976-85; Cedartown Comm Relations Council 1986; Wayside Inn Alcohol & Drug Residential Rehab Prgm, consultant 1986; board of directors, Georgia Assoc of Minority Entrepreneurs, 1988-. **HONORS/ACHIEVEMENTS:** Service Award Atlanta Medical Assn 1973; Service Award GA State Medical Assn 1975; President's Award GA County Welfare Assn 1982; Northwest Georgia MinorityBusiness Assoc, businessman of the yr 1986; Community Service Commendation, Georgia House of Representatives, 1988. **BUSINESS ADDRESS:** 812 South Main St, P O Box 508, Cedartown, GA 30125.

ANDERSON, BERNARD E.
Educator. **PERSONAL:** Born in Philadelphia, PA; children: Melinda D, Bernard E II. **EDUCATION:** Livingstone Coll, AB; MI State Univ, MA; Univ of PA PhD; Shaw Univ, LHD. **CAREER:** US Bureau of Labor Statistics, economist 1964-66; The Rockefeller Foundation, dir social scis 1979-85; Woodrow Wilson School, Princeton Univ, visiting fellow 1985; Wharton School, Univ of PA, asst to full prof 1970-79, sr economist 1986-. **ORGANIZATIONS:** Mem of bd Philadelphia Urban League 1970-76; mem former pres Natl Economic Assoc 1970-; mem bd NAACP Special Contributions Fund 1976-80; mem bd dirsMDRC Corp 1977-; consultant Ford Foundation and Major Corps 1985-; mem bd of economists Black Enterprise Magazine 1981-; mem Natl Commn Jobs & Small Business 1986. **HONORS/ACHIEVEMENTS:** Publs Black Managers in Amer Business 1980, Youth Employment and Public Policy 1981, "Economic Growth and Social Equity", The Changing Amer Economy 1986; keynote speaker dedication of new NAACP Natl Headquarters 1986. **MILITARY SERVICE:** AUS nco 2 yrs; Honorable Discharge w/Good Conduct Medal. **BUSINESS ADDRESS:** Senior Economist, The Wharton SchUniv of PA, 344 Vance Hall, Philadelphia, PA 19104.

ANDERSON, BRUCE ALLAN
Chief executive officer. **PERSONAL:** Born Nov 14, 1946, Sacramento, CA; married Nancy Van Vleet; children: Bron Charles, Nora Nan Moore. **EDUCATION:** Sacramento City College, AA 1967. **CAREER:** EDS, mgr 1969-74; VISA, dir of new product develop 1974-79; General Elec Consulting Svcs, mktg mgr 1979-83; Anderson Information Mgmt, pres 1984-. **ORGANIZATIONS:** Dir San Mateo Volunteers Bureau 1977-79; vice pres Marin Democratic Club 1982-83; pres Inst for Public Serv 1984-. **HONORS/ACHIEVEMENTS:** Outstanding State Dir CA Jaycees 1969. **BUSINESS ADDRESS:** President, Anderson Information Mgmt, 274 Flagstone, San Rafael, CA 94903.

ANDERSON, BRYAN N.
Business executive. **PERSONAL:** Born Jun 18, 1955, New Haven, CT. **EDUCATION:**

Univ of Connecticut, grad, 1977. **CAREER:** Sen Weicker, staff asst; Virgin Islands Legislative Improvement Project, St Thomas, US Virgin Islands, proj dir; former admin asst to chf dep Minority Leaders, Connecticut state senate; former Harlem mayor; Hamden CT, constable, 1973-80; Pace Advertising, coord of client svcs. **ORGANIZATIONS:** Former bd mem State Bd Higher Educ; dist leader Hamden Rep Town Com; mem Hamden Arts Cncl; Hamden League of Women Voters; mem Ripon Soc Natl Governing Bd. **HONORS/ACHIEVEMENTS:** Hamden Outstanding Youth Awd 1971; Comm Involvement Awd Greater New Haven Urban League 1973. **BUSINESS ADDRESS:** Coordinator of Client Serv, Pace Advertising, Woodbridge, CT.

ANDERSON, CAREY LAINE, JR.
Architect. **PERSONAL:** Born Jan 12, 1950, Louisville, KY; married Karen Elizabeth White; children: Latrice Elizabeth. **EDUCATION:** Univ of KY, BArch 1973. **CAREER:** Arrasmith Judd Rapp & Assoc Architects, architect draftsman 1973-77; Robert F Crump Architects, proj architect 1977-78; City of Louisville Pub Works Dept,city architect 1978-79; Larry E Wright & Assocs Architects, asso/project architect 1979-80; Anderson & Assocs Architects, architect 1980-. **ORGANIZATIONS:** Prog chmn Central KY Chap AIA; mem Construction Specification Inst; mem KY Soc of Architects; mem NAACP; mem Phi Beta Sigma Frat Inc. **HONORS/ACHIEVEMENTS:** First Black Architect License KY 1977; first Black Architect to establish architectural firm KY. **BUSINESS ADDRESS:** Architect, Anderson & Assoc Architects, 736 S First St, Louisville, KY 40202.

ANDERSON, CARL D.
Business executive. **PERSONAL:** Born Mar 27, 1931, Indianapolis, IN; married Sylvia Eaton; children: Steven, David, Michael. **EDUCATION:** Howard Univ, BA 1958; Georgetown Univ Law Sch, attended 1958-59; Amer Univ, attended 1964 1966 1968. **CAREER:** Natl Brewing co, br mgr 1966-68, mkt devel mgr 1968-69; United Way Met Wash DC, campaign dir 1969-72; Natl Urban Coalition, vice pres 1972-78; Media Assoc Inc, pres 1978-. **ORGANIZATIONS:** Local regional sales rep bd mem Ad Club of Metro Wash; Wash Chap Amer Marketing Assn; chmn exec com co-fndr Banneker City Club; past asst treas bd mem chap pres Natl Assn Market Developers; mem Natl Soc of Fund Raisers; Kappa Alpha Psi; adv bd Cromwell Acad; bd dir Triventure Corp; PDRC Intl Inc. **MILITARY SERVICE:** USAF. **HOME ADDRESS:** 1325 Geranium St NW, Washington, DC 20012.

ANDERSON, CARL EDWIN
Education administrator. **PERSONAL:** Born Sep 29, 1934, St Louis, MO; son of Raymond Anderson and Elizabeth Anderson; married Ida Bass; children: Carl Jr, Rhonda L, Sherri L. **EDUCATION:** Souther IL Univ, BA 1956, MS 1958; Univ of MD, EdD 1969. **CAREER:** Howard Univ, dir of student activities 1960-64, assoc dean of students 1964-69, acting dean of students 1969, vice pres for student affairs 1969-. **ORGANIZATIONS:** Bd of dir Amer Assoc of Univ Admin, Southern IL Univ Found, Howard Univ Found; mem Natl Assoc of Student Personnel Admin, Amer Assn for Counseling & Dev, Natl Vice Pres for Student Affairs Org; evaluator Middle States Assoc/Sec Schools & Coll; mem Natl Urban League, NAACP; endowment scholarship fundCommittee Kappa Alpha Psi Frat; Sigma Pi Phi Fraternity (Boule). **HONORS/ACHIEVEMENTS:** Disting Alumni Achievement Award Southern IL Univ 1972; Lamont Lawson Awd for Outstanding Contrib Kappa Alpha Psi Frat 1984; Serv to Southern IL Univ; Admin of the Year Student Council Howard Univ; Phi Delta Kappa Honor Society in Education; Pi Sigma Alpha Honor Society in Political Science; Psi Chi Honor Society in Psychology. **BUSINESS ADDRESS:** Vice Pres Student Affairs, Howard University, 2400 6th St Ste 201, Washington, DC 20059.

ANDERSON, CARLTON LEON
Director (corporate). **PERSONAL:** Born Jan 12, 1942, Ashland, VA. **EDUCATION:** VA State Coll, BA 1963. **CAREER:** Prudential Ins Co, coll relations consult 1972-73, mgr employment & col rel 1973-74, regl group mr 1974-76, sr group ins consult 1976, mgr group claims 1976-78, dir group claims 1978-. **ORGANIZATIONS:** Bd dir/mem Planned Parenthood Fed of Amer 1980. **HONORS/ACHIEVEMENTS:** Outstanding Leader in Bus YM/YWCA Chicago 1977. **MILITARY SERVICE:** AUS capt 1963-70; Bronze Star w/Oak Leaf Clusters; Army Commendation w/Oak Leaf Cluster. **HOME ADDRESS:** 14 Plymouth Ave, Maplewood, NJ 07040.

ANDERSON, CAROL BYRD
Economist, educator, banker. **PERSONAL:** Born Jun 07, 1941, Kansas City, MO; daughter of Hartwell Byrd and Elmira Byrd; married Dr Winston Anthony; children: Laura Elisabeth, Lea Elmira. **EDUCATION:** Coll of St Teresa, BA 1962; Boston Coll, MA 1964, PhD 1969. **CAREER:** Bur Labor Statistics, gen economist 1963-64; Fed Reserve Boston, economist 1969-70; First Natl Bank of Chicago, staff officer 1970-75; Howard Univ Wash, DC, assoc prof 1975-76; Fed Reserve Wash, DC, economist/bd of govs 1976-. **ORGANIZATIONS:** Mem Amer Econ Assn 1960-; Natl Econ Assn 1975-; mem Social Econ 1960-; trustee Coll of St Teresa 1975-81. **HONORS/ACHIEVEMENTS:** Woodrow Wilson Scholarship Award 1962; Outstanding Young People in US 1964; numerous publs 1st Natl Bank of Chicago 1971-73; Award, Chicago Jr C of C 1972. **BUSINESS ADDRESS:** Economist/Bd of Govs, Fed Reserve, 20th Constitution Ave NW, Washington, DC 20551.

ANDERSON, CHESTER R.
Educator, designer, consultant. **PERSONAL:** Born Jan 28, 1912, Weir, KS; married Charlene; children: Ercelle Johnson. **EDUCATION:** Univ of Pittsburg, KS, BS 1934; IA State Univ, MS 1949; Central MI Univ, LLD 1977. **CAREER:** Kansas City, MO Schl System, teacher 1934-68, gen coord voc end 1968-71; Amer Inst of Design & Drafting, consult 1971-. **ORGANIZATIONS:** Pres Ind Art Club & Vocational Educ 1940-50; MO State Disadvantaged and Handicapped Assn pres 1976-77, vice pres 1975-76; mem Pres comm for Disadv & Handicapped Task Force; life mem NAACP; bd of dir Amer Inst for Design and Drafting; chmn awards com Amer Inst for Design and Drafting. **HONORS/ACHIEVEMENTS:** Outstanding Serv Award MO Voc Assn 1977; Outstanding Serv Award MO Cncl for Local Adminstr 1977; Cert of Award Sch of Human Dignity 1977; Alumni Merit Achieve Award Pitts State Univ 1978; Maharishi Award 1980; Award from Friends of KEB Dubois Learning Center; Outstanding Lifetime Contrib to Kansas City, MO from Coca Cola Bottling Co of Mid-Amrica 1984; School Dist of Kansas City Award for Services as Member of Board of Educ 1980-84; Jefferson Award from AmerInst for Publ Serv by WDAFTV Kansas City, 1980; Award for Disting and Devoted Servs to Public Education in MO at 19 Ann Conf for MO School Adminstrs 1980. **BUSINESS ADDRESS:** Consultant, MO Correction Dept, Tulsa, OK.

ANDERSON, DAVID ATLAS
Educator/administrator. **PERSONAL:** Born Apr 28, 1930, Cincinnati, OH; son of Willie David Anderson and Mary Alice Anderson; married Ruth Joanine; children: David M, Kenwood M, Joanine C. **EDUCATION:** Rochester Inst of Tech, BFA 1960; Syracuse Univ, MA 1962; Union Grad School, PhD 1975. **CAREER:** Urban League of Rochester, deputy exec dir 1967-70; State Univ of NY Brockport, lecturer Afro-Amer studies; Rochester Inst of Tech, visiting asst prof 1981-, dir parent educ, Rochester City School District. **ORGANIZATIONS:** Assoc Comm Health Univ of Rochester Medical Sch 1970-82; bd mem vice pres Mental Health Assoc 1980-86; lecturer Correctional Institutions at Sonyea and Oatka NY 1983-85; bd of dirs Rochester Museum & Sci Ctr 1986-90; Natl Assn of Black Storytellers, 1988-89. **HONORS/ACHIEVEMENTS:** Community Leadership Awd Urban League of Rochester 1982; Outstanding Community Serv, Health Assn of Rochester 1984; Distinguished Volunteer, Mental Health Assn Rochester 1986. **MILITARY SERVICE:** USAF staff sgt 6 yrs. **BUSINESS ADDRESS:** Dir Parent Education, Rochester City School District, 131 W Broad St, Rochester, NY 14614.

ANDERSON, DONALD EDWARD
Business executive. **PERSONAL:** Born Nov 19, 1938, Los Angeles, CA; divorced; children: Donald E, Brian. **EDUCATION:** Los Angeles City Coll, 1956-58; UCLA, 1958-59; Western Electronic Inst, 1959-60. **CAREER:** TRW Systems Group, engineering designer 1958-65; Watts Manufacturing Co, manager 1965-68; Audio-Video Communications, Inc, pres 1968-72; Nat'l Cable TV Assoc, dir govt relations 1973-74; Home Box Office, Inc, sr vp. **ORGANIZATIONS:** Nat'l Broadcasting Club, bd of dir 1973-74; Black United Fund, bd of dir 1974; CA Cable TV Assoc, bd mem 1976-; Walter Kaitz FOundation, vice pres and mem of the exec committee 1982-; Los Angeles Urban League, bd of dir 1983-84. **HONORS/ACHIEVEMENTS:** YMCA, named black achiever in business & industry; Participant in Pres Jimmy Carter's Sponsored Prog for Minority Ownership and Control of Media, 1980; Time Inc, Andrew Heiskell awd for distinguished comm serv 1984. **HOME ADDRESS:** Hamilton Terrace, New York, NY 10031. **BUSINESS ADDRESS:** Senior Vice President, Home Box Office, Inc, 1100 Avenue of the Americas, New York, NY 10036.

ANDERSON, DOREATHA MADISON
Human resource. **PERSONAL:** Born Apr 03, 1943, Lynchburg, VA; widowed; children: Wanda M Taylor, Rae M Lamar, Raymond B Madison Jr, Doretha L Madison, Octavia D Madison. **EDUCATION:** VA Seminary Coll, BS 1968; VA Union Univ, BA 1984. **CAREER:** Juvenile Detention Home, youth care worker 1968-82; Bags Unlimited Inc, pres 1982-; NAACP, finance chmn 1982-84; Comm Educ Employment Svcs, prog mgr 1985-86; Youth Development Svcs, prog mgr 1986-. **ORGANIZATIONS:** Mem Diamond Hill Baptist Church 1944-; mem Usher Bd 1975-, Church Aid 1975-; recording sec Daughter Elk Chap 181 IPOEW 1975-82, Eastern Star 1980-82; pres Missionary Circle 1980-; asst treas Variety Garden Club Hill City Chap 1984-; mem Amer Business Women Assoc 1983, United Way 1986, Natl Assoc for Female Exec Inc 1986. **HOME ADDRESS:** 2114 Indian Hill Rd, Lynchburg, VA 24503.

ANDERSON, DORIS J.
Educator, counselor. **PERSONAL:** Born Oct 16, 1933, Reagan, TX; married Franklin D Anderson; children: Deborah, Daryl F, Caleb. **EDUCATION:** BA, 1962; MEd, 1966. **CAREER:** Teacher, 13 yrs; Bastian School, counselor. **ORGANIZATIONS:** Life mem NEA, TSTA; mem TCTA, HTA, APGA, TVGA, ASCA, NVGA, ANWC, TPGA, TACES, HSCA; treas Houston Tchrs Assn 1974-75; pres Houston Sch Counselors Assn 1975; Ct Vol WICS Vol; Sigma Gamma Rho Sor Inc 1962; Phi Delta Kappa 1975; Natl Cncl of Negro Women. **HONORS/ACHIEVEMENTS:** Sigma Woman of Yr 1975; Outstanding Serv Awd Houston Tchrs Assn 1975. **BUSINESS ADDRESS:** Counselor, Bastian School, 1415 Southmore Blvd, Houston, TX 77004.

ANDERSON, EDGAR L.
Educator. **PERSONAL:** Born Sep 24, 1931, New York, NY; married Gloria; children: David, Malcolm, Arnold. **EDUCATION:** AAS, BS, BSN, MS in Health Care Admin. **CAREER:** St Vincent's Med Center, chief nurse/anesthetist/resp care coord, 1967-70; State Univ of NY at Stonybrook, dir respiratory therapy educ, 1970-; School of Allied Health Professions Program, Div of Cardiorespiratory Schools, prof & chmn. **ORGANIZATIONS:** Chmn, App Promotions & Tenure Comm, Health Science Center, State Univ of NY at Stony Brook, 1972-73; bd dir, Amer Assn of Respiratory Therapies, 1973-76; bd dir, chmn, Fed Interagency Comm for AART; Amer Lung Assn, Nassau/Suffolk Counties, NY 1973-; Educ Comm, Amer Soc of Allied Health Prof, 1974-; mem, Amer Regis Resp Therapist 1970; regis professional nurse 1957; cert regis nurse anesthetist 1959; cert hypno-therapist mem, Soc for Critical Care Med, 1974; mem, Task Force Planning Comm, Univ Hosp Stonybrook; consultant, Northport VA Hosp in Resp Care and Anesthesia; natl consultant, cardiorespiratory therapy educ; consultant in hypnotherapy, Stress Center, Huntington NY, 1980-. **HONORS/ACHIEVEMENTS:** Outstanding Educators of Amer 1972 nomination; Cert of Appreciation Coner Day; Bronze Plate from Stony Brook Emergency Med Technicians. **BUSINESS ADDRESS:** Associate Professor & Chairman, State Univ of NY at Stonybrook, School of Allied Health, Stony Brook, NY 11794.

ANDERSON, ELIZABETH M.
Accountant, government official. **PERSONAL:** Born Nov 01, Paris, TX; daughter of Walter Mason and Emma McClure Mason; married Rev Harold Anderson, Oct 03, 1941; children: Andrew Anderson, Patricia Anderson Roper, Theresa Anderson Danzy, Portia Anderson Tucker. **EDUCATION:** Draughon Business Coll, 1955-58; Tulsa Univ, 1969-74. **CAREER:** Oklahoma Tax Commission, Tulsa OK, dir of personnel-supervisor of accounting; Anderson Amusement Corp, Tulsa OK, dir of personnel. **ORGANIZATIONS:** Mem, NAACP Tulsa Chapter, 1949-89; mem, Tulsa Urban League, 1950-89; mem, past pres, Jack & Jill of Amer, Tulsa Chapter, 1952-71, 1984-86; exec bd, Tulsa Pastor's Wives Council; mem, numerous state and city boards & committees; national board, Natl Council of Negro Women, Washington DC; natl council, Assault on Illiteracy, NY City; exec bd, YWCA, Tulsa OK; southern regional dir, Eta Phi Beta Sorority; natl pres, CEO, vice pres, Eta Phi Beta Sorority. **HOME ADDRESS:** 1724 Mohawk Blvd, Tulsa, OK 74110.

ANDERSON, ELLA L.
Educator. **PERSONAL:** Born Jul 04, 1917, Petersburg, VA; divorced; children: Rayfield, Mary C Ireland. **EDUCATION:** WVSC Inst WV, BS, BA; Univ Bridgeport, M 6th yr equivalency. **CAREER:** Bridgeport CT Bd of Educ, teacher. **ORGANIZATIONS:** Past bd mem bd trstees mem Comm Reg Coll; Advsry Cncl Housatnc Comm Coll; Bridgeport Bd Dir Comm Serv; Scholarship Commn State CT; past presNAACP; pres Girlfriends Inc Fairfield Co Chapt; 1st vice pres Cncl Negro Women; pres Les Treize Inc; mem United Jewish Cncl; Col Charles Young Post No 140; New Era Lodge No 291 BPOEW; bd trst Reg Comm Coll; Intrdnml Minstrl All; Doric Lodge 4 F&AM PHA. **HONORS/ACHIEVEMENTS:** Bridgeport NAACP Sojourner Truth Awd Natl Assn Negro Bus & Professional Women Club.

ANDERSON, ELOISE B. MCMORRIS
Educator. **PERSONAL:** Born Jan 26, Columbus, OH; divorced; children: Juanita B. **EDUCATION:** OH State Univ, BS 1943; Wayne State Univ, MEd 1947, EdD 1973. **CAREER:** Cleveland Jr High School, teacher 1944-63, exact sci dept head 1963-65; Western High School, Detroit MI, sci dept head 1965-70; Cass Tech High School, Detroit MI, asst principal 1970-; Denby High School, Detroit MI, principal 1983-84; Murray Wright High School, Detroit MI, principal 1984-. **ORGANIZATIONS:** Pres bd dir Detroit Teachers Credit Union; life mem Delta Sigma Theta; past mem bd of dir Afro-Amer Mus Detroit; Bethel AME Church; bd mem met Detroit Alliance of Black School Ed; life mem Natl Sci Teachers Assoc, Natl Alliance Black School Ed; bd dir Wayne State Univ Alumni Assoc; mem Natl & MI Assoc Secondary School Principal, Natl & MI Assoc for Suprv & Curriculum Devel, Professional Womens Network, Org School Admin & Suprv. **HONORS/ACHIEVEMENTS:** Anthony Wayne Awd Wayne State Univ 1979. **BUSINESS ADDRESS:** Principal, Murray-Wright HS, 2001 W Warren Ave, Detroit, MI 48208.

ANDERSON, EUGENE
Government official, company executive. **PERSONAL:** Born Mar 09, 1944, Diffee, GA; son of Velver Anderson Sr and Velma Anderson; married Mamie Jewel Sapp, Dec 03, 1966; children: Timothy E, Tamara E, Melanie J. **EDUCATION:** Wichita Tech Inst, radio, telephone communications 1971. **CAREER:** State of KS, state rep 1973-76; Congressman Dan Glickman, dist aide 1976-78; KS Commiss on Civil Rights, chairperson 1979-83; Black Democratic Caucus of KS, sec 1982-85; Rollin' & Smokin' Bar-B-Que Hut, owner/operator; KS Legislature, senator. **ORGANIZATIONS:** Pres Optimist Club of Northeast Wichita 1974-75; treas State Democratic Party KS 1985-87; mem Masonic Lodge, NAACP; ranking minority mem Fed & State Affairs; mem Confirmations Comm, Ed Comm, Public Health & Welfare Comm, Midwestern Conf of the Council of State Govts, Adv Council on Aging, Legislative Ed Planning Comm. **HONORS/ACHIEVEMENTS:** Community Serv Award Police Neighborhood Serv Center 1976; Coach of the Year Award The Salvation Army Biddy Basketball Program 1983. **MILITARY SERVICE:** AUS sp5 1962-65, Parachutist Badge. **HOME ADDRESS:** 1832 N Poplar, Wichita, KS 67214. **BUSINESS ADDRESS:** Owner, Rollin' & Smokin' Bar-B-Que Hut, 449 N St Francis, Wichita, KS 67214.

ANDERSON, FELIX SYLVESTER
Clergyman. **PERSONAL:** Born Oct 03, 1893, Wilmington, NC; married Bessie B Bezzell; children: Felix Sylvester Jr, Bishop Herman Leroy, Mrs Wright Robinson, Joseph D, Theodore M, Mrs Alfred Helena Haney. **EDUCATION:** Livingstone Coll, AB 1920; Hood Theol Sem, student 1920-21; Western Tehol Sem, attended 1922-24. **CAREER:** Ordained to AME Zion Ch Ministry; State of NC, pastor 1915-60; PW Moore HS Elizabeth City, tchr 1929-31; AME Zion Connection, bishop. **ORGANIZATIONS:** Pres Mobile Civic Orgn 1942-48; Louisville Civic Orgn chmn 1950-54; mem KY House of Rep 1954-60; life mem NAACP; KY Tchrs Assn; KY Fraternal Police Officers. **HONORS/ACHIEVEMENTS:** KY Genl Assn AME Zion Ministerial Alliance Plaque for Serv 1954-58.

ANDERSON, GARY
Professional athlete. **PERSONAL:** Born Apr 18, 1961, Columbia, MO; married Ollie; children: Antisha, Gary Jr. **EDUCATION:** Attended, Arkansas. **CAREER:** San Diego Chargers, running back/wide receiver 1983-. **HONORS/ACHIEVEMENTS:** Named MVP in three bowl games in coll career; named second team all-USFL by Coll and Pro Football Newsweekly 1984; all-Rookie first team honors from UPI, Football Digest and Pro Football Writers; mem 1987 Pro Bowl team. **BUSINESS ADDRESS:** San Diego Chargers, San Diego Stadium, PO Box 20666, San Diego, CA 92120.

ANDERSON, GEORGE A.
Business executive. **PERSONAL:** Born Nov 15, 1923, Chicago, IL; children: George Jr. **EDUCATION:** Attended, Howard Univ, Roosevelt Univ, Central YMCA Coll in Chicago. **CAREER:** Draper & Kramer, former branch office mgr; Lake Meadows Apts Chicago, mgr; Draper & Kramer Inc, vice pres. **ORGANIZATIONS:** Mem Chicago Real Estate Bd; Natl Real Estate Bd; Inst of Real Estate mgmt; Apt Bldg Owners & Mgrs Assn; South Side Planning Bd; supports LaRabida Children's Hosp, Jane Dent Home for the Aged. **BUSINESS ADDRESS:** Vice President, Draper & Kramer Inc, 500 E 33 St, Chicago, IL 60616.

ANDERSON, GLORIA L.
Educator. **PERSONAL:** Born Nov 05, 1938, Altheimer, AR; daughter of Charley Long (deceased) and Elsie Foggie Long (deceased); divorced; children: Gerald L. **EDUCATION:** AR AM&N Coll, BS 1958; Atlanta Univ, MS 1961; Univ of Chicago, PhD 1968. **CAREER:** SC State Coll, instr 1961-62; Morehouse Coll, instr 1962-64; Univ of Chicago, teaching & rsch asst 1964-68; SC State Coll, prof summer sch 1967; Lockheed GA Corp, NSF rsch fellow 1981, rsch consultant 1982; Air Force Rocket Propulsion Lab, SCEEE faculty rsch fellow 1984; Morris Brown Coll, assoc prof & chmn 1968-73; Callaway prof & chmn 1973-84; acting vice pres for academic affairs 1984-85, dean of academic affairs 1985-. **ORGANIZATIONS:** Mem, American Institute of Chemists, Amer Chem Soc, GA Acad of Sci, NY Acad of Sci, Amer Assn for Advancement of Sci, Natl Sci Tchrs Assn, Amer Assn of Univ Profs, Delta Sigma Theta Sor Inc, Natl Inst of Sci, Atlanta Univ Sci Rsch Inst, Natl Assn of Educ Broadcasters; mem of numerous adv bd comms & special projects; mem NAACP; author of numerous scientific publications; educ consultant US Dept of Educ 1976-88; mem ad hoc tech review group Natl Cancer Inst 1986. **HONORS/ACHIEVEMENTS:** Alpha Kappa Mu Natl Honor Soc; Beta Kappa Chi Sci Honor Soc; Alpha Kappa Mu Honor Trophy Coll All Expense Scholarship Highest Average in Freshman Class 1955; appointed by Pres Nixon mem of bd Corp for Pub Broadcasting 1972; honored by Atlanta Chap AR AM&N Coll Natl Alumni Assn 1973; honored by Atlanta Chap Delta Sigma Theta Sor Inc as one of 25 Atlanta Deltas "Breaking New Ground" 1974; Fellow Mem Amer Biographical Inst 1977; governor's appointee Public Telecommunications Task Force 1980; Atlanta Magazine "Atlanta's Best and Brightest Scientists," 1983; Arkansan of Achievement in Educ 1985; United Negro Coll Fund Distinguished Scholar 1985; NAFEO Natl Alumni Awd 1986; All-Star Excellence in Educ Award, Univ of Arkansas at Pline Bluff Alumni, 1987; 30 other honors and awards. **BUSINESS ADDRESS:** Dean of Academic Affairs, Morris Brown Coll, 643 Martin Luther King Jr Dr, Atlanta, GA 30314.

ANDERSON, GRADY LEE
Educator. **PERSONAL:** Born Dec 01, 1931, Ashby, AL; married Verna Frances Golson; children: Grady Marquis, Verma Celeste. **EDUCATION:** AL State Univ, BS 1956, MEd 1958; Univ of GA Athens, EdD (first black) 1968. **CAREER:** Montgomery Co Sch, tchr/counselor/prin 1956-61; Atlanta Bd of Educ, resource counselor 1962-66; Atlanta Public Sch, coord of testing 1968-69; GA State Univ, asst prof/assoc prof/1st Black dept head 1969-73; GA State Univ Atlanta, 1st black assoc dean/prof 1973-. **ORGANIZATIONS:** Past pres GA Personnel & Guidance Assn 1968-69; vis lectr Atlanta Univ 1968-73; chmn Comm Coord Child Care Atlanta 1973-75; trustee Eckerd Coll 1978; mem Alpha Kappa Mu, Alpha Phi Alpha, Phi Delta Kappa, Kappa Delta Pi, Frontiers Intl, NAACP; mem Amer Personnel & Guidance Assn. **MILITARY SERVICE:** USAF a/2c 1950-54. **BUSINESS ADDRESS:** Associate Dean & Professor, GA StateUniv, University Plaza, Atlanta, GA 30303.

ANDERSON, GRANVILLE SCOTT
Educational administrator. **PERSONAL:** Born Jul 25, 1947, Honolulu, HI; married Jennifer S Kato. **EDUCATION:** Queensborough Comm Coll, AAS 1971; Ruskin Coll, cert 1970; Queens Coll BA 1972. **CAREER:** City Univ, exec asst, 1972-82; CCNY, exec officer, 1982-87; Rsch Found, CUNY proj coordinator, 1987-. **ORGANIZATIONS:** Mem Univ Chancellor's Scholarship to Study in the UK 1969-70; Oscar Wilde Speaker's Tour to Belfast No Ireland 1969; administrator CUNY Pamela S Galiber Scholarship Fund 1976-86; mem exec bd Metro Squash Racquets Assoc 1977-80; Sports Management Consultant 1977-; chmn Referees Comm MSRA 1978; pres Queensborough Comm Coll Alumni Assoc 1979-86; squash professional Town Squash Inc 1980-. **HONORS/ACHIEVEMENTS:** John F Kennedy Award 1968; Nationally ranked amateur squash player US Squash Racquets Assoc. **HOME ADDRESS:** 218 East Fifth St, New York, NY 10003.

ANDERSON, HAROLD
Manager. **PERSONAL:** Born Oct 12, 1939, New York, NY; married Alice Campbell; children: Joi, Dwight. **EDUCATION:** Morehouse Coll, 1961-63; Queens Coll, BA 1966; NYU, 1967-69. **CAREER:** NY Life Ins Co, pub rel asst 1967-69; Interracial Cncl for Bus Oprt, dir pub rel 1969-70; ITT News Serv, writer 1970-74; ITT News & Pub Aff, admin 1974-76; ITT, mgr pub affairs 1977-86; Schomburg Ctr for Rsch in Black Culture NY Public Library, public relations officer 1986-. **ORGANIZATIONS:** Former bd mem Provide Addict Care Today; Rutgers Minority Invest Co; CCBE; Harlem Consumers Educ Cncl Inc; mem Natl Urban Affairs Cncl; Pub Rel Socof Amer; 100 Black Men; OIC NY Tech Adv Com; mem Nigerian/Amer Friendship Soc; visiting prof Natl Urban League Black Exec Exch Prgm Coord; Youth Motivation Task Force Living Witness Prgm; conslt Natl Urban League; Coll Awareness Prgm Black Achiever ITT 1976; bd mem Harlem YMCA of Greater NY. **HONORS/ACHIEVEMENTS:** Hon YMCA Black Achiever in Indus; Citations US Dept of Treas; Dillard Univ Louise Wise Services' Save our Schlrshp Com; Former prof singer, rec artist& song writer. **BUSINESS ADDRESS:** Public Relations Officer, NY Public Library Schomburg, Ctr for Rsch in Black Culture, 515 Lenox Ave, New York, NY 10037.

ANDERSON, HELEN LOUISE
Retail executive. **PERSONAL:** Born Feb 16, 1940, Luxora, AR; daughter of Ruby Lee Nunn. **EDUCATION:** Attended, Syracuse Univ, 1959-61, Fashion Inst of Tech 1965-67. **CAREER:** Eastern Airlines, flight attendant 1965-67; Fashion Barn, exec vice pres 1967-88, Anderson & Associates, pres. **ORGANIZATIONS:** Dir Fred J Rogers Foundation; mem Princess Grace Foundation, Exec Women of NJ, Coalition of 100 Black Women, Cornell Univ Medical Sch Comm for the Benefit of Minority Students; elected bd of dirs Fashion Barn 1987-; Network Support Group. **HONORS/ACHIEVEMENTS:** Twin Awd Natl Bd of the YWCA 1986. **BUSINESS ADDRESS:** President, Anderson & Associates, 1412 Broadway, New York, NY.

ANDERSON, J. MORRIS
TV producer, publisher, entrepreneur. **PERSONAL:** Born Jul 06, 1936, Greenville, SC; divorced; children: J Morris Jr, Gracelyn, Aleta, Kathy. **EDUCATION:** Amer Univ, BA 1961. **CAREER:** Miss Black Amer Beauty Pageant, Little Miss Black Amer, Tiny Miss Black Amer, Miss Black Am Teenager, Ms Black Amer, Mrs Black Amer, Miss Third World, founder/exec producer. **ORGANIZATIONS:** Pres Success Seekers Seminar; chmn & fndr Black Amer Radio & TV Network; chmn Miss Black Amer Beauty Ctrs; exec dir Rehab Inst of Amer; fndr J Morris Anderson Assn Investments Stocks & Bonds; mem Omega Psi Phi; bd mem several public orgns. **HONORS/ACHIEVEMENTS:** Author "Recipes for Black Togetherness", "The Seeds of Positivity", "The Secrets of Mind Control" Vol 1-12; received over 50 awds & citations. **BUSINESS ADDRESS:** Executive Producer, Ms Black Amer Beauty Pageant, 24 W Chelten Ave, Philadelphia, PA 19164.

ANDERSON, JACQUELINE JONES
Health care director. **PERSONAL:** Born Jul 13, 1935, Hartford, CT; divorced; children: Wilfred III, Gregory, Kevin, Kyle. **EDUCATION:** Art Inst Inc, 1959-61; Prince Reg Tech Sch, AI 1965-66; Univ of Hartford, 1966-71; Hartford Coll for Women, Cert 1971; SEDFRE, Cert 1972. **CAREER:** Anderson and Johnson Real, co-owner, 1960-62; Neighborhood Youth Corps, field staff sec, 1966-68, dep dir, Comm Renewal Team 1966-69, office mgr 1967-68; Hartford Hosp, dir health care dept, 1969-. **ORGANIZATIONS:** City councilwoman 1975-; bd of dir Ambul Health Care Plan Inc 1970-71; mem Amer Pub Health Assn 1969-; resour person Commun Health Serv Inc 1972-; steering comm mem Concerned Citizens for Health 1971-; pat edu comm CT Hosp Assn 1973-74; bd dir CT Pub Health Assn 1972-; mem CT Stroke Prog 1972-75; mem Drugs-Blue Hills Clin Task Force 1972-73; bd mem Get the Lead Out 1974-; task force Greater Hartford Councl on Alcohol and Drugs Inc 1973-; mem Mayor's Health Serv Comm 1973-; mem New Eng Pub Health Assn 1970-; bd dir PIT I Drugs 1972-; resource pers Plann Parenthood 1972-; bd dir TACT 1973-; mem Allian of Black Soc Workers 1971-; mem Black Caucus; mem Comm Councl 1973-; bd trustees Commun Renew Team of Hartford 1971-; Just of Peace Hartford Cnty 1972-; bd dir YMCA 1973-; consult Bd of Educ & Commun Renewal Team 1973; bd dir Child Guid Center 1974-; bd dir vice

chmn CONNTAC 1970-; resource pers Hartford Assn for Retarded Children 1972-74; resource pers Hartford Coll for Women 1970-74; chmn HEW Comm Proj STAR 1970-73. **HONORS/ACHIEVEMENTS:** CRT-Merit Award 1972; Univ of HHD Award 1974; W Ind Humanitarian Award 1975; UACO-Merit Award 1975. **BUSINESS ADDRESS:** Director, Health Care Dept, Hartford Hosp, 80 Seymour St, Hartford, CT 06115.

ANDERSON, JAMES ALAN
Educator. **PERSONAL:** Born Dec 13, 1948, Washington, DC. **EDUCATION:** Villanova Univ, BA 1970; Cornell Univ, PhD 1980. **CAREER:** Xavier Univ, asst prof of psychology 1976-80, chmn dept of psychology and assoc prof of psychology 1980-83; Indiana Univ of PA, assoc prof of psych 1983-87; prof of psych, 1987-. **ORGANIZATIONS:** Mem Assn of Black Psychologists 1982-, Assn of Black Women in Higher Educ 1983-, Amer Federation of Teachers 1983-; dir Benjamin E Mays Acad of Scholars IUP 1985-; editor Benjamin E Mays Acad of Scholars Monograph Series 1986-; American Psychological Society; National Assn of Developmental Education. **HONORS/ACHIEVEMENTS:** Grant to Develop Rsch Modules in Psychology Natl Sci Foundation 1976; Danforth Fellow 1980; grant Cross-Cultural Rsch Dillard Univ 1982; Rsch Travel Awd Intl Congress of Psychology 1984; Distinguished Black Alumni, Villanova Univ, 1987; Distinguished Black Pennsylvanian, 1988. **BUSINESS ADDRESS:** Prof of Psychology, IndianaUniv of PA, Dept of Pyschology, Clark Hall, Indiana, PA 15705.

ANDERSON, JAMES R., JR.
Educator. **PERSONAL:** Born Feb 25, 1922, Brazil, IN; son of James R Anderson and Eva Roberts Anderson; married Fern Gabenez Turner; children: James III, Reginald H, Stephen E, Pamela S, Carla J. **EDUCATION:** Indiana Univ, BS Soc Serv 1952, AM Soc Serv 1954; Michigan School of Public Health, attended 1965-68. **CAREER:** Indiana State Dept of Public Welfare, child welfare consultant 1954-55; VA Hospital Indianapolis, clinical social worker 1955-60; VA Hosp Dearborn MI, chief inpatient sect social serv 1960-61; Wayne State Univ School of Social Work, asst prof 1961-63, assoc prof 1963-68, asst to the dean for health scis & coord health care concentration, adj assoc prof health serv school of public health & comm med; Univ of Washington, assoc prof school of social work 1968-. **ORGANIZATIONS:** Consultant Multiple Sclerosis Soc King Co 1976-; mem adv com AMSA Found Interdisciplinary Team Proj 1977-79; consult ID Migrant Health Council 1979-; mem bd dir, pres, vice pres, Seattle Urban League 1971-73; mem adv com Midwifery Proj Health Coop of Puget Sound 1979-. **MILITARY SERVICE:** AAF t/sgt 1941-45; ETO Ribbon w/9 clusters. **HOME ADDRESS:** 12019 NE 67th St, Kirkland, WA 98033. **BUSINESS ADDRESS:** Associate Professor, Univ of WA, School of Social Work, Seattle, WA 98195.

ANDERSON, JANICE SCOTT
President/CEO. **PERSONAL:** Born Apr 22, 1949, Magnolia, MS; children: James Patrick, Christopher Scott. **EDUCATION:** Millsaps Coll, BA 1970; Univ of WI-Madison, MA 1972, MA 1974, PhD 1981. **CAREER:** WISN AM Radio, news analyst 1974-76; City of Milwaukee, writer 1975-76; Mayor Henry W Maier City Hall, staff consultant 1976-84; The Business Journal, columnist 1985-; HealthReach, president/ceo. **ORGANIZATIONS:** Founder/pres Reach for the Stars; pres Milwaukee County Mental Health Assoc; bd dirs YMCA of Greater Milwaukee, Leukemia Soc of WI, United Cerebral Palsy, Goals for Greater Milwaukee 2000; mem Sojourner Truth House, Amer Mgmt Assoc, WI Health Maint Organizations Assoc, Speech Comm Assoc of Amer, Milwaukee Press Club, Milwaukee Chap NAACP. **HONORS/ACHIEVEMENTS:** Headliner Awd Women in Communications 1986; "Just Between Us" Essence Magazine 1986; "In the News" Black Enterprise Magazine 1986; Readers Digest 1986; Hospital's Magazine 1986; Jet Magazine 1986; ABC's Good Morning America 1986; The '86 Most interesting People in Milwaukee, Milwaukee Magazine 1986; "Esquire Register" Esquire Magazine 1986.

ANDERSON, JAY ROSAMOND
Dentist/administrator. **PERSONAL:** Born Jan 06, 1953, Louisville, KY; married Katrina Kendrick; children: Tamika Laurie, Jay Rosamond Jr. **EDUCATION:** Centre Coll of KY, BS 1974; Univ of KY Coll of Dentistry, DMD 1978. **CAREER:** Louisville Chap Operation PUSH, chmn bd of dirs 1979-80; Louisville Chap NAACP, chmn health & welfare 1983-87; Falls City Medical Soc, vice pres 1985-87; Eritrean Relief Comm, adv comm 1987; Park DuValle Comm Health Ctr, dental dept dir. **ORGANIZATIONS:** Mem Alpha Phi Alpha Frat, Natl Dental Assoc; adjunct clinical instructor Univ of Louisville Dental Sch 1981-86. **BUSINESS ADDRESS:** Dental Dept Dir, Park Duvalle Comm Hlth Ctr, 1817 S 34th St, Louisville, KY 40211.

ANDERSON, JOHN A.
Radiologist. **PERSONAL:** Born Mar 09, 1937, Gary, WV; married Emilie Curtis; children: 3 children. **EDUCATION:** Univ of Chicago, BS 1958; Howard Univ Coll of Medicine, MS 1962; Howard Univ, AOA; UFAF Hosp Wright Patterson AFB, internship 1962-63; Wilford Hall USAF Med Ctr Lackland AFB TX, residency radiology 1965-68. **CAREER:** Davis-Monthan USAF Hosp Tucson, chief radiology 1963-65; Amer Bd Radiology, diplomat 1968; USAF Western Region, consult radiology 1968-71; David Grant USAF Med Ctr Travis AFB, radiologist & dir of educ dept of radiology 1968-71; Boulevard Genl Hosp Sumby Hosp, SW Detroit Hosp, radiologist 1971-; SW DetroitHosp, med consult in ambulatory care 1974; Goodwin Ervin & Assoc, radiologist; Highland Park Genl Hosp, ch radiology 1974-. **ORGANIZATIONS:** Med dir Model Neighborhood Total Health Care Inc 1974-; pres & fndr SW Medical Assoc Inc 1973-74; vestry man Grace Episcopal Ch Fairfield CA 1970-71;vice pres Ctr Sch PTA Fairfield 1969-70; sec treas Gesu Bus Com 1974-; vestryman All Saints Episcopal Ch Detroit 1974-. **MILITARY SERVICE:** USAFMC major 1961-71; Air Force Commendation Medal 1968. **BUSINESS ADDRESS:** Chief of Radiology, Highland Park Genl Hosp, 2401 20 St, Detroit, MI 48216.

ANDERSON, JOHN C., JR.
Retired probation officer. **PERSONAL:** Born Aug 12, 1917, Dwiggins, MS; married Celestyne L; children: Corrie Reginald. **EDUCATION:** Univ of Toledo, Toldeo OH, AB, 1940; Golden Gate Law Sch, LLB, 1953; Univ of California, post doctoral studies. **CAREER:** Civil Service, LeCarne OH, fed employee, 1941; Golden Gate Mutual Ins Co, 1946-47; Civil Service, Oakland CA, fed employee, 1946-52; Naval Supply Ctr, Oakland CA, 1952-53; Alameda Co Probation Dept, sr dep probation officer, 1953-. **ORGANIZATIONS:** Bd trustees Peralta Comm Coll Dist 1971-; bd trustees Beth Eden Bapt Ch; adv com Oakland Workshop for the Mentally Retarded; past pres Beth Eden Housing Inc; mem Omega Psi Phi Frat; mem Monarch #73 Prince Hall Masons; mem Bay Area Urban League; mem Oakland Br NAACP. **HONORS/ACHIEVEMENTS:** Men of Tomorrow, Oakland Man of Yr Beth Eden Bapt Ch 1962; Omega Cit of Yr Sigma Iota Chap Omega Psi Phi 1971. **MILITARY SERVICE:** OH NG pvt 1938-40; AUS m/sgt 1942-46.

ANDERSON, KATHLEEN WILEY
Government official. **PERSONAL:** Born May 22, 1932, Kansas City, KS; married Harvey L Anderson (deceased); children: Harvey, H Delon, Doryanna. **EDUCATION:** Univ of Kansas, Lawrence KS, BS, 1954, MS, 1955; Univ of Southern California, MPA, 1974; attended Wharton School, Univ of Pennsylvania, 1979. **CAREER:** Kansas City, hs tchr, 1954-56; Sch for the Deaf, tchr, 1958-63; California Inst for Women, adminstr, 1963-74; Correctional Training Facility, assoc supt act dep supt, 1974-76; California Inst for Women, supt, 1976-80; California Inst for Men, superintendent. **ORGANIZATIONS:** Mem United Black Correctional Workers Assn; CA Black Correctional Coalition; NAACP; Amer Correctional Assn; mem Alpha Kappa Alpha Sor; Eastern Star; Links Inc; guest instructor Simon Fraser Univ Banbury British Columbia, Wharton School; instructor Intl Women in Corrections. **HONORS/ACHIEVEMENTS:** Ombudsman type prog Ford Found Fellowship Fisk Univ, Univ of KS 1948-55; Ina B Temple Fellowship Univ of KS; 1st female correctional adminstr in male facility; 1st black woman correctional supr 1 in CA; listed Women in Corrections; listed in Book of Honors 1977-87, 2000 Notable Women 1977-87. **BUSINESS ADDRESS:** Superintendent, CA Inst for Men, PO Box 128, Chino, CA 91710.

ANDERSON, KENNETH RICHARD
Electrical engineer. **PERSONAL:** Born Aug 04, 1936, Philadelphia, PA; son of William and Dorothy; married Dorothy, Apr 17, 1987; children: Pamela, Veronica. **EDUCATION:** Drexel Univ, BSEE 1968; Central MI Univ, MA BA 1975. **CAREER:** Inselek, mgr test eng 1971-75; Aeroneutronic Ford, super comp engrg 1975-76; RCA Government Systems Div, mgr rel & test 1976-79; Siemens RTL, mgr IC design & test strategic planning, analysis & design of mfg syst. **ORGANIZATIONS:** Bd mem Willingboro Sch Dist 1971-74; governing bd IEEE Computer Soc 1979-; adjunct prof Widener Univ 1982-; 2nd vice pres & chmn Technical Activities Computer Society of IEEE 1987; president IEEE Computer Society, 1988-90. **HONORS/ACHIEVEMENTS:** Outstanding Young Men of America 1971/72; Distinguished Service Award US Jaycees 1972; Computer Soc Meritorious Service Awards 1981-85. **MILITARY SERVICE:** AUS specialist 4, 2 yrs. **HOME ADDRESS:** 158 Camber Lane, Mount Laurel, NJ 08054. **BUSINESS ADDRESS:** Manager of IC Design & Testing, SMTS, Siemens Corporate Research, 755 College Rd E, Princeton, NJ 08540.

ANDERSON, LEON H.
Corporate director. **PERSONAL:** Born Sep 22, 1928, Jacksonville, FL; married Mary T Taylor; children: Lisa, Leon R, Leah, Lori. **EDUCATION:** Morris Coll, BA 1956; Columbia Univ, M Pub Admin 1963. **CAREER:** Corbett HS, tchr 1956-58; Morris Coll, tchr 1958; Saltertown Elem Sch, prin 1958-61; Morris Coll, Tchr 1958; Saltertown Elem Sch, prin 1958-61; Morris Coll, tchr 1959; Moore Elem Sch, prin 1961-64; Ninth Ave HS, prin 1964-65; Los Pinos Job Corps Ctr Cleveland Natl Forest, dep dir for educ 1964-65; USDA Forest Serv San Fran, educ spec 1965-69; USDA Forest Serv Wash, educ spec 1969-70; USDA MO, liaison ofcr 1970-72; Human Resource Prog USDA,asst dir 1972-74; USDA Human Resources Prog Wash, dir 1974-. **ORGANIZATIONS:** Helped to develop a curriculum of therapeutic educ for a non-profit corp Assn for the Treatment of Troubled & Underachieving Children So CA 1969. **HONORS/ACHIEVEMENTS:** Cum Laude Morris Coll 1953; Who's Who in Amer Colls & Univs 1953; Superior Serv Awd USDA 1972; Superior Serv Awd Lincoln Univ 1974. **MILITARY SERVICE:** AUS corpl 3 yrs. **HOME ADDRESS:** 12320 Millstream dr, Bowie, MD 20715.

ANDERSON, LOUISE PAYNE
Educator. **PERSONAL:** Born Oct 18, 1923, West Virginia; widowed; children: Patricia, Cheryl. **EDUCATION:** Bluefield State Coll, BS 1945; WV Coll, MA; WV Univ, grad study. **CAREER:** Pentagon, sec 1946; Kanawha County Schools, teacher 1947-. **ORGANIZATIONS:** Mem NEA; WV Educ Assn; NEA Black Caucus; WVEA Black Caucus; sec Kanawha Co Educ Assn 1974-78; clk Bethel Bapt Ch 1955-; dir of youth Mt Olive DistAssn; WV BaptState Conv; chmn WVEA Human Relat Comm 1974-76; vice pres WV Br NAACP; mem Alpha Kappa Alpha Sor Inc 1943; Delta Kappa Gamma 1972; Natl Assn of Univ Women 1973.

ANDERSON, MADELINE
Producer, director. **PERSONAL:** Born in Lancaster, PA; daughter of William Whedbee and Nellie Whedbee; married Ralph Joseph Anderson; children: Adele, Rachel, Laura, Ralph Jr. **EDUCATION:** NY Univ, BA 1956. **CAREER:** Onyx Prod, pres 1975-; Infinity Factory Educ Devel Ctr, exec producer 1976-77; Children's TV Workshop, supervising editor prod dir 1971-75,TV producer/intl,1985-87. **ORGANIZATIONS:** Board of trustees, Intern Film Seminars, 1974-77; film panelist, NY State Cncl for the Arts 1975-79; mem Natl Acad TV Arts & Sci; board of Women Make Movies, 1986-. **HONORS/ACHIEVEMENTS:** Woman of the Yr Sojourner Truth Festival of the Arts 1976; Grand Prize Film "I Am Somebody" Media Women 1977; Grants NYSCA WNET Documentary Fund NEA & AFI; producer for "Al Manaahil" a literacy series for arabic children in the Middle East produced by the Children's TV Workshop working in Amman Jordan 1985-; Indie Awd 1985; Lifelong Achievement Awd from AIVF. **HOME ADDRESS:** 83 Sterling St, Brooklyn, NY 11225.

ANDERSON, MARCELLUS J., SR.
Business executive. **PERSONAL:** Born Jun 21, 1908, Anderson, SC; son of Edward Anderson; married Ada; children: Sandra Joy, Marcellus, Jr. **EDUCATION:** OH State Univ, AB; London Coll of Applied Sci England, doctor humane rel. **CAREER:** Livingstone Coll, Samuel Huston Coll, Huston-Tillotson Coll, former teacher; Pan TX Mortgage Invest Co Austin, TX, pres. **ORGANIZATIONS:** Pres Fedn of Masons of the World; dir comm Natl Bank of Austin; dir United Mortgage Bankers of Amer Inc. **BUSINESS ADDRESS:** President, Pan TX Mortgage Invest Co, 3724 Airport Blvd, Austin, TX 78722.

ANDERSON, MARCUS JACKSON
Professional athlete. **PERSONAL:** Born Jun 12, 1959, Port Arthur, TX. **EDUCATION:** Tulane Univ, Phy Ed 1983. **CAREER:** Memphis Showboats, wide rec 1984-; Chicago Blitz, wide rec 1984; Chicago Bears, wide rec; Detroit Lions, wide rec; LA Rams, wide rec. **HONORS/ACHIEVEMENTS:** Played with Chicago Blitz in 1984 and was teams's No 1 Rec with

46 catches 906 yards; set tulane rec for longest catch; participated in Liberty Bowls against Penn State; competed in 1980 Hall of Fame Bowl. **BUSINESS ADDRESS:** Memphis Showboats, 3767 New Getwell Rd, Ste 400, Memphis, TN 38118.

ANDERSON, MARIAN
Contralto. **PERSONAL:** Born Feb 27, 1902, Philadelphia, PA; married Orpheus H Fisher. **EDUCATION:** Private music educ in Philadelphia, New York & abroad; hon degrees from 24 Amer educ institutions and 1 Korean institution; Spellman Coll, degree 1979. **CAREER:** Began singing as child in Union Baptist Church Choir Philadelphia; began career 1924; debut in Un Ballo in Maschera Metropolitan Opera 1955; numerous US & European concert tours; US Delegate to UN 1955. **ORGANIZATIONS:** Mem Alpha Kappa Alpha; US delegate 13th Gen Assembly. **HONORS/ACHIEVEMENTS:** First prize at NY Lewisohn Stadium 1925; Bok Awd 1940; Finnish decoration "Probenignitate Humana" 1940; decorations from numerous US states & cities and from Sweden, Philippines, Haiti, Liberia, France; Yokus Lo Medal (Japan); first prize in competition with 300 others Lewisohn; author "My Lord What A Morning.". **HOME ADDRESS:** Danbury, CT 06810.

ANDERSON, MARJORIE
Public relations director. **PERSONAL:** Born Apr 10, Detroit, MI. **EDUCATION:** Univ of Detroit, BBA. **CAREER:** US Govt, EEO counselor, staff adv; D-Sace Charm Sch Comm, pub rel; Urban League Youth Assemb, pub rel dir; St Paul's Ch, pub rel dir; Afboney Mod & Fin Sch, pub rel dir; CANAC, pub rel dir. **ORGANIZATIONS:** Bd mem Det Soc for Adv of Cultur & Edn; bd mem Fisher YMCA; pres FEMS for Fisher YMCA; corr secy media coor Det Urban League Guild; Red Cross vol; coord child hops Sickle Cell Anemia prog; columnist Spirit of Det Tarcom Newspaper; bi-centennial chmn Det Urban League Guilds Fund Raising Proj; natl historian Gamma Phi Delta Sor Inc; edit in chief past Basileus Delta Nu Chap GPD Sor; youth dir Delta Nu's Rosebud Youth Group; US Govt coord Equal Oppty Day Upward Mobility Race Relat Unit Found Programs. **HONORS/ACHIEVEMENTS:** Comm Serv Award GPD Sor 1976; Comm Serv Award Det Urban League; Most Val Mem Award Urban League Guild 1976; Pres of the Year Gamma Phi Delta 1973; Outstanding Basileus GPD Natl Pres 1974; Bi-Centennial Award Delta Nu's Youth Group 1976.

ANDERSON, MARJORIE ELEANOR AMADO
Administrator, president. **PERSONAL:** Born Jan 30, 1939, Providence, RI. **EDUCATION:** Masasoit Comm Coll, associates 1974; Southestn MA Univ, BA 1976. **CAREER:** The Partng Ways Mus of Afro-Amer Ethno Inc, exec dir & founder 1974-; Plymouth Hd Strt Prog, prog 1970-72. **ORGANIZATIONS:** Chmn sub-com Plymouth Bicent Adv Com on Blck Hist & Cult 1974-80; blck hist & cul MA Bicent Comm 1974-80; rsrch & cont Town of Plym & Sch Sys 1974-; reg New Eng coord Afro-Am Mus Assn 1976; adv MA Hum Serv Bd 1980-. **HONORS/ACHIEVEMENTS:** Green Key Soc 1979-80; Who's Who in Am Coll 1974-75; Who's Who in Am Wom Marq Who's Who 1980. **BUSINESS ADDRESS:** Museum of Afro-American, Inc, PO Box 3651, Plymouth, MA 02361.

ANDERSON, MARVA JEAN
Social services/special assistant. **PERSONAL:** Born May 09, 1945, Morrilton, AR; children: Tamikko Afresa Green. **EDUCATION:** Los Angeles Trade Tech Coll, AA 1970; CA State Univ Dominguez Hills, BA 1973; UCLA, MSW 1978. **CAREER:** Communicative Arts Acad, admin asst 1972-76; Special Serv for Groups, asst dir prog devel 1976-82; YWCA Women Shelter, dir 1982-84; LA Co Dept of Childrens Svcs, special asst 1984-. **ORGANIZATIONS:** Vice pres 1980-81, pres 1982-83, treas 1984-87 Natl Assoc of Black Social Workers LA Chapt; natl rep Natl Assoc Black Social Workers 1984-87; commmem Image Awds NAACP Hollywood Chap 1984-86; vice pres Jenesse Inc 1986-88; bd mem NAACP Hollywood Chap 1987. **HONORS/ACHIEVEMENTS:** Plaque of Appreciation Assoc of Black Social Workers LA 1983; Recognition & Appreciation for Contribution to XXIII Olympics LA Olympic Organizing Comm 1984; Certificate of Commendation LA City Councilman Robert Farrell 1984; Leadership Awd LA Brotherhood Crusade 1985; Plaque of Recognition CA Assoc of Black Social Workers 1986. **BUSINESS ADDRESS:** Special Assistant, LA Co Dept of Childrens Serv, 1125 West Sixth St, Los Angeles, CA 90017.

ANDERSON, MARY ELIZABETH
Government official, educator. **PERSONAL:** Born in Andersonville, VA. **EDUCATION:** VA Union Univ, BS; Chicago Coll of Commerce, postgrad; Attended, Amer Univ; US Dept of Agric Grad Sch. **CAREER:** Office of Educ, fiscal officer 1965-70, women's prog coord 1975-; Union HS, tchr; VA UnionUniv Rept Women's Natl Adv Cncl, couns 1976-; HEW, specialist 1970-. **ORGANIZATIONS:** Affiliate Natl Alliance of Black Sch Educs; life mem NAACP, exec bd mem 1975-77; DC Women's Polit Caucus; Friends of Frederick Douglass Mus of AfricanArt; Alpha Kappa Alpha. **HONORS/ACHIEVEMENTS:** Outstanding Serv Awd NAACP 1976; Cit of Apprec NAACP 1974; Spl Cit US Civil Serv Commn 1973; publ "Sex Equality in Educ"; co-author "History of US Ofcof Educ & Fld Svcs". **BUSINESS ADDRESS:** Specialist, HEW, DHEW Ofc of Educ, 400 Maryland Ave SW, Washington, DC 20202.

ANDERSON, MICHAEL WAYNE
Public relations manager. **PERSONAL:** Born Feb 24, 1942, Wilmington, DE; married Yvonne Gloria Copeland; children: Kima-Joi Michaele. **EDUCATION:** CA State Univ LA, BS 1973. **CAREER:** YMCA Youthmobile of Metro Los Angeles, dir 1971-73; A Better Chance Inc, western states reg dir 1973-; Crenshaw Branch YMCA of Metro Los Angeles, exec dir 1975-77; CA FAIR Plan Assn, mgr public affairs 1977-. **ORGANIZATIONS:** Mem CA Arson Prevent Comm 1977-80; epres LA chap Natl Assn of Mkt Developers 1978-80; mem San Francisco Arson Task Force 1979-80; chmn speakers bur Pub Club of LA 1979-80; eligibil com chmn Pub Rel Soc of Amer 1980; rec sec PIRATES 1980; bd dirs Angeles Girl Scout Cncl 1980; pres Toastmasters Intl (WIIS) 1980; mem LA Mayor's Arson Supression Task Force; mem LA Chap NAACP; mem LA Chap Urban League; mem Crenshaw Neighbors. **HONORS/ACHIEVEMENTS:** Listed Who's Who Among Students in Amer Univs & Coll CA State Univ LA 1971-72; Cert of Apprec Co of LA 1972; Cert of Apprec City of LA 1974; Cert of Apprec LA Jr C of C 1974; Outstanding Young Men of Amer Wash,DC 1974; Disting Toastmaster Toastmasters Intl 1977; Speaker's Award Western Ins Information Serv 1978-80. **MILITARY SERVICE:** AUS E-4 1964-66. **BUSINESS ADDRESS:** Recruitment Coordinator, A Better Chance, Inc, 419 Boylston St, Boston, MA 02116.

ANDERSON, MITCHELL TERRELL
Professional athlete. **PERSONAL:** Born Sep 23, 1960, Chicago, IL. **EDUCATION:** Bradley, comm major 1982. **CAREER:** Utah Jazz, forward 1983-; Philadelphia 76er's, 1982-83.

ANDERSON, MONROE
Journalist. **PERSONAL:** Born Apr 06, 1947, Gary, IN; married Joyce Owens; children: Scott, Kyle. **EDUCATION:** Indiana Univ, BA 1970. **CAREER:** Chicago Tribune, journalist; Ebony Magazine, asst ed 1972-74; Natl Observer, staffwriter 1970-72; Post-Tribune, 1969; Newsweek Magazine, correspondent 1968-. **HONORS/ACHIEVEMENTS:** AP IL St Award for In-Depth Rptng 1976; Chicago Trib Edward Beck Spcl Award for Outst Invstgtv Rprtng 1976; First Place Inland Press Awd 1977; Jacob Scher Awd for Investigative Reporting 1979; Best Comm Serv Awd UPI 1980; Outstanding Print Journalism Awd Chicago Assoc of Black Journalists 1981; Outstanding Print Journalism Awd DuSable Museum 1982; Outstanding Commentary Chicago Assoc of Black Journalists 1985; NY State Bar Assoc Media Awd 1986. **BUSINESS ADDRESS:** Correspondent, Newsweek, 200 E Randolph Drive, Ste 7948, Chicago, IL 60601.

ANDERSON, MOSES B.
Clergyman. **EDUCATION:** Ordained 1958. **CAREER:** Titular Bishop of Vatarba; Detroit, auxiliary bishop 1982-. **BUSINESS ADDRESS:** Archdiocese of Detroit, 1234 Washington Blvd, Detroit, MI 48226.

ANDERSON, NICHOLAS CHARLES
Association president. **PERSONAL:** Born Feb 07, 1953, Gaston County, NC; son of Nicodemous Anderson and Fannie Mae Moses Anderson; married Darlene Davis, Mar 25, 1978; children: Brandye Nicole, Michelle Darlene. **EDUCATION:** Wayne State Univ, Detroit, MI, BA, 1981; Central Piedmont Community Coll, Charlotte, NC, 1971-72. **CAREER:** Piedmont Natural Gas Co, Charlotte, NC, mail clerk, 1971-74; Amer Tobacco Co, Charlotte, NC, sales representative, 1974-76, Detroit, MI, dist sales mgr, 1976-81; NAACP, Detroit Branch, MI, youth dir, 1981-83; NAACP, Natl Office, Highland Park, MI, regional dir, 1983-87; Detroit Urban League, Detroit, MI, president, chief exec officer, 1987-. **ORGANIZATIONS:** US delegate, Intl Youth Conf, Kingston, Jamaica, 1985; vice pres, Wayne State Univ Alumni Assn, 1985-; trustee, Henry Ford Hospital-Main Campus, 1988-; advisory bd mem, Natl Bank of Detroit, Community Devel Corp, 1989. **HONORS/ACHIEVEMENTS:** Outstanding Young Man of Amer, US Chamber of Commerce, 1982; Man of the Year, New Grace Baptist Church, 1987. **BUSINESS ADDRESS:** Pres, Chief Exec Officer, Detroit Urban League, 208 Mack Ave, Detroit, MI 48201.

ANDERSON, ODDIE
Psychiatric nurse. **PERSONAL:** Born Jan 20, 1937, Detroit, MI; daughter of Sam Brown and Annie Suggs Walker Brown; married Armstead Anderson, Jul 23, 1955; children: Cheryl Anderson-Hunter, Debra Anderson. **EDUCATION:** Highland Park Coll, Detroit, MI, AS, Nursing; Wayne State Univ, Detroit, MI, BA, Gen Studies. **CAREER:** Herman Kiefer Hospital; Detroit Receiving Hospital; Detroit E Community Mental Health Center. **ORGANIZATIONS:** Pres, Wayne County Partial Hospitalization Program, 1989, Chalmers Jr Block Club; mem, Great Lakes Regional Partial Hospitalization Assn, Amer Assn Partial Hospitalization Inc, United Sisterhood, Detroit Metropolitan District Young People's Dept; assoc, Detroit Black Nurses Assn; youth dir, St James Missionary Baptist Church; chairperson, Detroit E Client Fund Comm. **HONORS/ACHIEVEMENTS:** Heart of Gold, United Found, 1989; Sojourner Truth Award, Natl Assn Negro Business Women, 1989; Special Serv Award, Detroit Bd of Dir, 1989; Community Serv Award, Wayne County Mental Health Bd; Outstanding Serv Award, St James Baptist Church; Outstanding Youth Leader, governor James Blanchard; established "Take a Senior to Dinner" program, 1979; established Detroit chapter of "Just Say No to Drugs," 1988; established scholastic programs to monitor young people's report cards. **BUSINESS ADDRESS:** Program Supvr, Detroit E Community Mental Health Center, 9141 E Jefferson, Detroit, MI 48214.

ANDERSON, ORA STERLING
Educator. **PERSONAL:** Born Oct 15, 1931, Delta, AL; daughter of William Sterling and Mary Sterling; divorced; children: Sherri. **EDUCATION:** Spelman Coll, BA 1954; Atlanta Univ, MA 1969; Univ of Maryland, PhD, 1982. **CAREER:** Atlanta Public Schools, teacher/instructional coord 1954-72; Federal City Coll, reading dept chair 1975-78; Univ of the District of Columbia, asst prof of educ 1978-81; Coppin State Coll, prof & dept chair of C&I, 1981-88; dean Division of Education, 1988-. **ORGANIZATIONS:** 1st vice pres Natl Alumnae Assn of Spelman Coll 1982-86; mem editorial adv bd Innovative Learning Strategies Intl Reading Assoc 1985-86; pres Natl Alumnae Assn of Spelman Coll 1986-88; mem Alpha Kappa Alpha Iota Lambda Chap. **HONORS/ACHIEVEMENTS:** Mem editorial adv bd Reading World Coll Reading Assn 1982-84; mem US Delegation to the People's Republic of China US China Scientific Exchange 1985; fourteen articles published in educational journals 1979-89; published textbook Reading & Study Skills for the Urban College Student, Kendall/Hunt Publ 1984, 1988, 2nd ed; received NAFEO Distinguished Alumni Award, 1988. **HOME ADDRESS:** 9537 Kilamanjaro Road, Columbia, MD 21045. **BUSINESS ADDRESS:** Dean, Division of Education, Coppin State College, 2500 West North Ave, Baltimore, MD 21216.

ANDERSON, PATRICIA HEBERT
Community service organizer. **PERSONAL:** Born Aug 28, 1945, Houston, TX; daughter of Aldaah Augusta Hebert and Emma Jean Pope Hebert; married Rev Adolphus Anderson Jr, Jun 28, 1964 (deceased); children: Renee Hebert Ohia, Reginald, Adolphus III, Ruthalyn, Victor, Albert, Michael, Miriam. **EDUCATION:** TX Southern Univ, 1963; Houston Comm, 1972, 1984; Manpower Business Training, Key Punch Comp, 1974; Gulf Coast Bible Coll, AA Theol, 1975. **CAREER:** Harris City Democratic Exec Comm, precinct comm, 1976-; Glen Manor Weyburn Pl Civic Cl, pres 1979-; Gulf Coast Comm Serv, sec, bd of dir, 1980; North Forest ISD, sec, bd of dir, 1981; Natl Black Caucus of School Bd, sec, 1982, 1984, bd of dir, 1984; church musician & director 32 yrs; Star of Faith Grand Chap, OES #55 grand musician; North Forest School Dist, trustee; North Forest School Dist Bd of Educ, pres, 1988-89. **ORGANIZATIONS:** Comm coord, North East Comm Project Fund, 1972; chairwoman, New Hope Baptist Church Missionary Affairs, 1975; pres, Glen Manor Weyburn Pl, 1979-; alternate person, City Commr Jim Fontero, 1980; sec, Gulf Coast Comm, Serv 1981, BATTS Bd of Dir, 1982; admin asst, City Comm EA Squattylons, 1982; Harris County Black Elected Officials, 1986; bd mem, Evangelistic Bible Days Revival Church; secretary,

Natl Caucus of Black School Bd Members, 1986-; Houston Central Young Women Christian Council, 1987-89; bd mem, Greater Park Hill Church of God in Christ Evangelical Bd, 1987-. **HONORS/ACHIEVEMENTS:** Outstanding Young Woman of Amer, 1981; Community Serv Awd, City of Houston Mayor Whitemire, 1983; honored by Natl Black Caucus of School Bd Members, 1983; Woman of the Year, New Hope Baptist Church, 1983; Honor Award, Gulf Coast Community Serv, 1983; High Achievement, North East Comm Proj, 1984; Merit of Achievement, Legislative Black Caucus State Rep Harol Dutton, 1986; Mother of the Year, New Hope Baptist Church, 1986; Outstanding Black Elected Official, Wayside Church of Christ, 1986; Juneteenth Freedom Award, NAACP, 1987.

ANDERSON, PEARL CORINA
Nurse. **PERSONAL:** Born Aug 18, 1898, Gansville, LA; married John Wesley MD. **EDUCATION:** Coleman Coll, nursing cert 1917; Bishop Coll, Hon LLD 1958. **CAREER:** Grocery store owner/operator; Dallas Comm Chest, nurse/mgr of business investment vol. **ORGANIZATIONS:** Bd mem Moorland Br YMCA; dir Comm Cncl of Greater Dallas; bd mem Hexter Meml Lighthouse; vol Dallas Chap ARC; bd mem Marie Morgan Br YWCA; vol Goodwill Ind; trustee Bishop Coll; del White House Conf on Children & Youth 1960; mem Natl Assn of Negro Bus & Professional Women's Club; bd mem Dallas Day Nursery Assn; bd mem Dallas Cncl on Aging; bd mem Cath Charities; bd mem SERV; bd mem Vol Action Cntr. **HONORS/ACHIEVEMENTS:** Woman of the Year Kappa Zeta Sor 1955; Comm Serv Award Dallas Cncl of Soc Agency 1955-63; TX State Sen Resolution of Recogn of Outstanding Citizen 1955; Natl Sojourner Award Natl Assn of Negro Bus & Professional Women's Club 1956; Pearl C Anderson Day Nursery Dedicated 1958; Dedicated Pearl C Anderson Jr & HS of Dallas Ind Sch Dist (1st time DISD hon a living person) 1961; Acrete Award 1971; named life mem Dallas Chap ARC 1971; named life mem Dallas CoUnited Way 1972; Golden Deeds Award Exchange Club of Dallas 1973; Brotherhood Honoree Natl Conf of Christians & Jews 1977; Humanitarianism Award St James AME Temple 1977; Woman of the Year Dallas Comm of 100 1977.

ANDERSON, PEARL G.
Governmental administrator. **PERSONAL:** Born Oct 08, 1950, Richmond, VA; daughter of Howard H Green Jr and Mabel Fleming Green; divorced; children: Nicholas. **EDUCATION:** Randolph-Macon Woman's Coll, BA 1972. **CAREER:** City of Richmond, mgmt intern 1972-73, budget analyst 1973-78, sr budget analyst 1978-82. **ORGANIZATIONS:** Mem Amer Soc for Public Admin; mem Natl Forum for Black Public Admins; bd of Christian educ Fifth St Baptist Church; bd of dirs Young Women's Christian Assn 1973-79; bd of dirs Richmond Supplemental Retirement System 1973-79; mem Intl City Mgmt Assn 1978-82; bd dir Gr Richmond Transit Co. **HONORS/ACHIEVEMENTS:** Four Yr Scholarship at RMWC; Outstanding Jr Major 1971. **BUSINESS ADDRESS:** Dir Admin Services, VA Dept of Personnel-Training, 101 N 14th St, Richmond, VA 23219.

ANDERSON, RAY CHARLES
Law enforcement officer, former mayor. **PERSONAL:** Born Sep 04, 1954, Mexia, TX; married Delores Bluitt; children: Ray Jr, Christopher, Billi. **EDUCATION:** Navarro Jr Coll Corsicana; McClennan Comm Coll Waco, presently attending. **CAREER:** United Way Mexia, spokesman 1981; St Luke Mexia, chmn of admin board 1982-84; City of Mexia, council member 1979-84, mayor pro-tem 1982, mayor 1982-83. **HONORS/ACHIEVEMENTS:** Comm Service Awd St Luke Church 1978-82; articles published in local news Dallas Aff and Waco on numerous occasions. **HOME ADDRESS:** 505 W Main St, Mexia, TX 76667.

ANDERSON, REUBEN VINCENT
Judge. **PERSONAL:** Born Sep 10, 1942, Jackson, MS; married Phyllis Wright; children: Vincent, Rainall. **EDUCATION:** Tougalloo Coll, BA 1964; Univ MS, JD 1967. **CAREER:** Jackson MS, attorney 1967-75; municipal judge 1975-77; Hinds County, county judge 1977-81; 7th Circut court of MS, judge 1981-85; MS Supreme Court, judge. **ORGANIZATIONS:** Asembly Manufactor Corp, 1976-86; Trustmark Nat'l Bank, dir 1980-86; Jackson Chamber of Commerce, dir 1980-86; Piney Wood Sch, trustee 1980-; Tougaloo Coll, trustee 1981-; United Way, trustee 1983-. **BUSINESS ADDRESS:** Supreme Court Justice, Mississippi Supreme Court, PO Box 117, Jackson, MS 39205.

ANDERSON, ROBERT L.
Attorney. **PERSONAL:** Born Jan 26, 1940, Greenwood, MS; married Johnnie; children: Gail, Ivan, Robert Jr, Alison. **EDUCATION:** Chicago State Univ, B & grad work 1964; Chicago Kent Coll, JD 1973. **CAREER:** Atterbury Job Corp, dir training 1959-66; Chicago Pub Sch, tchr 1964-67; Chicago Urban League, dir apprenticeship prog 1967-71; IL Dept of Labor, mgr. **ORGANIZATIONS:** Vice pres Epsilon Pi Tau; historian Phi Delta Phi; mem Celestial Lodge #80; Urban League; NAACP; PUSH; Salvation Army; BSA. **BUSINESS ADDRESS:** Manager, IL Dept of Labor, 910 S Michigan Ave, Ste 1311-15, Chicago, IL 60605.

ANDERSON, RON
Professional athlete. **PERSONAL:** Born Oct 10, 1958, Chicago, IL. **EDUCATION:** Fresno State, 1980-84. **CAREER:** Cleveland Cavaliers, forward 1984-. **HONORS/ACHIEVEMENTS:** For Cavs' entry in the CA Summer League, led Cavs in scoring with an average of 187 points per game and was only NBA rookie named to league's All-Star team.

ANDERSON, RONALD EDWARD
Manager. **PERSONAL:** Born Aug 04, 1948, Indianapolis, IN; married Dolores Jean Benson; children: Ronald Jr. **EDUCATION:** TN State Univ, BS 1970; Graduate Work, Univ of Evansville 1976, Central Michigan Univ 1986. **CAREER:** State Farm Fire & Casualty Ins, admin & tech trainee 1971-72, sr claim rep 1973-75, claim specialist 1975-80, claim supt 1980-85; State Farm Mutual Automobile Insurance Co, claim supt 1985-. **ORGANIZATIONS:** Trustee New Hope Bapt Ch Evansville IN 1974-80; bd dir Transit System Evansville 1976-78; bd dir Carver Com Orgn Evansville 1976-80; v polemarch Evansville Alumni Chap Kappa Alpha Psi 1977-79; chmn finance com Evansville Black Expos 1979; secty/treas Flint îAlumni Chap of Kappa Alpha Psi 1982-86. **HONORS/ACHIEVEMENTS:** Good Neighbor of the Yr Awd IN Regional Office State Farm Ins Co W Lafayette IN 1978. **MILITARY SERVICE:** AUSR cpt 6 yrs. **HOME ADDRESS:** 6169 Pebbleshire Dr, Grand Blanc, MI 48439. **BUSINESS ADDRESS:** Claim Superintendent, State Farm Fire & Casualty, 4074 S Linden Rd, Flint, MI 48507.

ANDERSON, RUSSELL LLOYD
Physician. **PERSONAL:** Born Jan 12, 1907, Pittsburgh, PA; married Celeste Etta Johnson; children: Russell L Jr MD, Dorothy M Brickler, Dolores L Farr, Donald Louis. **EDUCATION:** Univ of Pittsburgh, BS 1928, MS 1930, PhD 1933; Howard Univ MD 1946. **CAREER:** Johnson C Smith Univ, prof of Biology 1930-43; FL A&M Univ, prof of Biology 1946-50; Anderson-Brickler Medical Clinic, physician 1956-. **ORGANIZATIONS:** Dir of student health serv FL A&M Univ 1950-67; life mem NAACP; mem NMA; mem Amer Medical Assn; mem AAAS. **MILITARY SERVICE:** AUS 1st lieutenant 1943-47. **BUSINESS ADDRESS:** Anderson-Brickler Med Clinic, 1705 S Adams St, Tallahassee, FL 32301.

ANDERSON, RUTH BLUFORD
Social work educator, government official. **PERSONAL:** Born Oct 28, 1921, Braden, OK; daughter of Ray Bluford and Josie Blocker Knowles; married James C Anderson, Jr; children: Eugene McKinnis, Carl, Valerie, Glennis Anderson Fox, Dennis, James, Keith McKinnis. **EDUCATION:** Lincoln Univ Jeff City, Mo, 1939-41; Univ of CA Berkeley, BA 1946; Columbia Univ NY, MSW 1956; Univ of Chicago, SSA, Summer Inst 1973-71; Smith Coll Northampton, MA, Workshop 1982. **CAREER:** Black Hawk Co Welfare Dept, dir 1963-67; Wartburg Coll Waverly IA, asst prof soc work 1967-1969; University of Northern Iowa, asst prof soc work 1969-73, assoc prof 1973-86, prof 1986-; acting head, dept of social work 1988-90. **ORGANIZATIONS:** Comm Gov Branstads Long Term Care 1984-; bd mem IA NB St Conf NAACP 1982-; mem bd of dir NE Coun on Substance Abuse 1985; mem National Assoc of Black SocialWorkers, 1989; Golden Life mem, Delta Sigma Theta Sorority; mem, North East Iowa Aids Coalition, 1987; mem, Gamblers Advisory Board, 1987. **HONORS/ACHIEVEMENTS:** Women's Hall of Fame 1982; Articles on Blacks and Substance Abuse; Author From Mother's Aid Child to Univ Prof, Auto of Amer Black Woman 1985; Jim Kraft Award, Governor's Conference on Substance Abuse, 1988; Women of Achievement, Networking Together IX, 1988.

ANDERSON, S. A.
Business executive. **PERSONAL:** Born May 31, 1935, Ennis, TX; married Betty; children: Monetta Kaye, Madeline Joyce, Arthur Girard. **EDUCATION:** Prairie View A&M Univ, BS 1956; attended Atlanta Univ, Texas Southern Univ, Univ of Oklahoma. **CAREER:** Pemberton HS Marshall TX, tchr/coach 1958-69. **ORGANIZATIONS:** Mem Natl Urban League; East Texas Coaches & Officials Assn 1958-69; Amer Soc Pub Admin; TX Assn Comm Action Agencies; chmn NAACP 1970-75; Natl Assn Comm Devel; Natl Comm Action Agency Exec Dir Assn; Assn Black Soc Workers Inc; mem Order of Arrow Boy Scouts of Amer 1962; mem bd dir East Texas Legal Serv Corp; mem Alpha Phi Alpha Frat; SW Baseball Umpires Assn; Amer Assn Retired Persons. **HONORS/ACHIEVEMENTS:** Man of Yr Reg Fellows Club 1970 1975; Natl Sci Found Grants 1960b 1962-64 1967; Excellence Awds East Texas Coaches & Officials Assn 1964 1968; Serv Awd Zeta Phi Beta 1972; Serv Awd Phi Beta Sigma 1971; Serv Awd AKA 1976; Outstanding Ach Awd TX St Conf NAACP 1971. **MILITARY SERVICE:** AUS capt 1956-58; Sr Parachutist Badge. **BUSINESS ADDRESS:** PO Box 1343, 214 E Houston St, Marshall, TX 75670.

ANDERSON, SARAH A.
Retired legislator. **PERSONAL:** Born in Jacksonville, FL; widowed; children: 6. **CAREER:** Philadelphia Public Schs, tchr; PA House of Reps, retired legislator 1954-72. **ORGANIZATIONS:** Chmn Hlth & Welfare Comm 193 Dist State Legislature; sponsored PA Equal Rights Amendment. **BUSINESS ADDRESS:** 226 N 52 St, Philadelphia, PA 19139.

ANDERSON, TALMADGE
Educator, writer. **PERSONAL:** Born Jul 22, 1932, Hazelhurst, GA; son of Viola Lee Baker Anderson; married Cerci Lee (divorced); children: Rose, Ramona, Talmadge, Rhunell, Raul. **EDUCATION:** Savannah State Coll, BS 1953; Atlanta Univ, MBA 1958. **CAREER:** Lane Coll, chmn dept of bus 1958-59; Allen Univ, asst prof 1959-62; St Augustine's Coll, asst prof/chmn 1963-65; Bethune-Cookman Coll, assoc prof 1966-67; WV Inst of Tech, asst prof 1968-70; Western Journal of Black Studies, founder & editor 1977-; Washington State Univ, assoc prof bus admin 1975-, dir assoc prof marketing & black studies 1970-. **ORGANIZATIONS:** Adv bd mem Employment Security Commn Washington 1975-77; exec bd mem Natl Cncl of Black Studies 1975-; exec cncl mem ASALH 1977-86. **HONORS/ACHIEVEMENTS:** 100 Most Influential Friends Awd Black Journal 1977; Cert of Achievement inst on Africa-Hamline Univ 1978; NW, NCBS Frederick Douglass Scholar Awd 1986. **MILITARY SERVICE:** AUS agt 1953-56. **BUSINESS ADDRESS:** Assoc Prof Black Studies, Washington StateUniv, Heritage House, Pullman, WA 99164.

ANDERSON, THOMAS JEFFERSON
Educator. **PERSONAL:** Born Aug 17, 1928, Coutesville, PA; son of Thomas J Anderson and Anita Turpeau Anderson; married Lois Ann Field; children: T J III, Janet, Anita. **EDUCATION:** WV State Coll, BM 1950; Pennsylvania State Univ, MEd 1951; Univ of IA, PhD 1958; Holy Cross Coll, DMA 1983; WV State Coll, D Mus 1984. **CAREER:** High Pt City Public School, NC; teacher, 1951-54; WV St Coll Inst WV, Instructor, 1955-56; Langston Univ, Langston OK, prof & chmn, 1958-63; TN State Univ Nashville TN, prof, music 1963-69; Atlanta Symphony Orchestra, composer in res 1969-71; Morehouse Coll, Atlanta, Danforth visiting prof of music, 1971-72; Tufts Univ Medford, ME, prof of music & chmn, 1972-80, Austin Fletcher prof of music, 1976- . **ORGANIZATIONS:** Founder/pres, Black Music Caucus MENC; Bd mem Elma Lewis School of Fine Arts 1975-; advisory bd, Meet The Composer, 1980; chp Comm of the Status of Minorities Coll Music Soc, 1976-80; mem Music Council the Arts & Humanities 1978-81; mem, Harvard Musical Assn, 1976-; assn mem, St Botolph Club 1980. **HONORS/ACHIEVEMENTS:** Fellow MacDowell Colony 1960-83; fellow Yhaddo 1970-77; Copley Found Award, Chicago 1964; Fromm Found Award, Chicago 1964-71; Phi Beta Kappa hon mem 1977; Over 50 published compositions; Artistic Resindency, Univ of Salvador, 1988; 60th Birthday Concert, Videmus, Harvard Univ, 1989; Fellow, John Simon Guggenheim Found, 1989; Bd mem, Harvard Musical Assn, 1989. **HOME ADDRESS:** 34 Grove St, Medford, MA 02155. **BUSINESS ADDRESS:** Austin Fletcher Prof of Music, TuftsUniv, Cohen Hall Dept of Music, Medford, MA 02155.

ANDERSON, TONY
Insurance company executive. **PERSONAL:** Born Jun 14, 1947, Dillon, SC; son of Mary Agnes Anderson; married Westley A Smith, Oct 22, 1983; children: Christopher, Natasha. **EDUCATION:** Western Connecticut State Coll, Danbury, CT, BA, 1979; Univ of New Haven, West Haven, CT, MBA, 1989. **CAREER:** Cititrust, Bridgeport, CT, securities trader, 1977-80; Equitable Life, New York, NY, vice pres funding operations, 1980-. **ORGANI-**

ZATIONS: NASD, 1977-; dir, Equitable Credit Union, 1988-. **HONORS/ACHIEVEMENTS:** Ford Found Scholar, 1976. **MILITARY SERVICE:** USAF, E-4, 1965-68.

ANDERSON, VINTON RANDOLPH
Bishop, clergyman. **PERSONAL:** Born Jul 11, 1927, Somerset, Bermuda;married Vivienne Louise Cholmondeley; children: Vinton R Jr, Jeffrey Charles, Carlton Lawson, Kenneth Robert. **EDUCATION:** Wilberforce Univ, BA, Payne Sem, MDiv 1952; KS Univ, MA 1962; Paul Quinn Coll, DD 1964; Wilberforce Univ, HHD 1972; Payne Sem DD 1977. **CAREER:** KS, MO, pastor; Presiding Bishop & Chief-Pastor, AL 1972-76, OH, WV, Western PA 1976-84; Office of Ecumenical Relations & Devel of the African Methodist Episcopal Church, dir, 1984-88; African Methodist Episcopal Church, presiding bishop, 5th Episcopal dist. **ORGANIZATIONS:** Chief organizer/spokesman Martin Luther King Memorial March; preached & lectured in Caribbean, S & W Africa; tours to Middle East Europe South Pacific & Russia; mem of team visiting New Zealand & Australia sponsored by World Council of Churches Prog to Combat Racism 1972; invited to visit Nationalist China by the Taiwanese govt 1976; delegate four World Methodist Conferences Norway 1961, England 1966, CO 1971, HI 1981; exec comm mem World Methodist Council; past chmn Wilberforce Univ Bd Trustees; chmn, bd of dir, Payne Theological Seminary; mem, Census Advisory Comm on the black population for the 1990 census. **HONORS/ACHIEVEMENTS:** First pastor to develop an Adult Educ Program; Urban League Awd of Merit; Disting Serv Awd NAACP; Profiles in Black Core 1975; Black on Black Crime Ebony Mag 1979. **BUSINESS ADDRESS:** Presiding Bishop, Fifth Episcopal District, African Methodist Episcopal Church, 4144 Lindell Blvd, Suite 222, St Louis, MO 63108.

ANDERSON, WILLIAM A.
Physician. **PERSONAL:** Born Jul 21, 1921, Atlanta, GA; son of Will and Mary; married Joyce McIntosh; children: Serena, Cheryle Posey, William A III. **EDUCATION:** Tuskegee Inst, BA 1942; Univ MI Med Sch, MD 1953. **CAREER:** Private Practice, dermatologist 1957-; Whitehall Labs NYC, assoc med dir 1965-69; Cornell Univ Med Coll, clin assoc prof med. **ORGANIZATIONS:** Consul Natl Acad Sci Natl Rsch Cncl 1965; pres Metro Derm Soc NY 1962; pres NJ Dermatological Soc 1963; fellow Amer Acad Dermatology 1959-; mem Natl Med Assn, AMA. **HONORS/ACHIEVEMENTS:** Rsch Fellow Div Virus Rsch Cornell Univ Med Coll 1957-61; Councilor Essex Co Med Soc NJ 1983-85; author, articles on clinical deramtology, immunology, virology. **MILITARY SERVICE:** AUS corpl 4 yrs; Combat Medical Badge 1945. **BUSINESS ADDRESS:** Clinical Assoc Prof of Med, Cornell Univ Medical College, 185 Central Ave, East Orange, NJ 07018.

ANDERSON, WILLIAM A.
Educator. **PERSONAL:** Born May 28, 1937, Akron, OH; children: 1. **EDUCATION:** Ohio State Univ, PhD 1966. **CAREER:** Kent State Univ, instr 1961-62; Disaster Rsch Ctr Ohio State Univ, rsch asst 1966-69; Minority Fellowship Prog, Amer Sociol Assn, dir 1974-75; AZ State Univ, assoc to full professor 1969-76; National Science Foundation, program director, 1976-. **ORGANIZATIONS:** Mem Natl Acad of Sci Panel on the Pub Policy Implications of Earthquake Prediction 1974-; mem Natl Acad of Sci Ad Hoc Comm on Minorities in the Sci 1975; mem Amer Sociol Assn; Pacific Sociol Assn; co-author of two books. **BUSINESS ADDRESS:** Program Director, National Science Foundation, Washington, DC 20550.

ANDERSON-JANNIERE, IONA LUCILLE
Insurance agent, retired educator. **PERSONAL:** Born Aug 28, 1919, Brooklyn, NY; married Ivan Lloyd Janniere, Jun 17, 1988; children: Wendie Anderson Peterson, Robert. **EDUCATION:** Hunter Coll, BA 1942; New York Univ, MA 1959; Heed Univ of FL, PhD 1976; City Univ of New York, Post Doctorate Study 1978-81. **CAREER:** Bd of Educ New York City, teacher of common branches 1945-69; Bank St College New York City, field rep 1969-70; Brooklyn Coll of CUNY, asst prof of educ 1969-74; City Univ of New York Medgar Evers Coll, assoc prof of educ 1974-85; Self-employed, writer/financial planner. **ORGANIZATIONS:** Education consultant Richmond Coll of CUNY 1973-75; chairperson Northeast Flatbush Comm Coalition 1977; comm rep New York City Planning Bd # 17 1978-83; evaluator of Early Childhood Programs for Bd of Educ District #73 1979-80 and District #9 1974-76; consultant on Eng as a Standard Dialect Bd of Educ New York 1983; reading consultant Houghton Mifflin Publishing Co 1983-84; mem bd dirs East New York Development Corp 1984-85; early childhood consultant PS Dist 17 New York 1984-85; financial planner Krueger Assoc North Port FL 1986-87; chair of Women's Issues, AAUW (Venice Branch) 1987-. **HONORS/ACHIEVEMENTS:** Fanny Lou Hamer Awd Medgar Evers Coll 1983; Sojourner Truth Awd Natl Business and Professional Women 1984; Special Awd New York State Tesol 1985; ESL Students in the Mainstream published in Integrative Approaches to ESL Teaching & Learning 1986. **HOME ADDRESS:** 5893 Mayberry Ave, North Port, FL 34287.

ANDERSON-TANNER, FREDERICK T., JR.
Educator. **PERSONAL:** Born Feb 17, 1937, Winston-Salem, NC; divorced; children: Allyson-Jenine, Frederick III. **EDUCATION:** Morgan State Univ, BS 1959; Atlanta Univ, MA 1964; VA Poly Inst & State Univ, EdD 1975. **CAREER:** Kathmandu Nepal, Fulbright scholar prof of English, 1962-63; Bd of Educ Sandersville GA, reading consult 1962; Clark Coll, instructor of English 1963-64; Morehouse Coll, reading specialist, 1965-66; Rosewood State Hosp, adult educ teacher 1966-67; Rosewood School for Retarded Children, vice principal, 1967-69; Coppin State Coll, Loyola Coll, visiting prof 1968; Bowie State Coll, prof 1968-69; Federal City Coll, dep dir skills center, 1969-70; State Dept of Health & Mental Hygiene, principal, 1970-72; Federal City Coll, assoc prof 1972-73; Gov Commn on Structure & Governance of Educ in MD, asst dir 1973-75; Gov of MD, educ aide 1975; Morgan State Univ, assoc prof of educ 1975-. **ORGANIZATIONS:** Life mem Alpha Phi Alpha; Masonic Order; Natl Educ Assn; Natl Cncl Tchrs of English; Cncl for Exceptional Children; Natl Rehab Counseling Assn; Phi Delta Kappa; natl Assn of State Dirs of Spec Educ; Assn for Supervision & Curriculum Devel; MD Consortium for Cooperative Planning in Spec Educ. **HONORS/ACHIEVEMENTS:** Fulbright Scholar to Nepal India, 1962-63; Natl Honor Soc; Exceptional Childrens Leadership Awd 1975; pres Black Caucus of Special Educators; Intl Council for Exceptional Children; 10 Yr Serv Award, State of MD; dissertation A Modified Delphi Study of Political Feasibility of Critical Issues Affecting Educ Reform in MD 1975. **BUSINESS ADDRESS:** Assoc Prof, Educ, Morgan State Univ, Coldspring Lane, Baltimore, MD 21207.

ANDREWS, ADELIA SMITH
Business executive. **PERSONAL:** Born Nov 07, 1914, New Orleans, LA; daughter of Christopher Columbus Smith and Adelia Beatty Smith; married Joseph H; children: Yolanda Reed, Joseph Reginald. **EDUCATION:** Professional Secretaries Intl; Certified Professional Secretary 1978. **CAREER:** Whiteway Cleaners & Dyers, sec 1933-36; State of California, sec 1936-42; Los Angeles County Probation Dept, sec 1942-44; A-Z Steno Serv, sec bookkeeper 1946-49; Los Angeles Urban League, admin asst 1949-53; Watkins Entrepeneurs Inc, admin asst 1953-63; California Museum of Science & Indus, admin asst 1963-84; Caribbean Childrenspace, St Croix US VI, admin asst 1985-. **ORGANIZATIONS:** Bd mem Childrens Dmnsn (Childrens Space) 1979-; project dir CMSI Black Achievement Exhibit 1973-78; mem Assn Women of Pepperdine Univ, Los Angeles Urban League, Professional Secretaries International 1971-. **HONORS/ACHIEVEMENTS:** 25 year pin State of California 1982. **HOME ADDRESS:** 754 W 109 Pl, Los Angeles, CA 90044.

ANDREWS, ADOLPHUS
Educational administrator. **PERSONAL:** Born Jan 19, 1943, Tampa, FL; son of Willie L Andrews and Marjoria Andrews; married Ruby Nell Brownlee; children: Adolphus William, Dawn Ingliss. **EDUCATION:** Howard Univ, BA Political Science 1964; Southern IL Univ Edwardsville, MS Political Sci 1970; OH State Univ, PhD Political Science 1982. **CAREER:** USAF Security Serv, flight commander 1965-67; USAF Scott AFB IL Military Airlift Command, special security officer 1967-70; USAF Squadron Officer School Air Univ Maxwell AFB, AL, section commander/instructor 1970-73; USAF Nakhon Phanom RTAFB Thailand, intelligence analyst dept of defense command briefing officer 1973-74; Sec of the Air Force Legislative Liaison, legislative liaison officer 1975; USAF Acad, instructor/asst prof Dept of Political Science 1974-76, asst prof/ personnel officer/ dir of Amer & policy studies 1979-81; Office of the Sec of the Air Force, speech writer 1984-85; USAF Acad Prep School, commander 1985-89; executive dir, Budget & Planning, Atlantic Community Coll. **ORGANIZATIONS:** Mem Air Force Assn 1978-; mem Amer Political Science Assn 1978-; mem Natl Conf of Black Political Scientists 1979-; mem Alpha Phi Alpha Fraternity Inc 1980-; Society of College and Univ Planners, 1989-. **MILITARY SERVICE:** USAF Col 1964-; Distinguished Military Graduate ROTC 1964; Outstanding Unit Award Citation USAF 1967 & 1973; Scott AFB Jr Officer of the Month USAF April 1970; USAF Commendation Medal 1970 & 1973, Joint Serv Commendation Medal 1974, Meritorious Service Medal 1984 & 1985; Legion of Merit, 1989.

ANDREWS, ALICE ELIZABETH
Computer consultant/marketing support. **PERSONAL:** Born Jul 28, 1954, Kansas City, KS. **EDUCATION:** Spelman Coll, BA (Cum Laude) 1975; Georgia Inst of Tech, MS 1977. **CAREER:** District Mktg & Support, mgr, exec briefing ctr. **ORGANIZATIONS:** Mem Delta Sigma Theta 1980-; local chap sec Natl Black MBA Assoc 1981-83,86-87; consult Project Bus Consult to Jr Achievement 1982-84; speaker/mem Toastmasters Pres's Chap 1983-84; speaker/student Atlanta Exchange 1983-85; mem The Comm at AT&T 1983-85; chairperson United Way (AT&T) 1983-85; mem pres ALTA/East Lake Chap 1984-85; cons/exhibitor Natl Urban League 1986; mem Women's League 1986-; mem Amer Mgmt Assoc 1987-; mem US Tennis Assoc 1987-. **HONORS/ACHIEVEMENTS:** Listed in Who's Who Among Coll & Univ Students 1974-76; Dean's List Spelman Coll 1974-76; Dean's List GA Inst of Tech 1976-77; Burrough's Fellow 1976-77; Chairman's Fund Awd Wang Laboratories Inc 1986. **BUSINESS ADDRESS:** Principal Consultant, District Mktg and Support, 30 Grant Ave, San Francisco, CA 94108.

ANDREWS, BENNY
Artist, educator. **PERSONAL:** Born Nov 13, 1930, Madison, GA; son of George C Andrews and Viola Perryman Andrews; married Nene Humphrey, Jun 14, 1986; children: Christopher, Thomas Michael, Julia Rachael. **EDUCATION:** Ft Valley State Coll, attended 1948-50; Univ of Chicago, attended 1956-58; Chicago Art Inst, BFA 1958; Atlanta School of Art, Honorary Doctorate 1984. **CAREER:** One man show Kessler Gallery Provincetown 1960-70; Queens Coll, assoc prof 1967-; New School for Social Rsch, instructor 1965-68; Studio Museum New York City 1970; Museum of Modern Art New York City 1968-71; ACA Gallery New York City 1972, UMD 1972; Aronson Midtown Gallery Atlanta 1973; Visual Arts Program Natl Endowment for the Arts, dir 1982-84; Natl Arts Program, dir 1985-; found in permanent collections in many museums and galleries. **ORGANIZATIONS:** Co-chmn Black Emergency Cultural Coalition 1969; bd dirs Children's Art Council. **HONORS/ACHIEVEMENTS:** John Jay Whitney Fellow 1965-67; NY Council Arts grantee 1971; contributed articles on black art culture to professional journals; NEA Fellowship Natl Endowment 1974; Bellagie Fellow, Rockefeller Foundation, 1987; Painting Fellowship, National Endowment, 1986. **MILITARY SERVICE:** USAF s/sgt 4 yrs. **BUSINESS ADDRESS:** Professor, Queens College, Kissena Blvd, Flushing, NY 11355.

ANDREWS, BERT J.
Photographer. **PERSONAL:** Born Mar 21, 1929, Chicago, IL. **CAREER:** Photographer, Equity Library Theatre, Actors Equity, Negro Ensemble Co, many off-Broadway & Broadway plays including, "Bubbling Brown Sugar," "Eubie," "Hair," "Canterbury Tales," "Pavlo Hummel," "Robeson," "Lovers & Other Strangers," "Ain't Supposed to Die a Natural Death"; Charles Stewart Photography NY, photographer 1953-57; Bert Andrews Photography, owner 1957-; "In the Shadow of the Great White Way," Images of Blacks in the American Theatre, Thunder's Mouth Press NY, 1989. **MILITARY SERVICE:** AUS staff sgt 1950-52.

ANDREWS, CARL R.
Retired association executive. **PERSONAL:** Born Apr 20, 1926, Williamsport, PA; son of Carl M Andrews and Georgie Bannister Andrews; married Jeanette M White, May 01, 1955; children: Carl R Jr, Keith R, Cheryl Y. **EDUCATION:** Lycoming Coll, 1946-48; Howard Univ, 1948-50; Rutgers Univ, Adj Urban Fellowship Program 1963-64; Yale Univ Drug Dependence Inst, 1971. **CAREER:** Boys' Clubs of Newark, NJ, club dir 1952-66; Boys' Clubs of Amer Natl Prgm & Training Svc, asst dir 1966-73; Boys' Club Assn of Indianapolis, IN, exec dir 1973-89. **ORGANIZATIONS:** Natl bd mem, Boys' Clubs of Amer, 1974-76, 1978-81; exec comm Boys Club Professional Assn; Chmn, BCA Midwest Region Steering Com; Natl Manpower Devel Comm; BCA Midwest Reg; Concerned Professional Assn of Boy's Club Workers; mem Comm Serv Cncl; IN Juvenile Justice Task Force; Kiwanis Intl; Greater Indianapolis Progress Com; Mayor's Soc Serv Adv Cncl; Alpha Phi Alpha Fraternity; HS Commencement Speaker 1944; chmn United Way Exec Cncl 1984-85; vice pres Marion Cnty Juvenile Cntr Adv Bd; steering comm Marion Cnty Juvenile Delinquency Prevention Council. **HONORS/ACHIEVEMENTS:** Mem, Natl Scholastic Hon Soc; NJ Afro-Amer Newspaper Award 1959; Man of Wk Award Prudential Ins Co 1966; Midwest Reg Heart & Soul Award 1978; Paul Lemmon Adminstr of Yr Award 1977; past pres award E Orange Comm Day Nursery 1973; Library dedicated in honor Newark, NJ 1982; Kiwanis Club of Indianapolis Career

Award 1980; State of Indiana, Sagamore of the Wabash, 1989. **MILITARY SERVICE:** USN 1944-46. **HOME ADDRESS:** 4924 Olympia Dr, Indianapolis, IN 46208.

ANDREWS, CYRIL BLYTHE
Business executive. **PERSONAL:** Born Jul 06, 1901, Apalachicola, FL; married Johna B Thompson; children: C Blythe Jr, William. **EDUCATION:** Atlanta Univ, BA. **CAREER:** Cent Life Ins Co, sec treas 1931-39; Lily White Sec Ben Assn, fndr pres 1939-; FL Sentinel-Bulletin Pub Co, pres editor 1945-. **ORGANIZATIONS:** Pres Alpha Phi Alpha; mem NAACP; adv coun US Civil Rights Comm; Hillsbrgh Co Civ Serv Bd 1965; Mayor's Hum Rel Comm; mem Beaulah Bapt Ch; mem bd dir Comm Fed Sav & Loan Assn; chmn bd Tampa Parks Apts; mem Small Bus Admin Cncl; Odd Fellows; Masons; Pythians; Elks; Shriners; hon Edward Waters Coll Jacksonville; FL Mem Coll St Augustine 1954; Kappa Alpha Psi 1956; mem Dem Voters League. **HONORS/ACHIEVEMENTS:** Awds Hillsborough Co Sch Sys 1965; FL A&M Univ 1965; Frontiers of Amer 1963; Mary McLeod Bethune Medallion Bethune-Cookman Coll 1965. **BUSINESS ADDRESS:** President/Editor, FL Sentinel-Bulletin Pub Co, 2207 21 Ave, Tampa, FL 33601.

ANDREWS, EMANUEL CARL
Elected government official. **PERSONAL:** Born Sep 09, 1956, New York, NY. **EDUCATION:** Medgar Evers Coll, BA 1978; Albany State Univ, MA 1981. **CAREER:** Black & Puerto Rican Caucus NYS Legislature, asst exec dir 1980-81; US Congressman Major Owens, specl asst 1982-84; NY State Assembly, special asst state assembly. **HOME ADDRESS:** 1185 Carroll St, Brooklyn, NY 11225.

ANDREWS, FRAZIER L.
Clergyman. **PERSONAL:** Born May 03, 1933, Mobile, AL; married Lula Tillett. **EDUCATION:** AL State Univ, BS 1955; VA Union Grad Sch of Rel, MDiv 1958. **CAREER:** First Baptist Church Hertford NC, pastor 1957-68; First Baptist Ch High Point NC, minister 1968-. **ORGANIZATIONS:** Treas High Point Ch Hsg Inc; fndr & pres Antil Enterp Inc; mem Head Start Pol Co Bd Guilford Co; mem ESAA Adv Com; High Point City Schs; mem exec bd Model City Comm; former bd mem SCLC; pres Minister's Conf High Point & Vic; chmn High Point Bus Dev Corp; pres Brentwood Shop Ctr; mem Legal Aid Bd & Fam Serv Bur; co-spon London Wood Dev low-mid-inc hsg dev; former mem NC Good Neigh Counc; pres Hertford Movement; stud at Urban Training Cent Chi. **HONORS/ACHIEVEMENTS:** Pastor of Yr Hertford NC 1966; holds sev Hon Degrees; rec'd sev Ford Found Grants. **BUSINESS ADDRESS:** Minister, First Baptist Church, 701 E Washington Dr, High Point, NC 27260.

ANDREWS, JAMES E.
Educator/psychologist. **PERSONAL:** Born Aug 06, 1943, Pensacola, FL; son of C Andrews and Emma Andrews; married Pat; children: Lisa, Marcus. **EDUCATION:** Compson Coll, AA, 1970; CA State Dom Hill, BA, 1972; UCLA, MA, 1974; Nova Univ, PhD, 1977. **CAREER:** Compson Unified Sch, psychologist 1973-75; Pomona Unified Sch, psychologist 1975-79; Psychological Assessment Lab, owner 1977-; Mt San Antonio College, psychologist 1979-. **ORGANIZATIONS:** Pres Southern California Assn of Black Psychologists 1975-76; consultant Dept of Rehabilitation 1975-; consultant CA Poly 1981-. **HONORS/ACHIEVEMENTS:** Published book Theories of Child Observation, 1974; published several articles on children and learning. **MILITARY SERVICE:** AUS sp/4 2 yrs.

ANDREWS, JAMES F.
Educator. **PERSONAL:** Born Oct 25, 1918, Council, NC; married Dollie Ellison; children: Audrey, Hal. **EDUCATION:** Fagetteville State Univ, BS 1949; NC A&T State Univ, attended 1961. **CAREER:** Plain View Elementary School, principal. **ORGANIZATIONS:** Pres Bladen Co Tchr Assn; pres Southeastern Schoolmasters Orgn 1975; sec Kappa Rho Chapt, Omega Psi Phi Frat Inc; mem Dev of Prin; em Fayetteville State Univ Natl Alumni Assn; mem Lodge #374 Prince Hall F&AM of NC; mem Young Dem of NC. **BUSINESS ADDRESS:** Principal, Plain View Elementary School, Rte 1 Box 144, Tar Heel, NC 28392.

ANDREWS, JUDIS R.
Attorney. **PERSONAL:** Born Aug 27, 1941; married W Deni. **EDUCATION:** AZ State Univ, JD 1972. **CAREER:** AZ Civil Rights Commn, asst dir 1964-67; Phoenix Coll, instr 1967-68; AZ State Univ, adminstrv asst to pres 1968-69; Joshua M Bursh II firm of Cunningham Goodson Tiffany & Weltch, law clerk 1968-69; Private Practice, attorney. **ORGANIZATIONS:** Dir Summer Youth Project Phoenix OIC 1969; dir Spl Serv Maricopa Co Comm Action Prog 1969; spl asst to dir of Housing at AZ State Univ 1969-70; dir Progs & Opers Seattle Oppors Indus Ctr Inc Seattle 1972-73; fndg mem first sec to bd dir Wm F Patterson Lodge IBPOE #447; Civil E Neighborhood Council fndg mem & initial bd mem; Negro Polit Action Assn of AZ State Pres 1966-67; NAACP Youth Pres Pinal Co; CORE chmn vice chmn sec treas; 50 Bus Man Club fndr 1st pres; Omega Psi Phi Frat AZ State Univ Scholarship Comm; mem bd dir AZ State Alumni Assn 1975; mem bd dir AZ Commn on Post Secondary Educ 1974-75. **HONORS/ACHIEVEMENTS:** Scholarship Awd Martin Luther King Ctr for Disadvantaged Youth Seeking Educ Oppors; Negro Polit Action Assn of AZ Man of Yr 1968; 50 Bus Man Club Man of Yr 1967-68.

ANDREWS, MALACHI
Educator, artist, African centric sports researcher. **PERSONAL:** Born Sep 11, 1933, Los Angeles, CA; son of William L Smith (stepfather) and Geneva Downing Smith; divorced; children: Kim Andrews Warnette, Sekou Eusi, Atiba Azikwe. **EDUCATION:** LA City Coll, AA 1953; Univ of AZ, BA 1956, MEd 1961; LA State Univ, ethnic intl study, Ethnic Kinesiology Research Inst, Ed DE, 1979. **CAREER:** Barstow Intermed Sch, tchr 1959-62; Barstow HS, tchr & coach 1962-66; Compton HS, art tchr & track coach 1966-68; CA State Univ Dept Kinesiology & Phys Edn, assoc prof 1968-79, prof 1979-; consultant, Melanin Healing and Movement of African Centric Sports Life and Health. **ORGANIZATIONS:** Rsch dir Thomas Ethnic Kinesiology and Sports Rsch Inst Tucson, AZ; mem 1956 Olympic Track Team; KM-WR Science Consortium, bd of dir, vice pres educ 1988-; bd of dir, Seymour-Smith Inc; Gymnastic Sports Training Dir California Special Olympics, 1987-. **HONORS/ACHIEVEMENTS:** All-Around State Gymnastic Champion 1955; 1st Black Head Track Coach at a major Univ in CA; recip of Professional Art Awards; author: "Psychoblackology," "Six Melanin Dollar Man and Zionic Woman," "Elastic Communication," "Color Me Right, Then Frame Me in Motion"; co-author "Black Language"; particip 2nd World Black & African Festival of Arts & Culture Nigeria 1977. **MILITARY SERVICE:** AUS Pfc 1956-58. **HOME ADDRESS:** PO Box 4742, Hayward, CA 94540-4742. **BUSINESS ADDRESS:** Professor, CA State Univ at Hayward, Dept of Kinesiology & Phys Educ, Hayward, CA 94542.

ANDREWS, MAXINE RAMSEUR
Educator. **PERSONAL:** Born May 17, 1934, Fayetteville, NC; daughter of Patsy Evans Ramseur; divorced; children: Dr Sabrina Andrews Molden, Gigi, Thurman J III. **EDUCATION:** Fayetteville State Univ, BS 1956; North Carolina Central Univ, MEd 1963; East Carolina Univ EdS 1975; Univ of NC at Greensboro, EdD 1985. **CAREER:** Cumberland County Schools, teacher 1956-66, school social worker 1966-69; Elizabeth City State Univ, title III coord 1969-71; Fayetteville State Univ, adj prof 1985-; Sincerely Yours Writing & Specialty Svcs, proprietor 1986-; Cumberland County Schools, elem supervisor 1971-84, supervisor secondary educ 1984-. **ORGANIZATIONS:** Mem Natl Educ Assoc, Assoc for Supervision and Curriculum Div, NC Assoc for Educators, Phi Delta Kappa, NC Assoc of Administrators; mem Delta Sigma Theta Sor; mem NC Historical Preservation Soc, Fayetteville State Alumni Assoc, Fayetteville Comm of One Hundred; vice pres elect Region 4 NC Assoc of Supervision and Curriculum Develop 1986-87. **HONORS/ACHIEVEMENTS:** Distinguished Alumnae Fayetteville State Univ Natl Assoc for Equal Oppor in Higher Educ 1986. **BUSINESS ADDRESS:** Supervisor Secondary Educ, Cumberland County Schools, P O Box 2557, Fayetteville, NC 28302.

ANDREWS, NELSON MONTGOMERY
Statistician. **PERSONAL:** Born Jul 09, 1951, Winston-Salem, NC; son of Clem Andrews Sr. and Frances Andrews; married Sharon Millicent Parrish; children: Elenora, Ava. **EDUCATION:** Johnson C Smith Univ, Physics, Math, 1969-73; Purdue Univ, Statistics, MSD 1977. **CAREER:** BF Goodrich, statistician 1977-78; Bell Laboratories NJ, statistician 1978-82; Bellcore Comm NJ, statistician 1982-84; GTF Deer Valley AZ, sr org statistician 1985-87; NEC, Mgr, Quality Statistics, presently. **ORGANIZATIONS:** Mem, Phi Beta Sigma Fraternity 1971-; participant Gistault Inst Career Devel Program 1978; career recruiter Bell Labs Bellcore NJ 1980-84; Affirmative Action Educ Career Developer 1982-84; charter mem, Boule, Sigma Pi Phi Fraternity 1986-. **HONORS/ACHIEVEMENTS:** Pres Beta Kappa Chi, Phi Beta Sigma, Johnson C Smith Univ; speaker on statistical abstracts 1986 Joint Statistical Meeting 1986; speaker Intl Communications Meeting Tokyo Japan 1987.

ANDREWS, RAWLE
Physician. **PERSONAL:** Born Feb 04, 1929; son of Mr and Mrs Lawrence Andrews; married Naomi Cox; children: Rawle, Rhetta, Ronald, Rhonda. **EDUCATION:** Hampton Inst, BS (w/Honors) 1956; URIU MI, postgrad 1956-58; Meharry Med Coll, MD 1963. **CAREER:** LA Co General Hospital, intern 1963-64; Charles R Drew School Houston, school physician 1964; William Jr & Sr High Houston, school physician 1965-67; General Practice Medicine Houston, physician 1964-; Rawle Andrews, MD Clinic Assn, general practitioner. **ORGANIZATIONS:** Vice pres Acres Home City Council 1969-70, pres 1970-72; mem advisory bd Riverside Natl Bank Houston; pres Houston Med Forum 1970-72; bd dirs Operation Breadbasket; co-chmn task force comm Houston Galveston Area Council 1970-; vice pres trustee Montessori School Houston 1970-71; bd dir So Christian Leadership Conf; mem advisiry bd Elizabeth Johnson Center for the Aged; Martin Luther King Center; mem AMA, Royal Soc Health; chmn, bd trustees, bd dirs Natl Med Assn. **HONORS/ACHIEVEMENTS:** Humanitarian Award Antioch Baptist Church, 1969. **BUSINESS ADDRESS:** General Practioner, Rawle Andrews, MD Clinic Assn, 7901 W Montgomery Rd, Houston, TX 77088.

ANDREWS, RAYMOND
Writer. **PERSONAL:** Born Jun 06, 1934, Madison, GA; son of George Cleveland Andrews and Viola Perryman Andrews. **EDUCATION:** Michigan State University, 1956-57. **CAREER:** KLM Airlines NY, res agent 1958-66; Pix Photographers NY, photo lbrn 1967-72; Archer Courier Sys NY, Acct 1972-84. **HONORS/ACHIEVEMENTS:** Books include Appalachee Red pub by Dial Press, NY 1978, Rosiebelle Lee Wildcat TN 1980, Baby Sweets 1983, The Last Radio Baby scheduled for 1990; received James Baldwin Award presented by Dial Press, 1979. **MILITARY SERVICE:** USAF amn 1c 1952-56. **HOME ADDRESS:** 2013 Morton Rd, Athens, GA 30605. **BUSINESS ADDRESS:** c/o Susan Anne Protter, 110 West 40th St., Suite 1408, New York, NY 10018.

ANDREWS, WILLIAM HENRY
Retired hospital administrator. **PERSONAL:** Born Oct 16, 1919, Wellston, MO; son of William H and Viola; married Mildred E Joyce; children: William, Brenda. **EDUCATION:** Lincoln Univ, BS 1941; WA Univ, MHA 1954. **CAREER:** Homer G Phillips Hospital, asst adminis 1941-52; People's Hospital, administ 1954-55; George W Hubbard Hospital Meharry Med Coll, admin 1955-59; Forest City Hospital, admin 1959-64; Kaiser Found Hospital, admin 1981-; Cleveland Metro General Hospital, asst dir, dep dir, dir 1969-81; Kaiser Found Hospital, admin 1981-86 retired. **ORGANIZATIONS:** Mem Faculty Hlth Serv Admin Grad Sch OH State Univ; cncl mem Natl Inst Arthritis & Metabolic Diseases 1968-71; mem Physicians Clinic; asst adv com Cuyahoga Comm Coll; personnel adv com & soc serv clearing house com Cleveland Fedn for Comm Plang; Cath Interracial Cncl Cleveland Arthritis Found; trustee Cleveland Hemophilia Found; Hough Norwood Family Hlth Care Prgrm; Commonwealth Fund Fellow 1952; Fellow Amer Coll Hosp Adminstrs; mem WA Univ Alumni Assn; mem Natl Assn Hlth Serv Execs; panel mem OH Hosp Assn; exec com Blood Bank Comm, House Staff Comm, Grtr Cleveland Hosp Assn; mem Kappa Alpha Psi; Rotarian. **HOME ADDRESS:** 2960 Ripley Rd, Cleveland, OH 44120.

ANDREWS, WILLIAM L., SR.
Company executive. **PERSONAL:** Born Dec 25, 1955, Thomasville, GA; son of Azell Andrews, Sr and Ethel Lee Glenn; married Lydia Elzy Andrews, Jan 01, 1980; children: William Andrews Jr, Micah Ryan Andrews, Khea D'ana Andrews. **EDUCATION:** Auburn. **CAREER:** Housing Specialists, executive; Atlanta Falcons, fullback 1979-87; The William Andrews Group Ltd 1987. **ORGANIZATIONS:** Special Olympics; Project CURE for leukemia research; Drug Abuse Programs. **HONORS/ACHIEVEMENTS:** Second player in NFL history to get over 2,000 yards rushing & receiving twice; NFL'S 26th most prolific rusher of all-time in 5 seasons; tied 3rd on Falcons' all-time scoring list with 240 points; named to Pro Bowl for 4 seasons; 12th player in league history to go over 1,000 yds in rookie season; All-NFL 1983; 2nd team All-NFL; Pro Bowl 1979, 1981 & 1983; Falcons' MVP 1980 & 1982; NFL All-Rookie; Falcons' Man of the Year 1983. **BUSINESS ADDRESS:** President/

CEO, The William Andrews Group Ltd, 1100 Johnson Ferry Rd, Perimeter 400 Center One, Suite 420, Atlanta, GA 30342.

ANDUJAR, JOAQUIN
Professional athlete. **PERSONAL:** Born Dec 21, 1952, San Pedro De Macor; married Walkiria; children: Jesse Joaquin. **EDUCATION:** Attended, San Pedro de Marcoris DR. **CAREER:** Bradenton, player 1970; Sioux Falls, player 1971; Three Rivers, player 1972-73-75; Indianapolis, player 1973; Houston Astros, professional baseball player 1976-79. **BUSINESS ADDRESS:** Oakland Alameda Coliseum, Oakland, CA 94621.

ANGELL, EDGAR O.
Physician. **PERSONAL:** Married Anita Roach; children: Thelma, Sheila. **EDUCATION:** Drake Univ, tchr diploma BA 1950; COMS, DO 1954. **CAREER:** Jamaica, tchr; Private Practice, Cleveland; Private Practice Jackson TN, physician 1970-. **ORGANIZATIONS:** Mem Amer Osteopathic Assn, OH Osteopath Assn, Cuyahoga Co Osteopathic Assn; TN Osteopathic Assn; mem ACGOP; mem NAACP; mem Civic Action Group of Jackson TN. **BUSINESS ADDRESS:** 346 Hays Ave, Jackson, TN 38301.

ANGELOU, MAYA
Author. **PERSONAL:** Born Apr 04, 1928, St Louis, MO; children: Guy Johnson. **CAREER:** So Christian Leadership Conf, coord 1959-60; Arab Observer Egypt, assoc editor 1961-62; Univ of Ghana, asst admin 1963-66; African Review, editor 1964-66; CA State Univ, Wichita State Univ, Wake Forest Univ, visiting prof, 1974; author. **ORGANIZATIONS:** Mem Directos Guild of Amer, Equity, AFTRA; adv bd Womens Prison Assoc; bd of trustees Amer Film Inst 1975, appt Reynolds Professor Wake Forest Univ, Winston-Salem NC 1981; commiss by Gov James B Hunt to Bd of NC Arts Counc 1984-85; contrib Ghanaian Times Radio Ghana. **HONORS/ACHIEVEMENTS:** Author "I Know Why the Caged Bird Sings" 1970, "Just Give Me A Cool Drink of Water Fore I Die" 1971, "Georgia, Georgia" 1972, "Gather Together in My Name" 1974, "Oh Pray My Wings are Gonna Fit Me Well" 1975, "Singin & Swingin & Getting Merry Like Christmas" 1976, "The Heart of A Woman" 1981, "Shaker, Why Don't You Sing" 1983; Woman of the Year Ladies Home Jrnl 1976; Natl Comm on Observance of Intl Womens Year named by pres Carter 1977; Amer Revolution Bicent Counc named by Pres Ford 1975-76; Tony Nomination for Best Supporting Actress role of Nyo Boto grandmother Roots 1977; hon degrees from Smith Coll, 1975, Mills Coll, 1975, Lawrence Univ, 1976, Wake Forest Coll, 1977. **BUSINESS ADDRESS:** Professor, Wake Forest University, Box 7314 Reynolda Station, Winston-Salem, NC 27109.

ANISE, LADUN OLADUNJOYE E.
Educator. **PERSONAL:** Born Mar 24, 1940, Nigeria. **EDUCATION:** Syracuse Univ, BA 1967, MA 1968, PhD Political Science 1970; Univ of Pittsburgh, MA 1975. **CAREER:** Syracuse Univ, African Studies-Minority Studies, lecturer 1968-70; Educ Policy & Resource Devel Center, Syracuse Univ, rsch assoc 1969-70; Univ of Pittsburgh, asst prof 1970-75; Univ of Ife Nigeria, visiting sr lecturer 1979-83; Hill Dist Catholic School System & Educ Devel Center, Pittsburgh PA, consultant 1972-75; Univ of Pittsburgh, assoc prof 1975-, African Studies Group, coord 1982-88, Black Studies Dept, chmn (summers) 1987, 1989. **ORGANIZATIONS:** Mem Current Issues Comm African Studies Assoc 1968-, Amer Political Science Assoc, Natl Org of Black Political Science, African Heritage Studies Assoc, NatlAcad of Social Science. **HONORS/ACHIEVEMENTS:** ASPAU Achievement & Scholastic Award 1967; Omecron Delta Kappa 1967; Maxwell Fellow 1967-70; Woodrow Wilson Doctoral Fellow 1970; Meritorious Achievement Award Univ of Pittsburgh 1974. **BUSINESS ADDRESS:** Associate Professor, Dept of Political Science, Univ of Pittsburgh, 4T25 Forbes Quad, Pittsburgh, PA 15260.

ANTHONY, CLARENCE EDWARD
Public business managment consultant. **PERSONAL:** Born Oct 10, 1959, Belle Glade, FL; son of Bill Anthony and Irene; children: Reidel V. **EDUCATION:** Palm Beach Jr Coll, AA 1979; FL Atlantic Univ, BA 1981, MPA 1982. **CAREER:** South FL Water Mgmt Dist, internship rsch asst; Treasure Coast Regional Planning Council, regional planner; Commissioner Ken Adams District V, admin asst; Dept of Equal Opportunity, dir; Palm Beach Co Bd of Commissioners, county commissioner; Anthony & Associates, pres. **ORGANIZATIONS:** Pres FL Atlantic Univ Alumni Assoc; bd of dirs Big Brothers/Big Sisters; mem District IX Mental Health Drug Abuse Planning Council; bd of dirs Leadership Palm Beach County; bd of dirs Hispanic Human Resources, Glades Area Retarded Citizens; mem FL League of Cities Urban Admin Comm; bd of dirs FL Inst of Govt; former pres and founder FAU Black Alumni Assoc; mem Omega Psi Phi Fraternity; chmn FL League of Cities Finance and Taxation Comm; bd mem Palm Beach County Area Planning Bd; mayor, South Bay Florida 1984-. **HONORS/ACHIEVEMENTS:** McKnight Foundation Black Doctoral Fellowship; FAU Distinguished Alumnus Awd; Palm Beach Jr Coll Distinguished Alumnus Award; Environmental Growth Mgmt Graduate Fellowship; Phi Theta Kappa Scholarship; Intl Youth in Achievement; 30 Leaders of the Future, Ebony Magazine, 1988. **HOME ADDRESS:** 310 SE 4th Ave, PO Box 23, South Bay, FL 33493.

ANTHONY, DAVID HENRY, III
Educator. **PERSONAL:** Born Apr 28, 1952, Brooklyn, NY; married Allison Anitra Sampson; children: Adey Tabita Frances. **EDUCATION:** NY Univ, AB 1968-72; Univ of WI-Madison, MA History 1975, DPhil History 1983. **CAREER:** Fulbright Fellow Dept of State, rsch assoc 1976-77; Univ of Dar es Salaam Tanzania, rsch assoc 1976-77; Clark Univ, visiting prof 1979; Coppin State Coll, instructor of history 1980-84. **ORGANIZATIONS:** Curr spec Madison Metro Sch Dist 1977-78; consul Swahili Anteiro Pietila Helen Winternitz 1980; rsch affiliate Univ of FL Ctr for African studies 1982; visiting prof History Dept Towson State Univ 1982-83; judge Gr Baltimore History Fair 1982-84; mem Phi Alpha Theta 1983-; mem Fulbright Alumni Assn 1981-. **HONORS/ACHIEVEMENTS:** Fulbright Hays Awd Fulbright Found Dept of State 1976-77. **BUSINESS ADDRESS:** Prof, Bd of Studies in History, Univ of California, Santa Cruz, CA 95064.

ANTHONY, JEFFREY CONRAD
Entertainment producer. **PERSONAL:** Born Jun 03, 1949, Washington, DC. **EDUCATION:** Georgetown Univ, BA 1976. **CAREER:** Natl Endowment for the Arts, sr program specialist 1980-85; Brooklyn Acad of Music, dir comm relations 1985-86; Freelance Consultant, independent production consultant 1986-. **ORGANIZATIONS:** Assoc producer Capital City Jazz Festival Washington DC 1982-85; assoc mem Smithsonian Inst; mem Natl Assoc of Jazz Educators; bd mem New Music Distribution Svcs; assoc mem Mgt Natl Jazz Serv Org 1984-; producer "Dance Africa" Brooklyn NY 1986; assoc producer "Black Family Reunion Celebration," Wash DC, Atlanta GA, Los Angeles CA, Detroit MI 1986-87; producer "1st Annual DIVA Found Awds" Kennedy Center, Wash DC 1987. **HONORS/ACHIEVEMENTS:** Certificate of Merit Outstanding Young Men of Amer 1983; Natl Endowment Arts, Sustained Superior Performance 1984, Special Act & Serv Awd 1984, Certificate of Appreciation 1985. **MILITARY SERVICE:** USMC sgt E-5 3 1/2 yrs; Silver Star, Bronze Star, Purple Heart (2), Vietnamese Service, Vietman Campaign Medal, Natl Defense Medal, Good Conduct Medal, Vietnamese Cross of Gallantry. **HOME ADDRESS:** 221 Clermont Ave2, Brooklyn, NY 11205.

ANTHONY, LEANDER ALDRICH
Elected government official. **PERSONAL:** Born Sep 21, 1917, St Joseph, LA; married Evelyn Minor; children: Elizabeth, Leander A Jr. **EDUCATION:** Southern Univ, BS; AUS Infantry, 2nd Lt; Tuskegee Inst, Dr's Degree of Veterinary Med. **CAREER:** Mad Parish Port Comm, chairperson; JTPA-Manpower Ctr, dir; City of Tallulah, mayor 1978-82 1982-86. **ORGANIZATIONS:** Mem North Delta Regional Planning Dist; mem Elks; mem Omega Psi Phi Frat. **HONORS/ACHIEVEMENTS:** Goodwill Ambassador State of LA; Man of the Year-Outstanding Black Omega Psi Phi Frat 1979. **MILITARY SERVICE:** 93rd Infantry 2nd lt 4 yrs. **HOME ADDRESS:** 800 Ethel St, Tallulah, LA 71282. **BUSINESS ADDRESS:** Mayor, City of Tallulah, 204 N Cedar, Tallulah, LA 71282.

ANTHONY, LILLIAN DELORES
Educator. **PERSONAL:** Born Nov 04, 1925, Indianapolis, IN; married Desmond. **EDUCATION:** Univ of MA, EdD 1976; Pittsburg Sem, MRe 1953; Lincoln U, BS 1951. **CAREER:** Univ of NE, chairperson & assoc prof; Minneapolis Civil Rights Dept, dir 1967-69; Univ of MN, assoc prof & asst chmn 1969-72; Towson State Univ, dean of minor student serv; US Dept of Labor Bureau of Work Programs MN & WI, dist dir 1965-67. **ORGANIZATIONS:** St dir Assn for Study of Afro-Am Life & Hist; consult Girl Scts of Am; Inst Serv Ed; Multi-Cltrl Inst; USA HEW; Lincoln Pub Sch; Inner Cities Studies Comm; Inst to Facil Desegra; bd dir YWCA; Franklin Comm Fed Cred Union; Girls Club of Omaha; Metro Arts Coun; Urban Leag of NE; mem Gamma Tau Chap of Iota Phi Lambda Sor; Sorop Intl of Am; Nat Coun of Negro Wmn Inc; Am Assn of Univ Prof; Am Pers & Guild Assn; rsrc prsn for Omaha Pub Sch Art Rsrc Ctr; Curric Revw Comm; mem Univ of NE at Omaha Educ Pol Comm & Fclty Senate. **HONORS/ACHIEVEMENTS:** UNO Goodrich Sch Prgm Award; award outst serv Girls Club of Omaha; spec recog award Franklin Comm Fed Cred Union; UMOJA award Boy Scts; grant NE Bi-Centnnl Res Grant to write profiles of Blks in NE 1976. **BUSINESS ADDRESS:** Staff Associate, General Assembly Council, EEO Presbyterian Church, 475 Riverside Dr, New York, NY 10115.

APEA, JOSEPH BENNET KYEREMATENG
President. **PERSONAL:** Born Aug 19, 1932, Aburi, Ghana;married Agnes Johanna Hinson; children: Kathleen Kyerewa, Adwoa Ofeibea, Abena Otwiwa, Akua Nyam. **EDUCATION:** IL Inst of Tech, BSCE 1968; Univ of IL, Arch. **CAREER:** Westenhoff & Novic Inc, Chgo, civil engr 1961-64; Kaiser Engrs, Chgo, stgruct engr 1964-65; Sargent & Lundy Engrs, Chgo, struct engr 1965-72; Samuels, Apea & Asso, Inc;; pres 1972-80. **ORGANIZATIONS:** Mbr Natl Soc Prof Engrs; mem Am Soc Civil Engrs; mem IL Asso Struct Engrs. **HONORS/ACHIEVEMENTS:** Community Leaders and Noteworthy Americans; frmwrk for rcnstrctn Ghana Citizens Org of USA & Canada 1984; positive attitude toward progress The Talking Drums UK 1985; chmn DBE/WBE Adv Cncl IL Dept of Transportation 1986. **BUSINESS ADDRESS:** President, Joseph Apea & Assoc Inc, 1313 S Michigan Ave, Chicago, IL 60605.

APPLEBY-YOUNG, SADYE PEARL
Educator. **PERSONAL:** Born Dec 18, 1927, Gainesville, GA; married Dr Harding B; children: Sybil Bernadette, Harding G, Angela, Gregory. **EDUCATION:** Tuskegee Inst (moton scholar), BS 1945; Cornell Univ (general educ bd fellow); MS, Child Devel 1946; GA State Univ (pi lambda theta), PhD Educ & Psychology, 1974. **CAREER:** UUniv of AR Pine Bluff, AR, div dir 1946-57; NC Central Univ Durham, NC, interim div dir 1958-60; Spelman Coll Atlanta, GA, dept chmn 1961-78; Morris Brown Coll, div dir, educ & psychology, 1978-. **ORGANIZATIONS:** Mem Alpha Kappa Mu Natl Hon Soc 1943-; sec Pi Lambda Theta Hon Soc 1978; Fac sec, Omicron Delta Kappa Natl Hon Leadership Soc 1983-; mem St Paul of the Cross Roman Catholic Church; rep, Catholic School of Educ; Acad Councils Work Related, Morris Brown Coll. **HONORS/ACHIEVEMENTS:** Moton Scholar Tuskegee Inst Tuskegee, AL 1945, Hon Soc 1943; Alpha Kappa Mu Nat; Frederick Patterson's Winner Oratory Tuskegee Inst 1945; All Expense Fellowship General Educ Bd to Cornell Univ, 1945; High School Class Valedictorian St High Gainesville, GA. **HOME ADDRESS:** 903 Falcon Dr SW, Audubon Forest, Atlanta, GA 30311. **BUSINESS ADDRESS:** Division Director/ Educ & Psy, Morris Brown Coll, 643 MLK Dr SW, Spelman Coll, Atlanta, GA 30314.

APPLETON, CLEVETTE WILMA
Social worker. **PERSONAL:** Born Jul 22, Louisville, KY; daughter of Cleve Appleton and Wilma Henry Appleton. **EDUCATION:** KY State Univ, BA 1971; Kent School of Soc Work Univ of Louisville, MSSW 1974. **CAREER:** Neighborhood Youth Corp, teacher asst 1966-67; Louisville Free Publ Library, clerk 1968-70; KY Dept of Human Resources, soc worker 1971-73; Metro Soc Serv Dept, student soc worker 1974; Bridgehaven, student soc worker 1974; KY Dept of Human Resources, soc worker grad I 1975; River Region Svcs, sr socialworker Univ of Louisville School of Med 1978-. **ORGANIZATIONS:** Mem NAACP, Council of Nephrology Soc Workers Network 17, Natl Kidney Found of Metro Louisville. **HONORS/ACHIEVEMENTS:** Natl Honor Soc of Secondary School 1967; Miss Wesley Club KY State Univ 1971; Maude Ainslie Scholarship 1967; KY Dept for Human Resources Grad School Stipend 1973. **HOME ADDRESS:** 3011 River Park Dr, Louisville, KY 40211. **BUSINESS ADDRESS:** Senior Social Worker, Kidney Disease Program, University of Louisville, Louisville, KY 40292.

APPLEWHAITE, LEON B.
Attorney. **PERSONAL:** Born Sep 04, 1927, Brooklyn; married Louise J Harley. **EDUCATION:** NY Univ, BA 1948; Brooklyn Law Sch, JD 1951; Brooklyn Univ Law Sch, LLM 1961. **CAREER:** Social Security Admin, claims authorizer 1955-59; Judge Francis E Rivers, legal sec 1959-63; NY State Comm for Human Rights, field rep; NY State Bd of Mediation, labor arbitrator & mediator 1964-67; NY State Workmen's Comp Bd, assoc coun 1967-68; NY State Pub Empl Relations Bd supervising mediator regional rep. **ORGANIZA-**

TIONS: Mem Assn of Bar of City of NY; Natl Academy of Arbitrators; Indus Relations Rsch Assn; Natl Bar Assn; Amer Arbitration Assn; Soc of Profls in Dispute Resolution. **MILITARY SERVICE:** AUS 1952-54. **BUSINESS ADDRESS:** Supervising Mediator, NYS Pub Emp Rel Bd, 342 Madison Ave, New York, NY 10017.

ARAUJO, NORMAN
Educator. **PERSONAL:** Born Mar 22, 1933, New Bedford, MA; son of Jose Joao Araujo and Julia Coracao Araujo; widowed. **EDUCATION:** Harvard Coll, AB (Magna Cum Laude, Phi Beta Kappa) 1955; Universite d'Aix-Marseille, Certificat d'etudes litteraires 1956; Harvard Univ, AM 1957, PhD 1962. **CAREER:** Univ of MA-Amherst, asst prof 1962-64; Boston Coll, asst prof 1964-68, assoc prof 1968-. **ORGANIZATIONS:** Mem Modern Language Assoc of Amer 1976-; chief advisor Cape Verdean News. **HONORS/ACHIEVEMENTS:** Fulbright Fellowship (France); Natl Defense Act Fellowship (Portugal); book "A Study of Cape Verdean Literature," 1966; book "In Search of Eden, Lamartine's Symbols of Despair and Deliverance," 1976; article "Emile Augier," in Magill's Critical Survey of Drama 1986. **BUSINESS ADDRESS:** Assoc Prof Romance Languages, Boston College, 302-C Lyons Hall, Chestnut Hill, MA 02167.

ARBERRY, MORSE, JR.
State legislator. **PERSONAL:** Born Mar 01, 1953, Oakland, CA; married Carol I Daniels. **CAREER:** Nevada State Assembly, Carson City NV, state assemblyman, District 7. **BUSINESS ADDRESS:** State Capitol, Carson City, NV 89710. *

ARBUCKLE, PAMELA SUSAN
Dentist. **PERSONAL:** Born Mar 12, 1955, Oakland, CA. **EDUCATION:** Laney College, AS 1975; Univ of CA, AB 1977, BS, DDS 1982, MPP 1984. **CAREER:** Univ of CA, teaching asst 1982-83; Congressional Rsch Service, policy analyst summer 1983; San Francisco Gen Hosp, staff dentist 1983-; Alameda Cty Health Care Serv Agency, staff dentist 1983-. **ORGANIZATIONS:** Sec Natl Dental Soc of the Bay Area 1983-84; comm Emeryville Comm Devel Adv Comm 1983-85; mem Alameda Cty Bd of Suprvs Subcomm on Dental Health 1983-85; prog comm mem Bay Area Black Consortium for Quality 1983-85; ed Network for Black Health Prof newsletter 1984-85; bd mem Berkelley Head Start Health Adv Bd 1984-85; vice pres CA Chap Natl Dental Assoc 1985; councilor UC CA Alumni Assoc 1984-87; bd mem City of Berkeley Maternal Child & Adolescent Health Bd 1985-86, Univ of CA Black Alumni Club; mem NAACP 1985; bd mem Holy Names HS Alumnae Bd 1983-. **HONORS/ACHIEVEMENTS:** Williard Fleming Scholarship Univ CA 1979; Regents Scholarship Univ of CA 1978-84; Comm Dentistry Service Awd Univ of CA 1982; Cert of Appreciation SF Area Health Educ Ctr 1984; recipient Outstanding Young Women of America 1984. **HOME ADDRESS:** 1262 Ocean Ave, Emeryville, CA 94608. **BUSINESS ADDRESS:** Dentist, Alameda Cty Hlth Care Svs, 470-27th St, Oakland, CA 94609.

ARBURTHA, LEODIES UYLESS
Educational administrator. **PERSONAL:** Born Dec 16, 1923, Warren, AR; son of Will Arburtha; married Mildred McGowan; children: Louise, LeNardias, Leodies, Alexis. **EDUCATION:** Tuskegee Inst, BS 1948; Chicago State Univ, MS 1966. **CAREER:** Chicago Vocational HS, tchr graphic arts 1959-70, asst prin 1968-72, principal 1972-. **ORGANIZATIONS:** YMCA; Intl Typographical Union; Phi Delta Kappa; reg dir IIEA Chicago; coord Area 5-J Phi Delta Kappa Intl 1976; natl rep NASSP Com on Asst Principalship 1974-78; pres Chicago HS Asst Principals Assn 1972-; mem NEA, IEA, AVA, IVA, Kappa Alpha Psi; dir & dist 5 rep Phi Delta Kappa Intl. **HONORS/ACHIEVEMENTS:** Amer Fed Tchrs Civic Awd, S Shore YMCA, 1974; special recognition plaque, Chicago HS Asst Principal's Assn, 1972, 1973. **HOME ADDRESS:** 8732 S Calumet Ave, Chicago, IL 60619.

ARCHER, CHALMERS, JR.
Educational administrator. **PERSONAL:** Born Apr 21, 1938, Tchula, MS; son of Chalmers Archer Sr (deceased) and Eva R Archer. **EDUCATION:** Tuskegee Inst, Alabama, BS 1972, MEd 1973; Auburn University, Alabama, PhD 1979; Univ of Alabama, postdoctorate study 1980-81; MIT, Cambridge MA, Certificate 1982. **CAREER:** Saints Jr College, asst to the pres, 1968-70; Tuskegee Inst, asst vice pres & asst prof 1970-83; Northern Virginia Community College, admin/assoc prof, 1983-; architect of Comp Counseling Ctr and Weekend College at Tuskegee Inst; Architect of Reading & Language Arts Special Emphasis Curriculum for public schools; developed successful multi-level Educ Alliance to Adv Equal Access with public schools; contributing editor Jackson Advocate, Jackson, MS; presented articulation model to Dept of Educ 1980; author of 22 educational and other publications. **ORGANIZATIONS:** Natl Assn of Coll Deans, Registrars, and Admissions Officers; Phi Delta Kappa; Kappa Delta Pi; APGA; NAACP; charter mem Kiwanis Intl of Macon Coll; AAUP; AACRAO; Southeastern Assoc of Community Coll; Cooperative Educ. **HONORS/ACHIEVEMENTS:** Honorary Doctorate of Letters, Saints Jr Coll, Lexington MS, 1970; Phi Delta Kappa's Award for Leadership; Exemplary Research & Program Development, 1981; vice pres, Saints Jr Coll Alumni; cited for community contribution; past bd mem, Natl Consortium for the Recruitment of Black Students from Northern Cities; past chairman, State of Alabama's Steering Committee for Advanced Placement of High School Students; lectured at Cambridge Univ, England, and five major universities on teaching and learning interdisciplinary studies, 1988-89. **MILITARY SERVICE:** AUS, Green Berets-Airborne, captain ten years; distinction of saving life of first Amer injured in Vietnam, 1957. **HOME ADDRESS:** 4522 Commons Dr, #40, Annandale, VA 22003. **BUSINESS ADDRESS:** Assoc Prof & Educ Admin, Northern Virginia Community Coll, 3001 N Beauregard St, Alexandria, VA 22311.

ARCHER, DENNIS WAYNE
Judge. **PERSONAL:** Born Jan 01, 1942, Detroit, MI; son of Ernest James Archer and Frances Carroll Archer; married Trudy DunCombe, Jun 17, 1967; children: Dennis Wayne Jr, Vincent DunCombe. **EDUCATION:** Wayne State Univ, Detroit MI, 1959-61; Detroit Inst of Tech, Detroit MI, 1961-63; Western Michigan Univ, BS, 1965; Detroit Coll of Law, Detroit MI, JD, 1970. **CAREER:** Gragg & Gardner PC, trial lawyer, 1970-71; Hall Stone Allen & Archer, trial lawyer, 1971-73; Detroit Coll Law, Detroit MI, assoc prof, 1978-78; Charfoos Christensen & Archer, trial lawyer, 1973-85; Wayne State Univ Law School, Detroit MI, adj prof, 1984-85; Michigan Supreme Court, assoc justice, 1986-. **ORGANIZATIONS:** Life mem, former pres Natl Bar Assn; mem Amer Bar Assn; mem Amer Judicature Soc; mem past pres State Bar of MI; mem Wolverine Bar Assn; mem Detroit Bar Assn; fellow Intl Soc of Barristers; mem MI Trial Lawyers Assn; mem Amer Trial Lawyers Assn; mem Thomas M Cooley Club; sec US Dist Court Monitoring Commissioner Detroit Sch Dist 1978; Old Newsboys Goodfellow Fund 1980-84; bd of dirs Legal Aid & Defenders Assn of Detroit 1980-82; mem Detroit Chamber of Commerce 1984-85; bd of dirs Metro Detroit Convention & Visitors Bureau 1984-87; mem Alpha Phi Alpha Frat Inc; mem The Fellows of the Amer Bar Assn; life mem NAACP; bd of trustees Detroit Coll of Law 1985-88; bd of dirs MI Cancer Foundation 1985-87; mem Detroit Coll of Law 50th Anniversary Commn 1986. **HONORS/ACHIEVEMENTS:** Co-winner Amer Bar Assn Personal Finance Annual Appellate Court Argument 1976; Western MI Univ Distinguished Alumnus Awd 1982; named as one of the 100 MostInfluential Black Americans by Ebony magazine 1984; publications including "Blackballed — A Case Against Private Clubs" Barrister 1983; cited in Natl Law Journal as one of the 100 most powerful attorneys in the US 1985; Community Serv Awd Detroit Urban Ctr 1985; Distinguished Achievement Awd NAACP Detroit Branch 1985; Probity Merit Awd Quinn Chapel AME Church 1986; Honorary Doctor of Laws Degree, Western Michigan University, 1987; Honorary Doctor of Laws Degree, Detroit College of Law, 1988; Honorary Doctor of Laws Degree, University of Detroit School of Law, 1988. **BUSINESS ADDRESS:** Associate Justice, Michigan Supreme Court, 1425 Lafayette Bldg, Detroit, MI 48226.

ARCHER, EVA P.
Nurse. **PERSONAL:** Born in Hackensack, NJ; daughter of Richard and Jennie Patrick; widowed; children: Reginald T Jr. **EDUCATION:** Lincoln School for Nursing, RN 1926; NYU, BS 1954. **CAREER:** Lincoln School for Nursing, operating room nurse 1927-28; New York City Health Dept, public health nurse 1928-69, public schools & prevention; Public School 92 Queens, educ asst 1970-73; Day Care Centers BCL, health advisor 1973-78. **ORGANIZATIONS:** Financial sec & treasurer Bd of Dir Langston Hughes Library Comm 1980-81; pres L I Seetem Natl Council Negro Women; past Moderator Corona Congressional Church; past Besilous Delta Clap Lambda Kappa New Sorority; pres No Shore Club Business & Professional Assn 1980-84; preseda NY Region Fedn of Colored Womens Club 1978-80; financial sec Queens Dist 369 Vet Assn Womens Div; cmdrs Daughters of Isis Aba Bekr Ct Brooklyn. **HONORS/ACHIEVEMENTS:** Bncnw Long Island Sec Citation for Leadership 1960-75; Ordinance of Eastern Star Serv Award 1961-79; Appreciation Award, No Shore Natl Assn Business & Professional Women 1984; Community Service Award, Natl Council of Negro Women 1987. **HOME ADDRESS:** 107 1/2 32nd Ave, East Elmhurst, NY 11369.

ARCHER, JUANITA A.
Physician. **PERSONAL:** Born Nov 03, 1934, Washington, DC; daughter of Roy E Hinnant and Anna B Blakeney; married Frederick Archer; children: Frederick II. **EDUCATION:** Howard Univ, Washington, DC, BS, 1956, MS, 1958, MD, 1965. **CAREER:** Freedman's Hospital, intern 1965-66; Howard Univ, resd 1966-68, flw 1970-71, instr 1971-75; Diabetes Investigative Grp, dir; Endocrine Metabolic Lab 1972-; Endocrine & Metabolic Diseases Sect, asst prof of medicine 1975-79, assoc prof medicine 1980-. **ORGANIZATIONS:** Coll of Medicine, admissions comm 1979-, Biohazards Comm 1981-, Comm to Review the Dermatology Dept 1980, mem Spec Awds Comm 1980, Srch Comm for Chmn of the Dept of Comm Health & Family Practice 1982, Rsch Comm 1978; Genl Clinical Rsch Ctr 1982, Alumni Awds Comm 1982; mem DC Med Soc; rsch comm Washington Area Affiliate of the Amer Diabetes Assn; mem Sigma Xi, Beta Kappa Chi, DC Med Soc, Amer Federation for Clinical Rsch, The Endocrine Soc, NY Acad of Sci, Delta Sigma Theta; mem Genl Clinical Rsch Comm NIH 1976-86; Biohazards & Biosafety Comm Howard U; consultant Arizona Research Council 1986, 1987. **HONORS/ACHIEVEMENTS:** Amer Men & Women in Science 1976; Josiah Macy Faculty Fellow 1974-77; Who's Who Black Amer 1978, 1979, 1981, 1982; mem Genl Clinical Rsch Ctr Comm NatlInstitutes of Health; Who's Who in Frontier Sci & Tech 1983, 1984; Physician's Recognition Award 1983-86; numerous publications including, Archer JA, Gorden P & Roth,J Defect in Insulin Binding to Receptors Clin Invest 55,166-175 1975; Archer, JA Knopp, R Olefsky, J Shuman, CR "Clinical Diabetes Update 11" Upjohn Monograph Jan 1980; Natl Podiatry Medical Award, 1989; Amer Red Cross Award, 1988; Amer Medical Assn Physicians Recognition Award; Moses Wharton Young Research Award, 1988. **BUSINESS ADDRESS:** Associate Professor of Medicine, Howard University, 520 W Street, NW, Seeley G. Mudd Building, Washington, DC 20059.

ARCHER, LEE A., JR.
Retired chairman. **EDUCATION:** Univ of CA at Los Angeles, Bachelor's degree; New York Univ, Master's degree. **CAREER:** Vanguard Capital Corp a Genl Foods MESBIC, first pres and then chairman; North St Capital Corp, chmn 1973; General Foods, mgr of corporate equal oppor affairs 1970, dir, corp vice pres of urban affairs (retired). **ORGANIZATIONS:** Guest lecturer in intl relations, geopolitics, military power and black history at various univs and colls in Central America, Europe and Southeast Asia; mem Intl Lions, United Nations Assoc, The Natl Business League, Columbia Univ's Brookdale Inst on Aging and Human Develop, Continental Africa Chamber of Commerce, Latin Amer Dance Theatre; founding mem Negro Airmen's Intl, Tuskegee Airmen's Assoc; mem bd of dirs Hudson Commercial Corp, McCall Corp, Caribbean Basin Broadcasting Corp, InterFuture, Boy's Clubs of Amer, OIC's of Amer, Cncl of Better Business Bureaus of Amer. **MILITARY SERVICE:** USAF deputy commander of bases Southern Command; attended Air Force Command and Staff Coll of the Air Univ 1956.

ARCHER, SUSIE COLEMAN
Educator, director. **PERSONAL:** Born Mar 29, 1946, Pembroke, KY; married Dennis Archer. **EDUCATION:** BS, 1968; MA 1969; Vanderbilt Univ, completed all course work for PhD. **CAREER:** Austin Peay State Univ, supvr women's dormitories 1969-74; Austin Peay State Univ, tchr 1969-75; Univ of MD European Br W Berlin Germany, instr 1975-77; Salt Lake City Sch Dist, supvr of counselors, 1978-80; UT Tech Coll at Salt Lake, dir of regis & admin, 1980-87; assoc univ registrar, Vanderbilt Univ, 1987-. **ORGANIZATIONS:** Mem Altrusa Club 1979; bd dir Travelers Aid Soc 1979-; mem Acad Governance Com; Discrimination & Unfair Grading Practices Comm; Affirmative Action Comm; Com to Revise Promotion & Tenure Policies; Comm Union for Women's Rights; mem Middle TN Educ Assn; mem APSU Women's Club; faculty adv Phi Alpha Theta 1971-72; faculty adv Alpha Mu Gamma; faculty adv Sr Classical League 1973-; faculty adv Circle K; faculty adv Alpha Phi; faculty adv Intl Students Assn; mem, Amer Assn of Collegiate Registrars & Admissions Officers, 1980-; pres, UT Assn of Collegiate & Admissions Officers, 1985-86; Mem, TN Southern Assn of Collegiate Registrars & Admissions Officers, 1987-. **HONORS/ACHIEVEMENTS:** Phi Alpha Theta Outstanding Student in History 1968; Outstanding Student in French 1967; Rene Descartes Medal in French Literature 1968; APSU Grad Assistantship 1968; Alpha Mu Gamma's Scholarship to participate in experiment in Intl Living Vanderbilts Chancellors Fellowship for Grad Study 1972-73. **BUSINESS ADDRESS:** Assoc Univ Registrar, Vanderbilt Univ, 242 Alexander Hall, Nashville, TN 37240.

ARCHIBALD, B. MILELE
Attorney. **PERSONAL:** Born Jul 04, 1945, New York, NY; married Faruq Muhammad; children: Nyota. **EDUCATION:** Bronx Comm Coll, AAS, 1968; Hunter Coll, New York NY, BA, 1973; Univ of California, Berkeley, JD, 1976. **CAREER:** Chief Judge DC Ct of Appeals, law clerk, 1976-77; Fed Trade Comm, Washington DC, staff atty, 1977-78; Overseas Private Investment Corp, spec asst to the pres, 1978-. **ORGANIZATIONS:** Mem Washington DC Bar Assn 1977-; mem Natl Assn of Black Women Attys 1978. **BUSINESS ADDRESS:** Special Assistant to President, Overseas Priv Investmt Corp, 1129 20th St NW, Washington, DC 20527.

ARCHIBALD, NATE
Professional basketball player. **PERSONAL:** Born Sep 02, 1948. **EDUCATION:** Univ of TX, attended 1970. **CAREER:** Cincinnati/KC Royals, basketball player 1970-76; NJ Nets, basketball player 1976-77; Buffalo Braves, basketball player 1977-78; Boston Celtics, professional basketball player 1978-. **HONORS/ACHIEVEMENTS:** Led league in socring & assists 1972-73; played in All Star Game 5 times; named NBA Comeback Player of Yr 1979-80; Fourth NBA passing 1980-81. **BUSINESS ADDRESS:** Boston Celtics, Boston Garden at N Station, Boston, MA 02114.

ARCHIE, CORNELL B., JR.
Business executive. **PERSONAL:** Born Sep 13, 1948, Okmulgee, OK; married Marian E Shavers; children: Kimberly G, Jammison C. **EDUCATION:** Univ of WA-Seattle, BA Bus Admin 1973. **CAREER:** Pilot House Realty, real estate Salesman 1971-72; WA Mut Savs Bank, mgmt training 1972-74, investment asst 1974-75, investment officer 1975-76, asst vice pres govt money 1977-78, vice pres & adminstr 1978-. **ORGANIZATIONS:** Mem Pacific NW Bankers Assn 1975-; mem Puget Sound Chap Financial Mgr for Savs Instn 1978-; mem Seattle Soc of Financial Analyst 1978-; mem Seattle C of C 1979-; life mem Alpha Phi Alpha Frat 1969-; pres EOP Alumni Assn of Univ of WA 1978-; bd mem E Madison YMCA 1978-; mem Evergreen State Coll Bus Adv Com 1979-. **HONORS/ACHIEVEMENTS:** Outstanding Volunteer Awd E Madison Br of Metro Seattle YMCA 1980; Outstanding EOP Alumni Awd Univ of WA 1980. **BUSINESS ADDRESS:** Vice Pres/Administrator, WA Mut Savings Bank, 1101 2nd Ave, Seattle, WA 98101.

ARCHIE, JAMES LEE
Artist. **PERSONAL:** Born Jun 28, 1922, Orlander, NC; son of Eddie Archie and Elizabeth Archie; married Marjorie Ann Booth; children: Victoria Esther, Olivia Rebecca, Daniel James, Enoch Lee. **CAREER:** Group Shows, Harlem Hosp 1968, Studio Mus New York City 1969, Mary Rogers Coll 1969; Works Include, Destitute Meets Tranquility 1969; Afro-Amer Art Festival 1969; Strength of Black Beauty 1969; Africa I'Leto Galleries New York City 1970; Youth Devel Agency Exhibit 1970; Countee Cullen Library 1970; Participant Westchester Panorama White Plaines, NY 1971; 1st Black Arts Exhibition Albany, NY 1972; 9th Annual Outdoor Afro-Amer Art Festival 1972; decorator for Broadway producer, David Merrick & actress Leslie Uggams; designer Apollo Theater Harlem, NY dressing rooms; mgr Wilfred G Goden Contracting Inc NYC. **ORGANIZATIONS:** Dir Creative Comm Workshop NYC; art therapist for adults in disadvantaged areas; mem Museum of Art NYC; Intl Platform Assn; Federated Cultural Comm; volunteer consultant to teachers to improve understanding of problems facing disadvantaged children; volunteer community consultant, museum arts projects in disadvantaged areas. **BUSINESS ADDRESS:** Artist/Designer, 61-15 98th St, Rego Park, NY 11374.

ARCHIE, SHIRLEY FRANKLIN
Association administrator, educator. **PERSONAL:** Born Apr 15, 1944, Philadelphia, PA; married Robert Lewis Archie Jr; children: Keita T, Kweli I. **EDUCATION:** Cheyney State Coll, BA 1966; Howard Univ, grad study 1967-69; Temple Univ, Urban Educ 1979-81. **CAREER:** DC School System, educator 1967-70; Philadelphia School System, educator 1976-; Temple Univ, instructor 1983-85; Sigler Travel Serv Inc, travel consult 1983-; Natl Barristers Wives Inc, natl pres. **ORGANIZATIONS:** Mem Links Inc, Alpha Kappa Alpha, Jack & Jill of Amer, Women's Leaders Team, African-Amer Inst Zimbabwe; bd of dir Girl Scouts of Amer 1982-; bd of trustees Springside School 1982-; commiss Camden Cty Commiss for Women 1983; commiss Philadelphia-Major's Commiss for Women 1985. **HONORS/ACHIEVEMENTS:** Distinguished Serv Award, Girl Scouts of Amer 1982; Commendation for Outstanding Teacher Philadelphia Syst 1982, 1984. **BUSINESS ADDRESS:** Natl President, Natl Barristers Wifes, 1330 W Olney Ave, Philadelphia, PA 19119.

ARDREY, SAUNDRA CURRY
Educator. **PERSONAL:** Born Aug 26, 1953, Louisville, GA; daughter of Earle Curry and Estella Curry; married William McCarty Ardrey MD. **EDUCATION:** Winston Salem State Univ, BA 1975; Ohio State Univ, MA 1976, PhD 1983. **CAREER:** Univ of North Carolina Chapel Hill, visting lecturer 1979-80; Jefferson Comm Coll Univ of Kentucky, instructor 1980-81; Furman Univ, asst prof 1983-. **ORGANIZATIONS:** Mem Amer Policical Science Assoc 1975-87, Natl Conf of Black Political Science 1978-87, Southern Political Science Assoc 1983-87, Amer Assn of Univ Prof 1983-85; bd mem Greenville City Urban League 1983-87, Greenville City United Way 1983-84; exec comm Greenville City Democratic Party 1984-85; pres Greenville City Young Democrats 1984-85; pres Bowling Green Natl Org of Women (NOW). **HONORS/ACHIEVEMENTS:** Outstanding Young Women of Amer 1984-85. **BUSINESS ADDRESS:** Asst Prof, Govt Dept, Western Kentucky Univ, Grise Hall, Bowling Green, KY 42101.

ARGRETTE, JOSEPH
Chief operating officer. **PERSONAL:** Born Apr 01, 1931, New York, NY; son of Joseph Argrette, Jr and Mariah Tucker Dawson; married June Parker; children: Kendelle Ruth. **EDUCATION:** Long Island Univ, Brooklyn, NY, BS, MS 1954. **CAREER:** Riverside Hospital, Bronx, NY, dir vocational counseling; Federal Govt Office of Equal Opportunity, Washington, DC, dir Region I; Natl Alliance of Businessmen, Washington, DC, dir community relations; Stone Craft Intl, New York, NY, pres; Argrett Enterprises Corp, New York, NY, pres, 1977-. **ORGANIZATIONS:** Dir, vice pres, Natl Assn of Minority Contractors, 1985-89; dir, Gen Bldg Contractors-Assoc Gen Contractor, Assoc Gen Contractors of Amer, 1980-89. **HONORS/ACHIEVEMENTS:** Outstanding Minority Contractor, New York State Dept of Environmental Conservation, 1984; delegate, White House Conf on Small Business, 1986; Outstanding Mem Award, Natl Assn of Minority Contractors, 1987; Distinguished Serv Award, Assn of Minority Enterprises of New York, 1987; Contractor of the Year Award, Westchester Minority Contractors of Westchester, New York, 1988. **BUSINESS ADDRESS:** Pres/CEO, Argrett Enterprises Corp, 133-43-35th Ave, Flushing, NY 11354.

ARINWINE, KENNETH WAYNE
Educator. **PERSONAL:** Born Mar 13, 1934, Wellston, OK; married Fayetta James; children: Sheilia, Sherry. **EDUCATION:** Langston Univ, BSc 1955; Mercy Hosp Sch of Med Tech, BS Med Tech 1960; Central State Coll, MEd Guid & Counseling 1970; Central State Univ, cert for adm 1971; OSU, cert in Secondary Admin 1974. **CAREER:** OK City, baseball coach 1956-58, teacher 1967-68, asst prin, dir night school 1972-73; Langston Univ, project dir Upward Bound Program 1976-. **ORGANIZATIONS:** Coach indus commer baseball league 1958-60; chief med tech OK City 1960-67; mem bd of commrs YMCA Upward Bound Proj; pres Polemarch OK City 1976-77; mem Natl Bd of Registry Med Tech & Am Soc of Clinical Pathologists; mem St Mary's Christian meth Epis Church; pres PTA Edison Elem Sch; mem NE Athletic Club; mem Langston Alumni Assn; mem Kappa Alpha Psi Frat. **HONORS/ACHIEVEMENTS:** Baseball scholarship Langston Univ 1952; Urban League Serv Awd 1975; Meritorious Awd US Dept of Commerce Bur of Census; cand Doctoral Degree in HigherEduc Admin OK State Univ.

ARKANSAW, TIM
Sculptor, songwriter, playwright, recording artist. **PERSONAL:** Born Oct 18, 1925, Anniston, AL; son of George Hudgons and Mattie Grace Hudgons. **EDUCATION:** City Coll of NY, BA voice-music, minor in business admin 1951. **CAREER:** Amer Federation of Musicians, musician 1961-85; Atlanta Public Schools, teacher of music 1972; Grady Memorial Hospital, pr admin 1973-74; Atsumhill Enterprises, founder, pres; artist in residence, Georgia Council for the Arts. **ORGANIZATIONS:** Admin yeoman MSC-LANT Navy Dept Brooklyn 1975-78; volunteer work Dekalb-Rockdale Chap GA 1976-85; comm worker Dekalb-Atlanta Voters Council 1970-85; volunteer worker Economic Opportunity Atlanta 1965-85. **HONORS/ACHIEVEMENTS:** Great Talent Search RCA Records WSB Radio Atlanta 1967; Bronze Jubilee Honoree in Music WPBA Ch 30 Atlanta 1981; composer, Children You're Our Tomorrow, Atlanta Public Schools, 1985; Martin Luther King Jr Community Serv Award, 1986. **MILITARY SERVICE:** USN chief petty officer 1943. **HOME ADDRESS:** 1344 Hardee St, NE, Atlanta, GA 30307.

ARKHURST, JOYCE COOPER
Librarian. **PERSONAL:** Born Oct 20, 1921, Seattle, WA; daughter of Dr Felix Cooper and Hazel James Cooper; married Frederick Arkhurst, Oct 03, 1959; children: Cecile Arkhurst. **EDUCATION:** Univ of Washington, Seattle, BA, 1944; Columbia Univ, New York, NY, MLS, 1957. **CAREER:** New York Public Library, children's librarian, 1947-58; Chicago Public Library, children's librarian, 1967-69; Fieldston School, Bronx, NY, librarian, 1971-74; Elisabeth Irwin School, New York, NY, 1978-83; New York City Bd of Educ, library teacher, 1983-. **ORGANIZATIONS:** Delta Sigma Theta Sorority, 1943-; Jack & Jill of Amer, 1964-79; NAACP, 1984-88; Amer Library Assn, 1983-85; Schomburg Corp, 1988-; sec membership comm, New York Black Librarians Caucus, 1983-. **HONORS/ACHIEVEMENTS:** Mortar Board, Sociology Honorary, Univ of Washington, 1944; author, The Adventures of Spider, 1964, More Adventures of Spider, 1971. **BUSINESS ADDRESS:** Library Teacher, New York City Bd of Educ, JHS 118, 155 E 179 St, Bronx, NY 10457.

ARLENE, HERBERT
Administrator. **PERSONAL:** Born Sep 05, 1917, Harrison, GA; married Emma; children: Herbert, Jr, Clara. **EDUCATION:** Philadelphia Bus Sch, grad. **CAREER:** Philadelphia 47th Ward, state rep, 1958-66, administrator; State of PA, retired senator, 1966-81. **ORGANIZATIONS:** Exec sec Dem City Com; past chmn Senate Labor & Industry Com; vice chmn Military Affairs & Aeronautics Comm; bd dir Wharton Neighborhood Comm Ctr; Greater Philadelphia Devel Corp; senate chmn Labor & Industry Comm; vice chmn Urban Affairs & Housing; senate comm Appropriations Ins Pub Health & Welfare & RuPes; mem of House 1958-66; senate 1967-80; N Philadelphia Business Men's Assn; Local #10 Laundry & Dry Cleaners Intl Union; AFL; YMCA; NAACP; Odd Fellows; Elks; Tuscan Morning Star #48; Prince Hall Masonic Order; Melchizedek Chap #25; Holy Royal Arch Masons; DeMolay Consistory #1; Ancient Accept Scottish Rite 33rd Degree; Pyramid Temple #1; Promotion Comm AEAO; Nobles of Mystic Shrine Inc; Philadelphia Athletic Club; mem bd dir Wharton Neighborhood Comm Ctr; trst Union AME Ch; Urban League; bd dir Temple Mental Health/Mental Retardation No Central Comm Organ Peoples Nghbrhd Med Ctr; bd trste Lincoln Univ, PA Coll ofPodiatric Med, Berean Inst; bd dir Philadelphia Assn for Retarded Citizens; del Model Cities Nghbrhd Council #15; officer Union AME Church; 32 Degree Mason. **HONORS/ACHIEVEMENTS:** First Black Senator in PA; Hon LLD Miller State Coll.

ARMISTEAD, MILTON
Attorney. **PERSONAL:** Born Jun 08, 1947, Indianpolis, IN; son of Mitchell Armistead and Margarette Armistead; married Susan Ward Phipps, Jun 18, 1982; children: Jeff, Milton. **EDUCATION:** Pasadena City Coll, AA 1967; San Jose State Coll, BA 1969; Univ of Southern CA, MS 1972, JD 1974. **ORGANIZATIONS:** Pres Wiley Manual Law Soc 1979-; correspondent Sacramento Observer 1981; mem CA Trial Lawyers Assoc, Defense Rsch Inst 1983; pres Toastmasters Capital IClub 1984; bd of dir Sacramento Claims Assoc 1984; vice pres Sacramento Black Chamber of Commerce 1985-; chmn Volunteers of Amer 1985; mem Black Ins Prof Assoc 1985. **HONORS/ACHIEVEMENTS:** Best Speaker Toastmasters 1984; Competent Toastmaster Award 1987; seminar speaker for Sacramento Claims Assn 1988. **BUSINESS ADDRESS:** Attorney, Law Office of Milton Armistead, 5777 Madison Ave, #630, Sacramento, CA 95841.

ARMOUR-LIGHTNER, ROSETTA AMELIA
Military administration. **PERSONAL:** Born Aug 30, 1937, Macon, GA; married William H Lightner Sr; children: William Jr, Anthony M. **EDUCATION:** Talladega Coll, AB (Cum Laude) 1958; Springfield Coll, MEd 1960; OH State Univ, MA 1974; USAF Maxwell AFB Air War Coll, 1984-85. **CAREER:** Air Force Bases in CA, OH, Okinawa, W Germany, personnel officer 1963-80; Bitburg AB W Germany, dep base commander 1980-82; Grambling State Univ, commanderafrotc 1982-84; USAF,chief airman assign div; AFMIL Pers Center, Randolph AFB, TX 1986-. **ORGANIZATIONS:** Mem Delta Sigma Theta 1955-; counselor Ballard Hudson HS 1960-62; mem, chmn Base Chapel Protestant Fund Council 1975-79; mem High Desert Fed Credit Union Bd of Dir 1976-79; mem Beta Sigma Phi 1980-, Phi Delta Kappa 1983-. **HONORS/ACHIEVEMENTS:** Alfred J Wright Awd Outstanding Student Org Advisor OH State Univ 1971-72; Outstanding Young Women of Amer OYWA 1973.

MILITARY SERVICE: USAF Col 1962-; Commend Medal 1970, Merit Serv Medal 1974,79,82,84; Equal Oppty Staff Ofcr Awd Tact Air Comm 1978; Lance Sijon Awd for Ldrshp 1981. **BUSINESS ADDRESS:** Dep Chief, Airman Assign Div, U S Air Force, Air Force Manpower & Pers Ctr, Randolph AFB, TX 78150.

ARMSTEAD, CHAPELLE M.
Social worker. **PERSONAL:** Born Aug 12, 1926, Monroe, AL; children: Marcia, Helen, Joseph, Dorothy. **EDUCATION:** Morgan State Coll, BS, 1950; Howard Univ, MSW, 1961. **CAREER:** Baltimore Cty Dept Soc Serv, caseworker, 1955-57, acting supr, 1957-59, stu caseworker, 1959-61, cs supr, 1961-64, dist supr, 1964-67; Maryland Soc Serv Admin, training spec, 1967-70, spec mnl polcy coordn, 1970-73, field supr, 1974-. **ORGANIZATIONS:** Organizer Women of Augesburg Lutheran Ch; mem bd Lutheran Soc Serv; pres Baltimore Alum Chap Delta Sigma Theta Inc; crdntr Reg Golden Life Membership Eastern Reg Delta Sigma Theta; mem Blk Admin in Child Welfare; mem NAACP, NCNW, NASW, YWCA. **HONORS/ACHIEVEMENTS:** Nom Who's Who in Human Serv 1973. **BUSINESS ADDRESS:** Field Supervisor, MD Soc Serv Admin, 1315 St Paul St, Baltimore, MD 21202.

ARMSTEAD, RON E.
Social work, urban planner. **PERSONAL:** Born Apr 12, 1947, Boston, MA; son of Leemon Smith and Ruby Smith; children: Tod, Kaili, Ronni. **EDUCATION:** Boston Univ Metro Coll, attended 1970-74; Boston State Coll, BA (with honors) 1975-79; Harvard Univ, Graduate School of Design, Certificate 1983; Massachusetts Inst of Technology, Cambridge MA, MCP 1989. **CAREER:** Teen Educ Center, educ counselor 1970-73; Model Cities Admin, community planner 1970-74; Veterans Center Veterans Admin, readjustment counselor, social worker 1979-87; Amistad Assoc, pres. **ORGANIZATIONS:** Bd of dirs William Joiner Center for the Study of War & Social Consequences; conference issue coordinator Speakers Conf on Vietnam Veterans; co-chmn Natl Black Veterans Working Group; coord Massachusetts Black Veterans Think Tank Group; mem Soc for Traumatic Stress Studies, Natl Assn of Black Social Workers, Assn for the Study of Afro-Amer Life & History 1985-; pres, bd of dirs Veterans Benefits Clearinghouse Inc 1975-85; mem Natl Assn of Social Workers 1980-, Senator John F Kerry's Black Advisory Comm 1989. **HONORS/ACHIEVEMENTS:** Commendation, Veterans Admin 1982; Commendation, Gov Michael L Dukakis 1983; Salute Award, Chelsea Soldiers Home 1986; Fellowship Massachusetts Inst of Technology 1987; Scholarship Award, Massachusetts Inst of Technology 1987; Certificate of Award, Massachusetts Office of Affirmative Action 1989; coordinated Black Veterans Workshops at Congressional Black Caucus Legislative Weekends 1985, 1987, 1988; presented Stress & Trauma Workshops at Natl Assn of Black Social Workers Conferences 1987-89. **MILITARY SERVICE:** USN E-4 1966-69; Vietnam Campaign Medal, Vietnam Serv Medal with 3/16" Bronze Star, Natl Service Defense Medal. **HOME ADDRESS:** 86 Thornton St, Roxbury, MA 02119.

ARMSTEAD, WILBERT EDWARD, JR.
Engineering administration. **PERSONAL:** Born Jun 23, 1934, Baltimore, MD; son of Wilbert E Armstead and Mary Josephine Hill Armstead; married Erma Shirley Cole; children: Barbara E, Valerie E, Sheryl J, Joann C, Jeri L, Angela M. **EDUCATION:** Johns Hopkins Univ, Bachelor Elect Engr 1955. **CAREER:** RCA Missile & Surface Radar, assoc mem engr staff 1955-58, mem engr staff 1958-62, sr mem engr staff 1963-74, unit mgr 1974-. **ORGANIZATIONS:** Mem 1967-79, vice pres 1979, pres 1980-86, Moorestown Township Board of Educ. **HONORS/ACHIEVEMENTS:** Community Serv Club Blue Chips 1975, Ed Comm & Baptist Church Moorestown 1977, NJ State Fed of Colored Women 1981. **MILITARY SERVICE:** AUS Corp of Engrs 2nd lt. **HOME ADDRESS:** 325 Farmdale Rd, Moorestown, NJ 08057.

ARMSTER-WORRILL, CYNTHIA DENISE
Educator, educational administrator. **PERSONAL:** Born Aug 07, 1960, Tokyo, Japan;daughter of Franksin Armster and Dorothy L Armster; married Dr Conrad W Worrill, Mar 07, 1987; children: Sobeenna Armster Worrill. **EDUCATION:** Emporia State Univ, BS 1982, MS 1983. **CAREER:** Emporia State Univ, job devel coordinator, 1982-83; Northern IL Univ, counselor, minority programs 1983-85; George Williams Coll, dir of academic support 1985; Chicago State Univ, dir of freshmen serv 1986-. **ORGANIZATIONS:** Chairperson Minority Personnel Concerns Comm 1984-85; prog chair 1985-86, membership chair 1986-87 Amer Coll Personnel Assoc; recording sec Alpha Kappa Alpha Sor Inc 1986-87; mem Natl Black United Front 1986-87; YWCA Chmn, Monarch Awards Found, 1989. **HONORS/ACHIEVEMENTS:** Outstanding Black Woman Black Student Union NIU, 1984. **HOME ADDRESS:** 7414 S Chappel, 2nd fl, Chicago, IL 60649.

ARMSTRONG, ERNEST W., SR.
Real estate broker/educator. **PERSONAL:** Born May 01, 1915, Soper, OK; son of Giles Armstrong and Vinnie Armstrong; married Irene C Pierce, May 21, 1976; children: Earl M Armstrong, Everett W Armstrong. **EDUCATION:** Dillard Univ, AB 1942; Howard Univ, MDiv 1946, MA 1947; Univ Heidelberg Germany, cert 1954; Univ OK, MEd 1969; Laurence Univ, PhD 1974; Prince Georges Community College AA 1979, 1981. **CAREER:** Natl YMCA NY Army-Navy Dept, student sec 1944-45; Howard Univ Washington, DC, chaplain 1947-48; Shiloh Bapt Ch Wash, DC, asst pastor 1947-48; Savannah State Coll, coll chaplain/asst prof soc sci 1948-49; US Army Chaplain 1949-69; Real Estate Broker 1984-. **ORGANIZATIONS:** Cnslr/inst Triton Comm Coll River Grove, IL 1969-70; asst pastor Enon Bapt Ch Baltimore, MD 1970-71; counslr Catonsville Comm Coll MD 1970-72; cnslr Livingstone Coll Salisbury, NC 1972-73; conslr Annapolis, MD Sr HS 1973-77; mem APGA, ACPA, AAMFC, MPGA, MCPA, Indiv Psy Assn DC, Natl Assn Black Psy, Omega Psi Phi Frat, Prince Hall Masons 33rd degree, US Chess Fedn. **HONORS/ACHIEVEMENTS:** Omega Man of the Year Frankfort, Germany Tau Chap 1962; Mason of the Year 1962 OK Prince Hall Grand Lodge; Licensed Marriage Counselor; Publ Army Chpln in Korea "The Oracle" Omega Psi Phi Frat Inc 1952; Doctoral Dissertation, Psychosocial factors & Academic Success in Black Colleges Santa Barbara Univ 1974. **MILITARY SERVICE:** AUS chpln 1948-69, colonel 1949-69. **BUSINESS ADDRESS:** Associate Broker, Century 21 David D Martin Real Estate Co, 5619 Annapolis Rd, Bladensburg, MD 20710.

ARMSTRONG, EVELYN WALKER
Director. **PERSONAL:** Born in Philadelphia, PA; daughter of J D Walker and Laurena Walker. **EDUCATION:** Howard Univ, BA 1949; Drexel Univ, MSLS 1956; Temple Univ, grad school of bus admin 1976. **CAREER:** Sharp & Dohme Inc, asst librarian 1950-53, assoc librarian 1953-57, chief librarian 1957-66; Drexel Univ Grad School of Library Sci, adjunct faculty 1963-66; Merck Sharp & Dohme Research Laboratories, mgr library serv 1966-81; Drexel Univ Grad School of Library Sci, visiting lecturer 1975-80; Merck Sharp & Dohme Research Laboratories, dir literature resources center 1981-. **ORGANIZATIONS:** Mem Adv Comm on Accreditation, Drexel Univ Grad School of Library Sci, 1974-75; mem Adv Comm on Library/Med Curriculum, Montgomery County Community College, 1973-; membership comm, Special Libraries Assn, 1972-73; mem Professional Studies Comm, 1965-67; chmn Pharm Div, 1963-64; past sec & exec bd mem of Sci Tech Div, Rankin Fund Comm, & Elect & Nom Comm, Special Libraries Council of Philadelphia, 1956-75; past adv bd mem & sec, Special Interest Group/Biol Chem Elect & Nom Comm, Amer Soc for Info Sci, 1965-73; chmn Regis Comm, Montreal Drug Info Assn 1973; conf comm mem, Boston, 1974; mem Div of Chem Info, Amer Chem Soc; steering comm mem Sci Info Subsection, Pharmaceutical Mfrs Assn, 1976-; adv bd mem Drexel Univ College of Info Studies, 1989-; bd mem Montgomery County Emergency Serv, 1988-. **HONORS/ACHIEVEMENTS:** Co-author "Computer Processing of Clinical Data for a New Drug Application" Drug Info Bulletin 1967; presented paper on Scientific Info Ctr Admin 12th Annual Natl Colloquium on Info Retrieval 1975; participant on panels of various mtgs of Special Libraries Assn, Drug Info Assn, Amer Soc for Info Sci; Black Achievers. **BUSINESS ADDRESS:** Dir, Lit Resources Center, Merck Sharp & Dohme Research Laboratories, Sunnytown Pike, West Point, PA 19486.

ARMSTRONG, J. NIEL
Retired education administration. **PERSONAL:** Born Jun 17, 1907, Rogersville, TN; married Jacquetta Sensabaugh. **EDUCATION:** Swift Mem Jr Coll, AA 1929; NC A&T State Univ, BS 1931; Univ of MI, MS 1939; OH State Univ, Univ of Chicago, Univ of NC at Greensboro, additionalstudy. **CAREER:** Pruitt Hill Elem School, teacher, principal 1932-33; Jr HS, principal 1933-34; Farmers Union School, principal 1934-37; Langston HS, principal 1937-54; NC A&T State Univ, dir summer school, assoc prof ed 1963-78, acting dean grad school 1965-66. **ORGANIZATIONS:** Mem Exec Comm So Assn Sec School & Coll 1940-55, Phi Delta Kappa 1955-, Natl Soc for Study of Ed 1955-80, Amer Assoc of Suprv & Curr 1956-78; natl dir ed Phi Beta Sigma 1969-75; mem Zoning Comm Greensboro 1970-77, Exec Comm Unied Way 1970-75; chmn Selective Serv Bd #51 1983-. **HONORS/ACHIEVEMENTS:** Pres East TN Teachers Assn 1952-53, NC Assn of Summer Session Dir 1966-67; hon life mem N Amer Assn of Summer Session Dir 1978; Disting Serv Key Triad Chap Phi Delta Kappa 1982-; vice pres N Amer Assn of Summer School Dir. **HOME ADDRESS:** 808 Bellaire, Greensboro, NC 27406.

ARMSTRONG, JOAN BERNARD
Judge. **PERSONAL:** Born Feb 15, New Orleans, LA; married Andrew Armstrong; children: David M, Anna K. **EDUCATION:** Xavier Univ, BA 1963; Loyola Univ School of Law, Juris Doctor 1967; Natl College of Juvenile Justice, college certificate 1974. **CAREER:** Orleans Parish Juvenile Court, judge 1974-84; State of LA Court of Appeal, 4th Circuit, judge 1984-. **ORGANIZATIONS:** Pres Community Relations Council 1972-74; pres LA League of Good Gov't 1972-74; member Visiting Comm Loyola Univ 1980-; charter member Natl Assn of WomenJudges 1981-; trustee Loyola Univ of the South 1984-; Bar Association memberships; served on numerous boards Family Service Society; Amer Red Cross; Legal Aid Bureau; LA Assn for Mental Health; Crisis Care Center. **HONORS/ACHIEVEMENTS:** Outstanding Young Woman New Orleans Jaycees 1974; member Visiting Committee Loyola Law School 1981; trustee Loyola Univ 1984; hon member Alpha Kappa Alpha 1974. **BUSINESS ADDRESS:** Judge, Court of Appeal, 4th Cir, State of Louisiana, 421 Loyola Ave, New Orleans, LA 70112.

ARMSTRONG, JOSEPH EARL
Elected official. **PERSONAL:** Born Nov 30, 1956, Knoxville, TN. **EDUCATION:** Univ of TN, BS 1981; Leadership Knoxville, 1986. **CAREER:** Armstrong Petrochemicals In, pres; Atlanta Life Ins Co, dist mgr present; Knox County Commn, vice chmn; Knox County, county commissioner. **ORGANIZATIONS:** Bd mem Community Action Comm 1983-present; bd mem Knoxville Opportunity Indus Ctr 1983-present; bd mem East TN Minority Purchasing Counsel 1985-present; vice-pres Jimmy's Who's Enterprises present; state democratic exec committeeman 7th Senatorial Dist 1986-; ward chmn Democrat Fourteen Ward Knox Co TN; mem Optimist Intl, Natl Democratic County Officials. **HONORS/ACHIEVEMENTS:** Outstanding Achievement in Politics, Black Alumnis of Univ of TN 1983; Outstanding Young Men of Amer 1985. **HOME ADDRESS:** 2624 Selma Ave, Knoxville, TN 37914.

ARMSTRONG, JOSEPH M.
Attorney. **PERSONAL:** Born Oct 13, 1943, Jefferson, TX. **EDUCATION:** Howard Univ, BA 1966; NY Univ Sch Law, JD 1969. **CAREER:** Davis Polk & Wardwell, attorney 1969-77; City of NY, atty human resources adminstrn. **ORGANIZATIONS:** Bd dir Pacific Psychotherapy Assn 1974-; legal cnsl Mayoralty Campaign AJ Cooper Mayor Pritchard 1972 1976; mem Fine Arts Collecting Com Studio Mus 1976; mem Alpha Phi Alpha Frat.

ARMSTRONG, JOSEPH N.
Business executive. **PERSONAL:** Born Jun 19, 1939, Little Rock, AR; married Ethel Hunter; children: Medgar, Joel, Courtney. **EDUCATION:** AM&N Coll, BS 1960; Roosevelt Univ, MBA 1969; Harvard Grad Sch of Credit & Fin, 1974; Gov State Univ, MS 1975; Chicago-Kent College of Law. **CAREER:** Amoco Oil Co, executive. **ORGANIZATIONS:** Omega Psi Phi. **HONORS/ACHIEVEMENTS:** Black Achiev of Industry Recog Award 1975; Harvard Exec Award 1974. **MILITARY SERVICE:** AUS 1962-64. **HOME ADDRESS:** 11417 S Bell, Chicago, IL 60643.

ARMSTRONG, MATTHEW JORDAN, JR.
Business administrator. **PERSONAL:** Born Dec 18, 1955, Rocky Mount, NC; son of Matthew J Armstrong Sr and Sarah Jane McDowell Armstrong. **EDUCATION:** Winston-Salem State Univ, Bachelor 1974-78; IA State Univ, Master 1978-. **CAREER:** Minority Student Affairs IA State Univ, rsch asst 1979-80, sec II 1980-82, sec III 1982, office coord 1982-84, admin asst 1984-85; Univ of Iowa Special Support Serv, outreach counselor 1986-; Univ of Iowa, Outreach Coordinator, 1986-. **ORGANIZATIONS:** Rsch asst history dept IA State Univ 1978-79; asst to pres Mid-Amer Assoc 1979-80; office asst III Minority Student Affairs IA State Univ 1979-; admin asst Spec Serv Prog 1980-; black cultural ctr Liaison/Black Cultural Ctr 1980-. **HONORS/ACHIEVEMENTS:** President's Awd, Mid-Amer Assoc, 1980; 1st Black Male Sec Office Coord & Admin Asst, Certificate of Recognition, MO-KAN-NE Chap of MAEOPP 1981. **HOME ADDRESS:** PO Box 848, Iowa City, IA 52244.

ARMSTRONG, NELSON
Educational administration. **PERSONAL:** Born Jan 07, 1950, Newport News, VA. **EDUCATION:** Dartmouth College, BA 1971. **CAREER:** Dartmouth College, counselor 1971-74; MIT, assoc dir of financial aid 1975-79, assoc dir of admissions. **ORGANIZATIONS:** Counselor-chairperson Boston NAACP Education Council 1975-80; co-chairperson 1977-78, member 1975-, Assoc Blk Admissions & Fin Aid Officers in Ivy League & Sister Schools; president Dorchester-Mattapan Comm Mental Health Center 1978-79. **HONORS/ACHIEVEMENTS:** Boston Black Achiever Boston YMCA 1985; MLK, Jr Award MIT 1983.

ARMSTRONG, WALTER
Product planning analyst. **PERSONAL:** Born Aug 25, 1948, Philadelphia, PA; son of Richard Armstrong and Roberta Lawrence Armstrong. **EDUCATION:** Winston-Salem State Univ, BA Political Science, History 1969-73; Univ of Louisville, graduate research 1974-75; Bradley Univ, MA 1975-77; Central MI Univ, MA 1977-79. **CAREER:** Frito-Lay Inc, product mgr 1973-75; Jefferson Cty Comm Devel Office, housing rehabilitation center coordinator 1975-76; Pabst Brewing Co, product supvr 1976-77; Ford Motor Co, program mgr 1977-. **ORGANIZATIONS:** Pres Groove Phi Groove Soc Fellowship Inc 1970-73; pres Pi Gamma Mu Natl Soc Sci Soc 1971-73; vice pres Phi Alpha Theta Natl History Soc 1972-73; recording sec Soc of Engrs & Applied Scientists 1977-78; recruiter Engrg Soc of Detroit 1979-82; recruiter Soc of Applied Weight Engrs 1985. **HONORS/ACHIEVEMENTS:** Mayor's Award Jefferson Cty KY 1975; Outstanding Leadership Award Pabst Brewing Co 1976; Speaking of People Feature Ebony Magazine 1983; Outstanding Young Men of Amer OYMA 1984. **HOME ADDRESS:** 7812 Raintree Dr, Ypsilanti, MI 48197. **BUSINESS ADDRESS:** Program Coordinator, Ford Motor Co, 17000 Rotunda Drive, PO Box 6010, Dearborn, MI 48121.

ARMSTRONG, WILEY T.
Physician. **PERSONAL:** Born Feb 11, 1909, Rocky Mount, NC; married Marguerite Carson; children: Brenda, Beverly, Wiley T Jr. **EDUCATION:** Shaw Univ, BS; Harvard Univ, grad work phys educ; Attended, Columbia Univ; Meharry Med Coll, MD 1944. **CAREER:** Private Practice, physician. **ORGANIZATIONS:** Sec treas Old N State Med Soc 1954-; pres NMA; chmn bd trustees NMA; chmn bd trustees NC Cntrl Univ 1973-; mem C of C Rocky Mount NC; Omega Psi Phi Frat; chmn bd trustees Nash-Rocky Mount ARC 1974. **HONORS/ACHIEVEMENTS:** Dr of Yr Old N State Med Soc 1954; Achievement Awd NMA 1972; Alumni Awd Meharry Med Coll 1972. **BUSINESS ADDRESS:** 128 E Thomas St, Rocky Mount, NC 27801.

ARNELLE, HUGH JESSE
Attorney. **PERSONAL:** Born Dec 30, 1933, New Rochelle, NY; son of Hugh Arnelle and Lynn Arnelle; married Carolyn; children: Nicole, Paolo, Michael. **EDUCATION:** PA State Univ, BA 1955; Dickinson School of Law, JD 1962; admitted to practice CA, PA, United States Supreme Court. **CAREER:** AU State Univ All-Amer Basketball, 1952-54; PA State Univ, honorable mention All-Amer Football 1953-54; NBA Ft Wayne Piston, 1955-56; NFL Baltimore Colts, 1957-58; Dept of Labor, atty 1962-63; Peace Corps, assoc dir 1963-65, dir 1965-66, staff 1966-67; FPC, asst to gen counsel 1967-68; IDEA Inc Chas F Kettering Found 1968-69; Morrison Foerster Holloway, atty 1971-73; US Dist Ct, asst federal public defender 1973-75; Arnelle & Hastie, civil litigation & public finance atty. **ORGANIZATIONS:** Mem Coll of Civil Trial Advocacy 1976; faculty Hastings Law School Criminal Trial Advocacy 1977; mem Hall of Fame NY 1977; commissioner San Francisco Redevelopment Agency 1981-; bd of dir SF Boys Club 1981-; mem Amer Bd of Criminal Trial Lawyers 1982-; exec commissioner, bd of trustees San Francisco World Affairs Council 1983-; bd of trust PA State Univ; exec comm PA State Univ; dir Renaissance Fund PA State Univ; mem Charles Houston Bar Assn; life mem Natl Bar Assn, Bar of PA, CA, Bar of US Supreme Court; diplomate Hastings Law School; mem Natl Panel of Arbit, Amer Trial Lawyers Assn, Westchester County Hall of Fame; adj prof Hastings Law School Coll of Advocacy; former pres Afro-Amer Hist Soc; bd of dir San Francisco Opera; bd of dir Bay Area UNICEF; pres World Centre. **BUSINESS ADDRESS:** Attorney, Arnelle & Hastie, Civil Litigation & Public Finance, 1160 Battery St, Suite 380, San Francisco, CA 94111-1204.

ARNETTE, DOROTHY DEANNA
Personnel administration. **PERSONAL:** Born Sep 19, 1942, Welch, WV; married Joseph; children: Kristina Nicole. **EDUCATION:** MI State Univ, BS 1965; Pace Univ, MBA 1979. **CAREER:** MI Natl Bank, asst branch mgr 1966-68; Metropolitan Life Ins Co, recruiting consult 1968-72; CIBA-GEIGY Corp, dir equal oppty affairs 1974-85; Amer CanCo, dir corp eeo & employ law 1985-. **ORGANIZATIONS:** Charter mem Fairfield Cty Chapter Links 1970-78; mem/pres Urban League Guild SW Fairfield Cty 1974-77; charter mem 1979-, pres 1985 Fairfield Cty Alumnae Chap DST; workshop leader legal issues Fairfield Cty Alumnae Chp DST 1981; mem, pres advisory council Coll of New Rochelle 1982-; advisory council Manhattan Ctr for Sci & Math 1983-84. **HONORS/ACHIEVEMENTS:** Outstanding Young Woman of Amer 1977. **HOME ADDRESS:** 492 Pepper Ridge Rd, Stamford, CT 06905. **BUSINESS ADDRESS:** Dir Corp EEO & Employ Law, Amer Can Co, Amer Lane, Greenwich, CT 06830.

ARNEZ, NANCY L.
Educator, author. **PERSONAL:** Born Jul 06, 1928, Baltimore, MD; daughter of Milton Emerson Levi and Ida Barbour Rusk; divorced. **EDUCATION:** Morgan State Coll, AB 1949; Columbia Univ, MA 1954, EdD 1958; Harvard Univ, post doctoral 1962; Loyola Coll, 1965. **CAREER:** Baltimore Pub Sch, English tchr 1949-58, dept head 1958-62; Morgan State Coll, dir student teaching 1962-66; Northeastern IL Univ, assoc prof/asst dir Cntr for Inner City Studies 1966-69, prof/dir Cntr for Inner City Studies 1969-74, co-founder, Cultural Linguistic, Follow Through Early Childhood CICS 1969-74; Howard Univ School of Educ, acting dean 1975, assoc dean 1974-, dept chairperson 1980-86, professor 1986-. **ORGANIZATIONS:** Congress of African People 1968-70; Amer Assn of School Admin 1968-87; Black Child Devel Inst DC 1971-74; Assn of African Historians Chicago 1972; Assn of the Study of Afro-Amer Life & Hist 1972-77; mem African Heritage Studies Assn, bd of dir membership sec 1973-77; Natl Alliance of Black Sch Educators 1973-87; Amer Assn of Sch Admin Resolutions Comm 1973-75; African Information Cntr Catalyst Chicago 1973-77; bd of dir DuSable Museum Chicago 1973-74; mem Black Women's Comm Devel Found DC 1974; Amer Assn of Coll Tchrs of Educ 1977; Natl Council of Negro Women 1977; mem Phi Delta Kappa Howard Univ Chap 1974-, editorial bd 1975-78; Journal of Negro Education, editorial bd 1975-80; AASA Professor, editorial bd 1981-84; NABSE Newsbrief, editor 1984-86; mem DC Alliance of Black School Educators 1984-, pres 1986-88. **HONORS/ACHIEVEMENTS:** Assn of African History Serv Award 1972; Alpha Kappa Alpha Sor Serv Award 1971; Appointed Hon Citizen of Compton, CA 1972; Howard Univ distinguished faculty research awd 1983; 4th place in the international competition for Phi Delta Kappa's biennial awd for outstanding research 1985. **BUSINESS ADDRESS:** Professor, Howard University, 2400 6th St, NW, Washington, DC 20018.

ARNOLD, ALTON A., JR.
Educator. **PERSONAL:** Born Aug 10, 1932, Little Rock, AR; married Ramona L Worlds; children: Anita Alton III, David. **EDUCATION:** Philander Smith Coll, BA Psych 1953; Univ of AR, ME Elem Ed 1954; Univ of CA LA, MA School Admin 1972; Univ of LA, EdD Ed Policy & Planning 1976. **CAREER:** Cty of LA, juvenile hall couns 1955-56; LA Unified School Dist, elem teacher 1956-69; Arnolds Shell Serv Shell Oil Co, owner 1959-65; LA Unified School Dist Div of Career & Continuing Ed 1970-72; LA Unified School Dist, adult school 1972-; Pepperdine Univ, adj prof ed 1975-76; Jordan-Locke Comm Adult School, principal 1976-. **ORGANIZATIONS:** Mem Alpha Phi Alpha Beta Chi Chap 1950, Phi Delta Kappa Ed Soc 1967; chmn, bd of dir LA Cty Model Cities/Model Neighborhood Prog 1972-76, LA Cty Econ Housing Devel Corp 1975-77, So Central Comm Child Care Ctr Inc 1979-80; mem CA State Vocational Educ Comm 1980. **HONORS/ACHIEVEMENTS:** Alpha Kappa Mu Natl Hon Soc 1951; Fellowship Ford Found 1953-54; HEW Fellowship US Dept of HEW 1970-72; Resolution LA Cty 1975; Citizens Part Awd Model Neighborhood Prog LA Cty 1976. **MILITARY SERVICE:** AUS pvt 1953-54; Good Conduct Medal; Marksman Medal. **BUSINESS ADDRESS:** Principal, Jordan-Locke Comm Adult School, 325 E 11th St, Los Angeles, CA 90061.

ARNOLD, CLARENCE EDWARD, JR.
Educational administrator. **PERSONAL:** Born May 18, 1944, Eastville, VA; son of Clarence E Arnold Sr and Nicey Press Arnold; divorced; children: Sherri Mignon. **EDUCATION:** VA State Univ, BS 1970, MEd 1973; Howard Univ, 1979. **CAREER:** Petersburg HS Petersburg, VA, home-sch coord 1970-71; McGuffy Educ Cntr Charlottesville, VA, tchr 1971-72; 16th Dist Ct Serv Unit, counsl juvenile & domestic rel 1973-74; VA State Univ, tchr educ TV prodn & photog 1977-78; J Sargeant Reynolds Comm Coll, instr/coord audio visual serv dept 1974-80; C E Arnold Photographic Services, free lance photographer, 1980-81; Virginia State Univ, Petersburg, VA, instructor/coordinator mass communications prog, 1981-88; Danville Community Coll, Danville, VA, 1988-. **ORGANIZATIONS:** Richmond Br NAACP, vice pres 1976-82; VA State Conf NAACP, bd dir 1976-82; mem Black Advisory Council, WTVR TV AM & FM, 1979-83; Assn for Educ Communications & Technology; Virginia Educ Media Assn; Community Coll Assn for Instruction and Technology; Virginia Television Representatives in Higher Educ; pres, Richmond Media Society, 1986-87; Natl Educ Assn; Virginia Educ Assn; Virginia State Univ Educ Assn; Kappa Alpha Psi Frat Inc. **HONORS/ACHIEVEMENTS:** R P Daniel Award & Trophy for Outstanding Mil Leadership & Scholastic Achievement in ROTC VA State Univ 1966; Grant NDEA Educ Media Inst for Trainers of Tchrs VA State Univ 1972-73; Black Arts Award for Visual Arts, BOTA, 1981. **MILITARY SERVICE:** AUS 1968-70; Reserves, Capt, 1970-79; Recipient Bronze Star/CIB, Vietnam Commendation Medal, Vietnam Serv Medal, Natl Defense Serv Medal, Expert Marksman Badge. **BUSINESS ADDRESS:** Director, Learning Resources Center, Danville Community Coll, 1008 S Main St, Danville, VA 24541.

ARNOLD, DAVID
Opera singer. **PERSONAL:** Born Dec 30, 1946, Atlanta, GA. **EDUCATION:** IN Univ, BA 1968, MA 1970; New England Conservatory, artist diploma 1972. **CAREER:** Opera Co Boston, Metropolitan Opera, Boston Symphony, New York City Opera, English Natl Opera, Amer Symphony, San Francisco Opera, American Composer Orchestra conducted by Leonard Bernstein, Atlanta Symphony, Wolf Trap Festival, Baltimore Symphony, Chautauqua Festival, Spoleto Festivals, Nashville Symphony, Tanglewood Festival, Chicago Symphony under Sir George Solit, Cincinnati May Festival conducted by James Conlon, Concertkebouw conducted by S Comissionaa; Tulsa Opera, opera singer; Metropolitan Opera, baritone singer. **HONORS/ACHIEVEMENTS:** Met Auditions Winner 1960; Sullivan Found Music Awd 1978; MYC Opera Gold Debut Awd 1980; Recordings include "Gurrelieder" on Philips, "The Magic World" on Leonarda, "Full Moon in March" on CRI; Walpurgisnacht on Arabesque. **BUSINESS ADDRESS:** c/o Grant House, 309 Wood St, Burlington, NJ 08016.

ARNOLD, ETHEL N.
Business executive. **PERSONAL:** Born Dec 20, 1924, Stillwater, OK; children: Nishua Bell, Renay Thigpen, Booker Jr, Myron, Geino. **EDUCATION:** Langston Univ, ICS Business Coll, Assoc; Northwestern Coll, BBA. **CAREER:** Cleve Cell & Post, news columnist; Picker Corp, tax specialist 1968; Harshaw Chemical, asst tax mgr 1970; Diamond Shamrock, acts asst 1973; OH Cel Pod Med, dir community relations 1976—84; Avant-Garde Models Inc, Modeling School & Agency, owner; R & E, pres & owner. **ORGANIZATIONS:** Natl pres Natl Assn Career Womens Civic Club Inc 1964-88; chm pp Natl Assn Negro Bus Prof Womens Club Cleve 1984-85; chp publicity Radio TV Cnclof Greater Cleve; mem Human Rsrch Comm. **HONORS/ACHIEVEMENTS:** Liberty Bell Awd Mayor of Philadelphia 1972; cong placque awdUniv S House Rep 1977; comm serv awd Ohio Cal Pod Med 1977, Bell Air Civic Club 1978, Mayor of Cleve 1977. **BUSINESS ADDRESS:** President, R & E, 14402 Kinsman, Cleveland, OH 44120.

ARNOLD, HARRIET AMELIA CHAPMAN
Elected city official. **PERSONAL:** Born Jul 03, 1937, Linden, NJ; children: Mercia, Regina, Christina. **EDUCATION:** Oberlin Coll, AB 1971; Case Western Reserve, MA 1974. **CAREER:** Lorain City Schools, teacher 1977-85; Oberlin, OH, Mayor 1984-. **ORGANIZATIONS:** Teacher Lorain City Schools 1974-85; mem NAACP, Urban League, Ohio Alliance Black School Educators. **HONORS/ACHIEVEMENTS:** Danforth Graduate Fellowship for Women Danforth Found 1972-74; Leadership Awd Lorain Cty Nordson Found 1985. **HOME ADDRESS:** 295 N Prospect St, Oberlin, OH 44074. **BUSINESS ADDRESS:** Mayor, City of Oberlin, So Main St, Oberlin, OH 44074.

ARNOLD, HASKELL N., JR.
Utility financial supervisor. **PERSONAL:** Born Jul 20, 1945, Savannah, GA; son of Haskell N Arnold Sr and Rosalyn Jackson Griffin; married Linda H Grayson; children: Shawn, Tia. **EDUCATION:** Hampton Inst, BS 1966; Harvard Bus Sch, MBA 1971. **CAREER:** H G Parks, controller 1972-74; Potomac Elec Power Co, mgr 1974-76; Pub Serv Broadcasting, vice pres 1977-80; MD Pub Serv Comm 1980-84; Commonwealth Tele Ent, controller 1984-85.

ORGANIZATIONS: Amer Inst of CPA's; MD Assn of CPA's; Harvard Bus Sch Club; Kappa Alpha Psi. **MILITARY SERVICE:** AUS 1st lt 2 yrs. **HOME ADDRESS:** 9078 Flamepool Way, Columbia, MD 21045.

ARNOLD, HELEN E.
Elected official. **PERSONAL:** Born Aug 02, 1924, Burlington, NJ; daughter of Samuel Ashley Crandall (deceased) and Lydia Rebecca Harvey Crandall (deceased); divorced; children: Cathy Dixx, Royal, Mona Diamond, Gale, John, Gary, Carla Anderson, Gerald, Donna. **EDUCATION:** Akron Sch of Cosmetology, 1500 hrs 1957; Black Univ, Pan Africanism 1968; attended Inst of Cultural Affairs-Global Acad, Chicago, IL; other courses, Akron Univ. **CAREER:** Beautician in self-owned shop 1959-62; Candeub Fleissig & Assoc, interviewer & surveyor 1964; City of Akron, neighborhood advisor; Partnership in small business 1970-73; UNCI, interim dir 1978-79; Summit Co Bd of Elections, employee 1982-; Dept of Human Svcs, community relations asst, employee 1985-; Bd of Educ Akron City Sch Dist, member 1978-89, past pres 1984, 1988-89, re-elected 3rd term. **ORGANIZATIONS:** Mem St Philips Episcopal Church 1950-; past mem, bd of dirs, Fallsview Mental Hosp; mem, past pres Akron branch 1970-71, NAACP; mem Summit Co Welfare Adv Bd; past financial officer Akron Summit Tutorial Prog; mem, Natl Assn of Black School Bd Educ, Large City Commn of Ohio School Bd Members, Natl Caucus of Black School Bd Members, Akron Univ Community Leaders Advisory Coucil; vice pres, Ohio Caucus of Black School Bd Members;. **HONORS/ACHIEVEMENTS:** Appreciation Awd NAACP 1968; Black Applause Awd Phi Beta Kappa 1983; Certificate from Akron Bd of Educ for Outstanding Serv as pres in 1984; Certificate from Akron Public Schools for Outstanding Serv & Effective Leadership 1985; Good Citizen Awd WHLO; Certificate from State of OH House of Reps for Meritorious Serv as Akron Bd of Educ Pres; articles Akron Reporter Newspaper; letters to editor Akron Beacon Journal; Awd Amer Cancer Soc 1985; Fund Raising Efforts Award Alpha Kappa Alpha 1986; Univ of Akron Awd Black Cultural Ctr 1986; Award from Ohio NABSE, 1987; Award of Appreciation, State of Ohio Welfare Rights Org, 1989; Award of Appreciation, State of Ohio Legislative Div, 1989. **HOME ADDRESS:** 413 Selzer St, Akron, OH 44310. **BUSINESS ADDRESS:** Personnel Div Social Worker Liaison Aide, Summit County Dept of Human Services, 47 N Main St, Bldg I, Room 616G, Akron, OH 44310.

ARNOLD, JAMES A.
Engineer. **PERSONAL:** Born Aug 10, 1936, Philadelphia, PA; married Janice M Kleckley; children: Alison Joy, Allen Jay. **EDUCATION:** PA State Univ, BS 1958; Rensselaer Polytechnic Inst, MS 1965, post masters courses 1965 1966; Univ of CA at LA, attended 1969. **CAREER:** Boeing Co Seattle WA, rsch engr 1958-61; United Technologies Corp Pratt & Whitney Div, project engr powerplant analysis 1961-. **ORGANIZATIONS:** Bd dir E Hartford Aircraft Fed Credit Union; speakers bur Pratt & Whitney Div of United Tech Corp; mem Amer Inst of Aero & Astro; chmn S WindsorBd of Educ 1972-73 mem 1966-73; sec S Windsor Jaycees 1963-66; mem S Windsor Dem Town Comm 1966-72; Omega Psi Phi Frat 1956-; Natl Urban League. **HONORS/ACHIEVEMENTS:** NAACP Achievement Awd for Serv S Windsor Sch System 1974.

ARNOLD, LARKIN
Business executive. **PERSONAL:** Born Sep 03, 1942, Kansas City, MO; divorced; children: Kevin Christopher, Derek Clinton. **EDUCATION:** Amer Univ Washington DC, BS 1966; Howard Univ Washington DC, JD 1969. **CAREER:** Capitol Records Inc, staff atty 1969-73; Capitol Records Inc, vice pres 1973-78; Arista Records Inc, sr vice pres 1978-80; CBS & Epic Records, vice pres & genl mgr 1980-. **ORGANIZATIONS:** Bd of dirs Black Music Assn 1979-; mem screening com Natl Acad of Records Arts & Scis (Grammies); mem Amer Bar Assn; mem CA Bar; mem LA Bar Assn; discovered & signed artists Natalie Cole, Peabo Bryson, Maze, Sylvers, GQ, Hiroshima, Busboys, Tavares, etc 1973-80. **HONORS/ACHIEVEMENTS:** Martin Luther King Exec Awd NY Chap 1978; Outstanding Grad Awd Howard Univ Law Sch 1979. **BUSINESS ADDRESS:** Vice Pres General Manager, Columbia & Epic Records, 1801 Century Park, Los Angeles, CA 90067.

ARNOLD, LIONEL A.
Educator. **PERSONAL:** Born Aug 30, 1921, Greenville, PA; son of J P Arnold and Gertrude Dowe Clark. **EDUCATION:** Thiel Coll, AB (Cum Laude) 1943; Anderson Coll, BTh 1943-44; Oberlin Grad Sch, MA BD 1947; Harvard Univ, STM 1955; Drew Univ, PhD 1969. **CAREER:** LeMoyne-Owen Coll, college pastor, 1947-64, dean, 1947-71; OK State Univ, prof 1971-86, prof emeritus. **HONORS/ACHIEVEMENTS:** Hon Doc Humane Letters, Thiel Coll Greenville, PA 1964. **HOME ADDRESS:** 2132 University, Stillwater, OK 74074.

ARNOLD, RALPH M.
Artist, educator. **PERSONAL:** Born Dec 05, 1928, Chicago, IL; son of Roy Arnold and Bertha Harris Arnold. **EDUCATION:** Univ of IL, attended; School of Art Inst of Chgo, attended; Hyde Park Art Ctr, attended; Roosevelt Univ, BA 1955; Art Inst of Chgo, MFA 1977. **CAREER:** Rockford & Barat Coll, teacher art; Art Inst of Chicago, mfa 1977; Loyola Univ, prof of fine art. **ORGANIZATIONS:** Appt mem IL Arts Council 4 yrs. **HONORS/ACHIEVEMENTS:** Partic in numerous group exhibits; one-man shows; works can be found in many pvt & publ collections. **BUSINESS ADDRESS:** Assistant Professor, Loyola University of Chicago, 6526 N Sheridan Road, Chicago, IL 60626.

ARNOLD, RUDOLPH P.
Attorney, appointed government official. **PERSONAL:** Born May 24, 1948, Harlem, NY; married Linda J Kelly; children: Preston, Rebecca. **EDUCATION:** Howard Univ, BA 1970; Univ of CT, JD 1975; NY Univ, LLM 1976. **CAREER:** Aetna Life & Casualty 1971-72; Legal Aid Soc of Hartford Cty, attny 1976-81; Arnold & Hershinson, atty 1982-84; Arnold & Assoc, atty 1985-. **ORGANIZATIONS:** Mem CT Bar Assoc, Hartford Bar Assoc; bd of dir Urban League 1977-79; dep mayor Hartford City Council 1979-83; bd of dir World Affairs Ctr 1983-88; chmn Hartford Comm TV 1986-89; bd dir Soc for Savings 1987-; mem Natl Bar Assoc, Amer Bar Assoc; lifetime mem NAACP 1987-; dir Natl Council for Internation Visitors 1989-. **HONORS/ACHIEVEMENTS:** Publ Intl Lawyer-Law 1974, Natl Bar Assoc 1980-; Outstanding Young Man in Amer 1979,82. **HOME ADDRESS:** 132 Terry Rd, Hartford, CT 06105. **BUSINESS ADDRESS:** Attorney, Arnold & Assoc, 80 Cedar Street, Hartford, CT 06106.

ARRINGTON, HAROLD MITCHELL
Physician. **PERSONAL:** Born Apr 09, 1947, Detroit, MI; son of Robyn Arrington and Irene Arrington. **EDUCATION:** Adrian Coll, BS 1968; Univ of MI Med Sch, MD 1972; Wayne State Univ Hosps, resident ob/gyn 1972-76; Amer Bd of Obstetrics & Gynecology, diplomate 1978. **CAREER:** Army Natl Guard Med Corps, Colonel 1972-; private practice, Ob/Gyn Detroit MI 1976-; Planned Parenthood League Inc, med dir 1976-; Detroit Bd of Educ, med dir 1978-. **ORGANIZATIONS:** Life mem NAACP; mem LPN Adv Comm Detroit, Amer Med Assn, Natl Med Assn; Natl Guard Association of United States. **HONORS/ACHIEVEMENTS:** Fellow Amer Coll of Ob/Gyn 1980; Fellow Intl College of Surgeons. **MILITARY SERVICE:** USNG, Colonel, 207th EVAC HOSP, 1972-. **BUSINESS ADDRESS:** 3800 Woodard, Ste 502, Detroit, MI 48201.

ARRINGTON, HENRY TERRELL
Director. **PERSONAL:** Born Feb 15, 1932, Montgomery, AL; married Evelyn; children: Michael, Karen, Alan. **EDUCATION:** Educ Inst, 1954-57; AL State Univ. **CAREER:** Dept Agriculture, Forest Serv Bur, ofc communications & distrb serv, 1968-69; Medical Care Vendor Acct Div, audit/verification & payment supr, 1969-71; Prince George's Co Model Cities, chf prgm oprtn, 1971-72; Gov Maryland, special asst, 1972-75; Maryland State Off of Minority Bus Enterprise, dir, 1975-79; APS Inc, dir real est devel, 1979-. **ORGANIZATIONS:** Mem Model Neighborhood Action Bd 1971; Prince George's Co Ad Hoc Comm; 5th Congr Dist Dem Caucus; precinct coord Alliance for Action Democratic Campaign; coord Citiz for Charter Prgm in Election Precinct; Hart for Congr Campaign in Precinct; poll worker Election Precinct; exec chmn DC Vet Assn; past pres Seat Pleasant Rec Cncl; past mem exec com Prince George's Co Chap NAACP; mem Prince George's Co PTA; Beulah Bapt Ch Deanwood Hts; Amer Vet Com; Dem Polit Excellence; mayor Seat Pleasant, MD; del Dem Conv 1972; mem Credentials Comm Dem Conv 1972; MD Comm Functions of Gov; chmn Prince George's Co Model Neighborhood Action Bd; bd dir Prince George's Comm Bank; bd trustees Heart Assn of So MD; assoc mem Model Cities Jaycees; at large mem Exec com MD Municip League; mem Natl conf of Black mayors; mem Natl Black Caucus of Local Elected Ofcls; bd dirs Cable Comm Inc of MD. **MILITARY SERVICE:** USAF E-3 1949-53. **BUSINESS ADDRESS:** Dir Real Estate Development, APS Inc, 6301 Addison Rd, Washington, DC 20027.

ARRINGTON, LLOYD M., JR.
Investment executive. **PERSONAL:** Born Dec 12, 1947, Montgomery, AL; son of Lloyd Arrington and Annie Arrington; married Brenda J Stovall;. **EDUCATION:** Fisk Univ, BA 1970; Stanford Univ, MBA 1973. **CAREER:** Bankers Tr NY Corp, asst treasurer 1973-77; Assoc for the Investigation of Mgmt, proj dir 1974-75; Pfizer Inc, mgr strategic planning 1978-79; US Small Business Admin, asst adv 1979-81; US Dept of Comm MBDA chief, capital devel 1981-82; Arrington & Co, pres; Economic Development Finance Corp., Investment Associate, 1988-. **ORGANIZATIONS:** Chm MD Small Business Devel Finance Authority 1986-; Natl Black MBA Assn; Omega Psi Phi; WA Soc of Investment Anlyst. **HONORS/ACHIEVEMENTS:** T J Watson Fellow Fisk Univ 1970-71; C E Merrill Fellow Stanford Univ 1972-73, COGME Fellow 1971-73; J Barlow Schlr Bd of Educ, Redding, CT 1966. **HOME ADDRESS:** 1602 Pebble Beach Dr, Mitchellville, MD 20716.

ARRINGTON, MARVIN
City council president. **CAREER:** City Council President, Atlanta, GA. **BUSINESS ADDRESS:** 68 Mitchell St SW, Atlanta, GA 30335. *

ARRINGTON, PAMELA GRAY
Professor. **PERSONAL:** Born Feb 28, 1953, Montgomery, AL; daughter of Mr & Mrs Willis E Gray; married Richard Arrington III; children: Gray. **EDUCATION:** Spelman Coll, BA 1974; The Univ of MI, MA 1975; George Mason Univ, DA 1987. **CAREER:** Talladega Coll, counselor 1976-77; Northern VA Comm Coll, counselor 1977-80, coord of affirmative action & grant develop 1980-88; Bowie State Univ, Human Resource Devel, associate professor 1988-. **ORGANIZATIONS:** Mem ASTD, OD; HRD Professors Network, Washington Metro Area; American Assn of Univ Prof. **HONORS/ACHIEVEMENTS:** Honor Scholarship Spelman Coll 1972-74; Psi Chi Spelman College 1974; Graduate Scholarship Univ of MI 1-74-75; Pi Lambda Theta 1975; Leaders for the 80's FIPSE/Maricopa Colleges 1983; Phi Delta Kappa 1983; Grad Rsch Asst & Scholarship George Mason Univ 1984-86. **BUSINESS ADDRESS:** Assoc Prof, Human Resource Development, Dept of Behavioral Sciences & Human Services, Bowie State Univ, Bowie, MD 20715-9465.

ARRINGTON, RICHARD, JR.
Mayor. **PERSONAL:** Born Oct 19, 1934, Livingston, AL; children: Anthony, Kenneth, Kevin, Angela, Erika Lynn. **EDUCATION:** Miles Coll, AB, 1955; Univ of Detroit, MS, 1957; Univ of Oklahoma, PhD, 1966. **CAREER:** Miles Coll, prof, 1957-63; Univ of Oklahoma, spl instr, 1965-66, prof, 1966-; Univ of Alabama, assoc prof, part-time, 1971-72; Miles Coll, counselor to men, 1962-63, dir summer sch & acting dean, 1966-67, dean of coll academic, 1967-70; Alabama Ctr for Higher Educ, dir, 1970-79; City of Birmingham AL, mayor, 1979-. **ORGANIZATIONS:** Mem Birmingham City Cncl 1971-75; mem Amer Inst of Biol Sci; OK Acad of Sci; Amer Assn for Advancement of Sci; Amer Soc of Zoologists; Phi Sigma Nat Biol Soc; Soc of Sigma Xi; Amer Assn of Coll Deans; mem adv bd Family Counseling Assn of Jefferson Co; mem Alpha Phi Alpha. **HONORS/ACHIEVEMENTS:** Ortenburger Award for Outstanding Work in Biology Univ of OK 1966; Alpha Phi Alpha Man of Yr 1969; Alpha Phi Alpha Achievement Award for Outstanding Comm Serv 1971; Man of Yr Awd AL Fedn of Civic Leagues 1971; Comm Civic Serv Award Druid Hill-Norwood Civic League 1972; Charles A Billups Comm Serv Award 1972; Comm Achievement Award 1972; Distinguished Alumni Award Miles Coll Alumni Assn 1972; Freedom Achievement Award Emancipation Assn 1973; Public Serv Award Birmingham Chapter Delta Sigma Theta 1974; Outstanding Educator Award Friends of Miles Coll 1973; Presidential Commendation Award Miles Coll Alumni Assn 1974; Distinguished Comm Serv Awd Birmingham Oppors Indus 1974. **BUSINESS ADDRESS:** Mayor, City of Birmingham, 710 20th St N, Birmingham, AL 35203.

ARRINGTON, ROBYN JAMES, JR.
Physician. **PERSONAL:** Born Jul 18, 1944, Detroit, MI. **EDUCATION:** Adrian Coll, BS 1966; Howard Univ Coll of Med Ob-Gyn, MD 1970. **CAREER:** Total Health Care of Detroit, med dir. **ORGANIZATIONS:** Bd of dir SE MI Red Cross. **MILITARY SERVICE:** AUS lt col 10 yrs; AUS NG. **BUSINESS ADDRESS:** Medical Dir, Total Health Care of Detroit, 3455 Woodward St, Detroit, MI 48201.

ARRINGTON, SAUL
Assistant director. **PERSONAL:** Born Nov 28, 1930, Chase City, VA; married Goldie Dickerson; children: Saul, Robin, Kim. **EDUCATION:** Univ of NE, BS 1966. **CAREER:** Frankfort, W Germany, provost marshall 1962-64; AUS Crime Lab Europe, commanding officer 1964-65; US Embassy Military Asst Command, joint US pub affairs ofcr Vietnam 1967-68; AUS Ammunit Procurement & Supply Agency, dir security & intelligence 1968-70; WA & OR Armed Forces Police, commanding officer 1970-72; WA State Orgn Crime Intelligence Unit, dep dir 1973-74; WA State Law & Justice Planning Office, admin 1974-77; WA State Jail Comm Dept of Licensing, asst dir/chmn 1977-. **ORGANIZATIONS:** Mem Intl Assn Chiefs of Police; WA State Assn Police Chiefs & Sheriffs; v chmn Natl Conf of State Criminal Justice Planning Adminstr 1975-76; pres Tee & Turf Golf Assn Tacoma, WA. **MILITARY SERVICE:** AUS Lt Col Retired 1948-72; Reicp Legion of Merit Award 1972; Bronze Star 1968. **BUSINESS ADDRESS:** Assistant Dir, WA State Jail Commn, Dept of Licensing, Hwy License Bldg, Olympia, WA 98504.

ARROYO, MARTINA
Opera singer. **PERSONAL:** Born in New York, NY; daughter of Demetrio Arroyo and Lucille Washington. **EDUCATION:** Hunter Coll, BA 1954; Marinka Gurewich, Mo Martin Rich, Joseph Turnau, Rose Landver, pupil; Kathryn Long Course Metro Opera, studies. **CAREER:** Metro Opera NY, Vienna State Opera, Paris Opera, Covent Garden; Teatro Colon; Hamburgische Staatsoper; Israel, La Scala, Milan, Munich Staatoper Berlin Deutsche Opera, Rome Opera, San Francisco, Chicago and all maj opera houses; soloist NY, Vienna, Berlin, Royal/London, Paris Philharmonics, San Francisco, Pittsburgh, Philadelphia, Chicago, Cleveland Symphonies; SAm, USA, Eur, perform; NY Philharmon "Andromaches & Farewell", debut 1963; LA State Univ Baton Rouge, visiting prof. **ORGANIZATIONS:** Former mem Natl Endowment of Arts WA; trustee Carnegie Hall. **HONORS/ACHIEVEMENTS:** First soprano in 20 hrs to sing 3 consecutive opening nights for the Met 1970-71,72; roles in Aida, Madame Butterfly, Un Ballo in Maschera, Cavalleria Rusticana; La Forza del Destino, Tosca, Macbeth, Don Giovanni, La Gioconoda, Vespri Siciliani; one of 4 natl win Metro Opera Aud of the & won guest contributor 1959; Hunter Coll Outstanding Alumna; Rec for Columb Lond Ang DGG Phil; Dr Honoris Cause of Human Letters Hunter Coll of NY Univ. **BUSINESS ADDRESS:** Thea Dispeker, 59th E 54th St, New York, NY 10022.

ARTERBERY, VIVIAN J.
Library director. **EDUCATION:** Attended, Howard Univ; Univ of So CA, MLS. **CAREER:** Space Tech Laboratories; Aerospace Corporation CA; Rand Corp Santa Monica, library dir; Natl Commn on Libraries and Information Sciences, exec dir. **ORGANIZATIONS:** Consultant US Office of Educ 1974-76; pres Special Libraries Assoc 1984-85; SLA rep Amer Library Assoc/US Dept of Educ Accreditation Project 1985-86; adv bd mem CA Library Assoc Councilor and Univ of So CA Library Sch.

ARTHOS, JOHN
Performing arts/producer. **PERSONAL:** Born Jan 15, 1956, Ann Arbor, MI. **EDUCATION:** Univ of MI, BA (High Distinction) 1978. **CAREER:** Amnesty Intl Bread for the World, human rights activist 1978-82; Interfaith Council for Peace, human rights activist 1978-82; Morehouse School of Medicine, videotape producer 1983-85; Channel 12 Public Access Atlanta, producer 1984; Grady School of Communications, instructor film/video/photography 1986-; Minority Film Serv, producer. **ORGANIZATIONS:** Pres Univ of MI Hunger Task Force 1975-77; dist coord Bread for the World 1976-82; city coord Amnesty Intl Urgent Action 1977-78; mem Assoc of Independent Video & Film Makers 1983-85; mem Image Filmmakers 1983-85; asst tennis coach Morehouse Coll 1982-; mem Inst of 3rd World Policies Morehouse Coll 1984-85; coach Grady HS Varsity Tennis 1987-. **HONORS/ACHIEVEMENTS:** Local Hunger Survey Ann Arbor News published 1978; Joint Bd Grant State Grant Awarded for Prod of Video on Old Age 1984; Caber Awd Prime Cable Atlanta 1984;Winner of the SE Media Fellowship 1985; Juror's Selection at the Festival of New Works New Orleans 1985; SCPA Photographic Competition winner 1986; CINS Excellence in Teaching 1987. **BUSINESS ADDRESS:** Producer, Minority Film Services, 2026 Hill St, Ann Arbor, MI 48104.

ARTHUR, GEORGE KENNETH
Elected administrator. **PERSONAL:** Born Jun 29, 1934, Buffalo, NY; son of William E Arthur and Jayne Potter; married Frances Bivens; children: George Jr, Janice, Hugh. **EDUCATION:** Empire State Coll, Pol Sci 1977. **CAREER:** Erie Cty Bd of Supervisors, suprv 1964-67; City of Buffalo, councilman 1970-77; city of Buffalo, councilman at large 1978-84, pres of common council 1984-. **ORGANIZATIONS:** Bd of dir Better Bus Bureau, Buffalo Philharmonic Orch, Kleinhans Music Hall, NAACP Life Mem; Jr Warden St John Lodge # 16; mem First Shiloh Baptist Church. **HONORS/ACHIEVEMENTS:** Man of the Year The Buffalo Club 1970; Man of the Year Afro Police 1973; Medgar Evers Awd NAACP 1984; Jackie Robinson Awd YMCA 1985. **MILITARY SERVICE:** AUS corpl 1953-55. **HOME ADDRESS:** 154 Roebling Ave, Buffalo, NY 14215. **BUSINESS ADDRESS:** President, Buffalo Common Council, Room 1315 City Hall, Buffalo, NY 14202.

ARTIES, ELVIRA YVONNE
Educator. **PERSONAL:** Born Aug 18, Pittsburgh, PA; daughter of Walter Arties and Catherine Arties. **EDUCATION:** Oakwood Coll, Huntsville AL, 1952-53, 1956-58; Univ of the Dist of Columbia, BA 1972; Howard Univ, Washington DC, 1972-74; George Washington Univ, 1983-84. **CAREER:** Dept of the Navy, Pers Spec 1964-69; Federal City Coll, Washington DC, staff asst 1969-72; Dept of Housing & Urban Devel, Washington DC, educ specialist 1973-74; Washington DC Public Schools, educator 1974-. **ORGANIZATIONS:** Mem Oakwood Coll Alumni Assoc 1958-; mem Univ of the Dist of Columbia Alumni Assoc 1981-; bd of dir WGTS-FM, Tacoma Park MD 1982-; chairperson Breath of Life Telethon Comm at Howard Univ 1983-; mem Washington DC Chamber of Commerce 1985; DC/DECA DC Public Schools 1985. **HONORS/ACHIEVEMENTS:** Mayor of the Dist of Columbia 1981; Certificate of Appreciation, Gov of the State of MD 1982; Graduate School Awardeeship, George Washington Univ 1982-83; Meritorious Award, Wilson Sr High School 1982; Certificate of Merit, Spingson Sr High School 1984. **BUSINESS ADDRESS:** Washington DC Public Schools, 24th & Benning Rd NE, Washington, DC 20016.

ARTIES, WALTER EUGENE, III
Producer, director, musician. **PERSONAL:** Born Nov 12, 1941, Pittsburgh, PA; married Beverly Ruth Deshay. **EDUCATION:** Faith Coll Birmingham, LHD 1977. **CAREER:** Walter Arties Chorale LA, dir/arranger 1961-71; Little Richard Gospel Singer Penniman, arranger 1961-63; Webber Button Co, office head 1961-71; Billy Graham Crusades Assn Minneapolis, guest tenor soloist 1971-; KHOF-TV & FM Radio, comm services dir 1971-74; Breath of Life Telecast, prod coord 1974-. **ORGANIZATIONS:** Bd of trustees 7th Day Adventist Radio & TV Film Center Thousand Oaks, CA 1974-; exec com mem N Amer Adv Com Wash, DC; SDA Radio Film Center Thousand Oaks, CA 1974-; bd dir RV Operations Thousand Oaks, CA 1974-; baseball particip LA Dept of Rec Univ SDC Ch LA 1966-67; singing particip World Evangilization Lusanne Switzerland 1974. **HONORS/ACHIEVEMENTS:** Recip Outstanding Music Accomplishment Award Grant Theol Sem Birmingham 1977; Mus Contributions for Singing Award Port Albernia Brit Columbia, Canada 1977; Outstanding Prodn Coord Award Breath of Life Comm Wash, DC MD Chap 1980. **BUSINESS ADDRESS:** Prod/Coordinator, Breath of Life Telecast, 1100 Rancho Conejo Blvd, Newbury Park, CA 91320.

ARTIS, ANDRE KEITH
Physician. **PERSONAL:** Born Oct 07, 1954, Brooklyn, NY; married Neva J; children: Ashley, Adrianne. **EDUCATION:** Oakwood Coll, BA 1976; Meharry Medical Coll, MD 1980. **CAREER:** Meharry Medical Coll, resident internal medicine 1980-83, instructor/chief resident 1985-86; Choctaw Health Ctr, dept of internal medicine chief medical officer 1983-85; US Public Health Service, senior surgeon; Univ of MO, post-doctoral fellow/cardiology 1986-88. **ORGANIZATIONS:** Associate Amer Coll of Physicians 1980-86, Amer Coll of Cardiology 1986-; commencement speaker Northeastern Conference Area Wide Elementary Schools 1986. **HOME ADDRESS:** 4408 So Pinebrook Lane, Columbia, MO 65201.

ARTIS, ANTHONY JOEL
Environmental designer. **PERSONAL:** Born Jan 11, 1951, Kokomo, IN; son of Myrle E Artis and Yvonne S Artis; married Iris Rosa; children: Andre Antonio, Claudia Lizet. **EDUCATION:** Miami Univ Oxford OH, B Environ Design 1975. **CAREER:** Musician/instrumentalist bass guitar various groups in IN & OH 1967-; Various architects in IN & OH, draftsman/designer 1974-79; Artis Environments, owner 1979-; Current Group "Directions" jazz/fusion 1985-. **ORGANIZATIONS:** Mem youth advisory council Center for Leadership Devel 1979-; speaker & mem exhibition comm Minorities in Engineering 1979-82; mem Meridian Kessler Neighborhood Assn 1981-; mem Natl Trust for Historic Preservation 1983-; mem volunteer staff Indianapolis City Center 1983-84; mem Indianapolis Chamber of Commerce 1984-; bd dirs Neighborhood Housing Serv of Indianapolis 1985-87. **HONORS/ACHIEVEMENTS:** Governors Trophy Indianapolis 500 Festival Parade Float Design Team Indiana Black Expo 1982; Black Achiever in Science, Childrens Museum, IN 1989. **BUSINESS ADDRESS:** Owner, Artis Environments, 3946 Guilford Ave, Indianapolis, IN 46205.

ARTIS, MYRLE EVERETT
Physician. **PERSONAL:** Born Sep 28, 1924, Kokomo, IN; married Pamela; children: Anthony, Mark. **EDUCATION:** IN Univ, AB 1953; IN Univ Med School, MD 1957. **CAREER:** Cty Bd of Health, pres; St Joseph Mem Hosp, pres of staff, internship, chief of med; Private practice, physician 1958-. **ORGANIZATIONS:** Mem Howard Cty Med Assoc, IN Med Assoc, AMA, Natl Med Assoc, Amer Acad of Family Practice Fellowships, Bd of Health, St Joseph Mem Hosp Found, Cty Library Adv Comm, C of C; mem dir Forest Park Convalescent Ctr Kokomo In; govt adv comm Sickle Anemia 1979-83, 1983-87; bd of dirs Kokomo Pal Club, Carver Community Ctr. **MILITARY SERVICE:** AUS 1943-46. **BUSINESS ADDRESS:** 402 S Berkley, PO Box 3067, Kokomo, IN 46901.

ARTISON, RICHARD E.
Law enforcement. **PERSONAL:** Born Jun 09, 1933, Omaha, NE; married Charleszine; children: Lisa, Richard Jr, Kelli. **EDUCATION:** Drake Univ, Sociol & Psych 1954; Univ of NE Law School, 1954-55; Cornell Univ, Ed for Publ Mgmt 1973-74. **CAREER:** US Army Counter Intelligence, spec agent 1955-58; Omaha NE Police Dept, police officer 1958-62; US Treas Secret Svc, spec agent 1963-67; Milwaukee Office Secret Svc, spec agent in charge 1974-83; Milwaukee Cty, sheriff 1983-. **ORGANIZATIONS:** Exec bd mem Milwaukee Cty Boy Scouts; bd of dir Amer Red Cross; past pres Fed Officials Assoc, past vice pres Milwaukee Frontiers Intl; mem Milwaukee Cty Metro Police Chiefs; charter mem Fed Criminal Invest Assoc. **HONORS/ACHIEVEMENTS:** Exemplary Achievement Kappa Alpha Psi; High Quality Awd US Treasury Dept. **MILITARY SERVICE:** AUS spec agent 3 yrs. **HOME ADDRESS:** 9365 N 67th St, Milwaukee, WI 53223.

ARTISST, ROBERT IRVING
Educator. **PERSONAL:** Born Jul 13, 1932, Washington, DC; children: Tawnya Alicia, Robert Irving II. **EDUCATION:** Howard U, BA 1959, MA 1969; Univ of DC, MA 1971. **CAREER:** Appalacian Reg Comm, public information/visual specialist 1966-71; Urban Inst, dir of pub 1972-71; Natl Assn of Black Manufacturing Inc, exec liaison officer 1972-73; Cooperative Extension Serv WTI, public information & comm coord 1973-76; Univ of Washington DC, assoc prof of media. **ORGANIZATIONS:** Asso prof Univ DC 1976-69; comm D C Homan Rights Comm 1978-84; comm Adv Neighborhood Comm 1975-85; chm of bd DC Capitol Head Start 1983-85; pres Brookland Civic Asso, Inc 1977-84; v chm Neighborhood Plng Cncl 1976-79; v pres DC Citizens for Better Pub Ed 1977-84. **HONORS/ACHIEVEMENTS:** Edtr/Writer Handbook for Tchrs of Adult 1971-72; spec awd Tchng Youth Operation Rescue 1982-84; spec accmdtn Mayor of the City for Services 1976-77, spec citation 1978-79. **MILITARY SERVICE:** AUS 1st lt Univ S 11th Airborne Div 5 yrs Wings/Calvary Star-Airman Star 1954. **BUSINESS ADDRESS:** Associate Prof of Media, Univ of Washington DC, 4200 Connecticut Ave, NW, Washington, DC 20008.

ASANTE, KARIAMU WELSH
Professor, choreographer. **PERSONAL:** Born Sep 22, 1949, Thomasville, NC; daughter of Harvey Farabee and Ruth Hoover; married Molefi K Asante; children: Daahoud, Khumalo. **EDUCATION:** State Univ of NY at Buffalo, BA 1972, MA 1975. **CAREER:** Black Dance Workshop, choreographer 1970-77; Center for Positive Thought Buffalo, NY, artistic dir 1971-81; Kariamu & Co, choreographer 1977-84; Natl Dance Co of Zimbabwe Harare, Zimbabwe, artistic dir 1981-83; Temple Univ, prof/choreographer. **ORGANIZATIONS:** Dir Museum of African Amer Art & Antiquities 1978-; editorial bd Journal of Black Studies 1982-; panel mem Buffalo Arts Cncl 1983-85; panel mem NYS Council on the Arts Spec Arts Serv 1984-85; consult Natl Dance Co of Zimbabwe 1984-; dir Institute of African Dance Research & Performance Temple Univ 1985-. **HONORS/ACHIEVEMENTS:** Natl Endowment for the Arts Choreography Fellowship 1973; NYS Creative Artist Serv Awd 1974; Choreographer Awd Clark Ctr for the Performing Arts NY 1977; Choreographers Fellowship

NYS Creative Artist Serv Awd 1978; Fulbright Scholars Fellowship Harare Zimbabwe 1982-83; Minority Choreographers Fellowship NY State Cncl on the Arts 1984; co-editor The African Culture, Rhythms of Unity 1985; Dance Historian Fellowship, Commonwealth of PA Council on the Arts 1988; editor The African Aesthetic: Keeper of the Traditions, Greenwood Press 1989; editor Journal of African Dance 1989. **HOME ADDRESS:** 707 Medary Ave, Philadelphia, PA 19126. **BUSINESS ADDRESS:** Professor/Choreographer, Temple University, Broad & Montgomery Sts, Philadelphia, PA 19122.

ASANTE, MOLEFI KETE (ARTHUR L. SMITH JR.)
Educator. **PERSONAL:** Born Aug 14, 1942, Valdosta, GA; son of Arthur L Smith Sr and Lillie B Wilkson Smith; married Kariamu Welsh; children: Kasina Eka, Daahoud, Molefi Khumalo. **EDUCATION:** Southwestern Christian Coll, AA 1962; Oklahoma Christian Coll, BA 1964; Pepperdine Univ, MA 1965; UCLA, PhD 1968. **CAREER:** CA State Polytechnic Coll, instr 1967; CA State Univ Northridge, instr 1968; Purdue Univ, asst prof 1968-69; Pepperdine Univ, visit prof 1969; Univ of CA LA, asst prof 1969-71; CA State Univ, visit prof 1971; Univ of CA LA, dir Center for Afro-Amer Studies 1970-73, assoc prof speech 1971-73; FL State Univ Tallahassee, visit assoc prof 1972; State Univ of NY Buffalo, prof communication dept; Center for Positive Thought Buffalo, exec dir; Univ of Ibadan, Univ of Nairobi, external examiner 1976-80; Zimbabwe Inst of Mass Communications, fulbright prof; Howard Univ, visiting prof 1979-80; Temple Univ Africana Studies, prof. **ORGANIZATIONS:** Consult Trans-Ethnic Educ/Communication Proj 1969-72, Spec in Black Rhetoric County Probation Dept LA 1969-; selection comm Martin L King Fellowships/Woodrow Wilson Fellowships 1970-72; textbook consult Cntr for Extending Am History 1971-73; consult CBS Bill Cosby Show 1972; pres SIETAR 1975-76; bd editors Black Man in Am; editorial assoc "The Speech Teacher"; editor "Journal of Black Studies"; adv bd Black Journal; mem Intl Soc for Gen Semantics; Intl Assn for Symbolic Analysis; Intl Comm Assn; Western Speech Assn; Central State Speech Assn; So Speech Assn; Natl Assn for Dramatic & Speech Arts; ed bds-Nigerian Journal of Political Economy, Afrodiaspora, Afrique Historie, Africa and the World, Urban African Quarterly, Journal of African Civilization; contributing writer for Buffalo Challenger, Philadelphia New Observer, Philadelphia Tribune; UNESCO reviewer for scholarly books 1985; consultant Zimbabwe Ministry of Information and Telecommunications; Intl Scientific Comm of FESPAC 1986-87 Senegal; chairperson, IMHOTEP 1987-; vice president, Natl Council for Black Studies, 1988-; vice president, African Heritage Studies Assn 1989-. **HONORS/ACHIEVEMENTS:** Author of 24 books; consulting editor for books; Contemporary Authors 1973-74; Christian Ed Guild Writer's Awards 1965; Outstanding Young Men of Amer 1970; LHD Univ of New Haven 1976; Outstanding Comm Scholar Jackson State Univ 1980; author of The Afrocentric Idea 1987; author of Afrocentricity, 1987. **HOME ADDRESS:** 707 Medary Ave, Philadelphia, PA 19126. **BUSINESS ADDRESS:** Professor, Temple University, Cladfelter Hall 809, Africana Studies, Philadelphia, PA 19122.

ASHBY, DOROTHY J.
Musician, composer. **PERSONAL:** Born Aug 06, 1932, Detroit, MI; married John Ashby. **EDUCATION:** Attended, Wayne State Univ. **CAREER:** Assists youth in developing skills in mus & theater 1957-; WJR, staff harpist 1960-63; WCHD-FM, radio show 1963-68; musicals produced by John Ashby & WileyThompson Detroit 1967, Toronto CAN 1968, Detroit 1970, Toronto 1970, Chicago 1971, Detroit 1972; professional harpist/composer. **ORGANIZATIONS:** Mem Amer Harp Soc; currently most recorded contemporary Harpist in world can be heard on virtually all albums of major pop artists, Johnny Mathis, Stevie Wonder, Natalie Cole, Bill Withers, Donald Byrd, Ramsey Lewis, Earth Wind & Fire, Black Byrds, Helen Reddy, Emotions, Jon Lucien, Freddie Hubbard etc; num commercials on radio & tv; mem Natl Acad of Recording Arts & Scis; Black Comm Theatre; Amer Fedn of Mus Local #47; Hollywood Local #5 Detroit; 12 LP Albums.

ASHBY, ERNESTINE ARNOLD
Educator. **PERSONAL:** Born Aug 20, 1928, Washington, DC; widowed; children: Ira Von. **EDUCATION:** Cortez Peters Bus Sch, bus cert 1947; Coppin State Tchrs Coll, BS 1950; Univ of MD, MEd 1967; Walden Univ, PhD candidate. **CAREER:** Baltimore City Public Schools, teacher 1950-69; Accomack County School System, reading spec 1969-. **ORGANIZATIONS:** Bd dir Emmanuel Christian Comm Sch Fed Credit Union Adv Cncl 1954-57; owner mgr Furniture Excng United Appeal Orgr Comm Chest 1955-57; bd mem YWCA; multi-media specialist 1968-; author co-author num children's stories & poems; mem NEA, VEA, AEA, IRA area chmn NAACP 1976,. **HONORS/ACHIEVEMENTS:** Awd in Recog Literary Guild; Cert of Achievement Small Bus Mgmt; Vol Serv Awd PTA.

ASHBY, LUCIUS ANTOINE
Business executive. **PERSONAL:** Born Feb 01, 1944, Des Moines, IA; son of Lucius A Ashby Sr and Ruth M Moore; married Victoria Lacy; children: Felecia, Armand. **EDUCATION:** Univ of Colorado Denver, BBA 1969; Harvard Univ, SCMP 1982-84. **CAREER:** Greast Western Sugar Co, management trainee program 1968-69; Arthur Anderson & Co sr accountant 1969-72; Ashby Armstrong & Co, managing partner 1973-; Ashby Jackson, Inc, chmn of bd. **ORGANIZATIONS:** Mbr Amer Inst of CPA's; bd of dir CO Soc of CPAW's Denver Partnerships, Assoc of Black CPA Firms, Ldrshp Denver Assn, Salvation Army 1975-; bd of dirs Downtown Denver Inc; chmn of bd, Colorado Invesco Inc, 1988-. **HONORS/ACHIEVEMENTS:** Rcpnt Barney Ford Eastside Action Mvmnt 1975; entrepreneur award United Negro Coll Fund 1980; achievement award Natl Assn of Black Accountants 1979. **MILITARY SERVICE:** AUS sp-5 e-5 1961-64. **BUSINESS ADDRESS:** Ashby Jackson Inc, 1900 Grant St, Suite 1050, Denver, CO 80203.

ASHBY, REGINALD W.
Business executive. **PERSONAL:** Married Ernestine C Arnold; children: Eugene Paula, Iravon. **EDUCATION:** Morgan State Coll, cert bus adminstrn. **CAREER:** Life Ins Career, 1936-; Universal Life Ins Co Norfolk, agent 1969-. **ORGANIZATIONS:** Mem VFW (1st Black exec offcr dist); pres Accomack Co, VA NAACP; orgn Neighborhood Boys Club Baltimore 1963; Grand Jury Baltimore 1968-69. **MILITARY SERVICE:** AUS 1946. **BUSINESS ADDRESS:** Agent, Universal Life Ins Co, 2802 Virginia Beach Blvd, Norfolk, VA 23504.

ASHCRAFT, BERNARD
Association executive. **PERSONAL:** Born Sep 02, 1941, Feyette, MO; children: Sonja, Darrell, Autumn. **EDUCATION:** San Diego Evening Coll, AA 1972; Univ of CA San Diego, 1973; Nat Univ San Diego, BS 1974, MPA 1975. **CAREER:** Action Interprs Devel Inc, pres; San Diego Urban Leag, supr of mnpwr prgm 1973-; Univ of CA San Diego, sr rsrch assoc 1969-70; Ford Med Ctr, x-ray & lab tech 1968-69. **ORGANIZATIONS:** Mem Crisis Ctr; Legal Aid Soc; San Diego Urban Leag; UCSD Black Caucus; Blk Action Com Inc; Mayor's Com on Housing; Comprhnsn Hlth Care Proj; Nghbrhd Hlth Orgn; Reg Empl Training Consortium. **HONORS/ACHIEVEMENTS:** Recip Citat from Nat Involvment Assn for Sickle Cell Anemia. **MILITARY SERVICE:** USN.

ASHE, ARTHUR R., JR.
Tennis professional. **PERSONAL:** Born Jul 10, 1943, Richmond, VA; married Jeanne Marie Moutoussamy; children: Camera Elizabeth. **EDUCATION:** UCLA, BS 1966. **CAREER:** Professional tennis player; ABC-TV, sports commentator; Author; Consultant. **ORGANIZATIONS:** UCLA alumni Assn Kappa Alpha Psi; Afr Stu Aid Fund; Natl Geo Soc US Men's Hart Ct Ch 1963; US Davis Cup team mem 1963-70, 1972,76,78, capt 1981-85; US Men's Clay Ct 1967; US Amateur Title 1968; US Open Tennis 1968; Australian Open Tennis 1970; French Open Doubles 1972; World Ch Tennis Singles 1975; Wimbledon Singles 1975; Australian Open Doubles 1977; bd of dirs Aetna Life and Casualty Co. **HONORS/ACHIEVEMENTS:** Won 2 US Inter-Coll Championships; US Jaycees TOYM 1969; ATP Player of the Year Awd 1975; Jefferson Awd 1982; Laurel Wreath Awd 1986; Graham-WindhamAwd 1987; Honorary Doctorates at VA Union Univ, St John's Univ, Princeton Univ, Dartmouth Univ, LeMoyne Coll. **MILITARY SERVICE:** AUS 1st Lt 1967-69. **HOME ADDRESS:** PO Box 447, Bedford Hills, NY 10507.

ASHFORD, EVELYN
Olympic runner. **PERSONAL:** Married Ray Washington; children: 1 daughter. **CAREER:** 1984 Olympics, runner. **HONORS/ACHIEVEMENTS:** 4 World Cup Titles; Flo Hyman Award, Women's Sport Foundation, 1989. **BUSINESS ADDRESS:** 818 Plantation Lane, Walnut, CA 91789. *

ASHFORD, LAPLOIS
Association executive. **PERSONAL:** Born Jul 18, 1935, McCool, MS. **EDUCATION:** Univ of Rochester, BA Hist 1957; NY State Univ, MA Soc Studies 1960; Univ of AK, attended. **CAREER:** Rochester Special Edn, teacher 1960-62; NAACP Youth & Coll Div, natl dirf 1962-65; City of Rochester, dep commr of pub safety 1965-67; Rochester Urban League, exec dir 1967-70; Chicago Urban League, exec dir 1970-72; Natl Urban Coalition, vice pres for Urban Edn. **ORGANIZATIONS:** Mem Natl Educ Assn; Amer Assn of Jr & Comm Colls; Amer Assn of State & Pub Inst of Higher Educ Commr of Schs Rochester 1967-69; pres Bd of EdnRochester 1968-69; chmn Action for Survival Chicago 1970-72; chmn UNCF of DC 1974. **HONORS/ACHIEVEMENTS:** Recip Outstanding Young man of the Year NY State Jaycees 1965; Leroy E Snyder Award for Outstanding Comm Serv Rochester 1967; Richard Allen Award AME Ch1970; Afro-Am Patrolmens League Testimonial Award Chicago 1971; Outstanding Serv Award Natl Urban Coalition 1974. **MILITARY SERVICE:** AUS 1957-59. **BUSINESS ADDRESS:** Vice Pres for Urban Education, Natl Urban Coalition, 2100 M St NW, Washington, DC 20037.

ASHFORD, NICHOLAS
Singer, musical arranger, composer. **PERSONAL:** Born 1943, Willow Run, MI; married Valerie Simpson; children: Nicole. **CAREER:** Songwriter-producer w/Valerie Simpson, Scepter Records then Motown Records; recording artist w/Valerie Simpson 1973-; songs cowritten, Your All I Need to Get By, Let's Get Stoned, Ain't No Mountain High Enough, Ain't Nothing Like the Real Thing; album Musical Affair, Is It Still Good To Ya, Stay Free; Hopsack & Soul;owner production co. **BUSINESS ADDRESS:** c/o William Morris Agency, 1350 Avenue of the Americas, New York, NY 10019.

ASHLEY, CORLANDERS
Secretary/treasurer. **PERSONAL:** Born May 09, 1951, Cleveland, OH. **EDUCATION:** OH Wesleyan Univ, attended 1969-71; Boston Univ, BS Business Admin 1971-73; Case Western Reserve, cand for MBA 1975. **CAREER:** ITT Headquarters NY, adm asst 1973-74; Ashley Distributors Inc, officer sec/treas 1975-. **ORGANIZATIONS:** Mem Cleveland Jaycees 1976-; bd mem Fam Bus Assn 1978-; bd trustee Cleveland Bus League 1980-81; Chi Chap treas Kappa Psi Frat 1971-73; mem Councilof Small Enterprises 1975-; mem Univ Serv Inst 1975-; Cert of Particip Univ Serv Inst 1975. **HONORS/ACHIEVEMENTS:** Outstanding Young Men of Amer Jaycees 1979. **BUSINESS ADDRESS:** Secretary/Treasurer, Ashley Distributors Inc, 19701 S Miles Rd, Warrensville Heights, OH 44128.

ASHLEY, LILLARD GOVERNOR
Educator. **PERSONAL:** Born May 01, 1909, Boley, OK; married Velma Dolphin; children: Lewis, Lillard Jr. **EDUCATION:** Langston Univ, BS 1933; OK State Univ, MS. **CAREER:** Bd of Educ Dist I-13. **ORGANIZATIONS:** Past pres Okfuskee Co Educ Assn; sec/treas Co Dem Assn; vice pres State Adv Council to St Bd of Voc & Tech Edn; mem/past pres Central OK Econ Devel Dist; past vice pres SW Reg Alpha Phi Alpha; sec Beta Epsilon Lambda Alpha Phi Alpha; mem OK Educ Assn; mem OK Assn of Sch Adm; treas Masonic Bene Assn Prince Hall Grand Lodge Jurisd of OH; past sec/treas Charity Comm Prince Hall Grand Lodge Jurisd of OK; Sunday Schl supt deacon Antioch Bapt Ch; chrt mem Boley Kiwanis Intl; past sec/treas Boley C of C; mem Okfuskee Co Fair Bd. **HONORS/ACHIEVEMENTS:** Special Recogn in ch 1954; Mason of the year 1968; Selected by Amer Assn of Sch Adm to visit schools in Germany 1973.

ASHLEY-HARRIS, DOLORES B.
Educator. **PERSONAL:** Born in Tuskegee, AL; daughter of Alonzo Ashley and Beatrice Ashley. **EDUCATION:** Tuskgee Inst, BS 1951; Univ of WI MS 1956; Arrowmont Sch of Arts, 197174; Penland Sch of Arts, Univ of Oslo, Sophia Univ Haystack Sch of Arts & Crafts. **CAREER:** Lincoln Univ, tchr edctr; Grambling, asst prof; Prairie View, asst prof; Murray St Univ, guest lecturer; TN St Univ design edctr. **ORGANIZATIONS:** Mbr exhbtr Nashville Artist Guild 1981-; ASIO Assoc Nashville Chptr Natl Surface Design Conf 1975-; banquet decor NAACP 1975-83; Natl Conf of Artist; exhbtns Dusable Museum Chgo, Schnectady Museum NY, FL A & M Univ; chairperson, Art Committee, Nashville Links Inc 1988-; impact and advisory committee, Cheekwood Fine Arts Museum, Harlem Renaissance Exhibit 1988-. **HONORS/ACHIEVEMENTS:** $1000 excellence in tchng TN St Univ 1974, St Dept Grant for Study W Africa 1975; $3000 schlrshp African Am Inst Howard Univ 1975; 1st place Fine and Folk Art Festival FL St U; purchase awd TN St Museum; schlrshps to Penland & Haystack Sch of Arts & Crafts; Humanities Scholar, Tennessee Humanities Society 1988-; Aristocrat of Bands Achievement Award, Tennessee State Univ Band 1989; Fulbright/

Hayes Research Abroad Fellow, Senegal, Cameroon, Liberia, Africa; Appointed Member of first Mayor's Task Force for the Cultural Arts, Nashville 1988; Artworks/vertical file, (Invitational) Women in Arts Museum, Washington DC 1986-; Art works in Contemporary Batik and Tie Dye, Dona Z. Meilach, Crown Publishers 1973; American Artists in Black vol 1, RMM Publishers 1982. **BUSINESS ADDRESS:** Professor of Related Art, TN StUniv, P O Box 320, Nashville, TN 37203.

ASHTON, VIVIAN CHRISTINA R.
Elected official, business executive, political activist. **PERSONAL:** Born Aug 14, 1910, Spokane, WA; daughter of Elijah J Reynolds and Madeline M Reynolds; married Lawrence Thomas Ashton (deceased). **EDUCATION:** Washington Lee Coll US Armed Forces, Cert 1945; Berne-Davis Business Coll, Certificate 1948; OH State Univ, Sociology 1948-50; Howard Univ, Sociology 1946-82. **CAREER:** The Wee-Angels Inc, chmn 1959-85; NOW, lobbyist 1975-76; Advisory Commission 5D DC govt, commiss 1981-85; League of Women Voters, speaker 1983-85. **ORGANIZATIONS:** Mem Col Charles Young Chap 3 DAV 1945-85, Prince Hall #5 OES Masonic Order 1950-85; public relat Club Intl 1960-80; chairperson crime comm Brookland Civic Assoc 1980-85; community liaison DC Comm Humanities Council 1981; chairperson Historical Comm ANC-5C 1981-85; mem, panel comment on Pres Reagan's address to nation TV Station 1981. **HONORS/ACHIEVEMENTS:** Letter of Appreciation Mayor Walter Washington 1975; Cert of Appreciation Spingarn Moreland Rsch 1975; Awd Active Bicentennial Program 1976; Singer 1st Pl DC Dept Talen Search 1979; Cert of Appreciation DC City Council 1985. **MILITARY SERVICE:** Sp E-2 personnel serv 1943-45; WAC WWII; WWII Victory Medal, Amer Campaign Med. **BUSINESS ADDRESS:** PO Box 4518, Washington, DC 20017.

ASKEW, BONNY LAMAR
Elected official & business executive. **PERSONAL:** Born Mar 04, 1955, Rome, GA; married Adrianne Denise Smith. **EDUCATION:** US Naval Acad, 1973-75; West GA Coll, BA Political Sci 1977. **CAREER:** South Rome Comm Assoc, co-founder 1979; 2nd Ward City of Rome, commissioner 1983-84; GA Kraft Co, laborer 1977-; Rome Council on Human Relations, vice chmn. **ORGANIZATIONS:** Mem Thankful Baptist Church; mem S Rome Comm Assoc; mem Starlight Lodge #433 FAAYM; comm mem GA Municipal Assoc Comm Dev 1983-84; comm mem Natl League of Cities Comm Dev 1983-84; mem Natl Black Caucus local elected official 1983-84; mem GA Assoc Black Elected Off 1983-84. **HONORS/ACHIEVEMENTS:** Who's Who Among Colleges & Univs 1977. **HOME ADDRESS:** 503 Cotton Ave, Rome, GA 30161.

ASKEW, JAMES R.
Business executive. **PERSONAL:** Born Apr 23, 1925, Gary, IN; married Essie; children: Linda. **EDUCATION:** Charles Stone Tlrng & Designing, grad 1950. **CAREER:** Carling Brewery, sales mgr & spec rep; Lowery Schlitz Dist Co, sales mgr; Askew Schlitz Distrib Co, pres & owner. **ORGANIZATIONS:** Fund Raising comm boy Scouts of Amer; mem & dir Chicago YMCA. **HONORS/ACHIEVEMENTS:** Award Chicago Assn of Commerce Comm Progress. **MILITARY SERVICE:** USN. **BUSINESS ADDRESS:** President, Askew Schlits Distrib Co, 5959 S Lowe St, Chicago, IL 60621.

ASKEW, ROGER L.
Educator. **PERSONAL:** Born Apr 07, 1931, Kansas City, KS. **EDUCATION:** Fisk Univ, BA 1953; Western Res Univ Cleveland, MA 1957. **CAREER:** Bennett Coll, instr of drama 1957; Cleveland Pub Sch, instr 1957-59; Karamu House Cleveland, dir of natural hist 1959-60; Fisk Univ, instr 1960-62; Republ of Guinea for Engl Lang Svcs, lang specialist 1962-64; Republic of Guinea, dep peace corps dir 1966; Republic of Cameroon, dep peace corps dir 1967-68; Republic of Guinea, dep peace corps dir 1966; Cleveland Job Corps for Women, supr recreation & life skills 1968-69; CW Post Coll, asst dean of students 1970-71; Fisk Univ, asst to pres spl programs/assoc prof; freelance actor, dir. **ORGANIZATIONS:** Quaker Intl Vol Serv 1953; dir & organizer of comm theatre in Conakry, Guinea 1963; dir comm theatre in Yaounde, Cameroon 1967; mem Smithsonian Inst; Natl Assn of Dramatic & Speech Arts; Metro Opera Guild; mem Alpha Phi Alpha Frat Inc. **HONORS/ACHIEVEMENTS:** Natl Jr Honor Soc 1946; Who's Who in Amer Coll & Univs 1953; Rockefeller Fellowship Karamu House Cleveland 1955. **MILITARY SERVICE:** AUS corpl 1953-55.

ASMA, THOMAS M.
Custom artist. **EDUCATION:** Layton Sch of Art, advertising art/design 1966-68; Coll of Lake Co, Liberal Arts 1975; Univ of IL, attended 1975-76. **CAREER:** Layson Prods, commercial artist 1970-71; Carlson Studios, commercial artist 1971-72; Lake Co Regional Planning Comm, planning tech 1972-73; Lake Co SafetyComm, graphic artist 1973-74; BALL Corp, palletizer genl factory 1976-78; Kitchens of Sara Lee, production sanitation 1978-80; Amer Heritage Indus, customartist 1980-. **BUSINESS ADDRESS:** American Heritage Industries, 3400 W Grand Ave, Waukegan, IL 60085.

ASOM, MOSES T.
Scientist. **PERSONAL:** Born Jul 27, 1958, Gboko Benue, Nigeria;son of Asom Ikyutor and Lydia Asom. **EDUCATION:** Univ of DC, Washington, DC, BSC (magna cum laude), Physics, 1980; Howard Univ, Washington, DC, MSC, 1982, PhD, 1985. **CAREER:** Univ of DC, Washington, DC, instructor, 1984; Howard Univ, Washington, DC, research asst, 1981-85; AT&T, Murray Hill, NJ, MTS, 1986-. **ORGANIZATIONS:** Comm mem, Educ Affairs, Amer Soc for Materials; mem, IEEE, American Physical Soc, Natl Technical Assn, Natl Org for the Advancement of Black Chemists & Chemical Engineers, Materials Research Soc. **HONORS/ACHIEVEMENTS:** NASA-HBCU, NASA, 1989; Black Engineer of the Year, 1989; published and presented over fifty technical papers and seminars in the past 3 1/2 years; special recruiter at Howard Univ. **BUSINESS ADDRESS:** Member of Technical Staff, Optoelectronic Dept, AT&T Bell Laboratories, 600 Mountain Ave, Rm GD-217, Murray Hill, NJ 07974.

ASSUE, CLARE MELBA
Chief executive officer. **PERSONAL:** Born Dec 27, 1922, New York, NY; widowed; children: Thea R, Laurie E, Charles A. **EDUCATION:** Hunter Clg of City of NY, AB 1949; Howard Univ Clg of Med, MD 1954; St Elizabeths Hosp Wash DC, Psychiatric Residency LLC Hosp, IN, 1958. **CAREER:** I Univ School Of Medicine, prof psychology 1958-; Peace Coprps Chili Sierra Leone, consultant 1962-63; V A Hospital, Indianapolis IN, consultant 1963-67; Midtown Comm Mental Health Center, consultant 1969-; LaRue D Carter Memorial Hospital, Superintendent. **ORGANIZATIONS:** Asso exmnr Am Bd of Psych & Nrulgy 70-; dir res I Univ Dept of Psych 1979-. **HONORS/ACHIEVEMENTS:** Bd dir Comm Serv Cncl of IN 1977; bd dir Julian Ctr for Women 1978. **BUSINESS ADDRESS:** Superintendent, LaRue D Carter Mem Hosp, 1315 W 10 St, Indianapolis, IN 46202.

ATAI, GRANT A.
Auto dealer executive. **CAREER:** Freedom Chrysler-Plymouth, Inc, Lancaster, TX, chief executive. **BUSINESS ADDRESS:** Freedom Chrysler-Plymouth, 940 North Beckley, Lancaster, TX 35146. *

ATCHISON, CALVIN O.
Business executive. **PERSONAL:** Born Sep 15, 1920, Millry, AL; married Amanda Rosetta McFadden; children: Antoinette, Calvin, II. **EDUCATION:** AL A&M Coll, BS 1944; Columbia Univ, MA 1949; IN Univ, EdD 1958. **CAREER:** Charlotte City Schools, school psych 1949-53; TN State Univ, assoc prof 1953-58, prof/coord of graduate studies & rsch 1958-64, prof of psych/asst grad dean 1964-67, acting dir rsch & devel 1968-69, devel officer 1969-72, vice pres for rsch planning & devel 1972-; TN State Univ Found, exec dir 1986-. **ORGANIZATIONS:** Mem Amer Psych Assn, Soc for Study of Projective Techniques, Psy Chi, Nashville Mental Health Assn, Better Bus Bureau of Nashville, Metro Nashville Housing & Urban Devel, Council for the Advancement & Study of Educ. **HONORS/ACHIEVEMENTS:** Danforth Teacher 1956-57; Outstanding Educator 1972-73; Amer Men of Sci; Who's Who in the S & SW; Administrator of the Year 1985. **MILITARY SERVICE:** USN Yeoman 2nd Class 1944-46. **BUSINESS ADDRESS:** Executive Dir, TN StateUniv Foundation, 3500 John Merritt Blvd, Nashville, TN 37202.

ATCHISON, LEON H.
Business executive. **PERSONAL:** Born Feb 27, 1928, Detroit, MI; son of A R Atchison and Rosy Lee Atchison; children: Aleta, Terrance, Erika. **EDUCATION:** MI State Univ, BA 1960; MI State Univ, MA 1962. **CAREER:** US Congressman John Conyers, admin asst 1965-71; Univ of Detroit, dir urban studies 1971-74, dir of purchasing 1974-75, dir parks & recreation 1975-79; MI Consol Gas Co, dir civic affairs 1979-. **ORGANIZATIONS:** Bd of gov Wayne State Univ State Wide Election 1970-; central business district board of directors 1981; mem Amer Assn of Blacks in Energy; bd of directors, Greater Detroit Chamber of Commerce, 1987-. **HONORS/ACHIEVEMENTS:** Man of the Year Awd Natl Assn Negro Bus & Professional Women's Clubs 1976; Outstanding Serv Awd United Cerebral Palsy Assoc 1978; Testimonial Resolution Outstanding Publ Serv Detroit City Council 1979; Proclamation, Outstanding Publ Serv Mayor City of Detroit 1979. **MILITARY SERVICE:** USN 3/c petty ofcr 1945-47; Good Conduct Medal, S Pacific Ribbon. **BUSINESS ADDRESS:** Dir of Civic Affairs, Michigan Consolidated Gas Co, 500 Griswold Ave, Detroit, MI 48226.

ATKINS, BRENDA J.
Educational administrator. **PERSONAL:** Born Jan 25, 1954, Washington, DC. **EDUCATION:** Loyola Marymount U, BA 1975; Georgetown Univ Law Ctr, JD 1978. **CAREER:** Georgetown Univ Law Center, asst dean 1978-; White House Office of Couns to the President, law clerk 1977-78; US Dept of Justice Tax Div, law clerk 1977; Lawy Com for Civil Rights Educ Proj, researcher 1976. **ORGANIZATIONS:** Org pan "Corp Divest in S Afr" 1979, "Palest Debate" 1979; mem ABA Sect on Leg Educ & Interntl Law; mem Nat Conf of Black Lawy; mem Nat Bar Assn. **HONORS/ACHIEVEMENTS:** Man ed "Am Crim Law Review 1977-78; auth "US Tax of For & For Tax" art 1980. **BUSINESS ADDRESS:** 1070 S LaBrea Ave, Los Angeles, CA 90019.

ATKINS, CAROLYN VAUGHN
Assistant professor, criminal justice. **PERSONAL:** Born Sep 21, 1930, St Louis, MO; daughter of George Vaughn Sr (deceased) and Eva Merritt Vaughn (deceased); divorced. **EDUCATION:** Fisk Univ Nashville, attended; Morgan State Univ Baltimore, BS 1951; So IL Univ Edwardsville, attended; Washington Univ St Louis, MA 1968; Central Missouri State Univ Warrensburg, MS Criminal Justice (pending); St Louis University, doctoral candidate, public policy, analysis and administration. **CAREER:** Mental Health Center of St Clair Co, counseling psychologist 1968-72; St Louis City Jail, consultant research eval & planning 1972-73; State Correctional Cntr for Women, supt 1974-76; Div of Corrections, prog specialist 1976-77, human relations officer 1977-78; Div of Probation & Parole Interstate Compact Admin, chmn & dir bd of probation & parole 1978-85; Lincoln University, asst prof, criminal justice; KLUM 98.9 FM, hostess, Criminal Justice Radiogram. **ORGANIZATIONS:** Mem Amer Corrections Assn, MO Corrections Assn; former sec/pres Acme Art & Culture Club 1964-; various offices Union Memorial United Meth Ch 1968-80; mem Psi Chi (scholastic hon psychology) So IL Univ 1969; chmn Soc Action Mental Health St Louis Alumnae Chap 1971-74; pres MO Chap Natl Assoc of Blacks in Criminal Justice 1979-80; MO reclamation coord Delta Sigma Theta Sorority 1980, pres Jefferson City Alumni Chapter 1988-89; alternate member Child Abuse and Neglect Review Board, State of Missouri 1988; life member NAACP. **HONORS/ACHIEVEMENTS:** Sigma Gamma Rho Comm Serv Award St Louis 1977; Comm Serv Award & Distinguished Women's Tea Union Memorial United Meth Ch St Louis 1978; MO Distinguished Citizen Award Union Memorial United Meth Ch 1979. **HOME ADDRESS:** 726 B Rock Hill Rd, Jefferson City, MO 65109. **BUSINESS ADDRESS:** Assistant Professor, Criminal Justice, Lincoln University, 313 Founders Hall, 820 Chestnut St, Jefferson City, MO 65101.

ATKINS, EDMUND E.
City planner. **PERSONAL:** Born Dec 06, 1944, Winston-Salem, NC; married Vera Clayton; children: Damien. **EDUCATION:** Grinnell Coll, BA, 1966; Univ of Oklahoma, MRCP, 1972. **CAREER:** San Francisco Redev Agency, asst planner, 1969; Oakland Model Cities, chief physical planner, 1970-71; US Dept HUD, urban planner, 1971-74; City of Berkeley, city planner, 1974-. **ORGANIZATIONS:** Assoc mem Amer Inst Planners; vice pres Natl Assn Planners; pres Bay Area chap New Niagra Movement Demo Club; treas Oakland Citizens Comm for Urban Renewal 1976-; mem Alameda Co Human Serv Cncl 1976-; CA Land Use Taks Force; life mem NAACP; vice pres Youth Council. **MILITARY SERVICE:** AUS Reserves 1968-74. **BUSINESS ADDRESS:** City Planner, City of Berkeley, 2030 Milvia St, Berkeley, CA 94704.

ATKINS, EDNA R.
Attorney. **PERSONAL:** Born Jan 22, 1945, Sicily Island, LA. **EDUCATION:** Univ of Omaha, BA 1967; Creighton Law School, JD 1970. **CAREER:** Legal Aid Soc of Omaha,

Council Bluffs Inc, staff atty 1970-. **ORGANIZATIONS:** Mem NE State Bar Assoc, Natl Bar Assoc, Amer Bar Assoc, Natl Assoc of Black Women Attny, NAACP 1970; gen counsel CARE Prog Inc 1973-. **BUSINESS ADDRESS:** Staff Attorney, Legal Aid Soc of Omaha, Council Bluffs Inc, 1613 Farnam St, Omaha, NE 68102.

ATKINS, FREDD GLOSSIE
City commissioner. **PERSONAL:** Born Jun 19, 1952, Sarasota, FL; son of Glossie Atkins; married Luethel Chochran Atkins, Oct 1985 (divorced); children: Nilaja, Amina, Baraka, Dumaka, Zakia. **EDUCATION:** Manatee Junior College, Bradenton, FL, AA, 1979; University of Southern Florida, Sarasota, FL. **CAREER:** Storefront Newtown Community Center, Sarasota, FL, assistant director, 1982-85; Genus Enterprises, Inc, Sarasota, FL, director of marketing, 1985-87; City of Sarasota, FL, commissioner, 1985-; Central Life Insurance, Tampa, FL, vice president, 1988-89. **ORGANIZATIONS:** Member, National Black Family Foundation; member, National Forum for Black Administrators; member, NAACP, Sarasota chapter; member, Southwest Florida Regional Planning Council; member, Florida League of Cities. **HONORS/ACHIEVEMENTS:** Political Academic Award, Kappa Alpha Psi, 1987; Martin Luther King Award for Service to Youth, 1988; NAACP Achievement Award, 1988; Human Rights and Achievement Award, Interdenominational Ministerial Alliance, 1988. **HOME ADDRESS:** 2896 Noble Avenue, Sarasota, FL 34234. **BUSINESS ADDRESS:** Commissioner, City of Sarasota, PO Box 1058, Sarasota, FL 34230.

ATKINS, HANNAH D.
Government official. **PERSONAL:** Born Nov 01, 1923, Winston-Salem, NC; daughter of James T Diggs and Mabel Kennedy Diggs; married Charles N Atkins, May 24, 1943 (deceased); children: Edmund, Valerie, Charles Jr. **EDUCATION:** St Augustine's Coll, Raleigh, NC, BS, 1943; Univ of Chicago Graduate Library School, BLS, 1949; Oklahoma City Univ School of Law, 1963-64; Univ of Oklahoma, 1968; John F Kennedy School of Govt; Harvard Univ, Program for Sr Exec. **CAREER:** Winston-Salem Journal and Sentinel NC, reporter, 1945-48; Atkins High School, NC, French teacher, 1945-48; Meharry Medical Coll, biochemistry research asst, 1948-49; Fisk Univ, reference librarian, 1949-50; Kimberly Park Elem School, NC, school librarian, 1950-51; Oklahoma City Public Library, branch librarian, 1953-56; Oklahoma State Library, Oklahoma City, reference librarian, 1962-63, chief gen reference div & acting law librarian, 1963-68, instructor of library science, 1967-68; Oklahoma City Univ, instructor of law, 1967; Oklahoma State Representative, 1969-80; US delegate to UN, 35th Gen Assembly, 1980; Oklahoma Dept of Human Serv, asst dir, 1983-87; State of Oklahoma, Sec of State, Cabinet Sec of Human Resources. **ORGANIZATIONS:** Exec bd Sunbeam Home & Family Serv, CAP-NAACP; past pres, Visiting Nurses Assn; Govt Comm on Status of Women; bd mem, Women Exec in State Govt; natl bd member, Trans-Africa; past pres, Oklahoma Chapter of the Amer Soc of Public Admin; former bd mem, Natl Amer Civil Liberties Union, Natl Black Child Devel Inst; founder and pres emeritus, Ntu Art Gallery, Oklahoma City; past chairperson, Oklahoma Advisory Comm of the US Commn on Civil Rights; vice pres, Oklahoma City Chapter of People to People; sec, Oklahoma Sister Cities; member, Executive Comm of the Oklahoma Chapter of UN/USA; member, Alpha Kappa Alpha, Assn of Law Librarians, Oklahoma Womens Political Caucus, Urban League. **HONORS/ACHIEVEMENTS:** Reference Librarian, Library USA, New York World's Fair, 1964; Outstanding Woman of the Year, Oklahoma Soroptomist Intl, 1965; Woman of the Year, Theta Sigma Phi, 1968; Outstanding Soror, Natl Founders Serv Award, Alpha Kappa Alpha Midwest Region; Legislative Conference, Rutgers Univ Eagleton Inst of Politics, 1972; Distinguished Serv Award, Natl Links Inc, 1972; Hibler Award for Distinguished Serv, 1973; Finer Womanhood Award, Zeta Phi Beta; Natl Public Citizen, Natl Assn of Social Work, 1975; Oklahoma Woman's Hall of Fame, 1982; Afro-American Hall of Fame of Oklahoma, 1983; scholar, Aspen Inst; legislative scholar, Eagleton Inst of Politics; Phi Beta Kappa; Doctor of Humane Letters, Benedict Coll. **BUSINESS ADDRESS:** Secretary of State, State of Oklahoma, 101 State Capitol, Oklahoma City, OK 73105.

ATKINS, NELSON LAWRENCE
Attorney. **PERSONAL:** Born May 27, 1939, Los Angeles, CA; married Barbara Walker; children: Lawren, Angelique. **EDUCATION:** CA State Univ of LA, BA 1961; Loyola Univ Law School, JD 1964. **CAREER:** LA City Attny, law clerk, dep city atty; Atkins Evans & Widener, partner atty. **ORGANIZATIONS:** Mem Amer Trial Lawyers Assoc, LA Cty Bar Assoc, CA Trial Laweyrs Assoc; bd of gov LA Trial Lawyers Assoc; mem Langston Law Club, Natl Bar Assoc, Criminal Courts Bar Assoc, NAACP, Urban League. **HONORS/ACHIEVEMENTS:** Outstanding Young Men of Amer 1972; Continuing Ed of LA Scholarship 1961.

ATKINS, PERVIS
Business executive. **PERSONAL:** Born Nov 24, 1935, Ruston, LA; children: Gerald, Christine, Gregory, Gayle. **EDUCATION:** NM State Univ, BA 1961. **CAREER:** LA Rams, WA Redskins, Oakland Raiders, professional football player 1961-68; KIIZ, TV sports commentator 1962; Southern California Edison Co, industrial psych 1963-66; Jack Fields & Assoc, theatrical agent; asst dir for motion pictures for ABC-TV; Artist Career Mgmt, vice pres; Atkins & Associates, owner. **ORGANIZATIONS:** Mem Pop Warner Football League; adv Concensus All Amer Football 1961; bd of dir Suisse Intl Entertainment. **HONORS/ACHIEVEMENTS:** Outstanding Citizen Ruston LA 1961; USO Commendation for Meritorious Serv 1971. **MILITARY SERVICE:** USMC, sgt 1954-57. **BUSINESS ADDRESS:** Owner, Atkins & Associates, 303 S Crescent Heights Blvd, Los Angeles, CA 90048.

ATKINS, RUSSELL
Poet, writer. **PERSONAL:** Born Feb 25, 1926, Cleveland, OH; son of Perry Kelly and Mamie Belle (Atkins). **EDUCATION:** Cleveland Sch of Art, Schlrshp 1943-44; Cleveland Music Sch Settlement, Pri Schlrshp 1943; Cleveland Inst of Music, 1944-45; Private Music Study, 1950-54. **CAREER:** Free Lance Mag, editor founder 1950-79; Sutphen Sch of Music, asst to dir 1957-60; Karamu House, writing instr 1973-; OH Poets Assn & Natl Endowment for Arts, writer in schools prog 1973-78. **ORGANIZATIONS:** Speaker, consultant OH Humanities Prog 1978; res workshops lectures Colleges & Univ 1963-78; consultant ETV WVIZ Cleveland 1970-72; mem Ltry Adv Panel OH Arts Council 1973-76; mem Intl Platform Assoc 1976-77; trustee Poets League of Greaster Cleveland 1978; writer-in-residence, Cuyahoga Community College 1973; writer-in residence, East Cleveland Public Library, 1979; writer-in-residence, Univ Circle, Inc., Cleveland Bd of Educ, 1988. **HONORS/ACHIEVEMENTS:** Hon doctorate Cleveland State Univ 1976; orig music theory intro Darmstadt Festival of Avant Gard Music, Germany 1956; ind artists fellowship OH Arts Council 1978; coord council of lit mag Grants 1970-77; invited to Bread Loaf Writers Conf 1956; published poetry books Here In The, Cleveland State Univ Press 1976, Heretofore, Breman Publishers, London England, 1968. **HOME ADDRESS:** 6005 Grand Ave, Cleveland, OH 44104.

ATKINS, SAM OILLIE
Urologist. **PERSONAL:** Born Aug 05, 1934, Decatur, AL; married Jeanne Cain; children: Courtland, April Melia. **EDUCATION:** Morehouse Coll Atlanta GA, BS 1957; Howard Univ Med Sch Wash DC, MD 1962. **CAREER:** Atlanta Med Assoc; pres 1978; Hughes Spalding Comm Hosp, pres med staff 1981-82; GA St Med Assoc, pres elect 1984-86; SW Atlanta Urology Assoc, urologist. **ORGANIZATIONS:** Mem bd of dir Woodward Academy Coll GA 1985-88, Med Assoc of Atlanta; mem adv bd Morehouse Med School; consult Atlanta Southside Comprehnsion Health Ctr; mem Morehouse Coll Alumnae Assoc; mem Alpha Phi Alpha; elder West End Pres Church. **HONORS/ACHIEVEMENTS:** 2nd place winner GA partners Exchange Prog Recife, Raz 1975; listed Outstanding Atlantans 1978-79; Unhearld Citizen Atlanta Omega Chap of Y's Men Intl 1980; Phys of Year Atlanta Med Assoc 1982. **MILITARY SERVICE:** Army colonel, res 1981- 3 yrs. **HOME ADDRESS:** 1021 Flamingo Dr S W, Atlanta, GA 30311.

ATKINS, THOMAS IRVING
Attorney. **PERSONAL:** Born Mar 02, 1939, Elkhart, IN; son of Rev & Mrs N P Atkins; married Sharon Annette Soash; children: Todd, Thomas, Jr, Trena. **EDUCATION:** Indiana Univ, BA 1961; Harvard Univ, MA 1963; Harvard Law School, JD 1969. **CAREER:** Boston NAACP, exec secretary 1963-65; Boston City Council, Boston city councilman 1968-71; Exec Office Communities & Dev (Governor's Cabinet), secretary 1971-75; NAACP, general counsel 1980-84; attorney; private practice. **ORGANIZATIONS:** Mem, ABA, Natl Bar Assn, Massachusetts Bar Assn; bd of dir, mem, Public Broadcasting Serv 1972-74; vice chmn, Federal Reserve Bank of Boston 1980-85. **HONORS/ACHIEVEMENTS:** Honorary PhD Northeastern Univ 1974; Honorary LLD New England School of Law 1982. **BUSINESS ADDRESS:** Attorney, 135 Eastern Parkway, #11-B-1, Brooklyn, NY 11238.

ATKINSON, CHARLES N.
President. **PERSONAL:** Born Apr 25, 1931, New Haven, CT; married Gladys Whitted; children: Cheryl, Lisa G Pitts, Patricia, Gregory L. **EDUCATION:** St John's Univ, Certificate 1979; Urban Business Assistance Corp, Certificate 1980; Univ of CT, Certificate 1980. **CAREER:** New Haven Minority Contractor, pres 1975-87; Home Builder Assoc of New Haven, dir 1978-85; Natl Assoc of Home, dir 1980-84; CT Chap NBL, pres 1984-87;Atkinson Builders Inc, pres. **ORGANIZATIONS:** Mem Black Republican Council Washington DC 1969-; notary public State of CT 1979-89; assistance register of voters City of New Haven 1983-85; justice of the peace State of CT 1981-85. **HONORS/ACHIEVEMENTS:** Delegate White House Conference on Small Business 1980,86. **MILITARY SERVICE:** AUS sgt 4 yrs; Korean Conflict Medal, European Medal 1952. **BUSINESS ADDRESS:** President, Atkinson Builders Inc, PO Box 1086, Torrington, CT 06790.

ATKINSON, CURTIS L.
Government official. **PERSONAL:** Born Sep 12, 1934, Brunswick, GA; son of Mr & Mrs Isreal Atkinson; married Dr Melvis Evans. **EDUCATION:** Howard Univ, 1953-54; Fort Valley State Coll, BS 1956; Columbia Univ, 1969. **CAREER:** Teacher, 1956-69; US Senate, staff 1969-80; State of Georgia, asst sec of state. **ORGANIZATIONS:** Exec comm, Georgia Special Olympics, 1984-85; bd of dir, Georgia Alliance for Children, 1980-; bd of dir, Southeast Regional/SERO/NSSFNS, 1980-; chmn/sec, State's Economic Develop Task Force, 1983-; bd of dir, Fort Valley St Coll Foundation, 1983-; trustee/bd, CME Church; Eta Lambda/Alpha Phi Alpha. **HONORS/ACHIEVEMENTS:** Roy Wilkins Award, Georgia NAACP, 1983; Public Serv Award, Alpha Phi Alpha, 1983; Outstanding Georgian, Fort Valley State Coll, 1984; Community Serv Award, Georgia Council of Deliberation, 1984; Res, Georgia House of Rep, 1983; Res, Georgia State Sen, 1983; City of Atlanta Proc, 1983; Hon from Georgia Young Farmers Assn, 1985; Leadership Award, Metro Atlanta Chap, FVSC Natl Alumni Assn, 1985; Political Leadership Award, Bronner Bros Intl, 1984. **MILITARY SERVICE:** AUS 1st lt 1951-53. **BUSINESS ADDRESS:** Assistant Secretary of State, Georgia State Government, Room 214 State Capitol, Atlanta, GA 30334.

ATKINSON, EUGENIA C. (JEANNE)
Chairman. **PERSONAL:** Born Jan 16, 1943, Laurens, SC; married Richard W Atkinson; children: Najuma, W Omari, Akilah, Jamila. **EDUCATION:** Youngstown State Univ, ABA 1971. **CAREER:** Hon Natlaniel R Jones Judge US Dist Court, sec 1960-63; Youngstown Sheet Tube Co, suprv sec-steno pool 1969-74; Youngstown Area Com Action Council, admin asst 1974-76, dir WIC prog 1976-79; Western Reserve Transit Auth, pres bd of trustees 1979-; Youngstown Civil Service Comm, chairman. **ORGANIZATIONS:** Scholarship com chmn Youngstown Chap OH Black Womens Leadership Caucus 1977-80; 1st vice pres YMCA 1978-80; mem Natl Afro-Amer Mus Plng Council 1978-80; bd trustee Career Devel Ctr for Women 1979-80; mem Youth Area Urban league, NAACP. **HONORS/ACHIEVEMENTS:** Dedication Commitment Awd Freedom Inc Youngstown OH 1972; Outstanding Admin Performance OH Dept of Health Cols OH 1978; Downtown Improvement Com Serv Youngstown Bd of Trade 1980. **BUSINESS ADDRESS:** Chairman, Youngstown Civil Service Comm, 26 S Phelps St, Youngstown, OH 44503.

ATKINSON, GLADYS W.
Government official. **PERSONAL:** Born Dec 08, 1932, Durham, NC; daughter of Edmond R Whitted Sr and Gwynetta Riley Whitted; married Charles N Atkinson (divorced); children: Milan Lucas, Joseph Lucas, Gwynetta Lucas, Allen E Lucas Jr, Cedric Lucas, Lisa, Patrick, Gregory, Cheryl. **EDUCATION:** Attended, Univ of DC 1969, Catholic Univ 1970-71, Department of Agriculture Graduate School, 1970-74. **CAREER:** US Dept of Agriculture, purchasing agent 1973-77; Natl Inst of Health, supervisory purchasing agent 1977-79; Celebrity Fashion Jewels, regional mgr 1971-81; Atkinson Builders Const Co, vice pres 1981-; Natl Insts of Health, small and disadvantaged business specialist 1979-. **ORGANIZATIONS:** Chairperson NBL Council of Women Business Owners 1984-; bd mem Black Business Alliance Baltimore 1984-; bd mem Natl Business League 1984-; bd mem Charlene Drew Jarvis Council for Women Business Owners Washington DC 1985-; bd mem Divas Foundation 1986-, Minority Business Adv Bd Port Amer MD 1986-; fund raising chairperson, National Assn of Black Procurement Officials 1989. **HONORS/ACHIEVEMENTS:** US Public Health Serv NIH Directors Awd 1983; President Reagan's Outstanding Business Woman Awd 1983; Outstanding Professional and Business Woman Awd Black Business Alliance 1985; Outstanding Serv Awd Blacks in Govt NIH Chap 1986; Superior Performance, NIH 1984; Outstanding Performance, Small Business Administration 1989. **HOME AD-**

DRESS: 3343 Hampton Point Dr, Silver Spring, MD 20904. **BUSINESS ADDRESS:** Small/Disadvantaged Bus Splst, Natl Institute of Health, 9000 Rockville Pike Bldg 31, Room 3C32, Bethesda, MD 20892.

ATKINSON, J. EDWARD
Public relations executive. **PERSONAL:** Born Jan 21, 1914, Denver, CO; married Antoinette; children: Edward Charles, Joy Priscilla. **EDUCATION:** Loyola Univ, BA. **CAREER:** Carnation Co, publ relat suprv, sr publ relat suprv, asst dir 1965-75; Carnation Co, mgr urban rel 1975-. **ORGANIZATIONS:** Mem Area Dv Bd to Mayor of City of LA; bd dir Loyola Univ Alumni Assoc, LA Chap NAACP, W Reg Urban League, Natl Assoc of Mkt Devel; bd of trustees Angelus Corp. **HONORS/ACHIEVEMENTS:** Author "Black Dimensions in Contemp Amer Art" 1971; recognized by Esquire Mag & Bus Com for the Arts for its outstanding contrib in promoting the arts; author of num pamphlets on employ, prenatal care & black hist; coord ed "Rising Voices", "Voces Que Surgen" 1974. **BUSINESS ADDRESS:** Manager of Urban Relations, Carnation Co, 5045 Wilshire Blvd, Los Angeles, CA 90036.

ATKINSON, LEWIS K.
Physician. **PERSONAL:** Born Nov 03, 1924, Georgetown, SC; married Theresa C; children: 6 children. **EDUCATION:** Howard Univ, BA 1950, MD 1956. **CAREER:** WA Hospital Center, attending physician; Howard Univ Hospital, attending physician, instr med 1961-; Private practice, physician. **ORGANIZATIONS:** Mem Med Staff SE Comm Hosp, Natl Med Assoc, Medico-Chirurgical Soc of DC, Amer Soc of Internal Med, So Med Assoc, Howard Univ Med Alumni Assoc, Century Limited Club, Daniel Hale Williams Reading Club, Natl Symphony Assoc, of Wash DC, Diabetes Assoc, DC Med Soc, NAACP, Friends Museum AfricanArts, Urban League. **MILITARY SERVICE:** AUS s/sgt 1943-46. **BUSINESS ADDRESS:** 5505 5 St NW, Ste 301, Washington, DC 20011.

ATKINSON, NOLAN N., JR.
Attorney, educator. **PERSONAL:** Born Jan 14; married Elizabeth Perry; children: Emily Elizabeth. **EDUCATION:** Boston Univ, AB 1964; Howard Univ Law School, LLB 1967; Univ of PA Law School, LLM 1969. **CAREER:** Herbert C Nelson, attny 1968-69; Brady & Flint, assoc attny 1969; Univ of PA School of Law, instructor 1969-70; Temple Univ School of Law, teacher; Zack Myers & Atkinson, attny. **ORGANIZATIONS:** Mem Bar of PA Supreme Court, PA Superior Court, Philadelphia Court of Common Pleas, Bar of US Court of Appeals, US Dist Court, Eastern Dist of PA, Philadelphia Bar Assoc, Amer Bar Assoc, Natl Bar Assoc, Barristers Club; pres bd dir Ardmore Commun Devel Corp 1970-; legal counsel Ardmore Prog Civic Assoc 1969-; membd dir Main Line Br NAACP 1969, Amer for Dem Action Philadelphia Chap 1970-; Philadelphia reg plng council Govs Justice Commun 1971-; mem Spec Funding Plnng Comm, Commun Crime Prevention Task Force, Corrections Task Force, Criminal Justice Task Force, Philadelphia Urban Coalition; mem bd dir World Affairs Council 1973-, Sigma Pi Phi, Sigma Delta Tau Legal Frat, asst eastern reg vice pres Alpha Phi Alpha 1963-64, St Thomas Episcopal Church, Lower Merion Twp Commiss 1973; campaign mgr Jesse F Anderson State Senate 1972; plng comm Hardy Williams for Mayor 1971; candidate Twp Commis of Lower Merion 1969; sub-area leader lower Merion Dem Party 1968-69; staff dir Robert F Kennedy Campaign Comm 1968; campaign mgr Lower Merion Dem Party Humphrey-Muski-Clark 1968. **HONORS/ACHIEVEMENTS:** Winner of the Amer Jurisprudence Awd for Excellence in UN Law 1968; Main Line Bus & Professional Womens Club Awd 1974; Mt Calvary Bapt Church Awd 1973; ZionBapt Church Awd 1973; Cit of Housing Achievement Awd 1972; Women of Ardmore Awd 1969; author of num publs. **BUSINESS ADDRESS:** Attorney, Zack, Myers & Atkinson, 42 S 15th St, Robinson Bldg Ste 320, Philadelphia, PA 19102.

ATKINSON, REGINA ELIZABETH
Social worker. **PERSONAL:** Born May 13, 1952, New Haven, CT; daughter of Samuel Griffin and Virginia Louise Atkinson Griffin. **EDUCATION:** Univ of CT, BA 1974; Atlanta Univ, MSW 1978. **CAREER:** Pal Beach Co Health Dept, medical social worker 1978-81; Glades General Hosp, dir social services 1981-. **ORGANIZATIONS:** Mem AHA Soc for Hospital Soc Work Directors, Comm Action Council, Florida Public Health Assn Inc, Glades Area Assn for Retarded Citizens, Natl Assn of Black Social Workers Inc, Natl Assn of Social Workers Inc, The Florida Assn for Health and Social Serv, The Natl Chamber of Commerce for Women Inc, National Association for Female Executives, Area Agency on Aging Advisory Council, NAACP. **HONORS/ACHIEVEMENTS:** American Legion Awd; Whitney Young Fellowship; DHEW Public Health Serv Scholarship. **HOME ADDRESS:** 525 1/2 SW 10th St, Belle Glade, FL 33430. **BUSINESS ADDRESS:** Dir Social Services, Glades General Hospital, PO Box 8002, Belle Glade, FL 33430.

ATKINSON, WHITTIER C.
Medical director. **PERSONAL:** Born Apr 23, 1893, Brunswick, GA; widowed; children: Whittier C (dec). **EDUCATION:** Brunswick & GA State Coll, Diploma; Howard Univ, BS 1921; Howard Univ Coll of Med, MD 1925. **CAREER:** Freedman's Hosp, intern 1925-26; Wash DC, physician 1926-27; Clement Atkinson Meml Hosp, med dir, founder 1932-77; Clement Atkinson Meml Hosp, physician 1927-. **ORGANIZATIONS:** Mem Hosp Study Comm for Commonwealth of PA Harrisburg; pres Natl Med Assoc 1951-52, Acad of Gen Practice of Chester Cty 1956-57, Chester Co Med Soc 1958; life mem NAACP; mem AMA 1928-; mem bd of dirs Chester Cty Tuberculosis soc 1957-. **HONORS/ACHIEVEMENTS:** Gen Practitioner of the Year PA Med Soc 1960; Coatesville Hall of Fame Coatesville Are C of C 1960; 50 Years of Serv as Physician Chester Cty Med Soc 1975.

ATLAS, JOHN WESLEY
Educator. **PERSONAL:** Born Aug 15, 1941, Lake Providence, LA; married Arthurlean Johnson; children: Mavis, Candace, Jamila, Amina. **EDUCATION:** Grambling Coll, BS 1963; Wayne State Univ, MEd 1968, EdD 1972. **CAREER:** LA Schools, music teacher 1963-65; Detroit Public Schools, music teacher 1965-67, guidance counselor 1967-70, asst prin 1970-72; Gov State Univ, prof 1972-73; Oakland Univ, assoc prof 1973-. **ORGANIZATIONS:** Mem Amer Personnel & Guidance Assn; mem Assn for Non-White Concerns in Personnel & Guidance; mem Omega Psi Phi Frat; Topical Conf on Career Educ for Handicapped Indiv 1979. **HONORS/ACHIEVEMENTS:** Publ "Consulting, Affecting Change for Minority Students" Jour of Non-White Concerns in Pers & Guidance Wash, DC 1975; publ "Effects of Crystal & Bolles on Vocational Choice" Jour of Emp Counsel Wash, DC 1977; publ "Career Planning Need of Unemployed Minority Persons" Jour of Emp Counseling Wash, DC 1978;book chap "The Role of Counseling & Guidance in Facilitating Career Educ Needs of Handicapped". **BUSINESS ADDRESS:** Associate Professor, OaklandUniv, Sch of Human & Educ Serv, Rochester, MI 48063.

ATTAWAY, JOHN DAVID
Educator. **PERSONAL:** Born Jan 30, 1929, Chicago, IL; son of Allen Attaway Sr DD and Pearl Holloway Attaway; married Paquita Anna Harris. **EDUCATION:** Central State Coll, BS 1950; Babson Coll, MBA 1956; George Washington Univ, DBA 1979. **CAREER:** US Dept of Commerce, policy analyst 1970-72; US Dept of Labor OFCCP, chief policy & procedures 1984; Univ of DC, assoc prof 1984-. **ORGANIZATIONS:** Pres Attaway Assoc 1978-; chairman The Dr Chester E Harris Medical Student Fund Inc 1978-; mem Sigma Pi Phi Fraternity Epsilon Boule 1985-; Kappa Alpha Psi Fraternity 1948-. **HONORS/ACHIEVEMENTS:** Grass Roots Award for Outstanding Civic Work DC Federation of Civic Assocs Inc 1970; Public Serv Award General Serv Admin 1976. **MILITARY SERVICE:** AUS major 14 yrs. **BUSINESS ADDRESS:** Associate Professor, Univ of District of Columbia, 900 F St NW, Room 914, Washington, DC 20004.

ATTLES, ALVIN
General manager. **PERSONAL:** Born in Newark, NJ; married Wilhemina Rice; children: Alvin III, Erica. **EDUCATION:** NC A&T. **CAREER:** Golden State Warriors, guard, coach 1970-. **HONORS/ACHIEVEMENTS:** Warriors' all-time winningest coach; NBA Championship (1974-75); two division titles (1974-75 & 1975-76); league's best record in 1975-76 (59-26); twice coached the NBA All-Star Western Conf team 1975-76; his 555-516 (518) coaching mark places him sixth among all-time winningest NBA coaches and last season he joinedRed Auerbach, Red Holzman, Jack Ramsey, Gene Shue and Dick Motta as the only mentors to coach in 1,000 NBA contests. **BUSINESS ADDRESS:** General Manager, Goldon State Warriors, Oakland Coliseum, Oakland, CA 94621.

AUBERT, ALVIN BERNARD
Educator, poet, editor. **PERSONAL:** Born Mar 12, 1930, Lutcher, LA; married Bernadine; children: Stephenie, Miriam, Deborah. **EDUCATION:** Southern Univ, BA 1959; Univ of MI, MA 1960. **CAREER:** Southern Univ, prof 1960-70; Univ of OR, prof 1970; State Univ of NY, prof 1970-79; Wayne State Univ, prof 1979-. **ORGANIZATIONS:** Book rvr Libr Journ 1972-74; eval NY State Poets in Schls 1974; adv ed Drama & Thr Mag 1973-75; adv ed Black Box 1974-; adv ed Gumbo 1976-78; adved Collaloo 1977-; ed & pub Obsidian, Black Literature in Review 1975-85; mem Modern Lang Assn; bd of dir Coord Councl for Literary Magazines 1983-86. **HONORS/ACHIEVEMENTS:** Undergrad Liberal Arts Schlrshp 1957-59; Woodrow Wilson Flwshp 1959-60; Schlrshp Bread Loaf Writers Conf 1968; Natl Endowment for the Arts Creative Writing Flwshp Grant 1973,81; CCLM Editors Flwshp 1979; poetry books, "Against the Blues" 1972; "Feeling Through" 1975; "New and Selected Poems" 1985; play "Home From Harlem, 1986; listed Broadside Authors & Artists; A Directory of Amer Poets; Black Amer Writers Past & Present; Contemporary Poets of the English Lang. **HOME ADDRESS:** 18234 Parkside Ave, Detroit, MI 48221.

AUBESPIN, FRANCIS BORGIA
Clergyman. **PERSONAL:** Born Oct 10, 1935, Opelousas, LA. **EDUCATION:** BA 1960; Theol studies finished 1965. **CAREER:** Divine Word Coll Philippines, appt dean of theol 1965, dir students affairs 1967, vice pres of coll 1970; Yazoo City MS, pastor 1973; St Rose Bay St Louis MS, pastor. **ORGANIZATIONS:** Mem NAACP 1972; mem adv bd RSVP of Bay St Louis 1973; elected mem Priest Senate for Diocese of Natchez Jackson 1973; chmn SUD Com for working among blacks in USA 1974. **HONORS/ACHIEVEMENTS:** Plaque for SVC Rendered as Moderator of Chap of Cath Action in Philippines 1971. **BUSINESS ADDRESS:** Pastor, St Rose Church, Bay St Louis, MS 39520.

AUBESPIN, MERVIN R.
Journalist. **PERSONAL:** Born Jun 30, 1937, Opelousas, LA; son of Henry Aubespin and Blanche Sittig Earsery; married Joan Wagner; children: Eleska. **EDUCATION:** Tuskegee Inst, BS 1958; IN State Univ, postgrad 1960; Columbia Univ, Spec Minority 1972; Univ of Louisville (KY), postgrad work 1973. **CAREER:** Courier Jrnl & Louisville Times, 1st black staff artist 1965-72; Courier Jrnl, reporter 1972-84; Courier Jrnl & Louisville Times, dir of minority recruitment, spec asst to exec editor; The Courier-Journal Newspapers, assoc editor development; Natl Assoc of Black Journalists, pres 1983-85. **ORGANIZATIONS:** Pres, founder Louisville Assoc of Black Comm 1979-80; dir reg 5 Natl Assoc of Black Jrnlst 1979-81; mem Bd of Overseers Bellarmine Coll 1980-81; vice pres Natl Assoc of Black Jrnlst 1981-83; pres Natl Assoc of Black Jrnlst 1983-; mem Minorities Comm Amer Soc of Newspaper Ed 1985; chair Minorities Comm The Soc of Professional Journalists; co-chmn Industry Wide Minority Issues Steering Comm 1985-; chmn Ida B Wells Jury 1986-88. **HONORS/ACHIEVEMENTS:** Leadership Awd West End Catholic Council 1970; Unity Awd Econ Reporting Lincoln Univ 1980; Outstanding Achievement Awd Louisville Branch Natl Assoc of Black Jrnlst 1980; Louisville Man of the Year Awd Louisville Defender Newspaper 1980; Unity Awd Civil Rights Reporting Lincoln Univ 1981; Outstanding Achievement Awd Natl Assn of Black Journalists 1981; Achievement Awd NAACP 1981; Spec Achievement Awd Reporting on the Concerns of Blacks; Leadership Awd Louisville Assoc of Black Communicators 1981; Meritorious Serv Awd Southern Reg Press Inst 1985; Disting Serv Award Inst for Journalism Educ 1985; Recp Mary HDunn Lecturship Univ of IL. **MILITARY SERVICE:** AUS E-4 2 yrs. **HOME ADDRESS:** 733 Southwestern Parkway, Louisville, KY 40211. **BUSINESS ADDRESS:** Associate Editor, Louisville Courier-Jnl Nwspapr, 525 W Broadway, Louisville, KY 40202.

AUGUSTINE, MATTHEW
Business executive. **PERSONAL:** Born Nov 11, 1944, Macon, GA; married Rita Guillory; children: Malcolm, Karanja. **EDUCATION:** Univ of SW LA, BS 1966; Harvard Univ, MBA 1971. **CAREER:** Polaroid, prod mgr 1971-73; Adugo Inc, matls mgr 1973-76; Eltrex Ind, pres, ceo 1976-. **ORGANIZATIONS:** Dir Serv Corps. **MILITARY SERVICE:** USMC sgt 1966-68. **BUSINESS ADDRESS:** President, Eltrex Ind, 65 Sullivan St, Rochester, NY 14605.

AUGUSTUS, FRANKLIN J. P.
Aerobatic air show pilot. **PERSONAL:** Born Mar 06, 1950, New Orleans, LA; son of Henry Augustus, Jr and Annie Cooper Augustus; children: Brandi Augustus. **EDUCATION:** North Carolina State Univ; AUS, Military Police, MPI, CID Narcotic Agent; NCSBI Schools & Conferences. **CAREER:** Terrebonne Parish Sheriff's Office, reserve deputy, in-

structor in acad; New Orleans Recreation Dept, LA, head of martial arts dept; Franklin JP Augustus Detective Agency Inc, New Orleans, LA, pres; Orleans Parish Civil Sheriff's Office, reserve duty; Super Air Shows Intl Inc, New Orleans, LA, pres. **ORGANIZATIONS:** Pres, Black Wing Pilots Assn; mem, Experimental Aircraft Assn, New Orleans and Slidell Area Chapters of the Experimental Aircraft Assn, Negro Airmen Intl, Intl Aerobatic Club, Intl Council of Air Shows; charter mem, Cajun Chapter #72 of the Intl Aerobatic Club, Crescent City Aviators; accident prevention counselor, FAA, 1985-. **HONORS/ACHIEVEMENTS:** Aerobatic license, FAA Unlimited Low Level; private license earned 1977; commercial license earned 1978; flight instructor certificate, 1979; certified in scuba, NOSD School, 1977-; Master of Martial Arts; movie stuntman; logged over 8000 flight hours. **MILITARY SERVICE:** AUS, sergeant. **BUSINESS ADDRESS:** Franklin JP Augustus, Pres, Super Air Shows Intl Inc, PO Box 50181, New Orleans, LA 70115.

AULD, ALBERT MICHAEL
Artist. **PERSONAL:** Born Aug 15, 1943, Kingston, Jamaica;married Rose A; children: Ian, Alexei, Kiros. **EDUCATION:** Howard U, BFA 1962-66, MFA 1978-80. **CAREER:** Lindo, Norman, Craig & Kummel, designer illustrator 1966-67; Natl Ed Assoc, designer illustrator 1967-73; USDA Graduate School, instructor 1967- Sidwell Friends School, art teacher 1973-77; Dept of Art, Howard Univ, lecturer 1977-82; Duke Ellington School of the Arts, instructor 1982-. **ORGANIZATIONS:** Co-founder dir A & B Assoc Adv 1973-79; co-fndr dir Opus 2 Gallery 1973-77; writer illstrtr for self-syndicated published comic strip 1967-72; freelance Ill designer The Design Co 1977-; cultural chm Caribbean Am Intercutl Org 1975-79; mem Africobra Natl Artists Coop 1977-; mem Intl Sculpture Conf 1983-; mem Natl Art Edctrs Assoc 1984-; mem Artists Equity, Natl Conf of Artists 1986-; mem bd of dirs Fondo del Sol Museum & Cultural Ctr 1986-. **HONORS/ACHIEVEMENTS:** Whos Who In Am Clg & Univ 1966; Folkloric Article titled Ananesem pub in the Jamarca Journal 1983; article on Africobra Artists Black Collegian 1967-; exhibited widely as a sculptgor 1967-; lectured on African Retentions in the Americas Oberlin, Smithsonian Inst, Natl Conf of Artists, NY Univ, Bronx Museum, NBCHs Tony Brown at Daybreak, local & overseas radio networks. **HOME ADDRESS:** 1519 Monroe St N W, Washington, DC 20010.

AULD, ROSE A.
Artist educator. **PERSONAL:** Born Oct 29, 1946, Washington, DC; married Albert Michael; children: Ian, Alexei, Kiros. **EDUCATION:** Howard U, BFA (cum laude) 1964-72, MA 1980; Georgetown U, Grad Work; Univ of the Dist of columbia, Grad Work; Catholic Univ, Grad Work. **CAREER:** A & B Assoc, illustrator designer 1970-75; Opus 2 Galleries, gallery Dir 1972-; DC Public Schools, curriclulum writer 1975-85, teacher fine arts dept head 1973-, chairperson. **ORGANIZATIONS:** Sec DC Art Ed Assoc 1982-87; artists bd of dir Centro De Arte Galeria Inti Assoc 1981-85, Fondo del Sol Art Gallery 1984-87; mem bd of dir Region D Fine Arts Cncl 1983-86; mem DC Tchrs Union 1976-85; mem Smithsonia Assoc Wash DC 1980-87; Artist Call mem ponsor of the E H Sch Stdnt Cncl NASC 1983-87; mem Amer Indian Soc of Washington DC Artitsts Equity. **HONORS/ACHIEVEMENTS:** Water color awd for otstndng work HowardUniv Wash, DC 1966; mural painting awd 1968; DC League of Women Voters Otstndng edctrs awd Wash DC 1980; Kiwanis Intl otstndng edctr awd Wash, DC 1981; numerous civic and prof awds 1964-87. **HOME ADDRESS:** 1519 Monroe St N W, Washington, DC 20010. **BUSINESS ADDRESS:** Art Teacher, Chairman, Dist of Columbia Pub Schs, Eastern Sr High School, 17th & East Capitol Sts N E, Washington, DC 20003.

AUSBY, ELLSWORTH AUGUSTUS
Artist, educator. **PERSONAL:** Born Apr 05, 1942, Portsmouth, VA; married Jemillah; children: Amber, Andra, Dawn, Kalif. **EDUCATION:** Pratt Inst, 1960-61; School of Visual Art, BFA 1965. **CAREER:** School of Visual Arts, instr. **HONORS/ACHIEVEMENTS:** One man shows, Cinque Gallery 1970, Artist House 1973, Soho Ctr for Visual Arts 1975; crit reviews, "Art in Amer", "Barbra Rose", 1970, "Henri Ghent" 1974, "Black Creations" 1972, "The School Weekly News by April Kingsley" 1975, "The Aldrich Museum of Contemp Art, Carles Dyer Dir", "The Soho Weekly News by April Kingsley" 1975; Amer Rep at "FESTAC" 2nd world Black Arts & Cult Festival Lagos Nigeria 1977; Fed Artist Grant CETA Title VI 1978; "Rock Paper Scissors" Port of Auth Publ Works Proj, "Space Odyssey" mural Howard Johnsons Queens Village NY 1980; CAPS Fellowship for Painting NYS Council on the Arts 1980; Exhibit the US Mission to the United Nations 1978; "Universal Units" exhibition at the Afro-Amer Hist & Cultural Mus Philadelphia 1979; "Afro-Amer Abstraction, Long Island NY 1980. **BUSINESS ADDRESS:** Instructor, School of Visual Arts, PO Box 15, Brooklyn, NY 11211.

AUSTIN, BOBBY WILLIAM
Educational administrator, author. **PERSONAL:** Born Dec 29, 1944, Bowling Green, KY; son of HH Austin Sr and Mary E Austin; married Joy L Ford; children: Sushama Meredith Cleva, Julian Sanjay Ford, Leah Mary Sajova, Aviana Joy Lalita. **EDUCATION:** Western Kentucky Univ, BA 1966; Fisk Univ, MA 1968; McMaster Univ, PhD 1972; Harvard Univ, Diploma 1986. **CAREER:** Univ of DC, exec asst to the pres; Georgetown Univ, asst prof 1971-72; Dept of Soc Georgetown summer term, chmn 1972; The Urban League Review Natl Urban League, editor; UDC Bd Vis Team Creative Prod Black Amer Folklore NETA-WASH PBS, pol spec & spec asst; pres Austin & Assoc. **ORGANIZATIONS:** Mem Natl Council for Accrdttn of Tchr Edn; mem Amer Soc Assn; Groves Conf on Marriage & the Family; Alpha Phi Alpha Frat; Natl Cong of Black Professionals; mem VOICE Inc; mem Alphi Phi Omega Natl Serv Fraternity; Peoples Congregational Church; Hannover Project, Germany; Academic Council on the UN Systems; Global Co-Operation for a Better World; UN Assn, DC Chapter. **HONORS/ACHIEVEMENTS:** Author of numerous publications; paper presented at the Assn for the Study of Afro-Amer Life & History New York, 1973; Smithsonian Inst 1976; published Natl Black Opinion ACRA Inc 1977; Kellogg Natl Fellow. **BUSINESS ADDRESS:** Austin & Associates, 6611 16th St NW, Washington, DC 20012.

AUSTIN, ERNEST AUGUSTUS
Physician. **PERSONAL:** Born Nov 26, 1932, Brooklyn, NY; son of Augustin Austin and Elrica Mildred Davidson Austin; married Margaret P Byrd, Aug 24, 1957; children: Vivian, Jean, Dunn, Alan. **EDUCATION:** St Johns Univ, BS 1953; Howard Univ, MD 1957. **CAREER:** SUNY, clinical instr surg 1962-69; Fordham Hosp, chief surg 1966-69; Bowman Gray School of Med, asst prof surg 1969-72; Reynolds Meml Hosp, dir of surg 1969-72; Univ of MD School of Med, asst prof surg 1972-79; Provident Hosp, chief of surg 1972-73; Univ of MD Inst for Emerg Med Shock Traum Ctr, chief of surg & traumatology 1974-76,78-79; Univ of MD Hosp, dir emergency serv 1977-78; Cooper Med Ctr Camden NJ, chief of traumatology, dir emergency med serv 1979-84; CMDNJ-Rutgers Med School, assoc prof of surgery 1979-84. **ORGANIZATIONS:** Founding mem Amer Trauma soc; bd of dir Amer Cancer Soc Forsyth Unit NC; bd dir Natl Found Forsyth-Stokes Chap NC; bd dir Amer Trauma Soc MD Chapt; diplomate Amer Bd of Surg; fellow Amer Coll of Surgeons. **HONORS/ACHIEVEMENTS:** Z Smith Reynolds Found Grant; publ 2 articles in Jrnl of Royal Coll of Surgeons 1975; publ Critical Care Med Jrnl 1979; editorial bd, "Trauma: Clinical Update for Surgeons" Vol 2 1983-86; visiting professor/lecturer at numerous universities & hospitals in US and Canada; author and publisher, The Black Amer Stamp Album 1988; "Thoracic Injuries," Camden County Medical Society Bulletin 1982; "Left Atrial Rupture 2 Degree Blast Injury," Journal Medical Society of NJ 1985. **HOME ADDRESS:** 3 Hunters Drive, Cherry Hill, NJ 08003.

AUSTIN, FRANK
Municipal official. **PERSONAL:** Born Mar 05, 1933, Newark, NJ; son of Sam and Louise; married Rubymae; children: Paul John, Frank Edward. **CAREER:** CAA/FAA, radio operator Philadelphia PA Nome & King Salmon AK 1956-60; King Salmon & Anchorage AK, control tower oper 1960-70; Civil Rights Specialist, 1970-72; Austins Rental & Svcs, owner operator 1970-; Civil Rights Staff, chief 1972-73; Anchorage AK, airport planner 1973-75; program analyst, 1977; Office of Equal Opportunity Municipality of Anchorage, dir 1982-83, dir dept of employee relations 1983-87; FAA, Planning & Appraisal Officer, Alaskan Region. **ORGANIZATIONS:** Commr AK Public Offices Comm 1981, 1983; commr AK Real Estate Comm 1976, 1981; bd mgrs Natl Congress of Parents & Teachers 1975, 1977; Municipal Personnel Review Bd; Bicentennial Comm; Comm Action Program; Head Start Prog; chmn Governors Blue Ribbon Commn on Collective Bargaining Between Teachers & Sch Bds in AK 1980; founder Anchorage Chap Black in Govt 1982; mem KTUU/TV Comm Adv Bd 1984-86; mem Crime Stoppers Br. 1988-; mem Neighbor to Neighbor Fund Br. 1988-. **HONORS/ACHIEVEMENTS:** FAA Anchorage Area Employee of the Yr 1969,74,81; First Black President AK Congress of Parents & Teachers 1975, 1977; Execitive of Yr 1984-85; Mildred Goodman Awd Region X Blacks in Govt 1986. **MILITARY SERVICE:** USAF staff sgt 1951-56. **BUSINESS ADDRESS:** Planning & Appraisal Officer, FAA Alaskan Region, 222 W Seventh Ave, #14, Anchorage, AK 99513.

AUSTIN, JAMES P.
Business executive, appointed official. **PERSONAL:** Born Apr 06, 1900, Jasper, TX; married Teresa Colvin. **EDUCATION:** FL A&M Univ, BS Voc Ed 1947; Amer-Gentlemens Designing School, Cert 1948; Mortgage Bankers Assn of Southwest FL, Cert 1962; Univ of Tampa FL, Cert 1964. **CAREER:** Austins Tayloring & Clothing, owner/oper 1948-52, 1968-75; Mid-FL Minority Contractors Assn, exec dir 1975-81; JP Austins Real Estate Co, re broker 1981-83; Polk Econ Devel Corp Inc, exec dir 1983-. **ORGANIZATIONS:** Pres NAACP 1954-; commander Amer Legion Post 213 1958-60; treas United Minority Contractors Assn 1975-81; bd chmn Polk Cty Oppty Council Inc 1980-82; bd mem Central FL Reg Planning Council 1982-83; treas FL Fed of CDC 1983-; bd mem FL Small Cities CDBG Adv Bd 1984-. **HONORS/ACHIEVEMENTS:** Loyalty & Dedication NAACP 1968-84; Mary Wolds Case Emperial 25 Club 1979; Citizen of the Year Polk Cty Law Enforcement Assn 1979; commiss City of Lake Wales 1981; vice mayor City of Lake Wales 1984-. **MILITARY SERVICE:** AUS sgt 3 yrs; Good Conduct, Sharpshooter 1943. **HOME ADDRESS:** 602 N Ave, Lake Wales, FL 33853.

AUSTIN, JANYTH YVONNE
Telecommunications. **PERSONAL:** Born Oct 29, 1958, Chicago, IL; daughter of Velma Gakins Austin. **EDUCATION:** Northwestern Univ, BSIE 1980; IL Inst of Tech, MBA 1986. **CAREER:** GD Searle & Co, engineering trainee 1977-79; IBT, engr distr serv 1980-83, engr network planning 1983-84, asst mgr capital recovery 1984-88, product manager, 1988-. **ORGANIZATIONS:** Mem Alpha Kappa Alpha 1977-, Inroads Alumnu Assn 1980-; mem, bd of dir Inez Harris Scholarship Program, 1984-; asst treasurer Natl Tech Assoc 1985-87; treasurer Chicago Chapter of the Natl Technical Assn, 1987-. **HONORS/ACHIEVEMENTS:** Up & Coming Black Business & Prof Woman Dollars & Sense Magazine 1986. **BUSINESS ADDRESS:** Product Manager, Illinois Bell Telephone Company, 225 W Randolph, Floor 22D, Chicago, IL 60606.

AUSTIN, MARY JANE
Supervisor of art education, Irvington Public Schools. **PERSONAL:** Born Apr 24, 1935, Orange, NJ; daughter of George W Greene Jr and Louise Margaret Street; married Harry Lester Austin, Dec 21, 1957; children: Sharon Milora, Sherrill Ruth. **EDUCATION:** Newark State Coll, BS 1957; Kean Coll, Grad work 1978; Bank St Coll Parsons School of Design, MS 1983. **CAREER:** Elizabeth Bd of Educ, layout artist 1973-78; Roosevelt Jr Schools, art consultant 1970-73; Elizabeth Public Schools, art educator 1953-79; William F Halloran Alternative Sch for the Gifted & Talented, art educator 1979-87. **ORGANIZATIONS:** Arts Educators of New Jersey; mem Natl Art Educ Assoc 1979-86; mem, The Independent Orders Foresters, associate for supervision and curriculum development; member, ASCD, 1987-89; treasurer, Citizen Awareness Group/Cranford, 1989-90; chairperson, Women's Day (Celebration of Womanhood), 1989-90. **HONORS/ACHIEVEMENTS:** Scholarship Artist Inst Stockton Coll NJ Council of the Arts 1980-81; Art Educ Awd Natl Council of Negro Women Inc 1981; participant Getty Conference Los Angeles Getty Ctr for Art Educ 1987; Governors Awd Governor Teacher Grant NJ State Dept of Educ 1987. **HOME ADDRESS:** 15 Wall St, Cranford, NJ 07016.

AUSTIN, RICHARD H.
Elected government official. **PERSONAL:** Born May 05, 1913, Stouts Mountain, AL; son of Richard Austin and Lelia Austin; married Ida; children: Hazel. **EDUCATION:** Detroit Inst of Technology, BS 1937. **CAREER:** Accountant private practice Detroit 1941-71; elected Wayne County Auditor 1966-70; State of Michigan, sec of state 1970-. **ORGANIZATIONS:** Mem Amer Inst of Certified Public Accountants; life mem NAACP; vice pres United Found of Metro Detroit; treasure Comm Found of Southeastern Michigan. **HONORS/ACHIEVEMENTS:** Michigan first Black CPA 1941; elect Sec of State 1970, re-elected 1974, 1976, 1982, 1986; Honorary Degrees Michigan State Univ, Detroit Inst of Tech, Detroit College of Business, Univ of Detroit. **BUSINESS ADDRESS:** Secretary of State, State of MI, Treasury Bldg, Lansing, MI 48918.

AUSTIN, SARAH SHORT
Business executive. **PERSONAL:** Born Sep 13, 1933, Alberta, VA. **EDUCATION:** Western Res U, MS 1962; Fisk U, BA 1954. **CAREER:** Greater Cleveland Roundtable, executive dir; Nat Urban Coalition, sr vP; Cities Operations Nat Urban Coalition, vice pres

1972-77; Sec Elliot Richardson Dept of HEW WA, fellow & spl asst 1971-72; Urban Systems Devel Corp, dir social planning 1969-71; Westinghouse Learning Corp, sr social scientist 1967-69; HowardUniv Sch of Soc Work, faculty 1964-67; YWCA, dir of youth serv 1956-60; Brimmer & Co Wash, dir. **ORGANIZATIONS:** Mem, bd of trustees Case Western Res U; mem, Bd of Overseers Morehouse Coll Med Educ Prgm; mem DC Manpower Serv Planning Adv Council; mem Child Health Bd Children's Hosp 1972-77; chpn of bd Christ Child Settlement House 1967-68; 1st vp, bd dir Metro YWCA 1967-71; Am Mgmt Assn Acad of Certified Soc Workers; Am Acad of Polit & Social Scis; Nat Assn of Soc Workers; Am Soc for Pub Adminstr Fellowship Western Res Univ 1960-62. **HONORS/ACHIEVEMENTS:** Who's Who Among Students in Am Colls & U's 1954; 1 of 75 black women honored for achvmt in Econ & Public Life of the 70's Black Enterprise 1974; publsComm Soc Serv Handbook 1974; Coalition Mission & the Silent Crisis of the 70's 1974.

AVENT, JACQUES MYRON
Political manager. **PERSONAL:** Born Nov 13, 1940, Washington, DC; married Loretta Taylor; children: James E. **EDUCATION:** Howard Univ, BS 1963. **CAREER:** Natl Assoc of Regional Councils, field dir 1969-71; Natl Urban Coalition, asst dir field opers 1971-72; NLC USCM, prog mgr 1972-74; League of CA Cities, spec Proj assoc 1974-75; Human Serv Inst, exec dir 1975; NLC, dir mem serv 1976-77, dir office of membership svcs. **ORGANIZATIONS:** Sec Natl Forum for Black Public Admin 1985; mem Amer Soc for Public Admin 1978-; bd mem Natl Forum for Black Public Admin 1983-. **HONORS/ACHIEVEMENTS:** Urban Exec Program Sloan Sch MIT 1973. **BUSINESS ADDRESS:** Dir Office Membership Serv, Natl League of Cities, 1301 Pennsylvania Ave NW, Washington, DC 20004.

AVERY, HERBERT B.
Obstetrician, gynecologist. **PERSONAL:** Born Oct 06, 1933; married Maunaloa T; children: Herbert Jr, Randy, Mark, Kenya Sasa, Libra J. **EDUCATION:** UCLA, 1951-56; Howard Univ, BS 1957; Howard Univ Med School, MD 1961. **CAREER:** UCLA & USC Schools of Publ Health, guest lect 1971-73; USC School of Med, asst prof; Martin Luther King Hosp, asst clin prof 1973; Private practice, ob/gyn 1966-. **ORGANIZATIONS:** Founder, dir Westland Health Serv Inc 1968; founder, chmn Univ Comm Health Serv 1975; founder, dir Amer Sicle Cell Soc Inc 1969; asst dir Ob/Gyn Serv John Wesley Cty Hosp, 1966-68; mem bd dir LA Reg Family Plng Council 1969-72; mem CA Interagency Council on Family Plng 1969-72, Pres Conf on Children & Youth 1972, Alpha Omega Alpha Honor Med Soc 1960-. **BUSINESS ADDRESS:** 4350 11th Ave, Los Angeles, CA 90008.

AVERY, JAMES S.
Oil company executive. **PERSONAL:** Born Mar 24, 1923, Cranford, NJ; son of John H Avery and Martha Ann (Jones) Avery; married Joan Showers; children: Sheryl, James Jr. **EDUCATION:** Columbia College, BA 1948, MA 1949. **CAREER:** Cranford NJ H S tchr 1949-56; Esso Standard Oil, Humble Oil, comm rel coord 1956-68; Humble Oil, Exxon Co USA, pub rel mgr 1968-71; Exxon Co USA, pub affairs mgr 1971-81, sr pub affairs consultant, retired 1986. **ORGANIZATIONS:** On loan assignment as exec vice pres Council on Municipal Performance 1981-83; vice chmn Natl Campaigns of UNCF 1962-65; vice chmn & chmn Vice Pres Task Force on Youth Motivation 1964-67; natl pres & bd chmn Natl Assn of Market Developers 1964-67; grand basileus Omega Psi Phi Frat Inc 1970-73; vice chmn Amer Pet Insts Offshore Sub-Comm, chmn NY St Pet Council 1978-79; mem of bd of trustees NY & NJ State Councils on Economic Educ 1975-86; vice chmn Philadelphia Reg Intro to Minorities to Engr. **HONORS/ACHIEVEMENTS:** Co-author of the Book of American City Rankings 1983; article on energy devlpmnt published by NY State Council for The Social Studies 1978; article on oil decontrol published by NY State Council on Econ Educ 1985; several major articles have been published in pamphlet form 1968-72. **MILITARY SERVICE:** AUS corp 3 yrs.

AVERY, WADDELL
Business executive. **PERSONAL:** Born Aug 16, 1928, Henderson, NC; son of Napoleon Avery and Hazel Avery; married Hilda Lee; children: Pamela K, Bryan W, Paula D. **EDUCATION:** Virginia State Univ, BS 1950; US Army/Baylor Univ, Grad Diploma Hospital Admin 1969; George Washington Univ, further study 1971. **CAREER:** Army Medical Dept, clinical biochem, bacteriologist 1950-54, helicopter pilot 1954-62, army hospital admin 1962-72; HEW Reg Medical Program Serv, public health adv 1972-73, supvr health serv & analyst 1973-78, hospital admin consultant 1974; US Dept HHS, grants management officer 1978-. **ORGANIZATIONS:** Mem Amer Coll of Hospital Admin 1974, Amer Hospital Assn 1968, Amer Medical Records Assn 1968, Natl Assn of Health Serv Exec 1971, Omega Psi Phi 1949, IBP Order of Elks 1951, Prince Hall Masons 33 Deg 1979, AEAONMS Inc 1969, NAACP 1964; life mem Retired Army Officers Assn 1972; ordained elder Presbyterian Church 1977; lecturer World Travel & Ancient History; Distinguished past pres Mt Vernon (VA) Kiwanis Club 1988-. **HONORS/ACHIEVEMENTS:** Certificate of Appreciation US Gen Comm on Chaplains & Armed Forces Personnel 1970; Citation of Honor Mound Bayou MS Comm Hospital 1974; USPHS Special Recognition Award HEW 1978; Superior Performance Award HEW 1975,77; Special Recognition Award, US Public Health Serv, 1979, 1986; Admin Citation Outstanding Serv, Health Resources & Serv Admin 1989. **MILITARY SERVICE:** AUS retired Lt Col 1950-72; Commendation Medals 1966,70; Army Merit Serv Medal 1972. **BUSINESS ADDRESS:** Grants Management Officer, US Dept HHS, 5600 Fishers Ln, Rm 11 A 18 Parklawn bldg, Rockville, MD 20857.

AXAM, JOHN ARTHUR
Administrator. **PERSONAL:** Born Feb 12, 1930, Cincinnati, OH; married Dolores Ballard, Sep 20, 1958. **EDUCATION:** Cheyney St Univ, BSE 1953; Drexel Univ, MSLS 1958. **CAREER:** Free Library of Philadelphia, librarian 1958-64, head, stations dept 1964-78, area adm 1978-. **ORGANIZATIONS:** ALA Cncl Am Lib Assoc 1971-72, various comm 1968; various comm PA Library Assoc 1964-; trustee United Way of So PA 1976-82; lay disciple Haven United Meth Ch 1965-. **HONORS/ACHIEVEMENTS:** Various articles in Library Prof Publications; Chapel of the Four Chaplains Awd; Certificate of Merit, Pennsylvania Library Association, 1988. **BUSINESS ADDRESS:** Area Administrator, Free Library of Philadelphia, Logan Square, Philadelphia, PA 19103.

AXT, VERONICA RENEE
Office manager. **PERSONAL:** Born Aug 05, 1960, Selma, AL; married Don Paris Axt. **EDUCATION:** AL State Univ, BA 1981. **CAREER:** WCOV TV & Radio, reporter/anchor 1981-83; Shaw Food Services Co, office mgr. **ORGANIZATIONS:** Life mem NAACP; mem Natl Assoc of Female Executives 1985-86; treasurer Cape Fear Civic & Social Org 1986. **HOME ADDRESS:** 6333 Lake Haven, Fayetteville, NC 28304.

AYALA, REGINALD P.
Hospital administrator. **PERSONAL:** Born Sep 07, 1931, Brooklyn, NY; son of Peter Ayala and Gladys Ayala; married R Winifred Covington; children: Kevin, Peter, Terrence, Kathyrn, Gladys, Gail. **EDUCATION:** Michigan State Univ, BA 1954, MBA 1970. **CAREER:** Harlem Globetrotters, professional basketball player, 1954-55, 1957; Detroit Parks & Rec, instr, 1958-59; Capri Convalescent Home, admin receiver,1962-65; Kirwood Gen Hosp, 1959-70; Boulevard Gen Hosp, 1970-74; Southwest Detroit Hosp, pres & CEO, 1970-. **ORGANIZATIONS:** Mem State Health Facilities Comm 1976-; fellow Amer Coll of Health Executives 1967, Amer Assn Med Admin 1960-, Hosp Financial Mgmt Assn 1960; past mem Dist II Michigan Hosp Serv Hosp Relations Comm, Natl Assn Health Serv Execs; bd trustees Michigan Hosp Serv; exec comm, assoc serv comm 1970-71 Greater Detroit Area Hosp Council; mem ed comm Greater Detroit Area Hosp Council 1970-71, Michigan Hosp Assn; public relations comm, Adv Comm on Occupational Safety & Health; chmn Personnel Comm, Michigan Cancer Found, House of Delegates, Amer Hosp Assn; chmn Ethics Comm, Amer Coll of Health Executives. **HONORS/ACHIEVEMENTS:** Citizen of the Year, Detroit Med Soc, 1975. **MILITARY SERVICE:** AUS 1st lt 1955-57. **BUSINESS ADDRESS:** President & CEO, Southwest Detroit Hospital, 2401 20th St, Detroit, MI 48216.

AYENSU, EDWARD SOLOMON
Plant biologist. **PERSONAL:** Born Aug 28, 1935, Sekondi, Ghana;married Dinah Ameley. **EDUCATION:** Miami Univ, Oxford Univ, BA Ghana Govt Scholar 1961; Univ of London, MSc Ghana Govt Scholar 1966, PhD. **CAREER:** Smithsonian Instr Washington, assoc curator 1966-69, curator 1970-. **ORGANIZATIONS:** Chmn dept botany 1970, dir Endangered species Prog; sec gen Intl Union of Biol Sci 1976-78; dir Office of Biol Conserv Smithsonian Inst 1978-; vstg prof Univ of Ghana 1969-; mem adv panel Systematic Biology NSF; trustee US Comm Intl Union Biol Sci; mem Inner Future NYC; fellow Ghana Acad Arts Sci, Linnean Soc London, Washington Acad Sci, Bot Soc Amer, Intl Assoc Plant Taxonomy, W African & Ghana Sci Assoc, AAAS, Amer Inst Biol Sci; exec dir 1969-71, pres 1977 Assoc for Tropical Biology; mem Bot Soc WA, Intl Soc Tropical Ecology, Intl Assoc Wood Anatomists, AAAS in Africa. **HONORS/ACHIEVEMENTS:** Author 9 books incl, Anatomy of the Monocotyledons, Dioscoreales 1972; co-author, Tropical Ecosystems in Africa & S Amer, A Comparative Review 1973, Commercial Timbers of Africa 1974, Endangered & Threatened Plants of US 1978, Med Plants of West-Africa 1978, Med Plants of the West Indies 1981; contrib over 100 articles to professional jrnls; rsch on comparative anatomy & phylogeny of angiosperms, vascular architecture & histology of monocotyledons, tropical biology, behavior of fruit-eating bats; Sci & Tech for Devel Countries.

AYERS, GEORGE E.
Educational director. **PERSONAL:** Born Nov 20, 1938, Quincy, IL; married Carolyn; children: Deanne, Danita, Darryl. **EDUCATION:** Quincy Coll, 1957-58; Western IL Univ, BS 1961; Univ of N CO, Master of Arts 1963, Dr of Educ 1965. **CAREER:** Cast Western Reserve Univ, instructor in phys med & rehab 1965-66; Mankato State Univ, rehabilitation counseling 1966-71; Metropolitan St Univ, vice pres & dean of college; Massasoit Comm Coll, pres 1978-82; Chicago State Univ, pres. **ORGANIZATIONS:** Chair bd of trustees Council for Advancement of Experiential Learning 1981-83; mem bd of dir President's Comm on Employ of the Handicapped 1975-; mem adv bd Lifelong Learning Harvard Univ 1981-; mem bd of trustees Milton Acad 1981-; mem bd of trustees Roseland Comm Hosp 1985-; mem bd of dir South Central Comm Services Chicago 1985-; bd of dir Assoc of American Colleges. **HONORS/ACHIEVEMENTS:** Cordelia Shelving Ellis Awd Natl Rehabilitation Assn 1969; Alumni Achievement Awd Western IL Univ 1981; 45 books articles & publications professional journals-mental retardation School Health Review Journal of Rehabilitation IL Change Journal Kappa Delta Pi Rehabilitation Counseling Bulletin; honorary Doctorate of Humane Letters State University of NY (Empire State College) 1986. **BUSINESS ADDRESS:** President, Chicago State University, 95th St at King Dr, Chicago, IL 60628.

AYERS, GEORGE WALDON, JR.
Dentist. **PERSONAL:** Born Sep 23, 1931, Lake City, FL; married Marjorie; children: Dwayne, Marva, Damian, Donald. **EDUCATION:** FL A&M Univ, BS 1956; Meharry Med Coll School Dentistry, DDS 1966. **CAREER:** Alachua Cty Health, 1969-70; Sunland Ctr, dental dir 1972-. **ORGANIZATIONS:** Mem Alachua Cty Dental Soc, Central Dist Dental, FL Dental Assoc, Amer Dental Assoc, FL Publ Health Assoc, So Assoc Intl Dentist. **MILITARY SERVICE:** Sgt 1951-54; capt 1966-68; Serv Medal; Korean War. **BUSINESS ADDRESS:** Dental Dir, Sunland Center, PO Box 1150, Waldo Rd, Gainesville, FL 32602.

AYERS, ROBERT G.
Railroad worker, farmer. **PERSONAL:** Born Jun 01, 1897, Summit, MS; married Helen Neeland; children: Marjorie A Clark. **CAREER:** City election commiss, 1968-76. **ORGANIZATIONS:** Master Boy Scouts 1942-61; agr extension serv Boy Scouts; mem Knights of Pythias, MW Stringer Grand Lodge No 23, NAACP; supt of AME Methodist Church; trustee Okolona Publ School Spec Awd in Forestry.

AYERS, TIMOTHY F.
Mayor, insurance agent. **PERSONAL:** Born Nov 19, 1958, Springfield, OH; son of Franklin R Ayers and Betty R Ayers; married Lisa J Henry-Ayers, Aug 31, 1985; children: Katheryne "Lindsay" Ayers. **EDUCATION:** Capital Univ, Columbus, OH, Political Science, 1977-81. **CAREER:** Ohio House of Representatives, Columbus, OH, legislative page, 1979, legislative message clerk, 1980-84; Ohio House Campaign Comm, Columbus, OH, 1982; Clark County Community Action Corp, Springfield, OH, 1984-86; City of Springfield, OH, mayor, 1984-; Reach Out for Youth Inc, Springfield, OH, foster care social worker, 1987-; Equitable, Springfield, OH, agent. **ORGANIZATIONS:** Licensed insurance agent, OH; bd mem, Amer Red Cross; mem, Truman-Kennedy Club, Clark County Democratic Exec Comm. **HONORS/ACHIEVEMENTS:** Outstanding Young Man in Amer, 1984, 1985. **BUSINESS ADDRESS:** Mayor, City of Springfield, 76 E High St, Springfield, OH 45502.

AYTCH, DONALD MELVIN
Educator. **PERSONAL:** Born Apr 17, 1930, Shreveport, LA; son of Sullivan Aytch and Della Aytch; married C Jean; children: Lynette, Don Jr, Cynthia, Neco. **EDUCATION:** Grambling State Univ, BS 1954; TX Southern Univ, MA 1969. **CAREER:** Bethune HS,

band dir 1957-68; Southern Univ, chmn 1969-. **ORGANIZATIONS:** Mem Louisiana Educ Assn, Natl Educ Assn, PAP, Natl Assn of Coll Professionals; public official Caddo Parish Police Jury 1966; comm Louisiana State Alcohol Commn 1964; Alpha Kappa Mu Hon Soc; mem Andante Con Expressive, Ark-La-Tex Focus. **HONORS/ACHIEVEMENTS:** 1st black Shreveport Symphony 1965. **MILITARY SERVICE:** AUS, S Sgt E7, 1954-56; received Good Conduct Medal. **BUSINESS ADDRESS:** Commissioner, Caddo Parish, District 7, P O Box 9124, Shreveport, LA 71109.

AZIZ, KAREEM A.
Educational admin. **PERSONAL:** Born Dec 15, 1951, Dayton, OH; married Nini Oseye; children: Jinaki Milele, Atiba Erasto. **EDUCATION:** Central State Univ, BA 1975; Univ of Dayton, M PubAdmin 1976; Morgan State Univ, Doctoral Student 1982-. **CAREER:** Comprehensive Manpower Ctr, admin asst to exec dir 1975-77; Clark Co Employment & Training Office, coord of comm PSE prog 1977-78; YMCA of Springfield OH, exec dir 1978-80; YMCA of Baltimore MD, exec dir 1980-81; Sojourner Douglass Coll, coord of inst rsch & planning 1981-. **ORGANIZATIONS:** Consultant New Day Assocs 1985; co-chair Natl Communications Comm Natl Black Independent Political Party 1983-. **HONORS/ACHIEVEMENTS:** "Key Statistics About Minorities in the Dayton Area" Dayton Human Relations Council 1973. **HOME ADDRESS:** 3302 Liberty Heights Ave, Baltimore, MD 21215. **BUSINESS ADDRESS:** Coord of Inst Rsch & Planning, Sojourner Douglass Coll, 500 N Caroline St, Baltimore, MD 21205.

B

BAAQEE, SUSANNE INEZ
Dentist. **PERSONAL:** Born Nov 24, 1952, Boston, MA; daughter of Everett Sabree and Inez Sabree; divorced; children: Shakir, Aneesah, Mikal. **EDUCATION:** Simmons Coll, BS, 1974; Tufts Dental School, DMD 1978; Harvard School of Dental Implantology, 1987. **CAREER:** Children's Hospital Med Center, immunology asst, 1972-75; Roxbury Comm Health Clinic, family dentist 1979-81; Harvard Biological Labs, rsch asst 1974; Implant & Family Dental Practice, dentist, 1980-. **ORGANIZATIONS:** Mem, MA Dental Soc, 1979-; Amer Dental Assn, 1979-; New England Soc Clinical Hypnosis, 1985-; bd mem, Dorchester Counseling Serv, 1983-86; treasurer, Amerislamic EID Assn, 1983-87; vice pres, Mattapan Comm Concern Group, 1984; mem, Amer Acad of Implant Dentistry, 1987-, Massachusetts Women's Dental Society, 1975-. **HONORS/ACHIEVEMENTS:** Girl of the Year Award, 1970; Scholastic Achievement, Natl Honor Soc, 1967-70, Alpha Kappa Alpha 1975-77, Links Soc, 1976-78. **BUSINESS ADDRESS:** Dentist, 1539 Blue Hill Ave, Mattapan, MA 02126.

BABB, VALERIE M.
Educator. **PERSONAL:** Born May 06, 1955, New York, NY; daughter of Lionel S Duncan and Dorothy L Babb. **EDUCATION:** Queens Coll, City Univ of New York, New York, NY, BA, 1977; State Univ of New York at Buffalo, Buffalo NY, MA, 1981, PhD, 1981. **CAREER:** Georgetown Univ, Washington DC, asst prof, 1981-. **HONORS/ACHIEVEMENTS:** Author, "William Melvin Kelly," Dictionary of Literary Biography, 1984; Award for Academic Excellence, Seek Program, City Univ of New York, 1985; "Black Georgetown Remembered: A Documentary Video," 1989. **BUSINESS ADDRESS:** Asst Prof of English, Georgetown Univ, Dept of English, 338 New North, Washington, DC 20057.

BABBS, JUNIOUS C., SR.
Educator. **PERSONAL:** Born Aug 15, 1924, Arkansas; married Bobbie; children: Junious C Jr, Dwayne, Jade. **EDUCATION:** BS, MS, EdS 1971; EdD 1984. **CAREER:** Cotton Plant Public Schools, coach, sci teacher, rec dir, principal, supt of school. **ORGANIZATIONS:** Chmn bd trustees Ash Grove Bapt Church; sec ECOEO; mem Cty Health Comm; mem Cty Adv Comm; mem City Council; chmn Finance Comm; mem NEAAA, AEA, State Principals Orgn for Admin; mem NCA State Comm; mem Adv Council on Secondary Ed, Cty Extension Bd; mem dir Cotton Plant Clinic; mem AR State Admin Assn, 32 Deg Mason, NAC; mem bd dir DAD; sec Mental Health Bd; deacon Ash Grove B Church; State Advisory Committee for Chapter II State Bonds & Facility Commission. **HONORS/ACHIEVEMENTS:** Man of the Year Awd 1969,73; Coach of the Year 1953,56,60,61,62; Biol Teacher Awd 1960-61. **BUSINESS ADDRESS:** Superintendent, Cotton Plant Public Schools, Church & Pine Sts, Cotton Plant, AR 72036.

BABER, CEOLA ROSS
Educator. **PERSONAL:** Born Nov 30, 1950, Selma, AL; daughter of Frederick Douglas Ross, Sr and Laura Stringe Ross; married Willie L Baber; children: Lorenzo DuBois, Tylisha Marie, Cheickna St Clair. **EDUCATION:** CA State Univ Sacramento, BA 1972; Stanford Univ, MA 1975; Purdue Univ, PhD 1984. **CAREER:** Sequoia Union HS Dist, teacher 1974-78; Tuskegee Univ, project coord/instructor 1979-80; Purdue Univ, rsch assoc 1980-81, dir/asst prof 1984-89; School of Educ, Univ of North Carolina-Greensboro, asst prof l989-. **ORGANIZATIONS:** Mem Greater Lafayette NAACP 1980-, Assoc for Supervision and Curriculum Devel 1984-; commissioner West Lafayette Human Relations Commn 1986-; consultant Southwestern Bell Telephone 1986; mem Natl Civil Rights Museum and Hall of Fame 1986-; mem Intl Black Women's Congress 1986-; pres Wesley Foundation Bd of Dirs 1987-88; mem publications/editorial committee, Natl Council for Black Studies l989-. **HONORS/ACHIEVEMENTS:** Ethnic Minority Fellowship & Grant 1982-84; invited fellow Amer Educ Rsch Assoc NIE seminar 1984; Comm Serv Awd Greater Lafayette NAACP 1985; Certificate of Appreciation Purdue Minority Student Union 1985; Indiana Comm on the Humanities Grant 1985-86; Special Recognition Awd Alpha Kappa Alpha Epsilon Rho 1986; CIES Fulbright Scholar-in-Residence Grant 1986-87; Lilly Endowment Grant 1987-88; certificate of Appreciation, Ft Wayne Minority Women's Network l989; "The Artistry and Artifice of Black Communication," book chapter l987; "Black Studies for White Students" article l987. **BUSINESS ADDRESS:** Asst Professor, Dept of Pedagogical Studies, School of Educ, Curry Bldg, Univ of North Carolina-Greensboro, Greensboro, NC 27412-5001.

BABER, LUCKY LARRY
Educator. **PERSONAL:** Born Apr 16, 1949, Ackerman, MS. **EDUCATION:** Grand Valley State Coll Allendale, MI, BS 1972; Central MI Univ, MA 1975; Bowling Green State Univ, PhD 1978. **CAREER:** Saginaw Big Brothers, asst dir 1972-73; Delta Coll, instructor 1973-74; Buena Vista High School, teacher 1974-75; Lincoln Univ Dept Soc, asst prof/chmn 1978-. **ORGANIZATIONS:** V chmn of Bd of Fellows Cent for Stydying Soc Welfare and Comm Devel Philadelphia 1979-80; chmn Bowling Green Chap Alpha Kappa Delta Natl Honor Soc 1977-78. **BUSINESS ADDRESS:** Assistant Professor/Chairman, LincolnUniv, Dept of Soc, Lincoln University, PA 19352.

BABERO, BERT BELL
Educator. **PERSONAL:** Born Oct 09, 1918, St Louis, MO; married Harriett King; children: Bert Jr, Andras Fanfiero. **EDUCATION:** Univ of Illinois, BS 1949, MS 1950, PhD 1957. **CAREER:** Artic Health Research Center AK, med prstlgst 1950-55; Ft Valley State Coll, Ga, prof of Zoology 1957-59; Southern Univ, Baton Rouge LA, prof of Zoology 1959-60; F Ed Emergency Sci Skeme, Lagos, Nigeria, lecturer Zoology 1960-62; School of Medicine Univ Baghdad, Iraq, prstlgst 1962-65; Grambling State Univ, prof of Zoology; Univ of NV Las Vegas, prof of Zoology emeritus. **ORGANIZATIONS:** Amer Soc of Prstlgst 1951-; Am Mcrscptcl Soc 1951-; Honorary Soc Phi Sigma Biological Soc; Beta Blgc Soc. **HONORS/ACHIEVEMENTS:** Comm NV St Equal Rights Comm 1967-68; Alpha Phi Alpha Fraternity 1957-; Sigma Xi Honorary Sci Soc Pres Local Chapter 1966-72; Phi Kappa Phi 1966-; fellow trop med Louisiana State Univ Medical School 1968; council Rep Amer Soc Prstlgsts 1981-85; honorary life mem Rocky Mt Conf Prstlgsts 1982; 80 science publication in Prstlgy in journals of many countries; Hall of Fame DuSable High School Chicago 1985. **MILITARY SERVICE:** AUS T4 1943-46; 3 overseas serv Bars; Am Cmpgn Medal; Asiatic Pac Cmgn Medal; Bronze Star; Good Conduct Medal; WWII Victory Medal. **BUSINESS ADDRESS:** Professor of Zoology, Univ of Nevada-Las Vegas, 4505 Maryland Pkwy, Las Vegas, NV 89154.

BACHUS, MARIE DARSEY
Educator. **PERSONAL:** Born Nov 29, 1940, St Joseph, LA; children: Maurice, Marcia. **EDUCATION:** Grambling State Univ, BS 1964; Southern Univ, ME 1974. **CAREER:** New Orleans, councilwoman, mayor pro-tem; Mabachus Record & Sweet Shop, owner; teacher. **ORGANIZATIONS:** Mem TEA, LTA, NEA; vice pres Grambling Alumni, PTSA, Athletic Club, Band Booster Club; sec Springfield MBC; dir Com Youth; Waterproof Schools Band Boosters. **HONORS/ACHIEVEMENTS:** Key to City of New Orleans 1975.

BACKUS, BRADLEY
Lawyer. **PERSONAL:** Born Sep 12, 1950, Kings County, NY; son of Thomas Backus and Bernice Smith; married Stephanie George (divorced); children: Crystal Olivia Backus. **EDUCATION:** Lincoln Univ, Oxford, PA, BA, 1972; George Washington Univ, Natl Law Center, JD, 1975. **CAREER:** Metropolitan Life, New York, NY, advanced underwriting consultant, 1977-80, dir Estate Planning, 1980-. **ORGANIZATIONS:** Pres, Bedford-Stuyvesant Lawyers Assn, 1980-81; bd mem, Bedford-Stuyvesant Community Legal Serv Corp, 1980-89; pres, Metropolitan Black Bar Assn, 1986-89; vice pres, MBBA Scholarship Fund Inc, 1987-89; bd mem, Comm for Modern Courts, 1988-; commr, NY State Judicial Commn on Minorities, 1988-; commr, NY City Korean Veterans Memorial Commn 1988-; commr, NY State Comm to Improve the Availability of Legal Services, 1988-. **BUSINESS ADDRESS:** Advanced Underwriting Consultant/Director, Metropolitan Life Insurance Company, One Madison Avenue, Area 4-H, New York, NY 10010.

BACOATE, MATTHEW, JR.
Business executive. **PERSONAL:** Born Feb 10, 1931, Asheville, NC. **EDUCATION:** Med Adminis Sch, attended 1951; Univ of So CA, bus admin 1953-55; Western Carolina Univ, Bus Admin 1970-71; NC State Univ CEU's, 1971-75. **CAREER:** Asheville Chamber of Commerce, gen mgr; Afran Inc, gen mgr; Asheville Commun Enter Inc, gen mgr 1973-; M Bacoate Disposable's Inc, pres. **ORGANIZATIONS:** Fndr & co-chmn Comm of Prog; mem bd of vis W Carolina Univ; mem Comm Int & Commit WLOS-TV; bd dir Asheville Chap Amer Red Cross; bd dir Commbs Museum of Fire Equip; mem Smithsonian Assn; mem Small Bus Adv Cncl 1978; bd dir Gov Western Residence Assn 1978; mem Priv Indsl Cncl (PIC) 1979; mem Employment Security Adv Cncl 1979; mem Central Asheville Optimist Club 1979; mem fund for self-devel of People Holston Presbyteria of US; steering comm Martin L King Prayer Break; mem Daniel Boone Council Boy Scouts of Amer 1978; mem bd dir Asheville Area C of C 1981; adv council US Small Bus Admin 1981; chmn bd Victoria Health Care Ctr 1981-; adv committee AB Tech Small Bus 1986. **HONORS/ACHIEVEMENTS:** Cert of Apprec Asheville Buncombe Tech Inst 1977; Cert of Recog City of Winston-Salem NC 1980-; Awd Ashville Area C of C Inc 1981; Cert of Recog Western Carolina Univ 1983; Outstanding Serv Inducted into the Chamber of Echoes Central Asheville Optimist 1984. **MILITARY SERVICE:** Army Med Corps 1951-56. **BUSINESS ADDRESS:** President, M Bacoate Disposables, Inc, 129 Roberta St, Asheville, NC 28801.

BACOATS, INEZ B.
Retired educator. **PERSONAL:** Born Nov 23, 1899, Spotsylvania Co, VA; married J Alvin (deceased). **EDUCATION:** Hartshorn Mem Coll, BS 1923; Leland Coll 1932; Univ of IA, MA 1943. **CAREER:** Benedict Coll, Columbia SC, instructor, dean of students retired. **ORGANIZATIONS:** Mem State & Natl Ed Assoc, Natl Council Negro Women, Natl Bapt Conv, Natl Assoc Ministers Wives, Alpha Kappa Alpha; charter mem Natl Assoc Personnel Workers; mem YWCA, SC Council Human Relations, Womens Voters League; exec bd Womans Bapt State Conv; past bd mem Gethsemane Womans Aux & Interagency Council of Aging. **HONORS/ACHIEVEMENTS:** Author "Echoes from a Well Spent Life" (biography of John Alvin Bacoats); Mother of Campus Awd 1962; Sr Membership & Serv Awd Sylvannah Bapt Church 1968; Pres Citation NAMW 1967; Cert of Awd Spotsylvania SS Union 1972; Cert of Appreciation Gethsemane Womens Aux 1973; Disting Serv Awd Benedict Coll Columbia.

BACON, ALBERT S.
Orthodontist. **PERSONAL:** Born Mar 01, 1942, LaGrange, GA; son of Albert Stanley Bacon Sr and Julia Spain Bacon. **EDUCATION:** Howard Univ, BS 1963, DDS 1967; certified in Orthodontics 1971. **CAREER:** VA Hosp, staff dentist 1969; private practice 1970; Community Group Health Found, staff dentist 1970; Howard Univ, asst prof 1971; private practice orthodontics 1971; Dept Comm Dentistry, acting chmn 1972; presently private group practice. **ORGANIZATIONS:** Mem Amer/Natl/So MD Dental Assns; Robert T Freeman Dental Soc; Amer Assn Orthodontists; Middle Atlantic Soc Orthodontists; Amer Acad of Group Dental Practice; Chi Delta Mu Frat; Young Adults of Washington; St Albans Soc; Canterbury Club; Howard Univ Alumni Assn. **BUSINESS ADDRESS:** West Office Bldg, Ste 308 Landover Mall, Landover, MD 20785.

BACON, BARBARA CRUMPLER
Educational administration. **PERSONAL:** Born Sep 07, 1943, Youngstown, OH; married Oscar; children: Robert, Jessica. **EDUCATION:** Youngstown State Univ, BA Sociology 1980. **CAREER:** Smithsonian Inst, eeo spec 1972-78; Mahoning Cty Transitional Homes, affirm action consult 1980, instr 1980-81; Youngstown State Univ, affirm action dir 1984-. **ORGANIZATIONS:** Bd mem Assoc Neighborhood Ctrs 1984-, YWCA 1985-; mem Links Inc 1985-; bd mem Gateways to Better Living 1985; Design Review Comm. **BUSINESS ADDRESS:** Dir Affirm Action, Youngstown StateUniv, Tod Admin Bldg Rm 209, Youngstown, OH 44555.

BACON, CHARLOTTE MEADE
Educator. **PERSONAL:** Born in Alberta, VA; daughter of Ollie Meade (deceased) and Pinkie Manson Meade (deceased); married Edward D Bacon Jr; children: Judith, Edward P, Susan, Detrick. **EDUCATION:** Hampton Inst, BS (Hon) 1946; Univ of Pittsburgh, MEd 1952. **CAREER:** Great Aliquippa YWCA, prog comm 1965-72; Aliquippa Ed Assoc, record sec 1969-72; Aliquippa Br of Amer Assoc of Univ Women, corres sec 1971-73; Aliquippa Negro Bus & professional Womens Club, pres 1960-62,63-77; PA State Fed of Negro Womens Clubs, pres 1969-73; Aliquippa School Dist, teacher. **ORGANIZATIONS:** Mem Delta Sigma Theta Sor, Natl Ed Assoc, PA St Ed Assoc, Holy Inst Bapt Church, NAACP, World Affairs Council of Pgh; life mem New Sheffield PTA; vchmn Mayors Comm on Civil Rights 1972-77; pres Willing Workers Mission Soc 1988, spon Jr Choir Holy Inst Bapt Church; pres Aliquippa Br Amer Assoc of Univ Women 1977-79; bd of dir Sewickley Comm Ctr; bd of dir 1976,82, spec task force 1978-83 Beaver Castle Girl Scout Cncl; state suprv PA State Fed of Girls Clubs 1974-79; Natl Assoc of Colored Womens Clubs; exec bd 1969-79, ed chrpsn NE Fed of Womens Clubs; chmn Consumer Affairs 1976-; mem Sewickley Intl Toastmistress Club 1976-82; dir Aliquippa NAACP Creative Dramatics Club; mem Sewickley NYPUM Prog Comm 1979-82; Black Womens Pol Crusade of Pgh 1987; 3rd vice pres Aliquippa Elem School PTA 1980-81; com munications comm Natl Assoc of Negro Bus & Professional Women's Clubs 1985; Women's History spkr PA Dept of Educ Speaker's Bureau on Black History Aliquippa Negro Bus & Professional Women's Club; mem Penn State Minority Recruitment Comm 1987-; 1st vice pres Aliquippa NBPW Club; second vice pres Aliquippa AAUW 1988, Women's History chairperson; Adult Literacy Council of Beaver County; recording secretary, Northcentral District NANBPWC 1988-; exec bd, Natl Assn Colored Women's Clubs 1988-; exec bd, Northeastern Federation of Negro Women 1987-88; historian, Modern Club Aliquippa PA 1987-; chaplan, Daniel B Mathews Historical Society 1987-; Girl Scout Leader Brownie Troop 77 1973-. **HONORS/ACHIEVEMENTS:** Woman of the Year Aliquippa NBPW Club 1970; Delta Sigma Theta Comm Involvement Awd 1971; Notable Amer of the Bicent Era 1976; Bict of Intl Biog 1971-76;Sojourner Truth Awd Natl Assoc of NBPW Clubs 1976; PA Woman of the Year Aliquippa Br AAUW 1981; Disting Serv Awd PA State Fed of Negro Womens Clubs Inc 1983; Appreciation Awd Beaver-Castle Girl Scout Cncl 1985; Aliquippa Elem Sch PTA Scholarship Awd 1986; Teacher of the Year Aliquippa Sch Dist 1987; 498 Hardworking Women of PA 1987; Co-Author, Four Drummers, poetry book 1989. **BUSINESS ADDRESS:** Teacher, Aliquippa Elementary School, 21 St, Aliquippa, PA 15001.

BACON, GLORIA JACKSON
Physician. **PERSONAL:** Born Sep 21, 1937, New Orleans, LA; married Frank C Bacon Jr; children: Constance Jackson, Judith Jackson, Phillip, Geoffrey, Stuart. **EDUCATION:** Xavier Univ, BS 1958; Univ of IL, Sch of Medicine MD 1962, Sch of Public Health MPH 1984. **CAREER:** Health/Hosp Governing Commn Cook Co, medical dir 1979; The Clinic in Altgeld Inc, founder/dir 1970-82; Provident Hosp and Med Ctr, vp/dev mktg 1985; Clinic Associates of Chicago Ltd, pres 1982-; Metro Care HMO, medical dir 1986-87; Provident Hosp & Med Ctr, pres/medical staff 1985-. **ORGANIZATIONS:** Mem bd of trustees Fisk Univ 1980-85, Gannon/Proctor Commn 1982-83; mem Natl Medical Assoc, The Chicago Network, Tech Adv Comm on School BAsed Adolescent Health Care Prog, Robert Wood Johnson Foundation. **HONORS/ACHIEVEMENTS:** Woman of the Year in Medicine Operation PUSH 1975; Candace Awd Comm of 100 Women 1984; publication "Is Love Ever Enough?" A Finial Press Champaign IL 1987. **BUSINESS ADDRESS:** President of Medical Staff, Provident Hosp & Medical Ctr, 500 East 51st St, Chicago, IL 60615.

BACON, LANDER MCCOY
Professional athlete. **PERSONAL:** Born Aug 30, 1943, Cadiz, KY; married Arlene Cleveland; children: Chanda, Tyrone. **EDUCATION:** Attended Jackson State. **CAREER:** Washington Redskins, def end 1978-; Cincinnati Bengals, player; Los Angeles Rams, player; San Diego Chargers, player. **HONORS/ACHIEVEMENTS:** Recov 11 fumb intercept 2 Pass scor 2 tchdwns NFL car.

BACON, RANDALL C.
Director. **PERSONAL:** Born Oct 02, 1937, Youngstown, OH; divorced; children: Randy, Keith, Kevin. **EDUCATION:** Los Angeles City College, AA 1958; CA State Univ, BS 1962; Univ of Southern CA, attended 1962-64; Loyola Law Sch, attended 1964-66. **CAREER:** Los Angeles County Social Svcs, fiscal officer 1965-69; Los Angeles County Pks & Rec, chief deputy dir 1969-74; Los Agneles County Adm Off, division chief 1974-79; San Diego County, asst chief adm off 1979-81, dir of social serv 1981-. **ORGANIZATIONS:** Mem Black Leadership Council of San Diego 1981-; chmn 44th Congressional Dist Adv Bd 1984-; natl pres Kappa Alpha Psi Frat 1985-; chmn CA Welfare Directors Assoc 1985-. **HONORS/ACHIEVEMENTS:** Published article "A Model Program for all California," Public Welfare Magazine 1986; 1987 Natl Public Serv Awd. **BUSINESS ADDRESS:** Dir of Social Services, San Diego County, 7949 Mission Center Ct, San Diego, CA 92108.

BACON, ROBERT JOHN, JR.
Psychiatrist. **PERSONAL:** Born Nov 20, 1948, Houston, TX; married Karen; children: Robyn, Kristen, Angelle. **EDUCATION:** Stanford Univ, BA 1970; Meharry Medical Coll, MD 1975. **CAREER:** TX Medical Foundation, physician advisor 1982-; Univ of TX-Houston, clinical asst prof 1984-; Ben Taub General Hosp, dir of psychiatric emergency serv 1984-; Baylor Coll of Medicine, asst prof 1984-. **ORGANIZATIONS:** Clinical consultant Harris Co Forensic Treatment Unit 1979-81. **BUSINESS ADDRESS:** Assistant Professor, Baylor College of Medicine, One Baylor Plaza, Houston, TX 77030.

BACON, WARREN H.
Business executive. **PERSONAL:** Born Jan 12, 1923, Chicago, IL; married Mary Lou; children: 3 children. **EDUCATION:** Univ Chicago, MBA 1951; Roosevelt Univ, BA 1948. **CAREER:** Supreme Life Ins Co, vice pres 1951-66; Inland Steel Co, mgr. **ORGANIZATIONS:** Dir Hyde Park Fed Savings & Loan Assn; dir Seaway Natl Bank; mem BLS Bus Rsch Adv Cncl; mem IL Bd of Higher Educ; trustee Russell Sage Found; mem Chicago Bd Educ 1963-73. **HONORS/ACHIEVEMENTS:** Alumni Awd Roosevelt Univ 1966; Alumni Awd Pub Serv Univ Chicago 1972. **MILITARY SERVICE:** AUS corpl 1943-46. **BUSINESS ADDRESS:** Manager, Inland Steel Co, 30 W Monroe St, Chicago, IL 60603.

BACON, WILLIAM LOUIS
Surgeon. **PERSONAL:** Born Dec 03, 1936, Austin, TX; married Donna Marie Harbatis; children: Tyra, William II, Donna, Mary, Jesse, Louise, Jonathan. **EDUCATION:** Morehouse Coll, 1956; Meharry Med Coll, 1962. **CAREER:** Fitzsimons Gen Hosp, intern 1962-63; Ireland Army Hosp, prespec surg 1963-64; Brooke Army Med Ctr, ortho 1964-67; Wash DC, course dir 1972-74; Miami, surg 1975-; private practice, physician. **ORGANIZATIONS:** Cert Amer Bd of Ortho Surg 1970; mem Amer Coll of Surg 1971; Amer Acad of Ortho Surg 1972; guest lecturer Univ of Miami 1976; staff consult Friedman's Hosp & Howard Univ; staff mem Mt Sinai Med Ctr, Cedars of Leb Hosp, Vict Hosp, Jack Mem Hosp; mem bd Cedars of Leb Hosp; mem Dade Co MedAssn, FL Med Soc, Amer Med Assn, Miami Ortho Soc, FL Ortho Soc; recert Amer Bd Ortho Surg 1983; commander 324th Gen Hosp USAR 1983-86. **HONORS/ACHIEVEMENTS:** Merit Serv Med 1970,74; Examiner Amer Bd Ortho Surg 1978-84. **MILITARY SERVICE:** AUS 1962-74; USAR 1975-; Army Commendation Medal 1972. **BUSINESS ADDRESS:** Physician, William L Bacon MD PA, 511 NE 15th St, Miami, FL 33132.

BACON RICHARDS, BILLE J.
Banking executive. **PERSONAL:** Born in Austin, TX; divorced; children: 3. **EDUCATION:** Houston-Tillotson Coll, BS 1962; Univ of TX Austin, 1963; Scarritt Coll, 1966; Univ of TX Arlington, MA 1974. **CAREER:** Ebenezer Baptist Church, dir of educ 1960-61; Dunbar HS, teacher 1961-64; Bethlehem Ctr, exec dir 1965-73; Fed Home Loan Bank Bd Ctr for Exec Develop, urban prog coord 1972-73; Neighborhood Housing Serv of Dallas, exec dir 1973-78; Dallas Fed Svgs & Loan Assn, sr vice pres urban lending 1978-. **ORGANIZATIONS:** N TX Conf of United Methodist Church Comm Ministries Comm 1972; adv comm mem Dallas Independent Sch Dist 1973; Minority Affairs Comm Adv Comm GradSch of Social Work Univ of TX 1973-74; mem Natl Assn of Black Social Workers 1973-76; mem Urban Reinvestment Task Force Natl Comm 1974-79; vice pres NHS Prof Assn 1976-78; mem North TX Council of Govts Human Resource Task Force 1976-; bd of dirs United Way 1979-82; United Way Admissions Comm 1982; memMayor's S Dallas Task Force 1983-84; bd of dirs & corporate mem Neighborhood Housing Services 1973-; mem N TX Council of Govts Housing Task Force 1976-;bd of dirs KERA 1977-; S Dallas Economic Development Comm 1982-; pres City of Dallas Indus Develop Corp Bd 1982-; US Savings & Loan League Urban Affairs Comm; co-chmn TX A&M Urban Institute Adv Council; finance comm Old City Park bd; mem Natl Assn of Urban Bankers Dallas; Sescquecentenial Intl Visitors Committee 1986; mem Visiting Nurse Assn 1984-86; Dallas Black Chamber of Commerce 1986-. **HONORS/ACHIEVEMENTS:** Rep Comm Ctrs throughout the nation at Natl Conf of the United Methodist Church New York 1970; Woman of the Year United for Action 1978; Comm Affairs Awd Committee of 100 1978; highlighted as one of channel 4's Dallas Women in their Dallas Women series 1979; Trailblazer Awd S Dallas Business & Prof Women's Organization 1979; Opportunity Dallas 1981; IA Credential Leadership Awd IA Dept of Job Service 1984; Soc of Internat'l Bus Fellows 1986.

BADGER, LLOYD, JR.
City councilmember. **PERSONAL:** Born May 25, 1950, Hiltonia, GA. **EDUCATION:** Rochester Inst of Techn, Indust Mgmt 1970-72. **CAREER:** Self-employed salesman; City of Hiltonia, city councilmenber 1983-. **ORGANIZATIONS:** Mem Johnson Grove Baptist Ch, NAACP, Optimist Club, Masons. **BUSINESS ADDRESS:** City Councilmember, City of Sylvania, Rt 1 Box 115-A, Sylvania, GA 30467.

BAETY, EDWARD L.
Attorney, judge. **PERSONAL:** Born Mar 13, 1944, Jacksonville, FL. **EDUCATION:** Morris Brown Coll, BS 1965; Howard Univ Sch of Law, JD 1968. **CAREER:** Atlant Leg Aid Soc, staff atty 1968-71; Equal Employ Opp Commn, dist coun 1971-72; Hill Jones & Farr, asso coun 1972-74; Hill Jones & Farr, part 1974-76; City of Atl Ct, asso jdg 1976-. **ORGANIZATIONS:** Mem Atl Bar Assn; Gate City Bar Assn; State Bar Assn of GA; Atlan Bus League; Vol Leg Serv Atty (Sat law); pres Atlan Spart Ath Clb; pst vice pres Phi Beta Sigma Frat Inc; Black Consort. **HONORS/ACHIEVEMENTS:** Lstd Who's Who in Am Coll & Univ 1965; outsdg yng man in Am 1970. **MILITARY SERVICE:** Ausr sp E-5. **BUSINESS ADDRESS:** City Court of Atlanta, 104 Trinity Ave SW, Atlanta, GA 30335.

BAGBY, RACHEL L
Composer, writer, performing artist, educator. **PERSONAL:** Born Feb 11, 1956, Philadelphia, PA; daughter of William H Bagby and Rachel Edna Samiella Rebecca Jones Bagby; married Martin Neal Davidson, Oct 03, 1987. **EDUCATION:** North Carolina AT&T State, Greensboro, NC, 1973-74; Univ of Pittsburgh, Pittsburgh PA, BA (summa cum laude), 1977; Stanford Law School, Stanford CA, JD, 1983. **CAREER:** The Wall Street Journal, San Francisco CA, writer 1979; freelance composer, writer, Stanford CA, 1979-; Philadelphia Community Rehabilation Corp, Philadelphia PA, asst dir, 1980-82; African and American Studies, Stanford Univ, program coord, 1983-85; Comm on Black Performing Arts, Stanford CA, program coord, 1983-85; Martin Luther King Jr, Papers Project, Stanford CA, assoc dir, 1985-; Bobby McFerrin's Voicestra, San Francisco CA, composer, performer, 1989-; pres, Outta the Box Recordings, 1989. **ORGANIZATIONS:** Mem & consultant, Natl Black Women's Health Program, 1986-; co-dir, Woman Earth Inst, 1986-; consultant, CA Arts Council, 1984-86; mem, CA Lawyers for the Arts (formerly Bay Area Lawyers for the Arts), 1982-. **HONORS/ACHIEVEMENTS:** Chancellor's Teaching Fellowship, V of Pitssburgh, 1975; admitted into master class with Bobby McFerrin, Omega Inst, 1988; composed and recorded "Grandmothers' Song," theme for a documentary on Alice Walker; chapters published in anthologies: "A Power of Numbers," Healing the Wounds, 1989, "Daughters of Growing Things," Reweaving the World: The Emergenance of Econfeminish, 1989; composed, recorded and produced anti-racism tape "Reach Across the Lines," on self-owened independent label, 1989. **BUSINESS ADDRESS:** Resident Fellow-ujamaa/ Associate Director, Martin Luther King, Jr Papers Project, Stanford University, Box 11066, Stanford, CA 94309.

BAGLEY, GREGORY P.
Engineer. **PERSONAL:** Born Sep 19, 1930, New York City, NY; son of Garrett P Bagley

and Carrie A Bagley; married Helen Smith; children: Gregory Jr, Carole, John. **EDUCATION:** Johns Hopkins Univ, BES 1958; Adelphi Univ, MS 1969. **CAREER:** Hazeltine Corp, electrical engr 1958-62; Sperry Gyroscope Cty, sr electrical engr 1962-68; Assoc Univ Brookhaven Natl Lab, rsch engr I 1968-. **ORGANIZATIONS:** Sec bd deacons Union Baptist Church Hempstead 1962-; sr mem IEEE; vice pres Franklin PTA 1972-73; mem bd Park Lake Devel Fund Corp 1970-. **HONORS/ACHIEVEMENTS:** Tau Beta Pi, Eta Kappa Nu Hon Engr Soc. **MILITARY SERVICE:** USAF a/1c 1950-53. **BUSINESS ADDRESS:** Research Engineer, Brookhaven Natl Lab, Bldg 902 B Brookhaven Nat Lab, Upton, NY 11973.

BAGLEY, JOHN
Professional athlete. **PERSONAL:** Born Apr 30, 1960, Bridgeport, CT. **EDUCATION:** Boston Coll, BA 1983. **CAREER:** Cleveland Cavaliers, guard 1983-. **HONORS/ACHIEVEMENTS:** As a Cavalier played in 68 games as a rookie in 1982-83, averaging 57 points per Game; scored in double figures 12 times. **BUSINESS ADDRESS:** Cleveland Cavaliers, The Colesium, Richfield, OH 44286.

BAGLEY, PETER B. E.
Educator, music conductor. **PERSONAL:** Born May 22, 1935, Yonkers, NY; married Bythema Byrd; children: Margaret R. **EDUCATION:** Crane Sch of Music SUNY/Potsdam NY, BS 1957; IN Univ Sch of Music, MM Chor Cond 1965, dM Chor Cond 1972. **CAREER:** Greenwich CT Public Schools, vocal music teacher 1957-61; First Baptist Church, Bloomington IN, dir of music 1964-66; New Paltz Concert Choir & Chamber Singers, conductor 1966-; All State Choruses of WV 1970-71, NH 1972, CT 1976, VT 1978, guest conductor; New England Festival Chorus, guest conductor 1980; State Univ of NY New Paltz, assoc prof of music 1966-. **ORGANIZATIONS:** Mem Amer Choral Dirs Assn; mem Amer Choral Found; mem Music Editor Natl Conf; mem Music Lib Assn; mem Natl Assn for Afro-Amer Educ; mem NY State Sch music Assn. **HONORS/ACHIEVEMENTS:** Listed Who's Who in the East 12th ed. **BUSINESS ADDRESS:** University of CT, 875 Country Rd, Storrs, CT 06268.

BAGLEY, STANLEY B.
Chaplain. **PERSONAL:** Born Sep 07, 1935, Trenton, NJ; son of Dr Samuel M Bagley (deceased) and Leomae Walker Bagley (deceased); married Ruth McDowell; children: Bernard, Sharon, Bryant, Brett. **EDUCATION:** Morehouse Coll, BA 1958; Crozer Theol Sem, BD 1961; Ashland Theol Sem, MDiv 1973; Univ of OK, grad study. **CAREER:** Galilee Bapt Ch Trenton NJ, asst pastor 1961-65; Calvary Bapt Ch, pastor 1965-67; Bapt Campus Ministry Langston Univ, dir 1967-70; Hough Ch, minister of educ comm 1970-71; VA Medical Center Brecksville OH, chaplain 1971-; Lakeside Bapt Ch E Cleveland OH, pastor 1972-1979. **ORGANIZATIONS:** Mem E Cleveland Ministeral Alliance 1975; Assn of Mental Health Clergy 1974; Amer Protestant Hosp Assn; chmn Evangelism Com Bapt Minister's Conf Cleveland OH; Dept of Metropolitian Ministry Cleveland Baptist Assn; life mem and golden heritage life mem NAACP; Omega Psi Phi Fraternity. **HONORS/ACHIEVEMENTS:** Christian Leadership Citation Bapt Student Union Langston Univ 1969; Outstanding Young Man of 1970 sponsored by Outstanding Amer Found; 33 Degree Free Mason; United Supreme Council 33 Degree Ancient and Accepted Scottish Rite of Freemasonry Prince Hall Affiliation. **HOME ADDRESS:** 2361 Traymore Rd, University Heights, OH 44118.

BAILER, BONNIE LYNN
Business executive. **PERSONAL:** Born Oct 11, 1946, New York, NY; daughter of Dr Lloyd Harding Bailer and Marvelyne Matthews Bailer; children: Miles Bailer Armstead. **EDUCATION:** Queens Coll of City Univ of NY, BA 1968, MS 1975. **CAREER:** Foreign Language Dept, New York City Public School System Jr High School, acting chmn 1970-75; Yellow-Go-Rilla Prod, Ltd, vice pres 1975-77; Manhattan Borough pres campaigns, political campaign admin 1977; NAACP, membership consultant 1978-79; The Talkshop Foreign Language Program for Children, founder & pres 1981-; The Gilbert Jonas Co Inc, professional fund raiser, vice pres 1979-86; United Nations Assn of the USA, dir capital campaign 1986-88; Bailer Studios, artists' agent & professional fund raising consultant 1988-. **ORGANIZATIONS:** Bd member, Morningside Montessori School 1979-82, The Grinnell Housein Defense Corp 1984-; certified building mgr City of NY 1979; press coord Annual Westside Comm Conf 1979-; consultant, Minisink City Mission Soc 1984; giving comm member, Cathedral School 1984-; member, Natl Assn of Female Exec, NAACP, Natl Soc of Fundraising Exec, Women in Financial Devel, Planned Giving Group. **BUSINESS ADDRESS:** Artists' Agent & Professional Fund Raising Consultant, Bailer Studios, 104 E 40th St, New York, NY 10016.

BAILER, KERMIT GAMALIEL
Attorney. **PERSONAL:** Born Apr 17, 1921, Detroit, MI; son of Lloyd E and Mabel E; married Penelope N Naylor; children: Mary Margaret Hill, Byron, Kelly, Ryan. **EDUCATION:** Wayne State Univ Law School, LLB 1949. **CAREER:** Univ S Dept of Housing & Urban Devel, asst admin 1963-67; City of Los Angeles, Berkeley CA, housing consultant 1968-75; Peat, Marwick & Mitchell, consultant 1969-70; City of Detroit MI, corporation counsel 1975-77; Ford Motor Co, sr trial counsel. **HONORS/ACHIEVEMENTS:** Pres Metro Detroit Youth Council 1980-84; pres Kenneth Jewell Chorale 1982-84; bd mem Detroit Symhony Orchestra 1986-; "Criminal Law Dev," Wayne Univ Law Review 1960; "Amendments to Age Act," Wake Forest Law Review; "Discrimination in Employment Legislation" 1980. **MILITARY SERVICE:** USAF 1st lt 1943-45. **BUSINESS ADDRESS:** Senior Trial Counsel, Ford Motor Co, 1 Parklane Blvd, Suite 300, PTW, Dearborn, MI 48126.

BAILEY, A. PETER
Editor. **PERSONAL:** Born Feb 24, 1938, Columbus, GA; children: Malcolm R. **EDUCATION:** Attended, Howard Univ, New Sch for Social Rsch. **CAREER:** Ebony Mag Johnson Pub Co, former assoc editor; Black Enterprise Mag NY, assoc editor. **ORGANIZATIONS:** Fndg mem Orgn Afro-Amer Unity; mem CORE Harlem Rent Strike Com; vet of 1960 human rights movement; contrib to numerous mags; made numerous public appearances; mem nominating comm Tony Awds 1975-76; chmn Awds Com AuDelco Awds. **HONORS/ACHIEVEMENTS:** Awd Anti-Narcotic Com 1971; Silver Medal Awd NY Chap Pub Relations Soc Amer Inc 1971. **MILITARY SERVICE:** AUS 1956-59. **BUSINESS ADDRESS:** Associate Editor, Reach Inc, 1230 5th Ave, New York, NY 10029.

BAILEY, ADRIENNE YVONNE
Foundation administrator, educator. **PERSONAL:** Born Nov 24, 1944, Chicago, IL; daughter of Leroy Bailey and Julia Spalding Bailey. **EDUCATION:** Mundelein Coll, BA 1966; Wayne State Univ, MEd 1968; Northwestern Univ, PhD 1973. **CAREER:** Chicago Bd of Educ, Deneen Elementary School, teacher Social Studies, English, French, Math 1966-67; So Shore YMCA, Chicago IL, neighborhood youth corps supvr 1967; Circle Maxwell YMCA, Chicago IL, program coordinator 1967-68; Detroit Bd of Educ, substitute teacher 1968-69; Gov Office of Human Resources, Chicago IL, educ coordinator 1969-71; Northwestern Comm Educ Proj, Northwestern Univ, univ coordinator 1972-73; Chicago Comm Trust, Chicago IL, sr staff assoc 1973-81; The Coll Bd NY, vice pres acad affairs 1981-. **ORGANIZATIONS:** Mem Gov Educ Adv Comm 1983-87,Natl Comm on Secondary Schooling for Hispanics 1983-85, Educ & Career Devel Advisory Comm Natl Urban league 1982-, visiting comm Grad School of Educ Harvard Univ 1977-83; advisory panel Phi Delta Kappa Gallup Poll of the Publics Attitudes Toward Public Educ 1984; policy comm School of Educ Northwestern Univ 1983-; bd of trustees Hazen Found, New Haven CT, 1977-87; bd of trustees So Educ Found, Atlanta GA, 1983-; Natl Task Force on State Efforts to Achieve Sex Equity 1980-83, chmn advisory comm Council on Found Internship & Fellowship Program for Minorities & Women 1980-82; adv comm Inst for Educ Finance & Govt Stanford Univ 1980-85; bd of dir Assoc of Black Found Exec 1975-87; mem IL State Bd of Educ 1974-81, pres 1978-79; Natl Assn of State Bds of Educ; commiss 1974-81, steering comm 1974-79, e xec comm 1977-75, 1978-79 Educ Commiss of the States; Natl Assessment of Educ Program Policy Comm 1976-80; task force Desegregation Strategies Project 1976-81; bd of dir Council on Foundations 86; META 86; editorial bd, The Kappan (Phi Delta Kappan); mem Governor's Advisory Comm on Black Affairs, New York, co-chair, Educ sub-Committee 1986-; mem, bd of dir The Negro Ensemble, New York 1987-; mem, bd of trustees Marymount Coll 1988-89; mem, bd of trustees The Foundation Center 1989-. **HONORS/ACHIEVEMENTS:** Merit Award, NW Alumni Assoc 1981; Diamond Jubilee Recognition, Phi Delta Kappa 1981; Certificate of Recognition, Phi Delta Kappa NW Univ Chapter 1980; Salute IL Serv, Federal Savings & Loan Bank 1980; Meritorious Serv Award, Educ Commission of the State NAEP 1980; Human Relations Award, IL Educ Assn 1980; attendance at White House Celebration for the Signing of S210 Creating a Dept of Educ, The White House 1979; Kizzy Award for Outstanding Contributions in Educ 1979; Outstanding Achievement Award in Educ, YWCA of Metro Chicago 1978; Distinguished Serv Award, Ed Commission of the State 1977; 1 of 10 Outstanding Young Citizens Award, Chicago Jaycees 1976; Community Motivation Award HU MA BE Karate Assoc 1975; 1 of 10 Outstanding Young Persons Award, IL Jaycees 1975; 1 of 100 Outstanding Black Women in Amer Award, Operation PUSH 1975; Commencement Speaker Mundelein Coll 19 75; Image Award for Outstanding Contributions in Field of Educ, League of Black Women 1974; Recognition Award, Black Achiever of Indust YMCA of Metro Chicago 1974; TTT Fellowship, Northwestern Univ 1971-73; MDEA Inst in French, Univ of ME 1966; numerous publications including, "Comm Coll Capability Project (A Statewide & Demonstration Project)" IL Bd of Higher Educ 1972, "Citizens in Public Ed in Chicago" Citizen Action in Educ 1976, "Agenda for Action" Educ Leadership 1984; "Top 100 Black Business & Professional Women," Dollars & Sense Magazine, 1985; Special Service Award, Natl Alliance of Black School Educators, 1987. **HOME ADDRESS:** 2951 S King Dr Apt 911, Chicago, IL 60616. **BUSINESS ADDRESS:** Vice President Acad Affairs, The College Board, 45 Columbus Ave, New York, NY 10023.

BAILEY, AGNES JACKSON
Educator. **PERSONAL:** Born Aug 18, 1931, Dallas, TX; divorced. **EDUCATION:** San Jose State Univ, BA 1951. **CAREER:** Hanford Joint Union High School, instructor 1954-58; Sacramento Sr High School, instructor 1959-74; California Youth Authority N Reception Center Clinic, math consultant 1967; Valley Area Constrn Opportunity Program, consultant & tutorial specialist 1970-; Sacramento Sr High School, Sacramento City Unified School Dist, counselor 1974-. **ORGANIZATIONS:** Mem CA Tchrs Assn 1954-; life mem Natl Educ Assn 1965; Sacramento City Tchrs Assn; pres Hanford HS Tchrs Assn 1957-58; mem CA Math Cncl 1956-; mem NAACP; Alpha Kappa Alpha; Delta Kappa Gamma Soc for Women in Educ; Amer Assn of Univ Women 1954-69. **HONORS/ACHIEVEMENTS:** First Black hs tchr at Hanford HS 1954; 2nd Black HS tchr in Sac City Unified Sch Dist 1959; honored by Stanford Univ Coll of Engrg 1966; Outstanding Secondary Educator of Amer 1975. **BUSINESS ADDRESS:** Counselor, Sacramento Sr HS, 2315 34 St, Sacramento, CA 95817.

BAILEY, ARTHUR
Government administrator. **PERSONAL:** Born in Wilkinsburg, PA; son of William Henry Bailey and Winifred Towers Bailey. **EDUCATION:** Pittsburgh Acad, 1947-49; Carnegie Inst of Tech, 1949-55; Dept of Agr Grad Sch Washington DC, 1955-56; Dept of Interior, Mgmt Training Prog 1955-56. **CAREER:** Dept of Interior Bureau of Mines, admin asst 1956-58, purchasing agent 1958-60; Holmes & Narver Inc, sec 1964-65; NASA Pasadena, CA, contract asst 1966-68; Social Security Admin, claims rep 1968-73, field rep 1974-81, claims rep 1981-. **ORGANIZATIONS:** Actor Pittsburgh Playhouse 1958-59; field rep journalist, public speaker Social Security Admin 1974-83; dir of public rel Black Porsche Inc 1976-78; mem, parliamentarian 1979-82, historian 1983-84 BPI 1973-; mem Porsche Club of Amer 1981-; mem bd of directors Federal Employees West Credit Union, Los Angeles, CA, 1986-; volunteer/coordinator Joint Action Community Services, Inc (c/o Job Corps), Los Angeles, CA, 1987-. **HONORS/ACHIEVEMENTS:** Sustained Superior Performance Awd Corps of Engrs 1960-61; Outstanding Performance Awd Socical Security Admin Huntington Park CA 1976; Superior Performance Awd Social Security Admin Los Angeles CA 1984; Outstanding Performance Award, Univ Village Office, Los Angeles, CA, Social Security Admin 1988; Public Service Award in Recognition of 40 years of service in the govt of USA, Commr of Social Security, Baltimore, MD, 1988; singer/tenor Downtown Chorale, Pittsburgh, PA, performed in 2-3 concerts a year in addition to performances with the Pittsburgh Symphony Orchestra and Wheeling Symphony Orchestra. **MILITARY SERVICE:** USAF sgt 1945-46. **BUSINESS ADDRESS:** Social Insurance Rep, Social Security Admin, 2021 S Flower St, Los Angeles, CA 90007.

BAILEY, BOB CARL
Business executive. **PERSONAL:** Born Oct 13, 1935, Colbert Co, AR; married Odessa Vaughn; children: Ramona, Tori, Jurado. **EDUCATION:** Attended AL A&M Univ Huntsville 1963. **CAREER:** WJOI Radio, announcer (1st Black) 1958-62; Bailey & Co, owner 1965-; Zelke Dodge, full-time auto salesman (1st Black in Muscle Shoals area) 1968-72; Bailey Used Cars, owner 1969-78; WOWL TV, full-time TV host (1st Black in Muscle Shoals area) 1975-76; WTQX Radio Sta Selma, AL, owner 1979-; Gov of AL, spec cabinetlevel post 1980-81; WZZA Radio/Muscle Shoals Broadcasting, owner/pres/gen mgr 1977-. **ORGANIZATIONS:** Mem Amer Legion Post 303 1969-; mem IBPOEW 1971-; pres Colbert Co Voter's League 1975-80; pres Shoals Area Bus Assn Inc; treas Coalition of ConcernedCitizens & Or-

ganizations 1987-. **HONORS/ACHIEVEMENTS:** Outstanding Perf as Broadcstr WEUP Radio & JLP Assoc Huntsville, AL 1973; Contrib Humna Dignity & Civil Rights Tri-Co Br NAACP 1974; Outstanding Businessman Campaign for Equal Devel 1975; Outstanding Achieve in Broadcasting Muscle Shoals Tuskegee Alumni Assn 1976; 1st Black Roastee of Muscle Shoals AreaLa Charmettes & Bona Fides Civic & Soc Club 1976; Ken Knight Award Black Radio & Music Jack the Rapper-Family Affair 1979; Achieve in Communications Omega Psi Phi Frat Inc 1979; Voice of Black People Kappa Nu Lambda Chap Alpha Phi Alpha 1980; Outstanding Contributions to Muscle Shoals Broadcasting Univ of North AL Broadcasting Assoc 1982; Outstanding Communications Coverage to Comm Shoals Talent Bank Inc 1984; Dedication to Comm Serv Rufus Slack Jr Scholarship Org 1985; Community Achievement Awd Muscle Shoals Area Chap Blacks in Govt 1985. **MILITARY SERVICE:** AUS Sgt 1953-56. **BUSINESS ADDRESS:** President/General Manager, WZZA Radio Muscle Shoals Brdcs, 1570 Woodmont Dr, Tuscumbia, AL 35674.

BAILEY, CALVIN
Artist. **PERSONAL:** Born Jun 14, 1909, Norfolk, VA; children: Calvin Jr (deceased), Cuma Bailey Barkley. **EDUCATION:** Newark NJ School of Fine Arts, 1932. **CAREER:** Amsterdam Newspaper in NYC, artist; Young & Rubican, caricature artist; NBC, caricature artist; KSAN, "Musi-Cal Sketch Book"TV show 1956; Universal Studios, artist 1969; United Airlines, caricature artist 1975-76. **HONORS/ACHIEVEMENTS:** Has captured caricatures of some of the great talents of our time including Bill Bojangles Robinson, Chief Justice Earl Warren, Edward G Robinson, Ella mae Bailey, Lena Horn; deisgning celebrity Christmas cards illustrating song title & brochure covers offering comm serv as a concerned citizen; has received many certificates of appreciation and awds of recognition. **HOME ADDRESS:** 3866 Willow Crest Ave, Apt #2, Studio City, CA 91604.

BAILEY, CHAUNCEY WENDELL, JR.
Editor. **PERSONAL:** Born Oct 20, 1949, Oakland, CA; married Robin. **EDUCATION:** Merritt College, Oakland CA, 1967; San Jose State, San Jose, CA, BJ 1972; Columbia Univ NYC, Summer Prog Minority Journalists 1974; Penn State Coll PA, minority Journalism speaker 1983-84. **CAREER:** Hartford Ct Courant, reporter 1974-77; San Francisco Sun Reporter, reporter 1972-74, Oakland Post Newspaper Group, reporter 1972; United Press Intl Chicago, reporter 1977; CA Voice, Oakland CA, editor 1978-80; COMPRAND, Inc, Chicago public relations 1980-81; Rep Gus Savage (D-IL), press sec 1982; Detroit News, Detroit, MI, reporter and editorial page consultant. **HONORS/ACHIEVEMENTS:** Exec dir Black Press Inst Chicago; mem Natl Assn Black Journalists; mem Natl Alliance Third World Journalists; mem Detroit Chapter NAACP; writer New Deliberations magazine (black political analysis), writer Black Press Review (overview key news items relating to blacks). **BUSINESS ADDRESS:** Reporter and Editorial Page Columnist, The Detroit News, 615 Lafayette, Detroit, MI 48231.

BAILEY, CLARENCE WALTER
Business executive. **PERSONAL:** Born Sep 25, 1933, Longview, TX; married Mavis Lean Blankenship; children: Sherry Lenel Smith. **EDUCATION:** Wiley Clg,bS 1954; Drake Univ, Mstrs 1959. **CAREER:** Baileys Ins Agency, mgr 1966-. **ORGANIZATIONS:** Life mem Million Dollar Round Table 1973-; dir Oil Belt Asso of Life Underwriters 1967-; sec LISD Sch Bd 1984-; dir Good Shephard Med Ctr 1983-. **HONORS/ACHIEVEMENTS:** Mem Civitan Club 1978-; dir Jr Achvmnt 1984-; Silver Beaver Awd BSA 1980; top ten prod Pres Cncl NWL 1971-; edctn Phi Delta Kappa 1981-; outstndng citizen awd NAACP 1978. **MILITARY SERVICE:** USAF E5 1954-57. **HOME ADDRESS:** 2307 Lilly St, Longview, TX 75602. **BUSINESS ADDRESS:** Divisional Sales Manager, Natl Western Life Ins Co, PO Box 7606, Longview, TX 75607.

BAILEY, CURTIS DARNELL
Specialist in marketing and communications. **PERSONAL:** Born May 21, 1954, Philadelphia, PA; son of Helena Bailey. **EDUCATION:** Temple Univ, BA 1976; Atlanta Univ, MBA 1978. **CAREER:** Benton & Bowles Inc, asst account exec 1978-79; Pennwalt Corp, advertising mgr 1979-84; DuPont Co, marketing communications specialist 1984-87; marketing and communications consultant 1987-89. **ORGANIZATIONS:** Mem Kappa Alpha Psi Frat 1983-; dir of communications Brandywine Professional Assoc 1986-87. **HONORS/ACHIEVEMENTS:** Bell Ringer Awd, Best Newsletter Business & Professional Advertising Assns, 1982, 1983; Top Ten Readership Ad Awd Chemical Processing Magazine, 1983, 1985. **HOME ADDRESS:** 2412 Aspen St, Philadelphia, PA 19130.

BAILEY, D'ARMY
Attorney. **PERSONAL:** Born Nov 29, 1941, Memphis, TN. **EDUCATION:** Clark Univ, AB 1964; Yale Univ, LLB 1967; Attended, Souther Univ 1959-62, Boston Univ 1964-65. **CAREER:** Field Found NY, prog adv 1970; City Council Bkly CA, 1971-73; Private Practice, attorney 1970-. **ORGANIZATIONS:** Staff atty Neighborhood Legal Assts Found 1968-70; natl dir Law Students Civil Rights Rsch Cncl 1967-68; bd dir Vollitine Boys Club 1974-; Council Legal Ed Prof Resp 1969-70. **BUSINESS ADDRESS:** Attorney, 161 Jefferson Ste 901, Memphis, TN 38103.

BAILEY, DIDI GISELLE
Medical doctor. **PERSONAL:** Born Mar 14, 1948, New York, NY; children: Jordan, Eleanor, Pete. **EDUCATION:** Howard Univ, BS 1968, MD 1972; Howard Univ Hosp, Cert Gen Psych 1975. **CAREER:** District of Columbia Govt, forensic psychiatrist 1974-79, med consult disability dept 1979-80; State of CA, med consult disability dept 1981-85; Didi G Bailey MD, psychiatrist 1975-. **ORGANIZATIONS:** Mem adv bd Alameda County Mental Health 1981-; mem No CA Black Women Physicians 1981-. **BUSINESS ADDRESS:** Psychiatrist, Didi G Bailey MD, 2700 E 14th St, Ste 31, Oakland, CA 94601.

BAILEY, DONN FRITZ
Educational administrator. **PERSONAL:** Born Feb 26, 1932, New Castle, IN; son of Walter F Bailey and Thelma Cottman Bailey; married Andrea June Bess; children: Donna, Marta. **EDUCATION:** IN Univ, BS 1954, MA 1962; PA State Univ, PhD 1974. **CAREER:** Chicago Bd of Educ Div of Speech Corr, speech therapist 1954-66; Center for Inner City Studies Chicago, asst dir 1966-68; PA State Univ Speech Comm Dept, research assoc 1968-70; Center for Inner City Studies Chicago, asst dir/asst prof 1970-74, dir/prof 1974-. **ORGANIZATIONS:** Vice pres of trustees Abraham Lincoln Center 1974-; exec dir Natl Black Assn for Speech Lang & Hearing 1978-80; sec bd of dir Coretta Scott King YWCA 1979-; chmn Comm on Communication Behaviors Amer Speech Lang & Hearing Assn 1976-; chmn, Monitoring Commn for Desegregation Implementation 1985-; chmn, brd, Natl Black Assoc for Speech, Language, Hearing; chmn, brd of dir, Open Lands Project 1987-; chmn 1st Congressional Dist Task Force on Educ 1988-. **HONORS/ACHIEVEMENTS:** Mem Kappa Alpha Psi Frat; Ford Advanced Study Grant Ford Foundation 1969-70. **MILITARY SERVICE:** AUS Capt 1954-56. **BUSINESS ADDRESS:** Director/Professor, Northeastern IllinoisUniv, 700 E Oakwood Blvd, Center for Inner City Studies, Chicago, IL 60653.

BAILEY, GRACIE MASSENBERG
Educator. **PERSONAL:** Born Feb 25, 1936, Waverly, VA; married Erling Sr; children: LaVetta F, Erling Jr. **EDUCATION:** VA State Coll, BS 1958; VA State Coll, Elem Ed 1963, Computer Mgmt 1969, MEd 1970; VA Polytechnic Inst and State Univ, DEd 1983. **CAREER:** VA State Coll, sec 1958-62; Amelia Cty School Bd, teacher 1958-60; Hartford Variable Annuity Life Insurance Co, salesperson 1960-79; Sussex Cty School Bd, teacher 1961-63; Dinwiddie Cty School Bd, business educ teacher 1963-74; Richard Bland Coll, dir of personnel, assoc prof business, asst to pres AA/EEO 1974-, registrar 1986-. **ORGANIZATIONS:** Mem Sussex Ed Assoc 1961-63; sec Dinwiddie Ed Assoc 1963-74; sec, treas Erling Baily Elect Contr 1966; mem & recording sec Amer Bus Women Assoc Dinwiddie Charter Chap 1971-84; mem Amer Assoc of Univ Profs 1974-79; mem Amer Assoc of Affirmative Action 1976-; mem adv cncl Educ Computing for the State of VA 1976-80; mem Coll and Univ Personnel Assoc 1978-; mem & rep Natl & VA Assoc for Women in Higher Ed 1978-84; recording sec VA Admissions Cncl on Black Concerns 1984-; mem Human Rights Comm for Hiram Davis Medical Ctr 1986-; mem VA Assoc of Coll Registrars and Admissions Officers, Southern Assoc of Collegiate Registrars and Admissions Officers, Amer Assoc of Collegiate Registrars and Admissions Officers 1986-. **HONORS/ACHIEVEMENTS:** Salutatorian Sussex Cty Training School 1954; Cert & Plaque of Apprec Future Bus Leaders of Amer 1972-74; Achievement Awds Dinwiddie Ed Assoc 1973-74; Outstanding Ed of Amer 1975; Listed in Who's Who in Amer 1980; Disting Amer 1981; Listed in Who's Who in the South & Southwest 1982, Who's Who of Women 1984. **BUSINESS ADDRESS:** Assistant to the President, Richard Bland Coll, Route 1 Box 77 A, Petersburg, VA 23805.

BAILEY, HAROLD
Educator. **PERSONAL:** Born Oct 15, 1946, McKinney, TX; married Patricia; children: Brandon. **EDUCATION:** Univ NM, BS 1969, MA 1971, PhD 1975. **CAREER:** Univ of NM, physical educ teacher, basketball/track coach 1969-70, asst dir, dir child devel program 1970-71, prof 1971-. **ORGANIZATIONS:** Consult Equal Empl Oppor; Human Rels; pub spkr Black Studies & Black Athletes; exec prod Black Experience; exec dir Uhuru Sasa African Dance Troupe 1974-; Afro-Studies Youth Enrichment Prog 1974-; karate instr AAS Summer Yth Prog 1970-; faculty adv Black Student Union Univ NM 1973-; dir Afro-Amer Studies 1974-; state chmn NM Black Studies Consortium; exec bd mem natl Cncl Black Studies 1975-; chmn Univ NM EEO Com 1974-77; life mem Omega Psi Phi Frat; NM Adv Com US Commn on Civil Rights Albq Black Coalition; Intl Black Merit Acad; NAACP; Natl Assn of Black Prof. **HONORS/ACHIEVEMENTS:** Outstanding Young Men Amer 1974; Paul Robeson Awd BALSA 1976; Omega Man Yr Omega Psi Phi 8th Dist 1977; apptd Hon Judge Lt Gov NM 1976; Watusi Awd 1975; Outstanding Dedication & Serv Sr Citz 1976; Outstanding Contrib Serv AAS Univ NM 1975. **BUSINESS ADDRESS:** Professor, Univ of NM, 1819 Roma NE, Albuquerque, NM 87131.

BAILEY, HARRY A., JR.
Educator. **PERSONAL:** Born Dec 19, 1932, Fort Pierce, FL; married Mary L; children: Harry III, Larry B. **EDUCATION:** FL A&M Univ, BA 1954; Univ KS, MA 1960, PhD 1964. **CAREER:** Univ of KS, asst instructor, 1960-62, asst instructor western civilization 1962-64, instr sociology, 1964; Temple Univ, asst prof, 1964-68, assoc prof & chmn dept political science 1970-73, prof dept political science 1973-75, prof & dir master of pub admin prog 1975-. **ORGANIZATIONS:** Mem Amer Polit Sci Assn; Amer Soc Pub Adminstrn; Ctr Study Pres PA Polit Sci & Pub Adminstrn Assn 1970-72; vice pres Northeastern Sci Assn 1971-72; pres bd gov Temple Univ Faculty Club 1972-73. **HONORS/ACHIEVEMENTS:** Editor "Negro Politics in Amer" Columbus OH Charles Merrill Publ 1967; co-editor "Ethnic Group Politics" Columbus OH Charles Merrill Publ 1969; Leonard D White Awd Com Amer Polit Sci Assn 1974-75; Pi Sigma Alpha Natl Polit Sci Hon Soc; Danforth Assoc 1975-81; editorial bd Journal Politics 1975-76; editor "Classics of the Am Pres" Oak Park IL Moore Publ Co 1980. **MILITARY SERVICE:** AUS 1st lt 1955-57, 2nd lt 1954-55. **BUSINESS ADDRESS:** Professor/Dir, TempleUniv, Dept Political Science, Philadelphia, PA 19122.

BAILEY, JACQUELINE
Social worker. **PERSONAL:** Born Jan 11, 1961; married Jonathan Kenneth Jefferson. **EDUCATION:** Rutgers Univ, BA, SW 1979-83; Atlanta Univ, MSW 1983-85. **CAREER:** Rutgers Univ Livingston Coll, student adv 1980-81, teaching asst 1982,83; Children Aid & Adoption Soc, childcare worker 1981-82; Rutgers Univ Sweet Shop,night mgr 1982-83; Fulton Cty Bd of Commiss, internee 1984; Atlanta Univ School of Social Work, treas 1984-85; Urban League for Bergen Cty, internee 1984-85; Atlanta Univ Payroll Dept, payroll asst 1984-, grad student 1983-, social worker. **ORGANIZATIONS:** Mem Urban League for Bergen Cty 1984-85; alumnus Rutgers Univ, Rutgers Univ School of Social Work, COOL JC Youth Group, Corp Social Workers at Atlanta Univ; dir teen pregnancy prog Mount Carmel Guild 1985; dir of social svcs, dir of admission New Community Extended Care Facility Inc 1986; youth counselor Refuge Church of Christ 1987. **HONORS/ACHIEVEMENTS:** Recipient COOL JC Scholarship, Atlanta Univ School of Social Work Scholarship; Deans List Rutgers Univ 1982, Atlanta Univ 1983,85.

BAILEY, JAMES L.
Professional athlete. **PERSONAL:** Born May 21, 1957, Dublin, GA; married Pamela Adams. **EDUCATION:** Rutgers Univ, BS Business, 1979. **CAREER:** Seattle, basketball player; NJ Nets, basketball player; Houston Rocket, basketball player; NY Nicks, basketball player. **HONORS/ACHIEVEMENTS:** Named to NBA Coaches All-Amer team in final two years. **BUSINESS ADDRESS:** NY Nicks, Madison Sq Garden, 4 Pennsylvania Plaza, New York, NY 10001.

BAILEY, JAMES W.
Judge. **PERSONAL:** Born Nov 12, 1922, Roanoke, VA; married Mary E; children: 4 children. **EDUCATION:** VA State Coll, AB 1942; Boston Univ, LLB 1948. **CAREER:** Private Practice, attorney 1948; Asst USDA, 1950-51; Boston Juvenile Ct, clerk pro tempore 1953-59; Comm MA, asst atty gen 1959-64; Boston Univ Sch Law, clin prof 1965-72; 3rd Dist

Ct Eastern & Middlesex, judge. **ORGANIZATIONS:** Mem former cncl Boston Bar Assn; former bd Natl Legal Aid & Defender Assn; former counsel Boston Br NAACP; mem Alpha Phi Alpha Frat; Phi Alpha Delta Legal Frat. **MILITARY SERVICE:** AUS 1942-46. **BUSINESS ADDRESS:** Judge, 3rd Dist Ct Estrn Middlesex, 40 Thorndike St, Cambridge, MA 02141.

BAILEY, JERRY DEAN
International business executive. **PERSONAL:** Born Sep 04, 1950, Colquitt, GA; son of Clarence Bailey and Wyolene Webb Bailey; married Cheryl Y Gould-Bailey, Aug 30, 1972; children: Jelani N Gould-Bailey, Camilah A Gould-Bailey. **EDUCATION:** Ohio University, Athens, OH, BA (cum laude), 1972; Boston Univ Law School, Boston, MA, JD, 1975; Massachusetts Inst of Technology, Cambridge, MA, MBA, 1979. **CAREER:** Boston Juvenile Ct, Boston, MA, asst clerk, 1975-77; Hewlett Packard Co, Palo Alto, CA, financial analyst, 1979-81; RJR Nabisco Inc, Winston-Salem, NC, assoc tax counsel, 1981-83; Winston-Salem State Univ, instructor in corp finance, 1982-86; RJR Nabisco Inc, Winston-Salem, NC, intl tax mgr, 1983-87; RJR Nabisco Inc, Atlanta, GA, sr intl tax counsel, 1987-89; World Trade Inst, seminar speaker, 1987-89. **ORGANIZATIONS:** Mem, Massachusetts Bar, 1975-89; area governor, pres, Toastmasters, 1980-89; treasurer, bd mem, Winston-Salem Junior Achievement, 1982-85; chapter pres, Optimist Club, 1984-87; mem, Tax Executives Institute, 1984-89; chmn, Soccer League, East Winston Optimist, 1986-87. **BUSINESS ADDRESS:** Dir, Intl Taxes, RJR Nabisco Inc, 300 Galleria Pkwy, Atlanta, GA 30339.

BAILEY, JOSEPH ALEXANDER, II
Physician. **PERSONAL:** Born Jul 22, 1935, Pine Bluff, AR; children: Ryan, Jana, Joseph III, Johathan, Jerad, Jordan. **EDUCATION:** Univ Of MI Ann Arbor, undrgrad 1953-55; Morehouse Clg, BS 1957; Meharry Med Sch, Med Degree 1961. **CAREER:** Los Angeles Co Hosp, internship 1961-62 hahnemann hosp phil pA, chf res 1964-66; st hosp for crippled children pA, chief res 1966-67; hosp for Joint Diseases NY, NY, sr res 1967-68. **ORGANIZATIONS:** Asso staff & prof San Bernardino Co Gen Hosp; independent med examiner for St of Ca; asso staff St Betnardines Hosp; chief of gen sect Acdmy of Ortho-Neuro Soc. **HONORS/ACHIEVEMENTS:** Flw Med Gen John Hopkins Hosp MA 1968-69; fellow Ortho Sur John Hopkins Hosp Baltimore 1968-69; fellow Am Clg of Surgeons 1971-; diplomate Am Bd ofOrtho Surgeons 1971; listed in best Drs of Am 1979; Comm Ldr Awd from Noteworthy Americans 1978; awd Black Voice News 1985. **MILITARY SERVICE:** USAF capt 1962-64. **BUSINESS ADDRESS:** President, JA Bailey II M D Prof Corp, 399 E Highland Ave #501, San Bernardino, CA 92404.

BAILEY, LAWRENCE R., SR.
Attorney. **PERSONAL:** Born Mar 31, 1918, Panama, CZ; son of Charles Wesley Bailey and Alma Smalls Bailey; married Norma Jean Thomas, May 20, 1961; children: Lawrence R Jr, Bruce, Lamont, Susan. **EDUCATION:** Howard Univ, AB, 1939, JD, 1942. **CAREER:** Asst Counsel to City Council Pres, New York City, 1952-53; Vice Chmn, Metropolitan Transportation Authority, 1970-present. **ORGANIZATIONS:** Dir & Pres, Harlem Lawyer's Assn; Regional Dir, Natl Bar Assn; Chmn, Constitutional Revision Comm; Mem, Amer Bar Assn; New York Lawyer's Assn; Arbitrator, Amer Arbitration Assn; Legal Counsel, Jamaica Comm Corp; Queen's Co Youth Athletic Center, Merrick Comm Center; Counsel & Mem of Bd, Queen's Urban League; Vice Chmn, Metropolitan Transportation Authority, New York State; Bd of Dir, Legal Aid Soc; NAACP; ACLU; Citizens Union Interview Panel. **HONORS/ACHIEVEMENTS:** Queen's Urban League Dedication; Soc of Afro-Amer Transit Employees, Adam Clayton Powell Award; Adam Clayton Powell Memorial Award, 1972; Humanitarian Award, Kennedy King Democratic Club; Alumni Award, Howard Univ; Achievement Award, Old Timers Jamaica Inc, 1968; Achievement Award, Kappa Alpha Psi Fraternity, 1952. **MILITARY SERVICE:** AUS, Chief Warrant Officer, Judge Advocate Dept, 1943-47; Bronze Star Medal. **BUSINESS ADDRESS:** Assistant Council, Pres Cty Cncl Rudolph Halley, 360 W 125 St, New York, NY 10027.

BAILEY, MAROLYN LESLIE
Business executive. **PERSONAL:** Born Jan 23, 1953, Philadelphia, PA. **EDUCATION:** Yale Univ, BA 1974; Harvard Business School, MBA 1978. **CAREER:** Philadelphia Cultural Alliance, prog dir 1974-76; Citibank, acct officer 1978-80; Harvard Business School Club, recruitment coord; Media Entertainment Ind, financial marketing consultant; Bedford Stuyvesant Restoration Corp, group mgr. **ORGANIZATIONS:** Mem Harvard Club of NY; mem Marketing Devel Assn; guest managing editor Mademoiselle Magazine 1972. **BUSINESS ADDRESS:** Group Manager, Bedford Stuyvesant Restoration, 1368 Fulton St 3rd Fl, Brooklyn, NY 11201.

BAILEY, MILDRED T.
Educator. **PERSONAL:** Born Oct 26, 1920, Athens, AL; married George W Bailey; children: Myrtle Lucille. **EDUCATION:** Talladega Coll, BMus 1942; Northwestern Univ, MMus 1952; Attended, KY State Coll, St Louis Univ, Univ of MO, WA Univ. **CAREER:** KY State Coll, instructor, 1942-45; Lincoln Univ, instructor, 1945-47; Univ of St Louis, instructor, registrar music & arts, 1950-54; Central Baptist Church, organist dir of choir 1950-; Bates Elementary School, classroom teacher & choir dir 1955-63; Turner Middle School, instructor vocal music & theory 1963-75, vocal music consultant 1975-. **ORGANIZATIONS:** Conducted guitar workshop for tchrs at Learning Ctr & guitar classes for Adult Educ 1974-; conducted ch music workshop for Regional Meeting of Natl Assn of Negro Musicians 1975; conducts music readiness prog at Music Ctr; training DCSAR (Gov Agency) Choir; mem NEA; MO State Tchrs Assn; St Louis Tchrs Assn;Ferrier Harris Home for the Aged; Annie Malone Children's Home; HELP Inc; Arsania M Williams Reading Club; Alpha Kappa Alpha. **HONORS/ACHIEVEMENTS:** Awd (silver tray) Epsilon Lambda Chap Alpha Phi Alpha 1968; plaque Chancel Choir Central Bapt Ch 1968; plaque Union Memorial United Methodist Ch 1968; Certificate Outstanding St Louis Club Women of Yr; 1st Prize Miss MO State Fedtn of Colored Women's Clubs 1970; listed Leaders of Amer Elem & Secondary Educ1971; Cert of Appreciation for directing Black Hist Pageant "Up From Slavery"; nominated to receive Outstanding Club Women of Yr City Federation of Colored Women's Clubs 1975; various other awds & citations. **BUSINESS ADDRESS:** Vocal Music Consul, Turner Middle School, 4235 W Kennerly Ave, St Louis, MO 63113.

BAILEY, MONA HUMPHRIES
Educational administrator. **PERSONAL:** Born Dec 14, 1932; married William Peter Bailey; children: Peter Govan, Christopher Evans. **EDUCATION:** FL A&M Univ Tallahassee, BS 1954; OR State Univ Corvalis, MS 1962. **CAREER:** Meany-Madrona Middle School, Seattle WA, principal, 1970-73; Univ of WA, instructor, 1973-74; Eckstein Middle School, Seattle WA, principal appointee, 1974-75; WA State Supt of Public Instuction, asst supt, 1974-. **ORGANIZATIONS:** Bd dirs Totem Girl Scout Cncl Seattle 1977-; chmn adv com Seattle Oppors Industrialization Ctr 1978; mem adv bd United Negro Coll Fund Inc Seattle1978-; Commn mem Gov's Commn on Criminal Justice 1974-; bd of trustees Pacific Sci Ctr Seattle 1975-; natl pres Delta Sigma Theta 1980. **HONORS/ACHIEVEMENTS:** Disting Serv Field of Educ Inner City Awd Carnation Co 1973-74; Achievement Awd Les Dames Bridge Club Seattle 1974; Disting achievement Serv to Youth Awd The Links Inc 20th Natl Assn Seattle 1976; Disting Comm Serv Awd Benefit Guild Seattle 1978. **BUSINESS ADDRESS:** Assistant Superintendent, WA State Supt of Pub Instn, Old Capitol Bldg FB-11, Olympia, WA 98504.

BAILEY, PEARL
Singer. **PERSONAL:** Born Mar 29, 1918, Newport News, VA; married Louis Bellson Jr. **CAREER:** Performed with Noble Sissle, Cootie Williams, Count Basie; Stage Debut St Louis Woman New York City 1946; Roles on Broadway, House of Flowers, Hello Dolly 1967-68; Motion Picture Roles, Carman Jones, Porgy & Bess, Variety Girl, St Louis Blues, Isn't I Romantic?, That Certain Feeling, All the Fine Young Cannibals, The Landlord, Lost Generation, Norman Is That You?; TV, star on Pearl Bailey Show ABC-TV 1970-71; guest appearances on variousTV programs; Contract Artist, Coral Records, Decca, Columbia Records; Night Club Engagements, Chicago, Hollywood, NYC, Boston, Las Vegas, London 1950-. **ORGANIZATIONS:** Mem ASCAP. **HONORS/ACHIEVEMENTS:** Citation from Mayor John V Lindsay; Donaldson Awd 1956; Entertainer of Yr Awd Cue Magazine 1969; Spl Tony Awd for Hello Dolly 1967-68; March of Dimes Awd 1968; USO Woman of Yr 1969; Nov 1975 joined UN Delegation; author "Raw Pearl" 1969, "Talking to Myself" 1971, "Pearl's Kitchen" 1973, "Duey Tale" 1975, "Hurry Up America & Spit" 1976. **BUSINESS ADDRESS:** c/o William Morris Agency Inc, 1350 Ave of Americas, New York, NY 10019.

BAILEY, RANDALL CHARLES
Minister. **PERSONAL:** Born May 26, 1947, Malden, MA; son of Mr Charles C Bailey and Ms Lorraine Margolis Bailey; married Dorothy Jean Lewis Bailey, Apr 07, 1973; children: Omari Lewis Bailey, Imani Akilah Bailey. **EDUCATION:** Brandeis Univ, Waltham, MA, BA (cum laude), 1969; Univ of Chicago, IL, AM, Social Serv Admin, 1972; Candler School of Theology, Atlanta, GA, MDiv (cum laude), 1979; Emory Univ, Atlanta, GA, PhD, Religion, 1987. **CAREER:** PCSAP Loop College, Chicago, IL, dir of educ prog, 1972-1973; Shelby Co Devel Coord Dept, Memphis, TN, assoc dir, 1973; Atlanta Univ School of Social Work, Atlanta, GA, asst prof, 1973-81; First Cong Church, UCC, Atlanta, GA, asst minister, 1980-81; Interdenominational Theological Center, Atlanta, GA, asst prof, 1981-. **ORGANIZATIONS:** Mem, Black Theology Project, 1986-; co-chair, Afro-Amer Theology & Biblical Hermeneutics Soc of Biblical Lit, 1987-; co-chair, Unity/Renewal Study, COFO/NCCCUSA, 1988-91; mem, Div Educ & Min/NCCCUSA, 1988-91, Bible Translation & Utilization Comm DEM/NCCCUSA, 1988-91, Soc for the Study of Black Religion, 1988-; mem, bd of dir, S DeKalb YMCA. **HONORS/ACHIEVEMENTS:** Distinguished Serv Award, Atlanta Natl Assn of Black Social Workers, 1978; Fellow, Black Doctoral Prog/FTE, 1979-81, 1984-85; "Litany for Beginning," Inauguration of Mayor Andrew Young, 1981; Fellow, United Negro Coll Fund, 1984-85; "1 & 2 Samuel," Standard Video Project, RSV, DEM/NCCCUSA, 1988; author, "Is That Any Name for a Nice Hebrew Boy: Ex 2:10..." JITC, 1989, David in Love and War: The Pursuit of Power in Sam 10-12, 1989. **BUSINESS ADDRESS:** Asst Prof of Old Testament and Hebrew, Interdenominational Theological Center, 671 Beckwith St SW, Atlanta, GA 30314.

BAILEY, ROBERT B., III
Educator. **PERSONAL:** Born Nov 09, 1929, Knoxville, TN. **EDUCATION:** Talladega Coll, BA 1951; Birmingham Univ, MA 1952; Univ Utrecht, PhD 1958; Univ Frankfort, attended 1953-55; Univ Munich, attended 1952-53. **CAREER:** Univ of WI, River Falls WI, instr to prof 1957-; Hamline Univ, St Paul MN, visiting prof 1970-; Univ of WI Dept Sociology, chmn 1965-. **ORGANIZATIONS:** Dir study abroad & progs; legal hypnotist with law firm; bd mem sec Cncl Intl Educ Exchange NY; bd mem Twin Cities Intl Progs for Social Workers & Students Minneapolis/St Paul; bd mem WI Chap Natl Assn Fgn Student Adv; organized Black Studies Prog MN State Prison Stillwater; mem Govs Commn Criminal Rehab. **HONORS/ACHIEVEMENTS:** Fulbright Scholarship to England 1951; Outstanding Educator Amer 1970; listed Who's Who Midwest, Who's Who Educ, Comm Leaders Amer, Intl Scholars Directory, Dictionary Intl Biography, Amer Men Sci. **BUSINESS ADDRESS:** Chmn Dept Sociology, University of WI-River Falls, River Falls, WI 54022.

BAILEY, RONALD W.
Consultant/planner. **PERSONAL:** Born May 21, 1938, Chicago, IL; son of Claude Bailey and Leona Z Smith Alexander; married Florentine Kelly; children: Darlene Butler, Ronald Jr, Charles. **EDUCATION:** Univ of WI, BS 1962; Northeastern IL Univ, MEd 1972; Univ of MI, Mgmt by Objective 1978; John Marshall Law School, Community Law Cert 1979. **CAREER:** Chicago Youth Centers, assoc exec dir; Northeastern IL Univ, instr; United Way of Chicago, planner; City of Chicago, child care manager; Cook County IL, manpower planner; United Way of Dade County, sr consultant, program manager, Community Renewal Soc. **ORGANIZATIONS:** Mem Chicago Urban League 1970-88; co founder/chmn Chicago Black Child Develop 1978-; mem Black Child Dev Inst Washington 1978-, Chicago Blacks in Philanthropy 1984-, Assoc of Black Fund Raising Execs 1984-; mem People United to Save Humanity 1984-88, Assoc Black Fundraising Execs 1986-88; vice pres, Roosevelt PTA; Steering Comm Neighborhood Capitol Budget Group; mem Chicago Council on Urban Affairs, Chicago Workshop on Economic Dev, Chicago Mgmt Assistance Program. **HONORS/ACHIEVEMENTS:** Superior Supervisor Awd SCOPE 1969-70. **MILITARY SERVICE:** AUS Corpl 2 yrs; Good Conduct Medal, Expert Marksman 1962-64. **HOME ADDRESS:** 125 Rice Ave, Bellwood, IL 60153. **BUSINESS ADDRESS:** Program Manager, Community Renewal Society, 332 S Michigan, #500, Chicago, IL 60104.

BAILEY, THURL
Professional athlete. **PERSONAL:** Born Apr 07, 1961, Seat Pleasant, MD. **EDUCATION:** NC State, Comm Major 1983. **CAREER:** Utah Jazz, forward 1983-. **HONORS/ACHIEVEMENTS:** Shot 500 or better from the field in 46 games.

BAILEY, WELTMAN D., SR.
Dentist. **PERSONAL:** Born Jan 26, 1927, Harveil, MO; married Margaret Barber; children: Sandra, Weltman Jr, Peter, Robert. **EDUCATION:** Univ WI, BS 1950; Meharry Med

Coll, DDS 1956; Univ MO, MPA, MPH 1973. **CAREER:** Staff numerous hosps health centers; Private Practice, dentist 1958-. **ORGANIZATIONS:** Mem Natl, Amer Dental Assns; Amer Pub Health Assn; Amer Soc Pub Adminstrn; Natl Rehab Assn; Amer Assn Hosp Dentists Inc; bd dirs Mid-Amer Comprehensive Health Planning Agency 1970-71; Rehab Inst; Reg Health Welfare Council 1969-70; med adv bd MO Div Family Health 1974-; fellow Royal Soc Health; mem Acad Gen Dentistry; Alpha Phi Alpha Frat; YMCA; Urban League; Bapt trustee 1967-. **MILITARY SERVICE:** AUS 1945-47. **BUSINESS ADDRESS:** 2514 E 27 St, Kansas City, MO 64127.

BAILEY, WILLIAM R.
Business executive. **PERSONAL:** Born Feb 19, 1935, Nashville, TN; children: Michelle Maria. **EDUCATION:** TN St Univ, BS 1956, Grad Stds in Guidance. **CAREER:** Metropolitan Pub Schs, tchr 1960-64; Pres War on Poverty Met Pub Schs, work training coord 1964-66; Metropolitan Life Ins Co, sales mgr 1966- 69; Metropolitan Life, sr sales rep 1969-. **ORGANIZATIONS:** Part time inst TN St Univ 1979-81; Sch of Bus; mem Kappa Alpha Psi, TN St Alumni Assoc, Agora Assn Qual; mem Million Dolloar Round Table. **HONORS/ACHIEVEMENTS:** Pres Buddies of Nashvl 1980-82; pres Nashville O I C 1982-84; bd of dir Citizens Savings Bank 1979-; Metro Plng Comm Metro Govt 1979-; mem Dollar-Round Table 1976-; man of the yr Mt Zion Baptist Ch 1969; citizen of the yr Alpha Phi Alpha Frat 1984. **MILITARY SERVICE:** UAS sp4 3 yrs. **HOME ADDRESS:** 2484 Walker Lane, Nashville, TN 37207. **BUSINESS ADDRESS:** Senior Sales Representative, Metropolitan Life Insurance, One Rorton Hills Blvd, Ste 370, Nashville, TN 37212.

BAILEY, WILLIAN H.
Director (corporate). **PERSONAL:** Born Feb 14, 1927, Detroit, MI; married Anna Porter; children: John Robert, Kimberley Ann. **EDUCATION:** Morehouse Coll, BA, 1947. **CAREER:** Count Basie Orchestra, featured vocalist, 1946-50; Las Palmas Theatre, Hollywood CA, entertainer, musical comedy, 1950-51; Natl & Intl Supper Club, tours, 1951-54; Moulin Rouge Hotel, producer, production singer, entertainer, 1955; Las Vegas ABC, CBS, PBS Affiliates, TV producer, 1955-65, 1985; Las Vegas Sun, newspaper columnist, 1955-57; First Securities Investment, broker-owner, 1962-72; Sugar Hill Inc, restaurant, lounge manager, retail merchant, 1964-71; Manpower Serv Las Vegas, dir, 1971; New Ventures "503", Cert Devel Co & New Ventures Inc, pres, exec dir; NEDCO Inc, pres, exec dir, 1972-. **ORGANIZATIONS:** Mem Las Vegas Bd of Realtors, Ctr for Bus & Econ Rsch, UNLV, Southern NV Econ Devel Council; exec bd mem So NV "Special Impact Area"; mem OEDP; pres Prospectors; exec bd mem Las Vegas C of C; mem White House Small Bus Conf 1980,86, NV Mktg Assoc, SW Equal Oppty Bd, Officers Assoc, NV Minority Purchasing Council, Las Vegas Press Club; exec bd mem NAACP, So Christian Leadership Conf; hon mem NV Assoc of Latin Amers; mem Uptown Kiwanis Club, Alpha Phi Alpha, 33 Degree Mason; exec bd mem Natl Assoc Black & Minority C of C; chmn NV Inst of Bus. **HONORS/ACHIEVEMENTS:** Recipient of over 80 awds, natl, state, local stature from professional & civic orgs; "Bob Bailey Day" Proclaimed for 30 Yrs Serv in State of NV. **BUSINESS ADDRESS:** Executive Dir, NV Econ Devel Co, 701 E Bridger Ave, Las Vegas, NV 89101.

BAIN, ERLIN
Clinical psychologist. **PERSONAL:** Born Sep 25, 1950, Nassau, Bahamas;son of Clifford Bain and Jennie Bain; children: Akilah-Halima, Kwasi Rashidi, Jamila Rashida. **EDUCATION:** Univ of Miami, BA 1980, PhD 1986. **CAREER:** Center for Child Develop, psychologist 1979-82; Miami Mental Health Ctr, dir of substance abuse 1982-84; Dept of Youth and Family Develop, clinical psychologist 1985-; Ujima Assocs Inc, exec dir 1986-. **ORGANIZATIONS:** Mem Mental Health Assn of Dade Co 1982-, Chiumba Imani African Dance Co 1983-, Natl Black Alcoholism Council 1984-; pres South FL Assoc of Black Psychologists 1986-; consultant Informed Families 1986, Switchboard of Miami 1986; mem Kuumba Artists Assoc 1986; consultant Family Health Ctr of Miami 1987. **HONORS/ACHIEVEMENTS:** Natl Minority Fellowship Grant 1978-83; Community Serv Award Welfare Mothers of Dade 1982; Appreciation Award Dade Co Sch Bd 1986 and Inner City Task Force 1986. **HOME ADDRESS:** 697 NW 56th St, Miami, FL 33127. **BUSINESS ADDRESS:** Executive Dir, Ujima Associates Inc, PO Box 470578, Miami, FL 33247.

BAIN, JOSIE GRAY
Educator. **PERSONAL:** Born in Atlanta, GA; married John C Bain; children: John David. **EDUCATION:** CA State Coll, MA 1954; Univ So CA, grad work; Attended, Immaculate heart Coll. **CAREER:** LA Unified School Dist, teacher, training teacher, vice principal, principal, acting admin asst, supr prin, coord prin, admin coord asst supr, area supt, supr, assoc supt instr 1946-. **ORGANIZATIONS:** Mem Delta Kappa Gamma, Delta Sigma Theta; Natl Cncl Negro Women; Natl Cncl Adminstr Women in Educ; vice chmn W Reg Bd United Way; exec bd Urban League; Comm Rel Conf So CA; mem Econ & Youth Oppor Agency; Family Serv Agency exec bd; coord Women's Soc Christian Serv. **HONORS/ACHIEVEMENTS:** Educ Awd Natl Cncl Negro Women 1966; Educator of Yr Beta Phi Chap Phi Delta Kappa 1967; Negro Hist Week Achiev Awd Out Authors Study Club 1968; Womenof Yr Zeta Phi Beta Natl Hon Soc 1969; Trailblazers Awd Natl Assn Bus & Professional Women 1969; US Congressman Augustus Hawkins Awd 1970; Comm Serv Awd W Div Federated Kings Daughters 1971. **BUSINESS ADDRESS:** Associate Superintendent, LA Unified Sch Dist, 450 N Grand Ave, Los Angeles, CA 90012.

BAIN, LINDA VALERIE
Management consultant. **PERSONAL:** Born Feb 14, 1947, New York, NY; married Samuel Green. **EDUCATION:** City Coll of NY, BA 1974. **CAREER:** NYS Dept of Labor, sec 1965-66; New York City Dept of Soc Serv, exec sec 1966-70; Manhattan St Hosp, prog coord 1970-73; Natl Coun of Negro Women's Ctr for Educ & Career Advancement, assoc dir 1973-79; Donchian Mgmt Serv, sr consultant 1980-85; Bain Assoc Inc, pres 1985-. **ORGANIZATIONS:** Mem Amer Soc for Training & Development 1981-; mem Natl & New York Org Develpment Network 1981-; bd of dir Friends of Alvin Ailey 1985; mem Natl Assn of Female Exec 1980-. **HONORS/ACHIEVEMENTS:** Mem & natl vice pres, Natl Coun of Negro Women 1963-; mem, Studio Museum of Harlem 1984-; mem, Coalition of 100 Black Women 1971-; mem, Alvin Ailey Amer Dance Theatre; Mary McLeod Bethune Achievement Award, Natl Coun of Negro Women; Outstanding Young Women of Amer 1976; mem, NY Urban League. **BUSINESS ADDRESS:** President, Bain Associates, Inc, P O Box 20789, New York, NY 10025.

BAIN, RAYMONE KAYE
Government official. **PERSONAL:** Born Apr 27, 1954, Augusta, GA. **EDUCATION:** Spelman Coll, Atlanta GA, BA Pol Sci, 1976; Georgetown Univ Law Ctr, JSD, 1983. **CAREER:** Asst to pres Jimmy Carter, 1974-81; Exec Ofc of Pres, spec asst to dir, 1977-81, trnstn asst, 1981; DC Dept Env Svc, lgs pnl anlst, 1982-84; Baskin & Steingut PC, assoc, 1984; Jackson & Bann PC, spts agt/atty. **ORGANIZATIONS:** Spts Lawyers Asso; Delta Sigma Theta Sor, Inc 1973-. **HONORS/ACHIEVEMENTS:** Outstndng Yng Wmn of Am; Pi Sigma Alpha Pol Sci Hon Soc; Ebony Mag 1978; 50 Future Blk Ldrs of Am; Whos Who Among Am Clgs & Univs; Citizen of Yr Augusta, GA 1977; Article Written "On Sports Violence" 1983; Contributions by Lynn Swann & Marvelous Marvin Hagler. **BUSINESS ADDRESS:** President, Jackson & Bain, P C, 1 Washington Sq, 1050 Connecticut Ave NW, Washington, DC 20036.

BAINE, HERMAN
Information processing researcher. **PERSONAL:** Born Sep 18, 1940, Delray Beach, FL; married Gary Veronica Chaney; children: Carlos C, Marc B. **EDUCATION:** KY State Univ, BA 1963; North Texas State Univ, Grad Study 1966; FL Atlantic Univ, MA 1968. **CAREER:** Buffalo Bills Football, defensive back 1963; Broward Co Bd of Educ, teacher/coach 1964-68; Palm Beach Co Bd of Educ, teacher/coach 1968; IBM, mgr/staff/planner 1968-. **ORGANIZATIONS:** Sustaining mem Republican Natl Comm 1980-87; layreader 1986-87, vestry mem 1987 St David's Episcopal Church; mem Kappa Alpha Psi Frat 1986-87. **HONORS/ACHIEVEMENTS:** Univ of FL Gator Medal of Honor Univ of FL 1984.

BAINES, HAROLD DOUGLAS
Professional athlete. **PERSONAL:** Born Mar 15, 1959, Easton, MD; married Marla Heney; children: Antoinette. **CAREER:** Chicago White Sox, outfielder 1980-. **ORGANIZATIONS:** Discovered as a 12 yr old by former White Sox Owner Bill Veeck when both lived on MD Eastern Shore. **HONORS/ACHIEVEMENTS:** 12th Batter in Pale Hose history reach double figures in extra base categories in one season; set major league record 22 game-winning RBI; led the AL in homers hit in winning games 18; drove in career high 105 runs at 23, became youngest player White Sox history to crack the 100 RBI barrier; ended longest game (8 hrs 6 min) in history on May 9 when he hit 753rd pitch into ctr field bullpen to give White Sox a 25 inning victory over Milwaukee, bat used sent to Baseball Hall of Fame At Cooperstown NY; homered three times at Minnesota Sept 17; hit 9th Inning sacrific fly to drive in the run that beat Seattle and clinched the White Sox AL West Div championship the franchise's first title s ince 1959; named to The Sporting News and UPI AL all-star teams at conclusion of season 1985;Amer League's top road batsman 1985; mem 1985 and 1986 All Star Team. **BUSINESS ADDRESS:** Chicago White Sox, Dan Ryan & 35th St, Chicago, IL 60616.

BAINES, TYRONE RANDOLPH
Educational administration. **PERSONAL:** Born Feb 22, 1943, Exmore, VA; married Shereatha; children: Tyrone R II, Tonita. **EDUCATION:** Morgan State Univ, AB 1965; Univ of PA, MSW 1967; Univ of MD, MA 1971, PhD 1972. **CAREER:** Community Programs Inc, consult 1971-72; MD School Syst, consult 1972; Fed Exec Inst, sr faculty mem 1974-75; NC Central Univ, dir of public admin 1975-78; NC Central Univ, dir of publ admin prog 1979-82; NC Central Univ, vice chancellor for univ relations. **ORGANIZATIONS:** Social worker Children's Serv Inc Philadelphia PA 1967; capt US Army Med Serv Corp 1967-69; consult US Congress House of Rep 1969-70; grad teaching asst Univ of MD 1969-70; personnel relations spec Office of Econ Opport Prog 1970-71; exec council Natl Assoc of Schools of Public Affairs & Admin 1985; bd of trustees Durham Acad; ed bd Political Sci, Southern Review of Public Admin; mem Citizens Advisory Comm for Durham Bd of Educ; bd of dir Natl Inst for Public Mgmt. **HONORS/ACHIEVEMENTS:** Conf of Minority Public Admin Natl Awd 175; Fellowship to attend Harvard Univ Inst for Ed Mgmt 1977; Selected to participate in 1977 Phelps-Stokes Fund West Africa Seminar 1977; Selected as an Amer Council on Ed Fellow in Ed Amin 1978; US Dept of Labor Cert of Recognition from Atlanta Reg 1979; Kellogg Natl Fellow Kellogg Found 1982-85. **MILITARY SERVICE:** AUS capt 1967-69; Superior Performance of Duty Awd 1969; Outstanding Achievement Awd 1969. **HOME ADDRESS:** 125 Wa Wee Nork Dr, #4C, Battle Creek, MI 49015. **BUSINESS ADDRESS:** Exec Asst to the Chancellor, North Carolina CentralUniv, Hoey Admin Bldg Rm 101, Durham, NC 27707.

BAIRD, KEITH E.
Educator. **PERSONAL:** Born Jan 20, 1923; children: Diana Baird N'Diaye, Marcia Baird-Johnson. **EDUCATION:** Columbia Univ, BS 1952; Union Grad School, PhD 1982. **CAREER:** Hunter Coll, prof dir Afro-Amer studies 1969-70; Hofstra Univ, prof of humanities 1970-73; SUNY Coll at Old Westbury, prof of humanities 1973-75; SUNY College at Buffalo, assoc prof anthropology 1975-. **ORGANIZATIONS:** Assoc fellow Ctr for Afro-Amer Studies Atlanta Univ 1973-; consult on lang GA Inst of Tech & Bass Community Org Humanities Fair 1973-74, mem 1976-77; SUNY Chancellor's Task Force on Afro Studies; mem SUNY Chancellor's Committee on Afro Amer Studies 1984; consult on Gullah Lang Sea Island Ctr Beaufort SC 1977;pres emeritus NY African Studies Assoc; assoc ed Freedomways; mem ed bd Jrnl of Black Studies, African Urban Quarterly; co-author "Names from Africa"; lecturer & consult on African & Afro-Amer Studies specializing in African cultural communities in the Americas. **HONORS/ACHIEVEMENTS:** Travel Seminar Grant Ford Found 1969; Publ "Names from Africa" Johnson Publ Co 1972; Summer Scholarship Grant US GOR Friendship Comm Univ of Jena 1981. **HOME ADDRESS:** 740 W Delavan Ave, Buffalo, NY 14222. **BUSINESS ADDRESS:** Assoc Prof Anthropology, StateUniv Coll at Buffalo, 1300 Elmwood Ave HB 115, Buffalo, NY 14222.

BAIRD, KERRY CALVIN
Professional athlete. **PERSONAL:** Born Oct 21, 1961, Franklin, KY. **EDUCATION:** Kentucky, 1980. **CAREER:** Michigan Panthers, 1984; Denver Gold, cornerback 1984. **HONORS/ACHIEVEMENTS:** Chosen Kentucky's "Outstndng Defensive Back" sr yr.

BAITY, GAIL OWENS
Human resources professional. **PERSONAL:** Born May 20, 1952, New York, NY; daughter of George A Owens and Ruth Owens; married Elijah A Baity, Apr 20, 1985; children: Allen J. **EDUCATION:** Spelman Coll, BA Psych 1970-74; Univ of WI Madison, MA Indust Relations 1974-76. **CAREER:** Corning Consumer Prod Div, prdn suprv 1978; Corning Info Serv Div, personnel dev spec 1978-80; Elmira Coll, instr 1980; Corning R&D Div, personnel suprv 1980-82; Corning Consumer Products Div, personnel suprv 1982-83; Corning

Personnel Div, human resource consultant; Corning Glass Works, human resource consultant, 1983-87. **ORGANIZATIONS:** Consult Career Devel Council 1982-; vice pres Soc of Black Professional 1982,86; treas Elmira Corning NAACP 1982-83; mem Soc of Black Profl, Elmira/Corning NAACP; chairperson policy comm Corning Children's Ctr 1986-87; member, Organizational Development Network (ODN), 1988-; member, American Society of Education and Training (ASTD), 1987-; member, National Black MBA Association, 1987-; board member, Career Development Council, 1988-; board member and chair person personnel policy comm, Corning Children's Center, 1986-. **HOME ADDRESS:** 18 Tall Meadow, Painted Post, NY 14870. **BUSINESS ADDRESS:** Human Resources Consultant, Corning Glass Works, Houghton Park, Corning, NY 14831.

BAKER, ANITA
Performer. **PERSONAL:** Born in Detroit, MI. **CAREER:** First solo album "The Songstress" and hit single from that album "Angel", second album "Rapture"; songwriter Watch Your Step, Sweet Love, Been So Long; performer at Montreux (Switzerland) Jazz Festival. **HONORS/ACHIEVEMENTS:** NAACP Image Awd for Best Female Vocalist and Best Album of the Year; Grammy Awards for best female singer and for best song "Giving You the Best That I Got," 1989. *

BAKER, BEVERLY POOLE
Attorney. **PERSONAL:** Born Jan 14, 1944, Birmingham, AL; daughter of Grafton L Poole and Minda Ingersoll Poole; married James K Baker, Nov 1968; children: Paige, Paula, Leslie. **EDUCATION:** Univ of Alabama at Birmingham, BA (summa cum laude), 1982; Cumberland School of Law, Birmingham AL, JD, 1985. **CAREER:** McMillan & Spratling, Birmingham, AL, atty, 1983-86; Haskell Slaughter & Young, Birmingham, AL, atty, 1986-. **ORGANIZATIONS:** Mem, American Bar Assn, Natl Bar Assn, Natl Assn of Bond Lawyers, Magic City Bar Assn, Birmingham Bar Assn, Leadership Birmingham Alumni Council, Camp Fire Boys & Girls, Children Can Soar, Alabama Council on Epilepsy, Jefferson County Medical Examiners Comm, Birmingham Museum of Art, Alabama New South Coalition, Public Affairs Research Council of Alabama, Operation New Birmingham. **HONORS/ACHIEVEMENTS:** Dean's Award, Univ of Alabama at Birmingham, 1981, 1982; Fellow, Amer Assn of Univ Women, 1984; "Perceptions and Propinquity on Police Patrol," SE Sociological Assn, 1982; "Privacy in a High-Tech World," seminar, 1985; "The Age Discrimination in Employment Act and Termination of the Public Sector Employee," Alabama Bar Inst Seminar, 1989. **BUSINESS ADDRESS:** Atty, Haskell Slaughter & Young, 800 First Natl-Southern Natural Bldg, Birmingham, AL 35203.

BAKER, DARRYL BRENT
Business executive. **PERSONAL:** Born May 05, 1955, Detroit, MI; son of Elliott Baker and Mary (Scott) Baker; children: Darryl Jr, Donnathon, LaKeisha. **EDUCATION:** General Motors Inst of Tech, attended 1973-75; Mott Community Coll, AS 1983; Univ of MI. **CAREER:** Baker Homes Co, president 1983-; General Motors Corp, supervisor 1977-88; First American National Securities, Atlanta GA, investment representative 1988-; A L Williams Home Mortgage Inc, Atlanta GA, sr regional mgr 1989-; General Motors Truck & Bus, machinist, machine repairer 1977-. **ORGANIZATIONS:** Owner income tax serv 9 yrs, investment consultant serv 7 yrs; cub scout/boy scout leader 7 yrs; dist exec Boy Scouts 1975-77; football/basketball coach Primary School 1981-81; mem Order of the Arrow; mem NAACP 1987-; chairperson, Employees Interested in Protecting Jobs 1987-; manager Little League & Pee Wee League Baseball Teams 1987. **HONORS/ACHIEVEMENTS:** Scouting Wood Badge Awd; movie producer Top Gun, 1989; Life-Accident-Health Insurance License and Securities Investment License 1988; Ex-cell, Home Mortgage License 1989. **BUSINESS ADDRESS:** Senior Regional Manager, A L Williams Inc, G-3163 Flushing Rd, Suite 208, Flint, MI 48504.

BAKER, DAVE E.
Educator. **PERSONAL:** Born Jun 18, 1943, Manhattan, KS; married Janice; children: Sherri Ann. **EDUCATION:** Emporia State Coll, BS Phys Educ 1968, MPE 1969. **CAREER:** Emporia State Coll, grad asst physical educ, asst baseball coach, 1969; Liberl Comm Jr Coll, head track coach, asst basketball coach, instructor physical educ, 1970; Creighton Univ, instructor physical educ, asst basketball coach, asst baseball coach, 1971-75, instructor physical educ, head baseball coach, 1972-. **ORGANIZATIONS:** Mem Phi Delta Kappa Frat; NCAA Coll World Series Games Comm 1972-75. **BUSINESS ADDRESS:** Physical Education Instructor, CreightonUniv Athletic Dept, 2500 California St, Omaha, NE 68178.

BAKER, DAVID NATHANIEL, JR.
Musician, composer, educator. **PERSONAL:** Born Dec 21, 1931, Indianapolis, IN; married Lida Margret Belt; children: April Elaine. **EDUCATION:** School of Jazz Lenox, MA, attended; studied trombone with JJ Johnson; IN Univ, BME, MME. **CAREER:** Performed as soloist with Boston Symphony Evansville, IN Philharmonic; guest conductor Indianapolis Symphony, The Indianapolis Civic Orch, IN Univ Symphony; composed 100 jazz & classical works; performed with Stan Kenton, Lionel Hampton, Wes Montgomery; former mem George Russell Sextet; toured Europe with Quincy Jones 1961; IN Univ Jazz Dept, chmn. **ORGANIZATIONS:** Chmn Natl Endowment for Arts; bd dir natl Music Council; mem AAUP; mem Natl Assn of Negro Musicians. **HONORS/ACHIEVEMENTS:** Author of 64 books on music improvisation; Recipient Dizzy Gillespie Scholarship 1959; Presidential Appointment to "The Natl Council of the Arts"; pres Natl Jazz Serv Org; nom Pulitzer Prize; nom for a Grammy; President's Awd for Disting Teaching IN Univ. **BUSINESS ADDRESS:** Chairman, Jazz Department, INUniv School of Music, Music Annex Room 309, Bloomington, IN 47405.

BAKER, DUSTY
Professional athlete. **PERSONAL:** Born Jun 15, 1949, Riverside, CA; married Harriet; children: Natosha. **EDUCATION:** Attended, Amer River Jr Coll Sacramento. **CAREER:** Atlanta Braves, outfielder 1968-76; Los Angeles Dodgers, outfielder 1976-83; San Francisco Giants, outfielder 1984; Oakland Athletics, player 1985-. **HONORS/ACHIEVEMENTS:** 3rd Natl Leag batting race with ML average 321 1972; career high 17 gme htg streak; led NL outfldrs tlt chances with 407 1973; Nat'l Leag ldrs GWRBIS 1980; Sporting News All-Star and Silver Slugger teams 1981; NL All-Star Third leag batting Glove helped Dodgers to World series Victory; mem All Star Team 1981,82. **BUSINESS ADDRESS:** Oakland Athletics, Oakland Alameda Cty Col, Oakland, CA 94621.

BAKER, EUGENE
Business executive. **PERSONAL:** Born Oct 04, 1938, Jacksonville, FL; son of Henry Baker and Mable Baker; married Vivian Hughes; children: Sedric, Sandy, Kenneth, Nina, David, Daniel. **EDUCATION:** Florida A&M Univ, BS 1960; Edward Waters Coll, LLD 1981. **CAREER:** Intl Book Inc, mktg dir 1962-65; Diversified Resources Inc, pres 1965-68; Diversified Plastic Inc, pres 1968-74; Natl Assn Black Mfrs Inc, pres 1974-82; Dyma Assn Inc, vice pres; Technology Resources Development, Inc, pres 1986-. **ORGANIZATIONS:** Natl Assn of Black Mfrs, dir 1976-83; Economic Rights Coalition, vice chmn 1977-79; Pres Advisory Council on Minority Business, vice chmn 1979; Tech Resource Syst, dir 1982-; Prince Georges General Hospital, Inc, dir 1984-; Educ Dynamic Research, Inc, dir; Quality Unlimited, dir; World Conf of Mayors, intl trade consultant; Natl Assn of Minority Printers, bd dir. **HONORS/ACHIEVEMENTS:** Comm Price Georges Hospital Comm 1980-83; dir Natl Business League PRC 1976-81; chm Coalition of Minority Trade Assn 1976-74; outstanding contributions White House Conf on Small Business 1979; outstanding assn exec NBL CJ Patterson Wd 1978; minority business leadership Rockwell Intl 1981; outstanding leadership Minority News Media Award 1980; outstanding achievement Natl Florida A&M Alumni Award 1972; co-author of book, Famanotophobia, 1987. **BUSINESS ADDRESS:** Vice President of Operations-COO, Phylco Inc, 1108 K Street, NW, Lower Level, Washington, DC 20005.

BAKER, FLOYD EDWARD
Dentist. **PERSONAL:** Born Mar 28, 1920, Auxvasse, MO; married Gertrude Andrews; children: Floyd E Jr, Teressa. **EDUCATION:** Lincoln Univ of MO, BS 1943; Meharry Coll of Dentistry, DDS 1946; Inst for Grad Dentistry, Post-Graduate 1956. **CAREER:** Mercy Douglas Hosp, staff dentist 1954-74, co-chair oral surgery 1970-74; New Era Dental Soc, bd mem. **ORGANIZATIONS:** Zone vice pres Natl Dental Assoc 1958-80; mem Mt Airy Presbyterian Church 1964-87; treas Bravo Investment Corp 1964-87; registrar Amer Dental Assoc Philadelphia County Dental 1978-85; mem Special Olympics 1983-87. **HONORS/ACHIEVEMENTS:** Forty Year Plaque Omega Psi Phi Frat 1984; Alumni of Year Awd Presidential Citation 1984; Life Membership Pin Amer Dental Assoc 1985. **MILITARY SERVICE:** AUS Dental Corp capt 2 yrs; Honorable Discharge 1948. **BUSINESS ADDRESS:** Board Member, New Era Dental Society, 1826 W Girard Ave, Philadelphia, PA 19130.

BAKER, HENRY W., SR.
Educator. **PERSONAL:** Born Apr 26, 1937, Valdosta, GA; son of Herbert Baker and Amie Lee Baker; married Rubye Veals, Jan 29, 69; children: Henry W, II, Michael De Leon, Debra Marie, Edith Marie. **EDUCATION:** Alcorn State Univ, BS 1964, Grad Study 1983; William Paterson College, Grad Study 1985. **CAREER:** Anchorage Jr HS, 1964-67; Natchez MI, tchr & coach phys educ; Eastside HS, phys educ tchr & basketball coach 1967-80; Passic Co Coll, head basketball coach 1978-83; Eastside HS, head coach girls tennis team coord phys educ 1983-84; Passaic County Community Coll, Head Basketball Coach, 1979-89, Paterson NJ; Eastside High School, head track coach (boys), 1988-89, Paterson NJ. **ORGANIZATIONS:** Dir Martin Luther King Comm Ctr Paterson 1970-76; founder/dir Black Youth Orgn Paterson 1971-77; pres/past vice pres Passaic Co Planned Parenthood Inc1976-79; vice pres bd of dirs Children Youth Serv Paterson NJ 1986-; vice pres Afrikan Amer Men Interested in Neighborhood Develop Inc 1986-; Brd of dirs Childrens Haven, 1985-89. **HONORS/ACHIEVEMENTS:** Comm Serv Awd Master Barber's Assn Unit 9 1975; Youth Serv Awd New Political Alliance Paterson1975; Basketball Coach of the Yr NY Dailey News 1975; Coach of the Yr Basketball Passaic Co Assn 1976; Coach of the Yr Girls Track Passaic Co Coaches Assn 1977-80; Junior College Coach of the Year 1985-86. **BUSINESS ADDRESS:** Assistant Athletic Director, Eastside High School, 150 Park Ave, Paterson, NJ 07501.

BAKER, HOUSTON A., JR.
Educator. **PERSONAL:** Born Mar 22, 1943, Louisville, KY; married Charlotte Pierce; children: 1 son. **EDUCATION:** Howard Univ, BA 1965; UCLA, MA 1966; Univ of Edinburgh, Scotland, doctoral work 1967-68; UCLA, PhD 1968. **CAREER:** Howard Univ, instructor 1966; Yale Univ, instructor 1968-69, asst prof 1969; Center for Adv Studies, Univ of VA, assoc prof mem 1970-73; Univ of VA, prof 1973; Univ of PA, prof/dir Afro-Amer Studies 1974-. **ORGANIZATIONS:** MLA Exec Council; assoc editor BALE; com on Scholarly Worth Howard Univ Press; visiting lectr; numerous publs in field. **HONORS/ACHIEVEMENTS:** Numerous academic awards & honors. **BUSINESS ADDRESS:** Prof/Dir Afro-Amer Studies, Univ of PA, 302 Bennett Hall, Philadelphia, PA 19104.

BAKER, JAMES E.
Government official. **PERSONAL:** Born Jan 21, 1935, Suffolk, VA. **EDUCATION:** Havenford Coll, BA, 1956; Fletcher Sch of Law and Diplomacy, MA, MALD, 1960. **CAREER:** SDept of State, Washington DC, frgn serv officer, 1960-84; United Nations, dir spec econ asst prog. **ORGANIZATIONS:** Sr rsrch asst Carnegie Endmnt 1978. **HONORS/ACHIEVEMENTS:** Cncl on Foreign Rltns; Am Foreign Serv Assoc. **MILITARY SERVICE:** AUS E-4 1957-59. **BUSINESS ADDRESS:** Dir Special Econ Asst Pgm, United Nations, United Nations, New York, NY 10017.

BAKER, JOEL L.
Psychologist, management consultant. **PERSONAL:** Born Mar 26, 1934, Fordyce, AR; divorced; children: Beverly, Cynthia, Jacquline. **EDUCATION:** Univ of AR at Pine Bluff, BS 1956; CA State Univ at Hayward CA, MS 1972; Univ of OR Eugene, PhD 1977. **CAREER:** City Coll San Francisco, counselor 1970-72; CA State Univ Hayward, prof 1971-73; Univ of OR, rsch asst 1973-74; Berkeley Unified Sch Dist, consult 1975-77; Delta Counseling & Guidance Ctr, psychologist 1978-79; Baker Enterprises Inc, pres 1979-. **ORGANIZATIONS:** Housing specialist Housing Devel Corp of AR 1977-78; exec dir Tri-Co Day Care Ctr 1977-; pres Local Branch of NAACP 1977-; pres Univ of AR Alumni Assn 1979; pres AR Assn of Black Psycholist 1980; Natl Sci Found William Jewel Coll Liberty MO 1960; Cooperative Internship Prog for Tchr & Counselors in Higher Educ Univ of CA Berkeley 1970. **MILITARY SERVICE:** AUS pfc 1956-58. **BUSINESS ADDRESS:** President, Baker Enterprises Inc, PO Box 461, Fordyce, AR 71742.

BAKER, LAVOLIA EALY
Insurance broker. **PERSONAL:** Born Nov 11, 1925, Shreveport, LA; married Luchan G Baker; children: Paul, Ronald, Luchan Jr. **EDUCATION:** Contra Costa, AA 1970; UC Berkeley Sch of Bus, attended 1968; Golden Gate Univ, attended 1972 1974. **CAREER:** L Baker Ins, owner/mgr 1974, fire & casualty ins broker. **ORGANIZATIONS:** Chairperson Oakland Metro Enterprises; chmn WAPAC; dir San Fran Indep Agents Assn 1975; dir

Black Brokers & Agents Assn; vice pres Natl Assn of Negro Bus & Professional Womens Club; pres bd chmn Alpha Phi Alpha Wives Aux; dir Sojourner Truth Housing Corp 1974; life mem NAACP; Bay Area Urban League; mem BOWOPA & E Bay Area Dem Club 1972; fndr The Ch By the Side of the Road 1955. **HONORS/ACHIEVEMENTS:** Bus Woman of the Yr. **BUSINESS ADDRESS:** Fire & Casualty Ins Broker, 1230 Fillmore St, San Francisco, CA 94115.

BAKER, MOOREAN ANN
Pediatric dentist. **PERSONAL:** Born Nov 22, 1953, Washington, DC. **EDUCATION:** Howard Univ, BS 1975, DDS 1980; ML King Hosp Los Angeles, Certificate in Pediatric Dentistry 1982. **CAREER:** Private Practice, pediatric dentist. **ORGANIZATIONS:** Mem Amer Assoc of Women Dentists 1981-, Amer Acad of Pediatric Dentistry 1981-, Amer Soc of Dentistry for Children 1984-, Robert T Freeman Dental Soc 1983-. **BUSINESS ADDRESS:** Pediatric Dentist, 1341 Pennsylvania Ave, Washington, DC 20003.

BAKER, OSCAR WILSON
Attorney. **PERSONAL:** Born Mar 29, 1911, Bay City, MI; married Robbie L; children: Gail, Cheryl, Christine. **EDUCATION:** Univ of MI, AB 1933, LLB 1935. **CAREER:** Baker, Baker & Selby, sr mem. **ORGANIZATIONS:** Chmn MI State Bar Comm on Civil Liberties 1952-54; mem MI State Bar Comm 1952-75; pres Bay Co Bar 1958; chmn MI State Bar Comm on Equal Justice 1966; Bay Co Bar Assn; MI Bar Assn; MS Civil Rights Voting Proj; MI NAACP; chmn St Legal Redress 1937-39; Bay City Charter Revision Com 1950; chmn mem Bay Co Rec Comm 1952-68; chmn Bay Co Red Cross 1964; pres Citizens League for Low Rent Housing 1951; Gov Comm on Migratory Labor 1966; Alpha Phi Alpha; Sigma Pi Phi; Iota Boule Chpt. **HONORS/ACHIEVEMENTS:** Special Award Bay City NAACP 1973; Saginaw Valley Coll Bd of Fellows 1973; Univ of MI Bd of Visitors 1970; Life Mem 6th Fed Circuit Jud Conf; Natl Lawyers Guild Award 1964-65. **BUSINESS ADDRESS:** Attorney, 504-10 Bay City Bank Bldg, Bay City, MI 48706.

BAKER, ROLAND CHARLES
Business executive. **PERSONAL:** Born Aug 12, 1938, Chicago, IL; married Addie Scott; children: Scott, Stephen, Stefanie. **EDUCATION:** Univ of CA, BS Bus Admin 1961; Univ of CA, MBA 1962; CPA licensed in CA 1971; Chartered Life Underwriter; Life Insurance Management Institute, Fellow. **CAREER:** N Amer Rockwell Corp CA, budget adminstr 1962-64; Ampex Corp Culver City, financial analyst 1964-65; Beneficial Standard Life Ins Co, staff asst/controller 1965-67, mgr corporate acctg 1967-68, asst controller 1968-69, vice pres & controller 1969-71, adminstrv vice pres & controller 1973-75, sr vice pres 1975-77; Colonial Penn Ins Co/Colonial Penn Franklin Ins Co/Colonial Penn Life Ins Co, exec vice pres bd dirs; Colonial Penn Group Inc, sr vice pres 1977-80; The Signature Group, chairman & ceo 1980-. **ORGANIZATIONS:** Mem CA Soc of CPA's/AICPA; bd dir Philadelphia Zool Soc 1979-80; bd dir Fund for an Open Society "OPEN" 1979-; com mem Central Allocations Com United Way Fund 1979-. **HONORS/ACHIEVEMENTS:** Fellow Life Mgmt Inst 1971; CLU Bryn Mawr PA 1976. **MILITARY SERVICE:** USMCR 1962-67. **BUSINESS ADDRESS:** Chairman, Chief Exec Officer, The Signature Group, 200 N Martingale Rd, Schaumburg, IL 60194.

BAKER, SHARON L.
Social worker. **PERSONAL:** Born Jan 18, 1958, New York, NY; daughter of Willie Baker Jr(deceased) and Lee Baker; children: Kendra. **EDUCATION:** Univ of NC at Charlotte, BA Sociology, Afro-Amer & African Studies 1979; Columbia Univ Sch of Social Work, MS Social Work, Minor in Business 1983; Baruch Coll Sch of Continuing Studies, Certificate in Business 1986. **CAREER:** Steinway Child & Family Developmental Center, social worker, 1983-84; South Bronx Mental Hlth Cncl Inc, psychiatric social worker 1984; Bedford Stuyvesant Comm Mental Health Ctr Inc, psychiatric social worker/recreation coord 1985; Victim Serv Agency, casework supervisor 1985-86; Bronx-Lebanon Hosp Ctr, psychiatric social worker 1986-. **ORGANIZATIONS:** Mem Natl Council of Negro Women 1979-, NY City Chap Assn of Black Social Workers 1981-; chairperson Black Caucus Columbia Univ Sch of Social Work 1982-83; corres sec Delta Sigma Theta NY Alumnae Chap 1983-87; mem Workshop in Business Oppors Alumni Assoc 1985-, Amer Enterpreneurs Assoc 1986-; professional licenses, NY State Certification in Social Work 1986-, NYC Bd of Education in school social work. **HONORS/ACHIEVEMENTS:** Outstanding Young Women of Amer 1984. **HOME ADDRESS:** 880 Colgate Ave #10H, Bronx, NY 10473.

BAKER, VINCENT S.
Business executive. **PERSONAL:** Born Jul 23, New York, NY. **CAREER:** NY amsterdam News, staff writer; NY Age, staff writer; NY Courier, staff writer; Big Red Newspaper, columnist, black historian. **ORGANIZATIONS:** Mem Fed Youth Clubs of Harlem, Modern Trend Group of Harlem YMCA, Harlem Christian Youth Council, March on Washington Movement, Congress of Racial Rquality; former officer Young Adult Fellowship of Salem Meth Church; chmn Salems Commiss on Christian Soc Concerns; former pres Young Adult Div NY Meth Conf; 1st vice pres 5 Boro Black Republican Council; parliamentarian, prog comm chmn Manhattan Republican Club; parliamentarian Manhattan Chap Assoc for the Study of Afro-Amer Life & History; chmn Anti-Crime Comm of the NY Br of NAACP; org, pres Citizens Mobilization Against Crime; ne reg dir Intl Black Writers Conf. **HONORS/ACHIEVEMENTS:** Cited for Leadership Intl Black Writers Conf 1979; Citation for Excellence in Ed Writing Lincoln Univ 1980; author The Republican Party & Black Amers, A Political History; co-editor The Black Writers publ by Intl Black Writers Conf.

BAKER, WANDA KAY
Consultant. **PERSONAL:** Born in Los Angeles, CA; children: Maury. **EDUCATION:** Univ of So CA, BS Educ 1954, MS 1958, PhD 1971. **CAREER:** Elem Schl, counselor 1961-67; ESEA Title V Prog, coord 1968; Div of Planning & Research, splst measurement & eval 1969; counselor 1970; Pacific Training & Tech Assist, gen consult 1971; Black Consult Serv, staff trainer 1971; Los Angeles Mgmt & Devel Corp, pres 1971; Model Cities, counselor coord 1973;CA Legislature Assembly Office of Research, consult 1973, prin consult 1974-; HUD administrative assistant to regional administrator, 1978-1981; chief-of-staff to state senator, 1989. **ORGANIZATIONS:** Intl Youth Oppor Bd 1964; research asst Pacific State Hosp 1960-61; tchr LACUSD 1954-60; mem Los Angeles Assn of Sch Psychologists & Psychometrist; pres Los Angeles City Counselors; adv bd NAACP; Black Alcoholics Assn; volunteer work in mental health agencies; Student Support Syst & Dist Atty; Childrens' Home Society Bd of Directors, Urban League Bd of Directors. **HONORS/ACHIEVEMENTS:** Youth Adv Bd Commendation, Assembly Resolutions, Top Real Estate Producer. **BUSINESS ADDRESS:** Chief-of-Staff, Office of State Senator Diane Watson, 4401 Crenshaw Blvd, Suite 300, Los Angeles, CA 90043.

BAKER, WILLIE J.
Elected official. **PERSONAL:** Born May 10, 1938, Birmingham, AL; married Barbara Ann Johnson; children: Barbara, Beverly, Carol Lynn Rance, Christopher, Dindi. **EDUCATION:** Graduated from IBM Computer Specialists, Control Data Corp, Univac Sperry Rand Peripherial Engrg, US Naval Electronics, Naval Nuclear Power Sch, Naval Leadership & Mgmt; Albany State Coll, M Astrophysics 1984; Alexander City JC, grad Magna Cum Laude. **CAREER:** Baker's Enterprises, pres; Macon Co Dist 1, co commissioner. **ORGANIZATIONS:** Mem Simmons Chapel AME Zion Church; vice pres Tuskegee Chamber of Comm; mem FOP; mem NAACP; mem Pres Council on Physical Fitness; mem AL Forest Farmers; pres Natl Assn of Landowners; mem Natl Assn of Black Co Officials; chmn Health & Human Serv Steering Comm; mem bd of dirs ACCA; pres AL Black Co Commissioners Assoc. **HONORS/ACHIEVEMENTS:** Bestowed Doctorate of Humanities Degree 1971; Young Man of the Year 1972; AL Democratic Conference Black Retail Businessman of the Year 1983; Who's Who in Amer Jr Colleges 1983; publications "The Dying Universe" 1981; "Cosmology and the Redshift" 1982; "Einsteins Theory of Relativity for the Layman" 1982; part in MGM's film "The Wind and the Lion" released 1974; Outstanding Student of the Year 1983. **MILITARY SERVICE:** USN data systems tech 1st class 20 yrs; 5 Navy Good Conduct Medals; Natl Defense Medal; Navy Achievement Awd Medal; Navy Chief Master-at-Arms. **BUSINESS ADDRESS:** County Commissioner, Macon Co Dist 1, PO Box 179, Tuskegee, AL 36083.

BAKER, WILLIE L., JR.
Labor union officer. **PERSONAL:** Born May 21, 1941, Sanford, FL; son of Willie L Baker and Ila Jessie Harris; married Madeline Dennis, Jan 26, 1966 (deceased); children: Kim, Keith. **EDUCATION:** Univ of Maryland Eastern Shore, Princess Anne, MD, BA, 1965. **CAREER:** UFCW Local 56, Bridgeton, NJ, recording sec, 1974-80, business agent, 1974-85, legislative-South Jersey, 1974-85, vice pres, 1980-85; UFCWIU, Washington, DC, intl vice pres, 1985-. **ORGANIZATIONS:** First vice pres, Coalition of Black Trade Unionists, 1986-; bd mem, Community Serv Comm AFL-CIO, 1986-; bd mem, Industrial Relations Council's Graduate Opportunities for Advanced Level Studies (GOALS), 1986-; pres, Univ of Maryland Eastern Shore Alumni Assn, 1987-. **HONORS/ACHIEVEMENTS:** Presidential Citation, Natl Assn of Equal Opportunity in Higher Educ, 1981; Alumnus of the Year Award, Univ of Maryland Eastern Shore, 1986. **BUSINESS ADDRESS:** Intl Vice Pres and Dir, Civil Rights Dept, United Food and Commercial Workers Intl Union, 1775 K Street NW, Washington, DC 20006.

BALDWIN, CYNTHIA A.
Lawyer, educator. **PERSONAL:** Born Feb 08, 1945, McKeesport, PA; daughter of James A Ackron and Iona Meriweather Ackron; married Arthur L Baldwin, Jun 17, 1967; children: James A , Crystal A. **EDUCATION:** Pennsylvania State Univ, University Park PA, BA, 1966, MA, 1974; Duquesne Univ School of Law, Pittsburgh PA, JD, 1980. **CAREER:** Pennsylvania State Univ, McKeesport PA, asst dean student affairs, 1976-77; Neighborhood Legal Serv, McKeesport PA, staff atty, 1980-81; Office of Attorney Gen, PA, deputy atty gen, 1981-83, atty-in-charge, 1983-86; Palkovitz and Palkovitz, McKeesport PA, atty; Duquesne Univ, Pittsburgh PA, visiting prof. **ORGANIZATIONS:** Exec Comm, Homer S Brown Law Assn, 1980-; vice pres, bd of dir, Neighborhood Legal Serv Assn, 1986-88; pres-elect, Penn State Alumni Assn, 1987-89; bd of dir, Greater Pittsburgh YMCA, 1987-; mem, Allegheny County Bar Assn, 1980-, Greater Pittsburgh Commn on Women, 1987-, Pennsylvania Bar Assn, 1988-, Pennsylvania Bar Assn House of Delegates, 1988-. **HONORS/ACHIEVEMENTS:** Poetry included in National Anthology of Poetry, 1977; Role Model Award, Chatham Coll, 1983; Tribute to Women Award in the Professions, YWCA, 1987; Humanitarian Service Award, Penn State Forum on Black Affairs, 1989. **BUSINESS ADDRESS:** Visiting Prof, Duquesne Univ School of Law, 900 Locust St, Hanley Hall, Pittsburgh, PA 15282.

BALDWIN, GEORGE R.
Attorney. **PERSONAL:** Born Oct 04, 1934, Brunswick, GA; children: Kirk. **EDUCATION:** Lincoln Univ, BA Economics 1955; Brooklyn Law Sch, LLB, JD 1964; NYU Law Sch, LLM 1976. **CAREER:** Private Practice NYC, attorney 1966-67; Danch, Rivers & Baldwin Westbury, NY, partner 1967-71; Legal Aid Soc NYC, atty-in-charge Comm Defender Office 1971-. **ORGANIZATIONS:** Mem Natl Bar Assn; mem Natl Conf of Black Lawyers; mem 100 Black Men Inc; JFK Dem Club; mem Metro AME Church. **MILITARY SERVICE:** AUS 1957-59. **BUSINESS ADDRESS:** Comm Defender Office, 1230 Fulton St, Brooklyn, NY 11216.

BALDWIN, JOHN H.
Business executive. **PERSONAL:** Born Oct 13, 1913, Clinton, MO; married Mae Hayden. **EDUCATION:** Two years college 1941; Phase 1 & 2 Busn Law completed; Real Estate & Appraisal course 1 completed. **CAREER:** Retired non-professional male model; Swanson's Hallmark, serv mgr. **ORGANIZATIONS:** John R McGruder Masonic AMFM Lodge; NAACP; steward CME ch; elected 1st Black Dist Gov Dist 260 MO Lions Lions Intl 1974; bd of govs MO Lions Eye Tissue Bank Columbia 1977; bd dirs Eye Research Found of MO Inc 1978. **HONORS/ACHIEVEMENTS:** Lion of the Year 1974; Outstanding Dist Gov Award 1975; Outstanding Layman Award 1974. **MILITARY SERVICE:** AUS CW0-W4 1941-61 retired; Serv Awards; Good Conduct Medal; Bronze Star; Meritorious Serv Medal.

BALDWIN, LOUIS J.
Business executive. **PERSONAL:** Born in New York, NY. **EDUCATION:** Ithaca College, Business Admin 1970. **CAREER:** Ithaca College, asst to the dir of admissions 1970-72; American Arbitration Assoc, asst dir 1972-73; Union Carbide Corp, administrator, recruitment & placement 1974-77; Allied Corporation, supervisor, employee relations 1977-82; Franklin Allen Consultants, employment consult 1983-84; Staten Island Cable, manager, human resources 1984-85; Amerada Hess Corp, personnel admin 1985-86; Amer Cablevision of Queens, mgr human resources 1986-. **ORGANIZATIONS:** Advisor Junior Achievement of NY 1976; board member Forum to Advance Minorities in Engineering, 1980-82; loaned executive United Way 1982; member the EDGES Group, Inc 1977-; member NAACP 1978-; principal & treasurer The TV Ten, Inc 1980-; member NY Chapter of Minorities in Cable 1984-; bd mem Harlem Dowling Childrens Serv 1986-; mem NY Urban League 1986-. **HOME ADDRESS:** 19727 Foothill Ave, Jamaica, NY 11423. **BUSINESS ADDRESS:**

Manager Human Resources, Amer Cablevision of Queens, 25-20 Brooklyn Queens Expwy, Woodside, NY 11377.

BALDWIN, WILHELMINA F.
Retired educator. **PERSONAL:** Born Aug 27, 1923, Anderson, SC; daughter of Charles Warwick Francis, Sr (deceased) and Almena Louise Martin Francis (deceased); married Bernard Joseph Baldwin, Sr, Jun 11, 1945 (died 1968); children: Bernard, Jr, Judith Dianne. **EDUCATION:** NC Coll for Negroes, BA 1944; Tuskegee Inst, MEd 1956. **CAREER:** Boggs Acad, instructor English, social studies, librarian 1944-46; John Andrew Hospital, information officer 1946-47; Cotton Valley School, jr high school instructor 1947-57; Macon County Bd of Educ, principal 1957-63; Maxwell Elementary School, librarian 1963-66; Title I ESEA Remedial Program, pilot reading teacher 1966-67; EPDA Projects, supvr dir reading & libraries 1967-69, dir 1969-70, dir career opportunitiess program 1970-72; Macon County Bd of Educ, educ, dir of Title I ESEA 1978; retired educ. **ORGANIZATIONS:** Member, AL Educ Assn, Natl Educ Assn, Macon County Educ Assn, Amer Library Assn, AL State Reading Assn, Natl Council of Negro Women, NABSE, Phi Delta Kappa; elder member, Session Westminster Presbyterian Church; bd of advisors Southern Vocational Coll Phi Delta Kappa; pres, Natl Sorority of Phi Delta Kappa Inc Upsilon Chapter; member, vice chair bd of dir, Central Alabama OIC, Montgomery. **HOME ADDRESS:** 2006 Colvert St, PO Box 1145, Tuskegee, AL 36088-1145.

BALL, JANE LEE
Educator. **PERSONAL:** Born Jun 02, 1930, Springfield, OH; daughter of Henry Lee and Luella Simpson Lee; married Wilfred R Ball, Apr 01, 1958; children: Janet, Carol B Williams, Wendy, Wilfred Cristan. **EDUCATION:** Wilberforce Univ, Wilberforce OH, 1946-47; Central State Univ, Wilberforce OH, BSEd, 1949; Howard Univ, Washington DC, MA, 1951; Washington Univ, St Louis, MO 1957; Ohio State Univ, Columbus OH, 1967. **CAREER:** Southern Univ, Baton Rouge LA, instructor, asst prof, 1951-58; Alcorn Coll, Lorman MS, asst prof, 1959-60; Ohio State Univ, Columbus OH, instructor, 1961, 1964-65; North Carolina Central, Durham NC, asst prof, 1963-64; Wilberforce Univ, Wilberforce OH, instructor, asst prof, assoc prof, prof, 1966-; Wiljoba Publishing Co, owner, 1989-. **ORGANIZATIONS:** AME Church, 1945-; Alpha Kappa Mu Honor Soc, 1948-; Delta Sigma Theta Sorority, 1949-; Coll Language Assn, 1955-; Wilberforce Univ Faculty Assn, 1975-80. **HONORS/ACHIEVEMENTS:** Teacher of the Month, 1982, Wilberforce Univ Faculty Merit Award, 1980, 1985, Wilberforce Univ; owner, Wiljaba Publishing Co, 1989-; co-author, College Writing, 1977; author, articles in Humanist, 1980, Critical Survey of Short Fiction; author, "Virginia Hamilton," "Gordon Parks," in Dictionary of Literary Biography, 1984; The Black Experience Perpetual Calendar, 1989. **BUSINESS ADDRESS:** Prof of English, Wilberforce Univ, Walker Center, Wilberforce, OH 45384.

BALL, RICHARD E.
Educator, legal economist, attorney. **PERSONAL:** Born Jul 18, 1918, Springfield, MA; married Edwinton Raiford. **EDUCATION:** NYU, BS 1946, MBA 1948; Brooklyn Law Sch, LLB 1954, JD 1967. **CAREER:** New York City Housing Authority; Dept of Welfare; New York City Bd of Educ; St Augustine's Coll, chmn/prof; NC Central Univ, bd trustees/acting pres/business mgr; NAACP, atty/legal editor/counsel/consultant; Episcopal Church, lay reader. **ORGANIZATIONS:** Mem Masons, shriners; Consistory; life mem Alpha Phi Alpha; life mem Amer Natl Bar Assn; NC, MA State Bar Assns; Natl Mgmt Assn; pres Alpha Phi Lambds Chpt. **HONORS/ACHIEVEMENTS:** Candidate for Superior Court Judge. **BUSINESS ADDRESS:** Ste 304 Odd Fellows Bldg, Raleigh, NC 27601.

BALL, WILFRED R.
Educator. **PERSONAL:** Born Jan 03, 1932, Chicago, IL; son of Wilfred Ball Sr and Mary SandersBall; married Jane L; children: Janet, Carol, Wendy, Cris. **EDUCATION:** Morehouse Coll, BS 1952; Atlanta Univ, MS 1955; OH State Univ, PhD 1965. **CAREER:** Southern Univ, instructor 1955-60; Alcorn Coll, asst prof 1960-61, 1968-69; Knoxville Coll, assoc prof 1969-70; Wilberforce Univ, assoc & prof 1972-. **HONORS/ACHIEVEMENTS:** NSF Fellowship, NSF, 1960-62; mem Beta Kappi Chi Honor Scientific Soc, Beta Beta Beta Biol Soc; President's Awd Outstanding Teacher Wilberforce Univ 1985. **BUSINESS ADDRESS:** Professor of Biology, Wilberforce University, Wilberforce, OH 45384.

BALL, WILLIAM BATTEN
Attorney, tax law specialist. **PERSONAL:** Born Aug 28, 1928, San Antonio, TX; son of William Henry Ball (deceased) and Lillian Edna Young Ball (deceased); married Charlie Mae Cooper, Nov 09, 1956; children: Jeffrey Christopher, Kathleen Lorraine, William Eric. **EDUCATION:** Woodrow Wilson Jr Coll, Chicago IL, 1944-45; Roosevelt Univ, Chicago IL, BS, Commerce, 1955, MBA, 1960; Chicago Kent Coll of Law of IL Inst of Technology, Chicago IL, JD, 1968. **CAREER:** IRS, revenue officer 1955-57; Supreme Life Insurance Co, accountant, jr exec 1957-59; State of IL Dept of Labor, auditor 1959; IRS, agent 1959-67, appellate appeals officer 1967-86; attorney, private practice, 1986-. **ORGANIZATIONS:** Member, Chicago & Cook Co Bar Assoc, IL State Bar Assn, Amer Bar Assn, Natl Bar Assn; chmn admin bd St Mark United Meth Ch 1973-77; troop committeeman BSA; member Order of the Arrow Natl Fraternity of Scout Honor Campers; member Order of Brotherhood; life member, Kappa Alpha Psi Fraternity Inc; member, bd of dir, Community Mental Health Council, 1982-87;. **HONORS/ACHIEVEMENTS:** Various Awards & Honors, BSA; Outstanding Performance Award, IRS; master's thesis, "Insurance Co Annual Statement Preparation/Instructions," Roosevelt Univ, 1960. **MILITARY SERVICE:** AUS Corpl 1951-53. **HOME ADDRESS:** 8355 S Perry Ave, Chicago, IL 60620.

BALLANCE, FRANK WINSTON, JR.
Attorney. **PERSONAL:** Born Feb 15, 1942, Windsor, NC; married Bernadine; children: Garey, Angela, Valery. **EDUCATION:** NCCU, BA 1963, JD 1965. **CAREER:** SC State Coll, librarian/asst prof 1965-66; prosecuting atty 1966-. **ORGANIZATIONS:** Dir Found Comm Devel 1973-74; chmn Warren Co Bd Educ 1974-76; past pres NC Assn Black Lawyers. **MILITARY SERVICE:** NC Natl Guard. **BUSINESS ADDRESS:** Prosecuting Attorney, 307 W Franklin St, Warrenton, NC 27589.

BALLARD, ALLEN BUTLER, JR.
Educator. **PERSONAL:** Born Nov 01, 1930, Philadelphia, PA; divorced; children: John, Alayna. **EDUCATION:** Kenyon Clg, BA 1952; Harvard Univ, MA, PhD 1961. **CAREER:** City Coll of NY, asst prof, assoc prof 1961-69; City Univ of NY, vice dean of faculty 1969-76. **HONORS/ACHIEVEMENTS:** Ford Fndtn, Natl Humanities Cntr, Motor Ctr Grants; Fulbright Schlr; Phi Beta Kappa 1952; Books "The Education of Black Folk" Harpar & Ron 1974; "One More Days Journey" McGraw-Hill 1984. **MILITARY SERVICE:** AUS corpl 1952-54. **BUSINESS ADDRESS:** Professor of Political Science, City College of New York, 137th & Convent Ave, New York, NY 10031.

BALLARD, BILLY RAY
Physician, dentist, educator. **PERSONAL:** Born Aug 15, 1940, Bossier City, LA; married Rose M Carter; children: Rachel, Percy. **EDUCATION:** Southern Univ, BS 1961; Meharry Med Coll, DDS 1965, MD 1980. **CAREER:** Dept of Oral Path SUNY at Buffalo, asst prof of oral pathology 1971-74; Meharry, assoc prof of pathology 1974-82; assoc prof & chmn of oral pathology 1981-82; UMC, assoc prof dept of oral pathology & radiology 1982-; Univ of MS Med Ctr, assoc prof dept of pathology 1982-; dir minority student affairs1982-. **ORGANIZATIONS:** Lay reader/vestry St Philips Episcopal Church; mem NAACP, Urban League, Amer Acad of Oral Pathology, Amer Assoc of Dental Schools, Amer Assoc of Medical Colls, Amer Dental Soc, Amer Medical Assoc, Amer Soc of Clinical Pathologists, Amer Soc of Cytology, Central MS Medical Soc, Intl Acad of Pathology, Intl Assoc of Dental Rsch, MS Medical and Surgical Assoc; bd of dir MS Div Amer Cancer Soc. **HONORS/ACHIEVEMENTS:** Fellowship NIH Hubbard Hosp Meharry St Univ of NY at Buffalo 1965-67; Fellowship NIH Amer Cancer Soc Buffalo 1967-69; Fellowship NIH NCI Roswell Park Buffalo 1967-70; Fellow Surgical Pathology & Cytopathology 1982-85 Dept of Pathology Univ of MS Medical Ctr; Fellow Amer Soc of Clinical Pathologists 1986-; Fellow Coll of Amer Pathologists 1986-; Bd of Certification, Diplomate Amer Bd of Dentistry, Fellow Amer Bd of Oral Pathology, Diplomate Amer Bd of Oral Pathology, Diplomate Amer Bd of Pathology Anatomic Pathology. **BUSINESS ADDRESS:** Minority Student Affairs Dir, Univ of MS Medical Center, 2500 N State St, Jackson, MS 39216.

BALLARD, BRUCE LAINE
Physician, psychiatrist. **PERSONAL:** Born Dec 19, 1939, Waverly Hills, KY; married Eleanor Glynn Cross; children: Tracy, Timothy. **EDUCATION:** Yale Univ, BA 1960; Columbia Univ Coll of Physicians & Surgeons, MD 1964. **CAREER:** Harlem Hospital Center - Dept of Psychiatry, assoc dir for training 1970-76; New York Hospital-Westchester Div, assoc dir - adult out patient dept 1976-81; Cornell Univ Medical Coll, assoc dean 1981-. **ORGANIZATIONS:** Amer Psychiatric Assn, chmn, selection/advisory comm for APA-NIMH fellowship program, 1974-80; chmn, comm of black psychiatrists, 1982-86. **HONORS/ACHIEVEMENTS:** American Psychiatric Assoc, fellow 1976. **MILITARY SERVICE:** US Air Force, captain 1968-70, commendation medal 1970. **BUSINESS ADDRESS:** Associate Dean, CornellUniv Med College, 1300 York Ave D-119, New York, NY 10021.

BALLARD, EDWARD HUNTER
Banker. **PERSONAL:** Born Apr 02, 1900, Lexington, KY; married Betty M Smith; children: Leslie Denise, Edward H Jr. **EDUCATION:** KS City, MO Gen Hosp, intern 1926-27; Howard Univ Wash DC, BS, MD. **CAREER:** Private Pract Birmingham, AL, physician 1927-49; Los Angeles, realtor 1950-64; Bank of Finance Los Angeles, organizer/chmn of bd 1964-, vice pres 1967-retirement. **ORGANIZATIONS:** Bd mem Watts Skill Center 1965-; adv council Dist Atty's Ofc 1965-; Comm Relations Conf So CA 1965-; exec bd Westside Br NAACP 1972-73; commrLos Angeles Co Health Facilities 1972-; bd dir Sickle Cell Disease Research Found 1965-73; chmn bd Men of Tomorrow 1967-69; bd dir Central City Comm Mental Health Center; mem Los Angeles C of C; Urban League; life mem Alpha Phi Alpha; mem AME Ch; Mason; Elks; former bd mem Morningside Hosp edevelProg; mem Community Relations conf; former mem United Way; bd life mem NAACP. **HONORS/ACHIEVEMENTS:** Awds from Howard Univ Alumni Assn of So CA; Awds Natl Assoc of Coll Women; Awd Miracle Mile Optimist Club; Awds Jesse M Unrah, Billy Mills, Mayor Tom Bradley, KDAY Radio Station Interdenominational Minister Alliance, Councilman Gilbert Lindsay.

BALLARD, GREG
Professional athlete. **PERSONAL:** Born Jan 29, 1955, Los Angeles, CA; married Donna; children: Lawrence, Gabrielle, Gregory Jr. **EDUCATION:** OR Univ, BS Commun Svc, Public Affairs 1977. **CAREER:** Washington Bullets, forward 1977-85; Golden State Warriors, small forward 1985-87. **ORGANIZATIONS:** Mem WA 1978 NBA World Championship Team; capt, player rep WA Bullets; hon chmn DC soc of Crippled Childrens Basketball Shootout. **HONORS/ACHIEVEMENTS:** Ranks among Bullets career leaders in games; inducted to Basketball Writers All-Amer Team; 1st team PAC-8 selection jr & sr yr OR Univ.

BALLARD, HAROLD STANLEY
Physician. **PERSONAL:** Born Nov 25, 1927, New Orleans, LA; married Gail; children: Harold Jr, Kevin. **EDUCATION:** Univ of CA, AB; Meharry Med Coll, MD. **CAREER:** Natl Heart Lung & Blood Inst, cons; Columbia Univ, clinical prof, physician & surgeon; NY VA Hosp, asst chf; physician. **ORGANIZATIONS:** Natl Inst of Health Cncl on Thrombosis; Amer Heart Assn Cert; Amer Bd of Intl Med; Hematology; oncology chmn policy bd Natural History Study of Sickle Cell Anemia. **HONORS/ACHIEVEMENTS:** Publ approx 30 scientific articles. **BUSINESS ADDRESS:** Physician, 408 1st Ave, New York, NY 10010.

BALLARD, JAMES M., JR.
Psychologist. **PERSONAL:** Born May 19, 1938, Petersburg, VA; married Natalie Dandridge; children: Tresa Melinda, James, III. **EDUCATION:** VA State Coll, BS 1963, MS 1964; attended IN Univ, Geo Washington Univ; Univ of MN, PhD Soc Psychol 1971. **CAREER:** Mid-Level Comm Clinical Psychology Prog, dir; Howard Univ, assoc prof; Univ of Manitoba, assoc prof; Bowie State Coll, first dir of Inst, Rsch & Eval; Crownsville State Hosp, staff psychol; BASS (Behavioral & Soc Sys), founder & pres. **ORGANIZATIONS:** Mem SE Psychol Assn; Amer Educ Research Assn; Assn of Black Psychologists; pres Eta Eta Lambda Chap Alpha Phi Alpha Frat; mem Psi Chi Psychol Hon Soc 1964. **HONORS/ACHIEVEMENTS:** Cited by NAACP for Svc/Inspiration/Support; Cert of Appreciation 1974. **MILITARY SERVICE:** USAF E-3 1955-59. **BUSINESS ADDRESS:** President, BASS Inc, PO Box 43, Arnold, MD 21012.

BALLARD, JANET JONES
University administrator. **PERSONAL:** Born Jun 09, 1930, New York, NY; daughter of

William Jones and Anna Jones; divorced; children: Ricki B Williams, Richard M Ballard III, Rodney J Ballard. **EDUCATION:** VA Union Univ, Richmond VA, BA, 1950; VA State Univ, Petersburgh VA, 1983-. **CAREER:** Richmond Dept of Welfare, Richmond VA, public asst case worker, 1956-61; Richmond Urban League, Richmond VA, exec dir, 1961-65; Richmond & Henrico Public Schools, Henrico County VA, substitute teacher, 1981-83; VA State Univ, Petersburg VA, alumni assn exec dir, 1983-84; VA State Univ, Petersburgh VA, dir alumni affairs, 1984-88; VA Union Univ, Richmond VA, dir alumni affairs, 1988-. **ORGANIZATIONS:** Mem, 1947-, supreme basileus 1986-, intl pres, Alpha Kappa Alpha Sorority Inc; bd mem, United Way Agencies, 1965-, United Negro College Fund Inc; mem, 1970-,natl parliamentarian, 1979-82, The Links Inc; bd of dir, Natl YWCA, 1970-82. **HONORS/ACHIEVEMENTS:** Citizen of the Year, Pan Hellenic Council of Richmond, 1972; Outstanding Woman of the Year in Volunteerism, City of Richmond, 1980; Distinguished Alumnus, NAFEO, 1988; volunteer service, YWCA, Richmond VA; publisher, "Hail State," VA State Univ Alumni Newsletter 1974-88, "Ivy Leaf Magazine," Alpha Kappa Alpha Sorority Quarterly, 1986-, "Interchange," Natl YWCA Quarterly Newspaper. **HOME ADDRESS:** 1726 Forest Glen Road, Richmond, VA 23228.

BALLARD, KATHRYN W.
Researcher. **PERSONAL:** Born Jun 10, 1930, Waverly Hills, KY. **EDUCATION:** Howard Univ, BS 1951; Univ of MI, MS 1953; Western Reserve Univ, MS 1959; Univ of So CA, PhD 1967. **CAREER:** Karolinska Institutet, visiting scientist 1968-70; Los Angeles County Heart Assn, sr investigator 1971-74; Univ of Southern CA, asst prof 1971-79; UCLA, assoc research physiologist 1979-; Univ of Southern CA Cardiovascular Rsch Lab, sr staff rsch assoc. **ORGANIZATIONS:** Mem Amer Heart Assn 1972-77; sec/treas Med Faculty Assn 1975-77; cncl Microcirculatory Soc 1974-77; faculty mem Med & Paramedical Seminars for HS Students; mem postdoctoral fellowship evaluation panel Natl Rsch Cncl 1977-; mem Faculty Senate 1977; attended several scientific meetings 1971-75; mem AAAS, Amer Physiol Soc, Microcirculatory Soc; elected to council on circulation Amer Heart Assn 1979; mem Arteriosclerosis Hypertension & Lipid Metabolism Adv Comm Natl Heart Lung & Blood Inst 1983-85. **HONORS/ACHIEVEMENTS:** Numerous articles & publns; grant recip NIH 1975-78; Weight Watchers Found Inc 1976-77; Amer Heart Assn 1976-77. **BUSINESS ADDRESS:** Senior Research Associate, Cardiovascular Research Lab, 1200 N State St, Res Bldg #1, Los Angeles, CA 90033.

BALLARD, MYRTLE ETHEL
Employment program manager. **PERSONAL:** Born Apr 20, 1930, Shreveport, LA; daughter of Henry Alexander, Jr and Roxanna Turner Gammage; married Thomas A Ballard, Jun 08, 1952; children: Thomas A Ballard, Jr, Roxane R Johnigan, Michael S Ballard,Alexandria Alicia Ballard. **EDUCATION:** Saint Mary's Coll, Moraga CA, BA, Public Mgmt, 1978. **CAREER:** CA State Employment Devel, Pleasant Hill CA, employment program mgr, 1967-. **ORGANIZATIONS:** Sec, Intl Assn of Personnel Security, 1971-73; sec, Black Personnel Mgmt Assn, 1972-75; pres, CA State Employees Assn, 1973-75; sec, Moneyworks, 1981-83; bd mem, CA Council on Children & Youth, 1973-75; mem, Lincoln Child Center, 1975-; bd chairperson, Sickle Cell Anemia Research & Educ, 1982-84; regional dir, Zeta Phi Beta Sorority, 1986-; loan exec, United Way, 1988. **HONORS/ACHIEVEMENTS:** Certificate of Appreciation, Sickle Cell Anemia Research, 1984; Zeta of the Year, Zeta Phi Beta Sorority, 1986; Those Who Care Award, Zeta Nu Chapter, Zeta Phi Beta, 1987; Noble Citizen, Phi Beta Sigma Fraternity, 1989. **HOME ADDRESS:** 2239 Dexter Way, Hayward, CA 94541.

BALLARD, WALTER W.
Dentist, educator. **PERSONAL:** Born Feb 12, 1928, Toledo, OH; married Joanne Marie Brown; children: Patricia Joan, Walter III. **EDUCATION:** Bowling Green State Univ, BA 1956; Notre Dame Univ, MS 1961; IN Univ, DDS 1963. **CAREER:** CO Univ, asst prof/oper dentist 1979-80. **ORGANIZATIONS:** Mem Amer Dental Assn, Natl Dental Assn, Chicago Dental Soc, IN Dental Assn 1963-80; mem CO Dental Assn 1966-80; pres trustee Southeastern CO Dental Assn 1974-75; chmn Cncl Jud Affairs CDA 1979-84; dist gov Lions Intl 1978-79; pres Peublo Symphony Assn 1979; Worshipful master Eureka #2 PHA F&AM 1979; Dentist Amer Soc Forensic Odontology 1971; Fellow Pierre Fouchard Soc 1974; Fellow Acad of Gen Dentistry 1978; Who's Who in SW 1978; Fellow Amer Coll of Dentists 1979. **MILITARY SERVICE:** USNR Lt 1946-73. **BUSINESS ADDRESS:** Asst Prof Oper Dentist, CO University, 1401 Elizabeth St, Pueblo, CO 81003.

BALLENTINE, KRIM MENELIK
Business executive. **PERSONAL:** Born Oct 22, 1936, St Louis, MO; son of Habib (Dickey) Ballentine and Rose Mae (Grimes) Ballentine; married Rosalie Erica Simmonds; children: Taraka T, Jabriel S. **EDUCATION:** Wayne St Univ, BS 1980; Univ of VA Quantico Continuing Educ Prog, Certificate 1980. **CAREER:** Pinkerton Natl Detective Agency, special investigator 1958-60; St Louis Airport Police, patrolman 1960-66; US Marshals Serv, chf dpty 1966-84 retired; St Thomas-St John Crime Comm, exec dir 1984-; ICOP Business Mgmt Consultant, exec officer 1984-. **ORGANIZATIONS:** Charter mem Natl Orgn of Black Law-Enforcement Exec; Intl Assn of Chiefs of Police; MO Peace Officers Assn; FBI Acad Assoc; vice pres Virgin Islands Boy Scout Council; US Navy League; Rotary Intl; IACP Police Support Serv Comm; Noble Drug Policy Comm; St Thomas-St John Chamber of Commerce; Disabled Amer Veterans; Intl Platform Assoc; Intl Assn of Law Enforcement Intelligence Analysts; life mem NAACP, Urban League; mem Northeast Regional Boy Scout Committee; pres Postal Customer's Council; exec dir Virgin Islands Republican State Committee. **HONORS/ACHIEVEMENTS:** Hon mem Mark Twain Soc; alum mem Wayne St U; Smithsonian Associates; contributing founder Natl Civil Rights Museum & Hall of Fame; 1988 delegate to Republican Convention; former local senatorial candidate; Order of the Arrow, Boy Scouts of America 1982; Silver Beaver, Boy Scouts of America 1983; book Krim's Simplistic Philosophies, Vantage Press Inc. **MILITARY SERVICE:** USAF & Army Res warrant officer 18 Yrs; National Defense, NCO Development Reserves Overseas Ribbon and Army Achievement Medal. **HOME ADDRESS:** PO Box 5396, St Thomas, Virgin Islands of the United States 00801. **BUSINESS ADDRESS:** Chief Executive Officer, ICOP, St Thomas, Virgin Islands of the United States 00801.

BALMER, HORACE DALTON, SR.
Professional sports executive. **PERSONAL:** Born May 28, 1939, Norfolk, VA; son of Martha W Balmer; married Pamela Walker, Horace D Balmer, Jr (divorced). **EDUCATION:** Norfolk State Univ, 1957-59; Virgina State Univ, 1959-60. **CAREER:** New York City Police Dept, detective, 1965-85; Natl Basketball Assn, asst dir of security, 1985-86, dir of security, 1986-89, vice pres & dir of security, 1989—. **ORGANIZATIONS:** Mem, Natl Org of Black Law Enforce Execs; mem, Intl Soc of Black Security Execs; mem, Intl Assn of Police Chiefs; mem, New York City Police Dept Guardians Assn; mem, NAACP. **HONORS/ACHIEVEMENTS:** Guardians Assn, 1985-87; Drug Enforcement Agency, 1986; 8 awards from New York City Police Dept, Elmcor-Youth Org, 1987. **BUSINESS ADDRESS:** Vice Pres & Dir of Security, Natl Basketball Assn, 645 Fifth Ave, 15th Fl, New York, NY 10022.

BALTHROPE, JACQUELINE MOOREHEAD
Educator. **PERSONAL:** Born Dec 02, Philadelphia, PA; married Robert G Balthrope, Sr (deceased); children: Robert G, Jr, Yvonne G, Robin B. **EDUCATION:** Central State Univ, BS (Magna Cum Laude) 1949; Case Western Reserve Univ, MA 1959, hrs on PhD; John Carroll Univ, Bowling Green State Univ, Cleveland State Univ, Kent State, post-grad work. **CAREER:** Cleveland Call-Post, free-lance writer/columnist; Chicago Defender, free-lance writer/columnist; Pittsburgh Courier Afro-Am, free-lance writer/columnist, 1960-69; Cleveland Public School System, teacher/supvr of student teachers; Cleveland Bd of Educ, Oliver Hazard Perry Elementary School, principal; Consultant, education. **ORGANIZATIONS:** Hon mem Entre Nous Club; mem/ofcr Royal Hearts Bridge Club; The Pair Ables Vol Homes for the Aged & Juvenile; active mem/ofcr Alpha Kappa Alpha Sor 1946-; Delta Kappa Gamma Soc 1972; Eta Phi Beta Sor 1972; Natl Sor of Phi Delta Kappa 1960; Natl Council Negro Women; Cleveland Chap The Carats Inc; Cleveland Squaws; The Jr League; mem local, state, natl Elem Sch Principals; active church worker St John AME Ch; vol Heart, Cancer, March of Dimes; UNICEF;Mental Health; United Negro Coll Fund; Girl Scouts Campaigns; Retarded Child; active mem/ofcr League of Women Voters; NAACP; YWCA; Phillis Wheatley Assn; Forest Hosp; Urban League & Guild; Phi Delta Kappa Natl Frat; organizer of Top Ladies of Distinction; Chums Inc; Project Friendship; Pi Lambda Omega; Amer Assoc of Univ Women. **HONORS/ACHIEVEMENTS:** Received scholastic, citizenship, civic and religious awards; Cleveland Tchr of the Year; Who's Who of the World; Who's Who of Amer Women; Who's Who in the Midwest; Outstanding Black Women of Cleveland OH; America's Outstanding Community Worker; Natl Honor Soc.

BALTIMORE, RICHARD LEWIS, III
Government official. **PERSONAL:** Born Dec 31, 1947, New York, NY. **EDUCATION:** MacMurray Coll, 1965-67; Geo Washington Univ, BA, 1969; Harvard Law Sch, JD, 1972. **CAREER:** Dept of State, fgn serv ofcr; US Embassy Lisbon, Portugal, polit/econ ofcr, 1973-75; US Embassy, Pretoria, S Africa, 1976-79; Dept of State, special asst, 1979-. **BUSINESS ADDRESS:** Special Assistant, Dept of State, Washington, DC 20520.

BALTIMORE, ROSLYN LOIS
Business executive. **PERSONAL:** Born Dec 17, 1942, New York, NY; daughter of Richard Baltimore, Jr. and Lois Baltimore; divorced; children: Richard. **EDUCATION:** Boston Univ, AB 1964; Harvard Graduate School of Educ, EdM 1970; Harvard Business School, MBA 1972. **CAREER:** Paul Sack Prop, asst devel 1972-73; Wells Fargo Bank, asst vice pres 1973-77; R L Baltimore Co, owner, pres. **HONORS/ACHIEVEMENTS:** Pres Handicapped Access Appeals Bd 1985; bd mem Reality House W 1978-; dir Bay Area Rapid Transit P; Business woman of yr Savvy Magazine 1984; proclomation Mayor of San Francisco 1985; Key to Evansville City of Evansville, In 1985; honorary mem Sigma Gamma Rho 1986. **BUSINESS ADDRESS:** President, Baltimore Mortgage Co, 699 Second St, Suite 110, San Francisco, CA 94107.

BALTON, KIRKWOOD R.
Business executive. **PERSONAL:** Born Jun 09, 1935, Birmingham, AL; married Juanita Jackson; children: Adriene. **EDUCATION:** Miles Coll, BS 1957; Stamford Univ, MBA 1970. **CAREER:** Bradford's Industrial Insurance Co, bookkeeper, 1957-59; Booker T Washington Insurance Co, bookkeeper, internal auditor, admin asst to pres & vice pres, 1959-73, executive vice pres, mem bd of dir 1973-; Booker T Washington Broadcasting Services Inc & A G Gaston Construction Co Inc, pres 1988-. **ORGANIZATIONS:** Jefferson Co Pensions & Sec; bd dir Birmingham Turf Club, Birmingham Area Chamber of Commerce, mem, Our Lady Queen of the Univ Catholic Church, Birmingham Broadcast Council, Rotary International, Leadership Birmingham Class of 1986-87, Natl Assn of Black-Owned Broadcasters, Jefferson Club, Alpha Phi Alpha Fraternity, Resolutions Committee-Camp Fire 1987; bd dir, A G Gaston Boys' Club Inc, All Amer Bowl, Jefferson County Department of Human Resources, Alabama School of Fine Arts Foundation, Metropolitan Development Board, Birmingham Historical Society Inc, Birmingham Area Council Camp Fire -past pres, Birmingham Turf Club Inc, Greater Birmingham Convention Bureau, Natl Camp Fire Inc, Lakeshore Inc and Lakeshore Hospital, Associated Builders & Contractors of Alabama Inc, Colonial Bank. **BUSINESS ADDRESS:** Executive Vice President, Booker T Washington Ins Co, PO Box 697, Birmingham, AL 35201.

BAMBARA, TONI CADE (TONI CADE)
Educator, author. **PERSONAL:** Born Mar 25, 1939, New York, NY; daughter of Helen Brent Henderson Cade. **EDUCATION:** Queens College, New York NY, BA, Theater Arts, 1959; City College of New York, MA, Lit, 1963; attended New York Univ and New School for Social Research. **CAREER:** New York State Dept of Social Welfare, New York NY, social investigatior, 1956-9; Metropolitan Hospital, New York NY, dir of recreation in psychiatry department, 1961-62; Colony House Community Center, New York NY, program dir, 1962-65; SEEK Program, City College of the City Univ of New York, New York NY, English instructor, 1965-69; Livingston College, Rutgers Univ, New Brunswick NJ, asst prof, 1969-74; Stephens College, Columbia MO, visiting prof of African Studies, 1975; Atlanta Univ, Atlanta GA, visiting prof, 1977, research mentor and instructor at School of Social Work, 1977, 1979; founder, 1976, dir, 1976-85, Pamoja Writers Collective; artist-in-residence for Neighborhood Arts Center, 1975-79. **ORGANIZATIONS:** Mem, screenwriters Guild of Amer, 1980-; mem, Natl Assn of Third World Writers; mem, African Amer Film Soc; mem, board of dir, Sisters in Support of South African Sisterhood; participant in lecture series (the Paul Robeson Scholar Series of Rutgers, the Ida B Wells Lecture Series of Univ of MD, The Reid Speakers Series of Barnard, the Ralph Bunche Scholar Series of Colby Coll); mem, board of dir, Sojourner Productions, Inc and Meridian. **HONORS/ACHIEVEMENTS:** Natl Assn of Negro Business & Professional Women's Club League Award for service to Black women; Child Develop Inst Award for service to Black children; George Washington Carver Distinguished African Amer Lecturer Award, Simpson College; Ebony Magazine Achievement In the Arts Award; Bronze Jubilee Award for Literature, WETV; Black Arts Award, Kaleidoscope Program of the Univ of Missouri; Rutgers Univ Sr Fellowship for curriculum work at Livingston College; Livingston College Comm Award for service to students; Theatre of the Black Experience Award; John Golden Award for fiction; Peter Pauper Press Award for journalism; TV documentary script writer and narration ; author of scripts The Bombing of Osage,

1986, and Cecil B Moore, Master Tactician of Direct Action, 1987; Langston Hughes Medallion, Langston Hughes Soc, City College of New York, 1986; Natl Endowment for the Arts Individual Literature Grant, 1980; author of award-winning works incl, The Salt Eaters (won the Amer Book Award in 1981), Random House, 1980; author of novel If Blessing Comes, Random House, 1987; editor of Tales and Stories for Black Folks, New American Library, 1975; The Mama Load, publ in Redbook (was a finalist for Best Amer Short Stories of 1978); anthology Tales and Short Stories for Black Folks (named Outstanding Book of 1972 in juv lit by New York Times; first collection Gorilla, My Love (won Black Rose Award from Encore Mag 1972); anthology The Black Woman pub in 1970 now in 18th edition; wrote several plays; over 50 articles and stories appeared in Negro Digest, The New York Times, MS, Redbook, Callaloo, First World and other publns; Best Documentary of 1986 Award from Pennsylvania Assn of Broadcasters and Documentary Award, National Black Programming Consortium, for The Bombing of Osage, 1986. **HOME ADDRESS:** 5720 Wissahickon Ave, Apt E12, Philadelphia, PA 19144. *

BANCROFT, RICHARD ANDERSON
Retired superior court judge. **PERSONAL:** Born Aug 30, 1918, Albany, NY; son of William Bancroft and Anna Bancroft; married Barbara; children: Richard, William, David, Kathleen. **EDUCATION:** Howard Univ, AB 1942, JD 1951; Univ of CA, LLM 1952. **CAREER:** Private pract, atty 1954-76; State of CA, superior court judge 1976-88; currently active as judge pro tem, arbitrator, referee, special master, and mediator, lecturer and seminar and panel leader, re bias and prejudice in and out of judicial system. **ORGANIZATIONS:** Trustee Alameda Co Law Libr; past dir Bay Area Rapid Transit; past bd mem Permit Appeals; past mem CA State Bar Assn; Amer Assn of Trial Lawyers; CA Assn of Trial Lawyers; CA Atty for Criminal Justice; past dir Mt Zion Hosp med Cntr; past pres San Francisco NAACP; past sec/treas Comm Bd Prog. **HONORS/ACHIEVEMENTS:** Published, "Practice & Procedure Before the Industrial Accident Commn" Univ of California Boalt Hall Law Review 1952; "Mainstreaming, Controversy & Consensus"; "Special Educ -Legal Aspects". **MILITARY SERVICE:** USMC Sgt 1944-46. **BUSINESS ADDRESS:** Retired Superior Court Judge, 640 Santa Barbara Road, Berkeley, CA 94707.

BANDO, THELMA PREYER
Retired educator. **PERSONAL:** Born Mar 11, 1919, Philadelphia, PA; daughter of Henry J Preyer and Katherine Person Preyer Perry; married McDonald M Bando, MD, Dec 27, 1947 (deceased). **EDUCATION:** Howard Univ, BA 1935; VA Sem & Coll, LHD; Columbia Univ, MA 1939; Univ of PA, postgrad 1940; Temple Univ, postgrad 1949-55. **CAREER:** Bishop Coll, chmn Educ Dept 1939-40; Dudley HS, chmn Eng Dept 1940-41; Morgan State Univ, assoc prof 1942-55, dean 1942-77 (retired). **ORGANIZATIONS:** Coll Woman's Assn; Alpha Kappa Alpha; natl pres Chi Delta Mu Wives 1949-53; Governor's Commn on Status of Women; pres Women's Med Auxil Balt, MD; commissioner Baltimore City Commission for Women; pres Philomathian Club; bd mem Pickersgill, Park Ave Lodge. **HONORS/ACHIEVEMENTS:** Received 2 major proclamations in Balt, MD; At Morgan Univ founder of, Women's Week, Charm Club, Mentor Syst, Coll Canteen; Author Handbook for Coll Res Hall Dir; Author Guide for Off Campus Housing; Author Handbook for Mentors; City Council Award; Morgan State Univ Meritorious Awd. **HOME ADDRESS:** 3506 Callaway Ave, Baltimore, MD 21215.

BANDY, RILEY THOMAS, SR.
Retired insurance agency director. **PERSONAL:** Born May 14, 1920, Beloit, WI; married Norma H; children: Riley Jr, Larry. **EDUCATION:** Lane Coll, AB 1947. **CAREER:** Wright Mutual Ins Co, asst vice pres 1981, conserv dir; Great Lakes Ins Co, mgr, assoc agency dir. **ORGANIZATIONS:** Mem & past pres Detroit Council of Ins Exec 1973-75; past vice pres Michigan NAACP; past pres Detroit Lane Coll Alumni; chmn trustee bd Carter Metropolitan CME Church Detroit 1976-77; mem Alpha Phi Alpha; life mem NAACP. **HONORS/ACHIEVEMENTS:** Outstanding Alumni Award Lane Coll, 1971; elected to Athletic Hall of Fame Lane Coll 1984. **MILITARY SERVICE:** USAC Sgt. **BUSINESS ADDRESS:** Agency Dir, 2995 E Grand Blvd, Detroit, MI 48203.

BANFIELD, ANNE L.
Public relations director. **PERSONAL:** Born May 27, 1925, Detroit, MI; married William J Banfield; children: DuVaughn, Bruce, William Credric. **EDUCATION:** Detroit Inst of Commerce Sec Sci, attended 1945; Wayne State Univ, 1 year; HP Coll, Univ of MI, Wayne Comm Coll. **CAREER:** AUS Signal Corps, tech sec/chf engr; Dr HM Nuttall, med sec; Julian Rodgers & Julian Perry, legal sec; Anne's Secretarial Svc, self-employed; YWCA, sec to exec dir; Detroit Inst of Commerce, asst admissions ofcr, asst ofc mgr; MI Chronicle, public relations dir. **ORGANIZATIONS:** Bd mem Natl Media Women; bd mem Mayor's Keep Detroit Beautiful Comm; mem Women's Econ Club of Detroit; mem Women's Conf of Concerns; mem Women's Comm United Negro Coll Fund; bd mem Randolph Wallace Kidney Found; Urban League; Natl Tech Assn Auxiliary; Concerned Boaters. **BUSINESS ADDRESS:** President, Anna Lue Enterprise, 21017 Green Hill Rd #260, Farmington Hills, MI 48024.

BANFIELD, EDISON H.
Surgeon. **PERSONAL:** Born Jun 25, 1924, Baltimore, MD; married Julia; children: Ava, Yvonne, Stephen, Edison, Jr. **EDUCATION:** Howard Univ, BS (cum laude) 1950, MD 1954. **CAREER:** Baylor Coll of Med, instr surgery; private practice, physician/surgeon. **ORGANIZATIONS:** Fellow of Amer Coll of Surgeons 1963. **MILITARY SERVICE:** AUS Corpl 1943-46. **BUSINESS ADDRESS:** Physician, 2914 Blodgett, Houston, TX 77004.

BANJO, CASPER
Artist. **PERSONAL:** Born Feb 13, 1937, Memphis, TN. **EDUCATION:** Laney Coll, AA 1970; SF Art Inst, BFA 1973, MFA 1975. **CAREER:** World Print Compt, staff 1976; self-employed artist, one man show Rockridge Medical Ctr Oakland CA 1977, Eastern Washington State Coll Spokane 1977, Wells Fargo Bank Gallery Traveling Show 1978, recent paintings and prints Los Medeno's Coll Pittsburg CA 1979. **ORGANIZATIONS:** Urban Art Prog 1972-73; instr Roosevelt Jr HS Commn Proj 1973-74; Black Cowboy in the West Oakland Museum 1974; spec proj Fillmore & Fell Corp 1975, Black Filmmakers Hall of Fame Handprints 1975-87; prog coord Rockridge Med Ctr Art Displays 1975-77; Dr Muse Bicentennial Intl Conf of Jazz 1976; Aesthetics of Graffiti Show SF Museum of Modern Art 1978; politics & social criticism Berkeley Art Ctr Berkeley Univ 1980; group exhibit Oakland Ensemble Theatre Exhibit 1980; mem N Oakland Planning Comm Libr. **HONORS/ACHIEVEMENTS:** Dr Karl Thomte Scholarship 1970; The Studio Museum in Harlem Traveling Exhib (Impressions/Expressions Black Amer Graphics) 1979-80; Impressions/Expressions Black Amer Graphics Howard Univ 1980; traveling exhibition Smithsonian Inst 1980-83; Toward Black Esthetic; Solano Comm Coll CA 1981; Laney Coll Expression in Brick on Papers Oakland CA 1985; The Written Word Twin Palms Gallery San Francisco CA 1985; "Black Artist on Art" Vol II 1971; "Hambone" Harmony House Stanford Univ 1974; "Three Afro-Amer Artists" Lagos, Nigeria Caralog, 1977.

BANKETT, WILLIAM DANIEL
Government official. **PERSONAL:** Born Dec 08, 1930, Oak Grove, VA; son of William Daniel Rich and Edna Weeden Rich; married Evelyn Robinson Bankett, Jun 25, 1955; children: Wendell, Kevin. **EDUCATION:** West Virginia State Coll, Institute WV, BS, 1954; George Washington Univ, Washington DC, 1957-58; Hampton Inst, Hampton VA, 1961; Massachusetts Inst of Technology, Boston MA, certified Urban Exec, 1972. **CAREER:** Natl Security Agency, Washington DC, 1954-55; Dept of Agriculture, Minneapolis, MN, examiner, 1955-57; Westmoreland County Schools, Oak Grove VA, principal, 1957-62; Prince William County Schools, Manassas VA, principal, 1962-67; Southeast House, Washington DC, exec dir, 1967-68; Southwest Community House, Washington, DC, exec dir, 1968-70; Redevelopment Land Agency, Dept of Housing & Community Devel, area dir, 1970-; chief exec officer, Dan the Man Mustangs Inc, 1973-. **ORGANIZATIONS:** Vice pres, Elementary Principals Assn, 1960-65; mem, Mayor's Economic Task Force, 1970-78; mem, VOICE, 1970-79; mem, Anacostia Economic Devel Corp, 1970-80,mem, Marlton Swim Assn, 1972-; mem Mustang Club of Amer, 1980-; mem Dept of Housing & Community Devel Assn, 1985-; vice pres at Johnson Alumni Assn 1986-. **HONORS/ACHIEVEMENTS:** Outstanding Mem Award, Amer Cancer Soc, 1985, 1986, 1987; Presidential Award, Amer Cancer Soc, 1988; Platinum Award for going 266% above the quota, DC One Fund, 1988; author, "Schools Without Grades," Virginia Educ Journal, 1967. **MILITARY SERVICE:** US Army corporal, 1945-47; Good Conduct, Sharp Shooter, 1946.

BANKHEAD, PATRICIA ANN
Educator. **PERSONAL:** Born Dec 30, 1947, Los Angeles, CA. **EDUCATION:** CA State Univ Los Angeles, BS Sociology 1972; Pepperdine Univ, MS School Mgmt 1976; San Jose State Univ, Certificate Aerospace Educ 1983. **CAREER:** Los Angeles Unified School Dist, elem teacher 1973-76; CA Lutheran Coll, lecturer 1977; Los Angeles Southwest Coll, instructor 1977-80; Los Angeles Unified School Dist, program coord 1977-80; State of CA, mentor/teacher 1984-87. **ORGANIZATIONS:** Sponsor Black Women's Forum Los Angeles 1980-87; mem adv bd United Negro College Fund 1981-87; official hostess City of Los Angeles 1983-87; mem NAACP 1984-87; mem Mentor Adv Bd LA Unified Schools 1984-87, CA Aerospace Assoc 1985-87, Delta Kappa Gamma Intl 1987; mem Natl Cncl of Negro Women 1987. **HONORS/ACHIEVEMENTS:** Black College Fair Black Women's Forum 1981; selected for Public Service TV spot State of CA Dept of Educ 1986; Letter of Appreciation for Serv Supt of Educ State of CA 1986; Certificate of Appreciation Mayor of Los Angeles for 200 service hrs; Letter of Recognition as Master Teacher City of Los Angeles. **BUSINESS ADDRESS:** Mentor Teacher State of CA, Los Angeles Unified Sch Dist, 1745 Vineyard Ave, Los Angeles, CA 90019.

BANKHEAD, PORTER LEE
Business executive. **PERSONAL:** Born Sep 28, 1941, Hickory Grove, SC. **EDUCATION:** SC State Coll, BS 1963. **CAREER:** NASA Goddard Space Flight Ctr, mathematician 1966-67; Dept of the Army, mathematician 1967; Computer Scis Corp, computer programmer 1967-69; Avco Systems Div, computer programmer/analyst 1969-73; Systems & Applied Scis Corp, chmn/ceo 1973-. **ORGANIZATIONS:** Vice chmn Aerospace & Electronic Systems Soc IEEE 1980-81; bd dirs Dem Bus Cncl Washington 1983; mem Dem Natl Conv Arrangements Comm Washington 1983; mem Armed Forces Comm & Electronics Assn; mem Air Force Assn; mem Natl Space Club; mem Kappa Alpha Psi. **MILITARY SERVICE:** AUS lt 1963-65. **BUSINESS ADDRESS:** President, Systems & Applied Science Corp, 1577 Springhill Rd, Vienna, VA 22180.

BANKS, ARTHUR C., JR.
Educator. **PERSONAL:** Born Nov 07, 1915, Columbus, OH; married Bertha Means; children: David, Dannett, Howard. **EDUCATION:** St John's Univ, BS 1939; NYU, MA 1945; Johns Hopkins Univ, PhD 1949. **CAREER:** NY Univ, lecturer, 1945; Southern Univ, Baton Rouge LA, instructor, 1945-46; Morehouse Coll, instructor, 1946-47; Fisk Univ, asst prof & lecturer, 1951; NC Coll, asst prof, 1951-54; Morgan State Coll, asst dean, 1954-57; Atlanta Univ, visiting prof, 1958-59; Morehouse Coll, prof, 1959-67; Emory Univ, exchange prof, 1965; Greater Hartford Comm Coll, pres, 1967-85. **ORGANIZATIONS:** Mem Amer Assn Comm & Jr Coll; New England Jr Coll Council; Amer Polit Sci Assn; New England Polit Sci Assn; numerous comm assignments & organizations. **BUSINESS ADDRESS:** President Emeritus, Greater Hartford Comm College, 61 Woodland St, Hartford, CT 06105.

BANKS, BEATRICE
Business executive. **PERSONAL:** Born Jul 24, 1936, Uniontown, AL; daughter of Mr & Mrs Robert Banks. **EDUCATION:** Wayne State Univ, BS 1963. **CAREER:** Detroit Bd Educ, tchr 1963; Residential & consumer Serv, advisor 1963-71, asst supvr 1971-72; Detroit Wayne Div Customer Marketing Serv, asst mgr 1972-74, mgr 1974-75, dir marketing serv Detroit Div 1975-79; dir, Customer & Marketing Srrv, Macomb Div, 1979-80; Detroit Edison Co, asst mgr 1980-. **ORGANIZATIONS:** Mem Women's Econ Club, Engrg Soc of Detroit, Greater Detroit C of C, Project Pride Board, Corp Urban Forum; bd dir Don Bosco Home for Boys, State of Michigan ivil Rights Commission 1979-84. **HONORS/ACHIEVEMENTS:** Headliner Awd Women of Wayne State Univ 1976; YMCA Minority Achievement Awd 1982. **BUSINESS ADDRESS:** Asst Mgr, Detroit Edison Co, 2000 Second Ave, Detroit, MI 48221.

BANKS, BRENDA L.
Physician. **PERSONAL:** Born May 18, 1953, Natchez, MS. **EDUCATION:** Southern Univ, BS 1977; Meharry Medical Coll, MD 1981. **CAREER:** Brooke Army Medical Ctr, internship 1981-82; King/Drew Medical Ctr, pgy III internal medicine. **ORGANIZATIONS:** General medical officer Army Medical Corp Martin Army Hosp Ft Benning 1982-85; assoc mem Amer Coll of Physicians, Amer Cancer Soc; cirriculum comm Meharry Medical Coll; mem Alpha Kappa Alpha Southern Univ. **HONORS/ACHIEVEMENTS:** Outstanding Young Woman of Amer 1984. **MILITARY SERVICE:** AUS Medical Corps capt

4 1/2 yrs; Army Achievement Medal 1985. **BUSINESS ADDRESS:** PGY III Internal Medicine, King/Drew Medical Ctr, 12021 So Wilmington Ave, Los Angeles, CA 90059.

BANKS, CARL A.
Attorney. **PERSONAL:** Born Jul 08, 1903, Washington, DC; son of Austin Banks and Elizabeth Banks; divorced; children: Ellen V, Carl A Jr. **EDUCATION:** Robt H Terrell Law School, LLB 1947. **CAREER:** Private practice, attny. **ORGANIZATIONS:** Past pres Armstrong Neighborhood Fed Credit Union; past legal counsel & mem bd of dir Amer Fed of Comm Credit Unions; chief legal counsel Church of God & Sts of Christ. **BUSINESS ADDRESS:** Attorney, 904 Euclid St NW, Washington, DC 20001.

BANKS, CARLTON LUTHER
Staff accountant. **PERSONAL:** Born Apr 09, 1958, Bronx, NY; married Creecy Seymore; children: Regina, Attallah. **EDUCATION:** Morgan State Univ, BA 1980; New York Univ, Certificate Direct Marketing 1985. **CAREER:** TroCar Realty Inc, vice pres 1981-85; The Greek Gallery, pres. **ORGANIZATIONS:** Keeper of finance 1987-, mem Omega Psi Phi Frat 1977-, Direct Marketing Club NY 1986-, NAACP 1987-. **HOME ADDRESS:** 676 Riverside Dr #10A, New York, NY 10031.

BANKS, CAROLINE LONG
City councilwoman. **PERSONAL:** Born Oct 30, 1940, McDonough, GA; daughter of Ralph A Long and Rubye Carolyn Hall Long; divorced; children: April Lynn, James H. **EDUCATION:** Clark College, Atlanta GA, BA, 1962; attended Univ of Hawaii, 1962-64; Georgia State Univ, MA, 1973. **CAREER:** Atlanta City Council, Atlanta GA, councilwoman, 1980-, vice-chair of Community Devel Comm, 1980-85, Human Resources Comm, 1983, and Transp Comm, 1984-87, chair of Comm on Coun, 1983, and zoning comm, 1986; Governor's Staff, Lt Col and Honorary Aide-de-Camp, beginning in 1983; Atlanta Univ Criminal Justice Center, mem of board of dir, beginning in 1982; Collections of Life and Heritage, member of board of dir beginning in 1985; Atlanta Preservation Task Force, chairwoman, beginning in 1986. **ORGANIZATIONS:** Area dir, 1980-86, treas, 1987, Natl Black Caucus of Local Elected Officials; sec, Georgia Black Elected Officials; mem, Public Safety Policy Comm, Georgia Municipal Assn, 1981-87; mem of public safety policy comm, Natl League of Cities, 1987; Delta Sigma Theta. **HONORS/ACHIEVEMENTS:** Bronze Woman of the Year, Iota Phi Lambda, 1980. **BUSINESS ADDRESS:** 68 Mitchell St S W, Atlanta, GA 30335. *

BANKS, CECIL J.
Attorney. **PERSONAL:** Born Sep 27, 1947, Des Moines, IA; married Dr Margot H Banks; children: Kimberly, Imani, Jamaal. **EDUCATION:** Sophia Univ Tokyo, Japan; Duquesene Univ, BA 1970; Univ of Pittsburgh Grad School of Public & Intl Affairs, MPA 1974; Rutgers Univ School of Law, JD 1976. **CAREER:** Newark Board of Educ, gen counsel 1978-82; City of Orange, legislative counsel 1980-, city atty 1984; Sills Beck Cummis, Zuckerman Radin Tischman & Epstein,partner 1984-. **ORGANIZATIONS:** Bd trustees United Comm Corp; chmn Young Lawyer's Com Essex Co Bar Assn; bd dir NAACP; mem Natl Bar Assn, Amer Bar Assn, Natl Assn of Bond Lawyers; bd mem Natl Assn of School Law Attys; bd of dir Community Coop Devel Found Bridgeport CT. **HONORS/ACHIEVEMENTS:** Serv Awd United Comm Corp; Serv Awd United Clergy of the Oranges; listed in Who's Who in Amer Law. **BUSINESS ADDRESS:** Partner, Sills, Beck, Cummis, Zuckerman, Radin, Tischman & Epstein, 33 Washington, Newark, NJ 07102.

BANKS, CHIP
Professional athlete. **PERSONAL:** Born Sep 18, 1959, Ft Lawton, OK. **EDUCATION:** Attended, Southern CA. **CAREER:** Cleveland Browns, linebacker 1982-. **HONORS/ACHIEVEMENTS:** Three year All PAC 10 team member; All NFL Rookie Team Choice 1982; Brown's Defensive MVP as selected by Cleveland TD Club; Awards for Performance in Pro Bowl 1983; Only fourth Brown to gain Pro Bowl honors as rookie; earned Pro Football Weekly Defensive Player of Week Awd 1983; All-NFL; 1st Team All-AFC; 2nd Team NFL All-Pro; Best Linebacker in AFC by NFL Players Assn; NFL Defensive Rookie of the Yr; 2nd Team All-AFC; AFC Defensive Rookie of the Yr; mem NFL Pro Bowl teams 1986,87. **BUSINESS ADDRESS:** Cleveland Browns, Cleveland Stadium, Cleveland, OH 44114.

BANKS, CULLEN W.
Government admin. **PERSONAL:** Born Jul 06, 1946, Baltimore, MD; divorced; children: Monifa, Keisha. **EDUCATION:** Morgan State Univ, BA 1968; Atlanta Univ, MA 1972. **CAREER:** NJ State Parole Bd, exec clemency investigator.

BANKS, DIANE LEWIS
Public administrator. **PERSONAL:** Born in New York, NY; daughter of George A Lewis and Alyce Morris Lewis; divorced. **EDUCATION:** Beaver Coll, Glenside PA, BA, 1969; Columbia Univ, New York NY, MS, 1977. **CAREER:** Natl Urban League, New York NY, project dir, 1970-73; Center for Urban Educ, New York NY, liaison, 1970-71; Trans Urban East, New York NY, consultant, 1972-73; Jamaica Urban Devel Corp, Kingston, Jamaica, West Indies, social planner, 1974-76; City of Oakland, Oakland CA, sr urban economic analyst, 1977-83, div mgr, 1983-. **ORGANIZATIONS:** Consultant, Trans Urban East Org, 1972-73; vice pres, Progressive Black Business & Professional Women, 1983-86; assoc mem, Urban Land Inst, 1984-; chair, Economic Devel Comm, BAPAC, 1984-86; past vice pres & sec, chmn nominations comm, Citicentre Dance Theatre, 1985-; mem, Niagara Movement Democratic Club, 1977-80, Natl Assn of Planners, 1978-, Black Women Organized for Political Action, 1983-84, Natl Forum for Black Public Admin, 1985-, Amer Soc of Public Admin, 1988-. **HONORS/ACHIEVEMENTS:** William F Kinne Fellowship, Columbia Univ, 1972, 1977; Intl Fellow, Columbia Univ, 1972-73; Intl Intern, Ford Found, 1973-74; speaker, Council of Minority Public Admin, 1988, Southeastern Conf of Public Admin, 1988, Amer Soc of Public Admin, 1989. **BUSINESS ADDRESS:** Mgr, Business Devel Div, City of Oakland, Office of Economic Devel & Employment, 1417 Clay St, Oakland, CA 94612.

BANKS, DWAYNE MARTIN
Educator. **PERSONAL:** Born Apr 07, 1961, Newport News, VA. **EDUCATION:** Norfolk State Univ, BS 1985. **CAREER:** NEA, teacher. **ORGANIZATIONS:** Bd mem SCA 1986-87, PTA 1986-87. **HONORS/ACHIEVEMENTS:** Deans List Norfolk State Univ 1985. **HOME ADDRESS:** 604 S Ave, Newport News, VA 23601. **BUSINESS ADDRESS:** Teacher, NEA, 4200 Marshall Ave, Newport News, VA 23607.

BANKS, ELLEN
Artist. **PERSONAL:** Born in Boston, MA. **EDUCATION:** MA Coll of Art, BA; School Museum of Fine Arts. **CAREER:** Dunbarton Galleries, painter/exhibits 1962; Boston Mus Fine Arts 1970; Smith-Mason Gallery 1971; Natl Ctr Afro-Am Artist. **HONORS/ACHIEVEMENTS:** Recipient Prix De Paris 1967. **BUSINESS ADDRESS:** 230 the Fenway, Boston, MA 02115.

BANKS, ERNEST (ERNIE)
Baseball coach. **PERSONAL:** Born Jan 31, 1931, Dallas, TX; married Marjorie; children: Jan, Jerry, Joey, Lyndel. **CAREER:** Negro Amer League, 1950-53; Kansas City Monarchs, 1953-54; Seaway Natl Bank, exec; Chicago Cubs, former player, first base coach 1954-. **ORGANIZATIONS:** Bd mgr Chicago Met YMCA; bd mem Chicago Transit Auth; bd mem LA Urban League; motivational lecturer. **HONORS/ACHIEVEMENTS:** Author "Mr Cub"; Named Most Valuable Player in Natl League 1958-59; Played in 13 All-Star Games; Named to TX Sports Hall of Fame 1971; Holds Natl Record forgrand slam home runs; Inducted into Natl Baseball Hall of Fame 1977. **MILITARY SERVICE:** US Army. **BUSINESS ADDRESS:** P O Box 24302, Los Angeles, CA 90024.

BANKS, FRED L, JR.
Circut judge. **PERSONAL:** Born Sep 01, 1942, Jackson, MS; son of Fred L Banks and Violet Mabery Banks; married Pamela Gipson, Jan 28, 78; children: Rachel, Jonathan, Gabrielle. **EDUCATION:** Howard Univ, BA 1965; Howard Univ Sch of Law, JD 1968. **CAREER:** Banks, Nichols Attys & Pred, 1968-84; Mississippi House of Rep, rep 1976-85; Banks Owens & Byrd Attys, partner 1985; 7th Circuit Court Dist of Mississippi, circuit judge 1985-. **ORGANIZATIONS:** Pres State Mutual Fed Savings & Loan Assn 1979-89; mem Mississippi Bd of Bar Admissions 1978-80; mem natl adv comm Educ of Disadvantaged Children 1978-80; mem natl bd of dir NAACP 1982-, Jackson Goodwill Industries 1985-. **HONORS/ACHIEVEMENTS:** Numerous civic awards from state and local organizations. **BUSINESS ADDRESS:** Circuit Judge, 7th Circuit Court Dist of Mississippi, Box 290, Jackson, MS 39205.

BANKS, GARNIE
Elected government official. **PERSONAL:** Born Oct 09, 1932, Elizabeth City, NC; married Alma Billups (deceased); children: Robin Banks, Sandra B Batise. **EDUCATION:** Elizabeth City State Univ, 1959; Coll of Albermarle, 1963; Good Year Trade Work Shop Williamsburg VA, Front End Alignment 1973; Inst of Governor Chapel HillNC, Training 1982. **CAREER:** Elizabeth City Boys Club, troop-leader 1956-57; Cornerstone Baptist Church, supt of ss 1957-72; Trustee Bd, vice chmn 1971-74; Deacon Bd cornerstone Baptist Church, vice chmn 1979-83; Public Works, vice chmn 1980; Perry Tire Store, alignment mgr; City of Elizabeth NC, city councilman. **ORGANIZATIONS:** Mem Pasquotank Cty ABC Bd 1979-81; Fireman's Relief Fund 1981, New Horizon 1981, Task Force Fair Housing; vice chmn, mem City Councilman Civic Affairs NAACP 1984; chmn Public Works Comm for City Council City of Elizabeth NC. **HONORS/ACHIEVEMENTS:** Man of the Year Cornerstone Baptist Church E City NC 1974; Cert of Honor Omega Psi Phi Frat E City NC 1979; Hunts Dinner Bell Governor Hunt's Dinner Bell Raleigh NC 1980; Men's Day Speaker Cornerstone Baptist Church. **MILITARY SERVICE:** AUS sgt 2 yrs; Good Conduct 1953-55. **BUSINESS ADDRESS:** City Councilman, City of Elizabeth City NC, 501 Elizabeth St, Elizabeth City, NC 27909.

BANKS, GENE
Professional athlete. **PERSONAL:** Born May 15, 1959, Philadelphia, PA; married Belle. **EDUCATION:** Duke Univ, BS 1981. **CAREER:** San Antonio Spurs, forward 1981-. **ORGANIZATIONS:** Walter Kennedy Citizenship Award 1984. **HONORS/ACHIEVEMENTS:** Season high 28 points with 13 rebounds 1984; 56 games with double points incl 12 with 20 plus led in steals 21 times, 17 in rebounds; 1984 Walter Kenendy Citizenship Award; career high of 568 shooting, 741 at the line, 256 fouls, 105 steals, 23 blocks, all were 1983-84; All-ACC as a senior and All-Amer; ACC rookieof the year and led Duke to NCAA finals. **BUSINESS ADDRESS:** San Antonio Spurs, Hemis Fair Arena, San Antonio, TX 78292.

BANKS, GORDON
Professional athlete. **PERSONAL:** Born Mar 12, 1958, Los Angeles, CA. **EDUCATION:** Stanford, Pol Sci. **CAREER:** New Orleans, 1980-81; Oakland Invaders, wide receiver 1984-. **ORGANIZATIONS:** Pres GBI Entr (company dealing in gold & silver commodities). **HONORS/ACHIEVEMENTS:** One of two players to have caught a pass in All 36 USFL regular season games; one of 6 players to have started all 36 Invaders games; holds club record for career receptions (125) and career receiving yardage (1,792); 4 yr letterman in both ftbl & track at Stanford.

BANKS, J. B.
Government official. **PERSONAL:** Born Mar 13, 1934, Missouri; married Annette. **EDUCATION:** Washington Univ, MA; Attended, Lincoln Univ. **CAREER:** State of Missouri, rep, 1966-76, senator 1976-. **ORGANIZATIONS:** Pres All Bank Bankers MO; chmn Urban Affairs & Housing Com Hlth Welfare Com; mem Alpha Kappa Phi; deacon Price Bapt Ch. **HONORS/ACHIEVEMENTS:** Man of the Yr Awd 1974.

BANKS, JAMES ALBERT
Educator. **PERSONAL:** Born Sep 24, 1941, Marianna, AR; son of Matthew Banks and Lula Holt Banks; married Cherry Ann McGee; children: Angela Marie, Patricia Ann. **EDUCATION:** Chicago City Coll, AA 1963; Chicago State Univ, BE 1964; MI State Univ, MA 1967, PhD 1969. **CAREER:** Joilet IL Public Schools, teacher, 1965; Francis W Parker School, Chicago, teacher, 1965-66; Univ of WA, assoc prof 1971-73; Univ of MI, visiting prof of educ summer 1975; The British Acad The United Kingdom, visiting lecturer 1983; Monash Univ Clayton Victoria Australia, visiting prof of educ 1985; Univ of WA-Seattle, prof of educ 1973-, chmn dept of curriculum & instruction 1982-87, prof of curric & instr. **ORGANIZATIONS:** mem, Natl Defense Educ Act; fellow, MI State Univ, 1966-69; Spencer fellow, Natl Acad of Educ, 1973-76; Natl fellow, WK Kellogg Found, 1980-83; Rockerfeller Found Fellowship, 1980; bd of dirs, Soc Sci Educ Consortium, 1976-79; bd dirs, Assn for Supervision & Curriculum Devel, 1976-80; vice pres, Natl Council for the Soc Studies, 1980; pres elect, Natl Council for the Social Studies, 1981, pres, 1982; bd of dir, Natl Council for the Social Studies, 1980-84. **HONORS/ACHIEVEMENTS:** Elected Honorary Mem Golden Key Natl Honor Soc 1985; named Disting Scholar/Researcher on Minority Educ Amer Educ Rsch

Assoc 1986; wrote numerous books including, We Americans, Our History and People, two volumes 1982; Teaching Strategies for the Social Studies, 4th ed, 1990; Multicultural Education in Western Societies, w/James Lynch 1986; Teaching Strategies for Ethnic Studies, 4th ed, 1987; Multiethnic Education Theory and Practice, 2nd ed 1988; March Toward Freedom: A History of Black Americans, 1978; Multicultural Education: Issues and Prespectives, w/ Cherry A McGee Banks, 1989. **BUSINESS ADDRESS:** Prof of Curric & Instr, Univ of WA Seattle, 122 Miller Hall-DQ-12, Seattle, WA 98177.

BANKS, JAMES S.
Business executive, attorney. **PERSONAL:** Born Jan 29, 1938, Detroit, MI; married Janice Diane Mitchell; children: James Jr, Diane Yvonne. **EDUCATION:** Wayne State Univ, BS Sociology 1964, JD 1970. **CAREER:** Procter & Gamble, sales rep 1964-66; Chrysler Corp, report proced analyst 1966-67; MI Blue Shield, 1967-70; City Natl Bank, employee relations ofcr personnel dept 1970-71, dir urban affairs 1972-74, vice pres corp responsibility 1974-. **ORGANIZATIONS:** Mem Amer Bar Assn; Amer Mgmt Assn; Natl Bus League; MI Bar Assn; Detroit Bar Assn; Urban Bankers Forum; Natl Bankers Assn; Phi Alpha Delta Law Frat; bd dir Merril-Palmer Inst 1975; pres of assn mem Natl Bankers Assn 1976; bd dir 1976 pres bd dir Adult Serv Ctr 1977; dir Human Resources & Personnel Adminstrn SE MI Transportation Auth; mem United Comm Svcs; Boy Scouts of Amer; Met Detroit Black Orchestra; Wayne State Univ Alumni; Detroit Urban League; NAACP; Wayne State Univ Law Alumni; Winship Jr High PTA; Childrens Aid Soc of Detroit; League for Handicapped; PTA Detroit Area Council; Peoples Comm Svcs; Selec Serv Bd #96; Region IV Sch Bd; Sr Citizen Ctr; Delta Home for Girls; Charlotte Rea Home for Girls; Fed of Girls Homes. **HONORS/ACHIEVEMENTS:** Varsity Debator Forensic Union Bronze, Silver, Gold Medals for Debating.

BANKS, JEFFREY LAURENCE
Designer, business executive. **PERSONAL:** Born Nov 03, 1953, Washington, DC. **EDUCATION:** Pratt Inst Brooklyn NY, attended 1971-73; Parsons Sch of Design NY, BA 1975. **CAREER:** Ralph Lauren/Polo, design asst to pres 1971-73; Calvin Klein/Calvin Klein Ltd, design asst to pres 1973-76; Nik-Nik Clothing & Sportswear, designer 1976-78; Jeffrey Banks Ltd, designer/president 1978-. **ORGANIZATIONS:** Mem Deisgners Collective New York City 1979-. **HONORS/ACHIEVEMENTS:** Spl Coty Awd for Men's Furs Coty Fashion Critics' Awd 1977; Coty nomination for Men's Design Coty Fashion Critics' Awd 1977; Excellence in Men's Wear Design Harvey's Bristol Cream Tribute to Black Designers 1978-79-80. **BUSINESS ADDRESS:** President, Jeffrey Banks Ltd, 1384 Broadway 25th FLoor, New York, NY 10018.

BANKS, JERRY L.
Medical artist, painter. **PERSONAL:** Born Nov 03, 1943, Sikeston, MO; married Olivia St James; children: Choi, Jerry Jr. **EDUCATION:** Worsham Sch Mortuary Sci, grad 1967; Lincoln Univ, BS 1969; Univ IL Sch Med Illustrations, med art degree 1972. **CAREER:** Hektoen Inst, pathology asst 1967-68; Chicago Bd Educ, tchr 1970-71; Univ IL Med Oppor Prog, rsch asst 1971-72; Univ IL Med Sch, dir anatomy museum 1972-; Worsham Mortuary Sch, instr 1972-. **ORGANIZATIONS:** Mem Alpha Phi Alpha Frat 1965; Dick Gregory Cosmetic Consult & Graphic Artists 1970; Afam Art Gallery 1972; med artist consult with Alexander Lane PhD; mem Natl Conf Artists 1974. **HONORS/ACHIEVEMENTS:** Publ on "Functional Human Anatomy, The Regional Approach" Black Artist Guild 1965. **BUSINESS ADDRESS:** Instructor, Worsham Mortuary School, 1853 W Polk, Chicago, IL 60612.

BANKS, JOYCE P.
Accountant. **PERSONAL:** Born Jul 17, 1930, Stillwater, OK; daughter of Louis Perry and Lucille Perry; married Thurml L Banks; children: Joyce Lynn, Toni Aileen. **EDUCATION:** Fisk Univ, BA 1953; OK State Univ, grad work. **CAREER:** Tuskegee Inst Carver Found, lab technician 1953-55; Univ of CA Med Ctr San Francisco, rsch assoc 1955-85; Touche Ross & Co, accountant 1987-. **ORGANIZATIONS:** Chmn Univ of CA Med Ctr Personnel Appeal Comm; adv bd Campus Planning, Affirmative Action Comm Hooper Found; com on Parking & Transp; San Francisco Regional Tumor Found; mem Natl Tissue Culture Assn; mem Women's Aux Natl Med Assn; chmn Mt Zion Hosp Evening Vols 1970-71; pres Women's Aux John Hale Med Soc 1970-72; bd dir Hamlin Sch; pres bd dir St Luke's Parish Sch; mem Links Inc; Jack & Jill of Amer Inc; bd of dirs, Volunteer Center of Marin. **HONORS/ACHIEVEMENTS:** Acad Senate Rsch Grant; publs in Natl Sci Journals; Rev Benedict M Blank O P Merit Scholarship, Dominican College 1985. **HOME ADDRESS:** 65 Corte Dorado Dr, Greenbrae, CA 94904. **BUSINESS ADDRESS:** Touche Ross & Co, 275 Battery St, San Francisco, CA 94111.

BANKS, KENNETH E.
Attorney. **PERSONAL:** Born Aug 13, 1943, Columbus, OH; children: Kenneth III. **EDUCATION:** John Carroll Univ, BA 1969; Case Western Reserve Univ Law Sch, JD 1973; Harvard Grad Sch of Bus Adminstr Exec Prog, attended 1979. **CAREER:** Cleveland Plain Dealer, reporter 1965-73; The Cleveland Trust Co (now AmeriTrust), ofc atty 1973-76; TRW Equip Group TRW Inc, legal counsel 1976-. **ORGANIZATIONS:** Mem Natl Security Indsl Assoc Legal Spec Task Subcom; mem Natl Bar Assn; mem Norman S Minor Bar Assn; instr Cleveland Bus Ctr 1965-73; mem Cncl on Human Relations; mem Black Professional Assn of Cleveland. **MILITARY SERVICE:** USMC corpl 1961-65; Letters of Appreciation & Commendation.

BANKS, LAURA N.
Business executive. **PERSONAL:** Born Jun 29, 1921, Tucson, AZ; married Jack L Banks. **EDUCATION:** BS, 1943; MEd, 1966; Univ of AZ, Educ Specialist Degree 1970, EdD 1981. **CAREER:** Univ of AZ, 5 summers, asst teacher workshops; Cavett Elementary School, elementary teacher 25 yrs, principal 6 yrs; Tucson Public School Dist #1, coord reading programs K-12; MariMac Corp, public relations dir; LNB Enterprises, pres/owner. **ORGANIZATIONS:** Coordinator, Neighborhood Youth Corp; lecturer, Peace Corp, Univ AZ; mem Natl Cncl of Women in Adminstrn; TEA, AEA, NEA; past & 1st chairperson Elem Prin Group; AZ Admin Assn; Natl Assn of Elem Prin; mem YWCA Natl Bd 1965-76; active on numerous committees in this field; NAACP; Tucson Urban League; Palo Verde Mental Health Found; bd dir Alumni Bd Univ AZ; organizer/pres local chapter, past far western reg dir, natl secretary, natl prog chmn, Alpha Kappa Alpha; Natl Council of Negro Women; Model Cities Neighborhood Housing Task force; pres Council United Way; Natl rec sec Links Inc 1974-78; Pima Coll Exec Com for Comm Affairs; mem, Women at the Top; adv bd Resources for Women; hon Soroptomist; bd of dirs Univ of AZ President's Club, Comm Housing Resource Bd. **HONORS/ACHIEVEMENTS:** Shriners Award of Excellence in Educ; NAACP Successful Business Awd; Black Economic Devel Certificate of Merit; Women on the Move Recognition YWCA; Pioneer in Educ Award The Links.

BANKS, LOUBERTHA MAY
Educator. **PERSONAL:** Born in Riderwood, AL; married Booker T Banks; children: Delores Foss, Carol, Brenda, Booker Jr, Christopher. **EDUCATION:** CA State Univ, BA, MA 1957; Univ of San Francisco, BA 1970, MA, Doctoral Cand. **CAREER:** Del Paso Heights School Dist, classroom teacher, 1957-67, master teacher, 1967-68, pre-school supr, 1968-69, dir of compensatory educ, 1969-70, vice principal, 1970-71, principal, 1971-73, consultant, 1971-73, dir of instruction ,1973-. **ORGANIZATIONS:** Mem CA Tchrs Assn; NEA; Delta Sigma Theta; Assn of CA Sch Adminstrs; Amer Assn of Sch Adminstrs; Assn of Sch Curriculum Dirs; Natl Assn of BlackSch Educators; NAACP; Sacramento Area Black Educators; Sacramento Black Sch Educators; Black Comm Ctr for Alcoholism; Robbie Robertson Comm Recreation Ctr; Alternate Classroom Mental Health Proj; Delta Sigma Theta's Bike Proj; Phi Delta Kappa; CA State Univ Sacramento Alumni Bd. **HONORS/ACHIEVEMENTS:** Delta Sigma Theta Scholarship Grant. **BUSINESS ADDRESS:** Dir of Instruction, Del Paso Heights School District, 575 Kesner Ave, Sacramento, CA 95838.

BANKS, MANLEY E.
Business executive. **PERSONAL:** Born Oct 12, 1913, Anniston, AL; married Dorothy M Jones; children: Manley E Jr, Jacquelyn A. **EDUCATION:** AL State Univ, BS 1937; Howard Univ, LLB 1949. **CAREER:** Perry Co Sch Uniontown AL, asst prin coach 1937-42; Afro Cab Co Inc Enterprises, co-fndr vice pres 1946-51; tchr, 1949-52; Banks Bicycle Shop, owner. **ORGANIZATIONS:** Elected chmn City Water & Sewer Bd 1976; 1st Black apptd City Adv Bd; mem ofcr Alpha Phi Alpha Frat Inc; mem Boy Scout Council Exec Bd 20 yrs; elder 1st United Presb Ch; mem legal adv Calhoun County Improvement Assn; NAACP; mem Human Relations Council 1964-70; City Adv Bd Water & Sewer Bd 1965-; Dist Adv Bd Salvation Army 1972-; treas deacon clerk United Ch Christ 1949-69. **MILITARY SERVICE:** AUS sgt 1942-45. **BUSINESS ADDRESS:** Banks Bicycle Shop, 112 W 10 St, Anniston, AL 36201.

BANKS, MARGUERITA C.
Journalist. **PERSONAL:** Born Sep 13, 1946, New York, NY; married Alfred Quarles. **EDUCATION:** Notre Dame Coll Cleveland, BA Engl & Fr Lit 1967. **CAREER:** Cleveland Press, reporter 1967-69, editor comm page 1969-70; WEWS-TV Scripps Howard Broadcasting, gen assignment reporter & consumer troubleshooter, host "Black on Black" 1970-; WEWS-TV Scripps Howard Brdcstg, co-host Edition Five 1986-. **ORGANIZATIONS:** Exec bd mem Amer Sickle Cell Anemia Assoc 1972-; adv bd mem Notre Dame Coll 1978-; exec bd mem Harambee Serv to Black Children 1979-; past bd trustee Big Bros of Greater Cleveland; past bd trustee Urban League Cleveland; past bd trustee Blacks in Commun, NE YWCA; mem Womens Equity Action League, Sigma Delta Chi; mem & ed Gamma Phi Delta Sor; former ballet & mod dance teacher local art centers; leadership Cleveland Class of '87. **HONORS/ACHIEVEMENTS:** Listed in Who's Who in Amer Coll & Univ 1967; Most Interesting People Cleveland Mag 1979; numerous Comm Serv Awds pamphlet "Buying Used Cars" distrib byCity of Cleveland Office of Consumer Affairs; "Punk Kids" series made into film distributed to comm groups by Cuyahoga Cty Juvenile Ct 1979; Notre Dame Coll Woman of the Year 1982; Female Broadcaster of the Year Natl Assn of Career Woman's Civil League 1982; Career Woman of Achievement Awd YWCA of Cleveland 1985; numerous press awds from Press Club of Cleveland and Women in Communications Cleveland Chapt. **BUSINESS ADDRESS:** Reporter, Host, WEWS-TV Scripps Howard Brdcstg, 3001 Euclid Ave, Cleveland, OH 44115.

BANKS, MARSHALL D.
Educator, urologist. **PERSONAL:** Born Dec 29, 1940, Richmond, VA; married Kathy; children: Marshall II, Martainn, Matthieu. **EDUCATION:** VA Union Univ, BS 1962; Howard Univ, 1963; Meharry Med Coll, MD 1970; Roswell Park Meml Inst, resd 1972-73; Wayne State Univ, 1975. **CAREER:** Detroit Rehabilitation Inst, cons; Coll of VA, rsch tech 1963-65; Maggie Walker High School, chem teacher 1964-65; Wayne State Univ, instructor urology 1975-76; Allen Park Veterans Hospital, chief urology 1976-; Wayne State Univ, asst prof 1976-. **ORGANIZATIONS:** Dir urogenital surg Allen Park VA Hosp; mem AMA; candidate Amer Coll surgeon; mem Wayne Cty med Soc, Detroit Surg Soc, Amer Urol Assoc, Natl Med Assoc, MI State Med Soc, Kappa Alpha Psi; surg resd yr Queens Med Ctr 1971-72. **HONORS/ACHIEVEMENTS:** 1st prize essay Buffalo Urol Soc 1973; publ "Topical Instillation of Adriamycin in Treatment of Superficial Bladder Cancer" Jrnl Urol 1977; co-investigator Natl Prostatic Cancer Proj 1978-79. **BUSINESS ADDRESS:** Assistant Professor, Wayne StateUniv, 1202 Oak St Ste 100, Richmond, VA 23220.

BANKS, PATRICIA
Attorney. **PERSONAL:** Born Feb 06, 1949, Marianna, AR. **EDUCATION:** Univ IL, BA 1969; Univ WI, JD 1972. **CAREER:** US Dept of Labor Chicago Region, 1972-73; Leadership Council for Met Open Comms, atty 1973-74; Sears Roebuck & Co, 1974-78; Private Practice, attorney 1978-. **ORGANIZATIONS:** Mem following Bar Assns, Cook Co, Chicago, Fed, WI, IL; mem Delta Sigma Theta Sor. **HONORS/ACHIEVEMENTS:** League of Black Women Awd US Marine Corps 1974; 1 of 10 Outstanding Young Citizens of Chicago-Chicago Jaycees 1977. **BUSINESS ADDRESS:** Attorney, 77 W Washington, Chicago, IL 60602.

BANKS, PRISCILLA SNEED
Federal government official. **PERSONAL:** Born Jul 13, 1941, Washington, DC; daughter of Excell Sneed and Mabel Sneed; widowed; children: Monica Banks. **EDUCATION:** Amer Univ. **CAREER:** Low Income Housing, tech instr; Low Rent Occupancy; US Dept Housing & Urban Devel, task force to desegregate public housing, housing program specialist; Anti-Drug Program for Public Housing; Civil Rights Act of 1964 and Title VIII, 1988. **ORGANIZATIONS:** Mem NAACP; Washington Urban League; Natl Welfare Mothers; NAHRO. **HONORS/ACHIEVEMENTS:** Public Service Awards; Miss HUD 1972; Special Achievement 1975-76 & 1978; Sustained Superior Performance 1969 & 1980; received 2nd highest award given by US Dept of Housing & Urban Devel - the Cert of Merit 1984; Outstanding Performance Awd 1984, 1985, 1986, 1987, 1988. **BUSINESS ADDRESS:** Housing Specialist, US Dept of Housing & Urban Development, 451 7th St SW, Suite 4206, Washington, DC 20410.

BANKS, REGINALD, SR.
Projectionist. **PERSONAL:** Born May 15, 1951, Little Rock, AR; married Willia Lorraine Smithey; children: Dennis Edward, Reggie Jr, Rian Christopher, Regan David. **EDUCATION:** Attended, Ohio State and Longview Coll 1979-85. **CAREER:** CBS/KCTV 5 Midwest Bureau, projectionist/engr 1970-87. **ORGANIZATIONS:** Pres # 170 Intl Alliance of Theatrical Stage, Emply, Moving Picture Machine Operators 1978-81; bd mem United Minority Media Assoc 1979-82. **BUSINESS ADDRESS:** Projectionist, CBS, 4500 Johnson Dr, Fairway, KS 66205.

BANKS, RICHARD L.
Attorney. **PERSONAL:** Born Nov 22, 1930, Boston, MA; married Catherine Martin; children: 3 children. **EDUCATION:** Harvard Coll, AB 1951; Harvard Law Sch, LLB 1958. **CAREER:** Boston Legal Aid Soc, atty 1958-60; Cardozo & Tucker, assoc 1960-69; Boston Lawyers for Housing, dir 1969-71; Unity Bank & Trust Co, conservator 1972-73; Municipal Ct Roxbury Dist Suffolk Co Boston, presiding justice. **ORGANIZATIONS:** Lectr Boston Univ Law Sch; mem MA Bd Educ 1965-72. **MILITARY SERVICE:** USNR lt 1953-57. **BUSINESS ADDRESS:** Presiding Justice, Municipal Ct Roxbury Dist, 85 Warren St, Roxbury, MA 02119.

BANKS, RONALD
Company executive. **PERSONAL:** Born Jun 19, 1951, Chicago, IL; son of Earl Banks and Geneva Martin Banks; married Vera D Lott; children: Janel, Lauren. **EDUCATION:** Loyola Univ of Chicago, BA 1973. **CAREER:** Montgomery Ward Chicago, buyer 1973-82; Sherwin Williams Co Cleveland, buyer 1982-84; Parks/Carver Tripp Cos, regional vice pres 1984-. **BUSINESS ADDRESS:** Vice President, Parks/Carver Tripps Co, PO Box 5, Somerset, MA 02726.

BANKS, RONALD TRENTON
Educator. **PERSONAL:** Born Sep 20, 1947, Knoxville, TN; son of Ralph Banks and Clara Banks; children: Rashondra Trenia. **EDUCATION:** Meharry Medical Coll, Certification in Mental Health 1971; Tenn State University, BS 1970; MS 1976. **CAREER:** Meharry Medical Coll, mental hlth tech trainees, pres 1970-71; Kentucky State Univ, co-chair rotating staff adv bd, vice pres 1983-84; Kentucky Tchrs Network, 1984-85 Cooperative Educ Handicap Comm, natl co-chairperson 1985-86. **ORGANIZATIONS:** Kentucky St Police, drug & alchol consultant 1976; Kentucky School System, consultant 1976-81; Frankfort Comm, dir crisis serv 1977- ; Kentucky St Univ, founder & dir Dial A Job prog 1978- ; (Kappa Alpha Psi) 1978; United Way, 1978; YMCA, Sr Citizens, Blind, Juvenille Deliq Mental Health Volunteer 1978; Cooperative Educ Assn of Kentucky, Awards Comm 1988-89; College Placement Assn, Cooperative Educ Assn. **HONORS/ACHIEVEMENTS:** Outstanding Young Men of Amer 1980; Most Loyal Co-Op Coordinator-KY 1982; Staff Awd KY Student Government KSU 1983; Cooperative Educ Appreciation Awd KSU 1983 & 1984; Most Outstanding Cooperative Educ Coordinator, State of Kentucky 1987; Kentucky Colonel 1987; State "B" Kentucky Racquetball Champion, Kentucky Racquetball Assn 1987; State "B" Senior Runner Up, Kentucky Racquetball Assn 1988; producer, Street Life of Drugs on a College Campus, 1989. **HOME ADDRESS:** 301 Forest Hill, Frankfort, KY 40601. **BUSINESS ADDRESS:** Asst Dir Counseling, Kentucky StateUniv, E Main St, Frankfort, KY 40601.

BANKS, RUTH R.
Attorney. **PERSONAL:** Born Sep 02, 1943, Washington, DC. **EDUCATION:** Morgan State Coll, BA; Howard U, JD 1968. **CAREER:** Off Gen Couns Civ Serv Comm, law clk 1968; Judges Tim Murphy Alfred Burka, law clk 1968-69; DC Just Dept, asst US atty 1969-73; Law, priv prac 1973-. **ORGANIZATIONS:** Mem Wash DC Bar Assn; mem Intnl Toastmsts Clb; mem Nat Bar Assn; vice pres Wom Div DC Chpt.

BANKS, SAUNDRA ELIZABETH
Appointed govt. official. **PERSONAL:** Born May 01, 1948, Baltimore, MD; married LeRoy Banks. **EDUCATION:** Morgan State Univ, BA 1974; Univ of Baltimore, 1979. **CAREER:** Baltimore City Schools, teacher 1975-77; WEAA, news reporter 1977-78; Court of Common Pleas, chief clerk 1978-82; Circuit Court Baltimore City, chief clerk 1982-. **BUSINESS ADDRESS:** Chief Clerk, Circuit Ct, 111 N Calvert St N, Baltimore, MD 21202.

BANKS, SHARON P.
Attorney, educator. **PERSONAL:** Born Sep 21, 1942, Washington, DC. **EDUCATION:** Morgan State Coll, BA 1964; Howard Univ Law Sch, JD 1967. **CAREER:** Neighborhood Legal Serv Program, 1967-72; Private Practice, attorney 1972-; Howard Univ, part-time teacher 1969-72, full-time teacher 1972-. **ORGANIZATIONS:** Mem Natl, Amer, DC Bar Assns; Howard Univ Law Alumni Assn; bd dir DC ACIU; Kappa Beta Pi Legal Sor. **BUSINESS ADDRESS:** Teacher, HowardUniv, Dept of Pol Sci, 112 Douglass Hall, Washington, DC 20001.

BANKS, TAZEWELL
Educator. **PERSONAL:** Born Jan 07, 1932, Washington, DC; married Myrtle Marie Trescott; children: Andrea, Gregory, Kelley. **EDUCATION:** Howard Univ, BS Chem 1953; Howard Med Clg, MD 1957. **CAREER:** Howard Medical Coll, clncl instructor 1966-68, asst prof 1968-71, assoc prof 1971-76, prof Med 1976-. **ORGANIZATIONS:** Published over 40 articles on Cardiovascular Diseases; prsntd over 100 Talks on Cardiovascular Diseases; bd of dir WA Heart Asso 1983-. **HONORS/ACHIEVEMENTS:** Chm Stdnt Rsrch Com WA Heart Asso mem Multiple WA Heart Asso Comms 1966-; meritorious serv DC Gen Hosp 1970; Citzns Adv Comm to DC Bar 1972-76; outstndng tchr Stdnt Cncl Awd Howard Med 1977; WA Heart Asso Golden Apple Awd 1983; DC General Hospital; outstanding physician award 1985-86. **MILITARY SERVICE:** AUS Med Corps capt 1956-61. **BUSINESS ADDRESS:** Professor of Medicine, Howard Medical College, Washington DC General Hospital, 19th & Mass Ave, SE, Washington, DC 20003.

BANKS, TERRY MICHAEL
Attorney. **PERSONAL:** Born Nov 20, 1947, Iowa City, IA; married Barbara Mahone; children: Lauren, Terry Jr, Natalie. **EDUCATION:** Univ MI, BS 1969; Catholic Univ, JD 1973. **CAREER:** Naval Air Systems Command, aerospace engr 1969-70; Ford Found, consult 1974; Hogan & Hartson, atty 1973-77; EOC, exec asst to the chair 1977-79; FCC, assoc gen counsel 1979-80, chief office of opinions & reviews 1980-82; Tepper & Edmundson, 1982-83; AT&T, atty 1983-. **ORGANIZATIONS:** Pres Lawyer's Study Group 1976-80; pres Washington Council Lawyers 1974-75 bd dirs 1974-86; mem DC Bar 1973-. **BUSINESS ADDRESS:** Attorney, AT&T, 1120 20th St NW, Washington, DC 20036.

BANKS, WALDO R., SR.
Educator, organization executive. **PERSONAL:** Born Mar 30, 1928, Beaumont, TX; married Anice D; children: Monica Diane, Natalie Anice, Waldo R. **EDUCATION:** Bishop Coll, BA 1951; Prairie View Univ, attended 1952; TX So Univ, MA 1957; IN Univ, EdS 1964; Claremont Grad Sch of Educ, PhD 1975. **CAREER:** S Park IN Sch Dist, psychol consult instr 1952-54; Orange IN Sch Dist, psychol consult instr 1954-56; So Univ, instr couns 1957-58; IN Univ, admins tchr rschr 1958-59; Knoxville Coll, dean dir asst prof adminstrv asst 1959-61; Gary Public Schs, dir fdr operation scholarship 1961-65, dir consult 1961-65; LA Bd of Educ, instr & couns 1965-66; CA St Univ, consult LA City Human Relat Bur asst prof couns dir 1965-67; PACE Proj, professional rschr writer 1967-69; Compton Unified Sch Dist, adminstr & dir 1967-75; UCLA, instr 1971-76; Global Oil Co Inc, pres 1975-77; Imperial Health Ctr Inc, dir 1975-77; Natl Employ Ctr, pres 1975-77; Amer Educ Found, pres 1970-80. **ORGANIZATIONS:** Consult to pres foreign & domestic affairs; consult dept of HEW Dept of Commerce Dept of Defense Dept of the Navy Dept of Labor Amer Soc of Mil History LA; Natl Adv Counc on Educ Profns Devel; mem Harry Walker Inc; Amer Prog Bur Inc; United Nations Spkrs Bur; mem Amer Assn of Coll Registrars &Admissions Officers; Amer Assn of Coll & Univ Deans; Amer Assn of Secondary Sch Prin; Amer Assn of Sch Adminstr; Amer Assn of Univ Profs; AmerColl Personnel Assn; Amer Educ Econ Asst Found; Amer Fed of Tchrs; Amer Jr Coll Assn; Amer Personnel & Guidance Assn; Amer Polit Sci Assn; Amer Sociol Soc; Amer Psychol Assn Boys Club of Amer; BSA; BPOE; CA Assn for Prog Dem; CA Fed of Tchrs; CA Person & Guid Assn; CA St Tchrs Assn; Intl Platform Assn; Masonic Lodge; NAACP; Natl Adv Cncl on EPDA; Natl Assn of Inter-Grp Relations Ofcls; Natl Cong of Parents & Tchrs; NEA; Natl Urban League; Phi Delta Kappa; So Christian Leadership Conf; YMCA. **HONORS/ACHIEVEMENTS:** Dr Joseph J Rhoads Schlrshp Grant Bishop Coll 1946-50; Adminstrv Rsch Asstshp Grant IN Univ 1957-58; educ grants Claremont Grad Sch of Educ 1972-74; pres USA appointee Natl Adv Cncl on Educ Profns Devel 1972-75; grant Natl Fellowship Fund Atlanta 1974-75; Personalities of the S 1970-77; Dict of Intl Biog 1971-77; 2,000 Men of Achvmt; Who's Who in the West 1975-77; numerous publications, research programs and projects; Natl Professional Serv Citation Pres Ford USA. **BUSINESS ADDRESS:** President, International Cougar Corp, 1806 E Turmont St, PH Ste No 300, Carson, CA 90746.

BANKS, WILLIAM JASPER, JR.
Physician/educator. **PERSONAL:** Born Jul 04, 1944, Richmond, VA. **EDUCATION:** VA Univ, BS 1965; VA Commonwealth Univ, MS 1966; Howard Univ, MD 1970; Univ of Edinburgh McMasters Coll, MA 1986. **CAREER:** DC Gen Hosp, med officer 1977-, vice pres med staff 1981-82; Howard Univ Hosp, chief orth clinics 1979-; 1979-; Howard Univ, instr surgery 1977-80, sec divof orth surg, asst prof surgery 1980-. **ORGANIZATIONS:** Fellow Amer Coll of Surgeons, Amer Acad of Ortho Surgeons, Intl Coll of Surgeons; mem AMA, DC Med Soc, Southern Med Soc; mem Arlington Hosp Foundation, Intl Oceanographic Foundation; sec Capital City Orth Found; fellow Royal Coll of Surgeons Edinburgh, Natl Geographic Soc Navl Inst; mem Southern Orth Soc, Eastern Orth Soc, Sigma Xi, Amer Assoc for the Advancement ofSci, NY Acad of Sci, Amer Philosophical Soc, Pan Amer Orth Group, Soc ofClinical Investigators. **HONORS/ACHIEVEMENTS:** Honorable Fellow JF Kennedy Library; Community Serv Silver Spring Boys Club; "Complications of Amputatim" Ortho Update Series; Osteoporosis Intl Conf Metabolic Bone Diseases-Rome Spec Citation Southern Poverty Law Center; Osteomyelitis A New Look At An Old Problem Jrnl of Diseases of Children. **MILITARY SERVICE:** USN rear adm; Legion of Honor, Presidential Citation, Vietnam Medal. **BUSINESS ADDRESS:** Asst Professor Surgery, HowardUniv, 2139 Ga Ave NW, Washington, DC 20060.

BANKS, WILLIAM MARON, III
Educator. **PERSONAL:** Born Sep 22, 1943, Thomasville, GA; married Karen Hembry; children: David, Tracey. **EDUCATION:** Dilalrd Univ, B 1963; Univ of KY, Doctorate 1967. **CAREER:** Attebury Job Corps Center, supr counselor & psychol 1967; Howard Univ, counselor psychol 1967-70, dept chairperson 1972-75; Univ of CA at Berkeley, prof 1970-. **ORGANIZATIONS:** Mem Soc for Psychol Study of Soc Issues; Soc for Study of Soc Problems; Amer Personnel & Guid Assn; chairperson Univ of CA Afro-Amer Studies Consortium 1979-81; Assn of Black Psychologists. **HONORS/ACHIEVEMENTS:** Summer Scholars Awd US Civil Serv Commn; Univ of CA Regents Fellowship; Instructional Improve Grant; num scholarly articles & monographs pub on effects of racial differences in psychotherapy & counseling. **BUSINESS ADDRESS:** Professor, Univ of CA, Afro Am Studies, 3335 Dwinelle Hall, Berkeley, CA 94720.

BANKS-WILLIAMS, LULA
Purchasing director. **PERSONAL:** Born Feb 23, 1947, Tallahassee, FL; daughter of Harry E Banks, Sr and Elizabeth Gaines Richardson; divorced; children: Felicia A Williams, Deanna M Williams. **EDUCATION:** Tallahassee Comm Coll, FL, AA 1985; attending Florida A&M Univ, Tallahassee, FL. **CAREER:** Indian River County School Board, Vero Beach, FL, teacher of adult educ, 1978; Brevard County School Board, Melbourne, FL, teacher of adult educ, 1979; Leon County Board of Commissioners and Leon County School Board, Tallahassee, FL, purchasing agent 1980-85, purchasing director 1985-. **ORGANIZATIONS:** Exec mem, Small Business Week Committee; mem, Natl Inst of Governmental Purchasing, FL Assn of Govt Purchasing Officers, Amer Soc of Public Admin, COMPA/ASPA, NAACP, Toastmaster, Philos of Sigma Gamma Rho. **HONORS/ACHIEVEMENTS:** FL Teacher Certificate, VOTECH, 1977; Professional Public Buyer, NIGP, 1984; Professional Manicuring/Pedicuring License, 1989; named Philo of Year, Sigma Gamma Rho, 1981, and 2nd place national runner-up, 1986.

BANKSTON, ARCHIE M.
Attorney, utility executive. **PERSONAL:** Born Oct 12, 1937, Memphis, TN; son of Archie M Bankston, Sr and Elsie Shaw Bankston; married Emma Ann Dejan; children: Alice; Louis Shaw. **EDUCATION:** Fisk Univ, BA 1959; Washington Univ School of Law, LLB 1962; Washington Univ Graduate School of Business Admin, MBA 1964. **CAREER:** General Foods Corp, asst div counsel 1964-67, product mgr Maxwell House Div 1967-69; Pepsico Inc, asst sec & corp counsel 1969-72; Xerox Corp, div counsel 1972-73; Consolidated Edison Co of NY, sec & asst general counsel 1974-89; sec & assoc general counsel 1989-. **ORGANIZATIONS:** Phi Delta Phi Legal Fraternity 1960-; admitted to practice law NY & MO; mem Securities Indu Comm; advisory group NY Reg Group; former chmn budget comm Amer Soc of Corp Sec Inc 1974-; former pres Stockholder Relat Soc of NY; Amer Bar Assn; NY State

Bar Assn; Assn of Black Lawyers of Westchester Co Inc; dir Beth Israel Med Center NYC; dir Mental Health Assn of Westchester Co; dir Amer Mgmt Assn; dir, Associated Black Charities; trustee, College of New Rochelle; mem 100 Black Men Inc; Beta Zeta Boule (Sigma Pi Phi Frat); Alpha Phi Alpha Fraternity; Westchester Clubmen Inc. **HONORS/ACHIEVEMENTS:** Recipient Black Achievers in Industry Award Harlem Branch YMCA 1971; Outstanding Young Men of Amer 1972; Merit Award for Black Exec Exchange Program Natl Urban League 1974; distinguished service commendation award, Mental Health Assn, 1987; 1st Black atty/product mgr Gen Foods 1964-67; 1st Black Sr Exec Officer Consolidated Edison 1974; 1st Black Corp Sec of a major US Co 1974. **BUSINESS ADDRESS:** Secretary, Associate General Counsel, Consol Edison Co of NY Inc, 4 Irving Pl, New York, NY 10003.

BANNER, MELVIN EDWARD
Educator, author. **PERSONAL:** Born Jul 16, 1914, McDonald, PA; son of Clyde Banner and Patricia Banner; married Patricia Duignan; children: Melvina Banner Ford. **EDUCATION:** Flint Jr Coll, AA 1936; Univ of MI, BA 1948, MA 1952; MI State Univ, grad studies. **CAREER:** Flint Dept of Recreation, 1934-36; Mott Found, adult ed rec 1938-48; Chevrolet Motor, 1936-38; Fisher Body, 1939; Buick Motor Div, foundry 1940-50; Flint Bd of Educ, tchr 1950-80. **ORGANIZATIONS:** Reporter MI Chronicle Flint 1936-38; asst ed Bronze Reporter 1940-55; editor Flint Spokesman 1956-58; editor Flint Mirror Urban League Circle 1961-63; treas 1966, pres 1971-72 United Teachers of Flint; bd dir 1970-72, exec bd 1971-72 MI Educ Assn; chmn Natl Educ Assn Comm Ed Finance 1971-74; vice pres Economic Crisis Ctr 1984-85; bd mem Comm Serv & Referral Ctr 1984; author "Black Pioneer in Mich" and "Reflections in Black Poetry"; East Lansing Human Rel Comm 1981-87; chmn Martin Luther King Commemoration 1987. **HONORS/ACHIEVEMENTS:** Heritage Awd Genesee Co Historical & Museum Soc; Liberty Bell Awd Law Day; Distinguished Serv MI, Natl Educ Assn; Big Brother Awd; Outstanding Newsmaker Awd Natl Assn of Media Women 1978; Reg 10 MI Educ Assn Tchr Hall of Fame 1982; Citation MI State House of Rep Tribute; MI State Legislature Senate Concurrent Resolution No 718; US Congressional Cert of Merit Educ & Author; Cert of Appreciation from The People of the City of Flint, Flint Comm Schs, Central Optimist Club Flint, Urban League of Flint; Outstanding Comm Serv Awd from United Fund of Genesee and Lapeer Counties; Cert of Honored Serv State Bd of Educ. **HOME ADDRESS:** PO Box 682, 1930 F Street, South Lake Tahoe, CA 95705.

BANNER, WILLIAM AUGUSTUS
Educator. **PERSONAL:** Born Sep 18, 1915, Philadelphia, PA; son of Zacharias Banner and Nannie Perry Banner; married Beatrice V Suggs; children: Beatrice Anne, William Perry. **EDUCATION:** PA State Univ, BA 1935; Yale Univ, MDiv 1938; Harvard Univ, MA 1944, PhD (Sheldon Traveling Fellow) 1947. **CAREER:** Bennett Coll, philosophy instr 1938-43; Howard Univ Sch of Religion, asst to assoc prof 1945-55, assoc prof of philosophy 1955-58, prof 1958-; Yale Univ, visiting prof 1964-65; Univ of Rochester, distinguished visiting prof 1970; Coll Liberal Arts, assoc dean 1971-75; Folger Institute, lect 1984-85; Howard Univ, department of philosophy, chairman 1976-81. **ORGANIZATIONS:** Mem Amer Philos Assn; Natl Humanities Faculty; Guild Scholars of Episcopal Ch; fellow Soc Religion in High Educ; mem Harvard Club. **HONORS/ACHIEVEMENTS:** Author, "Ethics, An Introduction to Moral Philosophy" 1968, "Moral Norms and Moral Order, The Philosophy of Human Affairs" 1981; contributor "Greece, 478-336 BC" a handbook 1982; Doctor of Humane Letters, Howard Univ 1988.

BANNERMAN-RICHTER, GABRIEL
Educator. **PERSONAL:** Born Oct 28, 1931, Oyo, Nigeria;married Jane Harvey-Ewusie; children: Anna, Jessica, Gabriel Jr, Matilda, Elizabeth. **EDUCATION:** CA State Univ, BA 1963-69; CA State Univ, MA 1969-70; Univ of CA Davis, 1970-72. **CAREER:** Sacramento City Coll, instr 1969-80; Univ of CA Davis, instr 1972-75; Univ of Cape Coast Ghana, vstg assoc prog 1976-77; CA State Univ Sacramento, prof 1969-. **ORGANIZATIONS:** Publ Gabari Publ Co 1982-. **HONORS/ACHIEVEMENTS:** Author "Practice of Witchcraft in Ghana" 1982, "Don't Cry My Baby, Don't Cry" 1984; NEH Scholar NEH Inst Univ of IN 1985; Author "Mmoetia, The Mysterious Dwarfs" 1985. **HOME ADDRESS:** 3612 21 Ave, Sacramento, CA 95820. **BUSINESS ADDRESS:** Professor Engl/Ethnic Studies, CA StateUniv, 6000 J St, Sacramento, CA 95819.

BANTOM, MICHAEL A.
Professional athlete. **PERSONAL:** Born Dec 03, 1951, Philadelphia, PA; married Bonita; children: Robbie Jamiele, Misha Mikel. **EDUCATION:** St Joseph's Coll, BS Food Processing 1973. **CAREER:** Phoenix Suns, mem 1973-75; Seattle Supersonics, mem 1975-77; NJ Nets, mem 1977; IN Pacers, player 1977-. **HONORS/ACHIEVEMENTS:** Mem All Rookie Team NBA 1973-74; MVP St Joseph's Basketball Team 3 yrs; Olympic Basketball Team 1972; Gold Medal Game at MSA US Olympics 1980. **BUSINESS ADDRESS:** IN Pacers, Market Square Center, Indianapolis, IN 46204.

BANTON, WILLIAM C., II
Brigadier general. **PERSONAL:** Born Nov 09, 1922, Washington, DC. **EDUCATION:** Howard Univ Coll of Liberal Arts & Sci, Howard Univ Coll of Med, mD 1946; Homer G Phillips Hosp, 1946-47; Robert Koch Hosp, 1947-49; USAF Gen Hosp, 1950-52; John Hopkins Univ Sch of Hygiene & Pub Health, 1970; St Louis Univ Schl of Med; USAF Sch of Aviation Med; USPHS; Sch of Aerospace Med; USN Med Sch; Armed Forces Inst of Pathology; Wash Univ Sch of Med; Def Atomic Support Agy; Sch of Awrospace Med; Boston U; Harvard U; Tufts Univ Sch of Med; Indsl Coll of Armed Forces. **CAREER:** Mitchell Air Force Base NY, med officer of internal med; 2230th AFR Floyd Bennett Naval Air Sta, flight surgeon 1951-52; St Louis Health Div Chest & TB Svc; part-time pvt prac in internal med; 8711th USAFG Hosp Scott Air Vorce Base, comdr & flight surgeon 1954-71; Hq USAF/SG Forrestal Bldg Wash, asst to surgeon gen 1971-; served on short active duty tours in So Vietnam 1968-69; Dept of Comm Health & Med Care St Louis Co MO, dir; St Louis Univ Sch ofMed, holds apptmnts as asst clinical prof of internal med. **ORGANIZATIONS:** Mem Reserve Officer's Assn; Air Force Assn; life mem Alpha Phi Alpha; Chi Delta Mu; Howard Univ Alumni Assn; life mem NAACP; bd dirs Koch Welfare Assn;Friends of City Art Mus of St Louis; Nat Geographic Soc; St Louis Zoo Assn; John Hopkins Univ Alumni Assn; Homer G Phillips Hosp Intern Alumni Assn. **HONORS/ACHIEVEMENTS:** Promoted Brigadier Gen Apr 6 1973; recipient WW II Victory Medal; Am Campaign Medal; Nat Def Serv Medal; Good Conduct Medal; Expert Marksman Medal; Armed Forces Longevity Serv Award; Award Forces Res Medal; S Vietnam Campaitn Medal. **MILITARY SERVICE:** AUS 1st lt 1946; USAFR capt 1950.

BAPTISTA, HOWARD
Association executive. **PERSONAL:** Born Nov 24, 1930, Nantucket, MA; married Margarit Von Steiger; children: Mark, Kim, Kevin, Stephan. **EDUCATION:** Bryant Coll, BA 1956; NY Univ, MA 1960. **CAREER:** Altman's Dept Store, jr exec; New York City Housing Auth, 1959-60; NY Bd Educ, 1960-62; Bedford Redevelop Auth, exec dir. **ORGANIZATIONS:** Vice pres SE Bank & Trust Co; incorporator NB Inst Savs Bank; dir Vol Amer; Comm Council; United Fund; New England Council NAHRO. **HONORS/ACHIEVEMENTS:** Eqalitarian Awd NAACP. **MILITARY SERVICE:** AUS cpl.

BAPTISTE, HANSOM P., JR.
Educator. **PERSONAL:** Born Jan 18, 1939, Beaumont, TX; married Mirabelle; children: 7 Children. **EDUCATION:** Attended Univ CA 1962, Univ Notre Dame 1964; Lamar State Coll, BS 1961; IN Univ, MAT 1966, EdD 1968. **CAREER:** Cuero Independent School Dist, 1961-63; Beaumont Independent School Dist, teacher 1963-65; IN Univ, asst prof 1968-72; Univ Houston, assoc prof. **ORGANIZATIONS:** Many workshops & seminars 1971-75; mem IN Univ Alumni Assn; Natl Sci Tchrs Assn; Natl Congress Parents & Tchrs; Phi Delta Kappa. **HONORS/ACHIEVEMENTS:** Educ Grant Career Oppor Prog 1970-72; Office Educ Title III grant training faculty doctorate level 1973-75; Valedictorian Scholarship 1957-58; Outstanding TchrAwd 1969-70; Natl Defense Educ Act Grant 1966-68; Natl Sci Found Academic Yr Grant 1965-66. **BUSINESS ADDRESS:** Associate Professor, University of Houston, College Education Rm 42, 3801 Cullen Blvd, Houston, TX 77004.

BARAKA, IMAMU AMIRI (LEROI JONES)
Writer. **PERSONAL:** Born Oct 07, 1934, Newark, NJ; married Amina; children: Kellie Elisabeth, Lisa Victoria Chapman, Obalaji Malik Ali, Ras Jua Al Aziz, Shani Isis, Amiri Seku, Ahi Mwenge. **EDUCATION:** Howard Univ, BA; Attended Newark, Rutgers; Columbia Univ New School, grad work. **CAREER:** New Sch Social Rsch, tchr; Columbia Univ, tchr; Univ Buffalo, tchr; San Francisco State, visiting prof; Yale Univ, vis lecturer afro-amer studies 1977-78; SUNY Stony Brook, assoc prof african studies 1983-, prof 1985-; professional writer publs numerous books plays. **ORGANIZATIONS:** Founder Yugen Mag and Totem Press New York City 1958; founder Black Arts Repertory Theatre Sch Harlem 1964; Spirit House Newark 1966; mem Black Acad Arts & Letters; mem United Brokers Newark 1967; com for Unified Newark; chmn Cong Arfrican People; co-gov Natl Black Polit Conv; sec Natl Black Polit Conv sec gen; mem Polit Prisoners Relief Fund; All African Games; African Liberation Day Comm; African Liberation Day Support Com; Pan African Federation Groups; 2nd Intl World Festival Black Arts; IFCO Intl Task Force; publ dir Jihad Press, Peoples War Publs; editor The Black Nation. **HONORS/ACHIEVEMENTS:** Whitney Fellow 1963; theatrical prod "Dutchman" Off-Broadway Awd Best Amer Play 1964; "The Slave" 2nd prize Intl Art Festival Dakar 1966; Guggenheim Fellow1965; Yoruba Acad Fellow 1965; Rockefeller Found Fellow 1981; Poetry Awd Natl Endowment for the Arts 1981, NJ Cncl for the Arts 1982, Drama Awd 1985. **MILITARY SERVICE:** USAF 1954-57. **BUSINESS ADDRESS:** c/o William Morrow & Co, 105 Madison Ave, New York, NY 10016.

BARANCO, BEVERLY VICTOR, JR.
Dentist. **PERSONAL:** Born in New Orleans, LA; widowed; children: 8 Children. **EDUCATION:** LA State Univ Dental Sch, DDS. **CAREER:** Private Practice, dental surgery. **ORGANIZATIONS:** Mem 6th Dist Dental Assn; Amer Dental Assn; LA Dental Assn; Pelcn State Dental Soc; pres chmn of bd of dir First Fed Sav & Loan Assn; Baton Rouge; mem Serra Club; Alpha Phi Alpha; Sigma Pi Phi; Chi Delta Mu; bd dir Blndn Home; bd dir Family Coun Serv; chmn bd dir Baranco-Clark YMCA; dir GoodSamaritans; mem Comm for Rehab of Penal Inst State of LA; mem St Agnes Roman Catholic Ch; mem Mayor's Bi-Rcl Comm Rel Comm. **HONORS/ACHIEVEMENTS:** Knights of St Peter Claver Awd; Knights of St Gregory the Great Pope Paul VI; Silver Beaver Awd BSA. **BUSINESS ADDRESS:** 1200 6 St, 2191 Main St, Detroit, MI 48226.

BARANCO, GORDON S.
Judge. **PERSONAL:** Born Feb 25, 1948, Oakland, CA; married Barbara N Gee; children: Lauren Barbara Baranco. **EDUCATION:** Univ of CA, BA 1969, JD 1972. **CAREER:** San Francisco, asst dist attny 1974-77; Neighborhood Legal Asst, managing attny 1977-80; Oakland, asst city attny 1980; Oakland Municipal Court, judge 1980-84; Alameda Cty Superior Court, judge. **BUSINESS ADDRESS:** Judge, Alameda County Superior Court, 1225 Fallon, Oakland, CA 94612.

BARANCO, GREGORY T.
Automobile dealer. **CAREER:** Baranco Lincoln-Mercury Inc, Duluth GA, chief exec. **BUSINESS ADDRESS:** Baranco Lincoln-Mercury Inc, 3265 Commerce Ave, Duluth, GA 30136. *

BARANCO, RAPHAEL ALVIN
Dentist. **PERSONAL:** Born Nov 19, 1932, Baton Rouge, LA; married Terry Bryant; children: Angela, Rachel, Raphael. **EDUCATION:** Xavier Univ, BS 1956; Meharry Med Coll, DDS 1961. **CAREER:** Jersey City Med Ctr, intern 1961-62; Meharry Med Coll Nashville, instr Prosthetic dentistry 1963-64; VA Hosp Tuskegee AL, dir clin dentistry 1964-68; Individual Practice, dentistry; 1968-. **ORGANIZATIONS:** Mem Amer Dental Assn; chmn Lafayette Parish Comm Action Cncl 1971; Lafayette Cncl on Human Relations 1968-; Lafayette Parish Sch Bd; Lafayette Parish Cncl of Govt; mem Sheriff's Adv Commn 1968-; bd dirs Tri-Parish Comm Action Agency; United Givers Fund; pres bd dirs Holy Family Sch 1971-; mem NAACP; chmn housing com; C of C; Alpha Phi Alpha; Alpha Phi Omega; Chi Delta Mu. **MILITARY SERVICE:** AUS 1953-55. **BUSINESS ADDRESS:** 1006 Surrey St, Lafayette, LA 70501.

BARBEE, LLOYD AUGUSTUS
State representative, attorney. **PERSONAL:** Born Aug 17, 1925, Memphis, TN; son of Ernest Barbee and Adlina Barbee; divorced; children: Finn, Daphne, Rustam. **EDUCATION:** LeMoyne Coll, BA 1949; Univ of WI Madison, JD 1956. **CAREER:** Industrial Commn of WI UC Dept, law examiner I 1957-62; Gov's Comm on Human Rights, legal consul 1959; NAACP, pres 1962-64; Milwaukee United Sch Integration Comm, chmn 1964-; WI Legislature, rep 1965-77; private law practice, attorney, 1956-. **ORGANIZATIONS:** Mem State Bar of WI 1956-; chmn Enrolled Bills comm 1965-66; mem Comm on Joint Finance 1965-73; chmn Assembly Judiciary Comm 1973-77; mem Comm on Transportation 1969-77; pres/pres emeritus WI Black Lawyers Assn 1965-80; chmn WI Black Elected & Apptd Officials 1972-76; minister Political Empowerment CommNatl Black Assembly 1973-75. **HONORS/**

ACHIEVEMENTS: Milwaukee Man of the Yr Alpha Phi Alpha Frat Inc 1965; Medgar Evers Awd Milwaukee Br NAACP 1969; Outstanding & Continuing Contrib to Milwaukee Black Business Comm 1976; Disting Civil Serv Milwaukee Frontiers 1978; Lawyer Scholar Pub Serv Milwaukee Theological Inst 1978; Serv in Educ Law & Govern St Mark AME Church 1979; Outstanding Serv as Law Sch Tchr Univ WI Madison Law Sch 1984; Univ of WI at Milwaukee, Coll of Letters & Sci Amer Studies Dept faculty award; Madison West HS, award for outstanding services toward improving civil rights in WI 1986; Wisconsin Black Political and Economic Development Council Award, 1987; Rufus King Educ Award, 1989. **MILITARY SERVICE:** USN sm 2/c 3 yrs; Asiatic-Pacific & Victory Medals. **BUSINESS ADDRESS:** Attorney, 2374 N Richards St #2, Milwaukee, WI 53212.

BARBER, HARGROW DEXTER
Oral/maxillofacial surgeon. **PERSONAL:** Born Aug 29, 1956, Alameda, CA; son of Hargrow Dexter Barber Sr and Jessie Singleton Barber; married Kimberly Higgins DDS. **EDUCATION:** Univ of California at Davis, BA 1978; Meharry Medical Coll, DDS 1983; Oral Surgery Residency Highland Hospital 1989. **CAREER:** Private practice, dentist 1983-85; Highland General Hosp, oral maxillofacial surgeon in residency 1985-89. **ORGANIZATIONS:** Mem Natl Dental Assn 1979-, Amer Acad of Oral Medicine 1983-, CA Dental Assn 1986-, Amer Assn of Oral and Maxillofacial Surgeons 1986-; Amer Dental Society of Anesthesiology 1989-, Maryland State Dental Assn 1988-; Amer Dental Assn 1986-. **HONORS/ACHIEVEMENTS:** Outstanding Achievement Award Amer Acad of Oral Medicine 1983; Honor Scholarship Award Meharry Medical Coll School of Dentistry 1983; Hospital Dentistry Award Meharry Medical Coll 1983; second black person accepted into the Oral and Maxillofacial Residency Program at Highland General Hospital in its fifty year history; Golden State Achievement Award 1988; published "Double Degree Oral Surgeons," Journal of Oral and Maxillofacial Surgery, Oct 1989, and "Orbital Infections," Journal of Oral and Maxillofacial Surgery, Nov 1989. **BUSINESS ADDRESS:** Highland General Hospital, Dept of Oral/Maxillofacial Surgery, 1411 E 31st St, Oakland, CA 94602.

BARBER, JAMES W.
Educator. **PERSONAL:** Born Sep 17, 1936, Alexandria, VA; married Doris; children: Laura, Tracy. **EDUCATION:** BS 1964. **CAREER:** High Meadows CT State Treatment Center, dir of educ & group life; AL Center for Higher Educ, sr group training consultant 1972; So CT State Coll, dir comm & minority affairs. **ORGANIZATIONS:** Consult New York City Bur of Youth Detention 1970, New Haven CT Publ School System 1971-72, State of CT Dept of Children Youth Serv 1975-77; chmn protem Eastern Alliance of Black Counselors 1975; pres Consumer Council So CT Gas Co; adv Org of Afro-Amer students at S CT State Coll; pres Assoc of Black Personnel in Higher Ed CT CHapt; mem High Meadows Child Study & Treatment Ctr; pres New Haven Scholarship Fund Inc; mem NAACP, Urban League, RIF. **BUSINESS ADDRESS:** Dir of Comm Min Affairs, So CT State Coll, 501 Casscent St, New Haven, CT 06515.

BARBER, JANICE DENISE
Dentist. **PERSONAL:** Born Nov 06, 1952, Alameda, CA; son of Mr Hargrow Barber and Mrs Hargrow Barber; married Russell J Frazier. **EDUCATION:** Mills Coll, BA 1974; Meharry Medical Coll Dental Sch, DDS 1979. **CAREER:** Hubbard Hosp, 1st yr general practice resident 1981, 2nd yr general practice resident 1983, asst instr in hosp dentistry 1981; New York City, assoc dentist 1983-86; Sydenham NFCC/Harlem Hosp, attending dentist 1984-86; Harlem Hosp, clinical floor coord 1985-86; Oakland CA, assoc dentist 1986-. **ORGANIZATIONS:** Mem Delta Sigma Theta, Acad of General Dentistry, Amer Dental Assoc. **HONORS/ACHIEVEMENTS:** Employee of the Year Harlem Hosp Dental Clinic 1985; Employee of the Month Harlem Hosp 1985; Harlem Hosp Attending of the Year Dental Clinic 1986; abstract "The Mental Foramen Injection" The NY Journal of Dentistry 1983; "Cosmetic Dentistry" Harlem Hosp Ambulatory Newsletter 1986. **HOME ADDRESS:** 2142 66th Ave, Oakland, CA 94621.

BARBER, JESSE B., JR.
Neurosurgeon. **PERSONAL:** Born Jun 22, 1924, Chattanooga, TN; married Constance Bolling; children: Clifton, Jesse III, Charles, Joye. **EDUCATION:** Lincoln Univ, BA; Howard Univ Coll of Medicine, MD 1948. **CAREER:** Freedmen's Hospital, intern & resident general surgeon, 1948-54; Howard Univ Coll of Med, instructor surgery, pathology 1956-58; McGill Univ Montreal Neurologic Inst, resident, 1958-61; Howard Univ Coll of Med, chief div of neurosurgery 1961-83, prof of surgery 1964-, prof of social medicine 1983-. **ORGANIZATIONS:** Founder, dir, Howard Univ Med Stroke Project, 1968-70; Natl adv comm Epilepsy Found of Amer; Exec comm for strokes Amer Heart Assn; mem, Kappa Pi, Alpha Omega Alpha; fellow, Amer Coll of Surgeons; pres, Natl Med Assn, 1978-79. **HONORS/ACHIEVEMENTS:** Howard Univ Alumni Fed Award for Meritorious Prof & Comm Serv 1970; Wm Alonzo Warfield Award 1974; Century Award YMCA 1974; Distinguished Serv Award Natl Med Assn, 1974; Outstanding Serv Award HTA 1982-86; Outstanding Serv Award Commn Public Health of DC 1985. **MILITARY SERVICE:** AUS pfc 1943-46; AUS Med Corps capt 1954-56. **BUSINESS ADDRESS:** Prof Social Med & Neurosurgery, HowardUniv Coll of Med, HowardUniv Hosp, 2041 9th Ave NW, Washington, DC 20060.

BARBER, WILLIAM, JR.
Building service supervisor. **PERSONAL:** Born Jan 04, 1942, Morristown, NJ; married Anita Clayter; children: William III. **EDUCATION:** Univ of NE, BE 1967. **CAREER:** Town of Morristown, recreational dir; M&M Mars, employment & comm relations rep; No Jersey Morris Catholic HS, 1st black wrestling coach, head track coach, 1967-73; Urban 4H, social comm worker, 1967-73; Morristown Neighborhood House, social rec dir, 1967-; Intl Harvester, sales trainee, school comm worker, social case & guidance counselor, 1967-73; Barber Maintenance Cleaning Contractor, pres; AT&T, mgr bldg operations, mgr public relations. **ORGANIZATIONS:** Counselor After Care Clinic Drug Rehabilitation Regions Clergy Council; chmn Juvenile Conf Bd; natl bd dir Morristown YMCA 1967-71; recreations commission 1967-69; mem Morris Community Coll 4H EOF, Cty Coll of Morris & St Elizabeth Coll 1969-72; More help bd of dir, scholorship comm Morristown Neighborhood House 1969; TYEFA dances 1972; local TV show "Cable-Whats Happening Now" 1973-; mem Plainfield NAACP 1974, Human Civil Rights Commiss; mem Morristown Kiwanis Club, Morris Cty NAACP 1980; 1st black volunteer fireman in Morristown 1980-; mem Morristown Memorial Hospital; parole bd State of New Jersey 1980; mem Intl Group Friendship Force; 2rd ward councilman, sr mem Town Govt; Market Street Mission Christian Counselling Training; bd of dir for Morris Habitat for Humanity. **HONORS/ACHIEVEMENTS:** Jaycees Distinguished Serv Award 1969; Outstanding Citizen 4-H Club Award 1970; Morris County Human Resource Award 1978; NAACP Comm Serv Award; Comm Serv Award for Ike Martin Book of Honors 1987; developed a private library with antique radios. **BUSINESS ADDRESS:** Bldg Serv Supvr, AT&T Bell Lab, Whippany Rd, Whippany, NJ 07981.

BARBOUR, JOSEPH PIUS, JR.
Psychiatrist. **PERSONAL:** Born Aug 16, 1923, Spartanburg, SC; married Elizabeth Louise; children: Russell, Warren, Joseph Pius III, Benjamin, Robert, Charlene. **EDUCATION:** Lincoln U, 1940-43; Meharry Med Coll, MD 1946. **CAREER:** Mercy Douglas Hosp Phila, intern 1946-47; Phila, pvt prac 1955-56; Cmmnwlth PA, sr psych 1956-; Philadelphia St Hosp, clin dir 1955-. **ORGANIZATIONS:** Mem training rsrch com psych & neurlgy 1959-; dir forensic psych, psych consult Eastern Corr Inst Phila; exec dir Philadelphia Psych Comm Mntl Hlth Ctr; asst clin prof Temple Univ Med Sch; dir Clncl Serv N Cntrl Philadelphia Comm Hlth Ctr; mem Am Psych Assn; PA Psych Soc Episc. **HONORS/ACHIEVEMENTS:** Contrib articles, professional jours. **BUSINESS ADDRESS:** Philadelphia Psychiat Comm Mnt, 3701 N Broad St, Philadelphia, PA 19140.

BARBOUR, WORTH L.
Business executive. **PERSONAL:** Born Mar 05, 1929, Spartanburg, SC; married Kristine Knous; children: Worth Littlejohn. **EDUCATION:** Shaw Univ, AB, 1951; Crozer Theol Sem, BD, 1954; Univ of North Carolina Grad School of Sociol, 1961; Univ of Pennsylvania Grad School of Soc Work, 1966. **CAREER:** Lecturer & guest speaker throughout eastern, southern & mid-western states; Natl Bapt Voice, contrib ed, 1952-54; A&T Coll Sociol & Soc Sci Survey Course, asst prof, lecturer & coord, 1960-65; State of PA, publ asst caseworker & psych soc worker; Voter Reg for NAACP, field rep, 1967; Curtis Park Comm Ctr, acting exec dir, 1970-71; Co div of Hwys, equal employment rep, 1971-76; US Equal Employment Opportunity Comm, equal opportunity spec, 1976-. **ORGANIZATIONS:** Mem Omega Psi Phi, NAACP; pres Mile High Chap CO Assoc of Publ Employees; pres CDOH Golf League 1973; chmn, comm Federal State & Local Compliance Officers within Metro-Denver Area. **HONORS/ACHIEVEMENTS:** Golfer of the Year 1972; State Fleet Golf Champion.

BARCLAY, CARL ARCHIE
Physician. **PERSONAL:** Born Jul 30, 1922, Nanticoke, MD; married Mae Neece Hodge; children: Carl Archie, Kenneth Dale. **EDUCATION:** Hampton Inst, BS 1942; Howard Univ, MD 1947. **CAREER:** Hampton Inst, teaching asst 1942-44; Homer G Phillips Hosp, intern St Louis 1947-48; Edwards Mem Hosp OK City, house physician 1948-51; OK City Bd of Ed, school physician 1949-59; OK City, gen practice 1951-; Guthrie OK Job Corps Ctr, physician 1971-. **ORGANIZATIONS:** Pres OK City Med De-Phar Soc 1962-65; pres OK Med Dental & Pharm Assoc 1965-66; chmn Met Outreach Dept Greater OK City YMCA 1971-75; mem OK Cty Med Soc 1971-, OK State Med Assoc 1971-, Amer Med Assoc 1971-; mem Natl Med Assoc; dir, treas, managing officer 1968-86, M-D-P Investment Fund Inc; mem OK City Urban League; life mem NAACP. **HONORS/ACHIEVEMENTS:** Metro Outreach Comm - Greater OK City YMCA, service awd 1975; Greater OK City YMCA Hall of Fame 1977; Eastside Branch-Greater OK City YMCA, outstanding volunteer awd 1979; OK Med Dental & Pharm Assn, life member awd 1983; China Painter, won several ribbins at the state fair of Oklahoma 1983. **HOME ADDRESS:** 2813 NE 19th St, Oklahoma City, OK 73111.

BARCLAY, DAVID RONALD
Business executive. **PERSONAL:** Born Aug 28, 1932, Oakland, CA; son of Fred and Margaret; married Pauline Brown; children: Steven, Danielle. **EDUCATION:** Los Angeles State College, BA 1961; UCLA Exec Prog, Cert 1982. **CAREER:** CA Fair Employment Prct Comm, supervisor, consultant 1967-71; Hughes Aircraft Co head EEO programs 1971, mgr urban afrs 1972-78, dir human resources. **ORGANIZATIONS:** Parole agent California Youth Authority 1964-66; soc case wrkr LA Co Bur of Pub Asst 1961-64. **HONORS/ACHIEVEMENTS:** Bd mem Natl Black United Fund; bd Mem L A Brotherhood Crusade; Outstanding Alumnus California State Univ - Los Angeles Black Support Group, 1988. **MILITARY SERVICE:** AUS cp 2 Yrs. **HOME ADDRESS:** 12638 Remington St, Pacoima, CA 91331. **BUSINESS ADDRESS:** Staff Vice President, Human Resources, Hughes Aircraft Co, 7200 Hughes Terrace, Los Angeles, CA 90045.

BARCLAY, LAWRENCE V.
Educator. **PERSONAL:** Born in Cleveland, OH; married Barbara; children: MeShelle, Lawrence, Terrence, Christopher. **EDUCATION:** John Carroll U, BS 1952; John Carroll U, MA 1955; Case Western Reserve U, MFA 1954. **CAREER:** Developmental Service Oberlin College, assoc dean; Coll Bd Prgm Assn, 1969-71; CWRU, dir of cnslr 1967-69; Educ Project CWRU, dir 1965-69; Cleveland Public Schools, teacher 1952-64; MIT, lecturer; Harvard Univ, lecturer; War Coll, lecturer; Oberlin Coll, lecturer; Cleveland State Univ, lecturer; Univ of NC, lecturer; Mississippi State Univ, lecturer; NAACP, cons; OE. **ORGANIZATIONS:** Mem NAACP; APGA; ANWC; ACE; NVGA; ASCA; AMEG; AAHE; NABSE; Teaneck Rec Ctr Comm NY Urban Leag. **HONORS/ACHIEVEMENTS:** Educ of yr Omega Psi Phi 1966; 1st elec pres Nat Orgn of Upward Bound Dir 1968; publ Teaching Urban Yth.

BARDEN, DON H.
Real estate developer, cable television executive. **PERSONAL:** Born Dec 20, 1943, Detroit, MI; son of Milton Barden, Sr and Hortense Hamilton Barden; married Bella Marshall, May 14, 1988; children: Keenan Barden. **EDUCATION:** Central State Univ, attended; Central State Univ, attended 1963-64. **CAREER:** Former city councilman, TV show host; The Don H Barden Co, pres; City of Lorain, councilman 1972-75; Don H Barden Co, owner/pres 1976-81; WKYC-TV NBC Cleveland, talk show host 1977-80; Barden Communications Inc, chmn, pres 1981-. **ORGANIZATIONS:** Pres Urban Action Inc; del White House Conf on Small Business Pres, Lorain Cty Comm Action Agency; exec comm Democratic Party; mem Ed Task Force; dir, Detroit Symphony Orchestra 1986-, Natl Cable TV Assoc IOB 1985-; dir, MI Cable TV Assoc 1987-, dir, First Independence Natl Bank 1987-; dir, Metropolitan Detroit Convention Bureau, 1988-. **HONORS/ACHIEVEMENTS:** Nominated Young Man of the Year. **BUSINESS ADDRESS:** President, Chairman, Barden Cablevision, 12775 Lyndon, Detroit, MI 48227.

BARDWELL, RUFUS B., III
Business executive. **PERSONAL:** Born Jan 25, 1937, Sylacauga, AL; married Barbara Vidrine; children: Andrea, Rufus IV. **EDUCATION:** Tennessee State Univ, BS, 1960; CCNY, advance studies. **CAREER:** Tuskegee Inst, intern, 1960-61; Home Ins Co, accountant,

1961; State of NY, tax accountant, 1961-62; IRS, New York NY & Dallas TX, revenue agent, 1962; DHUD, officer bus devel office, 1969-. **ORGANIZATIONS:** Mem Alpha Phi Alpha, Dallas Big Bro Assoc; bd mem Dallas Negro C of C. **HONORS/ACHIEVEMENTS:** AUS pfc 1954-56. **BUSINESS ADDRESS:** Officer Business Devel Office, DHUD, 1100 Commerce St, Dallas, TX 75202.

BAREFIELD, EDWARD EMANUEL
Educator, musician. **PERSONAL:** Born Dec 12, 1909, Scandia, IA; married Consuelo; children: Dolores, Patricia. **EDUCATION:** Northshore Conservatory of Music Joe Burns, studied clarinet; Joe Allard NY; NY Univ, Rudolf Schramm Schillinger Found; Julliard School. **CAREER:** Played with, Bennie Moten's KC Orchestra, McKinney's Cotton Pickers, Cab Calloway, Les Hite, Paramount Pictures, Fletcher Henderson, Ella Fitzgerald, Duke Ellington; ABC, staff mus arrgr, Don McNeil's Breakfast Club dir by Eddie Ballentine, others conducted for, Ella Fitzgerald's Orchestra; A Streetcar named Desire, Sarah Vaughn at Basin St E Loews State Theatre, Cab Calloway's Cotton Club Revue in NY, Brazil, Uraguay and Argentina; played at, Freedom Land in Bronx World Fair NY, PaulLavelle, Geo Seuffert Concert Band, Paul Toubman's All Amer Band, Sammy Spears Concert Band, musical revue Jazz train in Europe 1960, 9 countries and 22 citiesin Africa for State Dept with Dick Vance 1969; Broadway shows; freelance teaching. **HONORS/ACHIEVEMENTS:** Semi-Retired.

BAREFIELD, MORRIS
Educator. **PERSONAL:** Born Aug 15, 1939, Madison, IL; married Lun Ye Crim; children: Erik, Myla. **EDUCATION:** So IL Univ, BS 1961, MS 1965. **CAREER:** Eisenhower HS Blue Island IL, instr 1961-64; Richard HS Oak Lawn IL, instr 1964-66; New Trier East HS, instr 1966-. **ORGANIZATIONS:** Mem, Instructional Affairs Comm Natl Council of Teachers of Math, 1969-72, NEA, IL Educ Assn; treasurer, sec New Trier Educ Assn 1971-74; mem Glencoe Concerned Parents Assn; dir, student prog Rights & Responsibilities New Trier HS 1973-75; guest speaker Natl Council of Teachers of Math, 1972, regional speaker, 1971-72; faculty council pres New Trier HS 1987-88. **HONORS/ACHIEVEMENTS:** Award for Outstanding Effort in Human Relations IL Educ Assn 1974. **BUSINESS ADDRESS:** Instructor, New Trier East High School, 385 Winnetka Ave, Winnetka, IL 60093.

BAREFIELD, OLLIE DELORES
Educational administrator. **PERSONAL:** Born Dec 19, 1930, Teague, TX; married Henry B Barefield Sr; children: John Anthony. **EDUCATION:** Huston-Tillotson Coll, BA (Magna Cum Laude) 1950; Univ of No CO, MA 1966, EdS 1970. **CAREER:** Teague Independent School Dist, English teacher 1950-55; Bureau of Indian Affairs AZ, Bilingual teacher 1955-60; Denver Public Schools, elementary teacher 1960-70, elementary principal 1970-. **ORGANIZATIONS:** Mem Amer Assoc of Univ Women 1980, Ministers Wives Assoc 1980, Natl Assoc of Elem Principal 1980; bd of dir NAACP Denver 1980; mem Delta Sigma Theta1980, Natl Council of Negro Women Inc 1980; guest lecturer Rocky Mountain Book Festival 1970. **HONORS/ACHIEVEMENTS:** Teacher of the Year Denver Publ School 1969; listed in Who's Who in CO 1976; Woman of the Year Kappa Omega Chi Beauticians Sor 1980. **BUSINESS ADDRESS:** Principal, Denver Public School, 2480 Downing St, Denver, CO 80205.

BARFIELD, CLEMENTINE (NEE CHISM)
Organization founder, executive director. **PERSONAL:** Born Aug 19, 1950, Lexington, MS; daughter of Tolbert Chism and Malinda Baugh Chism; married Rev John J Barfield, Apr 04, 1967 (divorced); children: John, Ollie, Malinda, Derick (deceased), Roger. **EDUCATION:** Wayne State Univ, Detroit MI, BS, 1981. **CAREER:** Save Our Sons and Daughters (SOSAD,) Detroit MI, founder/exec dir. **ORGANIZATIONS:** Mem, Amer Humanics, Wayne State Univ; commr, Detroit City Council-Youth Advisory Commn; bd mem, Project Start; bd mem, Michigan Victim Alliance; mem, Natl Org of Victim Assistance (NOVA). **HONORS/ACHIEVEMENTS:** Community Service Award, Natl Assn Negro Professional and Business Women, 1987; Natl Black Journalist, 1987; Community Service Award, Amer Muslim Community, 1987; Community Service Award, Univ of Detroit, 1987; Black Professionals Award, Michelob Beer, 1988; honorary doctorate degree, Marygrove Coll, Detroit MI, 1988; Victims Advocacy Award, Pres Ronald Reagan, 1988; Special Tributes, City of Detroit/State of Michigan; Status of Women Awards, Top Ladies of Distinction; Public Citizen of the Year Award, Natl Assn of Social Workers, 1989. **BUSINESS ADDRESS:** Founder/Exec Dir, Save Our Sons and Daughters, 453 Martin Luther King, Detroit, MI 48201.

BARFIELD, JESSE LEE
Professional athlete. **PERSONAL:** Born Oct 29, 1959, Joliet, IL; married Marla; children: Joshua Laroy, Jessica. **CAREER:** Toronto Blue Jays, player 1979-. **HONORS/ACHIEVEMENTS:** BBWAA Awd for Rookie of the Year, 1982; Labatt's "Blue" Player of Month, April 1982, Aug 1985; AL Player of the Week, period ending Sept 4, 1982; first Blue Jay player to have 20 home runs and 20 stolen bases in same season; LaBatt's "Blue" Player of the Year and club's Player of the Year by Tor's BBWAA; named to Amer All-Star team which toured Japan after the 1986 season; became first Blue Jay player to reach the 100 HR mark 1986; Gold Glove and Silver Slugger Awd 1986; Blue Jay's Player of the Year, Toronto Chap BBWAA 1986; mem All-Star Team 1986. **BUSINESS ADDRESS:** Toronto Blue Jays, Box 7777, Adelaide St PO, Toronto, Ontario, Canada M5C 2K7.

BARFIELD, JOHN E.
Chief executive/president. **PERSONAL:** Married Betty; children: Jon, Aaron. **CAREER:** Univ of MI, janitor 1954; Part-Time Janitorial Svc, janitor 1954-69; ITT, mgr; realtor; consult to major corporations; Janitorial Serv 1975; Barfield & Assoc; Barfield Companies, chief exec/pres. **ORGANIZATIONS:** Mem Ypsilanti Chamber of Commerce; bd mem Eastern MI Univ Coll of Business. **MILITARY SERVICE:** AUS. **BUSINESS ADDRESS:** Chief Executive Officer, The Barfield Companies, 800 Lowell St, Ypsilanti, MI 48197.

BARFIELD, LEILA MILLFORD
Elected official. **PERSONAL:** Born Jun 16, 1923, Atlanta, GA; daughter of Eugene Millford and Leila Williams; married Quay F Barfield, Jun 19, 1970; children: Jeanne T. Meadows, William C. Terry (deceased). **EDUCATION:** Morris Brown Coll, BA 1952; Atlanta Univ, MA Educ 1962, EdS Reading 1968, EdS Admin 1970. **CAREER:** Atlanta Public Schools, curriculum coordinator, 1948-70; Lawton Public Schools, team teacher 1971-73; Bishop Elementary School, curriculum coordinator 1970-72; Univ of OK FAA Mgmt Training School, prof of History 1973-7; City of Lawton, councilwoman; Mayor Pro Tempore, formerly. **ORGANIZATIONS:** Clerk, sec Friendship Baptist Church, 1960-70; supvr, teacher, Atlanta Univ, C Morris Brown, Clark & Spelman Coll 1962, 1968; visiting prof Jackson State Coll 1968, 1969; chmn nominating comm, Amer Assn of Univ Women 1970-; facilitator workshops Univ of OK 1971, 1972; chairperson Bd of Family Health Care Serv 1971-73; nominated for 1st lady of Lawton 1972; mem Lawton-Ft Sill Comm Ed Citizens Adv Bd 1974-; sec NAACP 1979-84, Stewardess Bd Barnett Chapel AME Church 1979-; sunday school teacher Barnett Chapel Church 1979-; mem OK Municipal League 1979-; pres Women's Missionary Soc Barnett Chapel AME Church 1980-84; past pres Pan Hellenic Council 1980; exec bd Women in Municipal Govt 1981-; exec sec NAACP 1984; candidate State Legislature 1984; asst sec Usher Bd Barnett Chapel 1984-85; mem Women Involved in Global Issues Alpha Kappa Alpha Sorority, 1984-85; mem, Lawton Mobile Meals Bd, 1984; Mem, chairperson, sec, Alpha Kappa Sorority, Theta Upsilon Omega Chapter. **HONORS/ACHIEVEMENTS:** Full Scholarship for EdS Reading Ford Found 1968; Twice Outstanding Graduate Soror, Alpha Kappa Alpha 1980, 1984; Omega Citizen of the Year, Psi Upsilon Chapter, 1981, 1983; Consinious Support & Contribution to Comm & NAACP, 1982; Accomplishment in Political Awareness & Involvement Delta Sigma Theta Sorority, 1984; Wrote Proposal for City/County Teachers in Human Relations & Reading. **HOME ADDRESS:** 3304 Overland Dr, Lawton, OK 73501.

BARFIELD, QUAY F.
Business executive. **PERSONAL:** Born Aug 03, 1912, Hugo, OK; married Leila M. **EDUCATION:** Langston Univ, BA 1952. **CAREER:** Fort Sill, Fort Sill, OK, supply supervisor 1955-76. **ORGANIZATIONS:** Member Omega Psi Phi 1952-; trustee bd Barnett Chapel AME Church 1960-81; owner/mgr Barfield's Rentals 1968-; owner/mgr Barfield's Package Store 1970-; bd mem CEDAR 1972-81, Assoc of S Central OK Govt 1981-, NAACP; mem comm Natl Reclamation Comm Omega Psi Phi 1963-64; chmn 9th Dist Reclamation Comm Omega Psi Phi; 1st vice dist rep 9th Dist Omega Psi Phi 1963-64. **HONORS/ACHIEVEMENTS:** Greatest Master of Ceremony Froggs Civic & Social Club 1960-76; Outstanding Serv Psi Upsilon Chap Omega Psi Phi 1968-69; President Usher Board Barnett Chapel AME Church 1975-80; Best MC of Year Ladies Prog Social & Civic Club 1983; Dedicated Serv as President Natl Dunbar Alumni Assn 1979-83; MC East Side CommClub 1983; Dedicated Serv W Coast Region Cuney Booker T Washington HS Reunion 1984; Man of the Year Psi Upsilon Chaptger Omega Psi Phi; Commendation for Outstanding Performance of duties as supply clerk tactics Combined Amrs Dept USA Artillery & Missile School Ft Sill OK 11962-63. **MILITARY SERVICE:** Ordnance staff sgt 3 years 10 mo; Good Conduct 1942-46. **HOME ADDRESS:** 3304 Overland Dr, Lawton, OK 73501.

BARFIELD, RUFUS L.
Educator. **PERSONAL:** Born Nov 14, 1929, Hickman, KY; married Emma Crawford; children: Rufus Jr, Sheila, Joselyn. **EDUCATION:** KY State U, BA 1952; Univ of KY, MA 1956; Univ of Cinc, EdM 1966; OH State, adv grad wk 1967; Miami U, PhD 1972. **CAREER:** Rosenwald High School KY, teacher 1952-55; Lincoln Heights Schools OH, teacher 1955-56; Hoffman Schools, Cincinnati OH, teacher 1956-64; Schiel Schools, Cincinnati OH, teacher 1964-66, asst prin 1966-69; Colum Schools, prin 1969; Burton Schools, Cincinnati OH, prin 1969-71; KY State Univ, admin asst to pres 1972-74; Acad Affairs Univ of AR, vice chancellor 1977-; Acad Affairs KY State Univ, vice pres 1974-77. **ORGANIZATIONS:** Mem Nat Ed Assn; Am Assn of Sch Admin; Phi Delta Kappa; Nat Orgn on Legal Probl in Ed; Soc of Resrch Admin; ky Coun on Hghr Ed; Commn on Hghr Educ in KY commn on child srvcs; commn on voc ed for hghr ed; commd KY colonel. **HONORS/ACHIEVEMENTS:** Sel as Cit of Day Cincin Radio Sta; awd for merit serv as exec sec YMCA 1964; cert of awd for outstdng serv in Corryville Comm Coun of Cincin 1967; OH Dept of Elem Sch Prin Prof Growth Com; Cincin Sch Comm Assn Task Force; Cincin Hum Rel Aux Com; NDEA fellow OH StateUniv Crit Rdng & Child Lit 1967; dem tchrUniv of Cincin Tchr Coll at Schiel Sch 1964-66; invit from chmn Dept of Ed Admin Sch of Ed MiamiUniv to ent doct prog&tch cours in innov & ed; apptd KY Coll 1975. **MILITARY SERVICE:** AUS 1953-54. **BUSINESS ADDRESS:** U of AR, Pine Bluff, AR 71601.

BARKER, PAULINE J.
Business executive. **PERSONAL:** Born Apr 30, 1930, Ottawa, KS; daughter of John C. Wilson; married Keyton E Barker Jr; children: Sheila K Ewell, Brenda Lynn. **EDUCATION:** Washburn Univ, AA Business, 1950. **BUSINESS ADDRESS:** Pres, Web of Thread Inc, 220 SW 33rd St, Suite 2, Topeka, KS 66611.

BARKER, TIMOTHY T.
Teacher/coach. **PERSONAL:** Born Feb 03, 1948, Des Moines, IA. **EDUCATION:** Simpson Coll, BS 1970. **CAREER:** Des Moines Public Schools, teacher/coach. **ORGANIZATIONS:** Exalted ruler Hawkeye Elks Lodge # 160 1976-85; keeper of Peace Omega Psi Phi 1987-; mem Royal Dukes, Monarch Club, Sigma Phi Gamma, YMCA, NAACP, DMEA, SMB. **HONORS/ACHIEVEMENTS:** Youngest Exalted Hawkeye Elks Lodge #160 Ruler in the World. **BUSINESS ADDRESS:** Teacher/Coach, Des Moines Public School, 1800 Grand, Des Moines, IA 50317.

BARKLEY, CHARLES
Professional basketball player. **EDUCATION:** Attended Auburn University, Auburn AL. **CAREER:** Philadelphia 76ers, Philadelphia PA, professional basketball player. **BUSINESS ADDRESS:** Philadelphia 76ers Basketball Club Inc, P O Box 25040, Philadelphia, PA 19147. *

BARKLEY, MARK E.
Business executive. **PERSONAL:** Born Mar 15, 1937, Sprott, AL; married Arrie Ann Morton. **EDUCATION:** Alabama State Univ, BS 1961; Ohio State Univ, 1960; Atlanta Univ, 1961-63; Washington Univ, 1967; Work Oper Rsch, Computer Sci, Statistics 1967-. **CAREER:** AVSCOM Dir for S & CA, mathematician 1969-70; AVSCOM Dir for S&CA & P&P, oper rsch analyst 1970-72; AVSCOM Dir for Plans & Analysis, supr oper rsch analysis 1972-77; AVSCOM BLACK HAWK Proj Mgr, supr oper rsch analysis 1977-81, financial mgr; analyst 1976-77; Program Innovators Inc St Louis, pres, vice pres 1973-; AUS Aviation Systems Command, supvr oper rsch analyst. **ORGANIZATIONS:** Mem Asso for Comp Mchnry 1968; mem Operns Rsch Soc of Am 1972-; chm, bd of dirs Prg Innovators Inc St Louis, MO 1972-; sec, bd of dirs Gateway Fed Empls Co 1976; mem Soc of Logstcs Engrs 1977-; mem Army Avtn Asso of Am 1972-; deacon Antioch Bapt Ch St Louis, MO 1972; mem Cedar Vly Est Trustees 1983-; mem Free & Acptd Masons of AL 1960; mem Beta K. **HONORS/**

ACHIEVEMENTS: Hnrs grad AL StUniv 1957; Natl Sc Fnd fellow OSU, Columbus, OH; AU, Atlanta, GA 1960; long term training US Air Force & US Army 1967-68, 1975; cdrs awrd for Civ serv TSARCOM St Louis, MO 1983; Excptl Perf Awrd AVSCOM BLACK HAWK Proj Mgr 1984. **MILITARY SERVICE:** AUS pfc 1953-55; Armed Forced Exped Mdl Overseas Serv Mdl 1955-54. **HOME ADDRESS:** 12412 Cedarmoor, St Louis, MO 63131. **BUSINESS ADDRESS:** Financial Manager, Avscom, Black Hawk Proj Mgr, 4300 Goodfellow Blvd, St Louis, MO 63120.

BARKLEY, RUFUS, JR.
Freelance fashion designer & fashion illustrator. **PERSONAL:** Born Jan 11, 1949, New York, NY; son of Rufus Barkley, Sr and Sally Virginia Motron. **EDUCATION:** Parsons School of Design, NY City 1967-70. **CAREER:** Teal Traina, New York, designer; Oscar de la Renta Intl, asst designer; Geoffrey Beene Bag & Beene Shirt Bazaar, New York City, designer, 1973-74; Mollie Parnis Boutique & Couture New York City, asst designer, 1975-78; Beldoch Industries, New York City, designer Pierre Cardin blouses, 1982-83. **HONORS/ACHIEVEMENTS:** Don Simonelli Crit Awd; JC Penney Sports Awd; participant in The Ebony Fashion Fair 1969-79; "New Face of '72," article in Women's Wear Daily 1972; dress design, Bazaar Magazine, July 1972; "Soul on Seventh Ave," article in Time magazine, Aug 7, 1972; Designer of the Month, Essence Magazine, Nov 1972; dress design, cover of Cosmopolitan magazine, Jan 1973.

BARKSDALE, HUDSON L.
Business executive. **PERSONAL:** Born Jan 28, 1907, Barksdale, SC; married Katie; children: Jeanne Keith, Rev HL. **EDUCATION:** South Carolina State Coll, AB, 1936; Columbia Univ, MA, 1952. **CAREER:** Private practice, ins. **ORGANIZATIONS:** Pres Palmetto Ed Assoc 1962-64; pres elect Amer Teachers Assoc 1967; pres Spartanburg NAACP; chmn Natl Ed Assoc 1971; mem SC House Rep 1975-, Resolutions Comm; mem ethics comm NEA; mem Parliamentarian Civic League, Alpha Phi Alpha 1929. **HONORS/ACHIEVEMENTS:** Silver Beaver Awd BSA 1960; invited White House Conf Ed; Dossier Natl Ed Assoc Archives; Serv to Mankind Awd S Spartanburg Sertoma 1978; Recog of SvcCity of Spartanburg 1979; Humanitarian Awd Rutledge Coll 1980.

BARKSDALE, MARY FRANCES
Manager. **PERSONAL:** Born Apr 05, 1934, Richmond, IN; daughter of Charles Woodson and Mary A. Mitchell Woodson; married Wayne Edward Barksdale, Apr 18, 1953; children: Wayne E Jr, Stacey L McCampbell, Vickki A Morgan. **EDUCATION:** Attended, Earlham Coll, 1952-53, Indiana Univ, 1976-81. **CAREER:** Intl Harvester Co, employment asst, 1969-74, employment supvr, 1974-77, labor relations supvr, 1977-80, human resources mgr, 1981-83; Navistar Intl Corp, compensation & devel mgr, 1984-. **ORGANIZATIONS:** Bd mem, Parkview Memorial Hospital, 1971-74, 1976-79, 1985-88; bd of advisors, Indiana Univ, Purdue Univ, 1977-; bd mem, Urban League, Ft Wayne, 1979-85; mem, The Links Inc, 1979-; bd of school trustees, East Allen County Schools, 1979-; bd mem, United Way of Allen County, 1983-86. **HONORS/ACHIEVEMENTS:** Commander of the Garrison Award Community Service, Robert E Armstrong Mayor, City of Ft Wayne, 1979; Recognized for Community Service, Kappa Alpha Psi Fraternity, 1981; Community Service to City of Ft Wayne, The Gent's Club, 1983; Humanitarian Award, Fort Wayne Urban League, 1985; Helene Foellinger Award, Outstanding Contributions, 1989. **HOME ADDRESS:** 3424 Mono Gene Dr, Fort Wayne, IN 46806. **BUSINESS ADDRESS:** Compensation & Develop Mgr, Navistar Intl Corp, 2911 Meyer Rd, Fort Wayne, IN 46803.

BARKSDALE, RICHARD KENNETH
Educator. **PERSONAL:** Born Oct 31, 1915, Winchester, MA; son of Simon Barksdale and Sara Barksdale; married Mildred W; children: James, Adrienne Simkins, Calvin. **EDUCATION:** Bowdoin Coll, AB 1937; Syracuse Univ, AM 1938; Harvard Univ, PhD 1951; Bowdoin Coll, LHD 1972. **CAREER:** Southern Univ, instr Eng 1938-39; Tougaloo Coll, head, Eng dept 1939-42; NC Central, grad dean 1949-58; Morehouse Coll, head Eng dept 1958-62; Atlanta Univ, prof Eng & grad dean 1962-71; Univ of IL, assoc grad dean 1975-82, prof emeritus of English 1985. **ORGANIZATIONS:** Mem bd of overseers Bowdoin Coll 1974-86; mem Grad Record Exam Bd ETS 1982-86; mem univ press bd Univ of IL 1982-86; pres Langston Hughes Soc 1981-84. **HONORS/ACHIEVEMENTS:** Phi Beta Kappa Bowdoin Coll 1937; co-editor, Black Writers of Amer, Macmillan 1972; Langston Hughes Poet and His Critics, Amer Library Assn 1977; Langston Hughes Visiting Prof Univ of Kansas-Lawrence 1986; Tallman Visiting Professor, Bowdoin Coll 1986. **MILITARY SERVICE:** Field Artillery 2nd Lt 1943-46. **HOME ADDRESS:** 2207 Wyld Dr, Urbana, IL 61801.

BARKSDALE HALL, ROLAND C.
Historian. **PERSONAL:** Born Jul 30, 1960, Sharon, PA; son of Clarence Barksdale Hall (deceased) and Anna Steverson Barksdale Hall (deceased); married Drusilla L Sweeney, Nov 22, 1984; children: Rillis Celeste. **EDUCATION:** Univ of Pittsburgh, Pittsburgh, PA, BS, 1983; Univ of Pittsburgh, Pittsburgh, PA, MS, 1984; George Washington Univ, Washington, DC, 1987-. **CAREER:** Maxima Corp, Rockville, MD, librarian, 1985; Johns Hopkins Univ, Baltimore, MD, reference librarian, 1986-88; book review editor, Journal of the Afro-Amer Historical and Genealogical Soc, 1987-; Howard Univ, Washington, DC, coord of black health history, 1988-. **ORGANIZATIONS:** Mem, African Heritage Classroom Concept Comm, Univ of Pittsburgh, 1984; mem, Assn for the Study of Afro-Amer Life and History, 1986-; bd of dir, Afro-Amer Historical and Genealogical Society, 1988-; knight recorder, Prince Hall Knights of Pythagoras, Odell B Matthews Sr Council 11, 1975-82; mem Sphinxmen Club, 1980; bd of dir, Campus Christian Outreach Ministry, 1981; consultant, Bread for the World Educ Fund, 1984; keyworker, Combined Federal Campaign, 1988. **HONORS/ACHIEVEMENTS:** Mem, Quill and Scroll, 1979; Certificate of Merit, Grand Council Knights of Pythagoras, 1979; Certificate of Appreciation, Headquarters US Postal Service, 1987; Provost's Scholarship, Univ of Pittsburgh, 1984; Eagle Award, Combined Federal Campaign, 1988; author of "Rent Parties," poem, The Federal Poet, 1987; author of "Tracing Slave Ancestors," Coweta County Genealogical Society Magazine, 1987, author of "Staying a Little Ahead," Journal of the Afro-Amer Historical & Genealogical Society, 1987; author of Memories of PaSam, The Write Age, 1989; author of "Breast Cancer: Lighting Does Strike Twice," Sisters Magazine, 1989; author of "Our Harps Hang on the Willows," poem, Crisis Magazine. **MILITARY SERVICE:** US Army Reserves, spec fourth class, 1982-88; received Dept of the Army Certificate of Achievement, 1984. **HOME ADDRESS:** 2902 O Street SE, Washington, DC 20020.

BARKSTALL, VERNON L.
Executive director. **PERSONAL:** Born Aug 23, 1929, Cincinnati, OH; son of Nelson L Barkstall and Naomi Bailey Barkstall; married Carol Louise Benton, Jun 09, 1957; children: Jeffrey, Lisa, Karen. **EDUCATION:** OH State Univ, BS 1958, MA 1959. **CAREER:** Franklin Settlement Detroit, boys' group worker 1959-61; Columbus OH Pub Sch, tchr 1961-65; Lancaster OH Fairfield Sch for Boys, tchr recreation coord 1965-66; Urban League, exec dir 1966-69, exec dir social work 1969-. **ORGANIZATIONS:** Mem Champaign IL Rotary Club 1978-. **HONORS/ACHIEVEMENTS:** Sphinx-Senior Honorary, Ohio State Univ 1958; Award of Merit, Amer Assn of College Baseball Coaches 1973. **MILITARY SERVICE:** AUS corpl 1952-54. **HOME ADDRESS:** 704 Arlington Ct, Champaign, IL 61820.

BARKUM, JEROME PHILLIP
Athlete. **PERSONAL:** Born Jul 18, 1950, Gulfport, MS; married Linda; children: Laiysha. **EDUCATION:** Attended, Jackson State Coll. **CAREER:** NY Jets, tight end 1972-. **HONORS/ACHIEVEMENTS:** Played Pro Bowl 1973; 34 Straight Starts; Played in over 100 Games; 30 TD receptions; 223 Career Receptions. **BUSINESS ADDRESS:** NY Jets, 1000 Fulton Avenue, Hempstead, NY 11550.

BARLOW, GROVER S.
Community relations director. **PERSONAL:** Born Dec 25, 1934, New Orleans, LA; children: 6 children. **EDUCATION:** Wayne Univ, attended 1956. **CAREER:** Last Paragns H Inc Consult Firm, dir comm relations. **ORGANIZATIONS:** Mem Grand Juror's Assn; Comm Planning Bd for Manhattan; asst dist commr Boy Scouts Amer; vice pres Chambers Canal Civic Group; mgr Brunswick Corp; union counselor Cent Labor Councl; mem Membership Com YMCA Greater NY. **HONORS/ACHIEVEMENTS:** Black Achiever YMCA 1977. **MILITARY SERVICE:** USAF 1957-62.

BARNES, BENNY
Businessman. **PERSONAL:** Born Mar 03, 1951, Lufkin, TX; married Joyce; children: David, Damon, Deon, Christina. **EDUCATION:** Attended Stanford. **CAREER:** Dallas Cowboys, professional football player 1972-82; Owner & franchisee of 8 Kentucky Fried Chicken Stores. **ORGANIZATIONS:** Coach of Soccer Team. **HONORS/ACHIEVEMENTS:** Shares NFL Record for Most Safeties in Season with Two; Led Cowboys in Interceptions 1978. **BUSINESS ADDRESS:** Imperial Foods Inc, 9304 Forest Ln #119, Dallas, TX 75273.

BARNES, BOISEY O.
Educator, cardiologist. **PERSONAL:** Born May 16, 1943, Wilson, NC; married Bernadine. **EDUCATION:** Johnson C Smith Univ, BS 1964; Howard Univ, MD 1968. **CAREER:** Howard Univ Hospital, dir noninvasive echocardiography lab 1974-77; Howard Univ Hospital Cardiac Clinic, dir 1976-77; Howard Univ Hospital, asst prof med; Shaw E Corp; Boisey O Barnes, pres; Private Practice, cardiologist. **ORGANIZATIONS:** Professional educ com Amer Heart Assn 1977; lectr AHA 1975-77; past keeper records & seals Omega Psi Phi Frat 1975-77; pres Beta Kappa Chi Hon Soc 1963-64; mem Amer Inst Ultrasound 1975-77; Amer Soc Echocardiography 1977; adv bd Anacostia Congress Hghts Sect Red Cross 1977; mem DC Med Soc Diplomate Amer Bd Intl Med 1972. **HONORS/ACHIEVEMENTS:** Hon Mention Dept Prize Intl Med & Pediatrics Howard Univ 1968; develpr Echocardiography Lab Howard Univ 1973-74; Outstanding Young Men Amer 1970; publ "Echocardiographics Findings in Endocarditis in Heroin Addicts" Amer Journ Card 1977; "Echocardiography Abstracts, Echocardiography in Hypertensive Patients" "Echocardiography in Amyloidosis". **BUSINESS ADDRESS:** 413 G St SW, Washington, DC 20024.

BARNES, DELORISE CREECY
Educator, consultant. **PERSONAL:** Born Apr 02, 1947, Hertford, NC; daughter of William Creecy and Easter Creecy; married James M Barnes, Jun 08, 1968; children: Victor, Timothy, Stephen, Jonathan. **EDUCATION:** Livingstone Coll, BS (high honors) 1965-69; Univ of TN, MS 1970, EdD Vocational Tech Ed 1978; UT Knoxville-US Office of Educ Fellowship 1975-76. **CAREER:** Creecy's Poultry Farm, owner 1962-65; Oak Ridge Public Health & Welfare Dept, analyst/surveyor summer 1965; Oak Ridge Schools, adult ed instr 1973-76; Eureka Ctr Roane Co Schools, head office admin 1970-75; Roane State Comm Coll, prof of business. **ORGANIZATIONS:** Mem and advisor, Phi Beta Lambda RSCC 1976-; appt by Gov of TN mem, sec TN Commiss for Human Devel 1977-79; consult Univ of TN's Ctr for Govt Training 1980-87, Knoxville Prof Sec Intl 1983-87, Oak Ridge Schools 1983-88, Martin Marietta Energy Syst Inc 1984-; pres Alpha Kappa Alpha Xi Iota Omega; chmn-organized Homework Hot Lines in Oak Ridge Schools 1986-87; mem Natl Bus Ed Assoc, Amer Bus Comm Assoc, Delta Pi Epsilon, resource person Youth Enrichment Ctr; bd of dir Big Brother/Big Sisters 1985-88; secretary, Crown Monarch, auxillary of Girls Club 1988-; legislative liaison chmn, Tennessee Business Educ Association 1988-. **HONORS/ACHIEVEMENTS:** USOE grant UT Knoxville 1975-77; UT grant for a model office 1976; 6 articles in major publs between 1979-84; led a round table discussion at NBEA conv; selected as Outstanding Young Woman of Amer 1980; Dedicated Professional, Phi Beta Lambda, RSCC chapter 1988; Publication Award, The Writing Center, RSCC 1989; "Mobilizing for the Minority Teacher Educ Shortage" in The Balance Sheet, South-Western Publishing 1988; conducted communication workshops for industry; presented papers at Amer Business Communication Association, South East and Midwestern regionals 1989. **HOME ADDRESS:** 126 Barrington Dr, Oak Ridge, TN 37830. **BUSINESS ADDRESS:** Professor of Business, Roane State Community College, Patton Lane, Harriman, TN 37748.

BARNES, ERNEST EUGENE, JR.
Artist. **PERSONAL:** Born Jul 15, 1938, Durham, NC; divorced; children: Diedre, Michael, Sean, Erin, Paige. **EDUCATION:** North Carolina Central Univ, BA 1960. **CAREER:** San Diego Chargers, football player 1960-63; Denver Broncos, football player 1964-65; Amer Football League, afcl artist 1966; The Co of Art, artist/founder/pres 1970-. **ORGANIZATIONS:** Mem Screen Actors Guild; bd aldermen Atlanta, GA 1973; city govt Durham, NC 1973; California State Senate Rules Comm 1974; congr record of 93rd Congress. **HONORS/ACHIEVEMENTS:** "The Beauty of the Ghetto Exhibit" 1974; works include "Three Hustlers" 1970, "OJ" 1969, "Closed Set" 1970, "High Aspirations" 1971; one-man exhibitions held at Grand Central Art Gallery in NY, McKenzie Gallery in Los Angeles, Agra Gallery in Washington DC; Heritage Gallery in Los Angeles; works are part of numerous important private collections. **BUSINESS ADDRESS:** The Co of Art, 8613 Sherwood Dr W, Hollywood, CA 90069.

BARNES, EUGENE M.
Legislator. **PERSONAL:** Born Jul 24, 1931, Chicago, IL; married Melody; children: Vikki,

Eugina, Craig. **CAREER:** Dept of Sewers, comm; Illinois legislature, representative, 29th Dist, Chicago. **ORGANIZATIONS:** Mem IL Black Polit Caucus; past bd dir Nat Soc of State Rep; past mem bd dir Midwest Assn for Sickle Cell Anemia. **HONORS/ACHIEVEMENTS:** Introduced on of first legislative bills in support of sickle cell rsrch. **BUSINESS ADDRESS:** Commissioner Dept of Sewers, 121 N LaSalle St, Room 401, Chicago, IL 60602.

BARNES, FANNIE BURRELL
Librarian. **PERSONAL:** Born in New Orleans, LA; married Richard Alexander Barnes; children: Erica Arnetta, Maria Monique. **EDUCATION:** Dillard Univ, AB 1945; Atlanta Univ, MS 1950. **CAREER:** Gilbert Acad New Orleans, tchr Engl 1945-49; Atlanta Univ, asst libr summer 1950, 1957-61, 1967; Claflin Coll Orangeburg, SC, head libr 1950-54; tchr children's lit, 1957-; Atlanta Pub Libr Bookmobile, children's libr summer 1961; Clark Coll Atlanta, head libr 1954-. **ORGANIZATIONS:** Mem ALA, NEA, NAACP, Alpha Kappa Alpha. **BUSINESS ADDRESS:** Head Librarian, Clark College, 240 Chestnut St SW, Atlanta, GA 30314.

BARNES, JOHN B., SR.
Pedodontist. **PERSONAL:** Born Jan 15, 1922, New Iberia, LA; married Audra M Guyton; children: Audra Yvonne, John B Jr. **EDUCATION:** Meharry Med Coll, DDS 1952; LaSalle Ext Univ, LLB 1965. **CAREER:** Pedodontist. **ORGANIZATIONS:** Mem Amer Dental Assoc; Amer Soc Dentistry Children; Intl Acad Orthodontics Town Hall CA; Morehouse Alumni Assoc; bd dir Wesley Social Serv Ctr. **MILITARY SERVICE:** USAF Dental Bd Corp capt. **BUSINESS ADDRESS:** 12060 S Central Ave, Los Angeles, CA 90059.

BARNES, JOHN E.
City councilman. **PERSONAL:** Born Aug 22, 1933, Aliceville, AL; married Edna; children: John Jr, Debra, Darryl. **EDUCATION:** Attended, Bucknell Univ, Tuskegee Ins, GMI, Kent State Univ, Wooster Coll, Cleveland State Univ, Cuyahoga Comm Coll. **CAREER:** General Motors, former mgr; Lee-harvard Shopping Center Inc, vp; Barnes Enterprises, pres. **ORGANIZATIONS:** Mem White House Conf of Housing; sec of builders/bankers/realtors com; chmn Congr of Urban League Inc; pres 30th Ward Dem Club; vchmn SE Mental Health Adv; mem Dem Party Exec Com of Cuyahoga Ct; v chmn City Planning Com & Comm Devel; mem finance com St Use Com; mem Airport Aviation & Lakefront Devel Commn. **BUSINESS ADDRESS:** President, Barnes Enterprises, 13520 Miles Ave Playhouse, East Cleveland, OH 44105.

BARNES, JOSEPH NATHAN
Attorney. **PERSONAL:** Born Nov 29, 1950, Hermondale, MO; son of John Wesley Barnes and Lillie Mae Barnes; children: Julius. **EDUCATION:** Ibadan Univ Nigeria, Certificate in Intl Economics 1971; Antioch Coll, BA Finance & Commerce 1973; Univ of PA, MBA 1977; Univ of PA Sch of Law, JD1977. **CAREER:** Shearman & Sterling, assoc atty 1977-81; Zimet Haines Moss & Friedman, assoc atty 1981-82; Barnes & Williams, partner 1982-85; Barnes & Darby, partner 1985-. **ORGANIZATIONS:** Mem Natl Bar Assoc 1981-87; dir Black Entertainment & Sports Lawyers Assoc 1983-88; bd mem Urban League Manhattan Branch 1985-87; mem Metro Black Bar Assoc 1986-87, Natl Assoc of Securities Profls 1986-87; NY chmn telethon United Negro Coll Fund 1986, 1987, 1988; mem NAACP. **HONORS/ACHIEVEMENTS:** Rockefeller Grant 1968,73; Natl Fellowship Foundation Fellow 1973,74; First Black NY Law firm listed in Dir of Municipal Bond Dealers 1987. **HOME ADDRESS:** 150 West End Ave #19M, New York, NY 10023. **BUSINESS ADDRESS:** Founding Partner, Barnes & Darby, 11 Park Place Ste 903, New York, NY 10007.

BARNES, LEONARD C.
Chief executive officer. **PERSONAL:** Born Mar 26, 1922, Bogalusa, LA; married Doretha M Moss; children: Lenetta B Romar. **EDUCATION:** So Univ Baton Rouge, BS 1948; Univ of CO, MS 1954; attended, UC at Berkeley, Oak Ridge Inst, Univ of CO. **CAREER:** Central Louisiana Trade School, Alexandria LA, athletic dir & counsel 1948-49; Booker T Washington High School, head athletic coach 1949-65, asst prin of admin 1967; Southern Univ, Shreveport LA, dir student personnel 1967-71, vice pres 1971-77, chancellor 1978-. **ORGANIZATIONS:** Sec-treas Sewerage Dist #5 1965-69; commr of officials S Western Athl Conf 1967-79; vice pres Waterwork Dist #4 1970-80; bd dir Caddo-Bossier Assn for Retarded Citizens 1977-80; bd dir Shreveport C of C 1978-80; life mem Alpha Phi Alpha Frat. **HONORS/ACHIEVEMENTS:** Tchr of the Year Award Caddo Parish Tchr Assn 1964; Apprec Award Sigma Gamma Rho Sorority Inc Delta Lambda 1972; Disting Letterman Serv Award So Univ Athletic Dept 1974; Cert of Merit State of LA 1978. **MILITARY SERVICE:** AUS 1st Lt 1945-46; Asiatic Pacific Campaign Medal/Victory Amer Theater Campaign Medal. **BUSINESS ADDRESS:** Chancellor, Southern University, 3050 Cooper Rd, Shreveport, LA 71107.

BARNES, MARTIN G.
Councilman. **PERSONAL:** Born Mar 05, 1948, Paterson, NJ; married Diane Judith Grant; children: Gregory, Antoinette. **EDUCATION:** Seton Hall Univ, BS Edn. **CAREER:** Sterling Drug Co, sales & mgr 1968-72; HUD Target Proj Prog, coord dir 1975-77; Barnes Assoc Bus Mgmt Cons, pres 1975-; RP Vivino Esq, priv investigator 1975-; Passaic Co Dept Youth Svc, dir 1977-79; City of Paterson, councilman. **HONORS/ACHIEVEMENTS:** Outstanding Young Man Concerned Citizens of Paterson 1976; Hon Mem Bros in Blue 1976; Man of the Year Tombrock Coll 1977. **BUSINESS ADDRESS:** Councilman, City of Paterson, 155 Market St, Paterson, NJ 07522.

BARNES, MARVIN
Professional basketball player. **PERSONAL:** Born Jul 27, 1952, Providence, RI. **CAREER:** Detroit Pistons, player 1976-78; San Diego Clippers, player 1978-79.

BARNES, MATTHEW M., JR.
Engineering technician. **PERSONAL:** Married Clara M Lee; children: Danette LaTrise. **EDUCATION:** 4 yr apprenticeship; Comm Coll, 2 yrs; mgmt & job related courses; class D credential for teaching certain vocational subjects. **CAREER:** Mare Island Naval Shipyard, marine machinist 1951-55, machinist 1955-63, foreman machinist 1963-64, equipment spl 1964-65, engrg tech methods & standards 1965-66, foreman machinist 1966-73, engrg tech prev maint 1973-. **ORGANIZATIONS:** Mem Mare Island Supr Assn; Supr Toastmasters Club; pres Richmond Br NAACP; past vice pres Northern Area Conf NAACP; mem choir bd stewarts Davis Chapel CME Ch; past Sunday Sch tchr; past supt Sunday Sch; past chmn Scholarship Com Davis Chapel CME Ch; Richmond City Human Rel Speakers' Bur; chmn bd Richmond City Youth Serv Bur; mem Shipyard Commander's Equal Employment Opp Adv Com; pres The Original 21'ers Club. **HONORS/ACHIEVEMENTS:** First Black Supv Mare Island Naval Shipyard; First Black to hold present position. **MILITARY SERVICE:** AUS 2 years. **BUSINESS ADDRESS:** Engineering Technician, Mare Island Naval Shipyard, Richmond, CA 94806.

BARNES, N. KURT
Business executive. **PERSONAL:** Born Jan 11, 1947, Washington, DC; son of Norman H Barnes and Doris Boyd Barnes. **EDUCATION:** Yale Coll, BA 1968; Harvard Univ, MA 1973. **CAREER:** Rand Corp, assoc econimist 1968-73; Fortune Magazine, assoc editor 1973-75; Time Inc, financial analyst 1975-77; Inco Limited , financial analyst, dir investor relations, pres Inco Investment Management 1977-; chmn MacQuest Investment Counsel Ltd, 1989-. **ORGANIZATIONS:** Treas Hale Found 1974-; mem, Friends of Legal Defense Fund. **HONORS/ACHIEVEMENTS:** John Hay Whitney Fellow 1970-71; Harvard Graduate Prize Fellowship 1971-73. **BUSINESS ADDRESS:** President, Inco Investment Management, Inco Limited, 1 New York Plaza, New York, NY 10004.

BARNES, PAUL DOUGLAS
Government official. **PERSONAL:** Born Dec 20, 1946, Henderson, TN; married Bobbie Tyson; children: Richard, Michael. **EDUCATION:** Lane Coll, BS, 1968; Univ of South Carolina, MPA, 1977. **CAREER:** Soc Sec Administration, claims rep, 1968-70, admin ofcr, 1970-73, prog analyst, 1973-77, area dir, 1977-. **ORGANIZATIONS:** Mem Amer Soc for Pub Adminstrn; Omega Psi Phi; toastmasters Intl. **HONORS/ACHIEVEMENTS:** Spl Achievement Award 1971, 1974; Superior Perf Award 1975; Outstanding Young Men in Amer 1973, 1975. **BUSINESS ADDRESS:** Area Dir, Soc Security Administration, PO Box 6175, Macon, GA 31208.

BARNES, STEPHEN DARRYL
Lawyer. **PERSONAL:** Born May 29, 1953, Los Angeles, CA; son of John J Barnes and Marian E Barnes. **EDUCATION:** Univ of Southern California, BA 1978; Harvard Law School, JD 1981. **CAREER:** Covington & Burling, assoc 1981-86; Weissmann Wolff et al, assoc 1986-87; Strange & Nelson, partner, 1987-89; Bloom, Dekom & Hergott, partner, 1989-. **ORGANIZATIONS:** Mem Local Spiritual Assembly Baha'i Faith 1981-. **BUSINESS ADDRESS:** Partner, Bloom, Dekom & Hergott, 9255 Sunset Blvd, 10th Floor, Los Angeles, CA 90069.

BARNES, THOMAS
City mayor. **PERSONAL:** Married Francis. **CAREER:** Formerly Calumet Township Assessor; Mayor of Gary IN, 1988-. **BUSINESS ADDRESS:** Mayor, Municipal Building, 401 Broadway, Gary, IN 46402. *

BARNES, VIVIAN LEIGH
Elected government official. **PERSONAL:** Born Aug 09, 1946, Wilkinson, WV; married Leroy P Barnes; children: Charles Pershon, Jamila Kali, Nathifa Oni. **EDUCATION:** Saginaw Business Inst, Clerk Typist 1965; Delta Coll, AA 1979; Saginaw Valley State Coll, 1985. **CAREER:** Greater Omaha Comm Action Youth Prog, asst dir 1969-71; Oppty Indust Ctr, exec sec 1974-76; Delta Coll, Univ Ctr, admiss sec 1977-79; Buena Vista Charter Twp, twp clerk 1980-. **ORGANIZATIONS:** Exec bd mem Saginaw Cty Dem Party 1980-, MI Dem Black Caucus 1980-; alt delegate MI Dem State Central 1980-. **HONORS/ACHIEVEMENTS:** Community Service Delta Coll Black Honors Awd 1983. **HOME ADDRESS:** 151 Barbara Lane, Saginaw, MI 48601. **BUSINESS ADDRESS:** Township Clerk, Buena Vista Char Twsp, 1160 S Outer Dr, Saginaw, MI 48601.

BARNES, WILLIAM L.
Attorney. **PERSONAL:** Born Nov 28, 1936, Benton Harbor, MI; married Patricia Jean; children: Barbara. **EDUCATION:** LA City Coll, AA 1962; Van Norman Univ, BS 1965; USC Los Angeles CA, JD 1969. **CAREER:** Litton Sys, analyst 1963-65; Northrop Corp, buyer & contracts admin 1965-69; workmen's comp splst, 1969-71; Fibre-Therm, gen cnsl/vp; Barnes & Grant, atty 1971-. **ORGANIZATIONS:** Mem Natl Bar Assn, Amer Bar Assn, Nu Beta Epsilon Natl Law, Amer Trial Lawyers Assn, CA Lawyers for Criminal Justice, LA Trial Lawyers Assn, Kappa Alpha Psi. **HONORS/ACHIEVEMENTS:** Scholarship Balwin-Wallace Coll 1953. **MILITARY SERVICE:** USAF s/sgt, maj co-pilot B-47E (SAC) 1957; Outstanding Crew Chief 1955. **BUSINESS ADDRESS:** 111 N LaBrea Ave, Inglewood, CA 90301.

BARNES, WILLIE R.
Attorney. **PERSONAL:** Born Dec 09, 1931, Dallas, TX; married Barbara Bailey; children: Michael, Sandra; Traci, Wendi, Brandi. **EDUCATION:** UCLA, BA, Political Science, 1953; UCLA School of Law, JD 1959. **CAREER:** State of CA Dept of Corps, various attorney positions, 1960-68, supvr corps counsel 1968-70, asst commr, 1970-75, commr of corps, 1975-79; UCLA Alumni Assn, general counsel & dir, 1983-86; Manatt Phelps Rothenberg & Phillips, sr partner, 1979-88; Wyman Bautzer, Kuchel & Silbert, sr partner, 1989-. **ORGANIZATIONS:** Exec comm, Business & Corps Sec 1970-86; vp, dir UCLA Law Alumni Assoc 1973; mem Comm Real Estate Franchises Mutual Funds; chmn SEC Liasion Comm 1974-78; chmn Real Estate Investment Comm 1974-78; pres Midwest Securities Commiss Assoc 1978-79; 1st vice pres N Amer Securities Admin Assn 1978-79; co-managing ed, CA Bus Law Reporter 1983; mem Beverly Hills Bar Assn, Exec comm Corp & Commercial Law Sec; Bd of Governors of Century City Bar Assn, 1982-84; vice chmn, Comm on Corp; vice chmn, Oil Investment Comm; active leadership in directing the Securities Reg Prog of CA; mem vice chair Exec Committee Business Law Sec, California State Bar, 1983-86; mem Corp Banking & Bus Law, Fed Regulation of Securities, Commodities, Franchises & State Regulation Committies, Amer Bar Assn; chmn, bd of truste es, Wilshire United Methodist Church, 1986-. **HONORS/ACHIEVEMENTS:** Major role in developing uniform standards for real estate progs on nationwide basis; Acknowledged expert in real estate & oil & gas securities; Certificate of Appreciation, Practicing Law Inst, 1973; Alumnus of the Year UCLA Law School 1976; Resolutions of Commendation CA State Senate & CA Assembly 1979; chairman Knox Keene Health Care Service Plan Comm 1976-79; chmn, Leveraged Real Estate Task Force 1985-86; mem CA Senate Commission on Corporate Governance. **MILITARY SER-**

VICE: AUS pfc 1954-56. **BUSINESS ADDRESS:** Sr Partner, Wyman, Bautzer, Kuchel & Silbert, 2049 Century Park East, 14th Fl, Los Angeles, CA 90067.

BARNES, WILSON EDWARD
Military. **PERSONAL:** Born Jun 09, 1938, Richmond, VA; son of Ora Henderson; married Barbara Jones; children: Kaye, Lynette, Kimberly. **EDUCATION:** VA State Univ, BS Biology 1960, MS 1971; Univ of Southern California, Doctoral Studies. **CAREER:** AUS 18th Battalion 4th Training, commander 1976-78; Richmond Recruiting Battalion, commander 1978-80; Area IV First ROTC Region, commander 1982-84; Headquarters Dept of the Army ROTC Study Group, dir 1984-86; US Central Command, Deputy J-1 1986-88. **ORGANIZATIONS:** Member Association AUS; Virginia St Univ Alumni Assoc, NAACP; Retired Officer's Assn; Urban League. **MILITARY SERVICE:** AUS col 28 yrs; ARCOM; Bronze Star; Meritorious Service Medal; Defense Meritorious Service Medal. **HOME ADDRESS:** 403 E Carolina St, Apt 118, Tallahassee, FL 32302.

BARNES-SIMMONS, ANNE T.
Business executive. **PERSONAL:** Born Mar 10, 1940, Pitt Co, NC; married Robert G Simmons III; children: Darryl, Anita. **EDUCATION:** Corrine Brooks Hair Design Inst, diploma cosmetology 1957-58; Natl Beauty Culturist League Inc, BA Masters 1965, 1969; Norfolk State Univ, BA 1964; VA Union Univ Sch of Theology, certification 1979; Gulf Coast Seminary, Bachelor of Theology 1985. **CAREER:** LaBaron Hairstyling Salon, stylist 1958-61; Bett's Hairstyling Salon, stylist 1961-67; Anne's Beauty Acad, pres 1975-; Anne Barnes, Inc, pres 1967-. **ORGANIZATIONS:** Bd of dirs Tidewater Tele Adv Council; assoc min Garretts Comm Church; bd of dirs 100 Black Women Coalition; bd mem United Christian Front for Brotherhood; bd mem Hal Jackson Talented Teen; mem Natl Beauty Culturists League 1959-; bd mem Church St Merchant Assoc 1982-; bd mem Natl Teachers Educ Council 1983-. **HONORS/ACHIEVEMENTS:** Businessperson of the Year TABCA Norfolk; Awd of merit STOIC Norfolk 1981; Outstanding Citizen Awd Iota Phi Lambda Sor Inc 1984; Black Businesswoman of theYear Norfolk Journal & Guide Nwsp 1984; Outstanding Businessperson of the Year WRAP radio station Norfolk 1984. **HOME ADDRESS:** 1112 Rockingham St, Norfolk, VA 23523. **BUSINESS ADDRESS:** President, Anne Barnes Inc, 722 Chapel St, Norfolk, VA 23504.

BARNETT, ALFREDA W. DUSTER
Consultant. **PERSONAL:** Born Sep 03, 1904, Chicago, IL; widowed; children: Troy S, Charles E, Donald L, Alfreda D Ferrell. **EDUCATION:** Univ Chicago, PhB 1924. **CAREER:** Comm Rel Opport Ctrs, consult Present, dir 1967-75; IL Youth Commn, comm wkr delnqncy prevntn coord social 1947-65; House of Reps, sec approp comm 1953; Gen Assembly, sec to commn 1947. **ORGANIZATIONS:** Treas Alfreda Wells Duster Civic Club Asso of Rust Coll; mem womens bdUniv Chicago; mem YMCA; mem YWCA; mem Assn for the Study of Afro-Am Life & History; DuSable Mus of African-Am History. **HONORS/ACHIEVEMENTS:** Presented honorary doctor of humane letters Chicago StateUniv 1978; black book award Dollars & Sense Mag 1976; cit award Nat Council of Negro Women 1975; edited Crusade for Justice; The Autobiography of Ida B Wells 1970. **BUSINESS ADDRESS:** 1616 W 63rd St, Chicago, IL 60636.

BARNETT, ALVA P.
Educator. **PERSONAL:** Born May 04, 1947, Jacksonville, FL. **EDUCATION:** Bethune-Cookman Coll, BA 1969; Univ of Pittsburgh, MSW 1971, MPH 1978, PhD 1981. **CAREER:** North Central Comm MH-MR Ctr Crisis Ctr, asst adm dir 1971-72, soc work supervisor 1970-75; admin dir 1972-75; dir consultant social serv 1975-76; Univ of NE at Omaha, asst prof of social work. **ORGANIZATIONS:** Rsch consultant & prog evaluator Maternal & Child Health County Hlth Dept Pgh PA, United Methodist Comm Ctrs Inc; bd of dirs Social Settlement Assoc of Omaha 1982-; Chas Drew Health ctr 1986-, Head Start Child Develop Corp 1986-. **HONORS/ACHIEVEMENTS:** Listed in Dictionary of Intl Biography 1983; Visiting Scholar Quantitative Methods in Social Rsch Univ of MI Ann Arbor 1984; 2 book chapters and 2 articles published. **BUSINESS ADDRESS:** Asst Prof of Social Work, Univ of NE at Omaha, 60th and Dodge St, Omaha, NE 68182.

BARNETT, BUSTER CALVIN
Professional athlete. **PERSONAL:** Born Nov 24, 1958, Brooksville, MS. **EDUCATION:** Jackson State. **HONORS/ACHIEVEMENTS:** First team All-Southwestern Athletic Conf honors as a soph.

BARNETT, ETHEL S.
Government official. **PERSONAL:** Born Mar 07, 1929, Macon, GA; widowed; children: Prentis Earl Vinson. **EDUCATION:** Pioneer Busn Sch, attended 1947-50; attended Cheyney State Coll. **CAREER:** Supreme Lib Life Ins Co, ins agent 1954-55; City of Philadelphia Police Dept, officer 1961-71; Amer Found for Negro Affairs (AFNA), natr dir resource devel 1972; Commonwealth of PA, civil serv commr. **ORGANIZATIONS:** Bd dir Women for Greater Philadelphia 1978-; consult PECO Elec Co 1979-; 1st Black reg dir PA Fedn of Dem Women; natl dir Educ Dept (IBPOE of W) 1978-; mem Intl Personnel Mgr Assn; (IPMA); PUSH; Elks; NAACP; natl Assn Female Execs. **HONORS/ACHIEVEMENTS:** Comm Serv Award N Philadelphia Chap NAACP 1973; Humanitarian Award Bell Tel Co of PA 1976; Outstanding Woman of the Year Bright Hope Bapt Ch 1977; Who's Who in Amer Politics 1977-78; Patriots Bowl City of Philadelphia 1980. **BUSINESS ADDRESS:** Civil Service Commissioner, Commonwealth of PA, 320 S Office Bldg, Harrisburg, PA 17120.

BARNETT, ETTA MOTEN
Entertainer. **PERSONAL:** Born Nov 05, 1901, Weimar, TX; married Claude A Barnett (deceased); children: Sue Ish, Etta Traylor, Gladys Brooks. **EDUCATION:** Univ of KS, Music B 1931; Northwestern Univ Sch of Speech, further study 1949-50; Atlanta Univ Spelman Coll, Dr Hum Letters 1980-83. **CAREER:** Concert artist toured US & South Amer 1934-42; actress/singer starring role as Bess in "Porgy & Bess" 1942-45. **ORGANIZATIONS:** Co-owner Afro-Arts Bazaar 1950; vol work Intl Women's Decade Conferences 1975-85; mem Women's Decade Conference Nairobi 1985; mem Delta Sigma Theta Int Women's Conf Nassau 1987; mem Bd of Women Univ of Chicago; mem The African American Inst; mem the African Dia Intl Visitors Center; The Du Sable Museum; bd mem Alpha Kappa Alpha Sor; women's bds Univ of Chicago, Lyric Opera, The Field Museum, The Links Inc, Black Women's Agenda, Amer Assoc of Univ Women. **HONORS/ACHIEVEMENTS:** Honorary Doctorate Northeastern IL Univ 1981, Atlanta Univ 1983, Spelman Coll 1985, Univ of IL 1987; portrait commissioned by Alma Mater Univ of KS to be hung among Outstanding Alumnae in library on campus 1987. **HOME ADDRESS:** 3619 Martin Luther King Dr, Chicago, IL 60653.

BARNETT, EVELYN BROOKS
Educator. **PERSONAL:** Born Jun 04, 1945, Washington, DC; divorced; children: Nia Brooks. **EDUCATION:** Univ of WI Milw, BA(with honors); Howard Univ, MA 1974; Univ of Rochester, PhD(pending) 1981. **CAREER:** Milwaukee School System, high school teacher 1969-72; Howard Univ, Moorland-Springarn Research Center, manuscript rsch assoc 1974-75; Joint Center for Polit Studies, rsch consultant 1977-80; Simmons Coll, instructor 1979-80; Natl Council for Negro Women Bethune Proj, consultant 1979; Dartmouth Coll, asst prof 1980-; Harvard Univ Women's Studies Prog Div, resource assoc 1980-81; Harvard Univ WEB DuBois Inst for Afro-Amer Rsch, grad fellow. **ORGANIZATIONS:** Mem Alpha kappa Alpha Sorority; mem Natl Council of Negro Women; mem Assn for Study of Afro-Am Life & Hist; mem Amer Hist Assn. **HONORS/ACHIEVEMENTS:** Phi Alpha Theta Hist Honor Soc Univ of WI 1969; Kappa Delta Pi Educ Honor Soc Univ of WI 1969; Ford Fellowship for Grad Study Hist Dept Howard Univ 1972-74; Grad Fellowship Natl Fellowship Fund Atlanta, GA 1975-78; WEB DuBois Fellow Harvard Univ 1979-80; Author of "Changing Family Portrait of Afro-Am Slaves"; "Nannie Burroughs & Educ of Black Women"; "Class Rising but Race Remains". **BUSINESS ADDRESS:** Graduate Fellow, HarvardUniv, Canaday Hall B, Cambridge, MA 02139.

BARNETT, ROBERT
Administrator. **PERSONAL:** Born Apr 21, 1938, Fayetteville, GA; married Bessie Pearl Burch; children: R Terrance. **EDUCATION:** Morris Brown Coll, BA 1961; GA State Univ, MA pending (Deans List). **CAREER:** Atlanta Housing Auth, adminstrv intern 1966-67, bus relocation adv 1967-69, proj coord 1969-71, asst dir of redevel 1971-75, dir of redevel 1975-. **ORGANIZATIONS:** Basketball & football referee So Conf Ofcl Assn 1965-; mem Natl Assn Housing & Redevel Ofcls 1966-; mem resurgens 1971-; vice chmn Salvation ARmy Adv Cncl 1974-; mem Leadership Atlanta 1978-; first vice pres West Manor Elementary Sch PTA 1979-. **HONORS/ACHIEVEMENTS:** Ford Fellow Scholarship GA State Univ 1970; Annual Housing Awd Interfaith Inc Atlanta 1976; Cert of Appreciation for Outstanding Perf Atlanta Housing Auth 1977; Hall of Fame inductee Morris Brown Coll TAY Club 1978. **MILITARY SERVICE:** AUS e-4 23 months; Cert for Outstanding Serv & Achievements 1964. **BUSINESS ADDRESS:** Dir of Redevelopment, Atlanta Housing Authority, 739 W Peachtree St NE, Atlanta, GA 30308.

BARNETT, SAMUEL B.
Educator. **PERSONAL:** Born May 05, 1931, Philadelphia, PA; married Dorothy; children: Diane, Avonna, Christopher, Samuel, Donna. **EDUCATION:** Temple Univ, AA, BS; Newark State Coll, MA; Rutgers Univ, EdD candidate; Univ PA Woodrow Wilson Sch Princeton Univ, grad fels; Southeastern Univ, PhD 1979. **CAREER:** City of Philadelphia PA, police officer 1957-62; Philadelphia Area Delinquent Youth Program, project dir 1965-67; State of PA, parole officer 1967-68; Social Learning Lab Educ Testing Serv, prof assoc rsch div 1968-. **ORGANIZATIONS:** Mem Amer Personnel & Guidance Assn; Amer Soc Criminology; Natl Council on Measurement in Educ; Natl Assn Blacks in Criminal Justice System; bd dirs Timberlake Camp Charities Inc. **MILITARY SERVICE:** AUS 1946-49. **BUSINESS ADDRESS:** Prof Assoc Rsch Div, Soc Lrng Lab Educ Testing Serv, Rosedale Rd, Princeton, NJ 08540.

BARNETT, TEDDY
Accountant. **PERSONAL:** Born Mar 12, 1948, Freeport, NY; married Carol Ann Grier; children: Joell Carol, Jason Theodore, Jordan Dai. **EDUCATION:** Boston Univ, BS 1970. **CAREER:** Price Waterhouse & Co, sr accountant 1970-75; Bedford Stuyvesant Restoration Corp, dir intl audit 1976-78, dir fin admin 1978-79, vice pres fin & admin 1980-81, exec vice pres 1981-82, pres 1982-. **ORGANIZATIONS:** Bd dirs Enock Star Restoration Housing Devel Fund Inc; mem Stearns Park Civic Assn; mem Natl Assn Accountants; mem Natl Assn Black Accountants; bddir Brooklyn Arts Council, Amer Red Cross in Greater NY Brooklyn Chapt. **HONORS/ACHIEVEMENTS:** Black Achievers in Industry Awd 1974; Key Woman of Amer Achievement Awd 1984. **BUSINESS ADDRESS:** President, Bedford Stuyvesant Restoration, 1368 Fulton St, Brooklyn, NY 11216.

BARNETT, WILLIAM
Business owner. **PERSONAL:** Born Nov 29, 1917; married Edywna T. **EDUCATION:** YMCA Coll, law enforcement; Correspondence Sch, elec engrg. **CAREER:** Midwest Security Agency Inc Bd, pres; Chicago Police Dept, policeman; Cook Co Sheriff's Dept, sheriff's police; Chicago Sewer Dept, sewer insp; New 2nd Ward Regular Dem Orgn, alderman & committeeman. **ORGANIZATIONS:** Mem Ada S McKinnley Settlement House; exec dir 35th St Bus Men's Assn; mem 21st & 2nd Police Dist Steering Comm. **BUSINESS ADDRESS:** President, Midwest Security Agency Inc, 3430 S Prairie Ave, Chicago, IL 60616.

BARNEY, CLARENCE LYLE
Business executive. **PERSONAL:** Born Sep 19, 1934, New Orelans, LA; married Marie Dude Porter; children: Keith, Shawn. **EDUCATION:** So Univ, BS 1957; KS State, attended 1958; Tulane Univ, MSW 1970; MIT, rsch fellow 1973. **CAREER:** Franklin Co Welfare Dept Columbus OH, caseworker 1959; Magnolia HS Vacherie LA, tchr 1960; So Univ & Loyola Univ, instr 1964-75; US Equal Employment Oppor Commn, compliance officer 1966; Notre Dame Seminary & Dominican Coll, instr 1970; Urban League of Greater New Orleans Inc, pres. **ORGANIZATIONS:** Consult & lectr various orgns & univs 1963; mem Tulane Univ Bd of Visitors; mem New Orleans Chap Natl Assn of SW; mem C of C. **HONORS/ACHIEVEMENTS:** Publ "Housing Discrimination in New Orleans" 1969; publ "Leadership & Decision Making in New Orleans" 1969; publ "A Process for the Econ Devel of Black Ghetto Areas in the Urban South 1973. **MILITARY SERVICE:** AUS 1957-59. **BUSINESS ADDRESS:** President/ CEO, Urban League of Gr New Orleans, 1929 Bienville St, New Orleans, LA 70122.

BARNEY, WILLIE J.
Business executive. **PERSONAL:** Born Oct 10, 1927, Parkdale, AR; married Hazel Willis; children: Ronald, Reginald, Raymond, Reynaldo. **CAREER:** WISEC of C, pres/founder 1967-70; Consol Record Distrib, pres 1968-; Pyramid Intl, pres 1972-79; Barney's Records

Inc, pres. **ORGANIZATIONS:** Sr warden Masons Masonic Chicago 1959-69; mem marketing & com Black Music Assn 1978-; mem Westside Bus Assn 1973-75; treas Operation Brotherhood 1979-. **HONORS/ACHIEVEMENTS:** Businessman Awd FORUM 1975; Serv Awd Lu Palmer Found & Fernwood Meth Ch 1976; Serv Awd CBS Records 1978. **MILITARY SERVICE:** AUS pvt. **BUSINESS ADDRESS:** President, Barney's Records Inc, 3400 W Ogden Ave, Chicago, IL 60623.

BARNHILL, HELEN IPHIGENIA
Business executive. **PERSONAL:** Born Nov 10, 1937, Ponce de Leon, FL; daughter of Willie Ponds and Faustana Ponds; divorced; children: Carmen, Jerdie, Althea, Stanley, Hilliary, Kelli, Dana. **EDUCATION:** Marquette U, 1966; Lakeland Coll, hon dr of human letters 1975. **CAREER:** Milwaukee Urban League, caseworker 1962-65; Housing & Publ Accommodations State of WI, coord 1965-70; Proj Equality of WI, dir 1970-73; Barnhill-Hayes Inc, pres 1973-. **ORGANIZATIONS:** Bd trst Lakeland Coll; bd dir Better Bus Bur of Milw; corp mem United Way of Gtr Milw; bd dir Froedtert Memorial Lutheran Hosp, Hevi-Haul Intl, Competitive WI, WI MESBIC, Ind Bus Assn of WI; bd of trust Carroll Coll; Personnel-Indust Relations Assn of WI, Plymouth United Church of Christ; bd of governor, Mt. Mary Coll; bd Milwaukee Minority Chamber of Commerce. **HONORS/ACHIEVEMENTS:** B'Nai Brith Interfaith Awd Comm Serv 1969; Freedom of Residence Awd 1966; Outstanding Bus Achiev Awd WI Womens Polit Caucus 1976; YWCA Bus Ldr Awd 1977; WI Conf United Church of Christ 1977; WI Chap ASPA 1980; Midwest Region Soroptimist Intl 1982; Mary McLeod Bethune Awd WI Black Republican Council 1985; WI Assn for Sickle Cell Anemia 1985; Sales & Marketing Exec of Milwaukee 1985; St Francis Children's Center 1985. **BUSINESS ADDRESS:** President, Barnhill-Hayes, Inc, 788 N Jefferson, Ste 304, Milwaukee, WI 53202.

BARNWELL, HENRY LEE
Clergyman. **PERSONAL:** Born Aug 14, 1934, Blountstown, FL; married Shelie Yvonne Whiley; children: Aubrey, Cassandra, Timothy, Darlene. **EDUCATION:** Univ of MD, attended; AZ Coll of the Bible, BA 1978; St Stephens Coll, MS 1979; Carolina Christian Univ, Doctorate of Ministry 1984. **CAREER:** USAF, flight examiner 1954-70, recruiter 1971-74; Maricopa Cty Personnel, admin aide 1977-80; 1st new Life Missionary Baptist, clergyman. **ORGANIZATIONS:** Chmn Evangelism Bd Area I AB PSW 1970-83; exec bd mem Phoenix AZ PUSH Inc 1979-; chaplain Juvenile Dept of Corrections 1980-; exec bd mem Phoenix OIC1980-; moderator Area I Amer Baptist Pacific SW 1984-; pres Interdenominational Ministerial Alliance 1984-; reg dir Natl Evangelism Movement 1984-; religious adv council Maricopa Cty Sheriff Dept 1984-. **HONORS/ACHIEVEMENTS:** Community Serv Awd Williamsfield Air Force Base 1975-78; Hon Citizen of Tucson City of Tucson 1980; Outstanding Citizen Awd Citizens of Phoenix 1982; Appreciation Awd 82nd Flying Training Wing 1984. **MILITARY SERVICE:** USAF E-7 sgt 20 yrs; Airmans Medal, Air Force Commendation. **HOME ADDRESS:** 11633 N 49th Dr, Glendale, AZ 85304. **BUSINESS ADDRESS:** 1st New Life Missionary Bapt, 1902 W roeser Rd, Phoenix, AZ 85041.

BARON, NEVILLE A.
Physician. **PERSONAL:** Born Sep 14, 1933, New York, NY; married Cave-Marie Alix; children: Neilda, Collette, Marc, Rodney. **EDUCATION:** The OH State Univ, BSc 1955; Howard Univ Medical Sch, MD 1961; Howard Univ Serv Dist of Columbia Genl Hosp, rotating internship 1961-62. **CAREER:** Univ of MD Eastern Shore Div, medical dir 1962-68; Campbell Soup Inc, medical dir/consultant 1965-68; Univ of PA, residency training prog academic ophthalmology 1968; Univ of NJ Coll of Medicine, resident training prog clinical and surgical ophthalmology 1968-71; Warner Lambert Co, consultant/ophthalmology 1972-75; Private Practice, general ophthalmology 1972-85; Riverside Genl Hosp, chief of ophthamic dept 1976-85, chief of medical staff 1979-83; Westchester Ophthalmic Inst, clinical prof 1987-. **ORGANIZATIONS:** Mem Contemporary Oculoplastic Soc 1978-; pres The Continual Medical Ed Assoc of NJ 1982; pres NJ Chap Natl Medical Assoc 1985; clinical consultant Cooper Labs Inc 1987, Alergan Labs Inc 1987, Eye Technology Inc 1987. **HONORS/ACHIEVEMENTS:** Physician of the Yr Hudson Co NJ 1985; Howard Alumni Disting Accomplishment Awd 1985; mem China-Amer Scientific and Cultural Foundation 1986; 5 publications including "Ocular Chromophores-Topically Applies," (a new product for a newly-recognized ophthalmic need), Liquid Sunglasses 1986. **MILITARY SERVICE:** AUS ROTC OH State Univ completed w/Honors 1955, commissioned 2nd lt Chemical Corps 1955, officer Chemical Corps 1955-57; Honorable Discharge Medical Corps Reserves 1969. **HOME ADDRESS:** 146 Sandpiper Key, Secaucus, NJ 07094. **BUSINESS ADDRESS:** Clinical Professor, Westchester Ophthalmic Inst, 730 Marmaroneck Ave, White Plains, NY 11201.

BARR, LEROY
Police official. **PERSONAL:** Born Jul 01, 1936, New York, NY; married Virginia; children: Denise, LeRoy Jr, Nicole. **EDUCATION:** John Jay Coll, AA, 1970, BS, 1971; New York Univ, MA, 1973. **CAREER:** Youth House for Girls, couns 1959-64; New York City Bd of Educ, tchr 1971-73; Brooklyn Coll, couns 1973; New York City Police Dept, supr. **ORGANIZATIONS:** 100 Black Men; Assn of Black Psychologists; Amer Personnel & Guid Assn; Amer Acad for Professional Law Enforce; dir sec Black Family & marriage Couns Inc 1976-. **MILITARY SERVICE:** Sgt 1954-57. **BUSINESS ADDRESS:** Supervisor, New York City Police Department, One Police Plaza, New York, NY 10038.

BARRETT, JAMES A.
Association representative. **PERSONAL:** Born Dec 02, 1932, Cleveland, OH; married Edith Ransby; children: Zina, Jurena. **EDUCATION:** Attended, Kent State Univ, Cleveland State Univ. **CAREER:** City of E Cleveland, aptd city commnr 1969 elected 1970-72; E Cleveland Civil Svc, aptd commnr 1972-76; E Cleveland Pub Library, aptd trustee 1974-80; Blue Cross of NE OH, rep labor affairs. **ORGANIZATIONS:** Trustee E Cleveland PA, 1974; former bd mem E Cleveland YMCA 1972-73; mem E Cleveland Cits Adv Commn 1968-69; past pres Chamber-Mayfair Pres League. **BUSINESS ADDRESS:** Representative Labor Affairs, Blue Cross of NE OH, 2066 E Ninth St, Cleveland, OH 44112.

BARRETT, MATTHEW ANDERSON
Business executive. **PERSONAL:** Born Nov 13, 1947, Roanoke, VA. **EDUCATION:** VA Commonwealth Univ, BS Bus Admin 1974. **CAREER:** Univ Ford Motor Co, salesman 1969-70; Standard Drug Stores Inc, asst mgr 1970-72; VA Commonwealth Univ, computer programmer 1972-76; 3M Co, account rep. **ORGANIZATIONS:** Speaker Richmond Public Schools Speakers Bureau 1970-74; big brother Big Brothers Richmond 1970-75; treas Huntington Club Condominiums 1980-84; mem aircraft Owners & Pilots Assoc 1981-; scuba diver NAUI 1982-. **HONORS/ACHIEVEMENTS:** Salesman of the Year, 3M Co 1979, 1980; $100,000 Prod Awd 3M Co 1979; One of the Most Eligible Bachelors Ebony Mag 1983; Sales, Salesman of the Year, 1987; Apogee Award, 3M Co 1989. **HOME ADDRESS:** 53 Skyhill Rd #304, Alexandria, VA 22314. **BUSINESS ADDRESS:** Account Representative, 3 M Company, 1101-15th St NW, Washington, DC 20005.

BARRETT, RICHARD O.
Business executive. **PERSONAL:** Born Mar 04, 1923; married Vinella P; children: Richard Jr, Adrienne, Arlene, Yvonne. **EDUCATION:** Milwaukee Sch of Engrg, BA 1943, BSEE 1954; Univ of WI, MSEE 1955. **CAREER:** Kingston Tech School, instr 1946-50; Stearns Elec Corp, rsch engr 1955-59; Honeywell, devel engr 1959-65, systems analyst 1965-67, sr engr 1967-72, supr engrg. **ORGANIZATIONS:** Mem St Louis Park Rotary; registered professional engr MN; mem MN Soc of Professional Engrs 1966-72; pres Industry Section MN Soc of Professional Engrs 1969-75; corp bd mem Milwaukee School of Engrg 1979; commr Maplewood Planning Commn; mem bd dir St Paul Urban League; pres Minds for Prog Inc; pres Monitors (civic group); dir So MN 4-H Group. **HONORS/ACHIEVEMENTS:** NW Orient Airlines Outstanding Serv Awd 1971; Good Neighbor Awd WCCO Radio Northwest Ford Dealers; Engr of the Yr MN Soc of Professional Engrs 1970; Comm Serv Awd Honeywell 1976; Monitor of the Yr Civic Awd Monitor's Club 1977; Milwaukee Sch of Engrg Outstanding Alumnus Awd Class of 1954 granted 1984. **BUSINESS ADDRESS:** Supervisor Engrg Develop Lab, Honeywell Inc, 1625 Zarthan Ave, St Louis Park, MN 55416.

BARRETT, RONALD KEITH
Psychologist, educator. **PERSONAL:** Born Aug 17, 1948, Brooklyn, NY. **EDUCATION:** Morgan State Univ Baltimore, BS 1970; Univ of Pittsburgh, MS 1974, PhD 1977. **CAREER:** CA State Univ Dominquez Hills, asst prof psychology 1977-78; Loyola Marymount Univ Los Angeles, assoc prof, Psychology 1978-. **ORGANIZATIONS:** Consulting psychologist Inglewood Child Devel Cntr 1977-78; consult psychologist Soc Serv Bureau, City of Richmond 1978; consult pyschologist School of Business Central State Univ 1979; mem Natl Arts adv com for Natl Council of Negro Women (Western Reg Rep) 1979-; mem Catholic Big Brothers 1979-; mem Assn of Black Psychologists; mem, Am Psychological Assn. **HONORS/ACHIEVEMENTS:** Elected Psi Chi Natl Honor Soc, Psychology 1969; published "A Father's Love" interview Human Behavior 1978; published "Interpersonal Trust Among Coll Students"; Perceptual & Motor Skills 1979, "The Psychological Role of the Father in Early Child Devel, A Systems View". **BUSINESS ADDRESS:** Associate Professor Psychology, Loyola Marymount University, Department of Psychology, Los Angeles, CA 90045.

BARRETT, SHERMAN L.
Educator. **PERSONAL:** Born Aug 15, 1945, Charleston, SC; children: Larry. **EDUCATION:** Aurora Clg, BAE 1963-67; Adelphi U, 1966; UWM Milwaukee, 1975-83. **CAREER:** MTEA, ngtns 1969-72; WEA, crdntls 1970-72; NEA, del 1970-72; Black Teachers Org Milwaukee & Natl, vice pres 1970-72; Milwaukee Public Schools, teacher. **ORGANIZATIONS:** Dist dir A L Williams 1985; plygrnd/ctr dir Milwaukee Rcrtn 1967-81. **HONORS/ACHIEVEMENTS:** Coach/bsktbl 6th Graders/on own 1972-85. **HOME ADDRESS:** 1628 W Capitol Dr, Milwaukee, WI 53206.

BARRETT, WALTER CARLIN, JR.
Roman Catholic priest. **PERSONAL:** Born Sep 30, 1947, Richmond, VA; son of Walter Carlin Barrett, Sr and Elizabeth Norrell Barrett. **EDUCATION:** St John Vianney Seminary, diploma; St Mary's Seminary Coll, Catonsville MD, BA, Philosophy; St Mary's Seminary & Univ, Baltimore MD, MDiv, Theology. **CAREER:** Roman Catholic Diocese of Richmond, priest 1975-; St Mary's Catholic Church, assoc pastor, 1975-77; St Gerard's Catholic Church, Roanoke VA, pastor 1977-85; St Mary's Catholic Church, Norfolk VA, pastor, 1985-. **ORGANIZATIONS:** Member, NAACP, Natl Black Catholic Clergy Caucus, Black Catholic Commn, Black Catholic Clergy Conf; appointed to Diocesan Pastoral Council, Diocesan Priest Council; founder Richmond Black Catholic Caucus 1971-74; Exec Comm of Priests Council. **HONORS/ACHIEVEMENTS:** Winner Diocese/Deanery Public Speaking Contest Richmond Area 1965; Recognized for Outstanding Serv & Dedication by the Black Catholic Commn of the Roman Catholic Diocese of Richmond 1985. **BUSINESS ADDRESS:** Pastor, St Mary's Catholic Church, 1000 Holt St, Norfolk, VA 23504.

BARRON, REGINALD
Automobile dealer. **CAREER:** Barron Chevrolet Inc, Andover MA, chief executive. **BUSINESS ADDRESS:** Chief Executive, Barron Chevrolet, Rte 114, Andover, MA 01810.
*

BARRON, WENDELL
Automobile dealer. **CAREER:** Campus Ford Inc, Okemos MI, chief executive. **BUSINESS ADDRESS:** Chief Executive, Campus Ford Inc, 3003 E Michigan, Lansing, MI 48912.
*

BARROW, DENISE
Real estate executive. **PERSONAL:** Born Feb 03, 1943, New York, NY; daughter of Henry Barrow and Hazel Barrow. **EDUCATION:** Lebanon Hosp School of Nursing, LPN 1959-60; Bronx Comm Coll, 1963-65; Eastern Airlines Flight Attendant School, 1967; St Peters Coll, 1971-72; Queens Coll, 1979-80; Professional School of Bus, 1984. **CAREER:** Dr Eugene T Quash, nurse, med asst 1961-66; Eastern Airlines Inc, flight attendant 1967-86, inflight sup; Kennedy Kramer Inc, sales rep 1984-87; Kenedy & Kenedy Inc, sales & marketing exec 1988. **ORGANIZATIONS:** Bd mem Crotona Morrisania Civic Assoc 1964-67; mem League of Woman Voters 1964-67, Natl Coalescense of Flight Attendants 1983-86, Natl Board of Realtors 1986-, Natl Urban League 1986-, Teaneck Englewood & Vicinity Club of Natl Assoc of negro Bus & Professional Women 1987-; NY Coalition of 100 Black Women 1988. **HONORS/ACHIEVEMENTS:** Cert of Serv Awd United Negro Coll Fund. **BUSINESS ADDRESS:** Sales & Marketing Executive, Murphy Realty/Better Homes, 2035 Lamoine, Fort Lee, NJ 07024.

BARROW, LIONEL CEON, JR.
Business executive. **PERSONAL:** Born Dec 17, 1926, New York, NY; son of Lionel C Barrow Sr and Wilhelmina Brookins; children: Brenda, Rhonda, Aurea Nellie, K Erin, Leah Es-

trada. **EDUCATION:** Morehouse Coll, BA 1948; Univ of WI, MA 1958, PhD 1960. **CAREER:** Foote Cone & Belding Adv Agency NY, vice pres assoc rsch dir 1968-71; Univ of WI, prof mass comm & Afro-Amer studies 1971-75, chmn 1974-75; Howard Univ, dean sch of comm 1975-85; prof 1975-86; The Barrow Information Group, pres 1986. **ORGANIZATIONS:** Pres Journalism Council Inc 1970-79; mem adv bd Journalism Quarterly; consl Black Media; life mem NAACP; mem Natl Assn of Black Journalists, Capital Press Club; Sigma Delta Chi, Assn for Educ in Journalism; secretary, Elected Advocates, Maryland Conference on Small Business, 1987-89. **HONORS/ACHIEVEMENTS:** Chancellor's Awd, Distinguished Serv in Journalism, Univ of WI, 1971; publ "New Uses of Covariance Analysis" Journal of Advertising Rsch 1967; "Towards a Code of Ethics for Blacks in the Newsroom" Black Journal Review 1976; "History of the Black Press" Black Press Handbook 1977; author of "The Japanese: Are They Giving Us 'The Business'", Crisis, 1988. **MILITARY SERVICE:** AUS 1945-47 & 1950-53; Combat Infantry Badge, Korean Service Medal with five Bronze Stars, 1951. **BUSINESS ADDRESS:** President, The Barrow Informantion Group, P O Box 8118, Silver Spring, MD 20907.

BARROW, THOMAS JOE
Accountant, auditor. **PERSONAL:** Born Jan 12, 1949, Detroit, MI. **EDUCATION:** BS Acctg; MBA. **CAREER:** Arthur Andersen & Co, auditor 1971-75; Natl Assn Black Accountants, natl pres 1975-77; Commr of Intl Revenue, adv 1977-78; Barrow Coleman Aldridge & Co, partner 1978-. **ORGANIZATIONS:** Treas Acctg Aid Soc; pres Natl Assn of Black Accountants; mem MI Assn of CPA; mem Amer Inst of CPA; mem Natl Assn of Accountants. **BUSINESS ADDRESS:** Barrow Coleman Aldridge & Co, 750 David Whitney Bldg, Detroit, MI 48226.

BARROW, WILLIE B.
Business executive, clergyman. **PERSONAL:** Born Dec 07, 1924, Burton, TX; married Clyde Barrow; children: Keith (dec). **EDUCATION:** Warner Sch of Theol Portland, OR; Moody Bible Sch Chicago, IL; Univ of Monrovia Monrovia, Liberia, DD. **CAREER:** First Black Church of God Portland, OR, organizer; Vernon Pk Church of God, assoc min/bd trustees; Rev Jackson Pres Campaign, natl dep campaign & road mgr; Operation PUSH, natl exec dir. **ORGANIZATIONS:** Bd dir Malcolm X College 1976; commr Intl Women's Year 1978; mem Natl World Peace Cncl; chrpers IL Chap Natl Polit Congr of Black Women; mem NatlCncl of Negro Women 1945; mem Natl Urban League 1943. **HONORS/ACHIEVEMENTS:** Ordained Minister Ch of God of Anderson, IN; Human Serv Award Chicago Firefighters; Woman of the Year City of Chicago 1969; Image Award League of Black Women 1972. **BUSINESS ADDRESS:** Natl Executive Dir, Operation Push, 930 E 50th St, Chicago, IL 60615.

BARRY, MARION S., JR.
Mayor. **PERSONAL:** Born Mar 06, 1936, Itta Bena, MS; married Effi Slaughter; children: Christopher. **EDUCATION:** LeMoyne Coll, BS 1958; Fisk Univ, MS 1960; Univ of KS, postgrad 1960-61; Univ of TN, postgrad 1961-64. **CAREER:** City Council, mem-at-large 1975; Washington, DC, mayor 1979-. **ORGANIZATIONS:** Pres Washington DC Bd of Educ 1972-; dir of operations Pride, Inc 1967-; first natl chmn SNCC; chmn/bd dir/cofounder Pride Econ Enterprises 1968-; mem Third World Coalition Against the War; mem Alpha Phi Alpha Frat; pres Natl Conf of Black Mayors. **BUSINESS ADDRESS:** Mayor, Office of the Mayor, District Building, 14th & E Sts, Washington, DC 20004.

BARTELLE, TALMADGE LOUIS
Business executive. **PERSONAL:** Born in Darlington, SC; married Harriett Ruth Entzminger; children: Talmadge Jr, Barbara. **EDUCATION:** SC State Coll, BS 1949, LLB 1952; Amer Univ, MA 1965. **CAREER:** FAMU, asst prof of law 1952-54; Ft Ord CA, trial counsel 1955-58; France, asst staff judge adv 1959-62; Foreign Law & Status of Forces Br, chief 1965-67; Univ of MD, instr 1967-68; UN Command Korea, dep staff judge advocate 1967-68; JAGC Chf Tort Br Lit Div Dept of Army, lt col 1968-71; General Mills Inc, sr counsel 1971-. **ORGANIZATIONS:** Mem Supreme Court of SC; Supreme Ct of MN; US Dist Ct MN; Supreme Ct of the US; hearing examiner State of MN Dept of Human Rights 1976; mem Assn of Trial Lawyers of Amer; MN State Bar Assn; Hennepin Co Bar Assn; SC State Bar; Kappa Alpha Psi; bd dir Equal Employment Adv Council 1980; Northside Settlement Serv Inc 1976; allocations com United Way of Minneapolis Area 1975. **HONORS/ACHIEVEMENTS:** US Law Week Awd & Lawyers Coop Prizes for Schlrsp 1952; Legion of Merit 1971; publ "Counterinsurgency & Civil War" 1964; 1st Black to receive direct commnin the Judge Advocate Gen Corps 1954. **MILITARY SERVICE:** AUS lt col 1971. **BUSINESS ADDRESS:** Senior Counsel, General Mills Inc, 9200 Wayzata Blvd, Minneapolis, MN 55426.

BARTHE, RICHMOND
Sculptor. **PERSONAL:** Born Jan 29, 1901, Bay St Louis, MS. **EDUCATION:** Art Inst Chicago, attended 1924-28; Xavier Univ New Orleans LA, MA 1934; St Francis Coll Brooklyn, AFD 1947. **CAREER:** Represented in Whitney Museum, Metro Museum, IBM Collection NY, Tuskegee Univ AL, Yale Univ, Theosophical Soc Adyar India, Jamaican Public Lib St Ann's Bay Jamaica, Smithsonian Inst, num other museums; Carved large Frieze Kingsborough Housing Proj NY; Private Collections Austria, Italy, Spain, Rumania, Germany, Paris, England, Canada, Venezuela, Virgin Islands, Africa, Jamaica, Denmark, Switzerland, Morroco; One Man Shows, Women's City Club Chicago, Rankin Art Galleries Wash DC, Univ WI, Caz-Delbo Galleries NYC, Arden Galleries New York City 1939, So Side Art Ctr Chicago, Grand Rapids Art Gallery, Grand Central Art Galleries NY,Margaret Brown Galleries Boston, Montclair Art Museum NJ, num others 1930-59. **ORGANIZATIONS:** Awded Julius Rosenwald Fellowship 1922; Awded Guggemheim Fellowship 1940-41; Citation & Awd Amer & Natl Acad Arts & Letters 1945; Audubon Artists Gold Medal of Honor 1945; James J Hoey Awd Inter-Racial Justice 1945; rec'd Key to City Bay St Louis MS 1964; rec'd Key to City Hattiesburg MS 1977; listed in World Who's Who, Who's Who in Western Hemisphere, The Negro in LA, The Negro Handbook, Modern Negro Art, Brown America, Negroes In Our History, The Negro Genius, Who's Who in Amer Art, numerous others; sculptured Bust Booker T Washington, Dr George Washington Carver, Hall of Fame Great Amers 1976; sculptured bust & small figure Paul Robeson Theatre Awds of Actor's Equity. **BUSINESS ADDRESS:** 301 Beechwood Dr, Apt 9, Pasadena, CA 91103.

BARTHELEMY, SIDNEY JOHN
Mayor. **PERSONAL:** Born Mar 17, 1942, New Orleans, LA; son of Lionel Barthelemy and Ruth Fernandez Barthelemy; married Michaele Thibodeaux Barthelemy, 1968; children: Cherrie, Bridget, Sidney Jr. **EDUCATION:** Epiphany Apostolic Jr Coll, attended 1960-63; St Joseph Seminary, BA 1967; Tulane Univ, MSW 1971. **CAREER:** Admin asst, 1967-68, asst dir, 1969, Total Community Action; guidance counselor, interim dir, Adult Basic Educ Program, 1968-69; asst dir, New Careers Program, 1969; dir, 1969-71, dir social serv, 1971-72, Parent-Child Center; coord, Labor Educ Advancement Program, Urban League, 1969-72; dir, City of New Orleans Welfare Dept, 1972-74; assoc prof of sociology, Xavier Univ, 1974-86; state senator, Louisiana Legislature, 1974-78; councilman-at-large, New Orleans City Council, 1978-86; mayor, city of New Orleans, 1986-; pres, Natl Assn of Regional Coun, 1987-88; vice chmn for voter registration, Democratic Natl Party, 1988-89; second vice pres, Natl League of Cites, 1988-; pres, Louisiana Conference of Mayors, 1989-; adjunct prof, Kennedy School of Govt, Tulane Univ School of Public Health, Univ of New Orleans Coll of Educ. **ORGANIZATIONS:** Vice pres, Comm Org Urban Politics; member, Orleans Parish Democratic Exec Comm; chmn, Youth Assistance Council; bd dir, Central City Fed Credit Union, Family Serv Soc, St Bernard Neighborhood Comm Ctr, Comm Serv Ctr; member, City Park Commn, Democratic Natl Comm, Labor Educ Advancement Program, Louisiana Conf of Mayors, Louisiana Municipal Assn, Mississippi-Louisiana-Alabama Transit Commn, Natl League of Cities, NAACP, Natl Assn of Black Mayors, Natl Assn of County Officials, Natl Assn of Regional Councils, Natl Black Councils/Local Elected Officials, Natl Inst of Educ, New Orleans Assn of Black Social Workers, US Conf of Mayors. **HONORS/ACHIEVEMENTS:** Purple Knight Award Best All Around Student, 1960; Outstanding Alumnus of Tulane Univ, Social Worker of the Year, Louisiana Chapter of the Natl Assn of Social Workers, 1987; Amer Freedom Award, Third Baptist Church of Chicago, 1987; Amer Spirit Award, US Air Force Recruiting Serv, 1989. **BUSINESS ADDRESS:** Mayor, City of New Orleans, City Hall, 1300 Perdido St, Rm 2E10, New Orleans, LA 70122.

BARTHWELL, JACK CLINTON, III
Brewery executive. **PERSONAL:** Born Oct 16, 1950, Detroit, MI; son of Jack C Barthwell, Jr and Catherine McCree Barthwell. **EDUCATION:** Trinity Coll, Hartford CT, BA, 1972; Univ of Michigan Law School, Ann Arbor MI JD, 1976. **CAREER:** US House Comm on the District of Columbia, Washington DC, staff counsel, 1976-78; Hon Charles C Diggs, Jr, US House of Representatives, chief of staff, 1977-80; Hon George W Crockett, Jr, US House of Representatives, chief of staff, 1980-83; The Stroh Brewery Co, Detroit MI, dir, 1984-87, vice pres corporate communications & govt affairs, 1987-. **ORGANIZATIONS:** Mem of bd, Children's Museum Friends; mem bd Diversified Youth Serv Inc; mem bd, Project Pride-Detroit Chamber of Commerce; mem of govt & educ comm, New Detroit; mem, State Bar of Michigan, 1976-; mem, District of Columbia Bar, 1978-; mem, Eastern District of Michigan (Federal), 1980-, mem, NAACP. **HONORS/ACHIEVEMENTS:** Fellow, Thomas J Watson Found, 1972. **BUSINESS ADDRESS:** Vice Pres Corporate Communications & Govt Affairs, The Stroh Brewery Co, 100 River Place, Detroit, MI 48207.

BARTLETT, JEFFREY LEON
Administrator. **PERSONAL:** Born Jul 13, 1939, Parkersburg, WV; married Joy List Ellis; children: Jeffrey II, Jonathan. **EDUCATION:** WV State Coll, BA 1963; Univ of MN Law Sch, attended 1963-64; Coll of St Thomas, attended 1976-77. **CAREER:** Prudential Ins Co, claim examiner/job evaluator/asst mgr 1964-69, mgr ofc svc/ins serv 1969-78, affirmative act consult 1978-79, gen mgr 1979-. **ORGANIZATIONS:** Mem In-Plant Printing Mgmt Assn 1966-74; mem Minneapolis Postal Counc 1969-74; mem MN Affirm Action Assn 1978-79; mem Minn C of C 1978-80; reg vice pres & chap sec Minn Jaycees 1967-69; chmn MN Independent Rep 1975-; bd of dir Southdale YMCA 1977-79; vice pres Cornelia Sch PTA 1977; mem Natl Black Rep 1978-; adminstrv bd Oakland United Meth Ch 1980; vol Minn Area United Way; mem United Nations Assn of MN. **HONORS/ACHIEVEMENTS:** Who's Who Among Students in Amer Coll & Univs 1963. **BUSINESS ADDRESS:** General Manager, Prudential Insurance Company, 3701 Wayzata Blvd, Minneapolis, MN 55416.

BARTLEY, TALMADGE O.
Deputy officer, coordinator. **PERSONAL:** Born Dec 05, 1920, Arcadia, FL; married Louise; children: Katye, Ardlin. **EDUCATION:** US Intl Univ, BA, MA, PhD. **CAREER:** Free lanceTV writer "One Eye One"; Marine Corps Base, auto mech to foreman 1949-67; Marine Corps Base, comm relat spec & human relat ofcr 1967-71; CommEduc Vol Serv Prog, coord 1971-; Naval Ocean Sys Ctr, deputy equal employ oppor ofcr/coord. **ORGANIZATIONS:** Mem Inter Serv Task Force 1970; mem num ofcs, coms, social orgns. **HONORS/ACHIEVEMENTS:** Outstanding Deputy EEO Ofcr in NMC Chf of Naval material 1974; Navy Superior Civilian Serv Medal; num citations awds honors. **MILITARY SERVICE:** USMC. **BUSINESS ADDRESS:** Deputy Equal Employ Oppor Ofcr, Naval Ocean Sys Center, Naval Electronics Lab Ctr, San Diego, CA 92152.

BARTLEY, WILLIAM RAYMOND
Physician. **PERSONAL:** Born Dec 09, 1944, Daytona Beach, FL; married Freddye; children: Diallo, Rashida. **EDUCATION:** Knoxville Coll, BA 1968; Meharry Med Coll, attended 1975. **CAREER:** Equal Oppor Agency, staff; Little Rock VA Hosp, Lee Co Co-op Clinic, part time staff; Erlanger Hosp, intern 1975; USAF Sch Aerospace Med, 1976; USAF, flight surgeon. **ORGANIZATIONS:** Mem Little League Sports. **HONORS/ACHIEVEMENTS:** Natl Med Flwsp Awd 1970-72; Winn-Dixie Flwsp 1972; Jessie Noyles-Smith Ob-Gyn Fellowship 1973-74. **MILITARY SERVICE:** USAF capt 1976-. **BUSINESS ADDRESS:** Flight Surgeon, USAF Hosp, Little Rock, Jacksonville, AR 72076.

BARTOW, JEROME EDWARD
Business executive. **PERSONAL:** Born in Orange, NJ; married Louise Tolson; children: Sharon B Mitchell, Jerome E Bartow Jr. **EDUCATION:** VA St Univ, AB 1951; Columbia Univ, MA 1955, EdD 1968. **CAREER:** Various institutions of higher educ, 1955-64; NY Tele Co, various 1965-69; ITT World Headquarters, mgr exec placement 1969-74, dir employee rel opers 1974-77, dir personnel/industrial rel 1977-79, dir admin bsns systms & comm grp 1979; Hartford Ins Grp, senior vice pres & dir admin 1979-. **ORGANIZATIONS:** Chm exec adv comm BEEP Natl Urban League 1980-; mem bd of trus Natl Urbn League; mem bd of rgnts Univ of Hartford; mem bd of visitors Univ of CT; charter mem, bd of directors Exec Leadership Council. **HONORS/ACHIEVEMENTS:** Cert of Merit VA St Univ 1983; Cert of Merit Ft Valley State College 1981. **MILITARY SERVICE:** AUS lt 1951-53. **BUSINESS ADDRESS:** Senior Vice Pres & Dir of Admin, The Hartford Insurance Group, 690 Asylum Ave, Hartford, CT 06115.

BARZY, RAYMOND CLIFFORD, II
Lawyer. **PERSONAL:** Born Jun 25, New York, NY; son of Raymond Barzey and Elva Barzey. **EDUCATION:** City Coll City Univ of NYC, BA 1967; Atlanta Univ, MS 1968;

State Univ NY, MA 1970; NY Univ, PhD 1980; Seton Hall, JD, 1983. **CAREER:** Sterns Dept Store, asst buyer 1965-67; MN Mining & Mfg, production analyst 1968-71; Urban Develop Corp, assoc economist 1971-73; Housing Devel Corp, asst to exec dir 1974; Urban Devel Corp, assoc economist 1975; Harlem Urban Devel Corp, dir commercial devel 1976; Co of LA, sr budget analyst; City Univ of NY, Baruch College, NYC, adjunct asst prof, 1981-; NYC office of Economic Development, 1982; NJ Deputy Attorney General, 1983-. **ORGANIZATIONS:** Mem Amer Assn of Univ Profs; Amer Econ Assn; Amer Inst of Planners; Amer Library Assn; Amer Soc of Planning Officials; Natl Assn of Housing & Redevelopment Officials; Natl Econ Assn Amnesty Intl; Hospital Audience Inc; Inst for Mediation & Conflict Resolution; Natl Trust for Historic Preservation; Natl Urban League; Comm Urban Environment Project; 100 Black Men Inc; Planned Parenthood of NY; Amer Bar Assn, NJ Bar Assn. **HONORS/ACHIEVEMENTS:** Intl Student Com Deans List Atlanta Univ 1968; Martin Luther King Scholarship NY Univ 1975-77. **HOME ADDRESS:** 65 W 90th St, New York, NY 10024.

BASEY, OVETTA T.
Educator. **PERSONAL:** Born Mar 31, 1920, Birmingham, AL; married Robert Julian Basey; children: Robert Aulmon. **EDUCATION:** KY State Univ, AB 1945; Univ of KY, MA 1960; Univ of KY, post grad studies. **CAREER:** Hazard Bd of Educ KY, classroom teacher 1937-. **ORGANIZATIONS:** Grand Worthy Matron; Cecelia Dunlap Grand Chap KY Jurisdiction; KY Educ Assn bd dir 1974-78; commr KEA Human Relations Commn 1972-; chmn bd trustees Cecelia Dunlap Grant Chap 1975; Jurisprudence Com Cecilia Dunlap Grand Chap 1962-; mem Hazard City Planning & Zoning Commn; HEA; UKREA; KEA; NEA; Mayor'sadv com 1968-72; KY Area Devel Dist Human Resources Comm 1972-74; Commissioned a KY Col 1967. **BUSINESS ADDRESS:** Teacher, Hazard Bd of Educ, Roy G Eversole Elementary School, Broadway, Hazard, KY 41701.

BASHFUL, EMMETT W.
Educator. **PERSONAL:** Born Mar 12, 1917, New Roads, LA; married Juanita I; children: Cornell J Nugent. **EDUCATION:** So Univ Baton Rouge, BS 1940; Univ IL Urbana, MA 1947, PhD 1955. **CAREER:** FL A&M Univ, instr to full prof 1948-58; So Univ, prof of pol sci 1958-59; So Univ at NO, dean 1959-69, vice pres 1969-77, chancellor 1972-87. **ORGANIZATIONS:** Bd mem Metropolitan Area Comm; bd mem World Trade Ctr; adv bd Goodwill Ind; bd of dir Comm on Alcoholism of Greater NO United Way Agcy; bd memNO Chapter Natl Conf of Christians & Jews; bd dir Frey Fndtn. **HONORS/ACHIEVEMENTS:** Awd 10 Otstndng Ctzns of N O Inst for Human Undrstndng 1978; rcpnt Vol Activist Awd 1976; recpnt Silver Beaver Awd BSA 1967; citation FL Supreme Ct 1955. **MILITARY SERVICE:** AUS 1st lt 1942-46. **BUSINESS ADDRESS:** Chancellor, SouthernUniv at N O, 6400 Press Dr, New Orleans, LA 70126.

BASKERVILLE, CHARLES ALEXANDER
Educator. **PERSONAL:** Born Aug 19, 1928, Queens, NY; son of Charles H and Annie M; married Susan; children: Mark, Shawn, Charles. **EDUCATION:** The City Coll, BS 1953; NYU, MS 1958, PhD 1965. **CAREER:** NY State Dept of Transportation, 1953-66; McFarland-Johnson, soils engr 1967; Madigan-Hyland Engr, sr soils engr 1968; The City Coll, prof emeritus 1965-69, dean School of General Studies 1970-79; US Geological Survey, project Geologist Geologic Risk Assessment Branch 1979-. **ORGANIZATIONS:** Consultant Madigan-Hyland-Praeger-Cavanaugh-Waterbury 1969; consultant St Raymond's Cemetary 1970-76; mem Natl Advisory Comm on Minority Participant in Earth Science & Mineral Engr US Dept Interior 1972-75; Assn of Engr Geo 1973; consultant Consolidated Edison Co 1975; Tech Session subcomm for Natl AEG Convention 1976; chmn Marliave Scholarship Com 1976-77; chmn Natl Science Found Minority Graduate Fellowship Program 1979-80; mem Geological Soc of Washington; panelist Natl Science Found Graduate Fellowship Program; mem Sigma Xi; mem US Natl Comm on Tunnelling Technician Natl Acad of Engrg Natl Rsch Council; chmn Educ and Training Subcommittee; consultant IBM; consultant Eastmore Construction Co; New York City Corp Council consultant. **HONORS/ACHIEVEMENTS:** 125th Anniversary Medal, The City Coll; Founders Day Award, NYU; Presented & published numerous scientific papers; guest lecturer to schools & colleges; commonwealth visiting professor, George Mason Univ, Fairfax VA, 1987-89. **BUSINESS ADDRESS:** Proj Geologist, US Geological Survey, 922 Natl Center, Reston, VA 22092.

BASKERVILLE, PEARL
Educator. **PERSONAL:** Born Dec 09, 1929, New Bedford, MA; married Walden A Baskerville; children: Jill Louise, Jodi Ann, Judson Alan, Jinx Elaine. **EDUCATION:** William Penn Coll, BA 1951; Western Mi Univ, MA 1953. **CAREER:** Neighborhood Youth Corps Counselor, 1966-67; Western Michigan Univ, instructor basic studies program 1962-65, counselor, instructor, asst prof coll of genl studies & MartinLuther King program 1967-74, asst prof, counselor, coll of genl studies 1974-. **ORGANIZATIONS:** Founder/chairperson vice chairperson Western MI Univ Black Caucus 1969-75; professional vol to many civic orgns including League of Women Voters; YWCA; Human Relations Council; Amer Assn of Univ Women; NAACP; asst Operation Out-Reach Prog Kalamazoo; admin asst prog coord MI Independent Colleges Oppor Prog; pres Kalamazoo YWCA. **BUSINESS ADDRESS:** Asst Prof/Counselor, Western Michigan University, Coll of Gen Studies, 2090 Friedmann, Kalamazoo, MI 49008.

BASKERVILLE, PENELOPE ANNE
Personnel administrator. **PERSONAL:** Born Jul 09, 1946, South Orange, NJ; daughter of Robert L Baskerville and Yolanda Reaves Baskerville; divorced; children: Dylan Craig, Ailey Yolanda. **EDUCATION:** Brown Univ, BA 1968. **CAREER:** NJ Div on Civil Rights, field rep 1975-77; NJ Dept of Public Advocate Office of Citizen Complaints, field rep 1977-80; Princeton Univ, personnel admin 1980-86; Peterson's Guides Inc, personnel mgr 1986-89; Rider Coll, benefits manager, 1989-. **ORGANIZATIONS:** Mem Brown Univ Alumni Schools Comm 1971-; pres Bd of Trustees Princeton Nursery School 1977-82; mem Intergovernmental Drug Comm; Corner House 1982-; mem Bd of Ed Princeton Reg Schools 1982-85, ET Byrd Scholarship Fund 1983-; mem bd of trustees Princeton YWCA 1985-. **HOME ADDRESS:** 210 Birch Ave, Princeton, NJ 08542. **BUSINESS ADDRESS:** Benefits Manager, Rider College, Lawrenceville Road, Lawrenceville, NJ 08648.

BASKERVILLE, RANDOLPH
Attorney. **PERSONAL:** Born Jul 22, 1949, Henderson, NC; married Sarah McLean; children: Latoyia, Nathan. **EDUCATION:** Fayetteville State Univ, BS 1971; NC A&T State Univ, MS 1972; NC Central Univ School of Law, JD 1976. **CAREER:** Admin Office of the Courts, asst da 1979-84; Dept of Social Svcs, staff atty 1985-86; pvt practice, 1985-. **ORGANIZATIONS:** Mem NC Bar Assoc 1977-, Natl Bar Assoc 1977-; dir YMCA 1984-85, Amer Cancer Soc 1984-; pres Charles Williamson Bar Assoc 1985-86; dir NCNB Bank 1985-; dir C of C 1986-. **HONORS/ACHIEVEMENTS:** Outstanding Young Dem Young Dem of Vance Cty 1983; Contribs to Planning of YMCA Henderson/Vance YMCA 1983; Outstanding Contribs to Ninth Dist Ninth Judicial Dist Bar 1984; Outstanding Contribs to Black Comm Vance Cty Black Leadership Caucus 1984. **BUSINESS ADDRESS:** Attorney, PO Box 2224, Henderson, NC 27536.

BASKERVILLE, SAMUEL J., JR.
Physician. **PERSONAL:** Born Mar 02, 1933, Charleston, WV; son of Samuel Baskerville and Geraldine Baskerville. **EDUCATION:** Howard Univ Wash, DC, BS 1953; Meharry Med Coll, MD 1958. **CAREER:** Detroit Receiving Hosp, intern 1958-59; Kern County General Hospital, res internal med 1959-62, chief res internal med 1961-62. **ORGANIZATIONS:** Bd of dirs Kern Cty Med Soc 1964-, CA Med Assoc 1964-, Amer Medical Assoc 1964-, Natl Medical Assoc 1967-, Amer Soc Internal Med 1968-, Mercy Hosp Bakersfield CA 1984-; chief of staff Mercy Hosp Bakersfield 1973; bd dir 1979-81, pres 1987 Kern Cty Medical Soc; Omega Psi Phi Fraternity; Kern County Sheriff's Advisory Council 1988-. **HONORS/ACHIEVEMENTS:** Civil Serv Cmnsn Kern Cnty 1969-77. **MILITARY SERVICE:** USAF Med Corps capt 1962-64. **BUSINESS ADDRESS:** Internist, 2023 Truxtun Ave, Bakersfield, CA 93301.

BASKETT, KENNETH GERALD
Educator, businesss owner. **PERSONAL:** Born Nov 18, 1942, Kansas City, MO; son of W. Cletus Baskett and Rosella Kelly King; married Lynette; children: Charmel, Adrienne, Tiffany. **EDUCATION:** Tuskegee Inst, BS Accounting 1970-72; Alabama A&M, MS Personnel Mgt 1972-75; Command and Gen Staff Coll, Masters 1979. **CAREER:** US Army, captain/company commander Vietnam 1968-69; AL A&M Univ, asst prof 1972-75; Lincoln Univ, prof 1982-85; Lt Col USA Retired; owner Sparkle Cleaners. **ORGANIZATIONS:** Bd mem Optimist Club Jeff City 1982-85; Atlanta City Country Club; mem Alpha Phi Alpha Fraternity, 1989. **HONORS/ACHIEVEMENTS:** Numerous awds for combat service Vietnam 1968-69; #1 Bus Major Tuskegee Inst 1970-72, graduated with honors. **MILITARY SERVICE:** AUS infantry lt col 20 1/2 yrs; Air Medal, 3 Meritorious Service Awards 1966-86; captain/company commander, vietnam 1968-69; Retired 1986. **HOME ADDRESS:** 4584 Jamerson Forest Pkwy, Marietta, GA 30066. **BUSINESS ADDRESS:** Businessman, Sparkle Cleaners, 5344 Jimmy, Norcross, GA 30093.

BASKIN, ANDREW LEWIS
Educational administrator. **PERSONAL:** Born Feb 28, 1951, Maryville, TN; son of Jimmy Baskin and Eloise Baskin; married Symerdar Lavern Capehart; children: Thalethia Elois, Thameka La Cape. **EDUCATION:** Berea Coll, BA Hist 1972; VA Tech, MA Am Hist 1975. **CAREER:** Ferrum Coll, asst prof 1975-83; Berea Coll, dir of Blk Cultural Center1983-. **ORGANIZATIONS:** Mem Phi Alpha Theta 1975-; bd dir Mt Maternal Health League 1984-; treas Council of So Mts 1983-84; bd dir Berea Coll Credit Union 1985; editor, SCAASI's journal "The Griot" 1986-. **HONORS/ACHIEVEMENTS:** Hurt Faculty Achievment Award, Ferrum Coll 1976; James B St Award, Amer Hist, Berea Coll 1972. **BUSINESS ADDRESS:** Dir of Black Cultural Center, Berea Coll, CPO 134, Berea, KY 40404.

BASKIN, CLARENCE L.
Dentist. **PERSONAL:** Born Feb 27, 1927, Apopka, FL; married Thelma E Cobb; children: Clarence L. **EDUCATION:** Morehouse Coll, BS 1948; Howard Univ, Coll of Dent 1953. **CAREER:** Private Practice, dentist. **ORGANIZATIONS:** Life mem Kappa Alpha Psi Frat; mem GA, Natl, Amer Dental Assns; staff Med Ctr; chmn adv bd Wash Shores Fed Sav & Loan Assn Orlando FL; trustee St James AME Ch. **MILITARY SERVICE:** USNR. **BUSINESS ADDRESS:** 500 1/2 9th St, Columbus, GA 31907.

BASKINS, LEWIS C.
Business executive, dentist. **PERSONAL:** Born Jul 16, 1932, Springfield, AR; married Amanda J; children: Duane, Brian, Kevin, Holli. **EDUCATION:** AR AM & N Coll, BS 1956; Univ IL, DDS 1961. **CAREER:** Fuller Products Co, vice pres; Dentist. **ORGANIZATIONS:** Pres Chicago Chap AR AM & N Alumni; mem Amer, Chicago, Lincoln Dental Soc; Omega Psi Phi Frat; mem Mt Zion Bapt Ch. **MILITARY SERVICE:** AUS sp3 1953-55. **BUSINESS ADDRESS:** 6906 S Halsted St, Chicago, IL 60621.

BASRI, GIBOR BROITMAN
Educator. **PERSONAL:** Born May 03, 1951, New York, NY; married Jessica. **EDUCATION:** Stanford Univ, BSc 1973; Univ of CO, PhD 1979. **CAREER:** Univ of CO, rsch asst 1974-79; Univ CA, postdoctoral fellow 1979-82, asst prof 1982-88; Univ of California Berkeley, assoc prof 1988-. **ORGANIZATIONS:** Mem Amer Astronomical Soc 1979; mem Intl Astronomical Union 1984; mem Astronomical Soc of the Pacific 1984. **HONORS/ACHIEVEMENTS:** Chancellors Fellow Univ of CA 1979-81; several articles Astrophysical Journal 1979-. **BUSINESS ADDRESS:** University of California, Astronomy Dept, Berkeley, CA 94720.

BASS, ANTHONY DUANE
Marketing management. **PERSONAL:** Born Jul 14, 1960, Tuskegee, AL; married Angelette Waring; children: Tamara Leseon. **EDUCATION:** Cornell Univ Coll of Human Ecology, BS 1983; Cornell Univ Johnson Grad Sch, MBA 1986. **CAREER:** Neptune Soft Water Co, field sales rep 1978-79; Cornell Univ Minority Affairs, prog coord 1982-83; Old Ezra Investment Club, vice pres 1985-86; Montgomery Wards, sales mgr 1983-85; Procter and Gamble Co, marketing assoc 1986-. **ORGANIZATIONS:** Pres, bd of dirs Kappa Alpha Psi 1982-83; mem Black MBA Assoc 1986, Cornell Lightweight Football; pres IFC PANMFU Council; mem Amer Mktg Assoc, Most Worshipful Prince Hall Grand Lodge of OH, Free and Accepted Masons, Amer MBA Assoc. **HONORS/ACHIEVEMENTS:** Humanitarian Awd Cornell Univ 1981; Outstanding Student Leadership Awd; All-League Football Selection 2 yrs.

BASS, DON
Professional athlete. **PERSONAL:** Born Mar 11, 1956. **EDUCATION:** Attended, Houston. **CAREER:** Cincinnati Bengals, wide receiver. **HONORS/ACHIEVEMENTS:** To-

taled 724 yrds & three touchdowns on his 58 receptions 1979; Team Record (58 passes caught) 1979. **BUSINESS ADDRESS:** Cincinnati Bengals, 200 Riverfront Stadium, Cincinnati, OH 45202.

BASS, FLOYD L.
Educator. **PERSONAL:** Born Aug 11, 1921, Sullivan, IN; married Hazel B Huddleston; children: Floyd L Jr, Eileen C, Marc C, Lisa C Ealum. **EDUCATION:** Indiana State Univ, BS 1948, MS 1950; Univ of CO-Boulder, EdD 1960. **CAREER:** LeMoyne Coll, dean 1960-63; AL State Univ, dean 1963-64; CCNY, admin intern w/pres 1964-65; NC Central Univ, prof of educ 1965-68; The Univ of CT, prof of educ 1968-. **ORGANIZATIONS:** Dir The Ctr for Black Studies Univ of CT 1969-; pres Northeastern Chap CT Affiliate ADA 1982-84; pres Willimantic Rotary Club 1983-85; grand historian Grand Encampment Knights Templar 1985,87; pres CT Order of High Priesthood 1985,86; accreditation team mem NCATE 1983,84,85,86,87. **HONORS/ACHIEVEMENTS:** Ellis L Phillips Fellow; UNCF Fellow; John Jay Whitney Fellow; Thirty third Degree United Supreme Council AASR Freemasonry PHA Inc 1987. **MILITARY SERVICE:** USN 3rd class petty officer 1945-46. **BUSINESS ADDRESS:** Professor, Univ of Connecticut-Storrs, U-162 241 Glenbrook Rd, Storrs, CT 06268.

BASS, GEORGE HOUSTON
Educator, theatre artist. **PERSONAL:** Born Apr 23, 1938, Murfreesboro, TN; son of Rev Clarence C Bass (deceased) and Mabel Dixon Bass; married Ramona Wilkins; children: Kwame Noel, Khari Takeo, Ayana Vernice. **EDUCATION:** Fisk Univ, BA, 1959; New York Univ, Film School, MA, 1964; Yale School of Drama, 1966-68. **CAREER:** Landston Hughes, secretary, literary asst, 1959-64; Trustee for Langston Hughes Estate, literary executor, 1967-; On Being Black, a series of 13 original teleplays, WGBH-TV, Boston, assoc producer, story editor, 1968-69; Afro-Amer Studies Program, Brown Univ, artistic dir, founder, Rites & Reason, a rsch & devel theatre, 1970; Brown Univ, assoc prof, Theatre, Arts, Afro-Amer Studies, 1976-85; The Langston Hughes Review, founder, mng editor, editor, 1982-; Brown Univ, Prof, Theatre arts, Afro-Amer Studies, 1985-. **ORGANIZATIONS:** Mem, Univ Comm on the Arts, 1978-80, professional advisory bd, Theatre, Providence, Dept of Public Schools 1978; mem, Univ Comm on Women, 1980-81; vice chmn, RI State Council on the Arts, 1980-83; bd of dirs, Pembroke Center for Teaching & Rsch on Women, 1981; mem, Corp Comm on Minority Affairs, 1983-86; mem, Independent Study Comm, 1986-; mem, Bethel AME Church, Coll Language Assn, Alpha Phi Alpha Fraternity; bd of dirs, Langston Hughes Center for the Arts; RI Black Heritage Soc; mem, Dramatist Guild. **HONORS/ACHIEVEMENTS:** "George Bass Day" Yale School of Drama, 1967; Fulbright Rsch Scholar, India, 1977; Delta Sigma Theatre Comm Award of the Decade, 1980; Rockefeller Found Resident Fellowship Prog, 1986-89; Rhode Island Comm for the Humanities, 1986-88; Two productions of original plays; 30 plays directed at Brown Univ, 1970-89; Two TV directing credits; Numerous papers & public presentations; 6 articles published. **BUSINESS ADDRESS:** Prof Theatre Afro-Amer Studies, Brown University, Box 1904, Providence, RI 02912.

BASS, HERBERT H.
Educator. **PERSONAL:** Born Dec 26, 1929, Warsaw, NC; married Carrie L Ruff; children: Lori. **EDUCATION:** Shaw Univ, BA 1955; Antioch Univ, MEd Counseling 1972; Union Grad, PhD 1980. **CAREER:** Supreme Liberty Life Co, insurance agent 1956; Philadelphia School Dist, teacher 1957; City of Philadelphia, gang control worker 1959; PA Dept of Public Assistance, social worker 1960; Philadelphia Dept of Welfare, recreation supvr 1960; Philadelphia School Dist, counselor speciall educ 1961; Leeds & Northrup Co, coord of counseling (indsl) 1968-. **ORGANIZATIONS:** Consult Provident Life Ins Co 1965; vice chmn/trustee New Bethlehem Bapt Ch 1960-; commr Boy Scouts of Amer 1963-; mem Council for Exceptional Children; mem NAACP; mem YMCA. **BUSINESS ADDRESS:** Coordinator of Counseling, Leeds & Northrup Co, Sumneytown Pike, North Wales, PA 19454.

BASS, JAMES L.
Dental surgeon. **PERSONAL:** Born Mar 02, 1899, Stanton, FL; married Maria D; children: Gwendolyn. **EDUCATION:** Meharry Med Coll of Dentistry, DDS 1926. **CAREER:** Self-Employed, dental surgeon. **ORGANIZATIONS:** Mem FL State Med Dentl & Pharm Assn (pres 1959); mem ADA; NDA; mem Alibi Civic Club; NAACP; Natl Conf Christians & Jews; Urban League; Broward Co Human Rel Comm; Gov Askew's Broward Co Comm; Broward Co Jury Comm; pres Natl Employ the Handicapped Goodwill Oppor Com; Kappa Alpha Psi; charter mem Sigma Pi Psi Boule; Dem exec com 1971. **HONORS/ACHIEVEMENTS:** Southern Provincial Achievement Award Kappa Alpha Psi 1965; Outstanding Serv for Bethune Coll Dev Fund 1957; FL Lung Assn Hon Membership 1974; Service to Youth Award YMCA 1962; Dade Co Acad of Med; 1973. **BUSINESS ADDRESS:** PO Box 438, Fort Lauderdale, FL 33302.

BASS, JOSEPH FRANK
Administrator. **PERSONAL:** Born Jan 10, 1938, Phenix City, AL; married Jenean Brantley; children: Terence, Steven, Sandra. **EDUCATION:** Hartnell Coll, AA 1958; Carnegie-Mellon Univ, Cert in Transp 1972; Univ of Santa Clara, Cert in Mgmt 1977. **CAREER:** City of Salinas, engineering draftsman, 1958; City of San Jose, civil engr, 1962, sr civil engr, 1967, prin civil engr/head of transp planning, 1975-, dir dept of traffic, 1980-. **ORGANIZATIONS:** Regis civil engr CA 1966; mem Inst of Traffic Engrs 1970; mem Amer Pub Works Assn 1975; regis traffic engr CA 1977; mem NAACP 1980; mem BlackCoalition of Local Govt Empl 1980; mem No CA Cncl of Black Professional Engrs 1980. **HONORS/ACHIEVEMENTS:** Recip of Federal Grant to attend "Professional Program in Urban Transp" Carnegie-Mellon Univ 1972. **BUSINESS ADDRESS:** Director, Dept of Traffic, City of San Jose, 801 N First St, San Jose, CA 95110.

BASS, JOSIE A.
Administrator. **PERSONAL:** Born Jul 01, 1947, Washington, DC. **EDUCATION:** Bowie State Coll, BA Polit Sci 1971; Univ of Baltimore, JD 1978. **CAREER:** Prince George's Co MD Govt, spl asst to dir of human resources 1973, chief investigator law enforcement 1973-79; Gov Harry Hughes of MD, exec aide (1st Black female to hold this position) 1979-80; State of MD, adminstr for sec of personnel (1st Black female to hold this position) 1980; ACTION, spl asst to dir 1980-. **ORGANIZATIONS:** Pres Prince George's Co MD NAACP 1979-. **BUSINESS ADDRESS:** Special Assistant to Dir, ACTION, 806 Connecticut Ave NW, Ste 500, Washington, DC 20525.

BASS, KEVIN CHARLES
Professional athlete. **PERSONAL:** Born May 12, 1959, Redwood City, CA; married Elaine; children: Garrett Charles. **CAREER:** Milwaukee Brewers, outfielder 1981-82; Houston Astros, outfielder 1982-. **HONORS/ACHIEVEMENTS:** In minors named to Midwest League All-Star team 1978; tied a club record w/3 doubles in a game; led the Astros in pinch hits in 1981 (13) and 1983 (11); Playerof the Week for June 23-29 and Player of the Month for June 1986; mem League All Star Team 1986. **BUSINESS ADDRESS:** Houston Astros, P O Box 288, Houston, TX 77001.

BASS, LEONARD CHANNING
Physician. **PERSONAL:** Born Jul 23, 1941, Live Oak, FL; married Janet. **EDUCATION:** Meharry Med Coll, MD 1966; Genessee Hosp, intern 1967. **CAREER:** Private Practice, physician 1969-. **ORGANIZATIONS:** Mem FL Med Dent & Pharm Assn; Nat Med Assn; FL Med Assn; Broward Co Med Assn; pres FL State Med Assn; mem Am Heart & Assn; vice pres 1976. **HONORS/ACHIEVEMENTS:** Life mem, Alpha Phi Alpha Frat; Distinguished Serv Award Medical Dental & Pharmacy Assn, 1977; co-chmn, professional conf Amer Heart Assn 1976; one year, Vietnam Commendation Medal, USAF. **MILITARY SERVICE:** USAF MC capt 1967-69. **BUSINESS ADDRESS:** 2323 NW 19th St, Ste 3, Fort Lauderdale, FL 33311.

BASS, MARSHALL BRENT
Business executive. **PERSONAL:** Born in Goldsboro, NC; son of Marshall Bass and Estella Bass; married Celestine Pate Bass; children: Brenda, Marsha. **EDUCATION:** Univ of MD College Park, BS. **CAREER:** US Army, officer 1945-68; RJ Reynolds Tobacco Co, mgr personnel develop 1968-70; RJ Reynolds Industries, corporate mgr 1970-76, corporate dir 1976-82, vice pres 1982-; Sr Vice Pres, 1986. **ORGANIZATIONS:** Bd of dirs R J Reynolds Tobacco Co; bd of dirs Piedmont Federal Savings & Loan Assn; mem Natl Comm on Working Women; bd of dirs Winston-Salem/Forsyth Co YMCA; indus adv council Natl Newspaper Publishers Assn; bd of dirs Winston-Salem Urban League; bd of visitors NC Central Univ; chmn bd of dirs Winston-Salem State Univ Found; mem bd of trustees NC A&T State Univ; mem Phi Beta Sigma Fraternity Inc; mem Beta Epsilon Boule Sigma Pi Phi; sr warden St Stephen's Episcopal Church; lay leader chalice bearer Episcopal Diocese of NC; Board of Trustees NAACP Spec Contribution Fund; chmn, bd of trustees St Augustines Coll, Raleigh; chmn Advisory Bd Consortuim, Graduate Studies in Management. **HONORS/ACHIEVEMENTS:** Blackbook Natl Outstanding Business & Professional Award 1984; Several Honorary Degrees: Doctor of Civil Law, St Augustines Raleigh; Doctor of Humane Letters, Florida A&M Tallahasse FL; Doctor of Divinity, TN School of Religion, Detroit MI Division; LLD, Dr of Humane Letters, NC Central Univ, St Augustine Coll, Raleigh, NC, King Memorial Coll, Columbia, SC, Livingston Coll, Salisbury NC, Winston Salem State Univ. **MILITARY SERVICE:** AUS chief of army promotions 23 yrs; Legion of Merit; 3 Commendation Medals; Purple Heart; Combat Infantryman's Badge. **BUSINESS ADDRESS:** Sr Vice Pres, RJR Nabisco, Inc, Reynolds Blvd, Winston-Salem, NC 27102.

BASSARD, YVONNE BROOKS
Administrator. **PERSONAL:** Born Oct 27, 1937, Oakland, CA; married Edward Lee Jr; children: Edward Lee Jr, Margot Denise Walton, Daryl Lamont, Alicia Yvonne. **EDUCATION:** Patten Bible Coll, BS Theology 1973; St Stephens Coll, MA Health Sci 1975, PhD 1978. **CAREER:** Parks AFB Hosp, nurse 1956-57; Eden Hosp Castro Valley, CA, nurse 1960-62; St Rose Hosp Hayward, CA, nurse 1962-63; Patten Sch of Religion, sch nurse 1976-; Bassard Rehab Hosp, owner/adminst/nurse 1963-. **ORGANIZATIONS:** Mem Amer Coll of Nursing Home Adminstrs 1976-; mem Lic Voc Norses League 1977-; mem Consumer on Aging Comm CA Assn of Health Fac 1978-80; mem Smithsonian Inst. **HONORS/ACHIEVEMENTS:** Heart Award Patten Bible Coll 1969; Notable Amer 1976-77 & 1978-79; Who's Who in Amer Women 1977-78; Comm Leaders & Noteworthy Americans 1978; Who's Who world of Women 1979-80. **BUSINESS ADDRESS:** Administrator, Bassard Conval Hospital, Inc, 3269 D St, Hayward, CA 94541.

BASSEY, LINUS A.
Publisher. **PERSONAL:** Children: 2 children. **EDUCATION:** London Univ, cert 1963; Lincoln Univ, BA 1966; NYU, grad study 1966-. **CAREER:** African Pavillion NY World's Fair, sales mgr 1965; Lukens Steel Co, researcher 1966; Natl Maritime Union Amer 1967; Coney Island Fam Center, prog dir 1968; Econ Dev E NY, proj dir 1969-70; Vassar Coll, lectr 1970-72; African Progress Mag, publisher 1970-. **ORGANIZATIONS:** Pres Miss Black Universe Beauty Pageant 1972-; exec dir African Prog Speakers Bureau 1971-; bus consult Black Image Assocs 1971-; econ adv Africa Adventure Club 1970-; natl pres Nigerian Students Union in the Ams Inc 1969-70; pres United Nigerians for Industrialization 1968-; econ adv African Businessmen Coalition 1971-. **BUSINESS ADDRESS:** Publisher, African Progress Magazine, C/o Africa Adverture Club, 30 E 42nd St, New York, NY 10017.

BASTINE, LILLIAN BEATRICE
Educator. **PERSONAL:** Born in Houston, TX; married Volly C; children: Atty, Volly C, Raleigh W, Dwight (deceased). **EDUCATION:** Wiley Coll, BA 1943; TSU, MEd 1952; Syracuse U, 1961; Nova U, EdD 1980. **CAREER:** United Negro Coll Fund, bd mem 1954; State of TX, comm post sec ed plng; Houston Independent School Dist, prin. **ORGANIZATIONS:** Bd mem Un Negro Coll Fnd 1974; pnlst Rehab Serv Comm Un Way 1973; pgm chrmn YWCA Reunion Dinner 1985; comm on adm YWCA Blue Tri; Housto N Prin Assn HISD. **HONORS/ACHIEVEMENTS:** Robert Kneebone Un Way 1977; Blck Wmn Achvmnt Agnst Odds Houston Lghtng & Pwr 1985; door buster Zeta PH Beta Sor 1971; UNCF distinguished leadership awd 1987. **BUSINESS ADDRESS:** Principal, Houston Independent School Dist, 210 J W Mills Dr, Seabrook, TX 77586.

BATAILLE, JACQUES ALBERT
Physician. **PERSONAL:** Born Jul 11, 1926. **EDUCATION:** Faculty Med Haiti, MD 1953. **CAREER:** Provident Hosp, jr asst 1955-56; Homer G Phillips Hosp, 1956-57; Cumberland Hosp, resd 1957-58; Albert Einstein Med Coll, 1958-59; Port-Au-Prince, private pract 1960-69; Muscatatuck State Hosp, staff physician 1971-73, med dir 1974; Private Practice, physician 1974-77; Sharon Gen Hosp, 1974-. **ORGANIZATIONS:** Mem AMA; NAACP; Shenango Valley C of C; Mercer Co Heart Assn; PA med Soc; mem Smithsonian Inst. **HONORS/ACHIEVEMENTS:** Sharon Gen Hosp Continuing Educ Award AMA; Amer Citiz 1973. **BUSINESS ADDRESS:** Sharon General Hospital, 755 Division, Sharon, PA 16146.

BATCHELOR, ASBURY COLLINS
Business executive. **PERSONAL:** Born Nov 26, 1929, Leggett, NC; married William Ethel Stephen; children: Marlon Diane Whitehead. **EDUCATION:** A&T Univ Greensboro, NC, attended 1954-56; NC Central Univ Durham, NC, attended 1957; AUS Intelligence Sch, grad 1958. **CAREER:** NC Mutual Life Ins Co, agent 1957-61, sales mgr 1961-80; Western Dist Union, dir of training 1970-; Rocky Mount Devel Corp, sec 1973-; NC Mutual Life InsCo, asst to agency dir 1980-. **ORGANIZATIONS:** Past chmn/treas Rocky Mount Opport Industrializ Cntr 1974-; mem Amer Legion Post #323 1965; chmn pub rel Big Brothers/Big Sisters 1978; mem Rocky Mount Rotary Club 1979. **HONORS/ACHIEVEMENTS:** Man of the Year Award Mt Lebanon Masonic Lodge 1960; Staff Manager of the Year NC Mutual Life Ins Co 1963; Appreciation Award Coastal Plain Heart Fund Assn1968; Citation for Meritorious Serv Amer Legion Post #323 1979. **MILITARY SERVICE:** AUS 1st Sgt 27 years; Good Conduct Medal 1953. **BUSINESS ADDRESS:** Assist to Agency Dir, NC Mutual Life Ins Co, Mutual Plaza, Durham, NC 27701.

BATEMAN, CELESTE ANNE
Cultural affairs supervisor. **PERSONAL:** Born Sep 01, 1956, Newark, NJ; married Carter Mangan; children: Jamil. **EDUCATION:** Rutgers Univ, BA 1978. **CAREER:** New Community Corp, program dir 1978-79; Port Authority of NY & NJ, sec 1980-84; Newark Museum, program coord 1984-87; Cultural Affairs Newark, supervisor 1987-. **ORGANIZATIONS:** Mem Alpha Psi Omega, Alpha Epsilon Rho; selection comm mem Newark Black Film Festival 1984-; mem Friends of Newark Symphony Hall 1985-; mem adv cncl Newark Symphony Hall 1987-; vice pres Newark Festival of People 1987. **BUSINESS ADDRESS:** Supervisor, City Hall Room B23, 920 Broad St, Newark, NJ 07102.

BATEMAN, MICHAEL ALLEN
Business executive. **PERSONAL:** Born Apr 20, 1952, Louisville, KY; married Stephanie C Madison. **EDUCATION:** Univ of Louisville, BA 1974; Northwestern Univ, grad study 1975. **CAREER:** Louisville Defender Newspaper, typesetter 1969; Commonwealth of KY, legislative intern 1972; Courier-Jour Newspaper Louisville, gen assignment intern reporter 1972; WHAS-TV Inc News Dept Louisville, gen assignment reporter 1973-74; Univ of Louisville Pub Info Ofc, media prod 1975-79; Brown & Williamson Tobacco Co, minority affairs coord 1979-86, mgr of product publicity 1986-. **ORGANIZATIONS:** Bd mem Renaissance Devel Corp Louisville 1979; Kentucky Conf of NAACP Chapters 1983; natl pres Nat Nat Assn of Market Developers Louisville 1984; bd mem Louisville Urban League 1984. **HONORS/ACHIEVEMENTS:** Dean's List Univ of Louisville 1972; Outstanding Intern Louisville Urban League 1973; Pi Sigma Alpha Honor Soc Univ of Louisville Chap 1974; Corp Black Achiever Louisville YMCA 1980. **MILITARY SERVICE:** USNR Lt 1976-. **BUSINESS ADDRESS:** Manager of Product Publicity, Brown & Williamson Tobacco, P O Box 35090, Corporate Communications Dept, Louisville, KY 40232.

BATES, ALONZO W.
City employee. **PERSONAL:** Born Oct 07, 1939, Detroit, MI. **EDUCATION:** Alabama State Univ, BS, 1964; Wayne State Univ, grad study. **CAREER:** SChrysler Corp, mgmt trainee, 1964-66, labor rel rep, 1966-68, training adv, 1968-70, prog analyst, 1971-72; Dept Corrections, prog analyst; Detroit Dept Parks & Recreation, adminstrative asst. **ORGANIZATIONS:** Chmn Region 8 Bd Edn; mem Central Bd Educ Detroit Pub Schs; exec dir Civil Rights So Christian Leadership Conf; del Natl Sch Bd conf; chmn bdDetroit Chap Operation PUSH; mem Omega Frat. **HONORS/ACHIEVEMENTS:** Trophy Eastlake Bapt Ch Operation PUSH; Cert of Merit NAACP. **BUSINESS ADDRESS:** Administrative Assistant, Dept Parks & Recreation, Region 8 Bd Educ, 8131 E Jefferson, Detroit, MI 48214.

BATES, ARTHUR VERDI
Attorney. **PERSONAL:** Born Jan 16, 1916, New Haven, CT; married Ruthann Brennan; children: Jean, Arthur Jr. **EDUCATION:** Lincoln U, BA 1937; Howard Univ Sch of Law, JD 1940; Brooklyn Law Sch, L LM 1956. **CAREER:** Private Prct, atty 1948-67; The Legal Aid Scty, sr fmly law spclst retired 1986; Presently, legal consultant to various orgs and comm groups. **ORGANIZATIONS:** Muscian 1933-; bd mem Brooklyn Legal Srvcs Corp 1977-; cnsltnt Cntrl Brooklyn Coordng Cncl 1975-; pst pres Lincoln Civic Assn 1971-75. **MILITARY SERVICE:** AUS 1st lt 4 1/2 yrs; Brnz Star Mdl Cmbt Inf Bdg 1945.

BATES, CLAYTON WILSON, JR.
Educator. **PERSONAL:** Born Sep 05, 1932, New York, NY; married Priscilla Suzanne Baly; children: Katherine Arline, Christopher Thomas, Naomi Elizabeth. **EDUCATION:** Manhattan Coll, BEE 1954; Brooklyn Polytech Inst, MEE 1956; Harvard Univ, ME 1960; Washington Univ, PhD Physics 1966. **CAREER:** RCA, elect engr 1955; Ford Inst Co, 1955; Sylvania, phys 1955-57; AVCO, phys 1960; Varian Assoc, sr rsch engr 1966-72; Princeton Univ, vstg fellow 1978-79; Stanford Univ, assoc prof 1972-77, prof 1977-. **ORGANIZATIONS:** Fellow Amer Physical Soc, Optical Soc of Amer; sr mem IEEE, AAAS, AAUP, Soc of Photo-Optical Instr Engrs, Sigma Xi, Eta Kappa Nu, Sigma Pi Sigma, AmerCeramic Soc; chmn Affirm Action Comm of School of Engr Stanford Univ; fac adv Soc of Black Scientists & Engrs Stanford Univ; rsch fellow Black Theme House Stanford Univ 1973-76; past mem bd of dir Jr Achievement; past mem Natl Acad of Sci Eval Panel; mem adv panel on metall & matls Natl SciFound; vstg prof Univ of London 1968; professional model Demeter Agency San Francisco. **HONORS/ACHIEVEMENTS:** Sabbatical Awd Varian Assoc 1968; listed in Who's Who in the West, Who's Who in Amer Sci; publ 50 articles sci jrnls, 35 presentations sci mags. **BUSINESS ADDRESS:** Professor, StanfordUniv, Dept of Material Science, Stanford, CA 94305.

BATES, DAISY
Publisher, civil rights activist. **CAREER:** Worked with underprivileged people in the Office of Economic Opportunity Training Prog; Arkansas State Press, publisher/owner. **ORGANIZATIONS:** NAACP, former state pres; Mitchllnille OEO Self Help Proj, founder. **HONORS/ACHIEVEMENTS:** Univ of AR, honorary degree 1984; Washington Univ, honorary degree 1984; NAACP, Spingarn Medal 1958. **BUSINESS ADDRESS:** Publisher, Arkansas State Press, 1510 Izard St, Little Rock, AR 72202.

BATES, ERNEST ALPHONSO
Phycisian. **PERSONAL:** Born Dec 07, 1936, Peekskill, NY; children: Ernst R, Paul. **EDUCATION:** John Hopkins U, BA 1958; Univ Rochester Sch Med, MD 1962; Univ San Francisco Sch Med, Res 1967-71; Bd Cert Neurosrgy 1973. **CAREER:** Ernest A Bates MD Inc, neurosrgn 1970-; Am Shared Hosp Svc, pr & c Hm bd 1978-. **ORGANIZATIONS:** Mem bd gvnrs CA Comm Coll 1973; asst clncl prof Neurosrgy UCSF; mem Am Assn Neurlgcl Srgns; flwshp Am Coll Srgns 1978; flwshp Intl Coll ofSrgns. **HONORS/ACHIEVEMENTS:** Madam CJ Walken awd 1985. **MILITARY SERVICE:** USAF 3 yrs. **BUSINESS ADDRESS:** President/Chairman of Board, Am Shared Hosp Serv, 350 Parnassus Ave St 701, San Francisco, CA 94117.

BATES, GLADYS NOEL
Retired educator. **PERSONAL:** Born Mar 26, 1920, McComb, MS; married John M Bates; children: Kathryn Sue Gavin, John M Jr. **EDUCATION:** Tougaloo Coll, AB; WV Univ, MA Univ of CO, Univ of Denver, Further Study. **CAREER:** Jackson MS Public Schools, teacher; Mary Potter Acad, Osford NC, bookkeeper; MS Dist YWCA, sec; MS Teachers Assoc, asst exec sec; Denver Public Schools, teacher, dean of girls, asst principal for pupil serv, retired. **ORGANIZATIONS:** Life mem NEA; mem CO Ed Assoc, Natl Assoc for Women Deans Admin & Counselors, Denver Admin & Suprs Assoc, CO-WY Assoc for Women Deans Admin & Counselors; treas Denver Assoc of Secondary Women in Admin; past mem bd trustee Tougaloo Coll; past pres Natl Alumni Assoc, Tougaloo Coll, Delta Sigma Theta, Denver Chap Links Inc; past mem bd dir NAACP. **HONORS/ACHIEVEMENTS:** Precinct Com Recipient of Natl Ed Assoc Hum Rel Awd 1975; CO Ed Assoc established the Gladys & John Bates Hum Rel Awd to be awarded annually 1974; listed in Who's Who of Amer Women 1958-59; Merit Awd MS Teachers Assoc; Achievement Awd Alpha Phi Alpha; Finer Womenhood Awd Zeta Phi Beta; Pioneer Citation Delta Sigma Theta; Testimonial Banquet Awd Citizens Com of Jackson MS; Plaque of Appreciation Tougaloo Natl Alumni Assoc 1966; Teacher of the Year Denver Blade Newspaper 1964; DCTA Human Relations Awd 1979; Harriet Tubman Awd Esquire Club 1982.

BATES, HENRY MELVIN
Elected city official, retired service station owner. **PERSONAL:** Born Dec 20, 1918, Halifax, VA; married Henretta Villines; children: Max Bickford Richardson. **EDUCATION:** Person Co Training Sch, mechanic 1948; NC Central, electronics 1949. **CAREER:** Person Comm on Black Affairs, political action comm 1983-84; owned & oper serv station in Person Co for 30 yrs; City of Roxboro, retired mayor pro-tem. **ORGANIZATIONS:** Owner of the first Black Serv Station in Person Co operated for 30 yrs 1946; mem Sportsman Club 1950; mem Amer Legion 1950; steward bd treas 1973, chmn of men's day 1951-56 Quinn's Chapel AME Church; mem of health bd Caswell-Chathamslee Person Dist Bd of Health 1980; first Black to enter a baseball team in state championship. **HONORS/ACHIEVEMENTS:** Outstanding Leadership in Church Quinn's Chapel AME Church 1983; Outstanding Achievement in Business the Person Co Comm on Affairs of Black Citizens 1984. **MILITARY SERVICE:** AUS st sgt 4 yrs; Good Conduct Medal; Battlestar; European Oper Medal; Invasion of War Medal. **HOME ADDRESS:** 319 Ivy St, Roxboro, NC 27573.

BATES, JOHN MILTON
Retired educator. **PERSONAL:** Born Mar 27, 1914, Eastlake, AL; married Gladys; children: Kathryn, John. **EDUCATION:** WV State Coll, BS Mech of Arts 1937; WV Univ, AMEd; Univ Northern Coll, EdD. **CAREER:** Alcorn High School, teacher 1937-38; Attala Cty Training School, teacher 1938-39; Lanier High School, teacher 1939-42; Mary Potter Acad, teacher 1942-43; Lanier High School, teacher 1943-48; Empire Trade School, teacher 1948-52; Savannah State Coll, teacher 1952; So Christian Inst, teacher 1952-53; JP Campbell Coll, teacher 1954-60; Manual High School, retired teacher 1960-79. **ORGANIZATIONS:** Mem Denver Teachers Assoc, CO Ed Assoc; life mem Natl Ed Assoc; mem CO Vocational Assoc, Amer Voc Assoc, mem bd dir CO Ed Assoc 1969-; laymens activities comm Blenarm Br YMCA; trustee Pearl St AME Church; mem YMCA, United Givers Campaign; vice pres Gr Parkhill Comm Assoc; mem Stapleton Optimist Club; sponsor NE Parkhill Civic Assoc; mem bd dir E Denver YMCA 1967-; mem Com for Location of Metro Comm Coll; mem bd dir Modular Indust Inc; mem bd dir NEDCB Prog; mem NAACP; fin com Peoples Presbyterian Church; aging adv comm Denve Reg Council of Govts 1981-; mem Denver Co Council on Aging1985-; aging adv comm Zion Senior Center 1985-; adv bd on aging Montview Presbyterian Church 1987. **HONORS/ACHIEVEMENTS:** Candidate D of Ed 1980; Human Relations Awd CEA 1973-74; Volunteers of Amer; WV State Coll Athletic Hall of Fame Inductee 1985; Retired Sr Community SvcAwd; Cert of Merit Epilepsy Found of CO; Channel 9 TV Nine Who Care Awd 1986; WV State Coll Alumnus Awd 1986; CO Commission on Aging Serv Awd 1986.

BATES, LIONEL RAY, SR.
Commercial diver. **PERSONAL:** Born Oct 21, 1955, New Orleans, LA; married Karen M; children: Nicole M, Lionel R Jr. **EDUCATION:** Commercial Dive Ctr, air/mixed gas 1979. **CAREER:** Anatole's Garage, auto mechanic 1965-78; Sub-Sea Intl, tender 1979-80, commercial diver. **ORGANIZATIONS:** Bible student & minister Inst Divine Metaphysical Rsch Inc 1980-. **HONORS/ACHIEVEMENTS:** 1st Black to Graduate from Commercial Dive Ctr 1979; People & Places Ebony Magazine Jan 1984; 1st Black to do saturation diving to depth of 450 ft 1985. **BUSINESS ADDRESS:** Subsea Intl, 131 S Robertson, New Orleans, LA 70112.

BATES, LOUISE REBECCA
Business executive. **PERSONAL:** Born Sep 16, 1932, Cairo, IL. **EDUCATION:** Wilson Jr Coll, AA 1957. **CAREER:** Gold Blatt Bros Inc, clerk, buyer 1952-75; Evans Inc, buyer 1976-77; Louise Bates Jewelry Store, pres, mgr, owner. **ORGANIZATIONS:** Mem NAACP, Operation Breadbasket, Urban League, WTTW TV, United Negro Coll Fund; mem, pres Jr Hostess Council & Ed of newsletter USO; vol work Better Boys Found hostess Kup's Purple Heart Cruises; vol work & guest lectr Audy Juvenile Home Prog & Chicago Public School. **HONORS/ACHIEVEMENTS:** Woman of the Day 1975; Citation of Merit in REcog of Outstanding Contrib to Comm WAIT Radio St; Cert of Leadership Hon Leadership of Women in Economic Cultural & Civic Life of the Metro Chicago Comm, YWCA of Chicago 1972; Nathan Awd for Outstanding Buyer of the Year Goldblatts 1975. **BUSINESS ADDRESS:** President, Louise Bates Jewelry Store, 24 W Madison St, Chicago, IL 60602.

BATES, NATHANIEL
City official. **PERSONAL:** Born Sep 09, 1931, Cason, TX; married Shirley Adams; children: Michael, Gail, Larry, Steven. **EDUCATION:** San Francisco State Coll, BA 1963; CA State-Haywood 1975. **CAREER:** City of Richmond, councilman 1967-, mayor 1971-72, vice mayor 1975-76, mayor 1976-77, unit supervisor probation dept Alameda Co. **ORGANIZATIONS:** Pres E Bay Div League of CA Cities; vice chmn Human Resources Comm;

chmn Contra Costa Co Mayors Conf; mem Richmond Port Auth 1976-, Richmond Housing Auth 1976-; Richmond Redevel Commn 1976-; mem bd of dir Natl League of Cities; bd of dir League of CA Cities; Black Probation & Parole Assn; Natl Black Elected Officials Adv Bd; mem Natl Council on Alcoholism for Contra Costa Co; Regional Council on Criminal Justice; Bay Area Sewage Serv Agency 1973-; mem adv bd Mt Diablo Cncl Boys Scouts of Amer, Camp Fire Girls, Richmond Boys Club; pres Richmond Democratic Club 1986-87; bd of dir El Sobritate Girls Club 1986-87; West County YMCA 1986-87; Salesian Boys Club 1986-87. **BUSINESS ADDRESS:** Unit Supvsr Adult Div, Alameda Co Probation Dept, 400 Broadway, Oakland, CA 94607.

BATES, ROBERT E., JR.
Manufacturing manager. **PERSONAL:** Born Oct 12, 1934, Washington, DC; son of Robert E Bates Sr and Alice M Bates; married Gracia M Hillman; children: Dawne E Bates Collier, Brandon R, Hillman M. **EDUCATION:** Univ of IL, AB 1955. **CAREER:** US Census Bureau, statistician 1958-69; US Office of Economic Opportunity, mgmt info analyst 1967-69; Senator Edward Kennedy, legislative aide 1969-77; Mobil Oil Corp, mgr govt relations. **ORGANIZATIONS:** Bd mem United Black Fund; bd mem NAACP Energy Comm; bd mem Big Brothers of DC; mem NY Stock Exchange Fee Arbitration Bd; mem Amer Petroleum Inst; mem Chem Mfgrs Assn; Amer Assn of Blacks in Energy, bd of dirs. **MILITARY SERVICE:** AUS 1st lt 1955-58. **BUSINESS ADDRESS:** Manager of Govt Relations, Mobil Oil Corp, 1100 Connecticut Ave NW, Washington, DC 20036.

BATES, WILLIAM J.
Corporate architect. **PERSONAL:** Born Oct 05, 1952, Canonsburg, PA; son of George C Bates and Laura E Anderson-Bates; married Margaret M McDermott, Oct 27, 1977; children: Meaghan A, Owen P, Nora K. **EDUCATION:** Univ of Notre Dame, Notre Dame IN, BA 1975. **CAREER:** Shields Construction Co, Pittsburgh PA, designer, 1975; Celento & Edison Architects, Pittsburgh PA, intern architect, 1976, partner, 1978-84; Seluck Minnierly Group, Inc, Pittsburgh, PA, project architect, 1976-78; Westinghouse Electric Corp, Pittsburgh PA, consultant, 1984-88, design mgr, 1988—. **ORGANIZATIONS:** Pres, Pittsburgh Architects Woskshop, 1980-85; mem, Partnerships in Educ Speakers Bureau, 1980; founder, Allegheny Trails Architectural Career Explorer Post, 1983; pres, Pittsburgh chapter Amer Inst of Architects, 1987; sec, Pennsylvania Soc of Architects, 1989; chmn, Minority Resource Committee Amer Inst of Architects; mem, Allegheny County Airport Devel Commn, 1989—. **BUSINESS ADDRESS:** Design Mgr, Westinghouse Electric Corp, 11 Stanwix St, Rm 1433, Pittsburgh, PA 15222.

BATES, WILLIE EARL
Business executive. **PERSONAL:** Born Feb 19, 1940, Shaw, MS; married JoEllen; children: Roman Earl II, Patrice Simone. **EDUCATION:** TN State Univ, BS 1963. **CAREER:** Universal Life Ins Co, salesman, asst mgr, dist mgr, asst vp. **ORGANIZATIONS:** Mem Capital Investment Club, Met Bapt Church, Omega Psi Phi; chmn Bookter T Wash HS Class Reunion 1959. **HONORS/ACHIEVEMENTS:** Manager of the Year 1968; Cox Trophy Natl Ins Assoc 1969. **BUSINESS ADDRESS:** Assistant Vice President, Universal Life Insurance Co, 480 Linden Ave, Memphis, TN 38126.

BATES-PARKER, LINDA
Educator. **PERSONAL:** Born Feb 23, 1944, Cincinnati, OH; married Breland K; children: Robbin, Brandon. **EDUCATION:** Univ of Dayton, BS Eng 1965, grad teaching assistantship 1968; Univ of Cincinnati, MA English 1970. **CAREER:** Procter & Gamble, market research 1966-67; Shillito's Dept Store, training coord 1968-70; Univ of Cincinnati, head counselor, asst to dean 1970-75, asst to Vice Provost for Student Affairs 1975-76, assoc dir of career planning & placement 1975-81, assoc vice provost 1981-. **ORGANIZATIONS:** Pres consulting firm BCW Inc 1977-; bd mem Black Career Women's Resource Center 1983-; bd mem Cincinnati Local Devel Corp bd mem WCET Educ TV 1973-74; women's com Cincinnati Symphony Orch; mem Midwest Coll Placement Assn; past pres Jr Alliance for Soc/Civic Action; mem United Black Faculty & Staff Assn; mem Assn of Women Adminstrs; mem Middle Mgrs Assn; (UC) President's Commn on Domestic Affairs 1975; commentator OH Valley Kool Jazz Festival 1975; coord Professional Devel Sem for Black Women 1977; mem Cincinnati Charter Bd Com 1980-81; mem Mayor's Comm Relations Comm 1980; mem comm Chest Eval Comm 1980; hon mem Soc of Black Engineers 1980; mem Amer Personnel & Guidance Assn 1980-81; natl presentations APGA Atlanta/ACPA Boston/Coll Placement Counc; mem ACPA/AASPA Chicago. **HONORS/ACHIEVEMENTS:** Outstanding Young Women in Amer 1979; YWCA Career Woman of Achievement Award Recipient 1982; Women in Communications Advocate Award Recipient 1982; CincinnatiEnquirer Woman of the Year 1983; Who's Who of Amer Women 1984; cover story Elancee Magazine Sept 1984; Ethelrie Harper Awd Cincinnati Human Relations Commn1984; Top 100 Black Business and Professional Women in Amer Dollars and Sense Magazine 1985. **BUSINESS ADDRESS:** Associate Vice Provost, Univ of Cincinnati, Office of Vice Provost Student Affairs, Mail Code 159, Cincinnati, OH 45221.

BATH, PATRICIA E.
Physician, ophthalmologist. **PERSONAL:** Born Nov 04, 1942, New York, NY. **EDUCATION:** Hunter Coll NY, BA Chem 1964; Howard Univ Med Coll, MD 1968. **CAREER:** Sydenham Hosp of NYC, asst surg 1973; Flower & Fifth Ave Hosp NYC, asst surg 1973; Metro Surg NYC, asst surg 1973-74; NY Med Coll Dept of Ophthalmol, clinical instr 1973-74; UCLA Cntr for Health Sciences, asst attending 1974-; UCLA Sch of Med, assist prof ophthal 1974-; Charles R Drew Postgrad Med Sch, assist prof of opthalmol 1974-, assist prof of surg 1974-; Martin L King Jr Gen Hosp LA, dir clin serv & asst chf Div of Ophthal 1974-; Univ of Nigeria Med Sch, visit prof surg 1976-; Jules Stein Eye Inst Dept Ophthal, prog dir ophthalmic asst 1977-; Charles R Drew Postgrad MedSch LA, asst prof dept of comm med intl health sect. **ORGANIZATIONS:** Consult & chf ophthalmol Mercy Hosp Abak, Nigeria 1977; White House consult Natl & Intl Blindness Prevention Prog USA 1977-78; consult & rapporteur Onchocerciasis Sect 1st Gen Assemb of the Intl Agency for Prev of Blindness Oxford 1978; consult & rapporteur Prim Eye Care Sect WHO Meeting on Tech & Operatnl Approaches to the Prevent of Blindness Asilomar 1978; consult Fed Drug Admin Ophthalmic Devices Panel 1979-; mem Med Soc of Co of NY; mem Amer Med Assn 1973-75; mem Natl Med Assn 1973-; mem Amer Soc of Contemp Ophthalmol 1974-; mem Amer Pub Health Assn 1975-; mem Intl Agency for the Preven of Blindness 1975-; mem Soc of Eye Surg Intl Eye Found 1976-; fellow Amer Coll of Surgeons 1976-; fellow Amer Acad of Ophthalmology & Otolaryngology 1976-;Sci Found 1959. **HONORS/ACHIEVEMENTS:** Scholarship Alpha Kappa Alpha Sor 1965; NIH Fellowship 1965; NIMH Fellowship 1965; NIMH Fellow 1966; Fellowship Dept of HEW Childrens' Bur 1967; NIH Fellowship Dept of Ophthal Howard Univ 1968; Outstanding Student in Endocrinology Dept med Howard Univ 1968; Outstanding Student in Pulmonary Diseases (Payne Laurey) Dept of Med 1968; Outstanding Student in Ophthalmology (Edwin J Watson) Prize Dept of Surg 1968; Med Educ for Natl Def Prize for Outstanding Comm Serv Poor People's Campaign Wash, DC 1968; many publns 7 scientific papers. **BUSINESS ADDRESS:** Assistant Professor, Charles R Drew Postgrad Med Sc, 12021 S Wilmington Ave, Los Angeles, CA 90059.

BATHER, PAUL CHARLES
Elected official, businessman. **PERSONAL:** Born Jun 30, 1947, Brooklyn, NY; son of Charles Bather and Regina Bather; married Coretta Waddell, Jun 07, 1969; children: Amir, Omar. **EDUCATION:** Fairfield Univ, Fairfield CT, BA, 1968; City Univ of New York, New York NY, MSW, 1970; Univ of Louisville, Louisville KY, MBA, 1980. **CAREER:** Jefferson County, Louisville KY, treasurer, 1981-86; WJYL Radio, Louisville KY, gen mgr, 1986-88; gen partner, Louisville Communications, 1988-; limited partner, Louisville Radio, 1988-; The Bather Group, Louisville KY, pres, 1988-; City of Louisville, Louisville KY, alderman; Best Bet Magazine, Louisville, KY, pres. **ORGANIZATIONS:** Chmn, Economic Devel Comm, chmn Affirmative Action Comm; mem bd of dir, Downtown Devel Corp; life mem, Louisville NAACP; mem, Louisville Chamber of Commerce. **HONORS/ACHIEVEMENTS:** Eubank Tucker Award for Courage of Conviction, NAACP, 1984; Natl Alumnus of the Year, Amer Center for Intl Leadership, 1986; Outstanding Achievement, Kentucky Alliance Against Racism, 1988. **BUSINESS ADDRESS:** Alderman, City of Louisville, 601 W Jefferson St, Louisville, KY 40202.

BATINE, RAFAEL
Attorney. **PERSONAL:** Born Jul 20, 1947, Santurce, PR; married Patricia Estelle Pryde; children: Rafael Pablo. **EDUCATION:** St John's Univ Coll Bus Admin, BS 1969; St John's Univ Sch of Law, JD 1974. **CAREER:** Westbury Pub Sch NY, math tchr, 1969-73; Covington Howard Hagood & Holland NY, law clerk, 1973-74; Queens Dist Attys Office, asst dist atty, 1974-75; Rutledge Holmes Willis Batine & Kellam NY, pvt law practice, 1975-78; Georgia Office of Fair Employment, gen counsel, 1978-79; US Dept of Labor, atty. **ORGANIZATIONS:** 1st vice chmn Planning Bd 12 Queens NY 1977-78; sec/treas Macon B Allen Black Bar Assn 1975-78; legal redress chmn Jamaica NAACP NY 1976-78; admitted topractice law GA 1983, NY 1975, US Supreme Ct 1977. **HONORS/ACHIEVEMENTS:** Martin Luther King Scholarship St John's Univ Sch of Law 1971-74. **BUSINESS ADDRESS:** Attorney, US Department of Labor, Solicitor's Office, 1371 Peach Tree St NE, Atlanta, GA 30309.

BATISTE, EDNA E.
Registered nurse. **PERSONAL:** Born Aug 28, 1931, Detroit, MI; married Walter D Batiste; children: Lisa, Duane, Anthony. **EDUCATION:** Wayne State Univ, BS 1955; Univ of MI, MPH 1972. **CAREER:** Detroit Dept Health, staff nurse 1954-63, suprv publ health nurse 1963-66; Publ Health Nurse, dist suprv 1966-68; school health nursing consult 1968-70, asst dir. **ORGANIZATIONS:** Mem Wayne State Coll Nursing Alumni, Univ of MI Alumni Assoc, MI Nurses Assoc, Amer Nurses Assoc, Amer School Health Assoc, Wayne State Univ Alumni, Amer Publ Health Assoc, MI Publ Health Assoc, Chi Eta Phi, Year-round Head Start Parent & Pre-sch Adv Com; bd Well-Being Serv for Aging, Vstg Nurses Assoc Bd; policy adv com Mayors Human Resources Devel Group Health Sub-com; mem Detroit Council Publ Serv for Children & Youth, Delta Sigma Theta; parishrel Central Meth Church; mem Bagley commun Council, NAACP. **BUSINESS ADDRESS:** Assistant Dir, Public & Health Nursing, Detroit Health Dept, 2 Woodward Ave, Detroit, MI 48226.

BATISTE, MARY VIRGINIA
Hairstylist/instructor. **PERSONAL:** Born Jul 31, 1925, Alexandria, LA; children: Lela Virginia. **EDUCATION:** US Small Business Assoc, Management 1971; Univ of CA at Los Angeles, Vocational 1975, Educ/Voc 1977; Natl Beauty Culturists League; DEduc 1980. **CAREER:** CA State Bd of Cosmetology, examiner (first black) 1960-68; LA Unified School Dist, teacher 1975-87; Pacific Coast State Cosmetology Assoc, pres 1984-87;Natl Beauty Culturists League, asst dir educ 1985-87. **ORGANIZATIONS:** Educ consultant Summit Laboratories Deluxal Lect 1963-71; owner-oper Batiste Hair Modules Chain LA 1962-87; mem Mayor Tom Bradley Commn on Youth & Aged 1977-79; basileus Alpha Lambda Chap Theta Nu Sigma Sor 1979-81; first woman mem trustee bd Lewis Metropolitan CME Church 1981-87; mem bd of dirs NBCL Natl Inst 1984-87. **HONORS/ACHIEVEMENTS:** Madame CJ Walker NBCL Natl Awd 1978; Citation by State Assembly US Congress 1978; Woman of the Year Theta Nu Sigma Sor 1980; recipient of numerous first place trophies, awards, certificates, honors. **HOME ADDRESS:** 9246 So Hobart Blvd, Los Angeles, CA 90047.

BAT NAPHTALI, ASHIRAH SHOLOMIS (NKECHIELA CRUISE)
Business, finance and tax consultant. **PERSONAL:** Born Apr 06, 1950, Kingston, Jamaica;children: Teshaye Smith-Byroo. **EDUCATION:** New York Univ, BA 1979; Hofstra Univ, JD-MBA 1984. **CAREER:** Urban Devel, consultant/rsch asst, 1978-80; MAKKA Productions, mgmt consultant, 1980-82; Nassau County Office of Employment, legal asst, 1982-83; Colin A Moore Esquire, legal asst 1983; South Brooklyn Legal Svcs, law asst 1983-84; Michael M Laufer Esquire, assoc 1984; Helen Gregory Law Office, assoc 1987-; NACA Inc, pres 1984-; Law Office of Barbara Emmanuel, Queens, NY, associate 1989-. **ORGANIZATIONS:** Mem WIBO; mem NBA; mem Intl Soc of Financiers, 1986-; mem Amer Consultant League, 1986-; mem, Intl Soc of Financiers 1986-; mem, American Consultant League 1986-. **MILITARY SERVICE:** USAF sgt 1969-74; USAR sgt 1980-83. **BUSINESS ADDRESS:** CEO, NACA Inc, 161-10 Jamaica Ave, Suite 412, Jamaica, NY 11413.

BATSON, RUTH MARION
Educator. **PERSONAL:** Born in Boston, MA; children: Cassandra Way, Susan, Dorothy Owusu. **EDUCATION:** Boston Univ Psychology Dept, 1967; Univ MA Amherst, Masters Degree Candidate, 1972-73; Boston Univ School Educ, MEd 1976. **CAREER:** Commonwealth of MA, commr MA comm against discrimination 1963-66; Metro Council for Educ Opportunity, asst dir & ex dir 1966-70; BU Sch of Med Div of Psychiatry, dir consultant & ex 1970-75, dir school desegregation rsch project 1975-81, coordinator clinical task force 1981-; BU Sch of Med Div of Psychiatry, assoc prof 1986; Museum of Afro Amer History, pres and dir. **ORGANIZATIONS:** Bd mem New Englnd T V Corp 1978-; edtrl bd & mem WNEV-TV Ch 7 1978-; bd trustees MA General Hospital 1979-, Boston City Hospital 1970-76, Citizens Training Grp Boston Juvenile Court 1979-; mem corp MA General Hospital 1979-; co-chairperson NAACP Natl Convention, 1982; life mem exec bd NE Reg Conf NAACP; co-chair Natl Adv CommDocumentary Series Eyes on the Prize 1985-. **HON-**

ORS/ACHIEVEMENTS: Appreciation citation, Boston Branch NAACP 1982; M L King Awrd M L King Memorial Breakfast 1981; M Cass Black Achievement Award Black Achievers 1979; Woman 76 Awd Boston YWCA, 1976; Comm Contribution Citation Prince Hall Grand Lodge Boston 1976; Action for Boston Comm Devel Award 1985; Outstanding Commitment to Higher Educ Roxbury North Dorchester Area Planning Action Council Inc 1986; Visionary Leadership Wellesley Met Co Program, 1986. **HOME ADDRESS:** 250 Cambridge St, Apt 701, Boston, MA 02114. **BUSINESS ADDRESS:** President, Museum of Afro/Amer History, Abiel Smith School, 46 Joy St, Boston, MA 02114.

BATTEAST, MARGARET W.
Public relations director. **PERSONAL:** Born May 26, 1904, Chicago, IL; married Tracy W; children: Traceleanor McNamara, Zelma. **EDUCATION:** Northwestern Univ, BS 1937; DePaul Univ, grad work. **CAREER:** Shoop Elem Sch, tchr 1926; Public Sch, libr; Meliville W Fuller Sch, asst prin/acting prin; Chicago Bd of Edn, tchr; Sorority of Phi Delta Kappa, natl dir pub relations. **ORGANIZATIONS:** Past Matron Order of Eastern Star; first chmn Scholarship Com awarding first scholarship to needy student; past Basileus Mu Chap Chgo; pres Phidelka Found of Mu Chpt; mem Quinn Chapel AME Ch; delegate Chicago Annual Conf; deleg Gen Conf; sec Brotherhook of Quinn Chapel AME Ch; vice pres Paul Quinn Sr Missionary Soc; prom missionary educ chmn Chicago area Br Missionaries; supvr Young Adult Usher Bd of Quinn Chapel. **HONORS/ACHIEVEMENTS:** Recip Award for Outstanding Serv in Comm from 1942-69 Mellville W Fuller Sch PTA upon retirement.

BATTEAST, ROBERT V.
Business executive. **PERSONAL:** Born 1931, Rosetta, MS. **EDUCATION:** IN Univ, attended. **CAREER:** South Bend Devel Corp, vp; Batteast Constr Co Inc, pres. **ORGANIZATIONS:** Dir 1st South Bank. **BUSINESS ADDRESS:** President, Batteast Construction Co Inc, 430 LaSalle Ave, South Bend, IN 46617.

BATTEN, GRACE RUTH
Clergywoman. **PERSONAL:** Born Mar 22, 1943, Harbeson, DE; children: Earl William Jr. **EDUCATION:** Delaware Tech & Comm Coll, AAS 1976; Burke Bible Coll, BTh 1977; Wilmington Coll, BS 1986. **CAREER:** Adult Educ Satellite Prog, administrator 1979-; Natl Youth Conf, educ chairperson 1980-84; Mt Sinai Farm Develop Comm, chairperson 1986-; Mount Zion Holy Church Inc, pastor/president admin. **ORGANIZATIONS:** Life mem Natl Council of Negro Women 1977-; bd mem Delaware Assoc of A&C Educ 1982-; councilwoman/sec milton Town Council (first black) 1982-; mem Amer Soc of Notaries 1985-; vice chairperson Sussex Co Red Cross 1985-; mem Natl Assoc for Female Execs 1986-; bd mem People Place II Counciling Ctr 1986-. **HONORS/ACHIEVEMENTS:** Big Sister of the Year Sussex Co Branch of BB/BS 1981; Outstanding Citizen Awd Milton Chamber of Commerce 1983; Certificate of Appreciation Vica of Sussex Voc Tech Ctr 1986. **HOME ADDRESS:** 111 Orchard St, Milton, DE 19968. **BUSINESS ADDRESS:** Pastor/President Admin, Mount Zion Holy Church Inc, 325 Front St, Milton, DE 19968.

BATTEN, TONY
Motion picture director, producer. **PERSONAL:** Born Aug 17, 1935, New York, NY; son of Edward Batten and Olga Batten. **EDUCATION:** Coll City of NY, attended 1954-57; Univ of Xalapa Mexico, attended 1960-61; San Francisco Art Inst, attended 1961-62; San Francisco State Coll, BA 1967; Univ CA Berkeley, attended 1967-68. **CAREER:** Freelance photographer, Liberator, Trans-Action, San Franrancisco Magazine, Ramparts, Bohemia Magazine, NY Times Sun Magazine, Washington Post, Wilson Library Bulletin 1961-69; films for TV E Africa Ends & Beginning 1969; Bl Journal, mng editor 1968-70; MN Fats 1968; Karate Discipline & Dance 1967; The Toughest Labor Game in Town 1971; Bedlam in the Jails, special reports 1970; Ch 2 News prod 1970-71; The 51st State repoter 1971-73; Who Runs Newark? 1971; Ain't Gonna Eat My Mind 1972; The 1st Natl Bl Pol Conv 1973; Interface exprod & host 1974-76; A Prof of Paul Robeson 1975; Eubie Blake Long As you Live 1975; Guilty Until Proven Innocent 1975; Crisis in Paradise 1974; Bad Times on Gold Mtn 1974; ABC News Closeup 1977-79; T Batten Prod pres 1970-. **ORGANIZATIONS:** Chmn NE Reg Natl Assn of Black Media Prod 1969; NY Acad of TV Arts & Science; Intl Center for Photo; Dir Guild of Amer; Amer Fed of TV & Radio Artists; Writers Guild of Amer. **HONORS/ACHIEVEMENTS:** Awarded Emmy Ain't Gonna Eat My Mind 1972; 1st prize for Document Black Filmmakers Hall of Fame 1976; 1st prize for Document Natl Assn of Black Media Women 1976; included in permanent collections NY Schomburg Collection of negro Arts & Letters 1976; Intl Center for Photo 1976; Columbia Univ School of Journalism Dupont Award 1972, 1978 for ABC News Closeup "New Religions, Holiness or Heresy. **BUSINESS ADDRESS:** President, Tony Batten Production, PO Box 339, New York, NY 10019.

BATTIES, PAUL TERRY
Physician. **PERSONAL:** Born Jul 22, 1941, Indianapolis, IN. **EDUCATION:** IN Univ, AB 1961; IN Sch of Med, MD 1965. **CAREER:** Wayne State Univ Sch of Med, internship 1965-66; Wayne State Univ, resident internal med 1966-69, chief med resident 1969; physician private practice. **ORGANIZATIONS:** Cardiology fellowship Univ of KY Sch of Med 1971-73; bd of dir Assn of Black Cardiologists; bd of dir Marion Co Heart Assn; chmn Hypertension Com Marion Co Heart Assn; mem Kappa Alpha Psi Frat; Univ United Meth Ch; Am Assn Black Cardiologists. **HONORS/ACHIEVEMENTS:** Distinguished Citizen Award, IN 1976; has a cardiac transplant patient. **MILITARY SERVICE:** USAF Maj 1969-71. **BUSINESS ADDRESS:** 1633 N Capitol Ave, Ste 510, Indianapolis, IN 46202.

BATTLE, BERNARD J., SR.
Savings & loan executive. **PERSONAL:** Born Jun 26, 1927, Memphis, TN; son of Lewis Battle (deceased) and Lenora Tolbert Battle; married Corinne Stewart Battle, Nov 04, 1985; children: Maureen B Prillerman, Aaron S Battle, B J Battle, Jr, Edwin L Battle, Michelle T Battle. **EDUCATION:** Pioneer Inst, Philadelphia PA, diploma, 1951; A & T State Univ, Greensboro NC, Advance (Special); Guilford Coll, Greensboro NC; Amer Savings & Loan League, certificate Mgmt Training, 1972. **CAREER:** Palmer Memorial Inst, Sedalia NC, business mgr, 1951-62; Amer Federal Savings & Loan Assn, Greensboro NC, CEO/pres, 1962-. **ORGANIZATIONS:** Treasurer, 1962-84, pres, 1984-88, NAACP, Greensboro branch; treasurer, NAACP, State Conf, 1963-84; asst treasurer, NAACP, Natl Office, 1979-85; mem, NAACP bd of dir, 1982-88; pres, mem exec comm, Greensboro Citizens Assn, 1964-; mem, Greensboro Political Action Comm, 1965-; former vice chmn Greensboro War Memorial Coliseum Commn, 1979-88. **HONORS/ACHIEVEMENTS:** Serv Award, NC State NAACP, 1972; Serv Award, Greensboro Branch NAACP, 1972; Man of the Year, Region V NAACP, 1976; Man of the Year, Greensboro Young Men's Club, 1976; certificate, Youth Service Corp, Greensboro Branch, 1984; Man of the Year, Greensboro Branch NAACP, 1989; Welterweight (amateur) Boxing Champion, Middle-Eastern Serv Conf while in US Army, Fort Meyers VA, 1987. **MILITARY SERVICE:** AUS, seargent, 1945-48; Marksman Medal, Peace Medal. **BUSINESS ADDRESS:** Pres, Chmn of Bd of Dir, Amer Federal Savings & Loan Assn of Greensboro, 701 E Market St, Greensboro, NC 27401.

BATTLE, CHARLES E.
Business executive. **PERSONAL:** Born Aug 26, 1953, Shreveport, LA; married Elaine; children: Keisha L, Freadda C, Christin' Elisha. **EDUCATION:** CO Univ, 1970-71; Grambling, 1971-74; Coll for Financial Planning, 1982-83. **CAREER:** John Hancock Life Ins Co, ins agent 1975-76; Profesco of CO, owner 1977-82; Battle & Co Financial Planner, owner 1983-. **ORGANIZATIONS:** Mem NALU, CALU, DALU 1976-, ICFP 1982-; comm head CAMU 1982-; mem IAFP 1983-; bd mem Aurora Mental Health 1983-. **BUSINESS ADDRESS:** President, Battle & Company, 1957 Peoria St, Aurora, CO 80010.

BATTLE, GLORIA JEAN
Government official. **PERSONAL:** Born May 23, 1950, Deerfield Beach, FL; daughter of Eugene Battle and Joyce Thompson-Battle. **EDUCATION:** Bennett Coll, Greensboro NC, BA, 1972; Howard Univ, Washington DC, MUS, 1976; Florida State Univ, Tallahassee FL, 1985-. **CAREER:** Social Systems Intervention, Washington DC, research analyst, 1973-76; Mark Battle Assoc, Washington DC, consultant, 1976; Child Advocacy Inc, Miami FL, planner, 1977-79; Florida International Univ, Miami FL, dir, 1979-80; Broward County Govt, Ft Lauderdale FL, dir human relations div, 1981-. **ORGANIZATIONS:** Pres, Natl Assn of Human Rights Workers, 1981-, pres Deerfield Child Devel Center, 1981-82; first vice pres, NAACP, North Broward Chapter, 1984-85; mem, Intl Assn of Human Rights Officials, 1981-; mem, Community Housing Resource Bd, 1983-86; mem Forum for Black Public Admin, 1984-. **HONORS/ACHIEVEMENTS:** Davison-Foreman Scholarship, Bennett Coll, 1971; NIMH Fellowship, NIMH, Howard Univ, 1973; McKnight Fellowship, McKnight Found, 1985; Global Woman of the 80s, Charmettes, 1987; Liberty Bell Award, Broward County Bar Assn, 1989. **BUSINESS ADDRESS:** Dir, Broward County Human Relations Div, 115 S Andrews Ave, Rm 116, Ft. Lauderdale, FL 33301.

BATTLE, JOE TURNER
Elected government official. **PERSONAL:** Born Aug 25, 1941, Atlanta, TX; married Barbara L; children: Joe D, Kim C. **EDUCATION:** Dept of Defense Race Relations Inst, Cert 1975; CA State Univ Dominguez Hill, BS Bus Admin 1985. **CAREER:** Officer Training School Ft Sill, staff instr 1967-68; Schweinfurt Germany, equal oppty ed nco 1975-77; Lynnwood Unified School Dist, pres school bd mem 1983-85. **ORGANIZATIONS:** Chairperson, mem Lynnwood School Site Council 1980; mem Lynnwood USD Adv Council 1980-81; mem South Central Area Adv Council Catholic Youth Org 1981-85; pta legislative rep Lynwood PTA Council 1983-84; mem Cerritos Area Trustees Assoc 1981-85. **MILITARY SERVICE:** AUS sgt 1st class; 21 yrs; Bronze Star, Meritorious Serv Medal, Combat Infantry Badge, 3 Commend Medals, 5 Campaign Stars Vietnam, Vietnam Cross Galantry. **BUSINESS ADDRESS:** School Board Member, Lynwood Unified Sch Dist, 11331 Plaza, Lynwood, CA 90262.

BATTLE, KATHLEEN
Opera singer. **PERSONAL:** Born in Portsmouth, OH. **EDUCATION:** College Conservatory of Music Univ of Cincinnati, BMusic, MMusic. **CAREER:** Made professional debut at the invitation of Thomas Schippens appearing in Brahms "Requium" at Cincinnati May Festival 1972; regular guest soprano with the orchestras in New York, Chicago, Boston, Philadelphia, Cleveland, Paris and Berlin and at major opera houses including the Metropolitan, Paris, Vienna and the Royal Opera/Covent Garden; Le Nozze di Figaro will be videotaped forTV presentation on the PBS "Live from the Met" series 1985-86. **HONORS/ACHIEVEMENTS:** Hon Doctoral degree Westminster Choir Coll; Hon Doctoral degree Coll Conservatory of Music Univ of Cincinnati. **BUSINESS ADDRESS:** c/o Herbert Breslin Agency, 119 West 57th St, New York, NY 10019.

BATTLE, MARK G.
Educator, association executive. **PERSONAL:** Born Jul 28, 1924, Bridgeton, NJ; son of Edward M. Battle (deceased) and Mary Noble Battle (deceased); children: Erica, Kewana, Marcus. **EDUCATION:** Univ of Rochester, BA 1948; Case Western Reserve, MSSA 1950; Kings Pt Federal Exec Inst, Certificate, Federal Program Mgmt,1966. **CAREER:** Franklin Settlement, Detroit MI, exec dir 1960-64; Bd Work Trrgn Program US DOL, admin 1964-69; Mark Battle Assoc, chm bd dir 1969-83; Howard Univ School of Social Work, prof & chmn 1971-; Natl Assn of Social Workers, exec dir 1984-. **ORGANIZATIONS:** Mem House of Delegates CSWE; mem Amer Soc of Public Admin 1968-; Amer Public Welfare Assn 1975-85; Natl Urban League 20 yrs; mem bd dir Washington Council Agency 1981-85; life mem Natl Conf Social Welfare. **HONORS/ACHIEVEMENTS:** James M Yard Brotherhood Award NCCJ 1957; Distinguished Alumni Award Case Western Reserve SASS 1986. **MILITARY SERVICE:** USNR amm 3/C 3 yrs; USN V12 midshipman 1945-46. **HOME ADDRESS:** 10604 Woodbine Rd, Beltsville, MD 20705. **BUSINESS ADDRESS:** Executive Dir, Natl Assn Social Workers, 7951 Eastern Ave, Silver Spring, MD 20910.

BATTLE, THOMAS CORNELL
Librarian, administrator. **PERSONAL:** Born Mar 19, 1946, Washington, DC; children: Brima Omar, Idrissa Saville, Mensah Lukman. **EDUCATION:** Howard Univ, BA 1969; Univ of MD, MLS 1971; George Washington Univ, PhD 1982. **CAREER:** Fed City Coll, Sr Media Intern 1969-71; DC Public Library, readers advisor 1971; MSRC, ref librarian 1972-74; Sierra Leone Lib Bd, exchange librarian 1972-73; Moorland Spingarn Rsch Ctr, acting dir 1979-80; Howard Univ, curator of manuscripts 1974-86, MSRC dir 1986-. **ORGANIZATIONS:** Councillor-at-large 1980-83, treas 1983- African Amer Museum Assoc; bd mem museum of the City of Washington 1978 1981; chair task force on minorities Socof Amer Archivists 1982-; bd mem Washington DC Natl History Day 1983-; exec bd Black Caucus of the Amer Library Assn 1980-92; chair nominating comm, chair African & Caribbean Task Force Black Caucus of the Amer Library Assn 1980-92; bd mem DC Library Assn 1978-80; consul Natl Park Serv 1983-; mem Amer Library Assn; mem Mid-Atlantic Regional Archives Conf; field reviewer & panelist Natl Endowment for the Humanities 1976-85; bylaws comm Metro WashingtonCaucus of Black Librarians 1982-; prog comm 1986, nominating comm 1987 Mid-Atlantic Regional Archives Conf; prog comm Soc of Amer Archivists 1987. **HONORS/ACHIEVEMENTS:** Title IIB Higher Educ Act Fellowship 1970-71; Beta Phi

Mu Iota Chap 1971. **BUSINESS ADDRESS:** Dir, Howard Univ, 500 Howard Place NW, Washington, DC 20059.

BATTLE, TURNER CHARLES, III
Associate administrator & educator. **PERSONAL:** Born Mar 13, 1926, Oberlin, OH; son of Turner Battle and Annie McClellan; married Carmen H Gonzalez Castellanos; children: Anne E Mc Andrew, Turner IV, Conchita, Carmen. **EDUCATION:** Oakwood Coll, BA 1950; Temple Univ, MFA 1958; Columbia Univ, 1960; New York Univ, 1970; Columbia Pacific Univ, 1984; Wiley Coll, HHD, 1986. **CAREER:** Oakwood Coll, instructor 1946-50; US Navy Dept, auditor/acct 1950-55; Philadelphia School Dist, teacher 1955-66; Elmira Coll, asst prof 1966-68; Moore Coll of Art, assoc prof 1968-71; La Salle Coll, dir of special programs, 1969; Higher Educ Coalition, exec dir 1969-71; NYU, assoc prof 1970-72; Westmnstr Choir Coll, assoc prof 1971-74; United Negro Coll Fund, Inc, asst exec dir/sec corp; 1974-present. **ORGANIZATIONS:** Oakwood Coll Alumni Assn; Temple Univ Alumni Assn; visiting comm of educ Metro Museum of Art; mem Amer Soc of Assoc Exec, Sierra Club, Amer Museum of Natl History, Smithsonian Inst, Amer Assn Higher Educ; Phi Delta Kappa. **HOME ADDRESS:** 175 Adams St 7G, Brooklyn, NY 11201. **BUSINESS ADDRESS:** Asst Exec Dir/Sec Corp, United Negro Coll Fund Inc, 500 E 62nd St, New York, NY 10021.

BATTLE, WALTER L.
Clergyman. **PERSONAL:** Born Jul 01, Battle, MS; married Willa Lee Grant; children: Glarushia. **EDUCATION:** Univ of MI Northwestern Bible Coll, BTh 1950, grad studies; North Central Bible Coll, grad Theol. **CAREER:** Barber Shop, owner/oper 1948-61; On radio since 1953; Refuge Christian Youth Ctr, founder youth program 1959; TV minister since 1969; Pastor, 27 yrsvarious locations; House of Refuge Inc Deliverance Ch St Paul, pastor. **ORGANIZATIONS:** Mem Gov Human Rel Comm; State Counselling Com. **HONORS/ACHIEVEMENTS:** Hon DD Apostle's Mandate Autro Skinner 1961; Citation for Crusader of Peace 1966; Ed of Sentinel Newspaper. **MILITARY SERVICE:** AUS 1941-44. **BUSINESS ADDRESS:** Pastor, House of Refuge Inc, 247 N Grotto St, St Paul, MN 55104.

BATTLE, WILLIAM ELZIE
Clergyman, mayor. **PERSONAL:** Born Jun 29, 1899, Walls, MS; married Ernie Walker; children: Freddie, Amos (dec). **EDUCATION:** AR Bapt Coll, BTh 1941, AB 1941, DD 1955. **CAREER:** New Hope MB Church, minister; pastor 1934-; farmer until 1933; City of Sunset AR, mayor. **ORGANIZATIONS:** Mem NAACP, Mason. **HONORS/ACHIEVEMENTS:** Cert of Honor Forrest City Dist AME Church. **BUSINESS ADDRESS:** Mayor, City of Sunset, 10 Powell St, Marion, AR 72364.

BATTS, TERRY MILBURN
Clergyman. **PERSONAL:** Born Nov 02, 1914, Memphis, TN; married Mamye Crutcher; children: Terry M Jr, Harold, Carl. **EDUCATION:** Midwestern Grad Bible Sch, ThM 1960; Amer Div Sch Chicago, DD 1964. **CAREER:** Pastored churches in MS/AL/OH; moderator W AL Assn 17 yrs; AL State & Tri State Convs of AL/MS/TN, served as pres 17 yrs; The New Sarids Primitive Bapt Ch, pastor. **ORGANIZATIONS:** Affil with Bapt Ministers Conf of Mobile; 1st Prim Bapt minister to serve as pres of that orgn; former pres Interdenom Ministerial Alliance of Mobile;mem Bapt Conf & Pastors' Cncl of Greater Cleveland; pres mt Pleasant Ministerial Assn; mem NAACP; founder & pres Midwestern States Primitive Bapt Conv; pres Cleveland Bapt Mins Credit Union; editor Natl Prim Bapt Clarion; clk & dean of educ Chicago River Dist Assn; mem Intl Councl of Religious Edn; chmn publishing bd of Natl PB Conv. **HONORS/ACHIEVEMENTS:** Cited by Mobile Beacon & by AL State Coord Com for Regis & Voting for efforts to carry through full process of polit action stimulating voter regis; One of 1st Blacks to run for publ office in AL. **BUSINESS ADDRESS:** Pastor, The New Sardis Prim Bapt Churc, 3474 E 147 St, Cleveland, OH 44120.

BATY, REGINALD CLEMENT
Civil engineer. **PERSONAL:** Born Aug 12, 1937, Houston, TX; married Rachelle Johnson; children: Steven, Staci. **EDUCATION:** Prairie View A&M Coll, BS 1962; OK State Univ, Civil Engr 1964; Univ of CA, Soil Mech 1975; Univ of MO, Design of Embankment Dams 1973. **CAREER:** Highways & Railroads Sect Hydrologic & Hydraulics Sect, proj engr coord; Rathburn Lake, IA, proj engr coord; AL State Relocat & Co Relocat for HarryS Truman Dam & Res; MO MKT RR Relocat, proj engr coord. **ORGANIZATIONS:** Mem Soc of Civil Engrs; Amer Soc of Safety Engrs; MO Soc of Professional Engrs; Assn of Black Engrs & Applied Scientists. **HONORS/ACHIEVEMENTS:** Commendation Outstanding Serv in Equla Opp Prog 1969; Spec Achievements GE Processing Sys 1963; Techn Writing 1972; Work Techniques 1973; Supvsn & Perf 1973; Report Writing 1974. **MILITARY SERVICE:** AUS 1956-58. **BUSINESS ADDRESS:** Proj Engr Coordinator, 601 E 12 St, Kansas City, MO 64106.

BAUDUIT, HAROLD S.
Attorney. **PERSONAL:** Born Aug 27, 1930, New Orleans, LA; married Martie Branche; children: Harold III, Lianne, Cheryl. **EDUCATION:** US Naval Acad, BS Engrg 1956; Univ of CO, MA Economics, MS Mgmt, JD Law. **CAREER:** Univ of CO, instr bus law 1969-76, atty faculty 1972-76; Economics & Black Studies, lectr. **HONORS/ACHIEVEMENTS:** Sigma Iota Epsilon Hon Mgmt Frat Univ CO 1969-72; Martin Luther King Jr Fellow; Woodrow Wilson Natl Fellowship Found 1969-71. **MILITARY SERVICE:** USAF capt retired 1956-69.

BAUGH, FLORENCE ELLEN
Agency administrator. **PERSONAL:** Born Feb 02, 1935, Beaver Dam, KY; widowed; children: Delandria, Dallas, Christopher, Orville, Lynne. **EDUCATION:** Millard Fillmore Coll at SUNY, BA. **CAREER:** Comm Action Org, Erie Co, comm aide 1965-70; YWCA, dir racial justice public affairs 1971-72; Comm Action Org, Erie Co, dir, neighborhood servs dept 1972-. **ORGANIZATIONS:** Trustee Sheehan Mem Emer Hosp 1974-86, D'Youville Coll 1979-; mem at lrg Buffalo Bd Educ 1973-89; dir pres Ellicott Houses Inc 1978-; mem Univ Buffalo CAC 1982-; bd mem We NY Art Inst 1981-, Cncl of Grt City Sch Bds, sec treas 1978-89; Governor's appointee to 4th Dist Judicial Review Comm; Providence Bapt Church, organist, clerk, trustee; Pres, Council of Great City Schools, 1988-89. **HONORS/ACHIEVEMENTS:** Afro-American Policeman's Assn Comm Serv Award, 1972; Buffalo Chapter Negro Business & Professional Women Comm Serv Award 1973; Black Educators Assoc educ serv awd 1974; Citizen of Yr Buffalo Evening News 1975; Natl Org PUSH, woman of the year 1975; Buffalo Urban League Family Life Award 1976; Pres Distinguisheed Medal, Buffalo St Teacher Coll 1978; Univ Alumni Award Univ of Buffalo 1982; Natl Conf of Christians & Jews Educ award 1982; Medal of Excellence, NY State Univ, Bd of Regents 1984; Week of the Young Child, honorary chmn; Delta Kappa Gamma, Vernie Mulholland Friend of Ed Award 1986; St Univ Syst of NY St, Distinguished citizen awd 1986; Empire State Fed of Women's Clubs Comm Serv Award. **HOME ADDRESS:** 45 Woodward Ave, Buffalo, NY 14214. **BUSINESS ADDRESS:** Dir Neighborhood Service Dept, Comm Action Org Erie Co, 70 Harvard Pl, Buffalo, NY 14209.

BAUGH, JAMES EDWARD
Educator. **PERSONAL:** Born Dec 17, 1941, Lima, OH; married Veatrice DeWalt; children: Kendyl C, James R. **EDUCATION:** Western Michigan Univ, BS 1964; Univ of WI, MA 1971, PhD 1973. **CAREER:** Milwaukee Public School System, teacher 1964-68; Univ of WI, dir 1968-74, asst vice chancellor 1974-77; Univ of WI, System Admin, sr academic planner 1977-79; WI Council on Criminal Justice, exec dir 1980-. **ORGANIZATIONS:** Bd dir Natl Coord Councl for Educ Oppor 1974-; Natl Conf Adv Bd Natl Schlrshp Serv Fund for Negro Studies 1976-; adv bd Madison Neighbor Youth Corp 1970-74; civil rights consult WI Dept of Pub Instr 1971-76; consult HEW Trio Prgms 1969-; Kappa Alpha Psi 1962-; Madison Urban League 1970-; vol Milwaukee Boys Club 1964-68; mem Law Enforcement Training & Standards Bd 1979; mem Victim Compens Adv Bd 1979; mem Natl Crim Just Assn Liaison to Natl Jail Coalition 1980; Madison Zoning Bd 1973-74; Madison Reg Patient Comp Formal Panel 1976-; Madison police & fire commr 1977-; Amer Assn of Higher Educ 1971-; Amer Pers & Guid Assn 1972-; Natl Alliance of Black Sch Educators 1976-; Assn of Soc & Behav Sci 1975-; Med-Amer Assn of Educ Oppor Prgm Pers 1975-. **HONORS/ACHIEVEMENTS:** Basketball Scholarship W MI Univ 1960; Most Outst Tchr Milwaukee Pub Sch 1967; Outstn Achvmnt Award Kappa Alpha Psi 1972; Man of the Yr Kappa Alpha Psi 1973; Scroll of Honor Omega Psi Phi 1974; Outst Young Men of Amer 1977; Spl Serv Grant HEW Univ of WI 1975-77; Outstanding Serv Award Delta Sigma Theta 1978; Master of Ceremony WI Miss Black Amer Pageant 1979-80. **BUSINESS ADDRESS:** Executive Dir, Council on Criminal Justice, 122 W Washington, 4th Floor, Madison, WI 53702.

BAUGH, LYNNETTE
Associate executive. **PERSONAL:** Born Feb 22, 1949, Charleston, WV. **EDUCATION:** West Virginia State Coll, BA, 1971; Univ of Pittsburgh, MPA, 1972. **CAREER:** City of Chicago Pub Works Dept, planning analyst, 1973-74; Illinois Dept of Local Govt Affairs, area rep, 1974-76; Illinois Dept of Local Govt Affairs, area supr, 1976-77; Tacoma Intergovtl Affairs Office, dir, 1977; City of Tacoma Comm Devel Dept, asst dir, 1978-; Dept of Public Utilities, mgmt analyst, 1984-. **ORGANIZATIONS:** Mem Title 9 Sex Equity Adv Com 1978-81; bd mem Pierce Co Growth Policy Assn 1977-81; exec com & Vice Pres NAHRO Puget Sound Chap of NAHRO 1979-81; bd mem Tacom Urban League 1978-; mem NAACP 1978-; mem, vice pres Tacoma Alumnae Chap Delta Sigma Theta Sor 1979-81; mem Delta Sigma Theta Sor 1968-; mem Minority Concerns Task Force; mem Altrusa Intl 1981-, Kiwannianne 1984-86, ASPO, ICMA, APPA Task Force on Performance Indicators, Women in Govt 1984-, Accounting Advisory Comm. **HONORS/ACHIEVEMENTS:** RK Mellon Fellowship 1972; named Washington Potential Black Leader for the 1980's Northwest Conf of Black Pub Officials. **BUSINESS ADDRESS:** Management Analyst, Dept of Public Utilities, PO Box 11007, Tacoma, WA 98411.

BAUKNIGHT, TILLMAN
Dentist. **PERSONAL:** Born Nov 14, 1933, Cleveland, OH; married Vivian. **EDUCATION:** OH State U, 1957; Howard U, DDS 1964. **CAREER:** Self Employed, dentist; Ft Knox's Ireland Army Hosp, staff dent 1965-67; AUS, mil pol 1957-59. **ORGANIZATIONS:** Corp pres staff dent gen prac Dr Tillman Bauknight Dent Corp; past pres corp pres Drs Bauknight Bryant Gresham Reid & Co Coord Louis Stokes for Cong Com 8 yrs; mem Jimmy Carter Nat Fin Com 1 yr; chm bd SE Ren Inc 5 yrs co-chm tho ferguson for aud com 1 yr; mem Lee Harvard Area Civ Cncl 10 yrs; adv bd mem Oper Equal Urb League 8 yrs; camp mgr John Barnes for City Cndl. **HONORS/ACHIEVEMENTS:** Recpt Cleveland Bus League Inc; plaque for ded serv civ rhts; comm ldr am; list Who's Who in Am; sel Entrep of Yr Cleve Assn RE Brok Inc.

BAXTER, ALBERT JAMES, II
Government official, attorney. **PERSONAL:** Born Jun 22, 1935, Marshall, TX. **EDUCATION:** TN State Univ, BA 1956; TX So Univ, MA 1963, JD 1966; Attended, Univ of Denver Sch of Law, Univ of Madrid. **CAREER:** TX Southern Univ, instructor; FCC, attorney 1966-69, atty-advisor 1970-72, legal asst Comm Benjamin L Hooks 1972-76, asst chief cable TV bureau 1976-82; MA Media Bureau, 1982-85; Communications Consultant, 1985-. **ORGANIZATIONS:** Mem ABA, Fed Bar Assn, TX Bar Assn, DC Bar Assn; mem Omega Psi Phi Frat; Sigma Rho Sigma; Cedar Lane Theatre Group; part-time interior design consultant, Jarmon & Baxter. **HONORS/ACHIEVEMENTS:** Amer Law Student Assn Silver Medal 1966; winner of 3 Amer Jurisprudence Awds; starring roles "In White America", "The Fire Bugs". **MILITARY SERVICE:** USAF 1956-60. **BUSINESS ADDRESS:** Asst Chief Cable TV Bureau, Fed Comm Commission, 1919 M St NW, Washington, DC 20554.

BAXTER, AUGUSTUS, SR.
Business executive. **PERSONAL:** Born Dec 25, 1928, Philadelphia; married Dolores Hill; children: Deedra, Augustus, Jr, Donald, Stacey, Lisa. **EDUCATION:** Cheyney St Coll, BS, 1965. **CAREER:** Philadelphia Architects Workshop, pres, exec vp; Univ of Pennsylvania Sch of Fine Arts, staff; Philadelphia Big Bros Assn, cons, 1969-70; Primer for Comm Design Cntr, author, 1971; Philadelphia Housing Devel Corp, dir of comm serv, 1965-67; St Paul's Comm House Philadelphia, exec dir, 1961-65. **ORGANIZATIONS:** Lectr Royal Inst British Arch; mem Archit Assn; Ireland Archit Assn; Nat Assn Hsng Devel Officials 1970-; natl com Critical Minorities Problem Com; mem exec com Nat Urban Devel Cntr 1971-74; bd educ Sch Dist Philadelphia 1971-; bd dir Prints & Progress; bd Philadelphia Council for Com Advancement; 32 degree Mason; pres bd dir St Paul Comm House; vice pres bd dir Friend Nghbhd Guild; mem Philadelphia Civic Ballet. **HONORS/ACHIEVEMENTS:** Recip Whitney M Young Jr Cit 1973; hon APA awd Atlanta GA 1974; appointed by Philadelphia banks to study industrialized housing in London Stockholm CopenhagenParis 1971; rep Philadelphia Intl Expos 1976; England France Belguim Spain Africe 1971. **BUSINESS ADDRESS:** Philadelphia Architects, 401 N Broad, Ste 920, Philadelphia, PA 19108.

BAXTER, BELGIUM NATHAN
Clergyman. **PERSONAL:** Born Nov 03, 1921, Orangeburg, SC; married Augusta Ruth Byrd; children: Nathan, Charles, Larry. **EDUCATION:** Home Study Counseling 1970;

State and District Church Schools and Seminars 1960-85. **CAREER:** United Council of Churches, exec bd 1970; Faith Chapel Outreach Center, exec dir 1971-73; Hbg Adult Educ, bd member 1972-75; Hbg Bethesda Mission, bd member 1974-80; Neighborhood Center of UMC, staff member-counsellor 1973-83; Faith Chapel Church of God in Christ, pastor. **ORGANIZATIONS:** Pastor Faith Chapel Church of God in Christ 1953-85; state sect'y PA Churches of God in Christ 1965-85; Hbg dist supt Churches of God in Christ 1968-85. **HONORS/ACHIEVEMENTS:** Special achievement Office of Sec of Commonwealth 1971; special achievement Hbg Black Businessmen's Assn 1972; Martin Luther King Awd radio station WFEC 1980; Veteran's Acclaim Poet Laureate Gov Dick Thornburg 1980; special appreciation Pres Jimmy Carter 1980; special achievement PA House of Reps 1982; Publication of Pioneer Pastoral experience by Martin Luther King Fellows Press 1985. **MILITARY SERVICE:** AUS cpl-company clerk 2 yrs; Good Conduct Medal Meritorious Svs Awd 1945. **HOME ADDRESS:** 2213 Clayton Ave, Harrisburg, PA 17109.

BAXTER, CHARLES F., JR.
Physician. **PERSONAL:** Born Apr 23, 1959, Brooklyn, NY. **EDUCATION:** City College of NY, BS Chemistry 1981; Meharry Medical Coll, MD 1986. **CAREER:** Coll of Physicians & Surgeons of Columbia Univ, assoc fellow of surgery 1986-; Columbia Univ Coll of Physicians and Surgeons, surgical resident; Harlem Hospital Ctr, surgical resident. **ORGANIZATIONS:** Mem Amer Medical Assoc, Amer Chem Soc, The New York Acad of Sciences. **HONORS/ACHIEVEMENTS:** Minority Biomedical Studies Program CUNY Grant NIH 1979-81; Baskerville Chemistry Awd City Coll of New York 1981. **BUSINESS ADDRESS:** Surgical Resident, Harlem Hospital Center, 136th St and Lenox Ave, New York, NY 10037.

BAXTER, WENDY MARIE
Judge. **PERSONAL:** Born Jul 25, 1952, Detroit, MI; married David Ford Cartwright Jr; children: Samantha. **EDUCATION:** Eastern MI Univ, BBA 1973; Univ of Detroit School of Law, JD 1978. **CAREER:** General Motors, oil lease analyst 1977; Wayne Cty Criminal Bond, investigator 1978; Recorder's Court, court docket admin 1979; State Appellate Defender's Office, attny 1980; Private practice, attny 1982; 36th Dist Court, judge. **ORGANIZATIONS:** Bd of dir Wolverine Bar Assn, 1981; attny private practice Wendy M Baxter 1982; judge 36th Dist Court 1982; rules & forms committeewoman Dist Judges Assn 1982; 7th dist program dir Natl Assn of Women Judges 1985; life mem NAACP, Natl Bar Assoc, MI Assoc of Black Judges, State Bar of MI, Jim Dandies Ski Club. **HONORS/ACHIEVEMENTS:** Spirit of Detroit Detroit City Council 1981; Adoptive Parent Detroit Public School 1985. **BUSINESS ADDRESS:** Judge District Court, 36th Judicial Dist, 600 Randolph #132, Detroit, MI 48226.

BAXTER, ZENOBIA
Retired educator. **PERSONAL:** Born Feb 27, 1910, Shelbyville, TN; divorced; children: Frank IV. **EDUCATION:** Univ Chicago, PhB 1926; Chicago Coll Music, Mus B 1934; Northwestern Univ, MA 1942, post grad 1947; De Paul Univ 1949-50; Chicago Teachers Coll 1960-61; Northwestern Univ 1965. **CAREER:** Douglass Natl Bank of Chicago, bookkeeper/teller 1927-32, bookkeeper-in-charge 1932-36; Illinois, teacher 1936-38; Chicago Coll, teacher 1935-40; Ford Found, employment counselor 1959-63; Baxter Counseling, pres 1965-66; Chicago Bd of Edn, teacher counselor/guidance counselor 1938-72; Loyola Univ, educ lecturer 1965-72. **ORGANIZATIONS:** Mem R Nathaniel Dett Music Club 1935-50; NAACP 1935-70; Chicago Urban League 1950-60; NEA 1940-72; Amer Personnel & Guidance Assn 1942-72; Chicago Personnel & Guidance Assn 1942-72; Chmn Ctr COm S Parkway YWCA 1946-50; Univ of Chicago Alumni Assn, nw Univ Alumni Assn; Amer Assn of Retired Persons; Chicgo CHpt Nat'l Assn of Coll Women; Counselor Camp ILlini SUmmers 1951-53; sec 59th S Pkwy block & Club 1960-70; vol driver for Apolstolate of the Handicapped 1963-75; vol worker for travelers AId Soc 1963-; mem vols adv bd Travelers Aid SOc 1970-73,1976-79. **HONORS/ACHIEVEMENTS:** Silver Medal in piano contest Chicago Coll of Music 1933; Chicago Woman ofthe Year Natl Assn of Coll Women 1967; co author " Yoru Life in a Big City", 1967; Who's Who in Amer Women Recip, Award Outstanding Work in Educ Phi Beta Sigma Frat, Lola M Parker awd Iota Phi Lambda 1968; Nominated Sr Citizen of Year Chicago Mayors Comm 1976; Wrote & Publ natl song for Sigma Gamma Rho Sor, Scholarship named in honor "Zenobia Laws Baxter Scholarship" (mus/art/comm) Delta Sigma Chap of Sigma Gamma Rho Sor 1979.

BAYARD, FRANCK
Educator, economist. **PERSONAL:** Born Nov 05, 1917, Cayes; married Gislaine Duthier; children: Carole, Katia, Gislaine. **EDUCATION:** Univ of Haiti, LLB 1938; Howard Univ, MA 1962; Amer Univ, postgrad work 1962-66. **CAREER:** Army of Haiti, served from 2nd lt to col 1942-61; Washington, mil attach 1958-61; Washington Intl Center, lecturer 1961-62; Howard Univ, Washington DC, instructor Economics 1962-67; WV Wesleyan Coll, assoc prof chmn dept prof Economicss 1967-. **ORGANIZATIONS:** Mem Omicron Delta Epsilon; mem Omicron Delta Kappa; mem Pi Gamma Mu; mem Latin-Amer Ctr/Intl Social Rsch Cologne W Germany; Soc for Intl Devel; Amer Econ Assn Rsch with RW Logan Haiti & the Cominican Rep 1968. **HONORS/ACHIEVEMENTS:** Author "The Black Latin-Amer Impact on Western Culture" 1970; author "The Non-Orthodoxy of Latin-Amer Devel Thought" 1972; author "Haiti & the Other CaribbEcon" 1977; author "Recent Growth Trends in Energy Rich Region VII WV" 1978; author "Impact of WV Wesl Coll on Buckhannon's Economy" 1978; entry "Dictionaryof Amer Negro Biog 1980; author "WV's Region II Co, Past Growth Recent Prog Future Prospects" 1980. **BUSINESS ADDRESS:** West Virginia Wesleyan Coll, Buckhannon, WV 26201.

BAYE, LAWRENCE JAMES J.
Educator. **PERSONAL:** Born Oct 10, 1933, Houston, TX; children: Elizabeth Lenoa, Ursula Frances. **EDUCATION:** TX So U, BS, 1956, MS 1957; Univ of TX Austin, PhD Chem 1963; Univ of TN Knoxville, Post Dctrl Rsrch 1966. **CAREER:** TX Southern Univ Houston, asst prof Chemistry 1961-64; Knoxville Coll TN, assc prof dept head Chemistry 1964-67; Huston-Tillotson Coll Austin, TX, prof Chemistry 1967-. **ORGANIZATIONS:** Am Chem Scty; Scty of Sigma Xi; Beta Kappa Chi; Natl Org Prof Adv of Black Chemsts/Chem Eng 1980-; Blck Ctzns Task Force 1978-; Phi Beta Sigma Frat 1955-. **HONORS/ACHIEVEMENTS:** Rcpnt Robt A Welch Fndtn Rsrch Grnts; author 14 pblctns in Jour Am Chem Soc & other Major Chem Jrnls 1956-. **HOME ADDRESS:** 1729 E 38 1/2 St, Austin, TX 78722. **BUSINESS ADDRESS:** Professor of Chemistry, Huston-Tillotson Coll, 1820 E 8th St, Austin, TX 78702.

BAYLESS, PAUL CLIFTON
Educational administrator. **PERSONAL:** Born Nov 25, 1935, West Mansfield, OH. **EDUCATION:** OH State Univ Coll of Engrg, BIE (summa cum laude) 1966; OH State Univ, MSc 1970; Purdue Univ, post grad work. **CAREER:** Purdue Univ, facilities planning analyst 1966-74, assoc coord for space 1974-78, dir affirmative action 1978-. **ORGANIZATIONS:** Bd dirs Capsulated Systems Inc Yellow Springs OH 1974-; chmn Intl Assn 1975-77; facilities consult JF Blakesley & Assoc; mem Amer Assn for Advancement Sci 1977-; mem Amer Assn for Affirmative Action 1977-; mem Natl Tech Assn 1978-; Phi Eta Sigma; OH State Univ 1955; Alpha Pi Mu (Indus Engr Hon) OH State Univ 1965; Tau Beta Pi (Engr Hon) OH State Univ 1966; Phi Kappa Phi Purdue Univ 1973. **MILITARY SERVICE:** USNG capt 1957-66. **BUSINESS ADDRESS:** Dir of Affirmative Action, Purdue University, 401 S Grant St, West Lafayette, IN 47907.

BAYLOR, DON EDWARD
Professional athlete. **PERSONAL:** Born Jun 28, 1949, Austin, TX; children: Don Jr. **EDUCATION:** Miami Dade Jr Clge; Blinn Jr Clge Brenham TX. **CAREER:** Baltimore Orioles, 1970-75; Oakland A'S, 1976; CA Angels, 1977-82; NY Yankees, 1982-86; Boston Red Sox 1986-. **ORGANIZATIONS:** Raised money for Cystic Fibrosis Fnd the last 6 seasons. **HONORS/ACHIEVEMENTS:** 1985 winner Roberto Clemente Award; established major league record for most times caught stealing, inning, 2, June 15, 1974 (9th Inning); tied major league records for most long hits, most consecutive home runs; tied modern major league record for most at bats; tied AL record for most hits, two consecutive games; hit three home runs in a game 1975; led AL in sacrifice flies with 12; led AL in being hit by pitch with 13 in 1973, 20 in 1976, 18 in 1978, 23 in 1984, and tied for lead ith 13 in 1975; led intl League in being hit by pitch with 19 in 19 70 and 16 in 1971; led Intl League in total bases with 296 in 1970; led TX League in being hit by pitch with 13 in 1969; named AL MVP by Baseball Writers' Assc of Amer 1979; named AL Player of the Year by Sporting News 1979; named Appalachian League Player of Year 1967; named Minor L league Player of the Year by Sporting News 1970. **BUSINESS ADDRESS:** Boston Red Sox, Fenway Park, Boston, MA 02215.

BAYLOR, ELGIN
Professional athlete. **PERSONAL:** Born Sep 1934; married Elaine; children: Krystle. **EDUCATION:** Idaho, attended; Seattle Univ, attended. **CAREER:** Minneapolis Lakers, player 1958; Los Angeles Clippers, played and coached; New Orleans Jazz, asst coach 1974-77, coached 1978-79; Basketball Operations, executive vice pres 1986. **HONORS/ACHIEVEMENTS:** NBA's seventh all-time leading scoror; Rookie of the Year 1959; Co-MVP of the All-Star Game; Holds number of records for the most points scored in championshipseries, most field goals, most points in one half; Seventh Highest single-game point total in NBA History; mem Basketball Hall of Fame 1976. **BUSINESS ADDRESS:** c/o Los Angeles Clippers, 3939 Figueroa, Los Angeles, CA 90037.

BAYLOR, EMMETT R., JR.
Director. **PERSONAL:** Born Oct 18, 1933, New York, NY; married Margaret E; children: Kathryn R, Gladys E, Emmett R III, Steven G. **EDUCATION:** Wayne Cty Communn Coll, AA. **CAREER:** Maidenform, 1st black salesman 1963-75; Metro Life, sales rep 1975-77; Detroit Corrections Dept, dep dir 1977-81, dir 1981-. **HONORS/ACHIEVEMENTS:** Top 10 Salesman 1971-72; Top 15 Salesman 1967-70,73; Rookie of the Year Outstanding Sales & Service 1976.

BAYLOR, SOLOMON
Judge. **PERSONAL:** Born Apr 25, 1922, King William, VA; married Dr Ernestein Walker; children: Michael J, Michelle J Miles. **EDUCATION:** Coppin St Coll, 1939-42; Univ of MD, LLB 1951; Natl Judic Coll, Cert 1977 & 1979. **CAREER:** Mayor & City Council, asst city solicitor 1963-67, bd municipal & zoning appeals 1968-70; State of MD, judge dist ct 1970-78; Sup Bench of Baltimore City, assoc judge 1970-retirement. **ORGANIZATIONS:** Mem Natl Bar Assn; mem Monumental City Bar Assn; mem MD State Bar Assn; mem Engrg Soc of Baltimore Inc; mem Citizens Plan & Housing Assn; life mem NAACP. **HONORS/ACHIEVEMENTS:** Cert of Recogn Sunday Sch Bapt Training Union of MD; Cert of Recogn of Serv Enon Bapt Ch; Cert Greater Univ of MD Fund; Citation of Recogn Baltimore Area Counc Boy Scouts of Amer; Golden Heritage Citation NAACP; Citation Minority Scholarship & Leadership Guild Univ of MD for Outstanding Contribution Commitment & Generous Support 1986; Salute from Centennial United Methodist Church 1986. **MILITARY SERVICE:** AUS Corpl 1943-46; Good Conduct Medal WWII Victory Ribbon Battle of Normandy 1943-46; Citation 272nd Quatermaster Battalion & 4086 Quartermaster Co Vets for Unselfish Dedication & Devotion 1983.

BAYNE, HENRY G.
Microbiologist, priest. **PERSONAL:** Born Dec 02, 1925, New York, NY; married Gloria Loftin; children: Steven, Lisa, Gordon. **EDUCATION:** Brooklyn Coll, BA 1949, MA 1954. **CAREER:** Fellow in Biology, 1951-53; Brooklyn Coll, sanitarian 1953-55; New York City Dept of Health, bacteriologist 1955; St Mark's Episcopal Ch, assoc pastor 1963-; Mission of the Holy Spirit Episcopal Ch, vicar 1968-82; Western Regional Rsch Ctr Agr Rsch Serv, rsch microbiologist 1955-87. **ORGANIZATIONS:** Mem Standing Com Diocese of CA 1978-82, pres 1981-82; chmn Epis Diocese of CA Comm on Interracial & Ethnic Affairs 1977-79; mem Amer Soc for Microbiology; mem Amer Soc of Plant Psysiologists; AAAS; mem Alpha Phi Omega; Episcopal Conf of the Deaf; bd mem E Bay Counseling & Referral Agency for Deaf 1969-72; bd mem St Dorothy's Rest Assn 1966-70; mem bd Alzheimer's Disease and Related Disorders 1982-. **HONORS/ACHIEVEMENTS:** Harold Ramger Awd E Bay Counseling Agency for the Deaf 1973. **MILITARY SERVICE:** AUS 1944-46. **BUSINESS ADDRESS:** Microbiologist, Agr Rsch Service, 800 Buchanan St, Albany, CA 94704.

BAZIL, RONALD
Educator. **PERSONAL:** Born Mar 10, 1937, Brooklyn; married Bonnie; children: Lance, Tami. **EDUCATION:** Springfield Coll, BS 1958; Brooklyn Coll, MS 1964. **CAREER:** United States Military Acad, coach; Adelphi Univ, dir of intercoll athl 1972-; assoc dean of students 1970-72; dean of mem 1969-70; asst dean of student 1968-69; Health Educ, teacher 1959-68. **ORGANIZATIONS:** Mem exec council ECAC; pres exec council ICA; mem Concerned Cit of Westbury. **HONORS/ACHIEVEMENTS:** Indoor coach of yr USTFF 1974. **MILITARY SERVICE:** AUS reserve sp4 1958-63. **BUSINESS ADDRESS:** United States Military Acad, ODIA, West Point, NY 10996.

BAZILE, LEO
Public administrator. **CAREER:** Council District 7, Oakland, CA, council member. **BUSINESS ADDRESS:** 1 City Hall Plaza, Oakland, CA 94612. *

BEACH, WALTER G., II
Business executive. **PERSONAL:** Born Jul 23, Cataula, GA; married Marian C; children: Pennie, Pamela, Walter III, Bradford. **EDUCATION:** Univ of WI, BS Educ 1975; Marquette Univ Law Colloquium 1974-75; Univ of WI Law Sch, addtl studies. **CAREER:** Restaurant owner, 1963-64; news director; spec agent insurance; acting asst mgr dept store; Channel 18 (TV), news reporter 1974; WAWA AM & FM Radio, news &pub affairs dir. **ORGANIZATIONS:** Past pres local NAACP; chmn State Polit Action; pres/founder The New Image Concept Inc; pres Criminal Justice Assn Univ of WI; mem chmn NAACP; mem State Police Examining Bd;TV producer/v chmn Soc of Black Drama Heritage Inc; co-founder Com of Twenty-One; managing ed Harambee Newspaper; adv mgr Milwaukee Torch Newspaper; feature writer Echo Mag; mem steering com Model Cities; mem Midtown Kiwanis Club; Sickle Cell Anemia Found. **HONORS/ACHIEVEMENTS:** Man of the Year 1971; Youth Image Maker 1973; Congress Award 1974. **MILITARY SERVICE:** AUS; USN; Natl Guard. **BUSINESS ADDRESS:** News & Public Affairs Dir, WAWA AM & FM Radio, PO Box 2385, Milwaukee, WI 53212.

BEACHEM, CONSTANCE
Librarian, educator. **PERSONAL:** Born Jul 16, 1921, Washington, DC; children: Novert, Wimberly, William Wimberly, Ellen McKee, Emmanuel Humphries, Lincoln Beachem, Connie J. **EDUCATION:** AZ State Univ, BA 1964, MA 1966. **CAREER:** Phoenix Elementary School Dist, librarian 1964-. **ORGANIZATIONS:** Exec com AZ Educ Assn 1975-; bd dir NEA 1979-82; comm const NEA Bylaws-Rules 1979-84; mem AZ Educ Assn 1962-; mem Alpha Kappa Sor; mem NAACP; pres Cath Family & Comm Serv Diocese Phoenix 1978-80; mem Human Devel Counsel; dep registrar AZ Libr Assn. **BUSINESS ADDRESS:** Librarian, Dunbar School, 125 E Lincoln St, Phoenix, AZ 85004-2539.

BEACHEM, WILLIAM PERRY
Business executive. **PERSONAL:** Born May 04, 1932, E StLouis, IL; divorced; children: 3 children. **EDUCATION:** UCLA, Cert in Real Estate; CRB Educ Prog, Cert of Completion; Action in Real Estate Sales Course; Educ Prog in Real Estate. **CAREER:** Private Practice, promoter/mgr of entertainers; Brokerage Firm, former assoc broker/gen mgr; Great Western Investment Co, realtor 1960-; Bill Beachem & Assoc, pres. **ORGANIZATIONS:** Lectr on real estate & land invest/devel; mem Consol Realty Bd of Los Angeles Inc; CA Assn of Real Estate Brokers; Housing Com of Watts Model City; mem Atty Gen's Adv Council; mem DA's Adv Cncl & Curriculum Adv Com for LA Trade Tech Coll; mem Crucial Urban Issues Com; LA Co Urban League Inc of CA; Ancient Arabic Order of the Mystic Shrine Inc; Guidance Ch of Religious Sci; organizer/pres Black Rep Polit Educ Cncl of CA; apptd by Gov to Dept of Professional & Vocational Standards as pub mem on bd of Barber Examiners 1968; co-chmn Gov Minority Appointees Workshop Housing Comm. **HONORS/ACHIEVEMENTS:** First Black mem in state's history apptd by Gov to CA Real Estate Commn 1970; Recip Outstanding Citizen's Award Urban League; Back Patter's Citation Men of Tomorrow Inc. **BUSINESS ADDRESS:** President, Beachem Enterprises, 8703 LaTijera Blvd, Ste 209, Los Angeles, CA 90045.

BEAL, JACQUELINE JEAN
Banker. **PERSONAL:** Born Mar 06, 1960, Jamaica, NY; divorced. **EDUCATION:** DePaul Univ, BS 1982. **CAREER:** Amer Natl Bank, office occupations student 1977-78; The Northern Trust Co, inroads intern 1978-82, sr mktg rep 1981-84, financial serv officer/territorial mgr 1985-. **ORGANIZATIONS:** Grad chap mem Delta Sigma Theta Sor 1982-; policy setting bd mem Alumni Rep Inroads Inc 1983-87; mem Chicago Urban Bankers Assoc 1987-, Chicago League of Black Women 1987-; alumna Inroads Alumni Assoc 1987-; bd representative, Natl Inroads Alumni Assn. **HONORS/ACHIEVEMENTS:** Inroads Alumni Period Awd Inroads Inc 1985; Chicago's Up and Coming Black Business & Professional Women Awd Dollars & Sense magazine 1986. **BUSINESS ADDRESS:** Second Vice President, Cash Management Sales, Northern Trust Company, 125 S Wacker, Chicago, IL 60675.

BEALE, LARRY D.
Attorney,. **PERSONAL:** Born May 12, 1949, Southampton Cty, VA; married Patricia Warren; children: Patrice Luanda, Stefani Mandela. **EDUCATION:** VA Plytchnc Inst St U, BS Soc & Polit Sci 1971; Vlprs Univ Sch of Law, JD 1975. **CAREER:** Beale & Fleming, general legal practice 1982-; Beale Green & Hogan, gen legal practice 1980-82; Asso at Law, gen lgl prac 1977-80; Lgl Aid Soc of Lsvl,staff atty 1975-77; City of Gary IN, lgl adv intern law dept 1974-75, lgl intern lgl aid soc 1974. **ORGANIZATIONS:** Gen counsel Louisville Bd of Aldermen 1982-; asst dir of law City of Lsvl 1978-; exec dir KNBA Inmt Grvnc Mech; bd of dir Lsvl Br NAACP 1976; pres KY Nat Bar Assn; mem KY Bar Assn Lsvl 1975. **HONORS/ACHIEVEMENTS:** Rockefeller Grant; Reginald Heber Smithfellow; Louisville Natl Assoc of Real Estate Brokers Attorney of the Year Awd 1985. **BUSINESS ADDRESS:** Attorney, Beale & Fleming, 608 W Muhammad, Ste 403, Louisville, KY 40203.

BEAM, LILLIAN KENNEDY
Educational administrator. **PERSONAL:** Born Mar 17, 1924, Knoxville, TN; married Loudin J Beam; children: Loudin Jr, David, Susan Cooper, James, Mary, Robert. **EDUCATION:** OH State Univ, BA Engl 1947; San Diego State Univ, MA Engl 1970; US Intl Univ, PhD Human Behavior/Educ Leadership 1975. **CAREER:** San Diego State US Intl Univ, adj prof 4 years; San Diego Comm Coll Adult Center, dean 3 years; San Diego Comm Coll Dist, exec asst to chancellor 5 years, dir mgmt & support serv 5 years, pres Educ Cultural Complex. **ORGANIZATIONS:** Pres Gov's Commn on Vocational Edn; mem Assn of CA Comm Coll Adminstrn; mem San Diego Comm Colls Adminstr Assn; mem Amer Assn for Affirmative Action; mem Phi Beta Kappa OH State Univ 1948; mem Phi Delta Kappa San Diego State Univ 1969. **HONORS/ACHIEVEMENTS:** Woman of the Year Award San Diego 1976; Woman of Achievement Award San Diego 1976. **BUSINESS ADDRESS:** President, San Diego Community College, 3375 Camino del Rio S, Cultural Complex, San Diego, CA 92108.

BEAN, MAURICE DARROW
Ambassador. **PERSONAL:** Born Sep 09, 1928, Gary, IN; married Dolores Winston; children: Linda D, Karen M, Laura L, James W, Jennifer J. **EDUCATION:** Howard Univ, BA 1950; Haverford Coll, MA 1954; Johns Hopkins Univ, Cert 1959. **CAREER:** Foreign Operations Admin, Djakarta, Indonesia, program asst, 1951-53 & 1954-56; Intl Coop Adminstrn, asst, Laos desk officer, 1956-59; USOM Thailand, Bankok, asst program planning officer, 1959-61; Far East Peace Corps, dep reg dir, 1961-64, Phillipines, dir, 1964-66; Dept State, Malaysia, Singapore, country dir, 1966-70; Amer Embassy, Monrovia, Liberia, dep chief mission; Burma/Rangoon, ambassador. **ORGANIZATIONS:** Life mem Royal Bankok Sports Club; mem Omega Psi Phi Frat; Urban League; The Smithsonian Assn; mem Amer Foreign Serv Assoc, Amer Sch Assoc. **HONORS/ACHIEVEMENTS:** Christopher Reynolds Found Fellow 1953; Wm E Moshee Meml Scholarship 1961; Roosevelt Alumni Assn Achievement Award 1967; Outstanding Serv Awd Gary Host and Hostess Club 1979; Benjamin Hooks Awd NAACP 1980; named to Roosevelt HS Hall of Fame 1980. **BUSINESS ADDRESS:** State Department, AU/CAS Bldg 1401, Maxwell AFB, AL 36112.

BEAN, WALTER DEMPSEY
Retired educational administrator. **PERSONAL:** Born Oct 16, 1912, Midway, KY; son of James Ennis Bean and Lula G Rollins Bean; married Minnie Peck, Jan 02, 1982; children: Kenneth, Patricia Jenkins. **EDUCATION:** Kentucky State Univ, BS 1935; Butler Univ, MS 1954, Masters plus 30 hrs, 1960. **CAREER:** Indianapolis Public Schools, teacher 1935-56, asst principal & principal 1957-66, supvr personnel accounting 1966-68, supvr elementary teacher placement 1968-71, coord recruitment placement teacher personnel 1971-78. **ORGANIZATIONS:** First black & charter mem Phi Delta Kappa Fraternity Butler Univ 1956; 2nd black mem USA Amer Assn of School Personnel Admin 1966-78; various offices Assn of School, Coll & Univ Staff IN 1971-78; NAACP 1938-; Kappa Alpha Psi Fraternity 1935; life mem Kappa Alpha Psi Fraternity 1935-; advisory comm Red Cross Indianapolis Chapter 1961-66; mem Medicare Splmnt Advisory Group Blue Cross Blue Shield IN 1983-; Advisory Comm United Methodist Church 1970-75. **HONORS/ACHIEVEMENTS:** Annual Achievement Award, Kappa Alpha Psi Fraternity Indianapolis Alumni 1966; 1st Black Teacher Recruiter, Indianapolis Public School & IN Admin 1968; 2nd Black Teacher Recruiter, US Amer Assn of School Personnel 1968; IN Dist Citizen Award, Black Bicentennial Comm 1976; Certificate of Achievement Award, Kentucky State Univ Indianapolis Alumni 1981; IN Chamber of Commerce and Center for Leadership Development, Inc, Lifetime Achievement Award 1986; Kentucky State Univ Alumni Assn, selected one of 100 outstanding alumni 1986. **HOME ADDRESS:** Meridian Towers East, 25 E 40th St, Apt 3K, Indianapolis, IN 46205.

BEANE, PATRICIA JEAN
Educator. **PERSONAL:** Born Jan 13, 1944, Massillon, OH; married Frank Llewellyn; children: Frank Clarence II, Adam Tyler. **EDUCATION:** Ashland Coll OH, BS 1966. **CAREER:** Akron City Schools, teacher 1966-67; Massillon City Schools, teacher 1967-. **ORGANIZATIONS:** Mem Doris L Allen Minority Caucus 1984; mem Massillon Business & Professional Women 1977-80; mem Massillon Youth Ctr Bd of Trustees 1984; mem NEA 1966-76, 1979-; mem OH Educ Assn 1966-76, 1979-; mem E Cent OH Tchrs Assn 1966-76, 1979-; mem Massilon Educ Assn 1966-76, 1979-; mem Akron Symphony Chorus 1966-67; mem Canton Civic Opera Chorus 1969-79; sec bd of trustees Massillon YWCA 1972-76; mem Massillon Bus & Professional Women 1977-; mem OH Assn of Colored Women's Clubs 1978-; mem Natl Assn of Colored Women's Clubs 1978-; mem regional & local women's clubs. **HONORS/ACHIEVEMENTS:** Who's Who Among Students in Amer Univs & Colls 1965-66; guest soloist w/various choirs. **BUSINESS ADDRESS:** Teacher, Massillon City School, 724 Walnut St, Massillon, OH 44646.

BEANE, ROBERT HUBERT
County government official. **PERSONAL:** Born Mar 04, 1947, New York, NY; son of Sidney Beane and Lorrain Braithwaite; divorced; children: Craig J. **EDUCATION:** Fordham Univ College at Lincoln Center, BA 1974, Fordham Univ Grad School of Social Service, MSW 1976. **CAREER:** Mt Vernon Community Action Group; Westchester Comm Opportunity Prog, exec dir 1970-73; Westchester Urban Coalition, program dir 1973-74; Alcohelp Program, research & evaluation specialist 1974-76; Westchester County, program specialist 1976, Dept of Mental Health, center administrator 1976-79, asst to commissioner 1979-83, dir community service 1983-. **ORGANIZATIONS:** Comm for Protection of Human Subj NY Med Coll, mem 1980-; City of Yonkers Board of Education, trustee 1983-93, vice president 1983-93. **HONORS/ACHIEVEMENTS:** Alpha Sigma Lambda 1974; Woodrow Wilson Foundation, MLK fellow 1975 & 1976. **MILITARY SERVICE:** USAF, AFC. **HOME ADDRESS:** 412-13 North Broadway, Yonkers, NY 10701. **BUSINESS ADDRESS:** Director, Comm Service Oper, Westchester Cnty Dept of, Community Mental Health, 112 E Post Rd, White Plains, NY 10601.

BEARD, BUTCH
Athlete, assistant coach. **PERSONAL:** Born May 04, 1947, Hardinburg, KY. **EDUCATION:** Louisville Coll, 1969. **CAREER:** Atlanta Hawks, basketball player 1969-70; Seattle Supersonics, basketball player 1972-73; Golden State Warriors, basketball player 1973-74; Cleveland Cavaliers, basketball player 1971-72 & 1975-76; NY Knicks, professional basketball player 1975-78, asst coach 1978-. **HONORS/ACHIEVEMENTS:** Floor Leader playing in all 82 games & averaging approx 13 pts per game when Golden State Warriors won world championship 1974; NBA All-Star Game 1972. **BUSINESS ADDRESS:** Assistant Coach, New York Knicks, Madison Sq Garden, 4 Pennsylvania Plaza, New York, NY 10001.

BEARD, CHARLES JULIAN
Attorney. **PERSONAL:** Born Dec 24, 1943, Detroit, MI; son of James F Beard and Ethel C Beard; divorced. **EDUCATION:** Harvard Coll, AB 1966; Law School, JD 1969. **CAREER:** Boston Model City Program, asst admin comm serv 1970-74; Foley Hoag Eliot, associate 1974-78, partner 1979-. **ORGANIZATIONS:** Mem Gov's Judicial Nom Comm 1976-79; mem Commonwealth Housing Found 1975-; chmn bd trust Dr SC Fuller Comm; mem Mental Health Corp 1975-80; 2nd vice pres Boston NAACP 1976-79; dir Broadcast Capital Fund, Washington DC 1979-; trust Roxbury Comm Coll found 1985-; trust The Partnership Inc 1986-; dir Blue Cross of MA Inc 1986-; trustee Emerson Coll 1987-; trustee Boston Community Access and Programming Foundation 1981-. **BUSINESS ADDRESS:** Partner, Foley, Hoag & Eliot, One Post Office Square, Boston, MA 02109.

BEARD, ISRAEL
Educator. **PERSONAL:** Born Jun 27, 1932, Cairo, IL; married Gwendolyn Etherly; children: Lori L. **EDUCATION:** Lane Coll, BA 1958; Univ of WI-Milwaukee, MS 1973; Nova Univ, EdD 1980. **CAREER:** State Voc Training School, counselor 1958-59; Stigall HS, teacher 1959-61; Story School, teacher 1961-68; Opportunities Indust, dir 1968-69; Milwau-

kee Area Tech Coll, prof 1969-. **ORGANIZATIONS:** Pres Kappa Alpha Psi Frat 1968-70; pres Milwaukee Frontiers Intl 1975-78; thetsauristes Sigma Pi Phi Frat 1983; broker United Realty Co; mem Amer Vocational Assoc, WI Vocational Assoc; treas bd of dirs Child Comprehensive Day Care. **HONORS/ACHIEVEMENTS:** Presidential Awd Frontiers Intl 1976,77; Meritorious Awd Lane Coll 1981; Disting men of Milwaukee Top Ladies of Distinction 1986. **MILITARY SERVICE:** AUS corpl 3 yrs; Combat Infantry Badge, Good Conduct Medal 1952-55. **HOME ADDRESS:** 9619 W Beechwood, Milwaukee, WI 53224. **BUSINESS ADDRESS:** Professor of Basic Educ, Milwaukee Area Tech College, 1015 No 6th St, Milwaukee, WI 53224.

BEARD, JAMES WILLIAM, JR.
Attorney, educator. **PERSONAL:** Born Sep 16, 1941, Chillicothe, OH; married Gail LaVerne Rivers; children: James III, Ryan Jamail, Kevin Jarrard. **EDUCATION:** Hardin-Simmons Univ, BS 1967; TX So Univ, JD 1973; Univ of TX, LLM 1976. **CAREER:** Thurgood Marshall Law School, TX Southern Univ, assoc prof of law, assoc dean for academic affairs & programs, dir fed tax clinic. **ORGANIZATIONS:** Mem Amer Bar Assn, State Bar of TX; bd of govs Natl Bar Assn; chmn Sect of Taxation NBA; mem NAACP; past trust Houston Legal Found. **HONORS/ACHIEVEMENTS:** Outstanding Young Amer for 1977. **MILITARY SERVICE:** USAF A/2c 1959-63. **BUSINESS ADDRESS:** Assoc Prof Law/Dean Acad Aff, Thurgood Marshall Law Sch, TX Southern University, 3100 Cleburne, Houston, TX 77004.

BEARD, LARONCE D.
Attorney. **PERSONAL:** Born Jun 07, 1949, Augusta, GA. **EDUCATION:** Harvard Law Sch, JD 1975. **CAREER:** GA Legal Svcs, stf atty 1977-80. **BUSINESS ADDRESS:** Attorney, 1862 Central Ave, Augusta, GA 30904.

BEARD, LILLIAN MCLEAN
Physician. **PERSONAL:** Born in New York, NY; married DeLawrence Beard. **EDUCATION:** Howard Univ Coll of Liberal Arts, BS 1965; Howard Univ Coll of Medicine, MD 1970; Children's Hosp Natl Med Ctr, pediatric internship, residency, fellowship 1970-73. **CAREER:** Mary McLeod Bethune Infant Educ Ctr, pediatric consult 1972-73; Adams Comm Sch, sch hlth coord 1972-73; Children's Hosp Natl Med Ctr, child hlth ctr, pediatrician 1972-73; Burroughs Elem Sch, child dvlp consult 1972-73; Tubman Elem Sch, child dvlp consult 1972-73; Shaed Elem Sch, child dvlp consult 1972-73; HowardUnivUniv Without Walls, spec lecturer & pediatric consult 1972-73; Children's Hosp Natl Med Ctr, dir 1973-75; Geo WashUniv Sch of Med Dept ChildHlth & Dvlp, assoc clinical prof 1982; Howard U, clinical preceptor 1978-79; CatholicUniv Grad Sch of Nrsng, adj asst clinical prof 1978-82; HowardUniv Coll of Med, asst clinical prof 1979; private practice, pedatrician 1973-. **ORGANIZATIONS:** Bd of advisors The Women's Natl Bank of the Dist of Columbia 1980-; chmn nutrition task force Amer Acad of Pediatrics 1979-80; media spokesperson "Speak Up for Young People" Prog 1982-83 1983-84; various positions Amer Medical Women's Assn; admissions comm Geo Washington Univ Sch of Medicine 1978-; adv bd Dist of Columbia Gymnasts Inc 1977-81; bd dirs Family & Medical Counseling Serv Inc 1977-; adv bd Head Start Prog for the Washington Metro Area 1976-77; bd dirs Washington Home for Foundlings, 1972-79; mem med Soc of the Dist of Columbia; bd dirs Comm Psychiatric Clinic; life mem NAACP; mem Natl Urban League of Washington DC; mem Natl Medical Assn; mem Links Inc. **HONORS/ACHIEVEMENTS:** Presentations, Fast Food/Fast Society; Nutrition Prenatal Through The First Year of Life Motherhood Celebration Convention Seattle 1983; Counseling the Breast Feeding Mother Panelist Ross Laboratories Roundtable Chicago report published 1980; Innovative Approaches for Communicating w/Adolescents "Staying Alive" Adolescent Workshop 1979; One Pediatrician's Approach, The Role of the Pediatrician in Diagnosing Children With Learning Disabilities presented at the Intl Conf of the Assn for Children w/Learning Disabilities Washington 1977; Ann Bartsch Dunne Scholarship Awd 1968-69 1969-70; Dept Awd Dept of Obstetrics & Gynecology 1970; Citation Dept of Medicine 1970; Citation Dept of Pediatrics 1970; Sr Class Awd 1970; diplomate Natl Bd of Medical Examiners 1971; diplomate Amer Bd of Pediatrics 1976; 4 Awds Amer Medical Assn; Outstanding Young Women of Amer 1977; Comm Leaders and Noteworthy Amer Awd 1978; MD's Outstanding Young Women For the Yr 1979; One of the Ten Outstanding Young Women of Amer for 1979; Who's Who of Amer Women; Who's Who in the East; Directory of Amer Medical Specialists. **BUSINESS ADDRESS:** Assoc Prof Child Health, George Washington University, 5505 5th St NW, Washington, DC 20011.

BEARD, MARTIN LUTHER
Physician, educator. **PERSONAL:** Born Jul 15, 1926, Forrest Co, MS; married Delores; children: Myrna, Martin Jr. **EDUCATION:** Tougaloo Coll, BS 1953; Meharry Med Coll, MD 1960. **CAREER:** Kate B Reynolds Meml Hosp, intern 1960-61, resident 1961-64; Minneapolis VA Hosp, fellow 1964-67; MI State Univ, asst clinical prof 1967-; Private Practice, physician. **ORGANIZATIONS:** Dipl Amer Bd Surgery; fellow Amer Coll Surgeons; mem Optimist; Omega Psi Phi. **HONORS/ACHIEVEMENTS:** First Place Honor Award Excellence in Med Writing Bd MN Med 1969. **BUSINESS ADDRESS:** Assistant Clinical Professor, MI State University, 4250 N Saginaw, Flint, MI 48505.

BEARD, MELVIN CHARLES
Dentist. **PERSONAL:** Born Oct 28, 1935, Mobile, AL; married Patricia Ane Crawford; children: Kimberly, Melvin III. **EDUCATION:** TN A&I State U, BA 1958; Tuskepee Inst, MEd 1964; Howard U, DDS 1968; Univ of MI, MPH 1974; FAGD, Flwshp 1983; FRSH, Flwshp 1971; FADI, Flwshp 1984. **CAREER:** Syracuse NH Ctr, dntl dir 1969-72, admin 1971-72; Auburn Corr Facilty, dntl dir 1976-84; NYS Hlth Dept, rgnl hlth dir. **ORGANIZATIONS:** Affrmtv acct offcr CNY Hlth Syst Agncy 1981-; prnsl chprsn comm CNY Hlth Syst Agncy 1978-81; pres Syracuse Blck Ldrshp Congress 1983-85, Alpha Phi Alpha Frat 1978-84. **HONORS/ACHIEVEMENTS:** Pub Serv Awrd Natl Dntl Assn 1980; fellow Royal Scty/Hlth 1971, Acad Genl Dnstry 1983, Acad Dntl Intl 1984. **MILITARY SERVICE:** AUS spy 2 yrs; Hon Dschrg Battalion Rifle Tm Awrd 1964. **BUSINESS ADDRESS:** Regional Health Dir, NYS Hlth Dept, 499 S Warren St, Syracuse, NY 13208.

BEARD, MONTGOMERY, JR.
Real estate broker, company executive. **PERSONAL:** Born May 08, 1932, Brownsville, TN; son of Montgomery Beard and Hellen Beard; married Lou Etta Outlaw; children: Valencia Monetta, Helen Veronica, Michael Keith, Montgomery III. **EDUCATION:** TN State Univ, BS 1960, MS 1960. **CAREER:** Maury County Bd Educ, dir guidance & counseling 1959-64; Jewish Vocational Svc, counseling supvr 1964-68; Kansas City Reg Council for Higher Educ, dir student affairs 1968-69; Educ Projects Inc, exec assn, 1969-70; Natl Planning Assn, sr rsch assoc 1970-72; Intl Mgmt Resources Inc, vice pres 1973-76; Beard Enterprises Inc, CEO, 1989-present; Agent LTD, CEO, 1989-present. **ORGANIZATIONS:** Mem Amer Personnel & Guidance Assn; Amer Vocational Assn; chmn bd commrs Housing Auth Prince Georges Co 1972-76; candidate ho dels State MD Legislature 26th dist; chmn Zoning Comm; pres Millwood-Waterford Civic Assn 1975-77; mem Phi Beta Sigma Fraternity Inc; PTA; Upper Room Baptist Church; former com Boy Scouts; founder past pres Prince Georges Black Rep Club; former mem State Central Com Rep Party; past vice pres So Prince George Rep Club; mem, Young Reps; mem, bd of dirs, Prince Georges County Public Schools, Occupational Skills Found, 1987-present. **MILITARY SERVICE:** USN 1951-55. **BUSINESS ADDRESS:** President, Beard Enterprises Inc, 510 Millwheel St, Capitol Heights, MD 20743.

BEARD, VIRGINIA H.
Administrator. **PERSONAL:** Born Sep 09, 1941, St Louis, MO; married Otis C Beard; children: Bostic Charles, Bonji Lucille. **EDUCATION:** Harris Tchrs Coll, BA Educ 1964; So IL U, MS Guidnc 1968; St Louis U, PhD Cnslr Educ 1974. **CAREER:** St Louis Public Schools, teacher 1964-68; Univ City Public Schools, counselor 1968-72; St Louis Juvenile Center, behavoral counselor 1974-76; SLU Medical School, comm coord 1976-77; KingFanon Mental Health Center, acting dir 1977-78; Center Urban Living, exec dir 1978-80; Yeatman Un Sarah Mental Health Center, dir psychological services; dir student services, Clayton School Dist. **ORGANIZATIONS:** Thrpst Professional Cnslng Grp 1984-; mem Am Psych Assn 1977-; Am Assn Cnslng & Dvlpmnt 1985-; Adv Cncl KSDK-TV Comm Adv Bd 1982-; bd dir Annie Malone Chldrns Hm 1977-84; North City Am Cncr Scty 1983-; Conf on Educ 1980-Pres; mem Coalition 100 Blck wmn 1984-; Alpha Kappa Alpha. **HONORS/ACHIEVEMENTS:** Ford Fndtn Flw St Louis Univ Dctrl Stdy 1972-73; Gerontolgy Flw St Louis Univ Inst Appld Grntlgy 1973-74; Flw Ldrshp St Louis 1984-85; Co-author Cnslng Enhancing Well Being in Later Yrs 1982. **HOME ADDRESS:** 890 Berick Dr, St Louis, MO 63132. **BUSINESS ADDRESS:** Dir Student Services, Clayton School District, 7530 Maryland, St Louis, MO 63105.

BEASLEY, ALICE MARGARET
Attorney. **PERSONAL:** Born Apr 27, 1945, Tuskegee, AL. **EDUCATION:** Marygrove Coll Detroit, MI, BA 1966; Univ of CA Berkeley, JD 1973. **CAREER:** San Francisco Chronicle, writer 1970; Howard Prim Rice Nemerovski et al, atty 1973-74; Legal Aid Soc of Alameda Co, atty 1974-76; NAACP Legal Def & Educ Fund Inc, atty 1977-78; Erickson Beasley & Hewitt, atty/partner 1978-. **ORGANIZATIONS:** Bd mem San Francisco Lawyer's Com for Urban Affairs 1978-; bd mem Legal Aid Soc of Alameda Co 1978-; mem Litigation com Equal rights Adv; mem CA State & Fed Bar Assns 1973-; bd mem Stiles Hall Univ YMCA 1978-; mem Black Women Lawyers Assn; mem Charles Houston Bar Assn; mem & assoc editor CA Law Review 1972-73; lectr Civil Rights Practice for Pract Law Inst/Equal Oppty Employment Commn/CA Continuing Educ of the Bar. **BUSINESS ADDRESS:** Attorney, Erickson Beasley & Hewitt, 12 Geary St, San Francisco, CA 94108.

BEASLEY, ANNE VICKERS
Public accountant. **PERSONAL:** Born Sep 07, 1917, Orlando, FL; married William Beasley. **EDUCATION:** Manhattan Comm Coll, Associate Acctg 1965. **CAREER:** Union Theol Sem NYC, bookkeeping training teacher; notary public 30 yrs; real estate salesman 10 yrs; City of NY Housing Devel Admin, auditor 1973-74; St Nicholas Park Mgmt Corp, auditor, consult 1973; Bathgate Comm Housing Devel Corp, comptroller; Active VIP Bookkeeping Inc, owner-mgr. **ORGANIZATIONS:** Chmn Leadership Devel, Bd of Christian Ed, Convent Ave Bapt Church; staff instr Bapt Ed Ctr, Brooklyn & Long Island; mem NAACP, Natl Council Negro Women, Urban League, Carver Dem Club, YWCA, Church Women United, Womens Aux of the Army & Navy Union, Eastern Star, IBPOE of W, League of Women Voters. **HONORS/ACHIEVEMENTS:** Spec Leaderhip Awds in Church Order of Eastern Stars; IBPOE of W; listed in Intl Who's Who in Community Svc, Community Leaders & Noteworthy Amers.

BEASLEY, ANNIE RUTH
Educator, mayor. **PERSONAL:** Born Oct 06, 1928, Nashville, NC; daughter of Lucious Beasley and Lillie Alston Beasley. **EDUCATION:** Shaw Univ Raleigh, BA 1949; NC Central Univ, MA 1954-58. **CAREER:** Civil Service, file clerk 1951-53; S Nash Sr High, teacher; councilwoman, Town of Sharpsburg NC 1981-83; mayor, Town of Sharpsburg NC 1983-87. **HONORS/ACHIEVEMENTS:** Leader of Amer Secondary Educ 1972; Teacher of the Year Nash Co Teachers NC 1973-74; Human Relations Awd Nash Co Teachers NC 1978-79. **HOME ADDRESS:** PO Box 636, Sharpsburg, NC 27878. **BUSINESS ADDRESS:** Teacher English-French-Drama, S Nash Sr High, Rt 1 Box 318, Bailey, NC 27807.

BEASLEY, ARLENE AUDREY
Business executive. **PERSONAL:** Born Jun 03, 1943, Cleveland, OH; divorced. **EDUCATION:** OH Univ, BA 1965; Kent State Univ, grad 1967-69. **CAREER:** Cleveland Bd of Edn, tchr 1965-69; Sage Publications, artist 1969-70; KFI/KOST Radio, acct exec 1970-. **ORGANIZATIONS:** 1st Black woman pres Amer Women in Radio & TV 1977-78; bd of dir Merchandising & Exec Club of Los Angeles 1971-; mem & past vice pres Natl Assn of Media Women 1971-77; mem Costume Cncl Los Angeles Museum of Art 1974-. **HONORS/ACHIEVEMENTS:** Merit Award Amer Women in Radio & TV 1975; Outstanding Contr to Radio & TV Ind & Community; Joint Assembly Resolution CA State Senate 1974; Media Award Natl Assn of Media Women 1974; 1st one-woman art exhibit Polly Friedlander Gallery 1976. **BUSINESS ADDRESS:** 610 S Ardmore, Los Angeles, CA 90005.

BEASLEY, DANIEL L.
County commissioner. **PERSONAL:** Born Mar 22, 1910, Tuskegee, AL; children: 1 child. **EDUCATION:** Tuskegee Inst, BS, 1937. **CAREER:** Rosenwald Jr HS, Preston GA, prin, 1937-40; Farm Security Administ Linden, AL, 1940-42; Vet Administrn, clerk, 1946-68; Macon Co, county commr, 1971-75; Macon County, tax collector, 1977-91. **ORGANIZATIONS:** Pres Tuskegee Branch NAACP; mem Tuskegee Civic Assn. **HONORS/ACHIEVEMENTS:** Tuskegee's Man of Yr Award 1962. **MILITARY SERVICE:** AUS 1942-43.

BEASLEY, EDWARD, III
City manager. **PERSONAL:** Born in Omaha, NE; son of Dr Edward Beasley, Jr and Bessie Chandler Beasley. **EDUCATION:** Pittsburgh State Univ, Pittsburgh PA, 1976-77; Loyola Univ, BA, Political Science, 1980; Univ of Missouri, Kansas City MO, MPA, 1983; Pioneer Community Coll, Kansas City MO, 1984. **CAREER:** Jolly Walsh & Gordon, Kansas City MO, legal clerk, 1982-84; Federal Govt, Washington DC, aid to Senator Thomas Eagleton, 1983; City of Kansas City, Kansas City MO, mgmt trainee, 1984-85; City of Flagstaff, Flagstaff AZ, admin asst to city mgr, 1985-88; City of Eloy, Eloy, AZ, city mgr, 1988-. **ORGANIZATIONS:** Mem, bd of dir, Amer Cancer Soc, Pinal County AZ; bd mem, United Way of Northern Arizona, 1988, bd mem, Center Against Domestic Violence, 1988; bd mem, Impact Crisis Funding, 1988; mem, Intl City Managers Assn. **HONORS/ACHIEVEMENTS:** 30 Leaders of the Future, Ebony Magazine, 1988; Outstanding Young Men of America, 1986. **BUSINESS ADDRESS:** City Mgr, City of Eloy, 628 N Main St, Eloy, AZ 85231.

BEASLEY, JESSE C.
Optometrist. **PERSONAL:** Born Mar 11, 1929, Marshall, TX; married Ruth Adella Evans; children: Jesse II, Joseph, Janice. **EDUCATION:** LA City Coll, AA Ophthalmic Optics 1952; LA Coll of Optometry, OD 1956; Univ of CA, MPH 1971. **CAREER:** Assoc Pract, 1957; Private Practice, optometrist 1957-. **ORGANIZATIONS:** Passed state bd & lic as reg optometrist State of CA 1956; mem LA Co Optom Soc; pres-elect 1975 CA Optom Assn; Amer Optom Assn; elected to Fellow of Amer Acad of Optom 1969; mem Amer Pub Health Assn; chmn Comm Health Div 1973-74; chmn Div of Pub Health Optom 1972-73; Amer Optom Com of the Urban Optom 1969-70; Com on Urban Optom 1970-71; COA Bd of Trustees 1971; CA Optom Assn 1967; pres CA Optometric Assn 1976-77; pres Optom Vision Care Council 1968; chmn Comp Health Planning Com of So CA Optom Socs 1968; mem LA Co Optom Soc; mem Optom cosn in planning Optom; sec S Cntrl Multipurpose Health Serv Cntr 1976; proposal writer Optom Particip 1967; staff optom OEO Health Cntr 1968; mem Exec Com of med Staff Organ 1968; cond Free Vision Care Clinic in Jamaica gave RX glasses to indigent persons 1968; compl independ Med Records Abstract of Watts Health Cntr under contr to Geomet Inc 1971. **HONORS/ACHIEVEMENTS:** Has published & presented many papers on optometry; appointed to CA State Bd of Optometry by Gov Edmund G Brown Jr 1978-86; elected bd pres CA State Bd Optometry 1982,84. **MILITARY SERVICE:** USAAF Corp Sgt 1946-49. **BUSINESS ADDRESS:** Physician, Manchester Optometric Center, 130 W Manchester Ave, Los Angeles, CA 90003.

BEASLEY, PAUL LEE
Educational administrator. **PERSONAL:** Born Jan 10, 1950, East Point, GA; married Pamela Simmons; children: Deanna Estella. **EDUCATION:** Earlham Coll, BA 1972; Trenton State Coll, MEd 1973. **CAREER:** Trenton State Coll, dormitory dir 1973-74; Emory Univ Upward Bound, dir 1974-75; US Office of Educ, educ program specialist 1975-78; Univ of TN Chattanooga, dir special serv 1978-. **ORGANIZATIONS:** State rep SE Assn Educ Oppor Prog Personnel 1979-; com chmn TN Assn of Spl Prog 1978-; usher/bd mem First Bapt Ch Chattanooga 1979-; mem Toastmasters Intl 1979-. **HONORS/ACHIEVEMENTS:** Outstanding Young Men of Amer 1979; Award for Disting Serv SE Assn Educ Oppor Prog Personnel 1977; Outstanding Upward Bounder US Ofc of Educ 1976. **BUSINESS ADDRESS:** Dir of Special Services, Univ of Tennessee, 615 McCallie Ave, Chattanooga, TN 37402.

BEASLEY, ULYSSES CHRISTIAN, JR.
Attorney. **PERSONAL:** Born Jan 14, 2800, Arkansas City, AR; married Rose Jeanette Cole; children: Gayle, Mark, Erika. **EDUCATION:** Fresno City Coll, attended 1949-51; Fresno State Coll, attended 1951-53; San Francisco Law Sch, 1959-65. **CAREER:** Co of Fresno Welfare Dept, soc worker 1953-54; Fresno Police Dept, police officer 1954-59; Welfare Dept Contra Costa Co, soc worker 1959; State of CA, investigator 1959-66; Dist Atty Office Santa Clara Co, deputy dist atty 1966-. **ORGANIZATIONS:** Vp NAACP San Jose Br; bd dir Santa Clara Youth Village; mem Black Lawyers Assn. **MILITARY SERVICE:** USN 3rd Class Petty Officer 1945-48; Good Conduct Medal. **BUSINESS ADDRESS:** Deputy District Attorney, Dist Atty Santa Clara County, 70 W Hedding St, San Jose, CA 95110.

BEASLEY, VICTOR MARIO
Paralegal. **PERSONAL:** Born Feb 13, 1956, Atlanta, GA; son of Willie J Beasley and Mary L Beasley; married Linda Kaye Randolph; children: Cea Janay. **EDUCATION:** Morehouse Coll, BA 1979; Attended, GA Inst of Tech 1974-75, GA State Coll of Law 1984-85. **CAREER:** City of Atlanta Planning Bureau, planning asst 1977-78; Atlanta Bureau of Corrections, sgt/officer 1980-83; Atlanta Municipal Court, clerk/bailiff 1983-85; Atlanta Public Defender's Office, researcher/investigator 1985-. **ORGANIZATIONS:** Region I mem Morehouse Coll Alumni Assoc 1985. **HONORS/ACHIEVEMENTS:** Scholarship Atlanta Fellows and Interns 1977-78. **HOME ADDRESS:** 6794 Alexander Parkway, Douglasville, GA 30135-3581. **BUSINESS ADDRESS:** Leagl Researcher/Investigator, City of Atlanta Pblc Defender, 165 Decatur St, Atlanta, GA 30303.

BEATTY, CHARLES EUGENE, SR.
Educational administrator. **PERSONAL:** Born Apr 24, 1909, Asheville, NC; married Evelyn Douglas; children: Mary L Shorter, Charlotte Jordan, Charles, Jr. **EDUCATION:** Eastern Mich Univ, BS 1934; Univ of Mich, MA Ed 1962. **CAREER:** Ypsilanti Public Schools, teacher 1935-40, elementary principal 1940-74, school board mem 1975-. **ORGANIZATIONS:** Chairman Selective Service Comm 1965-75; president Boys Club of Ypsilanti 1966-74; president Eastern Mich Univ Alumni Assoc 1969-70; vice president Ypsilanti Board of Education 1977-78. **HONORS/ACHIEVEMENTS:** Outstanding Elem Principal Elem Principal Assoc Region II 1974; EMU Athletic Hall of Fame 1976; EMU Alumni Distinguished Service Award 1982; Univ of Pennsylvania Honored for 50th year winning 400 M Hurd 3 years in a row 1983; Michigan Education Hall of Fame 1985; co-founder internationally known LC PerryPre-School Ypsilanti, MI 1962. **BUSINESS ADDRESS:** School Board Member, Ypsilanti Pub Sch Dist, 1885 Packard Rd, Ypsilanti, MI 48197.

BEATTY, OZELL KAKASKUS
Retired educational administrator. **PERSONAL:** Born Mar 01, 1921, Newberry, SC; married Ellestine Dillard; children: Bryan E. **EDUCATION:** Livingstone Coll, BS 1943; Columbia Univ, MA 1949; Indiana Univ, NC State Univ, Natl Science Foundation Rsch Fellow. **CAREER:** Salisbury City Council NC, mem city council 1967-77; Livingstone Coll, govtl relations officer 1971-78; City of Salisbury NC, mayor pro tem 1971-73, 1973-75; Office of the Governor Raleigh NC, deputy dir office of local govt advocacy 1978-85. **ORGANIZATIONS:** Mem Alpha Kappa Mu Honor Soc, NAACP, Omega Psi Phi Frat, NC Black Leadership Caucus. **HONORS/ACHIEVEMENTS:** Livingstone Coll Alumni Meritious Serv Awd 1977; Salisbury-Rowan Negro Civic League Comm Meritorious Serv Awd 1978; Eastside and Westside Comm Meritorious Serv Awd 1978; Livingstone Coll Meritorious Serv Awd 1978; Inter-Greek Council Meritorious Serv Awd 1978; Livingstone Coll Distinguished Serv Award, 1979; NC Black Elected Municipal Officials Org Distinguished Serv Award 1984;. **MILITARY SERVICE:** AUS Medical Corps tech sgt 2 1/2 years; Asian Theater, Good Conduct, Overseas Service.

BEATTY, PEARL
Elected official. **PERSONAL:** Born Oct 03, 1935, Connellsville, PA. **EDUCATION:** Shaw Univ, BA (Cum Laude) Publ Admin; Vale School of Ins, Dipl Ins Corp Syst, Risk Mgmt. **CAREER:** Career Oriented Program for Employment, office mgr, exec sec; Urban League of NJ, exec sec; Ins Fund Commiss City of Newark, risk mgr. **ORGANIZATIONS:** Bd mem Natl Assoc of Cty Officials, Natl Assoc of Black Cty Officials, Natl Employment Steering Comm; mem 1984 Dem Platform Comm; bd mem, pres NJ Assoc of Counties; mem Essex Cty Women's Avd Bd, Essex Cty Correctional Adv Bd; chairperson Newark Housing Auth; mem Govt Risk & Ins Mgrs; pres NJ State Publ Welfare Bd. **HONORS/ACHIEVEMENTS:** Achievement Awd Newark Tenent Council; Sec Appreciation Awd Kenneth A Gibson Civic Assoc; Woman of the Year Awd South Ward Boys Club, Bronze Shieds Inc;Merit Awd Essex Cty Dem Women; Leadership Awd NJ Assoc of Housing & Redevel; Citation of Appreciaiton Amer Legion Guyton Callahan #152; Outstanding Leadership Awd CAHACO Inc; Pol Serv Awd Natl Council of Negro Women; Apprec Awd Essex Cty Coll; Essex Cty Admin Code Adoption Awd Cty of Essex; Positive Image Awd Positive Image Inc; Outstanding Citizen Awd Jerome D Greco Civic Assoc; Freeholder of the Year Central Parent Council 1984; Proclamation Pearl Beatty Day Nam 16 1985 Cty of Essex; Disting Serv Awd Natl Assoc of Black Cty Officials; Community Serv Awds Essex Cty Police Dept, Frontiers, Sickle Cell Ed & Serv Found, Women's Political Caucus of NJ; Kappa Alpha Psi, 22nd Delegation, High Park Gardens, Leaguers Inc, Essex Cty Freeholders, Allen Church. **BUSINESS ADDRESS:** Essex Co, 465 Martin Luther King Blvd, Newark, NJ 07102.

BEATTY, ROBERT L.
Business executive. **PERSONAL:** Born Sep 10, 1939, Turin, GA; married Marion L Bearden; children: Tara Patrice. **EDUCATION:** Univ of MD, BA Marketing 1961; Northwood Inst, Spl Diploma Mktg 1969. **CAREER:** WB Doner & Co Advertising Detroit, audio/vis dir 1965-72; Grey Advertising NY & Detroit, acct supr 1972-75; Ross Roy Inc Advertising Detroit, vp/acct supr 1975-. **ORGANIZATIONS:** Mem Adcraft Club of Detroit 1970-; exec bd com mem NAaCP Detroit Br 1977-; adv bd chmn MI Cancer Found 1978-; com mem New Detroit Inc 1978-. **HONORS/ACHIEVEMENTS:** CLIO Award (advt award equiv to movie industry's Oscar) Natl CLIO Adv Com 1978. **MILITARY SERVICE:** AUS Sgt 1958-61; Good Conduct European Command Award. **BUSINESS ADDRESS:** Vice Pres/Acct Supr, Ross Roy Inc Advertising, 2751 E Jefferson, Detroit, MI 48204.

BEATTY, VANDER L.
Government official. **PERSONAL:** Born Feb 05, 1941, Wilmington, NC; married Joyce; children: 3 children. **CAREER:** H Lehman Coll NYU, past prof; NY State Assembly, mem 1970-72; NY State, state senator 1972-. **ORGANIZATIONS:** Mem Prince Hall Masons; Kappa Alpha Psi; Natl Assn Univ Profs. **BUSINESS ADDRESS:** State Senator, State of NY, 670 Sterling Pl, Brooklyn, NY 11216.

BEATTY-BROWN, FLORENCE R.
Educator. **PERSONAL:** Born Dec 06, 1912, Cairo, IL; daughter of Webster Barton Beatty Sr and Mary Alice Titus; married Robert Duane Brown Sr (divorced); children: Robert Duane Jr. **EDUCATION:** Fisk Univ, AB (Cum Laude) 1933; Univ of IL Urbana IL, MA 1936, MS 1939, PhD 1951; Columbia Univ, Post Grad Work 1940-41; WA Univ, Post Grad Work 1954,66,67; St Louis Commun Coll Forest Park, AAS 1977; Georgetown University, S 1964; Washington Univ, F 1967; Mitchell College of Advanced Educ, Bathurst Australia, 1986. **CAREER:** Fayetteville State Teachers Coll, prof soc sci 1936-45; Lincoln Univ, prof soc sci 1945-47; Harris-Stowe Teachers Coll, Stowe Coll, prof soc sci 1949-60; Gen Bd of Ed Tuskegee Inst AL, guest prof, consult 1952-55; US Dept of State Liberia W AFrica, ed spec US Agency of Intl Devel 1960-63; Barnes/Jewish Hosp School of Nursing, assoc prof sociology 1964; Mark Twain Summer Inst Clayton MO, prof behavioral sci 1965-68; freelance writer; St Louis Comm Coll Meramec, professional emeritus, chmn behavioral/social sci 1963-. **ORGANIZATIONS:** Proposal writing Natl Endowment for the Humanities 1980-82; consult & eval No Central Accrediting Assoc of Inst of Higher Learning 1971-74; mem St Louis Writers Guild 1984-; chmn Book Review Discussion Club St Louis MO 1980; sec, bd mem Urban League of St Louis 1960-; consult Natl Sci Found, NCAA 1970-77; guest lecturer at num local univ & coll platforms, radio & tv; mem US Div of Laubach Literacy Intl; bd dir Intl Educ Consortium; So Conference on Afro, American Studies, 1983; member, St Louis Junior College Non-Certificated Retirement Plan Committee, 1988. **HONORS/ACHIEVEMENTS:** Natl Awd for 7 years commun serv Urban League of St Louis; Pub Mem/Foreign Selection Bd Dept of State Wash DC 1972; grant Natl Endowment for the Humanities 1979-81; Most Outstanding Instructor at Meramec Comm Coll Phi Thera Kappa Hon Soc 1980; Recognition Cert Amer Assoc of Univ Women; Certificate of Merit for Distinguished Service to the World Community, International Biographical Assn, Cambridge, England 1988; Australian Bicentennial: The Secrets are Out- The Crisis, 1988. **BUSINESS ADDRESS:** St Louis Community College at Meramec, 11333 Big Bend Blvd, Kirkwood, MO 63122.

BEAUBIEN, GEORGE H.
Executive director. **PERSONAL:** Born Nov 10, 1937, Hempstead, NY; married Lois Ann Lowe; children: Jacqueline II. **EDUCATION:** Compton Coll, AA 1956; Pepperdine Coll, BA 1958. **CAREER:** Golden State Mut Life Ins Co, staff mgr, 1960-64; IBM Corp, legal mktg rep, 1964-65, mktg mgr, 1965-71; Self-Employed, gen ins agency all lines of ins, 1971-76; Mayor's Office, Small Bus Asst, exec dir, 1976-. **ORGANIZATIONS:** Dir/pres Alpha Phi Alpha Frat; dir LA fire Dept Recruitment Prog; consult natl Bank United Fund Wash, DC/Norfolk, VA; chmn of bd LA Brotherhood Crusade 1968; pres New Frontier Dem Club 1969; pres LA bd of Fire Commr 1973-77. **HONORS/ACHIEVEMENTS:** Resolution of Appreciation LA City Council; Top Rookie Salesman of Year IBM corp 1971; Cert of Accomplish IBM Corp 1972-74; Exec of the Year LA Brotherhood Crusade 1976. **BUSINESS ADDRESS:** Executive Dir, Mayor's Office Small Bus Asst, 200 N Spring St, Los Angeles, CA 90012.

BEAUCHAMP, PATRICK L.
Beer distributor. **CAREER:** Beauchamp Distributing Co, Compton CA, chief executive. **BUSINESS ADDRESS:** Chief Executive, Beauchamp Distributing Co, 1911 S Santa Fe Ave, Compton, CA 90221. *

BEAUFORD, FRED
Publisher. **PERSONAL:** Born Nov 11, 1940, Neptune, NJ; married Cynthia Martinez; children: Danielle, Fred, Tama, Alexis. **EDUCATION:** NY Univ, BS 1971. **CAREER:** Black Creation, editor, founder 1969-73; Neworld Mag, editor, publisher 1974-81; Univ of So CA, sr lecturer 1977-81; Univ of CA Berkeley, vstg prof 1981-84; The Crisis Mag, editor 1985-. **HONORS/ACHIEVEMENTS:** Cert of Serv Inst of Afro-Amer Affairs NYU 1972; Outstanding Serv CA Conf of the Arts 1979. **MILITARY SERVICE:** AUS pfc 1958-60. **HOME ADDRESS:** 344 W 49th St, New York, NY 10019. **BUSINESS ADDRESS:** Editor, Crisis Magazine, 260 Fifth Ave 6th Fl, New York, NY 10001.

BEAVER, JOSEPH T., JR.
Author, publisher. **PERSONAL:** Born Sep 22, 1922, Cincinnati, OH; married Helen Mae Greene; children: Joseph T III, James Paul, Northe Lejana Olague, Wendla Tarascana Helene Coonan. **EDUCATION:** Univ of Cincinnati, Liberal Arts 1940-41; Univ WI Ext, Economics 1947; Univ Teuerife Spain, Economic Geography 1951; Foreign Serv Inst, Languages Labor Confs Public Speech Consular Officers Courses 1954, 1960-61, 1964-68, Sr Exec Seminar Course 1967; College of the Desert Palm Desert CA, Journalism 1978-79. **CAREER:** Govt career, retired 26 yrs in foreign service; Intl Review of Third World Culture & Issues, publisher/editor. **ORGANIZATIONS:** Life mem NAACP; bd mem Western States Black Rsch Ctr; bd mem Coachella Economic Develop Corp; mem Palm Springs C of C; mem Citizens for Freedom; affirmative action ofcr Coalicion Politica de la Raza; mem DEMAND; founder Friends of Jesse Jackson Coalition 1985; exec dir Black Historical & Cultural Socof Coachella Valley; lectured on foreign policy Africa & Latin America; chmn Martin Luther King Commemoration Comm Palm Springs. **HONORS/ACHIEVEMENTS:** Meritorious Honor Awd 1965; Trophy for Editorial Excellence in Journalism Coll of Desert CA 1978; author/columnist US & Abroad; author "Africa In Perspective", "The Best Neighbor"; named Exec Dir Black Historical and Cultural Soc of the Coachella Valley Palm Springs, CA 1984; Certificate of Appreciation for Significant Serv to the Comm and in observation of Black History month County of Riverside. **MILITARY SERVICE:** USMC sgt 1943-46. **BUSINESS ADDRESS:** Publisher/Editor, Intl Review of 3rd World Cul, PO Box 1785, Palm Springs, CA 92263.

BEAVERS, GEORGE A.
Business executive. **PERSONAL:** Born Oct 30, 1891, Atlanta, GA; married Lola Cunningham. **EDUCATION:** Univ of CA Extension Div of UCLA & USC, attended. **CAREER:** Amer Mutual Benefit Assn, supt 1922; Golden State Mutual Life Ins Co, co-organizer 1925, currently mem bd dir/chmn bd emeritus. **ORGANIZATIONS:** Mem Interim Comm Chicago Round Table of Commerce; mem bd govs Los Angeles Town Hall 1964-67; mem Grand Jurors Assn of Los Angeles Co; Phi Beta Sigma Frat; NAACP; mem bd dir Goodwill Ind of So CA; Dist Atty Adv Counc; State Atty Gen adv com; mem Men of Tomorrow; chmn Urban League Home Building & Finance Com 1951; commr LA City Housing Auth 1946-62, chmn 1953-62; pres Natl Ins Assn 1962-63; mem natl Adv Com 1957 Freedom Fund Campaign;finan sec NAACP LA Br 10 years; mem bd dir LA Fam Welfare Assn 8 yrs; pres Avalon comm Cntr 2 yrs; treas Health Assn 2 yrs. **HONORS/ACHIEVEMENTS:** Recip Cert of Apprec from FD Roosevelt 1943; Cert of Merit from Harry Truman 1946; Cert of Merit First AME Ch 1946; commended by mayor Fletcher Brown 1947; Carver Citation 1948; Crusade for Freedom Citation 1951; Phi Beta Sigma Frat Soc Action Achievement Award 1951; Gold Feather Award Comm Chest 1953; Human Rel Award Alpha Phi Alpha Frat 1954; Rheingold Civic Award 1955; Recogn for more than 10 years duty as Commr of Housing Auth LA 1957; George Washington Carver Meml Inst Gold Award 1960; Award of Merit for Comm Serv Welfare Planning Counc 1962; Recogn Award from Natl Ins Assn 1962-63; Scroll of HonorAward W LA Br NAACP 1966; Holman Meth Ch Award 1966; Resolution of Commendation LA 1968; Relations Award LA 1971; Pioneer Award LA Chap Natl Assn of Media Women 1974. **BUSINESS ADDRESS:** Chairman of the Board Emeritus, Golden State Mutual Life Ins, PO Box 2332, Terminal Annex, Los Angeles, CA 90051.

BEAVERS, NATHAN HOWARD, JR.
Clergyman, business executive. **PERSONAL:** Born Aug 06, 1928, Alexander City, AL; married Velma C; children: Vincent, Norman, Stephany, Rhonda, Lyrica. **EDUCATION:** Howard Univ Sch of Law, JD 1952, addtl studies; Hamma Sch of Theol, MDiv, PhD cand 1975-. **CAREER:** General Practice, civil & criminal law 1955-62; OH Eagle Newspaper, 1963-65; Cleveland, real est devel/gen contr/cons 1966-71; FHA St Univ of Coll Buffalo, lectr Natl Acad of Sci 1969; Affil Contractors of Amer Inc, fdr & natl exec dir 1971-; Faith Bapt Ch Springfield, co-pastor 1974-. **ORGANIZATIONS:** Past pres Soc of Registered Contractors 1968-70; mem Sigma Delta Tau Legal Frat 1951; fdr & 1st pres Omicron Lambda Alpha Chap 1950; pres Beta Chap 1949; fdr & 1st pres Zeta Delta Lambda Chap Alpha Phi Alpha Frat Inc 1957; mem Prince Hall Masons, Shriners, Knights of Pythias, Elks, Amer Legion; chrtr mem Frontiers Intl; bd of dir YMCA; Nutrition for the Elderly; Planned Parenthood 1975; con World Bank 1973; consult Urban League 1973-75. **HONORS/ACHIEVEMENTS:** Outstanding Contrib to Minority Econ Devel State of OH 1977; Outst Serv to Contractors Mayor Roger Baker 1976; Outst Serv Affiliate Contractors of Amer 1971-72; Outst Businessman of the Yr Urban League 1969; 1st & Outst FHA Multi-Fam Housing Proj HUD 1968. **MILITARY SERVICE:** USAF Cpt 1955. **BUSINESS ADDRESS:** Faith Bapt Church, 328 W Clark St, Springfield, OH 45506.

BECK, ARTHELLO, JR.
Artist. **PERSONAL:** Born Jul 17, 1941, Dallas, TX; married Mae Johnson; children: Marshariki Akiba, Hodari Amin. **CAREER:** Free-lance artist; Arthello's Gallery, owner. **HONORS/ACHIEVEMENTS:** One of 8 leading artists in Southwest 1964; Special Merit Award State Fair of TX 1974; 2nd Place So Western Ceramic Show 1974; 1st Place Black Art Exhibit Fort Worth 1972; Received Fine Arts Award Com of 100 Dallas, TX 1975. **BUSINESS ADDRESS:** Arthello's Gallery, 1922 S Beckley Ave, Dallas, TX 75224.

BECK, HERSHELL P.
Elected official. **PERSONAL:** Born Dec 19, 1940, Carthage, TX; married Ida Mae Reese; children: Lorengo Raoul, Jackie Deshun. **EDUCATION:** Tyler Barber Coll, 1960. **CAREER:** Poney League, coach 1977-83; Boy Scouts, leader 1977-85; Planning & Zoning Commiss, mem 1978-80; Human Devel Corp, bd mem 1980-84; City of Carthage, mayor pro tem. **ORGANIZATIONS:** Commisss city of Carthage TX 1980-; mem Turner Alumni Assoc 1980-; exec bd Turner Alumni Assoc 1980-; mayor pro tem City of Carthage TX 1983-; bd mem Devel Block Grant Review Comm 1983-; bd mem East TX Region Community 1984-. **HONORS/ACHIEVEMENTS:** Plaque HUDCO 1980; Cert Governor of TX 1984. **HOME ADDRESS:** 402 Highland, Carthage, TX 75633.

BECK, ROSWELL NATHANIEL
Physician. **PERSONAL:** Born in Georgetown, SC; married Barbara; children: Roswell Jr, MD, Janice, Celeste. **EDUCATION:** Fisk Univ, AB 1934; Meharry Med Coll, MD 1944. **CAREER:** Private practice, physician 1944-51, 1953-. **ORGANIZATIONS:** Mem Natl Med Assoc, So Med Assoc, Inter-Co Med Assoc; advisory mem SC Reg Med Program; mem SC Comm Alcohol & Drug Abuse; bd of visitors Med Univ of SC 1979; mem Mt Zion AME Church, Omega Psi Phi; chmn 6th Congressional Dist Voter Educ Project; past mem, advisory Group Title I on Higher Educ; chmn Florence Comm on Comm Affairs; past mem SC Comm Human Relations, NAACP. **HONORS/ACHIEVEMENTS:** Outstanding Community Service, Zeta Phi Beta Inc, 1972-73; Service Award, Masjid Muhammed of Florence SC, 1977; Leadership in Political Affairs, EC BDO Inc, 1980; Trustee of the Medical Univ at Charleston, 1983-88. **MILITARY SERVICE:** USMC capt 1951-53; Bronze Star. **BUSINESS ADDRESS:** 403 N Dargan St, Florence, SC 29501.

BECK, SAUL L.
Government official. **PERSONAL:** Born Jul 11, 1928, Greenwood, MS; married Elaine; children: 5 Children. **EDUCATION:** Attended, Chicago Tech Coll. **CAREER:** City Councilman, 1964-72; East Chicago Heights IL, mayor, 1973-. **ORGANIZATIONS:** Mem Intl Brotherhood Elec Workers; mem IL Bd of Comm & Econ Develop; past bd mem Prairie State Jr Coll; educ counselor mem Natl Conf Black Mayors 1976; pres IL Chap of Natl Conf of Black Mayors; del Dem Natl Conv NY 1980; bd of dir IL Municipal League; NBC LEO; NAACP; PUSH. **HONORS/ACHIEVEMENTS:** Appreciation Awd Order of Eastern Star; Humanitarian Awd Flwsp for Action; Comm Serv Awd CEDA. **BUSINESS ADDRESS:** Mayor, East Chicago Heights, 1501 E 13th Pl, East Chicago Heights, IL 60411.

BECK, THOMAS ARTHUR, III
Physician, educator. **PERSONAL:** Born Mar 04, 1929, Birmingham, AL; children: Cynthia, Stephen, Thomas IV. **EDUCATION:** Univ NE, BA 1952; Univ NE Coll Med, MD 1961. **CAREER:** Univ So CA Sch of Med, asst clinical prof. **ORGANIZATIONS:** Chmn Dept OB-GYN David M Brotman Mem Hosp; AMA; Natl Med Assn; CA med Assn Los Angeles Co Med Assn; Amer Pub Health Assn; Amer Fertility Soc Amer Geriatrics Soc; Kappa Alpha Psi Frat; bd cert OB-GYN 1968. **HONORS/ACHIEVEMENTS:** Med Student Fellow Natl Found. **MILITARY SERVICE:** USAF Capt 1956. **BUSINESS ADDRESS:** Assistant Clinical Professor, Univ So CA School of Medicine, 3756 Santa Rosalia Dr, Los Angeles, CA 90008.

BECKER, ADOLPH ERIC
Educational administrator. **PERSONAL:** Born Mar 16, 1925, East Rutherford, NJ; married Dorothy; children: Linda, Adolph II. **EDUCATION:** Univ So CA, BA 1952, MS 1956. **CAREER:** Jordan Locke Comm Adult School, principal 1974-77; Watts Branch NAACP Paramed Occupational Center, 1st on site admin 1977; Abram Friedman Occupation Center, principal 1977-83; Crenshaw-Dorsey Communty Ad School, principal 1983-. **ORGANIZATIONS:** Mem Alpha Phi Alpha Frat 1950; mem Nat Assn Pub Continuing & Adult Educ 1958-74; mem Crenshaw Neighbors Inc 1964-; co-founder, owner, dir, producer, with wife, Dorothy, Argo Center Cultural Arts 1969-74; chmn Adult HS Com of Nat Assn Pub 1975-; dir Nat Council of Urban Adminstrs Adult Educ 1975-; chmn Curr Council LA City Schs 1976-77; Phi Delta Kappa 1977-; charter mem & vice pres Prog Chmn Watts Willowbrook Rotary Club Intl Inc; mem Adult Sch PrinsAssn & Guid Council LA; chmn Scope & Sequence Com Curriculum Council LA City Schools. **HONORS/ACHIEVEMENTS:** Recipient Nat Med Assn Found Inc Award 1972; Co-Recipient Bahai Human Rights Award 1972; Best Principal of the Year Award Watts Star Review News 1975. **MILITARY SERVICE:** AUS Transp Corps WWII, Europe 1943-45. **BUSINESS ADDRESS:** Principal, Crenshaw-Dorsey Cmnty Ad Schl, 5010 11th Ave, Los Angeles, CA 90043.

BECKER-SLATON, NELLIE FRANCES
Professional writer, educator. **PERSONAL:** Born Aug 31, 1921, Providence, RI; daughter of Leslie Earl Becker and Nell Occomy Becker; married William H Slaton; children: Glenn, Shell, Baxter. **EDUCATION:** NY Univ, BS Occup Therapy 1946; CA State Clge at Los Angeles, Tchrs Credential 1952; Pepperdine Univ, MA 1975; Claremont Grad Schl, Doctoral Candidate; Claremont Graduate School, PhD 1988. **CAREER:** Hines VA Hosp in Chicago IL, Sawtelle VA Hosp in Los Angeles CA, occup therapist 1947-50; CA Eagle, family edit 1948-51; Pittsburgh Courier, contrib writer 1951-52; LA Unified Sch Dist Reg D, multicultural adult educ tchr 1972-77; Canfield Crescent Hts Elem Alt Sch, sci coord 1973-75; Westminster Elem Sch, multicultural coord 1978-79; Walgrove Elem Sch and Charnock Elem Sch, intgrtn coord 1979-80; LA Unified Sch Dist, educ prof writer. **ORGANIZATIONS:** Dir Comm Sci Workshops 1960-69; tchr Westminster Elem 1980-89; prof writer Bacteria and Viruses Pub by Prentice Hall 1965; co-author of textbook Harcourt Brace Jovanovich 1972, 1980; former pres Intl Scribbles West 1960-65; Chap 587 Council for Excep Children; former bd mem LA Reading Assn; Amer Folklore Soc; LA CA Genealogical Soc; EDUCARE; Linguistics Soc of Amer; Alpha Kappa Alpha Sor; founder Doctoral Support Group 1982; mem Western Folklore Soc, NAPPS and SCCLYP; Afro-Amer Genealogical Soc of Southern California. **HONORS/ACHIEVEMENTS:** Resolution comm work LA City Cncl 1985; Women of the Year LA Sentinel Newspaper 1962; author writers award Our Authors Study Club 1966; comm work Natl Assc for coll Women; Sci Authors Radio Station KDAY 1965; comm work Westminster Presb 1973. **HOME ADDRESS:** 2409 S Carmona Ave, Los Angeles, CA 90016.

BECKETT, CHARLES CAMPBELL
Government employee. **PERSONAL:** Born Jan 23, 1912, Philadelphia, PA; married Rubye L Rush; children: Sydney Ann. **CAREER:** VA, psychiatric soc worker 1939; Booker T Washington Comm Center Hamilton, OH, exec dir 1940-42; Washington Urban Leageu, exec dir 1947-50; Publ Housing Adm Philadelphia Field Office, exec dir racial rel officer 1950-51; Pub Housing Adm Washington, DC, dep dir racial relations 1951-58; SW Demonstration Proj Washington, DC, exec dir 1958-60; Dept of HUD Reg II, reg dir relocation div 1961-71, regional relocation adv 1971-. **ORGANIZATIONS:** Ordained elder AME Ch; mem natl

Assn of Housing & Redevel Officials; Natl Assn of Intergroup Rel Officials; Amer Acad of Pol & Soc Sci; past pres Urban League of Phila; bd mem Philadelphia Council for Comm Advancement; bd mem Philadelphia Fellowship House; bd mem Citizens Com on Publ Edn; bd mem PA Citizens Council; mem Human Services Task Force Philadelphia Poverty Program. **HONORS/ACHIEVEMENTS:** Recip of Citations from DC Fedn of Civic Assns; Interdenominational Ministers All; Urban League of Phila; Tioga Meth Ch; Disting Serv Award HUD 1971; Author of several published articles. **BUSINESS ADDRESS:** Regional Relocation Advisory, Dept HUD Reg III, 6 & Walnut Streets, Curtin Building, Philadelphia, PA 19106.

BECKETT, EVETTE OLGA
Marketing executive. **PERSONAL:** Born Sep 01, 1956, Glen Cove, NY; daughter of Arthur Dean Beckett and Ollie Leche Hall Beckett; married J Barrington Jackson. **EDUCATION:** Tufts Univ, BA 1978; Columbia Univ Graduate School of Business, MBA 1981. **CAREER:** Random House Inc, production asst 1978-79; Bankers Trust Co, corp lending officer 1981-82; Avon Products Inc, director of fragrance marketing 1982-. **ORGANIZATIONS:** Mem Natl Assoc of Female Execs 1986-87; bd mem Coalition of Black Professional Orgs 1986-87; mem Cosmetic Exec Women 1987; program chair NY Chap Natl Black MBA Assoc 1987; vice president operations, National Black MBA Assn, New York Chapter, 1987-88; board of directors, Children House, 1988-; program chmn, 100 Black Women of Long Island, 1987-. **HONORS/ACHIEVEMENTS:** Billie Holiday Performing Arts Awd Tufts Univ 1978; Outstanding Volunteer Awd Avon Products Inc 1984; Top 100 Black Business & Professional Women, Dollars & Sense Magazine, 1988; Black Achievers Award, Harlem YMCA 1989. **HOME ADDRESS:** 171 Ingraham Blvd, Hempstead, NY 11550. **BUSINESS ADDRESS:** Director Fragrance Marketing, Avon Products Inc, 9 West 57th St, New York, NY 10019.

BECKETT, SYDNEY A.
Educator. **PERSONAL:** Born Nov 20, 1943, Philadelphia, PA. **EDUCATION:** Temple Univ, BA 1965, MEd 1967. **CAREER:** Philadelphia School Dist, elementary teacher 1965-66; IBM, mktg support representative 1967-73; PA Comm on Status of Women, commr appointed by Governor 1972-; EI Dupont, training & devel 1974-. **ORGANIZATIONS:** Bd trustees Temple Univ 1974; bd dir Alumni Assn 1967; bd dir SW Belmont YWCA 1970; Amer Soc Training & Devel 1974; Phi Delta Gamma; mem AAUW 1977; mem Delta Sigma Theta Sor 1962. **HONORS/ACHIEVEMENTS:** Outstanding Woman of Yr Temple Univ 1970; Comm Serv Award IBM 1970-72; Dale Carnegie Inst 2 awards; Sr Recong Award of Pres & Faculty; Outstanding Sr Templar Yearbook; Greek Woman of Yr Temple Univ; Volunteer Serv Award; Treble Clef Alumnae Award; Campbell AME Ch Testimonial Dinner. **BUSINESS ADDRESS:** Training & Devel, EI Dupont, Concord Pl Webster Bldg, Wilmington, DE 19898.

BECKHAM, BARRY EARL
Educator and author. **PERSONAL:** Born Mar 19, 1944, Philadelphia, PA; son of Clarence Beckham and Mildred Williams Beckham; married Betty Louise Hope, Feb 19, 1966 (divorced 1977); children: Brian Elliott, Bonnie Lorine; married Geraldine Lynne Palmer, 1979. **EDUCATION:** Brown Univ, AB, 1966; attended law school at Columbia Univ. **CAREER:** Chase Manhattan Bank, New York, NY, public relations consultant, 1966-67, urban affairs assoc, 1969-70; Natl Council of YMCAs, New York City, public relations assoc, 1967-68; Western Electric Co, New York City, public relations assoc, 1968-69; Brown Univ, Providence RI, visiting lecturer, 1970-72, asst prof, 1972-78, assoc prof English 1979—, dir of graduate creative writing program, 1980—; visiting prof at Univ of Wyoming, 1972; mem of literature panel, Rhode Island Council on the Arts, 1980—; pres of Beckham House Publishers, Inc. **ORGANIZATIONS:** Exec bd, PEN, 1970-71; bd editors, Brown Alumni Monthly 1975—; mem, Authors Guild. **HONORS/ACHIEVEMENTS:** Author of books, including My Main Mother, 1969, Runner Mack, 1972, and Double Dunk, 1981; author of play, Garvey Lives! 1972; author of periodical publications, including, "Listen to the Black Graduate, You Might Learn Something," Esquire, 1969, "Ladies and Gentlemen, No Salt-Water Taffy Today," Brown Alumni Monthly, 1970, and "Why It Is Right to Write," Brown Alumni Monthly, 1978. **BUSINESS ADDRESS:** Department of English, Brown University, Brown Station, Providence, RI 02912. *

BECKHAM, EDGAR FREDERICK
Educational administrator. **PERSONAL:** Born Aug 05, 1933, Hartford, CT; son of Walter H Beckham and Willabelle Hollinshed Beckham; married Ria Haertl; children: Frederick H. **EDUCATION:** Wesleyan Univ, BA (honors) 1958; Yale Univ, MA 1959. **CAREER:** Wesleyan Univ, Instructor, German 1961-66, dir language lab 1963-66, 1967-74, lecturer in German 1967-, assoc provost 1969-73, dean of coll 1973-. **ORGANIZATIONS:** Comm on Institutions of Higher Educ 1981-84; dir Sentry Bank for Savings; secty, bd trustees Vermont Academy; Democratic Town Comm; bd of consultant Natl Endowment for Humanities 1975-84; corporator Liberty Bank for Savings 1977-82; bd of dir Middlesex Memorial Hospital 1976-, chmn 1983-85; bd dirs Rockfall Corp 1978-86, chmn 1985-86; chmn CT Humanities Council 1978-80; pres CT Housing Investment Fund 1981-83; bd trustees CT Public Broadcasting, 1980-, chairman 1980-; Educ Telecomm Corp 1980-; bd of dirs Amer Assoc of Colls 1987-; chmn bd of dirs Coll Venture Consortium. **MILITARY SERVICE:** AUS sp-3 1954-57. **BUSINESS ADDRESS:** Dean of The College, Wesleyan Univ, Wesleyan Station, Middletown, CT 06457.

BECKHAM, WILLIAM J., JR.
Government official. **PERSONAL:** Born Nov 07, 1940, Cincinnati, OH; married Mattie. **EDUCATION:** Detroit Inst Tech, 1960; Wayne State Univ, 1962, Cert, 1973; American Univ of Maryland, 1966. **CAREER:** Transport, dep sec 1979-; Ford Mtr Co, treas transp dept 1978-79; US Dept Treas, asst sec 1977-78; Dtrt MI, dep mayor dir myr's elct's trans dir eql oppt subcom hs educ & lbr com 1973-77; US Sntr P Hart, staff asst 1971-72, admin aide 1966-70, aide cmpgn asst 1965-66; US Cptl Plc, ofcr 1962-64. **HONORS/ACHIEVEMENTS:** Metro Dtrt Tch Ftbl Leag All Str Awd 1975, 1976; Over 30 Leag Bsktbl Awd City Dtrt 1975, 1976; Mayor-elect Sem on Urban Prblms 1973; plaque Fcs onDtrt Sem 1973; Butzel Ctr Recog of Serv Rndrd Comm & Hlth Life Devel 1974.

BECKLEY, DAVID LENARD
College executive. **PERSONAL:** Born Mar 21, 1946, Shannon, MS; married Gemma Douglass; children: Jacqueline, Lisa. **EDUCATION:** Rust Coll, BA 1967; Univ of MS, MEd 1975; Univ of MS, PhD 1986. **CAREER:** Rust Coll, purchasing agent 1968-69; US Army, public relations 1969-71; Rust Coll, dir public relations 1967-77, dir of devel 1977-81, interim provost 1984, dir advancement 1984-. **ORGANIZATIONS:** Cnstlnt Un Negro Coll Fund Lilly Endwmnt 1981-84; bd dir Holly Spgs MS Chmbr Comm 1980-86; sec Indust Devel Auth of Marshall Cty 1985-. **HONORS/ACHIEVEMENTS:** Kappan Yr Phi Delta Kappa Educ Frat 1984; Omega Man Yr Omega Psi Phi Frat Phi Rho Chptr 1983. **MILITARY SERVICE:** AUS E-5 2 yrs; Army Commdtn Vietnam Srvc Corp 1967-71. **HOME ADDRESS:** 385 S Craft St, Holly Springs, MS 38635.

BECKNELL, CHARLES E.
Government employee. **PERSONAL:** Born Jun 22, 1941, Levelland, TX; married Leora; children: Desiree, Valerie, Charles. **EDUCATION:** BS 1964, MA 1969, PhD 1975. **CAREER:** Publ School, soc studies teacher; SW Coop Ed Lab, dir, teacher trng; Gov Council on Criminal Justice Plnng, exec dir; Afro-Amer Studies Prog, Univ of New Mexico, dir; Criminal Justice in Gov Cabinet, sec; Corrections for State of New Mexico, sec; Gas Co of New Mexico, energy mgmt coord; City of Albuquerque, dir gen serv dept; Becknell & Assoc Inc, pres. **ORGANIZATIONS:** Vchmn Human Rights Bd City Albuquerque; bd trustees Univ of Albuquerque; mem NM Amer Revolution Bicentennial Comm; exec comm Albuquerque, Urban Coalition; past pres Univ of Albuquerque Alumni Assoc; state dir NM Black Leadership Conf, NAACP State Pol Action Chmn; bd mem United Way of Albuquerque. **HONORS/ACHIEVEMENTS:** Citizen of the Year Omega Psi Phi 1971; Cert of Appreciation Bicentennial Comm 1973; Black Merit Acad Awd 1972. **BUSINESS ADDRESS:** President, Becknell & Assoc Inc, 2620 San Mateo NE - E, Albuquerque, NM 87110.

BECTON, JULIUS WESLEY, JR.
Government official. **PERSONAL:** Born Jun 29, 1926, Bryn Mawr, PA; married Louise; children: Shirley Hill, Karen Johnson, Joyce Cokley, Renee, J Wesley III. **EDUCATION:** Prairie View A&M Coll, BS Math 1960; Univ MD, MA Econ 1966; Natl War Coll, 1970; Huston-Tillotson, D Laws 1982. **CAREER:** 1st Cavalry Div, cmdng gen 1975-76; US Army Oper Test & Eval Agncy, cmdng gen 1976-78; VII US Corps, cmdng gen 1978-81; USA Trngng Dctrn Comd, deputy cmdng gen & the Army inspctr of training 1981-83; Agency for Inl Dev Ofc of Frgn Diaster Asst, dir 1984-85; Federal Emergency Mgmt Agency, dir 1985-. **ORGANIZATIONS:** Dir Natl Assn of Unfrmd Serv 1969-71; mem Knight of Malta 1973-; The Ret Ofcrs Assn 1983-85; Fairfax Cnty Red Cross 1983-84; vice pres US Armor Assn 1982-; USO World Bd of Governors 1985-; bd of governors American Red Cross 1986-. **HONORS/ACHIEVEMENTS:** Top Hat Awrd Courier Inc 1973; Dstngshd Grad Prairie View A&MUniv 1975; Rock of Yr Rocks Inc 1983; G E Rush Awrd Natl Bar Assn 1984; Disting HonorAwd Agency for Intl Develop 1986. **MILITARY SERVICE:** AUS lt gen 39 Yrs; DSM, SS 2, LOM 2, DFC, BSN 2, AM 4, PH 2, ACM 2, Knights Cmdrs Cross FRG. **HOME ADDRESS:** 7737 Jewelweed Ct, Springfield, VA 22152. **BUSINESS ADDRESS:** Dir, Fed Emergency Mgmt Agency, Washington, DC 20472.

BECTON, RUDOLPH
Barber shop owner. **PERSONAL:** Born May 21, 1930, Eureka, NC; married Annie Veronia Wilson; children: Karen L. **EDUCATION:** Green County Training School Diploma 1950; Harris Barber Coll Diploma 1956; Sampson Tech Inst Certificate 1979; NC Argrcultural Extension Certificate 1984. **CAREER:** UNC Chapel Hill, emergency medical serv 1976 & 1978; James Sprunt Inst, communications police & patrol 1978; Winston Salem State Univ, hair styling & cutting techniques 1979; James Sprunt Tech Coll, fire apparatus & hose practice 1983; Becton Barber Shop, owner/operator. **ORGANIZATIONS:** President Magnolia Civic League 1967-; committee member Farmer's Home Admin 1970-73 & 1977-80; town commissioner Town of Magnolia 1974-; volunteer fireman/rescue Town of Magnolia 1977-; board member Duplin & Sampson Mental Health 1978-; mayor protem Town of Magnolia 1979-; board member Magnolia Fire Dept & pres Dupenza. **HONORS/ACHIEVEMENTS:** Trailblazer Boy Scouts of Amer, 1968; Humanitarian Magnolia Civic League, 1968-73; Human Relations Duplin Co Good Neighbor Council 1973; Distinguished Citizen Crouton III Boy Scouts of Am 1979. **MILITARY SERVICE:** AUS PFC two years The Quartermaster Corps (cooking); Honorable Discharge; Good Conduct Medal; Two Battle Stars. **HOME ADDRESS:** PO Box 86, Magnolia, NC 28453.

BEDELL, FREDERICK DELANO
Educator. **PERSONAL:** Born Apr 13, 1934, New York, NY; married Gail Smith; children: Karin, Kevin, Keith. **EDUCATION:** NYU, BS 1957, MA 1965; Univ of MA, EdD 1984. **CAREER:** Rockaway Beach, chief lifeguard 1953-56; White Plains Public Schools, 1957-68; White Plains, asst prin 1968-69; Bd of Coop Educ Serv, prin 1969-76; NY State Div for Youth, dir educ 1983-84; NY State Dept of Correction, asst comm and dir of Correct Industries 1983-84; White Plains Public Schools, asst supt for Pupil Serv 1984-. **ORGANIZATIONS:** Chmn Equal Oppr in Educ Com White Plains Tchr Assn 1966-68; deputy mayor & village trust Ossining 1973-76; v chmn Ossining Urban Revewal Bd 1973-76; presentations Severly Handicapped 1974; Intl Conv 1974; vice pres Cage Teen Ctr; bd mem St Mary's in the Field Sch; sec-treas bd of dir High Meadow Coop; Cub Scout Master Pack 104; life mem NY State Congress of Parents & Tchrs. **HONORS/ACHIEVEMENTS:** Jaycees Award. **BUSINESS ADDRESS:** Asst Supr for Pupil Services, White Plains Public Schools, 5 Homeside Lane, White Plains, NY 10605.

BEECH, HARVEY ELLIOTT
Attorney. **PERSONAL:** Born Mar 22, 1924, Kinston, NC; married Eloise Crowder; children: Pamela Michelle, Harvey Elliott Jr. **EDUCATION:** Morehouse Coll, BA 1944; Univ of NC, LLB 1952. **CAREER:** Durham NC, practiced law 1952-; Kinston NC, practiced law 1953-; Beech & Pollock, partner/law firm 1966-. **ORGANIZATIONS:** Past vice pres Southeastern Lawyer's Assn; mem Amer Bar Assn, Amer Judicature Soc, NC State Bar, Natl Bar Assn, Amer Trial Lawyers Assn; approved atty for, Lawyer's Title Ins Corp, Chicago Title Ins Corp, First Title Ins Co, US Dept of Agriculture, Farmers Home Adminstrn; vice pres Lenoir Good Neighbor Cncl; bd dirs Lenoir Co United Fund; bd dirs Lamp Inc; mem bd of commnrs Neuse River Economic Develop Commn; pres Lenoir Co Adv Cnc to theComm; vice pres Eastern Cncl of Comm Affairs; mem NC State Adv Comm on Public Educ; mem State Evaluation Comm on Tchrs Educ; mem State Govt Reorganization Commn; jr warden St Augustine Episcopal Ch; mem exec cncl & finance comm, mem cnslting comm Episcopal Dioscese of East Carolina; bd dirsWachovia Bank & Trust Co; mem NC Organized Crime Prevention Cncl; life mem legal advisor NAACP; mem bd trustees Pitt Co Memorial Hosp Inc; mem bd trustees E Carolina Univ; bd dirs secty-treas World-Wide Marketing Inc; chmn budget & finance comm E Carolina Univ; mem Univ NC at Chapel Hill Bd Vis. **HONORS/ACHIEVEMENTS:** One of three original Honorees named to Adkin Sr HS Hall of Fame Inc 1969. **BUSINESS ADDRESS:** Attorney, Beech & Pollock, 308 South Queen St, Kinston, NC 28501.

BEGUESSE, BARRY OSMUND, JR.
Obstetrician/gynecologist. **PERSONAL:** Born Feb 05, 1950, Chicago, IL; married Dr Pearl Carpenter; children: Kia, Kyla. **EDUCATION:** Yankton Coll, BS 1971; Meharry Medical Coll, MD 1974. **CAREER:** District of Columbia Genl Hosp, surgery/orthopedics internship 1975-76; General Practice, physician 1976-77; Mt Sinai Hosp, obstetrics-gynecology residency1977-79; Keesler Air Force Base, obstetrics-gynecology residency 1979-81; Providence Hosp, obstetrics-gynecology residency 1981-82; Private Group Practice, obstetrics/gynecology 1982-83; Comprehensive Health Serv of Detroit, obstetrics/gynecology practice 1982-83; Wayne State Univ Hosp Complex, attending staff; Univ of TN, faculty and clinical instructor 1983-84; Private Practice Inner City Knoxville TN, obstetrics/gynecology 1983-84; Memorial City Genl Hosp Houston, attending staff 1983-. **ORGANIZATIONS:** Mem Amer College of Sports Physicians, NAACP, Air Force Assoc, YWCA, SCCA, Reserve officers' Assoc; comm mem Knoxville Mental Health Bd Assoc, Univ ofTN Pre-med Enrichment Program, Univ Hospital Quality Assurance Bd; lectured at Chicago Public School System, Univ of TN Pre-med Enrichment Program, Knoxville Coll, Austin-East High School on Careers, Shephard Air Force Base; medical licenses TN, MI, MD. **HONORS/ACHIEVEMENTS:** Council for Bio-medical Careers 1971; Hill Family Foundation Scholar Univ of MN 1974; Amer Cancer Soc Professional Education Comm 1974. **MILITARY SERVICE:** USAF capt; Outstanding Unit Awd. **HOME ADDRESS:** 1715 Woodland Springs Dr, Houston, TX 77077.

BEHRMANN, SERGE T.
Business executive. **PERSONAL:** Born Jun 09, 1937, Port-au-Prince; children: Rachelle, Daphne, Serge. **EDUCATION:** Coll Simon Bolivar 1955; Brooklyn Tech; WI Univ, structural fab engrg 1972-73; Purdue Univ, structural fab engrg 1973-74. **CAREER:** Feinstein Iron Works, 1959-66; Behrmann Iron Works, structural fabricator. **ORGANIZATIONS:** Pres Ferrum Realty Corp. **BUSINESS ADDRESS:** Structural Fabricator, Behrmann Iron Works Inc, 832 Dean St, Brooklyn, NY 11238.

BELAFONTE, HARRY
Singer, actor, producer. **PERSONAL:** Born Jun 07, 1927, NYC, NY; married Julie Robinson; children: Adrienne, Shari, David, Gina. **EDUCATION:** Park Coll MO, DHL (hon) 1968; New School Social Rsch, HHD, DHL, HDA. **CAREER:** Broadway, Almanac 1953, Three for Tonight 1955; Motion Pictures include, Bright Road 1952, Carmen Jones 1954, Odds Against Tomorrow 1959, The Angel Levine 1969, Buck & the Preacher 1971, Uptown Saturday Night 1974; producer TV Specials, A Time of Laughter 1967, Harry and Lena 1969; performer, Tonight with Belafonte 1960 Emmy Awd; producer, Strolling Twenties TV, co-producer Beat St 1984; recording artist with RCA 1954-73; appeared on German TV spl I Sing What I See 1980; concert performances in Cuba Jamaica Europe Australia NZ US w/Can Symphony Orchs 1983; appeared at Golden Nugget Atlantic City and Las Vegas 1985,86; Belafonte Enterprises, pres. **HONORS/ACHIEVEMENTS:** Tony Awd 1953; Emmy Awd 1960; 1985 Recipient ABAA Music Award for efforts to aid African famine victims and for conceiving and giving leadership to USA for Africa, producing the album and video, "We Are the World"; Grammy Awd 1985. **BUSINESS ADDRESS:** Belafonte Enterprises Inc, PO Box 1700 Ansonia Sta, New York, NY 10023.

BELANCOURT, DUNET FRANCOIS
Physician. **PERSONAL:** Born Jun 09, 1928, Aquin, Haiti;married Lillian; children: Dunet Jr, Lisa, David. **EDUCATION:** St Martial Coll, Petit Seminaire 1949; Faculte de Medicine of Haiti, MD 1955. **CAREER:** Homer G Phillips Hosp, chf dept med 1962-74, chf renal div 1972-74; Central Med Cntr, med dir 1974-. **ORGANIZATIONS:** Pres Black Multi-Discip Group; mem exec com Mound City Med Forum; mem Natl Med Assn; AMA MO Med Assn; St Louis Med Assn; life mem NAACP. **HONORS/ACHIEVEMENTS:** Award for Stabilizing pvt predominately Black hosp N St Louis; Creator Renal Dialysis Serv Homer G Phillips Hosp. **BUSINESS ADDRESS:** Medical Dir, Central Med Center, 600 N Union Blvd, St Louis, MO 63108.

BELARDO DE O'NEAL, LILLIANA
Senator. **PERSONAL:** Born Jan 11, 1944, Christiansted, Virgin Islands of the United States;daughter of Gil Belardo Sanes and Paula Mendez Agosto; married Humberto O'Neal, Jan 30, 1986; children: Carlos Gill Ortiz. **EDUCATION:** Inter-Amer Univ, BA 1963; Univ of MI, MSW 1969; CA State Univ, NY Univ Puerto Rico Extension, presently in Doctoral Program University of Miami. **CAREER:** Dept of Social Welfare social worker 1964, probation worker 1970; Dept of Dept of Social Welfare Girls Training School dir 1971; State of CA youth authority worker 1975; Dept of Ed school guidance counsellor 1976; Legislature of the Virgin Islands legislator 1981-. **ORGANIZATIONS:** Mem board of dir Amer Red Cross St Crois Chapt; mem League of Women Voters, St Crois Lioness Club, Assoc of Social Workers, Business & Professional Women. **MILITARY SERVICE:** AUS NG Captain 5 years; dir Selective Serv for US Virgin Islands. **HOME ADDRESS:** PO Box 3383, Christiansted, St Croix, Virgin Islands of the United States 00820. **BUSINESS ADDRESS:** Senator of 18th Legislature, Virgin Islands Legislature, Christiansted, St Croix, Virgin Islands of the United States 00822.

BELCHER, LEON H.
Educator. **PERSONAL:** Born Aug 08, 1930, Mineral Springs, AR; married Mary S Randall; children: 2 sons. **EDUCATION:** BS 1955; MS 1957; PhD 1961; Post-doctoral Research Fellow ETS Princeton NJ 1966-67; LSU Univ of WI, further study. **CAREER:** Arkansas, teacher/jr high school counselor, 1955-60; AL A&M Univ, dean of students/prof, 1961-66; Princeton Univ, research psychologist, 1966-67; TX Southern Univ, prof/dir of testing/dir of Inst Research, 1967-71, prof of psychology. **ORGANIZATIONS:** Mem Amer Psychol Assn; Amer Personnel & Guidance Assn; Amer Educ Research Assn; Amer Coll Personnel Assn; editorial bd of Coll Student Personnel Journal; editiorial bd of Assn of Inst Research; licensed psychologist TX State Bd of Examiners; mem Cultural Affairs Comm of Houston C of C; Houston Coun of BSA. **HONORS/ACHIEVEMENTS:** Recip Wall St Journal Student Award 1955; Alpha Kappa Mu Natl Honor Soc 1955; Phi Delta Kappa 1960; HEW Post Doctoral Research Fellowship Award 1966. **MILITARY SERVICE:** AUS 1952-54. **BUSINESS ADDRESS:** Professor of Psychology, Texas Southern University, 3100 Cleburne, Houston, TX 77004.

BELCHER, LEWIS, JR.
Appointed government official. **PERSONAL:** Born Nov 06, 1931, McCormick, SC; married Jacquelyn E Meredith; children: Terri K, Toni K. **EDUCATION:** Univ of Washington, BA, 1972, MSW, 1974. **CAREER:** USAF, career mil worldwide 1951-71; North Seattle Comm Coll, veterans corrd 1974-; State of Washington, dir, cabinet mem, 1977-. **ORGANIZATIONS:** Mem Puget Sound Black Educ 1974-77; mem Council on Black Amer Affairs 1974-77; mem WA State Employ & Training Council 1977-; mem Natl Assn of Soc Workers 1972-; mem Masonic Lodge 1972-; mem AFSA 1971-. **HONORS/ACHIEVEMENTS:** Vet Serv Award Disables Amer Vet WA 1978; Nominated Outstanding Young Men of Amer 1979; Natl Council of Black Perspectives Tacoma, WA 1979. **MILITARY SERVICE:** USAF M Sgt served 20 years; Natl Comdrs Award Disabled Amer Vet WA 1980; Bronze Star; Commendation Medal w/Clusters USAF. **BUSINESS ADDRESS:** Dir Cabinet Member, State of WA, PO Box 9778 ED-11, Olympia, WA 98504.

BELCHER, MARGARET L.
Business executive. **PERSONAL:** Born May 11, 1922, Dallas, GA; married Ralph C Belcher; children: Brenda Vernelle. **EDUCATION:** Carpenters Busn Sch, 1951; LaSalle's Sch of Accounting; Columbus Coll. **CAREER:** Afro-Am Life Ins Co, cashier 1951-62; ABC Bookkeeping Serv, bookkeeper 1962-65; Belcher's Bookkeeping Serv, owner 1965-. **ORGANIZATIONS:** Bd dir YMCA 1962-; Amer Cancer Soc 1963-73; Goodwill Ind 1970-74; NAACP 1958-; Comm Cntr Inc 1958-; Columbus-Phenix City Club of Negro Bus & Professional Women various offices 1959-71; Continent Soc Inc 1970-; mem Metro-Columbus Urban League 1971-; past sec/mem Council on Human Rel 1961-; mem Columbus Manpower Planning Cncl 1973-; GA State Empl Planning Cncl 1974-; UN Assn 1970-72; pres bd dir Metro Colls Urban League 1975-77; Iota Phi Lambda; Alpha Phi Alpha. **HONORS/ACHIEVEMENTS:** Woman of the Yr Iota Phi Lambda 1960; Woman of Yr Alpha Phi Alpha; Sojourner Truth Award 1963; Meritorious Award GA Conf NAACP 1965; Merit Award Pres L B Johnson 1968; Red Triangle Award YMCA 1969; Who's Who of Amer Women 1974-75; Personalities of the So 1972-74; Intl Who's Who in Comm Serv 1973. **BUSINESS ADDRESS:** Belcher's Bookkeeping Service, 1323 1/2 Broadway, Columbus, GA 31901.

BELCHER, NATHANIEL L.
Attorney. **PERSONAL:** Born Aug 17, 1929, Plymouth, NC; married Estelle Thorpe. **EDUCATION:** NC Central Univ, AB 1952, LLB 1958, JD 1971. **CAREER:** CJ Gates, assoc atty 1958-61; Law Firm Bumpass & Belcher, 1961-67; Law Firm Bumpass, Belcher & Avant, 1967-. **ORGANIZATIONS:** Mem, George White Bar Assn, NC State Bar, Natl Bar Assn, Amer Bar Assn, Durham Busn & Professional Chain, Durham Chamber of Commerce, Omega Psi Phi Frat, 1950-; John Avery Boy's Club; NAACP 1948; trustee White Rock Baptist Church. **MILITARY SERVICE:** AUS 1952-55. **BUSINESS ADDRESS:** Attorney at Law, 1015 Red Oak Ave, Durham, NC 27707.

BELCHER, PAUL E.
Electronics engineer executive. **PERSONAL:** Born Mar 14, 1933, Enid, OK; married Daisy L Williamson; children: Phyllis, Paul Jr, Kerry, Jeanette. **EDUCATION:** MI Sch of Engr, BSEE 1957; W coast Univ, MSEE 1967; Univ of So CA, PhD studies. **CAREER:** Hughes Aircraft Co, sr applications engr/electron cons; Belcher Assoc, pres & founder. **ORGANIZATIONS:** Mem IEEE; mem New Frontier Dem Club; Crenshaw WMCA. **HONORS/ACHIEVEMENTS:** Two patents; many techn articles. **MILITARY SERVICE:** AUS 1953-55.

BELL, ALEXANDER F.
Pharmacist, researcher. **PERSONAL:** Born Nov 07, 1904, Casanova, VA; widowed. **EDUCATION:** PhC 1926. **CAREER:** Part-time inst Pharm Chem; Howard Univ, researching hist of Coll of Pharmacy. **ORGANIZATIONS:** Co-authored & pres research paper on Action Mercurial Diuretics to Pan Amer Congress of Pharm & Biochemistry Buenos Aires 1966; represented USA Pharm Section Problems in Pharm Educ & Possible Professional Fields Pharmacist to Fedn Asian Pharm Assn Seoul 1968; voting del APhA Intl Fedn Pharm Amsterdam 1964, Hamburh 1968; sec Grand chap Chi Delta Mu Frat 1946-68; since then grand historian; historian Natl Pharm Assn; apptd rep Amer Pharm Assn steering com of Intl Fed of Pharmacy Warsaw, Poland 1976, The Hague, Holland 1977; vestryman & historiographer St Mary's Church; mem Intl Fedn Pharmacy; Amer Inst History Pharmacy Amer Pharm Assn; Natl Pharm Assn; Urban League; Chi Delta Mu. **HONORS/ACHIEVEMENTS:** Plaque Grand Chap Chi Delta Mu Frat 1973; Citation Pan Amer congr Pharm & Biochem 1966; Research paper "The Analytical Determination of N-Acetyl p-aminiphonol, Its Metabolites & Related Compoinds in Biologic Fluids" Intl Fed of Pharmacy 1975; Articles co-authored, "The Problems Encountered in the Use of Mannitol Infection (25%)" AJHP 1980; "Drug Interactions I, Folic Acid & Calcium Gluconate" J Pharm Sci 1980. **BUSINESS ADDRESS:** Pharmacist, 518 Florida Ave NW, Washington, DC 20001.

BELL, CARL COMPTON
Psychiatrist. **PERSONAL:** Born Oct 28, 1947, Chicago, IL; son of William Yancey Bell Jr and Pearl Debnam Bell; married Dora Dixie; children: Erin, Audrey. **EDUCATION:** Univ of IL Chicago Circle, BS Biology 1967; Meharry Medical Coll, MD 1971; IL State Psychiatric Inst Chicago, psychiatric residency 1974. **CAREER:** Private Practice, psychiatrist, 1972-; Chicago Medical School, clinical instructor of psychiatry, 1975; Jackson Park Hospital Psychiatric Emergency Serv Program, dir, 1976-77; Human Correctional & Serv Inst, staff psychiatrist 1977-78; Chatham Avalon Mental Health Center, staff psychiatrist 1977-79; Chicago Bd of Educ, staff psychiatrist 1977-79; Comm Mental Health Council Day Treatment Center, staff psychiatrist 1977-79; Jackson Park Hospital Div of Behavorial & Psychodynamic Medicine, assoc dir 1979-80; Community Mental Health Council, med dir 1982-87, exec dir 1987-. **ORGANIZATIONS:** Biostatistician Matthew Walker Comp Health Center, Meharry Med Coll 1970-72; diplomat Natl Bd 1971; resident physician Dept of Mental Health, State of IL 1971-74; consultant/lecturer/panelist numerous meetings/confs workshops 1971-81; consultant Jackson Park General Hospital 1972-74; mem Pharmacy & Therapeutics Comm of Jackson Park Hospital 1977-78, Nurses Com 1979; mem Amer-Indian Asian-Pacific Am/Black & Hispanic Core Mental Health Discipline Advisory Com of Howard Univ Sch of Social Work 1980-; bd dirs Natl Commn on Correctional Health Care 1983; assoc prof of clinical psychiatry Univ of IL School of Medicine 1983-; chmn Natl Medical Assn Section on Psychiatry 1985-86; bd of dir American Assn of Community Mental Health Center Psychiatrists 1985-; diplomat, bd examiner; mem Shorei Go ju Karate soc-Rank 6th Degree Black Belt; mem Black Belt Med Soc of Phys icians Martial Arts Assn; editorial bd Journal of the Natl Medical Assn 1986-87; sec Natl Council Community Mental Health Center 1986-87; fellow Amer Psychiatric Assn 1986; mem Amer Coll of Psychiatry 1987. **HONORS/ACHIEVEMENTS:** Recipient of Grant, Dept of Health Educ & Welfare 1968; recipient Goldberger Fellowship (nutrition) 1969; Citation of Merit, Disabled Amer Veterans 1971;

Mosby Scholarship Book Award for Scholastic Excellence in Medicine, Meharry Medical Coll 1971; recipient Falk Fellowship of Amer Psychiatric Assn to Participate on Council of Natl Affairs 1972, 1973; Plaque for Contrbuting Efforts to Success of 2nd US Karate & Kung-Fu Championship Tour, IL Shaolin Krate & Kung-Fu Assn 1975; Certificate of Appreciation for Devoted & Invaluable Serv Rendered to Patients at Chatham-Avalon Community Mental Health Center 1979 and Plaque in Recognition & Appreciation for Outstanding Serv; elected to Gamma TN Chapter ALpha Omega Alpha Hon Medical Soc 1980; Scholastic Achievement Award, Chicago Chapter of Natl Assn of Black Social Workers 1980; numerous awards including, Amer Med Assn Physician's Recognition Award 1981; Am er Psychiatric Assn Certificate of Continuing Med Educ 1981; creator & producer of the animation "Book Worm" shown on PBS 1984, Monarch Award for Medicine, Alpha Kappa Alpha 1986; Ellen Quinn Memorial Award for Outstaning Individual Achievement in Community Mental Health 1986. **MILITARY SERVICE:** USNR Lt Commander 1975-76. **BUSINESS ADDRESS:** Medical Dir, Commun Mental Health Council, 1001 East 87th St, Chicago, IL 60619.

BELL, CHARLES SMITH
Educator & government official. **PERSONAL:** Born May 21, 1934, Capeville, VA; son of James A Bell, Sr and Martha Robinson Bell; married Sallie Annette parker; children: Charlette LaVonne, Mia Sallie, Angel Monique. **EDUCATION:** VA Union Univ, BS Biol 1954-57, 1970; Old Dominion Univ 1972; Norfolk State Univ. **CAREER:** Northampton Cty School Bd, teacher 1960-85; Northampton Cty Bd of Suprvs Eastville Magisterial Dist, teacher. **ORGANIZATIONS:** Mem exec bd Northampton Cty Branch NAACP 1960-85, Northampton Cty Voter's League 1960-85, Northampton Ed Assoc 1960-85; mem VA Ed Assoc 1960-85, Natl Ed Assoc 1960-85, Eastern Shore VA & MD Baptist Assn 1960-85; Dist Dep Grand MW Prince Hall Masons Inc 1960-85; master chmn bd of deacons 1st Baptist Church Capeville VA 1960-85; chmn scholarship comm Club Chautauqua 1961-85; chaplain Northampton Cty Bd of Suprvs 1982-85. **HONORS/ACHIEVEMENTS:** Teacher of the Year Northampton High School 1980,81,82. **MILITARY SERVICE:** AUS staff sgt 1957-59; Soldier of the Month, Presidents Medal of Honor. **HOME ADDRESS:** PO Box 554, Eastville, VA 23347.

BELL, DERRICK ALBERT, JR.
Educator. **PERSONAL:** Born Nov 06, 1930, Pittsburgh, PA; married Jewel A Hairston; children: Derrick 3d, Douglass, Carter. **EDUCATION:** Duquesne Univ, AB 1952; Univ of Pgh Law School, LLB. **CAREER:** US Dept of Justice, 1957-59; Pittsburgh Branch NAACP, exec sec 1959-60; NAACP Legal Defense & Educ Fund, staff atty 1960-66; Dept of Health Educ & Welfare, deputy asst to sec for civil rights 1966-68; Western Center on Law & Poverty, dir 1968-69; Harvard Law School, lecturer on law 1969, prof 1971-80; Univ of OR Law School, dean 1981-85; Harvard Law School, prof of law 1986-. **ORGANIZATIONS:** Mem of Bar in DC, PA, NY, CA and US Supreme Ct; US Courts of Appeal for 4th 5th 6th 8th & 10th circuits & several Fed Dist Courts. **HONORS/ACHIEVEMENTS:** Author "Race, Racism & Amer Law" pub second ed 1980, "And We Are Not Saved, The Elusive Quest for Racial Justice," 1987; editor "Desegregation Dialogue, Searching for Remedies Under Brown". **MILITARY SERVICE:** USAF 1952-54. **BUSINESS ADDRESS:** Professor of Law, Harvard University, Law School, Cambridge, MA 02138.

BELL, DIANA LYNNE
Program manager. **PERSONAL:** Born Apr 01, 1952, Baltimore, MD; daughter of Chester Bell and Mary E Hendershott Bell. **EDUCATION:** MI State Univ, BS 1973; Atlanta Univ, MBA 1975. **CAREER:** Hewlett Packard Co, rsch & devel engr 1975-80, marketing engr 1980-81, product support mgr 1982-84, product mktg mgr 1984-86, program mgr for vertical mkts 1987; product support mgr, 1988. **ORGANIZATIONS:** Instructor Junior Achievement Project Business 1984; regional coord HP United Way Campaign 1984; pres Women's League Church by the Side of the Rd 1985-86; pres Natl Black MBA Assoc SF Chap 1987-88; volunteer for Amer Heart Assn, OaklandEnsemble Theater; bd of trustees, Church by the Side of the Road, 1989. **HONORS/ACHIEVEMENTS:** Catalyst Awd Interracial Council for Business Oppor 1975; Outstanding Young Women of Amer 1984; MBA of the Year Award, San Francisco Chapter National Black MBA Assn, 1987. **BUSINESS ADDRESS:** Support Manager, Hewlett-Packard Co, 5301 Stevens Creek Blvd, Santa Clara, CA 95052.

BELL, EARNEST FRANKLIN
Retired teacher. **PERSONAL:** Born Dec 10, 1913, Taxarkana, TX; married Lorene Marie Gipson; children: Earnestyne Yvonne Bell Terry. **EDUCATION:** Prairie View A&M Univ, BS 1936, ME 1954; CO State College, advanced study 1937-38. **CAREER:** Dunbar High School, industrial arts, machine drafting 1934-44; Roseborough High School, industrial arts teacher 1937-40; Redwater High School, architectural drafting 1940-43; Veterans Trades School, carpentry teacher 1947-50; Texarkana ISD; building construction teacher 1950-84 (retired). **ORGANIZATIONS:** Mem Bd Christian Educ, Ch Brothers Prog Comm, Ch Career Educ Program; mem Baptist Church; bd mem YMCA, Economic Adv Corps; pres Neighborhood Comm Council; pres Bowie and Red River Councils; pres Links Inc; bd mem several local and state committees. **HONORS/ACHIEVEMENTS:** Outstanding Teacher JISD; Local Outstanding Citizen; Certificate for Sponsor of Most Outstanding Hi-Y Club in State; Outstanding Industrial Teacher State of TX 1963. **MILITARY SERVICE:** AUS staff sgt 2 yrs; Bronze Star, Good Conduct Medal, Sharp Shooter, Distinguished Serv Awd, Honorable Discharge. **HOME ADDRESS:** 1921 Goree St, Texarkana, TX 75503.

BELL, ELMER A.
Executive director. **PERSONAL:** Born Nov 17, 1941, Gurdon, AR; married Jo Ann Miller; children: Elmer II. **EDUCATION:** Univ of AR, BS 1964. **CAREER:** Univ of AR, counselor 1964; Pine Bluff Pub Sch, tchr; Ofc of Econ Oppor Pine Bluff, field rep, asst dir, exec dir. **ORGANIZATIONS:** Licensed professional funeral dir; bd mem bd sec Housing Develop Corp of AR Inc; mem Royal Knight Soc; life mem Kappa Alpha Psi Frat keeper of records; St John Meth Ch; bd dir Amer Red Cross; bd mem Big Bros of Amer. **HONORS/ACHIEVEMENTS:** Cert of Merit AR OEO Training Sch; Volt Tech Inst; Development Assoc Inc; Comm Serv Awd 1974. **BUSINESS ADDRESS:** Executive Dir, Office of Economic Oppor, 200 E 8 Ave, City Hall, Pine Bluff, AR 71601.

BELL, EVERETT THOMAS
Clergyman,mayor. **PERSONAL:** Born Jun 26, 1909, Winona, TX; married Edith Glaspie; children: Joe Everett, John F, Elayne Dedman. **EDUCATION:** Butler Coll, attended 1936-38; TX Coll, sales course 1938-39. **CAREER:** Universal Life Ins Co, salesman 1938-48; Benevolent Life, mgr 1955-66; clergyman 1965-; Afro-Am Life Ins Co LA, state supr 1972-74; Easton, TX, mayor. **ORGANIZATIONS:** Co-opener Universal Life Ins Co State of CA 1949; co-opener Afro-Am Life Ins Co of FL in State of LA 1972; rebuilt one church/pastored two/currently building another church; mem NAACP 1938-; mem Natl Negro Council Los Angeles 1946. **HONORS/ACHIEVEMENTS:** Recipient Numerous Awards Natl Assn of Ins; Increase Bonus & Awards Benevolent Life 4 years.

BELL, FELIX C.
Educator. **PERSONAL:** Born Jan 04, 1936, Senatobia, MS; married Eunice; children: Lolita, Kelvin, Jennifer, Kenneth. **EDUCATION:** Atlanta Univ, MS 1970; MS Indust Coll, BA 1958. **CAREER:** Tute Cty High School, instructor; Rust Coll, instructor. **ORGANIZATIONS:** Chmn dept Tute Cty HS 1967-70; pres Tate Cty Teacher Assoc 1968-70; chmn Tate Cty Leadership Assoc; mem Loyal Dem Party 1974-75; sr deacon Paradise Ch; mem Omega Psi Phi; master Mason Lodge 9 1958-75. **HONORS/ACHIEVEMENTS:** Runner Up Teacher Year Rust Coll 1975. **BUSINESS ADDRESS:** Instructor, Rust College, PO Box 121, Holly Springs, MS 38625.

BELL, GEORGE
Public administrator. **PERSONAL:** Born Mar 12, Pittsburgh, PA; children: George Jr, Christian, Kofi. **EDUCATION:** Cheyney State Coll, BS; Univ Detroit, MA. **CAREER:** Friends Select Sch Phila, tchr; Philadelphia Pub Schs, tchr; Harvou-Act Inc NYC, acting dir after sch study prog; United Ch of Christ, asst to dir & prog coord commn for racial justice; Shaw Coll, chmn div of social sciences; Mayor City of Detroit, exec asst. **ORGANIZATIONS:** Dir Child/Family Ctr City of Detroit; chmn Reg One Bd of Educ City of Detroit; pres Central Bd of Educ City of Detroit; chmn bd of trustees Wayne Co Comm Coll.

BELL, GEORGE ANTONIO
Professional athlete. **PERSONAL:** Born Oct 21, 1959, San Pedros de Macoris, Dominican Republic;married Marie Louisa Beguero; children: Christopher, George Jr. **CAREER:** Toronto Blue Jays, outfielder. **ORGANIZATIONS:** Music & Movies. **HONORS/ACHIEVEMENTS:** Named Labatt's Blue MVP; Labatt's Blue Player of Month for Aug; named Western Carolinas League All-Star Team 1979; Blue Jays Minor League Player of Month for June 1983; named Most Valuable Player of the American League. **BUSINESS ADDRESS:** Toronto Blue Jays, Box 7777, Adelaide St PO, Toronto, Ontario, Canada M5C 2K7. *

BELL, GREGORY LEON
Athlete. **PERSONAL:** Born Aug 01, 1962, Columbus, OH. **EDUCATION:** Univ of Notre Dame, Bachelor in Econ 1983. **CAREER:** Buffalo Bills, pro football 1984. **HONORS/ACHIEVEMENTS:** All AFC Rookie NFL 1984; Rookie of the Year Seagrams Football Digest 1984; Pro Bowler NFL 1985. **HOME ADDRESS:** 1 Bill Drive, Orchard Park, NY 14127.

BELL, H. B.
Educator. **PERSONAL:** Born Apr 13, 1938, LaRue, TX; married Susie Alice Davis; children: Diedrae Carron, Dionica Britte. **EDUCATION:** Prairie View A&M Univ, BA 1961, MEd 1967; East TX State Univ, EdD 1981. **CAREER:** Rust Coll, asst dean of men engrg tchr 1961-63; Dallas Independent Sch Dist, teacher sr high english 1963-68, asst principal 1968-73, educ planner 1973-74, dir teacher educ ctr 1974-76, deputy assoc supt personnel develop 1976-78, deputy assoc supt special funds acquisition and monitoring 1978-82, asst supt subdistrict II 1982-85, asst supt elem instruction 1985-. **ORGANIZATIONS:** Mem TX Educ Agency Eval Team evaluating The Univ of TX at Austin's Prog 1977; presented paper Competency-Based Teacher Educ in Dallas Assoc of Teacher Educators Conf Atlanta GA 1977; mem Southern Assoc Eval Team LG Pinkston HS 1977; adjunct prof East TX State Univ Dept of Admin and Supervision 1985,86; mem Dallas Sch Admin Assoc, Natl Assoc of Secondary Sch Principals, Natl Cncl of Teachers of English, Young Men's Christian Assoc Mooreland Branch, NAACP Dallas Branch, Alpha Phi Alpha Frat; bd of dirs Alpha Merit Group, Woodstream Property Assoc; mem Natl Assoc of Admin of State and Federal Educ-Progs, Amer Assoc of Sch Administrators. **HONORS/ACHIEVEMENTS:** Disting Alumnus Prairie View A&M Univ 1977; Outstanding Urban Educator for the Dallas Independent Sch Dist 1982; Disting Alumnus East TX State Univ 1983;Outstanding Admin Leadership in Educ Dallas Independent Sch Dist 1984; Outstanding Black Texan's Awd TX House of Rep Austin 1987; 5 publications. **HOME ADDRESS:** 6626 Harvest Glen, Dallas, TX 75248. **BUSINESS ADDRESS:** Asst Supt Elem Instruction, Dallas Independent Sch Dist, 3700 Ross Ave, Box 7, Dallas, TX 75204.

BELL, HOWARD EUGENE
Judge. **PERSONAL:** Born May 21, 1920, Norfolk Co, VA. **EDUCATION:** VA Union Univ, BBA 1944; Brooklyn Law School, LLB 1947. **CAREER:** NY City Private practice, attny 1948-58; Office Comptroller City of NY, attny 1958-60; Housing Devel Admin, asst counsel 1960-69; civil Court NY, judge 1969-. **ORGANIZATIONS:** Mem Natl Bar Assoc, NY & Cty Harlem Lawyers Assoc, NAACP, Omega Meml AME Church. **HONORS/ACHIEVEMENTS:** Supreme Court Justice in 1975 for State of NY for 14 yr term commencing 1976-.

BELL, HOWARD HOLMAN
Historian, educator. **PERSONAL:** Born Mar 13, 1913, Morland, KS; married Pauline Margaret Perrine. **EDUCATION:** Univ of CA Berkeley, BA 1941, MA 1947; Northwestern Univ, PhD 1953; Cath Univ of Amer, Grad Student 1955,64. **CAREER:** Country grad schools, teacher 1932-35; Dillard Univ, History instructor 1949-51; Amer Literature & Social Devel Library of Congress, manuscript specialist 1952-54, asst head gift sect 1954-56; TX Southern Univ, mem faculty & staff 1956-67, prof History 1962-67, librarian 1963-66; Morgan State Univ Baltimore, prof History 1967-. **ORGANIZATIONS:** Mem 1969-73, pres 1972-73 Senate State Coll; mem Amer Assoc Univ Prof; mem, pres 1965-66 TX Assoc Coll Teachers; mem Org Amer Historians, AssocStudy of Negro Life & History, Amer Hist Assoc. **HONORS/ACHIEVEMENTS:** Author "A Survey of the Negro Covention Movement 1830-1862" 1969; editor "Minutes of the Proceedings of the Natl Negro Conv" 1969, "Black Separatism & The Caribbean " James Theodore Holly & J Dennis Harris 1970; contrib articles to professional jrnls. **MILITARY SERVICE:** USNR 1942-45.

BELL, JAMES
Professional athlete. **PERSONAL:** Born May 17, 1905, Starksville, MS; married Clarabelle. **CAREER:** Mexican Leagues; Natl Negro Leagues, centerfielder 26 years; St Louis City Hall, retired night watchman. **HONORS/ACHIEVEMENTS:** Rated one of the fastest men on base paths; mem Baseballs Hall of Fame 1974; Credited with circling the bases in 131 seconds, four-tenths of a second faster than the accepted major league mark set by Evar Swanson; Stole 175 bases in one 200 game season; Credit with hitting over 400 several times. **BUSINESS ADDRESS:** c/o Baseball Hall of Fame, PO Box 590, Cooperstown, NY 11326.

BELL, JAMES A.
Educational administrator. **PERSONAL:** Born in Charleston, SC; married Sidney Silver; children: J Yvonne. **EDUCATION:** Hampton Univ, BS 1951; NY Univ, MA 1961. **CAREER:** Hampton Univ, asst prof 1952-70, dir career planning & placement 1970-. **ORGANIZATIONS:** Mem Amer Soc for Engineering Educ; pres VA College Placement Assn 1980-81; bd of dirs Southern Coll Placement Assn 1980-82; exec bd Episcopal Diocese of So VA 1984-86. **HONORS/ACHIEVEMENTS:** Certificate VA Coll Placement Assn 1975 & 1981; certificate Alpha Phi Alpha Frat 1980; certificate Natl Aeronautics & Space Admin 1980; certificate Southern Coll Placement Assn 1981. **MILITARY SERVICE:** AUS corpl 1943-46; European Service 2 Stars; Good Conduct Medal; WWII Victory Medal. **BUSINESS ADDRESS:** Dir Career Plng & Plcmt, HamptonUniv, Hampton, VA 23668.

BELL, JAMES EDWARD
Physician/radiologist. **PERSONAL:** Born Aug 31, 1926, Baltimore, MD. **EDUCATION:** Virginia Union Univ, BS 1951; Howard Univ Sch of Medicine, MD 1957. **CAREER:** Jewish Hospital Cincinnati, intern 1957-58; Veteran Hospital Ctr Milwaukee, radiology resident 1958-60; Univ of Chicago Hospital, radiology resident 1960-61; Marquette Univ Medical Sch, radiology instructor 1961-63; Marquette Univ Med Sch, radiology asst prof 1963-66, radiology assoc prof 1966-70, acting chmn radiology dept 1966-68; Univ of MD Medical School, radiology assoc prof 1970-; Radiology Imaging Assocs, pres. **ORGANIZATIONS:** Vice pres bd dir Baltimore City Medical Soc 1977-81; pres MD Radiological Soc 1981-83; chmn Public Relations Comm State Medical Soc 1983-. **HONORS/ACHIEVEMENTS:** Fellowship Awd Amer Coll of Radiology 1982; Alumni of Baltimore Howard Univ Baltimore Chap 1982; Baltimore Alumni VA Univ Baltimore Chap 1983. **MILITARY SERVICE:** USAF staff sgt 3 yrs. **HOME ADDRESS:** 721 Stoney Spring Dr, Baltimore, MD 21210. **BUSINESS ADDRESS:** President, Radiology Imaging Assocs, 2200 Garrison Blvd, Baltimore, MD 21216.

BELL, JAMES H.
Consultant. **PERSONAL:** Born Mar 21, 1916, Alabama; widowed; children: Thomas M, Minnie Ann Walker. **EDUCATION:** BA. **CAREER:** Cleveland City Counil, dean 18 yrs; real estate bus cons. **ORGANIZATIONS:** Dir Cedar Imp corp Inc, Welfare Fed; mem NAACP, Settlement Houses Assoc; dir, grand master Scottish Rite Masons; trustee St Phillips Luth Church. **BUSINESS ADDRESS:** Real Estate Bus Consultant, 2226 E 55th St, Cleveland, OH 44103.

BELL, JAMES L., JR.
Retired civil engineer. **PERSONAL:** Born Aug 04, 1921, Buffalo, NY; divorced; children: James L III. **EDUCATION:** Howard Univ, BSCE 1954; Univ of Buffalo, Cert of Mechanical Engrg 1949; Dept of Transportation Wash DC, certified bridge inspector 1973. **CAREER:** TVA, retired civil engr div power operations 1954-63, mech engr & asst mech maint supvr Widows Creek Steam Plant 1963-64, prin civil engr divisnl oil spill prevention & control coord 1964-. **ORGANIZATIONS:** Chattanooga Engr Club; chmn Educ Com; Order of the Engr; Equal Empl Oppor; chmn TVA Engrs Assn; Amer Soc Civil Engr Chattanooga Br TN Valley Sect past sec treas; Amer Concrete Inst; Physiography Judge Chattanooga Area Regional Sci Fair; engrg career guid couns Chattanooga HS; chmn Credit Com Chatanooga TVA Employees Fed Credit Union; TVA Chattanooga Comm Relations Com; past keeper of records & seals 5th dist Omega Psi Phi Frat Inc; past basileus Kappa Iota Chap Omega Psi Phi Frat Inc; Dist Commr Cherokee Area Cncl Boy Scouts of Amer; chmn Planning Com; Chattanooga Br NAACP; bd dir Chattanooga Hamilton Co Speech & Hearing Ctr & chmn Indsl Audiology Com; Lay Moderator & Ruling Elder Fairview Presb Ch; past pres Chattanooga Chap PanHellenic Council Inc; Boy Scout Adv; Alpha Phi Omega Serv Frat Boy Scouts of Amer; past dist commr Cherokee Area Counc; mem-at-large Merit Badge Couns. **HONORS/ACHIEVEMENTS:** Silver Beaver Awd Arrowhead Honor Commsrs Key Awd Order of the Arrow; 35 yr Vet Awd. **MILITARY SERVICE:** AUS capt 1942-46.

BELL, JAMES MILTON
Psychiatrist. **PERSONAL:** Born Nov 05, 1921, Portsmouth, VA; son of Charles Edward Bell, Sr. and Lucy Henrietta Barnes. **EDUCATION:** NC Coll Durham NC, BS 1943; Meharry Med Coll Nashville TN, MD 1947; Karl Menninger School of Psychiatry Menninger Found Topeka KS, training gen psych 1953-56; Menninger Found, child psych training 1957-58. **CAREER:** Harlem Hospital, intern rotating 1947-48; Winter Hosp Topeka, resident psych 1953-56; Community Mental Health Activity Keller Army Hosp West Point, col ret consult extended duty; Parsons Child & Family Ctr Albany NY, psychiatrist-child & adolescent; Albany Med Coll of Union Univ, clinical prof psych; Berkshire Farm Ctr & Serv for Youth, clinical dir, psychiatrist, sr child and adolescent psychiatrist 1986-. **ORGANIZATIONS:** Fellow Amer Orthopsychiatric Assoc; fellow Comm on the Stanley Dean Awd of Amer Coll of Psychiatry; charter mem Acad of Religion & Mental Health; mem Group for the Advancement of Psych; mem Council for the sections on Psych of Pan-Amer Med Assoc Inc; pres NY Capital Dist Council on Child Psych; fellow Amer Soc for Adolescent Psych, Council for Exceptional Children, Amer Acad of Political & Soc Sci, Menninger Found, NY State Capitol Dist Br of theAmer Psych Assoc, Natl Med Assoc, Amer Med Assoc, Med Assoc Natl Assoc of Training Schools & Juvenile Agencies, Assoc for Psych Treatment of Offenders, Assoc of the NY State Ed of the Emotionally Disturbed, NY State Soc for Med Rsch Inc, Rotary Club; life mem Reserve Officer Assoc of US; mem AmerMed Soc of Alcoholism 1982-, Assoc of Child Care Workers Inc, Alpha Omega Alpha; life fellow Natl Affairs of Amer Psychiatric Assoc, Comm on Psychiatric Facilities for Children and Adolescents; chair, Amer Psychiatric Assn; life fellow, Amer Acad of Child Psychiatry; life fellow, Amer Orthopsychiatric Assn; fellow, Amer Coll of Psychiatry; fellow, Amer Soc for Adolescent Psychiatry. **HONORS/ACHIEVEMENTS:** Listed in Who's Who in the East, Men of Achievement, Amer Men & Women of Sci-Med Sci, Leaders in Amer Sci, Directory of Med Specialists, The Blue Book, Dir of Intl Biography, The Natl Soc Dir, Who's Who in Community Svcs, US Dir (Geographical) The US Med Dir, Amer Psych Biographical Dir, 1975-76 Bicentenial Meml Ed of Community Leaders & Noteworthy Amers, Pediatric Dir, The Intl Register of Profiles, Intl Who's Who of Intellectuals Vol I, Book of Honor 10th Ed, Personalities of Amer 1978-79, Martin Luther King Meml Library, Intl Reg of Biographies; Disting Alumni in Medicine Meharry Medical Sch 1980, Who's Who in the World, Who's Who in America. **MILITARY SERVICE:** AUS col 1943-76; Army Commendation Medal, Meritorious Service Medal. **HOME ADDRESS:** Hudsonview, Old Post Road North, Croton-on-Hudson, NY 10520. **BUSINESS ADDRESS:** Senior Child/Adolescent Psych, Berkshire Farm Ctr/Serv Youth, Canaan, NY 12029.

BELL, JANET SHARON
Financial aid officer. **PERSONAL:** Born Jun 27, 1947, Chicago, IL; divorced; children: Lenny. **EDUCATION:** Chicago State Univ, BS Educ 1972; IL State Univ, MS Educ 1978. **CAREER:** Chicago Public Schools, teacher 1972-74; State Farm Insurance, coord 1974-76; IL State Univ, academic advisor 1981, counselor w/special serv program 1981-86, asst coord minority student serv 1986-88, asst dir, financial aid office 1988-. **ORGANIZATIONS:** Mem Striving for Affirmative Gains Effectively Bloomington-Normal Chap 1977-86; mem IL Assn of Educ Oppor Program Personnel 1977-86; mem Mid-Amer Assn of Educ Oppor Program Personnel 1981-; vice pres Assn of Black Academic Employees 1985-87; Midwest Assn of Student Financial Aid Administrators; The Illinois Assn of Student Financial Aid Administrators. **BUSINESS ADDRESS:** Assistant Director, Illinois State University, Financial Aid Office, 211 Hovey Hall, Normal, IL 61761.

BELL, JIMMY
Educator. **PERSONAL:** Born Jan 04, 1944, Indianola, MS; married Clara Mcgee; children: Sonya, Arlinda, Meredith, Rasheda. **EDUCATION:** MS Vly St U, BS 1966; MS St U, MA/ABD 1969; NY St Univ Albany, 1978. **CAREER:** Jackson State Univ, prof dept of criminal justice, criminal justice coord 1972-80, asst prof 1970; Lexington Bks DC Health, writer 1977-79. **ORGANIZATIONS:** Dir of rsrch Proj SCAN Indnl MS 1969; consult Nat Inst of Law Enforc 1975-77; consult IT&T 1970; consult lectr Jcksn Plc Dept 1974-80; chmn Dept of Sclgy MS Vly St Univ 1969; chmn Blck Caucus So Sclgcl Soc 1973; exec com mem Nat Assn of Blcks in Crmnl Jstc 1973-76. **HONORS/ACHIEVEMENTS:** Nat Fellow Nat Inst of Mtl Hlth 1966-70; 1st Blck Recip of MA Dgr MS St Univ 1968; Prsnlty of the So 1977; Otstndng Yng Men of Am Nom 1979. **BUSINESS ADDRESS:** Chairman, Jackson State University, Department of Criminal Justice, 1400 Lynch St, Jackson, MS 39217.

BELL, JOSEPH CURTIS
Executive director. **PERSONAL:** Born Mar 23, 1933, Huntington, WV. **EDUCATION:** St Johns Univ, BA 1956; St Maur's Theol Sem, MA 1961; Conception Coll, Cert Pastoral Affairs 1962. **CAREER:** St Maur Prep School, asst hdmstr 1962-65; St Maur Theol Library, admin 1965-67; USAF, chaplain 1967-70; Holy Cross Church, pastor 1970-72; St Maurs Theol Sem, assoc prof 1972-73; Resurrection School, principal 1973-76; Office of Black Ministry, exec dir 1976-. **ORGANIZATIONS:** Chrpsn Park Duvalle Serv Ctr 1971-73; founder, exec dir Fredrick Douglass Inst 1971-73; chief couns Manpower Unlimited Youth Prog, USAF Acad 1971. **HONORS/ACHIEVEMENTS:** Young Gifted & Black Comm Awd KY 1970. **MILITARY SERVICE:** USAF capt 1967-70. **BUSINESS ADDRESS:** Executive Dir, Office of Black Ministry, 1011 1st Ave, New York, NY 10022.

BELL, JOSEPH N.
Business executive. **PERSONAL:** Born Aug 15, 1948, Wilmington, NC; married Carolyn. **EDUCATION:** Shaw U, BS 1970; Univ of GA; Armstrng St Coll; Am Inst of Bnkng; BSA. **CAREER:** Shaw U, hd lncch 1970; Cntrl Trst Co, sr ana 1971; Crvr St Bk, exec vp. **ORGANIZATIONS:** Dir Svnnh Area C of C; dir Svnnh Bus Leag; dir Svnnh Trbn; mem Am Cncr Soc; Grnbr Chldrn Cntr; Cit Adv Com Chthm Urban Trans; Chthm Co Assn Rtrd Chldrn; Svnnh Area Mnrty Cntrctrs; Better Bus Bureau; NAACP; Omega Psi Phi Frat; dcn tst Cnnrs Temp Bapt Ch. **HONORS/ACHIEVEMENTS:** Man Yr Shaw Univ 1969. **BUSINESS ADDRESS:** Carver State Bank, PO Box 2769, Savannah, GA 31498.

BELL, KATIE ROBERSON
Librarian. **PERSONAL:** Born Jun 14, 1936, Birmingham, AL; married Leroy Bell Jr; children: Cheryl Kaye, Mada Carol, Janel E, Janet E. **EDUCATION:** AL State Coll, BS 1956, EdS 1977; Wayne State Univ, MSLA 1973; Univ of AL, PhD 1982. **CAREER:** Tuskegee Inst HS, librarian 1956-59; Parker HS, asst librarian 1959-70, librarian 1970-73; AL State Univ, asst ref lib 1973-74, coord of user serv 1974-75, coord lib educ 1975-; So AL Reg Inserv Educ Ctr, dir 1985; AL State Univ, assoc prof of lib educ 1985-. **ORGANIZATIONS:** Consultant ESAA Task Force ASU & Mobile Sch System 1979-82; mem Comm Tutorial Prog/Links Inc 1982-84; evaluator Natl Council for the Accreditation of Teacher Educ 1983-; bd mem pres elect AL Instructional Media Assoc 1984-; counselor Nu Epsilon Chap Kappa Delta Pi 1984-; evaluator S Assn of Schs & Colls 1985-; bd mem Montgomery Comm Council of the United Way 1985-. **HONORS/ACHIEVEMENTS:** Cert of Honor Birmingham Classroom Teachers Assoc 1970; Educator of the Year Area of Instructional Leadership/Univ of AL 1981; Identification of Activities in Staff Capstone Journal 1982; Development Progs for Secondary Educ Teachers. **BUSINESS ADDRESS:** Assoc Prof of Library Educ, Alabama State University, 915 S Jackson St, Montgomery, AL 36195.

BELL, KENNETH M.
Educator. **PERSONAL:** Born Apr 17, 1941, Bayboro, NC; married Geraldine P; children: Kenneth Jr, Sonji, Marcel. **EDUCATION:** Livingstone Coll, Ab 1964; NC State Univ, NC Central Univ, Grad Study; Duke Univ, MEd 1975. **CAREER:** NC Manpower Devel Corp Bayboro, dep dir; Pamlico Jr High School, teacher, social studies, school guidance counselor. **ORGANIZATIONS:** Past pres Local NC Teachers Assoc 1966; mem NC Ed Assoc, Assoc of Classroom Teachers, NEA, Local NAACP Chap 1964-; elected alderman Town of Bayboro NC 1969-73; founder Cty Youtharama Prog 1966; dir Local ABC-TV Gospel Music Show 1972-73; org 1st pres Agency Serv Council 3 Cty Areas 1970. **HONORS/ACHIEVEMENTS:** 1st black elected in Pamlico Cty as town alderman 1969; recog in Pamlico Cty Centen Cele Yearbook as one of most outstanding blacks in Pamlico Cty; vice pres Centennial Celeb for Pamlico Cty 1972; audition for Dick Cavett Show 1971. **BUSINESS ADDRESS:** Guidance Counselor, Pamlico Jr High School, Bayboro, NC 28515.

BELL, LEON
Clergyman, moderator. **PERSONAL:** Born Jul 14, 1930, Liberty, MS. **EDUCATION:** MS Bapt Sem, ThB 1957; Jackson State Univ, BS 1959; Univ of So MS, MS 1967; Wheaton Coll, Grad Stud Theol 1963,65,66; Univ of So MS, Further Study. **CAREER:** Springhill

Priestly Chap Fairview Bapt Church, Pilgrim Br Bapt Church, Monticello First Bapt, pastor 1954-68; Vctn Bible School MS Bapt Sem, state dir 1958-59; MS Bapt Sem, dean 1959-67; Jackson State Univ, chpln 1965-69, dir student actvts 1967-69, relig advsr, instr 1969-75; Jackson Dist Mission Bapt Assoc, moderator; New Mt Zion, Hyde Park Bapt Churches, pastor. **ORGANIZATIONS:** Chmn Jackson Bicent City-wide Simultan Reviv 1976; org Bell's All-Faith Lit Supplies 1975; chmn Curriculum Com for Convert Natchez Jr Coll into 4 yrsBible Coll 1976; moderat Jackson Dist Mission Bapt Assoc 1976-; mem Jackson Mnstrl Allian; bd mem MS Bapt Sem, Gen Bapt State Conv of MS, Progress Bapt State Conv, Phi Delta Kappa, Intl Platform Assoc, Op Shoestring; bd mem YMCA; inst rep Boy Scouts; clergy Laity Agst Crim; mem VFW, NAACP, Mason. **HONORS/ACHIEVEMENTS:** Listed in Who's Who in Religion 1975-76,77-78, Dictionary of Intl Biog 1976-77, Men of Achievement 1976-77, Comm Leaders & Noteworthy Amer 1976-77; Ambass Life Mag 1966; listed in Personality of the South 1976-77. **MILITARY SERVICE:** AUS 1952-54.

BELL, MARILYN LENORA
Corporate officer. **PERSONAL:** Born Apr 12, 1943, New York, NY; daughter of Dr Stephen A Bell and Audrey Cheatham Bell; children: Felicia Gray. **EDUCATION:** City Coll of NY Baruch School of Business, BBA 1966. **CAREER:** Brooklyn Coll of Business Enterprises, accountant 1966-68; Lucas Tucker & Co, auditor 1968-69; Harlem Commonwealth Council Inc, comptroller 1969-, sec treasurer 1971-; Commonwealth Holding Co Inc, comptroller 1970-, sec treasurer; Richards Consultants LTD, financial consultant 1988-89. **ORGANIZATIONS:** Treasurer United Black Political Action Comm; bd of dirs Magna Media; mem Pyramid Tennis Assn Inc 1976-; treasurer Dowdy Family Found 1979-; mem Coalition of 100 Black Women 1979-; mem Natl Council of Negro Women 1980-; bd of dir Freedom Natl Bank of NY. **BUSINESS ADDRESS:** Comptroller, Commonwealth Holding Co, Inc, 361 W 125th St, New York, NY 10027.

BELL, MARTHA LUE
Educator. **PERSONAL:** Born Oct 12, 1945, Monticello, FL; married Gerald Leon Bell; children: Marvin. **EDUCATION:** North FL Comm Coll, AA 1965; FL A&M Univ, BA 1967; Univ of MO, MA 1969; GA State Univ, EdS 1977; Univ of FL, PhD 1981. **CAREER:** Private Practice, educational consultant, speech and language consultant. **ORGANIZATIONS:** Instructor Exceptional Educ Univ of Central FL 1981-85; chmn Martin Luther King Jr Commemorative Observance Univ of Central FL 1981-85; certified trainer FL Performance Measurement System 1983-85; chmn nom comm Orlando Alumnae Chap Delta Sigma Theta Sor 1984-85; mem bd dirs Orange Co Mental Health Assoc 1984-85; founder The Saturday School (a community outreach prog) Mt Pisgah CME Church 1987; speech & language consultant Urban Serv Agency (Head Start) 1986-87. **HONORS/ACHIEVEMENTS:** Certificate of Minority Academic Achievement Univ of FL 1980; Postdoctoral Internship Amer Assoc of Colls for Teacher Educ 1985-86; McKnight Jr Faculty Fellowship McKnight Foundation 1985-86; numerous publications including "Quality and Equity in the Preparation of Black Teachers," Journal of Teacher Educ, 22 (2), 16-20 1986 (with C Morsink); "Minority Representation in Teaching," AACTE Briefs, 7(2), 10-12 1986. **HOME ADDRESS:** 9639 Axehead Ct, Randallstown, MD 21133.

BELL, MARY L.
Business executive. **PERSONAL:** Born in Nashville, TN; widowed; children: Iris Cox, Dorris Bass. **EDUCATION:** Walden Univ, Grad. **CAREER:** WCHB AM, WJZZ FM Bell Outdoor Advt, pres; Bell Broadcasting Corp, pres/chairperson. **ORGANIZATIONS:** Life mem YWCA, NAACP, Natl Cncl of Negro Women, Afro Amer Museum of Detroit, Bd of MI Cancer Foundation; mem Metro Chap March of Dimes, MI Cancer Foundation, Amer Women in Radio and Television, Womens Economic Club, Womens Advertising Club, Detroit Chap of Links Inc, Plymouth United Church of Christ, WorldServ Cncl of YWCA; vice chairperson Michigan UNCF; mem Sorosis Literary and Art Club, Womens City Club of Detroit. **HONORS/ACHIEVEMENTS:** Listed in Living Legends in Black 1974, Michigan Social Register 1977-, Afro American Museum Honor Roll 1984; NAACP Serv Awd 1978; Capitol Press Awd Washington DC 1979; Natl Black MBA 1981; 100 Black Women's Candace Awd 1984; A Salute to America's Top 100 Black Business & Professional Women 1985; Honorary mem Alpha Kappa Alpha Sor 1986. **BUSINESS ADDRESS:** President/Chairperson, Bell Broadcasting Corp, 32790 Henry Ruff Rd, Inkster, MI 48141.

BELL, MELVYN CLARENCE
Business executive. **PERSONAL:** Born Dec 13, 1944, Los Angeles, CA; married Eliza Ann Johnson. **EDUCATION:** CA State Univ at LA, BS 1971; Univ of So CA, MBA 1973. **CAREER:** KFOX Radio Inc, co-owner/vice pres 1979-; Security Pacific Natl Bank, vice pres 1971-. **ORGANIZATIONS:** Mem Univ S CA MBA Assn 1973; mem Natl Assn of Black MBA's 1976; mem Kappa Alpha Psi Frat 1969-; mem NAACP 1974-; mem LA Urban League 1977-; mem LA Black Businessmen's Assn 1979-; bd dirs LA So Area Boys Club 1979-; pres Kappa Alpha Psi Frat Upsilon Chap LA 1970-71. **MILITARY SERVICE:** USN yeoman 3rd 1966-68. **BUSINESS ADDRESS:** Vice President, Security Pacific Natl Bank, 33 S Hope St, Los Angeles, CA 90071.

BELL, NAPOLEON A.
Attorney. **PERSONAL:** Born Jun 17, 1927, Dublin, GA; married Dorothy J Lyman; children: Kayethel, Napoleon II. **EDUCATION:** Mt Union Coll, BA 1951; Western Reserve Univ Law Sch, LLB 1954. **CAREER:** Industrial Commn of OH, att examiner 1955-58; Bd of Tax Appeals, chmn 1971-74; Beneficial Acceptance Corp, pres & chmn bd; Bell White Saunders & Smallwood, atty 1958-. **ORGANIZATIONS:** Bd dir Columbus Area C of C 1970-73; bd dir Mt Union Coll; bd dir Columbus Urban League treas 1965-66, pres 1969-72; United Negro College Fund state chmn 1972; Columbus Bar Assn; spl counsel Att Gen State of OH 1972-74; bd dir Central OH Boy Scouts; life mem NAACP; chmn Concerned Cit for ColumbusCom 1969; 5th Ward Comm 1963; Franklin Co Dem exec com 1965; Dem Party Structure & Delegate Selection Com 1969; Dem State exec com 1971. **HONORS/ACHIEVEMENTS:** Awd of Merit OH Legal Ctr; Kappa Alpha Psi Man of Yr Awd 1964; Awd of Merit Mahoning Co Youth Club 1964; Awd of Merit United Negro Coll Fund; Seminar on Workmen's Compensation OH Legal Ctr; Mt Union Coll Alumni Chair Awd 1967; Gov Community Serv Awd 1974; NCAA Silver Anniversary Honoree Coll Athletic'sTop 10 1976. **MILITARY SERVICE:** AUS 1946-47. **BUSINESS ADDRESS:** Attorney, Bell White Saunders Smallwood, 180 E Broad St, Ste 816, Columbus, OH 43215.

BELL, PAUL, JR.
Chemist. **PERSONAL:** Born Sep 21, 1921, Lineville, AL; married Ruth Twyman; children: 6 Children. **EDUCATION:** Wilberforce Univ, BS 1947; Univ of Pgh, MS 1950; Grad Studies, Univ of Pgh, George Washington Univ. **CAREER:** Univ of Pgh, rsch assoc 1952-57; VA Hosp Martinsburg WV, biologist 1957-63; VA Hosp Aspinwall PA, histochemist 1963-67; VA Hosp Pgh, chemist 1967-. **ORGANIZATIONS:** Mem Phi Sigma; Sigma Xi; Soc of Experimental Biology & Med; Amer Assn of Clinical Chemist; polemark Kappa Alpha Psi; organized Charlestown Martinsburg WV chap NAACP. **HONORS/ACHIEVEMENTS:** Kappa Man of Yr 1971; Superior Performance Awd VA Hosp 1966 1971 1973; recognition for over 30 publs in med & chem rsch. **MILITARY SERVICE:** AUS 1943-46. **BUSINESS ADDRESS:** VA Hospital, University Dr, Pittsburgh, PA 15240.

BELL, RALEIGH BERTON
Business executive. **PERSONAL:** Born Dec 07, 1915, Clearwater, FL; son of Raleigh B. Bell, Sr. and Lillian Hocker Bell; married Ruth Nelson; children: Deveraux B, Sidney B. **EDUCATION:** Pinellas Indus Inst, graduated 1932; Edward Walters Coll, attended 2 yrs; Harlem School of Music, attended 1935-36. **CAREER:** 2357 Restaurant Corp, general mgr 1964-69; Centerfield Rest Corp, general mgr 1968-70; Jocks Rest Corp, general mgr 1971-72; Beveruth Rest Corp, pres 1973-85; Fairway Sports Inc, pres 1975-85; The Professional V Unlimited, pres; Sidney Bell Associates, consultant 1980-85; Bell Enterprises, pres. **ORGANIZATIONS:** Pres Harlem Citizens Comm 1977-85; pres trustee bd Cosmopolitan AME Church, 1979-87; 1st vice pres The Xmas Tree in Harlem Comm 1980-84; pres Floggers Golf & Tennis Club NYC, 1987; chmn Public Relations & Fund Raising Boys of Yesteryear Inc; bd mem Harlem Serv Center of The Amer Red Cross Harlem House of Commons; mem, Sickle Cell Disease Found of Greater NY; bd mem Community Bd #10; pres Boys of Yesteryear 1985-87; bd mem Comm Bd #10 New York City 1987; Pres, Christmas Tree in Harlem, 1987-present; mem, bd of dirs, Uptown Chamber of Comm, 1986-89. **HONORS/ACHIEVEMENTS:** Comm Serv Award, Amer Red Cross 1976,81; Communityman of the Year Boys of Yesteryear 1980; Baldwin E Sharpe Mem Award Xmas Tree in Harlem Comm 1983; Comm Serv Award Cosmopolitan AME Church 1983; Comm Serv Award Harlem Week 1984; Community Serv Award Central Harlem Senior Citizens Coalition 1986; Comm Citation, Manhattan Borough Pres, 1986; Harlem Community Serv Award, 1987. **HOME ADDRESS:** 2541 7 Ave, Apt 21D, New York, NY 10039. **BUSINESS ADDRESS:** President, Bell Enterprises, 2351 7 Ave, New York, NY 10030.

BELL, REVA PEARL
Educator. **PERSONAL:** Born Aug 17, 1925, Marshall, TX; married John Allen Bell; children: Michele A, Michael A, Sophia E, Ramona E, Jackson Kurtis L. **EDUCATION:** Bishop Coll, BS 1947; TX Christian Univ, MEd 1965; TX Woman's Univ, PhD 1980. **CAREER:** Ft Worth Public Schools, teacher, curriculum writer, curriculum content analyst, head teacher early childhood learning center; SW Educ Devel Lab, curriculum coord; TX Christian Univ, instructor. **ORGANIZATIONS:** Consult SW Educ Devel Lab; consult Indian & Migrants Div OCD; consult Early Childhood Parent Prog; treas/bd of dirs Winnie-the-Pooh Day Care Ctr 1978-79; day care ctr educ chairperson task force Amer Heart Assn 1979-; Curriculum Guide for Early Childhood Ft Worth Pub Schs 1972. **HONORS/ACHIEVEMENTS:** Concepts & lang prog co-author SW Educ Devel Lab 1974; Getting Started co-author Natl Educ Lab Publishers 1975; Natl Sic Found Grant N TX State Univ. **BUSINESS ADDRESS:** Instructor, Texas ChristianUniv, 2900 S University Dr, Fort Worth, TX 76129.

BELL, RICKY LYNN
Professional athlete. **PERSONAL:** Born Apr 08, 1955, Houston, TX. **EDUCATION:** Attended, Southern CA. **CAREER:** Tampa Bay Buccaneers, football player. **BUSINESS ADDRESS:** Tampa Bay Buccaneers, One Buccaneer Place, Tampa, FL 33607.

BELL, ROBERT L.
Psychologist, educator. **PERSONAL:** Born May 10, 1934, Bastrop, TX; married Mattye M; children: Allison E, Millicent P. **EDUCATION:** TX So Univ, BA 1953; Univ of TX, MA 1955, PhD 1961; Univ TX Sch Pub Health, MPH 1980. **CAREER:** VA Hospital Waco, clinical psychologist 1961-66; Baylor Univ, adj prof psychology 1965-66; VA Hospital, psychologist 1966-72; Rice Univ, consultant 1970-72; VA Hospital Houston Drug Abuse Prog, asst dir 1970-72; TX Southern Univ, assoc prof 1972; Riverside General Hospital Drug Abuse Program, psychologist 1972; Counseling Center Vassar Coll, clinical psychologist 1972-73; Rice Univ Houston, dir of student advising & prof psychology 1973-79; Rice Univ Houston, adj prof 1979-80; Private Practice, clinical psychol. **ORGANIZATIONS:** Mem Assn of Black Psychologists; Amer Psychological Assn; SW Psychological Assn; TX Psychological Assn; Houston Psychological Assn; Amer Group Psychotherapy Assn; Houston Group Psychotherapy Soc; SW Inst for Personal & Organizational Devel; NTL Inst of Applied Behavioral Scis; mem Alpha Phi Alpha Frat Inc; Prof Adv Com Ethnic Arts Ctr Hope Devel Inc. **HONORS/ACHIEVEMENTS:** Sup Perf Awd Vets Adminstrn 1964; Special Serv Perf Awd Vets Adminstrn 1968; Amer Psychological Assn cattell Fund Awd for Rsch Related to Psychol Consultation 1969; Outstanding Alumnus Awd TX So Univ 1972. **BUSINESS ADDRESS:** Clinical Psychologist, Medical Towers, Ste 1598, Houston, TX 77030.

BELL, ROBERT MACK
Judge. **PERSONAL:** Born Jul 06, 1943, Rocky Mount, NC. **EDUCATION:** Morgan State Coll, attended 1966; Harvard Law Sch, JD 1969. **CAREER:** Piper & Marbury, assoc 1969-74; Dist Ct of MD, judge 1975-. **ORGANIZATIONS:** Bd dir Villa Julie Coll; bd of dir Legal Aid Bureau; grader MD St Bar Examiners 1973-75; bd dir Afro Amer Newspaper 1973-74; bd dir Neighborhood Adolescent & Young Adult Drug Prog Inc 1974-75; Grievance Comm exec comm chmn memshp comm Baltimore City Bar Assn; MD State Bar Assn; chmn mem Bar Assn 1971-72; Bail Bond Commn 1973-77. **HONORS/ACHIEVEMENTS:** Dist Perf & Accompl Awd Morgan Alumni 1975; Distinctive Achiev Awd Phi Alpha Theta 1976; Comm Serv Awd Hiram Grand Lodge AF & AM 1976. **BUSINESS ADDRESS:** Judge, Dist Court of MD, 211 E Madison St, Baltimore, MD 21202.

BELL, ROBERT WESLEY
Building contractor. **PERSONAL:** Born Apr 10, 1918, Bethlehem, GA; married Louvenia Smith. **EDUCATION:** Welders & Mechanic School, 1940. **CAREER:** Afro-Amer Life Ins Co, agent 1955-75; State of GA, selective serv 1972-, 1st black dist commander of Amer Legion 1973-74, 1st black chmn of children & youth div of Amer Legion 1974-80; Economic

Opportunity of Atlanta, mem of fin comm 1980-84; Buford city Schools, elected mem of bd of ed 1981-85; People'sBank of Buford, 1st black mem of bd of dir 1983-85; Bell Brothers Constr Co, part owner; Buford City Schools, vice chmn bd of ed. **ORGANIZATIONS:** Mem deacon bd Poplar Hill Baptist Church 1940-85; church clerk Poplar Hill Baptist Church 1950-85; supt of Sunday School Poplar Hill Baptist Church 1950-85;asst clerk Hopewell Baptist Assoc 1974-85; staff mem Boys State Amer Legion 1976-85; appt mem Planning & Zoning City of Buford 1979-85; chmn Boy Scouts State of GA 1980-82; mem Gwinnett Clean & Beautiful Citizens Bd Gwinnett Cty 1980-83; amer chmn Amer Legion State of GA 1982-85. **HONORS/ACHIEVEMENTS:** Natl Achievement Awd Natl Amer Legion 1966; Man of the Year Buford Comm Org 1974; Gwinnett Clean & Beautiful Awd Gwinnett Cty Citizens Bd 1980. **MILITARY SERVICE:** AUS master sgt 1943-46; Asiatic Pacific Serv Medal, World War II Victory Medal, Amer Serv Medal, European-African Middle East Serv Medal 2 Bronze Stars. **BUSINESS ADDRESS:** Vice Chairman, Buford City Schools, 201 Roberts St, Buford, GA 30518.

BELL, ROSEANN P.
Educator. **PERSONAL:** Born May 02, 1945, Atlanta, GA; divorced; children: William David. **EDUCATION:** Howard Univ, BA 1966; Emory Univ, MA (Cum Laude) 1970, PhD (Cum Laude) 1974. **CAREER:** US Civil Service Commn, typist 1964-66; Atlanta Public School System, instructor 1966-70; various & part-time teaching positions; freelance editor of educ manuscripts 1970-; Spelman Coll, asst prof 1970-; Atlanta Voice Newspaper, columnist 1971; Cornell Univ, asst prof Afro-Amer studies. **HONORS/ACHIEVEMENTS:** Author of numerous published articles; Scholarship to Emory Univ 1968-70; Natl Inst of Humanities Fellowship 1971-73; Natl Fellowships Fund Fellowship FordFound 1973-74. **HOME ADDRESS:** 109 Fiddler Rd, Ithaca, NY 14850.

BELL, ROUZEBERRY
Dentist. **PERSONAL:** Born Jul 13, 1934, Pittsburgh, PA; married Alice McGhee; children: Cheryl, Karen, Jeffrey. **EDUCATION:** Univ of Pitts, BS 1959; Howard U, DDS 1970. **CAREER:** Pvt Prac, dentist 1973-; KW Clement Family Care Ctr, dental dir 1975-; Hough Norwood Family Care Ctr, staff dentist 1971-75; St Lukes Hosp, intern 1970-71; WA Hosp Ctr, pharmacist 1966-70; Univ Hosp of Cleveland, 1959-66. **ORGANIZATIONS:** Mem Forest City Dental Soc 1970-; Dept of Comm Dentistry Case Western Res Univ 1975-; bd of dir Forest City Dental Indep Prac Assn 1976-; Clevland Dental Soc; mem OH St Dental Assn; Nat Dental Assn; Am Dental Assn; Buckeye St Dental Assn; mem Big Bros of Am 1966-. **HONORS/ACHIEVEMENTS:** Flwsp Dept of Anesthesiology St Luke's Hosp 1971. **MILITARY SERVICE:** USN hospitalman 3rd class 1952-55. **BUSINESS ADDRESS:** Severance Medical Arts Bldg, 5 Severance Circle, Cleveland, OH 44118.

BELL, S. AARON
Educator. **PERSONAL:** Born Apr 24, 1924, Muskogee, OK; married Delores Orton; children: Pamela Lightsy, Aaron Wilson, Robin V. **EDUCATION:** Xavier Univ, BA Music 1938; New York Univ, MA Music 1951; Columbia Univ, MEd Music 1976, DEd Cmpstn 1977. **CAREER:** Duke Ellington Orchestra, arranger-bassist 1958-64; NBC NY, studio musician 1960-62; La Mama Theatre, res composer 1964-68; Essex County Coll, coll prof 1969-, chmn 1979-. **ORGANIZATIONS:** Bassist pianist cndctr Schubert Theatre Org 1964-70; res cmpsr R B Allen Theatre 1980-84; mem ASCAP 1955-85, Blck Caucus of NEA 1980-85, Natl Acad of the Arts 1975-85, Natl Scty of Lit Arts 1976-85. **HONORS/ACHIEVEMENTS:** Pnlst NY St Art Comm 1980, NJ Endwmt 1982, Jackie Robinson Fndtn Comm 1984; Ford Flwshp Columbia Univ 1975-76; Obie Nom Theatre Awd for CmpstnNew York City 1979; Outstndng Comm Srvc UNICEF Newark Chptr 1984. **MILITARY SERVICE:** USN mscn 1st cl 1942-46. **HOME ADDRESS:** 444 S Columbus Ave, Mount Vernon, NY 10553. **BUSINESS ADDRESS:** Chairman, Music Department, Essex County College, 303 High St, Newark, NJ 07103.

BELL, SHEILA TRICE
Attorney. **PERSONAL:** Born Aug 25, 1949, Pittsburgh, PA; married Howard W Bell Jr; children: Mayet Maria, Annora Alicia. **EDUCATION:** Wellesley Coll, BA 1971; Harvard Law Sch, JD 1974. **CAREER:** Pine Manor Jr Coll, faculty mem 1972-74; Hutchins & Wheeler, assoc lawyer 1973-77; Private Legal Practice, attorney 1977-79; Fisk Univ, univ counsel 1979-83; Northern KY Univ, acting univ counsel/affirmative action officer 1984-85, univ legal counsel 1985-. **ORGANIZATIONS:** Bd mem Family and Children's Services Nashville TN 1981-83; mem The Links Inc Cincinnati Chap 1984-; mem Jack and Jill Inc Cincinnati Chap 1984-; mem MA, TN, KY Bars, Amer Bar Assns; mem US Dist Courts of MA, the Middle Dist of TN and the Eastern Dist of KY, US Court of Appeals for the Sixth Circuit; bd mem Natl Assoc of Coll and Univ Attys 1985-88; bd mem The Program for Cincinnati 1986-88. **HONORS/ACHIEVEMENTS:** Equal Rights Amendment Commn for the Commonwealth of MA 1976; editorial bd The Journal of College and University Law 1982-83; Outstanding Young Woman of Amer 1982; Mayor's Special Task Force on Union Station Nashville TN 1982-83; publication "Protection and Enforcement of College and University Trademarks" co-authored w/Martin F Majestic in the Journal of College and Univ Law, Vol 10, No 1 1983-84. **HOME ADDRESS:** 40 Burton Woods Lane, Cincinnati, OH 45229. **BUSINESS ADDRESS:** Univ Legal Counsel, Northern KentuckyUniv, 834 Administrative Ctr, Highland Heights, KY 41076.

BELL, THEODORE JOSHUA, II
Escrow accountant. **PERSONAL:** Born Jan 08, 1961, Berkeley, CA; son of Theodore J Bell and Beverly Russ Bell. **EDUCATION:** St Mary's Coll of CA, BA 1983; CA Sch of Arts & Crafts, attended 1983-84; Heald Business Coll of Oakland, Career Business diploma 1985; Berkeley School of Computor Graphics, 1989-. **CAREER:** St Mary's Coll Basketball, VIP usher 1980-82; Marriott Boykin Corp, graphic illustrator/banquet waiter 1981-85; Equitec Financial Group, accountant 1985-88; First American Title Inc, escrow accountant, 1988-. **ORGANIZATIONS:** Donator/supporter St Mary's Coll Alumni 1983-; illustrator/volunteer Work of Love Program 1984-85; mem admin Heald Coll Business Club 1985; mem adv viewer Kron TV Adv Bd 1985-; mem supporter Natl Urban League 1986-. **HONORS/ACHIEVEMENTS:** Berkeley Marriott Employee of the Year Awd 1984; Investment in Excellence Commitment to Excellence Equitec Awd 1986. **HOME ADDRESS:** 2777 Park St, Berkeley, CA 94702. **BUSINESS ADDRESS:** Escrow Accountant, First American Title Company, 500 12th Street, Suite 210, Oakland, CA 94610.

BELL, THERON J.
Appointed official. **PERSONAL:** Born Jun 02, 1931, Junction City, KS; married Sonya M Brown; children: Kirk, Mark, Joy Pinell, Kimberly Good, Margo Goldsboro, Michele Brown. **EDUCATION:** Wayne State Univ, 1949-51. **CAREER:** CA Office of Economic Opportunity, dir 1967-69; Volt Info Sci, dir govt relations 1969-70; Chrysler Motors Corp, exec, 1970-72; Action Agency, various exec 1972-81; Minority Business Devel Agency, US Dept of Commerce, deputy dir. **ORGANIZATIONS:** Mem CA Assoc for Health & Welfare 1967-69, CA Job Training & Placement Council 1968-69, Erie Cty NY Environ Mgmt Council 1970-71, Alexandria VA Human Rights Commiss, Fed Interagency Comm on Fed Activities for Alcohol Abuse & Alcoholism, Alexandria VA Republican City Comm, CA Republican State Central Comm; life mem Republican Natl Comm; mem Alexandria VA Republican City Comm; Navy League of the US, American Legion, dir Fredrick Douglass Coalition. **HONORS/ACHIEVEMENTS:** Top Producer for One Year, consistently among the top producers for the co North Amer Life & Casualty Co San Francisco. **MILITARY SERVICE:** AUS pvt 8 mo. **HOME ADDRESS:** 803 N Howard St, Apt #435, Alexandria, VA 22304. **BUSINESS ADDRESS:** Deputy Dir, Minority Bussiness Develop, US Dept of Commerce, 14th & Constitution Ave NW, Washington, DC 20230.

BELL, THOM R.
Songwriter. **PERSONAL:** Born Jan 27, 1943, Philadelphia, PA; married Sybell; children: Cybell, Mark, Thom Jr. **CAREER:** Chubby Checker, band leader 1962-65; Cameo Pkwy Records, a&r man musician 1966-68; arranger/songwriter/producer 1968-80; Gamble Huff & Bell, mng partner. **ORGANIZATIONS:** Pres Mighty Three Music; mem AFM; opr Thom Bell Songwriter Workshop. **HONORS/ACHIEVEMENTS:** Ten BMI Awds; 2 Grammy nominations; 45 Gold Albums & 45's; 1 Grammy; 2 Number One Producers Awds; 2 Bus Awds Billboard Mag; 2 Number One Songwriter Awds Billboard Magazine; 2 Number One Producers Awds NATRA. **BUSINESS ADDRESS:** Producer, Philadelphia Intl Records, 309 S Broad St, Philadelphia, PA 19107.

BELL, TOM CALVIN
Professional athlete. **PERSONAL:** Born Nov 28, 1958, Middletown, OH. **EDUCATION:** Ohio State. **CAREER:** Chicago Bears, safety 1981-. **HONORS/ACHIEVEMENTS:** Named to Pfw all-NFC defensive team; earned game ball in season opening win over Tampa Bay; Natl Coaches Assn All-Strength Team; Prep all-Am linebacker at Middletown OH High. **BUSINESS ADDRESS:** Chicago Bears, Halas Hall, 250 N Washington Rd, Lake Forest, IL 60045.

BELL, TOMMY LEE, III
Chief executive. **PERSONAL:** Born Dec 03, 1948, Meridian, MS; son of Tommie Bell, Jr and Roselyn Wilson Bell; married Christiana C Attenson Bell, Oct 28, 1983; children: Antoine, Antanille. **EDUCATION:** Middleton Atten Center, Meridian MS; Glenville, Cleveland, OH. **CAREER:** TL Bell Power Clean, Inc, Cleveland OH, pres. **ORGANIZATIONS:** Vice pres, bd of trustees, Universal Church, 1984; pres, Successeeds, Inc, 1985-89; first vice pres, Martin Luther King Memorial Fund, 1988-89. **HONORS/ACHIEVEMENTS:** Outstanding Service Achiever, Cleveland Heights High School, 1978; Certificate of Achievement, MSMC Corp, 1986. **BUSINESS ADDRESS:** Pres, T L Bell Power Clean, Inc, 1700 E 13th St, Suite 4S E, Cleveland, OH 44114.

BELL, TRAVERS J., SR.
Chocolate manufacturer. **CAREER:** Cocoline Chocolate Co Inc, Brooklyn NY, chief executive. **BUSINESS ADDRESS:** Chief Executive, Cocoline Chocolate Co Inc, 689 Myrtle Ave, Brooklyn, NY 11205. *

BELL, TRENTON G.
Business executive. **PERSONAL:** Born Jun 13, 1924, Troy, OH; married Majorie Ann Chavis; children: Herbert A, Daryl Chavis, Linda Coleman, Sonja, Gordon G. **EDUCATION:** FL A&M Tallahasee, 1942-44. **CAREER:** Hobart Bros Co, mgr, human resources devel, 1950-. **ORGANIZATIONS:** St pres, IBPOE Elks 1960-69; pres Am Lung Assn 1978-; bd dir Lincoln Ctr; Troy Rec; Salvation Army 1969-; mem Bd of Elections Miami Cnty; chmn Miami County Democratic Party 1983-84; sec Ohio St Democratic Chmns Assn 1984; general mgr Grdn Mnr Housing Authority; mem bd of Health; pres, Troy Employment Svcs. **HONORS/ACHIEVEMENTS:** Serv to Mankind, Sertoma Club, 1981; Hon mem, Alpha Mu Sigma 1981; Key to City, Cleveland OH St Assn Elks; Key to City Youngstown, OH St Assn Elks. **MILITARY SERVICE:** AUS T/5 2 yrs. **HOME ADDRESS:** 1605 Henley Rd, Troy, OH 45373.

BELL, VICTORY
Supervisor. **PERSONAL:** Born Mar 07, 1934, Durant, MS; married Betty Ann; children: Jeffrey, Gregory, Victor, Michele. **CAREER:** I&M St Coin IL Bell Tele Co, supr pub serv; IL Bell Tele Co, consult affirm actn prog; Alderman, 1971; Nrthrn IL U, comm rep. **ORGANIZATIONS:** Mayor's appt Econ Devel Commn C of C; voice pres J Wattles Mtl Hlth 1971-; vol org to Imp Comm Efrts; pres PTA 1968-70; pres Comm Actn Wnnbg Poltcl Leag 1971-74; 1st vice pres IL Caucas 1977; coor IL St Blck Caucus; mem Spkrs Bureau Nrthrn IL U; bd mem Sthwst Improv Corp; mem Mayors Cncl for Yth Emp 1977; mem Plgrm Bapt Ch; bd mem Nrthrn IL Bus; bd mem Mark V Prdctns; mem Rckfrd Ctzn Adv Bd for Sch; chmn Cncl Sub Comm on Soc Serv Prog; chmn Rckfrd Comm Rnwl Com. **HONORS/ACHIEVEMENTS:** Man of yr recogn Natl Cncl Negro Wmn 1975; man of the yr Pltcl Chrstn Union Bapt Ch 1976; pnlst 1st Stwd Mnrty Conf for St of IL Sprngfld; del Pres Carter Nat Dem Conv 1980.

BELL, WARREN, JR.
Journalist. **PERSONAL:** Born Jun 18, 1951, New Orleans, LA; divorced; children: Kristina Marie. **EDUCATION:** Yale Univ, BA 1973. **CAREER:** WTNH-TV, reporter; WBAL-TV, reporter 1973-74; WDSU-TV, news anchorman. **ORGANIZATIONS:** Bd mem Big Brothers of New Orleans; bd mem Amer Fedn TV/Radio Artists; vice pres New Orelans Blacks in Communications. **HOME ADDRESS:** 716 Pauger St, New Orleans, LA 70122.

BELL, WENDOLYN YVONNE
Educational administrator. **PERSONAL:** Born Nov 21, 1928, Memphis, TN. **EDUCATION:** WV State Coll, BA (Cum Laude) 1948; Univ of WI, MA 1950; Univ of IA, PhD 1964.

CAREER: TN State Univ, instr of spanish 1950-51; Prairie View A&M Univ, instr of spanish 1951-53; FL A&M Univ, asst prof of spanish 1953-59, summer 1960; Univ of IA, grad asst 1960-63; TN State Univ, prof of spanish 1963-, asst dean 1976-79, assoc dean of arts 1979-82, acting dean 1982-. **ORGANIZATIONS:** Mem Amer Assoc of Teachers of Span & Port 1954-, Coll Lang Assoc 1954; reg vice pres Alpha Mu Gamma 1971-78; bd of dir Southern Conf on Lang Teaching 1974-78; consult Southern Assoc of Coll & Schools 1979-; exec comm TN Assoc of Coll for Teacher Ed 1983-85; mem of bd Natl Commiss on Arts & Sci 1983-88; mem Modern Lang Assoc; bd of dir Council of the Colls of Arts and Scis 1986-88; mem Literary Panel of the TN Arts Commn 1986-89. **HONORS/ACHIEVEMENTS:** Univ Scholar Univ of IA 1960-63; John Hay Whitney Fellow 1961-62; Book El Espanol Antiguo co-author with Dr George Zucker 1970; Article "Nomenclature and Spanish Literacy Analysis" CLA Jrnl 1974. **HOME ADDRESS:** 3804 Cravath Dr, Nashville, TN 37207. **BUSINESS ADDRESS:** Acting Dean, College of Arts & Sciences, Tennessee StateUniv, Nashville, TN 37203.

BELL, WILLIAM A.
City council president. **CAREER:** City Council President, Birmingham, AL. **BUSINESS ADDRESS:** City Hall, 710 North 20th St, Birmingham, AL 35203. *

BELL, WILLIAM CHARLES
Attorney. **PERSONAL:** Born Dec 28, 1945, Detroit, MI; married Jean Osbay; children: Michael Humbles. **EDUCATION:** Golden Gate Univ, BA 1973; Hastings Coll of Law, JD 1976. **CAREER:** San Francisco Co Jail Legal Assistance, atty 1978; Law Offices of William C Bell, pvt practice 1978-79; Bell Realty, real estate broker 1978; Holland & Bell, atty/partner 1979-. **ORGANIZATIONS:** Treas Wm H Hastie Bar Assn; mem bd dirs San Francisco Neighborhood Legal Assistance Found 1979-; bd dirs Charles Houston Bar Assn 1979. **HONORS/ACHIEVEMENTS:** Outstanding Young Man of Amer 1980. **BUSINESS ADDRESS:** Attorney, Holland & Bell, 390 Hayes St Ste 2, San Francisco, CA 94102.

BELL, WILLIAM JERRY
Government employee. **PERSONAL:** Born Apr 18, 1934, Chicago, IL. **EDUCATION:** Roosevelt Univ, BS Commrc 1958; Univ of IL; Univ of Chgo, PA. **CAREER:** IL Bur of Budget, sr budget analyst, 1969-72; IL Dept of Labor, mgmt specialist, 1972-75, financial rsch, 1975-79, asst comm unemployment insurance. **ORGANIZATIONS:** Partner, Fields Bell of Assoc Insurance Agency, 1970-83; consultant Small Business Assn, 1968-69; bd mem, Southside Comm Art Ctr 1985; adv Univ of IL Sch of Art & Dsgn 1981-83; founder/chmn bd, Talent Asst Pgm 1976-77. **MILITARY SERVICE:** AUS specialist, 1957-58. **BUSINESS ADDRESS:** Asst Comm Unemployment Insurance, IL Dept of Labor, 910 S Michigan Ave, Chicago, IL 60605.

BELL, WILLIAM MCKINLEY
Legal services administrator. **PERSONAL:** Born Aug 31, 1926, Grand Rapids, MI; son of William M Bell (deceased) and Mentie N Bell; married Patsy Ann Kelley. **EDUCATION:** Univ of Michigan, AB 1948, MBA 1954. **CAREER:** Johnson Publishing Co, salesman/merchandising rep 1956-57; William M Bell & Associates, president 1958-75; Equal Employment Opportunity Comm, consultant 1975-76; Bold Concepts, Inc, president 1976-82; US Navy, staff asst sec 1982-87; Legal Serv Corp, legislative asst to dir 1988-. **ORGANIZATIONS:** Member Omega Psi Phi Fraternity 1947; member Tabernacle Baptist Church Detroit, MI 1955-; member Univ of Michigan School of Business Alumni Assoc 1982. **HONORS/ACHIEVEMENTS:** Optimist of the Year, Optimist Club, Renaissance Chapter 1981; special tribute State of Michigan 1981. **MILITARY SERVICE:** AUS 1950-52. **BUSINESS ADDRESS:** Legal Services Corporation, 400 Virginia Ave, SW, Washington, DC 20024-2751.

BELL, WILLIAM VAUGHN
Senior engineer. **PERSONAL:** Born Jan 03, 1941, Washington, DC; son of William B Bell (deceased) and Willie M Vaughn Mullen; married Judith Chatters; children: William V II, Tiffany A, Anjanee N, Kristen V. **EDUCATION:** Howard Univ, BS Elect Engrg 1961; NY Univ, MS Elect Engrg 1968. **CAREER:** Martin Marietta Corp, jr engr 1961; US Army Electronics Command, proj engr 1963-68; IBM Corp, mgr 1968-83, tech asst 1983-, electrical engrg, elect engr mgr 1985-. **ORGANIZATIONS:** Mem IEEE 1961-; pres bd of dir UDI/CDC 1970-83; bd of dir NC School of Sci & math 1979-; cty commiss Durham Cty Bd of Commiss 1972-; chmn of bd Durham Cty Bd of Commiss 1982-; dir Durham Chamber of Commerce 1982-; bd of trustees, Durham County Hospital Corp 1984-; advisory bd, Duke Univ Hospital 1987-. **HONORS/ACHIEVEMENTS:** Community Serv Awd, State of NC 1981; Outstanding Citizen, Durham Committee on the Affairs of Blacks 1985; Community Serv Awd, Durham Chap Kappa Alpha Psi 1985; Outstanding Alumnus, Howard Univ Club of Research Triangle Pk 1985; Outstanding Citizen Award, Omega Psi Phi, Durham NC 1986; Alumni Award for Distinguished Post-Graduate Achievement, Howard Univ 1988; Service to Mankind Award, James E Shephard Sertoma Club 1989. **MILITARY SERVICE:** AUS Signal Corp 1st lt 2 1/2 yrs 1961-63. **HOME ADDRESS:** 1003 Huntsman Dr, Durham, NC 27713.

BELL, WINSTON ALONZO
Pianist/university professor. **PERSONAL:** Born Mar 24, 1930, Winchester, KY; married Marlita Peyton; children: Taimia Danielle. **EDUCATION:** Fisk Univ, BA 1951; Univ of Michigan, MusM 1955; Columbia Univ, EdD 1963; General Theol Seminary, StB 1964; studied at Cincinnati Conservatory of Music, Wells Theol Coll Wells England, Oxford Univ, Catholic Univ, UCLA, Univ of Louisville. **CAREER:** NY City School System, teacher 1955-60; Elizabeth City State Univ NC, instructor in piano 1953-55; Music Studio Nyack NY, pianist/teacher 1955-60; St Augustine Chapel NYC, curate 1963-64; St James the Less Jamaica NY, rector 1964-71; Winston-Salem State Univ NC, chmn dept of music 1972-; real estate broker 1981-. **ORGANIZATIONS:** Organist Holy Family Catholic Church; bd of dir Winston-Salem Symphony, Piedmont Opera Society; mem Suzuki Assoc of Amer, MENC, Phi Mu Alpha Sinfonia, Omega Psi Phi Frat, Coll Music Soc. **HONORS/ACHIEVEMENTS:** Rockefeller Theol Fellowship Fisk Univ; Piano Recitals Winchester KY, Louisville, Washington, San Juan, New York, Norfolk, Virginia Beach, Winston-Salem, St Louis, Ft Knox, Santo Domingo, Elizabeth City, London, Oxford, Paris, Heidelberg, Rome, Brussels. **MILITARY SERVICE:** AUS spl serv pfc 1951-53. **BUSINESS ADDRESS:** Professor of Music, Winston-Salem StateUniv, Columbia Heights, Winston-Salem, NC 27101.

BELL, YOLANDA MARIA
Government official. **PERSONAL:** Born Feb 24, 1949, Alliance, OH; children: William, Sidney, Jamie. **EDUCATION:** Kent State Univ, BS 1982. **CAREER:** WHBC Radio, receptionist/record librarian 1973; Security Forces Inc, security guard 1976-78; Superior Dairy Inc, equipment cleanup oper 1978-84; City of Canton, dir mayor's dept of consumer affairs 1984-. **ORGANIZATIONS:** Record secty/gate keeper Gladys Merrell Temple # 1049 IBPOEOW 1976-; mem 16th Congressional Dist Black Caucus; bd mem Special Adv Comm Alcohol & Drug Assistance Prog 1985-, Central State Co Mental Health Ctr 1986-. **HONORS/ACHIEVEMENTS:** Outstanding Young Women of Amer 1985. **HOME ADDRESS:** 1308 Cleveland Ave NW Apt 2, Canton, OH 44703. **BUSINESS ADDRESS:** Dir Mayor's Dept Consumer Afrs, City of Canton, 218 Cleveland Ave SW, Canton, OH 44702.

BELL-FOSTER, WILHEMENIA
Educator. **PERSONAL:** Born Jul 19, 1954, Detroit, MI. **EDUCATION:** Shaw Coll at Detroit, BA 1975; Univ of MI, BA 1975, MA 1978. **CAREER:** MI Dept of Corrections, correctional adult educator. **ORGANIZATIONS:** Club & district officer Toastmasters Intl 1981-; officer-steward St John CME Church 1981-; mem Corrections Educ Assoc 1984-, MI Reading Assoc 1985-; co-founder & coord Young Women's Sor 1985-; founder/organizer Cooley High Speakers Bureau 1986-. **HONORS/ACHIEVEMENTS:** Appreciation Awd 1984, Competent Toastmasters Awd 1984, Accomplished Toastmaters Awd 1985 all from Toastmasters Intl. **BUSINESS ADDRESS:** Correctional Adult Educator, MI Department of Corrections, 8110 E White Lake Rd, Clarkston, MI 48016.

BELL-SCOTT, PATRICIA
Educator. **PERSONAL:** Born Dec 20, 1950, Chattanooga, TN; daughter of Louis Wilbanks and Dorothy Graves Wilbanks; married Arvin U. **EDUCATION:** Univ of TN Knoxville, BS 1972; MS 1973; PhD 1976; JFK School of Govt Harvard Univ, Post Doctoral Fellow 1979-80. **CAREER:** Univ of CT School of Family Studies, assoc prof 1985-; MIT, asst equal oppty officer 1982-84; Wellesley Coll Center for Rsch on Women, rsch assoc 1980-84; Pub Policy Prog JFK Sch of Govt Harvard, fellow & rsrch asso 1979-; Child & Fam StudUniv of TN, asst dir black stud & asst prof 1976-79; Child & Fam StudUniv of TN, instr 1974-76. **ORGANIZATIONS:** Consult Women's Prog Off of Educ 1978; natl exec bd Nat Assn for Women Deans Adminstr & Counslrs 1978-80; consult Nat Adv Com on Black Higher Educ 1979;chrwoman AWA (Black Women's Comm Com) 1975-77; bd Black Comm Devel Inc Knoxville 1975-77; soc action com Delta Sigma Theta Knoxville Alumnae Chap 1977-78; vice pres for assoc relations natl Assoc for Women Deans & Admins 1980-82; co-founder SAGE, A Scholarly Jrnl of Black Women 1984; ed bd Jrnl of Negro Educ 1983-, Women of Power, A Jrnl of Feminism & Power 1984; guest ed Psychology of Women Quarterly, new Directions for Women 1982-83, Jrnl of the Natl Assn for Women Deans & Admins 1979-81; secretary, Family Action Section, Natl Council on Family Relations 1974-76; co-convener, Coordinating Council, Natl Women's Studies Assn 1977-78; bdmem, College Express Foundation 1989-. **HONORS/ACHIEVEMENTS:** Cit for Outstndg Serv UTK Chap of Mortar Bd 1977; Regl Finlst White House Fellow Prog 1977-78; author over 20 arts and two books; Cited as Outstndng Young Woman Outstndg Young Women in Am 1978; recip Disting Educ in CT Awd CT Chap of the Coalition of 100 Black Women 1986; recip Fourth Curriculum Matls Awd Women Educators 1983; recip Awd for Outstanding Contribution to Feminist Scholarship Nato Inst for Women of Color 1982; Cited for Outstanding Serv to the Univ of TN Knoxville Black Students Assoc 1978; Citation of Outstanding Contribution to the Psychology of Black Women, Div 35, American Psychological Assn 1988; Recipient, Esther Lloyd-Jones Distinguished Service Award of the National Assn for Women Deans, Administrators, & Counselors 1989; Guest Co-Editor, Special Issue on Black Adolescents, Journal of Adolescent Research 1989. **BUSINESS ADDRESS:** Associate Professor, Human Development & Family Relations, University of Connecticut, U-58, DRM Building, Storrs-Mansfield, CT 06268.

BELLAMY, ANGELA ROBINSON
Administrator. **PERSONAL:** Born Nov 25, 1952, Miami, FL; married Gregory Derek Bellamy; children: Gregory Robinson. **EDUCATION:** Fisk Univ, Nashville TN, BA, 1974; Vanderbilt Univ, Owen Grad Schof Mgmt, Nashville TN, MBA, 1976; Harvard Univ, John F Kennedy Sch of Govt, Program for Sr Executives in State and Local Govt, 1986. **CAREER:** City of Miami, admin asst, 1976-77, persnl ofcr, 1977-78, sr persnl ofcr, 1978-79, prsnl supr hum res, 1979, asst to city mgr, 1979-81, dep dir hum res, 1981-84, dir hum res, 1984-. **ORGANIZATIONS:** Sec 1978, vice pres 1979 IPMA S FL Chapt; co-ch host comm IPMA Intl Conf 1983-84; area coord FL Pub Persnl Assn 1984-85; mem Delta Sigma Theta Sor Inc, Natl Forum Black Pub Admin; chair IPMA Human Rights Comm 1985-86; mem IPMA Nomination Comm 1987. **HONORS/ACHIEVEMENTS:** Outstndng Yng Wmn of Am 1981; Who's Who and Why of Successful Florida Women 1984-85; Awd for Outstanding Achievement Personnel Assoc of Greater Miami 1987. **HOME ADDRESS:** 15800 SW 98 Court, Miami, FL 33157. **BUSINESS ADDRESS:** Dir of Personnel Mgmt, City of Miami, PO Box 330708, Miami, FL 33233.

BELLAMY, HERBERT L.
Business executive, councilman. **PERSONAL:** Born Apr 23, 1931, Burgaw, NC; married Irene Parham; children: Delphine, Jacquelyn Copeland, Darlene, Herbert Jr, Gwendolyn, John Wesley. **EDUCATION:** Dale Carnegie Inst, attended 1958; Buffalo State Coll, attended 1972. **CAREER:** Beth Steel Corp, 1950-56; Buffalo NY, civil serv commr 1965-77, councilman; Bellamy Enterp, owner. **ORGANIZATIONS:** Vice pres Buffalo C of C 1968-70; Jeff-Utica Bus Assn 1966-; dir Blue Cross Blue Shield 1973-; Blk Bus Dev Corp 1970-74; Long John Distng Merch Soc 1971; 3rd vice pres Ret Liq St Assn 1972-; dir Natl Jew Hosp 1974-; Cys Fib Res Found 1966-; dir Gr Bflo Dev Found 1966-; pres NY Civil Serv Officials 1975; dir Police Ath League 1968-; NY Blk & Puerto Rican Caucus; found pres 1490 Jeff Comm Ctr 1969-; Masten Dem Org 1964-; Un Way 1000 Plus Club 1969-; chmn pers com Bethel Hd St 1970-; dir Natl Assn of Christian & Jews 1974-; Erie Co Dem Fin Com 1965-; life mem NAACP 1965; dir Amer Red Cross; Coalition for Cap 1972-75; past pres E Side YMCA 1963-; 100 Club of Bflo 1965-; presiding co-chairperson Natl Conf of Christians & Jews Inc 1984-85. **HONORS/ACHIEVEMENTS:** Man of Yr Bflo Chngr 1965; Outstanding Serv to Youth Bflo Negro Schlshp Found 1965; Outstanding Serv to Elderly Mayor's Com 1966; Hi Lighters Awd Serv to Humanity 1963; Cert of Merit NAACP 1967; Silver Cup C of C 1969; Outstanding Cit of Bflo-Bflo Evening News 1972; Roberto Clemente Humanitarian Awd 1973; Outstanding Cit of Bflo Rosary Hill Coll 1972; Hon Cit Boys Town 1971; Family Life Awd Bflo Urban League 1983; President's Awd from Canisius Coll; 100 Black Men Awd

1984. **MILITARY SERVICE:** Hon USN Acad Adm Cnsl 1971; Hon Recr USAF 1973. **BUSINESS ADDRESS:** Bellamy Entp, 405 E Ferry St, Buffalo, NY 14208.

BELLAMY, IVORY GANDY
Educational administrator. **PERSONAL:** Born Feb 21, 1952, Tuscaloosa, AL; daughter of Mr & Mrs Iverson Gandy Sr; children: Cinnamon, Cecily. **EDUCATION:** Stillman College, BA 1974; Florida International University (Miami), further studies. **CAREER:** Dade Co Public Schools, instr 1978-79; Miami Dade Comm Coll, prog coord 1979-85; Univ of Miami, program dir for Minority Admissions 1985-. **ORGANIZATIONS:** District advisor FL Jr Coll Student Govt Assoc 1984-85; mem Southern Assoc of College Admissions Counselors 1985-86; mem Woodson, Williams, Marshall Assocs 1985-86; mem Network of Miami 1985; mem Leadership Miami 1986; Southern Assn for Admissions Counselors (SACAC). **HONORS/ACHIEVEMENTS:** Alpha Kappa Mu. **HOME ADDRESS:** 17501 NW 12th Ave, Miami, FL 33169. **BUSINESS ADDRESS:** Asst Dir of Admissions, University of Miami, PO Box 248025, Coral Gables, FL 33124.

BELLAMY, VERDELLE B.
Nursing administrator. **PERSONAL:** Born Mar 15, 1928, Birmingham, AL; daughter of Zephry Brim and Gladys Stovall; married Monroe Bellamy, Mar 17, 1950; children: Michael B. **EDUCATION:** Tuskegee University, BS, 1958; Emory University, Atlanta GA, MSN, 1963; Georgia State University, Atlanta GA, certificate in community gerontology leadership, 1984. **CAREER:** Tuskegee University, Tuskegee Institute AL, clinical associate, 1957-58; Grady Memorial Hospital School of Nursing, Atlanta GA, instructor, 1958-62; VA Medical Center, Atlanta GA, coordinator and supervisor, 1963-82, associate chief of nursing, 1982-; Georgia State University, member of board of counselors, gerontology, 1985-. **ORGANIZATIONS:** American Nurses' Association; National League of Nursing; American Cancer Society; state coordinator on the black family, National Council of Negro Women, 1987-89; NAACP; National Parliamentarian Association; board of directors, Georgia Nurses' Association, 1971-74; Georgia League of Nursing; charter member, Century Club, American Nurses Foundation, 1983; Emory University Alumni Assn; Tuskegee University Alumni Assn; Top Ladies of Distinction; board of directors, 1980-, natl secretary, 1984-86, vice president, 1986-, Nurses Organization of Veterans Administration; Supreme Basileus, Chi Eta Phi, 1973-77; Sigma Theta Tau; national executive board, 1979-86, 1988-, natl secretary, 1988-, Delta Sigma Theta. **HONORS/ACHIEVEMENTS:** Outstanding Service Award, American Nurses Assn, 1973; Mary McLeod Bethune Illuminated Scroll, Natl Council for Negro Women, 1976; Distinguished Ludie Andrew Service Award, Natl Grady Nurses' Conclave, 1977; Human Rights Award, American Nurses Assn, 1977; Natl Medical Assn and Natl Council of Negro Women service award, 1979; US Congressional Record for achievement, 1980; Distinguished Tuskegee Institute Alumni Merit Award, 1981; NAACP "Unsung Heroine" Award, 1981; Excellence in Health Care Professions Award, 1983, special achievement and community service award, 1984, Black Nurses Assn; Mary Mahoney Award, American Nurses' Assn; Distinguished Alumni Citation of the Year Award, Natl Assn for Equal Opportunity in Higher Education, 1985; NAACP Freedom Hall of Fame Award, 1986; Virginia Leadership Award, 1988; Federal Employee of the Year Award, 1988. **HOME ADDRESS:** 1824 Tiger Flowers Dr NW, Atlanta, GA 30314.

BELLAMY, WALTER
Retired professional athlete. **PERSONAL:** Born Jul 24, 1939, New Bern, NC; married Helen Ragland; children: Derrin. **EDUCATION:** IN Univ, BS 1961. **CAREER:** NBA, Chicago Packers, 1961-63, Baltimore Bullets, 1963-65, NY Knicks, 1965-69, Atlanta Hawks, 1970-74. **ORGANIZATIONS:** All-Amer mem, 1960 Olympic Basketball Team; NBA Player Rep 1971-74; vice pres, Natl Basketball Players Assn 1972-74; Senate Doorkeep GA General Assembly 1977-81; pres Atlanta Police Athletic League; vice chair Fulton County Democratic Party; Affirmative Action Com Dem Party; Alpha Phi Omega Serv Fraternity; mem Alpha Phi Alpha Fraternity; IN Univ Alumni Club Advisory Bd; mem Atlanta Comm Rel Commn; bd dirs SW YMCA; co-chmn Ad Hoc Com Gr Park, Atlanta; mem Atlanta Urban League; Lakestar HS PTA pres; bd mem SCLC; advisory bd mem MD Old Line Corp; Campbelton Ross Business Assn; vice chair Natl Scholarship Serv for Negro Children; NAACP memb drive; founder & first pres Men of Tomorrow Inc; Shaw Temple AME Zion Ch trustee; bd dirs United Youth Adult Conf; Southwest Youth Business Organiz bd mem. **HONORS/ACHIEVEMENTS:** NBA Rookie of the Year 1961-62; Atlanta Hawks MVP 1971-72 Award; Atlanta Salutes Walt Bellamy 1974; Bcame 9th NBA Player to reach 20,000 point career mark. **HOME ADDRESS:** 2884 Lake Shore Dr, Atlanta, GA 30337.

BELLE, CHARLES E.
Investment executive. **PERSONAL:** Born Sep 02, 1940, Chicago, IL; children: Cynthia Maureen, Charles Escobar. **EDUCATION:** Roosevelt Univ, BSBA 1963; Harvard Grad Sch of Bsns, MBA 1973. **CAREER:** Drexel Burnham Lambert, Inc, asst vice pres 1973-80; A G Edwards & Sons, Inc, investment broker. **ORGANIZATIONS:** Business editor Natl Newspaper Publishing Assn Washington, DC 1973-; professional lcenter Golden Gate Univ San Francisco 1975-; chmn Mayors Adv Comm for Community Devel of SF 1983-85. **HONORS/ACHIEVEMENTS:** Journalist, Natl Endowment for the humanities 1979; Econ for journalist, Brookings Inst, 1978; COGME Fellowship, Harvard Univ 1971-73. **HOME ADDRESS:** 270 Francisco St, San Francisco, CA 94133.

BELLE, EURIS E.
Management consultant. **PERSONAL:** Born Jun 28, 1955, Claxton, GA; divorced; children: Maurice Warren. **EDUCATION:** Northwestern Univ, BA Comp 1973-77. **ORGANIZATIONS:** Speaker Chicago Assoc of Commerce & Indust Youth Motiviation Program. **HONORS/ACHIEVEMENTS:** Black Achiever of Industry Awd YMCA Of Metropolitan Chicago 1984; Voted One of Chicago's Up and coming Black Business and Professional Women Dollars and Sense Magazine June/July Issue.

BELLE, JOHN OTIS
Educator. **PERSONAL:** Born Jun 08, 1922, Fort Worth, TX; married Joe Helen Hall. **EDUCATION:** Huston-Tillotson Coll, BA 1948; Our Lady of the Lake, MEd 1956; Attended, Univ of TX. **CAREER:** Rosewood Elementary School, teacher 1948-56; Sims Elementary School, prin 1956-72; Austin Independent School Dist, asst dir 1972-. **ORGANIZATIONS:** Mem TX Assn of Supv & Curclm Devel; TX Assn for Gifted Children; TX Elem & Prin Assn; TX State Tchrs Assn; Natl Elem Prin Assn; NEA; Austin Assn of Pub Sch Adminstr; Kiwanis Intl; mem Natl PTA Commn reg vice pres TX Cong of PTA; bd mem Austin Energy Commn; mem Curclm Adv Com KLRN-TV; NAACP; Austin Urban League; bd dir Austin Sym Soc; trustee Ebenezer Bapt Ch; adv bd Progm for Teenage Parents; mem Omega Psi Phi Frat; Phi Delta Kappa EducFrat; exec comm Huston Tillotson Coll Alumni Assn; life mem Natl & TX PTA. **HONORS/ACHIEVEMENTS:** Disting Serv Awd Jack & Jill of Amer; Outstanding Accomplishment in Educ; Zeta Phi Beta Sor; Disting Serv Awd Delta Sigma Theta Sor; Cert of Appreciation Child & Family Serv Awd of Amer; Dictionary of Intl Bio; Who's Who Biog Record; Sch Dist Officials; Personalities of the S. **MILITARY SERVICE:** AUS sgt 1943-46. **BUSINESS ADDRESS:** Assistant Dir, Austin Independent School Dist, 1607 Pennsylvania Ave, Austin, TX 78702.

BELLEGARDE-SMITH, PATRICK
Educator. **PERSONAL:** Born Aug 08, 1947, Spokane, WA. **EDUCATION:** Syracuse Univ, BA 1968; The Amer Univ, MA, PhD 1977. **CAREER:** Howard Univ Dept of Romance Languages, lecturer 1977; Bradley Univ Inst of Intl Studies, assoc prof 1978-86; The Univ of WI-Milwaukee, assoc prof of Afro-Amer Studies 1986-. **ORGANIZATIONS:** Mem Amer Assn of Univ Profs; mem African Studies Assn, mem Assn of Caribbean Studies; mem Natl Council for Black Studies; mem IL Council for Black Studies; mem Soc for Intl Devel; mem Natl Conf of Black Political Scientists; mem Midwest Assn for Latin Amer Studies; mem Latin Amer Studies Assn. **HONORS/ACHIEVEMENTS:** Numerous publications including, "In the Shadow of Powers, Dantes Bellegarde in Haitian Social Thought" Atlantic Highlands, Humanities Press 1985; "Haiti: The Breached Citadel," Westview Press 1989. **BUSINESS ADDRESS:** Assoc Prof Afro-Amer Studies, The Univ of Wisconsin, PO Box 413, Milwaukee, WI 53201.

BELLINGER, GEORGE M.
Company executive. **PERSONAL:** Born Aug 18, 1932, Brooklyn, NY; son of Mr & Mrs Richard E Bellinger III; married Barbara P; children: George, Randy, Rudolph, Patricia. **EDUCATION:** New Haven Coll, attended. **CAREER:** Bar-Pat Mfg Co Inc Bridgeport, founder 1970-. **ORGANIZATIONS:** Mem Metro Business Assoc; dir Bridgeport Hospital; dir Business Resource Center CT; dir Bridgeport Economic Devel Corp; advisory bd City Trust Co of Bridgeport; vice pres Black Corp Presidents of New England; Bridgeport Public Educ Fund, dir; Governor's High Technology Bd; Gov Partnerhsip for a Safe Workplace. **MILITARY SERVICE:** USAF 1949-53. **BUSINESS ADDRESS:** President & Chairman of the Bd, Bar-Pat Mfg Co Inc, 375 Howard Ave, PO Box 3062, Bridgeport, CT 06605.

BELLINGER, HAROLD
State government official. **PERSONAL:** Born Mar 28, 1951, New York, NY. **EDUCATION:** SUNY Farmingdale, AAS 1972; Rochester Inst of Technology, BS Social Work 1974; Univ of Pittsburgh, Masters of Public & Intl Affairs 1975; NY State Exec Chamber/NYS Affirmative Action Programs, Certificate of Completion 1982. **CAREER:** Legislative Commission on Expenditure Review, sr assoc 1976-79; NY State Senate Finance Comm/Minority, legislative budget analyst 1979-81; NY State Dept of Corrections, business affairs & contract compliance mgr 1981-82; New York State Correctional Industries, industries asst dir of marketing sales 1982-84; Economic Oppor Commn of Nassau County, asst dir YOU project 1984-85; State Univ of NY, asst to the pres affirmative action 1985-. **ORGANIZATIONS:** Mem Assoc of Minority Business Enterprises 1981-82; mem Albany Chamber of Commerce 1981-82; course instructor NYS Budget Process in sponsoring w/AL 1982; mem United Nations Assoc of the USA/Mid-Long Island Chap 1986. **HONORS/ACHIEVEMENTS:** City of Rochester Urban Fellowship Awd 1973-74; Univ of Pittsburgh Grad Student Awd Public and Intl Affairs Fellowship 1974-75; Ford Foundation UndergradScholarship Awd; State Univ of NY Office of Special Programs 1977. **BUSINESS ADDRESS:** Asst to the President, SUNY at Farmingdale, Ste 235 Administration Bldg, Melville Rd, Farmingdale, NY 11735.

BELLINGER, LUTHER GARIC
Corporate director. **PERSONAL:** Born Apr 24, 1933, Blackville, SC; divorced; children: Luther Garic Jr. **EDUCATION:** John C Smith Univ, BS 1955; Notre Dame Univ, MA 1965; Teamers Sch of Religion, DHL (hon) 1968; Universal Bible Inst, PhD (hon) 1978. **CAREER:** Edgefield SC, teacher 1959; Mecklenburg School System Charlotte NC, teacher 1959-63; South Bend IN Comm School Corp, teacher 1963-65; Bendix Corp Detroit, mgr EEO program, 1965-70; MI Lutheran Coll, part-time counselor 1968-69; McDonnell Douglas Corp, corporate dir EEO program 1969-. **ORGANIZATIONS:** Co-fndr & mem St Louis EEO Group 1972-; bd dirs United Negro Coll Fund 1972-75; bd dir Loretto Hilton Repetory Theater 1977-; sec MO Health Educ Facilities Auth 1978-80. **HONORS/ACHIEVEMENTS:** Scholarship Natl Sci Found 1961-63; author "A Guide to Slang" 1963; co-author primer for parents "An Internationally Circulated Tabloid on Modern Mathematics" 1964; Disting Serv Awd Commonwealth of VA Gov Linwood Holton 1970. **MILITARY SERVICE:** AUS spec 4th class 1956-58. **BUSINESS ADDRESS:** Corporate Dir, McDonnell Douglas Corp, Equal Employment Opportunity Program, PO Box 516, St Louis, MO 63166.

BELLINGER, MARY ANN (BIBI MSHONAJI)
Religious leader, freelance writer, humorist. **PERSONAL:** Born Jul 16, 1939, Cincinnati, OH; daughter of George W Allen and Mary Jane Banks Allen; divorced; children: Georgiana, Teresa, Lawrence, Maurice, Sheila Renee-Kinnard. **EDUCATION:** Andover Newton Theological School, Boston MA, MDiv, 1981; Bentley Coll of Accounting and Finance, Waltham MA, attended 1 1/2 years. **CAREER:** Wellesley Coll, Wellesley MA, asst chaplain, 1975-80; Andover Newton Theological School, Boston MA, adjunct faculty, 1978-80; Big Bethel AME Church, Atlanta GA, asst pastor, 1984-86; Grady Memorial Hospital, Atlanta GA, chaplain intern 1986-87; Newberry Chapel AME Church, Atlanta GA, pastor, 1987-89; The Atlanta Voice Newspaper, Atlanta GA, columnist/editor 1988-89. **ORGANIZATIONS:** Sec, The Racial Justice Working Group of the Natl Council of Churches, 1988-; SE regional vice pres, Partners in Ecumenism of the Natl Council of Churches; mem, board of dir, Christian Council of Metropolitan Atlanta, 1987-; faculty mem, chairperson first Year Class, AME Church Ministerial Preparaton; NAACP Atlanta Chapter; chairperson, Ecumenical Celebrations/Church Women United, 1987-88; mem, The Georgia Network Against Domestic Violence, 1988-89; mem, The Concerned Black Clergy of Atlanta. **HONORS/ACHIEVEMENTS:** Black Women In Ministry, Boston Ecumenical Commn, 1980; Boston YMCA Black Achiever Award, Boston YMCA, 1980; Salute to Women of the Clergy, Eta Phi Beta Sorority, Gamma Theta Chapter, 1988; sermons and articles published in The AME Christian Recorder; sermon published in Those Preachin' Women Vol I, 1985; ministerial delegate to Cuba, 1987, The People's Republic of Angola, Africa 1988; testified before The United Nations Committee Against Apartheid, 1989. **HOME ADDRESS:** 215 Piedmont Avenue, NE Suite 1709, Atlanta, GA 30308.

BELLINY, DANIEL S.
Business executive. **PERSONAL:** Born May 24, 1915, Jacksonville, FL; married Ella Walker. **EDUCATION:** Wilberforce Univ, BS 1936; Univ of Chicago, JD 1948. **CAREER:** IL Div of Unemployment Compensation IL Dept of Labor, employment interviewer, dep claims reviewer dept III, hearing referee & supr, 1st asst chief appeals sect 1940-. **ORGANIZATIONS:** Gen sec Cook Co Bar Assn 1968-; Natl Bar Assn; Chicago Bar Assn; NAACP; Operation PUSH. **HONORS/ACHIEVEMENTS:** Meritorious Serv Awd Cook Co Bar Assn 1973; 1st Black Vol Officer Candidate WWII 1942; 1st Black Hearings Referee IL Div of Unemployment Compensation Benefit Appeals. **MILITARY SERVICE:** AUS 2nd lt 1942-45. **BUSINESS ADDRESS:** 1st Asst Chief Appeals Sect, IL Dept of Labor, IL Div Unemploy Compensation, 6326 Cottage Grove Ave, Chicago, IL 60637.

BELLOW, CLEVELAND J.
Artist. **PERSONAL:** Born Jul 30, 1946, San Francisco. **EDUCATION:** CA Coll Arts & Crafts, attended 1969-71; BFA, MA 1971; CA Secondary Tchr Credential 1971; CA Comm Coll Credential 1972. **CAREER:** Alcorn A&M Coll, instr 1971-72; San Francisco Black Expo, art dir 1972-73; Laney Coll, 1972-73; deYoung Mus Art Sch, 1972-74; San Francisco Neighborhood Arts Prog, dist organizer 1972-74; Alameda Co, art commr 1977 1980; City of San Francisco, children's art specialist, artist, comm arts activist, art critic, guest speaker, cons. **ORGANIZATIONS:** Mem Bay Area Rapid Transit Art Council 1973-76; Contemporary Arts Cncl Oakland Museum; Natl Conf Artists; bd dirs Alpha Phi Alpha Frat; Educ Found 1971-73; bd advs Gwen Lewis Dance Co. **HONORS/ACHIEVEMENTS:** Numerous awds honors spl achievements; works included in many publs & pvt collections; Natl Endowment of the Arts Fellow 1979-80. **BUSINESS ADDRESS:** Earth N Arts Studio, 371 17th St, Oakland, CA 94612.

BELMEAR, HORACE EDWARD
Admissions officer/black student advisor. **PERSONAL:** Born Dec 12, 1916, Bardstown, KY; married Geraldine; children: Dianne, Derrick, Michael, Tracy. **EDUCATION:** WV State Coll, BA 1940; WV Univ, MS 1948; Postgrad, Univ of IL, Univ of Pgh. **CAREER:** Dunbar High School, teacher/coach 1946-55; AUS Missile Sect, dir of educ 1964-69; Allegheny County Community Coll, dir of admissions 1969-71; WV Univ, admissions officer/black student advisor 1971-. **ORGANIZATIONS:** Omega Psi Phi Frat; NAACP; mem Human Relat Bd of Fairmont WV; chmn Affirmative Action Comm WV Univ. **MILITARY SERVICE:** USN spec 1st class. **BUSINESS ADDRESS:** Assitant Dean of Admissions, West VA, Morgantown, WV 26506.

BELTON, C. RONALD
Financial consultant/investments. **PERSONAL:** Born Aug 28, 1948, Jacksonville, FL; son of Clarence A Belton Jr and Bettye Ruth Taylor Belton. **EDUCATION:** Hampton Inst, BA 1970. **CAREER:** Jacksonville Urban League, assoc dir 1970-76; Tucker Brothers, mortgage broker 1972-; Merrill Lynch Inc, financial consultant 1976-. **ORGANIZATIONS:** Mem Big Brothers & Sisters of Jacksonville 1972-; chmn of the bd Jacksonville Urban League 1983-84; vice chmn Jacksonville Downtown Develop Authority; sire archon elect Sigma Pi Phi Frat; co-chmn City Children's Campaign; life mem NAACP; mem Natl Eagle Scout Assoc; chmn, Jacksonville Downtown Development Authority 1987-; mem, Board of Governors, Jacksonville Chamber of Commerce 1988-91; bd mem, Jacksonville Symphony Assn 1988-91; mem, Advisory Board, Univ of North Florida School of Business 1988-91. **HOME ADDRESS:** PO Box 923, Jacksonville, FL 32201. **BUSINESS ADDRESS:** Financial Consultant, Merrill Lynch Inc, 121 Atlantic Place Ste 500, Jacksonville, FL 32202.

BELTON, EDWARD DEVAUGHN
Physician, association executive. **PERSONAL:** Born Jan 08, 1935, New Orleans; divorced; children: Lauren E, Gilbert D, Carole E. **EDUCATION:** Tuskegee Inst, BS 1954; Howard Univ, MD 1958; Freedmen's Hosp, internship 1958-59; VA Hosp, residency 1959-61. **CAREER:** FDA, dep dir div of cardiopulmonary renal drug prods 1968-72; Private Practice, cardiology; Howard Univ Med Sch, clinical instr med & cardiovascular disease 1966-; FDA Washington, dir cardiopulmonary renal drug prods 1972-. **ORGANIZATIONS:** Mem Inter-agency Task Force Natl Hypertension Info & Adv Comm; mem Medico-Chirugical Soc of DC; Natl Med Assn; mem Cncl on Hypertension; Med Soc of DC; Washington Heart Assn; Amer Coll of Cardiology. **HONORS/ACHIEVEMENTS:** Author articles for professional journals. **MILITARY SERVICE:** AUS Medical Corps capt. **BUSINESS ADDRESS:** Dir, Food & Drug Admin, Cardiopulmon Renal Drug Prod, 5600 Fishers Ln Rm 16 B45 HFD-, Rockville, MD 20852.

BELTON, HOWARD G.
Director, educator. **PERSONAL:** Born Mar 22, 1934, Muskogee, OK; married Ann Rempson; children: Consandra Denise, Sheryl Anne. **EDUCATION:** MI State Univ, BA, MS. **CAREER:** Michigan Dept of Social Services, case worker 1960-64; Lansing MI School Dist, teacher 1964-69; Michigan Educ Assn, human relations consultant 1969-72; Natl Educ Assn, organizational specialist 1972-73, dir employee relations 1973-. **ORGANIZATIONS:** Mem NAACP; Chicago Chap Operation PUSH. **HONORS/ACHIEVEMENTS:** Lansing MI Jaycees Outstanding Tchr Awd. **BUSINESS ADDRESS:** Director, Employee Relations, NEA, 1201 16 St NW, Washington, DC 20036.

BELTON, ROBERT
Attorney. **PERSONAL:** Born Sep 19, 1935, High Point, NC; son of Daniel Belton and Mary L Belton; married Joyce B Martin; children: R Keith, Alaina Yvonne. **EDUCATION:** Univ of CT, BA 1961; Boston Univ, JD 1965, LLB. **CAREER:** NAACP, Legal Defense & Educ Fund Inc, civil rights atty asst counsel; 1966-69; Chambers Stein & Ferguson Charlotte NC, atty 1969-75; Vanderbilt Univ School of Law, dir fair employment clinical law program 1975-77, assoc prof of law 1977-82; prof of law, 1982-; visiting prof of law, Harvard Law School, 1986-87. **ORGANIZATIONS:** Consultant TN Commn for Human Devel 1976-; editoral bd Class Action Reports 1978-; consult Equal Employment Opportunity Commn Trial Advocacy Training Programs 1979-; consultant Pres Reorganization Proj Civil Rights 1978; consultant Office of Fed Contracts Compliance Programs Dept of Labor 1979-80; NC Assn of Black Lawyers; Amer Bar Assn; NC Acad of Trial Lawyers; TN Bar Assn, NBA, ABA. **HONORS/ACHIEVEMENTS:** Awarded NC Legal Defense Fund Dinner Comm Plaque for successful litigation in area of employment discrimination 1973; counsel for plaintiffs in Griggs v. Duke Power Co., 401 US 424 (1971); Albemarle Paper Co vs. Moody, 422 US 405 (1975); published, Discrimination in Employment (west pub. 1986); "Mr Justice Marshall and the Sociology of Affirmative Action" 1989; Reflections on Affirmative Action after Johnson and Paradise, 1988. **BUSINESS ADDRESS:** Professor of Law, Vanderbilt School of Law, Nashville, TN 37240.

BEMPONG, MAXWELL A.
Educator. **PERSONAL:** Born Sep 14, 1938, Oda, Ghana;married Jacqueline B; children: Jeffrey Eugene, Kwabena Alexander. **EDUCATION:** MI State Univ, BS, MS, PhD 1967. **CAREER:** Journal of Basic & Appl Scis, Natl Inst of Science Transactions, editor-in-chief; Norfolk State Univ, prof of biology, dir biomedical rsch. **ORGANIZATIONS:** Mem Amer Genetic Assoc, Amer Coll of Toxicology, Amer Assoc for Advancement of Sci, Environmental Mutagen Soc, Torrey Botanical Club, Natl Inst of Sci, Sigma Xi, Beta Kappa Chi, Alpha Pi Zi; clinical consult Tidewater Ctr for Sickle-Cell Anemia. **HONORS/ACHIEVEMENTS:** MI State Univ Rsch Assistantship 1965-67; Phelps-Stokes Found Fellowship 1962-64; Cocoa Marketing Bd Fellowship 1964-67; Teaching Fellow Univ of NV Reno 1970. **BUSINESS ADDRESS:** Professor, Dir, Norfolk State College, Norfolk, VA 23504.

BENDER, BARBARA A.
Education administrator. **PERSONAL:** Born Nov 12, 1939, Milwaukee, WI; divorced; children: Lisa, Jason. **EDUCATION:** BA. **CAREER:** Admissions examiner; Milwaukee County Dept of Public Welfare, adoption social worker; Univ of WI, asst dir of instr support/experimental program in higher edn, dir of financial aid. **ORGANIZATIONS:** Mem Natl Adv council Amer Coll Testing & Svcs; Natl Task Force for Student Aid Problems; bd dir Curative Workshop of Milwaukee; pres bd dir Finan & Debt Counseling Svc; mem Midwest Assn of Student Financial Aid Administrators; mem WI Assn of Student Finan Aid Adminstrs; mem Delta Sigma Theta; Eta Phi Beta; NAACP; Fam Serv of Milwaukee. **BUSINESS ADDRESS:** Dir of Financial Aid, Univ of WI, Mellencamp Hall 162, 3203 N Downer, Milwaukee, WI 53201.

BENDER, DOUGLAS RAY
Personnel administration. **PERSONAL:** Born Jul 23, 1953, Chicago, IL; married Belinda Juanita Lipscomb; children: Douglas Ranier, Danitra Cheree, Nathaniel Frederick, Kevin Dante, Douglas Jr, Danielle Brean. **EDUCATION:** Alcorn State Univ, BA Pol Sci 1975; NC A&T State Univ, MBA Human Resources Counselling 1985; NC Central Univ School of Law, JD 1985-. **CAREER:** Miller Brewing Co, corp benefits analyst 1975-76, corp benefits coord 1976-77, corp recruiting admin 1977-78; Miller Brewing Co Reidsville Container Div, personnel rep 1978-80, indust rel rep 1980-82; Miller Brewing Co Eden Brewery, labor rel rep 1982-. **ORGANIZATIONS:** Mem Jr Achievement 1977-78, Amer Mgmt Assoc 1978-83, Amer Soc of Safety Engrs 1978-83, Reidsville NC-NAACP 1978-, Random Woods Comm Assoc 1978-, Amer Soc for Training & Devel 1978-83, Amer Soc of Personnel Admin 1978-; adv bd Rockingham Cty Reidsville HS Vocational Tech Schools 1978-83; adv bd Rockingham Comm Coll Adult Ed Prog 1979-; industry co-chair Alcorn State Univ Coll 1981-82; Personnel Admin Mag Editorial Review Comm 1982-. **HONORS/ACHIEVEMENTS:** Who's Who Among Black Wisconsins 1977; Jr Achievement Serv Recognition Awd 1977; Outstanding Community Serv Awd Reidsville NC NAACP 1980; Who's Who in the South and the Southwest 1982; Intl Biographical Centre Dir of Disting Amers 1982-83; Personalities of Amer 1982-83; Accredited Personnel Mgr Amer Soc of Personnel Admin 1982; Disting Alumni Awd Natl Assoc for Equal Opportunity in Higher Ed 1983; Jaycees Outstanding Young Men of Amer 1983. **HOME ADDRESS:** 4214 Chateau Dr, Greensboro, NC 27407. **BUSINESS ADDRESS:** Labor Relations Representative, Miller Brewing Company, PO Box 3327, Eden, NC 27288.

BENFORD, CLARE E.
Attorney. **PERSONAL:** Born Sep 16, 1939, Chicago, IL; divorced. **EDUCATION:** Wilson Jr Coll, AA 1961; Chicago-Kent Coll Law, JD 1966. **CAREER:** Legal Aid Bur United Charities of Chicago, staff atty 1967-71; Private Practice, atty with Geo C Howard 1971-. **ORGANIZATIONS:** Chicago Bar Assn; IL State Bar Assn; Natl Bar Assn; Cook Co Bar Assn; Chicago Council Lawyers; charter mem bd 1970-71; Chicago-Kent Alumni Assn; life mem ACLU; NAACP; United Federalists; chicago Peace Council; Women for Peace; Independent Voters of IL; Common Cause. **BUSINESS ADDRESS:** Attorney, 188 W Randolph St, Ste 1501, Chicago, IL 60601.

BENHAM, ROBERT
Law. **PERSONAL:** Born Sep 25, 1946, Cartersville, GA; son of Clarence Benham and Jessie Benham; married Nell Dodson; children: Corey Brevard, Austin Tyler. **EDUCATION:** Tuskegee Univ, BS 1967; Harvard Univ, 1966; Univ of GA, JD 1970. **CAREER:** State of Georgia, spec asst atty gen 1978-84; Georgia Court of Appeals, judge. **ORGANIZATIONS:** Cartersville Bar Assoc, president 1981-82; GA Conf of Black Lawyers, vice pres; Federal Defender Prog, board mem 1983-84; Amer Judicature Soc, mem. **HONORS/ACHIEVEMENTS:** Board of dir Cartersville Chamber of Commerce 1976; board chmn Coosa Valley APDC 1978; board mem Cartersville Devel Auth 1984; mem Georgia Historical Soc; Dent Awd Georgia Assn of Black Elected Officials 1986; outstanding service Cartersville Bar Assn 1984. **MILITARY SERVICE:** AUS reserve Capt 1970-77. **BUSINESS ADDRESS:** Judge, Georgia Court of Appeals, Judicial Bldg, Room 402, Atlanta, GA 30334.

BENJAMIN, ARTHUR, JR.
Business executive. **PERSONAL:** Born Feb 08, 1938, Wagener, SC; married Dorothy Carrington; children: Lisa Simone, Cecily Lyn, Stacy Elisabeth. **EDUCATION:** Natl Bsns Coll, Jr Acct Cert 1955; TN St Univ, BS 1959; Univ of CO, 1960; NY Univ, 1963-64. **CAREER:** Franklin Book Pgms, sr acct 1962-67; Amer Home Prod Corp, asst comptroller 1967-68; Whitehall Labs, asst treas 1968-72; ITT, sen fncl anlyst 1972-77; Wallace & Wallace Ent, vice pres & cmptrlr 1977-82; Unity Brdcstng Ntwrk, vice pres fnc. **ORGANIZATIONS:** Chmn bd Queensborough Scty for Prevention of Cruelty to Children 1981-83; pres Jamaica Serv Program for Older Adults 1979-81. **HONORS/ACHIEVEMENTS:** Blck Achvrs Harlem Branch YMCA 1978; Awrd of Hon TN St Univ Sch Bsns 1978. **MILITARY SERVICE:** AUS spec 4 3 Yrs. **HOME ADDRESS:** 115-101 222nd St, Cambria Heights, NY 11411.

BENJAMIN, CECIL R.
Educator. **PERSONAL:** Born Oct 19, 1945, Berbice, Guyana;married Ferryneisa L Hodge; children: Lawrence, Ofari. **EDUCATION:** Inter-American Univ, BS 1967; Temple Univ, MS 1971. **CAREER:** Ministry of Educ Guyana Govt, teacher 1960-63; VI Govt Dept of

Educ, teacher 1967-; Colelge of the Virgin Islands, instructor 1972-75; American Federation of Teachers, vice pres 1984-; St Croix Federation of Teachers, pres 1975-. **ORGANIZATIONS:** Mem VI Comm Action Agency 1978-80, VI Democratic Territorial Comm 1980-, St Croix Lions Intl Club 1980-; trustee/v chmn VI Govt Employees Retirement System 1980-86; pres Central Labor Cncl of the VI 1980-86; delegate VI 4th Constitutional Convention 1980-81; delegate AFL CIO Convention 1981-83; mem NCTR Legislative Comm 1984-86; exec mem VI Labor-Mgmt Comm 1985-; mem Industrial Develop Study Commn 1985-86, VI Task Force on Higher Educ 1987; mem NAACP, NABSE, Urban League, A Philip Randolph Inst. **HONORS/ACHIEVEMENTS:** Scholarship US Natl Science Foundation 1970-71; Citation Educ Leadership VI Dept of Educ 1977; Meritorious Serv Citation Amer Federation of Teachers 1980-85. **HOME ADDRESS:** #91 Sion Farm Box 2848 C'Sted, St Croix, Virgin Islands of the United States 00820.

BENJAMIN, DONALD F.
Sociologist, urban planner. **PERSONAL:** Born Sep 26, 1925, Port-of-Spain, Trinidad and Tobago;married Beverly A Brown, Aug 29, 1988; children: Dyanne, Allan, Stephen. **EDUCATION:** Univ of Cambridge, England, First Class School Certificate; Hunter Coll, City Univ of New York, BA 1958, MA 1960. **CAREER:** Dept of Planning, City of New York, community analyst 1959-62; Commission on Human Rights, City of New York, sr intergroup relations officer 1962-64; Central Brooklyn Coordinating Council, Bedford-Stuyvesant NY, exec dir 1964-68; Small Business Devel Center, Brooklyn NY, exec dir 1968-70; CLICK Inc, Brooklyn Navy Yard NY, chief exec officer 1970-73; Chaguaramas Devel Authority, Trinidad & Tobago, general mgr 1973-76; DFB Urban Devel Counsellors, Port-of-Spain, Trinidad and Tobago, pres 1976-79; Dade County Transportation Admin, Miami FL, team coordinator 1979-81, project mgr 1981-83; New Century Devel Corp, dir of devel 1983-86; Benjan Corp, pres 1984; Miami Dade Community Coll, Miami FL, adjunct prof English 1987; St John Community Devel Corp, Miami FL, exec dir 1987-88; Episcopal Diocese of Southeast Florida; asst to the Bishop for Social Concerns 1988-. **ORGANIZATIONS:** Governor, Brooklyn Children's Museum; governor, Brooklyn Acad of Music; trustee, Brook lyn Inst of Arts & Sciences, 1966-73; consultant, UN Roster of Experts—Sociology, Land Use Community Organization, 1970; charter mem, Amer Inst of Certified Planners, 1978-; mem, Overtown Advisory Bd, 1983-; mem, City of Miami Planning Advisory Bd, 1984-89. **HONORS/ACHIEVEMENTS:** Producer and moderator, half-hour television interview program on CTAP-TV, 1986. **BUSINESS ADDRESS:** Assistant to the Bishop for Social Concerns, Episcopal Diocese of Southeast Florida, 525 NE 15th St, Miami, FL 33132.

BENJAMIN, DONALD S.
Research analyst, deputy director. **PERSONAL:** Born Feb 13, 1938, New Orleans, LA; married Tritobia Hayes; children: Zalika Aminah. **EDUCATION:** So Univ, BS 1961; Howard Univ, MFA 1972. **CAREER:** US Army Engr Sch, artist/illustration 1961-63; Bailey's Cross Roads, asst art dir 1964-67; Defense Comm Agy, illustrator 1964-67; Naval Observatory, audio-visual spec 1967; PTAI/CDC S Vietnam, consult 1967-69; free-lance writer/artist/cons 1969-71; Comm Control Experimental Sch, coord 1973; Wash Tech Inst, research coord 1974-75. **ORGANIZATIONS:** Research analyst/dep dir/mem Natl conf Artists 1972-75; DC Bicentennial Heritage Comm 1974; vice pres United Culture Workshop Inc of Wash, DC 1973-76; execdir of United Cultural Assn Inc of Wash, DC 1975-76; vice pres United Multi-Arts Cultural Cntrs of Wash, DC 1974-76; econ devel cons/coord Paralel Econ Devel Projs 1971-76; art consult Bicentennial Bazaar Wash 1976; lectr Howard Univ Sch of Comm 1976-77; asst proj dir Afro-Am Datanamics CETA Intern Proj 1977-; alternate deleg to Natl Dem Conv NY 1976; asst Natl Coord for Natl Coalition of Involved People; media dir Afro-Am Datanamics Inc; research analyst conduct intl research on the multi-demensional profiles of African Lineage Artist 1974-76; conducting field research in the soc sci & culturally relevant areas 1974-76. **HONORS/ACHIEVEMENTS:** Exhibitions, Tribute to Carribean Independence Martin Luther King Libr Wash, DC 1977; Madam's Organ Gallery Exhibition Adams Morgan Comm 1977; 1st Ann Kappa Alpha Psi Scholarship Benefit 1977; Black Caucus Annex Exhibit of Wash Area Artists 1975-77; Project Dir EXPO '76; Compared to What Inc 1974. **BUSINESS ADDRESS:** President, Donald S Benjamin Artist Div, 3525 16th St NW, Washington, DC 20010.

BENJAMIN, ESTHER P.
Nurse, administrator. **PERSONAL:** Born Dec 04, 1910, Riverside, NJ; married Edward A Benjamin. **EDUCATION:** Mercy Hosp, RN 1934; Tchrs Coll Columbia Univ, BS 1946, MA 1948; Wayne State Univ, MS 1956. **CAREER:** Henry St Visit Nurse Assn, nurse; New Haven, CT visiting Nurse Assn, pub health nurse; US Pub Health Svc, sr pub health nurse; NC Coll, dir pub health nursing prog; Wayne State Univ Detroit, asst prof; Wayne Co Gen Hosp, dir nursing svcs. **ORGANIZATIONS:** Mem Natl League for Nursing; Amer Nurses Assn; Sigma Theta Tau; MI Reg Med Programs; life mem NAACP reserve officer US Pub Health Svc; appt State of MI Pub Health Adv Council. **BUSINESS ADDRESS:** Dir Nursing Services, Wayne Co General Hospital, Nursing Office, Eloise, MI 48132.

BENJAMIN, RONALD
Accountant, auditor. **PERSONAL:** Born Dec 31, 1941, New York, NY; married Carmen E Hodge; children: Nicolle, Danielle, Christopher. **EDUCATION:** Bernard M Baruch Coll, MBA 1974; Pace Coll, BBA 1968; Bronx Comm Coll, AAS 1966. **CAREER:** Main LaFrentz & Co CPA's, sr acct 1968-71; Union Camp Corp, sr auditor 1971-74; Ross Stewart & Benjamin PC CPA's, dir 1974-. **ORGANIZATIONS:** CPA 1971; mem Amer Inst of CPA; NY St Soc of CPA; NJ Soc of CPA; co-fdr Natl Assn of Black Accountants; adjunct prof Hostos Comm Coll; William Patterson & Essex Co Coll. **MILITARY SERVICE:** USAF e-3 1960-64. **BUSINESS ADDRESS:** Dir, Ross Stewart & Benjamin, 666 5th Ave, New York, NY 10019.

BENJAMIN, ROSE MARY
City official. **PERSONAL:** Born Apr 28, 1933, Pueblo, CO; married Orville B Benjamin; children: Darryl Kevin, Darwin Craig, Duane Carter, Benjamin. **CAREER:** Inglewood Unified Bd of Ed, pres 1982; Southern CA Reg Occupation, clerk 1983, vice pres 1984; CA Urban Assoc School Dist, sec exec bd 1985; Inglewood School Bd, vp. **ORGANIZATIONS:** Mem local chmn Coaltition Black School Bd 1983-84; dist chairperson coalition Advocating Reform in Ed 1984; sec exec March of Dimes Bd of Dir 1984; march of dimes rep Inglewood Council PTA 1984; bd of dir Centinela Child Guidance Clinic 1984; comm mem CA School Bd Hall of Fame Awd 1985. **HONORS/ACHIEVEMENTS:** Salute to Women Mornigside News Advertiser 1970; Martin Luther King Awd Holy Faith Episcopal Church 1970; Community Contrib Inglewood Neighbors 1973; Commendation Centinela & Professional Business Women 1983; Hon Serv CA Congress PTA 1985. **HOME ADDRESS:** 8711 3rd Ave, Inglewood, CA 90305. **BUSINESS ADDRESS:** Vice President, Inglewood School Board, 401 S Inglewood Ave, Inglewood, CA 90301.

BENJAMIN, TRITOBIA HAYES
Educator. **PERSONAL:** Born Oct 22, 1944, Brinkley, AR; married Donald S Benjamin; children: Zalika Aminah; Aminah Liani, Anwar Saleh. **EDUCATION:** Howard Univ, BA 1968, MA 1970; Univ of MD Coll Park, PhD Prog 1982-. **CAREER:** Georgetown Univ, instructor ,1970; Howard Univ, instructor, 1970-73, Cafritz guest lecturer, 1978; Afro-Am Inst NYC, guest curator "African Artists in Amer"; Howard Univ, asst prof art 1973-77, assoc prof art 1977-. **ORGANIZATIONS:** Judge Annual Sr & Jr Scholastic Awards The Hect Co Wash, DC 1970-74; lectures & seminars at various instns and organizatgions; comm mem Contemp AfricanExhibition for USA; rec sec Wash,DC Chap Natl Conf Artists; reg rep Natl Conf of Artists; mem Black Women's Comm Dev Found 1972-74; College Art Assn 1973-74. **HONORS/ACHIEVEMENTS:** Recipient Natl Endowment for the Humanities Fellowships in Residence for Coll Tchrs 1975-76; Spencer Found Research Award Howard Univ Sch of Educ 1975-77; Outstanding Young Women of Amer 1977; The World Who's Who of Women 1977; 2 summer publ, Haitian Art Newsletter & Africa Reports Mag; NEH Fellowship for Faculty of Historically Black Colls & Univs 1984-85; United Negro Coll Fund Facilty Grant/Fellowship Prog 1986-87; Hon Mem Eta Phi Sigma Sor 1986. **BUSINESS ADDRESS:** Associate Professor of Art, Howard Univ Dept Art, Washington, DC 20010.

BENN, ISHMAEL
Business executive. **PERSONAL:** Born Aug 18, 1919, Macon, GA; married Sarah Frances Walton. **EDUCATION:** Fenn Coll Cleveland, 1945-46; Cleveland Coll, 1951-52; Case Western Res Univ, 1969; OH Peace Officers Council, Cert of Grad. **CAREER:** US Post Office, clerk 1946-68; spl policeman 1957; US Post Office, foreman of mails 1968-70, foreman of sta operations 1970-72; pvt policeman investig/security/enforcement; real estate broker/salesman; acct svcs; US Post Office, asst mgr Annex Finance Sta 1972-. **ORGANIZATIONS:** Mem exec bd dir NAACP Cleveland Br; police Civil Def Dept 1965-69; past Exalted Rulers Council #15 Dist #1; IBPOE of W; OH State Assn IBPOE of W; active Exalted Rulers Council Reg #3; past Grand Exalted Rulers Council; Grand Lodge of the IBPOE of W 1952-; grand asst dir Beauty & Talent Dept. **MILITARY SERVICE:** AUS S/Sgt 1942-45; Silver & Bronze Star. **BUSINESS ADDRESS:** Assistant Manager, U S Postal Serv, Annex Finance Sta PP Annex Bld, 1000 W 9th St, Cleveland, OH 44113.

BENNETT, AL
Automobile dealer. **PERSONAL:** Married Yvonne. **CAREER:** Al Bennett Inc, Flint MI, chief executive. **BUSINESS ADDRESS:** Chief Executive, Al Bennett Ford Inc, 5510 Clio Rd, Flint, MI 48504. *

BENNETT, ARTHUR T.
Judge. **PERSONAL:** Born Feb 03, 1933, Corapeake, NC; married Josephine Adams. **EDUCATION:** Norfolk State Coll, Cert 1957; Howard Univ, BA 1959; Howard Univ Sch of Law, LLB 1963; Univ of Houston Natl Coll of District Atty, grad 1972. **CAREER:** BL Hooks, AW Willis Jr, RB Sugarmon Jr & IH Murphy Memphis, TN, assoc atty 1963-65; Natl Coll of Dist Atty, faculty adv 1973; Shelby Co, TN Gen Sessions Ct, judge 1976; Shelby Co, TN Criminal Ct, judge. **ORGANIZATIONS:** Mem Memphis & Shelby Co Bar Assns, Natl Bar Assn; legal dir & exec bd mem Natl United Law Enforcement Officers Assn; mem NAACP; mem bd dirsMemphis Branch NAACP; mem Memphis Chptr Assn for the Study of Afro-Amer Life & History; mem Title XX State Adv Councl Dept of Human Svcs; mem Natl Dist Atty Assn. **HONORS/ACHIEVEMENTS:** King of Cotton Makers Jubilee Memphis 1974; Natl Historical Honor Soc Phi Alpha Theta 1959; Natl Forensic Honor Soc Tau Kappa Alpha 1959. **MILITARY SERVICE:** AUS 1953-55. **BUSINESS ADDRESS:** Judge, Shelby County, 201 Poplar Ave, Memphis, TN 38103.

BENNETT, BESSYE WARREN
Association executive. **PERSONAL:** Born Aug 16, 1938, Praire View, TX; married Dr John H Bennett; children: Vera Elizabeth, John Stephen, Margaret Elaine. **EDUCATION:** Radcliffe Coll, BA(Cum Laude) 1958; Trinity Coll, MA 1967; Univ of CT Law Sch, JD 1973. **CAREER:** Psychiatric Residency Program, research sec 1958-59; Hartford Pub Schools, tchr 1964-69; Hartford Coll for Women, administ asst to pres 1970; Soc for Savings, assoc counsel/mgr equal oppty programs, asst vice pres 1973-83; Ct St Employees Retirement Comm, gen counsel 1983-84; Town of Bloomfield, dep town atty 1985-; private practice, atty 1983-. **ORGANIZATIONS:** Mem Am/CT/Hartford Bar Assns 1974-; mem Hartford Assn of Women Attys 1977-; mem Natl Assn of Bank Women 1978-; former pres Hartford League of Women Voters 1970-71; dir Univ of CT Law Sch Alumni Bd 1978-80; chmn CT Sr Civil Serv Bd 1980-87; chair Hartford Women's Network 1980-81; trustee CT Women's Legal & Educ Fund; past co-chmn & bd mem allocations comm United Way of Hartford; pres George W Crawford Law Assoc; trust Hartford Symphony Orchestra 1983-. **HONORS/ACHIEVEMENTS:** Women in Bus Awd Salvation Army 1975; Women in Bus Awd YWCA 1983. **BUSINESS ADDRESS:** Attorney, 120 Mountain Ave, Ste 210, Bloomfield, CT 06002.

BENNETT, BOBBY
Program director. **PERSONAL:** Born Jul 20, 1944, Pittsburgh, PA; married Connie Phillips; children: Eric Anthony. **EDUCATION:** George Heide Sch of Radio & TV Production, attended 1962. **CAREER:** DJ Promotions Concut Promo Organ, partner; WAMO Pittsburgh 1965; WZUM Pittsburgh 1965-67; Georgetown Univ Basketball, radio commentary; Sonderling Broadcasting WOL Radio, program dir 1967-. **ORGANIZATIONS:** Mem NAB; Urban League; NAACP; Black United Front; AFTRA; NATRA. **HONORS/ACHIEVEMENTS:** Black Radio's DJ of the Year Natl Bill Gayin Rpt; Black Radio's DJ of the Year Eastern Reg 1973 Billboard Mag; Announcer of the Year Washington, DC 1972; Announcers Air Personality of the Year Natl Assn of TV & Radio 1976; Man of the Year Faicoms 1976. **BUSINESS ADDRESS:** Program Dir, Sonderling Broadcasting WOL Ra, 1680 Wisconsin Ave NW, Washington, DC 20007.

BENNETT, COLLIN B.
Business executive. **PERSONAL:** Born Jun 08, 1931, St Andrew; married Winifred Tate; children: Michael, Adlia, Collin Jr, Sharon, Lisa, Dawn Colleen. **EDUCATION:** Attended Bus Coll Univ of CT Sch of Ins. **CAREER:** Justice of the peace; human relation commr; Collin Bennett Real Estate & Ins Agency, owner/pres. **ORGANIZATIONS:** Mem Metro Water Bur; adv bd Salvation Army; chmn Comm Renewal Team of Gr Hartford; vice pres

Redevel Agency for City of Hartford; former bd mem Urban League of Gr Hartford; former pres Barbour Sch PTA; councilman City of Hartford; chmn Housing & Planning & Governing Comm 8 years; regent Univ of Hartford; mem Electoral Coll; C of C of Gr Hartford; bd dir CT Savings & Loan Assn; Gr Hartford Bd of Realtors; Indpt Mutual Ins Agents; area prop mgr US Dept of Housing & Urban Devel; developer; sr warden St Monica's Epis Ch; vice pres St Monica's Day Care Entr; mem Visitors & Conv Bur of Greater Hartford; bd mem Mt Sinai Hosp. **HONORS/ACHIEVEMENTS:** W Indian Comm Award; Council of Negro Women Award; Humanitarian Award City of Hartford; mem Natl Bd of Realtors; recip Order of Distinction (one of highest honors bestowed) Govt of Jamaica, West Indies Outstanding Serv Rendered to Nationals abroad & surrounding areas. **BUSINESS ADDRESS:** President, Collin Bennett Real Est/Ins, 1229 Albany Ave, Hartford, CT 06112.

BENNETT, COURTNEY AJAYE
Educator. **PERSONAL:** Born Nov 17, 1959, New York City, NY. **EDUCATION:** HS of Music & Art, diploma/music 1972-76; Wagner Coll, BS 1980. **CAREER:** Health Ins Plan of Greater NY, marketing rep 1983; Ralph Bunch School, science coord/teacher 1983-. **ORGANIZATIONS:** Partner/oper JBR Discount Corp; pres/founder Sigma Phi Rho Frat 1978-80; bd of dirs Sigma Phi Rho Frat 1978-; advisor Sigma Phi Rho Frat 1981-; mem 100 Young Black Men 1985. **HONORS/ACHIEVEMENTS:** Wagner Coll Parker scholarship Music scholarship 1977 & 1978; Outstanding Young Man of America US Jaycees 1982; Outstanding service Sigma Phi Rho Frat 1983. **HOME ADDRESS:** 50 West 132nd St, New York, NY 10037.

BENNETT, DEBRA QUINETTE
Editor. **PERSONAL:** Born Feb 10, 1958, New York, NY. **EDUCATION:** Wagner Coll, BA English (dean's list) 1980. **CAREER:** Assn of Ship Brokers & Agents, asst exec dir 1980; Newsweek Magazine, researcher/reporter 1981-82; Mamaroneck Daily Times, reporter 1981; Scientific American Magazine, proofreader/copy editor. **ORGANIZATIONS:** Managing editor Sigma Phi Rho Frat Newsletter 1981-; sunday sch teacher Grace Episcopal Church 1984-; Zeta Phi Beta Sor Inc (mem & Finer Womanhood Comm mem). **HONORS/ACHIEVEMENTS:** Dean's List Wagner Coll 1980; Who's Who Among Students in Amer Univs & Colls 1980; Outstanding Young Woman of Amer Certificate 1980; Zeta Lady Awd for Scholarship & Serv Zeta Tau Alpha Frat Delta Epsilon Chap 1980. **BUSINESS ADDRESS:** Scientific American Magazine, 415 Madison Ave, New York, NY 10017.

BENNETT, DELORES
Community activist. **PERSONAL:** Born Nov 23, Clarksville, TN; daughter of Will Henry Caudle (deceased) and Carrie B Barbee-Caudle (deceased); married Eugene Bennett, Sr, Jun 15, 1951; children: Dr Ronda J Bennett, Eugene Bennett Jr, Mary Bennett-King,Esther M Bennett. **CAREER:** Wayne County, Michigan, Wayne County commr, 1978-82. **ORGANIZATIONS:** Bd of trustees, Henry Ford Hospital; chairperson of by-laws committee, Detroit Health Dept Substance Abuse Advisory Council; bd of dir, United Community Serv; lifetime mem, NAACP; bd of assembly, United Found; mem, Detroit Recreation Partners; founder/dir Northend Youth Improvement Council, 1964-. **HONORS/ACHIEVEMENTS:** Annual Adopt a Child for Christmas Program, 1965-; Resolution of Service, Detroit Bd of Educ, 1982; Proclamation of Dolores Bennett Day, Mayor of City of Detroit, 1982; MI State Senate Resolution, MI State Senate, 1982; Jefferson Award, Amer Inst for Public Serv, 1987; Michiganian of the Year, The Detroit News, 1988; Northend Youth Improvement Council (NEYIC), Mental Health Clothing Drive; Operation Green Thumb (NEYIC); Jobs for Youth Conf (NEYIC); NEYIC Youth Against Drugs. **HOME ADDRESS:** 111 King, Detroit, MI 48202.

BENNETT, DENNIS RAY
Reporter, journalist. **PERSONAL:** Born Mar 31, 1944, Wilson, NC; married Laurine Alethia Robinson; children: Alethia Rays. **EDUCATION:** Attended VA State Coll Univ. **CAREER:** WXEX-TV Richmond, reporter 1972-73; WRUA Radio Richmond, reporter 1973-74; WBAL-TV, reporter 1974-. **ORGANIZATIONS:** Adv MD Spl Olympics; adv MD Legal Aid Assn; mem NAACP; mem Black Media Workers Assn. **HONORS/ACHIEVEMENTS:** Emmy Plaque Baltimore/Wash Emmy Comm 1974; MD Sch Bell Award; Redeemer Palace Youth Award Redeemers Palace 1980. **BUSINESS ADDRESS:** Reporter, WBAL-TV, 3800 Hooper Ave, Baltimore, MD 21211.

BENNETT, GEORGE P.
Deputy chief police department. **PERSONAL:** Born Jun 22, 1927, Detroit, MI; married Tommie; children: George, Gary. **EDUCATION:** Completed Criminal Justice Inst Mgmt Trng; attended Wayne State Univ; grad Southern Police Inst. **CAREER:** Detroit Police Dept, served in all sworn ranks; currently deputy chief. **ORGANIZATIONS:** Instrum in initiating & devel Wayne Co Comm Coll Law Enforcement Adminst 1969; mem Intl Assn of Chiefs of Police; Wayne Co Comm Coll Law Enforcement Adv Com; founding mem Natl Assn of Black Police Officers; founding mem Guardians (Black Police Officers) of MI; founding mem/mem Mayor's Steering Comon reorgn of Detroit City Govt; mem New Detroit Drug Abuse Comm; bd dir Univ of Detroit HS; mem Fitzgerald Comm Council. **HONORS/ACHIEVEMENTS:** MI State Legisl Award for Outstanding Police Service; Award Natl Black Police Officers Assn; Major Contrib in field of Law Enforcement; Natl Bapt Conv Service Award; Annual Fitzgerald Club Outstanding Service Award; presented paper on Police Comm Relations to Natl Conf of Christians & Jews MI State Univ. **BUSINESS ADDRESS:** Deputy Chief, Detroit Police Dept, 1300 Beaubien, Detroit, MI 48226.

BENNETT, IVY HOOKER
Marketing manager. **PERSONAL:** Born Oct 30, 1951, Waterbury, CT; married Joseph Bryan Bennett. **EDUCATION:** Hampton Inst, BA 1973; Harvard Univ, MBA 1982. **CAREER:** Kaiser-Permanente Los Angeles, sr financial analyst 1975-80; Quaker Oats, mktg asst 1982-84; Kraft Inc, product mgr 1984-. **ORGANIZATIONS:** Mem Hoffmann Estates Chap of Links Inc; mem Alpha Kappa Alpha Sor, Second Baptist Church Evanston IL. **HONORS/ACHIEVEMENTS:** Chicago Top 50 Up and Coming Black Profls Dollars & Sense Magazine 1986. **HOME ADDRESS:** 127 Brandon Court, Palantine, IL 60067. **BUSINESS ADDRESS:** Product Manager, Kraft Inc, One Kraft Court, Glenview, IL 60025.

BENNETT, JULIA HUBERT
Educator, artist. **PERSONAL:** Born May 09, 1925, Sumter, SC; divorced; children: Horace A, Leanne V, Patricia R. **EDUCATION:** Benedict Coll, 1941-44; OH St U, BA 1946; OH St U, MA 1948. **CAREER:** Benedict Coll; Savannah St Coll, asst prof 1968-; Benedict Coll, instr; Jackson St Coll, instr; several Southeastern Coll, instr; artist featured in several exhibits in SE; Seminar in African Studies Savannah Coll, dir; Interant Curriculum Dev Prog under Phelps-Stokes Savannah Coll, coord 1969-; promise Lit Mag Jackson St Coll, adv; EXPRESSION 69 EXPRESSION 70 Savannah St Coll, adv; Windows of the World 1979 Savannah State Coll Lit Mag; Benedict Coll, residence hall dir. **ORGANIZATIONS:** Mem YWCA; NAACP; GA Poetry Soc; Nat Conf of Artists; Coll Language Assn; AAUP; Am Tcrhs Assn; Nat Council of Tchr of English. **HONORS/ACHIEVEMENTS:** Recip Gwendolyn Brooks Lit Awd ofr Poetry 1973. **BUSINESS ADDRESS:** Savannah State Coll, Savannah, GA 31404.

BENNETT, KEITH
Financial administrator. **PERSONAL:** Born Feb 21, 1956, McKeesport, PA. **EDUCATION:** Temple Univ, BA 1978; Univ of Pgh, M Pub Admin 1980. **CAREER:** City of Pittsburgh, community dev intern 1980; City of Kansas City, public mgmt intern 1980-81, interim budget analyst 1981, admin mgmt asst 1981-82; Cityof Pittsburgh, budget analyst 1982-. **ORGANIZATIONS:** Mem Intl City Mgmt Assn; mem Govt Finance Officers Assn; mem Amer Soc for Public Admin; mem Natl Forum for Black Public Adminis; mem Conf of Minority Public Adminis. **HONORS/ACHIEVEMENTS:** Graduate Fellowship provided by US Dept of Housing & Urban Develop at Univ of Pgh 1979-80. **HOME ADDRESS:** 475 Westover Hills Blvd #206, Richmond, VA 23225. **BUSINESS ADDRESS:** Budget Analyst, City of Pittsburgh, 202B City/County Bldg, Pittsburgh, PA 15219.

BENNETT, LERONE, JR.
Editor, author. **PERSONAL:** Born Oct 17, 1928, Clarksdale, MS; married Gloria Sylvester; children: Alma Joy, Constance, Courtney, Lerone III. **EDUCATION:** Morehouse Coll, BA 1949, DLetters 1966; Wilberforce Univ, DHum 1977; Marquette Univ, DLitt 1979; Voorhees Coll, DLitt 1981; Morgan State Univ, DLitt 1981; Univ IL, LHD 1980; Lincoln Coll, LHD 1980; Dillard Univ, LHD 1980. **CAREER:** Atlanta Daily World, reporter, city editor; Jet Chicago, assoc ed 1953; Ebony Mag, assoc editor 1955-57; author; Northwestern Univ, vis prof history 1968-69; Johnson Publishing Co, sr editor 1957-. **ORGANIZATIONS:** Mem Sigma Delta Chi; Kappa Alpha Psi; Phi Beta Kappa; Eighth Ward Citizens Com; mem Black Acad of Arts & Letters; Phi Beta Kappa; Kappa Alpha Psi; Sigma Delta Chi; bd dirs Chicago Pub Library; trustee Martin Luther King Jr Ctr for Social Change, Moorehouse Coll; bd dir Columbia Coll Chicago IL. **HONORS/ACHIEVEMENTS:** Author, "Before the Mayflower, A History of Black America 1619-1964"; "The Negro Mood" 1964; "What Manner of Man A Biography of Martin Luther King Jr" 1964; "Confrontation, Black and White" 1965; "Black Power USA" 1968; "The Challenge of Blackness" 1972 plus many more; Patron Saints Awd Soc Midland Authors 1965; Book of Yr Awd Capital Press Club 1963; AAAL Acad Inst Lit Awd 1978; Hon Dr of Letters Morris Brown Univ 1985, SC Univ 1986, Boston Univ 1987. **MILITARY SERVICE:** AUS 1st sgt 1951-52. **BUSINESS ADDRESS:** Senior Editor & Author, Johnson Publishing Co, 820 S Michigan, Chicago, IL 60606.

BENNETT, MAISHA B. H.
Clinical psychologist. **PERSONAL:** Born Sep 20, 1948, Russellville, AL; married Robert E Bennett; children: Kinshasa, Karega, Ayinde. **EDUCATION:** Mt Holyoke Coll S Hadley, MA, BA 1970; Univ of Chicago Chgo, IL, MA 1972, PhD 1973. **CAREER:** Kennedy King Coll Chgo, IL, cnslr 1971-72, instr 1972-73; IL Sch of Professional Psychlgy, adjnct fclty 1978-; Jcksn Pk Hosp Chgo, IL, dir outpat bhvr med clnc 1974-81, dir bhvrl sci training 1981-82; Private Practice, psychological serv corp 1977-; Chicago Dept of Health, deputy commissioner 1984-87. **ORGANIZATIONS:** Cnsltnt STEP Sch Chgo, IL 1982-84, Hlth & Hum Serv Wash, DC 1979-82, Englwd Comm Hlth Org Chgo, IL 1981; Safari Hse Drg Abuse Trtmnt Pgm Chgo, IL 1979-80; pres Natl Assn Blck Psychlgst 1978-79; ofcr Natl Assn Blck Psychlgst 1976-80; chmn Chicago Area Assn Blck Psych 1974-75; bd dir Chicago Area Assn Blck Psych 1973-; mem Am Psychlgcl Assn 1973-; Cngrsnl Blk Caucus Hlth Brain Trust 1977-; ofc bd dir Comm Mntl Hlth Cncl Inc 1983. **HONORS/ACHIEVEMENTS:** Outstndng Srvc Blk Comm Chicago Area Assn Blk Psych 1981; Comm Srvc Awrd Blk Stdnt Psych Assn 1983. **BUSINESS ADDRESS:** Deputy Commissioner, Chicago Dept of Health, 50 W Washington LL139, Chicago, IL 60602.

BENNETT, MARION D.
Clergyman, legislator. **PERSONAL:** Born May 31, 1936, Greenville, SC; married Gwendolyn; children: Marion Jr, Karen. **EDUCATION:** Morris Brown Coll, AB; Interdenom Theol Center, MDiv; studied at Univ of NV, Atlanta Univ, Switzerland Ecumenical Inst. **CAREER:** Zion United Meth Ch Las Vegas, NV, pastor. **ORGANIZATIONS:** Mem NV Legislature; bd dir Black Meth for Ch Renewal; chmn Health & Welfare Comm; mem Legislative Functions & Rules Comm; pres Las Vegas Br NAACP; 1963-67, 1971-73, vice pres 1967-69, treas 1969; chmn bd dir Operation Independence 1969-71; treas Econ Bd of Clark Co,NV 1969; dem. **BUSINESS ADDRESS:** Pastor, Zion United Methodist Church, 1911 Goldhill Ave, Las Vegas, NV 89106.

BENNETT, MAYBELLE TAYLOR
Urban planner. **PERSONAL:** Born Oct 19, 1949, Washington, DC; daughter of Raymond Bernard Taylor and Ruby Elizabeth Mills Taylor; married Robert Alvin Bennett, Apr 17, 1971 (divorced); children: Rebeccah Leah Bennett. **EDUCATION:** Vassar Coll, Poughkeepsie NY, AB (cum laude), 1970; Columbia Univ, New York NY, MSUP, 1972. **CAREER:** Lagos State Devel & Property Corp, Lagos, Nigeria, town planning officer, 1972-75; Joint Center for Political Studies, Washington DC, project mgr, 1975-78; Working Group for Community Devel Reform, Washington DC, dir of research, 1978-81; Natl Comm Against Discrimination in Housing, Washington DC, asst dir of program serv, 1982-84; District of Columbia Zoning Commn, Washington DC, vice chairperson, 1982-; Coalition on Human Needs, Washington, DC, dir of research, 1984-. **ORGANIZATIONS:** mem, Alpha Kappa Alpha Sorority, 1970-; mem, bd of dir, District of Columbia Mutual Housing Assn, 1987-; mem, Covenant Christian Community, 1982-; mem, Lambda Alpha Land Economics Soc, 1986-; mem, Amer Planning Assn, Natl Capital Chapter, 1987-. **HONORS/ACHIEVEMENTS:** Maryland Vassar Club Scholarship, Maryland Vassar Club, 1966; Carnegie-Mellon Fellowship for Graduate Studies, Carnegie-Mellon Found, 1970-71; HUD Work-Study Fellowship for Graduate Study, US Dept HUD, 1971-72; William Kinne Fellow Travel Fellowship, Columbia Univ School of Architecture, 1972; author, Community Development Versus Poor Peoples' Needs: Tension in CDBG, 1981, Citizen-Monitoring-A How-To Manual: Controlling Community Resources through Grass Roots Research & Action, 1981, Private Sector Support for Fair Housing: A Guide, 1983, Block Grants: Beyond the Rhetoric,

An Assessment of the Last Four Years, 1986, 1987, Block Grants: Missing the Target, An Overview of Findings, 1987.

BENNETT, PATRICIA A.
Attorney. **PERSONAL:** Divorced; children: Shandra Elaine. **EDUCATION:** Coll of Guam Agana GU, 1960-61; Riverside City Coll CA, 1967-70; Univ of CA, BA 1973; Hastings Coll of Law San Francisco, CA, 1973-76. **CAREER:** State of OH Dept of Finance, asst supr payroll div 1962-66; UCR Computing Ctr, prin clk 1967-71; Stanislaus Co Dist Atty's Office, legal researcher 1974; State of CA Dept of Water Resources, legal researcher 1975; Contra Costa Co Dist Atty's Office Martinez, CA, law clerk 1976-77; State Pub Utilities Comm, attorney. **ORGANIZATIONS:** Mem Urban League Guild 1970; mem UC Riverside Student Council 1971-72; volunteer San Francisco Co Legal Asst Prog San Bruno CA 1973; Council of Legal Educ Opport Scholarship 1973-76; Polit Sci Intern, Assemblyman Walter Ingalls Sacramento, CA 1973; Natl Dist Atty's Assn Intern 1974; mem Charles HoustonBar Assn 1976-; mem Nat Bar Assn 1979-. **BUSINESS ADDRESS:** Attorney, State Pub Utilities Comm, 350 McAllister St Rm 3157, San Francisco, CA 94102.

BENNETT, ROBERT A.
Educator, author. **PERSONAL:** Born Jan 11, 1933, Baltimore, MD; married Marceline M Donaldson; children: Elise Frazier, Mark, Malica Aronowitz, Ann, Michelle Aronowitz, Jacqueline Aronowitz. **EDUCATION:** Kenyon Coll, AB (magna cum laude) 1954; Gen Theo Seminary NYC, STB 1958, STM 1966; Harvard Univ, PhD 1974. **CAREER:** Episcopal Theo School/Divinity School, instructor/asst prof, 1965-74; Interdnmntnl Theo Center, Atlanta, visiting prof, 1973-77; Boston Univ School of Theology, visiting prof, 1975, 1982; Princeton Theo Seminary, visiting prof, 1975, 1983, 1986; Harvard Divinity School, visiting prof, 1976; Hebrew Univ, Jerusalem, Israel, fld arch stf supr, 1984; Episcopal Divinity Sch, prof Old Tstmt. **ORGANIZATIONS:** Trustee bd mem Interdenmntnl Theo Ctr, Atlanta 1973-77; vice-chr Stndng Litrgcl Commsn Episcopal Chrch 1982-; mem lctnry comm Natl Cncl Churchsof chrst 1982-; mem fnl slctn comm Fund for Theo Educ 1984-. **HONORS/ACHIEVEMENTS:** Phi Beta Kapa Kenyon Coll 1953; Fulbright Schlr Univ Copehagen, Denmark 1954-55; Vstng Rsrch Schlr Am Rsrch Ctr Cairo, Egypt 1979-80; Rsrch SchlrUniv Khartoum, Sudan 1980; Fld Stf Tel Dor, Israel Hebrew Univ 1984. **HOME ADDRESS:** 49 Hawthorne St, Cambridge, MA 02138.

BENNETT, WILLIAM DONALD
Educator. **PERSONAL:** Born Feb 19, 1939, Buffalo, NY; married Joyce Marie Echols; children: Craig, Jennifer. **EDUCATION:** Canisius Coll, BS 1961, MA 1967. **CAREER:** E High School, teacher, 1962-73, basketball coach, 1967, 1968, 1972, asst prin evening school, 1968-70, coord 1973-76; SUNY, instructor 1974-; Canisius Coll, instructor 1975-; E High School, principal 1976-. **ORGANIZATIONS:** Consortium com Canisius Coll 1977; pres 1060 Elmwood Ave Inc 1977; bd dir Buffalo Boys Town 1977; vice pres Black Tchrs Assn 1972; mem Di Gamma HonSoc 1973; pres Buffalo Secdr Prin Assn 1977. **HONORS/ACHIEVEMENTS:** Martin Luther King Citz Awd 1977; varsity basketbl & track Canisius Coll 1957-61. **MILITARY SERVICE:** AUSR capt 1962-68. **BUSINESS ADDRESS:** Principal, East High School, 820 Northampton, Buffalo, NY 14211.

BENNETT, WILLIAM RONALD
Educational administrator. **PERSONAL:** Born Jan 01, 1935, Parkersburg, WV; married Sarah L Clarkson; children: Denise Renee, Diane Elizabeth, Douglas Eugene. **EDUCATION:** Hampton Univ, BS 1956; John Carroll Univ, MEd 1972. **CAREER:** Cleveland Clnc, rsch tech 1960-62; Cleveland Bd Educ, sch admin 1962-72; Cleveland St Univ, dir, financial aid 1972-. **ORGANIZATIONS:** Pres, Natl Assn Student Financial Aid Admin, 1984-85; dir, Inroads N E Ohio Inc 1983-; treasurer, Inner City Renewal Soc, 1985; trustee Antioch Baptist Church 1985-88; pres Friendly Town Inc 1983-; mem CEEB Comm Pre Coll Guidance & Counseling, 1984-. **HONORS/ACHIEVEMENTS:** Article published NASFAA Journal; Man of Year, Alpha Phi Alpha Fraternity, 1982. **BUSINESS ADDRESS:** Dir of Financial Aid, Cleveland StateUniv, 1983 E 24th St, Cleveland, OH 44115.

BENNETTE, CONNIE E.
Editor. **PERSONAL:** Born Sep 09, 1951, Georgia. **EDUCATION:** Savannah State Coll Savanna, GA, BS 1973. **CAREER:** Coll TV News & Radio News Series Savannah, narrator/dir; The Medium Newspaper, reporter 1971-72; Univ of WA, supvr journalism interns; Tacoma True Citizen,editor; Tiloben Publ Co, vp; Mgt Bd YWCA, suvp hs newspapers; ABC News Seattle, monthly reporter 1974-. **HONORS/ACHIEVEMENTS:** Awards at Savannah State Coll, Alfred E Kennicker Journ Award; Columbia Sch of Journalism Award; Dean's List Recipient; Recip for Outstanding Scholastic Achievement; Med Newspaper Awards; Natl Newspapers Publishers Assn Merit Award for "Best New Story of 1974" 1975; Garfield HS Outstanding Publicity Award; Comm Serv Award; Unsung Heroine Honorable Mention Award. **BUSINESS ADDRESS:** Editor, PO Box 22047, Seattle, WA 98122.

BENNING, EMMA BOWMAN
Educator. **PERSONAL:** Born Oct 05, 1928, Columbus, GA; daughter of Ralph Bowman and Tinella Bowman; married Calvin C Benning, May 1946; children: Sheryl Ann Thomas, Nathaniel A, Eric A. **EDUCATION:** Cleveland State Univ, Cleveland OH, BS, MEd; Case Western Reserve Univ, Cleveland OH; Kent State Univ, Kent OH. **CAREER:** Cleveland Public Schools, Cleveland OH, principal, Benjamin Franklin Elementary, 1975-77, prinicpal, planner, 1979, dir, elementary schools, 1979-80, cluster dir, 1980-85, area supt, 1985-87, asst supt curriculum & instruction, 1987-. **ORGANIZATIONS:** Trustee, bd of dir, Children's Serv, 1969-; pres, Karamu House Bd of Dir, 1976-80; first vice pres, Jack & Jill of Amer Found, 1977-85, natl pres, 1985—; pres, Ludlow Community Assn, 1979-80; mem, Amer Assn of School Admins; mem, Amer Federation of Teachers; mem Ohio Assn of Elementary Principals; mem Delta Sigma Theta; mem, Natl Sorority of Phi Delta Kappa; mem, Links Inc. **HONORS/ACHIEVEMENTS:** Outstanding AME Woman of the Year; Good Neighbor Award; Outstanding Contributions to Jack & Jill of Amer Found; Outstanding Achievement Award, Cleveland Public Schools; author, Early Learning Laboratory Curriculum Guide, Early Childhood Education Guide Supplement, Education Program Guide for Inner City and EMR Children, Parent Guide, Get Into the Equation, AAAS. **HOME ADDRESS:** 3143 Ludlow Rd, Shaker Heights, OH 44120.

BENOIT, EDITH B.
Director of nursing. **PERSONAL:** Born Mar 07, 1918, New York, NY; married Elliot Benoit; children: Barbara, Lloyd. **EDUCATION:** Hunter Coll, AB 1938; Harlem Hosp Sch of Nursing, RN 1942; Tchrs Coll Columbia Univ, MA 1945, professional dipolma 1959. **CAREER:** Harlem Hosp, instr/supr/asst supt nurses 1942-51; VA Hosp Brooklyn, NY, supr/instr/asst chf nurse rsch & coord 1951-64; VA Hosp East Orange, NJ, assoc chf nursing serv for educ 1964-65; VA Hosp Bronx, NY, asst chf nursing serv 1965-67; Harlem Hosp NY,NY, dir nursing serv 1967-. **ORGANIZATIONS:** Chmn NY State Assn Comm to Study the Nurse Practice Act 1970; asst prof Columbia Univ 1967-; adj asst prof Pace Univ 1973-; bd dirs Natl League for Nursing; mem Open Curric Comm NLN 1972; mem Amer Nurses Assn 1942; Hunter Coll Alumnae Assn; mem bd dir Natl League for Nursing 1973-77; bd mgrsMinisink Town House New York City Mission Soc 1972-77. **BUSINESS ADDRESS:** Dir Nursing Serv Sch of Nurs, Harlem Hospital, 506 Lenox Ave, New York, NY 10037.

BENSON, GEORGE
Singer, composer, guitarist. **PERSONAL:** Born Mar 22, 1943, Pittsburgh, PA; married Johnnie; children: Robert, Marcus, Christopher. **CAREER:** Composed score for film "The Greatest"; album "Breezin" is largest selling jazz album of all time; Warner Bros Records, performer/singer/composer/guitarist. **HONORS/ACHIEVEMENTS:** Platinum Albums include, "Breezin," "In Flight," "Week-end in LA"; received Grammy Awd for Record of the Yr for "This Masquerade"; Grammy Awd for Best Record of Year 1977; Grammy Awd for Best Instrumental Performance, also for Best Engineered Recording 1977; Grammy Awd for Best Pop Instrumental Performance 1984. **BUSINESS ADDRESS:** c/o William Morris Agency, 151 El Camino Rd, Beverly Hills, CA 90212.

BENSON, GILBERT
Counselor, administrator. **PERSONAL:** Born Nov 01, 1930, Patterson, NJ; widowed; children: Michelle, Gilda. **EDUCATION:** Howard Univ Wash, DC, BS; Wm Paterson Coll Wayne, NJ, MA. **CAREER:** Family Planning Adm Youth Serv, welfare caseworker/youth worker 1960-74; Passaic Community Comm Coll, EOF counselor/admin; Council on Problems of Living, counselor/administrator; Bergen County Shelter for the Homeless, supervisor. **ORGANIZATIONS:** Past chmn Paterson NAACP; past affirm action chmn NJ State NAACP; chmn Paterson Coalition of Media Changes; chmn Passaic Co Citizens Vs Passaic Co Vocational Sch Bd; NOW Theatre of Paterson, NJ; mem Black Male Caucus of Paterson, NJ. **HONORS/ACHIEVEMENTS:** Comm Service Award NAACP 1973; Community Leader of America Award 1969; Passaic Co College Merit Award 1978. **MILITARY SERVICE:** AUS Reserves Reserve Capt. **BUSINESS ADDRESS:** Counselor/Admin, Paterson Board of Education, 33 Church St, Paterson, NJ 07505.

BENSON, HAYWARD J., JR.
Appointed official, educational admin. **PERSONAL:** Born Aug 29, 1936, Mt Dora, FL; son of Hayward J Benson Sr and Emily Smith Benson; married Mattie Jo Alexander; children: Stephan, Cameron. **EDUCATION:** FL A&M Univ, BS Elem Ed 1958; Univ of AZ, MS Educ 1965; Univ of FL, Cert Admin & Suprv 1968; FL Atlantic Univ, EdD 1984. **CAREER:** Broward Cty School Bd, dir office of comp planning for equal opport 1975-77; Nova Univ, adj prof part time; Broward Cty School Bd, admin asst to supt of schools 1977-83; Broward Cty Govt, dir public serv dept 1983-. **ORGANIZATIONS:** Mem Florida Assn for Health & Soc Serv, Broward Cty Human Relations div, State Univ System EEO Adv Comm Bd of Regents, Democratic Exec Comm; mem, bd of dir, Areawide Council on Aging, Amer Red Cross; chmn, bd of dir, Nova Univ Clinic; pres Florida Assn Comm Relations Prof, vice pres Natl Alliance of Black School Educ. **HONORS/ACHIEVEMENTS:** BCTA Teacher of the Year Awd 1966; BCTA Distinguished Serv Awd 1967; Certificate of Recognition Awd School Bd Broward Cty 1971; FEA Human Relations Awd 1972; LINKS Project Pioneer in Community Serv Awd 1975; Numerous other awds & citations for professional and community serv. **MILITARY SERVICE:** AUS capt 1959-65. **HOME ADDRESS:** 4410 NW 67 Terr, Lauderhill, FL 33319. **BUSINESS ADDRESS:** Dir Public Services, Broward County, 115 S Andrews Ave #433, Fort Lauderdale, FL 33301.

BENSON, JAMES RUSSELL
Educator, administrator. **PERSONAL:** Born Jan 19, 1933, Marks, MS; son of Escar Benson and Tressig V Benson; married Madgeolyn Warren; children: Barry Ray, Agnela Davis. **EDUCATION:** AL State Univ, BS 1963; Claremont Grad Coll, MA 1972, PhD 1977. **CAREER:** Radio Station WRMA Montgomery AL, news dir 1960-63; Urban League, dir teen post 1963-64; Lincoln High School, human relations dir 1964-66; Gow-Dow Experience, pres 1968-; Pomona Unified Sch Dist, dir of music; Palomares Jr High School, vice principal. **ORGANIZATIONS:** Bd of dirs JoAnn Concert Dance Corp 1984-85; bd of dirs NAACP 1986-87; dir MESA 1986-87. **HONORS/ACHIEVEMENTS:** Teacher of the Year Pomona Unified Sch Dist 1982-84; Langston Hughes Art Awd NAACP Pomona 1985; Bravo Awd LA Music Ctr 1985-86. **MILITARY SERVICE:** AUS Sp4 2 yrs; High Honor Trainee. **BUSINESS ADDRESS:** Vice Principal, Palomares Junior High School, 800 So Gary Ave, Pomona, CA 91767.

BENSON, RUBIN AUTHOR
Publication designer, educator, graphic artist. **PERSONAL:** Born Feb 08, 1946, Philadelphia, PA; son of Calvin Benson and Mable S Skinner; married Janet Wicks, Jul 10, 1978; children: Rubin, Heather, Badeerah. **EDUCATION:** Cheyney Univ, Cheyney PA, BS, 1969; Univ of Pennsylvania, Philadelphia PA, 1971; Parsons School of Design, New York NY, 1972. **CAREER:** Philadelphia School Dist, Philadelphia PA, graphic arts teacher, 1969-; Philadelphia Intl Records, art dir, 1982-84; First Impressions Design Group, Philadelphia, PA pres. **ORGANIZATIONS:** Judge, CEBA Awards, 1980-. **HONORS/ACHIEVEMENTS:** Award of Distinction, CEBA, 1983, 1984, 1985; Award of Excellence, CEBA, 1986. **BUSINESS ADDRESS:** Pres, First Impressions Design Group, 4920 Hazel Ave, Philadelphia, PA 19143.

BENSON, SHARON MARIE
Administrator. **PERSONAL:** Born Apr 20, 1959, Chicago, IL. **EDUCATION:** IL State Univ, BS 1981, MS 1983. **CAREER:** IL State Univ, rsch asst 1982-83; Goodwill Industries, vocational coord 1983-84; Operations Training Inst, job skills developer 1984-85; SAMCOR Dev Corp, administrator small business ctr. **ORGANIZATIONS:** Business consultant Westside Small Business Dev Ctr 1985-; mem MED Week Steering Comm 1985-; mem Chicago Assoc of Neighborhood Dev 1986-; mem Task Force on Small Business Needs 1986. **HOME ADDRESS:** 7918 South Escanaba, Chicago, IL 60617. **BUSINESS ADDRESS:**

Administrator Small Bus Ctr, SAMCOR Development Corp, 4 North Cicero Avenue, Ste 38, Chicago, IL 60644.

BENTLEY, ALBERT
Professional athlete. **PERSONAL:** Born Aug 15, 1960, Naples, FL. **EDUCATION:** Miami. **CAREER:** Oakland Invaders, fullback 1984-; Michigan. **HONORS/ACHIEVEMENTS:** 7-yard touchdown run in 1984 Orange Bowl proved to be winning score in Hurricanes 31-30 win over NE for natl chmpnshp.

BENTLEY, HERBERT DEAN
Business executive. **PERSONAL:** Born Jan 29, 1940, DeSoto, MO; married Judy Ann Lazard; children: Herbert, Karthryn, Karyn. **EDUCATION:** Harris Teachers Coll, AA 1958; So IL Univ, BS 1966; Amer Management Assn, Cert in Systems Design 1972. **CAREER:** New Age Fed Savings & Loan Assn, mng officer. **ORGANIZATIONS:** Pres PAS Mgmt Systems Inc; mem bd dir Gateway Natl Bank 1973-; mem bd dir New Age Fed Svngs & Loan Assn 1974-; bd dir Natl Assn of Black Accountants 1974-75; past officer bd mem Natl Assn of Black Accountants 1975-; mem bd dir Interracial Councl of Bus Oppty 1974-; mem bd dir Cntr Med Ctr 1976-; mem bd dir Christian Med Cntr 1976-; mem bd dir Oppty Indsln Cntr 1976-; mem bd dir Minority Bus Forum Assn 1976-; St Louis Tax Task Force for Congress of the US 1977. **HONORS/ACHIEVEMENTS:** Public Service Award Small Business Admin 1977. **BUSINESS ADDRESS:** Managing Officer, New Age Fed Savings & Loan, 1401 N Kings Highway, St Louis, MO 63113.

BENTON, CALVIN B.
Surgeon. **PERSONAL:** Born Aug 24, 1931, Morehead City, NC; married Jacqueline. **EDUCATION:** Agr & Tech Coll, BS 1953; Meharry Med Coll, MD 1963. **CAREER:** General Pract, surgeon. **ORGANIZATIONS:** Mem Natl Med Soc; Golden State Med Soc; pres Sinkler-Miller Med Soc; mem St Luke's Soc bd dir E Oakland Youth Center; Omega Phi Psi Frat. **MILITARY SERVICE:** USAF Capt 1953-59. **BUSINESS ADDRESS:** Surgeon, 10850 Mac Arthur Blvd, Oakland, CA 94605.

BENTON, GEORGE A.
President. **PERSONAL:** Born May 15, 1933, Philadelphia, PA; married Mildred Hogans; children: Anthony, Ondra. **CAREER:** Pro boxer 1949-70; Smokin' Joe Frazier, boxing trainer. **HONORS/ACHIEVEMENTS:** Outstanding Coach Award; Inducted in PA Hall of Fame 1979. **MILITARY SERVICE:** AUS Pfc served 2 years 14th Div Korea 1957. **BUSINESS ADDRESS:** President, Hardknocks, Inc, 2830 N Bailey St, Philadelphia, PA 19132.

BENTON, JAMES WILBERT, JR.
Attorney. **PERSONAL:** Born Sep 16, 1944, Norfolk, VA; married Faye L Young; children: Laverne Aisha. **EDUCATION:** Temple Univ, AB 1966; Univ of VA Law Sch, JD 1970. **CAREER:** Hill Tucker & Marsh, attorney; Court of Appeals of VA, judge. **ORGANIZATIONS:** Former bd mem, Friends Assn for Children; bd mem, VA ACLU; mem, VA State Educ Asst Authority; mem NAACP; former bd mem, Neighborhood Legal Aid Soc; former-mem Richmond Traffic Safety Comm; former bd mem, VA Educ Loan Authority; bd mem, VA Arts Comm; bd mem, VA Center for the Performing Arts. **BUSINESS ADDRESS:** Judge, Court of Appeals of Virginia, 101 N Eighth St, Richmond, VA 23219.

BENTON, JUANITA
Human services. **PERSONAL:** Born Nov 03, 1959, Vicksburg, MS. **EDUCATION:** Jackson State Univ, BS (Cum Laude) 1981, MS 1982. **CAREER:** Jackson State Univ, grad asst 1981-82; Rogers Cable Systems, sr customer service rep 1983-85; Metro State Univ, community faculty 1985-; Women Helping Offenders, counselor 1985-87. **ORGANIZATIONS:** Mem Jackson State Univ Marching and Symphonic Band 1977-80; mem Jackson State Univ Woodwind Choir 1977-80; mem Delta Sigma Theta 1979-85, NAACP 1983-86, Natl Assoc of Blacks in Criminal Justice 1986; mem MN Assoc of Women in Criminal Justice, Jackson State Univ Natl Alumni Assoc. **HONORS/ACHIEVEMENTS:** Regional Scholarship Awd Delta Sigma Theta 1981; 4 year Music Scholarship; mem Tau Beta Sigma Honorary Band Sor. **HOME ADDRESS:** 1418 Queen Ave, N, Minneapolis, MN 55411.

BENTON, LEONARD D.
Association executive. **PERSONAL:** Born Jul 01, 1939, Chickasha, OK; married Barbara Y Pointer; children: Quincy L. **EDUCATION:** Grambling Coll, BS 1961; IL Wesleyan Univ, MS 1964; Univ of Pittsburgh, MPA 1975. **CAREER:** Pub Schools Shreveport, LA & Chicago, instr 1961-65; Urban League, assoc dir 1967-69; Urban League Job Center, dir 1969-70; Urban League of OK City, pres. **ORGANIZATIONS:** Chmn Natl Balck Luth Lay Comm; exec sec Coalition for Civil Leadership OK city; chmn Soc Action Kappa Alpha Psi Frat; gen mgr SW Urban Devel Corp;sec Council of Exec Dirs So Region; Natl Urban League; chmn Soc Ministry OK Dist Luth Ch. **HONORS/ACHIEVEMENTS:** Natl Sci Found 1962-64; Serv to Mankind Award Seroma Club Okla City 1975. **BUSINESS ADDRESS:** President, Urban League of OK City, 3017 N Eastern, Oklahoma City, OK 73111.

BENTON, LUTHER
Business executive. **PERSONAL:** Born Jul 10, 1947, Morton, MS; married Juanita Johnson; children: Karen Diane, Christopher Wade. **EDUCATION:** Univ of IL, BSEE 1968; Pace Univ, MS Management 1979. **CAREER:** Bell Labs, mem tech staff 1968-70; IL Bell, engrg mgr 1970-76, div mgr 1978-84, dir 1984-; AT&T Gen Depts NJ, dist mgr 1976-79. **ORGANIZATIONS:** Vice pres Natl Tech Assn 1978-79; dir Circle Family Care Center 1983-; chmn Educ Subcomm Oak Park Racial Diversity Task Force 1983-; trustee Trinity Christian Coll 1983-; chmn IL Jr Engrs in Tech 1984-. **HONORS/ACHIEVEMENTS:** Professional Achievement Awd Natl Tech Assn 1983. **BUSINESS ADDRESS:** Dir of Marketing Services, Illinois Bell, 200 W Madison, Chicago, IL 60606.

BENTON, NELKANE O.
Business executive. **PERSONAL:** Born Jun 15, 1935, New York City, NY; married Thomas J Hill; children: Donna M. **CAREER:** KABC & KLOS Radio, dir pub affairs; Bing Crosby, pub rel/record promo; STEPInc, counselor; NKB Prod of Hollywood, exec dir; KABC-AM/KLOS-FM Am Broadcasting Corp, dir comm rel/dir ombudsman ser. **ORGANIZATIONS:** Mem KABC Radio Edn; bd mem, bd dir Consumer Credit Counsl of LA; bd dir LA Beautiful, Community Resources Development; mem Pacific Bell Consumer Adv Panel, Southern CA Gas Go Black Adv Panel. **HONORS/ACHIEVEMENTS:** Unity Award for Human Rel 1974; Mayor's Award Public Serv 1974; Outstanding Awds President Carter, Senator Alan Cranston, Supv Kenneth Hahn, State Senator Nate Holden 1976; Outstanding Employee Amer Broadcasting Co, Los Angeles Mayor Tom Bradley 1977,78; listed in Who's Who of Amer Women 1982-83. **BUSINESS ADDRESS:** Dir of Community Relation, Radio KABC-AM KLOS FM, 3321 S LaCienega, Los Angeles, CA 90016.

BENTON, QUINNIE ETTA
Retired educator. **PERSONAL:** Born Jun 25, 1898, Christian Co. **EDUCATION:** Lincoln Univ, BS Educ, MEd 1961. **CAREER:** Topeka KS Grade Sch, tchr 1926-32; Mexico Grade, grade sch tchr 1937-60; Garfield Sch, prin 1960-68; Garfield Mexico MO, tchr kindergarten 1968-71; Older Adult Transp Svc, pres. **ORGANIZATIONS:** Transp chmn Gov & Adv Com Cncl Jefferson City 1971-81; legislative mem Alert Chmn Mexico MO 1974-81; council mem MO Div of Aging Jefferson City 1974-81; Sr Citizen Chmn Audrain Older Adult Transp 1973-81; comm affairs Mexico Area Ret Tchrs 1974-81; professional adv cncl City-Co Health Unit Audrain Co 1974-81; elected mem Mexico Regional Mental Health Assn 1966; Del to White House Conf on Aging State of MO 1971. **HONORS/ACHIEVEMENTS:** Good Samaritan Awd Ch Women United Mexico 1973; Quinnie Benton Day Older Adult Transp 1979. **BUSINESS ADDRESS:** President, Older Adult Transp Serv, 601 Loop 70 W Parker Plaza, Columbia, MO 65201.

BENTON, SHIRLEY JEAN
Educator. **PERSONAL:** Born Aug 08, 1937, Carthage, TX; married Sammy L Benton; children: Reginald Jerome Knox. **EDUCATION:** Huston-Tillotson Coll, BA 1959; TX A&M Univ, summer study 1965; TX Women's Univ, Masters 1978; Harvard Univ, Ed Spec 1984. **CAREER:** North Side HS, vice principal; counselor; music teacher. **ORGANIZATIONS:** Pres Neighborhood Club 1971-; delegate NEA, TSTA, FWCTA 1974-; consultant High School Workshops 1982-; vice pres, pres Ft Worth Counselors Assoc 1983-84, 1984-85; consultant B&B Assocs 1984-; consultant Links Sororities 1984-85;NAACP,Zeta Phi Beta; Texas Assoc of Secondary principals, Ft Worth Admin Women, Phi Delta Kappa; Camp Fire Girls Board of Dir. **HONORS/ACHIEVEMENTS:** Honorary Life Mbrshp PTA 1975; Outstanding Teacher Awd H Ross Perot 1975; Fellowship Harvard Univ 1984; Outstanding Counselor of Yr North Texas CounselingOrganization 1985; Televesion Talk Shows KTVT Ch 11 1985; appeared in Jet Magazine article on Outstanding Counselor 1985. **HOME ADDRESS:** 5901 Eisenhower Dr, Fort Worth, TX 76112.

BEREOLA, ENITAN OLU
Editor. **PERSONAL:** Born Feb 16, 1947, Lagos, Nigeria;married Gwendolyn Jackson; children: Omotayo Omenike. **EDUCATION:** Coll San Mateo CA, AA 1969; San Jose State Coll, attended 1971; San Jose State, grad studies, 1971-72. **CAREER:** Occasionally lectures colls & schools; Impex Industries Corp, vice pres; KETH-TV, news reporter 1970-71; "Super Rap" weekly talk show KTAO-FM, co-host 1973-74; Ravenwood Post newspaper also Menlo Atherton Recorder sister newspaper, editor. **ORGANIZATIONS:** Fund raising coord Nairobi Schs Inc E Palo Alto CA 1973-74; play dir St John's Bapt Ch E Palo Also CA; taught class Comm Improvement Skills E Palo Alto & Belle Haven Students; soccer coach Black & Chicano Youths; E Palo Alto & Menlo Park CA. **HONORS/ACHIEVEMENTS:** Awarded John Swett Awd CA Tchrs Assn; Outstanding Editorial Interpretation Educ by Weekly Newspaper 1974; Cited Fairness Reportorial Sensitivity Mid-Peninsula Task Force Integrated Educ San Fran Bay Area CA; 1969 Awded Scholarship World Affairs Cncl No CA. **BUSINESS ADDRESS:** Editor, Ravenwood Post, 640 Roble Ave, Menlo Park, CA 94025.

BERKLEY, CONSTANCE ELAINE
Poet, educator. **PERSONAL:** Born Nov 12, 1931, Washington, DC; married Louis Berkley; children: Robert, Richard. **EDUCATION:** Columbia Univ, BA 1971, MA 1972. **CAREER:** Fordham Univ, one sem appt Black Drama 1971-72; Vassar Coll, literature lectr 1972-75; Ramapo Coll, appt african lit 1976; NY Univ Dept Near Eastern Lang & Lit, PhD; Fordham Univ, asst prof african afro-am & islamic lit 1979-. **ORGANIZATIONS:** Poet; mem Harlem Writer's Guild 1961-; NEC Dramatists Workshop Affiliate 1969-; lectr NY State Cncl of the Arts; Intl Poetry Soc; Assn Study Afro-Amer Life & History; Middle East Studies Assn; bd dir Natl Cncl Soviet Amer Friendship 1968; African Lit Assn; NY African Studies Assn; contrib ed Amer Dialog 1967; guest lectr "Islam in Africa" CBS/NYU Sunrise Semester Prog "1400 Yrs of Islam" 1980; guest lectr New Sch for Social Rsch 1980-81. **HONORS/ACHIEVEMENTS:** Author of poetry published in several anthologies; listed in Directory of Amer Poets 1975; Black Amer Writers past & present; The World Who's Who of Women 2nd & 3rd ed; Who's Who in Amer Women 1974; Intl Who's Who in Poetry 1974; Fisk Univ Biography of Living Black Writers. **BUSINESS ADDRESS:** FordhamUniv, Fordham Rd, Bronx, NY 10458.

BERKLEY, THOMAS LUCIUS
Attorney. **PERSONAL:** Born Aug 09, 1915, DuQuoin, IL; married Velda Maureen; children: Theon King, Gail, Miriam. **EDUCATION:** Fullerton Jr Coll, AA 1936; UCLA, BS 1938; Univ of CA Hastings School of Law, JD 1943. **CAREER:** Post Newspaper, publr; CA State World Trade Commiss, commiss; Private practice, attny. **ORGANIZATIONS:** Mem Alameda Cty Bar Assoc, CA State Bar Assoc, Amer Bar Assoc, Assoc of Trial Lawyers of Amer; mem Commiss of the Port of Oakland; mem bd dir Childrens Hosp Found, SF World Trade Club, SF Commonwealth Club, NAACP; past dir Oakland Unified School Dist; past mem, bd dir Oakland C of C; former regent John F Kennedy Univ; former mem adv council School of Bus Admin. **MILITARY SERVICE:** AUS 2nd lt 1943-46. **BUSINESS ADDRESS:** Attorney, 630 20th St, Oakland, CA 94612.

BERNARD, CANUTE CLIVE
Physician. **PERSONAL:** Born Jan 01, 1924, Costa Rica; married Daisy; children: Canute Jr, Carmen, Sonja, Arthur, Gregory. **EDUCATION:** Pharmacist Coll, degree pharmacist 1945; Howard Univ, BS 1949; NY Univ, MS 1951; Geneva Sch Med Univ Geneva, MD 1956. **CAREER:** Surgeon, Genl Practice; Jamaica Hosp, Queens Hosp Ctr, Harlem Hosp, Jamaica C of C, Health Systems Agency, NY State Workmen's Compensation Bd. **ORGANIZATIONS:** Third vice pres Natl Med Assn 1977-; bd of trustees Natl Med Assn; dir Med Bureau of NYS Workers Compensation Bd; bd secty/mem exec od Hlth Systems Agency; sec HSA Bd; mem HSA Exec Bd; mem Queens Clinical Soc NYC; past mem Chetto Med Prog; past pres Gamma Rho Sigma; past sec Queen's GGen Hosp; past pres Harlem Hosp; past v chmn Com Interns & Resd City NY; past chmn Pub Info Com MOTF for CHP; adv cncl York Coll;

bd adv cnclQueen's Urban League; mem NY State Health Planning Commn; Boro Pres's Cncl; mem CHPA Ad Hoc Task Force; v chmn Queens Med Hlth Prog; bd mem Friends York Coll; mem Queens United Dem Polit Club; S Jamaica Restoration Corp Bd; tstee Queens Med Sch; Queens Park Assn; mem Charter Revision Commn City NY 1977. **BUSINESS ADDRESS:** Surgeon, 107-60 Sutphin Blvd, Jamaica, NY 11435.

BERNARD, HAROLD O.
Educator, physician. **PERSONAL:** Born Jan 05, 1938; married Clara; children: Harold, Emily, Warren. **EDUCATION:** St Mary's Coll, attended 1955; Univ Manitoba, attended 1956-68; Fisk Univ, attended 1958-60; Meharry Med Coll, attended 1964. **CAREER:** Hubbard Hosp, intern 1964-65, resident 1965-68; Emory Univ Dept Ob-Gyn, assoc 1968-71; Meharry Med Coll, asst prof. **ORGANIZATIONS:** Mem Amer Bd Ob-Gyn & fellow Amer Coll Ob-Gyn; Morgagni Soc; consult Maternal & Infant Care Proj Grady Hosp; Maternal & Child Health Family Planning Meharry Med Coll; mem Natl Med Assn; RF Boyd Med Soc; Vol State Med Assn; Atlanta Med Soc; GA State Med Assn; TN State Med Found; YMCA Century Club. **HONORS/ACHIEVEMENTS:** Mem Beta Kappa Chi Hon Sci Soc; Alpha Omega Alpha Hon Med Soc; Prof Yr 1975. **BUSINESS ADDRESS:** Assistant Professor, Meharry Med Coll, 2209 Buchanan St, Nashville, TN 37208.

BERNARD, LOUIS JOSEPH
Surgeon, educator. **PERSONAL:** Born Aug 19, 1925, LaPlace, LA; married Lois Jeanette Mc Donald; children: Marie Jenkins, Phyllis Elaine Robison. **EDUCATION:** Dillard Univ, BA 1946; Meharry Med Coll, MD 1950. **CAREER:** Hubbard Hospital Nashville, intern 1950-51, resident 1954-56, 1957-58; Memorial Center NYC, resident 1956-57; Practice, med spec in surg, Oklahoma City OK, 1959-69, Nashville 1969-; Meharry Medical Coll, interim dean 1987-. **ORGANIZATIONS:** Nat'l Cancer Inst Rsch Fellow 1953-54; Amer Cancer Soc Clin Fellow 1958-59; mem Clinical Cancer Educ Comm NCI; mem Cancer Ctr Support Review Comm NCI; bd dir TN Div Amer Cancer Soc; mem staff of Hubbard, Nashville Hosps; clin asst prof surg Univ of OK 1959-69; assoc prof vice chair surg deptMeharry Med Coll 1969-73, prof chmn surg dept 1973-, assoc dean Sch of Med 1974-81; fellow Amer Coll of Surgeons; mem Southeastern Surgical Congress fellow; bd mem Nashville Acad Med; TN & Natl Med Assn; mem Soc of Surgical Oncologists; Soc of Surgical Chmn; OK Surgical Assn; OK City Surgical Assn; Commn on Cancer Amer Coll of Surgeons 1974-84; bd mem vice pres TN Found for Medical Care; mem Career Devel Comm Vet Admin; Clinical Fellowship Com Amer Cancer Soc; Alpha Omega Alpha; Alpha Phi Alpha; Sigma Pi Phi; TN Div Amer Cancer Soc, president elect. **MILITARY SERVICE:** USARMC 1st lt 1951-53. **BUSINESS ADDRESS:** Surgeon, Meharry Medical College, 1005-18 Ave N, Nashville, TN 37208.

BERNOUDY, JAMES LOGAN
Business executive. **PERSONAL:** Born Oct 28, 1919, Mobile, AL; married Barbara Wheeler; children: Jacquelyn Patterson, Jamesetta, Cheryl Marie Marbury, Barbara Elizabeth Dave. **EDUCATION:** Univ of CA at Los Angeles, construction mgmt & acct; Murphy Business Coll, contracting & bus admin; Los Angeles Construction Industry Coll of Estimating, attended, Cass Tech Sch, studies elec engrg. **CAREER:** Marvel Elec & Const Co, pres. **ORGANIZATIONS:** First black mem CA Contractors State License Bd; only black mem Amer Building Contractors Assn; mem Fair Employment Investigating Comm of the Assoc Electricians; mem bd dirs Minority Contractors Assn of LA; supervised tuition-free Electrical Technical Training Sch; Detroit Regional Dir Cub Scouts of Amer; represented Southern CA at 1971 White House Conf on Youth; mem Western Assembly on Black Economic Develop. **HONORS/ACHIEVEMENTS:** Harold Hammerman Awd Amer Building Contractors Assn - LA 1971; Outstanding in comm relations & remodeling in the US. **MILITARY SERVICE:** AUS corpl 4 yrs. **HOME ADDRESS:** 5033 Southridge Ave, Los Angeles, CA 90043. **BUSINESS ADDRESS:** President, Marvel Elec & Const Co, 2930 S La Brea Ave, Los Angeles, CA 90016.

BERNSTINE, DANIEL O.
Attorney, educator. **PERSONAL:** Born Sep 07, 1947, Berkeley, CA; children: Quincy, Justin. **EDUCATION:** Univ of CA, AB 1969; NW Univ Sch of Law, JD 1972; Univ of WI Law Sch, LLM 1975. **CAREER:** US Dept of Labor, staff atty 1972-73; Univ of WI Law Sch, teaching fellow 1974-75; Howard Univ Law Sch, asst prof 1975-78; Univ of WI Law Sch, prof 1978-; Howard Univ, asst vice pres for legal affairs. **HONORS/ACHIEVEMENTS:** Various publications. **BUSINESS ADDRESS:** Assistant Vice President, HowardUniv, 2400 6th St, NW, Washington, DC 20059.

BERRY, ALBERT G.
Educational administrator. **PERSONAL:** Born Jun 29, 1933, Indianapolis, IN; married Lillian F Pope; children: Wendell, Joyce, Alexis, Kenneth, Brian. **EDUCATION:** Butler U, BS 1959; IN Univ Med Cntr, MS 1964; Univ of TN, EdD 1975. **CAREER:** Meharry Med Coll, dir of gvmt rel; Meharry Med Coll, dir of office mgmt 1971-; Meharry Med Coll, asst dir 1969-71; Meharry Med Coll, instr 1967-69; IN U, instr 1962-67. **ORGANIZATIONS:** Mem TN Acad of Sci; Council on Arteriosclerosis; consult Phelps-Stores Fund; coord Nat Conf on Status of Hlt in Black Comm; Nat Conf on Mental Hlth;mem NAACP; life mem past dist rep past mem of supreme council Omega Psi Phi; treas Nashville Urban Kleag; deacon 15th Ave Bapt Ch; mem Sigma Xi Psi Delta Kappa; grad fellow Univ of TN; rschr grant IN Univ Found & US Pub Hlth Svc. **MILITARY SERVICE:** AUS 1st lt 1953-56. **BUSINESS ADDRESS:** Meharry Medical College, 1005 D B Todd Blvd, Nashville, TN 37208.

BERRY, ARCHIE PAUL
Business executive. **PERSONAL:** Born Nov 02, 1935, Akron, OH; married Sheila Yvonne Robinson; children: Troy Paul, Trent Anthony. **EDUCATION:** Univ Akron, BSEE 1963; Kent State Univ, MBA 1979. **CAREER:** Akron Standard Mold, elec engr 1963-64; IBM, systems engr 1964-65, market rep 1965-69, instr EXEC Educ 1969-71, instr mgr 1971, mgr info serv 1971-73, mgr computer serv 1973-76, mgr 1976-77, mgr castings & spl prods 1977-79, mgr prod educ. **ORGANIZATIONS:** Vice pres bus & finance Alpha Phi Alpha Homes Inc; NAACP; Urban League; Alpha Phi Alpha; vis prof Urban League's BEEP Prog; trustee Akron Regional DevelBd. **HONORS/ACHIEVEMENTS:** Man of Yr Alpha 1976; Four 100 Percent Sales Club Awds IBM 1966-69; Golden Cir Sales Awd IBM 1968. **MILITARY SERVICE:** USAF a/1c 1954-57. **BUSINESS ADDRESS:** Manager of Prod Educ & Training, Babcock & Wilcox, 20 S Van Buren Ave, Barberton, OH 44203.

BERRY, BENJAMIN DONALDSON
Educational administration. **PERSONAL:** Born Dec 22, 1939, Washington, DC; son of Benjamin D Berry Sr and Otis Holley Berry; married Linda Baker; children: Richard, Kathleen, Thena, Akuba. **EDUCATION:** Morehouse Coll, BA 1962; Harvard Divinity School, STB 1966; Case-Western Reserve Univ, PhD 1977. **CAREER:** Plymouth UCC, pastor 1966-68; Tampa Inner City Parish, dir 1968-70; Afro-Amer Studies Univ of So FL, dir 1969-70; Amer Studies Heidelberg Coll, asst prof 1970-74; Black Studies Coll of Woos, dir 1974-78; Skidmore Coll, dir of minority affairs; Prairie View A & M, assoc professor of history, honors. **ORGANIZATIONS:** Mem bd of dir Natl Amer Studies Faculty 1974-78; mem Bd of Ed 1981-; consult Berry Assoc. **HONORS/ACHIEVEMENTS:** Merrill Scholar Morehouse Coll 1961; Rockefeller Fellow Harvard Divinity 1962-66; Danforth Assoc Heidelberg Coll, 1972; Mellon Vstg Scholar Skidmore Coll 1978; Phi Beta Kappa, Morehouse College, 1987. **HOME ADDRESS:** 14522 Cypress Ridge Dr, Cypress, TX 77429. **BUSINESS ADDRESS:** Associate Professor of History - Banneker Honors College, Prairie View A & M University, Prairie View, TX 77446.

BERRY, CHARLES EDWARD ANDERSON (CHUCK BERRY)
Singer/composer. **PERSONAL:** Born Jan 15, 1926, San Jose, CA; married Toddy; children: Ingrid. **CAREER:** Musician guitar/saxaphone/piano; composer, Roll Over Beethoven, Maybelline, Memphis, Nadine, Johnny B Goode, Sweet Little Sixteen, Reelin' & Rockin', Rock 'n' Roll Music; popular rock & roll artist; rec artist Chess Records; concert &TV appearances 1955-; appeared in film "Go Johnny Go", "Hail! Hail! Rock n Roll". **HONORS/ACHIEVEMENTS:** Rock N Roll Hall of Fame; Grammy Awd for Lifetime Achievement 1984; autobiography "Chuck Berry". **BUSINESS ADDRESS:** Berry Park, 691 Buckner Rd, Wentzville, MO 63385.

BERRY, CHUCK **See BERRY, CHARLES EDWARD ANDERSON**

BERRY, FREDERICK JOSEPH
Educator. **PERSONAL:** Born May 29, 1940, Jacksonville, IL; married Quereda Ann Harris; children: Anthony, Frederick Jr. **EDUCATION:** Roosevelt Univ, 1961; Southern IL Univ, BMus 1962, MMus 1964; Stanford Univ, 1966-69. **CAREER:** S IL Univ Lab School, super of music 1964; Chicago Public School System, instructor 1964-66; Stanford Univ, asst dir of bands 1966-69; Coll of San Mateo, dir of jazz ensembles 1972-. **ORGANIZATIONS:** Mem Amer Fed of Musicians 1956-86; prof mus Amer Fed of Musicians 1960-85; mem San Fran 49ers Band 1970-85; mem Amer Fed of Teachers 1970-85; vice pres Amer Fed of Music Local 6 Credit Union 1973; mem CA Teachers Assn 1975-85; pres Berry Enterprises & Music Serv 1980-85; mem CA Music Educ Assn 1980-. **HONORS/ACHIEVEMENTS:** Guest soloist Oakland Symphony 1971; contractor Black Filmmakers Hall of Fame 1978-87; mem Golden Gate Theatre Orchestra 1982-87; musical dir Black Film Makers Hall of Fame 1983. **BUSINESS ADDRESS:** Dir of Jazz Ensembles, College of San Mateo, 1700 W Hillsdale Blvd, San Mateo, CA 94402.

BERRY, GORDON L.
Educator, author, lecturer. **PERSONAL:** Children: Gordon Jr, Steven, Cheryl, G Juanita. **EDUCATION:** Central State Univ, BS 1955; Univ of WI, MS 1961; Marquette Univ, EdD 1969. **CAREER:** Milwaukee Tech Coll, counseling psychologist; Marquette Univ, asst to academic vice pres; UCLA, asst dean 1970-76, prof 1976-. **ORGANIZATIONS:** Natl Assoc of Sch Psychologists 1970-; Am Orthopsychiatric Assn 1970-; Phi Delta Kappa; Bd of Southwest Lab for Research; Bd of Los Angeles Film Teachers Assn; mem Amer Psychological Assoc. **HONORS/ACHIEVEMENTS:** Research fellow Fanon Cntr of Charles Drew Med; fellow Inst for Study of Intercultural Commun Temple Univ; Ralph Metcalfe Chair Lecturer; Who's Who in Intl Svc. **MILITARY SERVICE:** AUS capt 1955-57. **BUSINESS ADDRESS:** Professor, Univ of CA Los Angeles, 405 Hilgard Ave, Los Angeles, CA 90024.

BERRY, JEROME
News reporter, sportscaster. **PERSONAL:** Born Aug 05, 1950, Tulsa; married Claudia; children: Carla Michelle, Kristen Lynette, Kayla Renee'. **EDUCATION:** Univ WY; Tulsa U; Bishop Coll. **CAREER:** Gulf Oil Co, 1970-73; KTUL TV, news reporter sportscaster 1973-74; KPRC TV Houston, news reporter, sportscaster 1974-79; WXYZ TV Detroit, anchor reporter 1982-. **ORGANIZATIONS:** NAACP; mem Black Communicators; co-chair Black United Fund. **HONORS/ACHIEVEMENTS:** Best Sportscaster in TX Assoc Press 1977; Best Feature in TX United Press Intl 1977; Outstanding Achievement "UPI" Sports Feature MI 1984; Emmy nom "When the Cheering Stops" 1984. **BUSINESS ADDRESS:** Sportscaster, WXYZ, PO Box 789, Southfield, MI 48037.

BERRY, LEE ROY, JR.
Educator. **PERSONAL:** Born Nov 05, 1943, Lake Placid, FL; married Elizabeth Ann Hostetler; children: Joseph Jonathan, Malinda Elizabeth, Anne Hostetler. **EDUCATION:** Eastern Mennonite Coll, BA 1966; Univ of Notre Dame, PhD 1976; IN Univ Bloomington Sch of Law, JD 1984. **CAREER:** Cleveland Public Schools, teacher, 1966-68; Goshen Coll IN, prof, 1969-79, leader of study serv trimester, 1979-80, assoc prof of History & Political Science, 1980-. **ORGANIZATIONS:** Mem Gen Bd of Mennonite Ch; chmn High Aim Comm Mennonite Bd of Missions; mem Relief & Serv Comm Mennonite Bd of Missions; mem Peace Sect MennoniteCentral Com. **HONORS/ACHIEVEMENTS:** Fellow John Hay Whitney 1970-71; Fellow Natl Fellowships Fund 1975-76. **BUSINESS ADDRESS:** Assoc Prof Hist/Polit Sci, Goshen College, South Main St, Goshen, IN 46526.

BERRY, LEMUEL, JR.
Educator/director. **PERSONAL:** Born Oct 11, 1946, Oneonta, NY; married Christine Elizabeth; children: Lemuel III, Cyrus James. **EDUCATION:** Livingstone Coll, BA 1969; Univ of IA, MA 1970, PhD 1973. **CAREER:** Sabin Elem Sch, 1971; Southeastern Jr High, 1972; Fayetteville State Univ, instr of week-end coll in serv tchrs 1975-76, chmn div of humanities 1973-75, chmn dept of music 1973-76; Langston Univ, chmn dept of music 1976-83, chmn dept of music & art 1981-83; AL State Univ, assoc prof sch of music 1983-86; Westchester Conservatory of Music, The Humphrey School of Dance, coord of curriculum & instr; Mercy Coll, chmn, prof dept of music & fine arts. **ORGANIZATIONS:** Natl pres Kappa Kappa Psi Natl Band Frat 1983-85; natl pres Rsch Assoc of Minority Prof 1983-86; bd of trustees Assoc of Concert Bands 1984-85; bd of trustees Southern Conf of Afro-Amer Studies 1983-87; cncl mem Cncl for Rsch in Music Educ 1978-, OK Arts Assoc 1982-84, N Central Tchr Certification 1982-84; state chairperson Natl Black Music Collequium 1979-80, AL Jazz

Educ Assoc 1984-; reviewer Amer Choral Dirs Assn 1984-. **HONORS/ACHIEVEMENTS:** Scholarship German Academic Rsch Scholar 1979; Who's Who in Music 1984; Intl Who's Who in Music 1976; Outstanding Educator 1975; Natl Endowment of the Humanities Grant Recipient 1985. **BUSINESS ADDRESS:** Professor, Mercy College, 555 Broadway, Dept of Music & Fine Arts, Dobbs Ferry, NY 10522.

BERRY, LEONIDAS H.
Physician. **PERSONAL:** Born Jul 20, 1902, Person County, NC; married Emma; children: Mrs Judith Berry Jones, ALvin E Harrison. **EDUCATION:** Wilberforce Univ, BS 1924, ScD (Hon); Univ of Chicago, SB 1925; Rush Med Coll of the Univ of Chicago, MD 1929; Univ of IL, MS 1933; Lincoln Univ of PA LLD (Hon) 1983. **CAREER:** Cook County, Michael Reese & Provident Hospitals, sr attending physician & gastroenterologist emeritus; private practice, Chicago IL, physician. **ORGANIZATIONS:** Pres Cook County Physician Assn 1950-; past pres Natl Med Assn 1965; diplomate Amer Bd of Intl Med; Subspeciality Bd of Gastroenterology; Natl Bd of Med Examiners; Amer Med Assn; Amer Gastroscopic Soc; mem Amer Coll Gastroenterology, Amer Soc Gastrointestinal Endoscopy; Natl Soc Gastroenterology France & Chile, SA, Japan Endoscopy Soc; mem Natl Med Assn; past pres NAACP; life mem Assn for the Study of Afro-Amer Life & History; Original Forty Club Chicago; fellow NY Acad of Medicine; life mem Alpha Phi Alpha; lecturer gastroenterology US Dept of State Foreign Cultural Exchange in Africa 1965, Japan, Korea, Philippines 1966, and Paris 1970. **HONORS/ACHIEVEMENTS:** Honorary ScD, Wilberforce Univ, 1945; prof Cook County Grad Sch of Med 1947-75 Fellow Amer Coll of Physicians 1950-; Distinguished Serv Awd, Natl Med Assn, 1958; Man of the Yr Awd, Orig Forty Club of Chicago, 1974; Schindler Awd, Amer Soc for Gastrointestinal Endoscopy, 1977; Prof Achievement Awd, Univ of Chicago Alumni, 1978; Alumni Citation for Pub Serv, Univ of Chicago; Certificate of Merit for Science Exhibits, Chicago Med Soc; Hon LLD, Lincoln Univ, 1983; author of numerous science articles in natl & state medical journals; sr author & editor of intl book on endoscopy; author of "I Wouldn't Take Nothin' for My Journey" (200 years of family history); Alpha Omega Alpha Med Hon Soc, Rush Med Coll; Leonidas Berry Soc for Digestive Diseases. **MILITARY SERVICE:** 1st Lt AUS Med Res 1930-40. **HOME ADDRESS:** 5142 S Ellis Ave, Chicago, IL 60615.

BERRY, LEROY
Educator. **PERSONAL:** Son of Lester Berry and Lubertha Foster; married Ruth Brothers Berry; children: Lorenzo Armstead. **EDUCATION:** Western Reserve Univ, Cleveland OH, 1946; UCLA-USC, Los Angeles, CA; UCLA, Los Angeles CA, BA, Sociology, 1957; CA State Univ, Los Angeles CA, MA, Elementary Teaching, 1961, MA, Elementary Admin, 1962, MA, Counseling, 1976. **CAREER:** Dept of Water & Power, Los Angeles CA, electr tester, 1948-54; Los Angeles Unified School Dist, Los Angeles CA, teacher 1957-77, substitute principal 1969-72, counselor 1977-80, teacher advisor 1980-82. **ORGANIZATIONS:** Mem, Kappa Alpha Psi Fraternity; life mem, NAACP; mem, Urban League, S Christian Lead Corp, Crenshaw Neighbors; alumni mem Univ of CA 1958-; pres Leimert Democratic Club, 1958-61; asst dist rep, CA Democratic Council, 1964-66; southern cred chmn, CA Democratic Council 1964-66; vice pres reg II CA Democratic Council 1966-68; representative, Democratic Council Committee, 1967-71; representative, State Democratic Committee 1967-73. **HONORS/ACHIEVEMENTS:** Appointed commr of Environmental Quality Bd, 1976, commr of Human Relations Comm, 1983, by mayor and city of Los Angeles. **MILITARY SERVICE:** AUS Coast Artill, corporal 1941-45; marskman, sharpshooter, good conduct medal. **HOME ADDRESS:** 3801 Welland Ave, Los Angeles, CA 90008.

BERRY, LISBON C., JR.
Attorney. **PERSONAL:** Born Apr 01, 1922, Washington, DC; son of Lisbon C Berry (deceased) and Annie J Berry; married Shirley Hart; children: Deborah E, Lisbon C III, Kimberly D. **EDUCATION:** NC Central Univ, BA 1950; Howard Univ School of Law, LLB 1957. **CAREER:** McKissick & Berry, Durham NC, atty 1957-60; Wilmington NC, atty 1960-67; US Dept of Justice & Civil Rights, senior trial atty 1967-82; Legal Serv Lower Cape Fear, exec dir 1982-87 (retired). **ORGANIZATIONS:** Life mem Natl Bar Assn; mem US Supreme Court Bar 1973; mem NC State Bar 1980; life mem NAACP; bd of dirs Public Radio 1985-, First Hanover Bank 1986-; mem North Carolina Assn of Black Lawyers 1982-, Cape Fear Area United Way 1987-; acting pres Southeastern Minority Business Assn 1988-; pres, bd of dir Community Boys Club 1988-. **HONORS/ACHIEVEMENTS:** Honored by North Carolina Assoc of Black Lawyers as Pioneer Civil Rights Attorney 1950-70; Special Achievement, US Dept of Justice 1975, 1980.

BERRY, MARY FRANCES
Professor of history and law. **PERSONAL:** Born Feb 17, 1938, Nashville, TN; daughter of George F. Berry and Frances Southall Berry. **EDUCATION:** Howard Univ, Washington, DC, BA, 1961, MA, 1962; Univ of Michigan, Ann Arbor, MI, PhD, 1966, JD, 1970. **CAREER:** Howard Univ, Washington, DC, tchng fellow in Amer history, 1962-63; Univ of Michigan, Ann Arbor, tchng asst, 1965-66, asst prof dept of history, 1966-68, asst and assoc prof, 1968-70; Univ of Maryland, College Park, assoc prof, 1969-76; Univ of Colorado, Boulder, acting dir of Afro-Amer studies, 1970-72, dir, 1972-74, provost of division of behavioral social science, 1974, chancellor, 1976-77; US Dept HEW, asst sec for educ, 1977-80; Univ of Colorado, prof of history, 1976-80; US Commn on Civil Rights, commr & vice chmn 1980—; Howard Univ, prof of history & law, 1980-87; Univ of Pennsylvania, Geraldine R Segal prof of Amer Social Thought, 1987—. **ORGANIZATIONS:** Mem, DC Bar Assn, 1972; consult to curator of educ, Natl Portrait Gallery, Smithsonian Inst; consult, Office Policy Planning HUD; Office for Civil Rights, HEW; US Civil Rights Commn; bd mem, Afro-Amer Bicentennial Corp; chmn, Maryland Commn Afro-Amer Indian Hist Culture, 1974; mem, exec bd, 1974-77, Org Amer Historians; exec bd, Assn Study of Afro-Amer Life History, 1973-76; mem, Amer Hist Assn; Org Amer Historians; Amer Bar Assn; Natl Bar Assn; natl panel of advisors, Univ of Mid-Amer; mem, Tuskegee Inst Bd of Trustees; bd of dir, DC Chap of ARC. **HONORS/ACHIEVEMENTS:** Civil War Round Table Fellowship Award, 1965-66; author of books, including Black Resistance/White Law: A History of Constitutional Racism in America, 1971, and Why ERA Failed: Women's Rights, and the Amending Process of the Constitution, 1986; assoc editor of "Journal Negro History" 1974—; Honorary Degrees from Central Michigan Univ, 1977, Howard Univ, 1977, Univ of Akron, 1977, Benedict Coll, 1979, Univ of Maryland, 1979, Grambling State Univ, 1979, Bethune-Cookman Coll, 1980, Clark Coll, 1980, Delaware State Coll, 1980, Oberlin Coll, 1983, Langston Univ, 1983, Marian Coll, 1984, Haverford Coll, 1984, Colby Coll, 1986, City Coll of the City Univ of New York, 1986, and DePaul Univ, 1987; Rosa Parks Award, Southern Christian Leadership Conf; Ebony Black Achievement Award; Ms. Magazine 1986 Woman of the Year. **BUSINESS ADDRESS:** Professor, University of Pennsylvania, 1000 Vermont Ave NS, Ste 300, Washington, DC 20005. *

BERRY, PAUL LAWRENCE
Reporter. **PERSONAL:** Born Feb 15, 1944, Detroit, MI; married Marilyn; children: Karen. **EDUCATION:** Attended, USAF Def Info Sch, Basic Med Sch, Basic Dental Sch. **CAREER:** WXYZ-TV, staff rep & co-anchor 1969-72; WMAL-TV, anchor st rep & mod 1972-75; WMAL-TV, st rep mod & co-anchor 1975-; Amer Black Forum, panelist; Paul Berry's WA, weekend anchor & host. **ORGANIZATIONS:** Wash DC Mayors Ad Hock Comm on Criminal Justice; DC Fed 524 Coun for Except Child; Sigma Delta Chi Prof Journ Soc; bd of dir Amer Digest Disease Assn; Lion Club of Wash DC. **HONORS/ACHIEVEMENTS:** Broadcasters Awd Chesapeake Assoc Press 1976; Metro Wash Mass Media Awd Amer Assoc of Univ Women 1976; Comm Awd MI Chap SCLC; Comm Serv Awd 1974;Comm Serv Awd Unit Cit Inc 1975; Media Awd Cap Press Club 1975; Natl Cap Area Health Assn Awd 1974; Outstanding Cit Awd MMEOC Assn 1976; Dept Comm Serv Awd Amer Amvets DC 1974; Comm Serv Awd Rap Inc 1976. **MILITARY SERVICE:** USAF staff sgt 1961-69. **BUSINESS ADDRESS:** Weekend Anchorman, c/o WJLA-TV Channel 7, 4461 Connecticut Avenue NW, Washington, DC 20008.

BERRY, PHILIP ALFONSO
Personnel consultant. **PERSONAL:** Born Jan 28, 1950, New York, NY; married Karen Bryan; children: Kiel, Maya. **EDUCATION:** Manhattan Comm Coll, AA 1971; Queens Coll CUNY, BA 1973; Columbia Univ Sch of Social Work, MS 1975; Xavier Univ of Cincinnati, MBA 1983. **CAREER:** Urban League of Westchester NY, dir 1975-78; Procter & Gamble, industrial relations mgr 1978-86; Digital Equipment Corp, human resources consultant 1986-. **ORGANIZATIONS:** NY State chmn Assoc of Black Social Workers 1975-78; fndr/pres Housing & Neighborhood Develop Inst 1976-78; pres The Delta Group & Berry Assoc Consulting 1983-; bd mem Cincinnati Comm Action Agency 1985-86; dean of pledges Alpha Phi Alpha Frat Alumni Chap 1986; mem Amer Soc for Training & Develop, World Future Soc; pres Black Student Union Queens Coll, Black Student Caucus Columbia Univ. **HONORS/ACHIEVEMENTS:** Ford Foundation Fellowship; Mayor's Proclamation "Philip Berry Day" Mt Vernon NY 1978; Outstanding Young Man of Amer US Jaycees 1979; Who's Who in the Midwest 1981. **BUSINESS ADDRESS:** Human Resources Consultant, Digital Equipment Corp, One Penn Plaza, New York, NY 10119.

BERRY, ROSCOE DAREWOOD, JR.
Business executive. **PERSONAL:** Born Jun 25, 1921, Chicago, IL; divorced; children: Sybil Lyn. **EDUCATION:** Loyola Univ, attended 1940-41; WV State Coll, attended 1941-43; Univ of PA, attended 1958-59; LUTC, grad study 1960-62; Natl Assn Security Dealers, licensed 1958; Travelers Ins Co Mgmt Training Sch, licensed 1968. **CAREER:** Commonwealth Edison, sales rep 1943-45; Met Mutual Life Assurance Co, debit agent 1945-55; Manhattan Life Ins Co, sales rep 1955-62; NY Life Ins Co, Philadelphia 1962-63; Manhattan Life Ins Co, LA 1963-67; General Agent, self-employed 1967-68; Travelers Ins Co, agency mgr 1968-72; RD Berry Jr & Assocs LA,gen agent 1972-; Occidental Life, gen agent 1972; Leimert Park Family Health Ctr, comptroller 1977-. **ORGANIZATIONS:** Pres Medical Econ Inc 1975; mem Urban League; exec com NAACP Philadelphia 1962-; mem Brotherhood Crusade; mem Manhattan Life Millionaire Club. **BUSINESS ADDRESS:** Comptroller, c/o Leimert Park Family Center, PO Box 8315, Attn: Dr Washington, Los Angeles, CA 90008.

BERRY, THEODORE M.
Retired attorney. **PERSONAL:** Born Nov 08, 1905, Maysville, KY; married Johnnie M Newton; children: 3 children. **EDUCATION:** Univ Cincinnati, AB 1928, LLB 1931. **CAREER:** Cincinnati City Council, council mem 1950-57; OEO, asst dir 1965-69; City of Cincinnati, mayor 1972-75; Tobias & Kraus, atty; Coll of Law Univ of Cincinnati, adj prof 1976-78; NAACP, interim gen counsel 1979-80. **ORGANIZATIONS:** Mem Amer, OH, DC Cincinnati, Sup Ct Bar Assns; dir Cedar Grove Homestead Assn; trust Cincinnati Better Hous League & Family Svc; Natl Dem Pol Comm; counsel West End Dev Corp; dir Southern OH Bank 1973-84; pres, trust Cincinnati Southern Railway 1977-; mem Lawyer's Del to China-Sponsor, Citizen Ambassador People to People Prog 1987. **HONORS/ACHIEVEMENTS:** Hon LLD Univ Cincinnati 1968; Humanitarian Awd ACTION 1973; bro chmn Natl Conf Christians & Jews 1973; Outstanding Citizen Awd Omega Psi Phi 1974; Natl Conf Christ & Jews Awd 1977; Hebrew Union Coll Doctor of Humane Letters 1979; NAACP Wm R Ming Advocacy Awd 1979; Disting Alumni Awd UC Coll of Law 1982; Cincinnati C of C Great Living Cincinnatian Awd 1984. **BUSINESS ADDRESS:** 414 Walnut St, Ste 911, Cincinnati, OH 45202.

BERRY, WELDON H.
Attorney. **PERSONAL:** Born Jan 04, Dallas, TX; married Lurlene Barnes. **EDUCATION:** TX Coll, AB 1941; TX So Univ Sch Law, LLB 1952. **CAREER:** Private practice, law. **MILITARY SERVICE:** USAF 2nd lt 1941-43. **BUSINESS ADDRESS:** Attorney, 711 Main St, Houston, TX 77002.

BERRYMAN, MACON M.
Retired lecturer. **PERSONAL:** Born Feb 17, 1908, Lexington, KY; married Dortha Hackett; children: James Henry. **EDUCATION:** Lincoln Univ PA, BA 1931; Atlanta Univ Sch of Social Work, MA 1933; Lincoln Univ PA, DCL 1967. **CAREER:** Casework Supr, investigator 1933-34; Burlington Co Emergency Relief Admin, dist adminstr 1934-36; NY State Training Sch for Boys, parole ofcr 1936-45; Sunnycrest Farm for Boys, exec dir 1945-50; Dept of Social Welfare, St Thomas VI, dir child welfare 1950-58; Social Welfare, actg commr 1958-59, ret commr 1959-74; Div of Social Sci Coll Of VI, guest lectr 1974-77; Retired. **ORGANIZATIONS:** Mem Nat Assn of Social Workers 1938-; fellow Acad of Cert Social Workers 1960-; Nat Cncl of State Pub Welfare Admin 1959-74; Nat & Intl Conf of Scl Wrk 1936-; Am Pub Wlfr Assn 1950-; mem bd of dir St Thomas & St John Chpt; ARC 1957-; mem Bd Dirs, St Thomas United Way 1959-85; chmn Bd ofDirs 1976-78; treas St Thomas Fed Credit & Union 1954-59; Civil Def Dir Welfare Disaster Serv 1958-74; consult VA Youth Commn 1950-59; VI Aging Commn 1959-74; mem Bd Dirs VI Cncl Boy Scouts 1964-; organizer & pres VI Chap Lincoln Univ Alumni Assn 1964-67; mem Alpha Phi Alpha Frat; Masonic Lodge; Episcopalian pres St Thomas Rotary Club 1966-67; sec Dist 404 Rotary Club 1978-79; founder St Thomas Rotary Club II 1979. **HONORS/ACHIEVEMENTS:** Citation for Distinguished Serv as Chmn; bd mem St Thomas, St John Chap ARC 1965; Citation in Recog of Outstanding Achievement in Serving Human Needsof Comm; St Thomas United Way 1957 & 1979; Citation in Apprec for interest in Serv to Youth of Comm; VI Cncl Boy & Scouts

1965; Silver Beaver 1969; Reg Cncl Boy Scouts Silver Antelope 1972; citation St Thomas USO 1966; citation St Thomas Women's League 1966; citation PR Cancer League 1966, 67, 72, 74; citation Am Bicentennial Res Inst 1974; awarded Paul Harris Fellow 1980. **HOME ADDRESS:** PO Box 3892, St Thomas, Virgin Islands of the United States 00801.

BERRYMAN, MATILENE S.
Attorney. **PERSONAL:** Born in Prince Edward Co, VA; divorced; children: D'Michele, Sherrill Diane Miller. **EDUCATION:** Attended, Bluefield State Univ WV; Howard Univ, attended 1945-46; Attended, PA State, UCLA, George Washington 1957-65; Amer Univ Washington DC, BMath 1957; Howard Univ Washington DC, JD 1973; Univ of RI, M Marine Affairs 1979. **CAREER:** US Naval Oceanographic Office Suitland, physical oceanographer 1955-63, oceanographer instructor 1963-68; Exec Office of Pres & Defense Documen Center, Alexandria VA, physical science admin 1968-70; Consortium for DC, dir marine science 1973-76; Univ of Washington DC, prof of marine science 1970-. **ORGANIZATIONS:** Chmn Enviromental Sci Dept Univ of DC 1971-78; financial sec Natl Assn of Black Women Atty 1975-; visiting prof Purdue Univ; mem PA State Bar 1974-; mem DC Bar 1975-; trustee Shiloh Bapt Ch Washington DC; bd dir DC Mental Health. **HONORS/ACHIEVEMENTS:** Who's Who in Amer Women 1976; nominated vice pres Marine Tech Soc 1978-79; Outstanding Serv to Marine Sci & Law Natl Assn of Black Women Atty 1978. **BUSINESS ADDRESS:** Prof of Marine Sci, Univ of DC, Van Ness Campus, 4200 Connecticut Ave NW, Washington, DC 20008.

BERTHOUD, KENNETH H., JR.
Business executive. **PERSONAL:** Born Dec 28, 1928, New York, NY; married Sara P Denby; children: Pamela, Kevin, Cheryl. **EDUCATION:** Long Island U, BA 1952; George Washington U, MS 1972. **CAREER:** Hdqtrs Marine Corps, dep dir 1975-77; MCDEC Quantico VA, ac of s supply 1977-78; CACI, dept of mgr 1978-80; Advanced Tech Inc, dep div gen mgr 1980-. **ORGANIZATIONS:** Bd mem Society of Logistics Engrs 1984-86. **HONORS/ACHIEVEMENTS:** Mayors Certificate of Appreciation City of New York 1969; Walter Milliken Awd Mem of the Year Soc of Logistics Engrs 1986. **MILITARY SERVICE:** USMC colonel 31 Yrs; LOM, MSM, JSCM, NCM Korean & Vietnam campaign medals. **HOME ADDRESS:** 708 S 26 St, Arlington, VA 22202. **BUSINESS ADDRESS:** Deputy Div General Manager, Advanced Technology Inc, 12001 Sunrise Valley Dr, Reston, VA 22091.

BERTRAND, JOSEPH G.
Business executive. **PERSONAL:** Born Oct 27, 1931, Biloxi, MS; married Joan Clara Tyler; children: Joan, Jason, Jeffrey, Joseph, Justin, Julian. **EDUCATION:** Notre Dame, AB 1954; Loyola, Post Grad Study. **CAREER:** Cook Cty Dept of Publ Aid, 1958-59; Chicago Comm on Youth Welfare, comm org 1959-61; Demert & Dougherty, dir of sales 1963-67; Standard Bank & Trust Co, vice pres 1966-70; Highland Comm Bank, pres, chmn of bd 1970-72; City of Chgo, treas; Gateway Natl Bank of Chgo, chmn, ceo. **ORGANIZATIONS:** Mem Highland Bus Assoc; exec comm, mem Small Bus Assoc, Bank Adv Comm; past pres Black Bankers of Chgo; mem Municipal Officers Assoc of US & CAN;mem Adv Council of Coll of Arts & Letters Notre Dame 1969; alumni bd Notre Dame 1970; reg council SBA; vchmn Govs Adv Council on Econ Oppty; bd memNAACP; bd chmn Rosenblum Chicago Boys Club; asst treas Chicago Boy Scout Council, Chicago Forum Talent Asst Prog, S End Jr C of C; chmn St Francis De Paula Holy Name Soc, St Philip Neri Holy Name Soc; mem Chicago Urban League, United Cerebral Palsy Assoc, Chicago Council on Foreign Rel, Econ Club of Chgo; bd mem WA Park YMCA of Metro Chgo; mem S Shore Comm, S Shore C of C, Variety Club of IL, Little Flower Men's Lay Bd; pres Sisters of the Blessed Sacrement Alumni Chicago Capt; committeeman Reg Dem Org 7th Ward; mem Kappa Alpha Psi; del Dem Natl Conv 1972; bd of regents Champion-Jesuit HS for Boys, Prairie Du Chien WI Polit Svc, Tuskegee Alumni Assoc. **HONORS/ACHIEVEMENTS:** Man of the Year Notre Dame Alumni Assoc 1974; One of the Top Ten Men of 1965 Chicago Jr C of C; State of Israel Prime Ministers Medal 1972; IL Basketball Hall of Fame 1973; listed in Who's Who in Midwest 1972-73; Spec Recog Awd Old Town Boys Club 1972; Honoree Chicago Conf on Brotherhood Inc 1972. **MILITARY SERVICE:** AUS 1956-58. **BUSINESS ADDRESS:** Chairman & Chief Exec Officer, Gateway Natl Bank of Chicago, 7853 S Stony Island Ave, Chicago, IL.

BERVIN-MITCHELL, GABRIELLE
Advertising sales executive. **PERSONAL:** Born Sep 12, 1955, Port-au-Prince, Haiti;married Attorney Leo K Mitchell; children: Chase K. **EDUCATION:** DePaul Univ, BA Polit Sci 1978; Attended, DePaul Univ Coll of Law 1979; Attended, Amer Mgmt Assoc 1982-84. **CAREER:** Chase Marketing Inc, private venture 1981-; Essense Magazine, account exec 1980; Essence Communications, midwest adv sales dir. **ORGANIZATIONS:** Mem Amer Mgmt Assoc, Natl Assoc for Female Execs, chicago Adv Club, Women in Print, Women's Adv Club, Black Women Form; mem Provident Hosp Committeeof Fifty, New Chicago Comm. **HONORS/ACHIEVEMENTS:** Fred Hampton Scholarship Fund Image Awd; Essence Commitment to Excellence Outstanding Sales Achievement 1980-81; Essence Sales Quarterly Awd for Outstanding Sales Achievement 1981; Essence President's Awd of Outstanding Performance of Ad 1981-84; Dollars and Sense Black Business & Professional Women Kizzy Awd 1987. **BUSINESS ADDRESS:** Midwest Adv Sales Dir, Essence Communications, 919 No Michigan Ave, Chicago, IL 60611.

BESHEARS, KELSY (KELSY BROWN COOPER)
Business executive. **PERSONAL:** Born Nov 01, 1898, Bluefield, WV; married Rufus Preston Beshears DDS (deceased); children: Jerry, Jean. **EDUCATION:** Howard Univ, BA 1937, attended 1944-45. **CAREER:** Bd Educ Bluefield WV, tchr 1916-18; Bur Census Wash DC, clk 1930-32; DC Bd Public Welfare, social wrkr 1932-37; Wash DC Pub Sch, cnslr 1937-46; Brookdale East Apts, owner/mgr. **ORGANIZATIONS:** Pres St Joseph Br NAACP 1948-76; MO Conf NAACP 1956-62; pres Ladies Aux Natl Dental Assn 1960-61; mem Natl Bd NAACP 1970-72; Commr St Joseph Zoning & Planning Commn 1976-81; bd mem MO Black Ldrsp Assn 1977; commr MO Housing Develop Commn 1977-81. **HONORS/ACHIEVEMENTS:** First black on jury Buchanan Co 1952; Natl Dental Aux Awd Human Rights 1963; Mayor's Awd 1964; first black commr St Joseph Housing Auth 1965-68; Ldrspin Housing NAACP 1970; Civic Achvmt Awd St Joseph C of C 1972; first black mem MO Com Humanities Inc 1972-; apptd by gov bd Law Enforcement Asst & Agency 1974-75; Meritorious Serv Yth Bros & Sisters United 1976; Continuous Serv Awd NAACP 1977. **BUSINESS ADDRESS:** Manager/Owner, Brookdale East Apts, 3414 Messame St, St Joseph, MO 64501.

BESSENT, HATTIE
Educator. **PERSONAL:** Born Dec 26, 1926, Jacksonville, FL. **EDUCATION:** FL A&M U, BS 1959; Nurs Educ IN U, MS 1962; Univ of FL, Intrnshp 1975, EdD 1970; Univ of FL Nurs Coll; Mtl Hlth Cnslt, Dipl 1971. **CAREER:** Vanderbuilt Univ School of Nursing, assoc dean grad affairs prof 1976-, prof psychist 1974-75; Univ of FL, psychol fnd teaching rsch 1971-76; Tulane Univ, consultant 1970-71; FL A&M Univ, asst prof psychist nurs 1962-67. **ORGANIZATIONS:** Am Educ Rsch Assn; Am Nurs' Assn; Am Pgtn Soc; Assn for Supvsn & Curr Devel; FL Nurs Assn; Nat Leag for Nurs; Delta Sigma Theta Sor; Alch Co Mtl Hlth Assn; Gnsvl Hum Relat Bd Sigma Theta Tau; Phi Lambda Theta; Phi Delta Kappa. **HONORS/ACHIEVEMENTS:** Career Tchrs Grant. **BUSINESS ADDRESS:** Deputy Executive Dir, American Nursing Assoc, 1030 15th St NW #716, Washington, DC 20005.

BESSON, PAUL SMITH
Attorney. **PERSONAL:** Born May 11, 1953, New York, NY; son of Frederick A. Besson and Patricia S. Besson. **EDUCATION:** Cornell Univ, BS Labor Relations 1975, MBA Marketing/Finance 1976; Northwestern Univ, JD 1980. **CAREER:** Cummins Engine Co, market planning analyst 1976-77; Jewel Companies, Inc, labor relations counsel 1980-82, mgr personnel/labor relations 1982-83; mgr labor relations, 1984-88, dir employee relations, 1988-, NBC Inc. **ORGANIZATIONS:** Mem Amer, IL, Chicago, Bar Assn; mem IL & NY Bars; bd of dir Cornell Club Assn 1982; pres Cornell Black Alumni Assn Chicago 1982-83; contributing writer Black Enterprise Magazine; Amer Arbitration Assn panel commercial arbitrations; hearing officer, Civil Serv Commn IL; bd of dir ABE Credit Union; pres, Cornell Black Alumni Assn, Washington, DC, 1989-. **BUSINESS ADDRESS:** Dir, Employee Relations, NBC Inc, 4001 Nebraska Ave, NW, Washington, DC 20024.

BEST, JENNINGS H.
Attorney. **PERSONAL:** Born Aug 05, 1925, Jacksonville, FL; married Elizabeth Blake; children: Valorie. **EDUCATION:** JD, 1956. **CAREER:** Knights of Pythias Jurisdic of FL, grand atty. **ORGANIZATIONS:** Mem DW Perkins Bar Assn; Natl Bar Assn; mem Phi Beta Sigma Frat. **MILITARY SERVICE:** AUS WW II 1944-46; Korean War 1950-52. **BUSINESS ADDRESS:** Grand Attorney, Knights of Pythias, 3410 N Myrtle Ave, Jacksonville, FL 32209.

BEST, JOHN T.
Urban planner, manager. **PERSONAL:** Born Jan 24, 1936, Philadelphia, PA; son of John Best and Mary Best; married Mary Ann Grady; children: J Toussaint, Johanna, Johnathan, Kevin, Deborah, Lydia Timmons. **EDUCATION:** Community Coll of Philadelphia, AGS 1972; Rutgers Univ, BA 1974; Univ of Pennsylvania, MCP 1976; attended Philadelphia Govt Training Inst 1972, Rutgers Univ 1980, Amer Mgmt Assn 1984, Franklin Inst 1984; Morris Arboretum, landscape design 1987. **CAREER:** Triangle Comm Develop Corp, chmn; Best Associates, urban-planner 1976-; City of Philadelphia, city planner II 1980-81; USPS, supervisor 1981-. **ORGANIZATIONS:** Mem Amer Planning Assoc 1976-, Society for the Advancement of Mgmt 1981-, Amer Mgmt Assoc 1981-; comm mem United Way 1981-; life mem Amer Legion; life mem 101st Airborn Assoc; life mem NAACP; mem Philaxis Soc; Lemuel Googins #129 Philadelphia. **HONORS/ACHIEVEMENTS:** Certificate of Awd USPA GPO Philadelphia PA 1972-75; Certificate of Appreciation, Motivation Counselor Philadelphia Prisons Philadelphia PA 1976; Certificate of Recognition, Basic Reading Tutor Ctr for Literacy Philadelphia 1978; Certificate of Appreciation Probation Counselor Camden Co NJ 1979; Certificate of Appreciation, United Way of Southeastern Pennsylvania. **MILITARY SERVICE:** AUS Airborne; Parachutists Badge, Natl Defense Medal 1954-57.

BEST, PRINCE ALBERT, JR.
Educational administration. **PERSONAL:** Born Feb 02, 1938, Goldsboro, NC; married Ernestine Flowers; children: Bryon, Selina, Gary. **EDUCATION:** A&T State Univ, BS Music 1959; East Carolina Univ, MA Ed 1971. **CAREER:** Johnston Cty Public School, band dir 1960-67; New Bern City Schools, band dir 1967-70; Goldsboro HS, counselor 1970-71; Johnston Tech Coll, counselor 1971-74; Wayne Comm Coll, admin 1974-, dean of human devel svcs. **ORGANIZATIONS:** Mem Alpha Phi Alpha 1957-, NAACP 1960-; bd of dir Alpha Arms Apts 1967-; bd mem Goldsboro Bd of Ed 1976-; mem Wayne Cty Pol Action Comm 1976-; bd of dir NC Employment & Training 1978-; chmn Goldsboro Bd of Ed 1984-. **HONORS/ACHIEVEMENTS:** Outstanding Citizen Awd Dillard HS Alumni Assoc 1984. **BUSINESS ADDRESS:** Dean of Human Devel Serv, Wayne Comm Coll, Caller Box 8002, Goldsboro, NC 27533-8002.

BEST, SHEILA DIANE
Physician. **PERSONAL:** Born Feb 23, 1956, Sacramento, CA; daughter of Eddie Best and Elizabeth Best. **EDUCATION:** Univ of CA Riverside, BA Biology 1978; Howard Univ Coll of Medicine, MD 1982. **CAREER:** Howard Univ Hosp, intern 1982-83, resident 1983-85; Independent Contractor, emergency medicine physician 1985-. **ORGANIZATIONS:** Mem Emergency Medicine Residents Assoc 1984-85, Amer Coll of Emergency Physicians 1985-, Action Alliance of Black Managers 1986-. **BUSINESS ADDRESS:** Emergency Medical Physician, 651 W Marion Rd, Mount Gilead, OH 43338.

BEST, WILLIAM ANDREW
Pastor. **PERSONAL:** Born Sep 17, 1949, Newburgh, NY; married Sharon Gerald; children: Cleveland, Andrew, Stephany, Shawn. **EDUCATION:** Mt St Mary Coll, BA 1975; Western Conn State Coll, attended 1981; Revelation Bible Inst, Certificate 1983. **CAREER:** Middletown Minority Ministerial Alliance, pres 1984-87; Church of God in Christ, regional pres 1986-; Inner Faith Council, vice pres 1986-87; YMCA, bd mem1987-; New York State Div for Youth, chaplain. **ORGANIZATIONS:** Mem Kiwanis 1986-87, NAACP; pres Middletown State Ctr 1985-86. **HONORS/ACHIEVEMENTS:** Certificate of Honor City of Middletown 1983; Citation State of NY Assembly 1985. **BUSINESS ADDRESS:** Chaplain, New York State Div for Youth, 137-139 Linden Ave, Middletown, NY 10940.

BEST, WILLIE ARMSTER
Accounting executive. **PERSONAL:** Born Dec 30, 1954, LaGrange, NC; married Joanne Loretta Jones. **EDUCATION:** NC Central Univ, BA 1973-77; Amer Univ, MPA 1979-81. **CAREER:** Roanoke Chowan Reg Housing Auth & Redevel Commiss, finance officer 1982-84; Natural Resources & Commun Devel, finance contracts & labor stds monitor. **ORGANIZATIONS:** Basileus Omega Psi Phi Frat Inc 1981-; sec Delta Lodge 436 Prince Hall 1981-; Roanoke-Chowan Consistory 276 1983-; mem Amer Soc for Public Admin 1984-85; Rosfelt Pasha Temple 175 1985-. **HONORS/ACHIEVEMENTS:** Serv Awd Prince Hall Mason

Delta Lodge 436 1982. **BUSINESS ADDRESS:** Monitor, Natural Resources & Comm Dev, Finance, Contracts & Labor Std, PO Box 27687, Raleigh, NC 27611.

BETHEA, EDWIN AYERS
Educational administrator. **PERSONAL:** Born May 15, 1931, Birmingham, AL; son of Mr & Mrs Monroe Bethea; divorced. **EDUCATION:** Knoxville Coll, BA 1953; Howard Univ, MSW 1962. **CAREER:** United Planning Orgn, comm organizer 1966-68; Youth Enterprises Inc, exec dir 1968-70; Volunteers for Intl Tech Ctr, dir/regional dir 1970-72; GA Tech Rsch Inst, sr rsch assoc/project dir 1972-. **ORGANIZATIONS:** Mem Southern Industrial Council 1974-, GA Industrial Developers Assoc 1974-; mem GA Tech Centennial Comm 1986. **HONORS/ACHIEVEMENTS:** Outstanding Contribution White House Conf of Small Business 1980; Certificate of Honor Mayor of Cleveland Contrib to Small Business 1984. **MILITARY SERVICE:** AUS pfc 1953-55; Korean Medal, Overseas Tour of Duty Medal. **HOME ADDRESS:** 50 Inwood Circle NE, Atlanta, GA 30309. **BUSINESS ADDRESS:** Director, University of Georgia, Office of Minority Business Development/SBDC, Chicopee Complex, Rm 2076, 1180 E Braod St, Athens, GA 30602.

BETHEA, GREGORY AUSTIN
Assistant city manager. **PERSONAL:** Born Sep 18, 1952, Hamlet, NC; son of Thomas Bethea and Annie Austin Bethea; married Hope Stelter Bethea, Aug 21, 1983; children: Ryan Stelter Bethea. **EDUCATION:** North Carolina Central Univ, Durham NC, BA, 1974. **CAREER:** Forsyth County, Forsyth County NC, asst to mgr, sr asst to mgr, intergovernmental relations & budget analysis, 1975-84; United Way, Forsyth County NC, deputy dir, 1984-85; City of Durham, Durham NC, asst city mgr, 1985-. **HONORS/ACHIEVEMENTS:** Edwin McGill Award, Univ of North Carolina Inst of Govt, 1980. **BUSINESS ADDRESS:** Asst City Mgr, City of Durham, 101 City Hall Plaza, Durham, NC 27701.

BETHEA, MOLLIE ANN
Financial administrator. **PERSONAL:** Born Oct 13, 1949, Mullins, SC. **EDUCATION:** NC A&T State Univ Greensboro, BS Bus Educ 1970; Francis Marion Coll, Florence, SC, MS Educ 1978. **CAREER:** So Packaging & Storage Co Mullins, SC, personnel officer, 1970-72; Francis Marion Coll, asst financial aid dir, 1972-78; Winthrop Coll, Rock Hill SC, financial aid dir 1978-. **ORGANIZATIONS:** Notary pub State of SC 1973-83; advisor to youth NAACP Francis Marion Coll 1977-78; advisor Delta Sigma Theta Sorority 1977-78; mem adv council Cumberland Day Care Prog 1977-78; sec SC Assn of Student Finan Aid Adminstr 1978-79; vice pres SC Student Finan Aid Admin 1979; faculty mem State Student Aid Training Prog 1979; presenter & organizer Financial Aid Workshops 1979; Judge Ability Counts Contest Mayor's Com of the Handicapped Rock Hill SC 1979-80; chairperson Prog Com of SC Assn of Student Financial Aid Admin 1979-80; mem So Assn of Student Financial Aid Administr; mem Medical Univ of SC/WinthropColl Satellite Nursing Prog. **HONORS/ACHIEVEMENTS:** Appreciation Award Delta Sigma Theta Sorority-Francis Marion College, Florence SC 1978. **BUSINESS ADDRESS:** Financial Aid Dir, Winthrop College, 638 Oakland Ave, Rock Hill, SC 29733.

BETHEL, JESSE MONCELL, SR.
Retired insurance agent, chemist. **PERSONAL:** Born Jul 08, 1922, New York, NY; son of Jesse M Bethel and Ethel Williams; married Claudia M Nichols, May 22, 1944; children: Marilyn Bethel-McAllister, Jesse M, Jr, Veronica Bethel-Johnson. **EDUCATION:** Huston-Tillotson Coll, Austin, TX, BS Chemistry 1944; UC Berkeley Graduate School. **CAREER:** Mare Island Naval Shipyard, analytical chemist 1944-61, nuclear chemist 1961-68, research chemist, 1968-73; State Farm Insurance, agent 1974-89. **ORGANIZATIONS:** Board of dir Vallejo Salvation Army; member NAACP; member Council of Navy League of US; member Vallejo Chamber of Commerce; member Friendship Baptist Church; board of directors Cal Coalition for Fair School Finance; past pres & board of directors Vallejo City Unified School Board 1969-85; past president Cal School Boards Assn 1976; member Alpha Phi Alpha Fraternity for 43 years; member Navy City Elks Lodge IBPOE of W. **HONORS/ACHIEVEMENTS:** Vallejo Citizen of the Year Omega Psi Phi Fraternity 1974; Man of the Year Western Region Alpha Phi Alpha 1976; Award Natl Caucas of Black School Board members 1977; Award NAACP Vallejo Branch 1982. **HOME ADDRESS:** 315 Pepper Drive, Vallejo, CA 94589.

BETHEL, LEONARD LESLIE
Educational administrator. **PERSONAL:** Born Feb 05, 1939, Philadelphia, PA; married Veronica Bynum; children: Amiel Wren, Kama Lynn. **EDUCATION:** Lincoln Univ, BA 1961; Johnson C Smith Univ Sch of Theology, MDiv 1964; New Brunswick Theological Sem, MA 1971; Rutgers Univ, DEd 1975. **CAREER:** Washington United Presbyterian Church, pastor 1964-67; Lincoln Univ, asst chaplain & dir counseling 1967-79; Bethel Presbyterian Church, pastor 1982-; Rutgers Univ Dept Africana Studies, faculty & staff 1969-80, chairperson & assoc prof 1980-. **ORGANIZATIONS:** Mem Bd of Trustees Rutgers Prep Sch 1971-84; fellow Rutgers Coll Rutgers Univ 1980-; mem Amer Assn Univ Profs Rutgers Univ 1980-; mem bd of dirsArmat Sch Graphic Arts 1980-; mem Frontiers Intl 1980-; mem Presbytery of Elizabeth 1982-. **HONORS/ACHIEVEMENTS:** Phi Delta Kappa Rutgers Univ 1975; Paul Robeson Faculty Awd Rutgers Univ 1978; NAFEO Pres Citation Lincoln Univ 1981; Woodrow Wilson Fellow Princeton Univ 1984. **HOME ADDRESS:** 146 Parkside Rd, Plainfield, NJ 07060. **BUSINESS ADDRESS:** Chrpsn Dept Africana Studies, RutgersUniv, Beck Hall 112 RutgersUniv, New Brunswick, NJ 08903.

BETTIS, ANNE KATHERINE
Market manager. **PERSONAL:** Born Jun 16, 1949, Newark, NJ. **EDUCATION:** Jersey City State Coll, BA 1972; Columbia Univ, MBA 1979. **CAREER:** Avon Products Inc, sr editor 1973-77; AT&T, acct exec 1979-82, natl acct mgr 1983-85, staff mgr 1985-. **ORGANIZATIONS:** Pres 8th Irving Park Condominium Assoc 1984-; mem Calvary Baptist Church, Natl Black MBA Assoc. **HONORS/ACHIEVEMENTS:** Achiever's Club AT&T 1982-84; Outstanding Young Women in Amer 1983,84; Who's Who of Amer Women 1986. **HOME ADDRESS:** 83 Boston St, Newark, NJ 07103.

BETTY, WARREN RANDALL
Physician. **PERSONAL:** Born Apr 21, 1931, Chicago, IL; children: Lisa C; Michael W. **EDUCATION:** Indiana Univ, AB 1954; Indiana Univ School of Medicine, MD 1959. **CAREER:** Richmond Co Prof Standard Review Organ, treasurer & bd of dir 1979-84; Health Ins Plan of Greater NY, mem bd of dir 1983-; Group Council Mutual Ins Co, mem bd of dir 1983-; Island Prof Review Organ, treasurer & bd of dir 1984-; Staten Island Med Group, medical dir. **ORGANIZATIONS:** Vice pres Richmond Cnty Med Soc 1983-84; asst clinical prof of pediatrics Albert Einstein Coll of Medicine NY 1965-; mem bd of dir Staten Island Urban League 1982-; mem Reg Advisory Council of The State Div of Human Rights. **HONORS/ACHIEVEMENTS:** Recipient Black Achiever Award Harlem Branch YMCA 1982. **MILITARY SERVICE:** USAF airman 2 c 1962-65. **BUSINESS ADDRESS:** Medical Dir, Staten Island Med Group, 4771 Hylan Blvd, Staten Island, NY 10312.

BEVEL, JAMES LUTHER
Clergyman, organization executive. **PERSONAL:** Born Oct 19, 1936, Ittabena, MS; married Diane Judith Nash; children: Sherrillyn Jill, Douglas John. **EDUCATION:** Amer Bapt Theol Sem, BA 1961. **CAREER:** Ordained to ministry Bapt Ch 1959; pastor in Dixon TN 1959-61; chmn Nashville Student Movement 1960-61; organizer Student Nonviolent Coord Comm 1961, field sec in MS 1961; organizer MS Free Press 1961; action prog of Albany Movement GA 1962; chief organizer dir Birmingham movement of So Christian Leadership Conf 1963, proj dir 1965; sponser Council Fed Orgns in MS 1962-64; dir AL movement in Selma March 1965; prog dir Westside Christian Parish Chicago. **HONORS/ACHIEVEMENTS:** Peace Awd War Resisters League 1963; Pesa Parks Awd So Christian Leadership Conf 1965; composer freedom songs Dod-Dog 1954; I Know We'll Meet Again 1969; Why Was A Darkly Born 1961. **MILITARY SERVICE:** USNR 1954-55. **BUSINESS ADDRESS:** SCLC, 334 Auburn Ave NE, Atlanta, GA 30303.

BEVERLY, BENJAMIN FRANKLIN
Manager. **PERSONAL:** Born Feb 27, 1938, Detroit, MI; children: Benjamin, Adrienne. **EDUCATION:** Univ of Detroit, BBA 1973. **CAREER:** Crocker Citizens Natl Bank San Francisco, customer serv rep 1962; Bank of the Commonwealth Detroit, asst vice pres 1966; Manufacturers Natl Bank Detroit,second vice pres 1972, sr staff anal 1973, asst dir urban affairs 1977-. **ORGANIZATIONS:** Former pres Urban Bankers Forum Detroit 1973; mem Natl Bus League 1973; former bd mem Black Family Devel Inc 1980; pres Livernois Seven Mile Local Develop Corp 1983; life mem NAACP 1982; mem Kappa alpha Psi Frat 1956. **HONORS/ACHIEVEMENTS:** AUS sgt spec 5 1959-62. **HOME ADDRESS:** 19424 Stratford, Detroit, MI 48221.

BEVERLY, CREIGS C.
Administrator/educator. **PERSONAL:** Born Sep 05, 1942, Selma, AL; children: Cheryl, Creigs Jr. **EDUCATION:** Morehouse Coll, BA 1963; Atlanta Univ, MSW 1965; Univ of WI, PhD 1972. **CAREER:** Atlanta Univ, assoc dean sw 1979-83; Univ of Ghana, acting coord 1984; Atlanta Univ, dean school of sw 1984-86, vice pres academic affairs 1986-87, sr prof social and behavioral science 1987-. **ORGANIZATIONS:** Special asst to the mayor Carnegie Foundation Fellow 1976-77; bd of dirs Council of Intl Programs 1985; mem Natl Assoc of Black Elected Officials, NASW,NABSW, CSWE, ACSW. **HONORS/ACHIEVEMENTS:** Achievement and Contribution Plaque City of Atlanta 1977; Fulbright Scholar West Africa 1983,84; Disting Alumni Citation Awd NAFEO 1986; Disting Youth Service Awd State of OK 1986; publication "The Black Underclass, Theory and Reality," 1986. **BUSINESS ADDRESS:** VP and Provost, Atlanta University, 223 James Brawley Dr SW, Atlanta, GA 30314.

BEVERLY, ROSE JACKSON
Educator. **PERSONAL:** Born Nov 13, 1938, Richmond, VA; divorced; children: Michelle. **EDUCATION:** Kings Co Hosp, RN 1959; Columbia Presb Hosp NYC, BSN 1970; Columbia Univ Tchr Coll NYC, MEd 1974. **CAREER:** Edwin Gould Found, clinical adminstr 1963-68; Downstate Med Centr, research asst 1968-70; Jewish Hosp, instr 1970-74; Long Island Univ, asst prof 1974-78; Martland Hosp, coord of Ambulatory Serv 1974-75; World Health Organ, short term consult 1976; Texas Christian Univ, asst prof 1978-. **ORGANIZATIONS:** Mem Am Pub Health Assn 1970-; mem Tarrant Co Black Hist & Geneal Soc 1978-; mem Recruitment Com TX Nurses Assn 1978-; com mem TX Health System Area 5, 1979; mem Am Nurse Assn 1980; mem Black Nurse Assn. **HONORS/ACHIEVEMENTS:** Leaflet pub. **BUSINESS ADDRESS:** Assistant Professor, John Peter Smith Hospital, Fort Worth, TX 76129.

BEVERLY, WILLIAM C., JR.
Attorney. **PERSONAL:** Born Jan 23, 1943, Los Angeles, CA; married Mona Birkelund. **EDUCATION:** Pepperdine Coll, BA 1965; SW Univ Sch Law, JD 1969. **CAREER:** Los Angeles Superior Court, judge; DPSS, soc wrkr & supvr 1965-70; Private Practice Law, attorney 1970-. **ORGANIZATIONS:** Mem CA & Long Beach Bar Assns; Langston Law Club; co-chmn Mil Law Panel 1971; instr Bus Law CA State Univ Long Beach; mem Langston Bar Assn; vice pres LA Co Commn on Human Relations. **BUSINESS ADDRESS:** Judge, Los Angeles Superior Court, 111 N Hill St, Los Angeles, CA 90012.

BEY, BEN
Artist, communicator. **PERSONAL:** Born Feb 19, 1938, Chicago, IL; children: Tiana A. **EDUCATION:** Cosmopolitan C of C Bus Sch, cert 1970; Chicago State Univ, BFA 1974. **CAREER:** YMCA Artist in Residence Prog, dir 1977-80; Silkscreen Training Prog at Special Serv Center, Goodwill Ind, City Coll of Chicago Adult Edn, Malcolm X Coll, dir 1983; The Ben Bey Experience Art Production Studio, owner 1968-. **ORGANIZATIONS:** Merchandise broker Goodwill Ind 1981-; real estate speculation 1980-; mem Operation PUSH 1969-; mem/volunteer Goodwill Ind 1980-; mem Natl Council of Artists 1970-. **HONORS/ACHIEVEMENTS:** Youth Positive Award Tranquility Comm Center 1978; Volunteer Award Goodwill Ind 1982; Community Award YMCA of Chicago 1980; Painting bought by State of NY Alban, NY 1976.

BIAGAS, EDWARD D.
Automobile dealership chief executive. **PERSONAL:** Born Oct 24, 1948, Lake Charles, LA; son of Alvin J Biagas and Veda Ovsot Biagas; married Lillie Belton Biagas, Aug 07, 1969; children: Edwin Jr, Shelley, Kevin. **CAREER:** Cities Service Oil, Lake Charles, LA, shift operator, 1972-75; Radford Buick, Lake Charles, LA, salesman, mgr,1975-81. **ORGANIZATIONS:** Bd mem, YMCA, 1986-, Chamber of Commerce, 1987-, Northern Ches County Nurses Assn, 1987-; chmn, PEP Comm, General Motors, 1988-; Minority Advisory Council, General Motors,1989-. **MILITARY SERVICE:** AUS E-5, 1969-71. **BUSINESS ADDRESS:** President, Biagas Pontiac-Buick, Inc, 639 W Bridge, Phoenixville, PA 19460.

BIASSEY, EARLE LAMBERT
Physician. **PERSONAL:** Born Jan 20, 1920, New Brunswick, NJ; son of Earl Henry Biassey and Lillian Craig; married Marie Davis; children: Sharon, Earle Jr, Eric, Sandra. **EDUCATION:** Upsala Coll, BS 1943; Howard Univ School of Medicine, MD 1947; Jersey City Medical Center, internship 1947-48, resident 1948-50; VA Hospital, 1950-51; Univ of MI Univ Hospital Ann Arbor, 1951-53; Horace Racham Graduate School, MS 1953. **CAREER:** Mental Hygiene Clinic, chief 1955-60; Woodfield Children's Home, psychiatric consultant 1957-62; Bridgeport Hospital, assoc attending 1959-67, sr attending chief psychiatric dept 1968-76; Weslyen Univ, psychiatric consultant 1970-; Whiting Forensic Inst, Middletown CT, psychiatric consultant 1976-; City Hospital, Bridgeport CT, sr attending physician; St Vincent Hospital, courtesy staff; Bridgeport Hospital 1957-87. **ORGANIZATIONS:** Mem Amer Psychiatric Assn 1950-, fellow 1969-; life fellow Amer Acad of Psychoanalysis 1966-; mem Soc of Medical Psychoanalysts; Fairfield Co Medical Soc; CT Medical Soc; Mental Hygiene Assn of Greater Bridgeport; mem Mental Health Council Com for Comm Mental Health Center; Stratford Rotary Club; Omega Psi Phi Fraternity; advisory bd Bridgeport Mental Health Center 1975; pres Fairfield Co Litchfield Chap CT Psychiatric Assn 1971; sec 1970-71, treasurer 1974-77 CT Psychiatric Assn; bd mem Bridgeport YMCA 1967-72; mem Com on Acad Educ Amer Psychiatric Assn 1971-74; Com on Social Issues Amer Acad of Psychoanalysis; Black Rock Congressional Church; chancellor Soc of Med Psychoanalysts 1969-74; chmn Professional Advisory Com Bridgeport Mental Health Assn; psychiatric consultant Bridgeport Educ System 1969-76; med adv bd Elmcrest Psychiatric Inst 1969-75; consultant Mental Health Serv & Afro-Amer Inst Wesleyan Univ 1971- ; Whiting Forensic Inst 1976-; mem Christian Med Soc 1971-; licensed NY, NJ, CT; life fellow Amer Psychiatric Assn 1984-. **HONORS/ACHIEVEMENTS:** Daniel Griffin Award, Bridgeport Mental Health Assn. **MILITARY SERVICE:** AUS capt 1953-55. **BUSINESS ADDRESS:** Psychiatric Consultant, Whiting Forensic Institute, 3200 Main St, Middletown, CT 06457.

BIBB, T. CLIFFORD
Educator. **PERSONAL:** Born Oct 29, 1938, Montgomery, AL; children: Tura Concetta. **EDUCATION:** AL State Univ, BS 1960, MEd 1961; Northwestern Univ, PhD 1973. **CAREER:** Rust Coll, chair English dept 1961-65; Daniel Payne Coll, chair English dept 1965-67; Miles Coll, English coord 1967-71; Northwestern Univ, English supr 1971-72; AL State Univ, chair advancement studies and dir four year plus curriculum prog. **ORGANIZATIONS:** Dir upward prog Northwestern Univ 1972-73; commiss, composition NCTE 1973-76; sec Peterson-Bibb Lodge 762 1974-; fac adv Alpha Phi Alpha 1981-; exec comm NCTE 1983-88; exec sec & bd mem Central Montgomery Optimists 1984-86; desoto commiss State of AL 1986-95. **HOME ADDRESS:** 5933 Provost Ave, Montgomery, AL 36116. **BUSINESS ADDRESS:** Chair Advancement Studies, Alabama StateUniv, PO Box 234, Montgomery, AL 36195.

BIBBS, JANICE DENISE
Management consultant. **PERSONAL:** Born Apr 23, 1958, Chicago, IL. **EDUCATION:** Purdue Univ, BS 1979. **CAREER:** Arthur Andersen & Co, manager 1979-. **ORGANIZATIONS:** Delta Sigma Theta; consultant Jr Achievement of Chicago 1985-87; special events adv bd Amer Cancer Soc 1985-87; bd mem Amer Foundation for the Blind Midwest Region 1986. **HONORS/ACHIEVEMENTS:** Outstanding Young Women of America 1982; Up & Coming Chicago Businesswoman Dollars and Sense Magazine 1985. **BUSINESS ADDRESS:** Manager, Arthur Andersen & Co, 33 West Monroe, Chicago, IL 60603.

BIBBY, DEIRDRE L.
Museum administrator. **PERSONAL:** Born Jun 09, 1951, Pittsburgh, PA. **EDUCATION:** MA Coll of Art, BFA 1974; City Coll of the City Univ of NY, MA candidate 1981-83. **CAREER:** ILEIFE Museum, dir/curator 1974-76; Afro-Amer Historical & Cultural Museumurator 1977-81; Mid-Atlantic Consortium, visual arts coordinator The Studio Museum n Harlem, assoc curator 1981-85; Schomburg Center for Rsch in Black Culture, arts coll mgr 1985-. **ORGANIZATIONS:** Mem African Am Museums Assn 1978-; co-chair Women's Caucus for Art 1985; mem Natl Conf of Artists 1978-. **BUSINESS ADDRESS:** Director-Curator, ILE-IFE Mus Afro-Am Culture, 2300 Germantown Ave, Philadelphia, PA 19133.

BIBBY, JAMES B.
Professional athlete. **PERSONAL:** Born Oct 29, 1944, Franklinton, NC; married Jacqueline Jordan; children: Tanya Norika, Tamara Nannette. **EDUCATION:** Fayetteville State Univ, attended 1962-64; Lynchburg Coll, BA 1977. **CAREER:** Raleigh-Durham Mets Carolina League, player 1968; Memphis TN TX League, player 1969; Tidewater, player 1969-70; St Louis Cardinals, player 1972; TX Christian Univ, publ relations 1974-; Cleveland Indians, player 1975-77; Pittsburgh Pirates, pitcher 1978-. **HONORS/ACHIEVEMENTS:** Rangers Pitcher of Yr 1973; One of 3 Pirates with a no-hitter credit 1973; Led Pirates in ERA with 280; Led NL in won & Lost percentage (750); played in World Series 1979; Played in NL Championship Games 1979. **MILITARY SERVICE:** AUS e-4 1966-67. **BUSINESS ADDRESS:** Pittsburgh Pirates, PO Box 1111, Arlington, TX 76004.

BIBLO, MARY
Librarian. **PERSONAL:** Born Dec 31, 1927, East Chicago, IN; daughter of James Davidson and Flora Chandler Davidson; married Herbert D Biblo, Aug 27, 1950; children: Lisa, David. **EDUCATION:** Roosevelt University, Chicago IL, BS, 1966; Rosary College, Chicago IL, MLS, 1970; Teachers College, Columbia University, 1984-85. **CAREER:** South Chicago Community Hospital School of Nursing, Chicago IL, medical librarian, 1966-67; Chicago Board of Education, Chicago IL, school librarian, 1967-70; University of Chicago Laboratory Schools, Chicago IL, head librarian, 1970—. **ORGANIZATIONS:** American Library Assn; past president, Children's Reading Round Table; Natl Caucus of Black Librarians; Natl Assn of Independent Schools; vice chair, minoriaty affairs committee, IL State Board of Education, 1988—; International Federation of Library Assns; American Assn of School Librarians; intellectural freedom round table, social responsibility round table, IL Library Assn; IL Assn for Media in Education. **HONORS/ACHIEVEMENTS:** Klingenstein fellow, Columbia University, 1984-85; master teacher, University of Chicago Laboratory School, 1985. **BUSINESS ADDRESS:** Head Librarian, University of Chicago Laboratory Schools, 1362 East 59th St, 101 High School, Chicago, IL 60637.

BICKERSTAFF, BERNIE LAVELLE
Professional athlete. **PERSONAL:** Born in Benham, KY; married Eugenia; children: Tim, Robin, Cydni, Bernard, John Blair. **EDUCATION:** Attended, Univ of San Diego. **CAREER:** Univ of San Diego, asst basketball coach; Wash Bullets, asst coach & scout 1974-; Sonics, head coach. **ORGANIZATIONS:** Charge of the team's summer devel program; serves as coach of Bullets Urban Coalition League Team; during summers runs a sucessful basketball camp in Baltimore, MD; coached Natil Puerto Rican team in the Aribbean Tour & won the Championship in 1976. **HONORS/ACHIEVEMENTS:** Turned down offer to play for the Harlem Globetrotters; youngest asst coach in the Natl Basketball assoc; assisted the team in making the playoffs 9 of 11 years; 3 conf Championships & one NBA title. **BUSINESS ADDRESS:** Head Coach, Seattle Supersonics, 190 Queen Anne Ave N, 2nd Floor, Seattle, WA 98109.

BICKHAM, L. B.
Educator. **PERSONAL:** Born Mar 02, 1923, New Orleans, LA; married Dorothy B; children: Luzine Jr, Nedra E. **EDUCATION:** Univ MI, BBA 1945, MBA 1947; Univ TX, PhD 1965. **CAREER:** Dillard Univ, instructor 1949; Watchtower Life Insurance Co, sec 1950; TX Southern Univ, instructor 1952; TX Southern Univ School of Business, dean 1969-. **ORGANIZATIONS:** Mem Amer Mktg Assn; bd dirs Std Savs & Loan Assn; TX So Fin; St Eliz Hosp Found. **MILITARY SERVICE:** AAC 1943-45. **BUSINESS ADDRESS:** Professor, TX Southern University, 3201 Cleburne St, Houston, TX 77021.

BIGBY-YOUNG, BETTY
Educational administrator. **PERSONAL:** Born Nov 08, New York, NY; daughter of Lucius Bigby and Dorothy Bigby; married Haskell I Young; children: Haskell I II (Chato), Jessica Melissa Bigby. **EDUCATION:** City Univ of NY Brooklyn Coll, BA 1970, MS 1972; Nova Univ, EdD, ABD. **CAREER:** Dept of State Foreign Serv Corps, admin asst foreign serv staff 1959-67; Office of the Mayor NYC, comm relations specialist 1968-71; CUNY Brooklyn Coll, dir model city TV training prog 1972-73; Model City Prog, comm relations specialist 1974-77; FL Intl Univ, dir univ relations & devel 1977-83; dir academic support prog 1983-. **ORGANIZATIONS:** Mem Natl Assn of Female Executives 1984-; Intl Platform Assn; Kappa Delta Pi Intl Honor Soc in Educ 1980-; founder/counselor Omicron Theta Chap KDP FIU 1981-; lifetime mem Alpha Epsilon Rho Radio TV Frat; Amer Assn of Univ Women; KDP Intl Honor Soc constitution/bylaws chairperson 1982-84; Amer Council on Educ; Southeast Dist Liaison for Minority Affairs PRSA; YWCA Women's Network; Mental Health Assn 1981-82; FL State Sickle Cell Found Inc 1978-83; White House Conf on Arts Testimony Congressional Hearing 1978; bd mem Art in Public Places Trust; pres Scott Lake Elem Sch PTA, Parkview Elem, Greynolds Park Elem; Congress of Black Scholars Dade Co 1982; radio talk show host WMBM Miami 1981-82; FIU Black Student Union Advisor founder 1978-; South FL Center for the Fine Arts; natl mem Smiths onian Assoc; mem Public Relations Soc of Amer, Council for Advancement and Support of Educ 1978-80; chief advisor Florida Black Student Assn Inc. **HONORS/ACHIEVEMENTS:** Community Service Award, Natl Congress of Parents and Teachers, 1989. **BUSINESS ADDRESS:** Undergraduate Studies, FL InternationalUniv, N Miami Campus, 151st St & Biscayne Blvd, North Miami, FL 33181.

BIGELOW, W. T.
Clergyman. **PERSONAL:** Born Mar 15, 1929, Yanceyville, NC; married Lillian; children: Ronnie, Patricia, Steve. **EDUCATION:** United Christian Coll, BT 1962, DDiv 1967, DE 1967. **CAREER:** First Bapt Ch New Hope Bapt, pastor; Grtr St Paul Bapt Ch, gospel singer 13 yrs, pastor. **ORGANIZATIONS:** Mem Drug Abuse Bd; past tchr Bible Training Inst; v moderator E Cedar Grove Assn NC; tour host Wholesale Tours Inc NY; bd mem Natl Bapt Conv Chicago;recdg artist "The Edge of Night"; mem Baptist Pastors Conference Columbus, OH; mem Lott Carey Baptist Foreign and Home Missionaries; mem Natl Baptist Evangelistic Assn; mem faculty Shaw Divinity School. **HONORS/ACHIEVEMENTS:** Plaque Mayor Durham 1973; Hob Record Co 1972; Dedicated Serv Radio Sta WSRC; fndr Interdenominational Ministers Conf; Cert Appreciation Columbus Bapt Pastor's Conf Columbus; Cert Fndr Interden Ministers Conf Durham; author "Evangelism-A Broad Open View," 1983. **BUSINESS ADDRESS:** Pastor, Greater St Paul Baptist Ch, 1102 Juniper St, Durham, NC 27701.

BIGGERS, SAMUEL LORING, JR.
Surgeon. **PERSONAL:** Born Nov 06, 1935, Crockett, TX; married Florestine A Robinson; children: Samuel L III, Shaun Denise, Sanford Leon. **EDUCATION:** Dillard U, AB (cum laude) 1956; Univ of TX Galveston, MD (cum laude) 1961. **CAREER:** Univ of TX Grad Sch, rsrch & teaching asst 1957-58; Orange Cnty GenHosp, intern 1961-62; USAF Med Corp, capt 1962-64; Univ of Southern CA Med, instructor clinical 1964-70; Los Angeles Cnty USC Med Cntr, asst prof clinical 1970-85; Charles R Drew Med Sch, assoc prof clinical 1974-85; Charles R Drew Medical Sch Martin Luther King Jr Hosp, vice chmn dept of neurological surgery; California Medical Ctr, vice pres medical staff; Samuel L Bigger & John J Holly Inc Neurological Surgery, pres. **ORGANIZATIONS:** Pres Samuel L Biggers, John J Holly MD Inc 1974-; Kappa Alpha Psi; Alpha Kappa Mu; Alpha Omega Alpha; Sigma Pi Phi; bd of trustees CA Medical Ctr. **HONORS/ACHIEVEMENTS:** Alumnus of the Year Dillard Univ 1985. **MILITARY SERVICE:** USAF capt 1962-64. **BUSINESS ADDRESS:** President, SL Biggers/JJ Holly Inc, 3756 Santa Rosalia Dr, Los Angeles, CA 90008.

BIGGS, CYNTHIA DEMARI
Songwriter. **PERSONAL:** Born Oct 02, 1953, St Pauls, NC. **EDUCATION:** Lincoln Univ Oxfrd PA, 1972; Temple Univ Phila, BA Commu 1975. **CAREER:** Philadelphia Intl Records, songwriter producer 1975-; Philadelphia Bd of Educ, substitute teacher 1975-77; The New Observer Newspaper, staff reporter 1974-78; Stlmnt Music Sch Madrigal Singers Philadelphia, vocalist 1969-71; Lincoln Univ Concert Choir, vocalist 1971-72; Ted Wortham Singers, composer vocalist 1972-. **ORGANIZATIONS:** Mem Sigma Delta Chi Nat Hon Soc 1970. **HONORS/ACHIEVEMENTS:** Amer Legion Awd for Girls, Amer Legion Soc Philadelphia Chap 1968; 1st Recip of the Art Peters Meml Scholarship for Journalism Philadelphia Inquirer Newspaper 1974; nominee Outstanding Young Woman of Amer, Outstanding Young Woman of Amer 1977-78. **BUSINESS ADDRESS:** Cindex Publishing, Inc, PO Box 18829, Philadelphia, PA 19119.

BIGGS, RICHARD LEE
Personnel administration. **PERSONAL:** Born Jan 16, 1949, Dyersburg, TN; married Linda D Warren. **EDUCATION:** TN State Univ, BS Biol 1971. **CAREER:** Questor Corp, mgmt coord 1974-81; Dyersburg Fabrics Inc, asst personnel dir 1981-; Dyer County, commissioner. **ORGANIZATIONS:** Mem Dyer Co Ed Comm 1978-86; clerk & trustee Tabernacle Baptist Church 1979-; advisor Dyersburg State Comm Coll Tech Dept 1980-84; chmn of bd Dyersburg Elect Syst 1980-; mem Dyer Co Budget Comm 1980-86; dir Private Ind Council 1983-86, West TN Investment Corp 1983-; dir C of C; pres elect Dyer County C of C 1988-89.

HONORS/ACHIEVEMENTS: Eligible Bachelor Ebony Mag 1980. **HOME ADDRESS:** 904 Central, Dyersburg, TN 38024.

BIGGS, SHIRLEY ANN
Educator. **PERSONAL:** Born Mar 09, 1938, Richmond, VA; married Charles F Biggs; children: Charles F Jr, Cheryl A. **EDUCATION:** Duquesne U, BEd 1960; Univ of SC, MEd 1972; Univ of Pittsburgh, EdD 1977. **CAREER:** Pittsburgh Public School, teacher, 1961-68; Benedict Coll, instructor, 1968-72, reading specialist consultant, 1972-; Univ of Pittsburgh, faculty in school of educ, 1974-, asso prof, asst dean for student affairs 1986-. **ORGANIZATIONS:** Coord Summer Communications Skills Project 1963-66; pres Gerald A Yoakam Reading Cncl 1978-79; chmn research div Pittsburgh Literacy Coalition 1984-; memIntl Reading Assoc 1973-; mem Nat Reading Conference. **HONORS/ACHIEVEMENTS:** Co-author Reading to Achieve, Strategies for Adult Coll 1983; co-author Students Self Questioning and Summarizing 1984; honored for literacy research activities by the Pittsburgh City Council 1986. **HOME ADDRESS:** 1126 N Euclid Ave, Pittsburgh, PA 15206. **BUSINESS ADDRESS:** Assoc Prof/Asst Dean, School of Education, Univ of Pittsburgh, 4h25 Forbes Quandrangle, Pittsburgh, PA 15260.

BIGGS, VERLON
Professional athlete. **PERSONAL:** Born Mar 16, 1943, Moss Point, MS; children: 2. **EDUCATION:** Jackson State Coll, BS 1965. **CAREER:** Little League Baseball, commr & organizer 1967-68; Census NY, mgr 1970; Dept Commerce, coord 1975; Washington Redskins, defensive end. **ORGANIZATIONS:** Mem Humane Soc; Prevention & Protection of Wildlife. **HONORS/ACHIEVEMENTS:** All Star Game 1967-69; SW Conf All Star Team 1965; NAIA & Pittsburgh Courier All-Amer Teams 1965; Black Rookie of the Yr Pittsburgh Courier 1966; Outstanding Defensive Player AFC All-Star Game 1966; MVP All Star Game 1969; Heede Awd Jet Teammates 1970.

BILAL, MELVIN ASIM
Business executive. **PERSONAL:** Born Sep 10, 1942, White Plains, NY; married Pamela Ann Brewer; children: Akobi, Nneka. **EDUCATION:** Univ of IL, BA 1965; attended NY Univ 1965; attended Univ of IL-Law 1970; Univ of PA Law Sch Grad Sch, JD 1972. **CAREER:** Dist Attorney's Office Phila, legal intern summer 1971; Catonsville Comm Coll, asst prof 1972; Howard Rsch & Devel, dir of security 1973; Security Amera Serv Inc, pres. **ORGANIZATIONS:** Bd of dirs MD Chamber of Commerce; mem Young President's Organ; mem Alpha Phi Alpha Frat; chmn Found & Devel Coppin State Coll. **HONORS/ACHIEVEMENTS:** All Amer Track Natl Collegiate Athletic Assn 1964; Man of the Yr Baltimore Marketing Assn Inc 1979; All Army Track Team. **MILITARY SERVICE:** AUS 1st lt 3 yrs served. **BUSINESS ADDRESS:** President, Security America Services Inc, 117 Water St, Baltimore, MD 21202.

BILLINGS, CHRISTINE D.
Educator. **PERSONAL:** Born May 01, Laurinburg, NC; married Donald Brooks. **EDUCATION:** Tchrs Coll Columbia Univ, Masters 1971; FL State Univ, PhD 1976. **CAREER:** FL A&M Univ, asst prof & chairperson bus educ 1974-76; Fayetteville State Univ, assoc prof & chairperson bus educ 1976-77, special consul 1978; State of FL Dept of Educ, educational; consultant II 1978-79; FL Dept of Labor & Employment Security, asst dir of administrative serv 1979-80, chief of workers' compensation rehab 1980-86; Office of Policy & Planning DC Government, deputy dir 1986-. **ORGANIZATIONS:** Mem Natl Rehab Assn; mem Intl Assn of Personnel in Employment Security; mem Adult Educ Assn of USA; mem Natl Bus Educ Assn; mem Southern Bus Educ Assn; mem Intl Soc of Bus Educators; mem Amer Vocational Assn; mem FL Adult Educ Assn; mem Natl Rehab Adminstrn Assn; mem FL Assn for Health & Social Svcs; natl bd mem Natl Assn of Black Adult Educators; state bd mem FL State Assn of Rehab Nurses; mem Phi Gamma Mu, Delta Pi Epsilon, PiOmega Bi; mem EEO Comm City of Tallahassee; mem NAACP; mem Zonta Intl, FL Women's Network; mem AKA Women's Sor; mem Tallahassee Urban League; mem Southern Christian Leadership Conf; mem League of Women Voters; exec dir & fndr Intl League of Black Voters Tallahassee FL 1981. **HONORS/ACHIEVEMENTS:** Kenyan Govt Serv Awd 1977; The Amer Educ Registry 1979; The Amer Govtl Registry 1979; NAACP Annual Serv Awd at the FL State Meeting 1978. **HOME ADDRESS:** 1820 Kalorama Road NW #3, Washington, DC 20009. **BUSINESS ADDRESS:** Deputy Dir, Office of Policy & Planning, DC Government, 801 N Capitol St, Washington, DC 20002.

BILLINGSLEA, EDGAR D.
Educator. **PERSONAL:** Born Jun 16, 1910, Canton, GA; married Anne Miller; children: Anne Beletta. **EDUCATION:** Tuskegee Inst, BS 1938; Atlanta Univ, MA 1953; West GA Coll Univ GA, grad study. **CAREER:** Various high schools in GA, principal since 1938; Project Headstart, dir 1964-69; Adult Night School, instructor 1973-74; Polk Sch Dist, coord E Polk County Vocational Educ Program 1970-75. **ORGANIZATIONS:** Mem PAE, GAE, NEA, Guid Div of GVA, AVA; pres GIA Dist 1 1963; chmn bd dir Tallatoona Econ Oppor Auth Inc 1972; pres Amer Cancer Soc E Polk Co1969-75; mem Natl All Black Educ 1973-75; sec Sarah D Murphy Home Inc 1970-74; deacon Friendship Bapt Ch 1974 (mem sr usher bd, mem hospitality Com, sunday sch tchr); apptd to gov's staff by Hon Jimmy Carter 1971. **HONORS/ACHIEVEMENTS:** Hon LLD 1974. **BUSINESS ADDRESS:** Coordinator Voc Educ Prog, Polk School District, 60 Hill St, Rockmart, GA 30153.

BILLINGSLEA, MONROE L.
Dentist, author. **PERSONAL:** Born Aug 03, 1933, West Palm Beach, FL; divorced; children: Brent, Christa. **EDUCATION:** Howard Univ Sch of Dentistry, grad 1963. **CAREER:** Coney Island Hosp Brooklyn, intern oral surgery 1963-64; Minot AFB ND, chief oral surgery 1964-65; Self-employed, dentist LA 1965-. **ORGANIZATIONS:** Mem NAACP, SCLC, Kendrin Mental Health. **HONORS/ACHIEVEMENTS:** Educational Achievement Awd USAF 1954; author "Smoking & How to Stop", "Better Health Through Preventive Dentistry & Nutrition". **MILITARY SERVICE:** USAF capt 1965-67. **BUSINESS ADDRESS:** 8500 S Figueroa #3, Los Angeles, CA 90003.

BILLINGSLEY, ANDREW
University executive. **PERSONAL:** Born Mar 20, 1926, Marion, AL; married Amy; children: Angela, Bonita. **EDUCATION:** Brandeis U, PhD Soc Wlfr 1964; Univ of MI, MS Soc 1960; Boston U, MS Soc Work 1956; Grinnell Coll, AB Polit Sci 1951. **CAREER:** Res Asst MA Soc for the Prevention of Cruelty to Children, soc worker 1960-63; Univ of CA, asst dean of students 1964-65, assoc prof soc welfare 1964-68, asst chancellor acad affairs 1968-70, vice pres 1970-75; Metro Applied Rsch Ctr Natl Urban League NYC, fellow 1968; Morgan State Univ, pres 1975-84; Univ of MD, prof of Afro-Amer studies 1985-87, prof, chmn dept family & community devel. **ORGANIZATIONS:** Ed bd Jrnl of Afro-Amer Studies 1969-; ed bd Black Scholar 1970-75; bd mem Govs Joint Ctr for Political Studies DC 1972-75; mem Caucus of Blk Soc ASA; Nat Assn of Blk Soc Wrkrs; chmn Fam Section ASA 1972-73; chmn Comm on Mgmt Howard Univ Press 1972-74; chmn adv bd for Jour of Abstracts; chmn Nat Assn of Soc Wrkrs 1973; mem Assoc of Black Sociologists, Natl Council on Family Relation, Groves Conf on Marriage and the Family, Natl Cncl on Family Relations. **HONORS/ACHIEVEMENTS:** 1st Bienneal Rsch Awd Natl Assn of Soc Workers 1964; Soc Sci Fellowship Metro Applied Rsch Ctr New York City 1968; The Michael Schwerner Meml Awd New York City 1969; Grinnell Coll Hon Doc of Humane Letters 1971; Afro-Amer Families & Comm Serv 1st Natl Leadership Awd 1972; Howard Univ Sci Inst Appreciation Awd 1974; recip Natl Council of Black Child Devel Appreciation Awd 1974; Hon DHL Mercy Coll 1982; author "Black Families in White America" 1968; co-author "Children of the Storm Black Children & Amer Child Welfare" 1972; author "Black Families and the Struggle for Survival" Friendship Press 1974. **MILITARY SERVICE:** AUS Quartermaster Corps personnel sgt 1944-46. **BUSINESS ADDRESS:** Professor/Chairman, University of Maryland, Dept of Family/Comm Development, Rm 1204 Marie Mount Hall, College Park, MD 20742.

BILLINGSLEY, ORZELL, JR.
Judge. **PERSONAL:** Born Oct 23, 1924, Birmingham, AL; married Geselda. **EDUCATION:** Tldg Coll, BA, 1946; Howard Univ, LLB, 1950. **CAREER:** Recorder's Ct, jdg; Roosevelt City AL, frmr mncpl jdg; pvt prac, atty; gen counsel, AL cities, co-orgn; Roosevelt City, fndr, 1967; civil rights Atty, 1968. **ORGANIZATIONS:** Orgn Afro Cntrctrs Assn of AL; consult corps Crdt Unions Coop; mem dem exec com of Jfrsn Co; bd dir AL St Conf of NAACP; bd dir Jfrsn Co Com for Econ Opp. **BUSINESS ADDRESS:** Maonic Temple Building, 1630 Fourth Ave, Birmingham, AL 35203.

BILLINGTON, CLYDE, JR.
State official. **PERSONAL:** Born Aug 29, 1934, Hartford, CT; married Malora W; children: Mark, Christal, Courtney. **EDUCATION:** Lincoln Univ, BA; Attended, Connecticut Univ, Maryland Univ. **CAREER:** Pratt & Whitney Aircraft, chem engr 1961-65; State of CT, rep; Clyde Billington Real Estate & Liquor Merchants Inc CT, owner/operator 1965-. **ORGANIZATIONS:** Area broker for US Dept HUD; mem Hartford Bd Realtors 1967-74; pres N Hartford Prop Owners Assn; pres Oakland Civic Assn; bd dir Businessmen's Assn; bd dir Pioneer Budget Corp; mem Amer Chem Soc; mem NAACP; mem Urban League; dir Gr Hartford Conv & Vis Bur; treas Dem Town Com; mem of othercivic & professional organizations. **HONORS/ACHIEVEMENTS:** Voted 1 of 1,000 Most Successful Black Businessmen Ebony Mag. **MILITARY SERVICE:** AUS SPP 1959-61. **BUSINESS ADDRESS:** Clyde Billington Real Estate, 919 Albany Ave, Hartford, CT 06112.

BILLOPS, CAMILLE J.
Artist, educator. **PERSONAL:** Born Aug 12, 1933, Los Angeles, CA; married James Hatch. **EDUCATION:** LA City Coll, AA 1955; LA State Coll, BA 1960; City Coll, MFA 1973. **CAREER:** NY Times, Amsterdam News, Newsweek, art articles; numerous exhibits US & abroad; Hatch-Billops Coll, co-founder; The Afro-Amer Bellwether Press NY, editor 1975-76; Rutgers Univ, City Coll City Univ NY, artist, art educator, lecturer. **ORGANIZATIONS:** Mem Natl Conf Artists 1972-; Natl Conf Art Teachers; NY State Council Arts 1973. **HONORS/ACHIEVEMENTS:** Huntington Hartford Found Grant 1963; MacDowell Fellowship 1975; author "The Harlem Book of the Dead" with James Van der Zee & Owen Dodson.

BILLS, JOHNNY BERNARD
Physician. **PERSONAL:** Born Oct 03, 1949, Hickory Valley, TN; married Hilda M; children: Jacqueline; Melissa; Johnny III. **EDUCATION:** Ashland High School Ashland, MS, Diploma 1967; Memphis State Univ, adv chemistry courses 1970; Rust College Holly Springs, MS, BS chem math 1971; Univ of Miss Medical Sch Jacksonm MS, MD 1977. **CAREER:** Ashland High School, mathematic teacher 1971-72; Rust College, lab technician 1972-73; University Hospital, intern 1977-78; Jefferson County Hospital, staff physician 1978-79; Madison, Yazoo, Leake Family Health Center, consultant physician 1979-80; Hospital Emergency Room, physician (several hospitals) 1977-; Bills Medical Clinic, medical dir 1980-. **ORGANIZATIONS:** Phi Beta Sigma Fraternity, member 1968-; American Medical Association, member 1977-; Jackson Medical Society, member 1977-; Mississippi Medical and Surgical Assoc,(secretary 1983-85) 1977-; Southern Medical Assoc, member 1980-; Methodist Hospital, Lexington, MS, chairman of infection control 1981-; Chamber of Commerse, member 1983-; mem NAACP, Jackson YMCA, New Hope Baptist Ch, Jackson Rust Coll Club, Baptist Haiti mission, World Concern. **HONORS/ACHIEVEMENTS:** Rust College, academic achievement award, science student of year 1971; Alpha Beta Mu Honor Society 1967-71; Friend of Children Citation-World Concern, United League of Holmes C Citation, member 1983. **HOME ADDRESS:** 140 Fairfield Dr, Jackson, MS 39206. **BUSINESS ADDRESS:** Medical Dir, Bills Medical Clinic, 115 China St PO Drawer 119, Lexington, MS 39095.

BILLUPS, FLORENCE W.
Educator. **PERSONAL:** Born Jan 16, 1921, St Louis; married Kenneth; children: Kathleen, Karla, Karyl, Ken Jr. **EDUCATION:** Stowe Tchrs Coll, BA 1941; Northwestern Univ, MA 1945. **CAREER:** Teacher, 1941-. **ORGANIZATIONS:** Mem MO State Tchrs Assn; past pres Assn Childhood Educ Intl Reading Assn; mem YWCA, NAACP, Urban League, Iota Phi Lambda Sor; past pres St Louis Music Assn; Top Ladies Distinction. **HONORS/ACHIEVEMENTS:** Woman Achievement St Louis Globe Dem 1974; Woman Yr Iota Phi Lambda St Louis Chap 1973; Woman Yr Regional 1974. **BUSINESS ADDRESS:** Teacher, Hamilton Br 3 Sch, 450 Des Peres, St Louis, MO 63131.

BILLUPS, MATTIE LOU
Elected official. **PERSONAL:** Born Mar 05, 1935, Bixby, OK; married Vernon S Billups Sr; children: Jacci Love, Jocelyn Palmer, Vernon Jr, Ricci Evans, Reginald Evans, Cheryl Lee, Robyn Evans, Murphy, Debi Cayasso, Beverly, Lesa Singleton. **EDUCATION:** BTW High School, 1954. **CAREER:** Branding Iron Saddle Club, treas 1972-85; Wagoner Cty Democratic Women, vice pres 1983-85. **ORGANIZATIONS:** Mem Church of Christ 1967-; treas Red Bird Park Fund 1977-80. **HONORS/ACHIEVEMENTS:** Most Outstanding Mayor for Black Mayors OK Conf of Black Mayor 1984. **HOME ADDRESS:** 679 S Market, Red

Bird, OK 74458. **BUSINESS ADDRESS:** Mayor, Town of Red Bird, PO Box 222, Red Bird, OK 74458.

BILLUPS, MYLES E., SR.
Union official. **PERSONAL:** Born Sep 25, 1926, Norfolk, VA; married Dorothy Vaughan; children: Darlene, Michael, Carolyn, Jean, Myles, Jr, Dorothy, Alma C. **CAREER:** ILA Lgl 1248, rec sec 1955; Pt of Hmptn Rds, de dist cncl 1961, vice pres dist cncl tst mrtm assn ILA wlfr pnsn fund sfty dir orgn 1967, pres lcl 1970-, pres dist cncl 1967-; Intl Lngshrmn's Assn AFL-CIO, intl vice pres 1975. **ORGANIZATIONS:** Vp mem bd VA Pt Athrty 1971-74; orgn bd dirs Atlntc Nat Bank; Prince Hall Mason; chmn bd dcns Bethl Bapt Ch; bd dirs Hlth Wlfr & Plng Cncl; Chld & Fmly Svcs; adv bd Estrn VA Med Sch; vice pres Tdwtr Chap Cystic Fbrss Soc; bd dirs Bnt Coll.

BINFORD, HENRY C.
Educator. **PERSONAL:** Born May 02, 1944, Berea, OH; son of Henry E Binford and Dorothy J Binford. **EDUCATION:** Harvard Univ, AB 1966, PhD 1973; Univ of Sussex England, MA 1967. **CAREER:** Northwestern Univ, asst prof 1973-79, assoc prof 1979-. **ORGANIZATIONS:** Dir Business and Professional People for the Public Interest 1985-; mem Sigma Pi Phi 1985-. **BUSINESS ADDRESS:** Assoc Prof of History, Northwestern University, History Dept, Evanston, IL 60201.

BING, DAVE
Retired professional basketball player. **PERSONAL:** Born Nov 29, 1943, Washington, DC; married Aaris; children: Cassaundra, Bridgett, Aleisha. **EDUCATION:** Syracuse Univ, grad 1966. **CAREER:** Detroit Pistons, player 1966-74; Washington Bullets, player 1975-77; Boston Celtics, player 1978; Bing Steel Inc, owner. **HONORS/ACHIEVEMENTS:** Named to first team NBA All Star 1967-68 1970-71; Rookie of the Yr 1967; All Amer Career at Syracuse Univ; leading scorer in Syracuse Univ History; All Star 6 times. **BUSINESS ADDRESS:** President, Bing Steel Inc, 1130 W Grand Blvd, Detroit, MI 48208.

BING, RUBELL M.
Librarian. **PERSONAL:** Born Jan 06, 1938, Rocky Mount, NC; daughter of Lonnie Moody and Alberta Green Moody; married Alex Bing Sr; children: Bonita, Tovoia, Yvonne, Alex J. **CAREER:** Girl Scout Council of the Nation's Capital, girl scout leader 1976-78; St Francis DeSales School, librarian; Adv Neighborhood Commn, recording sec 1980-82,correspondence sec 1982-. **ORGANIZATIONS:** Reading & library chmn Washington DC Parent-Teacher Assoc 1981-82; chairperson of publication PTA; suprv summer youth program Brentwood Sect 1981; leader Girl Scout Council Nations Capitol 1976-78; work with Washington DC Bd of Election & Ethics; St Anthony's After School Program; Dixie Leader 1970; St Anthony's Gospel Choir 1984-88; St Anthony's Sodality. **HONORS/ACHIEVEMENTS:** Girl Scout Council Award 1974; William R Spaulding Award Council of Washington DC 1981; Washington DC PTA Lifetime Membership 1975; ANC-5B Commissioners' Plaque for Outstanding Community Serv 1985-86; Dictionary of Intl Biography. **HOME ADDRESS:** 1228 Brentwood Rd NE, Washington, DC 20018. **BUSINESS ADDRESS:** Correspondence Secretary, Adv Neighborhood Commission, 2019 Rhode Island Ave NE, Washington, DC 20018.

BINGHAM, ARTHUR E.
Retired educator. **PERSONAL:** Born Jul 29, 1906, Fayette, MS; son of Max Bingham and Eva Bingham; married Olean; children: Natalie, Arthur, Max, Dorothy Hoye; Mardean Boykins. **EDUCATION:** Alcom A&M Coll, BSA, 1931. **CAREER:** Univ Life Ins, district auditor, 1932; high school principal, 20 yrs; vocational teacher, 10 yrs; County of Jefferson, notary public, 1980-84; Alcorn State Univ, dir of housing, 13 yrs; Jefferson County Bd of Education, mem, 1979-present; pres, District 77, State Teacher's Assn, 1953-55. **ORGANIZATIONS:** Alcom Coll basketball, 1927-31, baseball, 1928-31; secretary, Mason Mt Valley Lodge, 1933. **HONORS/ACHIEVEMENTS:** 4 Letter A's, Alcom Athletic Dept, 1927-31. **HOME ADDRESS:** PO Box 514, Fayette, MS 39069.

BINGHAM, DONNA GUYDON
Human resource manager. **PERSONAL:** Born Apr 04, 1961, Stuttgart, AR; married Porter B Bingham. **EDUCATION:** Clark Coll, BA Acctg (Magna Cum Laude) 1983; Atlanta Univ Grad Sch of Business, MBA (w/Highest Honors) 1985. **CAREER:** Equitable Life Assurance Soc of the United States, summer intern 1981; Marathon Oil Co, accountant 1982; YWCA of Greater Atlanta, asst accountant 1982-84; Atlanta Univ Grad Sch of Business, grad rsch asst 1984-85; Georgia Pacific Corp, grad intern personnel rep 1984-85; Jet Propulsion Lab, personnel rep 1985-. **ORGANIZATIONS:** Mem Delta Sigma Theta, Beta Gama Sigma Natl Honor Soc, Intl Assoc of Personnel Women, Assoc of MBA Execs; vice pres Soc for the Advancement of Management 1984-85; chairperson of membership Los Angeles Chap Natl Black MBA 1986; mem Amer Compensation Assoc, Amer Soc of Personnel Administrators. **HONORS/ACHIEVEMENTS:** Alpha Kappa Mu Natl Honor Soc Clark Coll 1982-83; Beta Gama Sigma Natl Honor Soc Atlanta Univ 1984-. **HOME ADDRESS:** 938 E Huntington Dr Unit M, Duarte, CA 91010.

BINGHAM, REBECCA JOSEPHINE (NEE TAYLOR)
Educator, librarian. **PERSONAL:** Born Jul 14, 1928, Indianapolis, IN; married Walter D Bingham; children: Gail Elaine Simmons, Louis Edward Simmons. **EDUCATION:** IN Univ, BS 1950; Univ Tulsa, MA 1961; IN Univ, MLS 1969. **CAREER:** Alcorn A&M Coll, asst librarian, 1950-51; Tuskegee Inst, serials librarian, 1952-55; Jarvis Christian Coll, acting librarian, 1955-57; Indianapolis Public Library, librarian school serv dept, 1957; Tulsa Jr High School, librarian, 1960-62; Russell Jr High School, English teacher 1962-63; Jackson Jr High School, librarian, 1963-66; Louisville Public Schools, supvr library serv ,1966-70, dir of media serv 1970-75; KY Public Schools, dir media serv Jefferson County 1975-. **ORGANIZATIONS:** Mem Alumni Bd Grad Library Sch; chmn Amer Assn of Sch Librns; Amer Sch Counselors Assn; Joint Media Com; mem KY Govs State Adv Coun on Libraries 1971-73; mem AA5L Natl Libry Week Com; Coun of Amer Libry Assn 1972-; ALA Com on Planning 1973-; vice pres pres-elect Alumni Assn of Grad Libry Sch 1973-74; KY Libry Assn Legislative Com 1973-74; sec treas So E Regional Libry Assn Resources & Tech Serv Div 1973-75; exec bd Amer Libry Assn 1974-78; pres Alumni Bd Grad Libry Sch 1974-75; chmn Amer Assn of Sch Librns/Ency Britannica Sch Libry Media Prog of Yr Awds; selec com exec bd KY Assn for Sprvn & Curriculum Develop 1976-77; KY Sch Supt Adv Counc for Suprvn 1977-; adv com for Bro-Dart Elem Sch Lib Collection 1975-77, Britannica Jr 1975-76, World Book 1977-79, White House Conf on Libraries & Information Serv 1978-79; pres Amer Assoc of School Librarians 1979-80; Louisville Jefferson Co Health & Welfare Cncl Bd Dirs; pres Southeastern Library Assoc 1984-86, Jefferson Co School of Administrators 1985-86. **HONORS/ACHIEVEMENTS:** Tangley Oaks Fellowship 1967; Beta Phi Lib Sci Hon; Outstanding Sch Librn KY Libry Trustees 1969; published article KY 1974 edition Amer Educator Ency;contrib 1974 edition Comptons Ency critical reviewer; Louise Maxwell Awd Outstanding Achievement field of Lib Sci Gra Lib Sch IN Univ; YWCA Woman of the Year Louisville 1978. **BUSINESS ADDRESS:** Dir Media Services, Jefferson County Public School, Darret Education Center, 4409 Preston Highway, Louisville, KY 40211.

BINNS, SILAS ODELL
Physician. **PERSONAL:** Born Nov 18, 1920, Newport News, VA; married Marion Edwina Calloway; children: D'Jaris, Claudette, Silas Jr, Darlene, Vincent. **EDUCATION:** VA Union Univ, BS 1942; Howard Univ, MD 1945; Homer G Phillips Hosp, intern 1945-46, asst res 1946-47, asst res urol 1947-48, res urol 1948-49. **CAREER:** Homer G Phillips Hosp, 1949-50; Hampton Genl Hosp, Whittaker Meml Hosp, urologist; Norfolk Richmond Comm Hosps, urological cons; JW Binns Corp, pres; Self-employed, urologist. **ORGANIZATIONS:** Mem Natl Medical Assn 1950; Peninsula Med Soc 1950-; Old Dominion Med Soc 1950-; NY Acad of Sci 1956-; Tidewater Urol Assn 1964-; Hampton Med Soc 1969-; VA Med Assn 1969-; Amer Urol Assn 1970-; AMA 1970-; Alpha Phi Alpha Frat; NAACP. **HONORS/ACHIEVEMENTS:** First black urologist VA 1950; listed Who's Important in Med 1952 1961; appt Med Malpractice Rev Panel Supreme Ct of VA 1976. **MILITARY SERVICE:** AUS 1943-45. **BUSINESS ADDRESS:** Urologist, 2901 Chestnut Ave, Newport News, VA 23607.

BINS, MILTON
Educational administrator. **PERSONAL:** Born Dec 11, 1934, Hazlehurst, MS; married Adrienne O King; children: Gregory Milton, Randall S Jackson. **EDUCATION:** Univ of IL, BS 1953-56; IL Inst of Tech, 1957-59; Univ of IL, BS 1960; Chicago State U, MS 1966; Univ of PA, MS 1972. **CAREER:** Cncl of The Great City Sch, senior asso 1974-81; White House Initiative on Historically Black Coll andUniv US Dept of Edn, exec dir & dir of the office of policy devel for postsecondary educ 1981-82; Cncl of The Great City Sch, senior asso 1982-. **ORGANIZATIONS:** Corporate dir John F Small Advertising Agency 1973-74; natl consultant & salesmn Harcourt Brace Jovanovich 1966-69; high sch math tchr Hyde Park High SchChicago Bd of Educ 1960-66; mem Alpha Phi Alpha Frat 1973-; communctns dir Cncl of 100 Black Republicans 1974-; chmn Council of 100 1986-. **HONORS/ACHIEVEMENTS:** Apptd by Sec of Commerce Malcolm Baldrige to serve a three term on the 1990 Census Adv Comm. **HOME ADDRESS:** 381 "N" St SW, Washington, DC 20024. **BUSINESS ADDRESS:** Senior Associate, Cncl of The Great City Sch, 1413 K St NW, Washington, DC 20005.

BIRCHETTE, WILLIAM ASHBY, III
Educational administrator. **PERSONAL:** Born May 09, 1942, Newport News, VA; son of William Ashby Birchette Jr and Sarah Birchette; children: William Ashby IV; Stacy Olivia. **EDUCATION:** St Augustine's College, BA 1964; VA State Univ, MEd 1973; Univ of VA, EdD 1982. **CAREER:** Wilson City Public Schools; Delaware Commun Coll; Banneker Jr HS, principal; DC Public Schools, asst to reg supt reg C; Magruder Middle School, principal 1983-87; Reservoir Middle School, principal 1988-. **ORGANIZATIONS:** Phi Delta Kappa; Assn of Super of Curriculum Devel; Natl Comm Educ Assn; VA Comm Educ Assn; advisory bd Hampton Roads Boys Club; bd of directors Youth Programs-Mall Tennis Club; Omega Psi Phi; member NAACP; pres Peninsula Council of Urban League; pres, PTPA. **HONORS/ACHIEVEMENTS:** Outstanding Leadership Awd 1978; editor Citizen Involvement in Education 1980; Charles Stewart Mott Fellow 1980; Education Fellow Univ of VA; Vanguard Middle School, VA Dept of Education 1989; Guidelines for Middle Schools in Virginia (VASSP Journal) 1988; Contributions (Executive Educator) 1988. **HOME ADDRESS:** 11741 Kingstowne Rd # 806, Newport News, VA 23606.

BIRCHETTE-PIERCE, CHERYL L.
Physician. **PERSONAL:** Born Sep 25, 1945, New Orleans, LA; married Samuel H Pierce II; children: Samuel Howard. **EDUCATION:** Spelman Coll, AB 1968; Meharry Medical Coll, MD 1972; Harvard Univ, MPH 1980. **CAREER:** Joslin Clinic, patient mgmt/instruction 1972-75; Lahey Clinic NE Deaconess Hospital, intern resident 1972-75; Peter Bent Brigham Hospital, ambulatory care doctor 1973-74; Harvard Univ Medical Sch, instructor in medicine 1973-80; NE Baptist Hospital, critical care cpr physician coord 1975-78; Roxbury Dental Medical Group, medical dir 1976-80; McLean Hospital, consultant internal medicine 1976-80; MIT-HMO Cambridge MA, dir health screening physician provider 1981-86; Private Practice, clinician. **ORGANIZATIONS:** Television/conference/health workshop appearances varied health issues 1974-; attending physician US Olympic Team Pan Amer Games 1975; sec house of delegates 3rd vice pres Natl Medical Assoc 1983-85, 1986-; work group participant Health Policy Agenda AMA 1985-86; mem Amer Public Health Assoc. **HONORS/ACHIEVEMENTS:** Merrill Scholarship Study & Travel Faculte de Medicine Univ of Geneva Switzerland 1966-67; Outstanding Young Women in Amer 1973; US Dept of Health Human Serv Fellowship 1980-81; Keynote/Founder's Day Speaker Delta Sigma Theta 1981. **HOME ADDRESS:** 407 Washington St #1, Brookline, MA 02146. **BUSINESS ADDRESS:** 91 Parker Hill Ave, Boston, MA 02120.

BIRDSONG, OTIS
Basketball player. **PERSONAL:** Born Dec 09, 1955, Winter Haven, FL. **EDUCATION:** Univ of Houston TX, attended. **CAREER:** Kansas City, basketball player 1977-81; New Jersey Nets, basketball player 1981-. **HONORS/ACHIEVEMENTS:** The Sporting News All-Amer First Team 1977; Named to All-NBA Second Team 1981. **BUSINESS ADDRESS:** Basketball Player, New Jersey Nets, Meadowlands Arena, East Rutherford, NJ 07073.

BIRTHA, JESSIE M.
Retired librarian. **PERSONAL:** Born Feb 05, 1920, Norfolk, VA; married Herbert M Birtha; children: Rachel Roxanne Eitches, Rebecca Lucille. **EDUCATION:** Hampton Inst, BS 1940; Drexel Univ, MLS 1962. **CAREER:** Penn School St Helena Island SC, secondary school teacher 1941-42; Norfolk, elementary school teacher 1942-46; Antioch Grade School, children's literature instructor, adjunct faculty Philadelphia Center, 1975-76; Free Library of Philadelphia, retired br librarian 1959-80. **ORGANIZATIONS:** Amer Library Assn; PA Library Assn; Publisher's consul for McGraw Hill Lang Arts Prog Am Lang Today 1974.

HONORS/ACHIEVEMENTS: Article published in PLA Bulletin, Top of News, McCann & Woodward The Black Am in Books for Children, 1972, Josey & Shockley Handbook of Black Librarianship 1977; Free Library Citation as Supvr of Year 1973; Chapel of Four Chaplains Legion of Hon Awd for Outstanding Work with Minority Children 1979; article published in Smith Jessie Carney Images of Blacks in Amer Culture 1987.

BISHOP, ALFRED A.
Educator. **PERSONAL:** Born May 10, 1924, Philadelphia, PA; married Maryann F; children: Janet L. **EDUCATION:** Univ of PA, BS 1950; Univ of Pgh, MS 1965; Carnegie Mellon Univ, PhD. **CAREER:** Naval Rsch, engineer, 1950-52; Fischer & Porter Co, engineer 1952-56; Westinghouse Corp, engineer, 1956-65, mgr thermal & hydraulic design & devel, 1965-70; Westinghouse Corp Nuclear Energy, consulting engineer 1970-73; BB Nuclear Energy Consultants, partner 1974-; Univ of Pittsburgh, assoc prof chemical engineering dir nuclear engineering program. **ORGANIZATIONS:** Lectr Carnegie Mellon Univ 1967-69; engr consult Westinghouse Advanced Reactors Div 1973-; mem ASME, AWS, ASEE, author of numerous publ in field of nuclearengrg heat transfer & fluid mechanics; mem bd dir PA Youth Ctrs 1973-; mem bd dir United Fund 1969-73; sr life master Amer Birdge Assn. **HONORS/ACHIEVEMENTS:** Natl Sci Found Awd 1975; Scholarships Rutgers & Lincoln Univ 1942; DuPont Rsch Awd 1971. **MILITARY SERVICE:** AUS t/4 1943-46. **BUSINESS ADDRESS:** Assoc Prof Chem Engrg, Univ of Pittsburgh, Pittsburgh, PA 15213.

BISHOP, CECIL
Clergyman. **PERSONAL:** Born May 12, 1930, Pittsburgh, PA; married Wilhelma. **EDUCATION:** Knoxville Coll, BA 1954; Howard Univ Sch of Religion, BD 1958; Wesley Theol Sem, STM 1960. **CAREER:** Ordained deacon 1955; elder 1957; Clinton AME Zion Ch, pastor 1957-60; Trinity AME Zion Church Greensboro NC, pastor 1960-. **ORGANIZATIONS:** Dir AME Zion Ch's Div of Preaching Ministries Dept of Evangelism; mem bd of Homes Missions; mem NC State Adv Com of US Commn on Civil Rights; chmn Greensboro Housing Authority. **BUSINESS ADDRESS:** Pastor, Trinity AME Zion Church, 631 E Florida St, Greensboro, NC 27406.

BISHOP, CLARENCE
Assistant supervisor. **PERSONAL:** Born Feb 19, 1959, Selma, AL; married Caroly. **EDUCATION:** Wayne College, BA 1980, M Spec Educ 1985. **CAREER:** Lake Park Day Care Ctr, counselor 1977-78; Mission of the Immaculate Virgin Group Home, sr counselor 1978-79, child care worker 1980-81; Wagner Coll, asst lead teacher 1980; NY State Division for Youth, asst supervisor 1982-; Sigma Phi Rho, founder. **ORGANIZATIONS:** Organized Lake View Park Basketball League for teenagers; founder/regional dir/advisor Sigma Phi Rho Frat; business mgr Natl Governors Council Sigma Phi Rho; mem Honorary Society of Art, Catholic Youth Organization Basketball League, Rutgers Univ Pro-Basketball League. **HONORS/ACHIEVEMENTS:** NY State Div for Youth's Regional Dir Awd for Academic Excellence and Career Development; Founders Achievement Awd Sigma Phi Rho Frat. **BUSINESS ADDRESS:** Founder, Sigma Phi Rho Fraternity, Inc, Wagner College, Staten Island, NY 10301.

BISHOP, DAVID RUDOLPH
Dentist. **PERSONAL:** Born Aug 20, 1924; married Joan; children: Robyn, Celeste, David. **EDUCATION:** Howard Univ, BS 1954, DDS 1958. **CAREER:** Howard Univ, instructor 1958-61; Self-Employed, DDS. **ORGANIZATIONS:** Mem pres Robert T Freeman Dental Soc 1972-74, sec 1968-69; mem Peer Review Comm DC Dental Soc 1972-75; dir Dental Serv Corp 1970-77; mem House of Del Natl Dental Assn 1972; pres DC Bd of Dental Examiners 1980; mem DC Health Planning Adv Com 1971-76; mem Task Force for Effective Health Care Delivery System DC 1973; mem "Hill-Burton" subcomm on hosp cert & need; mem State Adv Bd to Control Health Fees 1973; chmn adv bd United Natl Bank 1977; mem adv comm Armstrong HS Spec Educ Prog 1972-73; fellow Royal Soc of Health 1974; mem Robert T Freeman Dental Soc; mem ADA; NDA; Acad of Gen Dentistry; Chi Delta Mu Professional Frat; Amer Assn of Dental Examiners; mem DC Bd of Dental Examiners 1976; mem NE US Bd of Dental Examiners 1977; mem Pierre Fauchard Acad of Dentistry 1981; fellow Amer Coll of Dentistry 1984; pres DC Delta Dental Corp 1985; fellow, International College of Dentist 1989-. **HONORS/ACHIEVEMENTS:** Howard Dental Alumni Awd for Distinguished Serv to Profn & Comm 1979; DC Govt Certificate of Appreciation for Outstanding Performance as chmn & mem Bd of Dental Examiners 1983. **BUSINESS ADDRESS:** Dr of Dental Surgery, 2608 Sherman Ave NW, Washington, DC 20001.

BISHOP, JAMES, JR.
County official. **PERSONAL:** Born Jan 07, 1930, Humboldt, TN; married Ruby L Dickenson; children: James Gerald, Kathy L. **EDUCATION:** Attended, Univ of MI Ext Svc, Lewis Bus Coll. **CAREER:** Ford Motor Co, elected sec coke ovens blast furnace unit 1957-59, elected pres UAW 1959-73; UAW Natl Negotiation Com, elected 1961; Wayne Co Labor Relations Bd, dir secty. **ORGANIZATIONS:** Sec bd dir Rouge Employees Credit Union 1969; sec Van Dyke 100 Club; mem NAACP; Trade Union Leadership Council; mem Democratic Party of MI; delegate Intl Confederation of Free Trade Unionists UAW European Conf 1964. **MILITARY SERVICE:** AUS corpl 1953-55. **BUSINESS ADDRESS:** Director-Secretary, Wayne Co Labor Relations Bd, 728 City Co Bldg, Detroit, MI 48226.

BISHOP, RICHARD
Professional athlete. **PERSONAL:** Born Mar 23, 1950, Cleveland, OH; married Barbra. **EDUCATION:** Attended, Louisville. **CAREER:** Cincinnati Bengals, professional football player 1974; Hamilton Tiger Cats, professional football player 1974; Ottawa Rough Riders, professional football player 1975; CincinnatiBengals, professional football player 1976; Off Season, auto broker; New England Patriots, professional football player. **ORGANIZATIONS:** Mem New England Area Special Olympics; mem Boy Scouts; mem Boy's Clubs; mem Pres Task Force on Youth Employment. **HONORS/ACHIEVEMENTS:** Outstanding Lineman Jim Lee Hunt Meml Awd; Fan Club Unsung Hero Awd 1978.

BISHOP, VERISSA RENE
Police officer. **PERSONAL:** Born Nov 22, 1954, Houston, TX; daughter of Julia Lee Bishop. **EDUCATION:** Texas Southern University, BA, 1987. **CAREER:** Foley's Department Store, Houston, TX, receptionist/beauty operator, 1973-75; Houston Police Department, Houston, TX, clerk in dispatchers division, 1975-78, police officer, 1978—. **ORGANIZATIONS:** Board member, secretary, Afro-American Police Officers League; financial secretary, secretary, board member, National Black Police Association; YWCA; Phi Beta Lambda; City Wide Beauticians. **HONORS/ACHIEVEMENTS:** Member of year, Afro-American Police Officers League. **HOME ADDRESS:** 3829 Wichita, Houston, TX 77004. **BUSINESS ADDRESS:** Houston Police Department, 61 Riesner, Houston, TX 77001.

BISPHAM, FRANK L.
Retired government administrator. **PERSONAL:** Born Nov 02, 1924, Cambridge, MA; married Annie Larkins; children: Francine Harris, Gail Murphy, Jo-Ann Duke, Eric. **EDUCATION:** Lowell Inst Sch at MIT Cambridge, Engrg diploma 1965. **CAREER:** Office of Minority Business US Dept of Commerce, project officer 1970-78; Mattapan Enterprises, partner 1971-; NAACP Boston Branch, exec bd mem 1971-; Natl Business League, regional vice pres 1976-; Minority Business Develop Agency US Dept of Commerce, project officer 1978-82; Suffolk Univ, adv bd mem sch of mgmt 1986-; US Small Business Admin, asst regional administrator 1982-88; retired. **ORGANIZATIONS:** Mem Greater Boston Chamber of Commerce 1980-; vice chmn of bd Youth Business Initiative Prog 1985-. **HONORS/ACHIEVEMENTS:** Outstanding Civic Serv Boston Branch NAACP 1973; Outstanding Achievement Awd Natl Business League 1975; Citizern of the Year Awd Omega Psi Phi Frat 1979; Comm Serv Awd Boston Urban bankers Forum 1982. **MILITARY SERVICE:** USMC nco 31 months. **HOME ADDRESS:** 52 Violet St, Boston, MA 02126.

BISSON, WHEELOCK ALEXANDER
Retired physician. **PERSONAL:** Born Jan 05, 1898, Key West, FL; widowed. **EDUCATION:** FL A&M Univ, BS 1922; Harvard Univ, Grad Work; Meharry Med Coll, MD 1929. **CAREER:** Royal Circle Hosp, intern 1931-33; Memphis Health Dept, clinitian 1933-70; Private practice, physician 1933-1978 retired. **ORGANIZATIONS:** Mem Amer Thoracic Soc, TN Acad Sci, AAAS, Natl Publ Health Assoc; 2nd vice pres Natl Med Assoc, Bluff City Med Soc; past pres Vol State Med Assoc, Amer Med Assoc, Memphis Shelby Co Med Socs, TN State Med Assoc, Natl Publ Health Assoc, Natl Rehab Assoc, sec Bluff City Med Soc, treas, chmn Vol State med Assoc; mem Natl Sickle Cell Anemia Comm, Cynthia Milk Fund Comm, YMCA, BSA; life mem NAACP; past pres TN Elks, 33 Deg Mason; mem King Frederick Conis 38, Noble, Mystic Shrine, Psi Phi Frat, Emmanuel Epis Church; fellow Intl Biog Assoc; mem Intl Plat Assoc, Intercon Biog Assoc; worked with Memphis & Shelby Cty Health Dept for 40 yrs. **HONORS/ACHIEVEMENTS:** Merit Achievement & Awd FL A&M Univ 1964; Honored by City of Memphis for 35 yrs of unselfish serv 1965; Spec Citation & Golden Key to the City Mayor Wm Ingram; Plaque Memphis Health Dept; Letter of Commend TN Gov; Prac of the Year Awd Natl Med Assoc 1967; TN Dr of the Year Vol State Med Assoc 1962-63;Personalities of the South, Who's Who in the South & Southwest, Who's Who in Amer, TN Lives, Dict of Intl Biog, Comm Leaders of Amer, 2000 Men of Achievement, Natl Reg of Prominent Amer & Intl Notables; citations from US Presidents, Franklin D Roosevelt, Harry Truman, Dwight Eisenhower, John F Kennedy, L Johnson, Richard Nixon; Placque Outstanding Physician in the Field of Med Gov of TN 1978, State of TN, House of Reps 1977; Clinic named in honor of Wheelock Bisson by City of Memphis & Shelby Cty Health Dept.

BISWAS, PROSANTO K.
Educator. **PERSONAL:** Born Mar 01, 1934, Calcutta; married Joan; children: Shila. **EDUCATION:** Univ of Calcutta, BS 1958; Univ of MO, MS 1959, PhD 1962 (Charles Kiepe Scholar). **CAREER:** Univ of MO, res assoc 1961; Tuskegee Realty, pres; Tuskegee Inst, prof of plant & soil sci 1962-. **ORGANIZATIONS:** Chmn Macon Co Bd Educ. **BUSINESS ADDRESS:** Prof of Plant & Soil Science, Tuskegee Inst, Dept Agr Sci, Tuskegee, AL 36088.

BITTINGS, ROSEMARY BROOKS
Educator, publisher. **PERSONAL:** Born Jan 02, 1949, East Orange, NJ; daughter of Patrick Brooks and Ethel Field Brooks; divorced; children: Haven Michael, Ebony Mekia. **EDUCATION:** Claflin Univ, BA 1971; Seton Hall Univ, MA 1976; Kean Coll, Communication Certification 1978; Rutger's Union, MA Physical Fitness Specialist 1983. **CAREER:** East Orange Drug Center, substance abuse counselor 1975; Essex Valley School/The Bridge West, dir 1981-82; Second Chance Counseling Center, dir 1982-83; NJ Black Caucus of Legislators, lobbyist 1984-87; Irvington Board of Educ, Educator/History, 1984-; NJ Chapter Parents for Joint Custody, lobbyist 1985-87; Essex Co Fitness Program, specialist 1986-87; Irvington HS NJ Law & Psychology, instructor of history 1985-87; "Staying Fit" Exercise Program NJ Network, host, dir 1984-86; NJ Careers Council Irvington High, coordinator 1986-87; Irvington Bd of Educ, dir of history & law; Person to Person Greeting Cards, pres, writer, 1988-. **ORGANIZATIONS:** Educ comm chmn SOMAC Comm Council 1979-86; mem Governor's Council on Educ 1982-87; mem NJ State Bd of Lobbyists 1982-87, NJ State Bd of Fitness Specialist 1984-87; project chmn Maplewood PTA 1985-86; mem, treas Irvington Awareness Council 1986-87; dir Afro-History Soc Irvington HS 1983-87; writer/consultant, Sands Casino Atlantic City NJ, 1988-89; writer/consultant, Planned Parenthood NJ, 1988-89. **HONORS/ACHIEVEMENTS:** NAACP Award of Merit/Outstanding Educator 1980-81; creator/dir first black fitness program on cable in NJ/NY 1983-85; Citation for Excellence in Programming NJ State Assembly 1984; TV and radio appearances; feature writer Essence Magazine 1982-87, Focus Magazine 1984-87; choreographer "The Wiz" NJ Theatre Irvington 1986-87; Career Council Award for Outstanding Participation 1986-87; Person to Person Cards were recognized for its contributions to health, 1988-89. **HOME ADDRESS:** 95 Parker Ave, Maplewood, NJ 07040.

BIVENS, GYNA MACHELLE
Public relations manager. **PERSONAL:** Born Oct 16, 1954, Fort Worth, TX. **EDUCATION:** North TX State Univ, BA 1977. **CAREER:** KKDA-AM Dallas, anchor 1977-78; KBOX-KMEZ Dallas, anchor 1978-79; KCBD-TV Lubbock, anchor/reporter 1979-81; KMOL TV San Antonio, sr reporter 1981-82; City of San Antonio, public info mgr. **ORGANIZATIONS:** Mem Public Relations Soc of Amer, TX Public Relations Assoc; bd mem Amer Diabetes Assoc 1984-; bd mem NAACP. **HONORS/ACHIEVEMENTS:** Outstanding Achievement Jaycees-Lubbock; Serv Contributor Alpha Tau Omega San Antonio. **HOME ADDRESS:** 11311 Sir Winston, San Antonio, TX 78216.

BIVENS, SHELIA RENEEA
Registered nurse. **PERSONAL:** Born Jul 10, 1954, Pine Bluff, AR; daughter of Leon J King and Myrtle Jones Ervin King; widowed; children: Cory, Ronnie, Ronniesha. **EDUCATION:** Univ of AR Fayetteville, A 1974; Univ of AMS Coll of Nursing, BSN 1977. **CAREER:** Dr C E Hyman, nurse practitioner 1977-81; Jefferson Regional Medical Ctr, charge

nurse 1981-83; Univ of AMS Univ Hosp, staff nurse 1983-89, charge nurse 1989-. **ORGANIZATIONS:** Mem AR State Nurses Assoc 1977-; sec Little Rock Branch NAACP 1983-84, state sec 1984-; chap pianist 19 Electa Chap #5 OES 1984; mem AR Black Nurses Assoc 1987; mem Arkansas Perinatal Assoc 1987; mem Sigma Theta Tau Nursing Honor Society 1989-. **HONORS/ACHIEVEMENTS:** Outstanding Youth Awd Livingstone Coll Genl Educ of AME Zion Church 1970; Outstanding Serv Awd OES Electa Chap #5 1983; Five Year Service Award, UAMS 1989; Outstanding Black Employee of the Month UAMS 1989. **HOME ADDRESS:** 54 Saxony Circle, Little Rock, AR 72209.

BIVINS, EDWARD BYRON
Business executive. **PERSONAL:** Born May 11, 1929, Birmingham, AL; married Sarah Felton; children: Cheryl Ann, Janet Yvette. **EDUCATION:** Tuskegee Inst, BS 1951; OH State Univ, MA 1955; So IL Univ, Tuskegee Inst, further study 1961-63 summer. **CAREER:** Savannah State Coll, coll tchr 1955-64; Oppors Indus Ctr Philadelphia 1964-68; OIC Natl Inst, training dir, branch dir, natl dir of educ & trng, reg dir; Midwest Rsch Inst, sr staff 1968-69; Urban Coalition of Greater KC, exec dir 1969-70; Hallmark Cards Inc, dir of urban & minority affairs 1970-. **ORGANIZATIONS:** Mem C of C Small Bus Affairs Comm 1974-75; President's adv coun on Minority Bus Enterprise; MO State Dept of Educ Adv Comm; Bus Resources Ctr bdchmn 1974-75; mem KC MO Bd of Police Commr 1973-77; KC Region Manpower Council chmn; Downtown Kiwanis Club of KC; United Comm Serv treas; Children's Mercy Hosp bd; Greater KC Housing Inc secty; Family & Chidlren Serv Bd. **HONORS/ACHIEVEMENTS:** Kiwanian of Yr 1972-73; Kappa Alpha Psi Achievement awd Middlewestern Province 1973; Kappa Man of Yr KC Alumni Chap 1973; author of several publs. **MILITARY SERVICE:** AUS 1952-54. **BUSINESS ADDRESS:** Dir of Urban & Minority Affrs, Hallmark Cards Inc, 25 Mc Gee Trafficway, Kansas City, MO 64141.

BIVINS, OLLIE B., JR.
Judge. **PERSONAL:** Born Jul 07, 1923, Americus, GA; married Julia T Hawkins; children: Ollie B III. **EDUCATION:** Fisk Univ, AB 1950; Boston Univ Sch of Law, LLB 1953. **CAREER:** Atty Dudley Mallory, assoc 7 yrs; Flint MI, atty 1954; Genesee Co Pros, trial atty 1965, chief trial atty 1966-68; Municipal Court, aptd judge 1968; 68th Dist Flint, judge 1969; Dist Judge, elected 1971 8 yr term; Circuit Judge, aptd 1972; MI Ct of Appeals, judge 1976. **ORGANIZATIONS:** Bd dirs Genesee Co Legal Aid Soc; bd dirs Genesee Co Bar Assn; mem State of MI & Amer Bar Assn; past assoc mem Frat Order of Police; mem N Amer Judges Assn; MI Dist Judges Assn; Amer Judicatur Soc; lectr Dist Judges Seminary; served as Circuit Judge Circuit Ct of Genesee Co; served as Judge Detroit Recorders Ct; mem Kappa Alpha Psi Frat; Phi Delta Phi Legal Frat; Frontiers of Amer exec com Tall Pine Coun BSA; charter mem Y's Men's Club of Flint; past mem Sierra Club; bd dirs Cath Social Svcs; mem Knights of Columbus; hon chmn March of Dimes Walk-A-Thon 1972; bd dirs March of Dimes. **MILITARY SERVICE:** USN WW II. **BUSINESS ADDRESS:** Judge, MI Ct of Appeals, 7th Judicial Court, 900 S Saginaw, Flint, MI 48502.

BLACK, BARBARA ROBINSON
Educational administrator. **PERSONAL:** Born Aug 06, 1936, West Chester, PA; married Dr Samuel Hassell, Sr; children: Samuel H Jr, Chad R. **EDUCATION:** Cheyney State Coll, BS 1959; Kean Coll NJ, MA 1970; Cheyney State Coll, post graduate admin, 1971. **CAREER:** Rahway Sch Dist, tchr/cons 1963-68; NJ State Dept, cons/writer for black studies 1968; W Chester State Coll, asst prof black hist 1970-72, coord/counselor act 101 1972-79, asst dean of student devel/coord of greek life/student orgs 1979-. **ORGANIZATIONS:** Dir first prog Rahway NJ Comm Head Start 1968; counseling Chester PA Sch Dist 1972; treas BOLD Inc 1978; bd of dirs Friends Shelter for Girls 1970; charter mem Local Alpha Kappa Alpha Sor 1972; charter mem Local Twigs Inc 1973. **HONORS/ACHIEVEMENTS:** Delta Kappa Gamma Intl Hon Soc 1979; NJ State HS Hist NJ State Bd 1968; Tchr of the Yr Awd Rahway NJ; cons/writer Black History Elem/HS Unit Rahway NJ 1969; Rahway Civic Assn Awd Rahway NJ 1970; Act 101 Faculty Awd W Chester PA 1978; Outstanding Serv Awd West Chester State Acad Devel Prog 1979. **BUSINESS ADDRESS:** Asst Dean of Student Devel, West Chester State Coll, 204 Sykes Student Union Bldg, West Chester, PA 19380.

BLACK, BILLY CHARLESTON
Educational administrator. **PERSONAL:** Born Feb 01, 1937, Beatrice, AL; married Helen Ruth Jeenings; children: James Edward, Marla Jeaninne. **EDUCATION:** Tuskegee Inst, BS 1960; IA State Univ, MS 1962, PhD 1964. **CAREER:** Tuskegee Inst, lab instructor 1959-60; IA State Univ, rsch asst 1960-64; Albany State Coll, prof of chem 1964-; chmn dept of chem & physics 1966-80, chmn div of sci & math 1969-70, chmn div of arts & scis 1970-80, interim asst to the dean for academic affairs 1979-80, acting pres 1980-81, pres 1981-. **ORGANIZATIONS:** Consul Natl Sci Foundation 1966-; consul Natl Inst of Health 1966-; have served in the following capacities at Albany State Coll of GA coord Inst of Tech; prog dir Campus Action Prog; prog dir Natl Sci Found; proj dir NSF Grant; proj dir Natl Heart Inst; prog dir Interdisciplinary Biomedical Sci Rsch Prog; site development advocate Phelps-Stokes Albany State Coll Project; health develop advocate Phelps-Stokes Albany State Coll Project on Health Awareness; mem Albany State Coll Graduate Studies Council 1974-80; mem Amer Assn for the Advancement of Sci; mem Gamma Sigma Delta; mem Soc of Sigma Xi; mem IA Acad of Sci; mem Phi Lambda Upsilon; mem Amer Assn of Clinical Chemists; mem Amer Chem Soc; mem Amer Oil Chemists Soc; mem Amer Instof Chemists; mem GA Acad of Sci; mem Inst of Food Technologists; mem basileus Omega Psi Phi Frat 1980-; chmn bd of stewards Hines Memorial CME Church;chmn Council of Presidents SIAC 1984-; mem Natl Service Comm Amer Assoc of State Colls & Univs, NCAA President's Commn 1987-91. **HONORS/ACHIEVEMENTS:** Listed in Natl Register of Prominent Amers; listed in Who's Who in American Men of Scis; recipient of Amer Inst of Chemists Awd; Black Georgian of the Yr Awd 1980; listed in Personalites of the South 1981, 1982; listed in Personalities of Amer 1982; listed in Who's Who in GA 1982; listed in Who's Who in America 1983; 9 publications including "The Separation of Glycerides by Liquid-Liquid Column Partition Chromatography" Journal of Amer Oil Chemists Soc 1963; "The Isolation of Phosphatides by Dielectrophoresis" Journal of the IA Acad of Scis 1964. **BUSINESS ADDRESS:** President, Albany State Coll, 504 College Dr, Albany, GA 31705.

BLACK, CHARLES E.
Pilot. **PERSONAL:** Born Apr 02, 1943, Bainbridge, GA; divorced; children: Harriet, Michael. **EDUCATION:** Purdue Univ, BS 1964; GA State Univ, MS 1976. **CAREER:** Eastern Airlines Inc, pilot. **ORGANIZATIONS:** Mem Alpha Phi Alpha Frat 1961-65; Amer Soc of Pub Adminstrn 1971; mem Orgn of Blk Airline Pilots; coord SW Atlanta Comprehensive Comm Planning Workshops 1974. **HONORS/ACHIEVEMENTS:** Ford Fellow GA State Univ, 1971-73; Best All Around Student Washington HS 1960; Natl Honor Soc 1960. **MILITARY SERVICE:** USAF capt pilot b-52 1967-71; Air Medal with 2 Oak Leaf Clusters USAF 1970. **BUSINESS ADDRESS:** Eastern Airlines Inc, Flight Operations, Hartsfield Intl Airport, Atlanta, GA.

BLACK, CHARLIE J.
Publisher, educator, radio host. **PERSONAL:** Born Apr 19, 1934, Beatrice, AL; married Lola P; children: Lisa Yvonne, La Sonja Ann. **EDUCATION:** AL State Univ, BS Sec Ed 1956; Tuskegee Inst, 39 Sh Sc Ed 1959-60; Atlanta Univ, 24 Sh Sc Ed 1962-66; Southeastern Univ, MBPA Business Govt Relations 1978; Catholic Univ, Doctorial Stud Educ Admin 1979-80. **CAREER:** RR Moton High School, band dir 1956-58; Harrison High School, band dir & math teacher 1958-62; Atlanta Public Schools, Atlanta GA, math teacher 1962-63; Aero Chart & Info Center, cartographer 1963-65; US Army Educ Center, educ advisor 1965-66; St Louis Public Schools, St Louis MO, math teacher 1966; US Navy Publication Div, educ specialist 1966-67; Tracor Inc, technical writer 1967-68; Ogden Technology Lab, program dir 1968-71; Equitable Life Assurance Soc of US, ins rep 1972-73; Southern Aid Life Insurance Co, dist mgr 1973-75; DC Public Schools, math teacher 1976-79; Montgomery County Public School, math teacher 1981-84; The Washington Provider, publisher editor. **ORGANIZATIONS:** Pres Brightwood Comm Assn 1974-80; comm chrmn DC Fed of Civic Assoc 1974-80; vice pres Horizontes Investment Club 1976-78; mem Assoc of MBA Executives 1981-85; author, "Meeting the Mathematical Needs of Students in a Georgia Secondary School" published, 1971; "After the Fact, 20/20 Hindsight," published 1988; published column, "Upward Mobility" 1971-; pres West Elementry School PTA 1971-73; mem, Washington Teachers Union, 1976-80; chmn Georgia Ave Corridor Comm Devel Corp 1978-81; mem Intl Platform Assn 1989-. **HONORS/ACHIEVEMENTS:** Fellowship Natl Science Found 1959-60; 2 sales awards Equitable Life WA Dist Agency 1972; 2 service awards DC Chapter AL State Alumni Assn 1970-73; outstanding male DC Federation of Civic Assoc 1977; outstanding PTA pres DC Congress of Parents and Teachers 1973. **HOME ADDRESS:** 6435 13th St NW, Washington, DC 20012. **BUSINESS ADDRESS:** Publisher Editor, The Washington Provider, P O Box 5397, Takoma Park Station, Silver Spring, MD 20912.

BLACK, DANIEL L., JR.
Government official. **PERSONAL:** Born Sep 16, 1945, Sheldon, SC; married Mary Lemmon; children: Carlita. **EDUCATION:** SC State College, BA 1971; Univ of SC, MBA 1975. **CAREER:** IRS, Jacksonville, exam group mgr 1976-78, Atlanta, sr regional analyst 1980-81, exam branch chief 1981-82, Oklahoma City, chief appeals office 1983-85, Greensboro Dist asst district director. **ORGANIZATIONS:** Life mem Omega Psi Phi Frat 1978-86; mem Amer Inst of CPA's 1977-86; mem FL Inst of CPA's 1977-86; mem Sr Executives Assn 1985-86; Beta Alpha Psi Accounting Fraternity; Alpha Kappa Mu Natl Honor Soc. **HONORS/ACHIEVEMENTS:** Who's Who Among Students in American Univs 1970-71; Summa Cum Laude SC State Coll 1971; Distinguished Alumni Awd 1985. **MILITARY SERVICE:** AUS specialist E-4 1963-66; Good Conduct Medal; Vietnam Service and Defense Medal. **BUSINESS ADDRESS:** CPA,Asst District Dir, IRS-Greensboro District, 320 Federal Place, Greensboro, NC 27408.

BLACK, DON GENE
Public relations/advertising consultant. **PERSONAL:** Born Sep 06, 1945, Chicago, IL; son of Uster Black and Inez Franklin-Davidson; married Glenda Camp Black, Aug 14, 1966; children: Donerik, Shronda. **EDUCATION:** Sinclair Comm Coll, A 1967; Wright State Univ, BA 1970. **CAREER:** Dayton Express News, dir public relations 1967-68; Monsanto Rsch Corp, mktg 1968-70; Don Black Assoc Inc, pres 1970-77; Multi-Western Co, pres 1977-. **ORGANIZATIONS:** Bd mem Urban Youth Assoc 1976-81; pres OH Assoc of Blk PR/Adv/Mktg Co 1983-85; pres Dayton Chap Natl Business League 1983-86; advisory board, Goodwill Industries. **HONORS/ACHIEVEMENTS:** Achievement Awd Dayton Public School 1985; free lance writer. **BUSINESS ADDRESS:** President/Senior Consultant, Multi-Western Public Relations/Marketing, 7 East Fourth St, Suite 820, Dayton, OH 45402.

BLACK, FRANK S.
Educational administrator. **PERSONAL:** Born Feb 03, 1941, Detroit, MI; married Ruby S Lindsey; children: Piper L. **EDUCATION:** Central State Univ Wilberforce OH, BS (Cum Laude) 1967; OH State Univ, MA 1969, PhD 1972. **CAREER:** Columbus OH Public Schools, eval asst, 1969-71; OH State Univ, project dir, adjunct asst prof, 1972-73; TX Southern Univ, assoc prof, dir institutional rsch, 1973-77, assoc prof of educ, 1973-78; Murray State Univ, dean, 1978-84; Univ of Southern FL at Ft Myers, assoc dean for acad affairs 1984-. **ORGANIZATIONS:** Mem Amer Ed Rsch Assoc1971-75; mem exec comm Assoc for Inst Rsch 1977-79; mem Amer Assoc of Coll of Teacher Ed 1979, Murray KY Human Rights Comm 1979-; adv bd WKMS Univ Radio Sta 1979-; adv bd W KY Reg Mental Health & Retarded Bd 1979. **HONORS/ACHIEVEMENTS:** Grad Fellow Soc OH State Univ 1967-69; article publ Intl Reading Assoc 1975. **MILITARY SERVICE:** AUS sp4 1958-61. **BUSINESS ADDRESS:** Associate Dean Acad Affairs, University of South FL, 8111 College Parkway, SW, Fort Myers, FL 33919.

BLACK, FREDERICK HARRISON
Business executive. **PERSONAL:** Born Nov 11, 1921, Des Moines, IA; married Kay Browne; children: Joan Jackson, Lorna, Jai, Crystal. **EDUCATION:** Fisk Univ, BS Eng Physics 1949; Pepperdine Univ, MBA 1972; Univ of MA, DEd Personnel 1975. **CAREER:** USN, consultant to chief of naval personnel; President's Domestic Council, consultant; General Electric Co, missile project engr, marketing rep in Washington DC, corporate mgr EEO/safety & security; Watts Indus Park, exec dir; FH Black & Assocs, mng partner. **ORGANIZATIONS:** Diplomat Amer Personnel Soc; bd pres TRY US; mem bd ICBO; trustee Fisk Univ; published several articles. **MILITARY SERVICE:** AUS 2nd lt 3 1/2 yrs. **BUSINESS ADDRESS:** Managing Partner, FH Black & Assocs, 1377 K St, Washington, DC 20005.

BLACK, GAIL
Business executive. **PERSONAL:** Born Aug 29, 1950, Klamath Falls, OR; married Carl B Bowles; children: Amil Christopher Bowles, Teri Ruth Bowles. **EDUCATION:** Portland State Univ, attended 1970-71; Portland OIC, cert legal sec 1977. **CAREER:** Union Pac RR Co Law Dept, litigation specialist 1977-; Clairon Defender Newspaper, asst editor & pub 1970-. **ORGANIZATIONS:** Bd mem Knockout Industries Inc 1971-; exec bd charter mem Tenth Ave Irregulars Chap Toastmasters Intl Inc 1979-; dir Jimmy Bang-Bang Walker Youth Found 1969-; chmn Albina Rose Festival float com 4 prize winning floats Portland Rose Festi-

val Parade 1969-71; asst to Albina area coord United Good Neighbors 1970-73; United Way rep Union Pac RR Co 1979-80; parent adv com mem NE Christian Sch 1980-. **HONORS/ACHIEVEMENTS:** Dean's List Portland State Univ 1970-71. **BUSINESS ADDRESS:** Asst Editor & Publisher, Clairon Defender Newspaper, 319 NE Wygant St, Portland, OR 97211.

BLACK, JAMES TILLMAN
Dentist. **PERSONAL:** Born Feb 19, 1934, Guthrie, OK; married Joyce Toran; children: James Jr, Jeanine. **EDUCATION:** TN State Univ, BS 1955; Michael Reese Sch of Medical Tech, attended 1956; Central State Univ, MA 1960; Loyola Univ Sch of Dentistry, attended 1964. **CAREER:** Private Practice, dentist. **ORGANIZATIONS:** Ofcr LA Dental Soc 1977; LA Co Pub Health Serv 1964-71; mem NAACP; mem Amer Dental Assn; LA Dental Soc; Angel City Dental Soc; Kappa Alpha PsiFrat; Xi Psi Phi Dental Frat. **HONORS/ACHIEVEMENTS:** Publ "Dentistry in a Headstart Program" 1972; "Changes in Dental Concepts" 1976. **MILITARY SERVICE:** AUS spec 3 1956-58. **BUSINESS ADDRESS:** 3011 Crenshaw Blvd, Los Angeles, CA 90016.

BLACK, JOSEPH
Business executive. **PERSONAL:** Born Feb 08, 1924, Plainfield, NJ; married Bernice Reed; children: Uvonte, Joseph F, Marco, Toni, Martha J, Abduul. **EDUCATION:** Morgan State Coll, BS 1950; Shaw Coll at Detroit, Dr Humane Letters 1974; Central State Univ, Dr of Law, 1979; Miles Coll, Dr of Letters, 1982; Morgan State Univ, Dr of Public Works 1983. **CAREER:** Baltimore Elite Giants, Negro Natl League, pitcher 1944-50; Cuba, Venezuela Santo Domingo, pitcher 1947-51; Washington Senators Cincinnati Reds, Brooklyn Dodgers, pitcher 1952-57; Plainfield NJ, teacher 1957-63; special markets rep 1962-64; dir special markets 1964-67; Greyhound Lines, vice pres, special markets 1967-69. **ORGANIZATIONS:** Bd of trustees Jackie Robinson Found 1976; Natl Assn of Market Devel, pres, 1967-67, chmn bd 1968-68, 1972-73; bd of trustees Natl Assn for Sickle Cell Disease; bd of trustees Miles Coll; advisory panel US Census Bureau 1978-82. **HONORS/ACHIEVEMENTS:** Natl League Rookie of Year Brooklyn Dodgers 1952; New Jersey Sports Hall of Fame 1972; Morgan St Univ Hall of Fame 1972; Black Athletes Hall of Fame 1974; "Ain't Nobody Better Than You" Autobiography 1983; Central Intercollegiate Athletics Assoc 1986; Mid-Eastern Athletic Conf 1986; Martin Luther King Jr distinguished Serv Award, 1987. **MILITARY SERVICE:** AUS 1943-46. **BUSINESS ADDRESS:** Sr VP-Urban Affairs, The Greyhound Corp, Greyhound Tower, Phoenix, AZ 85077.

BLACK, LEE ROY
Law enforcement. **PERSONAL:** Born Jul 29, 1937, Oakland, MS; married Christine Gray; children: Lori Lynette, Colette Marie, Angela Denise, Lee Roy Jr. **EDUCATION:** Univ of IL Navy Pier, 1956-58; Roosevelt Univ, BA History 1962; Loyola Univ School of Law, 1969-70; OH State Univ, Fellow NPEL 1972-74; Union Grad School, PhD 1976. **CAREER:** Cook Cty Dept of Public Aid, caseworker 1953-62; Juv Ct of Cook Cty, probation officer 1963-67, suprv prob officer 1966-67; Chicago Dept Human Resources DiDiv Correctional Svcs, unit dir Lawndale-Garfield Corrections Unit 1967-70, asst dir 1967-70; UECU, dir Correctional Educ Prog 1970-72; Tchr Corps Youth Adv Prog US Off of Ed; field liaison rep 1975-76; UECU, spvsr 1975-76; IN Univ Dept of Forensic St, vstg asst prof 1975-76; St of IN Dept of Corr, dir Div Class & Treat 1976-77; St of WI Dept Hlth & Soc Serv, deputy admin Div of Corr 1977-81; St of MO Dept Cor & Human Res, dir 1981-. **ORGANIZATIONS:** Pres Midwest Assoc of Corrections Admin; bd of governors Amer Corrections Assoc; mem Natl Alliance for Shaping Safer Cities, NAACP, Natl Urban League,Alpha Phi Alpha, Natl Assoc of Blacks in Criminal Justics; chmn corrections subcommittee MO Governors Commiss on Crime; chmn/prog cncl ACA Natl Conf 1986. **HONORS/ACHIEVEMENTS:** Outstanding Achievers Awd MO Black Leg Caucus; Great Guy Awd for promoting youth leadership WGRT Radio Station Chicago IL; Fellow Natl Prog for Ed Leadership; Grad Scholarship Union for Experimenting Coll & Univ to Union Grad School Yellow Springs OH; Image Awd for Outstanding Contrib to Youth Career Youth Devel Milwaukee WI, Listed in Who's Who in Black Amer 1980-81; many publ incl "Perspectives in Community Corrections" Under grant from Law Enforcement Asst Admin Washington DC 1975. **BUSINESS ADDRESS:** Dir, MO Dept Correct & Human Resour, 2729 Plaza Dr, PO Box 236, Jefferson City, MO 65102.

BLACK, LEONA R.
States attorney administrative director. **PERSONAL:** Born Jan 05, 1924, Galveston, TX. **EDUCATION:** Prairie View Coll, attended; Roosevelt Univ, attended; Chicago Univ, attended; DePaul Univ, attended. **CAREER:** Cook Cty Dept of Public Aid, file clerk, finance clerk, head file clerk, office mgr, Chicago US Post Office, clerk supvr; Intl Harvester Co, equipment expeditor; AA Rayner Alderman 6th Ward, alderman's sec, admin asst; AR Langford Alderman 16th Ward, alderman's sec, admin asst; Donald Page Moore, polit org; State's Attorney of Cook County, political coordinator for Bernard Carrey; Fraud & Consumer Complaint Div Cook Cty, appt admin chief 1972; Cook County States Attorney Office, dir victim/witness asst proj 1974-. **ORGANIZATIONS:** Ombudsman States Atty Office; political activist, Natl Delegate 1972; lobbyist, Local Cty State for Consumer Protection Judicial Reform; advocate for, Criminal Justice, Consumerism, Judicial Reform, Child Abuse, Drug Abuse, Alcoholism; youth gr dir, founder, org SCAPY; bd of dir Natl Org of Victim Assn, 1976. **HONORS/ACHIEVEMENTS:** Set up Consumer Fraud classes within City Coll. **BUSINESS ADDRESS:** Dir Victim/Witness Asst, Cook Cty States Attny Office, 2600 S California Ave, Chicago, IL 60608.

BLACK, MALCOLM MAZIQUE (MIKE BLACK)
Educator, musician. **PERSONAL:** Born Nov 28, 1937, Vicksburg, MS; son of Fred Bell Black and Henriette Grace Smith Black; married Emma Kern Black; children: Varen Delois, Karen Barron. **EDUCATION:** Jackson State Univ, BME 1959; Univ of WI, MME 1967; Nova Univ, EdD 1975. **CAREER:** FL & MS HS, band dir 1959-69; FL Assn of Collegiate Registrars & Admission Officers, vice pres 1979; professional performances with Patti Page, Sam Cooke, Marilyn McCoo, Billy Davis, others; Broward Community Coll, registrar, dir of admissions 1969-79, dir of Jazz Studies & Bands. **ORGANIZATIONS:** Member, Placement Comm Amer Assn Collegiate Registrars & Admission Officers 1975, FL Veterans Advisory Council 1975, FL School Relations Comm 1975; vice pres FL Assn Coll Registrars & Admission Officers 1977; bd mem Broward County Housing Authority Advisory Bd 1978, Sunshine State Bank, Sistrunk Historical Festival Comm. **HONORS/ACHIEVEMENTS:** Plaque, FL Assn Coll Registrars & Admission Officers 1979; recognition as Broward County Black Pioneer, Links Inc 1980; plaque, 25 Years of Serv Omega Psi Phi Frat 1981; plaques, Sistrunk Historical Festival Comm 1981-85; Outstanding Florida Citizen, governor of Florida, 1986; Good Neighbor Award, Miami Herald Newspaper, 1986; Sharps & Flats to Freedom exhibit, Chicago, 1988. **HOME ADDRESS:** 2991 NW 24th Ave, Fort Lauderdale, FL 33311. **BUSINESS ADDRESS:** Dir of Jazz Studies/Bands, Broward Comm College, 3501 SW Davie Rd, Fort Lauderdale, FL 33314.

BLACK, MIKE See BLACK, MALCOLM MAZIQUE

BLACK, ROSA WALSTON
Urban planner, educator. **PERSONAL:** Born in Moyock, NC; children: Adrienne Vernice. **EDUCATION:** Norfolk State Coll, BS; Univ of VA, M Urban Planning. **CAREER:** Hampton Public School, teacher 1964-66; Portsmouth Public School, teacher 1966-70, suprv teacher 1967-68; Concentrated Employment Program, consultant, 1968-69; Central VA Comprehensive Health Planning Comm, researcher & statistician 1970-71; Charlotte Model Neighborhood Comm, dir of planning 1972; Baltimore Model Cities Program, consultant 1972; Dept of Devel & Planning, Gary IN, asst dir, 1973; Seat Pleasant MD, former city planning consultant; Antioch Coll, former chmn dept of health serv admin; City of Seat Pleasant, asst city admin. **ORGANIZATIONS:** mem, Amer Soc of Planning Officials, Natl Negro Business & Professional Womens Club, NAACP, Delta Sigma Theta. **BUSINESS ADDRESS:** Walston Research Inc, 1145 19th St, NW, Suite 717, Washington, MD 20036.

BLACK, WALTER KERRIGAN
Attorney. **PERSONAL:** Born Jan 27, 1915, Birmingham, AL; married Dorothy E Wickliffe. **EDUCATION:** Univ of IL, AB; John Marshall Law School, JD 1952. **CAREER:** McCoy & Black, partner 1952-59; Robbins IL, village atty 1952-69, E Chicago Heights IL, village atty 1952-59; McCoy, Ming & Leighton, partner 1959-64, 1965-77; Mitchell Hall Jones & Black PC, principal. **ORGANIZATIONS:** Gen counsel, Fuller Prod Co, 1968; gen counsel, Boyer Intl Lab Inc, 1968; sec & gen counsel, LaCade Prod Co, 1972; sec, dir, Lawndale Pkg Corp, 1974; hearing exam, IL Fair Practice Comm; panel arbitrator, Amer Arbitration Assn; mem gov bd, Cook County Legal Asst Found; co-counsel, Hon Richard Gordon Hatcher, 1967, 1971. **BUSINESS ADDRESS:** Principal, Mitchell, Hall, Jones & Black, 134 S La Salle St, Chicago, IL 60603.

BLACK, WALTER WELDON, JR.
Business executive. **PERSONAL:** Married Clairdean E Riley; children: Walter III. **EDUCATION:** Morgan State Coll, BS 1958; Amer Univ Law School, 1960-62. **CAREER:** Prudential Ins Co of Amer, spec agent; NAACP Spec Contrib Fund, urban prog dir 1968-69; Pinkett-Brown-Black Assoc, chmn bd 1969-72; Howard Univ, mkt rsch analyst 1972-76; Alaska Assoc Inc, Flennaugh Reliable Svcs, supt 1976-. **ORGANIZATIONS:** Pres MD State Conf of Br NAACP 1973-; dir of MD State Conf of NAACP 1965-68; vice pres DC Chap Morgan State Coll Alumni Assoc 1966-67; mem Alpha Phi Alpha. **HONORS/ACHIEVEMENTS:** Listed in Who's Who Among Students in Amer Coll & Univ 1957-58; Meritorious Serv Awd MD State Conf of Br NAACP 1973. **MILITARY SERVICE:** AUS 1st lt 1963-64.

BLACK, WENDELL C.
Business executive. **PERSONAL:** Born Jun 22, 1935, St Louis, MO. **EDUCATION:** Los Angeles City Coll, AA 1955; CA State Univ, BA 1961; Univ of CA, Grad Courses. **CAREER:** US Post Office, mail clerk 1958-59; Los Angeles Sheriff Dept, book clerk 1959-61; Los Angeles County Probation Dept, deputy probation officer 1961-68; RCA Serv Co, sr guidance counselor 1968-70, admin of comm relations corp staff 1970-72; Urban Strategy Center Chamber of Commerce of US, assoc dir 1972-. **ORGANIZATIONS:** Reg chmn Natl Urban Affairs Council 1972; mem Corp Urban Affairs Adv Com Natl Urban Coaliton 1972; mem Kappa Alpha Psi. **HONORS/ACHIEVEMENTS:** Author "Resource Coord" Jrnl Amer C of C Exec Mag 1974. **MILITARY SERVICE:** USAF 1955-58. **BUSINESS ADDRESS:** Associate Dir, Urban Strategy Center Chamber of Commerce, 1615 H St NW, Washington, DC 20062.

BLACK, WILLA
Businesswoman. **PERSONAL:** Born Jul 11, 1915, Cheraw, SC; married Luke; children: Margaret Buchan, Carolyn Smith, Carolyn Black. **CAREER:** Billies' Wholesale Distr, pres, owner 1946-. **ORGANIZATIONS:** Dist org Negro Bus & Professional Womens Club Inc; adv 4-H Club; mem Urban League, NAACP, Natl Council of Negro Women Inc. **HONORS/ACHIEVEMENTS:** Jobber of the Year OH Beautician Assoc 1957; Bus Woman of the Year Iota Phi Lambda 1967; N Central Gov Awd Negro Bus & Professional Women Club 1973; Ollie Porter Gold Awd (nat high awd) Negro Bus & Professional Women Club 1973; Spec Apprec Awd Youngstown Negro Bus & Professional Women Clubs Inc 1974; Youngstown Black Bus Women 1976. **BUSINESS ADDRESS:** President, Billie's Wholesale Distr, 533 W LaClede Ave, Youngstown, OH 44511.

BLACKBURN, ALBERTA
Government executive. **PERSONAL:** Born Apr 02, 1924, West Point, GA; married Edward Clinton; children: Mrs Vernyce Marvyne Jenrette, Edward Luther. **CAREER:** BB's Public Relations Agency, owner 1969; So Schaefer Nghbrhd City Hall, mgr, asst to Mayor Young serv & complaint dept. **ORGANIZATIONS:** Comm, bd of ed Urban League Guild; rel bd 12 Precinct Police Comm; rep Dem Black Caucus; mem Baptist Pastors Council, Girl Scouts of Amer; den motherBoy Scouts of Amer; pub rel dir, mem Gr New Mt Moriah Bapt Church; 25 yr vol March of Dimes; womens com Fashion Extravaganza; sr mother Lady Camille's Jr Temple; mem IBOPE of W; mem Gamma Phi Delta; chmn prog Baptist Con; del, bd mem Bus & Professional Women; assoc Municipal Professional Women; mem League of Women Voters; precinct del Wilberforce Alumni; mem pr coord, founding mem Women's Conf of Concerns; comm coord Natl Assoc of Media Women; mem Mother Waddles Perpetual Mission; bd of ed reg 5, housing bd, bd mem Kirwood Kosp Mental Health; dist Block Club Coord. **HONORS/ACHIEVEMENTS:** Outstanding Serv to Youth White Hous & John F Kennedy 1963; Outstanding Contribs to Detroit named Unsung Heroine of the Oustanding Civic, Community, Religious & Polit Contrib to Detroit Natl Grand Temple of Elks 1975; Intl Grandmohter of the Year 1979. **BUSINESS ADDRESS:** Asstto Mayor Coleman Young, City of Detroit/City Hall, 308 City County Bldg, Detroit, MI 48226.

BLACKBURN, BENJAMIN ALLAN, II
Prosthodontist. **PERSONAL:** Born Jun 10, 1940, Jackson, MS; married Sara Driver; children: Kellye, Benjamin III, Leigh. **EDUCATION:** Morehouse Coll, BS 1961; Meharry Med Coll, DDS 1965; Sydenham Hosp, intern 1966; NY Univ, Cert Prosthodontics 1968.

CAREER: Private practice, prosthodontist. **ORGANIZATIONS:** Fellow Amer Coll of Prosthdontist; mem Amer Prosthodontist Soc, SE Acad of Prosthodontist, Kappa Alpha Psi, NAACP, Urban League; diplomate Amer Bd Prosthodontists. **HONORS/ACHIEVEMENTS:** Hon Fellow GA Dental Assoc. **MILITARY SERVICE:** AUS Dental Reserve maj. **BUSINESS ADDRESS:** 75 Piedmont Ave NE, Atlanta, GA 30303.

BLACKBURN, CHARLES M.
Business executive. **PERSONAL:** Born Nov 04, 1937; married Mary L; children: Charles M III. **EDUCATION:** AL A&M Univ, 1960. **CAREER:** Capitol Vending Washington, mgr auto mach div 1960-61; Aprl Specialty Co Beltsville MD, counter div mgr 1964-68; Sigma System Inc MD, pres 1968-. **ORGANIZATIONS:** Mem Natl Fed of Independent Bus, Natl Assoc of Black Mfgs Inc, Alpha Gamma Mu Hon Soc. **MILITARY SERVICE:** Military 1961-64. **BUSINESS ADDRESS:** President, Sigma System Inc, 231 Westhampton Pl, Capitol Heights, MD 20743.

BLACKMAN, ROLANDO
Professional athlete. **PERSONAL:** Born Feb 26, 1959, Panama City, Panama; married Tamara; children: Valarie, Brittany, Briana. **EDUCATION:** Kansas St, majored in Marketing and Soc 1981. **CAREER:** Dallas Mavericks, guard 1981. **ORGANIZATIONS:** Community: Dallas Independent School District; Big Brothers and Big Sisters; Special Olympics; Muscular Dystrophy Assn; Children's Medical Center of Dallas; Just Say No Foundation; Summer Basketball Camp for youths. **HONORS/ACHIEVEMENTS:** Second All-time Leading Scorer-Dallas Mavericks; 3 Time NBA All-star; Most Popular Maverick Basketball Player; Team Captain; Bi-weekly Radio Show in Dallas; Olympic Team Member, mens basketball 1980; Pro Athlete of the Year 1986-87; 46 points 20 of 21 Fts (club records for makes and attemps) on 1/5/83 vs San Antonio in Reunion, scored 22 in the first Quarter. **BUSINESS ADDRESS:** Dallas Mavericks, Reunion Arena, 777 Sports St, Dallas, TX 75207.

BLACKMON, ANTHONY WAYNE
Business executive. **PERSONAL:** Born Feb 13, 1957, Newark, NJ; children: Terry. **EDUCATION:** Cornell Univ, NY SSILR, BS 1979. **CAREER:** WTKO Ithaca NY, broadcaster 1976-79; Meadowlands Sports Complex NJ, asst dir matrix opers 1976-79; Hollywood Park Racetrack, dir matrix oper 1979-; Blackmon Enterprises, pres, consult 1981-. **ORGANIZATIONS:** Mem Urban League, NAACP, Black Businessmans Assoc of LA, LA Better Bus Arbitrator. **HONORS/ACHIEVEMENTS:** Youngest & only black dir Matrix Oper Hollywood Park Racetrack. **BUSINESS ADDRESS:** President, Blackmon Enterprises, PO Box 1175, Inglewood, CA 90308.

BLACKMON, EDWARD, JR.
Attorney. **PERSONAL:** Born Jul 21, 1947, Canton, MS. **EDUCATION:** Tougaloo Coll, BA Political Sci 1967-70; George Washington Univ, Juris Doctorate 1970-73. **CAREER:** N MS Rural Legal Serv, staff atty 1973-74; Blackmon & Smith, partner 1974-. **ORGANIZATIONS:** State rep MS House of Rep 1979, 1984-; pres Magnolia Bar Assn 1984-; bd mem Natl Bar Assn 1984-. **BUSINESS ADDRESS:** Attorney, Blackmon & Smith, P O drawer 568, 232 W Peace St, Canton, MS 39046.

BLACKMON, MOSETTA WHITAKER
Corporation executive. **PERSONAL:** Born Jan 02, 1950, Homestead, PA; daughter of Garvis Whitaker and Elgurtha Spruill Whitaker; married Michael George Blackmon, Oct 19, 1975; children: Jason B., Jacqueline Renee, Jenelle Laraine. **EDUCATION:** University of Pittsburgh, Pittsburgh, PA, BA, 1970; American University, Washington, DC, MS, 1986. **CAREER:** Comsat Corp, Washington, DC, job analyst, 1974-76, employment manager, 1977-79; Marriott Corp, Bethesda, MD, senior compensation analyst, 1979-80; Mitre Corp, McLean, VA, employment manager, 1980—. **ORGANIZATIONS:** Member, American Compensation Association, 1975—; member, Washington Technical Personnel Forum, 1975—; member, Prince Georges Couty PTA, 1986—; member, board of advisors, US Black Engineer Magazine, 1988—; member, Black Human Resources Professionals, 1988—; Alpha Kappa Alpha. **HONORS/ACHIEVEMENTS:** Certified compensation professional, American Compensation Association, 1983; Outstanding Recruiter, Career Communications Group, 1988. **BUSINESS ADDRESS:** Manager of Employment and Employee Services, MITRE Corporation, 7525 Colshire Dr, McLean, VA 22102.

BLACKSHEAR, JULIAN W., JR.
Attorney. **PERSONAL:** Born Jul 09, 1941, Chattanooga, TN; married Margaret Ann; children: Jeffrey. **EDUCATION:** Morehouse Coll, BA 1963; Univ of TN Coll of Law, JD 1970. **CAREER:** NAACP Legal Defense & Ed Fund NY, coop civil rights attny 1970-; State Sen Avon N Williams Jr NASHVILLE TN, attny in gen prac law 1970-74; Petway Blackshear Hagwood & Thompson Law Firm, attny. **ORGANIZATIONS:** Mem Natl Bar Assoc, Amer Bar Assoc, Amer Trial Lawyers Assoc, TN Trial Lawyers Assoc, Delta Theta Phi, Natl Legal Aid & Defender Assoc; bd mem Nashville Urban League, Grace Eaton Day Care Ctr; supt Sunday School, John Calvin Presbyterian Church; sec Tau lambda. **HONORS/ACHIEVEMENTS:** Listed in Outstanding Young Amers 1974, Outstanding Amer of Southeast 1974; Individual Appellate Arguement Awd Univ of TN Coll of Law 1970; Outstanding Achievement Awd Freedom Found Valley Forge 1968; Individual Moot Ct Competition Awd Univ of TC Coll of Law 1970. **MILITARY SERVICE:** USAF sgt 1965-68. **BUSINESS ADDRESS:** Attorney, Petway, Blackshear, Hagwood, & Thompson Law Firm, Ste 1118 Parkway Towers, Nashville, TN 37219.

BLACKSHEAR, WILLIAM
Businessman. **PERSONAL:** Born Jun 01, 1935, Marianna, FL; married Betty Jean Booze; children: Bruce, Angelia, Edwina, Jeffery, Jacquline, Sylvia. **EDUCATION:** State of FL, Educ Cert 1963; Gen Elec Employ Educ, 1969. **CAREER:** Gen Elec Co, 1958-70; Wkly Challenger News, 1968-; Black Gold Inc, mgr. **ORGANIZATIONS:** Mem consult Black Media Inc; VAC; C of C; Black Gold of FL Inc; scout ldr 1950-53; pres PTA 1960-63; pres Home Improvement Commn 1961-67; pres HOPE 1965-67; pres Lincoln Nursery Assn 1961-67; elec city commn (1st black); pres SE Black Pub Assn Inc 1968; v chmn OIC of Suncoast; adv Youth of Amer NAACP; Urban League; Unity Temple Ch; Dem FL. **HONORS/ACHIEVEMENTS:** Citation Gen Elec Stud Guid Prog 1970; Citation Outstanding Efforts for Human Rights Ridgcrest Improv Assn 1966; Outstanding Comm Serv The Le Cercle Des Jeunes Femmes 1965; Key to City Pensacola FL 1969; Key to City Ft Lauderdale 1977.

MILITARY SERVICE: AUS staff sgt 1955-62. **BUSINESS ADDRESS:** Manager, Black Gold Inc, 2500 9th St S, St Petersburg, FL 33705.

BLACKWELL, ARTHUR BRENDHAL, III
County commissioner. **PERSONAL:** Born Jun 10, 1953, Detroit, MI; son of Robert Brendhal Blackwell and Florrie Love Willis Blackwell; married Zenobia Weaver, Oct 19, 1985; children: Mosii Mays Blackwell, Robert Brendhal Blackwell, II. **EDUCATION:** North Carolina A&T Univ, Greensboro, NC, BA, 1975. **CAREER:** Detroit Bank & Trust, Detroit, MI, asst branch mgr, 1978-79; 1980 Census, Detroit, MI, dir field oper, 1980; Wayne County Bd of Commr, Detroit, MI, commr, 1981-82, 1987-; Blackwell & Assoc, Detroit, MI, owner, 1983-86; Mayor Young's Re-election Campaign, Detroit, MI, headquarters coord, 1985-; Detroit Fire Dept, Detroit, MI, community admin coord, 1986-. **ORGANIZATIONS:** Chmn, Detroit/Wayne County Port Authority, 1988-; mem Natl Org of Black City Officials; Michigan Assn of County Officials, Detroit Windsor Port Corp, 1988-, mem First Congressional Dist Democratic Party; mem Michigan Democratic Party, City Resident Comm, The Young Alliance. **HONORS/ACHIEVEMENTS:** Father/Son Outstanding Achievement Award, Northern YMCA, 1981; Certificate of Appreciation, Wayne County Bd of Commr, 1982; Outstanding Performance for Oboe Solo in Quarter State Music Competition, 1969. **BUSINESS ADDRESS:** Wayne County Bd of Commr, 600 Randolph, Suite 450, Detroit, MI 48226.

BLACKWELL, DAVID HAROLD
Educator. **PERSONAL:** Born Apr 24, 1919, Centralia, IL; married Ann; children: 8 children. **EDUCATION:** Univ IL, AB 1938, AM 1938, PhD 1941; Honorary DSc, Univ of IL 1965, MI State Univ 1968, So IL Univ 1970. **CAREER:** Inst Advanced Study Princeton Univ, Post-doctoral Fellow 1941-42; Southern Univ, instructor 1942-43; Clark Coll, instructor 1943-44; Howard Univ, asst prof 1944-54, chmn dept statistics 1957-61; Univ of CA Berkeley, prof statistics 1954-. **ORGANIZATIONS:** Pres Inst Math Stat 1955, AAAS, Amer Math Soc; Rosenwald Fellow Inst Advanced Study Princeton Univ 1941-42; rsch fellow Brown Univ 1943; fellow InstMath Statistics 1947; mem Natl Acad Sci 1965; faculty rsch lecturer Univ of CA 1971. **BUSINESS ADDRESS:** Professor Statistics, Univ of California, Berkeley, CA 94720.

BLACKWELL, FAIGER MEGREA
Education administrator. **PERSONAL:** Born Dec 14, 1955, Reidsville, NC; divorced; children: Alexdria. **EDUCATION:** Winston-Salem State, 1974-76; UNC Chapel Hill, BS. **CAREER:** Jones Cross Baptist Church, chmn, trustee 1975-; NC Long Term Care Facilities, vice pres 1976-; Caswell NAACP; Caswell Cty Voters League, pres 1976; Caswell NAACP, bd mem 1978-. **ORGANIZATIONS:** Founder Blackwell Bros Florist 1974-; pres Blackwell Rest Home Inc 1976-; bd mem Wiz 4-H Club 1979-, Caswell Cty Planning Bd 1980-; pres Dogwood Forest Rest Home Inc 1980-. **HONORS/ACHIEVEMENTS:** Martin Luther King Jr Awd Caswell Sportsman Club; Leader of the Year NC Long Term Care; Outstanding Serv NC Long Term Care; Outstanding Serv Caswell Cty School Bd. **BUSINESS ADDRESS:** School Board Member, Caswell Co Pub Sch Dist, Rt 2 Box 218, Elon College, NC 27244.

BLACKWELL, FAYE BROWN
Educator, government official. **PERSONAL:** Born May 10, 1942, Monroe, LA; married Fred Blackwell. **EDUCATION:** Southern Univ, BA 1964. **CAREER:** Calcasiew Fed of Teachers 1978-82; Coalition for Comm Prog, pres of bd of dir 1983-85; Calcasiew Dem Assoc, pres 1984-85; Lake Charles City Council, vice pres 1984-85; Lake Charles City Council, council mem dist A. **ORGANIZATIONS:** Owner, oper Faye Brown Rental Inc 1968-85; pres Brown Enterprises P Monse LA 1978-85; sec Independent Invert Corp 1980-85; mem Women League of Voters, NAACP, Top Ladies of Distinction, Natl Assoc of Univ Women. **HONORS/ACHIEVEMENTS:** Community Serv Zeta Sor; Ed Exal Natl Assn for Univ Women; Woman of the Year, Martin L King Found, Los Angeles Municipal, School Los Angeles Municipal Assn. **BUSINESS ADDRESS:** Council Member, Lake Charles City Council, Lake Charles, LA 70601.

BLACKWELL, HARVEL E.
Educator. **PERSONAL:** Born Sep 25, 1937, Hulbert, OK; children: Carmella C, Howard E. **EDUCATION:** Compton Coll, AA 1959; CA State Univ Of Los Angeles, BA 1961; Univ of Southern CA, MS 1963, PhD 1968. **CAREER:** Southern Assoc of Coll & School, consultant 1970-; JSC NASA Lockhead Corp & Others, consultant 1975-; K-RAM Corp, bd of dir 1980-84; BSAS Abstract Subj Realism & Potrait, artist; Texas Southern Univ, prof of Physics. **ORGANIZATIONS:** Consultant Inst for Serv to Educ 1970-75; proposal review Nat Sci Found; visiting prof Lovanium U; bd of dir United Cerebal Palsy Gulf Coast 1978-80; mem Nat Tech Assoc; mem Nat Society of Black Physicists. **HONORS/ACHIEVEMENTS:** Grants Nat Sci Found & NASA; monographs Introd to Orbital Flight Planning, Lectures in The Natural Sci; articles Enter the Underprepared, to VUV as a Probe of Rare Gas Plasmas.

BLACKWELL, J. KENNETH
Educator. **PERSONAL:** Born Feb 28, 1948, Cincinnati, OH; married Rosa E; children: K Anika, Rahshann K, Kristin S. **EDUCATION:** Xavier Univ, BS 1970, MEd 1971, MBA 20 hrs; Harvard Univ, Prog for Sr Execs in State and Local Govts 1981. **CAREER:** Cincinnati Bd of Ed, teacher, coach 1971; Model Cities for Comm School Assoc, ed & consult 1973; Afro-Amer Studies Univ of Cincinnati, teacher; Xavier Univ Univ & Urban Affairs, instr, dir; Cincinnati City Council, mem 1977-; Community Relations, assoc vice pres 1980-; City of Cincinnati, vice mayor 1977-78, mayor 1979-80, vice mayor 1985-87. **ORGANIZATIONS:** Chmn Local Legislators Comm 1978-79; vchmn Transportation Comm 1979-80; mem Cable TV Task Force; mem Intl Econ Devel Task Force; steering comm Commission on Cities in the 1980's; co-chmn Labor Relations Adv Comm Natl League of Cities; mem, bd trust Public Tech Inc; state & local govt bd of advisors John F Kennedy School of Govt Harvard Univ; adv comm Amer Council of Young Political leaders; mem Jerusalem Comm; bd mem Natl Leg Conf on Arson; mem Rotary Intl, Cincinnati Fine Arts, Inst Bd, Cincinnati Opera, trustee Birthright of Cincinnati Inc; bd mem Gr Cincinnati Coalition of People with Disabilities. **HONORS/ACHIEVEMENTS:** Listed in Who's Who in Amer Coll 1970; Hon JD Wilberforce Univ 1980; HUD Public Leadership Fellow Harvard Univ 1981; Gordon Chase Meml Fellow Harvard Univ 1981. **BUSINESS ADDRESS:** Vice Mayor, City of Cincinnati, Room 3486 City Hall, Cincinnati, OH 45202.

BLACKWELL, JAMES E.
Professor. **PERSONAL:** Born Mar 04, 1926, Anniston, AL; married Myrtle Dapremont. **EDUCATION:** Attended Wilberforce Univ 1943-44; Western Reserve Univ, BS 1948, MA 1949; WA State Univ, PhD 1959. **CAREER:** Benedict Coll, instructor Biology, 1949-51; Shorter Coll, instructor Biology, 1951-52; Grambling State Coll, asst prof Social Science, Biology, 1952-55; WA State Univ, teaching fellow, acting instructor Sociology, 1955-59; San Jose State Coll, asst to assoc prof Sociology, 1959-63; Peace Corps, US fgn grd serv officer, 1963-69; US Peace Corps Tanzania, acting dir, 1963-64; US Peace Corps Malawi, dir, 1964-65; Univ of WI Milwaukee Center for Peace Corps Training & Rsch, dir, 1965-66; US Foreign Serv, res officer/nepal, 1966-69; Case Western Reserve Univ, assoc prof Sociology, 1969-70; Univ of MA, prof chmn Sociology, 1970-75; Univ of MA Boston, prof of Sociology, 1975-. **ORGANIZATIONS:** Pres Beta of WA Chap Alpha Kappa Delta 1956-57; pres Assn Grad Students of WA State Univ 1957-58; opp fellow John Hay Whitney Found 1958-59; pres SanJose NAACP 1962-63; comm chmn ASA SSSP & Eastern Sociological Soc 1961-63, 1969-; natl exec sec Soc for Study of Social Problems 1962-63; council mem Amer Sociological Assn 1970-71; pres Caucus of Black Sociologists 1970-72; consul So Educ Found 1973-; mem Rsch Comm Coll Entrance Exam Bd 1976-; mwm Heynl Blue Ribbon Panel on Higher Educ Desegregation 1977-; pres Soc for the Study of Social Problems 1980-81; mem Panel on Minority Concerns College Bd1980-84; pres Eastern Sociological Soc 1981-82; elected mem Sociological Rsch Assn 1984; mem NAACP, Urban League, Omega Psi Phi Frat, Amer Soc Assn, Caucus of Black Sociologists, Soc for Study of Social Problems, MA Sociological Soc, Eastern Sociol Soc. **HONORS/ACHIEVEMENTS:** Motion pictures &TV docum, "A Century After Emancipation" script-writer prod 1963; "The Peace Corps in Malawi" 1965; Outstanding Educator of Amer 1972; Danforth Found Asso 1974-; author "Comm Devel Focus" 1970; "The Black Comm, Diversity & Unity" 1975; "The Black Community, Diversity & Unity" 1975,85 "Black Coll as a Natural Resource" 1976; "The Participation of Black Students In Grad & Prof Schs" 1977; Spivak Awd Amer Sociological Assn 1979; Disting Scholarship Awd of the Univ of MA/Boston 1981; author Mainstreaming Outsiders, The Production of Black Professionals 1981,87; author Networking and Mentoring, A Cross-Generational Study of Black Experiences 1983, Cities Suburbs and Blacks (with Philip Hart) 1983; Outstanding Achievement Awd of the Univ of MA/Boston 1984; Alpha Kappa Delta Natl Honor in Sociology; Blue Key Natl Men's Hon; Chancellor's Medal Univ MA Boston 1986; DuBois-Johnson-Frazier Awd of Amer Soc Assn 1986; Benjamin E Mays Awd for Disting Scholarship Metro Boston YMCA Black Achievers 1987; 100 Influential Blacks in Boston 1987. **BUSINESS ADDRESS:** Professor of Sociology, Univ of MA at Boston, Boston, MA 02125.

BLACKWELL, LUCIEN E.
Legislator. **PERSONAL:** Born Aug 01, 1931, Whitset, PA; married Jannie; children: 4 children. **EDUCATION:** St Josephs Coll, attended. **CAREER:** Intl Longshoremens Assoc Local 1332, bus agt; PA House of Reps 188 Dist, former mem; Dist 3 City of Philadelphia, councilmember. **ORGANIZATIONS:** Mem Port Coord Council of Port Coord Council of Philadelphia, Dist Council Port of Philadelphia; committeeman, chmn labor comm 46th Ward; instr Supreme Council of Cadets of Amer; org Neighborhood Youth Council; mem Pyramid Temple No 1, Demolay Consistory No 1. **HONORS/ACHIEVEMENTS:** Won novice diamond belt championship as amateur boxer 1949; Light Middleweight Title of AUS 25th Infantry Div Korea 1953. **MILITARY SERVICE:** AUS. **BUSINESS ADDRESS:** Councilmember, City of Philadelphia Dist 3, 235 S Melville St, Philadelphia, PA 19139.

BLACKWELL, MILFORD
Neurologist. **PERSONAL:** Born Apr 02, 1921, Chicago, IL; divorced; children: Peter. **EDUCATION:** So IL Univ, BE 1943; Meharry Med Coll, MD 1948. **CAREER:** Harlem Hospital NYC, rotating intern, 1948-49; VA Hospital, Tuskegee AL, resident, 1949-50; Cushing VA Hospital, Framingham MA, resident, 1950-51; VA Hospital, Newington CT, resident, 1951-52; IN Univ Medical Center Indianapolis, resident, 1952-53; Natl Hospital, London England, resident, 1954, 1956-57; Bellevue Hospital NYC, clinical assoc visiting neurologist; Harlem Hospital NYC, assoc visiting psych; Sydenham Hosp NYC, assoc visiting neuropsych; Knickerbocker Bracie Sq Hospital NYC, courtesy staff; New York City Speech Rehabilitation Inst, Spencer-Chapin Adoptin Serv NYC, McMahon Memorial Shelter NYC, staff mem; NY Univ Med Coll, clinical instructor neurology, 1960-. **ORGANIZATIONS:** Consult neurologist Sydenham Hosp, Ken Garden Hosp NY, NY Foundling Hosp, Edwin Gould Found for Children; consult child psych Soc for Seaman's Children SI Foster Home Care Unit New York City Dept Social Svc; consult psych & neurology NY State Athletic Comm; panel psych NY State Dept Social Svc; comm Blind Vocational Rehab Serv Bur; disability determinations NY State Dept Social Svc; diplomate in psych, neurology, neurology with spec competence in child neurology Amer Bd Psych & Neurology; mem AMA, Amer Psych Assoc, Amer Epilepsy Soc, Amer Inst Hypnosis, NY State, NY Cty Med Soc; pres Neurol Disease Found 1966-. **MILITARY SERVICE:** USAF capt 1954-56. **BUSINESS ADDRESS:** 828 Hempstone Turnpike, Franklin Square, NY 11010.

BLACKWELL, NOBLE VIRGIL
Broadcast consultant. **PERSONAL:** Born Apr 19, 1934, Nashville, TN; married Katie Yvonne Betts; children: Michael Barry, Tracye Dionne, Sharnoa Renee, Wendy Valencia. **EDUCATION:** TN State A&I, 1952-54; Univ of TN, Certificate Small Business Admin 1962-63; Univ of MD Ext, Broadcast Mgmt Certificate 1979. **CAREER:** Night Train, host and exec producer 1963-65; Meharry Medical Univ, natl dir alumni affairs 1966-68; WVOL Radio Nashville, vice pres gen 1968-72; WCAU PU Philadelphia PA, dir of broadcasting 1972-75; CTS CBS, natl dir comm relations 1975-77; CBS Inc, dir corporate staff serv 1977-78; Radio Station WNJR Newark, vice pres gen mgr 1978-81; Marketing Concepts Inc, chmn of bd select; Lifestyle Productions Inc, pres & general mgr; consultant exec, NBN II, 1988-present. **ORGANIZATIONS:** Mem Founder of Minority Committee PRSA NY 1976-; mem Broadcast Pioneers 1973-; mem PTA Park Ridge High School 1975-; mem Northeast Advisory Club 1981-; mem Chamber of Commerce Scranton 1981-; deacon Mt Zion Baptist Church 1981-; bd of dirs Keystone Jr Coll; Intl Radio & TV Soc Inc; Public Relations Soc of Amer; Natl Assn of Black Owned Broadcast Operations. **HONORS/ACHIEVEMENTS:** Man of Year 1972 Natl Radio & TV Annc Assn 1972; Carbondale Pioneer Days Committee 1982; Pour Chaplius Legion of Honor Chapel of Poor Chaplius Philadelphia PA 1975; Neighborhood Crusades Inc 1973; NATRA Citation for Excellence in Broadcast Mgmt, Miami; Appreciation Award Community Serv Donelson Hermitage Jaycee's, Nashville, TN; TN State Univ, News Media Award; Black Associated Sports Enterprise, Sports Media Award, Philadelphia; Certificate of Appreciation, Natl Assn of Black Social Workers; Certificate of Merit & Appreciation, Military Dept; Nashville Broadcasters Award, Community Serv; Natl Television & Radio Announcers, Man of the Year Award; Appreciation of Community Serv, Neighborhood Youth Crusade; Appreciation of Serv, Meharry Med Coll; Four Chapel Legion of Honor Membership Award; Fund Raisers of Middle TN, Certificate of Serv Award; WVOL Radio Station, Community Serv Award; Carbondale Pioneer Days Valuable & Continued Support Award; Appreciation Award Sponsoring Radiothon for Tony Gabriel Surgical Fund; March of Dimes Birth Defects Found; The Congressional Record Award. **MILITARY SERVICE:** AUS spec 3 1956-69; SACOM special serv award; 11th airborne band award; European tour Germany citation 1956-59. **HOME ADDRESS:** 234 Vittorio Ct, Park Ridge, NJ 07656. **BUSINESS ADDRESS:** President/General Manager, Lifestyle Productions Inc, 127 Salem Rd, Carbondale, PA 18407.

BLACKWELL, PATRICIA A.
Business executive. **PERSONAL:** Born Aug 07, 1943, Metropolis, IL. **EDUCATION:** Southern Illinois Univ-Carbondale, 1962-65; Southern Illinois Univ-Edwardsville, 1966-67; Howard Univ Small Business Development Center, 1983-84. **CAREER:** Natl Urban League, WA Bureau, administrative asst 1971-72; John Dingle Associates, Inc, Washington rep/lobbyist 1972-73; EH White and Company, Inc, director, east coast operations 1973-74; Unified Industries Incorporated, program manager 1974-84; PA Blackwell & Associates, Inc, president 1984-. **ORGANIZATIONS:** Consultant DC Democratic Committee 1974; vice-president SIMBA Associates, Inc-Fund Raiser 1978-80; board member Regional Purchasing Council of VA 1978-; member Natl Conference of Minority Transportation Officials 1983-; member Natl Forum for Black Public Administrators 1984-; member Natl Assn of Female Executives 1984-; tutor Operation Rescue-Washington Urban League 1984-; mem Women's Transportation Seminar 1987; mem Natl Coalition of Black Meeting Planners. **HONORS/ACHIEVEMENTS:** Citation of Recognition Governor's Office-State of VA 1978; Certificate of Appreciation Virginia State Office of Minority Business Enterprise 1979; nominated Outstanding Young Women of America 1984. **HOME ADDRESS:** 1211 N Wall St, Carbondale, IL 62901-1740. **BUSINESS ADDRESS:** President, PA Blackwell & Assoc, Inc, 4700 King St Ste 300, Alexandria, VA 22302.

BLACKWELL, RANDOLPH TALMADGE
Administrative executive. **PERSONAL:** Born Mar 10, 1927, Greensboro, NC; married Elizabeth Knox; children: Blanche. **EDUCATION:** North Carolina Univ, BS Sociology 1949; Howard Univ, JD 1953; Amer Univ, Grad Study; Syracuse Univ, Grad Study. **CAREER:** Winston-Salem Teacher Coll NC, assoc prof of social sci 1953-54; AL A&M Coll Huntsville, assoc prof of econ 1954-63; Voter Ed Proj Inc Atlanta, field dir 1963-65; SCLC Atlanta, prog dir 1964-66; So Rural Action Atlanta, dir 1966-76; OMBE Wash DC, dir 1977-79; Ofc of Minority Enterprise Prog Devel Dept of Commerce, dir 1979-. **ORGANIZATIONS:** Lecturer MIT, Fed Exec Inst, Urban Training Ctr for Christian Mission Chgo; partic 3 White House Conf & 2 Natl Task Forces 1964; bd mem So Growth Policy 1965, Martin Luther King Jr Ctr for Social Change. **HONORS/ACHIEVEMENTS:** Cert of Merit HEW Dept of Commerce Dept of Labor 1973; Peace Prize Martin Luther King Jr Ctr for Social Change 1976; Equal Justice Awd Natl Bar Assoc 1978; Man of the Year Awd Natl Assoc of Minority CPA Forms 1978. **MILITARY SERVICE:** AUS pvt 1st class 1944-45. **BUSINESS ADDRESS:** Dir, Dept of Commerce, 275 Peachtree St NE Ste 150, Atlanta, GA 30303.

BLACKWELL, ROBERT B.
Consultant. **PERSONAL:** Born Nov 04, 1924, Meridian, MS; son of Dr & Mrs A B Blackwell; married Florrie Love Willis; children: Brenda B Mims, June Blackwell-Hatcher, Arthur Blackwell, Bobbi Blackwell. **EDUCATION:** Howard Univ, BA 1949; Detroit Coll of Law, 1965-68. **CAREER:** UAW, AFL-CIO, pres, local 889, 1955-62; City of Highland Park, city police & fire commissioner, 1958-63; Michigan Labor Relations Bd, exec dir, 1962-67; City of Highland Park, city councilman, 1963-67, mayor, 1967-75; US Dept of labor, special assistant under secretary, 1975-76; US Aid, Senate Dept, consultant, 1976-78; City of Highland Park, mayor 1980-88. **ORGANIZATIONS:** life mem, NAACP, Urban League, Kappa Alpha Psi Fraternity, Guardsmen, Boys Club of Amer; trustee, US Conf of Mayors; bd of dirs, Natl League of cities; 1st vice pres, Natl Conf of Black Mayors; chmn, labor comm, Michigan Municipal League. **HONORS/ACHIEVEMENTS:** Alumni of the Year, Howard Univ; Man of the Year, Little Rock Baptist Church; founder & first sr chmn, Natl Black Caucus of Local Elected Officers. **MILITARY SERVICE:** AUS, master sgt, 1942-48; Purple Heart.

BLACKWOOD, RONALD A.
Councilman, mayor. **PERSONAL:** Born Jan 19, 1926, Kingston, Jamaica;married Ann; children: Helen Marie. **EDUCATION:** Kingston Tech Inc, 1944; Kingston Commercial Coll, 1946; Westchester Comm Coll, attended; Elizabeth Seton Coll, Grad; Iona Coll New Rochelle NY, BBAMgmt. **CAREER:** Mount Vernon, NY, mayor (first elected black mayor in New York State). **ORGANIZATIONS:** Dir Mt Vernon Hosp Bd; dir Mt Vernon YMCA, boys Club; mem NAACP. **BUSINESS ADDRESS:** Mayor, City of Mt Vernon, Roosevelt Square, Mount Vernon, NY 10552.

BLACQUE, TAUREAN
Actor. **PERSONAL:** Born in Newark, NJ; children: Shelby, Rodney. **EDUCATION:** Attended, amer Musical and Dramatic Acad. **CAREER:** Made Broadway debut in The River Niger; also appeared on We Interrupt This Program; appeared with various Negro Ensemble Co productions; guest appearances onTV shows includeTV miniseries Backstairs at the White House 1979, Hill St Blues 1981; appeared inTV film The $520 an Hour Dream 1980; also in movie HouseCalls.

BLAIR, CHARLES MICHAEL
Philanthropy administrator. **PERSONAL:** Born Aug 05, 1947, Indianapolis, IN; widowed; children: Michael A, Tchad K. **EDUCATION:** Oberlin Coll, AB Communications 1970; Kean Coll, MA Stdnt & Personnel Admin 1972. **CAREER:** Lilly Endowment Inc, program evaluator 1973, asso pgm officer 1975, pgm officer 1977, senior pgm officer 1981-; President & Owner, Grand Slam Inc and Interlace Marketing Inc 1986-; Sports, entertainment & Mgmt Consultants. **ORGANIZATIONS:** Chmn Assoc of Black Found Exec 1980-83; founder & bd mem Madame CJ Walker Bldg Restoration Project 1979-; consult Fund Raising to Numerous Organ 1977-;chmn bd Blair Communications Indep Prod 1979-; bd of dir Big Bro Big Sisters Intl 1982-; bd of dir & Founder Youth Works Inc 1979-; Bd of dir & founder Ind Black Expo Found 1984-; Founder and Vice Chairman Bussiness Opportunities Systems, Inc, Vice Chairman Flanner Hous Inc Founder & president Youth Works, Inc. **HONORS/ACHIEVEMENTS:** Martin Luther King Award North Ward Cntr Newark NJ 1982; producer writer 5 Stage Plays, Middle Passage, Songs for Creator 1979-; Honored Spec Advocate for Girls Girls Club of Am New York City 1979; Community Service Award Center for Lead-

ership Devel Indianapolis 1984; roastee Indianapolis Links 1983. **BUSINESS ADDRESS:** President, Grand Slam Inc& Interlace Mkt, 3843 N Meridian, Indianapolis, IN 46208.

BLAIR, CHESTER LAUGHTON ELLISON
Attorney. **PERSONAL:** Born Jul 02, 1928, Corsicana, TX; married Judith K; children: Gregory, Bradford, Jefferson, Jan, Brent, Judy-Lee. **EDUCATION:** Chicago Teachers Coll, BEd 1952; John Marshall Law School, JD 1959. **CAREER:** Chicago Publ School, teacher 1952-54,56-59; Private practice, 1959-77; 7th congress Dist of IL, leg counselor 1974-; Chester L Blair Chtd, managing partner 1974-. **ORGANIZATIONS:** Mem bd of dir Metro Funeral Parlors; dir Joy Enterp Inc; mem Attys Reg & Discipl Comm of IL Rev Bd; real estate broker 1964,77; gen council, regagt Friendship Med Ctr 1976-77; pres Gr Lawndale Conserv Comm 1965-66; mem Kappa Alpha Psi; pres W Sub Br NAACP 1967; legal council 24th Ward Dem Org 1960-77; bd dir Ancona School Soc 1973-77; pres 1977, second vice pres Cook Cty Bar Assoc; mem Art Inst of Chgo; second vice pres Cook County Bar Assoc. **HONORS/ACHIEVEMENTS:** Black Awareness Awd Coll of St Thomas Min Prog 1977. **MILITARY SERVICE:** AUS spec 1st class 1954-56. **BUSINESS ADDRESS:** 122 S Michigan Ave, #1260, Chicago, IL 60603.

BLAIR, GEORGE ELLIS
Educator. **PERSONAL:** Born May 05, 1932, Braddock, PA; married Ann Schumieglow; children: Cheryl Ann, Stephanie Rene. **EDUCATION:** IN Univ, BA 1954; Adelphi Univ, MA 1959; St Johns Univ, PhD 1966; King Meml Coll, DHL; Church of Gospel Ministry, DD. **CAREER:** NY State Dept of Educ, asst dir, 1966-67, special asst to commiss of educ, 1967-68; NY Univ, visiting prof, 1968-69; NY State Dept of Educ, dir, 1968-69; Long Island Univ, vice pres, 1969-70; Teachers Coll, visiting prof, 1970-71; Human Affairs Rsch Center, pres, 1970-72; NY State Univ, dir, 1972-75, asst vice chancellor 1975-77, asst chancellor 1977-. **ORGANIZATIONS:** Mem amer Personnel Guidance Assoc, NY State Teachers Assoc, NEA, Amer Assoc for Publ Admin, NY State Acad of Public Ed, NY State Personnel Guidance Assoc; chmn NY State Ed Oppty Ctrs; mem bd trustee King Meml Coll; mem bd dir Ed Systems Inc, Friends of Addicts Rehab Ctr; mem NY State Senate Higher Ed Adv Comm; mem Cornell Inst for Occupational Ed Adv Com; Oppty Com, Natl Ministerial Alliance, Intl Ministerial Alliance; mem NY State Commiss of Ed Expanding Higher Ed Oppty Comm; arbitrator US Workers of Amer; ordained minister Amer Interdenominational Fellowship. **MILITARY SERVICE:** AUS 1st lt 1954-56. **BUSINESS ADDRESS:** Exec Asst to the Chancellor, StateUniv of New York, 60 East 42nd St, Ste 3025, New York, NY 10165.

BLAIR, JAMES H.
Business executive. **PERSONAL:** Born Oct 06, 1926, Pittsburgh, PA; married Murleen M; children: Keith J, Steven M. **EDUCATION:** Univ of Pittsburgh, BA 1950; Rutgers Univ, MA 1971, Doctoral Candidate 1971-72. **CAREER:** Essex Cty Probation Dept Newark NJ, sr probation officer 1953-64; United Comm Corp, comm action dir 1965-66, prog dir 1966-67; Ofc of Tech Asst Dept of Comm Affairs Trenton NJ, dir 1967-69; NJ Div on Civil Rights Newark, dir 1968; JH Blair Assoc, pres 1977-; Fair Housing Equal Oppty Dept of Housing & Urban Devel Wash DC, asst sec; MI Dept of Civil Rights, exec dir; MI Comm on Criminal Justice, commiss 1972-. **ORGANIZATIONS:** Mme bd dir NJ State C of C 1972-74; chmn Intl Assoc of Ofcl Human Rights Agys 1970-71; commiss NJ State Prof Occup License Study Comm 1970-71; mem State Adv Council Inst of Mgmt & Labor Rel Rutgers Univ 1969-73; mem bd dir Montclair NJ YMCA 1960-64,69-72; mem Gov Council on Urban Affairs NJ 1968-69; mem Kappa Alpha Psi 1947-, Frontiers Intl 1966-, NAACP. **HONORS/ACHIEVEMENTS:** Humanitarian Awd Montclair Br 1973; Outstanding Contribs Awd 1975 MI Civil Rights Comm; Kappa Alpha Psi Achievement Awd 1969. **MILITARY SERVICE:** USAAC 1944-47. **BUSINESS ADDRESS:** Commissioner, MI Commiss on Criminal Justice, 3625 Stonewall Court, Atlanta, GA 30339.

BLAIR, LACY GORDON
Physician. **PERSONAL:** Born Oct 10, 1937, Lynchburg, VA. **EDUCATION:** Hampton Inst, BS 1959; Meharry Med Coll, MD 1969. **CAREER:** Military Svc, lab tech 1961-64; Private practice, physician. **ORGANIZATIONS:** Writer, intl traveler; interested in Ethiopia's History and The Hebrews.

BLAIZE, MAVIS See THOMPSON, MAVIS SARAH

BLAKE, ALPHONSO R.
Clergyman. **PERSONAL:** Born Apr 23, 1935, Charleston, SC; married Doris Jackson; children: Sybil Renee, Alphonso Jr. **EDUCATION:** Amer Bapt Theol Sem, BA 1961. **CAREER:** WPAZ Radio, religious dir; Concentrated Employment Prog, counselor; Westwood Bapt Church Nashville, pastor; Morris St Baptist Church, pastor. **ORGANIZATIONS:** Pres Bapt Ministers Conf Charles Co; past pres, treas Charles Cty SS&BTU Congress; chmn exec com Charles Cty Bapt Assoc; past pres Charles Cty NAACP; trustee Charleston Cty School Dist, Morris Coll, Sumpter SC; chaplain Charleston Cty Jail. **HONORS/ACHIEVEMENTS:** NAACP Outstanding Freedom Fighter Citation; Omega Psi Phi Frat Scroll of Honor; Charles Cty Adult Ed Prog Citation. **MILITARY SERVICE:** AUS 1954-56. **BUSINESS ADDRESS:** Pastor, Morris St Baptist Church, Charleston, SC 29403.

BLAKE, CARLTON HUGH
Physician psychiatrist. **PERSONAL:** Born Apr 11, 1934, San Fernando, Trinidad and Tobago;son of Fitzevans Blake and Thelma Marshall Carty; married Carmelita, Oct 16, 1976; children: David. **EDUCATION:** Fatima Coll, Sr Cambridge Cert Grade 1; Queens Univ, MB, BCh, BaO 1960; NY School of Psychiatry, Cert Psych 1964. **CAREER:** Albert Einstein Coll, asst clinical prof 1969-71; Sound View-Throgs Neck Comm Mental Health Ctr, asst dir 1969-71; Sunrise Psychiatric Clinic, suprv psychiatrist 1971-75; Roosevelt Mental Health Ctr, comm psychiatrist 1972-74, med dir 1974-79; private practice, psychiatrist 1964-; Freeport School Dist, psychiatric consult 1974-; Nassau Ctr for Developmentally Disabled, med dir 1985-; Mercy Hosp, psychiatrist 1973-, attending 1971-; Nassau Co, Dept of Drug & Alcohol Abuse, Roosevelt NY 1988-; Mercy Hospital, Psychiatric Dept, Rockville Centre NY 1973-. **ORGANIZATIONS:** Mem NY Soc of Acupuncture for Physicians & Dentists, NY State Qualified Psych 1968-, NY State Qualified Acupuncturist 1975-; mem bd of vis Suffold Devel Ctr 1976-83, NY Cty Med Soc, Nassau Psych Soc, FRSH; faculty State Univ Stoney Brook; mem NMA, FAPA; diplomate Amer Bd of Psych & Neurol 1976-. **HONORS/ACHIEVEMENTS:** Many publ. **HOME ADDRESS:** 343 Washington Ave, Roosevelt, NY 11575. **BUSINESS ADDRESS:** Carlton H Blake MD, C H Blake MD, PC, 707 Broadhollow Rd, Ste F, Farmingdale, NY 11735.

BLAKE, ELIAS, JR.
Educational administrator. **PERSONAL:** Born Dec 13, 1929, Brunswick, GA; married Mona Williams; children: Michael, Elias Ayinde. **EDUCATION:** Paine Coll, BA 1951; Howard U, MA 1954; Univ of IL, PhD 1960. **CAREER:** Inst for Serv to Educ, dir of upward bound 1967-66, dir of evaluation 1969-67, pres 1969-77; Clark Coll, pres 1977-. **HONORS/ACHIEVEMENTS:** Outstanding tchr Coll of Liberal Arts Howard Univ 1964; meritorious achievement TN State Univ 1981; distinguished serv OH State Univ 1983; Honorary Doctorate, Paine College 1985; Documentary Film "The Story of One" 1986; Distinguished Achievement Awd Southern Univ 1986; Honors of the Assoc Southeastern Assoc of Educational Opp Program Personnel 1985. **BUSINESS ADDRESS:** President, Clark Coll, 240 Brawley Dr SW, Atlanta, GA 30314.

BLAKE, J. HERMAN
Educator. **PERSONAL:** Born Mar 15, 1934, Mt Vernon, NY; son of J Henry Blake and Lylace Michael Blake; married Maria W Brown; children: Vanessa E, Lylace Y, Audrey RA, Denise L, L Sidney Nathaniel. **EDUCATION:** NY Univ, BA 1960; Univ CA, MA 1965, PhD 1973. **CAREER:** Univ CA, asst prof 1966-70, assoc prof 1970-74; UCSC, prof 1974-84; Oakes Coll UCSC, founding provost 1972-84; Tougaloo Coll, pres 1984-87. **ORGANIZATIONS:** Mem Amer Sociol Assn, Population Assn of Amer, Pacific Sociol Assn; bd trustee Save the Children Fedn; bd trustee Penn Comm Serv Fellowships Woodrow Wilson 1960, John Hay Whitney 1963; mem Population Council 1964; Danforth Found 1964; Rockefeller Found 1965; Ford Found 1970. **HONORS/ACHIEVEMENTS:** Co-author "Revolutionary Suicide" 1973; named among Top 100 Emerging Young Leaders in Higher Educ Amer Council of Educ 1978. **BUSINESS ADDRESS:** Professor, Swarthmore College, Department of Sociology, Swarthmore, PA 19081.

BLAKE, J. PAUL
Public relations executive. **PERSONAL:** Born Mar 31, 1950, Neptune, NJ. **EDUCATION:** Drake Univ, BA 1972. **CAREER:** Univ of MN, assoc dir/asst dir of public relations 1976-83, asst to vice pres 1983-84, 1984-86; Pandamonium, pres 1986-. **ORGANIZATIONS:** Bd of trustees Council for the Advancement & Support of Educ 1982-84; first vice pres MN Press Club 1987; bd of dir US China Peoples Friendship Assoc MN Chapt; mem Public Relations Soc of Amer. **HONORS/ACHIEVEMENTS:** Volunteer Serv Awd, Minneapolis Urban League, 1977; Outstanding Young Man of Amer, Jaycees, 1979, 1982; Good Neighbor Awd, WCCO-AM Radio, 1982. **BUSINESS ADDRESS:** Dir of Public Relations, Seattle Univ, Seattle, WA 98122.

BLAKE, JAMES G.
Minister, executive director. **PERSONAL:** Born Dec 04, 1944, Charleston, SC. **EDUCATION:** Morehouse Coll, AB 1965; Boston Univ School of Theol, MTh 1968. **CAREER:** Gov of RI, spec asst 1968; Interfaith City-Wide Coord Com NYC, exec dir 1968-71; Union AME Church Little Rock, pastor 1971-72; Sen Hubert Humphrey, natl field coord 1972; SC Comm For Farm Workers Inc, exec dir. **ORGANIZATIONS:** Mem, natl vice pres NAACP; mem Selec Comm, US Youth Council; del World Assembly of Youth Leige Belgium 1970; del The World Council of Chs 1975; coord The Del of Black Religious Ldrs to Republic of China 1976; del 1st Pan African Youth Festival Tunis Tunisia 1972. **BUSINESS ADDRESS:** Pastor, Gr Zion AME Church, 134 Meeting St, PO 861, Charleston, SC 29402.

BLAKE, JOHN L.
Business owner. **PERSONAL:** Born Jun 11, 1921, Providence, RI; married Rose Marie; children: Kim R Wilcox, Edward M. **EDUCATION:** MI State U, BS 1961; Shaw U; Hon LLD 1972. **CAREER:** Marine Midland Bank, rochester asst sec NY 1966-69; US Dept of Labor, deputy manpower admin for employment security 1969-71; US Dept of Labor Job Corps, natl dir 1971-73; Marine Midland Bank, asst vice pres 1973-75; Rochester NY, mkt consult 1976-83; John L Blake Assoc Inc, pres owner. **ORGANIZATIONS:** Trustee Rochester Inst of Tech 1970-; trustee Rochester Reg Library Research Cncl 1984-; dir Rochester Bus Opport Corp 1983-; bd pres East House Corp Half-way Houses for Mental Patients 1973-. **HONORS/ACHIEVEMENTS:** Distinguished achievement US Dept of Labor 1972; "Job Corps Works" Building Trades Unions 1981; mgt training Am Manage Assoc 1967; aid to bus Nat Chamber of Commerce 1967; outstanding achievement Kappa Alpha Psi 1974. **MILITARY SERVICE:** USMC sgt 1943-46. **HOME ADDRESS:** 680 Claybourne Rd, Rochester, NY 14618. **BUSINESS ADDRESS:** President, John L Blake Assoc Inc, 195 St Paul St, Rochester, NY 14604.

BLAKE, MILTON JAMES
Labor/industrial relations manager. **PERSONAL:** Born Nov 11, 1934, Chicago, IL; married Beverly Marlene Skyles; children: Milton J Jr (dec), Robin. **EDUCATION:** Bradley Univ Peoria IL, BS Indust Arts 1957. **CAREER:** AUS Active & Res, infantry officer 1955-; Chicago Police Dept , human rel officer 1961-65; Continental Can Co, suprv indust rel 1966-72; Whittaker Metals,div mgr indust rel 1972-74; Gulf & Western Energy Products Group, group mgr employee rel 1974-78; Bunker Ramo Corp, corp mgr eeo & compliance mgmt 1979-; Amphenol Co, dir salary admin, org plnng & devel 1982-. **ORGANIZATIONS:** Mem indust rel adv comm Univ of WI 1971-; consult EEO, Gulf & Western 1979; youth adv St James Luthern Church 1961-66; mem Oak Brook Assoc of Commerce & Indust 1979-; mem Chicago Urban Affairs Council 1982; mem bd of dir Chicago Childrens Choir 1980; mem Alpha Phi Alpha, Alpha Phi Omega, Phi Mu Alpha. **HONORS/ACHIEVEMENTS:** Hon Mention Chicago Police Dept 1961; ;author "Supervisory Awareness Program" Continental Can Co 1969; vstg instr Affirm Action Prog Univ of WI 1977; Publ Affirm Action Prog Bunker Ramo Corp 1979; Good Conduct Medal AUS 1957. **MILITARY SERVICE:** AUS lt col 30 yrs; Armed Forces Reserve Medal 1976. **BUSINESS ADDRESS:** Dir Salary Administrator, Amphenol Co, 900 Commerce Dr, Oak Brook, IL 60521.

BLAKE, WENDELL OWEN
Physician. **PERSONAL:** Born Aug 09, 1940, Bartow, FL; married Mildred; children: Wendi, Michael. **EDUCATION:** Howard Univ, BS 1961; Meharry Med Coll, MD 1967. **CAREER:** Good Samaritan Hosp, intern 1967-68; Meharry Med Coll, resident 1968-72; Surg Oncology, fellow; Roswell Park Meml Inst, physician 1974-75; Private Practice, physician

genl surgeon. **ORGANIZATIONS:** Mem bd of dirs Boys Club of Lakeland; chief Genl Surgery Serv Lakeland Regional Med Ctr 1984; mem Soc of Abdominal Surgeons; mem FL Med Assn, Polk Co Med Assn of FL, natl Med Assn, FL Med Dental & Pharm Assn; staff mem Lakeland Regional Med Ctr; life mem Kappa Alpha Psi Frat; polemarch Lakeland Alumni Chapt; mem Kappa Alpha Psi Frat; diplomate Amer Bd of Surgery. **HONORS/ACHIEVEMENTS:** Awd for Achievement in recog meritorious performance of duty US Kenner Army Hosp 1972-74; publ "Thyroid Surgery at Hubbard Hosp" Jour Natl Med Assn;"The Changing Picture of Carcinoma of the Lung" Jour Natl Med Assn; Fellow Southeastern Surgical Congress. **MILITARY SERVICE:** AUS mc major 1972-74. **BUSINESS ADDRESS:** 1420 Martin L King Jr, Lakeland, FL 33805.

BLAKELEY, ULYSSES BUCKLEY, SR.
Retired clergyman. **PERSONAL:** Born Nov 29, 1911, Laurens, SC; son of Woolsey Blakeley and Ollie Blakeley; married Gwendolynne; children: Rebecca, Ulysses Jr, Gwendolynne. **EDUCATION:** Lincoln Univ, BA 1936, BST 1939; Harvard Univ Chaplains School, 1943; Temple Univ, Univ of PA, Parsons Coll, DD 1959. Princeton Univ, Masters in Theology 1948. **ORGANIZATIONS:** Exec sec Black Presybterian United; mem black caucus Presbyterian Church of Amer; co-founder The Woodlawn Org Chgo. **HONORS/ACHIEVEMENTS:** 1st black pastor 1st Presbyterian Church in Chgo; Exec Presbyter, Newark Presbytery. **MILITARY SERVICE:** Chaplain Corps, lt colonel, 1943-.

BLAKELY, CHARLES
Educational administrator. **PERSONAL:** Born Jan 31, 1951, Batesville, MS; son of Willie Blakely and Cora Edna Walton Blakely; widowed. **EDUCATION:** Coahoma Jr Coll, AA 1972; Jackson State Univ, BS 1975; attended MS State Univ one semester 1973, Delta State Univ two semesters 1981-82, Univ of MS one semester 1984. **CAREER:** Jackson State Univ, student admin clerk 1974-75; North Panola Vocatonal High School, substitute teacher 1975-78; Northwest Jr Coll Greenhill Elementary School, adult basic educ instructor 1981-88; Inst of Comm Serv, licensed social worker 1982-89; North Panola Consolidated School Dist I, pres school bd 1989-90. **ORGANIZATIONS:** Member, Cavalette Social Club; pres, Sardis Panola County Voters League 1980-88; asst supt of Sunday school, Miles Chapel CME Church 1982-; bd member, MACE affiliate local bd for continued educ 1983-85; bd member Selective Serv Local Draft Bd representing Panola County 1983-89; bd mem, Democratic Exec Comm for Panola County 1984-89; pres, North Panola School Bd of Educ 1989-90; member, Stewart Bd; member, part time Sunday school teacher, member of choir, Miles Chapel CME Church. **HONORS/ACHIEVEMENTS:** Certificate in recognition of noteworthy performance of serv MS United for Progress to the Black Comm 1980-81; certificate award Outstanding Serv in the Community NAACP 1982; outstanding serv and dedication and cooperation in the community Panola County Voter League Inc 1982; staff of the year, Inst of Community Serv Headstart Program, 1989. **HOME ADDRESS:** Rte 2 Box 374, Sardis, MS 38666. **BUSINESS ADDRESS:** School Board Pres, N Panola Consol Sch Dist 1, PO Box 334, Sardis, MS 38666.

BLAKELY, EDWARD JAMES
Educator. **PERSONAL:** Born Apr 21, 1938, San Bernardino, CA; son of Edward Blakely and Josephine Carter; married Maaike van der Slessen; children: Pieta, Brette. **EDUCATION:** San Bernardino Valley Coll, AA 1958; Univ of CA, BA 1960, MA 1964; Pasadena Coll, MA 1967; Univ of CA, PhD 1971. **CAREER:** UCLA Ext, training dir 1966-68; Western Comm Action Training Inc, exec dir 1968-70; US State Dept, special asst to asst sec 1970-71; Univ of Pittsburgh, asst to chancellor 1971-74; Univ of CA, dean, asst vice pres 1977-84, professor 1976-. **ORGANIZATIONS:** Consult US Agcy Intl Devel, United Nations & others; bd dir YMCA 1972-74; NAACP Pittsburgh 1972-74; Comm Devel Soc of Am 1976-; Intl Soc of Educ Planners 1977-. **HONORS/ACHIEVEMENTS:** All League Football & Basketball 1953-56; Young Man Yr San Bernardino 1955, 1958; hon mention Small Coll Coast Football 1959; Scholar Athlete Award Univ of CA 1959; Most Inspirational Player UC 1959; Coro Found Fellow 1960; Sgt Shriver Rural Serv Award 1968; NAACP Comm Serv Award 1970; Civic Serv Award Richmond, CA 1984; author of over 20 articles & 3 books on comm planning & devel. **MILITARY SERVICE:** USAF 1st Lt 1961-64; Outstanding Ofcr Training 1961. **BUSINESS ADDRESS:** Professor, University of California, Dept of City & Reg Planning, Berkeley, CA 94720.

BLAKELY, WILLIAM H., JR.
Executive search consultant. **PERSONAL:** Born Feb 12, 1927, Warren, OH; son of William Blakely Sr and Romelia Blakely; married Marcelle Wallace; children: Donna, Glenn. **EDUCATION:** NC A&T Univ, BS Sociology & History (w/honors) 1952; Rutgers Univ, postgrad. **CAREER:** Staff Univ Settlement NYC, mem 1952-62; Lillian Wald Recreation Rooms Settlement NYC, evening dir 1963-64; Urban League Skills Bank Newark, dir 1964-67; Engelhard Industries Newark, industrial relations rep 1967-74; Engelhard Mineral & Chem Corp Iselin NJ, corp mgr personnel; Phibro-Salomon Inc NYC, corp mgr employee relations 1981-85; WR Lazard & Co Inc, consultant 1985; Sandia Machine Co, consultant 1986; Salomon Inc, consultant 1986; Salomon Bros, consultant 1987; Radd Maintenance & Supply Co, pres 1987; H C Smith LTD, senior associate 1988; Strategic Financial Systems, consultant 1989. **ORGANIZATIONS:** Mem NJ Corps Comm United Negro Coll Fund; bd dirs past pres Urban League Essex Co 1968-75; mem chancellor's council NC A&T Univ; mem pres The EDGES Group Inc staff pres's office 1984-85; mem Newark Comm Affairs Group Businessmen Century Club of YMCA; trustee Kessler Inst Rehab; bd dirs Interracial Council Business Oppor, Better Business Bureau Project Pride, Harlem br YMCA, Black Achievers; pres bd dirs Urban Leaguers Inc; vice pres West Kenney Jr HS Scholarship Fund; commr juries Essex Co 1968-75; mem exec comm NCCJ; mem Natl Urban League Grant St Boys Assn C of C; mem Sigma Rho Sigma, Omega Psi Phi; bd of dirs General Machine Co 1985, Radd Maintenance & Supply Co 1986. **HONORS/ACHIEVEMENTS:** Achievement Awd Frontiersman Amer 1974; Awd Human & Civil Rights Assn NJ 1976; Awd Black Achievers in Industry 1976; Project Pride 1979; FOCUS Awd 1979; Awd United Comm Corp Union Co Urban League; NC A&T Univ Alumni Awd 1978; named to Athletic Hall of Fame 1978; Humanitarian Awd Essex Co Urban League Guild 1980; NCCJ Awd 1981; Larrie Stalk's Civic Assn Awd 1981; Black Achievers in Industry Awd 1975; Chmn's Plaque Congressional Black Caucus Found Inc 1982; NAACP Corporate Awd of Achievement 1986; Congressional Black Caucus 1986; Service Award, NAACP Oranges and Maplewood New Jersey 1988. **BUSINESS ADDRESS:** H C Smith, LTD, 3051 Van Aken Blvd, Cleveland, OH 44120.

BLAKEMORE, JERRY D.
Government official. **PERSONAL:** Born Jul 22, 1954, East Chiago Hts, IL. **EDUCATION:** Princeton Univ, BA 1976; John Marshall, JD 1980. **CAREER:** Washington, Kenner, Hunter, & Samuels, law clerk; US Dept of Health, Ed & Welfare, legal intern; Asst to Goveranor for Health & Human Services; Dir ofIntergovernmental Relations for GovJames R Thompson. **ORGANIZATIONS:** Chicago, Cook County, Nat'l & American Bar Assns, mem; Bar for US Dist Court and Ill State Supreme Court, mem; Pres Club; Urban League; NAACP, bddir; City Club of Chicago, mem. **HONORS/ACHIEVEMENTS:** Princeton Univ, frederick douglas awd 1976.

BLAKENSHIP, CHERYL L.
Educational & financial administrator. **PERSONAL:** Born Jul 25, 1950, New York, NY; children: Marne, Alex. **EDUCATION:** Univ of CA Berkeley, 1979-82; Mills Coll, BA 1972; Pepperdine Univ, MS 1985. **CAREER:** Mills Coll, asst dir of financial aid 1973-80; LA Coll of Chiropractic, dir of financial aid 1981-, dir of student affairs 1983-. **ORGANIZATIONS:** Mem west reg WASFAA Com on Minority Concerns 1984-85; mem Grad & Professional Fin Aid Com for CASFAA 1985-96. **HONORS/ACHIEVEMENTS:** Outstanding Young Women in Amer 1977; Coll Scholarship Recipient Pepperdine Univ 1984; GEP Scholarship Pepperdine Univ, 1985. **BUSINESS ADDRESS:** Dir of Student Affairs, Los Angeles Coll-Chiropractic, 16200 E Amber Valley Dr, Whittier, CA 90604.

BLAKEY, ART (ABDULLAH IBN BUHAINA)
Band leader. **PERSONAL:** Born Oct 11, 1919, Pittsburgh, PA. **CAREER:** Fletcher Henderson Orch, mem 1939; Mary Lou William's Band, mem 1940; Billy Eckstine Band, mem; Lucky Millinder's Band, mem; Buddy De Franco's Combo, mem; Birdland, drummer; The Jazz Messengers, organizer/band leader. **HONORS/ACHIEVEMENTS:** Grammy Award Best Acoustic Perf Group 1984; Appearances all over the world appearing at major festivals; toured with Dizzy Gillespie, Thelonious Monk, Sonny Stitt; historic drum battle with Max Roach, Buddy Rich & Elvin Jones at Radio City Music Hall during Newport Jazz Festival; Honored at Kool Jazz Festival with Jazz Messengers and alumni; Voted to Hall of Fame by readers of Downbeat Mag. **BUSINESS ADDRESS:** Art Blakey and the Jazz Messen, 77 Bleecker St, Apt 524E, New York, NY 10012.

BLAKEY, WILLIAM A.
Attorney. **PERSONAL:** Born Sep 01, 1943, Louisville, KY. **EDUCATION:** Knoxville Coll, BA 1965; Howard Univ Sch of Law, JD 1968; Georgetown Law Ctr, pursuing LLM. **CAREER:** Sen Daniel Brewster, exec asst/spl asst 1965-68; Dept of HUD, atty adv 1968-69; Natl Urban Coalition, exec asst to vice pres for field opers 1969-70; Transcentury Corp, vice pres sr assoc 1970-71; AL Nellum & Asssoc, sr assoc 1971-72; US Commn on Civil Rights, spl asst to staff dir 1972-74; KY Comm on Human Rights, lgl spclst/atty 1976-77; DHEW, dep asst sec for legis 1977-80; US Commn on Civil Rights, dir congressional Liaison 1974-. **ORGANIZATIONS:** Consult Neighborhood Consumer Information Ctr 1968; instr in Common Legal Problems Control Data Corp 1969 1971; mem KY, WA, Amer Natl Bar Assns; Omega PsiPhi Frat; Phi Alpha Delta Law Frat; Sen Waeden St Stephen Incarnation Episcopal; mem bd Louisville Br NAACP Legal Aid Soc of Louisville 1976-77; The Inner Voices Inc; chmn The Minority & Legislative Educ Proj chmn 1979-80; Natl Bar Assn 1975; Congressional Action Fund 1970-72. **HONORS/ACHIEVEMENTS:** Omega Psi Phi Dist Scholar 1965; Alpha Kappa Mu & Phi Alpha Theta Hon Soc; Who's Who Among Students in Amer Univs & Colls 1964 & 1965; Who's Who in Govt1974-75. **BUSINESS ADDRESS:** Senior Legislative Assistant, Senator Paul Simon, 462 Dirksen Senate Office Bldg, Washington, DC 20510.

BLALOCK, MARION W.
Educational director. **PERSONAL:** Born Dec 18, 1947, East Chicago, IN; married Roger; children: Erin Juliane. **EDUCATION:** Purdue Univ, BA 1969, MS 1973. **CAREER:** Parker Career Ctr, employment counselor 1970; Family Serv of Metro Detroit, family caseworker 1970-71; Purdue Univ, grad teaching asst 1971-73, asst dean of students 1974-75, dir mep and academic advisor freshman engrg 1975-. **ORGANIZATIONS:** Faculty advisor and mem natl adv bd Natl Soc of Black Engrs; mem Natl Assoc of Minority Engrg Program Administrators, Amer Soc for Engrg Educ, Black Colls Develop Comm; vice chair of steering comm Purdue Black Alumnmi Organization; bd dirs Tippecanoe Area Planned Parenthood Assoc 1985-88. **HONORS/ACHIEVEMENTS:** Dean M Beverly Stone Awd 1982; Hon member Golden Key Natl Honor Soc; Vincent M Bendix Minorities in Engrg Awd Amer Soc of Engrg Educ 1983; Reginald H Jones Disting Serv Awd Natl Action Council for Minorities in Engrg 1984; President's Affirmative Action Awd Purdue Univ 1985; Best Teacher Awd Dept of Freshman Engrg Purdue Univ 1985, 86; Outstanding Advisor of the Natl Adv Bd Natl Soc of Black Engrs 1986; Helen B Schleman Awd 1986; Hon member Iron Key; Hon member Natl Soc of Black Engrs Purdue Chapt. **BUSINESS ADDRESS:** Dir Minority Engrg, PurdueUniv, Room 211 ENAD Bldg, West Lafayette, IN 47907.

BLANCHET, WALDO WILLIE E.
Educator. **PERSONAL:** Born Aug 06, 1910, New Orleans, LA; married Josephine Lavizzo; children: Geri Therese, Waldo E Jr. **EDUCATION:** Talladega Coll, AB 1931; Univ of MI, MS 1936, PhD 1946. **CAREER:** Fort Valley N & I Sch, sci tchr 1932-35, dean 1936-39; Fort Valley State Coll, prof physical sci & adm dean 1939-66, pres 1966-73, retired pres emeritus. **HONORS/ACHIEVEMENTS:** Consultant to sci tchrs Adv Cncl on Educ of Disadvantaged Children 1970-72; sci research & sci teaching fellowship Atlanta Univ 1931-32; fellowship Genl Educ Bd Univ of MI 1935-36, 1938-39; Phi Kappa Phi Hon Scholastic Soc; Phi Delta Kappa Univ of MI; pres Natl Assn of Research in Sci Teaching 1957; Sci Educ Magazine Award; NARST Award. **HOME ADDRESS:** 508 Camelot Dr, College Park, GA 30349.

BLAND, ARTHUR H.
Government employee. **PERSONAL:** Born Dec 01, 1923, Milledgeville, GA; married Valerie Howard; children: Deborah, Stephanie, Angela. **EDUCATION:** Ohio State Univ, BS, 1950; Central Michigan Univ, grad study; Attended, Industrial Coll of Armed Forces, Air War Coll. **CAREER:** Dept of Defense, entire career has been within defense dept presently systems mgr. **ORGANIZATIONS:** Mem Amer Logistics Assn; bd mem Comm Serv Corp; mem adv bd Columbus Parks & Recreation; mem adv bd Columbus Metro Parks Dist Adv Bd; bd mem Central Comm House. **HONORS/ACHIEVEMENTS:** Meritorious Civilian Serv Awd 1968; Ten Outstanding Personnel Defense Constr Supply Ctr 1972 1975; inventor

hand computer 1968. **MILITARY SERVICE:** USAC flight officer. **BUSINESS ADDRESS:** Systems Manager, Dept of Defense, 3990 E Broad St, Columbus, OH 43215.

BLAND, EDWARD
Producer. **PERSONAL:** Born in Chicago, IL; divorced; children: Edward, Robert, Stefanie. **CAREER:** "Cry of Jazz", co-produced directed film 1959; composed many serious chamber works, articles in film culuture 1960; Mus of Modern Art, mus consult 1968-74; Brooklyn Acad of Music, mus consult 1973-75; innumerable mus scores for documentary & educ films; arranging and/or producing of record dates for Al Hirt Dizzy Gillespie, Lionel Hampton, Hesitations, Clark Terry, James Moody, Elvin Jones, Big Mama Thornton; Vanguard Records, exec producer. **ORGANIZATIONS:** Mus of Modern Arts Newsletter 1968. **MILITARY SERVICE:** USN 18 months. **BUSINESS ADDRESS:** Executive Producer, c/o Vanguard Records Inc, 71 W 23rd St, New York, NY 10010.

BLAND, HEYWARD
Business executive. **PERSONAL:** Born Oct 17, 1918, Tillatoba, MS; married Maemell Fuller; children: Patricia, Ronald (dec). **EDUCATION:** Shiloh Seventh-Day Adventist Acad, attended 1937. **CAREER:** Furniture Dealer, Chicago 1943-48; Real Estate Investor, 1948-; Shore Motel Corp, pres; 37th & Indiana Ave Bldg Inc, pres; Pacific Coast Bank, pres chmn bd. **ORGANIZATIONS:** Precinct capt 2nd Ward Dem Orgn 1962-68; co-sponsor Little League 1969 1970; mem bd dirs Girls' Club of San Diego 1974-; bd dirs PUSH Orgn of San Diego; organizer Pacific Coast Bank San Diego. **HONORS/ACHIEVEMENTS:** Honored as Business Man of Yr Women's Club of San Diego. **BUSINESS ADDRESS:** Chairman of the Board, Pacific Coast Bank, 5540 S Shore Dr, Chicago, IL 60637.

BLAND, ROBERT ARTHUR
Government official. **PERSONAL:** Born Jan 26, 1938, Petersburg, VA; married Shirley Thweatt; children: Angela Rene, Lael Gregory. **EDUCATION:** Univ of VA, BSEE 1959; CA State Univ, MA 1975; Nova Univ, EdD 1979. **CAREER:** Naval Weapons Ctr, proj engr 1959-71; Oxnard Comm Coll, counselor 1976-77, instr 1977-; Aquarius Portrait Photography, photographer 1983-; Naval Ship Weapons System Engrg Station, div head. **ORGANIZATIONS:** Instr Oxnard Comm Coll 1977-; mem Commiss on Ministry for Episcopal Diocese of Los Angeles 1980-; mem v chmn Ventura Cty Affirmative Action Comm 1982-; photographer Aquarius Portrait Photography 1983-; vestry St Patricks Episcopal Church 1985-. **HONORS/ACHIEVEMENTS:** First black undergrad to attend and/or grad from Univ of VA 1959. **HOME ADDRESS:** 3915 Crown Haven Ct, Newbury Park, CA 91320.

BLANDEN, LEE ERNEST
Educational administration. **PERSONAL:** Born Sep 16, 1942, Arcadia, FL; divorced; children: Teresa, Toni, Yvonne, Curtis. **EDUCATION:** Voorhees Jr Coll Denmark SC, AA 1962; Lane Coll Jackson TN, BA Elem Ed 1965; Univ of IL Urbana, MEd Admin & Suprv 1970, Post Grad Study Ed Admin & Suprv; Eastern IL Univ Charleston, Admin & School Law; IL Assoc of School Bd, Negotiations & School Law. **CAREER:** Gen Devel Corp summers 1958-60; Voorhees Jr Coll Denmark SC, maintenance 1960-62; Wildwood Linen Supply Wildwood NJ, laborer summers 1963-65; Lane Coll Jackson TN, library asst, asst varsity coach 1965-70; Danville Dist 118, elem teacher, asst principal 1965-70; Elementary Bldg, principal 1970-74; Danville Area Comm Coll, part time adult educ faculty 1970-74, dir of personnel 1974-80, asst to the pres, dean of student serv. **ORGANIZATIONS:** Mem Alpha Phi Alpha Frat Inc, Omicron Lambda Beta, Danville United Fund, Amer Soc for Personnel Admin; bd of dir, chairperson Laura Lee Fellowship House; trsutee bd, sanctuary choir, Second Baptist Church; ed admin Danville Rotary Intl; personnel mgr comm Danville Chamber of Comm; past master & sec Corinthian Lodge 31 F&AM; bd of dir Ctr for Children Svcs; bd of dir, treas Vermilion Cty Opportunities Indust Ctr Inc; bell ringer Salvation Army; school bd mem Danville Comm Consol School Dist 118 Bd Policy Revisions; chief negotiator Bd of Ed; consult & speaker Natl School Bd Annual Convention; attended several workshops. **HONORS/ACHIEVEMENTS:** Outstanding Educator of Midwest; Top 100 Administrators in North Amer 1980; Cited for Cost Containment Related to Personnel Absences. **HOME ADDRESS:** 4 W Bluff, Danville, IL 61832. **BUSINESS ADDRESS:** Assistant to President/Dean, Danville Area Comm Coll, 2000 E Main St, Danville, IL 61832.

BLANDING, LARRY
Government official, real estate associate. **PERSONAL:** Born Aug 29, 1953, Sumter, SC; son of Junius Blanding Sr (deceased) and Rosa Lee Williams Blanding; married Peggy Ann Mack, Dec 24, 1977; children: Dreylan Dre'Neka. **EDUCATION:** Claflin Coll, BA 1975; SC State Coll, MEd 19767; SC School of Real Estate 1988. **CAREER:** United Way of Jacksonville, campaign assoc 1975; United Way Richland & Lexington Cty, acting dir comm planning 1976; SC State Coll, head resident 1976-77; SC House of Representatives, state rep 1976-; Univ of South Carolina, guest lecturer 1983; Realty World Colonial-Moses, sales associate 1987-. **ORGANIZATIONS:** Mem Natl Caucus Black Leg 1976-; bd dir Sumter Learning Devel Center 1977-82; state dir Phi Beta Sigma 1979-83; mem Sumter Public Awareness Assoc 1977-; mem NAACP, Hon Soc, Pi Gamma Mu Iota Chapter Orangesburg SC; chmn SC Leg Black Caucus; mem St Paul Lodge 8, CC Johnson Consistory 136, Cario Temple 125; bd mem Sumter County Devel Bd 1983-; comm mem Southern Legislative Conference 1986-; bd mem Sumter Chamber of Commerce 1986-; mem Local, State & Natl Bd of Realtors 1987-. **HONORS/ACHIEVEMENTS:** Sigma Man of the Year Phi Beta Sigma Fraternity Inc 1977; Man of the Year Claflin Coll 1975; Citizen of the Year Omega Psi Phi Fraternity Gamma Iota Chapter 1976; One of Fifty Future Leaders of Amer Ebony Magazine 1978; Alumni Award, Claflin Coll 1987; Family Pioneer, Williams Family Reunion Comm 1989. **BUSINESS ADDRESS:** Representative, State of South Carolina, Blatt Building, 432-B, Pendleton St, Columbia, SC 29201.

BLANDING, MARY RHONELLA
Educational administrator. **PERSONAL:** Born Dec 21, 1950, Los Angeles, CA; children: Khamisi Rashad Woodyard. **EDUCATION:** Loyola Marymount Univ LA, BS 1973; Pepperdine Univ LA, MS 1975. **CAREER:** Southern CA Upward Bound Program, teacher/counselor, 1969-73; Ver bum Dei High School, teacher/counselor, 1973-74; Howard K Rasland Inc MD, medical office mgr, 1974-75; Loyola Marymount Univ, admin/instructor Afro-Amer Studies, 1975-78; Charles R Drew Medical School, admin faculty devel dept of family medicine, 1978-. **ORGANIZATIONS:** Consul Compton Unified Sch Dist 1978; consult Loyola Marymount Univ 1979; consult State Bd of Educ 1979; regional chairperson Coll Bounders Com Inc 1976-;com mem Nellie M Blanding Outstanding Serv Awds Comm 1977-; mem Natl Assn Negro Life & Hist 1978-80. **HONORS/ACHIEVEMENTS:** Carnation Scholar Carnation Co 1971-72; Afro-Amer Studies "Spl Mary Blanding" Awd Loyola Marymount Univ; Outstanding Serv to Students (Black) Loyola Marymount Univ 1978-79; Outstanding Serv to Young People Coll Bounders Com 1978-79. **BUSINESS ADDRESS:** Administrator, Charles R Drew Medical Sch, Dept of Family Medicine, 1621 E 120th St, Los Angeles, CA 90058.

BLANFORD, COLVIN
Clergyman. **PERSONAL:** Born Feb 06, 1938, Dallas, TX; son of John Hardee Blanford and Hattie Ellen Colvin Blanford; married Margaret Ann Tyrrell; children: Colvin II, Christopher. **EDUCATION:** San Francisco State Coll, BA 1960; Berkeley Bapt Div Sch, BD 1963; So CA Sch Theol, RelD 1969. **CAREER:** Third Baptist Church San Francisco, youth & asst minister 1956-63; Cosmopolitan Baptist Church San Francisco, pastor 1963-70; San Francisco Youth Guidance Ctr, prot chaplain 1963-70; Brooks House of Christian Serv Hammond IN, exec dir 1970-73; North Baptist Theol Sem, adj prof 1974-; First Baptist Church Gary IN, pastor 1973-81; Christ Baptist Church, organizing pastor 1981-. **ORGANIZATIONS:** Mem bd dir Morehouse School of Religion 1976-; Baptist Ministers Conf 1973-; Interfaith Clergy Council 1973-; bd mem, Gary NAACP 1986-; life mem NAACP 1980-. **HONORS/ACHIEVEMENTS:** Youth of Yr San Francisco Sun Reporter 1958; sermon publ in Outstanding Black Sermons by Judson Press 1976; represented the Baptist denomination as a participant in the Baptist-Lutheran dialogue on the meaning of baptism 1981; acclaimed by Dollars & Sense Magazine as one of the outstanding black ministers in Amer 1981; preaching missions to Liberia, Malawi, Swaziland, Republic of South Africa 1985, 1987, 1989. **BUSINESS ADDRESS:** Pastor, Christ Baptist Church, 4700 E 7th Ave, Gary, IN 46403.

BLANKENSHIP, EDDIE L.
City official. **PERSONAL:** Born Jan 22, 1925, Roanake, AL; married Mary L Bates; children: Donald E, Deborah J. **EDUCATION:** Booker T Washington Jr Coll, AAD 1949; Miles Coll, BS 1960; Southwestern Univ BS 1983. **CAREER:** US Postal Svc, mail handler 1953; US Dept of Commerce/Minority Bus Dev, ed & training spec 1973; Mayor's Office, spec admin asst 1976; US Dept of Commerce/Minority Bus Dev, dist officer 1983; City of Birmingham, city councillor. **ORGANIZATIONS:** Officer Minority Bus Opportunity; bd pres JCCEO, Urban Impact Inc; bd mem Pratt City Devel Corp. **HONORS/ACHIEVEMENTS:** Outstanding Supervisor Birmingham Urban League; Cert of Apprec Metropolitan Bus Assoc; Superior Accomplishment US Postal Svcs; Man of the Year Birmingham Sales Assoc. **MILITARY SERVICE:** AUS T/5 3 yrs. **HOME ADDRESS:** 1928 Center St South, Birmingham, AL 35205. **BUSINESS ADDRESS:** City Councilman, City of Birmingham, 710 N 20th St, Birmingham, AL 35203.

BLANKENSHIP, GLENN RAYFORD
Government official. **PERSONAL:** Born Aug 11, 1948, Memphis, TN; son of G Blankenship; married Zita R Jackson; children: Maia, Rayford. **EDUCATION:** Amer Univ Wash Semester Prog, 1968-69; LeMoyne-Owen Coll, BA 1970; Graduate Study in Public Administration, Syracuse Univ 1971, Univ of WI 1973, Univ of CO 1976. **CAREER:** US Dept of Housing & Urban Development, equal opportunity specialist 1971-74; Federal Energy Admin, equal oppor officer 1974-77; US Dept of Energy, equal oppor spec 1977-79; USDA Forest Service, eeo/affirmative action mgr 1979-89; USDA Forest Service, Historically Black Colls & Univs, program manager. **ORGANIZATIONS:** Life mem Kappa Alpha Psi Frat Inc; life mem NAACP; pres Atlanta Chap Natl Alumni Assoc LeMoyne-Owen Coll 1984-; registered football official Capitol City Officials Assoc 1985-; conference coord Sons of Allen-Atlanta/No Georgia 6th Episcopal District AME Church 1985-89; trustee Flipper Temple AME Church 1986-89. **HONORS/ACHIEVEMENTS:** Certificate of Appreciation Natl Alliance of Business 1983; Golden Parade of Alumni LeMoyne-Owen Coll Class of 86, 1985; Certificate of Appreciation The Martin Luther King Jr Ctr for Nonviolent Social Change Inc 1986; Certificate of Merit USDA Forest Service 1986; Presidential Citation NAFEO Disting Alumni 1987. **HOME ADDRESS:** P O Box 2808, Gaithersburg, MD 20886-2808. **BUSINESS ADDRESS:** Program Manager, Historically Black Colleges & Universities, USDA-Forest Service-RPE 904, P O Box 96090, Washington, DC 20090-6090.

BLANKINSHIP, G. L., JR.
Officer/wholesale distribution. **PERSONAL:** Born Oct 23, 1955, Kansas City, MO; married Kathryn Booker; children: Marcus, Adriane, GL III. **EDUCATION:** Rockhurst Coll, BSBA Mktg 1978, BSBA Mgt 1978. **CAREER:** Blankinship Distributors Inc, warehouse clerk 1970-74, sales rep 1974-77, vice pres 1977-84, pres 1985-. **ORGANIZATIONS:** Vchair UNCF Forty-Second Anniversary Dinner 1986, Douglass Bank Adv Bd; dir KC Minority Bus Adv Corp, Black Comm Fund; assoc mem Amer Health & Beauty Aids Inst; sec of the bd Urban League of Kansas City; pres Fr Benedict Justice School Bd; bd dir KC Chap for Sickle Cell Disease. **HONORS/ACHIEVEMENTS:** Eagle Scout Boy Scouts of Amer 1970; Alpha Phi Alpha Brother of the Year Awd for Missouri 1977; Wall St Journal Student Achievement Awd in Business 1978; Young Progressors Businessman on the Move Awd 1980; Outstanding Young Men of Amer 1981. **BUSINESS ADDRESS:** President, Blankinship Distributors, 1927 Vine St, Kansas City, MO 64108.

BLANKS, DELILAH B.
Educator. **PERSONAL:** Born Apr 05, 1936, Acme, NC; married Eddie W Blanks; children: Sherri Ann, Rhonda Fay. **EDUCATION:** Shaw Univ, AB English Soc Studies 1957; E Carolina Univ, AB Library Sci 1965; Univ NC, MSW 1972; Univ of NC, PhD in progress 1974-. **CAREER:** Wake County Bd of Educ, teacher, librarian, 1963-67; Whiteville City Schools, teacher Eglish, 1960-62; Brunswick County Bd of Educ, teacher, librarian, 1963-67; Neighborhood Youth Corps Whiteveill NC, counselor, 1967-68; Bladen County Dept of Social Services, child welfare worker, 1968-71; NC State Dept of Social Services, comm devel specialist I, 1971-72; Univ of NC, asst prof Sociology, Social Work, 1972-. **ORGANIZATIONS:** Income tax consult 1957-; notary public 1957-; mem Natl Assn of Social Workers 1974-; Natl Cncl on Social Work Educ 1974-; Delta Sigma Theta Sor; chmn EArcadia Bd of Town Councilmen; NAACP; first vice chmn Bladen Co Dem Exec Com; Bladen Co Improvement Assn; bd mem Wilmington New Hanover Headstart Inc; bd mem NC Comm for a Two Party Sys 1974. **HONORS/ACHIEVEMENTS:** Bladen Co Cit of Yr 1968; NC Senclander of Month 1974. **BUSINESS ADDRESS:** Asst Prof Sociology, Univ of NC, E Arcadia, S Coll, Wilmington, NC 28403.

BLANKS, LARVELL (SUGAR BEAR)
Professional athlete. **PERSONAL:** Born Jan 28, 1950, Del Rio, TX; married Rosemary Fay; children: Jeffery Wayne, Debra Lynn. **EDUCATION:** Attended, Misa AZ Coll.

CAREER: Savannah, player 1971; Atlanta-Richmond, player 1972-75; Cleveland, player 1976-78; TX, player 1979; Atlanta Braves, professional baseball player. **BUSINESS ADDRESS:** Atlanta Braves, PO Box 4064, Atlanta, GA 30302.

BLANKS, WILHELMINA E.
Government employee. **PERSONAL:** Born Nov 10, 1905, Decatur, AL; married Walter T Blanks; children: Wilhelmina Balla, Muriel Inniss. **EDUCATION:** Atlanta Univ, AB 1927; Attended, Loyola Univ, Northwestern Sch of Journalism, Univ Chicago. **CAREER:** Prairie View State Coll, tchr 1927-29; Cook Co Dept of Public Aid, 1936-74, asst dist office supr 1974-. **ORGANIZATIONS:** Organizer MI Ave Adult Educ Ctr 1965-; mem Tutoring Project for Mothers Univ of Chicago; mem Social Serv Guild of St Edmund's Episcopal Ch 1950-; bd mem City Asso of Women's Bd of Art Inst of Chicago; vice pres South Side Comm Art Ctr Chicago; mem Bravo Chap Lyric Opera Chicago; mem PUSH, NAACP, Chicago Urban League; vice pres Amer Friends of Liberia; mem Citizens Com Du Sable Museum of African Amer Hist; freelance writer. **HONORS/ACHIEVEMENTS:** Awd for Achievement in Public Welfare Intl Travelers Assn; 1972; Disting Serv Awd Dedication to Devel of Art in Blk Comm S Side Comm Art Ctr 1970. **BUSINESS ADDRESS:** Asst Dist Office Supr, Dept of Public Aid, 300 W Pershing Rd, Chicago, IL 60609.

BLANTON, JAMES B., III
Association executive. **PERSONAL:** Born Feb 06, 1949, Knoxville, TN; son of James B Blanton Jr and Martha Luckey Blanton; married Emily DeVoi Besley, Dec 25, 1977; children: Joseph, Sidney, James IV. **EDUCATION:** Knoxville Coll, BS Commerce 1971; Univ of TN, MBA. **CAREER:** Alpha Phi Alpha Frat Inc, exec dir 1977. **ORGANIZATIONS:** Asst exec sec Alpha Phi Alpha Frat Inc; dir of office serv TVA Knoxville 1966-73; asst state dir of TN Alpha Phi Alpha 1970-73; asst chief accountant US Postal Serv Knoxville 1971-73; dir of finances Our Voice Magazine Knoxville 1970-72; mem Amer Accounting Assn; life mem Alpha Phi Alpha; bd dir Boys Club; mem Pi Omega Pi; Phi Beta Lambda; Young Democrats of Amer; United Airline Exec Air Travel; US Jaycees; Urban League; YMCA; Knoxville Coll Alumni Assn; bd dirs Alpha Phi Alpha; mem Prince Hall Masons North Star Lodge #1 F&AM; life mem Knoxville Coll Natl Alumni Assn; Prince Hall Shriner Arabic Temple; Order of Eastern Stars; Western Consistory AASR of Freemasonry; United Supreme Council AASR Thirty Third Degree Mason; past potentate Imperial Council AEAONMS Inc; Holy Royal Arch Masons-Oriental; past master North Star F&AM; appt to bd of adv American Biographical Inst 1986; bd of dir Alpha Phi Alpha, bd dir Building Foundation; Natl Pan Hellenic Council Exec Committee. **HONORS/ACHIEVEMENTS:** Alpha Kappa Mu Natl Hon Soc; Bro of the Yr Award; Alpha Mu Lambda Chap; Alpha Phi Alpha 1975; Mary E Gilbert Scholarship Award for Grad Study 1972; MWPH Grand Lodge of IL-Grand Master's Award 1982; Clarence Clinkscales Award North Star Lodge 1985; Outstanding Young Men of America 1981 & 1985; Appreciation Award Chicago Society of Children & Families bd of dir 1985; Outstanding Serv Award Black Media Inc 1986; Best & Brightest Young Men in America 1987; Alpha Phi Alpha Presidential Award 1988. **BUSINESS ADDRESS:** Executive Dir, Alpha Phi Alpha Fraternity Inc, 4432 S King Dr, Chicago, IL 60653.

BLASSINGAME, JOHN W.
Educator, editor. **PERSONAL:** Born Mar 23, 1940, Covington, GA. **EDUCATION:** Ft Valley State Coll GA, BA 1960; Howard Univ, MA 1961; Yale Univ, PhD 1971. **CAREER:** Yale Univ, lecturer, 1970-71, asst prof, 1971-72, acting chmn Afro Amer Studies, 1971-72, assoc prof, 1972-74, prof 1974-. **ORGANIZATIONS:** Mem Phi Alpha Theta; Assn Behav Soc Scis; Assn Study Afro-Amer Life & Hist; So & Amer Hist Assn; orgn Amer Historian Contrib ed Black Scholar 1971-; adv bd Afro-Amer Bicentennial Corp 1971-; bd Centre Internationale de Recherches Africaines 1971-; mem Amer Hist Assn Rev Bd 1972-73; ed bd Reviews Amer Hist 1973-; Journal Negro Hist 1973-; exec cncl Assn Study Afro-Amer Life Hist 1973-; Amer Hist Assn 1974; chmn prog com Orgn Amer Historians 1974. **HONORS/ACHIEVEMENTS:** Pub books essays articles. **BUSINESS ADDRESS:** Professor, YaleUniv, Afro-Amer Studies Dept, New Haven, CT 06520.

BLAYLOCK, ENID V.
Educator. **PERSONAL:** Born Jan 24, 1925; married Lorenzo Blaylock; children: Andre, Dellis. **EDUCATION:** Loma Linda Univ, BSRN 1953; UCLA, MS 1959; Univ of So CA, PhD 1966. **CAREER:** White Memorial Hospital & St Vincent Hosp LA, staff nurse 1953-59; LA City School Dist, health supvr 1960-66; Inst for Intercultural Educ, dir 1974-; CA State Univ, assoc prof educ Psychology 1966-. **ORGANIZATIONS:** Lecturer UCLA Med Media Network 1969-; consult Vet Adminstrn Hosp 1970-74; Human Awareness Training Orange Co Personnel 1974; mem Professional Adv Bd Charles Drew Post Grad Med Sch 1973-; sec treas Assn of Black Coll Faculty & Staff of So CA 1972-; mem Women in Educ Leadership; Hon Assn for Women in Educ1970-. **HONORS/ACHIEVEMENTS:** Citation Distinguished Serv SDA So CA Conf Sch 1965; Ed Assn of Black Coll Faculty & Staff of So CA Newsletter 1972-74; author of article on drug abuse. **BUSINESS ADDRESS:** Assoc Prof Educ Psychol, CA StateUniv, 6101 E 7th St, Long Beach, CA 90840.

BLAYTON-TAYLOR, BETTY
Business executive, artist, arts administrator. **PERSONAL:** Born Jul 10, 1937, Newport News, VA; daughter of James Blain Blayton and Alleyne Houser Blayton. **EDUCATION:** Syracuse U, BFA 1959; City Coll; Art Student's League; Brooklyn Museum Sch. **CAREER:** Major exhibits 1959-; St Thomas, Virgin Island, art tchr 1959-60; City of New York, recreation leader 1960-64; Haryou Art/Graphics & Plastics, art supr 1964-67; The Children's Art Carnival, exec dir 1969-89, pres 1972-89; New York City Board of Education, consultant 1977-89. **ORGANIZATIONS:** Bd mem The Arts & Bus Council 1978-89; bd mem The Printmakers Workshop 1975-; founding mem The Studio Museum in Harlem 1965-77, mem bd Major Exhibit 1959-84; mem Commn for Cultural Affairs 1979-89; professional prof City Coll/Elem Ed Dept 1974; mem Nat Guild Sch 1982-; consult NYS Bd of Educ 1977-89; Natl Black Child Development Institute 1980-89. **HONORS/ACHIEVEMENTS:** Empire State Woman of the Yr in the Arts NYS Governor's Award 1984; Artist in Residence Tougoloo Coll MS 1982; Artist in Residence Norfolk State Coll VA 1980; Artist in Residence Fisk Univ TN 1978; Making Thoughts Become, publication 1978; Black Women in the Arts Award, Governor of New York 1988. **HOME ADDRESS:** 2001 Creston Ave, Bronx, NY 10453. **BUSINESS ADDRESS:** President and Executive Director, The Children's Art Carnival, 62 Hamilton Terr, New York, NY 10031.

BLEDSOE, CAROLYN E. LEWIS
Government planner. **PERSONAL:** Born Jan 31, 1946, Richmond, VA; married Rev Earl L Bledsoe; children: Katrina L, Tanya N. **EDUCATION:** VA State Univ, AB 1968, 36 hours towards MA degree. **CAREER:** King William Co Public Schools, teacher 1968-69; Richmond Public Schools, teacher 1969-71; Dept Developmental Progs, rsch analyst 1972-80; City Government,sr planner 1980-. **ORGANIZATIONS:** Vp bd of dirs Commonwealth Girl Scout Cncl of VA Inc 1976-84; 1979-81; secty/treas Northern VA Baptist Ministers' Wives 1981-83; chair scholarship comm the VA State Assn of Ministers' Wives 1981-84. **HOME ADDRESS:** 711 Wadsworth Drive, Richmond, VA 23236. **BUSINESS ADDRESS:** Senior Planner, Dept Planning & Development, 900 E Broad St Rm 500, Richmond, VA 23219.

BLEDSOE, FRANK S.
Judge. **PERSONAL:** Born Mar 28, 1891, Pulaski, TN. **EDUCATION:** Paul Quinn Coll Waco TX, BS 1916; Howard Univ Law Sch, LLB (Cum Laude) 1922. **CAREER:** Private Practice, law; Magistrate Ct MO, judge 24 yrs. **HONORS/ACHIEVEMENTS:** Valedictorian Class of 1916. **MILITARY SERVICE:** WW I pfc 1918-1919.

BLEDSOE, JAMES L.
City government official. **PERSONAL:** Born Dec 01, 1947, Tuskegee, AL; son of Willie James Bledsoe and Ada M Randle Bledsoe Jackson; married Clara A Fisher, Jun 14, 1975; children: Patrice Bledsoe. **EDUCATION:** Univ of West Florida, Pensacola, FL, BS, Marketing, 1972, MPA, 1974. **CAREER:** Dept of Budget, City of Miami, chief mgmt analyst, 1978-86; Dept of Solid Waste, City of Miami, asst to the dir, 1986; Dept of Solid Waste, City of Miami, asst dir, 1987; Dept of Budget, City of Miami, asst dir, 1988. **ORGANIZATIONS:** Mem, Amer Soc for Public Admin, 1978-, Natl Forum for Black Public Admin, 1982-, Amer Public Works Assn, 1986-; bd mem, Selective Serv System, 1987-.

BLEDSOE, MILTON HARGIS, JR.
Business executive. **PERSONAL:** Born Sep 25, 1941, Kansas City, KS; married Wanda Louise Scott; children: Milton, Michele. **EDUCATION:** Univ of MO, BBA 1969; Independence Comm Coll, AA 1961. **CAREER:** Douglass State Bank, asst cashier 1963-67; Swope Pkwy Natl Bank, asst vice pres 1968-72; Unity State Bank, pres, ceo, vice pres, cashier 1973-. **ORGANIZATIONS:** Dir first vice pres Dayton Urban League; Dayton Chap of Natl Bus League; bd dir Peanut Press; Amer Inst of Banking; Grtr Dayton Minority Purchasing Cncl; mem Westmont Optimist Club; Downtown Dayton Assn; Dayton Fund for Rehab; Dayton Racquet Club; mem Natl Honor Soc 1957-59. **MILITARY SERVICE:** AUSR 2nd lt 1963-69. **BUSINESS ADDRESS:** President/Vice President, Unity State Bank, P O Box 7277 Station B, Dayton, OH 45407.

BLOCK, CAROLYN B.
Psychologist. **PERSONAL:** Born Sep 07, 1942, New Orleans. **EDUCATION:** Xavier Univ, BS, 1963; Boston Univ, MS 1965, MA 1968, PhD 1971. **CAREER:** Private Practice, psychologist, 1977-; KQED-TV, content consult 1977-80; Fmly & Chld Crss Serv Mt Zion Hosp San Francisco, dir 1972-74; Children Youth Serv Wstsd Comm Mental Health Cntr, dir 1974-77; Center Univ of CA, psychological counseling 1970-72; Wstsd Mental Health Center, psychologist consultant, 1972-; Private Practice San Francisco, psychologist, 19773-. **ORGANIZATIONS:** Lecturer, Psychology Dept, Univ of CA 1973-; mem, Natl Assn of Black Psychologist, 1970-; San Francisco Red Cross; Am Psychology Assn 1972-; bd mem, San Francisco Com on Children's TV 1973-. **BUSINESS ADDRESS:** 1947 Divisadero St #2, San Francisco, CA 94115.

BLOCKER, HELEN POWELL
Retired accountant & volunteer. **PERSONAL:** Born Aug 15, 1923, Cape Charles, VA; married Adolphus; children: Preston, Kevin. **EDUCATION:** City Coll of NY, 1946; NY U, 1966; Pace Univ NYC, BPS 1983. **CAREER:** Mt Calvary Child Care Cntr, accountant 1953-78; Shiloh Baptist Ch, youth dir 1962-66; New York City Bd of Edn, family asst 1965-73; Scribner's Publishing, acctnt 1984; Shiloh Baptist Ch, dir of training; Vets Administration 306; fiscal accounts clerk-administration. **ORGANIZATIONS:** Tax cnslr aide AARP 1985-89; mem Inst of Internal Auditors 1982-; mem Nat Assn of Black Acctnts 1982-; exec bd Nat Cncl of Negro Women Inc 1980-87; sec Comm Planning Bd 5 Yrs; personnel chrmn Hunts Point Multi-Service Cntr 1980-87; personnel chair, Montefiore Medical Center Advisory Bd 1978-89; finance commission, South Bronx Mental Health Council 1989-. **HONORS/ACHIEVEMENTS:** 15 yr Achievement Nat Cncl of Negro Women Inc 1989; 100 yr Serv New York City Mission Soc Cadet Corps 1974; Black History #1 Sch Dist #7 Bronx 1974; Serv to Youth Shiloh Baptist Ch Sch 1981; Bronx NANBP Women's Club, Sojourner Truth Natl Awd 1986. **HOME ADDRESS:** 700 E 156th St, Bronx, NY 10455.

BLOCKSON, CHARLES L.
Educator. **PERSONAL:** Born Dec 16, 1933, Norristown, PA; children: Noelle. **EDUCATION:** PA State U, 1956; Villinova U, Hon Degree Educ 1979; Lincoln Univ, Hon Degree 1987. **CAREER:** PA Blk History Committee, dir 1976-; Historcl Soc of PA, bd mem 1976-83; PA Afro-Amer Hist Bd, dir 1976-; Governor's Heritage Pgm, governor's commissioner 1983-; TempleUniv Charles L Blockson Afro-Am Collectn, curator. **ORGANIZATIONS:** Mem NAACP 1974-; cncl mem PA State Univ Alumni Cncl 1982-; committee mem Temple Univ Centennial Committee 1983-; mem Urban League of PA; mem NAACP; mem Montgomery Cnty of PA Bicentennial Committee 1982-83. **HONORS/ACHIEVEMENTS:** PA St Quarterback Award PA State Quarterback Club 1984; PA Black History Book 1975; Blk Geneolgy Book 1977; Alumni Fellow Awd Penn State Univ 1979; Underground Railroad in PA 1980; Cover Story for Nat Geographic Mag "The Underground Railroad" 1984, "People of the Sea Island" 1987; The Underground Railroad First Person Narratives Book 1987; Lifetime Achievement Awd Before Columbus Foundation 1987. **MILITARY SERVICE:** AUS 1957-55. **BUSINESS ADDRESS:** Curator, TempleUniv, Broad & Berks St, Sullivan Hall, Philadelphia, PA 19122.

BLOOMFIELD, RANDALL D.
Physician. **PERSONAL:** Born Aug 03, 1923, New York City, NY; children: 2 children. **EDUCATION:** CCNY, BS 1949; Downstate Med Ctr, MD 1953. **CAREER:** Kings City Hospital, intern, surgeon 1953-54; Obs/Gyn, resident 1954-58; Kings City Hosp Brooklyn-Cumberland Med Ctr, dir; Private practice, physician. **ORGANIZATIONS:** Mem St John's Episcopal Hosp Mem, AMA, Kings Cty Med Soc; fellow Amer Coll OB/GYN; mem Amer Coll Surg, Brooklyn Gyn Soc, NY Observ Soc, Natl Med Assoc; diplomate Amer Bd

OB/GYN. **HONORS/ACHIEVEMENTS:** Cert Gynecol Oncology. **MILITARY SERVICE:** AUS WWII 1943.

BLOUIN, ROSE LOUISE
Educator. **PERSONAL:** Born Dec 13, 1948, Chicago, IL; daughter of Paul Blouin and Louise Blouin; children: Kimaada, Bakari. **EDUCATION:** Univ of IL Chicago, BA 1971; Chicago State Univ, MA 1983. **CAREER:** Chicago State Univ, staff assoc center for women's identity studies 1980-83, lecturer/English Composition 1983-87; City of Harvey IL, public relations dir 1984-86; Third World Press, assoc editor 1983-; photographer; Columbia Coll Chicago, English inst; co-owner, Spiraling Staircase, Inc. **ORGANIZATIONS:** Public relations consultant Inst of Positive Educ, African-Amer Book Ctr, Speak Up!, Communication Ctr Inc 1983-; freelance photography, Amer Airlines, Mary Thompson Hospital, Citizen Newspapers, various artists & arts organizations. **HONORS/ACHIEVEMENTS:** Co-author "Experiencing Your Identity" Developmental Materials 1982; Best Photography Awd Milwaukee Inner City Art Fair 1985; Purchase Award Museum of Sci & Industry "Black Creativity Exhibit" 1986; Purchase Award DuSable Museum of Afro-Amer History Art Fair 1986; traveling exhbiit acceptance "Roots, A Contemporary Inspiration," Evanston Art Center 1986-88; juried exhibit acceptance Atlanta Life Ins Natl Art Exhibit 1987; JB Speed Art Museum Louisville KY 1987. **HOME ADDRESS:** 8236 So Michigan Ave, Chicago, IL 60619. **BUSINESS ADDRESS:** English Inst, Columbia College, 623 So Wabash Ave, Chicago, IL 60605.

BLOUNT, CHARLOTTE RENEE
Journalist. **PERSONAL:** Born Mar 02, 1952, Washington, DC. **EDUCATION:** Catholic Univ Scholastic Journalism Inst, attended 1967; OH Univ, attended 1970-72; Amer Univ Washington DC, BA Journalism 1974, grad courses 1975-76. **CAREER:** WOUB-FM Athens OH, reporter/announcer 1971-72; Washington DC Voice & Visions Prods, freelance talent 1973-; WOOK-FM Washington, reporter/announcer 1973-74; WILD Boston, reporter/announcer 1974; Securities & Exchange Commn, writer 1974-75; George Washington Univ, assoc prof 1978-; Mutual Black Network, White House/state dept corres. **ORGANIZATIONS:** Mem Zeta Phi Beta Sor Beta Zeta Chap Washington. **HONORS/ACHIEVEMENTS:** Nominated Most Outstanding Young Woman 1976; Newswoman of the Yr Natl Assn of TV & Radio Artists 1976; Young Career Woman DC Natl Fed of Bus & Professional Women 1976; Nat Pub Relations Dir Zeta Phi Beta 1976-78. **BUSINESS ADDRESS:** Correspondent, Mutual Black Network, 1755 Jefferson Davis Hwy, Arlington, VA 22202.

BLOUNT, CLARENCE W.
Retired educator. **PERSONAL:** Born Apr 20, 1921, Richland, NC; married Gordine Chisolm; children: 3 children. **EDUCATION:** Morgan State Univ, BA 1950; Johns Hopkins Univ, MA. **CAREER:** Baltimore City Public Schools, educator 24 yrs; Community Coll Baltimore, admin asst to pres retired. **ORGANIZATIONS:** Mem MD Sen 1970-; 1st black chmn Balt City Senatorial Del; 1st black MD Del Natl Dem Comm; mem Acad Pol Sci, Acad Pol & Soc Sci, NEA, Morgan State Univ & Johns Hopkins Univ Alumni Assoc; chmn Urban Serv Conf 1958-; 1st black chmn Reg Bd Natl Conf Christians & Jews; bd Provident Hosp; bd Loyola HS; mem Baltimore Urban League, NAACP, Alpha Phi Alpha Hall of Fame, Douglass & Hunbar HS; majority leader MD Senate; former asst maj leader MD Senate 1979-82; former chmn MD Leg Black Caucus 1982-84. **HONORS/ACHIEVEMENTS:** Comm Serv Awd Druid Hill YMCA 1969; Citizenship Awd Modawmin Merchants Assoc 1970; Merit Awd Zeta Phi Beta, Phi Beta Sigma; Citizenship Awd Alpha Phi Alpha 1974. **MILITARY SERVICE:** WWII.

BLOUNT, LARRY ELISHA
Educator. **PERSONAL:** Born May 17, 1950, Vidalia, GA; married Sandra Grace Smith; children: Kendra Michele, Erin Nichole. **EDUCATION:** Univ of MI, BA Pol Sci 1972; Univ of Cincinnati Sch of Law, JD 1975; Columbia Univ Sch of Law, LLM 1976. **CAREER:** Univ of GA, asst law prof, 1976-79; Thurmond & Blount Attys Counselors at Law, partner of counsel, 1979-; Univ of GA, assoc law prof, 1979-. **ORGANIZATIONS:** Pres chmn BSR Economic Develop Corp Inc 1979-; pres chmn Comp Serv Bus Consult Corp Inc 1979-; bd chmn Athens Area Oppors Indsl Ctrs 1978-; bd mem OIC of Amer 1978-; com mem GA State Const Revision Commn 1979-. **HONORS/ACHIEVEMENTS:** Serv Awd Council on Legal Educ Oppor 1977; Serv Awd Abeneefoocoo Honor Soc 1978; Serv Awd Black Amer Law Students Assn 1978; Disting Serv Awd Leadership GA Inst Inc 1979. **HOME ADDRESS:** 120 Watson Dr, Athens, GA 30605.

BLOUNT, MELVIN CORNELL
Athlete. **PERSONAL:** Born Apr 10, 1948, Vidalia, GA; married Leslie; children: Tanisia, Norris. **EDUCATION:** Southern Univ Baton Rouge, Grad 1970. **CAREER:** Pittsburgh Steelers, professional football player 1976-84; NFL, dir player relations 1984-; Cobb Creek Farms, owner/oper; Mel Blount Youth Home Inc, founder; Mel Blount Cellular Phone Co, owner/oper. **ORGANIZATIONS:** Mem bd dirs Pgh Childrens Museum; mem policy Cncl Natl Ctr for Youth & their Families; mem bd dir Amer Red Cross; rep Red Cross on visit to Mauritania N Africa factfinding expedition; mem Paint Horse Assn, Amer Quarter Horse Assn, Natl Cutting Horse Assn. **HONORS/ACHIEVEMENTS:** NFL League Leader in Interceptions 1975; named MVP Pittsburgh Steelers 1975; NFL Player of the Yr 1975; MVP Pro Bowl 1976.

BLOUNT, WILBUR CLANTON
Educator. **PERSONAL:** Born Feb 05, 1929, Columbus, OH; married Elsie M; children: Elizabeth, Jacquelyn, Angela, Wilbur. **EDUCATION:** OH State Univ, BSc 1951, Grad Sch 1952, Coll of Medicine MD 1959. **CAREER:** Bur of Educ Rsch OSU, rsch assoc 1951-52; USAF Biodynamic Branch Aerospace Med Field Lab NM, rsch develop officer 1954-56; Radio Isotope OSU, chemist 1958-59; Inst Rsch in Vision OSU, rsch assoc 1964; Univ of KY Med Ctr, asst prof dir retinal serv 1971-77; Ophthalmologist. **ORGANIZATIONS:** Mem Acad of Medicine of Columbus & Franklin Co; assoc fellow Aerospace Med Assn 1969; life mem Air Force Assn; mem Amer Acad of Ophthalmology; mem Amer Assn for Med Systems Informatics; mem Amer Assn of Ophthalmology; fellow Amer Coll of Surgeons 1973; mem Amer Diabetes Assn; mem Amer Intra-Ocular Implant Soc; mem AMA; mem Assn of Military Surgeons of the US; mem bd trustees Central OH Diabetes Assn; mem Civil Aviation Med Assn; mem Columbus Ophthalmology & Otolaryngology Soc; mem Natl Med Assn; mem OH Ophthalmological Soc; mem Ophthalmic Photographers Soc; mem Order of Hipprocates The OH State Univ Coll of Medicine Med Alumni Soc; mem Pan Amer Assn of Ophthalmologists; life mem Reserve Officers Assn; mem Soc of Military Ophthalmologists; mem Soc of USAF Flight Surgeons, USAF Clinical Surgeons; life mem OH State Univ Alumni Assn; mem Pres's Club OH State Univ; mem military affairscomm Tuskegee Airmen Inc OH Chapt; mem bd trustees Vision Ctr of Central OH. **HONORS/ACHIEVEMENTS:** Disting Military Student OH State Univ Air Force Reserve Training Corps 1950; Disting Military Grad OH State Univ Air Force Reserve Training Corps 1951; Who's Who in Aviation 1973; Who's Who in the Midwest 1975-76 1982-83; Men of Achievement Intl Biographical Ctr Cambridge England 1976; Jane's Who's Who in Aviation and Aerospace US edition 1983 Natl Aeronautic Inst Publ; Who's Who in the World 1985 ed; Citation for Distinguished Achievement conferred by OH State Univ Office of Minority Affairs 1984. **MILITARY SERVICE:** USAF 1st lt air rsch develop command 1954-56; USAF Reserves & Air Natl Guard col oang 20 yrs. **BUSINESS ADDRESS:** 300 East Town St, Columbus, OH 43215.

BLOW, SARAH
Retired director. **PERSONAL:** Born Sep 14, 1921, Kennett Square, PA; daughter of Boston Parsons and Celia Carey; widowed; children: Roxine Louise, Michael Warren. **EDUCATION:** St Johns Univ, BS 1955; Col Univ, MA 1958. **CAREER:** Kings Cty Hosp Ctr, asst dir nursing 1966-68; Provident Clin Neighbor Health Ctr, dir nursing 1968-70; Concord Nursing Home, admiss 1972-74; Kings Cty Hosp Ctr, dir of patient serv 1977; White House Conf on Aging, gov appt delegate 1982. **ORGANIZATIONS:** Mem Amer Nurses Assoc 1948; founder, past pres Womens League of Sci & Med Inc 1960-75; lic nrsg home adm NY 1972; delegate UN for Natl Assoc of Negro Bus & Professional Womens Clubs Inc 1973; sec Brooklyn Assoc for Mental Health 1976; bd mem Marcus Garvey Nursing Home 1978; natl chmn Freedmens Nurses Alumni Clubs Reunion 1979; trustee Concord Baptist Church Brooklyn. **HONORS/ACHIEVEMENTS:** 1st prize NY NAACP Top Memshp Writer 1963; Brooklyn Disting Citizens Awd 1973; Prof Awd 1974; Comm Awd 1974; Humanitarian Awd 1975; So Journer Truth Awd 1978; Comm Serv Awd 1979; Apprec Awd for Outstanding Comm Partic & Leadership 1984; Apprec Awd from Shirley Chisholm Cultural Inst for Children Inc 1984; Humanitarian Awd (Alpha Cosmetologists) 1986; "A Black Woman Who Makes It Happen", Natl Council of Negro Woman Wueens Section, 1989; (non government) delegate to the United Nations for the Natl Assn of Negro Business and Professional Women Clubs Inc, 1988-. **HOME ADDRESS:** 312 Brooklyn Ave, Brooklyn, NY 11213.

BLUDSON-FRANCIS, VERNETT MICHELLE
Bank executive. **PERSONAL:** Born Feb 18, 1951, New York, NY; daughter of William Benjamin Bludson and Alfreda Peace Bludson; married Robert Francis, Sr, Aug 15, 1981; children: Robert Francis, Jr. **EDUCATION:** New York Univ, New York NY, BS, 1973, MPA, 1976. **CAREER:** Morgan Guaranty Trust, New York NY, mgmt trainee, 1973-75; Citibank, NA, New York, NY, vice pres, 1975-; Natl Minority/Women's Vendor Program, Citibank, NA, New York, NY vice pres & dir, 1977-. **ORGANIZATIONS:** Mem, Natl Urban Affairs Council, 1984-; financial sec, Harlem YMCA, 1985-; mem advisory bd, Natl Minority Business Council, 1986-; vice chmn of bd, New York/New Jersey Minority Purchasing Council, 1986-; bd mem, 1986-, fundraiser Benefit comm mem, 1987, Harlem Dowling-Westside Center for Children & Family Serv; bd mem, YM/YMCA Day Care Centers Inc, 1986-; corporate bd mem, Assn of Minority Enterprises of New York, 1987-; corporate bd mem, Caribbean-Amer Chamber of Commerce, 1987-; mem, EDGES, 1988-, mem, Coalition of 100 Black Women, mem, NAACP, mem,UBC, mem, Black Achievers in Industry Alumni Assn, mem, Images-Wall Street Chapter, mem, Cornell Univ Cooperative Extension Program, mem Natl Assn of Women Business Owners, mem, New York State Dept of Economic Devel Minority and Women's Business Div. **HONORS/ACHIEVEMENTS:** Black Achievers, Citibank/Harlem YMCA, 1984; Those Who Make A Difference, Natl Urban Affairs Council, 1985; Minority Advocate of the Year, US Dept of Commerce MBDA Regional Office, 1985; Mary McLeod Bethune Award, Natl Council of Negro Women, 1986; Public Private-Sector Award, US Dept of Housing and Urban Devel, 1986; Banker of the Year, Urban Bankers Coalition, 1987; Woman of the Year, Harlem YMCA, 1987; Cecelia Cabiness Saunders Award, New Harlem YMCA, 1987; Top 100 Black Business & Professional Women, Dollars & Sense Magazine, 1988; co-sponsor, Exec Banking programs with NMBC, 1983, 1984, 1985, Exec Banking Program with Westchester Minority Contractors Assn, 1986; Career Exploration summer internship program with Hunter Coll & Coalition of 100 Black Women, 1986; co-host, First Annu al BAI Alumni Fundraiser, 1986; co-chair, NUAC Student Devel Dinner, 1988; sponsor, Dept of Defense Symposium for the Vendor Input Comm, 1988. **HOME ADDRESS:** 65 W 96th St, Apt 20C, New York, NY 10025.

BLUE, DANIEL W., JR.
Business executive. **PERSONAL:** Born Apr 22, 1939, Dillon, SC; married Susie Wright; children: Daniel, III, Susan Danielle. **EDUCATION:** BA 1960; John Jay Coll of Crmnl Jstc. **CAREER:** City of Newark, exec dir office of mayor Newark human rights commn, responible for implementation of 1st affirmative action program; Newark Police Dept, admin asst to CO comm Organ 1970; Newark Police Acad, recruit patrolman 1973; Orangeburg SC, organ 1st successful boyscott to desegregate Woolworth dept store, bus terminal & other facilities 1959-60. **ORGANIZATIONS:** Mem Frdrck Dgls Training Prog 1970; orgn 1st St Wd Hum Rghts Orgn in St of NJ; mem NAACP; Upsln Phi Chap Omega Psi Phi; hon mem Brnz Shlds Mncpl Crrmn; mem Frntrs Internat; Newark Club; chmn Fund Rsng Com NAACP; Multi-prps Cntr Inc; Urban Leag; Intl Assn of Ofcl Humn Rghts Agy; Nat Assn of Hum Rghts Wrkrs; Hum Civ Rghts Assn of NJ; Am Soc for Pub Admin; Intrnat Chf of Polc; Inst of Soc Rels; Untd Nats Newark Chpt; So 17 St Blck Assn; Comm Agency Servg Alchlcs; Prsbytr of Newark Synd of NJ; Untd Presb Ch; elder in Clntn Ave Untd Prsbyn Ch; rep bd tst Untd Comm Corp. **HONORS/ACHIEVEMENTS:** Organized 1st Meet Your Mayor Night Newark; Certificate of inst in Mgmt Science; Certificate of Mrtrs Participation Newark; Commendation D Award for Outstanding Narcotics Arst 1969; Commendation C for Excellent Plc Duty 1969; Outstanding Achievement Award Central Ward Athletic Assn; E Rsvlt Intl Wrkshp; vice chmn Mayor's Policy Recruitment Comm. **MILITARY SERVICE:** AUS.

BLUE, VIDA
Professional baseball player. **PERSONAL:** Born Jul 28, 1949, Mansfield, LA. **EDUCATION:** Southern Univ Baton Rouge LA, attended. **CAREER:** Burlington, baseball player 1968; Birmingham, baseball player 1969; Oakland, baseball player 1969; Iowa, baseball player 1970; Oakland, baseball player 1970-77; Kansas City, baseball player 1982-83; San Francisco, 1978-81,85-86. **HONORS/ACHIEVEMENTS:** Led Amer League in shutouts with 8 in 1971; Named Amer League Pitcher of the Year by The Sporting News 1971; Named Amer League Most Valuable Player by Baseball Writers' Assoc of Amer 1971; Won Amer League Cy Young Memorial Awd 1971; Named lefthanded pitcher on The Sporting News Amer

League All-Star Team 1971; Named to Amer League All-Star Team 1977; Named Lefthanded pitcher on The Sporting News Natl League All-Star Team 1978; Named Natl League Pitcher of the Year by The Sporting News 1978; Named to Natl League All-Star Team 1980.

BLUFORD, GRADY L.
Personnel director. **PERSONAL:** Son of Atha Bluford; married Harriet; children: Michelle, Derrick. **EDUCATION:** Morningside Coll, BS. **CAREER:** St Luke's Med Ctr, med tech; Goodwill Ind Wall St Mission, vice pres of personnel, bd of dir; pastor, Westside Church of Christ. **HONORS/ACHIEVEMENTS:** Outstanding Young Man Award Jr Chamber of Commerce, 1965; past pres, Iowa Rehabilitation, 1989-90; pres, Suburban Rotary Club. **BUSINESS ADDRESS:** Dir of Personnel, Goodwill Industries, 3100 West 4th St, Sioux City, IA 51103.

BLUFORD, GUION STEWART, JR.
Air force officer, NASA astronaut. **PERSONAL:** Born Nov 22, 1942, Philadelphia, PA; son of Guion Bluford and Lolita Bluford; married Linda Tull; children: Guion Stewart III, James Trevor. **EDUCATION:** Pennsylvania State Univ, BS, 1964; Williams Air Force Base, Arizona, pilot training, 1964; Squadron Officers School, 1971; Air Force Inst of Technology, MS, 1974, PhD, 1978; Univ of Houston Clear Lake, MBA, 1987. **CAREER:** USAF F-4C pilot, Vietnam; instructor pilot, standardization/evaluation officer, asst flight commander, Sheppard Air Force Base, Texas, 1967; staff devel engineer, chief of aerodynamics & airframe branch, Wright-Patterson Air Force Base, Ohio, 1974-78; NASA astronaut, 1979-; mission specialist, STS-8 Orbiter Challenger, August 1983; mission specialist, STS 61-A Orbiter Challenger, October 1985; point of contact for generic Spacelab issues and External Tank issues, Astronaut Office, 1987; assigned technical duties, Astronaut Office. **ORGANIZATIONS:** Assoc Fellow, Amer Inst of Aeronautics and Astronautics; member, Air Force Assn, Tau Beta Pi, Natl Technical Assn, Tuskegee Airmen. **HONORS/ACHIEVEMENTS:** Leadership Award, Phi Delta Kappa, 1962; Distinguished Natl Scientist Award, Natl Soc of Black Engineers, 1979; two NASA Group Achievement Awards, 1980, 1981; Distinguished Alumni Award, 1983, Alumni Fellow Award, 1986, Pennsylvania State Univ Alumni Assn; NASA Space Flight Medal, 1983, 1985; Ebony Black Achievement Award, 1983; Image Award, NAACP, 1983; Distinguished Service Medal, State of Pennsylvania, 1984; Whitney Young Memorial Award, New York City Urban League; honorary doctorate degrees from Florida A&M Univ, Texas Southern Univ, Virginia State Univ, Morgan State Univ, Stevens Inst of Technology, Tuskegee Inst, Bowie State Coll, Thomas Jefferson Univ, Chicago State Univ, Georgian Ct Coll; logged 314 hours in space. **MILITARY SERVICE:** USAF, 1964-; distinguished Air Force ROTC graduate, 1964; Natl Defense Serv Medal, 1965; Vietnam Campaign Medal, 1967; Vietnam Cross of Gallantry with Palm, 1967; Vietnam Serv Medal, 1967; Ten Air Force Medals, 1967; three Air Force Outstanding Unit Awards, 1967, 1970, 1972; German Air Force Aviation Badge, Federal Republic of West Germany, 1969; T-38 Instructor Pilot of the Month, 1970; Air Training Command Outstanding Flight Safety Award, 1970; Air Force Commendation Medal, 1972; Mervin E Gross Award, Air Force Inst of Technology, 1974; Air Force Meritorious Serv Award, 1978; USAF Command Pilot Astronaut Wings, 1983; Defense Superior Serv Medal. **BUSINESS ADDRESS:** NASA Astronaut, Lyndon B Johnson Space Center, Code CB, Houston, TX 77058.

BLUITT, BENJAMIN
Coach. **PERSONAL:** Born Jul 28, 1924, Chicago, IL; married Doris Purvis; children: Alison, Benjamin Jr. **EDUCATION:** Loyola Univ, BS Zoology 1950. **CAREER:** St Anselm Comm Center, dir, 1957-65; Chicago Public School System, Biology teacher, Chemistry teacher, Physical Science teacher, 1953-69; Univ of Detroit, asst basketball coach, 1969-73; St Mary's of Redford, athletic dir, coach, counselor, 1974-75; Cornell Univ, coach 1977. **ORGANIZATIONS:** Big Brother Orgn; Kappa Alpha Psi Frat; Knights of Columbus; Rotary Club; Sci Club of Amer; Sci Tchrs of Amer; Optimists; Natl Educ Assn. **HONORS/ACHIEVEMENTS:** Loyola Univ Ath Hall of Fame 1976; pub articles Black Dig 1967 1968; North Amer Rev 1969; mem Natl Inv Basketball Tour 1949; Honorable Mention All Amer Bsktbl Sporting News & Helms Found 1949. **MILITARY SERVICE:** AAF 1943-46.

BLUNT, ROGER RECKLING
Building & construction business owner. **PERSONAL:** Born Oct 12, 1930, Providence, RI; son of Harry Weeden and Bertha Reckling Blunt; married DeRosette Yvonne Hendricks; children: Roger Jr, Jennifer Mari, Amy Elizabeth, Jonathan Hendricks. **EDUCATION:** USMA West Point, NY, BS 1956; MA Inst of Tech, MS 1962, MS 1962. **CAREER:** US Army Corps of Engr, officer 1956-69; Harbridge House Intl, senior asso 1969-71; Tyroc Construction Corp, CEO chmn 1971-; Blunt Enterprises Inc, CEO chrmn 1974-; Blunt & Evans Consulting Engr, managing partner 1979-84; Essex Construction Corp, chmn of bd, CEO 1985-. **ORGANIZATIONS:** Dir Potomac Electric Power Co 1984-; dir Greater WA Bd of Trade 1985; vice pres of finance and member, Northeast Region Boy Scouts of America; mem State of MD Water Resources Adv Commn; dir Univ of MD Foundation; dir District of Columbia Public Schools Foundation; dir Greater Washington Rsch Ctr; mem Natl & DC Socs of Professional Engrs; mem Amer Soc of Civil Engrs; bd of regents Univ of Maryland system; dir Association of Governing Boards of Universities and Colleges. **HONORS/ACHIEVEMENTS:** Comm serv Junior Citizens Corps Inc 1985; Reg Prof Engr Dist of Columbia 1963; Business Leadership Greater Washington Business Ctr 1976,78; Reg Prof Engr NY State 1981; Distinguished Serv Awd Natl Asphalt Pavement Assoc 1984; Whitney Young Award, Boys Scouts of America. **MILITARY SERVICE:** US Army Reserves major genl 1983; received Distinguished Service Medal, 1986. **BUSINESS ADDRESS:** Chairman of the Board/Pres, Blunt Enterprises Inc, 2018 5th St NE, Washington, DC 20002.

BLUNT-BATTLE, MADELYNE BOWEN
Publisher. **PERSONAL:** Born Apr 07, Providence, RI; daughter of William M. Davis and Ora Davis; married Cleon Battle; children: Rolanda Elizabeth. **EDUCATION:** Numerous special courses; Bryant Business Coll, RI; Case Western Reserve, Mgmt. **CAREER:** US Dept of Justice, traveling cons-media relations conf planner comm relations dept; Cleveland Call-Post, 1st full-time advertising sales woman 1959-60; Thomas J Davis Agency, admin asst; Kaiser WKBF-TV,TV producer 1968; Hurray for Black Women, prod, founder; Clubdate magazine, pres, owner, publisher. **ORGANIZATIONS:** Mem, NAMD, NHFL, NAACP; special program coordinator "Com of Concern" United Pastors Assoc; program producer "Devel of Consumer Conf", 'Hurray for Black Women" founder. **HONORS/ACHIEVEMENTS:** Recognition for Documentary "Black Peace" 1968; Business Woman of the Year, CSU 1975; Black Woman of the Year City Council 1979; Award of Excellence City Commiss 1979; Gov Business Award 1980; Key to the City Mayor of Omaha NE Media Conf Race Relations; AKA Award; Top Ladies of Distinction Award Serv Comm 1982; Business Award Black Media 1983; Leadership Cleveland 1985 as one of cities Most Valuable Resources; Outstanding Business Contribution media award United Way Sources 1986; Award for Outstanding Contribution WJMO Business 1986; Rosa Parks Award, Pioneer in Business, 1989; Cleveland Roundtable, Congressman Louis Stokes 21st Congressional Caucus Award, Outstanding Business, 1989.

BLYE, CECIL A., SR.
Attorney. **PERSONAL:** Born Nov 10, 1927, Gainesville, FL; son of Richard Blye and Janie Blye; married Alice; children: Cecilia, Cecil Jr, Steven. **EDUCATION:** Attended Clark Coll, Northwestern Univ, Univ of Louisville. **CAREER:** The Louisville Defender, editor 1958-68; Blye & Webb, sr partner 1972-79; Blye, Blye & Blye, attorney 1987-. **ORGANIZATIONS:** Mem Amer, KY, Louisville Bar Assns; gen counsel KY Elks; Louisville-Jefferson Co Fedn Tchrs & Amer Postal Workers Union; Louisville Br mem Alpha Phi Alpha Frat; chmn Louisville NAACP Legal Redress Com. **MILITARY SERVICE:** AUS 1st lt 1952-54. **BUSINESS ADDRESS:** Attorney, Blye, Blye & Blye, 247 S Shawnee Terr Blvd, Louisville, KY 40212.

BOAGS, CHARLES D.
Judge. **PERSONAL:** Born Jul 31, 1929, Brooklyn, NY; divorced; children: Lisa M, Martin R, Sarah E. **EDUCATION:** Long Island Univ, BA 1951; Brooklyn Law School, LLB 1956. **CAREER:** Compton Mun Ct Office, prel hearing dep 1958-61, supr ct trial dep 1961-71, dep in charge 1971-72; Cen Surpv Ct Trials Div LA Cty Publ Def Office, asst chief 1972-79; Beverly Hills Municipal Ct, judge 1979-. **ORGANIZATIONS:** Mem, pres adv comm SW Commun Coll 1974; mem Langston Law Club 1958-84, NAPP 1970-77; bd dir Ctr Study Racial & soc Issues 1970-77, CA State Bar Comm, Corr Facilities 1973-77, CA Bd Leg Spec 1973-77, Black Stud Psych Assoc 1969,70; adm NY State Bar 1956, CA State Bar 1958. **HONORS/ACHIEVEMENTS:** Cert Sp Crim Law 1973; Publ, Lectr, Vol Consult Cert of Apprec Awd Black Caucus Faculty, Admin & Staff Univ CA San Diego 1972; Cert of Apprec LA Cty Dist Attny's Youth Adv Bd 1973; Cert of Apprec Teem Post Youth Info Ctr 1974-76; Cert of Apprec Legal Aid Found of LA 1974; Trial Lawyer of the Year Langston Law Club 1975. **MILITARY SERVICE:** USMC 1951-53. **BUSINESS ADDRESS:** Judge, Beverly Hills Municipal Cout, 9355 Burton Way, Beverly Hills, CA 90210.

BOARD, DWAINE
Professional athlete. **PERSONAL:** Born Nov 29, 1956, Rocky Mount, VA. **EDUCATION:** NC A&T Greensboro, BS Ind Tech 1979. **CAREER:** San Francisco 49ers, Devensive End 1979-. **ORGANIZATIONS:** Niners most successful rookie ldng tm in sacks in 1979; 4 yr Starter for NC A&T linebacker; selected to Mutual Radio All-america Tm 3 times; All-mid-estrn Athletic Conf Tm selection his final 2 seasons; voted MEAC Def Player of Yr 1977; Clg & Pro Ftbl Wkly 49ers Player of Yr. **BUSINESS ADDRESS:** San Francisco 49ers, 711 Nevada St, Redwood City, CA 94061.

BOARDLEY, CURTESTINE MAY
Federal government training manager. **PERSONAL:** Born Dec 03, 1943, Sandersville, GA; daughter of William May and Zena Reaves May; married James E Boardley, Jul 27, 1968; children: Angela B, Zena Y. **EDUCATION:** Tuskegee Inst, BS 1965, MEd 1967. **CAREER:** Tuskegee Inst, admin asst to dean of women 1966-67; Howard Univ, residence counselor 1967-68; Public Sch of DC, counselor 1968; Vocational Rehab Admin of DC, vocational rehab counselor & acting coord counselor 1968-70; Fed Comm Commn, employee counselor 1970-73, dir EEO 1973-76; Civil Serv Commn, office of fed EEO 1976-79; Strayer Coll, Washington DC, instructor, 1987, 1989; US Office of Personnel Mgmt, EEO specialist, office of affirmative employ progs , mgr, personnel mgmt training div, 1979-. **ORGANIZATIONS:** Mem Amer Personnel & Guidance Assn 1968-; Natl Capitol Personnel & Guidance Assn 1969-71; APGA Assn for Non-White Concerns 1975-; DC Met EEO Council 1975; co-fndr Black Women for Social Action; mem Natl Cncl of Negro Women; mem, Rehoboth Baptist Church, 1971-87; mem, Ebeneezer AME Church, 1981-; vice pres, Fort Washington Charter Chapter, Amer Business Women's Assn, 1986-; mem, Amer Assn for Counseling & Devel, 1967-; mem, The Group, Washington DC Metropolitan Area, 1981-. **HONORS/ACHIEVEMENTS:** Nominee for 1975 Salute Black Women of the Met Area; Outstanding Grad Sr Tuskegee Inst YWCA 1965; participant in 1965 Natl Student YWCA Latin Amer Seminar to Chile & Peru; US Office of Personnel Mgmt, Meritorious Performance Award, 1985, Merit Pay Cash Award, 1988. **HOME ADDRESS:** 2902 Kingsway Rd, Fort Washington, MD 20744.

BOATWRIGHT, JOSEPH WELDON
Physician. **PERSONAL:** Born Jan 04, 1949, Richmond, VA; married Evelyn Donella Durham; children: Joseph Weldon IV. **EDUCATION:** Davis & Elkins Coll, BS 1970; Univ of VA Sch of Med, MD 1974; Med Coll of VA Grad Sch of Med Edn, residency 1978. **CAREER:** Private Practice, pediatrician. **ORGANIZATIONS:** Mem active staff St Mary's Hosp; mem active staff Richmond Meml Hosp; clinical instr Med Coll of VA; mem N Chamberlayne Civic Assn. **HONORS/ACHIEVEMENTS:** Hon Scholarship Davis & Elkins Coll 1966; Scholarship Univ of VA 1970. **HOME ADDRESS:** 8321 Futham Ct, Richmond, VA 23227.

BOATWRIGHT, MCHENRY RUTHERFORD
Concert artist. **PERSONAL:** Born Feb 29, 1928, Tenile, GA. **EDUCATION:** Attended, New England Conservatory. **CAREER:** Soloist New York Philharmonic, Philadelphia Orchestra, "The Visitation".

BOBBITT, LEROY
Attorney. **PERSONAL:** Born Nov 01, 1943, Jackson, MS; son of Leroy Bobbitt and Susie Bobbitt; married Andrea; children: Dawn, Antoinette. **EDUCATION:** MI State Univ, BA 1966; Stanford Univ Sch of Law, JD 1969. **CAREER:** Paul, Weiss, Rifkind, Wharton & Garrison, attorney 1970-74; Loeb & Loeb, attorney 1974, partner 1980-. **ORGANIZATIONS:** Mem State Bar of CA, Los Angeles Co Bar Assn, Amer Bar Assn; mem Los Angeles Copyright Soc, Black Entertainment & Sports Lawyers Assn. **BUSINESS ADDRESS:** Attorney, Loeb & Loeb, 10100 Santa Monica Blvd, #2200, Los Angeles, CA 90067.

BOBINO, RITA FLORENCIA
Educational administration, psychologist. **PERSONAL:** Born Jun 18, 1934, San Francisco, CA; daughter of Arthur Cummings and Urania Cummings; married Felix Joseph Bobino Jr;

children: Sharelle Denice Haqq, Michael J, Mario J, Mauricio Malaika J. **EDUCATION:** Laney Coll, AA 1973; Coll of the Holy Names, BS 1975; CA State Univ Hayward, MS 1977; The Wright Inst, PhD 1985. **CAREER:** Oakland Poverty Prog, 1960-71; Children Hosp Alameda Cty, dir women infants & childen's prog WIC 1973-76; Berkeley Mental Health Youth Prog, mental health worker 1976-77; San Francisco Streetwork Prog, counselor 1977-80; Oakland Unified Schools Youth Diversion Prog for HS, cities in schools dir 1980-84; Oakland Unified School Sr High, counselor, family therapist; on call-sexual assault therapist Highland Emergency Hospital Oakland; private practice in Oakland; Oakland Unified Schools Farwest High School, principal TSA, 1987-88. **ORGANIZATIONS:** Co-founder, dir BWAMU 1976-, Relationship Strategy 1978-; mem Bay Area Black Psych 1979; NAACP 1983-85, Juvenile Hall Diversion Program Lucy King; mem Alpha Nu Omega Chap Alpha Kappa Alpha; Oakland Black Educators; member, Oakland Educ Assn 1980-; licensed marriage family therapist, California, 1980-. **HONORS/ACHIEVEMENTS:** Social Science Honor Soc Pi Gamma Mu 1975; "Self-Concept of Black Students Who Have Failed" masters thesis; "African Amer Fathers & Daughters" doctoral dissertation completed. **HOME ADDRESS:** 3833 Elston Ave, Oakland, CA 94602.

BOBO, ROSCOE LEMUAL
County commissioner. **PERSONAL:** Born Nov 25, 1912, Abbeville Co, SC; married Jennie Shaw; children: Dennis, Jeannette. **CAREER:** MI Police Dept, patrolman to asst chief of police 1943-66; Wayne Co, legislative agent. **ORGANIZATIONS:** Chmn bd of commr Co of Wayne MI; chmn Wayne Co Detroit Criminal Justice Council 1 yr; mem Ecorse City Council; Mayor Pro-Tem City of Ecorse; Wayne Co Anicillary Manpower Planning Bd; mem NAACP River Rouge Ecorse; Intl Assn of Police Chiefs; past pres Beechwood Comm Ctr Men's Club. **HONORS/ACHIEVEMENTS:** Dem of Yr Wayne Co MI 1974. **BUSINESS ADDRESS:** Legislative Agent, Wayne Co, 726 City Co Bldg, Detroit, MI 48226.

BOCAGE, RONALD J.
Corporate counsel to insurance company. **PERSONAL:** Born Mar 18, 1946, New Orleans, LA; son of Charles L Bocage and Eva Charles Bocage; married Myrna DeGruy Bocage, Aug 16, 1969. **EDUCATION:** Univ of New Orleans, New Orleans LA, BA, 1968; Harvard Law School, Cambridge MA, JD, 1972. **CAREER:** Mintz, Levin, Cohn, Ferris, Glovsky & Popeo, Boston MA, assoc, 1972-74; John Hancock Mutual Life Insurance Co, Boston MA, atty, 1974-79, asst counsel, 1979-83, assoc counsel, 1983-86, sr assoc counsel, 1986, second vice pres & counsel, 1986-88, vice pres & counsel, 1988-. **ORGANIZATIONS:** Mem, Amer Bar Assn (Corporate Section), 1972-; mem, Massachusetts Black Lawyers Assn, 1976-; mem bd dir, Fund for the Arts in Newton, 1983-; Assn of Life Insurance Counsel, 1986-; mem advisory bd, Voluntary Action Center/United Way of Massachusetts, 1989. **MILITARY SERVICE:** US Army Reserve, E-7 (staff sergeant), 1969-75. **BUSINESS ADDRESS:** Vice Pres & Counsel, John Hancock Mutual Life Insurance Co, John Hancock Place T-55, PO Box 111, Boston, MA 02117.

BODDEN, WENDELL N.
Business executive. **PERSONAL:** Born Mar 08, 1930, New York, NY; married Natalie; children: Mark, Wendell Jr, Ingrid. **EDUCATION:** Attended, CW Post Coll, Armed Forces Inst. **CAREER:** Grumman Aerospace Corp, asst group leader & designer of structural systems 1966-68, dir cooperative educ & hS work/study progs 1968-74, mgr continuing educ sect 1974-. **ORGANIZATIONS:** Past vice pres Natl Cooperative Educ Assn 1973-74; chmn educ com NAACP Long Island; mem Wyandawch Devel Corp; Belmont Lake Civic Assn; Afro-Amer Rep; NY State Citz Adv Cncl on Occupational Educ 1975-; Nassau/Suffolk United Way Allocations Panel 1975-. **BUSINESS ADDRESS:** Manager, Continuing Educ Sect, Grumman Aerospace Center, Dept 327-Plant 39, Bethpage, NY 11714.

BODDIE, ALGERNON OWENS
Contractor. **PERSONAL:** Born Apr 03, 1933, Demopolis, AL; married Velma Fitzmon. **EDUCATION:** Tuskegee Inst AL, BS Indust Ed 1954. **CAREER:** St Judes Ed Inst Montgomery AL, teacher 1954-55; Boddie's Bldg Constr Inc, proprietor & estimator 1963-70; FHA Seattle, consult fee insp 1969-71; Tacoma Comm Devel, consult 1976-77; Boddie's Bldg Constr Inc, pres 1970-85. **ORGANIZATIONS:** Mem Tacoma Bldg & Fire Code Appeals Bd 1969-76; mem Tacoma Chap Assoc Gen Contractors of Amer 1974-85; pres Tacoma Publ Library Bd of Trustees 1978-79. **HONORS/ACHIEVEMENTS:** Comm Coop Awd Tacoma Publ Schools Div of Vocational Rehab 1971. **BUSINESS ADDRESS:** President, Boddie's Bldg Construction Inc, 2102 S 12th St, Tacoma, WA 98405.

BODDIE, ARTHUR WALKER
Physician. **PERSONAL:** Born Apr 21, 1910, Forsyth, GA; married Denise K Gray MD; children: Christopher, Nicholas. **EDUCATION:** Atlanta Univ, AB 1931; Meharry Med Coll, MD 1935. **ORGANIZATIONS:** Mem Kappa Alpha Psi 1933; mem Acad of Family Practice 1949, MI State Med Soc 1949, Natl Med Assoc, Amer Soc of Abdominal Surgeons 1960, Pan Amer Med Assoc 1968; exec comm Acad of Family Practice 1973-77; mem Plymouth Congr Church; life mem NAACP; examiner Selective Service; co-founder Detroit Med & Surg Ctr. **HONORS/ACHIEVEMENTS:** Citation Pres Roosevelt, Truman, Harper Grace Hosp, St Joseph Meml Hosp, Detroit Meml Hosp; fellow Amer Acad of Family Med.

BODDIE, DANIEL W.
Attorney. **PERSONAL:** Born Feb 10, 1922, New Rochelle, NY; married Annie Virginia Wise. **EDUCATION:** VA Union U, AB 1953; Cornell Law Sch, JD 1949. **CAREER:** Corp Counsel City of New Rochelle, 2nd asst; Law Sec; City Judge; Privat Practice. **ORGANIZATIONS:** Pres New Rochelle Bar Assn 1972; past chmn New Rochelle Hsng Auth; past legal & counsel NAACP; mem Omega Psi Phi; trustee Bethesda Bapt Ch. **MILITARY SERVICE:** AUS m/sgt 1945. **BUSINESS ADDRESS:** 515 North Ave, New Rochelle, NY.

BODDIE, GWENDOLYN M.
Educator. **PERSONAL:** Born Aug 04, 1957, Columbus, GA. **EDUCATION:** Mercer Univ, BA 1979; Tuskegee Inst, MEd 1981. **CAREER:** Tuskegee Area Health Educ Ctr, program coord 1981-83; Booker Washington Comm Ctr, program coord 1983; Atlanta Jr Coll, counselor 1983-85; Southern Univ, dir student recruitment 1985-. **ORGANIZATIONS:** Mem United Way 1983. **HONORS/ACHIEVEMENTS:** Kappa Delta Pi Lambda Delta 1980. **BUSINESS ADDRESS:** Dir Student Recruitment, Southern University, PO Box 9399, Baton Rouge, LA 70813.

BODDIE, LEWIS F., SR.
Physician. **PERSONAL:** Born Apr 04, 1913, Forsyth, GA; son of William F Boddie MD and Luetta T Sams Boddie MD; married Marian Bernice Claytor; children: Roberta, Lewis Jr, Bernice, Pamela, Kenneth, Margaret, Fredda. **EDUCATION:** Morehouse Coll, AB 1933; Meharry Coll, MD 1938. **CAREER:** Physician and surgeon, private practice. **ORGANIZATIONS:** Diplomate Natl Bd 1941, Amer Bd Obstetrics & Gynecology 1949; fellow Amer Coll Surgeons 1950, Amer Coll Obstetrics & Gynecology; chmn 1968-70, vice chmn 1965-67, Dept OB/Gyn; consult staff Queen of Angels Hosp; clinical asst prof Univ of So CA; dir, sec Vernbro Med Corp 1952-; dir State Bd Childrens Home Soc of CA 1952; pres Children's Home Soc 1968-70; dir Child Welfare League of Amer 1969-75; mem adv comm LA Welfare Planning Council 1958-61; mem Priorities Committee and Allocations Committee, United Way of Los Angeles 1985-. **HONORS/ACHIEVEMENTS:** Citation LA Cty Bd Supvr; Resolution of Appreciation LA City Council 1958. **HOME ADDRESS:** 1215 S Gramercy Pl, Los Angeles, CA 90019.

BODDIE, LOUISE
Business executive. **PERSONAL:** Born Feb 24, 1935, Winona, MS; married Thomas R; children: Jeanette, Dennis. **EDUCATION:** Kent State Univ, Bus Admin 1962. **CAREER:** 4th Dist Police Commun Rel, zone rep 1983-; Boddie Record Mfg & Rec Clevelend OH, vp. **ORGANIZATIONS:** Mem NBL 1966-, Council of Retail Merchants & Citizen League 1966-; sec Forest City Hosp Aux 1970-76; sec Businessmen Credit Union Cleveland 1972-79; vice pres Cleveland Bus League & Econ Devel Corp 1974-80; grand matron Daughters of Sphinx 1975-; bd mem Comm Relation Bd City of Cleveland 1977; mem SME 1978-; pres Cleveland Bus League 1978-81; bd mem Fed Minority Bus League Org 1980-; mem S East Area Women Caucus 1980-. **HONORS/ACHIEVEMENTS:** Serv Awd Cleveland Bus League 1973; Serv Awd City of Cleveland 1977; Outstanding Leadership Awds US Cong, OH Senate, City of Cleveland 1977-79; Woman of the Year Clubdate Mag 1979. **BUSINESS ADDRESS:** Vice President, Boddie Record Mfg & Rec, 12202 Union Ave, Cleveland, OH 44105.

BODRICK, LEONARD EUGENE
Educator. **PERSONAL:** Born May 17, 1953, Orangeburg, SC; married Sharon Trice; children: Jabari Talib, Nia Imani. **EDUCATION:** Johnson C Smith Univ, BA (Cum Laude) 1976; Univ of Pittsburgh, MPIA Pub Admin 1979; Univ of NC-Chapel Hill, PhD Prog 1980-83. **CAREER:** Three Rivers Youth Inc, staff counselor 1978-79; Southern Ctr Rural & Urban Develop, training dir 1979-80; Educ Oppor Ctr Roxboro NC, outreach coun 1983-85; Johnson C Smith Univ, dir upward bound prog. **ORGANIZATIONS:** Mem TransAfrica 1977-; finance chair 1985-87, conference chair 1987, NC Southern Area rep 1987-89 NC Council of Educ Oppor Progs; mem Amer Soc of Public Administrators, Conference of Minority Public Administrators; founding mem UNCF Inter-Alumni Chapt; founding mem managing editor GSPIA Journal; founding mem Exec Council Black Grad and Professional Student Caucus; mem Charlotte Council for Children, NAACP, SCLC, Charlotte Drop-Out Prevention Collaborative. **HONORS/ACHIEVEMENTS:** Horne Scholarship 1973; Babcock Scholarship 1974; Pre-Doctoral Fellowship 1976; Training Grant 1977; founding member/managing editor Univ of Pittsburgh GSPIA 1979; Teaching Assistantship UNC Chapel Hill 1981-82; Outstanding Young Men of Amer 1982. **HOME ADDRESS:** 2500 Eastway Dr, Charlotte, NC 28205. **BUSINESS ADDRESS:** Dir Upward Bound Program, Johnson C Smith University, 100 Beatties Ford Rd, Charlotte, NC 28216.

BOFFMAN, JAMES
Educator. **PERSONAL:** Born Feb 20, 1929, New York. **EDUCATION:** CCNY, BS Edn, special hons Romance Languages 1951, MA 1957; Univ of Lyon France, diploma 1952; Boston U, EdD. **CAREER:** NYC Bd of Educ, supt High School, 1970-(retired); Thomas Jefferson High School, prin, 1969; Ft Hamilton High School, chmn Foreign Languages, 1968; Dewitt Clinton High School, asst prin, 1967, teacher guidance counselor, 1959-67; Douglas Jr High School, teacher of French, 1952-59. **ORGANIZATIONS:** Mem Assn of Asst Supt 1970; chmn Assn of Foreign Lang 1968; Assn for Study of Negro Life & Hist 1967; asst examiner Bd of Examiners NYC, Bd ofEduc Ldr Operation Crossroads Africa 1966; interpreter US Dept of State 1970. **HONORS/ACHIEVEMENTS:** Idea Fellow Univ of San Diego 1977, Univ of San Francisco 1978, Harvey Mudd Coll 1979. **MILITARY SERVICE:** AUS corpl Signal Corps 1952-54.

BOGARD, HAZEL ZINAMON
Inspector. **PERSONAL:** Born Jan 08, 1925, Little Rock, AR; widowed; children: Jueroy, Veronica, Ike Jr, Victor, Rosemary, Debra, Hazel Jr. **EDUCATION:** Univ of CA, 1945; Livingstone Coll, 1974 & 1978. **CAREER:** Little Rock Br NAACP, pres 1979-81; Westinghouse, inspector 1964-80; NAACP, vice pres 1976-79. **ORGANIZATIONS:** Life mem NAACP; tchr Dramatic Interpretations Comm Little Rock; dist dir of Christian educ AME Zion Ch N AR Conf 1972-78; life mem Missionary Soc Ch AME Zion. **HONORS/ACHIEVEMENTS:** Life membrshp plaque NAACP Little Rock 1978. **BUSINESS ADDRESS:** Inspector, North American Phillips, Woodrow at Roosevelt St, Little Rock, AR 72206.

BOGGAN, DANIEL, JR.
Appointed government official. **PERSONAL:** Born Dec 09, 1945, Albion, MI; married Jacqueline Ann Beal; children: Devone, Daniel III, Dhanthan, Alike. **EDUCATION:** Albion Coll, BA 1967; Univ of MI, MSW 1967. **CAREER:** Starr Commonwealth for Boys, clinical supv 1968-70; Jackson MI, asst city mgr 1970-72; Flint MI, dep city mgr 1972-74; city mgr 1974-76; Portland OR, dir mgmt serv 1976-78; San Diego CA, asst cty admin 1978-79; Essex Cty NJ, cty admin 1979-82; Berkeley CA, city mgr 1982-; Univ of CA Berkeley, assoc vice chancellor business and admin serv 1986, acting vice chancellor business and admin serv 1986-87, vice chancellor business and admin serv 1987-. **ORGANIZATIONS:** Chmn Alameda Cty Mgrs Assoc 1984-85; chmn committee on minorities & women League of CA Cities 1985-. **HONORS/ACHIEVEMENTS:** Outstanding Young Men of America Jr Chamber 1973; Outstanding Public Admin Natl Soc of Afro-Amer Police 1975. **BUSINESS ADDRESS:** Vice Chancellor, University of CA Berkeley, Chancellor's Office, 200 California Hall, Berkeley, CA 94720.

BOGGS, JAMES
Author. **PERSONAL:** Born May 28, 1919, Marion Junction, AL; married Grace Lee; children: James, Wayman, Donald, Jacqueline, Thomasine, Ernestine. **CAREER:** Detroit Automobile Plant, former production worker 28 yrs; Author, "The Am Revolution, Pages from

a Negro Worker's Notebook" 1963, "Racism & the Class Struggle" 1970; co-authored, "Revolution & Evolution in the 20th Century" 1974, "Conversations in ME, Exploring Our Nation's Future" 1978. **BUSINESS ADDRESS:** 3061 Field St, Detroit, MI 48214.

BOGGS, NATHANIEL
Educator & educational administrator. **PERSONAL:** Born Dec 19, 1926, Anniston, AL; children: Paula, Cornell, Lynette, Andy. **EDUCATION:** Howard Univ, BS 1951, MS 1955, PhD 1963; UCLA, Post Doc 1969-70. **CAREER:** 155 AGF Band Grafenwohr Germany, dir 1946; Walter Reed, physiologist 1956-59; Natl Inst of Science, eastern reg vice pres 1970-71; Beta Beta Beta Biological Soc, sponsor 1971-73; Coll of Sci & Tech, dean vsu 1972-74, dean famu 1974-76; AL State Univ the Graduate School, interim dean asu 1984-. **ORGANIZATIONS:** Vstg prof zoology UCLA 1969-70; pres Nu Lambda Chap Alpha Phi Alpha Frat 1970-71; editor-in-chief Beta Kappa Chi Bulletin 1972-74. **HONORS/ACHIEVEMENTS:** Plaque Consortium for Black Prof Develop for Excellence in Biological Life and Marine Sciences 1977; trophy 1st place Strikes & Spares Bowling League 1983. **MILITARY SERVICE:** AUS corpl 2 yrs; Good Conduct Medal; ETO Medal; Expert Rifleman. **HOME ADDRESS:** 4060 Strathmore Dr, Montgomery, AL 36116. **BUSINESS ADDRESS:** Prof Biol-Inter Dean Grad Sch, Alabama State University, 915 S Jackson St, Montgomery, AL 36195.

BOGGUS, FRANCIS OLIVER
Attorney. **PERSONAL:** Born Nov 07, 1947, Omaha, NE; married Karen Solberg; children: Kimberly, Claire. **EDUCATION:** Univ of NE Lincoln, BS 1971; Univ of San Francisco, JD 1976. **CAREER:** Allstate Ins Co, claims 1977-81; attorney in private practice 1978-81; State of CA, attorney 1982-. **ORGANIZATIONS:** Vice pres Wiley Manuel Law Soc 1979-80; bd of dirs NAACP 1979-81; bd of dirs N CA Legal Serv Corp 1979-82. **BUSINESS ADDRESS:** Attorney, CA State Office of Admin Hear, 717 "K" St, Sacramento, CA 95814.

BOGHOSSIAN, SKUNDER
Education, artist. **PERSONAL:** Born Jul 22, 1937, Addis Ababa, Ethiopia;divorced; children: Aida Maryam, Edward Addissou. **EDUCATION:** St Martins Sch of Art London, 1955-57; Ecole des Beaux Arts Paris, vstng artst 1959-60; La Grande Chaumiere Paris, 1961-62. **CAREER:** HowardUniv Coll of Fine Arts, asso prof 1971-; One Man Sho & OHUniv Trisolini Gallery, lectr 1980; Atlanta Ctr for Black Art, instr in painting 1970-71; Addis Abada Fine Arts Sch Ethiopia, instr in painting & design 1966-69; Acad de La Grande Chaumiere Paris, asst to prof 1961-62. **ORGANIZATIONS:** Participant in seminar Afro-Am Studies Dept Harvard Univ 1974; chmn of selection com Exhibition of Cntmpryu Afrcn Art Howard Univ 1975; external exmnr Makerere Univ Kampala Uganda 1976; show African Art Today African Am Inst New York City 1974; grp show (cntmpry arts fstvl) Field Mus Chicago 1974. **HONORS/ACHIEVEMENTS:** Invited Partcpnt 2nd Cultural Moussem Asilah Morocco 1979; 1st prize for Cntmpry African painters Munich 1967; His Majesty Haile Selassie I & 1st Prize for Nat Contrbtn in the Field of Art Addis Abada Ethiopia 1967; 1st prize for Black Artist AU Atlanta GA 1970; commsnd to design a stamp "Combat Racism) UN New York City 1977. **BUSINESS ADDRESS:** Howard Univ Fine Arts, Washington, DC 20059.

BOGUES, LEON FRANKLIN
Government official. **PERSONAL:** Born Nov 08, 1926, New York City, NY; married Dorothy Johnson; children: Norma, Leon Jr. **EDUCATION:** Long Island Univ, AB 1952. **CAREER:** Dept Soc Svcs, soc investigator 1951-53; Magistrate Ct 1953; Domestic Relations Ct 1954-59; Bronx Supreme Ct 1954-59; NY City Dept of Probation, sr probation officer 1959-80; State of NY, senator 29th dist 1980-. **ORGANIZATIONS:** Vice pres bd dir W Side C of C 1975-77; exec bd mem Mid-Man NAACP 1975; chmn Polit Action Com 1975; 1st vice chmn Comm Planning Bd 1977; chmn Comm Planning Bd; chmn bd of trustees Welfare Fund Probation Officers Assn NYC. **BUSINESS ADDRESS:** Senator, State of NY Dist 28, Harlem State Ofc Bldg Rm 932, 163 W 125th St, New York, NY 10027.

BOGUS, DIANE
Educator, author & poet. **PERSONAL:** Born Jan 22, 1946, Chicago, IL; married C L Coleman. **EDUCATION:** Stillman Coll Tuscaloosa AL, BA 1968; Syracuse Univ Syracuse NY, MA 1969; Miami Univ Oxford OH, PhD 1985. **CAREER:** LA Southwest Coll, instructor 1976-81; Miami U, instructor 1981-84; WIM Publications, author 1975-, founder 1975-, publisher. **ORGANIZATIONS:** Mem Delta Sigma Theta Sorority 1965-; mem Nat Tchrs of Engl 1981-; mem Feminist Writer's Guild 1980-; mem COSMEP independent publishers 1975-. **HONORS/ACHIEVEMENTS:** Listed Who's Who Among Women Cambridge England 1983; honored by Art & Music Dept Trenton Public Lib 1983; works adapted into CA State Univ Archives 1982; nominated for Pulitzer Prize, Sapphire's Sampler 1982.

BOGUS, HOUSTON, JR.
Physician. **PERSONAL:** Born Sep 10, 1951, Knoxville, TN; son of Houston Bogus and Louise Bogus; married Dorris Loretta Gray; children: Alisha Dione, Houston III, Alyson Gray. **EDUCATION:** Univ of TN, BA 1973; Meharry Medical Coll, MD 1979. **CAREER:** United States Army, intern internal medicine 1979-80, resident internal medicine 1980-82, staff internist/chief of emergency serv 1982-83, fellow in gastroenterology 1983-85, staff internist/gastroenterologist 1985-. **ORGANIZATIONS:** Mem Omega Psi Phi Frat 1976-. **HONORS/ACHIEVEMENTS:** Mem Alpha Omega Alpha Honor Medical Soc Meharry Chap 1979-. **MILITARY SERVICE:** AUS major 10 yrs; Army Commendation Medal 1983. **HOME ADDRESS:** 94-444 Haiwale Loop, Mililani, HI 96789. **BUSINESS ADDRESS:** Staff Gastroenterologist, United States Army, Dept of Internal Medicine, Tripler AMC, Honolulu, HI 96859.

BOHEE, SUMNER T.
Physician. **PERSONAL:** Born Aug 16, 1928, Chicago, IL; married Elvira; children: Sumner III, Tiffany, Karl. **EDUCATION:** Franklin & Marshall Coll, BS 1950; Cornell Univ Med Coll, MD 1954. **CAREER:** Doctors Surg Ctr, med dir; Avalon Slauson Med Group, med dir; Fed Assets Mgmt Co Inc; pres; Metro Hosp, chief anesthesiologist 1958-71; Avalon Memorial Hosp, chief of staff 1970-85. **ORGANIZATIONS:** Bd dir Lafayette Inv Co; owner, opr Weight Reduction Med Clinics; fellow Amer Acad Family Practice; mem Natl Med Assoc, AMA, CA Med Assoc, LA Cty Med Assoc, Omega Psi Phi, Alpha Omega Alpha Downtown Mens Club, Urban League, Marina City Club, Los Angeles Club, CA Horseracing Assoc, Pacific Coast HorseRacing Assoc.

BOL, MANUTE
Basketballplayer. **EDUCATION:** Cleveland State Univ, 1984. **CAREER:** Washington Bullets, center; Golden State Warriors, center. **BUSINESS ADDRESS:** Golden State Warriors, Oakland Coliseum Arena, Oakland, CA 94621. *

BOLDEN, BETTY A.
Personnel administrator. **PERSONAL:** Born Dec 24, 1944, St Louis, MO. **EDUCATION:** Univ of Illinois, BA, 1965; DePaul Univ, MA, 1969. **CAREER:** US Dept of Labor, dep dir prsnl, exec asst 1976-78, supr prsnl mgmt spec 1975-76; US Civil Serv Commn Wash, DC, prsnl mgmt spclst 1973-75; US Postal Serv Chicago/Wash DC, prsnl mgmt spclst 1968-75; US Civl Serv Commn Chicago, career intern 1967. **ORGANIZATIONS:** Mem prnsl com Delta Sigma Theta 1979-81. **BUSINESS ADDRESS:** Special Asst to Asso Adm, Small Business Adm, 1441 L St NW Room 602, Washington, DC 20416.

BOLDEN, CHARLES E.
Program coordinator. **PERSONAL:** Born Feb 12, 1941, Alabama; married Dianne Nation; children: Charles R, Marva L. **EDUCATION:** AL State U, BS 1966; LaSalle Ext U, LLB 1975. **CAREER:** Nat Educ Assn Denver, orgnzng team coord 1970-74; Nat Educ Assn Chicago, fld rep 1968-70. **ORGANIZATIONS:** Orgnzr Publ Sch Tchrs for Collective Bargaining 1968-75; chmn Ft & Madison IA Hum Rel Comm 1967-68; orgnzd Human Rgts Ordinance Cmpgn Sigma Rho Sigma, Omega Psi Phi Frat; mem bd dirs Am Civil Libs Union PG Co MD 1975; vice pres PTA Ft Washington Forest Elem Sch 1975. **HONORS/ACHIEVEMENTS:** Tchr Advocate Awrd Compton CA 1973. **BUSINESS ADDRESS:** 1201 Sixteenth St NW, Washington, DC 20036.

BOLDEN, CHARLES FRANK, JR.
Astronaut. **PERSONAL:** Born Aug 19, 1946, Columbia, SC; married Alexis "Jackie"; children: Anthony Che, Kelly M. **EDUCATION:** United States Naval Acad, BS Elec Sci 1968; Univ of Southern CA, MS Systems Mgmt 1977. **CAREER:** NASA, astronaut candidate 1980-81, systems devel grp work on tile repair, SRB launch over pressure, launch debris prevention, shuttle autoland devel, astronaut office liaison for STS displays and controls, flight data file group, astronaut office safety officer, space shuttle software/hardware testing and verification at shuttle avionics integration lab, tech asst to the dir of flight crew opers, pilot on STS 61-C launched from Kennedy Space Ctr FL Jan 12, 1986, assigned pilot for Hubble Space Telescope mission, chief of safety div; Johnson Space Ctr, special asst to dir. **ORGANIZATIONS:** Has logged 146 hours in space; mem Marine Corps Assoc, Montford Point Marine Assoc, US Naval Inst; lifetime mem Naval Acad Alumni Assoc, Univ of So CAGeneral Alumni Assoc. **HONORS/ACHIEVEMENTS:** The Air Medal; Strike/Flight Medal; Univ of So CA Outstanding Alumni Awd 1982; Natl Tech Assoc Hon Fellow 1983; Hon Doctor of Science from Univ of SoCA 1984; Hon DHL Winthrop Coll 1986. **MILITARY SERVICE:** USMC col. **BUSINESS ADDRESS:** Chief of Safety Division, NASA Johnson Space Ctr, Houston, TX 77058.

BOLDEN, DOROTHY LEE
Business executive. **PERSONAL:** Born Oct 13, 1920, Atlanta; married Abram Thompson, Sr; children: Frank, Avon Butts, Dorothy Ingram, Altenmiece Knight, Abram, Anthony. **CAREER:** Natl Domestic Inc, pres, founder. **ORGANIZATIONS:** Dir Training Prog & Employment Agency 1968; contrib Ms Magazine, Essence Magazine, Atlanta Magazine; apptd to sec HEW Washington 1975; Commn on the Status of Women 1975; vice pres City NDP; vice pres Black Women Coalition of Atlanta; bd dir NAACP; mem Fulton County Democrats, legal aid & exec bd; mem Citizens Trust Bank Adv Bd. **HONORS/ACHIEVEMENTS:** Recip Atlanta Inquirer Mayors Awrd 1970; Wigo Adv Cncl Comm Action Awrd 1971-72; Wigo Basic Comm Awrd 1973; Econ Opportunity Atlanta Nghbrhd 1973; Omega Psi Phi Frat outstndng Comm Serv Awrd 1973; Black Womens Intl Awrd 1975; Concerned Citizens Awrd 1975. **BUSINESS ADDRESS:** Founder & Dir, Natl Domestic Workers Union, 52 Fairlee St NW, Atlanta, GA 30303.

BOLDEN, FRANK AUGUSTUS
Attorney, business executive. **PERSONAL:** Born Aug 07, 1942, Albany, GA; son of Augustus Bolden and Geraldine Bolden; married Carol Penelope Parsons; children: Brian, Ian. **EDUCATION:** Univ of VT, BA 1963; Columbia Univ Grad Sch of Bus, MBA 1972; Columbia Univ Sch of Law, JD 1972. **CAREER:** Columbia Univ, asst football coach 1971; Inst for Educ Devel, consult 1972; Cahill Gordon & Reindel, assoc 1972-75; Johnson & Johnson, atty 1975, intl atty 1976-85, sec 1984-86, vice pres corp staff 1986. **ORGANIZATIONS:** Dir Raritan Credit Union 1976-78; dir Winsor Minerals Inc 1976-87; dir Western Sources Inc 1979-87; dir Chicopee 1980; dir Inst Mediation & Conflict Resolution 1972-; adv Consortium of Met Law Sch 1972-73; sponsor Sponsors for Educ Opportunity 1973; dir NJ Assn on Corrections 1980-88; trustee Union County Coll 1983-; vice pres NJ State Opera 1984-; mem NJ Commission on Pay Equity 1984; mem NBA. **HONORS/ACHIEVEMENTS:** Matin Luther King Jr Fellowship Woodrow Wilson Found 1969-72; COGME Fellow 1970-72; Charles Evans Hughes Fellow 1971-72; Outstanding Young Man of Amer 1978. **MILITARY SERVICE:** AUS capt 1963-69. **BUSINESS ADDRESS:** Vice President Corp Staff, Johnson & Johnson, One Johnson & Johnson Plaza, New Brunswick, NJ 08933.

BOLDEN, JAMES LEE
Business executive. **PERSONAL:** Born Jun 14, 1936, Quitman, MS; married Margaret P Hardaway; children: James Jr, Sherry, Margery, Jeffery. **EDUCATION:** Topeka State Hosp, Cert 1959; LUCT Training Inst, Cert 1976; Washburn Univ, 1978. **CAREER:** Little Jim's Trucking Co, gen contractor 1958-71; Bolden Radio & TV Repair, mgr, owner 1958-66; Little Jim's Garage, mgr, owner 1969-; Four M Devel Co Inc, pres 1970-; Mid-Central Ins Cons, owner, gen agt 1974-; Mid-Amer Aviation Inc, pres. **ORGANIZATIONS:** Treas Mt Carmel Missionary Bapt Church 1966-; bd treas Black Econ Council of Topeka 1979-; chmn supervisory comm The Capital City Credit Union 1979-; bd mem Household Tech 1978-, Local Devel Corp 1979-; chmn membership comm NAACP 1979-; lecturer Enroute & Terminal ATC Procedures Oper Rain Check USA Dept of Trans Fed Aviation Admin 1980. **HONORS/ACHIEVEMENTS:** Cert of Appreciation KS State Conf of Br of NAACP 1979. **BUSINESS ADDRESS:** President, Mid-Amer Aviation Inc, 1800 Harrison, Topeka, KS 66612.

BOLDEN, JOHN HENRY
Educator. **PERSONAL:** Born Jan 10, 1922, River Junction, FL; married Bertha M Johnson; children: Richard. **EDUCATION:** FL Meml Coll, BS; FL A&M Univ, MS, MEd; IN

Univ, EdS, EdD. **CAREER:** IN Univ, rsch asst; Cheyney State Coll, dean of teachers; Duval Co, area dir; FL State Univ, assoc prof. **ORGANIZATIONS:** Pres Bolden's Coll of Music Inc; pres Bolden's Chorale Music Assn Inc; Bolden's BCM Educ & Labor Relations Ctr Inc; editor BCM Press; dir Bolden's Concert Choral; mem Amer Assn of Sch Admins; mem Phi Delta Kappa, Delta Kappa Pi, Natl Urban League, NAACP; Bolden's Academic Symposium Black Students Can Make It. **HONORS/ACHIEVEMENTS:** Nathan W Collier Meritorious Serv Awd; AASA-NASE Acad Prof Devel Awd Designing & Instructional Mgmt System, A Systematic Approach to Sch Mgmt; publications, "A Competency-Based Clinical Supervisory Module for Observing & Evaluating Teaching Performance"; "A Special Report, The Effective Mgmt Team"; "GettingEffective Results through School-Based Mgmt"; "Increasing the Effective of Personnel Mgmt in Educ"; "Balden's Songs of Faith"; "The Singing Black Church"; "A Cultural Resource and Songs of Jordan"; "Is Competency Testing the Black Students a Dilemma or an Opportunity" Select Issues & Answers; "Black Students are Achieving Excellence in Academic Achievement, Model Programs that made it Happen". **BUSINESS ADDRESS:** Associate Professor, FL StateUniv, Rm 113 Stone Blvd, Tallahassee, FL 32306.

BOLDEN, RAYMOND A.

Attorney. **PERSONAL:** Born Dec 17, 1933, Chicago, IL; children: Kathryn, Alan, Joseph. **EDUCATION:** Univ of IL, BS, LLB 1961. **CAREER:** Intelligence Div US Treas Dept, agt 1961-64; Will County, asst state atty 1964-68; Private Practice, atty. **ORGANIZATIONS:** Mem Natl & Will Cnty Bar Assns; pres Natl Blk Lwyrs Conf Joliet Br NAACP 1964-68; bd dirs Joliet-Will Cnty Comm Action Agency 1967-73; mem Will Cnty Legal Asst Prgm; chmn High Crime Redctn Comm Joliet 1975. **HONORS/ACHIEVEMENTS:** Distinguished Citizens Serv Awrd Black Student Union Lewis Univ 1975; awrd NAACP 1968. **MILITARY SERVICE:** USAF s/sgt 1953-57. **BUSINESS ADDRESS:** 81 N Chicago St, Joliet, IL.

BOLDEN, THEODORE E.

Educator. **PERSONAL:** Born Apr 19, 1920, Middleburg, VA; son of Theodore D Bolden and Mary Elizabeth (Jackson) Bolden; married Dorothy M Forde (deceased). **EDUCATION:** Lincoln U, AB 1941; Meharry Med Coll, DDS 1947; Univ IL, MS 1951, PhD 1958; Lincoln Univ, LLD (hon) 1981. **CAREER:** School of Dentistry, Meharry Med Coll, instructor, operative dentistry, pedondontics, periodontics 1948-49; Univ of IL School of Dentistry, instr pathology 1955-57, lecturer postgrad studies 1956; School of Dentistry Meharry Med Coll, spec lecturer 1956; Seton Hall Coll of Med & Dentistry, dentistry 1957-60; Med Ctr, attending pathology 1958-62, assoc prof oral diagnosis, pathology 1960-62; George W Hubbard Hosp Nashville TN, attending med & dental staff 1962-78; Meharry Med Coll School of Dentistry, prof dentistry, chmn oral path 1962-69, dir rsch 1962-73, assoc dean 1967-74; Univ of Med & Dentistry of NJ, dean 1977-78, acting chmn gen & oral path 1979-80, prof gen & oral path 1977-. **ORGANIZATIONS:** Trustee, adv Amer Fund for Dental Health 1978-85; mem, exec comm Amer Assn for Cancer Educ, 1977-78; chmn Dental, Amer Assn for Cancer Educ, 1976-77; chmn, rsch comm Acad of Dentistry for Children Natl Dental Assn 1974; pres Nashville Sect Amer Assn of Dental Rsch; mem sub-comm Curriculum Planning of Comm on Curriculum & Sched School of Dentistry 1972; councillor-at-large Amer Assn of Dental Schools 1971; chmn standing comm Alumni Assn Meharrry Med Coll 1970-73; vchmn 1969-70, chmn 1970-71 Amer Assn of Dental Schools; sec, treas George W Hubbard Hosp Med & Dental Staff 1968-70; rsch comm 1980-81,1983-84, admission comm minority sub-comm 1980-82 Univ of Med & Dentistry of NJ; co-chmn Montclair NJ Resd Crusade Amer Cancer Soc 1980-82; mem vice pres Newark Unit NJ Div Amer Cancer Soc Inc, 1983; editor, Outreach Natl Serv, 1975-82; consultant, VAH, Tuskegee, AL, 1958-, Brooklyn, NY, 1977-; trustee, Amer Fund for Dental health, 1978-86; chmn of bd, Newark Unit Amer Cancer Soc, 1984-85; trustee, Neighborhood Council, Montclair, NJ. **HONORS/ACHIEVEMENTS:** Pres Citation & Plaque Meharry Med Coll 1971; Plaque lecturer 3rd Carribean Dental Conv Tinidad 1964; Citation Personalities of the South 1970; Plaque & Citation Meharry Med Coll 1971; Cert of Apprec The Natl Dental Assoc Inc 1971; Citation The Neighborhood Council Fed Credit Union 1974; Citation Golden State Dental Assoc Inc 1974; Capital City Dental Soc & Pan-TN Dental Assoc Plaque 1977; Dentists of the Year Awd Natl Dental Assoc Inc 1977; Boss of the Years Plaque School of Dentistry Meharry Med Coll 1977; Serv to Community as Dean Plaque Natl Council of Negro Women 1978; Plaque The Univ of CT Carter G Woodson Collquim 1979; Outstanding Contribs Plaque CT Black Caucus Dentist 1979; Cert of Apprec for Serv 1979; PATCH Awd of Excellence to Theodore E BoldenDDS, PhD, FICD for Excellence & The Attainable Goal of CMDNJ-NJDS, # 1 Patch 1979; over 200 scientific publications including 10 books. **MILITARY SERVICE:** AUS sgt/1st lt DC 1943-44. **HOME ADDRESS:** 29 Montague Pl, Montclair, NJ 07042. **BUSINESS ADDRESS:** Professor of Pathology, UMDNJ NJ Dental School, 100 Bergen St, Newark, NJ 07103.

BOLDEN, WILEY SPEIGHTS

Educator. **PERSONAL:** Born Dec 18, 1918, Birmingham, AL; son of Wiley Lee Bolden Jr and Gertrude Mildred Speights Bolden; married Willie Creagh Miller, Sep 13, 1945; children: Millicent Ann, Lisa B Monette, Lelia E Crawford, Wiley Miller, Madeliene Ann. **EDUCATION:** Alabama State University, Montgomery AL, BS, 1939, further study, 1940; Atlanta University, Atlanta GA, 1941; Columbia University, Teachers College, New York NY, MA, 1947, EdD, 1957. **CAREER:** Shelby County Board of Education, Montevallo AL, principal of Almont Junior High, 1939-42; Mobile County Board of Education, Mobile AL, teacher, 1943-44; Clark College, Atlanta GA, associate professor of psychology, 1948-57, professor of psychology and chairman of department of education and psychology, 1957-63, dean of faculty and instruction, 1963-67; Southeastern Regional Educational Laboratory, Atlanta GA, associate director for research, 1967-69; Georgia State University, Atlanta GA, professor of educational foundations, 1970-87; Savannah State College, Savannah GA, acting president, 1988—. **ORGANIZATIONS:** Coordinator of research, Phelps-Stakes Fund, Cooperative Prefreshman Programs, Atlanta University Center and Dillard University, 1959-63; study director, Tuskegee University RoterScope Study, Academy for Educational Development, 1969-70; consultant, 1971-76, board of directors, 1978-82, United Board for College Development; board of directors, 1971-73, co-chairman of education committee, 1980-82, life member, 1980—, Atlanta chapter NAACP; member, Education Task Force, Atlanta Chamber of Commerce, 1972-76; member, Fulton County Grand Jurors Association, 1973-76; vice president for special projects and associate director of Title III, Advanced Institutional Development Project, 1975-77; board of directors, 1977-83, president, 1978-82, Southern Education Foundation; member of board, 1978-90, president, 1983-85, Georgia State Board of Examiners of Psychologists; member, Governor's Advisory Committee on Mental Health and Mental Retardation, 1980-83; member, advisory committee on education and career development, National Urban League, 1982—. **HONORS/ACHIEVEMENTS:** Salutatorian of graduating

class, Alabama State University, 1939; General Education Board fellow in clinical psychology, Teachers College, Columbia University, 1953-54; Phi Delta Kappa; Kappa Delta Pi; National Science Foundation science faculty fellowship, 1963-64; Roger C Smith Service Award, American Association of State Psychology Boards, 1988. **MILITARY SERVICE:** US Army, 1944-46; received Good Conduct Medal, 1945. **HOME ADDRESS:** 975 Veltre Circle, Atlanta, GA 30311.

BOLDER, J. TABER, JR.

Business executive. **PERSONAL:** Born Apr 26, 1926, Cleveland, OH; married Barbara A Williams; children: Lynn Ellen, Joseph Taber IV. **EDUCATION:** Springfield Jr Coll, 1946-47; Boston Univ, AB Psych 1950; Springfield Coll, MEd Guidance & Personnel 1953; Temple Univ, OD prog 1958-60. **CAREER:** Dept of Army Ordinance Corp Springfield MA, training officer (civilian) 1950-55; RCA Camden, training splst 1955-61; RCA Aerospace Systems Burlington MA, mgr, training & serv 1961-65; RCA Corp Staff Camden, admin training design & appl 1965-67; NBC NY, dir mgmt devel (OD) 1967-72; NBC Wash DC, dir personnel 1972-73;WRC-TV Wash DC, station mgr 1973-77; NBC-TV Stations Wash NY, vice pres station affairs 1977-. **ORGANIZATIONS:** Mem OD Org Devel Network 1963-77; vchmn Amer Soc of Trng; dir OD Div 1970-71; mem Natl Broadcasters Club 1975-79; exec comm Amer Friends Serv Comm 1959-61; exec comm Wash DC C of C 1974-79; trustee Natl Acad of TV Arts & Sci 1975-77; trustee Springfield Coll Springfield MA 1977-; pres Wash Jr Achievement 1978-79; 1st black dir, mgr, station mgr NBC; mem Alpha Epsilon Rho 1973. **HONORS/ACHIEVEMENTS:** Outstanding Achievement Awd 1st Black TV Station Mgr of Major Network by Capital Press Club 1976; Hallmark Awd for Outstanding Serv Jr Achievement of Metro WA 1977,79. **MILITARY SERVICE:** USN aircraft torpedo man 3/c 1944-46; WWII Pin, Pacific Theatre Pin 1944-46. **BUSINESS ADDRESS:** Vice President Station Affairs, NBC-TV Stations, 30 Rockefeller Plaza, New York, NY 10020.

BOLEN, DAVID B.

Ambassador/business executive—retired. **PERSONAL:** Born Dec 23, 1927, Heflin, LA; married Betty L Bolen; children: Cynthia, Myra White, David B Jr. **EDUCATION:** National War College; University of Colorado, BS, MS, 1950; Harvard University, MPA, 1960. **CAREER:** American Embassy, Monrovia, Liberia, administrative assistant, 1950-52; American Embassy, Karachi, Pakistan, economic assistant, 1952-55; U.S. Department of State, international economist at Japan-Korea desk, 1955-56; Afghanistan Desk Officer, 1957-59; American Embassy, Accra, Ghana, chief of economic section, 1960-62; staff assistant to Assistant Secretary of State for Africa, 1962-64; officer in charge, Nigerian affairs, 1964-66; American Embassy, Bonn, West Germany, economic counselor, 1967-72; American Embassy, Belgrade, Yugoslavia, economic/commercial counselor, 1972-74; ambassador to Botswana, Lesotho, and Swaziland, 1974-76; deputy assistant Secretary of State for Africa, 1976-77; American Embassy, East Berlin, East Germany, ambassador to German Democratic Republic, 1977-80; E I Du Pont de Nemours & Co, Inc, Wilmington, DE, associate director of international affairs, 1981-89; consultant, 1989—. **ORGANIZATIONS:** Member, Foreign Service Association, 1950—; member, National War College Alumni Association, 1967—; member, American Council on Germany, 1980—; vice president and director, Wilmington World Affairs Council, 1981—; director, Wilmington Trust Co, 1981—; member, Wilmington Club, 1982—; member, Rodney Square Club, 1983—; trustee, University of Delaware, 1983—; director, Urban Fund (USA), South Africa, 1987—; member, Delaware Council on Economic Education, 1987—; trustee, Medical Center of Delaware, 1987—. **HONORS/ACHIEVEMENTS:** Member, US Olympic Team, London, 1948; fourth place winner, 400 Meters, Olympic Games, 1948; Robert S. Russell Memorial Awards, 1948; Dave Bolen Olympic Award, University of Colorado, 1948; elected to Hall of Honor, University of Colorado, 1969; Norlin Distinguished Alumni Award, University of Colorado, 1969; superior honor award for outstanding and imaginative performance, Department of State, 1972-73; Department of Commerce Certificate for sustained superior performance, 1974; Alumnus of the Century Award, University of Colorado, 1977; Distinguished Alumni Service Award, University of Colorado, 1983. **HOME ADDRESS:** 26 Wesley Dr, Hockessin, DE 19707.

BOLIN, LIONEL E.

Broadcast labor rel counsel. **PERSONAL:** Born Oct 16, 1927, Poughkeepsie, NY; married Jean Rudd. **EDUCATION:** Williams Coll, BA 1948; New York Law Sch, LLB 1955. **CAREER:** First Natl City Bank (Citicorp), mgt trainee 1959-61; US Dept Justice Antitrust Div, trial atty 1961-67; New York City Law Dept, asst corp counsel 1967-69; Natl Broadcasting Co, sr attorney 1969-73, dir personnel & lab rel 1973-. **ORGANIZATIONS:** Mem NY and IL State Bar Assocs; dir & vice pres Portes Cancer Prevention Ctr 1976-, Chicago Area Project 1978-; dir ACLU of IL 1980-; trustee Williams Coll Williamstown MA 1985-89. **MILITARY SERVICE:** AUS corpl 1951-53. **BUSINESS ADDRESS:** Dir Personnel/ Labor Relations, Natl Broadcasting Co Inc, Merchandise Mart, Chicago, IL 60654.

BOLLES, A. LYNN

Anthropologist, professor. **PERSONAL:** Born Dec 04, 1949, Passaic, NJ; daughter of George Bolles and Augusta Beebe Bolles; married Dr James Walsh, Feb 09, 1980; children: Shane Bolles Walsh, Roberson James Walsh. **EDUCATION:** Syracuse University, Syracuse NY, AB, 1971; Rutgers University, New Brunswick NJ, MA, 1978, PhD, 1981. **CAREER:** Rutgers University, Livingston College, New Brunswick NJ, lecturer and teaching assistant, 1976-78, course coordinator for women's studies program, 1977; Bowdoin College, Brunswick ME, assistant professor, 1980-86, associate professor of anthropology, 1986—, director of Afro-American studies program, 1980—. **ORGANIZATIONS:** American Anthropological Assn; president, 1983-84, secretary-treasurer, 1988-90, Assn of Black Anthropologists; program chair, Assn of Feminist Anthropologists, 1989; board of directors, Assn for Women in Development, 1984-86; Caribbean Studies Assn; Latin American Studies Assn; National Council for Black Studies; Society for Applied Anthropology; Organization of Black Women Historians; New England Council of Latin American Studies; Northeast Anthropological Assn; Maine Commission on Women, Maine Humanities Council, 1983; editorial board, Feminist Studies; editorial and advisory board, Urban Anthropology. **HONORS/ACHIEVEMENTS:** Race Unity Day Award for Bowdoin Afro-American studies program, Spiritual Assembly of the Baha'is, 1983; Black History Maker of Maine Award, Augusta Black Community, 1984; Martin Luther King, Jr, Community Service Award, ME NAACP, 1988; numerous research grants. **HOME ADDRESS:** 1288 High St, Bath, ME 04530. **BUSINESS ADDRESS:** Afro-American Studies Program, Russwurm Afro-American Center, Bowdoin College, Brunswick, ME 04011.

BOLLING, BRUCE C.
City government official. **CAREER:** City Council President, Boston, MA. **BUSINESS ADDRESS:** 1 City Hall Square, Boston, MA 02201. *

BOLLING, ROYAL, JR.
Government official. **PERSONAL:** Born May 01, 1944, Boston, MA; married Marion; children: 2 Children. **EDUCATION:** Boston Univ. **CAREER:** State rep 1972. **ORGANIZATIONS:** House chmn Spl Comm on Arson Violence in Spectator Sports; mem Energy Comm; Black Caucus Office. **BUSINESS ADDRESS:** 6th Suffolk Dist, 115 Hazelton, Boston, MA 02126.

BOLTON, JULIAN TAYLOR
Elected official, telephone consultant. **PERSONAL:** Born Oct 28, 1949, Memphis, TN; married Joyce Walker; children: Julian II, Jared Walker. **EDUCATION:** Rhodes Coll, BA 1971; Memphis State Univ, MA 1973. **CAREER:** New Theatre South Ensemble, producer, dir 1978-; Bell System, systems design cons, telecommun; Shelby Cty Commiss, commissioner. **ORGANIZATIONS:** Producer New Theatre South Ensemble 1977-80; mem Memphis Black Arts Council 1981-; bd of dir Shelby Cty Comm Serv Admin 1982-; review comm Memphis ArtsCouncil 1985. **HONORS/ACHIEVEMENTS:** Producer, Dir of over 40 theatrical productions 1968-80; Fellowship Recipient consortium for Grad Study in Bus for Blacks 1971; Listed in Who's Who in AmerColl & Univ 1971. **BUSINESS ADDRESS:** Commissioner, Shelby Co Dist 2, 160 N Mid Amer Mall, Memphis, TN 38103.

BOLTON, RON
Professional athlete. **PERSONAL:** Born Apr 16, 1950, Petersburg, VA. **EDUCATION:** Norfolk St. **CAREER:** Clvlnd Browns, crnrbck 1976-; New Engl Ptrts, plyr 1972-76. **BUSINESS ADDRESS:** c/o Dee Rauch, NFL Players Association, 1300 Connecticut N W Ste 407, Washington, DC 20036.

BOLTON, WANDA E.
Educator. **PERSONAL:** Born Jul 14, 1914, Guthrie, OK. **EDUCATION:** Pittsburgh State Teachers Seminar, Certificate, 1963-64; Univ of MO Seminar, Certificate, 1964-65; Lincoln Univ, Cosmetology 3 1/2 yrs. **CAREER:** KC School Dist, instructor; Madame CJ Walker Mfg Co, cosmetology instructor; Prairie View Coll, Prairie View TX, cons-dean 1965-70; State Bd Cosmetology, state bd inspector, 1959-66. **ORGANIZATIONS:** mem, pres State Bd Dept Consumer Affairs, Cosmetology 1975-; practical testing; mem, Natl State Bds of Cosmetology, Cosmetology Accrediting Comm, Washington DC 1977-; mem Natl Interstate Council, Natl State Bds Cosmetology 1975-; mem Assn of Cosmetologists; mem OIC 1978-. **HONORS/ACHIEVEMENTS:** Recipient Beautician of Year Award 1971; Citizenship Award, 1973. **BUSINESS ADDRESS:** MO Sch Dist, 1215 E Truman Rd, Kansas City, MO.

BOMMER, MINNIE L.
Community services professional. **PERSONAL:** Born Feb 03, 1940, Covington, TN; daughter of Malcolm Yarbrough and Eula Ray Burrell; married John Samuel Bommer, Sr; children: Monica White, Gina, John Jr. **EDUCATION:** Univ of TN, continued educ 1976, 1983, 1984; TN State Univ, 1982; Spelman, 1983; Memphis State Univ, attending; Antioch University California, Rural Leadership Development Institute. **CAREER:** Tipton Cty Hosp, LPN 1968-73; Tipton Cty Human Svcs, elig counselor 1974-82; City of Covington, alderwoman (1st Black & 1st female to serve elected 1983);Douglas Health Clinic, maternal infant health outreach worker until 5/85; Tri-County Children & Family Services, director. **ORGANIZATIONS:** Chmn Tipton Cty Library Bd 1983-85; 1st vice pres TN State NAACP; mem Natl Black Women's Political Caucus, TN Women in Government; Rural West TN Minority Affairs Council; delegate, National Democratic Convention 1988; bd of directors, Tipton County Chamber of Commerce 1986-; bd of directors, Tennessee Housing Development Agency 1988-. **HONORS/ACHIEVEMENTS:** Mother of Year Canaans Church Group 1976; Delegate to White House Conf on Families State & Natl; served on Resolution Advance Drafting Comm NAACP 1985; Tennessee Women on the Move, Tennessee Political Caucus 1987; Distinguished Service Award, Tennessee Black Caucus State Legislators 1988. **HOME ADDRESS:** 707 Simonton Street, Covington, TN 38019. **BUSINESS ADDRESS:** Agency Director, Tri-County Children & Family Services Inc, James O Naifeh Building, 420 Long AveP O Box 45, Covington, TN 38019.

BONAPARTE, TONY HILLARY
Educational administrator. **PERSONAL:** Born Jun 13, 1939; son of Norman Bonaparte and Myra Bonaparte; married Sueli Fugita; children: Yvette. **EDUCATION:** St John's Univ, BBA 1963, MBA 1964; NY Univ, PhD 1967. **CAREER:** St John's Univ, asst prof 1964-68; Business Intl Corp, rsch assoc, mgmt syst 1968-70; Rapan Rsch Corp, exec dir 1970-73; Pace Univ, vice pres, dean, prof of intl bus 1968-85; Bentley Coll, vice pres for acad affairs/provost. **ORGANIZATIONS:** Dir Robert Schalkenbach Found 1975-, World Trade Inst Port Arthur 1977-, Brazil-Interpart Cabaatia Brazil 1979-; pres Middle Atlantic Assoc of Bus Admin1981-82, Fulbright Alumni Assoc 1983-84; chmn Intl Affairs Comm of the Amer Assembly 1983-; dir Assoc Black Charities 1983-. **HONORS/ACHIEVEMENTS:** Fellow Amer Assoc for the Adv of Sci 1969; Fulbright Sr Prof College Liberia 1973-74; Vstg Prof Univ of Strathdyde Univ of Edinburgh 1977; Co-Editor of book Peter Drucker Contribs to Bus Enterprise 1978; Hon DHL Southeastern Univ. **BUSINESS ADDRESS:** VP for Academic Affrs/Provost, Bentley College, Beaver & Forest Sts, Waltham, MA 02254.

BOND, ALAN D.
Business executive. **PERSONAL:** Born Jul 16, 1945, Jefferson City, TN; son of Frederick D Bond and Edna Coleman Bond; married Claudette Davis; children: Melinda Ann, Clayton Alan. **EDUCATION:** Central State Univ, BS Bus Admin 1967, post degree studies in law, business & insurance 1967-. **CAREER:** Detroit Pub Sch, instr part time; Ford Motor Co, prod planning & inven cont spec 1968-69; Control Data Corp, mat supr 1969-70; Xerox Corp, 1970-71; City of Detroit, police dept 1971-73; Chrysler Corp, prod systems & matl control specialist 1973-75; Equitable Life Assurance Soc of US, agent 1975-78; Detroit Edison Co, corp ins admin 1978-86, insurance consultant 1979-; Estate Enhancements, insurance & real estate consultant 1987. **ORGANIZATIONS:** Mem Natl Assn of Life Underwriters 1975-; trustee New Prospect Bapt Ch 1970-; mem Alpha Phi Alpha Frat 1963-; subscribing life mem NAACP 1984-. **HONORS/ACHIEVEMENTS:** Elected delegate Wayne Co Convention of Precinct Delegates 1972-; Hon Grad Natl Sales Develop Prog Xerox Corp 1970; participant Electric Passenger Car Promotion Prog 1982-83; numerous Public Serv Recog Awds Cambridge Univ England, Men of Achievement Directory, Ford Motor Co, Mayor City of Detroit. **BUSINESS ADDRESS:** Insurance/Real Est Consultant, Estate Enhancements, PO Box 32990, Detroit, MI 48232.

BOND, CECIL WALTON, JR.
Businessman. **PERSONAL:** Born Dec 30, 1937, Chester, PA; son of Cecil W Bond Sr and Frinsela P Bond; married Linette H Bond, Oct 10, 1986; children: Tracy, Cecil III. **EDUCATION:** Morgan State Univ, BS; Wharton Graduate School, two year mgmt program. **CAREER:** Central PA Natl Bank, vice pres; Southeastern PA Transportation Authority, dir of civil rights. **ORGANIZATIONS:** Urban Bankers Coalition; bd mem, Comm Accounts; bd mem, Greater Philadelphia Comm Devel Corp; Greater Philadelphia Venture Capital Corp. **MILITARY SERVICE:** US Army Military Police, major, 1961-70. **BUSINESS ADDRESS:** 714 Market St, Suite 502, Philadelphia, PA 19106.

BOND, GEORGE CLEMENT
Educator. **PERSONAL:** Born Nov 16, 1936, Knoxville, TN; son of J Max Bond and Ruth Clement; married Murray; children: Matthew, Rebecca, Jonathan, Sarah. **EDUCATION:** Boston U, BA 1959; London Sch of Econ London U, MA 1961, PhD 1968. **CAREER:** Univ of East Anglia England, asst lecturer 1966-68; Columbia U, asst prof 1969-74; Tchrs Coll Columbia U, prof 1975-. **HONORS/ACHIEVEMENTS:** Fellow Woodrow Wilson Cntr for Inter Scholars DC 1981-82; mem Inst for Advanced Studies, Princeton 1983-84; books "The Politics of Change in a Zambian Community" Univ Chicago 1976; bond African Christianity Acad Press 1979; Social Stratification and Educ in Africa 1981. **BUSINESS ADDRESS:** Professor of Anthropology, Tchrs Coll Columbia Univ, Box 10 Teachers College, ColumbiaUniv, New York, NY 10027.

BOND, GLADYS B.
Business executive. **PERSONAL:** Born Aug 26, 1914, Windsor, NC; married George L. **EDUCATION:** Temple Univ Sch of Liberal Arts; Craig Sch of Beauty Culture, grad. **CAREER:** Gladys Dress & Beauty Shop, owner 1946-67. **ORGANIZATIONS:** Dir The Center, A Place to Learn 1970-; pres Philadelphia Philos 10 yrs; past 3rd vice pres Bus & Professional Women of Phila; The Cotillion Soc; The Heritage House; City of Philadelphia Commn on Human Rels; The Chapel of Four Chplns; The Greater Philadelphia Press Wmn 1960-61; Unity Frankford Grocery Co; Pepsi Cola Co; Club Cornucopia; natl producer Miss All-Am Teenager Pageant. **HONORS/ACHIEVEMENTS:** The Tribune Chautier Ann Awrd The Gratz HS. **BUSINESS ADDRESS:** c/o Jacqueline Bond, 2235 North 19th St, Philadelphia, PA 19132.

BOND, HORACE JULIAN (JULIAN BOND)
Educator, former government official. **PERSONAL:** Born Jan 14, 1940, Nashville, TN; son of Horace Mann Bond and Julia Louise Washington Bond; divorced; children: Phyllis Jane, Horace Mann, Michael Julian, Jeffrey Alvin, Julia Louise. **EDUCATION:** Morehouse Coll, BA 1971. **CAREER:** Pappas Fellow, Univ of Pennsylvania, 1989; prof, History & Politics, Drexel Univ, 1988-89; Georgia House & Senate,1965-87; communications dir, Student Nonviolent Coordinating Comm, 1960-65; mng editor, Atlanta Inquirer, 1964. **ORGANIZATIONS:** pres, Atlanta NAACP, 1974-89; mem, Natl NAACP Bd. **HOME ADDRESS:** 6002 34th Pl, NW, Washington, DC 20015.

BOND, HOWARD H.
Consulting firm executive. **PERSONAL:** Born Jan 24, 1938, Stanford, KY; son of Frederick D Bond and Edna G Coleman Bond; married Ruby L Thomas, Jan 24, 1970; children: Sherman, Howard, Jr, Anita Warr, John, James, Edward, Alicia. **EDUCATION:** Eastern Michigan Univ, Ypsilanti MI, BS, 1965; Pace Univ, New York NY, MBA, 1974. **CAREER:** US Govt, Detroit MI, 1959-65; Ford Motor Co, Detroit MI, labor supvr, 1965-68; Gen Electric Co, Cincinnati OH, personnel mgr, 1968-69; Xerox Corp, Chicago IL, personnel dir, 1969-75; Playboy Enterprises Inc, Chicago IL, vice pres, 1975-77; Executech Consultants Inc, Cincinnati OH, pres, 1977-, corporate dir, 1977-89; Ariel Capital Mgmt Inc, corporate dir, 1983-89; Advent Bio Products, corporate dir, 1983-89. **ORGANIZATIONS:** mem, planning bd, United Way; mem, Cincinnati Bd of Educ, 1988-89; mem, Salvation Army, mem, Red Cross, Urban League of Greater Cincinnati, mem, Transafrica, mem, Kappa Alpha Psi, mem, Aleikum Temple. **HONORS/ACHIEVEMENTS:** Developed/implemented Xerox AA/EEO Strategies for Excellence, 1969; Special Recognition, Crusade of Mercy, 1976; Bd Mem of the Year, Lake County Urban League, 1976; Role Model, Cincinnati Friends of Amistad Inc, 1987; Black Business & Professional Award, Quinn Chapel AME Church, 1987; Achievers Award, Robert A Taft High School, 1988. **MILITARY SERVICE:** US Army, sergeant, 1953-58; Soldier of the Month, three times. **HOME ADDRESS:** 4040 Beechwood Ave, Cincinnati, OH 45229. **BUSINESS ADDRESS:** Pres, Executech Consultants Inc, 35 E Seventh St, Suite 714, Cincinnati, OH 45202.

BOND, JAMES ARTHUR
Educator. **PERSONAL:** Born Jul 11, 1917, Orangeburg, SC; married Ann Nordstrom; children: Sarah Louise. **EDUCATION:** Johnson C Smith Univ, BS 1938; KS Univ, MA 1942; Chicago Univ, PhD 1961. **CAREER:** Central Acad, math teacher, 1938-40; Langston Univ, Biology instructor, 1946-48; Chicago Univ & IL Univ School of Pharmacy, asst in zoology 1954-56; IL Univ, instr in biology, 1957-61, asst prof 1961-70, assoc prof 1971, asst dean library arts & science, 1974; LAS, asst dean 1977; IL Univ, assoc prof, Biology. **ORGANIZATIONS:** Ecology Soc of Amer; Amer Assn for Adv of Sci; Amer Soc of Zoology; Soc for Study of Evolution; Amer Inst of Biosciences; Biometric Soc of Amer; Soc for Genl Syst Res; Natl Assn Sci Teachers; Assn Field Museum; Assoc Smithsonian Inst; Art Inst of Chicago; Shedd Aquarium Soc; Contemporary Art Museum; DuSable Museum Soc of Sigma Xi; John M Prather Fellow, Chicago Univ, 1953; Fellow, AAAS, 1965. **HONORS/ACHIEVEMENTS:** Soc of Sigma Xi; John M Prather Fellow Chicago Univ 1953; Fellow of AAAS 1965. **MILITARY SERVICE:** Field artillery, 1942-46, 1952-53. **BUSINESS ADDRESS:** Associate Professor, Dept of Bio Sci, Univ of IL, Box 4348, Chicago, IL 60680.

BOND, JAMES G.
Educational executive. **PERSONAL:** Born Apr 17, 1924, Lorain, OH; married Lois A Leach; children: Constance, Michael, Timothy. **EDUCATION:** Baldwin Wallace Coll, BA 1948; Bowling Green State U, MA 1949; NY U, PhD 1954; Baldwin Wallace Coll, LLD 1969; Central New England Coll, DH 1973. **CAREER:** Lorain Co Mental Hygiene Clinic, staff psych, 1949-54; Toledo State & Receiving Hospital, 1950-51, chief psych, 1951-66; Univ of

Toledo, lecturer, 1954-56; Bowling Green State Univ, asst assoc prof, 1966-72; Student Affairs, vice pres, 1967-72; Amer Assn of State Colls & Univs, special consultant, 1972; CA State Univ, pres 1972-. **ORGANIZATIONS:** Mem Omicron Delta Kappa Natl Ldrshp Hon; Alpha Phi Omega; Nat Serv Frat; bd dirs Am Assn State Colls & Univs; Comstock Club; exec bd United Way; Golden Empire Boy Scouts Council; Sacramento Cnty Mntl Hlth Assn; bd dirs Am Hlth Assn; Am Justice Inst Numerous past activities. **BUSINESS ADDRESS:** 6000 J St, Sacramento, CA 95819.

BOND, JAMES G.
Politician. **PERSONAL:** Born Nov 11, 1944, Fort Valley, GA. **EDUCATION:** HS Grad, 1963. **ORGANIZATIONS:** Chmn Public Safety Com 1977; bd of dir Atlanta Legal Aid; elected Atlanta City Council 1973; chmn Com on Atlanta City Council 1975-76; chmn Labor Ed Advancement Project 1974; mem Bd of Resources Highlander Ctr; adv bd Nat Conf on Alternative State & Local Publ Policies; Voter Educ Project Fellow 1973;Southeastern dir of Youth Citizenshp Fund 1972. **BUSINESS ADDRESS:** City Hall, Atlanta, GA 30303.

BOND, JAMES MAX, JR.
Architect. **PERSONAL:** Born Jul 17, 1935, Louisville, KY; son of J Max Bond and Ruth Clement Bond; married Jean Davis Carey; children: Carey Julian, Ruth Marian. **EDUCATION:** Harvard Coll, BA (Magna Cum Laude) 1955; Harvard Grad Sch of Design, March 1958. **CAREER:** Ghana Natl Construction Corp, architect 1964-65; Univ of Sci & Tech Ghana, instructor 1965-67; Architect's Renewal Comm Harlem, exec dir 1967-68; Grad Sch of Arch & Plng Columbia Univ, asst prof to prof & chmn 1970-85; Bond Ryder James Arch PC, partner 1969-; City Coll/CUNY Sch of Environ Studies, dean/prof 1985-. **ORGANIZATIONS:** Commr New York City Planning Commn 1980-87; bd mem Studio Museum in Harlem 1984-, Municipal Arts Soc 1986-; mem Natl Orgn of Minority Architects. **HONORS/ACHIEVEMENTS:** Schomburg Center for Research in Black Culture, Harlem, New York 1980; Martin Luther King, Jr Center and Memorial, Atlanta Georgia, architect, 1980-82; Award of Excellence, Atlanta Urban Design Commission for Martin Luther King, Jr Center and Memorial 1982; Harry B Rutkins Memorial Awd AIA 1983; Whitney M Young Jr Citation Awd AIA 1987.

BOND, JOHN PERCY, III
Government official. **PERSONAL:** Born Dec 23, 1937, Washington, DC; married Eleanor Sawyer; children: Philip Sawyer, Johnna Carol. **EDUCATION:** Morgan State Univ, AB 1965; Wake Forest Univ Babcock Grad Sch of Mgmt, MBA 1975. **CAREER:** City of Winston-Salem NC, deputy city mgr 1971-78; City of Miami FL, asst city mgr 1978-79; City of Petersburg, city mgr 1979-84; Hillsborough Co FL, deputy county admin 1984; Durham Co NC, county mgr 1985-. **ORGANIZATIONS:** Past vice pres Intl City Mgmt Assoc; commr Commn on Accreditation and Law Enforcement Agencies; mem Amer Soc of Public Administrators; mem exec bd Natl Forum for Black Public Admins; president, Natl Forum for Black Public Administrators; Natl Advisory Council for Environmental Technology Transfer (EPA). **MILITARY SERVICE:** AUS capt 1960-67; Bronze Star. **BUSINESS ADDRESS:** County Manager, Durham County Government, 201 E Main St, Durham, NC 27701.

BOND, JULIAN See BOND, HORACE JULIAN

BOND, LESLIE FEE
Physician. **PERSONAL:** Born Feb 20, 1928, Louisville, KY; married Anita; children: Leslie Jr, Erik, Candace. **EDUCATION:** Univ IL, AB 1948; Meharry Med Coll, MD 1952; Am Coll Surgeons. **CAREER:** Metro Med & Hlth Serv Inc, pres; Washington Univ GI Endoscopy; asst clinical surg; Homer G Phillips Hosp, flw, resd, intern 1951-58. **ORGANIZATIONS:** Flw Am Coll & Surgeons; Intl Coll Surgeons; Soc Abdominal Surgeons; mem AMA; Natl Med Assn; St Louis Surg Soc; MO Surg Soc; pres Mound City Med Soc; MO-Pan Med Soc; Homer G Phillips Int Alumni Assn; St Louis Med Soc Cncl; sec chf staff Christian Hosp; mem Kappa Alpha Psi; Chi Delta Mu; Sigma Pi Phi; Frontiers Intl; fndr bd mem Gateway Natl Bank St Louis MO; tst Central Bapt Ch; choir mem Central Bapt Ch; team physician Country Day HS Ftbl Team; mem Page Park YMCA Bd. **HONORS/ACHIEVEMENTS:** Over 20 med articles publ. **BUSINESS ADDRESS:** 3400 N Kingshighway, St Louis, MO 63115.

BOND, LLOYD
Educator & scientist. **PERSONAL:** Born Nov 17, 1941, Brownsville, TN; married Sandra J Kras. **EDUCATION:** Hillsdale Coll, BS 1960-64; Johns Hopkins Univ, MA 1975, PhD 1976. **CAREER:** General Motors, personnel rep 1966-72; Univ of Pittsburgh Dept of Psych, asst prof 1976-82; Univ of Pittsburgh Learning R&D Ctr, assoc prof, sr scientist 1982-. **ORGANIZATIONS:** Mem NAS Committee on Military Testing 1983-, ETS Vstg Committee on Rsch 1983-; mem bd of trustees The Coll Bd 1984-. **HONORS/ACHIEVEMENTS:** Phi Beta Kappa Johns Hopkins 1977; APA Post Doctoral Fellow Amer Psych Assn 1982; Spencer Fellow Natl Acad of Ed 1980-83. **MILITARY SERVICE:** AUS E-5 1964-66. **BUSINESS ADDRESS:** Assoc Prof, Sr Scientist, Learning R&D Ctr, Dept of Psychology, 738 LRDC Bldg, Pittsburgh, PA 15260.

BOND, LOUIS GRANT
Educator. **PERSONAL:** Born Jan 06, 1947, Baltimore, MD; children: Jordan, Meredith. **EDUCATION:** Boston Univ, BA 1958; Harvard Univ, MTS 1972; Boston Coll, MEd, EdD 1974; CA Western Univ, PhD 1977. **CAREER:** Boston Univ, lecturer, instructor, 1969-; Educ Devel Social Studies, dir, parent educ, teacher trainer, curriculum developer, 1972-74; St Andres United Meth Church, pastor, 1973-; J LU-ROB Enterprises Inc, pres; B&R Corrugated Container Corp & B&R World Oil, pres, chmn of the bd. **ORGANIZATIONS:** Mem Black Meth for Church Renewal, Natl Assoc of Black School Admins, Amer Assoc of Jr & Comm Colls, Assoc of Black Psychologist, Amer Assoc of Gen Liberal Studies, Phi Beta Kappa, Harvard Univ Fac Club, NAACP. **HONORS/ACHIEVEMENTS:** Wm H Lemell Scholarship 1964; Martin Luther King Jr Grant 1970; Rockefeller Found Awd 1972; Fulbright Scholarship 1973; Hatcher Scholarship 1974. **BUSINESS ADDRESS:** President, Chmn of the Bd, B&R Corrugated Container Corp, Box 753, Millbury, MA 01527.

BONDS, BOBBY LEE
Professional athlete. **PERSONAL:** Born Mar 15, 1946, Riverside, CA; married Patricia Howard; children: Barry, Ricky, Bobby. **CAREER:** San Francisco Giants, 1968-74; NY Yankees, 1975; CA Angels, 1976-77; Chicago White Sox, 1978; TX Rangers, Cleveland Indians, 1979; St Louis Cardinals, 1980; Chicago Cubs, coach 1981. **HONORS/ACHIEVEMENTS:** Natl League's Player of the Year 1973 for hitting 283w/39 HRs, 96 RBIs & 43 steals; 3 Gold Gloves ('71,'73 & '74); All-Star 1971,73,75; 1st rookie to hit a grand slam HR in his 1st major league game in the 20th century 1968.

BONE, WINSTON S.
Clergyman. **PERSONAL:** Born Apr 07, 1932, New Amsterdam, Guyana;married Faye Alma O'Bryan; children: Alma Lorraine, Brian Winston. **EDUCATION:** InterAm Univ of PR, BA (summa cum laude) 1958; Waterloo Luth Sem, grad 1961. **CAREER:** Met NY Synod Luth Ch in Am, asst to bishop 1973-; Incarnation Luth Ch Queens, pastor 1968-73; Christ Luth Ch Brooklyn, pastor 1966-68; Luth Ch in Guyana, pres 1966; Ebenezer Luth Ch New Amsterdam Guyana, pastor 1961-66. **ORGANIZATIONS:** Chmn Admn Cncl Luth Ch in Guyana 1965-66; mem Mgmt Com Div for Professional Ldrshp 1972-80; bd of trustees Wagner Coll Staten Island NY 1969; bd of dir Luth Theol Sem at Gettysburg 1977-; chmn S Queens Luth Parish 1970-73; bd of dir Seamen & Intl House NY 1970-73. **BUSINESS ADDRESS:** Lutheran Church in America, 360tpark Ave S, New York, NY 10010.

BONET, LISA
Actress. **PERSONAL:** Born Nov 16, 1967, San Francisco, CA. **CAREER:** Appears as "Denise Huxtable" in theTV series The Cosby Show; first film Angel Heart.

BONEY, J. DON
University executive. **PERSONAL:** Born Mar 28, 1928, Calvert, TX; married Peggy; children: 3 Children. **EDUCATION:** Prairie View A&M Coll, BS 1948; Univ of TX, MEd 1957, EdD 1964. **CAREER:** Univ of Houston Downtown Coll, chancellor, 1975; Houston Community Coll System, pres, 1973-75; Houston Independent School Dist, chief of instr, 1971-72; Coll of Educ Univ of Houston, assoc dean of graduate studies, 1970-71; Univ of Houston, assoc prof of educ Psych, 1967-69. **ORGANIZATIONS:** Dir Project Upward Bound Univ of IL 1966-67; asso prof of educ Psych Univ of IL 1964-67; dir of testng Port Arthur Indpndnt Sch Dist 1959-64; coord of Guidance Temple Pub Sch 1956-59, tchr 1948-56; TX Pub Sch Mem, Am & Houston Psych Assn; Nat Training Lab Mem, Adv Educ Com, C of C, Houston; adv com Hope Cntr for Youth Houston; adv com Goodwill Indstrs Houston. **HONORS/ACHIEVEMENTS:** Outstndng Alumnus Awrd Prairie View A&M Coll 1966 & 1970; meritorious serv awd Bd of Educ Houston Indpndnt Sch Dist 1972; outstndng Educator Awrd Houston C of C 1972; Educ Awrd, & Cncl of Negro Wmn 1972; Distingshd TX Awrd Charles A George Dntl Soc 1973; Excellence in Educ Awrd Citizens for GoodSch 1973; Outstanding Educator Awrd Prairie View A&M Coll 1972; Distingshd Edctr Awrd Sigma Gamma Rho 1974. **BUSINESS ADDRESS:** 1 Main Plaza, Houston, TX 77002.

BONNER, ALICE A.
Judge, attorney. **PERSONAL:** Born Apr 11, 1941, New Orleans; married Al; children: Yvonne, Bernard, Lamont. **EDUCATION:** TX So U, BA 1963, JD 1966; Natl Coll Judiciary, grad; Am Acad Jud Edn, grad. **CAREER:** 80th Civil Dist Ct State of TX, judge 1979-; Co Criminal Ct at Law #6, judge 1977-78; Mun Ct Houston, judge 1974-77; Law Firm Bonner & Bonner, pvt prctnr family law spclst 1967-77. **ORGANIZATIONS:** Mem State Bd of Spclztn 1975; mem com on increase of female jvnl ofndrs 1967; mem pltfrm com State Dem Conv 1974; orgnzr-fndr-actng pres Black Women Lwyrs Assn 1975; bd mem Judicial Cncl Natl Bar Assn 1975-76; mem bd of govs Natl Bar Assn 1974-77; bd mem Houston Lwyrs Assn 1978; mem com for the indigent State Bar of TX 1980; dem cand for judicials races 1974 1978 1980; life mem Natl Assn of Negro Bus & Professional Women Inc, Phi Alpha Delta Legal Frat, Bapt Sisterhd of TX, City Wide Beauticians of Houston, Natl Cncl Negro Women, Blue Triangle Br YWCA, Women of Achvmnt; mem Eta Phi Beta Bus & Professional Sor; mem NAACP; coord Natl & Cncl Negro Women, Natl Med Assn, Natl Immnztn Prgm; numerous other civic & comm assns. **HONORS/ACHIEVEMENTS:** 1st Black Woman Judge Houston & Harris Co TX; 1st Black Civil Dist Ct TX; 1st Black Woman to win a country-wide election Harris Co TX succeeded to Co Criminal Ct Dem Primary 1978; Am Jrsprdnc Awrds Wills & Decedents Estates & Family Law TX SoUniv 1966; Atty of Year Tom Kato Models 1974; Bethune AchvrNatl Cncl Negro Women 1975; Cited Most Influential Black Woman in Houston Focus Mag 1978; Founders Awrd Black Women Lwyrs 1978; Outstndng Serv Mainland Br NAACP 1979; Black Hist Commemoration Philadelphia Bapt Ch 1979; Black Women Lwyrs Achvmnt Awrd 1979. **BUSINESS ADDRESS:** 80th Civil Dist Ct, 301 Fannin St Room 212 A, Houston, TX 77002.

BONNER, BESTER DAVIS
Educational administration. **PERSONAL:** Born in Mobile, AL; married Wardell; children: Shawn Patrick, Matthew Wardell. **EDUCATION:** AL State Coll Montgomery, BS 1959; Syracuse Univ NY, MSLS 1965; Univ of AL Tuscaloosa, further study. **CAREER:** Div of Educ Miles Co, chairperson, 1978-; Miles Coll, Birmingham AL, admin asst to pres 1974-78; AL A&M Univ Huntsville, asst prof Library media, 1969-79; Jacksonville State Univ Lab School AL, head librarian, 1965-69; Lane Elementary School, Birmingham AL, librarian & teacher of Literature, 1964-65; Westside High School, Talladega AL, librarian, 1959-64. **ORGANIZATIONS:** Mem Pub Rels Com AL Instrctnl Media Assn 1970-71; pres Dist AL Instrctnl Media Assn 1971-72; chrprsn Ecumenical Com Ch Women 1971-74; mem Am Lbry Assn 1972-74; del World Meth Conf Dublin Ireland 1976; vice chr AL State Ethics Commn 1977-81; exec bd Womens Missionary Cncl CME Ch; mem Kappa Delta Pi Ed Honor Soc; mem Thirgood CME Ch Birmingham AL Youth Adv Cncl Bd of Christian Edn; mem Alpha Kappa Alpha & Sor Mini-Grant for AV Rsrch pt 1 AL Cntr for Higher Educ 1974. **HONORS/ACHIEVEMENTS:** Author "Multimedia approach to Teaching & Learning" Birmingham News 1975; Mini-Grant for AV Rsrch Pt 2, AL Cntr Hghr Educ 1976; Citation UNCF 1977 1979; Lilly Endowmnt Fclty Imprvmnt Grant to study for PhD UNCF NY 1978; Citation (Womens Seminar) Miles Coll Comm Serv Awrds Zeta Phi Beta Sor Inc Birmingham 1980; Family Awrd (Outstndng tchr) Miles Coll 1980; Editor/Informer (Newsltr) CME Ch 5th Episcopal Dist; Rsrch Grant to Write Dissertation AL Cntr for the dev of Hghr Educ 1980. **BUSINESS ADDRESS:** Miles Coll, 5500 Ave G, Birmingham, AL 35208.

BONNER, CHARLES DOUGLASS
Physician. **PERSONAL:** Born May 01, 1917, New Haven, CT; married Frances E Jones MD; children: Carol, Dale. **EDUCATION:** Lincoln Univ PA, AB 1939; Boston Univ, MD 1944. **CAREER:** St Elizabeth's Hosp, asst in med 1956-62; Cardinal Cushing Rehab Ctr of Holy Ghost Hosp, physician-in-charge 1958-80, vice pres staff 1960-61, pres staff 1961-62; Tufts Univ, lecturer, phys med & rehab 1961; St Elizabeths Hosp, asst vstg phys in med 1962-,

consult phys med & rehab 1962-80; VA Hosp, cons, Northampton MA 1963-66; Cambridge City Hosp, cons, med 1967-; Holy Ghost Hosp, med dir 1968-80; Cambridge Hosp, chief phys med div 1968-80; Youville Hosp, pres med staff 1971-72; Boston City Hospital, attending staff 1949-86. **ORGANIZATIONS:** Diplomate Amer Bd Internal Med 1954; fellow Amer Coll of Physician 1956; adv bd School for Practical Nursing 1960-66; chmn Health & Soc Serv Comm Mass Council Aging 1961-65; vice pres 1961-65, pres 1965-67 Cambridge TB & Health Assoc; chmn 1965-67, bd dir 1964-; mem, pres Comm on Employment of Handicapped 1968; Stroke Comm, MA Heart Assoc; chmn Comm Programming in Low Income & Min Areas 1972; bd dir 1970-75, vice pres 1972-73 Amer Heart Assoc; natl chmn Conf on Partnership in Productivity 1973; bd dir MA Div Amer Cancer Soc 1970-72; adv bd 1958-60, mem 1957-62 United Comm Serv Rehab Council; med asst adv council Commonwealth of MA 1975; pres elect MA Heart Assoc 1976-; mem Gov Council Rehab & Chronis Disease Sect Amer Hosp Assoc; pres MA heart Assoc 1978-80. **HONORS/ACHIEVEMENTS:** Gen Alumni Awd Meritorious Serv Lincoln Univ 1958; Hon Mention Sci Exhibit Amer Med Assn 1959; Lincoln Univ Dsc Hon 1966; Cert of Meritorious Serv New England Region Natl Rehab Assn 1967; Better Life Awd MA Fed of Nursing Homes 1970; 17th Annual Distinguished Alumnus Awd Boston Univ School of Med 1971; Gen Alumni Awd Boston Univ 1973; Phys Recog Awd Amer Med Assn 1970-85; Awd of Merit Amer Heart Assn 1975; Cert Meritorious Serv MA Chap Natl Rehab Assn 1977; Louis B Russell Awd for Minority Involvement Amer Heart Assn 1978; Distinguished Leadership Awd MA Heart Assn 1982; Reg Reaffiliation Comm Amer Heart Assn 1982-84; over 80 publications, including 3 books. **MILITARY SERVICE:** AUS capt regimental surgeon 1946.

BONNER, DELLA M.
Educator. **PERSONAL:** Born Nov 25, 1929, Red Oak, IA; married Arnett Jackson. **EDUCATION:** Omaha U, BS 1961; Univ of NE at Omaha, MS 1969. **CAREER:** Omaha Public School teacher, 1962-68. **ORGANIZATIONS:** Dir, Greater Omaha Comm Action Inc, 1968-70; instructor, 1970-73; asst prof of Educ, Creighton Univ 1973-, chairperson, 1977, team mem, 1973, 1976 Natl Council for Accreditation of Teacher Educ; evaluator, Omaha Public School in Self-Study of Sr High School, 1970; counseling & guidance Jr HS 1971, Social Studies; chairperson, Human Rights Com NE Personnel & Guidance Assn 1972-74; faculty advisor, Coll of Arts & Sci 1970; exec faculty, 1972-73; Univ Com on Status of Women 1972-75; bd trustees Joint Conf Comm, 1973-74; Task Force on Resident Hall Life 1973-75; educ rep Boys Town Urban Prog Adv Bd 1980-, bd dir Urban League of NE 1964-72; chairperson Educ Task Force; recording sec Scholarship Com; bd dir Eastern NE Mental Health Assn 1969-74; volunteer Bureau of United & Comm Serv, exec com 1969-71; vice pres & mem Girls Club of Omaha 1973-77; chairperson, Natl Trends & Serv Comm Omaha Chapter of Links Inc; special advisory Comm, NE Educ TV Commn, 1971-72; Omaha Home for Gils study Comm for UC, 1974; Charter pres, Omaha Chapter Jack & Jill Of Amer Inc, 1970-71. **HONORS/ACHIEVEMENTS:** Candidate for Outstanding Young Educator Award, Nominee for Woman of Year, Omaha Women's Political Caucus Business & Professional Category 1974; vice chairperson, US Dist Ct Judges 10-mem Interracial Com 1975-76; Phi Delta Kappa 1976-. **BUSINESS ADDRESS:** Creighton Univ Dept of Educ, 2500 California St, Omaha, NE 68178.

BONNER, MARY WINSTEAD
Professor emeritus. **PERSONAL:** Born Apr 20, 1924, Nash Co, NC; daughter of Charles Edward Winstead and Mason Ann Winstead; married Thomas E Bonner, Aug 09, 1956. **EDUCATION:** St Pauls Coll, BS (Cum Laude) 1946; VA State Coll, MS 1952; OK State Univ, EdD 1968; Univ of KS, Post Doct 1974; St Pauls Coll, LhD 1979; Instde Fililogia Satillo Mexico, further study 1984. **CAREER:** Greensville Cty VA, instr 1946-52; So Univ, instr 1952-57; St Louis Publ Schools, instr 1957-64; OK State Univ, grad asst 1965-66; USC, vstg prof 1968; Norfolk State Coll, vstg prof 1971-73; Emporia State Univ, assoc prof, prof emeritus 1986. **ORGANIZATIONS:** Mem Sigma Gamma Rho, Amer Assoc of Univ Women, Natl Council of Negro Women, natl Spanish Hon Soc, Sigma Delta Pi 1979, International Platform Assn, Panel of American Women, KS Children's Service League, Retired Teachers Assn; asst dir, Hospital Auxiliaries of Kansas 1989-; secretary, Emporia Retired Teachers Assn 1988-89; bd of dirs, Societas Docta. **HONORS/ACHIEVEMENTS:** European Tour England, Belgium, Holland, Germany, France, Switzerland 1983; tour of Soviet Union & Warsaw Poland 1974, Spain 1976, Mexico 1979, Venezuela 1981,Caribbean 1986; Hall of Fame Sigma Gamma Rho; Cert of Achievement in Spanish Emporia State Univ 1978; languages Spanish, French, Russian; Outstanding Aluma St Pauls Coll 1979, 1984. **HOME ADDRESS:** 1008 Watson St, Emporia, KS 66801.

BONNER, THEOPHULIS W.
District manager. **PERSONAL:** Born Jul 25, 1917, Warm Springs, GA; married Blanche. **EDUCATION:** Ft Valley State Clge, AB 1943. **CAREER:** Atlanta Life Ins Co, dist sales mgr. **ORGANIZATIONS:** Mem sch bd 1972-; mem LUTC 1966; Liami mgmt 1968; LUTC Health 1971; mem NAACP. **MILITARY SERVICE:** Amvets s/sgt 1943-46. **BUSINESS ADDRESS:** 1008 State St, Box 837, Waycross, GA 31501.

BONTEMPS, JACQUELINE MARIE FONVIELLE
Artist, educator. **PERSONAL:** Born in Savannah, GA; daughter of William Earl Fonvielle and Mattie Louise Davis Fonvielle; married Arna Alexander Bontemps, Jul 05, 69; children: Traci, Arna, Fanon. **EDUCATION:** Fisk University, Nashville, TN, BA, 1964, MA, 1971; Illinois State University, Normal, IL, EdD, 1976. **CAREER:** Lane College, Jackson, TN, chair, 1966-68; Jackson Parks and Recreation, Jackson, TN, supervisor, 1968; South Side Community Center, Nashville, TN, director, 1969; Fisk University, Department of Art, Nashville, TN, administrative assistant, 1971; Tennessee State University, Department of Art, Nashville, TN, instructor, 1972-73; University of Tennessee, Department of Art, Nashville, TN, instructor, 1972-73, lecturer, 1973; Illinois State University, College of Fine Arts, Normal, IL, assistant to director, 1975-76, administrative assistant, 1976-77, assistant professor of art, 1976-78, associate professor of art, 1978-84; Hampton University, Department of Art, Hampton, VA, associate professor, chair of department, 1984—. **ORGANIZATIONS:** Trustee, American Association of Museums; American Association for Higher Education; American Council for the Arts; American Film Institute; American Association of University Professors; Association of Teacher Educators; member of committee, International Council of Museums; National Council for Black Studies; Delta Sigma Theta; Phi Delta Kappa; national arts research specialist, 1978-86, director for the arts, 1982-84, national secretary, 1988-90, The Links, Inc; member, Council of Arts Administrators of Virginia Higher Education, 1984-89; Inaugural National Blacks Art Festival, member of national blue ribbon panel, 1987-88; member, board of directors, Cultural Alliance of Greater Hampton Roads, 1987-91. **HONORS/ACHIEVEMENTS:** Curator and director of exhibit, "Forever Free: Art by African-American Women, 1862-1980," 1981-82; Pacesetter Award, Illinois Board of Education, 1981; certificate of special participation for community efforts, Illinois State University, 1982; Women in the Arts honoree, Virginia National Organization for Women, 1986; selected as one of "America's Top 100 Black Business and Professional Women," Dollars and Sense Magazine, 1986; curator and director of exhibit, "Choosing: An Exhibit of Changing Perspectives in Modern Art and Art Criticism by Black Americans, 1925-1985," 1986-87. **HOME ADDRESS:** No 1 Johnson Ct, Hampton, VA 23669.

BOOKER, ANNE M.
Public relations professional. **PERSONAL:** Born Feb 28, 1951, Spartanburg, SC; daughter of Claude C Booker and Tallulah Tanner Booker. **EDUCATION:** Michigan State Univ, B 1973, M 1986. **CAREER:** Ford Motor Co, electronic media specialist 1977-78, corporate news rep 1978-82, publications editor 1982-84, senior producer 1984-86, public affairs assoc 1986-88; assistant manager 1988-. **ORGANIZATIONS:** Mem Public Relations Soc of Amer 1978-; Women in Communications 1978-; Natl Black MBA Assoc 1983-; life mem NAACP; mem Fellowship Chapel Detroit; Amer Women in Radio-TV; Detroit Press Club 1978-. **HONORS/ACHIEVEMENTS:** Achiever in Industry YMCA Detroit; Aftra Golden Mike Awd; Kappa Tau Alpha Grad Journalism Honor Soc. **BUSINESS ADDRESS:** Assistant Manager, Ford Division Public Affairs, 300 Renaissance Center, P O Box 43303, Detroit, MI 48243.

BOOKER, CARL GRANGER, SR.
Fire marshal. **PERSONAL:** Born Aug 16, 1928, Brooklyn, NY; married Jacqueline Mayo; children: Carl G Jr, Adele Williams, Wendy. **EDUCATION:** Hampton Ins Univ 1948-50; Springfield Comm Coll MA 1977; US Fire Acad, MD 1979,80,82; Dartmouth, Yale, Quinsingamond Comm coll, structured coursesof more than 180 hrs. **CAREER:** City of Hartford CT Fire Dept, firefighter 1958-66, driver-pump oper 1966-67, fire prevention inspector 1967-68, fire prevention lt 1969-79, fire prevention capt/dep fire marshal 1979-81, acting fire marshal 1981-82, appointed fire marshal/fire prevention chief 1982-. **ORGANIZATIONS:** Bd of dir 1972-74, pres 1973, Child Guidance Clinic; pres Phoenix Soc Firefighters 1972-74; legislative rep CT Fire Marshals Assoc 1982-84; mem New England Assoc of Fire Marshals 1983-85; bd of dir Child & Family Serv 1983-; bd of dir Capitol Reg Assoc of Fire Marshals 1982-84; bd of dir Friends of Keney Park Golf Links 1984-85. **HONORS/ACHIEVEMENTS:** Front Page Weekly Reader 1972; Firefighter of the Year Phoenix Soc Firefighters 1972,76; Disting Serv Awd Radio WRCH 1975; Community Awd Makalia Temple 172CT 1983; Cert of Apprec US Consumer Products Comm Washington DC 1984. **MILITARY SERVICE:** AUS Infantry s-4 record spec 2 yrs. **BUSINESS ADDRESS:** Hartford Fire Department, 275 Pearl St, Hartford, CT 06103.

BOOKER, CLIFFORD R.
Pediatrician. **PERSONAL:** Born Nov 20, 1926, Liverpool, OH; son of Christopher C Booker and Cassie Marie Abbitt; children: Claudia, Tina, Cliff. **EDUCATION:** Howard Univ, BS 1949, MD 1955. **CAREER:** Howard Univ Med Sch, asst prof, tchr 1960-65; Georgetown Univ, clinical asst prof; Washington DC Govt, medical officer, 1987-. **ORGANIZATIONS:** Mem DC Med Soc; Kappa Pi Med Hon Soc; mem Med-Clie Soc; adv bd DC Med. **HONORS/ACHIEVEMENTS:** Research Award Sickle Cell Anemia. **MILITARY SERVICE:** USAAC 1945-47.

BOOKER, GARVALL H.
Dentist. **PERSONAL:** Born Apr 26, 1925, Washington, DC; married Doris L Wethers; children: Garvall III, Clifford, David. **EDUCATION:** Sarah Lawrence Coll, BA 1949; Dental Coll Howard Univ, DDS 1954; Sydenham Hosp NYC, resident 1954-56. **CAREER:** Speedwell Serv for Children, dir dentistry 1964-78; private practice, dentist 1956-. **ORGANIZATIONS:** Mem Amer & Dental Assn 1956-; mem NY Acad of Mem Amer Dental Assn 1956-; mem past pres Upper Manhattan Rotary Club 1968-; mem AAAS 1970; alumnae/trustee Sarah Lawrence Coll 1975-78; Paul Harris Fellow of Rotary Fnd Upper Manhattan Rotary Club 1975; adv council mem Harlem-Dowling Children's Serv 1979-; mem NY Acad of Sci 1980; mem Sigma Pi Phi Frat Zeta Boule, Reveille Club. **MILITARY SERVICE:** AUS t-3 1943-46; Bronze Star; Purple Heart; 3 Battle Stars 1945. **BUSINESS ADDRESS:** Dentist, Partner, 228 West 71st Street, New York, NY 10023.

BOOKER, GARY P.
Nuclear controls engineer. **PERSONAL:** Born Aug 29, 1959, Dillwyn, VA. **EDUCATION:** Electronic Technology, AS 1981, BS 1982. **CAREER:** Westinghouse Elec Corp, supervisor of shipbuilding quality assurance spec 1980, elec engrg tech 1981, engr nuclear controls 1982-. **ORGANIZATIONS:** Recording sec Alpha Phi Alpha 1986-. **HONORS/ACHIEVEMENTS:** Distinguished Alumni 1986. **BUSINESS ADDRESS:** Westinghouse Electric Corp, PO Box 164, New Hill, NC 27562.

BOOKER, IRVIN B.
Judge. **PERSONAL:** Born in Newark, NJ; children: 3 sons. **EDUCATION:** Rutgers Law Schl, JD 1963; Seton Hall Univ, BS 1960; Seton Hall Prep, Sci Dip 1949. **CAREER:** Newark Mun Courts, presiding judge trial judge 1970-; Newark NJ, atty 1965-; Military Hosp & others, radiograpllic tech 1953-65. **ORGANIZATIONS:** NJ State Bar Assc; Amer Bar Assc; Essex Cty & Bar Assc; Essex City Munc Judges Assc; Garden State Bar Assc; Natl Council on Alcoholism; Natl Bar Assc; Newark Crim Just Coord Counc; Newark Weequahic HS Fathers Club; Chancellor Ave Adult Rec Div. **HONORS/ACHIEVEMENTS:** Who's Who in Amer Univ & Clges 1959-60. **MILITARY SERVICE:** AUS med corp 1953-55. **BUSINESS ADDRESS:** 790 Broad St, Newark, NJ 07102.

BOOKER, JAMES AVERY, JR.
Physician, general surgeon. **PERSONAL:** Born May 26, 1936, Richmond, VA; son of James and Thelma; married Rita Tezeno; children: James III, Karla, Michael, Jarita. **EDUCATION:** Hampton Univ, BS, 1957; Med Coll of Virginia School of Dentistry, DDS, 1961; Howard Univ, Coll of Med, MD, 1968. **CAREER:** General surgeon, private practice, 1976-present; Oakland CA, city physician, 1976-77; USAF Hospital, Mather AFB, CA surgeon, 1974-76, chief of general surgery, 1975-76; internship & residency, 1968-74; Washington, DC; general dental practice, 1963-68; Armed Forces Entrance & Exam Sta, surgical consultant, 1971-78; Univ of California at Davis School of Med, preceptor principles of physical diagnosisl, 1974-76. **ORGANIZATIONS:** Past natl pres, Student Natl Med Assn, 1967-68; life mem, Alpha Phi Alpha Fraternity, 1955-; mem, Chi Delta Mu Med Fraternity, 1958-; Parl-

mtn Sinkler-Miller Med Soc component Golden State Med Assn & Natl Med Assn, 1977-; mem, Alameda-Contra Costa Med Assn; Component CA Med Assn, 1971-; vice pres, DC Chapter Natl Hampton Alumni Assn, 1965-67; Parlmtn Northern CA Chapter NHAA 1976-78; Diplomate Natl Bd of Dental Examiners 1961; Natl Bd Med Examiners, 1969-; Amer Bd of Surgery Inc, 1976, 1985; Amer Bd of Quality Assurance & Utilization Review Physicians, 1988; fellow, Intl Coll of Surgeons, 1980; fellow, Amer Coll of Surgeons, 1983; fellow, Amer Coll of Utilization Physicians, 1989-; fellow, Southwestern Surgical Congress, 1989-; chmn, Dept of Surgery, Memorial Hospital, San Leandro CA, 1985-88. **HONORS/ACHIEVEMENTS:** Virginia Dental License granted on basis of class standing, 1961; Appointed City Physician, Oakland, CA, 1976; Air Force Achievement Medical, 1988. **MILITARY SERVICE:** Colonel, US Air Force Reserves, 1985-present; Mobilization Augmentee to Commander, David Grant Med Center, Travis Air Force Base, CA, 1986-present. **BUSINESS ADDRESS:** 2844 Summit St, Ste 110, Oakland, CA 94609.

BOOKER, JAMES E.
Business executive. **PERSONAL:** Born Jul 16, 1926, Riverhead, NY; married Jean Williams; children: James, Jr. **EDUCATION:** Hampton Inst, 1943-44; Howard Univ, AB 1947; NYU & New Sch for Social Research, special courses; Armed Forces Information Sch & AUS Psychol Warfare Sch. **CAREER:** NY Amsterdam News, columnist & political editor 18 years; James E Booker Consultants (corporate & civil rights consultants), pres. **ORGANIZATIONS:** Chief Information Consult Nat Adv Commn on Civil Disorders; consult & dir of information 1966 White House Conf on Civil Rights; organized first natl conf ofblack elected officials in Chicago 1968; consult Dem Presidential campaigns 1968, 1972; consult NY State Commn on Human Rights; consult research specialist NY State Joint Legislative Commn. **HONORS/ACHIEVEMENTS:** Lecturer on numerous occasions; selectee Who's Who in Amer. **HOME ADDRESS:** 10 W 135 St, New York, NY 10037.

BOOKER, JOHN, III
Business executive. **PERSONAL:** Born Dec 28, 1947, Augusta, GA. **EDUCATION:** Paine Clge, His mjr 1969; NC Cntrl Univ Law Schl, LLB 1974; Univ of RI, Cert Mgmt 1980. **CAREER:** Amperex Electronic Corp N Amer Philips Co, asst persnl mgr 1980-; Speidel Div of Textron, employ mgr/Urban affairs coord 1977-80; Cntr Savannah & River Area EOA Inc, equal opport ofc 1976-77; Augusta Human Rel Commn, EEOC investigator/Field rep 1975-76; Atty John D Watkins, legal asst 1974-75. **ORGANIZATIONS:** Woonsocket C of C, act mem 1980; NAACP act mem 1980; co rep local minority & civil org 1980. **MILITARY SERVICE:** AUS e-4 1970-72. **BUSINESS ADDRESS:** Manager, Employee Relations, Amperex Electronic Corp, Div of North American Philips, One Providence Pike, Slatersville, RI 02876.

BOOKER, MERREL DANIEL, SR.
Educator. **PERSONAL:** Born Jul 09, Hackensack, NJ; married Erma Barbour; children: Marrel Jr, Sue. **EDUCATION:** Howard Univ, AB, BD; Boston Univ, STM; Union Theo Sem & Wash Schl of Psychiatry, attnd. **ORGANIZATIONS:** Dir pastoral serv Comm Hosp of Evanston; dir pastoral serv Provident Hosp of Chicago; adjunct prof Pastoral Psychology Garrett-Evangelical Theo Sem NWU; Detroit Council Chs; Detroit Gen Hosp; Normal Park Bapt Ch; Bd of Educ Chicago; New Hope Bapt Ch Dallas; Dean of Men Talladega Clge; Fed Bureau of Prison, Chillicothe Wash; Council of Chs; Freedmans Hosp; Fountain Bapt Ch Summit NJ; diplomat Amer Clge of Hosp Chaplains; assc suprv Clinical Pastoral Edn; suprv Council of Clinical Training for Theo Students; mem Alpha Phi Alpha Frat; Kiwanis. **HONORS/ACHIEVEMENTS:** Radio & TV Prog Detroit & Chicago; recip Mental Health Funding for Loneliness Proj Pilot Proj; co-author, "Cry At Birth" 1971, "Minister Speaks His Mind"; columnist for Informer chain of newspapers, writings in Mags & newspapers. **BUSINESS ADDRESS:** Garrett-Evangelical Theological Seminary, 2121 Sheridan Rd, Evanston, IL.

BOOKER, ROBERT JOSEPH
Executive director, newspaper columnist. **PERSONAL:** Born Apr 14, 1935, Knoxville, TN; son of Willie Edward Booker (deceased) and Lillian Allen (deceased). **EDUCATION:** Knoxville Coll, BS Educ 1962. **CAREER:** Chattanooga TN Pub Schools, teacher 1962-64; State of TN, elected mem of Legislature (3 terms) 1966-72; Mayor of Knoxville, TN, admin asst 1972-74; Stroh Brewery Co Detroit, market devel mgr 1974-77; Beck Cultural Exchange Ctr, exec dir 1978-84; City of Knoxville, personnel dir 1984-88; Knoxville Journal, weekly columnist, 1987-; Beck Cultural Exchange Center, executive director, 1988-. **ORGANIZATIONS:** Mem Phi Beta Sigma Frat; NAACP; VFW; American Legion; financial secretary, Martin Luther King Planning Committee; member, Knox County Metropolitan Historic Zoning Commission. **MILITARY SERVICE:** AUS 1954-57. **HOME ADDRESS:** 2621 Parkview Ave, Knoxville, TN 37914. **BUSINESS ADDRESS:** Executive Dir Beck Cultural Exchange Center Inc, 1927 Dandridge Avenue, Knoxville, TN 37915.

BOOKER, SIMEON S.
Journalist. **PERSONAL:** Born Aug 27, 1918, Baltimore, MD; son of Simeon Booker Sr and Roberta Warring; divorced; children: Simeon, Jr, James, Theresa. **EDUCATION:** VA Union Univ, BA 1942; Cleveland Coll, attended 1950; Harvard Univ, 1950. **CAREER:** Johnson Co Inc, chief; Jet Magazine, columnist; Washington Post, 1952-54; Westinghouse Broadcasting Co, radio commentator. **HONORS/ACHIEVEMENTS:** Publ "Man's King Taylor Black Mem", "Washington's Speaker's Office"; visited Africa with Pres Nixon 1957, US Attorney General Kennedy 1962, vice pres Humphrey 1968; Nieman Fellowship Journalism Harvard Univ 1950. **BUSINESS ADDRESS:** 1750 Pennsylvania Ave NW, Washington, DC 20006.

BOOKER, THURMAN D.
Physician. **PERSONAL:** Born Nov 08, 1937, Newark, NJ; married Lagretta; children: Carmen, Sharon, Rashida. **EDUCATION:** Temple Univ, BA 1959; Philadelphia Clge Osteopathic Med, DO 1964. **CAREER:** Physician gen prac 1965-; Eagleville Hosp & Rehab Ctr, addiction spec med staff 1966-, chf med 1973-. **ORGANIZATIONS:** Pres 1975-, bd, bd mem vice pres 1972-75 Human Srv Inst; bd mem OIC Montgomery Co 1968-71. **BUSINESS ADDRESS:** 1007 DeKalb St, Norristown, PA 19401.

BOOKER, VENERABLE FRANCIS
Banker. **PERSONAL:** Born Sep 23, 1920, Great Bend, KS; son of Venerable O Booker and Ora Ramsey. **EDUCATION:** Attended Portland State University. **CAREER:** Real estate broker; Amer State Bank, Portland OR, currently chief exec. **MILITARY SERVICE:** AUS corpl, 1942-46. **BUSINESS ADDRESS:** Chief Executive, Amer State Bank, 2737 NE Union Ave, Portland, OR 97212.

BOOKER, WALTER M.
Educator. **PERSONAL:** Born Nov 04, 1907, Little Rock, AR; married Thomye Collins; children: Walter M Jr, Marjorie H. **EDUCATION:** Morehouse Clge, BA 1928; Univ IA, MS 1932; Univ Chicago, PhD 1942. **CAREER:** Leland Coll, instructor, 1928-29; Prairie View Coll, instructor, 1932-43; Howard Univ, instructor, 1943-44, asst prof, 1944-48, assoc prof, 1948-53; acting dept head, 1953-54, prof, dept chmn, 1954-73, prof 1973-; Area B Mental Health Center, cons; Dept HEW Natl Inst on Drug Abuse. **ORGANIZATIONS:** Reviewer Addiction Research Fnd Fellow Amer Clge Cardiology 1973-; Univ Chicago Club of Wash Alumnus Award 1975; Sr Fulbright Schlr Belgium 1957-58; chrmn Univ Wide Com on Human Research HU 1970-73; bd dir Wash Heart Assc 1969-; rep Amer Soc for Pharm & Experimental Therapeutics to the Natl Res Council. **HONORS/ACHIEVEMENTS:** Publ in field. **BUSINESS ADDRESS:** PO Box 1027, Savannah, GA 31402.

BOOKERT, CHARLES C.
Physician. **PERSONAL:** Born Aug 08, 1918, Cottonwood, AL; married Mabel Berneice; children: Lisa. **EDUCATION:** Morris Brown Coll, BS; Meharry Med Coll, MD 1945. **CAREER:** Private practice, physician. **ORGANIZATIONS:** Pres Natl Med Assoc 1977-78, HSA Western PA; ed com Amer Acad Family Pract; past pres Gateway Med Group, McKeesport Acad of Med, Keystone State Med Soc; bd dir Allegheny Bd of Amer Cancer Soc; staff McKeesport Hosp Family Prac Dept; bd dir Allegheny Cty Comprehensive Health Care Com, Allegheny Rgnl Health Com, Allegheny Smoke Control, Allegheny Cty Med Soc, Med Soc of PA; ret mem Med Dept Westinghouse Elec Corp; mem Chi Delta Med, Phi Beta Sigma, Imperial Benevolent Proctective Order of Elks of World, Prince Hall Mason; trustee Mt Olive Bapt Ch; mem Rho Boule Sigma Pi 1977; del Dem Natl Conv. **HONORS/ACHIEVEMENTS:** Outstanding Alumnus Morris Brown Coll 1971; Athlete Hall of Fame 1974; Black Achiever OES 1974; Contemporary Black Leaders Yale Univ Press 1974; Hon Serv toAfro-Amer Youth in Ed Sears Roebuck Corp 1973; Hon Serv Gaetway Med Grp Keystone State Med Soc 1974-; Recipient Family Dr of the Year Awd NMA 1974; Honored McKeesport Br of NAACP 1977; Chi Delta Mu Frat for Serv to Black Youth 1978; Health Rsch Serv Found 1979; Clairton Br of NAACP 1979; Cert of Appreciation NMA 1979. **MILITARY SERVICE:** AUS pfc 1943-45; Med Corp capt 1953-55. **BUSINESS ADDRESS:** 471 Millen Ave, Clairton, PA 15025.

BOON, INA M.
Association executive. **PERSONAL:** Born Jan 06, 1927, St Louis, MO; divorced. **EDUCATION:** Oakwood Acad Huntsville AL, Grad; Natl Bus Inst; Tucker's Bus Clge; Washington Univ; WIU. **CAREER:** NAACP, dir Region IV 1973-, life mbrshp field dir 1968-73; St Louis Br NAACP, admin secr 1962-68; US Army Transp Corp & US Dept of Labor, former employee. **ORGANIZATIONS:** Mem St Louis Chap Natl Council of Negro Women; Natl Professional Women's Club; mem MO Univ adv coun; bd mem St Louis Minority Econ Dev Agcy; secr St Louis Mental Health Assc; 2nd vice pres Top Ladies of Distinction Inc; vice pres St Louis Chpt; vpv Natl Financial Secr. **HONORS/ACHIEVEMENTS:** Top Ladies of Distinction Inc Award for Distg Srv; St Louis Argus Newspaper Cancer Soc, St Louis Black Firefighters Inst of Racial Equality; Sigma Gamma Rho Sor; Kansas City KS Br NAACP; Kansas City MO Br NAACP & St Louis Globe Dem; Woman of Ach in Social Welfare 1970; Distg Srv Award Union Meml United Meth Ch 1977; Humanitarian Award; Human Dev Corp 1976; Outstanding Ldrshp & Admin Abilities 1973. **BUSINESS ADDRESS:** NAACP Ofc, 1408 N Kingshighway Blvd, St Louis, MO 63113.

BOONE, CAROL MARIE
Government official. **PERSONAL:** Born Nov 22, 1945, Pensacola, FL; daughter of Benjamin J Butler and Clarice Thompson Butler; married Dr Robert L Boone; children: Carlotta, Robert Jr. **EDUCATION:** Fisk Univ, BA 1966; Univ of Chicago, MA 1968; Vanderbilt Univ, EdD 1982. **CAREER:** IL Children's Home & Aid Soc, adoption counselor 1968-69; Dede Wallace Mental Health Ctr, branch dir 1970-80; TN State Dept of Mental Health, state employee assistance prog dir 1982-. **ORGANIZATIONS:** Mem Alpha Kappa Alpha Sor 1965-; mem Natl Assoc of Social Workers Nashville 1969-; mem, treas 1978-82 The Links Inc Hendersonville Chap 1976-; mem, sec 1977-; bd of dirs First Baptist Church Capitol Hill Homes Inc; mem, finan sec 1986-87 Jack and Jill of Amer Nashville Chap 1982-; mem Natl Assn of Labor-Mgt Administrators and Consultants on Alcoholism 1982-. **HONORS/ACHIEVEMENTS:** Social Worker of the Year Awd Middle TN Chap NASW 1977; Outstanding Professional Student Awd Vanderbilt Univ 1982; Outstanding Employee of the Year Awd TN Dept Mental Health 1986. **HOME ADDRESS:** 147 St Andrews Dr, Hendersonville, TN 37075. **BUSINESS ADDRESS:** Dir Employee Assistance Prog, Tennessee State Government, 706 Church Street Sixth Floor, Nashville, TN 37219.

BOONE, CHARLES
Police official. **PERSONAL:** Born Jul 05, 1930, Gary, IN; married Mary; children: Irene, Rodney, Tiffany. **EDUCATION:** Chicago Tech Clge; IN Univ; Calumet Clge. **CAREER:** City of Gary Police Dept, chief of police; B & W Security Agency Inc, pres. **ORGANIZATIONS:** Intl Assc of Chiefs of Police; IN Assc of Chiefs of Police; IN Crim Just Plan Agcy Region I; IN Crim Just Plan Agcy Law Enforc Statewide Task Force; US Dept of Just on Org Crim; Lake Co Coord Cound; Lake Co Law Enforc Coun; Natl Assc of Police Comm Rel Ofcr; mem Natl Council of Investigation & Security Svcs. **HONORS/ACHIEVEMENTS:** Natl Assc of Black Law Enforc Exec Merit Award Amer Fedn of Polcie Cert of Apprec; USN Recruit Serv Cert of Apprec Phi Alpha Delta law frat; Rev for Law Awd Frat Order of Eagles; cit Amer Leg Post 17; Recog Awd Tolle Mann Bus & Professional Assc; Cert of Merit Frontiers Intl. **MILITARY SERVICE:** USN. **BUSINESS ADDRESS:** President, B&W Security Agency Inc, 504 Broadway Ste 828, Gary, IN 46402.

BOONE, CLARENCE DONALD
Educational administrator. **PERSONAL:** Born Nov 23, 1939, Jackson, TN; married Louise May; children: Terrance A Beard, Torrance. **EDUCATION:** Lane Coll, BS 1961; Memphis State Univ, MEd 1977. **CAREER:** NAACP, treas 1957; Alpha Phi Alpha, mem 1959; United Teaching Prof, mem 1961; United Way, bd of dir 1980; West High School, principal. **ORGANIZATIONS:** Mem Ambulance Authority 1973, Cty Commn 1977, YMCA 1980; bd of dir Headstart 1980-83; mem JEA; bd of dir Lane Coll Natl Youth Sports. **HONORS/ACHIEVEMENTS:** Serv Awd Madison Cty Ambulance 1973-77; Alumni Awd Lane Coll

1978; Serv Awd State of Tennessee 1978; Educator of the Year Phi Delta Kappa 1984. **HOME ADDRESS:** 26 Brooks Dr, Jackson, TN 38301.

BOONE, CLARENCE WAYNE
Physician. **PERSONAL:** Born Aug 27, 1931, Bryan, TX; married Blanche O Lane; children: Terri, Clarence Jr, Brian. **EDUCATION:** IN Univ, AB 1953; IN Univ Schl Med, MD 1956. **CAREER:** Phys pvt prac 1964-; Homer G Phillips Hosp, resd 1957-61, internship 1956-57; Planned Parenthood Assc, med dir. **ORGANIZATIONS:** Mem Great Lakes Reg Med Adv Com Planned Parenthood Assc World Population 1974-; staff phys Meth Hosp of Gary; St Mary Med Ctr; pres Gary Med Specl Inc 1968-; mem Kappa Alpha Psi 1950-; Amer Clge of Observ & Gyn 1964-; Natl Med Assc 1967-; Homer G Phillips Alumni Assc; Assc of Planned ParenthoodPhys; Assc of Amer Gyn Laparoscopists; Amer Ferility Soc Diplomat Amer Bd Observ & Gyn 1964. **MILITARY SERVICE:** USAF capt 1961-64. **BUSINESS ADDRESS:** 2200 Grant St, Gary, IN 46404.

BOONE, CLINTON CALDWELL
Clergyman, educator, government official. **PERSONAL:** Born Feb 23, 1922, Monrovia, Liberia;son of Dr Clinton C Boone and Rachel Boone; married Evelyn Rowland Boone; children: Evelyn, Clinton III. **EDUCATION:** Houghton Coll, AB 1942; CW Post Center, MA 1973; Eastern Seminary; VA Union Univ. **CAREER:** Union Baptist Church, Hempstead NY, pastor 1957-89; Copiague Public School Mem, teacher; Town of Hempstead, Hempstead NY, commr 1982-89; former teacher 29 years VA, NC, NY. **ORGANIZATIONS:** Mem Alpha Phi Alpha Fraternity 1940; VA Union; bd of dir Natl Baptist Convention Inc, Hempstead Chamber of Commerce; vice pres Hempstead Community Development Comm, Park Lake Housing Develoment; mem 100 Black Men; Man of Year Hempstead Chamber of Commerce 1987. **HONORS/ACHIEVEMENTS:** CIAA Boxing Champion 1940; Unispan Award Hofstra Univ 1974. **BUSINESS ADDRESS:** Commissioner, Town of Hempstead, 250 Front St, Hempstead, NY 11550.

BOONE, ELWOOD BERNARD, JR.
Urologist. **PERSONAL:** Born May 07, 1943, Petersburg, VA; married Carol Fraser; children: Elwood III, Melanie. **EDUCATION:** Phillips Academy, 1961; Colgate Univ, AB 1965; Meharry Med Coll, MD 1969; Med Coll VA, internship 1970, surgery resident 1972, urology resident 1975. **CAREER:** Med Coll VA, clinical instr 1975-; Richmond Meml Hosp, staff physician 1975-. **ORGANIZATIONS:** Amer Bd of Urology 1977; Omega Psi Phi 1967; Richmond Med Soc; Old Dominion Med Soc; Natl Med Soc; Richmond Urological Soc; Richmond Acad of Med; Med Soc of VA; Fellow Surgery Amer Cancer Soc 1973-74; natl pres Student natl Med Assn 1968-69; mem VA Urological Soc; Fellow Amer Coll of Surgeons 1979; pres Old Dominion Medical Soc 1981-82; chief of surgery Richmond Memorial Hosp 1985,86. **HONORS/ACHIEVEMENTS:** Certified Amer Bd of Urology 1977. **MILITARY SERVICE:** USAR capt 1971-77. **BUSINESS ADDRESS:** President, Elwood B Boone Jr MD PC, 1400 Westwood Ave, Ste 304, Richmond, VA 23227.

BOONE, FREDERICK OLIVER
Pilot. **PERSONAL:** Born Jan 21, 1941, Baltimore, MD; married Penny Etienne; children: Vanessa, Frederick III, Kimberly, Sean. **EDUCATION:** Morgan State College, BS 1961. **CAREER:** Delta Airlines, flight engr 1969-70, 1st ofc 1970-79, capt 1980-86, capt/flight instructor and evaluator (B727) 1986-. **ORGANIZATIONS:** Mem Airline Pilots Assc Mem; Black Airline Pilots, sec org 1976-; So Christian Ldrshp Conf 1977. **HONORS/ACHIEVEMENTS:** Air Medal USN; Achv Award Wall St Journal. **MILITARY SERVICE:** USN lcdr o-4 Vietnam. **BUSINESS ADDRESS:** International Airport, Atlanta, GA 30320.

BOONE, RAYMOND HAROLD
Educator. **PERSONAL:** Born Feb 02, 1938, Suffolk, VA; married Jean Patterson; children: Regina, Raymond Jr. **EDUCATION:** Norfolk St Coll, 1955-57; Boston Univ, BS 1960; Howard Univ, MA 1985. **CAREER:** Suffolk, VA News-Herald, reporter 1955-57; Boston Chronicle, city editor 1958-60; Tuskegee Inst, deputy dir, public info 1960-61; White House, Afro-Amer reporter 1964-65; Richmond Afro-Amer, ed 1965-81; Afro-Amer Co, editor/vice pres, 1976-81; Howard Univ, visiting prof in Journalism 1981-83, lecturer, 1983-88, assoc prof, 1988-. **ORGANIZATIONS:** Bd dir exec comm Afro-Amer Co 1976-81; founder-pres Suffolk (VA) NAACP Youth Council 1953; edit Norfolk St Coll Spartan Echo 1956-57; co-founder Frederick Douglass Fellowship Program 1969; founder & ex-chmn Metro Richmond Jr Baseball League; sec VA St Educ Authority 1973-77; special advisory comm, US State Dept 1973-74; mem VA State Task Force on Study of Conditions in Jails 1974; ex-mem bd dir Richmond NAACP; Richmond Urban League; Richmond Chapter Sigma Delta Chi Prof Journalism Soc; bd dir Metro Baltimore YMCA 1980-87; bd of dir Virginia Forum 1985-87; mem, Kappa Alpha Psi Fraternity; mem, Guardsmen, Exec Comm, School of Communications, Howard Univ, 1985-. **HONORS/ACHIEVEMENTS:** Carl Murphy Comm Serv Award NNPA; 1st Place Robt Abbott Writing Award 1974, 1976; Distinguished Serv Award VA NAACP 1974; Unity Award for Pol Rpt Lincoln (MO) Univ 1975; Humanitarian of the Year Award Metro Richmond Business League 1976; VA State Coll Media Achievement Award 1976; Pulitzer Prize Juror 1978-79; Outstanding Suffolkian Morgan Memorial Library Suffolk, VA 1980; Metro Baltimore YMCA Outstanding Serv Award, 1986-87; Poynter Inst for Media Studies Award for Outstanding Teaching in Journalism, 1988. **BUSINESS ADDRESS:** Associate Professor, Howard Univ, Dept of Journalism, Washington, DC 20059.

BOONE, ZOLA ERNEST
Educational administrator. **PERSONAL:** Born Oct 16, 1937, Wisner, LA; married Arthur I Boone; children: Monica, Denise, Ivan. **EDUCATION:** MI State Univ, PhD 1972, MS 1970; Mt St Mary's, BA 1957; Inst for Educ Mgmt Harvard Univ, Cert 1975. **CAREER:** SDIP Coord Morgan State Univ, special asst to pres, 1979-; Morgan St Univ, dir center for curriculum improvement; Coppin State Coll, special asst to vice pres, 1975-76, prof, dept chairperson, 1973-75; Morgan State Coll, asst prof, 1972-73; Michigan State Univ, adv, 1970-71; Baltimore Public Schools, teacher, dept chmn, 1962-69. **ORGANIZATIONS:** Assc for Supv & Curr Dev 1972-77; Amer Assc of Higher Educ 1976-77; consult Curr Dev; Phi Kappa Phi Hnr Soc Delta Sigma Theta; pres The Links Inc 1977-78; Howard Co; Dem Coalition. **HONORS/ACHIEVEMENTS:** NAACP Ford Fellow MI State Univ 1971-72; Outst Serv Award Adult Educ Coppin State Clge 1975; Outst Young Women in Amer 1972; ACE Fellow 1978-79. **BUSINESS ADDRESS:** VP for Planning & Developmnt, Bowie State College, Jericho Park Road, Bowie, MD 20715.

BOONIEH, OBI ANTHONY
Writers bureau chief executive. **PERSONAL:** Born Jun 27, 1957, Onitsha, Nigeria;married Neka Carmenta White; children: Amechi. **EDUCATION:** Morgan State Univ, BA 1983; Northeastern Univ Sch of Law, JD 1986. **CAREER:** African Relief Fund, pres 1982-84; First WRiters Bureau Inc, managing editor 1986-. **ORGANIZATIONS:** Dir Mangrover & Co Ltd 1979-; mem Big Brothers & Sisters of Central MD 1980-83; dir African Relief Fund 1984-85; consultant/dir Culture Port Inc 1986-; mem NAACP, Phi Alpha Delta; dir Intl Pollution Control Corp 1986-. **HONORS/ACHIEVEMENTS:** Published article "Improving the Lot of Farmers," 1975; published book "A Stubborn Fate," ISBN#O-89260-146-9. **BUSINESS ADDRESS:** Managing Editor, First Writers Bureau Inc, 819 E Fayette St, Baltimore, MD 21202.

BOOTH, CHARLES E.
Clergyman. **PERSONAL:** Born Feb 04, 1947, Baltimore, MD; married Mary Jo Leverette. **EDUCATION:** Howard Univ, BA 1969; Eastern Bapt Theol Sem, MDiv 1973. **CAREER:** St Paul's Bapt Ch West Chester PA, pastor 1970-; Operation Explo Wilmington DE, dir 1969-70; New Shiloh Bapt Chr Baltimore, student asst minister 1966-69; Shiloh Bapt Chr Wash DC, student asst minister 1965-66. **ORGANIZATIONS:** Philadelphia Area Convener Black Amer Bapt Churchmen 1975; chrmn Com on Chr Work; mem West Chester NAACP 1973; adv council West Chester State Clge Higher Educ Prog 1973-; bd dir West Chester Comm Cntr 1972-. **HONORS/ACHIEVEMENTS:** Sermons published in 1974 issue of The Black Church, The Black Ecumenial Comm of MA; sermonic meditation publ in The Secret Place Mag of the Amer Bapt Conv. **BUSINESS ADDRESS:** Mt Olivet Baptist Church, 428 E Main Street, Columbus, OH 43215.

BOOTH, LAVAUGHN VENCHAEL
Clergyman. **PERSONAL:** Born Jan 07, 1919, Collins, MS; son of F A Booth and Mamie Booth; married Georgia Anna Morris; children: Lavaughn V Jr, William D, Anna M Metwally, Georgia A Leeper, Paul. **EDUCATION:** Alcorn State Univ MS, AB 1940; Howard Univ Sch of Religion, BD 1943; Univ of Chicago Div Sch, MA 1945; Wilberforce U, LHD 1964; Morehouse Coll, DD 1967; Univ of Cincinnati, LHD 1989. **CAREER:** First Bapt Warrenton VA, pastor 1943; First Bapt of Gary IN, pastor 1944-52; Zion Baptist of Cinci OH, pastor 1952-84; Univ of Cinci, first black bd mem 1968-; Baptist World Alliance, vice pres 1970-75; Prog Nat Bapt Conv, founder & former pres 1971-74; Hamilton Co State Bnk, founder & chrmn 1980; Olivet Bapt Cinci OH, pastor & founder 1984-. **ORGANIZATIONS:** Spec sec Am Bible Soc; first exec sec Prog Nat Bapt Conv 1964-69; founder of "Martin Luther King, Jr Sunday" 1972; founding mem Chan 12 TV Dialogue Panel 1965-; founder & chrmn Cinci OIC 1966-71; chrmn & org Cinci Black Bank 1974; mem bd of dir Martin Luther King Jr Center; mem bd of mgmt Amer Bible Soc. **HONORS/ACHIEVEMENTS:** Cert of Merit Cinci NAACP 1963; Disting Serv Award Churches of Detroit 1968; PNBC Founders Award Prog Nat Bapt Conv 1971; Operation PUSHS Award of Excellence 1974; Ebony's Success Library 1974. **HOME ADDRESS:** 6753 Siebern Ave, Cincinnati, OH 45236.

BOOTH, LE-QUITA
Administrator. **PERSONAL:** Born Oct 07, 1946, Columbus, GA; daughter of Joseph Reese and Hilda Reese; married Lester Booth; children: Joseph. **EDUCATION:** Columbus College, BS 1972; MBA 1977; Univ of Georgia Athens, EdD 1987. **CAREER:** Natl Bank & Trust, Commercial Officer 1974-77; Small Business Administration, Disaster Loan Spec 1977-78; Small Business Devel Ctr Univ of GA, Associate Dir 1978-; The National Science Center Foundation, assistant to the president for Educ 1988-. **ORGANIZATIONS:** Natl Business League, Board of Dir & Reg Vice Pres 1983-85; Georgia Assoc of Minority Entrepreneuers 1981-85; International Council for Small Business, Vice Pres for Minority Small Business 1984-86. **HONORS/ACHIEVEMENTS:** Wall St Journal, Award for Achievement 1972; Small Business Administration, Minority Advocate of the Year 1982; University of Georgia, Public Service Extension Award; International Council for Small Business Fellow 1986. **HOME ADDRESS:** 609 Zeron Drive, Columbus, GA 31907. **BUSINESS ADDRESS:** The National Science Center Foundation, PO Box 1648, 127 Seventh Street, Augusta, GA 30903.

BOOTH, WILLIAM H.
Attorney. **PERSONAL:** Born Aug 12, 1922, Jamaica, NY; son of William H and Mabel; married Suzanne Potter; children: Gini, Jeffrey, Ronald. **EDUCATION:** Queen's Coll, BA 1946; NY Univ Law Sch, LLB 1950, LLM 1954. **CAREER:** New York City Human Rights Commn, chmn 1966-69; New York City Criminal Court, judge 1969-76; NY State Supreme Court, justice 1976-82; Flamhaft, Levy, Kamins, Hirsch & Booth, partner 1982-. **ORGANIZATIONS:** Dir 100 Black Men of NY Inc; dir Amer Comm on Africa; dir Jamaica Serv Prog for Older Adults servicing 14 senior centers and core area of 70,000 senior citizens; pres 24-00 Ericsson St Block Assn; mem Intl Comm to Invest the Crimes of the Chilean Junta; mem of NY City Sickle Cell Found; mem bd dir Proctor-Hopson Post of the Veterans of Foreign Affairs; mem Queens Co Bar Assn; chmn Grievance Comm Supreme Ct Appellate Div Second and Eleventh Judicial Dists; mem Metropolitan Black Bar Assn; bd mem/asst treas Medgar Evers Found; mem Jamaica Br NAACP; charter mem Judicial Cncl of the Natl Bar Assn; mem Governor's Commn on Voluntary Enterprise; mem NYS Human rights Adv Cncl; mem Coalition for a Just New York; mem Adv Bd CUNY Law Sch Queens, NY; mem NYC Board of Correction. **HONORS/ACHIEVEMENTS:** Recipient of over 100 awards for public service; lecturer at numerous colleges and universities. **MILITARY SERVICE:** AUS Corp of Engineers M/Sgt served 4 yrs. **HOME ADDRESS:** 24-20 Ericsson St, East Elmhurst, NY 11369. **BUSINESS ADDRESS:** Attorney, 25-74 98th St, East Elmhurst, NY 11369.

BOOZER, EMERSON, JR.
Recreation administration. **PERSONAL:** Born Jul 04, 1943, Augusta, GA; married Enez Yevette Bowins; children: 1. **EDUCATION:** Univ of MD Eastern Shore, BS 1966. **CAREER:** CBS-TV, football analyst, 1976-77; Em Boozer's Pub Huntington Sta NY, owner/Oper; NY Jets, football player 1966-76; WLIB Radio, announcer 1971-74; LI Cablevision, sports analyst college & hs football games. **ORGANIZATIONS:** Mem Police Athletic League; mem Natl Football League Players Assn. **HONORS/ACHIEVEMENTS:** Actors Guild Meth Named Rookie of Year, Pittsburgh Courier 1966; All-Amer 1964-65; Outstanding Small Coll Athlete, Washington Pigskin Club, 1965; Named to Amer Football League All-Star Team 1966-68; AFC Scoring Touchdowns Champ 1972. **HOME ADDRESS:** 25 Windham Dr, Huntington Station, NY 11746.

BORDEN, HAROLD F., JR.
Artist. **PERSONAL:** Born Feb 03, 1942, New Orleans; married Barbara Sullivan; children: Tony, Tina. **EDUCATION:** LA City Clge, studied drawing under Norman Schwab; Trade Tech Clge LA, studied design; Otis Art Inst LA, studied drawing Charles White; sculpture under Racul Desota. **CAREER:** Krasne Co, designed jewelry 1969-71; Contemporary Crafts LA, exhibited 1972; H Borden Studios, master jeweler, sculptor artist owner. **ORGANIZATIONS:** Org Jua-Agr Ctr LA; mem Black Artists & Craftsman Guild LA; mem Amer Guild Craftsman; worked with Robert Nevis & Toshi Enami; worked with Thomas Green; bd mem Jua; design consult Black Artists & Craftsman Guild of LA. **HONORS/ACHIEVEMENTS:** Spec ach award Dept Recreation & Parks City LA 1972; participation award City of LA Day in the Park 1974. **BUSINESS ADDRESS:** 1255 1/2 S Cochran Ave, Los Angeles, CA.

BORDERS, MICHAEL G.
Educator, artist. **PERSONAL:** Born Oct 17, 1946, Hartford, CT; son of Thomas L Borders and Marjorie Davis Borders; married Sharon Armwood, Feb 04, 1984; children: Nicholas M A Borders. **EDUCATION:** Fisk Univ, BA 1968; Howard Univ, MFA 1970; attended Skowhegan School of Painting & Sculpture. **CAREER:** Fisk Univ, instructor 1970-71; Fox Middle School, math teacher 1971-72; S Arsenal Neighborhood Devel Sch, artist in residence 1974-78; Greater Hartford Comm Coll, art history instructor 1978; Freelance Artist, 1978-. **ORGANIZATIONS:** First Ann Fine Arts Exhibit 1968; First Annual Congreg Art Show 1968; Student Exhibit 1968; Student Exhibit Skowhegan School of Painting & Sculpture; One-Man Show Central Michigan Univ 1970; Joint Faculty Exhibit Fisk, Vanderbilt, Peabody 1971; display in lobby Phoenix Mutual Life Ins Co 1974; Unitarian Meetinghouse Hartford 1974; artist in residence Weaver HS 1973-74; lectr Loomis-Chaffee Prep Sch 1973; Lectr Trinity Coll 1973; portrait painter; works placed in local Washington galleries; billboard painter; Fisk Univ homecoming brochure covers 1967-68. **HONORS/ACHIEVEMENTS:** Two-man Show Natl Cntr for Afro-Amer Artists 1975; mural displayed in Hartford titled "Genesis of Capital City" (largest mural in New England - first permanent monument by Black Amer in Hartford); 18-month trip to Africa, Asia & Europe 1976-77; CT State Panorama of Business & Indus 1980; two mural panels City Hall, Hartford (2nd permanent monument by Black Amer in Hartford) 1980-85; three murals AETNA Insurance Co, Hartford, 1989; four murals AI Prince Regional Vocational Tech School, Hartford 1989; many conceptual paintings and portraits.

BORGES, FRANCISCO L.
Elected official. **PERSONAL:** Born Nov 17, 1951, Santiago, Cape Verde;son of Manuel Borges and Maria Lopes Borges; married Lynne MacFarlane Borges, May 28, 1988; children: Ryan. **EDUCATION:** Trinity Coll, BA 1974; Univ of CT, JD 1978. **CAREER:** Travelers Ins Co, associate counsel 1978-86; St Francis Hosp, corporator 1981-86; City of Hartford, councilman 1981-85, deputy mayor 1983-85; JPTA SteeringCommittee 1984-86; State of Connecticut, treas 1987-. **ORGANIZATIONS:** Mem Connecticut Bar Assoc 1979-; trustee Millbrook Schl 1979-; health ctr adv cnclUniv of Ct 1982-; mem Metropolitan District Commn 1983-; vice chmn Capitol Region Council of Governments 1984-; dir Hartford Ballet Co 1985-86; bd of regents Univ of Hartford 1986-; bd of trustees Hartford Grad Ctr 1986-. **HOME ADDRESS:** 77 Canterbury St, Hartford, CT 06112. **BUSINESS ADDRESS:** State Treasurer, State of Connecticut, 55 Elm St, Hartford, CT 06106.

BORGES, LYNNE MACFARLANE
Consumer goods company executive. **PERSONAL:** Born Oct 27, 1952, Middletown, OH; daughter of Victor MacFarlane, Sr and Charma Jordan; married Francisco L Borges, May 28, 1988; children: Ryan Elliot Jones. **EDUCATION:** Wesleyan Univ, BA Govt 1975. **CAREER:** Aetna Life & Casualty, mgr 1975-79; CT General Life Ins, asst dir 1979-82; CIGNA, dir 1982-85; Heublein Inc, dir 1985-. **ORGANIZATIONS:** Corporate adv comm Natl Assoc for Equal Oppor in Higher Educ 1983-; bd dirs CT Black Women's Educ/Rsch Foundation 1985-; org sponsor Human Resource Plnng Soc 1985-; women's exec comm mem Greater Hartford Chamber of Commerce 1986-; bd dir Greater Hartford Urban League 1986-; bd of trustees Mark Twain Memorial; advisory bd Hartford Stage Co. **HONORS/ACHIEVEMENTS:** State of CT Young Career Woman Bus/Prof Women's Federation 1979; Mary McLeod Bethune Awd Natl Council of Negro Women 1981; Outstanding CT Women of the Decade 1987; Outstanding Young Women of America 1987. **BUSINESS ADDRESS:** Dir Human Resources/Plng/Devel, Heublein Inc, 16 Munson Rd, Farmington, CT 06032.

BOROM, LAWRENCE H.
Social service administrator. **PERSONAL:** Born Feb 28, 1937, Youngstown, OH; son of Clarence H Russell and Cora Mildred Lewis Borom; married Betty J Fontaine, Nov 29, 1963; children: Martin Antoine Borom. **EDUCATION:** Youngstown State Univ, Youngstown, OH, BS in educ, 1954-58; Mankato State Coll, Mankato, MN, MA urban studies, 1970-71. **CAREER:** Cleveland Public Schools, Cleveland, OH, elementary teacher, 1962-63; St Paul Urban League, St Paul, MN, employment & educ dir, 1963-66; MN Governor's Human Rights Commn, exec dir, 1966-67; St Paul Urban League, commn, exec dir, 1967-74; Natl Urban League, New York City, NY, dir community devel, 1974-76; Urban League of Metropolitan Denver, Denver, CO, pres/CEO, 1976-. **ORGANIZATIONS:** Mem, Kappa Alpha Psi Fraternity, 1956-; mem, Advisory Comm Denver Mayor's Black Advisory Comm, 1985-; mem, pres, CO Black Roundtable, 1988-; mem, Advisory Comm, "A World of Differene" Project, 1988-; mem, bd of dir, CO African/Carribean Trade Office, 1989-. **HONORS/ACHIEVEMENTS:** Esquire Award, Esquire Club, 1984; Distinguished Service Award, UNCF, 1985; Distinguished Service Award, CO Civil Rights Commn, 1987. **MILITARY SERVICE:** US Army, Sp4. 1959-62. **HOME ADDRESS:** 355 S Oliver Way, Denver, CO 80224.

BORUM, REGINA A.
Educational administrator. **PERSONAL:** Born Jul 28, 1938, Dayton, OH; daughter of Robert Cortney Prear and Vivien L Hayes Prear; married Butler Borum, Oct 14, 1957; children: Joy Louise Middleton, Mark Randall, M Rodney. **EDUCATION:** Capital Univ, Columbus OH, BA, 1984; Union Graduate School, Cincinnati OH, doctoral work, 1988-. **CAREER:** Wright State Univ, Dayton OH, admin asst to dean, 1975-79, asst to Vice Pres for Health Affairs, 1979-81, dir univ & community events, 1981-88, dir conf & continuing educ, 1988-; Greene County Convention and Visitors Bureau, vice pres, 1987-. **ORGANIZATIONS:** Comm mem, YWCA Promotions and Publicity Comm, 1974-; mem, Dayton Urban League, 1979-; mem, NAACP, 1979-; bd mem, Meeting Planners Intl, 1980-, volunteer, Miami Valley Literacy Council, 1981-; mem, Amer Soc for Training & Devel, 1982; mem, Amer Assn for Univ Women, 1984; mem, United Way Allocations Comm, 1985-; Natl Coalition of Black Meeting Planners, 1986-. **HONORS/ACHIEVEMENTS:** Outstanding Volunteer, United Way, 1985; Serv Award, United Negro Coll Fund, 1985; Appreciation Award, Miami Valley Literacy Council, 1987; Appreciation Award, Delta Sigma Theta Sorority, 1988; Meeting Planner of the Year, Meeting Planners Intl, Ohio Valley Chapter, 1989. **BUSINESS ADDRESS:** Dir, Conferences and Continuing Educ, Wright State Univ, 3640 Colonel Glenn Hwy151 University Center, Dayton, OH 45435.

BOSCHULTE, JOSEPH CLEMENT
Physician. **PERSONAL:** Born Feb 05, 1931, Tortola Britich, VI; married Rubina; children: Cheryl, Jualenda, Joseph. **EDUCATION:** City Coll NY, BS 1954; Hwrd Univ Coll Med, 1958; Frdmn Hosp, Intern 1959, Resd 1967. **CAREER:** Pvt Prac, physcn 1972-; B Wash DC, chf inptnt serv area 1969-72. **ORGANIZATIONS:** Chmn Dept Psychtry Crtr SE Comm Hosp 1972-, mem 1968-; sr atdg psychtrst WA Hosp Ctr 1968-76; mem Prnc Grg's Hosp 1968-75; mem Am Psycht Assn; WA Psycht Soc; AMA. **HONORS/ACHIEVEMENTS:** DC Med Soc Flwsp Grant Nat Inst Mtl Hlth 1964-67. **MILITARY SERVICE:** AUS MC gen med of cr capt 1960. **BUSINESS ADDRESS:** 3330 Pennsylvania Ave SE, Ste 238, Washington, DC 20020.

BOSLEY, FREEMAN ROBERTSON, JR.
Elected official. **PERSONAL:** Born Jul 20, 1954, St Louis, MO. **EDUCATION:** St Louis Univ, Urban Affairs 1976, Pol Sci 1976, JD 1979. **CAREER:** Legal Serv of Eastern MO, staff atty 1979-81; Bussey & Jordan, assoc 1982-83; supreme Court Judiciary, clerk of the circuit court 1983-. **ORGANIZATIONS:** Mem Mound City Bar Assoc 1980, Metro Bar Assoc 1980, Bd of Jury Commiss; commissioner Child Support Commiss 1985-. **BUSINESS ADDRESS:** Clerk Circuit Court, Civil Court Bldg, 10 N Tucker, St Louis, MO 63101.

BOSLEY, THAD
Professional athlete. **PERSONAL:** Born Sep 17, 1956, Oceanside, CA; married Cherry Sanders. **EDUCATION:** Mira Costa Comm Clge. **CAREER:** CA Angels, outfielder 1977; Chicago White Sox, outfielder 1978-80; Milwaukee Brewers, outfielder 1981; Chicago Cubs, outfielder 1983-. **HONORS/ACHIEVEMENTS:** Named the CA League's Player of the Year in 1976; recorded a gospel contemporary album entitled "Pick Up the Pieces"; working on book of poem s for children. **BUSINESS ADDRESS:** Chicago Cubs, 1060 W Addison St, Chicago, IL 60613.

BOST, FRED M.
City official. **PERSONAL:** Born Mar 12, 1938, Monroe, NC; married Sara B; children: Sybil, Olantunji, Kimberly. **EDUCATION:** Bloomfield Coll, BS 1976; Cook Coll, Enviro-Health/Law 1979. **CAREER:** Elizabeth NJ Bd of Educ, chmn of title I 1970-72; Dept of Prop & Maint, asst mgr 1976-79; Township of Irvington, comm on drugs 1977-79; Essex Co, comm of youth/rehab comm 1977-80; ABC of Irvington, comm chmn 1982-84; Township of Irvington, councilman 1980-. **ORGANIZATIONS:** Pres of the Fred Bost Civic Assn 1975-81; rep for the Bureau of Indian Affairs 1976-78; public relations rep data processing 1977-79; pres East Ward CivicAssn 1979-81. **HONORS/ACHIEVEMENTS:** Concerned Citizen Awd PBA of Irvington 1980. **MILITARY SERVICE:** AUS sgt 2 yrs. **BUSINESS ADDRESS:** Councilmember, City of Irvington, 749 15th Ave, Irvington, NJ 07111.

BOSTIC, DOROTHY
Educator. **PERSONAL:** Born in Baltimore, MD; married Joseph; children: Joseph Jr, Lee, Debra. **EDUCATION:** Morgan State Coll, AB; NYU, MA; Temple Univ; Bank St Tchrs Coll. **CAREER:** Baltimore City Schools, instructor 3 years; Little Brown Schoolhouse, instr 4 years; Little School, founder & dir, 1952-63; Junior Academy, founder & dir, 1963-. **ORGANIZATIONS:** Mem Alpha Kappa Alpha Sor; Bus & Professional Women's Club; Natl Cncl Negro Women; Girl Friends Inc; Phi Delta Kappa Sor; Amer Assn of Univ Women; Girl Scouts Amer; Ch Women United; Brooklyn Mental Hlth; Comm Com of Brooklyn Mus; Brooklyn Protestant Cncl; Bedford-Stuyvesant Boys Club; NAACP; Brooklyn LINKS Inc;Natl Cncl Women of US; past sec & past pres Jack & Jill of Amer; past basileus AKA Sor; past pres Girl Friends Inc past sec tst bd Janes Meth Ch; 1st vice pres Brooklyn Home for Aged People; vice pres Brooklyn Prot Cncl; sec Brooklyn LINKS Inc; Cncl Ch Brooklyn Div; organized Girl Scouts Janes Meth Ch; mem Billy Holiday Theater Comm; natl pres Girl Friends 1948-50; chmn Ebony Fashion Fair Comm 1968-83; chmn Ebony Fashion Fair pres by Johnson Publns 1968-83. **HONORS/ACHIEVEMENTS:** Recip Woman of the Yr Award Bible Soc NY 1954; Achvmnt Award Alpha Kappa Alpha Sor 1955; 10 yr Serv Pin Girl Scout Ldrshp Phi Delta Kappa Sor 1955; Sojourner Truth Award Bus & Professional Women 1959; Women's Cncl Educ Award 1961; Natl Pres Achievement Award NY Girl Friends 1962; Flwshp Award Wesleyan Serv Guild 1963; Woman of the Yr Award Natl Cncl Christians & Jews 1969; Achvmt Award AKA Sor 1957; Educ Comm Ldrshp Award Brooklyn Div Cncl Churches 1972; Mayor's Award 1973; Comm Ldrshp & Noteworthy Amer Award 1976-77; Outstndg Contrib Field Educ PDK Sor 1976; 25 years Educ Excellence Jr Acad 1976. **BUSINESS ADDRESS:** Dir, Junior Academy, 856 Quincy St, Brooklyn, NY 11221.

BOSTIC, JAMES EDWARD, JR.
Director, scientist. **PERSONAL:** Born Jun 24, 1947, Marlboro Co, SC; married Edith A Howard; children: James E III, Scott H. **EDUCATION:** Clemson Univ, BS 1969, PhD 1972. **CAREER:** Clemson Univ, doctor flw 1969-72, graduate resident counselor 1969-72; Amer Enka & Rsch Corp, sr rsch science, 1972; Dept of Agriculture, special asst to sec of agriculture 1972-73, dep asst sec of agriculture 1973-77; Riegel Text Corp, corp regulat dir tech analyst, 1977-81, convenience products div 1981-85; Georgia Pacific, general mgr. **ORGANIZATIONS:** Mem Assn of Text Chem & Color; amer Chem Soc; Phi Psi Fraternity; Blue Key Natl Hnr Frat; Natl Acad of Engr 1975-76; bd trustees US Dept of Agriculture Graduate School 1976-77; mem Pres Commin on White House Fellowship Region Panel 1975-78; FFA Hnr Amer Farmer Deg 1976; council mem Clemson Univ Graduate School 1971-72; mem US Dept of Commerce Mgmt Labor Textile Advisory Com 1978-85; vice chmn & chmn SC Commn on Higher Educ 1978-83; chmn & mem Career Found Bd of Trustees 1978-; mem President's Commn on White House Fellowships 1981-; mem Clemson Univ, Bd of Trustees 1983-. **HONORS/ACHIEVEMENTS:** Ford Found Doc Fellowship for Black Students 1969-70; first black awarded PhD Clemson Univ; White House Fellow 1972-73; Distinguished Serv Award Greenville Jaycees 1979; Outstanding Public Servant of Year Award 1983 SC Assoc of Minorities for Public Administration. **MILITARY SERVICE:** USAR

2nd lt 1971-77. **BUSINESS ADDRESS:** General Manager, Georgia-Pacific Corp, Convenience Products Division, 33 Varen Drive, Aiken, SC 29802.

BOSTIC, LEE H.
Attorney. **PERSONAL:** Born Apr 17, 1935, Brooklyn, NY; married Gayle Spaulding; children: Lisa, Staci, Lee. **EDUCATION:** Morgan State Coll, AB 1957; Boston Univ Law School, LLB 1962. **CAREER:** Allstate Ins Co, claims adj 1964; Solomon Z Ferziger NYC, assoc atty 1964-65; Queens Co, asst dist atty 1966; private practice attorney 1967-. **ORGANIZATIONS:** Mem NY and Queens Co Bar Assocs; mem NAACP; male committeeman 29 AD Reg Rep Club Queens Co; mem NYS Bar Assoc, Macon B Allen Black Bar Assoc; bd of dirs Jr Academy League Inc. **MILITARY SERVICE:** AUS 1st lt 1957-59. **BUSINESS ADDRESS:** Attorney at Law, Lee H Bostic, PC, 22110 Jamaica Ave, 2nd Fl, Queens Village, NY 11428.

BOSTICK, LAURENCE HERBERT
Industrial technician. **PERSONAL:** Born Dec 02, 1913, Brookshire, TX; married Ruby Lee Vaughns; children: Ann R, Rosie M, Henry A, George D, Rita M. **EDUCATION:** Leadership Training Course 1968. **CAREER:** Exxon Co, maint spec & tech Katy Gas Recycling Plant TX, with co since 1944 in various positions. **ORGANIZATIONS:** Mem Manpower Adv Com of Houston-Galveston Area; council mem Brookshire Area Chamber of Comm 1967; Scoutmaster BSA 1945-55; councilman Brookshire City Council deacon zion hill bapt ch 1943-75; deputy grand master umw scottish rite grand lodge af&am of tX inc; secr trustee bd mt zion Lively Hope DistAssc 33 Deg Mason 1957. **BUSINESS ADDRESS:** 29003 Morton Rd, Katy, TX 77450.

BOSTON, ARCHIE, JR.
Art director, designer, educator. **PERSONAL:** Born Jan 18, 1943, Clewiston, FL; married Juanita; children: Michael, Jennifer. **EDUCATION:** CA Inst of the Arts, BFA 1965; Univ of So CA, MLA 1977. **CAREER:** Hixon & Jorgensen Inc, art dir 1965-66; Boston & Boston Design, partner 1966-68; Carson Roberts Inc, art dir 1968; Botsford Ketchum Inc, art dir 1968-77;CA State Univ, assoc prof 1977; Design Concepts, pres 1977-78. **ORGANIZATIONS:** Judge num award shows 1965-; pres Art Dir Club of LA 1973; mem Mt Sinai Bapt Church; bd of govs Art Dir Club of LA 1974-; com chmn Graphic Arts Bicent Black Achvmt Exhibit; instr Art Ctr Coll of Design 1976-77; instr CA State Univ 1971; inst CA Inst of the Arts 1966-68; NY Art Dir; San Fran & LA Art Dir Club Show; Type Dir & Aiga Show; Comncn Arts & Art Dir Mag Show; Graphis Annual & Typomondus 20. **HONORS/ACHIEVEMENTS:** Intl Exp of "Best Graphics of the 20th Century". **MILITARY SERVICE:** AUSR 1st Lt 1965-71. **HOME ADDRESS:** 5707 Aladdin St, Los Angeles, CA 90008.

BOSTON, GEORGE DAVID
Dentist, educator. **PERSONAL:** Born Nov 01, 1923, Columbus, OH; married Johanna Heidinger; children: George, Jr(dec), Donald, Darryl (dec). **EDUCATION:** OSU, BA 1949, DDS 1952. **CAREER:** Columbus State Hosp Dental Clinic, chief 1952-58; priv pract 1953-; OH State Univ, asst prof 1957-84. **ORGANIZATIONS:** Mem Columbus Dental Soc; OH Dental Assn; Amer Dental Assn; Natl Dental Assn; Buckeye State Dental Assn; Columbus Assn of Dentists & Physicians; partner Rosbos Leasing Aircraft Lessor, pilot; mem Omega Psi Phi Frat; Sigma Pi Phi Frat; Cavaliers Inc; Big Bros; bd dirs Beneficial Accept Corp; mem NAA CP; mem Natl Dent Honor Soc Omicron Kappa Upsilon; trustee bd mem Isabel Ridgway Nursing Center; mem Flying Dentists Assoc. **MILITARY SERVICE:** AUS 1st Lt QMC 1943-47. **BUSINESS ADDRESS:** 356 Taylor Ave, Columbus, OH 43203.

BOSTON, HORACE OSCAR
Dentist. **PERSONAL:** Born Jul 27, 1934, Clarksville, TX; married Iola. **EDUCATION:** So Univ, BS 1955; TX So Univ; Univ OK; Univ NM; Washingont Univ, DDS; Meharry Med Clg Sch, Dentistry 1973. **CAREER:** Private Practice, dentist; Wiley Coll, asst prof Biology; High School Science teacher; Midwestern Univ, asst prof; Several Nursing Homes, cons; WF & Evening Lions Club, pres. **ORGANIZATIONS:** Mem YMCA; bd dir Eastside Girls Clb; chmn adv bd Local Headstart Pgm; commr Wichita Falls Housing Authority; vice pres Wichita Dist Dental Soc; mem Am Dental Assn; mem TX Dental Assn; mem Kappa Alpha Psi Frat. **HONORS/ACHIEVEMENTS:** Inc publ "Prognathism A Rev of the lit" 1972; grant NSF. **MILITARY SERVICE:** USAR capt 1955-73. **BUSINESS ADDRESS:** 1004 Brook, Wichita Falls, TX 76301.

BOSTON, RALPH
Athlete, TV station owner. **PERSONAL:** Born May 09, 1939, Laurel, MS; son of Peter Boston and Eulalia Lott Boston; divorced; children: Kenneth Todd, Stephen Keith. **EDUCATION:** TN State Univ, BS, Grad Work. **CAREER:** Univ of Tennessee Knoxville, asst dean of students 1968-75; TV commentator, 1969; ESPC-TV, commentator 1978-85; Integon Insurance Corp, sales; South Central Bell Adv Systems, acct exec; WKXT-TV Knoxville, gen partner, 1988-. **ORGANIZATIONS:** Capt Natl Track & Field Team 1960-68; mem Olympic Teams 1960-68; lecturer Throughout US 1968-; field judge Special Olympics for East TN. **HONORS/ACHIEVEMENTS:** Broke Jesse Owen's 25 Yr Long Jump Record 1960; Gold Medal Rome Olympics 1960; titlist NCAA 1960; athelete of Yr N Am 1961; Helms Hall of Fame 1962; Silver Medal Tokyo Olympics 1964; Olympic Bronze Medal Mexico City 1968; world long jump record; TN Sports Hall of Fame 1970; Natl Track & Field Hall of Fame 1974; US Track & Field Hall of Fame 1975; first black inducted MS Sports Hall of Fame 1977; parks named in honor of, Laurel, MS 1978; first man to jump 26 ft indoors, 27 ft outdoors; 2nd Pl Team Championship NAIA Track Championship; Greatest Long Jumper of the Century 1979; All Time All Star Indoor Track & Field Hall of Fame 1982; Knoxville Sports Hall of Fame 1982; Mobile Oil Corp Track and Field Hall of Fame 1983; TN State Univ Athletic Hall of Fame 1983; Olympic Hall of Fame 1985; NCAA Silver Anniversary Awd, 1985.

BOSWELL, ARNITA J.
Educator. **PERSONAL:** Born Apr 19; married Dr Paul P; children: Bonnie B. **EDUCATION:** KY State Clg, BS Home Ec; Atlanta U, MSW; Columbia Univ Sch of Soc Work, Adv Cert Social Work; CO State U, Adv Ed. **CAREER:** Social Service Admin Univ of Chicago, assoc prof; Lincoln Inst KY, asst dean of students; Eastman Kodak, asst personnel dir; ARC Munich Germany, asst & clb dir, asst program dir; Family Serv ARC Chicago, sr case worker; Gov Hospital NYC, psychiatric social worker, medical social worker; Family Serv Bureau Unities Charities Chicago, case worker. **ORGANIZATIONS:** Lectr Roosevelt U; lectr Geo Williams Clg; sch soc worker ford found & bd of ed Greater Cities Improvement Proj Chgo; dir Soc Serv Proj Head Start Chgo; acting dir Soc Serv Proj Head Start Wash DC; dir Human Rights Ofc of econ Opp Region IV Chgo; spec cnslr Minority Stdnts Univ of Chicago Undergrad; dir Pub Welfare Curr Dev Proj; assc field work prof Grad Sch & of Soc Serv Admn Univ of Chgo; given many speeches & papers at various Seminars,Insts, Workshops, Radio, TV; consul for Organizing & Dev Soc Serv in Head Start at HI, PR, VI, MS, Appalachian & Spnsh Spkng Comm; chmn Training forDay Care White Hse Conf for Children 1971; co-chmn of Women's Div ChgoDr Martin Luther King in Solidarity Day Celebration Soldiers Field; consul First Unitarian Ch Chgo; mem numerous Local, Spec Local, Metro & Natl Com; consul HEW, OEO Poverty Comm Human Rights HUD & Metro Hsng & Plng Cnsl of Chgo. **HONORS/ACHIEVEMENTS:** Recip hon Alpha Gamma Pi for Professional Escellence in Soc Work, Soc Work Educ & Comm Svc; outstndg contribution to Comm Chgo; contrbtn to Youth Awrd, Phi Beta Sigma Frat; outstndg city awrd for Comm Serv Com of 100; outstndg alumni awrd KY State Clg; outstndg serv awrd OEO Work with Proj Head Start & Civil Rights; outstndg region prfmnc awrd OEO Chgo; faculty awrd Black Stdnts Univ of Chicago Work with all Stdnts; 1 of 6 outstndg women in Chicago YWCA HumanRelations Work; black child dev int for Involvement in Action & Progs Retlating to Early Childhood Ed; intrl traveler's awrd Work in Germany, Guam, Jamica, PR, VI, HI Legislativeley in Afrcn Afrs; great gal of day WGRT; natl inst of hlth awrd & spec contrbtn to Sickle Cell Disease Adv Com.

BOSWELL, ARTHUR W.
Association executive. **PERSONAL:** Born Jul 28, 1909, Jersey City; married Vivian S. **EDUCATION:** Howard Univ, AB, 1932; Columbia Univ, AM Dept Pub Law, Grad, 1935. **CAREER:** Dept HUD, rlty speclst 1950-75; Vet HS Jersey City, ret tchr 1948-50; Freno CA Newport RI, uso dir 1941-48; Dumber Comm League Sprngfld & MA, exec asst 1939-40; Xavier Univ New Orleans, athletic dir 1932-34. **ORGANIZATIONS:** Active mem AOA Frat 1930-; flw Acad of Pol Sci NYC; flw Am Acad Pol & Soc Sci Phila; exec com Local Br NAACP; tchr Adult Bible Class Mt Zion ofGermantown Stdnt of Dr Ralph Bunche. **HONORS/ACHIEVEMENTS:** Achvmnt awrd Alpha Sigma Howard U; masters thesis the Pol Theories & Policies of Negroes in Congress During Reconstruction.

BOSWELL, BENNIE, JR.
Personnel administrator. **PERSONAL:** Born May 04, 1948, Danville, VA; married Helen Thomas. **EDUCATION:** Williams Coll MA, BA cum Laude 1970. **CAREER:** Western Reserve Acad Hudson, OH, instr 1970-73; Williams Coll, asst dir of admissions 1973-75; A Better Chance Inc, assoc dir student affairs 1975; Wachovia Bank & Trust Co NA, vice pres employee relations & training 1976-. **ORGANIZATIONS:** Mem Amer Soc of Personnel Admins; mem black Exec Exch Prog; mem ASTD; vice pres & pres-elect Natl Assn of Bank Affirmative Action Directors; mem NAACP; bd chmn Fellowship Home of Winston-Salem; adv bd mem Duke Univ LEAD Prog; former mem exec comm Williams Coll Alumni Soc. **HONORS/ACHIEVEMENTS:** Francis Session Meml Fellowship Williams Coll 1970; Lehman Scholar Williams Coll 1967; Natl Achieve Scholar Natl Merit Found 1966. **BUSINESS ADDRESS:** VP Empl Relations & Training, Wachovia Bank & Trust Co, PO Box 3099, Winston-Salem, NC 27150.

BOSWELL, DOROTHYE HARRIS
Executive director. **PERSONAL:** Born Oct 12, Welch, WV. **EDUCATION:** Cleveland Clg of W Res U; LA City Clg; Univ of S CA Univ of CA. **CAREER:** Nat Assc for Sickle Cell Dis Inc, div exec dir; US Equal Oppty Commin, tech analy wrtr 1966-72; USAF, admn asst 1959-66; USN, supr 1950-59. **ORGANIZATIONS:** Mem Genetic Dis Advis Com State & Dept of Hlth 1977; mem Ad Hoc Com for Revis of Sickle Cell Regulat 1976-; advis co Sickle Cell Cnsl Dept of Hlth Serv 1977; life mem orgnzr Natl Assc of Negro Bus & Prof Women's Clb Inc; 1st vice pres Los Angeles Clb of Natl Assc of Negro Bus & Professional Women; mem Natl Assn of Media Women; 2nd vice pres Natl Assn of Mrkt Dev; mem bd of dir & sec Sickle Cell Dis Rsrch Found; mem NAACP; mem Los Angeles Urban League; mem New Front Dem Clb; mem Alpha Chptr; mem Lambda Kappa Mu Sor. **HONORS/ACHIEVEMENTS:** Dem Wormen's Forum Contrb "Sickle Cell Anemia-the Neglected Dis" 1973; outstndg comm serv awrd Help Pub Serv Found 1977; Who's Who Among Am 1973-74; Who's Who Am Women 1973-74; Who's & Who of Listed Women of World 1973-74; serv awrd Los Angeles Urban League Guild 1966; sup serv awrd Los Angeles Clb Bus & Professional Women 1965; sojrnr truth awrd Los Angeles Bus & Professional Women 1964; sup perform awrd USAF 1964. **MILITARY SERVICE:** USAF.

BOSWELL, PAUL P.
Physician. **PERSONAL:** Born Jun 12, 1905, Pittsburgh; married Arnita Young; children: Bonnie. **EDUCATION:** Lincoln U, AB 1930; Univ MN, BS, MB, MD 1940. **CAREER:** MD Prvt Prac, dr; Provident Michael Reese & Univ IL Hosp, dermatologist; IL State Legistalor; Gilleteee Co, derm cons; Union Hlth Svc, chgo bd hlth derm cons; Drexel & Home of Aged; Toni Co; Michael Reese Nrs Sch, lectr; Provident Hosp Nrs Sch; Michael Reese Hosep, sr atndng phys, Provident Hosp, MI Ave Hosp; Hlth Serv Chicago Cir Campus Univ of IL, asst prof. **ORGANIZATIONS:** Mem Nat Med Assc; mem Med Assc; mem Chicago Derm Soc; mem Am Acad of Derm; mem Pan Am Med Assc; mem Intrl Soc of Tropical Derm; mem Urban League; NAACP; dir IL Cncl for Mental Retard; Chicago Assc Retarded Children; Woodlawn Mental Hlth Svc; mem Hyde Park-Kenwood Comm; Unit Ch; Southside Comm Com; Hyde Park YMCA; Joint Negro Appeal; past mem Welfare Cncl of Metro Chgo. **HONORS/ACHIEVEMENTS:** Recip man of yr Lincoln U; best frshmn cit IVI; best legislators awrds IVI; IL Med & Soc Pol Activity Awrd; rep 74th Gen Assembly 1964-66. **BUSINESS ADDRESS:** 841 E 63 St, Chicago, IL.

BOTHUEL, ETHEL C.S.
University administrator. **PERSONAL:** Born Mar 18, 1941, Charleston, SC; children: Charles E Smith II, Arnold ASmith, Marvin II. **EDUCATION:** Atlantic Business College, Certificate 1958-60; Howard Univ, BA 1981. **CAREER:** Gallaudet Univ, asst to pres 1974-79; Self-employed, consultant 1979-, real estate assoc; George Washington Univ, dir eeo 1980-. **ORGANIZATIONS:** Mem Campbell AME Church 1961-; charter mem Washington Metro Area Affirmative Action Assoc 1980-; American Assn for Affirmative Action; Assn of Black Women in Higher Education; consultant Georgetown Univ 1980, Trinity College 1981, Natl Legal Aid & Defender Assoc 1982; real estate assoc Mt Vernon Realty Co Inc 1984-; mem NAACP; dir of choirs, Mathews Memorial Baptist Church 1981-. **HONORS/ACHIEVEMENTS:** Recognition Awd Gallaudet Comm Relations Council 1980; Appreciation Awd Federal Bureau of Investigation 1984; Outstanding Dedicated Serv Awds Campbell

AME Church, Matthews Memorial Baptist Church 1979-85. **BUSINESS ADDRESS:** Dir Equal Opportunity, George WashingtonUniv, 2121 Eye St NW Rice Hall, Washington, DC 20052.

BOUIE, MERCELINE
Educator. **PERSONAL:** Born Oct 18, 1929, St Louis, MO; daughter of Mr & Mrs Ray Morris; married Harry J Bouie; children: Ray Anthony, Pamela Sue. **EDUCATION:** Lincoln Univ, BA, Behavioral Sci, Physical Education, Health, 1953; Webster Univ, BA, Social Behavioral Science, 1972; MA, Social & Behavioral Science, 1973; Open Univ, PhD, Education, Social Behavorial Science, 1976. **CAREER:** St Louis Archdiocese Parochial School System, Elementary & High School Physical Education/Health Teacher, 1958-64; Venice, IL School System, Dept Chmn, Physical Education & Health Teacher, 1964-68; Wheeler State School, Dept Head, Young Adults, 1968-74; St Louis Bd of Education, Resource Specialist, 1974-82, St Louis Public Schools, Conductor of Workshops, 1979-83; Psychological Examiner, 1982-83, Learning Disabled Specialist, 1985-. **ORGANIZATIONS:** Member, AAUW; Exceptional child specialist counselor, Bouies Learning Center, 1978-85; 2nd Vice Pres, Learning Disability Assn, 1976-79; Advisor, Missouri Learning Disability Assn, 1976-80; Member, St Louis Assn of Retarded Children, 1979-; Mem, Intl Platform Assn, 1976-; Grandlady, Ladies Aux Peter Claver, 1979-82; Pro-life Committee, Our Lady of Good Counsel Parish; Advisory Bd, Human Rights Office of the Archdiocese; Judge, Intl Platform Assn Convention, Washington, DC, 1987; Advisor, State Rep of the 56th District; Chairperson, High Expectation, Effective & Efficient Schools, Soldan HS; Vice Pres, Mt Carmel School Bd, 1989-93; Vice Pres, Webster Univ Alumni Bd of Directors 1989-92; Coordinator, Soldan Parent's Organization, 1989-93. **HONORS/ACHIEVEMENTS:** Speaker's Award, Intl Platform Assn, 1979; Committee Leadership, Amer Assn Univ Women, 1977; Fourth Degree Award, Peter Claver, 1981; Special Education Award, Civic Liberty Assn, 1982; Oryx Press, Directory of Speakers, 1981, 1982; Community Leadership Award, 27th Ward Alderman; Amer Assn of Poetry Award, 1986; St Louis Symphony Ladies Assn Award, 1986; Article in North County Journal; Published Poem of Life, 1989, Parent Involvement, 1976 and Workbook, K-4, 1977. **HOME ADDRESS:** 1039 Melvin Ave, St Louis, MO 63137.

BOUIE, PRESTON L.
Retired assistant fire chief. **PERSONAL:** Born Jan 22, 1926, St Louis, MO; married Stella M Mosby; children: Sylvia N Saddler, Sheila N. **EDUCATION:** Vashon High School, 1944. **CAREER:** St Louis Fire Dept, private 1952-63, fire capt 1963-76, battalion fire chief 1976-78, deputy fire chief 1978-83, asst fire chief. **ORGANIZATIONS:** Trustee Washington Metropolitan AME Zion Church 1980-. **HONORS/ACHIEVEMENTS:** Inducted into-Vashon High School Hall of Fame, Vashon Hall of Fame Comm 1989. **MILITARY SERVICE:** US Navy AMMC 3rd class 2 years.

BOUIE, SIMON PINCKNEY
Clergyman. **PERSONAL:** Born Oct 03, 1939, Columbia, SC; married Willie Omia Jamison; children: Erich, Harold. **EDUCATION:** Allen Univ, BA 1962; Interdenomination Ctr, BD 1966; SC State Hosp, clinical ct 1968. **CAREER:** Metro AME Church, sr minister; Warwick Sch for Boys, first Black Chaplain 1972-74; Mother Bethel AME Church, sr minister. **ORGANIZATIONS:** Chairperson Salute to the Schomburg Ctr for Rsch in Black Culture, The Salute to Harlem Hosp, the Bethel Day Cae Center, the Ministerial Interfaith Assn Health Comm, The Harlem Civic Welfare Assn Comm Bd, NY AME Ministerial Alliance Social Action Comm, North Central Hospital Day; mem trustee bd of the NYAnnual Conference of the AME Church; mem 100 Black Men Inc; mem Alpha Phi Alpha Frat; NY Chap of the NAACP; bd of dirs NY City Council of Churches; NY Branch of the YMCA; Comm for the Soc for the Family of the Man Awd; mem Bd of NY State Council of Churches; pres Prince Hall Masons; pres HarlemCouncil; pres Richard Allen Ctr on Life. **HONORS/ACHIEVEMENTS:** NY Conf Outstanding Awd 1972; Lionel Hampton Awd 1975; Citizen of the Yr Awd Bi-Centennial 1976; Suffolk Day Care Awd 1978; Metro AME Church Outstanding Awd 1980; Distinguished Health & Hospital Corp Awd of NY 1980; first Disting Citizen Awd for North General Hospital 1982; DD Degree Interdenominational Theological Center 1982; DH Degree Monrovia College Monrovia W Africa 1984. **HOME ADDRESS:** 1135 Barringer St, Philadelphia, PA 19119. **BUSINESS ADDRESS:** Senior Minister, Mother Bethel Ame Church, 419 Richard Allen Ave, Philadelphia, PA 19147.

BOULDES, CHARLENE
Accountant. **PERSONAL:** Born May 05, 1945, Brooklyn, NY; children: Anthony, Christi, Minde. **EDUCATION:** Univ of Albuquerque, BSBA Accounting (Dean's List) 1981, BSBA Public Admin 1982; UNM, M Art 1983. **CAREER:** Grad Assistant UNM, researcher 1983; City/Co Task Force, financial advisor 1984-85; Univ of NM, acct supervisor accountant, US Forest Service, 1988. **ORGANIZATIONS:** Natl Assoc of Public Accountants, Univ of Albuquerque 1981; Amer Soc for Public Admin Univ NM 1982; graduate asst Univ NM Public Admin 1982-84; pres elect Civitan Intl 1984-85; mem NAACP 1951-, NAACP Youth Sponsor 1982-. **HONORS/ACHIEVEMENTS:** Scholarship Univ of Albany 1981; Phi Alpha Alpha Natl Honor Soc Univ NM 1984; Outstanding Graduate Student Univ NM Public Admin 1984. **HOME ADDRESS:** PO box 15752, Rio Rancho, NM 87124.

BOULWARE, FAY D.
Education association executive. **PERSONAL:** Daughter of William R Davis (deceased) and Fay H Davis; children: William H. **EDUCATION:** Hunter Coll CUNY, BA; Teachers Coll Columbia Univ, MA, Prof Diploma. **CAREER:** Teachers Coll Columbia Univ, assoc in admissions 1960-64; Insititue for Dev Stds New York Med Coll, adminstr coord/inst 1964-66; Inst for Devel Studies New York Univ, dir of adminstrn and research scientist 1966-71; Educ Studies Prgm Wesleyan Univ, lecturer 1971-75; African Am Inst Wesleyan Univ, dir 1971-75; Emmaline Productions, hist & literary researcher 1982; Merrill Lynch Pierce Fenner & Smith, prof writer 1983-; Chuckles Prod, dir story devel & research 1983-. **ORGANIZATIONS:** Consultant NY City Bd of Educ 1971-; consultant Acad Adv Bd Wesleyan Univ 1971-75; consultant to the Bd of Educ At Middletown, CT 1972-73, Lansing, MI 1971, Atlanta GA 1971, Charlotte, NC 1969-71, Model Cities, Pittsburgh, PA 1969, Univ Of Hawaii 1967, Virgin Isls Day Sch, St Croix, VI 1965. **HOME ADDRESS:** 25 W 132nd StApt 9P, New York, NY 10037.

BOULWARE, PATRICIA A.
Government relations. **PERSONAL:** Born Jan 29, 1949, Washington, DC; daughter of Etheridge H Boulware and Carrie Robbins Boulware; children: Kenyatta. **EDUCATION:** Washington Tech Inst, AA 1974; Univ of the District of Columbia, BA 1980. **CAREER:** United Cerebral Palsy Assoc, legislative analyst 1978-79, rsch asst 1980-81; Amer Assn for the Advancement of Sci, project asst 1981-82, program asst 1982-83, program assoc 1984-88; Tuskegee University, Federal Relations Office, assistant director 1989-. **ORGANIZATIONS:** Chair AAAS Subcommittee on Day Care/Child Develop 1985-88; mem Natl Black Child Develop Inst, Federation of Organizations for Professional Women, Amer Mgmt Assn; development educ advocate Natl Council of Negro Women; mem NAACP; member, United House of Prayer for all People; volunteer, Washington Area Council on Alcoholism and Drug Abuse 1988-. **HONORS/ACHIEVEMENTS:** Numerous publications including "Impact of Child Abuse on Neurological Disabilities," 1979, "Equity and Excellence Compatible Goals," (edited, et al) 1984, "Science, Technology and Women, A World Perspective," (edited, et al) 1985; Kappa Delta Pi; Model City Scholarship. **BUSINESS ADDRESS:** Assistant Director, Tuskegee University Federal Relations Office, 11 Dupont Circle, N W, Suite 220, Washington, DC 20036.

BOURGEOIS, ADAM
Attorney. **PERSONAL:** Born May 12, 1929, Chicago, IL; married Grace J Van Atta; children: 3 Children. **EDUCATION:** Loyola U, LIB 1951. **CAREER:** Adam Bourgeois Ltd, atty 1971-; OH State U, prof 1969-71; Human Res Gov's Ofc IL, exec dir 1968-69; W Coast Area Urban Coalition, exec dir 1968; Model Cities Mayor's Ofc St Louis, exec dir 1966-68; JOBS Proj Chicago & YMCA, admnstr 1962-65; Chgo, atty 1951-62. **ORGANIZATIONS:** Mem ABA & IL Bar Assc; Chicago Cncl Lwyrs.

BOURNE, BEAL VERNON, II
Funeral director. **PERSONAL:** Born Mar 29, 1950, Pulaski, VA; married Peggy Sharlotte Wright; children: Troy, Maurice, John. **EDUCATION:** Univ of MD, Cert History Major 1972; KY School of Mortuary Sci, diploma 1972-73; State of TN Funeral Dir & Embalmer, License 1972-74. **CAREER:** Amway, distributor 1973-80; Jarnigan & Son Mortuary, asst mgr 1973-75, mgr dir embalmer 1975-; Allen-Bourne-Cash Insurance Agency, part owner; Jarnigan & Son Mortuary, owner 1986. **ORGANIZATIONS:** Bd of dir Knoxville Big Brothers 1973-84; mem Knoxville United Way; Natl & State FD&M Assoc 1974; life mem DAV 1974; Christian Funeral Dir 1975; mem CC Russell Masonic Lodge 262 1976; dir of ed James E Derricks Elks Lodge 1977; Joe Jones Council 1978; mem Epsilon Nu Delta Mortuary Frat 1980; Lennon-Seney United Meth Church Fin & Trustee Bd 1980; mem Aux Knox Cty Sheriff Dept 1980; Knoxville Epileptic Found 1982; past pres & vice pres Chilchowee PTA 1982-84; bd of dir YMCA & YWCA 1982-85; mem E Knox Optimist Club 1983; vice pres 1983-84, pres 1984-85 E TN Funeral Dir; licensed ins agent State of TN 1984; KeblahTemple 78 Shriner 1984; mem House of Rep 1984-85, Natl Funeral Dir 1984-85; mem East Knoxville Advisory Bd. **HONORS/ACHIEVEMENTS:** UT Faculty Club 1980; Cert of Outstanding Serv Knoxville Big Brothers 1981; Notary State of TN 1982; Cert of Merit Knoxville YMVA 1983; Congressional VIP Card Natl Rep Comm 1983-84; Silver People to People Medic Blood Bank 1984; KY Col State of KY Col 1984; Col Aid De Camp TN 1984. **MILITARY SERVICE:** AUS sgt E-5 3 yrs; Hon Discharge, Cert of Apprec, Cert of Achievement 1972. **HOME ADDRESS:** 3002 Woodbine Ave, Knoxville, TN 37914. **BUSINESS ADDRESS:** Owner, Jarnigan & Son Mortuary, 2823 McCall Ave NE, Knoxville, TN 37914.

BOURNE, JUDITH LOUISE
Attorney. **PERSONAL:** Born Jul 02, 1945, New York City, NY; daughter of St Clair T Bourne and Gwendolyn Samuel Bourne. **EDUCATION:** Cornell Univ, BA 1966; NY Univ Law Sch, JD 1972, LLM Intl Law 1974. **CAREER:** Inst Culturale Peruano Norteamericano, English tchr 1965; NY Univ Clinic for Learning, comm asst 1966-67; New York City Human Resources Admin, special asst to the admin 1967-68; New York City Neighborhood Youth Corps, special consultant to dir for summer progs 1968; Bd for Fundamental Educ, prog assoc admin liaison to tech training 1968-69; Natl Council on Crime & Deliquency, legal intern 1970-71; NY State Spec Commn on Attica, ed staff 1972; NY Univ Sch of Continuing Educ, instr 1973; Emergency Land Fund, SC state coord 1974; private practice, SC atty 1974-77; Office of Fed Public Defender, asst federal public defender 1977-81; private practice, atty St Thomas US VI 1982-. **ORGANIZATIONS:** Junior fellow NY Univ Ctr for Intl Studies 1972-73; mem, natl co-chair 1976-79 Natl Conf of Black Lawyers 1973-; mem Intl Affairs Task Force SC State Dir 1973-76; chairperson Political Affairs Task Force 1979-80; mem Amer Trial Lawyers Assn; mem VI Bar Assn; mem Anguilla Virgin Islands Soc; mem Almeric L Christian Lawyers Assn; adv bd mem Div of Mental Health Comm Support Prog; mem Caribbean Develop Coalition; chair Virgin Islands Anti-Apartheid Commn 1985-; secretary, Virgin Islands Bar Assn 1983, treasurer 1984, secretary 1985, mem board of governers, 1987. **BUSINESS ADDRESS:** Attorney, PO Box 6458, St Thomas, Virgin Islands of the United States 00801.

BOUTTE, ALVIN J.
Business executive. **PERSONAL:** Born Oct 10, 1929, Lake Charles, LA; children: 4 children. **EDUCATION:** Xavier Univ, BS 1951. **CAREER:** Independent Drug Stores, pres 1956-64; Independence Bank, co-founder/vchmn 1964-70, chmn/ceo 1970-. **ORGANIZATIONS:** Pres 79th St med corp; bd mem Johnson Prods Co; bd mem BBB; bd gov's Urban Gateways; bd trustees Marion Bus Coll; bd mem Rehab Inst Chicago; Chicago State Univ Found; Jr Achievement; YMCA; Operation PUSH; past pres Small Busn Adminstrn; bd mem Chicago Bd Educ 1969-74. **HONORS/ACHIEVEMENTS:** Man of the Year Chicago Urban League 1971; Chicago Econ Dev Corp 1971. **MILITARY SERVICE:** AUS Capt. **BUSINESS ADDRESS:** Chairman/CEO, Independence Bank, 7936 S Cottage Grove, Chicago, IL 60619.

BOWDOIN, ROBERT E.
Business executive. **PERSONAL:** Born May 04, 1929, Los Angeles, CA; married Joan; children: Kimberly J, Robert G, Wendy M. **EDUCATION:** UCLA, BS 1951. **CAREER:** Pasadena Redevel Agy, dep adminstr tech serv redevel mgr; Bowdin Neal & Weathers, fdr; Fairway Escrow Co LA, co-owner mgr; Watts Svngs & Loan, real estate appraiser, loan officer, escrow officer; Family Savings & Loan Assoc, pres & ceo. **ORGANIZATIONS:** Bd mem United Way; Ginge Inc; Nat Archt Engr Firm; mem Brthrhd Crusade; past mem Altadna Lib Bd; bd mem CA Svngs & Loan Leag; mem Amer Savings& Loan League, US Savings & Loan League. **BUSINESS ADDRESS:** President & CEO, Family Savings & Loan Assoc, 3683 Crenshaw Blvd, Los Angeles, CA 90016.

BOWEN, CLOTILDE DENT
Retired US Army psychiatrist. **PERSONAL:** Born Mar 20, 1923, Chicago, IL; daughter of William Dent and Clotilde Dent; divorced. **EDUCATION:** OH State Univ, BA 1943; OH State Univ Med Sch, MD 1947; Harlem Hosp, intern 1947-48; NYC, residency in TB 1948-49; NY State, Fellowship in TB 1950; Albany Vets Admin Hosp, residency 1959-62; Amer Bd of Psychiatry & Neurology, diplomate certified in psychiatry 1966; 1st Black woman to graduate from OSU Med Sch & residency in psychiatry at Albany VA Hosp & Albany Med Cntr. **CAREER:** Priv pract 1950-55; VA Hosp, psych 1962-67; Active Reserve 1959-67; OCHAMPUS, chief rvw bd 1968-70; US Army Vietnam, neuropsych consult 1970-71; Fitzsimons Army Med Ctr, chief dept of psych 1971-74; HSC Region V Area, consult 1971-74;Univ of CO Sch of Med, assoc clin prof of psych 1971-85; US Probation Office Denver, psych consult 1973-85; Tripler Army Med Ctr, chief dept of psych 1974-75;Univ of HI, clin assoc prof 1974-75; Dept of Clinics Fitzsimons Army Med Ctr, liaison psych 1976-77; Fitzsimons Army Med Ctr, chief dept of primary care 1979-83; US Army Tripler Genl Hosp, chief of psych serv 1967-68, 1983-85; psychiatric consultant, Joint Commission on Accrediation of Healthcare Organizations, 1985-; chief psychiatry, Cheyenne (wyoming) Veterans Affairs Medical Center, 1987-. **ORGANIZATIONS:** Mem Amer Psychiatric Assn; mem Central Neuropsychiatric Assn; mem Alpha Epsilon Iota; mem Reserve Ofcrs Assn; mem CO Psychiatric Soc; mem Oregon Psychiatric Assn; Historical Archives CO Med Soc; exec mem Natl Endowment for the Humanities; mem APA Cncl on Emerging Issues; mem Acad of PsychosomaticMedicine; Fellow Intl Soc for Electrotherapy; mem Natl Medical Assn; Fellows of Menninger Found; mem Assn of Military Surgeons of the US; mem Joint Review Comm on Paramedic Standards; mem Amer Med Assn; psychiatric consul Joint Comm on Accreditation of Hospitals 1985-. **HONORS/ACHIEVEMENTS:** Scholarship for Achievement Delta Sigma Theta Sor 1945; Cert of Commendation Veterans Admin 1966; Natl Achievement Awd of Natl Assn of Negro Business & Professional Women's Clubs Inc 1969; Legion of Merit US Army 1971; Woman of the Yr Denver Business & Professional Women's Club 1972; OH State Medical Alumni Achievement Awd 1972; DeHaven-Hinkson Awd by the Natl Medical Assn 1972; Distinguished Awardee at 5th Annual Grad Sch Visitation Day OH State Univ 1975; Hall of Champions Champion Jr HS; Fellow Acad of Psychosomatic Medicine 1978; Fellow Amer Psychiatric Assn 1981; numerous publs; president's 300 Commencement Award OH State Univ, June 1987; Distinguished Black Alumni Award O.S.U. Student National Medical Assn 1987. **MILITARY SERVICE:** AUS col 30 yrs, first Black female MD Colonel US Army; Meritorious Serv Medal 1974. **HOME ADDRESS:** 1020 Tari Dr, Colorado Springs, CO 80908.

BOWEN, EMMA L.
Director. **PERSONAL:** Born Sep 30, 1916, Spartanburg, SC; widowed; children: Marian, Antionette, Gloria. **EDUCATION:** Fordham U, BA. **CAREER:** New York City Mental Hlth & Mental Retard Serv, dir 1966-; Black Citizens for Fair Media, pres; Wash Hghts W Harlem Inwood Mental Htlh Cncl Inc, v-chrmn; NY Amsterdam News, columnist 1973-74; NAACP Youth Cncl, youth adv & bd 1963-68. **ORGANIZATIONS:** Mem NY State Adv Com US Civil Girghts Commn 1980-82; mem bd advs WNET-TV NYC. **HONORS/ACHIEVEMENTS:** Respons for appt of first Black young man to serve as Page in US Senate 1965; Am Women in Radio & TV NY Chptr 1974; natl off awrd NAACP 1965; good citizen salute Radio Sta WWRL 1967; Central Harlem Comm 1967; cert of hon Oper Better Black Pgm 1968; West 129th St Black Assc & Proj Day Camp 1968; citof hon Vol Coord Cncl of New York City 1969; We Care Group 1970; awrds in black '72 1972; Boy Scouts of Am 1972; Natl Assc of Media Women 1976; "Upper Manhattan Resource Direct"; "Direct of Concerned Citizens" recip Reach Out Awrd & WCBS-TV New York City 1978; woman of yr awrd Morrisania Highbridge Women's Clb 1972. **BUSINESS ADDRESS:** 93 Worth St, New York, NY 10013.

BOWEN, ERVA J.
Retired sociologist. **PERSONAL:** Born Oct 12, 1919, Winfield, KS; daughter of Mr & Mrs D W Walker; married John R Bowen; children: Randy, John H, Gary. **EDUCATION:** Southwestern College, Teacher's Certificate, 1941; Univ of California at Berkeley, Certificate, Social Service, 1961. **CAREER:** Santa Cruz City Welfare Dept, Social Worker, 1958-72 (retired); Senior Outreach Counsellor, Family Service Assn, 1989. **ORGANIZATIONS:** Member, Del Assembly, California School Bd Assn, 1979-81; Pres, Santa Cruz City Schools Bd of Ed, 1976-77; Mem, Santa Cruz Housing Advisory Committee, 1974-76; Member, Citizen's Planning Advisory Committee, 1972; Chmn, Santa Cruz Workable Program Committee, 1969-70; Mem, Santa Cruz City Committee on Status of Women, 1973-75; California Social Workers Organization; California Alphi Phi Sigma Alpha; Mem, Bd of Dir, YWCA, 1960-64, 1974-75; Santa Cruz Branch, NAACP, Pres, 1962-66, 1968-70, Secretary, 1960-68, Vice Pres, 1968-74; Pres, Santa Cruz Church Women United, 1980-83; Pres, District 28 Amer Legion Auxiliary Dept of California, 1984-85; Member, Salvation Army Advisory Bd, 1986-. **HONORS/ACHIEVEMENTS:** NAACP Freedom Award, 1974; Women of Achievement, BPWC, 1974.

BOWEN, RAYMOND C.
Educational administrator. **PERSONAL:** Born Sep 19, 1934, New Haven, CT; married JoAnn; children: Raymond C III, Rebecca M, Ruth J, Rachel R. **EDUCATION:** Univ of New Mexico, MS 1962; Univ of CT, BA 1956, PhD 1966. **CAREER:** Community Coll of Baltimore, vice pres Harbor Campus 1976-78, vice pres academic affairs 1978-79, vice pres ACA & student affairs 1979-82; Shelby State Comm Coll, pres 1982-. **ORGANIZATIONS:** Mem ACE, AACJC 1981; bd dirs SACJC 1985; bd trustees Leadership Memphis 1985; bd dirs United Way 1985; vice chmn bd of dirs Bio-Medical Rsch Zone 1985. **HONORS/ACHIEVEMENTS:** Outstanding Educator in Pub Higher Educ Memphis Bd of Educ 1982; Separate Two-Year Systems Hurt Stu Opport Commercial Appeal 1982; Outstanding Services Eng Teachers Dist IV MCS 1985. **MILITARY SERVICE:** AUS sgt 1956-59. **BUSINESS ADDRESS:** President, Shelby State Community College, PO Box 40568, Memphis, TN 38174.

BOWEN, RICHARD, JR.
Business executive, educator. **PERSONAL:** Born Apr 20, 1942, Colp, IL; married Cleatia B Rafe; children: Gerald, Chantel. **EDUCATION:** VTI_Southern IL Univ, AA 1966; Southern IL Univ, BS 1969; Purdue Univ, MS 1971. **CAREER:** Restaurant Bar, owner 1964-71; Purdue Univ, teaching asst 1969-71; Lincoln Land Comm Coll, prof 1971-78; Pillsbury Mills, mgmt consult 1973-75; Lincoln Land Comm Coll, div chmn 1978-87; real estate sales 1985. **ORGANIZATIONS:** Leader Boy Scout Adv Bd 1978-80; sec Chrysler Customer Satisfaction Bd 1980-87; training officer Small Business Admin 1982-85; suprv comm Sangamon Cty Credit Union 1984-85; prog chmn Breakfasst Optimist Club 1985; bd mem Sangamon City Credit Union. **MILITARY SERVICE:** AUS E-4 training officer non commiss 2 yrs. **BUSINESS ADDRESS:** Division Chairman, Lincoln Land Community College, Shepherd Rd, Springfield, IL 62708.

BOWEN, RUTH J.
Business executive. **PERSONAL:** Born Sep 13, 1930, Danville, VA; married William. **EDUCATION:** Attened NY Univ UCLA. **CAREER:** Queen Booking Corp New York City Acts Include Aretha Franklin, Carolyn Franklin, Erma Franklin, Sammy Davis, Jr, the Impresions, Stevie Wonder, Redd Foxx, Jerry Butler, pres founder 1965-76. **ORGANIZATIONS:** Mem past pres Rinkydinks Clb; mem Operation PUSH. **HONORS/ACHIEVEMENTS:** Only Woman to Head Her Own Booking Agy.

BOWEN, WILLIAM F.
Government official. **PERSONAL:** Born Jan 29, 1929, Cincinnati, OH; married Delores Freeman (deceased); children: Linda, Kevin, William, Terrance, Nicole. **EDUCATION:** Attended, Xavier Univ. **CAREER:** Ohio House of Rep, state rep 1966-70; State of OH, state senator, past chmn Senate Finance Comm, currently ranking minority mem of Senate Finance Comm 1970-. **ORGANIZATIONS:** Past pres Cincinnati Br NAACP Hamilton Co Black Caucus; exec comm Dem Party Soc Serv Adv Council; mem Avondale Comm Council; Natl Conf of State Legislators; Outs Freshman Rep 107th Gen Assembly Mental Health Assn. **HONORS/ACHIEVEMENTS:** John F Kennedy Pub Serv Awd OH League of Young Dem; Outstanding Leadership 107th Gen Assembly; 1st Annual Awd OH Nursing Homes Assn for Outstanding Comm Svc; Cincinnati Ins Bd Outstanding Contrib during 108th Gen Assembly; NAACP Awd Outstanding & Dedicated Svcs; Black Excellence Awd PUSH; Cert of Recognition & Appreciation VIVA; resolution by 111th Gen Assembly Outstanding Contrib; Pioneer Awd Res Home for Mentally Retarded Hamilton Co; Pub Serv Awd OH Pub Trans Assn; Man of Yr Awd OH Pub Transit Assn; Ann Leadership Awd Concerned Citizens of OH; Ldrshp Awd All African Student Faculty Union OH State Univ. **BUSINESS ADDRESS:** State Senator & Chmn Finance, State of OH, 3662 Reading Rd, Cincinnati, OH 45229.

BOWENS, JOHNNY WESLEY
Educational administration. **PERSONAL:** Born Jun 02, 1946, Jacksonville, FL; married Monica Darlene Lewis; children: Torrence, Derick, Omari. **EDUCATION:** Dillard Univ, BA 1968; Univ of AZ, MEd 1973; Union Graduate School, PhD 1977. **CAREER:** Pima Community Coll, dir student activities 1970-86, coord financial aid 1986-. **ORGANIZATIONS:** Allocation chair Tucson United Way 1985-; 1st vice pres Tucson Branch NAACP 1985-87. **HOME ADDRESS:** 2170 W Rainbow Ridge, Tucson, AZ 85745.

BOWER, BEVERLY LYNNE
Librarian. **PERSONAL:** Born Sep 10, 1951, Washington, DC; daughter of James T Johnson and Bettylou Calloway Johnson; married Jack R Bower Jr. **EDUCATION:** Univ of KS, BS Ed 1973; Emporia State Univ, MLS 1980. **CAREER:** Lansing Jr High School, reading teacher 1973-74; Chillicothe HS, French/English teacher 1974-75; Dept of Defense Dependent Schools, French/English teacher 1975-80; Pensacola Jr Coll, librarian 1980-84; Pensacola Jr Coll, dir lrc serv 1985-. **ORGANIZATIONS:** Sec West FL Library Assn 1981-83; mem ALA-JMRT Minorities Recruitment Comm 1982-83, FL Library Assn 1982-; publ rep FL Assn of Comm Coll 1983,85; FL Library Assn, community college caucus chair/chair-elect 1986-88; FL Assn of Comm Coll, regional dir 1987; chapter president, Florida Assn of Community Colleges, 1988; bd of directors, YWCA Pensacola, 1989-91. **HONORS/ACHIEVEMENTS:** Natl Achievement Scholar; Article "A Survey of FL Comm Coll Libraries" Comm & Jr Coll Libr 1984; presentations, "FL Comm Coll Libraries" FACC 1983, FLA 1984, Southeastern Library Assn 1984; Leaders Program, Amer Assn of Women in Community & Junior Colleges, 1989. **BUSINESS ADDRESS:** Dir LRC Services, Pensacola Jr College, 1000 College Blvd, Pensacola, FL 32504.

BOWERS, CHARLES A.
Management consultant. **PERSONAL:** Born Apr 29, 1920, Skipwith, VA; married Mary A Hull; children: Mark C, Jill T, Joan M. **EDUCATION:** Attend Air U; NY U, 1938-40; OH State U, 1947-48; Sacramento State U, 1957-59. **CAREER:** CA State Dept of Veterans Affairs, dep dir 1968-75; Chiang Kei Chek Teipei Taiwan, chief educ & training advisory 1965-66; Chanute Tech Training Center IL, dir of oper & training 1962-64; USAF Graduate Navigator School, deputy commander. **ORGANIZATIONS:** CA chmn Gov Reagan's Task Force on Drug Abuse 1972-73; chrtr mem Tuskegee Airmen Assn past pres mem bd dir Sacremento Science Center & Jr Mus; exec bd dir Golden Empire Council BSA; bd dir Sacremento Urban League; bd dir United Way; mem NAACP First Black Person to Navigate a USAF Jet Bomber Across the Atlanta 1952. **HONORS/ACHIEVEMENTS:** Recip distngshd flying cross air medal with Six Oak Leaf Clusters; Korean Pres Citation; Chinese Pres Commendation; Chinese Air Force Pilot; US Pres Citation; awrds from VFW. **MILITARY SERVICE:** US AC col 1941-66.

BOWERS, MIRION PERRY
Physician. **PERSONAL:** Born Aug 25, 1935, Bascom, FL; married Geraldine Janis Nixon; children: Jasmine Anusha, Mirion Perry Jr, Jarvis Andrew, Jeryl Anthony. **EDUCATION:** FL A&M Univ Tallahassee, BA 1957; Meharry Med Coll Nashville, MD 1963. **CAREER:** AUS Gen Hosp Frankfurt Germany, chief otolaryngology svc; UCLA School of Med, asst prof dept of surgery (head-neck) 1972-73; Martin Luther King Jr Gen Hosp Div of Otolaryngology Charles R Drew Post Grad Med School, asst prof & chief 1972-73; UCLA School of Med, asst clinical prof dept of head-neck surgery, 1973-; Private practice, physician; USC School of Med, dept of otolaryngology, head & neck, clinical Prof. **ORGANIZATIONS:** Mem Taunus Med Soc Frankfurt Germany 1969-72; fellow Amer Acad of Ophthalmology & Otolaryngology 1970-, Amer Coll of Surgeons 1972-; mem Amer Med Assn 1972-, Natl Med Assn 1973-, Charles R Drew Med Soc 1973-, Amer Council of Otolaryngology; mem bd of dir Los Angeles Chap Amer Cancer Soc; mem Los Angeles Cty Med Assoc; chmn otolaryngology sect California Medical Center 1982-85; chmn otolaryngology 1976-, secretary/treasurer medical staff 1976-, secretary operating rm comm 1986-, mem bd of trustees 1989-, mem exec comm 1989-, The Hosp of the Good Samaritan. **HONORS/ACHIEVEMENTS:** Soc of the Upper Tenth, Meharry Medical Coll; numerous publications. **MILITARY SERVICE:** AUS Med Corps lt col 1963-72.

BOWIE, OLIVER WENDELL
Certified public accountant. **PERSONAL:** Born Jun 25, 1947, Detroit, MI; son of Ulvene Shaw; married Penelope Ann Jackson; children: Stephanie, Traci, Oliver II. **EDUCATION:** Eastern MI Univ, BBA 1972. **CAREER:** Michigan Dept of Treasury, revenue agent 1970-73; Coopers & Lybrand, sr accountant 1973-75; Natl Bank of Detroit, audit mgr 1975-77; Wayne County Community Coll, dir of accounting 1977-79; Garrett Sullivan Davenport Bowie & Grant, vice pres 1980-88; sole proprietor 1988-. **ORGANIZATIONS:** Mem Amer Inst of CPA's 1975-, MI Assoc of CPA's 1975-, NC Assoc of CPA's 1985-, Greensboro W-S HP Airport Auth 1985-; treas Triad Sickle Cell Foundation 1985-; pres Trial Natl Assoc of Black Accountants 1986-; chmn L Richardson Hosp 1986-. **HONORS/ACHIEVEMENTS:** Certificates of Appreciation Natl Assoc of Black Accts 1977, IRS 1985. **BUSINESS ADDRESS:** Oliver W Bowie, CPA, Box 22052, Greensboro, NC 27420.

BOWIE, SAM
Professional athlete. **PERSONAL:** Born Mar 17, 1961, Lebanon, PA. **EDUCATION:** KY State Univ, Commun 1984. **CAREER:** Portland Trail Blazers, center 1984-. **HONORS/ACHIEVEMENTS:** Led KY in rebounding as a sr with 92 average; 3rd on the Wildcats in scoring with 105 points a game. **BUSINESS ADDRESS:** Portland Trail Blazers, 700 NE Multnomah St, Portland, OR 97232.

BOWIE, WALTER C.
Educator. **PERSONAL:** Born Jun 29, 1925, Kansas City, KS; married Cornelia Morris; children: Carolyn Guiy, Colleen Wells, Sybil K. **EDUCATION:** KS State U, DVM 1947; Cornell U, MS 1955, PhD 1960. **CAREER:** Sch of Vet Med Tuskegee Inst, dean 1972-; Dept of Physiology Cornell U, adj prof 1972-73; Sch Vet Med Tuskegee & Isnt, assc dean 1971-72; Head Dept of Physiology Sch of Vet Med Tuskegee Inst, prof 1960-71;Univ Al Med Ctr, vis prof 1967-; Howard U, vis prof 1965-; Head Dept of Physio Sch of Vet Med Tuskegee Inst, assc prof; Vet Med Ti, instr 1947; Physio & Nicotine, cons; Vets Amdn Hosp Tuskegee, AL, rsrch 1965-. **ORGANIZATIONS:** Mem Deans Adv Cncl Va Hosp 1972-; consult Inst of Med NAS 1972-74; mem Commn on Hum Resources Nat Rsrch Cncl 1975-; %Mem Comm on Vet Med Sci Nat Rsrch Cncl 1975-; mem bd dir AL Heart Assc 1972-76; pres Am Soc Vet Physio & Pharmacologists 1966-67; sec World Soc Vet Physio & Pharm; chmn Cncl of Deans AAVMC 1977; consult Hlth Profn Ed Sec DHEW; consult Ford Motor Co S Africa 1974; adv screening com Cncl for Intl Exchange of Schlr Wash 1976-79; deleg Am Heart Assc 1970-72; deleg World Soc of Vet Physio & Pharms Paris 1968; rsrch Sec Ofc Am Vet Med Assc mem com Am Physio Soc 1970-73; consult NIH Arlington 1968-70; Sigman Xi; Phi Kappa Phi; Am Vet Assc; AL Vet Med Assc; mem Primate Rsrch Ctr Adv Com NIH 1972-76. **HONORS/ACHIEVEMENTS:** Prncpl invstgtr of following grnts, Pentose Metabolism in the Ruminant 1956-57, Further Stud on Absorp & Util of Pentose Sugar in Ruminants PHS 1956-57, The Cerebrospinal Fluid of Dogs, Its Physio Diag & Prognostic Eval Mark & L Morris Found 1961-62, Mechanisms of Infection & Immunity In Listeriosis NIH 1961-64, Movement of the Mitral Valve NIH 1964-72. **MILITARY SERVICE:** AUS 1st lt. **BUSINESS ADDRESS:** Sch of Vet Med, Tuskegee Institute, AL 36088.

BOWLES, BARBARA LANDERS
Business executive. **PERSONAL:** Born Sep 17, 1947, Nashville, TN; married Earl S Bowles; children: Terrence Earl. **EDUCATION:** Fisk Univ, BA 1968; Univ of Chicago, MBA 1971; CFA Designation, 1977. **CAREER:** First Natl Bank of Chicago, trust officer 1974-77, avp 1977-80, vice pres 1980-81; Beatrice Companies, avp 1981-84; Dart & Kraft Inc, vice pres 1984-. **ORGANIZATIONS:** Pres Chicago Fisk Alumni Assn 1983-85; Alpha Kappa Alpha Sorority; bd mem Chicago Girl Scouts; bd of dirs Hyde Park Bank. **HONORS/ACHIEVEMENTS:** Top 100 Black Business & Prof Women Black Book Delta Sigma Jul-Aug 1985; 10 Outstanding Business People Black Book 1981; 10 Outstanding Chicago Jaycees 1977. **BUSINESS ADDRESS:** Vice President, Kraft Inc, Kraft Court, Glenview, IL 60025.

BOWLES, HOWARD ROOSEVELT
City manager. **PERSONAL:** Born Oct 14, 1932, Roselle, NJ. **CAREER:** Parson Inst; Seton Hall Univ City Home Delivery WA Post, mgr; Baltimore News-Am, city mgr; Newark Evening News, dist mgr; Various Clg, auto salesman, sales mgr asst panel rep. **ORGANIZATIONS:** Mem Interstate Circulation Mgrs Assc. **HONORS/ACHIEVEMENTS:** Art awrd 32nd Degree Mason Prince Hall F&AM; mgmt & prodn awards. **MILITARY SERVICE:** AUS sgt 1952-55. **BUSINESS ADDRESS:** 1150 15th St NW, Washington, DC 20017.

BOWLES, JAMES HAROLD, SR.
Physician. **PERSONAL:** Born Jun 12, 1921, Goochland, VA; married Aretha Melton; children: Ruth Quarles, Jacqueline B Dandridge, James Jr MD. **EDUCATION:** VA Union Univ, BS 1948; Meharry Med School, MD 1952. **ORGANIZATIONS:** Pres Goochland Recreational Ctr Inc 1961-81; vice pres GRC Inc 1981-; v chmn Goodland Cty Bd of Suprv; mem Goochland NAACP; mem exec bd VA Assoc of Counties; treas Goochland Voters League; mem Goochland Democratic Comm; vp, bd of dir Citizen Devel Corp; mem Hazardous Waste Siting Comm of VA, Amer Legion, Goochland Cty soc Serv Bd; bd of dir Goochland Branch Red Cross; past chmn VA Assoc of Counties Comm on Soc Svcs; past mem Goochland Cty Planning Comm; past med examiner State of VA; mem Emmaus Baptist Church, Caledonia Lodge 240 F&AM PHA, Alpha Phi Alpha; past chmn, pres trustee bd Emmaus Baptist Church; teacher Intermediate Sunday School Class. **HONORS/ACHIEVEMENTS:** Outstanding Leadership Amer Red Cross 1969; Valuable Citizen Goochland NAACP 1978; Outstanding Serv Goochland Recreational Ctr Inc 1979; Appreciation BeulahBaptist Sunday School Convention 1979; Recognition Negro Emancipation Org Louisa & Adjacent Counties 1979; Appreciation Amer Heart Assoc VA Affil 1982. **MILITARY SERVICE:** AUS pvt 1944-46. **BUSINESS ADDRESS:** Family Practitioner, Sandy Hook, VA 23153.

BOWLING, FRANK
Artist, educator. **PERSONAL:** Born 1936, Guyana. **EDUCATION:** London Univ; The Slade School. **CAREER:** Royal Coll of Art, painter. **ORGANIZATIONS:** Boston Mus Fine Arts 1970; Whitney Mus Am Art 1966-71; First World Festival Negro Art 1966; Grabowski Gallery London 1962. **HONORS/ACHIEVEMENTS:** Recpt Guggenheim Flwshp 1967; Grand Prize First World Festival Negro Art 1966.

BOWMAN, EARL W., JR.
Educator. **PERSONAL:** Born Feb 07, 1927, Minneapolis, MN; married Jacqueline; children: Wayne, Scott. **EDUCATION:** Macalester Coll, BA 1950, MEd 1971. **CAREER:** Anoka MN, physical therapist, 1950-52; Phyllis Wheatley Settlement House, boys work dir, 1952-55; Minneapolis Public Schools, History teacher, coach of football/basketball/track, jr high principal, 1955-69; Macalester Coll, asst to pres, dir of devel, 1969-78; Minneapolis Community Coll, vice pres external affairs, pres. **ORGANIZATIONS:** Mem Mayor's Commn on Human Devel 1967-68; Assn of Afro-Amer Educators 1968-; Natl Alliance for Black Grad Level Educ 1970; bd mem Minneapolis Urban Coalition 1971; bd mem Gr Minneapolis Metro Housing Corp 1972; mem Natl Alliance of Black Sch Educators; pres mgmt com Exchange Inc; mem adv bd Lake St Office Northwestern Natl Bank; brd of trustees, St Peters AME Church brd mpls United Way, Brd TCOIC; brd Phyllis Wheatley Settlement House. **HONORS/ACHIEVEMENTS:** Bush Found Summer Fellow Inst for Educ Mgr Harvard Univ 1976; Recip Student Athlete Award 1950; Disting Alumni Citation 1968; Serv Award MN Track Coaches Assn 1975; Pres Award for Physical Fitness Prog. **MILITARY SERVICE:** AUS Pfc 1946-47. **BUSINESS ADDRESS:** President, Minneapolis Comm College, 1501 Hennepin, Minneapolis, MN 55403.

BOWMAN, JACQUELYNNE JEANETTE
Attorney. **PERSONAL:** Born Dec 04, 1955, Chicago, IL; married David Rentsch. **EDUCATION:** Univ of Chicago, BA 1976; Antioch Univ Sch of Law, JD 1979. **CAREER:** West TN Legal Svcs, staff attorney 1979-84; Greater Boston Legal Svcs, sr attorney 1984-87, managing attorney 1987-. **ORGANIZATIONS:** Mem Amer Bar Assoc 1979-, Natl Conf of Black Lawyers 1980-, Battered Women's Working Group 1984-; volunteer Project Impact 1984-; mem MA Bar Assoc 1986-, Boston Bar Assoc 1986-; subcomm chairperson Gov Comm on Foster Care 1986-. **HONORS/ACHIEVEMENTS:** Silver Key Awd ABA-LSD 1979; Certificate of Appreciation EACH 1982,83,84; George Edmund Haynes Fellow Natl Urban League 1982-83; Public Service Awd Project Impact 1985,86. **BUSINESS ADDRESS:** Managing Attorney, Greater Boston Legal Services, 68 Essex St, Boston, MA 02111.

BOWMAN, JAMES E., JR.
Pathologist, geneticist, educator. **PERSONAL:** Born Feb 05, 1923, Washington, DC; married Barbara Frances Taylor; children: Valerie June. **EDUCATION:** Howard Univ, BS 1943; Howard Med School, MfD 1943-46; Freedmans Hosp, internship 1946-47; St Lukes Hosp, resd 1947-50. **CAREER:** Univ of Chicago, asst prof, med dir blood bank, 1962-67, assoc prof, 1967-72, prof med & pathology, dir of labs 1971-81, comm on genetics, 1972-; Comprehensive Sickle Cell Center Univ of Chicago, dir, 1973-84; Kaiser Family Found Center for Advance Study in the Behavioral Science, Stanford CA, sr fellow 1981-82; The Univ of Chicago, asst dean of students div of bio scis & Pritzker School of Medicine, prof dept of pathology. **ORGANIZATIONS:** Fellow Hastings Ctr KY 1979-; mem Med Adv Comm, ARC; consult Path US Dept HEW, PHS; adv comm FDA Diagnostic Products, HEW, PHS; ed bd Lab Med Chgo;pres Metro Chicago Blood Council; vchmn Chicago Reg Blood Prog; chmn Subcom on Path & Hematology, diag Prod Adv Comm, FDA, PHS; consult Dept Publ Health State of IL; fellow Coll of Amer Pathologists, Amer Soc Clin Path, Royal Soc Tropical Med & Hygience; mem Amer Soc Human Genetics, AAAS; intern Congress of Hematology; mem comm on genetics, comm on african and afro-amer studies; consultant OTA (Congress), Fed Gov Nigeria; consultant Med Corps Laboratories, Defense Forces, United Arab Emirates 1987. **HONORS/ACHIEVEMENTS:** Author 80 scientific publ in field of human genetics; Spec Rsch Fellow Galton Lab Univ Coll London 1961-62; edited book "Dist & Evol of Hemoglobin and Globinloci"; mem Alpha Omega Alpha, Sigma Xi, Amer Bd of Pathology. **MILITARY SERVICE:** AUS pfc 1943-46; AUS capt 1953-55. **BUSINESS ADDRESS:** Professor of Pathology, The University of Chicago, 5841 Maryland Ave, Chicago, IL 60637.

BOWMAN, JANET WILSON
Educational administrator. **PERSONAL:** Born in Charleston, WV; daughter of Earl Wilson and Roberta Wilson; married Richard Bowman; children: Karen McAtee, M Earl McAtee, Chris, Cheryl, Patricia. **EDUCATION:** Tuskegee Inst, BS, 1954, MS 1956; Univ of CA at Berkeley, PhD, 1973; Postgraduate, Univ of Oregon, California State Univ, San Diego. **CAREER:** Merritt Coll, instructor, 1959-73; Univ of California, seismologist, 1960-73; Carnegie Found, Consultant, 1972-73; Diablo Valley Coll, Admin, 1973-85; Compton Coll, 1986-. **ORGANIZATIONS:** bd mem, NICM; org bd mem, Meridian Natl Bank, 1979; bd mem, Berkeley Comm Concert Group; mem, Tuskegee Alumni Assn; mem, Soroptemist Intl; UNCF InterAlumni Council; United Way Program Evaluator; mem, Compton Coll Patron Assn; mem, Black Women's Leadership Group. **HONORS/ACHIEVEMENTS:** George Washington Carver Fellowship, 1954-56; NSF Scholarship, 1970-71; Graduate Student Assistantship, Univ of California, Berkeley, 1957-59; Cerificate of Appreciation, Business Club, 1988; Cerificate of Commendation, Compton Coll Bd of Trustees, 1988. **HOME ADDRESS:** 5601 Sunlight Pl, Los Angeles, CA 90016. **BUSINESS ADDRESS:** Assistant Superintendent, Compton College, 1111 E Artesia Blvd, Compton, CA 90221.

BOWMAN, JOSEPH E., JR.
Business executive, educator, communicat. **PERSONAL:** Born May 22, 1950, Brooklyn, NY. **EDUCATION:** State Univ of NY, BA 1972; Nat Tchr Corp, MA 1975, MLS 1974; Columbia Teacher's Clg, edD Cand. **CAREER:** Olympic Village XIII Winter Games Lake Placid, fclty mgr/prod/dir/supr of entrmnt 1979-80; Schenectady Access Cable Cncl Channel 16 NY, location mgr 1979; Hamilon Hill Arts & Craft Ctr Schenectady NY, instr 1978-79; Siciliano Studio Schenectady, NY, photographer's asst 1978-79; WMHT TV, asst prod/dir 1977-78; WMHT Channel 17 Pub Afrs Div, asst prod 1975-77; Hamilton Hill Arts & Crafts Ctr, dir audio visual serv 1974-75; Educ Oppor Pgm Stdnt Assc State Univ of NY, telecommunications instr 1975. **ORGANIZATIONS:** Prt-time Lectr State Univ of NY 1974; camera & audio man & lighting WMHT-FM Channel 17 Schenectady 1972-75; asst tchr Schenectady Sch Systm 1975; radio ancr WMHT-FM 1975-76; host a jazz show World Media Arts 1970-75; pgmg engr & remote tech USUA Radio Albany 1971-74; Burundi African Dance & Drum & Troupe, NY State 1971-78; resident liason mem adv cncl on dugs & referral media cncl Youth Oppor Pgm NY State Dept of Mental Hygiene 1974-75; Middle Earth Pgm 1973; media publicity coord NY State Sesquicentennial Anv Celebration Albany 1977; media spclst/cncl RPI Troy NY 1978; cons/media spclst Dept of Ed NY State Summer Leadrshp Training Inst Siena Clg Albany 1979; media seminar Dept of Human Rsrcs Albany 1979; media cons/freelance photographer Harlem Children's Theatre New York City 1980. **HONORS/ACHIEVEMENTS:** Outstndg achvment awrd Schenectady Chptr NAACP 1975; pride in heritage awrd for Acad Achvmnt & Multi-Media Spclst; Theta Chap of Nat Sor Phi Delta Kappa 1978; awrd Intrnl Platform Soc 1980. **BUSINESS ADDRESS:** WMHT CHANNEL 17, Box 17, Schenectady, NY.

BOWMAN, PHILLIP JESS
Psychologist, educator. **PERSONAL:** Born Feb 18, 1948, Kensett, AR; married Jacqueline E Creed; children: Phillip, Frederick Dubois. **EDUCATION:** No AZ U, BS Psychology/Industrial Tech 1970; Univ of MI, ed S/MA (Prsnl Serv/Cnslng) 1971-74, phD/MA (Soc Psychology) 1975-77. **CAREER:** Inst for Soc Rsrch, asst prof of psychology/research scientist; Inst for Soc Research Univ of Michigan, research investigator, 1977-78; Delta Coll, instructor, 1973-77, counselor 1971-73; Northern AZ Unic, fin aid admin, 1969-70. **ORGANIZATIONS:** Dir Post-doctoral Training Pgm in Survey Rsrch 1978-80; faculty mem Ctr for Afro-am & Afrcn Studies 1978; consult pub Hlth Serv 1980; mem Assc of Black Psychologists; mem Am Psychological Assc; steering com mem Annual Conf on Ethnicity & Mental Hlth; study dir Natl Survey of Black Am Rsrch Pgm Inst for Soc Rsrch Univ of MI. **HONORS/ACHIEVEMENTS:** Post doctoral cert; Joint Inst for Labor & Indsl Relations Univ of MI/Wayne State Univ 1977; hat Is Black Psychology? Jour, of Contemporary Psychology 1980; Toward a Dual Labor Market Approach to Black on Black Homicide Pub Hlth Rprts 1980. **BUSINESS ADDRESS:** Institute for Social Research, University of MI, Ann Arbor, MI 48106.

BOWMAN, WILLIAM MCKINLEY, SR.
Clergyman. **PERSONAL:** Born Feb 07, 1914, Dorchester Co, SC; son of Joseph Bowman and Erline Windham; married Annie Mae (deceased); children: William Jr, Audrey, Joseph, Beverley. **EDUCATION:** AB & DD 1938. **CAREER:** Granger Baptist Ch Elloree, pastor 1938-46; Mt Carmel Bapt Church Cameron, pastor 1942-46; St Paul Baptist Ch Orangeburg, pastor 1946-49; WOIC Radio, religious dir 1952-72; Second Nazareth Baptist Church Columbia SC, pastor 1949-; Friendship Baptist Church, pastor 1960-86. **ORGANIZATIONS:** Pres Gethsemane Sunday Sch Conv Columbia; secty/treas Interracial Bapt Ministers Union Columbia; dir Pub Relations Black Baptist of SC; past pres Columbia Br of NAACP; past chmn Richland Lexington OEO; past pres Columbia Ministers Assn; past pres Interdenom Ministerial Alliance of Columbia; mem vice chairman Richland Co Dist Sch Bd 1979-; past vice chmn of Richland Co Democratic Party.

BOWMAN-WEBB, LOETTA
Systems analyst. **PERSONAL:** Born Dec 16, 1956, Fort Worth, TX; married Carl Webb. **EDUCATION:** TX Wesleyan Coll, BBA 1979; Univ of TX at Arlington; Tarrant Co Jr Coll. **CAREER:** City of Ft Worth, admin asst I 1980-81, admin intern 1981-82, admin asst II 1982-85, admin asst III 1985-. **ORGANIZATIONS:** Mem Urban Mgmt Assts of N TX 1981-; prog comm Conf of Minority Public Admins 1981-; mem Natl Forum for Black Public Admins 1984-. **BUSINESS ADDRESS:** Admininistrative Asst III, City of Ft Worth, 1000 Throckmorton, Fort Worth, TX 76102.

BOWSER, BENJAMIN PAUL
Educational administration. **PERSONAL:** Born Aug 20, 1946, New York, NY; married Judith A Little; children: Paul. **EDUCATION:** Franklin & Marshall Coll, BA 1969; Cornell Univ, PhD 1976. **CAREER:** SUNY Binghampton, asst prof, sociology 1973-75; Cornell Univ, asst dean grad school 1975-82; Western Interstate Commiss for Higher Ed, dir minority ed1982-83; Univ of Santa Clara, dir black student resources; Stanford Univ, asst to dir. **ORGANIZATIONS:** Assoc ed Sage Race Relations Abstracts 1981-; rsch assoc Soc for the Study of Contemporary Soc Problem 1982-; consult Western Interstate Commiss for Higher Ed 1983-; mem Committee on Applied Sociology Amer Sociological Assoc 1985-; mem Assoc of Black Sociologists; bd dir Martin Luther King Jr Center forSocial Change San Jose, Bayshore Employment Serv East Palo Alto CA. **HONORS/ACHIEVEMENTS:** Co-Editor "Impacts of Racism on White Amers" 1981, "Census Data for Small Areas of NY City 1910-60" 1981. **BUSINESS ADDRESS:** Assistant to Dir, StanfordUniv, Information Tech Serv, c/o Redwood Hall, Stanford, CA 94305.

BOWSER, CHARLES
Professional athlete. **PERSONAL:** Born Oct 02, 1959, Plymouth, NC. **EDUCATION:** Duke Univ, BS. **CAREER:** Miami Dolphins, linebacker 1982-; Real Estate, Partnership. **ORGANIZATIONS:** Voted Dolphin Rookie of Yr. **BUSINESS ADDRESS:** Miami Dolphins, 4770 Biscayne Blvd, Ste 1440, Miami, FL 33187.

BOWSER, HAMILTON VICTOR, SR.
Business executive. **PERSONAL:** Born Sep 20, 1928, East Orange, NJ; son of Edward T Bowser and Louise E Bowser; married Merle Charlotte Moses; children: Hamilton V Jr, Rebecca Louise, Jennifer Lynn. **EDUCATION:** NJ Inst of Tech, BS Civil Eng 1952, MS Civil Eng 1956; MA Inst of Tech, Grad Sch Civil Eng 1954; Licensed professional engr in NJ, NY, PA. **CAREER:** Porter Urgulart Eng, structural eng 1954-55; Louis Berger Assocs, sr bridge eng 1955-57; PARCO Inc, sr strucural eng 1957-59; Engineers Inc, v pres 1959-69; Evanbow Construction Co, pres 1969-. **ORGANIZATIONS:** Chairman bd Assoc Minority Contractors of Amer 1980-82; bd of dir and pres Natl Assoc of Minority Contractors 1988-; pres Natl Soc of Prof Eng Essex Chapter 1966-68; bd of dir Reg Plan Assoc of NY, NJ, CT 1981-; trustee & treas Essex County Coll 1971-74; bd chmn Orange YMCA Comm of Mgmt; Amer Soc of Civil Engrs; mem Prof Engrs in Construction Div of NSPE; mem Amer Concrete Inst, NJ Governors Council for Minority Business Develop, NJ United Minority Business Brain Trust; chmn Mayor's Task Force for Economic Develop of Newark NJ; rep NJ Solid Waste Disposal Commn; rep to White House Conf on Small Business; NJIT Adv Council on Civil and Environ Engrg; trustee New Jersey Institute of Technology. **HONORS/ACHIEVEMENTS:** Fellow Amer Soc of Civil Eng 1969; Natl Advocate Award for minority and small bus dev US Small Bus Admin 1984; Outstanding Alumnus Award NJ Inst of Tech 1985; NY Regional Contractor of the Year 1985 US Dept of Commerce; Outstanding Mem Awds of Natl Assn of Minority Contractors and NJ United Minority Business Brain Trust; NJIT Alumni Athletic Hall of Fame for Fencing; business included as one of Black Enterprise's Top 100 Service Firms 1988. **MILITARY SERVICE:** USMC pfc 2 yrs; USAFR captain 14 years. **BUSINESS ADDRESS:** President, Evanbow Constuction Co Inc, 67 Sanford St, East Orange, NJ 07018.

BOWSER, JAMES A.
Educator. **PERSONAL:** Born Nov 11, 1913, Norfolk, VA; married Margaret Smith; children: Barbara B Miller. **EDUCATION:** VA State Coll, BS 1935; PA State Univ, MEd 1952, DEd 1960. **CAREER:** High School teacher, 1936-37; Orange VA High School, prin ,1936-42; Norfolk State Coll, instructor bldg construction, 1947-54, voc indsl teacher, trainer 1954-60, prof Ind Educ & dir of Jr Coll Div, 1960-, dir of training 1962-64, chmn Div of Indsl Educ & Tech 1967-. **ORGANIZATIONS:** Proj dir US Ofc of Educ 1966; co-dir Project D-054 US Dept of Labor; mem bd dir Norfolk C of C 1971-74; Norfolk Housing Devel Corp; v-chmn Mayor's Comm of Job Oppor for Youth; bd dir Tidewater Minority Contractors Assn 1971-74; bd dir United Communities Fund; chmn Plans & Program Com; VA Adv Com on Vocational Edn; mem adv com 1202 Commn VA State Council of Higher Educ 1975; Comm on Specialized Personnel US Dept of Labor 1964-69. **MILITARY SERVICE:** AUS Capt 1942-46 & 1950-52. **HOME ADDRESS:** 2912 Hollister Ave, Norfolk, VA 23504.

BOWSER, MCEVA R.
Educator. **PERSONAL:** Born Nov 22, 1922, Elizabeth City, NC; married Dr Barrington; children: Angela. **EDUCATION:** Elizabeth City State U, BS 1944; VA Commonwealth U, MEd 1970. **CAREER:** Richmond VA Public Schools, curriculum specialist, elementary counselor, teacher; Sussex Co & Louisa Co, teacher. **ORGANIZATIONS:** Pres Richmond Med Aux 1956-58; pres Richmon Clb of Chi Delta Mu Wives 1966-68; natl vice pres Chi Delta Mu Wives 1970-72; mem REA, YEA, NEA, ASCD; pres Richmond Chptr Jack & Jill of Am 1964-66; past bd dir Jack & Jill of am Found 1968-70; tres Richmon Cphtr Links Inc 1977-; v-chrmn Regional Reading Commn 1977-; past pres Women of St Philip's Episcopal Ch 1964-68; mem Alpha Kappa Alpha Maymont Civic League. **HONORS/ACHIEVEMENTS:** Outstndg serv awrd Jack & Jill of Am Found 1972. **BUSINESS ADDRESS:** Bellevue Model Sch, Richmond, VA 23220.

BOWSER, ROBERT LOUIS
Business executive. **PERSONAL:** Born Dec 13, 1935, E Orange, NJ; son of Edward T Bowser Sr and Louise Bowser; divorced; children: David. **EDUCATION:** Newark Coll of Engr, BSCE 1958; Northwestern Univ, Certificate 1961; NYU, Certificate 1963. **CAREER:** City of Newark, city planner 1958-60; Town of Montclair traffic engr 1960-65; structural engr 1965-68; Bowser Engrs & Assoc, vice pres 1968-82; City of East Orange NJ, dir of public works 1986-; Robert L Bowser Assoc, owner 1982-. **ORGANIZATIONS:** Inst of Traffic Engr 1959-65; Natl Soc of Professional Engrs 1963; NJ Soc of Professional Engrs 1963; Land Surveyors Functional Sect NJ 1969; Licensed Professional Land Surveyor NJ 1969; Am Congress of Surveying & Mapping 1970; Licensed Professional Planner NJ 1973; vice chmn E Orange Rent Level Bd 1975-76; commr/fdr Essex Co Touch Football League 1975-89; pres Natl Assn Builders & Contractors NJ 1976; Public Works Assn 1986-; NJ Society of Professional Planners 1976-; bd of dirs, Girl Scout Council; National Council of Economic Development 1987; adjunct prof, Essex County College 1985-89. **MILITARY SERVICE:** USCG Reserve 1960-66. **BUSINESS ADDRESS:** Owner, Robert L Bowser Assoc, 67 Sanford St, East Orange, NJ 07018.

BOWSER, VIVIAN ROY
Educator. **PERSONAL:** Born Mar 24, 1926, Weimar, TX; married Jesse Hugh. **EDUCATION:** Prairie View A&M U, BS; TX So U, Cert; Univ of NM, Cert. **CAREER:** Houston Independent School Dist, teacher. **ORGANIZATIONS:** Pres Houston Class Tchrs Assc; pres Cent TX Dist Tchrs Assc; pres-elect Tchrs St Assc of TX; pres TX Class Tchrs Assc; pr & r com & legis com TX St Tchrs & Assc; pres Houston Alumnae, Delta Sigma Theta Inc; mem exec com NEA Tchrs Professional Pract Commn 1974-79; US Nat Commn to UNESCO 1974-78; gov commn on Early Child Ed 1974; Professional Pract Commn 1972-74; life mem YMCA, TX Women's Polit Caucus; life mem Natl Cncl Negro Women; golden life mem Delta Sigma Theta; Houston Tchrs Assc; TX Class Tchrs Assc; Dist IV TSTA; TX St Tchrs Assc; NEA. **HONORS/ACHIEVEMENTS:** Outst contrib in ed TX Legis 1973, 75; human rel awrd TX Class Tchrs 1976; Trailblazer in Educ SW Reg Delta Sigma Theta 1976. **BUSINESS ADDRESS:** 8701 Delilah, Houston, TX 77033.

BOX, CHARLES
Mayor. **PERSONAL:** Born 1951. **EDUCATION:** Graduated from Univ of Michigan Law School. **CAREER:** Mayor of Rockford, IL. **BUSINESS ADDRESS:** Mayor, City Hall, 425 East State St, Rockford, IL 61104. *

BOYCE, CHARLES N.
Business executive. **PERSONAL:** Born Jun 09, 1935, Detroit, MI; married Delma Cunningham; children: Terralyn, Tracy, Charles, LaShawn. **EDUCATION:** Attended, Wayne State Univ 1955-62, Univ of MI Grad School of Business 1981. **CAREER:** MI Bell Telephone, comm oper asst 1966-69, order unit mgr 1969-71, dist commer mgr 1971-76, gen customer relations mgr 1976-78, dir of public affairs1979-83, asst vice pres of urban affairs 1983-. **ORGANIZATIONS:** Alternate for bd of trust New Detroit Inc 1972-75,78-; bd of dir Assn of Black Bus & Engrg Students 1973-; commr Detroit Housing Commn 1976-; bd of dir 1078-, 1st vice pres 1985-86 NAACP Detroit; bd of dir MI League for Human Serv 1979-; mem Soc of Consumer Affairs in Bus 1979-; mem Million Dollar Club NAACP Detroit 1978 & 1979; bd dir Inner City Bus Improvement Forum 1987-89; mem African-Amer Heritage Assoc, Booker T Washington Bus Assoc, Bus PolicyReview Council, Corp Urban Forum, Detroit Area Pre-Coll Engrg Prog; bd dir Black Family Devel Inc, Concerned Citizens Council, Jazz Devel Workshop, March of Dimes SE MI Chapt, Neighborhood Serv Org. **HONORS/ACHIEVEMENTS:** Outstanding Serv Awd Oakland Co Urban League 1974; Serv Awd NAACP Detroit 1979; Outstanding Citizen Serv Awd Detroit Housing Commn 1979; Minority Achievers in Industry Awd YMCA 1980; "E" for Excellence in Marketing Awd AT&T 1982; Anthony Wayne Awd for Leadership Wayne State Univ 1983; Who's Who in Minority-Business Development 1983; E for Excellence in Marketing Awd AT&T 1982; Anthony Wayne Awd for Leadership Wayne State Univ 1983; Who's Who in Minority Bus Devel Minority Devel Agency 1983. **BUSINESS ADDRESS:** Asst Vice President, MI Bell Telephone Co, 444 Michigan Ave, Detroit, MI 48226.

BOYCE, JOHN G.
Educator. **PERSONAL:** Born May 06, 1935; married Erma; children: Mindora, Jane. **EDUCATION:** Univ Britsih Columbia, MD 1962; Columbia U, MSc 1971. **CAREER:** Gyn Oncology, dir; Downstate Med Ctr, prof. **ORGANIZATIONS:** Mem, Kings Co NY State Amer & Natl Med Assn; Am Coll Ob/Gyn; Soc Gynecologic & Oncologists. **HONORS/ACHIEVEMENTS:** Certified special Competence Gynecologic Oncology 1974. **BUSINESS ADDRESS:** Prof of OB Gyn, Div Gyn Onc, State Univ of NY, 450 Clarkson Ave, Brooklyn, NY 11203.

BOYCE, WILLIAM M.
Personnel administrator. **PERSONAL:** Born Jul 09, 1928, Brooklyn, NY; married Alice M Billingsley; children: David C, Lynne M. **EDUCATION:** Brooklyn Clg, AAS 1957; City

Clg of NY, AAS 1962, BBA 1965; Fairleigh Dickinson U, MBA 1976. **CAREER:** Kings Co Hosp Ctr, dir of prsnl 1974-. **ORGANIZATIONS:** Dir manpower task force New Urban & Coalition 1970-74; dir Ft Greene Neighborhood Manpower Cntr 1966-70; chmn Brooklyn Hlth Manpower Consortium 1975-77; mem Assc of MBA Exec 1975-; mem NY Assc of Hosp Persnl Admn 1977-. **HONORS/ACHIEVEMENTS:** Recipient of German Occupancy Medal AUS. **MILITARY SERVICE:** AUS pvt II 1951-53. **BUSINESS ADDRESS:** Kings Co Hospital Center, 451 Clarkson Ave, Brooklyn, NY 11204.

BOYD, CANDY DAWSON
Associate professor. **PERSONAL:** Born Aug 08, 1946, Chicago, IL; daughter of Julian Dawson and Mary Ruth Ridley Dawson; divorced. **EDUCATION:** Northeastern Illinois State University, BA, 1967; University of California, Berkeley, CA, MA, 1978, PhD, 1982. **CAREER:** Overton Elementary School, Chicago, IL, teacher, 1968-71; Longfellow School, Berkeley, CA, teacher, 1971-73; University of California, Berkeley, CA, extension instructor in language arts, 1972-79; St Mary's College of California, Moraga, CA, extension instructor in language arts, 1972-79; Berkeley Unified School District, Berkeley, CA, district teacher trainer in reading and communication skills, 1973-76; St Mary's College of California, Moraga, CA, lecturer to assistant professor, 1976-83, director of reading leadership and teacher effectiveness programs, 1976-87, tenured associate professor, 1983—. **ORGANIZATIONS:** Member, St Mary's College Rank and Tenure Committee, 1984-87; member, multiple subjects waiver programs committee, review committee, State of California Commission on Teacher Credentialing, 1985—, advisory committee for multiple subject credential with an early childhood emphasis, State of California Commission on Teacher Credentialing, 1986-87. **HONORS/ACHIEVEMENTS:** Authored Circle of Gold, Scholastic, 1984; Coretta Scott King Award Honor Book for Circle of Gold, American Library Association, 1985; authored Breadsticks and Blessing Places, Macmillan, 1985, published in paperback as Forever Friends, Viking, 1986; Outstanding Bay Area Woman, Delta Sigma Theta, 1986; authored Charlie Pippin, Macmillan, 1987. **HOME ADDRESS:** 1416 Madrone Way, San Pablo, CA 94806. **BUSINESS ADDRESS:** St Mary's College of California, School of Education, Box 4350, Moraga, CA 94575.

BOYD, CHARLES FLYNN
Educational administrator. **PERSONAL:** Born May 13, 1938, Pensacola, FL; married Marie Moore; children: Marie Therese, Carla, Charles Jr. **EDUCATION:** TX Southern Univ, BS 1956; FL A&M Univ MS 1964; Univ of OK, PhD Philosophy 1972. **CAREER:** School Dist of Escambia Co, sci teacher 1959-64, asst principal of hs 1964-70; Univ of OK, financial aide counselor 1970, secondary school principal 1971-78; School Dist of Escambia Co, dir fed proj 1972-. **ORGANIZATIONS:** Suburban West Rotary Club 1972-80; Pensacola Metro YMCA 1973-80; PJC Bd of Trustees 1981-; chmn Cert of Need Comm Northwest FL Comprehensive; Kappa Alpha Psi Frat; Phi Delta Kappa; Intl Reading Assn. **HONORS/ACHIEVEMENTS:** Who's Who Amer Educ 1970; Who's Who Personality of South 1972; Outstanding Educator of Amer 1973-74. **HOME ADDRESS:** 3370 Bayou Blvd, Pensacola, FL 32503. **BUSINESS ADDRESS:** Dir of Federal Projects, School District of Escambia Co, 301 W Garden St, Pensacola, FL 32501.

BOYD, DELORES ROSETTA
Attorney. **PERSONAL:** Born Apr 24, 1950, Ramer, AL. **EDUCATION:** Univ of AL, BA 1972; Univ of VA, JD 1975. **CAREER:** Judge John C Godbold, law clerk to Federal Judge, US Ct of Appeals 5th Circuit; US Ct of Appeals 11th Circuit, chief judge 1975-76; Mandell & Boyd, partner 1976-. **ORGANIZATIONS:** AL State Bar Bd of Bar Examiners, bar examiner 1979-83. **HONORS/ACHIEVEMENTS:** Featured in May 30, 1983 issue Time Magazine "The New Women in Court". **HOME ADDRESS:** 3 N Anton Dr, Montgomery, AL 36105. **BUSINESS ADDRESS:** Attorney, Mandell & Boyd, 25 S Court Sq, Montgomery, AL 36103.

BOYD, DENNIS RAY
Professional athlete. **PERSONAL:** Born Oct 06, 1959, Meridian, MS. **EDUCATION:** Jackson State Univ, attended. **CAREER:** Boston Red Sox, pitcher 1982-84. **ORGANIZATIONS:** Names KRHP on EL All-Star team, NYP All-Star pitcher in 1980. **BUSINESS ADDRESS:** Boston Red Sox, Fenway Park, Boston, MA 02215.

BOYD, EVELYN SHIPPS
Retired educator. **PERSONAL:** Born Aug 04, Birmingham, AL; daughter of Perry Shipps and Geneva White Shipps; married Gilbert M, Nov 28, 1948. **EDUCATION:** Baldwin Wallace Coll, BMusEd (cum laude) 1959; Cleveland Inst of Music, Master of Music Honor Grad 1970. **CAREER:** Cleveland Pub Schs, secretary 1942-55, teacher 1959-71; Cuyahagen Comm Coll, asst prof music 1971-81, dept head performing arts 1977-81; Cleveland Inst of Music, teacher 1970-76, retired. **ORGANIZATIONS:** Mem Bd of Managers Rainey Inst 1983; Women's Council Music Sch 1983; OH Music Teachers Assn 25 years, Music Educ Natl Conf 1961-; tape recorder for Cleveland Soc for Blind 1984-; secretary, Alumni Bd of Directors, Cleveland Institute of Music, 1987-; mem bd of trustees, Broadway School of Music, 1989-. **HONORS/ACHIEVEMENTS:** Besse Award for teaching excellence Cuyahoya Com Coll 1980; alumini merit award Balding Wallace Coll 1983; award for 1000 hours volunteer Univ Hosp SICU Unit 1985; Pi Kappa Lambda Music Honor Soc Cleveland Inst of Music; Baldwin-Walla Mu Phi Music Honor Sorority Dayton C Miller Honor Soc; Elizabeth Downes Award (Volunteer Award of Year) University Hospitals 1989.

BOYD, GEORGE ARTHUR
Scientist. **PERSONAL:** Born Mar 07, 1928, Washington, NC. **EDUCATION:** St Augustine Coll, BS; Amer Univ 1956-57; US Dept of Agriculture Grad Sch 1957; US Office of Personnel Mgmt Exec Inst, 1980, 1982. **CAREER:** US Naval Oceanographic Office, physical scientist, physical science tech 1956-57; Defense Mapping Agency, retired chief equal oppor officer. **ORGANIZATIONS:** Mem Sigma Xi the Scientific Rsch Soc 1972-; pres Mt Olivet Heights Citizens Assn 1975-; chairperson Gallaudet Coll Comm Relations Council 1977-; treasDC Federation of Civil Assns Inc 1981-; mem bd of trustees St Augustine Coll 1982-; chairperson Advisory Neighborhood Commission 5B 1986-. **HONORS/ACHIEVEMENTS:** Publication co-author "Oceanographic Atlas of the North Atlantic Ocean" 1965; Awd of Commendation Pres of the US 1970; resolution Bd of Trustees GallaudetColl 1981; Disting Alumni Awd Natl Assn for Equal Oppor of Higher Educ 1985. **MILITARY SERVICE:** AUS pfc 2 yrs. **HOME ADDRESS:** 1264 Owen Place NE, Washington, DC 20002.

BOYD, GREG CALVIN
Professional athlete. **PERSONAL:** Born Sep 15, 1952, Merced, CA. **EDUCATION:** San Diego St, 1975-76; Fresno Jr Coll. **CAREER:** New England Patriots, defensive end 1976-79; Denver Broncos, defensive end 1980-83; Green Bay Packers, defensive end 1983-84; New Jersey Generals, defensive end 1984-.

BOYD, JOSEPH L.
Educational administrator. **PERSONAL:** Born Dec 20, 1947, Columbia, SC; married Nellie Brown; children: Joseph Christopher, Michael Steven, Adrienne Kerise. **EDUCATION:** Univ of SC, BS 1969, MAcctg 1976, PhD 1977. **CAREER:** Johnson C Smith Univ, instructor 1972-74; Univ of SC, asst prof 1976-77; Univ of IL, asst prof 1977-78; NC A&T State Univ, assoc prof 1978-83; Norfolk State Univ, dean, school of business 1983-. **ORGANIZATIONS:** Mem Beta Alpha Psi, Beta Gamma Sigma, Omicron Delta Kappa, Amer Inst of CPA, Amer Acct Assoc, NC Assoc of CPA, SC Assoc of CPA, Natl Assoc of Accts,Natl Assoc of Black Accts, Amer Tax Assoc, Ins Selling Practices Comm, Curriculum Comm, Cluster Task Force, IRS Advisory Group; Amer Arbitration Assn. **HONORS/ACHIEVEMENTS:** Haskins & Sells Found Fac Fellow 1975; Doctoral Consortium Univ of SC Rep 1976; Amer Acctg Assoc Fellow 1976; Speaker on Unreasonable Compensation Amer Acct Assoc Meeting Portland OR 1977; Moderator of the Session on Tax Rsch Amer Acct Assoc Boston MA 1980; Grants from Alexander Grant & Co 1980, 1981,Deloitte Haskins & Sells 1980, 1981, Monsanto 1980, 1981, Standard Oil of OH 1982; Co-Chmn NC Ed Colloquium 1982; Program Chmn Acct Ed & Practitioners' Forum 1983; Faculty Internship Deloitte Haskins & Sells Intl Acctg Firm 1983; AICPA Faculty Summer Seminar on Teaching of Taxation; Instr Lambers CPA Review Course, Small Business Mgmt Seminar, IL Tax & Acctg Update; Consulting Speaker Devel of the Acct Curriculum at Livingstone Coll; Mem Advisor Council for theComm of IRS; Publications in The Tax Adviser, Oil & Gas Tax Quarterly, Taxes-The Tax Magazine, Prentice-Hall Tax Ideas Service, 1978, 1979, 1983. **BUSINESS ADDRESS:** Dean, School of Business, Norfolk StateUniv, 2401 Corprew Ave, Norfolk, VA 23504.

BOYD, LUCILLE I.
Educator. **PERSONAL:** Born Apr 03, 1906, San Antonio; married Frank. **EDUCATION:** Wiley Clg, BA 1928; Univ CA, MA 1939; Incarnate Clg, ME 1958; Trinity U, Post Grad 1960. **CAREER:** San Antonio, tchr. **ORGANIZATIONS:** Chmn TX Tchrs Welfare Com; Imperial Commandress Imperial Ct Dau Isis 1972-74; mem Zeta Phi Beta Sorority; founder & past basileus Alpha & Pi Zeta Chptr; mem NEA; Natl Retired Tchr Assc Bus & Professional Women's Clg; Order Eastern Star; past assc Worthy Matron; past choir mem youth %Dir St Paul United Meth. **HONORS/ACHIEVEMENTS:** Shriners region vi award 1974; Zeta of Yr 1971; NAACP Merit Awrd 1974; Isis Pub Relations Awrd 1973; Classroom Tchr Awrd 1969; Established Fund Mentally Retarded Child Isis Proj 1974.

BOYD, MILLER W., JR.
Psychologist. **PERSONAL:** Born Sep 16, 1934; children: Kevin, Kristin. **EDUCATION:** Fisk Univ, AB 1955; St Louis Univ, MS 1968; St Louis Univ, PhD 1970; Univ of TN, additional study 1955-56. **CAREER:** Parks Aeronautical Coll, gen psychology instructor, 1968; Project Follow Through & Head Start in St Louis, psychology consultant, 1968-69; Webster Coll, special educ instructor, 1968-69; Southern IL Univ, dir experiment in higher educ, asst prof 1969-71; Acad of Urban Serv St Louis, co-dir rsch, psychologist 1971-. **ORGANIZATIONS:** Mem Natl Assn of Educ of Young Children, Natl Council for Black Child Devel, Council for Exceptional Children, Amer Psychol Assn, Assn of Black Psychologists, Natl Caucus on the Black Aged, Child Day Care Assn of St Louis, Natl Assn of Non-White Rehab Workers, Southwestern Psychol Assn; author numerous papers for various publs.

BOYD, ROBERT NATHANIEL, III
Dentist. **PERSONAL:** Born Jan 31, 1928, Orange, NJ; children: Robert Brian DDS, Judith Karen, David Nelthropp. **EDUCATION:** Rutgers Univ, BS 1949; NY Univ Coll of Dentistry, DDS 1954. **CAREER:** NYU Coll of Dentistry, assoc prof dentl materials 1969-83, admissions comm 1969-83, asst dir admissions 1976-83; Dental Materials Group Ltd, vice pres 1983;Boyd Int Industries Inc, pres. **ORGANIZATIONS:** Fund raiser minority students NYU Coll of Dent; adv Natl Cncl of Negro Women 1979-83; mem Intl Assn of Dental Rsch, Amer Dental Assn, Essex Co Dental Soc, NJ State Dental Soc; panelist Natl Black Sci Students Organiz Conf 1970; consult LD Caulk 1970; consult Vicon Corp 1971; panelist Workshop Grad Oppty for Minority Students Loeb Center 1976; adv comm for Implementation of Task Force 1976; dir Minority Student Recruitment 1972-83; asst in devel of NYUposter and brochure for recruit of disadvantaged students. **HONORS/ACHIEVEMENTS:** Recip Senior Prize Amer Soc of Dentistry for Children 1954; Senior Prize Amer Acad of Dental Med 1954; Omicron Kappa Upsilon NYU Coll Dentistry Hon Soc 1954; 1st in class Dental Med NYU Coll of Dentistry; 1st in class Children's Dentistry NYU Coll of Dentistry; Who's Who in America 1974-75 & 1975-81; guestspeaker NYU Coll of Dentistry Alumni Assn Alumni Meeting and Dean's Day 1970; publications incl, with L Colin and GE Kaufman, A Survey of "Resin Systems for Dentistry" Abstract of Papers M25 - JD Res 42nd Gen Meeting IADR March 1964; Radio Broadcasts WLIB, WABC-AM, WNBC-AM, WNEW-TV 1973; Dental Forum White Plains NY 1975-76; NY Univ Continuing Dental Educ Instructor 1975; speaker CT State Dental Assoc 1977; Essayist Greater NY Dental Meeting 1981,83,85; speaker Commonwealth Dental Soc, Alpha Omega Study Club, North Bronx Central Hosp. **MILITARY SERVICE:** USAF Capt Dental Corps 1954-56. **BUSINESS ADDRESS:** President, Boyd Int Industries Inc, 2100 Millburn Avenue, Maplewood, NJ 07040.

BOYD, ROZELLE
Educator. **PERSONAL:** Born Apr 24, 1934, Indianapolis, IN. **EDUCATION:** Butler Univ, BA 1957; Ind Univ, MA 1964. **CAREER:** Marion Cty Dept of Public Welfare, caseworker 1957; Indianapolis Public Schs, teacher-counselor 1957-68; IN Univ, asst/assoc dean 1968-81; IN Univ, dir univ div 1981-85. **ORGANIZATIONS:** Indianapolis City councilman 1966-; Democratic Natl Committeeman; minority leader Indianapolis City Council; chmn Indianapolis Black Political Caucus. **HONORS/ACHIEVEMENTS:** Lily Fellow 1957; Freedom's Found Awd. **HOME ADDRESS:** 2527 E 35th, Indianapolis, IN 46218. **BUSINESS ADDRESS:** Director, University Division, Indiana University, Maxwell Hall 104 IU, Bloomington, IN 47401.

BOYD, RUTH R. (REID)
Business executive. **PERSONAL:** Born Dec 08, 1936, New York, NY; married Clyde H Reid. **EDUCATION:** Hunter Clg of NYC, BA Phi Beta Kappa 1957; Columbia Univ Sch of Social Work (summa cum laude), MS 1963. **CAREER:** Boyd & Associates, pres. **ORGANIZATIONS:** Spl consult to chief exec ofcr Girl Scouts of USA 1980-; asst natl exec dir Girl Scouts of the USA 1977-80; fclty mem chrmn Dept of Human Behavior Howard Univ Sch of Soc Work 1975-77; visiting fclty Univ of MN 1976; guest lectr Howard Univ Med Sch 1976; clinical instr & consult Environmental Medicine DownstateMed Sch 1965-67; del 23rd World Conf of World Assc of Girl Scouts Tehran Iran 1978; mem White House Adv Panel for Prod of Parental Films on Marijuana Use 1979-80; consult dept of HEW Ofc of Youth Dev Task Force on Runaway Youth 1975; consult Western PA Workshop Univ of Pittsburgh 1976; rsrch consult Kinte Library Proj Carnegie Found & San Jose Clg. **HONORS/ACHIEVEMENTS:** Citiation pres & ofcrs of Nat Bd GSUSA for Distingished Achvmnt & Contrb 1980; KIZZY Awrd Womafest & Chicago, IL 1979; most outsdng faclty mem awrd Human Bahavoir Soc Environment Sequence Nat Assc of Black Soc Workers; conceivedTV spot "Saluting the Women of the 80'S" Am Women in TV Which Received Pinnacle Awrd 1980. **BUSINESS ADDRESS:** Boyd & Associates, 502 G St SW, Washington, DC 20024.

BOYD, THEOPHILUS B., III
Corporate director. **PERSONAL:** Born May 15, 1947, Nashville, TN; married Yvette Duke; children: LaDonna Yvette, Shalae Shantel. **EDUCATION:** TN State Univ, BBA 1969; Shreveport Bible Coll, D Divinity 1980; Easonian Baptist Seminary, D Letters 1983. **CAREER:** Citizens Realty & Develop Co, pres 1982; Citizens Sav & Dev Co, president 1982-; Meharry Med Coll, mem exec bd of trustees 1982-; Natl Baptist Pub Bd, pres. **ORGANIZATIONS:** Mem bd of dirs March of Dimes TN Chapt; commnr human develop State of TN; bd of dirs Nashville Tech Institute. **HONORS/ACHIEVEMENTS:** Mem bd of governors Chamber of Commerce, the Nashville Symphony; life mem Kappa Alpha Psi Fraternity Inc; mem Chi Boule of Sigma Pi Phi Frat. **BUSINESS ADDRESS:** President, Natl Baptist Pub Bd, 7145 Centennial Blvd, Nashville, TN 37209.

BOYD, THOMAS
Employment practices/EEO administrator. **PERSONAL:** Born Apr 06, 1942, Philadelphia, PA; son of John Boyd and Thelma Archie Boyd; married Gwendolyn Lee, Dec 14, 1988. **EDUCATION:** Temple Univ, BA, 1970. **CAREER:** Remington Rand Inc, mgr, personnel, 1979; Computer Sciences Corp, mgr, equal employment opportunity, 1979-81; US Dept of the Navy, consultant, 1981-84; Hahneman Univ, mgr of employment, 1984-88; Syracuse Univ, employment practices administrator, 1988-. **ORGANIZATIONS:** Consultant Navy Dept, 1981-; consultant, Natl Guard Bureau, 1984-. **HOME ADDRESS:** 1118 Euclid Ave, Syracuse, NY 13210. **BUSINESS ADDRESS:** Syracuse Univ, Office of Human Resources, Skytop Office Bldg, Syracuse, NY 13244.

BOYD, WILLIAM STEWART
Attorney & accountant. **PERSONAL:** Born Mar 29, 1952, Chicago, IL. **EDUCATION:** Univ of IL, BS Accounting 1974; Northern IL Univ Coll of Law, JD 1981. **CAREER:** Legal Assistance Found of Chicago, clerk 1979; Boyd & Grant, clerk 1978-81; Arthur Anderson & Co, sr staff accountant 1974-77, 1981-83; Boyd & Boyd Ltd, attorney 1983-. **ORGANIZATIONS:** Bd of dirs Grant Park Recreation Assn; mem Young Executives in Politics; mem Natl Business League 1974; mem Amer Bar Assn 1981; mem Cook Co Bar Assn 1981; bd of dirs NIA Comprehensive Ctr Inc 1984. **HOME ADDRESS:** 436 W 100th Pl, Chicago, IL 60610.

BOYD-CLINKSCALES, MARY E.
Consultant, lecturer. **PERSONAL:** Born Aug 26, 1918, Haddocks, GA; married William F Clinkscales; children: Barbara Boyd Collins, Gerald F, Carl T. **EDUCATION:** Talladega Coll AL, BA 1936-40; Wayne State Univ Detroit, MI, MA 1956. **CAREER:** Lawrence N HS Indianpolis, IN, educator 1975-; Detroit Bd of Educ, educator (retired) 1982; Church of God, consultant/lecturer. **ORGANIZATIONS:** Curriculum coordinator, Natl Assn of the Church of God 1964-; dir, Leadership Training Inst Middlesex PA 1967-71; 1st black woman exec Natl Commn on Soc Concerns 1971-; proj dir IN Commn on Human Equality, 1974-75; pres Indianapolis Chap Talladega Alumni Assoc 1974-79; apptd bd dir Hoosier Capital Girl Scouts 1974; teacher, Anderson Coll, Anderson, IN 1974-75; lectr Educ & Reglion; consult Race Relations; adv com Women Affairs (Appointed by In Gov Bowen); life mem NAACP Indpls, IN 1979-; adv bd mem WFYI Channel 20 Indianapolis 1979-; pres/founder of Indiana Chap Ex-POSE (Ex-partners of Service Men and Women for Equality) 1980-; sec state bd of Christian Educ 1986-; editorial asst for Indiana Ministries publ Indianapolis IN 1986-. **HONORS/ACHIEVEMENTS:** Outstanding achievement award, Natl Assn of the Church of God, West & Middlesex, PA 1971; dramatic performance citation AUS Guam 1945-48; outstanding teacher award, AUS Guam 1945-48; salutatorian Ballard Normal HS Macon, GA 1936.

BOYD-FOY, MARY LOUISE
Manager. **PERSONAL:** Born Jun 30, 1936, Memphis, TN; daughter of Ivory Boyd (deceased) and Mamie Grey Boyd (deceased); married James Arthur. **EDUCATION:** Columbia Univ NY, BA 1977. **CAREER:** United Negro Coll Fund Inc, public info asst 1956-60; Foreign Policy Assoc, public info asst 1960-70; Columbia Univ Urban Center, office mgr 1971-73, asst to exec dean sch of engrg 1973-77, exec asst to vice pres personnel admin 1977-78; International Paper Co, rep northeastern sales accts 1978-80; Ebasco Serv Inc, coord legislative affairs 1980-86, corporate mgr subcontract compliance 1986-. **ORGANIZATIONS:** Mem Coalition of 100 Black Women 1980-; founding mem, former vice pres Natl Assoc of Univ Women Long Island NY Branch; member and past loyal lady, ruler Order of the Golden Circle, Long Island Assembly No 20, 1984-; mem, founder, and past matron Emerald Chapter No 81 Order of Eastern Star, Prince Hall Affiliation 1985-; mem, Daughters of Isis Abu-Bekr Court No 74, Prince Hall Affiliation 1986-; mem adv bd United Negro Coll Fund Inc 1986-; mem ad bd United Negro Fund Inc 1986-, Assn of Minority Enterprises of NY 1986-; first vice chmn and mem bd of dirs Amer Assn of Blacks in Energy 1986-88. **HONORS/ACHIEVEMENTS:** Woman of the Year Natl Assn of Univ Women 1984; Outstanding Woman of New York State NY Senate 1984; Outstanding Service Certificate United Negro Coll Fund Inc 1984; Recognition Awd; Distinguished Service Plaque United Negro Coll Fund Inc 1985-86: Appreciation Awd Concerned Women of Jersey City NJ Inc 1986; inducted into Queens, NY Registry of Distinguished Citizens 1989. **HOME ADDRESS:** 117-20 232nd St, Cambria Heights, NY 11411. **BUSINESS ADDRESS:** Corporate Mgr/EEO Subcontract Compliance, Ebasco Services, Inc, 2 World Trade Center, New York, NY 10048.

BOYER, HORACE CLARENCE
Educator. **PERSONAL:** Born Jul 28, 1935, Winter Park, FL; married Gloria Bernice Blue. **EDUCATION:** Bethune-Cookman Coll, BA 1957; Eastman School of Music Univ of Rochester, MA 1964, PhD 1973. **CAREER:** Monroe High School Cocoa FL, instructor 1957-58; Poinsett Elem Sch Cocoa FL, instructor 1960-63; Albany State Coll GA, asst prof 1964-65; Univ of Central FL, asst prof 1972-73; Univ of MA Amherst, prof of music 1973-. **ORGANIZATIONS:** Vice pres A Better Chance 1980-82; editorial bd mem Black Music Rsch Journal 1980-83; vice pres Gospel Music Assoc 1983-84. **HONORS/ACHIEVEMENTS:** Ford Foundation Fellow Eastman School of Music 1969-72; curator Natl Museum of American History Smithsonian 1985-86; United Negro Coll Fund Disting Scholar-at-Large Fisk Univ 1986-87. **MILITARY SERVICE:** AUS sp-4 1958-60. **HOME ADDRESS:** 92 Grantwood Dr, Amherst, MA 01002. **BUSINESS ADDRESS:** Professor of Music, Univ of Massachusetts, Dept of Music and Dance, Amherst, MA 01003.

BOYER, JAMES B.
Educator. **PERSONAL:** Born Apr 03, 1934, Winter Park, FL; married Edna Medlock. **EDUCATION:** Bethune-Cookman Coll, BS 1956; FLA&M U, MEd 1964; OH State U, PhD 1969. **CAREER:** FL A&M Univ, teacher, admin visiting prof, 1969; Univ of Houston, asst prof, 1969-71; KS State Univ, assoc prof, 1971-; College of Educ KS State Univ, prof of curriculum & instruc. **ORGANIZATIONS:** Dir Inst on Multi-Cultural Studies; mem Assn Afro-Am Life & Hist; Assn for Supr/Curric; Nat Alliance of Black Educ; Counc on Interr Books for Children; NAACP; Assn for Childhood Edn; Nat Counc for Soc Studies; Kappa Delta Phi; Phi Delta Kappa; edit bd Educ Forum; mem Human Rel Bd ; consult edit publs art in field. **HONORS/ACHIEVEMENTS:** Kelsey Pharr Awd 1956; Tchr of Yr 1957; Outstndg Churchman 1965, 1969; Danforth Assoc 1972. **MILITARY SERVICE:** AUS 1957-59. **BUSINESS ADDRESS:** Kansas State University, Bluemont Hall, College of Education, Manhattan, KS 66506.

BOYER, JOE L.
University president. **CAREER:** MS Valley State Univ, pres. **BUSINESS ADDRESS:** President, MS Valley State University, MVSU Campus, Itta Bena, MS 38941.

BOYER, MARCUS AURELIUS
Business executive. **PERSONAL:** Born Jul 10, 1945, Vado, NM; married Doris Ann Young. **EDUCATION:** WA Univ, MBA 1972; Univ of NM, BA 1967. **CAREER:** Small Bus Admin, trainee 1967-68, econ dev asst 1970, loan offcr 1971; Marine Midland Bank, asst ofcr 1973-74, ofcr 1974-76, asst vice prec ofcr 1976-77; Bank of Amer, vice president, Sr Account Officer. **ORGANIZATIONS:** Bd mem Natl Black MBA Assn 1973-76; pres NY Chap Natl Black MBA Assn 1975-76; NAACP; Assn of MBA Exec Fellowship; Consortium for Grad Study in Mgmt 1970. **HONORS/ACHIEVEMENTS:** Black Achiev in Ind Awd YMCA 1975. **MILITARY SERVICE:** AUS sgt E-5. **BUSINESS ADDRESS:** Vice Pres, Sr Acct Officer, Bank of America NT & SA, 335 Madison Ave, New York, NY 10017.

BOYER, SPENCER H.
Educator. **PERSONAL:** Born Sep 23, 1938, West Chester, PA. **EDUCATION:** Howard U, BS 1960; Geo Washington Univ Law Sch, LlB 1965; Harvard Law Sch, LlM 1966. **CAREER:** Howard Univ Law School, prof. **ORGANIZATIONS:** Dir Atlanta Leg Ed Oppor Pgm Summer 1971, 1972; dir Mid-Atlantic Leg Ed Oppor Pgm Summer 1970; vis prof Univ FL Clg Law 1968; patent & examiner Dept Commerce Washington 1964-65; mem Natl & DC Bar Assc; Am Cncl Ed Com; Natl Acad Sci Pubs; consult atty CHANGE 1967; com cit Participation Model Cities 1967-68; City Wide Natl Capitol Hous Auth 1967-69; asst dev HUMP; mem Assc Am Law Sch Com Minority Stdnt; Am Trail Lawyers Assc. **HONORS/ACHIEVEMENTS:** Who's Who in S & SW 1968-71; outstndg prof awrd 1973-74; Paul L Diggs Awrd; outstndg prof 1972-73; stud bar assc awrd Howard Univ Law Sch 1970-71.

BOYKIN, A. WADE, JR.
Educator. **PERSONAL:** Born Feb 07, 1947, Detroit, MI; married Jacquelyn M Starks; children: A Wade III, Curtis. **EDUCATION:** Hampton Inst, BA (Magna Cum Laude) 1968; Univ of MI Ann Arbor, MS 1970, PhD 1972. **CAREER:** Cornell Univ, asst to assoc prof, 1972-80; Rockefeller Univ, adjunct assoc prof, 1976-77; Howard Univ, prof 1980-. **ORGANIZATIONS:** Selection panel Natl Sci Found Grad Flwshp Prgm & Psych; NIMH Psychol Sci Flwshp Review Bd; Dir of Research CULS, Univ of MI 1971-72; Race Relations-Consultant Mental Hygiene Sci Div, Ft Sam Houston 1971; student supr psychology lab Hampton Inst 1967-68; mem Nat Assn of Black Psychologists; co-founder & plng comm mem Empirical Rsch Conf in Black Psychology 1974-; assoc ed Jrnl of Black Psych 1978-81; mem Natl Inst of Health Mental Retardation Rsch Comm 1983-; adv comm on testing NAACP 1981-, Amer Psych Assoc 1980-; mem Omega Psi Phi. **HONORS/ACHIEVEMENTS:** Omega Psi Phi, Whos Who Among Students in Am Coll & Univ 1966-68; 3rd Dist Schlr of Yr & Basileus of Yr Omega Psi Phi 1967-68; editorial bd Jour of Black Psychology 1974-; flw Rockefeller Univ 1976-; Comm Ldrs & Noteworthy Am 1975; Alpha Kapp Mu; fellow Ctr for Adv Study in the Behavioral Sci 1978-79; Spencer fellow Natl Acad of Ed 1978-81; scholar in resd Millersville Univ 1985; co-editor Rsch Dir of Psychologists 1979. **MILITARY SERVICE:** AUS Med Serv Corps 1st lt 1971. **BUSINESS ADDRESS:** Professor of Psychology, Howard University, Douglass Hall, Washington, DC 20059.

BOYKIN, JOEL S.
Dentist. **PERSONAL:** Born Jul 23, 1926, Birmingham, AL; son of Joel Allen Boykin and Juliett Watson Boykin; divorced; children: Stephan, George, Joels, Jr, Lisa Boykin Bolden, KristinaJoel Allen. **EDUCATION:** Morehouse Coll, BS 1948; Atlanta Univ, MS 1952; Meharry Med Coll, DDS 1956. **CAREER:** Dentist; Bullock County School System, teacher 1949-50; St Clair Co School System, 1949; Birmingham Public School System, 1948. **ORGANIZATIONS:** Mem Jefferson Co Dental Study Club, Nat Dental Assn, AL Dental Assn, Amer Dental Assn; past pres AL Dental Soc; soc mem Alpha Phi Alpha; deacon, 16th St Baptist Church. **MILITARY SERVICE:** AUS sgt 1945-46. **BUSINESS ADDRESS:** 2723 29th Ave N, Birmingham, AL 35207.

BOYKIN, RANDSON C.
Educator, poet, actor, art critic. **PERSONAL:** Born Sep 04, 1949, Chicago. **EDUCATION:** Columbia, BA 1974; Art Inst Chicago, 1973; Univ Chicago, postgrad. **CAREER:** Dunham Festivals, freelance poet, critic, actor, tchr 1968-; journl 1971-74; art cntr adminstr 1972-73; IL Arts Counc, lectr & poet 1971-73 ; Black Am Culture Chicago Pub Lib Orig, story-hour progs. **ORGANIZATIONS:** Mem Kuumba Lib Players 1970-72; mem Orgn

Black Am Culture; Culture Writers Wrkshp 1968-; gwendolyn Brooks Writers Wrkshp 1968-72; Black media rep; 1st pres Young Friends Art Youth Div IL Arts Counc 1973-74. **HONORS/ACHIEVEMENTS:** Nommo Poetry Pub Black Express; NSF awd 1967; lit awd Chicago Com Urban Oppor 1968; Lorraine Hansberry Meml awd Creative Writing 1972. **BUSINESS ADDRESS:** Dunham Festivals, 127 N Dearborn St, Room 620, Chicago, IL 60602.

BOYKIN, WILLIE
Educator. **PERSONAL:** Born Nov 07, 1916, Camden, SC; married Mable Violet Reese. **EDUCATION:** Morris Coll Sumter SC, BA 1942; Atlanta U, MA 1956. **CAREER:** City of Marion SC, coucilman; Marion School Dist #1, teacher 1951-; Mullins School Dist #2, teacher 1949-50. **ORGANIZATIONS:** Mem NEA 1952-80; mem SCEA 1952-80; pres Marion Co Educ & Assn 1972-74; pares Beta Alpha Sigma Chap Phi Beta Sigma Frat Inc 1975-79. **MILITARY SERVICE:** AUS s/sgt 1944 Good Conduct Medal & ETO Ribbon.

BOYKINS, ERNEST A.
Educator. **PERSONAL:** Born Oct 05, 1931, Vicksburg, MS; married Beverly Malveaux; children: Darryl, Rhea, Constance, Karen. **EDUCATION:** Xavier U, BS 1953; TX So U, MS 1958; Cell Biology Univ of CT, 1960; MI State U, PhD 1964. **CAREER:** MS Valley State Univ, pres, 1971-; Div Arts & Science Alcorn A&M Coll, 1970-71; Alcorn A&M Coll, prof, 1964-71; Michigan State Univ, instructor, 1964; Alcorn A&M Coll, instructor, 1959-61, acting head of Science Dept, 1958-59, instructor, 1954-57. **ORGANIZATIONS:** Mem Am Cncl on Educ 1954-57; Am Inst of Biological Sci; AAAS; Nat Cncl on Higher Edn; MS Conservation Educ Adv Cncl; Assn of SE Biologist; AmAssn for Higher Edn; mem Sigma Xi Scientific Hnr Soc; Nat Collegiate Hnrs Cncl; Phi Delta Kappa; Beta Kappa Chi; Omega Psi Phi; Alpha Kappa Mu; has had consult positions & com assignments on njmerous com & Commns including MS Select Com for Higher Educ 1973; Spl Health Career Oppor Prog Cons; Delta CnclBSA exec bd 1973; Greenwood-leflore Co C of & C 1974; Leflore Co United Givers Inc bd Mem 1974; Post secondary Educ Bd 1974. **HONORS/ACHIEVEMENTS:** Listed in Am Men of Sci 1964-; Outstanding Edctrs of Am; Outstanding Citizen of MS; Personalities of S 1973; Dstngshd Black Am 1973; Leaders in Educ 1973; Contemporary Notables 1974.

BOYLAN, DORIAN S.
Automobile dealer. **CAREER:** Gresham Dodge Inc, Gresham OR, chief executive. **BUSINESS ADDRESS:** Chief Executive, Gresham Dodge Inc, 855 NE Burnside, Gresham, OR 97030. *

BOYNTON, ASA TERRELL, SR.
Educational administrator. **PERSONAL:** Born May 20, 1945, Griffin, GA; married Evelyn Josephine Jordan; children: Asa Terrell Jr, Aaron Vernard, Antoine Debue. **EDUCATION:** Fort Valley State Coll, BS Bus Admin 1967; Univ of GA, MA Public Admin 1973. **CAREER:** Public Safety Div, St Petersburg, chief community relations 1973; Public Safety Div, Univ of Georgia, assoc dir, 1978, dir of public safety. **ORGANIZATIONS:** Pres, Assoc of Campus Law Enforcement Admin, 1976; pres, Alpha Phi Alpha Fraternity, Eta Iota Lambda, 1977; mem, Athens Rotary Club, 1983-; regional dir, Region 5, Intl Assn of Campus Law Enforcement Admin, 1983-; pres, Athens Breakfast Optimist Club, 1984. **HONORS/ACHIEVEMENTS:** Man of the Year, Alpha Phi Alpha, Eta Iota Lambda Chap, 1978; Mem of the Year, Georgia Assn of Campus Law Enforcement Admin, 1984. **MILITARY SERVICE:** AUS sgt, 2 years; Solider of the Month, Dec 1968. **HOME ADDRESS:** 135 Curtis Dr, Athens, GA 30605. **BUSINESS ADDRESS:** Dir of Public Safety, University of Georgia, Public Safety Division, Athens, GA 30602.

BOYNTON, ERNEST B., JR.
Educator. **PERSONAL:** Born in New York City. **EDUCATION:** City Coll NY, BA; Grad Sch Journalism Columbia U, MS; NY U, PhD candidate. **CAREER:** NY Amsterdam News, reporter, 1959; United Meth Bd Missions, researcher, 1960, staff writer, 1964, sr staff writer, 1966; City Coll of NY, lecturer, 1971-. **ORGANIZATIONS:** Mem Soc Professional Journalists; Sigma Delta Chi & Deadline & Club; Journalism Alumni pres Columbia U; chmn Minorities & Comm Div Assn for Educ in Jounalism1976-78; chmn Communications, Mass Media & Pub Policy Prgm 1977; The City Coll NY vP Jounalism Alumni 1978-79 Columbia U; mem Black Alumni Assn City Coll NY past pres NY Chap Religious Pub Relations Cncl; mem Coll English Assn; Pub Relations Soc Am Am. **HONORS/ACHIEVEMENTS:** Fac Serc Aw City Coll 1977; publs in field Mark of Excellence Awd 1974. **BUSINESS ADDRESS:** City College City Univ, New York, NY 10031.

BOZEMAN, BRUCE L.
Attorney. **PERSONAL:** Born Jan 21, 1944, Philadelphia, PA; married Patricia Johnson; children: Herman, Leslie, Patrick, Holly. **EDUCATION:** VA Union Univ, BA 1965; Howard Univ School of Law, JD 1968; NY Univ School of Law, LLM 1975. **CAREER:** Maxwell House Div GFC, asst counsel 1969-71, Birds Eye div couns 1971-73, beverage & breakfast foods div couns 1973-78, dir consumer affairs, asst gen couns; Norin Simen Inc, asst gen counsel 1981-83; private practice, atty; Bozeman & Roberts, PC, partner. **ORGANIZATIONS:** Mem Natl Bar Assoc, Amer Bar Assoc, NY Bar Assoc, Westchester Cty Bar Assoc, Assoc of Black Lawyers of Westchester Cty, Bar of DC 1968, NY 1969, US Ct of Appeals 1969, US Supreme Ct 1978; adj prof of law Pace Univ School of Law; mem Grievance Comm Westchester Cty Bar Assoc; chmn Black Dems of Westchester Cty; adjunct prof of law, CUNY Law School, Queens College. **BUSINESS ADDRESS:** Attorney, 100 East First St, Mount Vernon, NY 10550.

BOZEMAN, CATHERINE E.
Educator. **PERSONAL:** Born Mar 27, 1904; married Jerome Bozeman; children: 1 child. **EDUCATION:** Teachers Coll, EdD; Columbia Univ, PhD; Univ of TN, Early Childhood Educ; Univ of AL, Admin Curriculum Plnng. **CAREER:** Gamma Phi Delta, 1st anti-supreme basileus, supreme basileus 1977-86. **ORGANIZATIONS:** Pres Dallas Educators Credit Union; vice pres MS Soc 1st Bapt Ch of Selma, AL; worthy matron Phyllis Wheatly Chapter OES & Elks Lodge 919; life mem Natl Council of Negro Women; sec Econ Opportunities Selma; mem Natl Bd for March of Dimes; editor Title I Eval; bd mem Dallas Co Sch Bd; bd mem United Comm Serv Dallas Co; mem Century Club Claude Brown YMCA; trustee Gamma Phi Delta; architect for constitution rev 1976; golden life mem. **HONORS/ACHIEVEMENTS:** Featured as outstanding leader in Essence magazine 1981; first Black to be appointed to the Dallas Co School Bd; Finer Womanhood Awards from Aka & Zeta Phi Beta Sororities; Rose Pin Awardee 1973; Living Pearl Awardee 1973; Leadership Recogn from all chapters of GPD; supervised cornerstone ritual GPD Headquarters established; The Dr Catherine E Bozeman Scholarship Award Established in Delta Nu Chapter 1971; Dr Catherine E Bozeman Kindness Days recommended by Delta Nu'sYouth Group & voted by the bd to be a Natl Recognition Day; Supreme Basileus Emeritus Gamma Phi Delta Sor Inc 1986-87. **BUSINESS ADDRESS:** Supreme Basileus, Gamma Phi Delta Sorority Inc, 2657 W Grand Boulevard, Detroit, MI 48202.

BOZEMAN, MAGGIE SIMMONS
Educator. **PERSONAL:** Born Jul 24, 1929, Dancy, AL; married Clarence Eric. **EDUCATION:** AL St Univ Montgomery, BS 1951; IA St U, M 1953. **CAREER:** Tuskegee Inst AL, instructor, 1966; admin supvr headstart, 1965; Pickens County Bd of Educ, prin, 1950, Carrollton AL, elementary teacher, 1947. **ORGANIZATIONS:** Resolution Com AL Educ Assn AEA 1947-80; conv com /screening com AL Educ Assn 1947-80; steering com AKA Sor IWY; pres NAACP Aliceville Carrollton Br 1968-80; AL Dem conf coord Polit Black Caucus of AL ADC 1960-80. **HONORS/ACHIEVEMENTS:** Relgional Awd NAACP Atlanta 1968 75; Martin Luther King Jr Dream Awd AL Polit Black Caucus Montgomery ADC 1980; Minority People Cncl Epes AL 1980.

BRABSON, HOWARD V.
Educator. **PERSONAL:** Born Sep 18, 1925, Knoxville, TN; son of Alfred L Jones, Jr and Fannie R Burrough; married Rudiene Houston, Sep 13, 1952 (divorced). **EDUCATION:** Coll of Ozarks, BS 1956; Catholic Univ, Nath Catholic School of Social Serv, MSW 1962, DSW 1975. **CAREER:** Cedar Knoll School, asst supt 1958-62; Boys Industrial School Lancaster, admin vocational ed 1962-63; OH Youth Comm, dep commissioner 1963-65; VISTA Training Ctr, Univ of MD, asst proj dir 1965-66; VISTA E Eastern Region Washington DC, field supvr 1966-67; Great Lakes Region VISTA, prog mgr 1967-69; Univ of MI, prof of social work 1969-. **ORGANIZATIONS:** Community org consultant Neighborhood Groups 1965-; mem NABSW 1968-; chmn of bd Prog Mgmt & Devel Inc 1969-; Org MI Assoc BSW 1970; vice pres of OIC bd ACSW; VISTA training consultant Control Syst Rsch 1971-73; mem NABSW natl conf chmn 1973-74, vice pres 1974-76, pres 1978-82; pres emeritius 1982-. **HONORS/ACHIEVEMENTS:** Catholic Univ Fellow DSW 1970-71; Humanitarian Awd Willow Run Adversary Club 1977; Certificate of Appreciation for Outstanding Serv Univ of Toledo; Certificate of Appreciation NC ABSW 1979; Outstanding Comm Serv Awd MI ABSW 1979; Comm Serv Awd KY ABSW 1980; Distinguished Serv Awd Albany NY ABSW 1980; United Fund Special Awd; Faculty Recognition Awd Univ of MI 1981; author Job Satisfaction, Job Stress & Coping Among African-Amer Human Service Workers 1989. **MILITARY SERVICE:** AUS capt 1946-58; Commendation Ribbon. **BUSINESS ADDRESS:** Professor of Social Work, Univ of Michigan, 1065 Frieze Bldg, Rm 4097, Ann Arbor, MI 48109.

BRACEY, HENRY J.
Educator. **PERSONAL:** Born Jan 31, 1949, Grand Rapids, MI; son of Joe Bracey and Sheba M Davis Bracey; divorced; children: Anton J. **EDUCATION:** Western MI Univ, BS 1971; Univ of SC, MEd 1981. **CAREER:** SC Personnel and Guidance Assoc, mem exec council 1982; SC Sch Counselors Assoc, mem publicity comm 1982; SC Assoc of Non-White Concerns, pres and bdmem 1982; Southeastern Assoc of Educ Oppor Prog, personnel mgr 1983; Midlands Tech Coll, counselor. **ORGANIZATIONS:** Public relations dir Ms Black Columbia Pageant 1980-82; bd mem Columbia Youth Council 1982-84; bd mem Brothers and Sisters 1984-86; vice pres Coll Place Comm Council 1985-87; mem SC Tech Educ Assoc 1986-87; mem Southern Regional Council on Black Amer Affairs 1986-87; mem Omega Psi Phi; pres Heritage Comm Productions; student involvement coord Southern Regional Cncl on Black Amer Affairs Conf 1986; pres, Kuumba Circle 1988. **HONORS/ACHIEVEMENTS:** Published numerous articles on Cross-Cultural Counseling 1979-; Outstanding Young Men of Amer 1980; Outstanding Service Awd Ms Black Columbia Pageant 1980-82; designed and published Cross-Cultural Counseling Model 1980; Citizen of the Week (WOIC) 1981; Recognition Awd South Carolina Personnel and Guidance Assoc. **HOME ADDRESS:** 5016 Colonial Dr, Columbia, SC 29203. **BUSINESS ADDRESS:** Counselor, Midland Tech College, PO Box 2408, Columbia, SC 29202.

BRACEY, JOHN H., JR.
Educator. **PERSONAL:** Born Jul 17, 1941, Chicago, IL; son of John H Bracey and Helen Harris Bracey; married Ingrid Babb, Dec 19, 1975; children: Kali, Bryan, John Peter. **EDUCATION:** Howard Univ, attended; Roosevelt Univ, BA 1964; Northwestern Univ, NDEA Fellow ABD 1969. **CAREER:** Northeastern IL State Coll, lecturer 1969; Northern IL Univ, lecturer, hist 1969-71; Univ of Rochester, asst prof hist 1971-72; Univ of MA, chmn Afro-Amer studies 1974-79; Univ of MA, assoc prof Afro-Amer studies 1972-. **ORGANIZATIONS:** Mem Assn for the Study of Afro-Amer Life & History; life mem Org of Amer Historians; mem nominating comm Org of Amer Historians 1978-79; mem Phi Alpha Theta; contrib ed Jrnl of Ethnic Studies; mem standing comm on higher ed Natl Educ Assn; mem Amer Historical Assn. **HONORS/ACHIEVEMENTS:** Published 10 books, numerous articles, reviews on various aspects of the history & culture of Afro-Amers. **BUSINESS ADDRESS:** Associate Professor, Univ of Massachusetts, WEB Du Bois Dept Afro-American Studies, Amherst, MA 01002.

BRACEY, WILLIAM RUBIN
Chief of patrol. **PERSONAL:** Born May 11, 1920, Brooklyn, NY; married Louise Alleyne; children: Frances Kirton, William Jr, Gary. **EDUCATION:** Delehanty Inst, 1962; John Jay Coll of Criminal Just, 1966; Military Police Sch, compl Civil Disturbances Orientation Course 1973. **CAREER:** New York City Police Dept, asst chief 1977-79, dep chief 1973-77, inspector 1973, dep inspector 1972-73, capt 1970-72, lt 1959-70, sgt 195459, Patrolman 1945-54. **ORGANIZATIONS:** Past pres Guardians Assn of (Nyc Plice Dept; sec Nat Organ of Black Law Enforcement Exec; mem Intl Assn of Chiefs of Police; mem Captains Endowment Assn New York City Police Dept; mem St George Assn of New York City Police Dept. **HONORS/ACHIEVEMENTS:** Holder of 8 Police Dept Recognitions Awds for Otstndng Police Action in Field; recipient Unit Citation 1972; ltr of commendation from Police Comm New York City for outstanding contribution to success of Operation Sail & Bicent Celebration 1976. **MILITARY SERVICE:** AUS corpl 1943-45. **BUSINESS ADDRESS:** 1 Police Plaza, New York, NY 10007.

BRACEY, WILLIE EARL
Attorney, educational administrator. **PERSONAL:** Born Dec 21, 1950, Jackson, MS; son of Dudley Bracey and Anaretta; married Dianne Fullenwilder, Aug 15, 1987. **EDUCA-**

TION: Wright Jr Coll, AA 1970; Mt Senario Coll, BS 1973; Eastern IL Univ, MS 1976; Southern IL Univ, JD 1979. **CAREER:** Southern IL Univ, law clerk 1978-79; Southern IL Univ Ctr for Basic Skill, instr 1977-78; Southern IL Univ Law School, rsch asst 1977-78; Notre Dame Law School, teaching asst 1977; Western IL Univ, dir, student legal serv, 1979-, asst vice pres for student affairs special servs. **ORGANIZATIONS:** Mem NAACP, 1979-, ATLA 1979-, ABA 1979-, IBA 1979-, McDonough City Bar Assn 1979-, Natl Assn of Student Personnel Admin 1987-; faculty mem Blue Key Honor Soc; Housing Commissoner, McDonough County Housing Authority, appointment ends 1994. **BUSINESS ADDRESS:** Assistant Vice President, Western IllinoisUniv, Sherman Hall #315, Macomb, IL 61455.

BRACY, URSULA J.
Retired public health nurse. **PERSONAL:** Born Mar 09, 1908, Lake Charles, LA; married Jackson (deceased). **EDUCATION:** St Louis Univ, BS 1951; So Univ, 1928. **CAREER:** VNA of Greater St Louis, supvr 1951-73, staff nurse 1934-51; St Louis Chapter ARC; instr 1934. **ORGANIZATIONS:** Mem ANA 1946-; charter mem Nat League for Nursing 1952-; mem St Louis Univ Nursing Alumni 1951-; mem Lane Tabernacle CME Ch 1937; mem bd Vis Nurses Assn of Greater St Louis 1974-83; mem bd dir Annie Malone Childrens Home 1955-80; mem Sigma Theta Tau Natl Honor Soc of Nursing; attended several sessions Intl Council Of Nurses Congress various parts of world; rep Bi-state Chap ARC Melbourne Australia 1961. **HONORS/ACHIEVEMENTS:** Cited for 25 yrs Vol Serv; Bi-state Chapters ARC 1976; Plaque for 25 Yrs Dist Serv Annie Malone Childrens Home 1978; mem, Annie Malone Childrens Home Bd, 1955-80; mem, Sigma Theta Tau Intl Soc of Nursing Scholarship; life mem, bd of dir of The VNA of greater St Louis. **MILITARY SERVICE:** Woman of Achievement Award St Louis Globe Dem Newspaper 1978.

BRADDOCK, CAROL T.
Business executive. **PERSONAL:** Born Sep 07, 1942, Hamilton, OH; married Robert L; children: Ryan Lawrence, Lauren Patricia-Tipton. **EDUCATION:** Univ of Cincinnati, BA 1965, MA 1976; IN U, grad key 1980. **CAREER:** Fed Home Loan Bank of Cincinnati, vice pres comm investment officer 1978-, asst vice pres 1978, exec asst 1975; Fed Home Bank Bd, urban prog Coord 1973; Taft Broadcasting, prod coord 1972; McAlpins Dept Store , buyer 1969; Vogue Care Coll, instr 1971; Coll of Mt St Joseph, lectr 1973; Neighborhood ReinvestmentCorp, consult 1974. **ORGANIZATIONS:** Founder & past pres Womens Alliance 1966; exec comm mem WCET-TV Pub TV 1972-79; pres Minority Bus Devel Coalition 1980; ueen City Beauty, Cincinnati Enquirer 1973. **HONORS/ACHIEVEMENTS:** Otstndng Serv Awd Urban Reinvestment Task Force 1975; Black Achievers Awd YMCA 1978; Otstndng Young Women in Am 1980. **BUSINESS ADDRESS:** 2500 DuBois Tower, Cincinnati, OH 45202.

BRADDOCK, MARILYN EUGENIA
Comprehensive dentist. **PERSONAL:** Born Apr 25, 1955, Washington, DC. **EDUCATION:** Marquette Univ, BS 1977; Meharry Medical Coll, DDS 1982. **CAREER:** Cook Co Hosp, gpr 1982-83; Private Practice, dentist. **ORGANIZATIONS:** Mem Delta Sigma Theta Sor Inc 1980-; dental advisor Prince George Co Head Start Prog 1986-. **HONORS/ACHIEVEMENTS:** Flight Dentist Naval Air Station Andrews AFB Clinton MD 1984-85; Periodontology Fellowship US Navy Dental Corps 1985-86. **MILITARY SERVICE:** USN lt 3 yrs; USN Reserve Ctr presently dental officer Fort McHenry Baltimore MD. **HOME ADDRESS:** 29 E Laurel Ridge, Highway 54 Bypass, Chapel Hill, NC 27514.

BRADDOCK, ROBERT L.
Attorney. **PERSONAL:** Born Mar 21, 1937, Cincinnati, OH; married Gwendolyn Carol; children: Ryan Lawrence, Lauren Patricia Tipton. **EDUCATION:** Salmon P Chase Law Sch, JD 1972; Univ Cincinnati, BA 1964. **CAREER:** Morgan White Braddock & Brown LPA Co, Sr Partner; Manpower Planning Cty Cincinnati, asst dir 1971-72; OH Bur Emp Serv, mgr 1969-71; Lincoln Hgts & Pub & Sch, dir of social Work. **ORGANIZATIONS:** Mem Cincinnati Bar Assoc; OH St Bar; Amer Bar; mem City of Cincinnati Pub Sch Bd; pres Cty Cincinnati Pub Sch Bd 1976; mem Cincinnati RecreationComm; vice pres bd Camp Joy; pres Univ Cinti Coll of Arts & Scis Alumni Bd; mem Bd Trustees Tgraveler Aid; mem Bd Trustees Social Hlth Planning Council; Allocaltions Com Hlth Serv Cinti United Appeal 1972-74; Univ Cinti long range planning Com; mem Kappa Alpha Psi Frat; Referee Hamilton Co Municipal Ct OH 1980.

BRADEN, EVERETTE ARNOLD
Associate judge. **PERSONAL:** Born Nov 03, 1932, Chicago, IL; son of Zedrick Braden and Bernice Braden; married Mary Jeanette Hemphill; children: Marilynne. **EDUCATION:** Herzl Jr Coll, 1952; Northwestern Univ, BS 1954; John Marshall Law School, LLB 1961, JD 1969. **CAREER:** Cook Cty Dept Public Aid, caseworker 1966-69, property & ins consult 1966-69; Cook Cty Publ Defender Office, trial attny 1969-76, suprvising trial attny 1976-77; Circuit Ct of Cook Cty, assoc judge 1977-. **ORGANIZATIONS:** Mem Phi Alpha Delta Law, Natl Bar Assoc, IL State Bar Assoc, Chicago Bar Assoc, Meth Bar Assoc; bd of dirs IL Judges Assoc; mem Kappa Alpha Psi; 2nd vice pres, John Marshall Law School Alumni Assoc; charter fellow The IL Bar Found; mem, The Nominating Committee of the Circuit Court of Cook County. **HONORS/ACHIEVEMENTS:** Golden Key Awd S Shore Valley Comm Assoc; We Can Inc Awd; Black Gavel Awd for Outstanding Judge Black Lawyers Network 1984; Awd of Merit IL Judges Assoc; Disting Serv Awd John Marshall Law School Alumni Assoc, IL Judicial Council. **MILITARY SERVICE:** AUS sp4 1955-58.

BRADEN, HENRY E., IV
Attorney. **PERSONAL:** Born Aug 24, 1944, New Orleans, LA; married Michele Bordenave; children: Heidi E, Remi A, Henry E V. **EDUCATION:** Le Moyne Coll, BS 1965; Loyola Univ Sch of Law, JD 1975. **CAREER:** New Orleans Hometown Plan Urban League of New Orleans, author & dir 1974; Labor Educ & Advancement Prog, Total Community Action Inc, dir On-the-Job Training & Prog; Neighborhood Youth Corps Out of Sch Prog TCA Inc, dir 1966; LA Div of Employment Security, coord Huricane Betsy Disaster Relief Proj 1965; City ofNew Orleans, past dir Ofc of Manpower & Economic Devel ; Murray, Murray, Ellis & Braden, atty private practice. **ORGANIZATIONS:** Dem Nat Committeeman St of LA; Mem exec com Dem Natl Com Mem Met Area Com; LA Manpower Adv Com; columnist Op-ed; Page New Orleans States; exec vice pres Community Orgn for Urban Politics; New Orleans Industrial Devel Bd one of 3 blacks on LA Dem State Central Com; former pres St Augustines HS Alumni Assn; dir Building Dr St Augustines HS. **HOME ADDRESS:** 2453 Esplanade Ave, New Orleans, LA 70119.

BRADEN, STANTON CONNELL
Patent lawyer. **PERSONAL:** Born Mar 08, 1960, Chicago, IL; married Frances. **EDUCATION:** Univ of IL at Urbana-Champaign, BSEE 1982, JD 1985, MBA 1985. **CAREER:** Motorola Inc, elec engr 1982; Data Com Systems Corp, business/legal consultant 1985-86; General Elec Co, patent lawyer 1986-. **ORGANIZATIONS:** Mem Natl Eagle Scout Assoc 1975-, Inst of Electrical & Electronic Engrs Inc 1982-, Chicago and Amer Bar Assocs 1986-, Natl Black MBA Assoc 1986-. **HONORS/ACHIEVEMENTS:** Monsanto-Bechtel Incentive Awds for Academic Excellence 1980,82; first place Univ of IL Engrg Soc Debates 1982.

BRADFIELD, CLARENCE MCKINLEY
Attorney. **PERSONAL:** Born Jul 05, 1942, Vaughns, MS; married Linda; children: Clark, Carmen. **EDUCATION:** Wayne State Univ, BS 1964; Detroit Coll of Law, JD 1970. **CAREER:** Dept of Justice, asst US atty 1971-72; Clarence M Bradfield PC, private practice. **ORGANIZATIONS:** Wolverine Bar Assoc 1970-; vice pres Northwest Deroit Optimist Club. **BUSINESS ADDRESS:** Attorney, 2701 Cadillac Taver, Detroit, MI 48226.

BRADFIELD, HORACE FERGUSON
Physician. **PERSONAL:** Born Jul 15, 1913, Denver; married Marjorie Blackstone; children: John Michael, Gertrude, David Martin. **EDUCATION:** Univ of MI, BS 1933, MS 1934; MI State Life Teachers Cert, 1937; Wayne State Univ, MD 1948. **CAREER:** Detroit Publ Library, page 1928; Briggs Mfg Co, laborer 1928,39; Green Pastures Camp Urban League, camp counselor 1930-37; Detroit Publ Schools, teacher, attendance officer 1934-44; Detention Home for Boys Wayne Cty Juvenile Ct, suprv 1944-48; UAW-CIO Health Inst, examining physician 1950-54; Private practice, physician 1950-. **ORGANIZATIONS:** Mem Amer Acad of Family Practice, Amer Med Assoc, Amer Publ Health Assoc; asst prof clinical med Wayne State Univ 1976-; chmn Boys Work Comm YMCA 1934-38; chmn Rsch Comm Council of Social Agencies 1934-35; bd mem Detroit Fed of Teachers 1942-44, Delta Home for Girls 1954-60, Detroit Urban League 1957-67; bd trustees Wayne Comm Coll 1968-76. **BUSINESS ADDRESS:** 3008 E Grand Blvd, Detroit, MI 48202.

BRADFORD, ARCHIE J.
Educator. **PERSONAL:** Born Feb 06, 1931, Ripley, TN; married Mariejo Harris; children: Kyle, Kevin. **EDUCATION:** So IL U, BA 1960; Ball St U, MA Guidance & Counseling 1965; Univ of Notre Dame completed course work Pub Sch Adm 1974; St Marys Coll, internship business 1966. **CAREER:** Univ of Notre Dame, dir of Upward Bound; Siuth Bend Schools, elementary school counselor, 1961-69; Hodges Park Elementary School, prin, 1959-60. **ORGANIZATIONS:** Mem Am Personnel & Guidance Assn 1962-; Am Sch Counselors Assn 1962-61; Am Assn of Non-white Concerns 1971-; mem Mayors Commn on Educ 1972-74; St Joseph Co Lurban Coalition Bd 1972-; vice pres Urban Coalition 1974-; chmn Coalition Educ Task Force 1972-; Evaluation & Allocation Div of United Way 1974-. **HONORS/ACHIEVEMENTS:** Reclip Kappa Alpha Psi Fidelity Awd. **MILITARY SERVICE:** AUS corpl 1950-53; USAC A1c 1953-57. **BUSINESS ADDRESS:** Box 458, Notre Dame, IN 46556.

BRADFORD, ARVINE M.
Educator. **PERSONAL:** Born Feb 20, 1915, Harriman, TN. **EDUCATION:** Univ of Pittsburgh, AB 1941; Fisk U, MA 1943; Harvard U, pub hlth cert 1944; Howard U;; MD 1949. **CAREER:** Howard Univ, assoc prof; Georgetown Univ, Certified Am Coll OB-GYN, assoc prof 1964; private practice 1959-74. **ORGANIZATIONS:** Mem Am Coll OB-GYN 1965; Amm Med Assn; Nat Med & Assn; Chi Delta Mu; NAACP; Urban League; Mayors Com on Ageing; mem DC Gen Hosp adv com; mem Alpha Phi Alpha Frat Sig Skin Club. **BUSINESS ADDRESS:** 1718 7 St NW, Washington, DC 20001.

BRADFORD, CHARLES EDWARD
Clergyman. **PERSONAL:** Born Jul 12, 1925, Washington, DC; married Ethel Lee McKenzie; children: Sharon Louise Lewis, Charles Edward Jr, Dwight Lyman. **EDUCATION:** Oakwood Coll Huntsville AL, BA 1946; Andrews U, Berrien Springs MI;; DD 1978. **CAREER:** NA GenConf of Seventh-Day Adventists;; Vice Pres 1979-, asso sec 1970-79; Lake Region Conf of Seventh-day Adventists pres 1961-70; LA/TX/MON/NY, Pastor 1945-61. **ORGANIZATIONS:** Trustee Oakwood Coll/Andrews Univ 1961; trustee Loma Linda Univ 1979. **BUSINESS ADDRESS:** 6840 Eastern Ave NW, Washington, DC 20012.

BRADFORD, EQUILLA FORREST
Educational administrator. **PERSONAL:** Born Apr 11, 1931, Birmingham, AL; married William Lewis. **EDUCATION:** Wayne State UDetroit, BS 1954, M 1963; MI State Univ East Lansing, PhD 1972. **CAREER:** Westwood Community School Dist, supt of schools, 1979-, exec asst supt, 1974-77, asst supt personnel, 1971-74; McNair Elementary School, Westwood School Dist, prin, 1968-71; McNair & Daly Elementary Schools, Westwood School Dist, art teacher, 1966-68, teacher, 1955-66; Michigan Assn for Individually Guided Educ, Consult, 1970-; Eastern MI Univ, instructor/lecturer, 1979-; Wayne State Univ Detroit, consultant, 1979-. **ORGANIZATIONS:** Mem Alpha Kappa Alpha Sor Inc 1954-; mem Am Assn for Sch Adm 1968-; mem Detroit Econ Club 1979-; mem St Paul AME Ch Educator of Yr, Delta Sigma Theta Sor 1979. **HONORS/ACHIEVEMENTS:** Dist educator Nat Sor of Phi Delta Kappa Inc 1980 , Woman of Year; Alpha Kappa Alpha Sor Inc Inc Eta Iota Omega & Chap 1980. **BUSINESS ADDRESS:** 25913 Annapolis, Inkster, MI 48141.

BRADFORD, JAMES EDWARD
Accountant. **PERSONAL:** Born Jun 27, 1943, Jonesboro, LA; married Mae Lean Calahan; children: Roderick, Berkita, D'Andra. **EDUCATION:** Grambling State Univ, BS 1965; Wayne State Univ, summer 1966. **CAREER:** Sabine Parish School Bd, teacher 1965-66; Bienville Parish School Bd, teacher 1966-70; Continental Group, accountant 1970-76, super; Independent ConsultantsInc, pres 1980-85; Bradco Sales, pres 1984-85; Stone Container Corp, super of accounting. **ORGANIZATIONS:** Bd chmn Pine Belt CAA 1979-85; bd chmn, Jackson Council on Aging 1980-85; bd mem North Delta Regional Planning Comm 1983-85. **HONORS/ACHIEVEMENTS:** Outstanding Young Men of America Jaycees 1975; Outstanding Blacks in LA 1982. **HOME ADDRESS:** 709 Leon Drive, Jonesboro, LA 71251.

BRADFORD, MARTINA LEWIS
Telecommunications executive. **PERSONAL:** Born Sep 14, 1952, Washington, DC; daughter of Martin Lewis and Alma Ashton; married William Bradford, Dec 24, 1982; children:

Sydney. **EDUCATION:** Amer Univ, Washington, DC, BA, 1973; Duke Univ, Durhan, NC, JD, 1975. **CAREER:** Interstate Commerce Div Finance Div, Washington, DC, atty, 1976-78; Comm on Approporiations, US House of Representatives, Washington, DC, counsel, 1978-81; Interstate Commerce Comm, Washington, DC, chief of staff to vice chmn, 1981-83; AT&T Legal Dept, New York, NY, atty, 1983-85; AT&T Corp Public Affairs, Washington, DC, atty, 1985-88; AT&T External Affairs, New York, NY, vice pres, 1988-; corporate legal intern, Southern Railways, Inc, 1974-; adjunct prof, Amer Univ School of Law, 1982-. **ORGANIZATIONS:** Minority counsel, US House of Representatives, 1978-79, minority counsel, US Senate, 1979-80; founding vice pres, Women's Transportation Seminar, 1978; mem, Dist of Columbia Bar, 1976, Maryland Bar, 1983-, Women's Bar Assn, 1989; bd mem, INROADS Inc, 1989. **HONORS/ACHIEVEMENTS:** Deans List, Amer Univ, 1971-73; Scholastic Honorary, Economics, Amer Univ, 1973. **BUSINESS ADDRESS:** External Affairs Vice Pres, AT&T, 32 Ave of The Americas, Room 2604, New York, NY 10013.

BRADFORD, ZEE
Advertising executive. **PERSONAL:** Born Oct 10, 1953, Atlanta, GA; married Quentin Eugene Bradford Sr; children: Quentin Eugene Jr, Qiana Yvonne. **EDUCATION:** Morris Brown Coll, 1971-75. **CAREER:** QZ Enterprises Inc, public relations dir 1979-83; First Class Inc, public relations dir 1983-84, exec vice pres 1984-. **ORGANIZATIONS:** 1st Black Pres Shaker Welcome Wagon 1980-81; steering comm Mayor's Task Force on Educ 1984-; bd member Amer Diabetes Assn 1984-; steering comm Black Public Relations Soc 1984-; min affairs comm Public Relations Soc of Amer 1985-86; pr comm Atlanta Assoc of Black Journalists 1985-86; adv bd ML King Jr Center for Social Change 1985-86; prog dir Jack & Jill of America 1985-86; activities chmn Girl Scouts of Amer 1985-87; youth activities chmn ProvidenceBaptist Church 1985-;prog dir Collier Heights Elem School, PTA, Grade Parent 1985-; publicity rel comm Amer Heart Assoc 1986-87; commiss A Reginald Eaves Blue Ribbon Task Force on Strenghthening the Black Amer Family 1986-; econ devel task force Natl Conf of Black Mayors 1986-; mem UNCF, Natl Forum of Black Public Admins 1986-; comm United Way's Media Devel 1987; chmn SME 1987; comm YWCA Salute to Women of Achievement 1987. **HONORS/ACHIEVEMENTS:** Congressional Tribute US Congress 1981; Civic Awd United Way 1981; council resolution Cleveland City Council 1981; Cert of Merit Atlanta Assn of Black Journalists 1984; Collier Heights PTA 1985,86; Girl Scouts of Amer 1986; Who's Who In Society 1986; Leadership Atlanta 1986-87; NFL/AFL-CIO Community Serv Awd. **BUSINESS ADDRESS:** Executive Vice President, First Class Inc, 1422 W Peachtree St, Ste 816, Atlanta, GA 30309.

BRADLEY, ANDREW THOMAS, SR.
Counselor. **PERSONAL:** Born Jan 04, 1948, Johnstown, PA; married Annice Bernetta Edwards; children: Andrew T Jr, Elizabeth Lorine, James Christopher. **EDUCATION:** Shaw Univ Raleigh, BA (Magna Cum Laude) 1975; Univ of DC, MA 1982. **CAREER:** Seacap Inc, mainstream suprv 1968-69; Neuse-Trent Manpower Devel Corp, instr, counselor 1970-72; Craven Comm Coll, instr, counselor 1972-75; Neuse River Council of Govts, reg admin 1975-77; Natl Ctr on Black Aged Inc, dir, crises rsch 1977-81; Bradley Assoc, consult 1981-84; Family & Children Svcs, psychotherapist; Harrisburg Area Comm Coll, counselor acad found. **ORGANIZATIONS:** Trainer Spec Training on Abuse & Neglect of Children & Adults; consult Mgmt Awareness Training; presentor Needs & Problems of the Minority Aged, Practical Approcahes to Providing Social & Health Serv to the Rural Elderly; pastoral counseling Faith Temple First Born Church; teahing, suprv Crisis Intervention Counseling; chairperson Crime Prevention Task Force; mem Natl Assoc of Victim Witness Asst, Natl Assoc of Black Soc Workers, Natl Ctr & Caucus on Black Aged Inc, Natl Council on Aging, Amer Mental Health Counselors Assoc, Amer Assoc for Counseling & Devel, Harrisburg Area Hospice; bonds comm Harrisburg Human Relations Commiss; bd mem WIZZ Calbe FM 1005 Radio. **HONORS/ACHIEVEMENTS:** Outstanding Young Man in Amer Natl Jaycees; Graduate Scholarship Inst of Geontology Univ of the Dist of Columbia. **MILITARY SERVICE:** USAR sp4 6 yrs. **HOME ADDRESS:** 2152 N Sixth St, Harrisburg, PA 17110. **BUSINESS ADDRESS:** Counselor, Academic Found, Harrisburg Area Comm Coll, 127 Locust St, Harrisburg, PA 17110.

BRADLEY, DAVID HENRY, JR.
Educator, writer. **PERSONAL:** Born Sep 07, 1950, Bedford, PA; son of Rev David Bradley and Harriette Jackson Bradley. **EDUCATION:** Univ of PA, BA 1972; Univ London, MA 1974. **CAREER:** JB Lippencott Co, asst editor 1974-76; book reviewer New York Times, Philadelphia Enquirer 1975; Univ of PA, visiting lecturer 1975-76; Temple Univ, visiting lecturer 1976-77, asst prof 1977-82, assoc prof 1982-89, Colgate Prof of Humanities, 1988, prof 1989-; Dist Found Prof of Literature, Univ of N Carolina, Wilmington. **ORGANIZATIONS:** Member, Screenwriters Guild, Author's Guild, PEN. **HONORS/ACHIEVEMENTS:** PEN/Faulkner Award, 1982; Amer Book Award nominee, 1983; Acad Award Amer Inst of Arts and Letters; Guggenheim Fellowship, 1989; articles in Esquire, New York Times, Redbook, The Southern Review; author of novels, South Street, 1975, The Chaneysville Incident, 1981. **BUSINESS ADDRESS:** Associate Professor, English, TempleUniv, Dept of English, Philadelphia, PA 19122.

BRADLEY, EDWARD R.
News correspondent. **PERSONAL:** Born in Pennsylvania; divorced. **EDUCATION:** Cheyney State Coll PA, BS Educ 1964. **CAREER:** WDAS Phila, news reporter 1963-67; SCBS NY, news reporter 1967-71; CBS TV News, corres 1973-78, prin corres 1978, in Paris, 1971, Saigon 1972-74, Washington 1974, prin corres CBS Reports 1978-81, "60 Minutes" 1981-. **ORGANIZATIONS:** Anchorman various documentaries "Whats Happening in Cambodia", "The Boat People", "The Boston Goes To China"; White House corr CBS. **HONORS/ACHIEVEMENTS:** WDAS-FM Philadelphia Disting Commentator Awd NY Chap Nat Assn Media Women 1975; Assn Black Jour Awd 1977; Emmy Awd 1979,83; George Polk Journalism Awd 1980. **BUSINESS ADDRESS:** 60 Minutes, CBS News, 524 W 57th St, New York, NY 10019.

BRADLEY, HILBERT L.
Attorney. **PERSONAL:** Born Jan 18, 1920, Repton, AL. **EDUCATION:** Valparaiso Law Sch, Jd, LlB 1950. **CAREER:** Pvt Pract Atty; Div of Air Pollution, dep pros atty, corp counsel atty. **ORGANIZATIONS:** Made Documentary for Fed Gov on Role of a Witness; involved, prepared, filed & litigated several landmark civil rights cases; IN mem Thurgood Marshall Law Assn; Nat Black Bar Assn; life mem NAACP; mem IN Il Supreme Ct of US Bars. **MILITARY SERVICE:** AUS pvt 1947. **BUSINESS ADDRESS:** Lawyer, 2148 W 11 Ave, Gary, IN 46404.

BRADLEY, J. ROBERT
Music director. **PERSONAL:** Born Sep 11, 1920, Memphis, TN. **EDUCATION:** Trinity Coll London Eng, Mus 1955. **CAREER:** Bapt Conv USA Inc, Music Dir Sun Sch Publ Bd Nat; Nat Bap Training Union Bd, dir mus 1935; Nat Sun Sch & BTU Cong Nat Bap Conv USA Inc, intern famous rel concert artist. **HONORS/ACHIEVEMENTS:** Iron Ship Awd 1960, highest awd from Korea; Albert Schweitzer Gold Medal 1970; London Knight Grand Comm Monrovia Lib 1974, highest awd from Rep of Liberia. **BUSINESS ADDRESS:** 330 Charlotte Ave, Nashville, TN 37201.

BRADLEY, JACK CARTER
Retired music chairman. **PERSONAL:** Born Mar 14, 1919, Moline, IL; son of Earl Russell Bradley and Eva Melissa Carter Bradley. **EDUCATION:** Univ of Denver, AB 1941; Army Bandleaders School, 1946; Univ of Denver, BMus 1948, MMus 1949. **CAREER:** Violinist, Denver Jr Symphony, 1928-32, Denver Civic Symphony, 1937-41, Denver Symphony, 1940-41, 1946-49, Corpus Christi Symphony, 1967-, Beaumont Symphony, 1968; prof, 1949-84, chmn of Music Dept, 1965-84, Texas Southern Univ; co-composer, co-conductor, soundtrack for NETV series People are Taught to be Different, 1950s & 1960s; first violinist, dir, New Horizon String Quartet, Houston. **ORGANIZATIONS:** Member, Music Educ Natl Conf, Amer String Teachers Assn, Amer Assn of Univ Prof, Texas Assn of Coll Teachers, Amer Federation of Musicians, Amer Chamber Music Society, Kappa Kappa Psi Band Fraternity, Phi Beta Sigma Honorary Physical Educ Fraternity, Texas Assn of Music Schools, Coll Music Soc, Texas Fine Arts Commn, Kappa Alpha Psi, YMCA, Lutheran Campus Council for Houston, Jr Chamber of Commerce Denver, Houston Chamber of Commerce Cultural Affairs Comm, Ebony Tennis Club, Fondren Tennis Club, Houston Tennis Assn, Memorial Park Tennis Club, US Tennis Assn, Houston Ski Jammers, Houston Bicentennial Comm, Tablernacle Baptist Church Moline IL, Zion Baptist Church Denver CO, Augustana Lutheran Church Houston TX; past dir, Texas Music Educ Assn; bd of dir, Houston Friends of Music; member of advisory council, Miller Theater; bd of dir, Houston Youth Symphony, bd of trustees, Theatre Under the Stars. **HONORS/ACHIEVEMENTS:** Certificate of Recognition, Natl Urban League, 1948; Natl Assn of Negro Musicians, 1964; first black as a regular member of a professional Amer symphony; recognition as a major black contributor in Colorado, Denver Public Library, 1972; recognition as a pioneer in professional symphony, Music Assistance Fund, 1988. **MILITARY SERVICE:** USNA warrant officer 1941-46. **HOME ADDRESS:** 3316 Rosedale, Houston, TX 77004.

BRADLEY, JAMES GEORGE
Administrator. **PERSONAL:** Born Sep 17, 1940, Cleveland, OH; married Lela; children: Wyette, James, Candace, Jason. **EDUCATION:** UNM, BEd 1963; Univ of Utah, MBA 1973 PhD 1977. **CAREER:** Human Resources, manpower dev spec 1979; Clearfield Job Corps, dir 1970; Detroit Manpower Center, dir 1976-77; USDA, civil rights 1986. **ORGANIZATIONS:** Advisory Board Special Ed 1983; NAACP, pres 1985. **HONORS/ACHIEVEMENTS:** Alb Police Dept, special ser. **HOME ADDRESS:** 6013 Unitas Ct, NW, Albuquerque, NM 87114.

BRADLEY, JAMES HOWARD, JR.
Business executive. **PERSONAL:** Born Nov 26, 1936, Detroit, MI; married Juanita E Bass; children: Vanessa, Angela. **EDUCATION:** MI State Univ, BA 1959; Univ of MI, Grad Work. **CAREER:** Central Foundry Div Gen Motors Corp, budget analyst 1962-69; Gen Motors Corp, sr financial analyst 1969-70; Jim Bradley Pontiac-Cadillac-GMC Inc, pres 1970-. **ORGANIZATIONS:** Dir City of Ann Arbor Econ Devel Corp 1979-81; pres, bd of dir Ann Arbor Comm Central 1979-; dir of exec bd Boy Scouts of Amer Wolverine Council 1980; life mem NAACP; mem Kappa Alpha Psi. **MILITARY SERVICE:** AUS E-4 6 months. **BUSINESS ADDRESS:** President, Jim Bradley Pontiac-Cadillac, 3500 Jackson Rd, Ann Arbor, MI 48103.

BRADLEY, JAMES MONROE, JR.
Clergyman. **PERSONAL:** Born Aug 15, 1934, Mayesville, SC; married Nellie Chambers; children: James, III, Rosemary. **EDUCATION:** Claflin Coll, AB 1956; Gammon Theo Sem;; BD 1959; Drew Theo Sem adv study. **CAREER:** Trinity United Meth Ch Orangeburg SC, minister 1974-; Emmanuel Ch Sumter NC 1970-74; Orangeburg Dist, dist supt 1964-70; Spartanburg, minister 1962-63; Cheraw, 1960-61; W Camden, 1958-60; Aiken, 1956-58. **ORGANIZATIONS:** Ordained Elder 1959; full connecltion 1958; ordained Deacon 1957; mem SC Conf United Meth Ch On Trial 1955; mem NAACP; Phi Beta Sigma; Mason Past vp; NAACP; mem Sumter Co Bd Educ 1971-73; mem bd dirs Sumter Co Rehab Cntr; delegate World Meth MtngLondon 1966, followed by 9 week tour of Europe.

BRADLEY, JESSE J., JR.
Government employee. **PERSONAL:** Born Jul 07, 1929, Hope, AR; married Marie A Saunders; children: Shawn P, Gregory J. **EDUCATION:** BA Economics 1968; Grad Work Urban Affairs. **CAREER:** Dept Trans Fed Aviation Admin, equal employment opp splst; Bendix Corp, purchasing agent/asst minority bus coord 1971-74, prod planner 1968-71; USPost Ofc, postal clerk 1956-68, chmn adv com 1974; Mid-Am Minority Bus Expos, exec dir 1973-74. **ORGANIZATIONS:** Complied/published minority bus dir Bendix Corp; Black Econ Union Dept of Trans Fed Aviation Admin; mem NAACP; Freedom Fund Com 1973-74; parliamentarian Phi Beta Sigma Frat 1974; sw regnl chaplain Phi Beta Sigma Frat 1972-74. **HONORS/ACHIEVEMENTS:** Special Recog Awards Mid-Am Minority Bus Exposition 1974, Ldrshp Awrd 1973, Recog Award 1972; Outstand Serv Award SW Region Phi Beta Sigma Frat 1974; Comm Ldrs of Am Award 1973. **MILITARY SERVICE:** AUS pvt 1951-53. **BUSINESS ADDRESS:** Civil Rights Staff DOT-FAA Fed, 601 E 12 St, Kansas City, MO 64106.

BRADLEY, JESSIE MARY
Educational administrator. **PERSONAL:** Born Oct 20, Little Rock, AR; daughter of Jesse Alexander Godley and Ophelia Washington Godley; married William O Bradley, Jun 28, 1953; children: Edwin Geory Bradley. **EDUCATION:** Oakwood, BA 1948; So CT St Univ, BS 1956, MS 1960; Univ of CT, PhD 1973. **CAREER:** NE Acad, tchr 1948-53; New Haven, tchr 1956-58; So CT St Coll, instr 1958-67; New Haven Bd of Edn, prin 1967-73, Dir 1973-77, asst supt 1977-86; Connecticut State Dept of Education, consultant, 1987-. **ORGANIZATIONS:** Chamber of Commerce Educ Com; Phi Delta Kappa; Pi Lambda Theta; Am Assn of Sch Administr; Am Assn of Univ Women; Nat Cncl of Adminstrv Women in Educ dir So CT Chap Am Red Cross; dir Easter Seal Goodwill Ind Rehab Ctr; consultant day care nursery; World Cncl for Curr & Inst; Inter Reading Assn Am Temperance Soc; Intl Quota Club;

Arts Coun of Grtr New Haven; CT Assn for Bilingual Bicult Edn; Grtr CT Coun for Open Edn; pres Oakwood Coll Alumni Assn; Urban League; NAACP; United Way; New Haven Jewish Ctr; New Haven Human Rel Coun; Assn of Super & Curr Devel; Nat Coun of Negro Women; sponsor United Negro Club 1976; bd of governors, Univ of New Haven 1987-; trustee, Mt Zion SDA Church; dir, Bank of kBoston, 1977-92; dir, Harris & Tucker Day School. **HONORS/ACHIEVEMENTS:** Educ Award Omega Psi Phi 1976; serv awd Oakwood Coll Unit Stud Move 1976; educ awd Gr New Haven Bvs & Professional Assn 1975; serv awd New Haven Headstart 1975; Educ Award Pampered Lady Inc 1973; serv awd Harriet Tubman 1972; achiev awd Nat Fed Kings Dau 1970; career adv awd NAACP 1970; serv awd Oakwood Coll Alumni Assn 1970; Outstanding Comm Serv Award Order of E Star 1970; Distinguished Alumni, Natl Assn for Equal Opportunity in Higher Education 1984; Outstanding Black Educator, Connecticut Historical Society 1984; An Analysis of Bilingual Education Programs (Spanish & English) for Pre-ad Children in Six CT Cities 1973; Ford Foundation Fellow 1977; Friendship Force Ambassador, East & West Germany 1978; Travel Grant,Israel, 1979; Sister Cities Exchange (Ed), Avignon France 1982. **HOME ADDRESS:** 109 Stevenson Rd, New Haven, CT 06515.

BRADLEY, LONDON M., JR.
Executive administrator. **PERSONAL:** Born Mar 03, 1943, Chestnut, LA; married Olivia Woodfork; children: London, Byron, Bradley. **EDUCATION:** Southern Univ, BS 1964. **CAREER:** Parks & Recreation Dept KC, MO, recreation dir 1968-69; Bendix Corp, personnel interviewer 1969-71. **ORGANIZATIONS:** Master mason MW Prince Hall Grand Lodge 1963; mem NAACP 1976; referee Big Ten Basketball Conf 1977; Sunday school teacher Second Baptist Church 1984. **MILITARY SERVICE:** USAF s/sgt 4 yrs. **BUSINESS ADDRESS:** Assistant Vice President, Allstate Ins Co, 51 W Higgins Rd, South Barrington, IL 60010.

BRADLEY, M. LOUISE
Government employee. **PERSONAL:** Born Jun 18, 1920, Clarksville, GA; widowed; children: Jacquelyn B (webb), William F, Jr. **EDUCATION:** Clark Coll, AB 1959; Atlanta Univ Sch of Social Work, MSW 1968. **CAREER:** EEOC, Voluntary Prog Officer; Dept of Labor Washington DC, chief Outreach Comm Serv Womens Bureau 1973-74; Ofc of Economic & Opp Regional Ofc Region IV, dist supvr 1970-73; OEO;; dep supvr 1966-70; Special Educ Atlanta, tchr 1966-70; Fulton Co Dept Pub Welfare, casework supvr. **ORGANIZATIONS:** Mem Nat Assn of Negro Bus & Professional Women; Alpha Kappa Alpha Sor; Continental Societies of Am Inc; Nat Assn of Soc Workers; Atlanta Womens C of C Black Womens Comm Found; Black Womens Coalition of Atlanta; membshp comm of NAACP; bd mem Nat Domestic Workers Inc 1972-74. **HONORS/ACHIEVEMENTS:** Recip Outstanding Serv Awd Comm Acltion Agencies; Outstanding Serv Awd Nat Domestic Workers Inc; Outstanding Comm Serv Awd Negro Bus & Professional Womens Club; Flwshp Fulton Co Dept of Welfare. **BUSINESS ADDRESS:** EEOC Citizens Trust Bank Bldg, Atlanta, GA.

BRADLEY, MELVIN L.
Govt. executive. **PERSONAL:** Born Jan 06, 1938, Texarkana, TX; married Ruth A Terry; children: Cheryl, Eric, Jacquelyn, Tracey. **EDUCATION:** LA City Coll, attended 1955; Compton Coll, attended 1965; Pepperdine Univ, BS 1973. **CAREER:** Real estate broker 1060-63; LA Co, dep sheriff 1963-69; State of CA, consult to gov's office 1970-73; State of CA, asst to Gov Reagan mem gov's sr staff participant in cabinet meetings 1973-75; Charles R Drew Postgrad Med Sch LA, dir pub rel; United Airlines, asst to vice pres 1977-81; President of the US White House, sr policy advisor 1981-82, spl asst to pres 1982-. **ORGANIZATIONS:** Mem Kiwanis Club; Toastmasters of Amer Inc; mem Natl Urban League, NAACP. **HONORS/ACHIEVEMENTS:** Awd for Outstanding Contrib City of Los Angeles; Awded Mayor's Key to City Riverside CA; Awd for Contrib in Field of Comm Relations Compton CA; Comm Serv Awd Co of Los Angeles; Shaw Univ, Bishop Coll, Hon Dr of Laws; Disting Alumnus Awd Langston Univ.

BRADLEY, PHIL POOLE
Professional athlete. **PERSONAL:** Born Mar 11, 1959, Bloomington, IN; married Ramona; children: Megan, Curt. **EDUCATION:** Univ of MO, BA 1980. **CAREER:** Seattle Mariners, outfield 1983-. **HONORS/ACHIEVEMENTS:** Was selected by CA League managers as "Best Defensive Outfielder"; Mid-Season All-Star Team 1985; Post-Season Sporting News All-Star Team 1985; mem All Star team 1985. **BUSINESS ADDRESS:** Professional Athlete, Seattle Mariners, 100 S King St Ste 300, Seattle, WA 98104.

BRADLEY, TERRYE SINGLETARY
Social worker. **PERSONAL:** Born Jun 17, 1950, Tarpon Springs, FL; married Rudolph K Bradley; children: Adia. **EDUCATION:** Stetson Univ, BA 1972; FL State Univ, MSW 1976. **CAREER:** Juvenile Services Prog, coord counseling dept 1977; Juvenile Welfare Bd, coord youth serv adv 1978-79, asst dir planning & funding 1979-84; Johnnie Ruth Clarke Health Ctr, exec dir 1984-. **ORGANIZATIONS:** Adv bd Pinellas Co Coll Fund 1969-; mem St Petersburg Bd of Realtors 1981-; alumni & grad Leadership St Petersburg 1984-; bd trainer FL Council Primary Care Ctrs 1986-87; bd of dirs FL Council Primary Care Ctrs 1986-87; consultant Oasis Program for Youth 1986-87. **HONORS/ACHIEVEMENTS:** Outstanding Young Women in Amer 1982; featured in Tampa Bay's Most Influential Blacks 1982; listed in Who's Who Among Young Women in Amer 1983. **BUSINESS ADDRESS:** Executive Dir, Johnnie Ruth Clarke Hlth Ctr, 1310 22nd Ave So, St Petersburg, FL 33705.

BRADLEY, THOMAS
Mayor. **PERSONAL:** Born Dec 29, 1917, Calvert, TX; married Ethel Arnold; children: Lorraine, Phyllis. **EDUCATION:** Univ of California, Los Angeles, attended. **CAREER:** LA Police Dept, 1940-62; Private law practice, 1961-63; LA 10th Dist, councilman 1963-73; Los Angeles CA, mayor 1973-. **ORGANIZATIONS:** Mem CA State Bar Assoc, Natl League of Cities, So CA Assoc of Govts; founding past pres Natl Assoc of Reg Councils; mem Pres Fords Natl Comm on Productivity & Work Quality, Amer Cancer Soc of LA Cty, Greater LA Urban Coalition, LA World Affairs Council, United Nations Assoc of LA, Urban League of LA, Natl Energy Adv Council; founding mem Black Achievers Comm, NAACP; past natl pres Kappa Alpha Psi; bd dir natl Urban Fellows; mem of numerous other civic org. **HONORS/ACHIEVEMENTS:** Newsmaker of the Year Awd, Natl Assoc of Media Women 1974; Los Amigos De La Humanidad School of Soc Work Univ of So CA 1974; Alumnus of the Year Univ ofCA 1974; Thurgood Marshall Awd; Sword of the Haganah of State of Israel Israeli Ambassador Simcha Dinitz 1974; David Ben Gurion Awd for Outstanding Achievement 1974; NAACP Legal Defense & Ed Fund Dinner 1975; MEDIC Intl Humanitarian Awd 1978; CORO Found Awd 1978; Awd of Merit Natl Council of Negro Women Inc 1978; John F Kennedy Fellowship Awd New Zealand Govt 1978; 1983 Equal Justice Awds Dinner honoring Mayor Bardley 1983; City Employee of the Year 1983; Magnin Awd Rabbi Edgar F Magnin 1984; NAACP Spingarn Medal 1985; Hon Doct of Law Degrees, Brandeis Univ, Oral Roberts Univ, Pepperdine Univ, Wilberforce Univ, Whittier Coll, Yale Univ, Univ of South Carolina, Princeton Univ, Busan Natl Univ, Korea, Southwestern Univ, Antioch Univ, North Carolina Central Univ, California Lutheran Coll, Loyola Marymount Univ; Hon Doct of Philosophy Degree Humanity Rsch Ctr of Beverly Hills. **BUSINESS ADDRESS:** Mayor, City of Los Angeles, 200 N Spring St City Hall, Los Angeles, CA 90012.

BRADLEY, WALTER THOMAS, JR.
Corporate executive. **PERSONAL:** Born Oct 02, 1925, Midway, KY; son of Walter T Bradley, Sr and Sarah Craig Bradley; married Mollie Priscilla McFarland; children: Walter T III, Harry S. **EDUCATION:** Sprayberry Acad of Electronics, attended 1946-50; AUS Sch of Engrg, attended 1948-50; Univ of KY, attended 1984-85. **CAREER:** US Civil Service, electronic tech 1950-77; Lex Blue Grass Army Depot, electronics inspector 1950-77; KY Bapt UCLC, exec sec 1970-78; Star Gazer Gr Chap OES KY, p editor 1972-79; PH Conf of Gr Chap OES, southeast region rep 1976-; KY Mapping Div, draftsman 1978-80; Masonic Herald PHGL of KY, editor-in-chief 1979-; Phylaxis Soc, pres chap of editors 1984-; CCFC MW Prince Hall Grand Lodge F&AM KY, rw grand sec 1980-88. **ORGANIZATIONS:** Mem trustee Pilgrim Bapt Church 1936-86; mem PH Conf of Gr Chap OES 1973-; councilman Midway City Govt 1977-; Honorary Grand Master, MW Prince Hall Grand Lodge, 1986-; vice pres Midway Lions Club 1986-; mem Immanuel Bapt Church 1986-; mem Royal Arch Masons PHA KY, Royal & Select Masters R&SM Ohio, Knights Templars KT KY, Scottish Rite of Freemasonry KY PHA, TIM, William H Steward Council R&SM 1987-, PM & sec Lone Star Lodge 19 F&AM KY; Rt Ill Grand Recorder, M ILL Prince Hall Grand Council, 1989-. **HONORS/ACHIEVEMENTS:** Grand Worthy Patron Grand Chap OES PHA KY 1973-75; Coronated 33 Degree Scottish Rite Mason United Supreme Cncl SJ 1981; Certificate of Merit Phylaxis Soc1983; Medal of Excellence Phylaxis Soc 1984; Fellow Phylaxis Soc 1985; 100 Influential Black Masons of Amer; Hon Grand Sec MW Prince Hall Grand Lodge F&AM Dist of Columbia 1981-; Grand Master MW Prince Hall Grand Lodge F&AM of KY 1986-; author, Prince Hall Founder of Free Masonry among Black Men of America, 1988; Matthew A Henson Man on top of the world, 1989; Deacon Immanuel Baptist Church, 1989-; President Midway Lions Club, 1989-90. **MILITARY SERVICE:** AUS pfc 1948-50; Engrg Sch graduate 1949. **HOME ADDRESS:** 215 E Walnut St, PO Box 749, Midway, KY 40347.

BRADLEY, WAYNE W.
Police officer. **PERSONAL:** Born Aug 20, 1948. **EDUCATION:** Wayne State Univ; BA, 1972. **CAREER:** Detroit Police Dept, police officer 1970-; Cass Corridor Safety for Sr Proj, proj Dir 1974-75; Wayne Co Community Coll, instr 1972-; Western Reserve Fin Services Corp, sales rep 1973-; Sears Roebuck & Co, security 1973-74; Philco Ford Corp, accounts receivable & payable 1968-69; MI Consolidated Gas Co, collecltion rep 1969-70. **ORGANIZATIONS:** Appointed Notary Pub Co of Wayne MI 1974; mem Kappa Alpha Phi Frat; mem Trade Union Ldrshp Coun; second vice pres Nat Pan Helenic Coun; mem NAACP; coach 12th precinct bsbl team; coach Presentation Cath Sch Ftbl Team; mem 1st Precinct Comm Relations Assn; bd mem editorial bd & Community Reporter Newspaper; mem Detroit Police Officers Assn; police Officers Assn of MI; Guardians of MI; Concerned Police Officers for Equal Justice. **HONORS/ACHIEVEMENTS:** Recipient Military Order of Purple Heart Civilian Awd 1971; Detroit Police Dept Wound Bar 1971; Detroit Police Dept Highest Awd; Medal of Valor 1971; 12th Precinct Outstanding Service Awd 1972; Detroit Police Dept Citation 1972; listed in Leaders in Black Am. **BUSINESS ADDRESS:** 3165 Second Ave, Detroit, MI 48201.

BRADLEY, WILLIAM B.
Educator. **PERSONAL:** Born Nov 28, 1926, Rushville, IN; married Pearle E Poole; children: William, Philip, Annette, Catherine. **EDUCATION:** IN U;; BPE 1949, MPE 1955, PED 1959. **CAREER:** Western IL Univ, prof Physical Educ, 1970-; VA State Univ; dir dept of athletics & Physical Educ, 1964-70; Southern Univ, chmn, prof Physical Educ, 1960-64; Fayetteville State Univ, 1959-60; School of HPER IN Univ, grad asst 1958-59; Sumner High School, coach phys educ. 1955-58. **ORGANIZATIONS:** Am Allian for Hlth, PE & Rec; IL Assn for Hlth PE & Rec; VA Assn for Hlth PE & Rec; Am Assn of Univ Profs; Phi Epsilon Kappa Frat; Phi DeltaKappa Frat; IN Alum Assn; "I" Mens Assn of IN U; consult Nat Yth Sports Prog Pres Counc on Phys Fitness & Sports 1970-79; bd mdm McDonough Co YMCA 1970-73; mem US Olymp Bsbl Com 1972; US Olymp Wghtlftng Com 1968. **HONORS/ACHIEVEMENTS:** Alpha Phi Alpha Frat Qtr Cent Club Awd IL Assn for Hlth PE & Rec 1975; cert of apprec Kiwanis Club of Macomb 1974; serv awd YMCA 1972; cert of apprec McDonough Co Am Legion 1972; cert of Achiev VA State Coll 1970; CIAA Bsbl Coach of Yr 1968; mem All-big Ten Conf Track Team 1947; co-capt IN Univ Track Team 1947; "The Effects of Velocity & Repetition of Motion on the Devel of Isokinetic Strength of the quadriceps Muscle Group"; Rsch cncl IL Univ 1977; a Summary of the Visitat Rep & Evaluat of Nat Yth Sports Prog" 1972-79; NCAA 1977. **MILITARY SERVICE:** AUS 1st lt 1950-53. **BUSINESS ADDRESS:** Western Il Univ, Macomb, IL 61455.

BRADSHAW, DORIS MARION
Educational administrator. **PERSONAL:** Born Sep 23, 1928, Freeman, WV; daughter of Fred Merchant and Roberta Merchant; married Virgil Alanda Bradshaw; children: Victoria Lee, Gary Dwayne, Eric Alanda, Barry Douglas. **EDUCATION:** Concord Coll, BS Early Childhood Educ 1976; WV Coll of Grad Studies, MA Early Childhood Educ 1985. **CAREER:** Raleigh Co, volun Head Start 1966; RCCAA Head Start Prog, head start teach 1967-69, head start teacher asst dir 1969-70, head start dir 1969-. **ORGANIZATIONS:** 2nd vice pres WV Head Start Dirs Assn 1970-; mem WV Comm on Children & Youth 1981-; consul Head Start Review Team for the Educ & Admin portion of the Head Start Prog 1983-; mem bd of dirs Region III Head Start Assoc 1984-. **HOME ADDRESS:** 121 Sour St, Beckley, WV 25801. **BUSINESS ADDRESS:** Dir, Raleigh Co Head Start Prog, PO Box 3066 E Beckley Sta, Beckley, WV 25801.

BRADSHAW, GERALD HAYWOOD
Business executive. **PERSONAL:** Born Dec 13, 1934, Larned, KS; married Wylma Louise Thompson; children: Kim Elaine, Gerri Lynn, Douglas Haywood. **EDUCATION:** KS State Teachers Coll, 1952-56; Univ of CO, BS; Amer Savings & Loan Inst Denver, Hours on Master. **CAREER:** Equity Savings & Loan Assoc Denver, auditor, appraiser 1958-67; Denver Urb Renew Auth, real estate dir 1960-71; CO Springs Urb Renew Effort, exec dir 1971-76;

GH Bradshaw & Assoc, pres 1976-. **ORGANIZATIONS:** Past pres CO Chap Natl Assoc of Housing & Redevel Officials; sr mem Natl Assoc of Review Appraisors; broker Real Estate CO, mem bd dir Urban League of Pikes Peak Region; mem Downtown Rotary Club of CO Springs; former mem El Paso Comm Coll Site Selection Comm; former sec Denver Oppty; former chmn bd of adv comm Columbine Elem School US. **HONORS/ACHIEVEMENTS:** Pres Cert of Awd Serving on Sel Serv Bd. **BUSINESS ADDRESS:** President, GH Bradshaw & Assoc, PO Box 9744, Colorado Springs, CO 80932.

BRADSHAW, LAWRENCE A.
Educator. **PERSONAL:** Born Sep 23, 1932, Philadelphia, PA; married Mary Ellen Osgood. **EDUCATION:** Shippensburg State Coll, BS, MEd; Bucknell Univ, Grad Studies; Univ of VT; Ball State Univ; The Amer Univ, Doctoral Studies. **CAREER:** Shippensburg Area Jr High School, teacher, 1961-62; Shippensburg Area Sr High School, teacher of English & humanities, 1962-69; Shippensburg State Coll, asst dean of admissions, 1970-72, asst to vice pres for acad affairs, 1972-73, asst to pres, 1974-75, assoc prof of English. **ORGANIZATIONS:** Mem Phi Delta Kappa, Amer Guild of Organists, Natl Council of Teacher of English, Coll English Assoc, PA Council of English Teachers, Amer Assoc of Univ Admin, PA State Ed Assoc, Natl Ed Assoc, Kiwanis Club of Chambersburg PA; past pres Cumberland Valley Torch Club, Amer Assoc for Higher Ed; mem bd of dir United Fund of Chambersburg PA; bd dir Franklin Cty Sunday School Assoc; trustee Chambersburg Hosp; 1st pres Canterbury Club Shippensburg State Coll; 1st pres Amer Field Serv Shippensburg PA; head adv Class of 1968 Shippensburg Sr HS; mem Comm Concerts Assoc, vestryman & organist St Andrews Episcopal Church. **HONORS/ACHIEVEMENTS:** Hon Grad of Shippensburg State Coll; Rockefeller Fellowship in Univ Admin for 1973-74; Designated an Outstanding Ed of Amer 1974-75; listed in Who's Whoin the East 1977-78. **MILITARY SERVICE:** AUS sgt maj 1953-55. **BUSINESS ADDRESS:** Associate Professor of English, Shippensburg State College, Shippensburg, PA 17257.

BRADSHAW, WALTER H., JR.
Physician, educator. **PERSONAL:** Born Jul 15, 1938, New York, NY; married Mary E Curtin; children: Katherine, Douglas. **EDUCATION:** St Peter's Coll, BS 1960; State Univ of NY, MD 1964. **CAREER:** Dept of Psychiatry Howard Univ Hos, prof; self-empl psychtrst & ps Ychoanly; Howard Univ Coll of Med, asst prof; Howard Univ Coll of Med, dir rsdncy training 1971-77; Dept of Psychiatry Howard Univ Coll of Med, actng chmn 1973-74; Nat Inst of Mntl Hlth, staff psychiat 1968-71; priv pract 1970-. **ORGANIZATIONS:** Am Psychiat Assn 1968-; fellow Am Psychiat Assn 1977; com of Black Psychiat 1974-77; chmn 1976-77; bd of trustees consult Am Psychiat Assn 1976; Black Psychiat of Am 1971-; exec bd Black Psychiat of Am 1976-77; Am Psychoanalytic Assn 1974-; Intermit Consult US Gov Agency 1971-77; vstng lectshps Harlem Hosp 1974; Geo Wash Univ 1977; Am Grp Psychother Assn 1973; Am Psychiat Assn 1977; Sci papers publ Jour of Hosp & Comm Psyciatry 1972; sci papers pub Psychiatry Jour of Interprsnl Proc 1972; Am Jour of Psychiatry 1978; co-edtr "Soc & Psychol Dim of Behavior" 1974; USPHS 1968-70.

BRADSHAW, WAYNE
Chief executive of savings and loan association. **CAREER:** Founders Savings and and Loan Association, Los Angeles CA, chief executive. **BUSINESS ADDRESS:** Chief Executive, Founders Savings and Loan Assoc, 3910 W Martin Luther King Jr Blvd, Los Angeles, CA 90008. *

BRADY, CHARLES A.
Attorney. **PERSONAL:** Born May 01, 1945, Palestine, TX; married Ida A Powell; children: Kimberly, Charles A Jr. **EDUCATION:** Coe College, AB 1967; Howard Univ Sch of Law, JD 1970. **CAREER:** McDaniel Burton & Brady, attorney 1971-82; Charles A Brady & Assoc, attorney 1982-. **ORGANIZATIONS:** Sub instr Bus Law Federal City Coll; active in litigation of employment discrimination cases treas Inner-City & Investment Assn Inc; mem several Forensic & Legal Frat & Assns. **BUSINESS ADDRESS:** Attorney, Charles A Brady & Associates, 1343 Pennsylvania Ave SE, Washington, DC 20003.

BRADY, JULIO A.
Elected official. **PERSONAL:** Born Aug 23, 1942, St Thomas, Virgin Islands of the United States;married Maria de Freitas; children: Julie, Andrew. **EDUCATION:** Catholic Univ of Puerto Rico, BA English Philosophy 1964; New York Law School, JD 1969. **CAREER:** NY Legal Aid Soc, public defender 1969-71; District of the Virgin Islands, asst US attorney 1971-73, US attorney 1974-78; Federal Programs Office, coordinator 1979-82; Govt of the Virgin Islands, lt governor 1983-. **ORGANIZATIONS:** Pres Virgin Islands Bar Assn; cochairman United Way Campaign; state chairman Democratic Party of the Virgin Islands. **HONORS/ACHIEVEMENTS:** Amer Juris Prudence Awd for Excellence in Criminal Law New York Law School 1969. **BUSINESS ADDRESS:** Lieutenant Governor, Government of the VI, PO Box 450, St Thomas, Virgin Islands of the United States 00801.

BRADY, NELVIA M.
Chancellor. **CAREER:** Worked for nearly twenty years in education; City Colleges of Chicago, Chicago IL, interim chancellor, 1988, permanent chancellor, 1989-. **BUSINESS ADDRESS:** Chancellor, Chicago City Colleges, 1900 W Van Buren St, Chicago, IL 60612. *

BRAGG, JOSEPH L.
Reporter, journalist. **PERSONAL:** Born Jul 06, 1937, Jackson, NC; married Barbara Brandom. **EDUCATION:** Georgetown Univ Sch of Foreign Serv Diplo & Consular Affairs; Career Acad Sch of Famous Broadcasters 1967; City Univ NY, BA 1976. **CAREER:** WHN News City Hall Bureau Chief WHN Radio Storer Radio Inc, news rptr; McGovern & Nixon Pres Campaign, covered/pictures 1972; Carter & Ford Pres Campaign, covered 1976; Mutual Black Network, newsman; Mutual Broadcasting Sys, newscaster 1971; Nat Acad of TV Arts & Sci, journalist/mem 1974. **ORGANIZATIONS:** NY Chap Jonathan Davis Consistory #1 32 Deg AASR of Free Masonry So Juris Wash, DC; mem Black Cits for Fair Media 1971; pres Inner Circle; pres NY Press Club. **HONORS/ACHIEVEMENTS:** Top 100 Polit Writers in NY State. **MILITARY SERVICE:** AUS pvt 1957. **BUSINESS ADDRESS:** 400 Park Ave, New York, NY 10017.

BRAGG, ROBERT HENRY
Educator. **PERSONAL:** Born Aug 11, 1919, Jacksonville, FL; son of Robert Henry Bragg and Camille McFarland Bragg; divorced; children: Robert III, Pamela. **EDUCATION:** Illinois Inst of Tech, Chicago IL, BS 1949, MS 1951, PhD 1960. **CAREER:** Univ of CA, prof 1969-; Phys Metallurgy Lockheed Rsch Lab, mgr 1961-69; IL Inst of Tech Research Institute, sr physicist 1956-61; Portland Cement & Assn, assoc physicist 1951-56; Lawrence Berkeley Lab, principal investigator 1969-. **ORGANIZATIONS:** Life mem, NAACP; mem Amer Phys Soc; Amer Ceramic Soc; Amer Inst Metal Engr; Amer Carbon Soc; Amer Cryst Assn; AAUP; AAAS; Sigma Xi; Sigma Pi Sigma; Tau Beta Pi; Applied Space Products, dir 1969-73; Siemens-Allis, consultant; Natl Science Found, consultant; Natl Research Council, consultant; NASA, consultant; Lockheed Missiles & Space Co, consultant; faculty sponsor Black Engineering & Science Students Assn 1969-; mem Natl Technical Assoc 1978-; mem, Northern California Council of Black Professional Engineers, 1969-. **HONORS/ACHIEVEMENTS:** Published articles in technical journals & books; distingushed ser award AIME 1972, ACS 1982, NCCBPE 1985. **MILITARY SERVICE:** AUS 2nd lt 1942-46. **BUSINESS ADDRESS:** Professor, University of California, 370 Hearst Mining, Berkeley, CA 94720.

BRAGG, ROBERT LLOYD
Educator. **PERSONAL:** Born Nov 03, 1916, Jackson, MS; son of Jubie Barton Bragg Sr and Anna A Smith Bragg. **EDUCATION:** FL A&M Univ, BS 1936; Boston Univ, MA 1938; Columbia Univ, MD 1952; Harvard School of Publ Health, MPH 1955. **CAREER:** Human Rel Serv of Wellesley Inc, dir 1963-73; MA Genl Hosp, coord comm mental health training prog 1965-73; Harvard Med School MA Genl Hosp, asst prof 1970-73; Univ of Miami School of Med, assoc dean spec proj 1976-, dir 1974-, prof of psych 1979-. **ORGANIZATIONS:** Mem Amer Psych Assn, Dade County Med Assn, S FL Psych Soc, Behavioral Sci Inst of Miami Inc; Florida Medical Assn; Natl Medical Assn; Florida Medical; Dental Pharmaceutical Assn; Black Psychiatrists of America. **HONORS/ACHIEVEMENTS:** Distinguished Alumnus Awd FL A&M Univ 1964. **MILITARY SERVICE:** Med Adm Corps capt 1941-46. **HOME ADDRESS:** 1199 NW 88th Street, Miami, FL 33150.

BRAILEY, TROY
Legislator. **PERSONAL:** Born Aug 26, 1916, Lynchburg, SC; married Chessie; children: Alice Faye (Toriente), Norman. **EDUCATION:** New York Univ. **ORGANIZATIONS:** Mem Maryland Ho of Del; former rep Brotherhood of Sleeping Car Porters; vice-chmn Balti City Deleg to the House; chmn March on Wash 1963; former chmn Balti Chap Am Labor Cncl. **HONORS/ACHIEVEMENTS:** Hon as Unsung Hero MD Chap Am Labor Cncl 1965; 1st black ever named to one of city's 2 leadership positions 1970. **BUSINESS ADDRESS:** 2405 Baker St, Baltimore, MD 21216.

BRAITHWAITE, GORDON L.
Business executive. **PERSONAL:** Born in Atlantic City, NJ. **EDUCATION:** Hunter Coll; UCLA; Santa Monica Jr Coll; Herbert Berghof Acting Studios. **CAREER:** Natl Endowment for the Arts, dir/office of special projects; City of NY Dept Cultural Affairs, pgm spcl. **ORGANIZATIONS:** Mem adv com Comm Gallery Brooklyn Mus 1970-72; 100 Black Men Inc; NAACP. **BUSINESS ADDRESS:** C/O Nat Endowment for the Arts, Washington, DC 20506.

BRAITHWAITE, JAMES ROLAND
Educator, musician. **PERSONAL:** Born Feb 28, 1927, Boston, MA; married Alexandrina Stewart; children: Elisa Diane, Roland Alexander. **EDUCATION:** Boston U, MusB 1948, MA 1950, PhD 1967. **CAREER:** Talladega Coll, assoc prof of music, 1952-67, dir curriculum program 13 coll, 1967-71, head music dept, 1969-76, dean of the coll, 1974-81, acting dean of the coll, 1983-84, buel gordon gallagher prof of humanities & coll organist. **ORGANIZATIONS:** Organist St Mark Congregational Ch 1946-47; organist Trinity Lutheran Ch 1948-50, 1952; organist Episcopal Ch at Harvard and Radcliffe 1960-61. **HONORS/ACHIEVEMENTS:** Organ Recitals in Southeast and Boston Passim 1952-; participant NEH Summer Seminar for Coll Tchrs HarvardUniv 1982; NEH Fellowship for Coll Tchrs 1985; "A Minority Perception of Liberal Education" Liberal Edn; LXVII 3 1981; lecture "The Richard Allen Hymnals of 1801" Smithsonian Inst 1987; reprint "Richard AllenHymnal of 1801 with the Historical Commn Mother Bethel AME Church 1987; originality in the 1801 Hymnals of Richard Allen prepared for the Festschrift for Eileen Southern 1987. **MILITARY SERVICE:** AUS Artillery sgt 1st class 1950-52. **BUSINESS ADDRESS:** Professor of Humanities, Talladega Coll, Talladega Coll, Talladega, AL 35160.

BRAITHWAITE, MARK WINSTON
Dentist. **PERSONAL:** Born Jul 15, 1954, New York, NY; son of David and Grace; married Carlene V. **EDUCATION:** Bowdoin Coll, BA Biology 1976; Columbia Univ, attended 1977; State Univ of NY at Buffalo Sch of Dental Medicine, DDS 1982. **CAREER:** Private Practice Assoc, dentist/general practitioner 1983-85; NY City Dept of Health Bureau of Dentistry, general practitioner dentist 1984-87; Joint Diseases North Genl Hosp, general practitioner dentist 1985-; Sydenham Hosp Neighborhood Family Care Ctr, attending dentist 1987-; Harlem Hosp Ctr, attending dentist 1987-. **ORGANIZATIONS:** License/certification Northeast Regional Dental Boards 1982, Natl Dental Boards 1982; licensed in NY, MD, Washington DC; mem Natl Dental Assoc, Natl Soc of Dental Practitioners, Dental Health Serv Corp; mem Harlem Dental Soc, SUNY at Buffalo Sch of Dental Medicine Alumni Assoc; mem comm on pharmacy and therapeutics, antibiotic subcomm Joint Disease North General Hosp; mem Amer Dental Assoc. **HONORS/ACHIEVEMENTS:** Teaching assistant 1978 & 1979 State Univ of NY at Buffalo Sch of Medicine; teaching assistant 1981-82 State Univ of NY at Buffalo Sch of Dental Medicine 1981-82; Special Academic Achievement Periodontology 1981-82; Attending of the Year, 1988-89. **HOME ADDRESS:** 159 Midwood St, Brooklyn, NY 11225.

BRAMBLE, LIVINGSTON
Professional boxer. **PERSONAL:** Children: 1 son. **CAREER:** Fight against Ray Mancini, boxer lightweight champion. **BUSINESS ADDRESS:** c/o Lou Duva, New Jersey Sports Prod Inc, 214 Lackawanna Ave, West Paterson, NJ 07424.

BRAME, WALTER MELVYN
Association president and chief executive officer. **PERSONAL:** Born Mar 21, 1946, Henderson, NC; son of Walter Brame and Rosetta Jeffreys (deceased); married Veronica Watford, Jul 19, 1969; children: Kenyatta, Abayomi, William, Tamika. **EDUCATION:** North Carolina Central Univ, North Carolina, BA, 1968; Wayne State Univ, Detroit, MI, MA, 1973; Atlanta Univ, Atlanta, GA, 1984; Western Michigan Univ, Kalamazoo, MI, EdD, 1989. **CA-**

REER: Found for Community Devel, Durham, NC, dir, 1968-69; Univ of Maryland, Washington, DC, training officer, 1969; Wayne County Community Coll, Detroit, MI, Comm Coord, 1973-74; Detroit Urban League, Detroit, MI, dept dir, 1974-79; Grand Rapids Urban League, Grand Rapids, MI, pres/CEO, 1979-. **ORGANIZATIONS:** Mem, Grand Rapids Rotary Club, 1980-; founding mem, Comm for Representative Govt, 1982-; bd mem, Grand Rapids Area Transit Authority, 1985-; founder & chairperson, Grand Rapids Voter Coalition, 1985-; vice basileus, Omega Psi Phi Fraternity, 1985-; bd mem, St Marys Health Care Corp, 1987-, Kent County Defenders Office, 1987-; Grand Rapids Area Employment & Training Council, 1988-. **HONORS/ACHIEVEMENTS:** Distinguished Humanitarian, True Light Baptist Church, 1988; Phyllis Scott Activist, Grand Rapids GIANTS Comm, 1988; Man of the Year, Madison Park School, 1986; fellowship, Atlanta Univ, 1984; Excellence in Serv, US Dept of HUD, 1981; author, Competencies Needed by a Chief Exec Officer of a Local Urban League, 1989, A System of Accountability and Control, 1989, Required Reading for Educ Blacks, 1988, The Role of the Pres and Chairperson of the Bd, 1986. **MILITARY SERVICE:** USAF, sergeant, 1969-73; Air Force Commendation Medal for Outstanding Achievement in Human Relations. **BUSINESS ADDRESS:** President and CEO, Grand Rapids Urban League, 745 Eastern Avenue SE, Grand Rapids, MI 49503.

BRAMWELL, FITZGERALD BURTON
Educational administrator, chemist. **PERSONAL:** Born May 16, 1945, Brooklyn, NY; son of Fitzgerald Bramwell and Lula Burton Bramwell; married Charlott Burns; children: Fitzgerald, Elizabeth, Jill, Timothy. **EDUCATION:** Columbia Coll, BA 1966; Univ of MI, MS 1967, PhD 1970. **CAREER:** Esso Rsch & Engineering, rsch chemist 1970-71; NYU PREP Program Chem, chmn 1971; CUNY Doctoral Faculty, asst prof 1971-74, assoc prof 1975-79, prof 1980-, Graduate Studies and Research, acting dean. **ORGANIZATIONS:** Consultant Bell Labs; consultant Burgess Publishing Co; bd of dirs NY Section Amer Chem Soc 1983-84, 1988-89; chair/fellowship panel Natl Rsch Council 1983-84; advisory bd Staten Island Urban League 1984-88; consultant New York City Bd of Educ; dir-at-large NY Section Amer Chem Soc 1986. **HONORS/ACHIEVEMENTS:** IAESTE Intl Exchange Fellow 1966; Phi Lambda Upsilon 1967; Phillips Petroleum Fellow 1968; Allied Chem Fellow 1969; numerous rsch grants prof publications and textbooks 1970-; Sigma Xi Hon Rsch organ 1971; Rsch Grants in excess of $2,000,000 last two years; Natl Science Found Faculty Devel Grant 1977-78; Fellow of the Acad of Science & Human of the City Univ of NY 1980; 6 books 30 articles in areas of Physical Chem and Chem Educ; Fellow of Amer Inst of Chemists. **BUSINESS ADDRESS:** Dean Graduate Studies and Research, CityUniv of New York, Brooklyn College, Brooklyn, NY 11210.

BRAMWELL, HENRY
Judge. **PERSONAL:** Born Sep 03, 1919, Brooklyn, NY; son of Henry and Florence; married Ishbel W. **EDUCATION:** Brooklyn Law School, LLB 1948; Brooklyn Coll, LLD (Hon) 1979. **CAREER:** US Atty Office, asst atty 1953-61; NY State Rent Comm, assoc attny 1961-63; Civil Ct City NY, judge 1969-75; US Dist, judge 1975-. **ORGANIZATIONS:** Mem Natl Fed NY, Amer & Brooklyn Bar Assoc; mem bd of trustees Brooklyn Law School 1979. **MILITARY SERVICE:** Sgt 1941-45. **BUSINESS ADDRESS:** District Judge, US Courthouse, Brooklyn, NY 11201.

BRAMWELL, PATRICIA ANN
Social worker. **PERSONAL:** Born May 17, 1941, Brooklyn, NY; daughter of Arthur L Bramwell and Miriam Campbell Bramwell. **EDUCATION:** Ctrl State Univ, BA 1965; Fordham Univ Sch of Social Work, MSW 1969; Hofstra Univ, cert of managerial studies & labor relations 1980; Para Legal Cert. **CAREER:** The Society for Seamen's Children, foster home care 1966-70; E NY Mntl Health Clinic, grp therapy 1977; The City Coll SEEK Prog, psychol couns 1970-. **ORGANIZATIONS:** Assn of Black Soc Workers; cert State Soc Worker; vice chairperson Comm Sch Bd Dist 16 1975-77; asst sec Chama Day Care Ctr 1974-76; life mem Natl Council of Negro Women; bd of dir Forham Univ Sch of Social Serv Alumni Assn; Brooklyn Community Planning Bd #3; Community Bd Kings County Hosp. **BUSINESS ADDRESS:** Prof, Dept of Special Programs, City College of the City Univ of New York, 138th St and Convent Ave, NAC 4/137, New York, NY 10031.

BRANCH, ADDISON A., SR.
Educator. **PERSONAL:** Born Dec 19, 1903, Lynchburg, VA; daughter of Albert Branch and Alice Branch; married Rose Hayes Branch, Sep 15, 1924; children: Addison A Branch Jr. **EDUCATION:** VA Union Univ, BS Chemistry 1923, MA Educ 1925; Columbia Univ, MA 1930; Harvard Univ, Administration in Higher Educ 1956. **CAREER:** LeMoyne Coll, professional chem, chmn natural science div 1931-52; Tougaloo Coll, academic dean 1952-65, interim pres 1955-56, vice pres 1965-75. **ORGANIZATIONS:** Served on numerous bds of community activities; one of founders and first pres Memphis & Shelby Co Civic Clubs; chmn of local policy comm Headstart; officer of Boule, Sigma Pi Phi Frat; life mem Omega Psi Phi, NAACP; life & golden heritage mem NAACP; ch ed comm Shelby Co Historical Commission. **HONORS/ACHIEVEMENTS:** Silver Beaver Awd Boy Scouts of Amer 1964; Outstanding Educator of Amer 1971; Golder Heritage Membership NAACP; numerous community awds and plaques; Doctor of Laws, Tougaloo College, 1975. **MILITARY SERVICE:** Student Army Training Corp VA Union Univ.

BRANCH, B. LAWRENCE
Personnel administrator. **PERSONAL:** Born Sep 13, 1937, New York, NY; married Elva C; children: Erica Danielle, Gabrielle Angelique. **EDUCATION:** Univ of IL, 1956-59; S IL U, BS 1960-61. **CAREER:** Merck & Co Inc, dir equal employment affairs 1972-, asst to vice pres personnel 1968-72, employment supr 1966-68; Chesebrough-Ponds Inc, wage & salary analyst1964-66; Traveler's Ins Co, underwriter 1963-64; EEO Cornell Univ Sch of Ind & Labor Rel, prof 1972-; Nat Urban League BEEP Pgm, vist prof 1972-. **ORGANIZATIONS:** Bd mem Cncl of Concerned Black Exec 1968-70; bd mem Assn for Integration of Mgmt 1970-74; bd co-chmn Interracial Cncl for Bus Oppor NY 1973-78. **BUSINESS ADDRESS:** Merck & Company, PO Box 2000, Rahway, NJ 07065.

BRANCH, CLIFFORD
Athlete. **PERSONAL:** Born Aug 01, 1948, Houston, TX. **EDUCATION:** Wharton Co Jr Coll. **CAREER:** Univ Co LA Raiders, wide receiver 1972-. **HONORS/ACHIEVEMENTS:** Led NFL in pass recv yds 1092; in touchdown recpn 13; led NFL for td recpt 12 1976; Pro Bowl 1974, 75, 76, 77; AFC Chmsp Game 1973-76; NFL Chmsp Game 1976. **BUSINESS ADDRESS:** Los Angeles Raiders, 332 Center St, El Segundo, CA 90245.

BRANCH, DOROTHY L.
Clergywoman. **PERSONAL:** Born Feb 04, 1912, Chicago, IL; daughter of Nettie Sutton; married Lemmie. **EDUCATION:** N Baptist Theological Seminary, ThB; Northwestern Univ & Garrett Biblical Inst, MA; Divinity School Univ of Chicago, Scholarship Awardee; Burton Theological Seminary, ThD. **CAREER:** Commonwealth Comm Church, founder/pastor 1946-; Douglas Park Devel Corp, pres 1968-; Bd 508 Eight City Coll of Chicago, trustee 1967-; Rehabilitation Serv Public Asst, psychologist; Cook County Rehabilitation Servs, supvr; Inst Juvenile Research, counselor. **ORGANIZATIONS:** Co-founder Funeral Dir Wives Assn; pres Gr Lawndale Conservation; mem Gov Walker's Task Force; chmn Lawndale Residents Urban Renewal 1954-75; vice pres Citizen Housing Commn Chicago 1969-75; bd dir Scars YMCA 1963-; mem Council Religious Leaders Chicago Urban League 1970-75. **HONORS/ACHIEVEMENTS:** The Intl Yr of the Woman Citation Israeli Parliament for bringing 21 Goodwill pilgrims to Palestine after 6 day war 1967; liquidated $228,000 debt on Lanon Stone Church property 1964-74. **BUSINESS ADDRESS:** Commonwealth Comm Church, 140 W 81st St, Chicago, IL 60620.

BRANCH, ELDRIDGE STANLEY
Clergyman. **PERSONAL:** Born Oct 29, 1906, Houston, TX; married Delcenia Mangum. **EDUCATION:** Conroe Coll, AB 1928, BTh 1931, PD 1936. **CAREER:** Natl Bapt Foreign Mission Natl Baptist Conv of Amer, sec 1949-75; Fourth Mission Baptist Ch, pastor. **ORGANIZATIONS:** Exec edtr Globe Advoc Newsp; sec Foreign Mission Bapt Gen Conv of TX; vice pres bd dir Stand Sav Assn; YMCA; bd mem Conroe Coll; NAACP; bd trust Bishop Coll; 3 hous proj in TX. **HONORS/ACHIEVEMENTS:** Hon degree Bishop Coll. **BUSINESS ADDRESS:** Pastor, Fourth Mission Baptist Ch, PO Box 8147, Houston, TX 77004.

BRANCH, G. MURRAY
Clergyman, educator. **PERSONAL:** Born Apr 18, 1914, Prince Edward Co, VA; married Jamima Wall; children: Dianne Everett Branch Nunnally. **EDUCATION:** VA Union U, BS 1938; Andover Newton Theol Sch, BD 1941; Drew U, AM 1946; Hebrew Union Coll, further grad study 1951-52;additional grad study at Drew Univ 1952-53, 1958-59,1962-63. **CAREER:** First Baptist Church, Madison NJ, pastor, 1941-44; Natl Student & Coun YMCA, field sec, 1944-47; Morehouse Coll, asst to assoc prof, 1947-59; Interdenominational Theology Center, assoc prof, 1959-79; Morehouse School of Religion Interdenominational Theology Center, dir, 1963-66; Dexter Ave Baptist Church, Montgomery AL, pastor, 1966-72; Extension Dept ITC, dir, 1971-77; Dexter Ave King Memorial Baptist Church Montgomery, pastor, 1978-; Old Testament Emeritus Iterdenominational Theology Center, prof, 1980-. **ORGANIZATIONS:** Pres Morris Co, NJ NAACP 1942-44; mem Soc of Biblical Lit; Am Acad of Religion; Am Sch of Oriental Research; Soc for Values in Higher Edn; FriendshipBapt Church Atlanta GA 1947-;Kent Fellowship 1952; Soc for Scientific Study of Religion;Atlanta Brd of Educ Area I Adv Com 1954-57; vice polemarch Kappa Alpha Psi Frat Atlanta Alumni CHapt 1955-58; vice pres Comm of Southern Churchmen 1962-65; adv comm west side branch Butler St YMCA Atlanta 1963-66; bd dir Cleveland av YMCA Montgomery Al 1969-72; bd dir Koinonia Partners Inc Americus GA 1971-77; DD Honorary Benedict Coll Columbia SC 1973. **BUSINESS ADDRESS:** Pastor, Dexter Ave King Mem Bapt Chrch, 454 Dexter Ave, Montgomery, AL 36104.

BRANCH, GEORGE
Elected city official. **PERSONAL:** Born Oct 20, 1928, Seaboard, NC. **EDUCATION:** ICBO Rutgers Bus Admin Course, 1970; Rutgers Univ, Sociol & Vocab Improvement 1967-68, Urban Studies. **ORGANIZATIONS:** Dir Project Pride; past master Samson Lodge 66; bd mem Neward Bd of Ed; founder Supt Parents Students Forum; promoter Boxing Match Maker; trainer Prof Trainer for Boxers; mem of exec bd NAACP 3 yrs; pres W Distr Comm Precinct Council; mem United Comm Corp, N Jersey Transit Advisory Comm. **HONORS/ACHIEVEMENTS:** Outstanding Serv to the Youth of Newark Awd Queen of Angels Church 1970; Civic Awd for Comm Partic Beta Chap Theta Nu Sigma Natl Sor 1970; Man of the Year Awd Central Ward Boys Clubs 1973; Outstanding Achievement Awd Essex Cty of Black Churchmen 1974. **MILITARY SERVICE:** USNG corpl 2 yrs 3 mo. **HOME ADDRESS:** 185 Bruce St, Newark, NJ 07103. **BUSINESS ADDRESS:** Councilmember, City of Newark, 920 Broad St, Newark, NJ 07102.

BRANCH, GERALDINE BURTON
Physician. **PERSONAL:** Born Oct 20, 1908, Savannah, GA; married Robert Henry; children: Elizabeth Doggette, Robert Henry III. **EDUCATION:** Hunter Coll, BA 1931; NY Med Coll, MD 1936; UCLA, MPH 1961. **CAREER:** Private practice, physician ob/gyn 1938-53; LA Dept of Health Svcs, dist health officer 1964-71, reg dir health serv 1971-74; US CA, assoc clinical prof comm med 1966; Watts Health Found Inc, dir preventive health serv 1976-78, med dir 1978-. **ORGANIZATIONS:** Bd of govs LA Co Med Assn 1966-70; bd of dir Am Lung Assn 1970-76; pres Federated Kings Daughters Clubs 1966-70; mem Nat Med Assn 1968; Walter Gray Crump Fellowship NY Med Coll 1932-36. **HONORS/ACHIEVEMENTS:** Published "Study of Gonorrhea in Infants & Children" Public Health Reports 1964, "Study of Use of Neighborhood Aides in Control of a Diphtheria Outbreak" 1966; "Study of Use of Non-Physicians in HB Control" Preventive Med 1977. **BUSINESS ADDRESS:** Medical Dir, Watts Health Foundation, 10300 South Compton Ave, Los Angeles, CA 90002.

BRANCH, HARRISON
Educator, artist. **PERSONAL:** Born Jun 06, 1947, New York, NY; son of Harrison Branch Sr and Margaret Williams-Branch; married Jacqueline Susan Hyde; children: Harrison III, Alexander Hyde. **EDUCATION:** SF Art Inst, BFA 1970; Yale Univ Sch of Art, MFA 1972. **CAREER:** OR State Univ, asst prof art 1972-77; Owens Valley Photograph Workshop 1978-86; OR State Univ, assoc prof/prof art 1977-. **ORGANIZATIONS:** Guest lectr & photographer Univ of Bridgeport 1970-71; published photographs "Think Black" Bruce Publishing Co NY 1969. **HONORS/ACHIEVEMENTS:** Recip Alice Kimball Travelling Fellowship Yale Univ Sch of Art 1972; Research Grant OR State Found 1974; Research Grant OR State Univ Grad Sch 1976-77. **HOME ADDRESS:** 1104 N W 29th St, Corvallis, OR 97330. **BUSINESS ADDRESS:** Professor of Art/Photography, Oregon StateUniv, Dept Art, Corvallis, OR 97331.

BRANCH, OTIS LINWOOD
Educational administrator. **PERSONAL:** Born Sep 07, 1943, Norfolk, VA. **EDUCATION:** Chicago Conservatory Coll, MusB 1966; Chicago Mus Coll of Roosevelt Univ, MusM 1974. **CAREER:** LaGrange Park (N) Public Schools, chmn music dept, 1970-; Chicago

Conservatory Coll, dean admissions & records, 1979-82; Bremen High School, Midlothian IL, dir choral music & humanities, 1970-. **ORGANIZATIONS:** Curriculum writer State Bd of Educ Elem Mus IL; curriculum writer State Bd of Educ Allied Arts IL; evaluator N Central Assn and State Bd of Educ IL Music Educator's Natl Conf; Natl Educ Assn; Humanities Educators Assn;. **BUSINESS ADDRESS:** Dir Choral Music/Humanities, Bremen High School, 15203 S Pulaski Rd, Midlothian, IL 60445.

BRANCH, WILLIAM BLACKWELL
Playwright, producer, professor. **PERSONAL:** Born Sep 11, 1927, New Haven, CT; son of Rev James Matthew Branch and Iola Douglas; divorced; children: Rochelle Ellen. **EDUCATION:** Northwestern U, BS 1949; Columbia U, MFA 1958; Columbia U, Postgrad Study 1958-59; Yale Univ Resident Fellow, 1965-66. **CAREER:** Theatre TV & Motion Pictures, playwright 1951-; The Jackie Robinson Column in NY Post and Syndication, co-author 1958-60; Channel 13 Educ TV NYC, staff writer/producer 1962-64; Columbia Sch of Arts, assoc in film 1968-69; Universal Studios, screenwriter 1968-69; NBC News, producer 1972-73; William Branch Assocs, pres 1973-; Univ of Maryland, vstg prof 1979-82; Luce Fellow Williams Coll 1983; Cornell Univ, prof 1985-; Univ of California, regents lectr 1985. **ORGANIZATIONS:** New York City Bd of Educ, consult 1975-77; consult Ford Foundation Office of Communications 1976; natl adv bd Ctr for the Book Library of Congress 1979-83; The African-American Theatre Journal, founding mem, editorial bd 1987-; treasurer, Natl Conference on African American Theatre 1987-. **HONORS/ACHIEVEMENTS:** Hannah B Del Vecchio Awd Columbia 1958; Robert E Sherwood Awd for Light in the Southern Sky 1958; Blue Ribbon Awd for Still a Brother: Inside the Negro Middle Class, Amer Film Festival 1969; author "Fifty Steps Toward Freedom" 1959; works include (theatre) A Medal for Willie 1951, In Splendid Error 1954, A Wreath for Udomo 1960, To Follow the Phoenix 1960, Baccalaureate 1975; TV, Light in the Southern Sky 1958; Still a Brother, 1969 (Emmy Award nominee); documentary TV series Afro American Perspectives 1974-83; exec producer Black Perspective on the News, Pub Broadcasting System 1978-79; A Letter from Booker T 1987; screen, "Together for Days" 1971. **MILITARY SERVICE:** AUS 1951-53. **BUSINESS ADDRESS:** President, William Branch Associates, 53 Cortlandt Ave, New Rochelle, NY 10801.

BRANCH, WILLIAM MCKINLEY
Judge. **PERSONAL:** Born May 10, 1918, Forkland, AL; married Alberta; children: William, Thaddeus, Patricia, Alberta, Malcolm, Vivian, Wanda. **EDUCATION:** Selma U, AB 1944; Union Theol Sch Selma U, DD, LLD 1976; AL State U, BS 1956. **CAREER:** Ebenezer Bapt Ch, pastor. **ORGANIZATIONS:** Probate judge/chmn Greene Co Commn; co-chmn/past pres Greene Co Educ Assn; past chmn Greene Co Housing Auth; co-chmn Greene Co Dem Exec Com 1976-77; bd dir Greene Co Hlth Svc; mem Nat Assn Co Commr; AL Probate Judge's Assn; Assn Co Commn; Mental Hlth Assn AL; mem NACO Transp Steering Comm; chmn Rural Transp Comm; AL Law Enforcement Planning Agency State Supervisory Bd; mem State-Wide Hlth Cncl AL; mem Lt Gov Staff; Christian Valley Bapt Ch. **HONORS/ACHIEVEMENTS:** Cert of Merit Birmingham Urban League Guild; Cert Recog Fed Greene Co Empl; Leadership Award AugurnUniv Exten Svc; Distgsd Serv Award Greene Co Urban League; Award Outstand Courage S Polit Arena; Hon Lt Col Aide de Camp; Cert Apprctn TN Tombigee Waterway.

BRANCH-SIMPSON, GERMAINE GAIL
Educator. **PERSONAL:** Born Apr 25, 1950, Philadelphia, PA; daughter of Earl Joseph Branch and Germaine Lopez Jackson Branch; children: Kwadjo. **EDUCATION:** Bennett College, BA 1969; Montclair State Coll, MA 1971; Ohio State Univ, PhD 1984. **CAREER:** Orange, NJ Bd of Educ, teacher 1969-71; Guilford Co NC Neighborhood Youth Corps, ed specialist 1971-73; OH Dominican Coll Upward Bound, assoc dir 1973-77; Ohio State Univ, grad admin assoc 1978-82; OH Bd of Regents, rsch assoc 1980; Ohio State Univ, dir minority assistance program 1982-. **ORGANIZATIONS:** Mem Amer Personnel & Guidance Assoc 1978-; mem Natl Assn of Women Deans & Counselors 1978-; adv bd mem OSU Upward Bound 1979-; team sec Mifflin Youth Assn 1985; mem Natl Assn Student Personnel Admin 1985-; consultant State of OH 1986; mem Northwest Coll Placement Assn 1986; mem, Assn for the Study of Classical African Civilizations 1986-; mem, Assn of Black Psychologists 1985-. **HONORS/ACHIEVEMENTS:** Conference Presentation, Black Student Development, An Africentric Perspective 1988. **HOME ADDRESS:** 2607 Caralee Place, Columbus, OH 43219. **BUSINESS ADDRESS:** Director, Minority Assistance, Ohio State Univ-Coll of Bus, 1775 College Rd, Columbus, OH 43210.

BRANCHE, GILBERT M.
Government official. **PERSONAL:** Born Mar 16, 1932, Philadelphia, PA; son of Merwin E Branche and Wilma M Brown Branche; married Jean Overton; children: Andrea, Dolores. **EDUCATION:** Univ of PA, B of Political Sci 1968; PA State Police Exec Devel Course, Cert 1974; FBI Academy, Cert 1975. **CAREER:** Philadelphia Police Dept, policeman, sgt, lieutenant, captain 1957-74; Philadelphia Dist Atty Office, dep chief co detective 1970-74; Philadelphia Police Dept, inspector 1974-78; Philadelphia Dist Atty Office, chief co detective 1978-retired; Deputy Sec of Fraud and Abuse Investigation & Recovery for Commonwealth of PA. **ORGANIZATIONS:** Bd dir, vice pres Safe St 1968-80; police consult Assn Consult Wash, DC 1972-77; pres Blacks in Blue 1974-76; pres Natl Orgn of Black Law Enforce Exec 1979-; commr Standard & Accred of Police 1979-; past pres Circle NOBLE 1983-; Free & Accepted Mason. **HONORS/ACHIEVEMENTS:** Meritorious Serv Award Philadelphia City Council 1968; Man of the Year Award Voice Pub 1978; Humanitarian Award Chapel of Four Chaplains 1979; Distinguished Career Award Co Detective Assn of PA 1980; Humanitarian Awd Natl Orgn of Black Law Enforcement Exec 1983; Trail Blazer in Law Enforcement Awds State of PA 1985; James Reaves Man of the Year Awd 1986; inducted into PA Policeman Hall of Fame, International Police 1988. **MILITARY SERVICE:** USAF s/sgt 1951-55; Good Conduct Medal; Korean Serv Medal. **BUSINESS ADDRESS:** Deputy Secretary, PA Dept of Public Welfare, Fraud & Abuse Investigation, PO Box 8016 300 N Second St, Harrisburg, PA 17105.

BRANCHE, WILLIAM C., JR.
Scientist. **PERSONAL:** Born Sep 05, 1934, Washington, DC; son of William C Sr and Frances; married Eloise; children: Christine, Michael, Marc. **EDUCATION:** OH Wesleyan Univ, BA 1956; George Washington Univ, MS 1959; Cath Univ of Amer, PhD 1969. **CAREER:** Dept of Microbiology, virologist 1958-61; Gastroenteritis Stud Sec, chief 1961-68; Niesseria Meningitis Stud Sec, chief 1968-72; Walter Reed Army Inst ofRsch, safety officer div of comm dis & immun 1971-, safety officer dept of bact dis 1971-76; Inf Dis Serv Lab, chief 1972-76; USAMRD Ad Hoc Comm on Bact & Myopic Dis, asst proj dir 1974-; Walter Reed Army Inst of Rsch, health sci admin 1976-78; NIH Bacteriology & Mycology SS Div of Rsch Grant,health sci admin & exec sec 1979-. **ORGANIZATIONS:** Mem Equal Employment Opportunity Council Walter Reed Army Med Ctr 1969-, Walter Reed Army Inst of Rsch Inc Awd Comm 1969-73, Walter Reed Army Inst of Rsch Ed Bd 1969-; vp, bd of dir Pointer Ridge Swim & Rac, Club 1971-76; asst prof Fed City Coll & Natl Inst of Rsch Camp 1971-; chmn Walter Reed Army Inst of Rsch Inc Awd Comm 1973-; mem bd of dir South Bowie Boys & Girls Club 1976-; pres, bd of dir Pointer Ridge Swim & Rac Club 1976; mem Amer Soc of Microbiology, Sigma Xi, Amer Wildlife Soc; Staff Training in Extramural Programs Committee (STEP) NIH 1985-88. **HONORS/ACHIEVEMENTS:** 1st black Teaching Assistantship George Washington Univ 1956-58; Rsch Grant USN George Washington School of Med 1956-58; Citizen of the Year Awd Kiwanas Club of Bowie 1980; publ numerous articles; NIH Merit Award 1989. **BUSINESS ADDRESS:** Health Sci Admin, Exec Sec, Natl Inst of Health, Division of Research Grants, Bethesda, MD 20805.

BRAND, DOLLAR See IBRAHIM, ABDULLAH

BRANDFORD, NAPOLEON
Business executive. **PERSONAL:** Born Feb 23, 1952, East Chicago, IN; married Sharon Delores Bush. **EDUCATION:** Purdue Univ, BA 1974; Univ of S Calif, MPA 1978. **CAREER:** Union Carbide-Linde Air Div, summer intern 1970; Standard Oil of Indiana, Summer intern 1971-74; Pacific Telephone, asst transportation coordinator 1976-78; Dade County Finance Dept, asst finance dir 1978-83; Shearson Lehman Bros, Inc, vice president-public finance 1984-; Grigsby, Brandford Inc, dir public finance 1985-. **ORGANIZATIONS:** Member Natl Forum of Black Public Administrators 1983-; executive secretary Builders Mutual Surety Co 1984-85; board member Urban Economic Development Corporation 1984-; committee member Mayor's Advisory Committee for International Trade and Foreign Investment Program 1985-. **HONORS/ACHIEVEMENTS:** Basketball Hall of Fame East Chicago Roosevelt 1975; Employee Suggestion Award Dade Cty Manager's Office 1981; Recipient Leadership Miami Alumni Assoc 1982. **BUSINESS ADDRESS:** Dir Public Finance Div, Grigsby, Brandford Inc, 230 California St, San Francisco, CA 94111.

BRANDON, BRUMSIC, JR.
Cartoonist. **PERSONAL:** Born Apr 10, 1927, Washington, DC; married Rita Broughton; children: Linda M, Brumsic III, Barbara A. **EDUCATION:** NYU, 1945-46. **CAREER:** J R O'Brien Assoc, illustrator 1953-55; RCA Serv Co, asst art dir 1955-57; Bray Studios Inc Motion Pictures, designer animator 1957-69; WPIX TV, artist performer 1969-82; cartoonist. **ORGANIZATIONS:** Cartoonist LA Times Syndicate "Luther" Comic Strip 1970-; cartoonist Black Resources Inc 1976-; cartoonist Freelance 1970-; forum mem White House Conf on Children 1969-70; bd of dir Afro Am Bicentennial Corp 1976; bd of dir Intl Art of Jazz 1985. **HONORS/ACHIEVEMENTS:** 6 books Paul S Eriksson Inc; numerous articles Freedomways; article "The Crisis" 1981; work in many art exhibits Montreal CN Berlin Germany. **MILITARY SERVICE:** AUS sgt; German Occupation 1950-52.

BRANDON, CARL RAY
Therapist. **PERSONAL:** Born Nov 15, 1953, Port Gibson, MS; son of Alonzo Brandon and Marjorie Williams Brandon; married Debra Cynthoria Knox, Jun 02, 1984. **EDUCATION:** Alcorn State Univ, BS 1976; Alcorn State Univ, MS 1984; additional studies, Univ of Southern Mississippi, Alcorn State Univ. **CAREER:** Claiborne Cty Public Schools, counselor 1977-84; Southwest Mental Health Complex, case mgr II 1984-88, therapist 1988-; Thompson Funeral Home, Port Gibson MS funeral dir, 1971-. **ORGANIZATIONS:** Mem MS Assoc of Ed 1977-, MS Counseling Assn 1981-, MS Deputy Sheriffs Assn 1982-, MS Assn of Constable 1984-; Sunday school teacher, bd of deacon China Grove MB Church Port Gibson MS; Grand Gulf State Park, Port Gibson MS, bd of dirs 1988; State of Mississippi, Certified Hunter Safety, instructor 1981. **HOME ADDRESS:** Rte 01 Box 138, Port Gibson, MS 39150.

BRANDT, LILLIAN B.
Business executive. **PERSONAL:** Born Jul 04, 1919, New York, NY; married George W Sr. **EDUCATION:** City Coll NY. **CAREER:** James Daugherty Ltd, partner/vp/sec; Teal Traing Inc, 2 1/2 yrs; Sam Friedlander Inc, 27 yrs; Capri Frocks Inc, 2 yrs; Ben Reig Inc, 1 yr. **ORGANIZATIONS:** Mem Fashion Sales Guild; mem Fashion Cncl of NY Inc.

BRANHAM, GEORGE, III
Professional bowler. **PERSONAL:** Born in Detroit, MI. **CAREER:** PBA, professional bowler. **HONORS/ACHIEVEMENTS:** Southern CA Junior Bowler of the Year 1983; first Black to win a Professional Bowlers Assoc tournament.

BRANKER, JULIAN MICHAEL
Automobile dealer. **CAREER:** Mike Branker Buick Inc, Lincoln NE, chief executive. **BUSINESS ADDRESS:** Chief Executive, Mike Branker Buick Inc, 421 N 48th St, P O Box 30184, Lincoln, NE 68503. *

BRANN, HERMAN IVELAW
Educator. **PERSONAL:** Born Jan 23, 1942, Georgetown, Guyana;married Gloriana Maxfield; children: Ricky, Marlon, Collin. **EDUCATION:** Univ of West Indies Trinidad, BS 1967; Cornell Univ, MS 1971; Univ of West Indies Jamaica, PhD 1983. **CAREER:** Univ of the West Indies, lecturer 1971-80; Prairie View A&M Univ, asst prof 1980-86; Nova Univ, asst prof 1986-. **ORGANIZATIONS:** Mem Amer Economics Assoc, Amer Agricultural Economics Assoc, Caribbean Studies Assoc, Intl Assoc of Black Business Educators; mem United States Assocfor Small Business and Entrepreneurship, Assoc for Institutional Rsch. **HONORS/ACHIEVEMENTS:** Esso Fellowship, IIE Fellowship, Fulbright-Hays Fellowship; Merit Awd Univ of the West Indies 1978 and Prairie View A&M Univ 1981. **HOME ADDRESS:** 9725 NW 26th St # 1, Sunrise, FL 33322. **BUSINESS ADDRESS:** Professor of Economics, Nova University, 3301 College Ave, Fort Lauderdale, FL 33314.

BRANNEN, JAMES H., III
Pilot. **PERSONAL:** Born Dec 25, 1940, Queens, NY; children: Keree, Myia, Christopher. **EDUCATION:** Northrop Inst Tech, BS Aero Engrng 1964; Univ Baltimore Law Sch, JD 1975. **CAREER:** CT Legislature, mem 1973-75; US Patent Office, 1966-67; United Airlines, pilot flight mgr. **ORGANIZATIONS:** Cand US Sen Rep Party 1974; Rep Study Com, CT; bd dir Colchester Montessori Children's House 1973-; mem Rep Town Com 1972-; Jaycees

1972-. **BUSINESS ADDRESS:** SFOFO, United Airlines, San Francisco Intnl Airport, San Francisco, CA 94128.

BRANNON, JAMES R.
Insurance company executive. **PERSONAL:** Born Feb 26, 1943, Texarkana, TX; married Dorothy Williams; children: Sherrilyn C, Deanna E. **EDUCATION:** NC A&T State Univ, BS Economics 1967; Harvard Univ Grad School of Business Admin Program for Mgmt Devel, certificate 1975. **CAREER:** Liberty Mutual Insurance Co, business lines underwriter 1967-68, mgr Roxbury keypunch training center, 1968-69, commercial underwriter 1969-71, coordinator, equal employment 1971-78, asst vice pres, employee relations 1978-. **ORGANIZATIONS:** Mem, NAACP 1967-, A&T State Univ Alumni Assn 1967-, Harvard Business School Assoc of Boston 1976, Natl Urban League Boston 1980-; bd mem Freedom House Boston 1984-; comm mem Lexington Fair Housing 1985-; Bd Mem, Sportsmen Tennis Club; Lena Park Community Center. **HONORS/ACHIEVEMENTS:** Numerous articles written on career planning, preparation Black Collegian magazine. **HOME ADDRESS:** 380 Lowell St, Lexington, MA 02173. **BUSINESS ADDRESS:** Assistant Vice President, Liberty Mutual Insurance Group, 175 Berkeley St, Boston, MA 02117.

BRANSFORD, PARIS
Surgeon. **PERSONAL:** Born Jan 01, 1930, Huntsville, AL; married Gladys Toney; children: Paris, Toni, Traci. **EDUCATION:** TN St U, BS 1956; Mhry Med Coll, MD 1963. **CAREER:** Priv Prac, surgeon; NASA Hntsvl AL, res chem mssl prog; N Cntrl Gen Hosp, bd dirs chf of staff 1973-75; Rvrsd Gen Hosp, chf of emrgncy rm 1972-. **ORGANIZATIONS:** Vp sec Hstn Med Frm 1973-76; pres Med Asso Almd Med Sqr 1973-; mem Alpha Phi Alpha Frat; YMCA; NAACP; Harris Co Med Assn; Am Med Assn; TX Med Assn; Am Soc of Abdmnl Srgry; lectr Srs for Am Cncr Soc. **HONORS/ACHIEVEMENTS:** Recip serv to Chap Comm Delta Theta Lambda Chpts Alpha Phi Alpha Frat Inc 1971; cit of apprec Kappa Psi Phrmctcl Frat Serv to Comm 1975. **MILITARY SERVICE:** USAF 1950-53. **BUSINESS ADDRESS:** 6911 Almeda Rd, Ste 101, Houston, TX 77021.

BRANSFORD, WILLIAM L.
Clergyman. **PERSONAL:** Born Oct 13, 1924, Glasgow, KY. **EDUCATION:** Howard Univ, BA 1949; NY Univ, MA 1951; Yale Univ, MDiv 1954; Harvard Univ, postgrad 1954-55; So Bapt Theol Sem, attended 1958-59; Northwestern Univ Garrett Sem, attended 1960-64; DePaul Univ, attended 1968-69; Natl Coll of Educ, attended 1971-72; Chicago Baptist Inst, DD 1983. **CAREER:** Pond St Baptist Ch Providence RI, minister 1954-55; Christian Educ Mt Carmel Bapt Ch Washington, dir 1955-57; Howard Univ, instr 1957-58; Chicago Bapt Inst, instr 1963-; Cong Christian Educ Baptist State Conv, dean 1964-78; Baptist Bethlehem Dist Assn, sec 1965-; Christian Educ Bapt State Conv, dir 1973-78; Bethlehem Baptist Dist Cong Christian Educ, pres 1974-; Whitney M Young HS, reading tchr hearing impaired prog 1975-; Bethany Bapt Ch, pastor 1960-. **ORGANIZATIONS:** Mem Military Chaplains Assn; Intl Reading Assn; Assn for Supr & Curriculum Devel; Natl Council Tchrs English; Naval Reserve Assn. **MILITARY SERVICE:** USN 1943-46; 1951-52; Reserve Officers assn of the US. **BUSINESS ADDRESS:** Pastor, Bethany Baptist Ch, 1225 Elmwood Ave, Evanston, IL 60202.

BRANSON, HERMAN RUSSELL
Educator. **PERSONAL:** Born Aug 14, 1914, Pocahontas, VA; married Corolynne Gray Branson; children: Corolynne Gertrude, Herman Edward. **EDUCATION:** Univ of Pgh, attended 1932-34; VA State Coll, BS (Summa Cum Laude) 1936; Univ of Cincinnati, PhD Physics 1939. **CAREER:** Dillard Univ, instructor in Math & Physics 1939-41; Howard Univ, prof & head dept of Physics 1941-68; Central State Univ, pres 1968-70; Lincoln Univ, pres 1970-. **ORGANIZATIONS:** Mem Alpha Boule Sigma Pi Phi Frat; mem Alpha Phi Frat Inc; mem Amer Assn for the Advancement of Scis; mem Amer Assn of State Colls & Univs 1969-; mem Amer Found for Negro Affairs 1973-; mem Assn for the Study of Afro-Amer Life & History; mem Carver Rsch Found 1960-; mem Egypt Exploration Soc 1971-; mem MIT (various comm) 1979-; mem Middle Atlantic Consortium for Energy Rsch 1980-; mem Natl Acad of Scis; mem NAACP; mem Natl Assn for EqualOppor in Higher Educ 1969-; mem Natl Assn of Indepedents Colls & Univs; mem Natl Inst of Independent Colls & Univs; mem Natl Medical Fellowships Inc 1971-; mem Natl Sci Tchrs Assn; mem NJ Marine Scis Consortium; mem Oxford Area C of C 1982-; mem Philadelphia Bd of Public Educ; mem Rotary Club; mem Sea Grant Review Panel US Dept of Commerce 1980-; mem Sigma Xi Soc; Hon mem Smithsonian Inst; mem US Dept of Energy; mem Univ City Sci Ctr 1972-;mem Woodrow Wilson Natl Fellowship Found 1975-. **HONORS/ACHIEVEMENTS:** Sigma Pi Phi Scholarship Pgh 1933; Special Fellow in Physics 1936-37; Laws Fellow in Physics 1937-39 Univ of Cincinnati; ScD VA State 1967; ScD Univ of Cincinnati 1967; ScD Lincoln Univ 1969; LHD Brandeix Univ 1972; LLD Western MI Univ 1973; LHD Shaw Coll at Detroit 1978; LittD Drexel Univ 1982; Sigma Xi; Sigma Pi Sigma; Pi Mu Epsilon; Rosenwald Fellow Univ Chicago 1940; Sr Fellow Natl Rsch Cncl CA Inst of Tech 1948-49; Faculty Fellow Natl Sci Found Univ of Hamburg Germany & French Atomic Energy Comm (Saclay) 1962-63. **BUSINESS ADDRESS:** President, Lincoln University, Lincoln University, PA 19352.

BRANTLEY, BOOKER TERRY, JR.
Business executive. **PERSONAL:** Born Mar 09, 1935, Troy, AL; married Baby Ruth Griffith; children: Vanessa Terrene, Booker III. **EDUCATION:** Hoke Smith Tech Sch, 1960; Ford Marketing Inst, 1974. **CAREER:** Terry Motors Van Motores Greenbriar Lincoln Merc Sales Inc, pres/owner; Pure Oil, 1967; Brantley TV, 1965; Ole King Cole Bakery, 1965;Univ Drug Store, mgr 1962. **ORGANIZATIONS:** GA Auto Dealers Assn; GA Auto Auction; Atlanta Bus League; Small Bus Admn; sponser Miss Black GA 1975-76; W Manor Little League Football Team; Metro Tennis Classic 1976-77. **HONORS/ACHIEVEMENTS:** Poor Peoples Ach Awards Day 1977; Finance Com for Mayor Jackson 1977; Top Outstand Black Bus Men; Black Enterprise 1976; Sales Award Ford Motor Co 1976; Outstand Ach Award City of Atlanta 1976; Outstand Ach Award Nat Symposium on State of the Black Econ 1976; 1st Black to become a mem of Lincoln Mercury's 100 Club; Spcl Award for Outstand Serv to Atlanta Comm from Atlanta Omega Chap of Y'S Men 1977. **MILITARY SERVICE:** AUS pfc 1955. **BUSINESS ADDRESS:** 2770 Campeliton Rd, Atlanta, GA 30311.

BRANTLEY, EDWARD J.
Educator, association executive. **PERSONAL:** Born Dec 12, 1923, Lockland, OH; married Dr Laura Rowe; children: Edward J Jr. **EDUCATION:** Howard Univ, BS (cum laude) 1948; Columbia Univ, MA 1949; Univ CO, DEd 1960. **CAREER:** Clark Coll, prof educ, 1960-72, acting pres, 1969-70; Knoxville Coll, pres, 1972-75; Inst for Serv to Educ Inc, Washington DC, dir div of planning & mgmt, 1975-77, vice pres institute for servs to educ, 1977-78; US Office of Educ, div dir, 1978-. **ORGANIZATIONS:** Life mem Amer Personnel & Guid Assn; mem NEA; Amer Coll Pers Assn; Amr Educ Res Assn; Coop Coll Dev Prog; Phi Delta Kappa; Kappa Delta Pi; secty/treas Mid-Appalacia Coll Council 1973-; vice chmn Higher Educ Dept E Dept E TN Educ Assn 1973-74; chmn 1974-75, bd dirs Knoxville Knox Co Urban League; mem Knoxville Ctr City Task Force; Knoxville Min Bus Bur; adv coun Jr Achievement; ex-officio Hon Tr Dulin Gall Art;Lay Leader United Method Church Asbury; Brd Dir Asbury Senior Citizens Dwelling; Brd Dir Boys & Girls Club; Pres Washington Bridge Unit. **MILITARY SERVICE:** AUS 1943-46. **BUSINESS ADDRESS:** Division Dir, US Office of Education, 400 Maryland Ave SW, Washington, DC 20012.

BRANTLEY, MONTAGUE DELANO
Physician. **PERSONAL:** Born Oct 19, 1919, Wilmington, NC; divorced; children: Montague Jr, Todd, Aubie, Barron. **EDUCATION:** Morris Coll, AB, BS 1949; Howard U, MS 1951; Meharry Med Coll, MD 1955; Jewish Hosp NY Univ Harvard. **CAREER:** Private Pract, physician; NY Univ Harvard Med Sch, stdnt; Knickerbocker Hosp, chf med resd 1970-76; Jewish Hosp Bklyn, resd internal med 1968; Vassoi Bros Hosp, intern 1965. **ORGANIZATIONS:** Mem NY Cardinl Soc; AMA; SC Med Assn; Phi Beta Sigma Frat; atdng staff McLeod Meml Hosp; mem PSRO & PRSO Long Term Care; Lay Elder 7th Day Aventist; asso hlth sec S Atlantic Conf; bd dir Boys Club; mem Therapeutic & Pharm Com McLeod Meml Hosp. **HONORS/ACHIEVEMENTS:** WW II. **BUSINESS ADDRESS:** 1051 S Main St, Darlington, SC 29532.

BRANTON, LEO, JR.
Attorney. **PERSONAL:** Born Feb 17, 1922, Pine Bluff, AR; married Geri. **EDUCATION:** TN St U, BS 1942; Nrthwstrn U, JD 1949. **CAREER:** Pvt Prac LA, atty 1949-; Angela Davis, prtcptd in scsfl def 1972; Hlywd Entrtnrs, rprsntd as atty; Communists, rprsntd as atty; Poor Blcks Rblnin Watts, atty 1965; Blck Pnthr Prty, def mem in civ rights actvsts arstd in the so. **ORGANIZATIONS:** Mem ACLU; NAACP; St Bar of CA; Wilshire Bar Assn; J M Langston Law Club. **HONORS/ACHIEVEMENTS:** Recpt outsdng contrib to fld Crmnl Ltgtn Awd 1972; Lwyr of Yr 1974; Trl Lwyr of Yr J M Langston Bar Assn 1973. **BUSINESS ADDRESS:** Attorney at Law, 3460 Wilshire Blvd, Ste 410, Los Angeles, CA 90010.

BRASEY, HENRY L.
Educator. **PERSONAL:** Born Nov 25, 1937, Cincinnati, OH; married Anna; children: Darrell, Jenifer. **EDUCATION:** BS 1972; IBM Corp, Cert. **CAREER:** UUniv of Cincinnati, asst dir of computer serv/adjunct asst prof of engineering analysis; Regional Computer City of Cincinnati, programming proj leader; Full House Inc, pres; Withrow HS Data Processing Prog, curriculum adv. **ORGANIZATIONS:** Mem Assn for Computing Machinery; mem Kennedy Heights Comm Cncl; Ken-Sil Athletic Club; Pleasant Ridge PTA. **BUSINESS ADDRESS:** Director, Acad Computer Ser, University of Cincinnati, Mail Location 149, Cincinnati, OH 45221.

BRASHEAR, BERLAIND LEANDER
Judge. **PERSONAL:** Born Apr 18, 1934, Dallas, TX; married Johnnie Mae Blanton; children: Rhonda Elaine, John Henry, Bradley Nathaniel. **EDUCATION:** Prairie View Coll A & M, 1962; TX Southern Univ Sch of Law 1967. **CAREER:** Dallas Legal Svc, staff atty 1968; private practice 1969-75; municipal judge 1975-77; cnty criminal judge 1977-. **ORGANIZATIONS:** TX Bar Assn; Dallas Cty Bar Assn; TX Judges Assn; Am Judge Assn; bd of dir Operation PUSH; Negro Chamber of Commerce; Nat Bar Assn; bd of dir WestDallas Community Cntrs. **HONORS/ACHIEVEMENTS:** Am Acad of Judicial Edn; Negro Chamber of Commerce; J L Turner Legal Assn. **MILITARY SERVICE:** USMC pfc good conduct medal 1954-57. **BUSINESS ADDRESS:** Judge, Cnty Criminal Court #6, 600 Commerce, Dallas, TX 75202.

BRASWELL, PALMIRA
Educator. **PERSONAL:** Born Mar 23, 1928, Macon, GA. **EDUCATION:** Fort Valley State Coll, AB 1950; Teachers College Columbia Univ, MA 1959; Univ of GA, EdS 1969; Principals Ctr Harvard Univ, attended 1985. **CAREER:** Bibb Co Bd of Educ and NY Bd of Educ, teacher 1950-64; Bibb Co Bd of Educ, dir instructional materials ctr 1965-74, curriculum dir 1977-83, dir staff development 1983-. **ORGANIZATIONS:** Past mem Civil Service Bd City of Macon 1976-79; past basileus Epsilon Omega Omega-Alpha Kappa Alpha 1979-83; past mem Booker T Washington Comm Ctr 1979-83; mem curriculum council Mercer Univ Medical School 1979-80; past mem Middle GA Chap Amer Red Cross 1980-84; state sec Professional Assoc of GA Educators;pres Middle Georgia Chap Phi Delta Kappa 1986-. **HONORS/ACHIEVEMENTS:** 1st Black female radio announcer City of Macon GA station WBML 1956-58; Teacher of the Yr BS Ingram Elem Sch 1976; 1 of 20 Most Influential Women in Middle GA NAACP Macon Chap 1981; Disting Alumni Awd, Presidential Citation Natl Assoc in Higher Educ for Equal Oppor 1986. **HOME ADDRESS:** 3016 Paige Dr, Macon, GA 31211. **BUSINESS ADDRESS:** Director, Staff Development, Bibb County Bd of Educ, 2064 Vineville Ave, P O Box 6157, Macon, GA 31213.

BRAXTON, EDWARD KENNETH
Priest, educator, theologian, author. **PERSONAL:** Born Jun 28, 1944, Chicago, IL; son of Mr & Mrs Cullen L. Braxton, Sr. **EDUCATION:** BA, 1966; MA, 1968; M, Div, 1969; STB, 1968; PhD, 1975; STD, 1976; Univ of Chicago, Postdoctoral Fellowship. **CAREER:** Harvard Univ, 1976-77; Notre Dame Univ, visiting prof, 1977-78; Diocese of Cleveland, chancellor for theological affairs & personal theology; Archdiocese ofWashington, DC, chancellor for theological affairs, 1978-81; Rome North Amer Coll, scholar in residence, 1982-83; Univ of Chicago, Catholic Student Center, dir; William H Sadlier Inc, official theological cons; 1988 winter school lecturer, South Africa. **ORGANIZATIONS:** Mem, Amer Acad of Religion; Catholic Theological Soc of Amer; Black Catholic Clergy Caucus; Catholic Bishop's Committee on Liturgy & Doctrine; bd of dir, St Mary of the Lake Seminary, Chicago; keynote speaker, 43 Intl Eucharistic Congress, Nairobi, Kenya; theological advisor to bishops of Africa & Madagascan, 1984; del, writer & speaker for Historic Natl Black Catholic Congress, Washington, DC 1987. **HONORS/ACHIEVEMENTS:** Published, The Wisdom Comm; numerous articles on Catholic Theological Religion; forthcoming book, One Holy Catholic and Apostolic: Essays for the Community of Faith. **BUSINESS ADDRESS:** Official Theological Consultant, William H Sadlier Inc, 11 Park Place, New York, NY 10007.

BRAXTON, HARRIET E.
Elected official. **PERSONAL:** Born Jul 18, 1926, Charlotte, NC; married Paul A Braxton; children: Paula E Arp, Rosemary L Smith, Harriet A Price, Regina B Mitchell, Julia L, Diana A, Paul M. **EDUCATION:** William Penn HS, Cert Housing Inspectors 1970, Cert HAAC 1972; Latestart Uptown Sr Citizens, Cert 1982. **CAREER:** Mechanicsburg Naval Depot, clerk typist 1945-49; PA Dept of Revenue, addressograph op 1961-63; City of Harrisburg, housing inspector 1968-71; Harrisburg Housing Authority, housing coun/res ad 1972-73; City of Harrisburg, councilwoman appointed 1982, elected 1983-; Capital Cty Ret Cntr Inc, by-laws comm mem. **ORGANIZATIONS:** Comm chair Uptown Civic Assoc 1963-73; dir Harrisburg Opportunity Bd 1963-65; neighborhood aide Harrisburg Opportunity Program 1965-67; mem Mayor's Advisory Comm 1966-68; bookmobile asst Harrisburg Public Library 1967; inspector of elections Tenth Ward Second Precinct 1975-80; judge of elect 10th ward 2nd precinct 1980; bd mem YWCA 1977; bd mem YMCA 1968; mem of Our Lady of Blessed Sacrament Ch; mem OLBS School PTA. **HONORS/ACHIEVEMENTS:** Braxton Playground Uptown Civic Assoc & City 1965; Merit of Honor Sixth St Uptown Revit Eff 1978-85, Amer Red Cross 1977; Faces & Places Harrisburg Historical Soc 1984; Banneker Tennis Champion 1940; 2nd Place Winner AAU Basketball; 1st Natl Medal Set Baseball throw Fager Field (235 ft) Harrisburg, PA; Capt Soccer Team William Penn HS 1943. **HOME ADDRESS:** 2142 N 7th St, Harrisburg, PA 17110. **BUSINESS ADDRESS:** Councilwoman, Harrisburg City Council, City Government Center, Harrisburg, PA 17101.

BRAXTON, JOHN LEDGER
Attorney. **PERSONAL:** Born Feb 06, 1945, Philadelphia, PA. **EDUCATION:** PA State Univ, BS 1966; Howard Univ School of Law, JD 1971. **CAREER:** Wolf, Block Schorr & Solis-Cohen, assoc 1971-73; Braxton, Johnson & Kopanski, partner 1973-76; Blue Cross of Greater Philadelphia, assoc counsel 1976-78; Asst Dist Atty, chief 1978-81; Court of Common Pleas, judge. **ORGANIZATIONS:** Bd mem Fellowship Commission 1978-85; vice pres Child Psychiatry Center St Christopher's 1976-85; bd mem Judicial Council Natl Bar 1984-85; bd mem Philadelphia Citywide Devel Corp 1981-85; pres Homemaker Serv of the Metropolitan Area; Philadelphia Council Boy Scouts of Amer. **HONORS/ACHIEVEMENTS:** State of Black Philadelphia Philadelphia Urban League 1984; Outstanding Alumnus Howard Univ. **MILITARY SERVICE:** AUS 1st lt 1966-68; bronze star with 1st oak cluster 1968. **BUSINESS ADDRESS:** Judge, Court of Common Pleas, 203 One E Penn Square, Philadelphia, PA 19107.

BRAYNON, EDWARD J., JR.
Director of supplemental services (dentistry, pharmacy, and publications). **PERSONAL:** Born Jan 15, 1928, Miami, FL; son of Edward J Braynon and May Dell Jackson Braynon; married Ann Carey; children: Edward III, Keith. **EDUCATION:** Howard Univ, BS 1949, DDS 1954; Fisk Univ. **CAREER:** USAF, dental officer 1954-56; private practice, dentist 1956-; Family Health Center Inc, chief of dental serv. **ORGANIZATIONS:** Past pres Dade Cnty Acad of Med 1962-62; past pres Dade Cnty Dental Soc 1970-72; grand baseileus Omega Psi Phi Frat Inc 1976-79. **HONORS/ACHIEVEMENTS:** Outstanding serv to the community and poor Howard Univ Washington DC 1976; "Dr E J Braynon, Jr Day" City of Miami, FL 1976; Key to City Columbus, GA 1973; Key to City Fayetville, NC 1976; Key to City Spartanberg, SC 1977. **MILITARY SERVICE:** USAF capt 1954-56. **HOME ADDRESS:** 2271 NE 191st St, North Miami, FL 33180. **BUSINESS ADDRESS:** Chief of Dental Services, Family Health Center Inc, 5361 NW 22nd Ave, Miami, FL 33142.

BRAZEAL, BRAILLSFORD REESE
Educator, economist. **PERSONAL:** Born Mar 08, 1905, Dublin, GA; married Ernestine Vivian Erskine; children: Ernestine Walton, Aurelia Erskine. **EDUCATION:** Morehouse Coll, AB 1927; Columbia, MA 1928; PhD 1942. **CAREER:** Morehouse Coll, instructor Economics, 1928-34, chmn dept Economics/dean of men, 1938-48, acad dean, 1948-69, prof Economics, 1948-73; Emeritus Acad, dean & prof of Economics, 1973-. **ORGANIZATIONS:** Dir Mut Fed Savs & Loan Assn of Atlanta; former mem adv com Ctr for Study of Liberal Educ for Adults Exec Cncl Highlander Research/Educ Ctr; FultonCo Commn Employment Opportunity; Nat Cncl Comm Serv to Intl Visitors US Dept State; adv com Manpower Research & Devel Labs Div Behavioral Sci Nrc; former dir/chmn soc sci select com Nat & So Fellowships Funds; mem/exec com Am Conf Acad Deans; vice pres Assn Am Bapt Educ Instrs 1954-56; Assn Colls & Secondar Sch; chmn Commn on Colls & Univ 1956, pres 1957; mem Am Civil Liberties Union Adv Cncl Acad Freedom; Morehouse Nat Alumni Assn; Am Econos Assn; Am Acad Polit & Social Sci; Acad Polit Sci; com on labor mgmt Nat Cncl Chs; former dir s regnl cncl Am Assn Univ Prof; Phi Beta Kappa; Omega Psi Phi; Sigma Pi Phi; Delta Sigma Rho. **HONORS/ACHIEVEMENTS:** Bapt Soc Sci Research Cncl Fellow 1932-33; Rosenwald Fund Fellow 1938-39; Ctr for African & Afro-Am Studies Fellow; European Study-Travel Grantee AtlantaU 1955; Ford Found Research & Travel Grantee 1971-72; auther, "The Brotherhood of Sleeping Car Porters, It's Origin & Devel; 1946; chapter, "Desegregation &The Negro Coll" Yrbook Jour Negro Educ 1958; Studies of Negro Voting in 8 Rural Co of GA & 1 of SC 1960.

BRAZELTON, EDGAR, JR.
Business executive. **PERSONAL:** Born Jun 23, 1913, Birmingham, AL; married Elizabeth Weaver; children: Carolyn, Irene, Alice, Edgar III, Barbara. **EDUCATION:** Reforestation Exten Sch at Univ of MI, 1936; Boston Sch of Floral Culture, 1942. **ORGANIZATIONS:** Pres Brazelton's Florist Inc Detroit; founder Black Causes Assn Inc; pres Booker T Washington Bus Assn; past pres Retail Div of Allied Florists Assn; past pres Men's Club Ebenezer African Meth Episcopal Ch; past sec King Solomon Grand Lodge; past chmn Intl Florists Conv 1954; past chmn Flower & Garden Show 1966; recreation instr Detroit & River Rouge; pres Central HS Complex 1960-62; vice-chmn Fedn of Self-Determination 1967-68; mem Bishop Br YMCA;NAACP; MI State Florists Assn; Soc of Am Florists; Teleflora Wire Serv Worldwide; IBTOE of W; Detroit Urban League; MI Horticultural Soc; Cit of Equal Oppor; Attinson Ave Improvement Assn; Booker T Wash Businessmens Assn; Keep Detroit Beautiful Com; witness to Pres Nat Adv Panel of Ins in Riot Infected Areas; treas Inner City Bus Improvement Forum; Randolph Wallace Kidney Fund; financial sec Central Regnl Econ Cnsl; New Cntr Area Coun; DetroitBus & Civic League; Greater Detroit C of C; MI State Housing Devel Auth; founder Cotillion Club. **BUSINESS ADDRESS:** President, Brazelton Florist, Inc, 2686 W Grand Blvd, Detroit, MI 48202.

BRAZIER, MARTIN GEORGE
Business executive. **PERSONAL:** Born Feb 05, 1943, Houston, TX; married Janie Louise Fortune; children: Kimberly, Marty Jr, Trishia Nicole. **EDUCATION:** Pacific Lutheran Univ, 1968-70; Central Washington State Coll of Edn, 1973-74; Jackson State Univ, BS, 1977; Flight Training Sch, 1976-77. **CAREER:** FAA, special contract compliance ofcr 1972-; Civil Rights Div, chief; Dept of Justice, personnel staffing specialist, 1971-72, personnel mgmt specialist 1970-71; Thriftco Stores, supvr 1968-70; Safeway Stores Inc, supvr 1967-68; Jones & Brazier Bldg Maint Serv of Tacoma, partowner. **ORGANIZATIONS:** Pres Brazier Enterprises Intl; bd trustee/treas Pierce Cty Opp Indsln Ctrs of Am; mem Seattle NAACP Urban League 1977; bd trustee New Jerusalem COGIC; mem Christian & Black Airmans Assn; Aircraft Owners & Pilots Assn 1977; tchr Sunday Sch 1977. **HONORS/ACHIEVEMENTS:** Full Gospel Businessmens Fellow Toastmasters Intl 1977; Superior Performance Award Dept of Justice 1971; Fed Employee of Yr Civil Serv Commn Fed Exec Bd 1973; Outstanding Achievements EEO 1976. **MILITARY SERVICE:** USAF E-5 1961-66. **BUSINESS ADDRESS:** FAA Bldg, 9010 E Marginal Way, Seattle, WA 98108.

BRAZIER, WESLEY R.
Consultant. **PERSONAL:** Born Aug 20, 1917; widowed; children: Benita E, Ellen R. **EDUCATION:** MSW, AB; Dillard U, 1939; Atlanta Univ Sch of Soc Work, 1940-42. **CAREER:** Beeson Asso Inc, consult 1968-, now retired. **ORGANIZATIONS:** Exec dir Los Angeles Urban League 1948-68; DSA-DEFENSE Contract Admin Serv Region LA 1968-73; mem Nat Assn of Social Workers; Accredited Social WorkersAssn; organizer Men of Tomorrow; mem Los Angeles & Nat Urban League; life mem NAACP. **HONORS/ACHIEVEMENTS:** Recipient Cert of Achievement Dept of Def 1972; Men of Tomorrow Award 1962; First Equal Oppor Day Luncheon in recog of life-long dedication to the principles of equal oppor Los Angeles Urban League 1967; Resolutions from Los Angeles City Cncl Los Angeles Co Bd of Supr; Merit Serv Award State of CA Div of Apprenticeship Standards 1971. **MILITARY SERVICE:** AUS 1942-44.

BRAZIER, WILLIAM H.
Editor, publisher. **PERSONAL:** Born Aug 01, 1922, Xenia, OH; married Alice Marie; children: Tony, Michele. **EDUCATION:** Wilberforce, BS 1952; Teacher Coll Grad School, 1958; Bank St Coll Grad School, 1970-72; Hofstra Univ Grad School, 1975. **CAREER:** "Big Payoff," "Strike It Rich" shows,TV prod asst 1952-54; NY Amsterdam News, advertising rep 1953-56; New York City Bd of Educ Higher Horizons Proj, dir audio-visual instructional serv 1964-66; New York City Public School, admin 1984 retired; Long Island Weekly Voice, editor, publisher, founder; Long Island Voice Associates, president. **ORGANIZATIONS:** Natl vice chmn, public relations, Omega Psi Phi; dir public relations, 2nd Dist, Omega Psi Phi; editor, publisher Omegan Newspaper & Q-2 Monthly; bd dir, cofounder, Banneker Business Devel Corp; charter mem, Long Island Black Business & Professional Men's Assn; steering comm, Harlem Teacher Assn, Suffolk County CORE, LI Black Assembly, NAACP; mem, Bethel AME Church, Copiague NY; former lecturer, adv commun, CW Post Coll Black Studies Prog; commun adv, Stony Brook State Univ Black Studies Prog; producer, Stony Brook Black World Newspaper; life mem, Disabled Amer Vets; natl dir of public relations, Omega Psi Phi Frat Inc; mem editorial bd, The Oracle Magazine; bd dir, Suffolk County Black History Museum Assn; mem, Breezy Point Yacht Club, Huntington Boating Assn, Wilberforce Univ Alumni Assn, Central LI NAACP. **HONORS/ACHIEVEMENTS:** Omega Man of the Year LI 1974; 100 Black Men of Nassau Suffolk Inc; Second District and Natl Omega Man of the Year 1986 Chi Rho Chap. **MILITARY SERVICE:** AUS, Asiatic Pacific Theater 1943-45. **BUSINESS ADDRESS:** President, Long Island Voice Associates, PO Box 751, Amityville, NY 11701.

BRAZIL, ERNEST L.
Attorney. **PERSONAL:** Born Dec 16, 1943, Louisville, KY; married Rosemarie Yule. **EDUCATION:** OH State U, BA 1965; Harvard Law Sch, JD 1974. **CAREER:** Brae Corp, gen counsel/sec; Heller Ehrman White & McAuliffe Law Firm, asso atty 1974-77. **ORGANIZATIONS:** Asso mem Am Bar Assn; mem Am Soc of Corp Secretaries; mem Nat Bar Assn; mem Harvard Club; mem Barristers Club; mem Airplane Owners & Pilots Assn. **HONORS/ACHIEVEMENTS:** Martin Luther King Fellowship 1971; 2nd Place Award for Prose 1st Chap of "For Those In Peril" San Fran Bar Assn Creative Writing Contest. **MILITARY SERVICE:** USN lt 1966-71. **BUSINESS ADDRESS:** Brae Corp, 3 Embarcadero Center, San Francisco, CA 94111.

BRAZIL, ROBERT D.
Educator. **PERSONAL:** Born Mar 19, 1939, Memphis; divorced; children: Patrice, Alan. **EDUCATION:** Chicago Tchrs Coll, BEd 1960; DePaul U, MEd 1965. **CAREER:** Chicago, tchr 1960; Tesla Sch, prin 1966; Headstart, prin 1966-67; US Dept Juctice, Midwest educ cnsltnt 1967; Parkside Sch, prin 1971; HEW Office Edn, non fed pnlst 1974-75; Parker HS, prin 1975. **ORGANIZATIONS:** Mem Kappa Alpha Psi Frat; adj prof educ McGaw Grad Sch; Natl Coll Educ Past vol S Side Comm Com; mem Beatrice Caffrey Youth Svc; Betty Boys Found; Marillac Comm House;O. **BUSINESS ADDRESS:** Parker High School, 6800 Stewart, Chicago, IL 60621.

BRAZILE, ROBERT (DOC)
Professional athlete. **PERSONAL:** Born Feb 07, 1953, Pineland, AL; married Alice; children: Sherri, Robert III. **EDUCATION:** Jackson State. **CAREER:** Houston Oilers, linebacker. **HONORS/ACHIEVEMENTS:** Top Linebacker in AFC 1979; All-Pro by AP 1981; All-AFC by UPI 1981; Defensive Rookie of the Year 1975. **BUSINESS ADDRESS:** Houston Oilers, P O Box 1516, Houston, TX 77001.

BRAZINGTON, ANDREW PAUL
Dentist. **PERSONAL:** Born Jun 21, 1918, Philadelphia, PA; married Mabel Coffey; children: Andrew P. **EDUCATION:** Howard Univ DC, BS 1949, DDS 1957. **CAREER:** Philadelphia Dept of Hlth, clin dntst; Private Practice, dntst New Era Dntl Soc Phila, dntst 1971-. **ORGANIZATIONS:** Philadelphia Cnty Dntl Soc 1958-; PA Dntl Assn 1958-; Am Dntl Assn 1958-; treas vice pres Chrstn St & Y'S Mem Club; mem Olde Philadelphia Club; mem Med Com Cncrnd wth Civ Rgts; bd of mgrs Chrstn St YMCA 1973-; mem NAACP. **HONORS/ACHIEVEMENTS:** Omega Psi Phi Spec Serv Awrd Am Cancer Soc 1969; Serv Hon YMCA Philadelphia 1973-75. **MILITARY SERVICE:** AUS 1st lt 1941-46. **BUSINESS ADDRESS:** 5051 Chestnut St, Philadelphia, PA 19139.

BRECKENRIDGE, FRANKLIN E.
Attorney. **PERSONAL:** Married Cora Smith, Jun 13, 1964; children: Lejene, Franklin Jr, Emma Estel. **EDUCATION:** IN U, BS 1963, JD 1968. **CAREER:** Kokomo-Center Township Consolidated Schools, tchr 1963-65; Indianapolis Pre- Schools Inc, tchr 1965-66;

IN Dept Revenue, admin supr corporate income tax 1966-68; private practice, 1968-73; Miles Inc, sr atty & asst sec, associate council. **ORGANIZATIONS:** Mem Elkhart City Bar Assn, Indiana Bar Assn, Amer Bar Assn; Alpha Phi Alpha Social Frat; mem Phi Delta Phi Legal Frat; numerous offices and committees NAACP; pres IN State Conf of Brs NAACP; mem Natl Bar Assn; Dem Precinct Com for Eklhart Co 1975-77. **HONORS/ACHIEVEMENTS:** Numerous NAACP Awards. **HOME ADDRESS:** 54653 Briarwood Dr, Elkhart, IN 46514. **BUSINESS ADDRESS:** Miles Inc, 1127 Mrytle St, Elkhart, IN 46514.

BRECKENRIDGE, JOHN L.
Attorney, accountant. **PERSONAL:** Born Jun 12, 1913, Maysville, KY; married Eddye M DeFoor. **EDUCATION:** Youngstown State U, BS Bus Admin 1952, LLB 1958, JD 1969; Natl Coll of Advocacy, ATLA 1974. **CAREER:** Gen of OH, spcl cnsl atty 1971-; Private Practice, atty 1958-; reg pub accnt 1960-; pub accnt 1948-60. **ORGANIZATIONS:** Mem Am Arbtrtn Assn; The Assn of Trial Lwyrs of Am; OH State Bar Assn; Natl Assn of Crmnl Def Lwyrs; Trumbull Co Bar Assn; Mahoning Co Bar Assn; Nat Bar Assn; The AmS Judicature Soc Life mem NAACP. **HONORS/ACHIEVEMENTS:** Listed Who's Who ins Am Coll &Univ 1952; Alpha Tau Gamma Hon Accnt Frat 1952; recip Bancroft Whitney Law Sch Awrd 1955; Meritorious Serv Awrd United Negro Coll Fund 1959; Warren Rotary Club Cert 1960; Who's Who in OH 1961; Kiwanis Club of Warren Cert 1961; Omega Psi Phi 4th Dist Man of Yr 1|964; Urban League Comm Serv Awrd 1974. **MILITARY SERVICE:** AUS 1st sgt 1942-45. **BUSINESS ADDRESS:** 279 Second St, Warren, OH.

BREDA, MALCOLM J.
Educator. **PERSONAL:** Born Aug 14, 1934, Alexandria, LA. **EDUCATION:** Xavier Univ of LA, BS 1956; Univ of IN, MMEd 1962; Univ of So MS, PhD 1975. **CAREER:** NO Archdiocesan Music Progs, lectr & cons; recitalist accompanist adjudicator of musical activities throughout the US; AL A&M Univ, instr asst prof 1956-64; Boys Town NE, organist pianist-in-residence 1964-67; St John Prep Sch NO LA, dir choral activities 1967-73; Xavier Univ of LA, prof/chmn dept of music 1967-. **ORGANIZATIONS:** Mem Alpha Kappa Mu Honor Soc, Phi Mu Alpha Sinfonia Frat, Music Educators Natl Conf; mem Amer Guild of Organists, Afro-Amer Music Opportunities Assn; mem Natl Assoc of Schools of Music. **HONORS/ACHIEVEMENTS:** Sister M Cornelia Jubilee Awd 1952; Mother Agatha Ryan Awd 1956; ISSP Summer Fellowship Harvard Univ 1968; Natl Fellow 1973-75. **MILITARY SERVICE:** AUS sp4 1956-58. **BUSINESS ADDRESS:** Assoc Prof/Chmn, Dept of Music, Xavier Univ of LA, New Orleans, LA 70125.

BREEDEN, JAMES PLEASANT
Educator. **PERSONAL:** Born Oct 14, 1934, Minneapolis, MN; son of Pleasant Breeden and Florence Thomas Breeden; divorced; children: Margaret, Johanna, Frederick, Paul. **EDUCATION:** Dartmouth Coll, BA 1956; Union Theological Seminary NYC, MDiv 1960; Harvard Grad Sch of Educ, EdD 1972. **CAREER:** Comm on Church & Race MA Council of Churches, dir 1967-69; Harvard Grad Sch of Educ, assoc prof 1972-76; Univ of Dares Salaam Tanzania, prof in ed 1973-75; Boston Public Schs, sr officer planning policy 1978-82; Ctr for Law & Ed, dir 1983-84; Dartmouth Coll, dean Wm Jewett Tucker Found 1984-. **ORGANIZATIONS:** Canon St Paul's Cathedral Episc Diocese of MA 1963-65; asst dir Comm on Religion & Race Natl Council of Churches 1965-67; bd of trustees Episcopal Divinity Sch 1981-; bd New World Foundation. **HONORS/ACHIEVEMENTS:** Annual Awd MA Soc Worker Assn 1964; The Young Men of Boston Boston Jr Chamber of Commerce 1965; Alper Awd Civil Liberties Union MA 1978. **BUSINESS ADDRESS:** Dean, WM. Jewett Tucker Foundation, Dartmouth College, Hanover, NH 03755.

BREEDING, CARL L.
Educator, civil rights. **PERSONAL:** Born Aug 30, 1932, Indianapolis, IN; divorced; children: 4 children. **EDUCATION:** Indianapolis Univ, AB 1955; MI State Univ, MA 1970. **CAREER:** Summer Youth Oppor Prog, coord 1971-72, 1974; Jackson MI Public Schools, algebra teacher 1960-88. **ORGANIZATIONS:** MI State Conf of NAACP 2nd vice pres 1969-70, 1st vice pres 1970-71, pres 1971-; pres MI State NAACP 1971-; candidate for mayor Jackson 1972; chmn Region II Comm Action Agency 1978; mem bd of dirs NAACP 1982-; vice pres Natl NAACP 1986-; mem Jackson Educ Assn Legis Com; elected mem of Rep Assembly; mem MI Educ Assn; life mem Natl Educ Assn; life mem NAACP; mem Jackson Br Exec Comm; bd dir vice chmn Jackson-Hillsdale Area EOC; mem exec comm Summer Youth Oppor Adv Council; mem MI Dem Black Caucus; bd mem Jackson Co Legal Aid Soc; Notary Public; past mem Jackson Jaycees; former mem Jackson Human Relations Commn; adv comm Jackson Citizens Sch Bd; selective serv system Local Bd #39 & mcCulloch Sch PTA. **HONORS/ACHIEVEMENTS:** Outstanding Young Educator 1965; rec Resolution of Tribute from MI Legislature. **MILITARY SERVICE:** AUS 1956-57. **BUSINESS ADDRESS:** Algebra Teacher, Parkside Jr High School, PO Box 361, Jackson, MI 49204.

BREMBY, RODERICK LEMAR
Assistant to city manager. **PERSONAL:** Born Feb 04, 1960, Eufaula, AL; son of J B Bremby and Margaret J Robinson-Johnson; married April Lynne Harris, Jun 19, 1982; children: Rachel. **EDUCATION:** Univ of Kansas, Lawrence KS, BA, 1982, MPA, 1984. **CAREER:** City of Fort Worth, Fort Worth TX, mgmt intern, 1983-84, admin analyst I, 1984-85, admin analyst II, 1985, admin analyst III, 1985-86, asst to city mgr, 1986-. **ORGANIZATIONS:** Assoc mem, Intl City Mgmt Assn, 1983-; pres, Urban Mgmt Asst of N Texas, 1986; mem, City of Fort Worth Juneteenth Planning Comm, 1986-; mem, City of Forth Worth MLK Planning Comm, 1986-; mem, Leadership Fort Worth, 1987-; pres, 1989-, sec, 1986-89, Natl Forum for Black Public Admin, N Texas Chapter. **HONORS/ACHIEVEMENTS:** Outstanding Young Man of Amer, YMCA, 1983, 1986; R Scott Brooks Memorial Award, Univ of Kansas, 1984; author, "Voice Processing Applications in the City of Fort Worth," Town & City Magazine, 1988. **HOME ADDRESS:** 1720 Clover Ln, Fort Worth, TX 76107.

BREMER, CHARLES E.
Educator, administrator. **PERSONAL:** Born Sep 12, 1941, New Orleans, LA; married Jocelyn. **EDUCATION:** OH Univ BS govt & hist 1965; Kent State Univ, Certified vocational guidance & counselor, 1965; Southern IL Univ/Rutgers Univ, graduate of labor internship 1978. **CAREER:** A Philip Randolph Educ Fund/YEP, natl dir 1978-; RTP Inc-Manpower Training & Devel, dep exec dir 1968-74; So IL U, tchr/cnslr 1967; OH State Dept of Labor, voc guid couns 1966; Cleveland Publ Schs, tchr 1965; Contini & Riffs Retails Bus, pres 1974-78. **ORGANIZATIONS:** Bd mediation Inst for Mediation & Conflict Resolution 1971-; chmn schlrshp com WC Handy Schlrshp Club 1975-; bd finance Workers Defense League 1979-. **HONORS/ACHIEVEMENTS:** Clg schlrshp OHUniv 1960-65; Meritorious Awrd Cleveland Br RTP Inc 1974; Serv Awrd Minority Bus Ent Ctr Anchorage AK 1979. **BUSINESS ADDRESS:** Assistant Dir, Inter Union of Electronics, Soc Act Dept, 1126 Sixteenth St NW, Washington, DC 20036.

BRENSON, VERDEL LEE
Clergyman. **PERSONAL:** Born Feb 28, 1925, Cumberland City, TN; married Quintine Hayes; children: Beverly Elaine, Verdella Rene. **EDUCATION:** Natl Bapt Sem, 1946. **CAREER:** Bryant Temple AME Los Angeles, pastor 1968; Brown Memorial AME Pasadena, pastor 1955-68; Price Chapel AME Los Angeles, pastor 1952-55; St Paul AMEImperial Valley, pastor; 1st AME Pomona, pastor 1948-51; St Mathew AME Clarksville, pastor 1946-47. **ORGANIZATIONS:** Past pres Intrdnmntnl Mnstrs Alliance for Pasadena & Vicinity 1960-62; del to AME Gen Conf 1968 & 1972; mem AME Minstrl Alliance of Los Angeles &vicinity; Los Angeles Br NAACP. **HONORS/ACHIEVEMENTS:** Cited for comm ldrshp Los Angeles Cnclmn Robert Farrell 1974. **BUSINESS ADDRESS:** 2525 W Vernon Ave, Los Angeles, CA 90008.

BRENT, DAVID L.
Government official. **PERSONAL:** Born Jun 27, 1929, Forrest City, AR; married Estella Bryant; children: David Jr, Patricia, Mary, William, Jeanne. **EDUCATION:** Blackstone Coll of Law, LLB 1966; Missouri Univ, 1963-66; Kansas State Univ, 1966; Moody Bible Inst, 1954-57. **CAREER:** MO Dept of Mntl Hlth, chf hmn rel ofcr 1971-; St Louis Civil Rgts Law Enfcmnt & Agy, EEOC proj dir 1969-71; Aetna Life Ins Co, consult 1967-69; Washington DC, soc serv rep 1966-67; Prog Bapt Ch, mnstr 1957. **ORGANIZATIONS:** Bible tchr, orgn devel human rel communctns Affirmative Action Plng; Mgmt Principles & Practices; mem NAACP; MO Black Ldrshp Assn Inc; Am Mgmt Assn; US Civil Serv League; Gov Cncl on Affrmtv Action; MO Orgn Devel Network; bd dir MBLA Pub Prsnl Mgmt Awrd 1976; consult exec order on Fair Empmt Pracs 1973. **HONORS/ACHIEVEMENTS:** Human Rels Recg Awrd 1970. **MILITARY SERVICE:** USAF 1948-52. **BUSINESS ADDRESS:** 2002 Missouri Blvd, Jefferson City, MO 65101.

BRENT, JOHN CLINTON, JR.
Business executive. **PERSONAL:** Born Sep 28, 1937, Hopkingsville, KY; married Arnette J Harris; children: Portia, Shelley, Pamela, John, Frederick, Ronald. **EDUCATION:** TN State Univ, 1955-58; Univ of MD, 1962-64; Univ of CA, 1964-65. **CAREER:** USAF, intelligence spec 1968-67; Colt Industries, office serv mgr 1968-70; Friden Alcatel, sales mgr 1970-75; Brent's Mailing Equip Co pres. **ORGANIZATIONS:** Exec board Rock River Training Corp, Family Advocate Inc. **HONORS/ACHIEVEMENTS:** Agent of the Year Friden Alcatel Corp 1980; Black Enterprise Article Black Enterprise 1982. **MILITARY SERVICE:** USAF Tech Sgrt 10 years; Air Force Commendation Medal Award 1964. **BUSINESS ADDRESS:** President, Brent's Mailing Equipment Co, 129 Phelps Avenue, Rockford, IL 61108.

BREWER, ALVIN L.
Physician. **PERSONAL:** Born Nov 08, 1946, Chicago, IL. **EDUCATION:** Triton Coll, AA (hon) 1970; Univ of IL Chicago Circle Campus, BA 1972; attended Univ of IL Med Ctr; Rush Univ Presbyterian St Luke Med Ctr, MD 1979. **CAREER:** St Mary's Hosp, chief dept of emer med 1985; So MS State Hosp Laurel MS, chief dept of emer med 1985-86, hosp med dir 1986; Hughes Spalding Med Ctr, dir of emer med 1987-; Morehouse School of Med, asst prof. **ORGANIZATIONS:** mem, dir, editor Progressive Sec mag 1985-; contrib editor Functional Human Anatomy; mem Toastmasters, Optimist Intl. **HONORS/ACHIEVEMENTS:** Ford Found Scholarship Triton Coll 1970; Natl Med Fellowship 1975. **MILITARY SERVICE:** USAF sgt 1965-68. **HOME ADDRESS:** 5642 Southern Pine Court, Stone Mountain, GA 30087. **BUSINESS ADDRESS:** Asst Prof, Morehouse School of Medicine, 720 Westview Dr, Atlanta, GA 30335.

BREWER, CURTIS
Legal services corporation executive. **PERSONAL:** Born Sep 18, 1925, Cambridge, MA; son of Nathaniel Albert Brewer and Ethyl Myra Whitaker; married Bettie Anne Foster; children: Zakia Al-Ghuiyy, Geri Jefferson, Scott. **EDUCATION:** New Sch for Social Research, BA 1956; NY Univ Sch of Public Admin & Social Svc, 1957-61; Brooklyn Law Sch, JD 1974. **CAREER:** Community Serv Assoc, dir 1955-60; Self-employed, private ombudsman 1960-67; Untapped Resources Inc, exec dir 1964-74; NY Med Coll Neuropsychology Lab,administrator 1968-70; Untapped Resources Inc, exec dir & genl cnsl 1974-. **ORGANIZATIONS:** Mem natl advisory cncl Architectural & Transp Barriers Compliance Bd Dept of HEW 1977-78; mem bd of dir Nat Cntr for Law & the Handicapped 1975-77; mem advisory cncl Barnard Coll 1980-; mem advisory cncl In-Touch Radio Network 1979-; mem advisory cncl New York City Opera 1980-; mem, American Bar Assn 1975-; mem, New York City Bar Assn 1975-; mem bd of dirs, Fiduciary Insurance Co of America 1988-; mem, Manhattan Borough President's Adv Committee on the Disabled 1986-; mem, Natl Rehabilitation Assn 1976-. **HONORS/ACHIEVEMENTS:** Inductee Nat Hall of Fame for Persons with Disabilities 1983; Handicapped Am of the Yr Pres Comm Emplymnt of Handicapped 1980; Humanitarian Award R Kirzon Group for Handicapped Chldrn 1976; life mem NAACP 1974; Thurgood Marshall Award NY Trial Lawyers Assn 1972. **BUSINESS ADDRESS:** Executive Dir & Gen Counsel, Untapped Resources Inc, 60 1st Ave, New York, NY 10009.

BREWER, JAMES A., SR.
Utility executive. **PERSONAL:** Born Aug 26, 1931, Philadelphia, PA; son of James G Brewer and Virginia Lawson Anderson; married Lonnie Allen, May 03, 1959; children: Dominique L, James A, Jr. **EDUCATION:** Penn State Univ, University Park PA, BS, 1954; Temple Univ, Philadelphia PA, MEd, 1961. **CAREER:** GOIC, Philadelphia PA, branch mgr, 1965-68, regional dir, 1968-69 Brooklyn NY, dir, 1969-72 Detroit MI, exec dir, 1972-80; Mich Con Gas Co, Detroit MI, mgr customer information, 1980-81, dir customer information, 1981-87, vice pres customer & account serv, 1987-. **ORGANIZATIONS:** Trustee, HOSPICE of Southeastern Michigan, 1964-68; consultant, Dept of Health, Educ and Welfare, 1968-72; mem, Accounting Aid Soc, 1976-; mem, New Detroit Inc, 1976-; mem, Civic Searchlight, 1977-; trustee, budget chmn, Chapel Hill Missionary Baptist Church, 1977-; life mem, NAACP, 1978-; commr, Michigan Air Pollution Control Commn, 1979-80; chmn, dir, Private Industry Council, Detroit, MI, 1980-82; pres, Freeman Investment Club, 1986-88; consultant, Outreach Enterprise, 1988-. **HONORS/ACHIEVEMENTS:** Distnguished Serv Award, Greater OIC of Metro Detroit, 1983; Boss of the Year Award, Amer Business Women's Assn, 1987; Heart Light Award, Proving Grounds intl Inc, 1987; Man of the Year

Award, Minority Women Network, 1988; Community Serv Award, Michelob, 1989. **MILITARY SERVICE:** US Army, Specialist 3, 1954-57; Soldier of the Year, 1955; Commander's Trophy, 1956. **BUSINESS ADDRESS:** Vice Pres, Customer and Account Serv, Mich Con Gas Co, 500 Griswold St, 21st Fl, Detroit, MI 48226.

BREWER, JIM
Professional athlete. **PERSONAL:** Born Dec 03, 1951, Maywood, IL. **EDUCATION:** MN U, 1973. **CAREER:** Prtlnd Trlblzrs, professional bsktbl plyr; Detrt Pstns, professional bsktbl plyr 1979; Cleveland, professional bsktbl plyr 1973-78. **BUSINESS ADDRESS:** c/o NBA Players Association, 15 Columbus Circle, New York, NY 10023.

BREWER, MOSES
Business manager. **PERSONAL:** Born Mar 12, 1947. **EDUCATION:** Northeastern Jr Coll Sterling CO, 1966-67; Univ of Denver, BA 1967-71; Univ of Denver, MA 1975. **CAREER:** Baseball program for Denver boys, dir, 1969; St Anne's Elementary School, teacher, 1970; City Auditor's Office, coordinator of microfilm, 1969-71; Univ of Denver, coordinator recreational activities, 1971-72; Univ of Denver, asst dean of student life, 1972-73; Denver Univ, univ consultant-at-large, 1973-; Adolph Coors Co, asst natl program mgr; Denver Public Schools, consultant, 1974-75; Adolph Coors Co, asst natl prog mgr. **ORGANIZATIONS:** Mem All-Regional 9 Basketball Team 1966-67; mem Nat Assn Student Personnel Adminstr; mem Natl Speech Communication Assn; mem Pi Kappa Alpha Frat; United Negro Coll Fund; Black Caucus; Black Alumni Assn Univ of Denver; Western Regional Ombudsman Assn; Natl Scholarship Serv & Funds for Negro Students. **HONORS/ACHIEVEMENTS:** Outstanding Athlete Award 1968; Outstanding Faculty Admin Award 1974; Outstanding Personality Awd. **BUSINESS ADDRESS:** Asst Natl Program Mgr, Adolph Coors Company, 311 10th St #NH420, Golden, CO 80401.

BREWER, RON
Professional athlete. **PERSONAL:** Born Sep 15, 1955, Ft Smith, AR; married Carolyn; children: Ken, Candice. **EDUCATION:** AR, Phy Ed Major 1978; Westark JC, 1975. **CAREER:** San Antonio Spurs, guard 1980-; Portland Trail Blazers, 1978-80; San Antonio Spurs, 1984; Cleveland Cavaliers, 1982; Golden State Warriors, 1983. **ORGANIZATIONS:** Came to the Spurs 1/21/84 from Golden State; came to San Anotnio 12/U9/80 from Portland for Mike Gale; sent to Cleveland in Dec 1981 for Mike Mitchell; went form Cleveland to Golden State in Dec 1982 for World Free. **HONORS/ACHIEVEMENTS:** Led in Steals 3 Times, 2 in points; season high 23 points were 2/23/84 at Utah as a starter; season high 7 rebounds were 2/21/84 vs Phoenix; 1981-82 had career high points 1357 and average 188; career highs of 39, 40, 44 points; won 2 SWC titles; twice he was All-SWC; All-amer twice. **BUSINESS ADDRESS:** San Antonio Spurs, Hemisfair Arena, 777 Sports St, San Antonio, TX 78292.

BREWER, ROSE MARIE
Sociologist/educator. **PERSONAL:** Born Oct 30, 1947, Tulsa, OK; married Walter Griffin; children: Sundiata Brewer Griffin. **EDUCATION:** Northeastern State Coll, BA 1969; Indiana Univ, MA 1971, PhD 1976; Univ of Chicago, Post-Doctoral studies 1981-83. **CAREER:** Rice Univ, vstg lecturer 1976; Univ of TX, asst prof 1977-80, 1983-86; Univ of Chicago, post-doctoral fellow 1981-83; Univ of MN, asst prof 1986-. **ORGANIZATIONS:** Bd dirs, vice pres, pres elect Big Brothers/Big Sisters Austin 1984-; bd dirs Soc for the Study of Social Problems 1985-88; council mem Section on Racial & Ethnic Minorities 1985-88; comm mem Amer Sociological Socl 1986-87; chair Comm on Status of Racial and Ethnic Minorities Assoc 1986-87. **HONORS/ACHIEVEMENTS:** Ford Foundation Fellow 1972-73; NIMH Post-Doctoral Rsch Fellow 1981-83; articles "Black/White Racial Inequality," Humanities and Society 6 1980; "On Reproducing Racial Inequality," Humanities in Society 6 1983; plus many other articles. **BUSINESS ADDRESS:** Professor, University of MN, Afro-Amer Studies & Sociology, 909 Social Sciences, Minneapolis, MN 55455.

BREWER, WEBSTER L.
Judge. **PERSONAL:** Born May 11, 1935, Clarksville, TN; son of Marvin Brewer and Margie Brodie Brewer; married Patricia Freeman; children: Elaine, Pamela, Webster Jr. **EDUCATION:** IN U, BS 1957; IN Univ Sch of Law, JD. **CAREER:** Marion Co Superior Court #2, judge 1975-; Brewer Budnick & Sosin, mng lawyer private practice 1970-75; Indianapolis Lawyers Commn, exec dir 1968-70; United Dist Court for So Dist of IN, probation ofcr 1964-68; US Bur of Prisons, parole ofcr 1960-64; Marion Co Juv Ct, probation ofcr 1958-60; Marion Co Welfare Dept, caseworker 1957-58. **ORGANIZATIONS:** Mem Am Bar Assn; Indianapolis Bar Assn; IN St Bar Assn; Natl Bar Assn; past natl ofcr Phi Alpha Delta Legal Frat Group Leader Christamore Settlement House 1958-60; Juvenile Ct Adv Comm 1960-64; chmn of bd NAACP 1963-64; chmn Labor & Industry Comm Indianapolis Chap NAACP 1964-66; bd mem Forward Inc 1968-70; bd mem Indianapolis Legal Serv Orgn 1970-75; bd mem trustees & chmn Ways & Means Comm Bethel AME Ch 1973-; bd mem Marion Co Child Guidance Clinic 1973-; bd mem Marion Co Youth & Serv Bur 1974-76; bd mem Indianapolis Family Serv Agency 1977-; instr IN Univ Sch of Law seminar 1970; participated in numerous seminars spons by IN Judicial Study Ctr; special proj dir IN Judicial Study Ctr preparing Bench Book for IN judges on facilities avail at various IN penal institutions; mem Kappa Alpha Psi Frat; Trinity Lodge #18; F&AM, PHA; mem Sigma Pi Phi Fraternity 1971. **BUSINESS ADDRESS:** 443 City County Bldg, Indianapolis, IN 46204.

BREWER-MANGUM, ERNESTINE TYWANNA
Educator, librarian. **PERSONAL:** Born Aug 07, 1936, Durham, NC; daughter of Robert Brewer (deceased) and Patti Brewer (deceased); married Billy L Mangum, Jul 25, 1969. **EDUCATION:** NC Central Univ, BA Spanish, Library Sci 1957; Rutgers Univ, MLS 1965; Fairleigh Dickinson Univ, MA Human Devel 1982. **CAREER:** NJ Ed Assoc, mem 1957-; Natl Ed Assoc, mem 1957-; Civil Rights & Human Rights Comm, mem & officer 1963-; Elmwood Presbyterian Church, mem 1964-74; Mt Ararat Baptist Church, mem 1975-; school teacher/librarian. **ORGANIZATIONS:** Mem NJ Historical Soc 1960, NJ Media Assoc, NC Central Univ Alumni Assoc 1960-, Rutherford Educ Assoc 1962-; mem & officer Mt Ararat Women's Club 1974-; volunteer counselor in various self-help groups 1980; interviewed by three editors during Black History Month 1984. **HONORS/ACHIEVEMENTS:** Published article in NJEA Review 1970; Governor's Teachers Recognition Program 1986. **BUSINESS ADDRESS:** Rutherford Board of Education, 176 Park Avenue, Rutherford, NJ 07070.

BREWINGTON, RUDOLPH W.
Reporter. **PERSONAL:** Born Nov 02, 1946, New York City, NY. **EDUCATION:** Federal City Coll, MA (cum laude) 1973, grad study. **CAREER:** WRC/NBC Radio News Wash DC, reporter 1975-; WWDC Radio, news reporter edtr 1971-75; WOOK Radio, news dir 1970-71; WUST Radio, news reptr 1969-70; Washington, DC, bus operator 1969; Natl Syndctd TV Prgm "America's Black Forum", rsrch dir/pnlst 1978-79; Natl Syndctd Radio Prgm "The Black Agenda Reprts", pres/exec prod 1979-80; Asso Prsnl Inc Washington DC, dir pub rels 1980; USNR, pub afrs ofcr 1980. **HONORS/ACHIEVEMENTS:** Recipient Robt F Kennedy Jrnlsm Awrd Citation for ""Diagnosis, Desperate, A Report on Minority Hlth Care"" 1973; APHA Ray Bruner Sci Writing Fellowshp 1974. **MILITARY SERVICE:** USMC corpl e-4 1964-68. **BUSINESS ADDRESS:** 4001 Nebraska Ave NW, Washington, DC 20014.

BREWINGTON, THOMAS E., JR.
Ophthalmologist. **PERSONAL:** Born Oct 12, 1943, Dunn, NC; married Vyvien; children: Kathryne, Mitchelle. **EDUCATION:** Morehouse Coll, BS 1975; Meharry Med Coll, MD 1969; HG Phillips Hosp, intern 1969-70, resd 1970-73. **CAREER:** Prvt Practice, opthlmlgst 1976-; EENT Clinic AUS, chf 1973-75. **ORGANIZATIONS:** Diplmt Am Bd Ophthlmlgy; flw Am Acad & Ophth; mem Natl Med Assn; NC State Med Soc; Guilford Co Med Soc; Greensboro Acad Med; Greensboro Med Soc; Old N State Med Soc Exec bd Guilford Co Easter Seal Soc; mem Phi Beta Sigma Frat. **MILITARY SERVICE:** AUS maj 1973-75; recpt Commendation Medal. **BUSINESS ADDRESS:** PO Box 20346, Greensboro, NC 27420.

BREWSTER, LUTHER GEORGE
Aircraft maintenance manager. **PERSONAL:** Born Dec 16, 1942, Manhattan, NY; son of Donald F. Brewster and Alethia Samuels; married Theresa Maria Smart, May 08, 1965; children: Maria, Luther Jr., Renee. **EDUCATION:** Bronx Community College, Bronx NY, 1965-72; College of Aeronautics, Queens NY, AAS, 1974; Lehman College, Bronx NY, 1980-87; North Central College, Naperville IL, 1988—. **CAREER:** Pratt & Whitney Aircraft, Hartford CT, engine mechanic, 1964; Pan American, New York NY, aircraft & engine mechanic, 1965-77; Seaboard World Airlines, Frankfurt, West Germany, maintenance rep, 1977; American Airlines, Chicago IL, division mgr aircraft maintenance, 1977—. **ORGANIZATIONS:** Institute for Certification of Engineering Tech, Aviation Maintenance Foundation, American Management Association. **HONORS/ACHIEVEMENTS:** Honored by official resolution of Boston City Council, 1986; certificate of merit, youth motivation program, CACI, 1987-88. **MILITARY SERVICE:** US Air Force, technical sergeant, 1960-64; good conduct medal, expeditionary medal, outstanding unit award.

BREWTON, BUTLER E.
Educator, poet. **PERSONAL:** Born Feb 07, 1935, Spartanburg, SC; son of W O Brewton and J M Brewton; divorced; children: Seneca, Monica, Catrina. **EDUCATION:** Benedict, BA 1956; Montclair State, MA 1970; Rutgers, EdD 1978. **CAREER:** Montclair State Coll, assoc prof, English, 1970-. **ORGANIZATIONS:** Consultant, McGraw Hill Intl Press 1972; poet NJ State Council on the Arts 1970-76; speaker NCTE Kansas City 1978; writer book "South and Border States" The Literary Guide to the US; "Richard Wrights Thematic Treatment of Women" ERIC. **HONORS/ACHIEVEMENTS:** NDEA fellow SC State Coll 1965; poems "Tramp", "Lady of the Evening", "5 PM", "Discovered", "Pattern", "Barren", "Southbound", "Idol", "Yesterday Hangs", "The Custodial Hour", "Democracy", "The Kiss", "For A Reprieve", "Peach Orchard", "Full Measure", "At the General Store"; article New York Times "A Diploma Must Mean What It's Supposed to Mean" New York Times 1986; speaker, NCTE. **MILITARY SERVICE:** USAF A/2. **BUSINESS ADDRESS:** Assoc Prof of English, Montclair State College, English Department, Upper Montclair, NJ 07043.

BRICE, EUGENE CLAY
Retired government official. **PERSONAL:** Born Jun 18, 1929, Morristown, TN; married Vert; children: Eugene II, Alan, Alesia. **EDUCATION:** Morristown Jr Coll, 1949; MD State Coll, 1950. **CAREER:** US Govt, 1955-84; Wright-Patterson AFB, data processing 1964-69, computer supv 1969-77, mgr 1977-retired 1984. **ORGANIZATIONS:** Vp Springfield OH Frontiers Intl 1972-75; bd dir Springfield OH Urban League 1974-76; dist treas N Central Dist 1975-82; trustee Rose Devel Corp 1975-; mem Springfield OH Bd of Realtors 1975-80; pres Springfield OH Frontiers Intl 1976; vice pres Rose Devel Corp 1979-. **HONORS/ACHIEVEMENTS:** Player No 1 Football Team MD State Coll 1949; Wright-Patterson AFB Mgr of the Month 1975; Springfield OH Frontiersman of the Year 1978. **MILITARY SERVICE:** AUS 1951-53.

BRICE, PERCY A., JR.
Professional musician. **PERSONAL:** Born Mar 25, 1923, New York City, NY; married Pearl Minott. **EDUCATION:** Music Sch, 4 yrs. **CAREER:** Luis Russell Orch, 1944; Benny Carter Orch, 1945-46; Mercer Ellington, 1947; Eddie Vinson, 1947-51; Tiny Grimes Show Group, 1951-52; Harlems Savoy Bathroom with Lucky Thompson's 8-piece & Group; Billy Taylor Trio, 1954-56; George Shearing Quintet, 1956-58; Carmen McRae Sarah Vaughn, 1959-61; Harry Belafonte Troupe 1961-68; New Sound, leader plyng lounge circts around metro area. **ORGANIZATIONS:** Taugh drums 1969-71; mem Masonic Order 1949-. **HONORS/ACHIEVEMENTS:** Harlem Dist champ in table tennis.

BRICKUS, JOHN W.
Elected official. **PERSONAL:** Born Jul 28, 1919, Coatesville, PA; married Susan A Corley. **EDUCATION:** Howard Univ, attended 1937-41. **CAREER:** Commonwealth of PA, mgr of PLCB 28 yrs; Valley Twp, vice chr bd of super. **ORGANIZATIONS:** Mem Chester Co Twp Officials Council; mem bd of trustees Chester Co Dept of Welfare; mem Elks Lodge 159 Axe Grinders Charity Clubs; mem pastor's steward & choir mem St Paul AME Church; mem NAACP; mgr Brickus Funeral Home 1950-85; admin super Valley Twp 1979-85; life mem Amateur Trapshooting Assoc; mem Nat Rifle Assoc; mem Eastern Trapshooting Assoc. **HONORS/ACHIEVEMENTS:** Co-owner Susan A Brickus Funeral Home; chmn Township Bd of Adjustment & Appeals; Comm Serv Awd from Local Business & Prof Group 1982. **HOME ADDRESS:** 977 W Lincoln Hwy, Coatesville, PA 19320.

BRIDGEFORTH, BARBARA (BARBARA COLLIER LONG)
Government official. **PERSONAL:** Born Dec 18, 1943, Athens, AL; daughter of John Robert Collier and Eunice Louise Collier; married John Henry Bridgeforth; children: Tracey Dione. **EDUCATION:** Alabama A&M Univ, BS 1965. **CAREER:** Dept of Energy, compliance officer 1973-78; Dept of Labor, program analyst 1978-79, supervisor 1979-80, area of-

fice dir 1980-84, dir of regional operations. **ORGANIZATIONS:** Mem Fundraising Comm BACS 1982; past vice pres adv bd VEVA 1984; vice pres prof dev NABHRP 1986; mem NAACP, Zeta Phi Beta Sor; agent Realty World; pres TSB Ranch; vice pres Wakefield Estates; volunteer fundraiser United Negro Coll Fund; mem Amer Assoc Affirmative Action Officers; mem CA Assoc of Affirmative Action Officers; moderator Beth Eden Retreat Comm Workshop; rep Federal Women's Program; volunteer Ctr for Independent Living. **HONORS/ACHIEVEMENTS:** Special Recognition BACS 1982, VEVA 1984; Special Achievement Dept of Energy 1976, Dept of Labor 1984; Outstanding Young Women Women's Suffrage Awd 1984; Outstanding Young Women of Amer 1986. **HOME ADDRESS:** 2696 Rollingwood Lane, Atlanta, GA 30316. **BUSINESS ADDRESS:** Assistant District Director, U S Department of Labor-OFCCP, 1373 Peachtree Street NE, Suite 305, Atlanta, GA 30309.

BRIDGEMAN, DONALD EARL
Personnel/program administrator. **PERSONAL:** Born Mar 14, 1939, Grenville, Grenada;son of Julien Anthony Bridgeman and Madonna Theresa Bridgeman; married Dr Rosemary Malcolm; children: Winston, Selwyn, Joie, Edelyne. **EDUCATION:** Erdiston Teachers Coll, AA Educ 1960; Howard Univ, BSc 1968; Northwestern Univ, Cert Mortg Banker 1973; Southeastern Univ, MBPA (w/Honors) 1976. **CAREER:** Foundation for Coop Housing, dir hsg spec inst 1969-72; Howard Univ, dir ctr for housing and real estate 1975-77; US Dept of Housing & Urban Develop,employee develop spec 1977-84; Prince George's County Govt, deputy personnel officer 1984-. **ORGANIZATIONS:** Mem United Way Health and Welfare Cncl Washington DC 1965-76; co-founder of CHANGE Federal Credit Union Washington DC; co-founder Natl Assoc of Housing Specialists 1971; conf dir Joint Annual Minority Housing Conf 1974-80; consultant Winston-Salem State Univ, Southern Univ, and Texas Southern Univ on develop of housing mgmt curricula 1975-77; pres Housing Specialists Inst 1977-81; pres, Local Government Personnel Assn of the Baltimore-Washington Metro Area 1986-89. **HONORS/ACHIEVEMENTS:** Samuel E Sessions Awd Natl Assoc of Housing Specialists Housing Specialists Inst 1975; Realist of the Year Awd Washington Real Estate Brokers Assoc 1976; Superior & Excellent Performance Awds HUD Washington DC 1979,80; Personnelist of the Year, International Personnel Management Assn, Eastern Region 1989. **HOME ADDRESS:** 600 Dwyer Place, Largo, MD 20772. **BUSINESS ADDRESS:** Deputy Personnel Officer, Prince George County Govt, 425 Brightseat Rd, Landover, MD 20785.

BRIDGEMAN, JUNIOR
Professional athlete. **PERSONAL:** Born Sep 17, 1953, East Chicago, IL; married Doris; children: Justin, Ryan. **EDUCATION:** Louisville, Psychology 1975. **CAREER:** Los Angeles Clippers, guard 1984-. **HONORS/ACHIEVEMENTS:** Earned Acad and Athletic All-Amer honors in Sr year u of LA; in Sr year named Most Valuable Player MO Valley Conf. **BUSINESS ADDRESS:** Los Angeles Clippers, 3939 S Figueroa St, 777 Sports St, Los Angeles, CA 90037.

BRIDGES, ALVIN LEROY
Physician. **PERSONAL:** Born Jun 06, 1925, Dayton, OH; married Lois; children: Alvin Jr, Keith, Lori, Cornelius. **EDUCATION:** Univ Dayton, BS 1948; Meharry Med Coll, MD 1952; Kansas City Genl Hosp, intern 1952-53; Univ Cincinnati VA Hosp, resd 1953-54. **CAREER:** Community Hosp Alderson IN, chief of staff 1984; Private Practice, physician 1954-. **ORGANIZATIONS:** Charter diplomate Amer Bd Family Practice; recertified Amer Bd of Family Practice 1977, 1984; charter fellow Amer Acad Family Physicians; mem Intl SocIntl Medicine; Amer Acad Family Physicians; Natl Med Assn; life mem NAACP; Alpha Phi Alpha Frat. **MILITARY SERVICE:** AUS 1943-46. **BUSINESS ADDRESS:** 1302 S Madison Ave, Anderson, IN 46016.

BRIDGES, JAMES WILSON
Physician. **PERSONAL:** Born Feb 16, 1935, Valdosta, GA; married Earnestine Bryant; children: Sabrina, Lloyd, Mark. **EDUCATION:** Central State Coll, BS 1956; Meharry Medical Coll, MD 1960; Hmr G Phillips Hospital, intern 1961, chief resident 1966; Univ Miami, resident 1967. **CAREER:** Private practice, physician; Univ Miami, clinical asst prof; Cedars of Lebanon Health Care Center, chief; Christian Hospital, chief. **ORGANIZATIONS:** Diplomate, Amer Bd of Obstetrics & Gynecology, 1969; bd of trustees, Christian Hospital, 1973-76; bd dir, FL Div Amer Cancer Soc, 1972-77, FL Physicians Ins Rec, 1985, FL Physicians Ins Co, FL Political Action Comm; chmn, FL Div United Cancer Task Force, 1975-77; member, Beta Beta Lambda Chapter, Alpha Phi Alpha, NAACP, Comm Minority Affairs Univ of Miami School of Medicine. **HONORS/ACHIEVEMENTS:** Fellow Amer Coll of Obstetrics & Gynecolgy 1970; scholarship FL State Medical Coll 1959-60. **MILITARY SERVICE:** AUS medical corps captain 1961-63. **BUSINESS ADDRESS:** 8340 NE Second Ave, Ste 222, Miami, FL 33138.

BRIDGES, LEON
Architect, business executive. **PERSONAL:** Born Aug 18, 1932, Los Angeles, CA; married Eloise Avonne Jones; children: Vanessa Joy, Elise Gay, Leon Jr, Elliott Reynolds. **EDUCATION:** Univ of Washington, B Arch 1959; Urban Syst, post grad studies; Loyola College of MD, MBA 1984. **CAREER:** Intern asst city planner 1956; Leon Bridges Arch, owner 1963-66; Bridges/Burke Arch & Planners, partner 1966-72; The Archl Research Collabor Inc, owner 1976-; The Leon Bridges Co, owner 1972-. **ORGANIZATIONS:** Visit prof Hampton Inst 1971/1973/1975; visit prof Prairie View A&M 1972; particip Tuskegee Inst Comm Arch Design Charette sponsored by Endowment of the Arts 1971; mem Guild for Religious Architecture; panelist Mental Health Center Design sponsored by AIA and Natl Inst of Mental Health; mem AIA; mem Natl Urban League; mem MD State Arts Councl 1980-; bd dir Lutheran Hosp 1980-; bd dir MD Minority Contractors Assn 1981; chmn Morgan State Univ Urban Dev Comm 1981; bd dir Roland Park Place 1981; bd of advisors Univ of Knoxville TN 1981-; bd dir School for the Deaf 1981; bd of dirs The Amer Inst of Architects 1984-; Middle Atlantic Region Dir of The Amer Inst of Architects 1984-; assoc prof Morgan State Univ 1985-; vice pres The Amer Inst of Architects 1987-. **HONORS/ACHIEVEMENTS:** Honor Award The Amer Soc of Landscape Architects 1980; The Black Pages Award Recogn for Outstanding Contrib to the Economic Health of Minority Enterprise in Baltimore 1981; Merit Award The Amer Inst of Architects in Wash, DC; Recogn for Outstanding Contribution for Restoration of the Baltimore Pennsylvania Station 1981; Design Excellence Awd Natl Org of Minority Architects of the Baltimore/Penn Station 1983; Design Excellence Awd The Amer Inst of Architects Baltimore Chap Baltimore Penn Station 1985; Design Excellence Awd NOMA Lexington Market Subway Station 1985; Grand Conceptor Awd Amer Consulting Engrs Council Ft McHenry Tunnel East Ventilation Building & Opers Control Bldg 1986. **MILITARY SERVICE:** AUS Corpl 1952-54. **BUSINESS ADDRESS:** Architect, The Leon Bridges Company, 3000 Chestnut Ave, Ste 100, Baltimore, MD 21211.

BRIDGES, LUCILLE W.
Educator. **PERSONAL:** Born Jul 03, 1923, Virginia; married Stanley P; children: Stanley P Jr. **EDUCATION:** Howard U, BA (cum laude) 1945, JD 1949; SUNY, mEd Social Studies1970. **CAREER:** Law Related Educ Afro-Am History, History teacher cons; Author, conent writer teachers manual; Dept of Instructional TV, MD & State Bd of Educ, TV series "Afro-am Perspectives"; Handbook for DC Teachers, co-author 1960; Area Coll & Univ, lecturer in Urban Educ Methods & Afro-Amer History 1967-72. **ORGANIZATIONS:** Life Mem NEA; mem Natl Council for Soc Stud 1968-; fndr 1st pres Washington DC Cncl for the Soc Stds 1975; curriculum wrtr "Discover DC" 1976; sec Asbury United Meth Women 1976-77; lectr Juvenile Justice 1976; Title IV Engl Wkshp 1976-77; chmn History Dept Woodrow Wilson Sr HS 1977; mem Advisory Com Emergency Sch Aid Act Prgm 1976-77; Urban League; NAACP; Washington Tchrs Union #6; Capital Press Club; State Dir Wash DC ASALH; former mem Adv Bd Natl Jrsprdnce Club; mem Delta Sigma & Theta; Iota Phi Lambda; vice pres Alpha Wives of Washington DC; Asbury United Meth Ch; Mus of African Art; former Ed Bakers Dozen Newsletter; DCEA Nwsltr; Ft Totten Civic Assn Newsletter "The Asburyan". **HONORS/ACHIEVEMENTS:** Awrd for Excellence in Tchng US Dept of State 1964; NDEA Experienced Tchr Flwshp SUNY 1968-69; Cert of Serv Barney Nghbrhd House 1969; Serv Awrd Capital Press Club 1970; EDPA Flswhp Afro-Am Hist 1970-71; Taft Inst in Govt Flwshp AmUniv 1971; Title III Wrkshp DC Schs 1975. **BUSINESS ADDRESS:** Woodrow Wilson HS, Nebraska & Chesapeake St NW, Washington, DC 20016.

BRIDGETT-CHISOLM, KAREN
Computer consultant. **PERSONAL:** Born Mar 25, 1956, Jamaica, NY; married Darryl A Chisolm. **EDUCATION:** Pace Univ, BBA 1979. **CAREER:** EBASCO Serv Inc, programmer 1978-80; Computer Sciences Corp, mktg specialist 1980-83; Information Sciences Inc, product training mgr 1983-84; Sony Corp of Amer, project leader 1984-87; The Hunter Group Inc, consultant 1987-. **ORGANIZATIONS:** Mem Zeta Phi Beta Sor Inc 1978-, Human Resources Systems Profls Inc 1985-, The EDGES Group Inc 1985-; instructor LaGuardia Comm Coll 1986-. **BUSINESS ADDRESS:** Consultant, The Hunter Group Inc, 6 Landmark Square, 4th Floor, Stamford, CT 06901.

BRIDGEWATER, ALBERT LOUIS
Government official, scientist. **PERSONAL:** Born Nov 22, 1941, Houston, TX; son of Albert Bridgewater and Rita Narcisse Bridgewater; married Juanita Edington (divorced); children: Ramesi, Nicole, Ryan, Akin; married Hebe Milagros Candelario, Jul 06, 1988. **EDUCATION:** Columbia Univ, PhD 1972, MA 1967; Univ of CA, BA 1963. **CAREER:** Univ of CA, postdoctoral fellow 1970-73; Elem Particle Physics, asst prof officer 1973-74; Howard Univ, prof 1974-75; Natl Science Foundation, staff asst 1973-76, special asst 1976-86, acting asst dir for AAEO/NSF 1983-85, deputy assistant director, AAEO/NSF 1981-86, sr staff assoc 1986-. **ORGANIZATIONS:** Mem, Amer Physical Soc; Amer Geophysical Union; mem advisory board, LBL/SSU/AGMFF Science Consortium 1986-88. **HONORS/ACHIEVEMENTS:** Order of Golden Bear; Peace Corp volunteer, West Cameroon, 1963-65. **BUSINESS ADDRESS:** Senior Science Associate, National Science Foundation, 1800 G St, NW, Washington, DC 20550.

BRIDGEWATER, HERBERT JEREMIAH, JR.
Reservation sales agent. **PERSONAL:** Born Jul 03, 1942, Atlanta, GA; son of Herbert Bridgewater (deceased) and Mary Sallie Clark Bridgewater Hughes. **EDUCATION:** Clark Coll, Atlanta GA, BA, Business Admin, 1968; Atlanta Univ, 1968; Univ of Georgia, Inst of Govt & Center for Continuing Educ, 1978; Atlanta Area Technical School, Certificate of Completion, 1980; Federal Law Enforcement Training Center, 1980; Spelman Coll Inst for Continuing Educ, 1984. **CAREER:** Atlanta Public School Syst, teacher, Business & English Commun, 1964-67; Atlanta Housing Authority, relocation & family serv consultant, 1967-70; Federal Trade Commn, consumer protection specialist, dir of public affairs 1970-83; Atlanta Area Tech School, teacher 1978-; Clark Coll, assoc prof 1983-; Delta Airlines Inc, customer sales & serv 1984-. **ORGANIZATIONS:** Bd mem, GA Chapter, The Epilepsy Found of Amer, Mid-Atlanta Unit Amer Cancer Soc; bd chmn The Atlanta Dance Theatre; task force Just Us Theater; founding mem Intl Assoc for African Heritage & Black Identity; mem The Atlanta Jr Chamber of Commerce, The Big Brothers Council of Atlanta, The Natl Urban League, United Negro Coll Fund; host "Bridging the Gap" 1981-, "Confrontation" 1974-; owned & oper 1st all black professional placement serv in GA as Bridgewaters Personnel Serv 1971-75; columnist "Facts for Consumers"; former columnist "Unsung Heroes". **HONORS/ACHIEVEMENTS:** Received natl acclaim after successfully obtaining & delivering to the US Congress over 10,000 signatures of registered GA voters which were secured in 4 days in support of House of Reps Resolution to refrain former GA Gov Lester Maddox from passingout racially symbolized objects on the US House Capital ground 1969; individually won the struggle to have Black Coll athletic scores aired onTV stations in GA 1966; assisted the City of Atlanta & Consumer Affairs Office in preparing proposed Consumer Protection Ordinance for the City of Atlanta which is currently in existence; Outstanding Serv Award Martin Luther King Jr Center for Social Change in support of Kingfest 1984; Distinguished Supporter Top Star Awd 1983; Best Talk Show Host on Radio Award Atlanta Chapter Natl Assn of Black Journalist , 1983; Dr Herbert J Bridgewater Jr Day in Atlanta Proclaimed by Mayor Andrew Young, 1982; Super-Teacher Award, students at Atlanta Area Tech School, 1982; Numerous others; Meritorious Serv Award, GA Chapter, Epilepsy Found of Amer, 1981; Outstanding Serv & Coop Award, Amer Red Cross, 1981; Outstanding Serv, Atlanta Fed Exec Bd Minority Business Opportunity Comm, 1981; Distinguished & Dedicated Serv Award, Greater Travelers Rest Baptist Church, Decature GA, 1981; Outstanding Comm Serv Award, SW Career Counsel. **BUSINESS ADDRESS:** Reservations Sales/Serv Agent, Delta Airlines Inc, 1718 Peachtree St NW, Ste 1000, Atlanta, GA 30309.

BRIDGEWATER, PAUL
Public administration. **EDUCATION:** Saginaw Valley Coll, BA 1975. **CAREER:** Saginaw Bd of Educ, career advisor 1971; Poverty Peoples Alliance, outreach worker 1972-74; Opportunities Industrialization Ctr of Metro Saginaw, counselor 1974-75; Saginaw County Comm Action Committee, comm developer 1975-77; MI State Univ Cooperative Ext Svcs, ext 4-H youth agent 1977-80; Mayor Young's Farm-A-Lot Program, field coord 1980; Detroit Area Agency on Aging, supervisor 1980-. **ORGANIZATIONS:** Chairperson Comm for the Black Art Festival; mem MI State Fair Agriculture Comm; mem Optimist Intl Club of Central Detroit; mem Natl Caucus and Concernsfor the Black Aged; natl bd mem NCBA; mem

Mayor Young's Hunger and Malnutrition Task Force; mem Leadership Detroit VII; mem Chamber of Commerce. **HONORS/ACHIEVEMENTS:** Outstanding Young Men of Amer Jaycees 1981; Special recognition MI House and Senate for "Outstanding Serv to the Comm"; delegate MI White House Conference on Aging. **BUSINESS ADDRESS:** Supervisor, Detroit Area Agency on Aging, 3110 Book Building, 1249 Washington Blvd, Detroit, MI 48226.

BRIDWELL, HERBERT H.
Education administrator. **PERSONAL:** Born Aug 23, 1928, Jonesboro, TN; married Cue Tribble. **EDUCATION:** TN State A&I Univ Nashville, BS 1951; TC Columbia Univ NY, MS 1955; IN Univ, 1960-61; GA State Univ, FL A&M Univ, attended. **CAREER:** Twin Lake High School, Palm Beach City School Dist, teacher, principal sec dir, 1959-85; Palm Beach City School Dist, area supt north. **ORGANIZATIONS:** Pres Palm Beach Cty Principals Assoc 1975-76; bd dir Boy Scouts, YMCA, Rotary, Project Rescue 1975; chmn plng bd City of West Palm Beach 1979-81; chmnCity of West Palm Beach Plng Bd 1979-81; mem Urban League, NAACP 1960-85. **HONORS/ACHIEVEMENTS:** Omega Man of the Year Kappa Upsilon Chap Omega Psi Phi Inc West Palm Beach FL 1963. **MILITARY SERVICE:** AUS m/sgt 1951-53; Bronze Star 1952. **HOME ADDRESS:** 318 S Chillingworth Dr, West Palm Beach, FL 33409.

BRIEVE-MARTIN, ILA CORRINNA
Educator. **PERSONAL:** Born Mar 20, 1939, Newark, NJ; married Robert H Dean. **EDUCATION:** Bloomfield Coll Bloomfield, NJ, BA 1964; Rutgers Univ Grad Sch of Edn, EdM 1972, EdD 1975. **CAREER:** Central High Sch Newark, Spanish teacher 1964-67, title I coordinator 1967-70; US Dept of Justice Comm Relations Dept, consult 1968-70; Rutgers Univ GradSch of Edn, asst prof 1970-74; VA Commonwealth Univ Richmond, asst dean sch of educ 1975-80; VA State Univ, assoc prof div of Educ Leadership 1984-. **ORGANIZATIONS:** Consult US Dept of Justice Comm Relations Dept 1968-70; vice pres Bus & Professional Women 1967-69; bd of dir Richmond Area Programs for Minorities in Engineering 1977-; bd of dir Greater Richmond Transit Co 1978-80; mem Phi Delta Kappa 1973. **HONORS/ACHIEVEMENTS:** Fellowship Univ of AL 1979; Outstanding Educator Award PTA Richmond; various publications in area of creative dynamics. **BUSINESS ADDRESS:** Associate Professor, Virginia State University, 35 Ivy Lane, Petersburg, VA 23805.

BRIGGINS, CHARLES E.
Educator. **PERSONAL:** Born Nov 06, 1930, Helena, AL; married Mary Jones; children: Charles, Anthony, Tonya. **EDUCATION:** AL A&M U, BS 1956, MS 1961. **CAREER:** Huntsville City Schools, diversifiedd occupations coord; Huntsville AL, vctnl T&I coord, 1971; Decatur City Schools, teacher coord, 1958-71; KY State Coll, instructor, 1956-68. **ORGANIZATIONS:** Mem AL Educ Ass; AL Vocational Assn; Am Vocational Assn 1958; mem Alpha Phi Alpha; RE Nelms Elks Lodge #977; Masn; VFW; Am Legion. **MILITARY SERVICE:** AUS sgt 1951-54. **BUSINESS ADDRESS:** SR Butler HS, 2401 Homes Ave, Huntsville, AL.

BRIGGS, COLLIN
Educator. **PERSONAL:** Born Dec 11, 1920, Houston; married Hallie Mae Waddell; children: Brenda, Kenneth, Octavia. **EDUCATION:** Tuskegee Inst, BS 1942; TX So Univ, MEd 1948; Prairie View A&7 Univ, Admin Cert 1974. **CAREER:** Phillis Wheatley Houston, physical educ & coaching, 1946-68; Prototype Schools Project Houston, community coord, 1968-70; Educ Component Model Cities Proj Houston, community coord, 1968-69; Teacher Instr Program Houston, coord, 1969-70; Multi-Culstural Awareness Program Houston, asst program dir, 1969-70; Parent Adv Program, officer, 1970-71; CUSG Program Houston, acting coord, 1971-73; Model Cities Adult Learning Center Houston, admin asst, 1973-. **ORGANIZATIONS:** Mem TX State Tchrs Assn; Alpha Kappa Psi Frat; Houston Princs Assn; mem Bsktbll Cntry Club, winning over 100 games 1954. **HONORS/ACHIEVEMENTS:** Phillis Wheatley Man of Yr Awrd 1961; TX So Quarter Back Club Coack of Yhr Awrd 1963; Outstanding Achvmnt Awrd for Outstndng Ldrshp 1968; Alpha Kappa Psi Frat Kappa of Yr Awrd 1968; Resolution signed by Spkr of House Ben Barnes presented to Wheatley Wildcates for Tremendous Athletic Achvmnt & Collin Briggs for Guidance in Sportsmnshp & Athletic Skill; Jack Yates Sr HS Comm Serv Awrd 1969; May 16, proclaimed by Mayor Louis Welch as Collin Briggs Day 1969; Outstndng Achvmnt Awrd Tuskegee Inst 1973; During 23 yrs coaching 1947-69 608 wins 55 losses, won 13 state chmpnshps, runner up 1 yr & 3rd pl 1 yr; Attended Nat HS Tournmnt Nashville TN 3 yrs, 1st yr lost in Quartr Fnls, 2nd yr lost in Semi-fnls, 3rd yr won 2nd plc. **MILITARY SERVICE:** Sgt Transp Corps 1942-46. **BUSINESS ADDRESS:** 3830 Richmond Ave, Houston, TX 77027.

BRIGGS, PAUL W.
Retired superintendent. **PERSONAL:** Born Nov 23, 1912, Mayville, MI; married Arvilla; children: Betty, James. **EDUCATION:** Western MI, AB 1934; MI State U, MA 1943; Columbia, postgrad 1956; Baldwin-Wallace Coll, EdD 1964; Central State U; Cleveland State U; Case Inst Tech, LHD 1966. **CAREER:** Cleveland OH, supt of schools, 1964-; Parma Public Schools, 1957-64; Bay City, prin, 1943-53, teacher, 1940-42; Brown City, teacher, prin, 1934-40; OH State Univ, lecturer, 1963; Cleveland State Univ Bd, adjunct prof. **ORGANIZATIONS:** Mgrs Cleveland Metro YMCA 1964; mem exec bd BSA 1960-; mem exec com Nat Urban Coalition; mem Nat OH Educ Assn; sch admin rotarian OH Assn; past pres Bay City Mason; 33rd deg Shriner. **HONORS/ACHIEVEMENTS:** Recpt Ann Brotherhood Award; Nat Conf Christians & Jews 1974. **BUSINESS ADDRESS:** HQ 4 ROTC Region, Fort Lewis, WA 98433.

BRIGGS-GRAVES, ANASA
Senior producer, director of black ethnic affairs. **PERSONAL:** Born in Loma Linda, CA. **EDUCATION:** Univ of CA Riverside, 1968-70; Univ of CA Santa Barbara, BA Drama 1986; San Diego State Univ, Masters pending. **CAREER:** SD Unified School Dist, drama consult 1976-78; Grad School for Urban Resources, staff consultant 1977-78; Mozaic Repertory Theator, actress 1978-79; Barbizon School of Modeling, TV acting instr 1979; San Diego State Univ KPBS-TV, producer black ethnic affairs. **ORGANIZATIONS:** Pres San Diego Assoc of Black Journalists; chairperson exec bd, exec bd SD Black Leadership Council; Natl Med Assn; bd of dir Comprehensive Health Ctr; United Way Contact Team; SD County Human Relations Commission Advisory Bd for Media; regional dir, Natl Assn of Black Journalists 1987-89; bd of governors San Diego Chapter, Natl Acad of Television Arts & Sciences 1988-89; bd mem San Diego Opera 1989-91; bd mem Mayor's Black Advisor Bd 1986-89; bd mem Study Commn on Black Affairs 1985-89. **HONORS/ACHIEVEMENTS:** Achievement Nancy Wilson Found 1983; Bronze Medal Intl Film & TV Fest of NY 1983; Excellence in Journalism San Diego Chap NAACP 1984; Emmy Nominee Producer Category San Diego 1984; Old Glove Theater Best Supporting Actress in Lead Role 1975-76; 2nd Runner Up Miss San Diego; fellow Media Inst USC Mid Summer Inst in Broadcast Mgmt for Minorities 1982; fellow CA Public Broadcasting Commiss Mgmt Training 1983; SD Pres Club Best Documentary 1986; Natl Assn of Black Journalists1986; Best TV Feature Annual Award; Emmy 1986; Emmy nominee for Religious Program "The Spiritual Legacy of the Gospel" Emmy nominee for Entertainment Program " Water of your Bath". **BUSINESS ADDRESS:** Sr Producer Blk Ethnic Affairs, San Diego StateUniv, KPBS SDSU, San Diego, CA 92182.

BRIGHT, ALFRED LEE
Artist, educator. **PERSONAL:** Born Jan 09, 1940, Youngstown, OH; married Patricia; children: Leslie, Alfred Jr, Nichole, Steven. **EDUCATION:** Youngstown U, BS 1964; Kent St U, MA 1965. **CAREER:** Youngstown State Univ, dir black studies program & assoc prof art, 1985. **ORGANIZATIONS:** Mem St Dept of Edn, Advisory Com on the Arts; exec mem OH Arts Council; mem Natl Humanities Faculty; Art Blakey and the Jazz Messengers 1980; Jimmy Owens 1985. **HONORS/ACHIEVEMENTS:** Num one-man shows; exhbns; pvt colls, perm colls dev, "Total Walk-In Environmental Rooms", 1st & hon ment award Butler Art Inst, Youngstown 1967; best of show Haber-Gall 1966; 1st & 2nd awards, oils Village Cntr Fine Art Exhib, Niles OH 1964-67; consult Nat Humanities Faculty 1977-; co-author "An Interdisciplinary Intro to Black Studies"; Best of Show Butler Inst of Amer Art 1984; 1st place AAA Exhibit Butler Inst of Amer Art 1985; listed in Who's Who in Amer Art 17th ed; exhibitions, Butler Inst of Amer Art 1985, Roanoke Museum of Fine Arts 1986, Harmon-Meek Gallery Naples FL 1986. **BUSINESS ADDRESS:** Professor of Art, Youngstown State University, Black Studies Program, 410 Wick Ave, Youngstown, OH 44555.

BRIGHT, HERBERT L., SR.
Corporate executive. **PERSONAL:** Born Aug 20, 1941, Shelbyville, TN; son of Henry Bright and Alvirleen Buchanan; married Vera Foulks, May 08, 1965; children: Troy, Sonja, Yolanda, Herbert Jr., Kristi. **EDUCATION:** Thornton Junior College, Harvey, IL; Seton Hall University, South Orange, NJ. **CAREER:** Nabisco Brands, Inc, general clerk, 1963-65, operations manager, 1968-72, assistant accounting office manager, 1972-73, personnel policies specialist, 1973-75, corporate equal opportunity manager, 1975-79, senior manager of personnel services, 1979-83, director of personnel practices, 1983-87, director of personnel services, 1987—. **ORGANIZATIONS:** President, board of directors, Nabisco Brands Employee Credit Union; member, corporate advisory council, NAACP ACT-SO, Opportunities Industrialization Centers of America, Tom Skinner Associates' Industry and Labor Council; member, National Urban League Commerce and Industry Council, American Society for Personnel Administration, Union County Urban League Board, Virginia Union University Cluster, Howard University Cluster, Felician College Business Advisory Board. **HONORS/ACHIEVEMENTS:** Whitney M Young, Jr, Memorial Award, Morris County Urban League, 1985; national honoree, Afro-American History Award, 1987. **MILITARY SERVICE:** US Army, 1963-66. **BUSINESS ADDRESS:** Nabisco Brands, Inc, 6 Campus Dr, Parsippany, NJ 07054.

BRIGHT, JEAN MARIE
Educator, writer. **PERSONAL:** Born Sep 23, 1915, Rutherfordton, NC; daughter of John W Bright, Sr and Wollie Lynch Bright. **EDUCATION:** North Carolina Agricultural and Technical State Univ, Greensboro NC, BS, l9339; Columbia Univ, New York, NY, MA, l953. **CAREER:** North Carolina Agricultural and Technical State Univ, Greensboro NC, prof of English, 1951-78; lecturer, North Carolina Humanities Comm, 1977-79. **ORGANIZATIONS:** Mem, African Literature Assn; mem, Coll Language Assn; pres, Bright Forest Enterprises, Inc, 1980-89. **HONORS/ACHIEVEMENTS:** Co-editor, Images of the Negro in Amer, 1965; co-editor, Voices from the Black Experience, 1972. **HOME ADDRESS:** 1008 S Benbow Rd, Greensboro, NC 27406.

BRIGHT, WILLIE S.
Executive search consultant. **PERSONAL:** Born Feb 07, 1934, Houston, TX; son of Willie S Bright and Ovida Y Johnson; married Mildred Ball, Jun 04, 1960; children: Develous A, Nicole O. **EDUCATION:** Tuskegee Inst, Tuskegee AL, 1951-53; Texas Southern Univ, Houston TX, BA, 1955, MEd, 1964. **CAREER:** Houston Independent School Dist, Houston TX, teacher, 1959-66; Crescent Found, Houston TX, counselor, 1966-67; Concentrated Employment Program, Houston TX, training officer, 1967-68; Forenz Southeastern Inc, Houston TX, dir, 1968-71; The Urban Placement Serv, Houston TX, owner, 1971-. **ORGANIZATIONS:** Vice polemarch, bd mem, Kappa Alpha Psi, Houston Alumni 1954-; mem, Natl Assn of Personnel Consultants, 1971-; vice pres, dir, Houston Area Assn of Personnel Consultants, 1971-; bd of dir, Mental Health Assn of Houston, Harris County, 1974-80, mem, Univ Oaks Civic Club, 1979-; life mem, Kappa Alpha Psi, 1974; mem, Kiwanis Intl, Houston Metropolitan Chapter, 1985-; expert witness, Office of Hearing and Appeal, SSA, 1975-80; bd mem, Citizens for Good School, 1976-78; mem, Natl Assn of Market Developers, Houston Chapter, 1978; vice chmn, PPR Comm, Mt Vernon United Methodist Church, 1989. **HONORS/ACHIEVEMENTS:** Goodwill Ambassador Award, City of Houston, 1975; Meritorious Service Award, City of Houston, 1976; Certificate of Appreciation, Houston Area Private Employment Assn, 1977; Certified Public Consultant, 1978; Trailblazer Award, Kappa Alpha Psi, Houston Chapter, 1983; Certificate of Appreciation, Ensemble Theatre, 1987. **MILITARY SERVICE:** US Army, E-4, 1956-58. **BUSINESS ADDRESS:** Owner, Mgr, The Urban Placement Serv, 2211 Norfolk, #816, Houston, TX 77098-4044.

BRIMM, CHARLES EDWIN
Physician. **PERSONAL:** Born May 22, 1924; married Edith Mapp; children: Charles Jr, Linda Jean. **EDUCATION:** South Jersey Law School, 1947-48; Ottawa Univ, BS 1951; Ottawa Univ Med School, MD 1955. **CAREER:** Hahnemann Hosp, teaching 1974-; Family Practice, specialist 1975; Coll of Med & Dentistry of NJ, teaching 1977; Family Practice Hahnemann Hosp, instr 1978-79; General Practice, physician 1956-. **ORGANIZATIONS:** Mem BPUM 1978; founder Concept House Drug Rehab Settlement 1970; mem Camden Cty Heart Assoc; bd of trustees Camden Cty Coll; life mem NAACP; booster club Camden HS; mem Natl Med Assoc; consult Cooper Med Ctr, Dept of Neurology & Psychiatry, Dept of Intl Med, Dept of Family Practice. **HONORS/ACHIEVEMENTS:** Publ "Use of Fluplenazine Decanoate in Managing PCP Intoxication"; Physician of the Year Camden Cty Med Soc 1971; Diplomat of Bd, 1974, Elected an affiliate 1979 Royal Soc of Med by Queen of England 1979; Postgrad Med Rsch Awd 1979. **MILITARY SERVICE:** AUS chem war-

fare quartermaster 1943-46. **BUSINESS ADDRESS:** Councilmember-at-Large, 514 Kaighers Ave, Camden, NJ 08103.

BRIMMER, ANDREW F.
Economist. **PERSONAL:** Born Sep 13, 1926, Newellton, LA; married Doris Millicent Scott; children: Esther Diane. **EDUCATION:** Univ Washington, BA 1950, MA 1951; Univ Bombay, India, postgrad (Fulbright fellow) 1951-52; Harvard Univ, PhD 1957; numerous honorary degrees. **CAREER:** Fed Res Bank NYC, economist 1955-58; MI State Univ, asst prof 1958-61; Wharton Sch Finance & Commerce Univ of PA, asst prof 1961-66; Dept Commerce Washington, dep asst sec 1963-65, asst sec for econ affairs 1965-66; Fed Reserve Bd, member 1966-74; Grad Sch Bus Admin Harvard Univ, Thomas Henry Carroll Ford Found vis prof 1974-76; Brimmer & Co Inc, pres 1976-. **ORGANIZATIONS:** Bd govs/v chmn Commodity Exch Inc; dir Bank of Amer, Amer Security Bank, Intl Harvester Co, UAL-United Air Lines, Du Pont Co, Gannett Co Inc; mem Fed Res Central Banking Mission to Sudan 1957; consult SEC 1962-63; mem Trilateral Commn; chmn bd trustees Tuskegee Inst Com for Econ Devel; mem viscom NYU; co-chmn Interracial Cncl for Bus Oppty; mem Amer Econ Assn; Amer Fin Assn; Assn for Study Afro-Amer Life and History (pres 1970-73); mem Natl Economists Club, Cncl on Foreign Relations, Amer Statis Assn. **HONORS/ACHIEVEMENTS:** Author, "Survey of Mutual Funds Investors" 1963; "Life Insurance Companies in Capital Market" 1962; "Economic Development, International and African Perspectives" 1976; contribr articles to professional journals; named Govt Man of the Year Natl Bus League 1963; recip Arthur S Flemming Award 1966; Russwurm Award 1966; Capital Press Club Award 1966; Golden Plate Award Amer Acad Achieve 1967; Alumnus Summa Laude Dignatus Univ Wash Alumni Assn 1972; Natl Honoree Beta Gamma Sigma 1971; Horatio Alger Award 1974; Equal Oppty Award Natl Urban League 1974; One Hundred Black Men and NY Urban Coalition Award 1975. **BUSINESS ADDRESS:** President, Brimmer & Company, Inc, 4400 MacArthur Blvd NW, Washington, DC 20007.

BRINKLEY, CHARLES H., SR.
Educator, coach. **PERSONAL:** Born Nov 13, 1942, Gallatin, TN; son of Hutch and Ellen; married Gloria Johnson; children: Katrena, Anglea, Charles II. **EDUCATION:** Vally State Univ, BS, MS; Tennessee Technical Univ, Additional Study; Tennessee State Univ, MA, Education, 1989. **CAREER:** TEA Local Unit, Tennessee Prep School, Past Pres; Taft Youth Center, Principal, 1968-70; St Training School, Dept of Correctionss, Indianola, MS, Counselor, Teacher, 1967; Sumner County Election Commission, 1983-89, Chmn, 1985. **ORGANIZATIONS:** Local Rep, TPS Education Assn, Middle TN Council B S Assn; Mem, Tennessee Sheriff's Assn; Vice Chmn, General Ct Committee, 1975-77; Deputy Sheriff Command, 1975; 2nd Vice Pres, NAACP Gallatin Branch, 1977; Member, C of C, 1975; Notary Public at large, State of Tennessee, 1975-78; Mem, NEA, MTEA, TEA,TPSEA; Deacon, 1975-, Chmn, Deacon's Bd, 1985-, first Baptist Church. **HONORS/ACHIEVEMENTS:** Outstanding Service Presidential Award, TPS Education Assn, 1972; NSF Fellowship Grant, 1968; Outstanding Service Award, NAACP, 1989. **BUSINESS ADDRESS:** 1200 Foster Ave, Nashville, TN 37211.

BRINKLEY, NORMAN, JR.
Educational administrator. **PERSONAL:** Born Jul 07, 1931, Edenton, NC; married Pearl A Rozier; children: Franklin, Cassandra, Norman T, Carmellia, Christa A. **EDUCATION:** NC Agr & Tech Coll, BS 1950-54; NC Agr & Tech State U, MS 1973-74. **CAREER:** MS Valley State Univ, dean of students, 1970-; Lincoln Univ, Lincoln PA, activity dir & comm coord, 1969-70; Child Care Serv Media PA, social worker, 1965- 69; Children Serv Inc, Philadelphia PA, caseworker, 1963-64; State Of PA, youth supvr, 1961-63; City of Philadelphia, youth counselor, 1959-61; MS NASPA, state dir, 1979-80. **ORGANIZATIONS:** Mem Voters League 1970-80; mem MS Student Personnel Adminstrn 1970-80; officer M W Stringer Grand Lodge F & AM 1976-80. **HONORS/ACHIEVEMENTS:** Recipient Comm Relations AwardUniv of MS 1971; adminstrs for Developing Insts AwardUniv of WI 1972-73; Supervisory Leadership Skills Award So ILUniv 1975. **MILITARY SERVICE:** USAF 2nd lt 1955-58. **BUSINESS ADDRESS:** Dean of Student Affairs, Mississippi Valley StateUniv, Box 1239, Itta Bena, MS 38941.

BRINN, CHAUNCEY J.
Education administrator. **PERSONAL:** Born Mar 21, 1932, Kalamazoo, MI; married Elizabeth L. **EDUCATION:** BA 1963; MA 1975. **CAREER:** Western Michigan Univ, dir acad affairs & minority student affairs, asst to vice pres, 1971-, Special Prog Office of Student Financial Aids, coord, 1968-71, banking, branch mgr, minority recruitment, 1965-68; IBM Corp, admin, minority recruitment, 1963-65; Industry, chem lab tech, 1956-58; Assn of Western MI Univ, chem lab tech, resrch, past vice pres 1954-56. **ORGANIZATIONS:** Mem minority caucus Midwest Assn of Stdnt Fin Aid Admin 1971; mem Nat Assn of African Am Educators; Kalamazoo Co Prsnl & Gdnc Assn; MI Prsnl & Gdnc Assn; dir Region XI MI Stdnt Fin Aid Assn 1969-70; chmn Minority Affairs Com, MI Student Fin Aid Assn 1970-71; mem Midwest Assn of Std Fin Aid Admin; del, exec bd natl assn, fin aid admin dir Kalamazoo Comm Serv Cncl 1961-62; dir Citizens Teen 1960-62; dir Kalamazoo Jaycees 1964-66; dir Otsego-plainwell Jaycees 1966-67; chmn Grtr No Dist Explr Scouts 1967; Kalamazoo Chap NAACP 1965; chrmn Mar of Dime 1966; consult Civil Rights Commn Migrant Lbr 1969; mem MI Alliance of Black Educs 1976; state Pres, mem MI Assn for Non White Concerns; adv Affrm Act Bus & Ind 1972-75; Men of Achievement 1976. **HONORS/ACHIEVEMENTS:** Author publ "Going to College Costs Money". **MILITARY SERVICE:** USN 2d cl petty off 1950-54. **BUSINESS ADDRESS:** Western MIUniv, Administration Bldg, Kalamazoo, MI 49008.

BRISBANE, SAMUEL CHESTER
Physician. **PERSONAL:** Born Aug 08, 1914, Jacksonville, FL; married Martha Shields. **EDUCATION:** Lincoln Univ PA, BA 1937; Howard Univ Med Coll, 1949. **CAREER:** Columbia Univ Coll of Physicians & Surgeons, asst clinical prof anes 1963; Harlem Hosp Cntr, asso dir dept of anes 1963, attndng anesthesiolgst 1950;220 W 139 St, gen Prac 1950-. **ORGANIZATIONS:** Mem Nat Med Assn; mem Am Soc of Anesthesiolgsts AMA; past pres Manhattan Grdsmn Inc; mem Alpha Phi Alpha Frat. **HONORS/ACHIEVEMENTS:** Alpha Phi Alpha Frat Humanitarian Award; John Hunter Mem Camp Fund 1975; Humanitarian & Civic Award; Boys of Yesteryear Inc 1978. **MILITARY SERVICE:** AUS pvt 1943. **BUSINESS ADDRESS:** 506 Lenox Ave, New York, NY 10037.

BRISCO-HOOKS, VALERIE
Track and field athlete. **PERSONAL:** Born Jul 06, 1960, Greenwood, MS; married Alvin Hooks; children: Alvin. **EDUCATION:** Long Beach Community Coll. **CAREER:** Athletic Congress Natl Championships, 1984; Olympic Games, Los Angeles 1984, Seoul, Korea 1988; UCLA Invitational, 1984; Bruce Jenner Meet, San Jose CA, 1984; European Track Circuit, 1984, 1985; Millrose Games, 1985; Sunkist Invitational, Los Angeles, 1985; Times-Herald Invitational, Dallas, Texas, 1985; LA Times-Kodak Games, Inglewood, CA, 1985. **HONORS/ACHIEVEMENTS:** 3 Gold Medals, 1984 Olympics, Los Angeles; Silver Medal, 1988 Olympics, Seoul, Korea; ranked #6 in world 400 meters, ranked #2 in US 400 meters, ranked #4 in US 200 meters, Track & Field News, 1988; Outstanding Mother's Award, Natl Mother's Day Comm, 1986; co-chairperson, Minnie Riperton Cancer Week, 1986, 1987; 1st female asked to compete in Australia's Stalwell Gift Race, 1987. **BUSINESS ADDRESS:** Amateur Athlete, World Class Mgmt, PO Box 21053, Long Beach, CA 90801.

BRISCOE, EDWARD GANS
Physician. **PERSONAL:** Born Nov 18, 1937, Glenridge, NJ; son of Gans H Briscoe and Evelyn M Van Dunk; married Agatha Donatto, Jan 23, 1976; children: Valerie R Washington, Kurt G, Pamela Y Morant, Keith E, Deidre A, Allison M. **EDUCATION:** Howard Univ, BS 1959, MD 1963. **CAREER:** Howard Univ Dept of Surgery, chief div of anesthesia 1971-74; Martin Luther king Jr General Hosp, assoc prof of anesthesiology 1974-75; West Adams Comm Hosp, staff anesthesiologist 1975-76; Charles R Drew Postgrad Sch, assoc prof of anesthesiology 1976-77; Westside Comm Hosp of Long Beach, chief of anesthesia 1977; private practice, family medicine 1977-79; Hilo Medical Group, family practice 1979-82; Family Practice Treatment of Chronic Pain, 1982-87; Department of Health, US Virgin Islands 1987-. **ORGANIZATIONS:** Mem Amer Assn of Family Practice, Natl Medical Assn, Hawaii Federation of Physicians & Dentists, mem St Thomas-St John Medical Society 1988-; bd mem, Partners for Health, US Virgin Islands, 1989-. **HONORS/ACHIEVEMENTS:** Author "Diary of a Short Timer in Vietnam" 1970; Fellow Amer Coll of Anesthesiologists; Assoc Examiner Amer Coll of Anesthesiologists, Amer Bd of Anesthesiology; 11 papers presented including "Pain Control in an Isolated Clinical Environment," presented to annual meeting Golden State Medical Soc Honolulu, HI 1984. **MILITARY SERVICE:** USN lt cmdr 5 yrs; Vietnam Serv Medal, Combat Action Medal, Letter of Commendation, Navy Unit Citation. **HOME ADDRESS:** P O Box 10688, St Thomas, Virgin Islands of the United States 00801. **BUSINESS ADDRESS:** Chief of Anesthesiology, Saint Thomas Hospital, Department of Health US Virgin Islands, Sugar Estate Road, St Thomas, Virgin Islands of the United States 00801.

BRISCOE, LEONARD E.
Corporation executive. **PERSONAL:** Born May 22, 1940, Ft Worth, TX; married Rosita; children: Edward, Rosanna. **EDUCATION:** Pepperdine U, MBA 1975; Univ TX, Currently Studying PhD. **CAREER:** Expediters, pres; NAMCON, Briscoe-morrison, real est; Briscoe Consultant Serv, Rolling Hills Bldg & Devel, Universal Financial Corp, Interntl Mortgage Corp, exec v p; Real & Est Broker 1960-. **ORGANIZATIONS:** Local State & Nat Real Est Brokers Assns; mem Local State & Nat Home Bldrs Assns, Ft Worth City Cncl 1971-75; Nat League Cities; Ft Worth Comm Devel Cncl; pres Assn Mayors Cnclmn & Commrs. **BUSINESS ADDRESS:** 2016 Evans Ave, Fort Worth, TX.

BRISCOE, SIDNEY EDWARD, JR.
Business executive. **PERSONAL:** Born Oct 05, 1929, Jennings, LA; married Lana Pullman; children: Sidney III, Linda, Cora, Sheryl, Zannette, Darryl, Andrea, Maria, Bryan. **EDUCATION:** Southern Univ, BS 1951. **CAREER:** Insurance Agency, owner; Consumer Finance Co, mgr 1969-72; Jefferson Davis Public School Bd, teacher 1954-72, principal 1953-54; Evangeline Parish School Bd, dir 1952-53. **ORGANIZATIONS:** Mem LA Oil & Gas Msm; mem Jefferson Davis Parish Police Jury; pres NAACP Jefferson Davis Chapter 1976-; pres Local Comm Action Agency 1972-; vice pres Holy Name Soc 1974-. **HONORS/ACHIEVEMENTS:** Bishop honoree Cath Lafayette Diocese 1964; awrd ded serv to the Jeff Davis Parish 1975; cert Jeff Davis Com Action 1975. **BUSINESS ADDRESS:** PO Box 497, Jennings, LA 70546.

BRISCOE, THOMAS F.
Retired educational administrator. **PERSONAL:** Born May 25, 1910, Mitchell, AL; married Loretta Mc Kee; children: Carolyn, Nancy. **EDUCATION:** Western MI Univ, BS, 1937; Wayne State Univ, MA, 1940; Univ MI, postgraduate studies, 1960. **CAREER:** Admin Asst, Detroit Public Schools, 40 years, retired. **ORGANIZATIONS:** NAACP, Metro Detroit YMCA, Alpha Phi Alpha Fraternity, Commissioner, Michigan State Athletic Bd of Control, Recreation Dept, City of Detroit, First Pres, Brewster Old Timers Inc; Charter mem, Varsity Club, Inc. **HONORS/ACHIEVEMENTS:** Detroit Recreation Dept, Recognition of Appreciation for Outstanding Recreational Serv, 1989; WMU Athletic Hall of Fame, 1988; Leo Salakin Michigan Boxing Hall of Fame, 1985; IBF, Dean of Referees, 1985; Michigan Sports Sages, Humanitarian Award, 1983; Michigan High School Athletic Assn's First Annual Officials' Awards Banquet, 25 years of service, 1980; Michigan Amateur Sports Hall of Fame, 1980; Michigan Sports Sages, Pres, 1976; Alpha Phi Alpha Award, Outsstanding Contribution to Community & Fraternity, 1976; Several other awards. **BUSINESS ADDRESS:** 6550 W Warren Ave, Detroit, MI 48210.

BRISKER, LAWRENCE
Educational administrator. **PERSONAL:** Born Oct 05, 1934, St Louis, MO; married Flossie Richmond. **EDUCATION:** So IL U, BA 1959; Univ of NM, MA 1966; Case-Western Res U, PhD 1976. **CAREER:** Cuyahoga Community Coll, dean student life unit, 1978-, special asst to the chancellor, 1977-78, coord student assistance program, 1976-77; Cleveland Municipal Court, chief deputy clerk, 1975-76; OH Bell Telephone Co Cleveland, employment supvr & traffic mgr, 1964-70; Cleveland Public School System, teacher, 1962-64. **ORGANIZATIONS:** Bd mem Glen Oak Pvt Sch for Girls 1968-; mem Citizen's League 1978-; bd dir Cleveland Pub Radio 1979-; bd trustees Cleveland TB & Respiratory Fed 1966; mem Urban League's Emplymnt & Econs Com 1968; mem United Area Citizens Agency 1979-. **HONORS/ACHIEVEMENTS:** Spinix awrd So IL Univ 1958; Phi Delta Kappa Univ of NM 1960; natl defense ed act flwshp Case-Western Res Univ 1970; ahs flwshp awrd Case-Western Res Univ 1972. **MILITARY SERVICE:** AUS e-4 1958-60. **BUSINESS ADDRESS:** Cuyahoga Community College, 2900 Community College Ave, Cleveland, OH 44115.

BRITT, PAUL D., JR.
Educational administrator. **PERSONAL:** Born Feb 03, 1951, Franklin, VA; married Priscilla Harding; children: Pauleatha Clara, Taene Renita. **EDUCATION:** Norfolk State Univ, BA Social Service 1970-74; VA State Univ, M Educ Admin 1980-84. **CAREER:** Southampton Co Schools, teacher/coach 1975-79; Franklin City Schools, teacher/coach/social studies dept chmn 1979-84; Smithfield HS, asst principal 1984-. **ORGANIZATIONS:** Deacon First Baptist Church Franklin 1979-; councilmember Franklin City Council 1982-. **BUSINESS ADDRESS:** Asst Prin & Mem City Council, Smithfield High School, Rt4 Box 115, Smithfield, VA 23851.

BRITTAIN, BRADLEY BERNARD, JR.
Engineer, editor. **PERSONAL:** Born Mar 22, 1948, Arlington, VA; married Lenora C Robinson Freeman; children: Kandakai Freeman, Kini Freeman, Zina Freeman. **EDUCATION:** Attended, Howard Univ. **CAREER:** ABC Inc, engr editor newsfilm editor apprentice film editor desk asst 1972-; freelance photographer 1976-77; American Broadcasting Co, engr. **ORGANIZATIONS:** Life mem NAACP; Natl Rifle Assn; mem Natl Geog Soc; Radio & TV Corr Assn; Friends Natl Zoo; Natl Capital Velo Club; Assn Corcoran; mem Natl Acad TV Arts & Sci 1983-84-85; mem White House News Photographer Assn 1983-85; mem Capitol Hill Correspondents Assoc 1978-; public relations comm Northern Virginia Gun Club 1983-85; mem Smithsonian Resident Associates 1978-. **HONORS/ACHIEVEMENTS:** Achievement in TV Awd CEBA 1982-83. **HOME ADDRESS:** PO Box 2486, Fairfax, VA 22031. **BUSINESS ADDRESS:** Engineer, American Broadcasting Co, 1717 DeSales St NW, Washington, DC 20036.

BRITTON, ALBERT B., JR.
Physician. **PERSONAL:** Born Jan 17, 1922, Enterprise, MS; children: Albert B III, Tanya E, Camilla Lewis, Therese Britton-Decatur. **EDUCATION:** Tougaloo Coll, BS 1943; Howard Univ Sch of Medicine, MD 1947. **CAREER:** Child Develop Group, medical dir 1966-68; Self-employed, physician. **ORGANIZATIONS:** Mem MS Adv Comm US Commn on Civil Rights 1958-86; pres MS Med & Surgical Assoc 1966-67; Ntl Med Assoc vice pres 1966-67, board of dir 1967-74; colonel Governor's Staff 1976-80; mem Natl Medical Assoc. **HONORS/ACHIEVEMENTS:** Special Achievement Awd Natl Assoc Minority Medical Educators 1985; Special Achievement Awd NAFEEO 1986. **MILITARY SERVICE:** AUS Medical Corp capt 2 yrs; Bronze Star, Division Citation, 3 Battle Stars Korea. **BUSINESS ADDRESS:** 527 1/2 N Farish St, Jackson, MS 39207.

BRITTON, ELIZABETH
Professional registered nurse. **PERSONAL:** Born Jul 18, 1930, Gary, IN; children: Darryl T Gillespie, Tamara A Gillespie, John G Gillespie, Lisa M Roach, Anthony L, Alycyn M. **EDUCATION:** Mayfair-Chicago City Coll, AA 1969; Purdue Univ, BSN 1974; Portland State Univ, MS 1982. **CAREER:** Chicago Maternity Ctr, nursing serv admin 1970-73; Beverly Learning Ctr, health educ instructor 1972-74; Univ of OR Health Scis Ctr Sch of Nursing, instructor 1976-81; OR Health Scis Univ Office of Minority Student Affairs, asst prof 1981-. **ORGANIZATIONS:** Pres Willamette Valley Racial Minorities Consortium; mem Natl Assoc of Medical Minority Educators; bd dirs North Portland Nurse Practioner Comm Health Clinic; anti-basileus Alpha Kappa Alpha Sor Zeta Sigma Omega; mem Oregon Alliance of Black School Educators; bd of dirs, Oregon Donor Program 1988-; mem, The Link's Inc, Portland Chapter 1988. **HONORS/ACHIEVEMENTS:** Natl Honor Soc of Nursing Sigma Theta Tau 1976; Special Contribution to Indian Educ 1981, 82, 83; Certificate of Appreciation Ctr for Black Studies Portland State Univ 1983; Outstanding AKA Woman, Zeta Sigma Omega Chapter 1986. **BUSINESS ADDRESS:** Director, International & Ethnic Affairs, Oregon Health SciencesUniv, 3181 SW Sam Jackson Park Rd, Portland, OR 97201.

BRITTON, JOHN H., JR.
Public relations executive. **PERSONAL:** Born Jul 21, 1937, Nashville, TN; son of Rev John H Britton Sr and Martha Parrish Britton; married Betty J Thompson; children: John III. **EDUCATION:** Drake Univ, BS 1958; Syracuse Univ, MS 1962. **CAREER:** Atlanta Daily World, reporter 1958-62; Jet Mag, assoc editor asst mng ed 1962-66; US Civil Rights Commn, asst info officer 1966-67; Civil Rights Doc Proj Washington, assoc dir 1967-68; Jet Mag, mng editor 1968-71; Motown Rec Corp Detroit & LA, pub rel mgr 1971-73; Encore Mag, columnist 1974-75; The Washington Post, public relations mgr; Univ of DC, public affairs dir. **ORGANIZATIONS:** Mem Council for Advancement & Support of Educ; editorial adv bd Crisis Mag; Natl Black Media Coalition. **HONORS/ACHIEVEMENTS:** NNPA Merit Awd 1971. **BUSINESS ADDRESS:** Director of Public Affairs, University of DC, 4200 Connecticut Ave NW, Washington, DC 20008.

BRITTON, THEODORE R., JR.
U.S. government official. **PERSONAL:** Born Oct 17, 1925, N Augusta, SC; married Vernell Elizabeth; children: Theodore (dec), Renee, Warren, Sharon, Darwin. **EDUCATION:** New York Univ, BS, 1952. **CAREER:** Amer Baptist Mgmt Corp, pres 1966-71; HUD, act asst sec for rsch & tech 1973; ambassador Barbados & Grenada 1974-76; United Mutual Life Ins Co of NY, pres & chief exec officer 1978-79; mgmt consul 1979-80; Assn WI States, spec rep; Logical Tech Serv Corp, exec vice pres & secty; Housing & Urban Dev for Intl Affairs, asst to sec 1981; D Parke Gibson Intl Ltd, sr consul 1979-. **ORGANIZATIONS:** Chmn New York City Urban Renewal mgmt Corp 1968-71; vice chmn Sector Grp Urban Env Orgn for Econ Coop & Devel 1971-74; deacon & trustee Riverside Church in NYC1970-77; chair US/China Agreement on Housing 1981; vice chmn Group on Urban Affairs OECD 1982; dir Riverside Brdcstg Corp; mem Inst Real Estate Mgmt, Natl Assn Realtors, Amer Baptist Rep; bd of dirs Freedom Natl Bank 1978; exec sec US Agreement on Housing & Urban Develop with Canada Mexico & USSR. **BUSINESS ADDRESS:** Senior Consultant, D Parke Gibson Intl Ltd, 451-7th St SW, Ste 7114, Washington, DC 20410.

BROACH, S. ELIZABETH
Educational administrator. **PERSONAL:** Born in Little Rock, AR; married Hughes M; children: Jacqueline Johnson Moore, David M Johnson, Anita M. **EDUCATION:** Dunbar Jr Coll, Tchrs Cert 1940; Philander Smith Coll, BA Music Ed 1950; Univ of AR, MS Sec Ed 1953; CA State Univ at Hayward, Ed Psychology 1974. **CAREER:** Little Rock & Pulaski County Public Sch, music instructor 1955-65; SFUSD, music specialist 1967-69; Pelton Jr High Sch, dean of women 1969-70, asst principal 1970-72; Ben Franklin Jr High Sch, asst principal 1973-74; Wilson High Sch, asst principal 1975-77; McAteer High Sch, asst principal 1984-78; San Fran Unified Sch Dist, admin consultant. **ORGANIZATIONS:** Organist Beebe Meth Ch 1967-85; organist European Tour Voices of Beebe 1982; Natl Business & Prof Women; dir instructor Creative Arts Center San Fran; music dir Mt Pleasant Baptist Church Little Rock, AR; Natl Assn of Negro Musicians 1984-85; epistoleus Sigma Gamma Rho Sor; Phi Delta Kappa Ed 1978; Natl Council of Negro Women; educ comm NAACP 1984-85; Oakland Symphony Guild. **HONORS/ACHIEVEMENTS:** Diagnostic Counseling Learning Center SFUSD 1973; Commendation Merit Letter Bay Area Rapid Transit; Certificate of Merit CA Conf 9th Episcopal Dist; organ performance Bristol England, Chippenham Methodist Church; Outstanding Bay Area Organist, Natl Assn of Black Musicians. **HOME ADDRESS:** 7615 Hanson Dr, Oakland, CA 94605.

BROADNAX, MADISON
Government official. **PERSONAL:** Born Feb 14, 1914, Swords, GA; married Ruth Elaine Mitchell. **EDUCATION:** West Virginia State Coll, BS, 1940; Michigan State Univ, MS, 1942. **CAREER:** US Agency for Interl Dev, reg ofcr 1976-; Khartoum, ofcr 1973-75; USAID Dept of State, dir 1970-73; Dept of Agr, aid 1968-70; Suwon, rsrchr 1965-68;Intrl Corp & Agy, advsr 1958-65; W VA State Clg, prof 1949-58; WV State Clg, mgr 1943-47; farm mgr 1942. **ORGANIZATIONS:** Mem Am Forgn Serv Assc; Rural Sociological Soc; Beta Kappa Chi Sc Soc; Kappi Alpha Psi; Am Legion Mason; Nat Assc of Retired Tchrs Comdr; Col Chas Young Post 1946-49; v cmdr WV Dept Am Leg 1950; cnslr WV Boys State; mem Grace Epis Ch; mem Bachelor Benedict Clb; fndr Capitol City Civic Clb; bd dir Sudbury House Cond 1971-73; rep Org of Assc of Agr Clg 1972. **HONORS/ACHIEVEMENTS:** Serv awrd US Gov; achvmt plaque Kappa Alpha Psi 1975; sabbatical flwshp AID 1968; aluminus of yr WV State Clg 1975. **MILITARY SERVICE:** USAAC 1943-46. **BUSINESS ADDRESS:** Nairobi Dept of State, Washington, DC 20520.

BROADNAX, MELVIN F.
Educator. **PERSONAL:** Born Oct 21, 1929, Seaboard, NC; married Ruth Bracey. **EDUCATION:** Shaw U, BA 1963; A&T State U, MS 1963; Shaw U, LlD 1972. **CAREER:** Northampton Bd of Educ, teacher; Seaboard NC, town commr. **ORGANIZATIONS:** Mem Kappa Frat; deacon & trustee of Ch mem NAACP; NEA. **HONORS/ACHIEVEMENTS:** Ncta selected prsnlty of So 1969; kappa man of yr 1974. **MILITARY SERVICE:** AUS sgt Korean War.

BROADUS, CLYDE R.
Dentist. **PERSONAL:** Married Lorraine; children: Clyde R Jr, Reginold H. **EDUCATION:** Talladega Coll, BA 1944; Univ of PA, attended 1945; Meharry Med Coll, DDS 1949. **CAREER:** St Joseph Hosp, dentist/staff. **ORGANIZATIONS:** Mem Natl Dental Assn; Amer Dental Assn; Acad of Gen Dentistry; past pres Gulf State Dental Assn; pres NT Wallis Dental Soc of Fort Worth; past chmn of bd Gulf State Dent Assn 1962-70; past bd of dirs Natl Dental Assn; past vice pres Natl Dental Assn 1968-69; mem Laison Com Natl Dental Assn;bd trustees Natl Dental Assn; chmn bd trustees Natl Dental Assn 1969-70; laison Ft Worth Dist Dental Soc w/Ofc of Equal Opp 1968-70; pres Natl Dental Assn 1970-71; mem Dental Hygiene Adv Comm Tarrant Co Jr Coll Dist 1971-74; mem Dental Asst Adv Com Tarrant Co Jr Coll Dist 1971-74; mem Gen Adv Com for Health Occupations Coop Training Prog Trimble Tech HS 1972-73; mem bd dir McDonald Br YMCA 1958-69; bd dir Metro Bd YMCA Ft Worth 1967-69; bd dir Tarrant Co Comm Council 1968-69; bd dir Comm Action Agency 1968-69; educ com Ft Worth Comm Relations Commn; sec St Andrews United Meth Ch 13 yrs; bd trustees St Andrews United Meth Ch 9 yrs; Master Mason; mem Alpha Phi Alpha Frat. **HONORS/ACHIEVEMENTS:** Citizenship Awd Radio Sta KNOX 1968; Awd for Professional Ptcptn Vocational Health Occupation Educ 1972-73; Cert of Awd Occupation Inf Forums Tarrant Co JrColl 1972; Appreciation Cert devoted serv YMCA 1965-66; Cert of Merit & Apprec Tarrant Co Jr Coll 1971-72.

BROADWATER, TOMMIE, JR.
Senator. **PERSONAL:** Born Jun 09, 1942, Washington, DC; married Lillian; children: Tommie III, Tanya, Jackie, Anita. **EDUCATION:** Southern Univ; Prince Georges Comm Coll. **CAREER:** MD State, senator 1974-78; Broadwater Bonding Corp, owner; Prince Georges Comm Bank, vice pres 1976-77; Ebony Inn, owner 1974. **ORGANIZATIONS:** Cnclmn City of Glenarden 1967-73; Pince Georges C of C; tres MD Legislators Black Caucus; bD dir Prince George Comm Bank; bd dir PAR-LOT Entrprs Glenarden Boys Clb; spnsr Chapel Oaks Fire Dept Baseball Team; 25th Alliance Civic Grp; NAACP; Sr Citizens Adv Cncl. **HONORS/ACHIEVEMENTS:** Outst alumni awrd Fairmont Hts Sch 1976; outst leader in Prince Georges Co Civic Grps 1977. **BUSINESS ADDRESS:** 5611 Landover Rd, Hyattsville, MD 20784.

BROADY, EARL CLIFFORD
Judge. **PERSONAL:** Born Dec 24, 1904, Los Angeles, CA; married Anna Hall; children: Earl Jr, Elaine Pope. **EDUCATION:** Univ of So CA, Undergrad; LA Clg of Law, Law. **CAREER:** St of CA, superior ct judge 1965-; LA Co, chief dep dist atty 1965. **ORGANIZATIONS:** Mem Am Bar Assc; Legion Lex of Univ of So CA; frmr pres LA Criminal Cts Bar Assc; mem McComb & Com to study Watts Riot in 1965. **HONORS/ACHIEVEMENTS:** Hon by Criminal Cts Bar Assc for Outst Serv to Admn of Justice; hon by resolution of LA City Cncl Bd of Upr for Contbns to Citizens of LA Area. **BUSINESS ADDRESS:** 1003 Benedict Canyon, Beverly Hills, CA 90210.

BROCK, GERALD
Judge. **PERSONAL:** Born Aug 23, 1932, Hamtramck, MI; married Jacqueline B Holmes. **EDUCATION:** Eastern MI Univ, BS 1953; Detroit College of Law, LLB 1961. **CAREER:** Flint Public Schools, teacher 1953-57; Wayne County Training Sch, teacher 1957-61; Private Practice, attorney 1961-81; 36th District Court, judge 1982-. **BUSINESS ADDRESS:** Judge, 36th District Court, 421 Madison, Detroit, MI 48226.

BROCK, LILA MAE
Associate executive. **PERSONAL:** Born Jul 11, 1915, Lauren, SC; daughter of William Martin and Lila Martin Martin; married James D Brock (deceased); children: Jimmy, James D. Lilliam B. Fleming. **EDUCATION:** Greenville Tech Coll, Certificate 1982. **CAREER:** Greenville Cty Public Schools, luncheon operator 1941-76; Mt View Baptist Church, pres; Jr Church & Vacation Bible School, advisor, teacher; Christian Educ, organizer of acteens, mem; Southernside Center, dir. **ORGANIZATIONS:** Founder Southernside Comm Center 1980; mem Greenville City Advisory Bd 1985, Urban League Housing Advisory Bd, Housing Resource Bd, Greenville Council of Church Women, Advisory Commn for Comm Devel. **HONORS/ACHIEVEMENTS:** Jefferson Awards 1983; Share Comm Serv Award

1983; Max Heller Comm Asd Greenville 1984. **HOME ADDRESS:** 117 Asbury Ave, Greenville, SC 29601. **BUSINESS ADDRESS:** Director, Southernside Community Center, 846 W Washington St, Greenville, SC 29601.

BROCK, LOUIS CLARK
Business executive. **PERSONAL:** Born Jun 18, 1939, El Dorado, AR; divorced; children: Wanda, Lou Jr. **EDUCATION:** So Univ Baton Rouge LA, Attended. **CAREER:** Chicago Cubs, outfielder 1961-64; St Louis Cardinals 1964-79; Brock World St Louis, bus exec 1980-. **ORGANIZATIONS:** Invstr Various Bus Enterprs Active with Lou Brock Boys Clb St Louis World Championship Team St Louis Cardinals 1964-67; Led Cardinals in Base Hits (65) 1967-68; All & Star Team 1967, 72, 74; Played in World Championship Game 1968. **HONORS/ACHIEVEMENTS:** 1st in NL in doubles-triples-stolen Bases/Led Cardinals in Batting 298) At Bats (655) Hits (195) Doubles (33) Triples (10) Stolen Bases (53) 1969; Led Cardinals in runs (114) & 2nd in Doubles (29) & Hits (202) 1970; Led Cardinals in Doubles (37) & Major Legue in Runs Scored (126) 1971; 118 Stolen Bases 1974; Total of 753 Stolen Bases is 2nd Only to Terr Cobb's 892; Jackie Robinson Awrd Ebony Mag 1975; Roberto Clemente Awrd 1975; B'Nai Brith Brotherhood Awrd Man of Yr St Louis Jaycees; Inducted into Natl Baseball Hall of Fame 1985. **BUSINESS ADDRESS:** Brock World, St Louis, MO 63120.

BROCK, O. LEE
Educational administrator. **PERSONAL:** Born Mar 23, 1947, McKamie, AR; married Brenda Joyce Rye. **EDUCATION:** Univ of Wash, BA 1971, MEd 1974. **CAREER:** N Seattle Comm Coll, asst to assoc dean of continuing educ/dir minority affairs, 1971-; Univ of Wash, counselor financial aids, 1971; Oakland Raiders NFL, professional football player, 1970. **ORGANIZATIONS:** Bd mem Micro Bus Systems 1977; bd mem Job Skills Bank Seattle Urban League 1978; mem Univ of Wash Alumni Assc 1974-; mem Western Regional Cncl on BlackAm Afrs (Affiliate of Am Assc of Comm & Jr Clg) 1975-; mem Seattle Urban League 1978-; UPI-AP ALL Coast & ALL Am Univ of Wash (football) 1969. **HONORS/ACHIEVEMENTS:** Capt & inspiration award winner Univ of Wash (football) 1969; MVP (defense) EW Shrine Game 1969; statement of purpose, Puget Sound Regional Minority Affairs Consortium Ed Resources Information Ctr 1976. **BUSINESS ADDRESS:** N Seattle Comm College, 9600 College Way N, Seattle, WA 98103.

BROCKENBOROUGH, JOSEPH ANTONIO
Educator. **PERSONAL:** Born May 11, 1921, Edmonton, Alberta, Canada;son of Joseph A Brockenborough; married Stella May Ramsey; children: Joseph Brett, Rosalyn Lee Land. **EDUCATION:** Lewis & Clark Coll Portland, OR, BSc 1967; CA State Hayward Univ, MPE 1976, 1969-72. **CAREER:** Lewis & Clark Coll, head soccer coach 1963-67; School Dist #66 Lake Cowichan, tchr secondary & coach 1967-69; California State Hayward Univ, head soccer coach & asst baseball 1969-72; Ray Watkins Elem Sch K-7, phys ed dir & coach 1973-83; BC Retired Tchrs, retired phys ed inst & coach. **ORGANIZATIONS:** Soccer & softball Natl Coaching Certificate 1975-84; Clinician Levels I & II Program Canada. **HONORS/ACHIEVEMENTS:** Golden Key Lewis & Clark Coll Chptr Portland, OR 1967. **MILITARY SERVICE:** Royal Canadian Engr lance corporal 1942-46; war medal 1939-45. **HOME ADDRESS:** 1395 Dansey Avenue, Coquitlam, British Columbia, Canada V3K 3H7.

BROCKETT, CHARLES A.
Educator. **PERSONAL:** Born Jan 24, 1937, Princess Anne Co, VA; married Annette Lee; children: Troy Christopher. **EDUCATION:** VA State Clg, BS 1961; Old Dominion U, MS 1972; Norfolk State Clg Univ of VA. **CAREER:** Booker T Washington High School, Norfolk VA, asst prin, asst football coach, 1963-67, Biology teacher, 1963-70; Lake Taylor High School, Norfolk VA, 1979-86; Norview High School, asst principal, 1986-. **ORGANIZATIONS:** Mem Natl Assc of Sec Pincipals; Secondary Principal Assc of Norfolk; VA Assc of Secondary Prin; vice pres Dist L Prin Assc; natl bd mem Natl Black United Fund; pres Black United Fund of Tidewater; Kappa Alpha Psi; Chesapeake Men for Progrss; Chesapeake Forward; civic reg dir Kappa Alpha Psi Guide Right Pgm; Eastern Reg pres Kappa Alpha Psi. **HONORS/ACHIEVEMENTS:** Outstanding Serv Awd Kappa Alpha Psi; Outstanding Community Serv Awd 1973; Outstanding Community Serv 1986. **MILITARY SERVICE:** AUS sp 4 1961-63. **BUSINESS ADDRESS:** Assistant Principle, Norview High School, 1111 Park Ave, Norfolk, VA 23513.

BROCKETT, JOHN HENRY, JR.
Retired. **PERSONAL:** Born Apr 06, 1915, Yonkers, NY; son of John H Brockett and Julia Brockett; married Beulah Naomi Bick (deceased). **EDUCATION:** Livingston Coll, BS 1936; Univ of PA, MS 1948; NY U, Postgraduate Work 1952, 1956; Fairleigh Dickinson Univ, 1963-64, 1967-68; CCNY, attended. **CAREER:** Ch St HS Thomasville, NC, tchr dir athletics 1937-42, tchr 1946-47; Palmer Memorial & Inst Sedalia, NC, admn dean instr sci 1948-51; Livingston Coll, instr chem 1951-57, acting admn dean 1953-55, dir public relations 1954-57, acting pres 1957-58, assoc prof 1958-61; Midland Park HS NJ, tchr chem 1961-, retired chmn sci dept 1975-81. **ORGANIZATIONS:** Elem sci coord, mem admin comm, Commn on Higher Educ Natl Council of Churches 1957-58; bd dir City Recreation for Negroes Thomasville 1938-42; official visitor World Meth Conf Lake Junaluska, NC 1956; mem admn staff Civic Def Salisbury 1954-; mem NEA; Amer Assn of Univ Prof; NJ Ed Assn; NJ Sci Tchrs Assn; vice pres Midland Pk Educ Assn 1965-66; Natl Inst Sci; NC Tchrs Assn; NJ Sci Suprs Assn; Beta Kappa Chi; Phi Beta Sigma Dem; Meth Capt. **HONORS/ACHIEVEMENTS:** Winner Princeton Awd for Outstanding Secondary School Teaching 1974. **MILITARY SERVICE:** AUS capt 1942-46.

BROCKETT, RONALD
Chief executive of promotional advertising company. **CAREER:** Dover Graphics Ltd, New York NY, chief executive. **BUSINESS ADDRESS:** Chief Executive, Dover Graphics Ltd, 100 Sixth Ave, New York, NY 10013. *

BROCKINGTON, BENJAMIN
Educator. **PERSONAL:** Born Nov 22, 1933, Charleston, SC; married Wilhelmenia C McClain; children: Deborah Shenese, Daryl Benet. **EDUCATION:** SC State Clg, BS 1956, MEd 1966. **CAREER:** Burke High School, asst prin, chmn science dept, 1970-74, band dir, 1969-70, Biology teacher, 1966-69; Eastern High School, band dir & Science teacher, 1961-62; Spaulding High School, band dir & Science teacher, 1959-61; Simms High School, band dir, 1956-59. **ORGANIZATIONS:** Mem NEA; Charleston Co Ed Assc; SC Ed Assc; SC Assc of Classroom Tchrs; Cntrl Cncl of Charleston Tchrs; Charleston Co Sci Tchr Assc; mem Omega Psi Phi; Mason; Shriner; Charleston Co Polit Com on Ed (PACE); pres Charleston Co Ed Assc 1975-76; ppres Cntrl Cncl of Charleston Tchr. **HONORS/ACHIEVEMENTS:** Outst band awrds 1969; physics awrd SC State Clg 1955; outst scndry edctr of Am 1974. **BUSINESS ADDRESS:** Burke HS, 207 President St, Charleston, SC 29403.

BROCKINGTON, DONELLA P.
Government administrator. **PERSONAL:** Born Nov 08, 1952, Washington, DC; daughter of Josiah Armstrong Brockington and Harriet Brown Brockington. **EDUCATION:** Clark Univ, BA Math & Psych 1973; Howard Univ School of Ed, MEd Guidance Counseling 1974, M Urban Sys Eng 1976. **CAREER:** Health Sys Agency of N VA, health sys analyst 1976-80; DC Govt Office of the City Admin, sr oper analyst 1981-85; DC Govt Dept of Admin Serv, deputy real prop admin 1985-, assoc dir for real property 1987-88; Lockheed Datacom, vice pres for natl mktg 1988-. **ORGANIZATIONS:** Mem MI Park Civic Assoc 1977-; coord McKinley High School Alumni Orgn 1980; sec/tres Solar Eclipse Inc 1981-; sec Capital Ballet Guild Inc 1982; mem Natl Forum for Black Public Admin 1984-; mem Natl Assn of Business & Professional Women 1986-. **HONORS/ACHIEVEMENTS:** Distinguished Public Serv Awd DC Govt 1982; Outstanding Young Women in Amer 1983, 1984; 1989 Salute to African-American Business & Professional Women, Dollars & Sense Magazine 1989. **BUSINESS ADDRESS:** Vice President for National Marketing, Lockheed Datacom, 1350 Connecticut Ave NW Suite 700, Washington, DC 20036.

BROCKINGTON, EUGENE ALFONZO
Financial administrator. **PERSONAL:** Born Jun 21, 1931, Darien, GA; married Mable M; children: Eugene Jr, Karyn L. **EDUCATION:** Comm Coll of Philadelphia 1967-68. **CAREER:** DeMarco Printer Philadelphia, printing press oper 1951; Amer Fiber-Velop Co Collingdale PA, printing press oper 1954; Jones & Johnson Soft Ice Co, salesman 1956; US Postal Serv Philadelphia, postal source data tech 1958; Natl Alliance of Postal & Fed Employees, treas, comptroller, data proc mgr 1976-. **ORGANIZATIONS:** Fin sec NAPFE 1966; scoutmaster Boy Scouts of Amer Philadelphia Council 1968; lay leader Sayre Meml United Meth Church Philadelphia 1969; football coach Philadelphia Police Athl League 1969; treas bd of dir NAPFE Fed Credit Union Washington DC 1977; treas bd of dir NAPFE Housing Corp Wash DC 1979. **HONORS/ACHIEVEMENTS:** Legion of Merit Chapel of the Four Chaplins Philadelphia 1969; Merit Serv Awd Dist Five NAPFE 1973. **MILITARY SERVICE:** AUS corpl 2 yrs. **BUSINESS ADDRESS:** Treasurer, Comptroller, Natl Alliance of Post/Fed Empl, 1628 11th St, NW, Washington, DC 20001.

BROCKS-SHEDD, VIRGIA LEE
Library director. **PERSONAL:** Born Jun 22, 1943, Utica, MS; daughter of John Brocks, Sr and Flora Williams Brocks-Moore; married Charles Clifton Shedd, Feb 15, 1972 (divorced); children: Victoria Marie Shedd, Carla Lynette-Marie Shedd. **EDUCATION:** Jackson State Coll, Jackson MS, BS, 1964, ms, 1970; Atlanta Univ, Atlanta GA, MSLS, 1965; Fisk Univ, Nashville TN, certificate, 1970. **CAREER:** Jackson State Coll, Jackson MS, library asst, 1964; Atlanta Univ, Atlanta GA, graduate asst, 1964-65; Tougaloo Coll, Tougaloo MS, asst librarian, 1965-84, acting head librarian, 1984-86, head librarian, 1986—. **ORGANIZATIONS:** Mem, Mississippi Library Assn, 1965—; mem, Amer Library Assn, 1965—; founding mem, Soc of Mississippi Archivists, 1970—, councillor, 1983-85; founding mem, Mississippi Cultural Arts Coalition, 1978-86; participating founder of Jackson Writers' Group, 1978-86; pres, Piney Woods School Intl Alumni Assn, 1982-84, 1988—; mem, bd of dir, Jackson Maxwell Radio Group (WMPR) 1979-82; panelist/reviewer, Mississippi Arts Commn, 1985—; mem Southeastern Library Assn, 1986—, bd mem, Repertory Theatre of Mississippi, 1986—; mem, Mississippi Library Commn Bd commrs, 1988—; mem, Assn of Black Women in Higher Educ, 1988-; mem, NAACP. mem comms/confs, 1983—; Southern Rural Women's Network (SRWN), mem various steering. **HONORS/ACHIEVEMENTS:** Grants recipient for the establishment, housing and preservation of Civil Rights documents at Tougaloo, 1970, 1975, 1976, 1989; ACRL fellow, Amer Library Assn/Mt Holyoke Coll, 1978; pres, Piney Woods School Intl Alumni Assn, 1982-84, 1988-; Mississippi Woods, a chapbook of poems, 1980; Contributor/natl researcher; M Davis, contributions of black women to Amer, 1983; poem - "Southern Road, City Pavement" is Mississippi Writers: Reflections of Childhood and Youth, Vol III, 1988; "Anthology of Mississippi Black Writers; grant recipient, teachers & writers collaborative to work one-on-one with Margaret Walker Alexander; mem, Daughters of Margaret Performing Arts group. **HOME ADDRESS:** 3719 James Madison Rd, Jackson, MS 39213. **BUSINESS ADDRESS:** L Zenobia Colemen Library, Tougaloo Coll, Tougaloo, MS 39174.

BRODIS, NELLIE FANNIE
Retired educator. **PERSONAL:** Born Feb 28, 1916, Pittsylvania Cty, VA; children: Geraldine Adams Simonds, Robert Lawrence. **EDUCATION:** VA State Univ, BS 1935; Cornell Univ, MS 1937, PhD 1969. **CAREER:** Hartshorn Coll Richmond, adult he 1935-36; Alcorn A&M Coll, dept head of he 1937-38; Wiley Coll, dept head prof of family life 1938-39; Detroit Bd of Educ, hs teacher 1942-75; Self-employed, education consultant 1977-. **ORGANIZATIONS:** Mem Alpha Kappa Alpha Sor 1937-; mem VA State Coll & Cornell Univ Alumni Assoc 1969-; mem Groves Conf on the Family 1969; mem Natl Council on Family Relations 1970-; mem ACLU, NOW 1977-; mem AVA & Natl Assoc for the Adv of Black Amers in Vocational Educ 1980-; mem Detroit Assoc of Retired Teachers, Plymouth Congregational United Church of Christ Bd of Christian Educ 1981,86. **HONORS/ACHIEVEMENTS:** Invitation by World Health Org in a Nutritional Amendment at the Annual Meeting in Geneva Switzerland 1978-; charter mem Top Ladies of Distinction; First black woman to be assigned to a Vocational School in Detroit; charter mem Cite D' 'detroit Chap Top Ladies of Distinction Inc. **HOME ADDRESS:** 9345 Wildemere, Detroit, MI 48206.

BROKAW, CAROL ANN
Attorney, business executive. **PERSONAL:** Born Nov 14, 1946, Somerville, NJ; daughter of Thomas Brokaw and Annis Bryant Brokaw (deceased). **EDUCATION:** Cedar Crest Coll Allentown PA, BA 1968; Georgetown Law Ctr Washington DC, JD 1971; Hastings Coll of Law San Francisco, cert trial advocacy 1978. **CAREER:** Natl Labor Relations Bd Washington DC & Newark NJ, atty/labor 1971-73; ABC Co NYC, atty/labor 1973-79, assoc dir labor relations 1979-81, genl atty labor relations 1981-. **ORGANIZATIONS:** Mem Women's Natl Dem Club 1972-, DC Bar Assn 1972-; mem Cedar Crest Coll Alumnae Bd 1977-80; mgmt mem Membership & Finance Com Labor & Employment Law Sect Amer Bar Assn 1978-; participant Black Exec Exchange Prog Natl Urban League 1979; founder Plainfield Tutorial Project; bd mem, Children's Art Carnival New York City, NY 1987-. **HONORS/**

ACHIEVEMENTS: Outstanding Young Women's Awd NJ 1972, 1975, 1978; Black Achiever in Industry Awd Harlem Branch of the YMCA of Greater NY Amer Broadcasting Co 1986; Mary Bethune Award, Natl Council of Negro Women, 1988. **BUSINESS ADDRESS:** General Attorney, Capital Cities/ABC Inc, 77 W 66th St, New York, NY 10023.

BROMERY, RANDOLPH WILSON
Geophysicist, educator. **PERSONAL:** Born Jan 18, 1926, Cumberland, MD; son of Randolph and Edith; married Cecile Trescott; children: Keith M, Carol Ann Thompson, Dennis R, David T, Christopher J. **EDUCATION:** Univ of MI, 1944-46; Howard Univ, BS Math 1956; The American Univ DC, MS Geology & Geophysics 1962; The Johns Hopkins Univ, PhD Geology 1968. **CAREER:** US Geological Survey, exploration geophysicist 1948-67; Univ of MA, prof geophys & dept chmn 1968-70, vice chancellor 1970-71, chancellor 1971-79, commonwealth prof of geophysics; Westfield State College, acting pres 1988-; Weston Geophysical Intl Corp, pres, 1981-83; Geoscience Engineering Corp, pres 1983-. **ORGANIZATIONS:** Mem bd of dirs Exxon Corp, NYNEX Corp, Singer Co; Chemical Bank, John Hancock Mutual Life Insurance Co. **HONORS/ACHIEVEMENTS:** Gillman Fellow Johns Hopkins Univ 1965-67; Dr of Laws HON Hokkaido Univ Japan 1976; Dr of Sci Frostburg State Coll MD 1972; Dr of Humane Letters Univ of MA 1979; Dr of Educ Western New England Coll MA 1972; Distinguished Alumni, Howard Univ; Honorary Alumnus, Univ of Massachusetts; President, Geological Society of America. **MILITARY SERVICE:** USAF 3 medals. **HOME ADDRESS:** 75 Cherry Ln, Amherst, MA 01002. **BUSINESS ADDRESS:** Commonwealth Prof Geophysics, Univ of Massachusetts, Dept of Geology & Geography, Amherst, MA 01003.

BRONNER, JAMES ARTHUR
Physician. **PERSONAL:** Born Sep 09, 1935, Louisville, KY. **EDUCATION:** Lincoln Univ PA, BA 1957; Univ of Louisville Sch of Med, MD 1961. **CAREER:** Marion Co Gen Hosp Indianapolis, internship 1961-62; VA Hosp Buffalo, resident in gen surgery 1964-65; State Univ of NY at Buffalo, urology residency 1965-68; So CA Permanente Med Group San Diego, staff urologist 1968-70; Kaiser Found Hosp San Diego, chief of dept of urology 1968-83; So CA Permanente Med Group, urologist 1968-. **ORGANIZATIONS:** Mem Natl Med Assn 1970-; mem Western Sect of AUA 1976-; mem Amer Urological Assn 1978-. **MILITARY SERVICE:** USAF capt 1962-64. **BUSINESS ADDRESS:** Urologist, So CA Permanente Med Group, 4647 Zion Ave, San Diego, CA 92120.

BRONNER, NATHANIEL, SR.
Chief executive of hair-care products manufacturing company. **CAREER:** Bronner Brothers Cosmetics, Atlanta GA, chief executive. **BUSINESS ADDRESS:** Chief Executive, Bronner Brothers Cosmetics, 600 Trusco Way SW, Atlanta, GA 30310. *

BRONSON, FRED JAMES
Dentist & pastor. **PERSONAL:** Born Jan 10, 1935, Cincinnati, OH; married Barbara Dobbins; children: Fred Jr, Mark, Stefanie, Shellie, Shawn, Sharon. **EDUCATION:** Miami Univ Oxford OH, BA 1958; Howard Univ Washington DC, DDS 1982. **CAREER:** Cincinnati Dental Soc, chrmn peer review 1979-81, pres 1982, vice pres 1980, pres elect 1981; Temple Ch of Christ Written in Heaven, pastor 1984; Private Practice & Temple Church of Christ Written In Heaven, dentist & minister. **ORGANIZATIONS:** Delegate Ohio Dental Assn 1978-, mem 1963-; mem Nat Dental Assn 1962-, delegate & trustee 1962; instructor KY Dental Coll 1973-76; fellow, Intl Coll of Dentists, 1978, AmerColl of Dentists, 1983; mem, Alpha Phi Alpha 1957; chmn, Dentist Concerned for Dentists, 1980. **HONORS/ACHIEVEMENTS:** Distinguished Serv Residents of Lincoln Heights, OH 1969. **BUSINESS ADDRESS:** Private Practice, 4935 Paddock Rd, Cincinnati, OH 45237.

BRONSON, OSWALD P.
Educational administrator/president. **PERSONAL:** Born Jul 19, 1927, Sanford, FL; married Helen C Williams; children: Josephine S, Flora H, Oswald P Jr. **EDUCATION:** Bethune-Cookman Clg, BS 1950; Gammon Theol Sem (summa cum laude) Atlanta, BD 1959; Northwestern U, PhD 1965; St Paul's Clg Lawrenceville, VA, DD. **CAREER:** Interdenominational Theol Ctr Atlanta, vice pres 1966-68, pres 1968-75; Bethune-Cookman & Clg, pres 1975-. **ORGANIZATIONS:** Interdenom Theol Ctr 1968-77, vice pres 1968-77, dir field ed 1964-68; author lectr tchr mem Atlanta Univ Ctr; cncl pres bd trustees Carrie S Pitts Home; Hinton Rural Life Ctr; N GA Conf; Un Meth Ch; chmn N GA Conf Bd Ed; UMC; Mid-Atlantic Assc Profs Relig Ed; bd dir United Negro Clg Fund Inc; bd dir FL Assc of Clg & U; bd dir Work Oriented Rehabilitation Ctr Inc; bd dir United Way; bd dir Am Natl Red Cross; bd dir Natl Assc for Equal Opprty in Higher Ed; bd dir Daytona Bch Area C of C; mem Sch Bd of Volusia Co; gov's adv cncl Productivity; mem Indep Clg & Univ of FL Inc; mem Rotary Clb of Daytona Bch; bd mem Ministry of United Meth Ch; bd mem Ministry of FL Annual Conf; exec & com So Reg Ed Bd; mem Am Assc of Univ Prof; mem Phi Delta Kappa; mem Ministerial Assc of Halifax Area; mem Daytona Bch Area Exec Clb; adv com FL State Sickle Cell Foud Inc; mem Am Assc of Theological Sch; past mem State Bd of Indep Clg & U. **HONORS/ACHIEVEMENTS:** Alumni Awds Gammon Theol Sem Bethune-Cookman Clg; Crusade Scholar; United Negro Clg Fund Awd. **BUSINESS ADDRESS:** President, Bethune-Cookman College, 640 2nd Ave, Daytona Beach, FL 32015.

BRONZ, LOIS GOUGIS TAPLIN
Councilwoman, educator. **PERSONAL:** Born Aug 21, 1927, New Orleans, LA; daughter of Alex Gougis and Elise Cousin; married Charles Bronz; children: Edgar, Francine Shorts, Shelly. **EDUCATION:** Xavier Univ, BA 1942; LA State Univ, 1954; Wayne State Univ, MEd 1961; Houston Tillitson Coll, 1962; Coll of New Rochelle, 1974. **CAREER:** US Treasury Dept, proofreader 1950-51; Orleans Parrish School Bd, classroom teacher 1952-61; Xavier Univ, instru math, recruitment, job placement 1961-67; Natl Merit Comm, consult 1965-67; Civil Serv Commiss, personnel consult 1966; Manhattanville Coll, coll adv 1968-73; Greenburgh Central 7 Sch Dist, teacher 1968-82; Town of Greenburgh, councilwoman 1975-. **ORGANIZATIONS:** Founder League of Good Gov New Orleans LA, GROUP; mem League of Women Voters Greenburgh NY, Greenburgh Housing Council, Community Facility Comm, Woodhill Neighborhood Assoc, Xavier Univ Admiss Comm, Xavier Univ Admin Council, Inter-Alumni Council United Negro Coll Fund, Eds for Johnson & Humphrey, Black Dems of Westchester Cty, Afro-Amer Found, Greenburgh Dem Party; co-chrpsn Westchester Womens Council; vice pres Greenburgh Central #7 PTA; vol United Way of Westchester; mem bd of dir CO House Greenburgh, Union Child Day Care Ctr, Westchester Coalition; pres, bd of dir Westchester Comm Oppty Prog; life mem White Plains-Greenburgh NAACP; tutor Westchester Cty Penitentary; instr, rel ed Sacred Heart Church Hartsdale; vol Friends of Children's Village Dobbe Ferry; treas Greenburgh Teachers Assoc Welfare Bd; charter & exec mem Westchester Black Womens Political Caucus; pres Xavier Univ Natl Alumni Assoc; Childrens Village Dobbs Ferry, bd mem; Child Care Council of Westchester, v chair; Legal Awareness for Women, bd mem; NAACP, life mem; Alpha Kappa Alpha, charter mem of Pi Iota Omega chapter. **HONORS/ACHIEVEMENTS:** Panelist 1st NY State Womens Meeting; co-ord Westchester Womens Recog Day; panelist Panel of Amer Women; Natl Assoc of Negro Bus & Professional Womens Club Awareness Awd; Black Democrats of Westchester Political Awareness Awd; Westchester Black Women'sPolitical Caucus Awd; Westchester Advocate Newspaper Achievement Awd; dir Minority Task Force on Womens Issues, Minority Task Force Contractors Conf; revived & dir Human Rights Commiss; conducted meetings throughout the town & village of Greenburgh Saturday Listening Posts; established Sr Citizens Info Ctr; publ handbook/dir of info for sr citizens; obtained fed funds & established sr legal serv prog; mem Grey Panthers Task Force on Social Security; initiated & completed census of Greenburghs Elderly; NY state women's political caucus awd; Westchester Black Lawyers Assn, community service awd. **HOME ADDRESS:** 282 Old Tarrytown Rd, White Plains, NY 10603. **BUSINESS ADDRESS:** Councilwoman, Town of Greenburgh, Box 205, Elmsford, NY 10523.

BROOKE, EDWARD W.
Attorney. **PERSONAL:** Born Oct 26, 1919, Washington, DC; married Anne Fleming; children: Edward. **EDUCATION:** Howard Univ, BS, ML, BL 1941; Boston Univ Law School, ML 1948. **CAREER:** Commonwealth of MA, attny gen 1963-67; US Senate, senator 1967-79; Csaplar & Bok Boston, counsel; O'Connor & Hannan Wash DC, partner. **ORGANIZATIONS:** Chmn fin comm Boston 1961-62; mem Natl Council of BSA, Natl Bd of Boys Clubs of Amer, Amer Bar Assn, Massachusetts Bar Assn, Boston Bar Assn, AMVETS; chmn of bd The Opera Co of Boston Inc; fellow Amer Bar Assoc, Amer Acad of Arts & Sci; mem Spingarn Medal Commn; bd of dir Meditrust Inc Boston, Grumman Corp Bethpage NY; public mem Administrative Conf of the US; bd of dirs Washington Performing Arts Soc. **HONORS/ACHIEVEMENTS:** Spingarn Medal NAACP 1967; Charles Evans Hughes Awd Natl Conf of Christians & Jews 1967; Distinguished Serv Awd AMVETS; 30 hon deg from various coll & univ. **MILITARY SERVICE:** AUS capt 5 yrs. **BUSINESS ADDRESS:** Attorney, O'Connor & Hannan, 1919 Pennsylvania Ave NW, Ste 800, Washington, DC 20006.

BROOKER, MOE A.
Educator. **PERSONAL:** Born Sep 24, 1940, Philadelphia, PA; married Virginia Robinson. **EDUCATION:** PA Acad of Fine Art, Cert 1963; Tyler Sch of Fine Art Temple U, BFA 1970, MFA 1972. **CAREER:** Cleveland Inst of Art, assoc prof, 1975-; Tyler School of Fine Art, guest lecturer, 1975; Univ of NC, assoc prof, 1974; Univ of VA, asst prof, 1973; Tyler School of Fine Art, instructor, 1972, teacher asst drawing, 1971. **ORGANIZATIONS:** Bd mem New Orgn for Visual Arts 1978-; 1st Prize May Show Cleveland Mus of Art 1978; juror painting & drawing Scottsdale Ctr for the Arts AZ 1980; panelist OH Cncl of the Arts 1980. **MILITARY SERVICE:** AUS sp/4 1963-65. **BUSINESS ADDRESS:** 11141 E Blvd, Cleveland, OH 44106.

BROOKES, BERNARD L.
Health care executive. **PERSONAL:** Born Oct 01, 1950; married Glenda F Funderburg; children: Darrilyn. **EDUCATION:** Berklee Coll of Music, BM 1978; Boston Univ Grad Sch, MA 1980, PhD 1983; Boston Univ Sch of Mgmt, MBA 1985. **CAREER:** McLean Hospital, psychology intern 1981-82, psychologist/unit dir 1982-85; MA Dept Mental Health, dir clinical serv 1985-86; New Medico Assoc Inc, deputy dir of operations 1986-87; Basic Health Mgmt Inc, CEO. **ORGANIZATIONS:** Mem Amer Psychological Assoc 1984-, Natl Black MBA Assoc 1986-, MA Psychological Assoc 1986-; corp dir Douglas A Thom Clinic 1986-; consultant MA Dept Mental Health 1986-, New Medico Assoc Inc 1987-. **HONORS/ACHIEVEMENTS:** Martin Luther King Fellow Boston Univ 1979-81; Clinical Fellow Harvard medical Sch 1981-82; instructor in psychology Harvard Medical Sch 1983-. **BUSINESS ADDRESS:** CEO, Basic Health Management Inc, 636 Beacon St, Ste 607, Boston, MA 02215.

BROOKINS, BONITA COLEMAN
Public relations consultant. **PERSONAL:** Born Mar 26, 1950, Lake Charles, LA; married Bishop H Hartford Brookins. **EDUCATION:** CA State Univ Fullerton, BA 1976; Shorter Coll, D Human 1986. **CAREER:** Curtin & Henig Inc, dir of public relations 1976-80; Tobin & Coleman Public RElations Firm, partner 1978-86; Shorter Coll, dir of public relations 1986-; Park Lane Assocs, pres 1986-. **ORGANIZATIONS:** Consultant/fund raiser Friends of Tom Bradley 1982,84,86; mem CA Statewide Fundraising/Jesse Jackson for Pres 1984; supervisor 12th Episcopal Dist Women's Missionary Soc 1986-; bd of dirs Shorter Coll 1986; inaugural comm chair Gov Bill Clinton 1987; mem Natl Assoc Black Journalists, Natl Assoc of Media Women, Black Women's Forum, Black Public Relations Soc, NAACP. **HONORS/ACHIEVEMENTS:** Outstanding Young Women of Amer 1984; NAACP Image Awd 1984; Outstanding Citizen of Arkansas Gov Bill Clinton 1986; Humanitarian Commendation Sen Dale Bumpers 1986. **BUSINESS ADDRESS:** President, Park Lane Associates, 4625 Crenshaw Blvd, Los Angeles, CA 90043.

BROOKINS, DOLORES
Educator. **PERSONAL:** Born Mar 10, 1948, Memphis, TN. **EDUCATION:** Lane Coll Jackson TN, BS 1970; TN State Univ, MS 1973; The Ohio State Univ, PhD 1982. **CAREER:** Illinois Comm Coll Bd, assoc dir for instructional svcs. **ORGANIZATIONS:** Mem Phi Delta Kappa Honor Soc, NASPA, ACPA, SACSA, The Amer Assoc of Junio and Comm Colls, The Amer Soc for Training and Develop, Southern Assoc of Housing Officers; Ed Lum Educ Alumni mem OH State Univ; mem NAACP, PUSH, St John Methodist Church. **HONORS/ACHIEVEMENTS:** Natl Woodrow Wilson Internship Fellow 1980-82; Outstanding Faculty Staff Awd Univ of AR 1983; Outstanding Young Woman of Amer 1983-84; Outstanding Personality in the South 1983-84. **HOME ADDRESS:** 2639 Beech Ave, Springfield, IL 62703. **BUSINESS ADDRESS:** Assoc Dir/Instructional Serv, Illinois Comm College Board, 509 South 6th St, Springfield, IL 62701.

BROOKINS, H. HARTFORD
Clergyman. **PERSONAL:** Born Jun 08, 1925, Yazoo County, MS; married Bonita Coleman. **EDUCATION:** Wilberforce U, BA 1950; Payne Theol Sem, BD 1951, DD; Univ of KS, Attended. **CAREER:** St Paul & AME Church Wichita, KS, pastor 1950-59; First AME Church Los Angeles, pastor 1959-72; AME Church Ctr Africa, 1972-76; 5th Epis Dist AME Church, bishop 1976-84; 12th Epis Dist AME Church, 1984-. **ORGANIZATIONS:** Pres

SCLC Western Region; chmn bd S Los Angeles Dev Corp; immediate past chmn natl bd dir Operations PUSH; past Chmn Ecumenical Ministers Com of PUSH; exec bd mem & life mem NAACP; bd dir Bank of Fin Los Angeles; Los Angeles Cncl of Ch; bd trustees Joint Proj UCLA; adv bd USC Comm Cntr; execcom Men of Tomorrow Inc; mem LA Sister Cities; LA Psychiat Svc; LA Urban League; Alpha Phi Alpha Frat; Concerned Clergy; Pince Hall Masons; 32 Degrees part 6th Pan African World Congress Tanzania 1974; Organized Comm Primary Conv to Elect Los Angeles First Black City & Cnclmn; Convened a Scnd Comm Conv to Elect First Black Sch Bd Mem in 25 Yrs; mgr adv Successful Campaign of Thomas Bradley for Mayor of Los Angeles; adv in numerous Other Campaigns; founder Martin L King Stdnt Fund; organized the first Interfaith Serv at Hollywood Bowl 1971; first black pres Wichita Inter-Racial Ministerial Alliance; former vice pres Wichita, KS Cncl of Ch; frmr mem Wichita, KS Human Relations Commn. **HONORS/ACHIEVEMENTS:** Recipient awrd from Congress of US; NAACP Image Awd 1985. **BUSINESS ADDRESS:** Bishop, Twelfth Episcopal District, Office of the Bishop, 601 Locust St, North Little Rock, AR 72114.

BROOKS, A. RUSSELL
Retired educator. **PERSONAL:** Born May 19, 1906, Montgomery, AL; son of John Randolph Brooks and Eliza Brooks; married Sara Tucker; children: Dwight. **EDUCATION:** Morehouse Coll, BA 1931; Univ of WI, MA 1934; Univ of Edinburgh, 1938-39; Univ of WI, PhD 1958. **CAREER:** NC A&T Coll, chmn English dept 1934-44; Morehouse Coll, assoc prof of English 1946-60; KY State Coll, chmn Engl dept 1960-72 (retired). **ORGANIZATIONS:** Advisory editor CLA Journal 1960-85; mem Modern Language Assn 1958-85; mem Nat Cncl of Tchrs of Engl 1948-85; mem Coll Language Assn 1941-85. **HONORS/ACHIEVEMENTS:** Author of book "James Boswell" Twayne Publishers 1971; mem KY Arts Commission 1965-68. **HOME ADDRESS:** 415 College Park Dr, Frankfort, KY 40601.

BROOKS, ALVIN LEE
Government official. **PERSONAL:** Born May 03, 1932, North Little Rock, AR; married Carol Rich Brooks, Aug 23, 1950; children: Ronall, Estelle, Carrie, Diane, Rosalind, Tameisha. **EDUCATION:** Univ MO Kansas City, BA Hist & Govt 1959, MA Sociology 1973. **CAREER:** Kansas City Police Dept, detective & police officer; Kansas City Sch Dist, home sch coord 1964-66; Neighborhood Youth Corp of Cath Diocese of Kansas City St Joseph, dir out of school proj 1966-67; Kansas City, coord pub info & com interpr 1967-68; Human Relations Dept Kansas City, dir 1968-73, 1980-; City of Kansas City MO, asst city mgr 1973-80. **ORGANIZATIONS:** Mem past vice pres Bd of Regents Ctr MO State Univ 1975-82; chmn MO Commn on Human Rights 1975-82; chmn MO Black Leadership Assn 1979-82; National Assn of Human Rights Workers 1968-; International Assn of Official Human Rights Agencies 1969-; convenor, Ad Hoc Group Against Crime 1977; vice pres, Prime Heal Inc (HMO) 1987. **HONORS/ACHIEVEMENTS:** Man of the Yr Ivanhoe Club 1969; Outstanding Citizen of the Yr Beta Omega Chap Omega Psi Phi 1972; Outstanding Citizen of the Yr Young Progressives 1973; Alumni Achievement Awd Univ of MO at Kansas City 1975; Kansas City Tomorrow 1988; Natl Conference of Christians & Jews (NCCJ) 1989. **BUSINESS ADDRESS:** Dir of Human Relations Dept, City of Kansas City, Missouri, 414 E 12th St, City Hall, 4th Fl, Kansas City, MO 64106.

BROOKS, ARKLES CLARENCE, JR.
Salesman. **PERSONAL:** Born Aug 25, 1943, Detroit, MI; married Sarah L; children: Arkles III, Ira David, Alice Ruth, Sharon Louise. **EDUCATION:** Southern IL Univ, BA 1967; Wayne State Univ, MA 1976. **CAREER:** Natl Bank of Detroit, asst branch mgr 1968-70; Aetna Life & Casualty, career agent 1970-72; Detroit Bd of Educ, math, science teacher 1971-73; The Upjohn Co, hospital sales specialist 1973-; Allstate Insurance, Southfield, MI, sales assoc, 1987-. **ORGANIZATIONS:** Member, Wayne County Notary Public 1968-, Natl Assoc of Life Underwriters 1970-; pres, Varsity Club Inc 1971-; corp treasurer, 1972-, assoc pastor, 1985-, exec vice pres, 1989-, Gospel Chapel of Detroit Inc. **HOME ADDRESS:** 17101 Anna, Southfield, MI 48075.

BROOKS, AVERY
Actor. **PERSONAL:** Born 1949, Gary, IN; son of Samuel Brooks and Eva Lydia Crawford; married Vicki Lenora; children: Ayana, Cabral, Asante. **EDUCATION:** Indiana Univ; Oberlin College; Rutgers Univ, New Brunswick NJ, BA, MFA. **CAREER:** Rutgers Univ, assoc prof of theater; staged reading of Lord Byron's Manfred New England Convervatory's 1986 festival Music With Words; starred in Solomon Northrup's Odyssey PBS 1984; appears as "Hawk" inTV series Spenser, For Hire; star of own ABC-TV series A Man Called Hawk. *

BROOKS, BERNARD E.
Management consultant. **PERSONAL:** Born Jul 08, 1935, Camden, SC; son of James Brooks and Bertha Brooks; married Julia D Lyons, May 07, 1988; children: Bernard II, Sharon, Karen, Susan, Theresa. **EDUCATION:** Brooklyn Coll, AAS Accounting 1964; Fairleigh Dickinson Univ, BS Accounting 1973; Pace Univ, MS Mgmt 1978. **CAREER:** Chase Manhattan Bank, systems planning officer 1968-69; Trans World Airlines, dir data serv admin 1969-70; Arthur Young & Co, principal 1970-74; AT&T, mktg mgr 1974-78; Arthur Young & Co, partner; PA Exec Search, vice pres; MSL Intl Ltd, vice pres; Kearney Executive Search, vice pres. **ORGANIZATIONS:** Councilman Twp of Teaneck 1978-82; trustee St Vincents Hosp & Med Ctr 1982-; mayor Twp of Teaneck 1982-88. **HONORS/ACHIEVEMENTS:** Publ Intro to Telecomm 1978; Man of the Year N NJ Chap Negro Bus & Professional Women 1979. **MILITARY SERVICE:** USAF staff sgt 1952-56. **HOME ADDRESS:** 273 Glen Court, Teaneck, NJ 07666.

BROOKS, BERNARD W.
Artist. **PERSONAL:** Born Sep 06, 1939, Alexandria, VA. **EDUCATION:** Univ of MD, 1958-60; Philadelphia Mus Clg of Art, 1960-61; Corcoran Gallery Sch of Art, 1961-62; Howard U, 1962-65. **CAREER:** A&B Assc Washington, DC, assc dir; Howard Univ Clg of Dentistry , artist islstr; Opus 2 Galleries, assc dir. **ORGANIZATIONS:** Pblctn artist Am Chem Soc & Washington, DC; asst art dir Van Heusen Shirt Co; asst advertising mgr Grand Union Food Co Inc Landover, MD; tech illstr Atlantic Research Corp Alexandria, VA; silk screen tech Grand Union Food Co Landover, MD; ownr dir Bernard W Brooks Studio; vice pres DC Art Assc; WashingtonWatercolour Assc; pub rel dir Natl Conf of Artists; art exhibited Georgetown Graphics Gallery. **HONORS/ACHIEVEMENTS:** 1st prize D/C Rec Outdoor Art Show 1971; 1st prize Montgomery Mall Outdoor Art Show 1972; 1st prize George F Muth Awrd HowardUniv 1962; 2nd prize HowardUniv 1963; num profnl exhibtns; collections; Radio-tV Presentations . **MILITARY SERVICE:** USAR pfc. **BUSINESS ADDRESS:** 2315 M St NW, Washington, DC 20037.

BROOKS, CAROL LORRAINE
Government official. **PERSONAL:** Born Nov 23, 1955, Brooklyn, NY. **EDUCATION:** Univ of VT, BA 1977; Rutgers Univ, postgrad studies 1977-79; School for Intl Training, Exchange Student to Mexico 1975; Recipient of the Walter Russell Scholarship 1977. **CAREER:** CBS News Inc, project coord 1978-81; NJ Office of the Governor, special asst 1981-85; NJ Dept of Environ Protection, administrator 1985-. **ORGANIZATIONS:** Bd of dir Family Serv Assoc of Trenton/Hopewell Valley 1983-; commn mem NJ Martin Luther King Jr Commemorative Commn 1985-; mem Urban League Guild of Metropolitan Trenton 1986-. **HONORS/ACHIEVEMENTS:** 100 Young Women of Promise Good Housekeeping Magazine 1985; Employ Serv Awd 5 yrs NJ State Govt 1987; Outstanding Young Women of Amer 1986. **HOME ADDRESS:** 15 Winthrop Rd, Lawrenceville, NJ 08648. **BUSINESS ADDRESS:** Administrator, NJ Environ Protection, 440 E State St, Trenton, NJ 08625.

BROOKS, CAROLYN BRANCH
Research associate professor. **PERSONAL:** Born Jul 08, 1946, Richmond, VA; daughter of Charles W Branch and Shirley Booker Branch; married Henry M Brooks, Sep 28, 1965; children: Charles T, Marcellus L, Alexis J, Toni A. **EDUCATION:** Tuskegee Univ, Tuskegee AL, BS, 1968, MS, 1971; Ohio State Univ, Columbus OH, PhD, 1977. **CAREER:** Bullock County Bd of Educ, Union Springs AL, science teacher, 1968-69; Macon County Bd of Educ, Tuskegee AL, science teacher, 1971-72; VA Hospital, Tuskegee AL, research technician, 1972-73; Ohio State Univ, Columbus OH, graduate teaching asst, 1975-77; Kentucky State Univ, Frankfort KY, principal investigator & program dir, 1978-81; Univ of Maryland Eastern Shore, Princess Anne MD, research asst prof, 1981-. **ORGANIZATIONS:** mem, advisory bd, treasurer 1989-90, mem, Salvation Army Youth Club. **HONORS/ACHIEVEMENTS:** Outstanding Serv Award, Silhouettes of Kappa Alpha Psi, 1980; First Place Award, Competitive Paper Presentation, Seventh Biennial Research Symposium HBCU, 1987; Outstanding Faculty Award for Research, School of Agricultural Sciences, 1987-88; Chancellor's Research Scholar Award, 1988; Woman of the Year Award, Maryland Eastern Shore Branch of the Natl Assn of Univ Women, 1988; First Annual White House Initiative Faculty Award for Excellence in Science, 1988; invited speaker, "Symposium on Biotechnology," Alabama A&M Univ, 1988; invited visiting scientist, Hampton Univ, 1989; USDA Peer Review panelist, USDA Natl Needs Fellowship Program, 1989; author, articles for scientific journals, Tropical Agriculture, Journal of Invertebrate Pathology, others; researcher, Togo & Senegal, West Africa, 1984, 1985, Cameroon, West Africa, 1988. **BUSINESS ADDRESS:** Research Assoc Prof, Univ of Maryland Eastern Shore, Trigg Hall, Princess Anne, MD 21853.

BROOKS, CHARLOTTE KENDRICK
Educator, consultant. **PERSONAL:** Born Jun 05, 1918, Washington, DC; daughter of Swan Kendrick and Ruby Moyse Kendrick; married Walter Henderson Brooks; children: Walter (deceased), Joseph Kendrick. **EDUCATION:** Howard Univ, AB (Magna Cum Laude) 1939; NY Univ, MA 1954; Walden Univ, PhD 1976. **CAREER:** Baltimore Public Schools, teacher 1939-42; Wash DC Public Schools, teacher 1942-61; DC Public Schools, supvr 1961-73; The Amer Univ, asst prof, dir of commun studies 1974-78; DC Heath Public Co, natl lang arts cons; Brooks Assoc, consult in ed. **ORGANIZATIONS:** Consultant English Educ 1965-85; bd of dir Southwest House 10 yrs; chmn Youth Task Force of SW Assembly 1983-84; pres Natl Council of Teachers of English 1977; trustee Rsch Found NCTE 1980-81; mem Commn on the English Language NCTE 1980-81; comm Verbally Gifted & Talented NCTE 1978-81; local chairperson Secondary English Conf of NCTE 1973-74; mem trustee bd Ctr for Applied Linguistics 1972-75; mem Commn on Reading NCTE 1970-74; chairperson Nominating Comm for NCTE 1970; mem Commn on the Reading Process Intl Reading Assn 1969-72; mem Comm on Behavioral Objectives in English; rep White House Conf on Children NCTE 1969-70; partic Conf for Teachers of the Disadvantaged Staffordshire England 1968; partic TV progs on lang, NBC & BBC 1966-67; professional consultant in English & reading for US Office o f Educ Public School Systems Univ & State Dept 1965-85; public relations rep NCTE 1964-69; consultant, speaker for NCTE, IRA & others 1963-89; lecturer Ruskin & Balliol Coll, Oxford and other schools and professional organizations. **HONORS/ACHIEVEMENTS:** Alpha Kappa Alpha Awd for undergrad studies; Natl Conf of Christians & Jews; Eugene & Agnes Meyer Grant 1958; Fulbright Exchange Grant 1960-61; Coll Entrance Exam Bd Grant 1962; Winifred Cullis Lecture Fellowship 1963,64; Gulbenkian Grant 1968; Ford Grant 1972; NCTE Black Caucus Awd 1975; Cullis/Mair Lecture Fellowship 1980; num publs incl, "Tapping Potential, English & Language Arts for the Black Learner" CK Brooks editor The Natl Council of Teachers of English 1985, "African Rhythms" Simon & Schuster Publ Co 1974, "Communicating" DC Heath Publ Co 1973, "They Can Learn English" Wadsworth Publ Co 1972; Dist Black Women Ed BISA 1986; Named Dist Black Women and Photo & Bio on 1985 BISA Calendar. **BUSINESS ADDRESS:** Consultant in Education, Brooks Associates, 472 M St, SW, Washington, DC 20024.

BROOKS, CLYDE HENRY
Personnel administrator, librarian, industrial relations manager. **PERSONAL:** Born Sep 05, 1941, Danville, IL; son of George Brooks and Venie Brooks. **EDUCATION:** Western IL Univ McComb, BS 1958, MS. **CAREER:** Chicago Metro Chap So Christian Ldrshp Conf, pres 1972-. **ORGANIZATIONS:** Dir Natl EEO & Employee Relations Blue Cross/Blue Shield Assn 1973-; assc & exec dir/ manpower dir Cook County Office of Equal Opportunity Inc Chicago 1968-73; area dir Cook County Office of Equal Opportunity Inc Chicago 1966-67; dir Sears Roebuck Comm Coop Proj Chicago 1965-66; supr Dept of Ed JOBS Proj Chicago 1964-65; employment cnsl Il State Employment Serv Chicago 1964; cnsl Crane HS Chicago 1964; neighborhood worker Chicago Comm on Youth Welfare Ch 1961-64; probation ofcr Juvenile Ct of Cook Co Chicago 1959-61; tchr Wendel Phillips Evening Sch 1959-65; cnsl Marillac Settlement House 1963-66; cnsl Scott Foresman Pub Co 1969-; cnsl Il Drug Abuse Pgm 196971; vis prof Harper Clg 1970-77; pres bd chmn BRASS (Behavior Research in Action in the Social Sci) Chicago 1969-71; chmn Ed Labs Inc Elk Grove Vlg, IL 1969-71; tchr St Mary of the Lake Sem Mundelein, IL 1965; field work instr Univ of Chicago 1972-; pres & founder Minority Economic Resourses Corp 1972-; mem Chicago C of C & Inds 1973-; mem Il State C of C 1973-. **HONORS/ACHIEVEMENTS:** Pub "Rockwell Garden Comm Appraisal Study"; Chicago authority pub "Midwest Comm Teenage Study"; pub "The Negro in Amer.". **BUSINESS ADDRESS:** Minority Economic Resources Corporation, 1565 Ellinwood St, Des Plaines, IL 60016.

BROOKS, DAISY M. ANDERSON
Day care provider. **PERSONAL:** Children: Yolanda Denise, Wadell Jr, Cassandra An-

nette. **EDUCATION:** Natl Inst of Practical Nursing, Chicago, Practical Nurses Training; Northwestern Med School, Chicago, Training in Med Tech. **CAREER:** Tots & Toddlers Day Care Ctr Inc 2 Waukegan, IL, co-owner; Daisy's Nursery, co-owner/exec dir; Victory Meml Hosp, med tech; Phys & Surg Lab Waukegan, IL, supvry med tech. **ORGANIZATIONS:** Past pres N Chicago Dist 64 Band Parents Assc; Worthy Matron Order of Eastern Star 1974; ofcr Golden Cir 59; mem deaconess Shiloh Bapt Ch; past pres Music Dept; mem N Chicago Br NAACP; past pres Progressive Comm Organ of N Chgo; past sec Cntrl Grade Sch PTA; past treas N Chicago Black Caucas; bd dir Altrusa Intrl Clb/Day Care Crisis Cncl for State of IL; mem Citizen Adv Com Lake Co Area Voc Ctr (Child Care Sub Com) N Chicago HS Voc Adv Com; past vice pres N Chicago Great Lakes VA C of C; vice pres Day Care Crisis Cncl for State of IL/Citizens Adv Com N Chicago Comm Block Dev; chprsn Schlrshp Com; mem Mt Sinai Bapt Ch.

BROOKS, DELORES JEAN
College administrator. **PERSONAL:** Born Nov 13, 1944, Chicago, IL; divorced; children: Edward L Jr. **EDUCATION:** Northeastern IL Univ, BA 1977; Natl Coll of Educ, MS 1983. **CAREER:** Hyde Park Herald Newspaper, free lance reporter 1977-; Chicago Dept of Human Svcs, staff writer 1977-79; Dollars & Sense Magazine, contributing editor 1979-;City Colls of Chicago, coord of public relations and develop 1979-. **ORGANIZATIONS:** Mem Natl Assoc of Media Women Chicago Chap 1980-83, Fine Arts Acad 1981-83; subcomm chairperson/mem Publicity Club of Chicago 1984-; bd of dirs Northeastern IL Univ Alumni Assoc 1985-; mem Mayor's Commn on Women's Affairs 1985-; mem Chicago Assoc of Black Journalists 1986-. **HONORS/ACHIEVEMENTS:** Outstanding Volunteer Serv Chicago Park District 1980,81,83; Outstanding Young Woman of Amer Awd 1980; Outstanding Volunteer Serv DuSable Museum of AfricanAmer History 1981,83; One of Chicago's Up and Coming Black Business and Professional Women Dollars & Sense Magazine 1986. **BUSINESS ADDRESS:** Coord of Pub Relations/Dev, City Colleges of Chicago, 226 W Jackson Blvd, Chicago, IL 60601.

BROOKS, DON LOCELLUS
Business executive. **PERSONAL:** Born Oct 21, 1953, Galveston, TX; married Charlotte; children: Eric, Don Jr, Chris. **EDUCATION:** Galveston Coll, AA Mid Mgmt 1975; Univ of Houston, BS Mktg/Mgmt 1977; Univ of TX Austin, Finance Leadership 1976-78. **CAREER:** Guaranty Fed Savings & Loans, mgmt trainee 1976-78, reg savings coord 1978-80, asst vice pres 1980-81, vice pres savings 1981-. **ORGANIZATIONS:** Bd of trustees Galveston Park Bd 1982-; bd of dir Family Serv Ctr 1984-85; mem United Way Inc of Galveston 1984-85, Legislative Comm Galveston 1984-; council rep City of Galveston 1984-; chairperson Fiscal Auditing & Insurance Comm City of Galveston Park Bd of Trustees 1984-85; city council ex-officio Galveston Park Bd of Trustees 1984-85. **HONORS/ACHIEVEMENTS:** Two Pres Awd Cert Galveston Coll, 1973; Recipient of Hon Mention Mid-Mgmt Student Awd 1973; Elected to Who's Who of Amer Tech Schools & Coll Galveston Jr Coll 1973; Two Deans Awd Certs Galveston Coll 1974; Founder of Galveston Coll Key Club 1975; Highest Vote Getter Galveston City Council (4,013 votes)1984-85; Elected to Exec Comm United Way Inc of Galveston 1985. **HOME ADDRESS:** 5506 Ave P, Galveston, TX 77550. **BUSINESS ADDRESS:** Vice President, Branch Manager, Guaranty Fed Savings & Loan, 2121 Market St, Galveston, TX 77550.

BROOKS, GILBERT
Programming specialist. **PERSONAL:** Born Jul 03, 1934, Somerton, AZ; married Bernice Louise Stroud; children: Gilbert, Sharon, Brian, Jonathan, Catherine. **EDUCATION:** Univ of CA Berkeley, AA, BA 1955. **CAREER:** Lockheed Missiles & Space Co Inc, sci prog spec 1966-; Control Data Corp, computer prog/Analyst 1966-; Lockheed Missiles & Space Co, computer oper & sci prog 1960-65; Univ of CA Lawrence Radiation Lab, computer oper 1958-60; Univ of CA Berkeley, stud & sr libr asst 1954-58. **ORGANIZATIONS:** Mem Milpitas Schl Dist Bd Educ 1963-. **BUSINESS ADDRESS:** Lockhead Missiles & Space Co, 1111lockhead Way, Sunnyvale, CA 94088.

BROOKS, GWENDOLYN ELIZABETH
Author, lecturer. **PERSONAL:** Born Jun 07, 1917, Topeka, KS; daughter of David Anderson Brooks and Keziah Corinne Wims Brooks; married Henry Lowington Blakely, Sep 17, 1939; children: Henry Lowington III, Nora. **EDUCATION:** Wilson Jr Coll, Chicago, 1936. **CAREER:** Poet, novelist, lecturer; publicity dir, NAACP Youth Council, Chicago, 1937-38; taught poetry at numerous coll and univ; distinguished prof of the arts, City Coll of the City Univ of New York, 1971. **ORGANIZATIONS:** Bd member, Inst Positive Educ, Amer Acad of Arts and Letters, Natl Inst of Arts and Letters; member, Society of Midland Authors Chicago, Illinois Arts Council. **HONORS/ACHIEVEMENTS:** Grant in literature, Natl Inst of Arts and Letters, 1946; award for creative writing, Amer Acad of Arts and Letters, 1946; two fellowships, Guggenheim Memorial Found, 1946, 1947; Eunice Tietjens Memorial Prize, Poetry magazine, 1949; Pulitzer Prize in poetry (for book Annie Allen), 1950; Kuumba Liberation Award; Robert F. Ferguson Memorial Award, Friends of Literature, 1964; Thormod Monsen Literature Award, 1964; Anisfield-Wolf Award, 1968; named Poet Laureate of Illinois, 1968-; honored for outstanding achievement in letters, Black Academy of Arts and Letters, 1971; Shelley Memorial Award, 1976; poetry consultant to the Library of Congress, 1985-86; forty-nine honorary degrees from univ and coll; inductee, Natl Womens' Hall of Fame; Essence Award; Frost Medal, Poetry Soc of Amer; Lifetime Achievement Award, Natl Endowment for the Arts, 1989; published works include A Street in Bronzeville 1945, Annie Allen 1949, In the Mecca 1968, Bronzeville Boys and Girls 1956, and Maud Martha 1953. **BUSINESS ADDRESS:** Poet Laureate of Illinois, c/o Contemporary Forum, 2528a West Jerome, Chicago, IL 60645.

BROOKS, HAROLD W.
Financial administrator. **PERSONAL:** Born Aug 23, 1948, Los Angeles, CA. **EDUCATION:** Loyola Univ, BA 1970. **CAREER:** ARC, EFO dir financial dev 1977-; United Way Los Angeles, co-dir of campaign 1973-77. **ORGANIZATIONS:** Mem Natl Soc of Fund Raising Exec 1980. **BUSINESS ADDRESS:** 615 N St Asaph St, Alexandria, VA 22314.

BROOKS, HARRY W., JR.
Business executive. **PERSONAL:** Born May 17, 1928, Indianapolis, IN; son of Harry W Brooks, Sr and Nora E Brooks; married June Hezekiah, Nov 24, 1985; children: Harry W III, Wayne L, Craig E. **EDUCATION:** Univ of Oklahoma, Norman, MA; Univ of Nebraska, Omaha, BGE; attended US Army War Coll, Carlysle, PA. **CAREER:** US Army, private to major general, 1947-76, commanding general 25th Infantry Division, Hawaii, 1974-76; Amfac, Inc, senior vice pres and public affairs dir, 1978-82, exec vice pres and chmn of Horticulture group, 1982-84; Advanced Consumer Marketing Corp, chmn and chief exec officer, 1985-; Gurney Seed and Nursery Corp, chmn and chief exec, 1985-; Gurney Wholesale Inc, chmn and chief exec, 1985-; Western Compiter Group, Inc, chmn and chief exec, 1985-. **ORGANIZATIONS:** Trustee, Gannett Found, 1976-89; dir, Occupational Medical Corp of Amer, 1985-89; trustee, San Mateo Easter Seals, 1988-89; director, San Francisco Opera, 1988-89. **HONORS/ACHIEVEMENTS:** Distinguished Service Medal, 1976, Legion of Merit, 1970, Vietnamese Cross of Gallantry, 1967, all from US Army; Leonard H Carter Award, NAACP, Region I, 1988. **HOME ADDRESS:** 14 Parrott Ct, San Mateo, CA 94402. **BUSINESS ADDRESS:** President, Advanced Consumer Marketing Corp, 858 Burlway Rd, Burlingame, CA 94010.

BROOKS, HENRY MARCELLUS
Extension administrator. **PERSONAL:** Born Oct 16, 1942, Tuskegee, AL; son of Ewing Tipton Brooks (deceased) and Willie Ruth Jackson Brooks; married Carolyn D Branch, Sep 28, 1965; children: Charles Tipton, Marcellus Leander, Alexis Janine, Toni Andrea. **EDUCATION:** Tuskegee Univ, Tuskegee, AL, BS, 1965, MEd, 1966; Ohio State Univ, Columbus, OH, PhD, 1975. **CAREER:** Auburn Univ, Union Spring, AL, extension farm agent, 1967-73; Kentucky State Univ, Frankfort, KY, extension specialist, 1975-80; UMES, Princess Anne, MD, extension admin, 1980-; Univ of Maryland Coll Pk, College Park, MD, center head, LESREC, 1988-; center head, Univ of Maryland Coll Park, 1988-. **ORGANIZATIONS:** Grammateus, Sigma Pi Phi, 1984-89; polemarch, Kappa Alpha Psi, 1987-89. **HOME ADDRESS:** 1906 Kipling, Salisbury, MD 21801. **BUSINESS ADDRESS:** Extension Admin, Univ of Maryland Eastern Shore, Trigg Hall, Rm 122, Princess Anne, MD 21853.

BROOKS, HUBIE
Professional athlete. **PERSONAL:** Born Sep 24, 1956, Los Angeles, CA. **EDUCATION:** Mesa (AZ) Comm Coll; AZ State Univ, BS Health Sci. **CAREER:** NY Mets, infielder 1980-84; Montreal Expos, infielder 1984-. **HONORS/ACHIEVEMENTS:** 24 game hitting streak from May 1 to June 1, 1984 was personal career high and Natl League high for 1984; named NL Player-of-the-Week 2 times; finished third in Rookie of the Year balloting; named to every Rookie All-Star team at third base in 1981; selected Mets' Player-of-the-Year in 1982; Silver Slugger Awd winner 2times; Expo's Player of the Month April 1986; NL Player of the Month May 1986; mem 1986 All Star Team. **BUSINESS ADDRESS:** Montreal Expos, PO Box 500, Station M, Montreal, Quebec, Canada HIV 3P2.

BROOKS, HUNTER O.
Educator. **PERSONAL:** Born Sep 01, 1929, Bluefield, WV; married Barbara Boudreaux; children: Hunter, II, Christopher. **EDUCATION:** WV State Clge, BA; WV Univ, MA. **CAREER:** TX Southern Univ, asst prof History. **ORGANIZATIONS:** Mem Natl Council Soc Studies; Assc Study Negro Life & Hist; Oral Hist Assc Dir Amer Schlrs; Dict Intl Biography; Personalities So; Community Ldrs& Amer. **HONORS/ACHIEVEMENTS:** 2000 Men Ach Carnegie Flwshp 1966; mem Phi Alpha Theta; Sigma Rho Sigma Pubs Man & Civilization 1963; Black Ldrshp Amer 1973; Discovering Black Amer 1973. **MILITARY SERVICE:** AUS 1951-53. **BUSINESS ADDRESS:** TX Southern Univ, Houston, TX 77004.

BROOKS, JAMES O'NEIL
Business executive. **PERSONAL:** Born Aug 22, 1922, Greenville, MS; married Beria K; children: Geoffrey, Cynthia. **EDUCATION:** Univ Portland, BS 1952, BA 1966, MEd 1972. **CAREER:** Urban League, exec dir 1973-, dep exec dir 1970-73; Urban League LEAPD dir 1970-73; Urban League, employment dir 1965-67; Multnomah County Juvenile Ct, group work 1959-65; Maryhurst College, instr 1966-73. **ORGANIZATIONS:** Amer Assc of Univ Prof; Natl Assc of Housing & Redev Officials; Natl Assc of Human Rights Wrkrs; Kappa Alpha Psi; Billy Webb Lodge 3; F&AM PH NAACP; Irvington Comm Assc; St Philip's Episcopal Ch Bd commrs; Housing Authority of Portland; adv com Portland Publ Schl; pres Albina Lions Club. **HONORS/ACHIEVEMENTS:** Title VII Prog 22nd Annual Brotherhood Award B'nai B'rith Portland Lodge 65 1976. **MILITARY SERVICE:** USAAC engr gunner 1942-46. **BUSINESS ADDRESS:** Trainer, Private Industry Council, Rm 404 718 W Burnside, Portland, OR 97209.

BROOKS, JAMES ROBERT
Professional athlete. **PERSONAL:** Born Dec 28, 1958, Warner Robins, GA; married Simone Renee; children: James Darnell, Tianna Renee. **EDUCATION:** Attended, Auburn. **CAREER:** San Diego Chargers, all-purpose back 1981-83; Cincinnati Bengals, all-purpose back 1984-. **ORGANIZATIONS:** Baseball & Softball with Bengals Team. **HONORS/ACHIEVEMENTS:** Led the NFL in total yards, rushing, receiving, punt & kickoff returns 1981-82; All-Am at Auburn; High Sch All-Am on Nat Champion Warner-Robins, GA team; All Pro; mem 1987 NFL Pro Bowl team. **BUSINESS ADDRESS:** Cincinnati Bengals, 200 Riverfront Stadium, Cincinnati, OH 45202.

BROOKS, LARRY
Athlete. **PERSONAL:** Born Jun 10, 1950, Prince George, VA; married Colleen; children: Larry Jr. **EDUCATION:** Attended VA State Coll; Chapman Coll, educ degree. **CAREER:** Los Angeles Rams, def tackle 1972-83, assistant defensive line coach. **ORGANIZATIONS:** Partipant in AP'S first team Little All-Amer. **HONORS/ACHIEVEMENTS:** Lineman of Year VA State Coll; football & track star Prince George VA; played in NFC Championship Games 1974, 1976, 1979; played in Pro Bowl 1976, 1977, 1979; Sporting News NFC All-Star Team 1977, 1978; played in NFL Championship Game 1979. **BUSINESS ADDRESS:** Asst Defensive Line Coach, Los Angeles Rams, 2327 West Lincoln Avenue, Anaheim, CA 92801.

BROOKS, LEO AUSTIN
Military. **PERSONAL:** Born Aug 09, 1932, Washington, DC; married Naomi Ethel Lewis; children: Leo Jr, Vincent Keith, Marquita Karen. **EDUCATION:** VA St U, BS Instrmntl Mus Educ 1954; Cent St Univ Wilbeforce OH, Bus Adminstrn addtnl study 1960-62; George Wash Univ Wash DC, MS in Fin Mgmt 1964-66. **CAREER:** AUS Troop Sprt Agency Ft Lee VA, comdg gen 1978-; 13th Corps Sprt Cmmnd Ft Hood TX, comdg ofcr 1976-78; Sacramento Army Depot, cmdg ofcr 1974-76; Hdqrs Dept of the Army Wash DC, congrsnl coord 1967-70; Joint Chfs of Staff Wash DC, Cambodian desk ofcr 1972-74. **ORGANIZATIONS:**

Bd dir United Urban Leag Sacramento CA 1974-76; bd dir Gr Sacramento United Way 1974-76; bd dir United Serv Auto Assn (Usaa) 1978-; chmn bd of Advis Jesuit HS Sacramento CA 1974-76; past master Acacia Lodge #32 Prince Hall F&A Masons VA 1967-; pres Cntrl VA Chap Fed Exec Assn 1979-. **HONORS/ACHIEVEMENTS:** Fam of yr Freedom Found Vly Forge PA 1980; recip Legion of Merit; 2 Oakleaf Clusters; Bronze Star; Meritorious Serv Medal; Army Commndtn Medal, AUS. **MILITARY SERVICE:** AUS brig gen 1954-. **BUSINESS ADDRESS:** Hdqrts-Department of the Army, (DAPE-GO), Room 2E 749, The Pentagon, Washington, DC 20310.

BROOKS, MARCELLUS
Educator. **PERSONAL:** Born Jun 24, 1941, Senatobia, MS; married Lula M; children: Marcellus Vaughn Brooks. **EDUCATION:** Fisk Univ, BA 1964; NY Univ & Univ Madrid, MA 1965; Vanderbilt Univ, postgrad; Univ IL; Univ TN. **CAREER:** Fisk Univ, asst prof Spanish, instructor, 1965-. **ORGANIZATIONS:** Mem Sigma Delta Pi; Alpha Mu Gamma, Alpha Phi Alpha, Mod Lang Assc TN For Lang Assc Ford Fnd Grant Univ IL 1968-69, Coll Language Assoc. **BUSINESS ADDRESS:** Assistant Professor, Fisk University, Box 19, Nashville, TN 37203.

BROOKS, MARION JACKSON
Physician. **PERSONAL:** Born Feb 15, 1920, Ft Worth, TX; married Marie Louise Norris; children: Marian Bryant, Carol Eleanor Stroughter, Roy ChArles, Clearence Jackson, Marie Anne. **EDUCATION:** Prairie View A&M Clge, BS 1940; Howard Univ, MD 1951. **CAREER:** Freedmen's Hosp Wash, intern 1951-52; Ft Worth, gen prac med 1952-; St Joseph Hosp, mem staff; Harris Hosp, mem staff; All Saints Hosp, mem staff;Great Liberty Life Ins Co Dallas, dir; Neighborhood Action Inc, pres 1967-68. **ORGANIZATIONS:** Chmn Sickle Cell Anemia Assc TX; mem Ft Worth City Park & Recreation Bd 1963-67; Ft Worth Symphony Assc; Comm Action Agcy; Ft Worth-Tarrant Co; bddir Tarrant Co Prec Workers Coun; dir Eto TX Council Alpha Phi Alpha; Mason Shriner. **MILITARY SERVICE:** AUS 1st lt 1942-47. **BUSINESS ADDRESS:** 2200 Evans Ave, Fort Worth, TX 76104.

BROOKS, NORMAN LEON
Educational administrator. **PERSONAL:** Born Feb 21, 1932, Port Chester, NY; married Barbara EmmeLuth. **EDUCATION:** State Univ of NY Potsdam Crane Schl of Music, BS 1954; Tchrs Clge Columbia Univ, MA 1961; NY Univ, A & Sup Cert 1976. **CAREER:** City Schl Dist of New Rochelle, supr mus educ 1969-; New Rochelle HS, choral instr 1967-69; New Rochelle Pub Schl, vocal & gen mus instr 1958-67; Port Chester Pub Schl, instr 1954-58. **ORGANIZATIONS:** Choirmaster & organist St Peter's Episcopal Ch Port Chester 1958-70; asst conductor NY Collegiate Chorale 1970-73; prog chrmn Keynote Fund Com New Rochelle Library 1978-79; vestryman St Peter's Episcopal Church Peekskill 1987-; mem Phi Mu Alpha Sinfonia Hon Music Frat; mem NAACP New Rochelle. **HONORS/ACHIEVEMENTS:** Guest conductor Westchester Co Sch Mus Assc 1976-80; conductor & artistic dir New Rochelle All-City Chorale 1979-; guest pianist Benefit Concert for CommCh 1980; guest Pianist Stars over Port Chester 1980; NYSSMA Chairperson for multi-cultural Awareness Comm 1982,83. **BUSINESS ADDRESS:** District Supervisor Music Ed, New Rochelle School Dist, 515 North Ave, New Rochelle, NY 10801.

BROOKS, NORWARD J.
State employee. **PERSONAL:** Born Sep 10, 1934, New Iberia, LA; son of Cleo Brooks and Ivory Brooks; married Violet Caldwell; children: Norward, Jr, Cleoanna, David Eric Spencer. **EDUCATION:** Seattle Univ, BS 1955, MA 1971, MBA; Univ of WA, PhD, 1989. **CAREER:** The Boeing Co Seattle, various positions 1959-69; United Inner City Dev Fnd, exec dir, 1969-70; King Co Govt Seattle, dir records & elections dept 1970-73; Washington State Employment Sec Dept, commr 1973-77; Univ of Washington, dir admin data proc 1977-81; Model Capitol Corp, pres 1979-; Washington State Employment Security Dept, commissioner 1981-85; City of Seattle, comptroller 1986-. **ORGANIZATIONS:** Past pres Council for Minority Bus Enterprises in Washington State 1969-70; past pres Seattle Econ Oppor Bd Inc 1971-72; mem Govt Adv Council on Voc Educ; chmn Washington Occupational Info Consortium; trustee Washington State Assc of Co Officials 1971-72; co-chmn Washington State Co Auditors' Educ Com 1971-72; past pres Intl Thunderbird Little League Assc; past chrmn Minority Bus Dev Com Seattle Chamber of Commerce; past mem King Co Boys Club Bd Dir; past Mem United Way; mem bd dir Natl Conf of Christians & Jews; mem bd stewards 1st AMLE Ch; Alpha Phi Alpha. **HONORS/ACHIEVEMENTS:** Magna Cum Laude Southern Univ 1955; Golden Acorn Award Newport Hills PTA 1971; Urban League, Affirmative Action Award 1985; Employment Security Administrator of the Year 1985. **MILITARY SERVICE:** AUS 1st lt 1955-59; WA NG capt 1961-65. **BUSINESS ADDRESS:** Seattle City Comptroller, City of Seattle, 101 Municipal Bldg, Seattle, WA 98104.

BROOKS, PERRY
Professional athlete. **PERSONAL:** Born Dec 04, 1954; married Vergie; children: Ahmad, Krsunthia, Perry Jr. **EDUCATION:** So LA Univ, Agr Agronomy. **CAREER:** Washington Redskins, defensive tackle 1977-. **ORGANIZATIONS:** Consultant for Heritage Financial Group-an Alexandria, VA firm dlng in investments, real estate & stock, etc; worked in personnel dept of Giant Foods.

BROOKS, PHILLIP DANIEL
Business executive. **PERSONAL:** Born Mar 02, 1946, Charlottesville, VA. **EDUCATION:** Norfolk State Coll, BA 1969; VA Commonwealth Univ, MA 1971. **CAREER:** Norfolk Comm Hospital, admin 1971-, asst admins 1971. **ORGANIZATIONS:** Mem bd dir Blue Cross Blue Shield VA; Tidewater Hospital Council; Amer Hosp Assn; VA Hospital Assn, Amer Coll of Hospital Admin; Natl Assn of Health Serv Execs Mem; Tidewater Regional Political Assn; United Comm Fund Allocation Liaison Team 1977; chmn advisory com Hal Jackson's Miss US Talented Teen Pageant. **HONORS/ACHIEVEMENTS:** Award of Recognition Norfolk Comm 1976;, Health Mgmt Achievement Award Natl Assn of Health Serv Execs 1976. **BUSINESS ADDRESS:** 2539 Corprew Ave, Norfolk, VA 23504.

BROOKS, RICHARD LEONARD
Educator, city alderman. **PERSONAL:** Born Sep 15, 1934, Meridian, MS; son of Joe C. Brooks and Arlena H. Brooks; married Essie Stewart, May 08, 1967; children: Richard Jr, Gloria R. Watt, Randy, Fredrich, Ronald Maurice, Carolyn. **EDUCATION:** Tougaloo Coll, BA 1958; Jackson State Univ, cont study 1960; Lane Coll Jackson, cont study 1978; MS State Univ, cont studies 1981. **CAREER:** Teacher, Noxubee County High School, 1964-; boy leader, Explorer Post 110 Macon MS, 1973-83; Noxubee County Comm of Concern, bd of dir, 1980-83; Child Comm Devel Day Care Ctr, bd of dir, 1980-82; chmn, Admin Bd St Paul United Meth, 1980-83; city alderman, Macon, MS, 1981-. **ORGANIZATIONS:** Mem Gamma Rho Chap of Kappa Alpha Psi 1956-58, Metro Lodge 551 IBPIE 1968, Grant Lodge 123 NW Stringer Grand F&AM 1980; pres, Noxubee Ebony Performing Arts Assn Inc, 1981-; commr, Desota Trail, 1989-. **HONORS/ACHIEVEMENTS:** Letter of Commendation Pushmataha Area Council Boy Scouts of Amer 1977; Youth Leadership MS Youth & Govt Affairs 1977, 1978, 1979; Appreciation Award Noxubee Comm Concern Inc 1979-80; numerous other awards Boy Scouts of Amer. **HOME ADDRESS:** 205 S Washington St, Macon, MS 39341.

BROOKS, RODNEY NORMAN
Social service executive. **PERSONAL:** Born Jun 06, 1954, Asbury Park, NJ; married Gloria Jeanette Walker; children: Sheena Monique. **EDUCATION:** Bowling Green State Univ, BS Secondary Education 1976; Kent State Univ, 1981; Atlanta Univ, 1984. **CAREER:** Massillon Bd of Educ, sub teacher 1977-78; Supreme Life Ins Co, debit mgr 1977-78; Canton Urban League Inc, project dir 1978-83; Massillon Urban League, pres/chief exec officer. **ORGANIZATIONS:** Grand recording sec Buckeye Grand Lodge IF & AMM 1983-; directorship Planned Parenthood of Stark Co 1984-; directorship Westcare Mental Health Ctr 1984-; directorship Social Planning Council/United Way of West Stark 1984-; worshipful master Simpson Lodge #1 IF & AMM 1985. **HONORS/ACHIEVEMENTS:** Whitney M Young Jr Fellow NUL Inc/Atlanta Univ 1984. **BUSINESS ADDRESS:** Pres & CEO, Urban League of Racine & Kenosha Inc, 718 N Memorial Dr, Racine, WI 53404.

BROOKS, ROY LAVON
Legal educator. **PERSONAL:** Born Mar 07, 1950, New Haven, CT; married Penny Feller; children: Whitney. **EDUCATION:** Univ of CT, BA (magna cum laude) 1972; Yale Univ, JD 1975. **CAREER:** United States District Court, law clerk 1975-77; Yale Law Jrnl, editor 1975; Cravath Swaine and Moore, corporate attorney 1977-79; Univ of San Diego, law professor 1979-. **ORGANIZATIONS:** Bd of dirs Heartland Human Relations Assoc 1984-86; bd of dirs NAACP San Diego Chap 1987. **HONORS/ACHIEVEMENTS:** Publs "Foreign Currency Translations" 1980, "Small Business Financing" 1981, "Affirmative Action in Law Teaching" 1982. **BUSINESS ADDRESS:** Professor of Law, University of San Diego, Law School, San Diego, CA 92110.

BROOKS, SIDNEY JOSEPH
Manager. **PERSONAL:** Born Mar 17, 1935, St Genevieve, MO; married Geraldine Lois Cooper; children: Joey, Mike, Alison, Brett. **CAREER:** San Diego Chargers, equip mgr; BSA, asst cub master 1962-64; Am Jr Bowling Cong, hd coach 1966-68. **ORGANIZATIONS:** Mem Holy Name Soc 1965-68; panel mem Pre-Cane Conf 1966-68; hd coach Young Amer League Ftbl 1968-71; SOCSY & Awards Com 1968-71; chief judge CO Annual HS Indoor Easter Races 1969-71; protocol NCAA Ice Hockey Champships; asst track coach Corpus Christi Schl 1969-71; mem Rule Com Jr Parochial Annual Track& Field Meet 1969-71; dir 1st El Paso Co Amateur Athletic Union 1969-71; coord Rocky Mt AAU Track & Field Jr Oly Meet 1969; judge Green Thumb Com 1969; commr Amateur Athletic Union 1969-71; chrmn Natl AAU Jr Oly Chmpshp 1969-70; parish cncl mem AF Acad Parish 1970; dir Danang Field Day for Vietnamese Boys & Girls 1972. **HONORS/ACHIEVEMENTS:** Ourstdng active duty Airman of Year 1st AFR Region 1964; outstdng supply supr Alaskan Communications Region 1966; outstdng noncommn ofc of quarter AlaskanCommcn Reg 1967; oursdng sr NCO of Year USAF Acad 1969; outstdng Airman of USAF 1970; outstdng Young Men of Amer 1970; PACAF outstdng Airman of the Year 1972; Serv to mankind award Rocky Mt Sertoma Claub 1972. **MILITARY SERVICE:** USAF sr m/Sgt 1953-73. **BUSINESS ADDRESS:** San Diego Chargers, PO Box 20666, San Diego, CA 92120.

BROOKS, THEODORE ROOSEVELT, JR.
Physician, educator. **PERSONAL:** Born Aug 02, 1930, Jackson, MS; married Yolande Stovall; children: Leslie, Naida, Blair, Angelle. **EDUCATION:** Tougaloo Coll, BS summa cum laude 1951; Howard U, MD 1955; USC, MS Ed 1981, MS Gero 1983. **CAREER:** Private Med Practice, 1956-; Charles Drew Med Sch, assoc prof gerontology 1978-. **ORGANIZATIONS:** Pres Amalgamated Devel Assn 1980-87; pres TRB Corp 1984-87; AMA; NMA; Kappi Pi; Sigma Pi Phi; NAACP; Alpha Phi Alpha; diplomate Amer Bd of Fam Practice; Alpha Omega Alpha; Fellow Amer Acad of Fam Physicians; Amer Coll Of Medicine; Amer Coll of Gen Practice; Soc of Teachers of Fam Med; bd of dir PSA Martin Luther King Hosp LA CA; bd of dir Ambassador East Develpmnt Inc; bd of dir Allied Diversified Inc; bd of dir Omaha Inc; bd of dir Allied Inc; bd of dir Hypertensive Council of Los Angeles; physician's asst supervisor bd of medical quality assurance; physician's asst examining committee. **HONORS/ACHIEVEMENTS:** Listed in the following, International Who's Who of Intellectuals, Marquis Who's Who in the West, Community Leaders and Noteworthy Americans, Men of Achievement, Who's-Distinguished Citizens of North America. **MILITARY SERVICE:** USAF capt 1956-58. **BUSINESS ADDRESS:** Associate Professor, Drew Medical School, 3701 Stocker St 104, Los Angeles, CA 90008.

BROOKS, THOMAS E.
Police officer. **PERSONAL:** Born Jun 14, 1907, Monticello, AR; children: Thomas Jr, John. **EDUCATION:** Philander Smith Coll. **CAREER:** St Louis, playground supr 1929-34; Acad, student patrolman 1935; 8th Dist, student Patrolman 1935, prob patrolman 1935; Spec srv Div, patrolman 1936; Crime Prev, corpl 1947, sgt 1950; 10th Dist, sgt 1950; Spec Srv Div, lt 1952; 9th Dist, lt 1959; Bureau Investigation, capt 1960; Bureau Inspection, capt 1962; Chief's Office, capt 1962; 5th Dist, capt 1963; Annual Insp Div, capt 1965; 8th Dist, capt 1965; 5th Dist, capt 1968; 7th Dist, capt 1969;7th Dist, maj 1971; Bur Field Oper, maj 1971; Bureau Inspection, maj 1973. **HONORS/ACHIEVEMENTS:** Commendation Letter 1963; Commendation Letter Citation for Hnrbl Mention 1952; Letter of Commendation 1963; Sportmen Ath Assc; Mound City Youth Assc; Maj Tom Brooks Baseball League 1973; Culinary Soc Distg Pub Srv Award; Regal Sports Ach Award; Omega Man of Year Award; St Louis Argus Newspaper Outstndg Citizen Award; Aunt & Uncle Gold Shoe Award; St Louis Bd Educ Comm Srv Award; HCV Award.

BROOKS, TILFORD UTHRATESE
Educator. **PERSONAL:** Born Jun 13, 1925, E St Louis, IL; married Ethelyn; children: Gerri Lynn Brooks Dickerson, Denise, Tracey, Leslie. **EDUCATION:** Southern IL Univ, BS Mus Educ 1949; Wash Univ in St Louis, MA Mus Educ 1960, EdD Mus Educ 1972. **CAREER:** Washington Univ St Louis, chmn music dept, 1976-84, assoc prof Music, 1973-; E

St Louis IL School Dist, dir music educ, 1971-73, instructor media spec, 1966-71, instrumental music instructor, 1950-66. **ORGANIZATIONS:** Bd dir New Music Cir 1972-75; bd dir Young Audiences Inc 1973-78; southerwestern div rep to steering comm Black Music Caucus 1974-; mem Natl Assc of Negro Musicians; mem MO Music Educ Assc; mem Music Educ Natl Conf. **HONORS/ACHIEVEMENTS:** "Why Study Black Music?" Musart 1975, "The Black Musician & Amer Soc" The Music Jour 1975; "Afro-Amer Music & Its Roots, Silver Burdett Co Morristown NJ 1976; Amer's Black Mus Heritage Prentice-Hall Inc 1984. **MILITARY SERVICE:** USAF flight ofc 1943-45. **BUSINESS ADDRESS:** Assoociate Professor of Music, Washington University, Lindell & Skiuker Blvd, St Louis, MO 63130.

BROOKS, TODD FREDERICK
Physician. **PERSONAL:** Born Sep 01, 1954, New York, NY; son of Delaney Brooks and Effie C Brooks. **EDUCATION:** Drew Univ, BA 1976; Meharry Medical Coll, MD 1980; Univ of TN Health Science, Post Doctorate 1980-84. **CAREER:** Univ of TN, clinical instructor 1984-; Private Practice, ob/gyn 1986-; Memphis Health Ctr, chief ob/gyn 1984-. **ORGANIZATIONS:** Mem Bluff City Medical Soc, Univ of TN Ob/Gyn Soc; fund raiser Boy Scouts of Amer. **HONORS/ACHIEVEMENTS:** Publ "Perinatal Outcome," Journal of Ob/Gyn 1984. **BUSINESS ADDRESS:** 1211 Union Ave Suite 495, Memphis, TN 38104.

BROOKS, W. WEBSTER
Educator. **PERSONAL:** Born May 25, Orangeburg Co, SC; married McPhine Jenkins; children: Carl Edward, Sallie Belita, Lenior Lamar, Wanda Yvonne, Lisa Latanya. **EDUCATION:** SC State Clge, BS 1949, MS 1954; Cornell Univ, attnd 1956; FL State Univ 1968; Univ of SC 1974. **CAREER:** Jackson High School, Camden SC, Industrial Arts teacher, asst prin, coach, 1949-51; West Lee School, supt, 1952-57; West Lee Primary School, prin, 1958-; Rembert Educ dir of head start, 1968-70. **ORGANIZATIONS:** Mem SCEA; mem NEA; mem NEASP; mem SCASA; mem SCAPS Adult Educ; SCEA Standing Com PEA; PEA House of Delegates SCEA Delegates Assemble; Lee Co Educ Assc Chmn; Civic Educ of Six Congr Dist; pres Lee Co Educ Assc 1972-74; mem exec comm Mbrshp Chrmn Lee Co SCASA; discussion ldr NEASP 1973; legislative comm SCASA; immediate past pres LCEA; mem LCEA-SCEA Pace; chmn Civic Educ Com; mem Voter League; chmn Bi-racial Comm mem Jerusalem Bapt Ch; Deacon supt Clerk, Clerk of Lynches River Union; pres Brotherhood; secr Brotherhood Sumpter Assc; mem Kappa Alpha Psi; pres LCC of State Clge Alumni Assc; mem Sandy Bluff Lodge 44 Ashland Consistory 246 Crescent Temple 148; Delegate to NEA Conv; Chamber of Commerce of Bishopville SC. **HONORS/ACHIEVEMENTS:** Listed Who's Who in Amer Educ 1966; plaque highest percentage mbrshp in SC Educ Assc 1974. **MILITARY SERVICE:** USN 1943-45. **BUSINESS ADDRESS:** Rt 1 Box 360, Rembert, SC.

BROOKS, WADELL, SR.
Administrator. **PERSONAL:** Born Jan 20, 1933, Lexington, MS; married Daisy Anderson; children: Yolanda, Wadell Jr, Cassandra. **EDUCATION:** IL State Normal Univ, BS Bus Educ 1957; No IL Univ, attnd 1958. **CAREER:** Pub Works Ctr Naval Base Great Lakes IL, dept of equal employment opportunity ofcr 1979-, dir assignment/referral 1970-79; Naval Training Ctr Great Lakes Naval Base, educ specialist 1968-70; VA Hosp educ therapist 1957-68. **ORGANIZATIONS:** Pres Tots & Toddlers Day Care Ctr Inc 1974-; pres Amer Assn for Rehab Therapy Inc 1970; sec/treas Daisy's Nursery Infant Ctr 1979-; past master Rufus Mitchell Lodge 107 1972; pres NAACP N Chicago Br 1976-; bd dir Lake Co Urban League; life mem NAACP 1979; bd dir Great Lakes Credit Union Naval Base Great Lakes IL 1980-. **HONORS/ACHIEVEMENTS:** Superior Perf Award VA Hosp 1967; Superior Perf Award Rufus Mitchell Lodge 107 1975; Non-Fed Contrib Award Pub Works Ctr Great Lakes IL 1979; SuperiorAchvmt Award WE DO CARE Org Chicago 1980. **MILITARY SERVICE:** AUS spec/4 1954-55. **BUSINESS ADDRESS:** Public Works Center, Bldg 1 A, Great Lakes, IL 60088.

BROOKS, WILLIAM C.
Business executive. **EDUCATION:** Long Island Univ, BA; Univ of OK, MBA; Harvard Business Schools, advanced mgmt prog grad 1985. **CAREER:** Held several Federal Govt positions in office of Mgmt & Budget in the Exec Office ofth Pres , Dept of Defense, Dept of Labor, Dept of Air Force; General Motors Corp, public relations, genveral div of personnel. **ORGANIZATIONS:** General Motors Dey Exec to Fl A & M, mem; Nat'l Inst of Ed Advisory Panel on Employability, mem; 70001 Training & Employment; chairman, bd dir; Nat'lCoalition on Black Voter Particitpation, Inc, bd dir; OH State Univ Nat'l Center for Research and Vocational Ed; mem advisory bd; State of Ohio's Public Employment Advisory & Counseling, mem; Boy Scouts of American, dist chairman. **HONORS/ACHIEVEMENTS:** Articles Published in the Personnel Administrator, the Nat'l Training Lab Jornal on Social Change, and The Black Collegian; Awarded the Nat'l Assoc of Negro Bus and Prof Women's Ombudsman Appreciation Awd, 1979; CETA, bridge builders award 1979; Nat'l BLack MBA Assoc, outstanding MBA of the year award 1980; Awarded the 70001 Ltd Pathfinder Award 1981. **BUSINESS ADDRESS:** Asst Secretary of Labor, 200 Constitution Ave, NW, Washington, DC 20210.

BROOKS, WILLIAM P.
Administrator. **PERSONAL:** Born Nov 19, 1934, Newkirk, OK; son of Mr & Mrs Carl F Brooks Sr; married Sue Jean Johnson; children: Barry P, Leslie J Lykes, Terryl D Abington, William R, Virgil A. **EDUCATION:** Friends Univ Wichita KS, 1952-53; Wichita Univ, 1967. **CAREER:** Winfield State Hosp Training Ctr, laundry worker 1957, vocational teacher 1961, vocational training suprv 1966, unit b 1970, unit dir, admin officer I 1977-87 special asst to supt 1987-. **ORGANIZATIONS:** Youth comm Winfield Kiwanis Club 1972-; pres Winfield Quarterback Club 1974; adv comm Conley Cty Comm Coll & Voc Tech School 1975-; city plnng commiss City of Winfield 1978-; mem Winfield Police Reserve 1984-. **HONORS/ACHIEVEMENTS:** Disting Serv Awd Winfield Jaycees 1967; Outstanding Young Man KS State Jaycees 1967; Illustrious Potentate Emith Temple #30 Wichita 1975. **BUSINESS ADDRESS:** Soecial Assistant to The Superintendent, Winfield State Hosp & Training Ctr, N College, Winfield, KS 67156.

BROOME, PERSHING
Educator. **PERSONAL:** Born Sep 15, 1921, Utica, MS; married Annette E Chandler; children: Richard P, Robert P, Kimberly D, Michael E. **EDUCATION:** TN A&I State Univ, BS Sci Ed 1957; Roosevelt Univ, MA Ed Admin & Suprv 1972, MA Guid & Couns 1977. **CAREER:** Bur HS, chmn sci dept, instr chem & physics 1957-59; Chicago Bd of Ed, instr chem & physics 1959-64; Thornridge HS, instr physics 1964-70, dean 1970-84, counselor 1984-. **ORGANIZATIONS:** Treas Vlg of Phoenix 1967-75,80-; mem bd of ed & sec, pres School Dist 151 1970-; bd ed rep IL Assoc of School Bds 1975-; chmn So Cook Cty DivIL Assoc of School Bds 1984-; mem Faculty Assn Dist 205, IL Educ Assn, Natl Ed Assn, 1964-; elect del NEA Conv 1976-77, IEA Conv 1978; mem Res Off Assn of US, Amer Assn of Physics Teachers, IL Deans Assn, ATO, APTO. **MILITARY SERVICE:** AUS 1942-52; USAR 1952-73; retired AUS 1981; Good Conduct; WWII Victory Medals. **BUSINESS ADDRESS:** Counselor, Thornridge High School, 15000 Cottage Grove, Dolton, IL 60419.

BROOMES, LLOYD RUDY
Psychiatrist. **PERSONAL:** Born Feb 02, 1936; married Lauvenia Alleyne, Jun 02, 1963; children: Lloyda, Melissa. **EDUCATION:** Shell Tech School, 1950-55; Oakwood Coll, BA 1961; Loma Linda Univ, MD 1966. **CAREER:** Camarillo State Hospital, staff psychiatrist 1969-71; Meharry Alcohol Drug Abuse Program, asst prof 1972-75; Meharry Comm Mental Health Center, dir clinical serv; Nashville, private practice 1973-86; Tennessee Dept of MH & MR, A & D Division, asst commissioner 1988-89; Alvin C York VA Medical Center, Psychiatry Services, chief 1987-88; Madison Hospital, Department of Psychiatry, chief 1978-80; Carl Vinsan VA Medical Center, psychiatry services chief, 1989. **ORGANIZATIONS:** Mem, Amer Psych Assn; mem TN Psych Assn; TN Amer Med Assn Nashville Acad Med Hillcrest 7 Day Adventist Church 1972-; mem Govt Advisory Commn Alcohol & Drugs; Nashville Drug Treatment & Rehabilitation Center; Black Adventist Med; exec vice pres, Lupus Found of Amer, Nashville Chapter 1986-89. **HONORS/ACHIEVEMENTS:** Dental Assn Gold Medal Award Shell Tech School 1955; Fellow, Amer Psychiatric Assn, 1985; Amer Bd of Psychiatry & Neurology, Diplomat in Psychiatry, 1981. **MILITARY SERVICE:** Civilian Work Program 1969-71. **BUSINESS ADDRESS:** Chief of Psychiatry Service, Carl Vinson Veterans Admin Medical Center, Dublin, GA 31021.

BROOMFIELD, MARY ELIZABETH
Educator. **PERSONAL:** Born Apr 04, 1935, Helena, AR. **EDUCATION:** IL State Normal Univ, BA El Educ 1956; Roosevelt Univ, MA 1963. **CAREER:** NE IL Univ Residential Schl for Boys & Girls, supt 1973-, prin/Supt 1971-73; Bousfield Soc Adj Sch, asst dir 1969-70; Motley Soc Adj Schl, asst princ 1966-69. **ORGANIZATIONS:** Mem Phi Delta Kappa; mem Samuel B Stratton Prin Assc; Delta Kappa Gamma; Assc of Secondary Schl Prin; Natl Council of Juvenile Justice; mem Council on Comm Svc; League of Black Women.

BROSSETTE, ALVIN, JR.
Educator. **PERSONAL:** Born May 16, 1942, Montgomery, LA; married Delores Gipson; children: Derrie, Alicia, Kathy. **EDUCATION:** Grambling State Univ, BS El Educ 1962; Northwestern State Univ, MEd Admin 1970; Western MI Univ, EdD Educ Ldrshp 1975. **CAREER:** Wilmer-Hutchins Independent School Dist, gen supt, 1980-; Prairie View A&M Univ TX, dept head Coll of Educ Curriculum & Instr, 1976-80; Northwestern State Univ Los Angeles, asst prof Dept CI Coll of Educ, 1975-76; Kalamazoo Publlic Schools MI, program coord/(R&D), 1974-75; Grant Parish Public Schools, Colfax LA, asst prin/teacher, 1967-73; Winn Parish Public Schools, Winnfield LA, teacher, 1962-67. **ORGANIZATIONS:** Mem Natl Assc for Curriculum Dev 1976-; mem/Tchr ctn adv bd Prairie View A&M Univ TX 1979-; consult N Forest ISD Houston 1979-; mem Phi Beta Sigma 1968-; mem Phi Delta Kappa 1975-; mem Amer Assc of Sch Admin 1980-; pres Grant Parish Educ Assc 1972-73. **HONORS/ACHIEVEMENTS:** Flwshp-Grant Western MI Univ 1973-75. **BUSINESS ADDRESS:** 3820 E & Illinois Ave, Dallas, TX 75216.

BROTHERS, EDITH
Government official. **PERSONAL:** Born May 24, 1936, Brooklyn, NY; married Herbert Brothers; children: Kirk B, Derick J, Paulette S. **EDUCATION:** New York City Comm Coll, attnd 1973-76. **CAREER:** PE State Com Woman/Dist Ldr 40th Assembly Dist; Comm School Bd Dist 23, vice pres, 1977-; NY State Assemblyman Edward Griffith, govt liason 1974-77; Brownsville Neighborhood Activity Center, exec sec, 1971-77; Amer Home Prod, exec sec, 1968-71; Uhuru Dress Shop, owner/buyer, 1964-67. **ORGANIZATIONS:** Bd mem Medgar Evers Clge Coun 1978-80; bd mem Tilden Comm Ctr Pres Women's Aux of John F Kennedy Reg Dem Club; vice pres E Brooklyn Civic Alliance; fnd of Ldrs of concerned parents during Tilden-Carnasie struggle Comm Srv 1977. **HONORS/ACHIEVEMENTS:** Award for Srv Parents Children & Staff Comm Sch Dist 23 1980; Ldrshp & Srv Women on the Move 1980; Ldrshp E NY Youth Adv Counc 1980. **BUSINESS ADDRESS:** 40th Assembly Dist, Brooklyn, NY.

BROUGHTON, CHRISTOPHER LEON
Actor, magician. **PERSONAL:** Born Mar 04, 1964, Detroit, MI; son of Ronald Leon Broughton and Theodora Faye McCord-Broughton. **EDUCATION:** Mercy Coll of Detroit, attended, 1984. **CAREER:** Magician, Los Angeles CA, 1976-present; comedian. **ORGANIZATIONS:** Intl Brotherhood of Magicians, 1984-present; Mystics, 1976-89; SAG, 1984-89; AFTRA, 1984-89; ICAP, 1988-present. **HONORS/ACHIEVEMENTS:** Intl Brotherhood of Magicians Award (the world's greatest magician), was the first black to win this award, 1989; created a magical illusion to be marketed, 1989. **HOME ADDRESS:** 10458 Westover, Detroit, MI 48204.

BROUSSARD, ALLEN E.
Supreme court justice. **PERSONAL:** Born Apr 13, 1929, Lake Charles, LA; married Odessa; children: Eric, Craig, Keith. **EDUCATION:** Univ CA Berkeley, AB Plit Sci 1950, JD 1953. **CAREER:** San Francisco, Oakland CA, prvt practice 1954-56, 1956-59; Dist Ct Appeals 1st Appellate Dist 1st Div, rsch atty for presiding justice 1953-54; Wilson Metoyer & Sweeney, assoc 1959-61; Metoyer Sweeney & Broussard, mem firm 1961-64; Oakland-Piedmont Dist Mcpl Ct, judge 1964-65; Alameda County Superior Ct Oakland, judge 1975-81; CA Supreme Court San Francisco, justice 1981-. **ORGANIZATIONS:** Mem faculty CA Coll Trial Judges 1969-72,74, Golden Gate Coll San Francisco 1971, Univ San Francisco 1972; adv to exec comm Jud Council CA; vice pres governing com Ctr Jud Educ & Rsch; mem council judges Natl Council Crime & Delinquency; vice pres East Bay Big Bros Amer; bd dirs Alameda County Community Found; bd dirs, past chmn Oakland Men of Tomorrow, Black Bus & Professional Men's Service Orgn; exec bd 1970-71, pres 1972-73 Conf CA Judges; exec bd jud council Natl Bar Assn; vice pres Alameda County Bar Assn; past dir Alameda County Criminal Cts Bar Assn, Boalt Hall Alumni Assn; mem State Bar of CA, Phi Alpha Delta. **BUSINESS ADDRESS:** Court Justice, California Supreme Court, 4050 State Bldg, 350 McAllister St, San Francisco, CA 94102.

BROUSSARD, ARNOLD ANTHONY
Administrator. **PERSONAL:** Born Sep 26, 1947, New Orleans, LA; married Venita Lorraine Thomas; children: Danielle Lorraine, Darryl Anthony. **EDUCATION:** Tulane Univ, BA Soc 1965-69; Wharton Sch Univ of PA, MBA acct oper research 1969-71. **CAREER:** City of New Orleans, exec asst to Mayor's Ofc 1978-; J Ray McDermott & Co Inc, fin planning analyst 1975-78; Arthur Andersen & Co, sr consult 1971-75. **ORGANIZATIONS:** Co-coord Jr Achvmnt 1975-77; bd dir New Orleans Area Bayou River Health Sys Agcy 1975-78; mem Natl Assc of Black Acct 1976-. **BUSINESS ADDRESS:** 1300 Perdido St, New Orleans, LA 70112.

BROUSSARD, LEROY
Associate director. **PERSONAL:** Born Jan 28, 1948, Abbeville, LA; married Patricia. **EDUCATION:** BA 1970. **CAREER:** UUniv of WI, advisor, counselor experimental program higher educ, 1970-71; Dept Intl Scholars, assoc dir, 1971-; US Agency Intl Devel, counselor; Amer Assn Collegiate Reg & Admissions Officers, rsch team, 1973; YMCA, bd mem, 1974-. **ORGANIZATIONS:** Mem Acad Staff Assn Univ WI 1973-; mem Black Professional Assn 1973-; mem Alpa Phi Alpha 1977. **HONORS/ACHIEVEMENTS:** Recpt Univ of WI Milwaukee Div of Stdnt Serv Disting Awd. **BUSINESS ADDRESS:** Dept of Internal Scholars, U WI Milwaukee, Milwaukee, WI 53201.

BROUSSARD, VERNON
Educator. **PERSONAL:** Born Jan 30, 1934, Shreveport, LA; son of Leon Broussard and Verdie Brannon Broussard; married Ida Mae Macias, Aug 08, 1982; children: Peggy Anne, Tona Collette, Vernon Jr. **EDUCATION:** Southern Univ Baton Rouge, BS 1955; CA State Univ San Jose 1966; MI State Univ, PhD 1971. **CAREER:** School of Educ Univ of Southern CA, assoc dean program devel & operations 1978; Schooll of Educ Univ of Southern CA, assoc prof 1977-78; CA State Dept of Educ, chief bureau & of program devel 1971-77; Unified School Dist, asst supt 1968-71; Stockton Unified School Dist, math supvr 1966-68; Stockton Unified School Dist, classroom teacher 1958-66; Chicago Pub School, Lansing MI, and California Test Bureaus; planning consultant 1966-71; World Congress of Comparative Educ Soc London England/Mexico City, Vancouver BC, presenter/chmn 1977. **ORGANIZATIONS:** Life mem NAACP 1978-; guest seminar lecturer Nat Inst of Ed 1978; Alpha Kappa Mu, Southern Univ Baton Rouge 1955; Presidential Appointment (President Reagan), mem, The Natl Advisory Council on Vocational and Technical Educ 1982-85. **HONORS/ACHIEVEMENTS:** Published various articles 1963-; Natl Sci Found Fellow; NSF Math Washington DC 1965-66; Pres List MI State Univ 1977; State of Kuwait Invitation, Lecture/Tour of the Educational System, 1987. **MILITARY SERVICE:** AUS major 1955-63. **BUSINESS ADDRESS:** University Pk, Los Angeles, CA 90007.

BROWDER, ANNE ELNA
Business executive. **PERSONAL:** Born Mar 18, 1935, Vernon, AL; daughter of Eddie and Mary E.; divorced. **EDUCATION:** LaSalle Ext; Roosevelt U.niv. **CAREER:** NBC News, Chicago, Production Talent Mgmt, 1960-73; TV News Inc, Office Mgr, 1973-75; The Tobacco Inst, Asst to Pres, Natl Spokesperson, Tobacco Industry, 1976-86; A&W Intl Ltd, pres 1986-; The Exec Television Workshop, assoc, 1988-. **ORGANIZATIONS:** NAACP.

BROWN, A. DAVID
Personnel and labor relations executive. **PERSONAL:** Born Aug 04, 1942, Morristown, NJ; son of Arthur D Brown, Sr and Muriel Kyse Brown; married Joan Currie, Jun 22, 1980. **EDUCATION:** Monmouth Coll, West Long Branch NJ, BS, 1965. **CAREER:** Bamberger's New Jersey, Newark NJ, personnel exec, 1968-71, admin, personnel, 1974, vice pres, 1975; R H Macy & Co Inc, New York NY, vice pres, personnel, 1981, sr vice pres, personnel & labor relations, 1983, bd of dir, 1987. **ORGANIZATIONS:** Mem, Black Retail Action Group. **MILITARY SERVICE:** US Army Natl Guard, specialist fifth class, 1965-71. **BUSINESS ADDRESS:** Sr Vice Pres, R H Macy and Co Inc, 151 W 34th St, New York, NY 10001.

BROWN, A. SUE
Administrator. **PERSONAL:** Born Jun 28, 1946, Lauderdale, MS. **EDUCATION:** Bloomfield Coll, BS 1968; Rutgers Univ Grad Sch of Social Work, MSW 1969; Univ of PA, cert mgmt by objectives 1979; Harvard Univ Sch of Pub Hlth, Cert 1980. **CAREER:** Urban League-Essex Co Newark, dir health 1969-73; Coll Medicine and Dentistry Newark, health planner 1973-75; Newark Comprehensive Health Service Plan, acting asst dir then dir 1973-75; Martland Hosp Coll Medicine and Dentistry Newark, acting exec dir 1975-77; Coll Univ Hosp, Univ Med and Dentistry NJ, 1977-83; Inst Medicine Natl Acad Scis Office Congressman Richard Gephardt Washington, fellow 1983-. **ORGANIZATIONS:** Mem adv com Commn Pub Gen Hosps 1977; lectr NJ Med Sch Newark 1979-; mem acute care com Regional Health Planning Council 1980-82; mem NJ Comprehensive Health Planning Council; mem adv com Region II Health Services Mental Health Admin Comprehensive Health Planning; mem Amer Pub Health Assn; founding mem Natl Assn Pub Gen Hosps; mem Assn for Children of NJ; mem NAACP; mem Natl Council Negro Women; mem 100 Women for Integrity in Govt Baptist. **HONORS/ACHIEVEMENTS:** Scholar Scholarship Educ and Def Fund 1964-69; Citizenship Awd Bloomfield Coll 1968; Community Service Awd Natl Council Negro Women 1978; Leadership in Health Services Awd Leaguers 1978; named Woman of Achievement Essex County Coll 1979; mem Assn Am Med Colls (del); Amer Coll Hosp Adminstrs (nominee). **BUSINESS ADDRESS:** Long Term Care Administrator, Department of Human Services, Commission of Public Health, 200 Independence Ave, SW, Washington, DC 20201.

BROWN, ABNER BERTRAND
Insurance representative. **PERSONAL:** Born Jan 20, 1942, DeQuincy, LA; married Genevieve Mallet; children: Abner B Jr, Alvin D. **EDUCATION:** Southern Univ, BA 1964; TX Southern Univ, MEd 1972, MA 1974. **CAREER:** TX Southern Univ, instructor 1975-77; Family Serv Ctr, marriage & family counselor 1973-83; State Farm Ins Co, insurance agent 1983-. **ORGANIZATIONS:** Past pres Scenicwood Civic Club 1975-77; pres North Forest ISD 1983-85; mem Amer Assn of Marriage & Family Counselors 1975-. **MILITARY SERVICE:** AUS sp4 2 yrs; Good Conduct Medal; Vietnam ERA. **HOME ADDRESS:** 10500 Caxton, Houston, TX 77016.

BROWN, ALVIN MONTERO
Physician. **PERSONAL:** Born Jul 09, 1924, Prince George Co, VA; son of F Lee Brown and Lillian Brown. **EDUCATION:** Morgan State Coll, BS 1941-45; Columbia U, MA 1947; NY U, 1953-54; Meharry Med Coll, MD 1960. **CAREER:** Chester Co Hosp, intern 1960-61; Phil Gen Hosp, 1962-63; NY Med Coll, resident 1963-65; NY Med Coll, asst prof 1970-71; Emory U, 1969-70; Sinai Hosp Baltimore, staff psychiatrist 1966-69; VA Hosp, asst chf 1965-66; NY Med Coll, resident physician 1963-65; Mt Carmel Mercy Hosp, physician 1972-85; MeHarry Medical College, Nashville Tennessee, consultant physical medicine and rehabilitation 1987-. **ORGANIZATIONS:** Mem Natl Med Assn; AMA; Amer Congress Physical Med & Rehab; Amer Acad Physical Med & Rehab; Amer Coll Sports Med; pres MI Acad Physical Med & Rehab 1979-80; MI Rheumatism Soc; bd dir MI Kenny Rehab Found 1972-; MI Rheumatism Soc; staff mem Meharry Med Coll 1965-69; Howard Univ 1967-69; Univ MD 1967-69; Emory Univ 1969-70; NY Med Coll 1970-; Wayne State Univ 1973-; consultant Rehab Med VA Hosp 1969-; Metro Soc Crippled Children & Adults 1972-; bd tst Neuromuscular Inst 1973-; mem adv bd Comprehensive Health Ctr 1974-; bd dir Met Home Health Care Serv 1976-; clinical rep Wayne State Univ 1975-; sec/treas MI Acad Physical Med & Rehab 1975-, mem MI State Bd Physical Therapy Reg 1977. **BUSINESS ADDRESS:** Physician, 5121 Woodland Hills Drive, Brentwood, TN 37027.

BROWN, ALYCE DOSS
Educator. **PERSONAL:** Born in Tuscaloosa, AL; daughter of John A Doss (deceased) and Julia Doss; married Lelton C; children: Ouida, Kimberly. **EDUCATION:** Tuskegee Inst, BS 1956; Med Coll of GA, MSN 1975. **CAREER:** Mt Sinai Hosp, charge nurse 1956-57; Colbert County Hosp, charge nurse 1957-73; TVA, industrial nurse 1966-67; Univ of North AL, asst prof 1973-. **ORGANIZATIONS:** Mem Amer Nurses Assn; mem Natl League for Nurses; vice chairperson Human Rights Comm Alabama State Nurses Assn; pres Muscle Shoals Chap Tuskegee Alumni Assn 1985; dir Christian educ North Central Alabama Conf CME Church; dir of youth WK Huntsville Dist of the CME Church; member University of North Alabama Nursing Honor Society. **HONORS/ACHIEVEMENTS:** Phi Kappa Phi Hon Soc Chap 132 UNA 1977-; Lillian Holland Harvey Awd 1986-87; Martin Luther King Jr Human Relations Award, Alpha Phi Alpha Fraternity, 1987; Shoals Area Woman of the Year, Shoals Council of Women's Organizations, 1988-89; 2,00 Notable American Women, American Biographical Institute, 1989-90. **BUSINESS ADDRESS:** Asst Prof of Nursing, Univ of North Alabama, Box 5087, Florence, AL 35630.

BROWN, AMOS CLEOPHILUS
Clergyman. **PERSONAL:** Born Feb 20, 1941, Jackson, MS; son of Rev Charlie Daniel Brown Sr (deceased) and Mrs Loutta Bell Robinson-Brown; married Jane Evangeline Smith; children: Amos Cleophilus Jr, David Josephus, Kizzie Maria. **EDUCATION:** Morehouse Coll, BA 1964; Crozer Seminary, MDiv 1968; VA Seminary & Coll, DD 1984. **CAREER:** NAACP, field sec 1960-62; St Paul Bapt Church Westchester PA, pastor 1965-70; Pilgrim Baptist St Paul MN, pastor 1970-76; Third Baptist San Francisco CA, pastor 1976-. **ORGANIZATIONS:** Pres MS Youth Council NAACP 1956-59, Hi-Y Clubs MS 1958-59; natl chmn NAACP Youth Dept 1960-62; chmn Amer Baptist Black Caucus 1972-80, Natl Baptist Civil Rights Comm 1982-; mem Comm Coll Gov Bd 1982-; founding mem bd Black Amer Resp to African Crisis 1984. **HONORS/ACHIEVEMENTS:** Outstanding Young Man of Amer Jr Chamber of Commerce 1974-76; Martin Luther King Jr Ministerial Awd Colgate-Rochester Div School 1984; Man of the Yr San Francisco Business & Professional Women Inc 1985. **HOME ADDRESS:** 111 Lunado Way, San Francisco, CA 94127. **BUSINESS ADDRESS:** Pastor, Third Baptist Church, 1399 McAllister, San Francisco, CA 94115.

BROWN, ANDREW J.
Clergyman. **PERSONAL:** Born Nov 20, 1922, Duncan, MS; married Rosa Lee Nicholson. **EDUCATION:** Bishop Coll; Moody Bible Inst; Butler U; Natchez, MS, Hon DD; Cntrl Theological Sem, DD; Urban Training Cntr Christ Mission Chgo; Wesylan Theol Sem (ch devel & mgmnt). **CAREER:** St John Missionary Bapt Ch, pastor 33 yrs. **ORGANIZATIONS:** Past pres NAACP; IN Ministerial Alliance; bd mem IN Comm Serv Cncl; Intl Christ Univ Japan; IN Urban League; pres IN Chap SCLC; reg vice pres Nat SCLC. **HONORS/ACHIEVEMENTS:** Disting Man of the Yr. **MILITARY SERVICE:** AUS tch sgt & acting chpln 1942-46. **BUSINESS ADDRESS:** St John's Missionary Church, 1701 Martindale Ave, Indianapolis, IN 46202.

BROWN, ANNIE GIBSON
Tax assessor & collector. **PERSONAL:** Born Aug 12, 1944, Lexington, MS; married Charles. **EDUCATION:** S IL U; MS Valley St Univ 1966. **CAREER:** Holmes Co, tax assessor/collector 1976-; pub official dep 1971-75; bookkeeper 1969-71; sec 1966-69; preschool tchr 1966. **ORGANIZATIONS:** PTSA Order of E Star Daughter of Elks; Assessor-Collectors Assn State & Nat; vice pres MS Hlth Serv Agency. **BUSINESS ADDRESS:** PO Box 449, Lexington, MS 39095.

BROWN, ARNOLD E.
Business management consultant. **PERSONAL:** Born Apr 21, 1932, Englewood, NJ; son of John Scott Brown Jr and Hortense Melle Stubbs; married Lydia Barbara White, Jun 25, 1955; children: Crystal L Brown,Beverly M Brown-Fitzhugh, Dale E Brown-Davis, Arnol d E Brown II. **EDUCATION:** Bowling Green State Univ, BA 1954; Rutgers Univ Sch of Law, JD 1957. **CAREER:** Self-employed atty, Englewood NJ, 1957-86; Brown & Associates Consultants Inc, Englewood NJ, pres mgmt consultant firm 1986-. **ORGANIZATIONS:** Mem Gen Assembly NJ 1965-66; former pres Bergen Co Urban League; NAACP Bergen Co; bd mem Adv Comm Salvation Army Bergen Co; mem and former pres Kappa Theta Lambda Chap Alpha Phi Alpha Frat Inc; pres African American Business Enterprise Council of Northern New Jersey, Inc 1986-; bd mem The Applied Technology Center, Bergen Community Coll 1988-. **BUSINESS ADDRESS:** President, Brown & Assoc Consultants Inc, 106 W Palisade Ave, Suite A, Englewood, NJ 07631.

BROWN, BARBARA ANN
City official & photographer. **PERSONAL:** Born Aug 17, 1949, Lynchburg, VA. **EDUCATION:** Phillips Bus College, AA 1967; Cortez W Peters Bus College, AA 1971. **CAREER:** Bur of Natl Affairs, Inc, Data Entry Operator 1971-; New York Institute of Photography, student 1983-. **ORGANIZATIONS:** Member/recording sect'y Mayfair Mansions Res Coun 1971-; member 6th District Police-Citizens Advisory Council 1979-; correspondeng sect'y Marshall Hghts Comm Development Organ, Inc 1983-; member Citizens Advisory Comm DC Bar 1984-; member Professional Photographers of America, Inc 1985. **HONORS/ACHIEVEMENTS:** Outstanding Community Service ANC7A-Wash DC 1978-81; For Women Only Moorland-Spingarn Rsch 1983-; For Black Women Photographers Howard

Univ Wash DC 1984. **BUSINESS ADDRESS:** Chairperson, Adv Neighborhood Commission, 650 Anacostia Ave NE, Washington, DC 20019.

BROWN, BARBARA J.
Savings and loan association executive. **CAREER:** New Age Federal Savings and Loan Association, St Louis MO, chief executive. **BUSINESS ADDRESS:** Chief Executive Officer, New Age Federal Savings & Loan Assn, 1401 N Kingshighway Blvd, St Louis, MO 63113. *

BROWN, BARRI ANNE
Anthropologist. **PERSONAL:** Born Jan 02, 1961, New York, NY; married Kevin Moore. **EDUCATION:** Johns Hopkins Univ, BA Biology 1982; New School for Social Rsch, MA Medical Anthropology (Hon) 1986. **CAREER:** Dialectical Anthropology (journal), managing editor 1984-; New School for Social Research, dept of anthropology. **ORGANIZATIONS:** Mem Alpha Chi Sigma Professional Chemistry Fraternity 1979-82; mem Amer Anthropological Assoc 1985-. **HONORS/ACHIEVEMENTS:** Publication "The Production of Culture," published in Dialectical Anthropology Vol 10 1986. **BUSINESS ADDRESS:** Anthropologist, New School for Social Rsch, Dept of Anthropology, New York, NY 10003.

BROWN, BEATRICE S.
Educator. **PERSONAL:** Born Jul 14, 1950, Louisville, KY; daughter of Thomas J Brown, Sr and Irene Brown. **EDUCATION:** Columbia Univ, MA, PhD; Univ of Louisville, BM Ed, BLS, 1968-73. **CAREER:** Louisville's Sheltered Workshop for the Handicapped, 1977; The Holy Temple Church, music/choral dir 1978-; AC-BAW Center for the Arts, music dir 1982-84; Holmes Elementary School, dir/teacher of music 1983-84; NY State Council for the Arts, performing arts consultant 1984-; Mt Vernon NY African-American Music Arts Festival, founder/dir 1984-; Univ of Louisville, music choral dir and teacher 1969-75; Musical Arts of Creative Expression, dir and music dir 1972-; United Cerebral Palsy of New York State, 1985-; Brown Educational Institute, 1989. **ORGANIZATIONS:** Consultant NY State Council for the Arts 1984-; founder, pres, Brown Educational Institute. **HONORS/ACHIEVEMENTS:** Letter of Award Univ of Lousville 1970; No 1 Songwriter Award WLOU radio station Louisville 1971; award certificate Univ of Louisville 1974; Hon Appreciation Award African-Amer Music Arts Festival Comm 1984; Hon mem Natl Collegiate Sigma Gamma Rho Sorority; Award, Distinguished Leadership for Extraordinary Teaching Profession by the American Biographical Institute; Brown Seven Laws of Human Life Existence Principles for Positive Thinking & Behavior in Children & Adolescents, 1989; A Children's Collection of Music & Poetry; Music Synopsis; Twenty Great Black Leaders & Their Contributions to the Amer Society. **BUSINESS ADDRESS:** PO Box 203, Bronx, NY 10460.

BROWN, BENJAMIN LEONARD
City government official. **PERSONAL:** Born Sep 19, 1929, Baltimore, MD; divorced; children: Roslyn B Montgomery, Johanne R. **EDUCATION:** Lincoln Univ, PA, BA, 1951; Univ of Maryland Sch of Law, LLD, 1959. **CAREER:** State of MD, atty private pract 1960-71; Baltimore City, deputy states atty 1971-73; Dist Court of MD, judge 1973-74; City of Baltimore, city solicitor 1974-. **ORGANIZATIONS:** Pres Nat Inst Muni Law Ofcrs 1983-84, bd of dir 1975-; gen cnsl Municipal Employees Credit Union of Balto City 1975-; gen cnsl MD Credit Union InsCorp 1975-; bd of dir Ideal S & L Assn 1979-; bd of dir Provident Hosp, Inc 1976-85; vice pres Baltimore City Bar Found, Inc 1982-; mem Baltimore City, MD State Nat & Monumental Bar Assns 1960-. **HONORS/ACHIEVEMENTS:** Outstanding City Atty Nat Inst of Mun Law Ofcrs 1976; Outstanding Citizen Award Frederick Douglass High Sch Alumni 1979; Man of the Yr St Francis Acad1980; Cert of Appreciation Minority Bus Oppor; numerous articles & seminar presentations Committee of the Fed Exec Bd 1979-81. **MILITARY SERVICE:** AUS corporal 1951-53; leadership, combat support 1951-52. **BUSINESS ADDRESS:** City Solicitor, Baltimore City, 100 N Holliday St, City Hall Ste 101, Baltimore, MD 21202.

BROWN, BERNICE BAYNES
Program executive. **PERSONAL:** Born Jun 19, 1935, Pittsburgh, PA; daughter of Howard Baynes and Henrietta Hodges Baynes; married James Brown, May 04, 1963; children: Kiyeseni Anu. **EDUCATION:** Carnegie Mellon U, BFA 1957; Univ of Pittsburgh, MEd 1964. **CAREER:** Pittsburgh Public Sch, art tchr 1957-64; Carlow Coll, lecturer 1964-67; Bay Area Urban League, educ speclst 1967-68; San Fran Coll for Women, asst prof 1968-73; Lone Mountain Coll, dean of students 1973-76; The San Fran Found, program exec 1977-86; Educational Consultant. **ORGANIZATIONS:** Mem Assn of Black Educ Exec; mem Women & Found Corporate Philanthropy; trustee San Fran Bar Assn Found; trustee Sch of the Sacred Heart; bd mem Found for Community Serv Cable TV; quarterly chairperson Commonwealth Club of CA; mem State Adv Comm on Black Affairs. **HONORS/ACHIEVEMENTS:** Visiting Scholar Stanford Univ Stanford CT.

BROWN, BERNICE H.
Podiatrist. **PERSONAL:** Born Aug 23, 1907, Ronceverte, WV; widowed. **EDUCATION:** Bluefield State Coll; OH Coll Podiatric Med. **CAREER:** Private Pract, podiatrist. **ORGANIZATIONS:** Mem 4-H Club Extension Agr Housewife; act prof Negro Bus & Professional Women Assn; treas Altrusa Intl; mem Eta Phi Beta Sor; mem Civic Antioch Bapt Ch;NAACP; Urban League; Fifty-Plus Club. **HONORS/ACHIEVEMENTS:** Appreciation Award Bus & Professional Club 1972. **BUSINESS ADDRESS:** 7916 Cedar Ave, Cleveland, OH 44103.

BROWN, BETTYE JEAN (BETTYE JEAN CRAWLEY)
Organizing specialist. **PERSONAL:** Born Jan 30, 1955, Hazlehurst, GA. **EDUCATION:** FL State Univ, BS 1976,77; GA Southwestern Coll, MEd 1983. **CAREER:** Jeff Davis County Bd of Educ, educator 1977-85; South GA Coll, instructor 1983; GA Assoc of Educators, uni serv dir 1985-. **ORGANIZATIONS:** Founder/coord Student Involvement for Black Unity 1978-85; coord Upward Bound Prog 1981-85; pres Jeff Davis Co Assn of Educators 1982-84; sec NAACP 1984; pres Jeff Davis County Clients Council 1984-88; coord Non-Urban Organizing Project 1986-; vice pres Amer Assn of Univ Women; worthy matron Order of Eastern Star; conf coord Natl Black Staff Network; mem Natl Educ Assn, Natl Council of Social Studies; vice pres Delta Sigma Theta; mem Negro Business & Professional Women; mem Bulloch 2000 Comm; sec State Human Relations Comm; monitor GA Housing Coalition Comm Develop Block Grant Prog; designed & coord progs for Amer Educ Week, World Food Day, Martin Luther King Day, Natl Teacher Day, Black History Month, Y-Club Week, Model Comm, Miss Ebony Pageant; public spkr Jeff Davis Co Reapportionment Comm. **HONORS/ACHIEVEMENTS:** Outstanding Serv in Community Clients Council 1985; Outstanding Teacher Y Clubs Model United Nations Club 1985; Dedicated Service NAACP 1986; Outstanding Service Washington Co Assn of Educators 1986; Friend of Education Award, Washington County Association of Educators, 1989. **HOME ADDRESS:** 969 Georgetown Drive, North Augusta, SC 29841. **BUSINESS ADDRESS:** Executive Director, Georgia Association of Educators, 1399 Walton Way, Augusta, GA 30901.

BROWN, BOBBY
Professional athlete. **PERSONAL:** Born May 24, 1954, Turbeville, VA; married Leontine; children: Bonita. **CAREER:** Baltimore Orioles, outfielder 1972-76; NY Mets, outfielder 1978; Toronto Blue Jays, outfielder 1979; Seattle Mariners, outfielder 1982; San Diego Padres, outfielder 1983. **ORGANIZATIONS:** Summoned to starting lineup for Game 5 of LCS and World Series after McReynolds injured, 1st World Series action; 1979 batted 349 for Columbus & named the Intl League co-MVP.

BROWN, BOBBY
Singer. **PERSONAL:** Born 1966. **CAREER:** Former member of New Edition (music group); solo singer. **HONORS/ACHIEVEMENTS:** Singer on records King of Stage and Don't Be Cruel. **BUSINESS ADDRESS:** Bobby Brown, MCA Records, 70 Universal City Plaza, Universal City, CA 91608. *

BROWN, BOOKER T.
Director of recreation. **PERSONAL:** Born Aug 10, 1950, Macon, MS. **EDUCATION:** Forest Park Comm Coll, undergrad 1969-71; Boise St U, BSEd 1971-73. **CAREER:** Morrison-Knudsen Intl Co Inc, dir of recreation; ID 1st Nat Bank, loan ofcr 4 yrs. **ORGANIZATIONS:** Mem Optimist Club; MCU Sports Softball Team. **HONORS/ACHIEVEMENTS:** Dean List Award Boise St Univ 1973; article publ in Today's Psychology 1973; Outstanding Athlete of Amer Award 1973; Most Valuable Player Basketball 1970-71 & 1971-72. **BUSINESS ADDRESS:** Personnel Manager, Morrison-Knudson Corporation, PO Box 73, Boise, ID 83702.

BROWN, BUCK
Cartoonist. **PERSONAL:** Born Feb 03, 1936, Morrison, TN; married Mary Ellen Steverson; children: Robert, Tracy Elizabeth. **EDUCATION:** Wilson Jr Coll Chgo, AA 1962; Univ of IL, BFA 1966. **CAREER:** Chicago Transit Auth, bus driver 1958-63; Playboy Esquire Cavalier Tuesday Rogue Rudder & True, cartoonist 1961-. **ORGANIZATIONS:** Pres/founder Fat Chance Prodns Ltd; mem VP's Task Force on Youth Motivation 1968-70; mem Mag Chicago Jr C of C 1970. **MILITARY SERVICE:** USAF 1955-58. **BUSINESS ADDRESS:** c/o Playboy Magazine, 919 N Michigan Ave, Chicago, IL 60611.

BROWN, BURNELL V.
Business executive. **PERSONAL:** Born May 13, 1925, Richmond, VA; married Navy A; children: Burnell Vincent Jr, Navy Alice. **EDUCATION:** Busy B Supermarkets Inc, pres 1972-; Ebony Supermarkets, vp/dir 1970-71; Royal Farms Supermarkets, supr/dist mgr 1969-70; Food Pageant Supermarkets, supr/dir 1967-69; Waldbaum Supermarkets, clerk/asst mgr 1946-67. **CAREER:** Pres, Cambria Heights Chamber of Commerce, 1974-77, chmn of bd 1978, chmn mem com 1978; pres cambria Hts Alpha Phi Alpha Sr Center 1977-79; bd chmn Cambria Hts Kiwanis Club 1977, pres elect 1978-80. **ORGANIZATIONS:** Comm Serv Award 105th Precinct Comm Cncl 1976; The Annual Sportsman of the Yr Award Cambria Hts Sports Assn 1978. **HONORS/ACHIEVEMENTS:** AUSAF sgt maj 1943-46; AUSAF Sharp Shooter & Good Conduct Medals 1943-46.

BROWN, BYRD R.
Attorney. **PERSONAL:** Born Jul 26, 1929, Pittsburgh, PA; children: Patricia Stephens. **EDUCATION:** Yale U, BA 1951, LLB 1954. **CAREER:** Am Bar Assn, mem; Nat Bar Assn; Allegheny Cnty Bar Assn; Acad of Trial Lawyers of Allegheny Cnty, mem; Allegheny Cnty Bar Assn/U of Pittsburgh/Trial Advocacy, faculty mem; Lawyers Advisory Committee, mem; US Court of Appeals for the 3rd Circuit; Disciplinary Bd of Supreme Court of PA, mem; Law Offices of Byrd R Brown, senior partner/atty at law. **ORGANIZATIONS:** Elected to bd Pittsburgh Branch NAACP Cerca 1957; elected pres Pittsburgh NAACP Cerca 1958; pres Pittsburgh NAACP 13 yrs; founder United Negro Protest Committee; spokesman Black Construction Coalition; bd of dir PA State Conf NAACP; bd of dir Am for Democratic Action; bd of dir Centre Avenue YMCA; bd of dir Visiting Nurses Assn; charter mem Mayor's Commission on Human Resources/Community Action Pittsburgh, Inc; mem of bd Pittsburgh Brnch NAACP/AM for Democratic Action. **MILITARY SERVICE:** AUS sp 2 1954-56. **BUSINESS ADDRESS:** Senior Partner Atty at Law, Law Offices of Byrd R Brown, 515 Court Pl, Pittsburgh, PA 15219.

BROWN, C. B.
Professional athlete. **PERSONAL:** Born Aug 15, 1961, Jackson, MS; children: John Jr. **CAREER:** San Francisco Giants, player 1979-. **HONORS/ACHIEVEMENTS:** Led all NL third basemen with a 971 fielding percentage 1985; named to the Topps and Baseball Digest's All Rookie Squads 1985; mem All Star Team 1986. **BUSINESS ADDRESS:** San Francisco Giants, Candlestick Park, San Francisco, CA 94124.

BROWN, CALVIN ANDERSON, JR.
Educator, physician. **PERSONAL:** Born Sep 13, 1931, Athens, GA; son of C A Brown Sr; married Joy San Walker; children: JoiSanne, SannaGai. **EDUCATION:** Morehouse Coll, BBS 1952; Meharry Med Coll, MD 1958. **CAREER:** Hubbard Hosp Nashville, intern 1958-59; specialized family practice 1959; Atlanta Southside Comprehensive Health Ctr, dir 1968; Pineview Convalescent Ctr Atlanta, med dir 1968-74; Holy Family Hosp, Hughes Spalding Hosp Atlanta, mem staff; Martin Luther King Jr Nursing Ctr, chief of staff 1971-73; Fulton County Jails, chief physician 1971-83; Atlanta City Jail, chief physician 1980-85; Hughes Spalding Hosp Atlanta, dir of emergency room 1984-86. **ORGANIZATIONS:** Pres Natl Alumni Assn Morehouse Coll 1962-72; trustee Morehouse Coll 1969-; vchmn, bd trustees Morehouse Coll 1975-; asst prof preventive med Emory Univ Med School 1968-69; mem Task Force on Cardiovascular Disease Hypertension & Diabetes GA Reg Med Prog 1971; mem Atlanta Med Assoc; mem Alpha Phi Alpha 1975; vice chmn bd of trustees Morehouse Coll 1975-89; pres Kappa Boule of Sigma Pi Phi Frat 1983-84. **HONORS/ACHIEVEMENTS:**

Honorary Doctor of Science, Morehouse Coll 1987. **MILITARY SERVICE:** AUS 1952-54. **BUSINESS ADDRESS:** 1123 Gordon St South West, Atlanta, GA 30310.

BROWN, CARL ANTHONY
Company executive. **PERSONAL:** Born Apr 29, 1930, Philadelphia, PA; son of Percy Brown and Louise Somers West; married Kathleen Smith, Mar 10, 1956; children: William C Brown, Carl A Brown, Jr, Michael Brown. **EDUCATION:** Temple Univ, Philadelphia, PA, AB, Math, 1955, MA, Math, 1957, MA, Physics, 1960, doctoral studies, 1960-66. **CAREER:** Keystone Computer Assoc Inc, Ft Washington, PA, gen mgr div; Onyx Enterprises Inc, Palisades Park, NJ, pres, 1968-69; Kappa Systems Inc, Paoli, PA, program mgr, 1969-71; Amer Technical Assistance Corp, McLean, VA, pres, 1971-74; JRB Assoc Inc, McLean, VA, vice pres, 1974-76; Mandex Inc, Springfield, VA, pres, 1976-. **ORGANIZATIONS:** Bd member, Natl Urban Coalition. **BUSINESS ADDRESS:** Pres, Mandex, Inc, 8003 Forbes Pl, Springfield, VA 22151.

BROWN, CAROL ANN
Educator. **PERSONAL:** Born Jan 25, 1952, Ann Arbor, MI; married Marcellus B Brown; children: Brandon, Marc, Adam. **EDUCATION:** Univ of MI, bachelors 1974, masters 1975. **CAREER:** Ann Arbor Public Schls, instrumental music instr 1974-75; Joliet Public Schls, coordinator of music 1975-82; Augustana College, asst dean of student services 1982-. **ORGANIZATIONS:** Visiting Nurse Homemaker Assoc, bd of directors 1985-; Delta Sigma Theta, Inc Moline Davenport Alumnae, president 1985-, member 1972-; Sounds of Peace Ensemble, member 1984-; Zonta Interntl, member 1983-. **HONORS/ACHIEVEMENTS:** Outstanding Serv Awd Delta Sigma Theta, Inc 1985; Apprecian Awd Black Student Union, Augustana Coll 1983-85, Joliet Band Parents Assoc 1982, Joliet OrchParents Assoc 1982; Honorary Membership Ladies of Vital Essence Club 1984; Outstanding Service Awd Parent Teacher Assoc 1980. **BUSINESS ADDRESS:** Asst Dean of Student Services, Augustana College, Founders Hall 115, Rock Island, IL 61265.

BROWN, CAROLYN M.
Purchasing agent. **PERSONAL:** Born Oct 12, 1948, Seattle, WA; divorced; children: Cesha, Channelle, Clifton. **EDUCATION:** Anderson Coll, BA major Speech Educ, Sociology, minor Educ 1970; Ball State Univ, MA Speech Educ, Commun 1976; Univ of Berkeley, grad work educ; numerous educ & training seminars. **CAREER:** Indianapolis Publ School, teacher 1970-71; Delco Remy, clerk 1971, sec 1971, secy 1971-72, supv 1972-75, buyer 1975-83, sr buyer 1983-86, genl supv central stores 1986-. **ORGANIZATIONS:** Mem IN Reg Minority Purchasing Council 4 yrs; bd mem Natl Minority Supplier Devel Council 3 yrs; bd mem Channel 49; chairperson Telesale 2 yrs;TV personality 2 yrs; mem Women of the Church of God 3 yrs; alumni dir Anderson Coll 2 yrs; mem Ball State Alumni Assoc 5 yrs; capt Telethon Night Drive 3yrs; mem The Christian Center, Alpha Kappa Alpha, Alpha Psi Omega; mayoral appointed educ comm Blue Ribbon; mem Madison County Fine Arts Council, Urban League of Madison County 9 yrs; bd dir United Way 6 yrs, United Cerebral Palsy 4 yrs; mem NAACP 7 yrs; mem Natl Republican Comm, Career Guild Assoc 4 yrs, Amer Business Women of Amer 5 yrs; dir Youth Choir 10 yrs; Sunday School teacher 12 yrs; mem Kodiakanal/Woodstock Found 15 yrs; mrm Smithsonian Assoc 2 yrs; fellow, sponsor Anderson Coll; membership drive person Community Concert Series 3 yrs; mem IN Black Expo Inc 2 yrs; sponsor Theada Club of Anderson Coll 2 yrs; judge Black Ball State Pageant 3 yrs; Jr Miss of Madison County 2 times. **HONORS/ACHIEVEMENTS:** Sequentennial Queen 3rd Place; William B Harper Awd for Outstanding Community Serv to Madison County; Outstanding Young Woman of Amer 3 times; Outstanding Black of Amer 2 times; Outstanding Elementary Teacher of Amer; President's Awd Urban League of Madison County; Outstanding Conference Leader-NAACP Natl Convention in Anderson IN; Outstanding Lady of the Day AME Church Anderson IN; nom for Professional Achievers Awd; IN Reg Minority Supplier Development Council Achievement Awd; Natl Supplier of the Year Buyer Recognition Awd. **BUSINESS ADDRESS:** General Supervisor, Delco Remy div of Gen Motors, 2401 Columbus Ave, Anderson, IN 46012.

BROWN, CARROLL ELIZABETH
Appointed official, business executive. **PERSONAL:** Born Aug 31, 1942, Ft Worth, TX; married Ralph Theodore Brown Sr; children: Ralph Jr, Erik, Shawn. **EDUCATION:** Seattle Univ, 1960-63. **CAREER:** Toma Comm Youth Svcs, founder, dir 1967-77; Capital Temporaries Inc, placement mgr 1980-83; TRW Geometric Tool, personnel asst 1977-80; WADS Radio, radiobroadcaster, talk show hostess 1976-77; Shubert Theater, public community relations liaison 1983-. **ORGANIZATIONS:** 1st black pres West Haven PTA Council 1980-81; mem, bd of dir CT Assoc of Bds of Ed 1981-85; vice chmn West Haven Bd of Ed 1981-85; delegate, rep West Haven Bd of Ed 1982-; mem Amer Red Cross 1982-86; prog chmn, bd of dir Community Consult Ctr 1984-88; mem Delta Sigma Theta, West Haven HS Parents Club, Minority Adv Comm at WTNH TV; rcsc tutor West Haven School Syst; sub teacher West Haven School Syst; founder & dir Meadowbrook Comm Serv Youth Prog; mem West Haven Drug/Alcohol Task Force. **HONORS/ACHIEVEMENTS:** Nominee Jefferson Awd Community Serv 1975; Mrs Connecticut Second Runner-Up 1982; Outstanding Volunteer of the Year Bridgeport Public School System 1983; pres, founder CT Council of Black School Bd Mem 1984; mem State Racial Imbalance Adv Comm 1984-85. **BUSINESS ADDRESS:** Public Community Liaison, Shubert Performing Arts Center, 247 College St, New Haven, CT 06510.

BROWN, CECIL M.
Author. **PERSONAL:** Born Jul 03, 1943, Bolton, NC. **EDUCATION:** Attended A&T State Univ, Greensboro NC; Columbia Univ, BA English 1966; Univ of Chicago, MA 1967. **CAREER:** Univ of Illinois, English teacher; Univ of California at Berkeley, English teacher; Merrit College, English teacher; Merrit College, produced own plays; author. **HONORS/ACHIEVEMENTS:** Author of "The Life and Loves of Mr Jiveass Nigger," 1969; periodical publications, "I Never Raped One Either But I Don't Let It Bother Me" 1972, "A Few Hypes You Should Be Hip To By Now" 1975, "The Apotheosis of the Prodigal Son" 1968, "Bad Writing Or unclewillieandthebadpoet" 1972, "Interview with Tennessee Williams" 1978, "Blues for Blacks in Hollywood" 1981. **BUSINESS ADDRESS:** 1856 Dwight Way, Berkeley, CA 94703.

BROWN, CHARLES HENRY (KIPPY)
Football coach. **PERSONAL:** Born Mar 06, 1955, Sweetwater, TN; married Helene Deon Wilson; children: Robert Jerome; Jennifer Rai. **EDUCATION:** Memphis State Univ, BA 1977. **CAREER:** Memphis State Univ, asst football coach 1977-80; Univ of Louisville, asst football coach 1982-82; Univ of TN, asst football coach 1982-, receiver coach. **HONORS/ACHIEVEMENTS:** All State TSSAA 1971-72; 1st Black Quarterback Memphis State Univ 1973-77; 1st Full Time Black Coach Memphis State Univ 1977-80. **BUSINESS ADDRESS:** Univ of Tennessee Football, 258 Stokely Athletics Ctr, Knoxville, TN 37996.

BROWN, CHARLES SUMNER
Clergyman. **PERSONAL:** Born Sep 18, 1937, Plant City, FL; married Joan Marie Steed; children: Charles Jr, Gene Mitchell. **EDUCATION:** Morehouse Coll, AB 1956; United Theol Seminary, MDiv (Cum Laude) 1962; Boston Univ Sch of Theol, ThD 1973. **CAREER:** Wright-Patterson Air Force Base, mathematician fluid dynamics rsch branch 1956-59; Sheldon St Congregation Church Providence, pastor 1964-66; Ebenezer Bapt Ch Boston, interim pastor 1966-67; United Theol Seminary, prof of church & soc 1968-79; Yale Univ Divinity Sch, assoc prof of practical theol (w/tenure) 1979-83; Bethel Baptist Ch, pastor. **ORGANIZATIONS:** Sec The Soc for the Study of Black Religion 1978-; voluntary assoc prof Dept of Medicine in Soc Wright State Univ Med Sch 1984-; bd mem United Wayof Greater Dayton 1984-, Family Serv Assoc 1984-, Dayton Council on World Affairs 1985-, Dayton Art Institute 1986-; pres Metro Churches United 1986-; moderator Western Union Bapt Dist Assoc 1986-. **HONORS/ACHIEVEMENTS:** Ford Foundation Early Admission Scholarship to Morehouse Coll; Protestant Fellowship Awd Fund for Theol Educ 1961-62; Presbyterian Grad Fellowship United Presby Church USA 1966-67; ATS Basic Rsch Grant for Theol Sch 1975-76; mem Kappa Alpha Psi Frat, Sigma Pi Phi Boule. **HOME ADDRESS:** 625 Ridgedale Rd, Dayton, OH 45406. **BUSINESS ADDRESS:** Pastor, Bethel Baptist Church, 401 South Summit St, Dayton, OH 45407.

BROWN, CHARLIE
State representative. **PERSONAL:** Born Mar 08, 1938, Williston, SC; son of Charlie Brown Jr and Ruth A Hickson Brown; divorced 1972. **EDUCATION:** Cheyney State College, BS; Indiana University-Northwest, MPA, 1982. **CAREER:** Gary IN Public Schools, teacher, 1961-68; Gary Youth Services Bureau, dir until 1983; General Assembly, state representative, 1983-86; City of Gary, Gary IN, affirmative action officer and risk manager. **ORGANIZATIONS:** Mem bd of dir, National Civil Rights Museum and Hall of Fame. **BUSINESS ADDRESS:** Indiana Black Legislative Caucus, State House, Room 4-2, Indianapolis, IN 46202. *

BROWN, CHAUNCEY I., JR.
Housing director. **PERSONAL:** Born Oct 08, 1928, Paterson, NJ; married Betty; children: Cheryl, Porchia, Chauncey III, Clifford W. **EDUCATION:** Electronic Tech Inst, Los Angeles, 1952; Rutgers Univ, 1971; NJ Public Serv Inst, 1972; William Paterson Coll, present. **CAREER:** City of Paterson, dir of community serv, 1968-70, Action Now dir 1970-75, dep dir & CETA 1976-78, dep dir of housing 1978-85. **ORGANIZATIONS:** Co committeeman Dem Orgin of Passaic Co; scout m Troop #23 First AME Zion Ch; founder & pres SECA Orgin; Sgt of arms Rotary of Paterson; numerous others mem, Oldtimer's Assn; bd of dirs Boy's Club; hon mem Bros in Blue Paterson Police Dept; mem, Paterson Catholic School. **HONORS/ACHIEVEMENTS:** Special Award for Community Serv Oldtimer's Assn; Coaches Award, & Oldtimer's Jr Football League; Dedication to Youth Award, CETA Summer Program, 1976-77; honors by numerous religious & community assns. **MILITARY SERVICE:** USN, MMM 3/C, 2 Yrs. **BUSINESS ADDRESS:** Div of Housing, 125 Ellison St, Paterson, NJ 07505.

BROWN, CHRISTOPHER C.
Judge. **PERSONAL:** Born Nov 20, 1938, Pontiac, MI; son of Arthur Patrick Brown and Ardelia Christopher Brown; married Lillian Jean Twitty; children: Alesa Bailey, Tice C. **EDUCATION:** Wayne State Univ, BA 1962; Detroit Coll of Law, JD 1966. **CAREER:** Private practice, attorney 1966-73; 50th Dist Ct City of Pontiac, judge 1973-. **ORGANIZATIONS:** Mem NAACP, Urban League, Amer MI Wolverine Oakland Cty Bar Assns. **BUSINESS ADDRESS:** Judge, 50th Judicial Dist, 70 N Saginaw St, Pontiac, MI 48058.

BROWN, CLARENCE WILLIAM
Personnel administrator. **PERSONAL:** Born Mar 08, 1933, Lakewood, NJ; married Alberta L Hardy; children: Patricia, Valerie F. **EDUCATION:** New Mexico Western Coll, Cert Admin, 1951; Rutgers Univ, Cert Bd of Educ, 1969; Univ of Arizona, Tucson, Cert Early Child Educ, 1970. **CAREER:** Naval Air Engineering Ctr, dep equal employment oppor. **ORGANIZATIONS:** Chmn Citizens Adv Bd Lakewood Housing Auth 1960-66; chmn Better Community Assn of Lakewood 1960-64; pres Ocean Co Chap of NAACP 1961-66; cent Jersey Youth Adv NJ State NAACP 1963-65; chmn Lakewood Econ Action Pgm 1966-76; bd of dir Ocean Co Econ Action Now Inc 1967-72; vice pres Lakewood Bd of Educ 1969-76; mem EOF Bd Georgian Ct Coll 1974-76; adv bd Ocean Co Coll 1976-; v chmn & mem Lakewood Comm Sch Bd; mem Naval Civilian Admin Assn. **HONORS/ACHIEVEMENTS:** Man of the Yr Negro Bus & Professional Womens Assn 1971; Man of the Yr Lakewood C of C 1973; Meritorious Serv Award Lakewood Bd of Educ 1976; Outstand Serv &Contrib Lakewood Econ Action Pgm Inc 1976; 1st Black Elected to Bd of Educ in Ocean Co Lakewood, NJ. **MILITARY SERVICE:** USAF A/2c 1951-55. **BUSINESS ADDRESS:** Bldg 26, EEO Office, Lakehurst, NJ 08733.

BROWN, CLARICE ERNESTINE
Accountant. **PERSONAL:** Born Jun 08, 1929, Toledo, OH; daughter of Robert Durham (deceased) and Margaret Durham (deceased); married Bud Luther Brown; children: Gregory, Babette Jackson, Jocelyn. **EDUCATION:** Roosevelt Univ, BS Business Admin 1965; DePaul Univ, attended; Cortez Business Coll, attended. **CAREER:** US Treasury IRS, internal revenue agent 1960-84; Iota Phi Lambda Sorority Inc, past natl pres. **ORGANIZATIONS:** Leader, 1st vice pres of bd 1977-73, pres 1977-81; Girl Scouts 1964-81; pres 1973-71, parliamentarian 1985, Alpha Beta Chap Iota Phi Lambda; natl pres Iota Phi Lambda 1981-83; natl finance sec Top Ladies of Distinction 1985-88; mem NAACP, Oper PUSH 1985; court 142 jr daughter counselor, counselor for Catholic girls 7-18 Knights of St Peter Claver Ladies Aux 1985. **HONORS/ACHIEVEMENTS:** Fed Employee of the Year 1967; Outstanding Women St Columbanus 1972; St Anne's Medal 1973; Mother of the Year 1974; Volunteer of the Year; nominee for Aldermans Awd 1982; Cardinals Awd Parish Awd 1983; honoree Alpha Gamma Pi; citations from WAIT & WBEE; Albert Gallatin Awd Treasury Dept US Govt. **HOME ADDRESS:** 9134 S Lowe Ave, Chicago, IL 60620.

BROWN, CLARK S.
Business executive. **PERSONAL:** Born in Roanoke, VA; married Macie E; children: Clark

Jr, John T. **EDUCATION:** City Coll NY, attending; Renouard Coll of Embalming NY, 1930. **CAREER:** Real estate broker; Clark S Brown & Sons Funeral Home, pres. **ORGANIZATIONS:** Mem Most Worshipful Grand Lodge Prince Hall Masons, ABC Bd of NC; former mem, bd trustees NC Central Univ; bd mem Central Orphanage of NC, Salvation Army, Retail Merchants Assoc; former vchmn Dem Party of Forsyth Cty NC; former chmn Civil Preparedness Adv Council; bd trustees Shaw Univ Raleigh. **BUSINESS ADDRESS:** President, Clark S Brown & Sons Funeral, 727 N Patterson Ave, Winston-Salem, NC 27101.

BROWN, CLAUDELL, JR.
Association executive. **PERSONAL:** Born Jun 08, 1949, Jackson, TN; married Linda Ruth Brogden. **EDUCATION:** Lane Coll, BA. **CAREER:** Happy Children Multi-Svc, Center, Happy Children Day-Care, Inc, dir; Tipton Co Sch Sys, tchr 5th Grade 1974; Lane Coll, french tutor; WH Jones, prof;Bur of Comm & Relations, teen counselor 1969-71; Lane Coll, tutor, English, French Black Literature. **ORGANIZATIONS:** Upward Bound Proj, 1969-70; vp, Shelby Co Dem Voters Council; Precinct 40-2, 1974; bd dirs, Mid-South Med Cntrs Council, 1973; bd dirs, Memphis-Shelby Co Legal Serv Assn, 1973; comm adv com, Memphis-Shelby Co Legal Serv Assn 1973; Chelsea Comm coord com, 1972; Memphis Comm Singers, Inc; Nat Social Workers of Am, 1972; soc serv coord, dep dir Memphis-Shelby Co Comm Action Agency; Chelsea Nghbrhd Serv Cntr, 1972; Prog Rep, US Dept of Health, St Louis, 1971; Memphis Chpt, Lane Coll Alumni Assn, 1971; Basileus, Theta Iota Chap of Omega Psi Phi, Frat Inc, 1973-74; aptd to Pres & Adv Com to Slective Serv Bd of Tn, Operation PUSH, 1972; mem NAACP; Concert Choir; Pre-Alumni Club; Student Christian Assn; French Club; Social Sci Club; Student Tribune. **BUSINESS ADDRESS:** 709 Keel Ave, Memphis, TN.

BROWN, CLIFFORD ANTHONY
Business executive, accountant. **PERSONAL:** Born Sep 09, 1951, Danville, KY; married Mary Margaret; children: Marilyn F, Clifford A Jr, Jason T. **EDUCATION:** Northwood Inst, Assoc in Bus Mgmt 1971; Eastern MI Univ, BBA Accounting 1973; College of Business honors student 1972, 1973. **CAREER:** Arthur Young & Co, audit staff/sr 1973-78, audit mgr 1979-82; Widger Chem Corp, vice-pres finance 1982-83, exec vice-pres 1983-84; Arthur Young & Co, principal 1987-; CAB Industries, Inc, pres 1984-86. **ORGANIZATIONS:** Pres Detroit Chap Natl Assn of Black Accountants 1979-81; dir tech affairs Natl Assn Black Accountants 1982; dir long range planning Natl Assn Black Accountants 1984; cert pub accountant State of MI 1975-; membership comm MI Assn of Certified Pub Accountants 1975-; mem Amer Inst of Certified PublicAccountants 1975-; chmn finance Downtown Detroit YMCA 1981-; natl dir Natl Assn of Black Accountants 1982-; mem Macomb Comm Coll Accounting Curriculum Advisory Comm 1983-; natl dir Natl Assoc of Black Accts responsible for professional chap admin. **HONORS/ACHIEVEMENTS:** Outstanding member Natl Assn of Black Accountants 1982; achievement awd Natl Assn of Black Accountants 1983; minority achievers awd Detroit Metropolitan YMCA 1984. **BUSINESS ADDRESS:** President, Cab Industries Inc, One Kennedy Square, Ste 1230, Detroit, MI 48226.

BROWN, CONELLA COULTER
Educator. **PERSONAL:** Born Sep 26, 1925, Kansas City, MO; daughter of Charles P Coulter and Carrie Davis Coulter; married Arnold A Brown, Mar 25, 1956. **EDUCATION:** Ks City Cnsrvtry of Mus, 1949; Univ of MO Ks City, BA 1953; Case Wstrn Rsrv U, MA 1961; Lincoln U; OH U; Case-wstrn Rsrv U; Clvlnd St U; Bwlng Grn St U. **CAREER:** Cleveland Pub Sch, Cleveland OH, social studies teacher 1954-63, asst principal, Rawlings Jr HS, 1964-65, asst supervisor, office of human relations, 1965-66, admin asst to supt ofc of hum rel 1966-79, asst supt 1972-80; Ford Fnd Proj, coor in area of curr devel 1963-64; retired 1980. **ORGANIZATIONS:** Mem adv com Sch of Dent; mem vis com stud afrs Cs Wstrn Rsrv U; Delta Kappa Gamma; Am Assn of Sch Admin; Nat Assn for Supv & Curr Devel;bd dir Chrstn Chldrn Fund; bd tst Free Med Clin of Gtr Clvlnd; NAACP; Delta Sigma Theta; Urban Leag of Gtr Clvlnd; mem, trust St James AME Church; hon mem, Phi Delta Kappa. **HONORS/ACHIEVEMENTS:** Professional Awd for Leadership in Educ Cleveland Bus & Professional Women 1973; Outstanding Achievement Awd in Educ Cuyahoga Comm Coll 1973; Hon Life Mem Cleveland Council of Parent Teacher Assn 1974; 1st Woman Asst Supt of major OH SchoolDist; 1st Pres Awd Urban League of Greater Cleveland; Distinguished Educator Award, St James AME Church; "Conella Coulter Brown Day," City of Cleveland, and tribute from US Rep Louis Stokes, March 5, 1989.

BROWN, CONSTANCE YOUNG
Educator. **PERSONAL:** Born Aug 04, 1933, Leonardtown, MD. **EDUCATION:** Morgan State Coll, BS (cum laude) 1955; Univ of MD, MEd 1960, Masters plus 60 1973. **CAREER:** Western Placement Serv Bd of Educ, Baltimore County, mgr, 1974-; Bd of Educ Baltimore County, data processing instructor, 1971-74, distributive educ teacher & coord, 1969-71, business educ teacher, 1955-69. **ORGANIZATIONS:** Mem TABCO; mem MSTA; mem NEA; mem MVA; former sec/treas MADECA; pres Anne Arundel Co Br NAACP 1973-76, treas 1977-; 1st vice pres MD St Conf NAACP 1974-; basileus Delta Pi Omega Chap Alpha Kappa Alpha Sor 1977-80; Corresponding sec Southgate Comm Assn 1973-; anti-basileus Delta Pi Omega Chap Alpha Kappa Alpha Sor 1974-76; life mem NAACP; mem Nat Nom Com NAACP 1980. **HONORS/ACHIEVEMENTS:** DAR Award Citizenship 1950; Trustee & Senatoral Schlrshp Morgan State Coll; Plaque Who's Who in Human Resources; Dr Carl Murphy Award MD State Conf of BrNAACP 1974; NAACP Award Anne Arundel Co Br 1977; Hon 1st Women's Conf NY Naacp 1980; certs Gov of MD Mayor of Annapolis/Anne Arundel Co Exec.

BROWN, COSTELLO L.
Educator. **PERSONAL:** Born Oct 16, 1942, Mebane, NC; married Florida; children: Eric, Ninita. **EDUCATION:** Hampton Inst, BS 1963; IA State U, MS 1966, PhD 1968; Univ of IL, Postdoctoral 1969. **CAREER:** CA State Univ, asst prof, 1969-72, assoc prof, 1972-77, prof of Chemistry, 1977-; Univ of GA, visiting prof, 1972-; CA Inst of Technology, visiting fac assoc, 1975. **ORGANIZATIONS:** Mem S CA Section Am Chem Soc; exec com Sigma Xi Hon Soc; Am Chem Soc. **HONORS/ACHIEVEMENTS:** Woodrow Wilson Fellow 1963; Nat Inst Hlth Postdoctoral Fellowship 1969; NIH Marc Fellowship & Career Devel Award 1975. **BUSINESS ADDRESS:** Chem Dept CA State, Los Angeles, CA.

BROWN, COURTNEY COLERIDGE
Director. **PERSONAL:** Born Jul 29, 1924, New York, NY; children: Beverly, Courtney Jr. **EDUCATION:** Shaw U, BA 1954. **CAREER:** NY State Div of Human Rights, dir, reg dir, 1968-76; Urban League, asst exec dir, 1965-66, coord, 1966-68; Sarco Co, dept mgr, 1944-65; Graduate School of Social Work, asst prof; NY Univ, instructor; NY State Dept of Educ, counselor; Oral History USA, dir. **ORGANIZATIONS:** Clerk St Phillips Prot Epis Ch; vice pres St Phillips Housing Corp; mem Interparish Cncl; bd of dir Grace Episc Sch; mem Child Study Well Met Inc; Children's Prepartory Entr Prog; past pres Dunbar Tenants League; past owner The Negro World; past owner Harlem Daily; past editor Brown Mag. **BUSINESS ADDRESS:** 2 World Trade Ctr, New York, NY 10047.

BROWN, CRAIG VINCENT
Educational administrator. **PERSONAL:** Born Jul 22, 1943, St Louis, MO; son of Portia Brown and Laura Daniels Brown. **EDUCATION:** MacMurray Coll, Jacksonville IL, BA 1963; Illinois State Univ, Normal IL, MA 1969; Harris-Stowe State Coll, attended; St Louis Univ, attended. **CAREER:** St Louis Public Schools, teacher special educ 1968-72; City of St Louis, psychologist 1972-75; Univ of Missouri, Fontbonne Coll, Harris-Stowe State Coll, Forest Park Community Coll, Greenville Coll, adjunct faculty, special educ & psychologist 1971-87; Inst of Black Studies, research project coord 1978-80; Washington Univ, research assoc, project coord; Bellefontaine Rehabilitation Center, psychologist 1987-; St Louis Job Corps Center, mental health consultant 1988-. **ORGANIZATIONS:** Bd dir West End Community Conf 1968-80; mem Assn of Black Psychologists 1972-87; mem Assn for The Educ of Young Children 1974-87; mem, vice chmn Advisory Comm on Special Needs Adoptions, Missouri Div of Family Serv St Louis 1975-80; governor-at-large (intl exec comm) Council for Exceptional Children 1980-83; life mem, past natl pres Black Caucus of Special Educators; mem Black Child Devel Inst 1980-87; sec Eastern Region Advisory Comm, Comprehensive Psychiatric Serv Dept of Mental Health State of Missouri 1986-89. **HONORS/ACHIEVEMENTS:** Co-author, Johnson Brown Harris & Lewis "Manual of Black Parenting Educ St Louis Inst of Black Studies 1980. **BUSINESS ADDRESS:** Psychologist, Bellefontaine Habilitation Ctr, 10695 Bellefontaine Rd, St Louis, MO 63137.

BROWN, CURTIS CARNEGIE, JR.
Marketing manager. **PERSONAL:** Born Sep 14, 1951, Seattle, WA; married Patricia Ann Beale. **EDUCATION:** San Diego State Univ, BA 1970-73; Natl Univ Sch of Business, MBA 1976-77. **CAREER:** United Karate Fed San Diego, owner/mgr 1975-78; CT Gen Ins Corp San Diego, agent 1978; Merrill Lynch Pierce Fenner and Smith Inc, San Francisco sr acctexec 1978-84, Washington sales mgr 1984-. **ORGANIZATIONS:** Mem Optimist Club San Diego 1977/1978; vice pres Bay Area Urban Baker's Assoc 1981; pres Men's Christian Assoc St Pauls Church 1982; pres San Fran Chap Natl Black MBA Assoc 1982-83; bd mem Oakland Business Develop Corp 1983, 1984; bd mem Natl Black MBA Assoc 1984, 1985. **HONORS/ACHIEVEMENTS:** First Degree Black Belt 1974; Exec Club Merrill Lynch et al 1980 1981 1982; Pres Club Merrill Lynch et al 1983; Black Achievers in Industry Harlem YMCA 1983;Outstanding Young Men of Amer Jaycees 1984. **HOME ADDRESS:** 15104 Centergate Dr, Silver Spring, MD 20904.

BROWN, CYRIL H.
Dentist. **PERSONAL:** Born Oct 10, 1931; married Marva J Lee; children: Michael, Brian, Stephen. **EDUCATION:** Howard U, BS 1959, BDS 1963; Johns Hopkins U, MPH 1973. **CAREER:** DC Gen Hosp Dept of Human Resources, chief dental serv 1971-; Dept of Pedodontics Howard U, asst prof 1964-67; Freedmen's Hosp, oral surgery internship 1963-64. **ORGANIZATIONS:** Mem DC Dental Soc; Robert T Freeman Dental Soc; Am Soc of Dentistry for Cldrn; Am Dental Assn; Nat Dental Assn Found; past pres Trinidad & Tobago Assn of Wash, DC; vice pres DC & MD Soccer State Assn; past vice pres Caribbean-Am Intercultural Organ; mem Urban League; NAACP; mem/past pres Beta Kappa Chi. **HONORS/ACHIEVEMENTS:** Deans List HowardUniv Coll of Liberal Arts; Chem Hon Roll Howard U. **BUSINESS ADDRESS:** Chairman Dept of Dentistry, DC General Hospital, 19th & Mass Ave SE, Washington, DC 20003.

BROWN, D. JOAN
Insurance company executive. **CAREER:** Chief executive of Rhodes Life Insurance Company of Louisiana and National Service Industrial Life Insurance, both New Orleans, LA, and Rhodes Mutual Life Insurance Company of Alabama, Mobile, AL. **BUSINESS ADDRESS:** Chief Executive, Rhodes Mutual Life Insurance Company of Alabama, 402 Dr Martin Luther King Jr Ave, Mobile, AL 36603. *

BROWN, DALLAS C., JR.
Educational administrator. **PERSONAL:** Born Aug 21, 1932, New Orleans, LA; son of Dallas C Brown and Sydney Taylor Brown; married Elizabeth T; children: Dallas C III, Leonard G, Jan B, Karen L, Barbara A. **EDUCATION:** WV State Coll, BA History/Pol Sci 1954; IN U, MA Gov't 1967; US Army Command & General Staff Coll, 1967-68; US Army Russian Inst, 1968-70; US Naval War Coll, Dist Grad 1973-74. **CAREER:** US Army Field Statn Berlin Ger, commander 1977-78; USA FORSCOM Atlanta, GA, deputy chief of staff/intelligence 1978-80; Defense Intelligence Agency Wash DC, deputy vice dir 1979-80; US Army War Coll Carlisle, PA, deputy commandant 1980-84; WV State Coll, assoc prof of history. **ORGANIZATIONS:** Mem Alpha Phi Alpha 1951-89, Natl Eagle Scout Assn 1978-89, Assn of US Army 1978-89; chmn Greater Atlanta Armed Forces Day 1979; US Army War Coll Found 1981-89; Am Assn of Univ Prof 1984-87; mem Upsilon Boule Sigma Pi Phi 1984-89, Pi Sigma Theta Natl Political Sci Hon Soc 1985-89, Phi Alpha Theta Natl Historical Soc 1985-89, Rotary Club Intl 1987-. **HONORS/ACHIEVEMENTS:** Contributing author "Soviet Views on War and Peace, NDU 1982; WV State Coll Alumnus of the Yr 1978; WV State Coll ROTC Hall of Fame 1980. **MILITARY SERVICE:** USA brigadier general retired 30 yrs, July 1954-May 1984; DSSM; MSM 2 OLC; JSCM; ACM; master parachutist; air crewman. **HOME ADDRESS:** 400 Bibby St, Apt E, Charleston, WV 25301. **BUSINESS ADDRESS:** Associate Professor of History, WV State Coll, Box 162, W Va State College, Institute, WV 25112.

BROWN, DAVE STEVEN
Professional athlete. **PERSONAL:** Born Jan 16, 1953, Akron, OH; married Rhonda; children: Aaron, Sterling. **EDUCATION:** MI, Communications. **CAREER:** Pittsburgh Steelers, 1975; Seattle Seahawks, right cornerback 1976-. **ORGANIZATIONS:** Worked Ikndustrial Real Estate Broker for Andover Co; active with Multiple Sclerosis, The Variet Club, Big Brothers & United Cerebral Palsy, Cystic Fibrosis, Professional Athletes Outreach, Retail Leasing Specialist w/The Sherwood Group. **HONORS/ACHIEVEMENTS:** 1984,85,86 elected defnsv cptn by teammates prior to start of season; First-team All-NFL (NFL Films); second team All-NFL (AP, Coll & Pro-Football Newsweekly); second-team All-AFC (UPI); AFC Pro Bowl squad; AFC Def Plyr of Week; named 1982 Seattle Miller

High Life NFL Man Of The Year. **BUSINESS ADDRESS:** Right Cornerback, Seattle Seahawks, 5305 Lake Washington Blvd, Kirkland, WA 98033.

BROWN, DAVID EUGENE
Attorney & government official. **PERSONAL:** Born Dec 1938, Wichita, KS. **EDUCATION:** Univ of San Francisco, BA 1969; Lincoln Univ Sch of Law, JD 1974. **CAREER:** CA Dept of Corrections, staff counsel 1977-82; CA Bd of Prison Terms, chief counsel. **ORGANIZATIONS:** Mem State Bar Comm on Corrections 1981-; trustee Los Rios Comm Coll Dist 1981-; pres Wiley Manuel Bar Assn Sacramento Co 1983-; dir CA Comm on Athletics 1984-; dir CA Comm Coll Trustees 1984-. **MILITARY SERVICE:** AUS spec 3 3yrs. **BUSINESS ADDRESS:** Chief Counsel, CA Bd of Prison Terms, 545 Downtown Plaza Ste 200, Sacramento, CA 95814.

BROWN, DELORES ELAINE
Clergywoman. **PERSONAL:** Born Dec 10, 1945, Wildwood, FL; daughter of William Levy Robinson Sr and Mary Lee Howard Robinson; married Marshall L; children: Mare DeShall. **EDUCATION:** FL A&M Univ Tallahasee FL, pre-eng 1962-64; Tuskegee Inst Tuskegee AL, BSEE 1965-67. **CAREER:** Gen Elec/US Atomic Energy Commission, assoc engr 1967-68; FL Power Corp St Petersburg, FL, assoc engr 1968-70; Honeywell Aerospace Inc St Petersburg, FL, assoc engr 1971-75; E-Systems ECI Div St Petersburg, FL, quality engr 1975-78; Sperry Univac Clearwater, FL, engr; First Baptist Institutional Ch, minister 1981-; publisher/preacher, Lake Maggiore Congregation, Kingdom Hall of Jehovah's Witnesses, 1989. **ORGANIZATIONS:** Soc of Women Engrs 1973-75; Soc of Quality Cntrl 1975-77; mem Tuskegee Alumni Assn 1980-; mem Church Women United 1985. **HONORS/ACHIEVEMENTS:** EA Grant Award; Electronic Excellence Award, Tuskegee Inst AL 1966; Most Promising Female Engineering Student Award, Sch of Engineering Tuskegee Inst 1966; 1st female to grad from Tuskegee Inst in Engineering 1967; licensed to preach the gospel First Baptist Inst Ch St Petersburgh FL 1981. **HOME ADDRESS:** 2630 Queen St South, St Petersburg, FL 33712.

BROWN, DELORIS A.
Attorney. **PERSONAL:** Born Aug 16, Los Angeles, CA; children: Nitobi. **EDUCATION:** CA State Univ, BA 1964; Univ of So CA, MA 1970; Peoples College of Law, JD 1978. **CAREER:** Peace Corps Brazil, volunteer 1964-67; Attorney-at-Law. **BUSINESS ADDRESS:** Attorney, 808 North Spring St #622, Los Angeles, CA 90012.

BROWN, DENNIS SNOWDEN
Real estate executive. **PERSONAL:** Born Jul 07, 1954, Alexandria, LA; married Barbara; children: Destiny. **EDUCATION:** Southern Univ Baton Rouge LA, BS Accounting (Cum Laude) 1976. **CAREER:** Arthur Andersen & Co, auditor 1976-78; Sonat Offshore Drilling, sr accountant 1978-83; Texas Realty Ventures Inc, exec vice pres. **ORGANIZATIONS:** Mem Natl Notary Assoc, Natl Assoc of Black Accountants, The Planning Forum, Omega Psi Phi Frat. **HONORS/ACHIEVEMENTS:** Outstanding Young Men of America 1983.

BROWN, DIANA JOHNSON
Police officer, sergeant. **PERSONAL:** Born Jan 25, 1951, Dania, FL; daughter of Walter Rolle and Enith Gloria Johnson Mulkey; married Sherman Leon Brown, Mar 28, 1987; children: Shantel Ramsey, Laquantas Mulkey. **EDUCATION:** Broward Community Coll, Davie FL, Associate Science, 1983; Florida Atlantic Univ, Boca Raton FL, 1975-84. **CAREER:** Broward Community Coll, Davie FL, clerk-typist, admission clerk, sec to registrar, 1970-74; FAU-FLU Joint Center, Ft Lauderdale FL, clerk-typist, 1974-77; Broward County Sheriff's Office, Ft Lauderdale FL, corrections officer, 1977-79; City of Pompano Beach, Pompano Beach Fl, police officer 1979-88, sergeant, 1988-. **ORGANIZATIONS:** Mem, Fraternal Order of Police, 1979-; mem 1983-, secretary for State of Florida 1983-85, Natl Organization of Black Law Enforcement Executives; mem 1984-, financial secretary for southern region 1986-, Natl Black Police Assn; pres, Broward County Law Enforcement Organization, 1980-; mem, Police Benevolent Assn, 1983-; mem, steering committee, Preventing Crime in the Black Community, 4th Annual Conf. **HONORS/ACHIEVEMENTS:** Officer of the Month, City of Pompano Beach, 1982. **MILITARY SERVICE:** USAR, E-6 staff sgt, 1976-; Humanitarian Award 1980; Army Reserve Component Achievement Medal, 1981. **BUSINESS ADDRESS:** Sergeant Police, City of Pompano Beach, 100 SW 3rd Street, Pompano Beach, FL 33351.

BROWN, DONALD R., SR.
Dentist. **PERSONAL:** Born Jun 28, 1939, Kansas City, MO; married Ruby Brogden; children: Donna Grace, Donald Jr. **EDUCATION:** Univ MO, DDS 1965. **CAREER:** Priv Prac, dentist 1966-; Hollywood Presb Hosp, staff mem 1969-73. **ORGANIZATIONS:** Mem Wam Wam Pro Entertainment Prod Agy; West Coast Enter; It Club; Finan Mgmt Corp. **BUSINESS ADDRESS:** PO Box 1137, Reseda, CA 91335.

BROWN, DOROTHY LAVANIA
Physician, educator. **PERSONAL:** Born Jan 07, 1919, Philadelphia, PA; daughter of Samuel Redmon and Lola Redmon; children: Lola D, Kevin Edward. **EDUCATION:** Bennett Coll, BA 1941; Meharvy Med Coll, MD 1948; Fellow of Am Coll of Surgeons, FACS 1959; Russell Sage Coll, Hon DSc 1972. **CAREER:** Riverside Hosp, former chief of surgery 1960-83; Meharry Med Coll, clinical prof of surgery. **ORGANIZATIONS:** Mem Metro Bd Health Nashville TN; mem Natl Med Assn; consultant HEW Natl Inst of Health 1980-82; former rep TN State Legislature 85th General Assembly 1966-68; mem Negro Business & Professional Womens Club; life mem NAACP; mem Delta Sigma Theta. **HONORS/ACHIEVEMENTS:** Dorothy L Brown Bldg Meharry Med Coll Nashville TN 1970; Natl Sojourner Truth Award Nashville TN 1973; Amer Heritage & Freedom Fowler Historic Gallery, Chicago, IL 1979; Blazing Torch Award Inter Min Alli 1981; Certificate of Merit Music City BPW Nashville TN 1984. **HOME ADDRESS:** 3109 John A Merritt Blvd, Nashville, TN 37209.

BROWN, EARL RICHARD
Company executive. **PERSONAL:** Born Jul 11, 1952, Beaufort, SC; son of Tom David Brown Sr and Margaret Hampliton Brown. **EDUCATION:** Benedict Coll, BA (Cum Laude) 1971; Univ of IL, MBA (w/Honors) 1973. **CAREER:** US Dept of Labor Washington, manpower specialist 1971-72; Procter & Gamble Mfg Dallas, personnel mgr 1973-82; Xerox Corp Fremont, mgr personnel oper 1982-; Red Carpet Realty, real estate salesman 1988-89. **ORGANIZATIONS:** Consultant AL Nellum & Assocs 1971-80; mem bd Dallas Urban League 1976-82; vice chmn Park South YMCA Dallas 1979-81; mem Industrial Relations Rsch Assoc 1980-; mem Jobs Task Force Bay Area Urban League Oakland 1986-. **HONORS/ACHIEVEMENTS:** Mem Private Industry Council Dallas (apptd by Gov Mark White) 1980-85; Amer Soc of Personnel Administrators chmn of Employment Task Force Comm Dallas Urban League 1982-85. **BUSINESS ADDRESS:** Mgr of Employee/Industrial Relations, Xerox-Info Products Div, 901 Page Ave, Fremont, CA 94537.

BROWN, EDDIE C.
Investment counselor. **PERSONAL:** Born Nov 26, 1940, Apopka, FL; married Sylvia Thurston; children: Tonya Yvonne, Jennifer Lynn. **EDUCATION:** Howard Univ, BSEE 1961; NYU, MSEE 1968; IN Univ, MBA 1970; CFA 1979; CIC 1979. **CAREER:** T Rowe Price Assn Inc, investment counselor 1973-83; Irwin Mgmt Co, engr 1970-73; IBM, investments 1963-68; Brown Capital Mgmt Inc, pres 1983-. **ORGANIZATIONS:** Mem 3rd Circuit Judiciary Nominating Commission; Baltimore Security Analysts Soc; Financial Analysts Fed; panelist Wall St Week; dir Community Foundation of Greater Baltimore, MD Science Center; trustee Stovall/Twenty-First Consistent Return Trust; mem Governor's Task Force on South African Investments. **HONORS/ACHIEVEMENTS:** Fellowship Grant Consortium for Grad Study in Mgmt 1968. **MILITARY SERVICE:** AUS 1st lt 1961-63. **BUSINESS ADDRESS:** President, Brown Capital Mgmt, Inc, 519 N Charles St, Baltimore, MD 21201.

BROWN, EDWARD LYNN
Minster. **PERSONAL:** Born Apr 02, 1936, Madison Co, TN; married Gladys D Stephens; children: Alonzo, Cheronda. **EDUCATION:** Lane Coll, BS 1960; Interdenominational Theol Ctr, MDiv 1963; Miles Coll Birmingham, AL, Hon Dr Degree 1979. **ORGANIZATIONS:** Gen sec Bd of Pub Serv Christian Meth Episcopal Ch; mem Long Range & Planning Commn, Commn Pension; mem Genl Educ Bd CME Ch; rep World Meth Conf Evangelism Jerusalem 1974; bd dir mem OIC; bd dir mem Memphis NAACP; exec bd mem Nat OIC; bd dirs Memphis Urban League; past bd dir United Way Greater Memphis; mem Intl Soc Theta Phi; bd mem Orange Mound Comm Action Agy; mem Orange Mound Consolidated Civic Club; Dean S Memphis Dist Leadership Training Sch; bd mem Memphis Comm Educ Proj; bd chmn Orange Mound & Creative Involvement Pgm; mem Memphis & Shelby Co Welfare Commn; pres CME Min Alliance; vice pres Memphis Min Assn. **HONORS/ACHIEVEMENTS:** Outstand Serv Memphis NAACP 1973; Outstand Comm Serv Memphis Urban League 1973; Serv City Memphis Cert Merit Mayor Wyeth Chandler 1971; serv gen asst Commn Mayor Wyeth Chandler 1971; Big "S" Citation City Memphis Co Commn 1972; Outstand Religious Leader City Memphis Alpha Kappa Sor 1973; Outstand Comm Serv UMCAP; Cert Appreciation Comm Action Agency 1970. **BUSINESS ADDRESS:** 531 S Parkway E, Memphis, TN 38106.

BROWN, EDWIN C., JR.
Attorney. **PERSONAL:** Born Sep 20, 1935, Washington, DC; son of Edwin C Brown Sr and Pearl W Brown; married Martha; children: 3. **EDUCATION:** Howard Univ, BA 1957, LLB 1960. **CAREER:** Office US Atty Pres's Comm on Crime, asst US atty 1965; Brown Brown & Watkins, atty 1966-. **MILITARY SERVICE:** AUS, 1st lieutenant, honor graduate, Officer Candidate School. **BUSINESS ADDRESS:** Senior Partner, Brown Brown & Watkins, 320 N Fayette, Alexandria, VA 22314.

BROWN, EFFIE MAYHAN JONES
Educator. **PERSONAL:** Born Apr 08, 1922, Penhook, VA; widowed; children: Ethel Jaqueline, Ristina Etelle, Harry Alva III. **EDUCATION:** Bluefield St Coll, BS 1954; Marshall Univ, MA 1964; West Virginia Univ, grad study; Univ of Virginia; Georgetown Univ; Coll of Grad Studies. **CAREER:** Preston Elementary School, Wade Elementary School, kindergarten teacher, 1970-71; Stinson Elementary School, asst principal guidance, 1958-69. **ORGANIZATIONS:** Life mem NEA; West Virginia Educ Assn; 1st black woman pres Mercer Co Assn of Classroom Tchrs 1972-74; mem bd dir Mt Zion Baptist Church; church clerk, Mt Zion Baptist Church; pres Auxiliary Conv; finance sec West Virginia Baptist Congress of Christian Educ; bd mem Mercer Co Adv Comm 1970-73; mem bd dir United Way; chmn Mary C Reed Scholarship Fund; chmn Bible Auxiliary Club; mem Alpha Kappa Alpha, Phi Delta Kappa Frat for Educators Bluefield Virginia Chap. **HONORS/ACHIEVEMENTS:** Recipient Outstanding Elem Tchr of Amer Award 1974; author of This Twig We Bend: A Handbook for Parents and Faculty Handbook & Student Tchr Guide.

BROWN, ELLEN ROCHELLE
Journalist. **PERSONAL:** Born Mar 10, 1949, Denton, TX. **EDUCATION:** Broadcast & Film Arts, So Melth U, BFA 1971; Columbia U, cert 1972. **CAREER:** KDFW-TV Dallas, producer/hostess "Insights"; WROC-TV, anchor Noon News 1975-78; NBC News NY, researcher 1973-75; KERA-TV Dallas, TV reporter 1971-72. **HONORS/ACHIEVEMENTS:** Journalism Flw Columbia Univ 1972; Alfred I, DuPont Awd for Journalism KDFW-TV 1979; TX Sch Bell Awd Dallas 1979; Dallas Sch Adminstr Awd Dallas Sch Dist 1979. **BUSINESS ADDRESS:** 400 N Griffin, Dallas, TX 75202.

BROWN, EMMETT EARL
Administrator. **PERSONAL:** Born Jan 30, 1932, Chicago, IL; son of Joseph E Brown and Julia H Knox; widowed; children: Paula Davis, Patricia E, Emmett E Jr, Cecilia B, Alan C. **EDUCATION:** Pepperdine Univ, 1979. **CAREER:** SEIO AFL-CIO Local 660, bus agent; Central & West Basin Water Replenishment Dist, dir. **MILITARY SERVICE:** USAF A1/C 1950-53. **BUSINESS ADDRESS:** Director, Central & West Basin Water Replenishment District, 7439 E Florence Ave, Downey, CA 90240.

BROWN, ERNEST CALVIN
Engineer. **PERSONAL:** Born May 28, 1941, Winnsboro, LA; married Anne Mahone; children: Philip Calvin, Kelly Anne. **EDUCATION:** Chicago Tech Coll, BS 1963; Washington U, MS 1969. **CAREER:** McDonnell Douglas Corp, plant engr; RW Booker & Asso Inc, proj engr; II Sverdrup & Parcel & Asso Ltd, sr engr. **ORGANIZATIONS:** Am Soc of Civil Engrs; Engr Club of St Louis; IL Structural Engrs Assn bd dir deaconess hosp; alpha phi alpha frat inc. **HONORS/ACHIEVEMENTS:** The James B Eads Bridge at its Centennial 1972; The Journal of Engrs Club of St Louis.

BROWN, ERNESTINE M.
Educator. **PERSONAL:** Divorced; children: Richard Jr, Roger. **EDUCATION:** West-

ern CT St Coll, BS 1965; Harvard Univ Grad Sch Edn, MEd 1974. **CAREER:** Title 2 consult State Dept of Educ Vocational Tech Schools; CT Coll Dir, educ admin, 1970-79; Wooster School for Boys, project dir, 1968-69; Wooster Upward Bounds, follow-up asst dir;, apptd & dir, 1967-68, coord, follow up tutorial program, 1966-67; Danbury Public School System, teacher, 1963-66. **ORGANIZATIONS:** Mem pres adv com Student Affairs; Ad-hoc Com; Informal Com Black Faculty & Staff bd trustees New Ind HS; mem sec Waterford, CT Bd of Edn; exec bd Family Services, New London; New London Youth Serv Adv Com; pres Greater New London Com Interracial Educ & Coop; mem Executive Bd Planned Parenthood,Coordntr, Conn Lupward Bound Project Dir; mem of gen adv cncl Dept of Children & Youth Servs 1977; mem Sub-com Minority Involvement Higher Edn; Resource Com IV; dir Conn Humanities Council Project; mem & sec Bd Educ Middletown; exec bd & mem CT Assn, Bds Educ del Nat Sch Bds Assn State & Nat; chmn CABE Conf Seminar on Communications; lectr & coordintr; sec Regional Exec Council TGRIO Prog; Adminstrv asst to pres Natl Caucus Black Sch Bd Mem; del Conn Nat Del Assembly Nat Sch Bd Assn.

BROWN, EVELYN
City official. **PERSONAL:** Born May 15, 1930, Tifton, GA; married Macon (deceased). **EDUCATION:** Atkinson Cty HS Pearson GA, attended. **CAREER:** Cafeteria aide; Evelyn Spiritual Hour Radio Station WRMU FM, hostess 15 yrs; MCity of Alliance, councilwoman 1984-85. **ORGANIZATIONS:** Mem Gospel Announcer's Guild of Amer, Inc 1975; mem Democratic Exec Comm 1981; mem Christian Update TV 1985; mem Democratic Party 5 years. **HONORS/ACHIEVEMENTS:** First Black Councilwoman Nails of Thounder Soc Club 1984; Queen for a Day Comm Churches 1976; gospel announcer Gospel Music Workshop of Amer 1978; Woman ofthe Year Altrusic Club 1980. **HOME ADDRESS:** 110 1/2 S Freedom, Alliance, OH 44601.

BROWN, EVELYN DREWERY
Educational administrator. **PERSONAL:** Born Oct 29, 1935; children: Clinton O. **EDUCATION:** Morris Brown Coll, BS 1957; Atlanta U, MA 1969, further studies 1975. **CAREER:** Econ Opportunity Atlanta, program dir, 1970-; Atlanta Public Schools, dept chairperson & teacher, 1964-70; Economic Opportunity Atlanta, head start dir, 1965-69; Richmond County Bd of Educ, teacher, 1962-64; Columbia County Bd of Educ, teacher, 1957-62. **ORGANIZATIONS:** Mem GA Assn of Edctrs; mem Nat Assn for Children Under Six; consult & task force mem Parent & Child Centers; Nat 1st vice pres Zeta Phi Beta Sor 1978; pres Better Infant Birth/March of Dimes 1978-80; sec organizations & Communications, The Womens Missionary Cncl 1980-. **HONORS/ACHIEVEMENTS:** Comm Serv Awd, Zeta Phi Beta Sor Morris Brown; Otstndng Serv Awd in Edn; Zeta of Yr Awd; Otstndng Serv in Field of Religion, Holsey Temple CME Ch Atlanta. **BUSINESS ADDRESS:** Atlanta Parent & Child Center, 2071 Boulevard Dr SE, Atlanta, GA 30317.

BROWN, FLOYD A.
Announcer. **PERSONAL:** Born Nov 05, 1930, Dallas, TX; married Mary E Stephens; children: Floyd Keith, Diane Faye. **EDUCATION:** Northwestern Sch of Bus; Radio Inst of Chicago 1951. **CAREER:** TV WGN, staff announcer, personality on radio 1971-; NBC-WMAQ Chgo, prgm mgr announcer 1965-71; WYNR-WNUS Radio Chgo, 1962-65; WRMN, announcer chief engr prgm dir asst Mgr 1951-62. **ORGANIZATIONS:** Bd dir 1st Fed Savings & Loan; dir bd dir Selected Funds; Selected Am Selected Spec Mutual Funds & Selected Spec Money Mrt Fund; co-owner, pub rel & advertising Firm Rotary Intnl; bd dir YMCA; bd dir Fox Valley Council; Boy Scouts of Am; NAACP; Urban League; Elgin C of C; bd dir Larkin Home for Children Family Svcs; chmn bd deacons Elgin 1st Cong Ch; mem Elgin Citizens adv com Mental Health Assn. **MILITARY SERVICE:** AUS sgt 1953-55. **BUSINESS ADDRESS:** 2501 Bradley Pl, Chicago, IL 60618.

BROWN, FRANCHOT A.
Attorney. **PERSONAL:** Born Jul 11, 1943, Columbia, SC; son of Rupert A Brown Sr and Sara D Brown; children: Brian S Brown. **EDUCATION:** Howard Univ, Washington DC, BA 1965; Univ of South Carolina Law School, Columbia SC, JD 1969; Univ of Pennsylvania, Reginald Heber Smith Comm Lawyer 1969. **CAREER:** Legal Aid Serv Agency Columbia, 1969-72; private law practice, 1972-73; Columbia SC Magistrate, 1973-76; Franchot A Brown & Assoc, lawyer 1976-; Brown & Stanley, sr partner, 1976-. **ORGANIZATIONS:** Bd SC Blue Cross-Blue Shield; bd Greater Columbia Chamber of Comm; bd Victory Savings Bank; bd mem Drug Response Op; vocational rehab Midlands Center for Retarded Children; chmn Citizens Advisory Comm for Community Devel for the City of Columbia, SC 1975-. **BUSINESS ADDRESS:** Senior Partner, Brown & Stanley, Attorneys at Law, PO Box 543, Columbia, SC 29202.

BROWN, FRANK
Educator. **PERSONAL:** Born May 01, 1935, Gallian, AL; son of Thomas Brown and Ora Lomax Brown; married Joan Drake; children: Frank G, Monica J. **EDUCATION:** AL State Univ, BS 1957; OR State Univ, MS 1962; Univ of CA at Berkeley, MA 1969, PhD 1970. **CAREER:** Urban Inst CCNY, dir 1971-72; Cora P Maloney Coll SUNY Buffalo, dir 1974-77; SUNY Buffalo, prof 1972-83; School of Ed Univ of NC Chapel Hill, dean 1983-. **ORGANIZATIONS:** Assoc dir NY State Commiss on Ed 1970-72; vice pres Div A of American Ed Research Assn 1986-88; bd of dirs, American Assn of Colleges of Teacher Education 1988-92. **HONORS/ACHIEVEMENTS:** Grad Fellowship OR State Univ 1961-62; Grad Fellowship Univ of CA Berkeley 1968-70; Rockefeller Found Scholars Awd 1979-80; Publ 5 books, monographs & 80 articles; Fellow, Harvard Univ Institute for Educational Management 1988. **MILITARY SERVICE:** AUS spec 1958-60. **HOME ADDRESS:** 6523 Huntingridge Rd, Chapel Hill, NC 27514.

BROWN, FRED
Professional athlete. **PERSONAL:** Born Jul 07, 1948, Milwaukee, WI; married Linda Nelson; children: Fred Jr, Terik Jemal, Bryan Rashad. **EDUCATION:** Burlington IA Comm Coll, 2 yrs; Univ of IA, 2 yrs. **CAREER:** Seattle Supersonics, professional basketball player 1970-. **ORGANIZATIONS:** Mem Old Gold Club Univ of IA 1975; vice pres NBA Players Assoc 1980-; co-capt of Team 4 yrs. **BUSINESS ADDRESS:** Seattle Supersonics, 419 Occidental South, Seattle, WA 98114.

BROWN, FREDDIEMAE EUGENIA
Educator. **PERSONAL:** Born Oct 16, 1928, Racine, WI. **EDUCATION:** Univ of MI, ALMS 1959; Fisk U, 1951. **CAREER:** Detroit Public Library, asst to assoc dir branch serv ,1970-73, pre-profl librarian I, II, III chief of div, chief of dept 1956-70; Dept of Library Science Wayne State Univ, asst prof 1973-. **ORGANIZATIONS:** Mem Am Library Assn; Reference & Subscrition Books Com 1966-; MI Library Assn; womens Nat Book Com rec sec 1973-, Detroit Chapt; Am Assn of Higher Educ 1973-; Assn of Am Library Sch. **HONORS/ACHIEVEMENTS:** Listed in Whos Who in Am Women.

BROWN, GARY W.
Engineer. **PERSONAL:** Born Nov 07, 1944, Lawrenceburg, KY; married Wanda Johnson. **EDUCATION:** Lincoln Inst; United Electronics Inst, 1964. **CAREER:** Intl Bus Machines, gen systems field engr vice-chmn. **ORGANIZATIONS:** KY Black Caucus 1973; city cnclmn Lawrenceburg KY 1974-; little league commn bsbl 1975; mem NAACP. **MILITARY SERVICE:** USN radarman 2nd class 1965-69. **BUSINESS ADDRESS:** 1733 Harrodsburg Rd, Lexington, KY 40501.

BROWN, GEORGE HENRY, JR.
Judge. **PERSONAL:** Born Jul 16, 1939, Memphis, TN; married Margaret Solomon; children: Laurita, George III. **EDUCATION:** FL A& M, BS 1960; Howard Univ Sch of Law, 1967. **CAREER:** AA Latting, atty 1967-70; Equal Emp Opp Comm, dep dir 1969-70; Legal Serv Assoc, exec dir 1970-73; Brown & Evans Law Firm, atty 1973-; Shelby County Circuit Court, judge 1983-. **ORGANIZATIONS:** Chmn Memphis Bd of Ed 1974; mem ABA; mem NBA; mem Memphis & Shelby Cnty Bar Assn; comr Memphis Bd of Edn; vice-chrmn Steering Comm NSBA; trustee Lane Coll; trustee memphis Acad of Arts; mem bd of dir Memphis Chap Natl Bus League; bd of dir Memphis Chap NAACP; vice pres & bd mem Beale St Hist Found; mem Vollentine & Evergreen Comm Assn. **MILITARY SERVICE:** USAR Capt. **BUSINESS ADDRESS:** Shelby County Circuit Court, 161 Jefferson Ave, Memphis, TN 38103.

BROWN, GEORGE HOUSTON
Clergyman. **PERSONAL:** Born Oct 15, 1916, Finchburg, AL; son of A D Brown and Annie D Brown; married Amanda S; children: Marian Payne, LaVerne Bruce, Gwendolyn A Rothchild. **EDUCATION:** AL State Univ, BS 1953, MEd 1968; Inter-Baptist Theological Sem, DD 1967; Selma Univ, LLD 1982. **CAREER:** Free Mission Dist Congress, congress dean 1955-75; Coneuch-Monroe Community Action, bd member 1950-77; Monroe County Mental Health, bd member 1972-80; Tom Bigbee Regional Commission, bd member 1973-89. **ORGANIZATIONS:** Pres Monroe County-Ministerial Assn 1965-70; first vice-moderator Bethlehem No 2 Dist Assn 1963-85; congress dean Bethlehem No 2 Congress 1970-85; member Independent Order Universal Brotherhood 1936-; member Blue Lodge Masons 1940-; member Order of the Eastern Star 1941-; member Enoch Consistory No 222 1960-; mem of Jericho of Alabama 1961-; mem of the Monroe County Board of Educ 1980-. **BUSINESS ADDRESS:** Moderator, East Star Dist Assn, Rt 1 Box 59, Beatrice, AL 36425.

BROWN, GEORGE L.
Business executive. **PERSONAL:** Born Jul 01, 1926, Lawrence, KS; son of George L Brown Sr and Alberta Watson Brown; married Modeen; children: Gail, Cindy, Kim, Laura. **EDUCATION:** Univ KS, BS 1950; Univ CO, grad work 1959; Harvard Univ Business Sch, grad work. **CAREER:** CO House of Reps, 1955; State of CO, state senator 1956-74, lt gov 1975-79; Grumman Ecosystems, vice pres of mktg 1979; Grumman Energy Systems, sr vice pres of business devel 1979-81; Grumman Corp, vice pres Washington office 1981-; Denver Post, Denver CO, writer/editor, 1950-65; Denver Housing authority, asst dir, 1965-69. **ORGANIZATIONS:** Mem Legislatlures Joint Budget Comm 8 yrs; instr Univ CO; instr Univ Denver, Metro St Coll; 1st exec dir Metro Denver Urban Coalition 1969; chmn 1974 Gallup Poll Educ Survey; chmn St Legislative Comm, Senates St Affairs & Finance Comm, Dem Caucus; Natl Policy Council of US Dept of HEW; mem Exec Comm SW Regional Council of Natl Assn of Housing & Redevel Officials; chmn Citizens Adv Council for Denver's Model City Prog; mem Gov Coord Com on Implementation of Mental Health & Mental Retardation Planning; mem Dem Natl Comm; chmn Black Caucus of Dem Natl Comm; mem exec comm Natl Conf of Lt Govs; mem Natl Panel of Natl Acad of Pub Admin Found Neighborhood-Oriented Metro Govt Study; Natl Task Force for Secondary Educ Reform; Nutrition Adv Bd for CO Soc Serv Dept; chmn Natl Urban Coalition Steering Comm; bd dirs World Trade Ctr Washington; McLean VA Orchestra Bd; mem Bocle Fraternity; brd of trustees Davis and Elkins Coll, W. VA, 1988-. **HONORS/ACHIEVEMENTS:** Denver Met Br NAACP Exceptional Man Awd 1972; CO Black Caucus Achievement Awd 1972; Kappa Alpha Psi Achievement Awd 1974; Adam Clayton Powell Awd Polit Achievement Cong Black Caucus 1975; George Brown Urban Journalism Scholarship Est 1976; numerous other honors and awds. **BUSINESS ADDRESS:** Vice President, Grumman Corporation, 1000 Wilson Blvd, Ste 2100, Arlington, VA 22209.

BROWN, GEORGE PHILIP
Physician. **PERSONAL:** Born Feb 08, 1920, Arlington, VA; married Phyllis Glazer; children: George Sabree, Rodney, Craig. **EDUCATION:** Howard Univ, BS 1940; Howard Univ Coll of Med, MD 1944. **CAREER:** Mark Twain School, school psychiatrist 1971-72; Inst for Children, supt 1972; Private practice, physician 1947-. **ORGANIZATIONS:** Diplomate Amer Bd Pediatrics 1953, Amer Bd Neurology & Psychiatry 1962. **MILITARY SERVICE:** USAF capt 1951-53. **BUSINESS ADDRESS:** 11065 Little Patuxent Pkwy, Ste 112, Columbia, MD 21045.

BROWN, GEORGIA R.
Social service executive. **PERSONAL:** Born in Chicago, IL; divorced. **EDUCATION:** Wilson Jr Coll, 1937-38; Roosevelt Coll, BA 1947; Loyola Univ Inst of Soc Admn, MSA 1950; Wayne St Univ, post grad 1953. **CAREER:** Cook County Hosp Mental Health Clinic, sr case worker 1964-65; OEO, sup 1965-68; Mayors Commn for Human Resources Dev, asst dir act dir 1968-71; AL Nellum & Assoc Inc WA, sr consultant 1971; Cit & Conv for a New City Chtr MI, dir 1971-; Comm Un for Act Inc MI, exec dir 1972-74; Model Neighborhood Dept, exec dir 1974-75; Neighborhood Serv Dept Detroit, exec dir 1975-82; Samaritan Health Ctr, vice pres for primary care initiative 1982-84; Project Elite, dir 1985-87. **ORGANIZATIONS:** Mem NASW; bd mem Delta Sigma Theta Sor; 1st vice pres MI Metro Girl Scouts; mem Federation of Girls Homes, MI Chap Natl Alliance Against Racist and Political Repression, Wayne Co Foster Care Review Bd. **BUSINESS ADDRESS:** Dir, Project Elite, 2230 Witherell, Detroit, MI 48201.

BROWN, GEORGIA W.
Educational administrator. **PERSONAL:** Born Oct 01, 1934, St Francisville, LA; daughter

of Edward Watts and Mary Jones Calvin; married Ollie J, Aug 23, 1958; children: Pamel Karen, Oliver Joseph. **EDUCATION:** Southern Univ, BA 1957; LA State Univ, MS 1969. **CAREER:** Southern Univ, asst serials librarian 1957, serials librarian 1962-69, jr div librarian 1969-72, coordinator of readers serv 1972-75, acting dir of libraries 1975-76, dir of libraries 1976-. **ORGANIZATIONS:** Mem LA Library Assoc; chmn Acad Section LLA 1979-80; mem Amer Library Assoc, Southwestern Library Assoc, SW Rsch Center & Museum for Study of African Amer Life & Culture, Phi Delta Kappa, Advisory Council for Graduate School of Library Science LA State Univ; co-chmn Baton Rouge Bicentennial Comm 1974-76; chmn So Univ Bicentennial Comm 1974-76; mem Mayor-Pres Comm of the Needs of Women 1977-, Arts & Humanities Council, YWCA; Gov's comm of one hundred State of LA 1986-; LA Centseptequinary Commission; mem, East Baton Rouge Parish Library, Board of Control. **HONORS/ACHIEVEMENTS:** Public Service Award Baton Rouge Bicentennial Comm 1976; Public Serv Award Mayor-Pres City of Baton Rouge 1976; Serv Award Southern Univ 1976. **BUSINESS ADDRESS:** Dir of Libraries, Southern Univ Baton Rouge, Baton Rouge, LA 70813.

BROWN, GLENN ARTHUR
Health care executive. **PERSONAL:** Born Jan 27, 1953, Fort Knox, KY. **EDUCATION:** Harvard Univ, AB, 1975; Wharton School Univ of Pennsylvania, MBA, 1980; Univ of Pennsylvania, School of Dental Medicine, DMD, 1982. **CAREER:** Ambulatory Health Care Consult, mng partner, 1980-83; Dental Medicine Assoc, PC, pres, 1983-. **ORGANIZATIONS:** Treasurer, Walnut Hill Comm Devel Corp, 1986-; vice pres, West Philadelphia NAACP, 1989-91; vice pres, Philadelphia Chapter, Natl Black MBA Assn 1989-90; bd mem, Lutheran Children & Family Services 1989-91; bd mem, Greater Philadelphia Health Action 1989-91. **BUSINESS ADDRESS:** President, About Your Smile, 144 S 52nd St, Philadelphia, PA 19139.

BROWN, GLENN WILLARD
Chief executive officer. **PERSONAL:** Born Sep 23, 1918, New Franklin, MO; children: William, Lawrence. **CAREER:** Glenn Brown Corp;; pres 1978-; PEACE Inc, exec dir 1971-78; US Peace Corps, staff mem 1962-70. **ORGANIZATIONS:** Mem Govs Task Force on Aging 1974-75; pres NY St Comm Action Agency & Exec Dir Assn 1975-77; commr Metro Commn of the Aging 1971-78; mem Manpower Planning Cncl 1970-78; pres DA's Adv Cncl 1976-78; vice pres Cntrl NY Hlth Sys Agency 1974-78; bd of dirs United Way of Central NY 1972-77; pres Comm Hlth Info & Plng Servs Inc 1976-78. **HONORS/ACHIEVEMENTS:** Otst Comm Serv Awd Syracuse & Onondaga Co 1976; article Comm Action 10 yrs Later, Metro Opinion. **MILITARY SERVICE:** AUS maj 1941-62. **BUSINESS ADDRESS:** 811 E Washington St, Syracuse, NY 13210.

BROWN, GUY, III
Professional athlete. **PERSONAL:** Born Jun 01, 1955, Palestine, TX; married Jacqueline Vera Grimes. **EDUCATION:** Univ of Houston. **CAREER:** Dallas Cowboys, professional football player present; Davis Advertising Co, sales Rep 1980. **ORGANIZATIONS:** Mem Fellowship Christian Athletes.

BROWN, H. RAP See AL-AMIN, JAMIL ABDULLAH

BROWN, HAZEL EVELYN
Community service. **PERSONAL:** Born Sep 03, 1940, Eden, NC; daughter of Joseph Brown (deceased) and Mary Sue Hairston Brown. **EDUCATION:** Russell's Business School, Winston-Salem, NC, Certificate Sec, 1960; Winston-Salem State Univ, Winston-Salem, NC, BA Business Admin, 1977-82; Babcock Center Wake Forest Univ, Winston-Salem, NC, Certificate Mgmt Devel, 1978; NC Central Univ, Durham, NC, Certificate Counsel & Interviewing, 1982; A&T State Univ, Greensboro, NC, MS Adult Educ, 1983-85. **CAREER:** Winston-Salem Urban League, Winston-Salem, NC, vice pres, 1961-. **ORGANIZATIONS:** Mem, NAACP, 1972-; mem, Mt Zion Baptist Church, 1972-; mem, Winston-Salem State Alumni Assn, 1982-; mem, Up and Coming Investment, 1986-; pres, Natl Women of Achievement/Clemmons Chapter, 1987-; mem, Delta Sigma Theta Sorority, 1988-; mem, Housing Resource (Bd of Realtors), 1988-; mem, Urban Arts of Arts Council, 1988-; mem, Benton Convention Center Coliseum Comm, 1987-. **HONORS/ACHIEVEMENTS:** Girl Friday, Urban League Guild, 1970; Service Award, NAACP, 1987; Leadership Award, Winston-Salem Urban League, 1988. **BUSINESS ADDRESS:** Vice Pres, Winston-Salem Urban League, 201 W Fifth St, Winston-Salem, NC 27101.

BROWN, HENRY H.
Vice president. **PERSONAL:** Children: 4 children. **EDUCATION:** Attended, Xavier Univ New Orleans; Texas Southern Univ, Graduate. **CAREER:** Howard Univ School of Business and Industry, adjunct prof; Anheuser-Busch Inc, vice pres of mktg develop and affairs. **ORGANIZATIONS:** Developed Great Kings and Queens of Africa 1975; Anheuser-Busch's ambassador to major leading natl orgs; chmn Natl Business Policy Review; past imperial Potentate Prince Hall Shriners; also serves on several civic and comm org bds; mem Public Relations Soc of Amer, American Mgmt Assoc, Amer Mktg Assoc, NAMD, St Louis Ambassador and mem Royal Vagabonds. **HONORS/ACHIEVEMENTS:** Disting Awd 1982 World's Fair in Knoxville; Adolphus Awd for Excellence Anheuser-Busch; Disting Amer Awd & 1985 Professional Business Leadership Awd Dollars and Sense Magazine; Omega Man of the Year 1983 St Louis; Corporate Man of the Year NAACP; Marketeer of the Year NAMD; Par Excellence Awd Shielf Foundation; Daniel W Bowles Awd Alpha Phi Alpha; James Weldon Johnson Awd Phi Beta Sigma; Brotherhood Awd Chicago Conf of Human Relations; Disting Pioneer Awd Amer Black Artists; Corporate Executor Natl Assoc of Univ Women; Golden Palm Awd Harris Stowe State; Disting Alumni Awd TX Southern Univ; also various citations from the Links, Jack and Jill, and several municipalities for outstanding supportive svcs. **BUSINESS ADDRESS:** Vice President-Marketing, Anheuser-Busch, Inc, One Busch Place, St Louis, MO 63118.

BROWN, HERBERT R.
Insurance executive. **PERSONAL:** Born May 20, 1940, Ashville, NC; children: Cheryl, Adrian, Janice. **EDUCATION:** Intl Data Proc Inst, Cert 1961-62; Univ of Cincinnati 1967-69. **CAREER:** Western Southern Life, computer systems mgmt 1963-78, community affairs/personnel 1978-. **ORGANIZATIONS:** Consult Manpower Training Programs Inc 1978-82; mem & past pres Cincinnati Bd of Ed 1978-; trustee OH School Bds Assoc 1979-; mem Articulation Commiss OH Coll & Secondary Schools 1981-82; vice pres Community Chest United Way 1982-; pres OH Caucus of Black School Bd Mems 1983-; assoc staff dir Greater Cincinnati Found 1983-; bd of dir Amer Red Cross of Cincinnati 1983-; vice pres Private Industry Council of Cincinnati 1983-; pres Natl Caucus of Black School Bd Mems1985. **HONORS/ACHIEVEMENTS:** Outstanding Comm Serv Awd Community Chest of Cincinnati 1976; Jefferson Awd for Public Serv The Amer Inst Public Serv 1979; Leadership Awd Community Chest of Cincinnati 1981; Citizen of the Year Omega Psi Phi Cincinnati 1982. **MILITARY SERVICE:** AUS sgt E-5 1958-61. **HOME ADDRESS:** 2550 Hackberry, Cincinnati, OH 45206. **BUSINESS ADDRESS:** Community Affairs Coord, Western Southern Life, 400 Broadway, Cincinnati, OH 45202.

BROWN, HERMAN
Educator. **PERSONAL:** Born Jul 25, 1922, East Orange, NJ; divorced. **EDUCATION:** Morgan St Coll, BS 1947; NYU, 1949; Univ of MI, MS 1952; Harvard Univ, 1955; WA School of Pschiatry, 1957; WA Teacher Coll, 1958; George Washington Univ, 1958; WA State Univ; VA Coll & Sem, DHum 1969; Catholic Univ of Amer, PhD 1972; Hamilton State Univ, EdD 1973; Stanton Univ, Dr of Letters, 1975. **CAREER:** Washington DC Teachers Coll, acting dean, prof, 1976-; Fed City Coll, assoc provost, assoc prof, 1975-76; DC Teachers Coll, dean, assoc prof, 1974-75; Howard Univ, lecturer, 1970-75; DC Teachers Coll, assoc prof & dean, 1970-74; Howard Univ, instructor, 1960-70; Southern Univ, asst prof, 1958-63; Lincoln Univ, assoc prof, 1956; Morris Coll, rsrch consultant, 1951; MD State Teachers Coll, 1951-58; Bennett Coll, visiting prof, 1949-51; A&T Coll, 1948-51. **ORGANIZATIONS:** Numerous serv & com activities, DC Tchrs Coll; Natl Educ Assn; Amer Assn of Univ Profs; Assn for Supervision & Curric Devel; Harvard Tchrs Assn; Amer Assn of Sch Admins; Amer Psychol Assn; Amer Personnel & Guid Assn; Assn for Childhood Educ Intl; Assn for Higher Educ; Natl Assn of Sec & Elem Sch Prins; Educ Ldrshp Council of Amer Inc; LA Educ Assn; Natl History Soc; DC Psychol Assn; Soc for Coll & Univ Planning; Natl Alliance of Black Sch Educs; Black Child Devel Inst Inc; Assn for Study of Afro-Amer Life & History Inc; Natl Council of Univ Resrch Adminstrs; Assn for Innovation in Higher Edn; Nat Capital Personnel & Guidance Assn; Amer Heritage Studies Assn, natl alumni assn Morgan state Univ; consultant Howard Univ; nellums & co inc; litton Science Indus Inc; numerous others; mem Omega Psi Frat; bachelor Benedict Club; WA Urban League Inc. **HONORS/ACHIEVEMENTS:** Numerous Honors, achievements, appointments, publications; Alumnus of Year Award, Torch Club Morgan State Univ 1979. **MILITARY SERVICE:** AUS I&E officer, 1942-46. **BUSINESS ADDRESS:** 1100 Harvard St NW, Washington, DC 20009.

BROWN, HEZEKIAH
Educator. **PERSONAL:** Born Jul 29, 1923, Monticello, MS; married Rosa L S. **EDUCATION:** Tuskegee Inst, BS 1950; TN A&I St U, MS 1958; Delta St U, Educ Spec or AAA Cert 1973. **CAREER:** Simmons High School, group guidance instructor, 1970-75; Carver Elementary School, prin, 1963-70; Simmons High School, teacher, 1951-63; Eutaula, teacher, 1950-51. **ORGANIZATIONS:** Past & treas Sunflower Co Tchrs Assn; chaplain VFW Post 9732 1955-75; Dept chaplain Dept of MS 1974-75; mem Adv Bd CHP; bd of alderman; vice pres Washington Tchrs Assn 1970-75; mem Washington Co Solid Waste Com; VFW; MS Tchrs Assn; MS Vocational Guidance Assn; Alpha Phi Alpha; MS Municipal Assn; AVA; Military Order of Cooties SS #13. **HONORS/ACHIEVEMENTS:** Tchr Awd MS State 1975; life memshp VFW Post #9732. **MILITARY SERVICE:** AUS sgt 1943-46.

BROWN, HOYT C.
City administrator. **PERSONAL:** Born Nov 01, 1920, Andersonville, GA; married Marjorie Harmon; children: James F, Beatrice C. **EDUCATION:** So U, 1941; Compton JC, 1949; IN Univ NW Campus, 1969. **CAREER:** City of Gary, adminstr engr ofc bldg 1979-, baliff City Ct 1977-79; Lake Co IN, Justice of Peace, Dem 1962-77; Gary, IN, first black City Zoning & Adminstr 1960, first black City Chief Draftsman 1958; Crown Point, first black Chief Draftsman 1952; Lake Co, juvenile probation ofc 1951. **ORGANIZATIONS:** Pres IN St Assn of Justices of Peace; mem Mason IBOPE; Lake City Elks; Knights of Phythias; IN Black Caucus; Club Future; Steel Dust; Ol' Timers; NAACP; FAB; MADA; Kappa Alpha Psi; Brotherhood of Sleeping Car Porter; Laison of FEPC. **BUSINESS ADDRESS:** 401 Broadway, Gary, IN.

BROWN, IRMA JEAN
Attorney. **PERSONAL:** Born May 17, 1948, Los Angeles, CA. **EDUCATION:** Marymount Coll, 1970. **CAREER:** LA Co Pub Defenders Office, law clerk 1973; CA Assoc of Black Lawyers, secty; Greater Watts Justice Ctr Legal Aid Foundation of LA, law clerk, staff atty; Hudson Sndz & Brown, law firm partner; Los Angeles County Municipal Ct, judge. **ORGANIZATIONS:** Pres LA Negro Bus & Professional Wmns Club 1965-66; vice pres So Chap Blck Wmn Lwyrs Assn of CA 1975-76, pres 1976-77; sgt at arms JM Langston Bar Assn 1976-77; LA Co Bar Assn; CA Attys for Crmnl Jstc; treas Nat Conf of Blck Lwyrs 1976-77; Nat Bar Assn; Delta Sigma Theta Sor; Urban Leag; NAACP;Jrdn H S Almn Assn; New Frntr Dem Club; trustee First African Methodist Episcopal Church of Los Angeles; mem 100 Black Women of Los Angeles, Natl Assoc of Women Judges, CA Judges Assoc. **HONORS/ACHIEVEMENTS:** Grnt schlrsh Lgl Educ Oppty 1970-73; Delta Sigma Theta Schlrsh 1970; So CA Gas Co Schlrsh 1970; publ The Minor & The Juv Ct Lgl Aid Found of LA 1975; Certificates of Recognition for Achievement US Congress, CA Senate, City of Compton, Carson-Lynwood, Los Agneles County. **BUSINESS ADDRESS:** Judge, Los Angeles County Munic Ct, 200 W Compton Blvd, Compton, CA 90056.

BROWN, J. QUANTIN
Stockbroker. **PERSONAL:** Born in Baltimore, MD; married Dolores J; children: Mark J, Beverly J, Jonathan W. **EDUCATION:** Univ Denver, LlB. **CAREER:** Buyer Martin Co, 1957-62; Logictron Inc, founder; J Brown Corp Denver, chmn of bd 1960-70; Denver Comm Coll, recd prof econ & hist 1968-70; Sooner Securities Inc, mgr financial consult mgmt consult 1970-. **ORGANIZATIONS:** Mem Mensa & Nat Assn Securities Dlrs; author "The Black Sucker"; bd dirs Tulsa Urban League 1971; candidate for CO House of Reps 1968. **HONORS/ACHIEVEMENTS:** Received citation Mayor of Denver 1965; named Outstanding Citizen in Denver 1969. **BUSINESS ADDRESS:** PO Box 6034, Tulsa, OK 74106.

BROWN, JACQUELINE D.
Educator, orthodontist. **PERSONAL:** Born Oct 27, 1957, Nashville, TN; daughter of James H Brown, DDS and Birdie Faulkner Brown. **EDUCATION:** Brandeis U[illegible] tham, MA, BA, 1979; Meharry Medical Coll, Nashville, TN, DDS, 1983[illegible] Ann Arbor, MI, MS, 1985. **CAREER:** Howard Univ Dept of [illegible] DC, asst prof, 1985-; private practice, Silver Springs, MD, 198[illegible]

Dentistry, Advanced Gen Dentistry Program, consultant, 1986-; Howard Univ School of Dentistry, Gen Practice Residency Program, attending physician, 1986-. **ORGANIZATIONS:** Amer Assn of Orthodontists, 1983-; Intl Assn of Dental Research, 1983-; Middle Atlantic Soc of Orthodontists, 1983-; Omicron Kappa Upsilon Dental Honor Soc, 1983-; Metropolitan Washington Study Club, 1983-; Amer Assn of Women Dentists, 1987-. **HONORS/ACHIEVEMENTS:** Univ of Michigan Merit Fellowship, 1983, 1984; Patterson Dental Supply Award, 1983; William H Allen Award, 1983; Certificate of Appreciation, Howard Univ Coll of Dentistry Advanced Gen Dentistry Program, 1988; author, abstract, "The Development of the Oxytalan Fiber System of the Mouse Periodontal Ligament," IADR meeting, 1986.

BROWN, JAMES
Entertainer. **PERSONAL:** Born Jun 17, 1928, Augusta, GA; son of Joseph Brown; married Adrianne Brown; children: Deanna, Terry, Daryl, Venisha, Yamma. **CAREER:** Leader musical group Famous Flames, now solo performer; recordings include Original Disco Man, Please Please Please, Hot on the One, Poppa's Got a Brand New Bag; JB Broadcasting Ltd, pres 1968-; James Brown Network, pres 1968-. **ORGANIZATIONS:** Chmn bd James Brown Productions, James Brown Entertainment, and Man's World Augusta; his organizations include two recording companies, two real estate int & three radio stations. **HONORS/ACHIEVEMENTS:** Known as "Godfather of Soul" & Soul Brother #1; 44 Gold Records; Grammy Awd 1965; appeared in 3 films and in television and theatre productions; recorded first hit song 1956; received Humanitarian Award; Music & Perform Arts Lodge of B'nai B'rith New York City 1969; one of first ten musicians inducted into Rock n Roll Hall of Fame; hit songs include "Don't Be A Dropout" and "Say It Loud, I'm Black and I'm Proud"; author of autobiography James Brown, The Godfather of Soul. **BUSINESS ADDRESS:** c/o Brothers Mgmt Assocs, 141 Dunbar Ave, Fords, NJ 08863. *

BROWN, JAMES E.
Dental surgeon. **PERSONAL:** Born Feb 03, 1923, Holly Hill, SC; married Sarah L Burgess. **EDUCATION:** SC St Coll, BvS 1947; Howard U, DDS 1952. **CAREER:** Self Employed Dental Surgeon. **ORGANIZATIONS:** Mem Am Dental Assn; SC Dental Assn; Costal Dist Dental Soc; Palmetto Med Dental & Pharmaceutical Assn (pres 1967-68); pres Charleston Co Med Assn;dental staff McClellan Banks Mem Hosp; bd dir Franklin C Fetter Comprehensive Hlth Ctr; past pres Owis Whist Club; Owls Whist Club; treas Athenians Club; Omega Psi Phi; treas St Paul AME Ch; sec treas Midland Park Dem Precinct; mem Tri Dent C of C; chmn Task Force for Quality Edn; mem Charter Commn Charleston Co Consult Govt. **HONORS/ACHIEVEMENTS:** Recipient 2 Bronze Stars; honored as outstanding Black Professional Coll of Charleston 1975. **MILITARY SERVICE:** USAF t/4; 3 yrs. **BUSINESS ADDRESS:** 34 Morris St, Charleston, SC 29403.

BROWN, JAMES H.
Business executive. **PERSONAL:** Born Mar 16, 1935, Wake Co, NC; married Geraldine G; children: Deborah C, James H, Jr. **CAREER:** Raleigh Funeral Home, asst funeral dir 1955-57; Salesman, auto 1957-58; 1st Natl Bank, bank mess 1958-59; Wash Terr Apts, apt supt 1958-59; J W Winters & Co, real estate sales mgr 1961-66; Brown Realty Co, pres 1966-. **ORGANIZATIONS:** Chmn Political Action Comm; NAACP; Raleigh Citizens Assn; Raleigh C of C; precinct chmn Wake Co Democratic Party; chmn trustee bd, chmn bldg comm, chmn finance comm compl chrg of 300,00000 ch Ldc United Church of Chrst 1972-73; Chmn Mayoral Campaign. **HONORS/ACHIEVEMENTS:** 1st Black Mayor Elected in City of Raleigh 1973.

BROWN, JAMES MARION
Elected official. **PERSONAL:** Born Jul 30, 1952, Holdenville, OK; son of Clearnce Brown, Jr and Carrie Mae Knox Brown; married Clarice M Brown (divorced); children: James Jr, Tiffany. **EDUCATION:** East Central Univ, Ada, OK, BS; 12 hours on Masters. **CAREER:** McAlester High School, teacher 1977-; City of McAlester, Councilmember, 1982-86, 1988-. **ORGANIZATIONS:** Member, Special Service Board for State of Oklahoma Teachers, 1977-81; Member, Board of Directors, State of Oklahoma Teachers Convention Committee, 1977-81; Trustee, McAlester Health Authority, 1982-86; Trustee, McAlester Economic Devel Service, 1982-86; Member, Black Elected Officials, 1982-86; Board Member, Public Works Board, McAlester, Oklahoma; Appointed Member, Oklahoma Human Rights Commission, 1984; Board Member, McAlester Boy's Club, 1984-86. **HONORS/ACHIEVEMENTS:** Awarded Highest Grade Point Average of Alpha Phi Alpha, 1975; Member, Oklahoma Municipal League, 1982-86; Councilmember, McAlester City Council, 1982-86; Member, McAlester Youth Shelter, 1984; Member, State Attorney General Advisory Commission, 1985; Gov Committee Physical Fitness; NAACP Man of the Year Award, 1988-89. **MILITARY SERVICE:** Oklahoma Military Academy. **HOME ADDRESS:** 1208 North G St, McAlester, OK 74501. **BUSINESS ADDRESS:** Councilman, City of McAlester, 1 Buffalo Drive, McAlester, OK 74501.

BROWN, JAMES MONROE
Funeral home owner. **PERSONAL:** Born Jun 28, 1928, Pulaski, TN; son of John Brown and Theola Brown; married Ann McKissack. **CAREER:** Abraham McKissack Sr Citizens Homes Inc, chmn of the bd, pres; TN Voters Council, gen chmn; bd TN Black Leadership Round Table; Queen Ann Funeral Home, owner. **ORGANIZATIONS:** Mem Elks Lodge 1489; trustee State Coord TN Voters Council; mem TN Delegation Dem Natl Conventions 1968-72-76; former chmn Giles Co Dem; mem Campbell AME Church; former mem Consumer Affairs Comm So Bell Telephone for State of TN 1980-82. **HONORS/ACHIEVEMENTS:** Man of Yr Giles & Lawrence Cos 1968; Man of Yr Elks Lodge #1489 1973; Elks man of the Year Giles Co 1985. **MILITARY SERVICE:** USN 1944-46, 1951-55. **BUSINESS ADDRESS:** General Chairman, Tennessee Voters Council, 410 N 1st St, Pulaski, TN 38478.

BROWN, JAMES NATHANIEL (JIM)
Athlete. **PERSONAL:** Born Feb 17, 1936, St Simons Island, GA; divorced; children: Kim, Kevin, Jim. **EDUCATION:** Syracuse U, Grad. **CAREER:** Film Actor; Cleveland Browns, fullback 1957-65. **HONORS/ACHIEVEMENTS:** Recip Player of the Yr 1958, 63, 65; Hickoc Belt Athlete of Yr 1964; All Am 1956; named to every All-star Team 1963; holder rushing mark & greatest distance gained in one season; 18 films include "Rio Conchos" "Dirty Dozen" "Ice Station Zebra" "Slaughter"; TV Appearances; author "Off My Chest" Doubleday 1964.

BROWN, JASPER C., JR.
Attorney. **PERSONAL:** Born Mar 27, 1946, Columbia, SC; married Sandra Cox; children: Leslie, Douglass, Jasper David. **EDUCATION:** Hampton Inst, BS 1969; Cath Univ Columbus Sch of Law;; JD 1974. **CAREER:** NLRB Div of Advice, staff atty 1974-77; Gen Electric Co, prodn Mgr 1969-71. **ORGANIZATIONS:** Mem Nat Bar Assn 1974-; mem PA Bar Assn 1974-; mem NC Assn of Black Lawyers 1977-. **HONORS/ACHIEVEMENTS:** Opportunity fellow Council on Legal Educ Opportunity Scholarship Fund Washington DC 1971-74; Earl Warren fellow Earl Warren Found Scholarship Fund NY 1973. **BUSINESS ADDRESS:** Natl Labor Relations Board, 241 N Main St, Ste 447, Winston-Salem, NC 27101.

BROWN, JEFFREY LEMONTE
Clergyman. **PERSONAL:** Born Dec 22, 1961, Anchorage, AK; married Lesley A Mosley; children: Rayna Adair Brown. **EDUCATION:** East Stroudsburg Univ, BA 1982; Indiana Univ PA, MEd 1984; Andover Newton Theol Sch, MDiv 1987. **CAREER:** Amer Baptist Churches Inc, rep gen bd 1987-91; Union Baptist Church, senior pastor. **ORGANIZATIONS:** Student body pres 1981-82, black caucus pres 1980-81 East Stroudsburg Univ; student exec officer 1985-86, mem racism/sexism task force 1986-87 Andover Newton Theol Sch; corresponding secretary, United Baptist Convention of Maryland, Rhode Island, & New Hampshire 1988-; bd mem, Dept of Church and Society, Amer Baptist Churches of Massachusetts; bd mem, Board of Ministry, Harvard Univ 1989-92. **HONORS/ACHIEVEMENTS:** Jonathan Edwards Honor Soc Andover Newton Theol Sch 1985-87; Student Leadership Awd East Stroudsburg Univ 1982; Outstanding Achievement Awd PA EEO-Act 101 1986; Kelsey Merit Scholar Andover Newton Theol Sch 1986-87. **HOME ADDRESS:** 184 Raymond Street, Cambridge, MA 02140.

BROWN, JOAN P. (ABENA)
Foundation executive. **PERSONAL:** Born in Chicago, IL. **EDUCATION:** Roosevelt U, BA 1950; Hull House Fellowship, 1962; Univ of Chicago, MA 1963. **CAREER:** YWCA of Metropolitan Chicago, area dir 1963-65, consult human rel 1965-70, dir of program serv 1970-82; ETA Creative Arts Found, pres 1982-. **ORGANIZATIONS:** Pres Black Theatre Alliance Chicago IL 1978-84; pres Midwest Theatre Alliance 1982-86; chmn City Arts Policy Committee 1985-; mem/chmn Sub Committee on Pgm Mayor's Dept of Cultural Affairs 1985-; mem Interdisciplinary Panel Natl Endowment for the Arts. **HONORS/ACHIEVEMENTS:** Paul Robeson Award, Black Theatre Alliance of Chicago 1978; Governor's Award in the Arts IL 1981; monograph Politics of/and Black Theatre 1979; producer ETA Mainstage Prod 1983-; dir "Shango Diaspora," "Witness a Voice Anthology When the Wind Blows" 1981-; "Passenger Past Midnight.". **HOME ADDRESS:** 7637 S Bennett St, Chicago, IL 60649. **BUSINESS ADDRESS:** President/Executive Dir, ETA Creative Arts Found, 7558 S South Chicago Ave, Chicago, IL 60619.

BROWN, JOHN ANDREW
College educator, educational administrator. **PERSONAL:** Born Jul 17, 1945, Birmingham, AL; son of Kalop Todd Brown (deceased) and Elmira Kelsey-Brown (deceased). **EDUCATION:** Daniel Payne Coll, AA 1965; Miles Coll, BA 1967; Yale Univ Divinity Sch, MDiv 1970, STM 1972. **CAREER:** Yale Univ Divinity Sch, assoc prof 1970-73; Trinity Coll Hartford, asst prof rel/dir ICS prog 1973-76; CT Coll New London, vstg prof rel 1974-75;The Coll of New Rochelle at NY, theol sem adj prof rel 1980-; The Coll for Human Svcs, prof/adm 1979-. **ORGANIZATIONS:** Consultant Trinity Coll1973, Manchester Comm Coll1976; educ admin Bronx Extension Site-Coll for Human Serv 1986-; mem NY Urban League, Alpha Phi Alpha,NAACP, ASALH, Yale Alumni Associates of Afro-Americans, AAUP. **HONORS/ACHIEVEMENTS:** Carnegie Fellowship Columbia Univ 1966; Richard Allen Awd; Rockefeller Protestant Fellowship Theological Education 1967-70; Oliver E Daggett Prize Yale Corp 1969; Research Fellowship Yale Univ 1971-72; mem Pi Gamma Mu; Fellowship UTS Black Econ Develop Fund 1976; Biog sketch in Yale Univ 1985 Alumni Directory. **BUSINESS ADDRESS:** Asst Prof Ethics & Philosophy, College for Human Services, 345 Hudson St, New York, NY 10014.

BROWN, JOHN C., JR.
Business executive. **PERSONAL:** Born Jun 09, 1939, Camden, NJ; married Gloria Brown; children: Jay, Ernie. **EDUCATION:** Univ of Syracuse, BA 1962; Univ of Pittsburgh, attended 1972-74; Stonier Grad Sch of Banking, grad degree banking 1980. **CAREER:** Pittsburgh Nat Bank Oakland, dist mgr dist X 1980; Pittsburgh Nat Bank Oakland, vice pres 1979; Pittsburgh & Nat Bank Oakland, asst vice pres 1978; Pittsburgh Nat Bank Oakland, mgr Oakland ofc 1977; Pittsburgh Nat Bank Oakland, comm banking ofc 1974; Pittsburgh Nat Bank, credit analyst 1970-74; Cleveland Browns, professional football 1962-66; Math & English, tchr & counselor 1962-63; Firestone Tire & Rubber Co, franchise with Paul Warfield 1964; Pittsburgh Steelers, professional football 1966-72. **ORGANIZATIONS:** Bd of dir United Way YMCA; treas Nat Multiple Sclerosis Soc; mem NAACP; mem Rotary Oakland. **BUSINESS ADDRESS:** Pittsburgh Natl Bank, 4022 5th Ave, Pittsburgh, PA 15213.

BROWN, JOHN MITCHELL, SR.
Retired general officer, military history expert, real estate entrepreneur, economic & financial analyst, consultant. **PERSONAL:** Born Dec 11, 1929, Vicksburg, MS; son of Joeddie Fred Brown and Ernestine Helen Foster Brown; married Louise Yvonne Dorsey, Dec 14, 1963; children: Ronald Quinton, Jan Michelle, John Mitchell, Jay Michael. **EDUCATION:** West Point, US Military Academy, BS, Eng, 1955; Syracuse Univ, MBA, 1964; Univ of Houston, 1978. **CAREER:** US Army, 1955-88: Combat Duty Republic of South Vietnam; Asst Secretary of the General Staff to Chief of Staff Army, 1970-71; Battalion Commander, 8th Infantry Div, 1971-73; Sr Exec to Comptroller of the Army, 1973-77; Commander, 3rd Brigade, 2nd Div, Korea, 1976-77; Asst Commander, 2nd Infantry Div, Korea, 1979-80; Deputy Chief of Staff, Material Plans, Programs & Budget; Office of Army Rsch, Devel & Procurement, 1980-83; Comptroller, US Army Forces Command, 1983-85; Deputy Commander, III Corps & Fort Hood Texas. **ORGANIZATIONS:** Mem, Legion of Merit, Defense Meritorious Service, Republican Party, NAACP. **HONORS/ACHIEVEMENTS:** Two Meritorious Service Awards; Three Army Commendations, 1955-present; Published Defense Econ Analysis in Defense, Econ Analysis in the Army, 1969; City Proclamation Designating June 19, 1985 as "John M. Brown Day", State of Georgia. **MILITARY SERVICE:** AUS, 1955-88. **BUSINESS ADDRESS:** Long & Foster, 116 Old Largo Rd, Largo, MD 20772.

BROWN, JOHN OLLIS
Physician. **PERSONAL:** Born Oct 23, 1922, Colbert, OK; married Marie Louise Faulkner; children: John, Jr, William E, Gala Munnings, Lawrence F. **EDUCATION:** Univ of WI,

1939-43; Menarry Med Coll, MD 1950; VA Hosp Tuskesee, AL, residency 1951-55. **CAREER:** Cedars of Lebanon Hosp, physician; Jackson Mem Hosp, physician; Christian Hosp, physician. **ORGANIZATIONS:** Bd of dir Capital Bank 1976-80; trustee of Nat Med Assn 1979-80; mem Dade Co Med Assn; mem Am Med Assn; mem FL Med Assn; life mem NAACP; mem Sigma Pi Phi; mem Omega Psi Phi. **MILITARY SERVICE:** Inf 1st Lt 1943-46; Recipient Purple Heart & Oak Leaf Cluster Inf 1945. **BUSINESS ADDRESS:** 1001 NW 54th St, Miami, FL 33127.

BROWN, JOHN SCOTT
Architect. **PERSONAL:** Born Oct 04, 1930, Englewood, NJ; son of John Scott Brown (deceased) and Melle Hortense Stubbs Brown (deceased); married Brenda Lawson (deceased); children: Leigh Melle, Courtney Hughes, John. **EDUCATION:** Howard U, BArch 1965, Master ofc City Planning 1975. **CAREER:** IRS Dept of Treas, chief A & E sec; Reg Griffith Asso, sr arch urban planner 1974-78; United & Plan Org, dir office of prgm Dev 1973-74; Concept Design Div United Plan Org, head 1971-73; WA Plan Wrkshp Planner Met WA Planning & Housing Assn, dir 1969-71; Constrn Specs Inst, asst tech dir 1966-69; NAV FAC Dept of Navy, arch plan 1965-66; IRS Dept of Treas, chief building services section 1985-88, technical advisor 1988-. **ORGANIZATIONS:** Reg arch DC; mem Am Inst of Arch; mem Am Inst of Planners; Nat Assn of Comm Dev Pres bd of Commr Mayor Highland Beach Inc Anne Arundel Cty MD 1977-79; 1st vice pres bd dir Friends of Nat Zoo 1969-; mem DC Urban League; Howard Univ Alumni Assn HUDC Alumni Club; Nat Conf of Christians & Jews. **HONORS/ACHIEVEMENTS:** Ford Found Fellowship for Grad Study 1970-71. **MILITARY SERVICE:** AUS corpl 1952-54. **HOME ADDRESS:** 4225 17th St NW, Washington, DC 20011. **BUSINESS ADDRESS:** Technical Advisor, Internal Revenue Service/Dept of Treasury, 1111 Constitution Ave NW IGC 6326, Washington, DC 20224.

BROWN, JOHNNY MAC
Automobile dealer. **CAREER:** Three Star Chrysler-Plymouth Inc, Birmingham, AL, chief executive. **BUSINESS ADDRESS:** Chief Executive, Three Star Chrysler-Plymouth Inc, 2970 Lorna Rd, Birmingham, AL 35216. *

BROWN, JONEL LEONARD
Educator. **PERSONAL:** Born Jan 17, 1910, Port Gibson, MS; married Claudia O'Neal; children: Dr Jonel II, Dr Ashland O'Neal Brown. **EDUCATION:** Morehouse Coll, AB 1930; Univ WI, AM 1942, PhD 1946; NY Gen Educ Bd, flwshp 1945-46. **CAREER:** Riverside Natl Bank; dir business devel, 1973-retirement; Prairie View A&M Univ, retired dean educ, 1969-73; Netroes TX State Dept of Educ, asst state dir Educ, 1946-50; Prairie View A&M Univ; chmn dept Economics, 1944-69. **ORGANIZATIONS:** Mem bd dir Riverside Nat Bank 1967-; dir bus devel Riverside Nat Bank 1973-; chmn bd mgmt S Central YMCA 1959-; bd dir Bus & Professional Club; mem Mayors Manpower Area Planning Cncl Houston TX 1971; Urban Bankers Cncl; bd dir Zool Soc Houston; bd of dir Houston MESSBGC 1980-. **HONORS/ACHIEVEMENTS:** Recpt plaque YMCA; plaque Mayors CETA Adv Bd; plaque Prins Assn life mem vestry St Francis Episcopal Ch.

BROWN, JOSEPH CLIFTON
Administrator. **PERSONAL:** Born Oct 15, 1908, Jackson, MS; married Rubye L Threlkeld; children: Velma, Thelma, Selma, Reuben, Edwin, Edna. **CAREER:** Dusable Museum of African Am, adminstr; Taylor Voc Agr HS, prin 1934-40; Picayune HS, prin 1941; Oxford Training Schl, instr 1943-45; WPA, instr 1944; Rocessing Bureau Employment & Sec State of IL, oper Data Processing 1945-75; Dusable Museum of Afro-am History, admin staff mem 1970-77. **ORGANIZATIONS:** Mem Phi Beta Sigma Frat 1932; contr MS Black Educ Jrnl 1941-42; opr Data Processing 1946; chm Creative Writers Forum 1946-48; lay ldr Christ UM 1963-77. **HONORS/ACHIEVEMENTS:** Humanitarian Awd Christ Ch 1976.

BROWN, JOSEPH DAVIDSON, SR.
Administrator. **PERSONAL:** Born Dec 27, 1929, St Joseph, LA; married Cleola Morris; children: Ann Marie, Mitchell George, Ollie Mae Neely, Joseph Davidson Jr, Joyce Lavel Davis, Claude Ernest. **EDUCATION:** Eswege Germany School, mechanic 1951; Tyler Barber Coll, barber 1954; Triton Coll, supervision 1978. **CAREER:** Central Area Park Dist, police officer 1976-79, comm 1979-; Second Baptist Church, deacon 1984-; Village of Maywood, public works 1962-. **ORGANIZATIONS:** Mason Pride of Tensas #99 1954-. **HONORS/ACHIEVEMENTS:** Village of Maywood Code Enforcement Marshal; Natural Hazards Recovery Course (Inland); Emergency Mgmt Inst Emmitsburg MD. **MILITARY SERVICE:** AUS corp 1948-52. **HOME ADDRESS:** 223 South 12th Ave, Maywood, IL 60153. **BUSINESS ADDRESS:** Dir of Public Works, Public Works of Maywood, One Madison Plaza, Maywood, IL 60153.

BROWN, JOYCE
Educational administrator. **PERSONAL:** Born Aug 02, 1937, Lagrange, GA; daughter of Willis Storey and Nellie Kate Harris Storey; married Randolph F Brown; children: Randette J, Randolph J, Ronda J, Randal J. **EDUCATION:** OH State Univ, 1956-58; Sinclair Coll, 1958-59. **CAREER:** Citibank NA, asst mgr/FISG foreign exchange 1975-80, mgr/FMG/treasurer serv 1980-83, mgr/NABG/CSD/treasurer serv foreign exchange 1983-; Hempstead Public Schools, pres; Citibank/Citicorp, New York, asst vice pres, 1983-; NY State School School Board Assn, dir bd devel NYC community school bd improvement project, 1989-. **ORGANIZATIONS:** Chmn Advisory Com on Minority Affairs NY State School Bds Assn; mem bd dir Alliance Counselor for Drug & Alcohol Abuse; mem bd dir Natl Caucus of Black School Bd Members; mem Natl Business & Professional Womens Clubs Inc; pres, mem Hempstead School Bd, 1981-86; mem, Natl Alliance of Black School Educators, 1984-; vice pres, Natl Caucus Black School Board Members, 1986-87; chairperson, Governmental Affairs, Natl Assn of Black Business and Professional Women's Clubs, 1987-; mem, 100 Black Woment Inc, 1987-; pres, Hempstead Civic Assn, 1987-88; chairperson Hempstead Educ Committee, 1988-; life mem, NAACP. **HONORS/ACHIEVEMENTS:** Outstanding Service Award, 100 Black Men, 1984; Legislative Citation, Ohio State Assembly, 1984; Outstanding Service, Hempstead School District, 1986; Legislative Citation, New York State Assembly, 1989; Legislative Citation, Nassau County Elective, 1989. **HOME ADDRESS:** 254 Rhodes Ave, Hempstead, NY 11550. **BUSINESS ADDRESS:** New York State School Boards Association, 119 Washington Avenue, Albany, NY 12210.

BROWN, JULIUS J.
Business executive, educator. **PERSONAL:** Born Feb 17, 1907, Oak City, NC; married Roberta Lassiter; children: Robert D, Julia, Shearian. **EDUCATION:** A&T St U, BS 1937. **CAREER:** Self employed Real Estate Salesman; Mitchell Co Training Sch, prin tchr agr; Pitt Co Training Sch, tchr Agr; S Ayden Sch, tchr Agr; Ayden & Grift Sch, tchr Agr. **ORGANIZATIONS:** Pitt Co NC Precinct Chmn; Mason; mem Kappa Alpha Psi Frat; Knights of Pythian; NACW NEA Commnr Town of Ayden 1968-75; Mayor Pro-tem 1974; mem Mid E Exec Com 1970-74; mem Mideast Manpower & Finance Com 1974-; mem of Finance & Exec Com. **HONORS/ACHIEVEMENTS:** Recip Cert of Merit Pitt Co Schs; Cert of Appreciation in Occupational Educ at Ayden-grifton HS; cert of Appreciation Agr & Educ 30 yrs faithful serv NC Vocational Tchrs Assn; cert of Appreciation otstndng serv Mt Olive Bapt Ch 1970; Cert Meritorious Serv Pitt Co United Fund 1972; Achvmnt Awd Pitt Co Br of NAACP 1972; Certt of Merit A&T StUniv Dept of Vo-ag 1975. **BUSINESS ADDRESS:** PO Box 126, 218 W 3 St, Ayden, NC 28513.

BROWN, JULIUS RAY
Educational administrator. **PERSONAL:** Born Feb 18, 1940, Birmingham, AL; married Betty Jean; children: Laura, Kenyen. **EDUCATION:** Wayne State Univ, BA 1963, MEd 1971; Univ of MI, PhD 1973. **CAREER:** Project Equality of MI, exec dir 1969-71; Univ of MI, regional dir 1971-76; Wayne County Comm Coll, regional dean 1976-83; Comm Coll of Allegheny Co, vice pres exec dean 1983-. **ORGANIZATIONS:** Mem bd dirs Northside Chamber of Commerce 1984-; mem bd dirs Local Govt Acad 1985-; mem bd dirs St John's Hospital 1985-; program officer President's Roundtable AACJC 1986; mem Natl Convention Comm Church of Our Lord Jesus Christ 1986. **HONORS/ACHIEVEMENTS:** Outstanding Young Man of Amer 1976; State of MI Legislative Tribute 1981; Principals & Educators Awd BTWBA 1981. **BUSINESS ADDRESS:** Vice Pres & Executive Dean, Comm Coll of Allegheny Co, Allegheny Campus, 808 Ridge Ave, Pittsburgh, PA 15212.

BROWN, JURUTHA
Government administrator. **PERSONAL:** Born Apr 11, 1950, San Diego, CA; daughter of Fred Brown and Bertha Brown. **EDUCATION:** Occidental College, BS 1972; UCLA, Cert Executive Mgmt Program 1988. **CAREER:** Worked included test devel, selection rsch, classification prior to 1984; City of Los Angeles, chief fire selection div 1984-87, chief workers' compensation div. **ORGANIZATIONS:** Treas/sec Personnel Testing Council of So CA 1982/1984; chair, human rts comm Intl Personnel Mgmt Assoc 1985; mem bd dirs IMPA Assessment Cncl 1984-87, pres, vice pres, treas Western Regional Intergovt Personnel Assessment Council 1985-87; mem Natl Forum for Black Public Admin 1984-; pres Black Alumni of Occidental Coll; frequent speaker on test devel & test rsch, police recruitment. **BUSINESS ADDRESS:** Chief Worker's Compensation, City of Los Angeles, 111 E 1st St Rm G1, Los Angeles, CA 90012.

BROWN, JUSTINE THOMAS
Mayor. **PERSONAL:** Born May 12, 1938, Guyton, GA; daughter of J. W. H. Thomas, Sr. and Marie Easley Thomas; married Willie Brown, Jul 27, 1961; children: Rahn Andre, Willie Antjuan, Jatavia Anreka. **EDUCATION:** Savannah State College, Savannah GA, BS, 1959; Georgia Southern College, Statesboro GA, 1989. **CAREER:** Screven County Board of Education, Sylvania GA, teacher, 1959-89; mayor of City of Oliver GA, 1988—. **ORGANIZATIONS:** National Association of Educators, National Conference of Black Mayors. **HONORS/ACHIEVEMENTS:** Educator of the Year award, Screven County Rotary Club, 1988; First Black Mayor Award, City of Oliver GA, 1988. **BUSINESS ADDRESS:** City of Oliver, PO Box 221, Oliver, GA 30449.

BROWN, KENNETH EDWARD
Physician. **PERSONAL:** Born Aug 14, 1946, Lafayette, LA; married Cheryl Ann Trahan. **EDUCATION:** Dillard U, BA 1968; Howard U, MD 1972. **CAREER:** Private practice, MD; Lafayette Gen Hosp, chmn obstet gynecol Dept 1978. **ORGANIZATIONS:** Bd of dir Republic Fed Savings & Loan 1979; trustee City of Lafayette Pub Trust Authority; bd of dir Southwest Nat Bank of Lafayette; LA Perinatal CareCommn; mem LA State Med Soc; mem Lafayette Parish Med Soc; bd of dir Am Cancer Soc Lafayette; mem Omega Psi Phi Frat Inc; bd Of dir Acadiana Sickle Cell Anemia Found; bd of dir Holy Rosary Inst High Sch. **HONORS/ACHIEVEMENTS:** Outstanding black citizen award So Consumers Educ Found Lafayette 1975; Martin Luther King humanitarian award Lafayette Council on Human Relations 1978; man ofthe year Frontiers Intl Lafayette Club 1978. **BUSINESS ADDRESS:** 155 Hospital Dr, #304, Lafayette, LA 70503.

BROWN, KENNETH S.
Educator. **PERSONAL:** Born Jul 03, 1919, Macon; married Lillian Loving. **EDUCATION:** Coll of Pharmacy, BS; Howard U, 1955. **CAREER:** Rohm & Haas Chemical Co PA, control analytical chemist; Prvate Practics, pharmacy; PA, lecturer on dangers of drug abuse, jr high school students & parents, 1958-69; Pharmacy School & Temple Univ, clinical instructor. **ORGANIZATIONS:** Pharmacy coord & consult for Temple Univ Comprehensive Health Serv Prog; mem Nat Pharm Assn; mem Am Pharm Assn; mem Nat Pres; Chi Delta Mu Med Frat. **MILITARY SERVICE:** AUS 1943-46.

BROWN, LARRY
Professional athlete. **PERSONAL:** Born Jun 16, 1949, Jacksonville, FL; married Vanessa. **EDUCATION:** Univ of Ks, BS 1972; Howard Univ Dental Sch. **CAREER:** Pittsburgh Steelers, professional football player tight end. **HONORS/ACHIEVEMENTS:** Played in AFC Championship Game 1792-79; played in NFL Championship Game 1974-79.

BROWN, LAWRENCE, JR.
Athlete. **PERSONAL:** Born Sep 19, 1947, Clariton, PA. **EDUCATION:** Dodge City Comm Coll; KS State U. **CAREER:** WA Redskins, running back 1969-. **HONORS/ACHIEVEMENTS:** Led NFL in rushing yds w/1125 1970; in td scored W/14 1973; played Pro Bowl 1969-72; played NFL Chmpsp Game 1972. **BUSINESS ADDRESS:** Pittsburgh Steelers, 300 Stadium Cir, Pittsburgh, PA 15212.

BROWN, LAWRENCE E.
Business executive. **PERSONAL:** Born Jan 28, 1947. **EDUCATION:** Bryant Coll, BS 1969; Bentley Coll, Masters of Taxation 1979. **CAREER:** Peat Mawrick Mitchell & Co, supervising sr acctnt 1970-75; Lawrence E Brown CPA;s, owner/principal 1975-. **ORGA-**

NIZATIONS: Pres chmn bd dir S Providence Fed Credit Union 1971-; dir Bryant Coll Alumni Assn 1974-; treas Irreproachable Beneficial Assn 1976-; treas dir Accountants for Pub Interest of RI 1975-; treas dir RI Minority Bus Assn 1977-; city councilman Providence 1971-75; asst treas Providence Dem Com 1975-; mem RI Soc of CPA's & Amer Inst of CPA's; mem Phi Beta Sigma; bd dir Bannister House 1976-; mem RI Black Heritage Soc 1976-; co-chmn Natl Black Caucusof Local Elected Officials 1972-74; dir Oppty Indsln Ctr of RI 1970-74; dir Comm Workshops of RI Inc 1974-76; dir Headstart Adv Bd 1971-73; dir Challenge House Inc 1971-74; mem Urban League of RI; mem NAACP. **HONORS/ACHIEVEMENTS:** First Black CPA in RI 1972; 2nd Black City Councilman in Providence; S Providence Comm Serv Awd 1972. **MILITARY SERVICE:** USMC 1969-75. **BUSINESS ADDRESS:** Lawrence C Brown CPA's, 42 Weybosset St, 5th Floor, Providence, RI 02903.

BROWN, LAWRENCE M., SR.
Research chemist. **PERSONAL:** Born Oct 29, 1927, Boston; married Dorothy Morse; children: Lawrence, Jr, Catherine F. **EDUCATION:** Harvard Coll, BS 1948; Howard U, MS 1950; Cath Univ of Am, PhD 1964. **CAREER:** Mobil Research & Devel Co, sr research chemist 1964-; Nat Bur of Standards, physis chemist 1951-64; So Univ Baton Rouge LA, chemisty instr 1950-51. **ORGANIZATIONS:** Mem Am Phys Soc; am assn for Advancement of Sci.

BROWN, LEE PATRICK
Chief of police. **PERSONAL:** Born Oct 04, 1937, Wewoka, OK; son of Andrew Brown and Zelma (Edwards) Brown; married Yvonne C Streets, Jul 14, 1959; children: Patrick, Torri, Robyn, Jenna. **EDUCATION:** Fresno State Univ, BS 1960; San Jose State Univ, MS 1964; Univ of CA Berkeley, MCriminology 1968; DCriminology 1970. **CAREER:** San Jose CA, police officer 1960-68; Portland State Univ, prof 1968-72; Howard Univ, prof 1972-75; Multnomah Cty OR, sheriff 1975-76, dir of justice serv 1976-78; Atlanta GA, publ safety commiss 1978-82; Houston Police Dept, police chief 1982-. **ORGANIZATIONS:** VP Intl Assoc of Chiefs of Police 1984, Natl Org of Black Law Enforcement Exec 1984; mem Police Exec Rsch Forum, Harvard Univ Exec Session on the Police 1985, chmn Natl Minority Adv Council on Criminal Justice 1976-81; dir, Houston Rotary Club; NAACP; bd mem, The Forum Club of Houston; dir, Houston Boy Scouts of Amer; dir, Natl Black Child Devel Inst; dir, Houston Area Urban League; mem, Natl Advisory Commn on Criminal Justice Standards & Goals, Washington DC; mem, Natl Commn on Higher Educ for Police, Washington DC; chair, Natl Minority Council on Criminal Justice, Washington, DC; task force mem, Natl Center for Missing & Exploited Children; advisory bd, Natl Inst Against Prejudice & Violence; adjunct prof, Univ of Houston; adjunct prof, Univ of Texas Health Science Center at Houston; adjunct prof, Texas Southern Univ. **HONORS/ACHIEVEMENTS:** Honorary Doctorate FL Intl Univ 1982; Law Enforcement of the Year Awd Natl Black Police Officers Assoc 1982; Criminal Justice Professional Awd Natl Assoc of Blacks in Criminal Justice 1984; Hon Doct John Jay Coll of Criminal Justice 1985; Mgr of the Year Award, Natl Mgmt Assn, 1986; Communicator of the Year Award, Washington News Service, 1986; Robert Lamb Jr Humanitarian Award, Natl Org of Black Law Enforcement Execs, 1987; August Vollmer Award, Amer Soc of Criminology, 1988; Natl Public Service Award, Amer Soc for Public Admin & the Natl Acad of Public Admin, 1989; co-author of 2 books, editor of 3 books & author of numerous articles & book chapters. **BUSINESS ADDRESS:** Chief of Police, City of Houston Police Dept, 61 Riesner, Rm 330, Houston, TX 77002.

BROWN, LEO C., JR.
Clergyman. **PERSONAL:** Born Jul 17, 1942, Washington, DC; son of Leo Charles Brown Sr (deceased) and Mildred Vera Brown (deceased); married Barbara DeLespine; children: Cindy Fisher. **EDUCATION:** Seattle Comm Coll, Apprenticeship Cement Mason 1966-69; Tacoma Comm Coll, Bus & Psych 1972-73; Evergreen State Coll, BA 1974-77; Amer Bapt Sem of the West, MMA 1980-81; Hardy Theological Institute of Seattle WA, DD 1988. **CAREER:** Local 528 Cement Mason, cement mason 1964-72; True Vine Comm COGIC, pastor 1975-; Progress House Assoc, exec dir 1972-. **ORGANIZATIONS:** Pres Tacoma Ministerial Alliance 1982-; founder, pres True vine Multi-Serv Ctr 1979-; bd mem Family Broadcasting Station 1979-; vice pres United Brotherhood Fellowship 1977-; founder & pres True Vine Sr Citizen Ctr 1980-; co-founder, dir 1st Minority Christian Summer Camp 1965-; founder, dir Emmanuel Temple Prison Ministry McNeil Island WA 1968; vice pres Metro Devel Council 1973-75; chaplain Tacoma Fire Dept 1975-79; Taoma Urban Policy, bd mem 1979; Intl Halfway HouseAssoc; Amer Corrections Assoc, NAACP, Tacoma Urban League, Kiwanis Club, Prince Hall Masons, Acad of Criminal Justice Soc; bd mem United Way, Fellowship of Reconciliation A; mem Amer Correctional Assoc, Govs Public Safety Adv Group for State of WA; commissioner, State of Washington Housing Finance Commission 1985-. **HONORS/ACHIEVEMENTS:** Key to the City Mayors Office City of Tacoma 1977; Serv to Manking Awd Sertoma Club 1978; Nominee & runner-up for Rockefeller Found Humanity Awd 1979; Disting Citizens Awd Tacoma Urban League 1983; Newsmaker of Tomorrow Awd Time Mag 1983; Rev Leo C Brown Jr Day City of Tacoma Cty of Pierce & State of WA 1982; Disting Citizen Awd WA State Senate & Office of Lt Gov 1984; Doctor of Divinity, Hardy Theological Institute of Seattle 1988. **MILITARY SERVICE:** AUS sp4 1961-64. **BUSINESS ADDRESS:** Executive Dir, Progress House Assoc, PO Box 5373, Tacoma, WA 98405.

BROWN, LEROY
Assistant high school principal. **PERSONAL:** Born Dec 10, 1936, Buckner, AR; son of LeRoy Brown; married Dorothy Jean Hughey; children: Johnny Otis, Cinini Yvette, Titian Valencia, Leviano Regatte. **EDUCATION:** Univ of Ar Pine Bluff, BS Chem; E TX State U, MA. **CAREER:** Lewisville Sch Dist, middle sch prin 1978-; City of Buckner, mayor 1975-78; Lewisville Sch Dist, asst prin & math 1972-77; Lewisville Sch Dist, Foster HS prin 1970-71; Lewisville Sch Dist, Sci & Math tchr 1960-69; mayor & judge City of Buckner, 1975-78; alderman, City of Buckner, 1980-90; asst prin, math, Lewisville School Dist High School, 1983-90. **ORGANIZATIONS:** Mem Ar Educ Assn 1960-80; mem Nat Educ Assn 1970-80; vice pres Lafayette Co Alumni Assn 1977-80; mem St John Bapt Ch Buckner 1948-80; mem NAACP Buckner Hpt 1968-80; sr warden Rose of Sharon Lodge 1978-80. **HONORS/ACHIEVEMENTS:** Best School Award, Red River Vo-Tech School, 1981, 1982. **BUSINESS ADDRESS:** Lewisville Sch Dist, PO Box 550, Lewisville, AR 71845.

BROWN, LEROY BRADFORD
Physician. **PERSONAL:** Born Jun 05, 1929, Detroit, MI; married Ola Augusta Watkins; children: Leroy, Rene, Rita. **EDUCATION:** SC State Coll, BS 1954; Howard U, MD 1958. **CAREER:** Fresno County General Hospital, intern, 1958-59; Internal Med, resident, 1959-62; Prac Medicine, specializing in internal medicine, 1962-; Mercy Hospital, staff mem, 1962-; City of Sacramento, city physician, 1958-71; Medical Examiner, aviation, 1966-; UC Davis Medical School, clinic instr 1977. **ORGANIZATIONS:** Mem Am Ca & Sacramento Co Med Assns;am ca & sacramento co Socs Internal Med; dir Sacramento Co Heart Assn mem Notomas Union Sch Bd 1971-75; mem Ch ofGod. **BUSINESS ADDRESS:** 3031 G St, Sacramento, CA 95816.

BROWN, LEROY J. H.
Educator, architect. **PERSONAL:** Born Dec 14, 1912, Charleston, SC; married Angella. **EDUCATION:** Sc State Coll, BS; Howard U, BS; Cath U, MS. **CAREER:** Howard Univ & Propr Firm of Architects, Engineers & Planners in Washington, prof arch. **ORGANIZATIONS:** Mem Construction Specif Inst; Nat Tech Assn; Am Inst of Arch. **HONORS/ACHIEVEMENTS:** One of 11 black architects & engrs & contracted to survey bldgs for possible rehab in Washington & one of 7 black architects retained to make a preliminary study of the future campus of Fed City Coll Washington Office Am Inst of Architects. **BUSINESS ADDRESS:** 3310 Georgia Ave NW, Washington, DC 20010.

BROWN, LEROY RONALD
Educator. **PERSONAL:** Born Dec 18, 1949, Wadmalaw Island, SC; married Eva Elizabeth Choice; children: Tamyka M, Stephan L, Krystine V. **EDUCATION:** Benedict Coll, BS 1971; Univ of OK, EdM 1973; New York Univ, EdD 1982. **CAREER:** New York Univ, research assoc 1978-80; Denmark Tech Coll, dean of continuing educ 1980-82; Morristown Coll, exec vice pres & dean of coll 1982-83; Midlands Technical Coll, vice pres 1983-. **ORGANIZATIONS:** Mem AACD, NASDA, AAHE; sec of bd of dirs United Black Fund 1984-; mem bd of dirs Southern Region Council of Black Affairs 1985-; mem Columbia Comm Relations Council 1986; mem Leadership Columbia 1986. **HONORS/ACHIEVEMENTS:** Outstanding Young Men in America Jaycees 1976, 83; Presidential Citation NAFEO 1985; Citation Southern Council on Black Affairs 1985; Outstanding AdministratorMidlands Tech Coll 1985; listed in Who's Who in South and Southeast 1986. **HOME ADDRESS:** 225 Meadowlake Dr, Columbia, SC 29203. **BUSINESS ADDRESS:** VP Student Services, Midlands Technical College, 316 S Beltline Ave, Columbia, SC 29202.

BROWN, LEROY THOMAS
Educator. **PERSONAL:** Born Aug 08, 1922, Atlantic City, NJ. **EDUCATION:** SUNY, AA 1949; UCLA, BA 1954, MA 1957; Stanford Univ, PhD 1970. **CAREER:** Veterans Admin Hospital, med tech, 1954-65; UCLA, sr rsch tech, 1957-65; Pasadena High School, teacher, 1963-65; Foothill Jr Coll, instructor, 1965-67; SUNY, asst prof Anatomy, 1970-75; Univ WI Medical School, assoc prof Anatomy, 1975-82, asst dean, 1975-82; Univ WI Madison, asst vice chancellor, 1975-79; Drew Medical School, visiting prof, 1979-. **ORGANIZATIONS:** Mem NIH Scientific Prog Comm 1982-85; bd dir MARC Prog Drew Med School 1983-85; mem Amer Assoc of Anatomists 1970-85; officer communications US CoastGuard Aux 1984-85; vstg rsch fellow Univ WI 1969-70; guest scientists Brookhaven Natl Labs 1970-75, Univ WI Med School 1969-70; mem Soc Electron Microscopists 1971, SUNY Faculty Sub-com on Expanding Ed Oppty 1974-75; chmn SUNY Stony Brook Pres's Com on Equal Oppty; exec com Faculty Senate Partic 1stCong Black Profls in Higher Ed 1972. **MILITARY SERVICE:** AUS quartermaster 1942-44. **HOME ADDRESS:** PO Box 241951, Los Angeles, CA 90024. **BUSINESS ADDRESS:** Visiting Professor, Drew Medical School, 1621 E 120th St, Mail Point 27, Los Angeles, CA 90059.

BROWN, LESTER J.
Government official. **PERSONAL:** Born Aug 24, 0942, New York, NY; son of James Brown and Earlean Price Brown; divorced; children: Natalie Milligan, Omar A, Lesondra E. **EDUCATION:** Lincoln Univ, BA 1966; Attended, Fel's Inst of State & Local Govt 1969, State Univ of NY at Albany 1973, Antioch Coll New England Ctr, MEd Mgmt & Org 1978. **CAREER:** Philadelphia Model Cities Prog, manpower planner 1967-68; Philadelphia Sch Dist, teacher 1968-70; Schenectady Co Comm Coll, sr counselor 1970-76; New York State Div for Youth, prog mgmt specialist 1977-. **ORGANIZATIONS:** SMem economic develop & employment comm Broome Co Urban League; mem allocation panel Broome Co United Way; life mem Omega Psi Phi Frat Inc; mem Lincoln Univ Alumni Assoc; pres Price Brown Family Reunion Org; vice chmn, NYS Div for Youth Affirmative Action Adv Comm; Broome county NAACP. **HONORS/ACHIEVEMENTS:** District Service Omega Psi Phi Frat 1980-83. **HOME ADDRESS:** PO Box 2041, Binghamton, NY 13902. **BUSINESS ADDRESS:** Program Management Specialist, New York State for Youth, 164 Hawley St, Binghamton, NY 13901.

BROWN, LEWIS FRANK
Attorney. **PERSONAL:** Born Aug 04, 1929, Cleveland, MS; married Dorothy Jean Fitzerald; children: Lewis Gene, Orville Frank. **EDUCATION:** Vallejo Jr Coll, AA 1955; San Francisco State Univ, BA 1957; Lincoln Univ Law Sch, DJ 1964. **CAREER:** Vallejo Unified Sch Dist, educator 1957-64; CA Greenleigh Assn, asst dir 1964-65, dir 1965-66; Health Educ & Welfare, private consultant 1966-69; Member Amer Arbitration Assn, arbitrator 1972-; Brown & Bradley, att at law 1978-. **ORGANIZATIONS:** Elected Solano County Demo Central Committeeman 1959-66; Vallejo City Planning Commission 1963-65; Vallejo City Councilman 1965-69; Vallejo City Vice-Mayor 1967-69; golden heritage life mem NAACP; 173rd life mem NBA. **HONORS/ACHIEVEMENTS:** Dist Duvice Award Church of God in Christ 1982; Distinguished Record CA State Senate & Assembly Resolution Commending Lewis F Brown 1982; Civic Leader Award 1982; City of Vallejo Legal Commendation Award Dist Atty of Solano Cnty 1982; Resolution of Commendation, Jones County, Mississippi Board of Supervisors 1988; Resolution of Commendation, City Council of Laurel Mississippi 1988. **MILITARY SERVICE:** AUS pfc 1951-53. **BUSINESS ADDRESS:** Attorney, Brown & Bradley, 538 Georgia St, Vallejo, CA 94590.

BROWN, LINDA JENKINS
Government official. **PERSONAL:** Born Nov 08, 1946, Baltimore, MD; married Charles Edward Brown II; children: Charles Edward III. **EDUCATION:** Morgan State Univ, BS 1971; Univ of Baltimore, MPA 1980. **CAREER:** Baltimore County Bd of Educ, elem sch teacher 1971-73; Dept of Defense Ft Holabird MD, equal employ oppor specialist 1973-75; Federal Highway Administration, equal oppor spec 1975-78, regional compliance officer 1978-80, deputy chief int eeo div 1980-84, chief, intl eeo div 1984-, historically black colls and univs and univs coord 1985-. **ORGANIZATIONS:** Basileus Zeta Phi Beta Sor Inc Alpha Zeta Chap 1982-84; adv bd mem Natl Festival of Black Storytelling 1983-86; charter mem Assoc of Black Storytellers 1983-; mem NAACP 1983-; 2nd vice pres Howard Cornish Chap Morgan State Univ Alumni 1984-; adv bd mem US Office of Personnel Mgmt EEO Curriculum 1984-; presidential adv council mem Morgan State Univ 1985-; adv bd mem Atlanta Univ

Career Placement 1986-; asst boule marshall Zeta Phi Beta Sor Inc 1986-88. **HONORS/ACHIEVEMENTS:** Outstanding Women of Amer 1984; Outstanding Woman Awd Federally Employed Women 1984; Zeta of the Year Zeta Phi Beta Sor Inc Alpha Zeta Chap 1985; Secretary's Awd for Merit Achievement US Dept of Transportation 1985; Disting Alumni Awd Natl Assoc for EO in Higher Educ 1986. **HOME ADDRESS:** 2401 Poplar Dr, Baltimore, MD 21207. **BUSINESS ADDRESS:** Chief, Internal EEO Div, Federal Highway Administration, 400 7th St SW, Washington, DC 20590.

BROWN, LLEWELLYN DON
Consumer products executive. **PERSONAL:** Born Jul 15, 1945, Horatio, AR; son of Tommie L Brown and Snowie B Coulter-Brown; married Inez Waytt, May 04, 1968; children: Daria Akilah K, Ellynn Donisha, Dalila Jinelle. **EDUCATION:** Univ of Arkansas, Pine Bluff, AR, BS, 1966; Univ of Southwest Missouri, Springfield MO, 1971-72; Kutztown Univ, Kutztown PA, 1973-74; Univ of Penn, Philadelphia PA, 1987; Harvard Univ, Cambridge MA, 1987. **CAREER:** Howard County, Mineral Springs AR, instructor, 1966-68; State of Arkansas, Texarkana AR, job interviewer, 1968-69; Kraft Inc, Springfield MO, food technologist, 1971-72; Lehigh Valley, PA, gensupt, 1972-79; Glenview, IL, plant mgr, 1979-85, vice pres production operations & Technology, 1985-. **ORGANIZATIONS:** Mem, Amer Mgmt Assn, 1972; mem, Productivity Assn, 1975; mem, NAACP, 1978-84; mem, Urban League, 1978-84; head of Industrial Div, United Way, Dallas TX, 1984. **HONORS/ACHIEVEMENTS:** Outstanding Black Achievement, Chicago YMCA, 1982; Kraft Achievement Award, Kraft, Inc, 1982. **MILITARY SERVICE:** US Army, Spec 5, 1969-71, Commendation Medal-Vietnam Service. **BUSINESS ADDRESS:** Vice Pres Manufacturing, General Foods USA, 250 North Ave, White Plains, NY 10625.

BROWN, LLOYD
Social service director. **PERSONAL:** Born Jul 05, 1938, St Louis, MO; son of Charles W Brown Sr and Veldia B Sproling Brown Stinson; married Johnnie Mae Irvin; children: Marvin, Etoy, Rosalinda, Lloyd Jr, Donna, Tanya. **EDUCATION:** Forest Park Coll, AA 1974; Northeast MO State Univ, BS 1976. **CAREER:** Tandy Area Council, youth counselor 1974-76; Wellston School Dist, dep gen mgr 1976-81; Intl Revenue Svc, tax rep 1982-83; Human Devel Corp, branch mgr 1983-. **ORGANIZATIONS:** Community worker, VISTA (Volunteers in Service to America) 1972-74; mem Natl Assn of Housing & Redevel 1982-, MO Assn of Housing & Redevel 1982-; chmn Wellston Housing Bd of Commissioners 1982-, Wellston Land clearance for Redevel Bd of Commiss 1982-; vice president Wellston Bd of Ed 1983, 1986, 1989; mem MO State School Bd Assn 1983, Natl School Bd Assn 1983-. **HONORS/ACHIEVEMENTS:** Special Service Awd Mathew Dicky Boys Club 1968; Creator Writer & Performer The Messingers Inc 1969; Co-Founder Black Library of St Louis 1971; Student Service Awd Forest Park Coll 1972, 1973, 1974; Community Serv Awd Human Devel Corp 1972; Resolution-Outstanding School Board Member, Missouri State Legislature 1987; Youth Service Award, Providence Schools, St Louis, MO, 1985, 1986, 1987. **MILITARY SERVICE:** USAF airman 2nd class 1957-61. **HOME ADDRESS:** 6324 Ridge, Wellston, MO 63133.

BROWN, LLOYD ODOM, SR.
Judge. **PERSONAL:** Born Dec 12, 1928, Little Rock, AR; married Phyllis; children: Lloyd Jr, Raymond, Leslie. **EDUCATION:** OH State U, grad BA LLB JD 1955. **CAREER:** Cuyahoga Co Ct of Common Pleas Clevend OH, judge 1973; Cleveland Muncpl Ct, judge 1968-71; OH Sup Ct, assoc justice 1971-73; OH, asst atty gen 1958-59; Couyahoga Co, asst & prosecutor 1959-67; Cleveland, began law practice 1955. **ORGANIZATIONS:** Mem numerous professional & civic groups including Judicial Council of the Nat Bar Assn & Citizens League; area Chmn BSA; mgr Little League team; mem adv bd Cuyahoga Co Child Welfare; mem commn Public School Personnel Policies in OH. **MILITARY SERVICE:** USCG radioman 1946-49.

BROWN, LOUIS SYLVESTER
Mayor. **PERSONAL:** Born Oct 11, 1930, Navassa, NC; married Ruby Moore; children: Yvonne, Yvette, Roderick, Valorie. **EDUCATION:** Tyler Barber Coll, Barber 1959. **CAREER:** NAACP, bd of dir 1970-; Brunswick Cty Hosp, bd of dir 1975-81; Sencland, bd of dir 1978-85; Apri Inst, bd of dir 1979-; City of Wilmington, mayor. **ORGANIZATIONS:** Masonic Pride of Navassa Lodge 1965-85; noble Habid Temple 1970-85; v chmn Recreation bd 1975-. **MILITARY SERVICE:** AUS corpl 2 yrs. **HOME ADDRESS:** General Delivery, Navassa, NC 28404.

BROWN, MALCOLM MCCLEOD
Educator, artist. **PERSONAL:** Born Aug 19, 1931, Crozet, VA; son of Franklin Brown and Dorothy Brown; married Ernestine Turner, 1964; children: Malcolm, Jeffrey, Rhonda. **EDUCATION:** VA State Coll, BS 1956; Case Western Reserve Univ, MA 1969. **CAREER:** OH, internationally exhibited & acclaimed watercolorist; Shaker Heights Schools, art teacher, 1969-. **ORGANIZATIONS:** Mem Am Watercolor Soc; work shown museums & Colls throughout US under auspices AWS, Watercolor USA & Mainstreams Intl traveling exhibitions & represented numerous pvt collections; work viewed internationally through CA Watercolor Soc & Am Embassy, Nat exhibitions, Am Watercolor Soc, Nat Acad Design, Butter Inst Am Art, Watercolor USA, CA Watercolor Soc, Mainstreams Internat; Shaker Heights bd educ Evening Faculty Clev Inst Art; mem OH Watercolor Soc, NAACP, Urban League, Friends of Karama, Clev Museum Art, Nat Conf Artists, CA Watercolor Soc, Omega Psi Am Watercolor Soc 1973. **HONORS/ACHIEVEMENTS:** Larry Quackenbush Award 1980; Purchase Award Watercolor USA 1974; First Prize Watercolor VA Beach Boardwalk Show 1971-74; Second Prize Watercolor Canton Art Inst 1971; Henry O Tanner & Award Nat Exhbn Black Artists 1972; Award Excellence Mainstreams Intl 1970; award in Rocky Mt Nat Watermedia Exhib in Golden CO 1975; work featured Mag Art Review; Ohio Watercolor Soc Award, 1984, 1985. **MILITARY SERVICE:** First lt 1956-59. **BUSINESS ADDRESS:** Malcolm Brown Gallery, 20100 Chagrin Blvd, Shaker Heights, OH 44122.

BROWN, MARGERY WHEELER
Author and illustrator of children's books, retired educator. **PERSONAL:** Born in Durham, NC; daughter of John L Wheeler and Margaret Hervey Wheeler; married Richard E Brown, Dec 22, 1936 (deceased); children: Janice Brown Carden. **EDUCATION:** Spelman Coll, Atlanta, GA, BA, 1932; Ohio State Univ, special art student, 1932-34, 1935. **CAREER:** Hillside High School, Durham, NC, art instructor, 1934-35; Washington High, Atlanta, GA, art instructor, 1935-37; Spelman Coll, Atlanta, GA, art instructor, 1943-46; Newark Public School System, NJ, art instructor, 1948-74. **HONORS/ACHIEVEMENTS:** Author, illustrator, That Ruby, 1969, Animals Made by Me, 1970; author, The Second Stone, 1974, Yesterday I Climbed a Mountain, 1976, No Jon, No Jon, No!, 1981; illustrator, Old Crackfoot, 1965, I'm Glad I'm Me, 1971. **HOME ADDRESS:** 245 Reynolds Terrace, Apt C-1, Orange, NJ 07050.

BROWN, MARSHA J.
Physician. **PERSONAL:** Born Oct 27, 1949, Baltimore, MD; married Ray Brodie, Jr MD; children: Bradley Ray, Sean Elwooa. **EDUCATION:** Howard Univ, BS 1971; Univ of Maryland, MD 1975. **CAREER:** Mercy Hospital, internal medicine residency; Baltimore City Police Dept, physician; Private Practice, physician internal medicine. **ORGANIZATIONS:** Adv bd Central MD Comm Sickle Cell Anemia; bd of dir LM Carroll Home for the Aged, LM Carroll Nursing Home; Girl Scouts of Amer Teenage Pregnancy Task Force; medical consultant Glass & Assocs Mental Health, Baltimore City Police Dept; Baltimore City Civil Serv Commissioner 1982-; mem Bd Eligible Internal Medicine, Monumental City Medical Assocs, MD medical & faculty for the State of MD, Natl Medical Assoc, Baltimore City Chapter Links Inc, Alpha Kappa Alpha Sor. **HONORS/ACHIEVEMENTS:** Outstanding Young Women of Alpha Kappa Alpha Sorority 1980; Citizens Serv Recognition Award for Comm Serv 1986; Natl Assn Negro Women Humanitarian Award, 1986. **BUSINESS ADDRESS:** 844 N Carey St, Baltimore, MD 21217.

BROWN, MARSHALL CARSON
Retired educator. **PERSONAL:** Born Dec 13, 1918, Washington, DC; son of Frederick Brown and Louise Brown; married Clara Kersey Jackson (deceased); children: Clara Jones, Marshall Jr, Alice Joye. **EDUCATION:** VA State U, BS 1940; Columbia U, MA 1947; NY U, 6th yr Cert 1954-60. **CAREER:** Armstrong High Sch Richmond VA, tchr/coach 1942-49; VA Dept of Educ of all Black Sch, supr 1949-53; Plainfield High Sch NJ, tchr coach 1954-63; US Dept of State to Nigeria, track consult 1963-64; US Dept of State to Iraq, track consultant 1967; US Dept of State Sri Lanka, basketball consult 1967; US Dept of State Trinidad, track consult 1972; chmn coach of phy ed/track coach 1968-84. **ORGANIZATIONS:** Pres Plainfield NAACP 1967-69; chmn Labor & Industry Committee 1969-71; chmn Minorities Action Comm 1966-69; mem exec committee Am Comm on Africa 1968-. **HONORS/ACHIEVEMENTS:** Track Coach of the Yr NJ 1960; 5 book reviews for Freedomways 1978; 1st Black Track Coach in NJ High Sch & Coll 1954; 1st Black Teacher in Plainfield, NJ History 1954. **MILITARY SERVICE:** AUS sgt 1944-45. **HOME ADDRESS:** 1406 E Front St, Plainfield, NJ 07062.

BROWN, MARTHA HURSEY
Librarian. **PERSONAL:** Born in Bridgeton, NJ; children: Sally, Sherill, Saul T Jr. **EDUCATION:** State Tchrs Coll Glassboro NJ, BS 1949; Drexel Univ Philadelphia PA, MLS 1966; Carnegie-Mellon Pittsburgh PA, MA 1971, DA 1976. **CAREER:** Fisk & Norfolk Newspaper, public rel & journalism 1949-54; Bridgeton NJ, sch tchr/librarian 1954-67; Central MI U, history professor 1972-84; Langston U, dir of libraries 1984-. **ORGANIZATIONS:** Mem Human Rel Committee 1964-69; Am Friends Serv Comm; mem Personnel Committee Serv 1967-69; appointed NJ Civil Rights Commn 1968; organizer/pres Women's Civic League; publicity chrmn NAACP Bridgeton NJ 1962-67; mem usher bd Mt Zion AME Ch 1958-68. **HONORS/ACHIEVEMENTS:** Fellowship US Office of Educ 1969; fellowship Ford Found 1970; hon soc Phi Kappa Phi Carnegie-Mellon 1972; grants Summer Seminars NEH 1980-83. **HOME ADDRESS:** P O Box 127, Langston, OK 73050. **BUSINESS ADDRESS:** Dir of Libraries, LangstonUniv, Langston, OK 73050.

BROWN, MARVA Y.
Educational administrator. **PERSONAL:** Born Aug 25, 1936, Charleston, SC. **EDUCATION:** SC State Coll, BS bus adminstrn 1958; Univ of WA, MEd rehab couns 1970. **CAREER:** Servs for Handicapped Students Edmonds Community Coll, Lynwood WA, counselor, coordinator, 1971-; Poland Spring ME Job Corp Center, sr counselor, 1966-68; State of CT Walfare Dept/Health Dept, case worker/med & social worker, 1962-66; Park City Hospital, Bridgeport CT, asst bookkeeper, 1959-62; Berkley Training High School, Monks Corner SC, business educ instructor, 1958-59. **ORGANIZATIONS:** Mem NEA 1971; mem WA State Human Rights Commn 1977; mem Gov's Commn on Employment of the Handicapped 1977; mem Nat Assn Sex Educators & Couns 1975; mem Snohomish Co Alcoholic Commn 1978. **HONORS/ACHIEVEMENTS:** Del The White House Conf on Handicapped Individuals Wash DC 1977. **BUSINESS ADDRESS:** 20000 68th Avenue, Lynwood, WA 98036.

BROWN, MARY BOYKIN
Nurse instructor. **PERSONAL:** Born Feb 01, 1942, Sampson Cty, NC; married Franklin Der Brown; children: Franklin Jr, Franita Dawn. **EDUCATION:** Winston-Salem State Univ, BS Nursing 1963; Long Island Univ, MS Comm Mental Health 1978. **CAREER:** Long Island Jewish Med Ctr, instr inservice ed 1966-70; Harlem Hosp Ctr NY, instr school of nursing 1970-74; Midway Nursing Home, coord inservice ed 1974-75; Mary Gran Nursing Ctr Clinton NC, dir inservice ed 1975-76; Sampson Tech Coll Clinton NC, instr school of nursing 1976-. **ORGANIZATIONS:** Mem Amer Nurses Assoc 1964-, Natl League of Nursing 1964-, NC Nurses Assoc Dist 14 1976-, Council of Assoc Degree Nursing 1976-; teacher beginners classSt Stephen AME Zion Church 1976-84; chmn, sec Four Cty Med Ctr Bd of Dir 1981-85; police commiss Garland Town Bd 1983-; vice pres Browns Cleaners & Laundromat 1985-. **HONORS/ACHIEVEMENTS:** Outstanding Young Women Outstanding Young Women of Amer 1977; Most Outstanding 4-H Leader Sampson Cty 4-H Clinton NC 1977-78; Outstanding 4-H Volunteer NC Gov Raleigh NC 1980; Cert of Apprec Sampson Cty Voters League 1981. **HOME ADDRESS:** PO Box 296, Garland, NC 28441.

BROWN, MARY CATHERINE
Environmental administrator. **PERSONAL:** Born Oct 14, Vicksburg, MS; daughter of Elijah Brown and Macie Little Brown. **EDUCATION:** Tuskegee Inst, BS Social Science 1971, MEd Stu Personnel 1972; Jackson State Univ, MPA Public Policy & Admin 1982-85. **CAREER:** MS Employment Svcs, employment counselor 1972-73; Alabama A&M Univ, dir new women's residence hall 1973-74; Jackson State Univ, coord special serv 1974-82; Comm Housing Resources, dir 1982-84; Hinds Co Bd of Supervisors, comm and economic develop specialist; Special Project officer, Mississippi Bureau of Pollution Control 1989-. **ORGANIZATIONS:** Treas 1977-78, vice pres 1978-80 Jackson Urban League Guild; charter mem Vicksburg Chap Delta Sigma Theta Sor 1978; sec MS Assn of Educ Oppor Progs Personnel 1979-80; pres MS Caucus on Conseumerism 1979-81; treas Assn for Public Policy & Admin 1982-84; bd of dirs Jackson Urban League 1984-87; comm chairperson United Negro College Fund 1986; chmn of bd of directors, Jackson Community Housing and Resources Board,

1987-89. **HONORS/ACHIEVEMENTS:** Kappa Delta Pi & Phi Delta Kappa Honor Socs 1972; Cert of Appreciation Tampa Urban League 1978; Outstanding Serv Plaque Jackson State Univ Upward Bound Program 1980; Outstanding Serv Plaque Jackson State Univ Coronation Comm 1981; HUD Fellowship Jackson State Univ Dept Housing & Urban Develop 1982-84. **HOME ADDRESS:** 753 Wingfield St, Jackson, MS 39209.

BROWN, MARY ELIZABETH
Business executive. **PERSONAL:** Born Mar 07, 1932, Chicago, IL; married Floyd A; children: Keith, Diane. **EDUCATION:** St Francis Coll Joliet, RN 1954. **CAREER:** Quad Adv, co-owner; Quad Advt, pub relations advertising coordinator 1970-; Emergency Nurses Sherman Hosp Elgin IL, dir 1969; St Joseph Hosp Elgin, RN 1955;Sherman Hosp & PR Com, bd dir 1969; Cancer & Heart Fund City of Elgin, present chmn 1969; PTA Council, past pres 1970; Elgin Women's Club, pres 1974-76; Hemmens Civic Com Comm Facility, pub relations coordinator; Women's Symphony League, co-chmn benefit com fund raising. **ORGANIZATIONS:** Mem Easter Seal & Comm Chest 1979-. **HONORS/ACHIEVEMENTS:** Outstanding Solist for State of IL Chicago 1951; outstanding Woman of Elgin Altrusa Club of Elgin 1976; outstanding Woman in the Commerative Issue of Women inAdvertising 1978; 1st Place Award Winner Arden Shore Grand Prix Benefit Fashion Show 1978; listed "Who's Who in Am" 1980. **BUSINESS ADDRESS:** PO Box 804, Elgin, IL 60120.

BROWN, MARY LEE
Licensed practical nurse. **PERSONAL:** Born Oct 07, 1923, Powhatan, LA; married Frank E Sr; children: John Anthony, Donald, Ronah Marie, Marie Alice. **EDUCATION:** Caddo Parish Ksch of Nursing (honor student). **CAREER:** P & S Hosp, addictive diseases nurse 1980; Willis Knighten Hosp, emerg room nurse 1978; Schumpert Med Center, psychiatric nurse 1966-76; P & S Hosp, lpn 1959-66. **ORGANIZATIONS:** Juvenile couns Caddo Parish Juvenile Ct 1976; asst sec State of LA NAACP; mem LA State Conf/exec com/state bd NAACP; mem Steering Com for Equal Employment; sec NAACP; mem YMCA; mem Am Legion Aux 1978-; mem Council of Negro Women 1978-; organizer NAACP Youth Council of Shreveport LA 1979. **HONORS/ACHIEVEMENTS:** Comm Serv Awards NAACP Shreveport LA/NEW Orleans 1974 79; Effective Comm Orgn Diploma Nat NAACP Convention 1977; Comm Serv Award Nat CouncilNegro Women 1978.

BROWN, MATTIE R.
Business executive. **PERSONAL:** Born Nov 22, 1901, Gloster, MS; married Louis E Sr. **EDUCATION:** Alcorn A&M Coll, BS 1920; Merrill-Palmer Inst; Wayne State Univ; Hampton Inst; Tuskegee Inst. **CAREER:** Peter Pan Nursery of Detroit Inc, chmn bd dirs; Peter Pan Nursery, fonder first Detroit black nursery school non-profit & inst 1937. **ORGANIZATIONS:** Mem Detroit bd edn; Nat Youth Assn; field placements for students from Merrill-Palmer Inst, Wayne State U, Univ of MI, Oakland U, Wayne Co Comm Coll,Neighborhood Youth Corps; mem Detroit YWCA; alumni bd Merrill-Palmer Assn of Metro Detroit; child care coord Council of Wayne Co Inc; United Comm Svcsof Metro Detroit; MI Assn of Colored Women's Clubs; Sigma Gamma Rho Sor; Negro Coll Fund; NAACP; Nta Assn for Educ of Young Children; Day Care Child Devel Council of Am Inc; Detroit Metro Child Care Assn. **HONORS/ACHIEVEMENTS:** Intl Women's Com of Bicen Commn Recip Mother-Home-Child Award 1958; Greater Macedonia Bapt Ch Serv Award 1965; Merrill-Palmer Assn of Metro & Detroit Alumni Award of Merit 1971; Alcorn Agr & Mechanical Coll Merit Award 1971; Nat Pllice Ofcrs Assn of Am Appreciation Award 1973; Imperial Ct Daughtersof Isis PHA Human Rights Award 1973; Detroit Chap Jack & Jill of Am Inc Outstanding Contrib Award 1973; State of MI Hse Com on Youth Care Accolade ofTribute 1974; Hon Cit Award City of Highland Park 1973; Day Care & Child Devel Council of Am Quality in Child Care Award 1973. **HOME ADDRESS:** 6111 VanCourt, Detroit, MI 48210.

BROWN, MAXINE J. CHILDRESS
Elected official. **PERSONAL:** Born Aug 13, 1943, Washington, DC; married James E Brown; children: Scot, Nikki, Kimberly. **EDUCATION:** Springfield Coll, BS 1971; Univ of MA, MEd 1973. **CAREER:** Rochester Inst of Tech, asst prof 1973-74; State Coll Geneseo NY, asst prof, spec ed, dir learning disabilities 1975-78; People Helping People, dir 1978-80; City of Rochester Dept of Rec & Comm Svcs, dir of publ rel 1980-83; City of Rochester, councilwoman. **ORGANIZATIONS:** Natl cert interpreter for the deaf Amer Sign Lang 1970-85; vp, bd of dir Puerto Rican Youth Devel 1982-; mem adv bd, chmn ed comm NY State Div of Human Rights 1984-; mem & city council rep, adv bd Monroe Cty Office for the Aging 1984-; mem adv bd Ctr for Ed Devel; vp, bd of visitors State Ag & Indust School at Indust; mem bd of dir Prog for Rochester to Interest Students in Sci & Math; mem, former pres Metro Women's Network; chairperson Arts Reach Arts for Greater Rochester; bd of dir Rochester Area Multiple Sclerosis; mem Urban Ad Hoc Comm Home Econ Monroe Cty Coop Ext. **HONORS/ACHIEVEMENTS:** Nominated by Gov Carey & Approved by State Sen for Bd of Visitors State Ag & Indust School at Indust; 12 Publ including "About Time Mag", "Improving Police/Black Comm Relations", "A Not So Ordinary Man", "A Study Skills Program for the Hearing Impared Student" Volta Review Alexander Graham Bell Jrnl; Politician of the Year Eureka Lodge Awd 1984. **HOME ADDRESS:** 222 Chili Ave, Rochester, NY 14611. **BUSINESS ADDRESS:** City Councilwoman, City of Rochester, 30 Church St, Rochester, NY 14614.

BROWN, MILTON F.
Educator & administrator. **PERSONAL:** Born Apr 29, 1943, Rochester, NY; divorced; children: Damien. **EDUCATION:** SUNY Oswego, BS 1965; Columbia Univ Teachers Coll, MA 1973; EdD 1983. **CAREER:** Natl Inst of Ed, Educ Policy Fellow 1978-79; New York City Board of Ed, Asst Sup 1979-80; NY State Educ Dept, Dir 1980-82; NJ Dept of Higher Ed/Academic Affrs, Dir 1982-85. **ORGANIZATIONS:** Independent Consultant 1975-83; IUME Teachers Coll, Sr Research Assoc 1977-78; US Dept of Educ, Consultant 1975-83; vice pres Task Force on Youth Employment 1979-80; vice pres Mondale's Task Force on Youth Employment 1979-80. **HONORS/ACHIEVEMENTS:** George Wash Univ, Inst for Ed Leadership Ed Policy Fellow 1978-79; Teachers College Columbus Univ, Heft Fellow 1972-73. **MILITARY SERVICE:** USMCR, L/Corporal. **BUSINESS ADDRESS:** President, Malcolm X College (Chicago City College), 1900 West Van Buren, Chicago, IL 60612.

BROWN, MORGAN CORNELIUS
Sociologist, educational administrator. **PERSONAL:** Born Jul 26, 1916, Macon, GA; son of Morgan Cornelius Brown and Ida Moore Brown; married Anne L Boles; children: Morgan C III, Andrea E. **EDUCATION:** Paine Coll, BA 1937; OH State Univ, MA 1950, PhD 1954; Harvard Univ, post-doctoral research 1968-69. **CAREER:** So Univ, prof sociology 1954-60, chmn sociology dept 1960-68; Bridgewater State Coll, prof & chmn sociology dept 1969, dir & dean behavioral sciences div 1972-. **ORGANIZATIONS:** Mem NAACP; Urban League; Am Sociologists Assn; Eastern & MA Sociologists Assns; Alpha Kappa Delta; Pi Gamma Mu; Psi Chi; Alpha Phi Alpha; Christian Methodist Episcopal Church. **HONORS/ACHIEVEMENTS:** Research awards & grants NSF; Ford Found; Milton Fund; US Dept HEW. **MILITARY SERVICE:** AUS 1st Lt 1942-45; Bronze Star Award in Pisa, Italy 1945. **HOME ADDRESS:** 1462 Centre St, Newton, MA 02159.

BROWN, MORTIMER
Clinical psychologist. **PERSONAL:** Born Feb 20, 1924, NYC; married Marilyn Green; children: Frank, Mark. **EDUCATION:** Vanderbilt Univ, Nashville, PhD, 1961; City Coll of NY, BS, 1949. **CAREER:** IL Dept Mental Health, Springfield, IL, asst dir, 1961-69; FL State Univ, Tallahassee, prof, psychology, 1969-73; Florida Mental Health Inst, 1973-78; Independent Practice, 1978-present. **ORGANIZATIONS:** Various bd, comm, councils, Am Psychological Assn; Am Black Psychological Assn; bd, various Comm Southeastern Psychological Assn; bd & comm mem, Florida Psych Assn, pres, 1980, 1981. **HONORS/ACHIEVEMENTS:** DP, Bedford Univ, 1960. **MILITARY SERVICE:** USAF, 1942-46. **BUSINESS ADDRESS:** Univ Prof Center, 3500 E Fletcher, Tampa, FL 33612.

BROWN, NANCY COFIELD
Administrator. **PERSONAL:** Born Jul 25, 1932; married David; children: David, Stephen, Philip. **EDUCATION:** Pratt Inst, Grad 1954. **CAREER:** Trudy Rogers Co, asst designer 1955-57; Family & Child Svc, coord 1974-77; Town of Greenwich, dir comm dev 1978-. **ORGANIZATIONS:** Corp, dir CT Womens's Bk 1974-78; grants consult Town of Greenwich 1977; consult Affirmative Act Town of Greenwich 1977; dir Urban League of SW Fairfield CT 1970-74; mem Links-Fairfield CT 1980; trustee Stanford Found1980; mem CT Housing Fin Atuhority. **HONORS/ACHIEVEMENTS:** 10 outstndng women BRAVO Award; YMCA 1979. **BUSINESS ADDRESS:** Dir Community Development, Town Hall, 101 Field Pt Rd, Greenwich, CT 06830.

BROWN, NOAH, JR.
Educator. **PERSONAL:** Born Dec 05, 1925, Detroit, MI; married Velma; children: Diana, Sandra, Mrs Victoria Ramsey. **EDUCATION:** Wayne State U, SB 1949, MS 1952; Univ of MI, Educ Specialist 1970, Guidance & Counceling 1976. **CAREER:** Wayne State Univ, counselor to pres for ethnic relations, 1974-, vice pres student affairs, 1970-74, dir special projects & inner city relations, 1968-70; Detroit Bd of Educ, special educ teacher, 1949-68; Wayne State Univ, freshman basketball coach, 1957-66, Upward Bound, counselor, 1966-67, Higher Educ Opportunities Com, directing counselor, 1966-68. **ORGANIZATIONS:** Outreach Coll Recruitment Prgm of Talent Search; Kappa Alpha Psi Scholarship Prgm; Men Who Dare Scholarship Prgm; Varsity Club Scholarship Prgm; BrewstersOldtime Scholarship Prgm & Comm Activities for Sr Citizens & Youth; Youth for Understanding Prgm of Am 1969-71; Wayne Anthony Soc WSU; bd dirUniv of MIAlumni Assn; Detroit Tchrs Credit Union; mem, vice pres Detroit Counc of Polit Eldn; New Detroit Educ Com; Housing Com & Keep Detroit Clean Com; mem Plymouth Congregational Ch; Tabernacle Batp Ch. **HONORS/ACHIEVEMENTS:** Ldrshp & schlrshp Omicron Delta Kappa 1949; ldrshp in educ Phi Delta Kappa 1953; cert of com svc, Wayne State Univ 1967; cert of svc, Upward Bound, WayneState Univ 1968; Mackenzie Honor Soc 1969; Eductr of the Yr, Phi Delta Kappa 1971; Midwest 5th Regnl Serv Award for Trio Prgm 1976; Statewide Testimonial for Serv Rendered to Higher Educ & Com 1974. **MILITARY SERVICE:** AUS fld sgt 1944-49. **BUSINESS ADDRESS:** Detroit Board of Education, 5057 Woodward Ave, c/o Personnel Records, Detroit, MI 48202.

BROWN, NORMAN E.
Scientist, business executive. **PERSONAL:** Born Feb 20, 1935, Cleveland, OH; married Mary Lee Tyus; children: Karen, Dianne, Pamela, David, Robert. **EDUCATION:** Western Res Univ Cleveland OH, BA biology 1959; Univ of MN Minneapolis, MS biochem 1970. **CAREER:** Western Reserve Univ, rsch assoc 1957-64; Univ of MN, resch assoc; Hoffman-LaRoche Inc, asst sci II 1969-71, assoc sci 1971-73, mgr equal oppor 1973-78, asst dir equal oppor 1978-86; Tampa Bay Regional Planning Council, assoc housing planner 1986-. **ORGANIZATIONS:** Mem Edges Inc 1975-80; pres bd of trustees United Way Plainfield 1978-; vice pres bd of trustees United Way Union Co 1978-; pres 1984-85, mem Plainfield NJ School Bd 1982-85. **HONORS/ACHIEVEMENTS:** Black Achivers in Ind Award; YMCA Harlem Br; YNew York City 1974. **BUSINESS ADDRESS:** Associate Planner, Tampa Bay Regional Plng Cncl, 9455 Koger Blvd, St Petersburg, FL 33712.

BROWN, OLA M.
Educator. **PERSONAL:** Born Apr 07, 1941, Albany, GA. **EDUCATION:** Albany State Coll, BS 1961; Univ of GA, MEd 1972, EdS 1973, EdD 1974. **CAREER:** Thomas County Schools, Thomasville GA, teacher, 1961-67; Dougherty County Schools, Albany GA, teacher, 1967-71; Univ of GA Athens, grad asst, 1972-74; Valdosta State Coll GA, prof of educ 1974-. **ORGANIZATIONS:** Mem Phi Delta Kappa Educ Frat 1975-80; recording sec GA Council of Intl Reading Assn 1977-79; treas GA Assn of Higher Educ (GAE Affl) 1977-80; mem Amer Assn of Univ Prof 1977-80; vice pres 1979-80, pres 1980-81 GA Council of Intl Reading Assn. **HONORS/ACHIEVEMENTS:** Educ Instr of Yr Student GA Assn of Educ (VSC) 1975; WH Dennis Meml Awd Albany State Coll 1976; Ira E Aaron Reading Awd S Central GA Council of IRA 1977. **BUSINESS ADDRESS:** Professor of Education, Valdosta State College, Patterson St, Valdosta, GA 31601.

BROWN, OLIVIA
Actress. **CAREER:** Actress on Miami Vice. **BUSINESS ADDRESS:** c/o Light Company, 901 Bringham Ave, Los Angeles, CA 90049. *

BROWN, OTHA N., JR.
Educator, government official. **PERSONAL:** Born Jul 19, 1931, DeQueen, AR; daughter of Otha Brown and Elizabeth Gossitt; married L Evelyn Permenter; children: Darrick Othaniel, Leland Kendrick. **EDUCATION:** Central State Univ OH, BS (Cum Laude) 1952; OH State Univ Law School, 1955; Univ of CT, MA 1956; Univ of Bridgeport, Prof Diploma-Admin 1959; NY Univ, Cert Counseling 1965; Springfield Coll, Mass Cert Counseling 1966; Queens Coll NY, Cert in Counseling 1967; Boston Univ, Cert of Counseling 1969. **CAREER:** Wooster Jr HS Stratford CT, English & soc studies 1957-60; Rippowam HS Stamford CT, counselor 1961; City of Norwalk, city councilman 1963-69, 1977-81; CT Gen Assembly,

legislator 1966-72; 2nd Taxing Dist City of Norwalk, commissioner 1981-83, chmn 1982-; Fairfield Cablevision, vice pres; Biebel Travel Agency, vice pres; licensed notary, real estate broker; Stamford HS, counselor. **ORGANIZATIONS:** Regional dir Alpha Phi Alpha 1969-79; mem Amer Personnel & Guidance Assn, Amer School Counselors Assn, Natl & State Educ Assn, Phi Alpha Theta, Kappa Delta Pi; mem Dem Town Comm 1972-74; sec bd of trustees Univ of CT 1975-; founder & pres Norwalk Area Improvement League Inc 1978-; founder & pres Greater Norwalk Black Democratic Club & Coalition 1976-; pres & dep mayor Norwalk Comm Council 1980; bd dir, vice pres Fairfield Cablevision; founder & pres Southern CT United Black Fund 1983-; co-chmn Jesse Jackson for Pres Norwalk 1984; pres Connecticut State Federation of Black Democratic Clubs Inc 1972-76; State Task Force on Justice & the Courts, 1987-. **HONORS/ACHIEVEMENTS:** Man of the Year Alpha Phi Alpha 1969; Distinguished Serv Awd 1981; Past Pres Awd CT State Fed of Black Democrats 1979; Citizen of the Year Omega Psi Phi 1970; Young Man of the Year Jaycees 1967; NAACP Leadership Awd 1970; publications include "School Counselors, A New Role & Image" Connecticut Teacher Magazine 1972, Remembering: A Book of Poetry 1977, "Political Blackout" Connecticut Magazine 1979, "Fighting Apartheid UCONN Makes the Decision to Divest" The Stamford Advocate Viewpoint 1986, "Thoughts on Education" Sphinx Magazine, Vol 74 No 4, Alpha Phi Alpha Fraternity 1988; Politics & Service Award, Prince Hall Grand Chapter, Order of Eastern Star, State of Connecticut 1987; Official Citation, City of Hartford 1989. **MILITARY SERVICE:** AUS psychological warfare officer 1952-54. **HOME ADDRESS:** Shorefront Park, Norwalk, CT 06854.

BROWN, OTIS
Professional athlete. **PERSONAL:** Born Feb 03, 1960, Monroe, LA. **EDUCATION:** Jackson State, BS Finance. **CAREER:** Oakland Invaders, halfback 1984-. **HONORS/ACHIEVEMENTS:** Set club season records for kickoff returns (33) and kickoff return yardage (691).

BROWN, PAUL, JR.
Manager. **PERSONAL:** Born Oct 10, 1926, Chicago, IL; married Jean Pace. **CAREER:** Kicks & Co Chicago, mus lyrics & book writer 1961. **HONORS/ACHIEVEMENTS:** Appeared in Village Vanguard 1961; Apollo Theater 1961; Carnegie Hall 1962; Bule Angel 1962; Hungry I 1962; Crescendo 1962; Berns Stockholm 1963; & Waldorf Asteria 1963; Cool Elephand London Eng 1965; one-man shows Prince Charels Theater London 1963; Mus Box Theater Los Angeles 1964; Gramercy Arts Tehater New York City 1965; producer dir Joy '66, Happy Medium Theater; Summer in the City Harper Theater; Alley Theater; In de Beginin' 1977; composer Dat Der 1960; Brown Baby 1960; Work Song 1960; The Sanke 1963; Muffled Drums 1965; series host 13 Prog Pub TV Series "From Jumpstreet A Stroy of Black Music" WETA Wash DC; present mem Author's League Am. **BUSINESS ADDRESS:** Solid State Div, Route 202, Somerville, NJ 08876.

BROWN, PAUL D.
Business executive. **PERSONAL:** Born Feb 26, 1901, Cameron, TX; married Amalia O (deceased). **EDUCATION:** Paul Quinn Jr Coll, 1921-22; NY Bus Inst, 1939-40; Am Coll for Life Underwriters, Life Underwriters Ins Cert 1957. **CAREER:** Various insurance companies, life agt, asst dist mgr, dist mgr, state mgr, natl traveling supr, asst gen mgr, gen agt 1923-48; Paul D Brown, Inc, corporate pres & owner 1944-. **ORGANIZATIONS:** Mem Greater NY Ins Broker's Assn; Life Underwriter's Assn of Greater NY; Intl Assn of Health Underwriters; mem & past pres Allied Real Estate Bd Inc;mem Career Life Underwriter; life mem NAACP; bd of dir C of C of the Rockawrys; mem Lawrence-Cedarhurst Rep Club; Com on Civil Rights in Met NY Inc; Automobile Club of NY; Bethel AME Ch Far Rockaway; dir Inwood Prop Owner's Civic & Improvement Assn; past mem SCLC; mem Adv Bd of the NAREB Inc; bd of dir Negro Chamber Commerce Dallas; century mem & founder N Dallas Branch YMCA. **HONORS/ACHIEVEMENTS:** Red Cross Community Award Five Towns for fund raising 1957; Broker of the Year Allied Real Estate Bd Inc 1962; Comm Serv Award Allied Real Estate Bd & Ebony Oil Corp 1967; Recognition Award for 45 years input in Bus Natl Assn of Real Estate & NAACP 1972; Community Award for 74 years of membership AMECby BAMEC 1974; Community Award Allied Real Estate Bd Inc 1977. **BUSINESS ADDRESS:** Corporate President & Owner, Paul D Brown, Inc, 230 Lawrence Ave, Lawrence, NY 11559.

BROWN, PAUL E. X.
Business executive. **PERSONAL:** Born Dec 20, 1910, Weir, MS; married Verna. **EDUCATION:** Univ of MN, 1933; Columbia Coll, Moody Bible Inst, Attended. **CAREER:** Natl Assn of Market Devel Inc, exec dir 1985; Atlanta Coca-Cola Bottling Co, 1962-75; Radio WAOK, news public affairs dir, 1958-62; GA Edition, Pittsburgh Courier, ed, mgr; Radio Station WERD, program dir, announcer. **ORGANIZATIONS:** past pres, Atlanta Chapter, Natl Assn Market Devel; sr consultant, Triangle Assn, Inc chmn Adv Council; prince Hall mason Atlanta Emp Vol Merit Emp Assn; Shriner; Elk; Frontiers Int; Phi Beta Sigma; Imperial Dir; public relations Shriners; public Shriners Quarterly; radio nwscstr The Pyramid 1946; bd mem, George Washington Carver Boys Club; bd mem Goodwill Industries of Atlanta; Enterprises Now Inc; sec Pledging Found; past pres Adelphi Clb; mem DeLeg Assembly United Way; mem Task Force on Youth Motivation; NAB. **BUSINESS ADDRESS:** 201 Ashby St NW, Ste 306, Atlanta, GA 30314.

BROWN, PAUL L.
Educator. **PERSONAL:** Born Feb 18, 1919, Anderson, SC; married Lorene S Byron; children: Pauletta B, Gloria J, Nanola K. **EDUCATION:** Knoxville Coll, BS 1941, PhD 1955; Univ of IL, MS 1948. **CAREER:** Atlanta Univ, prof of Biology, 1978-; Clark Coll, dean of fac & instr, 1974-78; Natl Science Found, program mgr, 1974, 1963-64; Norfolk State Coll, chmn, natl science & math, 1958-74; FL A&M Univ, prof of Biology, 1958-59; Southern Univ, instructor of Biology, 1948-58; Atlanta Univ School of Arts & Science, dean 1982-. **ORGANIZATIONS:** Consult & sr prog Assoc Inst of Serv to Educ Soc of Sigma Xi; mem Beta Beta, Phi Sigma, Betta Kappa Chi, Phi Beta Sigma, Natl Inst of Sci, Am Zoologists, IL & VA Acad of Sci, Inst of Biol Sci, Am Micro Soc J Hay Whitney Flwshp, Am Med Assoc Flwshp. **HONORS/ACHIEVEMENTS:** Pub Am Midland Nat & other learned jrnls. **MILITARY SERVICE:** AUS european theater of oprtns 1942-45. **BUSINESS ADDRESS:** Dean, AtlantaUniv, 223 James P Brawley Dr, Atlanta, GA 30314.

BROWN, PHILIP ERSKINE
Educator. **PERSONAL:** Born Mar 26, 1949, Georgetown, SC. **EDUCATION:** Univ of Nantes France, attended 1970; Morehouse Coll, BA 1971; Univ of IL, MA 1972; Univ of MI, PhD 1983. **CAREER:** NY Times, natl desk, 1970-71; Dept of Housing & Urban Devel, public relations, 1971-72; Johnson Publishing Co, writer, 1976-78; Atlantic Records, writer, 1976-78; City Colleges of Chicago, educator 1972-. **ORGANIZATIONS:** Mem NAACP 1968-, IL Comm Colls Journalism Assoc 1971-; pres Skin & Bones Pro 1980-85; songwriter ASCAP 1981-; mem Intl Black Writers Conf 1982-; chiefexec PO Productions 1984-. **HONORS/ACHIEVEMENTS:** New Generation Prof Ebony magazine 1980; Fred Hampton Image Awd Fred Hampton Foundation 1982; Superior Public Serv Awd City Colls of Chicago 1984,85; Joseph Jefferson Awd Chicago Equity Theatre 1985; Outstanding Faculty Member Awd IL Comm Coll Trustee Assoc 1986. **BUSINESS ADDRESS:** Asst Prof of English, City Colleges of Chicago, Olive-Harvey College, 10001 So Woodlawn, Chicago, IL 60628.

BROWN, PHILIP RAYFIELD, III
Pastor, association executive. **PERSONAL:** Born Oct 07, 1917, New Orleans, LA; married Bertha Duckett; children: Philip IV, Eleanor Miller, Norma West, James. **EDUCATION:** Xavier U, BA; Union Theol Sem, MTH; United Theol Sem, DD. **CAREER:** New Orleans, US letter Carrier inspector; Pleasant Grove Bapt Ch, pastor 1948-59; Travelers Rest Bapt Ch, pastor 1959; Calvary Missionary Bapt Ch, pastor 1959-. **ORGANIZATIONS:** Exec dir Ouachita Multi-Purpose Comm Action Program 1966; pres Monroe NAACP 1961-63; pres La Sunday Sch Conv 1969-; instr Nat Sunday Sch Cong 1943-. **HONORS/ACHIEVEMENTS:** Highest City Award New Orleans 1957; Man of Yr Monroe 1970, 1974; Humanitarian of Yr 1972. **BUSINESS ADDRESS:** Calvary Miss Bapt Church, 201 South 9th St, West Monroe, LA 71291.

BROWN, RALPH H.
Administrative law judge. **PERSONAL:** Born Dec 13, 1919, Petersburg, VA; son of William H Brown and Lillian Brown; married Ollie M Brown; children: James A, Ralph K, Steven H, Leland M. **EDUCATION:** St. Augustine Coll; Franklin Univ Law, Capital Univ, Columbus, LLB, JD. **CAREER:** Postal clerk; pvt law practice OH; attorney; examiner PUCO OH; Bur Hearings & Appeals DHEW SSA, admin law judge. **ORGANIZATIONS:** Mem Alpha Phi Alpha Frat; mem St Phillips Episc Church; mem Columbus Civil Rights Assn; mem Amer, Natl Bar Assns; Robert B Ellist Law Club. **MILITARY SERVICE:** USAF 1943-46, 1962, 1968. **BUSINESS ADDRESS:** DHEW SSA, 50 W Broad St, Room 17, Columbus, OH 43215.

BROWN, RAYMOND MADISON
Business executive/construction group. **PERSONAL:** Born Jan 12, 1949, Ft Worth, TX; son of Raymond E Brown and Lutiel V Houston; married Linda, May 17, 1974; children: Derek, Christopher. **EDUCATION:** W TX St, BA 1971. **CAREER:** Life of GA, ins underwriter; Waldo Shirt Co, NY, sales rep; New Orleans Sts, professional 1977-; Atlanta Falcons, def sfty 1971-77; Real Estate Broker 1980-; Brown Boy II Properties Inc, constr co pres 1984-. **ORGANIZATIONS:** Mem Omega Psi Phi Frat. **HONORS/ACHIEVEMENTS:** Author of one novel. **BUSINESS ADDRESS:** President, Brown Boy II, Properties Inc, 133 Johnson Ferry Rd, Suite 111, Marietta, GA 30068.

BROWN, REGINALD ROYCE, SR.
Law enforcement officer. **PERSONAL:** Born Mar 18, 1946, Baton Rouge, LA; son of Walter J Brown Sr and Theresa M Bell; married Charlotte Ann Henderson, Feb 24, 1975; children: Reginald Jr, Tashera Patrice, D'Laniger Royce. **EDUCATION:** Southern Univ, NA, 1965. **CAREER:** 13th Amendment Band, pub relation dir & mgr; Governor's Office on Consumer Protection, program supr 1972-73; So Univ Baton Rouge LA, Centex dir 1972-75, asst to bus mgr 1973-; City Councilman Jospeh A Delpit, aide; Hon State & Sen of LA 1975; E Baton Rouge Sheriffs Office, admin asst, 1975-; Reginald Brown & Assocs Inc, pres, 1972-. **ORGANIZATIONS:** Honorary mem Baranco Clark YMCA; honorary mem NAACP; bd council of First Time Offenders; East Baton Rouge Civil Def Rescue Unit; spl dep of E Baton Rouge; mem LA Dem Assn; mem, Natl Sheriffs Assn, 1972-; mem, Natl Org of Black Law Enforcement Execs, 1983-; pres, Holiday Helpers of Baton Rouge Inc, 1987-. **HONORS/ACHIEVEMENTS:** Martin Luther King Award, Shady Grove Baptist Church, 1987; Honorary mayor Baton Rouge 1974; award Recognition for Outstanding Serv to SoUniv Student Body 1974; oustanding award for Contrib to SoUniv Marching Band 1974; award for Serv & Contbns to Sickle Cell Anemia Found & Retarded Childred Assn 1974; cmpgn coord 1st blk Woman Councilwoman in LA; letter of recognition from Pres of US on Drug Abuse; letter of recognition Honorabel Edwin W Edwards Gov of LA on Drug Abuse; letter of recognition Honorable W W Dumas Mayor of Baton Rouge on Duge Abuse; honorary colonel on Staff of Gov 1972; honorary dist atty 1973; awards for outstanding serv to Baranco Clark YMCA 1972; award of appreciation for serv & contbns to S Baton Rouge Neighborhood Serv Center 1971. **HOME ADDRESS:** Box 881, Baton Rouge, LA 70821.

BROWN, RICHARD
Educator. **PERSONAL:** Born Oct 24, 1927, Alexandria, LA; married Geralyn Simon. **EDUCATION:** Grambling St Univ Grambling LA, BS polt sci 1954; So Univ Baton Rouge, MA black hist 1970. **CAREER:** NAACP Lake Charles Branch, pres, 1979-; Calcasieu Parish School Bd, teacher, 1964-78, teacher & coach, 1954-64. **ORGANIZATIONS:** Pres & fndr DeQuincy LA Voter's League 1957-63; pres Gulf Asst-Prog 1974-78; pres Calcasieu Fed of Tchr & Cal Ed Assn 1977-78; 1st vice pres SW Sickle Cell Anemia Found 1978-; spoksmn for Civil Rights; NAACP 1954-; Mstr Mason; 32nd deg Mason & Shriner 1955-; mem Lk Charles Human Rel Cncl 1965-70; com mem Expl Div of Scouting BSA post 200 1976-78. **HONORS/ACHIEVEMENTS:** St bsktbl Coach of the Year 1962; Citizen of the Day; KLOU Radio Sta 1977; city of lake charles Cand for Mayor 1977; st of LA Del to St Dem Conv 1979-80. **MILITARY SERVICE:** AUS rec good conduct medal 1950-51; AUS sgt 1/c, 2 yrs srvd.

BROWN, RICHARD ALGER
Retired physician. **PERSONAL:** Born Nov 29, 1905, Steelton, PA; married Grace King Binford; children: Richard, Barbara Dunbar, Patricia Yancey. **EDUCATION:** Lincoln Univ, AB 1927; Howard Univ, MD 1932; Tufts Univ post-grad; NYU Med Sch; Albert Einstein Univ; Miami Med Sch. **CAREER:** Physician. **ORGANIZATIONS:** Mem Harrisburg Sch Bd 1949-67, vice pres 1961-67; past bd mem Dauphine Co Unit Am Cancer Soc; past mem Homemaker Serv Staff; mem Hgy Hosp; Emeritus advisory bd mem Douphin Deposit Bank & Trust Co; mem Central AL OIC Bd of Dir; co-founder Vitiligo Clinic of Harrisburg Hosp; charter fellow Am Ac Family Practice; mem Dauphine Co Med Soc; AMA; Nat Med Assn; mem E End Med Group; vice pres Harrisburg Sch Bldg Authority; bd mem Samuel L Abrams Scholarship; mem Rotary Club of Harrisburg; num other affiliations; 32 degree

Mason & Shriner; hon mem Frontier Intl Inc; Omega Psi Phi; trustee Wesley Union AME Zion Church.

BROWN, RICHARD EARL
Retired librarian. **PERSONAL:** Born Apr 01, 1922, Oakland, CA; son of John S Brown and Linnie M Coleman Richardson. **EDUCATION:** Univ of San Fran, BS 1960. **CAREER:** Oakland Public Lib, jr librarian 1951-60, sr librarian 1960-67; Berkeley Public Lib, dir of adult serv 1967-72, acting dir 1972-73, asst dir 1973-83, retired asst dir 1983-. **ORGANIZATIONS:** Dir of bd Oakland Municipal Civil Serv Assn; bd of dir Berkeley Municipal Credit Union 1973-81. **HOME ADDRESS:** 6363 Christie Ave, Emeryville, CA 94608.

BROWN, RICHARD JESS, SR.
Retired attorney. **PERSONAL:** Born Sep 02, 1912, Coffeeville, KS; married Jether Walker; children: Jacqualyn Roberts, Richard Jess Jr. **EDUCATION:** IL State Univ, BEd 1935; IN Univ, MS Ed 1943; LaSalle Univ, LLB 1948; TX So Law School, 1953. **CAREER:** Man Tr HS, educator; TX & Alcorn Coll, educator 1935-54; Brown, Alexander & Sanders, attorney; NAACP Legal Defense, coop atty. **ORGANIZATIONS:** Mem MS, Nat, Magnolia Bar Assns. **HONORS/ACHIEVEMENTS:** C Francis Straton Legal Defense Award; Nat Lawyers Guild Award; Elk's Award; NAACP Award; Phi-Beta Sigma Frat Award; Jackson State Univ Award; Jack HYoung Sr Award; Magnolia Bar Award. **HOME ADDRESS:** 5161 Gualt St, Jackson, MS 39209.

BROWN, RICHARD M.
City official, attorney. **PERSONAL:** Born Jun 20, 1940, Roanoke, VA; married Irene Spencer; children: Richard Jr, Kia Richelle. **EDUCATION:** Univ of San Francisco, BS 1962; Harvard Law Sch, JD 1968. **CAREER:** City of Hartford, cnclmn 1973-76; Aetna Life & Casualty Co Hartford, cnsl 1971-; Priv Prac, atty 1968-71; CT Bar Rev Course, lecturer 1969-70; Philadelphia DA Off, legal asst 1967; Subst Sch, tchr 1962-65. **ORGANIZATIONS:** Mem CT Bar Assn; Hartford Co Bar Assn; Am Bar Assn; Harvard Law Sch Assn; Ins Com of Hartford Co Bar Assn; co dir & pres ABA Joint Ins Subcom Hartford Econ Dev; Grtr Hartford Urban League 1974-; dir & bd chmn Ujima Inc 1973-74; commr Hartford Charter Revsn Commn; chmn Comm Serv Panel of United Way 1973; bd dir, various comm serv; Justice of Peace 1973-74. **BUSINESS ADDRESS:** Aetna Life & Casualty, Law Dept, 151 Farmington Ave, Hartford, CT 06115.

BROWN, RICHARD OSBORNE
Physician. **PERSONAL:** Born May 20, 1930, Detroit, MI; son of Richard Wells Brown and Flossie Eva Osborne Turner; married Martha Evelyn McGregor, Oct 06, 1973; children: Richard D, Kevin M, Vincent, Tiffany D. **EDUCATION:** Wayne U, BA 1953; Howard Univ Med Sch, MD 1959; Homer G Phillips Hosp, Ophth Residency 1962-65. **CAREER:** Ophthalmology, private prac 1967-; Southwest Detroit Hosp, active med staff; Samaritan Hlth Cntr, active med staff; Kirwood Gen Hosp, chief of staff 1974-76; New Center Hosp, active med staff; courtesy staff physician; courtesy med staff, Riverview Hospital 1987-. **ORGANIZATIONS:** Pres Detroit Med Soc 1978-80; pres Wolverine Med Soc 1982-; 2nd vice pres Natl Med Assn 1981-83, 1st vice pres 1983-85, bd of trustees 1985-; Alpha Phi Alpha Frat; life mem NAACP 1971. **MILITARY SERVICE:** AUS 1953-55. **BUSINESS ADDRESS:** 3800 Woodward 504, Detroit, MI 48201.

BROWN, ROBERT, JR.
Government official. **PERSONAL:** Born Mar 23, 1936, Lansing, MI; married Joy G Turnstll. **EDUCATION:** MI State Univ, BA social work 1958. **CAREER:** MI Dept of Corrections, parole officer 1962-67, dep warden 1967-70, dep dir 1970-84, dir 1984-. **ORGANIZATIONS:** Life mem Alpha Phi alpha 1955-, NAACP; exec bd mem Youth Devel Corp 1978-87; pres, life mem MI Correctional Assoc 1984; vice pres Midwest Assoc of Correctional Admin 1985-86; exec bd mem Chief Okemos Council Boy Scouts of Amer 1986-87. **HONORS/ACHIEVEMENTS:** Black Achievers Awd Phi Beta Sigma 1986. **MILITARY SERVICE:** USAF capt 1958-60,62. **BUSINESS ADDRESS:** Dir, MI Department of Corrections, Mason Building, PO Box 30003, Lansing, MI 48909.

BROWN, ROBERT CEPHAS, SR.
Master watch maker, diamond appraiser. **PERSONAL:** Born Dec 09, 1925, Meridian, MS; married Ranola Hubbard; children: Robert Cephas Jr, Ranola LaVohn, Michelle Lynette, Rochelle La Kaye. **EDUCATION:** Attended Van Slyke Sch of Horology (watchmaking); attended Gemological Inst of America. **CAREER:** Brown's Jewelers, owner/inventor/master watchmaker/ diamond appraiser 1950-. **ORGANIZATIONS:** Mem Downtown Merchant's Assn; vice pres Vallejo Revitilization Assn; mem Charter Review Com of Vallejo; mem NAACP. **MILITARY SERVICE:** AUS pfc 1944-46. **BUSINESS ADDRESS:** Brown's Jewelers, 316 Georgia St, Vallejo, CA 94590.

BROWN, ROBERT J., III
Educator. **PERSONAL:** Born May 31, 1919, Norfolk; married Blanche Randall; children: Jeanne, Catherine, Marcia. **EDUCATION:** Hampton Inst, BS 1939; Howard Univ, MS 1941, MS, MIT, MD, 1945. **CAREER:** Union Baystate Chemical Corp, chemist, 1943-46; Dept of Medicine, Howard Univ, asst prof, 1959-60; Veterans Benefits Office, medical officer, 1960-61; Howard Univ, fellow & Psychiatry, 1961-66; Howard Univ, asst prof, 1966; Clinical Operations Area B Community Mental Health Center, pres, asst dir, 1972-. **ORGANIZATIONS:** Pvt practice mem Am Psychiatric Assn 1966-; mem Med Soc Dist Columbia 1966-; mem Am Assn Advancement Sci Present Position DC Civil Servic. **HONORS/ACHIEVEMENTS:** Research Steric Hindrance & Enolization Acetylenic Precursors Vitamin A 1939-45; Theoretical Biology 1950; USNR LT JG MC 1955-56; LT 1956-57. **BUSINESS ADDRESS:** Acting Dir, Howard University Hospital, 2041 Georgia Ave NW, Washington, DC 20060.

BROWN, ROBERT JOE
Owner. **PERSONAL:** Born Feb 26, 1935, High Point, NC; married Sallie J Walker. **EDUCATION:** VA Union U, Attended; NC A&T St U, Attended. **CAREER:** B & C Intrntl Inc, chmn & pres 1979-; B & C Assoc, Inc, chmn & pres 1973-, fndr pres & chmn 1960-68; Minority Aff Pres of the US, spl asst1968-73; Harlem Freedom Assoc, prtnr 1967-; Fed Bur of Narcotics, agt 1958-60. **ORGANIZATIONS:** Bd of dir Oper PUSH Inc 1985; bd of dir MLK Cntr for Soc Change 1985; mem bd of dir Norfolk S Railway Co 1985; mem bd of dir Winston Mut Life Ins Co 1985; mem So Furniture Clb; life mem NAACP. **HONORS/ACHIEVEMENTS:** Dist Serv Award "Most Outstndng Man of the Year" High Pt NC C of C 1964; Most Outstanding Young Man in Am, Jr C of C 1965; achvmnt Award Natl Natl Dental Assn 1972; achvmnt award Nat Med Assn 1972; natl merit award Alpha Phi Alpha Frat 1972; natl exec br award OIC 1973; enabler's award Black Media Inc 1980. **BUSINESS ADDRESS:** B & C Asso Inc, 2033 M St NW, Washington, DC 20036.

BROWN, ROBERT LEE
Professional athlete. **PERSONAL:** Born May 21, 1960, Edenton, NC. **EDUCATION:** VA Tech, Phys Ed. **CAREER:** Green Bay Packers, defensive end 1982-. **HONORS/ACHIEVEMENTS:** All-South Independent 1st team choice; NEA & Coll & Prof Football Newsweekly 2nd team selection following sr season at VA Tech 1981; Voted VT's MVP; All-Amer Honors Chowan Jr Coll. **BUSINESS ADDRESS:** Green Bay Packers, 1265 Lombardi Ave, Green Bay, WI 54307.

BROWN, ROBERT LEE
Mayor. **PERSONAL:** Born Jul 31, 1947, Wetumpka, AL; son of Samuel Bernard Brown and Annie Pearl Moore Brown; married Donna Holland; children: Remington. **EDUCATION:** Central Connecticut State, Britain CT, BA Mathematics, Rutgers Law School, Newark NJ, JD. **CAREER:** Washington DC, counsel, 1973-76; Dept of Public Advocate, Newark NJ, asst deputy public defender; City of East Orange, corp counsel, 1980-81; Brown & Manns, Newark NJ, lawyer, 1981-83; Law Officers of Robert L Brown, Newark NJ, lawyer, 1984-; City of Orange NJ, mayor, 1984-; Comm on Judiciary, House of Rep, US Congress; Rutger's Univ, Newark NJ, mathematics instructor. **ORGANIZATIONS:** New Jersey Trial Lawyers Assn; New Jersey Bar Assn; Natl Criminal Defense; Amer Bar Assn; Criminal Trial Lawyers of New Jersey; Essex County Bar Assn; Roscoe Pound Found; NAACP; Omega Psi Phi. **HONORS/ACHIEVEMENTS:** Outstanding Contributions in Govt, Hillside Valley Presbyterian Church, 1988; Natl Trubute to Black Heritage, Prince Hall Grand Lodge Masons; Congratulations Award, Alif Muhammad Productions, 1988; Resolution of Congratulations, East Orange City Council, 1988; featured in Jet Magazine, Newark Star-Ledger, Orange Transcript, Greater News Perspectus. **BUSINESS ADDRESS:** Mayor, City of Orange Township, 29 N Day St, Orange, NJ 07050.

BROWN, ROBIN R.
Editor. **PERSONAL:** Born May 19, Pulaski, TN; married Betty. **EDUCATION:** Eastern MI Univ, attended; Univ of Louisville, attended. **CAREER:** WSPD-TV Storer Broadcasting Co, reporter, anchor 1969-72; KMOX-TV Columbia Broadcasting Syst, reporter, anchor 1972-73; WAVE-TV Orion Broadcasting, investigative reporter 1973-78; WDIA Radio Viacom Intl, dir news & publ affairs 1978-83; RKO Gen WHBQ-TV, assignments editor. **ORGANIZATIONS:** Past pres Memphis Black Arts Alliance 1983-84; v chmn Bd of Governors Memphis Health Ctr 1984-85; mem NAACP, Ctr for Southern Folklore, Natl Assoc of Black Journalists, KY Col. **HONORS/ACHIEVEMENTS:** Spec Awd Promoting Ethnic History Shelby County Historic Commiss 1981; Martin Luther King Awd Natl Assoc of Black Journalist 1982. **HOME ADDRESS:** 1867 Crump Cove, Memphis, TN 38107.

BROWN, RODERICK
Automotive engineer. **PERSONAL:** Born Apr 22, 1952, Newport News, VA; son of Robert Brown, Sr and Clara L Brown; divorced; children: Roderick F BRown. **EDUCATION:** Norfolk State Univ, BSEE 1975; Univ of MI, Grad Study in Elec Engineering 1984; Univ of Detroit, MEM, 1986, MBA, 1988. **CAREER:** NASA, rsch asst 1974; Atomic Energy Commn Fermi Natl Accelerator Lab, rsch asst 1974; Caterpillar Tractor Co, tech writer 1975, training instructor 1977; Caterpillar Tractor Co Field Serv Operations, asst to div mgr 1978; Caterpillar Tractor Co Serv Engineering Div, asst staff engr 1978; Ford Motor Co Product Develop Dept, prod develop engr 1979; Ford Motor Co Advanced Vehicle Pkg Control and Design Dept, product design engr 1983; Ford Motor Co Medium and Large Car FWD Design Engrg Dept, product design engr, 1985; Ford Motor Co Car Product Planning, product planning analyst, 1986. **ORGANIZATIONS:** Mem Phi Beta Sigma Fraternity Inc 1976-; speaker Local Career Programs 1976-; mem Natl Tech Assoc 1979-; mem Soc of Automotive Engrs Detroit 1980-, SAE Public Affairs Comm 1980-82, Natl Black MBA Assoc Detroit 1980-; speaker Detroit Area Pre-Coll Engrg Program 1980-; mem Engrg Soc of Detroit 1980-82; mem bd of trustees Metro Detroit Science and Engrg Coalition 1980-83; co-coordinator First Annual Detroit Technical and Business Career Conf 1980; financial coordinator 53rd Annual NTA Convention 1981. **HONORS/ACHIEVEMENTS:** Mem Beta Kappa Chi Natl Scientific Honor Soc 1975-; Outstanding Achievement Award Natl Technical Assoc 1986. **MILITARY SERVICE:** Army ROTC 1975-76. **HOME ADDRESS:** 22450 Lucerne Dr, Southfield, MI 48075.

BROWN, RODGER L., JR.
Real estate development. **PERSONAL:** Born Aug 15, 1955, Petersburg, VA. **EDUCATION:** Boston Coll, BA 1977; MIT, 1980-82. **CAREER:** IBM, marketing rep 1977-79; Sittler Assoc, consult 1979-80; United South End/Lower Roxbury Devel Corp, proj mgr 1980-83; Greater Boston Community Devel, proj mgr 1983-86; Cruz Devel Co, devel proj mgr 1986-. **ORGANIZATIONS:** Mem MA Minority Devel Assoc, Builder Assoc of Greater Boston, Citizens Housing & Planning Assoc, Jones Hill Civic Assoc 1986-. **HONORS/ACHIEVEMENTS:** US Dept of Housing & Urban Devel Minority Fellowship 1982-82. **BUSINESS ADDRESS:** Development Project Manager, Cruz Development Co, 1 John Elliott Square, Boston, MA 02119.

BROWN, RODNEY W.
Construction company executive. **CAREER:** Shelly's of Delaware Inc, Wilmington, DE, chief executive. **BUSINESS ADDRESS:** Chief Executive, Shelly's of Delaware Inc, 610 W Eighth, Wilmington, DE 19801. *

BROWN, ROLAND O.
Director. **PERSONAL:** Born Jun 28, 1929, Brazoria, TX. **EDUCATION:** Bishop Coll, BS 1950; Univ of So CA, MS 1957. **CAREER:** HISD, dir, hlth & phys edn, cntrl admin 1971-; Lockhart Elem, elem prin 1968-71; J Will Jones Elem, elem prin 1967-68; Doris Miller Elem, elem prin 1964-67. **ORGANIZATIONS:** Mem Am Alliance for Hlth Phys & Educ & Rec; TX Assn for Hlth Phys Educ & Rec; city & co dirs Health & Phys Edn; HPA; TSTA; NEA; mem adv bd BSA 1968-70; mem, bd dirs Houston Tennis Assn 1968-73; commnr SE Div of Youth Tennis League 1968-71; tchr Sunday Sch; exec dir Nat Jr Tennis League1971-73; Hiram Clarke Civic Clb; mem TX ALL Star Ftbl Team, Angel Bowl LA CA 1947. HON-

ORS/ACHIEVEMENTS: Recip JJ Sampson Award; cntrbtn to youth tennis Houston Tennis Assn 1971; citation, serv rendered Nat Alumni Fund Camp Bishop Coll 1972. **MILITARY SERVICE:** AUS pfc 1951-53. **BUSINESS ADDRESS:** Executive Dir, Houston I S D, 3830 Richmond, Houston, TX 77027.

BROWN, RON JAMES
Professional athlete. **PERSONAL:** Born Mar 03, 1961, Los Angeles, CA. **EDUCATION:** Attended, Arizona St. **CAREER:** L A Rams, wide receiver 1984-. **HONORS/ACHIEVEMENTS:** Won Medal in '84 Olympics as mem of US 4 X 100 Relay; Winner of annual Carroll Rosenbloom Awd as Ram Rookie of Yr; selected NAACP 1986 Sportsman of the Year by San Gabriel Valley Chap NAACP; AP, Pro Football Writers, NFL Alumni and Sporting News All-NFL as a kick returner 1985; mem 1986 NFL Pro Bowl team. **BUSINESS ADDRESS:** Los Angeles Rams, 2327 W Lincoln Ave, Anaheim, CA 92801.

BROWN, RONALD H.
Political party executive. **PERSONAL:** Born Aug 01, 1941, Washington, DC; son of William H Brown and Gloria Osborne Carter; married Alma Arrington, Aug 11, 1962; children: Michael, Tracey. **EDUCATION:** Middlebury Col, Middlebury VT, 1962; St. John's Univ School of Law, New York NY, 1970. **CAREER:** Natl Urban League, Washington DC, gen counsel, chief Washington spokesperson, deputy exec dir, vice pres Washington operations, 1968-79; US Senate Comm on Judiciary, Washington DC, chief counsel, 1980; Senator Edward Kennedy, Washington DC, gen counsel & staff dir, 1981; Patton, Boggs & Blow, Washington DC, partner, 1981—; Democratic Natl Comm, Washington DC chmn, 1989—. **ORGANIZATIONS:** Bar mem, US States Supreme Ct, State of NY, Dist of Columbia; mem, Standing Comm on Law and Electoral Process of the Amer Bar Assn; chmn, Sr. Advisory Comm. trustee, Univ of the Dist of Columbia, trustee, Middlebury Coll, Harvard Univ, John F Kennedy School of Govt, Inst of Politics. **HONORS/ACHIEVEMENTS:** JFK fellowship, Inst of Politics, Harvard Univ, 1980; Doctor of Laws, Hunter Coll, New York NY, 1989; Doctor of Public Serv, Rhode Island Coll, Providence RI, 1989; Doctor of Laws, St John's Univ, Jamaica NY, 1989. **MILITARY SERVICE:** US Army, captain, 1963-67. **BUSINESS ADDRESS:** Chmn, Democratic Natl Comm, 430 S Capitol St, SE, Washington, DC 20003.

BROWN, RONALD HARMON
Attorney. **PERSONAL:** Born Aug 01, 1941, Washington, DC; married Alma Arrington; children: Michael Arrington, Tracey Lyn. **EDUCATION:** Middlebury Coll, BA 1962; St John's Univ Sch of Law, JD 1970. **CAREER:** Natl Urban League, various positions 1968-78, vice pres for Washington Operations 1978-79; Kennedy for President, deputy campaign mgr 1979-80; US Senate Comm on the Judiciary, chief counsel 1980; Sen Edward Kennedy, genl coun & staff dir 1981; Democratic Natl Committee, dep chmn 1981-85 chmn, currently; Patton, Boggs & Blow, partner. **ORGANIZATIONS:** Dir Natl Environmental Controls 1982-; chmn bd dir Univ of the Dist of Columbia 1976-80 & 1983-; dir Community Found of Greater Wash; adv bd mem United Negro Coll Fund; dir Public Voice for Food & Health Policy; chmn Sr Adv Comm Institute of Politics John F Kennedy Sch of Govt Harvard Univ. **HONORS/ACHIEVEMENTS:** Fellow Inst of Politics John F Kennedy Sch of Govt at Harvard Univ 1980; recip Amer Jurisprudence Award Outstanding Achievement in Jurisprudence; Amer Jurisprudence Award for Outstanding Scholastic Achievement in Poverty Law. **MILITARY SERVICE:** AUS Capt served 4 years. **BUSINESS ADDRESS:** Chairman, Democratic National Committee, 430 S Capitol St, SE, Washington, DC 20003.

BROWN, RONALD PAUL
Educational administrator. **PERSONAL:** Born Mar 19, 1938, Ravenna, OH; married Joyce Anita Jones; children: Todd Mason, Lisa Kay, Paula Marie. **EDUCATION:** Univ of Akron, BS Hist & Govt 1967, MS Counseling & Guid 1969, PhD Counselor Educ 1974. **CAREER:** Univ of Akron, coord of dev serv & student adv 1969-74; Cuyahoga Co Bd of Mental Retardation, dir of habilitation serv 1974-80; Co of Summit, admin asst 1981-84; Kent State Univ, asst to the dean for minority & women affairs 1984-87; Kent State Univ Ashtabula Campus, asst dean and asst prof of counselor educ 1987-. **ORGANIZATIONS:** Mem Univ of Akron Alumni Council 1978-81; bd of trustees Cuyahoga Valley Mental Health 1982-84; Natl Cert Counselor Natl Bd for Certified Couns Inc 1984; bd of trustees St Paul AME Church 1978-; mem Alpha Phi Alpha Frat 1982-; bd of dirs Alpha Homes Inc 1982-; chap sec Natl Old Timers Inc 1984-87; treas Black Alumni Assoc 1987-; vice pres Comm Action Council Ashtabula OH; adv bd mem Ashtabula Salvation Army; dir Community Resource Economic Comm Ashtabula. **HONORS/ACHIEVEMENTS:** Chmn of the Educ Comm Eta Tau Lambda 1982-84; Outstanding Serv Awd Eta Tau Lambda 1983; "The Joys and Pain of Brotherhood: A Neophyte Expressed Himself" Alpha Newsletter 1983; chairman Univ of Akron's Black Alumni 1984. **MILITARY SERVICE:** AUS sp4 1961-63. **HOME ADDRESS:** 951 Kickapoo Ave, Akron, OH 44305. **BUSINESS ADDRESS:** Assistant Dean, Director of Continuing Studies, Asst Prof, Kent State Univ/Ashtabula Campus, 3325 West 13th St, Ashtabula, OH 44004.

BROWN, ROOSEVELT H., JR.
Professional football scout. **PERSONAL:** Born Oct 20, 1932, Charlottesville, VA; married Thelma. **EDUCATION:** Morgan St Coll, BS. **CAREER:** NY Giants, played with 13 yrs, coached offensive line 5 yrs, scout 1985, Mid-west & Big 10 Coll. **ORGANIZATIONS:** Mem Elks; Sholoh Lodge 1964-. **HONORS/ACHIEVEMENTS:** 8 times pro football all-pro Helms Hall of Fame; 10 times Pro-Bowl; Pro Football Hall of Fame. **BUSINESS ADDRESS:** New York Giants, Giants Stadium, East Rutherford, NJ 07073.

BROWN, ROSCOE C., JR.
Educator. **PERSONAL:** Born Mar 09, 1922, Washington, DC; divorced; children: Doris, Diane, Dennis, Donald. **EDUCATION:** Springfield Coll MA, BS; NY U, MA PhD. **ORGANIZATIONS:** Dir Inst of Afro-Am Affairs NYUniv Aurthor more than 50 articles on educ black studies, sports & phy fitness for various publs; host of weekly TV series "Black Arts" & a weekly radio series & "Soul of Reason"; co-host WCBS TV prog "Black Letters"; co-host WNBC TV A Black Perspective; co-editor Book "Negro Almanac" 1967; co-author "Classical Studies on Physical Activity" 1968; & "New Perspectives of Man in Action" 1969; co-author "Black Cultur Quib" 1971, 73. **HONORS/ACHIEVEMENTS:** Awards Emmy Citation 1973; distgd alumnus Springfield Coll 1973, NY Univ 1973; natl hon Am Alliance for Hlth PE & Rec; distgd flying cross & air medal USAF. **MILITARY SERVICE:** USAF 1943-45. **BUSINESS ADDRESS:** New York Univ, Washington Pl, New York, NY 10003.

BROWN, ROY HERSHEL
Educator. **PERSONAL:** Born Aug 02, 1924, Jamaica; married Lilly Berlinger; children: Geraldine, Lawrence, Christopher, Anthony, Andrew. **EDUCATION:** Fordham Coll, BS 1945-59; Univ Zurich Med Sch, MD 1950-56; NY Dip Med Lic, 1960; Dip Phys Med & Rehab, 1971. **CAREER:** Jamaica Hosp, dept of rehab med 1985; PM&R, diplomate, asst prof 1968-; Off of Voc Rehab, consult 1975-; Private Prac, 1960-66. **ORGANIZATIONS:** Mem, bd trustee The Barlow Sch; Suffolk Co Med Soc,; Nat Med Assn; Am Acad of Physical Med & Rehab; AAAS; NY Soc of PMYR; Am Geriatrics Soc. **HONORS/ACHIEVEMENTS:** Publ "Innovative Aspect of Stroke Prgm In Ghetto" 1971, "The Role of Med Sch in a Ghetto Population" 1971. **BUSINESS ADDRESS:** Sr Vice President, Total Health HMO, 1010 Northern Blvd, Great Neck, NY 11021.

BROWN, RUBY EDMONIA
Psychologist. **PERSONAL:** Born Sep 05, 1943, Pittsburghq, PA; married Ephriam Wolfolk Jr; children: Kenneth, Kevin, Keith. **EDUCATION:** Univ of CO, BA 1976-81; Univ of OR, MS 1981-82; Univ of OR, PhD 1982-87; Woodburn Comm Mental Health Ctr, Psych Intern 1985-86. **CAREER:** Pikes Peak Mental Health Ctr, mental health therapist 1976-81; Univ of OR, teaching asst, instr 1981-85; Woodburn Comm Mental Health Ctr, intern, psych 1985-. **ORGANIZATIONS:** Mem Phi Betta Kappa Hon Soc 1981-, Amer Psych Assoc 1984-; assoc mem Center for the Study of Women 1985-. **HONORS/ACHIEVEMENTS:** Minority Fellow Amer Psychological Assoc 1981-84; Grad Teaching Fellow Univ of OR 1981-85; Alumni & Friend Student of the Year Univ of CO 1981; Rsch Grant Center for the Study of Women Univ of OR 1987; Jane Grant Dissertation Fellowship Univ of OR 1987. **BUSINESS ADDRESS:** Psychologist, Woodburn Comm Mental Health, 3340 Woodburn Rd, Annandale, VA 22003.

BROWN, RUBYE G.
Educator. **PERSONAL:** Born Aug 20, 1923, Birmingham, AL; married Robert L; children: Gloria, Robin, Debbie, Carson. **EDUCATION:** Youngstown State Univ, Certificate, 1974. **CAREER:** Ft Leonard-Wood, dept head PX, 1959-60; Ft Leonard-Wood, substitute teacher, 1960-61; Renanos' Jewelry, 1st black credit mgr 1962-64; Mahoning Cty Church, dept treasurer, 1977; Princeton School, teacher, 1977; Youngstown Public School, Campbell School Syst-Catholic Diocese, substitute teacher. **ORGANIZATIONS:** 2nd vice pres trustee exec bd Internal Mgmt Project Review; bd trustee Educ Opportunity Youngstown; vice-chmn Consumer Protect Agency, mem NAACP; mem Urban League; past vice pres Comm Action Agy; mem Cavelle Club; mem bd dirs Negro Bus & Prof Club; bd mem State Health Dept OH 1980; com Planning & Devel State Health Dept; chr mem CAC; 1st black trustee Health Sys Agency E OH Valley; mem Nat Cncl of Negro Women; exec comm mem Dem party; precinct & committeewoman 5m; ran for mem Youngstown Bd Educ 1977; pres, Mahoning County Court-Watch; mem, police task force. **HONORS/ACHIEVEMENTS:** Only Black 19th dist del Pres Carter; Certificate for Community Involvement & Volunteer Work, Junior Civic League 1986; apptd by Gov Richard Celeste to State Health Bd of Columbus, OH 1986.

BROWN, SAMUEL FRANKLIN, JR.
Educational administrator. **PERSONAL:** Born Jun 19, 1921, New York, NY; married Mabel Nation Taylor; children: Samuel F III, Ronald Delano, Leigh Lani. **EDUCATION:** Shaw U, 1940-42; Eastman Sch of Music 1964; Univ of RI, 1965; Univ of MD European Div, 1966; Carthage Coll, 1970; St Martin's Coll, BA 1973. **CAREER:** HQ Tascom Band Europe, bandmaster, 1966-69; HQ 6th Army Symphonic Band, bandmaster, 1969-70; Republic of Vietnam Armed Forces Officers Band School, sr advisor, 1970-71; Am Infantry Div Band, bandmaster, 1971-72; Amer Assn of Minority Veterans Pgm Admin, dir region X, 1982-85; Nat Assn of Veterans Pgm Admin, dir region X 1984-85; Tacoma Community Coll, dir of veterans affairs. **ORGANIZATIONS:** Mem City Mayor's Veterans Task Force 1981-88; life mem NAACP 1983-; life mem Disabled Am Veterans DAV 1984-; mem Cassia Lodge No 5 F & A M 1948-85; mem Prince Hall Consistory No 67 1950-85; mem Beni Hassan Shriners Temple No 64 1951-85. **HONORS/ACHIEVEMENTS:** Medal d'Orleans City of Orleans, France 1969; Chairman's Award Am Assn of Min Vet Prog Admin 1983. **MILITARY SERVICE:** AUS chief warrant ofcr-4; legion of merit 1974; bronze star 1970; meritorious service medal 1969; army commendation medal 1959. **HOME ADDRESS:** 907 Manor Dr, Tacoma, WA 98466.

BROWN, SHARON MARJORIE REVELS
Media executive. **PERSONAL:** Born Sep 26, 1938, Detroit, MI. **EDUCATION:** Fisk U, 1953-57; Wayne State U, BA 1957-60; Coll of Edn, post-degree work 1960-61; MI Bd of Pub Instrn, Teaching Cert 1961; Wayne State U, 1966. **CAREER:** WXYZ-TV, comm rel dir 1974-; WKBD-TV, news & pub affairs sv 1972-74; Detroit Pub Sch Hutchins Jr HS, instr 1961-70;Univ of MI, resources Ctr Coord1970-71;Univ of MI, educ field consult 1969-70; Hutchins Jr HS, tchr coord 1964-65. **ORGANIZATIONS:** Bd dir Nat Cncl on Alcholism; mem Homes for Black Children; mem educ Com New Detroit Inc mem Urban Affairs Forum; mem Greater Detroit C of C; mem Keep Detroit Beautiful Com; mem Publicity Com United Negro Coll Fund; mem Women's Advertising Club; mem Am Women in Radio & TV; host "Ethnit-City"; chpn Publicity Com Afro-Am Mus of Detroit; publicity com Freedom Fund Dinner NAACP 1977; mem Alpha Epsilon Rho; mem MI Speech Assn; mem v Arious other professional orgns. **HONORS/ACHIEVEMENTS:** Frat sweetheart Kappa Alpha & Psi 1958-59; 3rd pl winner scholarship contest Miss Marracci Beauty-Talent Pageant Shriners.

BROWN, SHERMAN L.
Business executive. **PERSONAL:** Born Nov 18, 1943, Portland, OR; son of Bennie Brown (deceased); married Mable J; children: Sherman Jr, Stephen, Stanton. **EDUCATION:** BS, 1966; MSW, 1968. **CAREER:** St Elizabeth Hosp, psychiatric social worker 1966-67; Comm Action Agency, urban planner 1966-68; James Weldon Johnson Comm Ctr, prog dir 1968-70; Chase Manhattan Bank, vice pres 1970-80; MCAP Group Inc, pres. **ORGANIZATIONS:** Bd mem United Neighborhood Houses; bd mem Settlement Housing Fund; founder & bd mem Queens Youth Fedn NY; Bankers Urban Affairs Com, Kappa Alpha Psi Frat; chmn bd dir Neighborhood Housing Serv Jamaica Inc; bd mem S Jamaica Restoration Devel Corp; vice pres bd Bronx River Comm Ctr; bd mem Natl Scholarship Serv Fund for Negro Students; mem Univ S Civ Rights Comm; chmn bd Queens Urban League; bd mem NAHRO Washington DC; bd mem Natl Housing Conf Bd Washington DC; bd mem United Black Men of Queens Co; mem Natl Assn of Redevel Officials; chmn bd Queens Co Overall Econ Devel Corp. **HONORS/ACHIEVEMENTS:** 1973 Black Achiever in Indus Awd Harlem YMCA; Professional Serv Awd NY C of C 1973; instr in Urban Econ Amer Inst of Banking; lectr for Banks on Corporate Social Responsibility; lectr Medgar Evers Coll. **HOME AD-**

DRESS: 85-23 Edgerton Blvd, Jamaica, NY 11432. **BUSINESS ADDRESS:** President, MCAP Group Inc, 89-50 164th St, Ste 2B, Citibank Bldg, Jamaica, NY 11432.

BROWN, SHIRLEY ANN VINING
Educator. **PERSONAL:** Born May 17, 1936, Monroe, MI; daughter of Elmer Vining and Annie Vining; married Charles Lester; children: Caryn, Sandra, Garret. **EDUCATION:** Univ of MI, AB 1958, MSW 1969, MS 1972, PhD 1975. **CAREER:** MI Public Sch, teacher 1965; Ann Arbor Public Sch, social worker 1969-1970;Univ of MD, assoc prof 1975-; Nat'l Acad of Sci, proj dir 1986-87; Educational Testing Service, senior research scientist 1989-. **ORGANIZATIONS:** Proj dir Youth Enrichment Program Inc 1986; consultant Boysville of MI 1986. **HOME ADDRESS:** 5448 Newgrange Garth, Columbia, MD 21045.

BROWN, STANLEY DONOVAN
Elected official. **PERSONAL:** Born Feb 04, 1933, Washington, DC; married Helen Hampton; children: Kevin, Kimberly, Karla. **EDUCATION:** Southeastern Univ, BS, BA 1962; Amer Univ, Grad 1968. **CAREER:** Dept of the Army, supr, computer spec 32 years; Office of the Secretary of Defense, spec programs dir 1984-; Town of Glenarden, mayor. **ORGANIZATIONS:** Councilman Town of Glenarden 1967-73; chmn Glenarden Housing Authority 1974-75; councilman Town of Glenarden 1975-78, mayor 1983-. **HONORS/ACHIEVEMENTS:** Recognition of Civic Involvement MD House of Delegates 1978; Cert of Appreciation Boys Scouts of Amer 1980; Outstanding Loaned Exec CFC Dept of Army 1984, 11985; Citizen of the Year Omega Psi Phi Frat 1984. **MILITARY SERVICE:** USN quartermaster 2nd class 4 years; Korean Conflict Medal, Good Conduct Medal 1957. **HOME ADDRESS:** 7916 Grant Drive, Glenarden, MD 20706. **BUSINESS ADDRESS:** Mayor, Town of Glenarden, 8600 Glenarden Pkwy, Glenarden, MD 20706.

BROWN, STEPHEN H.
Educational administrator. **PERSONAL:** Born Aug 18, 1927, Chicago, IL; married Barbara Grand Pre; children: Stephen, Veronica, Mark, Eileen. **EDUCATION:** IL State Normal Univ, BS 1950; Loyola Univ, MEd 1955; Nova Univ, EdD 1975. **CAREER:** Chicago Bd of Ed, teacher 1950-64, asst principal 1964-66, coord dist human relations 1966-68, principal 1968-72, dist supt 1972-78, asst supt 1978-. **ORGANIZATIONS:** Mem Phi Delta Kappa, Amer Assn of School Admin, Natl Alliance of Black School Educators, Kappa Alpha Psi, Chicago Urban League, Assn for Supervision & Curriculum Devel, Chicago Alliance of Black School Ed, Oper PUSH; bd of dirs Chicago Access Corp. **HONORS/ACHIEVEMENTS:** Lamp of Learning Awd, Chatham Village Assn, Chicago Assn of Learning 1976; Man of the Year, Chicago Alumni; Educator of the Year, Phi Delta Kappa. **MILITARY SERVICE:** AUS sgt 1945-46. **BUSINESS ADDRESS:** Assistant Superintendent, Chicago Bd of Education, 1819 W Pershing Rd, Chicago, IL 60609.

BROWN, STEVE
Professional football player, actor. **PERSONAL:** Born May 20, 1960, Sacramento, CA. **EDUCATION:** Univ of OR. **CAREER:** Houston Oilers, professional football player (cornerback) 1983-. **ORGANIZATIONS:** Mem Screen Actors Guild. **HONORS/ACHIEVEMENTS:** Coll, returned kickoffs four yrs at Oregon; compl senior season with 70 tackles (collegiate best for season); Honorable Mention All-America by several publications; played in Hula Bowl following senior season; profl, streak of 25 consec starts; 47 solo and 18 assists for 65 total tackles; played in every game hisrookie season and recvd 10 starts; totaled 60 tackles (48 solos and 12 assists); had 81 yd return vs Tampa Bay in 1983; appeared in an episode of "Miami Vice". **BUSINESS ADDRESS:** Houston Oilers, Box 1516, Houston, TX 77001.

BROWN, THEOPHILE WALDORF
Clergyman. **PERSONAL:** Born Aug 24, 1925, Richmond, VA; son of Thomas Harvey Brown, Sr and Sarah Etta Taylor Brown. **EDUCATION:** St John's Univ, BA 1952; Univ of Ottawa, MA 1961; Sorbonne, Dipl me D'Etu des Fran aises; Institut Catholique, Paris, 1975; Middlebury Coll, MA French 1985. **CAREER:** St Augustine's, tchr 1956-71; St Augustine's, headmaster 1971-73; St Augustine's, head foreign language dept 1976-; St Augustine's Monastery, prior 1981-; St John's Abbey, benedictine monk & priest. **ORGANIZATIONS:** Asst principal Amer Inst for Foreign Study 1969-71; mem Classical League 1970-73. **HOME ADDRESS:** Box N3940, Nassau, Bahamas.

BROWN, THERESA F.
Retired business executive. **PERSONAL:** Born Oct 13, 1922, Baito, MD; married Roland V Brown. **EDUCATION:** Cortez Peters (Bus), 1940-42; Baltimore Comm Coll, 1954-56. **CAREER:** C&P Tele Co, bus office serv rep 1943-83. **ORGANIZATIONS:** Comm Adv Neighborhood Comm 1977; pres LeDroit Pk Preser Soc 1975-; dir Peoples Involvement 1977-; adv Natl Trust Historic Pres 1983-86; trustee United Planning Organ 1983-86.

BROWN, THOMAS EDISON, JR.
Fire chief. **PERSONAL:** Born Aug 22, 1952, Atlanta, GA; son of Thomas E Brown, Sr and Rosa Branham Brown; married Yolanda Smith, Sep 09, 1978; children: Brittany Joy. **EDUCATION:** DeKalb Community Coll, Clarkston, GA, Emergency Medical Serv, 1978, Fire Science, 1980; Brenau Professional Coll, Gainesville, GA. **CAREER:** Atlanta Fire Bureau, Atlanta, GA, deputy fire chief, 1972-85; DeKalb County Public Safety, Decatur, GA, fire chief, 1985-. **ORGANIZATIONS:** Intl Assn of Fire Chiefs, 1983-; Natl Fire Protection Assn, 1985-; Intl Assn of Black Professional Firefighters, 1986-; Natl Forum of Black Public Admin, 1986-; 100 Black Men of Atlanta, 1988-; South Decatur Kiwanis, 1988-. **HONORS/ACHIEVEMENTS:** Outstanding Alumnus, DeKalb Community Coll, 1986; Outstanding Serv Award, Toney Gardens Civic Assn, 1986. **BUSINESS ADDRESS:** Fire Chief, Deputy Dir of Public Safety, DeKalb County Public Safety, 4400 Memorial Dr Complex, Decatur, GA 30032.

BROWN, TILMON F.
Business vice president. **PERSONAL:** Born Jan 13, 1945, Buffalo, NY; married Jonnie R Kemp; children: Trina, Aaron, Melissa. **EDUCATION:** Univ of Buffalo, 1962-66. **CAREER:** Continental Baking, gen mgr 1974-77, regional sales mgr 1977-82, vice pres dir of sales 1982-83, regional vice pres 1983-. **ORGANIZATIONS:** Omega Psi Phi Frat 1964.

BROWN, TOMMIE FLORENCE
Educator. **PERSONAL:** Born Jun 25, 1934, Rome, GA. **EDUCATION:** Dillard Univ, BS(Cum Laude) 1957; Atlanta Univ School of Social Work, 1957; WA Univ St Louis, MSW 1964; Columbia Univ, DSW 1984. **CAREER:** TN Dept of Public Welfare, child welfare worker, 1957-64, case worker supvr/dir training, 1954-71; SOCW Univ of TN at Chatanooga, asst prof Sociology, 1971-73; Univ of TN Chattanooga, dir human serv, 1977-82; SOCW & Project Dir Univ of TN at Chatanooga, dept head, 1977-82; SOCW Univ of TN at Chatanooga, assoc prof 1982-. **ORGANIZATIONS:** Natl sec Natl Assoc Social Workers 1972-74; bd mem Chatta Psych Ctr 1982-, Chatta, Br NAACP 1964-; bd mem Chatta Model Cities Prog 1969-73; elected commiss Chatta/Hamilton Metro Charter; mem League of Women Voters 1968-70; steering comm mem Urban Forum 1980-81. **HONORS/ACHIEVEMENTS:** Woman of the Year Awd AKA Pi Omega Chap 1968-69; Social Worker of the Year SE TN Chap of Natl Assoc of Soc Workers 1970; Natl Social Worker of the Year Natl Assoc of Social Workers Inc 1970; Tommie Brown Day City of Chattanooga 1970; Disting Alumni Awd Washington Univ St Louis 1971. **BUSINESS ADDRESS:** Associate Professor Soc Work, Univ of Tennessee, Chattanooga, TN 37402.

BROWN, TONY (WILLIAM ANTHONY BROWN)
TV executive producer, educator, filmmaker, columnist, lecturer. **PERSONAL:** Born Apr 11, 1933, Charleston, WV; divorced. **EDUCATION:** Wayne State U, BA 1959; Wayne State U, MSW 1961; Univ of MI, LLD 1975. **CAREER:** Black Journal Nat Educ Tv, exec producer; The Detroit Courier, city Ed; Numerous Mag, pub & ed; Var TV Shows, host & moderator; Howard Univ Sch of Communications, first dean prof & founder; Howard U, communications Conf; Cntrl Wash State U, vis prof; Tony Brown Productions, founder/pres, 1977-; Tony Brown's Journal, exec producer/host, 1978-. **ORGANIZATIONS:** Founder/pres, Video Duplication Center, 1986; Founder/chmn, Buy Freedom Comm, 1985; Nat Assn of Black Media Producers; Nat Assn Of Black TV & Film Producers; bd of govnrs Nat Commnct Cncl; mem Adv Bd Nat Cncl for Black Studies; chmn of bd WHUR-FM radio 1971-74; bd mem Nat Cntr of Afro-AM Artists; Nat Black United Fund; mem Communications Com of Nat Inst of Mental Health; bd of dirs, Assn for the Study of Afro-Amer Life & History; bd of dirs, Natl Business League; bd of dirs, Harvard Found. **HONORS/ACHIEVEMENTS:** Living Legends In Black, 1976; Black Am Ref Book, 1976; Natl Urban League Pub Serv Award 1977;Intl Key Women Of Am Award 1977; 100 Most Influential Black Am Ebony Mag; Top 50 Nat Black & Newsmakers of Yr 1974; Natl Newspaper Pub Assn; Operation PUSH Communicator for Freedom Awd 1973; Frederick Douglass Liberation Award; Solomon Fuller Award, Amer Psychiatric Assn, 1989; Community Service Award, Black Psychologists, 1988; Special Image Award, Beverly Hills/Hollywood NAACP; producer/dir, The White Girl (motion picture), 1989. **MILITARY SERVICE:** US Army, corporal, 1953-55. **BUSINESS ADDRESS:** Pres, Tony Brown Productions Inc, 1501 Broadway, Suite 2014, New York, NY 10036.

BROWN, TONY
Professional athlete. **PERSONAL:** Born Jul 29, 1960, Chicago, IL. **EDUCATION:** AR Univ, 1982. **CAREER:** Indiana Pacers, guard/forward 1984; New Jersey Nets. **ORGANIZATIONS:** Invited to the Midwest Sumemr League. **BUSINESS ADDRESS:** Indiana Pacers, 300 E Market St, Market Square Arena, Indianapolis, IN 46204.

BROWN, TYRONE W.
Musician, composer, educator. **PERSONAL:** Born Feb 01, 1940, Philadelphia, PA. **EDUCATION:** Berklee Sch of Music, Certificate in Arranging & Composition. **CAREER:** Pep's Show Bar, house bassist 1964-69; History of Jazz Lecture & Concert Tours, staff bassist 1968-71; Audi Prodns TV Commercial Prodns & Louisvle, staff bassist 1970-72; Il State U, instr for jazz 1971; Brigham Young U, instr for jazz 1972; Bellermine Coll, instr for jazz 1975; Model Cities Cultural Arts Program, taught composition, advanced harmony & theory, improvisation & bass 1972-74. **ORGANIZATIONS:** Aptd dir Music Dept Model Cities Cultural Arts Program 1974; owner publ Nirvana Music Co; formerly with Grover Washington Jr,Catalyst,Billy Paul, Lou Rawls,Pat Martino, Sonny Fortune,Johnny Coles and Johnny Hartman Currently touring and recording with Max Roach. **HONORS/ACHIEVEMENTS:** 16 recorded albums; 2 gold albums; placed first Fred Miles Publ of Musicians Poll 1974;22 Albums to date.

BROWN, VERNON E.
Business executive. **PERSONAL:** Born Jun 15, 1943, Merced, CA; married Shirley; children: Sara, Kim. **EDUCATION:** BA, Bus & Econ 1973. **CAREER:** R & B, booked shows 1963; Golden State Mutual Life Ins Co, agt; Emmy Ins Agy; Continental Assurance Co, gen agt; Copley News Service, newspaper columnist. **ORGANIZATIONS:** Pres Am News Svc, World-wide Syndicate, 1975; pres Flain Co; Samson Fi Am Comm Property Devel, Inc; pres Vernon E Brown Mgmt & Consult Ltd; past mem Co Tax Assessment Tax Appeal Bd;pres, past treas, co-founder So Ca Minister Vanguard; nominee for congress 35th Cong Dist 1972. **HONORS/ACHIEVEMENTS:** Authored Constitutional Amendment Tax Relief On Dwellings-Retired & Disabled Owners 1974; appointed first black gen agt in Amby a major life ins co 1969. **BUSINESS ADDRESS:** P O Box 8865, Los Angeles, CA 90008.

BROWN, VIRGIL E., JR.
Business executive. **EDUCATION:** Case Inst of Tech, BS Physics 1968; Cleveland State Univ, JD-cum laude 1974. **CAREER:** Gen Elec, engr; Cleveland Growth Assn, consultant; Cleveland Business League, chairman. **ORGANIZATIONS:** Commissioner Ohio's Minority Financing Board. **BUSINESS ADDRESS:** Chairman, Cleveland Business League, 2136 Noble Rd, The Brown Bldg, Cleveland Heights, OH 44112.

BROWN, WALTER E.
Business executive. **PERSONAL:** Born Mar 04, 1931, St Thomas, Virgin Islands of the United States;son of Arthur Brown and Geraldine James Brown; married Cheryl Ann Johnson, Dec 31, 1985; children: Jason Walter. **EDUCATION:** CCNY, BBA 1958, MBA 1961; NY Univ, MPA 1972; Union Grad Sch OH, PhD 1978. **CAREER:** Shriro Inc NY, admin asst 1956-58; Dept of Health Govt of VI St Croix, admin 1962-71; NENA Comprehensive Health Serv Ctr; NY Univ HEOP, 1980-83; Hunter Coll School of Health Sciences CUNY, adjunct asst prof. **ORGANIZATIONS:** Lecturer Coll of VI St Croix Campus 1967-69, Univ of Cincinnati Community Health Prog 1973, Columbia Univ Sch of Continuing Educ 1973-75; mem Natl Assn of Health Serv Exec; mem Amer Pub Health Assn; Speaker of the House of Del Natl Assn of Neighborhood Health Ctrs 1972-74; pres Natl Assn of Neighborhood Health Ctrs 1974-75; pres Natl Assn of Neighborhood Health Ctr, 1975-76; pres Public Health Assn of NYC 1986-87; editorial consultant Journal of Public Health Policy; mem Com-

mittee on Ambulatory Care Amer Hospital Assn 1972-74; hon trustee NY Infirmary Beekman Downtown Hospital NY 1980. **HONORS/ACHIEVEMENTS:** 1st Morris De Castro Fellow Govt of VI St Thomas 1970; Certificate of Appreciation for Outstanding Contribution to & Promotion of Community Health Metro Boston Consumer Health Council Inc 1975; Past Pres Awd Natl Assn of Neighborhood Health Centers Inc 1976 past Aes Award; Public Health Assn of New York City, 1988. **MILITARY SERVICE:** AUS sgt e-5 1956-58. **BUSINESS ADDRESS:** Pres, WEBCO Assoc, 48 Candlewood Path, Huntington Station, NY 11746.

BROWN, WARREN ALOYSIUS
Journalist. **PERSONAL:** Born Jan 17, 1948, New Orleans, LA; married Maryanne; children: Tony, Binta Niambi, Kafi Drexel. **EDUCATION:** Xavier Univ of LA, BA 1969; Columbia Univ of New York, MSJ 1970. **CAREER:** Washington Post, natl labor writer 1976; Philadelphia Inquirer, city reporter/state rep 1972-76; Jet Magazine, assoc editor/educ & politics 1971-72; New Orleans States-Item, city reporter 1970-71; New York Times, natl news desk aide 1969-70; Garden City, Long Island NY, intern reporter 1969. **ORGANIZATIONS:** Regular panelist Am Black Forum 1979; mem XavierUniv Alumni Assn 1969. **HONORS/ACHIEVEMENTS:** Katharine Drexel Award Xavier Univ of LA 1969; NY Times Fellow NY Times 1969-70; LA/MS AP Award LA/MS Asso Press 1971; Duke Univ Fellow Wash Post 1978. **BUSINESS ADDRESS:** The Washington Post, 1150 15th St, NW, Washington, DC 20071.

BROWN, WARREN HENRY
Educator. **PERSONAL:** Born Jul 29, 1905, Jackson, TN; married Mattie. **EDUCATION:** Univ of WI, 1928; NY U, BS 1935;New Sch of Social Research, PHD 1941. **CAREER:** Amer Assn of State Coll & Univ, consultant, 1974-78; Graduate Faculty Bowie State Coll, prof of urban affairs, 1972-75; Dept of Sociology, Catholic Univ of Amer, adjunct assoc prof, 1971-72; US Govt Counselor of Cultural Affairs, foreign serv officer, 1960-70; City Coll of NY Univ, asst prof, 1947-60; Amer Univ at Cairo Egypt, fulbright prof, 1955-56; Broadcast Music Inc NYC, research consult 1956-57; UNESCO Mission to Syria, diplomat 1957-58. **ORGANIZATIONS:** Mem Mayor's Com on Puerto Rican Affairs New York City 1949-53; bd of dir Am Civil Liberties Union 1949-60; del Welfare & Health Council of New York City 1950-55. **HONORS/ACHIEVEMENTS:** Research grant Martha Chamberlin Found 1954; dist serv award Yale 1 1962; commendation for social serv Ministry of Health Guatemala 1963; meritorious medalof honor Dept of State US Govt 1965.

BROWN, WEBSTER CLAY
Physician/surgeon. **PERSONAL:** Born May 06, 1923, Marshall, TX; married June Elizabeth Borders; children: Lance, Lisa, Linda. **EDUCATION:** Wiley Coll, BS (Magna Cum Laude) 1942; Meharry Dental Sch, DDS 1945; Meharry Medical Sch, MD 1950. **CAREER:** Coney Island Hosp, intern 1950-51; Meharry Medical Sch, surgical resident 1951-54, instructor in surgery 1956-57; Emanuel, Good Samaritan, Providence Hospitals Portland OR, attending surgical staff 1957-86; Univ of OR Med Sch, instructor in surgery 1958-70; Private Practice, physician. **ORGANIZATIONS:** Attended Orient Medical Seminar in Tokyo Japan and Hong Kong 1971, African Medical Seminar in Rabat Morocco and Nairobi Kenya 1972, South Pacific Medical Seminar in Papeatee Tahiti, Sydney Australia and Auckland New Zealand 1984; mem, exec comm Urban League of Portland; mem Urban League; fellow and mem AMA, OMA, NMA, MCMS, FICS, FASAS, MWSS, FPAM 1957-; life mem NAACP; mem Kappa Pi and Kappa Sigma Pi Medical and Dental Socs. **HONORS/ACHIEVEMENTS:** First black to be appointed chief of surgery at any US military hosp 1954-7520 USAF Hospital London England. **MILITARY SERVICE:** USAF capt 1954-56; Chief of Surgery 7520th USAF Hospital London England. **HOME ADDRESS:** 8330 N Chautauqua Blvd, Portland, OR 97217.

BROWN, WESLEY ANTHONY
Navy civil engineer corps (retired). **PERSONAL:** Born Apr 03, 1927, Baltimore, MD; son of William Brown and Rosetta Shepherd Brown; married Crystal M; children: Willetta West, Carol Jackson, Wesley Jr, Gary. **EDUCATION:** US Naval Acad, BSME 1949; Rensselaer Polytechnic Inst, MCE 1951. **CAREER:** Navy Civil Engr Corps Officer, public works officer-in-charge of construction 1949-69; NY State Univ Construction Fund, project mgr 1969-74; NY State Dorm Authority, project mgr 1974-76; Howard Univ Office of Univ Planning, facilities master planner 1976-. **ORGANIZATIONS:** Chmn/CEO Natl Business Consultants Inc 1984-; alumni trustee US Naval Acad 1986-; life mem Alpha Phi Alpha Frat, Naval Acad Alumni Assoc, Assoc for the Study of Negro Life and History; mem Naval Inst, Navy League, Sigma Pi Phi Frat. **HONORS/ACHIEVEMENTS:** "The First Negro Graduate of Annapolis Tells His Story" Saturday Evening Post 1949; article "Eleven Men of West Point" Negro History Bulletin. **MILITARY SERVICE:** USN lt commander 20 yrs; Antarctic Service, Amer Theatre, Korean Serv World War II Victory, Sec of the Navy Commendation for Achievement Medal 1949-69. **HOME ADDRESS:** 6101 16th St NW #805, Washington, DC 20011.

BROWN, WILLARD L.
Attorney. **PERSONAL:** Born Jun 09, 1911, Boston; married Juanita. **EDUCATION:** WV State Coll, BA 1932; Boston U, JD 1935, LLM 1936. **CAREER:** Pvt Practice, atty; Pub Serv Commn State of WV, adminstr law judge; NAACP, state legal adv 1941; Elks, state legal adv 1949; City of Charleston, councilman 1947-54; Grand Lodge, Prince Hall Masons, past grand counselor 1958-66. **ORGANIZATIONS:** Past potentate of Shriners, Charleston; past mem Charleston Human Relations Commn; past basileus Gamma Chap Boston, Omega Psi Phi; past basileus Xi Alpha Chap Charleston, Omega Psi Phi; past mem State Adv B D Dept of Employment Security; pres Charleston Br NAACP 1950-66; mem Charleston Bus & Professional Mem's Club; coordinator Civil Rights Conf 1964. **HONORS/ACHIEVEMENTS:** Recipient TG Nutter Civil Rights Award, 1970; citizen of year Omega Psi Phi 1950; citation Women's Improvement League 1954; Omega Man of Year 1961. **BUSINESS ADDRESS:** 426 Shrewsbury at Lewis St, Ste 201 Brown Bldg, Charleston, WV.

BROWN, WILLIAM, JR.
Physician, surgeon. **PERSONAL:** Born Feb 05, 1935, New Haven; married Sarah Robinson; children: Kirsten, Kecia, Kollette, Karlton. **EDUCATION:** Univ CT, BA 1957; Howard Univ Coll Med, MD 1961. **CAREER:** Prvt prac; DC Ge Hosp, internship 1961-62; Crownsville Stae Mental Hosp, resident psychiatry 1962-63; Dept Family Prac & Howard U, asst clinical prof 1972. **ORGANIZATIONS:** Chi Delt Mu 1960; DC Med Soc; Beta Sigma Gamma; natl bd Nat Med Assn 1965; diplomate of am bd Of Family Practice 1971-. **MILITARY SERVICE:** AUS capt 1963-65. **BUSINESS ADDRESS:** 1210 Mapleview, Washington, DC 20020.

BROWN, WILLIAM ANTHONY See BROWN, TONY

BROWN, WILLIAM CRAWFORD
Educator. **PERSONAL:** Born Jun 03, 1925, Ruthville, VA; married Dr Jessie Lemon. **EDUCATION:** Hampton Inst, BS 1950; New York Univ, MA 1952, EdD 1960; William & Mary Coll, Postgraduate courses, Marketing & Admin. **CAREER:** DuPont, 1945-47; Hampton Inst, 1947-50; Baltimore Public Schools, 1951-52; Newport News VA Public Schools, 1952-55; Hampton Univ, 1955-65; Prairie View Univ, 1965-66; Hampton Univ, prof of mktg 1966-. **ORGANIZATIONS:** Grad sch prof (part-time) George Washington Univ; dir Project STEP Celanese Corp 1967-74; dir Small Business Ctr Hampton Univ 1973-78; consultant Peninsula Chamber of Commerce, Mayor's Comm on Consumerism, Natl Business League, Southern and Amer Mktg Assoc; life mem NAACP; mem Alpha Phi Alpha, Sigma PiPhi (Boule); mem Hampton Heritage Foundation; bd of dir Hampton Univ Credit Union, Amer Mktg Assoc, Common Cause, Natl Business League, Kiwanis Clubs of Amer. **HONORS/ACHIEVEMENTS:** Distinguished Scholarship Award, New York Univ 1962; mem Kappa Delta Pi, Phi Delta Kappa, Phi Beta Lambda; IBM Summer Internship Award 1978; Lindback Distinguished Teaching Award, Hampton Univ 1986. **MILITARY SERVICE:** AUS Airforce Engrs sgt 1943-45. **BUSINESS ADDRESS:** Professor of Marketing, Hampton University, Box 6444, Hampton, VA 23668.

BROWN, WILLIAM CREWS
Educational administrator. **PERSONAL:** Born Feb 28, 1920, Greenwood, SC; married Margaret Elizabeth Curry. **EDUCATION:** Allen U, BS 1942, LLD 1979; NY U, MA 1947, EdD 1960. **CAREER:** Higher Educ Opportunity, dir Inst Present; Fayetteville State Univ, vice chancellor acad affairs/prof of Educ, 1973-75; Higher Educ Opportunity, assoc dir, instructor, 1972; Barber-Scotia Coll, interim pres, 1971-72, dean of coll, 1967-71; SC State Coll, assoc prof/ prof & chmn dept of Health & Physical Educ, 1950-67. **ORGANIZATIONS:** Consult acad affairs United Negro Coll Fund 1971; mem educ adv com, US Mdl Dist Ct Macon GA 1973; mem natl adv com Inst for Socio-Tech Problems Jackson St Univ 1980; cons, state Agcys for Higher Educ Mem bd of control Allen Univ Columbia SC 1960-80; state dir Fellowsh For the Am Sch Health Assn 1960-67; mem exec com Charlotte Area Educ Consortium 1969-72; mem bd of & dirs United Serv Fund Fyttvl 1974-75; mem adv council Project Read DeKalb Co GA1977; mem adv com Allied Health Professions Spl Project Grant for Minority Recruitment & Retention 1977; chmn bd of trustees DeKalb Co Library System 1978. **HONORS/ACHIEVEMENTS:** Recipient of Am Serv Medal/EAME Serv Medal/ Good Conduct Medal/3 Bronze Stars/WWII Victory Medal AUS; Fellow Am Sch Health Assn 1961; Who's Who in Am Educ 1965-66; Community Leaders of Am 1968; Leaders in Educ 1971; Personalities of the South 1972; cert of appreciation Bd of Co Commrs of Cumberland Co NC1975; presidential Citation Nat Assn for Equal Opportunity in Higher Educ 1979. **MILITARY SERVICE:** AUS staff sgt 1943-45. **BUSINESS ADDRESS:** Southern Regional Education Bo, 130 6th St NW, Atlanta, GA 30313.

BROWN, WILLIAM F.
Dentist. **PERSONAL:** Born Jan 10, 1900, Lauderdale, MI; married Mary Douge Freeland (dec) (deceased). **EDUCATION:** Howard U, BS Lib Arts 1924, DDSColl of Dentistry 1929. **CAREER:** Priv Prac, dentist 1932-80 (retired). **ORGANIZATIONS:** Life mem Third Dist Dental Soc; State of NY Dental Soc; Am Dental Assn Mem, Alpha Phi Plpha Frat, Inc; Adv Com of Albany NY on Urban Rnwl; temporary & state commn on Cap City; 1st pres Albany NY branch NAACP 1932-34. **HONORS/ACHIEVEMENTS:** Selec Serv Bd Recip, Omicron Kappa Upsilon Nat Dental Hon Soc, 1952; cit Albany Inter-Racial Council 1973; cit Plaque Cit of Yr, Omega Psi Phi Frat 1975; Albany NAACP recognition awd 1985.

BROWN, WILLIAM H.
Educational administrator. **PERSONAL:** Born Oct 20, 1935, Washington, DC; married Dolores L Arthur; children: DeNaye D. **EDUCATION:** Morgan State U, BS 1957; Springfield Coll, MS 1958; Catholic U, PhD 1976. **CAREER:** Cardozo High School, asst prin, 1968-69; Washington DC Public Schools, coord youth serv, 1969-71; Spingarn High School, prin, 1971-77; Washington DC Public Schools, asst supt, 1977-. **ORGANIZATIONS:** Notary public Washington, DC 1976-; mem Am Soc of Notaries; mem Nat Alliance of Black Sch Educators 1982-; mem Nat Assn of Secondary Sch Prin 1970-;life mem DC Parent Tchr Assn; mem NAACP; vice pres Capital Children's Museum; cnslr Neighborhood Youth Corps 1967. **HONORS/ACHIEVEMENTS:** Mem Omega Psi Phi; vice pres Phi Delta Kappa AmUniv Chpt; mem Hall of Fame Morgan StateUniv Baltimore 1976; mem Hall of Fame Cardozo High Sch Washington DC 1978; listed in Who's Who in Washington DC. **MILITARY SERVICE:** AUS 1958-62. **BUSINESS ADDRESS:** Assistant Superintendent, DC Public Sch, 45th & Lee Streets, NE, Washington, DC 20019.

BROWN, WILLIAM H.
Educator. **PERSONAL:** Born Aug 09, 1929, Newark, NJ; married Rosetta; children: Geraldine, Michael. **EDUCATION:** Winston-Salem State U, BS 1953; Seton Hall U, MA. **CAREER:** Head Start Program, teacher, elementary school head teacher; Title I Project Coordinator; Dir of Community Relations; Newark Public Schools, admin asst; Newark State Coll of Elementry Schools & Curriculum & Independent Study of Educ, instructor; Newark Bd of Educ, asst supt in charge of elementry educ. **ORGANIZATIONS:** Mem 5 mem Nat Adv Bd Harcourt Brace Co; mem Omega Psi Phi Frat; former mem First Negotiating Team Nat Alliance of Black Sch Educators; Am Assn ofSch Adminstr; NJ Educ Assn Testimonial Dinner, Newark 1973; mem Selective Serv Draft Bd. **HONORS/ACHIEVEMENTS:** Recipient of numerous awards & plaques for serv to comm; Morton St Sch Named Lab "The William H Brown Reading Lab". **MILITARY SERVICE:** AUS spl svcs. **BUSINESS ADDRESS:** Asstistant Superintendent, Newark Board of Educ, 2 Cedar St, Newark, NJ 07101.

BROWN, WILLIAM H., III
Attorney. **PERSONAL:** Born Jan 19, 1928, Philadelphia, PA; son of William H Brown Jr and Ethel L Washington Brown; married D June Hairston, Jul 29, 1975; children: Michele Denise, Jeanne Marie. **EDUCATION:** Temple Univ, BS, 1952; Univ of PA Law School, JD, 1955. **CAREER:** Schnader, Harrison, Segal & Lewis, partner, attorney; Norris, Brown & Hall, partner, 1964-68; Norris, Green, Harris & Brown, partner, 1962-64; Norris, Schmidt,

Green, Harris & Higginbotham, assoc, 1956-62; EEOC, chmn, 1969-73; EEOC, commr, 1968-69; Deputy Dist Attorney, Dist Attorney, 1968; Dist Attorney Office, chief of frauds, 1968; chmn, Philadelphia Special Investigation Commn, 1985-86. **ORGANIZATIONS:** bd of dir, United Parcel Serv, 1983-; mem, Regional Bd of Dir, First PA Banking & Trust Co, 1968-73; bd dir, mem exec comm, Lawyers Comm for Civil Rights Under Law; founding mem, World Assn of Lawyers; permanent mem, 3rd Cir Judicial Conference; mem, Alpha Phi Alpha; Philadelphia, Am Fed & PA Bar Assn; Am Trial Lawyers Assn; Am Arbitration Assn; Am Law Inst; Nat Bar Assn; Inter-Am Bar Assn; mem, Commn on Higher Educ, Middle States Assn of Coll; mem, Natl Sr Citizen's Law Center; faculty mem, Natl Inst Trial Advocacy, 1980-present; faculty mem, Practicing Law Inst, 1970-85; pres, mem, bd of dir, Natl Black Child Devel Inst, 1986-present; mem, bd of dir, Community Legal Services; bd of dir, NAACP Legal Defense & Educ Fund. **HONORS/ACHIEVEMENTS:** Secondary School Award of Recognition, Alpha Phi Alpha, 1969; Handbook of Modern Personnel Admin, 1972; author of numerous articles; Philadelphia NAACP President's Award; Recipient, World War II Victory Medal. **MILITARY SERVICE:** USAF, 1946-48. **BUSINESS ADDRESS:** Attorney at Law, Partner, Schnader Harrison Segal Lewis, 1600 Market St Ste 3600, Philadelphia, PA 19103.

BROWN, WILLIAM J.
Business executive. **PERSONAL:** Born May 17, 1917, Harrisburg, PA; widowed; children: Natalie, Andrea. **EDUCATION:** BA 1942; MA 1953. **CAREER:** Talladega Coll, dean of mem 1947; William A Hunton Br YMCA, exec sec 1951; Detroit Urban League, vocational serv asst 1956; S Bend Urban League, exec dir 1961; Hartford & TTT Prog, dir 1970; Urban League of Greater Hartford, exec dir 1964-69 &71. **ORGANIZATIONS:** Mem bd dir Jr Achievement; bd dir CT Econ Edn; Greater Hartford Council of Chi; mem Dept Comm Affairs Adv Council; Univ of CT Health Ctr AdY Bd; bd dir Govtl Affairs Council; mem Metro AME Zion Ch Greater Hartford C of C; Rotary Internat; Social Workers Conf of CT; pres exec dir Council of United Way & Comm Council Agencies; former treas exec dir Council Nat Urban League Inc; bd dir World of Affairs Center; bd dir NCCJ Hartford Commr State of CT Parole Bd; commr on Human Rights & Opportunities; Bank Dir Bloomfield State Bank; vis guest lectr Univ of & CT Sch of Social Work. **MILITARY SERVICE:** AUS warrant officer jr. **BUSINESS ADDRESS:** Retired Dir, Urban League of Grtr Hartford, 1229 Albany Ave, Hartford, CT 06112.

BROWN, WILLIAM JAMES (GATES)
Athelete. **PERSONAL:** Born May 02, 1939, Crestline, OH; married Norma; children: Pamela, Willima Jr. **CAREER:** Detroit Tigers, coach 1978-, scout professional baseball player 1960-77; Minor Leagues, 1960-63. **HONORS/ACHIEVEMENTS:** Pinch hit champ, smokey burgess Am League 1949-67; hit home run as pinch hitter 1st time at bat in majors 1963; tied major leag record most home runs-consecat bats for a pinch hitter 2 1968; played in World Series 1968; played in AL Championship Series 1972; Freedom Found Awd 1973; est AL record most hits for a pinch hitter lifetime (107) & most home runs by a pinch hitter lifetime 16. **BUSINESS ADDRESS:** Tiger Stadium, Detroit, MI 48215.

BROWN, WILLIAM MCKINLEY, JR.
Health officer. **PERSONAL:** Born Jan 24, 1926, Chicago, IL; married Gloria G; children: William III, Joseph, Timothy, Anthony. **EDUCATION:** Roosevelt Coll, BS 1950; Meharry Med Coll, MD 1955; Univ MI, MPH 1959; internship gen prac Sacramento Co Hosp 1955-57; pub health resident LA1962-64. **CAREER:** Milwaukee, public health physician 1959-62; LA, dist health officer 1964-70; consul CA State Dept 1970-75; Pasadena, health officer 1970-75; Drug Treatment Prog, med dir 1975-; Charles R Drew Postgrad Medical Sch, asst prof comm medicine; Hubert H Humphrey Comp Health Ctr, preventive hlth officer. **ORGANIZATIONS:** El Monte Kiwanis Club 1966-68; Urban Health Conf MI State Univ 1971; trustee US Conf City Health Officers 1971-75; bd dir Pasadena Child Health Found 1973-76; assoc clinical prof Univ So CA Med Sch sec treas CA Acad of Preventive Med 1971-73, pres 1975; bd of dir High Blood Pressure Council LA; bddirs Casa Las Amigas; adv bd El Santos Nino Social Serv Ctr; adv bd Child Health and Disability Prog South Area; bd of dir Amer Cancer Soc San Gabriel Valley Unit; Foothill Free Clinic; Mental Assn of Pasadena; Pasadena Council on Alcoholism; Pasadena Humane Soc; Pasadena Lung Assn; Wesley Social Serv Ctr; Vis Nurses assn; diplomate Amer Bd of Preventive Med; fellow Amer Coll of Preventive Med; fellow Amer Pub Health Assn; commr City of El Monte Sister City; article Public Health Report 1966. **MILITARY SERVICE:** USNR phm 3/c 1944-46. **BUSINESS ADDRESS:** Preventive Health Officer, Hubert H Humphrey Hlth Ctr, 5850 S Main St, Los Angeles, CA 90003.

BROWN, WILLIAM MELVIN, JR.
Business executive. **PERSONAL:** Born Feb 19, 1934, Charleston, SC; married Juanita Washington; children: Tamara T, William Melvin III. **EDUCATION:** SC State Coll, BS 1955; Atlanta U, MS 1964; Webster Coll, MBA 1974. **CAREER:** Charleston Cnty Sch, tchr 1958-63; Metropolitan Life Ins, consult 1964-72; Charleston Cnty Auation Auth, dir; State Chamber of Commerce, dir; SC State Ports Auth, dir 1980-; North Carolina Natl Bank, dir; Bankers Trust of Charleston, dir; Am Devel Corp, pres/ceo. **ORGANIZATIONS:** Dir Charleston Museum; past pres Charleston Bus & Prof Assn; former chrmn City of Charleston Election Comm. **HONORS/ACHIEVEMENTS:** Distinguished Grad SC State Coll 1981; Outstanding Grad Among Black Coll NAFEO; Top 100 Black Comp Black Enter Mag 11 yrs; Top Mgr & Adminstr AUS 1979. **MILITARY SERVICE:** AUS sp/5 2 yrs; hon discharge 1958. **HOME ADDRESS:** 2311 Port Side Way, Charleston, SC 29407. **BUSINESS ADDRESS:** President/Chief Executive Ofcr, Am Devel Corp, 1930 Hanahan Rd, North Charleston, SC 29406.

BROWN, WILLIAM ROCKY, III
Elected official. **PERSONAL:** Born Oct 10, 1955, Chester, PA; children: Catrina J. **EDUCATION:** Cheyney State Univ, BA Pol Sci 1977; Martin Luther King Jr Ctr, Course in Non-Violence 1978-80; Eastern Baptist Seminary, MA Religion 1983; Jameson Christian Coll, DDiv 1986. **CAREER:** Chester-Upland School Dist, substitute teacher 1978-81; Calvary Baptist Church, asst pastor 1979-; State of PA, notary public 1980-; PA Legislature Dist 159, asst state rep 1982-83; First Baptist Church of Bernardtown Coatesville PA, pastor; City of Chester, city controller. **ORGANIZATIONS:** Founder, pres Chester Black Expo 1979-; exec bd Black Ministers Conf 1979-; exec bd Chester Branch NAACP 1979-; vice pres Chester Comm Improvement Project 1981-; pres Bill Dandridge Art Gallery 1982-; exec bd Kiwanis Club of Chester 1984-. **HONORS/ACHIEVEMENTS:** Columnist What's Happening Now Newspaper 1978-; Outstanding Young Man US Jaycees 1984; Johnson Freedom Awd Chester Branch NAACP 1984; Outstanding Alumni Natl Assn for Equal Opportunity in Higher Educ 1985. **HOME ADDRESS:** 214 Edwards St, Chester, PA 19013. **BUSINESS ADDRESS:** Controller, City of Chester, Municipal Building, 5th & Welsh St, Chester, PA 19013.

BROWN, WILLIAM T.
Scientist. **PERSONAL:** Born Jun 11, 1947, Columbus, MS; divorced; children: Kesha. **EDUCATION:** Dillard Univ, BS (cum laude) 1969; Univ of NM, MS, PhD 1984. **CAREER:** Los Alamos Sci Lab, tech staff physicist 1969-73; Sandia Natl Lab, tech staff physicist 1974-. **ORGANIZATIONS:** Bd dir Natl Technical Assoc 1983-; mem Natl Black Child Development Inst; pres bd dir Albuquerque Montessori Soc 1975-77; bd dir mem Natl Consortium for Black Professional Development 1976-79; mem Amer Physical Soc 1977-; mem AAAS 1978-; mem NAACP 1976-; mem NM Acad of Sci 1975-; mem Soc of Black Physicists 1978-; mem Natl Tech Assn 1979-. **HONORS/ACHIEVEMENTS:** Who's Who Among Students in Amer Colls & Univs 1968-69; Who's Who in Tech 1979. **BUSINESS ADDRESS:** Technical Staff Physicist, Sandia Natl Lab, Box 5800 Div 1533, Albuquerque, NM 87185.

BROWN, WILLIAM T.
Administrator, educator, scenic designer. **PERSONAL:** Born Mar 11, 1929, Washington, DC; son of William and Henretta; married Alfredine Parham (deceased); children: Camilla (Parham), Darrell, Kevin. **EDUCATION:** Howard Univ, BA 1951; Western Reserve Univ, MFA 1954. **CAREER:** Theatre Dept Univ of MD Baltimore Co, assoc prof & chmn 1970-75, 1982-; assoc prof drama, Howard Univ 1959-70, & dept chmn 1967-70; Theatre Univ of Leeds, visiting prof 1975; Theatre Univ of Ibadan Nigeria, sr & lecturer & consultant 1963-65; Karamu Theatre Cleveland, tech dir 1951-59. **ORGANIZATIONS:** Mem East Central Theatre Conference; mem, American Theatre of Higher Education; mem, Maryland State Arts Council 1988-89; mem, Howard County Artistic Review Panel 1987-89. **HONORS/ACHIEVEMENTS:** Gold Medallion Award of Excellence in Theatre Amoco Oil Co 1971; Hines-Brooks Award of Excellence in Theatre HowardUniv 1961; Distinguished Program Award, Maryland Assn of Higher Education 1988; creation of Mobil Stage Shakespeare On Wheels 1985. **BUSINESS ADDRESS:** UMBC Theatre Dept, 5401 Wilkens Ave, Baltimore, MD 21228.

BROWN, WILLIE
Defensive back coach. **PERSONAL:** Born in Yazoo City, MS; married Elizabeth; children: 3 children. **EDUCATION:** Attended, Grambling. **CAREER:** Denver Broncos, player 1963-66; LA Raiders, player 1967-78, defensive back coach. **HONORS/ACHIEVEMENTS:** Named to Pro Football Hall of Fame.

BROWN, WILLIE L.
Physician. **PERSONAL:** Born Jan 04, 1932, Laurel, MS; married Julia; children: Dr Willie L Jr, Glenn, Karma. **EDUCATION:** Bakersfield Jr Coll; Vallejo Jr Coll, AA; Univ of CA, BA 1954; Meharry Medical College, MD. **CAREER:** Private Practice, Fresno, CA, 1962-. **BUSINESS ADDRESS:** 2828 Fresno St, Ste 201, Fresno, CA 93721.

BROWN, WILLIE L., JR.
Assemblyman, speaker. **PERSONAL:** Born Mar 20, 1934, Mineola, TX; married Blanche Vitero; children: Susan, Robin, Michael. **EDUCATION:** CA State Univ San Francisco, BA 1955; Hastings Coll of Law, JD 1958. **CAREER:** San Fran law firm of Brown, Dearman & Smith, partner 1959-; admitted to practice before US Supreme Ct 1964; elected to CA State Assembly 1964; Assembly Com on Ways & Means, chmn 1971-74; Joint Com on Siting of Teaching Hosp, chmn 1973-74; CA Assembly, speaker 1980-. **ORGANIZATIONS:** Mem Assembly Com on Efficiency & Cost Contraol Elect & Reapportionment Govt Admin; Governor's Commn on Aging; mem Joint Comm on Master Plan for Higher Edn; Legislative Budget; Legis Space Needs Legis Audit; v chmn Select Com on Health Manpower; mem Select Com Deep Water Ports; co-chairperson CA Delegation to Natl Dem Conv 1972; co-chmn CA Delegation to Natl Black Polit Conv 1972; CA rep Credentials Com Dem Conv 1968; bd mem Natl Planned Parenthood Assn; Fellow of Amer Assembly; mem NAACP, League of Women Voters; adv bd mem CA & Tomorrow; honorary lifetime mem ILWU Local #10; San Francisco Planning & Urban Renewal Assn; Sunset Parkside Educ & Action Com; Fillmore Merchants Improvement Assn; Planning Assn for Richmond; Hight Ashbury Neighborhood Council; San Francisco Aid Retarded Children; Chinese for Affirmative Action. **HONORS/ACHIEVEMENTS:** Outstanding Freshman Legislator Press Award 1965; Man of the Year Sun Reporter Newspaper 1963; Children's Lobby Award Outstanding Legislative Efforts 1974; Leader of the Future Time Magazine 1974. **BUSINESS ADDRESS:** Speaker of the House, CA Assembly, State Capitol, Room 219, Sacramento, CA 95814.

BROWN, WILLIS, JR.
Retired educator. **PERSONAL:** Born Dec 15, 1924, Charleston, SC; son of Rev Willis Brown and Evelyn Kirlow Brown; married Bertha Adams Brown, Nov 25, 1950; children: Angela C Brown, Alford. **EDUCATION:** Benedict Coll, BS. **CAREER:** Science tchr 1953-79. **ORGANIZATIONS:** Referee Camden Co GA Juvenile CT; charter mem treas mgr Camden Co Comm Fed Credit Union; dir & past pres GA Science Teacher Assn Inc; mem CADRE-100; charter mem Epsilon chap of Omega Psi & Phi; Lambda Tau Grad chap keeper of records & seals; Prince Hall 33 Degree Mason; v chmn Zoning & Planning Commn; co-chmn Camden Co Comm Chest Dr; Coastal Area Planning & Develop Adv Council on Planning; grand secretary Most Worshipful Prince Hall Grand Lodge F&AM of Georgia; deputy of the Orient Georgia's All 32 Degree - 33 Degree Prince Hall Masons of Georgia. **HONORS/ACHIEVEMENTS:** Tchr of yr Camden Co teachers; cited by Am Nat Red Cross & GA Vet Serv. **HOME ADDRESS:** PO Box 475, Woodbine, GA 31569.

BROWN, ZACK BERNARD
Physician. **PERSONAL:** Born Feb 05, 1946, Camden, SC; married Janice Mills; children: Kimberly, Bernadette. **EDUCATION:** Morehouse Coll, BS 1967; Meharry Med Coll, MD 1973. **CAREER:** Private Prac, physician; Cook Co Hosp Chgo, internship 1974. **ORGANIZATIONS:** Omega Psi Phi 1965; AMA. **HONORS/ACHIEVEMENTS:** Detroit Med Soc Samdoz Award Meharry Med & Coll 1972.

BROWN-KNABLE, BOBBIE MARGARET
Educational administrator. **PERSONAL:** Born May 20, 1936, Knoxville, TN; married Norman Knable; children: Jacob. **EDUCATION:** Oberlin Conservatory of Music, BMus

1958. **CAREER:** Tufts Univ, asst prof dept of english 1970-74, dir of continuing educ asst academic dean 1974-77, assoc academic dean, dean of freshmen 1977-80, dean of students 1980-. **ORGANIZATIONS:** Bd of trustees Vermont Acad 1982-85; steering comm New England Alcohol Network 1983-; mem Natl Assoc Student Personnel Administrators, MA Assoc of WomenDeans Administrators and Counselors, Assoc of Coll Personnel Administrators, Amer Assoc of Higher Educ. **BUSINESS ADDRESS:** Dean of Students, Tufts University, Ballou Hall, Medford, MA 02155.

BROWN-NASH, JOAHN WEAVER
Educator & businesswoman. **PERSONAL:** Born Nov 27, 1935, Kansas City, KS; daughter of Theron Adveature Weaver and Edna Virgie Jones; married Monroe Chester Nash; children: Leander III, Brandon, Dwayne, Monte. **EDUCATION:** Fisk Univ Nashville TN, BA Bus Admin 1957; Chicago State Univ, MEd Counseling Psych 1964; Univ of Chicago, Ed Admin; Univ of San Francisco, PhD Orgn & Leadership 1978. **CAREER:** La Petite Acad, owner, dir 1969-75; Prescription Learning Corp, dir r&d 1970-75, exec vice pres 1975-; Educational Leadership Inst, pres 1975-; current position, sr vice pres, Prescription Learning Corp A Jostens Company. **ORGANIZATIONS:** Prof, asst dean Govs State Univ 1971-76; dir training Eastern IL Devel Serv 1968-71; dir Gifted Demo Ctr Chicago Public Schools 1958-68; Chief Consultant for Educational Charrett to Build Inner City Public Schools-Des Moines, IA 1971; staff leadership acad Delta Sigma Theta 1985; mem Alpha Gamma Pi 1985-; pres So Suburban Chicago Chap The Links 1985-88; National Chapter Establishment Officer, The Links, Inc 1988-. **HONORS/ACHIEVEMENTS:** Image Awd, League of Black Women 1974; Distinguished Prof, Gov State Univ 1976; Outstanding Black Women Awd, Fernwood Methodist Church 1976; Humanitarian Awd, New Hope Baptist Church 1977; Outstanding Educator, Woodson-Delong Fund 1982; Recognition & Appreciation Awd - Academic Olympic, Chicago Public Schls 1982; Outstanding Educator, Chicago Alliance of Black Educators 1983; Charles D Moody Distinguished Serv, Natl Alliance of Black School Educators 1984; Bethune-Tubman Truth Award, Black Women's Hall of Fame Foundation, Revelon 1989; Dare to Be Great Awwrd, Illinois Women Administrators 1988; Educational Excellence Award, Ohio State House of Representatives 1989. **HOME ADDRESS:** 30 E 150 St, Harvey, IL 60426. **BUSINESS ADDRESS:** Sr Vice President, Prescription Learning Corp, 900 N Franklin St, Ste 403, Chicago, IL 60610.

BROWN-WRIGHT, MARJORIE
Educator, home economist, social worker. **PERSONAL:** Born Jan 01, 1935, Little Rock, AR. **EDUCATION:** DePaul U, PHB 1956; Univ Il, MSW 1961; Tulane U, Advanced Stud Cert 1970; Or St U, PHD 1976. **CAREER:** St Elizabeth High School Chicago, 1956-57; Univ of Chicago, proj sec, 1957-58; IL Div Child Welfare Servs, child welfare worker, 1958-60; Champaign IL Public Schools, school & social worker, 1960-61; Lawndale Neighborhood Services Chicago, social group worker, 1962-63; Cook County Dept of Public Welfare, various social work, 1958-66; Univ OK, asst prof Social Work, 1966-70; Community Serv Univ of OR, asst prof, 1970-77; Community Devel & Human Rel Serv Consult Mass Media & Minority Group Rel Conf Tulsa US Dept Justice, presently consultant, 1970; Tulsa Model Cities Prog, social planning team committeewoman, 1968-71. **ORGANIZATIONS:** Nat bd mem & western reg campus coord Sigma Gamma Rho 1974-76; asso ed aurora mag Sigma Gamma Rho 1967-76; pres Lane Dist Nat & Assn Social Wrkrs 1971-72; governor's appointee state chairperson OR Community Coorinated Child Care Council 1974-77; pres Lane Co OR Child Care Council 1973-74; bd mem UN Assn Tulsa 1970-71. **HONORS/ACHIEVEMENTS:** OR Social Wrkr of Yr 1973; Outstanding Young Women in Am 1965; grad study scholarship awards Cook Co Il 1959-61; cen reg scholarship awardee Sigma Gamma Rho 1955; citation mayor Tulsa Contrib Model Cities Prgm 1970; Hall of Fame Educ Award Sigma Gamma Rho 1974; outstanding Human Serv Profs Am 1974; Vol Serv Awd OR Community Coord Child Care Counc 1975. **BUSINESS ADDRESS:** 20 Brae Burn Dr, Eugene, OR 97405.

BROWNE, DAVID A.
Business executive. **PERSONAL:** Born Mar 25, 1931, Brooklyn, NY; married Virginia Lee; children: Allyson, Lauren, Kyla. **EDUCATION:** Long Island Univ Brooklyn Coll NY, BA, Post Grad Study. **CAREER:** Programs Nat Urban Coalition, deputy to pres vp; Nat Cntr for Dispute Settlement Am Arbitration Assn, acting dir 1971-73; Gen Learning Corp, asso dir 1969-74; Mayors Ofc of Educ Liaison NYC, deputy dir 1968-69; United Fed of Tchr NYC, feild rep 1967-68; Comm Rel Service Dept of Justice, field rep 1967; bd of Edn, tchr 1956-66; Comm Relations Service, cons; Boston Housing Authority & Tennants Policy Coun, cons; KS Commn on Civil Rights, cons; Rochester Sch Mediations, cons. **ORGANIZATIONS:** Co-founder Negor Tchr Assn; former bd mem Nat Assn of Minority Consultants; former bd mem Volunteers in Tech Assistance; vice-chmn Domestic Com. **MILITARY SERVICE:** AUS. **BUSINESS ADDRESS:** 1201 Connecticut Ave NW, Washington, DC.

BROWNE, ERNEST C., JR.
Councilman. **PERSONAL:** Born Dec 26, 1925, Detroit, MI; married Evelyn Virginia James. **EDUCATION:** Wayne State U, BS 1967; Program for Urban Exec MIT, grad 1969. **CAREER:** Detroit Health Dept, pub health sanatarian 1949-64; Detroit Budget Bur, govt budget analyst 1965-69; Mayor's Task Force on Police Recruiting & Hiring, Detroit, staff dir 1968; Detroit, councilman 1970-75. **ORGANIZATIONS:** Pres MI Municipal League; chmn MI Municipal League Humasn Resources Com 1973-74; vice-chmn Revenue & Finance Com; Nat League of Cities; regional dir Nat Black Caucus of Local Elected Officials; vice pres Detroit Area Coun BSA; vice pres United Found; chmn Black Historic Site Com of Detroit Historic Museum; trustee Starr Commonwealth for Boys; MI adv comm on Criminal Justice & Law Enforcement. **HONORS/ACHIEVEMENTS:** Rec Silver Beaver Award, BSA 1960; Two Grand Awards, Employee Award Bd Detroit 1966. **MILITARY SERVICE:** USAAF. **BUSINESS ADDRESS:** 1340 City Co Bldg, Detroit, MI 48226.

BROWNE, LEE F.
Science educator, chemist. **PERSONAL:** Born Dec 18, 1922, High Point, NC; son of Lee Browne and Lula Winchester; married Dorothy G; children: Gail, Daryl, Adriene, Scott (dec). **EDUCATION:** Storer Coll, HS 1940, AA 1942; WVA State Coll, BS 1944; University of Pennsylvania, Navy V-7 Prog, 1946-49; UCLA, 1946-49; NYU, Doctoral Prog 1955. **CAREER:** UCLA, teaching fellow 1946-49; Tuskegee Inst, instr 1948-49; Knoxville Coll, div chmn 1950-51; Valley Jr Coll, chem instr 1952-56; Pasadena Schools, sci consult & chem 1958-68; Caltech, lecturer, dir 1969-. **ORGANIZATIONS:** Mem ACS, AAAS, AAUP, NSTA, Natl Assoc of Curriculum Spec, CCTA, Kappa Alpha Psi, Phi Sigma Biol Soc, Phi Delta Kappa Ed Hon Soc; bd of dir Pasadena Hall of Sci, Science Activities Mag, NACME Inc 1980-, Pasadena Boys Club 1981, NAMEPA Minority Engrg Prog 1980-; accred team WASA 1970; vice chmn, chmn MESA 1978. **HONORS/ACHIEVEMENTS:** LA Cty Sci & Engrg Soc Teachers Awd 1968; ACS HS Chem Contest Teacher of # 1 Team & # 1 Student 1968, 1969; Industry & Educ Council Teacher of the Year 1968; Amer Chem Soc Teacher of the Year 1970; Raymond Pitts Human Rel Awd Pasadena Star News 1970-76; CA Congress of Parent & Teachers Serv Awd 1970; Citizen of the Year 1980; Phi Delta Kappa Womens Sor 1971; Nominee to Pasadena Bd of Ed 1971; founder & ed Pasadena Eagle newspaper 1968-73; publ "Developing Skills for Coping" 1977, "Midpoint vs Endpoint" 1980; elected to Amer Inst of Chemists 1986. **MILITARY SERVICE:** USN v-7 cadet 1945-46. **HOME ADDRESS:** 871 W Ventura St, Altadena, CA 91001. **BUSINESS ADDRESS:** Lecturer, Dir of Secondary School Relations, Caltech, 10-63 Caltech, Pasadena, CA 91125.

BROWNE, ROBERT SPAN
Economist. **PERSONAL:** Born in Chicago, IL; son of William H Browne Jr and Julia Barksdale Patterson; married Huoi Nguyen; children: Hoa, Mai, Alexi, Marshall. **EDUCATION:** Univ of Chicago IL, MBA 1947; Univ of IL, BA Hon in Eco 1949; City Univ of NY, 1964-67. **CAREER:** Intl Cooperation Admin, pgm ofcr 1955-61; Fairleigh Dickinson U, prof 1965-70; Black Eco Research Cntr, pres 1969-80; African Devel Fund, exec dir 1980-82; Howard U, sr research fellow 1982-83; Subcommittee on Domestic Monetary Policy, staff dir 1986; Subcommittee on Interntl Development Institutions &Finance, staff dir 1987. **ORGANIZATIONS:** Bd mem Saxon Industries 1975-81; bd mem Harlem Commonwealth Cncl 1974-80; pres The 21st Century Found 1972-; chrmn Emergency Land Fund 1972-82; mem Eco Advisory Panel to Congressional Budget Off 1975-80; mem Governor's Commn on Welfare Mgmnt NJ 1976-80; mem Cncl on Foreign Relations 1976-; mem US Assn for the Club of Rome 1976-. **HONORS/ACHIEVEMENTS:** The Amistad Award NY Friends of Amistad 1984; co-authored "The Lagos Plan vs The Berg Report" 1984; co-authored "The Social Scene" 1972. **MILITARY SERVICE:** USAAF sgt 1944-46. **HOME ADDRESS:** 214 Tryon Ave, Teaneck, NJ 07666. **BUSINESS ADDRESS:** Staff Dir, Subcomm on Interntl Financl, Inst & Fin of House Bkg Comm, House Annex #2, Washington, DC 20515.

BROWNE, ROSCOE LEE
Actor, writer, director. **PERSONAL:** Born in Woodbury, NJ. **EDUCATION:** Lincoln Univ; Middlebury Coll VT, postgraduate; attended Columbia. **CAREER:** Scheneley Import Corp, natl sales rep, 1946-56; Lincoln Univ, literature & French instructor, 1952; NY Shakespeare Festival, 7 seasons; CBC Toronto; Spoleto Festival, guest artist; Broadway, Tiger Tiger Buring & Bright, The Cool World, General Seeger, The Ballad of the Sad Cafe, The Old Glory, The Connection, Black Like Me; dir, actor, A Hand Is On The Gate, Area da Capo, The Blacks; motion pictures, The Liberation of LB Jones, Uptight, The Comedians, The Cowboys, The World's Greatest Athlete, Superfly, TNT, Topaz, Uptown Sat Night, Logan's Run, Twilights Last Gleaming. **ORGANIZATIONS:** mem, AEA, AFTRA, SAG; trustee, Millay Colony Arts; mem, LA Free Public Theatre, KPFK Pacifica Radio. **HONORS/ACHIEVEMENTS:** track champion, 1000 yd indoors; Amateur Athletic Union 1949, 19511 named All-Amer (2); Obie Award, best actor in Benito Cereno; best actor, Dream on Monkey Mtn, LA Drama Critics; Black Filmmakers Hall of Fame 1977; author, short stories, poems. **BUSINESS ADDRESS:** c/o Georgia Gilly, 8721 Sunset Blvd, Ste 103, Los Angeles, CA 90069.

BROWNE, VINCENT J.
Educational administrator. **PERSONAL:** Born Jul 21, 1917, Washington, DC. **EDUCATION:** Howard U, AB 1938; Harvard U, AM 1941; PhD 1946. **CAREER:** Carnegie Corp, research asst, 1939-40; Howard Univ, Washington DC, Political Science instructor, 1941-42, asst prof, 1946-59, assoc prof, 1950-61, asst to pres, 1955-64, prof 1961-; dir affairs scholars & programs, 1964-67, civil rights document project dir & Fund for Advanced Educ dir, 1968-70, Coll Liberal Arts, dean, 1968-71. **ORGANIZATIONS:** Spl asst field relations Fed Civil Def Adminstrn 1951-53, consult 1954-55; pres's commn Vet Benefits 1955-56; mem Polit Sci Assn. **HONORS/ACHIEVEMENTS:** Soc Pub Adminstrn Contrib article to professional publs. **MILITARY SERVICE:** AUS 1941-46. **BUSINESS ADDRESS:** 3915 24 St NE, Washington, DC 20018.

BROWNE, VINCENT JEFFERSON, JR.
Account executive marketing/sales. **PERSONAL:** Born Mar 08, 1953, Washington, DC; son of Dr & Mrs Vincent J Browne; married Matrice W. **EDUCATION:** Brown Univ, BA 1975; Columbia Univ, MBA 1977. **CAREER:** Consolidated Rail Corp, mktg analyst 1977-78, business develop analyst 1978-86, account exec 1986-. **ORGANIZATIONS:** Mem Natl Black MBA Assoc 1982-, Assoc of MBA Execs 1986-. **HOME ADDRESS:** 7950 Henry Ave Apt 17C, Philadelphia, PA 19128. **BUSINESS ADDRESS:** Account Executive, Consolidated Rail Corp, 1126 One Liberty Place, Philadelphia, PA 19103.

BROWNE, VIVIAN E.
Artist, educator. **PERSONAL:** Born Apr 26, 1929, Laurel, FL; daughter of Henry Leonard Browne and Odessa Bryant Browne. **EDUCATION:** Hunter Coll of NYC, BS 1950, MA 1958; Art Stdnts League NYU; Pratt Inst; The New Sch for Social Research. **CAREER:** Booker T Wash HS Columbia SC, tchr of fine arts 1950-53; Brooklyn, Queens JHS, tchr of fine arts 1953-56; Newtown HS Queens NY, tchr of fine arts 1956-65; Bureau of Art Bd of Educ NYC, supt of art 1966-68, asst to dir of art 1968-71; Rutgers Univ Newark NJ, chrmn art dept 1975-78, assoc prof of art, prof of art 1985-. **ORGANIZATIONS:** Bd mem Women Artist & Series Douglass Coll 1979-; Feminist Art Inst 1984-; Women's Caucus for Art 1980-85; mem Nat Conf of Artists; Coll Art Assn; Assn of Univ Prof; Women's Caucus for Art; Printmaking Workshop. **HONORS/ACHIEVEMENTS:** Painting fellowship Huntington Hartford Univ 1964; Achievement Award Nat Assn of Bus & Prof Women 1965; painting fellowship MacDowell Colony 1980; visiting asso prof Univ of CA At Santa Cruz 1983-84; research cncl grants Rutgers Univ 1976-77; black artists rep Artists Delegation to The People's Republic of China 1976; Distinguished Teacher of Art, College Art Assn 1989; Artist Honoree of the Year, NYFAI 1988. **HOME ADDRESS:** 451 W Broadway, New York, NY 10012.

BROWNER, JOEY
Professional athlete. **PERSONAL:** Born May 15, 1960, Warren, OH; married Valeria. **EDUCATION:** USC, Public Admin. **CAREER:** Minnesota Vikings, safety 1983-. **ORGANIZATIONS:** Mem NEL Boys & Girls Club of AK Camp "87", camp confident Celebrity Tournament; mem Vikings Charity Basketball. **HONORS/ACHIEVEMENTS:** Selected first team All-Pac 10; UPI All Coast; College Pro Football Newsweekly second-team All-Amer; AP third-team All-Amer; USC's MVP; played captain in Japan Bowl 1983; MVP on

Defense Vikings 1985; mem Pro Bowl teams 1986,87. **BUSINESS ADDRESS:** Minnesota Vikings, 9520 Viking Dr, Eden Prairie, MN 55344.

BROWNER, ROSS
Professional athlete. **PERSONAL:** Born Mar 22, 1954, Warren, OH; son of Jimmie Sr and Julia G; married Shayla Simpson, Jun 14, 1986. **EDUCATION:** Attended, Notre Dame. **CAREER:** Cincinnati Bengals, professional football defensive lineman 1978-87; Green Bay Packers, professional football defensive lineman 1987; Coldwell Banker, Cincinnati OH, realtor 1989. **HONORS/ACHIEVEMENTS:** All-Amer Notre Dame; winner of Outland & Lombardi Trophies Notre Dame; Bengal MVP Bengal Fans 1978; HS All-Amer; Robert W Maxwell Trophy 1978. **BUSINESS ADDRESS:** Cincinnati Bengals, 200 Riverfront Stadium, Cincinnati, OH 45202.

BROWNING, GRAINGER
Educator. **PERSONAL:** Born Nov 05, 1917, Weldon, NC; son of James Henry Browning and Emma Browning; married Esther Merriman; children: Grainger, Jr, Cornelia Aida. **EDUCATION:** Shaw U, AB 1939; Boston U, MA 1945, PhD 1962. **CAREER:** A&T Coll, instr 1947-49; MA Inst Tech, 1952-53; Johnson C Smith U, asst prof 1954-58; United So Educ Settlements, community organizer 1958-62; Hampton Inst, asso prof 1961-66; Fitchburg State Coll, prof retired 1986. **ORGANIZATIONS:** Mem Mayor's Citizens Adv Comm 1964-66; pres NAACP Fitchburg 1968, exec comm 1969; bd of dirs Fitchburg Planning Bd 1969-; faculty senate Fitchburg State Coll 1969; mem Am Univ Profs; Am Sociological Assn; pres MA Sociological Assn 1971-72; bd dirs United Comm Serv 1973-; MICAH Housing Corp; MA Common Cause; Worcester N Savings Bank Corp 1977-; chmn educ com NAACP 1978-; bd dir Montachusett Opportunity Council 1979-; Omega Psi Phi Frat, Iota Chi Chpt; chmn Nat Achvmt Eek Celebration; pres Men's Fellowship Union Baptist Church Cambridge MA 1987. **HONORS/ACHIEVEMENTS:** Book of Golden Deeds Award, Exchange Club of Fitchburg 1969; Dist Serv Award, Fitchburg State Coll 1979; Omega Man of the Yr, Omega Psi Phi Frat Iota Chi Chap 1980,85; Pioneer Awd Massachusetts Sociological Assoc 1986; Martin Luther King Jr Human Relations Award, Massachusetts Teachers Assn 1982. **BUSINESS ADDRESS:** Professor of Sociology, Fitchburg State College, Sociology Department, 160 Pearl St, Fitchburg, MA 01420.

BROWNLEE, GERALDINE DANIELS
Educator. **PERSONAL:** Born in E Chicago, IN; daughter of Jerry Daniels and Nellie Cossey Daniels; married Brady Brownlee, Aug 04, 1957. **EDUCATION:** West VA State Coll, BA (cum laude) 1947; Univ of IL, grad 1949-50; Univ of MI, grad 1950; Chicago Teachers Coll, grad 1955; Univ of Chicago, MST 1967, PhD 1975; Univ of IN, post-doctoral study 1978-79. **CAREER:** Cook Co IL Dept of Pub Welfare, adv caseworker 1950-55; Chicago Public Sch, elem sch teacher 1955-66; Univ of Chicago, staff assoc 1968-70; Univ of Chicago Ford Found Training & Placement Prog, coord 1969-70; Univ of Chicago, asst dir trainer of tchr trainers prog 1970-71; Univ of IL Coll of Educ, asst dean, asst prof 1971-74; Park Forest IL Sch Dist, dir title VII proj 1975-76; Univ of IL, asst prof 1971-. **ORGANIZATIONS:** Consul US Off of Educ; consul Pk Forest Sch Dist 163 Amer Educ Res Assoc; Natl Soc for the Study of Educ; Amer Assn for Higher Educ; Alpha Kappa Alpha; Amer Assn of Univ Women; mem Links Inc, Education Network; natl vice pres Pi Lambda Theta Natl Honor Assn for Professionals in Educ; mem, Assn for Supervision and Curriculum Devel, 1988-89; mem, Assn of Teacher Educ; 1982-88; chairperson, Chicago Urban League Education Advisory Comm, 1983-; mem board of directors, Chicago Urban League, 1984-. **HONORS/ACHIEVEMENTS:** Pi Lambda Theta; John Dewey Soc; Alpha Delta Sigma; Beta Kappa Chi; Scholarship West VA State Coll; fellowship Rackham Sch of Soc Work Univ of MI; fellowship Univ of Chicago; Fellow ACE Amer Council on Educ in Acad Admin "The Role of the Cadre Liaison/Curriculum Coordinator"; papers Ford Training & Placement Prog Univ of Chicago Press 1970; "Correlates of Tchr Leadership & Change in Some Urban Pub Elem Schs" 1975; "Evaluation Nutrition Educ Progs" Thresholds in Educ 1978; "Characteristics of Teacher Leaders" Educ Horizons 1979; "Teachers Who Can Lead"; Alpha Delta Kappan 1980; "Parent-Teacher Contacts and Student Learning, A Research Report (with Iverson & Walberg) The Journal of Educ Rsch 1981; "Characteristics of Teacher Leaders" reprint in the Practising Administrator (Australia) 1980; "Identification of Teacher Education Candidates" in Career Long Teacher Educ 1985; Special Task Force Study "Instructional Management" in Chicago School System 1981; Fifteenth Annual Distinguished Rsch Awd, Assn of Teacher Educators, 1987; The Role of Teacher Career Stages and Professional Develop Practices in Determining Rewards and Incentives in Teaching 1987; Beautiful People Awd, Chicago Urban League, 1989; principal evaluator, FY88 and FY89 Truant's Alternative and Optional Educ Program Evaluation, Chicago Public High Schools, 1988-89; principal evaluator, Hispanic Dropout Program Evaluation, Chicago Public High Schools, 1988. **BUSINESS ADDRESS:** Assistant Professor, Coll of Educ Univ of IL Chicago, Box 4348, Chicago, IL 60680.

BROWNLEE, JACK M.
TV operations manager. **PERSONAL:** Born Jul 24, 1940, St Louis, MO; son of Clifford and Johnny; married Martha Diaz, May 23, 1987; children: Bryan, Michael. **EDUCATION:** San Diego City, grad; San Diego St Coll, grad. **CAREER:** KFMB TV, prod, supr 1975-, dir 1972-73; KFMB TV San Diego,TV oper mgr 1973-75. **ORGANIZATIONS:** Bd of Governors, Natl Assn of Television Arts & Sciences 1984-85. **HONORS/ACHIEVEMENTS:** Upper Level Div Scholarship Award; 1st black dir & 1st black on KFMB TV mng staff; Emmy Award, best entertainment show, Natl Assn of Television Arts & Sciences 1983. **MILITARY SERVICE:** USMC 1959-64. **BUSINESS ADDRESS:** Production/Operations Supervisor, Midwest Broadcasting, KFMB-TV, San Diego, CA 92111.

BROWNLEE, LESTER HARRISON-PIERCE
Educator. **PERSONAL:** Born Apr 25, 1915, Wakefield, RI; son of Rev Leonidas Brownlee (deceased) and Rosa Adele Latimer Brownlee (deceased); married Priscilla Ruth MacDouglass, Jul 05, 1987; children: Laird, Raymond, Curtis M, Gerick. **EDUCATION:** Univ of WI Madison WI, 1947-40; Medill Sch of Journalism NU, BSJ 1947, MSJ 1948. **CAREER:** Ebony Magazine, assoc editor 1946; self-employed, commercial photographer 1947; Chicago Defender, feature writer & adv mgr 1948-52; Chicago Daily News, 1st black news reporter 1950-52, 1953-58; Chain of Newspapers, Texas, Teacher, TX S U, mgr 1953; Chicago's Am, feature writer 1958-64; Radio Station WBEE, 1st news dir 1964; WLS-TV, 1st black TV reporter 1964; Urban Affairs, editor 1969; WLS-TV, 1st black TV exec 1972-75; Chicago Bd of Educ, media rel 1975-79; WSSD, mgr 1979-80; Chicago IL Fair Plan Assn, public relations advisor 1968-79; Columbia Coll, prof of journalism. **ORGANIZATIONS:** Jury All-Amer Cities 1975; founder Evanston Urban League 1961-63; vice chmn IL Commn on Human Relations 1962-74; vice chmn Governor's Insurance Advisory Bd 1974-76; pres Dewey Day Care Center 1975; bd of dir Evanston Mental Health Assn 1976; pres The Headline Club, Chicago Chapter, Society of Professional Journalists, Sigma Delta Chi. **HONORS/ACHIEVEMENTS:** Man of Yr Lincoln Univ 1952; feature photographer Sigma Delta Chi 1947; Stick-o-Type Award Chicago Newspaper Guild 1952; Emmy Natl Acad TV Arts & Sci 1975; Outstanding Achievement Cook County Bd of Educ; Natl Alliance of Business 1974. **MILITARY SERVICE:** AUS & USNG; lt col; Bronze Star; Legion of Merit; Croce di Guerra 1945. **HOME ADDRESS:** 1800 Dobson St, Apt 318, Evanston, IL 60202. **BUSINESS ADDRESS:** Professor of Journalism, Columbia Coll, 600 S Michigan Ave, Chicago, IL 60605.

BROWNLEE, VIVIAN APLIN
Editor/writer. **PERSONAL:** Born Sep 17, 1946, Haines City, FL; married Dennis James Brownlee; children: Lauren Denise Aplin. **EDUCATION:** OH Univ, BS 1968. **CAREER:** WEWS-TV, interviewer 1974-77; NY Times, Cleveland stringer; The Plain Dealer, suburban reporter, fed court reporter, gen assign reporter, spec reporting teams, subs suburban edit & assign edit, assoc edit, edit writer 1969-78; San Diego Union, asst city editor 1978-79; Dist Weekly/The Washington Post, editor 1979-81, natl staff 1982-. **ORGANIZATIONS:** Regional dir & exec bd mem Natl Assn of Black Journ; mem bd of adv Cleve Chap of Amer Arbit Assn, ESEA, Title IV-C Comm Proj Cleveland Bd of Educ; steward Amer Newspaper Guild. **BUSINESS ADDRESS:** Editor, Dist Weekly/Washington Post, 1150 15th St NW, Washington, DC 20071.

BROWNLEE, WYATT CHINA
Referee. **PERSONAL:** Born Mar 18, 1909, Hodges, SC; married Emma Roundtree; children: Wyatt Q. **EDUCATION:** Fenn Coll, 1937-40; John Marshall Law Sch, LLB 1940-44; Cleveland Marshall Law Sch, doc of law conferred 1968. **CAREER:** Cleveland Eviction Ct, referee, Small Claims Ct, Traffic Ct 1977. **ORGANIZATIONS:** Mem Judicial Cncl of NBA; asst law dir Cleveland 1973-77; asst Atty & Gen OH 1964-70; past pres Gamma Alpha Sigma Chap of Phi Beta Sigma Frat Inc; 1st pres, orgnzr Jr br NAACP; past exalted ruler of King Tut Lodge #389; asst grand legal adv IBPOE of W; asst st legal adv; St Asn of Elks; advto reg SSS Local Bd #23. **HONORS/ACHIEVEMENTS:** Mem various Bar Assns; outstsvc; legal prof & comm Cleveland Bar Assn; saluted by TA-WA-SI Schlrshp Clb; hon by Zeta Phi Beta Sor. **BUSINESS ADDRESS:** Justice Ctr, Cleveland, OH.

BROWNRIDGE, J. PAUL
Government official. **PERSONAL:** Born Jun 10, 1945, Macon, MS; son of James Brownridge and Arna M Moore Brownridge; married (Dr) Rose M; children: 4. **EDUCATION:** Jackson State Univ, Jackson MS, 1966-68; Univ of Akron, BS 1970, JD 1974; Indiana Univ, master's degree 1980; Harvard Univ, senior executives program 1987. **CAREER:** Goodyear Tire & Rubber Co, accountant 1971-73; Container Corp of Amer, tax attorney 1973-78; Clark Equip Co, tax attorney 1978-80; Phillips Petroleum, sr tax attorney 1980-82; Ideal Basic Industries, tax counsel 1982-84; City & County of Denver, deputy mgr of revenue 1984-86; City of Grand Rapids, treasurer 1986-88; City of Chicago, dir of revenue 1988-. **ORGANIZATIONS:** Bd mem Junior Achievement 1978-80; commissioner Denver's Commn on Aging 1984-86; chmn Denver's Tuition Reimbursement Prog 1984-86; mentor Colorado Alliance of Business 1985-86; chmn, Central Support Sub-cabinet mem, Executive Comm & Financial Policy Comm, City of Chicago. **HONORS/ACHIEVEMENTS:** Proclamation recipient for Outstanding Service Mayor of Denver 1986; Leadership Certificate US Postal Service 1987; elected to the Executive Bd of Government Finance Officers Assn of United States & Canada. **MILITARY SERVICE:** AUS sp4 3 yrs; various commendation medals Vietnam Vet 1963-66. **BUSINESS ADDRESS:** Director of Revenue, City of Chicago, 121 N LaSalle, Room 107, Chicago, IL 60602.

BRUCE, CAROL PITT
Federal government employee. **PERSONAL:** Born Dec 25, 1941, Elkton, MD; daughter of Ralph A Pitt and Elizabeth J Sawyer; married Don Franklin; children: Donna E Bowie, Keith, Kirk. **EDUCATION:** Morgan State Univ, BA 1964, MBA 1979. **CAREER:** Hartford Co Dept Social Svcs, asst dir income maint 1975-77; US Army 8th Inf Div ADAPCP, clinical supv 1977-79; US Army Civilian Personnel Ofc Ft Polk, personnel staffing spec 1981-84; US Army Civilian Personnel Ft Geo G Meade, chief tech serv 1984-85; Chemical Rsch Engrg & Dev Ctr Aberdeen Proving Ground, chief alcohol drug control/ea office 1985-. **ORGANIZATIONS:** Mem Exec Bd Baltimore Urban League 1976-79; me Natl Assoc Female Execs; mem Harford County Alumnae Chapter, Delta Sigma Theta Inc 1988-; Youth Program Dir, St. James AME Church 1987-. **HOME ADDRESS:** 525 Oak St, Aberdeen, MD 21001. **BUSINESS ADDRESS:** Chief Alcohol Drug Control Ofc, Chem Rsch Engrg & Dev Ctr, Aberdeen Proving Ground, Aberdeen, MD 21010.

BRUCE, JAMES C.
Educator. **PERSONAL:** Born Jul 15, 1929, Washington, DC; divorced; children: James C, Jr, Jason W. **EDUCATION:** Howard U, AB 1952, MA 1968; Univ Of Chicago, PhD 1963. **CAREER:** SC State Coll, German instructor, 1956-57; Univ of Chicago, German instructor, 1961-64, asst prof of German, 1964-69, assoc prof German, 1969-. **ORGANIZATIONS:** Mem Mod Lang Assn Of Am; sec Am Assn of Tchrs of German 1974; Midwest Mod Lang Assn; Literarische Gesellschaft Chicago; mem IL Commn Human Rel 1971-73. **HONORS/ACHIEVEMENTS:** Fulbright FellowshipUniv of Frankfurt am Main, Germany 1960-61; Inland Steel Fac FellowshipUniv of Chicago 1965. **MILITARY SERVICE:** AUS sp5 1953-55. **BUSINESS ADDRESS:** Associate Professor, Univ of Chicago, Dept of Germanic Languages, The Univ of Chicago, Chicago, IL 60637.

BRUCE, JOHN IRVIN
Director. **PERSONAL:** Born Aug 01, 1929, Ellicott City, MD; married Alease Sully; children: Shawn. **EDUCATION:** Morgan State Coll, BS 1953; Howard Univ, MS 1965, PhD 1968. **CAREER:** Walter Reed Army Inst of Rsch, parasitologist 1958-68, (Japan) chief composite drug screening unit 1968-71; US Civil Admin of Ryukyu Islands, consult, 1969-71; Walter Reed Army Inst, chief schistosomiasis rsch unit, 1971-73; Coll of Pure & Applied Sci, Univ of Lowell, dean, 1973-78; Aid for Intl Devel, dep asst, change of devel tech, 1978-80; Smithsonian Inst Mekong River Delta Proj, Thailand cons; consult to Surgeon General of AUS; Lowell Univ, prof, biosciences, dir, center for tropical diseases. **ORGANIZATIONS:** mem, US Schistosomiasis Delegation to People's Republic of China, 1975; Consultant to Group Review of Overseas Med Rsch Labs 1980. **HONORS/ACHIEVEMENTS:** Certifi-

cate of Achievement 406th Med Lab 1968-71; Outstanding Performance Awd Dept of Army 1969-70; Student Senate Recognition Award Outstanding Serv to Student of LTI, 1973-75; Co-author, monograph Mekong Schistosomiasis 1980. **MILITARY SERVICE:** USN 1946-48. **BUSINESS ADDRESS:** Prof Biological Services, LowellUniv, Ctr for Tropical Diseases, 450 Aiken St, Lowell, MA 01854.

BRUCE, KENNETH E.
Attorney. **PERSONAL:** Born Jul 20, 1921, New York, NY; married Rosalia Maria. **EDUCATION:** Cc NY, BA 1945; Columbia Law School, 1946; Fordham Law School, LLD 1950. **CAREER:** Human Resources Admin of NYC, legal consultant, 1950-82; State of NY, state certificate, social worker 1950; Solo Practitioner, atty at law. **ORGANIZATIONS:** mem, The Supreme Court of The US 1958, Lawyers Trail Assn, Amer Bar Assn, Westchester Bar, Natl Bar Assn, Bronx Bar, Black Lawyers of Westchester, Natl Bar of Black Lawyers; former sr arbitrator of Amer Arbitration Assn. **HONORS/ACHIEVEMENTS:** Physical Handicapped Man of The Yr Awarded by Bronx Women of Bronx Commnty 1982. **MILITARY SERVICE:** USNG 1938. **HOME ADDRESS:** 44 Livingston Rd, Scarsdale, NY. **BUSINESS ADDRESS:** Attorney, Solo Practitioner, 44 Livingston Rd, Scarsdale, NY 10583.

BRUCE, PRESTON, JR.
Government official. **PERSONAL:** Born Sep 10, 1936, Washington, DC; married Kellene Margot Underdown; children: Preston III, Kellene Elaine. **EDUCATION:** Lyndon State Coll, BS 1958; Univ of Massachusetts, EdD 1972. **CAREER:** Readsboro School, principal 1959-63; Office of Econ Opp admin asst dir 1964-67; Head Start, dir exec asst 1968-69; Office of Child Devel, dir 4-c prog 1969-71; Univ of MA, asst to chancellor 1971-74; Office of Child Devel, dir daycare 1974-83; ACYF-DHHS, dir NCCAN 1983-84; USDHEW/ACYF-CB dep dir Office of Families. **ORGANIZATIONS:** Mem Lion's Club 1958-63; mem Jaycees 1969-71; mem, vestry mem St Mark's Church 1971-74; board of dir Day Care Council of Amer 1975-83; board of dir Capitol Ballet Guild 1978-80; board of dir District of Columbia O/C 1978-82; chmn Howard Univ School of S/W Vstg Comm 1979-. **HONORS/ACHIEVEMENTS:** Professional baseball pitcher Pittsburgh Pirates 1958; horace mann lecturer Univ of MA 1971-72; disting alumnus Lyndon State Coll 1973; Athlete's Hall of Fame Lyndon State Coll 1985. **HOME ADDRESS:** 10341 Maypole Way, Columbia, MD 21044.

BRUIN, JOHN See BRUTUS, DENNIS VINCENT

BRUMMER, CHAUNCEY EUGENE
Attorney. **PERSONAL:** Born Nov 22, 1948, Louisville, KY; married Isabelle J Carpenter; children: Christopher, Craig. **EDUCATION:** Howard U, BA; Univ of KY, JD. **CAREER:** Louisville & Nashville RR Co, atty; Louisville Legal Aid, comm educ dir 1973-74; Reginald Heber Smith Fellow, Louisville Legal Aid Society. **ORGANIZATIONS:** Mem KY Bar Assn; Louisville Bar Assn; Nat Bar Assn Explorer advr; Law Explorer Post - #922 1974-; pres Shawnee HS Alumni Assn; mem Alpha Phi Omega. **HONORS/ACHIEVEMENTS:** Nat Serv Frat Pres Award 1976; The Big E Award 1976; Outst Alumnus Award, Shawnee HS 1975. **MILITARY SERVICE:** AUSR 1970-76. **BUSINESS ADDRESS:** 908 W Broadway, Louisville, KY 40203.

BRUNDIDGE, NANCY CORINNE
Retired educational administration. **PERSONAL:** Born Sep 27, 1920, Louisville, MS; daughter of Elijah Thompson (deceased) and Roberta (May) Thompson (deceased); married Maj Roy Lee Brundidge (deceased) (died 1987); children: Carlita J Nickson, Adrienne E Nickson. **EDUCATION:** IN Univ Gary IN, AA Soc & Ed 1956; Roosevelt Univ Chicago IL, BA Sociology & Psychology 1960, MA Urban Sociology 1973; Drug Ed Training Resource Ctr Cert 1974; Northwest IN Reg Addiction Authority, Cert 1974. **CAREER:** Cook Cty Dept Public Aid, suprv 1, caseworker 1,2 1960-69; Gary School Corp, school social worker 1970-71; IN State Employment, work incentive spec 1971-73; Hammond Public Schools, social worker & legal attendance 1973-86; Hammond School City, cert drug cons, social worker/suprv 1974-86; retired. **ORGANIZATIONS:** Mem Calvary Baptist Church 1939-; fin sec Amer West Indian Assoc Inc 1969-; mem Hammond Public Schools 1973-; legislative comm Northwest IN Council of Social Workers & Attendance Officers 1975-; coord Christmas cheer Salvation Army 1976-; past bd chairperson, exec bd mem Bethany Child Care & Devel Ctr 1976-; annual sci fair judge Purdue Univ Reg Sci Fair 1977-; reporter, mem Univ Women Calumet Area Branch 1978-; coord Thanksgiving baskets Lake Cty Econ Opport Council 1979-; assoc mem Bethel Temple Church 1981-; prog comm chairperson Adv Bd of Salvation Army 1982-; co-sponsor class 1986 Hammond HS 1982-86. **HONORS/ACHIEVEMENTS:** Bd of Governors Roosevelt Univ Chicago IL 1958-60; Cert of Achievement Lake Area United Way 1980; Guest Lecturer & Resource Person IN Univ Gary Ctr 1980-81; Baptist Woman of the Month Natl Baptist Voice 1981; Cert of Achievement Voluntary Action Ctr 1981; Nom for Florence O Alexander Ed Awd 1981; Cert of Recognition Bethany Child Care Ctr 1982; Dedication to mankind Salvation Army 1982; Cert of Merit IN Dept of Public Instr 1983; Outstanding Serv to Ed School City of Hammond 1983; IN Social worker of the Year State of IN 1984; Candidate Midwest Reg Social Worker for 1985 Award 1984. **HOME ADDRESS:** 137 Porter St, Gary, IN 46406.

BRUNER, VAN B., JR.
Architect, educational administrator. **PERSONAL:** Born May 22, 1931, Washington, DC; married Lillian E Almond; children: Scott V. **EDUCATION:** Univ of MI, BS 1954; Drexel Evening Coll, BS 1965. **CAREER:** Spring Garden Coll Dept of Architecture, dept chmn 1965-72, 1979-81; Natl Org of Minority Architects, charter mem 1972-; Amer Inst of Architecture, former natl vice pres 1972-74; Private Practice, architect 1968-. **ORGANIZATIONS:** Former mem NJ Hotel & Multiple Dwelling Health & Safety Bd 1971-; elder Philadelphia Evangelistic Ctr; field rep Full Gospel Businessmens Fellowship Intl. **HONORS/ACHIEVEMENTS:** Listed in Who's Who in the East; Hall of Fame (track) Woodbury HS NJ; Whitney Young Awd The Amer Inst of Arch 1975; Fellow (FAIA) The Amer Inst of Arch 1979. **MILITARY SERVICE:** USAF capt 3 yrs. **BUSINESS ADDRESS:** Architect, 506 W Park Blvd, Haddonfield, NJ 08033.

BRUNO, MICHAEL B.
Accounting firm executive. **PERSONAL:** Born Jul 25, 1948, New Orleans, LA; married Paulette Pinkins; children: Sean, Shannon, Shelton, Shane. **EDUCATION:** Souther Univ in New Orleans, BS 1971. **CAREER:** Ernst & Whinney CPA's, in-charge acct 1971-73; Otha Brandon CPA's, mgr 1973-76; Rochon & Staes CPA's 1977-78; Bruno & Tervalon CPA's, managing partner 1978-. **ORGANIZATIONS:** Bd mem AICPA Minority Recruitment & Equal Oppor Comm; mem Metro Area Comm Black Economic Develop Cncl, Chamber of Commerce Small Business Council. **HONORS/ACHIEVEMENTS:** Minority Small Businessman of the Year Awd 1984,85; Disting Service Awd Natl Assoc of Black Accountants Inc; Interracial Cncl for Business Oppor Businessman of the Month; United Negro Coll Fund Disting Serv Citation; Outstanding Young Men of Amer Awd; City of New Orleans Certificate of Appreciation. **BUSINESS ADDRESS:** Managing Partner, Bruno & Tervalon CPA's, 650 So Pierce St, Ste 203, New Orleans, LA 70119.

BRUNSON, DOROTHY EDWARDS
Business executive. **PERSONAL:** Born Mar 13, 1938, Glennsville, GA; children: Edward Ross, Daniel James. **EDUCATION:** St Univ of NY, BS. **CAREER:** Sonderling Broadcasting Corp, general mgr 1963-73; WWRL, New York, asst general mgr 1969; Inner City Broadcasting Corp, vice pres, general mgr 1973-79; WEBB Radio Baltimore, owner 1979-. **ORGANIZATIONS:** Panelist business & communications White House; dir adult Christian educ Pennsylvania Ave AME Zion Church; founder Afro-Amer Assn of Advertising Agencies; former Board Member: Institution for Mediation and Resolution Conflicts, First Woman's Bank New York, WNYC AM/FM Municipal Radio Station, United Way New York Special Allocation Committee, I CRY (Inner City Rountable of Youth), Park Heights Advisory Board, Baltimore Economic Devel Corporation, United Way of Central MD, John Hopkins Metro Center, Baltimore Symphony, Kennedy Institute for Handicapped Children; Present Member: Harlem Commonwealth Council, President's Roundtable, Greater Baltimore Committee, Foundation for Minorities in Media, HUB. **HONORS/ACHIEVEMENTS:** Honored by The Kiwanis, The Natl Assoc of Media Women, The Jaycees, HUB Inc, Baltimore's Black Pages; Outstanding Women of Amer Award Natl Council of Christians & Jews; Fair Media Award Black Citizens for a Fair Media; 1st Black Woman to Buy Radio Station in Amer Natl Assoc of Media Women; guest speaker in Africa on the need for greater input by women in business & industry; Mayor's Recognition Award; New York Women's Special Commission Recognition Award; Black Citizens for Fair Media, Pioneer Award, 1981; Outstanding Board Member, Harlem Commwealth Council, New York; NAACP Local/Nation Awards; Business Woman of the Year, Uptown Chamber of Commerce; HUB Inc Business Award, 1982; Baltimore Black Pages Business Award, 1982; Atlanta's Heritage Series; Natl Assn of Media Women; Kizzy Award, New York Chapter Kiwanis, New York Chapter Jaycees; Woman of the Year Bla-Africa Inc; honored as one of 50 outstanding Woman of America, Natl Conference of Christians and Jews; Amer Women in Radio and Television, first black women general manager, station owner, first black woman to co-own an advertising agency on madison avenue; Alpha Kappa Alpha for Dedicated Community Service, 1985; Miles Connors Chapter of Virginia Union; Governor Harry Hughes Award; Cystic Fibrosis, 1987; Business Woman of the Year, Business & Professional Women's Club of Baltimore; Congressional Certificate of Merit Senator Barbara Milkulski; Distinguished Service Award, Morgan State Univ Found, 1987; Natl Council of Negro Women, Distinguished Serve Award, 1987; Service to Scouting Award; Distinguished Service, Natl Convention of Blacks in Government; United Way of MD, 1987; United Negro College Fund of MD, 1986; Small Business Media Advocate of the Year, United States Small Businesss Admin; Committee to Save Sandtown Winchester, Community Award, 1987; Sickle Cell, Wilmington North Carolina, 1987; Delta Sigma Theta Natl Award 1986 Convention; MD Jr Achievement Hall of Fame; Dollar & Sense 100 Outstanding Black Women; Atlanta Univ Honorary Doctorate of Law; Morgan Homecoming Grand Marshall, 1988; Park Heights Streets Academy, Distinguished Service, 1988. **BUSINESS ADDRESS:** Brunson Communications, Inc, 3000 Druid Park Dr, Baltimore, MD 21215.

BRUNT, SAMUEL JAY
Financial administrator. **PERSONAL:** Born Jan 14, 1961, Baltimore, MD. **EDUCATION:** Howard Univ, BA 1979-83; Univ of Baltimore, MPA 1983-. **CAREER:** Comm Coll of Baltimore, admin asst, instr 1983-84; Baltimore Fed Financial, new accounts, investment clerk 1984-85; MD State Legislature, fiscal rschr 1984 interim & 1985 leg session. **ORGANIZATIONS:** Mem Natl Forum for Black Public Admin 1984-; advisor Youth Ministry Trinity Baptist Church 1984-; supt Trinity Baptist Church School 1985. **HONORS/ACHIEVEMENTS:** HUD Fellow-Baltimore Reg Plnng Council 1983-; Contestant 1983 Natl Pi Alpha Alpha Manuscript competition for Public Admin Literature; Delegate 4th Natl Model OAU at Howard Univ 1983; Recommended for profile in new natl publ Black Profiles.

BRUTON, BERTRAM A.
Architect. **PERSONAL:** Born May 18, 1931, Jacksonville, FL; son of George W Bruton and Lula C Bruton; married Dorothy Garcia; children: Michelle Yvette, Sabra Lee. **EDUCATION:** Howard Univ, BArch 1953. **CAREER:** Paul Rader AIA, job capot 1956-58; James H Johnson AIA, job capt 1958-59; Donald R Roark Denver, asso arch 1959-61; Bertram A Bruton & Asso, arch 1961-. **ORGANIZATIONS:** Mem AIA, NCARB, Natl Organ of Black Arch; Mitchell Sixty-Six Asso Devel; dir Salvation Army; dir Equity Federal Savings Bank; mem CO State Bdof Examiners of Architects; mem Kappa Alpha Psi; Kiwanis Club of Denver. **HONORS/ACHIEVEMENTS:** Awd of Merit AIA; Achievement Awd Kappa Alpha Psi; Denver Man of Yr 1974 and 1984; Barney Ford Awd. **MILITARY SERVICE:** USAF 1st lt 1953-56. **BUSINESS ADDRESS:** Architect (Principal), Bertram A Bruton & Asso Architects, 2001 York St, Denver, CO 80205.

BRUTUS, DENNIS VINCENT (JOHN BRUIN)
University educator. **PERSONAL:** Born Nov 28, 1924, Harare, Zimbabwe;son of Francis Henry Brutus and Margaret Winifred Bloemetjie; married May Jaggers, May 14, 1950; children: Jacinta, Marc, Julian, Antony, Justina, Cornelia, Gregory, Paula. **EDUCATION:** Fort Hare Univ, South Africa, BA 1947; Witwatersrand Univ, Johannesburg, South Africa, 1962-63. **CAREER:** Univ of Denver, Denver CO, visiting prof of English, 1970; Northwestern Univ, Evanston IL, prof of English, 1971-85; Univ of Texas, Austin TX, visiting profof English, African & African-Amer studies research, 1974-75; Amherst Coll, Amherst MA, visiting prof of English 1982-83; Dartmouth Coll, Hanover NH, visiting prof of African & African Amer studies 1983; Swarthmore Coll, Swarthmore PA, Cornell chair, 1985-86; Univ of Pittsburgh, Pittsburgh PA, prof of African literature & chmn dept of black community educ research & devel, 1986—. **ORGANIZATIONS:** Pres, South African Non-Racial Olympic Comm (San Roc), 1963—; founding mem, Troubadour Press, 1970—; vice pres, Union of Writers of the African Peoples, 1974; founding chair, African Literature Assn, 1975—; mem, Intl Jury Books Abroad Award, 1976; chmn, Africa Network, 1984—; advisory bd mem, African Arts Fund, 1985—; bd mem, Nicaragua Cultural Alliance, 1987-; advisory bd mem, Amer Poetry Center, 1988-; mem, Advisory Comm, Natl Coalition to Abolish the Death Penalty, 1989.

HONORS/ACHIEVEMENTS: Mbari Prize for Poetry in Africa, Mbari Press, 1963; Sirens, Knuckles, Boots, 1963; Thoughts Abroad, John Bruin (pseudonym), TX, 1970; A Simple Lust, 1972; Stubborn Hope, 1978; Doctor of Humane Letters, Worcester State Coll, Worcester MA, 1985; Doctor of Humane Letters, Univ of Massacussets, Amherst, MA, 1985; Langston Hughes Medallion, City Univ of New York, 1986; Paul Robeson Award for Artistic Excellence, Political Consciousness and Integrity, 1989; Airs & Tributes, 1989. **BUSINESS ADDRESS:** Chmn, Dept of Black Community Educ Research & Devel, Univ of Pittsburgh, 230 S Bouquet St, Forbes Quad 3T01, Pittsburgh, PA 15260.

BRYAN, ADELBERT
Elected official. **PERSONAL:** Born Aug 21, 1943, Frederiksted, Virgin Islands of the United States;married Jerilyn; children: Lecia, Adelbert, Scheniqua, Lori, Andrea, Lyrhea, Mia. **EDUCATION:** College of VI, AA Police Sci & Admin 1975; FBI Acad, grad 1978. **CAREER:** St Croix Police Dept, captain 1966-; Virgin Islands, senator 1983-. **ORGANIZATIONS:** Chmn Econ Develop & Affairs Comm 15th Legislature; chmn Educ Comm 16th Legislature; mem Olympic Shooting Team; delegate to 3rd & 4th Constitutional Conventions. **HONORS/ACHIEVEMENTS:** Medal of Honor Natl Police Awd; Policeman of the Year; 1st degree Karate Black Belt. **MILITARY SERVICE:** AUS 1961-63. **HOME ADDRESS:** PO Box D, Christiansted, St Croix, Virgin Islands of the United States 00820.

BRYAN, CLARICE
Attorney. **PERSONAL:** Born Apr 30, 1923, StThomas, VI; divorced; children: Charlene Smith. **EDUCATION:** Howard Univ, AB 1944; Howard Univ, LLB 1949. **CAREER:** VI Govt tax assessor 1950, asst atty gen 1961-68, asst commr labor 1968-70, dir consumer admin 1970-73; Private Practice, attorney. **ORGANIZATIONS:** VI Bar Assn 1950-77; Amer Bar Assn 1955-77; state pres VI Bus & Professional Women 1964-65; del UN Rep Intl Assn Women Lawyers 1965; dir Peoples Bank of VI 1971-75; VI Del Spl Disting Delgn Russia Hungary & Romania 1972; mem Natl Organ of Women, Natl Bus & Professional Women; del 1st constl conv of VI; publications "The Virgin Island Woman-What Was She Like?" 1967; "A Look Behind the Iron Curtain" 1972. **BUSINESS ADDRESS:** Attorney, PO Box 831, St Thomas, Virgin Islands of the United States 00801.

BRYAN, CURTIS
President. **EDUCATION:** Elizabeth City State Univ, BS 1960; Temple Univ, MEd 1968; New York Univ, PhD (Summa Cum Laude) 1977. **CAREER:** Virginia State Univ, dean of div of educ and dir of teacher educ 1978-80, exec vice pres 1980-82, interim pres 1982-83, vice pres for admin; Denmark Technical Coll, pres. **ORGANIZATIONS:** Mem Assoc of the United States Army, Natl Assoc for Higher Educ; apptd to City of Petersburg School Bd Adv Comm. **HONORS/ACHIEVEMENTS:** New York Univ Educ Fellow; City of Petersburg Educ Serv Awd 1980; Who's Who in the South and Southwest 1983; mem Kappa Delta Pi Honor Soc, Phi Delta Kappa, Sigma Rho Sigma; publications "Quality Control in Higher Education," 1973, "Faculty Personnel, Perspectives on the Academic Freedom," 1976. **BUSINESS ADDRESS:** President, Denmark Technical College, PO Box 327, Denmark, SC 29042.

BRYAN, DAVID EVERETT, JR.
Attorney. **PERSONAL:** Born Sep 30, 1947, New York, NY; married Jacqueline Alice Weaver. **EDUCATION:** St Johns Univ, BBA, 1965-70; St Johns Univ, School of Law, JD, 1972-75. **CAREER:** New York City Metro Council, NAACP, exec sec, 1978; US Securities & Exchange Commn, trial atty, 1975-77; SE Queens Comm Corp, asst exec dir, 1971-72; Westvaco Corp, admin asst, 1970-71. **ORGANIZATIONS:** mem, past pres, Kappa Alpha Psi, 1966; mem, past pres, Jamaica Branch, NAACP 1970; pres, Jamaica Branch, NAACP Employment Devel Program, 1975-76; mem, Macon B Allen Black Bar Assn, 1975; bd of dir, Carter Community Health Centre, 1978. **HONORS/ACHIEVEMENTS:** Martin Luther King Jr Scholarship, St John's Univ School of Law, 1972; Thurgood Marshall Award, NY State Trial Lawyers Assn, 1975; Merit Award, St Albans Chamber of Commerce, 1978; Professional Award, Natl Assn of Negro Business & Professional Women's Clubs, Laureltono Club, 1979.

BRYAN, FLIZE A.
Physician. **PERSONAL:** Children: Sylvia. **EDUCATION:** Univ of W Indies, Nursing 1956; Tuskegee Inst, BSC 1967; Pomona Coll, Diploma 1968; Howard Univ Med Sch, MD 1972. **CAREER:** Hlth Dept, nurse 1956-58; Beth Israel Hosp NYC, nurse 1958-60; Pvt Duty, RN 1960-66; Sydenham Hosp NY, surgeon 1977-; Met Hosp NY Med Coll, clinical instr surg 1979-; Sydenham & Hosp NY, dir emerg room 1980-; SNFCC Harlem Hosp, surgeon 1980-; Brooklyn Hospital, staff. **ORGANIZATIONS:** Mem Comm Bd New York City 1984-; delegate Doctors Cncl Union 1980-; mem Susan McKinley Assn 1983.

BRYAN, JESSE A.
Educational administrator, educator. **PERSONAL:** Born Jun 15, 1939, Red Springs, NC; son of Felix F Bryan (deceased) and Laney Osaka Smith Bryan Ward (deceased); married Virgie D Daniels Bryan, Sep 26, 1964; children: Tami, Jason. **EDUCATION:** Johnson C Smith Univ, Undergrad Degree 1964; Univ of GA, Grad Studies 1964; Temple Univ, MEd 1968; Univ of Toledo, PhD 1977. **CAREER:** Admissions Glassboro State Coll, numerous positions & assoc dir 1969-70; Student Field Experience Office Univ of Toledo, admin asst 1970-71; Univ of Toledo, dir upward bound 1971-73; Bloomsburg Univ, dir center for acad devel 1973-. **ORGANIZATIONS:** Mem Kappa Alpha Psi Fraternity 1961-; mem Phi Delta Kappa 1972-; dir Act 101 Program 1973-; mem Act 101 Exec Comm 1973-83; Black Conf on Higher Educ 1973-; mem Western Reg of Act 101 1978-; mem Kiwanis Intl 1979-; pres Equal Educ Oppor Program 1980-. **HONORS/ACHIEVEMENTS:** Special Recognition Ed Opportunity Ctr, Ctr for Acad Devel; Two Advisory Awards Third World Cultural Soc; Advisory Award Kappa Alpha Psi Lambda Alpha; Vol Leader Awd Young Men's Christian Assoc. **MILITARY SERVICE:** USN fire control tech 1956-60. **HOME ADDRESS:** 375 Hillside Drive, Wonderview, Bloomsburg, PA 17815. **BUSINESS ADDRESS:** Cairperson, Dir, Department of Developmental Instruction, Bloomsburg University, Waller Administration Bldg Room #14, Bloomsburg, PA 17815.

BRYANT, ANDREA PAIR
Intellectual property lawyer. **PERSONAL:** Born Jul 19, 1942, Baltimore, MD; daughter of James M Pair, MD (deceased) and Mamie Savoy Pair (deceased); married Melvin W Bryant, Oct 19, 1968; children: James Burnett West, Michael David. **EDUCATION:** Morgan State, BS Physics (high honor) 1965; Fulbright Fellowship Karlsruhe Germany 1965-66; Georgetown Univ Law Center, JD 1978. **CAREER:** IBM Corp, programmer 1967-73, programmer/instructor 1973-74, patent atty in training 1974-78, patent atty 1978-. **ORGANIZATIONS:** Mem Austin Area Urban League Bd of Dir 1983-; sec Natl Bar Assn Bd 1988-; pres Legal Aid Soc of Central TX 1988; treas Austin Black Lawyers Assn 1987-; second vice chair Austin Area Urban League 1988-; bd mem Paramount Theatre for the Performing Arts 1989-. **HONORS/ACHIEVEMENTS:** Leadership Austin Class 1983-84. **HOME ADDRESS:** 5202 Vista West Cove, Austin, TX 78731.

BRYANT, ANXIOUS E.
Broker, educator. **PERSONAL:** Born Jan 18, 1938, Nashville, TN; married Christie Tanner; children: Karen, Karl. **EDUCATION:** State Univ Nashville, BS 1959; Memphis State U, MS 1970. **CAREER:** Memphis One Inc Realtors, affiliate broker, 1980-; State Tech Inst Memphis, assoc prof, 1979-; Thompson & Miller Architects, architectural technician, 1978-79; Gassner Nathan Parners, architectural technician, 1977; Jones & Thompson Architects, architectural technician, 1973; Carver High School Memphis, teacher, 1959-70; Rust Coll, Holly Springs MS, part-time lecturer, 1980-. **ORGANIZATIONS:** Chmn exam bd, Shelby Co Plumbing Dept 1977-. **BUSINESS ADDRESS:** State Tech Inst, 5983 Macon Cove, Memphis, TN 38134.

BRYANT, CASTELL VAUGHN
Educator. **PERSONAL:** Born Mar 03, Jasper, FL; married Leonard Bryant Jr; children: Kathie Vaughn Howell, Craig Leonard. **EDUCATION:** Fl A&M U, BS; Fl A&M U, MS; Nova U, EdD. **CAREER:** Miami-Dade Community Coll, assoc dean/acad support 1978-, coordinator of curriculum/Job Placement STIP Grant 1978; Dade County Public School System, teacher 1975-78; FL A&M Univ, staff asst to dean 1973-75. **ORGANIZATIONS:** Mem NAWDAC; Dade FL/Nat Bus -edn Assn; Council on Black Am Affairs; mem Nat Council of Negro Women; com on fair repres Dade Co; mem NAACP; mem Nat Assn of Student Personnel Admin Serv Awards; FAMU Alumni Assn/(At Cncl of Negro Women/The Greyhound Corp; Grant Writing Team Miami-Dade Community Coll NWCC. **BUSINESS ADDRESS:** Dean of Students, Miami Dade Community College, 300 NE 2nd Ave, Miami, FL 33132.

BRYANT, CLARENCE
Circuit judge. **PERSONAL:** Born Jun 13, 1928, Lewisville, AR; son of Jehugh Bryant and Lucy Faulkner Bryant; married Doris L Hearns (deceased); children: Nelson T, Kevan L. **EDUCATION:** Roosevelt Coll, BA 1953; Chicago Kent Coll of Law (ITT), LLB 1956, JD 1969. **CAREER:** Circuit Court of Cook Co IL, elected circuit court judge 1982, assoc appointed judge 1976-; Wash Kennon Bryant & Hunter, atty partner 1960-76; Wash & Durham, atty assoc 1956-60. **ORGANIZATIONS:** Only black among first 9 mem Review Bd IL Atty Diciplinary System 1973-76; 1st vice pres Cook Co Bar Assn 1970-72; pres Cook Co Bar Assn 1973-74; mem Jud Council NBA 1976-. **HONORS/ACHIEVEMENTS:** Meritorious Serv Award Cook Co Bar Assn 1972. **MILITARY SERVICE:** AUS lt 4 years served. **BUSINESS ADDRESS:** Circuit Judge, Circuit Court of Cook County, Daley Center, Chicago, IL 60602.

BRYANT, CLARENCE W.
Electronic specialist. **PERSONAL:** Born May 22, 1931, Clarendon, AR; married Annie Laure Aldridge; children: Carolyn, Antonette, Sibyl, Johanna. **EDUCATION:** City Coll of San Francisco, 1949-50; City Coll of San Francisco, AS Elect 1976; CA State Univ San Fran, BA Design & Industry 1979, MA DAI/Transp 1981. **CAREER:** Maintenance Engrg Br Los Angeles CA, elect tech, installation 1958-60; Western Reg San Francisco AF Sector Field Office, SFIA, elect tech, commun 1960-68, Elect tech, radar 1974, elect tech 1974-78, elect tech regular relief 1978-79; Fed Aviation Admin, suprv elect egr mgr 1979-. **ORGANIZATIONS:** Mem San Fran Black Catholic Caucus 1972, Mayors Comm on Crime 1968-71, Arch-Bishops Campaign for Hum Devel 1969-72, Black Leadership Forum of San Francisco; exec bd Catholic Soc Svc, Top Flight Golf Club. **HONORS/ACHIEVEMENTS:** Awd of Achievement CA State Assembly 1968; Awd OMICA 1968; num tech awd FAA. **MILITARY SERVICE:** USAF a/1c 1950-54.

BRYANT, CUNNINGHAM C.
Major general. **PERSONAL:** Born Aug 08, 1921, Clifton, VA. **EDUCATION:** Howard U, 1940-43; Infantry Officer Candidate Sch, 1944; Food Serv Sch, mess mgmt course 1947; Infantry Ofcr Asso, basic course 1948; Engr Ofcr Asso,advanced course 1956; Command & Gen Staff Coll, sr ofcr civil disturbance orientation course 1968; Nat War Coll, def strategy sem 1969. **CAREER:** Active Duty, 1943, 2nd Lt 1944-Major General Feb 1975; DC Nat Guard, commanding gen 1974-; DC Guard, adj gen 1968-74; various other posts. **ORGANIZATIONS:** Mem Nat Guard Assn of US & DC; Assn of AUS; The Adjs Gen Assn. **HONORS/ACHIEVEMENTS:** Recipient of Bronze Star Medal; Army Commendation Medal; Purple Heart Medal; Army of Occupation Medal (Germany); WW II Victory Medal; Nat Def Serv Medal; European-African-Middle Eastern Campaign Medal with 2 stars; Am Campaign Medal; Combat Infantry Badge; 1st federally recognized black gen officer in Nat Guard. **MILITARY SERVICE:** USNG gen ofcr. **BUSINESS ADDRESS:** DC Nat Guard, Washington, DC.

BRYANT, DELORES HALL E.
Executive director. **PERSONAL:** Born Nov 06, 1935, Omaha, NE; married Robert. **EDUCATION:** Univ of Denver, BFA, 2 yrs legal edn. **CAREER:** Sacramento Urban League, exec dir; Denver Model Cities, 1969-70; Denver Juvenile Ct, probation counselor 1965-69; Denver Pub Sch, tchr 1963-65. **ORGANIZATIONS:** Mem Delta Sigma Theta 1964-; Sacto Chap Am Assn Council ofUniv Women 1973-; C of C mem natl counicl of negro women; naacp; mem CA state Council ofUrban Leagues; aptd to CA Manpower Serv Council by Gov Brown; vice pres Council of Exec Dir Nat Urban League. **HONORS/ACHIEVEMENTS:** Who's Who in Midwest 1969; Who's Who in the W 1970; prod wkly TV prgm "Urban League Presents" 225 half hour prgms since 1922.

BRYANT, DONNIE L.
Financial administrator. **PERSONAL:** Born Dec 20, 1942, Detroit, MI. **EDUCATION:** Walsh Inst of Accountancy, attended 1960-63; Wayne State Univ, BA 1970; Univ of MI, MPublic Policy 1972. **CAREER:** Public Admin Staff, staff assoc 1973-77; Neighborhood Reinvestment Corp, dir of finance & admin 1977-83; Govt of DC, deputy to the city admin.

ORGANIZATIONS: Mem Intl City Mgmt Assn 1972-; mem Natl Assn of Black Public Admins 1984-. **HONORS/ACHIEVEMENTS:** Graduate Fellowship US Dept of Housing/Intl City Mgmt Assn 1971-72. **HOME ADDRESS:** 2400 41st St NW #313, Washington, DC 20007. **BUSINESS ADDRESS:** Deputy To City Administrator, District of Columbia, 1350 Pennsylvania Ave NW, Washington, DC 20004.

BRYANT, EDWARD JOE, III
Aircraft power plant specialist. **PERSONAL:** Born Sep 19, 1947, Shreveport, LA; son of Moses B Bryant and Ester Lee (Harper) Bryant; married Bettye Jeane Gordon, Nov 1981; children: Lorie, Khristopher, Elizabeth. **EDUCATION:** Palmer College, Associate 1975; Baptist College, Bachelors 1978; Air Natl Guard & Air Reserve Academy, graduate 1972; Propulison Branch Management, Chanute IL. **CAREER:** USAF, jet specialist 1965-69; Sperry-Rand Corp, maintenance engr 1969-72; Dept of Defense, aircraft powerplant specialist 1972-; Federal Civil Service Employee, 1972-; North Charleston SC, counselor 1978-89. **ORGANIZATIONS:** Air reserve tech 1969-86; chmn of legal NAACP 1975-86; mem Air Force Assn SC Personnel & Guidance Assn 1978-80; counselor, guidance School System 1978-79; legal chmn NAACP 1980-86; legal staff, North Charleston Citizen Advisory Council 1986-87; State Legal Redress Committee NAACP 1988-89; local chaptr, Air Force Assn. **HONORS/ACHIEVEMENTS:** Sustained Superior Performance Awd 1983; South Carolina NAACP, Best Legal Activities & Staff 1986-87; Superior Performance Award (civil service) 1989; Black Heritage Certificates 1983-1988. **MILITARY SERVICE:** USAF, sgt 4 yrs; Good Conduct Medal; Meritorious Service Medal; Vietnam Ribbon Oversea Service Medal. **BUSINESS ADDRESS:** President, North Charleston SC NAACP, PO Box 10728, North Charleston, SC 29411.

BRYANT, FAYE B.
Educator. **PERSONAL:** Born Mar 15, 1937, Houston, TX. **EDUCATION:** Howard Univ, BA 1958; Univ of Houston, MEd 1967. **CAREER:** Houston Independent Sch Dist, tchr 1960-67, Title I counselor 1967-70; Houston Met YWCA, prog dir 1968-69; Bellaire Sr HS, counselor 1970-75; QIE, HISD field inf coord 1975; Supt for Instruction, prog admin 1976; Office of Supt for Inst, assoc dir 1977; Magnet Sch Prog, asst supt 1978; Magnet Sch Prog & Alternate Educ, assoc supt 1982, asst supt enrichment programs 1987; Houston Independent School Dist, deputy supt, personnel serv 1988-. **ORGANIZATIONS:** Mem Houston Professional Admins & Assn for Supervision of Curriculum Devel (local, state, natl); pres Houston Personnel & Guidance Assn 1975-76; 1974 Task Force on Human Concerns TX Personnel & Guidance Assn; chap senator Houston Met YWCA 1970-74; bd dirs Com of Admin of Blue Triangle Br; natl past pres Top Ladies of Distinct 1975, pres Houston Chap 1973-74; south central regional dir Alpha Kappa Alpha Sor 1968-72; vice pres Alpha Kappa Alpha Sor 1978; natl pres Alpha Kappa Alpha Sor 1982-86; mem NAACP 1982-86; mem Links Inc; mem NCNW Court of Calanthe; Houston C of C; bd mem Natl Negro College Fund; bd mem, natl chmn Assault on Illiteracy; mem Black Leadership Roundtable, Coalition of 100 Black Women. **HONORS/ACHIEVEMENTS:** Young Educator Awd Finalist 1967; TX Personnel & Guidance Assn Cert of Appreciation in Recog of Commitment & Serv to Statewide Enchancement of Counseling; TX Personnel & Guidance Assn Outstanding Counselor Awd 1975; 100 Most Influential Black Americans Ebony Magazine 1983-86; Community Serv Awd TX Southern Univ's Bd of Regents; Outstanding Alumni Achievement Award, Howard Univ 1987. **HOME ADDRESS:** 3215 Milburn St, Houston, TX 77021.

BRYANT, HARRISON JAMES
Clergyman. **PERSONAL:** Born Nov 20, 1900, Georgetown, SC; married Edith H; children: 6. **EDUCATION:** Allen U, AB 1932; Payne Theol Sem, BD 1935; Wilberforce U, Hon LLD & DD. **CAREER:** AME Chs SC OH KY MD, pstr 38 yrs; St John Ch Balt, rebuilt 1943-47; Bethel AME Ch Balt, pastor 1949-64; Bishop, elected 1964; AME Ch, Republic S Africa, bishop 1964-68; 5th Episcopal Dist, USA, AME Ch, bishop 1968-76. **ORGANIZATIONS:** 33rd degree Mason; past pres Council Bishops AME Ch; vice pres Gen Bd AME Ch; MO Council Chs; Cncl of Chs of MD 1974-; pres bd Wilberforce Inst Johannesburg S Africa 1964-65. **BUSINESS ADDRESS:** 7419 Harrison St, Kansas City, MO.

BRYANT, HENRY C.
Pathologist. **PERSONAL:** Born Feb 21, 1915, Birmingham, AL; married Barbara; children: Henry, Lisa. **EDUCATION:** Talledega Coll, BA 1936; Univ MI, MD 1940, MS 19478 PhD 1949. **CAREER:** Physicians Clinical Lab Co, dir pres; Univ MI, rsrch asst, rsrch asso, instr, lectr. **ORGANIZATIONS:** Dir St Joseph Mercy Hosp 1958-64; dir Peoples Comm Hosp 1958-64; dir Merrywood Hosp, Herrick Meml Hosp 1958-; Washtenew Co MI State Med Soc 1949; AMA 1949-; Nat Med Assn 1949-; NY Acad of Scis 1948-; Am Soc of Clinical Pathologists; MI Soc of Pathologists 1949-; MI Assn of Profs 1976-; NAACP 1945. **MILITARY SERVICE:** USAR 1941-48.

BRYANT, HUBERT HALE
Attorney at law. **PERSONAL:** Born Jan 04, 1931, Tulsa, OK; son of Dr Roscoe Conkling Bryant and Curlie Beatrice Marshall Bryant; married Elnora Roberson, Oct 25, 1952; children: Cheryl Denise Bryant Hopkins, Tara Kay Bryant-Walker. **EDUCATION:** Fisk Univ, BA 1952; Howard Univ Law Sch, LLB 1956. **CAREER:** City of Tulsa, OK, asst city prosecutor 1961-63, city prosecutor 1963-67; ND OK, asst US atty 1967-77; ND OK Dept of Justice, US atty 1977-81; City of Tulsa OK, municipal court judge 1984-86; private law practice 1986-. **ORGANIZATIONS:** Atty at law private practice 1956-61; trustee First Baptist Church N Tulsa 1970-75; bd Tulsa Urban League 1962-64; vice sire archon Sigma Pi Phi Alpha Theta Boule; exec bd Tulsa Branch NAACP; Alpha Phi Alpha. **HONORS/ACHIEVEMENTS:** Outstanding Alumni Howard Univ Sch of Law 1981; Outstanding Citizen Tulsa Branch NAACP 1981; Outstanding Citizen Masons 1978; Mason of Yr Masons 1963. **BUSINESS ADDRESS:** 2623 North Peoria, Tulsa, OK 74106.

BRYANT, ISAAC RUTLEDGE
Consultant. **PERSONAL:** Born Nov 04, 1914, Lawnside, NJ; married AnnaMae Jones; children: Isaac R Jr, Wayne R Esq, Mark K. **EDUCATION:** Attended Temple Univ Phila; US Army Officer Candid Sch Camp Lee VA. **CAREER:** Borough of Lawnside NJ, dist clerk & bus mang 1938-42; Lawnside NJ Sch Dist, dist clerk & bus mgr 1938-42; IRS, US Treas Dept 1942-74; Borough of Lawnside, adminis aide; Self Employed, consultant. **ORGANIZATIONS:** Pres of trustees & dir Camden Co YMCA 30 yrs; trustee United Way; pres Lawnside NJ Bd of Educ; life mem NAACP; mem adv council Camden Co NJ Employment & training Ctr; pres bd of trustees Mt Zion UM Church; chmn supervy comm Lawnside Fed Cred Union; chmn admin bd Mt Zion UM Church; dir Lawnside Cultural Comm; dir Lawnside Comm Ctr Inc; past mem bd of dir State of NJ Educ Oppor Fund and the Camden Co Comm Coll; past grand sr warden PrinceHall Grand Lodge F&AM State of NJ, past master Hiram Lodge No 5 F&AM. **HONORS/ACHIEVEMENTS:** The Youth of Mt Zion UM Church 1969; YMCA Man of the Yr Camden Co 1973; Gallatin Awd US Dept of Treas 1975. **MILITARY SERVICE:** AUS 1st lt 1942-45. **BUSINESS ADDRESS:** Consultant, 34 W Emlen Ave, Lawnside, NJ 08045.

BRYANT, JAMES W.
Educational administrator. **PERSONAL:** Born May 04, 1922, Sarasota, FL; married Ophelia Jeanette Quillin. **EDUCATION:** Philadelphia Coll of Art, BFA Educ 1951; Rutgers U, MEd 1959, 1965. **CAREER:** Camden City Bd of Educ, Lawnside NJ, dir adult & comm educ prog 1975-; Pyne Poynt Jr High School, prin 1968-75; Cooper-Grant Elementary School, prin 1964-68; Pyne Poynt Jr High School, asst prin 1962-64; Camden City Bd of Educ, art teacher 1953-62; Construction, 1939-53. **ORGANIZATIONS:** Rgstrd rep Mutual Funds Assos Inc Philadelphia 1959-69; elected councilman Lawnside NJ 1960-69; mayor Lawnside NJ 1975-; co committeeman Borough of Lawnside-Camden Co 1955-67; pres 1st Regular Dem Club of Lawnside 1956-60; mem NJ Hlth Dept Admin Bd 1969-72. **HONORS/ACHIEVEMENTS:** Anne E Sinnot excellence in teaching award Philadelphia Coll of Art 1951; Four Chaplains Legion of Hon Award for Serv to All People Philadelphia Chapel of Four Chaplains 1977; humanitarian award Club Anglers Philadelphia 1979; recipient 2 Battle Stars AUS; Good Conduct Medal, AUS; ETO Ribbon AUS. **MILITARY SERVICE:** AUS tec-gr5 1943-45. **BUSINESS ADDRESS:** Baird Ave & Park Blvd, Camden, NJ 08103.

BRYANT, JEROME BENJAMIN
Physician. **PERSONAL:** Born Aug 29, 1916, Adel, GA; married Lois. **EDUCATION:** Talladega Coll, AA 1939; Meharry Med Coll, MD 1943; FL Inst Tech, MS 1977. **CAREER:** AUS, chf physical exam, surg 1957-77; physician. **ORGANIZATIONS:** Mem GA Med Assn; Assn Mil Surgeons; mem Alpha Phi Alpha Frat; 32nd degree Mason. **HONORS/ACHIEVEMENTS:** Outstanding Commendation Award, Dir Gen Korean Nat RR 1969; Legion Merit Award 1977. **MILITARY SERVICE:** AUS Col 1957-77. **BUSINESS ADDRESS:** Ft Benning, Columbus, GA 31905.

BRYANT, JESSE A.
Business executive. **PERSONAL:** Born Aug 27, 1922, Supply, NC; married Eva Mae Fullwood; children: 4 children. **CAREER:** Sec Intl Longshoremans Assn; NAACP, president. **ORGANIZATIONS:** Pres Cedar Grove Br NAACP; vice pres SENC Land Chap of A Phillips Randolph Inst; mem exec bd Brunswick Co Cit Assn. **HONORS/ACHIEVEMENTS:** Twice crowned as the Most Outstanding Small Branch NAACP President in NC; crowned once as Mr NAACP of NC.

BRYANT, JOHN RICHARD
Pastor. **PERSONAL:** Born Jun 08, 1943, Baltimore, MD; son of Harrison and Edith; married Cecila Williams; children: Jamal, Thema. **EDUCATION:** Morgan State Coll, AB; Boston Univ Sch of Theol, ThM, MDiv 1970; Colgate Rochester Div Sch, DMin 1975; Virginia Seminary at Lynchburg, Honorary Doctorate; Wilberforce Univ & Payne Seminary Honorary Doctorate. **CAREER:** Preached on five continents; guest lecturer to various colleges & univs 1970-72; Peace Corps Liberia, teacher; Boston Urban League, comm organizer; St Paul AME Church, pastor; Bethel AME Church, pastor; AME Church, Monrovia, Liberia, bishop, 1988-. **ORGANIZATIONS:** Bd mem Natl Comm of Black Churchmen; Natl Council of Churches; Black Ecumenical Commn; World Methodist Council on Evangelism; bd mem Ecumenical Inst. **HONORS/ACHIEVEMENTS:** Springfield Outstanding Churchman Award Boston Jaycees; Outstanding Leader Award Winkey Studios; Man of the Year Award; contributed to Pastor's Manual and four other books; honored by Vanguard Organization, Delta Sorority; Boston Univ School Theology Outstanding Alumni Awd. **BUSINESS ADDRESS:** Pastor, Bethel AME Church, 1300 Druid Hill, Baltimore, MD 21217.

BRYANT, NAPOLEON, JR.
Educator. **PERSONAL:** Born Feb 22, 1929, Cincinnati, OH; married Ernestine C; children: Karen, Derek, Brian, David. **EDUCATION:** Univ Of Cincinnati, BS 1959; IN Univ, MAT, 1967, EdD 1970, NDEA Fellow, 1968-70. **CAREER:** Cincinnati Public School, teacher; Xavier Univ, Science Resource teacher, Prof, Educ, Dir, secondary educ 1974-79; NSF, pre-coll teacher devel projects, 1974-79, dir of minority affairs, 1984-86; Xavier Coll, prof of Educ. **ORGANIZATIONS:** Mem Shc Sci & Math Assn; OH Council of Elementary School Int; chmn Com for Local Arrngmnts; Rollman Psychist Hosp 1976-78; mem sev com Epic Diocese of So OH; life mem NAACP; Nat Sci Teachers Assn; mem Phi Delta Kappa, Natl Assn of Research in Sci Teaching Am Educ Rsch Assn; Consultant on Elem & Secondary Sci Educ for school & publsihing firms; co-organizer & participant Carribbean Regional Orgn of Assn of Sci Educators Barbados WI 1979; hon life mem Assn of Sci Teachers of Jamaica 1979; Cub Pack Master 1973-; Comm Athletic Assn; Cincinnati School Found 1972-81; ordained deacon Episcopal 1984; bd of dir Harriett Beacher Stow Preservation Comm, William Proector Conf Center; adv comm Cincinnati Acad of Math & Sci, Rockdale Sch Math & Sci, VIP NASA Educ Conf Danforth Fellow 1983; sci cons, sci adv comm State of OH. **HONORS/ACHIEVEMENTS:** "For What Have You Toiled?" Pride Mag 1978; "Action, A Model for Influencing Curricular & Instructional Changes for the Educ of Minorities in Sci" The Hoosier Sci Teacher 1979; "Non-Formal Teacher Educ in Sci" Sci Educ for Prog, A Caribbean Perspective 1980; "About Films" Jrnl of Geological Educ 1982; nom pres elect NSTA 1983; Natl Builders Awd Xavier Univ 1984; Keynote Speaker Annual ASTJ Conf Jamaica WI 1986. **BUSINESS ADDRESS:** Professor of Education, Xavier University, Department of Education, 3800 Victory Parkway, Cincinnati, OH 45207.

BRYANT, PRESTON
Educator. **PERSONAL:** Born Aug 08, 1938, Chicago; married Sandra; children: Carolyn, Beverly. **EDUCATION:** Chicago Tchrs Coll, BEd 1961; Roosevelt U, MA 1963; Nova U, EdD 1978. **CAREER:** Teacher, 1961-63; master teacher, 1963-67; Madison School, asst prin, acting prin 1968-70; EF Dunne Elementary School, prin 1971-73; George Henry Corliss High School, prin 1974-77; Chicago Bd of Educ, supt 1977-; Chicago Teachers Coll, instructor 1975; Union Graduate School, prof 1979; Gov State Univ, instructor 1980; District 10 Chicago IL, supt 1977-. **ORGANIZATIONS:** Mem Samuel B Stratton Educ Assn; IL Assn for Supr & Curriculum Dev; Chicago Prins Assn; Nat Assn Secondary Sch Prins; bd of dir George Howland Adminstrs Assn, former vp; Roosevelt Univ Alumni Assn; bd mem Roosevelt Univ Bd Govs; Roosevelt Educ Alumni Div; Citizens Schs Com; mem Nat Alliance of Black Sch Educators; mem advis counc Olive Harvey Coll Dept of Nursing; Nat Assn Black

Sch Edntrs; NAACP; PUSH; Phi Delta Kappa; mem Zion Evangelical Luth Ch, mem bd educ; mem Forum Civic Orgn. **HONORS/ACHIEVEMENTS:** Sch & community award 1974; outst serv in educ Edward F Dunne Sch Comm 1974; educators award Operation PUSH 1977; outst educators award Dr Roger's BelleTone Ensemble 1977. **BUSINESS ADDRESS:** 1830 S Keeler Ave, Chicago, IL 60623.

BRYANT, R. KELLY, JR.
Business executive. **EDUCATION:** Hampton Inst, BS 1940; NC Coll, 1941-42. **CAREER:** NC Mutual Life & Insurance Co, asst sec 1965-; Ordinary Dept, asst sec-mgr 1960-65, mgr 1956-60; Ordinary Dept NC Mutual Life Insurance Co, chief clerk 1944-56; Mutual Savings & Loan Assn Durham, bookkeeper 1941-44; Peoples Bldg & Loan Assn VA, bookkeeper 1940; Devel Training & Opportunities Corp Inc, sec 1972-77; Durham Business & Professional Chain, sec 1943-. **ORGANIZATIONS:** Mem Durham C of C; pres Chain Investment Corp; bd dir Goodwill Industries Inc 1968-76; bd dir Vol Serv Bur Inc; chmn Sch Improvement Com-Burton Sch PTA 1968-; chmn Educ Com-Durham Human Relations Commn 1968-; mem adv bd Emergency Sch Assistance Act Prog-Operation Breakthrough Inc 1972-77;trustee-chmn-auditing com White Rock Pabt Ch; sec AS Hunter Lodge #825 Free & Accepted Masons & First Worshipful Master 1961-; sec Durham Outboard Boating Club 1966-; registrar Burton Sch Voting Precint #3 1951-; scoutmaster Boy Scout Troop 187 1951-; fromer mem Study Commn on Pub Educ City & Co 1973-; mem Educ Com Durham Com on Negro Affairs; mem Nat & Durham Chap Nat Hampton Alumni Assn; treas NC Region; mem Auditing & Finance Com; Most Worshipful Prince Hall Grand Lodge of Free & Accepted Masons of Juridsiction of NC; vice pres Burton Comm Civic League; mem numerous other orgns. **HONORS/ACHIEVEMENTS:** Man of Yr Durham Housewives League 1958; NC Hamptonian of Yr 1957; Silver Beaver Award; BSA 1953; Alumni Merit Award Nat Hampton Alumni Assn 1969; Appreciation for Serv Award AS Hunter Lodge No 825 Free & Accepted Masons 1974; Most Outstanding Sec9 AS Hunter Lodge No 825 Free & Accptd Masons 1976; Spl Cert for 8 Yrs Serv on Durham Human Relations Commn Durham City Council 1977; Man of Yr Award Durham Outboard Boating Club 1978; Appreciation for Serv Award Nat Hampton Alumni Assn 1979. **BUSINESS ADDRESS:** NC Mutual Life Ins Co, Mutual Plaza, Durham, NC 27701.

BRYANT, REGINA LYNN
Financial analyst/corporate finance. **PERSONAL:** Born Dec 01, 1950, Memphis, TN; daughter of Al C Bryant and Mrs Dorothy Scruggs-Bryant. **EDUCATION:** TN State Univ, BA Foreign Lang 1974; Atlanta Univ, MBA Finance 1980. **CAREER:** IBM, marketing rep 1976-77; Amer Telephone & Telegraph, mgmt develop prog 1980-82; Comptroller of the Currency, asst natl bank examiner 1983-84; Credit Bureau Inc/Equifax Inc, financial analyst 1984-. **ORGANIZATIONS:** Mem Alpha Kappa Alpha Sor Inc 1971-; 2nd vice pres academics Natl Black MBA Assoc 1980-83; business consultant Jr Achievement of Greater Atlanta 1981-; pres Sch of Business Admin Assoc Atlanta Univ 1983-85; chairperson finance comm St Anthony's Catholic Church 1984-86; asst treas Animalife Inc 1984-86; youth motivator Merit Employment Assoc 1985-; chairperson St Anthony's Night Shelter Fund Raising Comm 1986. **HONORS/ACHIEVEMENTS:** Exxon Fellowship 1979; Outstanding Serv Awd Natl Black MBA Assoc 1982; Outstanding Young Women of Amer 1985. **HOME ADDRESS:** 200 26th St NW Q204, Atlanta, GA 30309. **BUSINESS ADDRESS:** Financial Analyst, Credit Bureau Inc/Equifax Inc, 1600 Peachtree St NW, Atlanta, GA 30309.

BRYANT, ROBERT E.
Seminar workshop leader, public speaker. **PERSONAL:** Born Feb 01, 1910, Chattanooga, TN; children: 3 children. **EDUCATION:** YMCA Coll, AB 1938; Kent Coll of Law, LLB 1941, JD 1969; Roosevelt Univ, MPA 1979. **CAREER:** Chicago Br NAACP, spec counsel 1941-46; Fed Dist Ct Chgo, practice law 1941-; Cook Cty IL, asst states attny 1953-55; IL State Fair Emp Practices Com,hearing officer 1962-64; IL Sec of State, hearing officer 1964-66; Legal Serv Bur War on Poverty Carbondale, org, dir 1966-67; Tabernacle Comm Hosp & Health Ctr, hosp admin, gen counsel 1972-76; workshop leader in industry. **ORGANIZATIONS:** Mem, asst pastor Tabernacle Missionary Bapt Church; mem Amer Soc of Hosp Attnys, Cook Cty Bar Assoc, Natl Bar Assoc, Amer Bar Assoc; author,"How to Grip and Hold Attention in Public Speaking". **BUSINESS ADDRESS:** Attorney, 3651 S Michigan Ave, Chicago, IL 60653.

BRYANT, ROBERT EDWARD
Architect. **PERSONAL:** Born Sep 14, 1931, Palmetto, GA; married Shirley Mae Smothers. **EDUCATION:** Howard Univ, BArch 1954. **CAREER:** Bernard L Frishman & Assoc, arch draftsman 1956-58; Edmund W Dreyfuss & Assoc, architect/assoc 1958-69; Bryant and Bryant, partner 1969-. **ORGANIZATIONS:** Mem Natl Ctr for Barrier Free Soc, Panel of Arbitrators of Amer Arb Assn 1982-85, Amer Inst of Architects 1964-85, Br of Dir Boys & Girls Clubs of Greater WA 1983-85. **HONORS/ACHIEVEMENTS:** Internation exchg delegate People to People 1982; NAACP Achvmnt Award NAACP Arlington, VA Chapter 1968. **MILITARY SERVICE:** USAF capt. **HOME ADDRESS:** 5524 4th St NE, Washington, DC 20011. **BUSINESS ADDRESS:** Architect, Bryant & Bryant/Architects, 4301 Connecticut Ave NW, Washington, DC 20008.

BRYANT, T. J.
Physician. **PERSONAL:** Born Dec 28, 1934, Wellston, OK; married Rosie L; children: Daryl, Gregory, Cynthia. **EDUCATION:** AR AM&N, BS 1957; Kansas Univ Med Schl, MD 1963; KUMC Menorah, Residency Training 1964-67. **CAREER:** Jackson County Med Soc, sec 1973-75; UMKC Sch of Med, assoc prof 1977-; UMKC Sch of Med, docent 1974-79; Dept of Med Bapt Med Center, chmn 1980-82; Dept of Med, Menorah Med Center, vice chmn 1980-; Menorah Medical Center, board of directors 1989; Missouri Board of Healing Arts 1989. **ORGANIZATIONS:** Mem MO State Med Assn 1963-, Jackson County Med Soc 1963-, Amer Coll of Gastroenterology 1972-, Amer Soc of Internal Med 1970-, NAACP Urban League 1980-81, Greater Kansas City Chamber of Commerce 1978-; American Medical Association. **MILITARY SERVICE:** USAAF a1c 1959-65. **BUSINESS ADDRESS:** 6724 Troost, Kansas City, MO 64131.

BRYANT, TERESENA WISE
City official, educational administrator. **PERSONAL:** Born Jan 19, 1940, St Petersburg, FL; daughter of Mose Gardner (deceased) and Mattie Cooksey Gardner; divorced; children: Donna Kaye Drayton. **EDUCATION:** Gibbs Sub Div, AA, 1960; Florida A&M Univ, BS, 1962; Howard Univ, Certificate of Completion Program Evaluation & Craftsmanship, 1976; NYU, MPA, 1977; Man Coll, 12 credits counseling psych; Fordham Univ, work toward PhD. **CAREER:** NYC, admin positions, 1974-81; State Senator, Bronx City NY, legislative asst, comm liaison, 1978-83; Office of the Mayor, New York City Youth Bureau, asst exec dir, 1981-83; NY State Tempy Comm to revise the SS Laws, contract mgr, sr program analyst, 1983-; St Senator, Jos L Galiber, campaign mgr, 1978-; Office of the Mayor, New York City Youth Bureau, dir of planning; campaign mgr, Robert Johnson, first black district attorney in NY state, 1988; special asst to Bronx City Central Board 1987-; mem, NYC Bd of Education. **ORGANIZATIONS:** Mem, Alpha Kappa Alpha, Tau Omega, 1975-; coordinator of Comm of Bronx Blacks 1977-; under legislative leadership of Sen Goliber responsible for securing of additional minority councilman and a Black assembly seat in Bronx Co redistricting lines; chairperson, Bronx Center for Program Serv Youth, 1981-; bd of dir, PR Representative, Urban League Bronx Aux Chap, 1982-; mem, Florida A&M Univ Alumni, Amer Assn of Univ Women, NY City Managerial Employees Assn, NAACP, Amer Soc for Public Admin, Natl Forum of Black Public Admin, Natl Assoc for Female Exec, William Inst CME Church, Stewart Memorial CME Church, NYC, St Petersburg, FL, Council of Concerned Black Exec, NY Univ Alumni NY Chapter; Former women advisor, NYC Youth Bureau; The NYS Temp Commission to Revise the Soc Serv Law; pres, chairperson, owner, founder, T Wise Enterprise Inc (major area political strategy); mem, Women Business Owners of NY; Bronx Black Assn of Educators. ; mem Women Business Owners of NY. **HONORS/ACHIEVEMENTS:** Martin L King Scholarship to NYU Graduate School of Public Admin, 1973-77; Saluted by 48th Comm Council Serv & Dedication 1971, PTA of PS 67 Serv Award, 1971; Certificate of Merit Vocational Adv Serv 1971; Scholarship to Howard Univ, 1976; St Augustine Coll Acknowledge the Loyal Support & Devoted Interest, 1976; Certificate for Contribution, Time, New York City, Central Labor Rehabilitation Council, 1978-83; SAVE, Dept of Labor Serv Award, 1981-83; Outstanding Civic Leadership Bronx Unity Democratic Club, 1981; Woman of the Year Morrisania Ed Council 1981; Service Award, Bronx Center for Program Service, 1982-84; Community Serv Award Each One Teach One 1983; Mid Brooklyn Health Soc "Project Helping Hand Outstanding Serv & Dedication to the Youth of Our Community 1983; Pres Award as Pres of Adlai Stevenson HS 1971-72; First Award from North Bronx Black Pol itical Women Org, 1985; Resolution passed NYS Senate & Assembly proclaiming for the leadership role in redistricting for Blacks in Bronx City, 1980; Distinguished Serv Award, NY State Assn of Black & Public Relation Legislators 1989; Community Srvice Award in Education, Community School District 9, 1988; Outstanding Service to PS 30, Community School District 7, 1989; Campaign Mgr, NY State's First Black Elected District Attorney, 1988. **HOME ADDRESS:** 950 Evergreen Ave Apt 16M, Bronx, NY 10473. **BUSINESS ADDRESS:** Special Asst, New York City Bd of Educ, 110 Livingston St, Rm 1130, Brooklyn, NY 11201.

BRYANT, WALLACE HENRY
Professional athlete. **PERSONAL:** Born Jul 14, 1959, Madrid, Spain. **EDUCATION:** San Fran, 1982. **CAREER:** Dallas Mavericks, center 1984-; Chicago Bulls, center 1982. **HONORS/ACHIEVEMENTS:** Helping his club win the European Cup; USF'S All-amer center; on USF'S all-time charts is fifth. **BUSINESS ADDRESS:** Dallas Mavericks, Reunion Arena, 777 Sports St, Dallas, TX 75207.

BRYANT, WAYNE R.
Attorney. **PERSONAL:** Born Nov 07, 1947, Camden, NJ; son of Isaac R Bryant Sr and Anna Mae Bryant; married Jean Woods; children: Wayne Richard Jr. **EDUCATION:** Howard Univ, BA 1969; Rutgers Univ Sch of Law, JD 1972. **CAREER:** Transportation & Communications Comm, vice chmn 1982-84, chmn 1984-; Independent Authorities & Commun Comm, mem 1982-84, vice chmn 1984-; State of NJ, assemblyman dist 5 1982-; Camden Co Council on Economic Oppor, solicitor 1982-; Borough of Somerdale, spec solicitor 1983-; Juvenile Resource Center, solicitor 1983-; Borough of Lawnside, bond counsel 1984-, solicitor 1984-; Capital Budgeting & Planning Comm, assembly rep 1984-; Camden Co Housing Auth, solicitor 1985-; Borough of Chesilhurst, spec solicitor 1985-; Freeman Zeller and Bryant, general partner, 1974-. **ORGANIZATIONS:** Natl officer, mem, exec bd of Natl Black Caucus of State Legislators; mem, Amer Bar Assn, NJ Bar Assn, Camden Co Bar Assn, Natl Conf of Black Lawyers, Phi Alpha Delta Law Frat, NAACP; Eastern Regional Council of State Govts; Amer Council of Young Political Leaders; Monorail Commn State of NJ; bd of dirs NJ Conference of Minority Trans Officials; mem US Supreme Court, US Court of Appeals for the Third Circuit Court of Appeals DC, Supreme Ct of NJ, US Dist Court for the District of NJ; bd of dirs Camden Co Urban League; bd of mgmt, asst sec, Camden Co YMCA; mem Camden Co Council on Economic Oppor Inc; mem Head Start Policy Council Camden Co; mem Educ Oppor Fund Comm Adv Bd Rutgers Univ; mem Lawnside Educ Assn; chmn Co State & Local Govts United Way Campaign of Camden Co; NJ State Democratic Platform Comm. **HONORS/ACHIEVEMENTS:** Recognition Award, Natl Political Congress of Black Women; Disting Serv Awd Camden Co Bd of Chosen Freeholders; Disting Serv Awd Camden Co Planning Bd; Awd of Merit NJ Co Trans Assn; Legislative Committment Awd Educ Improvement Ctr S Jersey Region; Outstanding Achievement Awd,Lawnside Bd of Educ; Awd of Merit Assn of Parking Authorities State of NJ; Comm Serv Awd Gloucester Co Black Political Caucus; Comm Serv Awd, Grace Temple Baptist Church; Comm Serv Awd, YMCA Camden Co; Mt Pisgah Man of the Year; Comm Serv Awd First Regular Democratic Club of Lawnside; Outstanding Serv to the Comm Brotherhood of Sheriff & Corrections Officers; Outstanding Serv Award, Good Neighbor Award, Juvenile Resource Ctr; Cert of Appreciation Camden City Skills Ctr; Outstanding Commitment to Human Serv Alternatives for Women Now Camden Co; Outstanding Serv to the Community Cert of Appreciation Awd Camden Comm Serv Ctr; adv bd Music Festival Rutgers; Hairston Clan Comm Serv Awd; Natl Business League Awd Disting Serv Awd Haddon Heights HS Afro-Amer Cultural Club; Citizen of the Year Alpha Phi Alpha Frat Inc Nu Iota Chapt; NJ Assn of Counties Achievement Awd; Cooper Hospital/Medical Ctr Outstanding Legislator. **HOME ADDRESS:** 79 LaPierre Ave, Lawnside, NJ 08045. **BUSINESS ADDRESS:** Assembly Member District 5, Freeman Zeller & Bryant, 309 Market St, Camden, NJ 08102.

BRYANT, WILLA COWARD
Retired educator. **PERSONAL:** Born Nov 21, 1919, Durham, NC; married Harry L Bryant (deceased); children: Mona, Maree, Shanklin. **EDUCATION:** NC Central Univ, AB 1951; Temple Univ, MEd 1961; Duke Univ, EdD 1970. **CAREER:** Durham City Schools, teacher 1954-61; NC Central Univ, asst prof ed 1961-69; Livingstone Coll, chairperson, div of ed & psych 1970-83. **ORGANIZATIONS:** Consult Coop School Improvement Prog 1964-66; pres Alpha Tau Chap of Kappa Delta Pi 1969-70, Triangle Reading Assoc 1970-72, NC Assoc of Coll for TeacherEd 1980-81; mem Bd of Ed Durham City Schools 1984-. **HONORS/ACHIEVEMENTS:** Southern Fellowship Found 1968-70; "Two Divergent Approaches to Teaching Reading" Amer Rsch Assoc 1970; "Crucial Issues in Reading" Views

on Elementary Reading 1973; Phelps Stokes Scholar 1975; mem Phi Delta Kappa Fraternity Carolina Chap 1987.

BRYANT, WILLIAM ARNETT, JR.
Physician. **PERSONAL:** Born Dec 31, 1942, Birmingham, AL; married Hidla R Timpson; children: Kristen, Lamont. **EDUCATION:** Clark Coll Atlanta, BA 1964; State Univ NY at Buffalo Sch of Medicine, MD 1975. **CAREER:** Pvt Practice of Pediatrics, physician 1979-; Univ of MD Hosp Dept of Pediatrics, intern/Resident/Chief Resident 1975-79; Buffao Med Sch, med student & SUNY 1971-75; Erie Cty Health Dept Buffalo, lab supr 1969-71; Erie Co Health Dept Buffalo, vd epidemiologist 1967-69; Provident Hosp Baltimore MD, asst chief of pediatrics 1980-. **ORGANIZATIONS:** Mem Nat Med Assn 1975-; Peace Corps Vol US Govt 1964-66; mem Chi Delta Mu Health Prof Frat 1977-; pres Baltimore Clark Coll Club 1979-. **BUSINESS ADDRESS:** 1532 Havenwood Rd, Baltimore, MD 21218.

BRYANT, WILLIAM B.
Judge. **PERSONAL:** Born Sep 18, 1911, Wetumpka, AL; married Astaire A Gonzalez; children: Astaire, William B. **EDUCATION:** Howard U, AB 1932, LLB 1936. **CAREER:** DC Asst US Atty, 1951-54; Houston Bryant & Gardner, partner 1954-65; US Dist Judge DC, 1965-; Howard U, law prof 1965-. **ORGANIZATIONS:** Sec, Bd Educ DC; mem Amer Bar Assn. **MILITARY SERVICE:** AUS 1943-47. **BUSINESS ADDRESS:** Sr US District Judge, US District Court, U S Courthouse, 3rd & Constitution Ave NW, Washington, DC 20001.

BRYANT, WILLIAM CULLEN
Athlete. **PERSONAL:** Born May 20, 1951, Ft Sill, OK; married Sandra. **EDUCATION:** Univ CO. **CAREER:** Los Angeles Rams, running back 1973-. **ORGANIZATIONS:** Mem Denver Inner City Rec Prgms. **HONORS/ACHIEVEMENTS:** All-Am defensive back UPI Coaches & Sporting News 1972; All-Big Eight AP & UPI polls; performer Sr Bowl Coll All-Star NFC Championship Game 1974 1976-79. **BUSINESS ADDRESS:** Los Angeles Rams, 10271 W Pico, Los Angeles, CA 90064.

BRYANT, WILLIAM HENRY, JR.
Design engineer. **PERSONAL:** Born Feb 10, 1963, Cleveland, OH; son of William Henry Bryant Sr and Ruth Earle Bishop-Bryant. **EDUCATION:** Kent State Univ, AAS 1984; Pacific-Western Univ, BS 1987. **CAREER:** AUS C Co 101 Aviation Battalion 101st Abn Div, crew engr 1986-; Cleveland Rebar, cost estimator 1989-; Veteran's Administration, Cleveland OH, records mgr 1989-. **ORGANIZATIONS:** Sec Amer Inst of Aero & Astronautics 1982-86; mem Aircraft Owners & Pilots Assoc 1982-; vice pres Phi Beta Sigma Frat Inc 1983-85; mem Soc of Manufacturing Engrs 1984-; jr deacon Starlight Baptist Church 1984-; mem Future Aviation Profls of Amer 1986-. **MILITARY SERVICE:** AUS specialist 4-1 1/2 yrs; Ohio Natl Guard, OCS cadet; received Letter of Commendation 101st Airborne 1986; Letter of Commendation 5th Group Special Forces 1986; 101st Aviation Battalion Achievement Award 1986; Good Conduct 1987;Army Commenmdation Award 1987; Army Achievement Award 1988; Overseas 1988. **HOME ADDRESS:** 3663 Severn Rd, Cleveland Heights, OH 44118.

BRYANT, WILLIAM JESSE
Dentist,educator. **PERSONAL:** Born Apr 08, 1935, Jacksonville, FL; son of Katie Bryant Brown; married Taunya Marie Golden Bryant, Feb 22, 1979; children: Kiwanis Linda, William, Deron, Vincent, Michael, Kimberly, Zachary, Jessica. **EDUCATION:** FL A&M U, BA 1960; AZ State U, 1962; Meharry Med Coll, DDS 1967; Boston U, Cert Orthodontics 1970; Boston U, ScD 1971. **CAREER:** N Eastern U, chmn assoc prof 1972; FL A&M, rsch asst 1961-63; NE U, instr 1969-71; Whittier Dental Clinic, orthodontist 1970-72; Chicago, chmn 1971-72; pvt practice 1970; Roxbury Comprehensive Community Health Ctr, dental dir 1971-78; Boston U, asst prof 1971-74; Boston U, assoc prof 1974; WPFL Stuart FL, private practice 1986. **ORGANIZATIONS:** Exec bd mem Roxbury Med Tech Inst 1972-74; dental consult HEW Boston 1974; exec bd mem United Way 1976; exec bd mem NAACP 1976; Commonwealth Dental Soc of Greater Boston; Am Assn of Orthodontists; NE Soc of Orthodontists; Internatl Assn for Dental Rsrch; Am Dental Assn; Nat Dental Assn; MA Dental Assn; Capital City Dental Soc; Nashville TN FL TN MA GA State Dental Bds; Am Soc of Dentistry for Children; Am Anesthesiology Assn; Soc of the Upper 10th; Alpha Phi Alpha; Guardsmen Inc; NAACP; exec bd mem Health Planning Council of Boston; Pub Health Council; bd dir United Way; bd mem Big Brother Inc Boston; bd member, St Michael's School Stuart FL; fellow, International College Craniomandibular Orthopedics. **HONORS/ACHIEVEMENTS:** Numerous awards & publications. **BUSINESS ADDRESS:** 203 West Ocean Blvd, Stuart, FL 34994.

BRYANT-MITCHELL, RUTH HARRIET
Business executive, librarian. **PERSONAL:** Born Jun 28, 1943, Birmingham, AL; daughter of Harrison Armstead Bryant and Ora Ardell Knight Bryant; married Ronald J Mitchell, Dec 03, 1966 (divorced); children: Sydney Adele Mitchell. **EDUCATION:** Attended, Hunter Coll NY. **CAREER:** City Hospital at Elmhurst, asst librarian 1964-65; Chem Construction Corp, asst librarian 1965-67; St Vincent's Hospital, asst librarian 1967-69; Ford Found, editorial & rsch asst 1969-71; Public Information & Research Library, dir 1971-79; Bedford Stuyvesant Restrant Corp, asst to pres for public relations 1979-80; Magnolia Tree Earth Center of Bedford Stuyvesant Inc, exec dir 1980-82; Brooklyn Acad of Music, dir of comm relations 1983-85; Natl Park Serv Gateway Natl Rec Area, coop activities specialist 1985-86; Bedford-Stuyvesant Early Childhood Devel Center, asst dir 1986-87. **ORGANIZATIONS:** Mem Soc for Preservation of Weeksville & Bedford-Stuyvesant History; mem Brownstoners of Bedford Stuyvesant; adv council Medgar Evers Coll School of Continuing Educ; adv council Empire State Coll; mem Bedford-Stuyvesant Jaycees; chairperson bd dir Bedford-Stuyvesant Early Childhood Devel Center; bd mem Jubilation Dance Co; mem 1st Family Theatre Co; dir HTUR Acting Co, Lionesses of Bedford-Stuyvesant. **HOME ADDRESS:** 4 Herkimer Ct, Brooklyn, NY 11216.

BRYANT-REID, JOHANNE
Vice president, corporate human resources. **PERSONAL:** Born Mar 11, 1949, Farmington, WV; daughter of Leslie Bryant and Jessie Scruggs Bryant. **EDUCATION:** West Virginia Univ, BS 1971. **CAREER:** Ran Assoc, gen mgr/recruiter 1971-78; Merrill Lynch, exec recruitment mgr 1978-81, vice pres corporate human resources 1981-. **ORGANIZATIONS:** Mem Council of Concerned Black Execs 1983-, Amer Soc of Personnel Admin 1983-, Employment Mgrs Assoc 1984-, EDGES 1985-; mem adv bd Natl Council Negro Women 1985-, Black World Championship Rodeo 1985-; adv bd mem Borough of Manhattan; adv bd mem Community Coll; bd mem James Robert Braxton Scholarship Fund. **HONORS/ACHIEVEMENTS:** Black Achievers Awd YWCA 1981. **BUSINESS ADDRESS:** Vice Pres, Corp Human Resources, World Financial Center, South Tower, 11th Fl, New York, NY 10080-6111.

BRYCE, HERRINGTON J.
Insurance executive, economist. **PERSONAL:** Married Beverly J Gaustad; children: Marisa Jeanine, Shauna Celestina, Herrington Simon. **EDUCATION:** Mankato State Univ, BA 1957-60; Syracuse Univ, PhD 1960-66; Amer Coll, CLU 1984-85, ChFC 1984-85. **CAREER:** Natl Planning Assoc, economist 1966-67; Clark Univ, faculty 1967-69; Urban Inst, sr economist 1969-70; Brookings Institution, fellow 1970-71; MIT, faculty 1972-73; Joint Center for Political Studies, dir of rsch 1973-76; Harvard Univ, fellow 1978; Academy for State & Local Govt, vice pres 1978-80; Natl Policy Inst 1980-85; Carlogh Corp/Coll of William and Mary, prof of business 1986-. **HONORS/ACHIEVEMENTS:** Honoarary Citizen City of Atlanta 1975; Minority Admin of Yr Conf of Minority Public Admins 1976; Honorary Citizen City of New Orleans 1976; Distinguished Alumnus Mankato State Univ 1982. **BUSINESS ADDRESS:** President, Carlogh Corp/Coll of Wm & Mary, Box 15678, Chevy Chase, MD 20815.

BRYCE-LAPORTE, ROY SIMON
Sociologist, educator. **PERSONAL:** Born Sep 07, 1933; son of Simon V Bryce and Myra C Laporte; divorced; children: Camila, Robertino, Rene'. **EDUCATION:** Panama Canal Coll, AA, 1954; Univ of Nebraska, MA, 1960, BS Ed, Social Science, Romance Lang (Hon), 1961; Univ Puerto Rico, Adv Cert, 1963; UCLA, PhD, Sociology (Hon), 1968; Yale Law School, MSL, 1985. **CAREER:** Hunter Coll, CUNY, asst prof soc, 1968-69; Yale Univ, dir assoc of sociology, 1969-72; Natl Inst of Mental Health, visiting sci, 1971-72; Smithsonian Inst, dir, research sociologist, 1972-82; Univ of Pennsylvania, visiting prof, 1974-; Howard Univ, guest prof, 1975-; Catholic Univ of Amer, dept of anthropology; Research Inst Immigration Ethnics Studies Inc, dir, pres, research cons, 1983-86; Guest Curator, Schomburg Center for Research in Black Culture, 1985-86; Prof of Sociology, Graduate Center & Dir, The center on Immigrant and Population Studies, Coll of Staten Island, City Univ of New York, 1986-. **ORGANIZATIONS:** Mem, Amer Sociologist Assn, Black Sociologist Assn, Caribbean Studies Assn, Alpha Phi Alpha Inc, Caribbean Amer Intercultural Assoc, Com World Soc Amer Soc Assn, 1974-78, Intl Soc Assn, Eastern & DC Soc for Study of Soc Problems, Intl Studies Assn, Caribbean Studies Assn; bd of dir, Caucus Black Sociologists, Amer Acad of Polit & Soc Scis; sec gen I Cong of Black Culture in the Americas Cali Colombia, 1979; chmn, Frazier-Johnson-Dubois Awds Comm Amer Soc Assn, 1978-79; mem, Alpha Kappa Delta, Pi Gamma Mu, Phi Delta Kappa, Mu Epsilon Nu, Phi Sigma Iota, Alpha Phi Alpha; mem adv bd, US Census Adv & Race Ancestry Minorities; Yale Law Schl Assn & Yale Club, Washington, DC; mem bd of mgr, Seamen's Children's Soc; mem advisory bd, Schonberg's Afro-Amer Scholar Comm. **HONORS/ACHIEVEMENTS:** City Council, Dist of Columbia, 1984, Mayors Award, 1982, Yale Alumni Assoc 1975, Intl Public Relations Assoc, 1984; Sociologist, 1978-79; editor, "New Immigration Vols I & II," Transaction Books, 1980; Caribbean Personalities, 1980; School Contrib Award Caribbean Amer Int Cultural Org, 1981; Mayor's Award for Contrib to the Arts, Washington, 1981; Achievement by Panamanians Award Dedicators Inc New York City, 1982; Arturo Griffith Award Afro Latino Inst Washington, DC, 1983; Recog Resolutions of 1984, City Council of Dist of Columbia, 1984; adv bd, Cimarron Journal Carib Stud Assocs, City Univ of New York, 1984; publs sr editor, "Contemporary Alienation" Praeger Publ, 1975; "Inequality & the Black Experience, Some Intl Dimensions" special issue "Journal of Black Studies"; sr editor, RIIES on New Caribbean Immigrations; Recognition Afro-Amer S tudies Yale Alumni of Afro-Amer Inc; Gelman Serv Awd Eastern Sociological Soc; charter fellow Woodrow Wilson Intl Center; "Man of the Year Award," Panamanian Council of New York, Inc, 1986; Guest Curator of special exhibition on "Give Me Your Tired, Your Poor?"; Voluntary Black Immigration to the US, Schomberg Center, New York; Centennial of Statue of Liberty, 1986. **BUSINESS ADDRESS:** Professor, Coll of Staten Island/Grad Ctr, 130 Stuyvesant Place, Staten Island, NY 10301.

BRYSON, DYAN CAROL
Professional medical representative. **PERSONAL:** Born Jun 19, 1956, Washington, DC. **EDUCATION:** Millersville State Univ, BA 1978. **CAREER:** John Wanamaker, buyer 1978-81; Danskin Inc, major acct mgr 1982-85; Ciba-Geigy Pharmaceuticals Corp, 1985-86, professional medical rep 1986-. **ORGANIZATIONS:** Me MBMBAA 1985-; vice pres of mktg & public relations Natl Black MBA Assoc 1987; mem Natl Council of Negro Women 1987, Alpha Kappa Alpha Sor Inc Omega OmegaChap 1987. **HONORS/ACHIEVEMENTS:** Outstanding Young Women of Amer 1978,86.

BRYSON, RALPH J.
Educator. **PERSONAL:** Born Sep 10, 1922, Cincinnati, OH; son of Ralph Bryson and Annie (Davis) Bryson. **EDUCATION:** Univ Cincinnati, BS 1947; Univ Cincinnati, MS 1950; OH State Univ, PhD 1953. **CAREER:** So Univ, instr English 1949; Miles Coll, instr English 1949-50; AL State Univ, asso prof English 1953-62; prof & dept head 1962-75, chmn div of humanities 1975-77, prof of English 1977-; Univ of AL, adjunct prof 1987. **ORGANIZATIONS:** Pres Assn Coll English Tchrs AL; AL Council Tchrs & English Exec Bd; bd dir Nat Council Tchrs English; Modern Language Assn; S Atlantic MLA; Coll Language Assn; Conf Coll Composition & Communication; Phi Delta Kappa; Lectr Author & Consult Kappa Alpha Psi; Editor Column Books & Such; chmn Nat Achievement Commn; officer, mem Province Bd Dir; Am Bridge Assn; chmn exec bd & sectional vice pres Montgomery; Seminar Arts; bd of trustees, Museum Fine Arts Assn. **HONORS/ACHIEVEMENTS:** Dexter Ave Baptist Church; Outstanding Journalistic Contributions & Achievement Kappa Alpha Psi; Outstanding Men of Yr & Montgomery; Cited Outstanding OH State Univ Graduate in They Came & They Conquered. **MILITARY SERVICE:** AUS 1942-45; European Theater of Operations 1943-45. **BUSINESS ADDRESS:** Professor of English, Alabama State University, 915 S Jackson St, Montgomery, AL 36101-0271.

BRYSON, SEYMOUR L.
Educator. **PERSONAL:** Born Sep 08, 1937, Quincy, IL; son of Claudine Jackson; married Marjorie; children: Robin, Todd, Keri. **EDUCATION:** Southern IL Univ Carbondale, BA Sociology 1959; MS, Rehabilitation Counseling 1961, PhD Educ Psychology, 1972. **CAREER:** St Louis State Hospital, rehabilitation counselor 1961-65; Breckinridge Job Corps Center, admin 1965-69; Devel Skills Program, dir 1969-72; Rehabilitation Inst SIU, asst prof 1972-75, assoc prof 1975-84, prof 1984; Coll of Human Resources, assoc dean 1977-78, 1980-

84, interim dean 1978-80, 1984; Coll of Human Resources, dean 1984-88; asst to pres, 1988-. **ORGANIZATIONS:** Gov appointee Dept of Rehabilitation Serv Advisory Council 1980, State Use Commission 1983-; chmn Racism Comm Amer Rehabilitation Counseling Assn 1972-74; senate Amer Rehabilitation Counseling Assoc Delegate to the Amer Personnel & Guidance Assoc in Personnel & Guidance 1976-78; pres IL Assn of Non-White Concerns 1984-85; mem Amer Assoc of Univ Admin, Assoc of Non-White Concerns, Amer Rehabilitation Counseling Assoc; bd dir Jackson Cty Comm Mental Health Center 1974-82; chmn, bd dir Jackson Cty Comm Mental Health Center 1980-82; Jackson County 708 Bd 1986-; bd dir, Res-Care, 1989-. **HONORS/ACHIEVEMENTS:** Phi Kappa Phi Natl Hon Soc 1972-; Rsch Award Assn of Non-White Concerns for Personnel & Guidance 1976; Certificate Appreciation Outstanding Contribution Specialized Student Serv; Special Award for Distinguished Serv ICBC-1985; NAACP Image Award for Education, Carbondale Branch. **BUSINESS ADDRESS:** Dean, Southern Illinois Univ, Coll of Human Resources, Carbondale, IL 62901.

BRYSON, WINFRED OCTAVUS, JR.
Business executive. **PERSONAL:** Born Apr 20, 1915, Chattanooga, TN; married Prima-Lee Woodall. **EDUCATION:** Morehouse Coll, AB 1936; Atlanta Univ, AM 1937; Univ of PA, PhD 1947. **CAREER:** Morgan State Univ, prof of Economics 1937-84; JB Blayton, CPA, accountant 1940-60; Frederick Douglass Memorial Hospital, business mgr 1945-47; Baltimore Branch NAACP, auditor 1947-66; Advance Fed Savings & Loan Assn, president. **ORGANIZATIONS:** Vp mem exec com Am Savings & Loan League 1968-71; mem bd dir Am Savings & Loan League 1968-75; treas chmn of finance com, mem bd dir MD Savings & Loan Serv Corp, Inc; departmental exec Grad Prgm Morgan 1972-83; certified mortgage underwriter 1977-. **BUSINESS ADDRESS:** President, Advance Fed Svngs & Loan Assn, 1405 E Cold Spring Ln, Baltimore, MD 21239.

BUCHANAN, OTIS
Television news reporter. **PERSONAL:** Born May 15, 1951, Battle Creek, MI; married Pamela. **EDUCATION:** Kellogg Community Coll, AA 1971; MI State U, BA 1973. **CAREER:** WKNR Radio News radio news anchor Battle Creek 1969; WUHQ-TV, TV anchor Battle Creek 1971-72; WXYZ Radio, radio reporter Detroit 1973; WJIM-TV, capitol corr Lansing MI 1973; WJBK-TV, st reporter Detroit 1974. **ORGANIZATIONS:** Mem AFTRA. **BUSINESS ADDRESS:** c/o WMAQ-TV News, Merchandise Mart, Chicago, IL 60654.

BUCK, IVORY M., JR.
Educational administrator. **PERSONAL:** Born Dec 25, 1928, Woodbury, NJ; married Ernestine; children: L'Tanya Ivy, Ivory Melvin III. **EDUCATION:** William Penn Bus Inst, Certificate Business Ad 1954-56; Glassboro State Coll, BA 1960, MA 1968. **CAREER:** Public Schools Deptford NJ, teacher 1958-64; Johnstone Training Rsch Ctr, teacher 1960-62; Jr High Sch Deptford, dir guidance 1964-68; Glassboro State Coll, asst registrar 1968-71; Gloucester Co Coll, counselor 1969-72; Glassboro State Coll, asst dir advisement ctr. **ORGANIZATIONS:** mem, Kappa Alpha Psi, Phi Delta Kappa Frat; Grand Master Prince Hall Free & Accepted Masons for NJ 1977-79; elected White House Conf for Library Serv 1978; alumni treas, Glassboro State Coll Bd of Dirs 1979; mem Evaluation Team for Sec ondary Educ 1980; sec gen Prince Hall Scottish Rite Masons 33 Degrees 1983; sec of bd of dirs Fitzwater Housing Project 1985; natl elected officer Prince Hall Shriners 1980-; bd dir Camden Co YMCA; Berlin bd Jr Chamber of Commerce; chairperson for Inclusion, Black Studies Monroe Township Public Schools; mem, NAACP, Elks. **HONORS/ACHIEVEMENTS:** Leadership Awd Marabash Museum New Egypt NJ 1978; Legion of Honor Awd for Leadership/Serv Shriners 1980; Distinguished Alumni Awd Glassboro State Coll 1981; The Chapel of Four Chaplains Awd Philadelphia PA 1964, 1984. **MILITARY SERVICE:** USAF s/sgt 4 yrs; Airman of the Month; Good Conduct Medal; Eastern Theatre & Korean Medals. **BUSINESS ADDRESS:** Asst Dir Advisement Ctr, Glassboro State College, Glassboro, NJ 08028.

BUCK, JUDITH BROOKS
Educator. **PERSONAL:** Born Mar 03, 1949, Norfolk, VA; daughter of Mr & Mrs George A Brooks, Sr; married Henry Buck Jr; children: Kimberly, Michael Henry. **EDUCATION:** Bennett Coll Greensboro NC, BA 1967-71; Univ of VA, M Educ 1986; Further study at: Norfolk State Univ, Old Dominion Univ, Hampton Univ, Alabama A&M Univ, Univ of AL. **CAREER:** Council for Exceptional Children, info spec 1972; Fairfax Cty Bd of Ed, leanring disabilities teacher 1972-74; Harford Cty Bd of Ed, crisis resource teacher 1974-76; Norfolk Public Schools, child devel spec 1976-77; USAF, child care ctr, preschool dir 1978-80; Norfolk Public Schools, learning disabilities teacher 1980-81; Huntsville Public School, alternative prog coord 1981-83; Norfolk Public Schools, spec ed teacher 1983-86; Huntsville City Schools, spec educ area specialist; Huntsville City Schools, principal. **ORGANIZATIONS:** Mem Shiloh Baptist Church 1959-, Delta Sigma Theta 1968-, Natl VA Ed Assoc 1976; mem Fed Women's Clubs of Amer 1984-85; assoc mem First Baptist Church1986. **HONORS/ACHIEVEMENTS:** Received scholarships for undergrad studies Bennett Coll 1967-71; Article publ Slow Learner Workshop Mag 1976. **HOME ADDRESS:** 2228 Briarcliff Rd, Huntsville, AL 35801. **BUSINESS ADDRESS:** Center for Developmental Learning, 2901 Fairbanks St, Huntsville, AL 35816.

BUCK, VERNON ASHLEY, JR.
Educational consultant. **PERSONAL:** Born Jan 10, 1920, Atlanta, GA; married Eutrilla Graham (dec) (deceased); children: Vernon,III, Rudolph, Cheryl. **EDUCATION:** Morehouse Coll, BA 1935-39; NY Univ, MS 1948; State Univ of NY at Albany, 1957-74. **CAREER:** W Charlotte High Charlotte, NC, math teacher & coord of distrib educ program 1946-48; Carver Jr Coll, dir chief adminstrative officer 1948-51, chairman math dept 1953-57; Hackett Jr High Albany, math teacher 1957-68; State Univ of NY at Albany, dir chief adminstr for EOP 1971-85 (retired); Veruch Co, Albany, pres, 1987-. **ORGANIZATIONS:** Inst systems analyst & designer/proj dir/vp Learning Techn Inc Albany 1968-71; mem natl Soc for Performance & Instr; NY State United Univ Profl; Rotary Intl; adj prof SUNYA School of Educ 1971-74; adj prof SUNYA Afr & Afro-Am Studies 1975-; mem adv comm 1982-, chmn adv comm 1986-87 Capital Dist Educ Oppors Prog; mem adv bd LaSalle School for Boys 1986-. **HONORS/ACHIEVEMENTS:** Proposal Reader Advanced Inst Develop Prog US Dept of Health Educ and Welfare, Office of Educ, Bureau of Higher and Continuing Educ 1978-82; "The MarketValue Approach to Property Appraisal" NY Bd of Equal & Assess 1972; co-author "Basic Spelling Skills" revised ed McGraw-Hill 1980; author of training system, SICON, Mich Heart Assn, 1972. **MILITARY SERVICE:** AUS Capt 1942-46 & 51-52; Org & Training Officer 1943-46; post-info & educ officer Ft Stewart, GA 1951-52.

BUCKHALTER, EMERSON R.
Physician. **PERSONAL:** Born Nov 10, 1954, El Monte, CA; married Veretta Boyd; children: Monica. **EDUCATION:** Univ of CA Los Angeles, BA 1976; Howard Univ Coll of Medicine, MD 1980. **CAREER:** Hawthorne Comm Med Group, physician 1983-86; St Francis Care Med Group, physician 1986-. **ORGANIZATIONS:** Mem Amer Medical Assoc 1980-. **HONORS/ACHIEVEMENTS:** Alpha Omega Alpha Honor Med Soc 1979; Natl Medical Fellowships; Henry J Kaiser Foundation Merit Scholar 1980. **HOME ADDRESS:** 5936 Croft Ave, Los Angeles, CA 90056. **BUSINESS ADDRESS:** 3680 E Imperial Hwy, Lynwood, CA 90262.

BUCKHANAN, DOROTHY WILSON
Marketing manager. **PERSONAL:** Born Jul 12, 1958, Sumter, SC; daughter of Ida Gregg; married Walt A Buckhanan, Aug 22, 1987. **EDUCATION:** Benedict Coll Columbia SC, BS Business 1980; Atlanta Univ Grad School of Bus, MBA 1982. **CAREER:** Xerox Corp, mktg asst 1982-84; SC Johnson & Son Inc, prod mgr 1984-. **ORGANIZATIONS:** Mem Amer Mktg Assn 1980-, Toastmaster's Intl 1980-82, Natl Black MBA Assn 1984-; vice president fundraising chmn, corresponding sec Alpha Kappa Alpha 1984-87; vice president Top Ladies of Distinction Inc 1985-88. **HONORS/ACHIEVEMENTS:** Outstanding Undergrad Awd Alpha Kappa Alpha 1979; Natl Deans List Atlanta Univ 1980-82; Exec Scholarship Fellow Atlanta Univ 1982-84; Employee Recognition Awd Xerox Corp 1983; Distinguished Alumni Awd Benedict Coll 1987; Service Award, Alpha Kappa Alpha, 1988; Outstanding Speaker Award, Dale Carnegie Institute, 1989. **HOME ADDRESS:** 7331 W Marine Dr, Milwaukee, WI 53223. **BUSINESS ADDRESS:** Product Manager Consumer Prod, SC Johnson & Son Inc, 1525 Howe St, Racine, WI 53403.

BUCKLEY, GAIL LUMET
Writer. **PERSONAL:** Born Dec 21, 1937, Pittsburgh, PA; daughter of Louis Jones and Lena Horne; married Kevin P Buckley, Oct 01, 1983; children: Amy Lumet, Jenny Lumet. **EDUCATION:** Radcliff Coll, Cambridge, MA, BA, 1959. **HONORS/ACHIEVEMENTS:** Author of The Hornes: An Amer Family, 1986; Doctor of Letters, Univ of Southern IN, 1987. **BUSINESS ADDRESS:** C/O Lynn Nesbit, 598 Madison Ave, New York, NY 10128.

BUCKNER, EDWIN R.
Business executive. **PERSONAL:** Born Feb 01, 1914, Dayton, OH. **EDUCATION:** Univ of Dayton, Univ of Cincinnati, attended 1949-51; Roosevelt Univ, attended 1952-54; Chicago Kent Law, attended 1954-56; Univ of IL, attended 1955; Chicago Tchrs Coll, attended 1958. **CAREER:** Mgr Liquor Store, 1947-49; Real Estate Salesman, 1953-55; State of IL, state minority groups rep 1960-65; Apprenticeship Info Ctr IL, dir 1964-65; Dept of Defense, personnel staff employment relations speclst 1966-68, equal employment oppor officer 1968-70, Office of Contract Compliance consult tech assist 1970-. **ORGANIZATIONS:** Organizer pres United Vet Orgn 1943; vice pres Amer Fed of State Co & Municipal Employees 1956-66; Dayton Youth Movement organizer & pres 1937-39; UrbanLeague, Amer Legion, Masonic Lodge. **HONORS/ACHIEVEMENTS:** Commendation for Recruitment of Federal Serv Employment Examinees US Civil Serv Commn IL 1967-68. **MILITARY SERVICE:** AUS m/sgt 1973.

BUCKNER, IRIS BERNELL
Public relations manager. **PERSONAL:** Born Sep 21, 1952, Columbus, GA. **EDUCATION:** Gustavus Adolphus Coll St Peter MN, BA/Polit Sci 1970-74; IN Univ Bloomington, MPA/Pub Mgmt 1974-76. **CAREER:** Census Bur, comm serv specialist 1979-; Comm Awareness Program Cols NAACP, coordinator 1977-79; Troy State Univ Ft Benning GA, instr 1977-78; State of IN, personnel examiner 1976; Region Iii - Comprehensive Health Planning Council, research asst 1975; Minority Groups Program IN Univ Bloomington IN, counselor 1975-76; Muscogee Sch Dist Columbus GA, sub tchr 1970-74. **ORGANIZATIONS:** Sec Cols Br NAACP Youth Council Adv 1976-; adv council Comprehensive Employment Training Adminstrn 1977-; commnr Columbus GA Clean & Green Bd Keep Am Beautiful 1979-; bus mgr Negro Bus & Professional Women 1979; Worthy Matron Nefertiti Chap Order of Eastern Star 1979-. **HONORS/ACHIEVEMENTS:** Comm Serv Award Young Adult Negro Bus & Professional Women 1979; Outstanding Young Woman in Am 1979; NAACP Appreciation Award Columbus Br NAACP 1980; Outstanding Opinion; Maker Columbus Times Newspaper. **BUSINESS ADDRESS:** Dept of Commerce Census Bureau, 1375 Peachtree St N E Ste 67, Atlanta, GA 30309.

BUCKNER, JAMES L.
Dentist. **PERSONAL:** Born Jul 29, 1934, Vicksburg, MS; son of Dr. Clarence E. Buckner and Florice Williams Buckner; children: JaSaun, Justina Jordan. **EDUCATION:** Univ of Illinois, BSD, 1957, DDS, 1959. **CAREER:** Private practice, dentist. **ORGANIZATIONS:** pres, Lincoln Dental Soc, 1965-66; sec, bd of dir, Natl Dental Assn, 1966-67; bd of advisors, Supreme Life Insurance Co, 1970-; trustee, WTTW, Channel 11, 1970-74,CityColl of Chicago 1971-76; chmn Chicago Dental Soc Comm on Public Aid 1971-80; vice chmn, Chicago Econ Devel Corp, 1972-75; mem, Pres Council on Minority Business Enterprise, 1972-75; Gov Walkers Public Health Transition Task Force, 1972-73; bd of adv, Midwest Sickle Cell Anemia Inc, 1972-; trustee, Univ of IL Dental Alumni Assn, 1973-75; co-chmn, Chicago United, 1973-75; mem, Illinois Dental Soc, Amer Dental Soc, Leg Interest Comm of IL Dentists, IL Dental Serv Corp, IL Dept of Public Aid Dental Adv Comm; pres, Chicago Urban League, 1973-76; chmn, Chicago Financial Devel Corp, 1973-76; chmn, Council of Natl Urban League Pres', 1975-76; pres, Trains & Boats & Planes Inc 1978-; The Foodbasket Inc, 1981, 1988-; mem, Amer Soc of Travel Agents; vice pres, Seaway Commun Inc, 1978-85; founder, mem bd of dir, Seaway Natl Bank, 1965-86; chairman, Seaway Comm Inc, 1985-; chairman, the Push Foundation, 1987-; vice chmn, Illinois Serv Fed Savings & Loan, 1988-. **HONORS/ACHIEVEMENTS:** 10 Outstanding Young Men Award, South End Jaycees 1965; Certificate of Achievement, Amer Inst of Banking, 1965, Natl Dental Assn, 1966; Plaque For Outstanding Contributions to Ed Jensen School, 1970; Certificate of Appreciation, Chicago Area Council of Boy Scouts, 1970; Community Serv Award, Big Buddies Youth Serv Inc, 1971; Man of the Year Award, Chicago Urban League, 1972; Certificate of Appreciation, Commonwealth Church, 1972; Certificate of Recognition, Council of Natl Urban League Pres', 1977; Outstanding Achievement Award, Women's Div, Chicago Urban League, 1985. **BUSINESS ADDRESS:** President, Trains & Boats & Planes Inc, 155 N Harbor Dr, Chicago, IL 60601-7328.

BUCKNER, MARY ALICE
Attorney. **PERSONAL:** Born Mar 03, 1948, Columbus, GA. **EDUCATION:** Mercer Univ, BA 1970; attended Emory Univ; Mercer Univ, JD 1973. **CAREER:** Randall & Turner Attys at Law, law clerk 1971; Bishop & Hudlin Attys at Law, law clerk 1973-75, assoc 1975-78; Troy State Univ, part-time instr 1977-79; Recorders Court (Pro Tem), judge 1984; GA Dept of Educl, regional hearing officer 1984; Bishop & Buckner Attys at Law, atty & partner 1978-. **ORGANIZATIONS:** Bd mem AJ McClung Br YMCA 1974-; bd mem Muscogee Co Chap ARC 1976-; mem Delta Sigma Theta Inc. **HONORS/ACHIEVEMENTS:** Natl Merit Semi-Finalist 1966; Who's Who Among High Sch Students 1966; Rockefeller Scholarship 1966-70; Emory Univ Pre-Law Prog Field Found of NY 1970-71;herbert Lehman Educ Fund Fellowship 1971-72; Lt Col Aid De Camp Gov's Staff 1976; Outstanding Young Woman of Amer 1976; Who's Who in Amer Law 1979. **BUSINESS ADDRESS:** Attorney, 1214 First Ave Commerce Bldg, Ste 370, Columbus, GA 31902.

BUCKNER, WILLIAM PAT, JR.
Educator. **PERSONAL:** Born Oct 05, 1929, Brazil, IN; married Irene Smith; children: Lawrence, Douglas. **EDUCATION:** De Pauw Univ, AB 1950; IN Univ, MS 1954, HSD 1969. **CAREER:** Southern Univ New Orleans, assoc prof, chmn dept of HPER 1959-70; Eastern MI Univ, assoc prof & health coord 1970-71; Prairie View A&M Univ, prof & head dept of HPER 1971; Baylor Coll of Medicine, lecturer comm med 1975-; Univ of Houston Univ Park, prof health sci & allied health 1972-. **ORGANIZATIONS:** Mem Assoc for the Advancement of Health Ed 1955-, Family Life Council of TX 1977-, Natl Forum for Death Ed & Couns 1977-; grief couns Life Threatening &Illness Alli 1972-; bd of dir Natl Sudden Infant Death Inc of Gr Houston 1973-79; adv bd ENCORE Gr Houston YWCA 1978-; mem Phi Delta Kappa Kappa Alpha Psi 1954; fellow Royal Health Soc 1966, Danforth Found 1972; editor Med Readings in Ecology 1976, Med Readings on Human Sexuality 1978; chrpsn nom & elections comm Amer Alliance for the Advancement of Health Ed, constitution comm for the Natl Soc for Allied Health Professions; mem exec council So DistAmer Alliance for the Advancement of Health Ed; mem Univ of Houston Univ Park Faculty Promo & Tenure Comm, Task Force for the Recruitment & Retention ofMinority Students; chrpsn Univ Faculty Devel Leave Comm; mem Univ Admissions Comm. **MILITARY SERVICE:** USMC 1951-53. **BUSINESS ADDRESS:** Professor of Health Science, Univ of Houston, Cullen Blvd, Houston, TX 77004.

BUCKNEY, EDWARD L.
Director. **PERSONAL:** Born Feb 28, 1929, Keokuk, IA; children: Edwin Darryl (dec). **EDUCATION:** Columbia Coll, BA 1957; IL Inst Tech, MP Admin 1970. **CAREER:** Chicago Police Capt Assoc, appt date 1954, sgt 1963, lt 1965, capt 1968, dist comdr 1970, asst dep supt 1974, watch comdr 1979, dir of training 1983-. **ORGANIZATIONS:** Sec Chicago Police Capt Assoc 1972-74. **MILITARY SERVICE:** AUS corpl 1951-53. **BUSINESS ADDRESS:** Dir of Training, Chicago Police Assoc, 1121 State St, Chicago, IL 60605.

BUCKSON, TONI YVONNE
Transportation administration. **PERSONAL:** Born Jun 05, 1949, Baltimore, MD; married James Buckson, Jr. **EDUCATION:** Coppin State Coll, BS 1971; Univ of Baltimore, MS 1978; Northeastern Univ, certificate 1985; Atlanta Univ, certificate 1985. **CAREER:** Mayor and City Council of Baltimore, CATV task force manager 1979-81; Natl Aquarium in Baltimore, group events coord 1981-82; Mass Transit Administration, ridesharing dir 1982-86; MD Trasportation Authority, ass't admin bridges 1986-. **ORGANIZATIONS:** Goucher Coll, cirriculum advisor 1975-78; Jr League of MD, board mem 1978-80; Natl Information Center on Volunteerism, trainer 1979-81; MD Food Bank, boardmem 1979-81; Future Homemakers of America, board mem 1980-81; Girl Scouts of Central MD, board mem 1982-84. **HONORS/ACHIEVEMENTS:** Girl Scouts of Central America; service award 1984; MD Dept of Transportation, affirmative action award 1984; Outstanding Young Women in America 1985; Natl Assoc for Equal Opportunity in Higher Education, presidential citation 1986. **HOME ADDRESS:** Six Tallow Court, Baltimore, MD 21207. **BUSINESS ADDRESS:** Asst Administrator, Bridges, MD Transportation Authority, PO Box 9088, Dundalk, MD 21222.

BUFFONG, ERIC ARNOLD
Physician. **PERSONAL:** Born May 11, 1951, Oranjestad, Aruba;married Gail Helena LaBorde; children: Erica, Nicole, Alicia. **EDUCATION:** Manhattan Coll, 1969-73; Howard Univ, MD 1977. **CAREER:** Harlem Hosp Cntr NY, resident & chief resident 1977-81, president house staff 1980-81; Albert Einstein Coll, of Medicine, fellow in reproductive endocrinology 1981-83, assoc prof dept gyn 1983-84; Private practice 1984-. **ORGANIZATIONS:** Board eligible Reproductive Indocrinology 1983; mem Amer Coll of Ob-Gyn 1986,87; diplomate/bd certified FACOG; mem Amer and Natl Medical Assocs; mem Old North State Medical Soc. **HONORS/ACHIEVEMENTS:** Board of dir NCNB of Jacksonville, NC 1986-; Eastern Area Sickle Cell Assoc board of dir 1986-; Vaginal Delivery of Quadruplets 1985. **BUSINESS ADDRESS:** Physician, Onslow Women's Health Ctr, 1703 Cntry Club Rd 203, Jacksonville, NC 28540.

BUFFORD, EDWARD EUGENE
Clergyman. **PERSONAL:** Born Jul 15, 1935, Birmingham; married Joyce Lyn E Jessie. **EDUCATION:** Miles Coll, BA 1970; M Div Gammon Theol Sem, 1973; D Div Union Bapt Theol Sem, 1974. **CAREER:** Centenary Un Meth Ch, minister; St Johns Un Meth Ch LA, 1972-74; Morning Star Un Meth Ch AL, 1969-72; Mt Moriah Un Meth Ch, 1967-69; Powell Chapel Lafayette AL, 1963-67; St Paul Jasper AL, 1962-63; St James, 1959-61; Watts Comm Ministries, dir 1972-74. **ORGANIZATIONS:** Mem NAACP; Masons; Alpha Phi Alpha Frat Inc. **HONORS/ACHIEVEMENTS:** Crusade Scholar 1971. **BUSINESS ADDRESS:** 584 E Mc Lemore Ave, Memphis, TN 38106.

BUFORD, JAMES HENRY
Association executive. **PERSONAL:** Born Jun 02, 1944, St Louis, MO; son of James Buford and Myrtle Margaret Brown Buford; married Helen Joyce Freeman, Jun 23, 1967; children: James H Jr, Jason. **EDUCATION:** Forest Park Community Coll, AA Business Admin; Elizabethtown Coll, Elizabethtown PA, BA Human Serv Admin. **CAREER:** Smith, Kline & French, St Louis MO, regional mktg representative, 1972-75; St Louis Community Coll, St Louis MO, program coord, 1975-76; 70001 Ltd, St Louis MO, vice pres, 1976-80; Intl Mgmt & Devel Group LTD, Washington DC, sr vice pres, 1980-81, St Louis MO, exec vice pres, 1981-85; Urban League, St Louis MO, pres/CEO, 1985-. **ORGANIZATIONS:** Mem, NAACP; bd mem, Leadership St Louis, 1985-88; mem exec comm, BlueCross/Blue Shield, 1986-; exec bd, Boy Scouts, 1986-; mem bd of dir, St Louis Comunity Coll Building Corp, 1986-; mem bd of regents, Harris Stowe State Coll, 1987-; bd mem, Confluence St Louis, 1987-; chair nominating comm, Sigma Pi Phi, 1988; mem, Personnel Advisory Comm, President George Bush, 1989-. **HONORS/ACHIEVEMENTS:** Order of the 1st State, Governor of Delaware, 1981; Humanitarian Award, Kappa Alpha Psi-St Louis, 1984; Professionalism Award, Kappa Alpha Psi-St Louis, 1986. **BUSINESS ADDRESS:** President/CEO, Urban League of Metropolitan St Louis, 3701 Grandel Square, St Louis, MO 63108.

BUFORD, KENNETH L.
Clergyman. **PERSONAL:** Born Aug 17, 1917, Pulaski, VA; married Lillian Glanton. **EDUCATION:** Livingston Coll, BA 1939; Bloomfield Sch Religion, BTh 1943; Miller Univ, Hon Degree Div 1960. **CAREER:** NAACP, AL state field dir 1966-; Butler Chapel AME Zion Ch, pastor 1956-66; Second AME Zion Ch, pastor 1947-56; St Luke AME Zion Ch New Castle, pastor 1943-57; St James AME Zion Ch Matawan, pastor 1940-43; Brighton Rock AME Zion Ch Portsmouth, pastor 1937-39. **ORGANIZATIONS:** Pres Tuskegee Ministerial Alliance 1956-; AL Annual Conf 1960-63; treas AME Zion Ch 1956-; trustee Lomax-Hannon Coll 1957-; mem AL Dem Conf 1963-; life mem NAACP 1937-; mem Intl Platform Assn 1973-; mem Tuskegee Civic Assn 1956-; vp1957-64; mem United Nat Assn USA 1972-; mem AL CoalitionBetter Educ 1974-; mem Tuskegee Area C of C 1974; mem Com Greater Tuskegee 1962-; hon mem AL State Atty Gen Staff Montgomery 1971-; vice pres New Castle &Br NAACP 1946-47; sec LA Interdenominational Ministerial Alliance 1950-54; mem exec com LA Br NAACP 1950-56; mem Tuskegee Inst Religious Life Council Chpln to Meth Students 1960-63; mem City Cncl Tuskegee 1964-66; Whos Who in Negro Clergy 1960; participated several White House confs 1963-67; Whos Who in Dem Party 1964. **HONORS/ACHIEVEMENTS:** Award Outstanding Political Achievement SE Regional conf NAACP 1965; plaque Outstanding Political Achievement by AL Coordntg Council 1965; Minister of the Yr by NAACP 1965; award Dedicated & Dynamic Leadership SE Regional Conf NAACP 1969; Whos Who in Am 1968; Personalities of the S 1972; certificate in recognition Outstanding Citizenship MI House of Rep 1972; award AL State Conf NAACP Brs Dedicated & Dynamic Leadership 1972; Dictionary Intl Biography for Distinguished Service Human Rights Advancement 1973; Cited for Outstanding Achievements by SE Regional Conf NAACP 1973 Listed Outstanding Profls Human Service by Am Acad Human Service 1974; Certificate Appreciation in recognition Distinguished Serv 1974; Dictionary Intl Biography for Men of Achievement Cambridge En 1974.

BUFORD, SHARNIA
Business executive. **PERSONAL:** Born Feb 02, 1939, Bryans Mille, TX; married Phyllis A Scott; children: Rhae Shawn, Bruce. **EDUCATION:** Univ NE, BA; Univ CO, postgrad; TX, CO Univ, DLaw 1983. **CAREER:** Urban Renewal Agency Kansas City KS, relocation adivser, mortgage fin officer 1966-67; Douglass State Bank Kansas City KS, vice pres 1967-68, sr vice pres 1968-72, pres, ceo 1972-77; Freedom Natl Bank NYC, pres, ceo 1977-. **ORGANIZATIONS:** Dir, former mem 29th Dist Jud Nominating Com KS; natl adv comm Natl Bank Washington; trustee Tyler Coll KS 1984-; mem, bd dir 1969-77, pres 1975-76 Natl Bankers Assn; Reville Lodge, Knights of Malta. **HONORS/ACHIEVEMENTS:** Named Ebony's List of 100 Most Influential Black Amers 1976; Disting Serv Awd Jr C of C 1973. **BUSINESS ADDRESS:** Pres, CEO, Freedom Natl Bank of New York, 275 W 125th St, New York, NY 10027.

BUFORD, WILLIAM P.
Banker. **PERSONAL:** Born Sep 27, 1936, New York, NY; married Minnie. **EDUCATION:** City Coll Of NY, AA 1959. **CAREER:** Vanguard Nat Bank Hempstead NY, vice pres Cashier; First Nat City Bank of NY, clk to asst vp. **BUSINESS ADDRESS:** 49 N Franklin St, Hempstead, NY 11550.

BUGG, GEORGE WENDELL
Physician. **PERSONAL:** Born Jun 17, 1935, Nashville, TN; children: George Jr, Michael Stanley, Kevin Gregory, Kisha Monique. **EDUCATION:** TN State Univ, BS 1958; Meharry Med Coll, MD 1962. **CAREER:** Self Employed, genl surgeon. **ORGANIZATIONS:** Chmn Cecil C Hinton Comm Ctr 1969-72; chmn W Fresno Fed of Neighborhood Ctrs 1972; chmn Comm Serv Amer Heart Assn 1972; pres Daniel H Williams Med Forum 1974-77; mem AMA, CMA, NMA, Surveyors, JCAH, Alpha Phi Alpha Inc, Fresno-Madera Med Found; mem Comm Cncl on Black Educ Affairs. **HONORS/ACHIEVEMENTS:** AMA Physicians Recognition Awd 1969. **MILITARY SERVICE:** AUS med corps maj 1967-69. **BUSINESS ADDRESS:** General Surgeon, 2045 Divisadero St, Fresno, CA 93701.

BUGG, JAMES NELSON
Dentist. **PERSONAL:** Born Jul 11, 1904, Savannah, GA; married Janie G. **EDUCATION:** Meharry Med Col, DDS 1930. **CAREER:** Nat Dental; Old N State Dental; AOA Frat; Meharry Alumni. **ORGANIZATIONS:** Passed GA NC & NY State Dental Boards. **HONORS/ACHIEVEMENTS:** Meharry Med TE 50 Yrs 1980; Old North State Dental 50 Yrs 1980; Meharry Medical Coll 55 Year Plaque 1985; life membership Old North State Dental Society, Natl Dental Assoc.

BUGG, MAYME CAROL
Attorney. **PERSONAL:** Born Apr 18, 1945, Portsmouth, VA. **EDUCATION:** Fisk Univ, BA Sociology 1966; George W Brown Sch of Social Work Washington Univ, MSW 1968; Cleveland State Univ, JD 1977. **CAREER:** Oberlin Coll, educ prog dir 1969-70; Cleveland City Hall, city planner 1970-71; Cuyahoga Comm Coll, asst to dept head 1971-74; Comm Action Against Addiction, court liaison 1976-77; United Labor Agy, proj dir 1977-79; Cuyahoga Co Juvenile Ct, referee 1979-. **ORGANIZATIONS:** Mem OH Bar 1978; mem League Park Neighborhood Ctr 1979-84; bd mem Harambee Serv to Black Families 1979-84, adv, comm 1985-; bd mem Citizens League of Greater Cleveland 1980-84; bd mem NAACP 1980-84; mem Drop-Out Prevention Comm, Cleveland Bd of Educ 1981-; Fisk Univ Cleveland Alumni Club 1983-; mem Cuyahoga Co Bar Assn 1983; bd mem Project Friendship 1983-; Bbd mem Project Redirection; mem Assn of Blacks in the Juvenile Justice System 1979-84; Leadership Cleveland (Class of 1983); Alpha Kappa Alpha Sor; bd mem Cmmty Youth Mediation Prog 1986-; graduate of United Way Serv Ldrshp Development Prog 1986;African -Amer Famlty Congress 1986-; allocations panel United Way Serv 1986-; Norman S Minor Bar Assn 1986-. **HONORS/ACHIEVEMENTS:** Who's Who Among Students in Amer Coll & Univs 1965-66; Office of Economic Oppor Scholarship Washington Univ 1967; Outstanding Young Women of Amer 1974; Cert of Recog Natl Assn of Black Social Workers

1979; Cleveland Chapter, Tots & Teens leadership awd 1986. **BUSINESS ADDRESS:** Cuyahoga Co Juvenile Ct, 2163 E 22nd St, Cleveland, OH 44115.

BUGGS, CHARLES WESLEY
Educator, microbiologist. **PERSONAL:** Born Aug 06, 1906, Brunswick, GA; married Maggie Lee Bennett; children: Margaret. **EDUCATION:** Morehouse Coll, AB 1928; Univ MI MS 1931, Rosenwald Scholar 1932, PhD 1934. **CAREER:** Dillard Univ, prof Biology, chmn div scis 1935-43, 1949-56; Wayne Univ School of Medicine, instr, assoc prof Bacteriology 1943-49; Howard Univ School of Medicine, prof Microbiology 1956-71, chmn dept 1958-70; Charles R Drew Postgrad Medical School, project dir faculty allied health scis 1969-72; Univ of Southern CA, 1969-73; CA State Univ Long Beach, prof Microbiology 1973-83; Special Rsch, resistance bacteria to antibiotics. **ORGANIZATIONS:** Fellow Washington Acad Scis; Amer Acad Microbiology; mem AAAS; Amer Soc Microbiology; NY Acad Scis; Assn Amer Med Colls; Amer Assn Dental Schs;Sigma Xi; Alpha Phi Alpha; Sigma Pi Phi. **HONORS/ACHIEVEMENTS:** Author, "Premedical Education for Negroes" 1949.

BUGGS, JAMES
Insurance executive. **PERSONAL:** Born Apr 27, 1925, Summerfield, LA; son of Clifton Buggs and Lucille Buggs; married Johnye; children: James F, Bruce J. **EDUCATION:** Spauling Business Coll. **CAREER:** Independent, Family Life Insurance Co, field mgr/mgr; real estate salesman 1973-; Caddo Parish Shreveport, LA, deputy tax assessor 1982-85; AL Willimas & Assoc, life insurance executive. **ORGANIZATIONS:** Past pres Shreveport Negro Chamber of Commerce 1972-73; deacon Galilee Baptist Church; bd dir Lighthouse Sec Investment Co Inc; mem Amer Legion 525; YMCA; current master Fred D Lee Lodge 259 1973-78; Civic League; VFW Worshipful Master Fred D Lee Lodge Prince Hall affiliation. **MILITARY SERVICE:** AUS Corpl 1943-46. **HOME ADDRESS:** 2839 Round Grove Ln, Shreveport, LA 71107.

BUHAINA, ABDULLAH IBN See BLAKEY, ART

BUIE, SAMPSON, JR.
Educational administrator. **PERSONAL:** Born Sep 18, 1929, Fairmont, NC; married Catherine O; children: Debra, Janice, Velma. **EDUCATION:** NC A&T State Univ, BS 1952; Univ of NC Greensboro, MEd 1973, Doctorate EdD 1982. **CAREER:** Boy Scouts of Amer, asst scout exec 1954-70; NC A&T State Univ, dir comm relations 1970-82, dir office of alumni affairs 1982-. **ORGANIZATIONS:** Bd of dir Greensboro Rotary Club 1969-; mem bd of visitors Shaw Univ Div School 1981-; mem NC Comm Devel Commiss 1982-; trustee Gen Baptist State Conv of NC 1982-; mem Coll & Grad Comm, Chamber of Commerce, Greensboro United Fund, Piedmont Triad Criminal Justice/Planning Unit; vice pres Gen Greene Council BSA; mem NC A&T State Univ Natl Alumni Assoc Inc, Phi Beta Sigma, Greensboro Citizens Assoc, Natl Univ Extension Assoc, Guilford Cty Recreation Commiss, Greensboro-Guilford Cty Pulpit Forum, Drug Action Council Personnel Search Comm, NC State Adv Comm on Recruitment of Minorities for State Criminal Justice System; mem at large Natl Council BSA; consult for Monitoring & Tech Asst Training Prof HUD, USHUD; project dir Univ Year for Action Prog; numerous professional paper incl "Andragogy vs Pedagogy, Characteristics of Adults That Impact on Adult Learning & Dev" 1983; "Lifelong Learning, A Necessity & Not a Luxury" 1983. **HONORS/ACHIEVEMENTS:** Nathaniel Greene Awd City of Greensboro 1969; Achievement Awd NC A&T State Univ Alumni Assoc 1969; United Negro Coll Fund Awd Bennett Coll 1972; Silver Beaver Awd BSA 1978; Minister of the Year Deep River Baptist Assoc 1983. **MILITARY SERVICE:** Infantry 1st lt 1952-54. **HOME ADDRESS:** 2111 Belcrest Dr, Greensboro, NC 27406. **BUSINESS ADDRESS:** Dir of Alumni Affairs, North Caroline A&TUniv, 1601 E Market St, Greensboro, NC 27411.

BULGER, LUCILLE O.
Business executive. **PERSONAL:** Born Sep 26, 1912; married Robert; children: Neil, Kent. **EDUCATION:** New Sch of Social Reasearch New York City Cornell Univ Extension, 1967-68. **CAREER:** Comm League of W 159th St Inc, exec dir 1966-. **ORGANIZATIONS:** Pres Comm League of W 159th St 1952-66; founder Comm League of W 159th St Inc 1952; pres Council Dist 6 1954-56; vice pres United Parents Assoc of NY 1957-61; mem Neighborhood Clean-Up Campaign Comm 1966-; bd mem Washington Heights W Harlem Inwood Mental Health Cncl 1969-; bd mem Central Harlem Meals on Wheels 1972; various comm com at ColumbiaUniv NYC; chmn Health Com of Ofc of Neighborhood Govt; mem Fed Grants Com of Addiction Serv Agy; Dist 6 Health Council 1973-75. **HONORS/ACHIEVEMENTS:** Recipient Certificate of Pub Serv State of NY 1959; New York City Dept of Health Certificate of Merit 1967; Nat Assn of Media Women Inc Awd 1967; New York City Dept of Health Certificate of Merit 1975. **BUSINESS ADDRESS:** Executive Dir, Comm League of W 159th St Inc, 508 W 159 St, New York, NY 10032.

BULLARD, EDWARD A., JR.
Educator, accountant, systems analyst. **PERSONAL:** Born Apr 02, 1947, Syracuse, NY; married Terrlyon D; children: Lan R, Edward III, Terron D. **EDUCATION:** Southern Univ, BS 1969; Syracuse Univ, MBA 1972; Univ of Detroit Law School, JD 1978. **CAREER:** Carrier Corp, analyst 1969; Ernst & Whinney, accountant 1969-72; Univ of MI Flint, prof; GMI, assoc prof acctg 1972-1987. **ORGANIZATIONS:** Bd mem Urban Legue Flint 1984, Flint Comm Devel Corp 1984; mem AICPA, Amer Acctg Assoc; adv Flint City Schools Bus Prog 1985; mem City of Flint Cable TV Advisory Panel; Small business consultant and urban analyst; mem Amer Business Law Assoc. **HONORS/ACHIEVEMENTS:** CPA NY 1977-; Outstanding Prof Univ of MI Flint 1979; mem Univ of Detroit Law Schl Moot Court Tax Team 1977. **HOME ADDRESS:** 3026 Concord, Flint, MI 48504. **BUSINESS ADDRESS:** Associate Professor of Acctng, GMI Engineering & Mgmt Inst, 1700 W 3rd Ave, Flint, MI 48502.

BULLETT, AUDREY KATHRYN
City supervisor, mayor. **PERSONAL:** Born Feb 12, 1937, Chicago, IL; daughter of Louis Hill and Eva Reed Hill; married Clark Ricardo Bullett, Jr, Sep 18, 1965 (deceased); children: Iris J. **EDUCATION:** Ferris State University, Big Rapids MI, AA, 1983, BS, 1984; University of Metaphysics, Los Angeles CA, MMs, 1986, doctoral candidate. **CAREER:** Lake County MI Veterans Trust Fund, authorized agent, 1969-80; Lake County, MI, deputy county clerk and deputy register of deeds, 1970-73, building and grounds manager, courthouse, 1970-80, public service employment program administrator, 1971-80, vice chair, county planning commission, 1975-76, chair 1976-80; TV 9/10, Cadillac MI, news correspondent, 1973-80; 78th District Court, Baldwin MI, court clerk and deputy magistrate, 1974-81; Yates Township, Idlewild MI, volunteer firefighter, 1969—, treasurer, Economic Development Corp, 1978—, township supervisor/mayor, 1984—; Dawn's Light Center, Inc, Idlewild MI, founder/president, 1985—; Mason County MI Central School District, adjunct teaching position, Adult Education Program, 1985—. **ORGANIZATIONS:** Chairperson, MI chapter, Natl Conference of Black Mayors, 1988—; advisory board member, Rural Businees Partnership Board, 1989—; secretary, West Central MI Community Growth Alliance, 1988—; Peacock Ladies Auxiliary, Veterans of Foreign Wars; chairperson, Lake County Democratic Party, 1975-78, 1985-86. **HONORS/ACHIEVEMENTS:** Robert F Williams Memorial Scholarship, 1983; Victor F Spathelf Award for leadership, 1984. **HOME ADDRESS:** 5197 South Broadway, PO Box 144, Idlewild, MI 49642.

BULLINS, ED
Playwright, producer, educator. **PERSONAL:** Born Jul 02, 1935, Philadelphia, PA. **EDUCATION:** Attended Los Angeles City College, San Francisco State Univ, New York School of Visual Arts, New School Extension, Vista College, Univ of California at Berkeley Extension; Wm Penn Business Institute, Philadelphia PA, general business certificate; Antioch University, San Francisco CA, BA, 1989; Sonoma State University, BA candidate. **CAREER:** Black Arts West, San Francisco CA, founder and producer, 1965-67; New Lafayette Theatre of Harlem, resident playwright and associate director, 1967-73; Black Theatre Magazine, New York NY, editor, 1968-73; New York Shakespeare Festival, writers unit coordinator/press assistant, 1975-82; New York Univ instructor in School of Continuing Education, 1979, instructor of dramatic writing, 1981; Berkeley Black Repertory, public relations director, 1982; The Magic Theatre, San Francisco CA, promotion director pro tem, 1982-83; Julian Theatre, San Francisco CA, group sales coordinator, 1983; City College of San Francisco, CA, instructor in drama, 1984-88; Antioch University, San Francisco CA, instructor of playwriting and administrative asst in public information and recruitment, 1986-87; The B ullins Memorial Theater, Emeryville CA, produce/playwright, 1988; lecturer at Sonoma State University, Rohnert Park CA, and University of California, Berkeley. **HONORS/ACHIEVEMENTS:** Recipient of 3 Obie Awards; 4 Rockefeller Foundation grants; 2 Guggenheim fellowships; Natl Endowment for the Arts grant; AUDELCO Award, Harlem Theater; New York Drama Critics Circle Award, 1975; author of numerous plays, including "The Taking of Miss Janie," 1974, "The Fabulous Miss Marie," 1970, "In New England Winter," 1968; author of Five Plays by Ed Bullins, Bobbs-Merrill, 1969, The Duplex, Morrow, 1971, The Hungered One, Morrow, 1971, Four Dynamite Plays, Morrow, 1972, The Theme Is Blackness, Morrow, 1973, The Reluctant Rapist, Harper, 1973. **HOME ADDRESS:** 3629 San Pablo Ave, Emeryville, CA 94608.

BULLOCK, BYRON SWANSON
Educational administrator. **PERSONAL:** Born Aug 04, 1955, Washington, DC; married Antoinette Langston; children: Melanie; Aaron. **EDUCATION:** Lincoln Univ, BA 1973-77. **CAREER:** Lincoln Univ, admin counselor 1977-79; Univ of Delaware, asst dir of upward bound 1979-85; James Madison Univ, asst dean of students 1985-. **ORGANIZATIONS:** Alpha Phi Alpha, area coord 1980, sec 1984-85; Delaware Personnel & Guidance 1981-85; Opp Prog Personnel, bd mem 1982-85; State Trio Assoc, pres 1983-85; Nat'l Council of Educational Opp, team leader 1984-85; Mid Eastern Assoc of Educational, tresurer 1985. **HONORS/ACHIEVEMENTS:** Martin Luther King, Jr, science awrd; Outstanding Young Men of America, 1983-86; Outstanding Young Personalities 1984. **HOME ADDRESS:** 888 Vine St, Harrisonburg, VA 22801. **BUSINESS ADDRESS:** Asst Dean of Students, James Madison University, Allinae Hall, Harrisonburg, VA 22807.

BULLOCK, CLIFTON VERNICE
Clergyman. **PERSONAL:** Born Feb 12, 1928, Lincoln Co, MS; married Voncile C Bowman; children: Vidette K, Kim V Joseph, Ivan A. **EDUCATION:** NE Wesleyan Univ, BS 1967; Perkins School of Theology, Southern Methodist Univ, ThM 1971; St Paul School of Theology, graduate work 1974-75. **CAREER:** Newman United Methodist Church, Lincoln, minister 1962-67; Eastwood Ministry Ft Worth, pastor-dir 1968-71; NE Wesleyan Univ Lincoln, chaplain/dir minority studies 1971-76; Washington Heights United Methodist Church, pastor/dir 1976-. **ORGANIZATIONS:** Mem N Central Jurisdiction Council on Ministries United Meth Ch 1976-; chairperson Religion & Race Commn W MI Conf United Meth Ch 1977-; mem Mayor's Coms on Youth Employment & Drug Abuse Ft Worth 1968-71; gov's appointee NE Arts Council & NE Crime Commn Lincoln 1971-76; bd of dir United Way, Urban League, Youth Employment Serv Battle Creek 1977-. **HONORS/ACHIEVEMENTS:** Senior Award Perkins School of Theology 1971; Special Awards Cereal City Lions Club & Lakeview Kiwanis Club 1978; Sojourner Truth Award Natl Org of Negro Business & Professional Women BC 1979; George Award Battle Creek Enquirer & News 1980. **MILITARY SERVICE:** AUS sgt 1st class 1948-52. **BUSINESS ADDRESS:** Pastor/Dir, Washington Heights United Methodist Church, 153 N Wood St, Battle Creek, MI 49017.

BULLOCK, DEBORAH LYNNE
Non-profit organization executive. **PERSONAL:** Born Nov 30, 1961, Chicago, IL; daughter of Edward Wright, Jr. and Donna L. Radford Wright; married Sam R. Bullock, May 12, 1988. **EDUCATION:** Howard Univ, Washington DC, BS, 1983; Roosevelt Univ, Chicago IL, paralegal certificate; Institute for Paralegal Trn, Chicago IL, certificate, 1984. **CAREER:** Winston & Strawn Law Firm, Chicago IL, corporate paralegal, 1984-85; Junior Achievement of Chicago IL, vice pres of ed serv, 1985-88, pres of ed serv, 1988—. **ORGANIZATIONS:** Robbins Youth Center, Michiana Advisory Council on Economic Education. **HONORS/ACHIEVEMENTS:** Named most outstanding student, school of human ecology, Howard Univ, 1983. **BUSINESS ADDRESS:** Junior Achievement of Michiana, 1201 Northside Blvd, South Bend, IN 46615.

BULLOCK, ELBERT L.
Correctional officer. **PERSONAL:** Born Jan 19, 1934, Houston; married Yvonne M; children: Paula, Jo Anna, Lauren. **EDUCATION:** Fresno State Coll, BA 1957. **CAREER:** CA Community Realese Bd, hearing rep; CA Med Facility CA Dept Corrections chief human relations section CA Dept Corrections, assoc supt 1972-74; Richmond Serv Center CA, mgr 1970-72; Richmond Serv Center, CA asst Mgr 1969-70; CA Dept Corrections, correctional consultant 1967-69; Cdc, parole agt 1965-67; tchr pub & state 1959-65. **ORGANIZATIONS:** Mem Counseliers W; CA Black Correctional Coalition; past mem Allied Peace Officers Assn Mem; Alpha Phi Alpha Frat; past mem City Richmond Model Cities Com 1968-71; chmn Mayors Cit Com Study Comm Relations Richmond CA 1969; All Conf team Fresno State Coll 1956; All Star Football team USMC 1958; devel first pre-serv ttng acad hiring &

training staff CA dept corrections; Affirmative Action plan Cdc. **MILITARY SERVICE:** USMC lance corpl 1957-59. **BUSINESS ADDRESS:** CA Community Release Bd, 714 P St, Sacramento, CA 95814.

BULLOCK, J. JEROME
Government official. **PERSONAL:** Born Jan 03, 1948, Hogansville, GA; son of Jerry L Bullock and Vivian Baker Bullock; married Alice Gresham; children: Brian Jerome, Alison Whitney. **EDUCATION:** Tuskegee Inst, BS Political Science 1969; Howard Univ School of Law, JD 1975. **CAREER:** US Marshal Serv, assoc legal counsel 1975-77, US Marshal 1977-82, assoc legal counsel 1982-84, chief congressional & public affairs 1984-85; Office of Internal Security, chief 1985-89; Office of the inspector General, US Dept of Justice, 1989-. **ORGANIZATIONS:** Vp Air Security Corp 1983-85; commercial pilot; FAA certified flight instructor; mem Natl Assoc of Flight Instructor 1984-, IA State Bar Assn, Phi Alpha Delta Law Fraternity, Intl Assoc of Chiefs of Police, Kappa Alpha Psi. **HONORS/ACHIEVEMENTS:** Meritorious Serv Award US Marshals Serv 1978; Tuskegee Alumni Award Tuskegee Inst 1979; Distinguished Military Grad Army ROTC Tuskegee Inst 1969; Special Achievement Award US Marshal Serv 1976; appt by Pres Carter US Marshal for DC 1977; Distinguished Service Award, US Marshals Service, 1987. **MILITARY SERVICE:** AUS capt 1969-72. **HOME ADDRESS:** 6127 Utah Avenue NW, Washington, DC 20015.

BULLOCK, JAMES
Educator, attorney. **PERSONAL:** Born Aug 22, 1926, Charleston, MS; married Lois; children: Joseph. **EDUCATION:** TX So U, BA JD 1970. **CAREER:** US Postal Service, supvr; TX Southern Univ, assoc dean law, assoc prof law. **ORGANIZATIONS:** Justice Greener Chap Phi Alpha Delta Legal Frat; TX Black Caucus; mem Am Bar Assn; Nat Bar Assn; State Bar TX; Houston Bar Assn; Houston Lwyrs Assn; Phi Alpha Delta Legal Frat; mem S & Central YMCA; NAACP; Harris Co Cncl Orgn; TX Assn Coll Tchrs. **HONORS/ACHIEVEMENTS:** Phi Alpha Delta Outstanding Alumnus. **MILITARY SERVICE:** USAF s/sgt 1947-56. **BUSINESS ADDRESS:** Associate Professor, Texas SouthernUniv, School of Law, 3100 Cleburne Avenue, Houston, TX 77004.

BULLOCK, JOSEPH MOSES
Dentist. **PERSONAL:** Born Jun 18, 1891, Tarboro, NC; married Lucille W Gilbert. **EDUCATION:** Meharry Med Coll, DDS 1923. **CAREER:** Dentist Hartford, CT, gen prac dentistry,. **ORGANIZATIONS:** Mem CT Am Dental Assn; mem Blue Hlls Civic Assn 1968; trustee Wmn's League Day Care Center; Alpha Phi Alpha; Sigma Pi Phi; Bapt. **MILITARY SERVICE:** AUS rep capt 1917-19. **BUSINESS ADDRESS:** 75 Pratt St, Hartford, CT 06103.

BULLOCK, SAMUEL CAREY
Educator, psychiatrist. **PERSONAL:** Born Oct 06, 1921, Washington, DC; children: Wallace, Anne. **EDUCATION:** Dartmouth Coll, AB 1943; NY Univ Coll of Med, 1946; Inst of Philadelphia Psychoanalytic Soc, 1969. **CAREER:** Hahnemann Medical Coll & Hospital, prof of psychiatry; Howard Univ, prof dept chmn 1974-77; Univ of Pennsylvania Medical School, private practice, psychiatry & psychoanalysis. **ORGANIZATIONS:** Mem Am Psychiatric Assn; Philadelphia Coll Of Physicians Career Tchng Flwshp; Nat Inst Of Mental Hlth 1955-58. **MILITARY SERVICE:** AUS pfc 1943-46, capt 1951-53. **BUSINESS ADDRESS:** 230 N Broad St, Philadelphia, PA 19102.

BULLOCK, THEODORE
Owner. **PERSONAL:** Born Aug 06, 1928, Pike Co, MS; son of Eugene Bullock and Willie Bullock; married Vivian Bridges; children: Brian Nichols, Reuben Nichols, Sherry Butler, Cynthia. **CAREER:** Piggly Wiggly Stores, clk 1948-56; Railway Express Agency, materials handler 1957-60; Veteran's Taxi, owner 1970-73; US Post Office, mail clerk 1961-70; Bullocks Washateria, owner 1972; Brnch & Recreation Inc, part owner 1979; Bullock's Food Mart, owner. **ORGANIZATIONS:** Bd mem Mccomb C of C 1975; bd mem Pike Co Bus League 1976; elected bd mem McComb City Council 1979; elected supervisor Pike Co District #1 1984. **HONORS/ACHIEVEMENTS:** Cert of Appreciation Gov of MS 1975. **BUSINESS ADDRESS:** Bullock's Food Mart, 130 St Augustine St, McComb, MS 39648.

BULLOCK, THURMAN RUTHE
Municipal government official. **PERSONAL:** Born Oct 06, 1947, Richmond, VA; son of Warren Bullock and Dorothy Hargrove Bullock; married Anne Leshner, Aug 31, 1976; children: Thurman Martin. **EDUCATION:** Franklin & Marshall Coll, Lancaster, PA, BA, 1970; Temple Univ, Philadelphia, PA, MS, 1979. **CAREER:** Comptroller of the Currency, Philadelphia, PA, asst natl bank examiner, 1970-75; Deloitte Haskins & Sells, Philadelphia, PA, auditor, 1977-80; Bell of Pennsylvania, Philadelphia, PA, internal auditor, 1980-82; City of Philadelphia Office of the Controller, PA, deputy city controller, 1982-. **ORGANIZATIONS:** Bd mem, Council of Intl Programs, 1981-, Intl Professional Exchange, 1981-, Opportunities Acad of Mgmt Training Inc, 1981-, Philadelphia Clearinghouse, 1989; business advisory bd, House of Umoja, 1986-; past sec, treasurer, 1980-89, pres elect, 1989-, Pennsylvania Inst of Certified Public Accountants; past pres, mem, Philadelphia Federation of Black Business & Professional Org, 1981-; past vice pres, former advisory bd mem, Community Accountants; mem, Natl Assn of Black Accountants, 1979, Amer Inst of Certified Public Accountants, 1980-, Govt Finance Officers Assn, 1981, Accounting Research Assn, 1989, Amer Soc for Public Admin, 1989, Assn of Local Govt Auditors, 1989. **HONORS/ACHIEVEMENTS:** CPA Certificate, 1979; Distinguished Public Serv Award, Inst of Certified Public Accountants, 1986; appeared in Pennsylvania Inst of Certified Public Accountants career video, "Is an Accounting Career in Your Future?", 1987. **BUSINESS ADDRESS:** Deputy City Controller, Philadelphia, Office of the Controller, 1230 Municipal Serv Bldg, 15th St and John F Kennedy Blvd, Philadelphia, PA 19102-1679.

BULLOCK, WILLIAM HORACE
Educator, physician. **PERSONAL:** Born Nov 06, 1919, Washington, DC; son of George Oliver Bullock and Rebecca Burgess Bullock. **EDUCATION:** Howard Univ, BA 1940, Howard Univ MD 1944; Univ of Michigan Simpson Memorial Inst. 1950-51. **CAREER:** Private practice, physician; Howard Univ, clinical instr 1944-50; Univ of Michigan, rockefeller fellow in hematology 1950-51; Howard Univ prof of med 1952-58; Howard Univ, assoc prof of med 1958-76, prof emeritus, 1977-. **ORGANIZATIONS:** Diplomat of Amer Bd of Internal & Med 1954; fellow of Amer Coll of Physicians 1958; fellow of Intl Soc of Hematology 1956; fellow of Amer Soc of Hematology 1958; mem Amer Intl soc of Internal Med; mem Amer Soc of Intl Med; mem Nat Sickle Cell Anemia Adv Bd 1971-75; mem bd dir Washington Chap of Amer Red Cross; mem adv bd DC Chapter of Amer Red Cross. **HONORS/ACHIEVEMENTS:** Student coun faculty award Howard Univ 1958; HEW award for service on Natl Sickle Cell Disease Adv Bd 1973; recipient Rockefeller Fellow. **BUSINESS ADDRESS:** Physician, William H Bullock MD FACP, 408 T St NW, Washington, DC 20001.

BUMBRY, GEORGE NORDLINGER
Clergyman. **PERSONAL:** Born Sep 28, 1922, Washington, DC; married Carrie Mae; children: Jeffery, Gary, Carolyn, Belinda, Estelle, Brian. **EDUCATION:** BDiv candidate 1975; VA Union Univ School of Theology Richmond, Religion Educ. **CAREER:** First Baptist Church Colonial Beach VA, minister 24 yrs. **ORGANIZATIONS:** Past EEO counselor NWL; past pres NAACP; mem King George Ministers Assn, Colonial Bch Ministers Assn; past dir of bd Indus Control Bd; mem Local Sickle Cell Assn, Masonic Lodge 212; bd dir Big Bros; funding chmn Local Sickle Cell Assn; former EEO counselor, NWL Dahlgren; pres No Neck Church & Sunday School Union 1979-80; mem sr vice commander VFW. **HONORS/ACHIEVEMENTS:** Awd Sickle Cell Assn; Presidential Citation 5 stars for World War II. **MILITARY SERVICE:** AUS WW II. **HOME ADDRESS:** Rt 3 Box 489, King George, VA 22485.

BUMBRY, GRACE ANN
Soprano. **PERSONAL:** Born Jan 04, 1937, StLouis, MO. **EDUCATION:** Boston Univ, student 1954-55; Music Acad West, student 1956-59; studied with Lotte Lehmann Northwestern Univ; several honorary degrees. **CAREER:** Paris Opera, operatic debut 1960; concert and operatic appear in Europe, Japan, Bayreuth, Germany and US; The White House, command perf; performed Met Opera NYC, Royal Opera House Covent Garden, London, La Scala Milan, Vienna Stateopera, Teatro Colon Buenos Aires, Chicago Lyric Opera, Berlin Opera, San Francisco Opera. **ORGANIZATIONS:** Mem Zeta Phi Beta; mem Sigma Alpha Iota. **HONORS/ACHIEVEMENTS:** Recording for Deutsche Grammophon, Angel, London and RCA; recip John Hay Whitney Award 1959, Richard Wagner Medal 1963; recip Awards from Natl Assn Negro Musicians, Boston Univ; Hon Citizen Baltimore, Los Angeles, Phila, St Louis.

BUMPHUS, WALTER GAYLE
Educator. **PERSONAL:** Born Mar 19, 1948, Princeton, KY; married Aileen Thompson; children: Michael, Brian, Fran. **EDUCATION:** Murray State Univ, BS 1971, MEd 1974; Univ of TX at Austin, PhD 1985. **CAREER:** Murray State Univ, counselor & dorm asst 1970-72, dir of minority affairs 1972-74; East AR Comm Coll, dean 1974-78; Howard Comm Coll, dean of students 1978-. **ORGANIZATIONS:** Reader Field Read for Office of Educ Title IV 1986; chairperson Middle Stated Accred Assoc Team 1986; vice pres Natl Assoc of Student Develop. **HONORS/ACHIEVEMENTS:** Richardson Fellowship Univ of TX at Austin 1983; Key to City Awd Princeton KY 1984. **BUSINESS ADDRESS:** Dean of Students, Howard Community College, Little Patuxent Pkwy, Columbia, MD 21044.

BUNDLES, A'LELIA PERRY
Journalist. **PERSONAL:** Born Jun 07, 1952, Chicago, IL; daughter of S Henry Bundles Jr and A'Lelia Mae Perry Bundles (deceased). **EDUCATION:** Harvard-Radcliffe Coll, AB (magna cum laude) 1974; Columbia Univ Grad Sch of Journalism, MSJ 1976. **CAREER:** Newsweek Chicago Bureau, intern 1973; WTLC-FM Indpls, anchor/reporter 1974; Du Pont Co, Wilmington, DE, staff asstnt 1974-75; NBC News NY, Houston & Atlanta bureaus, field producer 1976-85; NBC News Washington, DC, producer 1985-89; ABC News Washington DC, World News Tonight, producer 1989-. **ORGANIZATIONS:** Trustee Mme C J Walker Estate 1976-, Whitney Young Fdn 1979-81; sec Radcliffe Class of '74 1979-, Nat'l Assoc of Black Jrnlsts 1980-; comm advsry brd Clark Coll Sch of Comm 1981; planning comm Radcliffe Inst Symposium, Black Women 1973; trustee of Radcliffe Coll, bd of management 1985-89; dir, Harvard Alumni Assn 1989-; The Links Inc. **HONORS/ACHIEVEMENTS:** NBC/RCA Fellow at Columbia Schl of Jrnlsm 1975-76; summer resch Fellow Kennedy Inst of Politics Harvard 1973; freelance writer published in Parade, Ms, Sage, Ebony, Jr, Radcliff Quarterly, Seventeen, Indpls, Star, Indianapolis News; National Assn of Black Journalists 1st Place Features Award 1987; Aurthor, Biography of Mme C J Walker for Chelsea Press 1990. **BUSINESS ADDRESS:** Producer, ABC News, 1717 DeSales St NW, Washington, DC 20016.

BUNDY, JAMES LOMAX
Judge. **PERSONAL:** Born Mar 06, 1920, Bluefield, WV; married Sarah J; children: 4 children. **EDUCATION:** Bluefield State Coll, BS 1942; Univ MD Sch Law, LLB 1949, JD 1969. **CAREER:** City of Baltimore, asst city solicitor 1962-68; State of MD, asst atty gen 1968-74; District 1, judge. **ORGANIZATIONS:** Mem Natl, MD State Bar Assns; mem Bar Assn Baltimore City; mem Monumental City Bar Assn; mem Bluefield State Coll Baltimore Alumni Chap pres 1970-73; lectr Business Law Morgan State Coll Grad Sch 1970. **HONORS/ACHIEVEMENTS:** Afro-Amer Superior Comm Serv Awd 1958. **MILITARY SERVICE:** USAF sgt maj 195=42-45. **BUSINESS ADDRESS:** Judge, District 1, 221 E Madison St, Baltimore, MD 21202.

BUNKLEY, LONNIE R.
Real estate developer. **PERSONAL:** Born Aug 12, 1932, Denison, TX; son of C B Bunkley and Ruth Smith Bunkley; married Charlene Marie Simpson; children: Karen Annette, Natalie Anitra. **EDUCATION:** Prairie View Univ, BA 1952; CA State Univ LA, MS 1964; Univ of So CA, grad studies 1965. **CAREER:** LA Neighborhood Youth Corps Econ & Youth Oppor Agency, dir 1968; East LA Coll & Compton Coll, coll instr 1970-78; LA Co Probation Dept, div chief 1977; Pacific Properties, broker & Developer/pres; Commercial Devel Corp, president; commercial developer of Compton Plaza. **ORGANIZATIONS:** Mem exec comm Southside LA Jr C of C 1966; mem SE Welfare Planning Council 1973; bd of dir Compton Sickle Cell Anemia Educ & Detection Ctr; mem CA Probation & Parole Assn; mem Black Probation Officers Assn; bd of dir Natl Black United Fund; chmn bd of trustees Los Angeles Brotherhood Crusade; mem Omega Psi Phi Frat; ruling elder St Paul's United Presby Church; bd of directors, Black Support Group, California State University.. **HONORS/ACHIEVEMENTS:** Outstanding Serv Awd Brotherhood Crusade 1972; Certificate, Ctr for Health Urban Educ & Rsch 1982; Cert of Appreciation US Congress 1983; Awd LA Co Bd ofSupervisors 1984; Certificate Compton Sickle Cell Educ & Detection Ctr 1982; Prairie View Univ Alumni Awd 1970; Commendation Southside Jr Chamber of Commerce 1962; LA Co Bd of Supervisors Awd 1984; Commendatory Resolution City of Compton 1982. **MILI-**

TARY SERVICE: AUS educ specl 1953-55. **BUSINESS ADDRESS:** President, Commercial Develop Corp, 900 South Stoneacre Ave, Compton, CA 90221.

BUNN, WARREN J.
Union business executive. **PERSONAL:** Born May 13, 1914, Brooklyn, NY; married Amanda Carr; children: Barbara (dec), Warren, Jr. **EDUCATION:** Cornell Extension Sch, Abor-mgmt Relations & Union Functions Courses; New York City & Rutgers U, Lab Or Educ Center NJ. **CAREER:** Factory worker Various Locations 1935-38; New York, part-time salesman 1937-39; E R Squibb & Sons & Pharmaceutical Co Brooklyn, NY, 1939-50. **ORGANIZATIONS:** Oil, Chemical & Atomic-workers, Intl Union, AFL-CIO, 1950; NAACP, Life mem, former pres, Brooklyn NAACP 1962-70; NY State NAACP Labor Com, Chmn 1971-72; NY City Central Labor Council, AFL-CIO 1950 exec bd mem. **HONORS/ACHIEVEMENTS:** NAACP, Brooklyn Br Award 1964; JFK Library for Minorities, Am Heritage Award 1972; NY City Central Labor Council Comm Serv Award 1970; Concord Baptist Church Serv in Labor Movement Award 1974. **BUSINESS ADDRESS:** 1155 W Chestnut St, Ste 2 B, Union, NJ 07083.

BUNTE, DORIS
Administrator. **PERSONAL:** Born Jul 02, 1933, New York, NY; divorced; children: Yvette, Harold, Allen. **EDUCATION:** Boston U, Metro Coll, Univ MA Amhurst/Suffolk Univ 1969-73. **CAREER:** 7th Suffolk Dist, state rep 1972; Boston Housing Authority, comm 1969-75; So End Nghbrhd Action Program Boston, dir pers 1970-72; So End Nghbrhd ActionProgram & Boston, dir housing 1969-70. **ORGANIZATIONS:** Mem Dem Nat Conventions, 1972-76; mem, Electoral Coll Pres Election 1976; mem MALEG Black Caucaus; mem Third World Jobs Clearing Hse; mem MA Assn Paraplegics; mem Combined Black Philanthropies; mem MA Leg Women's Caucus; mem NAACP; mem Nat Order Of Women Legltr; mem Black Polit Task Force; mem MA Conf Human Rights; mem Citizen's Housing & Planning Assn; mem Solomon Carter Fuller Mental Health Ctr; mem Rosbury Multi-Serv Ctr Declaratoion & "Doris Bunte Day" 1975; Loeb Fellow, Harvard Grad Sch of Design 1975-76. **HONORS/ACHIEVEMENTS:** Citizen Of Y R Omega Psi Frat Inc Iota Chi Chap 1978; Citizen Of Yr Award Nat Assn Social Wkrs 1980; Notary Public, Commonwealth MA; Appointee Nat RentAdv Bd Phase II Econ Stabilization Act; Award Black Housing Task Force; Award Roxbury Action Prog; Published, Address To City Missionary, 1973; Publ Child Force; Award, Roxbury Action Prog; Published, Address to City Missionary 1973; Publ "Child Advocacy" a dependency cycle is not a goal" 1977; publ "our & Third World Comm Revitalization Through Access By Mandte Example & Monitoring"; Guest Lectr Boston Coll, Boston U, John F Kennedy Sch govt, Simmons Coll Suffolk U; So U; Univ of Ma. **BUSINESS ADDRESS:** Administrator, Boston Housing Authority, 52 Chauncy St, Boston, MA 02111.

BUNTON, HENRY CLAY
Clergyman. **PERSONAL:** Born Oct 19, 1903, Tuscaloosa, AL; married Alfreda; children: Mattye, Marjorie, Henry, Joseph. **EDUCATION:** A&M U, AB; Denver U, Sch of Theology MTh; Northwestern U, Garret Theol Sem; Meth U, Perkins Sch of Theology of So. **CAREER:** Christian Meth Episcopal Ch Seventh Episcopal Dist, bishop; Churchs in AL FL AR TX CO TN, former pastor; Miles Coll, Paine Coll KS-MO Annual Conf Trustee, former pres elder. **ORGANIZATIONS:** Mem NAACP; Phi Beta Sigma; mason; contrib editor Christian Index Christimeth Epis Ch1948-60; charter mem SCLC. **BUSINESS ADDRESS:** CME Ch, 557 Randolph St NW, Washington, DC 20011.

BUNYON, RONALD S.
Business executive. **PERSONAL:** Born Mar 13, 1935, Philadelphia, PA; married Josephine; children: Ronald Jr, Judith, Joann, Joyce, Jodetta. **EDUCATION:** Mitchell Coll, AS Engineering 1965; Univ of New Haven, CT, BS Business, 1969; Southern CT State Coll, MS Urban Devel. **CAREER:** Business Ventures Intl Inc, pres 1979-; Drexel Univ Philadelphia, asst vice pres 1979; Opportunities Ind Ctr Intl, mgmt spec 1976; Zion Investments Philadelphia, business mgr 1973; Natl Prog Asst for Econ Devel, reg dir 1972; Gen Dynamics Nuclear Ship Bldg, sr designer 1958. **ORGANIZATIONS:** Member, Export Council US Dept of Commerce, 1979, World Trade Assn Philadelphia, 1979; honor soc, Alpha Ki Alpha 1967; Leadership Comm Bd of Educ, Philadelphia 1978. **HONORS/ACHIEVEMENTS:** First in class, cum laude graduate, 1969. **BUSINESS ADDRESS:** PO Box 1324, Philadelphia, PA 19105.

BURCH, REYNOLD EDWARD
Physician. **PERSONAL:** Born Oct 03, 1910, August, ME; married Mary. **EDUCATION:** Bates Coll, BS 1933; Howard U, MD 1942. **CAREER:** Pvt practice 1946-72, 1976; MJ Med Schl, asso clinical prof 1972-76; Gardiner HS, sci tchr 1934; Booker Washington HS, chem tchr 1935; Bordentown Manual Training Schl, sci tchr; Maternal & Infant Care, NJ Med & Sch, dir. **ORGANIZATIONS:** Bd dir, Pub Serv Electric & Gas; bd trustee, Coll Med & Dent NJ 1972-74; AMA; NMA; United Hosps of Newark; Bethany Lodge 31; Prince Hall Foam Masons; bd dir, Essex Co Youth House 1949-54; adv bd Planned Parenthood Essex Co; chmn bd trustees, Leaguers Ind; 200 Club; NAACP; YMCA. **HONORS/ACHIEVEMENTS:** Diplomat, Am Bd of Obstetrics, 1963; Fellow, Am Coll of Surgeons; fellow Am Coll Obs-gyn; Alpha Phi Alpha; Sigma Pi Phi; Co-author "Heroin Addiction Among Pregant Women & Their Babies" author "A Plan For Family Planning"; 3 Meritious Serv awds, Essex Co Med Soc. **MILITARY SERVICE:** AUS Air Corps, cpt 1943-46.

BURCHELL, CHARLES R.
Educator. **PERSONAL:** Born Nov 24, 1946, New Orleans; married Paulette Martinez. **EDUCATION:** Tulane U, 1964-66; Southern U, 1966-68; LA State U, BA 1968, MA 1971, PhD 1977. **CAREER:** LA State Univ, instructor dept of Psychology 1971-; WRBT-TV,TV news & reporter 1972-74, 76; WXOK Radio Baton Rouge, radio announcer 1966-72. **ORGANIZATIONS:** Mem Southern Psychol Ass 1974-75; Psi Chi 1968; AFTRA 1970. **HONORS/ACHIEVEMENTS:** Recipient Welfare Rights Orgn Serv Award 1973. **BUSINESS ADDRESS:** LA State Univ, Dept of Psychol, Baton Rouge, LA 70803.

BURDEN, PENNIE L.
Community activist. **PERSONAL:** Born Nov 26, 1910, Waynesboro, GA; daughter of John W Bell and Sarah L Bell; married Sherman J Burden, Nov 04, 1959. **EDUCATION:** Wayne State Univ; Detroit Inst Musical Art; Lewis Business Coll. **CAREER:** Detroit Gen Hospital, desk clerk registration of patients for clinic, sec in oral surgery 1969-70, technician in radiology clinic patients, sr clerk business office. **ORGANIZATIONS:** Natl pres, Eta Phi Beta Sorority, Inc, 1962-66; Campfire Girl Leader, 1970-80; Campfire Girl Leader 197-80; Historic Sites Committee, 1980-; U.N.N.C.F. MI Con Sr Program, 1989; St Stephen AME Church Bd of Trustees asst sec; DABO bd of dir; Natl Council Negro Women; St Stephen Dir Sr Citizen; St Stephen pres Goodwill Club, 1989; Dir Sr Citizen Program St Stephen AME Church, 1980-89. **HONORS/ACHIEVEMENTS:** Life Membership, NAACP; sec Mortgage Fund, St Stephen AME Church, 1975; Golden Heritage, NAACP, 1988; Town Hall Forum, St Stephen AME Church; Out Reach Program, City Detroit Retirees, 1989. **HOME ADDRESS:** 13233 Vassar Dr, Detroit, MI 48235.

BURDEN, WILLIE JAMES
Administrator. **PERSONAL:** Born Jul 21, 1951, Longwood, NC; son of Emily H Burden; married Velma Stokes; children: Courtney. **EDUCATION:** Ohio Univ, Masters 1983; NC State U, BA 1974. **CAREER:** OH Univ, asst football coach 1982-84; Calgary Stampeders of CFL, prof athlete 1974-81; NC State Univ, asst to athletics dir 1976-82, asst Football Coach 1974-76; Tennessee Tech Univ, asst athletic dir 1984-88; Ohio Univ, asst athletic dir 1988-. **ORGANIZATIONS:** Sr cnslr Amer Legion Boys State TN 1984 & 1986; pres Friends of Distinction NC 1969-; big bro cnslr PHD Prevent High Sch Drop Outs Prog Raleigh, NC 1973-74; mem, Phi Delta Kappa 1987-; mem, Civilian Civic Organization 1988-. **HONORS/ACHIEVEMENTS:** Athletic endwmnt schlrshp honoree Univ of Calgary, Alberta, CN 1983-; all-star Canadian Football League 1975-79; mvp Canadian Football League 1975; mvp player of the year Atlantic Coast Conf Football 1973. **BUSINESS ADDRESS:** Athletic Department, Box 689, Ohio University, Athens, OH 45701.

BURFORD, EFFIE LOIS
Educator. **PERSONAL:** Born Feb 16, 1927, Learned, MS; children: Cecelia Adela Boler, Suzette Elaine, Maurice M. **EDUCATION:** Butler U, AB 1950; Christian Theol Sem, MA 1952 1955. **CAREER:** Indianapolis, teacher 1957-65; Language Arts & Spanish, teacher 1966; Language, Traveling Foreign teacher 1970; Zeta Phi Beta Sor Inc, state dir 1966, reg dir 1968-74. **ORGANIZATIONS:** Bd mem editor Mem Am Tchrs Spanish & Portguese 1974; IFT; bd mem 2nd Christian Ch; comm on ch devel in IN; life mem NAACP; natl chmn Reconciliation Christian Ch; mem Publicity Com. **HONORS/ACHIEVEMENTS:** Black women's intl conf award in journalism Columbia Scholastic Press Assn 1971; regional award Zeta Phi Beta Sor 1972; natl reg dir's award 1974. **BUSINESS ADDRESS:** 150 W 40th St, Indianapolis, IN.

BURGER, MARY WILLIAMS
Educational administrator. **PERSONAL:** Born in North Little Rock, AR; children: Nathaniel R III, Henry W. **EDUCATION:** Univ of AR Pine Bluff, BA magna cum laude 1959; CO State Univ, MA Eng Lit 1961; Washington Univ, PhD Mod Lit 1973; Harvard Univ, cert in ed manag 1978. **CAREER:** Lincoln Univ, instr of English 1961-66; Univ of MO, instr asst prof of English 1966-69, 1973-75; Univ of MD, asst provost/asst vice pres 1975-84; TN State Univ, vice pres for academic affairs, prof of English 1984-. **ORGANIZATIONS:** Consultant Natl Educ Assoc 1973; reviewer Middle States Assoc of Colls & Schools 1974-75; consultant Urban Behavioral Rsch Assoc 1974-79; consultant Midwest Ctr for EEO 1974-75; Alpha Kappa Mu Hon Soc; Alpha Kappa Alpha Sor; Phi Kappa Phi Hon Soc; Sister Cities of Baltimore-Garnga Liberia; Coll Lang Assn; State Planning Comm ACE/NIP. **HONORS/ACHIEVEMENTS:** Black Viewpoint New Amer Library 1971; Ford Foundation Fellow Washington Univ 1972-73; "Images of Black Women Sturdy" Black Bridges Doubleday 1979; "Improving Opp for Black Students" NAFEO Proceedings 1983; Sister Cities Intl TAP Grant Gbarnga Liberia 1983.

BURGESS, DWIGHT A.
Association executive. **PERSONAL:** Born Dec 16, 1927, Bailey's Bay; married Delores L Caldwell; children: Daphne, Danita. **EDUCATION:** Tuskegee Inst, BS 1952, MEd 1953. **CAREER:** Birmingham Urban League, aptd exec dir 1972-; Daniel Payne Coll, interim pres 2 months 1969, dean Acad affairs 1968; New Castle HS, head soc & sci dept, oratorical coach, athletic bus mgr 1966; Summer Basic Skills Workshop For Am Ethical Un, dir 1964-66; Hooper City HS, soc studies Tchr, jeff co bd educ 1955; Francis Patton Sch Bermuda, tchr english Tchr athletic Coach 1953-55. **ORGANIZATIONS:** Aptd to professional rights & responsibilities comm AL State Tchrs Assn 1963; pres Jeff Co Educ Assn 1963-65, exec comm mem 1966; aptd gr ldr soc studies tchrs Jeff Co AL 1968; mem Adv Com AL Cntr for Higher Edn; chmn Faculty Sharing Emp Com AL Cntr for Higher Educ 1968; aptd inst dep AL, Cntr for Higher Educ 1968; aptd Adv Bd Curbar Asso for Higher & Educ 1968; elected sec St John Fed Com 1969; aptd consult in educ Group Research 1969; aptdchmn Health Manpower Adv Com, Comm Health Planning Commn, Comm Serv Cncl of Jeff Co 1969; aptd outreach supvr Health Planner, Comm Serv Council 1970; aptd Comm Liaison Adv, Family Planning, Dept of OB-GYN of Univ of AL Med Sch 1971; cits adv com Birmingham Police Dept 1972; bd dirs Crisis Cntr 1972; coord Jeff Co Drug Abuse Com 1973; AL Com for Public Progs in Humanities 1973; Birmingham Manpower Area Planning Council 1973; C of C Manpower Voc Educ Com 1974; Birmingham Art Club 1974; Birmingham Youth 1974. **HONORS/ACHIEVEMENTS:** Recip Delta Sigma Theta Sor Comm Serv Award 1973; cert outstanding serv OIC 1974; selected Alpha Phi & Alpha Man of Yr 1974. **BUSINESS ADDRESS:** 505 N 17 St, Birmingham, AL 35203.

BURGESS, JAMES R., JR.
Attorney. **PERSONAL:** Born 1915, Putnam Co, TN; married Doris Antoinette Murray. **EDUCATION:** Univ of MD, BA 1961; Univ of IL, LLB 1965; Completed German Language Course in Oberammergau, Germany; Russian Language Course at Army Language Sch Presidio of Monterey, CA. **CAREER:** Army Officer 20 years; Champaign Co, state atty 1972-76, first asst state atty, supr atty; 1st black States Attorney in IL; 1st black US attorney Eastern/Southern Dist of IL 1977-82; private general law practice; Lawndale Legal Aid Office, inspector gen US Dept of Agriculture. **ORGANIZATIONS:** Pitched for semi-pro baseball Team; mem Pi Sigma Alpha Natl Honorary Soc; Phi Alpha Delta Law Frat; Urbana Rotary Club; First United Methodist Ch; various positions Boys' Club; bd mem Champaign Co Coun on Alcoholism; bd mem Champaign Co Children & Family Services; implemented Adult Diversion Prog as alternative to prosecution; introduced law-related education into Champaign Cty Public Schs; United Way, Champaign Cty, bd mem; visually impaired volunteer reader; mem, IL, Chicago & Federal Bar Assoc. **HONORS/ACHIEVEMENTS:** Selected Artillery OCS Trng; dean's list for Scholastic achievement Univ of MD; cited by Los Angeles Area Coun & Far East Coun BSA; cited for outstanding service Phi Alpha Delta Law Frat. **MILITARY SERVICE:** Army Officer 20 years, retired. **BUSINESS ADDRESS:** Attorney, 811 West Springfield, Suite 3, Champaign, IL 61820.

BURGESS, JOHN MELVILLE
Clergyman. **PERSONAL:** Born Mar 11, 1909, Grand Rapids, MI; married Esther; children: Julia, Margaret. **EDUCATION:** Univ of MI, AB 1930, MA 1931; Episcopal Theol Sch Cambridge, BD 1934; Hon Dr, Univ of MA, Univ of MI, Boston Coll, Trinity Coll, Colby Coll, Northeastern Univ, Suffolk Univ, Assumpton Coll, Berkeley Divinity Sch, Bryant Coll, St Augustine's Coll. **CAREER:** Began ministry in Grand Rapids 1934; Howard Univ, chaplain 1946-51; Washington Cahtedral, canon 1951-56; Episcopal City Mission, archdeacon Boston supt 1956-62; Diocese of MA, elected bishop coadjutor 1969, bishop 1970; Episcopal Diocese of MA, bishop retired 1976; Yale Divinity Sch, asst prof 1976-. **ORGANIZATIONS:** Mem Natl Council of Chs; MA Civil Liberties Union. **HONORS/ACHIEVEMENTS:** Editor "Black Gospel/White Church" 1982.

BURGESS, JOSEPH EDWARD
Health service administrator. **PERSONAL:** Born May 18, 1935, Kingstree, SC; son of Joseph Ting Burgess and Earline Burgess. **EDUCATION:** West Virginia State Coll, BA, 1958; New School for Social Rsch, MA 1983; Univ of MI, certificate, 1983. **CAREER:** AUS, military serv, 1958-63; Mobil Oil Corp, sr marketing rep, 1964-68; Natl Urban League, staff asst, military & vet affairs program, 1969-70, asst dir military & vet affairs program, 1970-71; Babcock & Wilcox Co, supervisor, minority affairs, 1971-72, mgr, minority relations, 1972-75, dir, minority relations, 1975-78; Anheuser-Busch Companies, dir, EEO affairs, 1978-79; GAF Corp, dir, equal employment opportunity, 1979-86; Metropolitan Life Insurance Co, asst vice pres, human resources, 1982-86; City of Yonkers NY, city councilman 1986-. **ORGANIZATIONS:** first vice pres, Yonkers Branch, NAACP, program chmn, NY/NJ OFCCP Liaison Group; mem, BEEP Program, Natl Urban League; mem, YMTF Task Force, Natl Alliance of Business; program comm, Natl Urban Affairs Council; advisory bd, Who's Who in Black Corporate Amer; mem, Westchester Co, Rent Guidelines Bd; 2nd vice chair, Yonkers Democratic Comm, 1986-; bd mem, Lower East Family Fund Inc, 1987-. **HONORS/ACHIEVEMENTS:** Community Leaders Award, West Virginia State Coll, Natl Alumni Assn, 1984; Natl Alliance of Business' Youth Motivation Task Force Chairperson Award, 1980-84; Omega Psi Phi Fraternity Service Award, 1982; Natl Urban Affairs Council Service Award, 1982; US Presidential Commendation, 1981; Natl Urban League Black Exec Exchange Program Award, 1974-79; Outstanding Among Blacks, 1984. **MILITARY SERVICE:** AUS, Captain, 6 yrs; Parachutist Badge; Ranger Tab; Expert Infantryman Badge. **HOME ADDRESS:** 300 Palisade Ave Apt 3N, Yonkers, NY 10703.

BURGESS, LORD See **BURGIE, IRVING LOUIS**

BURGESS, RAYMOND L.
Appointed official, clergyman. **PERSONAL:** Married Johnettra Rozier; children: Rayna Evon, Mira Yolanda. **EDUCATION:** Wilberforce Univ Zenia, BA Pol Sci; Payne Theol Sem, BDiv; Lutheran Theol Sem, D Ministry. **CAREER:** St James AME Church, assoc pastor, minister 1967; Baptist Bible Coll, instr pastoral care 1967-69; NAACP, dir black studies 1968; St Paul United MethChurch, sr pastor 1970-77; Century United Methodist, pastor 1977; Summity County Human Serv Comm, chmn. **ORGANIZATIONS:** Pres West Side Neighbors; vice pres NAACP; sec Akron Comm House; mem Young Men of Amer 1970; council mem 1st Charter Govt of Summitt Cty 198-84; mem Dist Council on Ministries, No OH Urban Learning Comm. **HONORS/ACHIEVEMENTS:** Outstanding Service in the Comm Mayor Ralph Perk & Cleveland City Council.

BURGESS, ROBERT E.
Business executive. **PERSONAL:** Born Oct 13, 1937, Lake City, SC; married Mary Elizabeth; children: W Michael Tiagwad, Tamara Tiagwad Wagner, Robert E Jr. **EDUCATION:** J M Wright Tech School, Electrical 1954-57; Norwalk Comm Coll Cert City Housing Planning & Devel 1973; IBM Mgmt Devel Prog for Community Execs 1983. **CAREER:** Self-employed band leader 1958-63; Norden Aircraft, inspector 1963-66; Self-Employed, restaurant owner 1966-69; Committee on Training & Employment, admin asst 1966-71; Norwalk Econ Opportunity Now Inc, employed 1970-, exec dir 1972-. **ORGANIZATIONS:** Chmn/organizer Fairfield Cty Black Businessmens Assoc 1969; organizer Norwalk Conn Fed Credit Union 1970; mem South Norwalk Comm Ctr Bd 1970, State Manpower Training Council Gov Meskill 1972; bd of dir Springwood Health Unit 1973; mem New England Comm Action Program Dir Assoc 1973, Natl Comm Action Agchmn/org dir Assoc 1973; chmn Norwalk Comm Devel Citizens Partic Comm Mayor Irwin 1974-; mem State Employment Training Council Gov Grasso 1978; pres CT Assoc for Community Action 1978-84; mem State Energy Adv Comm Gov Grasso 1979; State Negotiated Invest Strategy Team Gov O'Neill 1983; mem NAACP Exec Comm 1983-; legislative chmn CT Assoc for Comm Action 1984-; District Heating Comm 1984; mem Review Team ACVS Headstart 1984; mem Exec Comm, Action Housing 1989 (Vice Pres); mem Advisory Comm to CT Housing Finance Authority by Gov O'Neill 1989; CT Employment & Training Commission by Gov O'Neill 1989. **HONORS/ACHIEVEMENTS:** Roy Wilkins Civil Rights Awd CT State NAACP 1984; Awd for Outstanding Serv to Norwalk Corinthian Lodge 16 F&AM PHA 1982; Citizen of the Year Alpha Nu Chap Omega Psi Phi 1981; Dedicated Serv to Fairfield Cty Kappa Alpha Psi 1985. **MILITARY SERVICE:** AUS Reserve pfc 4 yrs. **HOME ADDRESS:** 37 Brooklawn Ave, South Norwalk, CT 06854. **BUSINESS ADDRESS:** Executive Dir, NEON Inc, 98 S Main St, Norwalk, CT 06854.

BURGEST, DAVID RAYMOND
Educator. **PERSONAL:** Born Dec 10, 1943, Sylvania, GA; married Loretta Jean Black; children: Juanita Marie, Angela Lynore, David Raymond II, Paul Reginald. **EDUCATION:** Paine Coll, BA 1965; Wayne State Univ, MSW 1968; Syracuse Univ, PhD 1974; Univ of Chicago School of Divinity, Postdoctoral studies 1984-85. **CAREER:** Central State Hosp Milledgeville GA, social work aide 1965-66; chief social worker 1968-69; Syracuse Univ, asst prof 1969-72; SUNY Upstate Med Coll Syracuse, assoc prof of psychology 1971-72; Univ of Nairobi Kenya, vstg prof of sociology 1980-81; Atlanta Univ Sch of Social Work, social work consultant 1986-87; Governors State Univ, prof 1972-80, prof of social work 1981-. **ORGANIZATIONS:** Consultant to various local natl and intl social serv orgs in America, Europe, Canada and Africa such as Dept of Family Svcs, Alcoholism Cncls, United Charities, vocational Rehab and others; founder/president Circle of Human Learning & Development Specialists Inc 1975-; licensed gospel minister 1976; editorialbd Black Caucus Journal of Natl Assoc of Black Social Workers 1979-80; prison ministry at Stateville Prison Joliet IL and other facilities in IL 1982-; consultant Suburban NAACP 1984-; editorial bd Journal of Pan-Africans Studies 1986-; elected Univ Park Library Bd 1987-91. **HONORS/ACHIEVEMENTS:** Presented various papers, workshops, and Institutes locally, nationally and internationally in Africa, America, Canada and Europe; published in such journals as Black Scholar, Social Work, Black Male/Female Relationships, Black Books Bulletin, Intl Social Work, Journal of Black Studies and many others; author of wordgame entitled Ebonics, Black Talk word game; Social Worker of the Year Awd 1968; author of several articles in professionaljournals 1973-; Everyday People Awd 1975; author "Social Work Practice with Minorities," Scarecrow 1983; Appreciation Awd Far South Suburban NAACP 1983; "Social Casework Intervention with People of Color," University Press of Amer 1985; Village of University Park proclaimed December "Dr David R Burgest Month" 1985; Man of the Year Awd for Excellence 1985. **HOME ADDRESS:** 1041 Monterey Ct, University Park, IL 60466.

BURGETT, PAUL JOSEPH
Educational administrator. **PERSONAL:** Son of Arthur C Burgett and Ruth Garizio Burgett; married Catherine G Valentine, Jan 01, 1982. **EDUCATION:** Eastman School of Music, Rochester NY, BM, 1968, MA, 1972, PhD, 1976. **CAREER:** Hochstein Memorial Music School, executive dir, 1970-72; Nazareth Coll of Rochester NY, lecturer, 1976-77, asst prof of music, 1977-81; Univ of Rochester, dean of students, 1981-88, vice pres & dean of students, 1988-. **ORGANIZATIONS:** Mem, chair, vice chair, Zoning Board of Appeals, 1981-86; dir, Governing Board Hochstein Memorial Music School, 1982-; dir, Corporate Board YMCA of Rochester and Monroe County, 1983-; mem, Natl Advisory Board, Center for Black Music Research, 1985-; dir, bd of trustees, Margaret Woodbury Strong Museum, 1987-; dir bd of dir, Urban League of Rochester, 1987-. **HONORS/ACHIEVEMENTS:** Vindication as a Thematic Principle in Alain Locke's Writings on the Music of Black Americans, 1989; Artistry in Student Affairs or Virtuisity in Practicing the Craft of Being Human, 1987; On the Tyranny of Talent: An Analysis of the Myth of Talent in the Art Music World, 1987; From Bach to Beethoven to Boulez and Very Few Women in Sight, 1987; ... On Creativity, 1982. **MILITARY SERVICE:** US Army, E5, 1969-75. **BUSINESS ADDRESS:** Vice President, University Dean of Students, University of Rochester, 500 Wilson Commons, Rochester, NY 14627.

BURGETTE, JAMES M.
Dentist. **PERSONAL:** Born Aug 18, 1937, Toledo, OH; married Carolyn Harris; children: Stephanie, James, Ngina. **EDUCATION:** Lincoln University, Pennsylvania AB 1959; Howard Univ, DDS 1964. **CAREER:** YMCA Pittsburgh, counselor 1958; Allegheny Co Health Dept Pittsburgh, 1960; US Post Office Washington DC, 1962; private practice, dentist 1968-. **ORGANIZATIONS:** Mem Natl Dental Assn; House of Delegates; Wolverine Dental Soc; Acad of Gen Dentistry; vice pres Orgn of Black Scientists; bd of trustees Comprehensive Health Planning Council of Southeastern MI; pres Wolverine Dental Soc 1975; bd govs DIAL; parliamentarian Natl Dental Assn 1975; deacon Shrine of Black Madonna; natl staff BCN Inc; committeeman BSA; bd trustees First Cong Dist MI Dem; Omega Psi Phi Chi Delta Mu. **MILITARY SERVICE:** USNR ensign 1960; USN lt 1964. **BUSINESS ADDRESS:** 23077 Greenfield Road, Southfield, MI 48075.

BURGIE, IRVING LOUIS (LORD BURGESS)
Composer, publisher. **PERSONAL:** Born Jul 28, 1924, Brooklyn, NY; married Page Turner; children: Irving Jr, Andrew. **EDUCATION:** Julliard Schl of Music, 1946-48; Univ of AR 1948-49; Univ of So CA, 1949-50. **CAREER:** Self-employed composer, lyricist; composed 37 songs for Harry Belafonte including Jamaica Farewell, Island In the Sun, Day O; composed Belafonte's Calypso Album, 1st album to sell 1 million copies; wrote Ballad for Bimshire, 1963. **ORGANIZATIONS:** Mem ASCAP 1956; Am Guild of Authors & Composers 1956; Local #802 Am Fed of Musicians; pres & publr Caribe Music Corp; life mem NAACP; mem Harlem Writers Guild; United Blk Men of Queens; hon chmn Camp Minisink; hd of Lord Burgess Caribbean Day Assembly Pgrms Publr; The W Indian Song Book 1972; writer of lyrics Barbados Nat Anthem 1966. **HONORS/ACHIEVEMENTS:** Numerous awards & citations; Silver Crown of Merit (Honorary), Barbados Government 1987; Honorary Doctor of Letters, Univ of the West Indies 1989. **BUSINESS ADDRESS:** 199-02 111th Ave, Hollis, NY 11412.

BURGIN, RUTH L. W.
Attorney. **PERSONAL:** Born in Asheville, NC. **EDUCATION:** Berea Coll, AB 1962; OH State U, MSW 1966; Univ of MA, PhD 1971; Valparaiso Univ Schl of Law, JD 1980; US Dist CT Hammond In, internship 1979-80. **CAREER:** Student Intership Program Univ of MA Amherst, MA, dir 1971-76; US Senate Wash DC, internship legislative asst 1970-71; Central State Univ Sociology Dept Wilberforce OH, lectr 1969-70; Supportive Council on Preventive Effort Dayton, OH, dep dir 1969-70; Health & Welfare Planning Council Dayton, OH, asso dir 1968; Health & Welfare Planning & Grantsmanship Program Developer & Guild Tri-Co Urban League Peoria, IL,, dir 1966-67; Health & Welfare Planning & Guild Advisor Urban League Dayton, OH, dir 1962-64. **ORGANIZATIONS:** Bd mem Social Heatlh Assn Dayton, OH 1962-64; financial sec Voter Reg Com DAYTON 1964-66; mem United Fund Adv Com Peoria, IL 1966-67; coordinator Univ of MA Nat Negro Coll Fund Amherst 1974-76; bd mem Urbaa League Springfield MA 1974-76; mem Phi Kappa Phi/Psi Chi/Pi Gamma Mu. **HONORS/ACHIEVEMENTS:** Nat hon socs for scholastic achievements Berea Coll Berea, KY 1958-59; natl urban league fellowship OH St Univ Columbus 1964-66, natl inst of mental health fellowship 1964-66, OH state Univ Fellowship 1964-66, cc stillman scholar 1964-66; ford foundation fellowship Univ of MA AMHERST, MA 1970-71.

BURKE, DEGRANDVAL
Retired clergyman. **PERSONAL:** Born Dec 25, 1909, Matthews, NC; married Mattie Cannon. **EDUCATION:** Johnson C Smith U, BS 1938; JC Smith Sem, BD 1944; McCormick Theol Sem, MA 1947. **CAREER:** Synod of the Piedmont, commr 1972-75; Gen Assembly of the United Presb Ch, commr 1948, 56, 75; Christian Life Prgm JC Smith U, dir of campus 1974-75; Dept of Rel JC Smith U, instr 1947-50 62-75; Emmanuel Presb Ch, pastor 1944-62. **ORGANIZATIONS:** Chmn Gen Council of Catawba Presbytery 1962-74; mem Gen Assembly's Com on Examinations for Sem Srs 1970-73; mem Alpha Kappa Mu Nat Honor Soc; mem Phi Beta Sigma; mem NC Assn of Religious Educators; mem Task Force on Christian Educ for Synod of the Piedmont, United Presb Ch 1972-75; moderator Catawba Presbytery 1950. **HONORS/ACHIEVEMENTS:** Jr prize contest gold medal JC SmithUniv 1937; personalities of the south 1972; minister of the year Catawba Synod 1948; post-grad work Garrett Theol Sem 1962-63; author "Innovations in Christian Edn" 1975.

BURKE, DENZER
Dentist. **PERSONAL:** Born Sep 22, 1933, Atlanta, GA. **EDUCATION:** Univ MI, BBS 1956; Howard U, DDS 1959. **CAREER:** Dentistry Texarkana, pvt prac 1953-. **ORGANIZATIONS:** Mem Am Nat Texarkana Dental Assns; v chmn TX State Adv Com to US

Commn on Civil Rights 1968-; sec exec com Bowie Co Econ Advancement Corp 1964-68; bd dirs Texarkana Comm Chest; Boxie Orgn & Loyal Dem; Texarkana Spl Educ Kindergarden Sch; Texans for Educ Excellence; chap sec-treas Kappa Alpha Psi 1967. **MILITARY SERVICE:** USNR 1959-63. **BUSINESS ADDRESS:** 523 W 3 St, Texarkana, TX 75501.

BURKE, EMMETT C.
Educator. **PERSONAL:** Born Jan 30, 1920, Montgomery, AL; son of William J Burke and Ethel Scott Burke; married Sarah L Scott, Aug 14, 1949. **EDUCATION:** Roosevelt Univ, AB, BS 1946; Loyola Univ, MA 1953; DePaul Univ, MEd 1954; IL Coll Optometry, OD 1947. **CAREER:** IL Welfare Dept, sr caseworker 1948-56; Chicago Publ Schools, instr spec ed 1957; Wm Carter School Chicago Bd of Educ, asst principal 1968-; Natl Coll of Ed Urban Campus Chicago, adjunct assistant prof 1973-; CSW, Illinois Certified Social Worker, private practice 1974-89. **ORGANIZATIONS:** Pres Chicago African-Amer Teachers Assn 1963-; cadre leader Great March on Wash, Selma to Montgomery March 1963; pres Assn for the Study of Afro-Amer Life & Hist Chicago Chap 1969-; mem bd of dir Chicago African-Amer Teachers Assn; mem, bd of dirs Wash Park YMCA, Afro-Amer Family & Comm Svcs, Council for Exceptional Children, Chicago Assn of Asst Principals, Civil Rights Activist, SCLC, NAACP, Urban League; mem Alpha Phi Alpha, Phi Delta Kappa, Amer Assn of Univ Profs, Church of the Good Shepherd. **HONORS/ACHIEVEMENTS:** Appointed Sr Delegate to World Centennial of YMCA Paris 1955; Scholarship to Univ of MI, IL Public Aid Comm 1961; IL License Cert Soc Worker Cert Publ School Admin. **MILITARY SERVICE:** WWII Aviation Cadet. **BUSINESS ADDRESS:** Assistant Principal, Wm Carter Public School, 5740 S Michigan Ave, Chicago, IL 60637.

BURKE, KIRKLAND R.
Promotion manager. **PERSONAL:** Born Jan 04, 1948, Chicago, IL; son of Alonzo Waymond Burke and Johnnie Irene Savage Burke. **EDUCATION:** Chicago Tech Coll, 1966; Chicago St U, BA 1986. **CAREER:** Holy Angels Roman Cath Sch, tchr 1973-74; Reliable Promotions, promotion mgr 1974-75; Warner, Elektra, Atlantic Corp, promotion mgr 1975-78; Warner Bros Records, midwest promotion mgr 1978-; Whitney Young Magnet High School, Girl's Basketball, asst coach 1987-. **ORGANIZATIONS:** Speaker Chicago Pub Sch Youth Motivation Prog 1972-; mem Natl Assoc of TV & Radio Announcers 1972-77; youth div asst to chm Operation PUSH 1972-75, Natl Choir 1972-75; mem Black Music Assoc 1978-; asst coach Near North High Sch Chicago IL Girls Basketball 1986-87. **HONORS/ACHIEVEMENTS:** 37 gold & platinum records Warner Bros Records 1975-; Am Legion Natl Chmpnshp Chicago Cavaliers D & B Corps 1969; VFW & Am Legion IL St Championship Chi Cavaliers 1969; Executive Producer, The Barrett Sisters Album "I Got a Feeling" 1986. **MILITARY SERVICE:** USN 3rd class petty officer E-4 1965-68; Natl Defense Serv Medal 1965-68. **BUSINESS ADDRESS:** Promotion Manager, Midwest Region, 500 Wall St, Glendale Heights, IL 60139.

BURKE, LILLIAN W.
Judge. **PERSONAL:** Born Aug 02, 1917, Thomaston, GA; married Ralph Burke; children: Bruce. **EDUCATION:** OH State Univ, BS 1947; Cleveland State Univ, LLB 1951; Cleveland Marshall Law Sch Cleveland State Univ, postgrad work 1963-64; Natl Coll State Judiciary Univ, grad 1974. **CAREER:** Cleveland, genl practice law 1952-62; sch teacher bus educ & social sciences; State of OH, asst atty gen 1962-66; OH Indus Commn, vice chmn mem 1966-69; Cleveland Community Coll Western Campus, teacher constitutional law; Cleveland Municipal Ct, aptd judge 1969, elected to full term judge 1969-. **ORGANIZATIONS:** Pres Cleveland Chap Natl Council of Negro Women 1955-57; past pres/former woman ward ldr 24th Ward Rep Club 1957-67; Cuyahoga Co Central Com 1958-68;secty E Dist Faily Serv Assn 1959-60; mem Council Human Rel Cleve Citizens League 1959-; pres Cleve Chap Jack & Jill of Amer Inc 1960-61; alternate delegate Natl Rep Conv in Chicago 1960; sec Cuyahoga Co Exec Comm 1962-63; Gov's Comm on the Status of Women 1966-67; bd, dirs chmn minority div Natl Fed Rep Women 1966-68; vice pres at large Greater Cleveland Safety Council 1969-; aptd to serve four yr term Adv Comm of Accreditation & Institutional Eligibility of Bur of Higher Educ 1972; mem Comm on accreditation 1980-; exec bd mem Amer Assn of Univ Women; past Grammateus Alpha Omega Chap Alpha Kappa Alpha Sor; Hon Adv mem Women Lawyers Assn; mem Cuyahoga Co, Cleveland Bar Assns; life mem past bd mem NAACP Cleve Chapt; mem Phyllis Wheatley Assn; bd trustees Consumer's League of OH; mem OH State, Amer Bar Assns; mem Am Judicature Soc, Natl Bar Assn Inc; trustee OH Comm on Status of Women. **HONORS/ACHIEVEMENTS:** Achievement Awd Parkwood CME Church Cleveland 1968; Career Woman of Yr Cleveland Women's Career Clubs Inc 1969; Martin Luther King Citizen Awd of RecogMusic & Arts Com Pgh 1969; Awd in Recog of Outstanding Ach in Field of Law Natl Sor of Phi Delta Kappa 1969; Awd Natl Council of Negro Women 1969; Outstanding Achieve Awd Te-Wa-Si Scholarship Club Cleve 1969; Outstanding Serv Awd Morning Star Grand Chap Cleve 1970; Lectr Heidelburg Coll Tiffin OH 1971; Salute from Amer Woodmen for First Elected Negro Female Judge Cleve 1970; Golden Jubilee Awd Zeta Phi Beta Sor 1970; Outstanding Serv Awd Morning StarGrand Chap 1970; Awd of Honor Cleveland Bus League 1970; Serv Awd St Paul AMe Ch Lima OH 1972; Woman of Achievement Awd 1973; Inter-Club Council 1973. **BUSINESS ADDRESS:** Judge, Cleveland Municipal Court, Room 13B Justice Center, 1200 Ontario St, Cleveland, OH 44113.

BURKE, OLGA PICKERING
Business executive. **PERSONAL:** Born Jan 06, 1946, Charleston, SC; daughter of Dr L Irving Pickering and Esther Robinson Pickering; married Philip C Burke Sr; children: Philip C Jr, Brian. **EDUCATION:** Johnson C Smith Univ, AB Economics/Accounting 1968; Natl Rural Development Leaders School, certificate 1976; Life Investors Inc Co, insurance license 1981. **CAREER:** HA Decosta Co, accountant 1969-70; Allied Chemical Corp, lost accountant 1970-72; Charleston Area Minority Assoc, fiscal officer 1972-75; Minority Development & Mgt Assoc, exec directory 1975-79; Affiliated Management Sys Inc, pres 1979-. **ORGANIZATIONS:** Martin Luther King Comm YWCA Charleston 1977-79; organizer SC Rural America 1979; economic adv council Clemson Univ 1978-81; first vice pres Regional Minority Purchasing Coun 1981; policy comm YWCA Charleston 1981; MBE Governor's Comm State of SC 1982; Business Development Sub-Committee City of Charleston 1982; mem Amer Soc of Professional Consultants 1983; mem Natl Assoc of Minority Contr 1983-; mem Charleston Business & Professional Assn 1980-83; bd of dirs/treas SC Sea Island Small Farmers Co-op 1981-83; Columbia Adv Council US Small Business Admin 1981-83; chairperson business comm Charleston Trident Chamber of Comm 1984. **HONORS/ACHIEVEMENTS:** Outstanding Overall Phi Beta Sigma Frat Beta Mu Sigma Chap Charleston 1977. **BUSINESS ADDRESS:** President, Affiliated Mgmnt Systems, 90 Cannon St, Charleston, SC 29403.

BURKE, SELMA HORTENSE
Artist. **PERSONAL:** Born Dec 31, 1900, Mooresville, NC. **EDUCATION:** Winston-Salem Univ, BA; St Augustine Coll, RN 1924; Columbia Univ, MFA 1941; Livingston Coll, PhD 1970. **CAREER:** Sculptress, present; AW Mellon Found Carnegie Inst, consultant 1967-76; Sidwell Sch/Haverford Coll/Livingston Coll/Swarthmore Coll, instructor in art & sculpture 1963-76; Friends School/George's School/Forrest House NYC, instructor in art & sculpture 1930-49; Selma Burke Sch of Sculpture NY, founder 1940; Selma Burke Art Center Pittsburgh, founder 1968. **ORGANIZATIONS:** Mem PA Council on Arts 1965-75; mem Nat Conf of Artists 1972; life mem NAACP; life mem League of Women Voters. **HONORS/ACHIEVEMENTS:** Hon degrees PhD Livingston Coll/U of NC/MOORE Coll of Art; winner Fine Arts Comm for DC Competition; profile of Pres Franklin D Roosevelt currently minted on US dime 1943; work appeared in over 25 one woman & group shows; commissioned to create over 20 bronze & wood sculptures; Pearl S. Buck Foundation Woman's Award, 1987. *

BURKE, VIVIAN H.
Govt. official. **PERSONAL:** Born in Charlotte, NC; married Logan Burke; children: Logan Todd. **EDUCATION:** Elizabeth City State Univ, BS; A&T State Univ, MS; certification Guidance Counseling Administration Curriculum Instructional Specialist. **CAREER:** City of Winston-Salem, alderman. **ORGANIZATIONS:** Bd of dirs Piedmont Health System Agency; minority interest grp for the NC Sch of Science/math; mem Trans Adv Council; chmn America's Four Hundredth Anniversary Comm; mem bd of trustees Elizabeth City State Univ; organized the Flora Buffs Garden Club; past pres PTA East Forsyth Sr HS; mem PTA Adv Council; experiment in Self-Reliance Bd; mem Forsyth Health Council; admin council Patterson Avenue YWCA; mem Recreation & Parks Comm; basileus Alpha Kappa Alpha Sor; natl membership chmn Alpha Kappa Alpha Sor; former chmn Carver Precinct; co-chair 5th Dist Council to elect Jimmy Carter; delegate to local StateDem Conv; NAACP; Alpha Kappa Alpha Sor; Forsyth Assn of Classroom Teachers; NC Assn of Educators; Top Ladies of Distinction Inc; 5th Dist Blk LdrshpCaucus; League of Women Voters; Flora Buffs; first woman and first black apptd public safety chmn City of Winson-Salem; one of first two women apptd to Public Wks Com; appt to St Dem Affirm Actn Comm 1983; Chmn Mondale for Pres Forsyth Co 1983; bd of dir 1983, mem-at-large 1984 League of Municipalities. **HONORS/ACHIEVEMENTS:** Recipient of a 4 yr academic scholarship Elizabeth City State Univ; RJR Scholarship Univ of VA; NAACP Outstanding Political & Comm Serv; AKA Sor Outstanding Woman of the Year, Pres of the Year, Grad Leadership Awd, Most Distinguished Political Awd; Outstanding Volunteer ESR; Outstanding Volunteer Heart Fund;Genl Alumni Outstanding Political Awd Elizabeth City State Univ; Gov's Order of Long Leaf Pine; Outstanding Political & Comm Serv Awd Black Political Action League; Outstanding Serv in Politics & Comm Northeast Ward; Dedicated Serv Awd 5th Dist Black Leadership Caucus Banquet Chmn; Serv Awd Forsyth Co Health Council; Distinguished Citizen Awd Sophisticated Gents; Outstanding Women's Achievers Awd Prof Business League. **HOME ADDRESS:** 3410 Cumberland Rd, Winston-Salem, NC 27105.

BURKE, WILLIAM ARTHUR
President of Marathon Company. **PERSONAL:** Born May 13, 1939, Zanesville, OH; son of Leonard Burke and Hazel Norris; married Yvonne Brathwaite Burke, Jun 14, 1972; children: Christine Burke, Autumn Burke. **EDUCATION:** Miami Univ, BS, 1961, BS; Boston Univ, 1963-64; Harvard Univ, 1963-64; Univ of MA, 1977, EdD. **CAREER:** Pres, The City of Los Angeles Marathon, Tennis Commr XXIII Olympiad; pres, Fish and Game Commr, State of CA; pres, Wildlife Conservation Bd, State of CA; chmn of the bd, Genesis Intl; pres of World Mining Devel Co Inc; deputy Los Angeles City Councilman 1966-69; pres, Amer Health Care Delivery Corp; pres, Batik Wine and Spirits Honorary Consul Gen for the Republic of Mali. **HONORS/ACHIEVEMENTS:** Dir of Legislative Radio & TV for CA State Legislature; Meritortous Service Award, City of Los Angeles; Certificate of A.U.S. Citation of Honor, CA State Senate; Alpha Epsilon Rho, Natl Radio and Television Honorary. **MILITARY SERVICE:** US Air Force, major, 1961-65. **BUSINESS ADDRESS:** President, Los Angeles Marathon Inc, 11110 W Ohio Ave, Suite 100, Los Angeles, CA 90025.

BURKE, YVONNE BRATHWAITE
Attorney. **PERSONAL:** Born Oct 05, 1932, Los Angeles, CA; daughter of James A Watson and Lola Moore Watson; married Dr William A Burke, Jun 14, 1972; children: Autumn Roxanne. **EDUCATION:** Univ of California, AA, 1951; University of California, Los Angeles CA, BA, 1953; Univ of Southern California, JD 1956. **CAREER:** CA State Assembly, mem, 1966-72; US House of Representatives, mem, 1972-79; Los Angeles County, supervisor, 1979-81; Kutak Rock & Huie, partner, 1981-83; MGM/UA Home Entertainment, mem bd dir; Burke Robinson & Pearman, partner 1984-87; Jones, Day, Reavis & Pogue, Los Angeles CA and Cleveland OH, partner. **ORGANIZATIONS:** Mem The Trusteeship, Urban League, Women's Lawyer's Assn; pres Coalition of 100 Black Women LA; vice chmn Univ of CA Bd of Regents; bd mem Educ Testing Svc; dir Los Angeles Branch Federal Reserve Bank of San Francisco; mem Bd of Educ Testing Svc; chair Los Angeles Branch Federal Reserve Bank of San Francisco; mem Ford Foundation Board of Trustee. **HONORS/ACHIEVEMENTS:** Loren Miller Award NAACP; Chubb Fellow Yale Univ 1972; Professional Achievement Award UCLA 1974; Future Leader of America Time Magazine 1974. **HOME ADDRESS:** 1970 Mandeville Canyon Rd, Los Angeles, CA 90049.

BURKETTE, TYRONE
College president. **CAREER:** Barber-Scotia College, Concord, NH, president. **BUSINESS ADDRESS:** President, Barber-Scotia College, Concord, NH 28025. *

BURKS, JAMES WILLIAM, JR.
Business executive. **PERSONAL:** Born Feb 04, 1938, Roanoke, VA; married Janice A Kasey. **EDUCATION:** Lincoln U, AB 1959; Univ of VA; NW U; Roanoke Coll; Lynchburg Coll. **CAREER:** Norfolk & Western Ry Co, asst mgr; Addison HS, Tchr. **ORGANIZATIONS:** V chmn Roanoke City Sch; bd, pres, bd of dir Gainsboro Elec Co 1970-; mem Omega Psi Phi Frat; bd dir Magic City Bldg & Loan Assn; City Plng Commn 1973-76; Human Relat Com; bd dir Roanoke Nghbrhd Devel Proj; past dir Roanoke Jaycees; Roanoke Valley Counc of Comm Serv 1974-77; Commn to Study Relatshp between Govtl Entities & Elec Utilities; bd of vis Norfolk Outst Serv Award, RKE Valley Counc of Comm Servs. **HONORS/ACHIEVEMENTS:** Outst serv award City Plng Commn; outst serv award Roanoke Jaycees; 1st black on city plng commn. **MILITARY SERVICE:** AUS spec-4 1960-63. **BUSINESS ADDRESS:** 8 N Jefferson St, GOBN, Roanoke, VA 24042.

BURKS, JUANITA PAULINE
Business executive. **PERSONAL:** Born Jul 02, 1920, Marion, KY; married Ishmon C; children: Lt Col Ishmon F, Donna S, Rev Robert C. **EDUCATION:** KY State Univ, 1940-42; Univ of Louisville, 1969-71. **CAREER:** Park Duvalle Welfare, social worker 1968-71; Metro United Way, suprv 1971-74; Burks Enterprises Inc, owner/pres, CEO 1974-. **ORGANIZATIONS:** Mem Louisville Urban League 1975-, Natl Christians & Jews 1982-, Professional Bus Womens 1983-, Governors Scholar Prog 1983-; bd dir Spaulding Univ 1984-. **HONORS/ACHIEVEMENTS:** Women in Business Game 1980; Woman of Achievement Prol Bus Women 1983; Mayor's Citation City of Louisville 1983; Black Enterprise Mag 1983; Comm Serv Eta Zeta 1984; Equality Awd Louisville Urban League 1984; Money Mag 1984. **BUSINESS ADDRESS:** Chief Executive Officer, Burks Enterprises Inc, 1602 Heyburn Bldg, Louisville, KY 40202.

BURLESON, HELEN L.
Writer, poet, educator, consultant, realtor. **PERSONAL:** Born Dec 08, 1929, Chicago, IL; daughter of Blaine Major Burleson (deceased) and Beatrice Hurley Burleson (deceased); divorced; children: Earl Fredrick III MD, Erica Elyce Fredrick. **EDUCATION:** Central State Univ, BS 1950; Northwestern Univ, MA 1954; Nova Univ, Dr of Public Adminstration 1984. **CAREER:** Lover's Lane Sweet Shop, part owner & mgr 1947-56; licensed real estate salesperson 1950-56; HS English, tchr 1951-56, 1958-61; HS Eng sponsor Yrbk & Newspaper Washington, tchr 1956-57; WBBM Radio Matters of Opinion, commntr; Bd of Educ Flossmoor IL, 1972-75, 1975-78, re-elected 1978-81; writer poet education consultant; Nurturing Experiences Enterprises, pres/founder 1987-; Century 21, Dabbs & Associates, broker-associate, Flossmoor Office. **ORGANIZATIONS:** Past pres Women's Aux of Cook County Physicians Assn 1956; mem AKA 1948; NAACP 1950-; Alpha Gamma Pi 1978; apptd IL State Bd of Educ 1981; apptd Gov's Task Force to Study Medical Malpractice 1985. **HONORS/ACHIEVEMENTS:** 1973 Alumni of Yr; Chicago Chap Central State 1974 Humanitarian Awd; St Matthews AME Ch; One of 100 Women Honored by PUSH Found 1975; Literary Achievement Awd Central State Univ 1976; Humanitarian Awd Dr Gavin Found 1977; Outstanding Civic & Freedom of the Arts Awd Links 1978; Outstanding Contrib to the Black Comm UNCF 1979; founded Women's Bd Wash Park YMCA 1979; 1974 pub verse "No Place is Big Enough to House My Soul" 1975; pub Where Did You Find Me? Anthology of Prose Poetry & Songs; Gold Medallion Award, for real estate sales in excess of $4,000,000, Northern Illinois Region of Century 21, 1988. **HOME ADDRESS:** 56 Graymoor Ln, Olympia Fields, IL 60461.

BURLESON, JANE GENEVA
Councilwoman. **PERSONAL:** Born May 22, 1928, Fort Dodge, IA; married Walter Burleson. **CAREER:** George A Hormel & Co, 1948-81; Ft Dodge School Syst, para professional 1982-; Ft Dodge City Council, council mem 1984-. **ORGANIZATIONS:** Rec sec P-31 United Food & Comm Workers 1974-75; mem League of Women Voters, Mayors Adv Comm 1980; pres A Phillip Randolph Inst Ft Dodge Chapt; memSuperintendents Adv Comm 1984; bd mem Jazz Festival 1984-85, Natl Camp Fire 1985-86; mem IA of Tommorrow Comm 1985-. **HONORS/ACHIEVEMENTS:** Comm on Status of Women Cert State of IA 1979; Cert of Apprec IA Devel Comm 1983, 1984; First Black Woman Elected to Ft Dodge City Council. **BUSINESS ADDRESS:** Councilwoman, Fort Dodge City Council, City Hall, 819 1st Ave So, Fort Dodge, IA 50501.

BURLEW, ANN KATHLEEN
Psychologist. **PERSONAL:** Born Dec 10, 1948, Cincinnati, OH; married John Howard. **EDUCATION:** Univ of MI, BA 1970; Univ of MI, MA 1972; Univ of MI, PhD 1974. **CAREER:** Univ of Cincinnati, assoc prof of psychology 1978-, asst prof of criminal justice & psychology 1972-78; Social Tech Sys, sr partner 1974-80. **ORGANIZATIONS:** Mem & chair Evaluation Com & YWCA Shelter for Battered Women 1977-79; mem Comm Develop Adv Com 1980; vice pres Cincinnati Assn of Black Psychologists 1979-80; mem CETA Adv Com of United Appeal 1979-80; bd mem United Appeal/Community Chest Planning Bd 1980; vice pres United Black Assn of Faculty & Staff 1980. **HONORS/ACHIEVEMENTS:** Summer faculty research grantUniv of Cincinnati 1977, 80; Co-author 2 Books "Minority Issues in Mental Health" & " Reflections on Black Psychology"; pub 7 Articles. **BUSINESS ADDRESS:** U of Cincinnati Dyer Hall, Mail Location #376, Cincinnati, OH 34221.

BURNETT, ARTHUR LOUIS, SR.
Judge. **PERSONAL:** Born Mar 15, 1935, Spotsylvania County, VA; son of Robert Louis Burnett and Lena Victoria Bumbry; married Ann Frisbieann Lloyd, May 14, 1960; children: Darnellena Christalyn, Arthur Louis II, Darryl Lawford, Darlisa Ann, Dionne. **EDUCATION:** Howard Univ, BA (Summa Cum Laude) 1957; NY Univ Sch of Law, LLB 1958 (Law Review & honors). **CAREER:** Asst US Atty DC 1965-68; Dept of Justice, attorney adviser criminal div 1958-65; MPDC (Met Police), legal advisor 1968-69; US Magistrate judge 1969-75; Legal Div US Civil Serv Comm, asst gen counsel 1975-78; Office of Personnel Mgmt, assoc gen counsel 1979-80; judge, US magistrate 1980-87; judge, Supreme Court of the District of Columbia 1987-. **ORGANIZATIONS:** Mem Amer Bar Assn; Natl Bar Assn; Fed Bar Assn; DC Bar Assn; Washington Bar Assn; Amer Judges Assn; Amer Judicature Soc; chmn Conf of Spl Court Judges ABA 1974-75; pres Natl Council of US Magistrates 1983-84; pres DC Chapter FBA 1984-85; chmn Federal Litigation Sect Admin of Justice FBA 1983-84; 1984-85; chmn Criminal Law & Juvenile Justice Comm Admin Law Sect ABA 1983-84, 1984-85. **HONORS/ACHIEVEMENTS:** Recipient Sustained Superior Performance Award Dept of Justice 1963; Recipient Fed Bar Assn Distinguished Serv Award as Chmn of Nat Criminal Law Com; Recipient US Civil Serv Commn Distinguished Serv Award 1978; Recipient Office of Personnel Mgmt Dir Meritorious Serv Award 1980; chmn FBA Natl Com on Utilization of US Magistrates in Fed Cts 1980-; Editor-in-Chief/Author FBA-BNA publ "Labor-Mgmt Relations Civil Serv Reform & EEO in the Fed Serv" 1980; author of numerous articles in law journals & reviews on role of US Magistrates in Fed Judiciary, on Federal Civil Practice, bail and search & seizure; Flaschner Awd Outstanding Special Court Judge in the United States Natl Conf of Special Court Judges Amer Bar Assoc 1985. **MILITARY SERVICE:** AUS 1958-60; AUS Reserves 1960-63. **BUSINESS ADDRESS:** Judge, Superior Court of the District of Columbia, 500 Indiana Avenue, NW, Room 1020, Washington, DC 20001.

BURNETT, CALVIN W.
Educator. **PERSONAL:** Born Mar 16, 1932, Brinkley, AR; married Gretta L Gordy; children: Vera A, Susan L, David G, Tywana. **EDUCATION:** St Louis U, BS 1959, PhD 1963. **CAREER:** St Louis State Hospital, research social psychologist 1961-63; Health & Welfare Council of Metro St Louis, research dir of special project 1963-66; Upward Bound Program, US Office Of Educ, consultant 1966-70; Natl Planning Org Washington, consultant 1967-68; Urban Sys Corp Washington, consultant 1967-69; Southern IL Univ, assoc prof 1969-70; Coppin State Coll MD, pres 1970-. **ORGANIZATIONS:** State rep Am Assn of State Coll & Univ 1970-74; mem bd of dirs Natl Assoc for Equal Oppor in Higher Educ 1985-, Amer Assoc of State Colls & Univs 1986-. **HONORS/ACHIEVEMENTS:** Recipient Outstanding Educ Of Am 1971; St LouisUniv Alumni Merit Award 1973. **MILITARY SERVICE:** AUS 1953-55. **BUSINESS ADDRESS:** President, Coppin State College, 2500 W North Ave, Baltimore, MD 21216.

BURNETT, LUTHER C.
Urban planner. **PERSONAL:** Born Aug 12, 1925, Detroit, MI; son of Jesse H Burnett and Caroline E Burnett; married Lucille Walston; children: L Carl Burnett. **EDUCATION:** MI State U, BS MS 1952. **CAREER:** Landcore Assoc, president, 1986-; retired from Civil Service 1986; US Department of Interior/Natl Park Service, Program Manager 1975-86; Natl Capital Parks-West, supt 1972-75; Conservation & Cultural Affairs US Virgin Islands, commr 1971-72; Natl Park Service Washington Office, urban planner 1969-70; Bur of Outdoor Recreation, & Interior Dept, urban planner 1960-69; Nat Capital Planning Commn Washington, urban planner 1957-60; Inkster, MI, dir of planning 1955-57; Detroit Regional Planning Commn, urban planner 1954-55; Detroit Met Area Traffic Study, urban planner 1953-54; Detroit Dept of Pub Works, land surveyor 1948-53. **ORGANIZATIONS:** Mem Amer Inst of Planners; Amer Soc of Planning Officials; mem Alpha Phi Alphpa Frat; mem Pigskin Club of Washington, DC; pres Blair-Shepard Neighbors 1961-63; 32 degree Mason, Prince Hall; Urban League Housing Comm 1957-61; bd dir March of Dimes 1972-73; Sigma Pi Hhi (Epsilon Boule). **HONORS/ACHIEVEMENTS:** Outstanding contrib award March of Dimes 1972; Washington Area Walk-A-Thon; gov outstanding service US Virgin Islands. **MILITARY SERVICE:** AUS 1943-46. **BUSINESS ADDRESS:** President, Landcore Associates, Washington, DC 20015.

BURNETT, MARY COGHILL
Association executive. **PERSONAL:** Born Jul 25, 1907, King George Co, VA; widowed; children: Sylvia J Williams. **EDUCATION:** Attended, Fredericksburg Normal Indus Inst, VA State Coll, VA Union Univ, Hampton Inst. **CAREER:** Southern Aide Ins Co, insurance agent; Westmoreland Co, bd of educ; King George Co, bd of educ; DC Health Dept, retired. **ORGANIZATIONS:** Area solicitor Amer Heart Assn, Amer Cancer Soc, TB Assn; area chmn Fredericksburg Area Chap Sickle Cell Anemia Assn; bd mem Rappohonack Agency onAging; life mem NAACP; AARP, political action comm King George co; area 13 chairperson NAACP 1975-83; delegate Democratic State Convention 1984; mem Rainbow Coalition; mem Salem Baptist Church; asst registrar Mt Bethel Baptist Learning Inst 1981-; finance asst Mt Bethel Baptist Assn Annual Session 1979-; mem Natl Baptist Convention USA Inc. **HONORS/ACHIEVEMENTS:** Sickle Cell Assn Awd 1973; NAACP Awd 1975, 1982, 1984; Mt Bethel Baptist Assn Civil Rights Awd 1984; Certificates from Mt Bethel Baptist Assn, Education Congress, Special Olympics.

BURNETT, SIDNEY OBED (BIG SID)
Dentist. **PERSONAL:** Born Dec 04, 1924, Apex, NC; married Faye Valeria Mc Daniel; children: Stephanie Gantt, Sydney Lee, Sharon, Aaron, Angela, Cassandra. **EDUCATION:** Morgan State Univ, 1942-45; Howard Univ Coll of Dentistry, 1945-49. **CAREER:** Freedmen's Hosp, surgical 1949-50; Dental Coll Howard Univ, instr 1950-51; Barrett School for Girls, dentist 1950-60; Private practice, dentist 1951-; Balt City Health Dept, dentist 1952-65; MD State Bd Dental Examiners, dentist, sec, treas. **ORGANIZATIONS:** Past sec, past pres MD Dental Soc; mem Balto City MD State & Amer Dental Assocs, Amer Assoc of Dental Examiners; past mem Mayors Comm for IntegratedHousing Balt; mem NAACP, Balto Alumnae Chap Kappa Alpha Psi, Kappa Alpha Psi; fellow Acad Dentistry Intl, Amer Coll of Dentists; consult examiner NE Reg Bd Dental Examiners 15 states. **HONORS/ACHIEVEMENTS:** Guardsmen Achievement Awd Balto Alum Kappa Alpha Psi. **BUSINESS ADDRESS:** MD State Bd Dental Examiners, 1318 N Caroline St, Baltimore, MD 21213.

BURNETTE, ADA PURYEAR
Educator. **PERSONAL:** Born Oct 24, Darlington, SC; married Thomas Carlos Burnette Sr; children: Paul Puryear Jr, Paula Puryear, Anita B Houser, T Carlos Burnette Jr, Diane B Day. **EDUCATION:** Talladega Coll, BA 1953; Univ of Chicago, MA 1958; FL State Univ, PhD 1986; attended Chicago State Univ, FL A&M Univ; FL State Univ, certified public supvr; FL State Univ, certified public mgr 1989. **CAREER:** Winston Salem NC Public Schools, high school math teacher 1953-54; Chicago Public Schools, elem school teacher 1954-58; Norfolk State, admin & teacher 1958-61; Univ of Chicago Reading Clinic, teacher 1958 summer; Tuskegee Inst, admin, teacher 1961-66; Fisk Univ, admin, teacher 1966-70; FL DOE, admin 1973-88; Bethune-Cookman Coll, admin, teacher, 1988-. **ORGANIZATIONS:** Pres Intl Read Assn Affiliate Concerned Educ of Black Students 1984-86; sec, treas Afro-Amer Research Assn 1968-73; bd dir Christian School Performing Arts; deacon Trinity Presbyterian Church; mem Leon Dem Exec Bd 1982-; pres teen sponsor Jack & Jill of Amer Tallahassee 1984-85; undergrad advisor, treas, sec, Alpha Kappa Alpha; pres, historian Drifters Tallahassee; pres, publicity chmn, initiation chmn Phi Kappa Phi, FSU; mem Phi Delta Kappa, Pi Lambda Theta; Natl membership chmn, Drifters, Inc; FL Elem and Middle Schools commr; Southern Assn of Coll and Schools newsletter editor; FL Council on Elem Educ; DOE liaison; sec, co-founder, Societas Doctas Inc, 1987-; FL Assn for Supervision and Curriculum Devel Bd, 1988-; pres, Les Beau Monde, 1989-. **HONORS/ACHIEVEMENTS:** Black Woman of the Year, Drifters Inc 1984; Head Start Honoree of the year for Florida 1985; Humanitarian of the year 1987; First Black Admin in FL Dept of Educ; Serv to Children and Educ Plaque, FL Council on Elementary Educ 1988; co-author, member of early childhood panel, Four and Five Year Old Programs in Public Schools; delivered hundreds of speeches. **HOME ADDRESS:** PO Box 15154, Daytona Beach, FL 32015. **BUSINESS ADDRESS:** Admin, Assoc Prof, Bethune-Cookman Coll, 640 Second Ave, Daytona Beach, FL 32015.

BURNEY, HARRY L., JR.
Educator. **PERSONAL:** Born Sep 29, 1913, Lakeland, FL; married Iona Mack; children: Harry L III, Sandra Burney. **EDUCATION:** Bethune-Cookman Coll, BS 1946; Univ of PA, MS 1954; Univ of PA; FL A&M U; OK U. **CAREER:** Tivoli High School, Defuniak Springs FL, prin 1946-47; Middleton High School FL, prin 1952-68; Bethune-Cookman Coll, admin asst to pres 1968-76; United Negro Coll Fund, FL St dir 1976-. **ORGANIZATIONS:** Mem Nat Educ Assn; FL Educ Assn; Nat Alumni Assn of Bethune-Cookman Coll; Alumni Assn ofUniv Qof PA; Alpha Phi Alpha Frat; chmn Scholarship & Loans Com Dayto-

na Beach Rotary Club; mem Daytona Beach Area C of C; Selective Service Sys Local Bd No 24; Guidance Cntr Bd; Mental Health Bd of Volusia District, Inc; Bethune-Cookman Coll; Edward Waters Coll; State Dept of Edn; Putnam Co Tchr Assn; Central Acad; Middleton High Sch; Alpha Phi Alpha Frat. **HONORS/ACHIEVEMENTS:** United way bd dir awards FL State Tchr Assn; Chapter of Eastern Star named for him. **MILITARY SERVICE:** AUS. **BUSINESS ADDRESS:** 444 Seabreeze Blvd, Ste 925, Daytona Beach, FL 32018.

BURNHAM, MARGARET ANN
Judge, attorney. **PERSONAL:** Born Dec 28, 1944, Birmingham, AL. **EDUCATION:** Tougaloo Coll, BA 1966; Univ of PA Law Sch, LLB 1969. **CAREER:** Boston Municipal Ct, justice 1977-; Burnham, Stern & Shapiro, atty 1973-77; Roxbury Defenders Com, staff atty 1972-73; Peo of State of CA v Angela Y Davis, co-counsel 1971-72. **ORGANIZATIONS:** Bd mem Nat Alliance Against Racist & Polit Repression; mem Nat Conf of Black Lawyers; MA Black Lawyers Assn; coord 3#Rd World Women's Orgn. **BUSINESS ADDRESS:** Boston Municipal Court, 380 Old Court House, Boston, MA 02108.

BURNIM, MELLONEE VICTORIA
Educator. **PERSONAL:** Born Sep 27, 1950, Teague, TX; married C Jason Dotson; children: Jamel Arzo. **EDUCATION:** N TX State U, BM Music Educ (Cum Laude) 1971; Univ of WI Madison, MM African Music Ethnomusicology 1976; Indiana Univ, PhD Ethnomusicology 1980. **CAREER:** Delay Middle School, Lewisville TX, dir of choral music 1971-73; Univ of WI, res asst 1973, acad adv 1973; Afro-Amer Choral Ens IN Univ, dir 1976-82; IN Univ Opera Theater, choral dir 1976 & 1980; Afro-Amer Studies IN Univ, prof. **ORGANIZATIONS:** Musical dir video tapes 2-30 min "The Life & Works of Undine S Moore" Afro-Am Arts Inst IN Univ 1979; musical dir WTUI Bloomington "Contemp Black Gospel Music" 1979; lect Dept of Afro-Am Studies IN Univ 1979-80; mem Alpha Lambda Delta 1968; mem Sigma Alpha Iota NTSU Denton TX 1969; chap vice pres Mortar Bd NTSU Denton TX 1970-71; mem Pi Kappa Lambda 1971. **HONORS/ACHIEVEMENTS:** Full Music Scholar NTSU Denton TX 1969-71; Natl Defense Foreign Language Fellow in Arabic Univ of WI 1973-74; fellow, Natl Fellowships Fund Univ of WI & IN Univ 1973-78; Eli Lilly Postdoctoral Teaching Fellow 1984; alternate for Natl Rsch Council Postdoctoral Fellowship, Washington DC 1984. **BUSINESS ADDRESS:** Assoc Prof Afro-Amer Studies, Indiana University, Memorial Hall E M30, Bloomington, IN 47401.

BURNIM, MICKEY L.
Educator. **PERSONAL:** Born Jan 19, 1949, Teague, TX; married LaVera Levels; children: Cinnamon, Adrian. **EDUCATION:** North TX State Univ, BA Economics 1970, MA Economics 1972; Univ of WI-Madison, PhD Economics 1977; The Brookings Inst Washington DC, post-graduate work 1980-81. **CAREER:** FL State Univ, asst prof/economics 1976-82; The Univ of NC/GA, asst vice pres for academic affairs 1982-86; UNC-Chapel Hill, adj asst prof/economics 1983-85, adj assoc prof/economics 1985-86; NC Central Univ, vice chancellor academic affairs 1986-. **ORGANIZATIONS:** Chmn educ comm NAACP 1979-80; mem bd dirs Tallahassee Urban League 1979-80; consultant Transcentury Corp 1986. **HONORS/ACHIEVEMENTS:** Brookings Economic Policy Fellow The Brookings Inst 1980-81. **BUSINESS ADDRESS:** Vice Chancellor Academic Afrs, North Carolina CentralUniv, 1801 Fayetteville St, Durham, NC 27707.

BURNS, ANN
Staff editor. **PERSONAL:** Born Feb 07, 1947, Charleston, SC; daughter of Walter Burns and Janie Williams Burns. **EDUCATION:** SC State Coll, BA 1969; New York Univ, Certificate 1978. **CAREER:** RR Bowker Co, booklister 1970-73, editorial asst 1974-78, asst editor 1979-81, editorial coord 1982-87; Cahners Publishing Co, staff editor, 1987-. **ORGANIZATIONS:** Women's International Bowling Congress. **HONORS/ACHIEVEMENTS:** Frederick Douglass Fellowship in Journalism. **HOME ADDRESS:** 1598 Unionport Rd #5d, Bronx, NY 10462.

BURNS, CHARLES THURGOODE
Business executive. **PERSONAL:** Born Aug 29, 1914, Baltimore, MD; married Juanita. **EDUCATION:** Morgan State Coll, 1935. **CAREER:** Comm Foods Inc, stockholder 1970-; Hilton Ct Pharmacy Inc, owner 1962; Dairy Farm, owner 1957; Bar & Restaurant "1017", owner 1946; Baltimore Shipyard, welder 1942; Grocery Store, owner 1936; Acme Markets, mgr 1936, Clk 1934. **BUSINESS ADDRESS:** Comm Foods, Inc, 336 E 25th St, Baltimore, MD 21218.

BURNS, CLARENCE DU
Government official. **PERSONAL:** Born Sep 13, 1918, Baltimore, MD; married Edith Phillips; children: Cheryl Turner. **CAREER:** City of Baltimore, mem city council 1971-82, vice pres city council 1977-82, pres of city council 1982-87, mayor 1987-. **ORGANIZATIONS:** Chmn exec bd Eastside Democratic Org 1967-87; chmn East Baltimore Comm Corp 1971-82; chmn East Baltimore Medical Plan 1973-82; delegate Democratic Natl Convention 1980,84; mem Regional Planning Council 1982-. **HONORS/ACHIEVEMENTS:** Service Awd MD Assoc of Equal Oppor Personnel 1983; Disting Serv Awd Central MD Comm Sickle Cell Anemia 1984; Awd for Contributions to Black Economic Develop The Hub Org 1985; Harry Bard Disting Citizenship Awd Comm Coll of Baltimore 1987; Andrew White Medal Loyola Coll in MD 1987. **MILITARY SERVICE:** AUS Air Corps sgt 1943-46. **BUSINESS ADDRESS:** Mayor, City of Baltimore MD, City Hall Room 250, 100 Holliday St, Baltimore, MD 21202.

BURNS, DARGAN J.
Business executive. **PERSONAL:** Born Feb 09, 1924, Sumter, SC; married Joyce Price; children: Dargan, Jr, Cedric Charles. **EDUCATION:** Hampton Inst, 1949; Boston Univ, MS 1952. **CAREER:** Burns Public Relations Serv, pres; AL State Coll, teacher & public relations; Advertising, Couyahoga Comm Coll. **ORGANIZATIONS:** Dir, public relations, Karamu House & Karamu Theater; bd mem, Public Relations Soc of Amer; Greater Cleveland Growth Assn; Cleveland Business League; pres, Cleveland Assn of Market Devel; bd mem BSA; Omega Psi Phi. **MILITARY SERVICE:** AUS 1942-46. **BUSINESS ADDRESS:** President, Burns Public Relations Service, 668 Euclid Ave, Ste 516, Cleveland, OH 44114.

BURNS, DENISE
Computer company executive. **CAREER:** World Computer Systems Inc, Laurel, MD, chief executive. **BUSINESS ADDRESS:** Chief Executive, World Computer Systems Inc, 340 Main Street, Laurel, MD 20707. *

BURNS, EMMETT C.
Educator. **PERSONAL:** Married Earlean Poe; children: Emmett III, Engel Dawson, Evers Allen. **EDUCATION:** Jackson State U, BS; VA Union Univ Sch of Religion, MD; Christian Edn, M; Presbyterian Sch Of Christian Edn; Univ of Pittsburgh, PhD. **CAREER:** Rogers High School, Canton MS, teacher 2 Yrs; New York City Program VA Union Univ, teacher 1 Yr; Baker Elementary School, teacher 1965-69; Richmond Public Schools, special educ 1968-69; Univ of Pittsburgh, academic advisor 1969-72. **ORGANIZATIONS:** Chmn grad coun of Students In Educ 1969-72; field dir NAACP; student asst Ebenezer Bapt Ch Richmond 1965; pastor Oak Grove Bapt Ch 1966; pastor Mosby Memorial Bapt Ch 1967-69; pastor New Second Bapt Ch 1969-71; pastor Mt Vernon Bapt Ch 1972-73; pastor New Hope Bapt Ch Jackson, MS; mem Omega Psi Phi Frat; Nat Bapt Conv Jackson Ministers Union; Jackson Clergy Alliance; Jackson Interfaith Alliance; Gen Bapt Conv of MS; Nat & Progressive Bapt Conv; Am Assn of Higher Edn; mem Sch Bd Christ the King Sch; natl chaplain Jackson State Coll Alumni Assn. **BUSINESS ADDRESS:** 7-1072 W Lynch St, Jackson, MS 39203.

BURNS, FELTON
Psychologist, educator. **PERSONAL:** Born Mar 12, 1936, Tillar, AR; married Verlene Dean; children: Gregory L, Pamele E. **EDUCATION:** Fresno St, BA 1962; CA St Univ, Fresno, MA 1972; Univ So CA, EdD 1977; Natl Bd Cert Cnslr, Inc, NCC 1983-. **CAREER:** County of Fresno, social worker 1962-65; Economic Opportunities Comm, asst dir 1965-68; CA State Univ Fresno, asst to dean of students 1968-71, staff counselor 1971-. **ORGANIZATIONS:** Dir Advncd Rsrch Tech 1978-83; pres Spectrum Asso 1977-85; mem Am Asso Cnslng & Dev 1985, CA Blck Fclty & Stf Asso. **HONORS/ACHIEVEMENTS:** Albright Endwd Chair for Exclnc 1st Rcpnt CA St Univ Fresno Stdnt Afrs Div 1984-85; Troy Awrd Educ Fresno Comm Srvc 1975; Who's Who in West US &Canada 1972-73; Who's Who in Fresno Grapevine Mag 1971. **HOME ADDRESS:** 6378 N 8th, Fresno, CA 93710. **BUSINESS ADDRESS:** Staff Counselor/Prof Rehab, CA State Univ, Fresno, 6378 N 8th, Fresno, CA 93710.

BURNS, JEFF, JR.
Business executive. **PERSONAL:** Born Dec 04, 1950, Varnesville, SC. **EDUCATION:** Howard Univ, BBA 1972. **CAREER:** Ebony Magazine, advertising director; Johnson Publishing Co, vice pres. **ORGANIZATIONS:** Mem PUSH Intl; bd of dirs Trade Bureau; mem Caribbean Tourism Organization; judge CEBA Awds; Howard University Alumni Assn of NY.. **HONORS/ACHIEVEMENTS:** Business Person of the Year, Natl Assn of Negro Business & Professional Women's Clubs 1989. **BUSINESS ADDRESS:** Vice President, Johnson Publishing Co, 1270 Ave of Americas, New York, NY 10020.

BURNS, LEONARD L.
Podiatrist, travel agent. **PERSONAL:** Born Jan 10, 1922, New Orleans, LA; son of George Burton Burns and Leona Galle Burns Gauff; married Phyllis Charbonnet Burns; children: Debra E Barnes, Gary M Burns, Lenette P Plummer. **EDUCATION:** Xavier Prep, Xavier Univ, New Orleans, LA, pre-med, 1947; Temple Univ, Philadelphia, PA, DPM 1951; Tulane Univ, New Orleans, LA, Leadership MPC, 1966. **CAREER:** Private medical practice, New Orleans, LA, 1951-; Four Corners Travel Agency, LA, pres, 1963-. **ORGANIZATIONS:** Bd of dir, NAACP, 1963-66; bd of dir, trustee, NAACP Special Contribution Fund, 1966-; pres, InterAmerican Travel Agents Soc, 1974-78; bd mem InterAmerican Travel Agents Society, 1986-; LA Tourist Devel Commn, pres, 1969. **HONORS/ACHIEVEMENTS:** Man of the Year, Psi Chapter Alpha Phi Alpha Philadelphia, PA, 1950; Honorary Award, civic activities, New Orleans United Clubs, 1962; Small Business Council Champion, New Orleans Chamber of Commerce, 1985; Award of Merit, LA/New Orleans Host Comm, 1988. **MILITARY SERVICE:** US Marine Corp, OCS/S-SGT,1941-46; Bronz Star/First Black Volunteer Eighth District. **BUSINESS ADDRESS:** 1813 N Rocheblave St, New Orleans, LA 70119-1403.

BURNS, OLLIE HAMILTON
Educator. **PERSONAL:** Born Jun 13, 1911, Monroe, LA; son of Ernest Hamilton and Charlotte Davis Hamilton Reed; married Rev Alex A Burns Jr, Nov 17, 1937; children: Alice, Alex III, Sylvia, Lawrence, Benjamin. **EDUCATION:** Grambling Univ, BS 1947; LA State Univ, MS 1957. **CAREER:** Jackson Parish Elementary School, teacher 1932-34; Quachita Parish Elementary School, teacher 1934-39; Quachita Parish HS, teacher 1947-60; Quachita Parish School, librarian 1960-76. **ORGANIZATIONS:** Mem Amer Library Assn; mem, Natl Educ Assn; Elec Comm NEA 1972; pres, Library Dept, LEA 1965; pres Quachita Educ Assn 1967-69; dir Quachita Parish Conf; past pres Quachita Human Relations Cncl; past vice pres Women in Politics; mem Quachita Multi-Purpose Comm Action Program, 1965-72; mem, Monroe Branch, Natl Assn of Univ Women; vice pres, Quachita League of Women Voter; Organizer & dir, New Way Center; mem, Parish Library Bd; Gov State Drug Abuse Advisory Council; Mayor's Ind Dev Comm; NAACP; consultant, NDEA Inst. **HONORS/ACHIEVEMENTS:** Articles publ "Library Services in Quachita Parish"; "Economic Contrib of Blacks in Quachita Parish 1803-1976"; Woman of the Year, NAACP, 1985; Natl Assn of Univ Women, Award, 1989. **BUSINESS ADDRESS:** Dir, New Way Center, 507 Swayze St, Monroe, LA 71201.

BURNS, RONALD MELVIN
Painter. **PERSONAL:** Born Feb 02, 1942, New York, NY; married Edith Bergmann; children: Elizabeth Bergmann, Alexi Bergmann. **EDUCATION:** School of Visual Arts. **CAREER:** Collections Museum of Modern Art; Lincoln Center; Art for the Working Place; Kaptensgarden-Borstahusen-Lankskrona-Sweden; Exhibitions, Provinceton Gallery-Paul Kessler-USA 1962; Gallery Sari Robinson, PA 1964; Passepartout-Charlotteborg 1966; Passepartout-Bergen 1969; Landskrona Konsthall 1969-70 & 1980; Galleri Heland-Stockholm 1970; Galerie Migros-Lausanne 1970; Teatergalleriet-Malmo 1970; Graphikbienale-Wien 1972; Corcoran Gallery of Art Washington, DC 1975; Gallerie Univorn 1975; Fundacion Rodriquez-Acosta-Granada 1977; Galleria II Traghetto-Venice 1977-80; Galerie Schindler Bern 1978; Hvidovre Bibliotek 1980; numerous others in the USA, Denmark, Sweden, and Switzerland. **ORGANIZATIONS:** Mem Artist's Exhibition Group AZ-Venice Italy; mem Artist's Exhibition Group-Gallery 2016 Switzerland. **HONORS/ACHIEVEMENTS:** Honorary Mem of Danish Acad of Art. **HOME ADDRESS:** HC Orsteds Vej 71, 1879-V Copenhagen, Denmark.

BURNS, SARAH ANN
Administrative officer. **PERSONAL:** Born Sep 20, 1938, Tupelo, MS; married Floyd Burns. **EDUCATION:** Univ of Akron, BS 1960. **CAREER:** Macomb County NAACP, pres 1978-84; US Senator Carl Levin Screening Committee for Military Academies, member 1980-; Natl Council of Negro Women-McLeod Sect, pres 1986-. **ORGANIZATIONS:** Bd of directors Turning Point 1982-; bd of directors League of Women Voters 1983-; member Natl Assn for Female Executives 1983-; pres Natl Council of Negro Women 1984-; member Amer Soc of Military Comptrollers 1984-. **HONORS/ACHIEVEMENTS:** Woman of the Year Natl Council of Negro Women 1981 & 1984; EEO contribution Detroit Federal Executive Bd 1981 & 1984; EEO contribution Army & Air Force Natl Guard Bureau 1984; Community Service Macomb County Branch NAACP 1984; Brotherhood/Sisterhood Awd 1986; Naval Air Facility Detroit Employee of the Year Awd 1986. **HOME ADDRESS:** 26450 Crocker Apt 301, Mount Clemens, MI 48045. **BUSINESS ADDRESS:** Personnel Administrator, Naval Air Facility US Navy, Naval Air Facility Detroit, Mount Clemens, MI 48043.

BURNS, TOMMIE, JR.
Service company executive. **CAREER:** Burns Janitor Service, Inc, Louisville, KY, chief executive. **BUSINESS ADDRESS:** Chief Executive, Burns Janitor Service, Inc, 1625 W Hill Street, Box 11395, Louisville, KY 40210. *

BURNS, W. HAYWOOD
Attorney/educator. **PERSONAL:** Born Jun 15, 1940, Peekskill, NY; married Marilyn Reynolds; children: Seth, Jeremiah. **EDUCATION:** Harvard Univ, BA, 1962; Cambridge Univ, England, Lionel de Jersey Scholarship, 1962-63; Yale Univ Law School, JD, 1966. **CAREER:** Paul Weiss Rifkin Wharton & Garrison, assoc, 1966; Hon Constance B Motley, US Dist Judge, law clerk, 1966-67; SUNY at Buffalo, visiting prof of law, 1974-75; NY Univ, assoc prof of law, 1975-77; NY Law School, adjunct prof; CUNY Law School at Queens Coll, adjunct prof of law, 1986; Rabinowitz, Boundin, Standard, Rinsky & Lieberman, counsel, 1987; Max & Filomen M Greenburg Center for Legal Educ & Urban Policy, City Coll of NY, provost & dir, urban & legal programs. **ORGANIZATIONS:** Dir, Natl Conf of Black Lawyers, 1970-73; bd of dirs, Natl Prison Project; bd of dirs, Center for Constitutional Rights; bd of dirs, VERA Inst for Justice; bd of dirs, Inst for Mediation & Conflict; pres, Natl Lawyer's Guild; co-chair emeritus, Natl Conference of Black Lawyers; Legal Action Center, NYC, emergency civil liberties comm; vice chair, Prisoner's Legal Services of NY; pres, The Natl Inst; New York City Criminal Justice Agency; Puerto Rican Legal Defense Fund; NYU Law Center Found; 21st Century Found; Natl Employment Law Project; pres, Natl Coll Advisory Service; Asian-Amer Legal Defense Fund; Lawyers Comm for Nuclear Policy; Boehm Found; Natl Coalition Against the Death Penalty; Fortune Soc; Advisory Council; fellow, NY Inst for the Humanities; Bronx Comm Coll Paralegal Studies Program; Advisory Comm. **HONORS/ACHIEVEMENTS:** Hon, History, Harvard Univ, 1962; Natl Founder's Award, Natl Conference of Black Lawyers, 1974; Best Teacher, New York Univ, School of Law, 1976; Lewisburg Prison Chapter, NAACP Dedicated Scholarship Award, 1979; Service Award, Black American Student's Assn, 1980; Karl Menninger Award, Fortune Soc, 1981; Coll President's Award, Malcolm-King, 1983; Civil Rights, Human Rights and Ordinary People's Rights Award, Portland Chapter, Natl Lawyer's Guild, 1985; Florina Lasker Award, NY Civil Liberties Union, 1986; Service Award, Prisoners' Legal Services of NY, 1986. **BUSINESS ADDRESS:** Dean, City Univ of New York, Law School at Queens, 65-21 Main St, Flushing, NY 11367.

BURNS, WILLIE MILES
Publishing executive. **PERSONAL:** Born in Lake Village, AR. **EDUCATION:** AM&N Coll, BS. **CAREER:** Johnson Pub Co Chicago, vice pres, agency mgr 1946-. **ORGANIZATIONS:** Mem State St Bus & Professional Women's Club; bd mem Sears YMCA; mem Cook Co Hosp Governing Commn. **BUSINESS ADDRESS:** 820 S Michigan Ave, Chicago, IL 60605.

BURR, LAWRENCE C.
Business executive. **PERSONAL:** Born Jun 18, 1913, Denton, TX; son of John Burr and Rhonda Burr; married Mildred S Caesar; children: LaRosa Lumpkin, Marial Burr, Marthal Burr. **EDUCATION:** Langston Univ, AB 1936; George Williams Coll, MS 1946; Columbia Univ, Doctoral study 1957-59; Lehman Coll, Real Estate Mgt 1982. **CAREER:** Deaf Blind & Orphan Inst, supt 1938-42; YMCA of Chicago, comm boys' work sec 1942-46; Intl Comm of YMCA's, staff mem 1946-53; NJ YMCA, assoc sec 1953-59; Forest Neighborhood Houses Inc, exec dir 1959-63; Afri-Amer Inst, program officer 1963-66; Comm Cncl of Greater NY, staff consultant 1967-68; State of NY Off Parks & Rec, staff consultant 1968-73; River Park Towers Housing Dev, mgr 1973-74; Chestnut House Assoc, gen partner 1977-; McKinley Square Merchants Assn, consult 1980-85; Burr Manor Assoc Inc, pres 1973-. **ORGANIZATIONS:** Pres WESTBRO Comm Dev Corp 1975-; foreign corresp Assoc Negro Press Madras, India 1946-52; mem Alpha Phi Alpha Frat; founding pres Beta Chi Lambda Muskogee, OK 1940; pres Bronx Cncl for Environ Quality 1975-; mem Bronx Soc of Science & Letters; mem African Methodist Epis Church; mem Comm Planning Bd Bronx, NY 1962-80; mem Bronx Overall Econ Dev Comm 1980-85. **HONORS/ACHIEVEMENTS:** NY State Assemb Citation Hon Gloria Davis 1984; America's Leading Exec Plaque 1984; Man of the Year Award McKinley Sq Merchants Assn 1984; Cert of Apprec US Environmental Agency 1979; Outstanding Serv Award New Jackson Democratic Club Bronx 1979; Achievement Award Bronx Club Natl Assn of Business & Professional Women's Clubs Inc 1970; Ford Found Fellow 1957; 300 Anniv Plaque City of NY Awarded by mayor 1965; publication, "The Historical Devel of the Wabash Ave Dept of the YMCA of Chicago", completed as a requirement for the MS degree at George Williams Coll Chicago, IL; Gov Morris Awd for Promoting Environmental Quality for Ourselves and Our Posterity Bronx Council for Environment Quality 1986. **HOME ADDRESS:** 218 North Oraton Pkwy, East Orange, NJ 07017. **BUSINESS ADDRESS:** President, Burr Manor Assoc Inc, 1135 Manor Avenue, Bronx, NY 10472.

BURRELL, CLINTON BLANE
Professional athlete. **PERSONAL:** Born Sep 04, 1956; children: Erica Renee. **EDUCATION:** LA State U, BS Business 1978. **CAREER:** Cleveland Browns, 2nd yr Defensive back 1979-. **BUSINESS ADDRESS:** Cleveland Browns Inc, Cleveland Stadium, Cleveland, OH 44114.

BURRELL, EMMA P.
Clergywoman. **PERSONAL:** Born Aug 09, Maryland; widowed; children: 1 Son (dec). **EDUCATION:** Howard U, AB, BD, MDiv 1959, DD 1965. **CAREER:** Tchr; Irwin, VA, prin; DC Census Bureau Engraving, govt employee; Good Hope United Meth Ch, pastor. **ORGANIZATIONS:** Mem C4 Colesville Comm Council Ch 1972-74; 1st woman receive full clerical rights & membership Annual Conf; Those Incredible & Meth; vp, trustee, Intl Assn of Women Ministers 1973-74; dist dir Rel & Race. **BUSINESS ADDRESS:** 14655 Good Hope Rd, Silver Spring, MD 20904.

BURRELL, GEORGE REED, JR.
Attorney. **PERSONAL:** Born Jan 04, 1948, Camden, NJ; married Doris; children: Stephen, Leslie. **EDUCATION:** Univ PA, LLD 1974; Wharton Sch, BS 1969. **CAREER:** Mayor Of Philadelphia, dep 1980-; Colonial Penn Ins Co, asst gen counsel 1978-80; Wolf Block Schorr & Solis-Cohen, atty 1977-; Goodis Greenfield, Henry & Edelstein 1974-77. **ORGANIZATIONS:** Mem Empire Sports Inc (Denver Broncos) 1969; mem Nat Bar Assn; reg dir bd dir Phil Baristers Assn; mem Am Judictre Soc; Am Bar Assn; Philadelphia Bar Assn; bd tstsUniv PA; bd dir World Affairs Cncl; bd mgrs Friends Hosp. **BUSINESS ADDRESS:** 10th Floor Packard Bldg, Philadelphia, PA 19102.

BURRELL, KENNETH EARL
Musician. **PERSONAL:** Born Jul 31, 1931, Detroit, MI. **EDUCATION:** Wayne State U, MusB 1955. **CAREER:** Oscar Peterson Trio, guitarist 1955-57; Benny Goodman Orch, 1957-59; Jimmy Smith Trio, 1959; Kenny Burrell Trio, Formed 1960; Kenny Burrell Quartet, 1963; Guitar Player Productions, exec dir; Jazz Heritage Found, pres 1975-78; UCLA, faculty 1978-79; 50 Records, recording artist. **ORGANIZATIONS:** Mem Kappa Alpha Psi; mem Phi Mu Alpha. **HONORS/ACHIEVEMENTS:** Recip Intl Jazz Critics Awards 1957, 60, 65, 69-73; winner Downbeat Reader's Poll 1968-71; Downbeat Critics Poll 1968-73; Swing Journal Poll 1970-72. **BUSINESS ADDRESS:** Prestige Records, 10 th Parker St, South Berkeley, CA 94710.

BURRELL, MORRIS
Clergyman. **PERSONAL:** Born Aug 04, 1908, New Orleans, LA; married Desmonia M; children: Morris, Alvin Peter, Joseph Leroy. **EDUCATION:** Dillard U, 1939-45; Leland Coll, AB 1947, DD 1953. **CAREER:** Union Bapt Theol Seminary, instr 1943; Bath House Commn Hot Spgs AR, mgr. **ORGANIZATIONS:** Mem Nat Bapt Conv; chmn Interracial Com LA Bapt State Conv & So Bapt Conv; sec-treas Dept Christian Edn; mem Finance Com LA MS Bapt State Conv; exec council Negro Div BSA; mem Big Bro Club Milne Municipal Boys Home;parole adv State LA Penal Inst; adv com Safety City New Orleans 1953; trustee Am Bapt Theol Seminary; mem NAACP; mem Interdenom Am Bapt Theol Seminary; mem Interdenominatl Ministerial Alliance; dir Federation Civic Leagues 1936; vice pres Ideal Missionary Bapt & Educ Assn; mem Orleans Parish Progressive Voters League; mem Urban League. **HONORS/ACHIEVEMENTS:** Dem hon deputy criminal sheriff Orleans Parish 1969. **BUSINESS ADDRESS:** 2200 2210 Dumaine St, New Orleans, LA 70119.

BURRELL, THOMAS J.
Business executive. **PERSONAL:** Born Mar 18, 1939, Chicago, IL; children: 3 children. **EDUCATION:** Roosevelt Univ Chgo, BA English 1961. **CAREER:** Wade Advertising Agency, mail room clerk, copy trainee, copywriter 1960-64; Leo Burnett Co Chgo, copywriter 1964-67; Foote Cone & Belding London, 1967-68; Needham Harper & Steers, copy suprv 1968-71; Burrel McBain Advertising, co-owner 1971-74; Burrell Advertising Inc, owner 1974-. **HONORS/ACHIEVEMENTS:** Has worked on accounts for Pillsbury, Swanson Frozen Foods, Vick Chem, Alka-Seltzer, One-a-Day Vitamins, Falstaff, Coca-Cola, Johnson Products Co, Joseph Schlitz Brewing Co, Proctor & Gamble, Jack Daniel Distillers, Stroh Brewing Co, McDonalds; 2 Clio Awds "St Song" Coca Cola 1978, McDonalds; other prestigious awds forTV & radio commercials & print advertising; 1985 Person of the Year Awd Chicago Advertising Club. **BUSINESS ADDRESS:** Chairman, Burrell Advertising Inc, 20 N Michigan Ave, Chicago, IL 60602.

BURRESS, JAMES R.
Retired federal executive, author, lecturer. **PERSONAL:** Born Aug 22, 1913, Hampton, VA; married Constance G; children: Melvin L, Cynthia K, Margaret J. **EDUCATION:** NC Agricultural & Tech Coll, BS 1937; Howard Univ & NYU, grad studies; Columbia Univ of Social Work, MS 1941; Wash Psychiatric Inst Univ of Northern CO, advanced studies; Fed Exec Inst, EdD 1972. **CAREER:** DHEW, vocational rehab counselor & dist supr 1943-51, vocational rehab spec adv 1951-59, assoc regional commr 1959-67, regional commr 1967-76; People to People Com for Handicapped Intl Prog, past dir 1976-80; James R Burress (self-employed), resources consultant soc & rehab serv 1981-. **ORGANIZATIONS:** Mem Natl Rehab Counseling Assn; natl conf for Social Welfare; Amer Pub Welfare Assn; Natl Assn of Soc Workers; Amer Soc for Pub Adminstrn; Amer Acad of Political & Social Sci; Natl Assn of Hearing & Speech Agy; St John's Episcopal Cathedral Parish; Denver chap Omega Psi Phi Natl Coll Frat; bd mem CO Rehab Assn 1963-67; numerous positions Natl Rehab Assn, natl pres 1971-72; natl bd mem Columbia Univ Sch of Soc Work Alumni Assn; bd mem program chmn/vp CO Conf of Social Welfare 1965-68; bd mem Denver Fair Housing Cntr 1967-70; prof adv com Laradon Hall Sch for Exceptional Children 1964-68; adv consult Western Interstate Commn on Higher Educ Rehab & Spl Educ 1965-68; exec policy com Denver Fed Exec Bd 1965-68; coord Field Training &Comm Orgn Smith Coll 1967-69; delegate 12th World Conf on Rehab of Disables 1972, 1976, 1980, 1984; delegate Intl conf on Social Welfare 1974. **HONORS/ACHIEVEMENTS:** Citation Alumni Assn Howard Univ Sch of Social Work 1960; Spl Serv Award Vocational Rehab Administration 1965; Gallery of Fame Denver Post Newspaper 1966 & 1968; Alumni Assn NC Agr & Tech Coll 1966; Omega Man of the Year Award 1966 & 1969; Superior Serv Award Soc & Rehab Serv 1968; Disting Serv Award US Dept of Health, Educ & Welfare 1970; Social & Rehab Serv Adminstr Award 1974; Recipient of 1st Annual Mary E Switzer Award Award from NRA for Rehab Leadership 1974; Recipient of "The Secretarys Special Citation" US Dept of HEW 1976.

BURRIS, BERTRAM RAY
Professional athlete, administrator, business executive. **PERSONAL:** Born Aug 22, 1950, Idabel, OK; son of Cornelius Burris and Clara Mae Vaughn-Burris; married Debra Marie Foots, Jan 24, 1986; children: Djemal Jermaine, Ramon Jerome, Damon Jevon, Deneen Janice, Bobby J. **EDUCATION:** Southwestern OK St Coll, BA, 1972. **CAREER:** Professional baseball player, 1972-87; Burris-Neiman & Assocs Inc, Canada, pres, 1983-; Neiman & Asso Inc Canada, pres 1983-; Burris-Neiman & Asso Inc US, pres 1985-; Burbrook invest-

ments, founder, 1988; Baseball Network, exec vice pres, 1987-; Milwaukee Brewers, admin asst, instructor, 1987-. **ORGANIZATIONS:** bd dir, Friendship Pentacostal Holiness Church,; bd of dir, Burris-Neiman & Assocs Inc, US, 1985; Citizen Advisory Bd, United Cancer Council; chmn, athletic Advisory Council; chmn, Fund Raising Comm, Metro Speedsters Educ & Athletic Assn; bd of dir, The Baseball Network, BNA- Canada; chmn, Fund Raising Comm, The Baseball Network; bd of dir, Mt Olive Baptist Church. **HONORS/ACHIEVEMENTS:** Player of the Month, Natl League, 1976; MVP, Oakland A'S, 1984; All-Amer, NAIA, Southwestern OK St Coll, 1971; Southwestern OK State Univ, Athletic Hall of Fame, 1985. **BUSINESS ADDRESS:** President, Burris-Neiman & Asso, Inc, 2304 Woodsong Trail, Arlington, TX 76016.

BURRIS, JOHN L.
Attorney. **PERSONAL:** Born May 05, 1945, Vallejo, CA; son of DeWitt C Burris and Imogene Terrell Burris; married Ramona Tascoe MD; children: Damon, Justin, Monique, Courtney, Jonathan. **EDUCATION:** Vallejo Jr Coll, AA 1965; Golden Gate Coll San Francisco, BS 1967; Univ of CA Grad Sch of Bus Berkeley, MBA 1970; Univ of CA Sch of Law, JD 1973. **CAREER:** Haskins & Sells San Francisco, acct/auditor 1967-69; Jenner & Block Chicago, assoc atty 1973-74; State Atty Office Cook Co Chicago, asst state atty 1975-76; Alameda Co DA Office Oakland, dep dist atty 1976-79; Alexander Burris Miller & McGee, atty; Law Office of John L Burris, atty. **ORGANIZATIONS:** Past pres CA Assn of Black Lawyers; mem bd of dir Charles Houston Bar Assn; spl consultant to pres Natl Bar Assn; mem Amer, Cook Co, IL Bar Assns; mem Amer Trial Lawyers Assn; mem CA DA's Assn; mem Alameda Co Criminal Cts Bar; mem Alameda Co Bar Assn; mem bd of dir Mile Square Health Ctr; mem Kappa Alpha Psi Frat; mem Black MBA Alumni Assn; mem bd of dir Clinton W White Youth Found specl investigation into fatal shooting of 15 yr old youth & entry into NAACP offices by Oakland Police Officers. **HONORS/ACHIEVEMENTS:** Outstanding Leadership Awd CA Assn of Black Lawyers 1980; James K Hollister Scholarship; lectr "Criminal Trial Practice" Natl Conf of Black Lawyers Annual Conf 1980; panelist "Media & the Law" CA Judges Assn Inc Berkeley 1980; Omegas Continental Boys Club Outstanding Leadership Awd 1986; Second Baptist Church, Martin Luther King Leadership Award Vallejo 1985; Clinton White, Californiaq Assn of Black Lawyers, Outstanding Contribution to Civil Rights Litigation, Charles Houston Bar Assn, 1987; Loren Miller, Outstanding Civil Rights Lawyer, 1989. **BUSINESS ADDRESS:** Attorney, Law Office of John L Burris, 1212 Broadway, 12th Floor, Oakland, CA 94612.

BURRIS, ROLAND W.
Comptroller, attorney, director. **PERSONAL:** Born Aug 03, 1937, Centralia, IL; married Berlean Miller; children: Rolanda Sue, Roland Wallace II. **EDUCATION:** So IL Univ, BA 1959; Univ Hamburg Germany, post grad 1959-60; Howard Univ, JD 1963. **CAREER:** US Treasury Dept, comptroller/natl bank examiner 1963-64; Continental IL Natl Bank & Trust, various positions from tax accountant to 2nd vice pres 1964-71; State of IL Dept Gen Svcs, cabinet appointee/dir 1973-76; Operation PUSH, natl exec dir 1977; State of IL, comptroller 1978-. **ORGANIZATIONS:** Mem Amer, IL, Chicago, Cook Co Bar Assns; Amer Inst of Banking; mem Independ Voters of IL; NAACP; Cosmopolitan Chamber of Commerce; Natl Business League; Chicago SoEnd Jaycees; Assembly of Black State Execs; Alpha Phi Alpha; vice chair Democratic Natl Comm; Natl Assn of State Auditors Comptrollers & Treasurers; immediate past pres & chmn Intergovtl Relations Comm. **HONORS/ACHIEVEMENTS:** Distinguished Serv Award, Chicago South End Jaycees 1968; One of Outstanding Young Men of Amer 1969; 1 of 10 Outstanding Young Men of Chicago 1970, 1972; Jr Chamber Intl Scholarship 1971; 1 of 1,000 Successful Black in Amer 1973; Cook County Bar Public Serv Award 1974-75; 1 of 10 Outstanding Black Business People Black Book Dir 1974; One of the 100 Most Influential Black Americans Ebony Magazine, 1979-86; Outstanding Alumnus Award Howard Univ Law School Alumni Assn 1980; Awd of Financial Reporting Achievement Govt Finance Officers Assn of the US & Canada 1985. **BUSINESS ADDRESS:** Comptroller, State of IL, 201 State Capitol, Springfield, IL 62706.

BURROUGH, GENE
Business executive. **PERSONAL:** Married Toni Burrough; children: Keenya, Luke, Dwayne. **CAREER:** Community Serv Div of Jacksonville FL, chief 1972-75; Pro Athletes Corp of Jacksonville FL, pres 1975-79; Argovitz & Assoc, partner 1979-83; Houston Gamblers, gen mgr, pro athletics 1983-.

BURROUGHS, BALDWIN WESLEY
Educator. **PERSONAL:** Born Feb 22, 1915, Houston, TX; children: Max Anton. **EDUCATION:** Wiley Coll, AB 1936; N Western U, AM 1938; Yale U, MFA 1950; Western Reserve U, PhD 1960. **CAREER:** Spelman Coll, retired 1979; Spelman Coll, prof 1950-77, prof lang & drama 1942-43; Tillitson Coll, prof 1939-42; Inst of African Studies, Univ Ghana, prof 1971-72. **ORGANIZATIONS:** Alpha-Phi Alpha; African Theatre; drama critic 1964-71; study grant Africa. **HONORS/ACHIEVEMENTS:** Governor's Award for Contribution to Drama 1979; Bronze Jubilee Award for Cotnribution to Drama 1980. **MILITARY SERVICE:** USN corpsman 3rd class 1943-45. **BUSINESS ADDRESS:** 350 Spelman Ln, Atlanta, GA 30314.

BURROUGHS, HUGH CHARLES
Business executive. **PERSONAL:** Born Feb 06, 1940, Trinidad; son of Mr & Mrs Vernon Burroughs; married Henrietta E Johnson; children: Kwame, Dawn. **EDUCATION:** Columbia Univ, BA, 1966, MA, 1969; Non-profit Mgmt, Harvard Univ, certified instructor, 1973. **CAREER:** Henry J Kaiser Family Found, vice pres, 1987-pres; Hewlett Foundation, program officer, 1977-87; John Hay Whitney Found, exec dir, 1971-77. **ORGANIZATIONS:** Prgm dir, Woodrow Wilson Natl Fellowshp Found, 1969-71; asst dean, Columbia Univ, 1966-69; chmn, bd of vis, Clark Coll; bd of overseers, Morehouse School of Med; bd of dir, Assn of Black Found Exec, 1973-77; bd of dir, Women & Found/Corp Philanthropy, 1977-80; commencement speaker, Texas Southern Univ, 1977; bd of dirs, Council on Foundations, Northern California Grantmakers, Natl Charities Information Bureau. **BUSINESS ADDRESS:** Vice President, Henry J Kaiser Family Foundation, 2400 Sand Hill Rd, Menlo Park, CA 94025.

BURROUGHS, JOHN ANDREW, JR.
Appointed government official. **PERSONAL:** Born Jul 31, 1936, Washington, DC; married Audrey C Shields. **EDUCATION:** Univ of IA, BA Polit Sci 1959; George Washington Univ, post-grad 1962. **CAREER:** Dept of State Washington, passport examiner 1960-63; Dept of Stte Bur of Econ Affairs, admin asst 1963-66; Dept of Navy Washington, employ relations spec 1970-77; Dept of Navy Washington, spl asst for equal employ 1970-77; Dept of State Washington, asst sec for equal employ oppor 1977-81; Republic ofMalawi, US ambassador 1981; Joint Ctr for Polit Studies, sr rsch fellow 1984-. **ORGANIZATIONS:** Pres bd of dir Ridgecrest Condominium 1964-70; mem Kappa Alpha Psi. **HONORS/ACHIEVEMENTS:** Civilian Superior Serv Awd Dept of Navy Washington DC 1977; Superior Honor Awd Dept of State Washington DC 1980. **MILITARY SERVICE:** AUS pfc 1961. **BUSINESS ADDRESS:** American Consul General, U S Dept of State, Dept of State 2201 C St NW, Am Con Gen - Cape Town, Washington, DC 20520.

BURROUGHS, LEONARD
Podiatric physician. **PERSONAL:** Born May 31, 1921, Evanston, IL; married Jeweline; children: Dorothy Carroll, Ellen D, Neal D, Nancy E. **EDUCATION:** Central YMCA Coll & Northwestern U1941-42; Univ of IL Urbana, predental 1946-47; IL Coll of Podiatric Medicine Chicago, Dr of Podiatric Medicine 1948-52. **CAREER:** US Treasury Dept, clk Fraud & Forgery Dept 1945-46; City Of Chicago Welfare Dept, podiatrist Div of Phys & Medicine of Rehab 1952-54; Foster G McGaw Hosp Loyola Univ of Chicago, clinical instructor in podiatric medicine; Schell Coll of Podiatric Medicine Chicago, adj prof podiatric medicine; Private Practice, podiatrist 1954-. **ORGANIZATIONS:** Mem & past pres IL Podiatry Soc; mem/alternate del Am Podiatry Assn; past mem bd of trustees IL Coll of Podiatric Medicine Chicago; past-pres AlumniEduc Found IL Coll of Podiatric Medicine; mem Kappa Alpha Psi Frat Inc 1942; 32nd Degree Mason Prince-Hall 1967; mem Title XIX Spl Proj Cook Co Dept of Pub Aid 1968-69; bd mem Chicago Assembly; mem Duffer's dozen Golf Club; mem St Edmund's Epis Ch Chicago; mem Amer Podiatric Medical Assoc; mem ILPodiatric Medical Soc; mem Acad of Ambulatory Foot Surgery; mem Natl Podiatric Medical Assoc. **BUSINESS ADDRESS:** 1525 Hyde Park Blvd, Chicago, IL 60615.

BURROUGHS, MARGARET TAYLOR (MARGARET TAYLOR)
Educator, museum director, artist, and author. **PERSONAL:** Born Nov 01, 1917, St Rose, LA; daughter of Alexander Taylor and Octavia Pierre Taylor; married Bernard Goss, 1939 (divorced 1947); children: Gayle Goss Toller; married Charles Gordon Burroughs, Dec 23, 1949; children: Paul (adopted). **EDUCATION:** Graduated from Chicago Teachers College (now Chicago State Univ), 1937; Art Inst of Chicago, BFA, 1944, MFA, 1948; attended Esmerelda Art School, Mexico City, 1952-53; graduate study at Teachers Coll, Columbia Univ, summers, 1958, 1959, 1960. **CAREER:** DuSable High School, Chicago, IL, teacher of art, 1946-69; Kennedy-King Community Coll, Chicago, prof of humanities, 1969-79; instructor in African and African-Amer art history at Chicago Inst of Art, 1968; also officer and mem bd of dir of South Side Art Community Center, Chicago, 1940—; dir, 1961-84, and dir emeritus, 1984—, of DuSable Museum of African-Amer History. **ORGANIZATIONS:** Founder, mem, Natl Conference of Negro Artists, 1959-63; mem, Phi Delta Kappa. **HONORS/ACHIEVEMENTS:** Author of Jaspar, the Drummin' Boy, 1947; NCA Award, 1963; Centennial Award, 1963; author of Whip Me Whop Me Pudding and Other Stories of Riley Rabbit and His Fabulous Friends, Praga Press, 1966; fellow, Amer Forum for Intl Study, 1968; author of What Shall I Tell My Children Who Are Black?, MAAH Press, 1968; New City Award, Better Boys Federation, 1971; AKA Award, 1973; Urban Gateways Honor Award, 1973; YMCA Leadership Award, 1974; Rockefeller Family Foundation Award; Awarded Doctorate of Humane Letters, Lewis Univ, 1974; Two Centuries of African Amer Art, Los Angeles Art Co Museum, 1976; author of Sketchbook 1976, 1976; selected 1 of 16 women to tour China, 1977; 1 of 10 black artists honored by Pres & Mrs Carter at White House, 1980; Ten Black Amer Artists Exhibition, Corcoran Art Galleries, 1980; Outstanding Alumnus from Chicago State Univ, 1982. *

BURROUGHS, ROBERT A.
Attorney. **PERSONAL:** Born Mar 30, 1948, Durham, NC; married Laverne Davis. **EDUCATION:** NC Central U, BA 1971. **CAREER:** State Of NC, magistrate 1970-71; USMC, defense counsel. **ORGANIZATIONS:** Trustee Mt Zion Bapt Ch; scoutmaster 1969-71; exec com JFK Young Dem Club 1971. **MILITARY SERVICE:** USMC 1st lt 1971-75. **BUSINESS ADDRESS:** Staff Judge Advocates Office, Force & Troops FMF LANT, Camp Le Jeune, NC.

BURROW, MARIE BRABHAM
Educational administrator. **PERSONAL:** Born Dec 14, 1915, St Louis, MO; married Artis N; children: Louvon B Brown. **EDUCATION:** Stowe Tchrs Coll, BS-edn 1937; So IL U, MS-guidance & coun 1965; MO U, cert-adminstr 1969. **CAREER:** St Louis Pub Schs, personnel spec Area IV 1979-, coord career educ 1978-79; Harris Stowe Tchr's Coll, cons-career educ 1975-79; St Louis Pub Schs dir-career educ 1973-78. **ORGANIZATIONS:** Consult Building Self-Concepts Work Study Hich Sch 1973; cons-mem-presenter Gov's Conf on Educ 1977; consult career educ Webster Coll St Louis 1978; life mem Delta Sigma Theta Sor 1936-; sec St Louis Met Urban Leage-Board of Dir 1973-81; commr MO Commnon Human Rights 1975; life mem NAACP 1977-; memChurch Counc-Pilgrim Congregational Ch 1978-. **HONORS/ACHIEVEMENTS:** Outstanding Educ Award Clark Sch Comm Assn 1976; 1st edit sch dist officials-marquais Who's Who Biographical Record 1976; Outstanding Workshop Award Nat Career Educ Conf 1977; Achievement Award in Educ Zeta Phi Beta Sor St Louis 1978; Intl Who's Who Comm Serv third edit 1979; Who's Who Personalities-W-Midwest Am Biog Inst 6th edit 1979. **BUSINESS ADDRESS:** 721 Pendelton Ave, St Louis, MO 63108.

BURROWS, CLARE
Public health administrator. **PERSONAL:** Born Sep 29, 1938, Kansas City, MO; married William L Burrows; children: James Michael Pickens, Joye Nunn Hill, Carla Nunn, Anita Nunn Orme, Maurice Nunn. **EDUCATION:** College St Mary Omaha, BS 1962; UCLA, MPH 1972. **CAREER:** Stanford Univ Palo Alto, compliance auditor 1975-78; Community Hosp Santa Rosa CA, dir medical records 1978-80; Univ SF UCSF, dir patient service 1980-82; CA Medical Review San Francisco, monitor 1982-86; Beverly Enterprises Inc, dir business admin. **ORGANIZATIONS:** Tutor Urban League 1980-82; consultant Medical Records Assoc 1980-84. **HONORS/ACHIEVEMENTS:** Outstanding Church Work Mt Hermon AME Church 1984. **MILITARY SERVICE:** USAR capt 6 yrs.

BURRUS, CLARK
Senior vice president. **PERSONAL:** Born Nov 05, 1928, Chicago, IL; married Lucille Thomas; children: James. **EDUCATION:** Roosevelt U, BSC 1954, MPA 1954. **CAREER:** First Nat Bank of Chicago, sr vp; City of Chicago Dept of Finance, fiscal ofcr/city comptroller 1973-79, 1st dep city comptroller/asst & comptroller/dir of acctng & asst dir of finance 1954-73. **ORGANIZATIONS:** Bd of dir & immed past pres Municipal Fin Off Assn

of US & Canada; bd of dir & past treas Options Inc; bd of dir Urban Gateways; mem of evaluation panel on HUD financial mgnt capacity sharing prog Nat Acad of Pub Adminstrn; bd of dir Trust Inc; mem State Comptroller's Commn for Analsyis & Review; vice chmn Mortgatge Revenue Bond Adv Com; mem adv com Grad Sch of Mgmt Northwestern U; bd of dir & past chmn region IV Am Cancer Soc; council mem & mem budget-finance com Chicago Heart Assn; mem exec com Boy Schouts of Am; mem NAACP; mem Alpha Phi Alpha. **HONORS/ACHIEVEMENTS:** Author of "Minorities in Pub-Finance" pub in Government mag 1972; ex Ec of yr Exec Develop Alumni 1974; man of yr Sertoma Intl 1975; Who's Who in Govt 1977-79; ten outstanding bus & professional people Blackbok Bus & Ref Guide 1979; author "Issues Concerning the Financing of Mortgages with Tax-exempt Bonds". **BUSINESS ADDRESS:** First Natl Bank of Chicago, One First Natl Plaza, Ste 0090, Chicago, IL 60670.

BURRUS, WILLIAM HENRY
Business executive. **PERSONAL:** Born Dec 13, 1936, Wheeling, WV; married Ethelda I; children: Valerie, Doni, Kimberly, Kristy. **EDUCATION:** WV State, 1957. **CAREER:** OH Postal Union, dir rsch & educ 1971, pres 1974-80; Amer Postal Workers Union, bus agent 1978-80, exec vice pres 1980-. **ORGANIZATIONS:** Labor del Cleveland Fed AFL-CIO 1977; vice pres Black Trade Labor Union 1977; mem OH Advisory Bd Civil Rights Comm 1979-81; vice pres A Philip Randolph Inst 1982-. **HONORS/ACHIEVEMENTS:** OH House of Rep 1981; Frederick O'Neal Award 1981; A Philip Randolph Achievement Award 1982; num union awds & recognition. **MILITARY SERVICE:** AUS sgt 3 years. **BUSINESS ADDRESS:** Executive Vice President, Amer Postal Wrks Union AFL-CIO, 817 14th St NW, Washington, DC 20005.

BURSE, LUTHER
Educator. **PERSONAL:** Born Jan 03, 1937, Hopkinsville, KY; son of Monroe Perry and Ernestine Perry; married Mamie Joyce Malbon; children: Luther Jr, Elizabeth N. **EDUCATION:** KY State Univ, BS 1958; Univ of IN, mEd 1960; Univ of MD, EdD 1969. **CAREER:** Cheyney St Coll, prof; Chicago Pub Sch, tchr 1958-59; Elizabeth City State U, instruct 1960-66; Univ of MD, research assist 1966-69; Chester Pub Sch, consultant, Philadelphia Bd of Exam; Fort Valley State Coll, pres 1984-. **ORGANIZATIONS:** Bd of dirs Amer Council on Industrial Arts Tchr Educ; PA State Educ Assn; bd of dirs Assn of State Coll & Univ Faculty; past pres Indus Arts Assn of PA; Natl Assn of Indus Tchr Educ; Delaware County Indus Arts Assn; Chester County Indus Arts Assn; past pres PA Assn for Voc and practical arts educ; Amer Voc Assn; mem NEA Higher Educ Caucus; mem NEA Black Caucus; NEA Women's Caucus; NEA Vocational Caucus Trustee Beta Pi Chap Epsilon Pi Tau Frat; adv Mu Eta Chap Alpha Kappa Mu Honor Soc; mem Omega Psi Phi Frat; Iota Lamda Sigma Frat; chmn Scholarship Comm Omega Psi Phi Frat Inc; life mem NAACP; Amer Council on Educ Leadership Comm; Council of 1890 Land Grant Institutions; bd of directors, Georgia Assn of Minority Entrepreneurs; Sigma Pi Phi Fraternity. **HONORS/ACHIEVEMENTS:** Omega Man of the Yr Nu Upsilon Chap; leadershp award in arts assoc; PA State Educ Assoc Serv Award; Outstanding Educ of Amer; Honorable KY Col Commonwealth of KY; Outstanding Alumnus, Kentucky State University. **BUSINESS ADDRESS:** President, Fort Valley State College, 805 State College Drive, Fort Valley, GA 31030.

BURSE, RAYMOND MALCOLM
Educational administrator. **PERSONAL:** Born Jun 08, 1951, Hopkinsville, KY; married Kim M; children: Raymond M Jr; Justin Malcolm. **EDUCATION:** Centre College of Kentucky, AB Chem & Math 1973; Oxford Univ, Grad work 1973-75; Harvard Law School, JD 1978. **CAREER:** Kentucky State Univ, pres. **ORGANIZATIONS:** Amer Bar Assn; KY Bar Assn; bd of directors Frankfort-Franklin Cty Chamber of Commerce; bd chmn Louisville Fed Reserve; bd mem State YMCA. **HONORS/ACHIEVEMENTS:** Rhodes Scholar; Fred M Vinson Honor Graduate, Centre College; John E Davis Award NAACP Legal Defense and Educational Fund. **BUSINESS ADDRESS:** Wyatt, Tarrant & Combs, 27th Fl, Louisville, KY 40202.

BURSTERMANN, JULIETTE PHIFER
Educator. **PERSONAL:** Born Jan 03, 1905, Charlotte, NC; married Louis C. **EDUCATION:** Winston-Salem State U, BS 1929; Tchr Coll Columbia U, MA 1933; NY U, PhD 1948. **CAREER:** Eastern CT State Coll, prof emeritus 1974-; On-Island Prog of Teacher Educ VI co-dir 1953-54; Willimantic State Coll, prof of educ 1949-74; Lab School Fayetteville State Coll, prin 1936-46; Adult-Educ 25 Counties Cen NC, govt supervisor 1935-36; Middle Grade Lab School Fayetteville State Coll, supvr, teacher 1933-34; Greensboro NC Public Schools, teacher Language Arts 1930-31; Mid Grd Elementary School, Method NC, teacher 1924-28. **ORGANIZATIONS:** Bd of dir State Mental Health 14 yrs; vol chmn Adv Comm Intergovt Activities for Newtown Friends School; mem Riverside Church New York City 1959-, Riverside Church Personnel Comm 1971-73, Bd of Deacons Riverside Dr 1975-85; vchair bd 1974-75, corresp sec 1975-78, mem 1975-, sec 1978-80 The Women's Soc of theRiverside Church; mem Black Christian Caucus of the Riverside Church 1975-. **HONORS/ACHIEVEMENTS:** Gen educ bd Fellowship for Post-grad Study 1937-38; Kappa Delta Pi hon key; Epsilon Nu Chap Eastern CT 1972; distinguished serv award St Mental Health 1974; distignuished serv award Alumni of Eastern St Coll Willimantic 1975; distinguished serv citation Borough of Manhattan Comm Coll of the CityUniv of NY 1980; listed in Who's Who in Educ 1959-60, Who's Who of Amer Women 1961-62, The Dictionary of Intl Biography 1974, The World Who's Who of Women 1976, Personalities of Amer, Honoring US Leaders 1981.

BURT, JAMES E.
Association executive. **PERSONAL:** Born Jul 18, 1946, Raleigh, NC. **EDUCATION:** St Augustine's Coll, BA 1969; NC State Univ Coord of Alumni Affairs St Augustine's College, addl study. **CAREER:** United Church of Christ NY, youth dir; Bennett Coll, vice pres institutional adv. **ORGANIZATIONS:** Mem Raleigh Hum Rel Com; YMCA; Raleigh Experimental Ministry; Raleigh Oratorio Soc; Local Govt & Inst; NAACP; Interdenom Men's Chorus; pres Laymen's League Laodicea United Ch of Christ. **HONORS/ACHIEVEMENTS:** Award for Devoted Serv to SNEA 1969; Award for Meritorious Serv St Augustine's Coll 1970; Outstanding Comm Serv Raleigh City Council 1970; Raleigh Comm Rel Award 1970; Local Govt Inst Award 1971; Outstanding Young Men of Amer 1972; Certificate of Appreciation; bd dir Amer Biographical Inst. **BUSINESS ADDRESS:** Area Development Director, United Negro College Fund, Inc, First Union Bank Bldg, Suite 630, Winston-Salem, NC 27101.

BURTON, CALVIN E.
Business executive. **PERSONAL:** Children: 1. **EDUCATION:** Morgan St Coll, BA 1964; Rutgers U, MBA. **CAREER:** NBC Stations, staff producer 1972-; KNBC, adminstr programs 1970-72; Eual Empl Prog, adminstr 1968-70; Direct Hire Prog, adminstr 1967-68; Prog RotatingAssign, corp training 1966-67; RCA Electr Comp Div, interviewer recruiter 1965-66; US Dept Health Educ & Welfare 1964. **ORGANIZATIONS:** Mem Morgan St NJ Alumni Assn; Nat Caht Ofc for Radio & TV; Hollywood Chap Nat Acad of TV Arts & Sci; Oper Breadbasket PUSH; Nat Urban League; pub affairs com LA Urban League; Am Mgnt Assn; chmn radio &TV com United Negro Coll Fund; exec bd mem NAACP; People United to Save Humanity; SCLC W Spl. **HONORS/ACHIEVEMENTS:** Spl consult Inst of Black Am Music; football schlrsp 4 yrs Morgan St Coll; first internal employe to be selected for 6 mo corp personnel training prog RCA Corp Staff; five day AMA Seminar; nominated for Emmy Award; awared resolution CA St Assembly; awared resolution for outstanding prod City Coun of Los Angeles; award for excellence Nat Assn of TV Program Exec 1973; outstanding contrib to Los Angeles Black Comm Los Angeles Urban League 1973; Salute dto Red FoxxABC; 2 spec in conjuction with Rev Jessee Jackson's Oper PUSH NBC; best local TV pub affairs prgm award 10th Annual NAACP Images Award Dinner. **BUSINESS ADDRESS:** 3000 W Alameda Ave, Burbank, CA 91523 915.

BURTON, CHARLES HOWARD, JR.
Army officer. **PERSONAL:** Born Sep 21, 1945, Richmond, VA; married Adline Mildred Johnson; children: Stuart Howard, Stacee Michelle, Stephanie Brouke. **EDUCATION:** VA State Coll, BS 1968; Meharry Medical Coll, MD 1975. **CAREER:** US Army, chief ob/gyn. **ORGANIZATIONS:** Fellow Amer College Ob/Gyn 1983, Amer College of Surgeons 1984; mem Omega Psi Phi Frat; 32 Degree Mason, Shriner. **MILITARY SERVICE:** AUS col 18 yrs; Army Commendation Medal 1978. **HOME ADDRESS:** 3852 Highgreen Dr, Marietta, GA 30068. **BUSINESS ADDRESS:** Chief Ob/Gyn, US Army, Martin Army Hospital, Fort Benning, GA 31905.

BURTON, CLARINDA MATTEA
Resident physician. **PERSONAL:** Born Jan 16, 1959, Philadelphia, PA. **EDUCATION:** Cheyney State Coll, BA (Summa Cum Laude) 1980; Meharry Medical Coll, MD 1984. **CAREER:** Meharry/Hubbard Hosp, third year resident. **HOME ADDRESS:** 1456 Snell Blvd, Nashville, TN 37208. **BUSINESS ADDRESS:** Third Year Resident, Meharry/Hubbard Hospital, 1008 Dr DD Todd Jr Blvd, Nashville, TN 37208.

BURTON, DAVID LLOYD
Accountant. **PERSONAL:** Born Aug 01, 1956, Detroit, MI; son of Freddie G Burton Sr (deceased) and C Lutressie Johnson-Burton; married Michele Lisa Simms-Burton, Dec 26, 1987. **EDUCATION:** Wayne State Univ, BS 1977, MBA 1980. **CAREER:** City of Detroit Employment & Training Dept, sr program monitor 1978-80; Arthur Young & Co CPA, auditor 1980-81; Barrow Aldridge & Co CPA, semi-sr auditor 1981-84; Ford Motor Co, internal auditor/operations rep 1985-88; Reeves & Associates, dealership operations coordinator, 1988-. **ORGANIZATIONS:** Mem Natl Assoc of Black Accountants 1979; Natl Black MBA Assoc 1981; Cascade United Methodist Church 1986. **HONORS/ACHIEVEMENTS:** Certified Public Accountant State of MI 1983. **BUSINESS ADDRESS:** Dealership Operations Coordinator/Comptroller, Reeves & Associates, 1710 North Expressway, Griffin, GA 30223.

BURTON, DONALD C.
Law enforcement officer. **PERSONAL:** Born Apr 21, 1938, Lawnside, NJ; son of William and Josephine; married Marcia E Campbell; children: Donald Jr, Barry D, Jay S, Robert T. **EDUCATION:** Camden Co Coll, AS 1969-74; Rutger State Univ, BA 1975-77. **CAREER:** Security consultant-private business 1973-; Cherry Hill Police Dept, polygraph oper 1973-, commander 1967-84; Camden Co Sheriff's Dept, undersheriff 1984-88; Bergen County Sheriff's Dept, undersheriff 1988-. **ORGANIZATIONS:** Pres Cherry Hill #176 PBA 1969-71; delegate NJ State PBA 1970-72; pres NJ Chap of NOBLE 1983-88; regional vice pres NOBLE 1987-88; trustee HOPE for Ex-Offenders. **HONORS/ACHIEVEMENTS:** Valor Awd Cherry Hill Township 1970; Commissioner Citation US Customs 1973; Alcohol Tobacco & Firearms Citation polygraph expert 1974; numerous awds from law enforcement organizations municipal and from county, state, and national groups. **MILITARY SERVICE:** AUS reserves 1957-67. **HOME ADDRESS:** 3402 Whittier Ct, Mahwah, NJ 07430. **BUSINESS ADDRESS:** Undersheriff, Bergen County Sheriff's Dept, Box 369, Hackensack, NJ 07601.

BURTON, IOLA BRANTLEY
Educator. **PERSONAL:** Born Oct 20, Ensley, AL; daughter of Willie Douglas Brantley and Cremonia D Watkins Brantley; married Herman L Burton, Apr 01, 1945; children: Constance Parma Pulliam, Laura J Odem. **EDUCATION:** Miles Coll, Birmingham, AL, AB, 1941; Columbia Univ, New York, NY, 1953; Univ of Denver, Denver, CO 1954-55; Univ of S CA, Los Angeles, CA, 1964. **CAREER:** Limestone County Bd of Educ, Athens, AL, teacher, 1941-43; Jefferson County Bd of Educ, Birmingham, AL, teacher, 1943-45, 1948-56; Los Angeles County Dept of Social Service, case worker, 1957-60; Centinela Valley Unified School Dist, teacher, 1963-83; Los Angeles City DPT Recreation & Parks, Los Angeles, CA, outreach consultant, 1983-85; Centinela Valley U.S.D., Hawthorne, CA, substitute teacher, 1985-. **ORGANIZATIONS:** Supreme Epistoleus, The Natl Sorority of Phi Delta Kappa Inc 1987-; Supreme Grammateus The Natl Sorority of Phi Delta Kappa, Inc. 1967-71; Clerk of Session , Westminster Presbyterian Church, 1984-; corres sec bd of dir, Natl Alumni Assoc Miles Coll, 1988-. **HONORS/ACHIEVEMENTS:** Service, Los Angeles City, 1974; Natl Sojourner Truth Meritorious Serv, Natl Assn of Negro Business & Professional Women, 1977; Service & Leadership, Natl Sorority Phi Delta Kappa Inc, 1980; Service, Los Angeles City Dept of Rec & Parks, 1985; Service 10 years, Our Authors Study Club/African Festival, 1989; author, The Way It Strikes Me, 1988, Yawl Come on Back Home Again, 1978. **HOME ADDRESS:** 3039 Wellington Rd, Los Angeles, CA 90016.

BURTON, JOAN E.
Association executive. **PERSONAL:** Born Sep 05, 1945, Fuguay-Varina, NC. **EDUCATION:** NC Central Univ, BA 1976; Howard Univ Sch Law, JD 1972. **CAREER:** Commerce Clearing House Inc, labor law editor 1972-73; US Dept Agr Wash, opportunity spec 1973-74; US Environ Protection Agncy Wash, equal empl opport spec 1974; Creative Univ Prod Inc, legal researcher. **ORGANIZATIONS:** Mem Phi Alpha. **HONORS/ACHIEVEMENTS:** Responsible for drafting proposed regulation prohibiting empl discrim

for commodity exch auth US Delta Legal Frat. **BUSINESS ADDRESS:** Office Civil Rights, 401 M St SW, Washington, DC 20460.

BURTON, JOHN FREDERICK
Retired. **PERSONAL:** Born Mar 26, 1913, Nashville, TN; married Rhunette Paul; children: John F Jr, Beverly Jean Jemison. **EDUCATION:** Fisk Univ TN St A&I Coll, Pre-med Course 1930-33; Meharry Sch of Phrmcy, PhC 1937; Meharry Sch of Med, MD 1941. **CAREER:** Lincoln Hosp, Durham, NC, rotating intrnshp 1941-43; Wayne Co Gen Hosp, Eloise, MI, pthlgy res 1950-52; VA Hosp, Dearborn, MI, pthlgy res 1952-54; Wayne Univ Coll of Med, Detroit, MI, instr in Cytology 1955; VA Hosp, Dearborn, MI, asso pthlgst 1955-58, chf Anatomic Path 1958-62; Cntys Chf Med Ex, retired. **ORGANIZATIONS:** Cert Am Bd of path (Anatomic Path) 1955, (Forensic Path) 1964; pthlgst Med Ex Ofc Wayne Co Detroit, MI 1962-67; chf Med Ex Ofc Wayne Co, Detroit, MI 1967-70, Oakland Co, Pontiac, MI 1970-76; mem St Crime Comm, Lansing, MI 1970-76. **HONORS/ACHIEVEMENTS:** Report of Actvts & Stats, 1960-69 "The Detroit Riot" 1970; Exchng Trainee to Scotland Yard, London, England 1970; 10 timely articles pblshd Ofcl Med Jrnls 1961-74; 5 wrthy prsntns before Natl Orgs 1965-73. **MILITARY SERVICE:** AUS mjr med corps 3 yrs; Meritorious Sv Unit Awrd 1945; Am Cmpgn Sv Mdl 1943; WW II Vctry Mdl European-Afrcn Mdl Eastrn Sv Mdl 1946. **HOME ADDRESS:** PO Box 317, Mercer Island, WA 98040.

BURTON, JOHN H.
Union negotiator. **PERSONAL:** Born Jul 18, 1910, St Louis, MO; married Willie. **EDUCATION:** Attended 2 yrs. **CAREER:** Intl United Auto Workers Union UAW, rep internat; Ypsilanti, mayor, former city councilman 18 yrs. **ORGANIZATIONS:** Mem bd of Controls Med Center of Univ of MI; bd trustees Chelsea Med Center; exec bd dir Comprehensive Planning Council. **HONORS/ACHIEVEMENTS:** Recipient man of yr award Ford Motor Car Co Ypsilanti & Rawsonville plants; law day award Washtenaw Bar Assn distignuished serv awards MI Assn of Black Women's Clubs & NAACP Office. **BUSINESS ADDRESS:** 9650 S Telegraph Rd, Taylor, MI 48180.

BURTON, JUANITA SHARON
Physician. **PERSONAL:** Born Sep 28, 1946, Philadelphia, PA; married Ronald A Burton, MSW,PhD. **EDUCATION:** Cabrini Coll Radnor PA, BS Biology 1973; Jefferson Medical Coll, MD 1977. **CAREER:** Presbyterian Univ of PA Med Ctr, internship 1977-78; Union Memorial Hosp Baltimore, resident ob/gyn 1978-80; Walter Reed Army Med Ctr DC, resident ob/gyn 1980-82; US Army MEDDAC Shape Belgium, staff physician 1982-85; US Army MEDDAC Ft Jackson SC, staff physician 1985-87, chief ob/gyn serv 1987-. **ORGANIZATIONS:** Mem Jr Fellow Amer Coll of Ob/Gyn 1980-; mem Assoc of Military Surgeons of US 1982-; mem Amer Med Women's Assoc 1986-. **HONORS/ACHIEVEMENTS:** US Army Commission Capt 1980; US Army Promotion Major 1983; Diplomate Amer Bd of Ob/Gyn 1985. **MILITARY SERVICE:** AUS major 7 yrs. **HOME ADDRESS:** 132 Parkshore Dr East, Columbia, SC 29223. **BUSINESS ADDRESS:** Chief Ob/Gyn Services, Moncrief Army Hospital, Fort Jackson, Columbia, SC 29207.

BURTON, LEROY MELVIN, JR.
Physician. **PERSONAL:** Born Sep 12, 1940, Statesville, NC; son of Mr & Mrs Leroy M Burton Sr; married Barbara Stokes Pannell; children: Randi Pannell, Lori, Albert Pannell II, Leslie. **EDUCATION:** Lincoln Univ PA, BA 1962; NC Coll, MS 1965; Meharry Med Coll, MD 1969. **CAREER:** Sunny Brook Med Center Raleigh NC, private practice internal med 1977; Meharry Med Coll, student health dir 1973-74; Meharry Med Coll, asst prof 1973-74. **ORGANIZATIONS:** Mem Nat Med Assn 1975; mem Old N State Med Soc 1975; mem LA Scruggs Med Soc 1975; mem Alpha Phi Alpha Frat 1959; mem Prince Hall Mason 1962. **HONORS/ACHIEVEMENTS:** Mem 32nd Degree Prince Hall Mason & Shriner 1976. **BUSINESS ADDRESS:** 100 Sunnybrook Rd, Ste 101, Raleigh, NC 27610.

BURTON, LEVAR
Actor. **EDUCATION:** Univ of Southern California. **CAREER:** Actor, Looking for Mr Goodbar 1977, Roots 1977, Almos' A Man 1977, Billy, Portrait of a St Kid 1979, Dummy 1979, The Hunter 1980, Guyana Tragedy, The Story of Jim Jones 1980; hosted 26 episodes of Rebop PBS series; actor, Liberty, NBC mini-series; host, PBS Reading Rainbow, 1983-. **BUSINESS ADDRESS:** Dolores Robinson Management, 7319 Beverly Blvd, Ste 7, Los Angeles, CA 90036.

BURTON, MICHAEL ANGELO
Automotive designer/stylist. **PERSONAL:** Born Aug 27, 1956, Lansing, MI; son of Denison Edward Burton and Jessie Lee Greene; married Sharon Mae Wesley, Dec 27, 1986. **EDUCATION:** Center for Creative Studies, Detroit MI, BFA, 1988. **CAREER:** Ford Motor Corp, Dearborn MI, automotive stylist, 1978-80; Chrysler Corp, Highland Park MI, automotive stylist, 1984—; minister of Greater Grace temple.

BURTON, PHILIP L.
Attorney. **PERSONAL:** Born Oct 28, 1915, Topeka, KS; married Octavia Walker; children: 2 children. **EDUCATION:** BBA 1939; JD 1948. **CAREER:** WA State Bd of Prison Terms & Paroles, atty 1961-63; Private Practice, attorney. **ORGANIZATIONS:** Mem Am Bar Assn; Nat Bar Assn; Nat Conf of Black Lawyers; Am Trial Lawyers Assn; WA State Bar Assn; Seattle-King Co Bar Assn; Loren Miller Law Club; NAACP; Urban League; United Way; mem King Co Wash Policy Dev Com; bd of trustees Seattle Comm Coll Dist 6. **HONORS/ACHIEVEMENTS:** Recipient William Robert Ming Advocacy Award 1978; Martin Luther King Humanitarian Award "The Medium Newspaper" 1979; Seattle Alumni Chap Award for Outstanding Serv to NAACP Kappa Alpha Psi 1979. **MILITARY SERVICE:** USAAF 1st Lt. **BUSINESS ADDRESS:** Attorney, Burton & Burton, 800 5th Ave, Ste 3500, Seattle, WA 98164.

BURTON, RONALD E.
Business executive. **PERSONAL:** Born Jul 25, 1936, Springfield, OH; married JoAnn Jourdain; children: Steven, Elizabeth, Ronald, Jr, Phillip, Paul. **EDUCATION:** NW U,bS Bus & Mktg 1960. **CAREER:** John Hancock Mutual Life Ins Co, pub rel exec 1966-; Wall St, stockbroker 3 yrs; Boston Patriots, running back 6 yrs; ABC-TV, sports commentators collgame of week 1969; ABC, commentator for Mon night game of week 1972; Pop Warner football league Charlestown, founder 1971. **ORGANIZATIONS:** Mem Republ St Fin Com; Framingham Pk Commn; mem Copr of Framingham Savings Bank; mem Hood Milk Phys Fit Prgm; Boy Scout Coun; Framingham YMCA; bddir Boston Evening Clinic; vice pres Northwestern Univ Club of Boston; advisory bd Salvation Army. **HONORS/ACHIEVEMENTS:** One of ten outs men in Boston 1967; various records & achvmts in football. **MILITARY SERVICE:** USNG & reserves 1960-65. **BUSINESS ADDRESS:** 200 Berkeley St, Boston, MA 02117.

BURTON, RONALD J.
Information services executive. **PERSONAL:** Born Jun 12, 1947, Montclair, NJ; son of Joseph Burton and Ruth Jackson Burton; married Carolyn Ievers, Oct 1975; children: Christopher, Alison. **EDUCATION:** Colgate Univ, Hamilton, NY, BA, History, Economics, 1969; Wharton School, Philadelphia, PA, graduate courses. **CAREER:** Dallas Cowboys, Dallas, TX, professional athlete, 1969; EI Dupont, Wilmington, DE, mktg mgr, 1969-74; RH Donnelley, New York, NY, mgr, 1975-87, vice pres, 1987-. **ORGANIZATIONS:** Bd mem, vice pres, Colgate Alumni Club, 1975-80, Montclair Public Schools, 1985-87; bd mem, George Jr Republic Assn, Ithaca, NY, 1979-85, Mountainside Hospital, Montclair, NJ, 1987-. **HONORS/ACHIEVEMENTS:** All-Amer Quarterback, Colgate, 1966-68; Maroon Citation, Colgate. **BUSINESS ADDRESS:** RH Donnelley, Dun & Bradstreet Co, 711 Third Ave, New York, NY 10017.

BURTON-JUNIOR, EVA WESTBROOK
Educator. **PERSONAL:** Born Jul 10, 1944, Yazoo City, MS; married EJ Junior Jr; children: Lori M Burton, Lesli M Burton. **EDUCATION:** TN State Univ Nashville, BS 1966, MA Ed 1972. **CAREER:** Catholic Schools Washington DC, lang arts teacher 1966-67, 1969-70; DC Public Schools, lang arts teacher 1967-69; Fed City Coll Wash DC, english instr 1968-69; Fisk Univ Nashville, reading instr 1974-75; Atlanta Public Schools Atltanta GA, english, reading teacher 1977-80; Spelman Coll Atlanta GA, english instr 1980-81; Fulton County Schools Atlanta GA, english teacher 1981-82; Morris Brown Coll Atlanta GA, english instr 1983-85; Ft Valley State Coll Ft ValleyGA, english instr 1986-. **ORGANIZATIONS:** Mem Modern Lang Assn 1968-70, Natl Educ Assn 1968-76, Delta Sigma Theta 1970-, Intl Reading Assn 1974-76, PTA of GA 1977-85 GA Assoc of Educators 1978-82; notary public-at-large Stae of GA 1978-; mem Girl Scouts of Amer 1979-84, Mayros' Task Force on Educ Atlanta GA 1982-84, Trinity Bapt Church 1986-. **HONORS/ACHIEVEMENTS:** Dean's List TN State Univ 1963-66; Excellence in Teaching Awd Atlanta Public Schools 1977-78; Cert of Outstanding Performance Morris Brown Coll Special Progs 1983-84-85; Cert of Outstanding Achievements and Appreciation for Dedicated Serv Alpha Phi Alpha, Iota Chapter, 1984 Morris Brown Coll. **HOME ADDRESS:** 103 Cochran Ct, Byron, GA 31008.

BURTON-LYLES, BLANCHE
Musician, educator. **PERSONAL:** Born Mar 02, 1933, Philadelphia, PA; daughter of Anthony Taylor-Burton and Blanche Taylor-Burton; married Thurman Wardell, Dec 07, 1957; children: Thedric Burton-Lyles. **EDUCATION:** Curtis Inst of Music, MusB 1954; Temple U, Phila, BMusEd 1971, MusM 1975. **CAREER:** Soc Orch of LeRoy Bostic's Mellowaires, pianist; tchr, concert pianist; society pianist. **ORGANIZATIONS:** Mem Delta Sigma Theta Sor 1954; Pro Arts Society. **HONORS/ACHIEVEMENTS:** 1st and youngest black piano soloist, NY Philharmonic Symphony Orch Carnegie Hall 1947; 1st black woman pianist to graduate, Curtis Inst of Music Philadelphia 1953; 1st black woman pianist to receive degree, Curtis Inst. **HOME ADDRESS:** 1118 S 19th St, Philadelphia, PA 19146.

BURWELL, WILLIAM DAVID, JR.
Educator. **PERSONAL:** Born Jan 09, 1942, Birmingham, AL; married Leslie; children: Edith, Anthony, Miata, Mandela, Shabazz. **EDUCATION:** San Fernando Valley State Coll, MA 1974, BA, 1970; Los Angeles Valley Coll, AA, 1967. **CAREER:** CA State Univ, chmn 1975-, asst prof 1969-75; San Fernando Valley State Coll, teacher operation & headstart, 1964-69, asst dir 1960. **ORGANIZATIONS:** Consult Southern CA Schl Dist; mem Southern CA Black Stud Alliance; consult Kent State Univ 1970; mem United Prof of CA 1969-; mem CA Assn of Black Faculty &Staff, 1976-; co-fndr CA State Univ Black Stud Union, 1967; chrm Afro Am of Pacoima, 1966; chrm La Valley Stud. **HONORS/ACHIEVEMENTS:** Recpt Civil Rights Org 1964 San Fernando Valley Youth Serv 1959; publ Right-on-Learning, 1975. **MILITARY SERVICE:** AUS sp4 1960-63. **BUSINESS ADDRESS:** 18111 Nordhoff St, Northridge, CA 91330.

BUSBY, EVERETT C.
Educator. **PERSONAL:** Born in Muskogee, OK. **EDUCATION:** Langston Univ Langston OK, BA Sociology, 1950; Univ of Norman, Cert in Social Work 1951; Univ of TX Austin, MSW 1953. **CAREER:** Fordham Univ Grad Sch of Social Svc, asso prof 1961-; Private Practice, supervising psychotherapist, triana & asso 1971-80; NIAAA HEW Wash DC, consult 1970-72; Seton Hall Coll of Medicine & Dentistry Jersey City NJ, instr & dept of psychiatry 1959-61; Kings Co Psychiatric Hosp NYC, psychiatric social worker 1956-59; US Army Med Serv Corps, psychiatric social worker 1953-55. **ORGANIZATIONS:** Consult training ed Bedford-Stuyvesant Youth in Act Brooklyn; consult training ed HARYOU-ACT NYC; mem bd %Educ & training Nat Council on Alcohol New York City Affl; mem Nat Assn of Black Soc Wrkrs 1985; mem Council on Soc Wrk Educ 1985; mem Am Assn of Univ Prof 1985; mem Nat Conf on Soc Welfare 1985; mem Nat Conf on SocWelfare 1985; mem Am Civil Liberties Union; mem Alpha Phi Alpha Frat. **MILITARY SERVICE:** AUS spec II 1951-53. **BUSINESS ADDRESS:** Fordham Univ Grad & Sch of Soc Sv, Lincoln Center Campus, New York, NY 10023.

BUSH, ANN
Educator. **PERSONAL:** Born Dec 05, 1939, Philadelphia, PA. **EDUCATION:** Cheyney State Coll, BS; Elem Educ Temple U, EdM; Elem & Urban Educ Temple U, EdD. **CAREER:** School Dist of Philadelphia, supt of schools; Univ School Relations Temple Univ, admin asst to dean; Philadelphia, Educ improvement cons; School Dist; Philadelphia School Dist, teacher; Temple Univ Coll of Educ, adjunct prof; School Dist of Philadelphia, reading teacher; Performance Appraisal of Admin & Suprs, spec cons; Temple Univ, competency based teacher educ. **ORGANIZATIONS:** Title 1 Review Com Educ Educ & Human Relat Com Assn for Field Serv in Tchr Edn; Black Educ Forum; Educ Equality Leag; Nat Counc of Adminstrv women in Edn; PA Assn for Supervsn & Curr Devel; PA Congress of Sch Adminstrs. **HONORS/ACHIEVEMENTS:** Phi Delta Kappa Serv Award TempleUniv 1975; bicentennial award Nat Assn ofUniv Women; awards of apprec Linpark Civic Assn Trevose PA; Morton Mcmichael SchPhiladelphia PA; charter mem PA Congress of Sch Adminstrs; Philadelphia Black Women's Educ Alliance. **BUSINESS ADDRESS:** HS for International Affairs, 4th & George Sts, Philadelphia, PA 19123.

BUSH, CHARLES VERNON
Business executive. **PERSONAL:** Born Dec 17, 1939, Tallahassee, FL; son of Charles Bush and Marie Bush; married Bettina; children: 3 children. **EDUCATION:** USAF Acad, BS Engrg 1963; Georgetown Univ, MA Intl Relations 1964; Harvard Univ Grad School of Business Admin, MBA Finance 1972. **CAREER:** USAF, intelligence officer 1963-70; White Weld & Co Inc, assoc corp financier 1972-74; Celanese Corp, asst treas 1974-78; Max Factor & Co, vp, treas 1978-80, vp, corp controller 1980-83; ICN Pharmaceuticals Inc, vice pres fin, CEO 1983-85; Greenberg, Glusker, Fields, Claman & Machtinger, exec dir 1985-87; Unicel Inc, executive vice president, 1987-89. **ORGANIZATIONS:** Bd of dir United Mutual Ins Co 1976-78; mem Financial Exec Inst 1978-; exec council Harvard Bus School Alumni Assn 1978-83; bd of dir Harvard Business School Southern CA Alumni Assoc 1981-84, Harvard Business School Black Alumni Assoc. **MILITARY SERVICE:** USAF capt; Bronze Star Medal, Joint Serv Commendation Medal, Air Force Commendation Medal with Oak Leaf Cluster. **HOME ADDRESS:** 23022 Mosby St, Woodland Hills, CA 91364.

BUSH, LENORIS
Executive director. **PERSONAL:** Born Jul 18, 1949, Colquitt, GA; married Helen. **EDUCATION:** Para-Prof Inst, Social Serv Aide 1969; Univ of UT, sociology 1975; Westminster Coll, BS Behavioral Science 1977; Univ of Phoenix, MBA 1984. **CAREER:** Probation Dept Juvenile Court, caseworker 1968-69; Granite Comm Mental Health Center, mental health aide 1969-70; Second Dist Juvenile Court, probation officer 1970-74; UT Opportunity Industrial Center, job developer/indust relations dir 1976, dir program operation 1977, deputy dir 1977-78, exec dir 1978-. **ORGANIZATIONS:** C of C Indust Dev Comm; UTA Adv Bd 1978-; Apprenticeship Outreach Bd 1977-; Co-Op Exoffender Pgm Bd 1977-80; Blacks Unlimited Bd Dir 1977-; CentralCity and Summer Sch Bd 1974; youth rep Salt Lake Cnty ETD Instit Task Force 1978; asst chairpers Support Serv Task Force for ETD 1978; asst chair Salt Lake Cnty Manpower Planning Cncl 1978; mem Exec Dir Assn of OIC's of Amer 1978; mem Reg Plann comm for OIC's of Amer 1978; mem PIC; bd mem Black Adv Cncl; Governor's Vocational Educ Adv Cncl; Natl Alliance of Businessmen 1980; NAACP 1980-; Black Adv Cncl State Bd of Edn; C of C 1979-; NAACP Scholarship Found 1981; mem Minority Coalition 1981; reg adv bd SBA 1983; Vocational Adv Bd Salt Lake Sch Dist 1985; 1st vice pres Salt Lake NAACP 1985; chmn Black Educ Scholarship Found 1982. **HOME ADDRESS:** 2528 Imperial St, Salt Lake City, UT 84109.

BUSH, MARY K.
Banker. **PERSONAL:** Born Apr 09, 1948, Birmingham, AL. **EDUCATION:** Columbia Univ, summer internship 1967; Yale Univ, summer internship 1968; Fisk Univ, BA econ 1969; Univ of Chicago, MBA fin 1971. **CAREER:** Chase Manhattan Bank NA, credit analyst 1971-73; Citibank NA, account officer 1973-76; Bankers Trust Co, vp, world corp dept 1976-82; US Treasury Dept, exec asst to dep secy 1982-85; Intl Monetary Fund, us alternate ed 1984-. **ORGANIZATIONS:** Vchair, treas Women's World Banking NY 1983-, Exec Women in Gov 1984-, Univ of Chicago Bus School 1979-; bd of trustees YMCA Washington DC 1985-. **HONORS/ACHIEVEMENTS:** Scott Paper Co Leadership Awd; Who's Who in Finance and Industry; Outstanding Young Women of Amer; Who's Who in Amer Coll & Univ. **HOME ADDRESS:** 4201 Cathedral Ave NW, Washington, DC 20016. **BUSINESS ADDRESS:** US Alternate Exec Dir, Intl Monetary Fund, 700 19th St NW Rm 13-320, Washington, DC 20431.

BUSH, NATHANIEL
Attorney. **PERSONAL:** Born Jan 19, 1949, Washington, DC; son of Thelmen Bush and Elouise Graves Bush; married Marsha Diane Jackson; children: Traci, Nathan. **EDUCATION:** Ripon Coll, BA 1973; Cleveland Marshall Coll of Law, JD 1977; Wharton Sch of Business, certificate 1984. **CAREER:** Distinguished visiting Prof of Law Cambridge Univ, grad asst 1976-77; Bureau of ATF Dept of Treas, attorney 1979-81; Univ of the District of Columbia, adjunct prof criminology 1982-84; DC State Campaign Jesse Jackson for Pres, general counsel 1983-84; DC Bd of Educ, vice pres; Ward VII rep. **ORGANIZATIONS:** Bd of dir Southeast Neighbors Citizens Assoc; bd of dirs Far East Comm Serv Inc; chmn bd of dirs Concerned Citizens on Alcohol & Drug Abuse; mem Bar of the State of OH 1977; mem Bar of the District of Columbia 1979. **HONORS/ACHIEVEMENTS:** Moot Court Bd of Govs Cleveland Marshall Coll of Law; 1st place Third Annual Douglas Moot Court Competition 1975; Jessup Intl Moot Court Competition 1976; Outstanding Young Men of America, 1984. **HOME ADDRESS:** 1119 44th Place SE, Washington, DC 20019. **BUSINESS ADDRESS:** Vice President, DC Bd of Education, 415 12th St NW, Washington, DC 20019.

BUSH, T. W.
Law administrator. **EDUCATION:** Morehouse Coll Atlanta GA, 1963-64; Univ of GA, Mgmt Devel 1982-; US Dept of Justice, Human Relations 1982; Southern Police Inst GA Police Acad, Admin Officers Varied in Serv Training, 1984. **CAREER:** Dekalb Cty Dept Public Safety, patrolman 1974-79, master patrolman 1979-80, sgt 1980-82, lt 1982-. **HONORS/ACHIEVEMENTS:** Numerous Commendations Intradepartmental; Police Officer of the Month DEK Civic Org 1980. **BUSINESS ADDRESS:** Lieutenant, Dekalb Cty Public Safety, 4400 Memorial Dr Complex, Decatur, GA 30032.

BUSKEY, JOHN
State legislator. **CAREER:** Alabama House of Representatives, Montgomery AL, state representative, district 77. **BUSINESS ADDRESS:** House of Representatives, State Capitol, Montgomery, AL 36130. *

BUSSEY, CHARLES DAVID
Public relations. **PERSONAL:** Born Dec 08, 1933, Edgefield, SC; son of Alex William Bussey, Sr and Mattie Lou Bussey; married Eva Lois Gray, Jul 01, 1967; children: Terri Lyn, Tonia Marie, Charles F. **EDUCATION:** A&T Coll of North Carolina, Greensboro, BS, English 1955; Indiana Univ, MA, Journalism 1970; Shippensburg State, MS, Communications 1974. **CAREER:** Chief Legislative Liaison HQ, Exec to the Chief, 1975-76; 2nnd Infantry Div, Korea, Commander, 2nd Brigade, 1976-77; OFC Chief of Public Affairs HQ, Chmn of Policy & Plans, 1977-80; 172D Inf Bde, Deputy Commander, Chief of Staff, 1980-82; HQ Dept of the Army, Dept Chief of Public Affairs, 1982-84, Chief of Public Affairs, 1984-87; HQ AMC, Dept Chief of Staff for Personnel, 1987-present. **ORGANIZATIONS:** Mem, Alpha Phi Alpha, 1953-present, Assn of US Army, 1955-present, A&T SU Alumni Assn, 1960-present, Indiana Univ Alumni Assn, 1970-present, Rocks Inc, 1975-present, PRSA, 1986-present. **HONORS/ACHIEVEMENTS:** ROTC Hall of Fame, A&T SU, 1969; Outstanding Alumnus, A&T SU, 1970; Distinguished Alumnus, Indiana Univ, 1983; Articles on Leadership, Management, Discipline & Training published in Army, Armor, Infantry, Military Review, & Buffalo Magazines; Order of the Palmetto, State of South Carolina, 1987; Accredited in Public Relations, PRSA, 1989. **MILITARY SERVICE:** AUS, Major General, over 30 years; Distinguished Service Medal, Legion of Merit; Bronze Star; Meritorious Service Medal; Air Medal; Army Commendation Medal; Combat Infantry Badge; Expert Infantry Badge; Parachutist Badge; Rok Order of Matl Security Merit. **HOME ADDRESS:** 6302 Martins Lane, Lanham-Seabrook, MD 20706.

BUSSEY, REUBEN T.
Attorney. **PERSONAL:** Born Mar 07, 1943, Atlanta, GA. **EDUCATION:** Morris Brown Coll, BA 1965; TX So Univ Law Sch, JD 1969. **CAREER:** Kennedy, Bussey & Sampson, ptnr 1971-76; Fed Trade Commn, Boston, atty 1969-71; Legal Aid Soc, Inc, Atlanta, staff mem 1969; St Bar of TX, admtd 1969; GA Bar, 1971. **ORGANIZATIONS:** Mem Hsg Task Force; Atlanta C of C; Gate City Bar Assn, & Atlanta; Nat Bar Assn. **HONORS/ACHIEVEMENTS:** Who's Who Among Stds in Am U's & Coll 1965, 1968-69; Outstndg Young Men in Am 1972; Who's Who in GA 1973; Who's Who in Am Law; Outstdng Personalities in the S. **BUSINESS ADDRESS:** 171 Ashby St SW, Atlanta, GA 30314.

BUSTAMANTE, JOHN H.
Attorney. **PERSONAL:** Born Aug 11, 1929, Santiago, Cuba;married Joy; children: Tuan, Sonali, Andre, Kamala, Joachim. **EDUCATION:** Boston Univ, AB, JD; Harvard Univ, LLM. **CAREER:** Harrison-Ross Mortuaries Inc; Higbee Co; N OH Redevel Corp; JW Wills Co, dir sec gen cnsl; PW Pub Co, dir vice pres gen legal cnsl; John H Bustamante Co LPA & Devel Intl Inc, dir chmn bd; OH Civil Rights Commn, state of hearing examiner; First Bank Natl Assn, chmn chief exec; Cleveland, attorney. **ORGANIZATIONS:** Mem Amer Bar Assn, Natl Bar Assn; bd trustees Central State Univ. **HONORS/ACHIEVEMENTS:** Booker T Washington Symbol of Service Awd The Business League's highest honor. **BUSINESS ADDRESS:** Terminal Tower #800, 50 Public Sq, Cleveland, OH 44113.

BUTCHER, GOLER TEAL
Attorney. **PERSONAL:** Born Jul 13, 1925, Phila; married George T; children: Lily, Georgette, George, Caryl. **EDUCATION:** Univ PA, AB 1946; Howard U, LLB 1957; Univ PA, LLM 1958. **CAREER:** Judge Hastie 3rd Circuit, law clerk 1958-59; Legal Aid, atty 1960-62; Library of Congress, legal analyst 1962-63; Dept of St, atty 1963-71; Ho Subcom on Africa, cons, Counsel 1971-74; Private Law Practice, 1974-. **ORGANIZATIONS:** Mem Dem Fgn-Affairs Task Force; co-chmn Dem Study Group on Africa; mem bd trustees Lawyers Com on Civil Rights Under Law; mem Com on Soc Respnsblty;exec council Episcopal Ch; mem exec council Am Soc of Interntl Law; mem Disciplinary Bd; DC Bar; mem Nat Conf Black Lawyers; Nat Assn Black Women Attys; Interntl Adv Cncl; African-Am Inst; African Legal Asst Proj Subcom, Lawyers' Com. **HONORS/ACHIEVEMENTS:** Phi Beta Kappa 1945. **BUSINESS ADDRESS:** 1156 15 St NW, Ste 302, Washington, DC 20005.

BUTCHER, PHILIP
Educator, writer. **PERSONAL:** Born Sep 28, 1918, Washington, DC; son of James W Butcher and Jennie Jones Butcher; married Ruth B; children: 2. **EDUCATION:** Howard Univ, AB, MA; Columbia Univ, PhD. **CAREER:** Opportunity, Journal of Negro Life 1947-48; Morgan State Coll, English tchr 1947-49, asst prof 1949-56, assoc prof 1956-59; SC State Coll, visiting prof 1958; Morgan State Univ, prof 1959-79, dean grad sch 1972-75, prof emeritus 1979-. **ORGANIZATIONS:** Mem Coll Language Assn; Modern Language Assn; Soc Study So Literature; Lectr many coll & univ. **HONORS/ACHIEVEMENTS:** Gen Educ Bd & John Hay Whitney Fellowship; Creative Scholarship Award Coll Language Assn 1964; many research grants; many citations, reference works; many books & articles pub. **MILITARY SERVICE:** AUS T/Sgt 1943-46.

BUTLER, ANNA M. (NEE LAND)
Educator. **PERSONAL:** Born Oct 07, 1901, Philadelphia, PA; married Floyd Butler; children: Maurice A Hayes Jr dec. **EDUCATION:** Trenton State Coll, 1922; Temple Univ, 1953; Univ of MD, 1942-45. **CAREER:** Pittsburgh Courier, newspaper corr 1936-65; Atlantic Publ School, teacher 1952-64; Mag Responsibility, ed 1955-59; Eastern Area Natl Links Jrnl, assoc ed 1967-70; Morris Child Care Ctr, head instr, dir 1969-72. **ORGANIZATIONS:** Pres Eastern Seabord Council Heritage House 1954-; vice pres NJ Org for Teachers, Episcopal Church; mem Philadelphia Cath Poetry Soc 1960-66, Bermuda Writers Club 1961; exec bd Atlantic City Ed Assoc 1962-64; mem Northside Bus & Professional Womens Club 1961-66; mem Ed Council Atlantic Human Resources Inc 1965, Amer Poets Fellowship Soc, Natl Soc Literature & the Arts 1975-, Intercontinental Biog Assoc, England Ed Writers Assoc; vice pres Atlantic Dist Epis Churchwomen Diocese of NJ; churchwomen St Augustines Church 1975; dist chmn Atlantic Dist NJ Episcopal Diocese & Atlantic Dist; recording sec, bd mem St Augustine Episcopal Church; charter mem, bd dir Philadelphia Cotillion Soc; charter mem Phi Delta Kappa Natl Soc Iota Chapt; mem Planning Comm Bal Masque, NJFed Colored Womens Clubs; mem bd Atlantic Cty Cultural & Heritage. **HONORS/ACHIEVEMENTS:** Versatile Teacher Awd 1953; Natl Links Inc Creative Achievement Awd 1960; Teacher of the Year Awd NJ Org of Teachers 1961; named Poet Laureate of EasternArea Links Natl Inc; Legion of Honor Awd Chapel of Four Chaplains 1963; Sachs Cert of Recognition 1963; Northside Bus & Professional Womens Achievement Awd 1963; Theta Phi Lambda Sor Womens Showcase Awd, Merit Awd 1964; Natl Assoc Sojourner Truth Awd 1966; Cert of Merit United Jaycees 1967; Theta Kappa Omega Chap AKA Black Women Comm Serv Awd 1970; Citation Creative Writing New Orleans 1972; Cert of Awd of Achievement Outstanding Negro Woman, Imperial Daughters of Isis 1972; Cert of Apprec Natl Links Inc 1972; Pres Serv Awd Atlantic City Chap Links Inc 1973; Citation Religious Leadership, Women of Valor, Unionof Amer Hebrew Congregations, Cultural Serv 1975; Eugene Wayman Jones Cultural Civil Awd 1975; listed in num Who's Who Publs, Who's Who of Intellectuals, Dictionary Intl Biography, Black Amer Writers Past & Present.

BUTLER, ANNETTE G.
Attorney. **PERSONAL:** Born Jun 23, 1944, Cleveland, OH; divorced; children: Christopher, Kimberley. **EDUCATION:** Case Western Reserve Univ, BA 1966; Cleveland State/Cleveland Marshall Law, JD 1970. **CAREER:** Civil rights specialist, D/HEW Office of Civil Rights, 1970-74; assoc atty, Guren, Merritt, Sogg & Cohen, 1974-81; dir legal affairs, Office of School Monitoring, 1981-82; asst US Atty, Atty Office ND OH, 1982-. **ORGANIZATIONS:** Trustee, vice pres grievance comm Cleveland Bar Assn; founder, past pres Black Women Lawyers Assn; bar admissions OH 6th Circuit Court of Appeals; Supreme Court of US; trustee, treas, vice-chmn, Cleveland State Univ; past pres Cleveland City Club; past pres

Cleveland Heights Univ Library Bd; bd of trustees Shaker Heights Recreation Bd. **HONORS/ACHIEVEMENTS:** Distinguished Serv Cleveland Jaycees; Outstanding Achievment Narrator Cleveland Chapter Natl Acad Arts & Sciences; Woman of Year Negro Business & Professional Club; Outstanding Achievement Cuyahoga County Bar Assn; Outstanding Young Woman of Amer; Distinguished Alumnus Award, Cleveland State Univ; member, Golden Key Natl Honor Soc. **HOME ADDRESS:** 13901 Larchmere Blvd, Shaker Heights, OH 44120. **BUSINESS ADDRESS:** Attorney, US Dept Justice Atty Ofc, 1404 E Ninth St, Cleveland, OH 44114.

BUTLER, B. JANELLE
Attorney. **PERSONAL:** Born Jul 26, 1949, Springfield, MA. **EDUCATION:** Howard Univ Sch of Business, BA 1971; Howard Univ Sch of Law, JD 1975; Admitted to Ohio State Bar 1975. **CAREER:** State of OH, asst atty gen 1975-78; Toledo Legal Aid Soc, exec dir 1978-. **ORGANIZATIONS:** Toledo Bar Assn Asst; bd of dir Zonta II of Toledo; pres Thurgood Marshall Law Assn. **HONORS/ACHIEVEMENTS:** Outstanding Young Women of Amer; Delta Sigma Theta Sor Toledo Alumnal Chpt. **BUSINESS ADDRESS:** Executive Dir, Toledo Legal Aid Society, 1 Stranahan Sq, Ste 540, Toledo, OH 43604.

BUTLER, BENJAMIN WILLARD
Surgeon. **PERSONAL:** Born Feb 27, 1933, Detroit, MI; son of Marvin L Butler and Millie L Butler; married Ernestine Laverne Carter; children: Kenneth, Kevin, Karla. **EDUCATION:** Univ MI, 1950-54; Meharry Med Coll, 1955-59. **CAREER:** VA Hosp, res; Childrens Hosp, 1964; Detroit Rec Hosp, intern 1959-60. **ORGANIZATIONS:** Cert Amer bd of Surgery; Amer Soc of Abdominal Surgery; fellow Am Coll of Surg; OH St Med Assn; past-pres Toledo Surgical Soc; Toledo Acad of Med; clinical assistant professor Med Coll of OH; Natl Med Assn, Society of Amer Gastrointestinal Endoscopic Surgeons. **HONORS/ACHIEVEMENTS:** Local pres Sigma Pi Phi; past-pres Frontiers Interntl; Kappa Alpha Psi; elder Grace United Presby Ch; mem NAACP; published "Bilateral Congential Lumbar Hernia" 1966-67; published "Successful Immediate Repair of a Traumatic Aorta-Inferior Vena Cava Fistula" 1974. **MILITARY SERVICE:** USN lt comm 1960-62. **BUSINESS ADDRESS:** Surgeon, 2052 Collingwood Blvd, Toledo, OH 43620.

BUTLER, BROADUS NATHANIEL
Retired educator. **PERSONAL:** Born May 28, 1920, Mobile, AL; married Lillian Rutherford, MEd; children: Bruce Nathaniel MD, Janet Cecile Reid PhD. **EDUCATION:** Talladega Coll, BA 1941; Univ of MI, MA 1947, PhD 1952. **CAREER:** St Augustine's Coll, instr 1953; Talladega Coll, dean of guidance & asst prof 1953-56; Wayne State Univ Detroit, asst to dean coll of lib arts 1956; US Commr of Educ & Assoc Commr for Higher Educ, special asst 1964-67; TX So Univ Houston, dean coll lib arts/prof philos 1969; Dillard Univ New Orleans, pres 1969-73; Amer Coun on Educ Washington, dir office of leadership devel in higher educ 1974-77; Robert R Moton Inst, pres 1978-81; NAACP Natl Bd, dir intl affairs 1981-83; KY State Univ Ely Lilly found Scholar, distinguished visiting prof 1984, retired 1985; John D and Catherine T McArthur Foundation UNCF distinguished scholar-at-large 1987-88; director of archives, Dr Martin Luther King, Jr Center for Nonviolent Social Change 1989. **ORGANIZATIONS:** Bd dir Natl Merit Schol Corp 1970-; life mem NAACP; bd dir Natl NAACP 1977; vice pres NAACP 1979; bd dir Publ Mem Assn Foreign Serv 1978; mem adv council to US Dept HEW & Natl Inst Health; mem Amer Assn for High Educ; bd mem Center for Study of the Presidency 1976-. **HONORS/ACHIEVEMENTS:** Grand Comdr Order of Star of Africa Liberia, W Africa 1971; numerous outstanding citizen awards/certificates of merit; Book: Lessons From the 1984 Presidental Candidacy of the Reverend Jesse Louis Jackson 1988; Book: Trilogy on Two Constitutions and Ex-Slave Frederick Douglas 1988. **MILITARY SERVICE:** USAF 332nd Fighter Group 1942-45. **HOME ADDRESS:** 1025 Marion Ave, Cincinnati, OH 45229.

BUTLER, CHARLES H.
Physician. **PERSONAL:** Born Feb 12, 1925, Wilmington, DE; married Barbara; children: Yvonne, Kathy, Charla, Leslie. **EDUCATION:** IN Univ; Univ PA; Meharry Med Coll, MD 1953. **CAREER:** Private Practice, physician. **ORGANIZATIONS:** Mem Nat Med Assn; Am Acad Faminly Physicians; PA E PA Med Soc; staff Coatesville Hosp; former health officer & Borough S Coatesville; med adv Loacl Draft Bd Pres PA State Conf NAACP; pres Coatesville Br NAACP; vice pres Unite Political Actin Com; Chester County; past pres Chester County Rep Club former exec com 32 deg Mason; mem Charles E Gordon Consistory #65; IBPOE Wilmington; treas past pres Pan-hellenic Assembly Chester County; past v polemarch Wilmington Alumni Chap Kappa Alpha Psi; mem Natl Bd NAACP. **HONORS/ACHIEVEMENTS:** Life mem Humanitarian Award SE; Chester Cou Bus and Prof Women's Culb Inc 1973; Mason & of Yr 1967; Citation Optimist Club of Coatesville 1972; Community Achievement Award Lily of the Valley Lodge #59 1973. **MILITARY SERVICE:** USN discharged as lt sr grade. **BUSINESS ADDRESS:** NAACP, 134 N 4th Ave, Coatesville, PA 19320.

BUTLER, CHARLES W.
Clergyman. **PERSONAL:** Born May 04, 1922, Dermott, AR; married Helen Odean Scoggins; children: Charles Jr, Beverly, Keith, Kevin. **EDUCATION:** Philander Smith Coll, BA 1939; Union Theol Sem, BD 1949, MDiv 1971; Columbia Univ, residence for PhD 1951; Interdenom Theol Ctr Morehouse School of Religion, DD 1980; Birmingham Bapt Bible School, 1980. **CAREER:** St James Presb Church NYC, asst to the pastor 1947-50; New York City Mission Soc, released time teacher 1950-51; Bapt Ctr NYC, teacher 1950-51; Morehouse Coll Atlanta, teacher Bible lit & religon 1951-54; Met Bapt Church Detroit, pastor 1954-63; New Calvary Bapt Church, pastor 1963-. **ORGANIZATIONS:** Pres MI Progressive Bapt Conv Detroit 1962-64; bd dir Interdenom Theol Ctr Detroit 1978-; mem Morehouse School Religion Atlanta; dir org 1st Ind Natl Bank Detroit 1970; chmn bd Police Comm City Detroit 1976; mem adv bd MI Consol Gas Co Detroit 1980-86; pres Progressive Natl Bapt Conv Washington 1982-84; pres Bapt Pastors Council Detroit 1987-; mem Alpha Phi Alpha; chmn bd, Congress of NationalBlack Churches, 1988. **HONORS/ACHIEVEMENTS:** Man of the Year MI Chronicle 1962. **MILITARY SERVICE:** AUS 1943-46. **BUSINESS ADDRESS:** Pastor, New Calvary Baptist Church, 3975 Concord St, Detroit, MI 48207.

BUTLER, CLARY KENT
Minister, broadcaster. **PERSONAL:** Born Jul 05, 1948, Charleston, SC; son of Carl Dallas Butler and Mary Capers Butler; married Patsy Swint Butler, Sep 20, 1970; children: Tammy R, Clary K, Jr, Cora L. **EDUCATION:** South Carolina State Coll, Orangeburg SC, BA, 1970; Webster Univ, Charleston (AFB) Branch, 1986-87. **CAREER:** Berkeley Broadcasting Corp. WMCJ Radio, Monicks Corner SC, 1984. **ORGANIZATIONS:** Mem, Omega Psi Phi, 1968—; mem/pastor, House of God Church, 1980-89; bd mem, Charleston County Branch (Amer Cancer Soc) 1985; mem, Berkeley County Chamber of Commerce, 1989; dir at large, SC Broadcasters Assn, 1989. **BUSINESS ADDRESS:** Pres, Berkeley Broadcasting Corp, WMCJ-AM, 314 Rembert Dennis Blvd, P O Box 67, Moncks Corner, SC 29461.

BUTLER, ERNEST DANIEL
Clergyman. **PERSONAL:** Born Jan 11, 1913, Connersville, IN; married Mary L Jones; children: Ernest E, Robert J, William D, Grayce L, Albert R, Florence M, Marye Anne, James L. **EDUCATION:** Simmons Univ, BS 1937; Franklin Coll; Simmons Univ; Moody Bible Sch; Central Theological Seminary Indianapolis, IN, DD 1981. **CAREER:** Mt Zion Bapt Ch, pastor 1934-49; 1st Baptist Ch, pastor 1949-59; 2nd Baptist Church, pastor. **ORGANIZATIONS:** Mem Natl Bapt Conv of Amer 1945-75; dir youth activ IN Shepherd Boy's League 1962-72; vice-moderator/moderator SE Dist IN Missionary Bapt 1964-73; moderator So Eastern Dist 1982-85; chmn IN Missionary Bapt State Educ Bd 1971-75; guest lectr Dept Guidance & Soc Serv IN Univ; Charter mem MU Sigma Chi 1934-73; dir Noblesville Boy's Club 1949-59; NAACP 1958-73; adv bd YMCA 1962-69; v chmn IN Citizens Fair Housing Com 1962-66 (chmn 1966-71); chrmn Mayor's Commn on Human Relations 1964-67; mem bd dir Comm Action Prog 1965-71; bd mem/chmn Family Serv Agency 1965-72; mem IN State Libr Adv Cncl Bloomington Traffic Commn 1973-75. **HONORS/ACHIEVEMENTS:** Recip Minister of Year Award Hamilton Co IN 1956; Man of the Year Monroe Co Serv Council 1962; Disting Serv Award Omega Psi Phi 1971; Disting Serv Award Joint Action for Comm Serv 1972; Chmn Monroe Cnty Comm Serv Cncl 1983-85; 14 years Disting Serv to Church 1973; Humanitarian Awd Indiana Governor's Volunteer Program 1987; Author poems Sat Evening Post; weekly & monthly sermons & lectures published in city & state publs. **BUSINESS ADDRESS:** Pastor, Second Baptist Church, 321 N Rogers St, Bloomington, IN 47401.

BUTLER, EUGENE THADDEUS, JR.
Educator. **PERSONAL:** Born Dec 03, 1922, Washington, DC; married Dorothy Mary Dickson; children: Eugene T. **EDUCATION:** Modesto Jr Coll, AA 1960; Stanislaus State Coll CA, BA 1965; SD State U, MEd 1969; SD State U, PhD 1980. **CAREER:** SD State Univ Brookings, EEO compliance officer/Title IX 1975-, Handicapped, coordinator; SD State Univ Brookings, grad research/Teaching asst 1970-73. **ORGANIZATIONS:** Vp & past sec Pi Gamma Mu Local (Nat Social Sci Honor Soc 1973; mem Alpha Kappa Delta Nat Sociology Honor Soc Gamma Sigma Delta #Pres; mem Nat Agricultural Honor Soc Phi Kappa Phi. **HONORS/ACHIEVEMENTS:** Co-author of various publ; recipient USAF Commendation Medal; recipient Air Medal with Oak Leaf Cluster/Ggod Conduct Medal/10 Year Combat Crew Duty Cert USAF1943-70. **MILITARY SERVICE:** USAF lt col 1943-70. **BUSINESS ADDRESS:** University Station, Brookings, SD 57007.

BUTLER, EULA M.
Educator. **PERSONAL:** Born Oct 15, 1927, Houston; married Henry C (deceased). **EDUCATION:** TX So Univ, BS 1954, MED 1958; Univ of TX, Grad Study; Prairie View Univ, Educ & Psy, Counseling & Guidance; TX So Univ, Spec Educ, Vstg Teaching, Counselor; Mount Hope Bihle Coll, DM 1984. **CAREER:** Region IV Educ Serv Center, TX Educ Agency; classroom teacher; visiting teacher, counselor, first teacher certified with Head Start Prog; writing demonstrator; workshop presenter; TX Southern Univ, public relations, community 1985-87; After School Tutorial Prog Inc, founder, dir, educ cons, mgr. **ORGANIZATIONS:** First State Coord Rehab & Prog for Fed Female Offenders; mem Delta Sigma Theta Sor; comm-counselor Parents & Students; mem YWCA Nat Cncl Negro Women Top Ladies of Distin; mem Am Judicature Soc; bd dirs ARC mem Harris Co Grand Jury 1974-; Harris Co bd dirs; Girl Scout bd dirs; mem Task Force Quality Integrate Educ Houston Independent Sch Dist; dir SW Region Delta Sigma Theta; past pres Houston Chap Delta Sigma Theta; Am PGA NEA TSTA Guid & Gounseling Assn; bd mem Natl Delta Rsch & Educ Found Inc, 1985-88, Vstg Nurses Assoc, The Light House of Houston, Natl Housing & Properties, DeltaSigma Theta, Houston Network For Family Life Education; mem of bd Houston Enrichment of Life Prog Inc; bd mem Metro Teacher Educ Ctr, Volunteers In Public School, Houston Independent School Dist. **HONORS/ACHIEVEMENTS:** Teacher of the Year Awd 1969; Comm Leadership Awd; Delta Sigma Theta Cert of Appreciation; United Negro Coll Fund Leadership Awd; Golden Life Mem Delta Sigma Theta Sor; Black History in the Making Awd 1986; Christian Serv Awd Beth Baptist Church 1985; Community Serv Awd Mt Corinth Baptist Church 1985; School After School Awd presented by School After School Faculty & Staff 1985; Recognition of Excellence Achievement Awd Phillis Wheatley High School 1985. **BUSINESS ADDRESS:** Dir & Founder, Schl After Schl Basic Skills, Tutorial Program Inc, PO Box 15757, Houston, TX 77020.

BUTLER, FREDERICK DOUGLAS
Attorney. **PERSONAL:** Born Nov 05, 1942, Philadelphia, PA; married Carolyn Gatlin; children: Frederick Douglas II. **EDUCATION:** Rutgers Univ, BA 1974; New York Univ, MA 1977; Univ of CA Hastings Coll of Law, JD 1986. **CAREER:** Newark Housing Authority, dir of family & comm serv 1973-80; White Plains Housing Auth, exec dir 1980-81; Govt of Trinidad & Tobago Natl Housing Auth,consultant 1984-85; Carroll Burdick & McDonough, attorney. **ORGANIZATIONS:** Mem World Affairs Counsel, Amer Soc of Public Administration, Inst of Real Estate Mgmt, Natl Assoc of Housing Officials, Afro-Amer Historical Soc; former pres United Comm Corp Newark NJ, Newark Citizen's Adv Bd, Soul-House Drug Abuse Prog, NJ Coll of Medicine & Dentistry. **HONORS/ACHIEVEMENTS:** Community Service Awds Newark TEnants Council, Service Employees Intl Union, Newark Central Ward Little League, Frontiers Intl; Amer Jurisprudence Awd. **MILITARY SERVICE:** USAF A2C 4 yrs; Good Conduct Medal. **HOME ADDRESS:** 370 Turk St #229, San Francisco, CA 94102.

BUTLER, HOMER L.
Educator, pharmacist. **PERSONAL:** Born Dec 23, 1934, Trenton, NJ; son of Homer Butler and Freda Sapp Belk; married Andrea Reule; children: Paul, Jeremy. **EDUCATION:** Temple Univ, BS 1958; Sangamon State Univ, MA 1980. **CAREER:** NJ State Hosp, psychiat tech 1951-52; sub postal clerk 1954-56; FMC Corps, lab tech 1958-61; Sangamon State Univ, asst dean 1970-71, assoc dean studentsvcs 1971-73, dean students 1973-79, dean of student serv 1979-. **ORGANIZATIONS:** Vol Peace Corps 1962-64; assoc dir Peace Corps Dakar 1964-66; dir Peace Corps Chad 1964-68; dep dir Peace Corps Ft Lamy Africa 1966-68; dir Div Specialized Recuriting Office of Vol Placement Peace Corps 1969-70; vice pres Sangamon Co United Way 1978-80; bd of dirs Girl Scouts 1980-86; Omega Psi Phi Frat. **HONORS/ACHIEVEMENTS:** Outstanding Alumni Awd Temple Univ 1967. **MILITARY SER-**

VICE: AUS sp-5 1956-58. BUSINESS ADDRESS: Dean of Students, Sangamon StateUniv, Shepard Rd, Springfield, IL 62794-9273.

BUTLER, J. RAY
Clergyman. **PERSONAL:** Born Aug 05, 1923, Roseboro, NC; married Marion C Lucas; children: Charles, Ellis, Larry, Vincent. **EDUCATION:** Shaw U, BA & BD; Friendship Coll, 1964; Southeastern Theol Sem 1966-67; Shaw U, DD 1973; Shaw Div Sch, MDiv 1974; McKinley Theol Sem LLD 1977; Southeastern Theol Seminary DTh 1969. **CAREER:** Ebenezer Bapt Ch Wilmington, pastor 1954-70; First Bapt Ch Creedmoor, pastor; Mt Olive Bapt Ch Fayeteville, pastor; New Christian Chapel Bapt Ch RoseHill, pastor; Shiloh Bapt Church Winston-Salem, pastor 1970-. **ORGANIZATIONS:** Past pres Interdenom Ministerial All; past pres Interracieal Minist Assn; past pres Wilmington Civic League; past pres PTA; 1st vice pres NAACP; bd of dirARC; mem Man Power Delvel; mem Citizens Coalition Bd; pres-at-large Gen Bapt State Conv; pres Bapt Ministers Conf & Asso; mem Forsyth Clergy Assn Chmn of Gen Bapt St Conv of NC Inc; mem extension tchg staff of Shaw U; exec bd of Lott Carey Bapt Foreign Missions & Conv; appointed bd of licensed gen contractors Gov Jim Hunt of NC. **HONORS/ACHIEVEMENTS:** Various tours in foreign countries; Who's Who Among Black Am; Pastor of Yr Award Midwestern Bapt Laymen's Fellowship Chicago 1975; elected Contbng Writer Nat Bapt Sunday Sch Publ Bd; Who's Who in the S & SW. **BUSINESS ADDRESS:** Shiloh Baptist Church, 916 East 12th St, Winston-Salem, NC 27101.

BUTLER, JEROME M.
Attorney. **PERSONAL:** Born Jul 15, 1944, Chicago, IL; married Jean Brothers. **EDUCATION:** Fisk U, BA 1966; Columbia U, JD 1969. **CAREER:** Tucker Watson Butler & Todd, Atty. **ORGANIZATIONS:** Mem Cook County Chicago Bar Assns.

BUTLER, JERRY
Professional athlete. **PERSONAL:** Born Oct 12, 1957, Greenwood, SC. **EDUCATION:** Clemons U, Rec & Parks Adm. **CAREER:** Professional Football Buffalo Bills, wide reciever. **HONORS/ACHIEVEMENTS:** Rookie of the Year Am Football Conf UPI/Football Digest. **BUSINESS ADDRESS:** Buffalo Bills, 1 Bills Dr, Orchard Park, NY 14127.

BUTLER, JOHN DONALD
Doctor. **PERSONAL:** Born Feb 02, 1910, Sewickley, PA; son of James E and Harriet G; married Charlita Elizabeth Whitby; children: Beverly Flavergneau, John G, Richard S, Diane, David, Michelle. **EDUCATION:** Lincoln U, PA, AB 1931; Meharry Med Coll, MD 1937; Univ of Pittsbrgh Sch Med, Res & Teaching Fellow Dermatology 1947-50. **CAREER:** Gen Prac Med, Montgomery, WV, 1939-41; Gen Prac Med, Pittsbrgh, PA, 1941-47, Detroit 1951; Wayne State Univ Med Sch, asst clin prof. **ORGANIZATIONS:** Adjunct Associate clinical prof dermatology, Wayne St Univ Med Sch; life mem Am Acad Dermatology; mem AMA, Natl Med Assn, MI Dermatology Soc; life mem NAACP; mem Alpha Phi Alpha Frat. **HOME ADDRESS:** 301 Orange Lake Dr, Bloomfield Hills, MI 48013. **BUSINESS ADDRESS:** 2175 W Grand Blvd, Detroit, MI 48208.

BUTLER, JOHN GORDON
Management consultant. **PERSONAL:** Born Apr 23, 1942, Pittsburgh, PA; son of John Donald Butler and Marjorie Johnson Butler; children: John Mason. **EDUCATION:** Harvard Coll, Cambridge MA, BA Economics, 1963; Harvard Graduate School of Business Admin, Boston MA, MBA, 1966; Graduate Management Inst, Union Coll, Schenectady NY, 1985-87. **CAREER:** Carver Federal Savings, New York City, admin asst, 1963-64; Mobil Intl Oil Co, New York City, financial analyst, 1966-68; Kaiser-Aetna Partnership, Oakland CA, dir of investment analysis 1970-71; Kiambere Ltd, Nairobi, Kenya, mng dir, 1971-83; State Univ Coll, New Paltz NY, visiting prof, 1983-85; John Butler Assoc, New Paltz NY, consultant, 1985-. **ORGANIZATIONS:** Mem, Alpha Phi Alpha Fraternity, 1963-; lecturer, Univ of Nairobi, Kenya, 1968-69; consultant, Bomas of Kenya Cultural Village, 1972-73; dir, Kiambere Bldg Soc, 1975-83; assoc, African Development Group, 1979-82; mem, Village of New Paltz Planning Bd, 1984-88; fellow, New York African Amer Inst, 1986-88; mem, New Paltz Democratic Comm, 1987-88; treasurer, Harvard Business School Black Alumni Assn, 1987-.

BUTLER, JOHN NATHANIEL
Educator. **PERSONAL:** Born Aug 09, 1932, Orlando, FL; married Fannie B Brooks; children: Karen, Kelvin, Kalestine. **EDUCATION:** FL A&M Coll, BS 1956; FL Technological U, MEd 1975; Stetson U; Albanystate; Univ of OK; FL State U, postgrad; Univ of FL. **CAREER:** Orange County, teacher, coord; Maitland Jr High School, instructor 1973-, guidance counselor 1969-73; Oak Ridge High School, teacher 1966-69; Phyllis-Wheatley High School, chmn of math dept 1956-66. **ORGANIZATIONS:** Trustee BL Lee Sem; vice pres Orlando Conf Lay Orgn 1973; life mem Kappa Alpha Pso Frat 1952-; steward bd Choir #1, Men's Bible Class, finan sec Mt Olive AME Ch 1976-; mem NAACP; vice pres United Tchrs of Orange; Nat Counc of Math Tchrs; FL Councof Math Tchrs; treas Orange Co of Tchrs 1962-66; polemarch Orlando Alumni Chap Kappa Alpha Psi Frat 1968-70; keeper of exchequer 1959-65; eval com State Adopted Textbooks 1967-75; Dunellron Eval Com Pub relat chmn Phyllis Wheatley HS 1963-64. **HONORS/ACHIEVEMENTS:** Plaques Christian Servs to Mt Olive AME Ch 1975; honor's & cers Albany State Coll Nat Sci Found 1957; lincensed minister African Method Episcopal Ch; Who's Who Among Balcks in Central FL; Who's Who in S & SW 1976-77. **BUSINESS ADDRESS:** 2620 Lake Sunset Dr, Orlando, FL 32805.

BUTLER, JOHN O.
Business executive. **PERSONAL:** Born Nov 28, 1926, Bristol, TN; son of Pinkey E Butler and Olivia J Butler; married Marjorie M Jackson; children: Deborah, David, Brian, Bruce. **EDUCATION:** Howard Univ, BS Mech Engrg (magna cum laude) 1950. **CAREER:** GE Co, design engr 1950-57; Raytheon Co, mgr indus engrg 1958-64; GTE Sylvania Inc, dir value engrg 1965-68; Deerfield Optics, founder/president. **ORGANIZATIONS:** Registered professional engr MA; mem MA Businessmen's Assn; Natl Soc of Professional Engrs; commr MA Gov's Exec Council for Value Analysis 1966-72; commr Framingham Housing Auth; dir Framingham Regional YMCA 1971-75; cooperator Framingham Union Hosp 1968-; mem Rotary Intl; mem Twn Repub Com 1972-; mem Tau Beta Pi Engrg Hon Soc 1952. **MILITARY SERVICE:** AUS tech fifth grade 1944-46. **HOME ADDRESS:** 6 Doyle Circle, Framingham, MA 01701.

BUTLER, JOHNNELLA E.
Educator. **PERSONAL:** Born Feb 28, 1947, Roanoke, VA. **EDUCATION:** Coll of Our Lady of the Elms, AB 1968; Johns Hopkins U, MAT 1969; Univ of MA Amherst, EdD 1979. **CAREER:** Towson State Univ, instructor 1970-84; Smith Coll, instructor 1974-79, asst prof 1979-81, assoc prof with tenure 1981-, instructor Afro-Amer studies 1974-76, asst to dean 1976-77, chairperson of dept 1977-79, chairperson of 5 Coll Black Studies Exec Comm 1978-79, asst prof, chairperson Afro-Amer Studies 1979-82, assoc prof (tenured) 1982, visiting lecturer Womens Studies Mt Holyoke Coll 1984. **ORGANIZATIONS:** Bd trustees Coll Our Lady of the Elms 1985-89; cnsltng Various Univs & Coll 1983-; Afro-Am Lit; Blck Stds; Wmns Stds;& Chorale 198-81; natl sec 1980-81, exec bd 1981-83 Natl Council for Black Studies; bd of trustees Coll of Our Lady of the Elms 1984-85; consult Womens Studies Prog Univ of IL Champaigne-Urbana 1984, Racism & Sexism Patterson Coll NJ 1984, Black Women in Amer Lit Courses Univ of IL DeKalb 1984, Black Studies & Womens Studies Carleton Coll Northfield MN 1984, Wellesley Ctr for Rsch on Women 1984, Womens Studies Faculty Devel Proj Coll of St Mary Omaha NE 1984; Drew Univ Faculty Devel Workshop 1984. **HONORS/ACHIEVEMENTS:** FIPSE Grnt Blck Stds/Wmns Stds 1981-83; $1/4 Million Frsty Dev Prjct Coord; Blck Stds Ped & Rev; Univ Press of Am, Wash, DC 1981; Studies & the Liberal Arts Tradition Through the discipline of Afro-Amer Literature" Univ Press of Amer 1981, "Toward a Pedagogy of Everywoman's Studies", Minority Womens Studies, Do We Want To Kill a Dream" Intl Women Studies Quarterly 1984; Ford Found Fellowship Johns Hopkins Univ 1968-69, Cazenovia Inst 1971; Smithsonian Conf Scholarship "Black Scholars & Black Studies" 1983. **BUSINESS ADDRESS:** Assoc Prof Afro-Am Studies, Smith Coll, Dept of Afro-Am Stds, Smith Coll, Northampton, MA 01063.

BUTLER, JOYCE M.
Government administrator. **PERSONAL:** Born Jun 12, 1941, Gary, IN; daughter of Robert W Porter and Dorothy Paige Porter; married Mitchell Butler, Jun 13, 1965; children: Stephanie Lynn, Adam Mitchell. **EDUCATION:** Wright Coll, Chicago, IL, AA, 1963; DePaul Univ, Chicago, IL, BA, 1976, MS, 1980. **CAREER:** Loop Coll, Chicago, IL, admin asst, 1963-78; City of Chicago Dept of Planning, Chicago, IL, city planner, 1978-83; City of Chicago, Mayor's Office of Inquiry & Information, Chicago, IL, program mgr, 1983-88, dir of program serv, 1988-. **ORGANIZATIONS:** Operation PUSH, 1972-; Natl Forum of Black Public Administrators, 1985-; Natl Assn of Female Exec, 1989; Soc of Govt Meeting Planners, 1988-; Publicity Club of Chicago, 1989. **HONORS/ACHIEVEMENTS:** Paul Cornell Award, Hyde Park Historical Soc, 1986; developer, initiator, annual Black History Fair, Murray Language Acad, Chicago, IL, 1985-. **BUSINESS ADDRESS:** Dir of Program Serv, City of Chicago, Mayor's Office of Inquiry and Information, 121 N LaSalle, Rm 100, Chicago, IL 60602.

BUTLER, KATHERINE ELIZABETH
Educational consultant. **PERSONAL:** Born Mar 19, 1936, New York, NY; daughter of Theodore Butler and Mary Butler; married Hubert Jones; children: Karen, Lauren, Harlan, Renee, Lisa, Hamilton, Cheryl, Tanya. **EDUCATION:** Mt Holyoke Coll, BA 1957; Simmons Coll, MS 1967; Harvard Univ, EdD 1980. **CAREER:** Boston Public Schools, teacher 1958-59; Newton Public Schools, coord for ed prog 1966-76; Simmons Coll, instr 1967-69; School Systems Public & Independent MA, consult 1968-; Wheelock Coll, instr 1976; Cambridge Elem Public Schools, supvr staff & prog 1977-81; self empl as ed cons. **ORGANIZATIONS:** Bd dir METCO 1966-73; bd trustees Mt Holyoke Coll 1973-78; 1st black mem Newton School Comm 1978-85; minority affairs comm Natl Assoc of IN Schools 1984-89; bd Boston Childrens Serv 1985-; bd Family Serv Assn 1986-, vice chairperson 1989-. **HONORS/ACHIEVEMENTS:** Ed Excellence Scholarship to Student Black Citizens of Newton 1976; Serv to METCO City of Newton 1976; Contrib to Integrated Ed METCO Boston Staff 1976; Serv Above Self Newton Chamber of Commerce 1974; Doctoral Dissertation School Consolidation in Newton 1980; Citizens Who Make a Difference Contrib to Mental Health MA Assoc of Mental Health 1982; Tribute to 350 years of Black Presence in Massachusetts Honoree, Museum of Afro-American History 1988. **HOME ADDRESS:** 1087 Commonwealth Ave, Newton, MA 02159.

BUTLER, LORENZA PHILLIPS, JR.
Administrator, investor. **PERSONAL:** Born Aug 03, 1960, Houston, TX. **EDUCATION:** Wiley Coll, Marshall, TX, BS, 1981; Clark Coll, Atlanta, GA, 1981. **CAREER:** The Butler Group, Pres, 1983-present; Central Life Insurance Co, Florida, Pres, 1987-89; JBSA, Vice Chmn, 1986-87; Lorenza Butler Tobacco Co, Pres, 1984-86; Eastex Wholesale Beer Inc, Pres, 1983-86; Miller Brewing Co, Regional Coll Coordinator, 1981-83; WCLK-FM, Clark Coll, Prod Asst, 1980; KRLY-FM, Intern-Promotion Asst, 1979; KHOU-TV, CBS, Intern/Community Affairs, News Dept, 1979; KBWC-FM, Wiley Coll, Program Dir, 1979; St Thomas Nursing Home/Convalescent Center, Intern/Adminstrative Asst, 1978; KBWC-FM, Wiley Coll, News Dir, 1978-79. **ORGANIZATIONS:** Pres, Texas State Conference of Youth Branches, 1978-81; Pres, Natl Pre-Alumni Council, United Negro, 1980-81; Parlimentarian, Natl Alumni Council, Coll Fund, 1980-81; Alpha Phi Alpha Fraternity Inc; Iota Beta Sigma Honorary Broadcasting Fraternity; bd of dirs, Central Life Insuance Co of Florida, 1987-, Wiley Coll Business Advisory Bd, 1987-. **HONORS/ACHIEVEMENTS:** Recipient, Benjamin L Hooks Award for Service, 1979; NAACP State Conference Award, 1979; Outstanding Service, NAPC/UNCF, Natl Pre-Alumni Council, 1980; IBS Service Award, Iota Beta Sigma Honorary Broadcasting Fraternity Inc, 1980; Prod uced, UNCF Film Movie on Studnets of the 41 Colleges & Universities, 1980; Congressional Black Caucus, Miller High Life Youth Award, 1982; PUSH Excel Student Leadership Award, 1982; Help Inc, Outstanding Young Houstonian, 1985; "30 Leaders of the Future", Ebony Magazine, 1985; Black History in the Making, Directory, Riverside General Hospital, Houston, 1986; Recognition of Contribution, Florida A&M Univ, 1988; Recognition, City of Tampa, 1988; Service Recognition, Tampa Housing Authority, 1988.

BUTLER, LORETTA M.
Educator. **PERSONAL:** Born in Forest Glen, MD. **EDUCATION:** Miner Tchrs Coll, BS 1937; Catholic Univ of Amer, MA 1946, PhD 1963. **CAREER:** Roosevelt Univ, assoc prof of educ emeritus 1971-80; Xavier Univ of LA, prof of educ 1963-71; Educ Res Ctr on Sch Deseg, assoc dir 1970-71; Univ of NE, visiting prof 1968-69; Paine Coll, visiting lectr 1968-71; Cath Univ of Amer, instr 1962; St Philip Elem Sch, tchr 1955-60; Friendship House, supvr 1953-55; Garrison Elem Sch, 1937-53. **ORGANIZATIONS:** Consultant Training prog for staffs of Model Cities Daycare Cntrs 1973; EDPA In-Service Workshop 1971; NCTE Ele Sch Language Conf 1971; EPDA Inst in Eng 1971; Inter-Instl Inst on Deseg 1967; Proj Headstart Madison WI 1966; NDEA Inst on Reading 1965; mem Natl Assn of Tchr Educ; Natl Council of Tchrs of English; Chicago Reading Assn; Assn of Afro-Amer Life & History.

HONORS/ACHIEVEMENTS: Author of numerous articles, book reviews, essays commenting on ednl, racial, social issues, especially in Comm Mag; named Danforth Asso 1974.

BUTLER, MARJORIE JOHNSON
Retired educator. **PERSONAL:** Born May 18, 1911, Oberlin, OH; daughter of Frank Johnson and Mary Jones; divorced; children: Beverly Lavergneau, John, Richard. **EDUCATION:** Oberlin Coll, AB 1930; OH State Univ; MA 1934; Univ Pittsburgh, PhD 1965. **CAREER:** WV State Coll, instructor 1930-31; Prairie View State Coll, 1931-37; Sumner High School, teacher 1937-40; 5th Ave High School 1955-58; Pittsburgh Public Schools, psychologist 1959-62; Univ of Pittsburgh, instructor 1961-65; State Univ of NY, asst prof 1965-67, assoc prof 1967-70, prof 1970-85; Vasser Coll, part-time prof 1971. **ORGANIZATIONS:** Mem Amer Psychology Assn; NY State Psychology Assn; Assn for Study of Afro-Amer Life & Hist; African Heritage Study Assn. **HONORS/ACHIEVEMENTS:** Mem, Alpha Kappa Alpha Sorority; Psi Chi; Pi Lambda Theta; Delta Kappa Gamma Hon Sorority.

BUTLER, MAX R.
Clergyman. **PERSONAL:** Born Jul 10, 1912, St Francisville, LA; married Leona Hickman; children: Angele B (evans). **EDUCATION:** New Orleans U, AB & BD 1935; Inter-Bapt Theological Sem, DD 1972. **CAREER:** Adult Edn, tchr, supv & parish dir 1937-41; US, letter carrier 1941-70; chemical mgf 1946-74; 10 Meth Ch, pastor 1933-74; Philips & Memi United Meth Ch, pastor. **ORGANIZATIONS:** Asst sec LA Annual Conf of United Meth Ch 1968-71; vice pres Dillard Univ Alumni Assn 1956; mem NAACP; Nat Urban League; 32 degrees Prince Hall Mason of New Orleans LA. **HONORS/ACHIEVEMENTS:** Honorary Atty Gen of LA 1973; New Orleans second most popular cit 1937; Boy Scout leadership award 1973; DD 1972; appntd by Gov Eswards mem adv council to Historical & Cultural Preservation Bd 1973. **BUSINESS ADDRESS:** 3236 Burdette Ave, New Orleans, LA.

BUTLER, MICHAEL EUGENE
Entrepreneur. **PERSONAL:** Born Jul 14, 1950, New York City, NY; son of Bernard Butler Jr and Myrtle Martin Butler; married Eileen Payne, Oct 10, 1982. **EDUCATION:** Pace U, NYC, BBA 1972; Univ of CA, Berkeley, MPH 1974. **CAREER:** New York City Hlth & Hosps Corp, asso exec dir 1975-80; NYS Comm Hlth Educ & Illness Prvntn, exec dir 1980-81; Comm Fmly Plng Cncl, exec dir 1981-82; NY St Div Yth, rgnl dir NYC; Executive Health Group, vice pres. **ORGANIZATIONS:** Mem 100 Black Men 1977-85; bd dir Pace Univ, Alumni Assoc 1983-86; mem Pace Univ Bd Educ Plcs Commn 1984-. **HONORS/ACHIEVEMENTS:** Outstndng Yng Men of Am; US Jaycees 1978; Trustees Awrd Pace Univ 1972.

BUTLER, MIKE
Professional athlete. **PERSONAL:** Born Apr 04, 1954, Washington, DC; married Darlene; children: Michelyn Cynthia. **EDUCATION:** KS Univ, attended. **CAREER:** Green Bay Packers, defensive end; Tampa Bay Bandits, defensive end 1984-. **HONORS/ACHIEVEMENTS:** Named 1st team All-USFL Coll & Pro Football Newsweekly; Earned 2nd team All-League honors USFL sportwriters & sportscasters; Named 1st team All-Amer SprotingNews 1976.

BUTLER, NEIL A.
Nursing administrator, former mayor. **PERSONAL:** Born Dec 03, 1927, Orange Heights, FL; son of Neil Butler and Bertha Butler; married Gracie Clarke; children: Neil Jr, Annette Mann, Archie, Danny, Andre' Lia. **EDUCATION:** Morris Brown Coll; Alachua Co Practical Nursing Program, diploma 1965; Univ of FL, BSN 1967; Univ of FL, MN 1971; Univ of FL, admitted to PhD program 1973. **CAREER:** Alachua General Hosp & Univ of Florida Hosp, staff LPN 1965-67; Veterans Admin Hospital Gainesville, staff nurse 1967-68; Univ of FL, head nurse pediatric unit 1968-69; Emmer Devel Corp, vice pres 1969-70; Univ of FL, grad rsch asst 1970-71; Univ of FL Coll of Med, instr dept of community health 1971-76; Gainesville, mayor 1971-72,74-75; Veterans Admin Med Center, admin. **ORGANIZATIONS:** Mem Amer Nurses Assn; FL Nurses Assn; bd dir Dist 10 FL Nurses Assn; Amer Nurses Assn Natl Honorary Be Involved Membership Comm; FL Nurses Assn Membership Comm; Amer Academy of Political & Social Scientists; Intl Paltform Assn; mem Omega Psi Phi & Fraternity, Basileus; exalter ruler Elks; mem VFW; Amer Legion; Gainesville Civitan Club; city commn rep on N Central FL Health Planning Council; pres New Gainsville Inc; adv bd League for Civic Action; vice-chmn Gainesville Progressive Devel Fund; adv rep Am Heart & Kindey Transplant Assn; bd dir Alachua Co Mental Health Assn; bd dir Muscular Dystrophy Inc; chmn Alachua Co Comprehensive Planning Comm. **HONORS/ACHIEVEMENTS:** Mem Sigma Theta Tau, Natl Nursing Honor Soc; Outstanding Citizen of Yr 1969; Awd for Contrib to Black Heritage Alpha Kappa Alpha 1971; comm Serv Awd Dist 10 FL Nurses Assn 1969; Awd for Meritorius Serv as Mayor Gainesville Club Council 1971; comm Serv Awd Mat Zion Ch 1973; Kappa Delta Pi Ed Hon Soc. **MILITARY SERVICE:** USN. **BUSINESS ADDRESS:** Administrator, Veterans Admn Medical Center, Tremont Ave, East Orange, NJ 07019.

BUTLER, OCTAVIA E.
Author. **PERSONAL:** Born Jun 22, 1947, Pasadena, CA. **EDUCATION:** Pasadena City Coll, AA 1968; CA State Coll LA, attended; UCLA, attended. **CAREER:** Author, Crossover" in Clarion edited by Robin Scott Wilson 1971; "Pattermaster" 1976,78; "Mind of My Mind" 1977,78; "Survivor" 1978,79; "Kindred" 1979-81; "Colay's Ark" "Near of Kin" in Chrysalis edited by Roy Torgeson 1979; "Wild Seed" 1980,81; "Bloodchild" 1984, "Speech Sounds" 1983 in Isaac Asimov's Science FictionMagazine; "Clay's Ark" 1984,85; short fiction "Dawn" 1987. **HONORS/ACHIEVEMENTS:** Periodical publs, "Future Forum" 1980, "Lost Races of Sci Fiction" 1980, "Speech Sounds" 1983; YWCA Achievement Awd for Creative Arts 1980; Hugo Awd Best Short Story 42nd World Science Fiction Convention 1984; Nebula Awd Best Novelette Science Fiction Writers of Amer 1984; Hugo Awd Best Novelette 43rd World Sci Fiction Convention 1985. **BUSINESS ADDRESS:** Freelance Writer, PO Box 6604, Los Angeles, CA 90055.

BUTLER, OLIVER RICHARD
Business executive. **PERSONAL:** Born Jul 03, 1941, New Orleans, LA; son of Richard Butler and Rose Butler; married Naurine M Jackson; children: Janee, Eric, Shann. **EDUCATION:** Xavier Univ of LA, BS Pharmacy 1958-62; Univ of IL Polk St Campus, Graduate Course in Organic Chem 1968; Univ of New Orleans, Graduate Business Courses 1975-77. **CAREER:** Walgreen Co Chicago, store mgr/pharmacist 1963-69; Bruxelles Pharmacy, store owner 1970-73; Ayerst Labs, sales positions 1974-78, dist mgr 1978-83, asst field sales mgr 1983-84, dir of sales opers 1984-88; Wyeth-Ayerst Labs (all divisions), Sales Administration, exec dir 1988-. **ORGANIZATIONS:** Mem New Orleans Comm/Human Relations 1970; mem exec comm LA High Blood Pressure Prog 1978; guest lecturer Xavier Univ Med Tech Dept 1978-81; adv bd Food/Drug Admin 1979; vice pres Ursuline Academy 1979-80; treas Acro I Gymnastic Club 1981-82; pharmacy dean search comm Xavier Univ Coll/Pharmacy 1981-82 adv comm Xavier Univ Coll of Pharmacy 1982-. **HONORS/ACHIEVEMENTS:** Achievement Awd Rexall Drug Co 1962; Man of the Year Chi Delta Mu Frat 1969. **BUSINESS ADDRESS:** Executive Director, Sales Administration, Wyeth-Ayerst Laboratories, 555 E Lancaster Ave, St Davids, PA 19087.

BUTLER, PATRICK HAMPTON
Business executive, attorney. **PERSONAL:** Born Jul 24, 1933, Gonzales, TX; married Barbara; children: Daphne, Ann Marie. **EDUCATION:** Univ CO Sch of Law, JD 1961; CO Coll, BA 1956. **CAREER:** Eli Lilly & Co, asst counsel; IN Univ asst pro of law 1966-68; US Dept of Labor, spec asst 19865-66; US Dept of Justice, trial atty 1962-65; Fed Trade & Comn 1961-62. **ORGANIZATIONS:** Bd govs Indianapolis Bar Assn 1972-74. **MILITARY SERVICE:** AUS 1st lt 1958. **BUSINESS ADDRESS:** 307 E Mc Carty St, Indianapolis, IN 46208.

BUTLER, RAY
Professional athlete. **PERSONAL:** Born Jun 28, 1956, Port Lavaca, TX. **EDUCATION:** Attended, Wharton County Jr Coll; Univ of So CA, degree in Speech 1980. **CAREER:** Baltimore, 1980-83; Indianapolis Colts, 1984-85; Seattle Seahawks, wide receiver 1986-. **BUSINESS ADDRESS:** Seattle Seahawks, 5305 Lake Washington Blvd, Kirkland, WA 98033.

BUTLER, REBECCA BATTS
Educator. **PERSONAL:** Born in Norfolk, VA; widowed. **EDUCATION:** Temple U, DEd 1965; Temple U, MEd 1958; Glassboro State Coll, BS 1942. **CAREER:** Camden Public Schools, elementary teacher 1937-51, supvr of guidance 1966-68, dir adult comm prog 1969-74; Camden Secondary School, teacher 1951-59; NJ State Dept of Educ, 1968-69; Glassboro State Coll, adj prof; Lincoln School for Unwed Mothers Camden City, organizor, director. **ORGANIZATIONS:** Chrm of Comm Tchr Educ and Prof Stand; natl editor-in-chief KRINON Natl Sor Phi Delta Kappa 1972-76; mem Natl Asso of Negro Bus & Prof Women 1974; dir Adult Cont Educ for NANPW; Girl Sct Leader 1941-60; mem Philadelphia Fellowshp House; organzr & 1st chrmn Comm on educ Chestnut St UAME ch; mem Civil Def Counc Camden City; mem exec bd Camden County Red Cross; mem of exec bd Vstng Nurses assoc; pres Assoc of Negro Bus and Prof Women of Camden and Vicinity; appt one of 1st mem bd of trustees & Thomas A Edison Coll 1973-75; panel men Unites Fund; past mem bd of dir Mary H Thomas Nursery; chmn Nat Adv Com on Comm Servs for Am Asso Ret Persons 1978-80; natl bd dirs AARP 1980; particant White House Briefing for Women 1980; initiative spokesperson for Amer Assoc of Retired Persons. **HONORS/ACHIEVEMENTS:** Woman of the Yr Awd Zeta Phi Beta 1977; Outstanding Citizen Afro-Amer Life & History of Camden County 1977; Volunteer of the Year Elks of Camden 1976; Citedfor Volunter Serv Camden County Red Cross 1976; Citation Spanish Spkg Commun of Camden 1974; Citation Camden Bd of Educ 1974; Cited for Commun Serv UnitedFund of Camden Cty 1974; Cited as Adult Educ of Yr Adult Educ of NJ 1973; Educ of Year Oppty Indn Cent 1972, Natl Achievement Awd & Natl Prog Awd Adult Cont Educ NABPW Clubs Inc 1977; Sojourner Truth Awd Camden B&P Club 1977; Outstanding Citizen of the Year Goodwill Ind 1972; Outstanding Citizen AwdAwds Comm of Ninth Annual Observ of Tenth St Baptist Church 1966; Cited for Community Serv Camden Commun Club 1965; Mae S Moore Awd natl Assoc of Bus& Professional Women of Camden & Vicinity 1964; Cited for Commun Serv Chapel of the Four Chaplains 1964; Bishop Awd 1954;v Chapel of the Four Chaplns 1964; Bishop Awd 1954; publ "Protraits of Black Role Models In The History of Southern NJ". **BUSINESS ADDRESS:** Educational Consultant, 15 Eddy Ln, Cherry Hill, NJ 08002.

BUTLER, VELMA SYDNEY
Retired educator. **PERSONAL:** Born Feb 06, 1902, Oakland, TX; daughter of P W Sydney and Henrietta Eason Sydney; married Payton Butler (deceased); children: Shirley Vel Butler Green. **EDUCATION:** Houston-Tillotson Coll Austin TX, BA; Univ of Denver Denver CO, MA 1953. **CAREER:** San Antonio Independent Sch Dist, elem dept; San Antonio Independent Sch Dist, dept spl educ 1930-69; Incarnate Word Coll San Antonio & TX, dept of spl educ 1969-70. **ORGANIZATIONS:** Exec bd Olive St Welfare Assn 1946-75; exec bd Welcome Home Blind & Aged 1946-75; exec bd Mt Zion First Bapt Day Care Center 1950-56; Alpha Phi Zeta Chap Basileus; life mem exec bd Zeta Phi Beta Sor Inc; exec Young Matrons Guild; dir So Reg Amicae; exec bd San Antonio Tchrs Council 1956-59; secYWCA; Interdenominational Courtesy Council; Woman's Pavilion for HemisFair 68, vp; exec bd Project FREE; first woman appointed on selective service bd in Bexar Co 1971-73; Eastside Neighborhood Devel Project; pres & vice pres Co Fed Credit Unoin 1950-77; bd mem Bexar Co Opportunities Industrialization Center Inc 1974-75; San Antonio & Bicentennial Com; region & natl bds & so region exec bd Zeta Phi Beta Sor Inc; natl exec bd Zeta Phi Beta Sor Ch Affiliations; mem Mt Zion First Bapt Ch; dir Mt Zion First Bapt Wednesday Morning Fellowship Hour; Ministers, Deacons, & Trustees Wives Aux; pres Mt Zion First Bapt Courtesy Comm; Retired San Antonio Tchrs Council; TX State Tchrs Assn; NEA. **HONORS/ACHIEVEMENTS:** Certificate of appreciation Pres of US; outstanding contrib in comm serv The Western Ares Links Inc; outstanding serv redered award from Local Regional & Nat Zeta Phi Beta Sor Inc; outstanding tchr of yr Alamo Dist C Of C; distinguished serv award Mt Zion First Bapt Ch; outstanding serv for city improvements City of San Antonio; comm serv Interdenominational Courtesy Council; outstanding leadership & contbns in educ polit comm civic ch life & toward struggle for women's rights State of TX House of Rep; appointed mem of Bicentennial Com by City Council 1974-76.

BUTLER, WASHINGTON ROOSEVELT, JR.
Executive director. **PERSONAL:** Born Jan 05, 1933, New Orleans, LA; married Maria A Hill; children: Landry, Luthuli, Leiah. **EDUCATION:** Clark Coll, BS 1953; Univ of TN Knoxville, MA 1964. **CAREER:** Urban & Ded Affairs State of TN, commr 1975-79; Riverside Hosp Nashville, TN, vice pres 1981-83; Self-Empl Madison, TN, devel consult 1979-; ADAM Inc, exec vice pres 1984-. **ORGANIZATIONS:** Bd dir Oakwood Coll Huntsville, AL 1977-82; bd dir Riverside Hosp Nashville, TN 1975-81; former sec-treas/bd mem Natl Assn for Comm Dev; former bd mem Southeastern Reg Assn of Comm Action Agencies; elect to two four-yr terms on City Cncl Oak Ridge, TN; served on Oak Ridge Reg Planning Commn; Oak Ridge Beer Board; Anderson Co Citizens Welfare Adv Bd; former mem Agricultural Ext Comm ; bd dir Memphis Opport Indust Center; Natl Busn League Memphis

Chpt; former pres Memphis Inter-Alumni Cncl of the United Negro Coll Fund; candidate for nom as Gov in Dem Primary of 1974; First Elder in Riverside Chapel Seventh-day Adventist Ch Nashville, TN; served as chrmn Building Comm FH Jenkins Elem Sch; former mem bd trustees Oakwood Coll Huntsville, ALand Riverside Adventist Hosp Nashville, TN. **HONORS/ACHIEVEMENTS:** Listed Who's Who in So and Southwest; Amer Honorarium; Who's Who in TN; Who's Who in Commerce and Industry; Natl Register of Prominent Amer and Intl Notables; Who's Who Among Students in Amer Univ & Colls; Beta Kappa Chi Natl Honorary Sci Soc. **MILITARY SERVICE:** AUS, USAREUR Command spec e-4 1953-56; USAR 5 years; Honorable Discharge. **BUSINESS ADDRESS:** Executive Vice President, Amer Div Asset Mngmt Corp, 230 Great Circle Rd, Ste 229, Nashville, TN 37228.

BUTLER, WENDELL HARDING
Dentist. **PERSONAL:** Born Oct 12, 1924, Carthage, TX; married Susie Sparron; children: Wanda Marie, Karen Diane, Carol Diane, Susan Jean. **EDUCATION:** Prairie View Coll, 1941-44; Howard U, DDS 1949. **CAREER:** HowardUniv Wash, instr 1950-51; Roanoke, prac dentistry 1953-. **ORGANIZATIONS:** Mem Am Dental Assn; dir sec treas NW Roanoke Corp 1965; bd dir & Hunton YMCA; v chmn Comm Roanoke Redevel & Housing Aurth 1968-70, 1973; Roanke Co Dem Committeeman 1970; mem Dem of VA Central Com 1972; mem Omega Psi Phi; Mason. **MILITARY SERVICE:** USAF capt 1951-53. **BUSINESS ADDRESS:** 721 11 St NW, Roanoke, VA 24017.

BUTTERFIELD, DON
Musician. **PERSONAL:** Born Apr 01, 1923, Centralia, WA. **CAREER:** Teddy Charles Charles Mingus, instrumentalist on tuba jazz tuba player 1950's; Radio City Mus Hall Orch NYC, prin tuba player for 18yrs; Am Symphony Orch, tuba player; free-lance rec artist with leading jazz musicians; spl perfmances including & nightclubs film performances with Dizzier Gillispie Orch 1962; Town-Hall concert with Charles Mingus 1962; Newport RI Jazz Festival 1963. **ORGANIZATIONS:** Mem faculty NY U; composer of study materials for low frequency mus instruments; pub through his own co DB Pub Co Office. **BUSINESS ADDRESS:** Nydam Lane, Wyckoff, NJ 07481.

BUTTS, CARLYLE A.
Business executive. **PERSONAL:** Born Nov 10, 1935, Richmond, VA; son of Thomas A Butts Sr and Coral P Butts; married Omeria A Roberts, Jun 11, 1966; children: Brian, Gregory. **EDUCATION:** Howard Univ, BS & EE 1963; USC, MBA 1969; UCLA, Executive Mgmt Program 1988. **CAREER:** Hughes Aircraft Co, assistant division manager, Ground Systems Group 1988; Hughs Aircraft Co, product operations manager 1987; Hughes Aircraft Co, dept mgr radar systems group 1978; Hughes Aircraft Co, proj mgr 1977; Hughes Aircraft Co, head facilities planning 1972-76; proj mgr 1970-72; head prod control 1969-70; various positions in material dept 1964-69; electronics test engr 1963-64; Howard Univ, electronic lab instr asst 1958-63. **ORGANIZATIONS:** Past mem Amer Marketing Assn; Natl Contracts Mgmt Assn; Intercollegiate Council of Black Colleges; Business Mgmt Consultant; mem Hughes Mgmt Club; past pres bd trustees Crenshaw Ch of Religious Sci 1974-77; den leader Webelos Pack 162c Holman Meth Chl 1978; pres Howard Univ Alumni Club of So CA 1971-73; pres Howard Univ Alumni Club of So CA 1980. **HONORS/ACHIEVEMENTS:** Howard Hughes Fellowship 1967; Los Angeles City Resolution for Service to Youth & Community 1983. **MILITARY SERVICE:** USAF a1/c 1954-57. **HOME ADDRESS:** 4906 Maymont Dr, Los Angeles, CA 90043. **BUSINESS ADDRESS:** Assistant Division Manager, Manager Product Operations, Hughes Aircraft Co, 1901 West Malvern Avenue, Bldg 607 Mail Station B219, Fullerton, CA 92634.

BUTTS, HUGH F.
Physician, psychiatrist, psychoanalyst. **PERSONAL:** Born Dec 02, 1926, New York, NY; son of Lucius and Edith; married Clementine; children: Lucia, Florence, Eric, by previous marriage; Sydney, Samantha, Heather. **EDUCATION:** City Coll NY, BS 1949; Meharry Med Coll, MD 1953; Morrisania City Hosp, intern cert 1955; Bronx VA Hosp, resd 1958; Columbia Univ Psychoanalytic Clinic, Cert Psychoanalytic Med 1962. **CAREER:** Hillcrest Ctr for Children, staff psych 1959-61; Private practice, psych 1959-74; Wiltwyck School for Boys, clinical dir 1961-63, chief in patient psych serv 1962-69; Private practice, psychoanalytic 1962-74; Harlem Hosp Ctr, assoc prof psych 1965-69; Columbia Univ Coll Phys & Surgeons, asst clin prof psych 1967-74; Albert Einstein College of Medicine, prof of Psychiatry 1974-81; Literary Mind Associates, pres 1986-; Clementine Publishing Company, Leeds NY, pres and founder 1989-; The New Hope Guild, Brooklyn NY, psychiatric consultant 1980-. **ORGANIZATIONS:** Consult The Neuropsychiatric Ctr NY 1957; psych consult Jewish Bd Guardians 1962; suprv training analyst Columbia Univ Psychoanalytic Clinic for Training & Rsch 1968-; psych consult Fieldston-Ethical Culture School 19709-74; staff psych Manida Juv Detention Ctr 1972-74; suprv psych Bronx State Hosp 1973-79; training analy, suprv analyst Post-Grad Ctr for Mental Health 1975-; act dir resd training Bronx State Hosp 1977-79; psych consult NY City Police Dept Psychol Clinic 1974-76; mem US Fed Ct 1970-75, Allegheny Cty Mental Health & Mental Retardation Assoc 1974-75; staff mem Gracie Sq Hosp 1961-66; mem Montefiore Hosp 1961-65; mem NY Psych Inst 1962-74, Beth-Isreal Hosp 1962-63, Harlem Hosp Ctr 1962-69, Vanderbilt Clinic Presbyterian Hosp 1963-65, NY State Dept Voc Rehab 1963-69, St Lukes Hos p 1958-74, Bronx State Hosp 1974-79, NY State Dept Mental Hygiene 1974-76, Natl Med Assoc, AMA, NY Cty Med Soc, Amer Psych Assoc 1970, Assoc for Psychoanalytic Med 1968-71, Amer Orthopsychiatric Assoc 1970-73, Alumni Assoc Psychoan Clinic for Training & Rsch; fellow NY Acad Med. **HONORS/ACHIEVEMENTS:** Num awds & citations & publs. **MILITARY SERVICE:** USAF, private 1st class 1944-45, Good Conduct Medal. **BUSINESS ADDRESS:** 350 Central Park West, New York, NY 10025.

BUTTS, WILSON HENRY
Scientist. **PERSONAL:** Born May 18, 1932, Elizabeth City, NC; married Geraldine High; children: Kevin Eric. **EDUCATION:** Fisk Univ, BA 1959. **CAREER:** Vanderbilt Univ Med Sch, instr surg research 1960-; Fisk Univ Chem Dept, organic research chemist 1959-60. **ORGANIZATIONS:** Mem Am Assn of Clinical Chem; mem AAAS; mem Omega Pso Phi Frat; officer Knights of Peter Claver & Council 5, 1978-. **HONORS/ACHIEVEMENTS:** Registered Clinical Chemistry Tech #690, Nat Registry in Clinical Chemistry; cert Instrumentation Labs 1965; cert Hewlett Packard 1967; cert Technicon 1967; cert Autoanalyzer 1969; cert AACC 1972; licensure Gen Lab Supr State of TN; numerous pub med jours 1969-78; recipent Good Conduct Medal USAF; sharp-shooter medal USAF. **MILITARY SERVICE:** USAF sgt 1951-55. **BUSINESS ADDRESS:** 21st Ave S, Nashville, TN 37232.

BYAM, MILTON S.
Consultant. **PERSONAL:** Born Mar 15, 1922, New York, NY; married Yolanda Shervington, Jan 18, 1947; children: Megan, Roger. **EDUCATION:** City Coll NY, BSS 1947; Columbia Univ, MS 1949; NYU, grad sch 1950-51; Columbia Univ Sch Library Sci, 1968. **CAREER:** Brooklyn Pub Libr, librarian trainee 1947-49, librarian 1949-50, asst br librarian 1950-51, br librarian 1951-56, supt br 1956-61; Pratt Inst, teacher 1956-67; Brooklyn Pub Libr, chief pub serv 1961-65, deputy dir 1965-68; chmn St Johns Univ Dept Library Sci 1968-72; dir DC Public Library 1972-74; dir Queens Borough Public Library 1974-79; Byam et al Inc, consultant 1979-. **HONORS/ACHIEVEMENTS:** Many publications; Friends Library Award Brooklyn Pub Library; Commendation Library Serv & Constrn Act DC Adv Council; Cert of Appreciation City of Philadelphia;Library Award Savannah State Coll; Bd of Regents NY State Univ. **MILITARY SERVICE:** Mil Serv 1943-45; Bronze Star. **BUSINESS ADDRESS:** Consultant, Byam et al Consultants, 162-04 75 Rd, Flushing, NY 11366.

BYARD, JOHN ARTHUR, JR.
Educator. **PERSONAL:** Born Jun 15, 1922, Worcester, MA; married Louise M Caruso; children: Denise, Diane, Gerald. **EDUCATION:** Comm Sch of Music Schillinger Sch of Music. **CAREER:** New England Conservatory of Music, music instr 1969-77; Hart Sch of Music, 1974-77; CCNX, 1974-76; SE of MA, 1974-76; Elma Lewis Sch, conductor 1972-76. **ORGANIZATIONS:** Instr Rotary Club & 1974-77; lectr Harvard Univ 1974-77; Univ of Pitts 197375; Univ of MD 1968-70; Bismark Jr Coll 1976-77; rec artist Prestige New Jazz 1959-67; Futura 1967-70; Victor 1971; Lechange; permc around world. **HONORS/ACHIEVEMENTS:** Hon mem Hartford Jazz Sox; Hot Club of France; Jazz Mus of NY; Vibration Soc; Roland Kirk; hon citz New Orleans 1969; cert of merit Black Stud Union of SE MA Univ 1975; act chmn AAS NE Conservatory 1972; tchr pvt Duke Ellington Flwsp Award 1977; talent recog Down Beat 1966. **MILITARY SERVICE:** AUS 1/sgt 1942-45.

BYAS, THOMAS HAYWOOD
Dentist. **PERSONAL:** Born Mar 10, 1922, St Louis, MO; son of Dr Thomas Haywood Byas and Rosetta Woolfolk Byas; married Ermine Casey Bush, Mar 25, 1950; children: Diane, Timothy. **EDUCATION:** Lemoyne Coll, BS 1943; Howard U, DDS 1951. **CAREER:** Univ of Rochester Sch of Med & Dent, asst prof 1978; St Mary's Hosp, 1978; Baden St Settlement, dentist 1954. **ORGANIZATIONS:** Mem Intl Coll of Dentist ADA 1979; mem Rochester & Acad of Med 1965; pres Chi-Psi Chap Omega Psi Phi 1942; pres Chi Delta Mu 1950; mem bd dir Montgomery Comm Ctr 1968; Dental Smilemobile Rochester 1970; dental dir Albion Ny Health Ctr 1972; mem bd dir Monroe Co Dntl Soc 1973; pres 1977-1978; Green Hills Golf Club 1970-73; Thunder Ridge Co Club 1976; co-chmn United Negro Coll Fund 1955; Rochester C of C 1966; pres Howard Univ Alumni Assn 1966; volunteer consult Operation Outreach 1976-; Dental Soc of NY; Amer Dental Assn 1953-; founder exec sec Seoul, Korea Dental Soc 1952; pres Seventh Dist Dental Society 1987; Sigma Pi Phi Frat, Gamma IOTA chapter, 1985-. **HONORS/ACHIEVEMENTS:** 32nd & 33rd degree mason 1963; award Alpha Phi Alpha 1977; Focal Infections in Periodontal Disease Howard Univ 1950. **MILITARY SERVICE:** AUS 1st lt 1943-1948; AUS 1st lt 1951-1953. **HOME ADDRESS:** 140 Gate House Trail, Henrietta, NY 14467. **BUSINESS ADDRESS:** 316 Chili Ave, Rochester, NY 14611.

BYAS, ULYSSES
Retired educator. **PERSONAL:** Born Jun 23, 1924, Macon, GA; son of Marie Byas Sharpe; married Annamozel Boyd, Jul 05, 1953; children: 4. **EDUCATION:** Fort Valley State Coll, BS 1950; Columbia Univ, MA 1952; further study, Atlanta Univ, NC Coll, Bennington Coll, Colorado Coll; Univ of MA, EdD 1976. **CAREER:** Elberton, tchr 1951-53; Hutchison Elem & HS, supr prin; Butler HS, EE 1957-68; GA Tchrs & Educ Assn, asst exec sec 1968; GA Assn Educ, dir 1970; Macon Co Bd of Educ, supt schs 1970-77; Roosevelt Union Free Sch Dist, supt schs 1977-87. **ORGANIZATIONS:** Mem, Amer Assn Sch Adminstrs, Natl Alliance Black Sch Educ, Nassau Co Chief Sch Assn, NY Assn Sch Adminstrs, Natl Assn Secondary Sch Prins, Phi Delta Kappa; exec comm hon chmn United Negro Scholarship; Lion Roosevelt Club; life mem Kappa Alpha Psi Frat; vice pres Long Island Cancer Council; participant 23rd Annual Amer War Coll Natl Security Forum; mem former chmn CME; past pres GA Cncl Secondary Sch Principals; past pres GA Tchrs & Educators Assn; past pres Natl Alliance of Black Sch Superintendents; mem, NY State Examinations Bd, NAACP, Lydia Hall Hospital Comm Bd; chmn Nassau Comm Coll Minority Recruitment Comm; consultant Univ of MA; adjunct prof Long Island Univ; past pres-elect, Nassau County NY Supt. **HONORS/ACHIEVEMENTS:** Ulysses Byas Elementary School, named by Roosevelt, NY Bd of Educ, 1987; Hall of Fame, Fort Valley Station Coll, 1988. **MILITARY SERVICE:** USN 1943-46.

BYAS, WILLIAM HERBERT
Educational administrator. **PERSONAL:** Born Nov 26, 1932, Macon; married Carolyn Kelsey; children: Yolanda E, William H. **EDUCATION:** TN State U, BS 1957; The Ft Valley State Coll, MS 1957; The Univ of TN, EdD 1971. **CAREER:** Univ of TN, dean of student servs 1979; Memphis State Univ, assoc prof/res 1978-79; Saginaw Valley State Coll, dir acad & support serv & assoc prof educ psychology 1973-78, dir student pers servs 1971-73; New Careers Inst Knoxville Coll, dir 1970; The Ft Valley State Coll, dir coll educ achievement proj 1966-70. **ORGANIZATIONS:** Mem Am Psychological Assn 1972; mem Nat Assn Student Pers Admin 1978; committeeman BSA 1966-69 bd of dirs big bros of am 1971; rotarian Rotary Intl 1971; mem Phi Delta Kappa 1971. **HONORS/ACHIEVEMENTS:** Recipient natl defense award Usn; doctoral fellowshipUniv of TN 1970-71;cert for outstanding serv So Assn of Colls & Schs 1973; couns students with splneeds Saginaw Valley State Coll 1974; consult US Officeof Educ 1975. **MILITARY SERVICE:** USN seaman 1950-52. **BUSINESS ADDRESS:** U of Tennessee, 3113 Circle Park Dr, Knoxville, TN 37916.

BYERS, MARIANNE
Educator. **PERSONAL:** Born Mar 29, 1941, Winston-Salem, NC; married Bennie J Byers; children: La-Lisa Scudder. **EDUCATION:** Barber-Scotia Coll, BS 1963; Queens Coll, MS 1971; Bowling Green State Univ, PhD 1985. **CAREER:** Longwood High School, teacher of English 1965-70; Bowling Green State Univ, teaching fellow, 1982-84; Suffolk County Community Coll, Prof, English, 1970-. **ORGANIZATIONS:** Editor & historian Gordon Heights Newsletter & Journal 1978-85; program coord Gordon Heights Comm Affairs Assoc Inc 1978-87; public relations Afro-Amer Comm Affairs Assoc Inc 1980-87; consultant Parent Advocacy Inc 1985-. **HONORS/ACHIEVEMENTS:** Graduate Teacher/Asst Awd Bowling Green State Univ 1982-85; textbook "Back to Basic Writing" CAT Publishing 1986; article "A Perspective of the Black Male in the Non-Fiction of Zora Neale Houston," Zora Neale Houston Soc 1987; numerous community serv plaques and certificates 1975-87. **HOME**

ADDRESS: 2 Cornwallis Ct, Coram, NY 11727. **BUSINESS ADDRESS:** Prof, English, Suffolk County Community Coll, 533 College Rd, Selden, NY 11784.

BYNAM, SAWYER LEE, III
Building contractor. **PERSONAL:** Born Sep 15, 1933, Houston, TX; married Betty Ann; children: Keith Wayne. **EDUCATION:** Tx So U, BS Certificate In Construction Planning & Estimating. **CAREER:** Gen & Sub-contractors Assn, contract dev, Est. **BUSINESS ADDRESS:** Gen & Sub-Contractors Assn, 2211 Wheeler St, Houston, TX 77004.

BYNES, FRANK HOWARD, JR.
Physician. **PERSONAL:** Born Dec 03, 1950, Savannah, GA; son of Frank H Bynes and Frenchye Mason Bynes; married Janice Ann Ratta, Jul 24, 1987; children: Patricia F Bynes, Frenchye D Bynes. **EDUCATION:** Savanna State Coll, BS 1972; Meharry Medical Coll, MD 1977. **CAREER:** US Air Force, internist, 1986-87; self-employed, internist, 1987-. **ORGANIZATIONS:** Mem Alpha Phi Alpha Frat 1969-, Amer Medical Assoc 1973-, New York Acad of Scis 1983-, AAAS 1984-, Amer Coll of Physicians 1985-, Air Force Assoc 1987-, Assoc of Military Surgeons of the US 1987-. **HONORS/ACHIEVEMENTS:** Outstanding Young Men of Amer 1978. **MILITARY SERVICE:** USAF major, 1986-87. **HOME ADDRESS:** 250 South End Avenue, Suite 6D, New York, NY 10280.

BYNOE, JOHN GARVEY
Retired federal executive, attorney. **PERSONAL:** Born Oct 25, 1926, Boston, MA; married Louise V Granville; children: Sandra M, John L, James G, Jonathan K. **EDUCATION:** Boston Univ New England School of Law, JD 1957. **CAREER:** Roxbury Comm Council, pres 1964-69; Unity Bank & Trust Co, dir 1968-76; Office Civil Rights Dept Health Ed & Welfare Reg I Boston, dir 1982 retired; attny, real estate broker 1982-; Real Estate Developer, 1987. **ORGANIZATIONS:** Former chmn of bd Urban League of Eastern MA 1979-80; former bd mem Freedom House Inc, Boston; past bd dir Legal Asst, Boston Legal Aid Soc; mem Alpha Phi Alpha; pres adv comm Museum of the Natl Ctr of Afro-Amer Artists Inc; bd mem MA Pre-Engrg Prog for Minority Students, Black Ecumenical Commiss Boston MA; senior warden, Widow Son Lodge #28 Prince Hall Grand Lodge Boston MA; legal counsel Natl Bus League Boston Chapt; chmn of the bd, Professional & Bus Club Boston MA; bd mem Natl Ctr of Afro-Amer Artists Inc; bd of dirs Resthaven Inc; mem Big Brother Assoc of Boston, Boy Scouts of Amer Boston Metro Chapt, Boston Branch NAACP 1987-88. **HONORS/ACHIEVEMENTS:** Honorary Doctor of Laws, New England School of Law, 1987; 33 Degree, United Supreme Council, Prince Hall Masons, 1989. **MILITARY SERVICE:** AUS sgt 1945-46.

BYNUM, HORACE CHARLES, SR.
Pharmacist. **PERSONAL:** Born Nov 02, 1916, New Orleans, LA; son of Henry Bynum, Jr and Amanda Medlock Bynum; married Ethel Frinkle, Feb 14, 1975; children: Adolph F, Horace C, Jr. **EDUCATION:** Xavier Univ, New Orleans, LA, BS Pharmacy, 1936. **CAREER:** US Post Office, New Orleans, LA, carrier 1936-46; Bynum's Pharmacy, New Orleans, LA, pharmacist. **ORGANIZATIONS:** mem, Alpa Phi Alpha Fraternity; pres, NAACP, New Orleans Branch, 1966-69; sec, New Orleans Branch NAACP 1955-66; treasurer, NAACP, State Branch, 1969-75; pres, Natl Pharmaceutical Assn, 1970-71, treasurer, Lafon Home Bd of Dir, 1969-89. **HONORS/ACHIEVEMENTS:** Pharmacist of Year, New Orleans, Progressive Assn; Man of the Year, Chi Delta MU Fraternity. **BUSINESS ADDRESS:** Pharmacist, Owner, Bynum's Pharmacy/DBA Bynum & Son, Inc, 3840 St Bernard Ave, New Orleans, LA 70122.

BYNUM, RALEIGH WESLEY
Optometrist. **PERSONAL:** Born May 27, 1936, Jacksonville, FL; married Thelmetia Argrett; children: Raleigh, Monjya, Zerrick. **EDUCATION:** FL A&M Univ, 1954-56; IL Coll of Optometry, BS OD 1956-60; Univ of SC, MPH 1975; Command & General Staff Coll AUS, certificate 1976. **CAREER:** Natl Optometric Assn, past pres/bd chmn 1979; Amer Acad of Optometry, vice pres NC chap 1980-85; Amer Opt Assn, trustee 1978-; Natl Optometric Foundatin, chmn of the bd 1980-. **ORGANIZATIONS:** Past pres bd of dirs Charlotte Bethlehem Ctr 1973; regional dir NOA Minority Recruitment Proj 1971-77; mem Natl HBP Coordinating Comm 1976-84; gen partner Westside Prof Assoc 1972-; vice chmn bd of dirs McCrorey Branch YMCA 1983-; vice chmn bd of dirs Charlotte Mint Museum 1983-. **HONORS/ACHIEVEMENTS:** Who's Who in the South & Southwest; Optometrist of the Year Natl Opt Assn 1980; deacon Friendship Baptist Church 1978-; pilot-instr rated single engine land airplane 1975-. **MILITARY SERVICE:** AUS med corpcol reserves 23 yrs. **HOME ADDRESS:** 6426 Heatherbrook Ave, Charlotte, NC 28213. **BUSINESS ADDRESS:** Chmn of the Board, Natl Optometric Foundation, 401 S Independ Blvd Midtown Sq, Charlotte, NC 28204.

BYNUM, VALERIE CALLYMORE
Musician. **PERSONAL:** Born Mar 09, 1942, Bronx, NY; married Louis Jr; children: Adam, Tanisha. **EDUCATION:** Itaca Coll Sch of Music, BS 1963. **CAREER:** Freelance Musician, 1965. **ORGANIZATIONS:** Mem Sym New World 1965-72; tchr Jr HS 1965-67; mem Radio City Music Hall Sym 1963-66; Recording with leading artist, concerts, broadway shows.

BYRD, ALBERT ALEXANDER
Educator. **PERSONAL:** Born Nov 06, 1927, Baltimore, MD; married Alice Muriel Poe; children: Karen Leslie Forgy. **EDUCATION:** Howard U, BA 1949; Temple U, 1959; Universidad Nacional Autonoma De Mexico, 1959; Istituto Statele D'Arte Per La Porcellana Sesto Florentino Italy, 1962; Instituto Statale D'Arte Porto Romano Florence Italy, 1962. **CAREER:** Sacramento City Coll, art instructor 1963; Baltimore Public School Dist, art teacher 1949-63. **ORGANIZATIONS:** Mem The Pacific Coast Africanist Assn, The Amer Fed of Teachers, Faculty Assn of CA Comm Coll, Kappa Alpha Psi, Howard Univ Alumni Assoc, Sierra Club,Sacramento Ethnic Arts Soc, Cousteau Soc, Wilderness Soc, Nature Conservancy, Natural Resources Defense Control, Planning & Conservation League. **HONORS/ACHIEVEMENTS:** Korean Serv Medal W 2 Battle Stars/Korean Serv Medal/United Nations Serv Medal/Nat Defense Serv United Nations Serv Medal/Nat Def Serv Endowment for the Humanitites Washington Dc 1972-73; Grant Am Forum For Intl Study ClevelandoH 1975. **MILITARY SERVICE:** AUS pfc 1951-53. **BUSINESS ADDRESS:** Sacramento City Coll, 3835 Freeport Blvd, Sacramento, CA 95822.

BYRD, ARTHUR W.
Social worker. **PERSONAL:** Born Dec 24, 1943, Washington, DC; son of Arthur W Byrd Sr and Doris Littlejohn Byrd; married Inez Marie Coleman Byrd, Nov 26, 1967; children: Arthur III William, Ashley Wendall, Allyn Winthrop. **EDUCATION:** Livingstone Coll, BS 1965; Univ NC, MSW 1972; Univ of KY, postgraduate; Univ of Chicago. **CAREER:** Clinch Valey Coll Univ of VA, faculty 1972; Longwood Coll Farmville VA, faculty 1972; Livingstone Coll Salisbyr 1974. **ORGANIZATIONS:** mem, Rowan Co Civic League, 1973; NC Neighborhood Workers Assn 1969; NASW 1970; CSWE 1970; So Assn of Undergrad SW Educ 1973; NAACP 1964; dir Neighborhood Corps 1965-68; Salisbury & Statesville NC; dir, Neighborhood Youth in School & out of School Programs Salisbury NC 1968-70; dir Outreach to Teenage Fathers Durham NC 1970; comm contact Rep Youth Serv Bureau, Winston Salem, NC 1971; state dir of Rsch Facility for Mentally Retarded; Adjunct J Sargent Reynolds Comm Coll, 1975. **HONORS/ACHIEVEMENTS:** Recipient, Babcock Fellow, 1970-72; Distinguished Serv Award, Salisbury Rowan Com Serv Coun; POP Award Coop School for Girls Durham NC; established 1st Afro-Amer Student Org Longwood Coll, 1972-73; established Social Work Action Group SWAG Livingstone Coll 1973-74. **HOME ADDRESS:** 6801 West Rd, Chesterfield, VA 23832.

BYRD, CAMOLIA ALCORN
Educator. **PERSONAL:** Born May 16, Baton Rouge, LA; married Lionel Patrick Byrd; children: Cheryl P, Lionel P Jr, Judith I, Roderick J, Janell M. **EDUCATION:** Souther Univ Baton Rouge, BA 1944; Central State Univ, MA 1964. **CAREER:** Oklahoma City Public Schools, teacher 1959-70, consultant 1970-76, asst coord 1976-80, coord 1980-86; "I Can" Reading/Math Center, dir 1987-. **ORGANIZATIONS:** Mem Assoc for Supervision and Curriculum Develop, Intl Reading Assoc and OK Reading Assoc, Teachers of English to Speaker of Other Languages & OK TESOL, Natl and Local Black Educators Assoc; mem Natl Council of Negro Women, Fed of Col Womens Club, Phi Delta Kappa Inc, Jack & Jill Inc, OK Eastside Culture Club, Alpha Kappa Alpha Sor, Assault on Illiteracy 1986, NTU Art Assoc, African Art Museum; campaign mgr Senator Vicki Lynn Miles LaGrange Oklahoma City OK 1986. **HONORS/ACHIEVEMENTS:** Eminent Women Phi Delta Kappa Inc Gamma Epsilon Chapter 1985. **HOME ADDRESS:** 6600 N Carol Dr, Oklahoma City, OK 73141.

BYRD, EDWIN R.
Educator. **PERSONAL:** Born Feb 23, 1920, Kansas City, KS; married Dorothy Wordlow; children: Terri E. **EDUCATION:** KS State Teachers Coll, BS; Univ of KS, ME 1950. **CAREER:** MO School Dist, 1946-81 retired, elementary school teacher 1946-55, jr high school teacher 1955-56, counselor jr & sr high schools 1956-60; Yates Elementary School, principal 1960-61; Dunbar School, principal 1961-63; Richardson School, principal 1963-68; Martin Luther King Jr High School, principal 1968-75; Nowlin Jr High School, principal 1975-. **ORGANIZATIONS:** Mem KC School Admin Assoc, NEA, MO State Teachers Assoc, MO Assoc of School Principals, Natl Assoc School Principals, Phi Delta Kappa, PTA, Amer Legion 149, NAACP, YMCA, Kiwanis Club; institutional rep Boy Scouts; elder Swope Pkwy United Christian Church; mem Alpha Phi Alpha, Rsch Acad of KC, Selective Serv Bd 49; mem adv comm Jr Red Cross; pres Inter-City Kiwanis Club 1983-84; mem Amer Assoc of Retired Persons. **HONORS/ACHIEVEMENTS:** Sigma Pi Phi Outstanding Secondary Educator of Amer 1974; listed in Who's Who in MO 1974; Athletic Serv Awd 1973; PTA Serv Awd 1968; YMCA Serv Awd 1962; Kin Comm Serv Awd 1975; Outstanding Mem Awd Beta Lambda Chap of Alpha Phi Alpha 1979; YMCA Super Quota Buster Awd 1984. **MILITARY SERVICE:** USAF sgt 1942-46. **BUSINESS ADDRESS:** Principal, Kansas City School District, Nowlin Jr HS, 2800 S Hardy, Independence, MO 64052.

BYRD, FREDERICK E.
Judge. **PERSONAL:** Born Mar 06, 1918, Marvell, AR; married Theresa Dooley; children: 4. **EDUCATION:** Northwestern Univ, BS, BA 1942; Wilson Jr Coll, 1938; Univ of Detroit Law School, JD 1948. **CAREER:** Traffic Ct, traffic ct 1961-73; Common Pleas Ct Detroit, judge 1973-. **ORGANIZATIONS:** Mem Michigan Bar Assn, Amer Bar Assn, Wolverine Bar Assn, Detroit Bar Assn; mem NBA; mem NAACP; mem Wayne County & Catholic Social Serv; adv bd Providence Hospital; bd mem Wayne County Mental Health Soc; Detroit Libr Comm; bd mem Delta Dental Plan of Michigan. **BUSINESS ADDRESS:** Judge, 36th District, 4068 Madison Center, Detroit, MI 48226.

BYRD, FREDERICK WAYNE
Reporter. **PERSONAL:** Born Jan 19, 1948, New York, NY. **EDUCATION:** Dartmouth Coll, BA 1969. **CAREER:** The Peace Corps, vlntr tchr 1969-71; The Star-Ledger, reprtr 1971-. **ORGANIZATIONS:** Mem Art Ctr of NJ 1971-; tutor YMCA 1972-73; host Shltr for Homeless 1983-. **HONORS/ACHIEVEMENTS:** Operation PUSH Professional Award 1975; Art Ctr of NJ Awrd 1978. **HOME ADDRESS:** PO Box 1751, Newark, NJ 07101.

BYRD, GEORGE EDWARD
General manager. **PERSONAL:** Born Sep 20, 1941, Troy, NY; son of George Byrd, Sr and Louise Collins-Byrd; married Alice Hill-Byrd, Jul 08, 1967; children: Sharon Collins, George Byrd III, Michael Byrd, Christopher Byrd. **EDUCATION:** Boston Univ, Boston MA, BS 1964; Univ of Michigan, Ann Arbor MI, Exec Mgmt Program, 1980. **CAREER:** Natl Football League (NFL) Buffalo Bills (NY) 1964-70, Denver Broncos (CO), 1970-72; Chrysler/Plymouth Corp, Atlanta GA sales mgr, New Haven CT, operations mgr, 1973-81; Polariod Corp, Oakbrook IL, regional marketing mgr/regional operations mgr, 1981-86, marketing mgr, 1986-87, gen mgr, 1987-. **ORGANIZATIONS:** Mem, The Partnership. **HONORS/ACHIEVEMENTS:** All-Pro, NFL, Buffalo Bills, 1965, 1966, 1968, 1969; man of the year, African Meeting Houses, 1989. **BUSINESS ADDRESS:** Gen Mgr, Polariod/Inner City, Inc, 716 Columbus Ave, 5th Fl, Boston, MA 02120.

BYRD, GILL ARNETTE
Professional athlete. **PERSONAL:** Born Feb 20, 1961, San Francisco, CA; married Marilyn. **EDUCATION:** San Jose State. **CAREER:** San Diego Chargers, cornerback 1983-; Aerospace Firm, fin anlyst. **HONORS/ACHIEVEMENTS:** 3rd plyr selected 1st round 22nd plyr chosen 83 draft round; played East-West Shrine Game & Blue Grey Game. **BUSINESS ADDRESS:** San Diego Chargers, San Diego Stadium, P O Box 20666, San Diego, CA 92120.

BYRD, HARRIET ELIZABETH
Retired elementary teacher. **PERSONAL:** Born Apr 20, 1926, Cheyenne, WY; married

James W Byrd; children: Robert C, James W II, Lindia C. **EDUCATION:** WV State Coll, BS Educ 1949; Univ of WY, MA Elem Educ 1976. **CAREER:** WY Educ Assn, WY TEPS Comm 1970-73; Marshall Scholarship Comm, comm mem 1972-79; WY State Adv Council, comm mem 1973-80; NEA Albuquerque, inserv training ctrs 1979; WY State Legislature, House of Representatives 4th term. **ORGANIZATIONS:** Mem Kappa Kappa Iota Sor Delta Kappa Gamma 1968; mem Instructional and Prof Develop Comm 1976-77; life mem Kappa Delta Pi 1977-; mem Laramie Co Coll Booster Club; mem WY State Adv Bd Health & Social Svcs; adv bd Laramie Co Senior Citizens; vice pres Laramie Co Democratic Women's Club; mem DePaul Guild, Intl Altrusa Cheyenne, NAACP, Univ of Wyoming Alumni, NEA Retired, WEA Retired, St Mary's Catholic Church. **HONORS/ACHIEVEMENTS:** Instructor Excellence in Teaching Awd Instructor magazine 1968. **BUSINESS ADDRESS:** Representative, Wyoming State Legislature, Wyoming State Capitol, Cheyenne, WY 82001.

BYRD, HELEN P.
Educator. **PERSONAL:** Born Feb 27, 1943, Waynesboro, GA; married Shedrick; children: Shedrick Tyrone. **EDUCATION:** Warren Wilson Coll, AA 1961; Berea Coll, BA 1963; Temple Univ, MEd 1965; Univ of CT, PhD 1972; Columbia Univ Teachers Coll, Postdoctoral Study 1973,76. **CAREER:** School Dist of Philadelphia, teacher 1963-65; Atlanta Public School System, teacher 1966-68; Atlanta State Univ, visiting prof 1968; Savannah GA State Coll, visiting prof 1971; Norfolk State Univ, prof special educ dept 1968-. **ORGANIZATIONS:** Sec membership chmn MR Div Comm on Minority-Council for Exceptional Children 1972-78; bd of trustees Boggs Acad 1976-83; mem prog agency United Presbyterian Church USA 1977-83; bd mem 1976-79, vchmn 1979-80 Norfolk Comm for Improvement of Ed; bd mem Hope House Found 1977-; mem Presbyterian Comm on Minority Educ 1982-; sec 1985, mem Norfolk Comm Serv Bd 1983-; bd mem Cultural Experiences Unlimited. **HONORS/ACHIEVEMENTS:** Scholr Wm H Hess Meml Scholarship Fund 1961; Fellow BEH-USOE Mental Retardation 1965-66; Fellow So Fellowship Fund 1970-72; Grant Recipient BEPD USOE Proj 1972-76; Grant Recipient BEH USOE Proj 1977-80; Education Awd Aurora 60 Order of Eastern Star 1983. **BUSINESS ADDRESS:** Professor Spec Education, Norfolk StateUniv, Spec Education Dept, Norfolk, VA 23504.

BYRD, ISSAC, JR.
Judge. **PERSONAL:** Born 1952. **CAREER:** Mississippi Board of Corrections, former vice chairman; chancery judge for state of Mississippi, 1989. **BUSINESS ADDRESS:** Owens & Byrd, 403 S State, Jackson, MS 39201. *

BYRD, JAMES W.
Marshall. **PERSONAL:** Born Oct 22, 1925, Newark, NJ; married Harriett Elizabeth Rhone; children: Robert, James, Linda. **EDUCATION:** Laramie Co Comm Coll. **CAREER:** Cheyenne Police Dept, 25 Yrs; Hwy Safety State of WY, dir 1975-77; US Marshall KC, 1977. **ORGANIZATIONS:** Life mem VFW Am Legion; Internatl Assn Chfs of Police; WY Peace Officers; IBPO Elks of WY Lawman of Year; Kiwanis Internatl 1968; Served In European Thtr; Ww Ii veteran; Koreanwar. **BUSINESS ADDRESS:** PO Box 768, Cheyenne, WY 82001.

BYRD, JERRY STEWART
Attorney. **PERSONAL:** Born Dec 11, 1935, Greenville, SC; son of Elliott Byrd and Ethel Byrd; married Paula Deborah Aughtry; children: Jerry Stewart Jr. **EDUCATION:** Fisk Univ, BA 1961; Howard Univ, JD 1964; Southeastern Univ, ASBA 1975. **CAREER:** Natl Labor Relations Bd Regional Adv Branch, atty 1964-65; Neighborhood Legal Serv, managing atty 1965-69 and 1974-81, dep dir 1970-71; Howard Univ, polit sci instructor 1971-72; Superior Ct of DC, hearing commissioner 1981-. **ORGANIZATIONS:** Mem Hearing Comm Bd of Professional Responsibility 1982-; mem Near Northeast Pub Interest Civic Assn; chmn Spec Bd of Inquiry Adams Comm Sch; mem bd dir Hospitality Comm Fed Credit Union; mem DC Consumer Goods Repair Bd 1974-77. **HONORS/ACHIEVEMENTS:** Publication, "Courts, Slums and Feasibility of Adopting the Warranty of Fitness The DC Housing Research Comm Report 1967; Important Cases, Thompson v Mazo 421 F 2d 1156, 137 US App DC 221 (1970) re'g 245 A2d 122 (DC App 1968); Durmu v Gill 227 A2d 104 (DC App 1970); Coleman v District of Columbia 250 A2d 555 (DC App 1968). **MILITARY SERVICE:** AUS Sp-4 served 3 years. **HOME ADDRESS:** 2110 T St SE, Washington, DC 20020. **BUSINESS ADDRESS:** Hearing Commissioner, Superior Court of DC, 500 Indiana Ave NW, Washington, DC 20001.

BYRD, JOSEPH KEYS
Education administrator. **PERSONAL:** Born Oct 03, 1953, Meadville, MS. **EDUCATION:** William Carey Coll, BS 1975, MEd 1980. **CAREER:** William Carey Coll, cnslr/instr 1980-82;Univ of New Orleans, devel specialist cnslr 1981-82; Xavier Univ of LA, gen cnslr 1982-83;Univ of New Orleans, asst dir dev ed 1983-86; Xavier Univ, asst dean student serv 1986-. **ORGANIZATIONS:** Cnslr/tutor coord William Carey Coll 1975-80; exec sec Sigma Lambda Chap Alpha Phi Alpha Frat 1982-; adv Omicron Delta Kappa 1978, Chi Beta Phi 1980; mem NAACP New Orleans LA 1984; president, Greater New Orleans Chapter National Pan-Hellenic Council Inc 1989; president, Louisiana Conference - Alpha Phi Alpha Fraternity Inc; steering committee, Greater New Orleans Foundation; bd of directors, Human Services on Cable. **HONORS/ACHIEVEMENTS:** Outstanding Young Educator William Carey Coll 1981; Outstanding Young Men of Amer 1979-80; Distinguished Service Award, Alpha Phi Alpha Fraternity Inc 1989; Advisor of the Year - Student Government, Xavier Univ. **BUSINESS ADDRESS:** Asst Dean Student Services, Xavier University, Box 101-C, New Orleans, LA 70125.

BYRD, KATIE W.
Supervisory management analyst. **PERSONAL:** Born Jun 26, Mobile, AL; children: Marcus Dalton, Taynetta Joy. **EDUCATION:** Alabama A&M Univ, BS, MS; Pennsylvania State Univ, PhD. **CAREER:** Previous positions include tchr educ specialist, counseling, equal oppty officer US army missile and munitions ctr and sch, equal employment opportunity program; US Army Missile Command, supervisory management analyst. **ORGANIZATIONS:** Mem Women's Equity Action League; mem Natl Assn Black Psychologists; Natl Assn Adminstr Counselors & Deans; Pi Lambda Theta; past president Huntsville Br NAACP; mem Natl Presbyterian Black Caucus; pres Women of Ch; elder Presbyterian Ch; chairperson Social Action-Delta Sigma Theta Sor; mem Women's Political Caucus; state recorder, vice pres Huntsville Chap AL New South Coalition. **HONORS/ACHIEVEMENTS:** Equal Employment Opportunity Awd; Outstanding Young Women of Amer; Outstanding Black in Human Services; Good Govt Awd Huntsville Jaycees; Outstanding Leadership Awd; Outstanding Comm Serv Awd.

BYRD, LUMUS, JR.
Marketing manager, chairman, president, ceo. **PERSONAL:** Born Apr 25, 1942, Clinton, SC; son of Lumus Byrd Sr and Mary J Byrd. **EDUCATION:** SC State Coll, BS Bio 1965, MS Bio 1969. **CAREER:** Charleston, SC Sch Dist #20, edctr 1965-70; Jos Schlitz Brewing Co, dist mgr 1970-74; Greyhound Lines, Inc, dir Sls 1974-78; The Greyhound Corp, mgr mkt dev 1978-82; Byrd Enterprises Inc, chmn, pres, CEO, 1989-; T & T Iron Works, pres, 1989-. **ORGANIZATIONS:** Vice pres Natl Asso Mkt Dev 1980; treas Am Mktng Asso 1982; vice pres Phoenix Advertising Club 1984; dir bd Valley Ldrshp Inc 1984; vice pres Alpha Hi Alpha Frat 1985; adv bd YMCA 1985. **HONORS/ACHIEVEMENTS:** Distinguished Alumni SC State Coll 1984; Man of the Yr Alpha Phi Alpha Frat 1983; Outstanding Mtr Toastmasters 1984. **BUSINESS ADDRESS:** President, Byrd Enterprises Inc, dba T & T Iron Works, 2453 Lewis Ave, Long Beach, CA 90806.

BYRD, MANFORD, JR.
Educational administrator. **PERSONAL:** Born May 29, 1928, Brewton, AL; son of Manford Byrd and Evelyn Patton Byrd; married Cheri; children: Carl, Bradley, Donald. **EDUCATION:** Central Coll, BA 1949; Univ of Chicago, MA 1954; Atlanta Univ, LHD (hon) 1969; Northwestern Univ, PhD, 1978. **CAREER:** Chicago Public Schools, teacher/principal, asst general supt, deputy supt, general supt, 1985-. **ORGANIZATIONS:** mem, bd of dir, Chicago State Univ Joint Negro Appeal, Chicago State Univ Found, Mid-America Chapter, Amer Red Cross; Sigma Pi Phi (Beta Boule) (Natl Treasurer of Sigma Pi Phi Fraternity, 1980); mem, Natl Alliance of Black School Educators; chmn, Christian Educ, Trinity United Church; mem, Large Unit Dist Assn (LUDA); mem, bd of dir, Council of the Great City Schools; mem, Found for Excellence in Teaching. **BUSINESS ADDRESS:** Superintendent of Schools, Chicago Board of Education, 1819 W Pershing Road, Chicago, IL 60609.

BYRD, NELLIE J.
Former alderman. **PERSONAL:** Born Jan 28, 1924, Rayvill, LA; married Leandreu Byrd; children: Bobbie Phillips, Marva Martin, Patricia Jackson, Larry Martin, Willie Martin, Travis Martin, Gerald Martin, Reginald Martin. **EDUCATION:** Chicoh Cty Training School, 1942. **CAREER:** City of Wrightsville, former alderman 1983-85, planning comm 1985-87. **ORGANIZATIONS:** Treas Esther Chap 384 OES; mem NAACP 1972-85, Natl Assoc of Colored Women Club 1982-85, Privident Relief Club Little Rock AR 1980-85. **HONORS/ACHIEVEMENTS:** 1st fin sec for 1st Bapt Church Wrightsville 1966-74. **HOME ADDRESS:** P O Box 2043, Wrightsville, AR 72183.

BYRD, PERCY L.
Company manager. **PERSONAL:** Born Jun 14, 1937, Hogansville, GA; son of Garland Byrd (deceased) and Ettarean Philpot Byrd (deceased); married Irene Stahler, Sep 21, 1977. **EDUCATION:** Morehouse Coll, Atlanta, GA, 1956-59; Savannah State Coll, Savannah, GA, BS (cum laude), 1961. **CAREER:** US Govt, St Louis, MO, Washington, DC, cartographer, geologist, mathematician, 1965-67; Planning Research Corp, St Louis, MO, San Antonio, TX, Washington, DC, sr tech staff mem, 1967-79, 1984; Sperry Univac, Washington, DC, computer salesperson, 1979-80; Magnavox Data Systems, Washington, DC, sr engineer, 1980-81; District of Columbia Govt, Washington, DC, branch mgr, 1981-83; SAIC, Washington, DC, dir, 1983-84; MAXIMA Corp, Washington, DC, Dayton, OH, Los Angeles, CA, sr vice pres, 1984-. **ORGANIZATIONS:** Bd of dir, treasurer, Black Business Assn of Los Angeles, 1989-90; mem, Los Angeles Urban League, 1987-89. **MILITARY SERVICE:** AUS, E-4, 1961-64.

BYRD, SHERMAN CLIFTON
Clergyman, former criminal investigator. **PERSONAL:** Born Dec 06, 1928, Mesquite, TX; married Dorothy Barksdale; children: Duane Edward, Dorothy Eleanor, James, Henry, Thomas, Nancy Ellen, Sandra Kay, Johnathan Earl, Joyce Jean. **EDUCATION:** St Philip's Coll, attended 1955-56 & 1966; Guadalupe Coll, B Div, DD 1962. **CAREER:** San Antonio Police Dept, various positions 1953-62; Bexar County DA's Office, criminal invest 1963-76; cert law enforcement instr; 1st Providence BaptistChurch, pastor; Holy Land Museum of the Americas, founder & president; Guadalupe Theological Seminary, chmn. **ORGANIZATIONS:** Providence Bapt Ch; pres founder United Counc of Civic Action; Christian Action for Prog; TX Bapt Min Union; EX Emancipation Day Commn; Comm Workers Council 1955; Bexar County Fed Credit Union 1964; coord San Antonio Child Care Assn, vice pres 1963. **HONORS/ACHIEVEMENTS:** Author "The Transplant"; est min wage law first city in TX. **MILITARY SERVICE:** USN 1948-50. **BUSINESS ADDRESS:** Pastor, 1st Providence Baptist Church, 1014 Clark Ave, San Antonio, TX 78203.

BYRD, TAYLOR
Educator. **PERSONAL:** Born Nov 02, 1940, Greene County, AL; married Katie W; children: Marcus Dalton, Taynetta Joy. **EDUCATION:** Al A&M U, BS 1963; Tuskegee Inst, MEd 1969; PA State U, PhD 1972. **CAREER:** Agribusiness Educ Dept, AL A&M Univ, Normal AL, chmn 1972-; PA State Univ, grad res asst 1970-72; TN Valley High School, instructor, asst prin 1966-70; Woodson High School, Andalusia AL, instructor, asst coach 1964-66; TN Valley High School, instructor, coach 1963-64; AL A&M Univ, NASA tech. **ORGANIZATIONS:** Evaluator of So Reg Agr Educ Conf Mobile, AL 1973; proj dir Cross-Cultural Skills & 2nterpresonal Effect in Urban Enviroment 1972; mem AVA, AVATA, NVATA, AATE, AEA, NEA, ALEA; mem Consistory #150 32 Mason IBPOE of W. **HONORS/ACHIEVEMENTS:** Student Council Avd Award TN Valley HS 1968; Tchr of Yr TN Valley HS1969; grad research assistantship 1970; Outstnading Achievement in Ed Phi Beta Sigma 1973; Listed in Outstanding Young Men of Amer 1973; Nat Alumni-normalite Assn Class Achievement Award 1973; Personalitires of the S 1974; Citation for Outstanding Contributions to Research Devel, Reg Adaptive Tech Cntr, Honolulu, 1975; appted chmn of Search Co for Dean of Sch of Bus AL A&MUniv 1975. **BUSINESS ADDRESS:** Dept of Agr Bus Educ, PO Box AL A&M Univ, Normal, AL.

BYRD, W. MICHAEL
Obstetrician-gynecologist. **PERSONAL:** Born Dec 26, 1943, Galveston, TX; married Mary Etta Davis; children: Michael Charles, Miles Eugene, Edward Ellington. **EDUCATION:** Morehouse Coll, BS 1964; Meharry Medical Coll, MD 1968. **CAREER:** Private Practice, obstetrician-gynecologist. **ORGANIZATIONS:** Mem Alpha Phi Alpha 1961-, Meharry

Alumni Assoc 1975-, Natl NAACP 1975-, Morehouse Alumni Assoc 1978-; expert on black health past and present NMA SpeakersBureau 1983-; consultant Black Health Affairs Natl NAACP 1983-; advisor to pres NMA Black Health Issues 1985-86; expert panelist Maternal & Child Health Cong Black Caucus Foundation Braintrust Workshop 1985-; resource person on black health issues US Congress 1985-; guest Karen Denard's "Evening Talk Show," KERA FM1985-; expert testimony Civil Rights Subcom of House Jud Com 1986. **HONORS/ACHIEVEMENTS:** Publications "Medical Care in America, A Tragic Turn for the Worst" w/GE Hairston, Crisis 1985; "1686178618861986, Over Three Centuries of Black Health Distress" paper presented at the annual meeting of the AL State Medical Assoc Birmingham 1986; "Peer Review, The Perversion of a Process" report prepared for the Subcommittee on Civil Rights of the House Comm on the Judiciary 1986; "An American Health Dilemma" Journal of the Natl Medical Assoc 1986. **MILITARY SERVICE:** AUS Medical Corps capt 2 yrs; Bronze Star Medal. **HOME ADDRESS:** 1021 Wesleyville, Nashville, TN 37217.

C

CABBELL, EDWARD JOSEPH
Association executive, editor. **PERSONAL:** Born Jun 26, 1946, Eckman, WV; married Madeline Harrell; children: Melissa Yvette, Winnia Denise. **EDUCATION:** Concord Coll, BS Ed 1970; Appalachian State Univ, MA 1983. **CAREER:** Upward Bound & Spec Serv for Disadvantaged Students, dir 1969-75; John Henry Folk Fest, dir 1975-; John Henry Records, producer 1978-; Black Diamonds Mag, editor 1978-; Appalachian Studies Concord Coll, adj prof 1984-; John Henry Mem Found Inc, founder, dir. **ORGANIZATIONS:** Advisory comm "We Shall Overcome" Fund Admin Royalties for "We Shall Overcome" Civil Rights Theme 1977; chmn City of Princeton Human Relations Commiss 1977-; pres Neighborhood Improvement Assoc Inc 1982-; advisory comm Folklife Festival 1982 Worlds Fair 1982; bd Council of the Southern Mountains 1984; bd mem Highland Rsch & Educ Center; gov appointee bd mem WV Martin Luther King Jr State Holiday Commiss 1986-. **HONORS/ACHIEVEMENTS:** Writer's Scholarship Breadloaf Writers Conf 1970; Black Studies Fellowship Univ of Louisville 1971; Appalachian Studies Fellowship Berea Coll 1980-,81; James Still Fellow in Appalachian Studies Univ of KY 1981; co-editor Black in Appalachia Univ Press of Kentucky 1985; Comtemporary Authors 1987. **HOME ADDRESS:** PO Box 1172, Morgantown, WV 26507. **BUSINESS ADDRESS:** Dir, John Henry Mem Found Inc, PO Box 135, Princeton, WV 24740.

CABRERA, ELOISE J.
Educator. **PERSONAL:** Born Dec 09, 1932, Evinston, FL; married Marion; children: Yolanda Alicia. **EDUCATION:** FL A&M Univ, BS 1954; IN Univ, MS 1963; study MI State Univ; Univ of S FL; Nova Univ Fort Lauderdale, EdD 1985. **CAREER:** Broward County School System, elementary teacher 1954-56; Hillsborough County School System, jr high core dept head 1958-63, head of Guidance dept 1963-66; Neighborhood Youth Corps, City of Tampa, asst proj dir 1966-69; Hillsborough County Community School Prog, supvr 1969-. **ORGANIZATIONS:** Mem Nat Comm Educ Assn; Am Assn of Univ Women; FL Assn for Comm Edn;bd dir Tampa Urban League; FL Adult Educ Assn; mem NAACP Nat Council of Negro Women; Tampa Alumnae Chap Delta Sigma Theta Sor, Corr Sec; Orgn for Concerned Parents. **HONORS/ACHIEVEMENTS:** Plaque for distn serv to FACE; Boy Scouts Award for Merit Svc; Cert for Outstanding Contribution to Hillsborough Comm Coll Adv Comm. **BUSINESS ADDRESS:** Instructional Serv Cntr, 707 E Columbus Dr, Tampa, FL 33602.

CADE, ALFRED JACKAL
Brigadier general. **PERSONAL:** Born Feb 04, 1931, Fayetteville, NC. **EDUCATION:** VA State Coll, BS Gen Psych; Syracuse Univ, MBA Comptrollership; Arty Sch; Quartermaster Sch; AUS Field Arty Sch; AUS Command & Gen Staff Coll;Indsl Coll of Armed Forces. **CAREER:** Over 25 years active commr svc; asst sector adv 1966-67; Phu Yen Province Vietnam, sector adv 1967; US Milit Command Vietnam, dep sr province adv 1967; Pacific-Vietnam, comdr 1st Battalion 92nd Arty 1967-68; budget operations ofcr 1968-69; Dir of Army Budget Wash, exec ofcr 1970-72; Material Command Wash, DC, asst comptroller for budget 1972; 210th Field Arty Group Europe, comdr 1973-74. **HONORS/ACHIEVEMENTS:** Promoted from 2nd Lt to Brigadier Gen Jan, 1954. **MILITARY SERVICE:** AUS Brig Gen; Recip Legion of Merit (with 2 Oak Leaf Clusters); Bronze Star Medal (with 3 Oak Leaf Clusters); Meritorious Serv Medal; Air Medal; Army Commend Medal; Combat Infantryman Badge; Parachutist Badge.

CADE, HAROLD EDWARD
Educational administrator. **PERSONAL:** Born Aug 25, 1929, Bonami, LA; married Josephine Lockhart; children: Deryl Vernon. **EDUCATION:** Prairie View A&M Univ, BA 1955, BS 1958; Univ of CO, MA 1960; North TX State Univ, MEd 1967. **CAREER:** VISD Gross HS, football coach 1960; VISD Victoria/Stroman HS, counselor 1965-; TSTA Dist 3, pres 1975; VISD Patti Welder Jr High, principal 1975-85. **ORGANIZATIONS:** Football coach Lockhart Public Schools 1953; football coach FW Gross 1955-66; counselor Victoria HS 1965-67; asst principal Stroman HS 1967; pres Victoria Kiwanis Club 1975; lt governor Div 25 TX/OK Dist 1977; pres Victoria TSTA 1978. **HONORS/ACHIEVEMENTS:** Pres TX State Teacher Assoc 1967; bd of dir Victoria Chamber of Com 1978; superintendent Palestine Baptist Church SS 1979-85; bd of dir YMCA Victoria 1980-85. **MILITARY SERVICE:** USMC lt 1954-57. **BUSINESS ADDRESS:** Principal, Victoria Public Schools, Patti Welder Jr High, 1500 E North St, Victoria, TX 77901.

CADE, HENRY
Business executive. **PERSONAL:** Children: Henry L, Crystal L, Jeffrey P. **EDUCATION:** Wayne St Univ Coll Pharmacy Allied Health Professions, BS Pharmacy 1948; Univ of Chicago Graduate School Business, MBA 1973. **CAREER:** Walgreen Co, various Mgmt positions 1959-79, mgr professional relations 1979-83, mgr public affairs prof relations 1983-87; dir, 1987-. **ORGANIZATIONS:** President Natl Assn Bds Pharmacy 1987-88, IL State Bd Pharmacy 1975-94; Editorial Advisory Bd US Pharmacist 1979-82, Chicago Blacks Phlnthrpy, Bureau School Attendance Advisory Council Chicago Public School; first black to serve in a leadership role in the 83 year history of the Natl Assn of Boards of Pharmacy; mem, bd of dir of Lawndale Community School, Chicago IL, 1986-; mem, Advisory Panel on Pharmacy Practice of Pharmacopeial Convention Inc, 1985-. **HONORS/ACHIEVEMENTS:** Distinguished Alumnus Wayne State Univ Coll Pharmacy 1979; Distinguished Serv Award Natl Pharmaceutical; IL Pharmacist of the Year Award, IL Pharmacists Assn 1987. **MILITARY SERVICE:** USNR seaman 1st cl 1 yr. **BUSINESS ADDRESS:** Dir Public Affairs & Professional Relations, Walgreen Co, 200 Wilmot Rd, Deerfield, IL 60015.

CADE, LIONEL C.
Government official. **PERSONAL:** Married Gladys; children: 4 Children. **EDUCATION:** Univ SF, BA; Univ So CA. **CAREER:** City cnclmn 1964-73; pub acct. **BUSINESS ADDRESS:** Compton City Hall, 205 S Willowbrook St, Compton, CA 90220.

CADE, MOSSY JACKSON
Professional athlete. **PERSONAL:** Born Dec 26, 1961, Eloy, AZ. **EDUCATION:** Texas. **CAREER:** Memphis Showboats, cornerback, rookie 1984-. **HONORS/ACHIEVEMENTS:** First-Team All-Amer choice in 1983; named to All-Amer teams by Assoc Press, Walter Camp Found and Sporting News; Southwest Conf Def Player of the Years; named second-team All-SWC. **BUSINESS ADDRESS:** Memphis Showboats, 3767 New Getwell Rd, Ste 400, Memphis, TN 38118.

CADE, TININA QUICK
Educational administrator. **PERSONAL:** Born Oct 15, 1949, Washington, DC; married Dr Ronald Evans Cade; children: Camille Topaz, Simone Nicole. **EDUCATION:** Univ of Cincinnati, BA 1971; OH State Univ, MA 1972; Univ of Pittsburgh, PhD 1977. **CAREER:** Univ of Pittsburgh, asst to provost 1972-77; OH State Univ, dir R&D eval 1977-80; VA Commonwealth Univ, asst dir of student activities 1980-81, asst dir of NSW off-campus program 1981-83; VA Union Univ, dean of students. **ORGANIZATIONS:** Mem Natl Assoc of Stud Personnel, 1971-, NAACP 1971-, Black Ed Assoc 1981-83. **HONORS/ACHIEVEMENTS:** Woman of the Year Delta Sigma Theta Sor 1982. **BUSINESS ADDRESS:** Dean of Students, Virginia Union University, 1500 N Lombardy St, Richmond, VA 23220.

CADE, TONI See BAMBARA, TONI CADE

CADE, VALARIE SWAIN
Educator. **PERSONAL:** Born Sep 16, 1952, Philadelphia, PA; daughter of William Arch Swain and Ena Lindner Swain; children: Ena Marietta, David Lloyd. **EDUCATION:** Penn State Univ, BA 1973; Temple Univ, MEd 1977, DEd 1978; Univ of PA, Philadelphia Child Guidance Clinic Post-Doctoral Family Therapy 1981; Wharton School Exec Educ Mngmt Prog 1987; Harvard University, IEM 1988. **CAREER:** PA State Univ, tutor 1971-72, peer counselor 1971-73; School Dist of Philadelphia, teacher language arts 1972-74; Camden Schools, language arts & reading teacher 1974-76; Camden County Comm Coll Learning Skills Ctr, administrator and study skills specialist 1976-77, counselor 1976-77; Dept of Educ, field reader & curriculum consultant 1976-; Rutgers Univ, asst prof of English 1976-78; Univ of PA, psychoeducational specialist 1978-80; Univ of PA, asst prof/lecturer 1978-82, faculty master WEB DuBois Coll House 1978-80, asst to vice provost for undergrad studies, dir commonwealth prog 1978-83, asst assoc provost 1983-85, exec asst provost 1985-86, asst provost 1986-88; assistant provost and assistant to the president 1989-. **ORGANIZATIONS:** PA coord Tri-State Council on Equal Educ Oppor 1978-81; eastern regional rep ACT-101 Adv Comm 1979-81; pres Mid-Eastern Assoc of Educ Oppor 1983; pres PA Assoc of Educ Oppor 1981-83; bd mem and Mid-Atlantic Regional Pres Emeritus Natl Council of Educ Oppor; exec bd mem Mid-Eastern Assoc of Educ Oppor; mem League of United Latin Amer Citizens Adv Bd; mem Amer Foundation for Negro Affairs Medical Steering Comm; mem National Assn for Educ Opportunity 1988. **HONORS/ACHIEVEMENTS:** Natl Merit Scholar 1969-73; NAACP Achievement Awd 1969; Dean's List Penn State and Temple Univs 1970-78; Youngest Black Woman in the US to run for Federal office 1972; Temple Univ Doctoral Fellow 1976-77; Onyx Senior Honor Soc Univ of PA 1979; PA Assoc of Educ Oppor Outstanding Achievement Awd 1983; Temple Univ Russell Conwell Ctr Awd 1983; PA State Univ Achievement Awd 1983; IEM fellowship, Harvard University 1988. **HOME ADDRESS:** 105 E Cliveden, Philadelphia, PA 19119. **BUSINESS ADDRESS:** Office of the President, University of Pennsylvania, 119 College Hall, Philadelphia, PA 19104.

CADE, WALTER, III
Artist, actor, singer, musician. **PERSONAL:** Born in New York, NY; son of Walter Cade and Helen Henderson Brehon. **EDUCATION:** Inst of Modern Art NY; private tchrs Lee Strasberg Sch of Dramatic Arts; Muse Drama Workshop. **CAREER:** Theatre, "Amen Corner" E River Players Repertory Co; "Hatful of Rain" Muse Drama Workshop; "Mateus" "Harle Quinade" others City Ctr Young Peoples Repertory Theatre; "Mary, Mary" Lexiton & London Barn Dinner Theatre; "Don't Bother Me I Can't Cope" Theatre for the Forgotten; movies, Cotton Comes to Harlem, Education of Sonny Carson, The Wiz, Claudine; TV, Joe Franklin Show, Positively Black, Soul, Sammy Davis Telethon, Musical Chairs, Big Blue Marble; Artist in NY WNYC; Controversy WLIB; singing in various inns in NY, Queens, Long Island, MA, WA. **ORGANIZATIONS:** Some exhibitions, CW Post Coll LIU Group Show 1968; Whitney Museum Annual Show 1969; Heckscher Mus Group 1969; Whitney Mus Contemporary Black Artist 1971; Fairleigh Dickerson Coll Group 1971; Corcoran Gallery Group 1972; Automation House Ten Black Artists 1973; Bedford Stuyvesant Restoration Ctr African Art & Afro-Amer Artist 1973; Black Expo 1973; Queens Cultural Ctr for the Arts Queens Talent 1973; Ocean Co Coll One Man Show 1977; Jackson State Univ One Man Show 1980; MS Mus of Art Group Show 1981; Tampa Museum Group Show 1982; Tucson Museum of Art Group Show 1983; permanent collections, Southeast Banking Corp; Rockefeller Found; Fine Arts Museum of the South; VA Beach Art Museum; Bruce Mus; City of Miami Beach.

CADORIA, SHERIAN GRACE
Military officer. **PERSONAL:** Born Jan 26, 1940, Marksville, LA; daughter of Cameron Joseph Cadoria and Bernice McGlory Cadoria. **EDUCATION:** Southern Univ, BS, Business Educ, 1961; AUS Command & General Staff Coll, Diploma, 1971; Univ of Oklahoma, MA, Human Relations, 1974; AUS War Coll, Diploma, 1979; Natl Defense Univ, Inst of Higher Defense Studies, 1985. **CAREER:** Women's Army Corps Sch & Ctr, instructor/human relations ofcr 1971-73; Women's Army Corps Branch, US Army Military Personnel Ctr, exec officer/personnel officer 1973-75; Law Enforcement Div Officer of the Deputy Chief of Staff for Personnel Headquarters Dept of the Army, personnel staff officer 1975-76; Military

Police Student Battalion, battalion commander 1977-78; Physical Security Div US Army Europe & 7th Army, division chief 1979-82; 1st Region Criminal Invest Command, brigade commander 1982-84; Dept of the Army, chief, Office of Army Law Enforcement 1984-85; Pentagon Organization of the Joint Chiefs of Staff, dir of manpower & personnel (Brigadier General) 1985-; US Total Army Personnel Command, deputy commander/dir for mobilization & operations 1987-. **ORGANIZATIONS:** Mem Intl Assn of Chiefs of Police; Assn of the United States Army; WAC Veterans Assn 1980-. **HONORS/ACHIEVEMENTS:** George Olmstead Scholarship Freedom's Foundation, Valley Forge, PA 1972; Social Aide to the President of the United States 1975-76; Distinguished Alumni Award Southern Univ 1984; author of, "Women in the Army, An Integral Part of America's Defense", Federal Women's Program, Ft Meade, MD 1984; One of Amers Top 100 Black Bus & Professional Women 1985; Distinguished Serv Medal, Hoffstra Univ 1986; Intl Black Woman of the Year, Los Angeles Sentinel 1987; one of 75 Black Women who helped change history in the I Dream A World photo exhibit in Corcoran Gallery, USA West/Life Magazine 1989. **MILITARY SERVICE:** AUS Brigadier General (served over 25 yrs); Legion of Merit, 3 Bronze Stars, 2 Meritorious Serv Medals, Air Medal, 4 Army Commendation Medals; Defense Superior Serv Medal 1987. **BUSINESS ADDRESS:** Deputy Commanding Gen/Dir for Mobilization & Operations, US Total Army Personnel Command, 200 Stovall St, Alexandria, VA 22332-0430.

CAESAR, HARRY
Actor, entertainer. **PERSONAL:** Born Feb 18, 1928, Pittsburgh, PA; son of Alec Caesar; married Marion K Bernot; children: Jacqueline, Valerie, Kimberly. **CAREER:** Worked as an extra 1953-69; pres starring in "Bird on A Wire"; earlier films include "Tanganyika" & "Carmen Jones"; first speaking role "The Graduate"; featured in "Emperor of the North" 1973; "The Longest Yard" 1976; "Casey's Shadow" 1978; "The Big Fix" 1978; "A Small Circle of Friends" 1980; "Barbarosa"1981, "Electric Boogaloo", "Breakin II" 1985, "From A Whisper to a Scream", 1987; TV shows, "Baretta"; "Cagney & Lacey"; "Hill St Blues", "L.A. Law"; featured vocalist with The Swingin' Honeydrippers (music of the '40's & '50's); album on "Route 66" label including "Going Down to the River", "Goodbye Baby" and 15 other blues hits recorded in early '50's. **ORGANIZATIONS:** Natl Rifle Assn; Amer Fed of Police; NAACP; Screen Extras Guild; Screen Actors Guild; Amer Fed of TV & Radio Actors. **HONORS/ACHIEVEMENTS:** Won Heavyweight boxing championship Fort Ord, CA 1950; Certificate of Achievement Acad of Science Fiction Fantasy and Horror Films for performance in "From a Whisper to a Scream" 1987.

CAESAR, LOIS
Musician, educator. **PERSONAL:** Born Apr 04, 1922, Texarkana, AR; married Richard C. **EDUCATION:** Wiley Coll, AB; State Univ IA, MA; State Univ of IA, MFA. **CAREER:** Europe & Am, concert pianist 1949-66; Paris, France debut Salle Gaveau 1950; Town Hall, NY Debut 1950; Fisk U, asst prof 1943-49; TN State U, artist in residence 1955-56; Monsieru & Ciampi, Paris repetitrice 1951-53. **ORGANIZATIONS:** Bd dir SF Symphony Found 1st black 1965-75; SF Symphony Assn 1st Black bd govs 1969-; SF Spring Opera 1st Black exec bd 1969-; SF Grand Jurists1972; 10 Outstanding Citizens judge 1972; Mayor's Crim Just Council 1st Black Woman exec bd 1974-; Juvenile Justice Commn 1st black 1st Woman 1st Minoritychmn 1976-78; SF WATF pres; SF Women's Aux Dental Soc 1st Black pres 1977; No State Dental Wives 1st Black pres-elect 1977; SF Links; NAACP life mem; Nat Newsletter of the Auxiliary Am Dental Assn chmn & Editory 1979; SF Bay Area United Way 1st Black exec bd. **HONORS/ACHIEVEMENTS:** First Black Recipient Thomas Jefferson Award for Public Serv Am Inst 1978; 6 Best Dressed Awards; 4 Outst Comm Svc, Incl 1 From City & Co of SF.

CAESAR, SHIRLEY
Singer, evangelist. **PERSONAL:** Born in Durham, NC; married Bishop Harold I Williams. **EDUCATION:** Shaw Univ, Business Mgmt 1984. **CAREER:** Joined Caravan Singers 1958; Shirley Caesar Outreach Ministries, opened to aid needy families in Durham NC 1969; recorded 30 albums; travels throughout the US singing to crowds of 8,000 to 35,000 people; Mt Calvary Holy Church Winston-Salem, co-pastor 1983-. **ORGANIZATIONS:** Active in various community & civic affairs; visits hosps regularly , sr citizen homes & schools; each yr she spends thousands of dollars buying food to feed the needy; host for the Gospel music indust; hon mem bd of dirs Divinity Sch Shaw Univ 1984; spokeswoman McDonald's Salute to Gospel Music 1987. **HONORS/ACHIEVEMENTS:** Grammy Awd for "Put Your Hand in the Hand of the Man From Galilee" 1972; several songs that sold over a million copies incl "No Charge", "Don't Drive Your Mother Away"; named Best Female Gospel Singer Ebony Magazine 1975; proclamation Oct and Nov as Shirley Caesar's Months in Durham NC 1978; performed at the WhiteHouse for Jimmy Carter 1979; Dr Martin Luther King Jr Drum Major Awd; Top Female Gospel Singer in the Country Ebony Mag Music Poll 1977; Stellar Awd by Peers in Gospel Music Industry 1987; 5 Grammy Awds; 3 Gold Albums. **BUSINESS ADDRESS:** P O Box 3336, Durham, NC 27702.

CAFRITZ, PEGGY COOPER
Television executive. **PERSONAL:** Born Apr 07, 1947, Mobile, AL; married Conrad Cafritz; children: Zachary Cooper. **EDUCATION:** George Washington U, BA 1968; Nat Law Center George Washington U, JD 1971; Woodrow Wilson Intl Center for Scholars, fellow 1972. **CAREER:** Post-Newsweek Stations Inc, special asst to pres; The Ellington HS of Fine & Performing Arts Washington DC, founder & developer 1968-; St for People Study to Plan Redevel of Pub Spaces in Downtown Washington, Washington project dir; Trustee Amer Film Inst, independent consult 1970-73; DC Arts Commn, exec comm chmn 1969-74. **ORGANIZATIONS:** Mem DC Bar 1972; mem exec com DC Bd of Higher Educ 1973; Arts Educ & Amer Natl Panel 1975-; exec bd 1980-86, planning comm 1986-, mem Natl Assembly of State Art Agencies 1979-; mem bd of trustees Atlanta Univ 1983-86; mem Washington Performing Arts Soc 1983-; bd of dirs PEN/Faulkner Foundation 1985-88; mem Natl Jazz Serv Org 1985-; bd of trustees Kennedy Ctr for the Performing Arts 1987; bd mem Women's Campaign Fund 1987. **HONORS/ACHIEVEMENTS:** Woodrow Wilson Intl Ctr for Scholars 1971; Presidents Medal Catholic Univ for Outstanding Comm Serv 1974; New York Black Film Festival Awd 1976; 27th Annual Broadcast Media Awd Aspen Inst Alvin Brown Fellow 1977; George Foster Peabody Award for Excellence in TV public affairs prod 1976; finalist Natl Emmy Award 1977; John D Rockefeller Intl Youth Award; Washingtonian of the Yr; Woman of the Yr Mademoiselle Mag.

CAGE, MICHAEL
Professional athlete. **PERSONAL:** Born Jan 28, 1962, West Memphis, AR. **EDUCATION:** San Diego State, 1984. **CAREER:** Los Angeles Clippers, forward 1984-. **ORGANIZATIONS:** Pres of Fellowship of Christian Athletes. **HONORS/ACHIEVEMENTS:** Named Western Athl Conf Player of the Year; second team All-Amer as voted by AP, UPI and Baksetball Weekly; UPI West Coast Player of the Year; DistEight selection by US Baksetball Writers; Sports Illustrated's collegiate Player of the Week for period ending Feb 13, 1984; invited to the US Olympic Team tryouts in Bloomington, IN in April. **BUSINESS ADDRESS:** Los Angeles Clippers, 3939 S Figueroa St, Ste 510, Los Angeles, CA 90037.

CAHILL, CLYDE S., JR.
Judge. **PERSONAL:** Born Apr 09, 1923, St Louis, MO; married Thelma Newsom; children: Linda Diggs, Marina, Valerian, Randall, Kevin, Myron. **EDUCATION:** Sch of Arts & Sci St Louis U, BS1949; Law Sch St Louis U, JD 1951. **CAREER:** City of St Louis, asst cir atty 1954-66; Office of Econ Oppor, reg atty 1966-68; Human Devel Corp, genl mgr 1968-72; Legal Aid Soc, genl counsel & dir 1972-75; St Louis Univ Law Sch, lecturer 1974-79; State of MO, circuit judge 1975-80; US District Court for the Eastern District of MO, dist judge 1980-. **ORGANIZATIONS:** Dir St Louis Urban League 1974; dir Met Y 1975-; dir Comprehensive Health Cntr 1975; dir Cardinal Ritter HS 1978; mem Met St Louis Bar Assn; St Louis Lawyers Assn; Mound City Bar; Am Bar Assn; Nat Bar Assn; Am Judicature Soc. **HONORS/ACHIEVEMENTS:** NAACP Disting Serv Awd; St Louis Argus Awd. **MILITARY SERVICE:** USAF,. **BUSINESS ADDRESS:** District Judge, Eastern District of MO, 1114 Market St, St Louis, MO 63101.

CAHN, JEAN CAMPER
Attorney. **PERSONAL:** Born May 26, 1935, Baltimore, MD; married Edgar S Cahn; children: Jonathan Daniel, Reuben Camper. **EDUCATION:** Swarthmore Coll, 1957; Newnham Coll England, 1959; Yale Law Sch, LLB 1961. **CAREER:** Urban Law Inst, dir/founder/prof 1968-82; Antioch Sch of Law, dean and prof 1971-80; Natl Clinets Cncl, Minna Shaughnessy Fellow 1981-82; Middlebury Coll, disting vstg prof 1984; London Sch of Economics Joint Apptmt Dept of Law and Intl Ctr for Economics and Related Disciplines, disting vstg scholar 1986; Fernandez Caubi Fernandez Aguilar Cancio & Berenguer PA, of counsel 1986-. **ORGANIZATIONS:** Consult Pres of Venezuela; consult President's Adv Cncl on Exec Reorg; adv bd Charles Stewart Mott Found on Comm Edn; mem Natl Adv comm for Legal Svcs; bd Wash Cntr for Metro Studies; mem Amer Bar Assn; mem Natl Bar Assn; dir Ford Found Publ Affairs Program; consult Neumeier Found; mem Judicial Conf for the Dist of Columbia 1976-; US Judicial Conf for the DC 1972-80; Natl Adv Council for Legal Svcs; Off of Econ Oppty; Wash Center for Metro Studies; Natl Inst for Consumer Justice (Presidential Appointee); Yale Univ Council; Adv Comm for Brookings Study of Priv Accredit and Publ Funding; US Administ Conf (Public Mem); mem Natl Legal Aid & Defenders Assn; State of CT Bar Assn; Natl Assn of Black Women Attorneys. **HONORS/ACHIEVEMENTS:** John Hay Whitney Fellow 1959-61; Benneke Scholar Yale Law School 1961; Fellow Ezra Stiles Coll Yale Univ; Who's Who Among Black Americans 1971-; Who's Who inAmerica 1971-; Founders Award Grad Class of the Antioch Sch of Law 1981; Resolution of Recog Cncl of DC 1969, 1980; Jefferson Award Amer Inst for PublSvc; Outstanding Serv Award Natl Clients Cncl 1969-71 and 1976; Resolution of Recogn Project Adv Group Legal Serv Program 1980; Bronze Award for Film on Repossession from the Information Film Producers of Amer; Chris Plaque for Films — "The Fact of the Matter", "Let the Buyer Beware" and "Repossession" 27th Annual Columbus Film Festival 1979; Citation as the Most Outstanding Law Teacher Amer Assn of Law Schools; Sigma Gamma Rho Sorority DC Chapter 1968; Woman Lawyer of the Year Howard Univ; Key to the City and Honorary Citizen of New Orleans; Natl Bar Assn Disting Serv Award 1968; Numerous Publications incl, "My Mother, the Lawyer" pub in Women and Careers; "Regionalization of Legal Svcs, An Examination of Problems and Issues"; "Power to the People or the Profession, The Public Interest in Public Interest Law" Yale Law Journ 1970; "What Price Justice, The Civilian Perspective Revisited" Notre Dame Lawyer 1966. **BUSINESS ADDRESS:** Attorney, 35 Edgewater Dr, Coral Gables, FL 33133.

CAILLIER, JAMES ALLEN
Educational administrator. **PERSONAL:** Born Sep 24, 1940, Lafayette, LA; married Geraldiner Elizabeth Raphael; children: Jennifer, Gerard, Sylvia. **EDUCATION:** Univ of Southwestern LA, BS 1964; So U, MS 1968; LA State U, Ed D 1978. **CAREER:** Univ of Southwestern LA, dean/prof jr div 1975-, dir/prof 1970-; Public Schools, Lafayette LA, supvr 1967-69, teacher 1964-67; US Office of Educ, natl field reader 1972-77, natl consultant 1974; Commr Lafayette Harbor Term & Indsl 1975-. **ORGANIZATIONS:** Bd of dirs Lafayette C C 1975-; Nat Sci Found Grant 1966-68.

CAIN, FRANK
Retired government official. **PERSONAL:** Born Sep 30, 1930, Mocksville, NC; son of Arthur Reece Cain and Ella Florence Eaton Cain; married Cecelia Ingram; children: DiShon Franklin. **EDUCATION:** A&T State Univ, BS 1956, MS 1967; Attended, NC State Univ, Univ of OK. **CAREER:** NC Agr Ext Svc, asst co agent 1957-62; USDA-FmHA, asst co sup 1962-66, co sup 1966-85. **ORGANIZATIONS:** Mem Black & Minority Employee Organization, NC Assoc of County Supervisors; chmn trustee bd, bldg fund Chinquepin Grove Baptist Church; mem Prince Hall Grand Lodge F&A Masons of NC; past pres of Alamance Co Chap A&T State Univ Alumni. **HONORS/ACHIEVEMENTS:** Certificate of Appreciation Human Rights Comm 1981; Certificate of Merit USDA-FmHA 1977,82; first black FmHA supvr in State of NC. **MILITARY SERVICE:** AUS spec E-4 1953-55; Natl Defense Service Medal, Good Conduct Medal, Letter of Commendation. **HOME ADDRESS:** 857 Dewitt Dr, Mebane, NC 27302.

CAIN, FRANK EDWARD, JR.
Attorney. **PERSONAL:** Born Feb 01, 1924, Blenheim, SC; married Dollie M Covington; children: Cherryetta, Anthony. **EDUCATION:** SC State Coll, BA; SC State Coll, LIB 1951. **CAREER:** Bennettsville, SC, atty priv prac; Kollock Elem Sch Wallace SC, tchr 1653-55. **ORGANIZATIONS:** Mem SC Bar Assn; SC State Bar; SC Black Lawyers Caucus; Marlboro Co Bar; past & Polemarch Cheraw Alumni Chapt; Kappa Alpha Psi Frat; Sr Warden Sawmill Masonic Lodge #375; vice pres Marlboro Co Br NAACP; past comm Am Legion Post 213; admitted to prac US Dist Ct for Dist of SC; US Ct of Appeals. **HONORS/ACHIEVEMENTS:** Pres W Bennettsvl Precinct Dem Party, Marlboro Co; Legal Adv to Reg of Local Bd No 34 Selec Serv Sys 1972; Recip Cert in Dist Educ SC Dept of Educ 1966; cert of Achievement Kappa Alpha Psi Frat 1966; Listed in SC Lives 1962; comm ldrs of Am 1969. **MILITARY SERVICE:** AUS Signal Corps corpl 1943-46. **BUSINESS ADDRESS:** 203 W Market St, Bennettsville, SC 29512.

CAIN, GEORGE M.
Author. **PERSONAL:** Born 1943, Harlem, NY; married Jo Lynne; children: Nataya. **EDUCATION:** Iona Coll New Rochelle, attended. **CAREER:** Author. **HONORS/ACHIEVEMENTS:** Author "Blueschild Baby" 1971 labeled by Addison Gayle in his NY Times review the most important work of fiction by an Afro-Amer since Native Son. **BUSINESS ADDRESS:** c/o McGraw Hill, 1221 Avenue of the Americas, Publicity Dept 35th Floor, New York, NY 10020.

CAIN, GERRY RONALD
Research analyst. **PERSONAL:** Born Dec 12, 1961, Ft Bragg, NC; son of Moses Cain and Katherine Cain. **EDUCATION:** Bowie State Coll, attended 1980; Prince George's Comm Coll, AA 1981-82; Univ of KS, BS Journalism 1983-85. **CAREER:** Freelance Researcher Consultant 1985-86; Mellwood Medical Labs, marketing rep 1985-86; Bernstien-Rein Advertising, analyst, marketing research dept 1985-. **ORGANIZATIONS:** Mem KUAD Club /Advertising Federation of America 1984-85; mem Natl Assoc of Black Journalists 1985-86; mem Univ of KS Alumni Assoc 1985-; mem, American Marketing Assn (Kansas City Chapter) 1988-. **HONORS/ACHIEVEMENTS:** Urban Journalism Workshop Recipient Univ of KS 1977; CLyde & Betty Read Scholarship Recipient Univ of KS 1983-84; Lucile Bluford Scholarship Recipient 1984-85. **HOME ADDRESS:** 3679 Summit St #2, Kansas City, MO 64111.

CAIN, HERBERT R., JR.
Judge. **PERSONAL:** Born Feb 20, 1916, New York, NY; son of Herbert Cain and Mayme Cain; married Louise G; children: Joanne C Fitzgerald, Herbert R III, Gerald R. **EDUCATION:** Lincoln Univ, AB (cum laude) 1938; Howard Univ Law Sch, JD 1941. **CAREER:** Court of Common Pleas First Judicial Dist of PA, judge 1969-. **ORGANIZATIONS:** Mem Amer, Philadelphia, Natl, Pennsylvania Bar Assns; PA Bar Assn Lawyer's Club of Phila; Amer Judicature Soc; Barrister's Club; mem bd dirs Natl Conference of Christians & Jews; mem bd dirs Teen-Aid Inc; Philadelphia Urban League Fellowship Commn; mem bd dirs Lankenau Hosp; mem Most Worshipful Prince Hall Grand Lodge Free & Accepted Masons of PA Phoenix Lodge No 3; DeMolay Consistory No 1 32 F&AM; Pyramid Temple No 1 Shriner; Holy Royal Arch Masons; IBPO Elks Leonard C Irvin Lodge No 994; Citizens League of West Phila; Central HS Alumni; Alpha Boule Sigma Pi Phi Frat. **BUSINESS ADDRESS:** Judge, Ct of Common Pleas, 1st Judicial District of PA, Judge's Chambers 504 City Hall, Philadelphia, PA 19107.

CAIN, JOHNNIE M.
Educator. **PERSONAL:** Born Jul 27, 1940, Shreveport, LA; married James O; children: Merion Edward, Nicole Rowlett, Phyllis Yevette. **EDUCATION:** Univ Maryland, BA 1964; Northern CO, MA 1964; Univ AZ & Univ NC, grad work. **CAREER:** Douglas Pur System, English teacher 1968-; ITT Hamiliton Corp, sales 1972; Cochise Co Hosp, nurse asst 1970-71; NC, home sch & social worker 1966; Am Dept Sch, kindergarten teacher 1964-65; AZ Informant, newswriter-rep; working toward PhD Child Care & Clinical Psychology; freelance poet writer poems appear in 13 anthologies Harlo Young Poets, Man When Born of Fire, Clover Book of Verse, Insearch of the Museum & others. **ORGANIZATIONS:** Only black woman mem Douglas Phi Delta Kappa; mem Poets's Study Club; Poetry Symposium Black Intl Writers Org Chicago; Natl Educ Assn; Douglas EdnAssn; Upward Bound coordinator Cochise Coll Advisory Bd of Upward Bound; mem Youth City Cncl Douglas Lecturd Black Writers Conf 1973; conducted Black Writers Workshop Urban League Phoenix Oct 1974. **HONORS/ACHIEVEMENTS:** Two poetry awards Clover Poetry Assn 1972-74; published two books "Poetrydo You Remember", "White Bastards", presently Celesterial Arts considering vol Poetry for publication; Northwoods Publication, Accepted vol poetry, publication Feb 1975. **BUSINESS ADDRESS:** Douglas High School, 1500 15 St, Douglas, AZ 85607.

CAIN, LESTER JAMES, JR.
Educator. **PERSONAL:** Born Mar 24, 1937, Pittsburgh, PA; son of Lester James Cain Sr and LeGertha Prince Cain; children: Stephanie Lynn. **EDUCATION:** US Armed Forces Inst, Certificate 1962; Connelly Skill Learning Ctr, GED 1977. **CAREER:** Operation Dig Pittsburgh Plan, field supervisor 1971-72, dir field super 1972-74; Univ of Pittsburgh, admin specialist 1977-. **ORGANIZATIONS:** Mem Pittsburgh Branch NAACP 1971-; bd mem Homewood-Brushton Revitalization & Devel 1983-; bd mem Homewood-Brushton Comm Improvement Assoc Inc 1984-. **HONORS/ACHIEVEMENTS:** Airco Tech Inst of Pittsburgh Certificate of Achievement 1978; Community Serv Awd East Hills Park 1983; Contributions to Educ Pittsburgh Public Schools 1984; Recruitment Awd Pittsburgh Branch NAACP 1985; United Negro College Fund Certificate of Appreciation 1985; Distinguished Leadership Awd UNCF Pittsburgh 1986; Univ of Louisville Certificate of Training 1986; Univ of Louisville Black Family in Amer Conference Continuing Studies Certificate 1986; Associates Program Joint Center for Political Studies 1986. **MILITARY SERVICE:** AUS E3 1960-66; Honorable Discharge. **BUSINESS ADDRESS:** Administrative Specialist, University of Pittsburgh, 3814 Forbes Ave, Pittsburgh, PA 15260.

CAIN, ROBERT R.
Health care delivery. **PERSONAL:** Born Mar 02, 1944, Chicago, IL; married Evelyn; children: Carla, Paula, Lisa. **EDUCATION:** Univ of NE, BS 1977, Northern CO MA 1979. **CAREER:** US Government Services, military career 1962-81; Superior Care of CA, clinic dir 1982-86; Northeast Clinical Svcs, chief exec officer. **ORGANIZATIONS:** Scottish Rite Mason Shriner 32 degree Mason 1976-86; mem Alpha Phi Alpha Frat 1982. **MILITARY SERVICE:** USN W-3 20 yrs; Vietnam Serv Medal, Armed Forces Expeolitionary Medal 1964-69. **BUSINESS ADDRESS:** Chief Executive Officer, Northeast Clinical Services, 2763 Windmillview Rd, El Cajon, CA 92020.

CAIN, SIMON LAWRENCE
Attorney. **PERSONAL:** Born Dec 19, 1927, Augusta, GA; married Ada Spence. **EDUCATION:** Howard U, BA 1949, LlB 1956. **CAREER:** Attorney. **ORGANIZATIONS:** Mem Wash Bar Assn, Am Bar Assn, Nat Bar Assn, DC Bar Assn; pres Lamond-Riggs Citizen Assn 1968-70; pres DC Fedn of Civic Assn 1969-71; chmn highways & transp Palisades Citizens Assn 1974. **HONORS/ACHIEVEMENTS:** Recipient Korean/United Nations 3 Battle Stars USAF 1950. **MILITARY SERVICE:** USAF lt col 26 Yrs Served. **BUSINESS ADDRESS:** 1621 New Hampshire Ave NW, Washington, DC 20009.

CAIN, WALDO
Physician. **PERSONAL:** Born Sep 29, 1921, Gadsden, AL; son of James L Cain and Evelyn Croft; married Natalia; children: Sheila, Anita. **EDUCATION:** Meharry Med Coll, MD 1945. **CAREER:** Cain-tanner Asso, pres, SW Detroit Hosp, chf surg; Wayne State U, asst prof surg; Meharry Med Coll, clinical assoc prof of surg 1946-52; Cain-Wood Surgical Assoc, pres. **ORGANIZATIONS:** Fndr First Independence Nat Bank Detroit; life mem NAACP; mem Am Coll Surgeons; Soc Military Surgeons; State MI Judicial Tenure Commn Physician Yr Detroit Med Soc 1969. **MILITARY SERVICE:** AUS MC capt 1953-55. **BUSINESS ADDRESS:** President, Cain-Wood Surgical Assoc, 4160 John R Road, Detroit, MI 48201.

CAISON, THELMA JANN
Physician. **PERSONAL:** Born Apr 26, 1950, Brooklyn, NY. **EDUCATION:** Winston-Salem State Univ, BS 1972; State Univ of NY at Buffalo Sch of Med, MD 1977. **CAREER:** Bd of Educ NYC, biol tchr 1972-73; Harlem Hosp Med Ctr NY, med externship trauma surgery & surgical ICU 1974, med externship obstet & gyn 1975; Downstate Med Ctr Kings Co Hosp Ctr NY, summer med externship in internal med 1976; Montefiore Hosp Med Ctr & N Central Bronx Hosp, physician 1977-83; Henry Ford Hosp Dept of Pediatrics/Div of Adolescent Medicine, division head 1983-. **ORGANIZATIONS:** Mem AMA 1970-80; mem Natl Med Assn 1979-80; mem Com for Residents & Interns 1979-80; mem State Univ of NY at Buffalo/Sch of Med Alumni Assn; mem Delta Sigma Theta Natl Sor; mem Winston-Salem Univ Alumni Assn. **HONORS/ACHIEVEMENTS:** Med Scholastic Hon State Univ of NY at Buffalo Sch of Med 1973-77; Pride in Heritage Awd in field of med Phi Delta Kappa Natl Sor 1978; guest speaker seminar in hypertension & nutrition Phi Delta Kappa Sor 1979; accomplished pianist. **BUSINESS ADDRESS:** Henry Ford Hosp, 2799 W Grand Blvd, Dept of Pediatrics, Detroit, MI 48202.

CALBERT, ROOSEVELT
Government official. **PERSONAL:** Born Nov 13, 1931, Philadelphia, MS; son of Jim Calbert; married Thelma Nichols; children: Debra C Brown, Jacquelyn C Smith, Rosalyn C Groce, Lori A. **EDUCATION:** Jackson State Univ, BS (Summa Cum Laude) 1954; Univ of Michigan, MA 1960; Univ of Kansas, PhD 1971. **CAREER:** Alcorn State Univ, physics prof 1960-63; AL State Univ, math & physics coord 1963-68; Univ of KS, rsch asst 1969-71; Inst for Services to Educ, dir coop academic planning 1971-75; Natl Sci Foundation, program dir. **ORGANIZATIONS:** Mem Phi Beta Sigma Frat 1951-; mem Alpha Kappa Mu Natl Honorary Soc 1952-; founder Heritage Fellowship Church 1978; bd chmn Community Investors Corp 1982-; mem AAAS 1984-. **HONORS/ACHIEVEMENTS:** Distinguished Alumnus Awd Jackson State Univ 1986. **HOME ADDRESS:** 11331 French Horn Lane, Reston, VA 22091.

CALBERT, WILLIAM EDWARD
Clergyman. **PERSONAL:** Born Jun 11, 1918, Lemoore, CA; son of William R Calbert and Sadie Hackett Calbert; married Madlyn Williams; children: Rose M Findley, Muriel L, Katherine E Jackson, Yvonne A, William E. **EDUCATION:** SF State Coll CA, AB 1949; Berkeley Baptist Divinity Sch CA, MDiv 1952; Tchrs Coll Columbia U, MA 1963; Amer Univ, Washington DC, Post Grad Stdy 1970-71. **CAREER:** US Army, US, Far East, Germany, unit & org chpln 1952-62; Concord Baptist Church Brooklyn, NY, dir chrstn educ part-time 1964-67; US Army Chpln Sch, Brklyn NY, staff & fclty 1963-67; US Army Cmds, Vietnam, stf chpln/dep Stf 1967-68; Hq 1st US Army, Ft Meade MD, asst Army chpln 1968-69; Far East Comm Srvs Anti-Pvrty Agncy, DC, asst dir/exec dir 1970-73; St Elizabeths Hosp, DC, stf chpln 1973-81; Shiloh Bptst Church, mnstr educ Washington, DC, 1982-86; Interim Dir, Chaplaincy & Pastorial Counselling Serv, Amer Baptist Churches, USA, Valley Forge, PA 1986-1987. **ORGANIZATIONS:** Pres Far NE Mnstrl Assn DC 1973-74, Natl Cptl Area Chptr Mltry Chplns Assn DC 1981-82, Washington DC Grad Chptr Alpha Phi Alpha Frat 1980-82; vice pres Mnstrl Assn CA, Fairfld, Vacavill, Travis AFB 1961-62; bd mem Hsng Dev Corp, DC 1972-76; mem Mayors Hlth Plng Adv Comm 1972-77; trustee Natl Mltry Chplns Assn 1984-1987; membership comm, Assn of Mental Health Clergy, 1988—. **HONORS/ACHIEVEMENTS:** Meritorious Srv Mdl US Army Ft Meade, MD 1969; Letter of Apprctn US Army Chf of Chplns Wash, DC 1969; DC Gov Cert Apprctn 1973; Frat Ldrsh Awrd Sigma Gammo Rho Sor 1983; author "Army Subjects Schedule 21-42" 1964. **MILITARY SERVICE:** AUS lt col 20 yrs; 15 mltry awrds & dcrtns incldng Meritorious Srv Medal 1969. **HOME ADDRESS:** 1261 Kearny St NE, Washington, DC 20017.

CALDWELL, BENJAMIN
Playwright. **PERSONAL:** Born Sep 24, 1937, New York, NY. **CAREER:** Free-lance writer. **HONORS/ACHIEVEMENTS:** Guggenheim fellowship for playwriting, 1970; author of Prayer Meeting; or, The First Militant Minister, New American Library, 1970; author of "What Is Going On," produced in New York City, 1973; author of "The World of Ben Caldwell," produced in New York City, 1982. **BUSINESS ADDRESS:** P O Box 656, Morningside Station, New York, NY 10026. *

CALDWELL, BESSIE ELLIS
Educator. **PERSONAL:** Born May 02, 1917, Kansas City, KS; married Robert Chester; children: Robert Ellis (dec), Aqualyn Colbert, Teree Lynn. **EDUCATION:** Univ WI Milwaukee, 1935-37; KS State Tchr Coll Pittsburg KS, BS 1938; KS State Tchr Coll Pittsburgh, KS, MS 1949; Tempole Univ Philadelphia, PA, 1969. **CAREER:** Marymount Coll, assoc prof 1969-; KS State Dance Council, bd of dir 1972; Marymount Coll, chmn of physical educ 1966; Marymount Coll, instructor 1956; City Bd of Educ, teacher 1939-46; Caldwell School of Dance, owner 1950-. **ORGANIZATIONS:** Mem Alpha Kappa Alpha Sorority 1937-80; mem KS Arts Commn Major Grants in Dance 1975; Fmem Central Area Arts Com Links 1980. **HONORS/ACHIEVEMENTS:** Nat Inst of Mental Health Grant Tempe Univ Philadelphia 1969; Study Tour Grant to Africa Phelps Stoke Found 1975; dance residency Salina Pub Sch 1975-80. **BUSINESS ADDRESS:** Marymount Coll, E Iorn & Marymount Rd, Salina, KS 67401.

CALDWELL, EDWIN L., JR.
Agency executive. **PERSONAL:** Born Mar 06, 1935, Durham, NC; son of Edwin Caldwell, Sr and Pearl Meritt Caldwell; married Eva Holmes, Dec 11, 1961 (divorced); children: Stacey Caldwell Thompson, Edwin Caldwell, III. **EDUCATION:** Hampton Inst, Hampton, VA, BS, 1952-57; Univ of NC, Chapel Hill, govt exec, 1980-, competion of requirements. **CAREER:** Orange-Chatham Comprehensive Health Serv Inc, asst dir 1973-78; NY Housing Finance Agency, Raleigh, NC, deputy exec dir, 1978-; Beaunit Fibers Research Triangle Park NC, chemist; Delafield Hospital Columbia Univ NY, asst supr; Delafield Hospital NY, biochemist; Delafield Hospital NY, biochemist. **ORGANIZATIONS:** Mem School bd; bd or-

ganizer Citizens Triangle United Bank; bd dir Chapel Hill Tennis Club; State Adv Council Title Iii Programs; bd dir NC School Board Assn; chmn, Chapel Hill Carrboro School Bd, 1981-83; chmn, Chapel Hill Housing Advisory Bd, 1987-89. **HONORS/ ACHIEVEMENTS:** Citizens of the year, Masonic Lodge, Kappa Frat, 1982-87; WTVD, Citizen of the Year, WTVD-TV, 1989. **MILITARY SERVICE:** US Army, Sp4, 1958-60. **BUSINESS ADDRESS:** Deputy Exec Dir, NC Housing Finance Agency (State Govt NC), PO Box 28066, 3300 Drake Circle, Suite 200, Raleigh, NC 27611.

CALDWELL, ELVIN R.
Councilman. **PERSONAL:** Born Apr 11, 1919; married Frank Harriette Webb; children: Elvin Jr, John Wilbur, Kenneth Clay, Frances Fuller. **EDUCATION:** Univ of Denver. **CAREER:** City & Co of Denver, councilman presently; Mayor's Cabinet Denver, first black mem; City & Co of Denver, mgr safety fire, police & sheriff depts. **ORGANIZATIONS:** Mem, Denver City Council, over 25 yrs; CO House of Rep, 3 terms; pres, Denver City Council, 5 terms; chief stat Remington Arms; special asst to prodn supr Remington Arms; asst to plant mgr Kaiser Industries; div accountant Ideal Cement Co Orgnr original pres Equity Savings & Loan Assn; orgnr pres Intl Oppty Life Ins Co Bd dir Metro YMCA; Metro Div Boy Scouts of Amer; NAACP; Oppty Industrialization Ctr; East Denver Improvement Assn Mayor's Comm on Comm Rel; Prodn Inc Dahlia Shopping Ctr; bd dir CO Municipal League; bd chmn Freedom House Job Placement Ctr; adv council to Bd of Health & Hospitals Chmn; bd dir Glenarm Br YMCA; chmn East Denver Dist; trustee Shorter AME Ch; vice pres Denver Urban League; budget comm United Fund; sec treas, Non-Pollution Chem Co. **BUSINESS ADDRESS:** Mgr of Safety's Office, 1331 Cherokee St, Denver, CO 80204.

CALDWELL, ESLY SAMUEL, II
Physician. **PERSONAL:** Born Sep 25, 1938, Lancaster, SC; married Judith Mary Slining; children: Esly II, Christina C, Robert S. **EDUCATION:** Howard Univ, Coll of Liberal Arts BS 1960, Coll of Medicine MD 1964; University of MI Sch of Public Health, MPH 1979. **CAREER:** Dougherty Medical Group, physician. **MILITARY SERVICE:** AUS Medical Group capt 2 yrs. **BUSINESS ADDRESS:** Dougherty Medical Group, 629 Oak St, Ste 503, Cincinnati, OH 45206.

CALDWELL, FRANK
Parole commissioner. **PERSONAL:** Born Jun 09, 1921, Denver; married Ruth Fayerman; children: Frank Jr, Cheryl, Clifton. **EDUCATION:** Univ Denver, JD 1947. **CAREER:** Nc Cntrl U, instructor 1947-50; Buffalo NY, prv practice 1951-59; NY St, comm parole 1959-. **ORGANIZATIONS:** Pompey Hls Country Club; Trinity Lutheran Ch; Alpha Phi Alpha; Dist Ctzns Cty Denver 1958.

CALDWELL, GEORGE THERON, SR.
Business executive. **PERSONAL:** Born Jun 05, 1939, Mississippi Co, AR; son of Harry Larnell Caldwell and Mary Alice Warren; married Jacqueline Romaine Hinch; children: Darri Alice, Jacqueline Michelle, George T II, Robert L, Richard D, Marilynn Kitt, Felecia, Terry, Delores S, Pammela, Shelly Murphy. **EDUCATION:** Gen Coll, Univ of MN, AA 1972; Coll of Liberal Arts, Honors Div, Univ of MN, BA (magna cum laude) 1976. **CAREER:** Affirmative Action Dept, County of Hennepin, rsch analyst 1973-76, asst dir 1976-80; Dept of Civil Rights, City of Minneapolis, exec dir 1980-84; Minnesota Valley Transportation Co Inc SW, owner 1984-86; Univ of Minnesota, asst dir EO/AA 1986-. **ORGANIZATIONS:** Bd of dirs Minneapolis Branch NAACP 1976-77; bd of dirs Benjamin E Mays Fundamental School 1977-81; trustee Mt Olivet Baptist Church 1978-80; chmn Intergovtl Compliance Inst 1978-81; pres MN State Affirmative Action Assoc 1979-80; founder/directorate MN Soc for Open Comm 1983. **HONORS/ACHIEVEMENTS:** NACo New Co Achievement Award, Natl Assn of Counties, 1977; Outstanding Leadership Award, MN Affirmative Action Assn, 1982; Proclamation GTC Day, City of Minneapolis, 1984; Citation of Honor, Hennepin County Bd of Commissioners. 1984; co-owner of one of the first black-owned railroads in US history, Minnesota Valley Transportation Co Inc, Southwest; featured in Ebony magazine, July 1984, and in Black Enterprize, June 1984, The Top 100 Black Businesses. **MILITARY SERVICE:** AUS spec 5/E-5 1958-64; Good Conduct Medal (1st & 2nd award); Seventh Army Citation Outstanding Soldier 1962. **HOME ADDRESS:** 787 Lafond Ave, St Paul, MN 55104.

CALDWELL, GLADYS EMANUEL
Educator. **PERSONAL:** Born Feb 17, Princess Ann, MD; divorced; children: Dr Lorena A Graves, Gladys G Woodland. **EDUCATION:** Poro Sch of Beauty Culture, operators & tchrs courses in beauty culture spec courses in barbering & beauty culture. **CAREER:** Gladine Beauty Prods, retired mfg; House of Good Shephard, planner tchr; Skidmore & Sch of Beauty Culture, supr tchr; Book Of Beauty Culture Written ForUniv of PA, consult 1944; Sch of Beauty Culture, owner tchr 1937-42; Beauty Shop, owner operator 1928-37. **ORGANIZATIONS:** Mem YWCA 1954-; mem NAACP 1956-; mem Lincoln Dames Aux of Philadelphia 1967-; charter mem Philadelphia Philos 1953-; pres 1953-57; parliamentarian 1957; life mem Nat Assn of Negro Bus & Professional Women's Clubs Inc 1937-; vice pres Local Chap of NANB & PWC Inc; chmn of num com; mem Nat bd of Dir Life Memshp Guild. **HONORS/ACHIEVEMENTS:** Nat Archieves Com Woman of Distinction Award Calvert Distillers NANB & PWC 1953f Merit Serv Award Tribune Charities 1957; Apprec Award Philadelphia Philos1958; Award Chapel of 1 & Chaplains 25 yr Serv Award Nat Chap NANB & PWC 1960; 25 Yr Faithful Merit Serv Award Local Chap NANB & PWC 1964; Serv Award Atlantic Dist NANB & PWC 1971; Serv Award Nat Chap NANB & PWC 1975.

CALDWELL, JAMES E.
Attorney. **PERSONAL:** Born May 22, 1930, Louisville, KY; son of George Caldwell and Emmie Lou Caldwell; married Dolores Robinson; children: Janelle, James, Randall. **EDUCATION:** Univ Of Pittsburgh, AB 1952; ROTC Univ of Pittsburgh, grad 1952; Howard Univ Sch of Law, JD 1958; Univ of Chicago, MBA 1973. **CAREER:** Standard Oil Co, tax counsel 1971-84; Amoco Oil Co, tax atty 1970-71; Chief Counsel's Office & IRS, sr trial atty 1959-70; Gen Counsel US Treasury Dept, honor Law Graduate Program 1959; Caldwell & Black, 1984-. **ORGANIZATIONS:** Mem, joint bd of trustees St Anne's & St Elizabeth Hospital; pres, Roseland Economic Devel Corp; mem bd of mgrs Chicago Bar Assn 1973-75; Chicago Bar Assn 1975-77; mem Cook Co Bar Assn; Nat Bar Assn; mem IL Bar, Supreme Ct, US Bar; mem bd dirs, Univ of Chicago Club XP Program MBA; alumni Grad Sch of Business, Univ of Chicago; mem bd trustees CBA Pension Fund; mem bd dirs CAM Health Trust; Commr Supreme Ct of IL; CLEO, pres. **MILITARY SERVICE:** AUSR colonel (retired). **BUSINESS ADDRESS:** 180 W Washington, Suite 300, Chicago, IL 60602.

CALDWELL, JOHN EDWARD
Life underwriter. **PERSONAL:** Born Feb 10, 1937, Newberry, SC; married Patricia Henderson; children: Sean Edward. **EDUCATION:** Benedict Coll, BS 1965. **CAREER:** Newberry Co Memorial Hosp, trustee 1970-80, chmn of trustee bd 1980-82; Newberry Co Council, councilman 1982-86, councilman 1987-91; Independent Life and Accident Ins Co, staff sales mgr. **ORGANIZATIONS:** Bd mem Newberry Co Task Force for Educ 1982-87; bd mem United Way of the Midlands 1983-86; bd mem Central Midlands Human Resources 1983-87; Newberry Co Coord for the United Negro Coll Fund 1983-87; bd mem Newberry Co Vocational Educ 1984-87; bd mem Piedmont Area Occupational Training 1986-. **HONORS/ ACHIEVEMENTS:** First Black elected to Newberry County Council 1983; Outstanding Alumni Newberry County Alumni Club 1985; Natl Sales Awd Independent Life & Accident Co Inc7 yrs; President's Club Independent Life & Accident Ins Co 8 yrs; First and only black staff mgr for Independent Life and Accident Ins Co. **MILITARY SERVICE:** AUS sp/4 1960-62; Outstanding Trainee. **HOME ADDRESS:** 711 McSwain St, Newberry, SC 29108. **BUSINESS ADDRESS:** Staff Sales Mgr, Independent Life/Accident Ins, 211 Montague, Greenwood, SC 29646.

CALDWELL, LEWIS A. H.
State representative. **PERSONAL:** Born Oct 12, 1905, Chicago; children: 2 Daughters. **EDUCATION:** BS 1933; Northwestern U, MS 1940. **CAREER:** Cook Co Welfare Dept, 1933-41; Cook Co Family Court, probation officer 1941-48; Lewis A H Caldwell & Assoc, pub relations consultant 1948-55; Baldwin Ice Cream Co, mgr 1951-61; Hawthorn Mellody Farms Dairy, sales rep 1961-68; General Assembly, former state rep IL; Cosmopolitan C of C, vice pres pub affairs 1968-; CES Travel, sr consultant. **ORGANIZATIONS:** Life mem Alpha Phi Alpha Frat 1930-; mem Chicago Area Project Youth Agency 1955-. **HONORS/ ACHIEVEMENTS:** Recip numerous honors & awards. **BUSINESS ADDRESS:** Senior Consultant, CES Travel, Inc, 405 Dearborn St, Chicago, IL 60605.

CALDWELL, M. MILFORD
Educator. **PERSONAL:** Born Feb 20, 1928, South Carolina; married Mazie Hammond. **EDUCATION:** SC State Coll, BS 1949; SC State Coll, MS 1950; OH State U, PhD 1959; OH State U, Post Doctoral Fellow. **CAREER:** DE State Coll, prof of educ; Elizabeth City State Univ, prof of educ 1961-62; OH State Univ, asst prof of educ 1959-61. **ORGANIZATIONS:** Pres Assn of Coll & Sch of Educ in State Univ & Land-Grant Colls; past pres DE Acad of Sci; mem Am Assn of Higher Edn; gov comm of Vocational Edn; mem Century Club YMCA; NAACP; Notary Public; Phi Alpha Theta; Gamma Sigma Delta; Phi Delta Kappa. **MILITARY SERVICE:** USAF. **BUSINESS ADDRESS:** DE State Coll, Dover, DE 19901.

CALDWELL, MARIA
Judge. **PERSONAL:** Born Aug 10, 1948, Mobile, AL; daughter of Hayward Frank Thomas and Cleo M Caldwell. **EDUCATION:** Tuskegee Inst, BS soc 1970; Univ of Southwestern School of Law, JD 1978. **CAREER:** District Attorney's Office, asst district attorney 1983-Dec 1986; Metropolitan Court, judge 1987-. **ORGANIZATIONS:** Mem Natl Council of Negro Women, Sunrise Civitan Club, League of Women Voters. **HONORS/ ACHIEVEMENTS:** Monroe N Work Awd 1970; Southwestern Univ Sch of Law Certificate of Disting Serv 1977; NAACP Legal Defense and Educ Fund Certificate of Honor. **HOME ADDRESS:** PO Box 26524, Albuquerque, NM 87124. **BUSINESS ADDRESS:** Judge, Metropolitan Court, PO Box 133, Albuquerque, NM 87103.

CALDWELL, MARION MILFORD, JR.
Educator. **PERSONAL:** Born Mar 11, 1952, San Antonio, TX; son of Mazie H Caldwell; married Priscilla Robertson; children: Priscilla Marina. **EDUCATION:** Delaware State Coll, BS 1978; Univ of the District of Columbia, MBA 1983. **CAREER:** Delaware Tech Comm Coll, instructor of Business 1984; Delaware State Coll, prof of Mktg 1984-. **ORGANIZATIONS:** Mem Omega Psi Phi Inc 1971-, Prince Hall Mason Prudence Lodge #6 1980-, Amer Mktg Assoc 1981-, Natl Black MBA Assoc Inc 1986-, MBA Exec Inc 1986-; mem NAACP; rep Faculty Senate; Intl Platform Assn; Prudence Lodge #6F&AM, PHA. **HONORS/ACHIEVEMENTS:** DE State Coll State Scholarship Award 1971; Omega Psi Phi Inc Psi Epsilon Chapter Service Award 1980. **BUSINESS ADDRESS:** Professor of Marketing, Delaware State College, Dept Econ & Business Admin, Dover, DE 19901.

CALDWELL, SANDRA ISHMAEL
Dentist. **PERSONAL:** Born Aug 23, 1948, Fort Knox, KY; children: Rhonda. **EDUCATION:** Howard Univ, BS 1971; Howard Univ Coll of Dentistry, DDS 1981. **CAREER:** Food & Drug Admin, microbiologist 1971-77; Ton Ron Productions, vice pres 1985-; Private Practice Silver Spring, dentist 1985-; Baltimore Medical Systems Inc, dentist 1982-. **ORGANIZATIONS:** Mem Natl Dental Assoc, Acad General Dentistry, Beta Kappa Chi Honor Soc, Prince George's Soc of Health Profls, Sigma Xi Scientific Rsch Soc; co-chair,secty Robert T Freeman Dental Soc; mem co-chair Delta Sigma Theta Sor Inc; dental alumni recruiter Howard Univ; mem Minority Women in Science. **HONORS/ACHIEVEMENTS:** Natl Health Serv Corp Scholarship 1978; Delta Sigma Theta Scholarship 1978; Outstanding Young Women of Amer 1980; Who's Who Among Students in Amer Univs & Colls 1981. **HOME ADDRESS:** 4505 Romlon St #103, Beltsville, MD 20705.

CALDWELL-SWISHER, ROZELLA KATHRINE
Retired educator. **PERSONAL:** Born Jan 31, 1908, Pittsburg, KS; married Laurence B Swisher (deceased). **EDUCATION:** Pittsburg State Teachers Coll, Life 1933, BS 1934, MA 1948. **CAREER:** Douglass Elem School, teacher 1931-34; Northeast Jr High, retired teacher 1934-76. **ORGANIZATIONS:** State sponsor KS Student NEA 1966; life mem Natl Assoc of Colored Womens Clubs 1972; founder Concerned Girls Women Kansas City 1975-85; chair allocations WyCo United Way 1975-80; commiss Kansas City Area Transportation Auth 1982-85; ed chair Region VII Greater Kansas City Area Coord Council 1984-85; founder Women in Transit Reg VII 1984; bd advisory Kansas City Branch NAACP 1985; dir KS Natl Silver-Haired Congress 1985-86; vchair Central States Coalition on Aging Proj Fund 1985. **HONORS/ACHIEVEMENTS:** Pittsburg State Univ Alumni Meritorious Achievement Awd 1976; Author Ethnic Study Guide Public School Kansas City Dist 500; Women of the Year Greater KC Womens Org 1983; Disting Older Adult State of KS By Governor 1983; Older Kansas Producer Kansas City Intergenerational Mem of Distinction 1984; One of 50 Celebration of Leadership 1986; KS City tommorrow Alumni 1986; 1987 Citizen Appreciation Awd 1987; United Way Significant Serv to the Community as a Senior Volunteer.

CALHOUN, CALVIN LEE
Educator. **PERSONAL:** Born Jan 07, 1927, Atlanta, GA; married Evelyn; children: Calvin jr. **EDUCATION:** Morehouse Coll, BS 1948; Atlanta U, MS 1950; Meharry Med Coll, MD 1960; GW Hubbard Hosp, internship 1960-61; GW Hubbard Hosp, residency 1961-62; Univ MN, neurology residency 1962-65; Univ MN, NIH rsrch fellow 1965-66. **CAREER:** Meharry Med Coll, prof 1966-73; Meharry, assc prof 1968-71; prof chmn 1971; Meharry Med Coll, chief 1966; Hubbard Hosp, dir 1966; Meharry, asst prof 1961-62; Meharry, instr 1951-57; Morehouse Coll, instr 1950-51. **ORGANIZATIONS:** Mem Am Acad of Neurology; Nat Med Assn; AAAS; Am Assn of Anatomists; TN Med Assn; volunteer State Med Assn; Am Assn ofUniv Profs Am Assn of Dental Schs; Assn ofUniv Profs of Neurology; Assn of Anatomy Dept; NY Acad of Scis; fellow Stroke Council Am Heart Assn; mem TN Anatomical Bd; bddir Nashville-Davidson Co Chap Am Nat Red Cross; So Soc of Anatomists Alpha Omega Alpha; Beta Kappa Chi; vis profUniv W Indies Med Sch 1975; resource Consult Elem Curriculum MN City Schs 1965-66;team Physician MN HS 1965; mem professional adv bd Epilepsy Found of Am; deacon 1st Bapt Ch; Am Men Of Sci 1967. **HONORS/ACHIEVEMENTS:** Who's Who in the S & SW. **MILITARY SERVICE:** AUS pvt 1945. **BUSINESS ADDRESS:** 1005 18th Ave N, Nashville, TN 37200.

CALHOUN, CECELIA C.
Educator & nurse. **PERSONAL:** Born Sep 22, 1922, New Roads, LA; married Noah R Calhoun; children: Stephen, Marc Michael MD, Cecelia Noel Domatilla BSRN. **EDUCATION:** Southern Univ, BS 1944; Catholic Univ, BS NEd 1950; Univ of Chicago, MS 1953; The Catholic Univ of Amer Washington DC, grad work in psychiatric nursing 1962. **CAREER:** VA Med Ctr, staff nurse, head nurse, supr, rsch nurse, skin integrity, nursing instr 1950-. **ORGANIZATIONS:** Consultant Life Styles for Wellness; participant Catholic Renewal Prog. **HONORS/ACHIEVEMENTS:** Pi Lambda Theta Univ Women of Higher Ed Univ of Chicago 1950; Incentive Awds for Work Improvement with VA 1960; board JB Nursing Home; Recognition as Woman of Culture 1974; Friend & Volunteer of the Kennedy Ctr 1974; AKA Sorority; Alpha Wives of Washington; Sigma Theta Tau Nurses Hon Soc. **BUSINESS ADDRESS:** Nursing Instructor, Veterans Admin Medical Center, 50 Irving St NW, Washington, DC 20422.

CALHOUN, DOROTHY EUNICE
Administrator. **PERSONAL:** Born Jul 16, 1936, Salitpa, AL; married Roosevelt; children: Michael W, Daryl T. **EDUCATION:** AL State U, BS 1957; Atlanta U, MLS 1972; Auburn U, 1973. **CAREER:** Clarke Co Bd of Educ, tchr 1957-59; Mntgmry Co Bd of Educ, tchr-Lbrn 1959-70; Maxwell AFB, AL, lbrn 1970-. **ORGANIZATIONS:** Mem Am Lbry Asso 1970-, AL Lbry Asso 1979-83, NEA 1959-70, Delta Sigma Theta Sor, Order of Eastern Star, Elite Social & Civic Clb 1970-84, Las Amigas Clb 1965-84. **HONORS/ACHIEVEMENTS:** 2 Sustained Superior Awrds USAF 1971-84; Lbrn of Yr ATC Cmd 1980; Tchr of Yr Clarke Co Bd of Educ 1958; Ten Year Cert of Serv USAF 1980; Theses, A Study of the Jr High Sch Lbry Fclts & Svcs, Atlanta Univ 1972. **BUSINESS ADDRESS:** Administrative Librarian, Maxwell Comm Library, Fl 3300 Bldg 28, Maxwell AFB, AL 36112.

CALHOUN, ERIC A.
Government official. **PERSONAL:** Born Nov 20, 1950, Gary, IN; son of William Calhoun; married Delores Brown Calhoun, Apr 22, 1983; children: Asha D Calhoun. **EDUCATION:** Wilberforce Univ, Wilberforce, OH, BS, Accounting, 1974; Kentucky State Univ, Frankfor, KY, MPA, 1982; Miles Law School, Fairfield, AL, Juris Doctorate (cum laude), 1989. **CAREER:** Central State Univ, Wilberforce, OH, admin, 1972-78; Wendy's Intl, Dayton, OH, store co-mgr, 1978-79; Kentucky State Univ, Frankfort, KY, admin, 1979-83; Miles Coll, Fairfield, AL, admin, 1983-85; City of Birmingham, Birmingham, AL, admin analyst, 1985-87; Mayor's Office, Birmingham, AL, admin asst, 1987-. **ORGANIZATIONS:** Mem, Drug Abuse Task Force, Bethel Baptist Church, 1989-. **HONORS/ACHIEVEMENTS:** Outstanding Young Men, Outstanding Young Men Org, 1987; Deans List, 1987. **BUSINESS ADDRESS:** Admin Asst to the Mayor, City of Birmingham, 710 N 20th Street, Birmingham, AL 35203.

CALHOUN, FRED STEVERSON
Educator. **PERSONAL:** Born Mar 20, 1947, McDonough, GA; son of Rev Willie M Calhoun (deceased) and Mattie Calhoun; married M Janice Wright. **EDUCATION:** Fullerton Coll, 1965-66; Cypress Coll, AA 1968-71; Univ of California-Irvine, BA Social Ecology 1971-73; California State Univ-Long Beach, MS Psychology 1974-77; Nova Univ, Ft Lauderdale FL, EdD, 1989. **CAREER:** Cypress Coll, Student Educational Development Center, work study jobs and recruitment coordinator 1968-71; UC Irvine/Social Ecology Dept, research asst 1971-73; Corbin Center, asst coordinator 1973; Cypress Coll, Student Educational Development Center, asst dir 1973-79, dir 1979-. **ORGANIZATIONS:** North Orange County Community Coll Affirmative Action Task Force; Cypress Coll Affirmative Action Comm, North Orange County Comm Coll District; Mgmt Group, North Orange County Comm Coll District; EOPS Advisory Comm, Cypress Coll; Extended Opportunities Programs and Services Assn. **HONORS/ACHIEVEMENTS:** Ford Foundation Upper Division Scholarship for Outstanding Minority Students, 1971; United States Army "Old Guard"; voted co-captain of Cypress Merit, North Orange County Comm Coll Bd of Trustees 1988; Devel Summer Readiness Program for pre-college students, 1980, scholarship program 1980, English as a second language conversational groups, 1981, Adult Literacy Program, 1987, and implemented classes in self-concept, 1987. **MILITARY SERVICE:** US Army, sergeant, 1966-68; received Good Conduct Medal. **BUSINESS ADDRESS:** Dir, Student Educ Develop Ctr, Cypress College, 9200 Valley View St, Cypress, CA 90630.

CALHOUN, JACK JOHNSON, JR.
Assistant jail administrator. **PERSONAL:** Born Sep 05, 1938, Canton, OH; son of Jack J Calhoun Sr and Jessie Mae Calhoun; married Constance Butler, Jun 02, 1979; children: Jack III, Leslie A, Lisa J, Rayetta J. **EDUCATION:** Central State, Wilberforce, OH, 1956-58; Kent State, Kent, OH, 1988-. **CAREER:** Republic Steel, Canton, OH, security guard, 1966-69; Canton Police Dept, Canton, OH, patrolman, 1969-79; Stark County Sheriff, Canton, OH, deputy sheriff, 1979-81; sergeant, 1981-85; lieutenant, 1985-. **ORGANIZATIONS:** Mem Buckeye Sheriff, 1979-; mem Amer Jail Assn, 1980-; mem Ohio Correctional Court Serv Assn (OCCSA) 1986-; consultant, TANO, State of Ohio, 1987-; pres Ebony Police Assn of Stark County, 1983-; Natl Black Police Assn, 1983-. **HONORS/ACHIEVEMENTS:** Stark County Amateur Baseball Hall of Fame, 1989. **MILITARY SERVICE:** AUS SP 4 1961-1965. **BUSINESS ADDRESS:** Assistant Jail Administrator, Stark County Sheriff Department, 4500 Atlantic Blvd NE, PO Box 9279, Canton, OH 44711.

CALHOUN, JOHN
Management executive. **PERSONAL:** Born Aug 06, 1937, Fort Oglethrope, GA; son of James Paul Calhoun and Geneva Fortson Calhoun. **EDUCATION:** Eastern NE Coll, BA 1965; Blackstone Sch of Law, LLB 1970; Edward Water Coll, JD 1975; Univ of ME, Amer Univ, Cath Univ, Univ of WI, US Armed Forces Inst, additional studies; Clayton Univ Intl, PhD finance & mgmt exec; Univ of East Asia Macau Grad Coll, Chinese Law Diploma 1987. **CAREER:** Massweiler Germany, newspaper editor 1956-58; AUS Recruiting Main Sta Detroit, record review clk 1958-59; NATO Izmir Turkey, intelligence analyst 1959; Stars & Stripes Newspaper, corres Germany 1959-60; Ft Myer Post, editor in chief 1961-63; Radio VUNC, news editor 1963-65; DOD Pub Relations for ME, NH, VT, supr1965-67; UN Tokyo Japan, pub affairs rep 1967-68; Military Dist of Washington DC, chief comm relations br 1969-70; Public Affairs Natl Farmers Union Green Thumb, dir 1970-71; Minority Comm Peace Corps, dir 1971-73; The White House, staff asst to the Pres 1973-74, special asst to the Pres 1975-77, dir for media relations 1975-77; Aaken-Calhoun Group Ltd APS, chmn of the bd. **ORGANIZATIONS:** Capitol Hill Club; Intl Platform Assn; Amer Mgmt Assn; Intl Comm Assn; author of The World Through TV 1967, 1969 Inaugural Parade Scenario, Green Thumb in Serv to Amer 1971, Mass Communications in Japan 1975; bd dir Bel-Pre Civic Assn; mem Disabled Vet's Assn; Montgomery Co Young Rep Club; mem Advertising Club of NY; mem DAV, Amer Legion, Washington Council on Foreign Affairs. **HONORS/ACHIEVEMENTS:** Middle Atlantic Assn of Indus Editors Awd 1961; Outstanding Newspaper Editors Awd Dept of Defense 1961; Rep of Korea State Commendation 1968; CLIO Awd Amer TV & Radio Commercials Festival Group 1972; Col Aide-De-Camp Gov of TN 1973; Hon Sgt at Arms House of Rep 1973; Commd Ambassador of Good Will Gov of AR1974. **HOME ADDRESS:** PO Box 70620, Washington, DC 20024.

CALHOUN, JOSHUA WESLEY
Psychiatrist. **PERSONAL:** Born Mar 21, 1956, Macon, GA; son of Dr E M Calhoun and Harriett Hixon Williams; married Deloris Davis, Dec 21, 1981; children: Joshua W II. **EDUCATION:** Yale Univ, BA 1978; Univ of Cincinnati, MD 1982. **CAREER:** Cincinnati General Hosp, medical internship 1982-83; MA Mental Health Ctr, resident in psychiatry 1983-87, chief resident in child psychiatry 1986-87; Harvard Medical School, clinical fellow in psychiatry; St Louis University Medical School, clinical instructor, 1987-. **ORGANIZATIONS:** Psychiatrist Norwood Hospital 1984-87, Brockton Multi-Service Ctr 1985-87, Winthrop Hospital 1986-87; adv bd Boston Adolescent Task Force 1986-; consultant, Annie Malone Children's Home 1988-; consultant, Children's Center for Behavioral Development, 1987-. **HONORS/ACHIEVEMENTS:** Fellow Amer Psychiatric Assoc, Natl Institute of Mental Health 1983-86; editorial bd Jefferson Journal of Psychiatry 1985-87. **HOME ADDRESS:** 7361 Princeton Ave, St Louis, MO 63130. **BUSINESS ADDRESS:** Southern Illinois Healthcare Foundation, 6010 Bond Avenue, Centerville, IL 62207.

CALHOUN, LEE A.
Educator. **PERSONAL:** Born Aug 16, 1947, Mobile, AL. **EDUCATION:** Univ Toledo, BA 1969; Notre Dame, MA 1971; Univ MI, MA 1972; Univ of MI, PhD Candidate. **CAREER:** Herring-Guerden Assoc, S Bend IN, consultant 1971; Dept of Sociology Notre Dame, teacher asst 1971; Dept of Sociology Univ MI, teaching fellow 1972; Afram Assoc, Ann Arbor MI, owner 1972; Howard Univ, lectr 1973-. **ORGANIZATIONS:** Mem Am Acad Polit & Social Sci; inst Soc Ethics Life Sci; Am Soc Pub Adminstrn; Nat conf Black Polit Scintists; Univ Toledo Alumni Assn; Notre Dame Alumni Assn Alpha Kappa Delta; Sociology Honor Soc; Who's Who Am Coll &U; NASSPAA Fellowship 1971-73; fellowship Univ MI 1972. **BUSINESS ADDRESS:** Dept Polit Sci, Howard Univ, Washington, DC 20059.

CALHOUN, LILLIAN SCOTT
Business executive. **PERSONAL:** Born in Savannah, GA; daughter of Walter S Scott and Laura McDowell Scott; married Harold; children: Laura, Harold Jr, Walter, Karen. **EDUCATION:** Ohio St U, BA. **CAREER:** Ebony-Jet Mag, assoc editor 1961-63; Chicago Daily Defender, feature editor, columnist 1963-65; Chicago Sun-Times, reporter 1965-68; Integrated Educ Race & Schools, managing editor 1968-71; Chicago Journalism Rev, columist 1969-74; Black Forum WLS-AM Radio, consultant, program moderator 1969-74; US Dept of Labor, information officer, dir Chicago regional information office 1971-73; The Chicago Reporter, co-editor 1973-76; WGN-TV "Issues Unlimited", semi-regular participant 1974-76; US Dept of Labor, writer-editor 1976-77; "The Business of Rights" Crain's Chicago Business, columnist 1978-80; "Matter of Opinion" WBBM-AM Radio, commentator 1979-80; Calmar Communications Inc, founder, pres 1978-. **ORGANIZATIONS:** Member Governor's Commn on Status of Women 1965-67; Governor's Advisory Council on Manpower 1973-75; past bd member Oppor Cntrs; Woman's Bd Chicago Urban League; Hyde Park Coop Society; Amer Civil Liberties Union; Erikson Inst For Early Educ; mem Alpha Kappa Alpha; Alpha Gamma Pi; Society of Midland Authors; Chicago Press Club; Publicity Club of Chicago; Arts Club of Chicago; life member NAACP; member bd of trustees, sec Chicago Educ TV Assn (WTTW-TV). **HONORS/ACHIEVEMENTS:** Second Prize Natl Negro Publisher's Assn Feature Competition 1963; second prize IL Associated Press Feature Competition 1966, 1967; Journalistic Excellence North Shore Chapter LINKS; Operation PUSH Communicator of Year 1975; YWCA Leader Award Communications 1984. **BUSINESS ADDRESS:** President, Calmar Communications Inc, 500 N Dearborn St, Chicago, IL 60610.

CALHOUN, NOAH ROBERT
Oral/maxillofacial surgeon. **PERSONAL:** Born Mar 23, 1921, Clarendon, AR; married Cecelia C; children: Stephen M, Cecelia N. **EDUCATION:** Dental Sch Howard U, DDS 1948; Tufts Med & Dent Coll, MSD 1955. **CAREER:** Med Ctr VA, asst oral surgeon 1964-72, asst chief dentist 1972-75, chief dental surgeon 1975-82, coord, Dental Rsch, Dental School Howard Univ; prof oral maxillofacial Surgery 1982. **ORGANIZATIONS:** Oral surgeon Med Ctr Tuskegee AL VA 1950-64; prof lecturer Georgetown Dental 1970-; consultant VA & Atena Ins Co 1982-; dir Red Cross Tuskegee Inst 1962-64; dir vice pres Credit Union VA 1982; adv comm Amer Bd Oral Surgery 8 yrs. **HONORS/ACHIEVEMENTS:** Fellow Amer Coll Dentistry; Fellow Intl Coll Dentistry; mem Inst of Med 1982; Dental Alumni Awrd Howard Univ 1972. **MILITARY SERVICE:** USAF cptn 2 yrs. **HOME ADDRESS:** 1413 Leegate Rd NW, Washington, DC 20012. **BUSINESS ADDRESS:** Prof Oral & Maxillofacial Surgery, Dental Sch Howard Univ, Washington, DC 20059.

CALHOUN, THOMAS
Medical educator. **PERSONAL:** Born Oct 06, 1932, Marianna, FL; son of Sylvia Barnes Thompson; married Shirley Kathryn Jones; children: Thomas Jr, Christine, Kathy, Maria. **EDUCATION:** Florida A&M Univ, BS 1954; Fisk Univ, grad school; Meharry Med Coll, MD 1963. **CAREER:** Fisk Univ, instr 1957-58; Tennis Circuit, amateur traveller 1958; US

Postal WA, employee 1958-59; Howard Univ, clinical assoc prof of surgery. **ORGANIZATIONS:** Mem Amer Tennis Assn; Amer Medical Tennis Assn; US Tennis Assn; District of Columbia Medical Soc; Bd of Surgeons Police Fire Dept; St Thomas Apostolic Catholic Church; Diplomate Amer Bd of Surgery 1971; fellow Amer Coll of Surgery 1972; fellow Amer Assn of Abdominal Surgeons 1977; med adviser Care-Plus, Delmarva Regional Pro; fellow Amer Coll of Nutrition. **MILITARY SERVICE:** AUS 2nd lt 1954-56. **BUSINESS ADDRESS:** Clinical Assoc Prof of Surgery, HowardUniv, 1140 Varnum St NW, Washington, DC 20017.

CALIP, BRAD CALVIN
Professional athlete. **PERSONAL:** Born Dec 12, 1962, Hobart, OK. **EDUCATION:** East Central Univ OK. **CAREER:** Denver Gold, slot back 1985-. **HONORS/ACHIEVEMENTS:** 1st team NAIA All-Am and NAIA Dist 9 Offensive Plyr of Year 1984.

CALLAHAN, SAMUEL P.
Dentist, clergyman. **PERSONAL:** Born Apr 15, 1924, Galax, VA; son of William Thomas and Nannie C; married Maude R Harris; children: Samuel, Maria, William, Angela. **EDUCATION:** Fisk U, BA; Meharry Coll, DDS; Wesley Theol Sem, MDiv. **CAREER:** Self employed dentist; Christ Is The Answer Deliverance Center, pastor; NAACP, chmn legal redress com. **ORGANIZATIONS:** Mem Anne Arundel Co Human Relation & Com; 32 Deg Mason; shriner; Alpha Phi Alpha. **HONORS/ACHIEVEMENTS:** Recipient Certificate for Creative Achievement in Dentistry. **MILITARY SERVICE:** USN 1944-46.

CALLAWAY, DWIGHT W.
Automotive component manufacturing executive. **PERSONAL:** Born May 22, 1932, Cincinnati, OH; son of H C Callaway and Virginia Moody Gordon (deceased); married Roberta F Leahr, Aug 06, 1955; children: Denise Callaway-Reistat, Gordon C Callaway, Dwight W Callaway II. **EDUCATION:** Morehouse Coll, Atlanta, GA, BS, 1953; Univ of Cincinnati, Cincinnati, OH, MS, 1956; Pennsylvania State Univ, eight week Exec Mgmt, 1979. **CAREER:** D H Baldwin Co, Cincinnati, OH, sr engineer, 1955-62; Electra Mfg Co, Independence, KS, mgr research & devel, 1962-64; Delco Electrical Div, GMC, Kokomo, IN, chief engineer, 1964-81; Youngwood Electric Metals, Murraysville, PA, exec vice pres, 1981-82; A C Rochester Div, GMC, Flint, MI, mgr intl operations, 1982-; bd of dir, Burnex Corp, Mexico City, Mexico, 1986; bd of dir, GM Luexenbourg, 1987; bd of dir, GM Australia, Melbourne, 1986-. **ORGANIZATIONS:** Pres, 1970-72, bd of dir, 1972-, Intl Soc for Hybrid Microelectronics; mem AIA Fraternity, 1952-; mem Sigma Pi Phi Boule, 1984-; mem All Port Authority, Flint, MI, 1986-; bd of dir, Flint School System Pic Engineering Program; bd of dir, Howard Community Hospital, Kokomo, IN, United Way, Kokomo, IN, YMCA, Calver Community center, Kokomo, IN; pres of bd, Kokomo OIC. **HONORS/ACHIEVEMENTS:** Engineer of the Year, Natl Electronic Production Conf, 1970; Daniel M Hughes Award, Intl Society for Hybrid Microelectronics, 1972; patent issued, "Plag/gold W B Semi conductors, 1969. **HOME ADDRESS:** 2620 Indian Bow Trail, Flint, MI 48507.

CALLAWAY, LOUIS MARSHALL, JR.
Plant manager. **PERSONAL:** Born Jan 22, 1939, Chicago, IL; married Duryea Dickson. **EDUCATION:** Drake U, BA 1961. **CAREER:** Ford Motor Co, plant mgr; Ford, asst plant mgr; Ford Truck plant, asst plant mgr; Ford, quality control mgr; Ford, pre-delivery mgr; Ford, supt; AAD Div, indsl rep. **ORGANIZATIONS:** Mem Chicago S C of C; dir Chicago Assn Commerce & Indus; coporate mem Blue Cross Blue Shield. **BUSINESS ADDRESS:** 12600 S Torrence Ave, Chicago, IL 60633.

CALLENDER, CARL O.
Commissioner, attorney. **PERSONAL:** Born Nov 16, 1936, New York, NY; married Leola Rhames. **EDUCATION:** Brooklyn Comm Coll Brooklyn NY, 1960-61; Hunter Coll Bronx NY, AB 1961-64; Howard Univ Sch Law Washington DC, JD. **CAREER:** Housing Litigation Bur NYC, dir 1975-76; Comm Law Ofcs Prgm, dir 1972-75; Comm Law Ofcs, deputy dir 1971-72; Comm Law & Ofcs, asso dir 1971; CALS Reginald Heber Smith Fellow Prgm NYC, COORD 1970-71; Regin Ald Heber Smith fellow Harlem Assertion of Rights Inc, 1969-70; Harlem Assertion of Rights Inc, staff atty 1968-69; Prentice-Hall's Federal Tax Service Bulletins NJ, legal edit 1968; Palystreet NYC, dir 1967; Hunter Coll NYC, asst libr aide 1966; Ebenezer Gospel Tabernacle, ordained minister 1972. **ORGANIZATIONS:** Chmn & pres Natl Young People's Christian Assn Inc; chmn & pres Christian Leaders United Inc; mem elec com of Student Bar Assnadministrv asst; Housing Research Com; Phi Alpha Delta Legal Fraternity. **HONORS/ACHIEVEMENTS:** "Student who made most & significant progress in senior year" 1967; Am Jurisprudence Award for Insurance 1967; half hour film on channel 2 "Eye On New York"; brief Biog; Sketch Life Entitled "Attorney For The Defenseless 1970. **MILITARY SERVICE:** USAF airman 1st class 1951-55. **BUSINESS ADDRESS:** 100 Gold St, New York, NY 10038.

CALLENDER, CLIVE ORVILLE
Educator, scientist. **PERSONAL:** Born Nov 16, 1936, New York, NY; son of Joseph Burke and Ida Burke; married Fern Irene Marshall; children: Joseph, Ealena, Arianne. **EDUCATION:** Hunter Coll, AB 1959; Meharry Med Coll, MD 1963. **CAREER:** Univ of Cincinnati, internship 1963-64; Harlem Hosp, asst resident 1964-65; Howard Univ & Freedmen's Hosp, asst resident 1965-66; Memorial Hosp for Cancer & Allied Diseases, asst resident 1966-67; Howard Univ & Freedmen's Hosp, chief resident 1968-69, instr 1969-70; DC Gen Hosp, med ofcr 1970-71; Port Harcourt Gen Hosp Nigeria, consult 1970-71; Howard Univ Med Coll, asst prof, dir 1973-76, prof 1982-; Howard Univ, prof vice chmn dept of surgery 1982-, dir transplant center 1974-. **ORGANIZATIONS:** Mem DC Med Soc; Soc of Acad Surg; Transplant Soc; Amer Soc of Transplant Surg; edtrl adv bd New Directions; bd dir Kidney Found Natl Capital ARea; Fellow of Amer Coll of Surg 1975; pres Natl Kidney Found of Natl Capital Area 1979-; chmn membership com Amer Soc of Transplant Surgeons; presMed Dental Staff of Howard Univ Hosp 1980; pres Alpha Phi Omega Frat 1959; pres Alpha Omega Alpha; Alpha Phi Alpha; dip Amer Bd of Surgery 1970. **HONORS/ACHIEVEMENTS:** Hoffman LaRoche Awrd 1961; Natl Med Assn Aux Scholarship 1961; Joseph Collins Scholarship Award 1961-63; Charles Nelson Gold Medal Meharry Med Coll 1963; Hudson Meadows Award Meharry Med Coll 1963; Natl Med Assn Scholarship Award 1963; Fellow Amer Cancer Soc 1965-66; Charles R Drew Rsch Award Howard Univ & Freedmen's Hosp 1968; Daniel Hale Williams Award Howard Univ & Freedmen's Hosp 1969; Spec Postdoctoral NIH Rsch Fellow 1971-73; Clin Transp Fellow Univ of MN 1971-72; numerous presentations, bibliographies & abstracts; Hall of Fame, Hunter College Alumni 1989. **BUSINESS ADDRESS:** Professor of Surgery, HowardUniv Med College, 2041 Georgia Ave, Washington, DC 20060.

CALLENDER, LEROY R.
Structural engineer. **PERSONAL:** Born Feb 29, 1932, New York City, NY; divorced; children: Eric. **EDUCATION:** City Coll City Of NY, BCE 1958. **CAREER:** Founder & owner of his own firm 1969-; draftsman 1950-52; during army service in Korea designed small office bldgs & other facilities; engr on first nuclear power plant built in East after discharge; has provided & consultation on $32 million dormitory & student union bldgs Mary Holmes Coll; $63 million Whitney M Young Complex; $30-million Lindsay-Bushwick Houses & $14 million Douglas Circle project. **BUSINESS ADDRESS:** 236 West 26th St, New York, NY 10001.

CALLENDER, RALPH A.
Dentist. **PERSONAL:** Born Mar 21, 1932, New York, NY; married Anita Pauline Goodwin; children: Ralph III, Richard, Randy. **EDUCATION:** Long Island U; Brooklyn Coll, AA 1958; Howard U, DDS 1962; Univ Rochester-Eastman Dental Ctr, pedodontic residency 1963; orthodontic grad cert 1965. **CAREER:** Pvt Practice, orthodontist 1965-; USC So & Central Health Ctr, dir orthodontics 1966-68; RAC Prodn, pres 1974-; Worldwide Films Inc, sales rep 1974; Bokari Films, producers rep 1974-; Am Transcontinental Pictures Inc, pres. **ORGANIZATIONS:** Mem Am Dental Assn; Nat Dental Assn; CA Dental Soc; ethics commn election Commn LA Dental Soc; mem vice pres sec treas Angel City Dental Soc; mem Indep Producers Assn Scoutmaster New York City 1955-58; chmn of bd S Central LA YMCA; mem Men of Tomorrow Kiwanis. **HONORS/ACHIEVEMENTS:** Martin Luther King Award 1976; Interntl of Dentists Award 1962; rsrch grant NIH 1960-61. **MILITARY SERVICE:** USAF a-1c 1951-55. **BUSINESS ADDRESS:** 3701 Stocker St, Los Angeles, CA 90008.

CALLENDER, VALERIE DAWN
Physician. **PERSONAL:** Born Oct 01, 1960, Port Chester, NY; daughter of Joseph H Callender and Nancy S Callender. **EDUCATION:** Bennett Coll, BS 1982; Howard Univ Coll of Medicine, MD 1986. **CAREER:** Health Science Acad Howard Univ Coll of Medicine, program asst coord 1983; Howard Univ Hospital, postgraduate physician 1986-87 internal medicine, 1987-89 dermathology. **ORGANIZATIONS:** Mem NAACP 1978-82, Amer & Natl Medical Assocs 1982-, District of Columbia Medical Soc 1983-, Amer Medical Women's Assoc 1984-; charter mem Natl Museum of Women in the Arts. **HONORS/ACHIEVEMENTS:** First prize Syntex Lab Outstanding Student Rsch Howard Univ Coll Medicine 1984; 2nd prize Student Natl Medical Assoc Rsch Forum, 1985; 2nd prize Howard Univ Residents Research Forum, 1988. **HOME ADDRESS:** 11409 Abbotswood Ct, Upper Marlboro, MD 20772. **BUSINESS ADDRESS:** Postgraduate Physician 3, Howard University Hospital, 2041 Georgia Ave NW, Washington, DC 20060.

CALLENDER, WILFRED A.
Educator, attorney. **PERSONAL:** Born in Colon, Panama;married Beth Robinson; children: Neil, Melissa. **EDUCATION:** Brooklyn Coll, BA 1954; Brooklyn Coll, MA 1963; Brooklyn Law Sch, JD 1969. **CAREER:** Boys High School Brooklyn, educator 1957-69; Dept Real Estate Commerce Labor Industry Corp Kings, asst dir 1969-70; Wade & Callender, atty 1972-; Hostos Community Coll, prof 1970-; Wade & Callender ESQS Practice of Law. **ORGANIZATIONS:** Mem Brooklyn Bar Assn; Bedford Stuyvesant Lawyers Assn; Natl Conf Black Lawyers; bd Trustees Encampment for Citizenship 1971-; pres Black Caucus Hostos 1972-; mem bd trustees Social Serv; bd NY Soc Ethical Culture. **MILITARY SERVICE:** AUS pvt 2 1954-56. **BUSINESS ADDRESS:** Assoc Prof of English, Hostos Community College, 500 Grand Concourse, Bronx, NY 10451.

CALLOWAY, CAB See CALLOWAY, CABELL

CALLOWAY, CABELL (CAB CALLOWAY)
Musician. **PERSONAL:** Born Dec 24, 1907, Rochester, NY. **EDUCATION:** Crane Coll Chicago. **ORGANIZATIONS:** Leader Alabamians Chicago 1928; New York City 1929; leader Missourians 1929; Cab Calloway Band 1930-48; appeared at Savoy Ballroom & Cotton Club; recorded Minnie the Moocher 1931; appeared motion & pictures Singing Kin Big Broadcast of 1933 Stormy Weather Sensations of 1945; toured US Europe with Porgy & Bess 1952-54; also appeared in Hello Dolly with Pearl Bailey; appeared night clubs with quartet numerous TV appearances; mem ASCAP 1942. **HONORS/ACHIEVEMENTS:** Ebony Lifetime Achievement Award for a career spanning more than 50 years and for pioneering in numerous areas for Blacks in the entertainment field, 1985.

CALLOWAY, CURTIS A.
Attorney. **PERSONAL:** Born Dec 09, 1939, Birmingham, AL; married Louise Ford; children: Curtis Shannon, Conrad Lamar. **EDUCATION:** Miles Coll Birmingham, AL, BA 1962; So Univ Sch Law, JD 1965. **CAREER:** Baton Rouge Legal Aid Soc, staff atty 1969-71; Law Firm of Lacour, Wilson & Calloway, attorney 1971-. **ORGANIZATIONS:** LA State Bar Assn; Baton Rouge Bar Assn; Natl Bar Assn; Amer Bar Assn; Amer Judicature Soc; Louis A Martinet Legal Soc; Lawyer Referral Proj; Consumer Affairs Com of Amer Bar Assn; pres Scotlandville Jaycees; pres bd Baton Rouge Legal Aid Soc; Baton Rouge Clients Couns Legal Advisor; bd dir Alsen Neighborhood Serv Center; LA Natl Bank adv bd; Kappa Alpha Psi. **HONORS/ACHIEVEMENTS:** LA Jaycees Outstanding Young Man Finalist 1973; Outstanding Alumnus So Univ Alumni Fedn 1974. **MILITARY SERVICE:** USMC Sgt. **BUSINESS ADDRESS:** Attorney, Lacour, Wilson & Calloway, PO Box 73588, Baton Rouge, LA 70807.

CALLOWAY, DEVERNE LEE
Legislator. **PERSONAL:** Born Jun 17, 1916, Memphis, TN; married Ernest Calloway. **EDUCATION:** LeMoyne-Owen Coll, AB 1938; Atlanta Univ & Northwestern U, grad studies in English. **CAREER:** 81st Dist St Louis, state rep for nine consecutive terms. **ORGANIZATIONS:** Mem of numerous city & state coms. **HONORS/ACHIEVEMENTS:** Fist black women to be elected in MO; commendation by St Louis Comm for efforts to educate average citizens in the effectiveness & need for polit participation on local state & fed Levels. **BUSINESS ADDRESS:** 4309 Enright, St Louis, MO 63108.

CALLOWAY, ERNEST
Educator. **PERSONAL:** Born Jan 01, 1909, Herberton, WV; married Deverne. **EDUCATION:** Brookwood Labor Coll, 1934-35; Ruskin Coll Oxford Univ Eng, 1948-49; Lincoln Univ Jefferson City MO, HHD. **CAREER:** Transport Serv Employees Union Chicago, gen organizer founder 1937-48; Natl CIO News, Washington DC, editorial staff 1944; CIO So Drive NC, staff 1949-50; St Louis Teamsters Joint Council, research dir 1951-59; Cent Conf Teamsters, assoc res dir 1959-73; Urban Problems St Louis Univ, lecturer 1969-72; St Louis Univ, educator 1973-. **ORGANIZATIONS:** Vice chmn St Louis City Plan Commn; lectr Race Relations Scott AFB IL Pres St Louis NAACP 1955-59; chmn Child Welf Adv Com; exec bd St Louis Civil Liber Commn; natl vice pres Negro Am Labor Council 1961-65; bd MO Assn Social Welf 1970; bd Am Dem Action St Louis 1960-70f research consult Am 2000 Found. **BUSINESS ADDRESS:** St Louis Univ, 221 N Grand Ave, St Louis, MO.

CALLUM, AGNES KANE
Genalogist, historian. **PERSONAL:** Born Feb 24, 1925, Baltimore, MD; daughter of Phillip Moten Kane and Mary Priscilla Gough Kane; married Solomon Melvin Callum, Jul 07, 1944 (deceased); children: Paul A Foster, Agnes H Lightfoot, Arthur M Callum, Martin J CallumMartina P Callum. **EDUCATION:** Morgan State Univ, BA, 1973; Univ of Ghana, West Africa, 1973; Morgan State Univ, MS, 1975. **CAREER:** Beauty Queen Co, Baltimore MD, sales manager 1954-58; North Carolina Mutual Life Insurance Co, Baltimore MD, 1958-62; Rosewood State Hospital, Ownings MD, practical nurse, 1962-66; US Postal Serv, Baltimore MD, review clk, 1966-86; Douglass High Evening School, Baltimore MD, teacher 1977-80; Coppin State Coll, Baltimore MD, teacher 1978. **ORGANIZATIONS:** Mem NAACP 1950-89; mem Assn for Study of Afro-Amer Life and History 1966-89; commn mem Baltimore City Hospital 1976-78; mem Maryland Genealogical Society 1978-89; corresponding sec Afro-Amer Historical & Genealogical Society 1986-89; historian Natl Alliance Postal & Federal Employees Local #202 1986-; historian St Francis Xavier Catholic Church 1988-; Advisory Committee Maryland State Archives 1989; mem Archive Committee Maryland Commn Afro-Amer Life & Culture. **HONORS/ACHIEVEMENTS:** City of Baltimore Mayor's Citation, Citizenship 1967; Author, Kane-Butler Family Genealogical History of a Black Family 1978; founder, editor Kane Family News Notes 1979; founder, editor, publisher, Flower of the Forest Black Genealogical Journal 1982-; author, Inscriptions From The Tomb Stones at Mt Calvary Cemetery 1926-1982, 1985; Senate of Maryland Award Outstanding Community Worker 1986; City Council of Baltimore Retirement 1986; Citizen Citation of Baltimore Leadership 1986; US Postal Service 20 year Service Award 1986; Natl Council of Negro Women Historian Award 1988. **HOME ADDRESS:** 822 Bonaparte Avenue, Baltimore, MD 21218.

CALOMEE, ANNIE E.
Educator. **PERSONAL:** Born Feb 02, 1910, Beaumont, MS; married Andrew; children: Doris, Gloria, Andrea. **EDUCATION:** Univ of So CA, BS MS; UCLA Pepperdine U, spl Study. **CAREER:** Multicultural Educ, teacher, consultant, lecturer; LA City School Dist Coord, teacher reading, splst coord; 1st workshop in Tech & Materials for Teaching Black History to classroom teachers LA City Schools, leadrr, consult 1967; inserv classes for teachers; Afro-Am History, consultant lecturer. **ORGANIZATIONS:** Life mem NAACP; Nat Counc of Negro Women; Assn for Study of Afro-Am Life & Hist; Nat Sor of Phi Delta Kappa; Women in Educ Ldrshp; CTA; NEA; United Tchrs of LA. **HONORS/ACHIEVEMENTS:** Woman of yr Ward African Meth Epis Ch Phi Delta Kappa 1965; City Counc Resolution for contrib to Am Hist; fdr chmn Negro Hist Workshop for Youth Pepsi Cola Bottling Co 1965; United Tchrs; plaque contrib to students & tchrs in Multicultural Edn. **BUSINESS ADDRESS:** Los Angeles School District, 450 N Grand, Los Angeles, CA 90012.

CALVIN, EARL D.
Clergyman. **PERSONAL:** Born May 26, 1934, Decatur, IL; son of Arless Calvin and Gladys Robinson Calvin; married Carol Matson, Apr 01, 1961 (divorced); children: Roger A, David E. **EDUCATION:** Attended, Univ of WI-Milwaukee; Bernie Robbins School of Rel Est, Milwaukee Wisconsin 1965. **CAREER:** Milwaukee Def, business mgr 1956-59; Milwaukee Courier, mgr editor 1964-68; Milwaukee Star Times, assoc publisher 1971-75; Racine Star Times, publisher 1975-76; Milwaukee Com Journal, expeditor 1976; Yellow Cab Cooperative, mem 1985-; licensed real estate broker WI, 1986-; Fellowship Comm Baptist Church, minister-asst pastor 1980-. **ORGANIZATIONS:** Mem WI Press Assn 1971-74; mem NNPA 1971-74; mem Milwaukee Ad Club 1973-; founder 1st dir Comm Pride Expo 1974; pres co-founder Crusaders Civic & Soc League 1957-58; vice pres Milwaukee United Sch Integration Comm 1963-66; mem N Central YMCA bd 1970-76; mem United Ministry Higher Educ 1963-75; chmn Milwaukee African Relief Comm 1973; vice pres SE Assn United Church of Christ 1969; co-founder & mem steering comm Jr Acad of Med and Engrg 1973-; mem NAACP Bd Racine WI 1976. **HONORS/ACHIEVEMENTS:** Scholarship 14th Annual Race Relations Inst Fisk Univ 1958. **BUSINESS ADDRESS:** Minister, Fellowship Comm Baptist Church, 2320 W Vine St, Milwaukee, WI 53205.

CALVIN, MICHAEL BYRON
Judge, attorney. **PERSONAL:** Born Feb 16, Nashville, TN; married Vanessa Ann Graham; children: Michael Langston, Justin Kinnard. **EDUCATION:** Hist/Govt Monmouth Coll, BA 1972; St Louis Univ Sch of Law, JD 1975. **CAREER:** City of St Louis, asso circuit judge; Black Am Law Students Assn BALSA Reports, editor . **ORGANIZATIONS:** Nat bd mem Law Student's Civil Rights Research Council; mem Mound City Bar Assn; mem MO Atty Gen Commn for Prevention of Crime 1980; scoutmaster All Saints Episcopal Ch; youth leader All Saints Episcopal Ch. **HONORS/ACHIEVEMENTS:** Outstanding young alumnus Monmouth Coll IL 1979; BALSA Alumnus Award Black Am Law Students St Louis Univ 1979. **BUSINESS ADDRESS:** Circuit Court Judge, State of MO, 12th & Market Sts, St Louis, MO 63101.

CALVIN, VIRGINIA BROWN
Educational administrator. **PERSONAL:** Born Jun 16, 1945, Lake Providence, LA; married Richmond E Calvin; children: Brent, Tremayne, Shannon D'Ann. **EDUCATION:** Alcorn State U, BS 1966; NM Highlands U, MA 1970; TX Wmns U, EdD 1973; North TX State U, 1970; IN Univ South Bend, 1979. **CAREER:** LA, NM & TX, teacher 1967-71; South Bend Community School Corp, counselor 1972-76, admin 1977-84. **ORGANIZATIONS:** State cnsltnt IN Head Start Training 1980; chprsn Validation-Head Start 1979; sec Delta Kappa Gamma Hnr Scty 1984; bd dir Jr League of So Bend 1984, Art Ctr 1985. **HONORS/ACHIEVEMENTS:** Wmn of Yr Plano, TX 1971; Monograph "Supt Intera" SBCSC 1979; Wmn of Yr SBCSC YWCA 1984. **HOME ADDRESS:** 1311 Berkshire Dr, South Bend, IN 46614. **BUSINESS ADDRESS:** Principal, Elem SBCSC, 1213 California, South Bend, IN 46628.

CALVIN, WILLIE J.
Clergyman. **PERSONAL:** Born Mar 31, 1913, Dallas, TX; married Bernice Fields; children: Willette Diane. **EDUCATION:** Bishop Coll, BA; Hampton Inst, LLD 1974. **CAREER:** Galilee Bapt Church, minister 10 years; Mt Zion Bapt Church Milwaukee, minister 1961-85; Greater Mt Zion Bapt Church, minister 1985-. **ORGANIZATIONS:** Bd mem YMCA; pres Milwaukee Inst of Theol; mem We, Milwaukeans; Com of Concern; past chmn Comm Relations Soc Devel Comm; 2nd vice pres NAACP of Milwaukee. **HONORS/ACHIEVEMENTS:** Guest Speaker Lacy Krik Williams Inst 1972; Guest Speaker "Distinguished Staley Award" Inst Hampton, VA 1974,76; listed Who's Who Among Bapt Ministers Howard's Library Wash, DC. **BUSINESS ADDRESS:** Minister, Greater Mt Zion Baptist Church, 4328 W North Ave, Milwaukee, WI 53210.

CAM, THEODORE VICTOR
Architect. **PERSONAL:** Born Sep 28, 1928, Philadelphia, PA; married Brigida P Deguzman; children: Marc, Theodore Jr, Jacinta, Anthony. **EDUCATION:** Drexel U, BS 1958. **CAREER:** Theodore V Cam PC & Assoc, owner pres; Drexel U, unstr 1967; Philadelphia Sch Sys, lectr 1966; Drexel U, critic 1966. **ORGANIZATIONS:** Mem Architect & Plng Commn 1964-65; chmn Architect Rev Commn 1963;jurist Drexel Univ 1961; corp mem Am Inst Arch Corp 1966-70; mem PA Soc Arch 1966-70; mem Am Arbit Assn 1968; consult Temple Univ & Comm 1967; dir Grtr Philadelphia Comm Devel Corp 1970; mem Grtr Philadelphia Enter Devel Corp 1970; consult Afro-Am Hist & Cult Mus 1976; adv bd Advoc Comm Devel Corp 1968; mem Coalition Meaningful Bicent 1968; mem City Wide Black Comm Counc 1968; mem United Property Commn 1969; commr Fair Housing Commn City of Philadelphia 1970-77; dir finan com Philadelphia Basic Adult Educ Acad 1976. **HONORS/ACHIEVEMENTS:** Afro-Am Hist & Cult Mus 1975; Spkr Afro-Am Hist & Cult & Mus 1976. **MILITARY SERVICE:** AUS 1945-47.

CAMBOSOS, BRUCE MICHAEL
Educator. **PERSONAL:** Born Jul 20, 1941, New Haven, CT; married Syleatha Hughes; children: Shanay. **EDUCATION:** George Washington U, 1961; Howard U, BS 1964; Howard U, MD 1969. **CAREER:** Ugast Treatment Center WA, staff psychiatrist 1976-; VA Hospital, staff pyschiatrist 1973-75. **ORGANIZATIONS:** Am Psy Assn; WA Psy Assn; St George Soc; Capital Med Soc Trustee. **HONORS/ACHIEVEMENTS:** Scholarship GWU 1959; tutorial scholarship HowardUniv 1965; ey Williams Award HowardUniv 1969. **BUSINESS ADDRESS:** 2041 Georgia Ave, Washington, DC 20060.

CAMERON, HOWARD K., JR.
Educator. **PERSONAL:** Born Dec 25, 1930, Talladega, AL; married Winifred Flanders; children: Carl. **EDUCATION:** Talladega Coll, AB 1954; MN Highlands U, MA 1956; MI State U, PhD 1963. **CAREER:** Howard Univ, dir of doctoral programs, prof of educ school psychology; Tuskegee Inst AL, educator 1956-58; FL A&M Univ Tallahassee, 1958-59; MI State Univ E Lansing, 1960-61; Southern Univ, Baton Rouge LA, 1960-61; Howard Univ, Washington DC, 1962-; US Labor Dept, consultant 1967-68. **ORGANIZATIONS:** Anns Black Psychol; Am Psychol Assn; Nat Assn School Psychol; Omega Psi Phi Nat Sci Found; Fellowship Univ CA Berkeley 1965. **MILITARY SERVICE:** AUS 1954-55. **BUSINESS ADDRESS:** PO Box 125, Adm Bldg Howard Univ, Washington, DC 20059.

CAMERON, JACK CALVIN
Professional athlete. **PERSONAL:** Born Nov 05, 1961, Roxboro, NC. **EDUCATION:** Winston-Salem. **CAREER:** Chicago Bears, wide receiver/defensive back 1984-. **HONORS/ACHIEVEMENTS:** Leb Bear kick-off return specialists & owned longest return of season 40 yds; appeared in both playoff games; All-conf, all-NAIA 1982-83; 4 year letterman at-Winston-Salem; holds school record for 3 interceptions in one game. **BUSINESS ADDRESS:** Chicago Bears, Halas Hall, 250 N Washington Rd, Lake Forest, IL 60045.

CAMERON, JOHN E.
Clergyman. **PERSONAL:** Born Jun 11, 1932, Hattiesburg, MS; married Lenora Woods; children: Jonetta, John Earl Jr. **EDUCATION:** Alcorn A&M Coll; Am Bapt Theo Sem, BTh 1956; Rust Coll, BS 1957. **CAREER:** Mt Calvary Bapt Ch, Minister; Mt Calvary Comm Devel Agency Inc, coord 1974-; Div of Youth Affairs at Gov's Ofc Jackson, coord 1972; Star Inc Jackson, job coach 1968-71; Star Inc Natchez, cntr dir 1966-68; Minister's Proj under auspices of Presb Commn on Religion & Race Hattiesburg , dir 1954-65. **ORGANIZATIONS:** Candidate US Congress 5th Congressional Dist of MS 1964; ambassador Cntrl Am 1954; pres Nat Bapt Student Union 1954; job Devel Specialist Star Inc 1969-71; sponsor Boy Scouts; Mason; historian for Progressive Nat Bapt Conv; commr Criminal Justice Sys for State Of MS Commr LEAA. **BUSINESS ADDRESS:** 901 Lynch St, Jackson, MS.

CAMERON, JOSEPH A.
Educator. **PERSONAL:** Born Apr 25, 1942, Fairfield, AL; married Mary E Stiles; children: Joseph Jr, Jozetta, Cecelia. **EDUCATION:** TN State U, BS 1963; TX So U, MS 1965; MI State U, PhD 1973. **CAREER:** TX Southern Univ, graduate teaching asst 1965; Dept of Biology Science, Grambling State Univ, instructor 1965-66, asst prof 1967-69; Dept Natural Science, MI State Univ, instructor 1969-73; Dept of Science, MI State Univ, asst prof 1973-74; Dept of Biology, Jackson State Univ, asst prof 1974-; Equal Opportunity Program, MI State Univ, faculty tutor 1969-71; High School Sci Teacher Grambling, consultant 1967-69; Natural Science Lab Manual, MI State Univ, contributing author 1971; published professional Journals; attended Numerous Science Professional Meetings & Presented Papers. **ORGANIZATIONS:** Mem Tri Beta Biol Honor Soc; Am Soc Zool; Am Assn Univ Prof; Tissue Culture Assn; Soc Sigma XI; AAAS; Miss Adad Sci Alpha Phi Aplha Frat Inc NSF Undergrad ResearchFellow TSU 1963; Tri-Beta Biol Honor Soc TSU 1964; research asst Dept Zool Univ IA 1966-67; Equal Opportunity Program Fellow MI State U1969; mem Sigma XI. **HONORS/ACHIEVEMENTS:** Academic Tuition Scholarship Univ IA 1966-67; Soc Sigma XI Award Meritous Research MSU 1973; apptd Fairfield Ind HS Hall Fame 1973; Personalities of So 1974; Dictionary of Intl Biography 1975. **BUSINESS ADDRESS:** Jackson State Univ, Jackson, MS 39217.

CAMERON, LENORE HOPEWELL
Government attorney. **PERSONAL:** Born Dec 20, 1945, Philadelphia, PA; married Daniel Jr; children: Stacey. **EDUCATION:** PA State U, BA 1967; George Wash U, 1968; Georgetown Univ Law Center, JD 1974. **CAREER:** US Dept of Justice, adv 1979-; US Dept of Justice, legal systems analyst 1977-79; Anne Blaine Harrison Inst Georgetown Univ Law Ctr, asst dir DC street Law & Program 1974-77; US Dept of Justice, law clk 1971-74; Vet Admin Central Office Wash DC, computer systems analyst 1967-70. **ORGANIZATIONS:** Corr sec Greater Wash Area Chap Women Lawyers Div Nat Barn Assn 1976-; dir & first vice pres Montgomery Child Day Care Assn Kensington MD 1976-; mem PA Bar 1979-; mem & vice chmn Fed Bar Assn Council on the Fed Lawyer Com on Managing Gov Law Offices 1979- ;commr Montgomery Co Commn for Women 1976-79; commr Montgomery Co Employment Devel Commn 1979-; Mem NAACP/Delta Sigma Theta Sorority. **HONORS/ ACHIEVEMENTS:** Mary Mccleod Bethune Award for Serv Black Am Law Students Assn Georgetown Law 1977; outstanding young woman of Am 1980; St Law "A Course in Practical Law" West Pub Co 1977.

CAMERON, MARY EVELYN
Educator. **PERSONAL:** Born Sep 08, 1944, memphis, TN; married Dr Joseph Alexander; children: Jozetta Louise, Joseph Alexander Jr, Cecelia Denise, Juanita Evette. **EDUCATION:** Marian Coll Indianapolis IN, BA 1962-66; Univ of IA Med Ctr, ADA Cert 1966-67; Jackson State Univ, MS 1979. **CAREER:** State of MS, nutritionist, mem of survey team 1967-68; Grambling State Univ; admin dietitian 1968-69; Sparrow Hosp, clinical dietitian 1969-74; Hinds Gen Hosp, clinical dietitian 1974-79; VA Med Ctr, clinical dietitian 1979; Univ of MS Med Ctr, asst prof 1979-. **ORGANIZATIONS:** Pre Central Dist Dietetic Assn 1978-79; rsch nutritionist Univ Med Ctr 1980-84; pres Nutritionists in Nursing Ed 1981-82; mem MS Heart Assn Professional Ed Comm 1982-84; chmn Nutrition Subcomm Professional Ed Comm 1982-85; nutrition consult Oper Headstart Prog 1982-85; mem MS Heart Ass Nutrition Comm 1983-; pres MS Dietetic Assoc 1983-84. **HONORS/ACHIEVEMENTS:** Outstanding Young Woman of Amer 1980; appt mem of Diocesan School Bd 1982-86; Reviewed several articles for professional jrnl 1982-84; Presented rsch abstract at Reg Hypertension Mtg 1983; Reviewed a major nutrition text Mosby Publ 1984; Publ article in professional referenced jrnl 1985; appt mem bd of CUP Univ S MS; mem Tri Beta Biological Hon Soc 1979-; mem Phi Delta Kappa Hon Soc; listed in Personalities of the South 1976-77. **BUSINESS ADDRESS:** Assistant Professor of Nursing, Univ of Mississippi Med Ctr, School of Nursing, Jackson, MS 39216.

CAMERON, RANDOLPH W.
Marketing & public relations consultant. **PERSONAL:** Son of Randolph W Cameron; married Martha; children: Randolph Jr, Michele. **EDUCATION:** Delaware State Coll, BS Business Admin 1958; New School for Social Rsch, MA Communications 1985. **CAREER:** D Parke Gibson Assocs Inc, vice pres 1962-72; Avon Products Inc, div sales mgr 1972-73, dir field sales support, dir of corp communications 1978-85; Cameron Enterprises, pres. **ORGANIZATIONS:** Bd mem Amer Cancer Soc 1978-; trustee McBurney School 1980-; mem NY Intl Assoc Business Communicators, NY Press Club. **HONORS/ ACHIEVEMENTS:** Black Achievers in Industry. **MILITARY SERVICE:** AUS pfc Military Intelligence. **BUSINESS ADDRESS:** President, Cameron Enterprises, 100 West 94th St, New York, NY 10025.

CAMERON, SAM ARCHIE
Archivist. **PERSONAL:** Born May 25, 1943, Chattanooga, TN; children: Sobuke Ibkey, Naima. **EDUCATION:** TN State Univ, BS 1970, MS 1972. **CAREER:** Fisk Univ, archivist 1972-84; Meharry Medical Coll, archivist 1984-. **ORGANIZATIONS:** Mem Soc of Amer Archivist 1978-; consultant Meharry Medical Coll 1983; mem Assoc for the Study of Afro-Amer Life and History 1985-. **HONORS/ACHIEVEMENTS:** Awarded grant from Natl Library of Medicine to update the Meharry Archives 1985-88. **MILITARY SERVICE:** USAF staff sgt 4 yrs; Good Conduct Medal 1966. **BUSINESS ADDRESS:** Director-Library Archives, Meharry Medical College, 1005 DB Todd Blvd, Nashville, TN 37208.

CAMERON, ULYSSES
Librarian. **PERSONAL:** Born Dec 04, 1930, Sanford Hts, NC; son of Archie Cameron (deceased) and Pearlie Cameron; married Ida R Womack; children: Sylvia, Byron, Cynthia Moorman, Myrna. **EDUCATION:** Howard Univ, BMusEd 1952; Atlanta Univ, MSLS 1965; Federal City Coll, MA 1974; VA Polytech Inst & State Univ, CAGS 1977, EdD 1984. **CAREER:** Enoch Pratt Free Library, librarian 1965-68; Federal City Coll Media Ctr, assoc dir 1968-74, deputy dir 1974-77; Univ of DC, assoc dir univ libraries 1977-82, head librarian, bus library 1982-84, head librarian educ library 1984-86, librarian & special proj dir serial library 1986-. **ORGANIZATIONS:** Mem Phi Delta Kappa. **HONORS/ ACHIEVEMENTS:** (cum laude) Howard Univ 1952; "Whats Wrong with our Library Schools" Cameron et al 1966. **MILITARY SERVICE:** USAF captain 1953-62. **HOME ADDRESS:** 4117 Raleigh Rd, Baltimore, MD 21208. **BUSINESS ADDRESS:** Librarian, Univ of DC, 4200 Connecticut Ave NW, Washington, DC 20009.

CAMERON, WILBURN MACIO, JR.
Dentist. **PERSONAL:** Born in Richmond, VA; married Jacqueline Amelia; children: Wilburn Macin III, Charles Anderson. **EDUCATION:** Virginia State, BS 1950; Howard Univ Grad Sch; Meharry Med Coll, 1956. **CAREER:** Richmond VA, private practice in dentistry, 1958-. **ORGANIZATIONS:** Past pres Peter B Ramsey Dental Soc 1967-75; Dr Wilburn M Cameron & Jr Professional Corp 1975-77; pres Old Dominion Dental Soc 1977-79; sec tres VA Acad Gen Dentistry 1977-79, vice pres 1979-; grand organizer Chi Delta Mu Frat 1967-73; bd of dir YMCA 1970-75; mem Richmond C of C Kappa Alpha Psi Frat. **HONORS/ ACHIEVEMENTS:** Fellowship VA, Acad of Gen Dentistry 1976; pres award Old Dominion Dentist Soc 1977, 1978. **MILITARY SERVICE:** AUS capt 1946-48, 1956-58. **BUSINESS ADDRESS:** 10 & 12 W Marshall St, Richmond, VA 23220.

CAMP, MARVA JO
Attorney, businesswoman. **PERSONAL:** Born Sep 17, 1961, Washington, DC; daughter of Fab Camp Jr and Ernestine Alford Camp. **EDUCATION:** Univ of Virginia, Charlottesville, VA, BA, 1983; Univ of Virginia, School of Law, Charlottesville, VA, JD, 1986. **CAREER:** Gartrell and Alexander Law Firm, Silver Spring, MD, atty, assoc, 1986-87; Congressman Harold E Ford, Washington, DC, legislative dir, tax counsel, 1987-88; Congressman Mervyn M Dymally, Washington, DC, advisor, 1988-; Congressional Task Force on Minority Business, Washington, DC, dir, legal counsel, 1987-; Crenshaw Intl Corp, Washington, DC, pres, CEO, 1988-/. **ORGANIZATIONS:** Legal counsel, Inst on Science, Space, and Technology, 1987-; consultant, Minority and Small Business, 1987; advisor, Democratic Natl Comm, 1988; legal counsel, Carribean Amer Research Inst, 1988; pres, bd of dir, Young Black Professionals, 1988-; co-chair, treasurer, African-Amer Political Fund, 1988; vice pres, bd of dir, Edward C Mazique Parent Child Center, 1986; bd of dir, 14th & U Coalition, 1988; advisor to pres, Congressional Black Assoc, 1988. **HONORS/ACHIEVEMENTS:** Soc of Outstanding Young Amer; Congressional Certificate of Recognition; author, Federal Compliance with Minority Set-Asides, 1988, Future of African-Amer, 1988.

CAMPANELLA, ROY, SR. (CAMPY)
Former professional athlete, executive. **PERSONAL:** Born Nov 19, 1921, Homestead, PA; married Roxie. **CAREER:** Negro Professional Baseball Teams, 1946; Brooklyn Dodgers, farm teams 1946-48; Brooklyn Dodgers Professional Baseball Team, catcher 1949-58; Roy Campanella Inc NYC, propr; Radio Interview Show "Campy's Corner", host. **HONORS/ ACHIEVEMENTS:** Set major league records for catcher with home runs & runs batted in 1953; named most valuable player in Nat League 3 times; named to Baseball Hall of Fame 1969; author "It's Good to be alive 1959. **BUSINESS ADDRESS:** Dodger Stadium, 1000 Elysian Park Ave, Los Angeles, CA 90012.

CAMPANERIS, BERT **See CAMPANERIS, DAGOBERTO BLANCO**

CAMPANERIS, DAGOBERTO BLANCO (BERT CAMPANERIS)
Athlete. **PERSONAL:** Born Mar 09, 1942, Matanzas; married Norma Prewitt; children: Carmen. **CAREER:** CA Angels, shortstop; KS City, Oakland & Texas Teams, 16 major league seasons. **HONORS/ACHIEVEMENTS:** Am League All-star 1968, 1972-77; World Series; 5 Championship Series.

CAMPBELL, BEATRICE MURPHY **See MURPHY, BEATRICE M.**

CAMPBELL, BLANCH
District manager, telephone sales/service center,. **PERSONAL:** Born Jan 24, 1941, Biscoe, AR; daughter of Oscar Louderdale and Luella Calbert; divorced; children: Tanja Marie Campbell. **EDUCATION:** Webster Coll, St Louis, MO, BA, 1981. **CAREER:** Southwestern Bell Telephone, St Louis, MO, serv asst, 1966-68, group chief operator, 1968-72, supvr business serv, 1972-74, supvr course devel, 1974-75, staff mgr training, 1975-78, district mgr, 1978-. **ORGANIZATIONS:** Pres, The Junior Kindergarten Bd, 1981-87; pres, Project Energy Care Bd, 1984; loan exec, United Way, 1984-85; pres elect, City North Y's Men Club, 1985-; mem, Monsanto YMCA Bd of Dir, 1989; chairperson, mem placement comm, Greater Mount Carmel Baptist Church; mem, Women in Leadership, 1984-; consultant, Emprise, 1988-. **HONORS/ACHIEVEMENTS:** Volunteer Serv Award, United Way of Greater St Louis, 1984; Outstanding Leadership, The Junior Kindergarten, 1984, 1985; Continental Soc Volunteer Award Educ Div, 1986; Y's Men of the Year, City North Y's Men, 1987, 1988; Youth Serv Award, Monsanto YMCA, 1989; Finalist, Missouri Mother/Daughter Pageant, 1989. **BUSINESS ADDRESS:** Dist Mgr-Sales/Serv Center, Residence, Southwestern Bell Telephone Co, 330 N Florissant Rd, Ferguson, MO 63135.

CAMPBELL, BOBBY LAMAR
City official & business executive. **PERSONAL:** Born Sep 30, 1949, Fairmont, NC. **EDUCATION:** Brooklyn Coll, BA 1975-79; Howard Univ, MCP 1980-82; Natl Inst Power Engrs, 3rd class engr 1984. **CAREER:** US HUD, prog analyst 1980-81; Howard Univ, researcher 1981-82; Polinger Mgt Co, resident mgr 1983-85; DC Mutual Housing Assn Inc, prop mgr 1985-. **ORGANIZATIONS:** Vet counselor Brooklyn Coll 1975-79; student rep Amer Planning Assn 1981-82; site coord Natl Capitol Health Fair Project 1982; steering comm mem DC office of planning 1983-84; pres Upper Northwest Civic Group 1984; ANC comm 4D Advisory Neighborhood Comm 1980-84. **HONORS/ACHIEVEMENTS:** Outstanding comm svs DC Recreation Dept 1983; contrib author Washington on Foot NCAC APA/Smithsonian Press 1983; outstanding comm svs 4D Advisory Neighborhood Comm 1984. **MILITARY SERVICE:** USAF SS6T 4 yrs; Air Force Accomendation Awd 1970-71. **BUSINESS ADDRESS:** Property Manager, DC Mutual Housing Assoc, Inc, 1436 Independence Ave, SE, Washington, DC 20003.

CAMPBELL, CALVIN C.
Judge. **PERSONAL:** Born Aug 20, 1924, Roanoke, VA; children: Cathleen. **EDUCATION:** Howard U, BA Econ 1948; Univ Of Chicago Law Sch, JD 1951. **CAREER:** Appellate Ct Of IL, justice 1978-; Circuit Ct, judge 1977-78; IL, asst atty gen 1957-77; Revenue Litigation, chief. **ORGANIZATIONS:** Mem Cook Co Bar Assn present; mem IL State Bar Assn; mem Forty Club of Chicago. **HONORS/ACHIEVEMENTS:** Recipient bronze Star; AUS 1945; outstanding lumni Chicago Howard Univ Alumni 1965; outstanding State of IL Employee Office of Atty Gen State Of IL 1976. **MILITARY SERVICE:** AUS pfc 1943-45. **BUSINESS ADDRESS:** Richard J Daley Center, 30th Floor, Chicago, IL 60602.

CAMPBELL, CARLOS, SR.
Production control supervisor. **PERSONAL:** Born Dec 23, 1946, Warrenton, VA; son of Albert Campbell and Martha Campbell; married Ethel Douglas; children: Carlos II. **EDUCATION:** US Army Air Defense School, Certificate of Completion Opers and Intelligence Specialist 1967; North AL Coll of Commerce, Certificate of Completion Business Admin and Accounting 1972; Alabama A&M Univ, BS 1975; Alabama A&M Univ, MBA graduate studies. **CAREER:** AL A&M Univ, univ recruiter 1975-76, dir of veterans affairs 1975-76; Chesebrough Ponds Inc Prince Matchabelli Div, production scheduler 1976-78, sr production planner 1978-80, supervisor of warehousing and inventory control 1980-86, senior production supervisor 1986-87; Consolidated Industries, production control manager 1989-. **ORGANIZATIONS:** Mem Madison Co Democratic Exec Comm, Exec Bd Madison Co NAACP; vice chmn AL Democratic Conf Exec Bd; chmn Univ and Industry Cluster AL A&M Univ; chmn bd of managers North West YMCA; chmn athletic exec bd AL A&M Univ; prof Black Exec Exchange Prog Natl Urban League; mem Youth Motivation Task Force Natl Alliance of Business; mem Alpha Phi Alpha Frat, Govtl Relations Comm AL A&M Univ; North Alabama Regional Hospital Board of Directors; exec bd Police Athletic Association. **HONORS/ACHIEVEMENTS:** Presidential Citation The Natl Assn for Equal Oppor in Higher Educ; Outstanding Leadership Awd Natl Alliance of Business Washington DC; Alumni of the Year Sch of Business AL A&M Univ; Distinguished Serv Awd, Outstanding Serv Awd AL A&M Univ; Citation the Natl Urban League, Natl Alliance of Business, AL Veteran Af-

fairs Assoc of AL; Distinguished Serv Awd Phi Beta Lambda Professional Business Frat; life mem 1814 Color Guard US Army Air Defense Command; Outstanding Young Man of America, US Jaycees. **MILITARY SERVICE:** AUS Air Defense Command 1966-72; Vietnam Vet 1970. **HOME ADDRESS:** 6726 Hollow Rd NW, Huntsville, AL 35810.

CAMPBELL, CARLOS CARDOZO
Banking executive. **PERSONAL:** Born Jul 19, 1937, New York, NY; married Sammie Marye Day; children: Kimberly, Scott. **EDUCATION:** MI State Univ, BS 1959; US Naval Post Grad School, Diploma Engrg Sci 1965; Catholic Univ of Amer, MA City & Reg Plnng 1968. **CAREER:** VA Polytech Inst & State Univ, adj prof summer 1974; Amer Revolution Bicentennial Admin, dep asst admin 1974-76; Carlos C Campbell & Assoc, principal & owner 1976-81; US Dept of Comm, asst sec for economic devel 1981-84; Inter-Amer Devel Bank, alternate exec dir design. **ORGANIZATIONS:** Sr systems analyst Control Data Corp 1968-69; spec asst US Dept of Housing & Urban Dev 1969-72; vice pres Corp for Comm Devel 1973-74; bd of dir Amer Soc of Plnng Officials 1973-74; bd of dir McLean Savings & Loan Assoc 1975-77; vice pres Amer Council on Intl Sports 1978-81; commiss Northern VA Reg Plnng Dist Comm 1980-82. **HONORS/ACHIEVEMENTS:** Grant Natl Endowment for the Arts 1972, Ford Found 1973; Author New Towns, Another Way to Live 1976; Book of the Month Club Alternate Selection 1976. **MILITARY SERVICE:** USN lt comm 1959-68; Naval Flight Officer, Navy Achievement Medal, Natl Defense Medal. **HOME ADDRESS:** 11530 Links Dr, Reston, VA 22090.

CAMPBELL, CARROL NUNN
Elected government official. **PERSONAL:** Born Dec 06, 1952, Brownsville, TN; married Lossie B Ivie; children: Anisha Carol, Letica. **EDUCATION:** Carver High School, 1970. **ORGANIZATIONS:** Bro esquire JS Evans Lodge 1559 1984; IBPO of EW. **MILITARY SERVICE:** NG sgt 10 years. **BUSINESS ADDRESS:** County Commissioner, Haywood County Court House, Rt 2 Box 39, Brownsville, TN 38012.

CAMPBELL, CHARLES EVERETT
Dentist. **PERSONAL:** Born Aug 13, 1933, Statesboro, GA; married Phyllis; children: Charles, Jacquline, Andrea. **EDUCATION:** Oakwood Coll, 1959; Meharry Med Coll, 1968; Univ NC, 1974. **CAREER:** Nghbrhd Hlth Ctr, staff dentist 1969-73; Hubbard Hosp & VA Hosp, dental intern 1968-69; VA Hosp, med tech 1960-64; Mt Sinia Hosp, 1959-60. **ORGANIZATIONS:** Mem Old N State Dental Soc; Durham Acad Med; Nat Dental Assn; Black Adventist Med Dental Assn; S Atlantic Conf SDA Dental Hlth Sec; mem Oakwo Od Coll Alumni Assn; Meharry Med Coll Alumni Assn. **HONORS/ACHIEVEMENTS:** Recpt Nashville Dental Prize; John Bluford Award; Sch Dentistry Meharry Med Coll 1968; Cumberland Chap Oakwood Coll Alumni Assn Award 1973. **MILITARY SERVICE:** AUS mc 1956-58. **BUSINESS ADDRESS:** 105 Ruberson St, Carrboro, NC 27510.

CAMPBELL, DICK C.
Foundation executive director. **PERSONAL:** Born Jun 27, 1903, Beaumont, TX; son of Richard Campbell (deceased) and Pauline Snow (deceased); married Beryl Murray, Oct 02, 1962. **EDUCATION:** Paul Quinn Coll, Waco, TX, BS, 1926; Teachers Coll, Columbia Univ, New York, NY, MS, 1934; Long Island Univ, New York, NY, 1963. **CAREER:** Negro Peoples Theater, Rose McClendon Players, dir, producer, New York NY, 1935-41; USO Campshows, World War II, producer, New York, NY, 1941-46; theatrical producer, director, New York, NY, 1946-57; US State Dept, African Affairs, field consultant, 1957-64; Operation Cross Roads Africa, New York, NY, dir public affairs devel, 1964-67; Human Resources Admin, New York, NY, Public Affairs, dir, 1967-72; Sickle Cell Disease Found, New York, NY, exec dir, 1972-. **ORGANIZATIONS:** Amer Soc of Assn Exec, Washington, DC; Amer Guild of Musical Artists, New York, NY; co-founder, African-Amer Guild of Performing Artists, New York, NY; bd mem, Schomburg Library Corp, New York, NY; Alpha Phi Alpha Fraternity. **HONORS/ACHIEVEMENTS:** Volunteer of the Year, President Ronald Reagan, 1984; Audelco Pioneer Award, Audience Development Co, 1986.

CAMPBELL, E. ALEXANDER
Minister. **PERSONAL:** Born Jan 31, 1927, Montego Bay, Jamaica;married Estelle Jones; children: Alexis, Paula, Edwin, Susan. **EDUCATION:** Cornwall Coll Jamaica, 1944; VA Union Univ, BA 1952; VA Union Theol Sem, MDiv 1955; Hartford Seminary Found, MA 1957; McCormick Theological Sem, DMin 1975. **CAREER:** Churches-in-Transition Proj, dir, prog devel; Urban Ch Strategy IN-KY Conf UCC, cons; Plymouth UCC Church, pastor. **ORGANIZATIONS:** Dorm dir, counselor for men VA Union Univ 1954-55; assoc conf minister RI Conf United Ch of Christ 1962-72; area chmn NE Comm of Church Leaders 1971-72; dir, host Church & Comm TV Prog RI; chairperson Oak River Forest HS Human Relations Comm; past pres Christian Ed Council United Church of Christ; past vice pres Greater Hartford Council of Church; past vice pres NE Comm of United Ministry in Highr Ed; bd dir United Church Bd for World Ministries; dir Black Church Empowerment Prog; past vice pres Barrington Prog for Action; past bd mem RI People Against Poverty; bd mem Ed Comm RI Childrens Ctr; bd dir Oak Park Housing Ctr; lecturer Negro Hist & Culture; mem Alpha Phi Alpha, Urban League; pres Louisville Interdenominational Ministerial Alliance; bd mem NAACP. **HONORS/ACHIEVEMENTS:** Citation UCC Churches in Chicago; Citation for Outstanding Leadership RI United Church of Christ Conf; Citation for Achievement in Bringing Understanding of Church & Comm through TV RI Council of Church. **BUSINESS ADDRESS:** Pastor, Plymouth UCC Church, 1630 W Chestnut St, Louisville, KY 40203.

CAMPBELL, EARL
Professional athlete. **PERSONAL:** Born Mar 29, 1955, Tyler, TX; married Reuna Smith; children: Earl Christian II. **EDUCATION:** Texas Univ, Deg in Speech Commun. **CAREER:** Pro Bowl, player 1978-81; AFC Champ Game, player 1978; Houston Oilers, football player 1978-84; New Orleans Saints, running back 1984-. **ORGANIZATIONS:** Active in charity work to benefit Sickle Cell rsch; co-sponsors annual golf tournament in Houston to raise funds to combat Sickle Cell disease. **HONORS/ACHIEVEMENTS:** Heisman Trophy 1977; Named Most Valuable Player in NFL 1978-80; SEC Offensive Player of the Decade 1970's. **BUSINESS ADDRESS:** New Orleans Saints, 1500 Poydras St, New Orleans, LA 70112.

CAMPBELL, EMMETT EARLE
Educator, physician. **PERSONAL:** Born Dec 22, 1927, Dayton, OH; married Geneva Sydney; children: Michael, Heather, Kimberly, Laura. **EDUCATION:** Univ Dayton, Pre-med 1948; Univ Cinn, MD 1953. **CAREER:** Am Coll Of Surgeons, fellow 1969; Am Acad Opthalmology & Otolaryngology, fellow 1966; Am Bd Of Otolaryngology, diplmt 1966; Temporal Bone & Lab NY Eye &Ear Infirmary, asst dir; Cleft Palate Clinic N Shore Univ Hosp, cons. **ORGANIZATIONS:** Mem Nassau Co Med Soc; Nassau Surgical Soc; AMA; Nassau Otolaryngol Soc; NY St Soc Of Surgeons; Empire Med Polit Action Com; Nassau Physicians-Guild; Am Council Of Otolaryngology; Nat Med. **HONORS/ACHIEVEMENTS:** Assn phy recognition award 1977; paper "Tympanoplasty Using Homograft Tympanic Membranes & Ossicles Nat Med Assn 1976. **MILITARY SERVICE:** USAF base flight surgeon 1954-57. **BUSINESS ADDRESS:** 131 Fulton Ave, Hempstead, NY 11550.

CAMPBELL, EMORY SHAW
Community service director. **PERSONAL:** Born Oct 11, 1941, Hilton Head Is, SC; married Emma Joffrion; children: Ochieng, Ayaka. **EDUCATION:** Savannah State Coll, BS Bio 1965; Tufts Univ, MS Env Eng 1971. **CAREER:** Harvard School of Public Health, Boston MA, rsrch asst 1965-68; Process Rsrch Cambridge, Boston MA, biologist 1968-70; Bramley Health Comm Center, Boston MA, asst dir1971; Beaufort Jasper Comprehensive Health, dir comm serv 1971-80; Penn Center, exec dir. **ORGANIZATIONS:** Plng comm Beaufort Co Plng Comm 1982-; bd dir Beaufort Jasper Water Admin 1978-82, Hilton Head Rural Water 1980-. **HOME ADDRESS:** 208 Spanish Wells Rd, Hilton Head Island, SC 29928.

CAMPBELL, EVERETT O.
Physician. **PERSONAL:** Born Nov 15, 1934, Chicago, IL; married Anne Big Ford. **EDUCATION:** Univ Of MI, MD 1958; Ucla, Chas Drew Post, Grad Med Schl. **CAREER:** Physician; Ucla, asst clinical prof; Chas Drew Post Grad Med Schl, asst prof; Martin Luther King Hosp. **ORGANIZATIONS:** Mem AMA; CA Med Assn; Los Angeles Co Med Assn; mem Applied Health Research. **HONORS/ACHIEVEMENTS:** Author of paper on cancer; organizing dept of Sexual studies at Martin Luther King Hosp; Who's Who in CA 1974. **MILITARY SERVICE:** AUS chf dept ob-gyn, 1962-64. **BUSINESS ADDRESS:** 1141 W Rodondo Beach Blvd, Gardena, CA 90247.

CAMPBELL, FRANKLYN D.
Airline pilot. **PERSONAL:** Born Feb 11, 1947, Washington, DC. **EDUCATION:** BS 1971. **CAREER:** The Flying Tiger Line, Inc, Airline Pilot 1974; Garrett Airesearch Aviation Co, test pilot 1974; Saturn Airways, Inc, aircraft planner 1971-72; Embry RiddleAero U, student flight dispatcher, tchr 1970-71; Page Airways, Inc, lineman 1970; Dept of Recreation, neighborhood yth corps coord 1969. **ORGANIZATIONS:** Mem, Nat Coll Flight Safety Council; mem NAACP; Brotherhood Crusade; Airline Pilot Assn; Negro Airman Internat, Inc. **HONORS/ACHIEVEMENTS:** Outstanding Flight Student 1970. **BUSINESS ADDRESS:** Flying Tigers, 7401 World Way West, Los Angeles, CA 90009.

CAMPBELL, GARY LLOYD
Educator. **PERSONAL:** Born Feb 15, 1951, Ennis, TX; married Alola McKinney; children: Phyllis, Traci, Bryan. **EDUCATION:** UCLA, BA Sociology 1973. **CAREER:** UCLA, asst coach 1976-78; Southern Univ, asst coach 1978-80; Howard Univ, asst coach 1981; Pacific Univ, asst coach 1982; Univ of OR, asst coach 1983-. **ORGANIZATIONS:** Mem Amer Football Coaches Assoc 1978-, Amer Congress on Real Estate 1984-. **BUSINESS ADDRESS:** Asst Football Coach, Univ of Oregon, McArthur Court, Eugene, OR 97403.

CAMPBELL, GEORGE LYNN
Administrator. **PERSONAL:** Born Nov 26, 1944, Washington, DC; married Barbara Jeanne Dawkins; children: Chadwick Michael Anthony. **EDUCATION:** Howard U, BArch 1969; Carnegie Mellon U, Graduate Work 1970. **CAREER:** Authority of Pittsburgh, Dir Rehab/New Construction Urban Redevel; ACTION-HOUS Inc, asso dir 1977-79; Comm Action Pittsburgh Inc, dir hsng & econ devel 1973-77; Urban Design Assoc, grad architect 1970-73; Design Const Cons, owner 1971; Ketterer Schinhofen Campbell Arch & Planners, partner-in-charge of mgmt 1976-78. **ORGANIZATIONS:** Bd mem Pittsburgh Architects Worshop 1970; bd mem Allegheny Co Air Pollution Adv Bd 1977-79; chmn Men of Holy Cross Ch 1978. **HONORS/ACHIEVEMENTS:** Gold Medal for Sr Design HowardUniv Wash DC 1969; Black Achievers Award Talk Mag Pittsburgh, 1973; Comm Devel Trophy, Homewood Brushton Citizens Renewal Council 1973; Fellowship-econ Devel Inter Nat Council for Equal Bus Opportunities 1976. **BUSINESS ADDRESS:** Dir of Development, Allegheny Housing Authority, 239 Fourth Ave, Pittsburgh, PA 15217.

CAMPBELL, GERTRUDE M.
Association executive. **PERSONAL:** Born Aug 03, 1923, Dallas; married Quintell O; children: Patricia. **EDUCATION:** Prairie View Coll, BS 1943; USC, 1968. **CAREER:** US Energy Res & Dev Adminstrn, dir ofc mgmt Serv 1st Female 1975;Oakland Adult Minor Proj, one of 1st Demon Projs US employ disadv Adults; brmgr; Berkeley Human Res Dev Cntr, 1st & female cntr mgr. **ORGANIZATIONS:** 1st Pres, Past Western Dist Gov & Life mem; E Bay Area Nat Assn Negro Bus & Prof Women's Clubs; Life mem Nat Coun Negro Wmn; Zeta Phi Beta; past matron Order Eastern Star; sec El Cerrito Br NAACP; mem Golden State Bus League; Prairie View Alumnae Assn; Bay Area Personnel Women; N CA Ind rel coun Who's Who Am Women 1971; com mem Gov's Commn Status Women. **HONORS/ACHIEVEMENTS:** 3 serv awards Zeta Phi Beta; commun serv award Order Eastern Star; empl awards Nat Assn Negro Bus & Prof Women. **BUSINESS ADDRESS:** 1333 Broadway, Oakland, CA.

CAMPBELL, GILBERT GODFREY
Clergyman. **PERSONAL:** Born Jan 16, 1920, Plainfield, NJ; married Bertha Vernice Morgan; children: Gilbert G. **EDUCATION:** Union Univ Richmond VA, AB 1941; Union Univ VA, MDiv 1944; Union Univ Va, DD 1967. **CAREER:** Moore St Bapt Ch, pastor; VA Union U, pastor 1971; 1st Gravel Hill Bapt Ch Rushmore & VA, pastor 1953-64; Chesapeake Pub Sch, prin/tchr 1950-64; Gethsemane Bapt Ch Suffolk, VA, pastor 1950-64; Grove Bapt Ch Portsmouth VA, pastor 1949-64; Theol Dept VA Sem & Coll, dean 1947-50; 1st Bapt Ch Cape Charles VA, pastor 1946-49. **ORGANIZATIONS:** Dir of Christian Educ Bapt Gen Convention of VA 1944-46; bd mem Richmond OIC 1965; pres Bapt Gen Convention of VA 1970-73; bd mem Richmond NAACP/Sickle Cell Anemia 1977-. **HONORS/ACHIEVEMENTS:** Outstndng leadershop Award VA Union Univ 1977; past pres Award

Bapt Gen Cvention Of VA 1979; Gold Key Award OIC 1980. **BUSINESS ADDRESS:** Moore St Baptist Church, 1408 W Leigh St, Richmond, VA 23220.

CAMPBELL, GRAHAM F.
Compensation manager. **PERSONAL:** Born Oct 20, 1939, Winston-Salem, NC; married Gloria Watson; children: Gregory, Gigi, Garry. **EDUCATION:** Johnson C Smith U, 1958-59; Winston-Salem State U, 1972-74; Dominican Coll, BS Mgmt 1982. **CAREER:** Joyce-Munden Co, Winston-Salem NC, warehouse mgr 1957-62, 1965-69; Hanes Knitwear, Winston-Salem NC, mgr-personnel admin 169-74; L & M Tobacco Co, Durham NC, asst dir personnel 1975-76; Grand Met USA, Inc, Montvale NJ, mgr compensation 1976-87; Guilford County School System, sr dir of personnel 1987-. **ORGANIZATIONS:** Am Mgmt Assn 1976-; Am Cmpstn Assn 1976-; dir & treas Am Scty Persnl Admin 1972-; Admin Mgmt Scty 1977-; chmn hsng task force Winston-Salem Model Cities Pgm 1967-71; Natl Urban League 1980-; Chmbr Comm Durham, NC 1975-79, Winston-Salem NC 1967-74. **MILITARY SERVICE:** AUS sgt E-5 1962-65. **HOME ADDRESS:** 6110 Westwind Dr, Greensboro, NC 27410.

CAMPBELL, JAMES A.
Exhibit specialist. **PERSONAL:** Born Oct 10, 1920, Charlotte, NC; married Ruth T; children: Colin, Richard, Jacqueline. **CAREER:** Smithsonia Anacostia Musm, exhibit spec. **ORGANIZATIONS:** Mem Boy Scout Of Am; mem YMCA; Men's Club; mem Advisory Ngh Comm 1976; mem Capitol E Com Crime Cncl 1976; mem Kiwanis Club of Capitol Hill 1976; memFriend's of jacko 1975; Capitols Childrens Museum, bd of dir 1979-80; mem Comm Adv Bd Com 1979-80. **HONORS/ACHIEVEMENTS:** 1st Elec Ngh Comm Black Assn 1976; 1st Y's Mem of the Yr YMCA 1965; Kiwanis of the Mo 1976.

CAMPBELL, JAMES W.
Clergyman. **PERSONAL:** Born Mar 17, 1945, Chicago, IL; married Anne; children: James, Jesse, Jared, Bridgett. **EDUCATION:** Wilson Jr Coll; Moody Bible Inst. **CAREER:** St James Ch God in Christ, supt State 1977; 5th Jurisdiction IL, sec 1973; dist supt 1972; pastorate 1970; ministry 1966. **ORGANIZATIONS:** Mem Resolution Com for Nat & Elders Cncl 1975-77; mem Westside br NAACP; Nat Petrolmans Assn; NACD; Intl bd Minister's; Intl Assn Pastor's; Nat Elder's Cncl. **HONORS/ACHIEVEMENTS:** COGIC spl citation City Chicago; pastor of the year Award Christian Guild Society 1979; Award for Dedicated & Faithful Servs as State Sunday Sch supt Sunday Sch Dept of IL 1980. **BUSINESS ADDRESS:** 4147 W Roosevelt Rd, Chicago, IL 60623.

CAMPBELL, MARGIE
Educator. **PERSONAL:** Born Jun 17, 1954, Musella, GA; married Kenneth Campbell; children: MeQuanta. **ORGANIZATIONS:** Mem Parker Chaptel AME Church; mem GA Municipal Assoc 1984; mem Gov's Project Steering Comm 1984. **HONORS/ACHIEVEMENTS:** Comm Leader Awd Gov's Project Competition Atlanta 1982; selected as one of the 50 most influential Black women in GA-GA Informer 1983. **HOME ADDRESS:** PO Box 61, Culloden, GA 31016.

CAMPBELL, MARY ALLISON
Educator. **PERSONAL:** Born Feb 18, 1937, Shelby, NC; married Fred N Campbell Sr; children: Alison Winifred, Fred N Jr. **EDUCATION:** Benedict Coll, BS 1960; Winthrop Coll, Early Childhood 1973. **CAREER:** Harold Fagges Assoc NYC, clerk 1963-68; Clover Town Council, councilmember; Clover Sch Dist, teacher 1968-. **ORGANIZATIONS:** Pres The Progressive Women's Club Inc 1970-75; assoc matron Magnolia Chap OES #144 1982-84; YCEA Pres, 1988-89. **HONORS/ACHIEVEMENTS:** School Yearbook Dedication Roosevelt Sch 1970; Appreciation Awd United Men's Club 1980. **HOME ADDRESS:** 104 Wilson St, Clover, SC 29710. **BUSINESS ADDRESS:** Teacher, Clover School District, 201 Pressly St, Clover, SC 29710.

CAMPBELL, MARY DELOIS
Administrator. **PERSONAL:** Born Jul 21, 1940, Greenville, TX; married David; children: Keith Devlin. **EDUCATION:** Jarvis Christian Coll Hawkins, Tx, BS Bus Admin 1957-62; Bishop Coll Dallas, 1962-63. **CAREER:** Housing Auth of City of Dallas, asst dir res selection 1980; Housing Auth of City of Dallas, asst dir of Soc Serv 1979-80; N Central TX Council of Govt, human serv & planner 1976-77; N Central TX Council of T, manpower planner 1971-76; City Of Dallas, asst youth coord 1969-71; Dallas Co Comm Action Inc, Neighborhood Center coord 1968-69; Bishop Coll Dallas Co Comm Action, clerical 1962-68. **ORGANIZATIONS:** Bd of dir Dallas Urban League 1974-77; mem Dallas Commn on Children & Youth 1975; pres bd of dir Dallas Urban League 1977-78; bd of dir Goals for Dallas 1977-79. **BUSINESS ADDRESS:** Housing Auth City of Dallas, 2525 Lucas Dr, Dallas, TX 75219.

CAMPBELL, MARY SCHMIDT
Executive director. **PERSONAL:** Born Oct 21, 1947, Philadelphia, PA; married George Campbell Jr; children: Garikai, Sekou. **EDUCATION:** Swarthmore Coll, BA English Lit 1969; Syracuse Univ, MA Art History 1973, PhD Humanities. **CAREER:** Nkumbi Intl Coll, Kabwe Zambia, instr, 1969-71; Syracuse New Times, art editor, 1973-77; Everson Museum, curator, guest curator, 1974-76; The Studio Museum Harlem, exec dir, 1977-; apptd by Mayor Edward I Koch as NY Commissioner of Cultural Affairs, 1987-. **ORGANIZATIONS:** Mem Womens Forum NYC, Assoc of Art Museum Dirs; mem, bd of trustees Coll Art Assoc; mem African Amer Museums Assoc; mem adv council The Harlem YWCA; mem bd of commissioners Housing Authority of New Brunswick NJ. **HONORS/ACHIEVEMENTS:** Author "Harlem Renaissance, Art of Black America"; Consultant to the Ford Found as part of their mid-decade reveiw; Lectures of Black Amer Art, The Studio Museum in Harlem and the issues involved in the Institutionalization of Diverse Cultures; author of numerous articles on Black Amer Art. *

CAMPBELL, MILTON
Athlete. **PERSONAL:** Born Dec 19, 1933, Plainfield, NJ. **EDUCATION:** Univ Mem, Olympic Teams 1952-56. **HONORS/ACHIEVEMENTS:** Co-holder World 120 Yd Hurdle Record; Won Ncaa & Aau 120 Yd Hurdle 1955; Decathlon Siler Medal H Elsinki Olympics 1952; Decathlon Gold Medal Melbourne 1956.

CAMPBELL, OTIS, JR.
Physician. **PERSONAL:** Born Sep 09, 1953, Tampa, FL; married Carol Y Clarke; children: Davin, Desmond, Donovon. **EDUCATION:** FL A&M Univ, BS Biology 1973; Meharry Medical Coll, PhD Pharmacology 1982; Meharry Medical Coll, MD 1986. **CAREER:** Special Medical Prog Meharry Medical Coll, instructor 1982-84; Biomedical Science Prog Meharry Medical Coll, instructor 1982-84; UNCF Fisk Univ Pre-Med Inst, 1982-84; TN State Univ Weekend Coll, prof 1982-86; Hubbard Hospital Dept of Internal Medicine, resident 1986-. **ORGANIZATIONS:** Mem Middle TN Neuroscience Soc; mem Amer Medical Assoc. **HONORS/ACHIEVEMENTS:** Post Doctoral Rsch Fellow in hypertension Vanderbilt Univ 1982,83,84,85 summers; Alpha Omega Alpha Medical Honor Soc 1986; Hall of Natural Scientists Florida A&M Univ 1987. **BUSINESS ADDRESS:** Internal Medicine Resident, Meharry-Hubbard Hospital, 1005 DB Todd Blvd, Nashville, TN 37208.

CAMPBELL, OTIS LEVY
Owner/manager. **PERSONAL:** Born Jan 09, 1935, Slidell, LA; married Lois Ziegler; children: Cherry Ann, Barry, Maynard, Lajuana. **EDUCATION:** Worsham Coll of Mortuary Sci, 1962; Christian Bible Coll Kenner La, BA/Theology 1980. **CAREER:** Campbell's Funeral Hm, mgr ownr 1952; O L Campbell Agy, broker/mgr 1952; St Tammany & Progressive Civic League, 1952-62. **ORGANIZATIONS:** Sec NAACP Local Chap 1952-62; Vice Pres CBC Citizens for a Better Comm 1974; Elected 1st Black Mem to Sch bd Saint Tammany Parish La 1978. **BUSINESS ADDRESS:** Campbells Funeral Home, 2522 4th St, Slidell, LA 70458.

CAMPBELL, ROGERS EDWARD, III
Pharmaceutical company executive. **PERSONAL:** Born Jul 14, 1951, Jersey City, NJ; son of Rogers E Campbell, Jr and Anne Mae Powell. **EDUCATION:** Saint Peter's Coll, BS 1973; Rutgers Univ, MBA 1974. **CAREER:** General Mills Inc, asst product mgr 1978-81; Mattel Electronics, product mgr 1982-83; Schering-Plough Corp, dir of marketing. **ORGANIZATIONS:** Admissions liaison officer US Military Acad 1984-; chmn public relations comm Rutgers Grad Sch of Business 1984-. **HONORS/ACHIEVEMENTS:** Distinguished Military Graduate. **MILITARY SERVICE:** AUS 1st lt 1974-77; Army Commendation Medal for Meritorious Svcs. **HOME ADDRESS:** 66 Highland Ave, Maplewood, NJ 07040. **BUSINESS ADDRESS:** Dir of Marketing, Schering-Plough Corp, 2000 Galloping Hill Rd, Kenilworth, NJ 07033.

CAMPBELL, SYLVAN LLOYD
Physician. **PERSONAL:** Born Oct 08, 1931, Boston, MA; children: 100831 Steven. **EDUCATION:** Boston Coll, AB 1953; Howard U, MD 1961. **CAREER:** Philadelphia Gen Hosp, intern 1961-62, res 1962-65; Boston, Pvt Practicemed, specializing in ob & gynecology 1965; Harvard U, Obstetrics Gynecology Obstetrics asst cl prof 1975. **ORGANIZATIONS:** Mem Attending Staff Beth & Israel Hosp Univ Hosp Boston; mem Am Bd Obstetrics-gynecology Boston Obstetrics Soc Lt JG. **MILITARY SERVICE:** USNR 1953-57. **BUSINESS ADDRESS:** President, Sylvan L Campbell, MD, Inc, 1539 Blue Hill Ave, Boston, MA 02126.

CAMPBELL, THOMAS W.
Musician. **PERSONAL:** Born Feb 14, 1957, Norristown, PA. **EDUCATION:** Berklee Coll of Music, Attended. **CAREER:** Dizzy Gillespie Band, professional jazz drummer 1985; Baird Hersey & Yr of the Ear, drummer; Own Group "TCB" Boston, drummer; Mar-Lena Shaw/Gap Mangione, drummer 1979; Webster Lewis, drummer 1978. **ORGANIZATIONS:** Big Brother Activities; org First Music Group & "The Mandells" 15 yrs; conducted music clinics Berklee Coll. **HONORS/ACHIEVEMENTS:** Recorded Album with Baird Hersey 1978; concert Berklee Performance Ctr 1979; toured US/Can/S Am/E Europe/Scandinavian Counties/Asia & Africa 1979-80. **BUSINESS ADDRESS:** Sutton Artists Corp, 119 W 57 Ste 818, New York, NY 10019.

CAMPBELL, WENDELL J.
Business executive. **PERSONAL:** Born Apr 27, 1927, East Chicago, IN; son of Herman Campbell and Selma Campbell; married June Crusor Campbell, Nov 06, 1955; children: Susan, Leslie. **EDUCATION:** IL Inst Tech, BA 1956. **CAREER:** Purdue Calumet Devel Foundation, staff architect & dir rehab; Wendell Campbell Assoc, Inc, owner; Campbell & Macsai Architects Inc, owner. **ORGANIZATIONS:** Pres lecturer Yale Univ MA Inst Tech, Univ IL; mem Urban Planning & Design Comm Amer Inst Architects; bd dir Chicago Amer Inst-Architects; mem Natl Organization Minority Architects; mem Chicago C of C; Chicago Assn Commerce & Ind; NAACP; Natl Urban League Devel Foundation. **HONORS/ACHIEVEMENTS:** Distinguished Bldg Award 1973; Construction Man Yr 1973; Engineering News Record 1973; AIA Whitney M Young Jr Medal 1976; Fellow Amer Inst of Arch 1979. **MILITARY SERVICE:** AUS sgt major. **BUSINESS ADDRESS:** President, Wendell Campbell Assocs Inc, 1326 S Michigan Ave, Chicago, IL 60605.

CAMPER, JOHN EMORY TOUSSAINT
Physician. **PERSONAL:** Born Feb 27, 1894, Baltimore, MD; married Florine Thompson; children: John Jr, Ellen Johns, Elizabeth Jones, Mary Cahn. **EDUCATION:** Howard U, BS, MD. **CAREER:** Physician, 1985; Howard U, line coach; Morgan St Coll, head ftbl coach 1921-22; Old Provident Hosp, vis staff. **ORGANIZATIONS:** Mem Nat, Monumental Med Soc Chmn March on Annapolis 1942; candidate US Congress 1948; former mem Jail Bd; chmn Citizens Com for Justice; former memGov Comm on Problems Affecting the Negro Pop; bd Crownsville St Mental Hosp; chmn Total War Employment Commission; NAACP. **HONORS/ACHIEVEMENTS:** Cert of merit Honor Roll; Afro-Am Newspaper 1948; merit award Citizens Com for Justice 1947; cert of merit EOE for all citizens; cert of merit HowardUniv Alumni 1949. **MILITARY SERVICE:** AUS 1917. **BUSINESS ADDRESS:** 639 N Carey St, Baltimore, MD 21217.

CAMPHOR, MICHAEL GERARD
Health services administrator. **EDUCATION:** Morgan State Univ, BA 1978; Univ of Baltimore, MPA Health Serv Admin 1984; Naval Health Sciences Education and Training Command, Certificate Financial/Supply Management 1986. **CAREER:** Columbia Rsch Syst, rsch asst 1976-77; N Central Baltimore Health Corp, center admin 1980-84; Dept Housing & Community Devel, project mgr 1983-84; Central MD Health Systems Agency, health implementor/liaison 1984-85; US Naval Hospital Philadelphia PA, comptroller/hosp administrator 1985-88; US Naval Hospital, Yokosuku Japan, Materials Management/Contracting, head officer. **ORGANIZATIONS:** Mem E Baltimore Comm Org 198-83, Waverly Human Serv Coord Council 1980-83; site coord Natl Health Screening Council for Volunteer Org

1980-83; mem Dallas F Nicholas Elem School Advisory Bd 1981-84; mem Johns Hopkins Hosp Comm Devel Advisory Bd 1983-84. **HONORS/ACHIEVEMENTS:** Senatorial Scholarship Sen Clarence Blount 1973-77; MJ Naylor Awd Highest Dept Average Morgan State Univ 1978; Admin of the Year N Central Baltimore Health Corp 1981; Outstanding Young Men of Amer Jaycees 1983; Recipient of Grad Studies Fellowship from Dept Housing & Urban Devel. **MILITARY SERVICE:** US Navy Med Officers Corp, Lt 1985-; Navy Achievement Medal 1988; Overseas Serv Ribbon. **HOME ADDRESS:** US Navy Hospital, Box 65-1645 Yokosuka, FPO Seattle, WA 98765.

CANADY, ALEXA I. (ALEXA CANADY-DAVIS)
Physician. **PERSONAL:** Born Nov 07, 1950, Lansing, MI; daughter of Clinton Canady Jr. and Hortense Golden Canady; married George Davis, Jun 18, 1988. **EDUCATION:** Univ of Michigan, Ann Arbor MI, BS, 1971, MD, 1975. **CAREER:** Univ of Pennsylvania, instructor in neurosurgery, 1981-82; Henry Ford Hosp, Detroit MI, instructor in neurosurgery, 1982-83; Wayne State Univ, School of Medicine, Detroit, MI, clinical instructor, 1985, clinical assoc prof, 1987—; Children's Hosp of Michigan, Detroit MI, asst dir of neurosurgery, 1986-87, dir of neurosurgery, 1987—. **ORGANIZATIONS:** American College of Surgeons, American Association of Neurological Surgeons, Congress of Neurological Surgeons, American Medical Association, National Medical Association, American Society of Pediatric Neurosurgery, Michigan State Medical Society. **HONORS/ACHIEVEMENTS:** Womens Medical Association citation, 1975; named teacher of the year, Children's Hospital of Michigan, 1984; Woman of the Year Award, Detroit Club of National Association of Negro Business & Professional Women's Club, 1986; Candace Award, National Coalition of 100 Black Women, 1986.

CANADY, HERMAN G., JR.
Judge. **CAREER:** Circuit Court, Charleston, WV, judge. **BUSINESS ADDRESS:** Hon Herman G Canady Jr, Judge of the Circuit Court, 4th Floor, Judicial Annex, Kanawha County Courthouse, 409 Virginia St E, Charleston, WV 25301. *

CANADY, HORTENSE GOLDEN
Educational administrator. **PERSONAL:** Born Aug 18, 1927, Chicago, IL; daughter of Alexander H Golden (deceased) and Essie Golden Perry (deceased); married Clinton Canady Jr, DDS; children: Clinton III, Alexa I MD, Alan L, Mark H. **EDUCATION:** Fisk Univ, BA 1947; Michigan State Univ, MA 1977. **CAREER:** Community Nursery School, dir 1947-48; Lansing Bd of Educ, elected bd mem 1969-72; Women's Commission State of MI, establishing comm 1967-71; Ausiliary to the NDA, natl pres 1976-77; Lansing Comm Coll, Director Lansing Community CollegeFoundation. **ORGANIZATIONS:** Commissioner Tri Co Regional Planning Comm 1974-77; natl pres Delta Sigma Theta Sor Inc 1983-88; natl bd YWCA 1976-82; bd dirs First of Amer Central Bank and First of Amer Corp Bd; charter mem Lansing-East Lansing Chapter Links, AAUW, NAACP, League of Women Voters, Women's Symphony Assoc; bd trustees Kalamazoo Coll; bds National Board Delta Sigma Theta Sorority. **HONORS/ACHIEVEMENTS:** DIANA Awd YWCA 1977; Sojourner Truth Awd Negro Bus & Professional Women; Black Book Awd 1984; 100 Top Black Business & Professional Women 1985; Hugo Lundberg Awd Lansing Human Relations Comm; Athena Award, Lansing Regional Chamber of Commerce. **BUSINESS ADDRESS:** Dir Lansing Community College Foundation, 419 N Capitol Ave, Lansing, MI 48901.

CANADY-DAVIS, ALEXA See CANADY, ALEXA I.

CANNADY, ALONZO JAMES See MUWAKKIL, SALIM

CANNON, ALETA
City official. **PERSONAL:** Born Jan 19, 1942, Greenville, MS; married Robert Lewis Dowell; children: Gerald, Marian, William, Gregory. **EDUCATION:** Garland Coll, AA 1968; Laney Coll, AA 1977; Univ of San Francisco, BS 1979. **CAREER:** Tufts Univ, sec 1968-72; CA Legislature, sec 1972-78, admin asst 1978-; City of Oakland, city councilmember. **ORGANIZATIONS:** Mem NAACP, CA Elected Women for Ed & Rsch, League of Women Voters, Natl Council of Negro Women. **HONORS/ACHIEVEMENTS:** Medal of Merit CA Natl Guard. **BUSINESS ADDRESS:** City Councilmember, City of Oakland, 1 City Hall Plz, Oakland, CA 94612.

CANNON, BARBARA E.M.
Educational administrator. **PERSONAL:** Born Jan 17, 1936, Big Sandy, TX; daughter of Archie Cannon and Jimmie Jones Cannon; married Booker T Anderson, Jr (deceased). **EDUCATION:** San Francisco State Univ, BA, 1957, MA 1965; Sorbonne Univ of Paris, Cert Pedagogipues, 1967; Alliance Francaise, Paris, Cert Pedagogiques, 1967; Univ of California, Berkeley, Admin Credit, 1973; Stanford Univ, MA, 1975, EdD, 1977. **CAREER:** Berkeley Public Schools, teacher, staff devel, assoc admin, 1958-74; Stanford Univ, teaching fellow, rsch assoc, 1974-75; Natl Teacher Corp, US Office of Educ, Washington, DC, educ policy fellow, 1975-76; Coll of Alameda, asst dean, 1978-85; Merritt Coll, asst dean, 1985-. **ORGANIZATIONS:** Urban Educ Inst, 1982-83; exec bd mem, East Bay Consortium of Educ Inst, 1982-84; mem, Sorptimist Intl Alameda, 1984-86; Business & Professional Women of Alameda, 1984-; Black Women Org Political Action 1981-; Women's Day Speaker, St Mark's United Methodist Church, 1983; Black History Speaker, Easter Hill United Methodist Church, 1984; Women's Day Speaker, Jones United Methodist Church, 1984; Women's Day co-chair, Jones United Methodist Church, 1985, Women's Day Chair, 1986; Assoc of California Community Coll Admin; Pi Lambda Theta; Phi Delta Kappa. **HONORS/ACHIEVEMENTS:** Theodore Presser Found Music Scholarship Recipient, San Francisco State Univ, 1956; Outstanding Sr of Yr, Mu Phi Epsilon, San Francisco State Univ, 1957; Sabbatical Berkeley Public School, 1966-67, 1974-75; govt fellow, Univ of CA, Univ of Ghana, 1968; educ policy fellow, Inst for Educ Leadership, Washington, DC, 1975-76; Status & Role of Women Shattuck Ave, United Methodist Church, 1987; Dissertation, School Community Councils: Parity in Decision Making, 1977; US Office of Education Monograph: Involvement: Parity in Decision Making, 1977. **BUSINESS ADDRESS:** Asst Dean, Student Serv, Merritt Coll, 12500 Campus Dr, Oakland, CA 94619.

CANNON, CALVIN CURTIS
Manager information systems. **PERSONAL:** Born Mar 02, 1952, Lenoir, NC; married Anna Laura Copney; children: Calvin IV. **EDUCATION:** Univ of MI Grad School of Business, BBA 1974; Attended, Wayne State Univ Sch of Engrg, Howard Univ Sch of Divinity. **CAREER:** Proctor and Gamble Co, client rep 1974-76; Vitro Laboratories, section leader 1977-79; Planning Rsch Corp, unit manager 1979-81; General Elec Information Serv Co, project coord 1981-83; Comp-U-Staff, staff mgr 1983-84; Executive Office of the President Washington DC, manager information serv 1984-. **ORGANIZATIONS:** Mem African Methodist Episcopal Zion Church. **HOME ADDRESS:** 10606 Wheatley St, Kensington, MD 20895.

CANNON, CHARLES EARL
Educator. **PERSONAL:** Born Jan 30, 1946, Sylacauga, AL. **EDUCATION:** AL A&M Univ, BS (w/Great Honors) 1968; Univ of WI-Milwaukee, PhD 1975. **CAREER:** Amoco Corp, rsch scientist 1974-85; West Aurora Sch Dist, educator 1985-86; Elmhurst Coll, adjunct faculty 1984-; IL Math & Sci Acad, prof of chemistry1986-. **ORGANIZATIONS:** Mem Amer Chem Soc Chicago 1974-; dir Natl Assoc of Negro Musicians 1975-; fellow The Amer Inst of Chemists 1979-; mem Executives Interested in Politics 1982-; past pres Natl Alumni Assoc AL A&M Univ 1984-86; co-chairman trustee bd Main Baptist Church Aurora 1985-; at-large 1987 Great Lakes Regional ACS Meeting Planning Comm 1986-. **HONORS/ACHIEVEMENTS:** Outstanding Young Men of Amer 1973,82; Who's Who in the Midwest 1982-83, 85; Merit Awd Public Service Cultural Citizen Foundation; J Org Chem 41,1191 (1976) Grignard Reagents Rearrangements ACS Natl Mtg Fall 1985, paper Semi-Automated Sep of Oils Resins Asphalcenes. **HOME ADDRESS:** 3 South 081 Barkley Ave, Warrenville, IL 60555. **BUSINESS ADDRESS:** Professor of Chemistry, IL Math and Science Academy, 1500 West Sullivan Rd, Aurora, IL 60506.

CANNON, DAVITA LOUISE
Editor. **PERSONAL:** Born Mar 17, 1949, Jersey City, NJ; daughter of James Cannon (deceased) and Bernice Cannon. **EDUCATION:** St Peters College, BS Marketing Management 1967-73; NYU Graduate School of Business, Advanced Mgmt Program 1979-83; America Computa, 1988. **CAREER:** JM Fields, dicta sec 1978-79; NJ Afro Amer, columnist 1980; Office Force Inc, exec sec admin asst 1979-83; Cannon Clues, editor/publisher 1981-, owner 1988-; public relations consultant/mktg specialist 1981-. **ORGANIZATIONS:** Pr chair NY metro Area Chapter Amer assn of Blacks in Energy 1983-84; mem US Rep Parren J Mitchell Brain Trust 1984; Natl Bd of Advisors Amer Biographical Inst 1985; Bayonne Youth Cntr, bd of dir 1974-; Governors Advisory Council on Minority Business Devel, reappointed councilmember 1987-; NJ Coalition of 100 Black Women, pr officer 1986-; Concerned Comm Women of JC, Inc, pr chair 1986-; Governor's Planning Comm; 1986-87; NJ Devel Authority for Samll Minority & Women's Business, commissioner 1987-; charter mem, Republican Presidential Task Force, 1989-. **HONORS/ACHIEVEMENTS:** Distinguished Serv Award Pavonia Girl Scout Council 1981; Mary McLeod Bethune Award Com-Bin-Nations Jersey City 1984; VIP Award Concerned Comm Women of Jersey City Inc 1984; Small Business Award Roselle Branch NAACP 1984; Jersey Journal, Woman of Achievement 1986; Governor's Conf on Minority Business Devel, keynote speaker 1986; Govs Conf on Small Business, panelist 1986; moderator; Concerned Comm Women of JC, Inc, women advancing through adversity 1986; Black Leadership Reception 100 Black Men of New Jersey, 1988. **HOME ADDRESS:** 528 Avenue A, Bayonne, NJ 07002.

CANNON, DONNIE E.
Business executive. **PERSONAL:** Born Oct 17, 1929, Magnolia, AR; married Chapman R Jr; children: Donald Chatman. **EDUCATION:** MME C J Walker Beauty Coll, Grad; Eugene Hairstyling Acad, Paris France; Myriam Carange Inst De Beaute Paris France; The Ophelia De Voores Modeling & Charm Sch, Grad. **CAREER:** Am Beauty Prod Co, Inc, co-owner & treas 1985; Johnson Prods, natl rep; La Roberts & Gray's Beauty Sch, NY. **ORGANIZATIONS:** Mem Alpha-Chi Pi Omega organized 1st chap in Hempstead; Tulsa Urban League Guild; Greenwood C of C; mem Tulsa Comm Devel Cntr; mem OK Beauty CulturistLeague; Tulsa Urban League, Inc. **HONORS/ACHIEVEMENTS:** Bus & Ind Award 1973; Service Award; Greenwood C of C 1974; Grand Basilleus; Alpha Chi Pi Omega; noted as Black Woman Mnf; Black Bus Women of OK. **BUSINESS ADDRESS:** 1623 E Apache, Tulsa, OK.

CANNON, EDITH H.
Educator. **PERSONAL:** Born Aug 08, 1940, Tougaloo, MS; married Dan Cannon Jr; children: Audra Charmaine, Portia Camille. **EDUCATION:** Tougaloo Coll, BS 1961; Boston State Coll, Grad Studies 1975-76; Bridgewater State Coll, Grad Studies 1982-83; Eastern nazarene Coll, MEd 1984. **CAREER:** Greenville MS Public Schools, elem teach 1961-65; Boston Head Start, educ dir 1969-73; Randolph Public Schools, elem teach 1973-81; North Jr HS, diagnostic prescriptive teach of reading 1981-. **ORGANIZATIONS:** Past vice chmn Randolph Fair Practices 1980-81; conference presenter MA Teachers Assn 1982-84; mem The Governor's Task Force on Educ Reform 1983-84; bd mem South Shore Council for Children 1983-85; mem Randolph Fair Practices 1973-; chair minority affairs comm MA Teachers Assn 1982-; bd dir Norfolk Co Teachers Assn 1983-; communication comm MA Teachers Assn 1984-. **HONORS/ACHIEVEMENTS:** Outstanding Serv Randolph Teachers assn 1980, 1981, 1982; Citation for Serv Gov Michael Dukakis 1983; mem Delta Kappa Gamma Soc Intl Honor Soc for Women Educators 1985. **HOME ADDRESS:** 38 Sunset Drive, Randolph, MA 02368. **BUSINESS ADDRESS:** Diag Prescr Teacher of Reading, North Jr HS, High St, Randolph, MA 02368.

CANNON, ELTON MOLOCK
Physician. **PERSONAL:** Born Aug 07, 1920, Caldwell, NJ; married Alice; children: Elton Jr, Adrienne, Alice. **EDUCATION:** Lincoln U, BA 1943; Howard Univ Med Sch, MD 1947; Lincoln U, 1940. **CAREER:** Hahnemann Hosp, Phy Self; Dept Pub Hlth, 1948-76; Norristown State Hosiptal, Pennsylvania 1978-88. **ORGANIZATIONS:** Charter mem Aerospace Med Sect Nat Med Assn 1970; asso flw Am Coll Chest Physician 1954; mem Am Thoracic Soc; Philadelphia Co Med Soc; Nat Med Assn; PA St Med Soc; Am Pub Hlth Assn; Four Chaplains; mem Alpha Phi Alpha; NAACP; Janes United Meml Meth Ch; Chi Delta Mu Frat. **HONORS/ACHIEVEMENTS:** Four Chaplains for Comm Serv Award 1951. **MILITARY SERVICE:** AUS col. **BUSINESS ADDRESS:** 6447 Chew Ave, Philadelphia, PA 19119.

CANNON, EUGENE NATHANIEL
Retired university administrator. **PERSONAL:** Born Sep 13, 1944, Wilmington, DE; son of Alice Henry; married Lillian; children: Eugene. **EDUCATION:** Delaware State Coll, BS 1972; Southern Illinois Univ, MBA 1976. **CAREER:** Bankers Trust, investment banking 1969-70; A Kelley Jr Construction Co, business mgr 1971-72; DE Opportunities Industrializa-

tion Ctr, dir of higher educprograms 1972-75; Penn State Univ, dir of business services 1976-84. **ORGANIZATIONS:** Mem Amer Mgmt Assn 1979-80; pres Int Rotary Club 1980-81; mem Assn of MBA Executives 1980-84; mem Natl Assn of College Bus Offices 1980-84. **MILITARY SERVICE:** USN Petty Officer 4 yrs. **HOME ADDRESS:** 2510 Pennington Way, Wilmington, DE 19810.

CANNON, H. LEROY
Attorney. **PERSONAL:** Born Jan 22, 1916, Georgetown, DE; married Eddie M; children: Muriel. **EDUCATION:** DE State Coll, BS 1933-37; Atlanta U, 1941-42; Hastings Coll of Law, JD 1949-52. **CAREER:** San Francisco Unified School Dist, legal advisor 1974-; City & County of San Francisco, deputy city atty 1963-74; Private Practice, atty 1952-63; United Methodist Church, supply pastor 1956-58. **ORGANIZATIONS:** Mem CA & State Bar; SF Bar Assn; bd of gov SF Lawyers Club; Nat Bar Assn; Am Bar Assn; Am Bar Assn; Charles Houston Bar Assn; CA Assn of Black Lawyers; Am Judicature Soc; past pres SW Conf on Intergp Relations 1968-72; past pres bd of gov SF Br NAACP; past pres Com on Religion & Race; CA-NV Annual Conf United Meth Ch; dist dir CA Dem Cncl 1961-63; bd of gov No CA Ecumenical Cncl JSAC; exec com Cncl on Ministries; past pres Civil Liberties Com; past chaplain LJ Williams Lodge. **HONORS/ACHIEVEMENTS:** First black legal advr SFUSD. **MILITARY SERVICE:** AUS CWO 1942-46. **BUSINESS ADDRESS:** 135 Van Ness Ave, San Francisco, CA 94102.

CANNON, KATIE GENEVA
Associate professor, theological ethicist. **PERSONAL:** Born Jan 03, 1950, Concord, NC; daughter of Esau Cannon and Corine Lytle Cannon. **EDUCATION:** Barber-Scotia Coll, BS, Elementary Education (magna cum laude), 1971; Johnson C Smith Seminary, Atlanta, MDiv, 1974; Union Theological Seminary, New York, NY, MPhil, 1983, PhD, Christian Ethics, 1983. **CAREER:** Episcopal Divinity School, asst prof; NY Theolological Seminary, dean, Religious Educ programs, 1979-; New York Theological Seminary, admin faculty, 1977-80; Ascension Presbyterian Church, first black female pastor, 1975-77; Yale Divinity School, visiting lecturer, 1987; Harvard Divinity School, visiting scholar, 1983-84. **ORGANIZATIONS:** Ecumenical dialogue, Third World theologians, 1976-80; Middle East travel guide, NY Theological Seminary, 1978-80; editor, Que Pasa, 1982-; member, Amer Acad of Religion, 1983-, Assn of Black Women in Higher Educ, 1984-; bd of dir, Women's Theological Center 1984-; member bd dir, Soc of Christian Ethics, 1986-90; member, Soc for the Study of Black Religion 1986-; World Alliance of Reformed Churches Presbyterian & Congregational, 1986-91. **HONORS/ACHIEVEMENTS:** Isaac R Clark Preaching Award, Interdenominational Theological Center, 1973; Rockfeller Prostestant Fellow Fund for Theological Educ, 1972-74; Rockefeller Doctoral Fellow Fund for Theological Educ, 1974-76; Ford Found Fellow Natl Fellowships Fund, 1976-77; Roothbert Fellow, 1981-83; Harvard Divinity School, woman research assoc, Ethics, 1983-84; Radcliffe Coll Bunting Inst, 1987-88; Episcopal Church's Conant Grant, 1987-88; Assn of Theological School Young Scholar Award, 1987-88; author, Black Womanist Ethics, Scholars Press, 1988; co-editor, Inheriting Our Mothers' Garden, Westminster Press, 1988. **BUSINESS ADDRESS:** Assoc Prof, Christian Ethics, Episcopal Divinity School, 99 Brattle St, Cambridge, MA 02138.

CANNON, PAUL L., JR.
Research chemist. **PERSONAL:** Born Nov 21, 1934, Harrisburg, PA; son of Paul L Cannon and Mildred A Mercer Cannon. **EDUCATION:** Lincoln Univ, AB 1956. **CAREER:** Harrisbrg Hospital, clinical chem 1956-58; PA Dept of Highways, chem 1958; Dept of the Army, rsrch chem 1958-. **ORGANIZATIONS:** Omega Psi Phi Frat; Sigma Xi. **HONORS/ACHIEVEMENTS:** Electrochem Patents US; published articles on electrochmstry & analytical chem. **MILITARY SERVICE:** AUS pfc 1958-1960. **HOME ADDRESS:** 21 N 15th St, Harrisburg, PA 17103. **BUSINESS ADDRESS:** US Army Chemical Research, Devel & Engineering Center, SMCCR-RSC-C, Aberdeen Proving Ground, MD 21010.

CANNON, REUBEN
Business executive. **PERSONAL:** Born Feb 11, 1946, Chicago, IL; married Linda Eisenhout; children: Tonya. **EDUCATION:** SE City Coll. **CAREER:** Univ Studios, mail room clerk, sec casting dept, casting dir 1970-77; Warner Bros, head ofTV casting 1977-78; casted roles for Roots II, The Next Generation, A Soldier's Story, The Color Purple, The A-Team, Hunter, Riptide, Moonlighting, Amen, Amerika, Ironside; Lichen Inc, co-owner producing musical called "Lifers"; producing "The Women of Brewster Place"; Reuben Cannon & Assoc, owner 1979-. **HONORS/ACHIEVEMENTS:** Emmy Roots II TV Academy 1979. **BUSINESS ADDRESS:** President, Reuben Cannon & Assoc, 2020 Avenue of the Stars, Los Angeles, CA 90005.

CANSON, FANNIE JOANNA
Educator. **PERSONAL:** Born Apr 26, 1926, Bainbridge, GA; married Robert L. **EDUCATION:** Spelman Coll Tuskegee Inst, BS 1945; Univ of OR, MS 1967, PhD 1967. **CAREER:** CA State Univ Sacramento, assoc prof; former high school teacher; univ admin dir; teacher corps Corrections Project; Natl Council of Chs, teacher; licensed marriage & family counselor. **ORGANIZATIONS:** Conducted numerous workshops self concept theories, curriculum in correctional instns & Personnel Panels for State of CA; mem Numerous professional & Civic Orgn teaching fellow Univ of OR. **BUSINESS ADDRESS:** CA State Univ, 6000 Jay St, Sacramento, CA.

CANSON, VIRNA M.
Association executive. **PERSONAL:** Born Jun 10, 1921, Bridgeport, OK; married Clarence B Canson; children: Clarence B Jr, Faythe. **EDUCATION:** Tuskegee Inst; Univ of WI; Credit Union Nat Assn Sch for Credit, Grad. **CAREER:** NAACP Credit Union Sacramento Br, treas/mgr 1953-; CA State Office of Econ Oppor, credit union & consumer educ & spec 1965-67; West Coast Region I NAACP, field dir & legislative advocate 1967-74, reg dir 1974-. **ORGANIZATIONS:** mem, People to People Sacramento Chapter, Oak Park United Church of Christ; Subscribing Golden Heritage life mem NAACP; mem Founders Club, Credit Union Natl Assoc; life mem Natl Council of Negro Women; mem Women's Civic Improvement Club Sacramento; mem comm adv panel, CA State Univ Syst. **HONORS/ACHIEVEMENTS:** 1st winner D D Mattocks Award for Serv to Comm Sacramento Branch NAACP; Bus Week Award Iota Phi Lamba 1957 & 1962; Outstanding Serv Award So Area Conf NAACP; Outstanding Serv Awd Natl Council of Negro Women; Service Awd Black Police Officers Assoc Los Angeles; El Cerrito Branch NAACP; CA Credit Union League; City of Long Beach; Operation Second Chance San Bernardino CA. **BUSINESS ADDRESS:** Dir West Coast Region, NAACP, 1975 Sutter St Ste #1, San Francisco, CA 94115.

CANTARELLA, MARCIA Y.
Executive director, nonprofit organization. **PERSONAL:** Born Oct 31, 1946, Minneapolis, MN; daughter of Whitney Young Jr and Margaret Buckner Young; married Francesco Cantarella, May 24, 1980; children: Mark Boles, step-children Michele Cantarella, Moratea Cantarella. **EDUCATION:** Bryn Mawr Coll, Bryn Mawr PA, BA (with honors), 1968; Univ of Iowa Law School, 1968; Simmons Coll, Boston MA, middle mgmt program. **CAREER:** Sen Robert F Kennedy's Washington Office, summer intern 1967; Rabat Amer School, Rabat Morocco, social studies teacher grades 6-8, 1970-71; Zebra Assoc, New York City, advertising, 1971-72; Avon Products Inc, New York City, dir sales devel, dir 1972-85; Mom's Amazing, New York City, pres, 1985-88; Natl Coalition for Women's Enterprise, New York City, exec dir. **ORGANIZATIONS:** Bd of dir New York City Police Foundation, 1988-; mem Vaseline Baby Care Council, 1987-88; dir Children's Museum of Manhattan, 1986-. **HONORS/ACHIEVEMENTS:** Woman of the Year, NCNW, 1976; published articles in Working Mother, McCalls , Essence, Working Parent, Boardroom Reports.

CANTON, DOUGLAS E.
Senator. **PERSONAL:** Born Jan 06, 1931, C'sted STX, Virgin Islands of the United States;married Pauline Edith; children: Denise, David, Douglas Jr, Danny, Leone, Dinah, Robert, Devin. **EDUCATION:** Central CT State Coll VI, Certificate. **CAREER:** Self-employed, carpenter 1953-60; Canton's Construction, contractor 1973; St Croix Central HS, vocational educ instructor 1973-86; Legislature of the Virgin Islands, senator. **ORGANIZATIONS:** Mem bd of dirs Amer Red Cross STX; mem St Croix Central HS Parent/Teacher Assoc; mem F'sted Citizen Assoc 1987-88; mem Majority Coalition 17th Legislature; vice chmn Housing & Planning; mem Educ & Youth Rules and Nominations. **MILITARY SERVICE:** USMC 3 yrs. **BUSINESS ADDRESS:** Senator, #1 Contentment Rd, C'sted, St Croix, Virgin Islands of the United States 00820.

CANTRELL, FORREST DANIEL
Business executive. **PERSONAL:** Born Dec 30, 1938, Atlanta, GA; married Cheryl Francis; children: John Daniel. **EDUCATION:** San Francisco State U, BA 1968; Univ of CA, MBA 1970; Harvard Bus Sch, AMP 1977. **CAREER:** Mile Sq Health Center Inc, pres, former proj dir, former admnstr; San Francisco Police Dept, former police & Officer; Vallejo Police Dept, patrolman; Dept of Corrections, corr ofcr. **ORGANIZATIONS:** Past pres Nat Asn of Neighborhood Health Cntrs Inc; pres bd dir Miles Sq Serv Corp; commr Chicago Hlth Planning & Resources Devel Commin; bd dir Chica United Black Appeal Fund. **MILITARY SERVICE:** USN airman 1955-58. **BUSINESS ADDRESS:** 2045 W Washington Blvd, Chicago, IL 60612.

CANTWELL, KATHLEEN GORDON
Physician/radiologist. **PERSONAL:** Born May 17, 1945, Beaumont, TX; daughter of Mildred Portis Gordon; children: Jennifer, John. **EDUCATION:** Univ of TX at Austin, BA 1967; Howard Univ Coll of Medicine, MD 1975. **CAREER:** Howard Univ Coll of Medicine, faculty 1979-80; Hadley Hospital, radiologist 1979-; Doctor's Hospital Lanham MD, radiologist 1980-83; Drs Press & Cantwell PC, radiologist/partner 1981-. **ORGANIZATIONS:** Sec 1983-85, pres 1985-86 DC Chap Amer College of Radiology; chmn Radiology Section Medical Soc of DC 1985-86; mem bd dirs Southeast House 1985-87; assoc clinical prof radiology George Washington Univ 1986-87; Chairman, Women Physicians Section, Medical Society of DC 1988-1989; member-at-large, Executive Board, Medical Society of DC 1989-1991; Alternate Councilor, D.C. Metropolitan Chapter, Amer College of Radiology 1989-. **HONORS/ACHIEVEMENTS:** Most Outstanding Resident Howard Univ Hospital 1979; 13 journal articles in radiology. **BUSINESS ADDRESS:** Radiologist, Drs Press and Cantwell, PC, 2041 M L King Ave SE, Washington, DC 20020.

CANTY, GEORGE
Chemical supervisor. **PERSONAL:** Born Dec 07, 1931, Manning, SC; married Mabel Lucille Scott; children: Andria G, Alison D. **EDUCATION:** Univ of Pittsburgh, BS Chemistry 1954; Am U, MS Physics & Chemistry 1966. **CAREER:** 3m Co St Paul MN, supr prod devel 1973-; Celanese Research Co Summit NJ, sr research chemist 1967-73; Gillete & Research Inst Wash DC, rsrch/develchemist 1965-67; Nat Bur of Standards Wash DC, chemist 1961-63; NIH Bethesda MD, chemist 1958-63. **ORGANIZATIONS:** Mem Am Chem Soc 1960-; mem MN Chem Soc 1973-; mem & past basileus NJ Chap Omega Psi Phi Frat 1953-; guest lectr Black Exec Exchange Prog Nat Urban League 1974-; pub "The Melting & Crystallization of Fibrous Protein in Non-Aqueous Media" J Physics Chemistry 67 1963; pub "Stereoregularity in Ionic Polyumerization of Acenaph-Thalene" J Nat Bur of Standrads 68a 1964. **HONORS/ACHIEVEMENTS:** Catalyst Club Award 3m Co Film & Allied Prod Div 1977; patented Photosensitive Composite Sheet Material 1979; Honorable Discharge USN. **MILITARY SERVICE:** USN seaman recruit 1952. **BUSINESS ADDRESS:** 3M Center, Bldg 236-1A, St Paul, MN 55101.

CANTY, MIRIAM MONROE
Educator, lecturer. **PERSONAL:** Born May 06, 1916, Savannah, GA; married E J. **EDUCATION:** CA State U, BA 1959; Mt St Mary's Coll, MS 1971. **CAREER:** Promotional Personnel, Los Angeles City Unified School Dist, consultant 1972-; Mt St Mary's Coll, instructor; Educ Professional Develop Act Internship Program, teacher, training coord 1969-72, special educ consultant 1968-69, special educ teacher 1963-68, first grade teacher 1960-63; Child Devel Center, dir 1948-60. **ORGANIZATIONS:** Charter mem CA Council for Exceptional Children; mem Nat Council for Exception Children; prof educ of Los Angeles; past mem Exec Bd Assn Tchrs of LosAngeles; co-chmn Delta Sigma Theta Golden Life Mem Com 1971-75; Ch of Christian Fellowship Achieve Funds 1975-77; chmn Ad Hoc Com Delta Reading Prog 1975-76; life mem Delta Sigma Theta; Nat Council of Negro Women Inc; CA State Univ Alumni Assn; mem Phi Delta Kappa; Alpha Chi Pi Omega; Magellan C Mars Am Leg Aux; CA Music Tchrs Assn. **HONORS/ACHIEVEMENTS:** Certificate of Serv Delta Sigma Theat 1971 & 1975; Los Angeles & Alumni Chap Delta Sigma Theta Leadership Award 1971-76; Certificates of Appreciation Ch of Christian Fellowship 1970-74; holder of six CA Credentials. **BUSINESS ADDRESS:** 8817 Langdon Ave, Sepulveda, CA 91343.

CANTY, RALPH WALDO
Clergyman. **PERSONAL:** Born Oct 09, 1945, Sumter, SC; married Jacqueline Wright; children: Ralph Jr, Serena. **EDUCATION:** Morris Coll, AB 1967, BD 1970, DD 1978. **CAREER:** Morris Coll, pub rel dir 1970-75; BF Goodrich (Elgin Plant), asst personnel dir 1975-78; Savannah Grove Bapt Ch, pastor. **ORGANIZATIONS:** Pres/chrm bd Job's Mortuary 1970-; pres Brenca 1976-; bd mem Natl Cncl of Churches 1980; bd mem Bapt World Alliance

1980; bd mem Morris Coll 1982. **HONORS/ACHIEVEMENTS:** Omega Man of the Yr Gamma Iota Chap 1985; Citizen of the Yr Key Publns 1980; Citizen of the Yr Gamma Iota Chptr 1979. **BUSINESS ADDRESS:** Pastor, Savannah Grove Baptist Church, Route 3 Box 475, Effingham, SC 29541.

CAPEHART, JOHNNIE LAWRENCE
Law enforcement. **PERSONAL:** Born Apr 02, 1947, Windsor, NC; son of Willie Cecil Capehart and Florence Slade Jordan; married Geneva Kendall; children: Gregory, Deloris, Willie. **EDUCATION:** Newport News Police Academy, Certificate Award 1971; Saint Leo College, AA 1978, BA 1979; FBI Academy Executive Development School, Quantico VA 1985. **CAREER:** Newport News Police Dept, police officer 1971-73; Christopher Newport College, campus police officer 1973-76; Williamsburg Police Dept, police detective 1976-78; Christopher Newport College, campus police chief. **ORGANIZATIONS:** Member Fraternal Order of Police 1971-; member Masonic Lodge 1973-; member Virginia Campus Police Chief Assn 1978-; member Virginia Crime Prevention Assn 1979-; member NAACP 1982-; member Intl Chief of Police Assn 1983-; member Conference of Minority Public Administrators 1983-. **HONORS/ACHIEVEMENTS:** Staff Member of Year Christopher Newport College 1975; 100 Club Award Sewart AFB, TN 1967; Airman of the Month USAF 1967; Candidate for Sheriff Bertie County, NC 1982. **MILITARY SERVICE:** USAF Staff Sgt (Admin Specialist), 1966-70; VA ANG Munition Specialist 1978-; USAF Accom Medal, Good Conduct Medal, Pres Citation, Airman of Month Awd, 100 Club Awd; Virginia Air National Guard, technical sergeant 1985-; Drug and Alcohol NCO. **HOME ADDRESS:** 548-103 Thorncliff Drive, Newport News, VA 23602.

CAPEL, FELTON JEFFREY
Business executive. **PERSONAL:** Born Feb 26, 1927, Ellerbe, NC; son of Acie Capel and Elnora Leak Capel; married Jean Walden, Jul 12, 1951; children: Jeff, Mitch, Ken. **EDUCATION:** Hampton Univ, BS 1951. **CAREER:** Salesman 1958-61, sales mgr 1958-61, reg sales mgr 1965-77, Century Metalcraft Corp; pres, Century Assn of NC 1977-85. **ORGANIZATIONS:** City councilman, Southern Pines 1959-68; dir, Carolina P & L Co 1972-85, Southern Natl Bank 1974-85, First Federal Savings & Loan 1978-85, North Carolina Assn of Minority Businesses Durham NC 1986, Durham Corp 1988-, Durham Life Insurance 1988-, North Carolina Citizens for Business and Industry Raleigh NC 1988, Wachovia Corp Winston-Salem NC 1989, Wachovia Bank and Trust Co NA Winston-Salem NC 1989; city treasurer and chmn of Moore County Bd of Elections 1980-86; dist governor, Rotary Intl 1981-82; chmn, Moore Co United Way 1983, Moore County Chapter Amer Red Cross 1983-85; member, North Carolina Comm for Educ, 1989. **HONORS/ACHIEVEMENTS:** Intl Mgr Sales Award Century Metalcrft 1962; Bd Mem of Year North Carolina Dept of Conservation & Devel 1971; chmn of the year, Sandhills Area Chamber of Commerce 1977; Delta Mu Delta Natl Honor in Business FSU 1983. **MILITARY SERVICE:** AUS staff sergeant two years. **BUSINESS ADDRESS:** PO Drawer 37, 1800 S Walnut St, Pinebluff, NC 28373-0037.

CAPEL, WALLACE
Physician. **PERSONAL:** Born Nov 12, 1915, Andalusia, AL; married Carrie Ford; children: Carolyn Capel Harrison, Jacqueline D, Denise L, Wallace Capel Jr. **EDUCATION:** Howard Univ, BS 1940, MD 1944; Baylor Univ, MHA 1970. **CAREER:** VA Medical Ctr, chief of staff. **ORGANIZATIONS:** Mem Amer and Natl Medical Assoc, 1970, Macon Co Medical Soc 1973. **HONORS/ACHIEVEMENTS:** Exec of Year Professional Secretaries Intl 1979. **MILITARY SERVICE:** AUS col 20 yrs; Legion of Merit w/Oak Leaf Cluster. **BUSINESS ADDRESS:** Chief of Staff, VA Medical Center, Drawer H, Tuskegee, AL 36083.

CAPERS, ELIZA VIRGINIA
Actress, singer. **PERSONAL:** Born Sep 22, 1925, Sumter, SC; children: Glenn S. **EDUCATION:** Howard U, 1943-45; Julliard Sch Music, 1946-50. **CAREER:** Actress in motion pictures, on stage, and on TV; singer; licensed agent. **ORGANIZATIONS:** Mem San Fernando Fair Housing Council; bd mem Muscular Dystrophy Assn; life mem NAACP; chmn CARE Intl Children's Party; World's Poet & Resources Ctr Inc; Meth Women; Women's Ort Lane Bryant for Operation Reach Out; mem Nat Acad TV Arts. **HONORS/ACHIEVEMENTS:** Lorraine Hansberry Fine Arts Award 1975; drama award Satellite Academy; Tony Award 1974. **BUSINESS ADDRESS:** C/O Lunt Fontanne Theater, 205 W 46 St, New York, NY 10036.

CAREW, COLIN A. (TOPPER CAREW)
Film & TV producer, musician, architect. **PERSONAL:** Born Jul 16, 1943, Boston, MA; married Alyce C Sprow. **EDUCATION:** Howard U, 1961-66; Yale U, barch 1970, march 1970; comm fellow MIT 1973; Comm Union Grad Sch, PhD 1974; Harvard Bus Sch NAEB Adv Mgt Prgm, 1976. **CAREER:** WGBH-TV, prgm mgr 1976; REBOP, exec prodr 1976; Say Brother Nat, exec prodr 1975; Say Brother, prodr host 1974; New Thing Art & Arch Ctr, fdr dir 1967-72; producer "The Righteous Apples" for PBS; producer "Two of Hearts" with grant from US Dept of Edn. **ORGANIZATIONS:** Founer Communications Inst of New England; consult Harvard Univ Ofc of Govt & Comm Afrs; Natl Urban Coalition; consult Inst for Contemp Art; consult Corp for Pub Broadcasting; consult Nat Ctr for Urban Ethnic Afrs; mem Black Caucus Brain Trust on Media; bd mem Mus of Afro-am Hist; bd mem Assn of Nghbrhd; bd mem MA Comm Sch; bd mem Trinidad & Tobago Assn; mem Sigma Pi Phi Frat. **HONORS/ACHIEVEMENTS:** Comm serv award Rosbury Action Prgm 1975; black achievers award YMCA 1976; disting comm fellow alumni award MIT 1976; citizen of Yr Award Omega Psi Phi 1977; 60 film & TV awards. **BUSINESS ADDRESS:** P O Box 93697, Los Angeles, CA 90093.

CAREW, RODNEY CLINE
Professional athlete. **PERSONAL:** Born Oct 01, 1945, Gatun, Panama;married Marilynn Levy; children: Charryse, Stephanie, Michelle. **CAREER:** MN Twins, second baseman 1967-78; CA Angels, 1st baseman, 2nd baseman 1979-86. **ORGANIZATIONS:** Works with underprivileged youth Atwood Rec Ctr Placentia CA; gives talks to schools in Orange Cty area regarding child abuse. **HONORS/ACHIEVEMENTS:** Rookie of the Year BBWAA 1967; bat champ 1969, 1972, 1973, 1974, 1975, 1978; Rookie of the Year Amer League 1967; Most Valuable Player Amer League 1977; Selected Top Hitter of Decade for Compiling a 343 Average 1979-79; selected to All-Star team for 18th consecutive season; won numerous awards by virtue of hitting 388 en route to winning the sixth of his seven batting titles; named AL's MVP Major League Player of the Year, MN Sports Personality of the Year, Roberto Clemente Awd, Calvin Griffith Awd; 1st player to win AL Player of the Month twice

in a season; 3 time winner AL Player of the Week; 4 time winner AL Player of the Month; all-time top vote-getter in All-Star balloting with total vote count approaching 32 million; set club record 339 average 1983; 16th player in major league history to get 3,000 hits Aug 4 1986. **BUSINESS ADDRESS:** Baseball Player, c/o California Angels, 2000 State College Blvd, Anaheim, CA 92806.

CAREW, TOPPER See CAREW, COLIN A.

CAREY, ADDISON, JR.
Educator. **PERSONAL:** Born Mar 10, 1933, Crescent City, FL; son of Addison Carey Sr and Laura Dowdell; married Clara Lee Parker; children: Leon, Alphonso, Pamela, Katrenia, Addison III, Michael, Douglas. **EDUCATION:** FL A&M Univ, BS 1958; The OH State Univ, MA 1960; Tulane Univ, PhD 1971. **CAREER:** Southern Univ at New Orleans, dir visiting scholars lecture series 1972-78, admin asst to the chancellor 1983-85, prof of political sci 1960-. **ORGANIZATIONS:** Bd mem YMCA 1978-; pres, Retired Military Assoc of New Orleans 1980-; pres Economic Develop Unit 1984-; mem Civil Service Commn City of New Orleans LA 1987-; past pres LA Political Science Assoc; mem Natl Conf of Black Political Scientists; mem, Pi Sigma Alpha Honorary Society; mem, African American Heritage Assn. **HONORS/ACHIEVEMENTS:** Ford Foundation Fellow; Southern Fellowships Foundation Fellow; Outstanding Professor Southern Univ at New Orleans 1965,74; Citations for work in voter registration drives YMCA and student organizations. **MILITARY SERVICE:** AUS pfc 3 yrs; Purple Heart, Korean Serv Medal, sigman Rhee Citation National Defense Medal 1950-53. **HOME ADDRESS:** 4844 Mendez St, New Orleans, LA 70126. **BUSINESS ADDRESS:** Professor of Political Science, SouthernUniv at New Orleans, 6400 Press Dr, New Orleans, LA 70126.

CAREY, ARCHIBALD JAMES, JR.
Judge. **PERSONAL:** Born Feb 29, 1908, Chicago, IL; married Hazel Harper; children: Carolyn Jones. **EDUCATION:** Lewis Inst, BS 1929; Garrett Theol Sem, BD 1932; Kent Coll, JD 1935; Wilberforce, honor DD 1943; John Marshall Law, LLD 1954. **CAREER:** Woodlawn AM E Ch, pastor 1930-49; Quinn Chapel 1949-67; minister emeritus 1967-; Private Practice, atty 1936-66; Supreme Ct of IL, judge 1966, 1980. **ORGANIZATIONS:** Pres bd mem IL Fed Svgs & Loan Assn 1957-66; pres IL Fed Svgs &N Assn 1957-66, bd mem 1936-70; past pres dir Cosmopolitan C of C; alderman 1947-55; US del to UN 1953; mem Alpha Phi Alpha; pres Theta Chap 1934-35; judges assn Judicial Countil Nat Bar Assn; bd mem Comm Fund Chgo; life trustee Garrett Theol Sem; trustee emeritus Interdenom Theol Sem; speaker, rep Nat Conv 1952. **HONORS/ACHIEVEMENTS:** Law scholarship Edmund Burke 1935; Alpha Phi Alpha Awrd of Honor 1953; usefful Cit AwardUniv of Chicago 1954. **BUSINESS ADDRESS:** 2002 Civic Center, Chicago, IL 60602.

CAREY, AUDREY L.
Elected official. **PERSONAL:** Born Nov 28, 1937, Newburgh, NY; widowed; children: Davina Henry, Dana, David C Jr. **EDUCATION:** St Luke's Hosp Sch of Nursing, Registered Prof Nurse (honors) 1961; NY State Dept of Educ, permanent certification sch nurse teacher 1971; NY Univ Graduate Sch of Educ, advanced degree admin & super 1971-76; UpState medical Coll SUNY, pediatric nurse practitioner certification 1980; State Univ Coll at Oneonta, BS Education/Nursing. **CAREER:** St Luke's Hosp, asst head nurse 1963-69; Headstart & N Jr HS, school nurse teacher 1966-69; Newburgh Sch Dist, drug educ coord 1969-74; Newburgh Free Academy, school nurse teacher 1975-80; Newburgh Free Academy HS, pediatric nurse practitioner 1980-; City of Newburgh, councilwoman. **ORGANIZATIONS:** Bd of dirs Orange Co Dept of Mental Health 1971-73; mem Inst of Black Studies Mt St Mary's Coll 1973-74; assoc coord Non-Credit Progs St Mary's College 1973-74; panelist NYS Bd of Regents Conf 1973-74; mem bd of dirs YWCA 1975-76; bd of trustees Orange Co Comm Coll 1973-82; panelist Robert WoodJohnson Found Sch Health Conf 1980-81; chmn Newburgh Comm Action Head Start Policy Advisory Council 1983-84; Newburgh City Councilwoman 1977-. **HONORS/ACHIEVEMENTS:** Professional Achievement Awd Omega Psi Phi Frat Upsilon Tau Chap 1961; Disting Serv Awd Jaycees 1973; Outstanding Comm Serv Awd Nimrod Lodge #82 AF&AM 1977; Continuous Serv Awd Black Commonwealth of Newburgh 1979; Disting Serv Awd NAACP 1981; Outstanding Comm Serv HVOIC Mary C Christian Awd 1982; Achievement Awd Newburgh Comm Action Head Start 1984; Comm Achievement Awd Black History Month 1985; Recognition Awd Newburgh Optimist Club 1985; publication"Adolescence, Feeling Good, Looking Fine, Acting Fit" Natl Sch Health Digest 1981. **BUSINESS ADDRESS:** Councilwoman, City of Newburgh, PO Box 4, Newburgh, NY 12550.

CAREY, CARNICE
Government contract compliance coordinator. **PERSONAL:** Born Dec 17, 1945, Chicago, IL; daughter of Joe Stephen and Ora Gardner Stephen; married Lloyd L Carey, Oct 29, 1966; children: Patrice Carey, Leslie Carey. **EDUCATION:** Loop Jr Coll, Chicago, IL; Northeastern Illinois Univ, Chicago, IL. **CAREER:** City of Chicago, Chicago, IL, contract compliance coord, 1972-75; Regional Transportation Authority, Chicago, IL, eeo officer, 1975-84; City of Chicago, Chicago, IL, contract compliance coord, 1985-. **ORGANIZATIONS:** Administrative bd, Redeemer Methodist Church, 1970; mem, Wesley Methodist Church, 1980-; consultant, Seventh Ward Democratic Org, 1988-.

CAREY, CLAIRE LAMAR
Manager. **PERSONAL:** Born Aug 11, 1943, Augusta, GA; daughter of Mr. & Mrs. P.W. Lamar; married Harmon Roderick; children: Roderick Lamar. **EDUCATION:** Fisk Univ, BS Chemistry 1964; OH Univ, graduate study, Chemistry, 1965; Univ of DE, mgmt certificate, 1975. **CAREER:** Hercules Inc, since 1965, presently, mgr, professional Devel, 1989-. **ORGANIZATIONS:** Pres, Alpha Kappa Alpha Sorority Inc Zeta Omega 1962-; mem Sigma Xi Sci Honor Soc 1969-; mem Amer Chem Soc Educ Comm 1974-; mem DE Tech Comm Coll Advisory Bd 1974-76; consult personnel affairs Human Resources Consultant; sec Gov's Commn Magistrates Screening; vice pres YWCA bd of dirs; mem NCCJ bd of dirs; pres, YWCA bd of dirs, 1987-89; mem, Boy Scouts bd of dirs. **HONORS/ACHIEVEMENTS:** Comm Serv Award United Way of DE 1975; Mem, Acquisition Award Wilmington DE Chapter NAACP 1976; Minority Achiever in Industry Award Wilmington Branch YMCA 1976; Leadership Award Alpha Kappa Alpha N Atlantic Region 1979; Outstanding Achiever in Industry-Brandywine Professional Assn 1985. **BUSINESS ADDRESS:** Manager of Training & Education, Hercules Inc, 910 Market St, Wilmington, DE 19899.

CAREY, HARMON RODERICK
Social services agency executive, businessman. **PERSONAL:** Born Jul 07, 1936, Wilmington, DE; married Claire D Lamar; children: Roderick. **EDUCATION:** Central State Univ, AB 1957; Univ of PA, MSW 1962, post grad; Temple Univ Law Sch, post grad 1963-65; Univ of DE, MA 1977; Univ of DE, doc candidate 1974-. **CAREER:** Dept Public Welfare Wilmington, caseworker 1958-60; YMCA, dir youth lounge 1959-64; Family Ct, supr 1960-65; Peoples Settlement Assn, prog dir exec dir 1965-70; Assn Greater Wilmington Neighborhood Ctrs, exec dir 1970-74; Pine Beverage Inc, pres; Bar-B-Que Pit Windsor Market & Deli, owner/operator; HaralRealty, treas; Human Resources Consultants, founder/pres; Afro-Amer Historical Soc of DE, founder/pres. **ORGANIZATIONS:** Mem bd dir Equity Farm Trust; instr Univ of DE Extension Div; founder King Collection; vice pres Communigraphics Inc; conf coord Natl Fed Settlements 1971; mem Natl Assn Social Workers, Acad Certified Soc Workers; mem NAACP, Black Alliance, Kappa Alpha Psi, Alpha Kappa Mu, Equity of DE Monday Club; numerous publications; founder Minority Business Assoc of DE; pres Carey Enterprises Unlimited. **HONORS/ACHIEVEMENTS:** Numerous honors & awds. **MILITARY SERVICE:** 2nd lt AUS 1957-58. **BUSINESS ADDRESS:** President, Afro-Amer Hist Soc of DE, 512 E 4th St, Wilmington, DE 19801.

CAREY, HOWARD H.
Association executive. **PERSONAL:** Born Jan 06, 1937, Lexington, MS; married Yvonne A Arnold; children: Melba, Rodney. **EDUCATION:** Morehouse Coll, AB 1957; Atlanta Univ, MSW 1963; US International Univ, PhD 1977. **CAREER:** San Diego Urban League, assoc dir 1963-66; Economic Oppor Commn, prog dev specialist 1966-69; Neighborhood House Assn, prog dir 1969-72. **ORGANIZATIONS:** Charter mem/treas LEAD; mem certification comm Natl Assn of Social Workers; mem Natl Assn of Black Social Workers; mem Alpha Phi Alpha Frat; mem Sigma Pi Phi Frat, Alpha Pi Boule; mem Alpha Kappa Delta; mem Morehouse Coll Alumni Assn San Diego Chapt; mem Natl Conf of Social Welfare; adv comm San Diego City Coll Adv Comm; mem US International Univ Alumni Assn; integration task force, mem human relations comm San Diego Unified Sch Dist; bd dirUnited Way Comm Serv Div; mem United Way Agency Executives Assn; mem held various offices United Neighborhood Centers of Amer; fndg mem Black Leadership Cncl; mem Congressman Jim Bates Adv Comm; mem Congressman Duncan Hunter's Black Affairs Sub-Comm; mem Black-Jewish Dialogue; mem Catfish Club; mem Bethel Baptist Ch; mem governing bd Physicians & Surgeons Hosp; sec Natl Head Start Friends Assn; mem Co of San Diego Child Care Task Force; mem bd ofdir Natl Head Start Assoc; mem Mayor O'Connor's Black Adv Comm; mem bd of visitors The Bishop's School,. **HONORS/ACHIEVEMENTS:** Cert of Appreciation as Educ Consul San Diego State Univ 1973-74; Special Thanks for Outstanding Contribs in Black Comm Black Federation of San Diego 1973; Significant Contrib to the Comm Educ Comm San Diego Urban League 1974; Citation for Dedication United Way of San Diego 1977; Thanks Coach Allied Gardens Little League 1977; Outstanding Achievement Awd Action Intrprises Develop 1980; Comm Serv San Diego Bd of Realists 1980-81; Dedicated & Outstanding Serv Neighborhood Home Loan Counseling Serv 1981; Cert of Honor Morehouse Coll 1957-82; Providing Competent Child Care Child Develop Assn 1983; Outstanding Leadership Neighborhood House Assn Bd dirs 1983; Concern for & Contributions Toward Well-being of Humanity Christ Church 1984. **MILITARY SERVICE:** USN e-5 4 yrs. **BUSINESS ADDRESS:** Executive Dir, Neighborhood House Assoc, 841 S 41st St, San Diego, CA 92113.

CAREY, JAMES WILLIAM
Educational administrator. **PERSONAL:** Born Jul 25, 1945, Detroit, MI; married Barbara Ann; children: Jason W. **EDUCATION:** Eastern MI Univ, BA 1969, MA 1970; North Texas State Univ, EdD 1977. **CAREER:** USN Recruiting Command, commander, education specialist 1973-77; USN Education and Training, chief education specialist 1977-84; US Coast Guard, asst chief of training and education. **BUSINESS ADDRESS:** Asst Chief of Training & Ed, US Coast Guard, 2100 Second St, SW, Washington, DC 20593.

CAREY, JENNIFER DAVIS
Educator. **PERSONAL:** Born Oct 02, 1956, Brooklyn, NY; married Robert J Carey, Jr; children: Michael. **EDUCATION:** Harvard & Radcliffe Coll, AB 1978; Harvard Graduate School of Educ, EdM, 1979. **CAREER:** Ohio Univ, asst dir student prog 1979-81; Harvard & Radcliffe Coll, dir of minority recruitment program, 1982-. **ORGANIZATIONS:** Albert Oliver Prog, mem, bd of dir 1983-; The Vista Group, partner 1986; NAACP, mem; Assoc of Afro-American Museums, mem 1986; Visions Foundation, mem 1986. **BUSINESS ADDRESS:** Dir Minorty Recruitment, Harvard and Radcliff College, Byerly Hall, 8 Garden St, Cambridge, MA 02138.

CAREY, MILTON GALES
Colonel, association executive. **PERSONAL:** Born Feb 15, 1926, Hugo, OK; married Barbara Anne Bryant; children: Linda Davies, Anthony P, Jo Anne, Reginald B. **EDUCATION:** San Francisco State U, BA 1961; Roosevelt Univ Chicago, 1966; AUS Command & Gen Staff Coll KS, grad 1967. **CAREER:** Assoc Minority Contractors of Amer, pres & founder 1975; Mars Gen Corp, pres 1972-75; Defense Lang Inst Wash DC, exec dir 1971-72; Balija-Marc Inc, pres 1978-; AMC Fed Credit Union, pres 1979-; The Carey Fnd, pres 1979. **ORGANIZATIONS:** Vice chmn Washington Area Construction Inds TV 1975-80; vice chmn DC Minority Business Opportunity Comm 1977-78; mem DC Adv Panel on Career Based Educ 1978-79. **HONORS/ACHIEVEMENTS:** Bronze star w/oak leaf cluster US Dept of Defense 1963-71; joint serv commendation ribbon Joint Chiefs of Staff 1970; meritorious serv medal US Dept of Defense 1970; legion of merit US Dept of defense 1971. **MILITARY SERVICE:** AUS lt col served 24 years. **BUSINESS ADDRESS:** 1111 Mass Ave NW, Ste 101, Washington, DC 20005.

CAREY, PATRICIA M.
University administrator. **PERSONAL:** Born May 03, 1940, Chicago, IL; daughter of Ezekiel J Morris, Jr and Mildred Fowler Morris; married Robert B Carey, Aug 28, 1965; children: Meredith Brooke, Jason Morris. **EDUCATION:** Michigan State Univ, East Lansing MI, BA, 1962, MA, 1963; New York Univ, New York NY, PhD, 1982. **CAREER:** Marketing Research, New York NY, psychologist, 1968-69; New York Univ, New York NY, counselor, 1970-76, dir of counseling services, 1976-79, dean of student affairs, 1979—. **ORGANIZATIONS:** American Association of University Women, American Psychological Association, Association of Black Women in Higher Education. **HONORS/ACHIEVEMENTS:** Distinguished service award, graduate school organization, New York University, 1987; distinguished alumnus award, New York University Black Alumni Association; outstanding leadership award, Higher Education Opportunities Program, New York University, 1987; named one of America's top 100 black business and professional women by Dollar & Sense magazine, 1988. **BUSINESS ADDRESS:** Dean of Student Affairs, New York University, 32 Washington Place, #31, New York, NY 10003.

CAREY, PEARL M.
Beauty consultant. **PERSONAL:** Born May 13. **EDUCATION:** Chatman Coll, AA. **CAREER:** Monterey Peninsula Unified School Dist, CETA coord; EDD, man-power specialist; Child Care Center, owner; Naval Post Graduate Cafeteria, supr; Youth Corps/Job Corps, employ interviewer; NYC, employ clerk. **ORGANIZATIONS:** Mem Comn on Status of Women; life mem & registrar PTA; pres Western States Golf Assn; past pres Dem Womens Club 1976; past pres life mem NAACP 1976; past pres Business & Professional Womens Club 1973; past exec bd mem YMCA; United Fund; Welfare Rights; Natl Council of Negro Women; CA Elected Womens Assn; Eskaton Aux Vol; past council woman Heart Fund & Infant Care Center 1970; Natl Dem Com Woman; Monterey Area Director, Pacific Women's Golf Assn, 1989-; Golf Course Rating Director, Pacific Womens Golf Assn, 1989-. **HONORS/ACHIEVEMENTS:** CA Woman of Achievement BPWC; valedictorian class 1974, MPC; 5 most activist women Monterey Peninsula Herald 1977; Outstanding Woman Monterey County, Monterey County Commission on Status of Women, 1988; Secretary, CA AARP State Legislative Committee, 1989; Monterey County Juvenile Justice Commissioner, 1989-.

CARGILE, C. B., JR.
Personnel administrator. **PERSONAL:** Born May 17, 1926, Bastrop, LA. **EDUCATION:** Rutgers State Univ NJ, BA Pol Sci 1973; Rider Coll, MA Mgmt 1980. **CAREER:** NJ State Govt, admin 1966-70; Ocean Cty Coll, asst dean of bus 1973-. **ORGANIZATIONS:** Exec dir Black Amer 1970-, Black Political Org; life mem NAACP, Alpha Phi Alpha; 1st black elected dem municipal chmn Lakewood NJ; 1st black cand for cty freeholder Monmouth Cty NJ; mem Ocean Cty Coll Speakers Bur; compliance chmn Toms River NJ Br of NAACP. **HONORS/ACHIEVEMENTS:** Disting Comm Serv Awd Concerned Citizens 1970; Pol Awareness Awd Camden NJ Action Council 1979; Disting Serv Awd for Five Yrs Serv as Chmn Ocean Cty CETA Adv Council. **MILITARY SERVICE:** AUS cwo3 1942-65; AUS Commendation Medal 1959; Oak Leaf Clusters 1963-64. **BUSINESS ADDRESS:** Assistant Dean of Business, Ocean County College, College Dr, Toms River, NJ 08753.

CARGILE, WILLIAM, III
Construction company executive. **CAREER:** William Cargile Contractor Inc, Cincinnati, OH, chief executive. **BUSINESS ADDRESS:** Chief Executive, William Cargile Contractor Inc, 2008 Freeman Ave, Cincinnati, OH 45214. *

CARGILL, GILBERT ALLEN
Government official. **PERSONAL:** Born Jun 04, 1916, Oberlin, OH; son of Edward Cargill and Mayora Mosby Cargill; divorced; children: Thomas Gilbert. **EDUCATION:** Oberlin Coll, AB, 1937; Case School of Science, 1959-60; Wayne State Univ, 1970-72. **CAREER:** US Army, flight instructor, 1945-46; Bd of Educ, teacher, 1946-66; Berz Aviation, charter pilot/flight instr, 1967-85. **ORGANIZATIONS:** Organizer, Airway Intruders Flying Club, 1945-67; Flight Instructor, Independent, 1967-85; FAA Designated Pilot Examiner, 1972-89; FAA Safety Counselor, 1972-89; natl pre, Negro Airmen Intl, 1976-78; pres, Detroit Chapter NIA, 1976-; mem, Tuskegee Airmen, 1976-; pres, Trojan-Hessel Block Club, 1981-82; production test pilot, Adams Industries, 1982; mem, British Methodist Episcopal Church, 1982-; sec of trustees of BME Church, 1984-; sec of stewards of BME, 1984-; treasurer of stewards of BME Church, 1984-; mem, Detroit Airport Advisory Commission, 1984-86; mem/chairman, Michigan Aeronautics Commission, 1985-; mem, Michigan Aviation Assn, 1987-88. **HONORS/ACHIEVEMENTS:** Great Lakes Region FAA Award for Outstanding Support of Safety Counselor Program, 1979; Aviation Radio Station "CARGL" named after me by the Federal Aviation Admin, 1981; Chapter Award given by the Detroit Chapter of NAI, 1982; Troy Citizenship Award given by City of Troy, MI, 1982; Detroit City Council Resoluti on, 1982; Mayoral Proclamation given by Mayor Coleman Young, 1982; C. Alfred Anderson Award given by NBCFAE (Natl Black Coalition of Federal Aviation Employees), 1983; Honorary Commission in thc AL State Militia given by Governor George Wallace, 1983; City of Holland Certificate given by the City of Holland, MI, 1986; Sesquicentennial Avaition Certificate given by MI Sesquicentennial Committee, 1987; MI Aeronautics Commission Leadership Award given by MI Aeronautics Commissio n, 1987; Elected to the MI Aviation Hall of Fame in November 1988, first black person to become enshrined in this organization, 1989. **MILITARY SERVICE:** Army Air Corps, f/o, 1945. **HOME ADDRESS:** 20213 Faust Road, Detroit, MI 48219.

CARGILL, SANDRA MORRIS
Contract management. **PERSONAL:** Born May 08, 1953, Boston, MA; married Ronald Glanville Cargill. **EDUCATION:** Univ of Redlands, BS Bus Admin 1984. **CAREER:** Amer Acquisitions Inc, admin asst 1976-77; Mode O Day Co, asst buyer, sec 1977-78; Loral (Xerox) Electro Optical Systems, sr contract admin 1978-85; CA Inst of Tech Jet Propulsion Lab, sr contract admin 1985-. **ORGANIZATIONS:** Pres, principal developer Xerox Electro Optical Systems Tutorial Prog 1980-83; mem Black Women's Forum 1980-83; lecturer Youth Motivation Task Force 1981-83; mem Loral EOS Mgmt Club 1983-85; gen mem 1983-85, bd dir logistics 1986-87, bd dir treas 1987-88 Natl Contract Mgmt Assoc San Gabriel Chapt; jrachievement comm 1984-85, mgmt devel comm 1984-85 Loral Electro Optical Systems Mgmt Club; exec adv Jr Achievement Prog 1984-85; mem Natl Mgmt Assoc CA Inst of Tech 1986-. **HONORS/ACHIEVEMENTS:** Outstanding Achievement in Contract Admin Xerox Electro Optical Systems 1981; Recognition for Leadership in Developing & Coord the XEOS Tutorial Prog Xerox Electro Optical Systems 1981; Recogniton for Volunteer Serv to Students Pasadena Unified School Dist 1981; Recognition for Volunteer Serv to Students Youth Motivation Task Force 1981,83; Recognition for Outstanding Contribs in Community Serv So CA Volunteers Assoc 1981; Recognition of Volunteer Serv Jr Achievement Assoc 1985; Recognition of Extraordinary Serv & Leadership Mgmt Devel Comm Loral EOS Mgmt Club 1985; Recognition of Volunteer Support to Students Jr Achievement Loral EOS Mgmt Club 1985. **BUSINESS ADDRESS:** Sr Contract Administrator, CA Inst of Tech, 4800 Oak Grove Dr, Jet Prop Lab, Pasadena, CA 91109.

CARL, EARL LAWRENCE
Educator. **PERSONAL:** Born Mar 23, 1919, New Haven, CT; married Iris Harris; children: Francine, Nina. **EDUCATION:** Fisk U, AB 1942, JD 1948; Yale Law Sch, LLM 1960. **CAREER:** Thurgood Marshall School of Law, TX Southern Univ, dean, prof, dean

of law 1958-59, prof of law 1960, assoc prof of law 1948. **ORGANIZATIONS:** Mem Nat Bar Assn Am Bar & Assn; vice pres in charge of legal affairs Phi Alpha Delta Parkwood Dr Civic Club; exec bd mem Houston Lighthouse for the Blind. **HONORS/ACHIEVEMENTS:** Alpha Phi Alpha Named Dstng Prof Bd of Trustees TX SoUniv 1974; named in Negroes & the Law Journal of Leg Educ 1965; publ articles, Negroes & the Law, Jrnl Leg Educ Vol 17 No 3 1965, The Shortage of Negro Lawyers, Jrn of Legal Educ Vol 20 No 1 1967; working on case book "Cases and Materials on Minorities and the law". **BUSINESS ADDRESS:** TX So Law Sch, 3401 Wheeler, Houston, TX 77004.

CARLINE, WILLIAM RALPH
Dentist. **PERSONAL:** Born Oct 21, 1910, Lake Charles, LA; married Gen. **EDUCATION:** Wiley Coll, BA; Meharry Dental Coll, DDS honors. **CAREER:** Carline Dental Clinic Corpus Christi Tx, practioner in dentistry. **ORGANIZATIONS:** Past pres Gulf State Dental Assn 1955; Phi Beta Sigma 1932; apptd citizens Com for revision of TX Constitution 1973; mem United & Methodist Ch; mem NatDental Assn; life mem NAACP; mem various other Local, State, Nat Orgns. **HONORS/ACHIEVEMENTS:** 1 of 5 chosen in nation Research Randolph Air Force 1956. **MILITARY SERVICE:** USAF group dental surgeon 1943-43. **BUSINESS ADDRESS:** 1211 Sam Rankin St, Corpus Christi, TX 78401.

CARLO, NELSON
Corporate executive. **CAREER:** Abbott Products Inc, Chicago, IL, chief executive. **BUSINESS ADDRESS:** Chief Executive, Abbott Products Inc, 3129 W 36th Street, Chicago, IL 60632. *

CARLOS, JOHN
Athlete. **PERSONAL:** Born Jun 05, 1945, New York, NY. **HONORS/ACHIEVEMENTS:** Mem US Olympic Team 1968; co-holder world 100 yd record; won gold me In 1967 w/20,5 in 200 m; 3rd pl 1968; worlds ldng sprntr in 100 yrd & 220 yd 1969.

CARLTON, PAMELA GEAN
Banker. **PERSONAL:** Born Oct 17, 1954, Cleveland, OH; daughter of Alphonso Carlton and Mildred Carlton; married Charles Jordan Hamilton Jr; children: Charles III, Samuel Aaron Hamilton. **EDUCATION:** Williams Coll, BA Pol Econ 1976; Yale Sch of Management, MPPM Business 1980; Yale Law School, JD 1980. **CAREER:** Cleary Gottlieb Stein & Hamilton, assoc counsel 1980-82; Morgan Stanley Co Inc, assoc investment banking 1982-85, vice pres investment banking 1985-. **ORGANIZATIONS:** Mem NY State Bar 1981-; bd mem Studio Museum in Harlem 1982-87; mem Westchester Bd Planned Parenthood 1987-; bd mem, Graduate School of City University of New York. **HOME ADDRESS:** 11 Salem Dr, Scarsdale, NY 10583. **BUSINESS ADDRESS:** Vice Pres Investment Banking, Morgan Stanley & Co Inc, 1251 Avenue of the Americas, New York, NY 10020.

CARMAN, EDWIN G.
Elected official. **PERSONAL:** Born Feb 13, 1951, New Brunswick, NJ; married Pamela M Vaughan. **EDUCATION:** Rutgers Univ, BA 1974. **CAREER:** Middlesex Cty Coll Found, bd mem 1980-; Middlesex Cty Econ Oppty Corp, bd mem 1975-, chmn 1981-84; City of New Brunswick, councilman 1975, council pres 1987. **ORGANIZATIONS:** Aide to the speaker of the house NJ Gen Assembly 1979-81; mem American Council of Young Political Leaders; bd mem NJ Foster Grandparents 1986. **HONORS/ACHIEVEMENTS:** Political Action Awd New Brunswick Area NAACP 1983. **BUSINESS ADDRESS:** Councilmember, City of New Brunswick, 78 Bayard St, New Brunswick, NJ 08901.

CARMICHAEL, BENJAMIN G.
Educator. **PERSONAL:** Born Jul 07, 1938, Atlanta, GA; married Dorothy; children: Christopher, Jennifer. **EDUCATION:** San Francisco St Coll, BA 1963; Univ of CA, MA 1972. **CAREER:** CA State Univ, prof 1969-; US Comm on Porno, princ invest; Transit Robby Study, Univ of CA, asst proj dir 1968-70; Univ of San Francisco, lecturer 1968-69; Hunters Pt Comm Devel Proj, proj dir 1966-68. **ORGANIZATIONS:** Dir Crim Just Admin Prgm CA St U; consul Law Enforce Assis Admin; advis bd me Admin of Just Prgm Ohlone Jr Coll Alpha Phi Alpha; Natl UrbanLeague; Natl Coun on Cr & Delinq Youth Cr in Urban Comm, St Hustlers & Their Crimes, Crime & Delinq Vol 21, 1975; The Hunters Pt Riot, Pol of theFrust, Issues in Crime, Vol 4 1969. **HONORS/ACHIEVEMENTS:** Fellow Natl Inst of Mental HlthUniv of CA 1966-68. **MILITARY SERVICE:** AUS 1957. **BUSINESS ADDRESS:** 25800 Hillary St, Hayward, CA 94542.

CARMICHAEL, CAROLE A.
Journalist. **PERSONAL:** Born Jul 09, 1950, Brooklyn, NY. **EDUCATION:** NY U, BA 1972. **CAREER:** Chicago Tribune, former careers editor; Clmb Coll Chicago, instr journalism 1978-79; Fairchild Publ Inc NY, news reporter 1976; UPI Omaha & NY, news reporter 1973-76; Stephen Decatur Jr High School, English tchr 1972-73; Philadelphia Daily News, news reporter. **ORGANIZATIONS:** Contrib wrtr Working Wmn Mag 1977-; contrib wrtr Essence Mag 1979; pres Chicago Assn of Blk Jrnlsts 1978-80; mem bd of dir YWCA Metro Chicago 1978-79. **HONORS/ACHIEVEMENTS:** Adv Study Fellow Econ for Jrnlsts Brkngs Instn Wash 1978; slctd as 1 of 50 ftr ldrs of Am Ebony Mag 1978; Sojrnr Truth Awd Nat Assn of Negro Bus & Professional Wmn NY 1980; Comm Serv Awd Nat Assn of Negro Bus & Professional Wmn Chicago 1980. **BUSINESS ADDRESS:** Philadelphia Daily News, PO Box 7788, Philadelphia, PA 19101.

CARMICHAEL, LEE HAROLD
Athlete. **PERSONAL:** Born Sep 22, 1949, Jacksonville, FL. **EDUCATION:** So Univ Coll. **CAREER:** Philadelphia Eagles, wide receiver. **HONORS/ACHIEVEMENTS:** Leads in most consec games receptions 112 & pass receiving yd NFL; played in Pro Bowl 1973, 1978, 1979; "Sporting News" NFC All-stars. **BUSINESS ADDRESS:** Philadelphia Eagles, Vet Stad Broad St & Pattison A, Philadelphia, PA 19148.

CARMICHAEL, STOKELY
Civil rights organizer and political activist. **PERSONAL:** Born Jun 29, 1941, Port-of-Spain, Trinidad and Tobago;son of Adolphus and Mabel F; married Miriam Makeba, Apr 1968 (divorced). **EDUCATION:** Howard University, BA, 1964. **CAREER:** Student Nonviolent Coordinating Committee (SNCC), Atlanta, GA, organizer, 1964-66, chairman, 1966-67; Black Panthers, Oakland, CA, prime minister, 1967-69. **HONORS/ACHIEVEMENTS:** Author of Black Power:The Politics of Liberation in America, Random House, 1967; author of Stokely Speaks: Black Power Back to Pan-Africanism, Random House, 1971; LLD, Shaw University. **BUSINESS ADDRESS:** Stokely Carmichael, c/o Random House, 201 East 50th Street, New York, NY 10022. *

CARNEGIE, RANDOLPH DAVID
Business executive. **PERSONAL:** Born Jan 23, 1952, Kingston, Jamaica;son of Anthony C Carnegie and Nola E Lindo. **EDUCATION:** Franklin and Marshall Coll, BA 1974; Pace Univ, MBA 1981. **CAREER:** Dow Jones & Co, account rep 1974-75; Time, Inc, account rep 1975-81; Conoco, Inc, senior analyst 1981-86; director T.A.G. Productions 1986. **ORGANIZATIONS:** NBMBAA - Houston Chapter, president 1985-86; Natl Conference Co-Chairmna NBMBAA 1988. **BUSINESS ADDRESS:** Carnegie, PO Box 1012, Bellaire, TX 77401-1012.

CARNELL, LOUGENIA LITTLEJOHN
Program analyst. **PERSONAL:** Born Mar 12, 1947, Memphis, TN; children: Gizele Montrece. **EDUCATION:** Dept of Agr Grad Sch; Catholic U; Univ of DC Chester. **CAREER:** Dept of Energy, prog analyst; Dept of Energy, personal asst to dep asst adminstr 1977-78; Interagency Council for Minority Business Enterprise Dept of Commerce, prsnl asst to exec dir 1975-76; Staff Chaplin Mil Dist Wash DC, admin sec steno 1973-75; MEECN Systems Engineering Office Def Communications Agency Wash DC, div sec steno 1971-73. **ORGANIZATIONS:** Mem Fed Women's Prof 1978-; 1st chmn Dept of Energy Task Force On Concerns of Minority Women 1979-80; mem Nat Council of Career Women 1979-; Nat mem Smithsonian Assos 1979-; med asst vol ARC Alexandria Chap 1973-76. **HONORS/ACHIEVEMENTS:** Key to City New Orleans 1975; recital WTOP-TV Wash DC 1975; cert & 3-yr serv pin ARC Alexandria Chap 1976; pub poetry & prose; 1st female in 108 yrs to be mem of bd of & trustees Mt Olive Bapt Ch Arlington 1977; first chmn Dept of Energy Task Force on Concerns of Minority Women Wash DC 1979; Peopleon the Move Black Enterprise Mag 1979; designated to address DOE-FWPMs Nat FEW Conf Seattle 1979; Women in Energy Newsletter 1979; cert of participation IL Ofc of Minority Bus Enterprise Statewide Annual Conf 1979; observance of black history month Prog Adv Dept of Energy. **BUSINESS ADDRESS:** 2000 M St NW, Washington, DC 20416.

CARNEY, ALFONSO LINWOOD, JR.
Attorney. **PERSONAL:** Born Aug 07, 1949, Norfolk, VA; married Cassandra E Henderson MD; children: Alison Lynette. **EDUCATION:** Trinity Coll Hartford CT, BA 1971; Univ of VA Sch of Law, JD 1974. **CAREER:** General Foods Corp, asst div counsel 1974-78, Washington counsel 1978-81, intl counsel 1981-86, sr intl counsel 1987-. **ORGANIZATIONS:** Mem Natl Bar Assoc 1976-, Amer Bar Assoc 1980-; chmn Law Dept Recruiting Comm 1983-85; mem Law Dept Mgmt Comm 1985; bd of dirs Volunteer Serv Bureau of Westchester 1985-. **HONORS/ACHIEVEMENTS:** Earl Warren Fellow Legal Defense & Educ Fund; Black Achiever Awd Harlem YMCA 1985; Financial Achievement Awd General Foods Corp 1986. **BUSINESS ADDRESS:** Sr International Counsel, General Foods Corp, 250 North St, White Plains, NY 10625.

CARNEY, CALLIE I.
Housing manager. **PERSONAL:** Born Jul 12, 1934, Alabama; married James; children: Kim, David, Joseph, Shrielle, Carolyn, James, Mary, Richard. **EDUCATION:** Sacramento City Coll, 1970-72. **CAREER:** Hsng & Redevel Agy, housing mgr; Sacramento Housing & Redevel Agy, community serv coor 1974-80. **ORGANIZATIONS:** Past consult mem Urban League; consumer rep & Sacramento Health Serv Corp 1973-; past v chmn bd Sacramento City Schs Vol 1960-; v pres mem Nat Comn on Consumer Law 1974-76; Sacramento City & County Liaison for Comp Employment & Training Act 1974-; charter mem Scaramento Nat Council of Negro Women; mem NAACP; past pres Upward Bound UC Davis Community Rep NAACP; cand City Council Dist 5; consumer mem Co Health Council; mem State Hypertension Prog; chmn Comm Adv Group on UCD Med Center Sacramento; trainer United Way Planning & Goal Setting; mem of Trustees United Way; office of Criminal Justice Proposal Review Comm; gov's adv commn on Urban & Problems; comm on Child Abuse; div Nursing Adv Comm CA State Univ DD. **HONORS/ACHIEVEMENTS:** Maddox Award 1972. **BUSINESS ADDRESS:** Rm 205 915 I St, City Hall, Sacramento, CA 95814.

CARNEY, ROBERT MATTHEW
Physician. **PERSONAL:** Born Feb 28, 1928, Steubenville, OH; married Loretta; children: Ruby, Darla, Wendi. **EDUCATION:** Univ of HI, attended; Univ of MI, attended; Fisk Univ, BA 1952; Meharry Med Coll, MD 1958; Mercy Hosp, intern 1958-59. **CAREER:** Private practice, physician. **ORGANIZATIONS:** Bd dir Brookhaven Nursing Home; staff sec Grinnel Gen Hosp; professional chmn Cty Chap Amer Cancer Soc, Poweshiek Cty Med Examiner; clinical tutorial staff Grinnel-Rush Med Students; assoc prof Alcohol/Drug Abuse Counselors; mem Poweshiek Cty Mental Health Assoc; lecturer HS Sex Ed; preceptor Univ IA Med Students; mem Amer Acad Family Physicians 1963-, Poweshiek Cty Med Soc 1959-, IA Family Practice Club, Amer Legion, United Presbyterian Church, Amer Bowling Assoc, Oakland Acres Golf Club; team physician HS Football 1960-, Army Tennis Team 1948-49. **HONORS/ACHIEVEMENTS:** Dr of the Day IA House & Senate 1976-77; Citizen Awd Prog 1969. **MILITARY SERVICE:** AUS 1946-49. **BUSINESS ADDRESS:** Family Physician, Box 109, 821 Broad St, Grinnell, IA 50112.

CAROLINE, J. C.
Football coach. **PERSONAL:** Born Jan 17, 1933, Warrenton, GA; married Laverne Dillon; children: Jayna. **EDUCATION:** BS 1967. **CAREER:** Univ of IL Athletics Assn, asst ftball coach 1966-; Chicago Bears, 1956-; Montreal Allouetts, 1955-56. **ORGANIZATIONS:** Bd of dir Don Moyers Boys Club. **HONORS/ACHIEVEMENTS:** All-am Football 1653; All Professional 1956. **BUSINESS ADDRESS:** 123 Assembly Hall, Champaign, IL 61820.

CARPENTER, ANN M.
Chiropractor, educator. **PERSONAL:** Born Jul 01, 1934, New York, NY; daughter of James Gowdy and Charity Gowdy; divorced; children: Karen, Marie. **EDUCATION:** City Coll of New York, MA/BS Educ 1956-60; NY Chiropractic Coll, DC 1978; Univ of Bridgeport CT, MS Nutrition 1980. **CAREER:** Harlem Prep Sch prin 1975; Harlem Prep Sch, admn asst tchr educ & curriculum 1968-75; Haaren Hs NY, chmn Eng dept 1967-68; Haaren HS NY, tchr Eng 1957-67; Beacon NY, chiropractor 1980. **ORGANIZATIONS:** Mem Natl Assn of Secondary Sch Admin 1979; mem NY Assn Mem Black Educators II 1978-;

mem Amer Chiropractic Assn 1975-; Bergen Co NJ Urban League of Bergen Co 1978; NY State Chiropractic Assoc 1979-; Amer Black Chiropractors Assoc 1985-; mem NY State Bd for Chiropractic 1985; pres NYSCA Dist Nine 1985-86, 1986-87; Chair NY State Bd for Chiropractic, 1988-89 . **HONORS/ACHIEVEMENTS:** Community service award Harlem Prep Sch 1976; youth guidance award Bergen Co Negro Bus & Professional Women 1974; Citizen of the Year Awards in Black; Service to profession, NY State Chiropractic Association, 1988. **BUSINESS ADDRESS:** Chiropractor, Beacon Chiropractic Office, 125 South Chestnut St, Beacon, NY 12508.

CARPENTER, JOSEPH, II
Educator. **PERSONAL:** Born Jul 21, 1937, Aliceville, AL; children: Martin, Brenda, Richard. **EDUCATION:** MATC, AA 1965; Marquette U, BA 1967; Fisk U, 1968-69; Marquette U, PhD 1970; Univ of IA, Post Doctorate 1972. **CAREER:** Univ of WI, prof Afro-Educ, soc research 1972-. **ORGANIZATIONS:** Dir Carthage Coll 1970-72; asst prof Lehman Coll Bronx Summer 1971; NEA Fellow Marquette Univ 1968-70; chmn City of Milwaukee Bd of Election Commr; chmn bd dir Northcott Youth Serv Bur for Prevention of Juvenile Delinq; chmn Univ of WI Afro-am Stud Comm Rel Comm; exec bd mem Social Studies Council of WI; consult State of NJ Dept of Ed; mem Phi Delta Kappa; alpha Psi Alpha; Milwaukee Frontiers Internat; bd dir Nat Council for Black Child Develop Inc. **HONORS/ACHIEVEMENTS:** Author of numerous articles; Distinguished Christian Fellowship Award for Comm Serv 1973; distinguished political serv Award 1974. **MILITARY SERVICE:** USAF comm spl 1955-60. **BUSINESS ADDRESS:** Dept of Afro Am Studies, U of WI, Milwaukee, WI 53201.

CARPENTER, LEWIS
Elected govt official. **PERSONAL:** Born Feb 01, 1928, Brantley, AL; married Myrtice Bryant. **EDUCATION:** Covington Cty Training School, AA 1956; LBW Jr Coll, Acct 1982. **CAREER:** Covington Cty Bank, custodian 1959-. **ORGANIZATIONS:** Mem Masonic Rose of Sharon Lodge 1965-, Advisory Comm LBW Jr Coll 1970-, Covington Cty Sheriff Reserve 1970-; mem advisory Local Draft Bd 1980-; advisory OCAP Comm 1982-. **HONORS/ACHIEVEMENTS:** 1st black City Councilman Andalusia City Council 1984. **MILITARY SERVICE:** AUS 1952-54 18 mos in Korea. **HOME ADDRESS:** 210 Lowe Ave, Andalusia, AL 36420.

CARPENTER, WILLIAM ARTHUR, II
Writer. **PERSONAL:** Born Oct 14, 1965, Fayettesville, NC; son of William Carpenter, Sr and Via Maria Randall-Carpenter. **EDUCATION:** Washington Saturday College, Certificate 1984-85; Univ of Dijon France, Certificate 1985; The Amer Univ, AA 1987. **CAREER:** Natl Conservative Political Action Commn, fund raiser 1983-84; Dept of Labor, claims reviewer 1984-85; Embassy of France, information asst 1986; Smithsonian-Natl Museum of Amer History, exhibit writer 1987; Bush/Quayle Campaign, Washington DC, campaign worker 1988-89; WYCB Radio, Washington DC, substitiute disc jockey 1988; Vietnam Veterans of Amer, Washington DC, press asst 1987; ILF Publications, Washington DC, features writer 1989-. **ORGANIZATIONS:** Assoc member, The Dramatists Guild 1984-86, Authors League of Amer 1984-86; member, Amer Film Inst 1985-86; editor/illustrator Curriculum Develop Ministry of ET 1985; instructor/tutor Evangel Temple Sch of the Bible 1985-; asst dir Tutoring Ministry of Evangel Temple 1987-88; editor, Gospel Highlights Newsletter, Mt Rainier MD, 1987-; professional member, Gospel Music Assn, Nashville TN 1987-. **HONORS/ACHIEVEMENTS:** Guest speaker on "In Our Lives" WDVM-TV channel 9 1983; Achievement Awd of Outstanding Serv Dept of Labor 1984; "Pretty Boy" Amer Poetry Anthology 1985; "Les Sortileges d'Amour & the Backyard" Amer Collegiate Poetry Anthology 1986. **HOME ADDRESS:** 4006 Bald Hill Terrace, Mitchellville-Willow Grove, MD 20716. **BUSINESS ADDRESS:** Features Writer, ILF Publications, Washington, DC.

CARPER, GLORIA G.
Educator. **PERSONAL:** Born Aug 10, 1930, Montclair, NJ; widowed; children: Gladyce, Terri. **EDUCATION:** Morgan State Coll, BS 1950; WV Univ, MA 1971. **CAREER:** WV Dept of Welfare, social worker 1961-64; WV Dept of Mental Health, welfare supvr 1964-67, admin asst med div 1967-72; Day Care Center, Mentally Retarded Children, Dept of Mental Health, dir 1972-73; WV State Coll, acting dir of guidance & placement, foreign student advisory, counselor for devel serv 1982-. **ORGANIZATIONS:** Mem natl Assoc for Retarded Children Inc, Kanawha Assoc for Retarded Children Inc; past pres Charleston Inst; mem Delta Sigma Theta, Charleston Inst Chapt, The Links Inc; bd mem Charleston Oppty Indust Ctr Inc; organist 1st Bapt Church. **HONORS/ACHIEVEMENTS:** Mother of the Year 1st Bapt Church 1972. **BUSINESS ADDRESS:** Foreign Student Adv, Couns, West Virginia State Coll, Developmental Serv, Institute, WV 25112.

CARR, CHARLES V.
Business executive. **PERSONAL:** Born Nov 09, 1903, Clarksville, TX; married Hortense; children: Carol, Charles, Leah, Cathleen. **EDUCATION:** Fisk U; Cleve State U, JD; Central State U, hon LlD. **ORGANIZATIONS:** Trustee Cleveland RTA; former mem Cleveland City Council 17th Ward; pres Quincy Savings & Savings & Loan Co 1952; Private Practice of Law 1929-; founder Dunbar Life Ins Company; mem John Harlan Law Club; clevel bar Assn mem Greater Cleve Growth Assn; Cleve Citizens League; life mem Elks; Masons; life mem NAACP. **BUSINESS ADDRESS:** 1380 Jasel Rd, Cleveland, OH 44106.

CARR, CLARA B.
Data entry inspector. **PERSONAL:** Born Aug 31, 1948, Opelika, AL; daughter of Ben Baker and Princella Ingram; married Lonnie Carr Jr, Jan 20, 1968 (divorced); children: Amy Arletha Carr, Amaris Artreja Carr. **EDUCATION:** Opelika State Technical Jr Coll, Business, 1966-67. **CAREER:** Ampex Corp, Opelika, AL, record insp II. **ORGANIZATIONS:** Past grand matron, Silver Queen Grand Chapter, Order of the Eastern Star, 1986-89; worthy matron, Queen Esther Chapter, Order of the Eastern Star, 1980-; food share unit clerk, Food Share, 1989; financial sec, Nazareth Baptist Church, 1988; sec, Mitchell Quarter Water System, 1983-88. **HOME ADDRESS:** Route 5, Box 202, Opelika, AL 36801.

CARR, JOSEPHUS CORNELIUS
Surgeon, banker, financier, teacher. **PERSONAL:** Born Nov 19, 1902, Chicago, IL; married Nellie & Gyndolyn Craige. **EDUCATION:** Howard U, BS (magna cum laude) 1921, MD 1925; Seton Hall Univ NY Med Coll, Post-grad & Research in Surgery & Coloproctology; Harvard Univ Med Sch, post-grad; Sir Reginald Watson Jones London, Ageis. **CAREER:** Montgomery, AL, surgeon in chief; Sev Hosp Newark, staff. **ORGANIZATIONS:** Founder dir & dir emeritus City Nat Bank Newark; founder & dir Bethune Savings & Loan Bank Newark; pres Six-O-Eight High St Inc; mem NJ Med Soc; Essex Co Med Soc; NJ State Med Assn; NMA; AMA; Intestinal Research Inst; Intl Acad of Proctology; Am Soc of Abdominal Surgery Mason 32 Degree; Elks; Knights of Pythias; Calanthes Atlanta Life & United Life Ins Co; past treas & pres Nat Chi Delta Mu Frat; mem Alpha Phi Alpha Frat; Sigma Pi PhiFrat; Boys Club of Am; Frontiers of Am; Urban League; life mem NAACP. **HONORS/ACHIEVEMENTS:** Who's Who in Medicines; Who's Who In E; Who's Who Among Black Am; most outstanding black physician State of NJ; recipient of numerous awards; recipient of 8awards Seton Hall U; author, numours publ.

CARR, KENNY
Professional athlete. **PERSONAL:** Born Aug 15, 1955, Washington, DC; married Adrianna; children: Cameron, Devon Roberts. **EDUCATION:** NC State Univ, 1978. **CAREER:** Los Angeles Lakers, forward 1977-79; Cleveland Cavaliers, forward 1980-81; Detroit Pistons, forward 1981-82; Portland Trail Blazers, forward 1982-. **HONORS/ACHIEVEMENTS:** 5th highest scorer in the nation 266 points a game sr yr NC State; Scored 798 point second only to David Thompson in NC State history; ACC's leading scorer & rebounder as a jr; Selected to the Sporting News 1st team All Amer squad; Gold Medal in Montreal with the US Olympic team 1976. **BUSINESS ADDRESS:** Portland Trail Blazers, 700 NE Multnomah St, Portland, OR 97232.

CARR, LENFORD
City official. **PERSONAL:** Born Sep 21, 1938, Haywood Co Bural, TN; married Ella R Porter; children: Vincent Louis, Bridgett Genese. **EDUCATION:** Knoxville Coll, 1957-58. **CAREER:** Humboldt City Park Comm, mem 1977-85; Humboldt City School Board, mem/secretary 1979-88. **ORGANIZATIONS:** Mem City Schools-Transportation-Building and Calendar Comm; mem Morning Star Baptist Church; mem NAACP Humboldt Chapt; pres Humboldt Demo Concerned Citizens Club; mem Gibson Co Demo Exec. **HONORS/ACHIEVEMENTS:** Plant Mgrs Awd Martin Marietta Aluminum Sales 1970; culinary serv Morning Star Baptist Church 1977; community serv NAACP-, IBPOWELK 1980-83; ed boardsmanship Humboldt City Schools Board 1983; Outstanding Citizen Political Involvement AKA Sorority 1983. **MILITARY SERVICE:** AUS Sp4 1961-64. **HOME ADDRESS:** 94 Maple St, Humboldt, TN 38343.

CARR, LEONARD G.
Clergyman. **PERSONAL:** Born Oct 25, 1902, Bridgewater, VA; married Juanita; children: Leonita. **EDUCATION:** Lincoln U, STB 1933; VA Theol Sem, DD 1949; Lincoln Univ PA, 1950. **CAREER:** Vine Meml Bapt Ch, founder pastor. **ORGANIZATIONS:** Treas, Nat Bapt Conv USA 20 Yrs; pres PA Bapt State Conv 1945; mem Eastern Keystone Assn; Home Mission Bd; YMCA; Lincoln Alumni Assn; Berean Inst; bd dirs Better Family Planning; Mason; mem Phi Beta Sigma. **HONORS/ACHIEVEMENTS:** Numerous honors & awards. **BUSINESS ADDRESS:** Vine Meml Bapt Ch, 5600 Girard Ave, Philadelphia, PA.

CARR, PERCY L.
Basketball coach. **PERSONAL:** Born Nov 19, 1941, Longview, TX; married Fredella Scott; children: Kacy. **EDUCATION:** CA State Univ, BS, Phys Educ 1968, MA, Phys Educ 1972. **CAREER:** San Jose City Coll, head basketball coach; Stanford Univ, asst basketball coach 1974-75; Edison HS, coach 1970-74; Tulare Union HS, 1968-70; Edison HS, teacher, asst vice principal & dean of boys 1970-74; Tulare Union HS, teacher & coach 1968-70; has worked in various basketball camps & clinics 1971-74. **ORGANIZATIONS:** Mem Masonic Lodge; Alpha Phi Alpha. **HONORS/ACHIEVEMENTS:** All metro coach of the Year, 1971; Coach of the Year, Central CA Basketball Coaches Assn, 1974; All metro coach of the year Fresno Bee 1974; Coach of the Year, 1976; Outstanding Teacher-Coach Award, 1988. **BUSINESS ADDRESS:** San Jose City College, 2800 Moorpark Ave, San Jose, CA 95128.

CARR, PRESSLEY RODNEY
Supervisor. **PERSONAL:** Born Oct 09, 1930, Cleveland, NC; married Sallie M Hargrove; children: Pressley Jr, Mondalyn, Bettye, Gregory. **CAREER:** Fiber Ind Inc, supr 11 yrs. **ORGANIZATIONS:** Deacon Allen's Temple Presb Ch; mem Ctrl Piedmont Criminal Plng Agy; mem Cleveland Town Bd 4 yrs; mem BSA 1966-69. **HONORS/ACHIEVEMENTS:** Obtained 1st full time pol ofcr for Cleveland 1974; 1st black mem Town Bd.

CARR, RODERICH MARION
Investment banker. **PERSONAL:** Born Nov 05, 1956, Birmingham, AL; son of Edgar A Carr; married Charlotte Bland. **EDUCATION:** Johns Hopkins Univ, BSEE 1978; Univ of Chicago Grad Sch of Business, MBA Finance & Marketing 1980. **CAREER:** Salomon Brothers Inc, vice pres 1980-. **ORGANIZATIONS:** Vice pres 1978-80, mem Natl Black MBA Assoc 1978-; speaker/lecturer Jobs for Youth 1986-. **HOME ADDRESS:** 2437 N Janssen Ave, Chicago, IL 60614.

CARR, SANDRA JEAN IRONS
Union president. **PERSONAL:** Born Jul 17, 1940, Middlesboro, KY; divorced. **EDUCATION:** Kentucky State Univ, Frankfort KY, BS 1960; Purdue Univ, West Lafayette IN, MAT 1965; Indiana Univ, Gary IN, MA plus 30 1980. **CAREER:** Gary Teachers Union Gary, IN, div pres 1971-; Gary Sch System Gary, IN, tchr 1961-71; State of OH Div Aid for Aged, social caseworker 1960-61. **ORGANIZATIONS:** Vp IN Fedn of Tchers 1971-; vice pres Am Fedn of Tchrs 1974-; trustee 1976-79, treas 1986 Lake Area United Way bd of trustees; co-chairperson/mem com NAACP 1977; Gamma Psi Omega Chap AKA; mem mayoral appt Gary Commn on the Status of Women; co-dir Christian Educ New Revelation Baptist Church Gary 1980-; mem Citizens Task Force on St Gangs & School Discipline 1983-; sec Gary Educ Devel Found 1984-; pres Mental Health Assoc in Lake County 1985-. **BUSINESS ADDRESS:** President, Gary Teachers Union, 1301 Virginia St, Gary, IN 46407.

CARR, VIRGIL H.
President/CEO. **PERSONAL:** Married Mygene. **EDUCATION:** Iowa State Univ, BA education-speech 1958-62; George Warren Brown School of Social Work-Washington University, MSW community development and administration. **CAREER:** Neighborhood Centers OEO Program, dir 1961-68, comm organizer 1961-68; Pruitt Igoe Housing, comm organizer 1961-68; Family Service of Omaha, director, multi-service program 1968-71; United

Charities of Chicago, dir of inner city operations 1970-75, dir of personnel 1975-76,assoc exec dir 1976-79; Family Service of Detroit and Wayne County, president 1979-85; United Way of Chicago, president and chief executive officer 1985-. **ORGANIZATIONS:** Appointed to Mayor Washington's Committee on Infant Mortality 1986; appointed to state advisory committee for the Illinois Dept of Public Aid 1986; HEW, nat'l consultant parent-child centers, nat'l task force to develope parent-child center standards; NIMH, nat'l consultant; MI Voluntary Agency Group Plan for Unemployment Compensation, Inc, board mem; Agape House, board mem; Family Financial Counseling Services, board mem; Black Human Service Administrators, co-founder and chairman; White House Conference on Families, governor's appointee; Select Committee of Childern, Youth, Families, appointed by Congressman SandorLevin to chair committee to plan for site hearings. **HONORS/ACHIEVEMENTS:** Family Service America, Grady B Murdock Humanitarian award 1979; Metropolitan Detroit Area, executive of the year 1983; George Warren Brown School of Social Work, Washington Univ, distinguished alumni award 1984; Chicago Committee for Excellence award 1985. **BUSINESS ADDRESS:** President/CEO, United Way of Chicago, 104 S Michigan Ave, 11th Floor, Chicago, IL 60603.

CARREATHERS, KEVIN R.
Educator. **PERSONAL:** Born Feb 26, 1957, Denison, TX; son of Raymond E Carreathers and Ernestine Thurston-Carreathers. **EDUCATION:** North Texas State Univ, BS 1979; Prairie View A&M Univ, MEd 1980. **CAREER:** Depauw Univ, asst to the dean of students 1980-82; East Texas State Univ, head resident advisor 1982-83; Texas A&M Univ, student dev specialist 1983-88; Texas A&M University, Coordinator Multicultural Services 1988-. **ORGANIZATIONS:** Life mem Alpha Phi Alpha 1976-; personnel admin TX Assoc of Univ and Coll Student 1982-; mem TX Assoc of Black Personnel in Higher Education 1982-; mem-minority recruitment and retention comm Coord Bd Texas Coll and Univ System 1985-88; T.A.M.U. National Youth Sports Program Advisory Board, Minority Leadership Development Advisory Board. **HONORS/ACHIEVEMENTS:** Certificate of Appreciation TX Assoc of Coll and Univ Personnel Administrators 1985; Certificate of Appreciation Prairie View A&M Univ 1985; Certificate ofRecognition Delta Sigma Pi 1986; Certificate of Appreciation Delta Sigma Theta Sor Inc 1987; Houston Young Black Achiever Human Enrichment Program 1988; John J. Koldus Faculty/Staff Award, Texas A&M University 1989. **BUSINESS ADDRESS:** Coordinator, Multicultural Services Center, Texas A&M University, 151 Bizzell-West, College Station, TX 77843.

CARREKER, WILLIAM, JR.
Educator. **PERSONAL:** Born Oct 17, 1936, Detroit, MI. **EDUCATION:** City Coll of San Francisco, AA 1964; Univ of CA, AB 1966, MSW 1968, MPH 1971; Univ of CA at Berkeley. **CAREER:** Columbia Univ School of Social Work, asst dir of admissions, financial aid officer; Golden State Medical Assn, proj dir 1972-73; Univ of CA Medical Center, staff asso 1971-72; Tufts-Delta Health Center, intern 1971; Alameda County Welfare Dept, child welfare worker 1968-70. **ORGANIZATIONS:** Vol couns Jr Ldrshp Prgm 1968; CA State Sch for Deaf & Blind 1971; Offenders Aid & Restoration 1974-75; Nat Assn of Black Soc Wrkrs 1974-77; publ article Comm Hlth Agency Partic in Plng; A Univ Ambulatory Care Prgm; contbd papers Am Pub Hlth Assn 1972. **MILITARY SERVICE:** 1955-59. **BUSINESS ADDRESS:** 622 W 113th St, New York, NY 10025.

CARRIER, CLARA L. DEGAY
Educator. **PERSONAL:** Born Jan 15, 1939, Weeks Island, LA; divorced; children: Glenda, Melvin T, Marcus W, Robby Bethel, Clarence (dec), Patrick R, Dawn Nicole. **EDUCATION:** Dillard Univ 1956-57; Univ of Southwestern Univ 1976-80. **CAREER:** JHH School Student Body, pres 1955-56; JB Livingston Elem PTC, sec 1961-67; Les Aimu Civic & Social Club, sec 1974-; Iberia Parish School Bd, exec mem at large 1979-82; Iberia Parish School Bd, 1st vice pres 1985-. **ORGANIZATIONS:** Mem NAACP 1963-65; teacher's aide Acadiana Nursery Head Start 1965; teacher's aide SMILE CAA Head Start 1970-76; social worker SMILE CAA 1976-79; teacher SMILE CAA 1979-; suprv New Iberia Recreation Dept 1980-; mem LA Caucus of Black School Bd Mems 1980-85; bd of dir Bayou Girls Scout Council 1983-84; mem LA School Bd Assoc, Natl School Bd Assoc. **HONORS/ACHIEVEMENTS:** USL Honor Soc Psi Beta Honr Soc 1978; Service to Youth Awd Park Elem 1982-84; The President's Awd Park Elem 1982-84; Cert of Recognition for Contrib tothe Comm Zeta Phi Beta Sor 1983; Omega's Citizen of the Year Omega Rho Omicron Chap 1983. **HOME ADDRESS:** 717 Elizabeth St, New Iberia, LA 70560. **BUSINESS ADDRESS:** 1st Vice President, Iberia Parish School Bd, 200 School Bd Dr, New Iberia, LA 70560.

CARRINGTON, CHRISTINE H.
Psychologist. **PERSONAL:** Born Jun 07, 1941, Palatka, FL; divorced; children: Michael, David, Lisa. **EDUCATION:** Howard Univ, BS 1962, MS 1965; Univ of MD, PhD Psychology 1979. **CAREER:** DC Public Schs, sch psychologist 1966-70, consult sch psychol 1971-72; Bowie State Coll, instr 1970-74; Fed City Coll, asst prof 1972; Bowie State Coll, rsch consult 1974-75; Howard Univ Hosp, Psychiatric Inst of Wash, Psychiatric Inst of Mont Co, consult psychologist privileges; Dept of Human Resources Washington DC, consulting psychologist; Howard Univ Couns Serv, couns psychologist. **ORGANIZATIONS:** Couns therapist Family Life Ctr Columbia MD; psychologist Rsch Team Howard Univ Med Sch; mem Amer Psychol Assn; Amer Assn for Psychologists in Private Practice; Assn of Counseling Ctr Training Dirs 1981-; Natl Assn Sch Psychol 1970-79; Amer Assn Univ Profs 1972-; Natl Assn Black Psychol 1970-; DC Psychol Assn 1969; bd of dirs Assn of Psychology Internship Ctrs; liaison to bd of APA; mem DC Assn of Black Psychol 1972-. **BUSINESS ADDRESS:** Cons Psychologist, HowardUniv, Counseling Center, Washington, DC 20059.

CARRINGTON, JAMES
Government official. **PERSONAL:** Born Apr 17, 1904, St Louis, MO; married Eysett; children: 2 Children. **EDUCATION:** Howard U. **CAREER:** Dist #67, St Louis, state rep 1972-; Moringing Globe, photographer. **ORGANIZATIONS:** Dir Yth Bridga. **HONORS/ACHIEVEMENTS:** Nom outsdng photographer Morning Globe.

CARROL, RAOUL LORD
Attorney. **PERSONAL:** Born Mar 16, 1950, Washington, DC; married Elizabeth Jane Coleman; children: Alexandria Nicole. **EDUCATION:** Morgan State Coll, BS 1972; St John's Univ Sch of Law, JD 1975; Georgetown Univ Law Center, 1980-81. **CAREER:** Dept of Justice, asst US atty 1979-80; US Bd of Veterans Appeals, assoc mem 1980-81; Hart Carroll & Chavers, partner 1981-86; Bishop Cook Purcell & Reynolds, partner 1986-. **ORGANIZATIONS:** Mem Amer1975-, Washington 1976-, Natl 1977- Bar Assocs; pres Black Asst US Attorney Assoc 1981-83; dir Conwest USA 1982-84; vice chmn Amer Ctr for Intl Leadership 1985-. **HONORS/ACHIEVEMENTS:** Outstanding Young Man of Amer 1978; "After the Dust Settles, Other Modes of Relief," The Advocate Vol 10 No 6 1978; listed in Who's Who in Amer Law 1984, Who's Who in the World 1986. **MILITARY SERVICE:** AUS capt 1975-79; Joint Serv Commendation Medal, Army Commendation Medal.

CARROLL, ANNIE HAYWOOD
Social service. **PERSONAL:** Born Sep 14, 1904, Raleigh, NC; married Richard Alexander Carroll Jr; children: Howard Livingston. **EDUCATION:** Fisk Univ; Shaw Univ, BA 1928. **CAREER:** Wake Cty Sch NC, teacher 1928-41; Acct Div Bureau of Empl Sec Dept Labor and Ind Harrisburg PA, clerk, supr 1943-69. **ORGANIZATIONS:** Exec com RSVP 1972-75; vol Radio Announcer Station WMSP Harrisburg PA 1973-74; mgr Capital Presby Sr Ctr 1984-. **HONORS/ACHIEVEMENTS:** Elder First Presbyterian Church of Honolulu 1987. **HOME ADDRESS:** 2333 Kapiolani Blvd #304, Honolulu, HI 96826.

CARROLL, CHARLENE O.
Business executive. **PERSONAL:** Born Apr 17, 1950, Boston, MA; married Ronald Carroll; children: Kiet, Robyn, Ronald. **EDUCATION:** La Newton Beauty Rama, Diploma 1971; John Delloria, certificate 1973; Chadwicks Masterclass NY, certificate 1979; Bruno's School of Hair Design, diploma 1980; Vidal Sassoon Hair Design, dipl 1980-82; Pivot Point, certificate 1981; Floyd Kenyetta/Fingertips Intl Workshop, certificate 1982; Jingles Intl, diploma 1978/83-84. **CAREER:** Black Hair Olympics Inc, pres 1985; Charlene's Hair Salon Inc, pres. **ORGANIZATIONS:** Platform artist & stylist Revlon Co 1978-79; mem Natl Hairdresser & Cosmotology Assoc 1980-85; traveling consultant Soft Sheen Co 1984; consultant Amer Beauty Products Co 1985. **HONORS/ACHIEVEMENTS:** Honorable recognition Greater Boston Cosmetologist Assoc 1975; honorable recognition Black Hair Olympics Silver Spring MD 1982; stylist of the year Black Hair Olympics Inc Washington 1984. **BUSINESS ADDRESS:** President, Charlenes Hair Salon, Inc, 634 Warren St, Roxbury, MA 02119.

CARROLL, CHARLES H.
Personnel officer. **PERSONAL:** Born May 31, 1910, Washington, DC; married Julia E Mack. **EDUCATION:** Howard U, BS 1943. **CAREER:** Univ of MD, personnel officer; Public Empolyees Safety Assn of MD, 3rd vp; City of Coll Park, MD, Councilman. **ORGANIZATIONS:** Mem Elks, Mason, Am Legion, Shriner; mem of Counicl of Gov't; Municpal League of MD; Transp Com of Met of Washington; pres Plutocrats Inc; pres Pub Employees Safety Assn of MD; mem 25 Club Inc. **MILITARY SERVICE:** Usn 1st class spl 1944-45. **BUSINESS ADDRESS:** Personnel Office, U of MD College, Park, MD 20742.

CARROLL, CONSTANCE MARIE
Educational administrator. **PERSONAL:** Born Sep 12, 1945, Baltimore, MD. **EDUCATION:** Duquesne U, BA 1966; Knubly Univ Athens Greece, cert 1967; Univ of Pittsburg, MA 1969; University of Pgh, PhD candidate. **CAREER:** Univ of Pittsburgh, teaching asst dept of classics 1968-69, academic advisor College of Arts and Scis 1969-70, College of Arts and Scis Adv Ctr 1970-71, dir of freshman adv and pre-profl programs College of Arts and Scis 1971-72; Univ of Maine Coll of Arts & Scis, asst dean 1972-73, asst prof of classics 1973-77; Marin Comm College District, interim chancellor 1979-80; Indian Valley Colleges Marin Comm Coll District, president 1977-83. **ORGANIZATIONS:** Mem CA Council for the Humanities; mem adv bd Inst for Leadership Develop; mem adv bd Policy Analysis of CA Education; mem Natl Humanities Faculty; mem CA Postsecondary Educ Comm Task Force on Women and Minorities; evaluator Western Assn of Schools and Colleges; mem Amer Philological Assn, Classical Assn of New England, Vergilian Soc of Amer, Natl Assn of Black Professional Women in Higher Educ, Council of Colleges of Arts & Scis, Comm for the Concerns ofWomen in New England Colls and Univs; bd mem Film Study Ctr of Portland; mem Commonwealth Club of CA, Comm for the Concerns of Women in CA Colls and Univs; mem Council on Black American Affairs Western Region, Assn of CA Comm Coll Administrators. **HONORS/ACHIEVEMENTS:** John Hay Whitney Scholarship Marshall Fellowship in Classics 1968; College of Arts & Scis Distinguished Teaching Awd University of Pgh 1971; Outstanding Educators of America 1975; Who's Who of American Women 1975; Excellence in Education Awd YWCA South Orange County 1984; numerous publications. **BUSINESS ADDRESS:** President, Saddleback College, 28000 Marguerite Parkway, Mission Viejo, CA 92692.

CARROLL, DIAHANN
Actress, singer. **PERSONAL:** Born Jul 17, 1935, Bronx, NY; married Vic Damone; children: Suzanne. **EDUCATION:** Attended NYU. **CAREER:** Starred in motion pictures "Carmen Jones", "Porgy & Bess", "Paris Blues", "Hurry Sundown", "Claudine", TV series "Julia"; featured in "Dynasty" 1984-. **ORGANIZATIONS:** Mem AEA, AFTRA, SAG. **HONORS/ACHIEVEMENTS:** Tony Award for Broadway role in "No Strings" 1962; 2 Emmy Nominations; Entertainer of the Year Cue Mag; Oscar Nomination for "Claudine" 1974; Recip NAACP 8th Image Award (Best Actress) Black Filmmaker's Hall of Fame 1976; Ten Intl Best Dressed List; Patron Performer John F Kennedy Center. **BUSINESS ADDRESS:** c/o Aaron Spelling Prodns, 1041 N Formosa Ave, Los Angeles, CA 90046.

CARROLL, EDWARD GONZALEZ
Educational administration. **PERSONAL:** Born Jan 07, 1910, Wheeling, WV; married Phenola Valentine; children: Edward Jr, Nansi Ethelene. **EDUCATION:** Morgan State Univ, AB 1930; Yale Univ, BD 1933; Columbia Univ, MA 1941. **CAREER:** Nat'l Student YMCA, assoc sec 1945-49; St Marks United Methodist Church, dir of christian ed 1949-53; Epworth United Methodist Church, pastor 1953-55; Sharp St Mem United Methodist Church, pastor 1955-62; Washington Conf Washington Dist, dist superintendent 1962-64; Baltimore Conf Washington W Dist, dist superintendent 1964-68; Marvin Mem United Methodist Church, pastor 1968-72; Boston Area United Methodist church, bishop 1972-80; Morgan Christian Ctr, retired interim dir. **ORGANIZATIONS:** Dir Black Methodists for Church 1972-; trustee Boston Univ 1972-80; hon Boston Univ 1980-; visiting prof and bishop in residence Boston Univ Sch of Theology 1980-81; interim dir Black Methodist for Church Renwal 1981-82; interim dir Morgan Christian Center Morgan St Univ 1983-84; life mem NAACP, Black Methodist for Church Renewal, Common Cuase, Torch Club. **HONORS/ACHIEVEMENTS:** LLD Morgan State Univ 1967; Alumnus of the Year Morgan St Coll Alumni Assoc 1973; DD Barrington Coll 1979; DLitt Univ of MA 1980; Children's Center;

honary trustee The New England Deaconess Hosp 1981.   **MILITARY SERVICE:** AUS chaplain maj 1941-45.

CARROLL, EDWARD M.
Educator.   **PERSONAL:** Born Dec 30, 1916, Corsicana, TX; son of Ezra Carroll and Estella Steward Carroll; married Arnell Lewis, Jul 13, 1941; children: Maria Vorcielle, Ednelvyn Lezette.   **EDUCATION:** Bishop Coll, BS 1939; Columbia U, MA 1952, EdD 1964.   **CAREER:** Educ NYU, prof math 1965-; Dwight Morrow HS NJ, math teacher 1958-65; Bishop Coll TX, asst to pres, dir of pub relations, prof of math 1946-57.   **ORGANIZATIONS:** Mem Mathematical Assn of Amer; Amer Educ Research Assn; Natl Council of Teachers of Math; Amer Math Soc.; mem NY Acad of Sci; trustee Social Serv Found, Englewood, NJ 1966-74; trustee & treas Greater Englewood Housing Corp 1969-; alumni of yr Bishop Coll 1965.   **MILITARY SERVICE:** AUS 1st Sgt 1944-46.   **BUSINESS ADDRESS:** Emeritus Professor of Mathematics Education, New York University, 933 Shimkin Hall, New York, NY 10003.

CARROLL, GEORGE D.
Judge.   **PERSONAL:** Born Jan 06, 1923, Brooklyn, NY; married Janie.   **EDUCATION:** Brooklyn Coll, BA (Cum Laude) 1943; Brooklyn Law School, JD (Cum Laude) 1950.   **CAREER:** Richmond City Council, councilmember 1961; City of Ricmond, mayor 1964; Gov Edmund E Brown, appt judge 1965; Bay Municipal Ct, judge 1970,76,82, retired 1985.   **ORGANIZATIONS:** Mem CA Bar 1953, NY Bar 1950, Jud Council of Natl Bar Assoc, CA Judge Assoc, Amer Bar Assoc, Jud Admin Sect; past pres Richmond Bar Assoc; life mem NAACP.   **HONORS/ACHIEVEMENTS:** John Russwurm Awd 1965; Man of the Year San Francisco Sun Reporter 1964.   **MILITARY SERVICE:** AUS s/sgt 1943-45.

CARROLL, HARRY MILTON
Government official.   **PERSONAL:** Born Aug 03, 1925, Baltimore, MD; married Irma G; children: Barbara Stancil, Joanne, Harry Jr.   **EDUCATION:** State Univ of IA, BS 1951.   **CAREER:** New York City Bd of Standards & Appeals, commr 1973-; New York City Bldg Dept, dep supt chief engr examiner 1961-73; New York City Dept of Pub Works, asst engr 1955-61; New York City Housing Auth, jr engr 1951-55; lic & professional engr NY.   **ORGANIZATIONS:** Mem 100 Black Men Inc; mem New York City Bldg Congress; bd of dir New York City Chap Assn for Help of Retarded Children; mem Kappa Alpha Psi Frat.   **MILITARY SERVICE:** AUS staff sgt 1943-46.   **BUSINESS ADDRESS:** Commissioner, Board of Standards & Appeals, 161 Broadway, New York, NY 10013.

CARROLL, JAMES S.
Attorney.   **PERSONAL:** Born Sep 17, 1945, Brooklyn, NY; son of James Carroll and Mabel Duncan Carroll; married Celia Antonia; children: Jason Sean, Jamaal Samuel.   **EDUCATION:** NY Univ, BA 1966; Howard Law Sch, JD 1970.   **CAREER:** Natl Conf of Black Lawyers, attorney 1970-72; Comm Devel Harlen Assertion of Rights, dir 1972-73; Private Practice, attorney 1973-79; Virgin Islands, asst US Attorney 1979-.   **ORGANIZATIONS:** Mem Nat Conf of Black Lawyers; Nat Bar Assn; Assn of Bar of City of NY.   **HONORS/ACHIEVEMENTS:** Recipient Root-Tilden Scholarship to NY Univ Law Sch; Reginald Heber Smith Fellowship 1970-72.   **BUSINESS ADDRESS:** US Attorney, Federal Bldg, St Thomas, Virgin Islands of the United States 00801.

CARROLL, JOE BARRY
Professional athlete.   **PERSONAL:** Born Jul 24, 1958, Pinebluff, AK.   **EDUCATION:** Purdue, BA 1980.   **CAREER:** Golden State Warrior, center 1980.   **ORGANIZATIONS:** Mem The Sporting News; mem Bay Area Special Olympics Prog.   **HONORS/ACHIEVEMENTS:** Joined Julius Erving & Bobby Jones as only mem of the Century Club; All-Amer his sr year at Purdue; first Team All-Big Ten his jr & sr years; captured theBig Ten scoring crown his jr season; Basketball Digest's Rookie-of-the-Year 1980-81; unanimous selection to NBA's All-Rookie Team 1980-81; Warrior's all-time career leader in blocked shots with 690 and ranks in the top ten in six other categories; played for SIMAC in Milan Italy and led team to both the Italian NatlChampionship and the 1985 European Kirac Cup Championship.   **BUSINESS ADDRESS:** Center, Golden State Warrior, Oakland Coliseum Arena, Kemper Arena, Oakland, MO 64102.

CARROLL, JUANITAELIZABETH P.
Clergyman.   **PERSONAL:** Born Dec 02, 1954, Rochester, NY.   **EDUCATION:** Brown Univ Providence RI, 1972-75; Univ of Rochester, BA Anthropology 1977; Colgate Rochester Bexley Hall Crozer Theol Sem, Masters of Div 1980; Leadership Mgmt & Devel Ctr USAF, Cert 1980,83; Univ of Illinois Coll of Medicine, currently matriculating.   **CAREER:** Nazareth Coll, lab asst microbiology 1971; Univ of Rochester, dept of preventive med 1972; Brown Univ, lab asst neurophysiology 1973-75; math tutor 1974-75; Univ of Rochester Med Ctr, oper room recept-clerk 1975-77; Immaculate Conception Parish, dir youth ministry prog 1979-80; USAF, chaplain 1980-84; 4th Episcopal Dist of the AME Zion Church, 1984-85; Christian Educ Evansville Dist, dist dir 1985-86.   **ORGANIZATIONS:** Dist dir Adult Christian Ed of AME Zion Church 1984-86; mem Carbondale Clergy Fellowship 1984-85; mem NAACP; mem Black Women in Church and Society; ITC (Interdenominational Theological Center) Atlanta, GA; mem Amer Assoc of Univ Women, Student Natl Medical Assoc; bd mem FDMHA.   **HONORS/ACHIEVEMENTS:** 1st black female student body pres, Colgate Rochester Bexley Hall Crozer Theol Sem 1979; 1st black female chaplain to USAF 1980; Outstanding Comm Serv AwdSafia Temple #188 1982; Outstanding Woman of 3201st ABC Eglin AFB FL 1983; Named 1 of 50 Young Leaders of the Future Ebony Mag 1983.   **MILITARY SERVICE:** USAF capt 3 1/2 yrs; Air Force Commendation Medal 1984; USAFR Chaplain, Capt 1984-.

CARROLL, LAWRENCE W.
Judge.   **PERSONAL:** Born Mar 07, 1923, Chicago, IL; son of Lawrence W Carroll and Lucille Blackwell Carroll; married Annie Lee Goode; children: Lawrence W III.   **EDUCATION:** Herzl Jr Coll, AA 1942; Univ of IL, 1942-44; Loyola Univ, JD 1950.   **CAREER:** USAF, multi-engine pilot 1944-46; Chicago Title and Trust Comp, lawyer & title examiner asst chief title officer Office Counsel 1950-82; Atty Reg Comm of the Supreme Court of IL, counsel to admin 1982-84; Circuit Court of Cook Cty IL, assoc judge 1984-.   **ORGANIZATIONS:** Chmn of bd Woodlawn Mental Health Ctr 1973-78; pres CEO TWO Hillmans Comm 1970-84; mental health corp State of IL 1973-80; bd mem Woodlawn Comm Develpment Corp 1976-85.   **HONORS/ACHIEVEMENTS:** Edward H Wright Award Cook Cty

Bar Assn 1981.   **MILITARY SERVICE:** USAF 2nd lt 1944-46.   **BUSINESS ADDRESS:** Associate Judge, Circuit Court Cook Cty IL, 16501 S Kedzie Parkway, Markham, IL 60426.

CARROLL, ROBERT F.
Business executive.   **PERSONAL:** Born Jun 18, 1931, Bartow, FL; son of Robert Carroll Sr (deceased) and Emma Harris Carroll (deceased); married Gwendolyn Jackson; children: Tosca, Denise, Robert III.   **EDUCATION:** FL A&M Univ, BA 1960; Univ of CT, further study 1961; Columbia Univ, MA 1963; Yale Univ, further study 1964-67.   **CAREER:** NY City Dept of Soc Services, deputy comm 1967-71; NY City Human Resources Admin, deputy admin 1971-74; City Coll of NY, vice pres 1974-78; Cong Chas B Rangel, chief of staff 1978-81; R F Carroll and Comp, chmn CEO.   **ORGANIZATIONS:** Bd mem WNET TV 1982-; chmn bd R F Carroll and Comp Inc 1981-; mem Public Rel Soc of Amer, Amer Assn of Political Scientists, Alpha Phi Alpha Frat; pres The Fellas 1970-73; Board of Governors, Mill River Country Club.   **HONORS/ACHIEVEMENTS:** Educ of year Assc of Black Educ 1975; distinguished srv award Univ of Taiwan 1979; public award srv US Dept HEW 1970.   **MILITARY SERVICE:** USAF t/sgt; srv medal 1955.   **HOME ADDRESS:** 37 Reynolds Rd, Glen Cove, NY 11542.   **BUSINESS ADDRESS:** Chairman/CEO, R F Carroll & Co, Inc, One World Trade Ctr, Ste 1251, New York, NY 10048.

CARROLL, SALLY G.
Association executive.   **PERSONAL:** Born in Roanoke, VA.   **EDUCATION:** Essex Jr Coll.   **CAREER:** Newark Police Dept, 1949-51; Essex Co Sheriff's Office, court attendant 1951-.   **ORGANIZATIONS:** Life mem 1970-, former sec treas pres Newark Br NAACP; trustee Bd of Gr Newark Urban Coalition; Newark Museum; Milt Campbell Youth Center; chmn Newark NAACP Day Care Bd; pres Batons Inc; mem Nat Assn of Negro Bus & Professional Women's Club; adv bd Profect COED; Hich Impact Anti-Crime Bd; Affirmative ActionReview Council; mem Citizens Adv Bd Mayor's Policy & Devel Office.   **HONORS/ACHIEVEMENTS:** Recipient Woman of the Year Award Frontiers Internat; Sojourner Truth Award Bus & Professional Women; Outstanding Negro Woman Imperial Court Of Isis PHA; 1st woman in hist of NJ apptd to NJ St Parole Bd by Gov Brendan T Bryne confirmed by NJ St Senate for 6-yr Term.

CARROLL, VINNETTE
Director, actress.   **PERSONAL:** Born in New York, NY.   **EDUCATION:** LI Univ, BA 1944; NYU, MA 1946; New Sch Social Rsch postgrad 1948-50.   **CAREER:** HS for Performing Arts NYC, drama tchr; Ghetto Arts Prog, former dir; NY State Cncl on the Arts, former cons; Actress, roles incl Caesar and Cleopatra 1955, Small War on Murray Hill 1956, Jolly's Progress 1959, Member of the Wedding 1960, Moon on a Rainbow Shawl London 1962; plays directed incl Dark of the Moon 1960, Ondine 1962, Black Nativity New York City 1962, Spoleto Festival of Two Worlds 1963, The Prodigal Son 1965, The Flies 1966, 74, Slow Dance of the Killing Ground 1968, Don't Bother Me I Can't Cope 1975, Step lively Boy 1973, Croesus and the Witch 1973, original dir, When Hell Freezes Over I'll Skate, 1979.   **HONORS/ACHIEVEMENTS:** Recip Obie Award for Disting Performance 1962; Emmy Award for conception and supervision of Beyond the Blues 1962; NY Outer Critics Circle Award; Los AngelesDrama Critics Awards; NAACP Image Award; Golden Circle Award 1979; Black Filmmakers Hall of Fame Award 1979; Tony nominee Don't Bother Me I Can't Cope 1975.

CARROLL, WILLIAM
University educator.   **PERSONAL:** Born Jan 04, 1936, Brooklyn, NY; son of Grover Cleveland Chatman and Willie Ann Carroll; married Thelma Ellen Young, Nov 26, 1966; children: William Stewart Carroll, Valinda Sue Carroll.   **EDUCATION:** Harvard Univ, Cambridge MA, 1964; Norfolk State Coll, Norfolk VA, BA 1965; Temple Univ, Philadelphia PA, MA 1967; Univ of North Carolina, Chapel Hill NC, PhD 1978.   **CAREER:** Norfolk State Univ, Norfolk VA, instructor 1967-73, asst prof 1974-77, assoc prof 1978-.   **ORGANIZATIONS:** Mem Alpha Kappa Mu Natl Honor Socity 1963-; mem Norfolk State Univ Alumni Assn 1965-; mem Coll Language Assn 1967-70, 1984-; mem Amer Assn of Univ Prof 1969-; vice pres Tidewater Fair Housing Inc 1969-70; mem Natl Council of Teachers of English 1975-86, 1988-; mem Sigma Tau Delta Intl Honor Society 1979-; mem NAACP 1982-; publicity dir Voter Registration 1982-84; mem United Council of Citizens & Civic Leagues 1982-; mem Middle Atlantic Writers Assn 1987-.   **HONORS/ACHIEVEMENTS:** Summer School Cooperative Scholarship, Harvard Univ 1964; Teaching Fellowship, Univ of North Carolina 1971; co-author Rhetoric and Readings for Writing 1981; author, "George Moses Horton," Dictionary of Leterary Biography, 1986; contributor, Fifty More Southern Writers.   **MILITARY SERVICE:** AUS specialist E4, 1959-62.   **BUSINESS ADDRESS:** Assoc Prof, Norfolk State Univ, 2401 Corprew Ave, 205 Madison Communication Building, Norfolk, VA 23504.

CARRUTHERS, GEORGE ROBERT
Research physicist.   **PERSONAL:** Born Oct 01, 1939, Cincinnati, OH.   **EDUCATION:** Univ of IL, BS 1961, MS 1962, PhD 1964.   **CAREER:** Space Sci Div NRL, research physicist 1964-82, head ultraviolet measurements brnch 1980-82, sr astrophysicist 1982-.   **ORGANIZATIONS:** Mem Amer Astronomical Soc, Amer Geophysical Union, Amer Inst of Aeronautics and Astronautics, Amer Assc for the Advancement of Science, Natl Tech Assc, chrmn edit review comm and edit of journal Natl Tech Assc 1983-.   **HONORS/ACHIEVEMENTS:** Arthur S Flemming Awd Washington Jaycees 1971; Apollo 16 excep sci achvmnt medal Natl Aeronautics & Space Admin 1972; Warner Prize Amer Astronomical Soc 1973; excep achievement awd Natl Civil Srv League 1973; honorary degree doctor of engr MI Tech Univ 1973; Samuel Cheevers Award Natl Tech Assc 1977.   **BUSINESS ADDRESS:** Senior Astrophysicist, Space Sci Div Naval Res Lab, Code 4109 Naval Research Lab, Washington, DC 20375.

CARRY, HELEN WARD
Educational administrator.   **PERSONAL:** Born Mar 22, Chicago, IL; widowed; children: Ronald, Julius J III.   **EDUCATION:** Xavier Univ New Orleans, LA, BA 1946; Loyola Univ Chicago, MEd 1963.   **CAREER:** Chicago Public Schools, teacher 1952, adjustment counselor 1962; Chicago Public Schools Head Start, coord 1965-69; Webster School, Chicago Public Schools, asst prin 1965, prin 1970; Christ Univ Temple, asst to minister 1976-; Johnnie Colemon Institute, dir 1976-.   **ORGANIZATIONS:** Consult David Cook Publishing; mem Delta Sigma Theta Sor.   **HONORS/ACHIEVEMENTS:** Alpha Kappa Mu Hon Soc New Orleans, LA 1945; Outstanding Principal Dist 8 Chicago Publ Schools.   **BUSINESS ADDRESS:** Dir, Johnnie Colemon Institute, 11901 S Ashland Ave, Chicago, IL 60643.

CARSON, BENJAMIN SOLOMON, SR.
Physician, neurosurgeon. **PERSONAL:** Born Sep 18, 1951, Detroit, MI; son of Robert Solomon Carson and Sonya Copeland Carson; married Lacena (Candy) Rustin Carson, Jul 06, 1975; children: Murray Nedlands, Benjamin Solomon Jr, Rhoeyce Harrington. **EDUCATION:** Yale Univ, New Haven CT, BA 1973; Univ of Michigan, Ann Arbor MI, MD 1977. **CAREER:** Johns Hopkins Univ, Baltimore MD, chief resident neurosurgery, 1982-83; Queen Elizabeth II Medical Center, Perth, Australia, sr registrar neurosurgery, 1983-84; Johns Hopkins Univ, Baltimore MD, asst prof neurosurgery 1984-, asst prof oncology 1984-, asst prof pediatrics 1987-; dir pediatric neurosurgery 1985-. **ORGANIZATIONS:** Mem Amer Assn for the Advancement of Science 1982-, Natl Pediatric Oncology Group 1985-, Natl Medical Assn 1986-; honorary chmn Regional Red Cross Cabinet 1987-; medical advisory bd Children Cancer Foundation 1987-; life mem Maryland Congress of Parents and Teachers 1988-; mem Amer Assn of Neurological Surgeons 1989-; mem Congress of Neurological Surgeons 1989-. **HONORS/ACHIEVEMENTS:** Citations for Excellence, Detroit City Council 1987, Philadelphia City Council 1987, Michigan State Senate 1987, Pennsylvania House of Representatives 1989, Detroit Medical Society 1987; American Black Achievement Award, Business and Professional, Ebony and Johnson Publications 1988; Clinical Practitioner of the Year, Natl Medical Assn Region II 1988; Certificate of Honor for Outstanding Achievement in the Field of Medicine, Natl Medical Fellowship Inc 1988; Honorary Doctor of Science Degrees, Gettysburg Coll 1988, Andrews Univ 1989, North Carolina A&T 1989, Sojourner-Douglass Coll 1989; Candle Award for Science and Technology, Morehouse Coll 1989; numerous scientific publications (books and journals 1982-; numerous natl network television appearances (medical and social issues) 1985-; performed first intrauterine shunting procedure for a hydrocephalic twin 1986, first successful separation of occipital craniopagus Siamese twins 1987; author of Gifted Hands (autobiographic sketch), scheduled for publication 1990. **BUSINESS ADDRESS:** Director of Pediatric Neurosurgery, Johns Hopkins Medical Institutions, Meyer 5-109, 600 N Wolfe, Baltimore, MD 21205.

CARSON, CURTIS C., JR.
Judge. **PERSONAL:** Born Feb 05, 1920, Cowpens, SC; married Vida Timbers; children: Curtis III, Gregory, Carol. **EDUCATION:** VA State Coll, AB; Univ of PA Law Sch, LLB. **CAREER:** Private Practice, attorney 1962-65; trial assistant district atty, 1952-58; atty 1958-71; Philadelphia NAACP, chief atty 1962-65; Ct of Common Pleas Commonwealthof PA, judge 1972-. **ORGANIZATIONS:** Mem Philadelphia PA Bar Assn 1946-77; bd rep Comm Legal Svcs; mem Philadelphia Co Bd of Law Examiners 1966-69; arbtr Amer Arbitration Assn; mem bd of dir Parkside YMCA 1948-73; pres bd of dir 1950-54; past mem Philadelphia Jr C of C; Big Bros Assn; elder Germantown Comm Presby Ch. **BUSINESS ADDRESS:** Judge, Ct Common Pleas Common PA, 113 One E Penn Sq, Philadelphia, PA 19107.

CARSON, DWIGHT KEITH
Physician. **PERSONAL:** Born Jul 27, 1951, Franklin, VA; married Maria Margaret Fisher; children: Shayla-Marie, Ilea Janelle. **EDUCATION:** Howard Univ, BS Zoology 1973; Meharry Medical Coll, MD 1977. **CAREER:** US Public Health Serv Hospital, internship 1977-78; West Baltimore Comm Health Care Corp, primary care physician 1978-80; Hahnemann Hospital, 2nd yr resident 1980-81; Norfolk General Hosp, 3rd yr resident 1982-83; Allen Memoiral Hospital, chairman infectious control comm 1986-; The Oberlin Clinic Inc, staff physician. **ORGANIZATIONS:** Guest lecturer local schools, churches etc 1983-; mem Lorain Co Medical Soc 1983-, Amer Medical Assoc 1983-; diplomate Amer Acad of Family Physicians 1984-91; appointee to public/profl relations comm OH Acad of Family Physicians 1984-; guest interviewee WBEA Radio subject-family health month 1985. **HONORS/ACHIEVEMENTS:** Outstanding Young Men of Amer Jaycees 1977,81,85,86. **HOME ADDRESS:** 203 N Prospect St, Oberlin, OH 44074. **BUSINESS ADDRESS:** Staff Physician, The Oberlin Clinic, Inc, 224 W Lorain Ave, Oberlin, OH 44074.

CARSON, HARRY DONALD
Professional athlete. **PERSONAL:** Born Nov 26, 1953, Florence, SC. **EDUCATION:** Attended, SC State. **CAREER:** New York Giants, linebacker 1976-. **ORGANIZATIONS:** Giant's rep 1985 nationally televised United Way Public Service Commercials. **HONORS/ACHIEVEMENTS:** Pro Bowl 5 times; All NFL Rookie team 1976; All NFL selection 7 times; NFL's Top Inside Linebacker Sports Illustrated 1980; NFC Linebacker of the Yr NFL Players Assoc; Kodak All-Am Hon; Little All-Amer by AP; Twice MVP of the Mid-East Conf; Eastern Airlines Award for the highest academic avg among Black Coll All-Amers; mem NFL Pro Bowl teams 1986,87. **BUSINESS ADDRESS:** New York Giants, Giants Stadium, East Rutherford, NJ 07073.

CARSON, IRMA
Law enforcement. **PERSONAL:** Born Jun 24, 1935, Monroe, LA; children: Sharon, Karen, Camille. **EDUCATION:** Bakersfield Coll, AA; CA State Coll, BA; Kern Co Law Enforcement Acad, Graduate; Univ of Santa Barbara, Certificate in Criminal Justice; Univ of CA, Cert of Instruction; CA Teaching Credential. **CAREER:** Bakersfield City Sch Dist; bd mem; Bakersfield City Police, police sgt. **ORGANIZATIONS:** Mem Amer Business Women's Assn; mem Kern Co Child Sex Abuse Treatment Comm; mem Black History Comm; mem BAPAC; mem NAACP; mem CFBL; mem King Memorial AME Church; co-author The Handbook for Battered Women; Rape Prevention Workshop; Parent's Rights & Responsibilities Workshop; Natl Political Inst Workshop 1984. **HONORS/ACHIEVEMENTS:** Officer of the Yr 1974; NAACP Comm Serv Awd 1979; People's Baptist Church Comm Serv Awd 1980; Black History Parade Grant Marshall 1980; The Golden West Leadership Awd 1981; Elks Lodge Comm Serv Awd 1981; CA Alliance of Black Educators Disting Serv Awd 1982; Comm Appreciation Reception 1982; Black History Parade Grand Marshall 1983. **BUSINESS ADDRESS:** Police Sergeant, Bakersfield Cty Police, 1601 Truxtun Ave, Bakersfield, CA 93301.

CARSON, JULIA M.
State senator. **PERSONAL:** Born Jul 08, 1938, Louisville, KY; divorced; children: 2 Children. **EDUCATION:** IU, 1970-72; St Mary of the Woods, 1976-78. **CAREER:** State of IN, state senator 1976-, state rep 1972-76; Cummins Engine Co, 1973-; House of Reps 1965-72. **ORGANIZATIONS:** Mem NAACP; Urban League; trustee YMCA; bd of dir Pub Serv Acad; Georgetown U; Nat Council Negro Women; Tabernacle Bapt Ch; committeewoman Nat Dem Party; vice pres Gtr Indianapolis Prog Com. **HONORS/ACHIEVEMENTS:** Woman of Yr IN 1974; Outstanding Leadership AKA; Humanitarian Award Christian Theol Sem. **BUSINESS ADDRESS:** State Capitol Bldg, Indianapolis, IN 46204.

CARSON, LOFTUS C.
Educator. **PERSONAL:** Born Oct 16, 1923, Marion, NC; married Marge B Wright; children: Loftus, II, Byran Ethan. **EDUCATION:** Livingstone Coll, BA 1946; Fisk U, MA 1952, Cert 1952; Boston U, grad study 1946-47; A&T State U, 1958; Brown Univ 1955-56. **CAREER:** Monroe Co Human Relations Commn, Rochester NY, exec dir 1961-, consultant police-comm & relations 1963-, consultant urban educ problems 1963-; Natl Council on Agr Life & Labor, Washington DC, assoc research dir 1952-53; Comm Center Addor, NC, dir 1952; Fisk Univ, research assoc 1951-52; McDowell County School System, principal 1948-51. **ORGANIZATIONS:** Mem Monroe Co Employee's Grievance Com; Urban League of Rochester; charter mem Rochester Jobs Inc; bd dir Legal Aid Soc; Am Judicature Soc; bd dir Consumer Credit Counseling Serv Inc; mem Rochester & Monroe Co Comm Chest; Otentiana Council BSA; chmn Scientists & Technicians of Tomorrow 1958-60; Advertising Council; City Club of Rochester Inc; Am Soc Pub Adminstrn. **HONORS/ACHIEVEMENTS:** Recipient Coll Achievement Award; College Scholarship Award & Omega Psi Phi Scholarship Award; Sidney Hillman Fellow Race Relations; Citizens Award for Outstanding Contributions to Better Race Relations; Man of Year Award Omega Psi Phi 1973. **MILITARY SERVICE:** AUS pvt 1943. **BUSINESS ADDRESS:** 350 E Henrietta Rd, Rochester, NY 14620.

CARSON, LOIS MONTGOMERY
Public administrator. **PERSONAL:** Born Jul 03, 1931, Memphis, TN; married Harry L Carson; children: Harry, Jr, William, Patricia, John, Brian, Felicia. **EDUCATION:** Wilberforce Univ; CA State Coll, BA 1967; Univ of CA, MA 1974; CA State, Secondary Teaching Credential 1970. **CAREER:** Freewalk Gazette, 1963-64; San Bernardino County Probation Dept, counselor 1964-68; precinct reporter 1964-69; San Bernardino County Schools, teacher 1968-72; Am News, 1969; Univ of CA, dir proj Upward Bound 1973-76; CA State Univ, prof English & Educ 1977-78; Comm Serv Dept, deputy dir 1978-80; Community Action Dept Riverside County, exec dir. **ORGANIZATIONS:** Mem CA Tchrs Assn 1968-73; CA Conf Black Elected Officials 1973-74; mem Military Acad Bd 38th Cong Dist 1973-74; past pres bd San Bernardino Comm Coll Dist 1973; state v chairperson CA Adv Health Council 1976-; Nat Bd Assn of Comm Coll Trustees 1978; mem Delta Kappa Gamma Intl Soc; Alpha KappaAlpha Sor; mem CA OEO Advisory Bd; sec Nat Bd Nat Council Negro Women. **HONORS/ACHIEVEMENTS:** Disting Achievement Award 1969; CA State Assembly Pub Serv Award 1973; Woman of Yr Inland Empire Sect NCNW 1973; Black Woman of Yr San Bernardino 1974; Women of Achievement of San Bernardino 1975; good citizenship award Alpha Kappa Alpha 1976; Outstanding Achievement Award Far Western Region 1979 & 84; Public Administrator of the Year 1980; CA State Distinguished Alumnus 1980. **BUSINESS ADDRESS:** Executive Dir, County of Riverside, Community Action Dept, 3556 Tenth St, Riverside, CA 92501.

CARSON, WARREN JASON, JR.
Educator. **PERSONAL:** Born Feb 12, 1953, Tryon, NC. **EDUCATION:** Univ of NC, AB 1974; Atlanta Univ, MA 1975; Univ of SC, 1976-. **CAREER:** Isothermal Community Coll, instructor 1975-76; Piedmont OIC, head of career prep div 1975-80; Rutledge Coll, dean for acad affairs 1980-84; Univ of SC at Spartanburg, prog dir. **ORGANIZATIONS:** Pres Polk Cty NAACP 1976-; chrmn Mayor's Adv Task Force 1980-; pres Tryon Schls PTA 1980-81. **HONORS/ACHIEVEMENTS:** Outstanding Young Men of Amer 1981; Who's Who Among Black Amer 1980; Church And Comm Award 1984; Outstanding Teacher Award Piedmont OIC 1980; Outstanding Teacher Award Rutledge Clge 1982-83. **HOME ADDRESS:** PO Box 595, Tryon, NC 28782. **BUSINESS ADDRESS:** Program Dir, U of SC Spar, Univ Of SC At Spartanburg, Spartanburg, SC 29303.

CARSON, WILLIS E.
Business executive. **PERSONAL:** Born Dec 23, 1912, Dallas; children: 2 Children. **EDUCATION:** Met Coll, 1943. **CAREER:** So Pacific RR, 1943; self-employed brokers office 1945; Consolidated Realty Bd So CA Inc, pres & founder 1949; Nat Assn Real Estate Brokers, regionalvp 1955, pres 1971-73; Prudential Life & Ins Co, managed properties & famous personalities; Fannie Mae, consult three days a week; Prevaled-upon Title Ins & Trust Co; George B Parks Devel Educ Program NAREB; Pub Soc Services LA, co commr; Co Appeal Bd, tax hearing officer. **ORGANIZATIONS:** Mem Fed Nat Mortgage Assn 1972-73; mem Ch Religious Sci Office. **BUSINESS ADDRESS:** Carson Realty Co, 3500-177 W Manchester Ave, Inglewood, CA 90305.

CARSWELL, ERNIE CALVIN
Professional athlete. **PERSONAL:** Born Dec 26, 1961, Brooklyn, NY. **EDUCATION:** Alabama State. **CAREER:** Denver Gold, strong safety 1984-. **HONORS/ACHIEVEMENTS:** Hornets third-leading tackler his sr yr.

CARSWELL, GLORIA NADINE SHERMAN
Accountant. **PERSONAL:** Born Dec 27, 1951, Cairo, GA; daughter of Eugene Martin Sherman and Mary Martin Sherman; married Willie F Carswell Jr; children: Mercedes Elaine, John Garfield. **EDUCATION:** Mercer Univ Macon GA, BS (Magna Cum Laude) 1972; FL State Univ, MA 1976. **CAREER:** Grady Cty Bd of Ed, math instr 1972-74; Deloitte Haskins & Sells, sr accountant 1976-81; Charter Oil Co, plng analyst 1981-82; The Charter Co, sr internal auditor 1982-83, mgr internal finance reporting 1983-86; AT&T American Transtech, mgr esop recordkeeping. **ORGANIZATIONS:** Mem FL Inst of CPA's, Amer Inst of CPA's; pres Jacksonville Chap Natl Assoc of Black Accountants 1979-81; bd dir Natl Assoc of Black Accountants 1979-81, Jacksonville Women Network , bd dir Volunteer Jacksonville Inc; All St Childcare Ctr, chairperson United Way of Northeast FL Agency Oper Comm Daycare 1983-87; bd dir Jr League of Jacksonville; bd dir Jacksonville Community Council, Inc. **HONORS/ACHIEVEMENTS:** Outstanding Leadership Award Jacksonville Chap Natl Assoc of Black Accountants 1981. **HOME ADDRESS:** 1634 Dunsford Rd, Jacksonville, FL 32207. **BUSINESS ADDRESS:** Manager ESOP Recordkeeping, AT&T American Transtech, 8000 Baymeadow Way, Jacksonville, FL 32216.

CARSWELL, THOMAS W., JR.
Physician. **PERSONAL:** Born Jan 01, 1949, Springfield, IL; divorced; children: Jennifer, Christopher, Michael. **EDUCATION:** Morehouse Coll Atlanta GA, BS 1972; Univ of IL School of Basic Med Sci, MD 1976; Howard Univ Hosp, Psych 1976-77, Family Practice 1977-78; Univ of IL Residency in Family Practice, Family Practice 1978-80; Chief Resident 1979-80. **CAREER:** St Francis Med Ctr, diener 1973-74; Methodist Med Ctr, emergency rm md 1974-76; Peoria Assoc for Retarded Citizens, med dir 1978-82; Carver Family Health

Ctr Methodist Med Ctr, acting med dir 1980-81; Univ of IL, asst dir 1980-84; Carver Familty Health Ctr, med dir 1981-84; Med First, staff physician 1983-84; Morehouse Familty Practice Ctr, med dir 1984-; Morehouse School of Med, med dir family practice/res 1984-. **ORGANIZATIONS:** Clinical instr, 1978-82, assoc clinical prof 1982, Univ of IL Coll of Med; asst prof Morehouse School of Med; mem Amer Bd of Family Practice 1982, Natl Med Assoc, AMA, IL State Med Soc, Peoria Med Soc, Soc of Teachers of Family Med; med exec comm, liaison comm for family practice residency, icu comm, Southwest Comm Hosp; curriculum comm, data processing adv comm, Morehouse School of Med; rsch comm, comm for equal oppty/affirm action, project impact adv bd, Univ of IL Coll of Med; health serv adv comm chmn, alcohol rehab council chmn Peoria Comm Action Agency; bd mem The Learning Tree School. **HONORS/ACHIEVEMENTS:** Natl Achievement Scholar 1967-72; Amer Psychiatric Assoc Natl Inst of Mental Health Fellow 1976-77; Univ of IL Fellowship in Family Practice. **HOME ADDRESS:** 214 Green Springs Dr, Palmetto, GA 30266.

CARTER, ALLEN D.
Educator, artist. **PERSONAL:** Born Jun 29, 1947, Arlington, VA; married Mae Ira; children: Flora Ophelia, Cecilia. **EDUCATION:** Columbus Coll Art & Design, BFA 1972; Amer Univ, Grad Study. **CAREER:** Adult Educ Program, art instructor; artist. **ORGANIZATIONS:** Mem Alexandria Art League 1974, Fairfax Art League 1974, Arlington Independence Day Celebration Comm 1974, Arlingto C of C 1974, Childrens Day SmithsonianInst 1974, Natl Portrait Gallery 1975. **HONORS/ACHIEVEMENTS:** 1st prize N VA Art League 1973; Disting Merit Awd 5th Annual Juried Athenaeum Show 1974; Kansas City key to the city 1986; Virginia Museum of Fine Arts fellowship award 1987.

CARTER, ALPHONSE H.
Management consultant. **PERSONAL:** Born Oct 03, 1928, Baton Rouge, LA; married Carolyn McCraw; children: Cynthia Susan. **EDUCATION:** Albany State Coll, 1956-57; Duquesne U, BS 1961; Univ of Cincinnati, PhD 1975. **CAREER:** Housing Authority City of Pittsburgh, interviewer 1961-62, asst mgr 1962;Kroger Co, mgmt trainee 1962-63, store mgmt 1963-65, div industrial engineering 1965-66, div personnel mgmt 1966-68, corp personnel coord 1968-72; Carter Carter & Assoc Inc, mgmt consult pres. **ORGANIZATIONS:** Mem Nat Alliance of Businessmen Coll Cluster 1969-72; bd mem Opportunities Industrialization Center 1969-72; block club pres Homewood-Brushton Improvement Assn 1958-61; bd mem Victory Neighborhood Serv Agency 1969-72; Community Chest 1970-72; Nat Urban League 1970-71; met dir Nat Alliance of Businessmen 1971; trustee Funds for Self Enterprise 1972-; mem Task Force ComUniv of Cincinnati Sch of Educ 1972;life mem NAACP 1946-; Soc for Advancement of Mgmt 1958-; Urban League 1958-; BOAZF & AM 1960-; Personnel Assn 1966-; bd mem Cit Com on Youth 1969; mem adv com Retired Sr Volunteer Program 1972-73;Alpha Mu Sigma Professional Fraternity in Mgmt Devel 1974; pres Churchill Area Kiwanis 1978-79; lt gov Kiwanis Div 6-A 1980-81; bd mem Allegheny Trails Boy Scout Council 1979. **HONORS/ACHIEVEMENTS:** Alpha Mu Sigma Award for Excellence in Scholarship Achievement in Mgmt 1975.

CARTER, ANTHONY CALVIN
Professional athlete. **PERSONAL:** Born Sep 17, 1960, Riviera Beach, FL; married Ortancis; children: Tara; Nikki. **EDUCATION:** Michigan. **CAREER:** Michigan; Oakland Invaders, wide receiver 1984-. **HONORS/ACHIEVEMENTS:** Clinched USFL title with 48-yd touchdown catch ending game with 9 catches for 179 yds & a touchdown; named All-USFL by Pro Football Weekly & also selected second team All-League; also named All-USFL as punt returner by Sporting News; became 1st USFL player to return a punt for a touchdown, a 57 ydr in 43-7 win vsTampa Bay; named teams MVP as Soph & sr.

CARTER, ARLINGTON W., JR.
Business executive. **PERSONAL:** Born Mar 13, 1933, Chicago, IL; son of Arlington Carter Sr and Martha Carter; married Constance E Hardiman. **EDUCATION:** IL Inst of Tech, BSEE 1961. **CAREER:** Seattle Housing Development, exec dir 1971-73; The Boeing Comp, program mgr 1973-77, general mgr 1977-81, prog mgr 1981-85, general mgr space systems 1985-88, Defense Systems Division, vice pres 1988-89, Missle Systems Division, vice pres & general mgr 1989-. **ORGANIZATIONS:** Pres Boeing Mgmt Assn 1982-84; mem Natl Space Club 1981-85; exec bd mem Seattle Comm Coll Foundation 1982-85; chmn King County Personnel Bd 1970-77; chmn Western Region of NAACP 1966; exec bd mem United Way 1978-82; mem Amer Defense Prepared Assoc; exec bd mem Metropolitan YMCA; mem Seattle Urban League; exec bd mem Seattle Hearing & Speech Center; sec/treasurer Northwest Chapter of Ill Inst Alumni Assn. **MILITARY SERVICE:** USAF staff sgt. **BUSINESS ADDRESS:** Vice President & General Manager, The Boeing Co, PO Box 3999, Seattle, WA 98124.

CARTER, ARTHUR MICHAEL
County commission chairman. **PERSONAL:** Born Apr 27, 1940, Detroit, MI; son of Arthur Carter and Alberta Carter; married Deborah Lightner. **EDUCATION:** Wayne State Univ, Detroit, MI, BA, 1962, MA, 1964, ED, 1971. **CAREER:** Detroit Public Schools, Detroit, MI, teacher; Wayne County Community Coll, Detroit, MI, dean; Wayne County Community, Detroit, MI, commr. **ORGANIZATIONS:** Executive producer, host, County Vision Cable TV Program; mem, Detroit Science Center; bd mem, Interim House; mem, Semcog Educ Comm. **HONORS/ACHIEVEMENTS:** Film, I Am Somebody, 1969; contributor, Career and Vocational Devel, 1972; author, Black Family Role in Political Educ, 1987. **BUSINESS ADDRESS:** Chairman, Wayne County Commission, County of Wayne, Wayne County Building, 600 Randolph, Suite 450, Detroit, MI 48226.

CARTER, BARBARA LILLIAN
Educator. **PERSONAL:** Born Jun 20, 1942, Mexia, TX. **EDUCATION:** Fisk Univ, AB 1963; Brandeis Univ, MA 1967, PhD 1972; Harvard Univ Inst of Educ Mgmt, attended 1984. **CAREER:** Federal City College, asst prof 1969-72, assoc provost and assoc prof 1972-77; Univ of District of Columbia, assoc vice pres and prof 1977-80, vice pres for academic affairs 1980-81; Spelman Coll, vice pres for academic affairs and dean 1981-, acting dean 1986-87. **ORGANIZATIONS:** Mem Amer Sociological Assoc 1969-; bd dirs YWCA of Atlanta 1982-; bd dirs United Way of Atlanta 1985-, Public Broadcast Assoc 1985-; bd trustees Atlanta Coll of Art 1986-; bd of trustees Chatham Coll. **HONORS/ACHIEVEMENTS:** Woodrow Wilson Fellow 1963; Phi Beta Kappa 1963; Fellow Natl Inst of Mental Health 1964-67; Aspen Institute for Humanistic Studies Fellowship 1981; co-author"Protest, Politics and Prosperity" 1978. **BUSINESS ADDRESS:** Vice Pres for Academic Afrs, Spelman College, 350 Spelman Ln SW, Atlanta, GA 30314.

CARTER, BETTY
Jazz singer/songwriter. **PERSONAL:** Born May 16, 1927, Flint, MI; children: Myles, Kagle. **EDUCATION:** Detroit Conservatory Music. **CAREER:** Lionel Hampton Band, singer 1948-51; Harvard Univ/Goddard Coll/Dartmouth Univ, conducted workshops; Performer, various nightclubs with Thelonius Monk, MuddyWaters, Miles Davis, Moms Mably, T-Bone Walker, Lincoln Center 1972; appeared in play "Don't Call Me Man" Billie Holiday Theatre 1975; Carnegie Hall, singer 1977; Newport Jazz Festival 1977-78; Shubert Theatre on Broadway (1st jazz singer to appear there); writer, compositions incl "I Can't Help It", "Who, What, Why,Where, When", "With No Words", "Happy", "Someone Else Will Soon Grow Old Too", "What Is It?", "New Blues", "Tight", "Sounds", "Open the Door", "We Tried". **HONORS/ACHIEVEMENTS:** Grammy Nominee, 1981; TV Appearances incuding, Saturday Nite Live, 1976; "But Then She's Betty Carter" PBS, 1980; Over Easy PBS, 1981; The Tomorrow Show NBC, 1981; Live At Resorts Intl Cable, 1981; "Call Me Betty Carter" CBS Cable, 1981; "A Tribute to Lionel Hampton" Kennedy Cntr White House CBS, 1981; radio programs incl,"All Things Considered" Natl Pub Radio Jazz Alive Natl Pub Radio; particip in festivals in Europe, US, Brazil, Japan; Recip Special Award Natl Assn Indep Record Distrib, 1981; Grammy Award for best female jazz vocal performance for her album "Look What I Got!," 1989. **BUSINESS ADDRESS:** Bet-Car Productions, 117 St Felix St, Brooklyn, NY 11217. *

CARTER, BILLY L.
Associate attorney. **PERSONAL:** Born in Montgomery, AL; married Brenda T. **EDUCATION:** Tuskegee Inst, BS 1967; Howard Univ Law School, JD 1970; Univ of VA, 1971. **CAREER:** Gray Seay & Langford, atty 1970-71; AUS Ft Meade, MD, chief defence counsel; Gray Seay & Langford, assoc atty 1974-; Recorder's Court City of Tuskegee, pros atty 1974-. **ORGANIZATIONS:** Mem ABA; NBA; Am Trial Lawyers Assn; AL Bar Assn; AL Black Lawyers Assn; DC Bar Assn; Kappa Alpha Psi. **HONORS/ACHIEVEMENTS:** Recipient Army Commendation Medal for Meritorious Serv 1974; Distinguished Military Graduate 1967. **MILITARY SERVICE:** AUS capt 1971-74. **BUSINESS ADDRESS:** PO Box 539, Tuskegee, AL 36083.

CARTER, BLANCHE NELSON
Educator. **PERSONAL:** Born Nov 27, 1907, Arkansas; widowed. **EDUCATION:** Santa Monical City Coll; Woodbury Coll; UCLA; USC. **CAREER:** Owner/operator dressmaking shop 10 yrs; teacher AR & LA. **ORGANIZATIONS:** Mem pres SM Bd Educ 8yrs; 2nd vice pres Woman's Aux Nat Bapt Ch 1961-;mem YWCA; Am Red Cross; Conf Christians & Jews; NAACP; Nat Cncl Negro Women; Salvation Army; WCTU; Ch Women United; Am Bible Soc Women Yr LA Sentinel newspaper; Citz Yr Rel Bd SM Inc.

CARTER, CHARLES EDWARD
Attorney. **PERSONAL:** Born Jun 20, 1925, Springfield, OH; son of Brimoley Carter and Mary Carter; divorced; children: Bette Brown, Norman. **EDUCATION:** Miami Univ OH, AB 1950; OH State Univ, LLB 1957, JD 1967. **CAREER:** City of Springfield, OH, law dir 1960-69; Mahoming Co Legal Serv Youngstown, OH, 1969-71; NAACP, assoc gen counsel 1971-86; Corporate Counsel 1986-. **HONORS/ACHIEVEMENTS:** Published "Civil Rights Handbook" NAACP 1979. **MILITARY SERVICE:** USN Yeoman 2nd Class 1943-46. **BUSINESS ADDRESS:** Corporate Counsel, NAACP, 4805 Mt Hope Drive, Baltimore, MD 21215.

CARTER, CHARLES MICHAEL
Attorney. **PERSONAL:** Born Apr 18, 1943, Boston, MA; married Jocelyne Hinfray; children: Brandon H, Chad F, Courtney C. **EDUCATION:** Univ of CA Berkley, BS 1967; George Washington Univ Schl of Law, JD 1973. **CAREER:** Winthrop, Stimson, Putnam, and Roberts, assc 1973-81; The Singer Comp, div counsel & finance staff and investment counsel 1981-83; RJR Nabisco Inc, sr corporate counsel 1983-. **ORGANIZATIONS:** Mem Amer Bar Assc, Natl Bar Assoc.

CARTER, CHESTER C.
Business executive. **PERSONAL:** Born Feb 14, 1921, Emporia, KS; married Claudia; children: Chester Jr, Marise, Carol. **EDUCATION:** USC, AB 1944, MA 1952; Loyola Law Sch, JD 1958. **CAREER:** Capitol City Liquor Co Wholesale, pres chmn of bd; US State Dept, ambassador Peace Corps 1962-68; Sup Ct of LA Co, juvenile traffic hearing ofcr 1956-62. **MILITARY SERVICE:** AUS 1st lt 1942-46, major 1950-52. **BUSINESS ADDRESS:** 645 Taylor St NE, Washington, DC.

CARTER, CLARENCE EUGENE
Professional athlete. **PERSONAL:** Married Jill Anne; children: Brandson. **EDUCATION:** IN Univ. **CAREER:** Los Angeles Lakers; IN Pacers; NY Nicks, bsktbl plyr. **HONORS/ACHIEVEMENTS:** 5th best scorer on team with 105 norm; co-MVP as jr 1979 Natl Invitation Torunmnt at Garden; scored winning points in OT when IN beat OH for 1980 Big Ten crown; Player of Year in HS 1976; All-State prepster as Jr. **BUSINESS ADDRESS:** NY Nicks, Madison Sq Garden, 4 Pennsylvania Plaza, New York, NY 10001.

CARTER, DAISY
Recreation program director. **PERSONAL:** Born Oct 17, 1931, Stuart, FL; daughter of Robert C. Carter and Lottie Simmions; children: Marilyn D Jewett. **EDUCATION:** St Joseph's Coll, Social Work, 1972; Temple Univ, BS, Recreation Admin, 1980. **CAREER:** Philadelphia Dept of Recreation, center recreation leader, asst day camp dir, drama specialist, dist coordinator for retarded program, 1968-71; Zion Church, ctr supvr, 1969-70, sr citizen's community worker, 1971-72; East Germantown Recreation Center, day camp dir, 1972-78; sr citizen's program supvr, sr citizen's program supvr, 1972-81; Penrose Playground, ctr supvr, 1981-82, 1983-88; Juinata Park Older Adult Center, program dir, 1981-88, therapeutic recreation program dir, 1989. **ORGANIZATIONS:** Mem, PA Park & Recreation Soc, PA Therapeutic Recreation Soc, Black Social Workers Assn, Natl Park & Recreation Assn, Natl Therapeutic Recreation Assn, Natl Recreation & Parks Assn Ethnic Minority Soc, Philadelphia YWCA, NAACP, Philadelphia People Fund, West Mt Airy Neighbors; chairperson, PA Park & Recreation Soc Minority & Women Comm; comm chairperson for State Rep David P Richardson Jr, Sr Citizens & Recreation Programs; bd dir, Ile Ife Museum; bd dir, Temple Univ Health, Physical Educ, Recreation, & Dance Alumni Comm Chmn; bd dir, HPERD Alumni to the Temple's General Alumni Bd; vice pres, Temple Alumni Bd of Dir. **HONORS/ACHIEVEMENTS:** East Germantown Sr Citizens Service Award, 1976; Commonwealth of PA House of Rep Citation, Sr Citizens & Comm Programs, 1976; finalist, NRPA

West Francis Audio Visual Contest, 1976; Citation Award, Natl Recreation & Park Ethnic Minority Soc, 1977, 1979; Natl Comm Leaders & Noteworthy Americans Award, 1977, 1980; Appreciation Award, Lincoln Univ, 1981; Admiration & Appreciation Award, East Germantown Sr Citizens, 1981; Certificate of Appreciation, Recreation Dept, Lincoln Univ, 1982; NRPA Ethnic Minority Soc Recognition Award, 1982; President's Certificatw, EMS, 1983; North Philadelphia Branch, NAACP, Youth Award, 1986; Philadelphia Child-Parent Assn, Serv Award, 1988. **BUSINESS ADDRESS:** Recreation Program Dir, Philadelphia Dept of Recreation, "L" St & Sedgley Ave, Philadelphia, PA 19133.

CARTER, DARLINE LOURETHA
Library administrator. **PERSONAL:** Born Dec 07, 1933, Pinola, MS; daughter of Gennie Carter and Cora Lee Carter. **EDUCATION:** Tougaloo Coll MS, BS Elementary Educ 1955; Syracuse Univ NY, MLS 1960. **CAREER:** Cleveland MS, school librarian 1955-59; Syracuse Univ, asst librarian 1959-60; Tougaloo Coll MS, circulation librarian 1960-62; West Islip Public Library NY, children's librarian 1962-66, asst dir 1966-69, library dir 1969-. **ORGANIZATIONS:** Member, Amer Library Week Comm, HW Wilson Awards Jury, Membership Comm Amer Libr Assn 1969-85, Exhibits Comm, Membership Comm NY Library Assn 1962-85; vice pres, recording sec, chmn Public Library Dir Assn 1969-85; pres, Spring Inst; exec bd Suffolk County Library Assn 1973-85, Univ of MD 6th Annual Library Admin Devel Program 1972; honorary life membership West Islip PTA 1971; reaccreditation comm Palmer School of Library and Information Science, Long Island Univ, CW Post Center 1983; pres, Suffolk Library Consortium Inc 1986-. **BUSINESS ADDRESS:** Dir, West Islip Public Library, Three Higbie Ln, West Islip, NY 11795.

CARTER, DAVID G., SR.
Educator, educational administrator. **PERSONAL:** Born Oct 25, 1942, Dayton, OH; married Lena Faye Smith; children: Ehrika Aileen, Jessica Faye, David George Jr. **EDUCATION:** Central State Univ, BS 1962-65; Miami Univ, MEd 1967-68; The OH State Univ, PhD 1969-71. **CAREER:** Dayton City Schools, 6th grade tchr 1965-68, asst prin 1968-69, elem prin 1969-70, unit facilitator 1970-71; Dayton Publ Schools, serv unit dir (dist supt) 1971-73; Wright State Univ, adj prof 1972; Penn State Univ, asst prof dept of educ admn 1973-75, assoc prof dept educ admn 1975-77; Univ of CT, assoc prof dept educ admin 1977-79, prof dept educ admn 1980-, assoc dean/sch educ 1977-82, assoc vice pres acad affairs 1982-; Univ of CT, Storrs, CT, assoc vice pres academicaffairs, 1982-88; Eastern CT State Univ, Willimantic, CT, president 1988-. **ORGANIZATIONS:** Consult Professional Devel Assoc 1979-80; consult Milwaukee Pub Schools 1980; consult Syracuse Univ Research Corp 1976; consult PA Dept of Educ 1973-77; consult So Ea Delco Sch Dist 1973-83; consult Booz-Allen and Hamilton Inc 1972-73; bd trustees Dayton Museum of Natl Hist 1973; mem Centre Cnty Mental Hlth and Mental Retardation Adv Bd 1974-76; mem Adv Cncl to the Bd of Mental Health for Program Dev 1977-80; mem Governor's Task Force on Jail and Prison Overcrowding 1980; bd dir New Engl Reg Exch 1981-; corporator Windham Meml Comm Hosp 1982; trustee Windham Meml Comm Hosp 1984; dir Windham Healthcare Sys Inc 1984; mem Phi Delta Kappa; mem Amer Educ Rsch Assn; mem NAACP; mem Pi Lambda Theta; mem Phi Kappa Phi; bd dir Natl Organiz on Legal Probl in Education 1980-83; ed bd Journal of Educ Equity and Leadership 1980; mem Good Samaritan Mental Health Adv 1968-73. **HONORS/ACHIEVEMENTS:** Selected Young Man of the Year Dayton Jr C of C 1973; published over 50 articles and chapters incl, "Students Rights and Responsibilities, Challenge or Revolt" The Penna School Master (Journal for Secondary Principals 1974; "Implications of Teacher Performance Appraisal" The Penna School Master 1975; "Minority Students, Ability Grouping and Career Development" Journal of Black Studies with Frank Brown and J John Harris 1978; "Race, Language and Sex Discrimination" in A Digest of Supreme Court Decisions Affecting Education 1978. **BUSINESS ADDRESS:** President, Eastern Connecticut State University, 83 Windham St, Willimantic, CT 06226-2295.

CARTER, DORVAL RONALD
Obstetrician, gynecologist. **PERSONAL:** Born Feb 13, 1935, Donora, PA; married Vivian Ann Johnson; children: Dorval Jr, Melanie. **EDUCATION:** Howard U, BS 1956; Howard Univ Coll of Med, MD 1962. **CAREER:** Self-employed ob/gyn; Freedmen's Hosp, medical intern; Cook Co Hosp, pathology resident, ob/gyn resident, sr attending physician 1970-73; Bethany MedCtr, dept chrmn Cons; St Francis Cabrini Hosp, dept chrmn; Columbus-Cabrini Med Center, cons; NW Univ Med Sch, clinical instr; Johnson Rehab Nursing Center, med dir & cons. **ORGANIZATIONS:** Mem AMA; Chicago Med Soc; Nat Med Assn. **HONORS/ACHIEVEMENTS:** Recipient Outstanding Black Achievement Award 1975; Fellow Am Coll of Ob/Gyn; Fellow Am Coll of Surgeons; Fellow Internatl Coll o Surgeons. **MILITARY SERVICE:** AUS Med Corp 1st lt 1956-58. **BUSINESS ADDRESS:** 500 S Racine Ave, Chicago, IL 60607.

CARTER, EDWARD EARL
Mayor. **PERSONAL:** Born Oct 09, 1939, Havelock, NC; son of Leander Carter and Nettie Morris Carter; married Evelyn Jean Carter, Jan 17, 1966; children: Regina Yvette Carter, Tonya Denise Carter, Jacquelyn Carter. **EDUCATION:** Virginia State Univ, Petersburg, VA, BS, 1963; Pitt Community Coll, Greenville, NC, AAS, 1979. **CAREER:** Hudson Labs Columbia Univ, Dobbs Ferry, NY, research asst, 1962-63; US Army, commissioned officer, captain, 1963-71; Burroughs Wallcourse Co, Greenville, NC, dept head admin serv, 1971-. **ORGANIZATIONS:** Life mem, Alpha Phi Alpha Fraternity, 1960-; master mason, Mt Calvary Masonic Lodge 669, 1973-; transportation policy communication safety comm, North Carolina League of Cities, 1988-89; transportation policy communication safety comm, Natl League of Cities, 1988-89; mem, Pitt County Mayors Assn, 1987-89; Black Natl Conf of Mayors, 1987-89, Black Mayors Conf, 1987-89; bd of dir, Governors Crime Commn of North Carolina, 1988-; bd of dir, Pitt-Greenville Chamber of Commerce, 1988-; bd of dir, Project Parenting, 1988-. **HONORS/ACHIEVEMENTS:** Appeared in army air defense movie, Nike-In-the-Attack, 1965; appeard in New York Times and New York Times Magazine army promotional, 1965; TAR-Heel-of-the-Week, Raleigh News & Observer, 1979; Gus Witherspoon Leadership Award, North Carolina Assn of Alpha men, 1975; Omega Psi Pi, Community Serv Award, 1975; Citizen of the Year, Mid Atlantic Region of Alpha Kappa Alpha Sorority, 1989. **MILITARY SERVICE:** AUS captain, 1963-71; two Bronze Stars, 1971, three Army Commendation medals, 1964, 1966, 1971; Vietmans Cross of Gallantry. **HOME ADDRESS:** 104 Fireside, Greenville, NC 27834.

CARTER, ENRIQUE DELANO
Physician, government official. **PERSONAL:** Born Jul 15, 1945, Ancon, Canal Zone, Panama;married Adalina E MD; children: Stephanie, Marshall, Brandon. **EDUCATION:** Gonzoga Univ, BSc Biology 1968; Gonzaga Univ School of Law 1969; Univ of WA, MD 1973. **CAREER:** Natl Ctr for Health Serv Rsch, health sci analyst 1982-83, acting dir 1983-84, dir 1984-. **ORGANIZATIONS:** Chmn Tech Coord Comm; tech info to ASH; hcfa physicians panel; liaison rep OMAR/NIH; coord comm Assessment & Transfer of Tech NIH; steering comm & objectives Amer Council on Transplantation; natl adv council Natl Med Emergency Disaster System; teach seminars Western Exec Seminar; participates in NatlHealth Policy Forum; presided over APHA panel on Tech Assessment Social Costs & Public Policy; chmn DHHS Steering Comm; mem Amer Coll of Physicians Assoc, Amer Gastroenterology Assoc, Northwest Assoc of Rehabilitation Med, Amer Soc of Intl Med; bd cert Natl Bd of Med Examiners 1973-, Amer Bd of Internal med 1976-, Amer Bd of Gastroenterology 1980-. **HONORS/ACHIEVEMENTS:** Outstanding Med Student Awd NW Assn of Rehab Med 1972; Wrote reports on Liver Transplantation, Pancreas Transplantation, Pacemaker Monitoring Guidelines, Computer Enhanced Electrocardiogram, Self Infusion of Antihemophilic Clotting Factors, Transtelephonic Pacemaker Monitoring; NW Soc of Rehab Med Outstanding Med Student Awd 1972; Spec Serv Awd, US Public Health Serv 1981-82; Unit Commendation Awd USPHS 1983. **MILITARY SERVICE:** US Public Health Serv commander 05 12 yrs; Spec Serv Awds, Unit Commendation, Meritorious Achievement 1985. **BUSINESS ADDRESS:** Dir, Natl Ctr Health Serv Rsch, Office of Health Tech Assess, 310 Park Bldg, 12420 Parklawn, Rockville, MD 20857.

CARTER, FRED LAVELLE
Professional athlete. **PERSONAL:** Married Jacqueline Carter; children: Stephanie, Mia, Christopher, Amee, Jason, Aaron. **EDUCATION:** St Mary's College Emmitsburg MD, Grad 1969. **CAREER:** Philadelphia 76ers, player; Chicago Bulls, asst coach; Baltimore Bullets, player, asst coach. **ORGANIZATIONS:** Instrumental this past summer in the development and instruct of Mayor Washington's innter-city basketball clinics; involved with Little City Foundation. **HONORS/ACHIEVEMENTS:** Played 8 seasons in The NBA scoring 9,000 plus points from 1969 through 1977; ended his career after 611 Games with a 152 scoring average; captained the 76ersfor 3 seasons; a player rep for 4 years. **BUSINESS ADDRESS:** Assistant Coach, Washington Bullets, Capital Centre, Landover, MD 20785.

CARTER, GENE RAYMOND
Educational administrator. **PERSONAL:** Born Apr 10, 1939, Staunton, VA; married Lillian Young; children: Gene Raymond Jr, Scott Robert. **EDUCATION:** VA State Univ Petersburg, BA 1960; Boston Univ, ME 1967; Teachers Coll Columbia Univ NY, EdD 1973. **CAREER:** St Emma Mil Acad & Norfolk Public Schools, teacher 1960-69; Campostella Jr High School, educ devel spec, intern principal 1969-70; Maury High School, Norfolk VA, asst principal for instr 1970-71; Englewood Public Schools NJ, admin asst for rsch & planning 1972-73; Norfolk Public Schools, supvr of curriculum resources 1973-74; School of Educ Old Dominion Univ, Norfolk VA, adj assoc prof 1974-; Norfolk Public Schools, reg asst supt 1979-83, supt of schools 1983-. **ORGANIZATIONS:** Bd mem Tidewater Juvenile Detention Home Adv Bd 1978-80; bd mem Comm of Mgmt Serv YMCA Norfolk 1978-80; pres, exec bd mem Sunrise Optimist Club of Norfolk VA 1979-80; pres Gene R Carter & Assoc Chesapeake VA 1979-; bd mem St marys Infant Home Norfolk 1980-. **HONORS/ACHIEVEMENTS:** Listed in Who's Who Among Students in Amer Univ & Coll VA State Univ Petersburg 1959-60; Natl Grad Fellow Training Teachers of Teachers-Techers Coll Columbia Univ 1971-72; Minority Student Scholarship Teachers Coll Columbia Univ NY 1972; Selected by Minority Affairs Adv Comm to serve as a resource in its Talent Bank of Consult Amer Assoc of School Admin 1979-; Optimist of the Year Sunrise Optimist Club Norfolk VA 1979-80. **BUSINESS ADDRESS:** Superintendent, Norfolk Pub Sch Admin Bldg, 800 E City Hall Ave, Norfolk, VA 23510.

CARTER, GEOFFREY NORTON
Commissioner. **PERSONAL:** Born Jan 28, 1944, St Louis, MO; son of Robert Carter and Daphne Louise Tyus Carter. **EDUCATION:** St Louis Univ School of Arts & Science, AB cum laude 1966; St Louis Univ Law School, JD 1969. **CAREER:** Atty private practice 1975-88; USAF, judge advocate 1970-74; Legal Aid Soc of St Louis, staff atty 1969-70; Oakland Municipal Ct, Oakland, CA, commr, 1988-. **ORGANIZATIONS:** Treasurer CA Assn of Black Lawyers 1978 & 1979; vice pres Charles Houston Bar Assn 1980; cmmr City of Oakland Citizens' Complait Bd 1980; mem, bd of dir, Heritage Trails Fund, 1987-. **HONORS/ACHIEVEMENTS:** Full tuition scholarship St Louis Univ School of Law 1966; USAF Commendation Medal 1974. **MILITARY SERVICE:** USAF captain 1970-74. **HOME ADDRESS:** 11136 Sun Valley Dr, Oakland, CA 94605.

CARTER, GILBERT LINO
Appointed official. **PERSONAL:** Born Jul 06, 1945, Richmond, VA; married Joyce Jones; children: Jana, Gilbert Jr, Ridgely. **EDUCATION:** Morgan State Univ, AB 1967; Howard Univ, JD 1970. **CAREER:** VA Commonwealth Univ, asst dean of student life 1971-73; Commonwealth of VA, asst dir 1973-75. **ORGANIZATIONS:** Exec dir Model Cities/City of Richmond 1975-77; vice-chair assts Intl City Management Assoc 1983-. **BUSINESS ADDRESS:** Exec Staff Asst City Mgr, City of Richmond, 900 E Broad StRoom 104, Richmond, VA 23219.

CARTER, GWENDOLYN BURNS
Educator. **PERSONAL:** Born Nov 21, 1932, Lufkin, TX; daughter of Robert Burns and Tressie Burns; married Purvis Melvin Carter, Jun 02, 1956; children: Purvis Melvin III, Frederick Earl, Burnest Denise. **EDUCATION:** Attended, Univ of Denver, Univ of CO, Univ of So IL, Univ of TX; Huston Tilloston Coll, BS 1954; Prairie View A&M Univ, MEd 1960. **CAREER:** Hempstead Elementary Sch, resource teacher. **ORGANIZATIONS:** Pres Jack and Jill of Amer Inc 1980-82; pres Waller Co Teachers Assoc 1983-84; mem Delta Sigma Theta Sor; career treas Top Ladies of Distinction Inc 1985-87; mem The Council for Exceptional Children, Natl Educ Assoc; mem adv council for Exceptional Children 1986-; mem youth develop comm Mount Corinth Baptist Church 1986-. **HONORS/ACHIEVEMENTS:** Outstanding Leadership Awd Girl Scouts 1984; San Jacinto Council Appreciation Awd 1984; Disting Serv Prairie View Local Alumni Assoc 1984; Certificate of Recognition Mt Corinth Baptist Church 1985; Human Relations Awd Waller Co Teachers Assoc 1986; Outstanding Serv Awd Top Teens of Amer Inc 1986; Certificate of Recognition Prairie View Local Alumni Assoc 1986; Top Lady of The Year, Top Ladies of Distinction 1989; International Directory of Distinguished Leadership 1989. **HOME ADDRESS:** 319 Pine St, PO Box 2243, Prairie View, TX 77446. **BUSINESS ADDRESS:** Resource Teacher, Hempstead Elementary School, Hempstead, TX 77445.

CARTER, HAZO
College president. **CAREER:** West Virginia State College, Institute, WV, president. **BUSINESS ADDRESS:** President, West Virginia State College, Institute, WV 25112. *

CARTER, HERBERT E.
Educator. **PERSONAL:** Born Sep 27, 1919, Amory, MS; married Mildred L Hemmons; children: Herbert E Jr, Gene Kay, Kurt Vincent. **EDUCATION:** Tuskegee Univ, BSc 1955, MEd 1969. **CAREER:** United States Air Force, fighter pilot 1943-44, group maintenance officer 1945-48, flight test maintenance officer 1948-50, prof air science 1950-55, deputy dir military adv group to German Air Force 1955-59, chief of maintenance 1959-63, 1963-65; Tuskegee Inst, prof aerospace studies 1965-69, assoc dean student services 1970-75, assoc dean admissions and recruiting 1975-84 (retired). **ORGANIZATIONS:** Mem Presidential Scholars Review Comm; mem Coll Bd Educ Testing Serv; mem Amer Assn Collegiate Registrars and Admissions Officers; mem Sigma Pi Phi, Kappa Delta Pi; mem Natl Assn Coll Admissions Counselors; pres Tuskegee Chap Tuskegee Airmen Inc; numerous speaking engagements over the past five years on "Professionalism, Commitment and Performance of Blacks in Aerospace Careers.". **HONORS/ACHIEVEMENTS:** Air Medal w/4 Clusters; Air Force Commendation Medal; Distingushed Unit Citation; European Theater Medal w/5 Bronze Stars; Natl Defense Medal w/1 Bronze Star; Air Force Longevity Awd w/5 Oak Leaf Clusters. **MILITARY SERVICE:** USAF lt col (retired). **HOME ADDRESS:** 2704 Bulls Ave, Tuskegee Institute, AL 36088.

CARTER, HOWARD
Professional athlete. **PERSONAL:** Born Oct 26, 1961, Baton Rouge, LA; married Allison; children: Kelly. **EDUCATION:** LA State, 1983. **CAREER:** Dallas Mavericks, guard 1984-. **ORGANIZATIONS:** Played for the gold meadal-winning team at '81 World Univ Games in Bulgaria. **HONORS/ACHIEVEMENTS:** Played in all 5 playoff games; scored a career-high 25 points on 1/18/84; two-time honorable mention All-Amer. **BUSINESS ADDRESS:** Dallas Mavericks, Reunion Arena, 777 Sports St, Dallas, TX 75207.

CARTER, HOWARD PAYNE
Educator. **PERSONAL:** Born Sep 09, 1921, Houston, TX; married Lolla Patterson; children: Vicki, Howard. **EDUCATION:** Tuskegee Inst bs 1966; columbia u, ma 1950; u CA, ma 1956; u WI, phd 1964; u CA, post doctral training 1966. **CAREER:** Tuskegee Inst, dean 1968-, prof Biology 1974, assoc prof Biology 1964-74, asst prof Biology 1957-64, instructor Biology 1957. **ORGANIZATIONS:** Mem Soc of Protozoologists; Am Soc of Parasitologists; Am Assn for Higher Edn; Am Inst of Biological Sci; Soc of Sigma Xi; Beta Kappa Chi Phi Boule; Alpha Phi Alpha; Scabbard & Blade; Tuskegee Civic Assn; NAACP numerous papers. **MILITARY SERVICE:** AUS 1st lt 1942-46. **BUSINESS ADDRESS:** Professor of Biology, Tuskegee University, Tuskegee, AL 36088.

CARTER, J. B., JR.
Manager. **PERSONAL:** Born Oct 05, 1937, Pascagoula, MS; married Mary Mallard; children: J B III, Joy Bonita, Janelle Betrice. **EDUCATION:** Tougaloo Coll, BA 1960. **CAREER:** Pub Schs MS, tchr coord; Litton Industries, labr Rltns, rep EEO coor mgr; Keesler AFB, mgmt specialist; MS St Employment Csecurity Com, employment interviewer; Jackson County Neighborhood Youth Corps, dir; Gulf Coast Safety Soc, sec 1975. **ORGANIZATIONS:** Adv bd Jackson County Salvation Army's Bldg Fund Drive 1975; mem Jackson County Civic Action Com 1969; decon, 1st Christian Ch; mem Omega Psi Phi Frat;chmn Paspoint Handicap Com 1972; co-chmn Bi-racial Com, Moss Point Sch System 1972; mem Jackson County Pres Task Force; sec bd trustees, Moss Point Municipal Separate Sch Dist 1975. **HONORS/ACHIEVEMENTS:** Outstanding Citizen, Jackson County Non-partisan Voters Leg 1974; Distinguished Serv Awd, Pas Point Jaycees 1972; Omega Man of Yr 1967.

CARTER, JAMES
Educator, mayor, businessman. **PERSONAL:** Born Jul 06, 1944, Woodland, GA; son of Jimmie L Carter and Mae Bell Carter. **EDUCATION:** Albany State Coll, Albany, GA, BS, Business, minor Math, PE; Georgia State Univ, Atlanta, GA; Univ of Georgia, Athens, GA, Finance. **CAREER:** City of Woodland, Woodland, GA, mayor, 1982-; Self-employed, small business manager; Homes of the South, Greenville, GA, contract writer, 1988. **ORGANIZATIONS:** Baptist Student Union; National Conf of Black Mayors; Joint Center for Political Studies-SBCC; Natl Towns and Townships-GRWA; Small Towns; Georgia Conference of Black Mayors; Master Mason. **HONORS/ACHIEVEMENTS:** Teacher of the Year, Central High School, 1979; Man of the Century Award, Concerned Citizens, 1988; Special Alumni Award, Albany State Coll, Albany, GA, 1989; appeared in Albany State Coll Magazine, Albany, GA, 1989.

CARTER, JAMES EARL, JR.
Physician. **PERSONAL:** Born Oct 13, 1943, Kansas City, KS; son of James E Carter Sr and Anna Sneed Carter; married Nina Sharon Escoe; children: Chisty, Kimberley. **EDUCATION:** UMKC, BS 1965; Univ MO, MD 1969; Walter Reed Hosp, intern 1969-70l; residency, Ventura County Hospital 1972-73. **CAREER:** Family practitioner 1975; Wayne Miner Health Ctr, family physician 1973-75; James E Carter, M.D., P.C. Kansas City MO, family physician & president 1975-. **ORGANIZATIONS:** Natl Med Assn; Jackson Co Med Soc; Amer Heart Assn Kansas City Chap; life mem NAACP; life mem Africare; Sunday School Teacher, Baptist Church; Metropolitan Medical Society; deacon, Paseo Baptist Church. **HONORS/ACHIEVEMENTS:** Fellowship Award Amer Acad of Family Practice 1975. **MILITARY SERVICE:** AUS med corp cpt 1969-72. **BUSINESS ADDRESS:** 7800 Paseo, Kansas City, MO 64131.

CARTER, JAMES EDWARD, III
Educational administrator. **PERSONAL:** Born Sep 03, 1938, Columbia, SC; son of Dr & Mrs James E Carter Jr; married Judy Luchey; children: James E IV, Mason Johnson III. **EDUCATION:** Howard Univ, 1958; Paine Coll, BS, 1958-60; South Carolina State Coll, MEd, 1971-73; Faith Coll, LHD, 1978. **CAREER:** Richmond County Bd of Educ, teacher, counselor, principal, 1960-73; AUS, AUSR, instructor of med corps, 1963-67; Franklin Life Insurance Co, agent, financial consultant, 1969-72; Med Coll of GA, recruiter, counselor, asst dean, Student Affairs, 1973-present. **ORGANIZATIONS:** pres, Belair Hills Assn, 1973-75; vice dist rep, 7th Dist, Omega Psi Phi, 1974-77; Black Heritage Comm, 1975-; pres, Alpha Mu Boule; Sigma Pi Phi, 1979-81; appointee Govenor's Advisory Council on Energy, 1980-82; Natl Assn of Med Minority Education, 1983-85; pres, Natl Assn of Student Personnel Workers, 1987-88. **HONORS/ACHIEVEMENTS:** United Negro Coll Found Distinguished Achievement Awards, 1977-; Paine Coll, Pres Alumni Award, 1979; Lucy C Laney High School Distinguished Alumni Award, 1983; governor, State of AR, AR Govenor's Award, 1984; Presidential Award, Natl Assn of Personnel Workers, 1985, 1989; Presidential Citation, Natl Assn of Med Minority Educators, 1982, 1984, 1985, 1987; Article, "The Need for Minorities in the Health Professions in the 80's: The National Crisis and the Plan for Action," 1986. **MILITARY SERVICE:** AUS, sp 5 E5; Good Conduct Medal, 1963; Honorable Discharge, 1969. **HOME ADDRESS:** 1528 Flagler Rd, Augusta, GA 30909. **BUSINESS ADDRESS:** Assistant Dean Student Affairs, Medical Coll of GA, DA 215 Medical College Of GA, Augusta, GA 30912.

CARTER, JAMES EDWARD, JR.
Retired dentist. **PERSONAL:** Born Jul 01, 1906, Augusta, GA; son of James Edward Carter and Emma Elizabeth Barnett; married Marjorie Butler, Jan 07, 1928; children: James III. **EDUCATION:** Haines Normal & Indust Inst, postgrad 1924; Howard Univ, DDS 1930; Fellow Amer Coll Dentistry 1972; Fellow Acad Gen Dentistry 1976; Fellow Royal Soc Health 1974; Fellow Acad of Dentistry Intl 1977. **CAREER:** Dentist 1930-81. **ORGANIZATIONS:** Mem Thankful Baptist Church 1918-, chmn trustee bd 1937-77, deacon 1960-; pres GA Dental Soc 1941; pres Natl Dental Assoc 1954-55; vice pres Natl Dental Assn 1952-53; chmn 9th St YMCA 1950-57; Boy Scouts of Amer del rep Natl Conv 1960; delegate Republican Natl Convention 1960; pres Stoney Med Dental & Pharm Soc 1961-63; bd dir Atlanta Richmond Co Lib 1967-71; mem Fedn Dentaire Internationale 1975; life mem Natl Dental Assn 1972-; Omega Psi Phi Frat Inc 1974; fellow Worldwide Acad of Scholars 1975; life mem Amer Dental Assn 1976; GA Dental Assn 1976; chmn Emeritus Thankful Bapt Ch 1977; life mem Amer Coll of Dentists 1978; mem Eastern Dental Assn; mem Intl Coll of Dentists 1981; mem Pierre Fauchard Acad 1983; pres John A Andrew Clinic Dental Sect; mem Club Frontiers, Optimist Intl; honora ble fellow GA Dental Soc 1987. **HONORS/ACHIEVEMENTS:** Omega Psi Phi past Basilius Psi Omega Chap 1936-37; treas 7th Dist Omega Psi Phi 1943-74; Achievement Awd Pub Serv Upsilon Sigma Chap Omega Psi Phi Frat 1949; Awd of Merit GA Dental Soc 1961; Achievement Awd Intl Human Relations Psi Omega Chap Omega Psi Phi 1963; Omega Psi Phi Frat Awds 40 yrs 1965, 50 yrs 1976, 60 yrs 1985; mem Sigma Pi Phi Frat 40 yr awd 1965, 50 yr awd 1975; 55 Yr Awd Thankful Baptist Ch 1973; GA Dental Soc Dentist of Yr Awd 1979-80; Whitney Young Awd Boy Scouts of Amer 1980; Achievement Awd Stoney Med/Dental & Pharm Soc 1980; Honorable Fellow Awd GA Dental Assn 1980; 50 Yr Awds GA Dental Soc, GA Dental Assn 1980; Fellow Intl College 1981; Howard Univ Coll of Dentistry Alumni Achievement Awd 1982; Stoney Med Dental and Pharmaceutical Soc Special Acknowledgement Awd f or 53 yrs 1983; mem Omicron Kappa Upsilon Hon Soc 1984; Eastern Dist Dental Soc of GA for Distinguished Serv as alternate and delegate for 10 yrs to the Amer Dental Assoc 1986. **HOME ADDRESS:** 2347 Fitten St, Augusta, GA 30904.

CARTER, JAMES HARVEY
Psychiatrist, educator. **PERSONAL:** Born May 11, 1934, Maysville, NC; married Jettie Lucille Strayhorn (deceased); children: James Harvey Jr. **EDUCATION:** NC Central Univ, BS 1956; Howard Univ Med College, MD 1966. **CAREER:** Walter Reed Army Hosp, internship 1966-67; Duke Univ Med Ctr, assoc prof 1967-83, prof of psychiatry 1983-; Dept of Corr Raleigh NC, sr psychiatrist 1984-. **ORGANIZATIONS:** Consulting psychiatrist Lincoln Community Health Ctr 1972-; consultant on minority mental health NIMH 1974-78; consultant on drug abuse NC State Univ 1970-71; 56 articles in Referred journals, 3 chapters in textbooks; commander 327th AUSR Hosp 1984-; chairperson Achievement Awards Bd Amer Psychiatric Assn 1984; mem US Senate on Aging and USAR Aged Blacks 1972-74; mem Committee of Black Psychiatrists 1984-86. **HONORS/ACHIEVEMENTS:** Macy Faculty Fellow Duke Univ Med School 1970-74; Faulk Fellow Amer Psychiatric Assn 1968-70, Fellowship 1980-; Fellow Orthopsychiatric Assn 1986; awarded the "A" Prof Designation by the Army Surgeon General Excellence in Psychiatry,. **MILITARY SERVICE:** AUSR col 1956-; Army Achievement Medal 1971; Army Comm 1980; Army Meritorious Serv 1986; Order of Military Merit 1988. **HOME ADDRESS:** 3310 Pine Grove Rd, Raleigh, NC 27610. **BUSINESS ADDRESS:** Professor of Psychiatry, Duke Univ Med School, Dept of Psychiatry, Box 3106, Durham, NC 27710.

CARTER, JAMES L.
Social worker. **PERSONAL:** Born May 20, 1933, Camden, NJ. **EDUCATION:** Howard U, BA; NY U, MSW. **CAREER:** Univ FL, clin soc worker 1975; Inst Black Culture Univ FL, fndr acting dir 1971-72; Student DevelUniv FL, asst dean 1971-72; Black Cultural Cntr Penn State U, dir 1972-73. **ORGANIZATIONS:** Mem Nat Assn Soc Workers; Assn Black Soc Workers; Acad & Cert Soc Workers; citizen adv com Alachua Co Div Corrections. **HONORS/ACHIEVEMENTS:** Radio sta WRUF Salute dist comm serv 1972. **BUSINESS ADDRESS:** Univ FL, Gainesville, FL.

CARTER, JAMES P.
Educator. **PERSONAL:** Born in Chicago, IL. **EDUCATION:** Northwestern U, BS; Columbia Univ Sch Pub Hlth, MS, PhD. **CAREER:** Dept of Nutrition & Nursing, Tulane Univ School of Public Health, chmn; Ibadan Univ, chmn; Egypt, staff pediatrician. **HONORS/ACHIEVEMENTS:** Numerous publ. **BUSINESS ADDRESS:** Tulane Univ, Dept of Nutrition, Sch of Pub Hlth & Trop Med, 1430 Tulane Avenue, New Orleans, LA 70112.

CARTER, JESSE LEE, SR.
Business executive. **PERSONAL:** Born Aug 01, 1926, Indianapolis; children: 3 Children. **EDUCATION:** Butler U; IN U; Howard U. **CAREER:** Owner dry cleaners & household maintenance svc9 1950-65. **ORGANIZATIONS:** Indianapolis C of C 1965-69; dir Indianapolis Urban League 1969-72; Manpower Commn1972-74; presently pres Devel Plus Mem; mem Indianapolis Alumni Chpt; Kappa Alpha Psi; Frat; Urban League; C of C; life mem NAACP. **MILITARY SERVICE:** AUS 1946; 1st lt IN Guard Reserve.

CARTER, JOAN ELIZABETH
Business executive. **PERSONAL:** Born Nov 20, 1937, Columbus, OH; married Panola Carter Jr; children: Kimberly Sue, Panola III, Karen Marie. **EDUCATION:** Shelby State Coll State Tech Inst, 1978-83; Memphis State Univ, 1980-83; OH State Univ 1984. **CAREER:** Defense Depot Memphis, chief emp servs 1971-80, equal employ specialist 1980-84, fed women's prog mgr 1980-84; Defense Construction Supply Ctr, federal women's program mgr, equal employment specialist 1984-. **ORGANIZATIONS:** Minister of music, chair annual women's day, chair Bd of Christian Ed, pastor's wife, ss teacher South Memphis Church of God 1971-84; toastmasters A-OK chap 1981-84; compliance chair Federally Employed Women 1982-83; chairperson Federal Women's Program Council of Memphis 1983; member-

ship chair Federally employedWomen 1984-; organizer & chairperson Intergovermental Council of Women's Program Managers of Columbus 1985. **HONORS/ ACHIEVEMENTS:** Letter of Commendation Defense Depot Memphis Office of Civilian Personnel 1977; Cert of Achievement Office of Civilian Personnel 1980; Outstanding PerformanceAppraisal Defense Depot Memphis Equal Opportunity office 1981; plaque 15 years of dedicated service S Memphis Church of God 1984. **HOME ADDRESS:** 5011 Coventry Ct N, Columbus, OH 43232.

CARTER, JOHN H.
Personnel administrator. **PERSONAL:** Born Sep 26, 1948, Thomaston, GA; son of Gus Carter and Rosa Carter; married Susan Gibson; children: Gregory L, Candace M. **EDUCATION:** Robt E Lee Inst, attended 1965-66; Morris Brown Coll, BA 1970; Univ of UT, MS 1977; Univ of Southern CA, MS 1989. **CAREER:** Cambridge Sch System, instr 1970; So Bell Tele & Teleg Co Atlanta, mgmt asst 1973, bus office mgr 1973-74, personnel supr 1974-76, bus office mgr 1976-77; Amer Tele & Teleg Co Basking Ridge NJ, dist mgr eeo goals/ analysis 1977-79; So Bell Tele & Teleg Co Atlanta, dist mgr personnel admin 1979-80; dist mgr assessment American Tel & Tel Co Atlanta GA 1980-81; Southern Bell dist mgr copr plg 1982-87 Operations mgr supplier relations; dir of purchasing 1987-88; BellSouth Fellow Univ of Southern CA 1988-89; general manager, property and service Southern Bell 1989-. **ORGANIZATIONS:** Visiting prof bus Paine Coll Augusta 1977; visiting prof bus Barber-Scotia Coll Concord NC 1978; pres Alpha Phi Alpha Frat 1969-70; pres Mt Olive Jaycees NJ 1977-78; chmn of admin bd SuccaSunna United Meth Ch 1978-79; bd dirs Atlanta Met Fair Housing 1983; loan exec Fulton Co Comm GA 1981; pres Huntington Comm Assn Atlanta 1981-82; vice pres Seaborn Lee Sch PTA Atlanta 1983-84; mem Clark Coll Allied Health Comm Atlanta 1981;Pres; Vice Pres Fulton Co Zoning Orgin Review Comm 1982 Pres; Econom Deve Advisory Brd 1985- ;Chrmn Douglas HS Bus Advis Cncl 1985-; Adult Schl Super Ben Hill United Mech Church 1986-87; Brd of Dir Renaisssance Capital Corporation 1987. **HONORS/ACHIEVEMENTS:** Natl Chap of Yr Natl Alpha Phi Alpha Frat 1970; Jaycee of Yr Coll Park Jaycees GA 1977; Outstanding Young Men in Amer 1978; Jaycee of Yr Mt Olive Jaycees NJ 1979; Outstanding Pres in Region NJ Jaycees 1978; BellSouth Services President's Award 1987. **MILITARY SERVICE:** AUS sp/5 1970-72; Good Conduct Medal. **HOME ADDRESS:** 3465 Somerset Trail, Atlanta, GA 30331. **BUSINESS ADDRESS:** General Manager, Southern Bell, 100 Perimeter Center West, Room 350, Atlanta, GA 30348.

CARTER, JOHN R.
Councilman. **PERSONAL:** Born Sep 02, 1941, Laurens County, SC; married Carrie; children: Anthony, Wadis, Kris. **CAREER:** Gray Ct, councilman; Gleams Human Res Comm, affirm action off; laborer 1960-69. **ORGANIZATIONS:** Bd mem Laurens Cty Serv Coun Sr Citizens; bd mem Gleams Weatherization Bd; pres SC Equal Opport Assoc; treas Southeast Reg Equal Opport Off & Assoc; past-pres Laurens Cty Chptr NAACP; worshpfl mstr Red Cross Masonic Ldg FMPHA; pres SC Equal Opport Assoc; former mem Laurens Cty Select Serv Bd Town Coun of Gray Court SC (2 yrs). **HONORS/ACHIEVEMENTS:** 1st black Gray Ct Council. **BUSINESS ADDRESS:** PO Box 196, Laurens, SC 29360.

CARTER, JOSEPH, JR.
Realtor. **PERSONAL:** Born May 12, 1927, Newark, NJ; married Ann; children: 5. **EDUCATION:** Grant Tech Coll, 1952-54; Am River Coll, 1955-56; Sacramento State Coll, 1957-59; Realtors Inst, grad 1972; Sacramento State U, housing mgmt 1972-73; Sacramento Jr Coll, ghetto econ 1973. **ORGANIZATIONS:** Mem NAACP; Urban League; Sacramento Bd of Realtors; CA Bd of Realtors; Sacramento Valley Chap of Inst of Real Estate Mgmt; Building Consultant Showcase Homes; Co-founder Minority Broker Assn; Co-founder New Start Inc; chmn Marketing Com; Operation Breakthrough; chmn Oak Park Redevel; Project Area Com; Sacramento City Housing Code Adv & Appeals Bd. **HONORS/ACHIEVEMENTS:** Sacramento Bd of Realtors Victory Medal. **MILITARY SERVICE:** USAF s/sgt 1945.

CARTER, JUDY SHARON
Personnel administrator. **PERSONAL:** Born Dec 22, 1951, Miami, FL; daughter of James Carter and Ola Carter. **EDUCATION:** Fisk Univ, BS (Magna Cum Laude, Dept Honors) 1969-73; Univ of MI, MA 1973-74, Coll of Financial Planning, AFP (CFP designation pending). **CAREER:** Dade Cty School Miami FL, teacher 1974-75; City of Miami FL, admin asst 1975-77, personnel officer 1977-78, sr personnel officer 1978-79, exec dir civil serv bd (1st Black & 1st Black woman exec dir) 1979-; Assoc Financial Planing (1st Black Woman in Dade County). **ORGANIZATIONS:** 1st black trustee Bd of Trustees City of Miami Pension Bd 1980; pres Natl Assoc of Civil Serv Commiss 1983; mem Leadership Miami Alumni Assoc; mem Natl Forum for Black Public Admin, Intl Personnel Mgmt Assoc, FL Public Personnel Assoc, Federal Selective Serv Syst Be, Natl Assoc of Female Exec; mem, Delta Sigma Theta Inc; sec Miami-Fisk Alumni Club; mem Young Adult Choir/New Way Fellowship Baptist; mem Natl Assoc of Negro & Professional Womens Club, Credit Union Loan Committee, Carver Young Mens Christian Assoc, Greater Miami Urban League, Amer Assoc of Individual Investors, Intl Assoc of Financial Planners; YWCA; Coordinator, Women's Growth Inst, New Way Fellowship Baptist; NAACP; Inst of Certified Financial Planners. **HONORS/ ACHIEVEMENTS:** Grad Class Leadership in Miami Greater Miami Chamber of Commerce 1980; article & publications, Carter, Judy S & Timmons, Wm M "Conflicting Roles in PersonalBds, Adjudications vs Policy Making "Public Personnel Mgmt, Vol 14, #2, 1985. **BUSINESS ADDRESS:** Executive Dir Civil Serv Bd, City of Miami, 1145 NW 11th St, Miami, FL 33136.

CARTER, LAMORE JOSEPH
Educator, psychologist. **PERSONAL:** Born Apr 18, 1925, Carthage, TX; married Lena Mae Jones; children: Greta Lisa, Kris-Lana. **EDUCATION:** Wiley Coll, 1946-47; Fisk U, AB 1950; Univ of WI, MS 1952; State Univ of IA, PhD 1958; Univ of Chicago, postgrad 1954; Univ of TX, 1966; Columbia, 1967; Emory U, 1970; Harvard U, 1976. **CAREER:** Grambling Coll LA, instructor 1952-54; asst 1961-66; State Univ of IA, rsch asst 1956-58; Institutional Research, admin 1966-68; Southern Assn of Colls & Schools, research fellow postdoctoral 1969-70; Morehouse Coll, visiting distinguished prof Psychology 1970; TX Southern Univ Houston, dean of faculties 1970-71; Grambling State Univ, assoc dean for admin 1971-76; consultant Peace Corps West Africa 1971-76; Southern Assoc of Colls & Schools, consultant 1971-82; Amer Council on Educ, fellow in academic admin 1976-77; Grambling State Univ, vice pres academic affairs 1977-. **ORGANIZATIONS:** Mem Am Educ Research Assn; diplomate Am Bd Professional Psychology; mem chap pres Am Assn Univ Prof 1960-63; consultant Headstart Program 1968-76; mem Am Southwestern; LA Psychol Assn; Am Assn for Higher Edn; Am Assn on Mental Deficiency; Nat Soc for Study Edn; LA Assn Mental Health; Nat Educ Assn mem; Phi Delta Kappa; Phi Beta Sigma; Dem; Meth; mem Amer Psychological Assoc; founder & pres Lions Club Intl 1981-84; bd of dirs United Campus Ministry. **HONORS/ACHIEVEMENTS:** Mason 32 degree; Fellow Amer Assoc on Mental Deficiency; Diplomate Amer Bd of Professional Psychology; cited in Who's Who in Amer; Licensed School Psychologistby LA Bd of Examiners of Psychologists; contrib articles to professional jours books monographs. **MILITARY SERVICE:** AUS; Bronze Star. **BUSINESS ADDRESS:** Vice Pres for Academic Affairs, Grambling State University, Grambling, LA 71245.

CARTER, LAWRENCE
University administrator. **PERSONAL:** Born Oct 04, 1942, Valdosta, GA; son of Mrs Isabell Beady Carter; married Mrs Marva L Moore, Jan 28, 1968; children: Mauri D Carter, Laurent L Carter. **EDUCATION:** Fort Valley State College, Ft Valley GA, BS, 1968; Tuskegee Institute, Tuskegee AL, MS, 1969; Florida State Univ, Tallahassee FL, EdS, 1973, PhD, 1976. **CAREER:** Goldkist Industries, Atlanta GA, mgr trainee, 1969-71; Tuskegee Inst, Tuskegee AL, asst prof of Adult Educ, 1973-74; Florida A&M Univ, Tallahassee FL, ext rural devel specialist, 1974-80, acting dir agricultural research, 1980-87, dir cooperative extension, 1980-. **ORGANIZATIONS:** Mem, Fort Valley State Coll Alumni Assn, 1968, Tuskegee Alumni Assn, 1969, Adult Education Assn of America, 1973, Florida A&M Univ Alumni Assn, 1974; consultant, Univ of Florida Int Program, 1980; dir, Steering Comm, Bethel Baptist Church, 1982-84; mem, bd of dir, Southern Rural Devel Center, 1987; pres, Phi Beta Sigma, Local Chapter, 1987; consultant, Kellog Project, North Carolina A&T Univ, 1988; mem, Policy Comm, Extension Serv, USDA. 1989. **HONORS/ACHIEVEMENTS:** Author, Thesis, "Adult Educ," 1969 The Effect of Readability on Comprehensive of Consumer Laws, 1976 A Package Approach for Rural Clientele, 1979 Small Farm Development in Florida's Vegetable Industry, 1979; Certificate of Appreciation, Governor's Office, State of Florida, 1981; Certificate of Appreciation, Florida A&M Univ, 1984; Strategic Planning for Cooperative Extension Involvement in International Programs, 1985; Meritorious Achievement Award, Univ of Florida, 1986; Certificate of Appreciation, Florida A&M Univ, 1987; Service Award, Florida A&M Univ, 1988. **MILITARY SERVICE:** AUS, Spec 4, 1961-65; Good Conduct Medal, 1964.

CARTER, LAWRENCE E., SR.
Clergyman, educational administrator. **PERSONAL:** Born Sep 23, 1941, Dawson, GA; married Marva Lois Griffin; children: Lawrence Edward Jr. **EDUCATION:** VA Coll, BA Soc Studies 1964; Boston Univ, MDiv Theol 1968, STM Pastoral Care 1970, PhD Pastoral Psych & Counseling 1978; Andover Newton Theol School, OH State Univ, Harvard Univ, GA State Univ, additional study. **CAREER:** Roxbury United Presbyterian Church, minister to youth 1965-67; Boston Public Schools, sub teacher 1966-77; Twelfth Baptists Church, minister of counseling 1968-71; Boston Univ Warren Residence Hall, resident counselor & asst dir 1968-71; People's Baptist Church, assoc minister 1971-78; Harvard Univ Divinity School, clergy teaching advisor 1976-77; Marsh Chapel Boston Univ, assoc dean 1978-79; Morehouse Coll, assoc prof, prof, dept of philosophy & religion 1979-; Martin Luther King Jr Intl Chapel Morehouse Coll, dean 1979-. **ORGANIZATIONS:** Mem Atlanta United Nations Assoc; bd of governors Natl Council of Chuches of Christ 1983-; mem Natl Assoc of Coll & Univ Chaplains, ACLU, Amer Acad of Religion, Assoc of Black Prof of Religion, Ministries to Blacks in Higher Ed, NAACP; coord Afro-Amer Studies Prog Simmons Coll, coord 1977-78; mem Soc for the Study of Black Religion, Class of Leadership Atlanta 1986. **HONORS/ACHIEVEMENTS:** Citizenship Medal of the Year VA Coll 1964; Recognition of Outstanding Achievement in the field of Religion & Humanitarianism Omega Scroll of Honor Morehouse Coll 1979; Natl Black Christian Student Leadership Consultation Awd in Appreciation for Support & Commitment to Devel of Black Christian Leadership 1980; Listed in Personalities of the South 1982; Delegate to United Nations Spec Committee Against Apartheid 1984; numerous radio &TV appearances including Ebenezer Church Serv WAGA Channel 5 Atlanta GA, "The Role of the Black Church" WAOK Interview Atlanta GA, WCNN Radio Anthony Johnson Commentary 1984, CNN Roy Patterson Interview 1984; Voted Faculty Mem of the Year Morehouse Coll Student Newspaper; Del to the 6th Assembly of the World Council of Churches 1983; Del to the World Baptist Youth Conf in Argentina 1984; Del to 4th Natl Council of Churches Dialogue between the Soviety Union Clergy & Amer Clergy in Moscow; Senate Concurrent Resolution by the State of MI in Honor of Dr Carter 1985. **BUSINESS ADDRESS:** Dean of M L King Jr Chapel & Prof of Philosophy & Religion, Morehouse College, 830 Westview Dr, PO Box 725, Atlanta, GA 30314.

CARTER, LEMORIE, JR.
Franchise owner. **PERSONAL:** Born Dec 09, 1944, Birmingham, AL; son of Lemorie Carter and Gloria Carter; married Joyce Goosby; children: Kristie, Ronnie, Lemorie III. **EDUCATION:** Morehouse Coll, 1963-65; Miles Coll, BA Soc Sci 1967; Life Underwriter Training Council, 1972. **CAREER:** Firestone Tire & Rubber Co, sales mgr 1968-70; Met Life Ins Co, sales rep 197-77; Lemorie Carter Ins Agency, Midland Natl Life Ins Co, ins broker, gen agent 1977-; AL Williams Fin Serv Org, sr vice pres 1983-; Carter-Carter Ins Agency, owner; Mayor Richard Arrington Jr Birmingham AL, admin asst 1977-; sr vice pres First Amer Natl Securities & The A L Williams Corp. **ORGANIZATIONS:** Adv bd Sickle Cell Anemia Screening Found 1979, Birmingham Creative Dance Co 1980; instr ins seminars Miles Coll, Daniel Payne Coll, Lawson State CommColl; treas Birmingham Urban League 1973-; initiated voter reg Birmingham 1973; publ rel dir Alpha Phi Alpha Omicron Lambda Chapt; budget comm Six Ave Bapt Church. **HONORS/ACHIEVEMENTS:** Num ins org awds, frat awd; Outstanding Young Men in Amer 1972-77; Outstanding Bd Mem Awd, Outstanding Serv Pin Birmingham Urban League 1975,78; several Financial Services Industry Awards. **BUSINESS ADDRESS:** 100 40th Street North, Avondale Commerce Park, Birmingham, AL 35222.

CARTER, LENORA
Publisher. **PERSONAL:** Born Mar 12, 1941, Corrigan, TX; widowed; children: Constance, Karen. **CAREER:** Forward Times Newspaper, chmn of bd, publisher. **ORGANIZATIONS:** Mem Riverside Hosp, Eliza Johnson Home for Aged, 20th Century Fund, Nat Assn Market Developers, Nat Newspaper Publishers Assn; sec NNPA; mem Am Red Cr, United Fund, United Negro College Fund, Eta Phi Beta, Gamma Phi Delta. **HONORS/ ACHIEVEMENTS:** Recipient Nat Emphasis Award NAMD; Fred D Patterson Leadership Award; Nat Assn of Media Women; Houston Med Forum Recognition Award; Outstanding CitizenState Of MI; listed Personalities of the South & Black Texans of Distinction. **BUSINESS ADDRESS:** Publisher, Chairman of the Bd, Forward Times, P O Box 2962, Houston, TX 77004.

CARTER, LEWIS WINSTON
Real estate broker. **PERSONAL:** Born Jul 16, 1920, Middletown, OH; children: 4 Chil-

dren. **EDUCATION:** Hampton Inst, grad 1944; Detroit Inst Tech, 1961; Univ Detroit, 1963. **CAREER:** Self-employed, real estate broker. **ORGANIZATIONS:** Sec Demo Dist #16; bd educ Region #2; mem United Citizens of SW Detroit; pres St Andrew & Benedict Dads Club; life mem NAACP; mem & Sts Andrew& Benedict Ch; mem Nat Lawyers Guild. **HONORS/ACHIEVEMENTS:** Police award 1960; Sch Achievement Award; State Legislature Common Council Detroit 1963. **MILITARY SERVICE:** USN 1943-46. **BUSINESS ADDRESS:** 2311 S Fort St, Detroit, MI.

CARTER, LISLE CARLETON, JR.
Attorney. **PERSONAL:** Born Nov 18, 1925, New York, NY. **EDUCATION:** Dartmouth Coll, AB 1945; St John's Univ Law School, LLB 1950. **CAREER:** US Dept of HEW, dep asst sec 1961-64; Office of Economic Oppty, asst dir for interagency rltns 1964-66; US Dept of HEW, asst sec for individual & family serv 1966-68; Natl Urban Coalition, vice pres for prog devel 1968; Cornell Univ, vstg prof of public admin 1968-70, vice pres for social & inviron studies 1969-71, prof public policy (tenured) 1970-74, dir of public policy & admin prog 1971-74; Atlanta Univ Center, chancellor 1974-77; Univ of Dist of Columbia, pres 1977-82; Verner Liipfert Bernhard McPherson & Hand, attorney partner 1982-. **ORGANIZATIONS:** Mem NY Bar 1950-, Pres Comm on Pension Policy 1979-80, Dist of Columbia Bar 1982-; mem bd dir Georgetown Univ 1982-; chmn The Charles F Kettering Found 1983-; mem bd of trustees Dartmouth Coll 1983-; mem DC Law Revision Comm 1985-; sec, bd mem Greater WA Rsch Ctr 1986-; mem bd dir The Prudential Ins Co of Amer 1987-. **HONORS/ACHIEVEMENTS:** Hon LLD Bethune-Cookman Coll 1976; Hon LLD George Washington Univ 1979; Hon LLD Dartmouth Coll 1979; Hon LLD Georgetown Univ 1982. **HOME ADDRESS:** 1307-4th St SW, Washington, DC 20024.

CARTER, MARGARET LOUISE
Elected official, educator. **PERSONAL:** Born Dec 29, 1935, Shreveport, LA. **EDUCATION:** Portland State Univ, BA; Washington State Univ, Post-Grad Studies, OR State Univ, MEd. **CAREER:** Albina Youth Opportunity School, instr 1971-73; Portland Comm Coll, counselor 1973-; business woman 1975-; House Educ Comm, mem 1985-; Conf Comm on Martin Luther King Jr State Holiday, co-chair 1985; Joint House-Senate Comm on Trade & Economic Development 1985-; Special Joint Comm on Health Care, mem 1986; OR House Human Resources Comm, vchair 1987-; OR State, state rep. **ORGANIZATIONS:** Mem OR Alliance for Black School Ed, Portland Teachers' Assoc, OR Assembly for Black Affairs, Amer Fed of Teachers, Spec Commiss for the Parole Bd on the Matrix Syst, NAACP, OR Political Women's Caucus, Alpha Kappa Sor; co-founder Black Leadership Conf 1986; gov appointee OR Task Force on Drug Abuse 1986-;gen adv comm Victims Rights 1986-. **HONORS/ACHIEVEMENTS:** Zeta Phi Beta Sor Awd; Musical Dir of the Joyful Sound Piedmont Church of Christ Portland; Appointed to OR State Commiss on Post-Secondary Ed; First blackwoman in history to be elected to OR Leg Assembly; Jeanette Rankin First Woman Awd OR Women's Political Caucus 1985; Jefferson Image Awd 1985. **BUSINESS ADDRESS:** Representative, District 18, 364 State Capitol, Salem, OR 97310.

CARTER, MARION ELIZABETH
Educator. **PERSONAL:** Born Jan 25, Washington, DC; daughter of James Martin Carter and Marion Jackson Carter. **EDUCATION:** Wellesley Coll; Howard Univ, MA; Middleburg Coll, MA; Georgetown Univ, MS; Catholic Univ, PhD; Georgetown Univ, PhD. **CAREER:** Wellesley Coll, visiting prof; Gordon Coll, prof; Teachers Coll, prof; Howard Univ, instructor; Barber Scotia Coll, instructor; Wiley Coll Stud Advisor, assoc prof; Univ of La Gaguna, lecturer; Amer Language Inst of Georgetown Univ, teacher; St Mary Univ Nova Scotia, lecturer. **ORGANIZATIONS:** Natl Assn of Foreign Student Affairs; mem Le Droit Park Civic Assn; mem Smithsonian Inst; past sec, Amer Assn of Teachers of Spanish & Portuguese; mem AAUP, AAUW, IBC, ABI. **HONORS/ACHIEVEMENTS:** Intl Biog Ctrt; Buena Aires Conv Award; Agnes Meyer Award; AATSP Award, Spain; Directory of Amer Scholars; Fulbright Award Spain; placque, Lifetime Bd of Governors, American Biographical Inst, Intl Hall of Leaders, IBC Book of Dedications.

CARTER, MARTIN JOSEPH
Clergyman. **PERSONAL:** Born Jul 31, 1930, High Point, NC. **EDUCATION:** Cornell Univ, MEd 1960, BA 1956; Emersin Coll, BA 1956. **CAREER:** Archdiocese Kingston, Jamaica, pastor 1976-; St Francis De Sales Church, 1975-76; St Joseph Comm Parochial School, tchr coord facilitator 1970-75; Harvard Univ, consult 1970-74; Dissemination Prog, participant 1971-72; Univ of Illinois Curriculum Studies in Math, model tchr. **ORGANIZATIONS:** Mem Natl Black Catholic Clergy Caucus 1968-77; Caribbean Ecumenical Const for Devel 1976-77; exec for Jamaica Council of Churches 1976-77. **HONORS/ACHIEVEMENTS:** Published "Teen-Age Marriage" 1974; "Homiletic & Pastoral Rev - Diocesan Policy on Teenage Marriages" 1975; "Dignitatis Humanae Declaration on Religious Freedom"; The New Catholic Encyclopedia 1979. **BUSINESS ADDRESS:** Church of Reconciliation, Kenton Ave, Bridge Port, Jamaica.

CARTER, MARY LOUISE
Elected official. **PERSONAL:** Born Jun 27, 1937, Clarksdale, MS; daughter of Mrs Julia M Turner; married Everett L Carter; children: Danny C, Eric L. **EDUCATION:** Coahoma Jr Coll, AA 1959; Alcorn Coll, 1959-60; Fontbonne Coll, 1977. **CAREER:** Sears Credit Central, CRT operator 1969-; City of Pagedale, alderperson. **ORGANIZATIONS:** Bd mem Normandy Mun Council 1981-88; bd mem Adult Basic Educ 1981-86; acting pres of bd City of Pagedale 1984-86; chairperson Public Awareness Adult Basic Educ 1984-85; acting mayor City of Pagedale 1984-85; Alderperson city of Pagedale 1981-. **HOME ADDRESS:** 1284 Kingsland, Pagedale, MO 63133. **BUSINESS ADDRESS:** Councilperson, City of Pagedale, 1404 Fergusond Ave, Pagedale, MO 63133.

CARTER, MATTHEW GAMALIEL
Mayor, business executive. **PERSONAL:** Born Oct 16, 1913, Danville, VA; married Frances A Hill; children: Bettye, Frances, Nanette, Carolyn. **EDUCATION:** Columbia U, grad student; Union Theol Sem NYC; Bloomfield Coll NJ honorary lLd 1969. **CAREER:** Bapt Ch, ordained to ministry 1939; Petersburg VA, minister 1940; Leigh St YMCA & Richmond, exec dir 1940-48; SW Area Council Nat Council of YMCA, assoc exec dir 1948-51; Spring St Br YMCA Columbus OH, exec dir 1951-58; Assn Pub Dept Nat Council of YMCA, asst dir 1958-69; Comm Affairs Hoffman-LaRoche Inc Nutley NJ, dir 1969-; Montclair NJ, bd chmn 1964-68; Montclair, mayor 1968-; Laymen's Nt Bible Com Inc, bd dir; First Fed Savs & LoanAssn, dir; NJ Conf Mayors, exec. **ORGANIZATIONS:** Mem NJ State League Municipalities; Commuter Adv Com; NJ Dept Transp; mem NJ Civil Rights Commn; bd dir chmn publs com; dir of com to affairs; Hoffman-LaRoche; Am Camping Assn rep. **HONORS/ACHIEVEMENTS:** Recipient NJ Fedn Negro Women's Club Award for being 1st Negro elected mayor of major NJ city 1968; Phi Delta Kappa Achievement Award 1968; Award for Outstanding Leadership in Govt; Montclair Chap Nat Council of Negro Women 1965; Man of the Yr Award Philadelphia YMCA; Y's Mens Club 1962; Distinguished Serv Award Bonkers Nat Life Ins Co 1969; Achievement Award N NJ Alumni Chap United Negro Coll Fund 1964. **BUSINESS ADDRESS:** Hoffmann La Roche Inc, Nutley, NJ 07110.

CARTER, MICHAEL
Professional athlete. **PERSONAL:** Born Oct 29, 1960, Dallas, TX; married Sandra Porter; children: Michelle Denee. **EDUCATION:** Southern Methodist Univ, Sociology degree 1984. **CAREER:** San Francisco 49ers, nose tackle 1984-. **HONORS/ACHIEVEMENTS:** The only four-time NCAA Indoor Shot Put Champ in history; won outdoor crown three times, placed second in the 1984 NCAA meet; All-Southwest Conference first teamer; second team UPI All-Amer selection in 1983; named Most Valuable Def Plyr in the 1980 Holiday Bowl; Silver Medal in Olympic shot put event; selected Second Team All-Pro by AP and College and Pro Football Newsweekly; mem 1986 NFL Pro Bowl team. **BUSINESS ADDRESS:** San Francisco 49ers, 711 Nevada St, Redwood City, CA 94061.

CARTER, MILTON O., SR.
Business executive. **PERSONAL:** Born Mar 17, 1912, St Louis, MO; married Ida M; children: Catherine ELindsey, Milton, Jr. **EDUCATION:** Wilson Jr Coll, attended 2 years; Central YMCA Coll, attended 2 years; George William Coll, attended 1 year. **CAREER:** St Charles School for Boys, rec dir 1983-41; Pine St YMCA St Louis, boys work sec 1941-45; N Webster YMCA St Louis, exec dir 1945-48; Wabash Ave YMCA Chicago, dir comm serv for outpost work 1948-50; Southtown YMCA Chicago, 1st Black staff mem 1951-53; Maxwell St YMCA Chicago, exec dir 1953-66; Wabash Ave YMCA, exec dir 1967-69; Univ of IL Chicago, spec asst to vice chancellor 1970-78; retired. **ORGANIZATIONS:** Mem adv bds, Near Westside Council, City wide Mental Health Bureau; chmn of Univ of IL Chicago Campus of Natl Youth Sports Program; Eisenberg Boy's Club Chicago. **HONORS/ACHIEVEMENTS:** Outstanding Work Award YMCA of Chicago 1958; Man of the Year Old Town Chicago Boy's Club 1975; Recognition Award Board of Trust Univ of IL Chicago 1977; Model Cities Chicago Comm on Urban Oppty Serv 1975; Humanitarian of the Year Near West Side Council 1977; Continuous Leadership Halsted-South Lawndale Citizens Adv Cncl to the City of Chicago 1978; Cert of Appreciation Dist 9 Chicago Bd of Educ 1978; Achievement Award for Vol Serv Chicago Police Dept 1978; Mayor Bilandic's Proclamation Day 1978; YMCA Olde Tymer Inc St Louis for Man of Compassion 1982; Apprec of Serv as Chmn of Adv Bd Salvation Army Chicago 1983.

CARTER, NANETTE CAROLYN
Professional artist. **PERSONAL:** Born Jan 30, 1954, Columbus, OH; daughter of Matthew G Carter and Frances Hill Carter. **EDUCATION:** L'Accademia di Belle Arti, Perugia Italy, 1974-75; Oberlin Coll, Oberlin OH, BA, 1976; Pratt Inst of Art, Brooklyn NY, MFA, 1978. **CAREER:** Dwight-Englewood School, Englewood NJ, teacher of printmaking and drawing, 1978-87; self-employed artist and painter, 1987-. **ORGANIZATIONS:** Mem, The Studio Museum in Harlem, 1984-, New York Artist Equity Assn Inc, 1987-, Free South Africa, 1987-; artistic bd, Cinque Gallery, 1988-89; mem, NARAL, 1988-, Amnesty Int, 1988-. **HONORS/ACHIEVEMENTS:** Jerome Found Grant, 1981; Natl Endowment for the Arts Grant, 1981; Solo Exhibition-Ericson Gallery, New York NY, 1983; Artist in Residence Grant, New York State Council on the Arts, 1984; New Jersey State Council Grant, New Jersey State Council on the Arts, 1985; Exhibition, Newark Museum, "Twentieth Century Afro-American Artist," Newark NJ, 1985; featured in The Christian Science Monitor, "Artist at Work-Nanette Carter," 1986; Exhibition, Studio Museum in Harlem, New York, NY, 1988; Solo Exhibition, Montclair Art Museum, Montclair NJ, 1988; Fellowship, Bob Blackburn's Printmaking Workshop, 1989.

CARTER, NELL
Actress, singer. **PERSONAL:** Born Sep 13, 1948, Birmingham, AL. **EDUCATION:** Bill Russell's School of Drama, attended. **CAREER:** Num radio &TV appearances in AL; num club appearances & concerts incl Los Angeles Philharmonic; Hair, Modern Problems 1981, Back Roads 1981, Baryshnikov onBroadway, The Big Show, Dude, Don't Bother Me, I Can't Cope, Jesus Christ Superstar, Bury the Dead, Rhapsody in Gershwin, Blues is a Woman, Black Broadway, Ain't Misbehavin', actress; Gimme a Break, star. **ORGANIZATIONS:** Mem AFTRA, Screen Actors Guild, Equity; life mem NAACP. **HONORS/ACHIEVEMENTS:** Tony Awd; OBIE Awd; Drama Desk Awd; Soho News Awd for Ain't Misbehavin'. **BUSINESS ADDRESS:** c/o Triad Artists Inc, 10100 Santa Monica Blvd, 16th Floor, Los Angeles, CA 90067.

CARTER, ORA WILLIAMS
Educator, artist. **PERSONAL:** Born Aug 25, 1925, Ferndale, MI; daughter of Samuel Williams and Emma Kinney Williams; married Walter H Carter (deceased). **EDUCATION:** Black Mountain Coll, Rosenwald Fellowship to attend summer art inst 1946; Clark Coll, AB 1947; Wayne State Univ, MEd 1963; Harvard Univ, Rosenwald Fellowship to attend summer inst in urban educ 1965. **CAREER:** Detroit Bd of Educ, teacher 1953-67; Communication Skills Center, instructor/diagnostician 1967-72; Bow Elementary School, instructor 1972-76; Roosevelt Elementary School, precision teacher 1976-81; Ora's Studio, artist 1978-. **ORGANIZATIONS:** Mem MI Assn of Calligraphers, Natl Conf of Artists, Met Detroit Reading Council 1965-81, Detroit Federation of Teachers; pres Detroit Alumnae Chapter Delta Sigma Theta Sorority 1973-75; charter mem Fred Hart Williams Genealogical Soc, Founders Soc & Friends of African Art; life mem NAACP; mem Museum of African Amer History, Bd of Mgmt YWCA 1972-79 1980-84; chairperson Bd of Mission Educ & Social Action Mayflower Congregational United Church of Christ 1976-80; mem Div of Mission Detroit Metro Assn United Church of Christ; chairperson Women's Day Comm Mayflower cong UCC 1984; mem bd dirs Delta Home for Girls 1968-78; mem bd of dirs Federation of Girls homes 1975-78; recording sec March of Dimes Fashion Extravaganza 1970-75; mem New Detroit Arts Comm 1982-; exhibited in juried calligraphy shows; 1st vice pres, Top Ladies of Distinction, 1987-88. **HONORS/ACHIEVEMENTS:** Artist of the Month Afro-Amer Museum of Detroit 1975. **HOME ADDRESS:** 19501 Hubbell, Detroit, MI 48235.

CARTER, OSCAR EARL, JR.
Physician. **PERSONAL:** Born Aug 02, 1922, Chesterbrook, VA; married Edna; children: Oscar III, Don, Donna, Kim. **EDUCATION:** Meharry Med Coll, MD 1952; Dillard U, BA 1948. **CAREER:** Lower 9 Methadone Clinic Inc, med dir sponsor; physician family prac 1959-76; Well Baby Clinics Eastside Hlth Dist, dir 1954-59; gen prac 1953-59; Lower 9 Methadone Clinic Inc, dir 1970-76; Desire Narcotics Rehab Ctr, med dir 1971-72; Com Alcoholism & Drug Abuse, med coord 1971-72. **ORGANIZATIONS:** Mem Sanity Commn Sect I Criminal Dist Ct 1971-72; Drug Abuse Rehab Team; consult SUNO'S Dept Drug Abuse; Dist I Adv Bd La; adv bd bur Drug Affairs New Orleans; New Orleans Med Soc; Nat Med Assn Cert Drug Abuse; Univ Miami Dept Urban Studies 1972; LSU Med Sch Dept Continuing Med Educ 1975. **BUSINESS ADDRESS:** 2017 Caffin, New Orleans, LA 70117.

CARTER, PATRICK HENRY, JR.
President. **PERSONAL:** Born Jan 08, 1939, Memphis, TN; married Mattie Pearl Bland; children: Kimberly, Patrick H III. **EDUCATION:** Attended, Mississippi Valley State Univ, Lemoyne Coll, General Motors Inst. **CAREER:** Exxon USA, instructor 1972; Pat Carter Pontiac Inc, president. **ORGANIZATIONS:** Exec bd Liberty Bowl 1982-86; pres Memphis Pontiac Group 1983; president Memphis Auto Dealers 1985; exec bd Leadership Memphis. **HONORS/ACHIEVEMENTS:** Achiever Pontiac Motor Div 1984-86; Top 100 Black Businesses Black Enterprise Magazine 1984, 1985, 1986, 1987; Small Business of the Year 25-75 employees, Memphis Business Journal 1988. **MILITARY SERVICE:** USN E5 4 yrs. **BUSINESS ADDRESS:** President, Pat Carter Pontiac, Inc, 3400 Elvis Presley Blvd, Memphis, TN 38116.

CARTER, PERCY A., JR.
Clergyman. **PERSONAL:** Born Jul 04, 1929, Hampton, VA; married Evelyn; children: Allen, Audrey, Mildred, Mark, Daniel. **EDUCATION:** VA Union U, AB 1949; Harvard Sch of Bus Adminstrn, 1951-52; M Div Andover-Newton, 1953; Boston Univ Sch of Theology, MST 1953; Harvard Divinity Sch,1953-55; Brown U, 1958-59. **CAREER:** Olney St Bapt Ch Providence RI, formerly pastored; Mt Calvary Bapt Ch Mansfield OH; Hosack St Bapt Ch Columbus OH, presently pastor. **ORGANIZATIONS:** Mem Bapt Pastor's Conf; mem Ministerial Alliance; mem Interdenom of Ministerial Alliance of Columbus OH; Met Area Church Bd Affiliate; broadcasts on radio weekly;previously served as substitue tchr on secondary level in pub sch; past chmn Mansfield Alliance for Progress; past chmn & founder Opport Indusl Cntr of Mansfield OH. **HONORS/ACHIEVEMENTS:** Contrib "What Jesus Means to Me", "Seven Black Preachers" 1971. **MILITARY SERVICE:** USAF 1963-68. **BUSINESS ADDRESS:** Pastor, Hosack St Baptist Church, 1160 Watkins Rd, Columbus, OH 43207.

CARTER, PERRY W.
Data systems officer. **PERSONAL:** Born May 24, 1960, Washington, DC; son of Charles P Carter and Viola Green Carter. **EDUCATION:** US Air Force Acad Prep School, Colorado Springs CO, 1978-79; US Air Force Acad, Colorado Springs CO, 1979-81; Temple Univ, Philadelphia PA, BA, 1985; Golden Gate Univ, Ft Myer VA, 1988-. **CAREER:** US Marine Corps, Washington DC, data systems officer, 1985-; Joint Education Facilities Inc, Washington DC, instructor, 1989-; Meridian Publishing, Washington DC, CEO, 1989-, chmn of the bd, 1989-. **ORGANIZATIONS:** Public affairs dir, Natl Naval Officers Assn, 1987-; asst editor, Journal of Black Data Processing Assoc, 1988-; editor, Articles of the Coalition, Washington DC Coalition of Black Professional Org, 1989-. **HONORS/ACHIEVEMENTS:** Cofounder, Temple Univ Student Chapter, BDPA, 1984; Outstanding Young Men of America, 1986, 1988; founding editor, NNOA Meridian, 1987, Articles of the Coalition, 1989; founder, chairman, CEO, Meridian Publishing Inc, 1989. **MILITARY SERVICE:** USAF, USMC, First Lt, 1978-; Certificate of Commendation, 1987. **BUSINESS ADDRESS:** United States Marine Corps, Company B, HQBN, HQMCCode (MMEA-51), Arlington, VA 22214.

CARTER, PHILIP W., JR.
Educational administration. **PERSONAL:** Born Feb 01, 1941, Widen, WV; married Beverly Thomas; children: Philippa, Stacey, Frederick. **EDUCATION:** Marshall Univ, BA Pol Sci 1964; Univ of Pittsburgh, MSW 1970. **CAREER:** Congress of Racial Equality, dir Cleveland 1967-68; Univ of Pittsburgh Graduate School of Public Intl Affairs, instr 1970-78; Comm Action Reg Training, dir 1972-73; Univ of Pittsburgh, asst to the provost 1979; DIGIT Inc, pres 1967-; Marshall Univ, dir soc work prog. **ORGANIZATIONS:** Consult Intercultural House Univ of Pittsburgh 1969-70; consult Clarion Univ of PA 1973,76,80,81,83,84,85; campaign mgr Mel King for Mayor in Boston 1979; bd mem Schuman Juvenile Ctr 1979-81; bd mem Human Relations Commiss 1982-; bd mem Barnett Day Care Ctr Huntington WV 1982-84; chairman Western PA Black Polit Assembly 1974-; campaign mgr Doris Smith for Judge Spring 1985. **HONORS/ACHIEVEMENTS:** Recipient Ford Found Fellowshp 1968; Outstanding Man of the Year Talk Mag 1974; Outstanding Contrib in Politics Black Republicans 1978; Outstanding Black Alumni Marshall Univ 1978; recognized by Herald Dispatch Newspaper as Major Architect of 1960's Student Movement 1983; Summa Cum Lauda in Tchng Excellence Marshall Univ Minority Affairs 1985. **BUSINESS ADDRESS:** Director, Social Work Program, MarshallUniv, 749 Smith Hall, Huntington, WV 25701.

CARTER, RAYMOND GENE, SR.
Educator, executive. **PERSONAL:** Born Nov 12, 1936, Youngstown, OH; married Virginia Averhart; children: Raymond Gene, John Amos, Dewayne Dwight. **EDUCATION:** Youngstown State U, BA 1959, MEd 1975; Univ of Pittsburgh, candidate PhD. **CAREER:** McGuffey Ctr Inc, admin dir, 1976-86; Youngstown State Univ, ltd serv faculty 1976-; Model City, dep dir; Curbstone Coaches, bd dir; Youngstown State Univ, limited serv faculty political & social sci dept. **ORGANIZATIONS:** Minority rep Stub Canal Private Sector; chmn Welf Adv Bd; Social Serv; bd dir Asso Neighborhood Ctr; vice pres bd dir Meth Comm Ctr; Eval Com - Area Health; bd dir C of C; mem Kiwanis Club; Big Brothers; bd dir Eastern Mental Health High Sch; mem Selective Svc; foreman Mahoning County Jury 1981. **HONORS/ACHIEVEMENTS:** Leadership & Citizenship Award; Coll Most Valuable Athlete; Curbstone Coaches Hall of Fame Youngstown; Athletic Achievement Awd Serv Awd Youngstown City Mayor; Community Serv Awd Black Knight Police Assoc; Choffin Career Ctr Award, 1988. **MILITARY SERVICE:** AUS 1960-62. **BUSINESS ADDRESS:** Limited Service Faculty, Youngstown StateUniv, Youngstown, OH 44503.

CARTER, ROBERT HENRY, III
Corporate executive. **PERSONAL:** Born Aug 02, 1941, Chicago, IL; married Marlene Y Hunt; children: Robert H IV, Kimberly, Brandon Robert. **EDUCATION:** Chicago City Colleges, attended 1962; Worshams Coll of Mortuary Science, attended 1963; IL Inst of Technology, attended 1964. **CAREER:** Lawndale Packaging Corp, sales mgr 1971-72; Chicago Minority Purchasing Council, purchasing specialist 1972-75; Robert H Carter, III & Assocs, Inc, pres 1975-; Group Insurance Administration Inc, pres 1982-. **ORGANIZATIONS:** Mem Cosmopolitan Chamber of Commerce 1972-, Chicago Urban League 1975-, Chicago Assoc of Commerce & Industry 1979-, Self Insurance Inst of Amer 1983, Soc of Professional Benefit Administrators 1984-, Professional Ins Marketing Assn 1986-. **HONORS/ACHIEVEMENTS:** Ten Outstanding Young Men of Chicago Jaycees (Chicago Area) 1974. **BUSINESS ADDRESS:** President, Group Insuance Admn Inc, 205 W Wacker Dr, Chicago, IL 60606.

CARTER, ROBERT LEE
Judge. **PERSONAL:** Born Mar 11, 1917, Caryville, FL; widowed; children: John, David. **EDUCATION:** Lincoln Univ, AB 1937; Howard Univ, LLB (Magna Cum Laude) 1940; Columbia Univ, LLM 1941; Lincoln Univ, DCL 1964. **CAREER:** Poletti, Freiden, Prashker, Feldman & Gartner, member of firm 1969-72; US Dist Ct So Dist, judge 1972-. **ORGANIZATIONS:** Mem NY Bar Assn 1941-; assp spl cnsl NAACP 1945-46; dir Vets Affairs Am Vets 1948-49; mem New York City Mayor's Jucic Comm 1968-72; educ bd NY Law Journ 1969-72; pres Natl Comm Against Descrim in Housing 1966-72; mem NY State Spl Comm on Attica, NY Ct Reform 1970-72; mem Natl Conf Black Lawyers. **HONORS/ACHIEVEMENTS:** Recipient Howard Univ Disting Alumni Award 1980; Fellow Columbia Urban Center 1968-69; Resenwald Fellow 1940-41. **MILITARY SERVICE:** USAF 2nd Lt 1941-44. **BUSINESS ADDRESS:** Judge, U S Dist Ct So District, U S Courthouse, Foley Square, New York, NY 10007.

CARTER, ROBERT T.
Business executive. **PERSONAL:** Born Mar 21, 1938, Cleveland; married Virginia; children: Robert John. **EDUCATION:** Baldwin Wallace Coll, BA 1959; Pepperdine Grad Sch of Business. **CAREER:** KFI Radio Inc, accnt exec 1968-; Hoffman LaRoche, sales & hosp rep 1966-68; Shell Oil Co Long Beach, sales rep 1964-66; Cleveland, tchr 1959-64. **ORGANIZATIONS:** Mem Natl Assn Market Developers; Radio Salesman of LA; mem Southern California Broadcasters; mem LA Brotherhood Crusade; New Frontier Dem Club; United Crusade Fund Raising Comm 1974-75; Leukemia Soc of Amer; Southern California Striders Track Club. **HONORS/ACHIEVEMENTS:** Martha Jennings Teaching Award 1963; Pharmaceuticals Sales Award LaRoche 1968; California delegate to Democratic Convention 1968; California Democratic Council 1968; Democratic State Central Comm 1968. **BUSINESS ADDRESS:** 610 S Ardmore, Los Angeles, CA 90005.

CARTER, ROBERT THOMPSON
Education program executive. **PERSONAL:** Born Mar 16, 1937, Cleveland, OH; son of Robert Carter (deceased) and Evelyn Carter (deceased); married Tessa Rosemary Felton; children: Robert, Jacqueline. **EDUCATION:** Dartmouth Coll, BA 1959. **CAREER:** Joseph T Ryerson & Son Inc, supervisor personnel admin 1967-68, mgr comm relations 1968-70; North Lawndale Econ Devel Corp, asst genl mgr 1970-72; Inland Steel Develop Corp, asst regional mgr & project mgr 1972-77, exec dir and sec 1981-86; Inland Steel-Ryerson Foundation, exec dir and sec 1981-86; Dearborn Park Corp, vice pres corp communications and corp sec 1977-81; Natl Merit Scholarship Corp, vice pres natl achievement scholarship prog 1987-. **ORGANIZATIONS:** Co-fndr Black Contractors United 1979; bd chairperson Just Jobs Inc 1982-86; dir Performance Comm 1982-86; vice pres Assoc of Black Foundation Execs 1984-86; founding mem/dir Indiana Donors Alliance 1984-86; corp adv bd Independent Coll Funds of Amer 1984-86; consultant, Lawndale Business and Local Develop Corp 1986-89; vice pres Music/Theatre Workshop 1986-; dir Brass Foundation Inc 1987; dir Blacks in Development 1987-; dir, Garfield Counseling Center 1986-; trustee, Gaylord & Dorothy Donnelley Foundation 1988-. **HONORS/ACHIEVEMENTS:** Leadership Awd Black Contractors United 1979; Beautiful People Awd Chicago Urban League 1980. **MILITARY SERVICE:** USAF capt 1959-66; Air Force Commendation Medal 1964. **BUSINESS ADDRESS:** Vice President of Achievment Prog, Natl Merit Scholarship Corp, One Rotary Center, Evanston, IL 60201.

CARTER, ROMELIA MAE
Chief executive officer. **PERSONAL:** Born Jan 01, 1934, Youngstown, OH; divorced. **EDUCATION:** Youngstown State Univ, BA 1974; WV Univ, MSW 1976. **CAREER:** Youngstown Comm Action Council, comm org 1967-70; Youth Devel Agency, proj dir children & family serv 1976-79; Assoc Neighborhood Ctrs, exec dir. **ORGANIZATIONS:** Mem Natl Assoc Black Soc Workers, Mattoning Cty Assoc of Counselors, Delta Sigma Theta Sor, Youngstown Urban League; issues chmn Youngstown Chap of OH Black Womens Leadership Caucus; mem Natl Council of Negro Women. **HONORS/ACHIEVEMENTS:** N Side Youth Serv Awd N Side Youth Council 1970; Serv Awd N Side Oldtimers 1972; Warren Black Youth Serv Awd Warren Black Youth 1974; listed in Who's WhoAmong Univ & Coll Students 1974; Civic Soc Awd OH Black Womens Leadership Caucus 1976; Comm Serv Awd Child & Adult Mental Health Ctr 1977. **BUSINESS ADDRESS:** Community Organizer, Assoc Neighborhood Centers, 755 Lexington Ave, Youngstown, OH 44510.

CARTER, RUBIN
Professional athlete. **PERSONAL:** Born Dec 12, 1952, Pompano Beach, FL; married Diana; children: Rubin Andre, Diandra Nicole. **EDUCATION:** Miami, Bus Admin. **CAREER:** Real estate salesman; Denver Broncos, nose tackle 1975-; Prudential-Bache Securities, investment banker. **ORGANIZATIONS:** Mem Fellowship of Christian Athletes; mem Pro-Athletes Outreach. **HONORS/ACHIEVEMENTS:** MVP on Defense Hula Bowl; Kodack All Amer; Coaches All-Amer Team 1975; Broward Co Hall of Fame; photo Sports Illustrated 1977; Ed Block Awd of Courage. **BUSINESS ADDRESS:** Denver Broncos, 5700 Logan St, Denver, CO 80216.

CARTER, RUTH DURLEY
Orthodonist. **PERSONAL:** Born Apr 01, 1922, LaFollette, TN; children: Ann, Bekka. **EDUCATION:** Meharry Med Coll Sch of Dentistry, DDS 1948; Orthodontic Sch St Louis U, post grad 1958. **CAREER:** Self-employed orthodontist; Mound City Dental Soc,. **ORGANIZATIONS:** Past pres Mound City Dental Soc; past pres Mid-Western St Dental assn; past mem Assoc Amer Women Dentists; Delta Sigma; Theta Sor; vice pres Comm Rel Educ Found 1966. **HONORS/ACHIEVEMENTS:** 1st female honored Mid-Western St Dental Assn; 1st black St Louis Dental Soc; mem Who's Who in Amer 1968. **BUSINESS ADDRESS:** 1326 Avalon Blvd, Wilmington, CA 90744.

CARTER, THEODORE ULYSSES
Attorney. **PERSONAL:** Born Oct 16, 1931, Birmingham; married Joyce A; children: Theodore N, Julia W. **EDUCATION:** Howard U, BA 1955; JD 1958; NY U, postgrad 1962-63. **CAREER:** PA NJ bars, atty; IRS Phila, atty 1961-; Glassboro NJ State Coll, adj prof justice. **ORGANIZATIONS:** Vol counsel Camden Legal Servs 1970-; mem Am Jud & Soc; Am Nat PA NJ Bar Assns; Howard Univ Alumni Assn.

CARTER, THOMAS ALLEN
Consultant. **PERSONAL:** Born Jul 12, 1935, Cincinnati, OH; son of Fernando Albert Carter and Mary Gladys Gover Carter; married Janet Tucker; children: Barry E, Duane A, Sarita A. **EDUCATION:** Jones Coll, AB (Cum Laude) 1980, BBA (Cum Laude) 1982. **CAREER:** Red Lobster Restaurant Const Dept, contract administrator 1976-78; Harcar, Inc, pres 1978-80; Blacando Develop Corp, exec sec 1980-84; DAMS Inc, project engr 1984-. **ORGANIZATIONS:** Consult cost estimating JH Dunlap Roofing Co 1978-84, Robinson's Custom Homes 1980-84; mem Bluejackets Choir USN, Bluejackets Octet USN, Amer Soc of Profl Estimators; Fleet Reserve Association. **HONORS/ACHIEVEMENTS:** Sailor of the Year 9th Naval Dist 1960; SeaBee of the Month Argentia Newfoundland Canada 1965. **MILITARY SERVICE:** USN master chief construction man E-9 22yrs; Navy Commendation Naval Unit Citation, Vietnam Expo, Good Conduct (5), Presidential Unit Citation, Expert Rifleman. **HOME ADDRESS:** 4128 Arajo Ct, Orlando, FL 32812. **BUSINESS ADDRESS:** Chief Project Engineer, DAMS, Inc, 5750 Major Blvd, Orlando, FL 32819.

CARTER, THOMAS CALVIN
Professional athlete. **PERSONAL:** Born Feb 05, 1961, Sun Valley, CA. **EDUCATION:** San Diego State. **CAREER:** Oakland Invaders, leftback 1984-. **HONORS/ACHIEVEMENTS:** Honorable mention All-WAC as a sr; voted teams Most Inspirational Plyr.

CARTER, THOMAS FLOYD, JR.
Educator. **PERSONAL:** Born Feb 04, 1927, Nacogdoches, TX; married Allene A Coleman; children: Jon Andre. **EDUCATION:** Shrivenham Amer Univ Shrivenham England, 1947; TX Coll Tyler TX, BA Engl 1950; TX So Univ Houston, MA Engl 1967. **CAREER:** Star-Post Dallas, sports editor 1951-52; TX City TX, high school teacher, coach 1952-69; Fiction TX, co-editor 1977-; Sidewinder, co-editor 1983; Coll of Mainland, prof 1969-. **ORGANIZATIONS:** Grants comm Moody Found Galveston 1970-72; commiss City of TX City TX 1978-; pres TX Coaches Assoc 1965-66; mem NAACP, MLA, CCTE, CEA, NCTE, SRCE, TJCTA,Kappa Alpha Psi. **HONORS/ACHIEVEMENTS:** Fellowship So Reg Ed Bd 1971; Piper Prof Piper Found San Antonio 1973; Fellowship Natl Endowment for Humanities 1976. **BUSINESS ADDRESS:** Professor, College of the Mainland, 8001 Palmer Hwy, Texas City, TX 77591.

CARTER, WARRICK L.
Educator, composer. **PERSONAL:** Born May 06, 1942, Charlottesville, VA; son of Charles Carter and Everlyn Carter; married Patricia McDonald; children: Keisha. **EDUCATION:** TN State Univ, BS; Blair Acad of Music, Advanced Percussion 1964-65; MI State Univ, MM 1966, PhD 1970; Univ of Chicago, Certificate in Fund Raising 1978. **CAREER:** Univ of MD, asst prof dept of music 1966, 1967, 1971; MI State Univ, dir dept of music 1970, 1971; Governors State Univ, coordinator in fine & performing 1971-76, coord music program 1976-79; Northwestern Univ, guest prof Afro-Amer Studies 1977-84; Governors State Univ, chmn div Fine & Performing Arts 1979-84; Univ of Santa Cantarina Florianopolis Brazil, guest lecture dept music 1980; Berklee Coll of Music, dean of faculty 1984-. **ORGANIZATIONS:** Visiting prof Music Dept CA State Univ LA 1983; guest lecturer School of Music Univ of Sao Paulo Brazil 1976; past pres NAJE 1982-84; "The Whistle" commissioned by the Natl Endowment for the Arts 1982-83; chmn Jazz Panel Natl Endow for the Arts 1982-85; co-chair Music Policy Panel Natl Endowment for the Arts 1983-84; natl sec Black Music Caucus 1974-78; ASCAP; bd mem Natl Jazz Cable Network 1982-84; bd mem Found for the Advancement of Music 1982; on adv bds of MusicFest USA and EPCOT Inst of Entertainment Arts. **HONORS/ACHIEVEMENTS:** Distinguished Teacher Award Gov's State Univ 1974; Best Drummer Award Collegiante Jazz Festival Notre Dame Univ 1970; Faculty Mem of the Yr Univ of MD 1967-68; Graduate Fellow Center of Urban Affairs MI State Univ 1969-70; named as one of ten Outstanding Music Educators by School Musician 1983. **BUSINESS ADDRESS:** Dean of Faculty, Berkelee Coll of Music, 1140 Boylston St, Boston, MA 02215.

CARTER, WEPTANOMAH WASHINGTON
Educator, author, executive. **PERSONAL:** Born Feb 15, 1937, Ossining; married Harold A; children: Weptanomah, Harold A, Jr. **EDUCATION:** Millersville State Tchr Coll, BS 1959; VA Sem Lynchburg, M of Divinity 1975; VA Sem Lynchburg, D of Lit 1977. **CAREER:** MD Bapt Sch of Rel, dean of church admin 1976-; MD Bapt Sch of Rel, instructor 1971-76; The Carter Foundation, pres. **ORGANIZATIONS:** Mem Bd of Trustees Community Coll of Baltimore 1977-83; co-ordinator of Christian Outreach New Shilow Bapt Ch1975-; announeer for radio ministry New Shiloh Bapt Ch; pres The Carter Found Inc. **HONORS/ACHIEVEMENTS:** Afro Honor Roll for Superior Service; Baltimore Afro-Am Newspapers 1971; author "The Black Ministers Wife"; Progressive Nat Pub Co 1976; Woman of the Year-Hon Mention Greyhound Corp 1976; Distinguished Serv Award Millersville Alumni Assn 1978; author "For Such A Time As Time" Gateway Press 1980.

CARTER, WESLEY BYRD
Psychiatrist. **PERSONAL:** Born Apr 22, 1942, Richmond, VA; married Norma. **EDUCATION:** VA Union U, BS 1964; Med Coll of VA, 1968; Med Coll of VA, pediatric internship 1969; Gen Psychiatry Residency, MCV 1971; VA Treatment Ctr for Children, child psychiatry fellowship 1973. **CAREER:** Richmond Pub Schools, psych cons; Friends Assn of Richmond, psych cons; Psych Med Coll of VA, asst clinical prof; Real School Richmond Pub Schools,spec cons; St Mary's Hosp, Stuart Circle, Richmond Meml, Richmond Comm Hosp, Richmond Metro Hosp, Westbrook Hosp, Psych Inst of Richmond, hosp appts; Psych Inst of Richmond Childrens Unit, med chief; Child Psych Ltd, child psych 1975-; Horizons Inc, pres. **ORGANIZATIONS:** Mem Yth Serv Commin Richmond; Spcl Educ Adv Com; Med Coll of VA Soph Med Curr Com; Richmond Acad of Med; past pres Richmond Med Soc; VA Counof Child Psychiatry; bd mem Neuropsychiatric Soc of VA; VA Soc for Adolescent Psychiatry; Med Soc of VA; Am Psychiat Assn; Am Acad of Child Psy; Black Psychiat of Am; Assn of Air Force Psychiat; Chi Delta Mu; Alpha Phi Alpha; past pres Psych Soc of VA. **HONORS/ACHIEVEMENTS:** Fellow Amer Psych Assoc, ACPHA, Kappa Mu, Beta Kappa Chi. **MILITARY SERVICE:** USAF 1975; Commendation Medal. **BUSINESS ADDRESS:** President, Horizons, Inc, 9200 Forest Hill Ave, Ste C-2, Richmond, VA 23235.

CARTER, WILL J.
Transportation company executive. **CAREER:** Carter Industrial Services Inc and Carter Express Inc, Anderson, IN, chief executive. **BUSINESS ADDRESS:** Chief Executive, Carter Industrial Services Inc, 2501 Fairview Street, Anderson, IN 46014. *

CARTER, WILLIAM BEVERLY, III
Educator administrator. **PERSONAL:** Born Feb 22, 1947, Philadelphia, PA; son of W Beverly Carter and Rosalie Terry Carter; married Kay Sebekos; children: Terence. **EDUCATION:** Univ Clge Nairobi Kenya 1965-66; Univ de Paris Sorbonne 1966; Howard Univ BA 1971; Johns Hopkins Univ Schl of Adv Intl Studies MA 1971-73. **CAREER:** US Comm on the Organization of Govt for Conduct of Foreign Policy, staff mem 1972-75; US Dept of State, escort interpreter 1972-75; Brookings Inst, res asst 1974-75; US Dept of Energy, foreign affairs officer 1976-81; Inst of Intl Educ, prog officer. **ORGANIZATIONS:** Mem bd dir Lupus Fnd of Greater Wash DC 1984-; mem Natl Genealogical Soc 1974-, Amer Assc of Individual Investors 1983-. **HONORS/ACHIEVEMENTS:** William C Foster Award JH Univ Schl of Advanced Intl Studies 1972-73, Rockefeller-luce Fellowship 1971-73. **MILITARY SERVICE:** AUS sgt; Bronze Star Ach 1967-70. **HOME ADDRESS:** 1201 Juniper St NW, Washington, DC 20012.

CARTER, WILLIAM THOMAS, JR.
Physician. **PERSONAL:** Born Apr 27, 1944, Norfolk, VA; married Juatina M Redd; children: William III, Dominique Michelle, Tiasha Malitha. **EDUCATION:** Fisk Univ, AB 1967; TN A&I State Univ, MS 1969; Meharry Medical Coll, MD 1973. **CAREER:** United States Navy, dir of emergency medicine. **ORGANIZATIONS:** Mem Kappa Alpha Psi Frat 1963-; dir of emergency medicine Natl Naval Medical Ctr 1980-82; mem Assoc of Military Surgeons of United States 1981-; ATLS instructor Amer Coll of Surgeons 1982-; mem Pigskin Club Inc 1984-, NAACP 1987-, Natl Medical Assoc 1987-, Amer Coll of Emergency Physicians 1987-. **HONORS/ACHIEVEMENTS:** Publication "Gunshot Wounds to the Penis," NY Acad of Urology 1979. **MILITARY SERVICE:** USN commander 9 yrs; Navy Commendation Medal, Meritorious Achievement 1984. **HOME ADDRESS:** 4411 Marquis Pl, Woodbridge, VA 22192. **BUSINESS ADDRESS:** Dir of Emergency Medicine, United States Navy, Naval Medical Clinic, Quantico, VA 22134.

CARTER, WILLIE A.
Carpenter, associate president. **PERSONAL:** Born Sep 05, 1909, Buckingham, CO; married Amanda Carey; children: Fannie, Ernest, James. **CAREER:** Prince Edward Co Br, pres. **ORGANIZATIONS:** NAACP; Mason; mem Human Relations; Prince Edward Co Voters League; Deacon Oak Grove Bapt Ch. **HONORS/ACHIEVEMENTS:** VFW award; NAACP; past Worshipful Master Mason.

CARTER, WILMOTH ANNETTE
Retired educational administrator. **PERSONAL:** Born in Reidsville, NC; daughter of William Percy Carter (deceased) and Margaret Lee Milner Carter (deceased). **EDUCATION:** Shaw Univ, BA 1937; Atlanta Univ, MA 1941; Univ of Chicago, PhD 1959; Shaw Univ, LHD 1986. **CAREER:** Univ of MI, research assoc 1964-65; Tuskegee Inst, research assoc 1965-66; Shaw Univ, chmn soc sci div 1966-69, educ devel officer 1972-73, dir of research 1969-72; vice pres inst research 1973-76, vice pres acad app acad affairs & research 1978-86. **ORGANIZATIONS:** Chmn soc dept Southern Univ New Orleans 1963-64, Shaw Univ Raleigh 1959-63; grad asst Dept of Soc Atlanta Univ 1943-47; mem Delta Kappa Gamma 1974-, Delta Sigma Theta Sor 1935-; Natl Council of Alpha Chi Scholarship Society 1977-1989. **HONORS/ACHIEVEMENTS:** Honor soc Alpha Omicron Shaw Univ 1936-37; Alpha Kappa Delta Atlanta Univ 1941-42; Rosenwald Fellow Study at Univ of Chicago 1947-49, Danforth Fellow 1957-59; Delta Kappa Gamma 1973-; Alpha Chi Honor Society 1979-; author of The Urban Negro in the South, published 1961; author of The New Negro of the South, published 1967; author of Shaw's Universe, published 1973. **HOME ADDRESS:** 1400 E Davie St, Raleigh, NC 27610.

CARTER, YVONNE P.
Educator, artist. **PERSONAL:** Born Feb 06, 1939, Washington, DC; daughter of Irving Lorenzo Pickering and Esther Robinson Pickering; married Joseph Payne (divorced); children: Cornelia Malisia. **EDUCATION:** Howard Univ, BA 1962, MFA 1968; Traphagen School Design, NY, certificate Interior Design 1959. **CAREER:** Dist Display Washington, DCD malisia display coord 1962-63; Howard Univ, Washington DC, library asst 1963-68, asst librarian 1968-71; fed city coll Washington, DC, asst prof of art; Art Dept Univ Dist of Columbia, prof; exhibitor, Howard Univ JA Porter Gallery, one-woman show 1973; Paintings WA Gallery Wash DC, two-woman show; Smith-Mason Gallery Nat Exhbn Black Artist Wash DC; selected group shows & performances: NJ State Museum black artist show; Howard Univ Art Gallery; Franz Bader Gallery Wash DC; Corcoran Gallery of Art; Miami-Dade Public Library; Los Angeles African-Amer Museum; Kenkelaba House, New York, NY; Baltimore Museum; Fendrick Gallery; Walters Art Gallery, MD. **ORGANIZATIONS:** Mem Coll Art Assn 1971-; Am Assn Univ Prof 1974-; DC Registery 1973-74; Am Soc African Culture 1966; Natl Assn Study Negro Life & History 1971-72; Artists Equity, 1987-; Women's Caucus for Art, 1976-. **HONORS/ACHIEVEMENTS:** Publ imprints by Amer Negro artists 1965; dasein 1962. **BUSINESS ADDRESS:** Assoc Prof, Univ of the District of Columbia, Art Dept, MB10-01, 4200 Connecticut Ave NW, Washington, DC 20008.

CARTER-MCCRAW, CAROLYN
Nurse, educator. **PERSONAL:** Born Nov 25, 1932, Monessen, PA; married Alphonse; children: Cynghia S. **EDUCATION:** St Francis Hosp Sch of Nursing, dip 1953; Univ of Pittsburgh Sch of Nursing, BSN 1958, MSN 1966; Univ of Pittsburgh Sch of Edn, doctoral candidate. **CAREER:** Univ of Pittsburgh School of Nursing, asst prof & dir of Minority Affairs 1976, asst prof & dir of Minority Nursing Prgm 1969-76; Hill Team Comm Mental Health Center, Western Psychiatric Inst & Clinic, nurs consult nom inst coord 1967-68, asst dir of nurs 1964-67; VA Hospital, staff head nurse & relief supvr 1954-62; St Francis Hospital, staff nurse 1953-54; Carter Carter & Assoc Inc, vice pres. **ORGANIZATIONS:** Mem Am Nurses Assn; bd dirs PA Nurses Assn; Human Rights Com Dist # 6 Nurses Assn; Nat League for Nursing; PA League for Nursing; Mercy Hosp Adv Com on Hlth Care; Chi Eta Phi Sor Inc; Alpha Kappa Alpha Sor Inc; Jack & Jill Inc; mem Pittsburgh Chap Girl Friends Inc;

mem Club 21; Churchill Woman's Club; St Francis Alumni Univ of Pittsburgh Alumni; Sigma Theta Tau; consult Spec Action Ofc of Drug Abuse Prevention Exec Ofc of White House 1973. **HONORS/ACHIEVEMENTS:** Outst Girl Grad Award Monessen Woman's Club 1950; Black Achievers Award Mon Valley 1974; wrote minority nurse recruitment training & manpower prgm which was awarded fed funds by Ctr for Minority Group Affairs Nat Inst of Mental Hlth 1975-80; commendation OH Senate 1976; WCIN Citz of Day 1976; Cincinnati MentalHlth Assn Reach Out Award 1976; picture hung un Univ of Cincinnati Coll of Nursing Library 1976; Mary Mahoney Award Am Nurses Assn 1976; World Who's Who Of Women 1977. **BUSINESS ADDRESS:** U of Pittsburgh, Sch of Nursing Room 329, Pittsburgh, PA 15261.

CARTEY, WILFRED G. O.
Educator. **PERSONAL:** Born Jul 19, 1931, Port of Spain, Trinidad and Tobago. **EDUCATION:** Univ of WI Jamaica, BA 1955; Columbia Univ NY, MA 1956; Columbia Univ NY, PhD 1964. **CAREER:** Columbia Univ NY, prof Comparative Literature 1963-70; Brooklyn Coll & City Univ of NY; prof 1972; Univ of WI Nassau, res prof extra-mural dept 1972; Afro-Amer Studies, Univ of CA Berkeley, visiting prof 1972; City Coll of NY, distinguished prof black studies 1973-. **ORGANIZATIONS:** Mem Black Academy of Arts & Letters; African Am Heritage Assn; mem African Heritage Studies Assn; Inst of Caribbean Studies; mem ColumbiaUniv Seminars; Inst of the Black Would; conf of Writers of Afr Descent Nat Endowment to the Humanities 1968-69; sr consult Urban Ethnic Affairs Urban Cntr; ColumbiaUniv NY 1968-70; consult Afr & Afro-Am Studies; CUNY NY. **HONORS/ACHIEVEMENTS:** Grants Rsch Found of CUNY 1985,86; author "Whispers From a Continent"; author "Suns and "Shadows", "Red Rain Waters of My Soul", "House of Blue Lightning"; Disting Professorship Martin Luther King Chair; CUNY; Fulbright Travel Grant; Bernard Van Leer Foun Fellowship; Columbia Univ Travel & Rsch Grant; publs BlackImages, Colonial Africa, Independent Africa, Embryos, Black Velvet Time, Children of Lalibela. **BUSINESS ADDRESS:** Professor, CCNY, Convent at 138th Sts, New York, NY 10031.

CARTHAN, EDDIE JAMES
Government official. **PERSONAL:** Born Oct 18, 1949, Tchula, MS; married Shirley; children: Cissye, Neketa. **EDUCATION:** MS Valley State U, BS 1971; Jackson State U, MS 1977; Univ MS. **CAREER:** Carthan's Convenience Store, owner mgr; Carthan's Pkg Store; Crystal Rest; Lexington Bus Serv Inc, bus specl 1973; Holmes Co Bd & Edn, pres 1973; St Coll, instr 1972. **ORGANIZATIONS:** Bd dir Delta Found; mem Gov Midas Com; King David Mason Lodge #112; Holmes Co Bd Edn; Holmes Co Elks. **HONORS/ACHIEVEMENTS:** Publ "The Last Hired & First Fired"; "Success & Hard Work"; editor "If Things Could Talk"; "We've Come A Long Way, Baby"; "Bus Ruralite". **BUSINESS ADDRESS:** PO Box 356, Tchula, MS 39169.

CARTLIDGE, ARTHUR J.
Educator. **PERSONAL:** Born Jun 28, 1942, Rolling Fork, MS; married Helen Rose King; children: Byron Darnell, Arthur J, Jr, Kirsten Jamille. **EDUCATION:** MS Valley State Univ, BS 1965; Delta State Univ, MS 1972; Spec Degree in Adm 1977. **CAREER:** T L Weston High School, teacher 1965-70; H W Solomon Jr High School, 1970-72, asst prin 1973-. **ORGANIZATIONS:** Mem Math Tchr Assn; Greenville Tchr Assn; Dist Tchr Assn; MS Tchr Assn; Nat Ed Assn; Nat Council of Secondary Prin; mem Uniserve Bd; #Jr warden Lake Vista Masonic Lodge; deacon; Mt Horeb Bapt Ch; mem Presidenths Comm; MVSU 1964-65. **HONORS/ACHIEVEMENTS:** Outs Tchr of Year Weston HS 1969-70; Outs Tchr of Year Solomon Jr Hi 1970-71. **BUSINESS ADDRESS:** 556 Bowman, Greenville, MS.

CARTRIGHT, LENORA T.
Educator. **PERSONAL:** Born Dec 21, 1936, Chicago, IL; married Richard Hunt. **EDUCATION:** Univ of Chicago, BA, MA; Layola Univ, MSW. **CAREER:** Urban Sci Univ IL at Chicago Cir, assoc prof 1968-; Cook Co Dept Pub Aid, soc wrkr; Dept of Human Serv City of Chicago, commissioner; Cartright & Assoc Mgmt Community Relations, pres. **ORGANIZATIONS:** Mem Am Pol Sci Assn; mem Am Publ Wel Assn; mem Am Orthopsy Assn mem Am Soc Behav Sci; mem Nat Assn Black Pol Sci; Mem Nat & Assn Black Soc Wrkrs; mem Nat Assn Soc Work; mem Nat Conf Soc Wel; mem Bd Dirs Blue Cross Blue Shield; Urban League; League Black Women; Consult Fifth City Commun Org; mem Joint Cntr Pol Study; mem Metro Hous & Plan Coun; mem Mid-West Commun Coun; mem Nat Conf Christians & Jews; mem YWCA; mem YMCA; mem W Side Health Planning Org; pres Commn Population& Am Future Pubs. **HONORS/ACHIEVEMENTS:** UNICEF Awd 1981; Black Book Awd 1981; Outstanding Alumnae Loyola 1982; Natl March of Dimes Outstanding Volunteer Awd 1982; Disting Leadership Awd YWCA. **BUSINESS ADDRESS:** President, Cartright & Associates, 401 E 32nd St, Chicago, IL 60616.

CARTWRIGHT, CAROLE B
Producer. **PERSONAL:** Born Aug 03, 1940, Chicago, IL; daughter of Donald Beard and Margaret Beard; married Eugene; children: Karen, Shari. **EDUCATION:** DePaul Univ, BS 1962. **CAREER:** KNBC-TV, dir of programing; WMAO-TV, mgr comm programs; "On Q" TV Program, WMAO-TV, exec producer/on air hostess, "As We See It-2- Us Dept of Health Educ & Welfare, project dir, exec producer, 1977-79; WMAQ-TV, producer, 1970-77; Public Affairs Channel 5, Sec, 1962. **ORGANIZATIONS:** Bd dir, Ada McKinley Org; mem, Amer Women in Radio & TV; mem, Natl Assn of Media Women; Natl Broadcast Assn of Fomm Affairs; bd dir, The Bedside Network; Bd of Governors, Academy of TV, Arts & Sciences. **HONORS/ACHIEVEMENTS:** Alpha Kappa Alpha Sorority Serv Award, Chicago School & workshop for Retarded, 1977; Outstanding Program Award, Natl Assn of TV Program Execs, 1976; Producer, Outstanding Children's Program Award, Medinah Shrine Temple, 1971. **BUSINESS ADDRESS:** KNBC-TV, 3000 W Alameda Ave, Burbank, CA 91523.

CARTWRIGHT, JAMES ELGIN
Business executive. **PERSONAL:** Born Jul 17, 1943, Memphis, TN; son of James Cartwright and Rachel Cartwright; children: Jennea. **EDUCATION:** San Diego State Coll, BA 1963; Stanford Univ of Law, 2 yrs 1963-66; Oxford Univ-Trinity Coll, M Intl Law 1968. **CAREER:** SEC, legal 1968-69; Shearson Hammil & Co, compliance examiner-legal 1969-71; 1st Harlem Securities Inc, investment exec 1971-75; Daniels & Cartwright Inc, exec vice pres 1976-84; Cartwright & Daniels Inc, pres, 1984-; Pres, Cartwright Securities Inc, 1985-present. **ORGANIZATIONS:** Consultant, Org of African Unity 1968-; consultant, Social & Econ Council UN, 1969; guest lecturer various high schools & colls in US, 1970-; mem, NAACP 1959-, Omega Psi Phi, 1970-, Council of Concerned Black Execs 1978-; mem NAACP 1959. **HONORS/ACHIEVEMENTS:** Oxford Fellowship Trinity Coll Oxford Eng 1966-68. **HOME ADDRESS:** 315 West 57th St #5H, New York, NY 10017.

CARTWRIGHT, JAMES WILLIAM
Professional athlete. **PERSONAL:** Married Sheri Johnson; children: Justin William, Jason James Allen. **EDUCATION:** Univ of San Fran, BA. **CAREER:** New York Nicks, basketball player 1979-. **ORGANIZATIONS:** Charity work Easter Seals. **HONORS/ACHIEVEMENTS:** Ranks 5th among NBA's all-time field goal perc shooters with his 557 Norm; matched the league record for most free throws without a miss going 19 for 19 vs KC at the Garden; first Knickerbocker ctr to start in every game; hattered USF single seas shooting perc mark with blistering 667 pace as a jr. **BUSINESS ADDRESS:** New York Nicks, Madison Sq Gardens, 4 Pennsylvania Plaza, New York, NY 10001.

CARTWRIGHT, MARGUERITE DORSEY
Educator research. **PERSONAL:** Born May 17, Boston, MA; married Leonard Carl Cartwright (deceased). **EDUCATION:** Boston Univ, BS, MS; NY Univ, PhD 1948. **CAREER:** Hunter Coll of the City Univ of NY, teacher, lecturer; communications, journalism other media; adv educ in foregin countries; Phelps Stokes Inst, rsch. **ORGANIZATIONS:** Mem Provisional Council of Univ of Nigeria; served on various delegations & com; covered intl conf including Bandung Middle East African States African Peoples; state guest several Independence Celeb in Africa; mem Govs & Vice Pres Overseas Press Club of Amer bd mem Intl League for Human Rights & various civic orgns; mem UN Corres Assn; Women in Communications Inc; World Assn of Women Journalists & Writers other organs. **HONORS/ACHIEVEMENTS:** Phi Beta Kappa other scholarly hons & awds; Headliners Awd 1975; Highest Natl Awd of Women in Communications Inc; Awds from Ford Found, Links, various civic & professional groups; Amoris Alumna Pax Pope Paul VI; Knight Commander Order of African Redemption Rep of Liberia; Keys to Cities Wilmington Xenia Zurich; street name in Nigeria for serv to Univ of Nigeria; subj of various feature articles. **BUSINESS ADDRESS:** Phelps Stokes Inst, 10 East 87th St, New York, NY 10028.

CARTY-BENNIA, DENISE S.
Educator. **PERSONAL:** Born Jun 28, 1947, Reed City, MI. **EDUCATION:** Barnard Coll Columbia U, BA 1969; Sch of Law Columbia U, JD 1973. **CAREER:** Northeastern Univ School of Law, prof of law; Wayne State Univ Law School, pres, assoc prof of law 1975-77; Kaye/Scholer/Fierman/Hays & Handler, assoc atty 1973-75. **ORGANIZATIONS:** Mem Am Bar Assn, NY State Bar Assn, mem Nat Bar & Assn 1974; mem bd of dir Affirmative Action Coordinating Center, 1978-; co-chmn bd of dir NCBL 1979-; Minority Group Sec Assn of Am Law Sch 1975-; Faculty & Legal Advisor Nat Black Am Law Students Assn 1977-; Cooperating Atty Cntr For Constitutional Rights Research Fellow Inst for the Stury of Educ Policy Howard Univ 1978. **HONORS/ACHIEVEMENTS:** Outstandint serv award Nat Black Am Law Students Assn 1979; presidents award, Nat Bar Assn 1979; revson fellow, Greenburg Center for Law & Soc Policy City Coll NY 1979-80; appreciation award, NE Region Black Am Law Students As, 1980; summer humanities seminar award, Nat Endowment for the Humanities, 1980. **BUSINESS ADDRESS:** Professor of Law, Northeastern University, School of Law, 400 Huntington Ave, Boston, MA 02115.

CARUTHERS, PATRICIA WAYNE
Educational administrator. **PERSONAL:** Born Aug 28, 1939, Kansas City, KS; daughter of Dr. Bertram Caruthers, Sr. and Mrs. Evelyn W. Caruthers. **EDUCATION:** Emporis State Univ, BS 1962; Univ of MO Kansas City, MA 1965, PhD 1975. **CAREER:** US Dist #500, teacher 1962-69; Kansas City KS Comm Coll, teacher 1969-72, asst dean of cont educ 1972-76, asst to the pres 1978-. **ORGANIZATIONS:** Comm KCK Planning & Zoning Bd 1975-85,87-; govt intern Office of Educ HEW 1976-78; past pres Alpha Kappa Alpha Sorority, 1981-83; chmn KC KS Economic Devel Comm 1980-; regent KS Bd of Regents 1982-; treasurer, Links Inc 1984-; mem Kanas City Zoning Appeals Bd. **HONORS/ACHIEVEMENTS:** Top Girl Winner Gr KC Science Fair 4th Place Tokyo 1957; Most Outstanding Young Woman in Amer 1976; Mary McLeod Bethune Alpha Phi Alpha Fraternity, 1982. **BUSINESS ADDRESS:** Assistant to the President, Kansas City KS Comm College, 7250 State Ave, Kansas City, KS 66112.

CARY, REBY
Educator. **PERSONAL:** Born Sep 09, 1920, Ft Worth, TX; married Madine S; children: Faith Annette. **EDUCATION:** Prairie View A & M, BA, MS 1948; TX Christian U, 1951-53; N TX State U, 1961-71. **CAREER:** McDonald Coll Industrial Arts, dir, teacher 1946-49; Tarrant County/Johnson County Vocational School, lead teacher 1954-64; Dunbar High School, counselor 1953-64, asst prof 1964-67; Tarrant County Jr Coll, asst prof 1966-69; Univ of TX Arlington, assoc dean student life, asst prof history 1969-78; TX House of Representatives, Dist 32-B State Legislature, state representative 1978-82. **ORGANIZATIONS:** Mem Nat Educ Found Bd; Alpha Phi Frat 1974-75; reg educ dir 1972-75; sec Ft Worth Independent Sch Bd 1974-75; trustee, choir dir New Rising Star Bapt Ch; bd dirs Boy Scouts Am; bd mem Tarrant County United Way; community dev bd city Ft Worth. **HONORS/ACHIEVEMENTS:** Man of yr Omega Psi Phi 1974; outstanding citizen award, St James AME Ch 1975. **MILITARY SERVICE:** USCG 1942-45. **BUSINESS ADDRESS:** 3307 B Miller Ave, Fort Worth, TX 76119.

CARY, WILLIAM STERLING
Minister. **PERSONAL:** Born Aug 10, 1927, Plainfield, NJ; married Marie B Phillips; children: Yvonne, Denise, Sterling, Patricia. **EDUCATION:** Morehouse Coll, BA 1949; Union Theolog Seminary, MDiv 1952; Morehouse Coll, DD 1973; Bishop Coll Dallas, TX, hon LLD 1973; Elmhurst Coll Elmhurst, IL, hon DD 1973; Allen Univ Columbia, SC, hon HD 1975. **CAREER:** Butler Meml Presbyterian Ch, pastor 1953-55; Intl Ch of the Open Door Brooklyn, NY, pastor 1955-58; Grace Congr Ch NYC, pastor 1958-68; Metro & Suffolk Assns NY Conf United Ch of Christ, area minister 1968-75; IL Conf of United Ch of Christ, conf minister 1975-. **ORGANIZATIONS:** Chr Comm for Racial Justice; mem gov bodies Cncl for Christian Soc Action and Off Communication; appointed by Pres Ford to 17 mem Task Force on Vietnamese Refugee Relocation; mem of 1977 UCC Cncl on Ecumenism; UCC rep to consult on Church Union; Natl Ministerial Adv Cncl; Chicago Theol Seminary Bd; Committee of Denominational Exec IL Conf of Churches; Exec Cncl United Ch of Christ; Church World Serv Comm; pres & vice pres Natl Cncl of Churches in Amer 1972-79; chr Council of Religious Leaders of Metropolitan Chicago; chmn Council of Religious Leaders, Chicago, 1987-88;

mem Council of Religious Leaders, Chicago. **BUSINESS ADDRESS:** IL Conf of United Ch of Christ, PO Box 7208, Westchester, IL 60153.

CASCONE, JEANETTE L.
Retired educator. **PERSONAL:** Born Aug 10, 1918, Gainesville, FL; married Anthony (deceased); children: Sally, Charles. **EDUCATION:** Barber-scotia Coll, Diploma 1939; Howard U, AB 1945; NY U, MA 1956; NY City U; Univ ME; Hunter Coll. **CAREER:** Seton & Hall Univ, asst prof of educ & black studies; Nigeria, W Africa, teacher; Univ of Ibadan, retired teacher. **ORGANIZATIONS:** Mem York City Bd of Educ; mem Bd Trustee, Barber-scotia Coll Concord NC; mem bd trustee, World Fellowship of Faiths; dir region 2 NJ State Assn Study of Afro-am Life & History; mem Nigeria hist Soc; mem NAACP; press Bergen Ct Br 1963-65;State Mem Ch 1964; mem Assn for Study of Afro-Amer Life & Histpres NY Br 1965-66; elected 2nd vice pres Nat Assn for Study of Afro-Am Life & Hist; mem 1968-, pres Assoc of Afro-Amer Life & History. **HONORS/ACHIEVEMENTS:** Honored by Nat Council Negro Women & Jr HS 55 Bronx for youth work; Educ of Yr Negro Book Club; Nat Sojourner Truth Meritorious Srv Award The Union CoNJ Club of the Nat Assn of Negro Bus & Professional Women's Clubs Inc; Honored by Roselle Poravch NAACP for Community work including teaching to sr citizens and the community Afro-Amer & African History. **BUSINESS ADDRESS:** Assistant Professor, Seton Hall University, 400 S Orange Ave, South Orange, NJ 07079.

CASE, ARTHUR M.
Dentist. **PERSONAL:** Born May 18, 1950, Philadelphia, PA. **EDUCATION:** Temple Univ, DDS 1979. **CAREER:** Private Practice, dentist; JFK Memorial Hosp, staff. **ORGANIZATIONS:** Mem Alpha Omega Frat, New Era Dental Soc. **HONORS/ACHIEVEMENTS:** Mem Oral Surgery Honor Soc, Peridontal Honor Soc. **BUSINESS ADDRESS:** 5555 Wissahickon Ave, Philadelphia, PA 19144.

CASEY, CAREY WALDEN, SR.
Minister. **PERSONAL:** Born Oct 12, 1955, Radford, VA; son of Ralph Waldo Casey Jr and Sarah Adline Coles Casey; married Melanie Little, May 15, 1977; children: Christie, Patrice, Marcellus. **EDUCATION:** Northeastern Oklahoma, Miami, OK, Physical Ed, 1974-76; Univ of North Carolina at Chapel Hill, BA Religion, 1979; Gordon-Conwell Theological Seminary, S Hamilton MA, MDiv, 1981; School of Theology Virginia Union Univ, Richmond VA, MDiv, 1984. **CAREER:** Northeastern Univ, Boston, MA, counselor for student athletes, 1980-81; Total Action Against Poverty, Roanoke, VA, youth employment coord, 1981; First Baptist Church, Petersburg, VA, minister in residence, 1982-83; Fellowship of Christian Athletes, Dallas, TX, urban dir, 1983-88; Mount Hebron Baptist Church, Garland, TX, interim pastor, 1984-85; Dallas Cowboys Football Club Training Camp, counselor, 1986-87; Proline Corp, Dallas, TX, consultant, 1987-; Fellowship of Christian Athletes, Kansas City, MO, natl urban dir, 1988-; Todays Image Inc, Dallas, TX, consultant, 1988-; Olympic Protestanc Chaplain, Seoul, Korea, 1988. **ORGANIZATIONS:** Comm, Martin Luther King Center, Dallas, TX, 1984-88; speaker, Athletes in Action, 1984-, Boys & Girls Clubs of Amer, 1986-, mem, NAACP, 1986-; consultant, Great Southwest Fire & Safety, Dallas, TX, 1986-; natl consultant, Salvation Army, 1988-; consultant to bd, International Sports Coalition, 1988-; steering comm, Kansas City Star-Times, 1989-. **HONORS/ACHIEVEMENTS:** Football Scholarship, Univ of North Carolina, 1976-79; Theological Scholarship, Billy Graham Evangelistic Assn, 1979; Outstanding Young Men of America, US Jaycees, 1980; NFL, Major League Baseball Chapel Speaker USA, 1980-; Juanita Craft Contribution to Sports in Comm, NAACP, 1984; L K Williams Inst Bishop Coll, Speaker, 1985; Proclamation Carey Casey Day, City of Louisvill, KY, 12/05/1988; World Congress on Sports, Seoul, Korea, Speaker, 1988. **BUSINESS ADDRESS:** National Urban Director, Fellowship of Christian Athletes, 8701 Leeds Rd, Kansas City, MO 64129.

CASEY, CLIFTON G.
Retired police commander. **PERSONAL:** Born Oct 22, 1924, Yolande, AL; divorced. **EDUCATION:** FBI natl Acad, 1972; Wayne State Univ, BS 1974; Tuskegee Inst, attended. **CAREER:** Detroit Police Dept, promoted through the ranks to police commander 25 yrs, retired; State of Michigan Liquor Control Commission, deputy dir retired 1989. **ORGANIZATIONS:** Mem Intl Assoc Chiefs of Police, MI Assoc Chiefs of Police, Natl Acad Assoc, FBI; life mem NAACP; mem Amer Legion, Tuskegee Airman. **MILITARY SERVICE:** USAF fighter pilot 1943-46.

CASEY, EDMUND C.
Physician. **PERSONAL:** Born in Marion, IN; married Liliane Winkfield; children: Yvette, Yvonne, Amie. **EDUCATION:** Attended Earlham Coll 1942-43, Univ of PA 1943; Meharry Med Coll, MD 1948; City Hosp of Cleveland, internship 1948-49, residency pulmonary diseases 1949-50, internal medicine 1950-52; Post Grad Courses, Cook Co Hosp Grad Sch of Medicine 1958 1960 1961 1965, Amer Coll of Physicians 1965 1966. **CAREER:** Bethesda Hosp, admin tchng staff; Christ Hosp, assoc staff; Univ of Cincinnati, asst clinical prof of medicine; Private Practice, physician internal medicine 1954-. **ORGANIZATIONS:** Mem Natl, Amer Medical Assns; mem former pres Cincinnati Med Assn; mem Acad of Medicine in Cincinnati; pres OH Thoracic Soc 1970-71; mem (various pos held) Natl Med Assn; co-dir of med 1969-71 co-dir of sect on internal med 1970-72 dir of coronary & intensive care units Bethesda Hosp; mem Dean's Comm on Admissions of Minority Students Univ of Cincinnati 1968-72; life mem Amer Radio Relay League, NAACP, Alpha Phi Alpha Frat; rep dir at large Amer Lung Assn 1972-; mem of cncl on health manpower AMA 1971-74; mem (various positions held) Acad of Medicine; mem chmn Natl Adv Comm Sickle Cell Anemia Program of the Natl Inst of Health Dept of Health Educ & Welfare; pres SW OH Lung Assn 1977; mem bd trustees Central State Univ; mem bd trustees Mt Zion United Methodist Ch; chmn of comm on prog & budget 1976-77 pres 1981-82 Amer Lung Assn; vice pres 1981, mem OH Lung Assn 1982,84; pres 1983, chmn 1982-84 Natl Commn on Certification of Physician's Assistants. **HONORS/ACHIEVEMENTS:** Hon DL Central State Univ 1983. **BUSINESS ADDRESS:** 437 Melish, Cincinnati, OH 45229.

CASEY, FRANK LESLIE
Television reporter, journalist. **PERSONAL:** Born Jan 29, 1935, Stotesbury, WV; son of Conston Casey and Mary; married Lenore Thompson, Apr 16, 1988; children: Zauditu, Tamarat, Bakaffa, Charles Arnold. **EDUCATION:** WV State Coll, BS 1962. **CAREER:** WPIX-TV New York City, TV reporter; New York City Dept of Welfare, social worker 1969; Repub Aviation, tech illustrator 1963. **HONORS/ACHIEVEMENTS:** Good Conduct Medal; New York Area Television Academy Award, The National Academy of Televlision Arts & Scienced 1976-77; Uniformed Firefighters Association Award for excellen e in T.V. coverage for fire fighting 1971; Humorous Writing Award, Society of the Silurians, New York 1986; Honorary Membership for Fair & Impartial Reporting for Police Stories, Retired Dectectives of the Police Dept of the city of New York Inc 1984. **MILITARY SERVICE:** AUS sp2 1954-57. **BUSINESS ADDRESS:** News Reporter, WPIX TV, 200 E 42nd St, New York, NY 10017.

CASEY, JOSEPH F.
Physician. **PERSONAL:** Born Mar 14, 1914, Weaver, IN; married Amye; children: 1 Child. **EDUCATION:** IL Coll, Podiatric Med 1937. **CAREER:** Private Practice Podiatric Med, dr. **ORGANIZATIONS:** Mem IN State Parole Bd 1953-58; mem IN State Podiatry Assn pres 1972; staff consult Podiatry for VA Hosp; past pres Marion Urban League 1955, 1965; mem Exchange Club Metro Marion; Marion C of C; bd trustees & past pres Bd of Educ 1966-75. **HONORS/ACHIEVEMENTS:** 33 deg Mason No Jurisdiction Mason of Yr 1960; Podiatrist of Yr 1970. **MILITARY SERVICE:** USN 1943-46. **BUSINESS ADDRESS:** 127 River Dr, Marion, IN 46952.

CASH, ARLENE MARIE
Educator. **PERSONAL:** Born Feb 19, 1955, Boston, MA; married Edward Richard Cash Jr. **EDUCATION:** Keuka Coll, BA 1976; Kent State Univ, MA 1983. **CAREER:** Kent State Univ, grad recruiter 1978-84; Brandeis Univ, assoc dir of admissions 1984-87. **ORGANIZATIONS:** Mem YWCA Cass Task Force 1985-. **HOME ADDRESS:** Brandeix Box 2655, Waltham, MA 02254. **BUSINESS ADDRESS:** Assoc Dir of Admissions, Brandeis University, 415 South St, Waltham, MA 02254.

CASH, BETTYE JOYCE (NEE MOORE)
Business executive. **PERSONAL:** Born Feb 19, 1936, Fort Worth, TX; divorced; children: Ardranae, James Jr, Anthony, Lisa, Janine. **EDUCATION:** Contra Costa Coll, 1963, AA 1975. **CAREER:** W Contra Costa Co, dist hosp dir. **ORGANIZATIONS:** Mem 2nd yr of 2nd 4 yrs term Natl Womens Pol Caucus, Black Bus & Professional Assoc, Church Missionary, CA Hosp Assoc, Med Staff, Assoc of W Hosp, AmerHosp Assoc, Assoc of Dist Hosps Dist Hosp; dir W Contra Costa Hosp. **HONORS/ACHIEVEMENTS:** 1st & only black elected female W Contra Costa Cty 1974; Woman of the Year Honor Soc 1976-77; num other honors. **BUSINESS ADDRESS:** District Hospital Dir, W Contra Costa Hospital Dist, 2000 Vate Rd, San Pablo, CA 94806.

CASH, DAVID, JR.
Athlete. **PERSONAL:** Born Jun 11, 1948, Utica, NY; married Pamela; children: Carmen. **CAREER:** San Diego Padres, 1980; Montreal Expos, 1977-79; Philadelphia Phillies, 1974-76; Pittsburgh Pirates, 1970-73. **HONORS/ACHIEVEMENTS:** NL All-Star 1974; led Expos in at bats (650) hits (188) stolen bases (21) & runs (91) doubles (42) in 1977; holds Major League Record for at bats in a season(699 in 1975); Led League in hits runs scored & doubles in 1975; 3 All Star Games; 4 Championship Series; 1 World Series. **BUSINESS ADDRESS:** San Diego Padres, PO Box 2000, San Diego, CA 92120.

CASH, JAMES IRELAND, JR.
Educator. **PERSONAL:** Born Oct 25, 1947, Fort Worth, TX; married Clemmie; children: Tari, Derek. **EDUCATION:** TX Christian Univ, BS mathematics and computer science 1969; Purdue Univ, MS computer science 1974, PhD management information systems & accounting 1976. **CAREER:** TX Christian Univ Computer Ctr, systems programmer 1969; Langston Univ, dir of computer ctr 1969-72, instructor/asst professor in vo-tech program 1969-72; Arth Drug Stores, Inc, systems analyst & programmer consultant 1973-76; Inst of Educational Management, exec educ course MIS instructor 1977-79; Harvard Grad School of Bus Admin, asst prof 1976-81, instructor in exec educ course 1978-; IBM Systems Research Inst, adjunct prof 1980; Harvard Grad School of Bus Admin, assoc prof of bus admin 1981-85, prof of bus admin 1985-. **ORGANIZATIONS:** Bd of advisors Amer Accounting Assoc; Assoc for Computing Machinery; Quality Assurance Inst; adv bd Society for Information Management; Strategic Management Society; US Dept of State Advisory Comm on Transnational Enterprises 1976-83; Index Systems, Inc 1978-; bd of trustees The Park School 1983-; adv bd BOSCOM 1983-; editorial bd Harvard Business Review 1983-; MA Governor's Advisory Comm on Information Processing 1983-; bd of dirs Affiliated Publications 1984-. **HONORS/ACHIEVEMENTS:** 3 books and 13 papers published; All American Academic Basketball team 1968; Outstanding Instructor Awd Vo-Tech Dept of Langston Univ 1971; Purdue Univ fellowship 1972; Phi Kappa Phi 1974; Hall of Fame TX Christian Univ 1982; 1st Century Disting Alumni Ft Worth Independent School Dist 1983. **BUSINESS ADDRESS:** Prof/Business Administration, Harvard Grad Sch Bus Admin, Anderson # 14, Soldiers Field, Boston, MA 02163.

CASH, PAMELA J.
Librarian. **PERSONAL:** Born Oct 26, 1948, Cleburne, TX; daughter of James Cash, S and Juanita Beatty Cash; married Gervis A Menzies, Sr, Sep 17, 1983; children: Gervis A Mensies, Jr. **EDUCATION:** Univ of OK, BA 1970; Univ of IL, MS Library Sci 1972. **CAREER:** Univ of IL, asst Afro-Amer bibliographer 1970-71, librarian of Afro-Amer studies 1971-72; Univ of TX, humanities librarian 1972-73; Johnson Publishing Co, librarian. **ORGANIZATIONS:** Mem Black Caucus of Amer Library Assn, Special Library Assn, Assn of Black Librarians of Chicago. **BUSINESS ADDRESS:** Librarian, Johnson Pub Co, 820 S Michigan Ave, Chicago, IL 60605.

CASH, WILLIAM L., JR.
Educator. **PERSONAL:** Born May 31, 1915, Savannah, GA; son of William L Cash; married Burnit Rhetta; children: William L Cash III, Marcia, Lisa, Audrey, Olivia. **EDUCATION:** Fisk Univ, AB 1937; Oberlin Grad Sch of Theology, BD 1940; STM, 1950; Univ of MI, MA 1952, PhD 1954. **CAREER:** YMAC, traveling Sec 1946-49; Prairie View A&M Univ, prof psychology dir counseling ctr 1953-60; Univ of ND, US Office of educ prof of psychology & dept 1960-65; NDEA Couns & Guidance inst Br, chief 1965-68; Bur for the Handicapped, assoc dir of planning and evaluation 1968; Univ of MI, asst to pres prof emeritus. **ORGANIZATIONS:** Vice pres bd dir Educ Skills Devel Corp 1969-76; consult US Office of Educ 1969-75; bd dir Natl Vocational & Guidance Assn 1970-72; licensed psychol 1970-; educ testing serv 1971-73; consult editor Journal of Counseling Psychology 1972-75; Amer Inst for Rsch 1972-76; pres Assn for Counselor Educ & Supv 1972-73; consult editor Amer Personnel & Guidance Journal 1978-81; vis prof Univ of WI, Univ of So CA, Univ of HI, Univ of NV;

mem Amer Psychol Assn, Amer Personnel & Guidance Assn, Phi Delta Kappa, Sigma Xi, Psi Chi, Phi Kappa Phi, editor of "Black Economical Devel Analysis & Implications" 1975. **MILITARY SERVICE:** AUS capt 1942-46. **HOME ADDRESS:** P O Box 2798-2101 Pauline Ct, Ann Arbor, MI 48106.

CASH-RHODES, WINIFRED E.
Retired educator. **PERSONAL:** Born in Savannah, GA; daughter of Rev William L Cash Sr and Mrs Clifford Brown Cash; married Augustus H Rhodes; children: Eva Carol, Lydia Ann, Victoria Elizabeth. **EDUCATION:** Fisk Univ, AB 1934; Univ of S California, MS 1959; New York Univ, Fellowship 1970; Univ of California-Berkley, fellowship 1960. **CAREER:** Tchr of Secondary Math, 1935-40, 1945-52; Dept Chairperson Math, 1957-65; Los Angeles Unified Sch, supr of secondary Math tchrs 1966-68, Spclst in Resch & Dvlpmnt 1968-78. **ORGANIZATIONS:** Sec Baldwin Hills Homeowners Assoc 1976-82; dir Far Western Rgnl Dir Alpha Kappa Alpha Sor Inc 1970-74; mem Exec Council of United Church of Christ representing So, CA and NV (first black) 1981-87; chmn Nominating Comm, Southern California Ecumenical Council 1987-; mem Southern California Interfaith Coalition on Aging Board 1989-. **HONORS/ACHIEVEMENTS:** Natl Sci Fdn US Gov't 1957-59; research fellowship New York Univ 1970; Article "What Jesus Means to Me" United Church of Christ New York 1982. **HOME ADDRESS:** 4554 Don Felipe Dr, Los Angeles, CA 90008.

CASON, DAVID, JR.
Urban planner. **PERSONAL:** Born Jun 20, 1923, Selma, AL; son of David and Mattie; married Armene B. **EDUCATION:** BA 1950; MA 1959; Wayne State U, MUP 1966; Univ of Manchester Eng, 1972; Univ of MI, PhD 1976. **CAREER:** Univ of MI, adj prof 1977-; CRW Assoc Consult in Planning Detroit, pres 1977; Univ of MI, lectr in urban planning; Research Assoc Environmental Research Inst of MI, 1972-73; Univ of MI Dept of Urban Planning, instr 1970-; MI Dept of Corrections Program Bureau, asst bureau chief 1985-. **ORGANIZATIONS:** Dir Model Neighborhood Agency Detroit 1967-70; tchr Merrill-Palmer Inst 1975; proj mgr Neighborhood Conservation Housing Commn 1962-65; dir Urban Renewal Ypsilanti 1961-62; pub aide worker Receiving Hosp Detroit 1956-61; part-time work in studies field Wayne State Univ 1966-67; past mem Natl Assn of Redevel & Housing Officials; MI Soc of Planning Officials, Amer Inst of Planners; has written several articles; past trustee Met Fund Detroit; co-vice chairperson Southeastern MI Regional Citizens; bd mem MI Council of Girl Scouts, Detroit Area Agency on Aging, Center for Humanistic Studies; mem Alpha Phi Alpha. **MILITARY SERVICE:** AUS quartermaster corp 1943. **BUSINESS ADDRESS:** Assistant Bureau Chief, MI Dept of Corrections, Stevens T Mason Bldg, PO Box 30003, Lansing, MI 48909.

CASON, JOSEPH L.
Business executive. **PERSONAL:** Born Mar 24, 1939, Anderson County, SC; married Margaret Johnson; children: Ajena Lynette, Kenneth Todd, Shawn Douglas, Valerie Kay. **EDUCATION:** Hampton Inst, BS. **CAREER:** Roanoke Valley Bus League, exec dir 1973; Cason Enterprises, owner 1970-; Eli Lily Corp, indsl engr tech 1968-70; City of Roanoke, proj engr 1967-68; Better Housing Inc, mgr 1965-67. **ORGANIZATIONS:** Charter mem pres Roanoke Vly Contractors Assn 1970; dir Roanoke Valley Bus League; charter mem vice pres Afro-Am Builders of VA 1973; bd mem SW VA CommDevel Fund 1971-75; mem Roanoke C of C; mem Hunton YMCA; group chmn United Fund 1977; mem Minority Bus Oppty Com Mem Kappa Alpha Psi; mem Comm Orgn for Rsrch & Devel; mem Nat Bus League; mem dir Nethel AME Ch; mem Hampton Inst Alumni Assn; mem US Army Res; 1st black professional hired by City ofRoanoke 1967; instrumental in orgnizing 3 minority contractros assns in VA; 1st State Registerd Gen Contractor in SW VA; originiated & administrated 4 yrs Office of Minority Bus Enterprise Prgr for SW VA. **MILITARY SERVICE:** AUS capt 1963-65. **BUSINESS ADDRESS:** 2318 Melrose Ave NW, Roanoke, VA 24107.

CASON, MARILYNN JEAN
Corporate officer. **PERSONAL:** Born May 18, 1943, Denver, CO; daughter of Eugene M Cason and Evelyn Clark Cason; married P Wesley Kriebel, Dec 12, 1987. **EDUCATION:** Stanford Univ, BA Polit Sci 1965; Univ of MI Law Sch, JD 1969; Roosevelt Univ, MBA 1977. **CAREER:** Dawson Nagel Sherman & Howard, assoc atty 1969-73; Kraft Inc, attorney 1973-76; Johnson Prods Co Inc, managing dir 1980-83, corp counsel 1976-86; vice pres intl 1986-88; vice pres & gen counsel DeVry Inc. **ORGANIZATIONS:** Dir Arthritis Found IL Chap 1979-. **BUSINESS ADDRESS:** Vice President & General Counsel, DeVry Inc, 2201 Howard St, Evanston, IL 60202.

CASON, UDELL, JR.
Educational administrator. **PERSONAL:** Born Jul 30, 1940, Glasgow, MO; married Emma R Bothwell; children: Carmen Q, Udell Q. **EDUCATION:** Drake U, BS 1965; Drake U, MS 1970. **CAREER:** Des Moines Pub Sch, prin 1972-, coord 1970-72, tchr 1968-70; City of Des Moines, admin asst 1965-68. **ORGANIZATIONS:** Chmn & v chmn & trustee bd Union Bapt Ch 1965-; pres United Black Fedn 1967-69; sec chmn prin DMPS; pres Kappa Alpha Psi Frat 1980-81; chmn board of directors, Iowa Children and Family Services 1984-89; board of directors, Des Moines YMCA 1982-89. **HONORS/ACHIEVEMENTS:** Task force award State of Iowa 1968; mayor task force award City of Des Moines 1968; outstanding achievement Kappa Alpha Psi 1975; Double D Award Drake Univ 1979; Service to Youth Award YMCA 1988; Tae Kwon Do Instructor YMCA 1979-. **BUSINESS ADDRESS:** Elementary School Principal, Des Moines Public Schools, 1800 Grand Avenus, Des Moines, IA 50307.

CASSIS, GLENN ALBERT
Educational administrator. **PERSONAL:** Born Nov 11, 1951, Jamaica, NY; married Glynis R; children: Glenn Jr. **EDUCATION:** Univ of Ct, BA pol sci 1973; Univ of CT, MFA arts adminstrn 1974. **CAREER:** N Adams State Coll, dir of campus center 1978; Oakland Center, Oakland Univ, Rochester MI, asst dir 1976-78, asst dir student act 1974-76; Jorgensen Auditorium, Univ of CT, Storrs CT, admin asst 1973-74; Assoc of Coll Union-Intl, region I comp coord 1979-. **ORGANIZATIONS:** Bd of dir Nat Entertainment and Campus Act Assoc 1972-74; co-founder minority affairs comm Nat Entertainment and Campus Act Asso 1973; advisory bd Salvation Army 1980-; mem Min Counc on Comm Concerns 1980-. **HONORS/ACHIEVEMENTS:** Founders award Nat Entertainment & Campus Act Assoc 1974; black faculty & admin service award OaklandUniv Rochester MI 1977. **BUSINESS ADDRESS:** North Adams State College, North Adams, MA 01247.

CASSON, LUELLA HOWARD
Administrator, educator. **PERSONAL:** Born Nov 27, 1935, Montgomery, AL; divorced; children: Sandranetta. **EDUCATION:** AL St U, BS, MEd 1957; Cast Western Reserve, 1960; Univ of NC, 1961; OH St U, 1961; Univ of MO, 1964; Memphis St U, 1971-72. **CAREER:** IN State Univ, dir of affirmative action 1977-; Univ of AR Little Rock, dir of placement 1975-77; Philander Smith Coll, dir of placement coop educ 1965-75; Harris Jr Coll, chmn of social science dept 1957-65. **ORGANIZATIONS:** Consult OCR HEW 1973-74; coord CPS title III prog Coll Placement Serv 1974-75; mem bd of dir Coll Placement Serv 1973-76; mem Gov Commn of Status of Women 1971-74; vice pres treas Urban Leag of Grtr Little Rock 1974-77; pres of bd Charles T Hyte Comm Ctr 1979-80. **HONORS/ACHIEVEMENTS:** Hon soc Alpha Kappa Mu; hon soc Kappa Delta Pi; hon soc Sigma Rho Sigma; RJ Reynold fellowUniv of NC 1961; NDEA fellow OH StUniv 1961; NSF fellowUniv of MO Ford Found Fellow Memphis StUniv 1970-71.

CASTENELL, LOUIS ANTHONY
Educational administrator. **PERSONAL:** Born Oct 20, 1947, New York, NY; married Mae E Beckett; children: Louis C, Elizabeth M. **EDUCATION:** Xavier Univ of LA, BA Educ 1968; Univ of WI Milwaukee, MS Educ Psych 1973; Univ of IL, PhD Educ Psych 1980. **CAREER:** Univ of WI-Milwaukee, academic adv 1971-74; Xavier Univ, dir alumni affairs 1974-77, asst prof 1980-81, dean grad sch. **ORGANIZATIONS:** Educ Task Force Urban League 1984; chair Human Rights and Academic Freedom AERA 1985-86; consultant Sch of Educ 1980-; bd mem Ronald McDonald House of Louisiana, 1987. **HONORS/ACHIEVEMENTS:** Craig Rice Scholarship Xavier Univ 1968; Fellowship Univ of IL 1977-78; Fellowship Natl Inst of Mental Health 1978-80; over 15 published work on aspects of educ. **MILITARY SERVICE:** AUS sgt 2yrs. **BUSINESS ADDRESS:** Dean, Graduate School, Xavier University of Louisiana, 7325 Palmetto St, New Orleans, LA 70125.

CASTER, CAROLEIGH TUITT
Tax law specialist. **PERSONAL:** Born Jan 25, 1947, Bronx, NY; daughter of James M Tuitt and Carmen L Charles Tuitt; married Dwight O Caster, Mar 30, 1985. **EDUCATION:** Howard Univ, BA 1968, JD 1972. **CAREER:** IRS, tax law specialist 1972-; OEO, law clerk 1971; Harlem Assertion of Rights, law asst 1970; DC Public Schools, substitute teacher, 1970-72; Library of Congress, library tech 1968-69. **ORGANIZATIONS:** Mem Howard Univ Law School Alumni Assn; Natl Bar Assn; Kappa Beta Pi Intl Legal Sorority 1971-72; mem, Greater Washington Area Chapter, Women's Division National Bar Assn, 1972-; mem DC Law Students in Ct Comm Income Tax Clinic 1971-72; pres Howard Law Alumni Assn, Greater Washington Area, 1988-. **BUSINESS ADDRESS:** Internal Revenue Service, 1111 Constitution Ave, NW, Washington, DC 20224.

CASTERLOW, CAROLYN B.
Computer consultant. **PERSONAL:** Born Jul 16, 1948, Rich Square, NC; daughter of Jesse Casterlow and Zeophia Casterlow. **EDUCATION:** Fayetteville State Univ, BS Business 1970; State Univ of NY at Albany, MS Business 1972; Georgia State Univ, advanced grad business courses 1976-78; GA Institute of Technology, Atlanta, GA, MS Information and Computer Sc. 1989-91. **CAREER:** Georgia Real Estate License, salesperson 1974-77, broker 1977-83; Atlanta EREB Chap of Women's Council, treasurer 1980-82; Atlanta Empire Real Estate Bd, sec 1981-83; City of Atlanta, Atlanta, GA, Consultant 1988-. **ORGANIZATIONS:** Owner/broker VIP Realty Co Atlanta 1977-83; mem Atlanta Bd of Realtors 1978-82; mem GA Assoc of Realtors 1978-82; treasurer Natl Women's Council of NAREB 1981-83; mem Assoc of MBA Execs 1985-86, Amer Assoc of Univ Women 1985-86; mem National Political Congress of Black Women 1988-; Owner/Senior Consultant, Consultants Unlimited, Atlanta, GA 1988-. **HONORS/ACHIEVEMENTS:** Mem Phi Theta Kappa Honor Soc 1986-; mem Who's Who In Professional and Executive Women 1989. **BUSINESS ADDRESS:** Senior Consultant, Consultants Unlimited, PO Box 311217, Atlanta, GA 30331.

CASTLE, KEITH L.
Corporate executive. **CAREER:** Phase One Office Products Inc, Cambridge, MA, chief executive. **BUSINESS ADDRESS:** Chief Executive, Phase One Office Products Inc, 89 Fulkerson Cam, Cambridge, MA 02141. *

CASTLEBERRY, EDWARD J.
Newscaster. **PERSONAL:** Born Jul 28, 1928, Birmingham, AL; son of Edward Castleberry and Lillian Castleberry; married Frances Bassett (deceased); children: Terrie Wade, Sharon Bryant, Susan, Bradley. **EDUCATION:** Miles Coll Birmingham, AL, 1950-51. **CAREER:** WEDR, WJLD Birmingham, AL, disc jockey, 1950-55; WMBM, Miami, FL, prog dir, disc jockey, 1955-58; WCIN, Cincinnati, OH, disc jockey, newsman, 1958-61; WABQ, Cleveland, OH, disc jockey, newsman, 1961-64; WVKO, Columbus, OH, program dir, disc jockey, 1964-67; WHAT, Philadelphia, PA, disc jockey, 1967-68; WEBB, Baltimore, MD, disc jockey, newsman; Mutual & Natl Black Networks, anchorman, entertainment editor. **HONORS/ACHIEVEMENTS:** Newsman of the Year, Coalition of Black Media Womrn, NY, 1980; Newsman of the Year, Jack the Rapper Family Affair, Atlanta, 1980; Outstanding Citizen Award, AL House of Representatives, Montgomery, 1983; Honored, Smithsonian Institute, Washington, 1985; Part of the first black newsteam to broadcast a presidential election, 1972. **MILITARY SERVICE:** USN Yeoman 3rd Class, served three years; WWII Victory Medal, 1945-47. **BUSINESS ADDRESS:** Anchorman/Entertainment Editor, Natl Black Network, 41-30 58th St, Woodside, NY 11377.

CASTLEBERRY, RHEBENA TAYLOR
Educational administrator. **PERSONAL:** Born Nov 17, 1917, Wilson, NC; daughter of Armstrong Taylor and Alice Taylor; married Henry A Castleberry; children: Dr Curtis A Leonard. **EDUCATION:** Cheyney State Coll, BS 1941; Temple Univ, MEd 1948-49, Doctoral Studies 1949-51; Univ of HI, Cert in Asian Studies 1968. **CAREER:** Ft Valley Coll Lab School, elem teacher 1941-42; Martha Washington School, elem teacher 1949-65, grad chmn & supr 1965-75; Natl Assn of Univ Women, natl pres; commr Philadelphia Fellowship Commn; mem bd dir Natl Conf of Christians and Jews; mem PA Coalition of 100 Black Women; mem bd dir, exec comm of Natl Polit Congress of Black Women; mem Mayor's Commn for Women. **ORGANIZATIONS:** Consultant to Dept of Christian Educ African Methodist Episcopal Church 1964-72; natl pres Natl Assn of Univ Women 1982-; mem of bd of dir Natl Conf of Women Christians & Jew 1983-; vice pres PA Council of Churches 1984-; bd dir Philadelphia Fellowship Commn. **HONORS/ACHIEVEMENTS:** Outstanding Serv Award Chapel of Four Chaplains 1980; Dedicated Serv in Secular & Christian Ed Awd AME Church 1981; Woman of Year Award Natl Assn of Univ Women 1982; Churchwoman

of the Year African Methodist Episcopal Church 1984; Woman of the Year Award, Jones Tabernacle AME Church.

CASTLEMAN, ELISE MARIE (NEE TUCKER)
Social worker. **PERSONAL:** Born May 30, 1925, Duquesne, PA; daughter of Guy L Tucker (deceased) and Fannie M Ridley (deceased); divorced; children: John II. **EDUCATION:** Howard Univ, BA 1947; Univ of Pittsburgh, M 1949. **CAREER:** Family & Childrens Agency, social worker 1949-53; DC General Hospital, social worker 1953-58; Wayne County General Hospital & Consulting Center, social worker 1958-59; United Cerebral Palsy, social worker 1960-66; Mental Hygiene Clinic Veterans Admin, social worker 1967-; Defense Construction Supply Center, mgmt analyst 1982-85. **ORGANIZATIONS:** Mem Columbus Bd of Ed 1971-79; exec adv comm Office of Minority Affairs OH State Univ 1972-73; adv bd Martin Luther King Serv Ctr 1963-67; Howard Univ Womens Club 1953-58; exec comm OH School Bds Assn; bd mem YWCA 1974-76; bd mem Columbus Civil Rights Council 1973-, OH School Bd Assn 1972-, NAACP, Black Womens Leadership 1973-76; fellowship for graduate study in social work Family Serv Assn 1947-49. **HONORS/ACHIEVEMENTS:** Public Serv Award 1979; Public Serv Award Inner City Sertoma Club 1978; Public Serv Award NAACP Columbus Chapter 1980; Cert of Appreciation for Serv & Leadership in the Field of Public Educ KEDs Kent State Univ 1980; Award for Distinguished Community Serv OH House of Rep 1981.

CASWELL, CATHERYNE WILLIS
Councilwoman, teacher. **PERSONAL:** Born Aug 27, 1917, Troy, AL; divorced; children: James, Leon, Bettye. **EDUCATION:** AL A&M U, BS 1946, M 1962. **CAREER:** Geneva Cty Pub Sch Sys & Montgomery Cty, teacher; Catheryne's Rec Ctr, owner & dir; G & W Grocery & Market, owner; Toliver's Place, owner; G & W Rec Ctr, owner. **ORGANIZATIONS:** Pres Geneva Cty Teachers Assoc; advisory coun mem ACT-NEA; mem AL St Teachers' Assn; 8 6 mem Natl Democ Party AL; mem dir United Mem Natl Bank; dirc West Side Improve Assn; rep Minority Prob on Democ Comm; capt Tuberculosis Heart and March of Dimes Drives. **HONORS/ACHIEVEMENTS:** Teacher of yr award Geneva Teachers Assoc; only Negro to serve actively with Democ 30 yrs ago. **BUSINESS ADDRESS:** 2032 Day, Montgomery, AL 36108.

CATCHINGS, HARVEY
Professional athlete. **PERSONAL:** Born Sep 02, 1951, Jackson, MS; married Wanda; children: Kenyon Doran, Tauja Dionne, Tamika Devonne. **EDUCATION:** Hardin-Simmons 1974. **CAREER:** Forward-Center, Milwaukee Bucks, New Jersey Nets, Philadelphia 76ers, Los Angeles Clippers 1984-. **ORGANIZATIONS:** Chmn NAACP Phila; mem Youth Orgn Phila. **HONORS/ACHIEVEMENTS:** Hon Mention as All-American 4 years; 9th on Milwaukee's all-time games played list; 7th on Milwaukee's all-time rebounding scrolls (1,918); career scoring average of 33 ppg; total of 3,377 career rebounds in 10-year NBA career for a 52 average per contest. **BUSINESS ADDRESS:** Los Angeles Cuppers, 3939 So Figuerosa St, Los Angeles, CA 90037.

CATCHINGS, HOWARD DOUGLAS
Insurance salesman. **PERSONAL:** Born Jun 19, 1939, Copiah County, MS; married Danella Brownridge; children: Sebrena, Douglas, James, Daniel. **EDUCATION:** Jackson State Univ, BEd 1963, MEd 1973. **CAREER:** Jackson Public Schools, teacher 1963-80; United Founders Ins Co, rep 1967-68; Natl Old Line Ins Co, rep 1968-. **ORGANIZATIONS:** Pres Jackson State Univ 1984-88; regional vice pres MS Assn of Life 1985-89; comm mem Million Dollar Round Table 1986-89; pres Jackson GAMA 1986-87; mem bd dirs Junior Achievement; mem State Job Training Coordinating Council; council mem Business/Industry/Educ Regional Council; board member, Jackson Chamber of Commerce; Regional Officer, GAMC. **HONORS/ACHIEVEMENTS:** Outstanding Teacher in Human Relations Jackson Public Schools 1972; Outstanding Achievement Awd Jackson State Univ Natl Alumni Assn; Natl Sales Rep 1986,No 1 Salesman (Nationally) 1986 Natl Old Line Ins Co; one of top ten agents 1971-89. **BUSINESS ADDRESS:** General Agent, Natl Old Line Insurance Co, PO Box 2509, Jackson, MS 39207.

CATCHINGS, WALTER J.
Automobile dealer. **PERSONAL:** Born Nov 08, 1933, Drew, MS; son of Walter Catchings Sr. and Mable Deshazer-Trotter; married Bobby Catchings, Jan 03, 1987. **CAREER:** Kessler Buick, Detroit MI, salesman, 1960; Shore Severs Cadillac, Detroit MI, salesman, 1972; Dick Harris Cadillac, Detroit MI, salesman, 1978, general sales manager, 1979-86; Eldorado Ford/Lincoln-Mercury Inc, president, 1986-. **ORGANIZATIONS:** Mem, Boys Club, Eldorado AR, Kiwanis Club, Eldorado AR.

CATCHINGS, YVONNE PARKS
Educator. **PERSONAL:** Born in Atlanta, GA; daughter of Andrew Walter Parks and Hattie M Brookins Parks; married James Albert A Catchings; children: Andrea Hunt Warner, Wanda Hunt McLean, James A A Jr. **EDUCATION:** Spelman Coll, AB 1955; Tchrs Coll Columbia, MA 1958; Univ of Michigan, MMP 1971, PhD 1981. **CAREER:** Spelman Coll, instr 1956-57; Marygrove Coll, instr 1970-72; Specialist; Detroit Bd of Educ, instr 1959-; Valdosta State Coll, assistant professor of art 1987-88; Detroit Board of Education, specialist 1988-. **ORGANIZATIONS:** Presenter Natl Art Educ Assn 1956-; natl treasurer, The Smart Set 1976-78; archivist pub rel MI Art Therapy Assn 1981-; reg art therapist Amer Art Therapy 1981-; prog chr bd mem Detroit Soc Genelogical Research 1965-; chmn Heritage Archives Delta Sigma Theta Sor 1983-; bd chr peace Amer Assn Univ Women 1981-; art chr The Links 1981-. **HONORS/ACHIEVEMENTS:** James D Parks Award Natl Conf of Artist 1979; Pres Spec Award Natl Dental Assoc 1973; 1st Award Art & Letters Delta Sigma Theta Sorority 1978; Mayor's Award of Merit Mayor Coleman Young 1978; Fulbright Hayes Award Study in Zimbabwe 1982; Outstanding Black Woman in Michigan 1785-1985, Detroit Historical Museum 1985; Service Award, Afro American Museum, 1983. **BUSINESS ADDRESS:** Instructional Specialist, Detroit Bd of Educ, Woodward Ave, Detroit, MI 48202.

CATER, ANNA L.
Vocalist. **PERSONAL:** Born Feb 09, 1933, Los Angeles, CA. **CAREER:** Toured US States with Amos & Andy, King Fish Concert Tour; traveled & toured with own show US Special Serv in Orient; TV Channel 9 Sidney Australia, vocalist; Louie Jordan, vocalist; Mom & Pa Davis Brass Rail Club LA with Hot Ashes Comedian, LuWanda Page, LeRoy & Skillet Commedians, Red Foxx, 1952-56; T Bone Walker, The Road Review Show, vocalist 1956-59; Elegant Four Plus One, Clyde Dunn, Peewee Jurnigan, Bill Willis, Don Coleman, vocalist; Fashion Shows, vocalist; Mini Red Carpet Rolls Royce Svc, vocalist. **ORGANIZATIONS:** Founder, staff writer Hawaii's Musicians Union. **HONORS/ACHIEVEMENTS:** Japan's 1st black female jazz singer in "Japanese"; Jazz Singer of the Year Musicians Honor 1965; Beverly Hills Postal Employee of the Year; wrote birthday composition for King, Banghok Thailand; 1st female vocalist incorp into "The Ink Spots" prod a/k/a "Lady Ink Spot of George Holmes Ink Spot '70"; performing "Lady Ink Spot Presents" 1980.

CATES, SIDNEY HAYWARD, III
Government official. **PERSONAL:** Born Mar 10, 1931, New Orleans, LA; married Betty; children: Sidney IV, Kim. **EDUCATION:** Loyola U, BA 1968. **CAREER:** Housing Authority of New Orleans, exec dir; LA Dept of Justice, atty gen gss inc, vice pres-gen mgr; Hibernia natl bank, mrktng off; City of New Orleans, asst chief admin off; New Orleans Police Dept, deputy & chief for admin. **ORGANIZATIONS:** Bd of dir Loyola U; Red Cross; Boy Scouts of Amer; United Way; Goodwill; St Claude Gen Hosp; mem Mid Winter Sports Assoc (Sugar Bowl); 4th degree Knights of St Peter Claver; Equestrian Knights of th E Holy Sepulchre; pres Studs Club; mem Chamber of Comm; vice-chrm Bicentennial Comm City of New Orleans; consul Law Enforce Ass Admin alfred e clay award; children bureau city of new orleans; charles e dunbar (hon mention); st of LA Carger Civil Ser Award. **MILITARY SERVICE:** Sgt 1951-53. **BUSINESS ADDRESS:** 234 Loyola Ave, Rm 821, New Orleans, LA 70112.

CATHCART, GEORGE W.
Retired educator. **PERSONAL:** Born Sep 16, 1910, Birmingham, AL; married Mary A Minter; children: George Arthur, Eloise Katherine, Ann Lytha. **EDUCATION:** Wayne State Univ, MA 1940; Atlanta School of Social Work Atlanta, MA 1936; Morris Brown Coll, AB 1934. **CAREER:** Todd Phillips Home for Boys Detroit, social worker; Detroit Public Schools, teacher 31 1/2 yrs, school teacher, social worker retired. **ORGANIZATIONS:** Mem Kappa Alpha Psi, NAACP, Natl Black Rep Council; chmn, trea Mid-West Masons; past master Doric #21; past IL Pot Marracci #13 Detroit Scholarship NSF; fellowship human rel Natl Assoc of Christians & Jews. **HONORS/ACHIEVEMENTS:** Athl Hall of Fame Morris Brown Coll Atlanta.

CATLETT, ELIZABETH
Sculptor/printmaker. **PERSONAL:** Born Apr 15, 1919, Washington, DC; daughter of John H. Catlett and Mary Carson Catlett; married Francisco Mora, May 31, 1946; children: Francisco, Juan, David. **EDUCATION:** Howard University, Washington DC, BS, 1935; State University of Iowa, Iowa City IA, MFA, 1940; Art Institute of Chicago, Chicago IL, 1941, Art Students' League, New York NY, 1943; privately with Ossip Zadkine, New York, NY, 1943; Esmeralda, Escuela de Pintura y Escultura, Mexico City, 1948. **CAREER:** Teacher in Texas, Louisiana, Virginia, and New York City; National School of Fine Arts, National Autonomous University of Mexico, professor of sculpture, 1959-73; free-lance sculptor/printmaker. **HONORS/ACHIEVEMENTS:** First prize in sculpture, Golden Jubilee Nation Exposition (Chicago IL), 1941; Tlatilco Prize, First Sculpture Biannual (Mexico), 1962; Xipe Totec Prize, Second Sculpture Biannual (Mexico), 1964; first prize in sculpture, Atlanta University Annual, 1965; first purchase prize, National Print Salon (Mexico), 1969; prize to study and travel in West Germany, Intergrafic Exhibition (Berlin), 1970; Alumni Award, Howard University, 1979; award from Women's Caucus for Art, National Congress (San Francisco), 1981; Brandywine Workshop Award, Philadelphia Museum of Art, 1982; purchase prize, Salon de la Plastica Mexicana, Drawing Salon (Mexico), 1985; honoree, National Sculpture Conference: Works by Women (Cincinnati OH), 1987. Numerous individual exhibitions throughout U.S. and Mexico. **HOME ADDRESS:** 375 South End Ave, New York, NY 10280-1018.

CAUTHEN, CHERYL G.
Ophthalmologist. **PERSONAL:** Born Nov 13, 1957, Flint, MI. **EDUCATION:** Attended, Howard Univ 1974-77; Howard Univ Coll of Medicine, MD 1981. **CAREER:** DC General Hosp, intern-medicine 1981-82; Howard Univ Hosp, resident ophthalmology 1982-85; Howard Univ Coll of Medicine, instructor dept of surgery ophthalmology div 1985-86; Norfolk Eye Physicians & Surgeons, physician 1986-. **ORGANIZATIONS:** Mem Amer Acad of Ophthalmology, Natl Medical Assoc, Amer Medical Assoc, Norfolk Medical Soc, Norfolk Acad of Medicine, Old Dominion Medical Soc, The Medical Soc of VA. **HOME ADDRESS:** 5881 Northampton Blvd, Virginia Beach, VA 23455. **BUSINESS ADDRESS:** Ophthalmologist, Norfolk Eye Physicians & Surg, 1005 May Ave, Norfolk, VA 23504.

CAUTHEN, RICHARD L.
Educator, attorney. **PERSONAL:** Born Dec 04, 1944, Canonsburg, PA; son of John Cauthen Sr and Mazella Bester Cauthen; married Glenda Joyce Wilson; children: Akowa Lashawn. **EDUCATION:** Wabash Coll, BA 1966; Wayne State Univ Law Sch, JD 1975. **CAREER:** Gary Froebel HS, Spanish tchr/dept head/head wrestling coach 1966-68; Detroit Public Schs, English history Spanish instr 1968-80; AIM Enterprises Assoc, curriculum coord 1971; Project CHILD, asst supvr Latch Key Prog 1972; CETA Summer Youth Prog, asst coord 1973-75; Comm Educ & Training Prog Coord, clients council policy bd 1976-77; Detroit Non-Profit Housing Corp, prog coord & office adminstr 1977-80, deputy dir 1979-84; Jordan Coll, instr acctg & bus law 1982-83; DMCC, financial consul 1982-; Mackenzie HS Detroit, bilingual instr. **ORGANIZATIONS:** Tech adv Brush Park Subdiv Property Owners Assn 1980-84; sec bd dirs Wayne Co Neighborhood Legal Serv Inc 1977-80; mem citizens adv comm Mayors Comm for Human Resources Develop 1971-76; chmn Citizens Adv Cncl MCHRD 1970-71; mem Amer Assn of Tchrs of Spanish & Portuguese, Amer Bar Assn, Detroit Bar Assn, Detroit Energy Corp Consortium, MI Assn of Profls, MI Federation of Housing Counselors, MI State Clients Cncl, Natl Black Caucus, Natl Caucus & Ctr on Black Aged, Natl Fed of Housing Counselors, Phi Alpha Delta Legal Frat, State Bar of MI, Tau Kappa Epsilon Frat, Wayne Co Clients Cncl Policy Bd, Wayne State Univ Alumni Assn, Wolverine Bar Assn; bd of governors Christian Love Fellowship; mem Citizens for Better Govt. **HONORS/ACHIEVEMENTS:** Mem Student Bd of Govs Wayne State Univ Law Sch 1971-72; Outstanding Young Men of Amer 1971. **HOME ADDRESS:** 18934 Ohio, Detroit, MI 48221. **BUSINESS ADDRESS:** Bilingual Instructor; Yearbook Advisor, Mackenzie High School, 9275 Wyoming Ave, Detroit, MI 48204.

CAVE, ALFRED EARL
Physician. **PERSONAL:** Born Jan 23, 1940, Brooklyn, NY; son of Alfred and Theodora; married Jeanne Byrnes; children: Christine. **EDUCATION:** Columbia Coll, BA 1961;

Downstate Medical Ctr, MD 1965. **CAREER:** Downstate Medical Ctr, instructor 1971, asst prof surgery 1971-77; Kings County Hosp Brooklyn, attending physician 1971-77; Long Beach Memorial Hosp, attending surgeon 1976-79; Lydia Hall Hosp, attending surgeon 1977-78; Nassau Co Med Ctr, attending surgeon 1978-; Syosset Comm Hosp, attending surgeon 1978-. **ORGANIZATIONS:** Mem Sigma Pi Phi Frat. **HONORS/ACHIEVEMENTS:** Natl Medical Fellowship Awd 1961; New York State Medical Scholarship 1961. **MILITARY SERVICE:** US Army Reserve capt 6 yrs; Honorable Discharge 1972. **HOME ADDRESS:** 1 Hutch Ct, Dix Hills, NY 11746.

CAVE, CLAUDE BERTRAND
Physician. **PERSONAL:** Born Jan 29, 1910, Brooklyn, NY; married Nora Elizabeth Wallace; children: Claude Bertrand II, Carol Ann, Curtis Bryan. **EDUCATION:** Coll of the City of NY, BS 1932; Loma Linda U, MD 1938. **CAREER:** Prt Practice, family physician 1965-75; Kingsbrook Flatbush Gen Lefferts Gen Hosp, asst surg 1956-74; Brookdale Hosp Unity Flatbush Lefferts Empire MedGroup, staff physician 1950-74; Harlem Hosp, staff member 1939-44. **ORGANIZATIONS:** Mem Kings Co Med Soc; NY State Med Soc 1944-; pres Provident Clinical Soc 1945-46; mem AMA; AAFP; NMA 1949; Charter Fellowship, AAFP Nat Group NY Chap 1974; life mem Kappa Alpha Psi Brooklyn LI Chap 1974. **HONORS/ACHIEVEMENTS:** Award of Excellence; Woodrow Lewis Assemblyman. **BUSINESS ADDRESS:** 1349 Dean St, Brooklyn, NY 11216.

CAVE, HERBERT G.
Physician, educator. **PERSONAL:** Born Jul 16, 1922, Colon, Panama;married Francis; children: Herbert Jr, LaVerne. **EDUCATION:** Coll of NYC, 1940-42; Howard Univ Washington Dc, 1942-44; Howard Univ Coll of Med, MDD 1947; Harlem Hosp Ctr, internship 1947-48. **CAREER:** Col U, assoc prof anestesolgy 1973-; Harlem Hosp, dir anestesolgy dept 1961-; Mitchell AFB Hosp, conslt 1959-61; Italian Hosp, attndg anesthesolgst 1957-61; Manhattan State Hosp, attndg anesthesolgst 1956. **ORGANIZATIONS:** Past mem House of Del NMA 1960; past mem Anesthsia Study Commn NY Co Med Soc 1633-64; past chmn Adv Coun of Med Bds Dept of Hosp 1969-70; mem Blk Caucus of Harlem Hlth Wrks NY 1969-; mem 369th VA Westchester Dist; chmn Educ Com 369th VA; mem Mt Vernon Narc Gdnc Coun 1969-; past mem Mayor's Com for Recptn of New Res Mt Vern 1970-71; past mem Sel Serv Be #10 1968-76; past participation Med Presence MS 1964; commr Mt Vern Plng Bd 1967-68; chmn Mt Vern Com Actn Grp 1976-; past host WLIB Radio Stn NY wkly show Hlth Your Grtst Invst 1972; past mem Com for Hlth Careers forDisadvantaged Manhattan 1968; mem Econ Devel Coun of Mt Vern 1976-; mem NAACP Articles a comprsn of Thiopental Sodium & Methohexital Sodium in Shrt Surgl Prcks SAA NA 1962; Anesthesia Prblms in Emerg Srgy JAANA 1964; Anesthetic Mgmt of Drug Addict Med Aspts of Drug Abuse 1975. **HONORS/ACHIEVEMENTS:** Dist serv aw Caucus of Blk Legltrs St of NY 1971; natl com aw Nat Assn of Bus and Prfsnl Wmns Clubs Inc 1972; humanitarian aw Key Wmn of Am Mt Vern Br. **MILITARY SERVICE:** AUS Med Corps capt 1952-54. **BUSINESS ADDRESS:** Harlem Hosp Ctr, Anesthesia Dept, 506 Lenox Ave, New York, NY 10037.

CAVE, PERSTEIN RONALD
Educational administrator. **PERSONAL:** Born Sep 24, 1947, Brooklyn, NY; married Jeanette; children: Christopher, Joscelyn, Jerilynn. **EDUCATION:** Kingsborough Comm Coll, AA 1967; The City Coll of NY, BA 1970; The Univ of Hartford, MBA 1981. **CAREER:** The Aetna Life & Casualty Ins Co, expense coord 1977-80; ESPN/ABC Television, special Projects consultant 1980-85; Asnuntuck Comm Coll, business mgr/assoc dean 1985-. **ORGANIZATIONS:** Ministerial servant Windsor CT Congregation of Jehovah's Witnesses 1980-; mem Natl Assoc of Accountants 1980-, Natl Black MBA Assoc 1982-, Minorities in Cable Broadcasting 1982-85; comm mem Asnuntuck Comm Coll Affirmative Action Comm 1985-. **HONORS/ACHIEVEMENTS:** Citation for Outstanding Community Service. **HOME ADDRESS:** 20 Maythorpe Dr, Windsor, CT 06095.

CAVE, VERNAL G.
Physician. **PERSONAL:** Born in Colon, Panama;married Natalie Helene Jacobs. **EDUCATION:** City Coll of NYC, BS 1941; Howard Univ Sch of Med, MD 1944. **CAREER:** Bureau of VD Control New York City Dept of Health, physician; Private Practice, physician Presently; Am Bd of Dermatology & Syphilology, diplomate 1956; NY Med Coll Ctr for Disease & Control USPHS, asst clinical prof 1972-; Sch of Med Howard U, former clinical instr; NY Univ Post Grad Med Sch, former clinical instr; Am Coll of Physicians, fellow; St Johns Epis Hosp of Brooklyn, atndng dermatologist; Coney Island Hosp, former asso atndng & current cons. **ORGANIZATIONS:** Mem bd dirs New York City Health & Hosp Cor P mem State Pub Health Council NY State Dept of Health; pres bd trustees former chmn former exec com Nat Med Assn Pres 1974-; mem b dirs exec com Hse of Delegates Nat Med Assn Found; mem chmn various other med assn; life mem NAACP; former mem bd dirs Brooklyn Br NAACP; mem Bd Dirs NY Urban League; founder mem bd dirs v chmn & Bedord-stuyvesant Restoration Corp; mem Bd Dirs Training Resources for youth. **HONORS/ACHIEVEMENTS:** Citation Plaque for Achievement The Surface Line Operators Frat Organ Brooklyn 1968; cert of apprecition luscheon Guest of Honor Section on Dermatology NatMed Assn Houston 1970; testimonial dinner An Evening with Dr Vernal G Cave People to People for Dr Vernal G Cave Sept 25; Many other cert plaques for prof & comm achievement. **MILITARY SERVICE:** AUS med ofcr 1947-52; also USAF capt.

CAVENS, SHARON SUE
Director. **PERSONAL:** Born Feb 15, 1942, Manhattan, KS; daughter of Royal H Cavens and Rosezella P Henderson; divorced; children: Ray Jr, Carl, Robert Beard, Michael Boone, Joseph Harris. **EDUCATION:** Washburn Univ, psychology, gerontology. **CAREER:** Kansas City MO, MDTA training sch, sales work, hostess, modeling, bookkeeper, 1965-68; OEO Mainstream Prog, outreach worker promoted to Fam Serv Spec 1968; Human Rel Commn City of Topeka, comm coord 1970-72; Capital Area Agency on Aging City of Topeka, field coord Friendly Neighbors Aging Nutritional Prog 1972-76; Shawnee County Community Asst & Action, outreach worker, outreach coord supv 1976-79; exec dir East Topeka Council on Aging 1979-. **ORGANIZATIONS:** Coord com Black Comm Credit Union; bd dir CCBC; mem Aging Task Force; Mayor's Commn of Status of Women; bd dir Big Bro & Big Sister; bd dir Kommunity Klothes Kloset; mem Sr Organized Cit of KS; mem Topeka Exodusters Awareness Inc, KS Sr Ctr Dirs Assoc, Topeka Black Women's Network, Natl Rainbow Coalition, Shawnee Cty Advocacy Council on Aging, Sigma Gamma Rho Inc; executive bd Topeka Exoduster Awareness, Inc 1979-; advocacy bd Shawnee County Advocacy Council On Aging 1987-. **HONORS/ACHIEVEMENTS:** Community Thanksgiving Day Dinner 1968; Coordinating Committee for the Black Community Credit Union 1971; Awd Big Bro & Big Sister 1973; CCBC Credit Union; Friendly Neighbors 1974; nom Woman of Yr for civic work Topeka KS 1975; KS Dept on Aging Commendation 1978; Sunset Optimist Recognition 1981; The Voluntary Work Diversion Prog of the Third Dist Court Serv Cert of Appreciation 1982; Retired Srs Vol Prog Cert of Appreciation 1982; Exoduster of the Year Awd for Outstanding Contrib to Exodusters Awareness 1984; Black Econ in KS, What is our Destiny (1985 KS Black Leg Conf) Cert of Appreciation; Sigma Gamma Rho Outstanding Women of the Twentieth Century Recognition 1986. **BUSINESS ADDRESS:** Executive Dir, E Topeka Council on Aging Inc, 1114 E 10th St, Topeka, KS 66607.

CAVER, CARMEN C. MURPHY
Retired business executive. **PERSONAL:** Born Oct 20, 1915, Auvergne, AR; married Scipio G Murphy; children: Robert C, Scipio, Jr. **EDUCATION:** Wayne Univ, attd; Mary Hall Acad. **CAREER:** House of Beauty, ret fnd & head 1948-74; Carmen Cosmetics, beauty/Travel consult 1955-; House of Beauty Record Co 1957-. **ORGANIZATIONS:** Consult Amalgamated Press; beauty consult Detroit Bd Educ resource adv 1960-; mem Com of 1000 Women; Serv Guild Blvd Gen Hosp Detroit; bd dir Detroit YMCA; Detroit Urban League Guild. **HONORS/ACHIEVEMENTS:** Recipt Bus Award Wilberforce Univ 1967; 7-Up Co 1968; Booker T Washington Bus Assc & Cham of Comm Top Ten Working Women Award 1970; mem Wilberforce Univ Alumni; Natl Assc Negro Bus & Prof Women's Clubs; NAACP; Women's Aux to Natl Med Assc chrt mem Detroit Med Soc Aux 1937; pres Detroit Med Soc Aux 1978-80; bd dir Sickle Cell Detection & Info Prog Inc; vol ARC Southeastern MI Chpt; chmn Women's Com United Negro Clge Fund 1979; chrt mem; Natl Assc Market Developers; Natl Assc Fashion & Accessory Designers; Natl Assc Media Women; Women's Econ Club; others; listed Who's Who in Amer; Who's Who of Amer Women; Who's Who in Bus & Finance; Who's Who in the Midwest.

CAVIN, ALONZO C.
Educational administrator. **PERSONAL:** Born Jul 17, 1939, Savannah, GA; son of Willie Cavin Dale; married Gwendolyn Mary Wells; children: Alonzo, William. **EDUCATION:** Cheyney State College PA, BS 1961; West Chester State College PA, MA 1969; Temple Univ, EdD 1979. **CAREER:** Bayard Middle Schl, eng tchr 1965-69; PMC Clge, dir proj prepare 1972-78; Widener Univ, dir state and fed prog 1979-. **ORGANIZATIONS:** Mem Assn for Supv and Curriculum Dev 1972-, PA Assn for Supv and Curriculum Dev 1972-, Mid-Eastern Assn of Educ Opportunity Prog Personnel 1972-; pres Chester PA Rotary Inc 1985; bd mem DE Governor's Council Exceptional Citizens 1979-, Wallingford Chester Amer Red Cross 1985. **HONORS/ACHIEVEMENTS:** Legion of Honor Chapel of Four Chaplains 1980; publ Cognitive Dissonance affective Domain ERIC 1979, Affective Variable Indicating Acad Success ERIC 1978, Pre College Exper, An Oppor Assessment PA Dept Educ 1974; Chairman Chester-Wallingford American Red Cross 1989-90; Service Award Omega Psi Phi Fraternity, Inc Epsilon Pi Chapter 1987. **MILITARY SERVICE:** USN lt jg 1961-65. **BUSINESS ADDRESS:** Dir State Federal Program, WidenerUniv, Sparrow Hall WidenerUniv, Chester, PA 19013.

CAVINESS, E. THEOPHILUS
Clergyman. **PERSONAL:** Born May 23, 1928, Marshall, TX; married Jimmie; children: Theophilus James, Theodosia Jacqueline. **EDUCATION:** Bishop Coll, BA; Eden Theol Sem, BD; VA Seminary & Coll, DD. **CAREER:** Greater Abyssinia Bapt Ch, pastor; 1961; Greater Abyssinia Bapt Ch Fed Credit Union, pres. **ORGANIZATIONS:** Historian & mem bd dir Nat Bapt Conv USA Inc; pres OH Bapt State Conv; pres Bapt Min Conf; exec asst Mayor of Cleveland Office. **BUSINESS ADDRESS:** Greater Abyssinia Bapt Ch, 1161 E 105 St, Cleveland, OH 44108.

CAVINESS, LORRAINE F.
Educator. **PERSONAL:** Born Apr 08, 1914, Atlanta; married Clyde E; children: Muriel E. **EDUCATION:** Spelman Coll, BA 1936; Atlanta U, postgrad study 1947-48; Am U, 1951-52; DC Tchrs Coll, 1959-60. **CAREER:** Winston-Salem Teachers Coll, asst teacher 1936-37; Vocational High School, teacher 1937-38; US Govt Dept of Labor, research asst 1942-44; Dept of Army, 1947-51; Washington DC Public Schools, 1946, 1963-64. **ORGANIZATIONS:** Mem Spelman Coll Alumnae Assn; mem Century Club Spelman Coll 1977; DC Nat Retired Tchrs Assns; Washington Urban League; mem Brightwood Community Assntreas 1968-70; del Beautification Com; Educ Com precinct chmn 1969; Federaton Civic Assns; mem Adv Neighborhood Council; Task Force which defined areaboundaries Summer 1975. **HONORS/ACHIEVEMENTS:** Honorable serv award US Dept Labor 1958; Wash Real Estate Brokers Award 1970; Grass Roots Honoree Award DC Federation Civic Assns 1969.

CAYOU, NONTSIZI KIRTON
Educator. **PERSONAL:** Born May 19, 1937, New Orleans; married William. **EDUCATION:** SF State U, AB 1962; SF State U, 1963; Univ Ca; SF State U, MA 1970;-73; tchr guest artist 1969-70; SF State U, tchr dance prgm 1963 , 65, 67; SF Unifed Sch Dist & Woodrow Wilson HS, dancer choreographer revues supper clubs dance theatres mus 1955. **CAREER:** San Francisco State Univ, coord dance program Presently; Stanford Univ, 1976-77; Univ of San Francisco 1972-73; teacher guest artist 1969-70; San Francisco State Univ, teacher dance program 1963, 1965, 1967; San Frnacisco Unified School Dist & Woodrow Wilson High School 1963; dancer choreograper revues supper clubs dance theatres museums 1955. **ORGANIZATIONS:** Dir founder Wajumbe Cultural Ensemble 1969; chmn Oakland Dance Assn 1966-68; chmn Comm of Black Dance 1969; CA Dance Educators Assn; Nat Dance Assn; Griot Soc Publ "The Dance is People" New African article 1965; article "Origins of Jazz Dance" Black Scholar 1970; book "Modern Jazz Dance" 1973. **BUSINESS ADDRESS:** 1600 Holloway Ave, San Francisco, CA 94132.

CAZENAVE, NOEL ANTHONY
University professor. **PERSONAL:** Born Oct 25, 1948, Washington, DC; son of Herman Joseph Cazenave and Mildred Depland Cazenave; married Anita Washington, Jun 20, 1971; children: Anika Tene. **EDUCATION:** Dillard Univ, BA Psychology (Magna Cum Laude) 1970; Univ of MI, MA Psychology 1971; Tulane Univ, PhD Sociology 1977; Univ of New Hampshire, Post-Doctoral Study 1977-78. **CAREER:** Invited Lecturer, Temple Univ conf on violence and discipline in society 1979, organizer and presider panel on "The Current Status of Theories of Black Family Life" 1980, Philadelphia State Hospital Conference on Violence 1980, Natl Conference on Family Violence Researchers 1981, organizer and presenter "Black Male-Black Female Relationships" 1982, Wellesley College Ctr for Rsch on Women 1983 1985, Tulane Univ Law School 1984, Organized North Philadelphia Centennial Confer-

ence 1985, coordinated with Nancy Kleiniewski Colloquium on Grass-Roots Resistance to Oppression in Minority Communities 1986; Temple Univ, assoc prof dept of sociology. **ORGANIZATIONS:** Mem Amer Sociological Assoc, Soc for the Study of Social Problems; mem Jessie Bernard Awds CommAmer Sociological Soc. **HONORS/ACHIEVEMENTS:** Numerous articles, book reviews, and academic papers published; editor special issue of Alternative Lifestyles Vol 3 No 4 1980; published report "Black Families at the crossroads? Retrospect and Prospect," report included in the Philadelphia Urban League's The State of Black Philadelphia 1983 pp 7-28; Natl Science Found grant; mem, Natl Endowment for the Humanities Urban Amer History seminar, 1989. **BUSINESS ADDRESS:** Associate Professor, Temple University, Department of Sociology, Philadelphia, PA 19122.

CEDENO, CESAR
Professional athlete. **PERSONAL:** Born Feb 25, 1957, Santo Domingo; married Cora Lefevre; children: Cesar Jr, Cesar Roberto, Cesar Richard. **CAREER:** Houston Astros, outfielder 1970-81; Cincinnati Reds, outfielder 1982-. **HONORS/ACHIEVEMENTS:** Only player in major league history to hit 20 or more homers and steal 50 or more bases in the same season three years in a row; had 5 0 or more steals six years in a row; named to the NL All-Star team four times; Gold Glove winner for defensive excellence in the outfiel d five years in a row 1972-76; named to the post-season NL All-Star team by Sporting News three times.

CELESTIN, TOUSSAINT A.
Physician. **PERSONAL:** Born Nov 17, 1930, Cap Haitien, Haiti;married Jessie; children: Nadhia, Ramses, Marthe, Marie, Toussaint, Victoria. **EDUCATION:** Lycee Nat Philippe Guerrier, BA 1950; Faculte de Med Univ Haiti, MD 1956. **CAREER:** Howard Univ Coll Med, asst prof psychiatry 1974-; Albany M Ed Coll Union U, 1971-74; Columbia Univ Coll & Physicians & Surgeons, staff psychiat 1964-71; Columbia Univ Coll Phusicians & Surgeons Harlem Hosp, resd psychiat inst 1964-67; post grad 1961-63; Univ Haiti, physician 1956-68; Area C Mental Hlth CtrDept Human Resources DC, dir in-patient serv; Clinical Hypnosis Inst Harvard U, dir; Intl Soc Papplied Studies Transcultural Adaptation Inc pres; St Thomas RC Ch, consult 1971. **ORGANIZATIONS:** Mem Shiloh Bapt Ch 1973; All Angels Episcopal Ch 1973; Christ Ch Meth; publ "Adaptation of the Haitian Physician & His Family to the Am Soc". **BUSINESS ADDRESS:** 2041 Georgia Ave, Washington, DC 20060.

CHAFFERS, JAMES A.
Professor of architecture. **PERSONAL:** Born Nov 30, 1941, Ruston, LA; married Geraldine; children: Pedra, Michael. **EDUCATION:** So Univ Baton Rouge, BArch (cum laude) 1964; Univ of MI, MArch 1969, DArch 1971. **CAREER:** Coll of Arch & Urban Plng, prof; Wastenaw Co, commnr 1970-71; Nathan Johnson & Asso, arch; So U, tchr 2 yrs; Univ of MI, 2 yrs. **ORGANIZATIONS:** Chmn So Univ Dept of Arch; dir Comm based Design Wrkshps N Cntrl Ann Arbor & SW Detroit; cntrbn author to "The Blk 70'S". **HONORS/ACHIEVEMENTS:** Recip Woodrow Wilson Fellow; outst tchr award So Univ 1971-72. **MILITARY SERVICE:** AUS Corps of Engr capt 5 yrs. **BUSINESS ADDRESS:** University of Michigan, College of Architecture, Ann Arbor, MI 48103.

CHALLENOR, HERSCHELLE
United nations official. **PERSONAL:** Born Oct 05, 1938, Atlanta, GA; divorced. **EDUCATION:** Spelman Coll, BA; Univ Grenoble, attended; Sorbonne Univ, attended; Johns Hopkins, MA; Columbia Univ, PHD. **CAREER:** Political Sci Dept Brooklyn Coll, asst prof 1969-72; Amer Pol Sci Assoc, cong fellow 1972-73; Div Ed & Rsch Ford Found, prog officer 1973-75; UN Ed Sci & Cultural Org Wash Liaison Office, dir 1978-. **ORGANIZATIONS:** Consult Sub-com on Africa; mem UN Assoc Council on Foreign Rel, Amer Pol Sci Assoc, Natl Conf Black Pol Sci, Bd of Oper Crossroads Africa; bd mem Intl Block United Fund; mem Spelman Coll Scholarship. **HONORS/ACHIEVEMENTS:** Charles Merill Study Travel Awd; Woodrow Wilson Fellowship; John Hay Whitney Fellowship; NY State Merit Fellowship; Amer Assoc Univ Women Fields Rsch Grant; Fellow Adli Stevenson Inst Intl Affairs Chgo; Ford Found Travel & Study Awd. **BUSINESS ADDRESS:** Dir, UNESCO, 2 United Nations Plaza, Room 900, New York, NY 10017.

CHALMERS, THELMA FAYE
Government official. **PERSONAL:** Born Feb 21, 1947, Shreveport, LA; daughter of Leonard Hampton and Ivy Williams Hampton; married Jimmy Chalmers; children: Troy, Douglas, Celeste. **EDUCATION:** Chandler College, Associates Degree 1966. **CAREER:** St Clair County Intergovermental Grants Dept, program monitor 1979-81, program planner 1981-83, special assignment supvr 1983-86, program mgr 1986-; St Clair County Grants Dept, Belleville IL, div mgr 1988-. **ORGANIZATIONS:** Equal employment opportunity officer St Clair County Grants Dept 1982-; staff liason Service Delivery Area 24 Private Industry Council 1984-; mem Illinois Employment & Training Assn 1988-. **HONORS/ACHIEVEMENTS:** Assertive Mgmt Certificate, Southern Illinois Univ Edwardsville School of Business 1985; Image and Communication Skills Certificate, The Business Women's Training Institute 1986. **BUSINESS ADDRESS:** Program Manager, St Clair County Intergov Grant, 512 E Main St, Belleville, IL 62222.

CHAMBERLAIN, WILT N. (WILT THE STILT)
Businessman, former professional basketball player. **PERSONAL:** Born Aug 21, 1936, Philadelphia, PA. **EDUCATION:** KS Univ, 1956-58. **CAREER:** Harlem Globetrotters, player 1958-59; Philadelphia Warriors, player 1959-65; Philadelphia 76ers, player 1965-68; LA Lakers, star center 1968-73; Big Wilt's Smalls Paradise Niteclub, owner; actor in various movies and adv endorsements. **HONORS/ACHIEVEMENTS:** Rookie of the Year 1960; led NBA League in total points scored per season 7 years straight; holds all-time professional lead-in points scored (more than 30,000); most points scored by individual in one game (100 Points) 1962; named NBA MVP 4 times; averaged 301 points per game and led League in rebounds 11 times; 14 years of professional basketball; mem Basketball Hall of Fame. **BUSINESS ADDRESS:** Los Angeles Lakers, 3900 W Manchester Blvd, Inglewood, CA 90306.

CHAMBERS, ALEX A.
College president. **CAREER:** Lane College, Jackson, TN, president. **BUSINESS ADDRESS:** President, Lane College, Jackson, TN 38301. *

CHAMBERS, CLARICE LORRAINE
Elected official, clergyman. **PERSONAL:** Born Oct 07, 1938, Ossining, NY; daughter of Willie Cross (deceased) and Louise McDonald Cross; married Albert W, Jun 09, 1962; children: Albert W Jr, Cheryl L Fultz. **EDUCATION:** Manna Bible Inst, Teachers Cert 1965; Trinity Coll of Bible, B Biblical Studies 1983; International Bible College & Seminary, Orlando FL, Masters Biblical Theology 1986. **CAREER:** Naval Supply Depot, master data spec 1957-65; dir of training Tri-Cty OIC 1970-72; PA State Dept of Revenue, asst public info dir 1972-79; Antioch Tabernacle UHC of A, pastor 1979-; Harrisburg School Bd, pres. **ORGANIZATIONS:** Sec Tri-Cty OIC Bd 1980-; mem Tri-Cty United Way Bd 1983-89, South Central PA Ford Bank Bd 1983-89; bd mem, YMCA 1989-; bd mem, Delta Dental 1989-. **HONORS/ACHIEVEMENTS:** Volunteer Comm Serv Tri-Cty OIC 1977; Community Serv Awd Natl Assoc Black Accountants 1984; Cert of Recognition Christian Churches United 1984; African-American Comm Service Award, Harrisburg Chapter Black United Fund of Pennsylvania 1989; Service Award, National School Boards Assn 1989. **HOME ADDRESS:** 147 Sylvan Terr, Harrisburg, PA 17104. **BUSINESS ADDRESS:** President, Harrisburg School Board, 1201 N 6th St, Harrisburg, PA 17101.

CHAMBERS, DONALD C.
Physician. **PERSONAL:** Born May 17, 1936; married Jacqueline; children: Christopher, Kimberly, Bradley. **EDUCATION:** NY U, BA 1957; Howard U, MS 1961. **CAREER:** Ings Co Hosp Ctr, res training 1961-66; StUniv NY, asst prof 1964-66; Baltimore Pvt Prac, 1968-; Sinai Hosp, physician; Provident Hosp, physician; Lutheran Hosp, physician. **ORGANIZATIONS:** Mem Pan Am Med Soc; Am Soc Abdominal Surgeons; mem NAACP; Monumental City Med Soc; Hlth Care Standards Com; MD Found Hlth Care. **HONORS/ACHIEVEMENTS:** Contrib author Urban Hlth Mag; fellow Am Coll Abstericians Gynecologists 1969; fellow Am Coll Surgeons 1973; fellow Royal Soc Hlth. **MILITARY SERVICE:** USAF cpat 1966-68. **BUSINESS ADDRESS:** 2300 Garrison Blvd, Ste 200, Baltimore, MD 21216.

CHAMBERS, DORIS FOSTER
Educator. **PERSONAL:** Born Aug 28, 1929, Pine Bluff, AR; married Fredrick Chambers; children: Ivie Cecilia, Fredrick Foster. **EDUCATION:** Palmer Mem Inst, 1946; Talladega Coll, AB 1950; Univ of TN, MSSW 1960. **CAREER:** NV Cty & Jefferson Cty, teacher 1950-53; Jefferson Cty AR, social worker 1953-55; Univ of AR Pine Bluff, coll prof 1963-71; Kent State Univ, asst profsocial work 1971-. **ORGANIZATIONS:** Teacher Boliver Cty MS 1955-57; social worker Memphis Urban Legue 1957-59; mem Alpha Kappa Alpha, The Links Inc, The League of Women Voters. **HOME ADDRESS:** 2010 Carlton Dr, Kent, OH 44240. **BUSINESS ADDRESS:** Asst Professor Soc Work, Kent StateUniv, 109 Lowry Hall, Kent, OH 44242.

CHAMBERS, FREDRICK
Educator. **PERSONAL:** Born Mar 28, 1928, Waterloo, IA; married Doris Foster; children: Ivie Cecilia, Fredrick Foster. **EDUCATION:** Univ of AR at Pine Bluff, BA 1955; Univ of AR, MEd 1959; Ball State U, EdD 1970. **CAREER:** Kent State Univ, assoc prof 1971-; Univ of AR at Pine Bluff, assoc prof 1959-71; Ball State Univ, teaching fellow History 1967-70; Phelix High School, social science teacher 1957-59; Mound Bayou High School, social science teacher 1955-57; AR Boy's Ind School, counselor 1955; Natl Teachers Ex Educ Testing Service, supr 1960-63. **ORGANIZATIONS:** Commr AR on Higher Educ 1970; exec com AR Conf of AAUP 1965-67; state sec & bd mem OH Am Civil Liberties 1976-. **HONORS/ACHIEVEMENTS:** Author "Histories of Black Coll" Journal of Negro History 1972; Black Higher Educ in the US Greenwood Press Inc 1978. **MILITARY SERVICE:** AUS pfc 1952-54. **BUSINESS ADDRESS:** Associate Professor, Kent State University, 404 White Hall, Kent, OH 44242.

CHAMBERS, HARRY, JR.
Financial partner. **PERSONAL:** Born Jul 04, 1956, Birmingham, AL; son of Harry Chambers Sr and Bessie Chambers; married Linda Giles; children: Hali Alexandria, Harry Alonzo III. **EDUCATION:** Alabama State Univ, BS 1979; Samford Univ, MBA 1985; Dale Carnegie, Human Relations & Leadership Training. **CAREER:** US General Accounting Office, co-op student 1976-77; Bank of Amer NT & SA, intl auditor Europe 1979-80; Amsouth Bank NA, div accounting officer opers 1980-86; US Treasury, IRS agent 1987-; Chambers Consulting Ltd, financial partner, 1987-. **ORGANIZATIONS:** Life mem Kappa Alpha Psi 1980-; 1st vice pres Natl Black MBA Assoc Birmingham Chap 1985-; Sunday school teacher Sixth Ave Baptist Church 1985-; presiding partner CBSA Investment Club 1985-; financial partner Chambers Consulting Ltd 1986-; deacon Sixth Ave Bapt Church 1986-; fund-raising capt Boy Scouts of Amer 1987; financial bd mem, Academy of Fine Arts Inc, Birmingham AL. **HONORS/ACHIEVEMENTS:** Woodrow Wilson designee Woodrow Wilson Fellowship Found 1985. **HOME ADDRESS:** 1040 50th St, Birmingham, AL 35208.

CHAMBERS, JAMES R.
Retired educator. **PERSONAL:** Born May 07, 1915; children: 4 Children. **EDUCATION:** KY State Coll, BS 1941; WV U, MA 1953. **CAREER:** Educ Talent Search, project dir. **ORGANIZATIONS:** Mem numerous offices coms; Broward County Guidance Assn; Am Personnel & Guidance Assn; Gvs Ad Hoc Task Force on Educ Problems FLhs Disadvantaged; Faculty Senate; ch The Incarnation; Met Dade County Fair Housing & Employment Commn; Diocese SE FL; Task Force on Pub Serv Employment; Community TV Found; So FL Inc; Kappa Alpha Psi Frat; Sigma Pi Phi Boule Cons; Equal Access/Equal Opportunity Community Coll System Workshop 1974-.

CHAMBERS, JULIUS LEVONNE
Attorney. **PERSONAL:** Born Oct 06, 1936, Montgomery Co, NC; son of William Chambers and Matilda Chambers; married Vivian Verdell Giles; children: Derrick, Judy. **EDUCATION:** NC Central Univ Durham, BA History (summa cum laude) 1958; Univ of MI, MA 1959; Univ of NC Sch of Law, JD 1962; Columbia Univ Sch of Law ML 1963. **CAREER:** Columbia Univ Sch of Law, assoc in law 1962-63; NAACP Legal Def & Educ Fund Inc, legal intern 1963-64; Harvard Univ Law Sch, lecturer 1965; Univ of VALaw Sch, guest lecturer 1971-72; Univ of PA Sch of Law, lecturer 1972-; Chambers Stein Ferguson & Becton PA, pres 1964-84; NAACP Legal & Educ Fund Inc, dir counsel 1984-. **ORGANIZATIONS:** Mem numerous cts of practice 1962-; mem Amer, Natl, 26th Judicial Dist NC Bar Assns; NC Assn of Black Lawyers; mem Amer Bar Assn Section on Indiv Rights & Responsibilities; adv com Natl Bar Assn Equal Employment Oppor; mem NC Bar Assn Com on Rules of Appellate Procedure; mem NC State Bar Assn Const Study Com; mem various NAACP brs; mem vari-

ous legal assns; bd of dirs Epilepsy Assn of NC; mem various Univ bds; mem various alumni assns; mem various frats; mem Friendship Baptist Church Charlotte. **HONORS/ACHIEVEMENTS:** WEB DuBois Awd Scotland Co 1973; Hall of Fame Awd NAACP 1975; numerous hon LLD degrees; various distinguished serv awds, frats & Assns. **MILITARY SERVICE:** USNR 1960-63; AUSR 1963-66. **BUSINESS ADDRESS:** Dir, NAACP Legal Def & Educ Fund, 99 Hudson St, 16th Floor, New York, NY 10013.

CHAMBERS, MADRITH BENNETT
Appointed official. **PERSONAL:** Born Oct 23, 1935, Beckley, WV; married Robert E Chambers; children: Stephanie M Rosario, Gregory B, Patrick M, Jennifer E, Sharri L. **EDUCATION:** Bluefield State College, AS Law Enforcement, BS Criminal Justice Adm 1985. **CAREER:** Social Security Admin, contact representative. **ORGANIZATIONS:** Councilwoman City of Pax 1972-74; vice-pres Amer Legion Women's Aux 1982-84; chairperson City of Beckley Human Rights Comm 1978-; pres Beckley Chap Bluefield St Coll Alumni Assn 1983-; mem Alpha Kappa Alpha. **HONORS/ACHIEVEMENTS:** DHHS Special Award Social Sec Admn 1980; Outstanding Service Awd Bluefield St Coll Alumni Assn 1984; Mountain State Bar Assn Citation Mt State Bar Assn 1984. **BUSINESS ADDRESS:** Contact Representative, Social Security Adm, 214 N Kanawna St, Beckley, WV 25801.

CHAMBERS, OLIVIA MARIE
Goverment service. **PERSONAL:** Born Sep 27, 1942, Denver, CO; married Bill D Chambers; children: Maria. **EDUCATION:** Dale Carnegie Crs Human Rel, Cert 1977; Univ of Denver, Mgmt Cert Prog 1983; CO Univ Ext Cntr and Comm Clge. **CAREER:** State of CO Interstate Dept of Employ and Training Unit, mgr 1976-77; State of CO Dept of Employ and Trng, chief of benefits 1977-84. **ORGANIZATIONS:** Mem IAPES; bd mem Comm Homemaker Suc 1981-83. **HONORS/ACHIEVEMENTS:** Citation hnrbl mntn Distgnshd State Serv Award Denver Federal Exec Bd 1981; rec Ebony Mag Speaking of People 1979. **BUSINESS ADDRESS:** Dept of Employment & Training, 251 E 12th Ave, Denver, CO 80203.

CHAMBERS, PAMELA S.
Police sergeant. **PERSONAL:** Born Nov 05, 1961, Gasden, AL; daughter of Hurley Chambers and Mildred Douglas Chambers. **EDUCATION:** Ferris State College, Big Rapids MI, AA pre-law, 1982. **CAREER:** City of Pontiac MI, police cadet, 1982, police officer, 1982, police sergeant, 1988. **ORGANIZATIONS:** Sec, Soc of Afro-American Police; bd mem, The Natl Black Police Assn; assoc mem, Natl Org of Black Law Exec (NOBLE). **HONORS/ACHIEVEMENTS:** Distinction of being the first black woman promoted to police sergeant in the history of the city of Pontiac; also the youngest person ever to be promoted to sergeant in the city of Pontiac. **HOME ADDRESS:** 593 Pearsall St, Pontiac, MI 48053. **BUSINESS ADDRESS:** Sergeant, Pontiac Police Department, 110 E Pike St, Pontiac, MI 48053.

CHAMBERS, RUTH-MARIE FRANCES
Counselor, educator. **PERSONAL:** Born Apr 07, 1953, Chicago, IL. **EDUCATION:** Southern IL Univ, BA 1974; Chicago Hearing Soc, 1975-76; Lycee Kassai Africa, Certificate 1978; Franco-Nigerien Cultural Ctr, 1979; Southern IL Univ, MS 1982; Cosumnes River College, Sacramento CA, Equine Technology Program 1988-. **CAREER:** Southern IL Univ, residence coord/counselor 1974-75; US Peace Corps Niger Africa, volunteer; Chicago IL, artist-in-residence 1975-78; Goodwill Rehab Training Ctr, vocational counselor-evaluator 1975-76; Austin Industries Rehab Facility, chief evaluator 1976-78; Natl Sch of Admin Africa, lecturer/asst prof 1978-80; Rehabilitation Inst Southern IL Univ, rsch asst 1981-82; Univ of CA-Berkeley, admin analyst 1984; Work Experience Prog San Leandro Sch Dist, coord 1984-86; Orange Grove Adult School, adult educator; Cosumnes River College, counselor 1988-. **ORGANIZATIONS:** Developed Annual Talent Show for Disabled Citizens in Chicago, Pedagogical Workshop Coord, chair of Special Projects Team; job develop consultant JD Consortium Oakland CA 1984-86; comm volunteer crisis counselor Oakland/Berkeley CA 1985-86; adv comm Handicapped for the County of Sacramento 1987; mem Alumni Assoc SIU, NAACP, Bay Area Black United Fund, Natl Urban League, Natl Rehab Assn; Natl Council of Negro Women; Sacramento Black Women's Network; bd mem, YWCA Sacramento CA 1988. **HONORS/ACHIEVEMENTS:** Sphinx Club Hon Leadership SIU 1974; Outstanding Young Women of Amer 1975; Special Mention for Serv to Disabled Children Minister of Sports and Culture, Africa 1980; Special Mention for Serv to Gamkale Equestrian Club Niger Africa 1980; Letters of Recognition from Ambassador Chicago City Councilman Mayor of Aurora IL for Outstanding Citizenship and Serv to the Community 1980-81; 4 publications "International Year of Disabled Persons, Past, Present and Implications for Tomorrow," 1982; "Speech and Pronunciation," presented at Intl Teacher's Conference Zinder, Niger Africa 1979; "Le Sahel in Retrospect" 1987; Shadow Program participant with Assemblyman Lloyd Connelly, California State Legislator 1988; The Porcelain Throne 1989; Equestrain comp etition 3rd & 4th place winnings. **BUSINESS ADDRESS:** PO Box 2991, Sacramento, CA 95812.

CHAMBERS, WALLACE
Athlete. **PERSONAL:** Born May 15, 1951, Phenix City, AL. **EDUCATION:** KY State U, degree in PE; M Communications; Off-Seasons Studies. **CAREER:** Tampa Bay Buccaneers, defensive end 1978-; Chicago Bears, defensive end 1973-78. **HONORS/ACHIEVEMENTS:** 4 Yr Letterman E KY; MVP E KY 1972; AP; NFL Rookie of Year 1973; Pro Bowl 1973, 1975, 1976; Coll All-Amer on Sporting News Team; N-S Sr Bowl & Coll All-Star Team Mem; All NFC Sporting News & UPI 1976. **BUSINESS ADDRESS:** Tampa Bay Buccaneers, One Buccaneer Pl, Tampa, FL 33607.

CHAMBERS, YJEAN S.
Educator. **PERSONAL:** Born Dec 09, 1921, Bluediamond, KY; daughter of Thomas H Staples and Hester Hutcherson Staples; married Herman; children: Lanel R. **EDUCATION:** Illinois State Univ, BEd, 1943; Purdue Univ, MA, 1973. **CAREER:** School Madison Illinois, 1943-45; Roosevelt HS Garn Indiana, 1945-71; PurdueUniv, Calumet Campus, guest lecturer, 1969-71; grad instructor, 1971-73; Purdue Univ, Calumet Campus, asst prof, 1973-79, acting dept head, 1981-83, assoc prof 1979-. **ORGANIZATIONS:** pres, Gamma Psi Omega Chapter (Alpha Kappa Alpha Sor Inc), 1960-64; Gen Chmn, 29th & 39th Central Region Conf of AKA; Program Com Co-Chairperson; Gary Br, NAACP life mem com; pres, Gary Bd of School Trustees, 1974-; bd mem, Indiana School Bd Assn; mem, Central State Communication Assn; mem, Van Buren Baptist Church; dir, Miss Gary Scholarship Pageant, 1969-73; bd of dirs, Methodist Hospital; adv bd, Bank One; bd of dirs, vice pres, Gary Educ Devel Found; apptd by Gov Robt Orr Calumet Township Control Bd; dir, Miss Black Indiana Pageant, 1980-85; acting head, communication & creative arts dept, Purdue University, Calumet, 1981-83; co-chmn, bd of dirs, Steel City Hall of Fame 1988-; chmn, Quality Assurance Comm & Asst Secretary, bd of dirs, Methodist Hospital, Inc 1985-;mem, Speech Communication Assn, 1971; ;mem, Popular Culturel/Amer Culture Assns, 1987-. **HONORS/ACHIEVEMENTS:** NAACP 10 yr Merit Awd 1973; Outstanding Citizen Awd Mayor Richard G Hatcher 1975; Appreciation Award Christian Debutante Mstr Commin African Meth EspisCh 1977; INFO Newspaper Outstanding Citizen Award 1975 76; Outstanding Teacher in Sch of Hess Purdue Univ Calumet 1980; Amoco Foundation Outstanding Teacher of Undergraduates 1974, 81; Outstanding Educator Awd Natl Sor of Phi Kappa Delta, Beta Nu Chap 1985; Gary City Council Resolution A Tribute in Academic Contributions to IN Youth & Adults 1986; Bethune Achievement Awd in Communication Miller Sect Natl Council of Negro Women 1986; named by IN Speech Assoc as one of Three Top Communication Educators in the State 1987; distinguished service award, Purdue University Alumni Assoc Calumet, 1987; Edgar L Mills Communication Award, The Communi cators of Northwest Ind 1988; The Golden Apple Award, Gary Ambassadors of Education 1988; Educational Vision Award, IU Dons & Donnetts, 1988; "Pronunciation Needs Attention", The Times, 1986; "Good Speech and the Job Interview" The Times 1988; "Gary Ind, remembered in the Diamond Time" (a narrative poem with musical interpolations) excerpted in The Skylark public performance, 1983; "Reverent Resonaces: M L King Remembered" public performance 1986. **BUSINESS ADDRESS:** Associate Professor, Purdue University-Calumet, Lawshe Bldg, Hammond, IN 46323.

CHAMBLISS, CHRIS
Professional athlete. **PERSONAL:** Born Dec 26, 1948, Dayton, OH; married Audra; children: Russell, Jonathan. **CAREER:** Atlanta Braves, first baseman 1979; Yankees, first baseman. **ORGANIZATIONS:** 37 doubles in 1980 tied the Atlanta record set byt Hank Aaron; Indian's No 1 pick in the Jan 1970 free agent draft; frmer mem Air Natl Guards. **HONORS/ACHIEVEMENTS:** Gold Glove award while with the Yanbkees; Pro Rookie to win a Triple-A batting title; AL Rookie Of The Year 1971. **BUSINESS ADDRESS:** Atlanta Braves, P O Box 4064, Atlanta, GA 30302.

CHAMBLISS, IDA BELLE
Educator. **PERSONAL:** Born Jun 10, 1935, Tuskegee, AL. **EDUCATION:** AL State Coll, BS Health & Physical Educ 1954; Univ of WI Milwaukee, M Soc Work 1966. **CAREER:** Foster Care Training, N Seattle Community Coll Home & Family Div, project coordinator 1975-; YWCA King Co Job Corps, job placement counselor 1967-69; YWCA Seattle King Co, program dir 1969-73; Univ of Washington School of Social Work, instructor & lecturer 1970-75; US Govt Santiago Chile SA, Peace Corps volunteer 1962-64. **ORGANIZATIONS:** Mem WA State Bd of Health State of WA 1979; pres Group Health Cooperative of Puget Sound 1978-; mem NAACP; Seattle Urban League; AKA; US Commr UNESCO. **HONORS/ACHIEVEMENTS:** Edwin T Pratt Annual Serv Award, Seattle Urban League 1979. **BUSINESS ADDRESS:** N Seattle Community Coll, 9600 College Way N, Seattle, WA 98103.

CHAMPION, JERRYE G.
Librarian. **PERSONAL:** Born Aug 23, 1940, Prentiss, MS; married Fred M; children: Christopher John. **EDUCATION:** Tougaloo Coll, BA 1961; Univ of OK, MLS 1965. **CAREER:** Scottsdale Pub Libr, libr dir 1973-77; Scottsdale Pub Library, asst library dir 1971-73; Scottsdale Pub Library, head of pub serv div; State Library of AZ, pub library consult 1966-67; Phoenix Pub Library Sys, reference librarian 1965-66; Tougaloo Coll, reference librarian 1964-65; Union Academy Columbus MS, tchr librarian 1962; Webster High Eupora MS, tchr librarian 1961-62. **ORGANIZATIONS:** Pres AZ State Library Assn; past pres Pub Libraries Div; past pres Pub Libraries Section; League of AZ Cities & Towns; exec bd SW Library Assn; mem Am Library Assn; mem Nat Exec Bd; Delta Sigma Theta Inc; pres Phoenix Chpt; mem exec bd Needy Children's Soc Inc; ch steward & chairwoman ofComm on Membership & Evangelism; AME Ch Who's Who of Am Women 1972 & 1974; Nat Reg Prominent Ams & Intl Notables 1976-77; Notable Ams 1976-77; Dict of Intl Biography 1977; Wold Who's Who of Women 1974; Intl Who's Who in Comm Serv 1975. **BUSINESS ADDRESS:** Scottsdale Pub Library, 3839 Civic Center Plaza, Scottsdale, AZ 85251.

CHAMPION, JESSE
Director, reporter. **PERSONAL:** Born Aug 27, 1927, Dolomite, AL; divorced; children: Hermenia Gwynette, Sharmayn Lil Margo, Jesse II. **EDUCATION:** AL A&M U, grad 1951. **CAREER:** WERC Radio, dir; news report; Southwestern HS, instr 1963-71; Council Elem Sch, tchr 1954-63; Carver HS, tchr 1950-54. **ORGANIZATIONS:** Mem AL Educ Assoc; mem Nat Educ Assn 1950-63; mem Amer Fed of Tchrs; Flint Tchrs Assn 1963-71; mem Amer Fed of Musicians; mem Prof Journalism Soc; NAACCP; B'ham Urban Leag; B'ham Press Club; Knights of Columbus; Alpha Phi Chap; ed past chrm Omega Psi Phi Frat; Sigma Delta Chi. **HONORS/ACHIEVEMENTS:** Outstanding Clarinetist, Morehouse Coll Award 1946; Acad Award, AL A&MUniv dram club; Fellowship Grant;Univ of Notre Dame 1951; Outst Newsman Award, B'hamFirefighters 1973; Best Public Affairs Dir, State Assn Press 1975; hon mention Active Partic during Civil rights struggle 1962-63. **BUSINESS ADDRESS:** PO Box 10904, Birmingham, AL 35202.

CHAMPION, TEMPII BRIDGENE
Speech/language pathologist. **PERSONAL:** Born Sep 02, 1961, Brooklyn, NY. **EDUCATION:** Northeastern Univ, BS 1983; Hampton Univ, MA 1986. **CAREER:** Bd of Educ New York, speech therapist 1983-84; Northern Westchester Ctr for Speech Disorders, speech therapist 1986-87; Federation Employment & Guidance Svcs, speech therapist 1987-. **ORGANIZATIONS:** Mem Amer Speech & Hearing Assoc, New York City Speech & Hearing Assoc, Natl Assoc of the Deaf, NAACP; mem Black Speech Language Hearing Assoc. **HONORS/ACHIEVEMENTS:** Graduate Fellowship 1984-86; Who's Who Among Outstanding Young Women of Amer 1985; Cert Speech Lang Pathologist (ASHA); NYS Lic Speech Language Pathologist. **HOME ADDRESS:** 334 Eastern Parkway, Brooklyn, NY 11225. **BUSINESS ADDRESS:** Speech/Language Pathologist, Federation Employ & Guid Serv, 510 6th Ave, Manhattan, NY 10011.

CHANCE, KENNETH BERNARD
Academician/endodontist. **PERSONAL:** Born Dec 08, 1953, New York, NY; son of George E Chance and Janie Bolles Change; married Sharon L Lewis; children: Kenneth B II, Dana Marie, Christopher Weldon. **EDUCATION:** Fordham Univ, BS 1975; Case West-

ern Reserve Univ Dental Sch, DDS 1979; Jamaica Hospital GP Residency Prog, Certificate 1980; NJ Dental School, Certificate in Endodontics 1982; PEW Natl Dental Educ Prog, Certificate 1986. **CAREER:** Harlem Hosp, attending 1981-; North Central Bronx Medical Ctr, asst attending 1982-; Jamaica Hosp, asst attending 1982-86; Kings Co Medical Ctr, chief of endodontics 1983-; Kingsbrook Jewish Medical Ctr, asst attending 1985-; NJ Dental Sch, dir of external affairs 1985-, assoc prof of endodontics 1987-; Univ of Medicine & Dentistry of New Jersey, asst dean for external affairs & urban resource devel, 1989-. **ORGANIZATIONS:** Mem Amer Assoc of Endodontists 1980-86, Natl Dental Assoc 1980-; minister of music and sr organist Sharon Bapt Ch 1983-; mem Intl Assoc of Dental Rsch 1984-; pres elect Greater Metro Dental Soc of NY 1985-; consultant Commonwealth Dental Soc of NJ 1985-. **HONORS/ACHIEVEMENTS:** Dr Paul P Sherwood Awd Case Western Reserve Dental Sch 1979; Awd for Excellent Serv Jamaica Hosp 1981; Rsch Awd The Foundation of the UMDNJ 1985; Exceptional Merit Awd NJ Dental Sch 1986; Nom for Excellence in Teaching Awd NJ Dental School 1985. **HOME ADDRESS:** 87 Victory Blvd, New Rochelle, NY 10804. **BUSINESS ADDRESS:** Assoc Prof of Endodontics, Univ of Med & Dentistry NJ, 100 Bergen St, Newark, NJ 07103.

CHANCELLOR, CARL EUGENE
Attorney. **PERSONAL:** Born Mar 01, 1929, Cleveland, OH; married Joyce Marshall; children: Carl C, Bruce E, Steven E, Yvette. **EDUCATION:** OH State Univ, BA 1951; Case Western Res Law School, JD 1954; Univ of MI Grad School of Bus Admin, Publ Utility Exec Prog Cert 1973. **CAREER:** Cleveland Electric Illuminating Co, assoc attny, attny, sr attny, gen suprv attny claims 1954-72, mgr legal serv dept 1972-82, asst gen counsel 1982-, sec and general counsel 1986-. **ORGANIZATIONS:** Spec counsel Attny Gen of OH 1953-69; sec, bd of dir Raymilton Land Co Coal Mining 1956-64; labor adv comm OH C of C 1977-; pres Self Insurers Group of OH 1965-70; chmn Edison Elec Inst Claims Comm 1985-86, Frankfort Pol Action Comm 1977-84; exec bd, life mem Cleveland Br NAACP; mem Alpha Phi Alpha. **HONORS/ACHIEVEMENTS:** Cert of Appreciation Vice Pres Humphreys Plans for Prog Comm 1969; Meritorious Serv Awd Cleveland Bar Assoc 1972; Legal Study Scholarship Rainey Found 1951-54. **BUSINESS ADDRESS:** Secretary and General Counsel, Cleveland Elec Illuminating Co, 55 Public Sq, Cleveland, OH 44113.

CHANDLER, DANA C., JR. (AKIN DURO)
Artist, educator, lecturer. **PERSONAL:** Born Apr 07, 1941, Lynn, MS; married Deborah; children: Dahna, Rene, Hope, Dana, Janis, Colby. **EDUCATION:** MA Coll of Art, BS Art Educ 1976; Univ Of MA, grad student. **CAREER:** Simmons Coll, Afro-Amer art critic; Bay State Banner, asst prof of art & art hist 1971-; Northeastern Univ, artist in residence 1974-, dir of AAMARP. **ORGANIZATIONS:** Comm organizer Jamaica Plain Are Planning Action Council 1065-67; rsch spec Lemberg Ctr Brandeis Univ 1967-68; asst dir Youth Dept Model City Admin 1968-70; art curriculum devel spec Model City Admin 1970; acting dir Art Dept Model City Consortium Coll 1970-71; dir African Art Curriculum Project Educ Devel Ctr 1970-71; mem Natl Conf of Black Artists Boston Black Artists Assn, natl Soc of Lit & the Arts, Natl Conf of Artists, Boston Union of Visual Artists, Amer Assn of Univ Prof, NAACP. **HONORS/ACHIEVEMENTS:** Man of the Year Awd NAACP 1970; Black Big Brother of Boston Awd 1971; recip Natl End of the Arts Awd 1973; Citation for Mural Work Kevin White Mayor of Boston 1973; Roxbury Action Prog Comm Serv Awd 1974; listed in Who's Who in the East 1972-, Who's Who in Amer Art 1976, Amer Art Dir 1976, Comm Ldr & Natl Personalities 1977-; has been the subject of many books & magazine articles; has a large no of group & one man shows; has lectured and had exhbn at many coll & univ. **BUSINESS ADDRESS:** Dir of AAMARP, NortheasternUniv, 11 Leon St, Boston, MA 02115.

CHANDLER, DENNIS COURTLAND
Business executive. **PERSONAL:** Born Dec 21, 1893, Duluth, GA; married Lena E Eubanks. **EDUCATION:** Morris Brown Coll. **CAREER:** Supreme Life Ins Co, ret vice pres consult 1965-; Supreme Life, vice pres 1959-65; Dunbar Life, pres 1956-59, vice pres 1945-56; Dunbar Mutual, vice pres orgnr 1930-45; SupremeLife & Casualty, asst sec, sorganizer 1921; Fireside Mut Ins, state mgr; Adelphi Bldg & Loan Co, pres 1920-25; Fireside Mut Ins, agent 1916. **ORGANIZATIONS:** Moderator Mt Zion Congregational Ch 1932-51; vice pres Congregational Union 1947-48; vice pres Cleveland Ch Fed 1950-51; historian Nat Negro Ins Assn 1962; chmn Anti Inflation Com; treas Cleveland Urban League. **HONORS/ACHIEVEMENTS:** Anti-Inflation com award, Pres Harry H Truman 1946; Mt Zion Congregation Ch award 1951; cert of Recognition Ins Mgrs Council of Cleveland 1951; Cleveland Bus League 1959; cert of Merit, Supreme Life Ins Co of Am 1961; 50 yrs of svc, Nat Ins Assn 1965; Outst Serv Award, Fed Shopping Mall & State of OH City of Cleveland 1974; Sr Citizens Award, Cleveland 1974; Nat Assn of Life Underwriters; Trial Blazers Award 1976. **BUSINESS ADDRESS:** 7609 Euclid Ave, Cleveland, OH 44103.

CHANDLER, EFFIE L.
Business executive. **PERSONAL:** Born Aug 13, 1927, Houston, TX; divorced; children: Donald C. **EDUCATION:** Massey Bus Coll, 1967-68; TX So U, BA 1966; TX So U, MEd 1975; Franklin Beauty Coll, Cosmetology TX License 1945. **CAREER:** US Postal Svc, dist EEO splst 1973-; asso employee devel advisor 1973; asst learning counselor 1971-73; acting & employment asst 1968-74; Personnel Section, clk steno 1965-68; scheme instr 1963-65; job instr 1963-65; distribution clk 1959-63. **ORGANIZATIONS:** Mem Nat Council of Negro Women; YWCA; Nat Assn of Postal Supr Br 122; Fed Minority Bus Opportunity Com; instr EEO Div, So Region Headquarters chrtr mem Cit Against Drug Abuse Com; past society editor for Houston's Oldest Black Weekly Newspaper, Effie's Excerpts 1973-74; sec Cambridge Civic Club 1967; sec treas 1968-69; pres Cambridge Village Civic Club 1973-74; chmn exec adv bd Anti-Basileus for Gamma Phi Sigma Chpt; Sigma Gamma Rho Sorority; campus advisor Alpha Lambda Chpt; Sigma Gama Rho Sorority TX So Univ 1974-. **HONORS/ACHIEVEMENTS:** Outstdng Serv to Comm, Cambridge Village Civic Club 1977; The Lt Col Cleveland Roy Petit Merit Award; Cert of Appreciation in recognition of performance in interest of improved Postal Svc, US Postal Svc, So Region; recipient Certificate & cash award for adopted suggestion, US PO 1967; Superior Accomplishment Award with cash award, US PO 1968; Quality Step Increase 1968; nominated for Fedl Women's Award 1975. **BUSINESS ADDRESS:** 401 Franklin Ave, Houston, TX 77201.

CHANDLER, EVERETT A.
Attorney. **PERSONAL:** Born Sep 21, 1926, Columbus, OH; son of Everett P Chandler and Mary Turner Chandler; married Mittie R, Mar 20, 1987; children: Wayne B, Brian E, V Rhette, Mae Evette. **EDUCATION:** Ohio State Univ, BSc in Educ 1955; Howard Univ Law School, JD 1958. **CAREER:** Juvenile Ct Cuyahoga County, referee, support dept 1959; City of Cleveland OH, hous insp 1960; Cuyahoga County Welfare Dept, legal inv 1960-1964; Cuyahoga County OH, asst cty pros 1968-1971; City of Cleveland OH, chief police prosecutor 1971-1975; Private Practice, attorney 1975-. **ORGANIZATIONS:** Bd mem Cedar Branch YMCA 1965, Comm Action Against Addiction 1975-1980, bd chrmn 1980-; bd mem Legal Aid Soc of Cleveland 1980; polemarch and bd chmn Kappa Alpha Psi Inc 1976 1980-1983; NAACP and Urban League; bd mem and past bd pres CIT Mental Health; mem Excelsior Lodge #11 F&AM. **HONORS/ACHIEVEMENTS:** Book review vol 21 #2 Cleveland State Law School Law Review 1972; main speaker banquet Frontiers Intl Columbus OH 1972. **MILITARY SERVICE:** USN qmq2. **HOME ADDRESS:** 3491 W 159th St, Cleveland, OH 44111-2967. **BUSINESS ADDRESS:** 815 Superior Ave, Ste 2020, Cleveland, OH 44114.

CHANDLER, HAROLD R.
Librarian. **PERSONAL:** Born Sep 08, 1941, Louisville, KY; son of Joseph F. Chandler and Nellie M. Chandler. **EDUCATION:** Morehouse Coll, BS, Biology 1965; Atlanta Univ, MSLS 1965; Univ of TN Med School, Certified Med Librarian 1972; Memphis Theological Sem, MDiv 1978, MAR 1987. **CAREER:** Memphis Theological Seminary, librarian-acquisitions/minister; Univ of TN Center for Health Science, rsch bibliographer 1972-76; Watkins Chapel CME Church Memphis, minister of music; Regional Med Center, Memphis, med librarian 1984-; Teaches class on ministry to the terminally ill. **ORGANIZATIONS:** HEW Fellowship for Science Librarians 1971-72; mem Memphis Ministerial Assn 2 yrs; steering com 1st Annual Lecture Series LeMoyne-Owen Coll 1980; post grad librarian fellowship Univ TN Med School; delegate to the World Methodist Conference Nairobi Kenya 1986; mem, Memphi, 1989. **HONORS/ACHIEVEMENTS:** Outstanding young man of year 1978; Commendation medal USAF; Honored for teaching class on death & dying, Mt Vernon Baptist Church Westwood; Organized the Black History Program at the MED, 1985-present. **MILITARY SERVICE:** USAF staff sgt 4 years served. **BUSINESS ADDRESS:** Reg Med Center at Memphis, 877 Jefferson Ave, Memphis, TN 38104.

CHANDLER, J. KING, III
Educator, clergyman. **PERSONAL:** Born Apr 10, Bessemer, AL; married Doris Tolbert; children: Joseph King IV (dec), Franklin King, Yvonne Jeanette. **EDUCATION:** Wilberforce Univ Wilberforce OH, BS 1948; Tchrs Coll Columbia Univ NY, MA & EdS 1954; Monrovia Coll Monrovia Liberia, DPed 1955. **CAREER:** Jefferson State Jr Coll Birmingham, minister & prog coordinator urban studies 1967; Cheyney State Coll PA, asso prof 1958; Daniel Payne Coll Birmingham, pres 1950; Talladega Coll Talladega AL, asst prof psychology 1949; Prairie View A&M U, asso prof educ (visiting prof) 1966; SC State Coll, asso prof educ (visiting prof) 1969; Grade Tchr Darien CT, summer field rep. **ORGANIZATIONS:** Chmn Youth Guidance Free & Accepted Masons 33rd Last Degree 1962; chmn bd of dirs Grand Lodge Knights of Pythias 1975; chmn Birmingham-Talladega Area United Negro Coll Fund Campaign 1976-77. **HONORS/ACHIEVEMENTS:** Recipient good conduct medal & squadran leadership plaque ACC; listed Who's Who in Am Educ 1969; listed "Who's Who in Religion"; listed Who's Who in Am Coll& Univ Adminstrn 1971; outstanding educator of Am Higher Educ Wash DC 1973; outstanding mem Bd of Govs Am Educ Life Ins Co 1974; hon 33rd last degreeSo Jurisdiction Free & Accepted Masons. **MILITARY SERVICE:** AAC sgt 1943-46.

CHANDLER, JAMES P.
Attorney, educator. **PERSONAL:** Born Aug 15, 1938, Bakersfield, CA; married Elizabeth Thompson; children: Elizabeth Lynne, James Jr, Isaac, Dennis Augustine, Ruth Rebekah. **EDUCATION:** Univ CA, AB, JD; Havard U, LLM. **CAREER:** The Natl Law Center, George Washington Univ, prof of law 1977-; Univ CA, research asst; Boston Univ Law School, instructor 1970-71; Univ of MD Law School, asst assoc prof 1971-75; Univ of MS Law Center, distinguished visiting prof of law 1976; Univ CO Law School, visiting prof of law 1977. **ORGANIZATIONS:** Mem DC Bar; mem Am Soc Intl Law 1969-; Am Assn Univ Profs 1971-; Am Soc Law Profs 1974-; Alpha Phi Alpha Frat 1961-; bd dirs Ch God Evening Light Saints 1972-; Computer Law Assn 1974-; Woodbourne Ctr Inc 1974-76; sect council mem Am Bar Assn; consult Adminstrn Officer Cts St MD 1974-76; USGen Acctng Office 1973-.

CHANDLER, RORY WAYNE
Accountant. **PERSONAL:** Born Jan 15, 1959, Washington, DC. **EDUCATION:** Dillard Univ, BA 1981. **CAREER:** Arco Oil & Gas Co, adp 1981-82, accountant 1982-86, assoc acctg analyst 1986-. **ORGANIZATIONS:** Sec and dean of pledges Alpha Phi Alpha Xi Tau Lambda Chap 1985-86; sec TX Council of Alpha Chapters 1986-. **HOME ADDRESS:** 11363 Amanda Apt 349, Dallas, TX 75238.

CHANDLER, SHARON KAY
Educational admin. **PERSONAL:** Born Aug 06, 1957, Concord, MA. **EDUCATION:** Southeastern MA Univ, BFA 1979; Fitchburg State Coll, 9 credits toward MEd. **CAREER:** SMU Residence Hall, resident asst 1977-79; Action/Foster Grandparent Prog, prog develop 1979; Brockton Public Schools, art teacher 1979-81; Fitchburg State Coll, asst dir of admissions 1981-84; Swain School of Design, dir of admissions 1984-. **ORGANIZATIONS:** Mem Minority Educs Public Colleges & Univs 1981-84; mem NAACP 1979-; mem NEACAC 1981-; mem NACAC 1981-. **HONORS/ACHIEVEMENTS:** Art opening/recept Harvard Public Library 1979. **HOME ADDRESS:** Whitney Rd, Harvard, MA 01451.

CHANDLER, THEODORE ALAN
Educator. **PERSONAL:** Born Sep 19, 1949, St Louis, MO. **EDUCATION:** Northwest MO State Univ, BS 1973; Southern IL Univ Edwardsville, MA 1980; Univ of FL, PhD 1986. **CAREER:** Cleveland HS, secondary teacher 1976-79; New Student Life-SIU Edwardsville, consul 1980; SIU Edwardsville, grad teaching asst 1979-80; Univ of FL, grad teaching asst 1980-83; Sex Equity in Voc Ed, project asst 1983; FL Keys Comm Coll, prof & ea/eo coord 1983-. **ORGANIZATIONS:** Mem FL Speech Comm Assn 1981-; mem Speech Comm Assn 1980-; mem Southern Speech Comm Assn 1981-; mem FL Assn of Equal Oppor Profs 1983-; mem Tennessee Williams Fine Arts Ctr 1985; mem Founders Soc Key West. **HONORS/ACHIEVEMENTS:** Top Ranked Competitive FL Speech Comm Assn 1982; Outstanding Young Men of Amer Jaycees 1984; Teaching Excellence Awds SIU-E Univ of FL 1980, 1983. **BUSINESS ADDRESS:** Prof & EA/EO Coord, Florida Keys Comm College, 1 Junior College Rd, Key West, FL 33040.

CHANDLER, WESLEY SANDY (CHANT)
Professional athlete. **PERSONAL:** Born Aug 22, 1956, New Smyrna Beach, FL; married Bridget; children: Lamar Saxton. **EDUCATION:** Univ of FL, BS 1978. **CAREER:** New Orleans Saints, wide receiver 1978-81; San Diego Chargers, wide receiver 1981-. **ORGANIZATIONS:** Founder Bd of Distinction New Orleans; Chargers rep to Muscular Dystrophy; hon chmn New Orleans Rec Dept. **HONORS/ACHIEVEMENTS:** Seagram's Seven Crowns of Sport Awd as Outstanding Player in NFL 1982; 2nd Team All NFC by UPI 1979; Seagrams 7 Crowns of Sports Awd 1982; named FL ProflAthlete of the Yr FL Sports Hall of Fame 1982; mem 1986 NFL Pro Bowl Team. **HOME ADDRESS:** 5860 Louis Prima Dr, New Orleans, LA 70127.

CHANEY, DON
Assistant coach. **PERSONAL:** Born Mar 22, 1946, Baton Rouge, LA; married Jackie; children: Michael, Donna, Cara. **EDUCATION:** Univ of Houston, grad 1968. **CAREER:** Boston Celtics, player 1968-75 1978-80; Los Angeles Lakers, player 1976-78; Detroit Pistons, asst coach; LA Clippers, asst coach. **BUSINESS ADDRESS:** Head Coach, Los Angeles Clippers, 3939 Figueroa St S, Los Angeles, CA 90037.

CHANEY, JOHN
Head coach. **EDUCATION:** Bethune-Cookman (BS, Education) Antioch (Master's Degree). **CAREER:** Cheyney State Coll, basketball coach; Temple Univ, basketball coach. **HONORS/ACHIEVEMENTS:** Philadelphia Public League's MVP Player 1951; NAIA All-Amer at Bethune-Cookman.

CHANNELL, EULA L.
Business assistant. **PERSONAL:** Born Jan 29, 1928, Greenville, SC; daughter of Caesar Channell and Ruby Davenport Channell (deceased). **EDUCATION:** Benedict Coll; Greenville Tech Coll, AA 1974. **CAREER:** Allen Music Co, mgr sheet music dept; SC Commn on Aging Greenville, office worker 1972; Phillis Wheatley Assn Greenville, girls worker 1965-69; Recreation Dept City of Greenville, supvr 1955-65. **ORGANIZATIONS:** Mem Greenville Urban League; mem NAACP; mem ARC; mem Bethel Church of God; Blu Triangle Garden Club; Lend-A-Hand Federated Club; Greenville Dem Women; SC Literacy Assn; YWCA; Adv Housing Com; Girl Scout Leader; Greenville Chapter of Human Services; mem SC Fed of Women and Girls' Club; pres Lend-A-Hand Fed Club; mem PTA; delegate to state convention Guille County Dems; charter mem, sec Greenville Chap Top Ladies of Distinction. **HONORS/ACHIEVEMENTS:** Honored for serv rendered Family Planning Assn; Citizen of week Focus Newspaper; received letter of congratulations US Senator James R Mann; Camp for Pregnant Girls; Girl Scouts; Boy Scouts; Cancer Soc; 1st runner up Woman of Yr Greenville Chap NAACP; hon Mayor of City vol Serv in recreation; rec'd of award vol serv by exec dir of Phyllis Wheatley Assn; part in City wide voter registration proj Political Action Com; Heart Fund; Arthritis Found; March of Dimes; United Fund. **HOME ADDRESS:** 144 Catlin Circle, Hyde Park, Greenville, SC 29607.

CHAPELLE, ANTHONY EARL
Magazine writer. **PERSONAL:** Born Jul 01, 1954, Oakland, CA; married Carla-Beth Paden; children: Clyde-Keith, Isom Charles. **EDUCATION:** Arizona State Univ, BS Broadcasting 1978; Amer Univ Washington DC, broadcast mgmt course 1978; Grad Sch of Journalism Columbia Univ, MS 1984. **CAREER:** US Sen Dennis DeConcini AZ, press intern 1978-79; Southwest Envelope Co AZ, paper baler 1981-83; Celebrity Register Who's Who Magazine, freelance print journalist 1984-85; Ebony Man Magazine Johnson Publishing Co, living editor. **ORGANIZATIONS:** TV reporter/producer "Get It On" show KPHO-TV Phoenix AZ 1977-82; anchorman WAMU-FM Washington DC 1978-79; camerman Smithsonian Inst Museum Programs Washington DC 1979; mem Adult Christian Alliance Abyssinian Bapt Church New York City 1984-; organizer 114th St Drug Crackdown East Harlem 1986; mem NY Assoc of Black Journalists 1986-. **HONORS/ACHIEVEMENTS:** Natl winner Radio & TV News Directors Assoc Documentary contest 1978; numerous articles for Ebony Man, Black Enterprise and United Methodist Church magazinesand Religious News Serv 1984-; co-author "My Light's Still Shining," autobio Martha Pryor Anderson 1987. **BUSINESS ADDRESS:** Living Editor, Ebony Man Magazine, Johnson Publishing Co, 1270 Avenue of the Americas, New York, NY 10020.

CHAPMAN, ALICE MARIAH
City government official. **PERSONAL:** Born Dec 31, 1947, New York, NY; daughter of Elijah Chapman Sr and Elizabeth Brooks Chapman. **EDUCATION:** City Univ of NY, Liberal Arts 1969; New York Univ, Business Admin 1974. **CAREER:** WOR Radio, dir public serv & comm affairs 1978-80; Waxy Radio, dir public affairs & comm relations 1980-83; RKO General Inc, corp equal employment compliance mgr 1976-78, corp dir equal employment oppor 1983-87; City of NY, deputy city personnel dir-equal employment opportunity 1987-. **ORGANIZATIONS:** Mem bd of trustees Staten Island Children's Museum; mem bd of governors Veterans Hosp Radio & TV Guild; mem bd of dirs New York Coalition of 100 Black Women. **HONORS/ACHIEVEMENTS:** Black Achievers in Industry Awd Harlem YMCA 1979; Cecelia Cabiness Saunders Awd New Harlem YWCA 1985; Corporate Recognition Awd Metropolitan Council of NAACP Br 1987. **HOME ADDRESS:** 330 East 39th St #8P, New York, NY 10016. **BUSINESS ADDRESS:** Deputy City Personnel Director, Equal Employment Opportunity, City of New York, 220 Church St, New York, NY 10013.

CHAPMAN, CHARLES F.
Health care. **PERSONAL:** Born Jul 11, 1947, Charlottesville, VA; married Kathy Williams; children: Weusi, Kia. **EDUCATION:** Rutgers Univ, BA 1971. **CAREER:** Ramapo Coll of NJ, dir community affairs 1972-75; NJ Dept Comm Affairs, EEO officer 1975-78; Legal Serv Corp, dir civil rights 1978-83; CNT, partner, consultant 1982-; Durhan Co Hospital Corp, compliance advisor 1984-. **ORGANIZATIONS:** Bd dirs NJ Public Policy Rsch Inst 1976-; commissioner NJ Commission EEO & Affirmative Action 1976-80; advisory bd Willingboro, NJ Township 1977-78; vice pres Natl Congress of Affirmative Action Assocs 1978; Amer Bar Assn Task Force on Minorities in the Profession 1982-84; consultant, Natl Legal Aid & Defenders Assoc 1983; consultant Puerto Rico Legal Services Inc 1983-84; president NC Chapter Amer Assn for Affirmative Action 1985-; mem NC Health Manpower Advisory Council 1985-; mem Triangle Area Business Advisory Council 1986-; admin NC Girls Olympic Devel Soccer Program 1986-. **HOME ADDRESS:** 3516 Manford Dr, Durham, NC 27707.

CHAPMAN, CLEVELAND M.
Construction company executive. **CAREER:** Englewood Construction Co, Chicago, IL, chief executive. **BUSINESS ADDRESS:** Chief Executive, Englewood Construction Co, 340 W 110th Place, Chicago, IL 60628. *

CHAPMAN, DAVID ANTHONY
Attorney. **PERSONAL:** Born Nov 06, 1949, Akron, OH; married Sharon Gail McGee; children: Brandon. **EDUCATION:** Univ of Akron, BA 1972; Univ of Cincinnati Coll of Law, JD 1975. **CAREER:** City of Cincinnati Law Dept, asst city solicitor 1975-; Civil Practice Cincinnati, atty gen 1975. **ORGANIZATIONS:** Mem Mayor's Tack Force on Minority Bus Enterprise 1978; mem OH State Bar Assn 1975; mem Cincinnati Bar Assn 1975; mem Black Lawyers Assn of Cincinnati1975. **BUSINESS ADDRESS:** City of Cincinnati Law Dept, Room 214 City Hall, Cincinnati, OH 45202.

CHAPMAN, DOROTHY HILTON
Librarian. **PERSONAL:** Born Sep 04, 1934, Victoria, TX; divorced; children: Dessalyn, Karen. **EDUCATION:** Tuskegee Inst, BS 1958; Carnegie Inst, MLS 1960. **CAREER:** Richard B Harrison Pub Lib, cataloger 1960-61; St Augustines Coll Benson Lib; TX SoUniv Lib, curator spl collections 1969-. **ORGANIZATIONS:** Mem Am & TX Lib Assns; TX Assn Coll Tchrs; mem Wheeler Bapt Ch Index Black Poetry GK Hall & Co 1974. **HONORS/ACHIEVEMENTS:** Index to Poetry by Black Amer Women Greenwood Press 1986. **BUSINESS ADDRESS:** Curator Special Collections, Texas SouthernUniv Library, 3201 Wheeler Ave, Houston, TX 77004.

CHAPMAN, FRANK
Civil rights administrator. **PERSONAL:** Born Sep 12, 1942, St Louis. **EDUCATION:** Univ of MO at Rolla, Bachelor's degree (cum laude) 1975; Washington Univ, Masters 1978. **CAREER:** Amer Friends Serv Comm, St Louis field sec 1978-80; Natl Alliance Against Racist & Political Repression, exec dir 1980-. **ORGANIZATIONS:** Bd mem AFSC Thid World Coalition; natl exec bd US Peace Council; founded first NAACP chap in a state penal inst; founding mem NAARPR. **HONORS/ACHIEVEMENTS:** Author of numerous articles which have appeared in the Journal of Negro Education; Presence Africaine; Freedomways of which he is a contributing editor. **BUSINESS ADDRESS:** Executive Dir, NAARPR, 126 W 119th St, Ste 101, New York, NY 10026.

CHAPMAN, GEORGE WALLACE, JR.
Educator. **PERSONAL:** Born May 14, 1940, Somerville, TX; son of George W Chapman and Angelona Goin Chapman; divorced; children: Craig, Kevin, Jennifer. **EDUCATION:** Prairie View A&M Univ, BS 1957; Howard Univ, MD 1966. **CAREER:** Univ of Iowa, asst prof 1981-83; Boston Univ, asst prof 1983-85; Louisiana State Univ, asst prof 1985-89; asst prof Univ of CA-Irvine 1988-. **MILITARY SERVICE:** AUS Medical Corp capt 1966-67. **BUSINESS ADDRESS:** Assistant Professor, UC-Irvine Medical Center, 101 The City Drive, Orange, CA 92668.

CHAPMAN, GILBERT BRYANT, II
Materials characterization engineer. **PERSONAL:** Born Jul 08, 1935, Uniontown, AL; married Loretta Woodard; children: Annie L, Bernice M, Gilbert B III, Cedric N, David O, Ernest P, Frances QH. **EDUCATION:** Baldwin Wallace Coll, BS 1968; Cleveland State Univ, MS 1973. **CAREER:** NACA Lewis Rsch Ctr, propulsion test tech 1953-58; NASA Lewis Rsch Ctr, matls characterization engr 1961-77; Ford Motor Co Rsch, project engr leader 1977-86; Chrysler Corp Engrg, adv matl testing specialist 1986-. **ORGANIZATIONS:** Vice chair & prog chair Cleveland Sect SAS 1977; lay leader SDA Church of Southfield 1983-86; chairman Detroit Sect ASNT 1985-86; bd mem Mt Vernon Acad;mem AAAS, ACS, APS, ASC, ASM ASNT, ASTM, NTA, SAE, SAS, SME, Sigma Pi Sigma; mem industrial adv comm Central State Univ, Henry Ford Com, Iowa State Univ. **HONORS/ACHIEVEMENTS:** Apollo Achievement Awd NASA 1969; Group Achievement Awd to Outstanding Employees Actively Participating in the EEO Prog NASA-Lewis 1970; Kent State Univ Chap Natl Physics Honor Soc; mem Sigma Pi Sigma 1975; Excellence in Oral Presentation Awd SAE 1982; Henry Ford Tech Awd nom Ford Motor Co 1981,82; Fellow Amer Soc for Nondestructive Testing 1987. **MILITARY SERVICE:** USAF Aviation cadet s/sgt 1959-61; Honorable Discharge. **HOME ADDRESS:** 17860 Bonstelle, Southfield, MI 48075. **BUSINESS ADDRESS:** Adv Matls Testing Specialist, Chrysler Corporation, PO Box 1118, Detroit, MI 48288.

CHAPMAN, JOSEPH CONRAD, JR.
Physician. **PERSONAL:** Born Nov 18, 1937, Poplar Bluff, MO; son of Joseph Chapman and Louise Chapman; married Myrna Loy; children: Joseph, Christopher. **EDUCATION:** Howard Univ, BS 1959, MD 1953; Georgetown Univ Hosp, residency 1968. **CAREER:** Private practice, otolaryngologist. **ORGANIZATIONS:** Mem Medico-Churgical Soc of DC, Med Soc of DC, Natl Med Assn, Amer Acad of Otolaryngology, Amer Council of Otolaryngology; asst clinical prof Howard Univ; mem Alpha Phi Alpha; fellow Amer Bd of Otolaryngology 1970. **MILITARY SERVICE:** USN lt cmdr 1968-70. **BUSINESS ADDRESS:** 106 Irving St NW, Ste 315, Washington, DC 20010.

CHAPMAN, JULIUS
Educator. **PERSONAL:** Born Apr 01, Kellyton, AL. **EDUCATION:** Tuskegee Inst, BS 1961, MEd 1967; Loyola Coll, EdS 1974. **CAREER:** Towson State Univ Baltimore, assoc dean 1969; Wilberforce Univ, assoc dir of admissions 1968-69; Residence Life Tuskegee Inst, counselor, dir 1966-68; Case-western Reserve Univ, research tech 1962-64; Assn for African-Amer Studies, dir co-founder 1972-; Amer Assn of Higher Educ; MD Black Coalition for Higher Educ. **ORGANIZATIONS:** Mem Baltimore-tuskegee Alumni Assn; Am Coll Personnel Assn; Omega Psi Phi Frat. **BUSINESS ADDRESS:** Voorhees College, Denmark, SC 29042.

CHAPMAN, LEE MANUEL
Business executive. **PERSONAL:** Born Aug 04, 1932, Chesterfield, SC; married Emily Bernice; children: Victoria Lenice, Leander. **EDUCATION:** Temple U, BS 1954, grad study. **CAREER:** NC Mutual, employed 1957-60; Equitable Life, 1960-73; Lee M Chapman Assos, 1973-75; Chapman & Chapman Agencies, prin partner. **ORGANIZATIONS:** Pres Waymar Inc; Owner Super Market 1966-; pres Horizon Devel Assos 1965-; chmn bd Human Devel Assos 1971; vice pres Cmnty Serv of PA past mem bd Benedix Coll; past vice pres Philadelphia JC; pres Northwest Devel Assos. **HONORS/ACHIEVEMENTS:** Recipient Nat

Assn Am Fellow Award Chaplin of 4 Chaplains; Young Man of Year JC Awards 1967. **MILITARY SERVICE:** AUS 1st Lt 1954-56. **BUSINESS ADDRESS:** President, Lee Manuel Chapman & Assoc, 6850 Anderson St, Philadelphia, PA 19119.

CHAPMAN, MARTIN ODES
Educator. **PERSONAL:** Born Feb 05, 1922, Milledgeville, GA; married Mary Virginia McDavid; children: Michael, Roberta. **EDUCATION:** Univ of Akron, BD 1947, MS 1952, grad study; Rutgers U. **CAREER:** Garfield High School, prin 1973-; Goodyear Jr High School, prin 1972-73; Margaret Park Elementary, prin 1969-72; Firestone Tire & Rubber Co, coll rel mgr 1968-69; Crouse Elementary School, prin 1964-68; Secondary Summer School, prin 1962-64; jr high school, asst prin 1956-64; jr high school, teacher, counselor 1954-56; teahcer, football coach 1947-54. **ORGANIZATIONS:** Dir Grp One Brdcstg Co 1969-; mem Nat Mus of Afro-Am Hist & Culture Plng Cncl 1975-; vice pres Akron Br NAACP 1976-77; contrib United Negro Coll Fund life; life mem NAACP; Alpha Phi Alpha Frat; mem Adron Hlth Commn; life mem OH PTA; mem past pres Phi Delta Kappa; chtr mem "A" Assn; exec bdpast pres Akron Touchdown Club; 32nd Degree Mason; hon mem Akron Coaches Assn Pioneered in asm & coaching Akron Pub Sch. **HONORS/ACHIEVEMENTS:** Akron's Distgd Citz Award 1972; Am Educ Gold Medal Freedoms Found at Valley Forge 1972; Hall Of Fame Summit Co 1973; Hon Alumnus Award Akron Univ 1973. **MILITARY SERVICE:** AUS corpl 1943-46. **BUSINESS ADDRESS:** 435 N Firestone Blvd, Akron, OH 44301.

CHAPMAN, MELVIN
Association executive. **PERSONAL:** Born Mar 16, 1928, Detroit, MI; married Elizabeth Patton; children: Carolyn, Melvin. **EDUCATION:** Wayne State U, BA 1949, MEd 1953, EdSpec 1965, EdD 1973. **CAREER:** Detroit, teacher 1949; Northwestern High School, counselor 1962; Wayne State Univ, dir high educ opportunity com 1964; Central High School, asst prin 1966; Northwestern High School, prin 1967; Detroit Public Schools, asst supt 1970-. **ORGANIZATIONS:** Mem Corporate Body MI Blue Shield; Trio Adv Com; Nat Alliance Black Sch Edn; MI Assn Children with Learning Disabilities; Met Detroit Soc Black Educ Adminstrs; Am Assn Sch Adminstr; mem NAACP; Kappa Alpha Psi USC of C. **HONORS/ACHIEVEMENTS:** Leaderhip award Chrysler Corp & NW HS 1968. **BUSINESS ADDRESS:** Region 4 Office, 14111 Puritan, Detroit, MI 48227.

CHAPMAN, ROBERT L., SR.
Bishop, clergyman. **PERSONAL:** Born Apr 13, 1923, Saluda, SC; son of Furman Chapman and Florence Chapman; married Geraldine Chisholm; children: Robert L Jr, Jacques, Harold, Irwin. **EDUCATION:** Erma Lee's Barber Coll 1951; attended Cleveland Coll 1949-51, Cleveland Bible Coll 1956, Mary Beach Sch of the Bible, Cleveland State Univ 1974. **CAREER:** Church of God in Christ, supt of sunday sch 1947, pres young people willing workers 1953, licensed minister 1953, dir religious educ 1954-58; Church of God in Christ Kent OH, pastorate appt 1957; Church of God in Christ Ashtabula, pastorate appt 1959; No OH Church of God in Christ, state pres young people willing workers 1960-66; founded E 116th St Church of God in Christ Cleveland 1966; No OH Ch of God in Christ, prog chmn 1967; R Chapman Realty Cleveland 1953-74. **ORGANIZATIONS:** Institutional rep for Boy Scouts of Amer 1952-55; vice chmn Intl Youth Congress Steering Comm 1966-68; admin asst to bishop NW OH 1967-72; dist supt OH NW Buckeye Dist 1968; asst pastor to bishop Jonas Temple Church of God in Christ Cleveland 1972-73; hon mem Fraternal Order of Police 1972-74; mem Urban League1974; mem YMCA Bus Men Club 1974; mem NAACP 1974; bd dir for the C H Mason Bible Coll 1974; consecrated bishop NW OH Jurisdiction 1974; personal adminasst to the natl chmn of the Genl Assembly of the Church of God in Christ Inc 1982-. **HONORS/ACHIEVEMENTS:** Letter of Commendation for Outstanding Comm Serv City of Ashtabula OH 1967; nominated for Honorary Dr of Divinity Degree Trinity Hall Coll 1973-74; Proclamation of May 4, 1974 as "Robert L Chapman Day" by Mayor Ralph J Perk City of Cleveland; resolution of congratulations Cleveland City Council 1974; commendations Howard M Metzenbaum US Senate 1974; commendations Louis Stokes US House of Rep 1974; commendations Intl presiding Bishop J O Patterson & Gen Bd of Bishops of Ch of God in Christ Inc 1974; Awd of Merit Emanuel Ch of God in Christ Harrisburg PA 1974; Letter of Congratulations US Dept of Labor 1974. **MILITARY SERVICE:** AUS 1943-46. **BUSINESS ADDRESS:** 11814 Buckeye Road, Ste 200, Cleveland, OH 44120.

CHAPMAN, ROSYLN C.
National accounts manager. **PERSONAL:** Born Mar 10, 1956, Richmond, VA. **EDUCATION:** Hampton Inst, BA 1978. **CAREER:** Johnson Products Co, sales rep 1979-80, key acct mgr 1980-81, dist mgr 1981-83, regional mgr 1983-84 natl accts mgr 1984-85; Alberto Culver Co, natl accts mgr 1985-. **ORGANIZATIONS:** Mem New Chicago Comm, Young Execs in Politics, Delta Sigma Theta Sor, Natl Black MBA, PUSH. **HOME ADDRESS:** 3930 No Pine Grove #2610, Chicago, IL 60613.

CHAPMAN, SAMUEL MILTON
Dentist. **PERSONAL:** Born Sep 10, 1920, Mangham, LA; son of Frank Chapman and Idella Ross Chapman; married Pauline Earl; children: Gregory Milton, Greta Michaele, Frances Delano, Pamela Chapman Wallace. **EDUCATION:** Morehouse Coll, BS 1947; Meharry Medical Coll, DDS 1951. **CAREER:** Private Practice, dentist. **ORGANIZATIONS:** Mem Sigma Frat 30 yrs; life mem NAACP. **HONORS/ACHIEVEMENTS:** 25 Year Awd Meharry Medical Coll 1976. **MILITARY SERVICE:** Infantry Medical Corps m/sgt 1943-45. **HOME ADDRESS:** 3917 W Bethany Home Rd, Phoenix, AZ 85019.

CHAPMAN, SHARON JEANETTE
Marketing executive. **PERSONAL:** Born Oct 25, 1949, St Louis, MO; children: Leslie Michelle Lee. **EDUCATION:** Southern IL Univ, BS 1970; College of St Thomas, MBA 1981. **CAREER:** Famous Barr Dept Store, asst buyer 1971-72; Donaldson's Dept Store, dept mgr 1972-75; IBM, systems engr 1976-83, mktg rep 1983-86; Job Trak Systems Inc, dir of mktg & sales 1986-. **ORGANIZATIONS:** 2nd vice pres 1983-85, pres, bd mem 1985-87 Twin Cities Chap Black MBA's; trustee Pilgrim Bapt Church 1984-87; bd of dirs Survival Skills Inst 1985-;chapter pres Delta Sigma Theta 1987-; mem Minneapolis Urban League, St Paul NAACP. **HONORS/ACHIEVEMENTS:** Outstanding Young Women of Amer 1982,85,86; Who's Who in Professional and Exec Women 1987. **HOME ADDRESS:** 4745 Zenith Ave South, Minneapolis, MN 55410. **BUSINESS ADDRESS:** Dir of Mktg & Opers, Jobtrack Systems Inc, 7269 Flying Cloud Dr, Eden Prairie, MN 55344.

CHAPMAN, TRACY
Singer, songwriter. **PERSONAL:** Born Mar 30, 1964, Cleveland, OH; daughter of George Chapman and Hazel Winters Chapman. **EDUCATION:** Tufts Univ, Medford, MA, BA (cum laude), Anthropology, 1986. **HONORS/ACHIEVEMENTS:** Received Academic Scholarship to high school through A Better Chance Program; singer, composer, Tracy Chapman, Elektra Records, 1988; Amnesty Intl Human Rights Now! Tour, 1988; Grammy Awards, Best New Artist, Best Contemporary Folk Recording, Best Female Pop Vocal Performance, Natl Acad of Recording Arts and Sciences, 1988; Best Selling Album by a New Artist, Best Selling Album by a Female Artist, Natl Assn of Recording Merchandisers, 1988; Best Intl Newcomer, Best Intl Female Artist, The Brits, 1989; Amer Music Award, Favorite New Artist Pop/Rock, 1989.

CHAPMAN, WILLIAM TALBERT
Neurologist. **PERSONAL:** Born Oct 15, 1944, Camden, NJ; married Ingrid; children: William Jr, Marcus, Blaire, Leigh. **EDUCATION:** Rutgers Univ, BA 1966; Howard Univ Coll of Medicine, MD 1971. **CAREER:** 97th General Hospital, asst chief neurology 1976-78; Silas B Hayes Hosp, chief of neurology 1978-79; Private Practice, neurologist 1979-. **ORGANIZATIONS:** Mem Natl Medical Assoc 1971, Amer Bd of Neurology 1977, Amer Bd of Electroencephalography 1985, Amer Medical Assoc 1987. **HONORS/ACHIEVEMENTS:** Alpha Omega Alpha Med Hon Soc. **MILITARY SERVICE:** AUS major 1976-79; Army Commendation Medal 1979. **HOME ADDRESS:** 3951 The Hill Rd, Bonita, CA 92002. **BUSINESS ADDRESS:** Neurologist, 2340 East 8th St, Ste G, National City, CA 92050.

CHAPMAN, WILLIE R.
Research scientist. **PERSONAL:** Born Sep 02, 1942, Memphis, TN; married Marion N Evans; children: William Eric, Lamont Everett. **EDUCATION:** LeMoyne Owen Coll, BS Chemistry (Cum Laude) 1964; Memphis State Univ, MAT Chemistry 1975. **CAREER:** Schering/Plough Inc, sr rsch chemist 1965-77; Chattem Inc, mgr/rsch and devel 1977-87; Chattanooga State Technical Comm Coll, instructor of Chemistry. **ORGANIZATIONS:** Soc of Cosmetic Chemists mem conduct & ethics comm, chapter affairs comm 1982, chmn professional relations and status 1983, area dir 1984-86, chmn educ comm 1986-; Alpha Phi Alpha founder/minority leadership conf 1985-87, social chmn 1985-86, chair educ comm 1986-87; mem Sigma Phi Fraternity, NAACP, Explorer Program/BSA, Alpha Phi Alpha Fraternity, Urban League. **HONORS/ACHIEVEMENTS:** Golden Parade Gallery LeMoyne Coll 1982; guest lecturer Summer enrichment workshops Univ TN Chattanooga 1984-; Role Models for Chattanooga Afro-Amer Museum 1986-87; author "Cosmetic Creams and Lotions for Dark Tone Skins," March 1980, Cosmetics and Toiletries; "The Development of Skin Lighteners" May 1983 Cosmetics and Toiletries; Phi Delta Kappa 1987; Leadership Chattanooga 1987. **HOME ADDRESS:** 707 Stone Crest Cir, Chattanooga, TN 37421.

CHAPPELL, EMMA CAROLYN
Banking executive. **PERSONAL:** Born Feb 18, 1941, Philadelphia, PA; daughter of George Bayton, Sr. and Emma Lewis Bayton (deceased); married Verdayne; children: Tracey, Verdaynea. **EDUCATION:** Berean Business Inst, Temple Univ, Amer Inst of Banking, Stonier Graduate School of Banking, Rutgers Univ. **CAREER:** Continental Bank Philadelphia, 1959-present, currently vice pres, community business loan devel. **ORGANIZATIONS:** Mem, Amer Bankers Assn; Natl Bankers Assn; Robert Morris Assn; Natl Assn for Amer Found of Negro Affairs; Natl Business League; Philadelphia Urban League; Ntl Assn of Bank Women Inc; Natl bd mem, PUSH; bd dir, Girl Scouts of Greater Philadelphia Inc; bd mem, Philadelphia Indus Devel Corp; mem, vice pres, admin & treasurer, Natl Rainbow Coalition; Founded/chair, Women's Network for Good Govt; Bd mem, Temple Univ, Coll of Arts & Sciences, Chestnut Hill Coll Pres' Council, Cheyney Univ Found, United Way of Southeastern Pennsylvania, United Negro Coll Fund, Philadelphia Chapter, PA Economic Devel Partnership Bd, March of Dimes, Delaware Valley Chapter; Vice Chmn, African Devel Found. **HONORS/ACHIEVEMENTS:** Motivational Speaking Exec Leadership & Professional Salesmanship Achievement Award Dale Carnegie Inst; Achievement Award Philadelphia Police Dept; Certificate of Appreciation Soc for Advancement of Mgmt; Couns Selling Achievement Award Larry & Willson; Achievement Award N Philadelphia Action Branch of NAACP; Pres Award Nat Assn of Colored Women's Clubs Inc; Recognition Award PA Contractors Coalition Inc; Achievement Awd Club VIP; Honored as One of America's Top 100 Black Business & Professional Women by Dollars and Sense Magazine 1986; Business & Professional Award, Blackbook Magazine, 1987; Bishop R. R. Wright Humanitarian Award, Ward AME Church, 1987; Achievement Award, West Philadelphia Economic Devel Corp, 1988. **BUSINESS ADDRESS:** Vice President, Continental Bank, Main & Swede Streets, Norristown, PA 19401.

CHAPPELL, RUTH RAX
Management consultant. **PERSONAL:** Born Apr 20, 1932, Los Angeles, CA; daughter of George Rax and Helen Finley Rax; married Joseph Chappell; children: Valinda, Patricia, Jerome, Kevin, Michael, Michelle, Sakeenah. **EDUCATION:** CA State Univ, BS 1977, MA 1986. **CAREER:** State Personnel Bd, training officer 1976-79, mgr admin serv 1979-81, asst mgr statewide women's program 1981-82, mgr appeals div 1982-83; Private Consultant, 1983-87. **ORGANIZATIONS:** Mem Natl League Women Political Caucus; chairperson Human Right Comm CA State Employees Assoc 1987-; mem NAACP. **HONORS/ACHIEVEMENTS:** Certificate of Merit CA State Govt. **BUSINESS ADDRESS:** Communications Consultant, CA State Personnel Bd, 2551 5th Avenue, Sacramento, CA 95818.

CHAPPELLE, THOMAS OSCAR, SR.
Clergyman. **PERSONAL:** Children: 2. **EDUCATION:** Bishop Coll, attended; Amer Baptist Theol Sem, Grad; Honorary Degrees, Wright School of Religion Memphis, DD 1953, Morris Booker Coll Dermott AR, DD 1955, Birmingham Baptist Coll Birmingham, DD 1962, OK School of Religion Langston, DD 1964, Bishop Coll Dallas TX, LLD 1972, TN School of Religion, LLD 1981, Univ of Central Amer 1983. **CAREER:** OK Baptist State Convention, pres; Natl Baptist Congress of Christian Ed, pres. **ORGANIZATIONS:** Mem bd of regents Tulsa Jr Coll; mem bd of dir OK State Nursing Home Assoc, Northside State Bank; mem bd of trustees N Tulsa Hosp Assoc, Bishop Coll; mem adv bd St John Hosp; mem bd of dir Moton Comprehensive Health Assoc; natl chmn Church Rel Bd Bishop Coll; chmn of bd of trustees OK School of Religion; life mem NAACP, Hutcherson Br YMCA, Greenwood C of C, Tulsa Urban League; mem Omega Psi Phi. **HONORS/ACHIEVEMENTS:** Traveled in all 50 states & made 6 trips abroad visiting Europe, Asia, Africa, Holy Land, Australia, Japan, Philippines; Disting Serv Awd Bishop Coll 1970; Disting Serv Awd OK State Nursing Home Assoc 1970; Disting Serv Awd Youth Rally of Natl Sunday School & BTUniv

Congress 1975; Omega Psi Phi Frat Awd 1977; Disting Serv Awd Carrie B Neely Art Guild 1978; MN Taylor Awd Tulsa Urban League 1978; Good Shepherd Awd Boy Scouts of Amer 1980. **BUSINESS ADDRESS:** Pastor, Morningside Baptist Church, 1014 E Pine St, Tulsa, OK 74106.

CHARBONNET, LOUIS, III
Mortician, state representative. **PERSONAL:** Born Mar 12, 1939, New Orleans; married Simone Monette; children: Kim Marie. **EDUCATION:** Commonwealth Coll of Svc, BS 1957. **CAREER:** Labat-Charbonnet Funeral Home, funeral dir embalmer; LA, state rep. **ORGANIZATIONS:** Mem Cresent City Funeral Dir Assn; bd dir Treme Cultural & Enrichment Ctr; bd mem Criminal Justice for State of LA; v chmn Bd of Appropriations Stateof LA; bd dir LA State Museum Bd; bd dir Total Comm Action. **HONORS/ACHIEVEMENTS:** Floor leader New Orleans Delegation to LA House of Rep; founder Treme Political Imp. **MILITARY SERVICE:** AUS. **BUSINESS ADDRESS:** 1615 St Phillip St, New Orleans, LA 20116.

CHARGOIS, JENELLE M.
Executive director. **PERSONAL:** Born Nov 19, 1949, Lafayette, LA; daughter of Alton J Alfred and Effie Jeanlouis Alfred; married Paul R; children: Jared Kiburi, Maisha Z Chargois. **EDUCATION:** Zavier U, 1 yr; Univ of Southwestern, 3 yrs; Spencer's Bus Coll, Accounting Cert. **CAREER:** So Coop Devel Fund, dir of pub relations; People's Enterprise, mgr 1972; So Comsumers Educ Found, dir 1971. **ORGANIZATIONS:** Mem St Paul's Credit Union; So Consumer Coop; People's Enterprise; So Consumer Educ Found; volunteer; counselor Scholarship Bd; mem Lafayette Juvenile; League of Women Voters; Black LA Action Comm; NAACP; Women Involved in Comm; Lafayette Comm Devel Program; adv council Lafayette Bi-Racial Comm; chmn Labor & Industry Comm; vice pres Black Alliance for Progress; sec So Coop Council; counselor Young Gifted Black Youth. **HONORS/ACHIEVEMENTS:** Key To City Lafayette 1972; 1st place honors Dist & State Competitions (Spanish) 1966-67; outstanding youth 1966; outstanding black citizen award 1972; comm orgn award 1972. **BUSINESS ADDRESS:** POBox 3005, Lafayette, LA 70502.

CHARITY, LAWRENCE EVERETT
Business executive. **PERSONAL:** Born Jun 21, 1935, Washington, DC; married Suzanne G Leach; children: Alexander PL, Danika N. **EDUCATION:** Rhode Island School of Design, BFA/Int Arch Des 1953-57; Cranbrook Academy of Art, MFA/Design 1957-58. **CAREER:** Skidmore, Owings & Merrill, designer 1958-68; Sewell & Charity Ltd Designers, principal 1968-74; Interior Concepts, Inc, principal 1974-. **ORGANIZATIONS:** Adjunct asst prof/design Rhode Island School of Design 1972-73; current member Alumni Council Rhode Island School of Design; current full member Industrial Designers Society of America 1974-. **HONORS/ACHIEVEMENTS:** Canopy design US Patent 214,226 issued 1969; chair design US Patent 224,856 issued 1972; door pull design US Patent 3,894,760 issued 1975. **MILITARY SERVICE:** AUS sp4 1959-62. **HOME ADDRESS:** 8 Gracie Sq, New York, NY 10028. **BUSINESS ADDRESS:** Principal/Designer, Lawrence E Charity Design, 12 West 29th St, New York, NY 10016.

CHARITY, RUTH HARVEY
Consultant, attorney. **PERSONAL:** Born in Pittsylvania Count, VA; married Ronald K Charity; children: Khris Wayne. **EDUCATION:** Howard Univ, BA, JD. **CAREER:** Formerly asst to dir President's Cncl on Consumer Affairs; Indust Rel Analyst Wage Stabil Bd; law prof formerly pract law under name of Ruth L Harvey; former Dem Natl Committeewoman; 1st Black woman South of Mason Dixon line to serve this capacity and as mem of Natl Dem Exec Comm. **ORGANIZATIONS:** Mem Pres's Comm on Civil Rights under the Law; past pres Old Dominion Bar Assn (1st woman to serve this capacity); mem Natl Bar Assn; formerly vice pres of Natl Bar Assn(1st woman to serve as vice pres of NBA at time of election); organiz Women's Sect Natl Bar Assn (1st natl orgn of Black women lawyers); mem Intl Fedn of Women Lawyers; past pres of Natl Assn of Black Women Lawyers; founder/pres VA Assn of Black Women Lawyers; past mem trustee bd Howard Univ;past mem trustee bd Palmer Meml Inst; mem bd of VA Seminary; past chrpsn VA State Adv Com US Civil Rights Comm (1st woman in VA to serve as chrpsn); mem Amer Assn of Univ Women; League of Women Voters; NOW; past mem Legal Staff State Conf NAACP; past natl parliamentarian Natl Cncl of Negro Women; past grand legal advisor Grand Temple Daughters IBPOE of W; past pres Chums Inc. **HONORS/ACHIEVEMENTS:** To date 1st and only Black woman elected to Danville, VA City Council 1970-74; Founder/President Black Women for Political Action; Charter Mem natl Women's Chamber of Commerce; numerous awards received from various organizations and groups including, Natl Fedn of Dem Women Mid-Atlantic Region; Alpha Kappa Alpha Sor; NAACP; Listings include, Who's Who in American Politics, Who's Who in American Law, Biography of Charlotte Hawkins Brown, Rights on Trial; Lecturer and consultant to political and civil rights and educational groups. **BUSINESS ADDRESS:** Consultant, 514 S Main St, Danville, VA 24543.

CHARLES, BERNARD L.
Educator. **PERSONAL:** Born Feb 27, 1927, New York, NY; married Eleanor; children: Bernard II, Dominique, Bridgette. **EDUCATION:** Fisk U, BA 1952; Yeshiua U, MS 1965; Rutgers Univ Grad Sch of Edn. **CAREER:** Livingston Coll Rutgers Univ, prof of educ, chmn dept urban educ 1970-; Town of Ramapo, councilman & deputy supvr 1966-74; Rockland Co Legis, vice chmn 1975-77; Dem Natl Comm NY State Voter Reg Drive, dir 1976; NY State Council of Black Elected Democrats, treas 1965-77; Office of Master Plan Bd of Higher Educ City Univ of NY, coordinator 1968-70. **ORGANIZATIONS:** Dir of spl projects Human Resources Admin 1968; dep dir Office of Civil Rights Region II NY 1966-68; dir of Life Skills Educ Training Resources for Youth 1965-66; asst to dir Jr Guidance Classed Program New York City Bd of Educ 1962-66; tchr Pub Sch 613 Brooklin Pub Sch 614 Bronx 1955-62; street club worker New York City Youth Bd 1954-55; co-dir Univ of Summer workshop for tchrs of Emotionally & socially maladjusted childred; guest lecturer; mem Assn of Tchr Edn; Am Assn of Higher Edn; Am Assn of Univ Prof; Am Assn of Sch Administr; Nat Advisory Council; Nat Advisory Health Council; treas Inst for Mediation & Conflict Resolution; pres Broadjump Inc; dir Action Priorities Inc; Rockland Comm Action Council; bd of dir World Rehabilitation Fund; Bulova Watchmaking SchState Cord Gov Samuels Campaign 1974; chairman New York State Governor's Advisory Comm for Black Affairs. **BUSINESS ADDRESS:** Livingston College, New Brunswick, NJ 08903.

CHARLES, DOREEN ALICIA
Newspaper publisher. **PERSONAL:** Born Apr 15, 1960, Chicago, IL. **EDUCATION:** Univ of NE-Lincoln, BA Journalism 1982. **CAREER:** Operation PUSH, youth comm 1982-84; Chicago Black United Comm, youth chmn 1982-84; Black United Front, sec 1982-83; Task Force for Black Political Empowerment, sec 1982-83; Intl Communications Corp, president. **ORGANIZATIONS:** Mem PUSH Intl Trade Bureau 1984-, Intl Black Writers 1984-, NAACP 1985-, Urban League 1985-; delegate Natl Small Business Conference 1985-86. **HONORS/ACHIEVEMENTS:** Outstanding Leadership Awd Afrikan People's Union 1982; Certificate of Achievement Operation PUSH Political Education 1983; published book "Til Victory is Won," book of political poetry 1984; wrote and acted in one-woman show "Sojourner Truth," 1986. **BUSINESS ADDRESS:** President, Intl Communications Corp, Printer's Square, 600 So Federal Ste 124, Chicago, IL 60605.

CHARLES, JOSEPH C.
Probation officer. **PERSONAL:** Born Jan 12, 1941, Lake Charles, LA; married Doris J Charles; children: Caron Scott. **EDUCATION:** BA AA 1969. **CAREER:** Mitchell Pacific Devel Corp, pres; San Diego Co Probation Dept, dep probation officer II; Webchar Construction Corp, pres. **ORGANIZATIONS:** Mem Black Businessmen Assn; Black Investors Inc; sec Reserve Officers Assn; charter mem Black Student Union San Diego State Coll; mem San Diego Co Emp Assn; mem CA State Corrections Assn. **HONORS/ACHIEVEMENTS:** Recipient Fed & State Commissions as Nat Guard Lt 1966. **MILITARY SERVICE:** USAR capt. **BUSINESS ADDRESS:** 6580 Mac Arthur Dr, San Diego, CA 92045.

CHARLES, LEWIS
Welder. **PERSONAL:** Born Aug 24, 1945, Jackins Co, GA; married Rosetta W; children: Tracy C. **EDUCATION:** Atlana U, 1 yr. **CAREER:** Fulghum Industrial Mgt Co, demonstrator; Hudson Mortuary Wadley, GA, asst mgr. **ORGANIZATIONS:** Mem GA State Fireman of Wadley, GA No 2217; mem Dem Party of GA 1972; mem Free & Accepted Mason; mem Brinson Hill Bapt C; life mem GA Municipal Assn; mem Wadley & Borlow Cit League; mem Nat Pilots Assn; ciy-councilman 1970-. **HONORS/ACHIEVEMENTS:** Award Wadley & Borlow Cit League 1972; spl award Brinson Hill Bapt Ch 1973. **BUSINESS ADDRESS:** Fulghum Industrial Mfg Co, Wadley, GA.

CHARLES, RAY (RAY CHARLES ROBINSON)
Singer, arranger, composer, band leader. **PERSONAL:** Born Sep 23, 1933, Albany, GA; son of Bailey Robinson and Reatha Robinson; married Della; children: Ray Jr, David, Robert. **CAREER:** At 7 yrs old began playing piano while attending school for deaf & blind; began touring with dance bands at 15 yrs old; Atlanta Records, 1952-59; signed on with Florida Playboys 1954, recorded 1st major hit "I Got A Woman 1954"; ABC Paramount, 1959-65; wrote "What I Say" 1959; formed Maxim Trio in Seattle; recorded 1st major; RPM Intl, owner; recorded country album featuring Willie Nelson "Friendship" 1984; Ray Charles Enterprises, owner; Crossover Records, 1973-. **HONORS/ACHIEVEMENTS:** Bronze Medallion presented by French Republic; 10 Grammy Awds; New Star Awd Down Beat Critic's Poll 1958, 1961-64; No 1 Male Singer Int Jazz Critics' Poll 1968; Playboy Jazz & Pop Hall of Fame; Songwriters' Hall of Fame; Hon Life Chmn Rhythm & Blues Hall of Fame; Ebony Black Music Hall of Fame; Gold records include, "Ray Charles Greatest Hits", "Modern Sounds in Country & Western Music", "Ray Charles A Man and His Soul"; B'nai B'rith Man of the Year; Kennedy Center Honors Medal 1986. **BUSINESS ADDRESS:** Singer, Ray Charles Enterprises, 2107 W Washington Blvd, Los Angeles, CA 90018.

CHARLES, RODERICK EDWARD
Psychiatrist. **PERSONAL:** Born Sep 04, 1927, Baltimore, MD; married Mamie Rose Debnam; children: Kimberly Anne, Roderick Todd. **EDUCATION:** Howard Univ, BS 1951; Univ of MD, MD 1955. **CAREER:** Mil City Gen Hosp, internship 1955-56; Meyer meml Hosp, psych resident 1956-59; NYS Fellow, 1959-60; Erie County Med Center (formerly Meyer Hosp), att psychiatry 1960-66; SUNY Brooklyn Sch of Medicine, asst clinical prof 1966-; Private Practice, psychiatry 1966-. **ORGANIZATIONS:** Asst psych Buff Gen Hosp; dir Migrant H clinic 1968-71; BUILD Acad H Progm 1971-75; mem state council Met H Plan 1977-81; pres WNY Psych Assn 1967-68; Fedr Citizens Council Human Rel 1964; Fellow Amer Psych Assn; mem Black Psychiatrists of Amer; Natl Med Assn; advisor SMNA Univ of Buffalo 1975; consultant Gowando State Hosp 1982-87. **MILITARY SERVICE:** USN 1944-46. **BUSINESS ADDRESS:** 142 N Pearl, Buffalo, NY 14202.

CHARLESTON, GOMEZ, JR.
Physician/cardiologist. **PERSONAL:** Born Mar 19, 1950, Chicago, IL; son of Gomez Charleston and Margie Williams Charleston; married Robin Prince, Jun 21, 1975. **EDUCATION:** Univ of Chicago, BA, 1971, MD, 1975. **CAREER:** Stony Island Medical Associates, Chicago IL, partner, 1980—; Michael Reese Hosp, Chicago, attending physician caridology, 1980—, dir of cardiac catheterization lab, 1987-88, Pritzker School of Medicine, Univ of Chicago, asst clinical prof of medicine, 1980—. **ORGANIZATIONS:** American Medical Association, Illinois Medical Society, Chicago Cardiology Group. **HONORS/ACHIEVEMENTS:** Sigmund E. Edelstone fellow in cardiology, Michael Reese Hospital & Medical Center, 1980; fellow of American College of Cardiology, 1982. **BUSINESS ADDRESS:** Stony Island Medical Assoc, 9000 South Stony Island, Chicago, IL 60617.

CHARLTON, CHARLES HAYES
Pastor. **PERSONAL:** Born Dec 22, 1904, Radford, VA; married Janet Lee Lewis; children: Charles. **EDUCATION:** Christiansburg Inst, 1959; VA Seminary, attended; E TN State Univ, attended; ETSU, BS 1982, M Ed 1984. **CAREER:** Radford City School Bd, 1972-74; Town of Radford VA, mayor 1974-76; Friendship Bapt Church, pastor. **ORGANIZATIONS:** Moderator Schaetter Meml Assoc of SW VA 1974-77; treas Bethel Dist Assoc; vice pres Radford Jaycees; moderator Bethel Dist Assoc of TN 1982-; dean ed Emmaus Bible Inst & Seminary Elizabethton TN 1984-; dir Pastors Conf of the TN BM&E Convention 1984-. **HONORS/ACHIEVEMENTS:** Radfords Outstanding Youn Men Radford Jaycees 1973; publ 2 weekly religious columns Radford News Jrnl.

CHARLTON, JACK FIELDS
Engineer executive. **PERSONAL:** Born Apr 30, 1928, Bellaire, OH; son of Harold L Charlton and Grace Stone Charlton; married Audrey Perry; children: Michael, James Eric. **EDUCATION:** Fenn Coll, BMechEng 1957; Tufts Univ, BMetEng 1963; Case Inst of Tech, MS 1965. **CAREER:** Euclid, div of GMC superintendent 1966-70, sub of White Motor dir 1970-

77, sub of Mercedes-Benz vice pres 1977-84; Mercedes-Benz Truck Co, dir quality assurance 1984-87; Freightliner Corp Dir Gov't Proj 1987-. **ORGANIZATIONS:** Special Task Force on Youth Motivation, vice pres of US; McGill Univ, lecturer 1968; Nat'l Professional Engrs, mem 1973, treasurer 1975/79; Cleveland Public Sch, advisor in economic education 1980; Ohio State Board of Education, advisor in economic education 1981; pres Williamsburg Mens Club 1988; engineer consultant NATO 1988. **HONORS/ACHIEVEMENTS:** Royal Canadian Soc of Engrs, fellow 1978; Soc of Military Engrs, fellow 1979. **MILITARY SERVICE:** AUS col corp of engrs 20 yrs. **HOME ADDRESS:** 42 Whittakers Mill, Williamsburg, VA 23185. **BUSINESS ADDRESS:** Director Government Projects, Freightliner Corp, 2400 Mercedes Dr, Hampton, VA 23661.

CHARTON, GEORGE N., JR.
Retired executive director. **PERSONAL:** Born Apr 12, 1923, Pittsburgh, PA; son of George N Charlton Sr and Mildred F Woods Charlton; married H Nadine Branch; children: George N III, Diana C Jones, Susan C Harrison, Ronald, Lena Coleman. **EDUCATION:** Univ of Pittsburgh, BBA 1955. **CAREER:** AUS, clerk-typist 1943-45, transfer unit asst suprv, analyst admin div 1945-48; VA Pittsburgh, regis clerk 1948, collec officer, collec div 1948-51; US Treas Dept IRS Intell Div Pittsburgh, spec agent 1953-63; Pittsburgh Private practice, spec investigator 1964-65; Commonwealth of PA Dept of Revenue Bur of Sales & Use Tax Harrisburg, spec audit staff 1965-67; Opps Indus Ctr Inc Pittsburgh, dir admin serv 1967-68; Homewood-Brushton Neighborhood HealthCtr Inc Pittsburgh, bus mgr 1968-71; Pittsburgh Model Cities, asst exec dir 1971-73, exec dir 1973-76; Public Parking Authority of Pittsburgh, exec dir 1976-88, retired. **ORGANIZATIONS:** Mem, treas, bd dir Housing Auth Pittsburgh; mem Mayors Econ Manpower Adv Comm; mem, treas Comm Action Pittsburgh Bd; mem Reg Personnel Serv Ctrof SW PA; life mem Kappa Alpha Psi; mem Reserve Officers Assoc, AUSA, PA Assoc of Notaries, UACM; mem, 1st vchmn Bd Mgmt of Homewood-Brushton YMCA Prog Ctr; exec dir Pub Parking Auth 1976; Province Polemarch, East Central Province, Kappa Alpha Psi Frat Inc 1971-84; mem Grand Bd of Dirs Kappa Alpha Psi Frat Inc 1985-88; bd of governors, mem, co-vice chmn, National Parking Assn 1983-88; mem, United Way of Pittsburgh 1986-89; exec mem, Urban League of Pittsburgh Inc 1986-89; mem, St Cyprian-Alpha Lodge #13 F & A M 1970-; life mem, NAACP 1981. **HONORS/ACHIEVEMENTS:** Man of the Year Achievement Awd Pittsburgh Alumni Chap 1971; Meritorious Serv Opp Indus Ctr Inc Pittsburgh 1972; Achievement Delta & Delta Zeta 1973; Serv to Youth Black Achievers Awd YMCA of Pittsburgh 1973; Outstanding Achievement E Cntrl Province 1974; Leadership Dayton Kappa League 1974; Meritorious Serv Medal 1976; Honor Black Cath Ministers & Laymen's Council 1976; Comm Leader Awd 1977; Citation 26 yrs of serv AUS 1976; Outstanding Achievement 4th Ed ofMen 1976; selected as 1 of 25 most influential blacks in Metro Pittsburgh Talk Mag 1975; Elder Watson Diggs Achievement Award, Kappa Alpha Psi Frat Inc 1986; Certificate of Achievement, National Parking Assn 1987. **MILITARY SERVICE:** AUS lt col retired WWII Vet 23 yrs; received Army Meritorious Service Medal, 1976. **HOME ADDRESS:** 1714 Lincoln Ave, Pittsburgh, PA 15206.

CHASE, ARNETT C.
Business executive. **PERSONAL:** Born Apr 05, 1940, Green Cove Spgs, FL; married Dianne J Thomas; children: Avis Chiquita. **EDUCATION:** Am Acad Funeral Serv, 1963; Univ FL, Certified Ophthalmology 1972. **CAREER:** Apprentice embalmer & funeral dir 1965, mgr 1970. **ORGANIZATIONS:** Mem Nat Funeral Dir & Morticians Assn; mem State Auditor FL Morticians Asn; chmn 4th Regional & Dist Morticians Assn; sec SDW Smith Lodge 481 F &AM; mem Jaycees; mem USO Council; mem Council Aged; mem Ancient City Charity Club. **HONORS/ACHIEVEMENTS:** Award FL Morticians Serv 1974; certificate appreciation St Paul AME Ch 1973. **MILITARY SERVICE:** AUS sp/5 1963-65. **BUSINESS ADDRESS:** Funeral Dir, Leo C Chase Funeral Home, 262 W King St, St Augustine, FL 32084.

CHASE, JAMES
Mayor. **PERSONAL:** Married Eleanor; children: Roland. **CAREER:** Barber shop porter; mgr auto body shop 40 yrs; City of Spokane, former mayor to 1985. **BUSINESS ADDRESS:** Former Mayor, City of Spokane, City Hall, 808 W Spokane Falls Blvd, Spokane, WA 99201.

CHASE, JOHN S.
Architect. **PERSONAL:** Born Jan 23, 1925, Annapolis, MD; married Drucie Rucker; children: John Jr, Anthony, Saundria. **EDUCATION:** Hampton Inst, BS 1948; Univ of TX, MArch 1952. **CAREER:** TX Southern Univ, asst prof; John S Chase FAIA Architect Inc, pres/chmn of the bd. **ORGANIZATIONS:** Mem AIA; mem TX Soc of Architects; notable contr to the advcmt of archt Coll of Fellows AIA 1977; pres Nat Orgn of & Minority Architects; consult architect to TX So Univ Bd of Regents; mem bd Huston-Tillotson Coll; mem bd Standard Savings & Loan Assn; mem Houston Engineering & Sci Soc; memUniv of TX Adv Council; sec Greater Houston Convention & Visitors Council; mem bd Houston Visitors & Convention Council; mem bd of trustees Herman Hospital, Hampton Univ; served on the US Commn of Fine Arts; mem bd of trustees Antioch Bapt Ch; mem bd of trustees Univ of Houston Foundation; mem TX Southern Univ; served on Univ of TX Presidential Search Comm; mem bd of dirs Golden State Mutual Life Ins Co; bd of dir TX Southern Univ Foundation. **HONORS/ACHIEVEMENTS:** Nu Phi Chap of Omega Si; trustee Antioch Bapt Ch; Whitney M Young Citation; NOMA Design Excellence Awd; John S Chase Scholarship in Architecture; McGraw Hill Publishing Co Golden 100 Fleet Awd. **MILITARY SERVICE:** AUS. **BUSINESS ADDRESS:** President/Chmn of the Board, John S Chase FAIA Arch Inc, 1201 Southmore, Houston, TX 77004.

CHASE-RIBOUD, BARBARA DEWAYNE (D'ASHNASH TOSI)
Author and sculptor. **PERSONAL:** Born Jun 20, 1939, Philadelphia, PA; daughter of Charles Edward Chase and Vivian May West Chase; married Marc Eugene Riboud, Dec 25, 1961; children: David, Alexis; married Sergio Tosi, 1981. **EDUCATION:** Temple Univ, BFA, 1957; Yale Univ, MFA, 1960. **CAREER:** One-woman shows include those at The Kunstmuseum, Freilburg, West Germany, 1976, The Musee Reattu, Arles, France, 1976, European Drawings, Berlin, West Germany, 1980, five-museum tour in Australia, 1980-81, and many more; selected group exhibitions include "Documenta 77" Kessel, West Germany, 1977, Museum of Contemporary Crafts, New York, 1977, Smithsonian Inst Renwick Gallery, 1977, Noeuds et Ligatures Fondation Nationale des Arts, 1983, California Museum of Afro-Amer Art, 1985; selected public collections at The Philadelphia Art Alliance, The Schoenburg Collection New York, New York State Council on the Arts, St John's Univ, Harlem State Office Bldg, The Metropolitan Museum of Art, New York, The Natl Collections, France. **HONORS/ACHIEVEMENTS:** John Hay Whitney Foundation Fellowship, 1957-58; Academic of Italy with gold medal, 1978; Janet Kafka Award for Best Novel by an American Woman, 1979; Honorary Doctorate of Arts & Humanities, Temple Univ, 1981; author of numerous publications, including From Memphis to Peking (poems), Random House, 1974; Sally Hemings (novel), Viking, 1979; La Virginienne (French translation of Sally Hemings), Albin Michel, 1981; Valide (novel), Morrow, 1986; Echo of Lions, Morrow, 1989. **BUSINESS ADDRESS:** Pres, Hessmayling Corp, B-10150 Brussels, Belgium. *

CHATMAN, ALEX
Educator, magistrate. **PERSONAL:** Born Oct 06, 1943, Greeleyville, SC; son of Alex Oscar Chatman and Alma Montgomery Chatman; married Mariah Williams Chatman, Sep 26, 1986. **EDUCATION:** Williamsburg County Training Sch 1962; Benedict Coll, diploma 1965; SC State Coll, BS 1973; Univ RI, ME 1966; Univ SC, Certificate 1970. **CAREER:** Tchr 1965-; Greeleyville, magistrate 1973-81; Williamsburg County Council, supervisor, chmn 1982-. **ORGANIZATIONS:** Pres Williamsburg County Educ Assn 1974-75; mem Credential Com State Dem Conv 1971 & 1974; pres Greeleyville Br Nat Bus Leauge 1970-; mem NAACP; mem United Teaching Professional; mem Nat Bus League; mem Official Black Caucus Nat Educ Assn; mem SC Magistrate's Assn; chmn 6th Congressional Dist Polit Action Com for Educ 1974; SC Assn of Counties 1982-; Governor's Council on Rural Devel 1982-86; SC Private Industry Council 1984-87. **HONORS/ACHIEVEMENTS:** Award Phi Beta Sigma Frat 1973; award SC Educ Assn 1975; Presidential Citation, Natl Assn for Equal Opportunity in Higher Education 1985; Citizen of the Year for Outstanding Public Service, Delta Rho Chapter Omega Psi Phi Frat 1982; Distinguished Service Award, Williamsburg Branch NAACP 1985; Certificate of Appreciation, Kingstree Kiwanis Club 1988.

CHATMAN, ANNA LEE
Administrator. **PERSONAL:** Born Aug 21, 1919, Monroe, GA; married Rev Marcellus; children: Marcella Ann McElroy, Ruby Marie Alexander. **EDUCATION:** Cuy Comm Coll, Cert Comm Org 1969, Bus Admin 1969. **CAREER:** 21st Cong Dist Caucus, exec dir 1969-; Congressman Louis Stokes, cong aide 1976-; Harvest Day Care Ctr, admin 1969-. **ORGANIZATIONS:** Dir MC Chatman Meml Found 1978-; mem Zoning Bd of Appeals Cleveland 1977-; pres Bapt Ministers Wives & Widows 1972-; mother of the church Harvest Missionary Bapt Church 1978-; co-sponsor Womens Com Leadership Defense Fund 1979. **HONORS/ACHIEVEMENTS:** Leadership Awd Cleveland Br NAACP; Congressional Awd Cong Louis Stokes; Recipient of numerous awds. **BUSINESS ADDRESS:** Administrator, Harvest Day Care Center, 1240 E 9th St, Cleveland, OH 44199.

CHATMAN, DONALD LEVERITT
Physician. **PERSONAL:** Born Dec 27, 1934, New Orleans, LA; married Eleanor; children: Lynn Ann, Eleanor Louise, Eric Leveritt. **EDUCATION:** Harvard U, AB 1956; Meharry Med Coll, MD 1960; Cooper Hosp NJ, rotating intrnshp 1960-61; Michael Reese Hosp, resident 1965-69. **CAREER:** Chicago, ob gyn 1969-; Lake Charles LA, gen Prac 1961-63; Dept of Ob Gyn Michael Reese Hosp & Med Cntr, asst Attndng 1969-74; Dept Ob GynUniv of Chicago-Pritzker SchDiamine Oxidase in Prgncy, clncl instr; USAF, cpt 1963-65. **ORGANIZATIONS:** Mem Chicago Med Soc; pres Chicago Med Soc S Chicago Br 1969-70; mem Am Assn of Gynecologic Laparoscopists 1974-; mem IL State Med Soc; mem Am Med Soc; mem NMA; mem Am Coll of Ob & Gyn Diplomate AmBd of Ob & Gyn 1972; rsrchr of, "Endometriosis & the Black Female" Am Jour of Ob & Gyn 1976, "Endometriosis & the Black Woman" Jour of Reproductive Med 1976, "Endometriosis & the Black Female" Adio-Digest 1976, "Laparoscopy-Falope Ring Sterilization" Am Jour of Ob & Gyn 1978, "Commentary on Inaugural Thesis-Laparscopic Cautery of Endometriotic Implants" Am Jour of Ob & Gyn 1979, "Pelvic Peritoneal Defects & Endometriosis-Allen-Masters Syndrome Revisited" in press, Direct Trochar Falope Ring Sterilization in press; presently resrchng, Laparoscopic Evaluation & Functional Classification of Endometriosis, The Concept of Pre-Clinical or "Emerging" Endometriosis, The Long Term Effectiveness & Complications of Falope Ring Sterilization, The Efficacy of Direct Trochar Laparoscopic Falope Ring Sterlization. **MILITARY SERVICE:** USAF capt 1963-65. **BUSINESS ADDRESS:** 8811 S Stony Island, Chicago, IL 60617.

CHATMAN, JACOB L.
Pastor. **PERSONAL:** Born Aug 05, 1938, Patterson, GA; married Etty; children: Mario. **EDUCATION:** FL Meml, BS 1963; Eastern Theol Sem, MDiv 1968; Univ of Ma, DEd 1974. **CAREER:** Scnd Bapt Ch Coatesville PA, pastor; organized coordinated tutorial progs for socially deprived children; written training curr for employabel disadvantaged of Chester; counseling drop-outs, drugs, planned parenthood, family counseling, organizer Day Care, chmn comm support. **ORGANIZATIONS:** Dir Pinn; mem Center PA Chmn Title I Coatesville Sch Dist; mem Am Assn ofUniv Profs; Coatesville Area Clergy; Kappa Alpha Psi Frat; trustee Cheyney State Tchrs Coll; pres Commn to Disadvantaged Eastern Sem; bd mgrs, exec bd PA DE Chs of Am Bapt Conv; Task Force on Foreign Mission; Black Churchmen of Am Bapt Conv; vice pres Coatesville Opp Council; chmn Non-profit Hsng Corp Scnd Bapt Ch; past chmn Comm Support Day Care; Coatesville vice-chmn Task Force on World Hunger; Am Bapt Conv; rotary mem. **HONORS/ACHIEVEMENTS:** Recip citizenship YMCA 1955; Eagle Scout 1955; Chapel of Four Chaplains Award 1969; cit award Mt Labanon HRAM of PA 1972; FL mem coll outsanding serv award 1972; Humanitarian Award 1973; outstanding youth man of Am 1972; cited by Coatesville Record for Outstanding Serv 1970-74. **BUSINESS ADDRESS:** St John Missionary Church, 34 W Pleasant St, Springfield, OH 45506.

CHATMAN, MELVIN E.
Educator. **PERSONAL:** Born Feb 09, 1933, Springfield, TN; married Velma R; children: Vera, Melvin Jr, Carol, Bobby, Jeff, Karl. **EDUCATION:** Lane Coll, BS 1955; Fisk Univ, MA 1963; Univ of TN, EdS 1975. **CAREER:** Bransford High School, teacher, coach 1957-68; Springfield High School, teacher 1968-70, asst principal 1970-73, supvr special educ 1973-. **ORGANIZATIONS:** Mem NEA, TEA, Robertson Cty Teacher Assoc, Council for Excpetional Children, TN Assoc for Suprv & Curriculum Devel; former mem Mid-Cumberland Council Gov, Mental Health Harriett Cty; mem num offices, coms Dem Party Selected Serv Bd; mem TN Voter Council, Cty Ct 1972-74, 33 Deg Mason, Shriner, Alpha Phi Alpha, Beard Chapel Baptist Church. **MILITARY SERVICE:** AUS 1955-57. **BUSINESS ADDRESS:** Supervisor Spec Ed, Robertson County Schools, 22 & Woodland Sts, Springfield, TN 37172.

CHATMON, LINDA CAROL
Educator. **PERSONAL:** Born Nov 13, 1951, Louisville, KY; daughter of L C Fox and

Betty A Savage; children: Dana Marie. **EDUCATION:** Univ of Louisville, BA 1980, MSSW 1982; currently pursuing EdD in Educational Administration, Univ of Louisville. **CAREER:** Creative Employment Project; counselor 1982-84; Univ of Louisville, coord of cooperative educ 1984, instructor/counselor 1984-89; Univ of Louisville, College of Urban and Public Affairs, dir of student services, 1989-. **ORGANIZATIONS:** Mem comm chair Urban League 1982-, Youth Performing Arts School 1983-; consultant GYSG Corp 1986-. **HONORS/ACHIEVEMENTS:** Martha Davis Scholarship for Grad Study Univ of Louisville 1980-82; Outstanding Young Women of America 1984. **HOME ADDRESS:** 1940 Goldsmith Ln, Bldg #7, Louisville, KY 40218. **BUSINESS ADDRESS:** Director of Student Services, College of Urban and Public Affairs, Univ of Louisville, Belknap Campus, Louisville, KY 40292.

CHATTERJEE, LOIS JORDAN
Bank officer. **PERSONAL:** Born Aug 04, 1940, Nashville; married Dr Suchindran S Chatterjee. **EDUCATION:** TN State U, BS 1962; Univ TN, 1963. **CAREER:** Commerce Union Bank, bank officer bus devel 1972-; Model Cities Prog, evaluator 1971; St Dept Corrections, couns youthful offenders 1966-70; Juvenile CtDavidson Co, legal sec 1962-66. **ORGANIZATIONS:** 1st black female mem Met Council 1971-; mem Negro Bus & Professional Womens League; Middle TN Bus Assn; Nat Bus League; sec SE Nashville Civic League; charter mem Dudley Park Day Care Cntr; bd dirs Goodwill Indus; The House Between; mem Nashville C of C; League Women Voters; YWCA; Nat Council Crime & Delinquency; Nat League Citizens. **HONORS/ACHIEVEMENTS:** Who's Who in Am Politics 1969-70; TN Lives 1970; Personalities of S 1970; Comm Ldrs Am 1972; Who's Who Women of World 1973; pub Essence mag 1974. **BUSINESS ADDRESS:** Educator, Metropolitan School System, 2601 Bradford Ave, Nashville, TN 37204.

CHAUNCEY, MINION KENNETH **See MORRISON, K. C.**

CHAVIS, THEODORE R.
Educator. **PERSONAL:** Born Jun 14, 1922, Asheville, NC; son of Theodre and Anna; married Montios; children: 2 daughters. **EDUCATION:** Talladega Coll, AB 1942; Atlanta Univ, MSW 1951; Smith Coll School of Soc Work, Grad Studies; Univ of MI School of Soc Work, attended. **CAREER:** NC Employment Security Comm, interviewer 1947-49; VA Guidance Ctr Atlanta GA, trainee 1949; Bur of Mental Hygiene Wash DC, 1950-51; Percy Jones Army Hosp, soc worker 1951-53; VA Hosp Battle Creek MI, asst chief soc work serv 1953-65; MI State Univ, School of Soc Work, past coord practicum instructim prof; MI State Univ School of Social Work, East Lansing MI, Professor Emeritus, 1988-. **ORGANIZATIONS:** Mem MI Chap Professional Standards Comm, ACSW, Natl Assoc of Social Workers, Council on Social Work Ed, mem Budget Panel United Way; past bd mem, chmn serv comm Big Brothers/Big Sisters; bd mem Capitol Area Child & Family Svc; mem, past chap chmn, treas Natl Assembly Delegate NASW; Legislative Task Force, MI Chap AARP; coordinator Capitol City Task Force, MI State Legislative comm, AARP 1987-. **HONORS/ACHIEVEMENTS:** Outstanding Performance Awd VA Hosp Battle Creek MI 1957. **MILITARY SERVICE:** AUS 1942-46. **BUSINESS ADDRESS:** Professor, Michigan StateUniv, School of Social Work, Lansing, MI 48824.

CHAVOUS, BARNEY LEWIS
Executive. **PERSONAL:** Born Mar 22, 1951, Aiken, SC; married Odessa; children: Shedric, Jasmine, Nikeya Monique. **EDUCATION:** SC State U, Phys Ed. **CAREER:** Denver Broncos, defensive end 1973-1986; Minority Arts & Education Foundation, chairman 1986. **HONORS/ACHIEVEMENTS:** Pittsburgh Courier's NFL Defensive Lineman of the Yr 1978; NFLPA Defensive Rookie of the Yr Hon 1973; All-Conf & defensive MVP at SC State; All-Am by AP;collegiate Defensive Lineman of the Yr; North-South Game; The Senior Bowl; Coaches' All-Am Game. **BUSINESS ADDRESS:** Chairman, Minority Arts & Ed Foundation, PO Box 4076, Englewood, CO 80155.

CHEATHAM, ADOLPHUS A. (DOC)
Musician. **PERSONAL:** Born Jun 13, 1905, Nashville, TN; married Amanda Ochoa; children: Alicia, Marshall. **CAREER:** Professional Musician, 1924-; recorded with "Ma" Rainey 1926; performed with Chick Webb, Cab Calloway, Teddy Wilson, Benny Carter, Fletcher Henderson, Basie only in The Sound of Jazz Film; toured Africa with Wilbur De-Paris & Herbie Mann Orch; Sam Wooding Orchestra, musician 1927-30 in europe; McKinnes Cotton Pickers,musician 1931; Machito European Festivals-Geowiem, musician; Teddy Wilson Orchestra, musician 1949; worked with Latin Amer Bands such as Perez Prado in 1950's& 60's. **HONORS/ACHIEVEMENTS:** Toured Europe & Africa; regular with Benny Goodman 1966-67; performed at the White House Jazz Party 1978; performed with Pee Wee Russell, Juanita Hall; author of booklet on improvisation.

CHEATHAM, BETTY L.
Appointed official. **PERSONAL:** Born Dec 05, 1940, South Carolina. **EDUCATION:** Benedict Coll, BS Bus Admin 1962. **CAREER:** Intl City Mgmt Assn, prog mgr 1974-80, minority prog dir 1980-83; DC Dept of Public Works, chief office of contract admin. **ORGANIZATIONS:** Mem Coalition of Black Public Admins 1982-85; mem Black Public Admins Forum 1984-85; mem Intl City Mgmt Assn 1983-85. **HONORS/ACHIEVEMENTS:** Awd Coalition of Black Public Admins 1982. **HOME ADDRESS:** 859 Venable Place, Washington, DC 20012. **BUSINESS ADDRESS:** Chief Office of Contract Admin, DC Public Works Department, 2000 14th St NW 5th Fl, Washington, DC 20009.

CHEATHAM, DELLA M.
Retired supply analyst. **PERSONAL:** Born Nov 25, 1920, Nashville; divorced; children: Gary M, Gregory S. **CAREER:** Vet Adminstrn Detroit, med stenographer 1945-47; Army Tank Automotive Command, inventory mgmt specialist. **ORGANIZATIONS:** Mem Sr Inventory Mgrs Club; columnist Tank Automotive; mem Urban League Guild; vice pres Detroit Drifters; Delta Nu Chap Gamma Phi Delta Sor; Highland Caucus Club; Urban Alliance; pres Intl Platform; Founders Soc; mem 1st Nighters; mem Detroit Jet Setters; Sagicornians; Lemacs. **HONORS/ACHIEVEMENTS:** Plaque Dexter YMCA.

CHEATHAM, HENRY BOLES
Broadcasting. **PERSONAL:** Born Oct 05, 1943, Bentonia, MS; married Helen M Hughes; children: Tonita R, Jomo K. **EDUCATION:** Columbia Coll, BA 1973; Univ of IL at Chicago, MA 1980. **CAREER:** Ford Motor Co, utility man 1965-73; WISH-TV Indianapolis, tv-production 1973; WSNS-TV Chicago, prod dir camer oper 1973-. **ORGANIZATIONS:** Union steward ex bd NABET 1980-; mem Chicago Area Broadcast Public Affairs Assoc 1980-83; mem Natl Black United Front 1983-, Operation PUSH 1983-. **HONORS/ACHIEVEMENTS:** Image Awd Fred Hampton Foundation 1983; article published in following publications, NABET-NEWS, Beverly Review, Chicago Defender. **MILITARY SERVICE:** AUS E-4 2 yrs; Honorable Discharge 1965. **BUSINESS ADDRESS:** Producer/Director/Camera Oper, WSNS TV, 430 W Grant Place, Chicago, IL 60614.

CHEATHAM, LINDA MOYE
City official. **PERSONAL:** Born Nov 02, 1948, Richmond, VA; married Harold D Cheatham, Jr; children: Michelle, Maxanne, Harold,III. **EDUCATION:** Wheaton Coll, BA, 1970; Virginia Commonwealth Univ. **CAREER:** City of Norfolk, planner 1970-72; City of Richmond, planner 1972-75, operations mgr 1975-79, senior budget analyst 1979-84, dir of general serv 1984-87, budget dir 1987-. **ORGANIZATIONS:** Mem, Intl City Mgmt Assn, 1980-; bd of governors, William Byrd Community House, 1983-; mem, Conf of Minority Public Admin 1983-; bd of dirs, City of Richmond, Fed Credit Union, 1984; chapter council VA Chapter Amer Soc of Public Admin, 1984-; treasurer, John B Cary PTA 1985-88. **HONORS/ACHIEVEMENTS:** Outstanding Woman of 1984; North Richmond YMCA Black Achiever 1985. **HOME ADDRESS:** 3112 Rendale Ave, Richmond, VA 23221. **BUSINESS ADDRESS:** Budget Dir, City of Richmond, 900 East Broad St, Richmond, VA 23230.

CHEATHAM, ROY E.
Educator. **PERSONAL:** Born Sep 14, 1941, Memphis; married Gertie Brenell Wilson; children: Roy III, Gina Rochele. **EDUCATION:** Lincoln U, BA 1965; St Louis U, MA 1969; St Louis U, PhD 1975. **CAREER:** Metropolitan College, dean; St Louis Univ, dir special acad prog, dir coll assistance prog & upward bound 1970-73; Coll of Arts & Science, St Louis Univ, asst to dean 1969-70; Human Dev Corp, adult & educ coord 1966-67; adult educ curriculum specialist 1969. **ORGANIZATIONS:** Mem Am Coll Pesonnel Assn's Commn XIV 1973-76; mem Basic Educ Oppor Grant Planning Com 1972; Reg VII Office of Higher Edn; pres Roy Cheatham & Asso; mem Financial Aid Panel 1973; pres 1976-77; bd educ Univ City Pub Sch Dist 1974-77; v-chmn bd dir Inroads Inc 1973-76; commr Mark Twain Boy Scout-Dist; mem bd dir Comm Learning Ctr; mem bd dir Sophia House; Educ Enrichment Prog 1972-75. **HONORS/ACHIEVEMENTS:** Comm serv award Orgn of Black Entrepreneurs 1972; meritorious serv award LincolnUniv Alumni Assn 1973; outstanding serv award Black Students of St Louis U1973; NDEA Fellow St Louis &Univ 1967-69. **BUSINESS ADDRESS:** St Louis University, 221 N Grand Blvd, St Louis, MO 63103.

CHECKER, CHUBBY **See CHECKER, ERNEST**

CHECKER, ERNEST (CHUBBY CHECKER)
Recording artist. **PERSONAL:** Born Oct 03, 1941, Philadelphia. **CAREER:** Appeared in night clubs, movies, theatres; popularized "The Twist" dance; TV appearances Midnight Spl Am Bandstand Mike Douglas Discomania; recordings include The Twist, Let's Twist Again, Pony Time, Limbo Rock. **ORGANIZATIONS:** Mem ASCAP; appeared at Peppermint Lounge & Madison Sq Garden; 4 films. **HONORS/ACHIEVEMENTS:** Grammy Award 1961.

CHECOLE, KASSAHUN
Publishing administrator. **PERSONAL:** Born Jan 22, 1947, Asmara, Ethiopia;married Nevolia E Ogletree; children: MuluBirhan, Senait. **EDUCATION:** SUNY Binghamton, BA Hnrs 1974, MA 1976. **CAREER:** Rutgers Univ, instructor 1979-85; Africa Research and Publishing Proj, dir 1979-; El Colegio De Mexico, research prof 1982-; The Red Sea Press, publisher 1982-; Washington School Inst for Policy Studies, lecturer; Africa World Press, publisher. **ORGANIZATIONS:** Vice chrmn Eritrean Relief Comm Inc 1983-85; editorial bd Saga Race Relations Abstracts, Horn of Africa; editor RSP current issues series. **BUSINESS ADDRESS:** Publisher, Africa World Press, PO Box 1892, Trenton, NJ 08607.

CHEEK, DONALD KATO
Educator. **PERSONAL:** Born Mar 24, 1930, New York, NY; married Calista Patricia Duff; children: Don Jr, Gary, Alan, Stephan, Donna. **EDUCATION:** Seton Hall Univ, BS 1953; Fordham Schl of Soc Srv, MSW 1955; Temple Univ, PhD 1971. **CAREER:** Lincoln Univ PA, vice pres student affairs, dean, lecturer 1967-69; Claremont Coll CA, dir of black studies 1969-73; CA Polytechnic State Univ, prof 1973-; rehabilitation counselor 1984-; ordained minister 1987-. **ORGANIZATIONS:** Consult spkr wrkshp facilitator Milwaukee WI Mental Health Ctr, Orangeburg SC Annual Guidance Conf NY Salomon Brothers, Las Vegas NV Amer Personnel & Guidance Assc Conv, New Orleans LA Assc of Blk Soc Wrks, Dallas TX Drug Educ Prev and Treatment, Daytona Bch FL, Bethune Cookman Clge, Emporia KS State Univ, Omaha NE Crighton Univ, Sanford FL Seminole Comm Clge, Xenia OH Cty Mental Health, Evansville IN Human Rel Comm, Univ of Cincinnati Clge of Nursing, Cleveland OH Urban Minority Alcoholism Outreach Proj, SC Schl of Alcohol and Drug Studies, City of Portland OR, Univ of ND, LA Black Prof Engrs. **HONORS/ACHIEVEMENTS:** Invited pres sci paper Intl Congress of Behavior Therapy Uppsala Sweden 1977; recipient of Natl Inst Mental Health Grad Flwshp 1967; presenter Intl Consult Counslng and Ethnic Minorities Univ of Utrecht Netherlands 1985; publ Assertive Black Puzzled White. **HOME ADDRESS:** PO Box 1476, Atascadero, CA 93423. **BUSINESS ADDRESS:** Professor, CA Polytechnic StateUniv, San Luis Obispo, CA 93407.

CHEEK, DONNA MARIE
Equestrian. **PERSONAL:** Born Dec 05, 1963, Philadelphia, PA. **EDUCATION:** CA Polytech State Univ, attending. **CAREER:** "One More Hurdle" Autobiography NBC TV, starred in one hour drama 1984; "Profiles in Pride" NBC TV, starred 1985; equestrian; Exhibition Equestrian, Coors. **ORGANIZATIONS:** Corp sponsorship Univox CA Inc, Pro-Line Corp, Quincy Jones Prod, Ed Lara's Westside Distr; spokesperson Involvement for Young Achievers Inc 1982-. **HONORS/ACHIEVEMENTS:** Financial Grant Black Equestrian Sports Talent 1980-, Avon Found NY 1983; Publ "Going for the Gold-The Story of Black Women in Sports" 1983-; NAACP Immage Awd "One More Hurdle-The Donna Cheek Story" 1984. **HOME ADDRESS:** PO Box 1476, Atascadero, CA 93423.

CHEEK, JAMES E.
Educator. **PERSONAL:** Born Dec 04, 1932, Roanoke Rapids, NC; married Celestine

Juanita Williams; children: James Edward, Janet Elizabeth. **EDUCATION:** Shaw U, BA 1955, LHD 1970; Colgate-Rochester Div Sch, M Div 1958; Drew U, PhD 1962, LLD 1971; Trinity Coll, LHD 1970; A&T State U, LLD 1971; L'Universite d'Etat d'Haiti, DHC 1972; Providence Coll, EdD 1972; DE State Coll, LLD 1972. **CAREER:** Drew Theology School, teaching asst 1959-60; Union Jr Coll, instructor Western History 1959-61; VA Union Univ, asst prof NT hist theology 1961-63; Shaw Univ, pres 1963-69; Howard Univ, pres 1969-89, pres emeritus 1989-. **ORGANIZATIONS:** Bd mem, trustee, and advisory bd mem of numerous professional and civic associations and committees; mem Alpha Theta Nu; Alpha Phi Alpha; Sigma Pi Sigma. **HONORS/ACHIEVEMENTS:** Outstanding Young Men in Amer 1968. **MILITARY SERVICE:** USAF 1950-51. **BUSINESS ADDRESS:** President Emeritus, Howard University, 2400 6th St, NW, Washington, DC 20059.

CHEEK, KING VIRGIL, JR.
Educator, attorney. **PERSONAL:** Born May 26, 1937, Weldon, NC; married Annette Walker; children: King Virgil III, Kahlil, Antoinette. **EDUCATION:** Bates Coll ME, BA 1959; Univ of Chicago, MA 1960; Univ of Chicago Law School, JD 1964. **CAREER:** Shaw Univ Raleigh, NC, asst econs prof 1964-65, acting dean 1956-66, dean 1966-67; private practice law Raleigh 1965-69; Shaw Univ, vice pres acad affairs 1965-69; Citizinship Lab, lectr 1968-69; Shaw Univ, pres 1969-71; Morgan State Coll, pres 1971-74; Union for Experimenting Colls & Univs, vice pres for planning& devel 1976-78; New York Inst of Tech, exec dir ctr for leadership and career develop 1978-85; New York Inst of Tech, Ctr for Leadership and Career Develop, vice pres, dean of grad studies, exec dir 1985-. **ORGANIZATIONS:** Bd of dir Baltimore Contractors 1974-; bd of dir Inst for Econ Devel 1978-; bd of trustees Martin Center Coll; bd of trustees Shaw Coll Detroit; bdof visitors Univ of Chicago Law Sch; bd of trustees Warnborough Coll Oxford England. **HONORS/ACHIEVEMENTS:** Grand Commdr of Order of Star Africa 1971; Top Young Leaders in Amer Acad Change Magazine 1978; Disting Civilian Award AUS 1973; LLD DE State Coll 1970,Bates Coll, Univ of MD 1972; LHD Shaw Coll at Detroit 1983. **BUSINESS ADDRESS:** Attorney/Educator, NY Institute of Technology, Old Westbury, New York, NY 11568.

CHEEK, ROBERT BENJAMIN, III
Dentist. **PERSONAL:** Born Sep 12, 1931, New York, NY; married Geraldine M Manley; children: Albert, Sonseeahray. **EDUCATION:** NC Coll, BS 1954; Howard Univ, DDS 1962. **CAREER:** Robert B Cheek DDS PC, pres 1956-; Am Airlines, sales rep 1956; Underwood Corp, sales rep 1954. **ORGANIZATIONS:** Mem Nat Dental Assn; mem Acad of Gen Dentistry; mem Bridgeport Dental Assn; mem Guardsmen; life mem NAACP. **HONORS/ACHIEVEMENTS:** Fighter Wings USAF 1956. **MILITARY SERVICE:** USAF 2nd lt 2 yrs. **BUSINESS ADDRESS:** President, 1211 Reservoir Ave, Bridgeport, CT 06606.

CHEEKS, CARL L.
Dentist. **PERSONAL:** Born Jul 07, 1937, Poplar Bluff, MO; married Beaulah Brittain; children: Darryl. **EDUCATION:** Fisk Univ Nashville, BA 1960; Meharry Med Sch, DDS 1965. **CAREER:** Self-Employed Evanston IL, dr dntl surgery 1967-. **ORGANIZATIONS:** Am Dental Assn; Nat Dental Assn; Northshore Dental Assn; Lincoln Dental Soc; Am Acad Gen Dentistry; mem Relative Analgesia Seminars; Chicago Dental Soc; life mem NAACP; life mem Kappa Alpha Psi Frat; mem & song leader Evanstron Ch Christ; bd dir United Community Services Evanston 1969-71; chmn nominating com Martin Luther King Lab Sch PTA 1975; mem Black Bus & Professional Assn; exec com Evanston Sch Bd 1969-71; mem Fisk Jubilee Singers; servedspl bd recruitment black hs male students Naval Acad; served com human relations Great Lakes, IL. **HONORS/ACHIEVEMENTS:** Certificate merit Minority Youth Motivation 1968-74; Chessman Club Award aid their civic program; certificate Council Nat Bd Dental Examiners. **MILITARY SERVICE:** USN dental & lt 1965-67. **BUSINESS ADDRESS:** Box AA 1408, Evanston, IL 60204.

CHEEKS, MAURICE EDWARD
Professional athlete. **PERSONAL:** Born Sep 08, 1956, Chicago, IL; children: West TX State: 1978. **EDUCATION:** Philadelphia 76er's, guard 1978-. **ORGANIZATIONS:** Especially known for great quickness and speed, when leading the fast break; only player other than Oscar Robertson to make All-Missouri Valley Conf 3 times. **BUSINESS ADDRESS:** Philadelphia 76ers, Veterans Stadium, 777 Sports St, Philadelphia, PA 19141.

CHEESE, PAULINE STATEN
Educator. **PERSONAL:** Born in Fernandina Beach, FL; widowed; children: Lee, Jr. **EDUCATION:** FL A&M U, BS 1954; Pepperdine U, MA 1973. **CAREER:** Los Angeles City Unified Schools, teacher 1962-; Peck High School, card counselor 1954-61. **ORGANIZATIONS:** Mem CA Tchrs Assn; Nat Educ Assn; CA Tchrs Assn; Black Educators; Zeta Phi Beta Sor; Polit Action Com Educators Mem; Women for Good Govt; Nat Assn Media Women; bd dirs Wesley Social Serv; mem Nat Council Negro Women; adv council Assemblyman Julian Dixon; CA Dem Council; Am Inst Parliamentarians; exec com SW Coor Council; mem New Frontier Dem Club; Dem State Central Com 1975-78; mem Phi Delta Kappa; Women for NAACP; Urban League; Ebony Press Club; adv bd Oaks Found; Nat Women's Polit Caucus; CA Dem Council; State Council of Edn; Sen Nate Holden's Educ Task Force Com; Bethel AME Ch; women's editor CRS Mag. **HONORS/ACHIEVEMENTS:** Commendation certificates LA County Dem Central Com; A Phillip Randolph Inst; Black Political Assn CA 1972; Outstanding Contribution to Community Award1974; Outstanding Volunteer Award LA Human Relations Comm 1975; Outstanding Vol Award High Blood Pressure Found 1977; listed in World Who's Who of Women 1977; Notable Americans 1977; Noteworthy Americans 1977. **BUSINESS ADDRESS:** 830 W 77 St, Los Angeles, CA.

CHENAULT, MYRON MAURICE
Vice chancellor. **PERSONAL:** Born Mar 03, 1949, Richmond, IN; married Vivian Michelle Chiles; children: Myron. **EDUCATION:** Manchester Coll, BA 1971; Valparaiso Univ Sch of Law, JD 1974. **CAREER:** Bowling Green Univ, asst vice pres 1978-80, assoc vice pres legal staff cont rel 1980-82; Winston-Salem State Univ, vice chancellor 1982-. **ORGANIZATIONS:** Bd mem Winston-Salem Housing Foundation 1984-, Greater Winston-Salem Chamber of Commerce 1984-; bd mem Southeastern Ctr for Contemporary Art 1985-, NatureScience Ctr 1985-; mem Phi Alpha Delta, Omicron Delta Kappa, Phi Beta Sigma, Leadership Winston-Salem; mem Ohio, America Bar Assocs; mem Council for Advancement and Support Educ; mem Ohio US Dist Court Northern Div. **BUSINESS ADDRESS:** Vice Chancellor, Winston-Salem StateUniv, PO Box 13325, Winston-Salem, NC 27110.

CHENAULT, WILLIAM J.
Business executive. **PERSONAL:** Born Sep 20, 1928, Cincinnati, OH; son of James Chenault and Dora E Hill Chenault; married Betty R; children: Lisa Ann, Constance Louise, Karla Ann, Kenneth Luther, Edward Alan. **EDUCATION:** Univ of Cincinnati, BBA 1959. **CAREER:** City of Cincinnati, city council mem 1968-75, vice mayor 1971, 1973, 1975; Chenault and Assoc Real Estate Appraisal and Consulting, owner & CEO 1971-; State of Ohio Dept of Tax Equal, appraisal supr 1977-84; J Ruth Corp Holding Company, pres & CEO 1982-89. **ORGANIZATIONS:** Instr, Univ of Cincinnati Evening Coll, 1978-81; chmn of admissions comm, Natl Assn of Independent Fee Appraisers, Cincinnati Chap, 1973; mem, Ohio, Kentucky, Indiana Regional Planning Commn, 1971-75; pres & treas, Cincinnati-Hamilton County Criminal Justice Regional Planning Unit, 1969-75; pres & founding mem, Political Action Programming Assembly, 1963-65; vice pres & bd dir, Jaycees Greater Cincinnati, 1960-62; vice pres, Hamilton County Democratic Party, 1969-75; first vice pres 1985-87, pres 1987-88, public relations comm chmn 1988-89, Columbus Chap, Amer Soc of Appraisers, 1985-87. **HONORS/ACHIEVEMENTS:** Public Serv Award, Prudential Insurance Co of Amer, 1967; Recognition of Serv, Ohio, Kentucky, Indiana Regional Planning Commn, 1975; Honorary Citizen of State of Tennessee, 1975; Honorary Sergeant-at-Arms, Tennessee State Legislature, 1975. **MILITARY SERVICE:** AUS Med Corps pfc; Good Conduct Medal; honorable discharge. **HOME ADDRESS:** 6433 Kennedy Ave, Cincinnati, OH 45213. **BUSINESS ADDRESS:** CEO and Owner, Chenault & Assoc, 2280 Henderson Rd, Suite 211, Columbus, OH 43220.

CHENEVERT, PHILLIP JOSEPH
Physician. **PERSONAL:** Born Feb 15, 1948, Detroit, MI; son of Wendell Sr (deceased) and Mary Chenenert Pembroke; married Judith Grandy; children: Belen, Amber. **EDUCATION:** Highland Park Comm Coll, AA 1970; North Carolina Central Univ, BS (Cum Laude) 1974; Meharry Medical Coll, MD 1978; Children's Hospital of Michigan, Residency 1978-81. **CAREER:** Private Practice, physician 1981-86; Cigna Health Plan of TX, pediatrics 1986-; Univ of Texas Southwestern Medical Center, Dallas Fellow Developmental and Ambulatory Pediatrics 1988-91. **ORGANIZATIONS:** Bd of dirs AYD Youth Job 1982-83; chief of pediatrics L Richardson Memorial Hosp 1982-86; med dir United Way Greensboro NC 1983-84; bd of dirs Amer Diabetes Assoc Greensboro NC 1985-86; volunteer Medical Instructor PA Prog Bowman Gray Sch of Medicine 1985-86; bd of dirs Arlington Charities 1986-. **HONORS/ACHIEVEMENTS:** Fellowship Natl Inst of Health; Outstanding Young Men of Amer 1986. **HOME ADDRESS:** 6517 Devine Dr, Arlington, TX 76017.

CHENIER, PHIL
Athlete. **PERSONAL:** Born Oct 30, 1950, Berkeley, CA. **CAREER:** WA Bullets, player. **HONORS/ACHIEVEMENTS:** NBA All Star Team 1974, 75, 77. **BUSINESS ADDRESS:** WA Bullets, Capital Ctr 1 Harry S Truman D, Landover, MD 20786.

CHENNAULT, MADELYN
Educator. **PERSONAL:** Born Jul 15, 1934, Atlanta, GA. **EDUCATION:** Morris Brown Coll, BS 1957; Univ of MI, MA 1961; IN Univ, PhD; Univ of GA, Post Doctoral Study in Clinical Psychology; Univ of MS Med Ctr, Post Doctoral Internship. **CAREER:** Public Schls GA, CA, MI, educator 1957-62; Albany State Coll, asst prof of Pychology 1962-64; IN Univ, rsch asst 1964-66; Atlanta Univ, asst prof educ 1966-67; Ft Valley State Coll, assoc prof educ 1967-70, prof educ 1970-72, callaway prof educ & psychology; Chennault Enterprise, pres 1974-. **ORGANIZATIONS:** Counsel Exceptional Children's Regional Meeting; consul Atlanta GA 1967; spl educ consult Grambling Coll 1968; educ psych consult Univ of CT 1969; elementary educ consult AL A&M Univ 1969; mental retardation consul GA State Dept Educ 1969-71; sch integration consul Americus GA Pub Schs 1970; spec educ visscholar NC Central Univ 1971; Natl Sci Found Visit Scientist AL State Univ 1971; Head Start consul for Heart of GA Project 1970-71; spec serv proj consult Ft Valley State Coll 1971-72; Natl Sci Found Vis Scientist Talledega Coll 1972; main speaker Alpha Kappa Alpha Sor Founders Day Prog 1972; spec educ consult & psychometrist Peach Co Pub Sch 1972; So Regional Rep Assn Black Psychologists 1972-74; served on exec adv com of Comm-Clinical Psych Project So Reg Educ Bd Atlanta 1972-75; consult psych Jackson Hinds Comm Mental Health Ctr 1973; psych consul MS State Univ 1973; mem Assn Adv of Behav Therapy, Am Assn on Mental Def, Am Assn of Univ Profs, Amer Psych Assn, Am Rsch Assn, GA Psych Assn; Nat Educ Assn, Alpha Kappa Alpha Sor. **HONORS/ACHIEVEMENTS:** Pub Law Fellowship 88-164 1964-66 IN Univ Bloomington; 4-yr Coll Scholarship Morris Brown Coll Atlanta; Post Doc Fellowship in Clinical Psych Univ of GA; Callaway Chair Prof Ft Valley State Coll 1979-84; Chair Psych Dept Morehouse Coll Atlanta; published numerous articles. **BUSINESS ADDRESS:** Callaway Prof Educ & Psych, Fort Valley State College, Box 1367, FVSC, Fort Valley, GA 31030.

CHEROT, NICHOLAS MAURICE
Attorney. **PERSONAL:** Born Jun 30, 1947, Ann Arbor, MI. **EDUCATION:** Univ of MI, BA 1969; NYU Sch of Law, JD 1972. **CAREER:** Autumn Industries Inc, sec-treas 1977-; Autumn-Everseal Mfg Co Inc, sec-treas 1979-. **ORGANIZATIONS:** Dir-partner Powell Blvd Holdin Co Inc & Powell Blvd Assoc 1979-; mem Harlem Lawyers & Assn NYC; mem NY Co Lawyers Assn; Natl Bar Assn; mem Black Allied Law Students Assn Invitations, law jours. **BUSINESS ADDRESS:** Cherot & Michael, PC, 305 Broadway, Room 600, New York, NY 10007.

CHERRY, ANDREW JACKSON
Clergyman. **PERSONAL:** Born Feb 08, 1927, Harrellsville, NC; married Bernice Britt; children: Vivian L Carter, Andrew J, Jr, Ada E. **EDUCATION:** Shaw University, AB 1950; Shaw Divinity School, BD 1950, DD, 1984. **ORGANIZATIONS:** President Bertie United Concerned Citizens 1953; president Bertie NAACP Branch 1954-56; member West Roanoke Missionary Baptist Assn 1944-85; member Roanoke Missionary Baptist Assn 1952-85; member Bertie Board of Education 1976-84. **HOME ADDRESS:** Rt 1 Box 65-B, Windsor, NC 27983.

CHERRY, CASSANDRA BRABBLE
Education specialist w/federal govt. **PERSONAL:** Born May 29, 1947, Norfolk, VA; married Capt Maurice L Cherry (deceased). **EDUCATION:** Bennett Coll, BA 1969; VA State Univ, MEd 1974; Richard Bland Coll of the Coll of Wm and Mary, Management diploma 1975; Nova Univ, EdD 1980. **CAREER:** US Army Quartermaster School, educ specialist 1974; US Army Logistics Ctr, educ specialist 1974-78; US Army Training Support Ctr, educ specialist 1978-79;Naval Supply Ctr, employee develop specialist 1979; Defense Activity for

Non-Traditional Educ Support, mgr instructional delivery programs 1980-. **ORGANIZATIONS:** Mem Phi Delta Kappa 1980-; bd dirs Minorities in Media 1982-83; mem Federally Employed Women 1985-; publicity chmn Equal Employment Oppor Council Pensacola Naval Complex 1985, 86; mem Amer Inst of Mortgage Brokers 1986-; mem NAACP 1986-. **HONORS/ACHIEVEMENTS:** One Woman Art Exhibit at Bennett College 1969; Who's Who in the South and Southwest 1982-83. **HOME ADDRESS:** 7811 Bay Meadows Court, Pensacola, FL 32507.

CHERRY, CHARLES WILLIAM
Publisher. **PERSONAL:** Born Oct 13, 1928, Americus, GA; married Julia Troutman; children: Charles II, Glenn, Cassandra. **EDUCATION:** Morehouse Coll, BA 1949; AL State U, MA 1953. **CAREER:** Daytona Times, pub 1977-; Bethune Cookman Coll, dir & asst prof 1961-79; Volusia Co Com Coll, mgr 1958-61; Claflin Coll, mgr 1956-58; Bethune Cookman Coll, acct 1953-56. **ORGANIZATIONS:** Mem Nat & Campgn Staff of Sen McGovern Pres 1971-72; pres Volusia Cnty NAACP 1972-76; pres FL State Conf NAACP 1974-; mem Nat Bd of DirNAACP; chrm of bd RV Moore Comm Ctr Inc; mem SHCC. **MILITARY SERVICE:** AUS 1950-52.

CHERRY, DERON LEIGH
Professional football player. **PERSONAL:** Born Sep 12, 1959, Riverside, NJ. **EDUCATION:** Rutgers Univ, attended. **CAREER:** Kansas City Chiefs, 1981-. **HONORS/ACHIEVEMENTS:** Tied NFL record for most interceptions game 4 against Seattle Seahawks 1985; Played in Pro-Bowl NFL All-Star Game following 1983-85 seasons. **BUSINESS ADDRESS:** Safety, Kansas City Chiefs, One Arrowhead Drive, Kansas City, MO 64129.

CHERRY, DONALD E.
Musician. **PERSONAL:** Born Nov 18, 1936, Oklahoma City. **CAREER:** Ornette Coleman Quintet NYC, played trumpet 1959; Sonny Rollins, 1963; Donald Cherry Quintet Europe, leader; recorded With Rollins Coleman Coltrane & Steve Lacy.

CHERRY, EDWARD EARL, SR.
Business executive. **PERSONAL:** Born Apr 14, 1926, Greenville, NC; son of Jasper Cherry and Velma Smith Cherry; married Mary Jean Jordan (deceased); children: Edward Jr, Todd J; married Tarah Stanton, May 31, 1987. **EDUCATION:** Howard Univ, BArch 1953. **CAREER:** Edward Cherry Architect, pres 1963-; Yale Univ School of Architecture, asst prof 1971, visiting critic 1972-81. **ORGANIZATIONS:** Founder, bd dir, pres, Greater New Haven Business Prof Assn 1964-; pres, Heritage Hall Devel Corp 1980; corporate mem, Connecticut Soc of Architects, AIA 1960-; worshipful master, Oriental Lodge No 6, F&AM PHA 1966-68; New Haven Consistory No 7, AASR PHA 1968-; mem, past basileus, Omega Psi Phi Frat 1957-; mem, State Review Bd, Connecticut Historical Comm 1980-; grand inspector general, AASR, PHA, Northern Jurisdiction 1986; archon, Beta Tau Boule, Sigma Pi Phi 1986; bd dir, Foundation for the New Haven Green 1986-. **HONORS/ACHIEVEMENTS:** AIA Design Award, Connecticut Soc Arch, AIA; Man of the Year, New England States, 1st Dist, Omega Psi Phi Frat, 1979; serv award, Grand Basileus, Omega Psi Phi, 1979. **MILITARY SERVICE:** AUS pvt 1945-46; Victory Medal, Occup Medal 1946. **HOME ADDRESS:** 22 Pine Ridge Rd, Woodbridge, CT 06525. **BUSINESS ADDRESS:** President, Edward E Cherry AIA Arch, PC, 60 Connolly Pkwy, Hamden, CT 06514.

CHERRY, LEE OTIS
Researcher. **PERSONAL:** Born Nov 20, 1944, Oakland, CA; married Lauran Michelle Waters; children: Aminah Louise. **EDUCATION:** Merritt Comm Coll, AA 1965; San Jose State Univ, BSEE 1968. **CAREER:** Intl Business Machines, systems analyst 1968-69; Pacific Gas & Electric Co, electrical engineer 1969-79; Dept of Defense, project mgr 1979-; African Scientific Inst, exec dir 1967-. **ORGANIZATIONS:** Sr consultant Develop Consultants and Assocs 1972-; proprietor L & L and Assocs Network Marketing 1980-. **HONORS/ACHIEVEMENTS:** Published "Technology Transfer," a monthly magazine 1979-83; Developer of "Blacks in Science Calendar" annually 1986-; produced general and technical conferences; performed public speaking; made numerousTV appearances and radio shows; written articles for various newspapers and magazines; Publisher, "Sci Tech," nationally distributed newspaper about developments in science and technology. **BUSINESS ADDRESS:** Exec Dir, African Scientific Institute, PO Box 12161, Oakland, CA 94604.

CHERRY, ROBERT LEE
Educational administrator. **PERSONAL:** Born Feb 17, 1941, Barrackville, WV; married Anna Luckett; children: Mary Elizabeth, Robert Lee, Ebon Michael. **EDUCATION:** Wittenberg U, EdB 1964; Wright State U, EdM 1973. **CAREER:** Clark Tech Coll, dir student serv 1975; DMVC-EDNL Opportunity Center, exec dir 1975; Clark Tech Coll, admissions officer 1973; Upward Bound Program Wittenberg Univ, program dir 1968; Intl Harvester Co, supr 1964. **ORGANIZATIONS:** Past mem & pres OH Assn of Upward Bound Dir 1970; certification com mem OH Assn of Student Financial Aid Adminstr 1974; mem OH Assn of Student Serv Dir 1977; bd mem Opportunities Industrialization Center 1974; chmn Clark Co 648 Mental Health & Retardation Bd 1975; city commnr Springfield OH 1974. **HONORS/ACHIEVEMENTS:** Comm merit award Springfield Frontiers Intl 1962; Outstanding Young Men of Am OYMA Bd of Advisors 1970; comm Serv award St John Bapt Ch 1980. **BUSINESS ADDRESS:** PO Box 570, Springfield, OH 45505.

CHERRY, THEODORE W.
Elected government official. **PERSONAL:** Born Dec 05, 1932, Woodland, NC; married Evelyn Maggett; children: Theodore Jr. **EDUCATION:** NC Central Univ, BS 1952-56; Hampton Inst, MS 1965-66. **CAREER:** Ralph J Bunche School, Weldon NC, chmn sci & math 1958-59; James Weldon Johnson School, Yorktown VA, chmn sci & math 1959-67; Hampton Inst VA, teacher 1966-67; Crossroads School, Monmouth Jct NJ, chmn sci dept 1967-87; Horizon for Youth PA, NY, UT, dir 1969-72; US Dept of Intl Youth Conservation Corp 1973; S Brunswick Township, mayor 1979-81, committeeman until 1990; MCEOC, dir 1981-. **ORGANIZATIONS:** Mem NAACP 1967-, NEA, NJEA, MEA, SBEA 1967-, Sci Club of Amer 1968; mem South Brunswick Township Lions Club 1986-. **HONORS/ACHIEVEMENTS:** Meritorious Teacher of the Year Awd VA Teacher Assoc 1965; Outstanding Educator Awd Jaycees of S Brunswick 1975; Mayors Apprec Awd S Brunswick Twp Com1976; Outstanding Citizens Awd NAACP 1979. **MILITARY SERVICE:** AUS sp5 1956-58. **BUSINESS ADDRESS:** Dir, MCEOC, Municipal Bldg, Monmouth Junction, NJ 08852.

CHERRY, WARREN W.
Educator. **PERSONAL:** Born Sep 12, 1942, Chicago, IL; married Cheryl; children: Michael. **EDUCATION:** BA 1966; MA 1967. **CAREER:** Evanston School Dist 65, prin 1974-, assoc prin 1971-74, teacher 1968-70. **ORGANIZATIONS:** Mem Phi Delta Kappan; NAACP; Black Alliance for Educators; IL Prins Assn; Nat Assn of Scndry Sch Prins. **BUSINESS ADDRESS:** 828 Main St, Evanston, IL 60202.

CHESS, ROBERT HUBERT
Physician. **PERSONAL:** Born May 20, 1930, Greenville, MS; married Gloria; children: Faye, Robert Jr. **EDUCATION:** TN State U, AB 1953, MS 1954; Meharry Med Coll, MD 1959; Xavier U, MBA 1976; Rollman Psych Inst, Resd Psychiatry 1968. **CAREER:** Rollman Psychiatric Inst, med dir 1979-;Univ of Cincinnati, clncl prof psy; Rollman Psychiat Inst, out-patient serv 1971-80; Rollman, chf male serv 1968-71; family prac med 1960-65. **ORGANIZATIONS:** Pres Cincinnati Psychiatric Soc 1978-79; cert mental hlth adminstrn Am Psy Assn 1976; diplomat Am Bd Psychiatry & Neurology 1972; consult psychiatrist Human Involvement Prgm 1972-79; Central Comm Helath Bd 1973; N KY Comp Care Ctr 1969-78; Ct Psychiat Ctr 1970; Proctor & Gamble 1973; mem MNA; AMA; APA; Am Orthopsychiat Assn; Am Mgmt Assn;bd tst Calvary United Met Ch 1967-79; bd dirs Chldrn Psych Ctr 1972-78; bd of dirs SW RegionalCouncil on & Alcoholism 1974-78; bd dirs Assn Home Care Agys 1974-78; adv bd Eden House; life mem NAACP; KAY; 32nd degree Mason; Shriner; Sigma Pi Phi Frat Outsdng Alumni TN State Univ 1962; flw Am Psychiat Assn 1974; Outsdng Greenvillian Citation 1975; pres elect Cincinnati Psy Soc 1977-78; publ "Goldie Cooper, Chess & Freeman "Effect of Radioactive Isotopes on Free Tumor in Peritrneal Cavity " 1958. **BUSINESS ADDRESS:** 3280 N Whitetree Cr, Cincinnati, OH 45236.

CHESS, SAMMIE, JR.
Attorney. **PERSONAL:** Born Mar 28, 1934, Allendale, SC; married Marlene Enoch; children: Eva, Janet. **EDUCATION:** NC Central U, LLB 1958. **CAREER:** Pvt Practice, atty 1960-71; spl superior ct judge 1971-75. **ORGANIZATIONS:** Mem NC Bd Higher Educ 1968-71; mem High Point Parks & Recreation Commn 1962-65; High Point Bar Assn; Am Assn; trustee Winston-Salem State U. **HONORS/ACHIEVEMENTS:** Outstanding & serv award High Point Bus & Professional Members Club; award of merit NC CentralUniv 1973; citizen of yr award Alpha Phi Alpha Frat. **MILITARY SERVICE:** AUS 1958-60. **BUSINESS ADDRESS:** 1222 Montlieu Ave, High Point, NC 27260.

CHESTANG, LEON WILBERT
Educator. **PERSONAL:** Born May 16, 1937, Mobile, AL; married Aurelia C Taylor; children: Nicole, Yvette. **EDUCATION:** Blackburn College, AB 1959; Washington Univ, MSW 1961; The Univ of Chicago, PhD 1977. **CAREER:** IL Dept of Children and Family Serv, supervisor 1961-65; IL Dept of Public Aid, social casework instr 1967-68; Family Care of Chicago, dir of casework services 1968-71; Univ of Chicago, asst prof 1971-78; Univ of Alabama, prof 1978-81; Wayne State Univ, dean and prof 1981-. **ORGANIZATIONS:** Bd mem Childrens Aid Soc of Detroit 1984-; bd mem Detroit Urban League 1985-; bd mem Natl Assn of Social Workers 1985-88. **HONORS/ACHIEVEMENTS:** ACE Fellow 1979; Distinguished Commonwealth Prof VA Univ Commonwealth 1984-86; Disting Lydia Rapaport Prof Smith Coll 1985; Disting Service Awd MI Assnof School Social Workers 1986. **HOME ADDRESS:** 682 Pallister Ave, Detroit, MI 48202. **BUSINESS ADDRESS:** Dean, Professor, Wayne StateUniv, School of Social Work, Detroit, MI 48202.

CHESTER, JOSEPH A., SR.
Legislator. **PERSONAL:** Born Mar 04, 1914, Wilson, NC; married Pearl V Brothers; children: Joseph, Jr, Fannie C. **ORGANIZATIONS:** Mem Mt Royal Dem Club; New Era Dem; Eastside Dem; deacon Wayland Bapt Ch; former chmn bd Hue Chemical Jantorial Supply; mem Old Timers Sound & Club; Fed Neighborhood Impro 1958-; pres The New Era Demo Club; vice-chmn Deacon Bd of Wayland Bapt; vice-chmn Health Confinement Sub Com; legislator State of MD Baltimore City 45th Sup Dist 1967. **MILITARY SERVICE:** USN 1944-45.

CHESTER, RAYMOND THOMAS
Athlete. **PERSONAL:** Born Jun 28, 1948, Cambridge, MD. **EDUCATION:** Morgan St Coll. **CAREER:** Baltimore Colts, tight end 1973-; Oakland Raiders, 1970-73. **HONORS/ACHIEVEMENTS:** Pro Bowl 1970-72. **HOME ADDRESS:** 4374 Turner Ave, Oakland, CA 94605.

CHESTNUT, DENNIS EARL
Educator, psychologist. **PERSONAL:** Born May 17, 1947, Green Sea, SC. **EDUCATION:** East Carolina Univ, BA Psych & Soc 1965-69, MA Clinical Psych 1971; Univ of utah, Doc Prog Clin Psy 1971-74; NY Univ, PhD Comm Psych 1982. **CAREER:** Camden Co MH Ctr, psychological consul 1974-75; Neuse Mental Health Ctr, qual assurance consult 1975-77; Medgar Evers Coll CUNY, instr psychology 1979-81; East Carolina Univ, asst prof psychol 1974-, prof of psychol. **ORGANIZATIONS:** Pres Young People's Holiness Assoc United Pentecostal Holiness Churches of Amer Inc; Alpha Phi Alpha Frat; natl treas Assoc of Black Psychologists 1983-84; organizational liaison Assoc for Humanistic Psychology 1983-84; s regional rep Assoc of Black Psychologists 1984-85; mem at large bd of dirs Assn for Humanistic Psychology 1984-85; reg rep NC Group Behavior Soc 1981-; vice bishop United Pentecostal Holiness Churches of Amer 1981-; pastor Mt Olive Holiness Church Tabor City NC 1984-; treas NC Assoc Black Psychologists; mem Pitt Cty Mental Health Assoc; pres NC Chap Assoc Black Psychologists 1986-87; dir Minority Affairs Assoc for Humanistic Psychology 1986-; co-chmn Natl Black Family Task Force of the Assoc of Black Psychologists. **HONORS/ACHIEVEMENTS:** Who's Who Amer Colls & Univs E Carolina Univ 1969; Outstanding Sr Dept of Sociology E Carolina Univ 1969; NIMH Fellow Univ Utah 1971-74; NIMH Fellow NY Univ 1978; NEH Summer Stipend for study of Southern Black Culture 1982. **HOME ADDRESS:** 1801 East Fifth St, Greenville, NC 27834. **BUSINESS ADDRESS:** Prof of Psychology, East CarolinaUniv, Dept Psychol, Greenville, NC 27834.

CHESTNUT, EDWIN, SR.
Insurance company executive. **PERSONAL:** Born Jan 14, 1924, Louisville; married Jacqueline Eades Chestnut, Nov 17, 1979. **EDUCATION:** Univ Louisville, BS 1952. **CA-**

REER: Mammoth Life & Accident Ins Co Louisville, vice pres cont 1975-, various pos. **ORGANIZATIONS:** 23 yrs mem Ins Acct & Stat Assn; Nat Accountants Assn; pres USO 1975; former sec Musicians Local #637. **MILITARY SERVICE:** USN petty officer 1st class 1942-45. **HOME ADDRESS:** 629 S 41st Street, Louisville, KY 40211.

CHEW, BETTYE L.
Secretary. **PERSONAL:** Born Dec 10, 1940; children: Gordon W, Cheryl L, Donna V. **EDUCATION:** Rosenwald Comm Jr Coll, 1959; Cortez W Peters Bus Sch, Grad 1964; Bowie State Coll, Spec Student. **CAREER:** Bowie State Coll, Bowie MD, Office of Dean, sec 1972-; Univ of MD Cooperative Extension Serv, Annapolis MD, sec 1969-72; Annapolis Urban Renewal & Program, sec 1967-69. **ORGANIZATIONS:** Corr sec 1966-70; rec sec 1974-; NAACP; reg rep of Annapolis Sr HS Citizens Adv Com 1974-; sudnay sch tchr First Bapt Ch 1964-; Offender Aid & Restoration Counselor at Anne Arundel Co Detention Cntr; chmn Citizen Adv Com Annapolis Sr HS 1976-77; mem Human Rel Com Annapolis Sr HS 1977; proj coord Am Issues Forum Prgm Bowie St Coll 1976; ldr Girl Scout Troop 43 1974-. **HONORS/ACHIEVEMENTS:** Certificate for serv NAACP 1974; employee of month award Bowie State Coll 1974; 5 yr serv award Bowie State Coll 1975. **BUSINESS ADDRESS:** Bowie State Coll, Office of Dean, Bowie, MD 20715.

CHEW, ROBERT L.
Clergyman. **PERSONAL:** Born May 15, 1935, Bryan, TX; married Keiko Sagisaka; children: Robert L, II. **EDUCATION:** CA Bapt Coll, BA 1962; Golden Gate Bapt Theol Seminary, MRE 1964; MDiv 1964; CA Grad Sch Theol, PhD; Urban Ch Inst, 1969-70. **CAREER:** Christian Fellowship Bapt Ch, pastor 1975-; Cochran Ave Bapt Ch 1971-75; Mt Moriah Bapt Ch 1967-70; Mt Zion, promotional asst 1965-67; San Quentin, chaplaincy 1960-65. **ORGANIZATIONS:** Coordinator Sugar Ray Robinsons Youth Found; dir Youth Actiities; mem Nat Bapt Conv Am; Black Am Bapt Churchmen; Am Bapt Ch; Nat Am Bapt Black Churchman; Black Urban Study Cntr Com; bd Educ Council Ch; asst dir House Agape; mem Comm Adv Comn; Oral Review Bd; Pasadena Police Dept; dir New Face; comm Council; Worshipful Master; sterring com concern Clergy election of Tom Bradley Police Comm Relation Commn. **HONORS/ACHIEVEMENTS:** Editors Citation Coll Yearbook; Deans scholastic hon roll; citation 5 yrs Distiguished Serv San Quentin 1964; AAC Pauline Award; Who's Who Religion 1975; Outstanding Negro Ministers HowardUniv 1975; Outstanding Young Men of Am 1970; meterious serv award Nat Bapt Youth Conv 1960.

CHICOYE, ETZER
Director of research. **PERSONAL:** Born Nov 04, 1926, Jacmel, Haiti;married Dolores Bruce; children: Lorena, Rigaud. **EDUCATION:** Univ of Haiti Port Au Prince, BS 1948; Univ of WI Madison, MS 1954; Univ of WI, PhD 1968. **CAREER:** Chicago Pharmacal, chemist quality control 1955-57; Julian Labs, prod chemist 1957-62; Julian Labs Chgo, chemist r&d 1962-64; Miller Brewing Co, chem rsch suprv 1968-72, mgr rsch 1972-77, dir of rsch 1977-. **HONORS/ACHIEVEMENTS:** Black Achiever Harlem YMCA 1979. **BUSINESS ADDRESS:** Dir of Research, Miller Brewing Co, 3939 W Highland Blvd, Milwaukee, WI 53201.

CHILDERS, TERRY L.
Government official. **PERSONAL:** Born Dec 31, 1952, Abilene, TX; married Essie Charles; children: Jonathan, Adam. **EDUCATION:** Abeline Christian Univ, BA 1974; North EX State Univ, M Pub Admin 1976. **CAREER:** City of Celina, city administrator 1975-76; City of Austin, asst to the city mgr 1976-78; City of Tyler, asst city mgr 1978-82, acting city mgr 1982; City of Austin, sr asst city mgr. **ORGANIZATIONS:** Bd dirs TX City Mgmt Assn; future horizons comm Intl City Mgmt Assn; adv bd Abeline Christian Univ; public serv div chmn Greater United Way Tyler1980-82; loaned exec Greater United Way Tyler 1979; pres Kiwanis Intl 1982; dir of church educ N Tenneha Church of Christ 1978-82; nom comm TX City Mgmt Assocs 1984-85. **HONORS/ACHIEVEMENTS:** Clarence E Ridley City Mgmt Scholarship TX City Mgmt Assn 1975; Hatton W Sumner Fellowship 1975. **BUSINESS ADDRESS:** Sr Asst City Manager, City of Austin, PO Box 1088, Austin, TX 78767.

CHILDRESS, ALICE
Playwright, novelist, actress, and director. **PERSONAL:** Born Oct 12, 1920, Charleston, SC; married Nathan Woodard, Jul 17, 1957. **EDUCATION:** Radcliff Inst, graduated, 1968. **CAREER:** Author of plays, screenplays, and novels, including Gold Through the Trees (play), 1952, Trouble in Mind (play), 1955, Like One of the Family, 1956, Wedding Band (play), 1966, Wine in the Wilderness (screenplay), 1969, Mojo (play), 1970, A Hero Ain't Nothin' but a Sandwich (novel), 1973, When the Rattlesnake Sounds (play), 1975, Let's Hear It for the Queen (play), 1976, Sea Island Song (play), 1977, A Short Walk (novel), 1979; Amer Negro Theatre, Harlem, NY, actress and director for eleven years; has also performed on Broadway and television; research for NBC-TV script "Life of Fannie Lou Hamer," MS, 1978; lecturer at universities and schools. **ORGANIZATIONS:** Bd mem, Frances Delafield Hospital; mem, Intl PEN Club; mem, Amer Federation of TV and Radio Artists; council mem, Dramatists Guild, 1980; council mem, Writers Guild of Amer, East, 1980; mem, New Dramatists Screen & TV Writers, East. **HONORS/ACHIEVEMENTS:** Obie Award for "Trouble In Mind," 1956; Jane Addams Children's Book Honor Award, 1974; Sojourner Truth Award, Natl Assn of Negro Business & Professional Women's Clubs, 1975; Lewis Carroll Shelf Award, Univ of Wisconsin, 1975; named honorary citizen of Atlanta, GA, for opening of "Wedding Band," 1975; Virgin Islands Film Festival Award, 1977; 1st Paul Robeson Award for outstanding contributions to performing arts, Black Filmmakers Hall of Fame, 1977; "Alice Childress Week" officially observed in Charleston and Columbia, SC, 1977, to celebrate the opening of "Sea Island Song.". **BUSINESS ADDRESS:** c/o FloraRoberts Inc, 157 W 57th St, Penthouse A, New York, NY 10019. *

CHILDS, FRANCINE C.
Educator. **PERSONAL:** Born Feb 08, Wellington, TX; children: Jimmy Fenley. **EDUCATION:** Paul Quinn Coll, BS 1962; East TX State Univ, MEd 1970, EdD 1975. **CAREER:** Wiley Coll, dean of students 1970-72; East TX State Univ, part-time project dir special svcs/full time doctorial student 1972-74; Ohio Univ, prof afro-amer studies 1974-85, chair/prof afro-amer studies 1985-. **ORGANIZATIONS:** Local pres & advisor OH Univ Chap NAACP 1971-; mem League of Women Voters 1977-; educ chair OH Conf of Branches NAACP 1978-; natl coord Booker T Washington Alumni Assoc 1982-; prayer coord Athens Christian Women Club 1984-86; workshop leader Ohio Bapt Women Aux Convention 1985-; local conf host and progcomm Natl Cncl on Black Studies 1987. **HONORS/ACHIEVEMENTS:** Paul Quin Coll Outstanding Alumni 1982; Individual Witness for Peace & Justice Awd 1985; OU Higher Educ Mgmt Develop Prog 1985-86; Outstanding Black Alumni Awd 1986; Fulbright Hays Scholarship 1986. **BUSINESS ADDRESS:** Chair/Prof Afro-Amer Studies, Ohio University, 302 Lindley, Athens, OH 45701.

CHILDS, JOY
Attorney. **PERSONAL:** Born Apr 10, 1951, Wilmington, NC; daughter of Joseph Childs and Mable Childs. **EDUCATION:** UCLA, BA 1973, MA 1975; Georgetown Univ Law Ctr, JD 1981. **CAREER:** Screen Actors Guild, contract admin 1981-83; Atlantic Richfield Co Legal Dept, paralegal 1983-84; Peace Officers Rsch Assoc of CA, labor relations rep 1984-86; CA State Univ, employee relations admin, 1986-. **ORGANIZATIONS:** Mem KCET Comm Adv Bd 1984-, UCLA Black Alumni Assn 1985-, Black Labor Attorneys of LA 1985-, Black Entertainment & Sports Lawyers Assn 1986-; Women of Color, 1987-. **HOME ADDRESS:** 2031 Dunsmuir Ave #1, Los Angeles, CA 90016.

CHILDS, OLIVER BERNARD, SR.
Non-profit organization executive. **PERSONAL:** Born Jan 15, 1933, Philadelphia, PA; son of Edmond A Childs Sr and Ogetta Faust Childs; married Dorothy Collins, Feb 07, 1953; children: Renee Olivia, Oliver Jr, Sean Vincent. **EDUCATION:** Cheyney State Teachers Coll, Cheyney PA, BS, El Educ, 1958; Univ of Utah, Salt Lake City UT, MS, Human Resource Mgmt, Economics, 1980. **CAREER:** Philadelphia Board of Educ, Philadelphia PA, teacher, 1958-65; Opportunities Industrialization Centers, Philadelphia PA, dir training, 1965-66, Los Angeles CA, exec dir, 1966-68; OIC Inst, Philadelphia PA, asst dir Ext Serv, 1968-71; OIC America, Dallas TX, regional dir, 1971-74, Philadelphia PA, dir Fund Devel, 1974-83; OIC Intl, Philadelphia PA, dir Resource Devel, 1984-. **ORGANIZATIONS:** Mem, Kappa Alpha Psi Fraternity, 1956-, Natl Soc Fund Raising Exec, 1976-, NAACP, Philadelphia PA, 1978-; chmn, Troop Comm, Boy Scouts of Amer, Philadelphia PA, 1980-; vice pres, bd of dir, Natl Coalition Black Mtg Planners, 1983-; bd mem, Independent Charities of America, 1989-; Minority Advisory Comm, Philadelphia Visitors & Convention Bureau, 1989-. **HONORS/ACHIEVEMENTS:** Mayoralty Awards, Los Angeles CA, 1968, New Orleans LA, 1972, Lubbock TX, 1972; Honorary State Senator, State of Louisiana, 1973. **MILITARY SERVICE:** AUS, corporal, 1952-54. **BUSINESS ADDRESS:** Director, Resource Development, Opportunities Industrialization Centers Intl, Inc (OICI), 240 W Tulpehocken St, Philadelphia, PA 19144.

CHILDS, THEODORE FRANCIS
Educator. **PERSONAL:** Born Feb 17, 1921, Jamaica, NY; married Marie J; children: Sheila Childs Berg, Theodore W. **EDUCATION:** Shaw Univ, BS 1944; State Univ IA, RPT 1948; Columbia Univ, MA 1958; Masonic Congress, Honorary Doctorate 1972; Columbia Univ, EdD 1976. **CAREER:** Brooklyn VA Hospital, chief pt 1955-65; US Comm Rehab Africa, vol exec dir 1962-75; NY Univ Medical Center, dir pt servs 1965-68; Long Island Univ, dir spec educ 1968-75; Nassau Coop Educ, school bd mem 1970-76; Tuskegee Inst, dir health science 1975-83; United Cerebral Palsy Assn, civil vice pres 1982-; AL State Univ, assoc prof, dir interdisciplinary studies program. **HONORS/ACHIEVEMENTS:** Man of the Year Westbury NY 1971; Brooklyn Hall of Fame Brooklyn NY 1973; Travel Flwshp Natl Fnd Europe and Africa 1957. **MILITARY SERVICE:** AUS lt col 1944-46; Assc Pacific Theatre of War WWII 1944-76. **BUSINESS ADDRESS:** Associate Professor Dir Stud, AL StateUniv, 125 S Jackson St, Montgomery, AL 36195.

CHILDS, WINSTON
Attorney, board chairman, chief executive officer. **PERSONAL:** Born Feb 14, 1931, Savannah, GA; son of Wendell Childs and Inez Childs; children: Evan, Julie, Stephanie. **EDUCATION:** Amer Univ, AB 1957, JD 1959. **CAREER:** Booker T Washington Found, special counsel; Minority Consult & Urbanologists, natl assn; GEOC, CIO Labor Union, pres; stock broker; private law pratice; DC Republican Central Committee, gen counsel; Natl Business League, gen counsel; Graham Building Associates Real Estate Development Company, pres; Amer Univ Law School, adjunct prof; MSI Services Inc, a systems engineering and mgmt consulting firm, Washington DC, founder, chairman, CEO. **ORGANIZATIONS:** DC Bar Assn; Amer Management Assn; Armed Forces Communication and Electronics Assn; Republican Senatorial Inner Circle; DC Metropolitan Boys/Girls Club; bd mem, Georgetown Symphony Orchestra; John Sherman Myers Society. **BUSINESS ADDRESS:** Board Chairman & CEO, MSI Services, Inc, 1925 K St, NW, Washington, DC 20006.

CHINN, JOHN CLARENCE
Writer, audio programmer. **PERSONAL:** Born Dec 15, 1938, Meadville, PA; son of Horace P Chinn and Marquerite Lucas Chinn. **EDUCATION:** Bowling Green Univ, BA 1960; Syracuse Univ, MS 1962. **CAREER:** J Walter Thompson NYC, advertising copywriter 1963-67; First Edition radio book discussion prog, assoc prod creative dir 1973; freelance writer for feature film, TV & radio drama, scripts, short stories & poetry; Inflight Serv Inc NYC, dir audio prog; freelance writer/radio producer. **ORGANIZATIONS:** Joined bd of editors of Literary Guild of Amer Book Club; created music entertainment channels; mem Writer's Guild of Amer; Natl Acad of Rec Arts & Sci; Airline Entertainment Assn; poetry published in NY Quarterly. **HONORS/ACHIEVEMENTS:** Author "Jelly Roll" musical on Jelly Roll Morton; produced series of multiple record albums entitled, Body & Soul-Five Decades of Jazz Era Song Satchmo-Louis Armstrong 1900-1971, A Silver Screen Symphony, Broadway Babies, others in coop with Columbia Spec Prod Div & Literary Guild 1970.

CHISHOLM, CLARENCE EDWARD
Assistant library director. **PERSONAL:** Born Sep 17, 1949, Charlotte, NC; son of Clarence Chisholm and Sarah M Fields-Chisholm. **EDUCATION:** Johnson C Smith Univ, Charlotte NC, BA, 1976; Atlanta Univ, Atlanta GA, MSLS, 1978; North Carolina A&T State Univ, Greensboro NC, MA, 1984. **CAREER:** Columbus Public Library, Columbus OH, head of branch, 1978-79; Wilberforce Univ, Wilberforce OH, head of reference, 1979-80; North Carolina A&T State Univ, Greensboro NC, head of reference, 1980-84; Eastern Michigan Univ, Ypsilanti MI, Humanities Librarian, 1984-86; Clinch Valley Coll, Wise VA, dir, 1986-88; Ohio Univ, Athens OH, asst dir, 1988-. **ORGANIZATIONS:** Mem, Amer Library Assn, 1978-; exec mem, NAACP, 1980-; chair, ACRL-Black Studies Librarian Discussion Group, 1987-, Ethnic Librarians Forum, 1987-; mem, ALA Council on Minority Concern, 1987-; exec mem, Black Caucus of ALA, 1987-; mem, Ohio Library Assn, 1988-, NAACP, Ohio, 1988-; advisor, Alpha Phi Alpha, 1988-. **HONORS/ACHIEVEMENTS:** Service Award, New Light Baptist Church, 1982; Rookie of the Year, Greensboro Jaycees, 1982; Affirmative Action: A Selective Bibliography, 1983; Outstanding Young Men of America, Jaycees, 1984,

1986; author, Affirmative Action: A Selective Bibliography, 1983, School Closings: A Bibliography, 1985, Health Care Construction: A Bibliography, 1985, The Nation's Environmental Laws Conflict, 1986 Export-Credit: A Bibliography, 1986. **HOME ADDRESS:** 1-H Station St, Athens, OH 45701. **BUSINESS ADDRESS:** Assistant Director of the Library, Ohio University, Alden Library, Park Place, Athens, OH 45701.

CHISHOLM, JOSEPH CARREL, JR.
Physician. **PERSONAL:** Born May 16, 1935, Detroit, MI; son of Joseph Chisholm and Maizie Jones Chisholm; married Maurita; children: John, Lynn, Kim, Kelly. **EDUCATION:** Univ Chicago, BS 1958, MS 1960; Meharry Med College, MD 1962. **CAREER:** VA Hosp Wash DC, consultant 1968-77; US Dept of State, consultant 1970-; DC Soc Internal Med, mem exec bd 1972-80; DC VNA, mem exec bd 1982-; Amer College of Physicians Washington DC, governor's bd 1984-; physician. **ORGANIZATIONS:** Mem DC Soc Internal Med 1970, Southern Med Soc 1980-, NY Acad Sci 1975-, Alpha Phi Alpha Inc 1957, Alpha Omega Alpha Honor Soc 1960-, NAACP 1978-, NMA, DC Thoracic Soc, Amer Lung Assn 1970-, DC Heart Assn, DC Med Soc, Amer Heart Assn 1970; mem Sigma Pi Phi Frat, 1986-. **HONORS/ACHIEVEMENTS:** Rockefeller Research School Allergy Immunology 1959-61; Pulmonary Research School NIH 1965-66; Fellow Amer College of Physicians 1970-; Order of the C Univ Chicago 1954-; mem Pigskinners of Washington DC 1980-. **MILITARY SERVICE:** USN comdr 1962-68; Korean Serv Medal; Vietnam Serv Medal 1966-68. **BUSINESS ADDRESS:** Physician, 106 Irving St NW, Ste 206, Washington, DC 20010.

CHISHOLM, JUNE FAYE
Clinical psychologist, educator. **PERSONAL:** Born Apr 29, 1949, New York, NY; daughter of Wallace Chisholm and Luretta Brawley Chisholm. **EDUCATION:** Syracuse U, BA Psych 1971; Univ of MA Amherst, MS Psych 1974; Univ of MA, PhD Psych 1978. **CAREER:** NY Univ Med Centr Bellevue, intern psych 1975-77; Harlem Hospital NY senior psychologist 1982-; Pace Univ NY asst prof 1986-; private practice, 1980-; adjunct prof NYU Medical Center 1984-. **ORGANIZATIONS:** Mem NY Assn of & Black Psychol 1977-; mem Am Psychol Assn 1979-; mem NY Society of Clinical Psychologists 1980-; mem NYSPA 1980; mem EPA 1988-. **HONORS/ACHIEVEMENTS:** Teaching flwshp NY Univ Med Cntr 1976-77. **BUSINESS ADDRESS:** 260 W 72 St, Ste 1-B, New York, NY 10023.

CHISHOLM, REGINALD CONSTANTINE
Educator. **PERSONAL:** Born Oct 13, 1934, Jamaica, WI; married Cecilin Coy. **EDUCATION:** Howard U, BS 1962, MD 1966. **CAREER:** Howard U, chief med oncology; NCI-VA Oncology Serv WA, fellow clinical assoc 1971-73; Freedmens Hosp, residency internal med 1967-70, intern 1966-67; Shaw Comm Health Clinic, internist 1970-71; Cancer Screening & Detection Clinic, chf 1977; Howard U, assoc dir 1977. **ORGANIZATIONS:** Mem DC Med Soc; WA Soc of Oncology; Nat Med Assn Publ "Hypercalcitonemig in Cancer of the Breast" 1975. **HONORS/ACHIEVEMENTS:** Post-grad fellowship 1971-73. **BUSINESS ADDRESS:** HowardUniv Hosp, 2041 Georgia Ave NW, Washington, DC 20060.

CHISHOLM, SHIRLEY
Educator. **PERSONAL:** Born Nov 30, 1924, NYC; married Arthur Hardwick Jr. **EDUCATION:** Brooklyn Coll, BA (cum laude); Columbia U, MA. **CAREER:** 12th Cong Dist NY, US representative; Veterans Affairs Com House Education & Labor Com Select Education, served; Mt Holyoke Coll MA, purington chair 1983-. **ORGANIZATIONS:** General Education & Agricultural Labor Subcommittees; mem comm on rules Sec of Dem Caucus; mem of Congressional Black Caucus Candidate for President of US 1972; first woman to ever actively ever run for president; member of numerous civic & professional organizations including League of Women Voters, Brooklyn Br NAACP, Delta Sigma Theta, Nat Bd of Americans for Dem Action, Adv Council, NOW, Hon Com Mem United Negro College Fund, Natl Assoc Coll Women, Brooklyn Coll Alumni, Key Women. **HONORS/ACHIEVEMENTS:** Recipient Clairol's "Woman of Year" award for outstanding achievement in pub affairs 1973; gallup poll's list of ten most admired women in the world 3 yrs; recipient of numerous honorary degrees; author "Unbought & Unbossed 1970; "The Good Fight". **BUSINESS ADDRESS:** Mt Holyoke College, South Hadley, MA 01075.

CHISM, HAROLYN B.
Financial administrator. **PERSONAL:** Born Jan 04, 1941, Columbia, SC; divorced; children: John Patrick, Sharon Elizabeth. **EDUCATION:** Benedict Coll, BS 1967. **CAREER:** US Dept of Commerce Minority Bus Devel Agency, budget ofcr 1978; USDA-animal & Plant Health Insptn Serv & Food Safety And Quality Serv, supr bdgt analyst 1972-78; USDA-Office Of Mgmt Serv, budget analyst 1967-72; IRS, sec 1964-65; Fed Power Commn, clk typist 1963-64; Gen Accounting Office, clk typist 1962-63. **ORGANIZATIONS:** Mem Am Assn of Budget and Program Analyst 1980; sec Boy Scouts of Am T351 1973-75; EEO counsellor USDA APHIS and FSQS 1974-78; bd mem USDA Credit Union 1977-78. **HONORS/ACHIEVEMENTS:** Incentive award Fed Power Commn 1964; cert of merit USDA/APHIS 1975; cert of merit USDA/FSQS 1978. **BUSINESS ADDRESS:** 14th & Constitution Ave NW, Washington, DC.

CHISM, VIRGINIA LARK
Labor relations specialist. **PERSONAL:** Born Apr 21, 1953, South Bend, IN; married Eldridge Louis Jr; children: X. **EDUCATION:** IN Univ At S Bend, BS, MPA 1979. **CAREER:** Meml Hosp of S Bend, employee relations specialist 1979; S Bend Human Rights Commn, exec dir 1977-79, actng dir 1977, staff invstgtr 1976-77; S Bend-mishawaka Area C of C Ldrshp Prgm, alumni 1979-80. **ORGANIZATIONS:** Bd of dir 1st United Meth Day Care Ctr 1978-79; bd of dir YWCA 1979; advis com Cmprhnsv Assessmnt & Prgrm Plng System Com for Math. **BUSINESS ADDRESS:** Yale Child Study Ctr, 333 Cedar St, New Haven, CT 06510.

CHISOLM, GRACE BUTLER
Professor, educational administrator. **PERSONAL:** Born in New Orleans, LA; daughter of Washington Butler and Althea Butler (deceased); children: Olethia Elise. **EDUCATION:** Xavier Univ, BS Music Educ 1958; Northwestern Univ, MM Music Educ 1962; Queens College, Sixth Yr Certificate in Educ Admin and Supervision 1972; NewYork Univ, PhD Educ Admin & Supervision 1976. **CAREER:** Queens College, adjunct lecturer dept of grad programs in educ serv 1974-75; OH State Univ, adjunct asst prof academic faculty of educ admin 1977-78; North Texas State Univ, assoc prof educ admin 1978-83; Texas A&M Univ, assoc prof educ admin educ 1983-86, prof educ admin 1986-, asst to the pres 1985-87. **ORGANIZATIONS:** Adv bd Univ Council for Educ Admin Prog Ctr for Educ Public Relations 1984-; TX A&M Univ president's adv council chair 1985-, task force on sexual harrassment chair 1985-, minority faculty network chair 1985-, career develop inquiry group co-chair 1986-, interim bd of dirs Univ Faculty Club 1986-; mem Delta Sigma Theta Sor Inc; mem Amer Assoc of Univ Women, Amer Educ Rsch Assoc, Brazos Valley Symphony Soc, Natl Assoc for Women Deans Admins and Counselors, Natl Conf of Profs of Educ Admin, Phi Delta Kappa Frat, TX Profs of Educ Admin; Natl org of Legal Professors of Educ (NOLPE). **HONORS/ACHIEVEMENTS:** Certificate for Outstanding Serv to Intl Educ North TX State Univ International Programs Staff 1982; selectee Leadership Brazos Program 1985-86; nomerous publications, articles and presentations including "Enhancing the Undergraduate Experience, Focus on Minority Students," Annual Symposium of the Ctr for Teaching Excellence, TX A&M Univ 1986, "Affirmative Action Progress Report" TX A&M Univ System Affirmative Action 1986, "Opportunities for Career Advancement as Perceived by Teachers and Administrators," Natl Forum of Educ Administration and Supervision Journal 1986; Honorary Society of Phi Kappa Phi, TX A&M Univ Chapter 1987; Phi Beta Delta Honorary Society for Intl Scholars, Alpha Eta Chapter, 1988. **BUSINESS ADDRESS:** Educational Administration, Texas A&M University, M T Harrington Bldg, College Station, TX 77843-4226.

CHISSELL, HERBERT GARLAND
Physician. **PERSONAL:** Born May 24, 1922, Petersburg, VA; married Robbie; children: Herbert, III, Robert. **EDUCATION:** VA State, BS 1942; Meharry Med Coll, MD 1946. **CAREER:** Monumental Hlth Pln & PA, exec vice pres med dir 1975; Provident Hosp, head dept fmly prac 1961-68, bd tsts 1960-. **ORGANIZATIONS:** Mem Nat Med Assn; AMA; Med Chirurical Fclty; MD Med Soc; Baltimore Med Soc; Monumental City Med Soc; Alpha Phi Alpha; Chi Delta Mu Mayor's com Med Facilities; gov com Drug Abuse Narcotics & Alcoholism. **MILITARY SERVICE:** AUS MC maj 1954-56. **BUSINESS ADDRESS:** 940 W North Ave, Baltimore, MD 21217.

CHISUM, GLORIA TWINE
Psychologist, director. **PERSONAL:** Born May 17, 1930, Muskogee, OK; married Melvin Jackson. **EDUCATION:** Howard Univ, BS 1951, MS 1953; Univ of PA, PhD 1960. **CAREER:** Univ of PA, lecturer in psych 1958-68; Naval Air Devel Ctr, rsch psych 1960-65, head vision lab 1965-80, head environ physiol rsch team 1980-. **ORGANIZATIONS:** Trsutee Philadelphia Saving Fund Soc 1977-85; dir Fischer & Porter Co 1978-; bd mem Arthritis Found of E PA 1972-80; trustee Univ of PA 1974-; bd mem WorldAffairs Council of Philadelphia 1977-80, Free Library of Philadelphia 1979-, Philadelphia Orch Assoc 1979-; dir Meritor Financial Group 1985-. **HONORS/ACHIEVEMENTS:** Raymond F Longacre Award Aerospace Med Assn, 1979; Distinguished Daughter of Pennsylvania 1983; Oklahoma Hall of Fame 1984. **BUSINESS ADDRESS:** Head Environmental Phys Rsch Team, Naval Air Devel Ctr, Warminster, PA 18974.

CHITTY, M. ELIZABETH
Librarian. **PERSONAL:** Born May 28, 1928, Pittsburgh, PA; widowed; children: Treka, David. **EDUCATION:** Columbia, BS 1961. **CAREER:** VA Somerville Supply Depot, admin lib & chief books & periodicals 1973; Lyons VA Hosp, chief cataloging sect med lib 1969-73. **ORGANIZATIONS:** Mem Negro Business & Professional Women's Clubs; African Women's Conf; bibliothrpst-founder Plainfield & Reading Prog; Model Cities Educ Task Force; Plainfield Bd Educ, mem 1969, pres 1974; NJ School Bds; ALA; Catholic Library Assn; Hosp & Inst Lib Assn; Amer Benedictine Acad Fellow; Plainfield Cit Adv Comm; vice pres finance NJSBA; bd dir NJ School Bd Assn 1973-77; Natl Commn Child Abuse & Neglect (Educ Commn of States); Union County Legislative Comm Lisle Fellowship student, Univ of Colorado; Delta Sigma Theta Sor. **HONORS/ACHIEVEMENTS:** Plainfield Public High School Library named M Elizabeth Chitty Library, 1977; Margaret C Scroggins Award, young adult lib; NY Public Library Merit Award. **BUSINESS ADDRESS:** Dir, Library Management Agency, 1228 South End Parkway, Plainfield, NJ 07060.

CHIVIS, MARTIN LEWIS
Banker. **PERSONAL:** Born Oct 05, 1952, Washington, DC; daughter of Samuel Lewis Chivis and Odesa Penn Chivis. **EDUCATION:** Drexel Univ, BS 1976; American Inst of Banking, graduated, 1983; Stonier Greaduate School of Banking, 1988. **CAREER:** NASA, aide 1969-70; Comptroller of the Currency, fellowship 1971-72; Peat Marwick Mitchell, pre pro intern 1973-74; Covington & Burling, coll co-op 1975-76; Continental Bank, exec trainee 1976-89; Industrial Bank, funds mgr. **ORGANIZATIONS:** Mem NABA, NBMBA, BDPA; bd mem Urban Bankers; mem Concerned Black Men, 21st Century PAC; jr deacon, 12th St Christian Church. **HONORS/ACHIEVEMENTS:** Most Outstanding Employee OCC 1971; Outstanding Professional Business Exchange Network Inc 1987. **HOME ADDRESS:** 611 Edgewood St NE, Apt 820, Washington, DC 20017. **BUSINESS ADDRESS:** Funds Manager, Industrial Bank, 4812 Georgia Ave NW, Washington, DC 20011.

CHOLMONDELEY, PAULA H. J.
Financial analysis manager. **PERSONAL:** Born Apr 19, 1947, Kingston, Jamaica. **EDUCATION:** Howard U, BA 1970; Wharton Sch of Fin, MS 1971. **CAREER:** Intl Paper Co, finan analysis mgr 1974; Zebra Asso, treas 1973-74; Arthur Anderson & Co, auditor 1971-73; Natl Assn of Black Accntnts, treas vp. **ORGANIZATIONS:** Mem Indus Government Com & AICPA 1977; BEEP; mem Small Bus Dev Com AICPA 1975-77; mem Int Operations Com NYSCPA 1977; exec exchange prgm ASWCPA. **HONORS/ACHIEVEMENTS:** Outstdng Young Women of Am 1977; outstanding mem Nat Assn of Black Accntnts 1977; salute to women in bus YWCA 1977. **BUSINESS ADDRESS:** 220 E 42nd St, New York, NY 10017.

CHONES, JIM
Athlete. **PERSONAL:** Born Nov 30, 1949, Racine, WI. **CAREER:** Los Angeles Lakers, professional basketball player; Cleveland Cavaliers, Former Basketball Player. **BUSINESS ADDRESS:** Los Angeles Lakers, PO Box 10, Inglewood, CA 90306.

CHOWNING, FRANK EDMOND
Dentist. **PERSONAL:** Married Edith Mae Jenkins. **CAREER:** Morgan Health Ctr, dentist. **ORGANIZATIONS:** Mem Kappa Alpha Psi Frat; mem Sigma Pi Phi Frat; past pres Ethical Culture Soc; past pres Nat Dntl Assn; past trustee Natl Dntl Assn; trustee & past asst supr Allen Chapel AME Ch; bd of dir Alpha Home; bd of Dir Citizens Forum; past bd mem

YMCA Exec Bd; mem Clncn Nat Dntl Assn; mem Clncn IN State Dntl Assn; past Polemarch Kappa Alpha Psi; mem Sigma Pi Phi; life mem NAACP; past pres IN State Med Dntl & Pharm Assn; past pres Indianapolis Frntrs Serv Clb; past mem Peer Review Com. **HONORS/ACHIEVEMENTS:** Dentist of the Yr Nat Dental Assn; fellow Am Coll Dentists; fellow Intenat Coll of Dentists; mem Am Dental Assn; mem Am Prosthodontic Soc.

CHRETIEN, GLADYS M.
Business executive. **PERSONAL:** Born Dec 16, Texas; divorced; children: Joseph P, III, Perry Duncan. **EDUCATION:** Prairie View Coll; Wiley Coll. **CAREER:** Salesman 1961; broker 1962; Gladys M Chretien Realty Co, real estate broker, realtor & realtist; Consolidated Realty Bd, 2nd women to serve as pres in 27 yrs of existence 1976; Multiple Listing, one women chmn; Wash Escrow Co, pres elect, part owner & vp; Wall St Enterprises & Wash Reconveyance Corp,part owner & stockholder; Century 21 Chretien Realty, owner. **ORGANIZATIONS:** Mem Ch Christ; LA Co Tax Appeals Bd Fndrs 3 yr term. **HONORS/ACHIEVEMENTS:** LA Co Tax Appeals Bd Fndrs Achvmnt Awrd Consolidated Rlty Bd 1969-70; Top Ten Cntrbtrs Consolidated Rlty; many sales awards. **BUSINESS ADDRESS:** 3754 W 54 St, Los Angeles, CA.

CHRICHLOW, LIVINGSTON L.
Church administrator, lay (retired). **PERSONAL:** Born May 13, 1925, Brooklyn, NY; married Mary Atkinson; children: Gordon H. **EDUCATION:** Queens Clge City Univ NY, BA 1975; Baruch Clge City Univ NY, MPA 1979. **CAREER:** Dept of Defense, contract admin 1951-80; Lutheran Immigration and Refugee Srv, coordinator 1980-82; Lutheran Church in Amer, dir urban ministry 1982-1987. **ORGANIZATIONS:** Sec Assn of Black Lutherans 1979-; chmn Finance Comm New Hope Church 1975-; dir Proj Equality NY 1980-1987; mem chmn Minority Concerns Comm NY Synod 1979-1987; pres Parkhurst Civic Assc 1984-; past pres Better Comm Civil Assn 1955-57; mem vice pres Comm Schl Bd 27 Queens 1965-70; sec Boy Scouts of Amer Alumni 1980-. **HONORS/ACHIEVEMENTS:** Distinguished discipleship Metro NY Synod Lutheran Church in Amer 1970; Distinguished Citizen Springfield Gardens Sr Citizens 1980. **MILITARY SERVICE:** USN elec mate 2nd class; Good Conduct Amer Theatre USN 1944.

CHRICHLOW, MARY L.
Interfaith education and human relations consultant. **PERSONAL:** Born May 27, 1927, Greenville, NC; married Livingston L Chrichlow; children: Gordon H. **EDUCATION:** Univ of CA at Berkeley, AS, Business Admin, 1946; CUNY-Queens Coll, BA Ed 1960, Adelphi Univ, Human Relations certificate 1964; Mercer School of Theology, cand certificate Christian Educ, 1984-. **CAREER:** Natl Conf of Christians & Jews, exec dir LI area 1958-83; human relations consultant 1984-; Adelphi Univ, co-dir workshops in human relations & police community relations 1962-81; private practice, human relations consultant. **ORGANIZATIONS:** Bd of trustees, Franklin General Hospital 1975-; mgmt comm div for professional leadership Lutheran Church in Amer 1983-; bd dirs MPCA Sr Citzens Holding Corp 1983-; bd dirs Lutheran Theological Seminary, Philadelphia 1980-; bd dirs Parkhurst Civic Assn 1982-; life mem NAACP; bd dirs Queens Fed of Churches 1982-; chairperson Christian Educ, New Hope Lutheran Church 1976-83; chair transition team Metro NY Synod/Evangelical Lutheran Church in Amer. **HONORS/ACHIEVEMENTS:** Certificate Amer Acad for Professional Law Enforcement, 1974; Woman of the year, Zeta Phi Beta 1975; special tribute Queens Interfaith Clergy Council 1979; leadrship citation Queens & Hempstead 1983; Distinguished Citizen Springfield Gardens Sr Citizens 1985. **HOME ADDRESS:** 2232 Leighton Rd, Elmont, NY 11003.

CHRISTIAN, ALMERIC L.
Retired chief judge. **PERSONAL:** Born Nov 23, 1919, St Croix, Virgin Islands of the United States;son of Adam E Christian (deceased) and Elena L Davis Christian; married Shirley C Frorup; children: Donna Marie, Adam Gregory, Rebecca Therese. **EDUCATION:** Columbia U, AB 1942, LLB 1947. **CAREER:** Chief judge 1970; Dist Ct VI, judge 1969; VI, US atty 1962-69; US Ct of Appeals 3 circuit; Supreme Ct; Pvt Pract, 1947-62. **ORGANIZATIONS:** Mem bd Of visitors of Columbia Univ Sch of Law; mem VI Bar Assn; mem Jr & Sr Warden All Saints Episcopal Ch 1966-67; Dist Committeeman; BSA; Missionary Diocese VI; gen chmn Diocesan Fund Dr; Commn propose Amendments 1936 Organic Act Testiomonial St Lukes Anglican Ch 19 74; hon VI Bar Assn 1968. **MILITARY SERVICE:** 1st lt 1942-54. **HOME ADDRESS:** 19-0 Solberg Box 7157, St Thomas, Virgin Islands of the United States 00801.

CHRISTIAN, CORA LEETHEL
Physician. **PERSONAL:** Born Sep 11, 1947, St Thomas, Virgin Islands of the United States;married Simon B Jones-Hendrikson; children: Marcus Benjamin, Nesha Rosita. **EDUCATION:** Marquette Univ Milwaukee WICS, BS 1967; Jefferson Med Coll Phila, PA, Medical Dr 1971; Johns Hopkins Univ Baltimore, MD, M Pub Hlth 1975. **CAREER:** Howard Univ Family Practice, admin chief resident 1973-74, instr 1974-75; Ingeborg Nesbitt Clinic Dept of Hlth, physician in charge 1975-77; VI Med Inst, exec dir/med dir 1977-; VI Dept of Hlth, asst commr 1977-81, asst commr for ambulatory care serv 1981-87; asst commr prevention, health promotion & protection 1987-. **ORGANIZATIONS:** Dir of family planning VI Dept of Hlth 1979-, proj dir Frederiksted Hlth Ctr 1978-80, act dir MCH 1982-, chief staff 1983; delegate Am Pub Hlth Assn; mem League of Women Voters VI 1979; pres Charles Harwood Mem Hosp Med Staff 1978-79, vice pres 1977-78; sec VI Med Soc 1976-77, treas 1980-81 & 1983-84,pres 1985-; pres Am Acad Family Pract 1978-. **HONORS/ACHIEVEMENTS:** Wilmont Blyden Scholarship VI 1963; John Hay Whiney Fellowship John Hay Whiney Found 1969; Nat Urban Coalition Fellowship National Urban Coalition Found 1974. **HOME ADDRESS:** PO Box 1338, Frederiksted, St Croix, Virgin Islands of the United States 00841. **BUSINESS ADDRESS:** Assistant Commissioner, VI Dept of Health, 6 & 7 Diamond Ruby, Christiansted, St Croix, Virgin Islands of the United States 00820.

CHRISTIAN, DOLLY LEWIS
Business executive. **PERSONAL:** Born in New York, NY; daughter of Daniel Lewis and Adeline Walton Lewis; divorced. **EDUCATION:** Manhattan Comm Coll. **CAREER:** The Sperry & Hutchison Co, dir civic affairs, personnel mgr, supvr, special project & records, employment specialist; IBM Corp, program mgr affirmative action program. **ORGANIZATIONS:** Chmn bd NY Urban League 1977-85; Panel of Arbitrators Amer Arbitration Assn 1978; bd mem Coalition Of 100 Black Women 1979; past vice pres The Edges Group Inc; mem Council of Concerned Black Exec; Natl Urban Affairs Council Office; mem Mngmt Assistance Comm Greater NY Fund; commissioner, New York City, Commission on Human Rights, 1987-90. **HONORS/ACHIEVEMENTS:** Scroll of Honor Natl Council of Negro Business & Professional Women's Clubs; Community Serv Award; Ambudswoman Award; Youth Salute to Black Corp Exec Awd. Natl Youth Movement; Corp Recp of Mary McCleod Bethune Awd; Natl Council of Negro Women; Spec Corp Recognition Award; Metro Council of Brances; NAACP; Woman Achiever, YWCA of NY; Black Achiever, Harlem YMCA. **BUSINESS ADDRESS:** Program Manager, IBM Corporation, 2000 Purchase St, Purchase, NY 10577.

CHRISTIAN, GAIL P.
Broadcast news director. **PERSONAL:** Born Feb 20, 1940, Los Angeles, CA; children: Sunday Barrett. **EDUCATION:** Pepperdine Univ, attended 1957-59; UCLA, attended 1959-60. **CAREER:** NBC News, correspondent 1975-77; KCET (Los Angeles), news dir 1977-79; Chronicle Broadcasting, Washington corres 1979-81; Public Broadcasting Serv, dir of news 1981-. **ORGANIZATIONS:** Mem Delta Sigma Theta. **HONORS/ACHIEVEMENTS:** (3) Emmys; (1) Columbia Dupont. **BUSINESS ADDRESS:** Dir of News, Public Broadcasting Service, 1320 Braddock Place, Alexandria, VA 22314.

CHRISTIAN, GERALDINE ASHLEY MCCONNELL
Pharmacist. **PERSONAL:** Born May 01, 1929, Denver, CO; daughter of Frederick Douglas Ashley and Mary Owens Ashley; widowed; children: Conrad P McConnell. **EDUCATION:** Univ of Denver, 1946-47; Univ of CO, BS 1950. **CAREER:** Rocky Mountain Arsenal Dept Army Chem Corps, phrmst 1951-55; VA Outpatient Clinic, Portland OR, pharmacist 1957-68, 1973-78; Crestview Hospital, pharmacist manager, 1968-73; retired 1978. **ORGANIZATIONS:** Mem, bd of dir, Urban League of Portland, 1974-78; first female pres, bd of State of Oregon; Portland Chapter, The Links Inc, 1965; Jacks & Jill of Amer, 1957-67; Alpha Kappa Alpha Sorority, 1947-; School Board Advisory Committee, 1973-75; Young Audiences Board, 1966-68; appointed by Governer to Amer Revolution Bicentennial Commission, 1974-77; appointed by Governer to Oregon Commission on Black Affairs, 1980-83. **HONORS/ACHIEVEMENTS:** Recipient Alpha Kappa Alpha Award 1966; named woman of year, Portland Fedn Women's Orgns; Superior Performance Award; numerous awards, certificates. **BUSINESS ADDRESS:** 426 SW Stark St, Portland, OR 97204.

CHRISTIAN, JERALD CRONIS
Business executive. **PERSONAL:** Born Apr 22, 1933, Marietta, GA; divorced; children: Lorraine. **EDUCATION:** OH Univ, BSC 1960; IN Univ, MSW 1965. **CAREER:** Indianapolis Public School System; State of IN Dept of Corrections, dir adult basic educ prog. **ORGANIZATIONS:** Exec dir CASA; mem NAACP, Urban League, Natl Black Polit Caucus, Mid-town Comm Mental Health Ctr, Better Sch Comm; mem Natl Assn Crime & Delinq; mem Natl Fedn Settlements; mem Natl Assn Comm Devel; mem Natl Assn Social Workers & Black Social Workers. **MILITARY SERVICE:** USN petty ofce 2nd class 1952-56.

CHRISTIAN, MAE ARMSTER
Educator. **PERSONAL:** Born Dec 22, 1934, Thomasville, GA; divorced; children: George C Armster, Earle A Armster. **EDUCATION:** NY Univ, BS 1963; Bank State Coll of Ed NYC, MS 1968; Univ of GA Athens, Doctorate 1977. **CAREER:** NY Univ Rehabilitation Center Child Div, asst to supvr 1959-63; Thomasville City Schools, Thomasville GA, teacher 1963-68; Univ of GA, Atlanta Public Schools, instructor early childhood educ 1968-71; GA State Univ, Univ of GA, Early Childhood Educ Inst, dir 1970-73; US Office of Educ & Govt VI Head Start School System, consultant 1971-73; Univ of GA, Atlanta Public Schools, assoc dir, teacher corps 1971-73; Multicultural Inst Univ of NE, Prairie View Coll, consultant 1975-76; Governors Task Force, Office of the Governor, State of GA, consultant 1975-76; Atlanta Public Schools Dept Gen Educ, dir 1980; Univ of GA, Atlanta Teachers Corp, dir 1973-. **ORGANIZATIONS:** Pres GA Assoc on Young Children 1976-77; mem, com chmn Delta Sigma Theta Sor Atlanta Alumnae Chap 1977-; governing bd mem Natl Assoc Ed of Young Children 1979-83; adv bd ASCN 1984; mem NAACP, AAUP, Phi Delta Kappa, ACEI, GAYC. **HONORS/ACHIEVEMENTS:** Ed Scholarships NY Univ & Bank St Coll 1960-63, 1967-68; NDEA Fellow Univ of GA 1965; Ford Found Leadership Fellow Ford Found 1967-68; Bronze Woman of the Year City of Atlanta 1976; Two citations Outstanding Ed Achievement Atlanta Const 1976-79. **BUSINESS ADDRESS:** Dir, Univ of Georgia, Atlanta Teacher Corps, 2930 Forrest Hill Dr SW # 205, Atlanta, GA 30315.

CHRISTIAN, SPENCER
Weatherman, co-host, and interviewer. **PERSONAL:** Born in Charles City, VA; married Diane; children: Jessica, Jason. **CAREER:** Reporter for a television station in Richmond, VA, 1971, weatherman, 1972-75; weatherman in Baltimore, MD, 1975-77; WABC-TV, New York, weatherman, 1977-86, weatherman, co-host, and interviewer on Good Morning America, 1986-. **BUSINESS ADDRESS:** Good Morning America, ABC-TV, 1330 Sixth Ave, New York, NY 10019. *

CHRISTIAN, THERESA
Educator. **PERSONAL:** Born Feb 10, 1917, Philadelphia, PA. **EDUCATION:** Freedmen's Hosp Sch Of Nursing, Diploma; Loyola U, BS; Univ Of Toronto, Cert; Univ of Chicago, MS u of mN, cert. **CAREER:** Provident Hospital School of Nursing, supvr instructor 1939-45; Univ of Chicago Clinics, 1945-47; Univ of KS, supvr asst & prof 1947-52; Cornell Univ, instructor, supvr 1952-58; Villanova Univ, assoc prof. **ORGANIZATIONS:** Mem Acad Policy Com & Admissions & Promotions Com Villanova U; treas Am Assn ofUniv Profs; Am Council of Churches; Am Nurses Assn; Black Conf on Higher Education; pres Beta Chap Chi Eta Phi; bd mgrs Ellen Cushing Jr Coll; Freedmans Hosp Alumni Assn; Nat League for Nursing; PA Nurses' Assn; SigmaTheta Tau;Univ of Chicago Alumni; Women's League of Voters; Womens Missionary Soc; bd of dir Philadelphia Nat League of Nursing; mem Nat L League for Nursing Comm; rep Am Bapt Women. **HONORS/ACHIEVEMENTS:** Recipient Citation for Citizenship Three Chaplains Philadelphia 1969; grant Am Inst of Pakistan Studies 1975; grant Rockefeller Found 1941; author of articles for professional publ listed Who's Who of Am Women 1977-78. **BUSINESS ADDRESS:** Associate Professor, VillanovaUniv, College of Nursing, Villanova, PA 19085.

CHRISTMAS, ROBERT H.
Executive director. **PERSONAL:** Born May 09, 1941, Aurora, IL. **EDUCATION:** Univ of Ill, BA 1968; Univ of Chicago, MBA 1970. **CAREER:** Sydenham Hosp NYC, exec dir 1974; Univ Of CA, asst hosp admin 1970-74; Augustana Hosp Chicago, med tech 1965-70; St Bernard Hosp Chgo, med tech 1960-65; St Joseph Hosp Aurora, 1955-60. **ORGANIZA-**

TIONS: Mem Nat Assn & Health Serv Exec. **BUSINESS ADDRESS:** 565 Manhattan Ave, New York, NY 10027.

CHRISTOPHER, JOHN A.
Microbiologist, immunologist. **PERSONAL:** Born Aug 19, 1941, Shreveport, LA. **EDUCATION:** Bishop Coll, BS 1964; Baylor U, MS 1967; IA State U, PhD 1971; TX S U, NIH Undergrad Research Fellow 1963. **CAREER:** Univ TX SW Med Sch, research tech 1964-65; Inst Of Baylor Univ, grad research fellow 1965-67; IA State U, grad research/tchr asst 1967- 71;Univ MN Med Sch, postdoctoral research fellow 1971-73; SoUniv Mem Soc for Microbiology, prof dept chm. **ORGANIZATIONS:** Am Assn For The Advancement of Sci; Soc of Sigma Xi; So Cntrl Br Am Soc for Microbiology; mem YWCA; NAACP; Community Cncl Inc; Natl Fnd March of Dimes. **BUSINESS ADDRESS:** So Univ, 3050 Cooper Rd, Shreveport, LA 71107.

CHUBB, LOUISE B.
Business executive. **PERSONAL:** Born Jun 15, 1927, Bronwood, GA; married Edward; children: Mrs Charles l Mc Coy. **EDUCATION:** Ft Vly State Coll, BS 1957; Ga State Univ, MS 1975; Smith Coll Grad Sc Hl Univ TN; GA State Univ. **CAREER:** GA School for the Deaf, retired English dept chairperson; Success, Inc, sales dir. **ORGANIZATIONS:** Community Youth Worker; mem NEA; CAID; GA Assn Edn; GA Educ Hearing Impaired; United Meth Ch; Minority Bus Assn; Delta Sigma Theta; Natl Council NegroWomen. **HONORS/ACHIEVEMENTS:** Sr class pres & miss summer sch Ft Vly State Coll 1957; tchr yr GSD 1963; outstanding state serv 1960, 65, 70, 75; Personalities S. **BUSINESS ADDRESS:** Sales Dir, Success, Inc, 1185 Chubb Rd, SW, Cave Springs, GA 30124.

CHUNN, JAY CARRINGTON, II
Educator, researcher. **PERSONAL:** Born Dec 26, 1938, Atlanta, GA; son of Jay Carrington Chunn Sr and Carrie Reid Morgan; married Brenda, Oct 18, 1987; children: Tracy, Jay III, Lauren Ruth. **EDUCATION:** Ohio Univ, BS 1957, BA 1961; Case Western Reserve Univ, MS 1965; Univ of MD, PhD 1978. **CAREER:** Community Coordinated Child Care, staff coordinator 1970; Council for Economic Opportunity in Greater Cleveland, child devel coordinator 1970; Natl Child Devel Day Care and Child Develop of Amer, pres 1970-71; Natl Child Devel and Day Care Consultants, president 1971-73; Howard Univ, prof 1972-74, dean of social work 1974-84; Medgar Evers Coll, president 1984-. **ORGANIZATIONS:** Natl pres Natl Assoc of Black Social Workers CA 1974-76, re-elected in Baltimore, MD for term ending in 1978; chairman 100 Black Men Intl Affairs Comm 1985-; mem 100 Black Men, Inc 1986-; mem Governor's Adv Comm for Black Affairs 1986. **HONORS/ACHIEVEMENTS:** Author "The Black Aged and Social Policy" in Aging 1978, "Mental Health & People of Color, Curriculum Development and Change," Univ Press 1983; "Stress Management and the Black Female in Corporate Environment," 1983. **MILITARY SERVICE:** Marine Reserves 6 months. **BUSINESS ADDRESS:** Director/Professor of Research & Development, Hunter College, 425 E 25th St, New York, NY 10010.

CHURCH, ROBERT T., SR.
Retired city councilman & county agricultural agent. **PERSONAL:** Born Sep 26, 1909, Athens, GA; son of Arthur Church and Pearl Billups Church; married Ruby Summers, Jun 26, 1938; children: Robert T Jr, Ruby A. **EDUCATION:** Hampton Inst, BS Agr 1934; Tuskegee Inst, MS Agr Educ 1958. **CAREER:** Washington GA Bd of Educ, asst principal & vocational agricultural teacher, 1934-36; Millen GA Bd of Educ, principal & voc agr teacher, 1936-38; Jenkins Co, co agent, 1938-46; Clarke Co, co agt 1946-48; Peach Co Ft Valley, co agt 1948-69; Ft Valley, GA, city councilman 1974-82 (retired); farmer, 1969-86; Church's Enterprises, Mgr, 1969-89. **ORGANIZATIONS:** Sponsored 4H winner of local/state & natl contest; keeper of fin Lambda Phi Chap Omega Psi Phi; mem Ft Valley City Council; chmn bd dir Div of Peach Co Family & Child Svcs; mem Deacon Bd Trinity Bapt Ch; Epsilon Sigma Phi 1968; Grammatues Beta Chi Boule 1984; appointed to Peach Cty Jurors Commission, 1986; Pres, Central GA Chapter of Hampton Univ Alumni Assn, 1985-; President, Tabor Hts Community Club, 1986-. **HONORS/ACHIEVEMENTS:** Omega Man of the Year Awd 1968; Plaques for Distinguished Serv GA Agr Ext Serv 1969; Peach Co Bd of Commrs 1969; Silver Serv Farmers of Peach Co 1970; Omega Citizen of the Year Award 1975; Man of the Year Award Trinity Bapt Ch 1975; Personalities of the South Award 1976-77; Public Serv Awd 1980; Houston Stallworth Awd for Outstanding Leadership from Citizens Ed Commiss 1982; Southeastern Region Natl Hampton Alumni Assoc Inc Awd for Outstanding Unselfish & Dedicated Serv 1986; Certificate of Appreciation for Outstanding & Dedicated Serv, Peach Co Div of Family & Children Serv, 1988; Fifty Year Award, Omega Psi Phi Fraternity, 1988. **HOME ADDRESS:** 901 S Carver Dr, Fort Valley, GA 31030.

CHURCHWELL, CAESAR ALFRED
Dentist. **PERSONAL:** Born Nov 26, 1932, Newton, GA; married Ruth; children: Caesar Jr, Gabrielle, Eric. **EDUCATION:** Mt Union Coll, BS 1956; Howard Univ Coll Dentistry, DDS 1967. **CAREER:** Self-Employed, dntst. **ORGANIZATIONS:** Mem ADA; SFDS; CDS; Western Peridontal Soc; SF Dental Fnd 1975; SF Dental Forum; Acad Gen Dentistry; No Chap Med; Dental & Pharm Assn; past pres NCNDA 1974; mem Bicentennial Com So SF 1975-76; Co San Mateo 1975-76; mem NAACP; personnel com mem NAACP Urban League Bd Dir 1971-72; adv bd Fulcrum Saving & Loan 1973; mem Black Ldrsp Forum; Men of Tomorrow; Black Unity Cnsl; past pres W Twin Peaks Lions Club 1973; actvty chm BSA 1974. **MILITARY SERVICE:** AUS pvt 1955-56. **BUSINESS ADDRESS:** 933 Geneva Ave, San Francisco, CA 94112.

CHURCHWELL, CHARLES DARRETT
Administrator. **PERSONAL:** Born Nov 07, 1926, Dunnellon, FL; married Yvonne; children: Linda, Cynthia. **EDUCATION:** Morehouse Coll, Math BS 1952; Atlanta U, MS Library Sci; Atlanta U; Univ IL, Library Sci 1966; City Coll; Hunter Coll; NY U. **CAREER:** Prairie View A&M Coll, library science instructor 1953-58; NY Public Library, discuss ion leader on great books 1960-61; Miami Univ, Oxford OH, dir of libraries 1969-72, chmn adv task force on acad priorities 1971-72, assoc provost for academic serv 1972-77; Brown Univ, librarian 1974-78; Washington Univ, St Louis, dean of library services. **ORGANIZATIONS:** Life mem Am Library 1960-61; mem Am Assn Of Higher Edn; life mem NAACP Office. **HONORS/ACHIEVEMENTS:** Auther of "A History Of Education For Librarianship". **BUSINESS ADDRESS:** BrownUniv, Library, Providence, RI 02912.

CISSOKO, ALIOUNE BADARA
Educational administrator. **PERSONAL:** Born Jun 15, 1952, Kolda Casamance, Senegal;children: Moussa Balla, Fatou. **EDUCATION:** Univ Dakar Inst Arts, BA 1975; RI Schl Design, MFA 1979; Univ RI, Arts Mgmt Cert 1982; Northeastern Univ, MA 1984, PhD candidate; certified case manager. **CAREER:** Intl House RI, prog asst 1978-80; Soc Cons, arts consult 1979-; Amer Sociological Assc, mem 1983-; Amer Anthropological Assc, mem 1983-; Northern RI Community Menthal Health Center Psychiatric Counselor Crisis Beds, psychosocial counselor & therapist; Southeastern MA Univ, publ rel prof of arts 1985-. **ORGANIZATIONS:** Fine artist Performing Arts RI 1977-; folk artist artist in educ RI State Council on Arts 1980-; listed Talent Bank NEA Wash DC 1983-; mem RI Black Heritage Soc 1979-, Intl House of RI 1979-; mem Natl Council on Creative Educ Therapy; mem & co-founder Black Artists of RI. **HONORS/ACHIEVEMENTS:** Citation State of RI and Providence Plantations 1984; fndr of Dougouto Ngnagnya African Drums and Dance Ensemble 1982-; RI State Council Awd on Creative Educ Therapy. **HOME ADDRESS:** 43 Doyle Ave, 2nd Rear, Providence, RI 02906. **BUSINESS ADDRESS:** PO Box 3227, Providence, RI 02906.

CLACK, DORIS H.
Educator. **PERSONAL:** Born Mar 24, 1928, Wakulla, FL; married Harold Lee Clack; children: Harold Levi, Herek Lerron. **EDUCATION:** FL A&M Univ, AB 1949; attended Univ of MI 1956; Univ of Pgh, PhD 1973; Univ of Toronto, certificate 1981. **CAREER:** Shadesville HS, teacher 1952-54; FL A&M Univ, librarian 1955-68; Univ of Pgh, lecturer 1969-70; Univ of IA, vstg prof 1978-80 summers; Library of Congress, cataloger 1984; Univ of Maiduquri Nigeria, vstg prof 1987-88; FL State Univ Sch of Lib & Info Studies, prof 1973-. **ORGANIZATIONS:** Mem Amer Lib Assn; chairperson ALA/RTSD Council of Regional Groups; mem ALA Rsch Comm RTSD/CCS CC,DA; Frontiers Intl Aux NAACP; mem Bethel BaptistCh; chair ALA/RTSD Cataloging & Classification Section; councillor SELA. **HONORS/ACHIEVEMENTS:** Title II Fellowship Univ of Pgh 1970-73; Who's Who 1979; Disting Alumni Awd Univ of MI 1979; Beta Phi Mu Hon Frat. **BUSINESS ADDRESS:** Professor, FL StateUniv, Sch of Library & Info Studies, Tallahassee, FL 32306.

CLACK, FLOYD
Educator. **PERSONAL:** Born Dec 21, 1940, Houston, TX; married Brenda J Jones; children: Monica Michelle, Michael Christopher Floyd, Mia Clarissa Brendan. **EDUCATION:** TX So Univ, BS 1965; TX So Univ School of Law, 1966; Eastern MI Univ, MA 1974. **CAREER:** McCoy Job Corps Ctr Sparta WI, teacher social studies 1967-68; Flint Bd of Educ, teacher social studies 1968-; House of Representatives, state rep 1982-. **ORGANIZATIONS:** Mem United Teachers of Flint 1968-; del rep MI Educ Assoc 1975; charter vice pres Flint Inner City Lions Club 1974-76; pres Flint Br NAACP; mem, rep NEA 1978; city council Flint MI 1979-; elected state rep 80th Dist MI 1982, relected state rep 1984; mem Kappa Alpha Psi, Jack & Jill Inc; initiator Mott Found Appreciation Comm; del Natl Conf on Correction Policy; panelist The Speaker's Conf on Crime Prevention & Inst for Training School Teams for the Prevention of Child Abuse & Neglect. **HONORS/ACHIEVEMENTS:** Outstanding Serv Awd Flint Br NAACP 1979; Man of the Year Flint Inner City Lions Club 1980; Supportive Serv Awd Metro C of C; Toll Fellowship Award, Council of State Governments 1987; Key to City of Flint. **BUSINESS ADDRESS:** State Representative, House of Representatives, State Capitol, Lansing, MI 48909.

CLAIBORNE, EARL RAMSEY
Physician. **PERSONAL:** Born Aug 16, 1921, Charleston, SC; married Marie; children: 2 Children. **EDUCATION:** Avery Inst, 1939; Talladega Coll, AB 1943; Howard Univ Sch Med, 1947; Stanford U, MD 1953-54. **CAREER:** Pvt Prac, drmtlgst 1959-; Parks AFB, chf drmtlgy 1954-58, resd 1951-54; Flight Surgeon Sch, stdnt 1949; Talladega Coll, sch physician 1948-49; Homer G Phillips Hosp, intern 1947-48. **ORGANIZATIONS:** Mem Am Coll Nursing Home Adminstr; consult HEW-Long Term Care Br; adminstr WA Nursing Home; bd dir LA City Nursing Home Assn; mem NAACP Urban League; Common Cause; United Nations Assn; Pacific Derm Assn; Am Acad Dermatology; tchr Avery Inst; coach SC State, City, & Nat Negro HS Champions Bsktbl. **HONORS/ACHIEVEMENTS:** Man month Watts Hlth Clinic. **MILITARY SERVICE:** USAF lt col 1949-58. **BUSINESS ADDRESS:** Dermatologist, A Medical Corporation, 3756 Santa Rosalia Drive, Ste 602, Los Angeles, CA 90008.

CLAIBORNE, LLOYD R.
Government official. **PERSONAL:** Born Feb 15, 1936, Newport News, VA; son of John Claiborne and Alma E Dennis; married Dorma J Robinson; children: Renee, Cheryl, Denise, Lloyd II. **EDUCATION:** City Coll of NY, BS 1958. **CAREER:** FDA NY, food & drug insp 1958-67, suprv food & drug insp 1967; DHEW/PHS/FDA Bureau of Compliance Washington, prog analyst FDA exec devel prog 1968-71; DHEW/PHS/FDA Kansas City, dep & reg food & drug dir 1971-72; DHEW/PHS/FDA, reg food & drug dir 1972-. **ORGANIZATIONS:** Mem NAACP 1971-; mem Assoc of Food & Drug Ofcls 1971-; chmn DHEW/PHS/FDA Field Med Device Adv Comm 1978-83; chmn DHEW/PHS/FDA Mid-Level Career Dev Prog Comm 1978-84. **HONORS/ACHIEVEMENTS:** Commendable Service Award, US Food & Drug Admin 1985; Commissioner's Special Citation, US Food & Drug Admin 1985. **BUSINESS ADDRESS:** Regional Food & Drug Dir, DHEW/PHS/FDA, 50 United Nations Plaza, San Francisco, CA 94102.

CLAIBORNE, VERNAL
Business executive. **PERSONAL:** Born Feb 01, 1946, Chicago, IL; married Sandra. **EDUCATION:** Grambling Coll, BS; Success Motivation Inst Inc, Cert; SBA, Cert; Am Inst of Banking; Univ of CA, MBA Cand. **CAREER:** Bank of Finance, pres 1977-, vice pres 1976-77; Imperial Bank, asst vice pres 1975; Home Bank, asst vp, mgr 1971-75; So CA 1st Nat Bank, asst mgr 1971. **ORGANIZATIONS:** Dir Compton Comm Devel Corp; dir Compton Rotary Club; bd of dir Jammes T Heard Inc; Mcdonalds; v chmn WFPC; mem Macedonia Bapt Ch; mem Epslon Kappa Frat; finan chmn BSA. **HONORS/ACHIEVEMENTS:** Ftbl schlrshp Grambling Coll 4 yrs; Deans List 3 times. **BUSINESS ADDRESS:** 2651 S Western Ave, Los Angeles, CA 90018.

CLAIR, AREATHA G. (NEE ANDERSON)
Educator. **PERSONAL:** Born Sep 05, 1931, Jacksonville, FL; married Alford; children: Andre, Armand. **EDUCATION:** FL A&M Univ, BS 1953; Chicago Teachers Coll, attended; CO Coll, attended; Univ of CO Springs, Grad Studies; Western State Coll, Type D Admin Cert, MA. **CAREER:** Chicago Public School, teacher 1962-65; CO Springs Teacher Assoc, prof negotiator 1970-72; Zebulon Pike Elementary School, principal 1977-78; Garfield Elementary School, principal 1978-80; Mark Twain & US Grant Schools, elem asst principal; CO

Springs School Dist 11, teacher; Taylor Elementary School, principal 1980-. **ORGANIZATIONS:** Pres CO Springs Alumnae Delta Sigma Theta; past comm Woman Dem Party CO Springs; del Delta's Natl Conv Atlanta 1972, CO Dem State Conv Denver 1974; writer for Drug Curr 1970; team leader CO Springs School Dist 11, Univ of So CO Teacher Corps Proj 1975; bd mem UCCS Alumni Assoc. **BUSINESS ADDRESS:** Principal, Taylor Elementary School, 900 E Buena Ventura St, Colorado Springs, CO 80907.

CLANAGAN, MAZZETTA PRICE
Social service. **PERSONAL:** Born Oct 14, 1920, Rankin, PA; married Robert A Clanagan (deceased); children: Robin Clanagan Moore. **EDUCATION:** Keller Schl Dressmaking & Design, Certf Grad 1943; Grad Schl of Pblc & Intrntl Affairs Univ of Pgh, Master Pblc Admn 1971, Doctoral Candidate Deferred1975; Regional Prsnl Serv Cntr of Southwestern PA, Cert Prsnl Law 1977. **CAREER:** Bureau of Emplymnt Security PA, manpower speclst emplymnt intrviewer emplyr reltns rep 1960-70; Univ of Pittsburgh, admsns ofcr 1971-74; Allegheny Cnty Gov't Pittsburgh PA, EEO spclst & contract compliance ofcr 1974-78; Claybar Intrntl, Inc Pittsburgh, PA Claybar Constrctn & Contrctrs Equip Corp, vice pres 1978-80; Allegheny Cnty Govt, soc serv cordinator. **ORGANIZATIONS:** Mgmt cnsltnt self-emplyd penal reform consltnt & coal broker Mazzetta Price Clanagan Co Pittsburgh, PA 1971-; co-owner-partnrshp P&M Assc Pgh PA 1978-80; cnsltnt-filming of documentary KDKA TV Channel 2 1973; Councilwoman Borough of Rankin, Rankin, PA 1976-84; mem Natl Black Caucus of Local Elected Pblc Offcls 1976-84; oral examiner PA State Civil Serv Comm 1972-; guest lecturer Univ, of Pittsburgh; pblc spkr Churches Univ Etc. **HONORS/ACHIEVEMENTS:** Jessie Smith Noyes Foundation & Carnegie Foundation flwship Grad Schl of Intrntl Affairs Univ of Pittsburgh 1969-71; author Article "Forgotten Inmates-Women" Commission for Racial Justice Reprtr. **HOME ADDRESS:** 300 Third St Apt #4, Rankin, PA 15104.

CLANCY, MAGALENE ALDOSHIA
Elected official. **PERSONAL:** Born Jan 02, 1938, Midway, GA; children: Eric G, Delia A. **EDUCATION:** Johnson C Smith Univ, 1957-59. **CAREER:** Liberty Elem School, sub teacher 1962-65; Liberty Co, oeo worker 1966-68; Ft Stewart GA, nurses asst 1968-. **ORGANIZATIONS:** Usher bd, chmn youth group, Midway 1st Presbyterian Church. **HONORS/ACHIEVEMENTS:** Outstanding Awd Ft Stewart USAH 1978; 15 Yrs Cert Ft Stewart USAH 1983. **HOME ADDRESS:** PO Box 166, Midway, GA 31320.

CLANTON, EARL SPENCER, III
Association executive. **PERSONAL:** Born Sep 22, 1919, Alliance, OH; divorced; children: Doris. **EDUCATION:** Kent State U, AB 1950; Kent State U, MA 1972. **CAREER:** Hampton Inst dir of public relations 1976-80; kappa alpha psi frat inc, asst exec sec 1974-76; TN state u, 1974; u relations fisk u, dir 1972-74; Kent State U, instr 1970-72; Sports Inf Dir TN State U, dir of publications 1952-70; Color Mag Charleston, asso editor 1949-52; freelance writing 1953-;Jet & Ebony Mags, wrtr & photo; Nashville Banner & Nashville Tennessean. **ORGANIZATIONS:** Interntl Sports Reporting; Sports Illus Mag Russian Winter Festival 1972; orgnr News Media Workshop Prgm 1970; mem Football Writer's Assn of Am; Coll Sports Inf Dir Assn; Kent State Univ Jour Alumni Assn; Eastman House Found; Sigma Delta Chi Jour Soc; Pub Relations Soc of Am; life mem Kappa Alpha PsiFrat; Master Mason; Toastmasters Internat; Sorts Car Club of Am; Jaguar Clubs of N Am; Mem Chi Pi; mem Clark Meml Meth Ch; mem Traffic & Safety Commn 1971; Grand Jury 1968-69. **HONORS/ACHIEVEMENTS:** Editor "The Jour"; coll football cent award, coll sports inf dir cert 1969; coll sports publ of the year Atlanta's 100 Percent Wrong.Club 1956,59; bestsports game prgm coll sports inf dir assn 1959; hon mention sports inf publ Am Coll Pbu Relations Assn 1955; 2nd place Publicity Photography Am Coll Pub Raltions Assn 1955; 1st place Institutional Photography Am Coll Pub Relations Assn 1955. **MILITARY SERVICE:** AUS sgt 1943-45.

CLANTON, LEMUEL JACQUE
Physician. **PERSONAL:** Born Mar 11, 1931, New Orleans, LA; married Barbara Guy; children: Mark, Lynn, Justine, Lemuel J, Leslie. **EDUCATION:** Howard U, BS 1952; Meharry Med Coll, MD 1956. **CAREER:** Med Asso, physician. **ORGANIZATIONS:** Bd Certified Surgeon; Am Bd Of Surgery; mem AMA; mem Nat Med Assn; bd mem Lafon Home for Aged 1975. **BUSINESS ADDRESS:** 517 Newton, New Orleans, LA 70126.

CLANTON, RANDOLPH J.
Business executive. **PERSONAL:** Born Aug 24, 1944, Augusta, GA; children: Marcia Liana. **EDUCATION:** Central State Univ OH, BS 1966. **CAREER:** Cincinnati Opportunities Industrialization Cntr Inc, fiscal dir 1969-72; Proctor & Gamble Co, traffic dept analyst 1972-. **ORGANIZATIONS:** Mem Soc for Advancement of Mgmt 1963-66; volunteer accounting instr Progressive Assn of Economic Devel 1970; bd mem Millvale Non-Profit Daycare Corp 1973-75. **MILITARY SERVICE:** AUS 1st lt Finance Corp 1967-69.

CLARDY, WILLIAM J.
Manager. **PERSONAL:** Born May 01, 1935, Newalla, OK; married Patricia Ann Lomax; children: D Vincent, Terri Lynette, William Gerald. **EDUCATION:** OK St U, ass eng degree 1960; USN Comm Tech Class A Sch; Iowa St U, 1971-72. **CAREER:** Lennox Ind Inc Pacific Div, terr mgr htg & air cond equip, instr; LA Unified Sch Dist, instr; Lincoln Job Corp Ctr Northern Sys Co, sr instr htg & air cond; Cal-Poly Workshop, made presentation 1972; Annual Ed Con CARSES, made presentation May 1974; Utah Sheet Metal Con Assn, conducted workshop Aug 1971. **ORGANIZATIONS:** Bd dir Marshalltown Chap Jaycees; bd dir Marshalltown Chap Am Field Ser; bd dir YMCA Omaha; mem Marshalltown, IA Optimist Club Intl. **MILITARY SERVICE:** USN tech 3 class 1952-56. **BUSINESS ADDRESS:** 2041 S Saybrook Ave, Los Angeles, CA 90022.

CLARK, AMEERA H.
Retired principal, representative. **PERSONAL:** Born Sep 21, 1919, Kansas City, MO; married John E Clark. **EDUCATION:** Los Angeles Comm Coll, 1939; UCLA, 1949; E LA Jr Coll 1951; LA Bd Ed 1956. **CAREER:** Los Angeles Unified School Dist, principal 1969-retirement, Classified Emp Relation Council, representative 1970-. **ORGANIZATIONS:** Mem Beta Pi Sigma, New Frontier Dem Club, Wilfandel Club, NAACP LA Chapt, Merry-Go-Rounders; served on comm to obtain yes vote, removal restrictive clause prohib, negro membership AFL.

CLARK, ANDREW LEE
Administrator. **PERSONAL:** Born Nov 24, 1942, Atlanta, GA; married Sandra Elaine Green; children: Andrew L Jr (dec), Keisha La Shawn. **EDUCATION:** Attended TN State A&I Univ 1961. **CAREER:** Band leader 1958-63; Atlanta, police officer 1964; Lockheed Aircraft Corp, machine oper 1964-66, machinist apprentice 1967-69, machinist 1970; Western Elec Mfg, machinist 1971-77; Comm Workers of Amer, dir ethnic affairs hdqrs staff 1977-. **ORGANIZATIONS:** Mem Golden Heritage; life mem Million Dollar Club; mem ad-hoc labor com NAACP; mem operating com A Philip Randolph Inst; mem exec com DC Chap Coalition of Black Trade Unionists; mem Natl Urban League; mem Labor Council for Latin Amer Advancement; contribut mem Dem Natl Comm; mem Natl Dem Club; mem Amer Civil Liberties Union; mem So Poverty Law Ctr; mem Touchdown Club of Wash DC; mem Trans Africa; mem Natl Black Comm Coalition; mem Com on Polit Educ Quorum; mem Oper PUSH; mem Natl Low Income Housing Coalition; mem Smithsonian Assoc; mem Natl Bd Natl Coalition on Black Voter Participation Inc; mem Natl Bd of Dirs A Philip Randolph Inst. **HONORS/ACHIEVEMENTS:** Leadership Skills Awd AFL-CIO Labor Studies Ctr 1977; New Staff Training Awd Comm Workers of Amer 1978; Awd of Appreciation Postal Telegraph & Telephone 7thPan-African Seminar Mauritius Indian Ocean 1979; Awd of Appreciation Nat Black Comm Coalition 1980; Nelson Jack Edwards Awd Coalition of Black Trade Unionists 1980. **HOME ADDRESS:** 4505 Rena Rd #102, Forestville, MD 20746.

CLARK, AUGUSTA ALEXANDER
Attorney, elected official. **PERSONAL:** Born Mar 05, 1932, Uniontown, AL; married Leroy W Clark; children: Mark, Adrienne. **EDUCATION:** WV State Coll, FS Bus Admin (Cum Laude) 1954; Drexel Univ, MS Library Sci 1958; Temple Univ, JD 1976; Drexel Univ, Hon Doctorates Degree 1985. **CAREER:** Fed Defense Installations & Free Library of Phila, librarian 1958-66; Gen Elect Co RESD, market rsch analyst 1967-69; Auerbach Corp, consult 1970-71; Philadelphia Model Cities Prog, admin 1971-73; Gen Elect Co, affirm action requirement mgr 1973-75; City Council of Philadelphia, councilwoman-at-large, attny. **ORGANIZATIONS:** Bd of dir Friends of Free Library of Philadelphia, New Horizons Rsch Inst, Horizon House, Shalom Inc, North Central Branch YWCA, Organization for Women & Girls Offenders, PILCPO; bd of trustees Philadelphia Coll of Arts; advisory bd PA Women's Campaign Fund; law comm Amer Baptist Churches USA Inc; founder &co-chair Bright Hope Survival Prog; sponsor The Month of the Woman 1983; delegate Natl Women's Conf Houston; co-chair PA Intl Women's Year Coord Comm; mem Barristers, PA Bar Assoc, Alpha Kappa Alpha Sor, West of Broad St Coalition, WV State Alumni, Steering Comm for Chessfest, Black Women's Network; organizer Jefferson Manor Tenant Assoc; counsel Minority Contractors Advisory Comm. **HONORS/ACHIEVEMENTS:** Oustanding Serv in the Community Nu Sigma Natl Sor 1980; Alumnus of the Year & Outstanding Citizen & Humanitarian WV State Coll Theta Chap of Theta 1981;Support to Delta Iota Chap Alpha Kappa Alpha Sor Inc 1983; Sponsored a number of Bills & Resolutions to assist in improving the quality of life. **BUSINESS ADDRESS:** Councilwoman-at-Large, City Council of Philadelphia, City Hall Room 580, Philadelphia, PA 19107.

CLARK, BENJAMIN F.
Dentist. **PERSONAL:** Born Sep 19, 1910, Charleston, WV; son of Mr & Mrs Benjamin F Clark Sr; married Alice Robinson. **EDUCATION:** WV State Coll, BS 1933; Howard Univ Sch of Dentistry, DDS 1944; Univ of MI Sch of Dentistry, Grad Work 1948. **CAREER:** WV gen practice, dentistry; Lakin State Hosp, dir dental serv. **ORGANIZATIONS:** Past pres Capital City Med Soc Bachelor Benedict Club; past post commander & exec bd mem Col Charles Young Post 57 of Amer Legion; mem exec, past state dept vice commander WV Dept of Amer Legion; past state vice pres Natl Dental Assn; mem Amer Assn of Hosp Dentists; dir Dental Prog of State Assn of IBPOE of World; mem NAACP; Omega Psi Phi Frat; Chi Delta Mu Med Frat; assoc mem Chicago Dental Soc; sec-treas WV Med Soc; vice pres Economic Comm Housing Opportunity; past treas and mem of trustee bd, First Baptist Church. **HONORS/ACHIEVEMENTS:** Recip Doctor of Yr Award WV Med Soc 1973. **MILITARY SERVICE:** AUS capt Dental Corps 1944-47.

CLARK, BERTHA SMITH
Educator. **PERSONAL:** Born Sep 26, 1943, Nashville, TN; married Phillip Hickman Clark; children: Phillipa Jayne, Margaret Ann, Sheryll Clark Nelson. **EDUCATION:** TN State Univ, BS (High Distinction) 1964; George Peabody Clg for Tchrs, MA 1965; Natl Inst of Mental Hlth, Pre Doctoral Fellow 1978-80; Vanderbilt Univ, PhD 1982. **CAREER:** Bill Wilkerson Hearing & Speech Center (BWHSC), head tchr OE #1 project 1965-70, speech pathologist 1965-78, 1980-; TN State Univ, supvr of clinical practicum 1969-78, 1980-; Mama Lere Parent Infant Home, Bill Wilkerson Hearing & Speech Center, parent-infant trainer 1982-86; Vanderbilt Univ, div of hearing and speech sciences. **ORGANIZATIONS:** Board of dir League for the Hearing Impaired 1973-, The Childrens House (A Montesson Preschool) 1984-, advsry Cmt Early Devel & Assistance Project Kennedy Cntr 1984-; co-chrprsn mem YWCA 1985; mem Delta Sigma Theta Sorority, Inc 1962-; admin comm, vice pres for educ TN Speech and Hearing Assoc 1985-87; chairperson Cochlear Implant Scholarship Comm; mem Compton Scholarship Comm Vanderbilt Univ 1985-; bd of dirs Peabody Alumni 1986-89. **HONORS/ACHIEVEMENTS:** Honors grad Haynes HS 1960, TN State Univ 1964; predoctoral flwshp Natl Inst of Mental Hlth 1978-80. **BUSINESS ADDRESS:** Assistant Professor, Vanderbilt Univ/TN StateUniv, VanderbiltUniv Sch of Med, Div of Hrg & Spch Scis, Nashville, TN 37235.

CLARK, BETTIE I.
Retired physician. **PERSONAL:** Born Feb 12, 1927, Mt Holly, NJ; daughter of Norman Norwood Graves and Viola Edna Stanley Graves; married Dr Ross J Clark (deceased); children: Ross James Jr, Patricia Leigh, Robyn Marie. **EDUCATION:** Morgan State Coll Baltimore, BS 1949; Howard Univ Coll of Med, MD 1954; Johns Hopkins Univ, School of Hygiene & Publ Health, MPH 1973. **CAREER:** Howard Univ Coll of Med, clinical instr dept of ped 1957-60; DC Govt Ambulatory Health Care Admin, pediatric med officer 1960-80; Coll of Med Howard Univ, asst clinical prof of ped 1966-80, retired. **ORGANIZATIONS:** Mem Amer Acad of Ped, DC Med Soc, Pan Amer Med Assoc, Amer Publ Health Assoc, Howard Univ Med Alumni Assoc; pres bd of dir Metro Lab Inc Wash DC 1974-78; sec, treas DC Chap Amer Acad of Ped 1976-79; bd of dir Columbia Hosp for Women Wash DC 1979-; cert in ped Amer Bd of Ped 1961; fellow Amer Acad of Ped 1962; apptd trustee The Holton-Arms School Bethesda MD 1982-.

CLARK, BRUCE
Professional football player. **PERSONAL:** Born Mar 31, 1956, New Castle, PA; married Sandra; children: Justin, Rachel Lauren. **EDUCATION:** Penn State Univ. **CAREER:**

Green Bay Packers, defensive end 1980-82; New Orleans Saints, defensive end 1982-. **ORGANIZATIONS:** Assists Amer Heart Assn with fund-raising and promotional projects. **HONORS/ACHIEVEMENTS:** Coll, Consensus All-America 1978-79; Lombardi Trophy winner 1978; finalist for Lombardi Trophy three yrs; Outland Trophy finalist 1978; started six games freshman season at LB; profl, voted to 1985 Pro Bowl; voted by teammates 1984 Most Valuable Defensive Player. **BUSINESS ADDRESS:** New Orleans Saints, 1500 Poydras St, New Orleans, LA 70112.

CLARK, CAESAR A. W.
Clergyman. **PERSONAL:** Born Dec 13, 1914, Shreveport, LA; married Carolyn Elaine Bunche, Apr 16, 1987; children: Caesar Jr. **EDUCATION:** Bishop Coll, BA, BTh, LLD, DD. **CAREER:** Good St Baptist Church Dallas, pastor; nationally known evangelist; National Baptist Convention USA Inc, vice pres at large; Baptist Missionary and Education Convention of Texas, pres. **ORGANIZATIONS:** Mem bd dir Nat Baptist Conventionnv; numerous other church & civic groups. **HONORS/ACHIEVEMENTS:** Recipient of numerous citations & awards. **BUSINESS ADDRESS:** 3110 Bonnie View Rd, Dallas, TX 75216.

CLARK, CHARLES WARFIELD
Physician. **PERSONAL:** Born Dec 06, 1917, Washington, DC; married Savanna Marie Vaughn. **EDUCATION:** Univ of MI, BS 1939; Howard Univ, MD 1944; internship Freedmen's Hospital 1944. **CAREER:** Sr attending urologist Howard Univ Hospital, Washington Hospital Center, Children's Natl Med Center Washington; Trinity Hospital, house physician 1944-46; Freedman's Hospital, chief resident urology 1952-53; Howard Univ School of Medicine, clinical instructor in Urology 1946-52, 1955-59, clinical asst prof of Urology 1960-. **ORGANIZATIONS:** Author of three publications; mem Mid-Atlantic Section of Amer Urologic Assn; mem Amer Assn of Clinical Urologists, Amer Urologic Assn, natl Med Assn, Medico-Chirurgical Soc of DC, Med Soc of DC, Amer Med Assn, Washington Urologic Soc, Soc Internationale d'Urologie; fellow Amer Coll of Surgeons; mem Sigma Pi Phi Fraternity Epsilon Boule; mem Amer Fertility Soc; mem Chi Delta Mu Fraternity, Friends of Kennedy Center, Mus of African Art, Pigskin Club of Washington, Smithsonian Assoc; mem Urban League, NAACP, YMCA; natl social dir Omega Psi Phi Frat; mem Plymouth Congregational Church. **MILITARY SERVICE:** AUS med corps capt 1953-55. **BUSINESS ADDRESS:** Clinical Asst Prof Urology, Howard Univ Sch of Medicine, 106 Irving St NW, Ste 406, Washington, DC 20010.

CLARK, CHRISTINE PHILPOT
Attorney. **PERSONAL:** Born Dec 27, 1937, Philadelphia; children: Chad, Kimani. **EDUCATION:** Bryn Mawr, AB 1960; Adelphia Bus Sch, 1960-61; Yale U, JD 1965. **CAREER:** Bryn Mawr Coll, consult dean, lectr 1969-72; Metro Applied Research Center, proj dir 1967-68; Atty, private prac 1971-73; CBS Inc, atty 1973-; Author numerous books mongraphs & articles; Nat Conf Black Lawyers, fundraiser. **ORGANIZATIONS:** Mem Council of Concerned Black Execs; bd consult Bryn Mawr Coll 1973-76; bd mem Legal Aid Soc. **HONORS/ACHIEVEMENTS:** Recipient of fairfax educ award 19760; outstanding young woman of am 1968; moir-cullis lecture fellow British-Am Assos London 1975. **BUSINESS ADDRESS:** CBS 51 W 52 St, New York, NY 10019.

CLARK, CLARENCE BENDENSON, JR.
Dentist. **PERSONAL:** Born Jun 15, 1943, Nashville, TN; married Jeana; children: Clarence III, Dominick. **EDUCATION:** Loyola Univ, BS 1965; Meharry Med Coll, DDS 1974. **CAREER:** Private practice, dentist. **ORGANIZATIONS:** Mem MS Dental Soc, N MS Med, Dental, Pharm Soc. **BUSINESS ADDRESS:** 1737 E Alexander, Greenville, MS 38701.

CLARK, CLAUDE LOCKHART
Artist, educator, businessman. **PERSONAL:** Born Mar 28, 1945, Philadelphia, PA. **EDUCATION:** CA Coll of Arts & Crafts, BA 1968; Univ of CA Berkeley, MA 1972. **CAREER:** House of Vai African Imports, owner 1977-; San Jose St Univ Afro-Am Studies Dept, instr crafts course 1974-; UC Berkeley Afro-Am Studies Dept, "Black artin the new world" 1974, 77; CA Coll of Arts & Crafts, instr 1970-; Coll of Alameda, instr 1971-72; Oakland HS, instr 1969-70; Univ of CA Berkeley, SOS upward bound prog; Craftsman, photography, painting, lithography, ceramics, jewelry, wood carving, murals,; numerous one man & group shows since 1962. **ORGANIZATIONS:** Mem, Smithsonian Inst 1980, World Print Council 1979; participant, 1st Natl African-Amer Crafts Conf & Jubilee Memphis 1979; mem, Music Publications of Amer 1947; Acts of art gallery NYC 1973; mem, Amer Federation of Arts 1976; catalogue exhibits Emanuel Walter & Atholl Mcbean Galleries San Francisco Art Inst 1976; Amistad II Afro-Amer art, Dept of Art, Fisk Univ, 1975-76; west coast 1974 the black image, eb crocker art gallery 1974-75; A third world painting/sculpture echibition San Francisco Museum of Art 1974; Tuesday Club Picture Rental Serv Sacramento 1972; catalogue ehibits Black Artist Huntsville AL 1979; Contemporary African-Am Crafts Exhibition Brooks Memorial Art Gallery Memphis 1979; mosaic exhibit Meml Union-Art Gallery UC Davis CA; freein' the spirit-the chin the black comm exhibit. **HONORS/ACHIEVEMENTS:** "The Complete Annotated Resource Guide to Black Am Art" 1978; included Numerous Private Collections 1971-; recipient 3rd prize Nat Ford Indus Arts Contest; 1st prize Oakland Art Museum's Exhibit for Public Schools; elected citizen of the day KABL Radio San Francisco; scholarship CA Coll of Arts & Crafts 1963. **BUSINESS ADDRESS:** Houst of Vai, PO Box 8172, Oakland, CA 94662.

CLARK, DAVE
Company executive. **PERSONAL:** Born Mar 06, 1913, Jackson, TN; children: William David. **EDUCATION:** Lane Coll, BSc 1934; Julliard School of Music, Special Class Music Appreciation 1939. **CAREER:** Duke-Peacock Records, dir of promotion 1954-71; Stax Records, natl promotion mgr 1971-76; TK Records, natl promotion mgr 1976-80; Malaco Records, vp-dir of black music 1980-. **ORGANIZATIONS:** Regional promotions Chess Records, 1947-51; Apollo Records, 1952-53; United Records, 1953-54; Columnist, Good Publications; mem Young Black Program Coalition, Black Music Assn, Natl Assn for Equal Opportunity in Higher Educ, Natl Black Media Coalition. **HONORS/ACHIEVEMENTS:** Achievers Awd Black Radio Exclusive, Jackson Music Assoc; BMI writer 50 songs published; Black Music Hall of Fame Chicago 1981; Citation Gov LA, TN, City ofHouston. **HOME ADDRESS:** 119 Somerset Dr, Jackson, MS 39206. **BUSINESS ADDRESS:** Vice President, Malaco Records, 3023 W Northside Dr, Jackson, MS 39206.

CLARK, DONALD LEWIS
Educator. **PERSONAL:** Born May 29, 1935, Philadelphia, PA; children: Dwayne, David. **EDUCATION:** Cheyney State Univ, BS Educ 1956; Glassboro State Univ, MA Spec Educ 1963; Fairleigh-Dickinson Univ, EdD Educ Leadership 1973. **CAREER:** Trenton State Coll NJ, asst prof spec educ 1964-68; Urban Schools Develop Council NJ, asst exec dir 1968-71; Rutgers Univ Livingston Coll Div, assoc prof & dept chair educ 1971-75; Urban Develop Assoc Inc, sr partner 1974-79; PA Dept of Educ, dir educ planning & testing 1979-. **ORGANIZATIONS:** Bd mem Tri County United Way Program for Female Offenders, Girls Clubs of Amer, WITF Black Adv Comm 1982-87; educ comms NAACP, Urban League Harrisburg Area 1982-87; mem Natl Alliance of Black School Educators; mem comm chair Juvenile Justice Adv Commn, Black Adv Panel, WITF (PBS Harrisburg), Sigma Pi PhiFrat Omega Psi Phi Joint Ctr for Polit Study; consultant Nat School Bds, Natl Alliance Black School Educs, Natl Chap I Parents et al. **HONORS/ACHIEVEMENTS:** Service Awds, Achievement, Merit, Man of the Year and Recognition (18 during the years 1982-87) Natl Coalition Title I Parent and E5 County/State Title 5, Natl Caucus on Black Aging, United Way, Girls Club, PA Voc Educ, Cont on Black Basic Educ; Carter G Woodson Achievement Awd. **MILITARY SERVICE:** AUS sp5 1957-59; Commendation for Development of On-Duty Schools Ft Campbell KY 101st Airborne 1958-59. **HOME ADDRESS:** 301 Chestnut St, Harrisburg, PA 17101. **BUSINESS ADDRESS:** Dir Educ Planning & Testing, PA Dept of Education, 333 Market St, Harrisburg, PA 17126.

CLARK, DOUGLAS L.
Educator. **PERSONAL:** Born May 02, 1935, Swedesboro, NJ; married Ellen; children: Douglas Jr, Dana Lynn. **EDUCATION:** Glassboro State Tchrs Coll, BS 1956, MA 1970; Laurence U, PhD 1975. **CAREER:** Glassboro State Coll, dir educ opportunity program 1970-, asst dir 1968-70; NJ Rural Manpower Prog, educ specialist 1967-68; jr high school NJ, instructor 1956-67; Real Estate, licensed salesman 1963-. **ORGANIZATIONS:** Mem Mt Calvary Bapt Ch; Businessman Assn 1975-; NJ Dirs Assn EOF; mem NAACP; bd dirs UYA. **BUSINESS ADDRESS:** La Spata House, Glassboro State Coll, Glassboro, NJ.

CLARK, EDWARD
Artist. **PERSONAL:** Born May 06, 1926, New Orleans, LA. **EDUCATION:** Art Inst Chgo, 1947-51; L'Academie de la Grande Paris, attended. **CAREER:** Univ of DE, Univ of OR, Art Inst Chgo, Showkegan School of Painting & Sculpture, OH State Univ, LA State Univ, vstg artist 1969-78. **ORGANIZATIONS:** Bd of dir Org of Independent Artist NY; bd of adv Cinque Gallery NY. **HONORS/ACHIEVEMENTS:** Numerous exhibits & one-man shows Cont Arts Ctr New Orleans, NC A&T Univ, Randall Gall NYC, Mus of Solidarity Titograd Yugoslavia, Art Salon NYC, LA StateUniv, "Contemp Black Art" FL Intl Univ, Sullivant Gall OH State Univ, James Yu Gall NYC, Acad of Arts & Letters NYC, Whitney Mus NYC, Lehman Coll NYC, Afro-Amer Exhib Mus of Fine Arts Boston, Morgan State Coll, Mod Mus Tokyo, Stockholm, Nova Gall Boston, Amer Ctr Artists, Amer Embassy Paris, Gall Creuze Paris, Salon d'Automne Paris, num others 1952-; Adolph Grant 1981, Natl Endowment Grant 1982.

CLARK, GARY
Professional athlete. **PERSONAL:** Born May 01, 1962, Dublin, VA. **EDUCATION:** Attended, James Madison Univ. **CAREER:** Washington Redskins, wide receiver 1985-. **HONORS/ACHIEVEMENTS:** Team MVP sr yr coll; Coll Offensive Player of the Yr in VA James Madison Univ 1983; Redskins Offensive Player of the Game against Cleveland 1985; Redskins leading receiver four times with three 100 yd games; mem 1987 Pro Bowl team. **BUSINESS ADDRESS:** Washington Redskins, PO Box 17247, Dulles Intl Airport, Washington, DC 20041.

CLARK, GRANVILLE E., SR.
Physician. **PERSONAL:** Born Jun 14, 1927, Santiago, Cuba;married Mary; children: Granville Jr, Robert, Joseph, James. **EDUCATION:** Institute DeSegunda Ensenanta De Santiago, BS 1947; Univ Havana, MD 1954. **CAREER:** Pvt Prac, physician 1959; Resd Gen Hosp, physician 1957-59; Norfolk Comm Hosp, physician 1955-57; Provident Hosp, intern 1954-55. **ORGANIZATIONS:** Mem SW Pediatric & Soc; KC Me Soc; Pan-MO State Med Soc; NMA; Jackson Co Med Soc; MO Med Assn; Cncl Selection Med Sch; bd mem Lead Poison Prgm; KC Sickle Cell Anemia; past mem Mid-Am Comprehensive Hlth Planning Agy; chmn Med Exec Com Martin Luther King Hosp; pediatrician consult KCMC DayCare Ctr; adv bd Douglas State Bank; pres Metro-Metic Clinic; life mem NAACP; mem YMCA; Grtr KC Boys Club. **HONORS/ACHIEVEMENTS:** Num awards & recognitions. **BUSINESS ADDRESS:** 3718 Prospect, Kansas City, MO 64128.

CLARK, HARRY W.
Physician, educator. **PERSONAL:** Born Sep 06, 1946, Detroit, MI. **EDUCATION:** Wayne State U, BA 1969; Univ of MI Med Sch, MD 1973; Univ of MI Sch of Public Hlth, MPH 1974. **CAREER:** Exec asst Div of Mental Hlth Serv Prgms, Comm Mental Hlth Serv, Nat Inst of Mental Hlth; Psychiatrist. **BUSINESS ADDRESS:** Room 11 C 23 Parklawn Bldg, 5600 Fisher's Ln, Rockville, MD 20852.

CLARK, HATTIE GILES
Educator/librarian. **PERSONAL:** Born Apr 02, 1938, Meridian, MS; married Rep William "Bill" Clark; children: William H, Reginald A. **EDUCATION:** Bishop State Jr Coll, AS 1959; AL State Univ, BS 1961; Atlanta Univ, MS Library Sci 1967. **CAREER:** Mobile Co Public Sch Syst, librarian 1961-70; Mystic Realty Inc 1972-74; Property Realty Inc, real estate appraiser, entrepreneur 1974-; SD Bishop State Jr Coll, librarian/instructor 1970-81, instructor/library tech 1981-, dir of private funds, training & develop 1981-84, alumni dir 1981-. **ORGANIZATIONS:** Mem Mobile United 1981-87; bd of dirs Mobile Mental Health Found 1981-; bd of dirs Mobile Mental Health 1981-; mem Natl Assn Realtors. **HONORS/ACHIEVEMENTS:** Salutatorian AL State Univ summer 1961; Sales Associate of the Yr Mystic Realty Inc 1974; Delta of the Yr Delta Sigma Theta Sor 1978; president's award, Bishop State Community Coll, 1985; certified in fund raising, Natl Soc of Fund Raising, 1985. **HOME ADDRESS:** 711 South Atmore Ave, Prichard, AL 36610. **BUSINESS ADDRESS:** Executive Director, Property Realty, Inc, 1556 St. Stephens Rd, Mobile, AL 36604.

CLARK, JAMES IRVING, JR.
Manager, clergyman. **PERSONAL:** Born Apr 18, 1936, Patterson, NJ; married Shirley Lorraine Matthews; children: James I III, Renee Therese, Rhonda Ellise. **EDUCATION:** Am Divinity Sch, BTH 1966; Baruch Coll, 1966-68; Columbia U, MBA 1973. **CAREER:**

Pfizer Diagnostics, mgr training & devel 1978, mgr professional placement 1975-78, personnel rela mgr 1973-75; New Era Learning Corp, exec vice pres 1969 -71; Slant/Fin Corp, asst ind rela mgr 1962-69; Christ Temple Ch, pastor 1969; Ch of Christ Bible Inst, acting dean 1971. **ORGANIZATIONS:** Pres vice pres 1st black pres pro tem Grad Bus Assn Columbia Univ Grad Sch of Bus 1971-73; COGME Fellowship Columbia Univ 1971. **HONORS/ACHIEVEMENTS:** Serv award Columbia Univ Grad Sch of Bus 1973; black achiever award Pfizer In & YMCA NY 1974. **MILITARY SERVICE:** USAF a/2c served 3 1/2 years. **BUSINESS ADDRESS:** Pfizer Diagnostics, 235 E 42nd St, New York, NY 10017.

CLARK, JAMES N.
Dentist, consultant. **PERSONAL:** Born Sep 16, 1934, Brooklyn, NY; son of Luther Clark and Augusta Neale Clark; married Patricia; children: Melissa, Holly, James II. **EDUCATION:** CCNY, BS 1956; Columbia Univ, DDS 1964; Acad of Gen Dentistry, FAGD (Hon) 1974; AM Coll of Dentists, FACD (Hon) 1980-. **CAREER:** ITT, dental dir 1965-69; Private practice, dentist; World Wide ITT, dental consult 1969-. **ORGANIZATIONS:** Mem NAACP, Omega Psi Phi 1955-; sec Commonwelath Dental Assoc 1969; Newark Beth Israel Hosp Attendant 1969; Civil Defense 1972-79; pres Amer Assoc of Indust Dentists 1973; co-chmn United Way 1973; sec Central Pkwy Assoc 1974; mem 100 Black Men 1975; Life mem Omega Psi Phi 1976; pres Ad Hoc Comm Orange Central YMCA 1976-80; sec 100 Black Men 1980; fellow Amer Coll of Dentists 1980-; bd of trustees Rampo Coll 1982-; pres Dental Assting Advisory Bd 1986-; Chairman - Board of Trustees Ramapo College 1988-; Vice President - External Affairs - 100 Black Men, Inc. 1988-. **HONORS/ACHIEVEMENTS:** John Hay Whitney Fellowship 1963; Smith & Noyes Scholarship 1960,64; Gold Foil Awd 1st Prize Dental Student Exhibit; Superstar Awd YMCA 1979. **MILITARY SERVICE:** AUS pvt E-2. **BUSINESS ADDRESS:** DDS, 185 Central Ave Suite 301, East Orange, NJ 07018.

CLARK, JESSE B., III
Director. **PERSONAL:** Born Feb 12, 1925, Philadelphia, PA; married Lucille Field; children: Bruce, Kevin, Blair, Cynthia. **EDUCATION:** PA State Univ, BA 1950; Grad Work Univ of PA, 1951-52. **CAREER:** Urban League, dir vocaliors 1954-59; Campbell Soct Co, persnl speclst 1959-62; Abbotts Dairies, dir pblc rltns 1962-1964. **ORGANIZATIONS:** Pres & board chrmn St Edmonds Home for Children 1983-; trustee St Charles Seminary Archdiocece of Philadelphia 1984, Mercy Catholic Medical Cntr 1974-; past pres Serra Club of Philadelphia 1972; tres Catholic Soc Serv Board 1974-; trustee Villanora Univ Villanora PA 1974-84; commissioner Charter Revision Commn Philadelphia 1976; board mem Natl Catholic Stwrdshp Cncl 1983-; bd mem Institutions for Mentally Retarded 1985-; sec Natl Adv Comm US Conference of Bishops 1987. **HONORS/ACHIEVEMENTS:** Knight of the Order Saint Gregory the Great 1977; Commandor Knight of the Order Saint Gregory the Great 1986. **MILITARY SERVICE:** USNA s/sgt. **BUSINESS ADDRESS:** Dir of Development, Archdiocese of Philadelphia, Rm 1100 222 N 17th St, Philadelphia, PA 19103.

CLARK, JESSIE
Professional athlete. **PERSONAL:** Born Jan 03, 1960, Crossett, AR. **EDUCATION:** LA Tech, attended; AR Univ, Criminal Law, M Public Relations. **CAREER:** Green Bay Packers, fullback 1983-87. **HONORS/ACHIEVEMENTS:** Packers #3 rusher & #4 receiver 1984; Special teams standout as a rookie registering 13 unassisted tackles on coverage units; capt of Green Bay Packers 1985; 2nd Leading Rusher 1985. **BUSINESS ADDRESS:** Fullback, Green Bay Packers, 1266 Lombardi Ave, Green Bay, WI 54307.

CLARK, JIMMY E.
College president. **PERSONAL:** Born Feb 20, 1934, Tyler, TX; married Norma J Tilley; children: Chandron E. **EDUCATION:** TX Coll, BS 1950; So Meth Univ, BD 1959; Univ of IL, MS 1962; Wayne State Univ, PhD 1972. **CAREER:** CME Churches TX & MI, minister 1952-72; Southern Methodist Univ, staff librarian 1959-63; Interdenom Theology Center Atlanta, asst prof 1964-68; TX Coll, vice pres 1968-69; Wayne State Univ, asst prof 1969-73; Highland Park Comm Coll, dean student serv 1973-80; TX Coll, pres 1980-. **ORGANIZATIONS:** Mem Amer Assn Higher Educ 1969-; Amer Assn Univ Profs 1969-73; Natl Assn Student Personnel Adminstr 1973-; N Central Assn Colls consult eval 1974-80; mem bd dir Tyler Area C of C; United Way of Greater Tyler; East TX Fair Assn; chmn Tyler Sr Citizen Adv Council, bd chmn 1981-83; TX Assn of Developing Colleges; bd mem Independent Colleges and Univs in TX and sec of Member Presidents; United Negro College Fund; bd dir United Negro College Fund Inc; founder & 1st pres Tyler Organization of Men; Kappa Alpha Psi; Alpha Kappa Mu; Beta Kappa Chi. **HONORS/ACHIEVEMENTS:** Lilly Found Award 1961-62; Ford Found Award 1969; Kellogg Found Award 1971-72; Outstanding Young Men 1968; Listed in "They made It - So Can You" Francis A Kornegay; Detroit Urban League 1971. **BUSINESS ADDRESS:** President, Texas College, Tyler, TX 75702.

CLARK, JOE LOUIS
Educator/secondary school principal. **PERSONAL:** Born May 07, 1939, Rochelle, GA; son of Rhomie Clark and Maggie Majors Clark; married Hazel, Jun 10, 1970; children: Joetta, Joe, Jr., Hazel. **EDUCATION:** William Paterson College, Wayne NJ, BA, 1960; Seton Hall University, South Orange NJ, MA, 1974. **CAREER:** Board of Education, Paterson NJ, teacher, 1960-74, coordinator of language arts, 1976-79, elementary school principal, 1979-82, secondard school principal, 1982—. **ORGANIZATIONS:** National Association of Secondary School Principals, NAACP, New Jersey Principals and Administrators Association, Paterson Principals Association. **HONORS/ACHIEVEMENTS:** NAACP Community Service Award (Paterson NJ), 1983; named New Jerseyan of the Year, Newark Star Ledger, 1983; named outstanding educator, New Jersey Monthly magazine, 1984; distinguished alumnus award, Seton Hall University, 1985; distinguished service award, Fairleigh Dickinson University, 1985; honored at presidential conference on academic and displinary excllence at White House, 1985; Principal of Leadership award, National School Safety Center, 1986; Humanitarian Award, National Black Policemen's Association, 1988. **MILITARY SERVICE:** US Army Reserve, E5, 1958-66. **BUSINESS ADDRESS:** Eastside High School, 150 Park Ave, Paterson, NJ 07501.

CLARK, JOHN JOSEPH
Business manager. **PERSONAL:** Born Jun 26, 1954, Pittsburgh, PA; son of Anna (Bluett) Clark. **EDUCATION:** Northeastern Univ Boston, BS, BA 1977; Univ of Chicago, MBA 1985. **CAREER:** Arthur Andersen & Co, auditor 1977-80; Bell & Howell, sr auditor 1980-81; Baxter Travenol Labs, mktg mgr 1981-86; Clark & Associates, pres 1986-. **ORGANIZATIONS:** School coord Chicago Assoc of Commerce & Industry Youth Motivation Program 1977-; mem 1978-86, treas 1980 Natl Assoc of Black Accountants; mem Natl Black MBA Assoc 1985-; bd mem Hollywood Tower Condo Assoc 1986-; mem Greater Pittsburgh Chamber of Commerce 1987, Pittsburgh Regional Minority Purchasing Cncl 1987; mem Alumni Assocs, Chicago Council Foreign Relations. **HONORS/ACHIEVEMENTS:** Beta Alpha Psi 1975-77; drafted by Boston Celtics in Natl Basketball Assoc 1976; Outstanding Young Men of Amer 1985; Certificate of Appreciation Chicago Assoc of Commerce 1986; inducted into Northeastern University Athletic Hall of Fame 1987. **BUSINESS ADDRESS:** President, Clark & Associates, 120 S Whitfield St, Pittsburgh, PA 15206.

CLARK, KENNETH BANCROFT
President. **PERSONAL:** Born Jul 24, 1914; son of Hanson Clark and Mirian Clark; widowed; children: Kate Miriam Harris, Hilton Bancroft. **EDUCATION:** Howard Univ, AB 1935; Howard Univ, MS 1936; Columbia Univ, PhD Psychology 1940. **CAREER:** Pyschology Emeritus City Clg, distinguished prof 1942-75; Columbia Univ, visiting prof; Univ Of CA, Berkeley, visiting prof; Harvard Univ, Ambridge, visiting prof. **ORGANIZATIONS:** Fndr/dir Northside Center for Child Devel 1946-; fndr/pres Metropolitan Applied Research Ctr 1967-75; mem NY State Board of Regents 1966-86; trustee Chicago Univ; mem Phi Beta Kappa, Sigma Xi; past pres Amer Psychological Assn, Soc for Psychological Studies of Social Issues, Metro Applied Rsch Ctr; trustee Woodrow Wilson Intl Ctr for Scholars; fndr Harlem Youth Oppor Unlimited. **HONORS/ACHIEVEMENTS:** Springam Medal 1961; Kurt Lewin Memorial Award 1965; Disting Professor of Psychology City College 1971; clg board medar of distngshd serv in education honorary degrees Several Colleges & Univ 1980; Sidney Hilman Award Dark Getto 1965. **HOME ADDRESS:** 17 Pinecrest Dr, Hastings-on-Hudson, NY 10706. **BUSINESS ADDRESS:** President, Kenneth B Clark & Assoc, Inc, 615 Broadway, Hastings-on-Hudson, NY 10706.

CLARK, LARON JEFFERSON, JR.
Educational administration. **PERSONAL:** Born Dec 06, 1937, Altanta, GA; son of Laron Jefferson Clark, Sr. and Doshia Mary Alice Blasingame; married Mary Ellen Smith; children: Laron III, Jeremy, Allison. **EDUCATION:** Morehouse Coll, AB 1961; Atlanta Univ, MS 1965; Univ of Tulsa, 1968. **CAREER:** Langton Univ, dir of devel 1968-72; Atlanta Univ, exec dir, univ relations & devel 1972-75; Hampton Univ, vice pres for devel 1975-. **ORGANIZATIONS:** Adult serv librarian Brooklyn Public Library 1961-63; suprv branch librarian Queensborough Public Library 1963-66; chief librarian & assoc prof Langston Univ 1966-68; trustees Hampton Rd Acad 1978-; mem Kiwanis Club 1979-, Tidewater Longshoremen Scholarship Cmte 1982-, Soc of Fund Raisers 1980-; mem bd of dirs Cultural Alliance of Greater Hampton Roads 1985-; Secretary - Board of Directors - Cultural Alliance of Greater Hampton Roads; member - Fund Raising Committee - Virginia Air and Space Center Museum. **HONORS/ACHIEVEMENTS:** Acad Scholarship Morehouse Coll 1956; Fellowship Univ of Tulsa 1968. **HOME ADDRESS:** 533 Ferry Rd, Hampton, VA 23669.

CLARK, LAWANNA GIBBS
Government official. **PERSONAL:** Born Feb 05, 1941, Calvert, TX; daughter of Wilbert Gibbs and Mildred Bunns; divorced. **EDUCATION:** Attended, Texas Southern Univ 1958-59, Univ of NV 1959-60 1972, Nevada College of Commerce 1961; ofc of Personnel Management Executive Semninar Center. **CAREER:** Energy Rsch & Devel Admin, exec asst to mgr 1975-77; Dept of Energy, exec asst to asst sec 1977-79, exec asst to under sec 1979-81, staff asst to sec 1981-85, special asst to mgr and eeo program mgr 1985-88; Equal Employment Specialist 1988-. **ORGANIZATIONS:** Leadership Las Vegas Chamber of Commerce 1986-87; life mem NAACP, Natl Council of Negro Women; mem Metropolitan Baptist Church, Washington, DC. **HONORS/ACHIEVEMENTS:** Special Citation for Outstanding Performance Dept of Energy 1981; Monetary Awd for Spec Act or Service Dept of Energy 1981; Certificate of Appreciation Dept of Energy 1985; Monetary Awd for Superior Performance Dept of Energy 1986; Good Service Awd Second Baptist Church 1986; Monetary Award for Superior Service, 1987, Dept of Energy; Quality Step Increase, Dept of Energy, 1988. **BUSINESS ADDRESS:** Equal Opportunity Specialist, US Dept of Energy, 1000 Independence Ave SW, Rm 4B-112, Washington, DC 20585.

CLARK, LEON HENRY
Pilot. **PERSONAL:** Born Aug 08, 1941, Hallandale, FL; married Pearlie; children: Tangela, Robbie. **EDUCATION:** TN State A&I U, BS 1965. **CAREER:** Delta Airlines, flight engr, co-pilot; sub sch tchr 1970-71. **ORGANIZATIONS:** Dir FL State; mem Negro Airmens Internat; mem Black Airline Pilots Assn; Broward Co Affirmitive Action Coalition. **HONORS/ACHIEVEMENTS:** Viet Nam Serv Medal. **MILITARY SERVICE:** AUS instr 1971-72; USN lt jg 1966-69. **BUSINESS ADDRESS:** Co-Pilot, Delta Airlines, Miami Intl Airport, Miami, FL.

CLARK, LEROY D.
Union executive. **PERSONAL:** Born Nov 19, 1917, Canal Zone, Panama;married Alzada Bradley; children: Leroy Jr. **CAREER:** So Region United Furn Workers of Am, AFL-CIO, vice pres 1970-; Intl Rep Chicago & Southern Reg 1957-70; Local Union Organizer NY, 1940-41; Factory Worker NY, 1937-40. **ORGANIZATIONS:** Mem Am Negro Labor Council; mem Memphis Chap A Philip Randolph Inst; mem Coalition of Black Trade Unionists; vice pres TN State Labor Council AFL-CIO; presMemphis Br NAACP 1969-72; Shelby County Dem Club 1964-73; Shelby Co Dem Voters Council 1973; Shelby United Neighbors 1970. **MILITARY SERVICE:** AUS sgt 1941-45. **BUSINESS ADDRESS:** Ste 132, 2881 Lamar, Memphis, TN 38114.

CLARK, LOUIS JAMES
Manager. **PERSONAL:** Born Apr 28, 1940, Camden, SC; married Beverly Jean Smith; children: Marcia, Louis, Christopher. **EDUCATION:** Wayne State U, BS 1973; IA State Univ Engring, 1973; Univ of MI Bus Admin 1979-. **CAREER:** MI Bell, dist eng mgr 1978-, design engr 1977-78, methods engr 1975-77, supervising engr 1973-, area engr 1973-74. **ORGANIZATIONS:** Mem Engineering Soc of Detroit 1975; contributor of articles Nat Electric Inst 1975; mem bd of dir Detroit Alumni & No Province of Kappa Alpha Psi 1975-; pres sch bd Presentation Sch 1975-. **HONORS/ACHIEVEMENTS:** Service award No Providence Kappa Alpha Psi 1979; Vietnam Service & Combat Award 1966. **MILITARY SERVICE:** AUS e-4 1964-66. **BUSINESS ADDRESS:** Michigan Bell Telephone Co, 100 S Gratiot, Mount Clemens, MI 48043.

CLARK, MAJOR
Retired military historian. **PERSONAL:** Born Dec 07, 1917, Headland, AL; widowed; children: William Marcus, Vivian Noreen, Gregory Lewis. **EDUCATION:** Ft Sill OK, Field Artillery School, Officer Candidate Course 1942, Artillery Officer Adv Course 1953-54; Ft Leavenworth KS, Command & Gen Staff Coll, Assoc Command & Gen Staff Officer Course 1955, Spec Weapons Course 1956, Sr Officers Nuclear Weapons Employment Course 1958. **CAREER:** FABN 597, battery commander, batallion intelligence officer, unit historian 1942-45; Hampton Inst VA, asst PMS&T 1947-51; Korea, sr artillery advisor 3d ROKdiv 1951-52; Dept Chief of Staff Military Oper Pentagon, army gen staff officer 1956-60; McDonnell Douglas Tulsa, 1962-79. **ORGANIZATIONS:** Mem, Retired Officers Assn, Assn AUS, Tulsa Urban League, NAACP, YMCA; author, Black Military History material. **HONORS/ACHIEVEMENTS:** Chungmu Medal with Gold Star & ROK Presidential Unit Citation Korea 1952; Inducted into Field Artillery OCS Hall of Fame Ft Sill OK 1980. **MILITARY SERVICE:** AUS lt col 1940-60; Bronze Star Medal & Cross for Merit of War Italy 1945; Oak Leaf Cluster-Bronze Star 1952; Army Commendation Medal 1960.

CLARK, MAJOR L., III
Educator. **PERSONAL:** Born May 31, 1946, Salisbury, NC; married Lynn Carole; children: Leonard. **EDUCATION:** A&T State U, BS 1968; Univ of IA, JD 1971, MS Urban Planning 1972. **CAREER:** Morgan State Univ, assoc prof of urban planning 1973; HEW Title I Project, land use & housing consult assoc dir 1973-75; Univ of MD Div of African-Am Studies, faculty 1972-73; OEO IA, atty 1971-72. **ORGANIZATIONS:** Mem Am Inst of Planners; Am Soc of Planning Officials; Assn of Collegiate Schs of Planning; Urban Land Inst; Phi Alpha Delta; Nat Assn of Planners; Governor's Human Resources Task Force MD; adv panel MD Health Cost Review Commn; adv editor Journal on Black Health Perspectives; mem WBAL-TV Adv Communication Council 1974-75; consult Pro Bono Rosemont Multi-Purpose Comm Orgn 1974-75; mem Comm Health Council of MD 1975-. **HONORS/ACHIEVEMENTS:** RecipientUniv of IA Faculty Award 1971; Reginald Herber Smith Comm Lawyer Felo 1971-72; Outstanding Young Mem in Am 1974-75; Sigma Rho Sigma Soc Sci Honor Soc 1967; NC Summer Intern 1966. **BUSINESS ADDRESS:** Morgan State Univ, Baltimore, MD 21239.

CLARK, MAMIE PHIPPS
Retired executive director. **PERSONAL:** Born Oct 18, 1917, Hot Springs, AR; married Kenneth; children: Kate, Hilton. **EDUCATION:** Howard U, BS 1938, MS 1939; Columbia U, PHD 1944; Pratt Inst, LLD 1974. **CAREER:** Northside Center Child Devel, former exec dir; Yeshiva Univ, experimental methods & rsch design 1958-60; Riverdale Children's Assn, psychologist 1945-46; US Armed Forces Inst, rsch psychologist 1945-46; Amer Public Health Assn, rsch psychologist 1944-45. **ORGANIZATIONS:** Bd of dir ABC Inc 1974; bd dir Union Dime Savings Bank 1975; mus Collaboratives Inc 1975; sec NY City Mission Soc 1962; chmn NY Pub Library, 110th St Plaza Housing Devel Corp; United Fund of Gtr NY; splAllocations Fund Com; mem Gov's Commn on Libraries; Palisades Interstate Pk Commn; proj dir Think Prgm 1968-70; Careers Proj 1974-75; Pre-School Prevention Prgm 1975. **HONORS/ACHIEVEMENTS:** Alumni award HowardUniv 1958; alumni award ColumbiaUniv 1972; Grad Fellow 1938-39; Rosenwald Fellow 1940-43; Phi Beta Kappa; fellowship award Am AssnUniv of &Women 1973; Dr of Humane Letters Williams Coll 1972. **BUSINESS ADDRESS:** 1301 Fifth Ave, New York, NY 10029.

CLARK, MARIO SEAN
Business owner, former professional athlete. **PERSONAL:** Born Mar 29, 1954, Pasadena, CA; son of Oscar Clark and Lois Prince Clark; married Lisa Clark Adkins; children: Taylor Alexander Clark. **EDUCATION:** Univ of Oregon, Studied Interior Design 1972-76. **CAREER:** Buffalo Bills, San Francisco 49ers, Defensive Back; owner Clark's Auto Upholstery, 1985-. **ORGANIZATIONS:** bd mem George Steuart Memory Football Camp 1985; consultant Boys Club of Pasadena 1985; counselor of disadvantaged youth, Pride. **HONORS/ACHIEVEMENTS:** All-rookie team Buffalo Bills 1976; all-pro Buffalo Bills 1980; super bowl winner San Francisco 49ers 1985. **BUSINESS ADDRESS:** Clark's Auto/Furniture Upholstery, 1566 N. Fair Oaks Avenue, Pasadena, CA 91103.

CLARK, MICHELE ARLEEN
Pay cable programming executive. **PERSONAL:** Born Jul 29, 1954, Pennington, NJ; daughter of Arthur Clark and Winifred Clark; children: Winifred Sarah. **EDUCATION:** Princeton Univ, BA 1976; NY Law School, JD 1982. **CAREER:** HBO, wirter/producer 1977-80, dir bus affairs 1980-. **ORGANIZATIONS:** Founding mem Council to support Afro-Amer Culture 1986-, Dance Theater of Harlem Guild 1986; community liaison Hyland Residential Center 1986-. **HONORS/ACHIEVEMENTS:** Andrew Heiskell Awd Time Inc 1986; project dir, producer of video, King Holiday commemorative recording honoring the first Martin Luther King holiday celebration 1986. **BUSINESS ADDRESS:** Director, Business Affairs, Home Box Office, Inc, 1100 Avenue of the Americas, 14th Floor, New York, NY 10036.

CLARK, MILDRED E.
Educator. **PERSONAL:** Born Dec 16, 1936, Columbus, GA; married Henry L; children: Henry L, Kenneth. **EDUCATION:** Lane Coll, 1954-57; Stautzenberger Coll, 1954-56; Toledo U, 1957-58; Wayne State U, BA 1963. **CAREER:** Toledo, legal sec 1958-59; Realty Co, sec 1960-61; Rossford Ordinance, clerk typist 1961-63; Eli B Williams Sch, educator 1963-65; Anna Pickett & Elementary Sch, educator 1963-. **ORGANIZATIONS:** Founder Ghanited Neighborhood Org 1970-; Toledo Fed of Teachers 1973; The Black Caucus of Toledo Teachers; Frederick Douglass Comm Assn NAACP; mem Toledo Educ Assn 1965-72; Black African Peoples Assn; Black Historical Soc; Sec PTA; chmn Human Relations Bd Toledo Educ Assn, 1966-67. **HONORS/ACHIEVEMENTS:** Outstanding serv Doer's Awd Toledo Educ Assoc. **BUSINESS ADDRESS:** Anna Pickett Sch, Vance & Hoag St, Toledo, OH 43607.

CLARK, MORRIS SHANDELL
Oral & maxillofacial surgeon. **PERSONAL:** Born Nov 27, 1945, Princeton, WV; son of Willie R Clark Sr and Clarie Clark; married Maureen Pamela Mercier; children: Gregory Morris, Angela Maureen. **EDUCATION:** WV State Coll, BS 1967; Univ of CA, BDS 1973, DDS 1973. **CAREER:** Upward Bound Program WV State, asst dir 1968-69; Columbia Univ, instructor oral surgery 1973-76, internship & residency 1976; Univ of Medicine & Dentistry, asst prof oral & maxillofacial surgery 1976-81; Univ of CO, assoc prof of otolaryngology, school of dentistry assoc prof oral & maxillofacial surgery & school of medicine dir of anesthesia 1982-. **ORGANIZATIONS:** Fellow Amer Soc of Oral and Maxillofacial Surgery, Amer Soc of Dental Anesthesiology, Intl Soc of Oral and Maxillofacial Surgery; consultant Amer Assn for the Advancement of Anesthesia in Dentistry 1979-, Veterans Admin Hosp 1981-82, Coors Biomedical Co 1985-. **HONORS/ACHIEVEMENTS:** Excellence in Teaching Awd 1981; Fellow Amer Coll of Dentists 1986; over 40 publications in medical & dental literature; 15 major research projects; spoken and lectured in USA, Europe, Canada, Asia, South Amer, Australia. **HOME ADDRESS:** 17 Cherry Hills Farm Drive, Englewood, CO 80110. **BUSINESS ADDRESS:** Assoc Prof/Dir of Anesthesia, Univ of Colorado Health Sciences Ctr, 4200 E 9th Ave, Box C-284, Denver, CO 80262.

CLARK, NEHEMIAH
Business executive. **PERSONAL:** Born May 06, 1941, Macon, GA; married Marion L Wilson-Clark; children: Neal Anthony Clark. **EDUCATION:** Morehouse Coll, BS 1963; Stanford Univ School of Finance, certificate 1978. **CAREER:** Wells Fargo Bank, asst vice pres 1971-78; Citizens & Southern Natl Bank Atlanta, vice pres 1978-83; Chemical Bank NY, vice pres 1983-. **ORGANIZATIONS:** Bd dir San Francisco Florence Crittenton Found 1976-78;Fulton Cnty(Atlanta) Brd of Family & CHildren Services 1981-83; Fee Arbitrator-State Bar of Georgia 1981-83. **BUSINESS ADDRESS:** Vice President, Chemical Bank, 52 Broadway, New York, NY 10014.

CLARK, RANDOLPH A.
Architect. **PERSONAL:** Born Nov 25, 1939, Marshall, TX; married Mae A Wesley; children: Dawn, Randalyn. **EDUCATION:** Prairie View A&M U, BS 1961. **CAREER:** Randolph A Clark & Asso Architects, owner 1973-; Hex Learning Ctr Urban Six Prtnship, owner; Gen Serv Adminstrn, architect 1963-73. **ORGANIZATIONS:** Mem AIA Nat Orgn of Minority Architects Rotary Intl Ft & Worth C of C; mem Alpha Phi Alpha Inc; bd dir Hex Learning Center. **HONORS/ACHIEVEMENTS:** Who's Who In Am 1974. **MILITARY SERVICE:** AUS capt 1963. **BUSINESS ADDRESS:** 3113 S Univ Dr, Fort Worth, TX.

CLARK, ROBERT G.
Legislator. **PERSONAL:** Born Oct 03, 1929, Ebenezer, MS; married Essie; children: Robert Jr, Bryant. **EDUCATION:** Jackson State Coll, BS; MI State Univ, MA. **CAREER:** State of MS Holmes & Vazoo Counties Dist 47, rep 1968-. **ORGANIZATIONS:** Founder & bd mem Central MS Inc of Comm Action Progs; mem Intl Bd of Basketball Officials; past pres Central MS Bd of Athletic Officials; fellow Inst of Politics John F Kennedy School of Govt Harvard Univ 1979; dem party nominee Congressional Seat 1982,84; past pres Fine Housing Enterprises; chmn ed conn House of Reps; mem appropriations comm House of Reps; sec rules comm House of Reps; pres bd of trustees Childrens Ctr of Lexington; mem Natl Coalition of Advocates for Students; mem Dem Natl Comm Voter Participation Task Force; co-chmn MS Del So Reg Council. **BUSINESS ADDRESS:** Representative, State of Mississippi Dist 47, Box 179, Lexington, MS 39095.

CLARK, RONALD C.
Association executive. **PERSONAL:** Born Sep 19, 1935, Los Angeles, CA; divorced; children: PAUL. **EDUCATION:** Marjorie Webster Coll Washington DC, AA 1973; Gov's Coll Chicago, BA 1 975. **CAREER:** RAP, Inc, exec dir & pres bd dirs 1970-; Antioch Coll Baltimore, asst prof 1972-73; Addiction Res & Treatment Corp NYC, therapist & clin dir 1969-70; Phoenix House NYC, facility & dir 1968-69; Synanon Los Angeles, asst dir 1962-68. **ORGANIZATIONS:** Mem Nat Com Black Drug Wrkrs; panelist Nat Drug Abuse Confs 1973-75; neighborhood adv bd Washington Rep Nat Black Pol Conv 1972. **HONORS/ACHIEVEMENTS:** Spl recog award Nat Inst Drug Progs Webseter Coll; award appreciation Nat Jr C of C. **BUSINESS ADDRESS:** Executive Dir, RAP, Inc, 1731 Willard St NW, Washington, DC 20009.

CLARK, ROSALIND K.
Singer, actress. **PERSONAL:** Born Nov 16, 1943, Dallas, TX. **EDUCATION:** TX So U, BMus 1965. **CAREER:** Las Vegas Hilton, nightclub performer; Playboy Club, nightclub performer; Jackson's Penthouse, nightclub performer; After Dark, nightclub performer; Studio One, nightclub Performer; The Tonight Show, Guest; Merv Griffin, Guest; Dinah, Guest; Paul Lynde, Toured. **ORGANIZATIONS:** Vp Celebration Soc Inc 1970-74; Alpha Kappa Alpha Sor. **HONORS/ACHIEVEMENTS:** Entertainment hall of fame awards The Wiz, Hair, Two Worlds & It's About Time. **BUSINESS ADDRESS:** c/o Actors Equity, 165 West 46th St, Attn: Jackie Veglie, New York, NY 10036.

CLARK, RUTH
Business executive. **PERSONAL:** Born Oct 16, 1942, New York, NY; divorced. **EDUCATION:** George Wash HS NYC, 1957-60. **CAREER:** Hour Power-Temp Employ Agency 1972-74; Clark Unltd Placement, pres 1977; Cup Stars Inc Talent Agency, franchised agent 1977; Clark Unltd Personnel-TempEmployment, pres 1974-. **ORGANIZATIONS:** Mem NY Assoc Temp Serv 1979; mem bd Natl Barch of Dimes 1980, Womens Forum 1978, Edges Group 1978; partic in spec prog Hunter Coll 1978; mem bd Women Bus Owners of NY, Natl Assoc of Female Exec, Edwinn Gould Serv for Children; adv bd Natl Minority Bus Council; entrepreneurship panel for Harvard Univ; sponsored To Be Ambitious, Gifted & Black prog; addressed num insts incl PA State Univ, Wharton School of Bus; keynote speaker at Networking TogetherConf Milwaukee WI, NY Univ & Citibank's 1984 Bus Career Forum for Minority Undergrad Students. **HONORS/ACHIEVEMENTS:** Hall of Fame PS 113 1978; Small Bus Skills Devel Prog Medgar Evers Coll 1979; bus Awd Black Retail Action Group 1979; appeared on severalTV shows such as, Midday Live, Hour Mag, Inside Bus Today, The Essence Show, Sonya Show in Detroit; featured in natl publs, Money Mag, Better Bus, New Woman, Jet, Savvy, Ebony, Class, Essence Mag; daily publ, USA Today, The New York Post, NY Daily News, NY Time; listed in Who's Who Among Amer Women 1980, Who's Who of Disting Amer 1983, 5,000 Personalities of Amer 1983; Bus Woman of the Year Natl Assoc of Negro bus; Role Model Awd New Future Found; The Pacesetter Awd New Dawn Leadership for Women Assoc; The Cecelia C Saunders Awd Outstanding Entrepreneurship of 1982 Harlem YWCA; Mary McLeod Bethune Recognition Black Woman Entrepreneur Awd Black Women Entrepreneurs Assoc 1984; Spec Recognition Awd New York City Commiss on the Status of Women; nominated for Natl Emily Warren Roebling AwD, Crystal Awd 1984 Natl Assoc of Negro Bus, Professional Womens Clubs, Philip Morris Inc. **BUSINESS ADDRESS:** Division President, Clark Unlimited Personnel, Employment, 527 Madison Ave, New York, NY 10022.

CLARK, SANZA BARBARA
Educator. **PERSONAL:** Born Jul 03, 1940, Cleveland, OH; daughter of Dewell Davis and Gladys Sanders Davis; divorced; children: Msia. **EDUCATION:** Kent State Univ, BA 1967; Duquesne Univ, MA 1970; Howard Univ, CAS 1980; Univ of IL, PhD 1985. **CAREER:** Univ of Pittsburgh, Swahili instructor 1969-72; Tanzanian Min of Natl Educ, educ officer IIA 1972-78; OH State Univ, Swahili instructor 1983-84; Cleveland State Univ, asst prof educ/rsch 1985-. **ORGANIZATIONS:** Statistical consultant Univ of IL 1980-83; pres Orchard Family Housing Council 1981-83; pres Parents for Quality Educ 1986-87; chmn, Mali Yetu Alternative Educ School 1988-; trustee, Center for Human Services, 1989-. **HONORS/ACHIEVEMENTS:** Mem Phi Delta Kappa Professional Soc; mem Phi Kappa Phi Honor Soc; Guide-Formulas-Hypothesis Testing Univ of IL 1982; Effects-Parental Educ & Sch on Ach Univ of IL 1985; Ed Refugees in Tanzania Comp & Intl Educ Soc 1986. **BUSINESS ADDRESS:** Prof of Education/Research, Cleveland StateUniv, Dept Curr & Fds, 1451 Rhodes Tower, Cleveland, OH 44115.

CLARK, SAVANNA M. VAUGHN
Professor. **PERSONAL:** Born Mar 10, 1927, Hutchinson, KS; daughter of Charles T Vaughn and Helen Grice Vaughn; married Charles Warfield Clark. **EDUCATION:** Prairie View A&M Univ, Prairie View TX, BS, 1949; Univ of Oklahoma, Norman OK, MEd; Oklahoma State Univ, Stillwater OK, postgraduate and doctoral studies. **CAREER:** Southern Univ, Baton Rouge LA, instructor, 1954-60; Ponca City Public Schools, Ponca City OK, instructor, 1960-65; North Carolina Central Univ, Durham NC, instructor, 1965-67; Langston Univ, Langston OK, asst prof, 1967-69; Univ of the District of Columbia, asst prof, 1974-. **ORGANIZATIONS:** Amer Public Health Assn; Amer Alliance for Health, Physical Educ, Recreation and Dance; Natl Educ Assn; Amer Medical Auxiliary Assn Inc; founding mem, Phi Delta Kappa, Univ of the District of Columbia Chapter; Delta Sigma Theta Sorority; founding mem, Friends of the Kennedy Center; vice pres, Women's Comm, Washington Ballet; patron, Museum of African Art; donor, Museum of Women in the Arts, Washington DC; exec bd mem, YWCA, Washington DC area, 1974; founder 1979, pres 1981, Capital City Links Inc, Washington DC; chairperson, Northwest Quadrant, Amer Cancer Soc, 1984; chairperson, Fund-Raiser for the Arts, Children's Museum, 1988;. **HONORS/ACHIEVEMENTS:** Award of Appreciation, Prairie View Univ Student Body; Award of Contribution and Presidents Club, Prairie View Univ; fund-raiser chairperson, raised $100,000 for Gems Program for Minority Medical Students, Georgetown Univ Medical School; honoree, Georgetown Univ Medical School, 1988, 1989;. **HOME ADDRESS:** 2922 Ellicott Terrace, NW, Washington, DC 20008.

CLARK, SHEILA WHEATLEY
Account executive. **PERSONAL:** Born Sep 04, 1948, Houston, TX; daughter of Reuben Wheatley and Helen Wheatley; divorced. **EDUCATION:** University of North Texas BBA Acctg 1969, MBA Acctg 1972. **CAREER:** Shell Oil Co, gas accountant 1969-70; Peat Marwick Main & Co, audit partner 1972-. **ORGANIZATIONS:** Memberships Amer Inst of Certified Public Accountants; Natl Assn of Black Accountants; Amer Women's Soc of CPA's; Comm on Tech Standards TX State Bd of Public Accountancy; TX Soc of CPA;s; TASBO; N TX State Univ Dept of Acctg; held various offices in Delta Sigma Theta Sor Inc; Houston Bus Forum; BOLD the Black Organ for Leadership Develop; NAACP; Houston Chamber of Comm; United Way of Houston; YWCA; Prof Christian Women Assn; Natl Coalition of 100 Black Women; INROADS; acctg instructor TX Southern Univ 1977-78; teaching fellow N TX State Univ; instructor TX Soc of CPA's Continuing Prof Educ seminars 1976-; auditing instructor Miller CPA Review Courses 1980-82; guest lecturer AICPA summer seminar 1978 & 1983; bd of regents TX State Univ System 1986-; Chairman of Board, Inroads Houston, Inc 1987-. **HONORS/ACHIEVEMENTS:** Natl Acctg Achievement Awd NABA; Acctg Achievement Awd NABA Houston Chapt; Who's Who in Amer Colls & Univs 1972; Outstanding Young Women in Amer 1979; Cert of Appreciation NABA 8th Annual Convention 1981; Alumni of the Yr Phillis Wheatley Sr HS 1982; NABA Achievement Awd NY Chap 1982; Outstanding Alumni Awd North TX State Univ 1987; Women on the Move Houston Post, Texas Executive Women 1986; Eagle within Award, Inroads 1986. **BUSINESS ADDRESS:** Partner, Peat, Marwick, Main & Co, 700 Louisiana, 3100 Republic Bank Bldg, Houston, TX 77210.

CLARK, SHIRLEY LORRAINE
Business executive. **PERSONAL:** Born Oct 26, 1936, Boston, MA; married James I Jr; children: James I III, Renee T, Rhonda E. **EDUCATION:** Am Bible Coll, BRE 1961; CPCU Coll of Insurance, 1978; Am Inst for Prop & Liability Underwriters, 1978. **CAREER:** EG-Bowman Co Inc, asst vice pres 1978, mgr 1975, supr 1974. **ORGANIZATIONS:** Mem NY Chap Soc of Chartered Pro and Casualty Underwriters 1979-80; di christian educ Christ Temple Inc of the Apostolic Faith 1975-80. **HONORS/ACHIEVEMENTS:** 1st black woman in US to receive CPCU Designation Chartered Prop/Casualty Underwriter 1978. **BUSINESS ADDRESS:** 97 Wall St, New York, NY 10005.

CLARK, TAMA MYERS
Judge. **EDUCATION:** Univ of PA Law School, JD 1972; Univ of PA Grad School, MA City Planning 1972; Morgan State Univ, BS 1968. **CAREER:** Office of the Dist Attny for the City & Cty of Philadelphia, asst dist attny 1973-80; Human Serv Div City of Philadelphia Law Dept, dep city solicitor 1980-83; Court of Common Please Criminal Trial Div, judge 1984-. **ORGANIZATIONS:** Mem PA State Conf of Trial Judges; bd of dir Comm Serv Planning Council, Prisoners; Family Welfare Assoc; mem The Links Inc, Coalition of 100 Black Women, Women & Girl Offenders Task Force, Mayor's Comm for Women. **HONORS/ACHIEVEMENTS:** Woman of the Year Natl Sports Found 1984; Morgan State Univ Disting Alumni of the Year Natl Assn for Equal Opport in Higher Ed 1984; Outstanding Woman of the Community Bright Hope Baptist Church Women's Comm 1984; Disting Alumnus Philadelphia Chap Morgan State Univ Alumni Assoc 1984. **BUSINESS ADDRESS:** Judge, Court of Common Pleas, 1 E Penn Square Rm 1503, Philadelphia, PA 19107.

CLARK, THEODORE LEE
Mayor. **PERSONAL:** Born Aug 29, 1907, Osceola, AR; married Bernice Walker; children: Theoplis, LeEvertt, James, Lorene Mc Cullough, Theodore Jr, Margarie McGee, Ardeen, Charles, Gloria Adams, David, Linda Rosten. **CAREER:** Village of N Lilbourn, mayor; AME Ch, minister 38 yrs; PTA, pres 14 yrs; Master Masons, sr warden 28 yrs. **ORGANIZATIONS:** Treas Bootheel Mayors Assn 2 yrs. **HONORS/ACHIEVEMENTS:** Ebony Mag 1975. **BUSINESS ADDRESS:** PO Box 139, Lilbourn, MO 63862.

CLARK, VEVE A.
Educator. **PERSONAL:** Born Dec 14, 1944, Jamaica, NY. **EDUCATION:** Univ of CA Berkeley, PhD; Queens Coll NY, MA; Univ de Nancy France, Cert d'Etudes Superieures; Queens Coll NY, BA. **CAREER:** Univ of CA Berkeley, lecturer 1974-79; Tufts Univ, assoc prof 1980-. **ORGANIZATIONS:** Archivist The Katherine Dunham Fund 1977-; coord Africa & The New World Program at Tufts Univ 1981-; bd mem Fenway Comm Devel Corp 1981-83. **HONORS/ACHIEVEMENTS:** Natl Endowment for the Arts Grants for Maya Deren Proj & Katherine Dunham Proj 1980-81; Merrill Ingram Found Writing Grant for Deren Proj 1982; Mellon Faculty Rsch Awd Tufts Univ 1983-84; Co-editor The Legend of Maya Deren, Film Culture NY 1985. **BUSINESS ADDRESS:** Associate Professor, Tufts University, 316 East Hall, Medford, MA 02155.

CLARK, VINCENT W.
Government official. **PERSONAL:** Born Apr 11, 1950, Bronx, NY; married LaVerne McBride; children: Derrick, Noelle. **EDUCATION:** LaGuardia Comm Coll, AS 1979; York Coll, BA 1983; New York Univ, MPA 1987. **CAREER:** New York City Bd of Education, asst director, management analyst, business manager, budget director. **ORGANIZATIONS:** Mem Amer Soc of Public Administrators 1982-, Assoc for School Bus Officials. **HONORS/ACHIEVEMENTS:** Mayor's Scholarship New York Univ 1985-86; Top 40 Program New York City 1986-87. **HOME ADDRESS:** 120 Maryton Road, White Plains, NY 10603. **BUSINESS ADDRESS:** Budget Dir, New York City Bd of Education, Division Special Education, 110 Livingston St, Brooklyn, NY 11201.

CLARK, WALTER H.
Business executive. **PERSONAL:** Born Jun 05, 1928, Athens, GA; married Juanita E Dillard; children: Hilton P, Jaunine C. **EDUCATION:** So IL Univ, BBA 1951; DePaul Univ, MBA 1958; Harvard Univ, Postgrad 1971. **CAREER:** IL Fed Savings & Loan Assoc 1952,54-55; 1st Fed Savings & Loan Assoc Chgo, exec vp, mem bd of dir 1955-; Citicorp, 1983-. **ORGANIZATIONS:** Mem Invest Comm YMCA Metro Chgo; bd dir Better Govt Assoc; mem adv council Coll Bus Admin; mem Univ of IL Urbana, Natl Soc Controllers & Financial Officers, Financial Exec Inst Econ Club Mem, Travelers Aid Soc Serv League 1967, Alpha Phi Alpha, Union League Club; bd dir Harvard Bus School, Snakes Soc Club; trustee Park Manor Congreg Church. **HONORS/ACHIEVEMENTS:** Black Achievers of Indust Recog Awd YMCA 1974. **MILITARY SERVICE:** AUS sgt 1952-54. **BUSINESS ADDRESS:** Citicorp, 7 S Dearborn, Chicago, IL 60603.

CLARK, WILLIAM
Elected official. **PERSONAL:** Born May 16, 1937, Meridian, MS; married Hattie Giles; children: William H, Reginald A. **EDUCATION:** Dillard Univ, BA 1961; Tuskegee Inst, MEd 1967; AL State Univ, EdS 1978. **CAREER:** Mobile Co Training Sch, teacher/coach 1961-70; Vigor HS, asst principal 1972-73; Property Realty Inc, pres 1974-; Citronelle HS, asst principal 1977-86, principal 1986; State of AL, state rep. **ORGANIZATIONS:** Mem Elks 1980-, Mobile United 1982-85, Phi Delta Kappa 1982-85. **HOME ADDRESS:** 711 Atmore Ave, Prichard, AL 36610. **BUSINESS ADDRESS:** Representative Dist 98, PO Box 10434, Prichard, AL 36610.

CLARK, WILLIAM ELGAN, JR.
Insurance administrator. **PERSONAL:** Born Apr 05, 1948, Martinsville, VA; married Rosemary Skipper; children: Jason Robert, Jennifer Lyn. **EDUCATION:** WV State, BA 1966-70. **CAREER:** Travelers Insurance Co, sr underwriter, 1970-77; Hancock Chicago, field rep, 1977-83; John Hancock Houston, mgr 1983-. **ORGANIZATIONS:** Salesman or consult for fin planning Natl Assoc Securities John Hancock Distr 1983-; treas Atascocita Civic Assoc 1984. **HONORS/ACHIEVEMENTS:** Production Leader, John Hancock Co, 1982-85. **HOME ADDRESS:** 6027 Upper Lake, Atascocita, TX 77346. **BUSINESS ADDRESS:** Manager, John Hancock Mutual Life Ins, 2218 North Park, Kingwood, TX 77379.

CLARK-THOMAS, ELEANOR M.
Educator. **PERSONAL:** Born Sep 18, 1938, Houston, TX; daughter of Alberta Palmer Henderson; married Bob Thomas; children: Natalie, Brandon, Shannon. **EDUCATION:** Kent St Univ, BS 1960; CA St Univ, MA 1973; ASHA, Certificate Clinical Competence Speech Pathology, Certificate Clinical Competence Audiology; Univ So CA, EdD pending. **CAREER:** Stockton Unified School Dist, speech & hearing therapist 1960-61; Ella School Dist & Olivehurst, speech & hearing therapist 1961-63; Sacramento City Unified School Dist, speech & hearing specialist 1963-76; St Dept of Educ, consultant, educ of communicable handicapped 1976; CA St Univ Northridge, assoc prof 1985; Folsom Cordova School Dist, speech therapist; Sacramento Co Schools, speech therapist for children, admin asst special educ. **ORGANIZATIONS:** Mem Delta Kappa Gamma 1977; mem CA Speech & Hearing Assn 1986-87; selected mem, bd dir Sacramento Hearing Soc 1974-; mem Amer Speech & Hearing Assn; mem, treasurer, coordinator council Sacramento Area Speech & Hearing Assn; mem NAUW, NBLSHA, NASDSE; pres, LA South Bay Alumnea Chapter, Delta Sigma Theta, 1989-. **HONORS/ACHIEVEMENTS:** Sustained Superior Accomplishment Award State Dept of Educ 1983-85; State Guidelines for Language-Speech Specialists, 1989. **BUSINESS ADDRESS:** Administrative Assistant, Dept of Education, 601 W 5th St, Ste 1014, Los Angeles, CA 90017.

CLARKE, ALYCE GRIFFIN
State legislator. **PERSONAL:** Born Jul 03, 1939, Yazoo, MS; daughter of Henry Griffin and Fannie Merriweather Griffin; married L W Clarke Jr, Jun 24, 1972; children: DeMarquis Clarke. **EDUCATION:** Alcorn State Univ, Lorman MS, BS, 1961; Tuskegee Univ, Tuskegee AL, MS, 1965; Mississippi Coll, Clinton MS, 1977-79; Jackson State, Jackson MS, 1982. **CAREER:** Washington County Public Schools, Leland MS, teacher, 1961-68; Mississippi Action for Progress, Jackson MS, nutritionist, 1969-71; Jackson Hinds Health Center, Jackson MS, nutritionist, 1971-87; Mississippi State Legislature, Jackson MS, state representative, 1985-. **ORGANIZATIONS:** Mem, Alcorn State Univ Alumni, 1961-89, Mississippi Assoc Community Health Centers, 1971-89, Natl Society of Nutrition, 1980-89, Mayor's Advisory Comm, 1980-89; bd mem, Mississippi Multiple Sclerosis Natl Soc, 1984-89; Mississippi Food Network, 1985-89; mem, Natl Women's Political Caucus, 1985-89; bd mem, United Way, 1986-89, Southeastern Educ Improvement Lab, 1986-89; chmn, Jackson Crime Prevention Comm, 1988. **HONORS/ACHIEVEMENTS:** WIC Coord of the Year, Mississippi Bd of Health, 1984; Employee of the Year, Jackson Hind Health Center, 1984; Outstanding Serv to Educ, Intl Alumni Council, 1984; Mississippi Woman of the Year, Hind County Federation

of Democratic Women, 1985; Distinction of being the first black woman legislator in Mississippi, 1985; Alcornite of the Year, Alcorn State Alumni, 1987; Leadership & Serv Award, Alpha Kappa Alpha Sorority, 1987.

CLARKE, ANGELA WEBB
Physician. **PERSONAL:** Born Nov 04, 1932, Baltimore, MD; daughter of Luke Webb and Cora Webb; divorced; children: Wuan, Indranee, Tarita. **EDUCATION:** Univ of MD School of Med, MD 1961. **CAREER:** UCLA Dept Comm Med, assoc prof 1970-76; Univ of NE Medical School, assoc prof; Amer Bd of Family Practice, diplomate 1972-. **MILITARY SERVICE:** WAAF, USAFR Lt col 1951-87. **HOME ADDRESS:** 3020 Bel Air Drive, Las Vegas, NV 89109.

CLARKE, BENJAMIN LOUIS
Personnel supervisor. **PERSONAL:** Born Mar 05, 1944, Springfield, OH; married Janet; children: Bryan, Darryl. **EDUCATION:** Lincoln Univ, BS Social Science 1966; Xavier Univ, MEd Counseling 1972; Univ of Cincinnati, MA Industrial Relations 1984. **CAREER:** Ford Motor Company, supervisor of personnel. **ORGANIZATIONS:** Pres Lincoln Univ Alumni Chap Dayton OH 1981-84; mem Northwestern Toastmasters 1985-; vice pres Just Us Indiv Investment Club 1985-; unit comm Detroit Boy Scout Leader 1985-. **MILITARY SERVICE:** AUS capt 2 1/2 yrs; Army Commendation Medal 1967. **BUSINESS ADDRESS:** Supervisor of Personnel, Ford Motor Company, 21500 Oakwood Blvd, Dearborn, MI 48121.

CLARKE, DONALD DUDLEY
Educator, scientist. **PERSONAL:** Born Mar 20, 1930, Kingston, Jamaica;son of I Dudley Clarke and Ivy Burrowes Clarke; married Marie B Burrowes; children: Carol, Stephen, Paula, David, Ian, Sylvia, Peter. **EDUCATION:** Fordham Clg, BS (cum laude) 1950; Fordham Univ, MS 1950-51, PhD 1951 univ of toronto, post doctoral res 1955-57. **CAREER:** NY Psychiatric Inst, research assc 1957-62; Columbia Univ Med Schl, sr res scientist 1960-62; Fordham Univ, assc prof 1962-70, prof 1970-. **ORGANIZATIONS:** Consultant Natl Inst of Mental Hlth 1972-76, Natl Inst of Hlth 1981-85; chmn chem dept Fordham Univ 1978-84; chmn, councillor NY sect Amer Chemical Socy 1976-; co-chmn Kingsbridge Manor Neighborhood Assn 1980-84. **HONORS/ACHIEVEMENTS:** NIH special fellowship Univ of PA to Research Publications in Professional Journals 1971-72. **BUSINESS ADDRESS:** Professor of Chemistry, FordhamUniv, Chemistry Dept, Bronx, NY 10458.

CLARKE, ELEANORA NORWOOD
Manager. **PERSONAL:** Born Oct 14, 1927, Norwalk, CT; divorced; children: Lynda, Leigh. **EDUCATION:** Howard Univ Wash DC, BA Political Sci 1949; Howard Univ Law Sch Wash DC,JD 1952. **CAREER:** ITT Continental Baking Co Rye NY, mgr EEO admin 1976-, asso consel law dept 1963-76; Remington Rand S Norwalk CT, legal asst legal patent div 1956-62. **ORGANIZATIONS:** Mem Nat Urban Affairs Council NE Region 1977-; mem Nat Urban League Black Exec Exchange Program 1977-; mem Rippowan Chap Bus & Prfl Women 1977-; sec Norwalk Chap NAACP; sec Carver Found Norwalk CT; mem Planned Parenthood; mem League of Women Voters; mem United Fund; mem Jack & Jill; mem The Links Inc; mem United Ch Women; mem Cibs Inc. **HONORS/ACHIEVEMENTS:** Black achievers award Harlem YMCA NY 1978; black achievers award ITT Ny 1978; black women's achievers award Carver Found Norwalk CT 1979. **BUSINESS ADDRESS:** Halstead Ave, Rye, NY 10580.

CLARKE, EUGENE H., JR.
Judge. **PERSONAL:** Born Jul 26, 1920, Philadelphia, PA; married Anne B; children: Shirley Franklin, Step-children: Ernestine Cheeves, Beverly Williams. **EDUCATION:** Howard Univ, BA 1940; Howard Univ Sch of Law, LLB 1943. **CAREER:** NAACP, chief legal counsel 1945-47; John M Langston Law Club, pres 1947; US Selective Bd, 1948-49; Criminal Justice Sect Philadelphia Bar Assn, chmn 1979; Court of Common Pleas, judge. **ORGANIZATIONS:** Pres Prisoner Family Welfare Assn 1983; chmn of Bd Women's Christian Alliance 1984; pres Philadelphia. **HONORS/ACHIEVEMENTS:** Distinguished Alumnus Awd Howard Univ 1978; J Austin Norris Barrister's Assn 1979; Philadelphia Bar Assn Criminal Justice Sect 1979 & 81; Award of Merit Olde Philadelphia Club 1980, 1983. **BUSINESS ADDRESS:** Judge, 1st Judicial Dist, Room 229 City Hall, Philadelphia, PA 19107.

CLARKE, EVEREE JIMERSON
Educator. **PERSONAL:** Born Jul 06, 1926, Merritt Island, FL; divorced; children: Frances Yvette. **EDUCATION:** Attended, Lincoln Univ 1945-48, Julliard Sch of Music 1952-54, Nova Univ 1979-82. **CAREER:** Everee Clarke Sch of Charm and Dance Inc, pres 1960-; Tri County Chap NBL, pres elegante intl; Natl Business League, natl sec 1972-76, asst regional vice pres 1986-, pres/ceo 1987. **ORGANIZATIONS:** Professional beauty/talent pageant consultant; consultant Frances Bright Women's Club Debutante Cotillion, "The Children's House" early childhood development prog, Palm Beach Co Cities in Schools prog 1985-86; mem Broward Co Republican Exec Comm 1985-88; mem City of West Palm Beach HCD Educ Comm 1987; mem BrowardCo Cncl for Black Economic Develop; mem Urban League, NAACP, Voters League. **HONORS/ACHIEVEMENTS:** Service Awd Natl Business League Washington DC 1977; Founder/Service Tri-County Chap NBL 1986. **HOME ADDRESS:** 4290 NW 19th St, Fort Lauderdale, FL 33313. **BUSINESS ADDRESS:** President and CEO, Tri-County Chapter NBL Inc, 1710 Old Okeechobee Rd, West Palm Beach, FL 33406.

CLARKE, FLETCHER JAMES
Editor. **PERSONAL:** Born Dec 09, 1942, Philadelphia, PA; married Vivian L Simmons; children: Owyda Denyse. **EDUCATION:** Temple Univ, 1963-64. **CAREER:** Philadelphia Bulletin, copy boy 1961-62; Philadelphia Bulletin, reporter 1962-72; Summer Program for Minority Journalists, dep admin 1972-73; Dem & Chronicle Rochester NY, copy editor 1973-74; Gannett News Svc, editor 1974-77; Niagara Gazette, mng editor; Gannett News Svc, copy editor 1977-80; Courier-Post Camden NJ, natl editor 1980-82; USA Today, various editing jobs 1982-84; Gannett News Service, copy editor 1984-86, business editor 1986-. **ORGANIZATIONS:** Mem Assoc Press Mng Editors 1977-, Amer Soc of Newspaper Editors 1977. **MILITARY SERVICE:** AUS sp4 1964-66. **BUSINESS ADDRESS:** Business Editor, Gannett News Service, PO Box 7858, Washington, DC 20044.

CLARKE, GRETA FIELDS
Physician/dermatologist. **PERSONAL:** Born in Detroit, MI; divorced; children: Richard. **EDUCATION:** Univ of MI, BS 1962; Howard Univ, MD 1967. **CAREER:** Harlem Hospital New York, internship 1967-68, residency internal medicine 1968-69; NY Univ Medical Ctr, residency dermatology 1969-72; Private Practice NY, dermatologist 1972-77; Arlington Medical Group Oakland CA, dermatologist 1977-79; Private Practice Berkeley CA, dermatologist 1979-. **ORGANIZATIONS:** Mem Amer Acad of Dermatology 1974-, Natl Medical Assoc 1976-, CA Medical Assoc 1977-, San Francisco Dermatological Soc 1977-; mem Jack and Jill of Amer 1977-; founding mem Northern CA Black Women Physicians 1981-; chmn Council on the Concerns of Women Physicians NMA 1983-; bd of dirs Bay Area Black UnitedFund 1985-; mem The Links Inc 1985-; chmn Region VI Natl Medical Assoc 1986-; mem Comm on Women in Med CA Med Assoc 1986-. **HONORS/ACHIEVEMENTS:** Who's Who Among Amer Women 1983; Certificate of Merit Natl Medical Assoc 1985; Professional Achievement Awd Sinkler Miller Med Assoc 1986; Founders Awd No CABlack Women Physicians 1986; Amer Spirit Awd 1987. **BUSINESS ADDRESS:** Dermatologist, 2500 Milvia St Ste 124, Berkeley, CA 94704.

CLARKE, HENRY LOUIS
Educational administrator. **PERSONAL:** Born May 28, 1908, Pickens, MS; married Dorethea Doris Falconer; children: 9 children. **EDUCATION:** Alcorn State Univ, BSA 1953; Tuskegee Inst, ME 1963; MS State Univ Further Study. **CAREER:** Holy City MB Church, sec 12 yrs; Cty ECM, sec 1980-85; Sec State Task Force Comm, mem 1984-85; State Election Commiss, adv bd election commissioner 1984-85. **ORGANIZATIONS:** Mem Democratic Party 1985, State Cty Retired Teachers Assn 1985, NEA Assn. **HONORS/ACHIEVEMENTS:** Elected Vice Pres of the State Election Comm March, 1985; 32nd Degree Mason. **HOME ADDRESS:** Rt 1 Box 173, Pickens, MS 39146.

CLARKE, JAMES ALEXANDER
Retired educator. **PERSONAL:** Born Jul 04, 1924, Jacksonville, FL; son of Rev Henry J Clarke (deceased) and Josephine Jones Clarke; married Mary Ada Zeigler, Jan 26, 1946; children: James Alexander Clarke II. **EDUCATION:** Morehouse Coll, attended 1946-47; Johnson C Smith Univ, BS 1949; NC A&T State Univ, MS 1954; Columbia Univ, MA 1963; Univ of NC-Chapel Hill, EdD 1976. **CAREER:** Kannapolis City Schools, teacher 1949-51; Rowan Co Schools, principal 1951-56; Charlotte-Mecklenburg Schools, principal & program dir 1956-72; Asheville City Schools, assoc supt 1972-77; NC Dept of Public Instruction, state dir 1977-82;Halifax County Schools, superintendent 1982-86 (retired). **ORGANIZATIONS:** Pres Div of Superintendents NC Dist VIII 1975-76; dir exec bd Natl Alliance of Black School Educators 1976-82; mem bd dirs Natl Community Educ Assoc 1980-82; deacon Martin St Baptist Church Raleigh 1980-; regional dir SE Region of Phi Beta Sigma Frat Inc 1981-84; mem AASA, NCASA, NCAE, NSBA, Sigma Pi Phi Frat, NASSP, NAACP; NC state housing coord, AARP, 1988-; deacon Martin Street Baptist Church, Raleigh, NC, 1982-; natl dir of educ, Phi Beta Sigma 1987-. **HONORS/ACHIEVEMENTS:** First black associate superintendent in NC; first black superintendent of Halifax County Schools; The Order of the Long Leaf Pine presented by Gov James Hunt of NC 1982; Educ Service Awd Phi Beta Sigma Frat 1984; Distinguished Alumni Awd Natl Assn of Equal Oppor in Higher Educ 1985; Outstanding Educ Leadership Award, Phi Beta Sigma, 1989. **MILITARY SERVICE:** AUS tech sgt 2 yrs. **HOME ADDRESS:** Box 37067, Raleigh, NC 27627.

CLARKE, JOHN HENRIK
Editor, writer, lecturer, reviewer. **PERSONAL:** Born Jan 01, 1915, Union Springs, AL; son of John Clarke and Willella Mays Clarke; married Eugenia Evans, Dec 24, 1961; children: Nzingha Marie, Sonni Kojo. **EDUCATION:** New York University, 1948-52; New School for Social Research, 1956-58; University of Ibadan, Nigeria, University of Ghana. **CAREER:** Co-founder and associate editor of Harlem Quarterly, 1949-51; New School for Social Research, New York NY, teacher of African and Afro-American history, 1956-58, developer of African Study Center, 1957-59, assistant to director, 1958-60; feature writer for Pittsburgh Courier, 1957-58, Ghana Evening News, 1958; editor of African Heritage, 1959; assistant editor of Freedomways magazine, 1962-82; director of HARYOU-ACT Heritage Teaching Program, 1964-69; Hunter College of the City University of New York, New York NY, associate professor of Black and Puerto Rican studies, 1970-86. **ORGANIZATIONS:** International Society of African Culture, African Studies Association, American Society of African Culture, founding member of Black Academy of Arts and Letters, Association for Study of Negro Life and History, American Historical Society, American Academy of Political and Social Science, African Heritage Studies Association, African Scholars Council, founding member of Harlem Writers Guild. **HONORS/ACHIEVEMENTS:** Carter G. Woodson Award, 1968, for creative contribution in editing, and 1971, for excellence in teaching; National Association for Television and Radio Announcers citation for meritorious achievement in educational television, 1969; LHD from University of Denver, 1970. **MILITARY SERVICE:** US Army Air Forces, master sergeant, 1941-45. **HOME ADDRESS:** 223 West 137 St, New York, NY 10030.

CLARKE, JOSEPH LANCE
Business executive. **PERSONAL:** Born Apr 06, 1941, New York, NY; married Marion Joyce Herron; children: Bernadette, Leslie, Lancelot. **EDUCATION:** So IL Univ Carbondale IL, 1960-63; City Coll of NY, BA 1967; NYU, 1967-68. **CAREER:** Fashion Fair Cosmetics, exec vice pres 1974-, dir of sales 1973-74; Supreme Beauty Products, dir of sales 1971-73; Livingstion Inst, mgr 1966-67. **ORGANIZATIONS:** V p Alpha Phi Alpha Frat Beta Eta Chap 1962-63; vice pres Young Dem of Mt Vernon NY 1966-68. **HONORS/ACHIEVEMENTS:** Plaque for Exemplary Serv AUS 1963-66; Letter of Accommodation AUS 1963-66; bus award Supreme Beauty Products 1970. **MILITARY SERVICE:** AUS spec/e5 1963-66. **BUSINESS ADDRESS:** 820 S Michigan Ave, Chicago, IL 60605.

CLARKE, LEON EDISON
Hospital administator. **PERSONAL:** Born Nov 17, 1949, Monrovia; married Fatu; children: Tanya, Nina, Lee Ann. **EDUCATION:** George Washington Univ, MD, 1975; Hospital of the Univ of PA, Surgical Residency, 1975-77; Medical College of PA, 1977-80; Surgical Oncology, Medical College of PA, 1980. **CAREER:** Veterans Administration Hospital, Philadelphia PA, consultant, 1981-; Medical College of PA, attending surgeon, 1981-; West Park Hospital, staff surgeon, 1985-; Mercy Catholic Medical Center, dir of surgery, 1988-. **ORGANIZATIONS:** The Medical Coll of PA, instructor of surgery, 1981-82; Assistant Professor of Surgery, 1982-; Medical Director of Surgical Procedure Unit, 1985-. **HONORS/ACHIEVEMENTS:** Valedictoria (Dux) High School; Phi Sigma Biology Honorary Society Washington & Jefferson Coll Graduatation Cum Laude; Student Representative on the Committee for New Chairman, Dept of Anatomy, George Washington Univ School of Medicine;

Golden Apple Award 1978-79, two consective academic yars Senior Medical Students Selection of the Best Teacher The Medical College of PA; Summer Research 1973; Histamine Release from Mast Cells: The Possible Effect of Papain on Bee Venom George Washington Univ School of Medicine. **BUSINESS ADDRESS:** Director of Surgery, Misericordia Hospital, 53rd & Cedar Avenue, 5th Floor, Philadelphia, PA 19143.

CLARKE, LEROY P.
Artist, poet. **PERSONAL:** Born Nov 07, 1938, Port-of-Spain, Trinidad and Tobago;divorced; children: Kappel, Ra-nkosane. **CAREER:** Artist; poet; tchr 1959-67. **ORGANIZATIONS:** Numerous exhibits 1969-; one-man exhibition, Studio Mus 1972; artist-in-residence, Studio Mus 1973-76. **HONORS/ACHIEVEMENTS:** Published portfolios of drawings, Fragments of a Spiritual 1972; Douens 1976; poems & drawings, Taste of Endless Fruit 1974; drawings, In a Quiet Way 1971; one-man exhibition, Douens at Howard Univ 1976; complete Douens' series exhibition, Port-of-Spain, Trinidad 1979.

CLARKE, RAYMOND
Organization executive. **PERSONAL:** Born Aug 02, 1950, Cincinnati, OH; son of William Clarke (deceased) and Genie Johnson Clarke (deceased); married Debra Ray Clarke, Dec 29, 1984; children: Terri Hunter, Paul Ray Clarke. **EDUCATION:** Univ of Arizona, Tucson AZ, BS 1973, MS, 1978. **CAREER:** Univ of AZ, counselor, youth, 1971, 1972; Pima County Juvenile Court Center, deputy dir, probation, 1973-84; Governor Bruce Babbitt, exec dir, health council 1984-86; Tucson Urban League Inc, pres/ceo Agency 1986-. **ORGANIZATIONS:** Mem, Pi Lambda Theta, 1977-; pres, Tucson Chapter Natl Assn of Black Social Workers, 1978-79; mem, AZ Small Businessmen Assn, 1979; consultant, Student Athletes Univ of AZ, 1980-81; mem, Mayor's Task Force, Economic Development, 1988-89; mem, Governor's Task Force on Welfare Reform, 1988-89; mem, Regents Ad-Hoc Committee, Minority Access and Retention, 1988-; mem, State Supreme Court Taskforce, 1989; mem, Tucson Community Foundation Grants Committee, 1988-. **HONORS/ACHIEVEMENTS:** One of the Youngest Administrator in the Juvenile Justice System, 1977; Co-Founder of the Tucson Chapter of the Natl Assn of Black Soc, 1978; Development and Implemention of an Educational and Career Development, 1979; Meritorious Recognition/Natl for Juvenile Delinquency Prevention, 1980; State Image Award, NAACP, 1980; Outstanding Young Men, OYM of America, 1980, 1982; Service to Youth, Foundation, Pima County, 1983; Service to Community, Optimist Club, Tucson, 1983; Service to Black College Students, UFA Black Alumni, 1988; Panelist, Documented Forum, Program for Student Athletes on Civil Rights in AZ, 1989. **BUSINESS ADDRESS:** President and Chief Executive Officer, Tucson Urban League, Inc, 2305 S Park Avenue, Tucson, AZ 85713.

CLARKE, RICHARD V.
Business executive. **PERSONAL:** Born Jun 11, 1927, New York City, NY; divorced; children: Tracy, Chip. **EDUCATION:** City Coll of NY City. **CAREER:** Richard Clarke Assos Inc, pres 1964-; Hallmark Employment Agy, fdr 1957; consult to fed, state & pvt agencies. **ORGANIZATIONS:** Mem NY State Econ Devel Bd; mem NY State Bd of Tourism; bd dirs NY State Council of the Arts. **BUSINESS ADDRESS:** President, Richard Clarke Assoc, Inc, 9 West 95th St, New York, NY 10001.

CLARKE, THEODORE HENSON
Podiatric physician & surgeon. **PERSONAL:** Born Feb 18, 1923, Martins Ferry, OH; married Ada Miller; children: Jeffrey Allen, Wendell Howard. **EDUCATION:** Sumner Coll KS City MO, Pre-podiatry 1943; IL Coll of Podriatric Med, DPM 1950. **CAREER:** Podiatry Clinic Ltd, doctor of podiatric med 1950-; Meridian & Foot Clinic Indianapolis, part owner 1972-. **ORGANIZATIONS:** Past pres/Mem Am Podiatry Assn 1950-; past pres & mem IN State Podiatry Assn 1950-; past pres/Fellow mem Am Acad of Podiatric Adminstrn 1956-; fellow mem Am Coll of Foot Surgeons 1970; past liaison & present mem bd of trustees Nat Podiatry Assn 1972; fellow mem Acad of Ambulatory Foot Surgery 1975; past pres & mem Alumni EdnFound ICPM 1967-; mem bd of trustees ICPM; past mem action bd/Present mem governing council Am Pub Health Assn; mem IN Pub Health Assn; mem bd trustees Howard Co Diabetes Assn; mem Am Acad of Human Serv; mem Intl Physician's Fellowship; mem Am Acad of Podiatric & Sports Medicine; mem Am Assn of Hosp Podiatrists; fellow mem Am Soc of Podiatric Medicine; other present & past professional ofcs. **HONORS/ACHIEVEMENTS:** Numerous honors; author of many pub lectures books & papers; editor Yearbook of Podiatric Medicine & Surgery Futura Publs. **BUSINESS ADDRESS:** Podiatry Clinic, Ltd, 320 E Taylor St, Kokomo, IN 46901.

CLARKE, THOMAS P.
Appraiser of american books & manuscript. **PERSONAL:** Born May 03, 1917, E Orange, NJ; married Bahrel Daly; children: Marlene, Stuart. **CAREER:** Sotheby Parke Bernet Inc, asst vice pres 1972, asst dir 1975; appraiser Wm Randolph Hearst Castle; appraiser Mrs Murial Vanderbilt Adams; appraiser MrsMarion Deering; appraiser Mrs Marjorie Tamayo Mansion; Sotheby Parke Bernet Inc, consul dept of books & manuscripts. **ORGANIZATIONS:** Mem AB Bookman's Weekly; mem Masons; mem Grolier Club. **MILITARY SERVICE:** AUS s/sgt 1942-45. **BUSINESS ADDRESS:** Consultant, Sothebys Dept of Books, 1334 York Ave, New York, NY 10021.

CLARKE, VELMA GREENE
Educator/administrator. **PERSONAL:** Born Sep 20, 1930, Chicago, IL; daughter of Sherman L Greene Jr. and Zadie Morgan Greene; divorced; children: Gwendolyn Clarke-Sills. **EDUCATION:** Fisk Univ Nashville, AB 1957, MA 1961; The Univ of MI, ABD 1973. **CAREER:** Talladega Coll, dean of women 1960-62; Edward Waters Coll, dir prof 1962-65; Shaw Univ, dir prof 1965-71; Eastern MI Univ Coll of Arts & Scis, adminis assoc. **ORGANIZATIONS:** Bd dirs Amer Assoc on Higher Educ 1972-74; mem Executive Comm on Higher Educ AME Church 1973-76; Delta Sigma Theta Sorority 1987-. **HONORS/ACHIEVEMENTS:** Ford Foundation Advanced Study Fellowship 1971-74; The Univ of MI Rackham Awd 1972-73. **BUSINESS ADDRESS:** Administrative Associate, Eastern MI University, College of Arts & Sciences, Ypsilanti, MI 48197.

CLARKE, WILLIAM DECKER
Attorney. **PERSONAL:** Born Jul 25, 1925, Cleveland, OH; married Edwina F Gilman; children: Lynda Mychelle, Leigh Decker, Ondre Decker, Renauld Gillman. **EDUCATION:** Samuel Huston Coll, BA 1947; Catholic Univ of Amer, MA 1949; Howard Univ School of Law, JD 1952. **CAREER:** Carver Fed Savings & Loan Assoc, gen counsel 1963-67; City of NY Housing Dev Admin, dep comm 1967-70; Commonwealth Insurance Co, counsel 1971-75; Centennial Abstract Corp, pres 1975-80; Scene Magazine, atty, pres, publ. **ORGANIZATIONS:** Sec, treas LH Stanten Publs Inc 1980-; chmn bd dir Sickle Cell Anemia Found of NY 1967-79; eastern vice pres Alpha Phi Alpha 1969-71; mem bd dir Citizen Advocate for Justice NY 1983-. **HONORS/ACHIEVEMENTS:** Over 25 awds for civil & public serv from various orgs.

CLAY, CAMILLE ALFREDA
Educational administrator, mental health counselor. **PERSONAL:** Born Aug 21, 1946, Washington, DC; daughter of James Clay and Doris Coates CLay. **EDUCATION:** Hampton Inst, BA 1968; Univ of DC, MA 1974; Psychiatric Inst Ctr for Group Studies, certificate 1972-74; George Washington Univ, EdD 1984. **CAREER:** DC Comm Mental Health Dept, mental health specialist 1971-72; SW Interagency Training Ctr, manpower develop specialist 1972-74; Private Practice, group therapist 1973-79; City of Bowie MD Youth Serv Bureau, asst dir 1974-76; Private Practice, mental health and career counselor 1983-; Towson State Univ, couns/sr counselor 1977-85, asst vice pres for minority affairs 1986-. **ORGANIZATIONS:** Mem NAACP, Phi Delta Kappa, Alpha Kappa Alpha; bd dirs Alfred Adler Inst of DC; past pres DC Mental Health Counselors Assoc; mem Amer Assoc for Counseling and Develop, DCACD, Assoc for Multi-Cultural Counseling and Develop; mem Alpha Kappa Alpha, Amer Mental Health Counselors Assoc; Assn of Black Psychologists; past president, DC Assn for Counselors and Develop 1987-88; chairperson, Licensure DCACD 1988-. **HONORS/ACHIEVEMENTS:** Study in Germany, Experiment in International Living 1966; Outstanding Young Women of Amer 1979; mem Omicron Delta Kappa Honor Leadership Society 1988; published dissertation, The Psychosocial Development of Middle Class African American Men & Women 1984; certification, Natl Certified Counselor NBCC/AACD, 1983. **BUSINESS ADDRESS:** Asst Vice Pres for Minority Affairs, Towson State University, Towson, MD 21204.

CLAY, CASSIUS See ALI, MUHAMMAD

CLAY, CLIFF
Artist. **PERSONAL:** Born in Greenwood, MS. **EDUCATION:** Cleveland Inst Art; Cooper Art Sch. **CAREER:** Prof Paul Travis, aprntc; Self Employed, painting tanned animal skins various other forms of painting. **ORGANIZATIONS:** Hon yet offcl deputy sheriff in Kay Co OK; mem The Karamu House; mem NAACP; Urban League Hon Amer Indian Pow-Wow 1969; hon mem 101 Ranch Ponca &City OK; me report on health conditions of Am Indian Am Med Assn 1974; bd mem 101 Ranch Restoration Found Ponca City OK; bd mem Afro Am Hist & Cult Museum, Cleveland OH; guest speaker & instr; has had various exhibits & one man hsows; scout for Red Carpet County; promote Hist Landmarks in 19 Counties inNW OK. **BUSINESS ADDRESS:** 10605 Chester Ave, Cleveland, OH 44106.

CLAY, ERIC LEE
Attorney. **PERSONAL:** Born Jan 18, 1948, Durham, NC; son of Austin Clay and Betty Allen Clay (deceased). **EDUCATION:** Univ of NC, BA 1969; Yale Univ Law School, JD 1972. **CAREER:** Lewis, White & Clay, atty 1973-; US Dist Ct for the Eastern Dist of MI, law clerk 1972-73; State of MI, special asst atty general 1974-75; Lewis White & Clay PC, dir, atty. **ORGANIZATIONS:** Arbitrator Amer Arbitration Assn 1976-; mem MI Soc of Hospital Atty 1978-; life mem 6th Circuit Jud Conf 1979; mem State Bar of MI 1972-, Wolverine Bar Assn 1973-, Amer Bar Assn 1973-, Detroit Bar Assn 1973-; mem Phi Beta Kappa; life mem Natl Bar Assn; life mem NAACP; mem Natl Assn of Railroad Trial Counsel; mem State Bar of MI Insurance Law Comm 1984-; trustee Detroit Bar Assn Foundation 1985-; mem, Eerit Selection Panel on Bankruptcy Judgeships, 1986-87; mem, Sixth Circuit Committee on the Bicentennial of the Constitution, 1986-; mem, Executive Committee, Yale Law School Assn, 1989-. **HONORS/ACHIEVEMENTS:** Admitted to practice State of MI 1972, US Dist Ct for the Eastern Dist of MI 1972, US Ct of Appeals for the Sixth Circuit 1978, US Supreme Ct 1977. **BUSINESS ADDRESS:** Attorney, Lewis, White & Clay PC, 1300 First Natl Building, Detroit, MI 48226.

CLAY, HAROLD R.
Engineer. **PERSONAL:** Born Dec 14, 1936, Philadelphia, PA; married Jeannette Bouden; children: Jennifer, Allison. **EDUCATION:** Drexel U, BS 1959, MS 1964. **CAREER:** GE Nuclear Energy Div, mgr control room design engineering 1971-; GE, sr engr control room design 1970-71; Lockheed Missiles & Space Div, design specialist1969-70; GE Space Systems & Div, supr engr 1967-69; GE Adv Space Proj Dept, vehicle design engr 1965-67; GE, structural analysis engr 1960-63; NAm Aviation, structural analysis engr 1959. **BUSINESS ADDRESS:** 175 Curtner Ave, San Jose, CA.

CLAY, HENRY CARROLL, JR.
Clergyman. **PERSONAL:** Born Jun 08, 1928, Yazoo City, MS; married Effie Husbands; children: Henry III. **EDUCATION:** Rust Coll, AB, MS 1952, DD 1969; Gammom Theol Sem, BD 1956. **CAREER:** Central United Meth Ch Jackson MS, min 1978-; Jackson Dist & United Meth Ch, dist supt 1967-73; Christian Educ MS Conf, exec sec 1959-67; St Paul UMC, pstr 1961-67; St Mark UMC, pastor 1956-61; MS Ann Conf, full connection 1956, on trail 1954; UMC, elder 1956, deacon 1954; Pub Sch, tchr 1952-53. **ORGANIZATIONS:** Staff mem MS Conf Cncl on Ministries United Meth Ch 1973-78; mem MS Conf Bd of Ministry 1968-76; Gen Bd of Discipleship UMC 1972-; staff mem UMC 1973-; pres MS Religious Ldrsp Conf 1975-76; del Gen Conf UMC 1976-80; 13th World Meth Conf; chmn Rust Coll Bd of Tst 1971-77; mem Bethlehem Ctr Bd Dir 1967; bd dir MS Cncl on Human Rels; mem Operation Shoestring Bd Dir; mem NAACP; bd dir Mississippians for Educ TV; MS YMCA Nat Meth Schlrsp 1954-55; Gammon Faculty & Schlrsp9 195. **HONORS/ACHIEVEMENTS:** Citz yr award Omega Psi Phi Frat; outstsdng religious ldr award MS Religious Ldrsp Conf. **BUSINESS ADDRESS:** 500 N Farish St, Jackson, MS 39203.

CLAY, NATHANIEL, JR.
Educational administrator. **PERSONAL:** Born Nov 09, 1943, Charleston, WV; married Margaret Z Walton; children: Victoria Anne, Lezlie Denise. **EDUCATION:** Bluefield State Clg, BS 1964; MI State Univ, MAT 1974; Univ of MI PhD 1980. **CAREER:** Pontiac Public Schools, elementary teacher 1964-68, dir of eary childhood educ 1968-70, asst dir state/fed programs 1970-74; Jackson Public Schools, dir state/fed programs 1974-78. **ORGANIZATIONS:** Pres MI Assc State/Fed Fed Speclst 1981-82; boardmem Schl Alliance Poltcl Action 1980-; mem Am Assc of Schl Admn 1980-; bd mem Land O'Lakes Scout Cncl 1983-, Jackson

Poltcl Action Caucus 1979-, Ella Sharp Museum 1981-. **HONORS/ACHIEVEMENTS:** Otstndg Young Edctr Pontiac Paraprfsnl Assc 1974; Spec Achvmnt Negro Bus Prfsnl Women 1983; Spec Serv MI Assc State/Fed Prg Spclsts 1982. **HOME ADDRESS:** 3396 Hathaway Ln, Jackson, MI 49201. **BUSINESS ADDRESS:** Deputy Superintendent, Jackson Pblc Schls, 1400 West Monroe, Jackson, MI 49201.

CLAY, PATRICIA ANN
Accountant. **PERSONAL:** Born Feb 01, 1963, Wichita Falls, TX. **EDUCATION:** Univ of TX at Austin, BBA Accounting 1985. **CAREER:** ARCO Oil & Gas Co, revenue accountant. **ORGANIZATIONS:** Mem bd of dirs Natl Business League 1984-85; pres Delta Sigma Theta Epsilon Beta Chap 1984-85. **HONORS/ACHIEVEMENTS:** Scholarship Amer Inst of CPA's 1984; Scholarship George M Kozmetsky Presidential School 1984-85; Scholarship Peat Marwick & Mitchell 1983; Scholarship TX Achievement Awd 1981-85. **BUSINESS ADDRESS:** Revenue Accountant, ARCO Oil & Gas Co, PO Box 2819, Dallas, TX 75221.

CLAY, REUBEN ANDERSON, JR.
Physician. **PERSONAL:** Born Feb 08, 1938, Richmond, VA; son of Rueben R Clay and Sue Clarke Clay; married Ardelia Brown, Jun 17, 1987; children: Raymond Alan, Adrienne Beth. **EDUCATION:** Amherst Coll, BA 1960; Univ of Rochester, MD 1964. **CAREER:** San Francisco Gen Hosp, internship 1964-65; Cornell Univ Med Ctr, resd 1967-68; Univ of CA, resd ob-gyn 1968-71; private practice, physician; UCSF, assoc clin prof 1981-; Ralph K Davies Med Ctr, chief of gynecology 1982-86. **ORGANIZATIONS:** Mem San Francisco Cty Med Soc, CMA, NMA, AMA, Amer Fert Soc; diplomate Amer Bd Ob Gyn 1973; fellow Amer Coll of Ob Gyn 1974; asst clin prof UCSF 1974-; mem San Francisco Gyn Soc; pres Parnassus Hts Ob Gyn Med Group Inc 1979-89; sec Dist IX Amer Coll of Ob Gyn 1981-88. **MILITARY SERVICE:** USAF capt 1965-67. **BUSINESS ADDRESS:** Pacific Gynecology and Obstetrics Medical Group, 2100 Webster St #319, San Francisco, CA 94115.

CLAY, ROSS COLLINS
Educator. **PERSONAL:** Born Dec 15, 1908, Conehatta, MS; married Ollie Dolores Billingslea; children: Ross, Jr. **EDUCATION:** Jackson State U, Atnd 1934; Fisk U, MA 1940; Northwestern U, MUSM Educ 1953; IN U, Study 1961-62; MS Southern U, Workshop 1970. **CAREER:** Jackson State Univ, dir music educ, tutorial teacher 1953-74; Lane Coll, dir music 1948-53; Philander Smith Coll, dir music 1946-48; Friendship Jr Coll, dir music defense worker 1943-46; Geeter High School, music educ 1940-43; AR Baptist Coll, music educ 1936-38; Humphries Co Tr School, music educ 1935-36; Corinth Hihg School, dir music 1934-35; Dir Music Educ Tutorial Teacher, composer ch music, piano, organ, instruments, voices. **ORGANIZATIONS:** Mem Music Educators Nat Con; mem NEA; mem MTA; mem Am Assn of Univ Profs; mem Nat Council of Sr Cits; AARP. **HONORS/ACHIEVEMENTS:** Recip NART Cert Merit JSU1974; plaque in honor of retirement Farish Bapt Ch 1974; trophy Student Chap MENC; guest performer Retired Cits Paterson NJ 1975; Who's Who in S & SW 1970-75; Mem of Achievement 1975; 32 deg Mason.

CLAY, RUDOLPH
Elected govt. official. **PERSONAL:** Born Jul 16, 1935, Gary, IN; married Christine Swan Clay; children: Rudolph Jr. **EDUCATION:** IN Univ, 1956. **CAREER:** State of IN, state senator 1972-76; Lake Co IN, county councilman 1978-85, recorder 1985-, county commissioner 1987-91. **MILITARY SERVICE:** AUS. **HOME ADDRESS:** 4201 W 10th, Gary, IN 46404.

CLAY, STANLEY BENNETT
Writer, producer, director. **PERSONAL:** Born Mar 18, 1950, Chicago, IL. **EDUCATION:** Banning High School, diploma 1968. **CAREER:** Motion Pictures, TV Shows, Commercials, Stage Plays, 200 starring, co-starring roles 1968-; Argo Reportory Co, artistic dir 1971-74; One Flight Up Theatre Co, resident dir playwright 1974-80; Preceptor Communications, producer/director/playwright; Los Angeles Theatre Review, theatre critic 1989-, producer/dir/co-writer, 2nd Annual NAACP Theatre Awards 1989, producer/dir, Los Angeles Black Family Reunion Concerts sponsored by Natl Council of Negro Women 1989, dir 7th Annual Ira Aldridge Awards 1989. **ORGANIZATIONS:** Mem exec comm NAACP Beverly Hills Hollywood Branch 1977-80; entertainment editor Sepia magazine 1981; publisher/editor-in-chief SBC Hollywood monthly magazine 1983-; Amer corres for London's Blues and Soul magazine 1984-87; mem bd of dirs The Intl Friendship Network; producer dir and author of "Ritual" at Theatre of Arts LA; vice pres, bd of dirs The Los Angeles Black Theatre 1989-; mem Los Angeles Black Playwrites 1988-. **HONORS/ACHIEVEMENTS:** Three Drama Logue Awds for Disting Writing Direction Production of "Ritual" 1982; Drama Logue Awd/Best Actor starring in "Zoomen and the Sign" 1984; NAACP Image Awd/Best Actor for starring in "Anna Lucasta" 1986; 3 NAACP Theatre Awards, NAACP 1987; author of novel, Diva (Holloway House) 1987; author of play, The Night The Queen of Outerspace Played Z, produced at Inner City Cultural Center 1988. **BUSINESS ADDRESS:** Producer/Director/Playwright, Preceptor Communications, 8033 Sunset Blvd Ste 707, West Hollywood, CA 90046.

CLAY, THEODORE ROOSEVELT, JR.
Educational administrator. **PERSONAL:** Born Jun 06, 1931, Huntsville, AL; married Eunice Johnson; children: Carla Latrice. **EDUCATION:** Alabama A & M, BS 1955; Chicago ST Univ, MsEd 1970; Univ of Sarasota, EdD 1980. **CAREER:** US Govt, Redstone Arsenal, tech writer 1955-62; Creiger Voc HS, English teacher 1962-65, counselor 1965-70, asst principal 1970-. **ORGANIZATIONS:** Omega Psi Phi; regional vice pres AL A&M Alumni Assoc; Natl Soc of Minority Writers; IL Voc Guidance Assoc; mem Bethany Lodge #63 F&AM Prince Hall; mem Elder Park Manor Christian Church; mem bd of trustees Univ of Sarasota. **HONORS/ACHIEVEMENTS:** Outstanding Service Awd So Shore Valley Cmmty 1974, Cregier Voc HS 1985; Outstanding Service Afro Amer Org 1977; NAFEO Dist Alumni of the Year AL A&M 1986; CSU's Outstanding Alumni Teacher's Awd Chicago St Univ 1986. **MILITARY SERVICE:** US Air Force sgt 1949-53. **HOME ADDRESS:** 8931 S Euclid Ave, Chicago, IL 60617. **BUSINESS ADDRESS:** Administrator, Chicago Board of Education, 2040 W Adams St, Chicago, IL 60612.

CLAY, TIMOTHY BYRON
Project director, Birmingham Minority Business Development Center. **PERSONAL:** Born Sep 22, 1955, Louisville, KY; son of Bernard H Clay and Louise Middleton Clay; married Phyllis Wells Clay, May 11, 1978; children: Jacqueline Simone Clay, Arielle Christine Clay. **EDUCATION:** Oakwood Coll, Huntsville AL, BS 1976-78; Univ of AL, Birmingham AL, MBA 1978-82. **CAREER:** Bell South Svcs, staff analyst 1978-86; Protective Industrial Ins Co, controller 1986-; Protective Indus Insurance Co, Birmingham AL, comptroller, 1986-87; Porter White Yardley Capitol Inc, Birmingham AL, project dir 1987-. **ORGANIZATIONS:** Sec Business Assocs of Amer Inc; instructor Miles Coll; writer Birmingham Times; mem Big Brothers/Big Sisters; mem Birmingham Assn of Urban Bankers, 1988-. **HONORS/ACHIEVEMENTS:** Leadership Award, Birmingham AL, 1989. **BUSINESS ADDRESS:** Project Director, Porter White Yardley Capital Inc, 2100 16th Ave S, #203, Birmingham, AL 35205.

CLAY, WILLIAM A. L.
Clergyman. **PERSONAL:** Born Feb 20, 1899, Selma, AL; married Anna Pearl; children: William A. **EDUCATION:** Selma U, BS; Duncan Coll, AB; Duncan Sem & Coll, BD, DD; Union Theol Sem, AM; Columbia U, AM Edn; Temple U, PhD Pending. **CAREER:** US Civil & Serv, 20 yrs; Businessman, 30 yrs; Philadelphia Pub Sch, 10 yrs; Religious Service, found pastor resurrection sanctuary 1915-. **ORGANIZATIONS:** 1st black dept chaplain Am Legion 1972-73; sec 3 Ministerial Conferences & Assn; chaplain & trustee Worshipful Master Masons 16 yrs; mem 1st African BaptCh. **HONORS/ACHIEVEMENTS:** Awards from WW II & Am Legion; Chapel of the Four Chaplains. **MILITARY SERVICE:** AUS col 20 yrs.

CLAY, WILLIAM L.
Congressman. **PERSONAL:** Born Apr 30, 1931, St Louis, MO; married Carol A Johnson; children: Vicki, Lacy, Michelle. **EDUCATION:** St Louis U, BS 1953. **CAREER:** Elected Alderman, 1959-1963; St Co & Municipal Employees Union; bus rep 1961-1964; 26th Ward, dem committeeman 1964-; 1st Dist MO, congressman. **ORGANIZATIONS:** NAACP; CORE; St Louis Civil Serv; Opened many unions for Blacks; House Com Ed & Labor; chmn Labor Mgmt Relations Subcom; Com Post Office & Civil Service; committee on House Admin. **BUSINESS ADDRESS:** Congressman, House of Representatives, Washington, DC 20515.

CLAY, WILLIAM LACY, JR.
Government official. **PERSONAL:** Born Jul 27, 1956, St Louis, MO; son of William L Clay and Carol A Clay; married Leslie Renee. **EDUCATION:** Univ of MD, BS Political Sci 1983, Cert in Paralegal Studies 1982. **CAREER:** US House of Rep, asst doorkeeper 1976-83; real estate salesman; Missouri General Assembly, representative. **HOME ADDRESS:** 6136 Washington, St Louis, MO 63112. **BUSINESS ADDRESS:** Representative, MO General Assembly, State Capitol Bldg, Rm 115B, Jefferson City, MO 65101.

CLAY, WILLIAM ROGER
Judge. **PERSONAL:** Born Oct 16, 1919, Phoenix, AZ; married Jacqueline Laura Banks; children: William R III, Benjamin R. **EDUCATION:** Southwestern Univ, LLB 1956. **CAREER:** LA Police Dept, policeman 1946-66; LA Co Publ Defenders Off, atty 1966; LA Neighborhood Legal Serv Soc, atty 1966-68; LA Superior Ct, referee 1968-70; LA Co, comm 1970-73; Inglewood Municip Ct, judge 1973-76; LA Co Superior Ct, judge 1976-. **ORGANIZATIONS:** Past pres Congr 1971; chrmn Parish Educ Bd; mem trustee bd Men's Club; comm Lutheran Ch & Ascension Luth Ch; mem Crenshaw YMCA & Y's Men's Club; bdmem YMCA; bd mem Boy's Club; mem LA Co Bar Assn; mem Natl Bar Assn; Judicature; mem CA Judges Assn; mem Retired Police Officer's Assn; NAACP mem Urban League. **HONORS/ACHIEVEMENTS:** Citation LA City Council. **MILITARY SERVICE:** AUS Staff Sgt 1940-44; AUS Reserves 1st Lt 1944-45, Major 1945-56. **BUSINESS ADDRESS:** Judge, Kenyon Juvenile Justice Center, 7625 S Central, Los Angeles, CA 90001.

CLAY, WILLIE B.
Minister. **PERSONAL:** Born Feb 16, 1929, Yazoo City, MS; married Ruth Davis; children: Gladys, Willie Jr, Jonathan, Margo, Lara. **EDUCATION:** Rust Coll, Grad; Gammon Theol Sem, Grad; Wiley Coll, DD. **CAREER:** North IL Conf Unit Meth Ch, council dir 6 yrs; MS, pastorates; IN, pastorates; IL, pastorates; Chic So Dist of North IL, dist supt 6 yrs; Gorham United Methodist Church, minister. **ORGANIZATIONS:** Mem Bd of Trustees N Cent Coll; mem Gammon & Theol Sem; del Gen Conf & Juris Conf of Unit Meth Ch; mem Rotary Club of Chic. **BUSINESS ADDRESS:** Minister, Gorham UM Church, 5600 S Indiana Ave, Chicago, IL 60637.

CLAYBORN, RAY DEWAYNE
Professional athlete. **PERSONAL:** Born Jan 02, 1955, Fort Worth, TX; son of Adell Clayborn and Jessie Wilson Clayborn; married Cindy Cavazos Clayborn, Nov 12, 1984; children: Lindsey Marie. **EDUCATION:** University of Texas, Austin, TX; B.S. Communications, 1977. **CAREER:** New England Patriots, corner back 1977-. **HONORS/ACHIEVEMENTS:** As rookie named to Pro Football Weekly's All-AFC and All-Pro squads as a kickoff returner; set 5 Patriot kickoff return records as a rookie; 2nd team All-AFC by UPI; 2nd team All-Pro by Coll and Pro Football Newsweekly; 2nd team All-NFL by NEA; mem Pro Bowl teams 1984,86,87; mem, Natl Found and Hall of Fame. **BUSINESS ADDRESS:** New England Patriots, Sullivan Stadium Route 1, Foxboro, MA 02035.

CLAYBORN, WILMA W.
Educator, business executive. **PERSONAL:** Born Aug 21, Louisville, KY; daughter of Louis Albert Westfield and Loreta Kline Westfield; widowed; children: Terrence A, Jocelyn L Clayborn Raymore. **EDUCATION:** KY State Univ, BS 1960; Catherine Spalding Univ, MEd 1971; IN State Univ SE, grad work; Univ of Louisville, post grad. **CAREER:** Grace Gospel Music Co, entrepreneur/publisher/promoter 1969-; Jefferson Co Public Schools, science tchr 1974-76, instructional coord 1976-78, tchr of biology science 1963-; Math, Science, Technology Magnet Science Resource Consultant, Jeff Co Public School 1987-89 (retired); Lincoln Found Math/Science Program, teacher, 1984-. **ORGANIZATIONS:** Mem Natl C of Gospel Choirs & Choruses Inc, NEA, KEA, LEA; chairperson Minority Involv Caucus; LEA 1971-74; coord Human Relations Workshop 1972-74; mem bd dir KY Assn for Progress in Sci 1974; natl reg local directress Youth & Young Adult Choirs Ch of God 1967-; directress various gospel choirs; mem Religious Radio Announcers Guild 1977-; officer Louisville Gospel Choral Union 1968-88. **HONORS/ACHIEVEMENTS:** Outstanding Young Educator Awd Louisville Jaycees 1972; Citation Pioneer in Educ for Innovations in Educ 1970-71; Outstanding Secondary Educators Amer 1973; Words & Music to song: "Jesus Is The Sunshine

of My Life". **BUSINESS ADDRESS:** Owner/Entrepreneur, Grace Music Co, PO Box 2138, Louisville, KY 40201.

CLAYBORNE, ONEAL
Elected official. **PERSONAL:** Born Dec 17, 1940, DeKalb, MS; married Deborah Roberts; children: Michelle, Shaneal. **EDUCATION:** Whisenton High Dekalb MS, diploma. **CAREER:** Pct #48 E St Louis, pct committeeman 1979-87; Aldermanic Pub Safety Comm, chmn 1981-85; City of E St Louis, alderman 1979-87. **ORGANIZATIONS:** Chmn Project ONEAL Citizen Patrol Neighborhood Watch 1982-85. **HONORS/ACHIEVEMENTS:** Special Achievement Awd Natl Coalition to Ban Handguns 1982. **HOME ADDRESS:** 840 N 79th St, East St Louis, IL 62203.

CLAYBOURNE, EDWARD P.
Educator. **PERSONAL:** Born Apr 07, 1927, Chattanooga, TN; married Earnestine Crawford; children: Kimberly, Karen, Kaye, Kenneth. **EDUCATION:** TN State U, BS 1952, MS 1968. **CAREER:** Harrison HS, asst prin/dean 1980; Harrison HS Evansville, asst 1975-; Central HS Evansville IN, counselor 1966-75; Lincoln HS Evansville, coach & tchr 1957-62; Educator, coach & tchr 1952-57; I & II Regional Tournament, football play-off champs. **ORGANIZATIONS:** Mem NEA; IN Tchr Assn; TN Tchr Assn; Evansville Tchr Assn; Assn Tchr Educators; HPER Assn Counselor Assn 33 deg Mason; mem NAACP Frofl Contract; coll soph LA Rams; 1st Black Coach Predom White Sch. **BUSINESS ADDRESS:** 5400 N First Ave, Evansville, IN.

CLAYE, CHARLENE MARETTE
Art historian. **PERSONAL:** Born Apr 06, 1945, Chicago, IL; divorced. **EDUCATION:** Univ of Bridgeport, BA 1966; Univ of Paris, certificate 1968; Howard Univ, MA 1970. **CAREER:** Univ of DC, instructor, 1970, 1973; Howard Univ Washington, instructor, 1970 1973; Spelman Coll Atlanta, instructor, 1971-72; Clayton Jr Coll, instructor, 1972-; New Muse, exec dir 1974-78; CA Afro Amer Museum, exec dir 1982-83; Mariposa, proprietor. **ORGANIZATIONS:** Pres Natl Conf of Artists 1976-78; assoc dir African Cultural Serv 1970; Amer Soc for Aesthetics. **HONORS/ACHIEVEMENTS:** Pubished curator "The Black Artist in the WPA" 1933-43; article on symbollism of African Textiles Contemporary Weavers Assn of TX; cover design for Logic for Black Undergrad; Curator permanent exhibit on "The Black Contrib to Devel of Brooklyn 1660-1960"; grants, Travel for Mus Professional Natl Mus Act 1976; Aid to Special Exhibitions Natl Endowment of the Art 1976; Planning Grant Natl Endowment for the Humanities 1976; Aid to Special Exhibitions Natl Endowment for the Arts 1977. **HOME ADDRESS:** 3209 Ewing St, Houston, TX 77004.

CLAYTON, CHARLES M.
Attorney. **PERSONAL:** Born Jul 26, 1889, Clayton, AL; married Francis D; children: Sylvia Francis, Sheila Denise. **EDUCATION:** Morehouse Coll, BS 1914; Atlanta U, MA 1936; LaSalle Ext U, LLB 1941. **CAREER:** Walden D'Antignac, asso atty 1975-; Decatur GA, prin city sch 1932-53; Sylvia Bryant Bapt Inst, 1915-32. **ORGANIZATIONS:** Adminstr to Bar 1944; mem Gate & City Bar Assn; GA Bar Assn; Atlanta Bar Assn; adv bd Hughes Spalding Pavillion; Decatur Civic League; Butler St YMCA;Deacon Wheat St Bapt Ch Built 1st Black High Sch Decatur 1932. **BUSINESS ADDRESS:** 195 1/2 Auburn Ave NE, Atlanta, GA 30303.

CLAYTON, CONSTANCE
Educational administrator. **EDUCATION:** Temple Univ, BA Elem Edn, MA Elem Sch Admin; Univ of PA, PhD 1981. **CAREER:** Harrison Elementary School Philadelphia, teacher; US Dept of Labor Women's Bur, reg dir 1971-72; Early Childhood Progs, dir & exec dir; Philadelphia School Dist, assoc supt, supt 1982-. **BUSINESS ADDRESS:** Superintendent, Schl District of Philadelphia, 21st & Parkway, Philadelphia, PA 19103.

CLAYTON, INA SMILEY
Educator. **PERSONAL:** Born Mar 02, 1924, Montrose, MS; married OL Clayton; children: Felicia. **EDUCATION:** Jackson State Univ MS, BS 1946; Syracuse Univ, MA 1955; USI Univ, PhD 1977; Pepperdine Univ, 72 hrs. **CAREER:** Smith Co Tri-School, head teacher 1946; Covington Co MS, jeanes super 1947-54; Laurel City School, head teach & principal 1955-67; LAUSD, teacher 1967-. **ORGANIZATIONS:** Sponsor Future Teachers of Amer 1964-66; mem NEA-CTA & UTLA 1967-; hostess Dist Science Assn Laurel MS 1966; vice pres & pres Methodist Women Spiritual Growth Grp 1980-83; mem Urban League & NAACP; mem Sigma Gamma Rho; mem Town Hall Los Angeles CA 1983-. **HONORS/ACHIEVEMENTS:** A dissertation The Relationship Between Busing & Attitudes Among Urban Elem Sch Students Parents & Personnel 1977; Who's Who of the West 1982-83; Who's Who of America 1982-83; Who's Who of Women 1984, Who's Who Among Intl Women 1984, Personalities of Amer. **BUSINESS ADDRESS:** Teacher, LAUSD, 1963 E 103rd St, Los Angeles, CA 90002.

CLAYTON, JAMES HENRY
Educator. **PERSONAL:** Born Jul 10, 1944, Marianna, AR; married Dorothy; children: Kamillah, Keith, Denise. **EDUCATION:** IL State U, BS 1967, MEd 1972. **CAREER:** CA State, dir educ opportunity program; Special Recruitment & Asmissions Program, dir 1974-75; Special Progress Parkland Community Coll, coord 1972-74; Upward Bound Univ of IL, dir 1970-72; Special Educ Opportunity, co-dir 1969-70. **ORGANIZATIONS:** Dir CA Assn of EOPDir; pres CA State Dom Hills Black Faculty & Staff Assn; proposal consult Carson Comm Thtr Mem NAACP; Intl Reading Assn; Phi Delta Kappa; chmn Comm Support; adv bd Carson Employment Readiness Support Ctrco-author, musical play Cinderella Brown 1976-77. **BUSINESS ADDRESS:** California State University, 1000 E Victoria, Long Beach, CA 90747.

CLAYTON, KATHLEEN R.
Business executive. **PERSONAL:** Born Jun 04, 1952, New Orleans, LA; married Lawrence Clayton Jr; children: Lisa, Lawrence III, Wesley. **EDUCATION:** Rice Univ, BA Behavioral Sci 1976. **CAREER:** Prudential Ins Co, cost analyst 1976-79; Bank of New Orleans, asst vice pres & mgr 1980-83; Liberty Bank & Trust Co, vp, human resource dir. **ORGANIZATIONS:** Mem Amer Compensation Assoc 1984-85, Black Heritage Comm New Orleans Museum of Art 1984-. **BUSINESS ADDRESS:** AVP, Human Resource Dir, Liberty Bank & Trust, 3939 Tulane Ave, New Orleans, LA 70119.

CLAYTON, LLOYD E.
Association executive. **PERSONAL:** Born Jul 08, 1921, Mobile, AL; married Lela Maxwell; children: Kenneth R, Robert L, Carole M. **EDUCATION:** Howard Univ, BS 1955. **CAREER:** Walter Reed Army Inst Res, res chemist 1951-68; Task Force Health Care Disadvantaged, dep chmn 1968-71; Task Force Health Care Disadvantaged 1968-71; Status Health Black Comm, proj officer 1971; Status Dental Health Black Comm, proj officer 1972; Minority Physician Recruitment Natl Health Serv Corps, proj officer 1973; Sickle Cell Disease Prog, proj officer 1976; Black Congress on Lealth & Law, proj officer 1980, staff consultant 1980-. **ORGANIZATIONS:** Vol coord trnsp between Poor People's Campaign HQ & Resurrection City 1968; mem Assoc Sports Intl Track Club 1967; official timer Natl Invitational Track Meet 1967-68. **HONORS/ACHIEVEMENTS:** Appreciation and Gratitutde Awd for Outstanding Leadership in the field of sickle cell anemia San Juan PR 1978; spec presentation for Contrib to the health field Black Congress on Health and Law Dallas TX 1980; Superior Serv Awd Natl Black Health Planners Assoc Wintergreen VA 1986. **MILITARY SERVICE:** AUS tech sgt 1944-46.

CLAYTON, MARK
Professional athlete. **PERSONAL:** Born Apr 08, 1961, Indianapolis, IN. **EDUCATION:** Attended, Univ of Louisville. **CAREER:** Miami Dolphins, wide receiver 1983-. **ORGANIZATIONS:** Founder Clayton's Kids. **HONORS/ACHIEVEMENTS:** Named All-South Independent and team MVP 1982; appeared on cover of Sports Illustrated 9/10/84; top NFL receiver 1984; Football News first-team All-AFC selection; named team's outstanding receiver for second straight campaign 1985; post seasons honors incl AP second team All-Pro; AFC Pro Bowl and USA Today first teamAll-Pro; mem 1986 Pro Bowl team. **BUSINESS ADDRESS:** Miami Dolphins, 4770 Biscayne Blvd, Ste 1440, Miami, FL 33137.

CLAYTON, MATTHEW D.
Counsel. **PERSONAL:** Born Mar 05, 1941, Philadelphia, PA; married Ramona Carter; children: Rebecca, Janice, Matthew D III. **EDUCATION:** Univ of MD, 1960-61; Uof MN, 1962-63; PA State U, BA 1966; Howard Univ Sch of Law, JD 1966-69. **CAREER:** Philadelphia Prisons System, correctional officer 1963; Philadelphia Crime Presention Assoc, staff 1966; Small Business Admin, legal asst 1968; US Dept of Labor, regional trial atty 1969-72; Counsel Corp Law, 1972-74; Smith Kline Corp, corporate employee relations & litigation counsel 1974-. **ORGANIZATIONS:** Mem Natl Bar Assn; Am Bar Assn; Fed Bar Assn; PA Bar Assn; Philadelphia Bar Assn; Indsl Relat Resrch Assn; mem sec of labor study on young professional US Dept of Labor 1970-72; coord US Dept of Labor; mem Nat Urban League; Natl Panel of Arbitrators; Am Arbitration Assn; Am Mgmt Assn; Am Trial Lawyers Assn; mem Barristers Club; fdng mem World Lawyers Assn. **HONORS/ACHIEVEMENTS:** Outstanding Academic Achievement Amer Jurisprudence Awd; Outstanding Legal Service Small Business Admin. **MILITARY SERVICE:** USAF 1959-63. **BUSINESS ADDRESS:** Corporate Empl Relations Cnsl, Smith Kline Beckman Corp, One Franklin Plaza, Philadelphia, PA 19101.

CLAYTON, MAYME AGNEW
Business executive. **PERSONAL:** Born Aug 04, 1923, Van Buren, AR; married Andrew Lee Clayton; children: Averyie, Renai, Lloyd. **EDUCATION:** UWW Berkeley, BA 1974; Goddard Coll, grad prog 1974; AR Baptist Coll, attended 1940-41; Lincoln Univ MO 1944-46; Univ of So CA, attended 1958-59; UWW, PhD 1983. **CAREER:** UCLA, asst lib for engrg lib 1956-59, dir of circulation & spl serv asst for law lib 1959-71, consult librarian for Afro-Amer Study Ctr 1970-71; UWW Berkeley, natl field rep adjunct faculty 1972-74; Universal Books, co-owner 1971-72; Special Black Achievement, consul & lectr; Third World Ethnic Books, owner/pres (largest black collection on W Coast OP specialist) 1972-. **ORGANIZATIONS:** Founder Black Amer Cinema Soc 1974-; producer Black Talkies on Parade 9th Annual Film Festival 1987; consult Claremont Coll Black Oral History Dept 1973-74; organizer of Intl Black Bookdealers 1973; African Work & Study Proj 1971; KCOP TV Minority Comm Rsch & Historian 1974-; KNBC-TV "What It Is" Rsch & Consult 1973-74; mem Iota Phi Lambda Sor Inc; Gamma Mu Chap LA 1973; Natl News Media Women Hollywood/Beverly Hills Chap 1973; founder Black Amer Cinema Soc 1976; art & cult coord Dist 8 Councilmatie; LA Coin Club 1974; founder Black Cultural Entertainment Network 1982; Producer Black Progs for TV & Cable; founder, exec dir Western States Black Research Center 1975 (nonrpofit); bd of dir Sierra Univ Santa Monica, CA. **HONORS/ACHIEVEMENTS:** Woman of the Yr Awd Iota Phi Lambda 1973; Feature article Third World Book Store Owner Black Profile Sepia Mag June 1974; Black Filmmakers Awd. **BUSINESS ADDRESS:** President, Third World Ethnic Books, 3617 1/2 Mont Clair St, Los Angeles, CA 90018.

CLAYTON, MINNIE H.
Librarian. **PERSONAL:** Married Robert L; children: Robert J III. **EDUCATION:** AL State U, BS 1954; Atlanta U, MLS 1970. **CAREER:** Atlanta Univ, asst archivist 1980-; Southern Regional Council Archives Proj, Atlanta Univ Dept Archives & Records Mgmt, proj archivist 1978-80; Martin Luther King Center for Social Change Atlanta, library archivist 1969-78; Lectures & Life of Martin Luther King Jr; Black history & Bibliography of Civil Rights 1954; Dev & Book Coll on Porton (all ages), cons. **ORGANIZATIONS:** Mem ALA; GA Lib Assn; Metro-Atlanta Lib Assn; Nat Hist Soc; Soc Am Archivist; mem Am Assn of Univ Prof/African Am Family Hist Assn; GA Archivist. **HONORS/ACHIEVEMENTS:** Coretta King Awd Com; League Women Voters; NAACP Jessie S Noyes Fndtn Grant 1966-68; State Historical Rec Adv Bd of GA; cert Archival Adm Emory Univ 1973; Danforth Found Assn, 1966-67; Traveled Canada & Mexico.

CLAYTON, ROBERT L.
Personnel manager. **PERSONAL:** Born Dec 06, 1938, Morris Station, GA; son of Henry Clayton and Willie Mae Mercer Clayton; married Sharon Cage, Mar 25, 1966; children: Robert, Angela. **EDUCATION:** Central State Univ, Wilberforce, OH, BS, Business Admin, 1962; Akron Univ, Akron, OH, post-graduate studies, 1965-66. **CAREER:** Co-op Supermarkets, Akron, OH, comptroller, 1965-73; Fiberboard, San Francisco, CA, sr financial analyst, 1973-79; Chzm Hill, San Francisco, CA, dist admin personnel mgr, 1979-. **ORGANIZATIONS:** Mem, Amer Soc Personnel Admin, 1980-, Natl Assn of Minority Engineering Program Admin, 1983-, Natl Assn of Black Public Admin, 1984-, UCLA Advisory Bd, 1986-, Industrial Technical Advisory Bd, Statewide MESA, 1986-, Univ of California Fullerton, Minority Engineering Bd, 1988-. **MILITARY SERVICE:** AUS, First Lt, 1962-66. **BUSINESS ADDRESS:** District Personnel Manager, Chzm Hill, 6425 Christie Ave Suite 500, Emeryville, CA 94608.

CLAYTON, ROBERT LOUIS
Educator. **PERSONAL:** Born Feb 25, 1934, Pensacola, FL; married Minnie Harris; children: Robert, Myrna. **EDUCATION:** Talladega Coll, AB 1955; Hood Sem, BD 1959; Interdenom Theol Ctr, STM 1965. **CAREER:** AL A&M Univ, prof, chaplin; Office of Educ, cons; ITC, sem instructor; Livingston Coll, dir; The Amer Coll Testing Program, dir minority program; The Metropolitan Business League, exec dir/CEO; Oak St AME Zion Church, pastor; Moton Inst, prog dir; VA State Univ, coord of recruitment & mktg. **ORGANIZATIONS:** Bd dirs WJ Walls Found; past pres Assn of Non-White Concerns in Personnel & Guid; govt contact person & rep Reg Coord Cnc of APGA; mem ACPA, APGA, Natl Urban League; NAACP, Alpha Phi Alpha Inc, AMEG, NVGA, NAHRW, ASCA, ACES, Black Educs Think Tank; NACUC, Concerned Citizens of SW Atlanta, African Meth Epis Zion Ch; consultant Black Colls, US Virgin Islands. **HONORS/ACHIEVEMENTS:** First black sem intern Danforth Found; Campus Ministry Grant Danforth Found; dir Grantmanship & Proposal Writing; lectr num schs; author num journ articles; several Honorary Doctorate degrees; author "Counseling Non-White Students in an Era of Integration". **BUSINESS ADDRESS:** Coord of Recruitment, VA State University, Petersburg, VA 23803.

CLAYTON, THEAOSEUS T.
Attorney. **PERSONAL:** Born Oct 02, 1930, Roxboro, NC; married Eva McPherson; children: Joanne A, Theaoseus T, Jr. **EDUCATION:** Johnson C Smith U, AB 1955; Central Univ Sch of Law, JS, JD 1958. **CAREER:** Theaoseus T Clayton PA Inc, pres 1979-; Clayton & Ballance, sr partner 1966-78; Theaoseus T Clayton, sole propietorship 1963-66; Gilliland & Clayton, jr partner 1961-66; McKissick & Berry Durham, NC, atty 1961. **ORGANIZATIONS:** Mem Nat Bar Assn; mem Am Bar Assn; mem NC State Bar; mem NC Bar Assn; mem NC Trial Lawyers Assn; mem NC Assn Black Lawyers; mem Nat Conf Black Lawyers; past sec/treas 9th Jud Dist Bar Assn; pres Charles Williamson Bar Assn; chief counsel Floyd B McKissick & Floyd B McKissick Enterprises Inc Life mem/past state vice pres NAACP; mem Warren Co Dem Party; mem Warren Co Polit Action Council; mem 2nd Congressional Dist Black Caucus; past v chmn NC Bd Youth Devel. **MILITARY SERVICE:** AUS corpl 1952-54.

CLAYTON, WILLIE BURKE, JR.
Police captain. **PERSONAL:** Born May 04, 1922, Sparta, GA; married Peggy Joyce; children: Eric, Craig, Deirdre, John, Kevin, Anthony, Peggy. **EDUCATION:** NJ Coll of Commerce, 1951; Temple U, 1952-59; MI State U, Cert 1968; Trenton State Coll, 1973; Montclair State Coll Grad Sch, 1973; Am Intl Open U, PhD Cand; Stockton State Coll, BA 1973; Atlantic Comm Coll, Resd Study Course 1974; Glassboro State Coll, MA 1974; Univ of DE, Cert Grad 1977. **CAREER:** Roy E Hager Acctnts, pub acct 1968; You're in Touch WUSS Radio Sta, host 1976; Community Relations Unit, dir; Atlantic City Police Dept, capt; AtlanticCity Police Dept, col & comdr of serv bur 1979-80; Atlantic City NJ, elected city commr 1980-84; Atlantic City, commr & dir of publ safety 1980;; Atlantic County Transportation Auth, sec 1987. **ORGANIZATIONS:** Vp bd of dir Atlantic Bus Comm Devel Corp; 1st pres NJ Conf of Police Professional 1976; treas Superior Ofcrs Assn ACPD 1977; past Nat treas Nat Counc of Police Soc Inc; charter mem Nat Orgn of Black Law Enforcement Exec 1977; pres NJ Statewide Assn of Comm Relat Ofcrs 1977; prgm advr Atlantic Comm Coll Bd; dir Boys Club of Am 1977; bd of trustees Nat Multiple Sclerosis Soc; life mem NAACP; mem League of Women Voters of Atlantic Co vpRing #12 of Nat Vet Boxers Assn 1977; assisted in orgn Atlantic City Jr Police; assisted in establ & comdg ofcr Police Athletic League; mem Intl Assoc of Chiefs of Police IACP; pres Mothers Against Drugs Inc; golden heritage mem NAACP; vice pres Mainland Br NAACP. **HONORS/ACHIEVEMENTS:** Plaque for Serv Rendered to Comm 3 R's Social Club 1975; Outstanding Serv in Human Realt Bus & Professional Women of NJ 1975; Cert of Honor Mainland Br NAACP 1975; listed in Who's Who in Atlantic City 1976; Policeman of the Year 1977; Plaque Miss Black Amer Beauty Pagent of NJ for Outstanding Serv 1979; Plaque Natl Multiple Sclerosis Soc Greater Chap Outstanding Volunteer of the Year 1980; Plaque Atlantic City Taxicab Assoc 1980; Plaque K-9 Corps Awd AC Police Dept 1980; Plaque Black Atlantic City Mag Awd 1982; Martin Luther King Awd 1983; Mainland Br NAACP Martin Luther King Awd Plaque 1986; 27 commendations for merit serv Atlantic City Police Dept. **MILITARY SERVICE:** AUS tech/5 1944-46. **BUSINESS ADDRESS:** Secretary, Atlantic City Police Dept, Tennessee & Arctic Avs, Atlantic City, NJ 08401.

CLAYTON, XERNONA
Television executive. **PERSONAL:** Born Aug 30, 1930, Muskogee, OK; daughter of Rev & Mrs James Brewster; married Paul Brady. **EDUCATION:** TN State U, BS 1952; Ru-Jac Sch of Modeling Chgo. **CAREER:** "The Xernona Clayton Show" WAGA-TV, hostess; Atlanta Voice, newspaper columnist; Chicago & LA, tchr pub schs; photographic & fashion modeling. **ORGANIZATIONS:** Mem Atlanta Women's C of C; State & Manpower Adv Com for GA Dept of Labor; Nat Assn of Market Developers; Arts Alliance Guild; Am Women in Radio & TV;Nat Assn of Media Women; Nat Assn of Press Women; Atlanta Chap of Sigma Delta Chi; Atlanta Broadcast Exec Club; founder Atlanta Chap Media Women; mem Nat Academy of TV Arts & Sci; mem Ebenezer Bapt Ch; Alpha Kappa Alpha Sorority; bd dir Greater Atlanta Multiple Sclerosis Soc; honorary asso So Ballet. **HONORS/ACHIEVEMENTS:** Outstanding Leadership Award winner Nat Assn of Market Developers 1968; First Negro Woman in TV Award Women's Orgn of Allen Temple AME Ch 1968; Bronze Woman of Yr in Human Relations Award Phi Delta Kappa Sorority 1969; Hadassah Women planted tree in her honor in Freedom Forest in Israel 1969; recipient GA Associated Press Award for Superior TV Programming 1969-71; awarded Excellence in TV Programming Los Angeles Chap of Negro Business & Professional Women 1970; Mother of Yr Future Homemakers of Am of Douglas HS 1969; Flying Orchid Award Delta Airline; included in Leadership Atlanta C of C 1971; named Atlanta's Five Best Dressed Brentwood Models Assn 1971; named Atlanta's Ten Best Dressed Women Women's C of C 1972; appointed by Gov of GA to Motion Picture & TV Commn for 4-yr term 1972-76; co-starred in major motion picture "House on Skull Mountain.". **BUSINESS ADDRESS:** Corporate Vice President Urban Affairs, Turner Broadcasting System, One CNN Center, Atlanta, GA 30303.

CLAYTOR, CHARLES E.
Association executive. **PERSONAL:** Born Jun 02, 1936, Hotcoal, WV; son of Harvey and Fairy; married Annette Broadnax; children: Dreama, Charles Jr, Brien. **EDUCATION:** NYCC. **CAREER:** Local 2947 United Brotherhood Carpenters, pres 1967-. **BUSINESS ADDRESS:** 87-80 153 St, Jamaica, NY 11432.

CLEAGE, ALBERT B., JR.
Clergyman. **PERSONAL:** Born Jun 13, 1911, Indpls, IN; divorced; children: Mrs Pearl Lomax, Mrs Kristin Williams. **EDUCATION:** Wayne State U, AB; Oberlin Grad Sch of Theol, BD. **CAREER:** Shrine of Black Madonna Detroit, minister. **ORGANIZATIONS:** Nat chmn Black Christian Nationalist Ch Inc; mem natl bds of interreligious Foun for Comm Rogn; Nat Com of Black Churchmen; Comm for Racial Justice. **HONORS/ACHIEVEMENTS:** Author "The Black Messiah"; "Black Christian Nationlism". **BUSINESS ADDRESS:** Pan African Orthodox Christian, 13535 Livernois, Detroit, MI 48238.

CLEAVER, ELDRIDGE
Lecturer, author. **PERSONAL:** Born Jun 05, 1935, Little Rock, AR; married Kathleen Neal; children: Maceo, Toju. **CAREER:** Ramparts Mag, ed and contrib. **HONORS/ACHIEVEMENTS:** Publications, "Soul on Ice" 1968; "Post Prison Writings and Speeches" 1969; "Eldridge Cleaver's Black Papers" 1969; "Soul on Fire" 1978. **BUSINESS ADDRESS:** Lecturer, Author, c/o Random House, 201 E 50th St, New York, NY 10022.

CLEAVER, EMANUEL, III
Clergyman, elected official. **PERSONAL:** Born Oct 26, 1944, Waxahachie, TX; married Dianne; children: Evan Donaldson, Emanuel III, Emiel Davenport, Marissa Dianne. **EDUCATION:** Prairie View A&M Coll, BA; St Paul School of Theology Kansas City, Masters; St Paul School of Theology, Doctorate of Social Ethics. **CAREER:** St James-Paseo United Methodist Church, pastor; Kansas City City Council, councilman. **ORGANIZATIONS:** Bd of dir De La Salle Ed Ctr; mid-central reg vice pres Southern Christian Leadership Conf; pres, bd of trustees Leon Jordan Scholarship Fund; bd of trustees St Paul School of Theology; council on finance United Methodist Conf; bd of dir, former Chmn of bd Freedom Inc; mem Alpha Phi Alpha, NAACP. **HONORS/ACHIEVEMENTS:** 41 achievements & honors incl Man of the Year Alpha Phi Alpha 1968; Community Leaders in Amer 1971; Builder of Boys Awd Boys Club of Amer 1976; White HouseGuest of Pres Jimmy Carter 1977; Recognition of Thanks Woodland Elem School 1983; Apprec Awd NAACP 1984; Black History Awd Univ of MO-Kansas City 1984; Disting Serv Awd Exceptional Leadership & Devoted Serv to Civil Rights Alpha Phi Alpha 1984; Awd for Outstanding Serv Freedom Inc 1984; Citizen of the Year Omega Psi Phi. **BUSINESS ADDRESS:** St James-Paseo United Meth Ch, 5540 Wayne, Kansas City, MO 64110.

CLECKLEY, BETTY J.
Educational administrator. **EDUCATION:** Marquette U, BS Sociology 1958; Smith Coll, MSS Soc Work 1960; Brandeis U, PhD Soc Welfare 1974. **CAREER:** Univ of TN Knoxville, School of Social Worker, assoc dean & assoc prof 1974; Dept of Family Comm Med, asst prof; Intl Allied Health Manpower Training Maternal & Child Health/Family Planning Training & Research Center, Meharry Medical Coll Nashville, coord; Social Welfare NE Univ, lectr; San Francisco Dept of Public Health, new careers corrdinator; Maternal & Infant Care Proj, Dept of Public Health San Francisco, sr psychiatrist, social worker; School of Social Work Univ of CA at Berkeley, field work supvr; Office of Child Devel Dept of HEW Region I, program cons. **ORGANIZATIONS:** Chmn The Commn for Blacks Univ of TN Knoxville; bd of dirs Helen Ross McNabb Center Knoxville; mem Knox Co Juvenile Ct Adv Bd Knoxville; mem TN Dept of Human Servs Region II Title XX Regional Adv Council; bd of dirs Goodwill Industries Knoxville; mem Acad of Certified Social Workers; mem Am Pub HealthAssn; mem Nat Assn of Social Workers; mem Nat Conf on Social Welfare; mem Council on Social Work Edn; mem US Com of the Intl Council on Social Welfare Inc; mem ACE/TN Women in Higher Educ Planning Com; pres Knoxville Links Inc 1978-80; chmn Nat Links Inc Central Area Com on Intl Trends &Servs 1980; mem Alpha Kappa Delta Hon Sociology Society 1957. **HONORS/ACHIEVEMENTS:** Recipient Mental Retardation Felloship 1969-72; So Fellowships Fund Scholarships 1972-73; listed "Oustanding Young Women of Am" 1973; pub numerous social welfare articles paper 1973-; presenter Workshop on Social Policy & Planning for Experienced Tchrs the Council on Social Work Educ Annual Prog Meeting Philadelphia 1976; various others; traveled E & W Africa Mexico Cananda & US. **BUSINESS ADDRESS:** Univ of Tennessee, 2914 Lake Ave, Knoxville, TN 37916.

CLEGG, LEGRAND H., II
Attorney. **PERSONAL:** Born Jun 29, 1944, Los Angeles. **EDUCATION:** UCLA, BA 1966; Howard Univ Sch Law, JD 1969. **CAREER:** City of Compton CA, deputy city atty; Compton Community Coll, instructor; Robert Edelen Law Offices, atty 1975-; LA, legal aid found 1972-74; Compton CA, admin asst 1970-72; Dept Justice Washington, legal intern 1968-69. **ORGANIZATIONS:** Mem LA Bar Assn; CA Lawyers Criminal Justice; Langston Law Club; Nat Conf Black Lawyers; Compton Cultural Commn; Assn Black Psychol; Pilgrim Missionary Bapt Ch. **HONORS/ACHIEVEMENTS:** Who's Who in CA 1974; Outstanding Young Mem of Am 1974; pubs LA Times 1974; current bibliography on African Affairs 1969, 1972; guest lecturer Vassar Coll/NY U/UCLA/U of So CA 1978-79. **BUSINESS ADDRESS:** Compton City Hall, Compton, CA 90224.

CLEMENDOR, ANTHONY A., IV
Catalog executive. **PERSONAL:** Born May 30, 1961, Washington, DC. **EDUCATION:** Tufts Univ, BS 1982; Harvard Grad Sch of Business Admin, MBA 1986. **CAREER:** Environmental Industries, sales mgr 1982-83; Xerox Corp, sales rep 1983-84; Hidden Heritage Catalog, pres 1986-; Tymely Ventures Inc, pres/ceo 1986-. **ORGANIZATIONS:** Mem Direct Marketing Assoc 1987-, Natl Conf of Artists 1987-. **BUSINESS ADDRESS:** President, Tymely Ventures Inc, 1923 1/2 Westwood Blvd Ste 1, Los Angeles, CA 90025.

CLEMENDOR, ANTHONY ARNOLD
Physician, educator. **PERSONAL:** Born Nov 08, 1933; son of Anthony Clemendor and Beatrice Stewart Thompson; married Elaine C Browne; children: Anthony A, David A. **EDUCATION:** NY Univ, BA 1959; Howard Univ Coll Med, MD 1963. **CAREER:** NY Med College, clinical assoc prof dept OB-GYN dir office minority affairs, assoc dean. **ORGANIZATIONS:** Life mem NAACP; mem 100 Black Men Inc; mem NY Urban League; bd mem Elmcor; fellow Amer Coll OB-Gyn; mem Amer Pub Health Assn; pres Student Amer Med Assn Chapter Howard Univ 1961-62; dir Office of Minority Affairs NY Med Coll 1974-; pres, New York Gynecological Society Inc 1988; bd of directors, Caribbean American Center 1988; secretary, New York County Medical Society 1989. **HONORS/ACHIEVEMENTS:** Publ "Transient Asymptomatic Hydrothorax in Pregnancy" 1976; "Achalasia & Nutritional Deficiency During Pregnancy" 1969; SNMA Award Univ of Buffalo Chap 1984; T & T Alliance Award Trinidad & Tobago Alliance of NA 1984; Trinidad & Tobago Nurses Assn of America

Inc Award 1988. **BUSINESS ADDRESS:** Assoc Dean/Clinical Assoc Prof, NY Medical Coll, 125 East 80 St, New York, NY 10021.

CLEMENT, JOSEPHINE DOBBS
County commissioner. **PERSONAL:** Born Feb 09, 1918, Atlanta, GA; daughter of John Wesley Dobbs and Irene Thompson Dobbs; married William Alexander Clement, Dec 24, 1941; children: Alexine Jackson, William Jr, Wesley, Arthur, Kathleen, Josephine. **EDUCATION:** Spelman Coll, Atlanta GA, BS 1933-37; Columbia U, New York, NY, MA 1937-38. **CAREER:** Durham City Bd of Educ, chmn; GA State Coll, tchr; NC Central Univ; GA State Coll, Savannah GA, instr, 1938-41; Morris Brown Coll, Atlanta GA, instr, 1943-45; North Carolina Central Univ, NC Inst, 1951-57. **ORGANIZATIONS:** Mem Durham Co Libr; NC Symphony; editorial bd Negro Braile Mag; Durham City Co Chrtr Commn 1971-74; Delta Sigma Theta; Links; docent Duke Univ Mus of Art; mem and chmn, Durham City Bd of Educ, 1973-83; bd mem Shaw Univ; bd mem Z Smith Reynolds Found. **HONORS/ACHIEVEMENTS:** Doctor of Humane Letters, Shaw Univ; Distinguished Award, Durham Chamber of Commerce; Women of Achievement, YWCA; Citizens Award, NAACP. **HOME ADDRESS:** 206 Pekoe St, Durham, NC 27707.

CLEMENT, WILLIAM A.
Business executive. **PERSONAL:** Born May 06, 1912, Charleston, SC; son of Arthur J Clement and Sadie K Jones Clement; married Josephine Dobbs; children: Alexine C, William A Jr, Wesley, Arthur, John, Kathleen Ophelia, Josephine Millicent. **EDUCATION:** Talladega Coll, BA 1934. **CAREER:** NC Mutual Life Ins Co, agency dir 1961, vice pres 1962, agency vice pres in charge of field opers 1966, sr vice pres 1969-75, retired exec vice pres 1975-78. **ORGANIZATIONS:** 33 Degree Mason Prince Hall 1945; earned CLU designation 1953; mem bd of dir NC Mutual Life Ins Co 1961-85; pres Durham's United Fund 1970; mem bd dir Wachovia Bank & Trust Co; dep grand master Prince Hall Grand Lodge 1975; chmn trustee bd NC Central Univ 1975; trustee Durham Co Gen Hosp Corp 1976; mem Raleigh-Durham Airport Auth 1979; grand master Prince Hall Grand Lodge of NC 1981; chmn Raleigh-Durham Airport Authority 1985; trustee Amer Coll Bryn Mawr PA; dir NC Mutual Life Ins Co; mem Durham Rotary Club; Durham Bus & Professional Chain; mem exec comm Durham Comm on Negro Affairs; mem bd dir Scarborough Nursery. **HONORS/ACHIEVEMENTS:** Silver Beaver Awd BSA 1966; Durham Chamber of Commerce Civic Awd 1987; Honorary Degree, North Carolina Central University Doctor of Law. **BUSINESS ADDRESS:** Executive Vice President, NC Mutual Life Ins Co, 411 W Chapel Hill St, Durham, NC 27701.

CLEMENT, WILLIAM A., JR.
Business executive. **PERSONAL:** Born Jan 22, 1943, Atlanta, GA; married Ressie Guy; children: Anika P. **EDUCATION:** Morehouse Coll, graduate; Wharton Sch of Finance & Commerce Univ of PA, MBA; Amer Coll of Life Underwriters, CLU. **CAREER:** North Carolina Mutual Life Ins Co, life insurance agent; Robinson Humphrey/American Express Inc, stockbroker; Prudential-Bache Securities Inc, stockbroker;North Carolina Natl Bank, credit analyst/commercial loan officer; Citizens Trust Bank, vice pres & sr loan officer; US Small Business Administration-Carter Administration, assoc administrator; Dobbs Corporation, pres/ceo; Dobbs Ram & Co, chairman/ceo. **ORGANIZATIONS:** Bd of dirs Dist of Columbia Develop Corp, Dist of Columbia Investment Corp, Dobbs Associates Inc, Dobbs Corporation, Natl Bank of Washington, Natl Consumer Cooperative Bank; chmn bd dirs USEP Inc; mem bd dirs Business League, Atlanta Urban League, Butler St YMCA, Big Bros of Atlanta, Rsch Atlanta &Southwest Community Hosp; vice pres and sr loan officer Citizens Trust Bank Atlanta; pres Atlanta Business League; bd mem Research Atlanta, The Boys Club of Atlanta, The Atlanta Exchange, The Alliance Theatre Co; mem Leadership Atlanta, The Atlanta Coalition of 100 Black Men, The Soc of Intl Business Fellows; chmn bd of trustees The Tabernacle Baptist Church. **BUSINESS ADDRESS:** Chairman & CEO, Dobbs, Ram & Co, 1422 W Peachtree St NE, Ste 814, Atlanta, GA 30309.

CLEMENTS, GEORGE H.
Clergyman. **PERSONAL:** Born Jan 26, 1932, Chicago, IL. **EDUCATION:** St Mary of the Lake Sem, BA; St Mary of the Lake Sem, MA philosophy. **CAREER:** Quigley Sem, 1st black grad ordained in 1957; Holy Angels Ch, pastor; Black Clergy Caucus, organizer; Afro/Am. **ORGANIZATIONS:** Oranized Black Clergy Caucus; chaplain Afro-Am Patrolmen's League; Afro-AmFiremen's League; Postal Workers' League; highly active in civic & comm affairs & has organized several neighborhood assns; mem bd SCLC's Operation Breadbasket; NAACP; Urban League; Better Boys Found; Black Panther party Malcolm X Coll. **BUSINESS ADDRESS:** Holy Angels Roman Catholic Ch, 607 E Oakwood Blvd, Chicago, IL 60653.

CLEMENTS, WALTER H.
Attorney. **PERSONAL:** Born Oct 28, 1928, Atlanta, GA. **EDUCATION:** Morehouse Coll, BA 1949; Univ of MI Law School, JD 1952. **CAREER:** Private practice, attny 1953-59; Vet Admin, adjudicator 1962-65; Small Bus Admin, asst area counsel 1966-69; State of MI, asst attny gen 1969-73; Southeastern MI Transp Auth, gen counsel 1973-. **ORGANIZATIONS:** Mem State Bar of MI, Wolverine Bar Assoc, Natl Bar Assoc, Amer Arbitration Assoc; referee MI Civil Rights Comm. **BUSINESS ADDRESS:** General Counsel, Southeastern MI Transp Auth, 211 W Fort St, PO Box 333, Detroit, MI 48231.

CLEMMONS, CLIFFORD R.
Retired branch chief probation. **PERSONAL:** Born in Kansas City, KS; son of H. B. Clemmons and Constance Clemmons; married Jimmie E Hill; children: Jennifer M Johnson, C Robert Jr. **EDUCATION:** Oakwood Jr Coll, Huntsville, AL, Diploma, 1939; Central State Univ, Wilberforce OH, BS, Social Work, 1948; OH State Univ, Masters of Social Admin, 1950; NYU, Columbia Univ, attended. **CAREER:** Greenpoint Hospital, Med Social Worker 1950; Probation Dept NY, Probation Officer, 1951-66, Supvr Probation Officer 1966-82; City of NY Dept of Probation, branch chief 1982-87. **ORGANIZATIONS:** Chmn, bd dir, Sickle Cell Disease Found, Greater NY 1972-89; vice pres bd dir Muncipal Credit Union, 1971-77; chmn bd of dir, Federation of Negro Serv Org Inc, 1968-77; state dir, Alpha Phi Alpha Fraternity Inc 1971-88. **HONORS/ACHIEVEMENTS:** Middle to Spike Harris Award Counseliers Inc NY 1978; Commr of Probation Merit Award, Probation Dept NY, 1980; Alpha Award of Merit, Alpha Phi Alpha Fraternity Inc, Queens Chapter, 1972; Comm Serv Award, Leadership Bell Park Manor Terrace Comm Council Inc, 1964; over 35 awards & citations. **MILITARY SERVICE:** AUS 1st sgt. **HOME ADDRESS:** 4345 Senna Dr, Las Cruces, NM 88001.

CLEMMONS, JACKSON JOSHUA WALTER
Pathologist, educator. **PERSONAL:** Born Mar 24, 1923, Beloit, WI; son of Henry Clemmons and Ora Clemmons; married Lydia; children: Jackson, Lydia, Laura, Jocelyn, Naomi. **EDUCATION:** Univ of WI, BS Biochem 1947, MS Biochem 1949, PhD Biochem & Exper Pathology 1955; Western Reserve Univ, MD, 1959. **CAREER:** Univ of WI Madison, WI, rsch asst, Biochem, 1942-43, res assoc in biochemistry/exper pathology 1947-52; Karolinska Inst of Biophysics & Cell Res Stockholm, Sweden, res fellow 1950; Sloan Kettering Inst for Cancer Res NY, special rsch fellow 1953; Univ of WI Madison, WI, project assoc in exper pathology 1953-55; Amer Cancer Soc Inst of Pathology, Western Reserve Univ, Cleveland OH, postdoctoral fellow 1956-57, fellow of pathology 1957-61, Helen Hay Whitney fellow 1961-64; Univ of VT Coll of Med, Burlington VT, asst prof, Pathology 1962-64. **ORGANIZATIONS:** Amer Bd of Pathology Anatomic Pathology 1964; Am Med Assn; Am Assn of Path & Bacteriologists; VT State Med Soc; Chittenden Co Med Soc; New England Rheumatism Soc; Sigma Xi Hon Science Soc; Phi Lambda Upsilon Hon Chem Soc; Gamma Alpha Hon Biological Soc; Am Soc for Experimental Pathology; Intl Acad of Pathology; Am Soc for Clinical Chem; NY Acad of Science; Am Soc of Clinical Pathologists; Univ of VT Radioisotope Com 1968-; Exec Com Graduate School Faculty 1969-71; vp Univ of VT Chap of Sigma Xi 1971-72, pres 1971-72; Univ of VT Admin Policy Com 1971-76; admissions com Univ of VT Coll of Med, student affairs com 1974-; admissions com Univ of VT 1977-, exec com 1977-; school dir Champlaing Vlly Union HS 1967-74, vice chmn Gov Advisory Comm to Council on Aging 1970-72; deleg VT White House Conf on Children & Youth 1971; mem, pathology training comm of Natl Inst General Med Science, 1971-73; mem, natl advisory council Health Professional Educ, 1975-78. **HONORS/ACHIEVEMENTS:** Publications, "An Improved Historadiographic Apparatus" 1953; "An Accurate Ref Sys for Quantitative Historadiography" 1953; "The Technique of Quantitative Historadiography" 1954; "Historadiographic Stud of the Calcifying Cartilage Matrix" 1954; "Procedures & Errors in Quantitative Historadiography" 1955; "The Influence in Estrogen on Nuclear Volumes & Chemical Composition" 1955; "Thermoluminescence & Fluorescence in Alkai Halide Crystals Induced by Soft X-Ray" 1955; "The Occurrence of Multiple Fractures in Suckling Rats Injured with B-Aminopropionitrile" 1957; "Quantitative Historadiography" 1957; "Inhibition of Cytochrome Oxidase by Aminoacetonitrile" 1962; "Proline Metabolism Collagen Formation & Lathyrism" 1966; "The Effect of Lathyrogenic Compounds on Oxygen Consumption of Devel Chick Embroys" 1966; Radiorespirometer for the Study of C14-Labeled Substance Administered to Chick Embryos" 1971; "Ornithine as a Precursor of Collagen Proline & Hydroxyproline in the Chick Embryo" 1973; "Embryonic Renal Injury-A Possible Factor in Fetal Malnutrition" 1977; "Electrolytic Radiorespirometer for Continuous Monitoring of Chick Embryo Devel" 1979; "Fetal-Maternal Hemorrhage, A Spectrum of Disease" 1980. **HOME ADDRESS:** Green Bush Rd, Charlotte, VT 05445. **BUSINESS ADDRESS:** Professor of Pathology, Univ of VT, College of Medicine, Burlington, VT 05405.

CLEMONS, FLENOR
Business executive. **PERSONAL:** Born Aug 30, 1921, Chicago, IL; married Thomasine Crisler; children: Felicia, Dwayne. **CAREER:** Clemons Cartage, owner; IL St Empl Bur; Ammun Cont Corp, ship clerk. **ORGANIZATIONS:** Bd of auditors Bremen Twnship; bd of ed Posen Robbins Sch Dist; pres Clemons Real Est mem Robbins Ind Comm; mem Robbins Human Rel Res Commn. **BUSINESS ADDRESS:** Clemons Cartage, 3707 W 135 St, Robbins, IL 60472.

CLENDENINN, NEIL J.
Physician. **PERSONAL:** Born Apr 07, 1949, New York, NY; married Mary Lavinia Neely. **EDUCATION:** Wesleyan Univ, BA 1971; New York Univ, MA, MD, PhD 1977. **CAREER:** Univ of WA Affiliated Hosp, residency 1977-81; Natl Inst of Health/Natl Cancer Inst, clinical pharmacology fellow 1981-83, oncology fellow 1983-84, medical staff 1984-85; Burroughs Wellcome, sr clinical research scientist 1985-. **ORGANIZATIONS:** Trustee Wesleyan Univ 1984-. **HONORS/ACHIEVEMENTS:** Numerous scientific articles and book chapts. **BUSINESS ADDRESS:** Senior Clinical Rsch Scientist, Burroughs Wellcome, 3030 Cornwallis Rd, Research Triangle Park, NC 27709.

CLERMONT, VOLNA
Medical director, physician. **PERSONAL:** Born Sep 15, 1924, Jeremie, Haiti;married Hazel Baggett; children: Karen, Kimberly, Christopher. **EDUCATION:** Lycee Petion of Port-au-Prince Haiti, BA 1943; Ecole Nationale de Medecine et de Pharmacie Univ d'Haiti Port-au-Prince Haiti, MD 1949. **CAREER:** Childrens Hosp of MI, pathologist 1960-69; Compr Neighborhood Health Ctr, chief pediatrics 1969-72; SW Detroit Hosp, chief of staff; DMIC-PLRESCAD, med dir 1972-; Private Practice, pediatrician. **ORGANIZATIONS:** Mem Detroit Med Soc; life mem NAACP; Natl Med Assn; Detroit Pediatric Soc; Dip of Bd of Pediatrics Wayne Co Med Soc; MI State Med Soc; mem medical staff Hutzel Hosp, Children's Hosp, Grace Hosp; mem Urban League, Founders Soc of MI; African Art Gallery, Intl African Museum Soc; Alpha Phi Alpha Frat. **BUSINESS ADDRESS:** 3800 Woodward, Detroit, MI 48203.

CLEVELAND, CLYDE
Councilman. **PERSONAL:** Born May 22, 1935, Detroit. **EDUCATION:** Wayne State Univ. **CAREER:** Detroit City councilman, 1974-; Comm Devel Div, New Detroit Inc, proj dir 1971-1973; Comm Org, New Detroit Inc, specialist, 1970-71; Inner City Business Improvement Forum, comm planner 1968-70; Comm of Human Resources Devel, community serv mayor, 1965-68; public aid worker 1958, 1960-64. **ORGANIZATIONS:** mem, MI Democratic Party, various committees in first dist Democratic Party; Nacirema Club; Trade Union Leadership Council; MI Comm on Law & Housing; Assn for Study of Negro Life & History; Assn of Black Soc Workers; Booker T Washington Business Assn; Advisory bd of Black Caucus; NAACP; Operation PUSH. **HONORS/ACHIEVEMENTS:** Has received numerous service & community awards. **MILITARY SERVICE:** AUS sp 4th class 1958-60. **BUSINESS ADDRESS:** City Councilman, City of Detroit, City County Bldg, Detroit, MI 48226.

CLEVELAND, GRANVILLE E.
Librarian. **PERSONAL:** Born Nov 25, 1937, Springfield, OH; married Juanita; children: Granville, Tivonnia. **EDUCATION:** Tougaloo So CC, attnd 1956-57; Central State Coll, 1957-60; Wittenberg U, 1963. **CAREER:** Univ Notre Dame Law Sch, asst law lib & faculty mem 1969-; Springfield Bar & Law Lib Assn, lib & exec sec 1963-68. **ORGANIZATIONS:** Mem Am Assn Law Libs 1964-; mem & past pres OH Reg Assn Law Libs 1964-; mem Affirmative Action Com Univ Notre Dame 1973-; past sec Community Wel Council; chmn Housing &Jobs Human Rel Com; adult adv Springfield Youth Club; Legal Aid Soc; United Appeal

Fund; vice pres Young Rep; adv & supr City Rec Dept;mem Planned Parenthood; YNCA; basketball referee; acting dir Black Studies Univ Notre Dame 1972-73; chmn Black Student Affairs Com 1973-74; asst dir Civil Rights Center 1973-74. **HONORS/ACHIEVEMENTS:** Black am law studies assn awd Univ Notre Dame Law Sch 1973-74. **MILITARY SERVICE:** Air Nat Guard sgt 1956-60. **BUSINESS ADDRESS:** Asst Law Librarian, Notre Dame Law School, Notre Dame, IN 46556.

CLEVELAND, HATTYE M.
Retired therapist. **PERSONAL:** Born Sep 22, 1911, Laurens, SC; daughter of William Guy Johnson (deceased) and Rosalee Fuller Johnson (deceased); married John M Cleveland, Aug 29, 1936 (deceased). **EDUCATION:** Shaw Univ, BS Sci/Home Economics 1935; NY Univ, graduate cert Occup Therapy 1956; Pace Univ, cert mgmt of Vol Orgns/Issues in Comm Devel 1975; Westchester Comm Coll/Fordham Univ Lincoln Center, attended bus seminars 1978; Westchester Comm Coll, attended Women in Pol II Lobbying Sem 1978; Mary Mt Manhattan Coll, blissymbolics 1979. **CAREER:** Willowbrook State Sch, therapist 1956-60; Beth Abraham Home, sr therapist 1960-65; Monte-Mor Affil, asst supr occupational therapy 1965-72; Monte-Mor Affil, supr occupational therapy 1973-76; Montefiore Hospital N Central Bx Affil, head occupat therapy serv 1976-77; (retired). **ORGANIZATIONS:** Charter mem Delta Sigma Theta Sor Alpha Rho Chap Shaw Univ 1934; mem Am OTA 1956-89; S Side Res Assn 1966-67; World Fedn Occ Therapy 1970-89; pres Westchester Co Natl Council Negro Women mem 1970-74, life mem 1970-87; Women's Task Force 1974-78; Amer Biog Assn 1977-87; Intl Platform Assn 1977-80; mem pub chmn Friends of Mt Vernon Public Library 1978-89; mem IFABI 1979, ABIRA 1980-89; rscher no 370 for the Amer Cancer Soc CPSII 1982-86; mem League of Women Voters 1985; NY State & NY Dist OTA; Nat'l Alumni Assoc & Alumni Club Shaw Univ; mem Grace Baptist Church 1989; mem of exec bd, chair, Scholarship Fund; life mem, Mt Vernon Branch NAACP 1988; committee mem, Home Health Care of Mt Vernon NY Inc 1988-90. **HONORS/ACHIEVEMENTS:** Cert Honor & Loyalty Shaw Univ Alumni Assn Brooklyn 1965; Mary McLeod Bethune Centennial Awd Natl Council of Negro Women Inc 1975; Cert of Attendance at seminar on Visual Perception Auditory Perception; pin 10 yrs Cont Dedicated & Outstanding Serv Montefiore Hosp & Med Ctr 1976; Comm Apprec Awd Morrisania City Hosp Emp Council 1976; Alumni Achievement Awd Admin Comm Ldr & Humanitarian Shaw Univ Natl Alumni Assn 1976; Spec Awd of Loyalty Grace Baptist Ch 1979; Hon Appt to the Natl Adv Bd ABI 1982; Cert of Recog as sustaining mem Democratic Natl Comm 1982-87; Appreciation Awd for Serv Church Supt Council of Westchester Co 1984; 5 yr & 10 yr Serv Awd Montefiore Hosp & Med Ctr; 3 yr & 5 yr Serv Awd Beth Abraham Home; United Way of Mt Vernon, NY, citation for community service 1985-86; Westchester County Dept Mental Health Community Systems, mental health award 1985; John F Kennedy Library, honorary fellow, 1988. **HOME ADDRESS:** 22 Union Ave, Mt Vernon, NY 10550.

CLEVELAND, JAMES
Clergyman, recording artist, organizatio. **PERSONAL:** Born Dec 05, 1931, Chgo, IL. **EDUCATION:** Roosevelt U. **CAREER:** Conerstone Institutional Bapt Ch LA, pastor; Savoy Records, gospel recording artist; Gospel Music Workshop of Am, natl pres & founder. **ORGANIZATIONS:** Piano accompanist for Caravans & Roberta Martin Singers; had own group The James Cleveland Singers. **HONORS/ACHIEVEMENTS:** Recipient of several gold records & numerous Awards. **BUSINESS ADDRESS:** 3701 Northland Dr, Los Angeles, CA 90008.

CLEVELAND, TESSIE ANITA SMITH
Social worker. **PERSONAL:** Born Sep 17, 1939, Loverne, AL; married Lawrence J. **EDUCATION:** AL State Coll, BS 1959; Atlanta U, MSW 1964; Univ of CA at Los Angeles, postgrad 1968-69. **CAREER:** Tuskegee VA Hosp, asst sec chief med serv 1959-62; Los Angeles Co Gen Hosp, med social worker diabetic serv 1964-66; Home Care Prog, sr med social worker 1966-67; Met State Hosp Norwalk CA, psychiataric social worker 1966-67; Allison Home for Girls Los Angeles, psychiatric social worker 1966-; Shaw's Home for Girls Los Angeles, psychiatric social worker 1969-. **ORGANIZATIONS:** Dir Med Social Serv 1970-; dir Comm Outreach Prog 1971-; med soc work consult Teen Pregnancy Project 1968-70; mem prog session TB & Heart Assn 1969; mem Assn Balck Social Workers; Nat Assn Social Workers; bd dir SE Welfare Planning Council; mem Nat Council Negro Women; Iota Phi.

CLEVERT, CHARLES N., JR.
Judge. **PERSONAL:** Born Oct 11, 1947, Richmond, VA; married Leslie Ann Johnson; children: Charles N III, Melanie Adia. **EDUCATION:** Davis & Elkins Coll Elkins WV, BA 1969; Georgetown Univ Law Center Washington DC, JD 1972. **CAREER:** Milwaukee Cty Dist Atty's Office, asst dist atty 1972-75; US Atty's Office Eastern Dist of WI, asst US atty 1975-77; US Bankruptcy, judge 1977-86; US Bankruptcy Court Eastern Dist of WI, chief US bankruptcy judge 1986-. **ORGANIZATIONS:** Mem WI Bar Assn, Milwaukee Bar Assn, WI Black Lawyer's Assn, 7th Circuit Bar Assn, Alpha Phi Alpha, Judicial Council NBA; mem bd of govs Natl Conf ofBankruptcy Judges; mem Natl Bar Assoc; treas & mem bd of dir Milauke Council on Alcoholism, Milwaukee Forum 1981-86, African methodist Episcopal Church. **BUSINESS ADDRESS:** Chief Judge, US Bankruptcy Court, 216 US Courthouse, Milwaukee, WI 53202.

CLIFFORD, CHARLES H.
Human relations consultant. **PERSONAL:** Born Sep 08, 1933, Sacramento, CA; married Claudean Akers; children: Carla, Carolyn, Caren. **EDUCATION:** Sacramento Jr Coll, AA 1958; Sacramento State Coll, BA 1965. **CAREER:** Dept of Corr State of CA, human rel consult 1964-. **ORGANIZATIONS:** Mem area pres Black Corr Coalition; past pres CA Corr Officers 1969-72; mem Urban League, Black Caucus, NAACP, CA Young Dems. **HONORS/ACHIEVEMENTS:** Co-author Dept Corrs Affirmative Action Plan; 1st black dep sheriff Sacramento Co 1960; 1st black corr sgt Folsom Prison; 1st black Lt Folsom 1970. **MILITARY SERVICE:** USN 1951-55. **BUSINESS ADDRESS:** 719 P St, Sacramento, CA.

CLIFFORD, MAURICE C.
Educational administrator. **PERSONAL:** Born Aug 09, 1920, Washington, DC; son of Maurice C and Rosa Linberry Clifford; married Patricia; children: Maurice C III, Jay PL, Rosemary Clifford McDaniel. **EDUCATION:** Hamilton Coll Clinton NY, BA 1941; Univ of Chicago, MA 1942; Meharry Med Coll, MD 1947. **CAREER:** Obstetrics & Gynecology, private practice 1951-78; Med Coll of PA, vice pres med affairs 1978-79, acting pres 1979-80, pres 1980-86; Dept of Public Health City of Phila, commissioner. **ORGANIZATIONS:** Trustee Meharry Med Coll 1963-; mem bd of mgrs Germantown Savings Bank 1968-; trustee Acad of Natural Sci Philadelphia 1974-85, Philadelphia Museum of Art 1983-; mem Bd of Ethics City of Philadelphia 1984-86. **HONORS/ACHIEVEMENTS:** Martin Luther King Jr Awd Operation PUSH Philadelphia 1981; Natl Serv Awd Salem Baptist Church Philadelphia 1982; George Washington Carver Awd G Washington Carver Committee Philadelphia 1982; Disting Serv Awd Frontiers of Amer 1983; Frederick D Patterson Awd Philadelphia Inter Frat Counc UNCF 1985; Doctor of Humane Letters LaSalle University 1981; Honorary Degree Hamilton College 1982; Doctor of Science Honorary Degree Hahnemann Univ 1985; Doctor of Laws Honorary Degree Medical College of Pennsylvania 1986. **MILITARY SERVICE:** AUS capt 1952-54. **BUSINESS ADDRESS:** Commissioner, City of Philadelphia, Dept of Public Health, 540 Municipal Serv Bldg, Philadelphia, PA 19102.

CLIFFORD, PAUL INGRAHAM
Psychologist. **PERSONAL:** Born Jan 22, 1914, Martinsburg, WV; son of J Paul Clifford and M Grace Clifford; married Margaret Washington. **EDUCATION:** Shippensburg Univ, BS 1938; Atlanta Univ, AM 1948; Univ Chicago, PhD 1953. **CAREER:** Tuskegee Army Air Field, Tuskegee, AL, Admin, 1941-45; Paine Coll, prof 1947-48; Atlanta Univ, instructor 1948-51, asst prof 1952-54, registrar 1954-66, prof dir summer school 1957-68; US Office Educ Washington, consultant 1961-68; Emory Univ, visiting lecturer 1964-66; Univ CA, 1968-69; Amer Mgmt Psychols Inc, staff psychologist 1966-70; Prof Serv Amer Mgmt Psychols Inc, regional dir 1970-71, natl dir 1971-72; SC State Coll, prof dept chmn 1972-76; Career Mgmt of Atlanta Inc, psychologist. **ORGANIZATIONS:** Special lecturer, numerous institutions of higher learning; fellow, AAAS; GA Psychology Assn; mem Alumni Assn of Shippensburg Univ; Amer Acad Political & Social Science; Amer Assn School Admins; Amer Assn Univ Profs; Amer Educ Rsch Assn; Amer Assn for Counseling & Devel; Amer Psychol Assn; Assn for Higher Educ of Natl Educ Assn; GA Branch Assn for Counseling & Devel; IL Psychology Assn; Midwestern Psychology Assn; Natl Alumni Assn; Atlanta Univ; Natl Council on Measurements Used in Educ; communicant Protestant Episcopal Church; life mem Univ Chicago Alumni Assn; mem Natl Soc for Study of Educ; NY Acad Sciences; Omega Psi Phi Fraternity Inc Eta Omega Chapter; PA Psychology Assn; Phi Delta Kappa Zeta Chapter; Soc for Psychol Study of Social Issues; SC Psychology Assn; charter mem SE Psychols Assn; contributor, journals, papers, author in field; mem numerous bds & comms; independent practice counseling/clinical/consulting psychogist 1962-. **HONORS/ACHIEVEMENTS:** Numerous honors; numerous publications in educational and psychological journals .

CLIFFORD, THOMAS E.
PERSONAL: Born Mar 09, 1929, Washington, DC; married Edith Sanders; children: Maria, Edwin, Larry, Mark. **EDUCATION:** Howard Univ, BA (Cum Laude) 1949; George Washington Univ, MBA 1963. **CAREER:** US Air Force, jet fighter pilot and officer 1949-79; General Motors Corp, plant mgr 1979-86; Self-Employed, automotive consultant 1986-. **MILITARY SERVICE:** USAF major genl 30 yrs.

CLIFT, JOSEPH WILLIAM
Physician. **PERSONAL:** Born Apr 24, 1938, Patoka, IN; son of Cecil William Clift and Mary Esther Lucas Clift; married Ulyssine Gibson Clift, Aug 10, 1989; children: Kory Grant Clift, Nathalie Louise Clift. **EDUCATION:** TX So Univ, BS 1959; Univ TX Med Br, MD 1965. **CAREER:** Physician self employed. **ORGANIZATIONS:** Pres Delta Theta Chap Alpha Phi Alpha Fraternity 1959; pres Alameda Contra Costa Co Diabetes Assn 1975; mem bd dir Samuel Merritt Hosp 1976-79; diplomate Amer Bd of Internal Med 1978; pres of medical staff Highland General Hospital 1983-84; pres East Bay Soc of Internal Med 1984-; mem Nat Med Assn; AMA; CA Med Assn; mem, counselor Alameda-Contra-Costa Med Assn. **HONORS/ACHIEVEMENTS:** Resident of the Year, Highland General Hospital 1971. **MILITARY SERVICE:** USAF MC captain 1967-69; Commendation Medal USAF 1969. **HOME ADDRESS:** 14030 Broadway Terr, Oakland, CA 94611. **BUSINESS ADDRESS:** 3300 Webster, Ste 308, Oakland, CA 94609.

CLIFTON, IVERY DWIGHT
Educator. **PERSONAL:** Born Apr 06, 1943, Statesboro, GA; son of B J Clifton and Rosetta B Clifton; married Patricia A Davis, Aug 24, 1967; children: Kalisa, Kelli. **EDUCATION:** Tuskegee Inst, BS 1965; Tuskegee Inst, MS 1967; Univ Of IL, PhD 1976. **CAREER:** Univ of GA, prof and vice pres for Academic Affairs, 1988-; US Dept of Agriculture, Washington DC, agricultural economist 1970-76; AUS VA and Vietnam, officer advisor 1967-70; TVA AL, agricultural economist 1967. **ORGANIZATIONS:** Speciall asst to & vice pres for acad affairs Univ of GA 1977-78; consult Resources for the Future 1979; sec Alpha Phi Alpha 1975; pres Stewart Bd First AME Church 1979-80. **HONORS/ACHIEVEMENTS:** AUS commendation bronze star Natl Defense 1967-70; achievement award USDA 1971; Chi Gamma Iota Univ of IL Chapter Urbana 1975; Phi Kappa Phi Univ of GA Chapter Athens 1979; gamma sigma delta Univ of GA Chapter Athens 1980. **MILITARY SERVICE:** AUS qm ltc(p) reserves 20 years served. **HOME ADDRESS:** 305 Idylwood Dr, Athens, GA 30605.

CLIFTON, LUCILLE
Poet, author, educator. **PERSONAL:** Born Jun 27, 1936, Depew, NY; daughter of Samuel L Sayles Sr and Thelma Moore; married Fred J Clifton, May 10, 1958 (deceased); children: Sidney, Fredrica, Channing, Gillian, Graham, Alexia. **EDUCATION:** Howard Univ, Washington DC, 1953-55; Fredonia State Teachers College, Fredonia, NY, 1955. **CAREER:** New York State Div of Employment, Buffalo, NY, claims clerk, 1958-60; US Office of Educ, Washington, DC, literature asst for Central Atlantic Regional Educ Laboratory, 1969-71; Copper State College, Baltimore, MD, poet in residence, 1971-74; Columbia Univ School of the Arts, visiting writer; George Washingtron Univ, Jerry Moore Visiting Writer, 1982-83; Univ of California, Santa Cruz, prof of literature and creative writing, 1985-; St Mary's College of Maryland, St Mary's City, MD, distinguished visiting prof, 1989-91. **ORGANIZATIONS:** Mem, Intl PEN, Authors Guild, Authors League of Amer. **HONORS/ACHIEVEMENTS:** Discovery Award, New York YW-YMHA Poetry Center, 1969; Natl Endowment for the Arts fellowships, 1970, 1972; honorary degrees from Univ of Maryland and Towson State Univ; Poet Laureate of the State of Maryland, 1979-82; nominated for Pulitzer Prize for poetry, 1980, 1988; Juniper Prize, Univ of Massachusetts, 1980; Coretta Scott King Award, Amer Library Assn, 1984; author, 21 children's books, including The Black BCs, 1970, All Us Come Cross the Water, 1973, Three Wishes, 1976, Everett Anderson's Goodbye, 1983; author, seven books of poetry, including Good Times: Poems, 1969, An Ordinary Woman, 1974, Next: New Poems, 1987; author, Generations: A Memoir, 1976; contributor to anthologies and periodicals.

CLIMMONS, WILLIE MATHEW
Educational administrator. **PERSONAL:** Born Mar 18, 1923, Magnolia, MS; married Vera Lois Chachere; children: Gwendoly Faye. **EDUCATION:** Leland Coll Baker LA, BS 1952; TX So Univ Houston, MEd 1960; LSU Baton Rouge LA, reading courses 1968-69. **CAREER:** Plaquemine Point Elementary School, St Landry Parish School Bd, prin 1958-; St Landry Parish School Bd, teacher Math, Chemistry, Biology & Science 1952-58. **ORGANIZATIONS:** Treas St Landry Parish Educ Assn Fed Credit Union 1962-; treas St Landry Parish Educ Assn 1967-; pres 7th Dist JK Haynes Found & Legal Defense FundInc 1977-; past pres & state dir Frontiers Intl past m & chmn audit com Keystone Lodge No 196 Opelousas LA; 1st lt comdr CF Ladd Consistory No 80. **HONORS/ACHIEVEMENTS:** Recipient good conduct medal & eto ribbon & 5 battle stars AUS 1943-46; natl sci found grant TX So Univ Houston 1958; Frontiersman of the year award Frontiers Intl Opelousas LA 1975; black outstanding educator awards SRRYHO 1975; disting serv award Dist 5 Frontiers Intl 1979; past exalted ruler degree 33rd Degree of Masonary PHA 1979. **MILITARY SERVICE:** AUS pfc 1943-46. **BUSINESS ADDRESS:** PO Box 850, Opelousas, LA 70570.

CLINE, EILEEN TATE
Educational administrator. **PERSONAL:** Born Jun 25, 1935, Chicago, IL; daughter of Herman Tate and Inez Duke; married William P (deceased); children: Jon Christopher, Joy Michele. **EDUCATION:** Geneva C Robinson Chicago Musical Coll, priv piano study 1947-52; Univ of Chicago, liberal arts 1950-52; Helen Curtis Chicago Musical Coll, class piano course 1950; Rudolph Ganz scholarship student, priv piano study 1956-58; Oberlin Conserv of Music, BMus Ed 1956, B Mus piano perf 1956; Univ of CO Boulder, MMus piano perf 1960; IN Univ Sch of Music Bloomington, IN, Doctor Mus Educ 1985. **CAREER:** Univ of CO, coord of cont educ piano 1965-75; Neighborhood Mus Sch New Haven, CT, exec dir 1980-82; Peabody Conserv of Mus The Johns Hopkins Univ, assoc dean 1982-83, dean 1983-. **ORGANIZATIONS:** Founder/dir Boulder Children's Choir 1972-75; student activities chmn CO State Music Teachers' Assn; prog chmn Boulder Area Music Tchrs' Assn; Music Prog Professional Training Panel Natl Endowment for the Arts 1980-; pres Young Musicians of Boulder; alumni-elected trustee Oberlin Coll 1981-; bd trustees Hopkins Sch1981-82; bd mem Natl Guild of Comm Schools of the Arts 1982-88; exec bd CO State Music Teachers' Assn; natl Keyboard Comm Music Educators Natl Conf; adv bd YWCA Univ of CO; Music Comm CO Council for the Arts and Humanities; Coll Bd Theory AP Test Devel Comm ETS 1983-; Eval Team Middle States Accredit Assn 1983-; mem MTNA, MENC, Coll Music Soc, Natl Guild of Piano Teachers, Society for Values in Higher Education, Amer Assn of Univ Professors. **HONORS/ACHIEVEMENTS:** Research grants, IN Univ Found, IN Univ Office of Rsch and Grad Devel; Oberlin Coll Alumni Rsch Grant; academic scholarships and honors Univ of CO 1958-60, Oberlin Coll 1953-56; Danforth Found Fellowship 1975-; "Reflections of Cultural Synthesis and Social Reality as Seen in George Walker's Sonata No 2" Soc for Values in Higher Education Conf Dickinson Coll 1979; "The Competition Explosion, Impact on Higher Education" MTNA Natl Convention 1980; "Education Relationships to Professional Training and Career Entry" NASM Conv Dallas, TX 1981; published, "The Competition Explosion, Impact on Education" The American Music Teacher Parts I-III Jan-March 1982; lectures, performance competitions; Outstanding Woman Awd Natl Exec Club 1984; Outstanding Alumni Awd Univ of Colorado College of Music 1985. **BUSINESS ADDRESS:** Dean, Peabody Conservatory of Music, 1 East Mount Vernon Place, Baltimore, MD 21202.

CLINKSCALES, JERRY A.
Educator. **PERSONAL:** Born Sep 25, 1933, Abbeville, SC; married Jerrolyn Holtzclaw; children: Mary, Jerry, David, Stephen. **EDUCATION:** SC State Coll, BSA 1956; Tuskegee Inst, DVM 1960; Univ IL, advanced training 1972. **CAREER:** Tuskegee Inst, instructor 1960; USDA, poultry insp div 1966; Tuskegee Inst, instructor 1967; head small animal clinic 1968; asst prof 1971-. **ORGANIZATIONS:** Mem Am Vet Me Assn 1960-; Am Assn Vet Clinicans 1961-; Am Animal Hosp Assn 1965-; mem Tuskegee Area C of C; Omega Psi Phi Frat; Phi Zeta Hon Vet Frat; adv City Recreation Detp; City Canine Control Center. **HONORS/ACHIEVEMENTS:** Outstanding tchr of yr award Norden's 1972-73. **MILITARY SERVICE:** AUSR 1956-.

CLINKSCALES, JOHN WILLIAM, JR.
Clergyman. **PERSONAL:** Born Mar 05, 1925, Chicago, IL. **EDUCATION:** VA Union U, AB 1946; McCormick Theol Sem, MDiv 1950. **CAREER:** Beth Eden Bapt Ch, asst min 1946-55; Lebannon Bapt Ch, min 1955-; St Bernard Hosp, chaplain 1974-80; Chicago Baptist Inst, instr 1980-. **ORGANIZATIONS:** Mem Amer Bapt Ministers Assn; vice pres Chicago Chapter VA & Union Univ Alumni Assn; bd mem Morgan Park Coop Credit Union; bd mem Englewood Quality of LifeNetwork; mem Chicago Heights Alumni Chap Kappa Alpha Psi; adv council Harper HS; neighborhood adv council Ogden Park; neighborhood social serv adv council Chicago Urban League; mem Southwestern Ministers Assoc; treas Interdenominational Ministers Alliance. **MILITARY SERVICE:** USAR retired col chaplain.

CLINTON, THOMAS R.
Salesman. **PERSONAL:** Born Aug 22, 1909, Cincinnati; married Bernice Holliday; children: Lorna, Helen, Tom, Jr. **CAREER:** Real est & ins salesman 1964-; Cincinnati, postal supvr 1957-64; postal field serv 1928-57. **ORGANIZATIONS:** Mem Kiwanis Gaines Meth Ch; NAACP; Cincinnati Real Est Bd; 1st Black Council Silverton 1967-; mem Nat Alliance Postal & Employees; Nat Fed Retired PO Employees. **BUSINESS ADDRESS:** 3407 Montgomery Rd, Cincinnati, OH 45207.

CLIPPER, MILTON CLIFTON, JR.
President. **PERSONAL:** Born Feb 03, 1948, Washington, DC; son of Milton Clipper, Sr and Gladys Robertson Clipper; divorced; children: Faith Ann Clipper,Jaime Marie Clipper. **EDUCATION:** Montgomery Coll; Corcoran Sch of Art. **CAREER:** WA Post, graphic designer 1976-; Corcoran Sch of Art, art tchr 1976-; WJXT-TV, art dir 1974-76; WTOP-TV, artist 1970-73; WDVM TV 9 Washington DC, Asst Promotions Mgr, 1985. **ORGANIZATIONS:** Editorial bd WJXT-TV 1975-76; mem Metro Art Dirs & Club of WA; guest lectr TV & Newspaper Graphics; mem Black Ski; Washington Urban League; mem Amer Film Inst; advisory bd mem Big Brothers of the Natl Capital area. **HONORS/ACHIEVEMENTS:** 2nd place Metro Art Dirs Club 1972; exhibition of abstract art 1973; Gold Award, Broadcast Designers Assn, 1984; Finalist Intl Film Festival, 1984. **BUSINESS ADDRESS:** Pres, Design Concepts Inc, 300 I St NE, Suite 212, Washington, DC 20002.

CLOSE, HARI P.
Multi-meeting planner. **PERSONAL:** Born Feb 07, 1961, Lynn, MA; children: Travis, Hari III. **EDUCATION:** Tuskegee Inst, BS Business Admin 1983; Attended, Auburn Univ Business Grad Sch. **CAREER:** Sheraton St Johns Place, marketing rep 1983-84; Sheraton Inner Harbor, pre-opening sales mgr 1984-84; Potomac Hotel Group, natl Sales mgr 1986; Close & Assocs Inc, pres 1986-. **ORGANIZATIONS:** Bd mem Boy Scouts of Amer ARea Cncl 1984-86; mem Natl Coalition of Black Meeting Planners 1985-; bd mem Big Brothers & Sisters of Amer Central MD 1985-86; consultant City of Baltimore/State of MD 1986-; intl pres Intl Assoc of First Friday Inc 1986-; conference coord Natl Funeral Directors & MorticiansAssoc 1986-. **HONORS/ACHIEVEMENTS:** Outstanding Young Men of Amer US Jaycees 1982,83,85,86; intl Directory of Disting Young Leadership 1987; Resolution from the City Council of Baltimore City "Generous Contribution to the Plight of the Homeless" 1987.

CLOSURE, VANILLA THREATS
Elected official. **PERSONAL:** Born May 14, 1946, Lake Providence, LA; married James Closure; children: Terral, Carla, Ronald, Tonja, Jacqueline. **EDUCATION:** Grambling State Univ, BS 1971; Univ of FL, DA 1982. **CAREER:** HIEFSS, asst dietitian 1982; East Carroll School Bd, bd mem 1983-; Shady Lake Nursing Home Activity Director 1986-. **ORGANIZATIONS:** Church musician East Carrol Musician 1962; prog chmn Lake Prov Grambling Alumni Assoc 1972; asst dir East Carrol Baptist Recreation Assoc 1982; pres 1964 class organization 1987-. **HONORS/ACHIEVEMENTS:** Outstanding Woman of the Year Grambling Alumni Assoc 1980. **HOME ADDRESS:** 810 4th St, Lake Providence, LA 71254.

CLOUD, ERIC WILLIAM
Attorney. **PERSONAL:** Born Feb 26, 1946, Cleveland, OH; married Carole Anne Henderson; children: Andre, Sharrieff. **EDUCATION:** Morris Brown Coll, BA (cum laude) 1973; Dag Hammarskjold Coll, fellowship (highest honors) 1974; Antioch Sch of Law, JD 1977; George Washington Law Sch, LLM Intl & Comparative Law 1980. **CAREER:** Pvt Practice Intl Law, atty; Intertax Inc (Intl Tax Consult Firm), pres; US Dept of Treasury, consult 1979-80; US Dept of Labor, spl asst to intl tax counsel 1976-78. **ORGANIZATIONS:** Mem Am Bar Assn 1977; mem Nat Bar Assn. **HONORS/ACHIEVEMENTS:** Good Samaritan of the Year Mayor Carl Stokes 1968; fellowship Dag Hammarskjolld Coll Dag Hammarskjold Found 1973; article to be published this year in GeorgeWashington Law Review "Tax Treaties the need for the us to extend its treaty network to developing countries in light of the new Intl Economic and Polit Realities". **BUSINESS ADDRESS:** 1511 K St NW, Washington, DC 20215.

CLOUD, SANFORD, JR.
Attorney. **PERSONAL:** Born Nov 27, 1944, Hartford, CT; married Diane Brown; children: Adam, Christopher, Robin. **EDUCATION:** Univ of Az; Howard U, BA 1966; Howard Univ Sch of Law, JD cum laude 1969. **CAREER:** Cloud & Ibarguen, partner 1977-; Robinson Robinson & Cole, atty 1970-76; CT General Assembly, couns 1971-72; Aetna Life & Casualty Law Dept, atty 1969; Covington & Burling, law clk 1968-69; US Sen Thomas Dodd, res asst 1964-67. **ORGANIZATIONS:** Mem Urban Leag; United Way; mem Prog Adv Com WFSB-TV 1972-; mem Bd RegentsUniv of Hartford 1972-; mem bd dir C of C; mem bd dir CT Savings & Loan Assn; mem Am Bar Assn; NBA; CT Bar Assn. **HONORS/ACHIEVEMENTS:** Recip man of month CT Mut Life Ins Co WKND Radio 1974; outstnd young men of Am 1974; oustsnd serv awd 1966; prod TV show "The Year 1973 Perspective in Black"; listed Who's Who Among Students in Am Coll & Univ 1966.

CLOUDEN, LAVERNE C.
Music director. **PERSONAL:** Born Dec 06, 1933, Cleveland, OH; married Aubrey B Clouden; children: Norman, Karen, Nathan. **EDUCATION:** Case Western Res U, BS (cum laude) 1966; MA 1970. **CAREER:** Buckeye State Band, dir 1958-; F D Roosevelt Jr High School, instructor, dir 1966-72; Music Dept Nathan Hale Jr High School, chmn 1972-74; John F Kennedy High School, music dir 1974-85; East High School, fine arts dept chmn/instructor, dir/vocal dir 1985-. **ORGANIZATIONS:** Mem Mt Pleasant Symphony Orch Parma Symphony; Cleveland Women's Symphony; Buckeye State Band; Mt Pleasant Musician's Guild; dir Musicians Umion #4; MusicEducators Nat Conf OH Music Educators Assn; Women Band Dirs Nat Assn; mem Nat Band Assn; mem Intl Platform Assn; mem Nat Assn of Music Therapy; mem Mu Phi Epsilon. **HONORS/ACHIEVEMENTS:** Congrats resolution Mayor & City Cleveland 1975; feat newspapers & Mags; apptd Natl Bd of Am Youth Symphony& Chorus; 1st female marching band band dir Cleveland HS. **BUSINESS ADDRESS:** Fine Arts Dept Chairman, East High School, 1349 E 79th Stv, Cleveland, OH 44103.

CLOUSER, ERNEST Z.
Public citizen, retired educator. **PERSONAL:** Born Sep 28, 1922, Galveston, TX; married Margaret Phelps; children: 2 Children. **EDUCATION:** Prairie View A&M U, BA 1943; TX Southern U, MEd 1951. **CAREER:** Houston Independent School Dist, former prin; P L Dunbar Elementary School, retired prin; asst prin 1957-61; USO dir; Houston, teacher Adult Educ; Phillis Wheatley Sr High School Houston, teacher; Atlanta Life Insurance Co, life underwriter. **ORGANIZATIONS:** Life mem Professional Administrs; Nat Assn of Elem Sch Prins Chmn Com Traffic & Transportation Houston Cits C of C 1975-80; former mem Governing Bd De Pelchin Faith Home; Negro Child Cntr; mem Prairie Viewn A&M Univ Alumni Asn; Common Cause; Public Citizen Houston Citizens C of C; Knights of St Peter Claver & Alpha Phi Alpha Frat Inc; Precinct 136 Dem Caucus; headed Several clubs & coms; guest speaker on numerous occasions; Houston Cit C of C. **HONORS/ACHIEVEMENTS:** Disting serv awards 1975-76; presided 1975 ground brkng ceremony for S Freeway construc; led successful moves resulting in easing rigid Fire Zone #2 restric in depressed areas & opened up channels for improvements in old nghbrhds. **BUSINESS ADDRESS:** 2808 Wheeler, Houston, TX 77004.

CLUSE, KENNY JOSEPH
Educator. **PERSONAL:** Born Sep 25, 1945, Houston, TX; son of McKinley Cluse and Elsie Green Cluse. **EDUCATION:** Texas Southern University, BA 1971; Univ of Houston, BA Radio TV 1973. **CAREER:** KCOH-AM Houston, Texas, newscaster 1973-75; KTSU-FM radio Houston, TX, sportscaster 1977; HISD Houston Texas, teacher 1978-89; KCOH Radio Houston, newsman. **ORGANIZATIONS:** Mem Sigma Delta Chi Journalistic Soc 1972. **HONORS/ACHIEVEMENTS:** Plaque Lynn Eusann Inst 1973; certificate of Appreciation Prairie View A&M Univ 1974. **HOME ADDRESS:** 4514 Oats Street, Houston, TX 77020.

CLYBURN, ELAINE MARIE
Educator. **PERSONAL:** Born Oct 16, 1934, Buffalo, NY. **EDUCATION:** Le Moyne Coll Syracuse NY, BS 1956; Howard Univ Wash DC, MSW 1958. **CAREER:** Villa Maria Coll, educator 1977-; CO State Univ, asst prof 1973-77; ARA, admin 1969-72; School Dist of Syracuse NY, school social worker 1965-60; Syracuse NY Community Day Care, exec dir 1964-65; NY State Commn for Human Rights, field representative 1961-64; Cath Welfare Bur Los Angeles, social worker 1958-61. **ORGANIZATIONS:** Bd of dir Community House 1979; second vice pres Planning/Allocations Div United Way Erie Co 1979-80; bd of dir Hospice Orgn of Metro Erie 1980; vol consult Am Nat Red Cross 1973-; membership chmn PA State Chap Nat Assn Soc Workers 1979-80; advis bd Health Systems Inc 1979-80; Pi Gamma Mu Le Moyne Coll 1954; Gamma Pi Epsilon Le Moyne Coll 1955. **HONORS/ACHIEVEMENTS:** Gold Key Award Syracuse Sch Vol Com 1963; hon mem 25th Inf Div Republic of Vietnam 1970. **BUSINESS ADDRESS:** 2551 W Lake Rd, Erie, PA 16505.

CLYBURN, JAMES E.
Government employee. **PERSONAL:** Born Jul 21, 1940, Sumter, SC; son of E L Clyburn and Almeta Clyburn; married Emily; children: Mignon, Jennifer, Angela. **EDUCATION:** SC State Coll, BA 1962; USC Law Sch, 1972-74. **CAREER:** St Human Affairs Commin, commr; Gov John C West of SC, spec asst (for human resource devel) 1971-74; SC Commn for Farm Workers Inc, exec dir 1968-71; Neighborhood Youth Corps, dir 1966-68; SC Employee Sec Commn, couns 1965-68; high school history teacher 1962-65. **ORGANIZATIONS:** Mem of numerous political & civic orgns. **HONORS/ACHIEVEMENTS:** 1st black pres SC Young Democrats; recipient of 36 citations & awards. **BUSINESS ADDRESS:** State Human Affairs Commin, PO Box 11009, Columbia, SC 29211.

CLYBURN, JOHN B.
Business executive. **PERSONAL:** Born Oct 22, 1942, Sumter, SC; married Vivian Hilton; children: Jeffrey, Erica, Kimberly. **EDUCATION:** SC State Coll, BS 1964; Northeastern Univ, MEd 1968; Univ of WI, PhD Urban Ed. **CAREER:** Wiltwyck School for Boys Inc, sr counselor; New England Home, weekend suprv; Hayden Goodwill Inn School for Boys, exec asst; SC Vocational Rehab Dept, vocational rehab counselor; ESC, natl coord 1969-70, proj dir 1970-71, vice pres 1971-72, exec vice pres 1972-73; Decision Info Systems Corp, chmn. **ORGANIZATIONS:** Mem Natl Assoc Market Developers, Amer Mgmt Assoc, Child Care Proj Adv Comm, Natl Rehab Assoc, Day Care & Child Devel Corp Amer, Natl Assoc EdYoung Children, Delta Psi Omega; lecturer Natl Head Start Conf, Natl Assoc Black Social Workers, Natl Conf Inst Svc. **HONORS/ACHIEVEMENTS:** Deviant Youth; "Use Your Aides Effectively" interview, edited & publ Tech Asst Bulletin; "Challenge Pre-School Ed" promo brochure; "New Horizons Migrant &Seasonal Farm Worker Youths" Publ Idea Exchange 1970. **BUSINESS ADDRESS:** 1425 K Street, NW, Ste 1000, Washington, DC 20005.

CLYMER, LEWIS W.
Retired judge. **PERSONAL:** Born Dec 16, 1910, Neosho, MO; married Janet L Blackwell; children: Willa Lynn. **EDUCATION:** Lincoln Univ, 1928-29; Howard Univ, 1935-36; Howard Univ School of Law, LLB 1939. **CAREER:** State of MO, asst attny gen 1935-60; War Manpower Comm Region 9 AR, KS, MO, OK, minorities placement spec 1941-45; Kansas City MO, gen practice 1945; Jackson Cty MO, asst pros 1948-52; Municipal Court MO, apptd judge 1960; Municipal Cty Mar, elected judge 1963; Non-partisan Ct Plan, re-elected 1967-71; 16th Judicial Circuit of MO 1970, judge retired 1980. **ORGANIZATIONS:** Former bd mem N Amer Judges Assoc, MO Munic & Magistrate Judges Assoc; mem Amer Bar Assoc, KC Bar Assoc, Jackson Cty Bar Assoc, Natl Bar Assoc, Cts & Judiciary Comm, The MO Bar & Adv Comm on Cit Ed, The MO Bar; mem bd of dirs urban League of KC, Blue Cross of KC; bd curators Lincoln Univ; vice pres Trumon Amer Eye Ctr; bd dir Gr KC Chap ARC; bd dir Acad of Health Prof; mem MO Statewide Prof Standards Review Council; bd mem at largeSchool Dist of Kansas City MO.

CLYNE, JOHN RENNEL
Lawyer, senior foreign service officer. **PERSONAL:** Born Feb 25, 1926, New York, NY; son of Reginald Clyne and Urielle Linard Clyne; married Jessie MacFarlane, Dec 28, 65; children: Diana, Reginald, Robert. **EDUCATION:** St Johns Univ School of Law, LLB 1958; St Johns Univ School of Law, JD 1968. **CAREER:** US & W Indies, engr 1958; private practice NY, lawyer 1958-62; New York City Transit Auth, attny 1963-65; US Agency Intl Devel Nigeria, Brazil, Nicaragua, Honduras, regional legal adv 1965-83; US Agency Intl Devel, asst general counsel 1983-; self-employed, econ devel consultant. **ORGANIZATIONS:** Dir Amer Intl School Managua, Amer Intl School Lagos. **HONORS/ACHIEVEMENTS:** Nominated Fed Exec Sr Sem 1977; Sr Foreign Serv Awd 1984; Secretary of State's Tribute of Appreciation for Distinguished Service in Foreign Disaster Assistance 1985. **MILITARY SERVICE:** USN 1944-46. **HOME ADDRESS:** 2200 Eugenia Ct, Oviedo, FL 32765.

COACHMAN, WINFRED CHARLES
Educator. **PERSONAL:** Born Oct 08, 1927, McDonald, PA; divorced; children: Winfred, Tonya, Sherrie, Sandy. **EDUCATION:** Univ of PA, MEd; Univ of PA, Cert Doctrl Cand. **CAREER:** Human Serv Neighborhood Centers Assn, dir 1977-; PA Bd of Educ Manchester Floating Classroom, prin; PA Blk Action Drug Abuse Center Inc, durg counselor, co-ord educ therapy 1970-71; Com Sch Partnership Program, co-ord 1970; Black History Bidwell Cultural Training Center, instructor 1968-70. **ORGANIZATIONS:** Chmn Manchester Comprehensive Educ Com; mem St Joseph's Comm Sch Bd Dir; mem Advsry Com Act 101 Allegheny Comm Coll; mem PA Br NAACP; memAdvsry Com and Sec Task Force PA Bd of Edn; mem N Side Com on Humn Resrcs Inc; mem PA Drug Advsry Task Frc Com Aw Manchester Fltng Clsrm 1975; com aw N Side Comm ; testimonial N Side Resdnts Co-wrks and Sch Persnl; achvmnt aw Manchester Fltng Clsrm. **HONORS/ACHIEVEMENTS:** Biol art SCOPE Allis Chalmers publ 1973. **MILITARY SERVICE:** AUS 1945-47. **BUSINESS ADDRESS:** 1439 N Franklin St, Pittsburgh, PA 15233.

COATES, JANICE E.
Optometrist. **PERSONAL:** Born Aug 27, 1942, Zanesville, OH; daughter of Urschel Mayle and Bessie Mayle; children: Stephanie, Stephlynn, Melissa, Tischa. **EDUCATION:** Marion Coll, undergrad work 1960-62; Wright State Univ, BS Comprehensive Sciences and BS Secondary Educ 1974; Indiana Univ, Dr of Optometry 1979. **CAREER:** Dr Frederick Grigsby, urologist asst 1963-65; Sanders Stone Ins Agency, insurance rater 1965-66; Montgomery Co Welfare Dept, welfare worker 1967-69; Dayton Bd of Educ, substitute teacher 1969-74, science teacher 1974-75; Capital Univ, educator 1980-82; optometrist private practice 1980-. **ORGANIZATIONS:** Prog coord 1982-83, treas 1983-84 Amer Bus Womens Assn; mem of minority recuirt Amer Optometric Assn Ohio Optometric Assn 1980-; liasion to state rep Miami Valley Soc of Optometrists 1981-; mem Gem City Med Soc 1982-; trustee Natl Optometric Assn 1983-; mem NAACP 1983-;NOA Secretary 1985-86/1986-87;exec bd mem of NOA 1983-89; exec bd for Youth Engaged for Success 1985-89. **HOME ADDRESS:** 1000 Amherst Pl, Dayton, OH 45406. **BUSINESS ADDRESS:** Optometrist, N O A, 1204 Salem Ave, Dayton, OH 45406.

COATES, SHELBY L.
Business executive. **PERSONAL:** Born Mar 25, 1931, Washington, DC; married Lysette D'Amours. **EDUCATION:** Dept of Agr Grad Sch, Cert 1965-66; Inst of Computer Tech, Cert 1965-66; USAF Supply Analysis & Design Sch, Cert 1969. **CAREER:** MISSO Serv Corp, pres, CEO 1976-; AUSNG, computer specialist 1966-78, computer systems analyst 1948-55. **ORGANIZATIONS:** Mem DAV 1970-; mem Republican Natl Finance Comm EAGLE. **HONORS/ACHIEVEMENTS:** Recipient 3 outstanding performance awards AUS 1971, 1974, 1978. **MILITARY SERVICE:** AUS pfc 8 yrs. **BUSINESS ADDRESS:** President & CEO, MISSO Services Corp, 5201 Leesburg Pike, Ste 1200, Falls Church, VA 22041.

COATIE, ROBERT MASON
Educator. **PERSONAL:** Born May 19, 1945, Mound City, IL; son of Rev Dixon C Coatie and Georgia B Mason Coatie; married Birdeen Golden, Jun 29, 1968; children: Dionne, Robert M II. **EDUCATION:** Ball State Univ, BS 1968, MA 1972. **CAREER:** Muncie Comm Sch Corp, tchr 1967-68; IN Civil Rights Commission, proj dir 1968-69; Ball State Univ, assc dir minority student development 1969-84; Univ Louisville, dir Center for Academic Achievement. **ORGANIZATIONS:** Bd mem Hooisers for Excellence 1983-85; past chmn, tres Area VI Council on Aging 1974-84; mem Kappa Alpha Psi Frat 1964-, Natl Assn Dev Educ 1985-, Southeastern Assn Educ Prog Personnel 1986-, Amer Assn Counseling & Devel 1987-, Natl Assn Student Personnel Admin 1987-; mem Assoc for Supervision and Curriculeum Development 1987-; mem YMCA Black Achiever's Parent Advisory Committee 1986-89; vice president Central High School Parent Teachers Assoc 1985-89; secretary Brown School Parent Teachers Association 1986-. **HONORS/ACHIEVEMENTS:** Observer White House Conf on Aging 1981; mem Outstanding Young Men of Amer 1975; Black Achiever, Muncie, Indiana 1988; Athletic Hall of Fame, Delaware County (Indiana) 1988; mem, Kappa Delta Pi 1974-. **HOME ADDRESS:** 1381 South 4th Street, Louisville, KY 40208. **BUSINESS ADDRESS:** Dir, Univ of Louisville, Strickler Hall 448, Louisville, KY 40292.

COAXUM, CALLIE B.
Educator. **PERSONAL:** Born Jun 07, 1930, Clinton, NC; married Lymon A Coaxum; children: Donald, Ronald, Kelvin. **EDUCATION:** Johnson C Smith Univ, BA (cum laude) 1949; SC State Coll, MS 1960; VA State Coll, post grad 1963; IN Univ, post grad 1964; Univ of SC, post grad 1969; SIU, DPhil in Educ 1976. **CAREER:** Porter Elementary School, prin 1951-52; St Helena High School, teacher, counselor 1955-69; Coll Counseling & Asst Dean of Students, dir 1970-72; Winston-Salem State Univ, prof of English, asst to vice chancellor for academic affairs 1977-83, vice chancellor for academic affairs 1983-. **ORGANIZATIONS:** Informal consul Ford Found Leadership Dev Prog 1972; pres Lady's Island Dem Precinct 1968; Alpha Kappa Alpha Sor; SC Coll Student Pers Assoc 1970-; Amer Coll Pers Assoc Summer Fellowship French VA State Coll 1963; Contrib articles to ed magazines & publishers. **HONORS/ACHIEVEMENTS:** Who's Who of Amer Women; The World Who's Who of Women 4th ed; mem Phi Kappa Alpha. **BUSINESS ADDRESS:** VP Chancellor for Acad Affrs, Winston-Salem StateUniv, Winston-Salem, NC 27102.

COAXUM, HENRY L., JR.
Business executive. **PERSONAL:** Born Jan 27, 1951, Charleston, SC. **EDUCATION:** Talladega Coll, BA History, Pol Sci 1969-73; IN Univ, MPA 1973-75. **CAREER:** City of Chicago, planning analyst 1975-79; DuSable Museum African-Amer History, devel officer 1979-81; Southtown Planning Assoc, exec dir 1981-83; AmistadRsch Ctr, dir of devel 1983-84; McDonalds Corp, mgr. **ORGANIZATIONS:** Pres Chicago Talladega Coll Alumni Club 1977-81; mem Natl Soc of Fund Raising Exec 1980-84, Comm Arts Comm of Chicago Council on Fine Arts 1981-82. **HONORS/ACHIEVEMENTS:** Cert Chief Planning Analyst City of Chicago Dept of Personnel 1979; Alumni Devel Robert R Moton Inst VA 1981; Commercial Redevel Natl Devel Council Atlanta 1982; Comm Exec Prog IBM Corp NY 1982. **BUSINESS ADDRESS:** Manager, McDonald's Corp, 10001 I-10 Service Rd, New Orleans, LA 70127.

COBB, BERNICE COAR
Educator. **PERSONAL:** Born Jun 19, 1938, Salem, AL. **EDUCATION:** Miles Coll Birmingham, BA (cum laude) 1960; Fisk Univ Nashville, MA 1963; Pudue Univ W Lafayette IN, PhD 1977. **CAREER:** Talladega Coll, Talladega AL, dir of health careers opportunity program, assoc prof of biology 1979-; Miles Coll Birmingham, natural science prof 1968-79; Parks Jr High School Atlanta, chmn, science teacher 1965-68; Carver High School, Columbus GA, biology teacher 1963-65; Sanford High School, Opelika AL, teacher, chmn of science dept 1960-62. **ORGANIZATIONS:** Dir of tchr training wkshop Miles Coll 1975-76; dir of CAUSE PROJ Miles Coll B-Ham 1978-79; chmn of natl sci dept Miles Coll 1978-79; chmn of career day program; Delta Sigma Theta Sorority Inc 1978-79. **HONORS/ACHIEVEMENTS:** Outstanding educator or Am OEA Organ 1975; Phelps Stokes Fund HEW Nat Health Service Corps 1976; outstanding contributions to Comm Editorial Bd of Am Biog Inst 1976; delta's award for outstanding academic achievement Delta Sigma Theta Inc 1978.

COBB, CHARLES E.
Association executive. **PERSONAL:** Born Sep 28, 1916, Durham, NC; married Martha Kendrick. **EDUCATION:** BA 1940; BD 1944; STM1954; DD 1972. **CAREER:** KY State Coll, chaplain dean men;St Mark Social Center, dir; St John AME Ch, pastor; St Johns Congregational Ch; Charlotte Edition Carolina & Times,mgn editor; Commn for Racial Justice United Ch Christ, exec dir. **ORGANIZATIONS:** Mem Ministers for Racial & Social Justice; Nat Council Chs; Commr Pub Welf Springfield; chmn spl com Black Clergy 1966 Omega Psi Phi Frat; UCC United Black Christina; Black ExecS in Denominations Religious Orgns & Communions Orgn Sch Civic Resopnsibility Springield 1952; bd dirs Child & Family Serv 1955-66. **HONORS/ACHIEVEMENTS:** Man Of Yr Omega Psi Phi New England Reg Award 1954; NAACP New England Reg Award 1958; Frederick Douglas Citation 1972;

City Wide Clergy Award 1971; Nazarene Brotherhood Award 1972; Richard Allen Brotherhood Award 1964. **BUSINESS ADDRESS:** Commission for Racial Justice, 105 Madison Ave Ste 1102, New York, NY 10016.

COBB, ETHEL WASHINGTON
Elected official. **PERSONAL:** Born Jun 10, 1925, Ravenel, SC; married Shedrick Cobb; children: Seven children. **CAREER:** City of Ravenel, bd of execs 1970-. **ORGANIZATIONS:** Mem St John Baptist Church, recording sec & pres The Pulpit Aid Bd, mem Missionary Bd, mem church choir; founder/chmn St John Day Care Ctr; mem Yonges Island Headstart Bd; mem Daycare Ctr Bd; mem Rural Mission Council; mem Biracial Comm Charleston Co Comm Develop Bd; vol firefighter Sea Island Prog; Clemson Univ Ext Comm Develop Progs; mem Democratic Party, exec comm, poll mgr for Primary & Presidential Elections; precinct chmn Pol Action Comm Dist 116; mem Democratic Council 1984; mem Budget Proposal Comm; represented Ravenel in Charleston Berkley & Dorchester Comm; represented Ravenel in Firemen Assn; mem Eastern Star; elected First Black Woman to the Bd of Execs in Ravenel. **HONORS/ACHIEVEMENTS:** Civil Defense Awd; 5 yr Recognition Awd Clemson Univ Ext Prog; Outstanding Assistance Awd, Who's Who Among Southern Americans; Outstanding Assistance Awd for the Baptist Hill HS Athletic Dept; Who's Who Among Black Elected Officials; Outstanding Democratic Female; cert from Gov's Rural School. **BUSINESS ADDRESS:** Councilmember, Rt 1 Box 9, Ravenel, SC 29470.

COBB, GARRY WILBERT
Professional football player. **PERSONAL:** Born Mar 16, 1957, Carthage, NC. **EDUCATION:** Univ of So CA, attended. **CAREER:** Detroit Lions NFL, football player 1979-84; Philadelphia Eagles, linebacker 1985-. **BUSINESS ADDRESS:** Linebacker, Philadelphia Eagles, Philadelphia Veterans Stadium, Broad St & Pattison Ave, Philadelphia, PA 19148.

COBB, HAROLD
Clergyman, elected official. **PERSONAL:** Born Jul 20, 1941, Covington, GA; son of Toy Q and Mary A; married Reta Jean Davis; children: Sheila, Shermekia, Harrell. **EDUCATION:** Atlanta Area Tech School, 1970; Marsh-Drangron Bus Coll, 1971-72; Oxford Coll of Emory Univ 1978; DeKalb Comm Coll 1981-. **CAREER:** City of Covington, lab analyst, water treatment 1974-78; Ford Motor Co, lab analyst, water treatment 1978-; City of Covington, commission; United Methodist Church, minister. **ORGANIZATIONS:** Masonic Lodge Friendship #20 F&AM 1969-; pres & founder Newton Cty Voter League 1970-77; founder & owner Cobb's Printing 1971-80; pres Cousins Middle School PTO 1973-75; bd of dir Newton Cty Mental Health 1974-76, Washington St Comm Ctr 1980-83; bd mem Newton Cty Public Defenders 1980-; founder-owner C&C Rental 1984-; co-founder Newton County King Scholar Prog Emory Univ of Oxford Coll 1986-. **HONORS/ACHIEVEMENTS:** Outstanding Serv to God & Country 1981; Inkind Contrib Headstart 1977; Outstanding Progress to Newton Cty 1978; Appreciation Awards Recreation Dept Supporter 1981-84; Gaithers Chapel United Methodist Church Appreciation 1983; Support of Industrial Growth Newton Cty Chamber Commerce 1984. **MILITARY SERVICE:** USAF E-3 4 yrs. **HOME ADDRESS:** 5224 Avery St, Covington, GA 30209.

COBB, JEWEL PLUMMER
Cancer researcher, university president. **PERSONAL:** Born Jan 17, 1924, Chicago, IL; daughter of Frank V Plummer and Carriebel Cole Plummer; married Roy Cobb, Jul 04, 1954 (divorced); children: Jonathan Cobb. **EDUCATION:** Talladega Coll, Talladega AL, BA, 1944; New York Univ, New York NY, MS, 1947, PhD, 1950. **CAREER:** New York Univ, New York City, instructor, 1955-56, asst prof, 1956-60; Hunter Coll, visiting lecturer, 1956-57; Sarah Lawrence Coll, Bronxville NY, biology prof, 1960-69; Connecticut Coll, New London CT, zoology prof, dean, 1969-76; Rutgers Univ, Douglass Coll, New Brunswick NJ, biology prof, dean, 1976-81; California State Univ, Fullerton CA, pres, 1981-. **ORGANIZATIONS:** Mem bd trustees, Inst Educ Mgmt, 1973-; developer & dir, Fifth Year Post Bacc Pre-Med Prog; bd dir, Amer Coun Educ, 1973-76; bd dir, Educ Policy Center, New York City; Natl Acad of Sciences, Human Resources Commn, 1974-; Natl Science Found, 1974-; bd dir, Travelers Insurance Co, 1974-; bd dir, 21st Century Found; trustee, Natl Fund for Minority Engineering Students, 1978-; bd dir, Californians Preventing Violence, 1983-; bd dir, First Interstate Bancorp, 1985-; bd dir, Amer Assembly of Barbard Coll, 1986-; bd mem, Newport Harbor Museum. **HONORS/ACHIEVEMENTS:** Research grant, Amer Cancer Soc, 1969-74, 1971-73, 1974-77; honorary doctorates from Wheaton Coll (1971), Lowell Technical Inst (1972), Pennsylvania Medical Coll (1975), City Coll of the City Univ of NY, St Lawrence Univ, Coll of New Rochelle, Tuskegee Univ, Fairleigh Dickinson Univ; author of Filters for Women in Science, 1979, Breaking Down Barriers to Women Entering Science, 1979, Issues and Problems: A Debate, 1979. **BUSINESS ADDRESS:** President, Callifornia State University, Fullerton, 800 North State College Blvd, Fullerton, CA 92634.

COBB, JOHN HUNTER, JR.
Lawyer. **PERSONAL:** Born May 05, 1953, Rocky Mount, NC; son of John H Cobb and Annie Lee Cobb; married Regina LaVerne Payne. **EDUCATION:** Hampton Univ, BA 1975; Howard Univ, JD 1979. **CAREER:** Michie Company, senior editor 1979-85; Robinson Buchanan & Johnson, associate 1985-; Virginia Union University, business law prof 1985-86; solo practicioner 1988-. **ORGANIZATIONS:** Mem Old Dominion Bar Assoc 1979-; Young Lawyers Conf VA State Bar 1979-; legal advisor Time Investment Corp 1985-; mem VA Trial Lawyers Assoc 1985-; comm mem Guardian Ad Litem Seminar 1987. **HONORS/ACHIEVEMENTS:** Litigation Section VA State Bar 1985-. **HOME ADDRESS:** 5509 Cardiff Court, Richmond, VA 23227. **BUSINESS ADDRESS:** 2025 E Main Street, Richmond, VA 23223.

COBB, MARVIN LAWRENCE
Athlete. **PERSONAL:** Born Aug 06, 1953, Detroit, MI; married Susan Elizabeth; children: Quentin. **EDUCATION:** Univ of S CA, BS BA 1975. **CAREER:** Cincinnati Bengals Inc, football plyr; CA Museum of Science & Inds, plnr 1976. **ORGANIZATIONS:** Mem All Pacific-8 Conf Team 1974; mem Skull & Dagger; mem All Pacific-8 Conf Team 1974; mem Assn Press All-Amer team (3rd). **HONORS/ACHIEVEMENTS:** Plyr of the wk S CA Sports Writers Assn 1974; most impr back varsity team 1974; distric award Am Asn of Coll Baseball & Coaches Collegiate All-Amer team 1975; player award Coll Sports Info dor of Amer Academic All-Amer Baseball 1975; scholar award Dean's List 1975; outstanding sr student athlete award 1975; The Jess Hill Heritage Trophy 1975; The Trojan Diamond Award 1975; NCAA top five student athlete award 1975; NCAA postgrad scholarship 1975; most valuable rookie Conn Bengals 1975; bengal plyr of the wk 1975,76; grand marshall Black Hsty Wk Parade 1977; honoree Perris Black Comm Scholarship Comm 1977; Nat Merit Scholar. **BUSINESS ADDRESS:** 200 Riverfront & Stadium, Cincinnati, OH.

COBB, NATHANIEL E.
Association executive. **PERSONAL:** Born Jun 20, 1939, Chattanooga, TN; married Alva Starling. **EDUCATION:** TN State U, BS 1969; Univ of OK, MPA 1972. **CAREER:** Urban League of Metropolitan Trenton, bd of dir; Trenton NJ, dir of health, recreation & welfare 1974; Trenton Model Cities Prog, dir 1972-74; Trenton, asst bus adminstr 1971-72; human resources prog mgr 1970-71; senior evalutor 1969-70. **ORGANIZATIONS:** Mem Am Soc of Publ Adm; Nat Moedl Cities; mem Comm Devel Assn; bd dir, mem Am Pub Health Assn; delaware Valely United Way; Trenton Salvation Army; pres Merco Co Big Bros & Big Sisters Assn; mercer Co Red Cross; pres Gr Trenton Urban League; Trenton NAACP; adv com Trenton State Coll; adv comMercer Co Comm Coll; mem Omega Psi Phi Frat. **MILITARY SERVICE:** USAF capt 1962-69.

COBB, ROBERT S.
Educator. **PERSONAL:** Born Jul 25, 1920, Dalton, MO; son of Robert S Cobb and Elizabeth Myers Cobb; divorced; children: Joyce Renea, Linda Michele, Robert III. **EDUCATION:** Lincoln U, BS 1942; OH State, MA1949; OH State, PhD 1951. **CAREER:** Sch Health Educ Univ of MN, professor of physical education & recreation 1975-; Head Dept Health Sci Mankato State U, prof 1968-75; Head Dept HPER IN A & I State U, prof 1953-68; HPER FL A&M U, prof 1951-53; OH State U, teaching asst 1949-51; lecturer & consultant to many schools & univs; author of numerous articles, reviews, appearing in professional publs 1956-. **ORGANIZATIONS:** Mem Amer Alliance for Health Physical Educ, Recreation & Dance; Amer Sch Health Assn; Amer Public Health Assn; participant Natl Conferences on Physicians & Schools AMA Chicago; mem Task Force on Black Studies Mankato State Coll; 1968-70; vice pres AAHPER (SHE) 1973-74; mem AAHPERD Pres Com 1970-71; chmn (Health) MN Assn for HPER 1971-72; mem Professional Adv Comm for TV Program "Inside Out" 1971-; mem, officer of numerous civic & professional orgns. **HONORS/ACHIEVEMENTS:** Recipient Award for Outstanding Service Cen Dist AAHPERD 1974; Lou Keller Award MAHPER 1978; Professional Serv Award AAHE 1980. **MILITARY SERVICE:** CIC special agent 1942-46. **BUSINESS ADDRESS:** University of Minnesota, 111 A Cooke Hall, 1900 University Ave, SE, Minneapolis, MN 55455.

COBB, THELMA M.
Educator. **PERSONAL:** Born Apr 03, Portsmouth, VA; married Henry E Cobb. **EDUCATION:** Hampton Inst, BS 1941, MA 1946; Univ of Houston, EdD 1976; Temple Univ Univ of CT, Furthur Study. **CAREER:** Tuskege Inst, instructor 1948-52; FL A&M, asst prof 1952-55; Southern Univ, prof 1958-. **ORGANIZATIONS:** Consultant Black Lit, Multicultural Studies, Women's Lit; reg dir Delta Sigma Theta; CLA Delta Sigma Theta, YWCA, Phi Delta Kappa, Pi Gamma Mu, NCTE; admin bd Camphor Memorial United Methodist Church; The Links,INC. **HONORS/ACHIEVEMENTS:** Gen Educ Bd Fellow; Outstanding Woman in Educ Baton Rouge Delta Sigma Theta; Tchr of the Yr Southern Univ and Alumni Fed. **BUSINESS ADDRESS:** Professor of English, SouthernUniv, Box 9984 SouthernUniv, Baton Rouge, LA 70813.

COBB, W. MONTAGUE
Physical anthropologist, anatomist. **PERSONAL:** Born Oct 12, 1904, Washington, DC; son of William Elmer Cobb and Alexzine Montague Cobb; married Hilda B Smith (deceased); children: Carolyn Wilkinson, Hilda Amelia Gray. **EDUCATION:** Amherst Coll, AB 1925, ScD 1955; Marine Biol Lab Woods Hole MA, cert in embryology 1925; Howard Univ, MD 1929; Western Reserve Univ, PhD 1932; Morgan State Coll, LLD 1964; Washington Univ, attended US Nat Mus; Univ of the Witwatersrand, LLD 1977; Georgetown Univ, ScD 1978; Med Coll of WI, ScD 1979; Howard Univ, DHL 1980; Brown Univ, DMedSc 1982; Univ AR, ScD 1983; Colby Coll, ScD 1984. **CAREER:** Howard Univ, instr embryology 1928-29; Freedmen's Hosp Washington, intern 1929-30; Howard Univ, asst prof anatomy 1932-34, assoc prof 1934-42, prof 1942-69, dept head 1947-69, distinguished prof anatomy 1969-73, emeritus 1973-; Stanford Univ, visiting prof anatomy 1972; Univ of MD, 1974; Univ of AR for Med Scis, distinguished univ prof 1979. **ORGANIZATIONS:** Mem Pub Health Adv Council of DC 1953-61, chmn 1956-58; fellow in anatomy Western Reserve Univ 1933-39, assoc anatomy 1942-44; Amer Anthrop Assn Fellow Gerontol Soc AAAS; Rosenwald Fellow 1941-42; Freedmen's Hosp Bd Chief Med Examiner 1941; consult AUS surgeon gen 1945; mem White House Conf Health 1965; mem Amer Assn Phys Anthropologists vice pres 1948-50, pres 1957-59; Anat Soc Great Britain & Ireland; Amer Eugenics Soc dir 1957-68; Amer Assn Anatomists; Natl Med Assn state vice pres 1943, pres 1965, editor 1949-77; mem Natl Urban League health specialist 1945-47; NAACP chmn natl med com 1950, dir 1949-; natl pres 1976-82; Amer Soc Mamalogists; Assn Study of Negro Life & History; Amer Assn History of Medicine; Anthrop Soc of Washington; Washington Soc for Hist of Med; Medice-Chirurgical Soc DC; Anthropol Soc Washington; Omega Psi Phi, chmn scholarship comm 1939-48; Alpha Omega Alpha; Sigma Xi. **HONORS/ACHIEVEMENTS:** Citations from Oppor Mag 1947, Washington Afro-Amer & Chicago Defender 1948; Distinguished Serv Awd Medice-Chirurg Soc DC 1952; Natl Med Assn DSM 1955; Med Soc of DC Meritorious Serv Awd 1968; Govt of DC meritorious Pub Serv Awd 1972; Distinguished Public Serv Awd USN 1978; Henry Gray Awd Amer Assn of Anatomists 1980; founder Bull of Medico-Chirurg Soc DC 1941, editor 1945-; author monographs articles.

COBBIN, GLORIA CONSTANCE
Elected official. **PERSONAL:** Born Dec 02, 1939, Detroit, MI; widowed; children: Darryl, Lynnette. **EDUCATION:** Labor School, Cert 1972; Wayne State Univ, 1973-76. **CAREER:** City of Detroit Human Rights Dept, office mgr 1962-82; MI AFSCME Council, political action coord/lobbyist 1982-; Detroit Bd of Educ, vice pres; Detroit Bd of Educ, pres 1987-. **ORGANIZATIONS:** Chairperson City-Wide School Bd Mem Caucus 1978; mem exec bd SACVE 1979; Newly Structured Detroit Bd of Ed 1982; delegate Natl Dem Convention 1984; chair Women's Comm; 1st dist adv & org 1st Dist Young Dems Comm; mem MI Dem Party Women's Comm; exec vice pres AFSCME #1329; co-founder Young Individualists for COPE; mem, steering comm Coaliton of Labor Union Women; mem South Martindale Block Club; former spokesperson Women United for Action; mem Policy Adv Comm Catholic Soc Serv Head Start Prog; moderator Bd of Educ Digest WDET FM 909; vice pres Central Region Natl Caucus of Black School Bd Members; secretary-treasurer, Metropolitan Detroit AFL-CIO (first female) 1988-; dir, Collaborative on Offender Training and Employment 1989-. **HONORS/ACHIEVEMENTS:** Conducted study of state boards of educ; received Awd for Outstanding Dem Woman of the Year; Harriett Turman Awd; Martin Luther King Awd MI AFSCME; first black female president Detroit Bd of Educ. **BUSINESS AD-**

DRESS: Vice President, Detroit Board of Education, 5057 Woodward Ave #358, Detroit, MI 48202.

COBBIN, W. FRANK, JR.
Business executive. **PERSONAL:** Born Jul 02, 1947, Youngstown, OH; married Deborah Walk; children: Kevin, Kimberly. **EDUCATION:** Cleveland State Univ, BA Psych, English 1971; IN Univ Exec Program, Prof Mgr & Bus Functions 1980-81. **CAREER:** OH Bell Telephone Co, mgr bus office 1973-77, mgr installation 1977-78, dist mgr installation 1978-79, mktg mgr 1979, dist mgr 1979-82; AT&T AmericanTranstech, dir telephone response ctr 1982-83, exec dir mktg svc, vice pres direct mktg serv 1987-. **ORGANIZATIONS:** Mem Direct Mktg Assoc, Telemarketing Assoc, Mayor's Econ Devel Council, Jax Urban League Bd; Basileus Omega Psi Phi Frat Inc; mem United Way, Univ of North FL Business Adv Cncl, Jacksonville Univ Career Beginnings Prog. **MILITARY SERVICE:** Reserves staff sgt 6 yrs; #1 in class NCO Acad. **BUSINESS ADDRESS:** Vice President, AT&T American Transtech, 8000 Baymeadows Way, Jacksonville, FL 32216.

COBBS, DAVID E.
Educator. **PERSONAL:** Born May 26, 1940, Nashville, TN; married Margaret; children: Amy Elizabeth. **EDUCATION:** TN State U, BS; MI U, MMus; Univ of MA, MMus; No TX State Univ USC, Grad Study. **CAREER:** Music Conservatory Compton Community Coll, dir 1970-; Prairie View Coll, 1963-70; Edward Waters Coll, Jacksonville FL, 1962-63; Univ of MA, teaching asst 1967-68; USC, teaching asst 1971-73. **ORGANIZATIONS:** Mem bd dir Compton & Comm Symphony; western rep Black Music Caucus Mu Sic Educ Nat Conf. **HONORS/ACHIEVEMENTS:** Award instrumental music; award asst dir of marching bands. **BUSINESS ADDRESS:** 1111 E Artesia Blvd, Compton, CA 90221.

COBBS, PRICE MASHAW
Business executive, psychiatrist. **PERSONAL:** Born Nov 02, 1928, Los Angeles, CA; son of P Price Cobbs and Rose Mashaw Cobbs; married Frederica; children: Price Priester, Marion Renata. **EDUCATION:** Univ of CA Berkeley, BA 1954; Meharry Med Clg Nashville, TN, MD 1958. **CAREER:** San Francisco Gen Hosp, intern 1958-59; Mendocino State Hosp, psychiatric Res 1959-61; Langley Porther Neuropsychiatric Inst, psych Res 1961-62; Pacific Mgmt Systems, pres 1967-, CEO; fellow American Psychiatric Association, board certified 1966. **ORGANIZATIONS:** Mem Natl Medical Assoc, Certified Consultants Inc; life mem NAACP; consultant to many Fortune 500 companies, govt agencies and comm groups. **HONORS/ACHIEVEMENTS:** Mem at Large Inst of Med Natl Acad of Sci; outstanding psychiatrist, Black Enterprise magazine 1988. **MILITARY SERVICE:** AUS corporal. **BUSINESS ADDRESS:** Chief Executive Officer, Pacific Mgmt Systems, 3528 Sacramento St, San Francisco, CA 94118.

COBBS, SUSIE ANN
Retired educator. **PERSONAL:** Born Feb 08, 1924, Toledo, OH; married Dr Therion D Cobbs; children: Therion, Therman, Jonathan. **EDUCATION:** Central State Univ, BS 1948; Univ of MO Kansas City, attended; Univ of KS, MS Ed; George Peabody Coll, attended; Central State Univ, BS; Univ of KS, MS. **CAREER:** Kansas City MO, physical educ teacher; San Diego School Dist, teacher; Fisk Univ, recreation dir, assoc prof retired. **ORGANIZATIONS:** Mem Alpha Kappa Alpha Sor, AME Ministers Wives Alliance; pres Progressive Matrons Club, Water Safety Instr; 1st aid instr ARC; mem St Philips AME Church, Womens Civic Forum of Nashville, The Assoc of Coll Women of Nashville, The TN Coll Womens Soports Fed, The Natl Assoc of Health Phys Ed & Rec; former staff mem, rec dir Martha O'Brian Comm Ctr; sub teacher Nashville Bd of Ed. **HONORS/ACHIEVEMENTS:** Natl ARC Serv Awd Frist Aid 1973; Adv of the Year Pi Chap of Alpha Kappa Alopha Sor 1974; listed in Who's Who Among Amer Women 1975-.

COBBS, WINSTON H.B., JR.
Fellow pulmonary diseases. **PERSONAL:** Born May 07, 1955, Flushing, NY; married Valerie Crouch; children: Noelle Bianca. **EDUCATION:** Boston Univ, BA Biology 1976; Meharry Medical Coll, MD 1980. **CAREER:** Long Island Jewish Medical Ctr, internship internal medicine 1980-81; Nassau Co Medical Ctr, residence in internal medicine 1983-85; Booth Memorial Medical Ctr, fellow in pulmonary medicine 1986-88; in private practice 1988-. **ORGANIZATIONS:** Mem Amer Soc of Intl Medicine, Amer Thoracic Soc; assoc mem Amer Coll of Physicians, Amer Coll of Chest Physicians. **HONORS/ACHIEVEMENTS:** Martin Luther King Scholarship Awd for Excellence in Education; Publications, "The Effects of Phospho-Diesterase on Insulin Metabolism," A Research Study The Diabetes and Endocrinology Ctr Nashville 1972; "The Spirometric Standards for Healthy Black Adults," A Research Study Meharry Medical Coll Nashville, The Journal of the Natl Medical Assoc 1981. **HOME ADDRESS:** 18-15 215 St #1-G, Bayside, NY 11360.

COCHRAN, DONNIE L.
Naval aviator. **PERSONAL:** Born Jul 06, 1954, Pelham, GA; son of I C Cochran and Addie B Cochram; married Donna F Townsell, Mar 18, 1978; children: Donnie L Jr, Destiny L. **EDUCATION:** Savannah State Coll, BS Civ Engr 1976. **CAREER:** VT-27, VT-23, VT-21 (Training Command), student aviator 1976-78; VFP-63 DET-5 RF-86, detach operation officer 1978-80; VF-124 F-14A, fleet replacement pilot 1980-81; VF-213 F-14A, fleet pilot 1981-85;VF-124 F-14A, instructor pilot 1985; Blue Angels, pilot number three 1986; Blue Angel #3 1987; Blue Angel #4 1988; US Navy NAS MIRAMAR, LCDR. **ORGANIZATIONS:** Mem Tail Hook, Natl Naval Officers Assoc 1976. **HONORS/ACHIEVEMENTS:** First Black Pilot to fly with the Blue Angles 1985-89; Black Engineer of The Year 1989. **MILITARY SERVICE:** USN, Lt Comm 1976-; Meritorius Unit Commendation; Navy Expeditionary Medal; Meritorius Service Medal. **BUSINESS ADDRESS:** VF-2, USS Ranger, FPO, San Francisco, CA 92145.

COCHRAN, EDWARD G.
Telecommunications manager. **PERSONAL:** Born Jun 16, 1953, Chicago, IL; married Barbara Porter; children: Rashida, Marcus. **EDUCATION:** Lake Forest Coll, BA (w/ Honors) 1975; DePaul Univ, MBA 1985. **CAREER:** Continental Bank, operations analyst 1975-77; IBM, systems engr 1977-81; Sears Communications, telecomm mgr 1981-. **ORGANIZATIONS:** Consultant Telecommunications 1984-; adjunct faculty Mundelein Coll (undergrad) 1986-, DePaul (grad) 1987-. **HONORS/ACHIEVEMENTS:** Several articles and papers published on Telecommunications. **BUSINESS ADDRESS:** Manager, Sears Communications, 95 West Algonquin, Arlington Heights, IL 60005.

COCHRAN, HERSCHEL J.
Dentist. **PERSONAL:** Born Jul 12, 1928, Dublin, GA; married Gail M Yancey; children: Sharon, Dawn. **EDUCATION:** WV State Coll, BA 1951; Howard U, MA 1956; Howard U, DDS 1961. **CAREER:** Priv Prac, doctor of dental surgery; Case Western ReserveUniv Dental Sch, clinical instr 1970-75; Beth Israel Hosp NY, staff 1962-63; Harlem Hosp NY, internship 1961-63. **ORGANIZATIONS:** Mem Alpha Phi Alpha; bd dir Cleveland Comm Dental Project; bd dir Hough-Norwood Multi Purpose Health Cntr; past pres Forst City Dental Study; Negro Nat Golf Assn. **MILITARY SERVICE:** AUS 2nd lt 1951-53. **BUSINESS ADDRESS:** 14101 Kinsman Rd, Cleveland, OH 44120.

COCHRAN, JAMES DAVID, JR.
Pediatrician. **PERSONAL:** Born Oct 24, 1951, Muskegon, MI. **EDUCATION:** Univ of MI, BS 1973; Howard Univ, MD 1977. **CAREER:** Howard Univ Hosp, pediatric resident 1977-80; Natl Health Serv Corps, medical officer 1980-83; Collier Health Svcs, staff physician 1983-84; Collier Health Serv Inc, medical dir 1984-. **ORGANIZATIONS:** Mem local vice polemarch Kappa Alpha Psi Frat 1980-; mem Amer, Natl Medical Assocs 1981-; mem Collier County Medical Soc 1983-; counselor Collier County Youth Guidance 1985-; mem Big Bros Collier County 1985-. **HONORS/ACHIEVEMENTS:** Publication "Study of Sickle Cell in an Animal Model," Journal of NMA 1980. **BUSINESS ADDRESS:** Medical Dir, Collier Health Serv Inc, 419 N First St, Immokalee, FL 33934.

COCHRAN, S. THOMAS
Sales manager. **PERSONAL:** Born Jun 08, 1950, Columbus, OH; son of Sylvester M Cochran and Dorothy Saunders Cochran; married Lynne Rankin; children: Clanci Marie, Camille Alexandra, Cameron Thomas. **EDUCATION:** OH U, BSC 1972. **CAREER:** WOUB-Radio, newscaster 1971-72; Taft Broad WTVN-TV, dir film & Ed floor dir 1972-75; Taft Broad WGR-TV, prod dir 1975-77; Langston Hughes Ctr for Vis & Perform Arts, adv 1976; Astro Adv Agency, consultant 1976; WGR-TV Taft Bdcst, acct exec; Buffalo State Coll, part-time prof of communications 1978-80;SUNY Buffalo, part-time prof of communications 1978-; TV for Black Hist, prod dir independent proj; WGRZ-TV, sales mgr local and Canadian. **ORGANIZATIONS:** Conduct seminars for Buffalo Black Media Coalition; mem Professional Communicators of WNY; minority bd rep WGRZ-TV; mem Buffalo Area Chamber of Commerce; bd of dir William-Emslie YMCA. **HONORS/ACHIEVEMENTS:** Guest speak for comm stud at coll & u wk; Black Acheivers Award in Ind 1976; Sales Achievement Awards Taft Broadcasting Co 1978-80. **BUSINESS ADDRESS:** Sales Manager, WGRZ-TV, 259 Delaware Ave, Buffalo, NY 14206.

COCHRAN, TODD S.
Business executive. **PERSONAL:** Born Sep 01, 1920, San Francisco, CA; married Inis; children: Todd, Walter. **EDUCATION:** Du Sable High School Chicago, graduate. **CAREER:** Bethlehem Steel, elect 1944-45; Nichols Dodge, auto salesman & mgr 1963-65, fleet mgr 1965-68; KC Dodge Inc, pres, owner 1968-. **ORGANIZATIONS:** Mem Natl Auto Dealers Assoc, SF Auto Dealers Assoc, Dodge Dealer Assoc, Driver Training Prog for San Francisco, Kiwanis Club; dir Bay Area Dealer Adversting Assoc, Chrysler Black Dealers Assoc; mem Natl Assoc of Minority Dealers. **HONORS/ACHIEVEMENTS:** Grand Awd for Dodge Sales 1964-67; Oldest Black Dealer for Chrysler Corp. **BUSINESS ADDRESS:** President, KC Doge Inc, 3030 Mission St, San Francisco, CA 94110.

COCKERHAM, HAVEN EARL
Personnel administrator. **PERSONAL:** Born Aug 13, 1947, Winston-Salem, NC; married Terry Ward; children: Haven Earl Jr, Audra. **EDUCATION:** NC A&T, BS Economics 1969; MI State, MBA 1979. **CAREER:** GMC, personnel admin exec comp 1978-79, admin personnel 1979-80; Fisher Body, genl offices gen admin 1980-82, Pgh plant dir personnel 1982-83; GeneralMotors, world headquarters dir personnel 1983-84, gen dir personnel. **ORGANIZATIONS:** Pres Detroit Chap Natl Black MBA Assn 1981; bd mem Natl Black MBA Assn 1981; mem Mon-Yough Chamber of Commerce Pgh 1982-83; leadership mem Leadership Detroit Chamber of Comm; bd mem Detroit South Macomb Hosp; chmn east central sec Detroit Area Council Boy Scouts of Amer. **HONORS/ACHIEVEMENTS:** Outstanding Leadership Detroit Chap Natl Black MBA Assoc 1982; Outstanding Serv Detroit Area Bou Scouts. **HOME ADDRESS:** 28346 Harwich, Farmington Hills, MI 48018. **BUSINESS ADDRESS:** General Dir Personnel, Fisher Guide Div GMC, 6600 12 Mile Rd, Warren, MI 48090.

COCKRELL, MECHERA ANN
Insurance sales. **PERSONAL:** Born Jul 08, 1953, Brookshire, TX; married Thomas Cockrell; children: Twanna Nicole Randle. **EDUCATION:** TX Southern Univ, BS 1975, MA 1978; Espanola's Beauty Coll, Licensed Cosmetologist 1978; Leonard's Sch of Insurance, Group II license 1986. **CAREER:** Cockrell Insurance, general agent. **ORGANIZATIONS:** Mem Teachers Educ Assoc 1975-; advisor Jack & Jill of Amer 1985-; teacher 4H Prairie View Chap 1985-; mem Home Economics Educators of Amer. **BUSINESS ADDRESS:** General Agent, Cockrell Insurance, 33405 Reynolds Rd, Simonton, TX 77476.

CODY, HENRY LEROY
Educator. **PERSONAL:** Born May 22, 1922, Tuscaloosa, AL; married Betty Frazier; children: Henry Leroy Jr, Patricia Elaine, Cynthia Jane. **EDUCATION:** NC A&T Univ Greensboro, BS 1957; OH State Univ Columbus, MA radio & TV 1959;Teacher Coll Columbia Univ NY, EdD 1978. **CAREER:** NC A&T Univ Greensboro, prof, military science & tactics 1954-58; AUS Signal School Ft Monmouth NJ,TV prod off 1959-62; AUS Pictorial Center NYC, motion picture off 1964-65; Amer Forces Network Europe, commanding officer 1966-68; AUS SE Asia Signal School Vietnam, commanding officer 1969-70; Brookdale Comm Coll, affirm action officer. **ORGANIZATIONS:** mem, 32nd Degree Mason Greensboro Consistory 106 NC 1956-85; pres Laymens Movement Seacoast Missionary Baptist Assn, 1977-85; past pres, NJ Assn for Affirm Action in Higher Educ, 1980-81; vice pres at large Natl Laymens Movement Natl Baptist Convention USA Inc 1983-85; pres, Laymens Movement General Baptist State Convention NJ. **HONORS/ACHIEVEMENTS:** Educ Bd Div of News Publications Co 1971; Considerations for Textbook Selection Teacher Coll Columbia Univ 1978; Elected Councilman of Laymens Movement of Men's Dept Bapt World Alliance 1980-85. **MILITARY SERVICE:** AUS lt col 29 yrs; Natl Serv & Legion of Merit 1971.

CODY, WILLIAM L.
Clergyman. **PERSONAL:** Born Jun 09, 1934, Philadelphia, PA. **EDUCATION:** Univ PA, AB 1951-55; Temple U, STB 1955-58; Monrovia Coll, DD; St Davis Sem, DD. **CAREER:** St James AME Ch, pstr 1972-; Grant AME Ch, 1966-72; Fisk Chpl AME Ch, 1964-66; Vernon Tmpl AME Ch, 1960-64; Union AME Ch, 1958-60; St Paul AME Ch Malvern, 1956-58; St Paul AME Ch Ben Salem, 1955-56. **ORGANIZATIONS:** Past pres Grtr Boston Inter-Denominational & Inter-Racial Ministers Alliance; past bd dir Boston Br NAACP; Cooper Comm Ctr; Conv Cncl Black Ecumenical Commn; past tst BostonUniv Without Walls; past pres bd dir Grant Manor Apts; past mem Black Studies Com Boston Theol Inst; Steering Com Metro Boston Com Black Chmn Act; presiding elder Atlantic City Dist African Met Epis Ch; 1st vice pres Atlantic City NAACP; pres Atlantic City Chap Frontiers Internat; tst Atlantic Comm Coll; mgr Bright's Villa N & Bright's Villa S; chmn NAACP Atlantic City Housing Corp.

COELHO, PETER J.
Business executive. **PERSONAL:** Born May 10, 1921, E Providence, RI; married Julia; children: Jean, Carol, Julie, Sheila, Susan. **EDUCATION:** Inst of Applied Sci, 1944-45; Univ RI, 1961-62. **CAREER:** RI Housing Investment Fund, exec dir 1972-77; Homes for Hope Found, 1968-72; PJ Coelho Painting Co, owner 1947-65. **ORGANIZATIONS:** V chmn RI Housing & Mortgage Fin Corp; past dir Blue Corss of RI 1973-76; chmn com on corp RI Ho of Reps; past pres chmn bd Cape verdean ProgCtr; area cat num maj fund drives. **HONORS/ACHIEVEMENTS:** First black elected RI Gen Assembly 1966; re-elected Biennialcy. **MILITARY SERVICE:** USAAF sgt 1942-46. **BUSINESS ADDRESS:** 155 Leonard Ave, East Providence, RI 02914.

COFER, JAMES HENRY
Mortician & city official. **PERSONAL:** Born Mar 24, 1925, New York, NY; married Marion D Willis; children: James H III, Linda S Hawkins. **EDUCATION:** Amer Acad of Mortuary Science, 1961. **CAREER:** Ft Monmouth NJ, electronic tech 1947-50; Long Branch Police Dept, patrolman 1951-60; Long Branch NJ, vice pres city council. **ORGANIZATIONS:** Mem NJ State Funeral Directors 1964-73; owner-mgr Cofer Memorial Home 1976-; pres Cofer-Willis Corp 1976-; dir Cofer-Hawkins Funeral Home 1981-; bd mem United Way, Red Bank Rotary Club, Cancer Soc, Second Baptist Church of Long Branch, Amer Red Cross, Long Branch Public Health; vice pres Long Branch City Council; former trustee BBA Local #10. **HONORS/ACHIEVEMENTS:** Lewis R Peet Awd NY 1961; NY State Merit Cert NY 1961; Conf FS Examining Bd of US 1961; Natl Conf of Christians & Jews. **MILITARY SERVICE:** AUS corpl 3 yrs. **BUSINESS ADDRESS:** Vice Pres City Council, Long Branch NJ 07740, 240 Shrewsbury Ave, Red Bank, NJ 07701.

COFFEE, LAWRENCE WINSTON
Dentist. **PERSONAL:** Born Apr 29, 1929, Detroit, MI; married Juanita; children: Lawrence Jr, Roderic, LaJuan. **EDUCATION:** Wayne State Univ, BS 1957; Meharry Medical College, DDS 1961. **CAREER:** Private practice, dental surgeon; Children's Hospital of Michigan, medical tech 1955-57; Detroit First Aid Co, drug shipper 1953-55; Chrysler Corp, machine operator 1949-51. **ORGANIZATIONS:** Mem Michigan Dental Assn; Amer Dental Assn; Natl Dental Assn; Wolverine Dental Soc; Detroit Dist Dental Soc; past trustee St Stephen AME Church; mem BSA; past dist commr Chi Health & Safety 1968-77; bd mgmt Meharry Medical College Alumni Assn; pres Meharry Medical College Alumni Assn. **HONORS/ACHIEVEMENTS:** Dentist of the Year 1972; trophies BSA 1966-67; Dentist of the Year, Meharry Detroit Chap 1972. **MILITARY SERVICE:** AUS mc corpl 1951-53. **HOME ADDRESS:** 8155 Sorrento, Detroit, MI 48228.

COFFEY, BARBARA J.
Educator. **PERSONAL:** Born Nov 24, 1931, Omaha, NE; daughter of Earl L Waldron, Sr and Eva Williams Waldron-Cooper; divorced; children: William Jai III. **EDUCATION:** Univ of NE, BA 1951; Fisk Univ, MA 1953; Univ of NE, PhD 1976. **CAREER:** US Dept of Commerce, Chicago Regional Office, survey statistian 1963-65; United Comm Serv Omaha, planning assoc 1965-67; Greater Omaha Comm Action Inc, dep dir 1967-70; Univ of NE Omaha, assoc dean of students & instrutor of sociology 1970-71; US Dept of HEW, consultant region VII 1971-; Univ of NE Syst, asst to pres, equal opportunity coordinator 1971-78; Northwestern Bell Telephone Co, supvr mgmt training 1978-81; Metro Communtiy Coll, south campus mgr 1981-84, dir of mktg 1984-. **ORGANIZATIONS:** Grad rsch fellowship Fisk Univ, 1951-53, State Univ of IA 1954-55; bd of dir United Comm Serv 1972-74; past vp, found dir NE Civil Liberties Union; mem Omaha Metro NAACP, Hon Soc; mem Natl Assoc of Women Deans Admin & Couns; chairperson NE Equal Opportunity Comm; mem Alpha Kappa Delta, Alpha Lambda Delta, Phi Delta Kappa; pres Omaha Chapter Links Inc; charter mem Omaha Chapter Jack & Jill Inc; mem Delta Sigma Theta Sorority, United Methodist Comm Center, Urban League of NE, Episcopal Church of Resurrection; mem vestry, layreader; bd dir Omaha Head Start Child Devel Corp; bd dir United Way of the Midlands, 1988-. **HONORS/ACHIEVEMENTS:** One of Outstanding Black Women of Omaha Quinn Chapel AME Church 1975; Omicron Delta Kappa Natl Leaderhip Honor 1986. **BUSINESS ADDRESS:** Dir of Marketing, Metropolitan Community College, PO Box 3777, Omaha, NE 68103.

COFFEY, GILBERT HAVEN, JR.
Government official, physician. **PERSONAL:** Born Nov 27, 1926, Lackawanna, NY; married Madelyn Elizabeth Brewer; children: Denise E. **EDUCATION:** Univ of Buffalo, BA 1952; certificate in phys therapy 1955; Meharry Med Coll, MD 1963. **CAREER:** Wayne Co Gen Hosp Eloise MI, phys therapist 1956-59; intern 1963; VA Hosp Buffalo, resident 1964-67; asst chief phys medicine & Rehab serv 1967-69; chief phys medicine & rehab serv 1969-70; Central Ofc VA Washington, prog devel policy chief phys medicine & rehab 1970; Univ of Buffalo Med Sch, prof 1968-70; Howard Univ Med Sch Washington 1971; George Washington u med sch, asst dir prof 1971-; diplomate am Bd Phys Medicine & Rehab; Nat Med Assn; Am Congress Rehab; Am Acad Phs Medicine & Rehab Commr Parks & Recreation Inster, MI 1958-59. **ORGANIZATIONS:** Mem Alpha Phi Alpha; Rep; Mason 32nd degree; contrib articles professional jours. **MILITARY SERVICE:** AUS 1946-47. **BUSINESS ADDRESS:** Howard University Hospital, Medical School, Dept PMER, 2041 Georgia Ave Nw, Washington, DC 20060.

COFFEY, WILLIAM L.
Engineer. **PERSONAL:** Born Sep 08, 1924, Stanford, KY. **EDUCATION:** BS (omega psi phi, alpha kappa mu, beta kappa ki, kentana honorary elec) 1950. **CAREER:** Environmental Protection Agency EPA, engr; HEW, elec engr; AUS Signal Corps, elec engr; Signal Corps, sr instr tech; USN, radio tech. **ORGANIZATIONS:** Mem Bd Dirs Dillards Bar-B-Q Inc; distr ISA & Masonic Lodge. **HONORS/ACHIEVEMENTS:** Recip Sup Sub Perf award; several cash awards for suggestions. **MILITARY SERVICE:** AUS Corps of Engrs.

COFIELD, ELIZABETH BIAS
County official, educator. **PERSONAL:** Born Jan 21, 1920, Raleigh, NC; married James; children: James Edward, Juan Medford. **EDUCATION:** Hampton Inst, BS; Columbia U, MA; diploma in adminstrn & supervision. **CAREER:** Wade County Bd of Commrs, Juan Medford co commr 1972; Shaw Univ, prof of educ. **ORGANIZATIONS:** Elected to Raleigh Sch Bd 1969-72. **BUSINESS ADDRESS:** Professor of Education, Shaw University, 118 E South St, Raleigh, NC 27602.

COFIELD, JAMES E., JR.
Business executive. **PERSONAL:** Born May 16, 1945, Norfolk, VA; son of Mr & Mrs James E. Cofield, Sr; married Joyce; children: Nicole. **EDUCATION:** Univ NC, BS 1967; Stanford Univ Grad Sch of Bus, MBA 1970; Attended, howard Univ Law Sch. **CAREER:** Cofield Properties, Inc, Brookline, MA. **ORGANIZATIONS:** Bd of dir Greater Boston Chamber of Commerce; bd of dirs MA Assn of Realtors; trustee WGBH Educational Foundation. **HONORS/ACHIEVEMENTS:** Outstanding Comm Serv Annual Awds Com of Boston 1979; Ten Outstanding Young Leaders Boston Jaycees 1980. **BUSINESS ADDRESS:** President, Cofield Properties, Inc, 10 Brookline Place West, Ste 308, P O Box 522, Brookline, MA 02147.

COGDELL, PARTHENIA D.
Educational administrator. **PERSONAL:** Born Sep 12, 1938, Wayne County, NC; daughter of Nathaniel Cogdell and Geneva Herring Cogdell; divorced; children: Samuel George Sanders III. **EDUCATION:** Fayetteville State NC, BS 1959; Trenton State NJ, MA 1971; Glassboro State NJ, 1973-74; Hunter Coll NY, 1982. **CAREER:** Burlington Co Special Servs, principal 1974-76, program dir 1976-79; NJ Dept of Educ, admin asst 1979-81, bureau dir 1981-. **ORGANIZATIONS:** project dir, Low Incidence Handicap Project, 1979-80; reader, US Dept of Educ & special educ Office 1974-79; chairperson, NJ State Advisory Council Handicap, 1974-76; bd dir, Council for Exceptional Children Found 1983-; pres, Intl Council for Exceptional Children 1978-79; pres, Delta Sigma Theta 1988-90; Phi Delta Kappa; pres, Rancocas Valley, Delta Sigma Theta Sor, 1988-90; pres, Intl Council for Exceptional Children, 1978-79; vice pres, Found for Exceptional Children, 1988-90. **HONORS/ACHIEVEMENTS:** Dan Ringeheim Award of Excellence, NJ State Federation; Outstanding Special Education, Intl Council for Exceptional Children. **BUSINESS ADDRESS:** Bureau Dir, NJ Dept of Educ, CN 500, 225 W State St, Trenton, NJ 08610.

COGGS, GRANVILLE COLERIDGE
Physician. **PERSONAL:** Born Jul 30, 1925, Pine Bluff, AR; son of Randy and Nammie; married Maud; children: Anita, Carolyn. **EDUCATION:** Univ of Nebraska, BS 1949; Harvard Medical School, MD 1953. **CAREER:** Univ of Texas Health Science Center, prof radiology dept 1975 -; Univ Ca1ifornia School of Medicine, assoc clinical prof 1971-75; asst chief 1969-71; Kaiser Hospital, staff radiologist 1959-71; Univ of California, resident 1955-58; Letterman Gen Hospital, intern 1954; Murphy Army Hospital, 1953-54. **ORGANIZATIONS:** Mem Harvard Medical School Alumni Survey Comm 1973-78; assoc mem Sigma Xi; mem Amer Coll of Radiology 1959-; fellow AMA 1972; Amer Inst Ultrasound Medicine 1972-; Amer Thermographic Soc 1972-; mem Phi Beta Kappa 1949. **MILITARY SERVICE:** USAAC 1943-46; USAF 1953-55; USAFR lieutenant Colnel 1956-85 (retired). **BUSINESS ADDRESS:** 7400 Merton Minter Blvd, San Antonio, TX 78284.

COGSVILLE, DONALD JOHN
Chief executive officer. **PERSONAL:** Born May 16, 1927, New York, NY; married Carol; children: Rachel, Donald Jr. **EDUCATION:** Mt Union Coll, BA 1963. **CAREER:** Harlem Urban Devel Corp, pres & chief exec 1971-; Office of Economic Opportunity deputy dir 1968-71; Econ Devel State of NJ, dir 1968-71; Harlem Urban Devel Corp, general mgr; NY State Urban Devel Corp, affirmative & action of Cr. **ORGANIZATIONS:** Mem Natl Task Force on Educ & Training for Minority Business; affirmative action advisor Clark-Phipps-Clark & Harris Consult Enter Firm; pres NY Urban League Trenton, NJ. **MILITARY SERVICE:** AUS spec 4th class 1958-60. **BUSINESS ADDRESS:** Harlem Urban Devel Corp, 163 W 125th St 17th Fl, New York, NY 10027.

COHEN, AMAZIAH VANBUREN
Dentist. **PERSONAL:** Born Nov 08, 1916, Miami, FL. **EDUCATION:** FL A&M U, 1943; Meharry Med Coll, DDS 1947. **CAREER:** Fulton Co Health Dept, dentist 1947-; prv prac. **ORGANIZATIONS:** Mem GA Dental Assn; Am Dental Assn; Nat Dental Assn; Acad of Gen Dentistry; mem YMCA; NAACP. **MILITARY SERVICE:** Spl assignment 1943-45. **BUSINESS ADDRESS:** PO Box 92541, Atlanta, GA 30314.

COHEN, VINCENT H.
Attorney. **PERSONAL:** Born Apr 07, 1936, Brooklyn, NY; son of Victor Cohen and Marion Cohen; married Diane Hasbrouck; children: Robyn, Traci, Vincent Jr. **EDUCATION:** Syracuse Univ, BA 1957, LLB 1960. **CAREER:** Consol Edison Co NY, 1960-62; US Dept of Justice, 1962-67; EEOC, 1967-69; Hogan & Hartson, partner 1969-. **ORGANIZATIONS:** Admission NY Bar 1960, US Supreme Ct 1966, OH 1967, DC 1968; mem Amer, Natl NY State Bar Assns; Justinian Law Soc; Natl Jud Conf DC Circuit 1972, 1975; sec Commn Med Malpractice; bd visitors Syracuse Univ Coll of Law; bd of gov's DC Bar; bd dirs ACLU; Young Lawyers Sect Bar Assn DC; Neighborhood Legal Serv Prog. **HONORS/ACHIEVEMENTS:** Helms Found All-Amer Basketball Team; AP All Amer; UP All-Amer 1957; Syracuse Law Review; Order of the Coif. **MILITARY SERVICE:** 1st lt 1957-65. **BUSINESS ADDRESS:** Attorney, Hogan & Hartson, 555 13th Street, NW, Suite 13W202, Washington, DC 20004-1109.

COLBERT, BENJAMIN JAMES
Educator. **PERSONAL:** Born Jun 02, 1942, Savannah, GA; children: Edwin. **EDUCATION:** Savannah State Coll, BS 1963; Univ of GA, MFA 1971. **CAREER:** Metro Atlanta Talent Search Progrm, dir; Natl Scholarship Serv & Fund for Negro Students; assoc regional dir; Univ of GA, admissions counselor, instructor; Savannah Bd of Educ, teacher, assoc program dir admissions testing program; HHS Fellow 1980-81; Educ Testing Svc, assoc dir spon-

sored scholaship program, 1981-. **ORGANIZATIONS:** Consultant Coll Entrance Exam Bd & US Office Educ Trio Program; advisory bd, Southern Educ Found, Human Relations Comm, Natl Assn of Coll Admissions Counselors, Natl Scholarship Serv & Fund for Negro Students; mem NAACP, APGA, Alpha Phi Alpha; deacon Witherspoon Presbyterian Church. **HONORS/ACHIEVEMENTS:** Callaway Found Award, Painting, 1970. **BUSINESS ADDRESS:** Associate Dir, Educational Testing Serv, Rosedale Rd, Princeton, NJ 08540.

COLBERT, ERNEST, SR.
Business manager. **PERSONAL:** Born Aug 02, 1916, Lettsworth, LA; married Gloria Kelly; children: Claudette, Barbara, Ernest Jr, Zanda. **EDUCATION:** Loyola Univ, Tulane Univ, attended. **CAREER:** Union 689, bus mgr constr & gen labor 1934-. **ORGANIZATIONS:** Vice pres LA AFL-CIO; chmn Local 689; bd mem Grtr New Orleans AFL-CIO; state pres LA A Philips Randolph Inst; sec treas SE LA Laborers Dist Cncl;past mem Commerce & Ind Bd; past commr LA Stadium & Exposition Dist; mem IBPOEW, Bon Temps Soc Club. **HONORS/ACHIEVEMENTS:** Awd Human Relations Dept Loyola Univ. **BUSINESS ADDRESS:** Bus Mgr, Union 689, 400 Soniat St, New Orleans, LA 70115.

COLBERT, GEORGE CLIFFORD
Educational administrator. **PERSONAL:** Born Mar 22, 1949, Cedar Rapids, IA; married Marion Patricia Clark; children: Bridget Lynette Clark, Donta Kami. **EDUCATION:** Kirkwood Comm Coll, AA 1972; Mt Mercy Coll, BA 1974. **CAREER:** IA State Men's Reformatory, correctional officer II 1975-76; Rockwell Intl, security guard 1976-78; Kirkwood Community Coll, outreach worker employer school program 1978-. **ORGANIZATIONS:** Chmn Genl Mills, FMC Minority Scholarship Prog 1978; vice pres NAACP 1978; founder/chmn Higher Educ minority Scholarship Prog 1979. **HONORS/ACHIEVEMENTS:** Cert Vol Serv Awd Jane Boyd Comm House 1974; Cert Vol Probation Officer Linn Co Juvenile Ct State of IA 1974; Humanities Awd NAACP Freedom Fund Banquet 1979; Appreciation in Recog of Serv Student Affairs Kirkwood Comm Coll 1979. **MILITARY SERVICE:** USMC E-3 1967-69; Natl Defense Serv Medal; Purple Heart; Pres Citation; Vietnam Campaign; Vietnam Serv Medal. **BUSINESS ADDRESS:** Outreach Worker Emp Sch Prog, Kirkwood Comm College, 6301 Kirkwood Blvd SW, Cedar Rapids, IA 52406.

COLBERT, JAMES D.
Football coach. **PERSONAL:** Born Nov 26, 1939, Los Angeles; married Cornelia; children: Karen, Dean, Donald, Kimberly. **EDUCATION:** Adams State Coll Alamosa, CO, BA 1961; MA 1964. **CAREER:** Green Bayb Packers, def backfield coach 1975-; Portland Storm WFL, def coord 1974; San Jose State U, dif backfld coach 1973; Fresno St U, 1969-72; Colorado Springs HS, tchr Coach 1963-68. **ORGANIZATIONS:** Mem Black Coaches Assn CA; Nat Football Coaches Assn; NAACP. **BUSINESS ADDRESS:** 1265 Lombardi Ave, Green Bay, WI 54304.

COLBERT, THELMA QUINCE
Attorney. **PERSONAL:** Born Nov 20, 1949, Bay Springs, MS; married Winfred T Colbert Sr; children: Winfred T Jr, Kristina Margaret. **EDUCATION:** Jackson State Univ, BA 1971; Southern Univs Sch of Law, JD 1975. **CAREER:** US Dept of Justice, trial atty 1975-83; Norwalk Comm Coll, asst prof 1985-; Quince-Colbert Law Offices, sr partner 1984-. **ORGANIZATIONS:** Mem bd of governors Natl Bar Assoc 1979-; vice pres 1985-86, treas 1986-87, pres/co-founder South CT Lawyers Assoc 1984-85; sec Minority Students Adv Bd Univ of CT/Stamford 1985-; vice pres Alpha Kappa Alpha Sor Inc Omicron Upsilon Omega Chap 1986-87; legal counsel Coalition of 100 Black Women/LowerFairfield Co 1986-; regional dir Region II Natl Bar Assoc 1987. **HONORS/ACHIEVEMENTS:** Special Recognition Awd US Dept of Justice 1980; President's Awd Natl Bar Assoc 1985; Special Recognition Awd Region II Natl Bar Assoc 1986. **HOME ADDRESS:** 247 Soundview Ave, Stamford, CT 06901. **BUSINESS ADDRESS:** 29 5th St, Stamford, CT 06905-5013.

COLBERT, VIRGIS W.
Company executive. **PERSONAL:** Born Oct 13, 1939, Mississippi; son of Quillie Colbert (deceased) and Eddie Mae Colbert; married Angela Johnson; children: Jillian, Alyssa. **EDUCATION:** Central MI Univ, BS; Graduate of Earlham College executive Institute. **CAREER:** Chrysler Corp, gen mfg superintendent 1977-79; Miller Brewing Co, asst to plant mgr 1979-80, production mgr 1980-81, plant mgr 1981-87, asst dir can mfg 1987-88; Director Can Mfg 1988-89; Vice President Materials Manufacturing 1989-. **ORGANIZATIONS:** Dir Mental Health Assoc of Milwaukee, Planned Parenthood of WI Inc; adv comm Industrial Tech Prog Southern Univ; exec comm Frontier's Intl, Mental Health Assoc of Milwaukee; mem Omega Psi Phi, Prince Hall Masons, Shriners, NAACP; NUL Black Exec Exchange Prog; Executive Advisory Committee, Sigma Pi Phi. **HONORS/ACHIEVEMENTS:** Scott High School Hall of Fame Toledo OH; Black Achiever Milwaukee YMCA; Role Model Natl Alliance of Business; Silver Ring Merit Awd Philip Morris Co Inc; Role Model Several Black Colleges. **BUSINESS ADDRESS:** Vice Pres. Materials Manufacturing, Miller Brewing Co, 3939 W Highland Blvd, Milwaukee, WI 532010482.

COLE, ADOLPH
Clergyman. **PERSONAL:** Born Jul 18, 1923, Shreveport; married Elizabeth. **EDUCATION:** Univ So CA. **CAREER:** "Shadows of the Future" & many religious tracts, author. **BUSINESS ADDRESS:** 3635 W Slauson, Los Angeles, CA.

COLE, ARTHUR
Educator. **PERSONAL:** Born Nov 06, 1942, Buffalo, NY; married Alice Bailey; children: Arthur, Brandon. **EDUCATION:** State Univ Coll at Buffalo, BS 1964; State Univ of NY Buffalo, MS 1968, PhD 1974. **CAREER:** State Univ Coll at Buffalo, counselor 1967-68, rsch asst 1968-70, personnel dir libraries 1973-75; US Office of Educ, educ prog specialist 1975-79; The White House, asst to deputy asst to pres 1979-80; US Dept of Educ, deputy dir Horace Mann Learning Center. **ORGANIZATIONS:** Vice pres Earmark Inc 1979-; chap sec Omega Psi Phi 1967-69; mem Phi delta Kappa 1967-; mem Amer Lib Assn 1973-. **HONORS/ACHIEVEMENTS:** Fellowship State Univ of NY Buffalo 1968; Fellow Dept of HEW 1975. **BUSINESS ADDRESS:** Dep Dir H Mann Learning Ctr, US Dept of Education, 400 Maryland Ave SW, Washington, DC 20202.

COLE, CHARLES ZHIVAGA
Association secretary. **PERSONAL:** Born Oct 07, 1957, Birmingham, AL; son of Mr Howard Hover Cole and Mrs Louise Cole. **EDUCATION:** McNeese State Univ, (law major). **CAREER:** NAACP Cameron, assoc sec 1978-85; CBC Organ & McNeese, former mr calendar/rep 1978; Student Govt NAACP Christian Educ, natl youth ambassador 1980-84; John G Lewis Consistory, 32nd degree mason natl 1981-85; S Bapt Convention, travels local state and natl ambassador of goodwill, speaks lectures and teaches, natl volunteer consultant. **ORGANIZATIONS:** Musician dir Music Ministry NJ Bapt LC Religious Inst Local State & Natl 1985; North Lake Charles Kiwanis 1977; McNeese State Lions Club 1978; civil rights activist NAACP 1984-; natl ambassador speaker Christian Educ Special Scientific Olympic 1984-; ROTC 1977-78; Sr Reserve Training 1978; minister of music choir & workshop Cheron Chapel, Star of Bethlehem Baptist Center; Macedonia Baptist, Cameron LA. **HONORS/ACHIEVEMENTS:** Cited for Outstanding Accomplishments Govt Dave C Treen 1981; All Star Drum Major 1973-74; Mr Calendar 1978 McNeese State; Natl Delegate Lobbyist 1980-84; Pres Dr Jack Doland 1985; Governors Award; Outstanding Leadership Award for Serv to Comm; LA State Senatorial Award Hon State Senator Clifford L Newman 1986. **MILITARY SERVICE:** ROTC 1976-77. **HOME ADDRESS:** 2817 1/2 Fitz/M.L. King, Lake Charles, LA 70601.

COLE, CURTIS, JR.
Engineer. **PERSONAL:** Born Jan 19, 1953, Norfolk, VA. **EDUCATION:** Old Dominion Univ, AS Engrg Design 1973, BS Civil Engrg Tech 1975. **CAREER:** City of Portsmouth VA, civil engr 1975-77; Turner Const Co, proj mgr. **ORGANIZATIONS:** Mem Washington Urban League; mem Minority Supplier Develop Council MD/DC 1982-84; mem Kappa Alpha Psi Frat Inc 1974-; mem Natl Assn of Minority Contractors 1982-; pres Curtex Corp 1983-. **HONORS/ACHIEVEMENTS:** NCAA II Champion Basketball Old Dominion Univ 1975; 1st Black Athlete to rec degree in Engrg at Old Dominion Univ 1975; Speaking of People Ebony Magazine 1983; Outstanding Bachelor Washington Living Magazine 1983. **HOME ADDRESS:** 18 T St NE, Washington, DC 20002.

COLE, EDYTH BRYANT
Educational administrator. **PERSONAL:** Born in Detroit, MI; children: Charles R, Constance A, Leslie B. **EDUCATION:** Eastern MI U, BA 1945; Eastern MI U, MA 1952; Univ of MI, EdD 1972; Univ of Toledo OH. **CAREER:** NC State Univ, Elizabeth City, chmn dept of educ & psychology 1972-, dir of summer sessions 1973-80; Highland Park MI Public Schools, admin asst for curriculum 1969-71; Wayne County MI Intermediate School Dist, educ consultant redesegregation 1966-69; Ypsilanti MI Public Schools, teacher 1945-66; Wayne Coutny Intermediate School Dist, shared learning experiences program 1967-69; Natl Resolutions Comm, assn for supervision & curriculum devel 1971-74. **ORGANIZATIONS:** Chmn of tchr educ Elizabeth City StateUniv 1972-78; former chap basileus Alpha Kappa Alpha Sorority 1976-78; former pres L'Esprit Club; bd of dir Mus of Albermarle 1977-79; Scholarship Social Studies Ypsilanti MI Pub Sch; NDEA GrantUniv of Toledo 1965; pub article re curriculum changes "Curriculum Trends" Croft Pub Co 1974. **BUSINESS ADDRESS:** Elizabeth City State Univ, Parkview Dr, Elizabeth City, NC 27909.

COLE, HARRY A.
Judge. **PERSONAL:** Born Jan 01, 1921, Washington, DC; children: Susan, Harriette, Stephanie. **EDUCATION:** Morgan State U, AB 1943; Univ of MD, LlB 1949. **CAREER:** Ct of Appeals Annapolis, judge Presently; Baltimore, asso judge 1968; Asst Atty General 1953; Sub Magistrate 1952; Justice of Peace 1951; State Senate of MD, Elected 1954-58. **ORGANIZATIONS:** Mem Exec Com US Nat Commn for UNESCO; chmn MD Adv Com on Civil Rights; mem Adv Bd Dept Parole & Probation; mem Monumental City Bar Assn Baltimore Bar Assn MD Bar Assn; NBA; Am Judicature Soc. **HONORS/ACHIEVEMENTS:** Life member NAACP; man of the year Alpha Phi Alpha; Alpha Kappa Mu Nat Honor Soc. **MILITARY SERVICE:** AUS 1st lt 1943-46. **BUSINESS ADDRESS:** 6th Judicial Circuit, Calvert & Fayette Sts, Baltimore, MD 21202.

COLE, JAMES O.
Attorney. **PERSONAL:** Born Feb 06, 1941, Florence, AL; married Ada; children: James, Jr, Barry. **EDUCATION:** Talladega Coll, BA 1962; Harvard Univ Law Sch, JD 1971. **CAREER:** The Clorox Co Oakland, sr atty presently; Kirkland & Ellis Chicago, atty 1971-73; Mayor's Office Boston, manpower dir 1968-71; Honeywell Inc Chicago, prod planning mgr 1963-68; Union Carbide Sheffield, chemist 1962-63. **ORGANIZATIONS:** Mem IL Bar Assn Cook Co Bar Assn Charles Houston Law Club; Nat Bar Assn; Am Bar Assn; Alpha Phi Alpha; pres bd of dir E Oakland Youth Devel Cntr; pub dir Cultural & Ethnic Affairs Guild Oakland Museum Assn pres Black Family Assn; mem Concord Comm Dev Task Force; past asso gen counsel Oper PUSH; mem Urban League NAACP Talent Assist. **HONORS/ACHIEVEMENTS:** Program Award for Volunteer Legal Service. **BUSINESS ADDRESS:** Charles Houston Bar Assoc, of Oakland, Oakland, CA 94623.

COLE, JOHN L., JR.
Association executive. **PERSONAL:** Born Nov 08, 1928, Johnstown, PA; children: Keia D. **EDUCATION:** Millard Fillmore Coll Univ of Buffalo, attended 1956-58; attended, Graduate Bryant & Stratton Coll. **CAREER:** Dept Comm Devel, exec asst; City of Cleveland, contract compliance officer 1966-72; Metro Atlanta Rapicl Transit Auth, asst gen mgr. **ORGANIZATIONS:** Bd dir Greater Cleveland Growth Assn 1971-72; bd of dir Cleveland Urban League 1971-72; Amer Public Transit Assn Comm Minority Affairs; comm chmn Urban League Cleveland. **HONORS/ACHIEVEMENTS:** Outstanding Serv Awd 1971; NAACP Cleveland Branch, Meritorious Public Serv Municipal Govt in Pursuit True Dem Ideals 1971. **MILITARY SERVICE:** AUS pfc 1951-53. **BUSINESS ADDRESS:** Assistant General Manager, Metro Atlanta Rapicl Trans, Ste 2200, 104 W Peachtree St, Atlanta, GA 30308.

COLE, JOHNNETTA BETSCH
Educator. **PERSONAL:** Born Oct 19, 1936, Jacksonville, FL; divorced; children: David, Aaron, Che. **EDUCATION:** Oberlin Coll, BA 1957; Northwestern Univ, MA 1959, PhD 1967. **CAREER:** WA State Univ, asst prof & instructor Anthropology, dir of dlack studies 1964-70; Univ of MA, faculty in anthropology & Afro-Amer studies 1970-84; Hunter Coll, Rusell Sage visiting prof Anthropology 1983-84, prof Anthropology 1984-; Spelman Coll Atlanta, pres. **ORGANIZATIONS:** Fellow Amer Anthrop Assn 1970-; bd mem Ctr for Cuban Studies 1971-; contrib & adv ed The Black Scholar 1979-; pres Assn of Black Anthropologists 1980. **HONORS/ACHIEVEMENTS:** Outstanding Faculty Mem of the Year,

WA State Univ 1969-70; conducted anthrop field work Liberia Cuba & Afro-Amer Comm in US. **BUSINESS ADDRESS:** President, Spelman College, 350 Spelman Lane SW, Atlanta, GA 30314.

COLE, JOSEPH H.
City official. **PERSONAL:** Born Feb 13, 1913, Philadelphia, PA; married Laura; children: Mrs 5Sylvia Ann Mackey, Mrs Kathleen Teresa Hopkins. **EDUCATION:** Howard U, BS 1935; Howard Univ & NY U, addl study toward master's degree; Cath U, studied human rel; Holy Cross Coll, coaching. **CAREER:** Park & Recreation, retired consult 1975-80; DC Dept of Recreation, dir 1966-75; started with dept in 1938 as playground dir, area dir, dir of city-wide programs; asst supt. **ORGANIZATIONS:** Mem Nat Recreation & Park Assn; mem Brookland Civic Assn; exec bd Police Boy's Club; C & O Canal Commn; HowardUniv Alumni Assn; NAACP; Omega Psi Phi. **BUSINESS ADDRESS:** 3149 16 St NW, Washington, DC 20010.

COLE, MACEOLA LOUISE
Physician. **PERSONAL:** Born Jun 18, 1934, Brentwood, MO; daughter of Maceo Cole and Anna Tibbs Cole. **EDUCATION:** St Louis U, BS 1954, MD 1958. **CAREER:** St Louis Univ Schl Med, asst 1961-; Cardinal Glennon Memorial Hosp, pediatrics attending phys 1961-; solo practitioner, pediatrician. **ORGANIZATIONS:** Mem Natl med Assoc; mem Mound City Forum; mem St Louis Pediatric Soc. **HONORS/ACHIEVEMENTS:** Diplomate Am Bd of Pediatrics 1964. **BUSINESS ADDRESS:** Solo Practitioner, 2715 N Union Blvd, St Louis, MO 63113.

COLE, NATALIE
Entertainer. **PERSONAL:** Children: Robert Adam. **CAREER:** Capitol Records, recording artist 1975-. **HONORS/ACHIEVEMENTS:** Gold Record "Inseparable"; Grammy Awds "Inseparable" & "This Will Be"; Gold Album "Natalie", "Unpredictable". **BUSINESS ADDRESS:** Singer, c/o Capitol Records, Inc, 1750 N Vine St, Hollywood, CA 90028.

COLE, ROBIN
Professional athlete. **PERSONAL:** Born Sep 11, 1955, Los Angeles, CA; children: Robin Jr, Jeremy. **CAREER:** Pittsburg Steelers, linebacker 1977-; Robin C Construction, owner 1981-. **ORGANIZATIONS:** Chmn March of Dimes Walk-a-Thon 1983. **HONORS/ACHIEVEMENTS:** Honorary Citizen in WV by Gov Jay Rockefeller; Back-up & Special Teams Player as Rookie 1977. **BUSINESS ADDRESS:** Pittsburg Steelers, Three River Stadium, 300 Stadium Circle, Pittsburgh, PA 15212.

COLE, THOMAS W., JR.
College president. **PERSONAL:** Born Jan 11, 1941, Vernon, TX; married Brenda S Hill; children: Kelley S, Thomas Winston. **EDUCATION:** Wiley Coll Marshall TX, BS 1961; Univ of Chgo, PhD 1966. **CAREER:** Atlanta Univ, mem faculty 1966-82, prof chem, chmn dept 1971-82, Fuller E Callaway prof 1969-80, proj dir resource ctr sci & engrg 1978-82, univ provost, vice pres acad affairs 1979-82; Univ of IL, vstg prof 1972; MIT, vstg prof 1972-74; Miami Valley Lab Procter & Gamble Co, summer chemist 1967; Celanese Corp Charlotte NC, chemist; UNCF, lecturer 1975-84; WV State Coll Inst, pres 1982-86; WV Bd of Regents, chancellor 1986-. **ORGANIZATIONS:** Mem Leadership Atlanta; mem Amer Chem Soc, AAAS, Natl Inst Sci, Natl Org Professional Advancement Black Chemists & Chem Engrs, Sigma Xi, Sigma Pi Phi, Alpha Phi Alpha, Rotary; adv bd United Natl Bank; dir C&P Telephone Co; trustee Natl Assoc of Public TV Stations; mem So Reg Educ Bd; mem Fund for theArts, United Way, Natl Inst of Chemical Studies. **HONORS/ACHIEVEMENTS:** So Regional Fellow summer 1961; Woodrow Wilson Fellow 1961-62; Allied Chem Fellow 1963. **BUSINESS ADDRESS:** President, Clark College, 240 Chestnut St SW, Atlanta, GA 30314.

COLE, THOMAS WINSTON, SR.
Educator. **PERSONAL:** Born Oct 24, 1915, Navasota, TX; married Eva M Sharp. **EDUCATION:** Wiley Coll, BS 1934; Univ of WI, MS 1947; Univ of TX, EdD 1955. **CAREER:** Dean of Acad Affairs for Instr Serv & Univ Ombudsman, Univ of FL, asst dean 1971-72; Wiley Coll, pres 1958-71, prev dean reg & prof 1948-58; Graduate Extension Program Prairie View Coll, dir grad 1950-71; Wash Elementary School, prin 1944-50; Wash High School, prin 1934-44. **ORGANIZATIONS:** Apptd by Pres of US to Advisory Com on Developing Institutions 1965-66; appted by Pres Commn on Presidential Scholars 1969-74; appted by Pres Nat Commn on Equality of Educational Opportunity 1972-76; delegate to World Conf of Meth Ch Oslo, Norway 1961 & London 1966; visited as rep of Bd Educ of Meth Ch all major universities in Europe & British Isles including Univ of Leningrad, Moscow & Kiev; Univ of Rome; the Sorbonne etc 1960; chmn work area on higher educ FL Conf United Meth Ch 1973-75; sec program Commn on Gen & Conf United Meth Ch 1968-76; numerous local state & federal appointments; mem Phi Delta Kappa; pres Alpha Phi Alpha; Sigma Pi Phi; Masonic Lodge; Rotary Internt; Omicron Delta Kappa Phi Kappa Phi; pres council Am Inst of mgmt; Am Assn of coll; Various others Listed in numerous biog publs; author "Duties of Acad Deans in Meth Ch Related Coll" 1955; co-author "Quality Edn" 1974. **BUSINESS ADDRESS:** 231 Tigert Hall, U of FL, Gainesville, FL 32611.

COLEBROOK, GEORGE, JR.
Manager. **PERSONAL:** Born Mar 30, 1942, New York, NY; married Pollia Jane Mundell; children: Sean Paul, Dawn Elizabeth, James Jay, George Lecoy III. **EDUCATION:** NY U, 1969; So W Coll, BA 1970; Pace Grad Sch, 1970-72. **CAREER:** The Arizona Bank, mgr 1976-; Irving Trust Co, asst sec 1970-76. **ORGANIZATIONS:** Tournament chmn Desert Mashie & Golf Club 1979-80; bd of dir Maryvale Men's Club 1979-80; mem Theta Phi Delta Frat; black achiever Harlem YMCA 1974. **MILITARY SERVICE:** USAF sgt 1959-67.

COLEMAN, ANDREW LEE
Elected official. **PERSONAL:** Born Jan 30, 1960, Humboldt, TN; son of Lennie Coleman and Doris Lovelady. **EDUCATION:** Vanderbilt Univ, BS Political Science, Sociology 1982; Dyersburg Comm Coll, principles of real estate. **CAREER:** Humboldt City Parks, asst supvr summer 1977; Jones Mfg Co, laborer summer 1978-79; Foster & Creighton Const Co, laborer summer 1981; Denver Broncis of NFL, professional player 1982; New Orleans St of NFL, professional player 1982; Classic I Kitchenware Inc, sales distr 1983; Humboldt Schools, sub teacher 1983; City of Humboldt, alderman 1983; Gibson Cty Vote Coord, get out the vote coord for Albert Gore Jr 1984; Jesse Jackson for Pres, coord 1984; The Drew Enterprise (publ rel/pers svcs), pres 1985-; Jonah, Inc, organizer/office mgr 1985; Al Williams, Inc, sales rep 1986; TN Bd of Paroles, parole officer/counselor, 1986; Morgan & Assocs Realtors, affiliate broker 1987; co-chairman Humboldt Strawberry Patch, 1988. **ORGANIZATIONS:** Volunteer/coach Special Olympics; Notary Public; mem TN Black Elected Officials 1984-, TN Voters Council 1984-, Gibson Cty Voters Council 1984; newspaper columnist Courier Chronicle The Drew Point; lecturing knight WJO Lee Elks #1290 1985-; mem NAACP; mem Jonah; W30 Lee Elks 1290, financial sec; Celestial Lodge #80; mem in dept of health & environment Amer Probation & Paroles 1988; bd mem, decatur co community corrections advisory bd 1988-; patron Order of Eastern Star 1988; mem Gibson Co fraternal order of police 1988-. **HONORS/ACHIEVEMENTS:** Most Valuable Player Vanderbilt Football 1980; voted Most Athletic Class of 1982; All Amer Middle Linebacker Vanderbilt Univ 1982; Amer Outstanding Names & Faces Natl Org 1982. **HOME ADDRESS:** 1610 Osborne, Humboldt, TN 38343.

COLEMAN, ARTHUR H.
Business executive, physician, attorney. **PERSONAL:** Born Feb 18, 1920, Philadelphia, PA; son of Jessie Coleman and Virgina Hines Coleman; married Renee Dorsey, Nov 21, 1987; children: Ruth Karnell, Patricia, John, Kurt. **EDUCATION:** PA State U, BS 1941; Howard U, MD 1944; Golden Gate Coll, LlB 1956; Golden Gate Coll, JD 1968. **CAREER:** Medicine, pvt practice 1948-; San Francisco Med Assoc, pres. **ORGANIZATIONS:** Bd dir Sec Drew Inv Corp 1952; pres co-founder Amer Health Care Plan 1973; bd dir Fidelity Savings & Loan Assn 1966; co-founder pres SF Med Assn Inc; exec dir Hunters Point Baypoint Comm Health Serv 1968-72; chmn SF Econ Opportunity Council 1964-67; pres chmn of bd Trans-Bay Fed Savings & Loan Assn 1964-66; guest lectr Golden Gate Coll of Law 1958-60; lectr Univ CA 1968; mem Pathway Comm for Family Med Univ CA Med Ctr 1970; internship Homer G Phillips Hosp 1945; mem AMA 1948; mem CA Med Assn 1948; mem SF Med Soc 1948-; pres Natl Med Assn 1976-77; pres John Hale Med Soc 1970-71; fellow Amer Acad of Forensic Sci 1958; fellow bd of govs Amer Coll of Legal Med 1961; pres Northern California Med Dental Pharm Assn 1964; pres bd Dir Golden State Med Assn 1970-74; mem World Med Assn 1971-; mem CA Acad of Med 197 1; coord com SF Alliance for Health Care; vice pres Amer Cancer Soc 1969-71; bd of dir SF Hunters Point Boys Club; bd dir adv council SF Planning & Ren Assn 1969-75; pres Amer Coll of Legal Medicine 1983-84; vice pres bd of dir Drew Medical Univ 1987; pres Port of San Francisco 1984-87. **HONORS/ACHIEVEMENTS:** Bay Area Howard Univ Alumni Award 1966; SF Bay Area Council Certificate 1965-67; SF bd of supres Certificate of Award 1968; SF Dept of Health Commendation 1976; Omega Psi Phi Award for Distingushed Serv 1973; numerous articles and otherpublications; Distinguished Alumnus, Penn State Univ 1977. **MILITARY SERVICE:** USAF capt 1945-48. **BUSINESS ADDRESS:** President, San Francisco Medical Assoc, 6301 Third St, San Francisco, CA 94124.

COLEMAN, AUDREY RACHELLE
Educational administrator. **PERSONAL:** Born Aug 26, 1934, Duquesne, PA; daughter of Dave Ward and Ola Dixon Ward; married William Franklin Coleman Sr; children: William Franklin Jr. **EDUCATION:** Youngstown Univ, BMus 1956; Boston State Coll, MEd 1965, Advanced Admin 1978. **CAREER:** Youngstown OH Public Schools, teacher 1957-61; Boston Public Schools, teacher 1961-75, asst principal 1975-76, admin 1976-, asst dir. **ORGANIZATIONS:** Natl First Anti-Basileus Lambda Kappa Mu 1976-79; conductor Natl Workshops Lambda Kappa Mu 1976-; conductor Citywide Workshops Boston Public Schools 1977-; mem MA State Review Team Chap I Prog 1978; grand basileus Lambda Kappa Mu 1981-85; bd of dir Natl Coalition-Black Meeting Planners 1984-86; natl bd mem, Lambda Kappa Mu (past natl pres); natl vice pres, American Federation of School Admin. **HONORS/ACHIEVEMENTS:** Certificate of Achievement & Leadership Urban League 1979; Mary M Bethune Awd Natl Council Negro Women 1982; Distinguished Serv Key Awd Lambda Kappa Mu 1983; featured on front cover of Black Monitor Magazine 1984; Dollars & Sense Magazine Award to Outstanding Afro-American Women 1989; Mayor of Boston Award for Leadership 1988. **HOME ADDRESS:** 35 Colgate Road, Needham, MA 02192. **BUSINESS ADDRESS:** Assistant Dir, Boston Public Schools, 26 Court St, Boston, MA 02108.

COLEMAN, AVANT PATRICK
Educator. **PERSONAL:** Born Jun 16, 1936, Rocky Mount, NC; married Willa Monroe; children: Jacqueline, Elliotte, Wanda. **EDUCATION:** Agr & Tech State Univ, BS 1960; NC State Univ, MS 1978. **CAREER:** Lenoir Cty Bd of Ed, teacher, vocational agr 1960-61; Greene Cty Bd of Ed, teacher, vocational agr 1961-62; NC Agr Extension Svc, extension agent 4-H 1962-. **ORGANIZATIONS:** Sec NC State 4-H Agents Assoc 1972-73; city council 1975-77, 1980-85, mayor pro tem 1982-89 City of Wilson; pres Kiwanis Club of Wilson All Amer 1981-82; pres Men's Civic Club 1982; bd mem United Way of Wilson Cty Inc 1983-85; 1st vice pres Red Cross Wilson County Chapter 1986-87; chapter chairman, Wilson Chapter American Red Cross, 1987-88; bd mem, NC Housing Partnership NC League of Municipalities, 1987-; vice chairman, Regional L Council of Governments, 1987-; bd mem, Small Cities Council Natl League of Cities, 1988-89; 3rd vice pres, NC League of Municipalities, 1988-89. **HONORS/ACHIEVEMENTS:** Distinguished Serv Award State Natl Assoc of 4-H Agents 1975; Certificate of Appreciation Mid-Atlantic Reg MD-NC 4-H Caravan Six Weeks 1977; Distinguished Serv Award Alpha Kappa Alpha Sorority 1982; Distinguished Humanitarian Award Gamma Beta Omega Chap Alpha Kappa Alpha Sorority 1982; Tour of United Kingdom Natl 4-H Council Washington DC; NCNB, bd of dir; NC League of Municipalities, bd of dir 1986-87; appointed to the Natl League Comm & Economic Devel Comm 1986-87; 25yr Service, Natl Assn of Extension 4H Agents, 1987. **HOME ADDRESS:** 2406 Belair Ave, PO Box 4185, Wilson, NC 27893.

COLEMAN, BARBARA SIMS
Social service psychiatry. **PERSONAL:** Daughter of Hugh N Sims and Rossa V Sims; married Julian D Coleman Jr, Aug 08, 1953; children: Julian, Hugh, Mark. **EDUCATION:** Howard Univ, BS 1953; Univ of WI, MSSW 1956. **CAREER:** Larue Carteer Memrl Hosp, asst dir soc work 1957-73, sprvr 1957-73, psychiatric soc worker 1957-73; asst dir soc work/psychiatry Riley Child Psychiatry Clinic 1973-. **ORGANIZATIONS:** Consltnt sprvsr Christian Theological Smnry Pastoral Cnslng Pgm 1972-; mem of bd Plnd Parenthood Cntrl IN 1981-; mem bd pres Raines Cnslng Cntr 1968-84; Natl Assn of Social Workers & Academy of Certified Social Workers. **HOME ADDRESS:** 4370 Knollton Rd, Indianapolis, IN 46208. **BUSINESS ADDRESS:** Asst Dir Soc Work/Psychtry, Riley Child Psychiatry Clnc, 702 Barnhill Dr, Indianapolis, IN 46223.

COLEMAN, BEN CARL
Educator. **PERSONAL:** Born Apr 01, 1927, Kansas City, KS; children: Cheryl L Williams, Kevin S, Tania Z. **EDUCATION:** Univ of WI, BA 1952; Loyola Univ Chgo, MA 1962; Univ of Chgo, PhD 1972. **CAREER:** Publishers Digest Inc, advertising copywriter, advertising prod mgr; Bankers Life Ins Co, ins salesman; Cook Co, social worker, family court consultant; Loop Jr Coll, instr of Spanish; UNI CICS, asst prof; East Coast Univ, foreign language consultant; NE Illinois Univ, asst prof, assoc dean of students, coord of community serv, assoc prof, prof of Afro-Hispanic Amer studies. **ORGANIZATIONS:** Sigma Delta Pi Spanish Hon Soc 1952; Alpha Delta Sigma Profsnl Frat 1952; Kappa Alpha Psi Soc Frat 1951; Chimexla & Union Puerto Rican Stdnts 1985. **HONORS/ACHIEVEMENTS:** Publications, "Black Themes & Subtitles in the Literature of the Caribbean" 1973; "Uso inteligente del poder de compra" 1974; "The Teaching of Afro-Hispanic Expression in Puerto Rican Lit" 1974; "A Critical Review of The Autumn of the Patriarch or El ontono del patriarca" 1978; "El aprendizaje del espanol y su relevancia para con el alumno negro" 1973; "The Teaching of Afro-Hispanic Literature" 1974; "Afro-Hispanic Influences in the Western Hemisphere" 1975; "The Black African in the Western Hemisphere, African/Am Links" 1975; "African Influence in the Lit of the Caribbean" 1975; "Striving for Excell" TV Show 1977; "Afro-Hispanic Religion & Black Mysticism" 1977; "Blackness, As it Pertains to the Caribbean" 1978; "Negritude & World Lit" 1978; "Afro-Hispanic Am Poetry, Past, Present& Future" 1982; "Afro-Hispanic Am Lit, New Dimensions" 1982; "A Critical Review of Afro-Hispanic Am Lit, Implications for the Future" 1983; "Literatura Afro-Hispanoamericana, Su Reflejo en la Sociedad" 1980; "The Role of Woman in Contemporary Afro-Hispanic American Prose, A Male Perspective" 1986. **MILITARY SERVICE:** AUS n comdg ofcr; Good Conduct 1945-48; Sharpshooter. **BUSINESS ADDRESS:** Professor, Northeastern IL Univ, 5500 N St Louis Ave, Chicago, IL 60625.

COLEMAN, CAESAR DAVID
Episcopal bishop. **PERSONAL:** Born Oct 04, 1919, Pickens, MS; son of Rev Ira Lee Coleman (deceased) and Mrs Eddye Love Coleman (deceased); married Elizabeth Luellen, Nov 11, 1955; children: Rev Daryll H Coleman. **EDUCATION:** Mary Holmes Jr Coll, West Point, MS; Mississippi Industrial Coll, Holly Springs, MS, AB, 1947; Lincoln Univ, Lincoln Univ, PA, BD, 1950. **CAREER:** Miles Chapel CME Church, Sardis, MS, pastor, 1952-57; Mississippi Industrial, Holly Springs, MS, prof of religion & philosophy, 1952-57; Christian Methodist Epis Church, N Mississippi Conf, presiding elder, 1956-58; General Bd of Christian Educ, CME Church, Chicago, IL, exec sec, 1958-74; Christian Methodist, Dallas, TX, presiding bishop, 1974-; Episcopal Church, Dallas, TX, sr bishop & CEO, 1986-. **ORGANIZATIONS:** Founder & trustee, Interdemonational Theology Center, 1960-76; chmn, bd of trustees, Texas Coll, 1974-; Dallas Area Ministers' Alliance, 1974-; chmn & chief endorser, Comm on Chaplaincy, 1978-86; pres, Gen Bd of Personnel Serv, 1982-86; sec, Coll of Bishops, vice pres, The Natl Congress of Black Churches, 1982-86; treasurer, Texas Conf of Churches, 1982-86; patron bishop, Women's Missionary Council CME Church, 1986-; dir, AMI Securities, 1988-; life mem, Natl Urban League, Consultation on Church Union, Urban Ministries Inc; mem, NAACP, Greater Dallas Community of Churches. **HONORS/ACHIEVEMENTS:** Doctor of Divinity, Lane Coll, 1960; Doctor of Laws, Mississippi Indus Coll, 1967; Doctor of Divinity, Interdemonational Theology Center, 1976; 100 Most Influential Black Amer, Ebony Magazine, 1986-; Trailblazer Award, South Dallas Business & Professional Women's Club, 1987; Outstanding Minister, Dallas Interdemonational Ministers' Alliance, 1988; Honorary Mayor, Kenny Dill, Mayor of West Point, MS, 1989; author, The CME Primer, Beyond Blackness to Destiny, Organizational Manual & Guide for Christian Youth Fellowship, CME Church; editor in chief, Civil Rights. **MILITARY SERVICE:** US Armed Forces, WW II, commissioned officer. **BUSINESS ADDRESS:** Bishop, Eighth Episcopal Dist Headquarters, Christian Methodist, 2323 W Illinois Ave, Upper Level, Dallas, TX 75224.

COLEMAN, CECIL R.
Business executive. **PERSONAL:** Born May 15, 1934, Centralia, IL; married Betti Thomas; children: Karla M, Mark C. **EDUCATION:** Northwestern U, BBA 1970; Northwestern U, Grad Sch of Mgmt. **CAREER:** Harris Trust & Savs Bank, dir 1980-; Harris Trust & Savs Bank, vice pres 1978-80; Harris Trust & Savings Bank, former asst mp 1965; Mammoth Life Ins Co, sales rep asst & mgr & mrg 1954-65. **ORGANIZATIONS:** Mem Chicago Chap AIB Bd Regents; TAP Cons; Alpha Delta Sigma; Human Resources Com IL State C of C chmn; Chicago Student Symposium ; Sci & Math Conf 1973; bd dir Chatham YMCA; mem Comm Fund Review Panel; mem Old Town Boys Club. **HONORS/ACHIEVEMENTS:** Chicago black achiever 1974; WGRT Radio "Great Guy Award 1973"; jacee of the month Chicago Chap 1969; Chicago merit Employee of week 1967; num Nat Ins Assn awards for sales achievement. **MILITARY SERVICE:** AUS sp/4 1956-58. **BUSINESS ADDRESS:** Harris Trust & Sav Bank, 111 W Monroe St, Chicago, IL 60690.

COLEMAN, COLUMBUS E., JR.
Corporate officer. **PERSONAL:** Born Jul 13, 1948, Wharton, TX. **EDUCATION:** Univ of TX, BS 1970; Univ of NC, MBA 1973-75; Univ of San Francisco, Law Courses 1978-79. **CAREER:** Wells Fargo Securities Clearance Corp, exec vice pres & gen mgr 1979-; Wells Fargo Bank, asst vice pres 1977-79; First Nat Bank in Dallas, corporate banking officer 1975-77; Gulf & Oil Co, elec engr 1970-71. **ORGANIZATIONS:** Adv capt Am Cancer Assn Dr 1977; Small Bus Assn 1978-; adv Jr Achievement 1978; pres Alpha Phi Alpha Epsilon Iota Chap 1970-71; mem & participant Big Brothers Assn 1978-; mem NAACP 1979-. **HONORS/ACHIEVEMENTS:** Hon mem Phi Theta Kappa Frat 1967-; Consortium Fellow 1973-75; Soldier of Year AUS 1971. **MILITARY SERVICE:** AUS spec-5 1971-72. **BUSINESS ADDRESS:** 45 Broad St, New York, NY 10004.

COLEMAN, DON EDWIN
Educator. **PERSONAL:** Born May 04, 1928, Ponac City, OK; married Geraldine J Johnson; children: Stephanie Lynn. **EDUCATION:** MI State Univ, BS 1952, MS 1956, MA 1958, PhD 1971. **CAREER:** Flint MI Schools, teacher 1954-67; Doyle Comm School, prin 1966-68; MI State Univ, teacher, coach 1968-69, asst dean graduate school 1978-. **ORGANIZATIONS:** Pres MI Health Council 1980; mem Amer Pub Health Assn; mem Amer Coll Pers Assn; mem Natl Assn Student Pers Admin; past mem Natl Comm Sch Dir Assn 1963-67; past mem MI Elem Principal Assn 1967-68; mem Phi Delta Kappa; mem Alpha Phi Alpha Frat 1949; past pres Epsilon Upsilon 1965-67; past pres fdr Kappa Delta Lambda 1972; Red Feather United Fund 1964-68; past dir BS of Amer 1965-68; Prince Hall Masonic Order 1954; Elks Genesee Temple 1956-68; NAACP 1954; mem Urban League 1954; exec comm Planned Parenthood 1952-60; mem Flint Jr Chamber of Comm 1960-64; bd mem Listening Ear 1970-73; Air Pollution Bd 1970-74; past mem Tri-Co Plng Comm 1974-76; MI State Univ Athletic Coun 1975; life mem Alpha Phi Alpha Frat 1980; exec dir Black Child & FamilyInst 1986; chmn Ingham County Bd of Helth 1987. **HONORS/ACHIEVEMENTS:** 10 Yr Awd Big Brothers of Amer 1955-68; Blue Key Natl Scholastic Honor; Unanimous All-Amer Tackle 1950-51; Outstanding Lineman 1951 1952; Coll All Star game 1952; 1st football jersey (78) retired at MSU 1952; Outstanding Lineman Hula Bowl Silver Anniv 1971; inductee Natl Football Found & Hall of Fame 1975; NCAA Silver Anniv Awd 1976. **MILITARY SERVICE:** AUS 1st lt 1952-54. **BUSINESS ADDRESS:** Asst Dean Grad School, Michigan State University, 535 E Fee, Coll of Osteopathic Medicine, East Lansing, MI 48824.

COLEMAN, EDWIN LEON, II
Educator, African American literature. **PERSONAL:** Born Mar 17, 1932, El Dorado, AR; married Charmaine Joyce Thompson; children: Edwin III, Callan. **EDUCATION:** City Coll of San Francisco, AA 1955; San Francisco State Univ, BA 1960, MA 1962; Univ of OR, PhD 1971. **CAREER:** Melodyland Theatre, technician 1960; Chicago State Univ, Speech Dept, asst prof, 1963-66; Univ of OR Dept of English, dir Ethnic Prog, professional musician. **ORGANIZATIONS:** Bd Campus Interfaith Ministry 1975-; bd Sponsors Inc 1980-; bd Clergy & Laity Concerned 1980-; bd OR Arts Found 1981-84; pres OR Folklore Soc 1983-84; consul Natl Endowment for the Arts 1983-; faculty Natl Humanities; mem Amer Folklore Soc; NAACP; Kappa Alpha Psi. **HONORS/ACHIEVEMENTS:** Ford Fellow Educ Grant 1970; Danforth Assoc 1977-; Distinguished Black Faculty 1978; Outstanding Faculty Natl Mag OR Art Commission 1982; Fredrick Douglass Scholarship Awd Natl Council of Black Studies 1986; Charles S. Johnson Service Award. **MILITARY SERVICE:** USAF staff sgt 1951-56. **BUSINESS ADDRESS:** Professor of English, Univ of Oregon, Dept of English, Eugene, OR 97403.

COLEMAN, ELIZABETH SHEPPARD
Performing arts director. **PERSONAL:** Children: Nedra, Andre, Jalinda, Angela, Aretha. **EDUCATION:** Muskegon Comm Clg, Assc 1973; Grand Valley State Clg, BS 1975, Masters Gen & Urban Educ 1979. **CAREER:** Advisory Cncl Muskegon Hghts Police, mem 1975-77; Muskegon Hghts Bd of Educ, trst sec 1975-81; Muskegon Cnty Cncl of Black Orgn, mem sec 1975-77; Muskegon Cnty Human Resrc Cmt, mem 1977-79; Muskegon Cnty Repertory Cntr, dir 1976-85; Naacp, civic serv mem. **ORGANIZATIONS:** Mem & sec Muskegon Co Black Orgn 1977-79; mem Muskegon Co Human Resource 1979-; mem Muskegon Co NAACP. **BUSINESS ADDRESS:** Dir, Muskegon Cnty Repertory, 706 Overbrook Dr, Muskegon, MI 49444.

COLEMAN, EMMETT See REED, ISHMAEL SCOTT

COLEMAN, ERIC DEAN
Elected official, attorney. **PERSONAL:** Born May 26, 1951, New Haven, CT; son of Julius Coleman and Rebecca Ann Simmons Coleman; married Pamela Lynette Greene, May 19, 1979; children: Trevonn Rakeim, Lamar Ericson, Erica Lynette. **EDUCATION:** Columbia Univ, BA 1973; Univ of CT, JD 1977. **CAREER:** Hartford Neighborhood Legal Svcs, staff atty 1977-78; CT Div of Pub Def Services, asst public defender 1978-81; Aetna Life & Casualty, consultant 1981-86; CT General Assembly, state rep 1983-. **ORGANIZATIONS:** Mem Greater Hartford Urban League 1974-, Greater Hartford NAACP 1974-, Amer Bar Assoc 1978-, CT Bar Assoc 1978-, George Crawford Law Assoc 1978-, Action Plan for Infant Health 1984-, Early Childhood Task Force 1984-; state adv comm US Civil Rights Commiss 1984-; mem Oper PUSH 1974-, Charter Oak Lodge of Elks 1982-, Omega Psi Phi, Bloomfield Dem Town Comm 1984-, Greater Hartford Black Dem Club 1978-, Metro AME Zion Church. **HONORS/ACHIEVEMENTS:** Citizen of the Year Omega Psi Phi Frat Tau Iota CT, 1982; Citizen of the Year Omega Psi Phi Frat Delta Lambda CT 1983; Outstanding Young Man, Outstanding Young Men of America 1984, 1985; First Report (Weekly Neighborhood Newspaper Column) 1983-; Marital Deduction Planning under ERTA 1981. **HOME ADDRESS:** 77 Wintonbury Ave, Bloomfield, CT 06002.

COLEMAN, EVEROD A.
Consultant. **PERSONAL:** Born Sep 24, 1920, Mounds, LA; married Willie Mae Dixon; children: Everod Coleman Jr, Rene Edwards. **EDUCATION:** Lincoln Univ, BS 1947; Attended, Wayne State Univ, Univ of Detroit. **CAREER:** White & Griffin Arch & Eng, steel designer 1947-49; City of Detroit, coord phys devel comm & econ devel dept (retired 1980); City of Inkster MI, interim chief bldg inspector & consul 1982; Architects Intl, consultant. **ORGANIZATIONS:** 1st black building insp City of Detroit 1949-; housing consul bd dir Phoenix Housing Corp; mem SMED; Natl Assn of Housing Rehab Officials; Natl TechAssn Omega Psi Phi Frat; NAACP; past elder & trustee Calvary Presby Ch; mem Detroit Housing Corp. **HONORS/ACHIEVEMENTS:** Father of Yr 1955 United Christian Ch. **MILITARY SERVICE:** Vet WW II. **HOME ADDRESS:** 4058 Clements St, Detroit, MI 48238.

COLEMAN, FREDERICK M.
Attorney. **PERSONAL:** Born Dec 27, 1917, Lilly, GA; married Mary; children: Frederick David. **EDUCATION:** Cleveland Coll Western Res Univ, 1946-49; Cleveland-Marshall Law School, JD 1949-53, LLM 1953-57. **CAREER:** US Post Office, letter carrier 1937-57; Private Practice, attny 1953-67; Public Defender Office, 1st asst 1963-67; Cleveland Mun, judge 1967-70; N Dist OH, US attny 1970-77; Cuyahoga Cty Court of Common Pleas, judge 1977-. **ORGANIZATIONS:** Mem OH Bar, Cleveland Bar, Cuyahoga Cty Bar, John M Harlan Law Club, OH Judicial Conf, Fed Bar, NBA, Amer Judicature Soc Bd & Comm, YMCA; bd of gov USO, pres Fed for Comm Planning, Urban League; mem Emeritus NAACP; bd trustees Amer Cancer Soc; mem Businessmens Interracial Comm; bd mem Blue Cross;mem Natl Conf Christians & Jews, Prince Hall Masonic Lodges, Elks Lodge; Cpm. **MILITARY SERVICE:** AUS 1943-46; USAR, OH Natl Guard 1946-. **BUSINESS ADDRESS:** Judge, Cuyahoga Cty Crt Common Pleas, The Justice Center, 1200 Ontario St, Cleveland, OH 44113.

COLEMAN, GARY
Actor. **PERSONAL:** Born Feb 08, 1968, Lima, OH. **CAREER:** TV commercials; guest starred, Good Times, The Jeffersons, The Johnny Carson Show; TV pilot, Little Rascals 1978; co-star Different Strokes; featured actor in several TV & feature films. **ORGANIZATIONS:** Honorary Gift of Life Chmn Natl Kidney Foundation. **HONORS/ACHIEVEMENTS:** Biography "Gary Coleman-Medical Miracle". **BUSINESS ADDRESS:** C/O Victor Perillo Talent Agcy, 9229 Sunset Blvd, Los Angeles, CA 90069.

COLEMAN, GEORGE EDWARD
Tenor, alto, soprano saxophonist. **PERSONAL:** Born Mar 08, 1935, Memphis, TN; son of George Coleman and Indiana Lyle; married Carol Hollister, Sep 08, 1985; children: George, Gloria. **CAREER:** Tenor alto and saprano saxophonist; mem BB King Band 1952, 1955; mem Max Roach Quintet 1958-59, Miles Davis Quartet 1963-64, Lionel Hampton Orch 1965-66, Lee Morgan Quintet 1969, Elvin Jones Quartet 1970; writer arranger of mus shows; Lenox MA Jazz Sch of Mus, consult 1958-; George Coleman Quartet & George Coleman Octet, mem 1974-; Consultant, New York Univ, Long Island Univ, New School for Social Research. **HONORS/ACHIEVEMENTS:** Selected by Intl Jazz Critics Poll 1958; Artist of the Yr Record World Mag 1969; Knight of Mark Twain 1972; Beale St Mus Festival Awd 1977; Tip of the Derby Awd 1978, 1979, 1980; New York Jazz Awd 1979. **HOME ADDRESS:** 63 East 9th St, New York, NY 10003.

COLEMAN, GILBERT IRVING
Educator. **PERSONAL:** Born Jan 20, 1940, Fredericksburg, VA; married Pearlie Ball; children: Darryl Langston. **EDUCATION:** VA Union Univ, BS 1956-60; Howard Univ, MS 1960-62; Univ of VA, DEd 1980-. **CAREER:** Microbiological Assoc, rsch assoc 1962-63; Natl Institutions of Health, rsch asst 1963-64; Smithsonian Inst, jr rsch analyst 1964-68; Spotsylvania SrHS, biology teacher 1968-70; Germann Comm Coll, instructor 1970-73, asst prof 1973-76, assoc prof 1976-, div chmn arts sciences & nursing. **ORGANIZATIONS:** Mem Shiloh Baptist Church 1949-; mem Personnel Bd Mary Washington Hosp 1984-; mem of the bd Rappahannock Serv Corp 1984-. **HONORS/ACHIEVEMENTS:** Man of the Year Veterans of Foreign Wars 1984; Man of the Year Fraternal Order of Police 1984. **HOME ADDRESS:** 335 Glover St, Fredericksburg, VA 22401. **BUSINESS ADDRESS:** Div Chair Arts Sci & Nrsng, Germanna Community College, PO Box 339, Locust Grove, VA 22508.

COLEMAN, GREG
Professional athlete. **PERSONAL:** Born Sep 09, 1954, Jacksonville, FL; married Eleanora; children: Cara, Greg. **EDUCATION:** Florida A & M, BA. **CAREER:** Cleveland, punter 1977; MN Vikings, punter 1978-; WCCO-TV, broadcaster. **ORGANIZATIONS:** Boys Club; Special Olympics; Am Heart Asso; Flwshp of Christian Athletes; Muscular Dystrophy Asso ; Big Brothers. **HONORS/ACHIEVEMENTS:** Led NFL in punting.

COLEMAN, HARRY A.
Theologian. **PERSONAL:** Born Aug 03, Piedmont, WV; married Helen T Price; children: Harry A. **EDUCATION:** Johnstown Cntr Univ of Pittsburg, 1955; WV U, AB 1957; Boston Univ Sch of Theology, MDiv 1960. **CAREER:** WV Wesleyan Coll Sociology Inst; Logan Memorial United Methodist Ch, 1960-62; Ebenezer Un Meth Ch, 1962-65 Huntington, WV; John Stewart & United MethCh Bluefield, WV, 1966-68; Simpson United Ch, 1968-74; WV State Coll, campus pastor 1968-72; Morris Harvey Coll, instructor sociology 1972-74. **ORGANIZATIONS:** Fin sec Charleston Business and Pro Men's Club 1968-72; mem Brotherhood of Christians and Jews 1960-62 Parkersburg, WV; offices within WV Annual Conf United Methodist Ch. **MILITARY SERVICE:** AUS pfc 1953-55. **BUSINESS ADDRESS:** The Chapel, WV Wesleyan College, Buckhannon, WV 26201.

COLEMAN, HARRY THEODORE
Dentist. **PERSONAL:** Born Jul 06, 1943, Somerville, TN; married Olivia Jackson; children: Brian, Chandra. **EDUCATION:** Johnson C Smith U, BS1965; Meharry Med Coll, DDS 1970. **CAREER:** Self, dentist; Hubbard Hosp, intership 1970-71. **ORGANIZATIONS:** Mem Nat Dental Assn; Shelby Co Dental Soc; Pan-TN Dental Assn; Am Dental Assn; mem Memphis Jr C of C; Kappa Alpha & Psifrat; NAACP YMCA; bd dir Boys Club. **MILITARY SERVICE:** USN lt 1971-73. **BUSINESS ADDRESS:** 3087 Park Ave, Memphis, TN 38111.

COLEMAN, HERMAN W.
Association executive. **PERSONAL:** Born Sep 10, 1939, Brookhaven, MS; married Kay G; children: Hope, Michelle. **EDUCATION:** Alcorn A&M Coll Lorman, MS, BS 1962; Western MI Univ Kalamazoo, MI, 1965 & 1968; Eastern MI Univ Ypsilanti, MI, 1968-69. **CAREER:** Michigan Ed Assn Assoc, exec sec; Div of Minority Affairs, exec sec; Urban Ed Prog Rochester & Public Sch Rochester, NY, dir. **ORGANIZATIONS:** Critic guest lecturer and/or consultant atUniv of MI MI StateUniv and Harvard U; consultative resource to US Off of Ed Nat Ed Assn & St Assn; Fmem State Com on Security & Privacy 1974; Urban League; NAACP; Omega Psi Phi Frat; MASCD; NEA; MEA; Nat Assn of Black Sch Adm; nom for alumni of yr award 1973-74; Mott Foundation Fellowship in Ed Admin 1968-69; 1st black exec sec of a St Ed Assn. **BUSINESS ADDRESS:** 1216 Kendale Blvd East, Lansing, MI 48823.

COLEMAN, HURLEY J., JR.
County parks and recreation director. **PERSONAL:** Born Apr 14, 1953, Saginaw, MI; son of Hurley J Coleman Jr and Martha Chatman Coleman; married Sandra Morris, Jul 18, 1981; children: Natoya Dinise, Hurley J III, Tasha Noel. **EDUCATION:** Eastern Michigan Univ, Ypsilanti, MI, BA, Com Recreation Admin, 1977. **CAREER:** Washtenaw County Parks & Recreation Com, Ann Arbor, MI, program specialist, 1977-78; Saginaw County Parks & Recreation Com, Saginaw, MI, recreation program coord, 1979-85; City of Saginaw Recreation Div, Saginaw, MI, recreation admin, 1985-89. **ORGANIZATIONS:** Comm mem, Michigan Recreation & Park Assn; mem, Michigan State Univ, Natural Resources/Public Policy, 1986-88; mem exec bd, Saginaw County Leadership Saginaw Program, 1987-88; chmn, Governor's Recreation Advisory Comm, 1988-; pres-elect, Michigan Recreation & Park Assn, 1988; mem, Michigan State Univ, Michigan Outdoor Recreation Task Force, 1988; comm mem, Natl Recreation & Park Assn; mem, Natl Forum for Black Public Admin, United Way of Saginaw County, Kappa Alpha Psi Fraternity; various church affiliations; past mem, Saginaw Human Relations Comm, Optimist Club, Lions Club. **HONORS/ACHIEVEMENTS:** Ten Outstanding Young People in Michigan, Jaycees, 1986; Distinguished Alumni, Eastern Michigan Univ, 1988; Community Service, A Phillip Randolph Inst, 1988. **BUSINESS ADDRESS:** Wayne County Parks and Recreation Dir, 33175 Ann Arbor Trail, Westland, MI 48185.

COLEMAN, JEAN ELLEN
Librarian. **PERSONAL:** Born in Brooklyn, NY. **EDUCATION:** Hunter Coll, AB, MS; Pratt Inst, MLS; Rutgers Univ, postgrad. **CAREER:** Apache Indian & Multi-Handicapped Children, teacher; Lexington School for the Deaf, librarian; Cen Brooklyn Model Cities Program, library admin bookmobile serv; ALA, dir libray outreach, serv coord coalition for literacy 1973-. **BUSINESS ADDRESS:** Outreach Service Coordinator, ALA, 50 E Huron St Am Lib Assn, Chicago, IL 60611.

COLEMAN, JOHN B.
Physician. **PERSONAL:** Born Nov 25, 1929, Houston; married Gloria Jones; children: Kathleen, John, Jr, Garnet. **EDUCATION:** Fisk U, BA 1951; Howard U, MD 1956. **CAREER:** Ob/Gyn, self Empld; Riverside Hosp, chief of ob/gyn 1974; Riverside Hosp, chief of staff 1972-73; Freedmens Hosp Wash DC, internship Residency (ob/gyn & cardiovascular) 1956-62; private practice since 1962. **ORGANIZATIONS:** Mem bd gr Houston Cable TV 1973-74; vice pres Houston Med Forum 1971-72; owner pres Cullen Women's Center 1973-74; Fpres KCOH Radio Houston; Almeada Med Center chmn; Houston Div UNCF; bd prof United Leadership 1972-74; mem Houston bd of SCLC; mem Adv Bd Houston Independent Sch System; mem Omega Psi Phi. **HONORS/ACHIEVEMENTS:** Spl serv award Houston UNCF 1973; service award Houston Med Forum 1973; listed Who's Who in TX; Who's Who in Am Coll 1951. **BUSINESS ADDRESS:** 1902 Biodgett, Houston, TX 77004.

COLEMAN, JOHN H.
Government employee. **PERSONAL:** Born Jul 29, 1928, Memphis; married Willa Nicholson; children: Patrice, Sylvia, John, Jr, Elissia, Tracey. **EDUCATION:** IN U, BS phys educ 1951; IL U. **CAREER:** Quad Co IL Dept of Pub Aid, bldg operation supvr 1974-; adminstrv asst 1972; ofc mgr 1969; caseworker 1959; worked steel mills post ofc 1955-59. **ORGANIZATIONS:** Mem planning com IL Welfare Assn; bd mem Strong Cntr; Maple Park United Meth Ch; prog chmn Maple Park Meth Men's Club; vice pres 116 Ada St Block Club; mem Maple Park Homeowners Assn. **MILITARY SERVICE:** USAF 1951-55. **BUSINESS ADDRESS:** 624 S Michigan, Chicago, IL.

COLEMAN, JOSEPH E.
Councilman. **PERSONAL:** Born Oct 08, 1922, West Point, MS; married Jessie L Bryant; children: 3 Children. **EDUCATION:** BS chem 1948; MS 1952; LlB 1963; LlD 1967; LHD 1969; AHC 1972. **CAREER:** Celanese Corp NY Hdq, patent atty 1962-65; USDA, res chem; City Council Philadelphia city planner 1965-71, councilman 1972, pres of council 1980-. **ORGANIZATIONS:** Mem Philadelphia Bar Assn; PA Bar Assn; mem all comm & civic organ in 8th Councilmanic Dist. **HONORS/ACHIEVEMENTS:** Recip Gold Bond Awdd Am Oil Chem Soc 1957. **MILITARY SERVICE:** USAF cpl. **BUSINESS ADDRESS:** President, Philadelphia City Council, Room 494, City Hall, Philadelphia, PA 19107.

COLEMAN, KENNETH L.
Executive administrator. **PERSONAL:** Born Dec 01, 1942, Centralia, IL; married Caretha; children: Kennetha, Karen, Kimberly, Kristen, Kenneth. **EDUCATION:** OH State Univ, BS Indus Mgmt 1965, MBA 1972. **CAREER:** Hewlett-Packard Co, corp staffing mgr division personnel, mgr northern European personnel, mgr 1972-82; Activision Inc, vice pres human resources, vice pres prod develop 1982-. **ORGANIZATIONS:** Mem St of CA MESA Bd 1984-85; bd mem Bay Area Black United Fund 1984-85; mem Univ of Santa Clara Indus Adv Comm 1984-85; mem OH State Bus Adv Bd 1984-85; mem past pres Peninsula Assoc of Black Pers Admin 1975-. **HONORS/ACHIEVEMENTS:** Awd for Excellence in Comm Serv San Jose CA 1981. **MILITARY SERVICE:** USAF capt 1968-72. **BUSINESS ADDRESS:** Vice Pres Prod Development, Activision Inc, 3885 Bohannon Dr, Menlo Park, CA 94025.

COLEMAN, LEMON, JR.
Councilman, educator. **PERSONAL:** Born Jan 14, 1935, Pineville, LA; married Dorothy Ruth Wilson; children: Valerie. **EDUCATION:** Grambling State Univ, BS 1957; So Univ, EdM 1968. **CAREER:** Pinecrest State School for the Mentally Retarded, teacher, recreation worker 1957; CC Raymond High School Lecompte, coach, teacher 1960-69; Lincoln State Hospital, rec sup therapist 1964; Boyce High School, coach, teacher 1969-71; Rapides High School, asst principal 1971-72; Slocum High School, asst principal 1972-73; Pineville High School, asst principal 1973-80, principal 1980. **ORGANIZATIONS:** Mem Natl Ed Assoc 1957, LA Ed Assoc 1957, Rapides Parish Ed Assoc 1957; asst exec dir Rapides Parish Poverty Agency 1965; mem Central LA Hosp Bd 1970-, Goals LA Comm 1970, Priorities for LA Conv 1979; mayor pro-tem 1979,83; del 8th Cong Dist Dem Party Natl Conv 1980; mem NAACP; bd of dir Family Serv Agency; mem Reg VI mental Health Bd, Omega Psi Phi, Bro & Sisters Solidarity, Pineville Neighborhood Council, N Rapides Civic & Polit Org, Natl Black Caucus; bd of dir Boys Club of Alexandria-Pineville. **HONORS/ACHIEVEMENTS:** 1st Negro Mem City Pineville Recreation Bd; 1st Negro City Councilman History Pineville; 1st Negro Mem Central LA Hosp Bd Dir. **MILITARY SERVICE:** USAR E-3. **BUSINESS ADDRESS:** Principal, Pineville Jr High School, 501 Edgewood Drive, Pineville, LA 71360.

COLEMAN, LOUIS H.
Association director. **PERSONAL:** Born Nov 21, 1943, Louisville; married Carolyn Morten; children: Andrea, Racheal. **EDUCATION:** KY State U, MA 1967; Univ of Louisville, MS 1971; Presb Sem, MDiv currently studing. **CAREER:** Housing & Urban Affairs Dept Louisville Urban League, dir; Shelby Cong Ch Shelbyville, KY, minister. **ORGANIZATIONS:** Mem Sr Kappa Alpha Psi; Pittsburgh Pirates card carrying mem; INUniv Mans Club; YMCA. **HONORS/ACHIEVEMENTS:** Recipient Louisvle Jaycees Man of Yr 1975; Louisvle Def Black Honor Roll 1975.

COLEMAN, MARIAN M.
Educator. **PERSONAL:** Born Aug 07, 1948, Laurens Co. **EDUCATION:** Friendship Jr Coll, AA 1967; Claflin Coll, BS 1969. **CAREER:** Gleams Community Action Inc, counselor 1974-; Comprehensive Employment Training Act, couns; Laurens Community Action Inc, social worker 1973-74; Pamplico Middle School, instructor 1970-72; Benning Terrace Recreation Center, recreational specialist 1970; Palmetto High School, instructor 1969-70. **ORGANIZATIONS:** Mem SC Head Start Assn 1975; mem SC Educ Assn 1969-73; advisor Youth Chap NAACP 1974; asst sec April Shower Chap 184 OES 1974-75; asst sec Usher Bd White Plain Bapt Ch 1973-75. **BUSINESS ADDRESS:** PO Box 1001, Laurens, SC.

COLEMAN, MELVIN D.
Psychologist. **PERSONAL:** Born Oct 09, 1948, Cleveland, OH; son of James Coleman and Neda Coleman. **EDUCATION:** Univ of WI Stout, BS 1969, MS 1974; Univ of MN Extension, cert beh analysis 1978. **CAREER:** Youth Employment Org, youth counselor summers

1967-68; Cuyahoga County Welfare, social worker 1969-70; OH Youth Commn, parole officer 1970; Univ of WI Stout, teaching asst 1970-71; State of MN, med disability adj 1971-72, vocational rehab 1972-79; Harley Clinic of MN, psychologist 1978-. **ORGANIZATIONS:** Mem MN Behavioral Analysis Assoc 1978-87; consult Pilgrim Baptist Church 1984-87, Bryn Mawr & Queen Nursing Homes 1985-87. **HONORS/ACHIEVEMENTS:** Basketball All Amer 1st Team Natl Assoc Inter Coll Ath 1969; 3rd Round Draft Choice Carolina Cougars BAsketball ABA 1969; 6th Round Draft Choice Cincinnati Royal Basketball NBA 1969; Univ of WI Stout Basketball Hall of Fame 1978; Outstanding Young Men of Amer 1983; established Gestalt Publications as distribution outlet for positive black literature; The Black Gestalt 1987; Reclaiming The Black Child 1989; Florence Meets Africa: A Jazz Concerto 1988. **HOME ADDRESS:** 3828 Clinton Ave So, Minneapolis, MN 55409.

COLEMAN, ORNETTE
Composer, saxophonist. **PERSONAL:** Born Mar 09, 1930, Ft Worth, TX. **EDUCATION:** Sch of Jazz Lenox MA, 1959. **CAREER:** Tenor alto savophone trumpet violin basson; Don Cherry, Eddie Blackwell & Charlie Haden, toured with; Clarence Samuels, toured with 1949; Pee Wee Crayton, toured with 1950; New Port, Monterey Jazz Fests, New York City Town Hall, 1962; New Orleans, LA, Ft Worth,, appeared; Columbia Records, on contract. **HONORS/ACHIEVEMENTS:** Resc include Something Else, Best, The Shape of Jazz to Come, Free Jazz, John Lewis Presents Jazz Abstractions; recip no 1 jazz man of the yr Jazz & Pop 3rd Annual Readers Poll 1968; Guggeheim Found Felow 1967; devel theory concept called "Harmoldic" for composer & players; pioneered use of double quartets; notedfor atonal style; over 100 compositions for small jazz groups & larger ensembles; works for string quartet & woodwind quintet recorded for London Symphony Orchestra.

COLEMAN, RAYMOND CATO
City official. **PERSONAL:** Born Jun 17, 1918, Ennis, TX; children: 7 Children. **CAREER:** So Pacific RR Co, 1943-64; City of Ennis, policeman 1965-72; Ennis, city marshall 1973-. **ORGANIZATIONS:** Mem Ennis Evening Lion's Club; Intl Police Chief's Assn. **HONORS/ACHIEVEMENTS:** 1st Black Elected City Marshall in State of TX. **BUSINESS ADDRESS:** 119 W Brown, Ennis, TX 75119.

COLEMAN, ROBERT A.
City official, mailman. **PERSONAL:** Born Feb 08, 1932, Hopkinsville; children: Dominic Joseph. **EDUCATION:** Paducah Community Coll. **CAREER:** US Postal Serv, letter carrier; Paducah, city commissioner 1973-. **ORGANIZATIONS:** Mem Nat Assn Letter Carriers, pres Paducah Br #383 1971, 73; chmn exec bd KY State 1974; mayor protem 1980-81; mem bd of dir Paducah McCrackenCounty Red Cross Chpt; mem bd of dir Boys Club of Paducah; mem advisory bd Paducah Community Coll; mem bd of dir Opportunity Industrilization Cntr; mem bd of dir Family "Y" of Paducah mem KY Crime Commission. **HONORS/ACHIEVEMENTS:** 32 Degree Mason; past master Stone Sq Lodge #5; former editor Masonic Herald. **MILITARY SERVICE:** USAF sgt 1950-54. **BUSINESS ADDRESS:** US Post Office & City Hall, Paducah, KY 42001.

COLEMAN, RODNEY ALBERT
Auto company executive. **PERSONAL:** Born Oct 12, 1938, Newburgh, NY; son of Samuel C Coleman and Rebecca Belden Coleman; divorced; children: Terri Lynne Coleman, Stephen A Coleman. **EDUCATION:** Howard Univ, Washington, DC, BArch, 1963; Univ of Michigan, Ann Arbor, MI, Exec Mgmt Program, 1988. **CAREER:** US Air Force, captain/project architect, 1963-73; The White House, Washington, DC, White House fellow, 1970-71; District of Columbia City Council, Washington, DC, exec asst to chmn, 1973-78; Pennsylvania Ave Devel Corp, Washington, DC, design consultant, 1978-80; General Motors Corp, Saginaw, MI, dir of Govt Relations, 1980-85, Detroit, MI, dir of Municipal Govt Affairs, 1985-. **ORGANIZATIONS:** Mem, The White House Fellows Assn, 1971-; mem bd of dir, Natl Council for Urban Economic Devel, 1986-; corporate representative, The Natl League of Cities, 1986-, The US Conference of Mayors, 1986-; alternate representative to bd, New Detroit Inc, 1986-, Detroit Economic Growth Corp, 1986-; mem, Urban Affairs Comm, Greater Detroit, Chamber of Commerce, 1986-, corporate representative, Natl Forum for Black Public Admin, 1987-. **HONORS/ACHIEVEMENTS:** Pony Baseball man of the Year, Pony League, Newburgh, NY, 1960. **MILITARY SERVICE:** USAF, Captain, 1963-73, The Air Force Commendation Medal, 1965; The Air Force Meritorious Service Medal, 1968; Republic of Vietnam Honor Medal, 1972; The Bronze Star Medal, 1972. **BUSINESS ADDRESS:** Director, Municipal Government Affairs, General Motors Corporation, 11-138 General Motors Building, 3044 West Grand Blvd, Detroit, MI 48202.

COLEMAN, RONALD GERALD
Educator & association executive. **PERSONAL:** Born Apr 03, 1944, San Francisco, CA; son of Jesse Coleman and Gertrude Coleman Hughes; children: Danielle D, Joron S, Cori D. **EDUCATION:** Univ of UT, BS Sociology 1966, PhD History 1980; CA State Univ Sacramento, CA teaching certificate secondary 1968, MA Social Science 1973. **CAREER:** General Mills Inc, grocery sales rep 1966-67; San Francisco Unified Sch Dist, faculty teacher social studies phys ed 1968-70; Sacramento City Coll, faculty instructor social science 1970-73; Univ of UT, dir of Afro-Amer studies 1981-, coord of ethnic studies 1984-; CA State Univ Haywood, visiting prof Afro-Amer studies 1981; Univ of UT, prof of history. **ORGANIZATIONS:** Consultant UT State Cultural Awareness Training Prog 1974-76; consultant UT State Bd of Educ 1981; consultant UT State Historical Soc 1981; mem UT Endowment for the Humanities 1982-88; commissioner Salt Lake City Civil Service Comm 1983-; chairperson Salt Lake City Branch NAACP Educ Comm 1984-85; mem UT Chapter American Civil Liberties Union 1989-. **HONORS/ACHIEVEMENTS:** "Blacks in Pioneer Utah 1847-1869" UOMOJA Scholar/Journal of Black Studies 1979; "Blacks in Utah History: An Unknown Legacy" The Peoples of Utah 1976; "The Buffalo Soilders, Guardians of the Uintah Frontier 1886-1901" Utah Historical Quarterly 1979; Martin Luther King Jr: Apostle of Social Justice, Peace and Love pamphlet printed for Univ of Utah Martin Luther King Jr Comm 1985; Phi Kappa Phi 1979; Merit Society for Distingushed Alumni George Washington High School. **BUSINESS ADDRESS:** Professor of History, University of Utah, Deptof History, Salt Lake City, UT 84112.

COLEMAN, RUDOLPH W.
Counselor, clergyman. **PERSONAL:** Born Aug 19, 1929, Live Oak, FL; son of Dr & Mrs D C Coleman; married Cecile Bryant; children: Princess, Cheryl. **EDUCATION:** Wilberforce U, BS 1954; Payne Seminary, BD 1956; Princeton Seminary, ThM 1968. **CAREER:** DE State Coll, academic counselor & coll chaplain; Mt Zion AME Ch; Var Chs, pastor 1956-74; Kent, Co, adminstrv coord & counselor for adult basic adn 1968-71. **ORGANIZATIONS:** Chaplain Rotary Intl 1978; Chaplain Tuskegee Airmen Inc 1989. **HONORS/ACHIEVEMENTS:** Outstanding citizenship award DE State Coll 1970; AME Ch Award 1972. **MILITARY SERVICE:** USAF corpl 1945-48. **BUSINESS ADDRESS:** DE State Coll, Dover, DE 19901.

COLEMAN, RUTH M.
Accounting assistant. **PERSONAL:** Born Jan 29, 1917, Elizabeth, NJ; widowed; children: A Bradford. **CAREER:** US Postal Serv, acctg asst 1975-. **ORGANIZATIONS:** Sec Nat Coun Negro Women; Intl Toastmistress Cl; past pres NY Postal Toastmistress Cl; past treas Council 4, Col Reg Intl Toastmistress Club; Bd Trustees FORE. **HONORS/ACHIEVEMENTS:** Merit serv award NCNW 1966.

COLEMAN, SINCLAIR B.
Statistician, economist. **PERSONAL:** Born Feb 17, 1946, Halifax, VA; son of N. Wyatt Coleman and Bessie Bowman Coleman. **EDUCATION:** Hampton Inst, BA 1967; Univ of Chicago, MS 1970; Rand Graduate Inst, PhD, 1975. **CAREER:** US Congress Budget, analytic staff 1976-78; The Rand Corp, rsch staff/consultant, 1968-76, 1978-. **HONORS/ACHIEVEMENTS:** Woodrow Wilson Fellow, Univ of Chicago, 1967-68; Published numerous articles, reports & reviews; seminars & briefings at univs, rsch institutions, govt agencies, confs, & professional meetings. **BUSINESS ADDRESS:** The Rand Corporation, 1700 Main St, Santa Monica, CA 90406.

COLEMAN, VICKI DOREE
Psychologist. **PERSONAL:** Born Apr 20, 1950, Detroit, MI. **EDUCATION:** Univ of IA Iowa City, BA 1971; Univ of IA, MA 1972; No IL Univ, MS Ed Dekalb 1974; Rutgers Univ New Brunswick NJ, EdD 1979. **CAREER:** Rutgers Univ, Douglass Coll, counselor-in-resd 1974-75; Rutgers Univ, Coll, counselor 1975-76; Rutgers Univ, New Brunswick NJ, rsch asst 1975-76; Educ Testing Serv, Princeton NJ, asst examiner & intern 1975-76; Bear River Work Force Consortium. Logan UT, prog admin, vocational counselor 1979-80; UT State Univ,counseling psych & asst prof of psychology 1976-80; Northwestern Univ, Evanston IL, counselor & asst prof of educ 1980-83; Pro-Professional Careers Proj, Univ of IL Chicago, 1981-82; Career Mgmt Dept Lodge Center YWCA, dir 1982-84; Jones Brothers Construction, admin affirm action prog 1984-; The Coleman Group, pres 1983-. **ORGANIZATIONS:** Cons-post doctoral intern Bear River Com Mental Health Ctr Logan UT 1978-80; sr cert coord Personal Dynamics Inst Minneapolis 1979-; state coord Amer Mental Health Counselors Assoc 1979-80; vice pres Cache Valley Bus & Professional Women's Club Logan UT 1978-80; hosp chprsn Delta Kappa Gamma 1978-80; state membership liaison Amer personnel & Guidance Assoc 1978-80. **HONORS/ACHIEVEMENTS:** Listed in Personalities of the West & Midwest 1977-78; Outstanding Young Woman of Amer 1977-78,82-83, Notable Amers 1978-79, Who's Who in the West 1978-81, Comm Leaders & Noteworthy Amers 1978, Comm Leaders of Amer 1980, Intl Who's Who on Comm Serv 1980.

COLEMAN, WANDA
Author. **PERSONAL:** Born Nov 13, 1946, Los Angeles, CA; daughter of George Evans and Lewana Evans; children: Anthony, Tunisia, Ian Wayne Grant. **EDUCATION:** California State Coll, Los Angeles, CA, 1964; Los Angeles City Coll, Los Angeles, CA, 1967. **CAREER:** "Days of Our Lives," NBC-TV, staff writer, 1975-76; medical transcriber and insurance billing clerk, 1979-84; Pacific Radio, interview program co-host, 1981-; writer and performer. **ORGANIZATIONS:** Writers Guild of America, West, 1969-; PEN Center, West, 1983-. **HONORS/ACHIEVEMENTS:** Open Door Program Hall of Fame, 1975; Emmy Award, Academy of Television Arts & Sciences, 1976; author, Art In The Court of The Blue Fag (chapbook), 1977; author, Mad Dog Black Lady, 1979; Grant, Natl Endowment for the Arts, 1981-82; author, Imagoes, 1983; Guggenheim Fellowship, Poetry, 1984; author, Heavy Daughter Blues: Poems & Stories 1968-86, 1987; author, A War of Eyes and Other Stories, 1988; Vesta Ward, Writing Woman's Building/LA, 1988; published over 300 poems and gave over 300 performances in the past 20 years.

COLEMAN, WARREN B.
Educator. **PERSONAL:** Born Aug 08, 1932, Swarthmore, PA; married Carole Berry; children: Warren, Kim, Fawn, Carole. **EDUCATION:** Hampton Inst, BS 1956; PA State U, MED 1974. **CAREER:** PA State Univ, asst prof of physical education 1968-; Carver High School, Newport News VA, head football & track coach 1956-68. **ORGANIZATIONS:** Real Estate Asso; mem bd dir PSU Black Christian Fellowship; originator of Black Cultural Center PA State U. **MILITARY SERVICE:** AUS 2d lt. **BUSINESS ADDRESS:** Pennsylvania State University, Room 60 Recreation Bldg, University Park, PA 16802.

COLEMAN, WILLIAM T., JR.
Attorney. **PERSONAL:** Born Jul 07, 1920, Germantown, PA; married Lovida Hardin; children: William T III, Livida Hardin Jr, Hardin L. **EDUCATION:** Univ of PA, AB (summa cum laude) 1941; Attended, Harvard Bus Sch; Harvard Law Sch, LLB (magna cum laude) 1946. **CAREER:** Judge Herbert F Goodrich US Ct of Appeals for 3rd Circuit, law sec 1947-48; Justice Felix Frankfurter Assoc Judge Supreme Ct, law sec 1948-49; Paul Weiss Rifkind Wharton & Garrison NY, assoc 1949-52; City of Phila, spl counsel transit matters 1952-63; Dilworth Paxson Kalish Levy & Coleman, partner law firm 1956-75; retained by Gov Scranton to represent Atty Gen of PA & Commonwealth of PA in litigation to remove racial restrictions at Girard Coll 1965; US Dept of Trans, sec 1975-77; SE PA Trans Auth, spl counsel 1968-; O'Melveny & Meyer, sr partner 1977-. **ORGANIZATIONS:** Dir Pan Am World Airways Inc; dir IBM; dir Pepsi Co; dir Chase Manhattan Corp; dir Amax Inc; dir CIGNA Corp; dir Philadelphia Elec Co; vice pres Philadelphia Museum of Art; chmn bd NAACP Legal Defense & Educ Fund; trustee The Rand Corp; trustee The Brookings Inst; fellow Amer Coll of Trial Lawyers; mem Trilateral Commn Council on Foreign Relations; officer French Legion of Honor; council Amer Law Inst; Amer Bar Assn; Amer Bar Assn Task Force on Judicial Admin; Philadelphia Bar Assn; DC Bar Assn; mem Amer Arbitration Assn; mem numerous public serv orgns. **HONORS/ACHIEVEMENTS:** Author co-author contributor numerous legal writings. **BUSINESS ADDRESS:** O'Melveny & Meyer, 1800 M St NW, Washington, DC 20036.

COLEMAN, WINSON
Educator. **PERSONAL:** Born Sep 10, 1905, Oskaloosa, LA; married Theodora Dugas; children: Grace Mauvene (Edwards), Winson, Edwina Elaine (clark. **EDUCATION:** Penn

Coll, BA 1928; Haverford Coll, MA 1929; Univ of Chicago, PhD 1950. **CAREER:** Johnson C Smith Univ, Charlotte NC, faculty mem 1929-, philosophy prof, 1950-74, acad dean, 1962-69; Univ of CO, visiting lecturer 1960; Quarterly Review Higher Educ Among Negroes, editor 1963-; Gen Educ Bd. **ORGANIZATIONS:** Mem Am Conf Acad Deans; Am Philos Assn; Mind Assn; Nat Educ Assn Presbyn. **HONORS/ACHIEVEMENTS:** Fellow philosophUniv Of Chicago 1947-49; Univ Fellow Philosophy 1949-50; Author of Article.

COLEMAN, WISDOM F.
Dentist. **PERSONAL:** Born Jun 20, 1944, Batesville, MS; married Veronica Freemon; children: Wisdom III, Daivd, Anthony. **EDUCATION:** Howard U, BS 1965, DDS 1969. **CAREER:** Emory Coll of Dentistry, instructor; VA Hospital, Atlanta GA, dentist 1970-71; VA Hospital St Louis, internship 1969-70. **ORGANIZATIONS:** Dental dir Memphis & Shelby Co Head Start 1974-77; exec sec Pan TN Dental Soc; pres Shelby Co Dental Soc 1974-77. **HONORS/ACHIEVEMENTS:** Dean's hon socUniv TN 1976. **BUSINESS ADDRESS:** 3087 Park Ave, Memphis, TN 38106.

COLEMON, JOHNNIE (JOHNNIE COLEMON NEDD)
Clergyman. **PERSONAL:** Born in Centerville, AL; married Don Nedd. **EDUCATION:** Wiley Coll, BA 1943, DD 1977, DHL. **CAREER:** Chicago Mkt Cntr, price analyst; Chicago Pub Schools, teacher; Christ Univ Temple, fdr; Christ Univ Temple for Better Living, pastor. **ORGANIZATIONS:** Elect pres (1st Black woman) of exec bd Unity Sch of Christianity; orgn of Univ Found for Better Living (UFBL); guest spkr Festival of Mind & Body in London, Eng; guest spkr & consult seen on radio & TV shows; mem Intl Thought Alliance; dist pres & bd of dir chrprsn 60th anniv INTA Congress; dedication of largest New Thought Church in the World 4,000 seating 1985; guest speaker AKA Boule 1986; guest speaker Prayer Breakfast Atlanta GA. **HONORS/ACHIEVEMENTS:** Tremendous "Ten Years" Unity Chicagoland Assoc 1966; Deep Appreciation of Unity Assoc of Unity Churches 1969-70; major contributions Assoc of Unity Churches1970; Golden Anniv Awd Alpha Kappa Alpha Sor 1972; Recognition Awd Serv to Humanity 1st CP Church 1972; Serv to Youth YMCA 1973; Outstndg Achvmnt in Gospel Ministry Youth for Christ 1974; Love with Sincere Appreciation Award Hillside Chapel & Truth Ctr 1974; Outstndg Christian Serv Civic Liberty League of IL1974; Women's Day Annual Black Excell Operation PUSH 1974; "The Year of the Woman" Award PUSH Found 1975; Cert of Apprec Chicago Cncl BSA 1975;Cert of Appreciation Comm Civic & Cultural Affairs 1975; Outstanding & Dedicated Serv as chairperson 60th Anniversary INTA Congress 1975; Blackbook's Humanit Awd Blackbook Bus & Ref Guide 1976; Excellence in Religion PUSH Foundation 1977; 100 Outstanding Black Women Dallas 1985; Blackbook's Par Excellence 1986; Dr Martin L King Drum Major Awd 1987; Awds and Key to the Cities Brooklyn NY, Atlanta GA, Detroit MI, Chicago IL; Candace Awd 1987; "A Woman Called Johnnie" TV Channel 2. **BUSINESS ADDRESS:** Pastor, ChristUniv Temple Better Liv, 11901 So Ashland Ave, Chicago, IL 60643.

COLES, ANNA B.
Nurse, educator. **PERSONAL:** Born Jan 16, 1925, Kansas City, KS; daughter of Alonzo Bailey and Lillie Bailey; children: 3 children. **EDUCATION:** BS, 1958; MS, 1960; PhD 1967. **CAREER:** VA Hosp, 1949-52; VA Hosp Topeka KS, tchr 1950-52; VA Hosp Kansas City MO, supr 1952-58; Freedmens Hosp, nursing admin 1960-68, asst dir 1960-61, admin asst 1961-66; Nursing Service, assoc dir 1966-67; Freedman's Hosp, dir nursing 1967-69; Howard Univ Coll of Nursing, dean 1968-86. **ORGANIZATIONS:** Mem Nurses Examining Bd; DC League Nursing; mem bd of dir Natl League for Nursing; Task Force Comm Planning Nursing DC; adv comm Visiting Nurses Assn; Amer Nurses Assn Nat Com Legislation; Health Planning Adv; Amer Assn Med Coll; Natl Urban Coalition; Natl League Nursing; Amer Congress Rehab Med; Inst Med Natl Acad Science; consult bd regents State Univ System of FL; adv council Status Health Sci Inst Serv Educ. **HOME ADDRESS:** 6841 Garfield Dr, Kansas City, KS 66102.

COLES, DARNELL
Professional athlete. **PERSONAL:** Born Jun 22, 1962, San Bernadino, CA; married Shari; children: Deanna. **CAREER:** Seattle Mariners, infielder 1983-85. **HONORS/ACHIEVEMENTS:** Named Southern CA HS Athlete of the Year 1980; M's 1st pick 6th player overall 1980.

COLES, JOHN EDWARD
Chief executive officer. **PERSONAL:** Born Jul 18, 1951, Roanoke, VA; married Jerelena Perdue; children: Caron N, Jonlyn E, John E Jr, Christin N. **EDUCATION:** TN State Univ, 1969-70; Hampton Univ, BS Bus Mgmt 1973; Golden Gate Univ,. **CAREER:** Citizens Bdgt Advsry Cmt, mem 1980-81; Consumer Crdt Cnslng of Peninsula, mem 1982 bd of educ City of Hampton, VA, mem 1982-83; A Bldrs of VA, dir1983-; People's Sav & Loan, chief exec ofcr. **ORGANIZATIONS:** Mem VA Peninsula Econ Dev Cncl 1982-; life mem NAACP, Omega Psi Phi Frat, Inc; tres Peninsula Assc for Mental Retrdtn 1982-84; pres Citizen's Boys' Clb of Hampton 1982-84; keeper of fin Omega Psi Phi Frat Zeta Omicron 1977-80. **HONORS/ACHIEVEMENTS:** Otstndg Young Men of Am Awrd 1981; Distngshd Ldrshp Awrd United Negro Clg Fund 1982; Omega Man of Yr Omega Psi Phi Frat Zeta Omicron Chptr Hampton, VA 1982. **HOME ADDRESS:** 7 Balmoral Dr, Hampton, VA 23669.

COLES, JOSEPH C.
Trustee. **PERSONAL:** Born Aug 26, 1902, South Boston, VA; married Ruth White; children: Joseph C, Jr. **EDUCATION:** Paine Coll; Howard U. **CAREER:** Bankruptcy, trustee; MI Civ Serv Comm, hearings offcr & mediat 1969-72. **ORGANIZATIONS:** Asst dir Detroit Comm on Human Rights Fdr; vchmn & mem Bd of Natl Assn of Intergroup Rel Officials; mem Bd of Nat Alumni Coun of Unit Negro Coll Fund for 10 Yrs; official Office of Price Adminstrn in WA, WW II; founder vice chmn MI Chap of Unit Negro Coll Fund; bd mem SW Gen Hosp; memexec bd of Paine Coll Natl Alumni Assn Natl Leader, Dem 30 yrs; mem ex-chmn Freedom Fund Dinner of the NAACP for 20 yrs. **HONORS/ACHIEVEMENTS:** 1st black del to St Dem Conv 1928; cited by NAACP at Natl Conv, Atlantic City for raisiing highest amount to date 1968; cited by Natl Alumni CounUnit Coll Fund at Ann Conv in New Orleans 1967; cited comm leadership Booker T Wash Bus Assn 1964; inv to White House in honor of Prime Min of Australia Pres Johnson 1964; attend Civil Rights Meet at White House Pres Johnson; mem JFK staff Natl Dem Conv 1960; consult Unit Conf of Mayor's Dept of Race Rel for several yrs; guest of Pres Truman on his train from Grand Rapids to Det, 1st black to be so honored 1948; honored at Testimonial Dinner 1974.

COLES, JOSEPH CARLYLE, JR.
Clergyman. **PERSONAL:** Born Feb 15, 1926, Washington, DC; married Geneva R Hamilton; children: Rubie G, Jocelyn D, Joseph III. **EDUCATION:** Howard Univ, BA 1947, BD 1950; NY Theol Seminary, STM 1971; MS Indus & Kittrell Coll, DD (Hon) 1974-75. **CAREER:** St Paul CME Ch Halifax VA, pastor 1949-50; Ebenezer CME Ch So Boston VA, pastor 1950-53; Lane Met CME Ch Cleveland, pastor 1953-63; Williams Inst CME Ch NY, pastor 1963-74; Amer Studies Ramapo Coll of NJ, adj lectr 1972-74; Christian Methodist Episcopal Ch, bishop 1974-. **ORGANIZATIONS:** Bd of trustees Paine Coll 1974-; pres GA Christian Council 1982-84; mem Atlanta Univ Ctr Bd of Trustees; bd of trustees Interdenominational Theol Ctr 1977-; Vice Chairman Bd of Trustees Phillips Sch of Theology 1979-; life mem NAACP; mem Alpha Phi Alpha 1952-; mem Cleveland Bd of Educ 1962-63; bd of dir S Christian Leadership Conf 1979-; Commencement Speaker MS Ind Coll 1975; Commencement Speaker Ft Valley State Coll 1976; mem US Delegation to Funeral of Golda Meir 1978; mem & pres World Methodist Council 1979-. **HONORS/ACHIEVEMENTS:** Honorary DD Interdenominational Theol Ctr 1986; Commencement Speaker Paine Coll Augusta GA 1986. **BUSINESS ADDRESS:** Christian Methodist Episcopal Church, 2001 Martin L King Dr SW, Atlanta, GA 30310.

COLES, ROBERT TRAYNHAM
Architect. **PERSONAL:** Born Aug 24, 1929, Buffalo, NY; son of George Coles and Helena Coles; married Sylvia Rose Meyn; children: Marion B, Darcy E. **EDUCATION:** MIT, MArch 1955, BArch 1953; Univ of MN, BA 1951; Hampton Inst, attended. **CAREER:** Perry Shaw Hepburn & Dean 1955-57, Shepley Bulfinch Richardson & Abbot 1957-58, Carl Koch & Assoc 1958-59, designer; Boston Architectural Ctr 1957-59, NY State Univ Coll 1967, Hampton Inst 1968-70, Univ of KS 1969, teacher; Adv Planning Assoc, assoc 1959-60; Techbuilt Inc, design mgr 1959-60; Deleuw Cather & Brill Engrs, coord architect 1960-63; Robert Traynham Coles Architect PC, pres 1963-; Amer Inst Architects, dep vice pres minority affairs 1974-75. **ORGANIZATIONS:** Fellow AIA 1981; consult Union Carbide Corp 1963; lecturer many coll & univ; treas 1975-77, vice pres 1977-79 Natl Org of Minority Architects; sec bd of dir Preservation League of NY State Inc 1976-,82; mem AIA, Comm Planning Assistance Ctr, Assoc Comm Design Devel Ctrs, NY State Assoc Architects; mayors adv com Buffalo Urban Caucus, BANC, Cit Adv Council, Goals Met Buffalo, comm Urban Univ, E Side Comm Org, Ellicott Talbert Study Comm, NY State Sub-Com US Comm Civil Rights, Com Community Improvement, Friendship House Study Comm; vice pres Buffalo Arch Guidebook Corp 1979-82; pres Amer Arch Mus & Resource Ctr 1980-82; trustee Western NY Public Broadcasting Assoc 1981-; mem NY State Bd for Architecture 1984-; commissioner, Erie County Horizons Waterfront Committee 1989-94. **HONORS/ACHIEVEMENTS:** Whitney E Young Awd AIA 1981; Outstanding Prof Achievement Urban League 1961; many scholarships; Langston Hughes Distinguished Professor of Architecture & Urban Design, Univ of Kansas 1989. **BUSINESS ADDRESS:** President, Robert Traynham Coles Arch PC, 730 Ellicot Square, Buffalo, NY 14203.

COLEY, DONALD LEE
Educator. **PERSONAL:** Born Feb 25, 1953, Baltimore, MD; son of Letell Sessoms and Emma Harrell Sessoms; married Linda Carol McNair, Jun 23, 1979; children: Natasha Shenee Coley. **EDUCATION:** St Augustine's Coll, BS (Cum Laude) 1975; East Carolina Univ, MAEd 1983. **CAREER:** Wake County Schools, teacher/coach 1975-79; Bertie Co Schools, coach/director alternative adjustment 1980-83; New York Yankees, scout 1978-. **ORGANIZATIONS:** Mem State of NC AAA Championship Basketball Team 1971; head coach of championship teams baseball 1976,78, football 1978, basketball 1980, 1982; chairperson Bertie County Youth Task Force 1981-87; mem Palestine Masonic Lodge 1982-; rep NC Extended Day Assoc 1985-87; mem NCAE, NEA 1986-87, Kiwanis Intl 1986-, NC Employment & Training Assoc 1986-; consultant/dropout prevention Weldon City Schools 1986; commentator of weekly radio program "Extended Day School Highlights"; mem NC Employment and Training Assoc; vice pres, NC Dropout Prevention Assn, 1988-; pastor, St John 2nd Baptist Church, 1987-; asst pastor, Indian Woods Baptist Church, 1988-. **HONORS/ACHIEVEMENTS:** Phi Beta Signia Scholarship 1973; Drop Prevention Leadership Exchange, NC Dept of Public Instruction, 1988; Exemplary Program in Dropout Prevention, NC State Bd of Educ. **HOME ADDRESS:** PO Box 7, Powellsville, NC 27967. **BUSINESS ADDRESS:** Bertie Co Schools, Windsor, NC 27983.

COLEY, ESTHER B.
Food service director. **PERSONAL:** Born Jun 09, 1915, Montgomery, AL; children: 2 Children. **EDUCATION:** LA Trade Tech Coll, AA 1968; LA Coll, BA. **CAREER:** School Food Serv in School Dist of CA, 1st black woman supvr 1952-66; Food Serv Willowbrook School Dist, Compton Unified School Dist, 1st black woman dir 1966-; Hunt-Wesson Foods, 1st black home economist; Ebony Magazine, wrote full-page article 4 yrs; "EBC's of Food Entertaining Around the Clock", wrote full book. **ORGANIZATIONS:** Lectures & demonstrations on food/mgmt; 1st black mem in CA Sch Food Serv Assn & 1st to hold an ofc; taught Food Mgmt & Catering for 10 yrs; mem Jack & Jill 1956-65; mem Urban League Guild; Nat Bus & Professional Women's Orgn; NAACP; Child Study Giuild; Lullaby Guild; Children's Home Soc; pres Nat Assnof Media Women 1973-74. **HONORS/ACHIEVEMENTS:** Recip LA Sentinal Woman of Yr 1952; LA Mother of Yr 1958; award for outstanding achievement in food serv, Nat Restaurant Assn 1970; award for humanitarian serv Willowbrook Bd Trustees; award for serv LA Boys Club; woman of yr LA Media 1971; award for achievement serv Boys Market. **BUSINESS ADDRESS:** 1623 E 118 St, Los Angeles, CA 90059.

COLEY, GERALD SYDNEY
Physician. **PERSONAL:** Born Jan 23, 1914, St Elizabeth, Jamaica. **EDUCATION:** Dillard Univ, New Orleans, LA; Howard Univ, BS 1950; Univ of Berne, Switzerland, grad 1960. **CAREER:** Govt Med Serv, physician; private practice, physician 1965-. **ORGANIZATIONS:** Past pres Med Assn of Jamaica 1972; mem Rotary Club of Montego Bay; past master English Free Mason 1973. **BUSINESS ADDRESS:** 38 Bernett St, Montego Bay, Jamaica.

COLIN, GEORGE H.
Business executive. **PERSONAL:** Born Apr 15, Cleveland, OH. **EDUCATION:** Coll Conservatory of Music Cincinnati, Mus B; Temple Bible Coll, AB; Miami U, AM; Temple Bible Coll & Sem, SMD. **CAREER:** Geo H Colin Mortuary, owner; Cincinnati, min music 22 yrs; Cincinnati, tchr music 15 yrs. **ORGANIZATIONS:** Pres Buckeye State Funeral Dirs & Embalmers Assn; bd dirs NAACP & Cincinnati Br; trustee Temple Bible Coll; bd mem Small Business Found Cincinnati; mem Phi Mu Alpha Frat; Hamilton Co Black Caucus;

Amer Guild of Organists; Local, State, & Natl Funeral Dirs Assn. **HONORS/ACHIEVEMENTS:** Recip Hon Dr of Music 1962. **MILITARY SERVICE:** AUS sp4.

COLLEY, NATHANIEL S.
Student, organization executive. **PERSONAL:** Born Jun 08, 1956, Sacramento; married Toni Denise Conner; children: Jasmine Nicole, Aishah Simone. **EDUCATION:** Univ MI, BA 1977; Univ MI Law Sch, JD 1979. **CAREER:** Colley-Lindsey & Colley, partner 1980; Sextus Prods(Entertainment), partner 1974-; WCBN-FM Ann Arbor MI, gen mgr 1979, prog dir 1978, talk show host 1976-78, disc jockey 1974-76. **ORGANIZATIONS:** Admitted to CA Bar 1980; Am Legion Boy's State CA 1973; CA Youth Senate 1973; memUniv MI Assn of Black Communicators 1974; vice pres Sacramento NAACP Youth Council 1973-74; mem natl bd dirs NAACP 1972-75; mem Black Music Assn 1979-. **HONORS/ACHIEVEMENTS:** Nat Merit Scholarship Finalist 1974. **BUSINESS ADDRESS:** 1810 South St, Sacramento, CA 95814.

COLLIE, KELSEY E.
Educator, playwright, talent agent. **PERSONAL:** Born Feb 21, 1935, Miami; son of James G Collie and Elizabeth Moxey Collie; divorced; children: Kim Denyse, Vaughn Hayse. **EDUCATION:** Hampton Inst, AB 1967; George Washington Univ, MFA 1970; Howard Univ, PhD. **CAREER:** Library of Congress, accessioner & documents librarian 1960-70; Coll of Fine Arts Drama Dept, prof, asst dean 1976-79; Kelsey E Collie Playmakers Repertory Co, artistic dir 1976-; Diva Productions, artistic dir 1986-; Howard Univ Children's Theatre, playwright; Kelsey E Collie Talent Assoc, talent mgr; Howard Univ, prof of drama 1973-. **ORGANIZATIONS:** Bd dir Pierce Warwick Adoption Serv 1973-; mem Amer Community Theatre Assn 1977-; pres Washington Theatre Arts Productions Inc 1980-; mem Artist-in-Educ Panel DC Commission on the Arts 1983-; mem Amer Council on the Arts 1985; mem Black Theatre Network 1986-. **HONORS/ACHIEVEMENTS:** Community Serv Award, Salisbury Cultural Arts Comm, 1978; Distinguished Serv Award, Univ Without Walls, 1980; Coalition of Professional Youth on the Move Award, 1981; appreciation award, Syphax School, Washington DC, 1989; director, Night of the Divas: Tribute to Marian Anderson, J F Kennedy Center, 1985. **MILITARY SERVICE:** AUS Sp4 1958-60. **HOME ADDRESS:** 2236 R St, NE, Washington, DC 20002. **BUSINESS ADDRESS:** Professor, Howard University, Drama Department, Washington, DC 20059.

COLLIER, ALBERT, III
Educator. **PERSONAL:** Born Jul 26, 1926, Newark, NJ; married Juanita Malia Augustono; children: Albert IV, Byron Joel. **EDUCATION:** Howard Univ, BA, 1951; Seton Hall Univ, MA 1956; Teachers Coll Columbia Univ, Prof's Diploma, 1961. **CAREER:** Friendly Neighborhood House, NJ, Groupleader, 1951-54; Cleveland Jr HS NJ, teacher, 1954-62; Somerset Public Schools NJ, dir special educ, 1963-66; Orange Public Schools NJ, dir spec serv 1967-70; Piscataway NJ, admn asst pupil personnel, 1970-75, asst supt schools 1975-. **ORGANIZATIONS:** NJEA; NEA; Amer Personnel & Guidance Assoc; NJ Assoc Pupil Personnel Admn; Council For Exceptional Children; Intern Assn Pupil Personnel Admin; Phi Delta Kappa; trustee Kean Coll NJ 1973-79; Bd of Educ, Highland Pk NJ 1969-72; pres NJ Assc Pupil Personal Admin 1980-82; mem Salvation Army, Urban League, Mental Health Alpha Phi Alpha Frat. **HONORS/ACHIEVEMENTS:** NDEA Fellow Columbia Univ Teachers Coll, 1960-61. **MILITARY SERVICE:** USN. **BUSINESS ADDRESS:** Assistant Superintendent, Piscataway Public Schools, Willow Ave & Scott St, Piscataway, NJ 08854.

COLLIER, CLARENCE MARIE
Educator. **PERSONAL:** Born in St Francisville, LA. **EDUCATION:** Southern Univ, BS; Tuskegee Inst, MS; Louisiana State Univ, MS; Grambling State Univ; New York Univ System. **CAREER:** Southern Univ, vice pres; Teacher Corps Program, admin; Parish School System, elementary principal, supvr of educ. **ORGANIZATIONS:** Mem Assn of Supr & Curriculum Devel; Phi Delta Kappa; NEA; Louisiana Educ Assn; Natl Alliance of Black School Educators; Amer Council on Educ; Natl Assn of Women Deans, Administrators, & Counselors; SW Assn of Student Personnel; admin co-chmn Louisiana Commn on Observance of Intl Women's Yr; Delta Sigma Theta; State & Natl Women's Political Caucus; Leauge of Women Voters; Women in Politics; Natl Council of Negro Women; Comm Assn for Welfare of Sch Children; bd of dir YWCA. **HONORS/ACHIEVEMENTS:** Operation Upgrade Advancement of Women Award Natl Orgn for Women; Arts & Letters Award Delta Sigma Theta Inc; Certificate of Merit Gov of Louisiana; Certificate of Recognition E Baton Rouge City Parish Council; cit of outstanding contrib to educ Prince Hall Masons. **BUSINESS ADDRESS:** SouthernUniv, Baton Rouge, LA 70813.

COLLIER, EUGENIA W.
Educator. **PERSONAL:** Born Apr 06, 1928, Baltimore, MD; daughter of H Maceo Williams and Eugenia Jackson Williams; divorced; children: Charles Maceo, Robert Nelson, Philip Gilles. **EDUCATION:** Univ of MD, PhD 1976; Coll Univ, MA 1950; Howard Univ, BA (Magna Cum Laude) 1948. **CAREER:** Balt Dept of Public Welfare, case worker 1950-55; Morgan State Univ, asst prof 1955-66; Comm Coll of Baltimore, prof 1966-74; So IL Univ, visiting prof 1970; Atlanta Univ, visiting prof 1974; Univ of MD, assoc prof 1974-77; Howard Univ, assoc prof 1977-87; Coppin State Coll, prof, 1987-. **ORGANIZATIONS:** Chmn Assn for the Study of Negro Life & History 1966; chmn Coll Language Assoc 1969; consult Workshop of Center for African & Afro-Amer Studies 1969; consultant Call & Response Workshop at Karamu House 1970; mem Middle St Evaluation Team for Lehigh Comm Coll 1970; consultant Black Studies Comm Coll Lang Assoc Pine Manor Jr Coll 1970; elect to comm Coll of Baltimore Sen Exec Comm 1970; attended meeting of Coll Language Assn 1971, So Amer Studies Assn 1972; comment for session at meeting of Center for African & Afro-Amer Studies 1972; consultant at Bond Human Fair 1973-74; recording sec Comm Coll of Baltimore Sen Exec C; lecture on TV in series "The Negro in History" Morgan State Univ. **HONORS/ACHIEVEMENTS:** Gwendolyn Brooks Award for Fiction 1969; Outstanding Educ of Amer 1972-75; creative prod TV Series on Black Amer Folklore; published numerous books. **BUSINESS ADDRESS:** Professor of English, Coppin State College, 2500 W North Avenue, Baltimore, MD 21216.

COLLIER, H. M., JR.
Physician. **PERSONAL:** Born Aug 07, 1916, Savannah; married Mozella B Gaither; children: Vincent L, Roberle E, Henry M. **EDUCATION:** Savannah State Coll, 1935; Meharry Med Coll, MD 1942. **CAREER:** Savannah, pvt pract med 1943-; St Josephs Hosp Warren A Chandler Hosp, staff. **ORGANIZATIONS:** Pres bd dirs William A Harris Hosp & Nurs Home; exec vice pres Savannah State Coll Nat Assn; chmn Savannah State Coll Fndtn 1973-; trustee YMCA; mem AMA. **HONORS/ACHIEVEMENTS:** GA med soc fellow, Am Soc Abdominal Surgs; recipient silver beaver awd Boy Scouts of Am 1970; recipient greene awd, meritorious serv So Region Alpha Phi Alpha Frat Inc 1976; recipient man of yr Mutual Benevolent Soc Inc 1977. **MILITARY SERVICE:** USAF 1952-55. **BUSINESS ADDRESS:** 900 W Broad St, Savannah, GA 31401.

COLLIER, JULIA MARIE
Administrative faculty. **PERSONAL:** Born Aug 23, 0949, Athens, AL; daughter of John Robert Collier Sr and Louise Bluford Collier. **EDUCATION:** Berea Coll, BA 1971; Temple Univ, MEd 1973; Eastern KY Univ, MA 1979. **CAREER:** Ministry of Educ, faculty 1973-76; Manchester Coll, faculty 1978-79; Franklin Wright Settlement, admin coord 1979-80; Aldine Independent Sch Dist, counselor 1980-83; Kennesaw Coll, asst dir of admissions. **ORGANIZATIONS:** Comm mem Southern Assoc of Collegiate Registrar & Admission Offices 1985; conference presenter Southern Assoc of Collegiate Registrar & Admission Offices 1986-87; workshop presenter ELS Language Ctr 1986; comm mem GA Educ Articulation Comm 1987-89; chmn, Georgia Assn for Foreign Student Affairs, 1989-90; bd mem, ELS Language Center. **HONORS/ACHIEVEMENTS:** Outstanding New Professional, Georgia Assn for Collegiate Registrars & Admissions Officers 1988. **BUSINESS ADDRESS:** Asst Dir of Admissions, Kennesaw College, PO Box 444, Marietta, GA 30061.

COLLIER, LOUIS MALCOLM
Educator. **PERSONAL:** Born May 19, 1919, Little Rock, AR; son of Albert Collier and Ludia Lewis Collier; married Pearlie B May Collier; children: James Bernard, Irving Orlando, Albert Jerome, Phillip Louis, Eric Wayne. **EDUCATION:** Grambling State Univ, BS 1954; OK State Univ, MS 1960; Cornell Univ, postgraduate 1961; OK State Univ, 1962-64. **CAREER:** Central HS Calhoun LA, teacher, chmn Science & Math dept 1955-62; So Univ, instructor Physic & Math 1962-65; Grambling Coll, instructor of Phys & Chem 1966-67; Hopewell HS Dubach LA, chmn Sci & Math dept; So Univ, assoc prof phys, chmn of dept 1967-75; So Univ Shreveport, chmn Physics 1975-; Caddo Parish School Bd, Shreveport, LA, pres, 1986. **ORGANIZATIONS:** Exec bd mem Amer Inst Physics; pres Ouachita Ed Assoc; dir 8th Dist LA Acad Sci; 2yr coll rep Natl Council Teachers of Math; mem Shreveport Cof C, Shreveport Negro Chamber of Commerce, LA Ed Assoc, Amer Assoc of Univ Prof, AAAS; exec bd mem, sec YMCA 1972; mem Kiwanis Club 1974; chmn advisory bd Caddo Parish School Bd 1974; vice pres Newton Smith PTA 1973; pres Cooper Rd Health Club 1973; bd mem Caddo Parish School Bd 1980-86; deacon, trustee Little Union BC 1973-; AARP, Minority Affairs, spokesperson, 1986-; State Leadership Team Forla-AARP, 1988-. **HONORS/ACHIEVEMENTS:** Science Educ Leadership Award LA Educ Assoc 1973; Selected by Gov of LA to serve as 1st & only Afro-Amer mem of LA Sci Found Bd; Teacher of the Year Freedom Found 1962; Shell Merit Fellowship Award Stanford Univ 1962; Ed Leadership Award LA Ed Assoc 1973; Outstanding Club Leadership Award N Shreveport Kiwanis Club 1975; Comm Leadership & Serv Award 1975; Comm Serv Awd Phi Beta Sigma Frat 1976; Leadership Awd Caddo Ed Assoc & Caddo Teachers Assoc 1977; Distinguished Serv Award, Gulf Coast Region (LA & TX) IBE, Phi Beta Sigma Fraternity, Inc, 1978; Distinguished Educ Award, Gulf Coast Region (LA & TX); Phi Delta Kappa, membership, 1987. **MILITARY SERVICE:** Sgt WWII. **BUSINESS ADDRESS:** Chairman, Physics Department, SouthernUniv, 3050 Cooper Rd, Shreveport, LA 71107.

COLLIER, TORRENCE JUNIS
Physician. **PERSONAL:** Born Sep 03, 1932, Texarkana, AR; married Gisele. **EDUCATION:** Morehouse, BS; Meharry, MD; Harvard, MPH. **CAREER:** Schering Plough Pharm Corp, dir, med liaison ; Preventive Med NY Med Coll, instr 1963. **ORGANIZATIONS:** Mem Drug Info Assn; Mental Hlth Assn; Meaning of Global Econ to Western Econ & Culture; past mem NMA; mem Urban League; Human Rights Commn; Adv Youth Rec Ctr; need for differentiated self-acknowledged & implemented role of black lawyers in pvt prac especially to "Get Down" & become accessible; mem Politics of Hlth Care. **HONORS/ACHIEVEMENTS:** Hon grades Morehouse; Harvard; Brook Army Med Ctr 1957; RooseveltUniv 1948-49; Sorbonne 1960. **MILITARY SERVICE:** AUS 1957-61.

COLLIER, TROY
Educator. **PERSONAL:** Born Apr 19, 1941, Nacogdoches, TX; married Claudette Liggns. **EDUCATION:** Phoenix Coll, AABus Adminstrn 1962; UT State U, BS Social Work 1964; S Meth U, MLA 1971; Nova U, Sutd Toward PhD. **CAREER:** Univ of Southern FL, asst to vice pres for sudent affairs; Clearfield Job Corps Center, res life counselor 1969-71; Youth Programs Coord & Neighborhood, organizer supvr 1968-69; City of Pheonix AR, youth programs coord & neighborhood organizer, supvr 1967-68; Harlem Globetrotters Basketball Team, professional basketball player 1964-67. **ORGANIZATIONS:** Bd of dir DACCO; mem Citizens Adv Com, Hillsborough Co Sch Bd; Am Civil Liberties Union, State Bd & Tampa Chpt; bd mem Nat Assn Human Rights Workers; So Assn Black Adminstr; Am Assn Affirmative Action; Tampa Urban League; NAACP; Tampa-Hillsborough Manpower Council. **BUSINESS ADDRESS:** 4202 Fowler, Tampa, FL 33620.

COLLIER, WILLYE
Educator. **PERSONAL:** Born Sep 26, 1922, Hattiesburg, MS; married Cisero. **EDUCATION:** Tuskegee Inst, BS 1943; John AAMHosp Tuskegee Inst, intern 1944; Univ of WI, MS 1946. **CAREER:** Bakersfield Coll, prof Food & Nutrition 1964-; San Luis Obispo City Schools, teacher 1960-64; Los Angeles Paso Robles & San Luis Obispo, consult diet 1956-57; Southern Univ, dir dietetics 1949-56; SC Public Schools, home economics teacher 1946-49. **ORGANIZATIONS:** Chmn Home Econ Dept Benedict Coll; Liasion Rep, Home Con Assn to CA Tchrs Assn/NEA; mem Amer Dietetic Assn; mem Amer Pub Hlth Assn; mem Amer Home Econ Assn; Intnl Fed of Home Econ; chmn bd Kern County Hlth Assn 1976-; chmn Nut Com KC Heart Assn 1970-76; mem of the Bd Kern Co MentHlth Assn 1974-80, organizer, pres 1977-79; chmn of bd Kem Co Mental Hlth Assn 1980-81; Links of Bakersfield 1977; mem NAACP; Basileus, Gamma Alpha Sigma Chap Sigma Gamma Rho Inc, 1976-78. **HONORS/ACHIEVEMENTS:** Who award CA Higher Educ 1976; sigma of the yr Sigma Gamma Rho Sor 1975; outstanding Contrib Kern County Heart Assn 1974. **BUSINESS ADDRESS:** 1801 Panorama Dr, Bakersfield, CA 93305.

COLLINS, BARBARA ROSE
City official. **PERSONAL:** Born Apr 13, 1939, Detroit, MI; widowed; children: Cynthia, Christopher. **EDUCATION:** Attended Wayne State Univ. **CAREER:** Wayne State Univ, business mgr, physics dept, 9 yrs, office asst in equal opportunity office, neighborhood relations; Detroit School Region I, bd mem 1970-73; House of Rep 21st Dist of Detroit, legislator

1974-82; City of Detroit, councilwoman 1982-. **ORGANIZATIONS:** Regional coord Michigan, Ohio Natl Black Caucus of Local Elected Officials 1985; trustee Michigan Municipal League 1985; bd mem Comprehensive Health Planning Council of Southeastern Michigan 1985; trustee Intl Afro-Amer Museum; chairperson Region I Political Action Comm; mem City-Wide Citizens Action Council, Democratic Party, ACLU, League of Women Voters, Amer for Democratic Action, Kenyatta Homeowners & Tenants Assoc, Black Teachers Caucus, Black Parents for Quality Educ, Inner-City Parents Council, Natl Order of Women Legislators; bd mem Detroit Black United Fund; mem Special Comm on Affirmative Action, Shrine of the Black Madonna Church, IWY State Coord Comm Natl Intl Women's Year Comm, Michigan Delegate to IWY Convention; chairperson Constl Revision & Women's Rights Comm; principal sponsor of bills which were later passed, including The Food Dating Bill, The Sex Educ Bill, The Pregnancy Insurance Bill; past mem Detroit Human Rights Comm; regional dir Natl Black Caucus of Local Elected Officials. **HONORS/ACHIEVEMENTS:** Feminist of the Year Awd, 1977; featured in "How Michigan Women Make It Happen," Redbook Mag, 1978; Woman of the Year Awd, Eta Phi Beta Sor Inc, Eta Lambda Zeta Chap, 1979; Invaluable Serv, Pershing High School, Detroit Public Schools, 1985; Devoted Serv, Metro Boy Scouts of Amer, 1984; Valuable Serv, Intl Freedom Festival, 1983; Distinguished Serv, Shrine of the Black Madonna Pan African Orthodox Christian Church, 1981. **BUSINESS ADDRESS:** Councilwoman, City of Detroit, 1340 City County Bldg, Detroit, MI 48226.

COLLINS, BERNICE ELAINE
Circus performer. **PERSONAL:** Born Oct 24, 1957, Kansas City, KS; daughter of William H Collins and Wanda Coby Collins. **EDUCATION:** Ringling Brothers Barnum Bailey Clown Coll, Diploma 1977; Transworld Travel Coll, Kansas City, KS, Diploma 1985. **CAREER:** Dr's Office, receptionist 1975-77; Ringling Brothers Barnum Bailey Circus, clown 1978-79, dancer/showgirl 1980-84, apprentice tiger trainer 1983; Trans World Airlines,Intl flight attendent 85-86; Kansas City Riverboat, entertainer/asst mgr; Kansas City Riverboat, Kansas City, MO, singer/asst mgr 1986-87; Ringling Brothers Barnum & Baily Circus, dancer/showgirl 1988-. **HONORS/ACHIEVEMENTS:** Gold Key Awards HS Art Award 1974-75; 1st black woman clown Ringling Brothers Barnum & Bailey Circus 1978, 1st black woman tiger Trainer 1983. **HOME ADDRESS:** 3507 Oak Ave, Kansas City, KS 66104.

COLLINS, BERT
Insurance executive. **PERSONAL:** Born Nov 09, 1934, Austin, TX; married Carolyn Porter; children: Suane, Carolyn Collins Suggs, Bert. **EDUCATION:** Huston-Tillotson Coll, BS Bus Admin 1955; Univ of Detroit, MBA 1959; North Carolina Central Univ Law School, JD 1970; Univ of North Carolina-Chapel Hill, Young Exec Prog. **CAREER:** Sidney A Sumby Meml Hosp, chief accountant 1956-61; Austin Washington & Davenport CPA's, sr staff accountant 1962-67; North Carolina Mutual Life Insurance Co, admin asst 1967, asst vice pres, official staff 1970, elected vice pres, controller 1974, bd dir, exec comm 1978, finance comm 1979, sr vice pres, controller 1982, sr vice pres, admin 1983, appointed chmn of securities comm 1983, chmn field comm 1986, exec vice pres, COO 1987-. **ORGANIZATIONS:** Mem, Durham Rotary Club, Kappa Alpha Psi, Sigma Pi Phi Boule'; vice chmn, bd dir, First Church of Christ Scientist; mem, Michigan Assn of CPA's, North Carolina Assn of CPA's, Amer Inst of CPA's, Amer Bar Assn, North Carolina State Bar, George White Bar Assn; vice chmn, bd dir, exec comm NCM Capital Mgmt Group Inc; bd dir, Amer Citizens Life Insurance Co; business advisory council, School of Business, North Carolina Central Univ; mem, Durham Comm on the Affairs of Black People, Durham Business & Professional Chain, Durham Chamber of Commerce; bd dir, treas, former pres, State Easter Seal Soc; exec comm, bd dir, Mutual Savings & Loan Assn; bd dir, United Durham Inc; advisory bd, North Carolina Central Univ Law School; bd dir, Kate B Reynolds Found; advisory bd, Duke Univ NC Business; bd dir, NC Amateur Sports; chairman, RDU-Intl Airport; bd mem, Africa News; appointed to Bd of Arts and Humanities (NC). **BUSINESS ADDRESS:** Exec VP, COO, North Carolina Mutual Insurance Co, 411 W Chapel Hill St, Durham, NC 27701.

COLLINS, BONIETHA INEZ
Executive director. **PERSONAL:** Born Jul 06, 1961, Chicago, IL. **EDUCATION:** Drake Univ, BA Public Admin 1983; Univ of IL-Chicago Graduate Sch, attended 1985. **CAREER:** United States Senate Alan J Dixon (IL), project specialist 1982-86; IL Assoc of Housing Authorities, exec dir. **ORGANIZATIONS:** Mem Natl Political Caucus Black Women, Executives' Club of Chicago, Metropolitan Bd of Chicago Urban League. **HONORS/ACHIEVEMENTS:** Outstanding Student Awd Drake Univ 1982; Youngest First Black Female to Head IL Assoc of Housing Authorities 1986.

COLLINS, CARDISS
US congresswoman. **PERSONAL:** Born Sep 24, 1931, St Louis; married George Collins (deceased); children: Kevin. **EDUCATION:** Northwestern Univ, grad 1967. **CAREER:** IL Dept of Revenue, revenue auditor; House of Representatives, mem 93rd 98th congresses from 7th IL Dist. **ORGANIZATIONS:** Mem, Comm on Govt Ops, Subcomms on manpower and housing, energy & commerce comm, subcom on telecommunications; mem, House Select Comm Drug Abuse & Control; past chairwoman Mems of Congress for Peace through Law Subcomm on Africa; chairwoman Congressional Black Caucus; Democratic committeewoman 24th Ward Chicago;mem NAACP, Chicago Urban League, Natl Cncl Negro Women, Natl Women's Political Caucus, Alpha Kappa Alpha (hon). **BUSINESS ADDRESS:** Congresswoman, House of Representatives, 2264 Rayburn House Office Bldg, Washington, DC 20515.

COLLINS, CARTER H.
Educator. **PERSONAL:** Born Mar 13, 1928, Torresdale, PA. **EDUCATION:** Amer Univ, EdD 1972; Georgetown Univ, doctoral studies 1960; Univ de las Americas, MA 1958; LaSalle Coll, BA 1953. **CAREER:** Washington DC & Philadelphia PA, tchr 5 yrs; USIA, cultural affairs & educ 3 yrs; State/AID, intl relations officer 2 yrs; CSA, prog mgmt, formulation, evalation, presentation, supervision 7 yrs. **ORGANIZATIONS:** Vice pres Paul Jr HS Adv Council; consult Brightwood Elem Sch Parent Council; proj officer SW Educ Devel Lab; Educ Equity Officer. **HONORS/ACHIEVEMENTS:** Govt Career Serv Award; Rotary Scholarship; produced or contributed numerous govt reports, papers, training manuals, audio-visual packages.

COLLINS, CHARLES MILLER
Real estate executive. **PERSONAL:** Born Nov 22, 1947, San Francisco, CA; son of Dr Daniel A Collins and Mrs Daniel A Collins; married Paula Robinson; children: Sara, Julia. **EDUCATION:** Williams Coll, BA (w/Honors) 1969; Certificate 1971; MIT, MCP 1973; Harvard Law School, JD 1976. **CAREER:** Private law practice, attorney 1976-79; State of California, deputy sec business 1980-82; WD6 Ventures Ltd, managing general partner 1987-89; Western Develop Group Inc, owner/principal 1982-; Pres, WDG Ventures, Inc. 1989-. **ORGANIZATIONS:** Trustee Howard Thurman Educ Trust 1976-; mem Alpha Phi Alpha, Sigma Pi Phi; trustee, Natl Urban League 1989-. **HONORS/ACHIEVEMENTS:** Thomas J Watson Foundation Fellowship 1969-71. **BUSINESS ADDRESS:** Western Development Group Inc, 3 Lagoon Dr Ste 250, Redwood City, CA 94065.

COLLINS, CONSTANCE RENEE WILSON
Executive director. **PERSONAL:** Born Nov 25, 1932, New York, NY; married Alphonzo S; children: Michael Alan, Tonilyn. **EDUCATION:** Skidmore Univ 1975; Harvard U, MEd 1979. **CAREER:** CT United Labor Agency of New Britain, exec dir 1982-87; Poor People's Fedn Inc, exec dir 1972-80; Silver Strands System Inc Consult Firm, dir of Adminstrn 1976-80; Arsenal Devel Corp, asso dir 1969- 72; United & Elec Workers of Am Local 207, pres 1965-69. **ORGANIZATIONS:** Alderman City of New Britian 1969-75; bd of advs Burrit Bank of New Britain Ct 1975-80; dir City Plan Commn 1978-80; grand dist dep IBPO of Elks of the World 1961-80; natl bd mem Opportunites Indsl Ctrs of Am 1972-80; organizer bd chmn OIC of New Britain, CT 1976-80; alderman City of New Britain1985-. **HONORS/ACHIEVEMENTS:** Recipient Dedication Award for Serv Bd & Staff Poor People's Fedn Inc 1974; Torch Bearer Award OIC's of Am 1976; Martin Luther King Comm Serv Award MLK Monument Com 1977; Elk of the Yr Award; New Eng Sts & Eastern Canada Assn IBPOE of W 1979; Outstanding Woman of the Year Awd State of CT Gov Ella Grasso 1979; Leader of the Month of Greater Hartford CT Mutual Ins Co 1979; One of CT Outstaning Woman in Labor CT Historial Cos 1984. **BUSINESS ADDRESS:** Executive Dir, CT United Labor Agency, 272 Main St, Ste 302, New Britain, CT 06051.

COLLINS, CORENE
Government administrator. **PERSONAL:** Born Apr 20, 1948; married Tony Collins; children: Craig, Kisten. **EDUCATION:** FL A&M Univ, BA Sociology/Criminology 1970; Rutgers Univ, MA Criminal Justice Admin (Outstanding Thesis). **CAREER:** Youth Serv Bureau East Orange NJ, dir 1974-78; United Way Comm Plnng & Devel Newark NJ, dir 1978-80; Div of Comm Serv Tampa FL, dep dir 1981-85; Divof Cultural Serv Hillsborough Cty, dir. **ORGANIZATIONS:** Exec dir volunteer Oper PUSH 1977-79; producer & host volunteer Black Spectrum TV Show 1978-79; public relations coord & newsletter co-editor Tampa Org of Black Affairs 1980-84; pres Tampa Bay Investment Club 1982-85; mem Natl Forum for Black Publ Admin, Tampa Chamber of Commerce Govt Comm; bd mem, Amer Cancer Society. **HONORS/ACHIEVEMENTS:** Natl PUSH Awd for Outstanding Chap Devel 1978; Outstanding Young Woman of Amer 1979; Selected 1 of 33 Women Achievers Tampa Tribune Newspaper 1982; Selected Minority Woman of the Year Zeta Phi Beta Sor 1984; Up and Comers Awd- price waterhouse. **HOME ADDRESS:** 4708 Soap Stone Dr, Tampa, FL 33615. **BUSINESS ADDRESS:** Dir, Hillsborough County, Division of Cultural Services, P O Box 1110, Tampa, FL 33601.

COLLINS, CORNELIA FAYE
Social worker. **PERSONAL:** Born Sep 30, 1963, Ennis, TX; daughter of Virgil L Collins, Sr. **EDUCATION:** Texas Woman's Univ, B Social Work 1985. **CAREER:** Federal Correctional Inst Seagoville TX, correctional intern 1984; TX Woman's Univ Police and Safety, student police aid 1985; Martin Luther King Jr Comm Ctr, social worker intern 1985; Big Brothers & Sisters of Metro Dallas, caseworker 1986-. **ORGANIZATIONS:** Mem Young Democrats TWU campus 1982-83; mem NAACP TWU Campus 1982-85; mem Alpha Omega Social Club TWU 1983-84; mem Delta Sigma Theta Sor Inc 1983-; mem Social Sciences Soc TWU Campus 1985; mem Natl Assoc of Social Workers 1985-88, Natl Assoc of Black Social Workers 1985-. **HONORS/ACHIEVEMENTS:** Natl Dean's List 1985-86; Outstanding Young Woman of Amer 1986. **HOME ADDRESS:** 805 E Arnold St, Ennis, TX 75119.

COLLINS, DAISY G.
Administrative judge. **PERSONAL:** Born Feb 05, 1937, Butler, AL; daughter of Booker T Collins Sr (deceased) and Luevinia Mitchell Collins; divorced. **EDUCATION:** OH State Univ, Acct major, 1955-58, BS Business Admin (cum laude) 1958; Howard Univ Sch of Law, Juris Dr (cum laude) 1970. **CAREER:** General Foods Corp, white Plains ost & bdgt anal 1964-66; N MS Rural Legal Serv Greenwood, stf atty 1970-71; OH Turnpike Comm, asst gen cnsl & stflwyr 1973-74; No Dist of OH, asst us atty 1975-77; Capital Univ Law Sch, vis assc prof of law 1981-82; Priv Prac of Law, atty at law; Equal Employment Oppor Commn Cleveland Dist Office, administrative judge 1986-. **ORGANIZATIONS:** Student asst to asst legal advisor, US State Dept, African Affairs, 1969; acct, City of Detroit, 1960-64; mgmt trainee, Commonwealth Edison Co, Chicago, 1958-60; part-time instructor, Business Law & Acct, Cleveland State Univ & Cuy CC; exec sec Cleveland Branch NAACP 1979-80; trustee Second Calvary Missionary Baptist Church, 1975-85; former trustee, Legal Aid Soc of Cleveland 1976-81; mem Ohio State Bar Assn, NS Mnr Bar Assn, Natl Bar Assn, Cleveland Women Lawyers Assn, Alpha Kappa Alpha Sor, NAACP. **HONORS/ACHIEVEMENTS:** Hon Mention, Cleveland Federal Exec Bd for Community Service, 1976; Cleveland Bar Assn Meritorious Serv Awards, 1972-73; Six Am Jurisprudence Awds for Exc Achievement; articles published in Howard Law Journal & Crnt Bibliography of African Affairs; HLJ Notes Editor Apprciation Award Law Journal Notes Editor 1970; Beta Gamma Sigma Natl Comr Hon 1956; Beta Alpha Psi; Phi Chi Theta Scholarship Key Most Outstanding Grad Woman Coll C & Admin. **HOME ADDRESS:** 12501 Brooklawn Ave, Cleveland, OH 44111.

COLLINS, DANIEL A.
Business executive, dentist. **PERSONAL:** Born Jan 11, 1916, Darlington, SC; married DeReath C James; children: Daniel Jr, Edward J, Charles M, Craig S. **EDUCATION:** Paine Coll Augusta, GA, AB 1936; Meharry Med Coll Nashville, TN, DDS 1941; Univ of CA, MS Dentistry 1944; Guggenheim Dental Clinic NYC, Cert in Chldrns Dentistry 1941; Armed Forces Inst of Pathlogy, Cert 1958; Am bd of Oral Pathology, Diplomat 1958. **CAREER:** Bay Area Dental Prac Coll of Dentistry Univ of CA, research asst/research fellow/instructor/asst prof 1942-60; Comprehensive Dental Hlth Care Project Mt Zion Hosp, co-dir; Div of Urban Educ San Fran Ofc Harcourt Brace Jovanovich New York, NY, pres. **ORGANIZATIONS:** Mem Am Dental Assn; Nat Dental Assn; Omicron Kappa Upsillon; Sigma Chi Iota; House of Delegates CA State Dental Assn; Am Acad of Oral Pathology; dental staff Mt Zion Hosp San Fran, CA; Intl Assn of Pathology; La Fed Dentaire Intl; The Royal Soc of Hlth; lecturer/clinician Univ of CA Dental Coll Alumni Assn; CA State Dental Assn; Meharry Med Coll; Howard U; Georgetown U; Stanford Med Coll; Annual Convention of ADA

& NDA; bd of dir San Fran Dental Soc; bd of trustees Meharry Med Coll; bd of dir Paine Coll; bd of dir Golden Gate U; World Coll West; fellow Intl Coll of Dentists; Fellow Am Assn for the Advancement of Sci; trustee Am Fund for Dental Edn; founder Oral-Facial Consultative Svc; founder & sec Beneficial Savings & Loan Assn; dir Harcourt Brace Jovanovich Inc; dir Natomas Co; consult chmn Harcourt Brace Jovanovich; Western Devel Group Inc; partner San Fran Airport Parking Group. **HONORS/ACHIEVEMENTS:** Citation of Merit Paine Coll; Disting Alumni Award United Negro Coll Fund; Alumnus of the Yr Meharry Med Coll; Cited Am Men of Sci; Disting Serv in Trusteeship Award The Assn of Governing Bds of Univ & Coll. **MILITARY SERVICE:** USAR Armed Forces Inst of Pathology lt col Honorable Discharge 1958.

COLLINS, DOROTHY LEE
Educator. **PERSONAL:** Born Jan 19, 1932, Nacogdoches, TX; married Samuel M Prin. **EDUCATION:** TX So U, 1952; Our Lady of the Lake U, MEd 1973; Trinity U, postgrad 1976-77. **CAREER:** Las Palmas Elementary School San Antonio; Edgewood Independent School Dist, prin 1973; jr high school, counselor 1971-73; Edgewood Independent School Dist, elementary teacher 1957-71. **ORGANIZATIONS:** Mem TX State Tchrs Assn/Nat Educ Assn 1966-; TX Elem Prins Assn 1973-; vice pres San Antonio Leag of Bus & Professional Women Inc 1971-76; mem State Bd ofExam for Tchr Educ 1975-77; adv bd educ dept Our Lady of Lake Univ 1976-77; Nat Educ Assn Task Force on Testing 1972-75; pres Edgewood Classroom Tchrs Assn 1969-71; pres Edgewood Admin & Servs Personnel Assn 1976-77; exec com TX State Tchrs Assn 1971-77; life mem Nat Council of Negro Women Inc 1979; vice pres San Antonio Chap Our Lady of the Lake Univ Alumni Asn 1979-80; chmn TX Educ Agency Tchr Educ Evaluation Team Visit to Hardin-Simmons Univ Abilene 1979; treas Dist XX TX Elem Prin & Supr Assn 1980-81; mem exec com United Negro Coll Fund Inc 1980-; bd of dir Young & Women Christian Assn 1966-69;Ella Austine Comm Ctr 1969-77; adv bd Edgewood ISD 1970-75; rep proj area com San Antonio Devel Agency 1973-78; bd of dir Bexar Co Opptys Indslzn Ctr 1974-; life mem NAACP spec state mem com TX State Tchrs Assn. **HONORS/ACHIEVEMENTS:** Hon roll cert TX So Univ 1951; 1st black to Integrat Tchng Profn Edgewood ISD 1963; Citation-Historical Achvmt Among Negroes of San Antonio Smart Set Club 1965; citation Woman's Pavilion Hemisfair 68 Vol Guide 1968; hon & life mem TX Congress of Parents & Tchrs 1969; 1st black pres TX State Tchrs AssnAffiliate 1969-71; cit outst work with Youth City of San Antonio 1970; ambassador of Good Will Sstate of TX 1970; past pres award Edgewood Classroom TchrsAssn 1971; disting educ serv award Prince & Princess Soc & Civic Club Inc 1971f cit Ella Austin Comm Ctr 1973,77; outst educ award Zeta Phi Beta Sor1973; TX Classroom Tchrs Assn Serv Award 1973; disting serv award Task Force on Testing Nat Educ Assn 1976; miss black san antonio bd of dir model comm ldrs award 1976; serv award TX State Thcrs Assn 1977; cert of apprec TX State Tchrs Assn 1977; 1st black mem TX Classroom Tchrs Asn Bd of Dirs Rep Dist 1973-73; boss of the yr Mission City Chap Am Bus Women's Assn 1978; educ adminstr of the yr Delta Rho Lambda Ch Alpha Phi Alpha Frat 1978; cert of apprec Edgewood Inde Sch Dist 1978.

COLLINS, ELLIOTT
Educational administrator. **PERSONAL:** Born Mar 18, 1943, Eastman, GA; married Carol Jones. **EDUCATION:** Univ of DE, BA 1966; NY U, MPA 1971. **CAREER:** Passaic Cty Community Coll, dean of students 1974-; Upsala Coll, Drew Univ, lecturer political ascience 1974-; Pusala Coll, asst dean for acad counseling 1974-77; Upsala Coll, affirmative action officer 1974-77; Educ Opportunity Fund Program Upsala Coll, dir and coordinator 1970-77; City of E Orange NJ, asst city planner 1969. **ORGANIZATIONS:** Vp United Way & Community Serv Council 1971-75; vice pres bd of dir Rotary Club of E Orange NJ 1971-72; bd of trustees Family Servs & Child Guidance Center1975-76. **HONORS/ACHIEVEMENTS:** Alpha Phi Alpha Scholarship 1962063; young man of the year Unity Club Wilmington DE 1965; Martin Luther King Scholarship 1968. **BUSINESS ADDRESS:** College Blvd, Paterson, NJ 07509.

COLLINS, ELSIE
Educator. **PERSONAL:** Born Apr 25, Durham, NC; divorced; children: Leslie Jean, Kimberly Ruth. **EDUCATION:** DE St Coll, BA 1945; Columbia U, MA 1952; Union Grad Sch, PhD 1977. **CAREER:** Trenton State Coll, asst prof 1971-; Trenton, NJ, asst dir of COP 1971; Natl Teachers Corp, Trenton NJ, team leader 1968-71; Core Curr Jr High School, Trenton NJ, teacher 1961-62, 1964-68, demonstration teacher 1965-68; Trenton State Coll, supvr summer semester for teachers 1965-75; Dover DE Jr & Sr High Schools, teacher 1945-59; Beth Jacob Jewish High School New York City, teacher 1960-61; Consult Serv & In-serv Workshops Trenton; Teahcer Educ NJ State Dept Higher Educ 1967-72; Afro-Amer Studies 1969-76; Urban Educ Curriculum Spec 1972-. **ORGANIZATIONS:** Mem Community Leaders & Noteworthy Am 1979; mem Doctorate Assn of NY Educators 1980; mem Amer Assn Univ Women 1954-60; current membrshp New Jersey HistSoc Am Assn Negro Mus; NAACP; Urban Leag Couns of Soc Studies NEA NJEA Poverty Law Ctr AKA Assn for Superv & Curriculum Devel. **HONORS/ACHIEVEMENTS:** Valedictorian high sch schlrship high honor DE St Coll; scholarship student of music Tchrs Coll Columbia Univ 1950-57; soloist St Paul United Meth Ch Trenton 1967-; publ "Poverty & the Poor" 1968; contributed to Devl of Urban Educ Series Prob of Amer Soc 1966-68; special award World Who's Who of Women in Educ 1977-78; Internatl Who's Who of Intellectuals 1979; Internatl Artists & Fellows of Distinction 1980. **BUSINESS ADDRESS:** 371 Education Bldg, Trenton St Coll, Trenton, NJ 08625.

COLLINS, GORDON GEOFFREY
Public relations executive. **PERSONAL:** Born Nov 07, 1958, Bronx, NY; son of Clyde Rogers Collins and Nellie Faison Collins. **EDUCATION:** The Coll of St Rose, Albany, NY, BA, 1982; Baruch Coll, New York, NY, MPA, 1988. **CAREER:** Town of Hempstead, Dept of Occupational Resources, Hempstead, NY, educ and training monitor, 1978; New York State Alliance of Comm Action Programs Inc, Albany, NY, public information specialist, 1981-84; Office of the Mayor, Cleveland, OH, exec asst to the Mayor, 1984-85; Collins Assoc, Elmony, NY, pres, 1985-; Springfield Gardens High School, Springfield Gardens, NY, dean of students, 1986-; Queensborough Comm Coll, Bayside, NY, adjunct lecturer of Social Science, 1988-. **ORGANIZATIONS:** Mem, Amer Political Science Assn, 1985-, Amer Soc for Public Admin, 1985-, New York State United Teachers, 1986-, New York Alliance of Black School Educators, 1987-; delegate, United Federation of Teachers Delegate Assembly, New York, NY, 1987-; mem, New York Urban League, 1988-; conf coord, Second Annual Black Man and Family Conf, New York, NY, 1988-89; mem, Queens Summit on Racial and Religious Harmony, New York, NY, 1988-; bd mem, Positive Images Found Inc, Cambria Heights, NY, 1989-; mem, Queens Martin Luther King Memorial Commn, New York, NY, 1989-. **HONORS/ACHIEVEMENTS:** Martin Luther King Scholarship Award, Nassau Community Coll, 1978; editor, New York State Alliance of Comm Action Programs Newsletter, 1981-84; Presidential Award, NAACP, Albany, NY, 1983; Natl Urban Fellow, Natl Urban Fellows Inc, 1984; Sidney Langsam Award, Springfield Gardens High School, New York , NY, 1988. **HOME ADDRESS:** 186 Arthur Ave, Elmont, NY 11003.

COLLINS, HYACINTH ROXANE
Attorney. **PERSONAL:** Born Apr 18, 1948, Washington, DC. **EDUCATION:** Catholic U, Ba in English 1970; Columbus Sch of Law Catholic U, JD 1973. **CAREER:** Sen Joseph Biden, Jr Washington,DC, leg asst (Sept) 1973-75; DC Govt, hearing examiner (Mar-july) 1973; Maritime Admin Washington DC, atty. **ORGANIZATIONS:** Mem Am Bar Assn; Nat Black & Women Polit Ldrship Caucus; World Peach Thr Ough Law student del to Ivory Coast 1973. **HONORS/ACHIEVEMENTS:** Apt by mayor Wash, DC Commn on Hum Rights 1974-75; outstanding young woman 1979.

COLLINS, JAMES DOUGLAS
Educator. **PERSONAL:** Born Dec 11, 1931, Los Angeles, CA; married Cecilia Lyons; children: Keith, Jelana Carnes, Jenine. **EDUCATION:** Univ Of CA, BA 1957; Univ of CA, MA 1959; Emharry Med Coll Nashville, MD 1963. **CAREER:** UCLA, assoc prof in radiology 1976-; UCLA, resident in radiology 1964-68; LA City General Hospital intern, 1963-64; Vet Admin (Wadworth/Spelveda), attending radiologist 1972-; Martin Luther King Jr Gen Hosp LA, attending radiologist 1973-; Olive View Mid-Valley Hosp Van Nuys, attending radiologist 1976-; Martin Luther King Jr Hosp, attending physician 1969-. **ORGANIZATIONS:** Mem Search Committee for Chmn of Radiology Dept of Martin Luther King Jr General Hosp 1969-70; vol Venice Community Health Center. **MILITARY SERVICE:** AUS corpl 1954-56. **BUSINESS ADDRESS:** 405 Hilgard, Los Angeles, CA 90024.

COLLINS, JAMES H.
Personnel manager. **PERSONAL:** Born Feb 01, 1946, Moline, IL; son of Alphonso and Mattie (Pennington); married Karen J Raebel; children: James Jr, Kimberly, Candace, Anthony, Kevin. **EDUCATION:** St Ambrose Coll, BA Sociology 1969. **CAREER:** Proj Now Comm Action Agy, exec dir 1968-71; John Deere, industrial relations rep 1971-74, EEO crdtr 1974-75, mgr prsnl 1975-83; Deere & Co, dir affirmative action. **ORGANIZATIONS:** Vice pres Milan, IL C of C 1981; advisor Jr Achvmt 1975; vice pres Quad Cities Merit Employment Council 1975; chmn Dubuque, IA Human Rts Comm 1973; bd Quad Cities United Way 1975-78; pres Quad Cities Council on Crime & Delinqncy 1978-79; chmn Human Rights & Empoyment Practices Comm Iowa Assoc of Bus & Ind; chmn PIC/JTPA; chmn, Business Advisory Council, Illinois Dept of Rehabilitation Services 1988-90; commissioner, Iowa Civil Rights Commission 1989-92. **HONORS/ACHIEVEMENTS:** Amer Legion Rock Island, IL 1961, Rotary 1964; Athletic Hall of Fame St Ambrose Coll 1984; Citizen Community Rehabilitation Service Award, Illinois Rehabilitation Assn 1989. **BUSINESS ADDRESS:** Dir of Affirmative Action, Deere & Co, John Deere Rd, Moline, IL 61265.

COLLINS, JANET
Choreographer, educator. **PERSONAL:** Born Mar 02, 1917, New Orleans, LA. **EDUCATION:** Los Angeles City Coll & Art Cntr Sch; Cath Community Cntr; studied dance under Charlotte Tamon, Dorothy Lyndall, Carmelita Maracci, Lester Horton, Mia Slavenska & Adolph Bohm. **CAREER:** Los Angeles Musical Productions, principal dancer 1940; toured with Kathryn Dunham Dance Co, 2 yrs; presented first concert at Las Palmas Theatre in Los Angeles 1948; Young Mens Hebrew Assn, performed in concert; Cole Porter Musical "Out of This World", principal dancer 1950-51; solo concert dance tours of US & Canada under Columbia Artists Mgmt 1952-55; Modern Da Nce Scho of Am Ballet, tchr 1949-52; St Joseph Sch for Deaf, 1959-61; Marymount Manhattan Coll NY, 1959-69; Manhattanville Coll of Sacred Heart NY 1961-65; Mother Butler Memorial HS, 1966. **HONORS/ACHIEVEMENTS:** Recipient Scholarship in Ballet Mm Toscanini; scholarship in Modern Dance Hanya Holm; Scholarship in Choreography Doris Humphry; Dance Magazine Award 1949 ; Mademoiselle Magazine Award woman of yr 1950; Donaldson Award 1950-51.

COLLINS, JOANN RUTH
Educational administrator. **PERSONAL:** Born Jan 26, Nashville; married John H; children: John K, Guy R. **EDUCATION:** MI State U, BS 1971; MI State U, MA 1973; MI State U, PhD Candidate. **CAREER:** Dept of Civil Serv, State of MI, women's training officer; MI State Univ, coord college work study program; Breckinridge Job Corps Center KY, dir family servs, dir & nursery & kindergarten. **ORGANIZATIONS:** Pres Nat Assn of Financial Assistance to Minority Students 1974-; mem Nat Task Force on Student Aid Problems; mem Black Faculty & Adminstrn MI State U1973; mem bd dir Lansing Senior Citizens Inc 1974-76; mem women's steering com MI State Univ 1973; mem adv com to bus & office Educ Clubs MI HS 1974-.

COLLINS, KENNETH L.
Attorney. **PERSONAL:** Born Aug 23, 1933, El Centro, CA; married Beverly Jean Sherman; children: Kevin, Leslie. **EDUCATION:** UCLA, BA 1959; UCLA, JD 1971. **CAREER:** LA Co, probation ofcr 1957-68; San Fernando Valley Juvenile Hall, acting dir; Fed Pub Defenders Office, pub defender 1972-75. **ORGANIZATIONS:** Mem Langston Law Club; CA Attys for Criminal Justice; CA State Bar; chmn bd dir Black Law Journal; past pres Kappa Alpha Psi Upsion 1957-58; co-founderBlack Law Journal; distinguished serv. **HONORS/ACHIEVEMENTS:** UCLA Chancelors Award 1971. **MILITARY SERVICE:** AUS corpl 1953-55. **BUSINESS ADDRESS:** 3701 Wilshire Blvd, Ste 700, Los Angeles, CA 90010.

COLLINS, LENORA W.
Consultant. **PERSONAL:** Born Feb 25, 1925, Fayette, MS; married Joe H. **EDUCATION:** Univ Sarasota, EdD 1977; Governors State Univ, MA 1974; Xavier Univ, BS 1946; DePaul U, advance study. **CAREER:** Lorman Comm Devel Org Lorman MS, exec dir; Dept of Public Aid State of IL, economics cons; Bur of & Home Economics Cook County Dept Public Aid, asst chief 1964-73; spr home economics 1962-63; supv caseworker 1959-61; Chicago Bd of Educ, home economics teacher 1948-54. **ORGANIZATIONS:** Life mem Am Home Economics Assn; life mem IL Home Economics Assn; v chmn Human Serv Section; chmn Health & Welfare Sect IL Home Econ Assn 1968-69; pres Chicago Home Econ Assn; 1970-71; Chicago Nutrition Assn; Am Public Welfare Assn; bd mem Chicago Met Housing Council Tenant Proj; trustee Jefferson Co Hosp; sec Jefferson Co Hosp 1979-80; mem Nat Negro Bus & Professional Women's Club; mem Delta Sigma Theta; Wacker Neighbor-

hood Assn Chicago Urban League; NAACP. **HONORS/ACHIEVEMENTS:** Recipient Finer Womanhood Award Zeta Phi Beta 1967; Silver Jubilee & Alumnus Award Xavier Univ 1971; listed Chicago Almanac & Reference Book 1973; Who's Who of American Women; World Who's Who of Women Dictionary of Intl Biography 1976 ed.

COLLINS, LEROY ANTHONY, JR.
Government official. **PERSONAL:** Born Jan 30, 1950, Norfolk, VA; son of Leroy Collins and Thelma Taylor-Collins; divorced; children: Kisten Collins. **EDUCATION:** Howard Univ, 1967-70; Rutgers Univ, BS, 1973; Temple Univ School of Business, 1980-81. **CAREER:** City of Newark, NJ, asst budget dir, 1974-78; City of Miami, FL, asst to city mgr, 1978-80; Penn Mutual Life Insurance Co, sr investment analyst, 1980-83; City of Tampa, FL, mgr of econ devel, 1983-86; City of St Petersburg, FL, dir of economic devel. **ORGANIZATIONS:** Trustee, Black Business Investment Board, 1988-; advisor, Governor's Council of Economic Advisor's, 1988-. **HONORS/ACHIEVEMENTS:** Focus Development, Penn Mutual Life, 1982; Leadership Tampa, Tampa Chamber of Commerce, 1985; Service Award, City of Tampa, 1986. **MILITARY SERVICE:** USMC E-4, 1970-73; Amer Spirit of Honor Award, 1971. **BUSINESS ADDRESS:** Director of Economic Development, City of St Petersburg, PO Box 2842, St Petersburg, FL 33731.

COLLINS, LIMONE C.
Educator. **PERSONAL:** Born Aug 14, 1921, Gonzales, TX; married Billye J Peters; children: Cheryl M Anderson, Limone C Jr, Tyrone J. **EDUCATION:** Prairie View A&M Univ, BS 1947, MS 1953; Univ of Iowa, PhD 1961. **CAREER:** OJ Thomas HS, head sci dept 1947-49; Prairie View A&M Univ, instructor of biol 1953-59, prof/head of biol dept 1961-73; Johnson C Smith Univ, vpfor academic affairs 1973-84; Davidson Coll, prof of biology 1984-. **ORGANIZATIONS:** Bd of dirs Goodwill Industries of Amer 1982-; bd of dirs Amer Red Cross; fellow TX Acad of Science; sr warden St Francis Episcopal Church TX; consultant and proposal reviewer NIH & NSF. **HONORS/ACHIEVEMENTS:** Danforth Fellowship; publications Amer Journal of Physiol 1962, TX Journal of Science 1972, Jour Amer Oil Chem Soc 1973. **MILITARY SERVICE:** AUS T/5 1943-45, 1950-51. **HOME ADDRESS:** 8310 Knights Bridge Rd, Charlotte, NC 28210.

COLLINS, MARVA DELORES NETTLES
Educator. **PERSONAL:** Born Aug 31, 1936, Monroeville, AL; daughter of Alex L Nettles and Bessie Maye Knight Nettles; married Clarence Collins, Sep 04, 1960; children: Cynthia Beth, Eric, Patrick. **EDUCATION:** Clark Coll, BA 1957; Northwestern Univ. **CAREER:** Monroe Co Training Sch Monroeville, AL, tchr 1958-59; Delano Elem Sch, tchr 1960-75; Westside Prep Sch, founder/dir 1975-; Delano School, teacher 13 years; Westside Preparatory School 1975-. **ORGANIZATIONS:** Dir Right to Read Found 1978; Sunday sch tchr Morning Star Bapt Ch 1978-79; mem President's Commn on White House Fellowships 1981-; mem Alpha Kappa Alpha, NAACP; President's Citizens' Group 1989-. **HONORS/ACHIEVEMENTS:** Fred Hampton Image Award Fred Hampton Found 1979; Watson Washburne Award Reading Reform Found 1979; Educator of the Year Award Phi Delta Kappa 1980; Endow a Dream Awd 1980; Jefferson Natl Awd 1981; Amer Public Serv Awd Amer Inst for Public Serv 1981; featured on TV's "60 Minutes"; subject of a made-for-TV movie "The Marva Collins Story" 1981; publs including Marva Collins' Way 1982; Honorary Degrees from: Washington Univ, Amherst, Dartmouth, Chicago State Univ, Howard Univ, Central State Univ; published book Marva Collins Way, 35 other professional articles. **BUSINESS ADDRESS:** Dir, Westside Prep School, 4146 Chicago Ave, Chicago, IL 60651.

COLLINS, MAURICE A.
Music educator. **PERSONAL:** Born Jan 27, 1936, Memphis; married Constance Rupert; children: Dominique M, Alan L, Kenneth F, Jonathan R. **EDUCATION:** Chicago Teachers Coll, BS 1964; Roosevelt U, MMus 1967; So IL U, PhD 1971. **CAREER:** Chicago State Univ, assoc prof of Educ; First AME Church, Gary IN, minister of Music; professional choral cond spec in the performance & of oratorios by Haydn, Mozart, Mendelssohn, & Brahms. **ORGANIZATIONS:** Founder Chorale/Omega & Orchestra 1963; mem Am Choral Directors Assn Phi Mu Alpha Sinfonia; Phi Delta Kappa; Kappa Delta Pi; John Dewey Soc; Philosophy of Educ Soc; Nat Assn of Coll Tchrs of Edn. **HONORS/ACHIEVEMENTS:** Recipient most outstanding dir Award Chicago Music Assn 1965; dir of the year Bapt SS & Training Union Congress of IL 1967; John Dewey Scholar & Lectr. **BUSINESS ADDRESS:** 95 St at King Dr, Chicago, IL 60628.

COLLINS, OTIS GRANT
Business executive. **PERSONAL:** Born May 02, 1919, Canton, MS; married Earlean Collins; children: Dwarrye Grant. **EDUCATION:** Wilson Coll, 1940; Roosevelt U; Chicago Tech; IIT. **CAREER:** Otis G Collins Gen Bldg & Elec Contractors, owner; IL House of Reps, 1964. **ORGANIZATIONS:** Mem IL Atomic Energy Commn 1968-69; mem sec IL State Property Ins Comn Consult IL & Citizens Com for Fair Ins & Consumer Practices; mem Black Legislators AAD-HOC Com; exec bd NAACP 1947-48; sec charter mem UAW Local 281; chmn Chicago Lawndale Citizens Schs Com; vice pres Greater Lawndale Conservation Commn; Chicago W Bldg & Edec Contractors Assn; Nat Acad of Polit & Social Scientist IL Res. **MILITARY SERVICE:** Milita 1943-44. **BUSINESS ADDRESS:** 1626 S Central Park Ave, Chicago, IL 60623.

COLLINS, PATRICIA HILL
Educator. **PERSONAL:** Born May 01, 1948, Philadelphia, PA; married Roger L Collins; children: Valerie Lisa. **EDUCATION:** Brandeis Univ, AB 1969, PhD 1984; Harvard Univ, MAT 1970. **CAREER:** Harvard UTTT Program, teacher/curriculum spec 1970-73; St Joseph Community School, curriculum specialist 1973-76; Tufts Univ, dir African Amer Ctr 1976-80; Univ of Cincinnati, asst prof of Afro-Amer studies, assoc prof of Afro-American Studies 1987-, assoc prof of Sociology 1988-. **ORGANIZATIONS:** Chair Minority Fellowship Program Comm 1986-1989; mem Amer Sociological Assn. **BUSINESS ADDRESS:** Assoc Prof of Afro-Amer Studies, Univ of Cincinnati, Dept of Afro-American Studies, ML 370, Cincinnati, OH 45221.

COLLINS, PAUL
Artist. **PERSONAL:** Born Dec 11, 1936, Muskegon, MI; married Candace Brown; children: Michael, Michelle, Scott, Eric, Chauvon. **CAREER:** Paintings Children of Harlem 1976-78; Joseph P Kennedy Found, spl olympics drawings & paintings 1976-79; paintings & book Great Beautiful Black Women 1976-78; mural Famous Moments in Black Amer History 1978-80; paintings Working Americans 1980-83; mural & book Gerald R Ford, A Man in Perspective 1976; Collins Fine Art, fine artist 1945-84; numerous others; paintings-Voices of Israel 1986-89; paintings, drawings and book- Black Portrait of an African Journey 1969-71. **ORGANIZATIONS:** Bd of trustees Robeson Players 1972-80; mem Amer Indian Movement 1972-84; adv bd John F Kennedy Ctr for the Perf Arts 1976-80; co-chrmn for Western Michigan - United Negro College Fund 1989-90. **HONORS/ACHIEVEMENTS:** Designer Martin Luther King Jr Non-Violent Peace Prize Medal 1979-80; Mead Book Awd 1972; Paul Collins Humanist Am Artist 1976; St named "Rue Monsieur Paul Collins" Govt of Senegal Africa 1977; Official Naming Ceremony Pine Ridge SD "Bright Eagle" 1977; 20 Outstanding Figure Painters & How They Work 1979; Arts Council Awd Grand Rapids Arts Council 1979; Black Achievement Awd 1979; People's Choice Awd Amer Painters in Paris 1976; 40th Anniversary Symbol for Israel 1988-89; American Woman Commemorative Plaque 1983. **BUSINESS ADDRESS:** Collins Fine Art, 615 Kent Hills Rd NE, Grand Rapids, MI 49505.

COLLINS, PAUL L.
Association executive. **PERSONAL:** Born Apr 19, 1931, Shreveport; married Shirley Alexander; children: Paula, Darryl. **EDUCATION:** So U, BA & MEd 1958; GWU, EdD 1976. **CAREER:** Branches & Dir of Office of Human Rights, asso exec intl relations, governmental reseach policy & analysis-registered lobbyist for Profnl Develop Prgms; Non White Concerns, dir; Div & International Relations, staff asso 1971-73; Wash Tech Inst, asso prof 1968-71; Roosevelt HS, dir guidance 1965-68; Wash Jr HS, tchr 1962-65; BTW HS, prof Military Sci 1959-62; Carver Jr HS, 1958-59. **ORGANIZATIONS:** Pres CESS Inc; DC Sch Counselors Assn 1968-70; Nat Capital PGA 1971-72; chrpsn APGA Nat Commn Human Rights 1969-70; dir & chmn bd of Religious Educ Mt Moriah BC; v chmn DC Career Educ Adv Council 1978-; mem Mayors Youth Com; Comm Adv EEO; Hiring Handicapped; Nat Task Force; St Moriah Bapt Ch. **HONORS/ACHIEVEMENTS:** Outstanding tchr award 1960; outstanding leadership award 1962; outstanding leadership vocational guidance 1970; Christian Leadership 1967; United Nations USA Award 1971-72. **MILITARY SERVICE:** 1st lt 1954-56. **BUSINESS ADDRESS:** 5203 Leesburg Pike, Falls Church, VA 22041.

COLLINS, PAUL V.
Educator. **PERSONAL:** Born Sep 07, 1918, Philadelphia, PA; married Margaret Anne Chambers; children: Paula L, Pamela E, Richard Paul, Margaret Nicole. **EDUCATION:** Livingstone Coll Salisbury NC, BA 1941; NY Univ New York, Ma sociology 1948; TN State Univ Nashville, MS Health & PE 1958; NY Univ New York, Doctoral Studies 1968-69. **CAREER:** CA State Univ Hayward, assoc prof Educ & coordinator multi cultural Educ 1973-; Weaver High School, Hartford CT Bd of Educ, prin 1970-73; US Office of Educ, Washington DC, educ program specialist 1969-70; NY Univ, instr in Educ 1968-69; IS 201 Manhattan, New York City Bd of Educ, master teacher 1966-68; JHS 139 Manhattan, NY Bd of Educ, dean of boys 1965-67; Wiley Coll, Marshall TX, head basketball coach & asst prof Sociology 1961-65; Lane Coll, Jackson TN, head basketball coach & assoc prof Health & Phsical Educ 1960-61. **ORGANIZATIONS:** Dir Pacific Center Educ Reserach & Devel Castro Vally PA 1974-; multicultural educ adv com CA State Dept of Educ 1977-78; ad hoc com Racial Isolation in Sch CA State Dept of Educ 1977-78. **HONORS/ACHIEVEMENTS:** Superior serv Award & HEW Office of Educ 1972; Phi Delta Kappa Hartford CT 1973; various papers pub. **MILITARY SERVICE:** USN amm 3/c 2 years served. **BUSINESS ADDRESS:** CA State University, Hayward, CA 94542.

COLLINS, ROBERT FREDERICK
Judge. **PERSONAL:** Born Jan 27, 1931, New Orleans, LA; son of Frederick Collins and Irma Anderson; married Aloha M; children: Francesca McManus, Lisa Ann, Nanette C, Robert A. **EDUCATION:** Dillard Univ, BA (Cum Laude) 1951, LLD (Hon) 1979; LA State Univ, JD; Univ of NV Natl Judge Coll, 1973. **CAREER:** Augustine Collins Smith & Warren New Orleans, partner 1956-59; So Univ, instr law 1959-61; Collins Douglas & Elie New Orleans, sr partner 1960-72; New Orleans Police Dept, asst city attny, legal adv 1967-69; Traffic Court New Orleans, judge ad-hoc 1969-72; State of LA, asst bar examiner 1970-78; Housing AuthNew Orleans, attny 1971-72; Criminal Dist Court Orleans Parish LA, judge magistrate sect 1971-78; US Dist Court, judge 1978-; instructor Southern Univ Law School, Baton Rouge LA 1981-89. **ORGANIZATIONS:** Trustee Loyola Univ 1977-83; mem LA Bar Assoc; mem ABA; mem Alpha Phi Alpha, Sigma Pi Phi, Phi Alpha Delta. **HONORS/ACHIEVEMENTS:** Passed Bar, LA 1954; Alpha Kappa Mu, Honor Society 1950. **MILITARY SERVICE:** AUS 1954-56. **BUSINESS ADDRESS:** Judge, US Dist Court, 500 Camp St, Ste 465, New Orleans, LA 70130.

COLLINS, ROBERT H.
Cleryman, educator. **PERSONAL:** Born Jul 10, 1934, Chicago, IL; children: Robert, Pamela. **EDUCATION:** Wilson Jr Clg Chicago IL, AA 1954; Michael Resse Sch of Med Tech, MT 1955; Roosevelt Univ Chicago IL, BS 1957; Concordia Theology Smnry Springfield, IL,BD 1964, MDiv 1965; Concordia Smnry St Louis, Master of Sacred Theology 1974. **CAREER:** Univ of IL R&E Hospital, medical tech 1955-56; Northwestern Univ, research chemist 1956; Lab of Vit Tech, chem quality control 1957-59; Concordia Seminary, Springfield IL, 1959-63; Bethlehem Luthern Church, Col GA, pastor 1963-73; St James Luthern Church, Bakersfield CA, pastor 1973-77; Northern IL Dist LC-MS, missionary-at-large; Corcordia Theological Seminary, Ft Wayne IN, prof of prctl theology counseling 1977-85. **ORGANIZATIONS:** Mem Scan 1982-; vacancy pstr Shepherd of the City Luth Ft Wayne 1983-; mem Resolve; vol chpln Parkview Meml Hosp Ft Wayne, IN; part-time chpln Cnty Jail; vacancy pastor Mount Calvary Luth Church; consultant cross-cultural ministry Trinity Luth Church. **HONORS/ACHIEVEMENTS:** Meritorious Serv City of Col GA 1971, 72-73; Cert of Aprctn Pres Nixon GA State Advsr Com on Edc 1972; Cert of Aprctn TB Assc, Legal Aid Soc, Sr Citizens; mem Bd of Dir 1972-73. **BUSINESS ADDRESS:** Professor of Counseling/Evng, Concordia Theological, 6600 N Clinton, Fort Wayne, IN 46825.

COLLINS, ROSECRAIN
Dentist. **PERSONAL:** Born Feb 14, 1929, Nashville, TN; married Elizabeth; children: Michelle, Adrienne. **EDUCATION:** TN State U, BS 1952; Meharry Med Coll, DDS 1958. **CAREER:** Chicago Child Care Soc, Dentist 1976-; Chicago Dept Pub Aid, dental consult 1977-; Martin Luther King Hlth Ctr, dentist 1971-74; Kennedy, Ryan & Monigal Realtors, asso 1973-. **ORGANIZATIONS:** Treas Great Western Investment Ltd 1969-; dir Intl Sporting Club 1974; partner Forestry Recycling Mill 1975-; mem Dental Hlth Screening Chicago Pub Sch 1961-63; mem Lincoln Dental Soc 1959-; memChicago Denatl Soc treas 1970-74; IL Dental Soc 1959-; Am Dental Soc 1959-; Nat Dental Soc 1959-; Acad Gen Dentistry 1974-. **HONORS/ACHIEVEMENTS:** Citation pub serv City Chicago 1962-63. **MILI-**

TARY SERVICE: AUS sgt 1952-54. **BUSINESS ADDRESS:** 1525 E 53rd St #903-R, Chicago, IL 60615.

COLLINS, SYLVIA DOLORES
Registered nurse. **PERSONAL:** Born Nov 17, 1934, Philadelphia, PA; daughter of Frank Durnell and Catherine Sanford; children: Dawn Catherine. **EDUCATION:** Episcopal Hospital, RN 1955; Univ of PA, BSN 1959; Temple Univ, MEd 1973. **CAREER:** Children/Youth Prog, chief project nurse 1970-72; Southeast Philadelphia Neighborhood Health Ctr, dir of nursing 1972-76; Philadelphia Health Plan, consultant 1976-79; Lutheran Home, instructor insvcs educ 1977-79; ACT Drug Rehab, staff nurse 1981-82; Comm Coll, vstg lecturer 1978-80; Philadelphia Corp for Aging, consultant/health prom 1981-86. **ORGANIZATIONS:** Dir North Central YWCA 1976-86; dir Black Alumni Soc Univ of PA 1982-86; chairperson Professional Adv Comm Opportunity Towers Philadelphia 1982-86; faculty Nursing East Continuing Educ 1983,84; mem vice chairperson Ethnic Nurses of Color 1984-86; sec Gratz St Neighbors 1984-86; mem prof ed comm Amer Cancer Soc 1985-86; mem Council of Neighborhoods 1985; mem Public Educ Comm Arthritis Assoc; mem Alpha Kappa Alpha Sor, Omega Omega Chapt, Amer Public Health Assoc, Chi Eta Phi Sor Theta Chapt; life mem NAACP. **HONORS/ACHIEVEMENTS:** Author article University of Pennsylvania 1986, BAS Newsletter; Sigma Theta Tau, Kappa Chi Nursing Honor Society 1988; 7 appearences Radio & TV 1981-89. **HOME ADDRESS:** 6245 No Gratz St, Philadelphia, PA 19141. **BUSINESS ADDRESS:** Consultant Health Promotion, Philadelphia Corp for Aging, 111 North Broad St, Philadelphia, PA 19107.

COLLINS, TESSIL JOHN
Educator/producer. **PERSONAL:** Born Aug 29, 1952, Boston, MA; son of Tessil A Collins and Evelyn A Gill Collins; married Barbara Clayton, Jul 23, 1988; children: Dionna Collins. **EDUCATION:** Boston Latin Sch, 1971; Tufts Univ, BA English 1975; Boston Univ, Exec Prog Cert Small Bus Dev Prog 1985. **CAREER:** WBZ Radio Boston, producer 1973-75 & 1976-78; WBCN Radio Boston, account exec 1978-80; Rep MHKing, campaign mngr 1978-79; WILD Radio Boston, acct exec 1975 & 1980-81; RCA Records, field merchandiser 1981-83; Beantown Music natl promoter 1983-84; Boston Public Schls Humphrey Occup Res Cntr, instructoraudioTV prodn 1984-; Spectrun Management, exec dir representing Butch Tavares, Yvette Cason 1984-. **ORGANIZATIONS:** Mem Boston Black Media Coalition; mem New England DJ Assoc; mem Prince Hall Grand Lodge F&AM; mem Boston NAACP; co-chmn Tufts Univ Black Alumni Assoc; bd mem MA Rock Against Racism; bd mem Young Artists Develop Inc. **HONORS/ACHIEVEMENTS:** Cert Media Technology MA Dept of Educ Div of Occup Educ 1985; position at Beantown announced in Black Enterp May & Feb 1984; producer video on student diversity "I'm Different, You're Different, We're All Okay" Tufts Univ 1985; producer of video for Mrs Black Boston Pagent 1986; Grand Prize Florida Citrus Commission Music Video Competition 1987; producer The Comedy Train. **HOME ADDRESS:** 650 Huntington Ave #11A, Boston, MA 02115.

COLLINS, THEODICIA DEBORAH
Attorney. **PERSONAL:** Born Feb 19, 1959, Brooklyn, NY. **EDUCATION:** SUNY Old Westbury, BA 1981; Univ of Bridgeport, JD/MBA 1986. **CAREER:** Univ of Bridgeport, acctg dept accts asst 1983-84, sch of law legal rsch asst 1984-85, sch of business grad rsch asst 1985-86, tax clinic legal intern 1986. **ORGANIZATIONS:** Mem Black Entertainment & Sports Lawyers Assoc 1985, NY Investors Network 1985. **HONORS/ACHIEVEMENTS:** Certificate of Awd Bd of Educ Bridgeport CT 1985; Certificate of Awd Outstanding Young Women of Amer 1986. **BUSINESS ADDRESS:** Entertainment Attorney, 401 Broadway, Suite 300, New York, NY 10013.

COLLINS, WARREN EUGENE
Educator. **PERSONAL:** Born Jan 26, 1947, Memphis; married Joyce Powell; children: Evangeline Monique, Warren Gabriel. **EDUCATION:** Christian Bro Coll, BS 1968; Vanderbilt U, MS 1970; Vanderbilt U, PhD 1972. **CAREER:** Southern Univ Baton Rouge, 1972-73; Fisk Univ Nashville, 1973-77; Vanderbilt Univ, rsch assoc 1974-75; Southern Univ, Baton Rouge LA, prof, chmn dept of physics 1977-. **ORGANIZATIONS:** Am Assn Physics Tchrs AAPT; Am Physical Soc APS; AAUP; Sigma Xi; officer trustee Spruce St Bapt Ch 1975; mem Beta Kappa Chi Sci Soc; mem ACLU; memAAAS. **HONORS/ACHIEVEMENTS:** Listed in Who's Who Among Sutdents Amer Univ & Coll 1958; Physics Abstracts publs 1970-; Outstanding Youn Men of Amer 1975. **MILITARY SERVICE:** AUSR 1st lt 1972-75. **BUSINESS ADDRESS:** Chairman, Professor, SouthernUniv, Physics Dept, Baton Rouge, LA 70813.

COLLINS, WILLIAM, JR.
Clergyman. **PERSONAL:** Born Jul 03, 1924, St Louis; married Margaret Elizabeth Brown; children: Sylvia, Deirdre, William, III. **EDUCATION:** St Louis U, BS 1956; Colgate Rochester Div Sch, BD 1960; Univ Rochester, MEd 1960; Colgate Rochester Div Sch, MDiv 1972; E NE Christian Coll , DD 1972; St Louis U, PhD 1973. **CAREER:** Antioch Bapt Ch St Louis, pastor 1961-; Bluefield State Coll, dir pub relations & asst registrar 1961; Antioch Bapt Ch St Louis, minister christian educ 1960-61; Second Bapt Ch Leroy NY, student pastor 1959-60; US Postal, employee 1951-56; MO Dept Welfare St Louis, caseworker 1948-51. **ORGANIZATIONS:** Bd trustees St Louis Jr Coll Dist elected 6 yr term 1975; mem Am Bapt Conv; Task Force; Intl Ministries Africa 1971-; bd mem Annie Malone Childrens Home St Louis 1970-; bd Health & Hosp St Louis 1968-; St Louis Municipal Nurses bd 1970-; Landmark & Urban Design Commn St Louis 1968- 72; Adult Welfare Commns St Louis 1970-; Eagle Scout 1939; Alpha Phi Alpha Frat 1947; Preaching Mission Am Bapt El Salvador & Nicaragua Latin Am 1966; Missionary Involvement Tour; Am Bapt W Africa 1972. **MILITARY SERVICE:** AUS sgt 1943-46. **BUSINESS ADDRESS:** 4213 W North Market, St Louis, MO 63113.

COLLINS, WILLIAM KEELAN
Dentist. **PERSONAL:** Born Oct 30, 1914, Seat Pleasant, MD; married Eleanore; children: William Jr, John. **EDUCATION:** Howard U, BS 1935; Howard U, DDS 1939; Georgetown Univ Coll Dnstry, DSc 1974. **CAREER:** Pvt Pract, dnstry 1939-. **ORGANIZATIONS:** Past pres Am Assoc Dntl Exmnrs 1976-77; mem exec coun AADE 1972-; sec treasr N E Regnl Bd & Dentl Exmnrs 1969-; chmn bd dir Untd Natl Bnk WA 1964-; bd trustee HowardUniv 1968-. **HONORS/ACHIEVEMENTS:** Harry Struther Aw NY Univ Coll Dnstry 1972; dnst of yr DC Dntl Soc 1970. **MILITARY SERVICE:** AUS 1st lt. **BUSINESS ADDRESS:** 4645 Deane Ave NE, Washington, DC 20019.

COLLINS-BONDON, CAROLYN R.
Educational fiscal analyst. **PERSONAL:** Born Mar 30, 1949, Jackson, MS; daughter of Mr & Mrs Roma Collins; children: Celeste. **EDUCATION:** Western Michigan Univ, BS 1971, MA 1980, EdD 1983. **CAREER:** Grand Rapids Public Schools, teacher 1972-74; Fairfax Co School, lang arts res teacher 1974-79; Western Michigan Univ, administrator 1981-84, lobbyist 1984-87; Higher Educ Fiscal Analyst, 1987-. **ORGANIZATIONS:** Mem bd dirs YWCA 1980-86; WMU Black Caucus Western MI Univ 1981-; mem Amer Soc Trainers and Developers 1983-; pres Training/Learning/Development/Design 1983-; speaker NCEOA Chicago 1985, Washington DC 1986; speaker Evaluation Conference ENET; mem Alpha Kappa Alpha, Natl Assoc Women's Deans & Admin. **HONORS/ACHIEVEMENTS:** Charles Stewart Mott Fellowship Mott Foundation 1981-82; Award for Achievement and Excellence in Educ Natl Assoc of Negro Business & Professional Women 1985. **BUSINESS ADDRESS:** House Fiscal Agency, Michigan House of Representative, 222 Seymour St, Lansing, MI 48909.

COLLINS-GRANT, EARLEAN
Elected official. **PERSONAL:** Born in Rollingfork, MS; married John Grant; children: Dwarrye. **EDUCATION:** Univ of IL, BS Soc & Ed. **CAREER:** Collins Realty & Ins Agency, self employed 1969-72; State of IL Dept of Children & Familty Svcs, soc serv admin 1972-76; State of IL, senator. **ORGANIZATIONS:** Mem Westside Business Assoc, Natl Assoc Soc Workers, Natl Conf State Leg, Conf of Women Leg, Intergovernmental Coop Council. **HONORS/ACHIEVEMENTS:** Best Legislator Awd Independent Voters of IL; IL Business & Professional Women's Awd; IL Ed Assoc Awd; Amvet's Awd. **BUSINESS ADDRESS:** Senator Dist 9, Illinois State Senator, 5943 W Madison St, Chicago, IL 60644.

COLLYMORE, EDWARD L.
College administrator. **PERSONAL:** Born Jan 05, 1938, Cambridge, MA; son of Percival Collymore and Eulah Collymore; married Marcia L Burnett; children: Sandra, Edward Jr. **EDUCATION:** Villanova Univ, BS, Econ, 1959, MA, Counseling, 1971; Univ of PA, EdD Admin, 1984. **CAREER:** Cambridge Public Sch, Substitute teacher, 1963; Liberty Mutual Ins Co, casulty underwriter, 1963-66; Third Dist Ct Cambridge; juvenile probation officer, 1966-69; Office Soc Action Program, Villanova Univ, asst dir, dir, 1969-;. **ORGANIZATIONS:** Bd Rosemont Optimist 1983; bd vice pres Comm Action Agency Delaware CO 1984. **HONORS/ACHIEVEMENTS:** Co-holder, World Record, 60yd dash, AAU Track, 1957; All-Amer 220 yard dash NCAA Track 1957-59; rep US Track Europe, Russia AAU, 1957-58; Soc Action Award VU, 1978; Hall of Fame, VU Alumni Assn, 1980; Distinguised Alumnus Black Cultural Soc, 1982; Rosemont Optimist Man of the Year, 1985; Comm Action Agency of DE County Bd, Mem of the Year, 1985. **MILITARY SERVICE:** USMCR col. **BUSINESS ADDRESS:** Dir Social Action Program, VillanovaUniv, VillanovaUniv, Villanova, PA 19085.

COLLYMORE, WALTER ARTHUR
Business executive. **PERSONAL:** Born May 19, 1933, Chicago, IL; married Jane M Humbert; children: Lisa, Terri, Glen. **EDUCATION:** CA State U, MBA 1968; Loyola Univ Haw Sch, 1965; Univ of IL, BSEE 1961. **CAREER:** P F Ind Inc, pres 1977-; Control Data Corp, vice pres 1968-77; ARINC Res Corp, asst gen mgr 1966-68; Rockwell Internat, prgm mgr 1962-66; Hughes Aircraft Co, engr 1961-62. **ORGANIZATIONS:** Mem Am Mgmnt Assn; Am Trucking Assn; Nat Assn of Wholesalers & Distbr; Rubber Mfg Assn; Am Mgmt Assn; bd dir Nat Conf of Christians & Jews Southeastern New Eng Region; Beta Gamma Sigma Hon Bus Soc; mem Gov Com on Govt Ind & Labor for RI; past pres Orange Co NAACP; past pres Orange Co Fair Housing Cncl; past Chmn Orange Co Dem Cncl Publ. **HONORS/ACHIEVEMENTS:** Sev articles on micro electronics leading trade mag. **MILITARY SERVICE:** USAF 1953-57.

COLSON, JOSEPH S., JR.
Telecommunications executive. **PERSONAL:** Born Sep 27, 1947, Washington, DC; son of Joseph S Colson, Sr and Bernice Brett Colson; married Rosemary Elizabeth Rogers, Jul 18, 1969; children: Angela, Joseph Michael. **EDUCATION:** North Carolina State Univ, Raleigh, NC, BSEE, 1968; Stanford Univ, Palo Alto, Ca, MSEE, 1969. **CAREER:** AT&T Bell Laboratories, Greensboro, NC, MTS, 1968-71, Columbus, OH, supvr 1971-77, Naperville, IL, supvr, 1977-79, dept head, 1979-82, dir, 1982-87, exec dir, 1987-; AT&T Campus Executive, North Carolina Agricultural & Technical State/Univ, 1982-. **ORGANIZATIONS:** Mem, Executive Advisory Council, Natl Communications Forum 1987-; mem, IEEE, North Carolina Agricultural & Technical State Univ Industry Advisory Group (School of Engineering); mem, bd of trustees, North Carolina School of Science & Mathematics 1988-; mem, bd of overseers, Illinois Inst of Technology School of Business 1988-; mem, Congressman Harris Fawell's Technology Advisory Comm 1989-. **HONORS/ACHIEVEMENTS:** Phi Eta Sigma, 1964-68; Eta Kappa Nu, 1964-68; Tau Beta Phi, 1964-68; Phi Kappa Phi, 1964-68; one of top 25 black exec in the US, Black Enterprise Magazine, 1988; black engineer of the year for professional achievement, Black Engineer Magazine 1989. **BUSINESS ADDRESS:** Exec Dir, AT&T Bell Laboratories, 200 Park Plaza, Room 2Y-201A, Naperville, IL 60566.

COLSTON, FREDDIE C.
Educator. **PERSONAL:** Born Mar 28, 1936, Gretna, FL; married Doris Marie; children: Deirdre, Charisse. **EDUCATION:** Morehouse Clg, BA 1959; AT Univ, MA 1966; OH State Univ, PhD 1972. **CAREER:** So Univ Baton Rouge, LA, assc prof pol sci 1972-73; Univ Detroit Detroit, MI, assc prof pol sci & blk stds 1973-76; Dillard Univ New Orleans, LA, chrm div soc sci 1976-78; Delta Clg Univ Cntr,MI, asst prof pol sci 1978-80; Exec Semnr Cntr US Ofc Prsnl Mgmt, assoc dir 1980-87; prof and coordinator of graduate studies Inst of Govt, TN State Univ 1987-88; professor and coordinator of graduate studies NC Central Univ 1988-89; dir public admin prog NC Central Univ 1989-. **ORGANIZATIONS:** Mem Natl Conf Blck Pol Sci 1971-, Natl Forum Blck Pblc Admn 1984-, Am Pol Sci Assc 1968-, Ctr for the Study of Presdency 1976-, Am Soc Pblc Admn 1983-, Omega Psi Phi Frat 1956; bd mgmt YMCA Metropolitan Detroit 1976; rptr & mem Govt Subcmt Task Force 2000 Midland, MI 1979; mem Amer Assn for Higher Educ 1987-; mem Amer Mgmt Assn 1988-. **HONORS/ACHIEVEMENTS:** Intntl stds summer fellow Ford Found Duke Univ 1967; tchg assc Dept of Pol Sci OH State Univ 1968-71; fellow So Flwshp Fund Atlanta, GA 1968-71; mem Pi Sigma Alpha Natl Pol Sci Hon Soc 1958-; mem Alpha Phi Gamma Natl Jrnlst Hon Soc 1958-. **HOME ADDRESS:** 126 Hazleton Ln, Oak Ridge, TN 37830.

COLSTON, MONROE JAMES
Business executive. **PERSONAL:** Born Sep 05, 1933, Richland, TX; married Frances V Brown; children: Rhonda Wardlow, Marietta. **EDUCATION:** Univ MN, AA; Nat Exec Inst, Grad; Univ CO. **CAREER:** Urban Affairs Gtr Des Moines C of C, mgr; Boy Scouts of Am, exec dir 1968-71. **ORGANIZATIONS:** Real estate commr State of IA; bd dir IA Soc for Mgmt Nat; mem & Metro Assistance Team; Nat Alliance of Businessmen; mem Brain Trust to Congressional Balck Caucus; chmn co-founder Blacks in Mgmt; council mem Boy Scouts of Am; Kappa Alpha Psi; com person IA Career Edn; Civilian Serv Club; mem Am C of C. **HONORS/ACHIEVEMENTS:** Dist scouter of year; IA All Am Family 1970; outst serviceman AUS 1 954. **MILITARY SERVICE:** AUS corpl 1954-56. **BUSINESS ADDRESS:** 800 High, Des Moines, IA 50307.

COLTER, CYRUS J.
Attorney/writer. **PERSONAL:** Born Jan 08, 1910, Noblesville, IN; married Imogene Mackay (dec) (deceased). **EDUCATION:** Chicago Kent Coll of Law, 1940; Univ of Chicago Circle Campus, Hon Litt D 1977. **CAREER:** State of IL, commerce commissioner 1951-73; Northwestern Univ, prof of humanities 1973-78; attorney/writer. **ORGANIZATIONS:** Bd trustees Chicago Symphony Orch; served with Adminis Conf of US for Study of Exec Agencies of Fed Govt; IL Res Planning Comm; Railroads Comm of Natl Assn of Reg & Utility Commrs; mem Friends of Chicago Schs Comm; Kappa Alpha Psi. **HONORS/ACHIEVEMENTS:** Novelist and short story writer, "The Beach Umbrella" (awarded the Univ of IA Sch of Letters Award 1970); "The Rivers of Eros" 1972; "The Hippodrome" 1973; "Night Studies" 1980. **BUSINESS ADDRESS:** 1115 S Plymouth Ct, Chicago, IL 60605.

COLTRANE, ALICE TURIYA
Musician. **PERSONAL:** Born Aug 27, 1937, Detroit, MI; married John Coltrane (deceased); children: John (deceased), Ravi, Oran, Michelle. **EDUCATION:** Attended, Detroit Inst of Technology. **CAREER:** Jowcol Music, owner. **ORGANIZATIONS:** Director/founder The Vedantic Ctr 1976-; owner Avatar Book Inst 1978-. **HONORS/ACHIEVEMENTS:** Record albums ABC, MCA, Warner Bros 1968-78; books, audio, video tapes 1978-. **BUSINESS ADDRESS:** Owner, Jowcol Music, 12424 Wilshire Blvd, Ste 1000, Los Angeles, CA 90025.

COLVIN, ALONZA JAMES
Elected official. **PERSONAL:** Born Jul 08, 1931, Union Springs, AL; married Charlene A Bacon; children: Judy Webb, James E, Jimmie, Chris, Mark, Elizabeth. **EDUCATION:** GED only. **CAREER:** General Motors, general labor 1950-75; Saginaw Model Cities Inc, chmn 1967-71; Valley Star News, editor-publisher 1967-73; Buena Vista Charter Township, trustee 1980-. **ORGANIZATIONS:** Mem Natl Newspaper Publishers Assn 1967-73; producer/dir Autumn Leaves Pageant 1967-73; bd of dirs Police-Comm Relations Comm 1970-83; bd of dirs Saginaw Economic Development Corp 1971-72; bd of dirs Big Brothers of Saginaw 1972-76; vice pres Miss Saginaw Co Pageant 1970-. **BUSINESS ADDRESS:** Trustee, Buena Vista Char Twnshp, 1160 S Outer Dr, Saginaw, MI 48601.

COLVIN, ERNEST J.
Dental surgeon. **PERSONAL:** Born Jan 20, 1935, Chester, SC; married Shirley Beard; children: Ernest J, II. **EDUCATION:** Morgan State Coll, BS 1956f Howard Univ Sch Dentistry, DDS 1968. **CAREER:** Howard Univ Sch Dentistry, taught part time 1968-71; Self-employed, dr dental surgery. **ORGANIZATIONS:** Bd dir Horseman's Benevolent Protective Assn WV; Chi Delta Mu Frat; Am Dental Assn; MD State Dental Assn fin sec; Baltimore City Dental Soc; Am Indodontic Soc; Am Dental Soc Anesthesiology; Am Soc Gen Dentistry; Kappa Alpha Psi Frat; Columbia Chap Jack & Jill Am Inc; Columbia NAACP Am Cancer Soc; Com Health Council Baltimroe City; bd dir NW Baltimore Community Health Care; St Johns Evagelist Roman Cath Ch. **MILITARY SERVICE:** AUS pfc 1956-58. **BUSINESS ADDRESS:** 4413 Park Heights Ave, Baltimore, MD 21215.

COLVIN, WILLIAM E.
Educator. **PERSONAL:** Born May 27, 1930, Birmingham, AL; son of Lucius Will Colvin and Lucille White Colvin; married Regina A Bahner, Jun 09, 1956; children: Felicia Imre, Gracita Dawn. **EDUCATION:** AL State Univ, BS 1952; IN Univ, MS 1960; Academic Affairs Conf of Midwestern Univs, cert of administration; IL State, EdD 1971. **CAREER:** Stillman Coll, chair dept of art 1958-69; Illinois State Univ, dir of ethnic studies 1974-78; Illinois State Univ, prof of art 1971-; visiting prof, Eastern Illinois Univ 1987-. **ORGANIZATIONS:** Elected rep to US/Brazilian Mod Art Soc 1981-; dir career program IL Comm on Black Concerns in Higher Educ 1983-; mem Natl Conf of Artists; mem Natl Art Educ Assn; mem Phi Delta Kappa Hon Soc in Educ. **HONORS/ACHIEVEMENTS:** Rockefeller Fellow 1973-74; Phelps-Stokes Fund Grant 1973; publs exhibitions in field; Martin Luther King BLM Normal Human Relations 1983; Outstanding Artist in the Field AL State Univ 1985; Outstanding Service Awd IL Committee on Black Concerns in Higher Educ 1985; Fulbright Lecture/Rsch Fulbright Brazil 1981-85; univ grant to Belize for research, 1989. **HOME ADDRESS:** 507 N Grove St, Normal, IL 61761. **BUSINESS ADDRESS:** Professor of Art, Illinois State University, Normal, IL 61761.

COMBS, JULIUS V.
Medical management company executive, physician. **PERSONAL:** Born Aug 06, 1931, Detroit, MI; son of Julius Combs and Everlee Dennis Combs; married Alice Ann Gaston, Dec 27, 1956; children: Kimberly A, Julius G. **EDUCATION:** Wayne State Univ, BS 1953; MD 1958 Wayne State Univ Affilated Hospital, 1964; Am Bd Ob-Gyn, diplomate 1967; fellow AGOG. **CAREER:** Vincent & Combs Bldg Corp, pres ; Wayne State Univ School Med, clinical asst, 1976-; Omni Care health Plan, dir 1973-; MHMO Plans Inc, chmn bd of dir 1980; Aso Med Develop Corp, vice pres 1979-; MHMO Plans Inc, exec com. **ORGANIZATIONS:** Detroit Med Soc; chmn Region IV NMA 1975-77; mem Am Fertility Soc; NMA; Detroit Med Soc; MI State Med Soc; Wayne Co Med Soc; Am Assn Gyn Laparoscopists; Am Coll Ob-Gyn; Detroit Inst Arts Founders Soc; life mem NAACP; mem Kappa Alpha Psi Frat; mem House Del NMA 1967-. **BUSINESS ADDRESS:** Chmn/CEO, United American Healthcare Corporation, 7650 Second Ave, Detroit, MI 48202.

COMBS, SYLVESTER LAWRENCE
Educator. **PERSONAL:** Born Nov 15, 1925, Bristow, OK; married Willa Ryan. **EDUCATION:** Langston Univ, BA; OK State Univ, MA. **CAREER:** Stillwater Middle School, OK, teacher indus arts educ chmn faculty council 1967-; Slick HS OK, teacher, coach, principal, 1957-67; L'Overture HS OK, prin 1955-57; L'Overture HS, teacher coach, 1946-55; Waddell Reed & Natl Distributors of United Group of Mutual Funds & United Investors Life Insurance Co, registered rep. **ORGANIZATIONS:** mem, OK Educ Assn; Nat Educ Assn; Stillwater Educ Assn; Iota Lambda Sigma Professional Fraternity; mem exec bd Stillwater YMCA; mem United Supreme Council Sovereign Grand Inspectors; general 33rd Degree Ancient & Accepted Scottish Rite of Free Masonry Prince Hall Affiliation; mem Alpha Phi Alpha Fraternity; Stillwater Evening Kiwanis Club; Rogers Chapel Baptist Church; offered mem Phi Beta Kappa. **BUSINESS ADDRESS:** 315 S Duck, Stillwater, OK 74074.

COMBS, WILLA R.
Educator. **PERSONAL:** Born Aug 11, 1925, Oklahoma City, OK; married Sylvester. **EDUCATION:** Langston Univ, BS 1947; Oklahoma State Univ, MS 1955; Colorado State Christian Coll, PhD 1973; Oklahoma State Univ, EdD 1974. **CAREER:** Attucks High School, Vinita OK, vocational home economics teacher 1947-49; Chandler High School, Chandler OK, 1949; L'Overture High School, Slick OK, home economics teacher 1949-57; Southern Univ, Baton Rouge LA, home economics, home mgmt instructor 1960-61; Slick High School, Slick OK, teahcer 1957-66; Human Resource Devel Cooperative Extension Serv, Oklahoma State Univ, Stillwater OK, cooperative extension specialist 1966-76; Langston Univ Study Tour of W African Countries Liberia Ivory Coast Chana via Portugal Canary Islands, prof & chmn 1972-73; Langston Univ, prof, chmn home economics, agr research 1976-82, prof emeritus 1982-. **ORGANIZATIONS:** Chmn Reactor Panel Natl Educ Leadership Conf, Tuskegee Inst AL 1971; mem Central Coord Com on Amer Home Econ Issues, Pres EEO Com Oklahoma State Univ 1967-76; group leader Oklahoma Coalition for Clean Air 1970; mem Payne-Noble Co Health Advisory Com; trainee Head Start Program Oklahoma State Univ 1966-70; Natl 4-H Club Congress Chicago IL 1968; chmn State Home Econ Family Econ Home Mgmt Sect 1968-70; chmn Family Home Econ Home Mgt Sec of Amer Home Econ Assn Com on World Food Supply; vice pres Prog Phi Upsilon Omicron 1975-76; sec AAUW Stillwater Branch; Anti-Basileus 1970-75; NAACP; Langston Univ Alumni Assn; alumni council & treas Langston Univ Home Econ; Oklahoma State Univ Alumni Assn; charter mem, vice pres Langston/Coyle Business & Professional Women's Club 1984-85; black heritage comm Oklahoma Historical Soc 1984-88; citizen review comm Librar y Improvement Program 1985-88. **HONORS/ACHIEVEMENTS:** Outstanding Alumnus 1975; Distinguished Women's Club Award; Farm Found Scholarship, Colorado State Univ; cum laude Langston Univ OH; Two Thousand Women of Achievement 1970; Named to Natl Register of Prominent Amers & Intl Notables 1975; Named Outstanding Educator of the Year, Prince Hall Grand Lodge 1978-80; Named Outstanding Woman of the Year, AAUW Stillwater Branch 1978; Septima Poinsette Clark Award, Beta Omicron Omega Chapter of Alpha Kappa Alpha 1986. **BUSINESS ADDRESS:** Professor Emeritus, Langston University, Dept of Home Econ, Langston, OK 73050.

COMEGYS, DAPHNE D. **See HARRISON, DAPHNE DUVAL**

COMER, JAMES PIERPONT
Educator. **PERSONAL:** Born Sep 25, 1934, East Chicago, IN; son of Hugh Comer and Maggie Nichols Comer; married Shirley Ann Arnold; children: Brian Jay, Dawn Renee. **EDUCATION:** Indiana Univ, AB 1956; Howard Univ Coll of Med, MD 1960; Univ of MI Sch of Pub Health, MPH 1964. **CAREER:** St Catherine Hospital, E Chicago, Intern 1960-61; U.S. Public Health Service DC, Intern 1961-63; Natl Institute of Mental Health DC, staff mem 1964-68; Yale Univ Child Study Center CT, asst prof 1968-70; co-dir Baldwin-King Program 1968-73; assoc prof 1970-75; dir School Development Program 1973-; prof of Psychiatry 1975-; Maurice Falk Prof of Child Psychiatry 1976-; Yale School of Medicine CT assoc Dean 1969-. **ORGANIZATIONS:** Dir Conn Energy Corp 1976-; trustee Conn Savings Bank 1974-; dir Field Foundation 1982-88; trustee Hazen Foundation 1977-80; trustee Wesleyan Univ 1978-84;co-founder, vp, pres Black Psychiatrists of Amer 1968; mem Amer Acad of Child Psychiatry 1971 (council mem 1977-80); Amer Psych Assn 1970-; Ad Hoc Com Black Psychiatrists of APA 1970-71; Natl Med Assn 1967-; Am Orthopsychiatric Assn 1968-; chmn Council on Problems of Minority Group Youth 1970-71; chmn Adolescent Comm 1974-77; num articles; books: Beyond Black & White 1972, co-author Black Child Care 1975, School Power 1980, Maggie's Amer Dream 1988; columnist Parent's Mag 1978-. **HONORS/ACHIEVEMENTS:** Disting Alumni Award Howard Univ 1976; Outstanding Serv to Mankind Award Alpha Phi Alpha E Region 1972; Rockefeller Public Serv Awd 1980; John & Mary Markle Scholar in Acad Med 1967-74. **MILITARY SERVICE:** AUS Lt Col 1968. **BUSINESS ADDRESS:** Professor of Child Psychiatry, Yale Child Study Ctr, PO Box 3333, Yale Medical School, New Haven, CT 06510.

COMER, MARIAN WILSON
Educational administrator. **PERSONAL:** Born Nov 26, 1938, Gary, IN; married Richard Comer; children: Lezlie Jo Thompson, Samuel Grady Wilson, Michael, Denise Garnett. **EDUCATION:** Roosevelt Univ Chicago, BS 1966; IN Univ Bloomington, MAT 1969; Univ of IL Urbana, PhD 1975; Natl Inst of Health, Postdoctoral study. **CAREER:** St Margaret Hosp Hammond, IN, clinical chem med techn 1964-66; Pub Sch System Gary, IN, teacher 1966-68; Univ of IL Circle Campus, teaching asst 1970-74; IN Univ NW, assoc faculty mem 1972-74; Amer Council on Educ Chicago State Univ, post doctoral fellow 1974-84; NIH, extramural assoc 1978; Chicago State Univ, asst to vice pres research & devel 1978-79, acting dean student devel 1979-81, assoc vice pres academic affairs 1981-84; Inst of Transition Gary IN, ceo 1984-; Chicago State Univ, prof of biology 1984-. **ORGANIZATIONS:** Mem, Amer Inst of Biological Scientist, Botany Soc of Amer, Biology Soc Cert, Chicago State Univ, Alpha Kappa Alpha; Horticultural Soc; bd mem, Save the Dunes Council. **HONORS/ACHIEVEMENTS:** Distinguished Minority Speaker Univ of CA Berkeley Devel Program Grad Level; Dr Marian Wilson Scholarship, Chicago State Univ, Biological Soc; Acad Excelence Award, IN Univ. **BUSINESS ADDRESS:** Professor of Biology, Chicago StateUniv, 95th St at Dr M L King Drive, Chicago, IL 60628.

COMER, NORMAN DAVID
Educational administrator. **PERSONAL:** Born Dec 08, 1935, East Chicago, IN; married Marilyn Gaines; children: Norman, Karen. **EDUCATION:** Northwestern Univ, BS 1958; IN Univ, MS 1965; Loyola Univ, EdD 1974. **CAREER:** E Chicago Public Schools, english teacher 1960-66; Army Medical Corps, chief wardmaster 1961-62; E Chicago Public Schools, asst prin 1966-70, asst supt 1970-. **ORGANIZATIONS:** Evaluator "Princeton Desegregation Plan" (Jackson MI Bd of Educ) 1973; chmn N Central Assn Evaluations (Gage Park & Hirsch HS Chicago) 1973-74; consult Chicago Pub Sch (Yr Round Sch Study) 1974; mem Alpha Phi Alpha 1958; mem Phi Delta Kappa 1972; mem Assn of Supervision & Curriculum Develop (ASCD) 1972; mem Rockefeller Eval Task Force (E Chicago Pub Sch); various articles published. **MILITARY SERVICE:** AUS m sgt E-8 1960-65. **BUSINESS AD-**

DRESS: Assistant Superintendent, East Chicago Public Schools, 210 E Columbus Dr, East Chicago, IN 46312.

COMER, ZEKE
Elected official. **PERSONAL:** Born Sep 12, 1938, Hertsboro, AL; married Louise. **EDUCATION:** Purdue Univ, AA Elect Tech. **ORGANIZATIONS:** Serving 4th 2-yr term as Precinct Committeeman of Gary 3-9 Precinct; former treas Third Dist Precinct Org; mem NAACP, Urban League, Local 1010 US Steel Workers of Amer, Teamsters Union 142; advisory council Third Dist Comm Org; former pres Evening Star Missionary Baptist Church Choir for 10 yrs. **HONORS/ACHIEVEMENTS:** Man of the Year Invahoe Tennant Council 1977; Employee of the Month Electrical Dept Inland Steel Co 1976; Many community serv awds during 4-yr term as Precinct Committeeman; Elected by the Precinct Council to serve out term of previous 3rd Dist council person; Elected to 4-yr term at 3rd Dist Councilman. **BUSINESS ADDRESS:** Councilmember, Gary IN Common Council, Municipal Bldg, 401 Broadway, Rm 209, Gary, IN 46402.

COMFORT, NEMO ROBERT
Educator. **PERSONAL:** Born Apr 03, 1932, Kyle, TX; married Sofronia W; children: Robert, Reggie, Roslyn, Patricia, Donald. **EDUCATION:** Tillotson Coll, BA; TX So U, MEd; Univ of TX, Cert; Prairie View A&M U,; TX A&M U, PhD. **CAREER:** Calvert Independent School Dist, prin 1967-; Calvert High School, teacher. **ORGANIZATIONS:** Mem 21 Mem State Adv Comm on Instructional Resources & TX Educ Agy; mem TSTA/NEA; TEPSA; PTA; bd of dir exec com BVDC Calvert City Counc; Calvert C of C; Robertson Co Mental Hlth Adv Com; cub scout instnl rep Prospect Lodge #300; civic deacon supt sun sch co-chmn deacon bd sun sch tchr Bethel Bapt Ch; hon mem Flower Lovers Garden Club; hon mem Alpha Gamma Mu Nat Frgn Lang Hon Soc. **HONORS/ACHIEVEMENTS:** Certs for serv on Local Draft Bd #13, Former Pres Nixon; Outst Sec Tchrs of Am; Who's Who in Am S & SW; Personalities of S. **MILITARY SERVICE:** AUS corpl. **BUSINESS ADDRESS:** PO Box 7, Calvert, TX 77837.

COMPTON, JAMES W.
Business executive. **PERSONAL:** Born Apr 07, 1939, Aurora, IL; married Marilyn; children: Janice H, James, Jr. **EDUCATION:** Morehouse Coll, AB 1961; Univ of Grenoble Grenoble France; Loyola Univ Grad Work, 1969; Chicago Tchrs Coll. **CAREER:** Broome Co Urban League Binghamton NY, exec dir 1969-70; Opportunities for Broome Broome Co Urban League & Bingham NY, interim exec dir 1970; W Side Project Urban League, dir 1968-69; Comm Serv Dept Chicago Urban League, dir 1968-69; Specialist-in-charge W Side Office Employment Guidance Dept Chicago Urban League, 1967-69; On-the-job Training Rep Chicago Urban League, 1965-67. **ORGANIZATIONS:** Tchr Literacy Program for Welfare Recipients Chicago Bd Educ 1961-65; tchr Upper Grade Social Studies Chicago Bd Edn; pres Chicago Urban League; dir Chicago Com Urban Opportunities; dir Chicago Regional Purchasing Council; dir Comm Fund of Chicago; dir Leadership Council for Metro Open Comm; dir RooseveltUniv Coll of Edn; dir Union Nat Bank of Chicago Chicago & Alliance for Collaborative Effort, Steering Com; Chicago Manpower Area Planning Council; mem adv bd WNUS AM/FM; mem deans adv bd Coll Educ Roosevelt U; Chicago Press Club; The Chicago Forum; Citizens Com for Employment; Citizens Com of Greater Chicago Inc; Com on Foreign & Domestic Affairs; Mayor's Commn on Sch Bd Nominations; Concerned Citizens for Police Reform; Congressional Blue Ribbon Panel; The Group; Nat Conf on Social Welfare; NE IL Plan Ning Commn; WBEE Radio Comm Needs Comm; WGN Continental Broadcasting Co. **HONORS/ACHIEVEMENTS:** 10 outstanding young men award Chicago Jr Assn Commerce & Industry 1972; S End Jaycees certification of Appreciation 1972; S End Jaycees Chicago 10 & outstanding young men award; merrill schollar 1959-61; student mem Cultural Exchange Program. **MILITARY SERVICE:** US & USSR 1959. **BUSINESS ADDRESS:** Chicago Urban League, 4510 S Michigan Ave, Chicago, IL 60653.

COMVALIUS, NADIA HORTENSE
Obstetrician, gynecologist. **PERSONAL:** Born Jan 21, 1926; daughter of Rudolf B W Comvalius and Martha James. **EDUCATION:** Univ Utrecht, MD 1949; Bd Certified Ob Gyn 1970. **CAREER:** Jewish Memorial Hospital, dir of Gyn present; Lenox Hills Hosp NYC/Beth Israel Hosp NYC, attending Ob-Gyn; Hahnemann Med Coll, cancer rsch 1959-61; Planned Parenthood Westchester, med dir 1970-72; Private Practice USA, retired; Petromin Medical Ctr Yeddah K Saudi Arabia, consultant Ob/Gyn. **ORGANIZATIONS:** Mem Intl Platform Assn; Zonta New Rochelle NY; United Nation Assn; Am Heritage Soc; mem Am Med Women's Assn; Comm Workers Amer; Nat Social Register.

CONCEPCION, DAVID ISMAEL
Athlete. **PERSONAL:** Born Jun 17, 1948, Oeurrare de la Co, Venezuela. **EDUCATION:** Augustin Codazzi Coll. **CAREER:** Cinc Reds, infielder. **ORGANIZATIONS:** Nat League All-Star Team 1975-79; Championship Series 1970-72, 1975-76, 1979; World Series 1970, 1972, 1975-76.

CONE, CECIL WAYNE
Educational administrator. **PERSONAL:** Born May 21, 1937, Bearden, AR; married Juanita Fletcher; children: Cecil Wayne, Leslie Anita, Charleston Alan. **EDUCATION:** Shorter Clg, AA 1953-55; Philander Smith, BA 1955-57; Garrett Theological Sem, MDiv1958-61; Emory Univ, PHD 1969-74. **CAREER:** Union AME Little Rock, pastor 1964-69; OIC Little Rock, exec dir 1964-69; Turner Theological Seminary, dean 1969-77; Edward Waters Coll, Jacksonville FL, pres 1977-. **ORGANIZATIONS:** Mem Soc for Study of Blck Rel, Blck Theology Proj of Theology of the Am, NAACP, Alpha Phi Alpha Frat, Natl Urban League, Etc; bd of govr Cof C Jax FL 1978-81; St ethics cmsn State of FL 1979-81; bd of dir Jacksonville Symphny Assc 1984-85, Mayor's Cmsn on High Tech 1984-85. **HONORS/ACHIEVEMENTS:** Author The Identity Crisis in Blck Thelgy 1975; Distnghd Serv Awrd United Negro Clg Fund 1984; Otstndg Edctr of Yr Jacksonville Jaycees 1985; Hon Doctorates Temple Bible Clg Sem & Philander Smith Clg. **HOME ADDRESS:** 2955 Ribault Scenic Dr, Jacksonville, FL 32208. **BUSINESS ADDRESS:** President, Edward Waters Clg, 1658 Kings Rd, Jacksonville, FL 32209.

CONE, JAMES H.
Professor. **PERSONAL:** Born Aug 05, 1938, Fordyce, AR; widowed. **EDUCATION:** Philander Smith Coll, BA 1958, LLD 1981; Garrett Theol Seminary, BD 1961; Northwestern Univ, MA 1963, PhD 1965; Edward Waters Coll, LLD 1981. **CAREER:** Philander Smith Coll, asst prof 1964-66; Adrian Coll, asst prof 1966-69; Union Theol Seminary, prof of theology 1969-. **ORGANIZATIONS:** Union Theological Quarterly Review, The Journal of Religious Thought; mem Amer Theological Soc, Soc for the Study of Black Religion, Amer Acad of Religion, Ecumenical Assoc of Third World Theologians, Black Theology Project of the Theology in the Americas. **HONORS/ACHIEVEMENTS:** Contributing editor, Christianity & Crisis, Review of Religious Research, Journal of the Interdenominational Theological Ctr; 8 book publications including, "Black Theology & Black Power" 1969. **BUSINESS ADDRESS:** Professor of Systematic Theol, Union Theological Seminary, 3041 Broadway, New York, NY 10027.

CONE, JUANITA FLETCHER
Medical doctor. **PERSONAL:** Born Nov 13, 1947, Jacksonville, FL; married Cecil Wayne Cone PhD. **EDUCATION:** Howard Univ, BS 1968, MD 1974. **CAREER:** Private Practice, medical doctor. **ORGANIZATIONS:** Mem Amer College of Physicians, Jacksonville Medical Dental and Phar Assoc, Natl Medical Assoc; mem Jacksonville Chamber of Commerce, Natl Council Negro Women, Jacksonville Chapter Links Inc. **HONORS/ACHIEVEMENTS:** Diplomate Amer Bd of Internal Medicine 1979. **HOME ADDRESS:** 2955 Ribault Scenic Dr, Jacksonville, FL 32208. **BUSINESS ADDRESS:** 1833 Boulevard Ste 510, Jacksonville, FL 32206.

CONEY, HYDIA LUTRICE
Assistant bank vice president. **PERSONAL:** Born Dec 24, 1963, New Orleans, LA; daughter of Jimmie Lee Coney and Mertis Marie Flanders Coney. **EDUCATION:** Louisiana State Univ, Baton Rouge, LA, BS, Management. **CAREER:** First Union, Jacksonville, FL, asst branch mgr, 1988-. **ORGANIZATIONS:** Mem, Chamber of Commerce 1988-; mem, Civitan, 1989-, mem, Sertoma, 1989-; third vice pres, Zeta Phi Beta Sorority Inc, 1982-; Project Business Inst, Jr Achievement 1989-. **HONORS/ACHIEVEMENTS:** Outstanding Young Women of Amer, 1987; Natl Collegiate Greek Merit Award, 1987; Zeta of the Year, Zeta Phi Beta Sorority Inc, 1986. **HOME ADDRESS:** 9765 Southbrook Dr, Apt 4016, Jacksonville, FL 32256.

CONEY, LORAINE CHAPELL
Educator. **PERSONAL:** Born Feb 08, 1935, Eustis, FL; son of Francis Coney (deceased) and Julia M Graham; married Bettye Jean Stevens; children: Gessner, Melodi. **EDUCATION:** FL A&M U, BS 1958. **CAREER:** Sumter Co Bd of Pub Instrn, band & choral dir present; Sumter Co Music Tchrs, chmn 1973-77; Streep Music Co, sales rep 1964-69; Omega Psi Phi, bas Gamma Tau 1965-67. **ORGANIZATIONS:** Chmn FL Band Dirs 1963-67; chmn Music Educs Nat Conf 1958-77; Sumter Co Educ Assn NAACP; Omega Psi Phi; Masonic Lodge; guest woodwind tutor LCIE Univ FL 1971, 1974. **HONORS/ACHIEVEMENTS:** 1st Award Winning Co Band Dir 1959; Orgnzd Band & Prod Superior Performers;1st Black Instrument Salesman FL 1964-69; known as the Sch Band Man of Sumter Co 1959-77; FL Bandmasters Assn Adjudicator 1986. **BUSINESS ADDRESS:** PO Box 67, Bushnell, FL 33513.

CONGLETON, WILLIAM C.
Counselor. **PERSONAL:** Born Feb 13, 1935, Mt Sterling, KY; married Norma Peterson. **EDUCATION:** Marshall U. **CAREER:** Huntington Post Office, EEO counselor present; NAACP, pres 5 yrs, vice pres chmn labor com; Parish Council, St Peter Claver Cath Ch, pres 1972-73, adv 1974; Cabell County Parks & Recreation Commn, vice pres 1974-; Community Coll, adv 1975; Marshall U, com 1975, speaker 1976 & 79; Huntington High Sch, speaker 1977-78. **ORGANIZATIONS:** Mem Huntington Human Rights Commn 1979; commodore Ship of State WV 1979; bd of dirs Action Inc; mem Region II Planning & Devel Council - 6 Co Area; voice Black History WGNT Radio 4yrs; loan officer Nat Alliance of Businessmen; main speaker & chmn Hal Greer Blvd Dedication; chmn Huntington Human Rights Commn 1980; Active in Little League. **MILITARY SERVICE:** AUS corpl 1953-56.

CONLEY, CHARLES S.
Judge. **PERSONAL:** Born Dec 08, 1921, Montgomery, AL. **EDUCATION:** Univ of MI, BS 1948, MA 1947; NY U, JD 1955. **CAREER:** FL A&M Coll, prof; AL State U, 1962-64; Dr Martin Luther King SCLC, counsel; Recorder's CT, judge 1968-73; Macon County CT Common Pleas, 1972-. **ORGANIZATIONS:** Mem Am Nat AL Bar Assns. **BUSINESS ADDRESS:** 315 S Bainbridge St, Montgomery, AL.

CONLEY, ELIZABETH-LUCY CARTER
Retired elementary school principal. **PERSONAL:** Born Sep 26, 1919, Indianapolis, IN; married John E Conley. **EDUCATION:** Butler Univ, BS 1940, MS 1950, MS 1973; IN State Dept of Public Instruction, Adult Educ Certificate 1967. **CAREER:** Kokomo IN Public Schools, teacher 1941-42; Indianapolis Public Schools, teacher 1942-64, asst principal 1964-73, principal 1973-82. **ORGANIZATIONS:** Educ comm tutoring program 1987, mem Mt Zion Baptist Church 1938-; mem Alpha Kappa Alpha Sor 1939-; life mem Central IN Retired Teachers Assoc 1982-; treasuer, Marion Co Retired Teachers 1983-84; mem NAACP 1986; program committee, Crispus Attucks Alumni Class of 1936, 1986-87; sustaining mem Fall Creek YMCA. **HONORS/ACHIEVEMENTS:** Man of the Year Fall Creek YMCA 1962; SFIE Principal Awd 1977; Certificate for Distinguished Serv Indianapolis Assn of Elementary School Principals 1982.

CONLEY, EMMITT JEROME
Mayor. **PERSONAL:** Born Jun 16, 1922, Arkansas. **EDUCATION:** Attended AR Baptist Coll. **CAREER:** Southwestern Veneer Co; Warwick Electronics (now Sanyo); Hallett Construction Co, truck driver; City of Cotton Plant AR, mayor. **ORGANIZATIONS:** Consultant, Planters Bank & Trust Co; mem of bd, White River Planning and Devel; Northern AR Human Serv; appointed by Governor Clinton to AR Industrial Commn 1982; member, Woodruff County Hospital Bd; accomplished as mayor, three housing projects, water and sewer projects, an industrial park, street and drainage projects, medical complex and community center; USDA Citizens Advisory Commn Equal Opportunity Federal; bd of dir, Woodruff County Hospital & Nursing Home; White River Revolving Loan; White River Nurses Inc. **HONORS/ACHIEVEMENTS:** Oldest black Republican mayor in the US; Man of the Year Award, Black Mayors Assn of AR, 1984. **MILITARY SERVICE:** USN 1944-46. **BUSINESS ADDRESS:** Mayor, City of Cotton Plant, Town Hall, Cotton Plant, AR 72036.

CONLEY, HERBERT A.
Government official. **PERSONAL:** Born Oct 04, 1942, Monroe, LA; son of Lavelle

and Eunice R; married Elmira Tucker; children: Mark Warren, Starling David Hunter, Eric Wendell Hunter. **EDUCATION:** Univ of Washington, BA 1973, MBA 1975, PhD 1980. **CAREER:** State of FL, dir div of treasury. **ORGANIZATIONS:** Mem Amer Mgmt Assn 1970-, Amer Mktg Assn 1970-, Sales & Mktg Execs Assn 1970-, Southern Mktg Assn 1980-; general chairperson United Negro Coll Fund Phoenix AZ 1982-; mem Telecommunications Task Force Public Utilities Comm 1983-84; mem FL Govt Finance Officers Assn 1984-, Intl Foundation of Employee Benefit Plans 1984-, Natl Assn of Securities Professional 1985-; mem Rotary 1986-. **HONORS/ACHIEVEMENTS:** Faculty Grant-in Aid Program 1981-82; publications Proceedings NE Aids Conference San Diego CA 1982, Proceedings NE Aids Conference Boxton MA 1984. **HOME ADDRESS:** 808 Braeburn Dr, Fort Washington, MD 20744. **BUSINESS ADDRESS:** Dr Herbert A Conley, 7931 Orchid St NW, Washington, DC 20012-1133.

CONLEY, JAMES MONROE
Retired educational administrator. **PERSONAL:** Born Aug 18, 1915, Livingston, AL; married Ellie M Banks; children: Eddie R, Judy Conley Goldthree, James R, Janis E. **EDUCATION:** Tuskegee Inst, BS 1941; TN State Univ, MEd, 1963. **CAREER:** TN State Univ, res counselor 1963-69; Metropolitan Nashville Public Schools, guidance counselor, 1970-72, vocational program dir, 1972-80. **ORGANIZATIONS:** Deacon, Mt Olive Baptist Church, Nashville, TN 1964-, Sunday school supt 1978-81; basileus Gamma Phi Chapter, Omega Psi Phi Fraternity, 1974-76; pres Optimist Club Central Nashville, TN 1980-81; lt governor TN Dist Optimist Intl 1983-84, Chaplain, 1987-89; Counselor, 5th Dist Omega Psi Phi Fraternity, 1983-88. **HONORS/ACHIEVEMENTS:** Omega Man of the Yr Omega Psi Phi Fraternity, Gamma Phi Chapter, Nashville, TN, 1976-82; Honor Club Pres, Optimist Intl, 1988; Outstanding Sec/Treasurer, TN Dist Optimist Intl, 1985. **MILITARY SERVICE:** USAF major, 1942-63. **HOME ADDRESS:** 912 38th Ave N, Nashville, TN 37209.

CONLEY, JAMES S., JR.
Business executive. **PERSONAL:** Born Jun 07, 1942, Tacoma, WA; son of James S Conley and Vera Dixon Conley; children: Kimberly, Kelli, James III, Ward James W Martin, Jr. **EDUCATION:** Univ of Puget Sound, Tacoma, Washington, 1960-61; US Military Academy, West Point, NY, BS, Engineering, 1961-65; New York Univ, GBA, New York, NY, MBA, Finance 1976-82. **CAREER:** Delco Moraine, Dayton, Ohio, plant mgr, 1985-88, various positions, 1982-85; Avon Products, New York, NY, dir sales coordination 1982-82, various positions 1974-81; CEDC, Inc, Hempstead, NY, vice pres, 1972-74; Capital Formation, New York, NY, exec dir 1970-72. **ORGANIZATIONS:** Mem, bd of dir, Natl Devel Council, 1973-80; trustee, bd of dir, Assn of Graduates, US Military Academy, 1975-; lifetime mem, West Point Society of New York; mem, Society of Automotive Engineers, 1986-. **MILITARY SERVICE:** US Army, captain, 1965-70; Bronze Star for Valor, 1966; Bronze Star Meritorious, 1967; Army Commendation Medal, 1970; Presidential Unit Citation, 1967, Airborne and Ranger, 1965.

CONLEY, JOHN A.
Attorney, educator. **PERSONAL:** Born Mar 10, 1928, Springfield, IL; married Beverly J. **EDUCATION:** Univ of Pgh, BS 1952, JD 1955, MSW 1961. **CAREER:** Univ of Pittsburgh, prof 1969-; housing developer. **ORGANIZATIONS:** Mem Hill House Assn 1955-69; Neighborhood Ctrs Assn 1963-65; Allegheny Co, PA Bar Assns; bd dirs Pgh Public Schs; Freedom House Enterprise Inc; chmn bd Neighborhood Rehab Inc. **BUSINESS ADDRESS:** Housing Developer, 6959 Thomas Blvd, Pittsburgh, PA 15218.

CONLEY, MARTHA RICHARDS
Business executive, attorney. **PERSONAL:** Born Jan 12, 1947, Pittsburgh, PA; married Charles D Conley; children: David, Daniel. **EDUCATION:** Waynesburg Coll, BA 1968; Univ of Pittsburgh School of law, JD 1971. **CAREER:** School Dist of Pittsburgh, asst solicitor 1972-73; Brown & Cotton, attny 1973-74; US Steel Corp, asst mgr labor rel, arbitration, asst mgr compliance 1984-85, compliance mgr 1985-87, atty 1987-. **ORGANIZATIONS:** Mem Homer S Brown Law Assoc, Allegheny Cty Bar Assoc; life mem NBA, Amer Bar Assoc, Alpha Kappa Alpha; bd dir Louise Child Care Ctr 1973-77; commiss Prog to Aid Citizen Enterprise 1973-78; bd dir Health & Welfare Planning Assoc 1978-84; mem NAACP; former mem Intl Toastmistress Club inc; pres Aurora Reading Club of Pittsburgh 1984-85; admitted to practice before bar of Supreme Ct of PA 1972, Supreme Ct of US 1977; resource devel comm YWCA of Pittsburgh 1983-. **BUSINESS ADDRESS:** Attorney, US Steel Corp, 600 Grant St Room 1580, Pittsburgh, PA 15230.

CONNALLY, C. ELLEN
Judge. **PERSONAL:** Born Jan 26, 1945, Cleveland, OH; daughter of George L and Gwendolyn J; married Dale P Johnson; children: Seth George. **EDUCATION:** Bowling Green State Univ, BS 1967; Cleveland Marshall Law School, JD 1970; Natl Judicial Coll, Reno, NV, 1980-84; Ohio College of Jucicial Education,1980-84. **CAREER:** Cuyahoga County Court of Appeals, law clerk for Judge Krenzler 1971-73; Coyahoga County Court of Common Pleas, general trial referee 1973-79; Cleveland Municipal Court, judge 1979-. **ORGANIZATIONS:** Vice pres Bowling Green State Univ Alumni Assn 1977-78; president Black Women Lawyers Assn of Cleveland 1977-79; PUSH 1979-; member Cuyahoga County Bar Assn 1979-; advisory committee Cleveland Board of Education 1981-; board of trustees Community Action Against Drug Addiction 1983-; Ohio delegate Natl Judicial Conference on Rights of Victims 1983; Natl Bar Assn; Natl Conference of Black Lawyers; American Judges Assn; pres bd trustees Cleveland Public Theatre 1984-; mem bd trustees Cleveland Soc of the Blind OH Judges Assoc; University Trustee-Bowling Green State University, Bowling Green, Ohio, 1988-. **HONORS/ACHIEVEMENTS:** Supreme Court Excellent Judicial Service 1980; Supreme Court Outstanding Jucicial Service 1981; Supreme Court Excellent Judicial Service 1982; Awarded Certificate of Achievement Amer Academy of Jucicial Education 1982; Supreme Court Outstanding Judicial Service 1983; Elected Admin Judge Cleveland Municipal Court 1987. **BUSINESS ADDRESS:** Cleveland Municipal Court, P.O. Box 94894, Cleveland, OH 44101-4894.

CONNELL, CAMERON
Business executive. **PERSONAL:** Born Sep 13, 1944; married Barbara. **EDUCATION:** St Anthony's Coll, 1963. **CAREER:** Hudson-W Radio Inc, vice pres bus mgr 1974-; Harlem Savings Bank, head teller 1971-74; Freedom Nat Bank, teller 1969-71; Barbados WI, tchr 1963- 68; Coco Cola NY, asst ofc mgr 1973-74. **ORGANIZATIONS:** Mem New Rochelle Cricket Club 1970-75.

CONNER, GAIL PATRICIA
Law enforcement. **PERSONAL:** Born Mar 20, 1948, Detroit, MI. **EDUCATION:** Exchange student to Bates College, 1967; Wilberforce Univ, BA 1969; Antioch College, MA 1970. **CAREER:** Detroit Public Schools, teacher 1971-73; State of MI, state probation/parole 1973-77; US Courts-Detroit, US probation/parole officer 1977-. **ORGANIZATIONS:** Quinn AME Church 1948-; member NAACP 1971-; Fed Probation Officers Assoc 1977-; Erma Henderson re-election steering comm 1978; vice president WilberforceAlumni Assoc 1978-82; board member YWCA Detroit 1983-; natl dir for education Natl Assoc Negro Bus & Prof Womens Club, Inc 1983-; Natl Assn of Black Alumni Steering Comm. **HONORS/ACHIEVEMENTS:** Spirit of Detroit City of Detroit 1981; Scroll of Distinction Negro Business & Prof 1982; Appreciation Award Jr Achievement 1982; NANBPW Yellow Rose Awd Natl 1982; Appreciation Awd Mott Comm Coll 1983; Natl Black Monitor Hall of Fame 1985; MI Women Resource Guide 1785-1985; Wilberforce Univ Dist Alumni Serv Award 1985; NANBPW Club Woman of the Year 1982; AOID Hall of Fame 1985; Outstanding Alumni of WU 1985. **HOME ADDRESS:** 2082 Hyde Park Dr, Detroit, MI 48207. **BUSINESS ADDRESS:** Probation/Parole Officer, US Justice Department, 415 Federal Building, Detroit, MI 48226.

CONNER, LUCY SHULL
Appointed official. **PERSONAL:** Born Feb 02, 1938, Fayetteville, TN; children: Reggie D, Kim A. **EDUCATION:** St Mary's College, BA 1978. **CAREER:** Mesa Lutheran Hosp, med tech 1964-70; Heard Museum of Art, membership coord 1972-77; Black Theatre Inc, bus mgr 1978-80; AZ Dept Economic Secty, progspecialist 1983-84; US Senate, legislative asst 1984-. **ORGANIZATIONS:** Mem AZ Townhall; precinct committeeperson Maricopa Co; advisor AZ Women's Task Force; mem Black Senate Staff Caucus; pres Phoenix Chap Delta Sigma Theta;bd mem Valley Christian Centers; pres POIC Women's Aux. **HONORS/ACHIEVEMENTS:** Published booklet "The Fundamentals of Finding Funds" for small arts groups. **BUSINESS ADDRESS:** Legislative Assistant, US Senate, 328 Hart Senate Bldg, Washington, DC 20510.

CONNER, MARCIA LYNNE
City manager. **PERSONAL:** Born Feb 26, 1958, Columbia, SC; daughter of Edward Eugene Conner and Joan Delly Conner. **EDUCATION:** Talladega Coll, Talladega, Alabama, B.A. 1980; Univ of Cincinnati, Cincinnati, Ohio, M.C.P., 1982. **CAREER:** City of Opa-locka, Opa-locka, FL, asst city mgr, 1985-87, city mgr, 1987-; Metropolitan Dade County Miami, FL, mgmt intern 1982-83, budget analayst, 1983-85. **ORGANIZATIONS:** Mem, American Society for Public Administrators, 1982-; mem, Intl City Manager's Assn, 1982-; mem, Leadership Miami, 1986-; sec/bd mem, Greater Miami YWCA, 1987-; bd mem, Big Brothers & Sisters of Miami, 1987-; bd mem, Natl Forum for Black Public Administrators, 1987-. **HONORS/ACHIEVEMENTS:** Outstanding Young Professional, South Florida American Society for Public Admin, 1982; One to Watch in '88, South Florida Magazine, 1988; Up & Comers Award, South Florida Business Journal, 1989. **BUSINESS ADDRESS:** City Manager, City of Opa-locka, 777 Sharazad Blvd, Opa-locka, FL 33054.

CONNOLLY, ALLAN BURNON
Educator. **PERSONAL:** Born Dec 07, 1919, Tazewell, VA; married Thelma Trigg; children: Allan, Jr, Madeline, Michael. **EDUCATION:** Bluefield State Coll, BS 1939; Atlanta U, MS; Hampton Inst, Grad Study; Howard U; Rutgers U; Univ WI; Temple U; VA State Coll. **CAREER:** Bluefield High School, teacher; City of Bluefield, vice mayor 1971-. **ORGANIZATIONS:** Past natl pres Bluefield State Coll & Alumni Assn 1954-58; WV State Tchrs Assn 1950-51; sec treas Summit City Amusement Enterprises 1972-75; mem KappaAlpha Psi Frat; Sigma Pi Phi Frat; Nat Educ Assn; pres Mercer County Assn Classroom Tchrs 1968; bd dirs Bluefield City 1969.

CONNOR, DOLORES LILLIE
Electronics and defense manager. **PERSONAL:** Born Sep 15, 1950, Mineral Wells, TX; daughter of Walter Malone Connor and Alpearl Sadberry Connor. **EDUCATION:** Univ of Texas at Arlington, TX, B.S. 1975; Amber Univ, Garland, TX, M.S. 1989. **CAREER:** Vought Systems Div of LTV, Dallas, TX, material control analyst 1969-76; Recognition Equipment, Irving, TX, buyer, 1975-77; Texas Instuments, Dallas, TX, buyer, 1977-78, small/minority business liaison officer, 1978-87, intl offset, 1978-80; mgr, small busines programs 1987-. **ORGANIZATIONS:** Mem, Zeta Phi Beta Honor Fraternity/Communications, 1975; Ft Worth Negro Business & Professional Women's Club 1975-77; bd mem, Dallas Urban League, 1979-80; mem, Richardson Business & Professional Women's Club, 1979-86; mem, Leadership Dallas, 1980-; bd chmn, D/FW Minority Purchasing Council, 1980-83, mem, Texas Governor's Committee for Employment of Disabled, 1981; bd mem, Mayor's Committee for Employment of the Disabled, 1981-85; exec dir, Loan-D/FW Minority Purchaisng Council, 1983; captain, Neighborhood Watch, Richardson, TX, 1983-87. **HONORS/ACHIEVEMENTS:** Young Careerest, Richardson Business & Professional Women's Club, 1980; sponsor of the largest fund raiser viewing party for the United Negro Coll Fund, 1982-86; Youth Motivator, Natl Alliance of Business, 1983; Supporter of Entrepreneurs, Venture Magazine & Arthur Young, 1987. **BUSINESS ADDRESS:** Manager, Small Business Program, Texas Instruments Inc, PO Box 650311, MS 3933, Dallas, TX 75265.

CONNOR, GEORGE C., JR.
State official. **PERSONAL:** Born May 18, 1921, Baldwin, LA; married Marjorie Breard; children: Jan, George, Terri. **EDUCATION:** Xavier U, BS 1950; Bradley U; VA State Coll; Dillard U; Lamar U. **CAREER:** LA, state rep. **ORGANIZATIONS:** Mem Crescent City Coaches 1952-65; Nat HS Coaches Assn; Alpha Phi Alpha Frat; Holy Name Soc; Knights of Peter Claver; mem So Reg Educ Bd; Educ Commn for States; bd dirs YMCA; St Bernard Area Community Ctr; Interracial Counsel for Business Opportunities; bd trustees Narconon New Orleans. **MILITARY SERVICE:** AUS 1942-46. **BUSINESS ADDRESS:** 2647 Havana St, New Orleans, LA 70119.

CONNOR, JAMES RUSSELL
Business manager. **PERSONAL:** Born Oct 30, 1940, Lima, OH; son of Russell T Connor and Esther Rowe Connor; married Beryl Dixon, Aug 25, 1973; children: Steven Eric Connor, Jeffrey Allan Connor. **EDUCATION:** Bowling Green State Univ, Bowling Green OH, 1969-71; Defiance Coll, Defiance OH, BS in Business 1972; Indiana Univ, Bloomington IN, MBA (consortium fellowship) 1974. **CAREER:** Ford Motor Co, Lima OH, quality control superintendent 1980-81; Kelsey-Hayes Co, Marlette MI, manufacturing manager, 1981-82, plant manager 1982-84; New departure Hyatt, General Motors Corp, Sandusky OH, director

quality assurance 1984-88, director engine & powertrain systems 1988-89; Saginaw Div General Motors Corp, Saginaw MI, director engine & powertrain systems, 1989-. **ORGANIZATIONS:** Bd mem, Fireland Community Hospital, 1986-87; bd mem, Community Action Program 1986-87; co-chairman, United Way Fund Drive, 1987; chairman, selection committee LEADS, 1988. **HONORS/ACHIEVEMENTS:** Beta Gamma Sigma, Bowling Green State Univ, 1971; Consortium Fellowship, Consortium for Graduate Study in Management, 1973. **MILITARY SERVICE:** USMC, sgt E5, two meriotorous promotions (pfc in 1961, corporal in 1963) 1961-66. **BUSINESS ADDRESS:** Dir of Engine & Powertrain Business Unit, Saginaw Division, General Motors Corp, 3900 Holland Road, Saginaw, MI 48601.

CONNOR, ULYSSES J., JR.
Educator. **PERSONAL:** Born Dec 13, 1948, New Orleans, LA. **EDUCATION:** Adelphi Univ, BA 1970; Syracuse Univ, JD 1974. **CAREER:** Syracuse Univ, programs coord 1974-75, dean of students 1975-82; Univ of MD, asst to vice chancellor 1982-85, dir/dev educ 1985-. **ORGANIZATIONS:** Bd of dirs Syracuse Ctr for Dispute Settlement 1976-81; allocations comm mem DC United Way 1986-. **HONORS/ACHIEVEMENTS:** Blue Book of Greater Syracuse 1981; Omicron Delta Kappa Honor Soc 1986. **MILITARY SERVICE:** USAF capt. **BUSINESS ADDRESS:** Asst to the Dean, Univ of Maryland, Undergraduate Studies,, Hornbake Library, Rm 1115, College Park, MD 20742.

CONRAD, EMMETT J.
Physician. **PERSONAL:** Born Oct 06, 1923, Baton Rouge, LA; married Eleanor; children: Cecila. **EDUCATION:** So Univ, BS 1944; Meharry Med Coll, 1948. **CAREER:** Private practice, gen surgeon. **ORGANIZATIONS:** Mem Dallas Ind School Bd Tst 1967-77; chmn Career Ed Comm State TX.

CONRAD, JOSEPH M., JR.
Business executive. **PERSONAL:** Born Jan 16, 1936, New Orleans; married Bernadine Barard; children: 3 Children. **EDUCATION:** Xavier U, BS 1962. **CAREER:** Office of Prog Planning & Control US Small Bus Adm, 1968-. **ORGANIZATIONS:** Mem bd dir Black Sec Catholic Archdiocese of Washington Bdc; permanent deacon Catholic Archdiocese 1971. **HONORS/ACHIEVEMENTS:** Recip 24th An Wm A & Jump Meml Awd 1973; SBA Med for Meritorious Serv 1970. **MILITARY SERVICE:** AUS 1955-58.

CONTEE, CAROLYN ANN
Dentist. **PERSONAL:** Born Feb 14, 1945, Washington, DC; married Dr James E Lassiter Jr; children: Lisa C Butler. **EDUCATION:** Howard Univ, BA (Cum Laude) 1969, MEd 1973, DDS 1981. **CAREER:** DC Public Schools, elem tchr 1969-77; Private Dental Practice, dentist 1981-86; Upper Cardozo Comm Hlth Ctr, staff dentist 1982-86; Shaw Comm Health Ctr, staff dentist 1982-86; Fairleigh Dickenson Coll of Dentistry, asst prof 1987; Airport Dental Ctr, asst dir 1986-. **ORGANIZATIONS:** Dir of continuing educ exec bd Robert Freeman Dental Soc 1982-84; house of delegates 1982-86, exec comm 1986, asst treas 1986 Natl Dental Assoc; bdof trustees Natl Dental Assoc Foundation 1983-, Potomac Chap of Links Inc 1984-. **HONORS/ACHIEVEMENTS:** Outstanding Serv Robert T Freeman Dental Soc 1984; Outstanding Serv Capital Headstart Certificate 1985. **BUSINESS ADDRESS:** Assistant Dir, Airport Dental Center, Newark Intl Airport Bldg 51, Newark, NJ 07101.

CONWAY, WALLACE XAVIER, SR.
Retired museum curator. **PERSONAL:** Born Jun 11, 1920, Wash, DC; son of Ewell Lucas Conway Jr and Jessie Taylor Conway; married Jessie Elizabeth Dedeaux; children: Dianne Pettie, Wallace X Jr, Stephanie Victorian. **EDUCATION:** Miner Teacher Coll, BS, 1941; Cooper Union Sch of Arts & Sciences, 1942; US Dept of Agr Grad School, 1953; Trenton State Coll, 1953; Mercer Community Coll, 1977-79; Paris-American Academy, Univ of Paris, 1977; NYU, MA, 1987. **CAREER:** Co-Art Studios (Visual Communications), owner/dir 1950-64; US Weather Bureau, graphic artist, 1964-65; Smithsonian Inst, graphic supvr, 1965-69; Afro-Amer Museum Assoc, Washington DC, advisor 1980-; NJ State Museum, curator, chmn exhibits, 1969-88 (retired). **ORGANIZATIONS:** Consultant, Dept of Educ, NJ, 1962-82; adjunct faculty, Trenton State Coll, NY, 1978-80; chmn, cultural comm Cable TV Network, NJ 1983-85; consultant, Afro Amer Museum, Philadelphia, PA 1981-83, NJ Civil Serv Comm 1981-84, Afro-Am Museum Assn, 1981-85, Bedford-Stynt Hist Assn Brooklyn, NY; chrtr mem Beta Kappa Chap KAU 1945-85; mem Rotary Intl 1975-; artist, author, lecturer, 1970-; validating comm Presbytery of New Brunswick NJ, YWCA Comm Cultural Enrichment Prog Trenton; tech consultant Martin Luther King Natl Holiday Memorial Mural unveiled on site Martin Luther King Library, Washington DC 1986; artist Don Miller making of mural traveling exhibit, 1986-87; Consultant, Rouse Associates, 1987-88; Consultant, Church & Dwight, 1988-89; Consultant, Merrill Lynch, 1987-88; Bd of Dir, Trenton YMMCA, 1988-; Advisory Bd, Minority Arts Assembly, 1988-. **HONORS/ACHIEVEMENTS:** Major Art Retrospective Exhibit, City of Trenton Museum, 1989; 19 Black Artists of Mercer City Exhibit, Mercer County Coll, 1989; fellowship, Kellog Found, Field Museum, Chicago, 1987. **MILITARY SERVICE:** USCG seaman 1/c; Honorable Discharge. **HOME ADDRESS:** One Chester Ave, Trenton, NJ 08619.

CONWILL, GILES A.
Clergyman. **PERSONAL:** Born Dec 17, 1944, Louisville, KY. **EDUCATION:** San Diego U, BA 1967; Athenaeum of OH, MDiv 1973. **CAREER:** St Rita's Bd Dirs Comm Crisis Center, Catholic priest. **ORGANIZATIONS:** San Deigo Black Lay Cath; mem Minority & Ethnic Comm VI San Diego Diocesan Synod; Diocesan Com Black Caths; vice pres SE San Diego Interdenominational & Ministerial Alliance; Expansion & Review Com 4-H Youth Program; NAACP; Diocesan Vocation Coordinator.

CONYERS, CHARLES L.
Educator. **PERSONAL:** Born Sep 08, 1927, Cyrene, GA; married Mary Foster; children: Charles C, Andrie B, Brian K. **EDUCATION:** Savannah State Coll, BS 1949; VA State Coll, BS, MS 1949-58; Univ of IL, Grad Study; Univ of VA, Grad Study. **CAREER:** Migrant Educ & Title I, asst supr, supr 1966-; JJ Wright School, principal 1963-66; Central Academy, principal 1961-63; VA High Schools, teacher 1949 -61. **ORGANIZATIONS:** Mem VEA; NEA; Masonic Lodge #322; Phi Delta Kappa; life mem Phi Beta Sigma; mem Deacon 1st African Bapt Ch RA 1945-47. **BUSINESS ADDRESS:** State Dept of Educ, PO Box 60, Richmond, VA 23216.

CONYERS, JAMES E.
Educator. **PERSONAL:** Born Mar 06, 1932, Sumter, SC; son of Emmett and Crenella; divorced; children: Judy, Jimmy, Jennifer. **EDUCATION:** Morehouse Coll, AB 1954; Atlanta Univ, MA 1956; WA State Univ, PhD 1962.. **CAREER:** IN State Univ, prof 1968-; Atlanta Univ, assoc prof 1964-68; IN State Univ, asst prof 1962-64; WA State Univ, teaching asst 1958-61; Lemoyne Coll, teacher, 1955-56. **ORGANIZATIONS:** Chmn, Caucus of Black Sociologists in Amer 1973-74; pres, Assn of Social and Behavioral Scientists, 1970-71; mem, Selection Comm for Natl Fellowship Fund Graduate Fellowships for Black Amer, 1973-78; mem, Advisory Panel for Sociology NSF, 1975-77; mem, Nominating Comm North Central Sociology Assn, 1979; mem, Young Men Civic Club Terre Haute, 1970-; mem, exec comm Vigo Co Black Political Caucus, 1971; mem, NAACP Terre Haute; mem, NAACP Natl; comm chmn, Participation & Status of Racial & Ethnic Minorities in the Prof of the Amer Sociological Assn, 1971-72. **HONORS/ACHIEVEMENTS:** Various articles published in Sociology & Social Research; Sociol Inquiry/Journal of Negro Educ; Co-editor, Sociology for the Seventies, 1972; Co-author, Black Elected Officials, 1976; WEB Dubois Award, Assn of Social & Behavioral Scientists, 1981. **BUSINESS ADDRESS:** Professor of Sociology, Indiana State University, Terre Haute, IN 47809.

CONYERS, JOHN, JR.
Congressman. **PERSONAL:** Born May 16, 1929, Detroit, MI. **EDUCATION:** Wayne State Univ, BA 1957, JD 1958; Wilberforce Univ, Hon LLD 1969. **CAREER:** Congressman John Dingell, legislative asst 1958-61; Conyers Bell & Townsend, sr partner 1959-61; MI Workman's Compensation Dept, referee 1961-63; US House of Reps, representative. **ORGANIZATIONS:** Vice chmn Natl Bd of Amer for Dem Action; vice chmn Natl Adv Bd Amer Civil Liberties Union; dir educ Local 900 UAW; exec bd mem Detroit br NAACP; mem Wolverine Bar Assn; gen council Detroit Trade Union Ldrship Council; mem Tabernacle Baptist Ch; Kappa Alpha Psi Frat; publs in field. **HONORS/ACHIEVEMENTS:** Rosa Parks Awd 1967. **MILITARY SERVICE:** AUS 1950-54. **BUSINESS ADDRESS:** Representative, US House of Representatives, 2444 Rayburn House Office Bldg, Washington, DC 2055.

CONYERS, NATHAN G.
Business executive. **PERSONAL:** Born Jul 03, 1932, Detroit, MI; married Diana Callie Howze; children: Nancy, Steven, Susan, Ellen, Peter. **EDUCATION:** Wayne State Univ, LLB. **CAREER:** Colven Snowden Smith & Keith Detroit, mem firm 1960-63; Keith Conyers & Anderson, partner 1964-67; Conyers Anderson Brown & Wahls, sr partner 1967-70; Conyers Ford Inc, pres 1970-. **ORGANIZATIONS:** Spec asst attny gen State of MI 1967-70; mem 1967, chmn 1971 MI Bd State Canvassers; mem, pres Natl Black Auto Dealers Assoc. **MILITARY SERVICE:** AUS 1953-55. **BUSINESS ADDRESS:** President, Conyers Ford, Inc, 2475 West Grand Blvd, Detroit, MI 48208.

COOK, CHARLES A.
Physician, consulting firm executive. **PERSONAL:** Born Jun 19, 1946, Biloxi, MS; son of Norman Cook, Sr and Eleanor Posey Shelby; married Shirley A Bridges Cook, Oct 23, 1967; children: Timothy, Tamotha, Torryhe. **EDUCATION:** Tougaloo Coll, Tougaloo MS, BA 1971; Tufts Univ School of Medicine, Boston MA, MD 1975; Harvard Univ School of Public Health, Boston MA, MPH, 1975; Univ of North Carolina, Chapel Hill NC, Government Executive Business Certificate, 1982. **CAREER:** State of MA, Boston MA, special asst, mental health 1974-75; State of Mississippi, Jackson MS, asst chief, disease control 1979-80; Univ of Mississippi Medical Center, asst prof of medicine, 1979-80; State of North Carolina, Raleigh NC, chief adult health, 1980-85; Univ of North Carolina at Chapel Hill, School of Public Health, adjunct-assoc prof, 1987-. **ORGANIZATIONS:** Bd mem, Amer Heart Assn of North Carolina, 1980-89; bd mem, Amer Cancer Society of North Carolina, 1980-85; pres, Associated Resources Consulting Group, 1984-89; mem, North Carolina Insurance Trust Commission, 1988-89. **HONORS/ACHIEVEMENTS:** Airman of the Month, US Air Force, 1965; Doctor of the Year, Hinds County Medical Society, 1979; Tarheel of the Week, Raleigh News & Observer 1983; Honored Volunteer, NC Diabetes Assn 1983; Volunteer of the Year, State Baptist Convention, 1984; author of "Anti-Hypertensive Drug Compliance In Black Males," Journal of the Natl Medical Assn 1984, "Hypertensive Therapy in Blacks," Journal of Clinical Hypertension, 1986, "Pathophysiologic and Pharmacotherapy Considerations-Black Hypertension," Amer Health Journal, 1988. **MILITARY SERVICE:** USAF, sgt, Airman of the Month (April 1967), 1964-68. **BUSINESS ADDRESS:** Pres, Assoc Resources Consulting Group, 3392 Six Forks Road-Park Place, Raleigh, NC 27609.

COOK, CHARLES CONWAY
Dancer, teacher. **PERSONAL:** Born Feb 11, 1917, Chicago, IL. **CAREER:** Dance Teacher, Yale Univ, Duke Univ, Long Island Univ, Amer Univ Washington DC, CETA Clark Ctr for the Arts; vaudville dance team Cook & Brown; toured w/Euke Ellington & Count Basie Orch; appeared in "Kiss Me Kate" Broadway; appeared in Dance Theatre Workshop "Shoot Me While I'm Happy" 1979; appeared in Brooklyn Acad of Music "Step In Time" 1979; appeared in "An Evening with Charles Cook and Friends" Aaron Davis Hall City Coll 1984. **ORGANIZATIONS:** Mem Copasetics Inc; mem Cultural Council Found; lecture demonstrations & creating routines CETA Artists Project; Dance & theatre credits all over the world.

COOK, FRANK ROBERT, JR.
Attorney, accountant. **PERSONAL:** Born Aug 19, 1923. **EDUCATION:** BS 1945, JD 1949, LLM 1955, BCS 1963, MCS 1964, PhD 1951, DD 1967. **CAREER:** Frank R Cook Jr, attny pub acct & mngmt cnslt, real property appraiser 1950; Chldrn of Ch of Christ, minister 1966-; RE Broker, bus chance broker 1945-; Integrity Adjustment Co, owner 1944-49. **ORGANIZATIONS:** Mem WA Bar Assn; Nat Soc Pub Acct Adm Planned Parnthd & Sex/Mar Cnslng Prog 1967. **BUSINESS ADDRESS:** 1715 Eleventh St NW, Washington, DC 20001.

COOK, FRED HARRISON, III
Athlete. **PERSONAL:** Born Apr 15, 1952, Pascagoula, MS; married Valerie; children: Frederick Ramon. **EDUCATION:** Univ So MS. **CAREER:** Baltimore Colts, def end 1974-.

COOK, HANEY JUDAEA
Clergyman. **PERSONAL:** Born Nov 05, 1926, Little Rock, AR; married Osa L Jones; children: Cecilia Cook Pryor, Millicent, Hancy Jr, Veda. **EDUCATION:** AR Baptist Coll, BS

1958, DDivinity 1962; TN Baptist School of Religion, Hon Doctor of Letters 1974; Intl Bible Inst & Seminary Orlando FL, MBible Theology 1983. **ORGANIZATIONS:** Organizer of North Shore Baptist Ministers Alliance 1962; trustee Waukegan Twp 1977-85; founder & sponsoring committee Lake Cty Urban League; life mem NAACP; bd of dir EC Morris Inst Little Rock AR, Bethlehem Bapt Dist Assoc of IL; vice pres United Bapt State Convention of IL; large faculty mem McKinley Theological Seminary North Shore Extension. **HONORS/ACHIEVEMENTS:** Freedom Awd Alpha Phi Alpha Frat Inc Kappa Chi Lambda Chap 1979; Cert of Recognition IL House of Rep 1980. **MILITARY SERVICE:** USN 2nd class petty officer 4 yrs; 4 Battle Stars, 2 Campaign Ribbons, Asiatic & Phillipine Liberation. **HOME ADDRESS:** 809 New York, Waukegan, IL 60085. **BUSINESS ADDRESS:** Pastor, Gideon Missionary Bapt Church, 1000 Yeoman St, Waukegan, IL 60085.

COOK, HAROLD J.
Administrative judge. **PERSONAL:** Born Feb 02, 1946, Richmond, VA. **EDUCATION:** Howard Univ, BA 1968; Attended, Amer Univ Law Sch; Howard Univ Law Sch, JD 1971. **CAREER:** HUSA Howard Univ, vice pres 1967-68; Val Viola Memorial Found Washington, dir 1973; JCD Enterprises Inc, dir 1973; Pace Assoc Inc, dir 1974; Coll & Comm Consult Inc, 1975; administrative judge. **ORGANIZATIONS:** Natl exec sec Omega Psi Phi Frat Inc; mem Phi Alpha Delta Law Frat Inc 1972; officer Omega Psi Phi Frat Inc Wash DC; mem Howard Alumni Assn 1974; life mem Omega Psi Phi Frat Inc 1972; mem NAACP; Natl Legal Aid Defender's Assn 1968; mem Natl Leadership Conf on Civ Rights; NE Comm Orgn Kappa Psi Chap Omega Psi Phi Frat; mem Lamond-Riggs Civic Assn 1975; mem Big Bros; mem Boy and Girls Clubs; mem DC Alumni; Operation Crossroads Africa. **HONORS/ACHIEVEMENTS:** Keys to Cities of Bossier 7 Shreveport LA 1977, Norfolk 1975, Birmingham 1975; Appreciation Awd 1972; participant Operations Crossroads Africa Ghana 1967; Hon Cit Spartanburg SC 1974; six time winner CORE Scholarship 1965-71; Grad Basileus of the Yr Third Dist Omega Psi Phi Frat Inc 1971; Alpha Chap Omega Psi Phi Frat Inc Man of the Yr Awd 1967; Kappa Psi Chap Omega Psi Phi Frat Inc Man of the Yr Awd 1969; Vol of the Yr Bureau of Rehab 1982; Big Brother of the Yr Natl Capital Area 1983; Region III Big Brother of Yr 1983; Pan Hellenic Citizen of Yr 1983; Omega Psi Phi Frat Inc Washington DC Citizen of the Yr 1983; City Council Resolution 1984; tribute Congressional Record 1984; vice pres Shiloh Branch Boys an d Girls Clubs 1986-89; pres Skill Shot Racquetball Club 1988-. **BUSINESS ADDRESS:** Administrative Judge, 1522 U St, NW, Washington, DC 20001.

COOK, HENRY LEE, SR.
Dentist. **PERSONAL:** Born Sep 07, 1939, Macon, GA; married Mamie R Richmond; children: Cathy L, Henry L II. **EDUCATION:** Tuskegee Univ, BS 1962; Meharry Medical Coll, DDS 1969. **CAREER:** Private Practice, dentist. **ORGANIZATIONS:** Chairman of bd Minority Asst Corp 1977-87; mem Col Bd Health 1978-87; pres Alpha Phi Sigma, Phi Beta Sigma 1980-87, L & L Sports Unlimited 1980-87; vicechmn bd YMCA 1982-87; treas GA Dental Soc 1983-87; natl vice pres Tuskegee Natl Alumni 1985-87; natl trustee Natl Dental Assoc 1986-87. **HONORS/ACHIEVEMENTS:** Cited in Who's Who Among Amer Colls & Univs; Outstanding Young Man of Amer; Civil Rights Awd Natl Dental Assoc; Governor apptd Statewide Health Coord Council. **MILITARY SERVICE:** USAF 1st lt 1962-65. **BUSINESS ADDRESS:** 1190 Martin L King Blvd, Columbus, GA 31906.

COOK, JAMES E.
Clergyman, dean. **PERSONAL:** Born Mar 25, 1925, Lancaster, SC; married Mildred C Washington; children: Diaon, Gloria, Roslyn. **EDUCATION:** Livingstone Coll, AB 1948; Hood Theological Seminary, 1951; AL St U; VA Union Theol Sem. **CAREER:** Butler Ch AME Zion, minister 1961-; Lomax-Hannon Jr Coll, acad dean 1967-, dean of religion 1961-67; Warner Temple AME Zion Ch Lancaster, pastor 1950-51; Baum Temple AMEZion Ch Summerville, pastor 1951-61; Moore's Chapel AME Zion Ch, asst pastor 1949. **ORGANIZATIONS:** Acting presiding elder of Greenville Dist S AL Conf; mem Bd Trustees Lomax-Hannon Jr Coll; mem of bd Christian Educ AME Zion Ch; mem Bd of Evangelism AME Zion Ch; mem Ministers & Laymen Assn AME Zion Ch; mem 33 Degree Mason; United Supreme Council Class of 1972; Wingfiled Lodge #23a & Consistory #19; Chancellor Comdr Eagle Lodge KP; Omega Psi Phi; mem bd dir Recreation City of Greenville; Organized Comm Action Program. **HONORS/ACHIEVEMENTS:** Certificate for outstanding work in religion Daniel Payne Coll 1966; Plaque For Outstanding Work In Local Church & Community. **BUSINESS ADDRESS:** Lomax Hannon Jr Coll, Greenville, AL 36037.

COOK, JOYCE MITCHELL
Appointed government official. **PERSONAL:** Born Oct 28, 1933, Sharon, PA. **EDUCATION:** Bryn Mawr Coll, AB 1955; Oxford U, BA 1957, MA 1961; Yale U, PhD 1965. **CAREER:** White House Staff, staff asst 1977-; Howard Univ, dir of honors prog, mem dept of philosophy 1966-68, 1970-76; CT Coll, dept of philosophy 1968-70; Office of Economic Opportunity, publ Head 1965-66; US Dept of State, foreign serv reserve officer 1964-65; Wellesley Coll, dept of philosophy 1961-62; Yale Univ, dept of philosophy 1959-61. **ORGANIZATIONS:** Mng editor Review of Metaphysics 1959-61; consult Inst for Serv ot Educ 1972-76; mem Am Philosophical Assn; Com on Blacks in Philosophy 1970-76; prog com Eastern Div 1974-76. **BUSINESS ADDRESS:** White House Staff, The White House, Washington, DC 20500.

COOK, JULIAN ABELE, JR.
Judge. **PERSONAL:** Born Jun 22, 1930, Washington, DC; son of Julian Abele Cook and Ruth McNeill Cook; married Carol Annette Dibble; children: Julian Abele III, Peter Dibble, Susan Annette. **EDUCATION:** PA State Univ, BA, 1952; Georgetown Univ, JD, 1957; Univ of Virginia, LLM, 1988. **CAREER:** Private Practice, attorney, 1958-78; East Dist of MI, US Courthouse, Detroit, US Dist Judge, 1978-; Trial Advocacy Workshop, Harvard Univ, instructor, 1988-present. **ORGANIZATIONS:** Amer & Natl Bar Assns; Am Bar Found; co-chmn, Prof, Devel Task Force, MI Bar Assn; MI Assn of Black Judges; co-chmn, Cont Legal Educ Comm, Wolverine Bar Assn; Fed Bar Assn; pres, master of the bench, Am Inst of Courts, Detroit; chmn, Cont Legal Educ Comm, Oakland County Bar Assn, 1968-69, vice chmn, Judicial Liaison, Dist Court Comm, 1977, Cont Legal Educ Comm, 1977, Unauthorized Practice of Law, 1977; MI Supreme Court Defense Serv Comm, 1977; special asst, attorney general, State of MI, 1968-78; Judge, Arthur E Moore Law Clerk, 1957-58; mem, exec bd of dir, past pres, Child & Family Serv of MI; mem, bd of dir, Todd-Phillips Children's Home; chmn, Sixth Circuit Comm on Standard Jury Instruction; bd of dirs, Amer Heart Assn of MI, Ashland OH Theological Seminary, Brighton Health Serv Co rp, Child & Family Serv of MI, Georgetown Univ Alumni Assn; Judicial Conference of the US Judicial Ethics Comm, 1988-present; life mem, NAACP. Georgetown Univ Law Ctr; Hutzel Hosp & Pennsylvania State Univ Alumni Assoc. **HONORS/ACHIEVEMENTS:** Distinguished Citizen of the Year, NAACP, Oakland County, MI, 1970; Citation of Merit, Pontiac, MI Area Urban League, 1971; chmn, Civil Rights Commn A Resolution of Tribute of Julian Abele Cook Jr, State of MI, House of Representatives, 1971; Boss of the Year, Oakland County, MI, Legal Secretary Assn, 1973-74; Pathfinders Award, Oakland Univ, 1977; Serv Award, Todd-Phillips Home Inc, Detroit, MI, 1978; fellow, Am Bar Found, 1981; Focus & Impact Award Oakland Univ, 1985; Distinguished Alumnus Award, Pennsylvania State Univ, 1985; Distinguished Alumnus Award, John Carroll Award, Georgetown Univ, 1989; Augustus Straker Award, Wolverine Bar Assn, 1988; Absalom Jones Award, Union of Black Episcopalians, Detroit Chapter, 1988; Bench-Bar Award, Wolverine, Detroit Bar Assn, 1987; Presidential Award, North Oakland County, NAACP, 1987; fellow, Michigan State Bar Found, 1987; Justice Frank Murphy Honor Soc, Univ of Detroit School of Law, 1981; B'Nai B'rith Barrister, 1980; Federal Bar Assn, 1978; Published, "Jurisprudence of Orignial intention: A Critical Evaluation," co-author, Mark S. Kende, 1986, "A Quest for Justice: Effective and Efficient Alternative Dispute Resolution Processes, 1983, "Some Current Problems of Human Administration, co-author, Allen Sultan, 1971. **MILITARY SERVICE:** AUS, Signal Corps, 1st lt, Honorable Discharge, 1952-54. **BUSINESS ADDRESS:** US Judge, Eastern Dist of MI, 2nd Floor US Courthouse, Detroit, MI 48226.

COOK, LADDA BANKS
Business executive. **PERSONAL:** Born Aug 22, 1935, Lancaster, SC; married Jessie Lee Oliver; children: Anita, Deborah. **EDUCATION:** Johnson C Smith Univ, BS 1957; Amer Coll of Life Underwriters, CLU 1972, CHFC 1986. **CAREER:** New York City Dept of Hosp & Health, asst chemist 1960-65; Gen Agents & Mgrs Assoc Brooklyn Chapt, pres 1976; NY Life Ins Co, gen mgr 1965-. **ORGANIZATIONS:** Bd of dirs Natl Assoc of Life Underwriters 1977, Amer Soc of Chartered Life Underwriters 1972-; mem 100 Black Men 1977, NAACP 1979, Kiwanis Club 1971; bd of disting visitors Johnson C Smith Univ 1979; pres Johnson C Smith Univ Alumni Assoc 1969; dir Reg I 1969; 2nd vice pres Natl Alumni Assoc 1977; basileus Omega Psi Phi, Alpha Upsilom Chap 1984; elder Siloam Presbyterian Church 1977; bd of trustees Claflin Coll 1984. **HONORS/ACHIEVEMENTS:** Robert Brown Mem Scholarship Awd 1957; Black Achievers in Industry Awd, YMCA of Gr NY 1971, NY Lifes Pres Trophy 1972. **MILITARY SERVICE:** AUS 1958-60. **BUSINESS ADDRESS:** General Manager, New York Life Insurance Co, 888 7th Ave, Ste 500, New York, NY 10106.

COOK, MARY MURRAY
Educator. **PERSONAL:** Born May 07, 1936, Winston-Salem, NC; married Rev Payton B Cook; children: Pamela, Lisa, Melanie. **EDUCATION:** Winston-Salem State Univ, BSN 1958; Univ of MD, MS 1970. **CAREER:** Comm Hosp Wilmington NC, instructor 1958-59; DC General Hosptial, head nurse pediatrics 1959-62; Central State Hosp Milledgeville, instructor inservice 1965-68; GA Coll, assoc prof nursing. **ORGANIZATIONS:** Pres 1978-80, treasurer 1980- 14th Dist GA Nurses Assoc; bd of ed Baldwin Cty 1984-; sr cadette Girl Scout Leader; undergrad advisor Delta Sigma ThetaSor. **HONORS/ACHIEVEMENTS:** Mem Alpha Kappa Mu Hon Soc, Alpha Phi Sigma Hon Frat, Sigma Theta Tau Hon Soc; Nurse of the Year 14th Dist GA Nurses Assoc 1980. **HOME ADDRESS:** 1100 Dunlap Dr, Milledgeville, GA 31061.

COOK, MATTIE (MATTIE COOK FISHER)
Educator. **PERSONAL:** Born Sep 15, 1921, Bedford Hills, NY; married Wilbur Fisher; children: Louis Wilbur, Allyson Debra. **EDUCATION:** VA State Univ, BS 1945; Columbia Univ Teacher's Coll, MA 1950; Coll of Mt St Vincent, LHD 1971; Marymount Manhattan Coll, LittD 1973; Fordham Univ, LHD 1976. **CAREER:** Pub Priv Agency NYC, child care worker 1945-64; New York City Bd of Ed, pub school teacher 1964; Addie Mae Collins Head Start & Comm Svc, exec dir 1964; Malcolm-King, Harlem Coll Ext, admin dir & co-founder 1968; Inst for Child Devel, teacher, trainer 1970; Malcolm-King Harlem Coll Ext, ceo/pres. **ORGANIZATIONS:** Mem Convent Ave Baptist Church; mem Assn for Comm Based Educ Washington, DC; NY State Dept of Educ-Regents External Degree Faculty; mem NY Hospital Burn Treatment Ctr; mem Central Harlem Assn of Montessori Parents; mem Comm of Independent Colls and Univs; mem Public Service Science Ctr; bd mem NatlAssn of Independent Colls and Univs 1985; bd Natl Assn of Independent Colls and Univs; bd Assn of Black Charities; bd Uptown Chamber of Commerce. **HONORS/ACHIEVEMENTS:** Received numerous community service awds in areas such as educ, correction, drug abuse treatment and economic development; Dr Humane Letters Coll of Mt St Vincent 1971; Dr Literature (Honoris Causa) Marymount Manhattan Coll 1973; Dr Humane Letters Fordham Univ 1975; Candace Awd Natl Coalition of 100 Black Women 1983; NY State Corning Glass Leadership Awd 1983; NY Assn of Black Educator Comm Awd 1985; Daily News Front Page Awd 1985; Outstanding Alumni Awd VAState Univ 1986. **BUSINESS ADDRESS:** President, Malcolm-King Harlem Coll Ext, 2090 Adam Clayton Powell Jr Bl, New York, NY 10027.

COOK, NATHAN HOWARD
Educator. **PERSONAL:** Born Apr 26, 1939, Winston-Salem, NC; married Thelma Vernelle Upperman; children: Carlene Y, Erika Y. **EDUCATION:** NC Central Univ, BS 1961, MA 1963; Univ of NC Greensboro, 1964; NC State Univ, Grad Credit 1965; OK State Univ, PhD 1972. **CAREER:** Barber-Scotia Coll, asst prof of biology 1962-68; Wica Chemicals Inc, faculty intern 1968; OK State Univ, grad teaching asst 1968-69; Lincoln Univ, prof & head of biology dept. **ORGANIZATIONS:** Chmn Sickle Cell Adv Comm MO Div of Health 1972-79; eval panelist Natl Science Found 1976; mem bd of dirs Amer Cancer Soc Cole Unit 1981-85; consultant/review panelist Natl Institutes of Health/div of Rsch Resources 1982; mem Environ Quality Comm 1981-; pres elect MO Acad of Science 1984-85; presSunrise Optimist Club of Jefferson City 1984-85. **HONORS/ACHIEVEMENTS:** Ford Found Fellow 1969-71; listed in Amer Men & Women of Science 1975; listed in Who's Who in MO Education; Blue Tiger Awd US Army ROTC Unit Lincoln Univ1982. **HOME ADDRESS:** 2908 Sue Dr, Jefferson City, MO 65101. **BUSINESS ADDRESS:** Prof of Biology, LincolnUniv, 820 Chestnut St, Jefferson City, MO 65101.

COOK, RUFUS
Attorney, investor. **PERSONAL:** Born Nov 22, 1936, Birmingham; divorced; children: Bruce. **EDUCATION:** Talladega Coll, BA 1956; Univ Chgo, LLD 1959. **CAREER:** Judge Luther M Swygert US Dist CT, law clerk 1959-60; Private Practice, Lawyer 1963. **ORGANIZATIONS:** Pres bd chmn Continental Inst Tech Inc; pres Phoenix Realty Inc; partner Cook Apts Assos; pres Pinnacle & Graphics Corp; chmn bd Hyde Park -Kenwood Comm Conf 1966-68; bd mem Chicago Fedn Settlements 1967-69; Daniel Hale Williams U; mem Nat Moot Ct TeamUniv Chicago 1958-59. **HONORS/ACHIEVEMENTS:** Prize Univ Chica-

go 1958; USAF Commendation Medal 1963. **MILITARY SERVICE:** USAF capt 1963-66. **BUSINESS ADDRESS:** 180 N La Salle St, Ste 3018, Chicago, IL.

COOK, SAMUEL DUBOIS
Educator. **PERSONAL:** Born Nov 21, 1928, Griffin, GA; married Sylvia M Fields; children: Samuel Jr, Karen. **EDUCATION:** Morehouse Coll, AB 1948; OH State Univ, MA 1950, PhD 1954; Morehouse Coll, Hon LLD 1972; OH State Univ, Hon LLD 1977; Duke Univ, Hon LLD 1979; IL Coll, Hon LLD 1979. **CAREER:** Southern Univ, prof 1955-56; Atlanta Univ, chmn 1956-66; Duke Univ, prof 1966-74; Univ of IL, visiting prof 1962-63; The Ford Found, program officer 1969-71; Dillard Univ, pres 1975-. **ORGANIZATIONS:** Bd tstees Martin Luther King Ctr for Soc Change 1969-; editorial bd Amer Polit Sci Rev; editorial bd Jour of Polotics; editorial bd Jour of Negro History; bd of dir So Christian Ldrsp Conf; bd dir Amer Cncl of Library Resources; bd of tst Cncl on Religion in Intl Affairs; past pres So PolitSci Assn; mem Mayor's Charter Revision Comm; bd of dir Inst for Serv to Educ; mem Exec Council Amer Polit Sci Assn; past vice pres Amer PolitAssn; mem Phi Beta Kappa; Pi Sigma Alpha; mem Natl Cncl for Humanities, Omicron Delta Phi, Omega Psi Phi, Sigma Pi Phi; trustee Duke Univ. **HONORS/ACHIEVEMENTS:** Outstanding Prof Awd Duke Univ; Disting Achvmt Awd St Augustine's Coll; Citation of Achvmt Awd OH State; Torch of Liberty Awd Anti-Defamation League; contrib articles to professional journals and anthologies. **MILITARY SERVICE:** AUS 1953-55. **BUSINESS ADDRESS:** President, DillardUniv, 2601 Gentilly Blvd, New Orleans, LA 70122.

COOK, SMALLEY MIKE
Writer-producer/theatre & film. **PERSONAL:** Born Mar 10, 1939, Chicago, IL. **EDUCATION:** Univ of Massachusetts, MA 1972; Union Grad Sch, PhD 1977. **CAREER:** Image Alliance, writer/producer 1974-; Univ of Iowa, professor of drama 1987-. **ORGANIZATIONS:** Consultant Chicago Urban League 1973-; consultant Chicago Dept of Cultural Affairs 1983-; founder Dramatic Arts Repertory Ensemble for Youth 1986-. **HONORS/ACHIEVEMENTS:** Writer-Producer "Drums of the Night Gods," staged, Los Angeles Cultural Ctr 1981; Goodman Theatre Chicago 1983, Chicago Cultural Ctr 1983; Writer-Producer "The Fire and the Storm" Lindblom Park Dist Chicago 1986. **MILITARY SERVICE:** AUS spl/4 3 yrs; European Svcs. **BUSINESS ADDRESS:** Professor of Drama, Univ of Iowa, 303 English-Philosophy Bldg, Iowa City, IA 52242.

COOK, TONI RAE
Administrator/organizer. **PERSONAL:** Born Jan 14, 1944, Denver, CO; children: Leslie Morrison, Arlene. **EDUCATION:** Univ of CA-Los Angeles, BA (Cum Laude) 1970, MA 1973. **CAREER:** Dept of Human Resources Gov of DC, sr program planner 1973-74; The Orkand Corp, sr staff mgmt consultant 1974-75; Charles R Drew Postgrad Medical School/ Martin L King Jr Gen Hosp, assoc project dir 1975-76; Office of the Mayor Gov of the Dist of Columbia Office of Criminal Justice Plans & Analysis, deputy dir 1979-81; Howard Univ Sch of Arch & Planning, assoc dean 1981-84; Office of Councilman Robt Farrell, chief deputy 1984-85; Bay Area Black United Fund, exec dir 1985-. **ORGANIZATIONS:** Mem Tech Adv Comm DC Comprehensive Plan 1982-83; natl dir of advance Jesse L Jackson for Pres Comm 1983-84; mem Natl Black Leadership Roundtable 1985-; mem bd of dirs Oakland Boys Club 1986-. **HONORS/ACHIEVEMENTS:** Meritorious Serv Awd Women in Architecture & Planning Howard Univ Chap Washington DC 1983.

COOK, WALLACE JEFFERY
Clergyman, dentist. **PERSONAL:** Born Jul 14, 1932, El Reno, OK; married Martha; children: Cheryl, Jeffery, Jeryl. **EDUCATION:** AZ State U, BA 1954; Howard U, DDS Coll of Dentistry 1957; Crozer Theol Sem, MDiv 1964; Union Theol Sem Richmond VA, D Ministry 1978; VA Union U, DD 1973. **CAREER:** Ebenezer Bapt Ch Richmond VA, pastor 1971; Providence Public Schs, dentist dept of health 1970; Joseph Samuels Dental Clinic, dentist 1969; Ebenezer Baptist Church Providence RI, pastor 1964-71; 1st Baptist Church Yardley PA, pastor 1963-64; USAF, Dentist 1957-61. **ORGANIZATIONS:** Richmond Comm Sr Center 1975; Urban League 1970; Urban Coalition 1970; Richmond Oppty Indus Ctrs 1976. **MILITARY SERVICE:** USAF capt 1957-61. **BUSINESS ADDRESS:** 216 W Leigh St, Richmond, VA 23222.

COOK, WILLIAM WILBURT
Educator. **PERSONAL:** Born Aug 04, 1933, Trenton, NJ. **EDUCATION:** Trenton State Coll, BS 1954; Univ of Chicago, MA (w/Honors) 1976. **CAREER:** Trenton Public Schools, teacher of English/social studies 1954-61; Princeton Regional Schools, teacher of English/ chair of English dept 1961-73; Dartmouth Coll, dir African and Afro-Amer studies 1977-84, 1985-, assoc prof of English-prof of English 1973-. **ORGANIZATIONS:** Humanities consultant Natl Faculty of Arts & Scis 1976-; bd of dirs Amer Folk Theater 1982-; patron/dir North Country Theater 1983-; chair adv comm on minority affairs Conf on Coll Comp & Communications 1983-; children's media consultant Natl Endowment for the Humanities 1984-; adv bd Natl Civil Rights Museum 1986-. **HONORS/ACHIEVEMENTS:** Disting Alumni Citation Trenton State Coll 1977; Danforth Assoc 1979-85; has published poetry, literary criticism; edited 3 books. **MILITARY SERVICE:** AUS sp-4 1957-59. **BUSINESS ADDRESS:** Professor of English, Dartmouth College, Dept of English, Hanover, NH 03755.

COOK, YVONNE MACON See POWELL, YVONNE MACON

COOKE, ANNA L.
Retired librarian. **PERSONAL:** Born in Jackson, TN; daughter of Thurston Lee and Effie Lee; married James A; children: Elsie Cooke Holmes. **EDUCATION:** Lane Coll, BA 1944; Atlanta Univ, MLS 1955. **CAREER:** Douglas Jr High School Haywood County TN, principal 1944-46; Jackson City School, teacher 1947-51, librarian 1951-63; Lane Coll, catalog librarian 1963-67, PR & Alumni dir 1966-69, head librarian 1967-88. **ORGANIZATIONS:** Mem Amer Library Assn 1964-; bd of dir Amer Cancer Soc 1967-73; sec bd of dir Jackson Arts Council 1974-76; bd dir Reelfoot Girl Scout Council 1974-86, 1st vice pres 1983-86; bd trustees Jackson Madison Co Library 1984-; TN Library Assn; West TN Library Assn; Southeastern Library Assn; Delta Sigma Theta Sorority Inc; Links, Inc; NAACP; bd of dirs Jackson Volunteer Ctr. **HONORS/ACHIEVEMENTS:** Library Sci Lane Coll 1966; Hon Fellow Philosophical Soc of England 1969; Alumni Plaque Lane Coll 1975; Action Awd Radio Station WJAK 1982; Serv PlaqueCity of Jackson 1972; Girl Scout Friendmaker Awd 1985; Serv Plaque Delta Sigma Theta Sor; authored "History of Lane College," 1987; Distinguished Service Award, State of Tennessee 1988; Diamond Jubilee Service Award, Delta Sigma Theta Sorority 1988; Certificate of Merit, Lane Coll 1988. **BUSINESS ADDRESS:** Head Librarian, Lane Coll, 545 Lane Ave, Jackson, TN 38301.

COOKE, LLOYD M.
Former organization executive. **PERSONAL:** Born Jun 07, 1916, LaSalle, IL; married Vera; children: Barbara Anne, William E. **EDUCATION:** Univ WI, BS 1937; McGill Univ, PhD 1941; Coll of Ganado, LLD (hon). **CAREER:** McGill Univ, lectr 1941-42; Corn Prods Refining Co Argo IL, sect leader 1942-46; Films Packaging Div Union Carbide Corp Chgo, grp leader 1946-49, dept mgr 1950-54, asst to mgr tech div 1954-57, asst dir rsch 1965-67, mgr planning 1967-70; NYC, dir urban affairs 1970-78, corp dir univ relations 1973-76; corp dir comm affairs 1976-77; sr consult 1978-81 (retired 1983). **ORGANIZATIONS:** Mem Natl Sci Bd 1970-82; consult Office of Tech Assessment US Congress 1972-79; vice chmn Econ Devel Council of NY 1978-81; pres Natl Action Council on Minorities in Engrg 1981-83, pres emeritus 1983; contrib articles to professional jours; mem Comm Conf Bd Downers Grove IL 1968-70; trustee McCormick TheolSem 1976-80; mem NY Acad Scis; mem Amer Chem Soc, AAAS, Sigma Xi, Phi Kappa Phi, Beta Kappa Chi, Chicago Chemists Club; NY Chemists Club. **HONORS/ACHIEVEMENTS:** Proctor Prize Sci Sci Rsch Soc Amer 1970; Fellow Amer Inst Chemists (honor scroll Chicago).

COOKE, PAUL PHILLIPS
Consultant, educator. **PERSONAL:** Born Jun 29, 1917, New York, NY; son of Louis Philip Cooke and Mamie K Phillips Cooke; married Rose Clifford, Aug 22, 1940; children: Kelsey C Meyersburg, Paul, Anne Katherine. **EDUCATION:** Miner Tchrs Coll, BS 1937; NY Univ, MA 1941; The Cath Univ of Am, MA 1943; Columbia Univ. **CAREER:** Miner Teachers College & DCTC, prof of English 1944-74; District of Columbia Teachers College, president 1966-74; Amer Assn of State Colleges & Univs, dir of intl programs 1974-75; AASCU, special consultant 1974-. **ORGANIZATIONS:** Consultant World Peace through Law Ctr 1974-78; consultant Amer Bar Assn Standing Committee on World Order under Law 1975-77; consultant Howard Univ Dept of Physics 1976, 81; consultant, School of Education 1979, 1988; consultant Anacostia Neighborhood Museum for 3 exhibits 1979-85; special asst to the pres of the Univ of the District of Columbia for Historical Rsch 1982-83; consultant Beacon College 1984-85; participant World Veterans Federation General Assemblies 1963, 65, 67, 76, 82, 85, 88; life mem NAACP; life mem Kappa Alpha Psi Fraternity. **HONORS/ACHIEVEMENTS:** Am Vet Com Bessie Levine Award 1960; Nat Sor of Phi Delta Kappa Award 1975; numerous publications including, "The Centennial Drama, A History of Miner Teachers College", "Civil Rights in the United States", "The Cooke Lecture Series"; Educ of the Disadvantaged in the Model Sch Div 1965; 23 articles in the Journal of Negro Education 1949-82 and other articles in the Negro History Bulletin 1958-82, Negro Educational Review, Mid-West Journal; establishment of the Paul Phillips Lecture Series 1979, Paul Phillips Scholarship 1984, at the Univ of the District of Columbia; Pope John Paul II Papal Medal, Pro Ecclesia et Pontifice 1984; Doctor of Laws Degree, Honoris Causa, Univ of District of Columbia 1986; Editor-In Chief, 1988 Assn for the Study Afro Life & History Kit. **MILITARY SERVICE:** USAF corpl 1945-46.

COOKE, THOMAS H., JR.
Business development executive. **PERSONAL:** Born Oct 13, 1929, Camden, SC; married Audrey E Wilson; children: Bonnye A Jefferson, Julie L, Michael W Thomas III. **EDUCATION:** NY Univ, BSc 1954; Montclair State Coll, MA 1974. **CAREER:** US Veterans Admin Hosp, corrective therapist 1957-58; Newark Bd of Educ, victoria plan coord 1958-77; City of East Orange, mayor 1978-85; McLaughlin PivenVogel Inc, sr govt bond specialist 1986-87; Maintenance Mgmt Specialists Inc, pres 1987-. **ORGANIZATIONS:** Bd of dirs/ 2nd vice pres Natl Conf of Black Mayors 1978-85; mem govt relations comm Natl United Way 1979-; bd of dirs/exec comm US Conf of Mayors 1981-85; bd of dirs/finance comm Natl League of Cities 1981-85; commissioner NJ Martin L King Commemorative Commn 1983-; commissioner NJ Drug Adv Commn 1983-; bd of dirs NJ Multi Housing Industry 1987-; life mem NAACP, Natl Cncl of Negro Women, Natl Cncl of Jewish Women. **HONORS/ACHIEVEMENTS:** Completion of Downtown Renewal Prog (40 yrs in the making) 1981-85. **MILITARY SERVICE:** USNR asst psychologist 1954-56; Honor Man Grad Co 1954. **HOME ADDRESS:** 74 Hawthorne Ave, East Orange, NJ 07018. **BUSINESS ADDRESS:** President/Managing Partner, Maintenance Mgmt Specialists, 576 Central Ave Ste LL-7, East Orange, NJ 07018.

COOKE, WILCE L.
Elected official. **PERSONAL:** Born Jun 18, 1939, Benton Harbor, MI; married Beverly. **EDUCATION:** Oakland Comm Coll School of Practical Nursing, 1968; Inst for Adult Ed Instr, Ed Prof Devel Act 1970; Lake Michigan Coll, AA 1975; Western MI Univ,BS 1976, MA 1985. **CAREER:** City of Benton Harbor, mayor. **ORGANIZATIONS:** Adv bd Tri-Gan; former suprv comm Peoples Comm Fed Credit Union; former bd of dir, org Self-Help Co-Operative; former charter revision commiss BentonHarbor Charter Commiss; treas mercy Hosp Staff Council 1977-82; mem Phi Theta Kappa; Benton Twp Black Coalition; bd of dir Berrien Cty Heart Unit MI Heart Assoc; trustee bd, asst sunday school supt Bethlehm Temple Pentecostal Church; mem Alpha Kappa Delta. **HONORS/ACHIEVEMENTS:** Natl Upper Div Scholarship Competition 1976; Outstanding Serv Awd Benton Harbor Concred Citizens; Berrien Cty Medical Soc for spear heading drive in retaining Open Heart Surgical Unit at Mercy Hosp in Southwestern MI 1978. **HOME ADDRESS:** 1130 Salem, Benton Harbor, MI 49022. **BUSINESS ADDRESS:** Mayor, City of Benton Harbor, 200 East Wall St, Benton Harbor, MI 49022.

COOKE, WILHELMINA REUBEN
Attorney. **PERSONAL:** Born Dec 13, 1946, Georgetown, SC; married Edmund Douglas Taylor Jr; children: Wilhelmina Nilaja, Shani Malika. **EDUCATION:** Duke U, BA 1967; Harvard U, PhD Candidate 1968; Univ of MI Law Sch, JD 1973. **CAREER:** Citizens Communications Center, staff Atty 1977-; Wilmer Cutler & Pickering, asso Atty 1973-77; Orange Co Bd of Educ Orlando FL, social studies tchr 1968-69. **ORGANIZATIONS:** Mem Nat Conf of Black Lawyers/Nat Bar Assn/Nat, Assn of Black Women Attys/Am Bar Assn Nat Media Reform Com, Nat Orgn for Women, 1980-;phi sigma alpha DukeUniv Chap 1966; phi kappa delta DukeUniv Chap 1966; phi beta kappa DukeUniv Cpt 1967. **HONORS/ACHIEVEMENTS:** Woodrow Wilson scholar 1967-68; John Hay Whitney fellow 1970-71.

COOKE, WILLIAM BRANSON
Cartographer. **PERSONAL:** Born Mar 11, 1927, Spencerville, MD; married Theresa M Johnson. **EDUCATION:** Miner Tchr Coll, BS 1951; Am U. **CAREER:** Geological Sur-

vey Interior Dept, supr cartographer. **ORGANIZATIONS:** Mem Antarctican Soc; mem Nat Congress on Surveying & Mapping 1st Vice Pres DC Br NAACP. **HONORS/ACHIEVEMENTS:** Presidential award for outstanding serv DC Br NAACP. **MILITARY SERVICE:** AUS pfc 1946-47. **BUSINESS ADDRESS:** Geol Survey Interior Dept, 1925 Newton Sq E, Reston, VA 22090.

COOKS, STONEY
Congressional assistant. **PERSONAL:** Born Feb 23, 1943, Uniontown, AL; married Shirley; children: Caleb Quaye. **EDUCATION:** Anderson Coll, 2 1/2 yrs. **CAREER:** SCLC, exec dir. **ORGANIZATIONS:** Adm asst pres Ralph D Abernathy; mem Natl Council Fellowship Reconciliation. **BUSINESS ADDRESS:** 332 Cannon HOB, Washington, DC 20005.

COOLEY, JAMES F.
Clergyman, civic worker, educator. **PERSONAL:** Born Jan 11, 1926, Rowland, NC; son of Rev James F Cooley and Martha Buie Cooley; married Carolyn Ann Butler; children: Virginia M Cooley Lewis, Gladys M Cooley Taylor, James Francis, Franklin Donell, Stephen Lamar, Stetson Laron. **EDUCATION:** Johnson C Smith Univ Charlotte, NC, AB Soc Sci 1953, BD Theol 1956; Interdenom Theol Center Atlanta, GA, DM 1973; World Univ Tucson, AZ, PhD Soc Sci 1982; Life Science Coll, DD 1972; St John Univ NE, MA Sociology 1972; Law Enforcement Official, certified; Law Enforcement Instructor of Jail Opers and Jail Admin, certified. **CAREER:** Grant Chapel Presb Ch, minister 1956-57; St Andrews Presb Ch, minister 1957-69; Forrest City Spec Sch Dist #7, 1957-69; St Francis Co, juv prob ofcr 1959-68, assoc juv judge 1963-64; Shorter Coll, polit sci dir/minister of svc/dean of men/acad dean 1969-73; State Rep Art Givens Jr, chf legisl on comm affairs; 5th Div Circ Ct for Judge Jack Lessenberg, prob ofcr; Tucker Prison, first black chaplain in AR 1971; Attorney Genl's Office, agent consumer protection; Pulaski County, deputy registrar; County Contact Comm Inc, founder/exec dir. **ORGANIZATIONS:** Police commr Wrightsville PD 1984; chaplain Pulaski Co Sheriff Dept 1985; roster of fellow mem Amer Biographical Inst 1985; selected to work on Admin Policy Comm on consolidation for Pulaski Co Sch Dist 1985; AR Teacher's Assn; Intl Platform Assn; SANE; Amer Security Cncl; Natl Comm of Black Churchmen; Omega Psi Phi Frat; NAACP; AR Cncl on Human Rel; Natl Hist Soc; Urban League; The Early Amer Soc; Natl Conf of Christians and Jews Inc; Postal Commem Soc; Natl Black Veterans Organ Inc; major genl Natl Chaplains Assoc; foot distrib for the poor AR Food Bank Network; mem Amer Legion, Natl Sheriff's Assoc; sr warden, comm mem 33rd Degree Mason; mem Boy Scouts of Amer; bd of dirs AA AWARE Drug and Alcohol Prevention Prog; Worshipful Master, Welcome Lodge #457 masonic 1987-. **HONORS/ACHIEVEMENTS:** Dr JF Cooley Day in AR 1977, at Shorter Coll 1978, Little Rock 1982, Rowland NC 1985, Jacksonville AR 1986, Wrightsville AR 1987; Dr JF Cooley Week in N Little Rock; Dr J F Cooley Month in N Little Rock 1977; Hon DD Shorter Coll No Little Rock; Hon D Civil Law E NE Christian Coll; Order of the Long Leaf Pine by Gov of NC 1986; Medallion of Honor by AR Gov Bill Clinton 1986; Cert of Appreciation Natl Chaplain's Assoc 1987; Certificates of Merit and letters of highest Commendation from Atty Genl Steve Clark, Sheriff C Gravett, Sec of State Bill McCuen; State Auditor Julia Hughes, Co Clerk Carolyn Staley, Sen Dale Bumpers, US Congressman Tommy Robinson; Dr. J. F. Cooley Day in Arkansas 1988 by Gov Bill Clinton; NAACP Community Service Award Jacksonville AR NAACP Chapter 1989. **MILITARY SERVICE:** AUS 1944-46; several decorations and 2 Battle Stars, 6 Bronze Stars; WWII Victory Medal 1985. **BUSINESS ADDRESS:** Minister, County Contact Comm Inc, PO Box 5150, North Little Rock, AR 72119.

COOLEY, NATHAN J.
Artist, educator. **PERSONAL:** Born Aug 24, 1924, Indianapolis, IN. **EDUCATION:** Ball State Univ, BS 1951, MS 1955; IN Univ NW, grad study; educational tour of Europe 1969; Univ of Ghana, studied 1970. **CAREER:** AL A&M Univ, prof of art 1951-55; City of Gary, educ 1955; IN Univ NW, assoc prof of art; City of Gary, dir of beautification 1955-. **ORGANIZATIONS:** Designer Life Membership Pin Kappa Alpha Psi; bd of dir N Cent Prov Kappa Alpha Psi Frat, mem bd of dir Save the Dunes Coun; mem bd of dir Lake MI Fed; mem NAACP; Kappa Alpha Psi; Phi Delta Kappa; 32 Degree Mason; Amer Fed of Tchrs; IN Fed of Tchrs; Black Merit Acad (founder); Educators to Africa Assn; Amer Soc of Planning Officials; Kiwanis Intl; vice pres Greater Gary Art Council; pres Greater Gary Art Council. **HONORS/ACHIEVEMENTS:** Kappa Man of the Yr 1968-69; C Leon Wilson Awd 1964; Serv to the Comm Awd NAACP 1972; Kappa of the Year 1974; Serv Awd IFTA 1976; Outstanding Citizen Awd Art Council 1984-85. **MILITARY SERVICE:** AUS s/sgt 1943-45. **BUSINESS ADDRESS:** Art Teacher, Marguette Park Pavilion, 1 North Grand Blvd, Gary, IN 46407.

COOLEY, VANESSA LYNNE
Director. **PERSONAL:** Born Sep 26, 1952, Providence, RI; children: E Jamal Cooley. **EDUCATION:** Univ of RI, BS 1974; MS 1987. **CAREER:** Univ of RI, hall dir 1974-77; educ counselor 1977; Southeastern Mass Univ educ cnslr 1977-78; program dir 1978-86. **ORGANIZATIONS:** Mass Disadvantaged Stdnt Prgm Directors, 1st vice chair; Mass Educ Opport Assoc, 1st chair; NE Minority Women Administrators, member; American Federation of Teachers, member; RI Advisory Comm on Women, commissioner; RI Black Women's Alliance, first pres; RI Leadership; member Delta Class and Program Comm mem 1987; Urban League of RI past bd member; mem SMU Black Coalition. **HONORS/ACHIEVEMENTS:** RI Black Achievement Awd, 1982; Outstanding Young Woman of Amer 1982. **BUSINESS ADDRESS:** Executive Dir, Times 2 Inc, 480 Charles St #204, Providence, RI 02904.

COOMBS, FLETCHER
Business executive. **PERSONAL:** Born Jul 08, 1924, Altanta, GA; son of Fletcher Coombs and Pearl Magnolia Floyd; married Helen Grimes, May 21, 1955; children: Toni, Kei. **EDUCATION:** Morehouse Coll, AB; Atlanta Univ School of Bus Admin, MBA; Indiana University Bloomington, Ind, Graduate School of Savings & Loan, Certificate 1971. **CAREER:** Mutual Fed Savings & Loan Assoc, various positions 1953-73, pres 1973-. **ORGANIZATIONS:** Fin chmn Butler YMCA; bd mem Sadie G Mayes Nursing Home. **HONORS/ACHIEVEMENTS:** Boss of the Year Golden Dome Chap Amer Bus Women Assoc. **MILITARY SERVICE:** 2nd lt reserves, t/sgt active duty. **BUSINESS ADDRESS:** President, Mutual Fed Savings & Loan Assn, 205 Alburn Ave NE, Atlanta, GA 30303.

COOMBS, HARRY JAMES
Business executive. **PERSONAL:** Born Sep 19, 1935, Washington, DC; married Barbara Ann Parrish. **EDUCATION:** Armstrong High Sch, 1952. **CAREER:** Philadelphia Intl Records, exec vice pres 1971-; Tangerine Records Corp, natl field rep 1970-71; Capitol Record Dist Corp, e coast regional prom rep 1969-70;CBS Records Inc, e coast regional promo rep 1969-69; Ramsel Productions, dir 1968-68; Schwartz Bros Whis Rec Dist, local promotions mgr 1965-67. **ORGANIZATIONS:** Mem exec council Black Music Assn 1978. **MILITARY SERVICE:** AUS spec 4 1954-56.

COOMBS, ORDE
Writer, editor. **EDUCATION:** Yale U, BA 1965; Clar Coll 1965-66; NY U, MA 1971. **CAREER:** NY Mag, writer contbs editor; Mccall Pub Co, sr editor 1969-71; Doubleday & Co, asso editor 1966-69; Black Conversations WPIX-TV, co-host 1975; NY U, adj lectr 1973. **HONORS/ACHIEVEMENTS:** Alicia Patterson Award PRSA 1974; media award for pub serv reporting 1974; edited "Is Massa Day Dead?" 1974; ed "What We Must See, Young Black Storytellers" 1971; "We Speak as Liberators, Young Black Poets" 1970; "Do You See My Love For You Growing" 1974. **BUSINESS ADDRESS:** 755 2nd Ave, New York, NY 10016.

COOPER, ALBERT, SR.
Business executive. **PERSONAL:** Born Sep 22, 1934, Americus, GA; married Josephine Wiggins; children: Albert Jr, Booker Alphonse, Jerel Boyd. **EDUCATION:** Sumter Cty Comprehensive High School, night school 1984-85. **CAREER:** Cooper's Groc & Mkt, 1979-83; Cooper's Const Co, owner 1970-85. **ORGANIZATIONS:** Councilman Americus GA 1979-85; elected mayor protem 1982, 1985; mem Early Bird Ctn 1980; bd of governors Chamber of Comm 1981; zoning bd City of Americus1978-85. **HONORS/ACHIEVEMENTS:** Excellence in Business Awd Ed Bryant 1978; Disting Serv Male Awd Oscar Marwell 1979; Men Bus League Awd 1984; Volunteer work providing housing for the poor 1984.

COOPER, ALMETA E.
Executive assistant & attorney. **PERSONAL:** Born Dec 27, 1950, Durham, NC; married Herbert A Nelson. **EDUCATION:** Wells Coll, BA 1972; Northwestern Univ Sch of Law, JD 1975. **CAREER:** Vedder Price Kaufman & Kammholz, assoc 1975-77; Amer Med Assn, asst dir of health law div 1977-82; Tuggle Hasbrouck & Robinson, partner 1980-82; Meharry Medical Coll, exec asst to pres/gen con, corp sec & gen counsel. **ORGANIZATIONS:** Lecturer Joint Comm on Accreditation of Hospitals; lecturer Amer College of Hospital Administrators; lecturer New England Hosp Assembly; mem Amer Soc of Hospital Attorneys; bd of dir Minority Legal Educ Resources; alternate mem Hines Veterans Admin Cooperative Studies Prog Human Rights Comm; pres bd of dir IL Family Planning Council; mem Renaissance Women; appointed mem Nashville Private Industry Council; fin comm League of Women Voters Nashville; mem Leadership Nashville 1986-87, Music City Chap of the Links, TN Bar Assn, Napier-Looby Bar Assn, Amer Acad of Hospital Attorneys. **HONORS/ACHIEVEMENTS:** Chicago Urban League; Alumnae Assns of Wells & Spelman Colleges; Outstanding Alumna Spelman Coll; Outstanding Volunteer Chicago Urban League; Outstanding Young Woman of 1981; Natl Finalist White House Fellowship 1982; publications have appeared in Journal of the Amer Med Assn and in St Louis Univ Law Journal. **BUSINESS ADDRESS:** Legal Counsel, St Thomas Hospital, 4220 Harding Rd, PO Box 380, Nashville, TN 37202.

COOPER, AUGUSTA MOSLEY
Association executive. **PERSONAL:** Born Aug 08, 1903, Wilmington, NC; daughter of Levie McKoyand Mosley and Ida Chestnut Mosley; widowed. **EDUCATION:** Howard Univ, BS 1930; Catholic Univ of Amer, grad study 1939. **CAREER:** NC Pub Schs, tchr 1924-25; Emergency Relief Admin of Phila, caseworker 1931-32; Emergency Relief Admin of New Hanover Co, supvr 1932-36; New Hanover Co Social Serv Dept, caseworker 1936-63; New Hanover Co Social Serv Dept, supvr 1963-66. **ORGANIZATIONS:** NC Conf of Social Serv 1939-;chrtr mem Delta Sigma Theta 1940-; Natl League of Women Voter 1959; mem Amer Pub Welfare Assn 1957-; PACE First Coord Com 1967; organizer Homeowners Improvement Assn of Wilmington 1968-; trustee Chestnut St United Prebyterian Ch 1968-72; mem Redevel Commn Adv Com 1968; mem SE Regional Commn Inc Cape Fear Council of Govts 1972-; mem Blue Cross Blue Shield NC Subscriber Adv Council 1975; mem NAACP; Mayor's Preservation Task Comm of Wilmington NC; Gr Wilmington Chamber of Comm Govt Affairs Comm; Preservation Preservation Net Work 1987; New Hanover County Museum Foundation, Inc, 1985; bd Pine Forest Cemetery 1982. **HONORS/ACHIEVEMENTS:** Certificate of merit NC Caseworkers Assn 1960, Citizen of Yr Delta Sigma Theta 1968 & Omicron Alpha; Citizen Adv Comm for a Workable Prog for Wilmington Comm Improvement 1968-70; first Black woman candidate City Council Wilmington NC 1969; first woman Wilmington Human Relations Commn 1971-; first vice chwmn New Hanover Co Dem Party 1972; Distingushed Serv Prince Hall Grant Lodge Free & Accepted Masons of NC 1972; Gr Wilmington C of C New Hanover Wilmington Human Relations Commn Outstanding Cit 1973; Golden Life mem Delta Sigma Theta 1973; Hist Preservations of Amer 1977; Comm Leaders & Noteworthy Amer Amer Biog Inst 1976-77; Zeta Phi Beta Awd for Outstanding Comm Serv 1983; New Hanover Co Democratic Party Awd for Distingushed Serv 1984; Susan B Anthony Awd for Lifetime Achievement sponsored by New Han over Co Natl Org for Women, 1984; award for outstanding service (preservation), Pine Forest Cemetery.

COOPER, BARBARA JEAN
Deputy inspector general for investigations. **PERSONAL:** Born in North Carolina; daughter of Jasper Cooper and Ezola Manly Britt. **EDUCATION:** Hampton Univ, BS (Highest Honors); Michigan State Univ, MBA; Stanford Univ, Graduate Certificate. **CAREER:** Portsmouth VA School System, teacher; Central Intelligence Agency, special asst to the deputy director, deputy dir of personnel; deputy inspector general for investigations. **ORGANIZATIONS:** Mem Exec Women in Govt; mem Alpha Kappa Alpha Sorority; mem, Natl Hampton Alumni Assn; vice pres Northern VA Chapter Natl Hampton Alumni Assn 1984-86. **HONORS/ACHIEVEMENTS:** Public Affairs Fellowship, Stanford Univ. **BUSINESS ADDRESS:** Deputy General, Central Intelligence Agency, Office of Inspector General, Washington, DC 20505.

COOPER, BOBBY G.
Educator. **PERSONAL:** Born Nov 03, 1938, Bolton, MS; married Della M Larkin; children: Christopher, Demetria, LaCarole. **EDUCATION:** Tougaloo Coll Touglaoo, MS, BS 1961; Univ of IL Urbana, MS 1970; Univ of CO Boulder, EdS 1971; Univ of CO Boulder, EdD 1977. **CAREER:** Humanitites Div Utica Jr Coll, Utica MS, chairperson 1972-; Special Educ Opportunity Univ of IL Urbana, counselor 1969-70; Camp Tree Tops, Lake Placid NY, counselor 1968-69; E T Hawkins High School, Forest MS, music tech 1961-68. **ORGANIZATIONS:** Mem Music Educators Nat Conf; mem Am Choral Dirs Assn; mem Music Com Meth Ch 1976; Fmem Phi Delta Kappa; organist Asbury United Meth Ch Bolton, MS 1961-; trustee Asbury United Meth Ch Bolton, MS 1975-. **HONORS/ACHIEVEMENTS:** Music scholarship Tougaloo Coll 1958; leadership devel grant Ford Found 1968; music scholarshipUniv of IL 1969; grant Office of Educ 1971. **BUSINESS ADDRESS:** Utica Jr College, Utica, MS 39174.

COOPER, CANDACE D.
Judge. **PERSONAL:** Born Nov 23, 1948, Los Angeles, CA. **EDUCATION:** Univ of Southern CA, BA 1970, JD 1973. **CAREER:** Gibson Dunn & Crutcher, atty 1973-80; Los Angelos Municipal Court, judge 1980-87. **ORGANIZATIONS:** Mem CA Assoc of Black Lawyers 1975-87, Black Woman Lawyers of Los Angeles 1975-87, Natl Assoc of Women Judges 1980-87; life mem Natl Bar Assoc; mem NAACP; bd of dir Watts/Willowbrook Boys & Girls Club 1982-87, Exceptional Childrens Found 1982-87. **HONORS/ACHIEVEMENTS:** Outstanding Alumni Ebonics/Univ of S CA 1982; Woman of Achievement Bus & Professional Women Los Angeles Sunset Chap 1985; Bernard S Jefferson Judge of the Year Awd 1986; Beta Pi Sigma Sor Inc Alpha Chap Outstanding Black Achievement Awd 1986. **BUSINESS ADDRESS:** Judge, Los Angeles Municipal Court, 110 N Grand Ave, Los Angeles, CA 90012.

COOPER, CECIL (COOP)
Professional athlete. **PERSONAL:** Born Dec 20, 1949, Brenham, TX; married Octavia; children: Kelly. **EDUCATION:** Attended, Blinn Jr Coll, Prairie View A&M Coll. **CAREER:** Boston Red Sox, 1971-76; Milwaukee Brewers, infielder 1977-. **ORGANIZATIONS:** Column "Coop's Corner" in club magazine "What's Brewing?". **HONORS/ACHIEVEMENTS:** MVP and Wisconsin Sports Personality of Yr 1980; named AL Player of the Month in August and Player of the Week in Sept 1980; set World Series record with 10 assists by a first baseman 1982; Distinguished Athlete Awd 1982; Roberto Clemente Awd 1982; earned team MVP & HR Awd 1983; named AL Player of the Week twice and Player of the Month in August 1983; 3 Silver Bat Awds from Sporting News; 3 time winner Harvey Kuenn Awd; named club's MVP 1985; club's Home Run Awd 1985; Athlete for Youth's "Good Guy" Awd 1985; 2 Golden Glove Awds. **BUSINESS ADDRESS:** Milwaukee Brewers Basball Club, Milwaukee County Stadium, Milwaukee, WI 53214.

COOPER, CHARLES W.
Physician. **PERSONAL:** Born Jun 13, 1929, Hayti, MO; married Bobbye Jean Hollins; children: Terri Lyn, Janis Kaye, Karyl Jean, Daryl Dean, Alan Jeffrey. **EDUCATION:** Lincoln Univ MO, BS 1951; Univ of Wichita, grad study 1956; Meharry Med Coll, MD 1964. **CAREER:** Phys present. **ORGANIZATIONS:** Pres Lincoln Univ Found 1972-73; trustee Quinn Chapel AME Ch 1967-. **HONORS/ACHIEVEMENTS:** Good conduct medal USAF 1954; Nat Meth Scholar Meth Ch 1962-63; mead johnson awd Mead Johnson Pharm Co 1966; dipl Am Acad Fam Phys 1973; fello AmAcad Fam Phys 1977. **MILITARY SERVICE:** USAF s/sgt 1951-55. **BUSINESS ADDRESS:** 300 E Dunklin St, Jefferson City, MO 65101.

COOPER, CLARENCE
Judge, attorney. **PERSONAL:** Born May 05, 1942, Decatur, GA; married Shirley; children: Jennae, Corey. **EDUCATION:** Clark Coll, BA 1960-64; Emory Univ Sch Law, JD 1965-67; MIT Comm Flws Prgm, flwsp 1977; Harvard Univ John F Kennedy Sch Govt Pub Admin, 1977-78. **CAREER:** Atlanta Legal Serv Prog, atty 1967-68; Fulton Co GA, asst dist atty 1968-76; Atlant Muncpl Ct, assoc judge 1976; Fulton County Superior Ct, judge. **ORGANIZATIONS:** Mem Natl Bar Assn, Gate City Bar Assn, Natl Conf BLack Lawyers, State Bar GA, Atlanta Bar Assn; mem exec bd Atlanta Br NAACP; mem Natl Urban League; bd dir Amistrad Prod, EOA's Drug Prog; past mem Atlanta Judicial Commm. **HONORS/ACHIEVEMENTS:** Schlrsp Clark Coll 1960-64; publ "The Judiciary & It's Budget an adminstrv hassle". **MILITARY SERVICE:** AUS E-6 1968-70; Bronze Star, Certificate of Commendation. **BUSINESS ADDRESS:** Judge, Fulton County Superior Ct, 136 Pryor St, Atlanta, GA 30303.

COOPER, CLEMENT THEODORE
Attorney. **PERSONAL:** Born Oct 26, 1930, Miami, FL; married Nannie Coles; children: Patricia, Karen, Stephanae, Bridgette, Stacey. **EDUCATION:** Lincoln Univ, AB 1952; Boston Univ, attended 1954-55; Howard Univ Sch of Law, JD 1958; CO State Christian Coll, Hon PhD 1973; Hastings Coll of Law Univ of CA, first natl coll of advocacy 1971. **CAREER:** Private Practice, attorney-at-law 1960-. **ORGANIZATIONS:** Mem MI State Bar 1960; mem DC Bar 1960; mem US Sup Ct Bar, US Ct Appeals, DC & Tenth Cir CO, US Ct Mil Appeals, Third Cir Phila, US Ct of Claims, US Second Circuit Ct of Appeals, US Fourth Circuit Ct of Appeals, US Sixth Circuit Ct of Appeals, US Ct of Appeals for Federal Circuit; mem Natl Bar Assn; Amer Bar Assn; Amer Trial Lawyers Assn; mem Amer Judicature Soc; Amer Civil Liberties Union; Pub Welfare Adv Council 1966-68; mem Ch of the Ascension & St Agnes Wash DC; mem Alpha Phi Alpha. **HONORS/ACHIEVEMENTS:** Author "Sealed Verdict" 1964; author "Location of Unpatented Mining Claims" CA Mining Journal Jan-May 1975 Vol 44; contrib editor Natural Resources Section Amer Bar Assn "Significant Adminis Legislative & State Court Decisions Affecting the Petrol Ind in States E of the MS River" 1979-80. **MILITARY SERVICE:** AUS 1952-54. **BUSINESS ADDRESS:** Attorney, Law Offices of C T Cooper, 918 F St NW, Washington, DC 20004.

COOPER, CONSTANCE DELORIS
Educator. **PERSONAL:** Born in Detroit, MI; children: Chauncey Lance. **EDUCATION:** Univ of MI, BA Hist 1958; Wayne State U, MA Admin 1963, EdD Leadership in Curr K-12 1971. **CAREER:** Detroit Public Schools, teacher, dept head 1958-66; Teacher Corps, Wayne State Univ, instructor 1966-68; Wayne State Univ, adjunct prof 1968-70; Intergroup Relations, Detroit Public Schools, asst dir 1968-71; Detroit Public Schools, regional admin 1971-77; Govt Funded Programs Dist 147 Illinois, dir 1977-78; School Mgmt Northern IL, asst prof, educ admin 1978-79; Dept of Doctoral Studies, Seattle Univ, asst prof 1979-83; Coppin State Coll, dean div of grad stud. **ORGANIZATIONS:** Pres TASK Inc Balti 1985; vice pres Travel Intl Inc Detroit/Shaker Hgts 1962-74; consult US Dept of Labor Region IV Seattle 1981; consult OIC'S of Am Region IV Seattle 1980-81; advis com to pres Minority Recruitment & RetentionUniv of MI Alumni Assn; co-chmn MD State Dept of Educ Pgm Eval Com; MD State Dept of Educ Profsnl Devel Com; AACTE Task Force on Human Serv & Tchr Edn; state planning com Am Cncl of Educ Nat Identifctn Pgm; ASCD; NAWDAC; AERA; NABSE;Univ of MI Alumni Assn; Delta Sigma Theta Sor; Eta Phi Beta Sor; Phi Delta Kappa. **HONORS/ACHIEVEMENTS:** Regents Alumni Scholar Univ of MI; Grad Fellowship Wayne State U; Pyces Award for Comm Serv Detroit 1977; chmn Civil Rights Commn City of Detroit 1975-77; Helping Women Advance Professionally The Am Assn of Sch Admin/Ford Found Fellowship 1978-79; Outstand Women in Admin Am Assn of Sch Admin 1977; Outstand Women Educators Award Nat Women Trial Lawyers Assn 1977; Who's Who in Educ Admin 1980-82. **HOME ADDRESS:** 14 W Cold Spring Ln, Baltimore, MD 21210.

COOPER, CONSTANCE MARIE
Educator. **PERSONAL:** Born Dec 16, 1952, Lorain, OH; married Hewitt J Cooper; children: Candace, Adrienne, Hewitt Jr. **EDUCATION:** Univ of MI, BBA 1975, MBA 1977. **CAREER:** Univ of Cincinnati, assoc prof of acctg. **ORGANIZATIONS:** Mem bd of dirs Victory Neighborhood Serv Agency 1981; mem bd of trustees Goodwill 1986; mem metro bd of dirs YMCA Hamilton Co 1986. **HONORS/ACHIEVEMENTS:** CPA Ohio 1984. **BUSINESS ADDRESS:** Assoc Prof of Accounting, Univ of Cincinnati, University Coll ML #207, Clifton Ave, Cincinnati, OH 45221.

COOPER, CURTIS V.
Business executive. **PERSONAL:** Born in Savannah, GA; son of Joshua Cooper; married Constance Hartwell; children: Custis, Allyson. **EDUCATION:** Savannah State Coll, BS 1955; Savannah State Coll, Spectal Studies Chem 1965-66; Armstrong State Coll, Entomology 1966; Univ of MI Ann Arbor, MPH 1977. **CAREER:** Guaranty Life Ins Co, debit mgr 1955; Toomer Realty Co, RE salesman & rents mgr 1957; USDA, rsch asst 1959; Westside Comprehensive Health Center, exec dir 1972; Westside Urban Health Ctr, exec dir 1980. **ORGANIZATIONS:** Dir Savannah Port Authority 1976-82; dir bd trustees Memorial Med Center 1979-; mem Natl Assoc of Comm Health Centers; past dir Savannah Area Chamber of Commerce 1980-84; pres Savannah Branch NAACP 1976-; CCFC & 33 mason Most Worshipful Prince Hall Grand Lodge GA 1977-. **HONORS/ACHIEVEMENTS:** Founding dir Westside Urban Health Center 1972; Alpha Man of the Year Beta Phi Lambda Chapter Alpha Phi Alpha Fraternity Comm Serv Award GA Council of Deliberation Prince Hall Masons; Freedom Award Savannah Chapter NAACP. **BUSINESS ADDRESS:** Executive Dir, Westside Urban Health Center, Inc, 115 E York St, PO Box 2024, Savannah, GA 31401.

COOPER, DANEEN RAVENELL
Engineer. **PERSONAL:** Born Oct 27, 1958, St Albans, NY; daughter of James Ravenell and Carrie Ravenell; married Maurice N Cooper; children: Elana Simone Cooper Kellen Marsalis Cooper. **EDUCATION:** Columbia Univ Sch of Engrg and Applied Science, BSEE 1980. **CAREER:** Bell Labs, sr tech assoc 1976-79; New Jersey Bell, engr 1980-85; United Parcel Service, data communications mgr 1985-. **ORGANIZATIONS:** Counselor Sponsors for Educ Oppty 1982-84; pres Council of Action for Minority Professionals 1983-87; mem Consortium of Telecommunications Execs 1985-86; mem Coalition of 100 Black Women 1985-; pres Council of Action for Minority Profls 1984-85; mem Black Data Processing Assoc 1989-; mem IEEE 1989-. **HONORS/ACHIEVEMENTS:** Bell Laboratories Engrg Scholarship Program 1976-80. **HOME ADDRESS:** 25 Highland Ave, Maplewood, NJ 07040.

COOPER, EARL, II (SKIP)
President. **PERSONAL:** Born Feb 04, 1944, Oakland, CA. **EDUCATION:** Merritt Coll Oakland CA, AA 1968; Golden Gate Coll San Francisco, BA 1970; Univ of So CA, MBA 1973. **CAREER:** IMPAC, business analyst 1972-74; Jim Dandy Fast Foods Inc, mkt rep 1974; Los Angeles Economic Develop Corp, exec deputy dir 1974-83; EC II & Assocs, pres 1979-. **ORGANIZATIONS:** Mem Natl Black MBA Assoc LA Chap 1974-, US Small Business Admin REgion Adv Comm 1978-; pres Black Business Assoc of Los Angeles 1979-; mem Los Angeles Co Private Industry Cncl 1979-84; mem Mayor's Office of Small Business Assistance 1980-; commissioner Housing Auth of Los Angeles 1984-86; vice presNAACP Los Angeles Branch 1986-. **HONORS/ACHIEVEMENTS:** CA delegate to the White House Conf on Small Business 1980,86; Resolution from CA speaker of the assembly for exemplary service to the comm & state for promoting the growth & develop of business 1981; Natl Educ for Business Develop Awd 1983; Natl Awd of Excellence from SBA 1983; US Small Business Admin Minority Business Advocate of the Year for the State of CA 1985. **MILITARY SERVICE:** AUS spl 4 1965-67; Natl Defense Service, Vietnam Service Medal, Combat Medical Badge, Marksman Rifle 10/S Bar 1965-67. **BUSINESS ADDRESS:** President, EC II & Associates, 727 So Ardmore Ave Ste 1006, Los Angeles, CA 90005.

COOPER, EDWARD L., SR.
Civic leader/volunteer. **PERSONAL:** Born in Washington, NC; married Thelma. **EDUCATION:** Virginia Union Univ, Sociology degree. **ORGANIZATIONS:** Former exec dir Boston Urban League, NAACP Boston Chapt; pres Highland Park 400, Metropolitan Boston chap of Natl Caucus and Ctr on Black Aged Inc; pres Boston Urban Gardeners; chmn adv comm Boston Commn on Elder Affairs; chairperson of bd of dirs Roxbury Action Prog; cochmn Minority Elderly Coalition; mem Bd of NCBA.

COOPER, EDWARD SAWYER
Educator. **PERSONAL:** Born Dec 11, 1926, Columbia, SC; son of Dr and Mrs H H Cooper, Sr; married Jean Marie Wilder; children: Lisa Cooper Hugdins, Edward S Jr (deceased), Jan Cooper Jones, CharlesW. **EDUCATION:** Lincoln Univ PA, AB 1946; Meharry Med Coll, MD 1949; Univ of PA, MA (honors) 1973. **CAREER:** Philadelphia Gen Hospital, internship medical residency 1949-54, fellow in cardiology 1956-57, pres of medical staff 1969-71, chief of medical serv 1972-76; Univ of PA, prof medicine 1973-. **ORGANIZATIONS:** Certified and recertifield Amer Bd of Internal Medicine 1957-74; fellow Amer Coll of Physicians 1960; co-dir Storke Research Center Philadelphia Gen Hospital 1968-74; chmn & member bd of dir Stroke Council Amer Heart Assn 1982-; chmn talent recruitment council & member editorial bd journal of Natl Med Assoc 1959-77; member of the council Coll of Physicians of Philadelphia 1970-84; member bd of dir Blue Cross of Greater Philadelphia 1975; member bd of dir Amer Foundation Negro Affairs 1977. **HONORS/ACHIEVEMENTS:** Hartley Gold Medal highest honors Meharry Medical Coll 1949; Distinguished Alumnus Award Lin-

coln Univ PA 1959; Distinguished Alummus Award Meharry Medical Coll 1971; Alpha Omega Alpha Honor Medical Soc 1962; Charles Drew Award for Distinguished Contributions to Medical Educ 1979; Amer Heart Assn, award of merit 1986. **MILITARY SERVICE:** USAF captain 1954-56; Chief Medial Serv, 6208 USAF Hospital. **BUSINESS ADDRESS:** Professor of Medicine, Univ of Pennsylvania, Univ of Pennsylvania Hospital, 3400 Spruce St, Philadelphia, PA 19104.

COOPER, EMMETT E., JR.
Postmaster. **PERSONAL:** Born Jun 03, 1921, Cleveland; married Ermelda Mohr; children: Emmett, Gerald, Hewitt. **EDUCATION:** Harvard Univ Adv Mgmt Prog, grad, BS 1951, MS 1954. **CAREER:** Cleveland Post Office, supt training 1954; Wage & Salary Admin, supt 1956, office personnel dir 1957; Cuyahoga Comm & Coll, teacher 1958-66; Postal Mgmt Br USPS HQ, dir 1970; Detroit Postal Dist, mgr 1971; Chicago Post Office, post master 1973-77; Eastern US Reg, postmaster gen 1977-78; Southern Region Memphis TN, retired postmaster gen 1978-83; Harte-Hanks Direct Mktg Group, dir postal affairs. **ORGANIZATIONS:** Mem Chicago Fed Exec Bd Campaign for Chicago Area; mem bd dirs Highland Comm Bank; Nat Assn Postmasters US Mem Chicago Assn Commerce & Industry; Chicago Urban League; Chicago Br NAACP; Christmas Seal Campaign; Chicago Lung Assn. **HONORS/ACHIEVEMENTS:** Postmaster of Year 1974. **MILITARY SERVICE:** AUS 1944-47.

COOPER, ERNEST, JR.
City planner, educator. **PERSONAL:** Born Jun 19, 1941, Toone, TN; married Marva Harper; children: Jeanine, Ernest III, Keita. **EDUCATION:** Lincoln Univ MO, BS 1963; Howard Univ, M City Plnng 1970; Univ of PA, PhD ABD, City Plnng. **CAREER:** Nia Group, pres; Univ of Dist of Columbia, chmn & prof urban plnng; Adult & Vocational School Cairo IL, math instr 1965-68; Washington Tech Inst, asst prof, math 1968-70; Washington Tech Inst Conceptualized Urban Plnng Tech Prog, train para-prof; Urban Inst, consult to eval staff 1971; ECA Inc Planner & Designers Urban & Reg Planning, pres 1971-. **ORGANIZATIONS:** Mem Amer Planning Assoc, Natl Assoc Planners, Amer Assoc Univ of Prof Curators School Lincoln Univ. **HONORS/ACHIEVEMENTS:** ML King Jr Study Grant Woodrow Wilson Found 1969-70, 1971-72; Grad Asst in Rsch & Recruit Howard Univ 1969; Urban Trans Ctr Fellow 1970; Voorhees School Natl Cap Area by AIP 1970; Fontaine Fellow Univ of PA. **BUSINESS ADDRESS:** President, ECA Inc Planners & Designers, Urban & Regional Planning, 916 6th St, N WSte 312, Washington, DC 20001.

COOPER, ETHEL THOMAS
Educator. **PERSONAL:** Born Mar 02, 1919, Abbeville Co, SC; married Rev B J Cooper; children: Joethel, Sandra. **EDUCATION:** Allen U, AB 1939. **CAREER:** Greenville Co, teacher 1964; Chrelston Co 1959-64; Spartanbury 1957-59; Dillon 1948-57; Marion 1947-48; Williamsburg 1944-46; Florence 1940-44; Edgefield 1939-40. **ORGANIZATIONS:** Pres Greenvl Co & Assn of Classroom Tchs 1973; exec bd SC Educ Assn 1975; bd of dir SC Educ Assn 1974; bd of dir NEA; chmn Credentials Comm SCEA; basileus Epsilon Iota Zeta; basileus Gamma Zeta; antapokritis SE reg ZOB Sor 1972-76; Greenvl Co Friends of Educ 1974-76; spkr United Meth Ch; mem NAACP. **HONORS/ACHIEVEMENTS:** Runner-up Citz of Yr Greenvl Co; Zeta Phi Beta Awd; ACT pres Awd; Greenville Co ACT Awd. **BUSINESS ADDRESS:** SCUM Conference, Columbia, SC 29605.

COOPER, EVELYN KAYE
Judge. **PERSONAL:** Born Jun 23, 1941, Detroit, MI. **EDUCATION:** Univ of Detroit, BBA 1968; Wayne State U, post grad Math; Wayne State Univ Law Sch, JD 1973. **CAREER:** Recorder's Ct, judge 1978-; Detroit Traffic Ct, traffic ct referee 1977-78; Self-employed, atty law office 1974-77; Detroit Jr High Sch, bd of educ 1966-70. **ORGANIZATIONS:** Mem Nat Assn of Women Judges; mem MI State Bar Assn; mem MI Judges Assn; mem Womens Lawyers Assn; mem Women's Conf of Concerns; mem NAACP 1976-;mem March of Dimes; Mem Delta Sigma Theta Sorority; judicial mem Nat Bar Assn 1974-; mem Wolverine Bar Assn. **BUSINESS ADDRESS:** Recorders Court, 1441 St Antoine, Detroit, MI 48226.

COOPER, GARY T.
Physician. **PERSONAL:** Born Jul 06, 1948, Washington, DC; married Cheryl Douglas; children: Michelle, Justin. **EDUCATION:** Marquette Univ, BS 1970; Howard Univ Coll of Medicine, MD 1975. **CAREER:** Planned Parenthood of Washington, med dir, 1979-80; Howard Univ Hospital, resident coordinator 1980-; instructor, 1980-86; ast prof 1986-87; Private Practice, physician Ob/Gyn. **ORGANIZATIONS:** Mem, Amer Coll of Ob/Gyn 1978-; Diplomate, Amer d of Ob/Gyn 1983-; mem, Washington Gynecological Soc 1981-, Kappa Alpha Psi Fraternity, Mem, Med Soc of the District of Columbia, 1979-. **BUSINESS ADDRESS:** 1140 Varnum St, NE, Suite 105, Washington, DC 20017.

COOPER, GORDON R., II
Attorney. **PERSONAL:** Born Mar 22, 1941, Wallisville, TX; married Barbara Ellison; children: Gordon R III. **EDUCATION:** Texas So U, BA 1965; JD 1970. **CAREER:** Humble Oil Co, labor relations dept; Ins Underwriter Pvt Practice. **ORGANIZATIONS:** Mem TX Am Houston Jr Bar Assn; regional dir Nat Bar Assn; Alpha Phi Alpha Frat; Phi Alpha Delta Legal Frat; Harris County Crim Lawyers Assn. **BUSINESS ADDRESS:** 2614 Two Houston Ctr, Houston, TX 77002.

COOPER, IRIS N.
Educator. **PERSONAL:** Born Oct 30, 1942, Ahoskie, NC. **EDUCATION:** NC Central U, BA 1964; Howard U, grad study; Univ of VA; Coll of William & Mary. **CAREER:** Portsmouth School System, instructor; Norfolk State Evening Coll, instructor 1968-69; Palmer Memorial Inst, instructor 1964; Project Upward Bound, Norfolk St Coll, instructor 1968-71. **ORGANIZATIONS:** Mem NEA; VA Educ Assn; Portsmouth Educ Assn; VA Assn Fof Classroom Tchrs; Portsmouth Assn of Classroom Tchrs; Am Assn of Women; Tidewater Alliance ofBlack Sch Educators; Am Assn of Tchrs of Spanish &Portuguese; mem Ebenezer Bapt Ch; NCCU Alumni Assn; Norfolk Players Guild; Portsmouth Chap Delicados Inc; Gamma Delta Omega Chpt; Alpha Kappa Alpha. **HONORS/ACHIEVEMENTS:** Outstanding young woman of America 1974. **BUSINESS ADDRESS:** Churchland HS, Portsmouth, VA.

COOPER, IRMA JULIAN See RAYBON, IRMA JULIAN

COOPER, JEROME GARY
Commissioner. **PERSONAL:** Born Oct 02, 1936, Mobile, AL; son of Algernon Cooper (deceased) and Gladys Cooper (deceased); divorced; children: Patrick, Joli, Shawn. **EDUCATION:** Univ of Notre Dame, BS; George Washington Univ, grad study; Harvard Sch of Bus, attended 1979. **CAREER:** House of Reps, State of AL, legislator 1974-80; USMCR, bgen 1985-87; David Volkert & Assoc, vice pres marketing, 1983-87; AL Dept of Pensions & Security, commissioner. **ORGANIZATIONS:** Mem bd of reg, Springhill Coll; chmn bd, Opp Indus Ctr; mem , bd of ARC; YMCA; OPERATION; Comm Chest & Counc; mem Mobile Ment Health Ctr; Dearborn St Comm Ctr; mem Spring Hill Coll; chmn bd of OIC; mem Public Welfare Assn; mem Natl Assn of Social Workers; Commonwealth Natl Bank. **HONORS/ACHIEVEMENTS:** 1st Black to lead infantry co into combat USMC 1967; selected as Outstanding Man in the US 1971; apptd Commanding Officer of 4th Battalion 14th Marines Headquarters Birmingham AL; Citizen of the Yr Omega Psi Phi 1974; Man of Yr Nonpartisan Voters League 1977; Highest Award Given by Sec USN for Public Serv 1978; MO BealeScroll of Merit for Good Citizenship Mobile Press Register 1979; Univ of Notre Dame Alumni Awd 1987. **MILITARY SERVICE:** USMC major general; 2 Purple Hearts; 3 Vietnamese Cross of Gallantry; Bronze Star; Legion of Merit. **BUSINESS ADDRESS:** Vice President Marketing, David Volkert & Assoc, Inc, P O Box 7434, Mobile, AL 36607.

COOPER, JOSEPH
Business executive, attorney. **PERSONAL:** Born Dec 20, Hemingway, SC; children: Kenneth. **EDUCATION:** Univ of Utah Sacramento City Coll, AA 1965; Mcgeorge Law Sch Univ of Pacific, JD 1969. **CAREER:** Cooper Realty Co, owner 1965; Self-employed, atty gen pract 1969-. **ORGANIZATIONS:** Mem bd dir CA Trial Lawyers Assn; mem adv bd United Bus League of CA; past pres Sacramento Chap Urban League 1971-72. **HONORS/ACHIEVEMENTS:** Distinguished serv award City of Sacramento 1972-73; resolution of commendation CA Legislature. **MILITARY SERVICE:** AUS 1960-62. **BUSINESS ADDRESS:** 2210 K St, Sacramento, CA 95816.

COOPER, JOSEPHINE H.
Educator. **PERSONAL:** Born Apr 07, 1936, Salinas, CA. **EDUCATION:** BA MA MA PhD; US CA Univ of San Francisco, research. **CAREER:** Educ Svcd Inst, asst dir; Programs for Mentally Handicapped, head teacher; Meritt Coll, GED prgm 1968; Low Income Housing Program in Vocational Counseling; Peralta Coll Dist, presently dean of educ occupation. **ORGANIZATIONS:** Mem CA Tchrs Assn; mem NAACP; United Taxpayers & Voter's Union CA; Alameda Co Contra Costa Co Com for Equal Oppor in Apprenticeship Tng; Berkeley Dem Club; Nat Council Negro Women Inc. **HONORS/ACHIEVEMENTS:** Numerous scholarships grants for further study; mem CA Comm & Jr Coll Assn on "Minorities and the Voc Disadv in Occupational Prgms in CA Comm Coll Trade Tech Schs". **BUSINESS ADDRESS:** Laney Coll, 900 Fallon St, Oakland, CA 94607.

COOPER, JULIUS, JR.
Police officer. **PERSONAL:** Born Jan 08, 1944, Sarasota, FL; son of Julius Cooper, Sr and Johnnie Mae Ramey; married Barbara Irene Campbell; children: Julius, Julian, Adrienne, Tara, Taheim. **EDUCATION:** Essex County Coll, A 1977; Natl Crime Prevention Inst, attended 1983; Security Mgmt & Admin Inst, attended 1984; Rutgers Univ, BS 1985; Seton Hall Univ Masters 1990. **CAREER:** Essex County Police Dept, breathalyzer oper 1973-, affirmative action officer 1982-, supervisor 1983-84, instructor 1983-85, crime prevention coord 1983-86,sergeant. **ORGANIZATIONS:** Deacon/co-chmn Mt Zion Bapt Church 1984-; vice pres Ebony Six Cooperation; life mem NAACP; mem PBA. **HONORS/ACHIEVEMENTS:** Certificate Awd US Dept of Health & Human Serv 1985; Achievement Awd Essex Co PBA Conference 1985; Achievement Awd Essex Co Bd of Freeholders 1986; Valor Award Essex Co Bd of Freeholders 1987. **BUSINESS ADDRESS:** Sergeant, Essex County Police Dept, 115 Clifton Ave, Newark, NJ 07104.

COOPER, KELSY BROWN See BESHEARS, KELSY

COOPER, LARRY B.
Communication company manager. **PERSONAL:** Born Jul 25, 1946, Fordyce, AR; married Carolyn Coleman; children: Sherri Jean. **EDUCATION:** Las Vegas HS, 1965; Univ of AR at Pine Bluff, BS 1969. **CAREER:** Kansas City Schl Dist, teacher/coach 1969-72; Southwestern Bell Tele Co, mgmt trainee 1972-73, engineer 1973-74, sr engineer 1974-77, mgmt dev supv 1977-79, dist stf mgr-Pers/Budgets 1979-81, stf mgr Mgmt Dev 1981-83; dist stf mgr Res Serv 1983-85; dist manager Res Serv 1985-. **HONORS/ACHIEVEMENTS:** Exec bd of directors Boy Scouts of Amer 1985-; bd of directors Southwest City Civitan 1985-; mem Kappa Alpha Psi alumni assoc 1972-; president Tall timberHome Owners 1978-79; commissioner Tall Timber Imp Dist 1986; Distinguished Alumni Awd NAFEO 1986; distinguished achieve award Kappa Alpha Psi fellow 1985; Greater LR Leadership Inst 1986. **HOME ADDRESS:** 5112 Timberlane Drive, Little Rock, AR 72204. **BUSINESS ADDRESS:** District Manager-Res Serv, Southwestern Bell Telephone Co, 4th & Ringo, Room 500, Little Rock, AR 72203.

COOPER, LINDA G.
Manufacturing company executive. **PERSONAL:** Born Jun 01, 1954, Jacksonville, FL; daughter of Benjamin H Groomes and Freddie Lang Groomes. **EDUCATION:** FL State Univ, BS 1974; Indiana Univ, MBA 1977. **CAREER:** Hallmark Cards Inc, budget analyst 1977-81, mktg budget mgr 1981-85, dir minority affairs 1985-. **ORGANIZATIONS:** Mem Alpha Kappa Alpha Sor 1972-, Defense Adv Comm on Women in the Serv 1984-87; pres bd of trustees Greater KC Black Economic Union 1984-; pres Natl Assoc of Market Developers 1985-; mem Natl Black MBA Assoc; bd mem YMCA 1987-. **HONORS/ACHIEVEMENTS:** Outstanding Young Woman of Amer 1983; SCLC Black Achiever in Business & Industry 1984; President's Award, Black Chamber of Commerce of Kansas City, 1988. **HOME ADDRESS:** 4010 NW Claymont Dr, Kansas City, MO 64116. **BUSINESS ADDRESS:** Dir, Hallmark Cards Inc, 2501 McGee, Kansas City, MO 64108.

COOPER, LOIS LOUISE
Transportation engineer. **PERSONAL:** Born Nov 25, 1931, Vicksburg, MS; married Wardell; children: Wyatt E, Christopher. **EDUCATION:** Tougaloo Coll MS, 1949; CA State Univ Los Angles, BA Math 1954; Post Graduate Civil Engineering CA State Univ 1975-81. **CAREER:** Div of Hwys (Caltrans), eng aid 1953-58, jr civil eng 1958-61; Caltrans, asst transp eng 1961-84, assoc transportation engineer 1984-88; Sr Transportation Engineer 1988-. **ORGANIZATIONS:** Past Brd of dir sec Los Angeles Council of Eng of Sci; adv brd Minority

Eng Pgm CSULA; past co-ch career guidance Scty of Women Engrs 1985; pres LA Cncl of Black Professional Engrs 1975-76, v pres 1974-75, sec/treas 1972-74; ASCE, NSPE. **HONORS/ACHIEVEMENTS:** Trail Blazer Natl Asso Negro Bus & Prof Womens Inc 1964; fellow Inst for the Adv of Engr 1982; First Black Woman to attain a Professional Engineers License in Civil Engineering in CA 1978; First Black Woman to achieve all positions at Caltrans 1983; Fellow, Society of Women Engineers 1989. **HOME ADDRESS:** 14324 Clymar Ave, Compton, CA 90220.

COOPER, MATTHEW N.
Psychologist, educator. **PERSONAL:** Born Oct 29, 1914, Macomb, IL; married Ina B; children: Matthew, John. **EDUCATION:** Western IL State Tchr Coll, BEd 1940; Univ of IL, MA 1946; NY U, PhD 1955. **CAREER:** TX So U, prof 1947; Lovejon IL Sch Dist, 1941-46; Riverside Gen Hosp Drug Abuse Clinic, 1972-; Private Practice, psychologist 1958-. **ORGANIZATIONS:** Mem Am Psychol Assn; Am Personnel & Guidance Assn. **BUSINESS ADDRESS:** 2601 Prospect St, Houston, TX 77004.

COOPER, MAUDINE R.
District government official. **PERSONAL:** Born Sep 30, 1941, Benoit, MS; divorced; children: Maria Teresa, grandchild - Malissa Rachelle Cooper. **EDUCATION:** Howard Univ Coll of Liberal Arts, BA Business Admin 1964; Howard Univ Sch of Law, JD 1971. **CAREER:** Natl Urban League, deputy dir 1976-79, asst vice pres public policy 1979, vice pres for Wash Oper 1980-83; DC OHR & Minority Business Oppor Commn, exec dir; DC Officeof Human Rights, dir 1983-89; staff director, Office of the Mayor. **ORGANIZATIONS:** Mem bd of dirs Natl Bar Assn 1979-80; mem bd of dirs Centennial One Inc 1982-87; vice pres for legislative affairs Black Women's Agenda 1983-; legal advisor MCAC/Delta Sigma Theta Sor 1985-88; treas Washington Chap Natl Assn of Human Rights Workers 1986-87; mem several bar Associations; mem bd of dirs, The Doug Williams Foundation. **HONORS/ACHIEVEMENTS:** One of the Women to Watch in the 80's Ebony Magazine 1982; Alumna of the Year Howard Univ Law Alumni Assn 1984; Woman of the Year Capitol Hill Kiwanis Club 1985; America's Top 100 Black Business & Professional Women Dollars and Sense Magazine 1986. **BUSINESS ADDRESS:** Dir, DC Office of Human Rights, 2000 14th St NW 3rd FL, Washington, DC 20009.

COOPER, MERRILL PITTMAN
Business executive. **PERSONAL:** Born Feb 09, 1921, Charlestown, WV. **EDUCATION:** Storer Coll, 1938. **CAREER:** TWU, intl exec bd 1965-68; Local 234, sec, treas, vice pres 1968-77; Transport Workers Union, intl vice pres. **ORGANIZATIONS:** Mem Negro Trade Union Ldrsp Cncl; NAACP; vice pres Philadelphia AFL-CIO 1977-; intl vice pres Transport Workers Union 1977-; mem Urban League. **HONORS/ACHIEVEMENTS:** Outsdng Man of Comm 1977. **BUSINESS ADDRESS:** Vice President, Transport Workers Union, 80 West End Ave, New York, NY 10023.

COOPER, MICHAEL GARY
County government administrator. **PERSONAL:** Born Jan 11, 1954, Cleveland, OH; son of Clifford Cooper Sr and Fletcher Lee Cooper; married Corrinne Crockett, May 26, 1984; children: Stacy, Michael Fletcher, Malik. **EDUCATION:** Univ of Pittsburgh, BA 1975; Atlanta Univ, MA History 1979, MSW Social Work 1979. **CAREER:** Young Men's Christian Assn, asst dir 1975-76; Atlanta Univ, admin intern 1977-79; City of Atlanta, field coord 1979; DeKalb Co Commission Office, affirmative action officer 1979-80; Fulton County Govt, director/contract compliance/EEO, Atlanta GA, 1988-. **ORGANIZATIONS:** Mem Amer Assoc for Affirmative Action Workers 1982-; mem Natl Forum for Black Public Adminis 1983-; treas Region IV Amer Assoc for Affirmative Action 1983-; mem Natl Assoc of Human Rights Workers 1986. **HONORS/ACHIEVEMENTS:** Governor's Intern Program 1978; Outstanding Young Men of Amer 1984; Disting Serv Awd Univ of GA Extension Serv 1985. **BUSINESS ADDRESS:** Director, Deptartment of Contract Compliance/EEO, Fulton County Government, 42 Spring St, Suite 210, Atlanta, GA 30303.

COOPER, MICHAEL LAVELLE
Professional athlete. **PERSONAL:** Born Apr 15, 1956; married Wanda; children: Michael Jr, Simone. **EDUCATION:** Pasadena City Coll; univ of NM, 1978. **CAREER:** Los Angeles Lakers, guard/foward. **ORGANIZATIONS:** Mem NAACP; NM State chrprsn sickle cell anemia. **HONORS/ACHIEVEMENTS:** Averaging 59 assists, second best on the club. **BUSINESS ADDRESS:** Los Angeles Lakers, P O Box 10, Ste 510, Inglewood, CA 90306.

COOPER, SAMUEL H., JR.
Elected government official. **PERSONAL:** Born Feb 02, 1955, Nassawadox, VA; son of Samuel H. Cooper, Sr. and Margaret C. Cooper; married Sandra; children: Cedrick, Shenae. **EDUCATION:** Norfolk State Coll, 1973-75; John Tyler Coll, AAS 1975-77. **CAREER:** CC Humbles Funeral Servs, mortician 1977-83; Accomac County Circuit Court, clerk. **ORGANIZATIONS:** Mem, Macedonia AME Church; Bd of dir, NAM Hospital, 1986-, Delmarva Advisory Council, 1989-. **BUSINESS ADDRESS:** Clerk Circuit Court, Accomac County Circuit Court, PO Box 126, Accomac, VA 23301.

COOPER, SYRETHA C.
Social worker, educator. **PERSONAL:** Born Nov 15, 1930, Youngstown, OH; married Murray A Cooper; children: Carole Bailey, Frances, Corrine, Louise, Murray Jr, Marvin. **EDUCATION:** Youngstown Coll, BA 1952; Western Reserve Sch App Soc Sciences, MS 1954. **CAREER:** Fam Serv Soc Youngstown, social worker; Woodside Receiving Hospital, psychologist, social worker 1957-61; Adult Mental Health Clinic, chief psychologist, social worker 1961-71; Youngstown State Univ, asst prof of social work 1971-. **ORGANIZATIONS:** Mem Natl Assn Social Work; mem Acad Certified Social Workers; registered in clinical social work registry 1976; mem Younstown OH Alumnae Chap Delta Sigman Theta Sor; case consult Youngstown Pub Sch Home Visitation Prog; mem Mcguffey Centre Bd Trustees; chrtrd bd mem P & C Prod of Youngstown; mem United Counc of Negro Women Negro Bus & Prof Women. **HONORS/ACHIEVEMENTS:** Chi omega alumnae award Outstanding Stud Soc Sciences 1952; St Andrews AME Ch Outstanding Woman in Prof Svc. **BUSINESS ADDRESS:** Youngstown State, 410 Wick Ave, Youngstown, OH.

COOPER, VALERIE ANTIONETTE
Investment banking. **PERSONAL:** Born Oct 18, 1961, Stamford, CT. **EDUCATION:** Morgan State Univ, BS 1983; Columbia Univ Grad Sch of Business, MBA 1987. **CAREER:** The Travelers Co, computer programmer 1983-85; Goldman Sachs & Company, associate. **ORGANIZATIONS:** Mem Alpha Kappa Alpha Sor Inc 1980-, Natl Black MBA Assoc 1985-, The Network Inc 1986-. **HONORS/ACHIEVEMENTS:** Outstanding Young Woman of Amer 1984; COGME Fellowship 1985. **HOME ADDRESS:** 84 Courtland Ave, Stamford, CT 06902.

COOPER, WALTER
Research associate, chemist. **PERSONAL:** Born Jul 18, 1928, Clairton, PA; son of Alonzo Cooper and Lula Cooper; married Helen E Claytor; children: Robert B, Brian P. **EDUCATION:** Washington & Jefferson Coll, BA 1950; Univ of Rochester, PhD 1956; Washington & Jefferson Coll, ScD, 1987. **CAREER:** Eastman Kodak Co, research chemist 1956; sr research chemist 1964; Action for Better Comm, assoc dir 1964-65; Rsch Assoc, 1966; US Small Business & Admin Special Consultant to Admin, 1968-69; Easman Kodak Co Rsch Assoc, 1969; Sigma Xi, 1956; ACS, 1959; AAAS, 1960; NYAS, 1970; APS, 1974; NY State Adv Comm to US Civil Rights Commn 1966; Eastman Kodak Co, Mgr of Office of Tech Communications, 1985-86; Retired 1986; Consultant, 1987-. **ORGANIZATIONS:** Bd trustees Washington & Jefferson Coll 1975; bd of Governors Genesee Hosp 1966; bd dir Rochester Area Found 1975; Genesee Regional Health Planning Council 1974; Urban Suburban Pupil Transfer Program 1973; Urban League of Rochester 1965-71; NAACP 1960-65; Celanese Corp of Am Fellow 1952-54; Nat Sci Found Fellow 1955-56; NY State Bd of Regents, 1988. **HONORS/ACHIEVEMENTS:** Rochester Jr Chamber of Commerce Leroy E Snyder Award 1966; Outstanding Achievement Award & Rochester Club of Natl Negro Professional & Business Women Inc 1966; Rochester Chamber of Commerce Devel Award, 1966; Washington & Jefferson Coll Distinguished Alumni Award 1968; Achievement Award Intl Org of Eastern Stars 1974; Knight of the Natl Order of the Republic of Mali, 1982; Rochester Chamber of Commerce Intl Relations Award; 3 patents in Photographic Science & Technology; 25 scientific & technical publications. **BUSINESS ADDRESS:** 68 Skyview Lane, Rochester, NY 14625.

COOPER, WILLIAM B.
Business executive. **PERSONAL:** Born Sep 05, 1956, Washington, DC; married Sandra F Burrus. **EDUCATION:** Control Data Institute, 1975-76; University of Maryland, 1978-80. **CAREER:** Control Data Corp, systems analyst 1974-79; TYMSHARE, Inc, applications consultant 1979-80; CGA Computer Assoc, Inc, 1980-84; Cray Research, Inc, analyst-in-charge 1984-. **ORGANIZATIONS:** Precinct chairman Montgomery County Republican Party 1979-80; member Association for Computing Machinery 1979-; member natl Panel of Consumer Arbitrators 1980-; deacon Plymouth Congregational UCC 1981-; cubmaster Cub Scout Pack 340 1981-; president Cooper & Associates 1982-. **HONORS/ACHIEVEMENTS:** Commissioner Advisory Neighborhood Commission 1982-85; delegate DC Statehood Constitutional Convention 1982-85; Outstanding Young Men of America 1983.

COOPER, WILLIAM M.
Chief executive. **CAREER:** ABBA Distribution Services Inc, Cincinnati, OH, chief executive, 1985-. **BUSINESS ADDRESS:** ABBA Distribution Services Inc, 644 Linn, Cincinnati, OH 45203. *

COOPER, WINSTON LAWRENCE
Advertising executive. **PERSONAL:** Born Oct 27, 1946, Port-of-Spain, Trinidad and Tobago;married Jeanne A Cox-Cooper; children: Zara. **EDUCATION:** Trinity Coll WI, GCE 1963; Univ of the West Indies, BA 1967. **CAREER:** Ogilvy & Mather Inc, acct suprv 1970-77; Case & McGroth Adv Inc, mgmt suprv 1977-79; Uniworld Group Inc, vice pres mgmt suprv 1982-85. **HOME ADDRESS:** 510 E 86th St, New York, NY 10028.

COOPER-LEWTER, NICHOLAS CHARLES
Consultant, psychotherapist, clergyman. **PERSONAL:** Born Jun 25, 1948, Washington, DC; son of R C Lewter Jr and Majel Hoage; married Marcia Wyatt; children: Michelle Marie, Sonia Renee, Sean Darcy, Nicholas Jr. **EDUCATION:** Ashland Coll, BA 1970; Ecumenical Ctr, Black Church Studies, Adv Studied, DMin Prog 1978; Univ of MN, MSW 1978; CA Coast Univ, PhD 1988; Teamer School of Religion, LHD (Hon) 1978. **CAREER:** Univ of MN, teaching asst 1974-75; City of St Paul Human Rights Dept, field investigator 1974; Cooper Lewter Hypnosis Ctr NB, dir owner 1978-83; Garden of Gethsemane LA, pastor 1985; CRAVE Christ Ministries Inc, founder, psychotherapist, author. **ORGANIZATIONS:** Founder 1st basileus Xi Theta Chap Omega Psi Phi 1966-70; rsch spec Ctr for Youth Devel Rsch Univ of MN 1972-73; consultant various Christian Churches 1976-; bd dir Amer Acad Med Hypnoanalysis 1977-84; sr vice pres Full Human Potential Enterprises 1978-; consultant various Olympic Team Members 1980-, US Jr Olympic Team NRA 1983-, CA State Fullerton Football Prog 1983-84, UCLA Basketball Prog 1984-85; judge Los Angeles Olympics 1984; lecturer Bishop College, LK Williams Inst 1985, SMU Perkins School of Theol 1986; mem NASW, NUL, NAACP, AAMH. **HONORS/ACHIEVEMENTS:** Deans Grad Fellowship Univ of MN School of Social Work 1974; Cert Hypnotherapist HEC Hypnotist Examining Council 1978-; Outstanding Young Men of Amer 1983; co-author "Soul, A Working Theology" Harper & Row 1986; publ "Concerns of Working Youth" People Human Svs MN 1974, "Working Youth, Selected Findings from Exploratory Study" Jrnl Youth & Adolescence 1974, "Sports Hypnotherapy, Contenderosis & Self Hate" Jrnl of Med Hypnoanalysts 1980; "The Initial EnvironmentalExperience, A Powerful Took for Psychotherapy & Hypnotherapy" Journal of Medical Hypnoanalysts 1981. **BUSINESS ADDRESS:** Pastor/Psychotherapist/Author, CRAVE Christ Ministries Inc, 4790 Irvine Blvd, Irvine, CA 92720.

COPAGE, MARC DIEGO
Performer. **PERSONAL:** Born Jun 21, 1962, Los Angeles, CA. **EDUCATION:** Attended college, 1 yr. **CAREER:** Actor singer comedian TV & stage since age 5; Metromedia Records, rec artist; Avco Records & Sussex Records, rec artist. **ORGANIZATIONS:** Mem Screen Actors Guild; mem AFTRA. **HONORS/ACHIEVEMENTS:** Nominated Best Actor NAACP Image Awards 1971; Human Rights Award NEA 1970; Communications Award CA Tchrs Assn; award BSA; award Goodwill Indus; award Salvation Army; numerous others.

COPE, DONALD LLOYD
Government official. **PERSONAL:** Born May 16, 1936, Kansas City, KS; married Eddie L. **EDUCATION:** Weber St Coll, BS 1973. **CAREER:** Gov Scott M Mattheson, ombudsman, pres; Ogden City Police Dept, comm relat ofcr 1971-72. **ORGANIZATIONS:** Con-

sult & lectr, race rel Weber St Coll, Cont Ed Dept 1973; govt intern prog Brigham Young U; Univ of UT Soc Dept; Weber St Coll Black Std Union; NAACP; Ogden Brkfst Exchng Clb; pres League of UT Consumers 1974-75; mem dinner com 7th Anual Congsnl Black Caucus Dinner 1977; past mem, adv NewsBd for KTUX, Chan 4 1974; mem Gov Policy Standard & Goals Task Force; bd of dir St Girl Scout Cncl Comm. **HONORS/ACHIEVEMENTS:** Serv award NAACP 1975; comm achvmt award Ogden Comm Action Agency 1977; publ brochure Govs Black Adv Cncl; Black Resource Cat On Blacs in UT; orgnzr Black Coll Std Intern Prog. **BUSINESS ADDRESS:** 110 State Capitol, Salt Lake City, UT 84114.

COPELAND, BARRY BERNARD
Auditor. **PERSONAL:** Born Jan 08, 1957, Paterson, NJ; son of Albert Copeland and Levonia Copeland; married Canary Gasaway; children: Eric, Antoine, Elise, Timothy, Malcolm. **EDUCATION:** Prairie View A&M Univ, BBA 1979. **CAREER:** Internal Revenue Serv, IRS agent 1979; AUS, accountant 1980-82; Corpus Christi Army Depot, auditor 1982-85; Beeco Acctg Svcs, owner/accountant 1985-; Defense Contract Audit Agency, sr auditor 1985-; Barry B Copeland, certified public accountant 1988-. **ORGANIZATIONS:** Mem Alpha Phi Omega 1977-, NAACP 1986-; Assn of Govt Accountants 1988. **HONORS/ACHIEVEMENTS:** Exceptional Performance Award Corpus Christi Army Depot 1985. **MILITARY SERVICE:** AUS SP/4 E-4 2 yrs; Army Commendation Medal. **HOME ADDRESS:** 16327 Dew Drop Lane, Houston, TX 77095-1507. **BUSINESS ADDRESS:** Senior Auditor, Defense Contract Audit Agency, 2320 Labranch Box 12, Houston, TX 77002.

COPELAND, BETTY MARABLE
Health services consultant. **PERSONAL:** Born Aug 31, 1946, Durham, NC; divorced; children: Abosede O. **EDUCATION:** NC Central Univ, BA, Psych 1975; NCCU, MA, Psych 1980. **CAREER:** Durham Tech Inst, part-time instructor, 1978-80; Mental Retardation & Substance Abuse Durham County, forensic screening examiner, 1980-; Rural Day Care Assoc of Northeastern NC Div of Mental Health, training consultant, 1983-; Durham County Community Mental Health Ctr, psychotherapist. **ORGANIZATIONS:** Chairperson NC Assoc of Black Psych, 1980-; mental health consultant, various organizations, 1982-; mem, NC Test Study Commn, 1982-; mem, NC Black Leadership Caucus, 1982-, Natl Black Child Devel Inst Durham Affiliate, 1982-; co-chair health comm Durham Comm on Affairs of Black People 1983; mem Durham NC City Bd of Educ 1983-; advisory bd mem Creative Arts in Public Schools 1984-; mem NCNW Durham Affiliate 1984-; state treas natl Council of Negro Women NC 1984-; serv unit mgr central unit Durham Cty Pines of Carolina Girls Scouts 1984-; founder & coord Coalition for Prevention of Adolescent Pregnancy 1984-; mem Natl Org for Legal Problems in Educ 1984-, Natl Assoc of Female Executives 1985-, bd nominating comm YWCA Durham, 1987; mem, Greater Durham Chamber of Commerce Human Relations Educ Comm, 1985-87; vice chmn, Durham City Bd of Educ, 1987-present. **HONORS/ACHIEVEMENTS:** Advocate of the Year Admin Category NC School Counselors Assoc 1984; Woman in Leadership Durham Comm on Affairs of Black People Natl Council of Negro Women 3rd Annual Bethune Recognition Luncheon 1984; Service Awd Durham Comm on Affairs of Black People 1987; Certificate of Advanced Achievement, NC School Bd Acad, 1987; Outstanding Leadership & Service as Black Elected Official, NC Leadership Conf, 1986; Serv Award, Interdenomination Health & Human Services, 1988. **HOME ADDRESS:** 2138 S Roxboro St, Apt D, Durham, NC 27707. **BUSINESS ADDRESS:** Psychotherapist, Durham County Community Mental Hlth, 414 E Main St, Durham, NC 27701.

COPELAND, ELAINE JOHNSON
Educator. **PERSONAL:** Born Mar 11, 1943, Catawba, SC; daughter of Aaron J Johnson and Lucille Hawkins Johnson; married Robert M Copeland; children: Robert M Jr. **EDUCATION:** Livingstone Coll, BS (with honors) 1964; Winthrop Coll, MAT 1971; Oregon State Univ, PhD (with high honors) 1974; Univ of IL Urbana-Champaign, MBA 1987. **CAREER:** Wilson Jr High School, biology teacher 1964-65; Jefferson High School, biology teacher 1966-70; Oregon State Univ, counselor/instructor 1970-74; Univ of IL, assoc dean/asst prof 1975-. **ORGANIZATIONS:** Pres Girls Club of Champaign County 1977; pres Univ of IL YWCA 1979; pres Univ of IL Chap Honor Soc of Phi Kappa Phi 1982; pres Champaign-Urbana Alumnae Chap Kappa Phi Delta Sigma Theta Sor 1984-86; affirmative action rep Div E counseling and devel Amer Educ Rsch Assoc 1984-86; vice pres Assoc Relations Natl Assoc for Women Deans Administrators & Counselors 1985-87; president National Association for Women Deans, Administrators and Counselors 1988-89. **HONORS/ACHIEVEMENTS:** Distinguished Service Awd College of Agriculture 1979; "Cross-Cultural Counseling and Psychotherapy, An Historical Perspective, Implications for Research and Training," Personnel and Guidance Journal 1983; Distinguished Alumni Presidential Natl Assoc for Educ Oppor in Higher Educ 1986; co-authored The Production of Black Doctoral Recipients, A Description of Five States Title IV Regulation, Problem and Progress, Teachers College Press 1988. **BUSINESS ADDRESS:** Assoc Dean Graduate College, Assoc Prof, Dept of Educational Psychology, Univ of IL at Urbana-Champaign, 202 Coble Hall, 801 S Wright, Champaign, IL 61820.

COPELAND, EMILY AMERICA
Educator, business executive. **PERSONAL:** Born Apr 12, 1918, Tifton, GA. **EDUCATION:** Spelman Coll, AB 1937; Atlanta U, BSLS 1942; Columbia U, MSLS 1948; NY U, attended; Columbia U, attended; Univ So CA, Attended. **CAREER:** Tift Co Independent High School, teacher 1937-38; Finly High School, librarian 1938-40, 1942; Spelman Coll Library, asst 1941-42; Gamon Theological Seminary, head librarian 1942-44; Atlanta Univ, librarian, asst ref 1944-46; NY Pubkuc Library, ref, school work asst 1945-46; SC State Coll, Dept of Library Science, head 1946-51; FAMU, library serv 1951-71. **ORGANIZATIONS:** Fndr, pres Black Res Inf Coord Svc, Inc 1942-; mem numerous off & coms Am Libr Assn; FL Libr Assn; Nat Small Bus Assn 1977-. **HONORS/ACHIEVEMENTS:** Carnegie Grant to study at Atlanta Univ 1948; awards by gen educ bd to conduct orkshps in Library Sci at SC St Coll; Spellman Coll Merit Achiev Award 1968; Alumni Citation, Columbia Univ 1970; Rosalyn Carter Cert 1978; Cert of Recognition, Nat Alumnae of Spelman Coll 1978; Cert of rec for Cntrbtn to Afro-Am Heritage; sec of State FL 1979; Cert of Appreciation, Std Parents & Friends 1979. **BUSINESS ADDRESS:** PO Box 6353, Tallahassee, FL.

COPELAND, KATHLEEN (NEE MAXWELL)
Attorney, accountant. **PERSONAL:** Born Jun 24, 1915; married Alfonso. **EDUCATION:** Wayne State Univ, BS 1949, JD 1958. **CAREER:** Allen Bookkeeping Svc, owner 1949; gen practice atty 1962; State of MI Civil Rights Commn, referee 1973; Wayne Co Juv Ct, referee 1976; self-employed, atty/accountant. **ORGANIZATIONS:** Mem Amer Bar Assn; 1st vice pres Highland Park C of C 1977, pres 1978-; Grievance Comm St Bar of MI 1962; mem Detroit Bar Assn 1962; 1st vice pres 1975, mem Women Lawyers of MI 1962; ofcr/bd mem Wolverine Bar Assn 1962; mem Natl Bar Assn 1966; assoc mem Real Estate Brokers Assn; past mem Trial Lawyers Assn 1969-70; Detroit Econ Club 1975; life mem NAACP; ofcr/dir MI Credit Union League; past Basileus Alpha Theta Sor; mem Natl Small Busn Assn 1977-78. **HONORS/ACHIEVEMENTS:** Admitted practice before US Tax Court 1975; admitted practice before US Supreme Court 1965; admitted practice before US Court of Appeals 1972. **BUSINESS ADDRESS:** 12223 Hamilton, Highland Park, MI 48203.

COPELAND, KEVON
International banker. **PERSONAL:** Born Mar 29, 1953, Pittsburgh, PA; son of Edward S Copeland Jr and Mary Jo Copeland. **EDUCATION:** Connecticut Coll, BA 1976; Univ of Pgh Sch of Business, MBA Finance 1980. **CAREER:** Pittsburgh Natl Bank, acct officer for China Hong Kong Singapore Malaysia Indonesia Thailand India 1981-86, acct officer for Japan Korea China 1986-. **ORGANIZATIONS:** Pres vice pres sec Natl Black MBA Assoc Pgh Chapt; mem One Hundred Black Men of Western PA; steering comm Pittsburgh Natl Bank Voluntary Polit Action Comm; mem Japan Amer Friendship Soc; co-chair Minority Alumni Committee CT Coll 1987-; exec bd Alumni Assn CT Coll 1987-. **BUSINESS ADDRESS:** Assistant Vice President, Pittsburgh Natl Bank, Intl Div-169, Pittsburgh, PA 15205.

COPELAND, LEON L.
Educator. **PERSONAL:** Born Sep 14, 1945, Portsmouth, VA; married Mary B; children: Leon, Jr. **EDUCATION:** Norfolk St Coll, BS 1968; VA St Coll, MEd 1973; VA Tech, EdD 1977. **CAREER:** Univ of MD, asst prof 1977-; VZ Tech, co-op counselor 1975-77; Oscar Smith High School, Chesapeake VA, teacher 1968-75. **ORGANIZATIONS:** Mem Ind Arts Assn 1973-; mem Phi Delta Kappa 1977-79; mem Am Vocatnl Assn 1977-; mem Kappa Alpha Psi Frat 1968-; mem Emergency Sch Aid Adv Com 1978-79; mem Salisbury Housing Rehab Com 1980. **HONORS/ACHIEVEMENTS:** Recp Outstng Young Men of Am Award; US Jaycees 1979; Dept Instr of the Yr,Univ of MD 1979; pub journal article Nat Assn of Indsl Tech Tchr Educ 1979; cited One of Ten Nat Leaders in Ind Arts VA Tech 1979. **BUSINESS ADDRESS:** U of MD Eastern Shore, Princess Anne, MD 21853.

COPELAND, MARY SHAWN
Association executive. **PERSONAL:** Born Aug 24, 1947, Detroit. **EDUCATION:** Madonna Coll, BA 1969. **CAREER:** Black Theol Proj-Theol, prog dir 1976-; NBSC, exec dir 1973-76, assoc dir 1973, dir 1971-73, instr 1969-71. **ORGANIZATIONS:** Mem Bd Dir Nat Off for Black Catholics 1971-73; mem Ad-Hoc Com for Ch Observance of Bi-Centennial 1973-; mem Adv Com Seminary Quarter, Grailville; mem Network; mem Religious Com for Integrity in Gov. **HONORS/ACHIEVEMENTS:** Recip KAWAIDA Award, NBSC 1971;Sojourner Truth Award, Black Woman's Comm Dev Found 1974; Outstndng Young Woman of Am 1974; Interntl Biography, Who'sWho 1977; The Am Cath Who's Who 1976-77; reg semi-finalist White House Flwshp Comp 1975; Who's Who in Rel in Am 1975; listed Who's Who in Am Coll & Univ 1969. **BUSINESS ADDRESS:** 3508 Fifth Ave, Pittsburgh, PA 15213.

COPELAND, RAY
Music educator. **PERSONAL:** Born Jul 17, 1926, Norfolk; married Edna E Garrett; children: Keith, Darrin. **EDUCATION:** Wurlitzer Sch of Music NY. **CAREER:** Kaercea Music Enterprise, Inc, pres; Nassau & Suffolk County Schools, fac artist & clinician; NJ High Schools, fac artist & clinician; Jazz Workshops, Wilmington DE, fac artist & clinician; NY State School Music Assn, lect, demos; NY Brass Conf, lect, demos; The Creative Art of Jazz Improvisation, cond seminar, lect, & demos 1975; Wilson Concert Hall, cond classes, clinics 1975; Monterey & Newport Jazz Festivals, jazz soloist, featured in US & Europe, jazz tours in 14 countries. **HONORS/ACHIEVEMENTS:** Composer "Classical Jazz", "Ste in Six Movements"; author "Ray Copeland Meth & Approach to Creative Art of Jazz Improvisation"; commnd by Nat Endowment for Arts; underscore strings, woodwind, precussion accomp to Jazz Suite, Cape Cod MA 1975; commnd Hedgerow, E Sandwich MA. **BUSINESS ADDRESS:** Kaercea Music Enterprises, PO Box 62, St Albans, NY 11412.

COPELAND, ROBERT M.
Educator, administrator. **PERSONAL:** Born May 12, 1943, Hendersonville, NC; son of Aggie McDaniel Copeland and Florie Jeter Copeland; married Elaine Johnson; children: Robert McDaniel Copelan, Jr.. **EDUCATION:** Livingstone Coll, BS, 1964; Oregon State Univ, MS, 1971; Oregon State Univ, PhD, 1974. **CAREER:** Coll of Liberal Arts & Sciences, Univ of IL, asst dean, 1974-; Oregon State Univ, teacher, counselor, 1971-74; Ebenezer Ave School Rock Hill SC, teacher, 1968-70; Sunset Park School, Rock Hill, SC, teacher, coach, 1964-68; Univ of IL, Coll of Liberal Arts & Sciences, assoc dean, 1986-present. **ORGANIZATIONS:** mem, Natl Science Teacher's Assn, Natl Educ Assn, Assn for Educ of Teachers of Sci, Urbana Council Comm for Training of Teachers of Science, Alpha Phi Alpha, Phi Delta Kappa Hon Soc, Amer Coll Personnel Assn, Assn for Council & Devel. **HONORS/ACHIEVEMENTS:** fellow, Natl Science Found, 1970-71, Ford Found, 1971-72, Natl Fellowships Fund, 1972-74; Pres, Natl Assn of Acad Affairs Administrators 1987. **BUSINESS ADDRESS:** University of Illinois, 270 Lincoln Hall, 702 S Wright, Urbana, IL 61801.

COPELAND, TERRILYN DENISE
Speech pathologist. **PERSONAL:** Born May 02, 1954, Toledo, OH; daughter of Bernice Copeland-Thomas. **EDUCATION:** Kent State Univ, BS, 1976; Bowling Green State Univ, MA, 1980. **CAREER:** Lucas Co Bd of Mental Retardation, speech pathologist, 1978-81; Speech & Language Serv Inc, speech pathologist, 1981-86; Upjohn Healthcare Serv Inc, speech pathologist, 1984-86; Lucas Co Children's Serv Bd, speech pathologist, 1985-86; St Francis Rehab Hospital, staff speech pathologist, 1986-88, Flower Memorial Healthpley, 1988-89, staff speech pathologist, 1988-89; St Francis Rehabilitation Hospital, dir of speech pathology and audiology, 1989-present; Toledo Mental Health Center, sppech pathologist, 1985-. **ORGANIZATIONS:** Mem, Delta Sigma Theta Sor, 1973-, The Amer Speech & Hearing Assn, 1980-, The Aphasiology Assn of OH, 1982-, The Amer Assn of Univ Women, 1986-, The League of Women Voters, 1986-, The Natl Found For Head Injuries, 1986, OH Speech & Hearing Assn, 1980-, NW OH Area Representative for the Aphasiology Assn of OH, 1987-; Mem, Amer Business Womens Assn, 1989-. **HONORS/ACHIEVEMENTS:** Certificate of Clinical Competence (CCC), Amer Speech & Hearing Assn, 1981. **BUSINESS ADDRESS:** Dir of Speech Pathology & Audiology, St Francis Rehabilitation Hospital, 401 N Broadway, Green Springs, OH 44836.

COPELIN, SHERMAN NATHANIEL, JR.
Corporate director. **PERSONAL:** Born Sep 21, 1943, New Orleans, LA; married Dr Maxine Jackson; children: Sherman Nathaniel III, Michon Jerel. **EDUCATION:** Dillard U, BA 1965; Loyola U, New Orleans, adv study psychology 1966, adv study real est investmnt 1978. **CAREER:** Corporate Mgmt Ltd, pres 1978-; LA Sports Inc, sec mngng prtnr 1978-; Superdome Srvs Inc, pres, chief exec off 1973-; Copelin & Assos, pres 1973-;Mayor New Orleans, dir, model cities/Spl asst 1969-73; Orleans Parish Sch Bd, tchr 1966-69. **ORGANIZATIONS:** Steering com Am Soc of Planning Ofcls 1971; resource person Nat League Cities US Conf of Mayors 1971; mem Com on Minority Involvement C of C; execbd Areawide Health Planning Cncl; chmn Manpower Area Planning Cncl; tech adv com Reg Plng Forum; std adv, pres Lyndon Johnson 1964; grad fellow Loyola Univ Inst of Politics; pioneer, estblshd new vistas of opp for minority firms Nat Bus League 1977; Design Excellence in Econ Deprived Areas, & MinorityArchs Inc Bus League. **HOME ADDRESS:** 163 Parkside Ct, New Orleans, LA 70127.

COPPEDGE, ARTHUR L.
Artist, lecturer. **PERSONAL:** Born Apr 21, 1938. **EDUCATION:** Brooklyn Coll, attended; Brooklyn Mus Art School, attended; Pratt Graphic Art Ctyr, attended; Art Stu League, attended. **CAREER:** Amer the Beautiful Fund, artist in resd; teacher art classes, private studio; Brooklyn Mus Art School, teacher; Walden School NYC, teacher; NY Soc for Ethical Culture, teacher adult ed; Brooklyn Coll, Cornell Univ, Natl Conf of Artists, Amer Assoc of Mus Waldoft Astoria Hotel, lecturer; Inst of Jamaica, painting & drawing teacher. **ORGANIZATIONS:** Mem Bicentennial Proj US Dept of Interior, Univ of PA; commiss Art in Embassies Prog US Dept of State; mural Servo-Mation Corp; publ NY Times, Washington Post, Cultural Post, Amer 1976, Black Enterprise, Essence, Attica Black, Viking Press; crit reviews NY Times, Wash Post, Art Worker News, The New Yorker,Art News; bd mem Hilton Hotel; pres Brooklyn Consortium for Artists & the Arts; founder, established Brooklyn Artists Coalition; 1st dir exhibition dept New Muse Comm Mus; art consult The Gallery NYC; hon chmn Com to Honor Judge Bruce Wright; former chmn BACA ReGrant Bd; chmn Ed Comm 8; mem comm Brooklyn Comm Plnng Bd; estab art dept NY Soc for Ethical Culture; establ artists series, slide collection New Muse Mus; art consultant African-Amer Caribbean Cultural Center, Brooklyn NY; bd mem Brooklyn Downtown Development Corp. **HONORS/ACHIEVEMENTS:** Exhibits Mus of Mod Art NYC, Brooklyn Mus, Smithsonian Inst, Inst of Contemp Art Boston, Fogg Mus Boston, Randall Gallery NYC, Natl Acad Galleries NYC, Hudson River Mus Yonkers, Allied Artists NYC, Amer Acad of Arts & Letters NYC, NY Cultural Ctr, Hunter College; Awds Judge Wash Sq Art Exhibit NYC; numerous publications.

CORBIE, LEO A.
Acting president of university. **CAREER:** Medgar Evers College, Brooklyn, NY, acting pres. **BUSINESS ADDRESS:** Medgar Evers College, Brooklyn, NY 11225. *

CORBIN, ANGELA LENORE
Physician. **PERSONAL:** Born Nov 19, 1958, Washington, DC; daughter of Maurice Corbin and Ruby Corbin. **EDUCATION:** Howard Univ, BS 1980; Meharry Medical Coll, MD 1984; Univ MD Hospital resident 1984-87; Univ MD Hospital nephrology 1987-89. **CAREER:** Univ of MD Hospital, resident 1984-. **ORGANIZATIONS:** Mem Amer Coll of Physicians, Amer Medical Assoc. **HONORS/ACHIEVEMENTS:** Listed in Who's Who Among Students in Amer Colls 1983; mem Alpha Omega Alpha Medical Honor Soc 1984. **HOME ADDRESS:** 9413 Mellenbrook Rd, Columbia, MD 21045.

CORBIN, EVELYN D.
Administrator. **PERSONAL:** Born Sep 25, 1923, New York, NY; daughter of Eustace Augustus Dixon and Beulah Talbot Dixon; married Eustace E MD, Dec 31, 1948; children: Pamela Joy, Patricia Jill. **EDUCATION:** Westchester School of Nursing Valhalla NY, RN 1948; Hunter Coll CUNY, BE 1961; Queens Coll CUNY, MLS 1972. **CAREER:** Elmont Public Library, Adult Services Program Coordinator 1986-89; Lakeview Pub Lib, Nassau Co, Long Island NY, founding dir 1975-86; Elmont Pub Library Nassau Co, adult serv librarian 1973-75; Franklin Gen Hosp Valley Stream NY, RN 1967-68; St Albans Naval Hosp, RN labor & del 1958-59; LI Jewish Hosp, nurse ob serv 1954-56; Beth-El Hosp, Brooklyn NY, head nurse labor & del 1945-52. **ORGANIZATIONS:** 4-H Leader 1960-67; PTA 1960-67; Girl Scouts 1960-67; Church board of Trustees 1960-67; editor Church Newsletter 1961-63; chmn Friends of the Lake View library 1963-71; chmn Lakeview NAACP 1965-67. **HONORS/ACHIEVEMENTS:** L Marion Moshier Award, NY Lib Assn 1976; Community Service Award, Central Nassau Club of Natl Assn of Negro Business & Professional Women's Clubs Inc 1977. **MILITARY SERVICE:** WAC pvt 1943-44. **HOME ADDRESS:** 75 Edgewood Rd, Lakeview, Rockville Centre, NY 11570.

CORBITT, JOHN H.
Clergyman. **PERSONAL:** Born Aug 24, 1941, Salley, SC; son of John Corbitt and Thelma Corbitt; married Betty Starks; children: Bruce, Terry. **EDUCATION:** SC State Coll, AB 1962; Interdenominational Tehol Ctr, MDiv 1966; Vanderbilt Univ Div Sch & Yale Div Sch, additional study; McCormick Theol Sem, DMin 1979. **CAREER:** Bells Chapel Baptist Church, pastor 1966-67; Owen Coll, coll minister & prof of religion 1966-67; Philander Smith Coll, coll chaplin & prof of religion & philosophy 1970-74; Mt Pleasant Baptist Church Little Rock, pastor 1967-74; Springfield Baptist Ch, pastor. **ORGANIZATIONS:** Consult Natl Student Ministries So Bapt Conv 1969-87; mem Natl Assn of Coll & Univ Chplns; Ministries to Blacks in Higher Educ; pres Interdenominational Ministerial Alliance of Greater Little Rock; natl dir Natl Baptist Student Union Retreat 1973-; mem NAACP; bd of adv Little Rock Urban League; mem Foreign Mission Bd Natl Baptist Convention USA Inc 1968-74; dean Natl Baptist Congress of Christian Educ 1984; apptd by Gov Rockefeller to Gov's Comm on First Offenders State of AR 1969; apptd Gov Dale Bumpers to Bd of Pardons & Parole State of AR 1971; apptd by Gov James B Edwards to Greenville Area Bd of Mental Health; pres Enoree River Congress of Christian Educ 1975-79; pres Gr Greenville Ministerial Assn 1980-81; attended World Baptist Alliance meeting in Toronto Canada 1980 and Los Angel e s CA 1985; attended Baptist World Youth Congress Buenos Aires Argentina 1984; pres SC State Congress of Christian Educ 1986-. **BUSINESS ADDRESS:** Pastor, Springfield Bapt Church, 600 E McBee Ave, Greenville, SC 29601.

CORDELL, LA DORIS HAZZARD
Judge. **PERSONAL:** Born Nov 19, 1949, Bryn Mawr, PA; daughter of Lewis Hazzard and Clara Hazzard; divorced; children: Cheran, Starr. **EDUCATION:** Antioch Coll, BA 1971; Stanford Law School, JD 1974. **CAREER:** NAACP Legal Defense & Educ Fund, staff attorney 1974-75; attorney private practice 1975-82; Stanford Law School, asst dean 1978-82; State Court of Appeal Sixth Dist, justice pro tem 1986-87; Municipal Ct Santa Clara Co, judge 1982-88; Superior Ct Santa Clara Co, judge 1988-. **ORGANIZATIONS:** Mem Black Women's Lawyers Assn CA Chapt; mem NAACP; mem CA Judges Assn; mem CA Women Lawyers; chairperson bd of dirs Manhattan Playhouse East Palo Alto 1980; bd of dirs & steering comm Natl Conf on Women and the Law 1980, 1984-85; policy bd Center for Rsch on Women Stanford Univ 1980-82; chairperson bd of dirs East Palo Alto Comm Law Project 1984-87; bd of trustees, United Way of Santa Clara County 1987-; bd of dir, Police Activities League (PAL), San Jose Chapter 1987-, Natl Conf of Christians & Jews Inc, Santa Clara County 1988-. **HONORS/ACHIEVEMENTS:** Black History Award Tulip Jones Womens Club 1977; nominated for Black Enterprise Magazine annual Achievement Award in under 30 category 1977, 1978; Comm Involvement Award East Palo Alto Chamber of Comm 1982, 1983; Public Serv Awd Delta Sigma Theta 1982; Public Serv Awards Natl Council of Negro Women 1982; Outstanding Mid-Peninsula Black Woman Award Mid-Peninsula YWCA 1983; Political Achievement Award CA Black Women's Coalition & the Black Concerns Assn 1982; Featured twice in Ebony Magazine 1980, 1984; Implemented a minority recruitment program at Stanford Law School as asst dean; First Black Woman Judge in Northern CA; elected presiding judge of the Municipal Court 1985-86 term; author of "Before Brown v Bd of Educ—Was It All Worth It?" Howard Law Journa l Vol 23 No 1 1980; coauthor, "The Appearance of Justice, Judges' Verbal and Nonverbal Behavior in Criminal Jury Trials" Stanford Law Review Vol 38, No 1, 1985; "Black Immigration, Disavowing the Stereotype of the Shiftless Negro" Judges' Journal Spring 1986; Achievement Award from Western Center on Domestic Violence 1986; Santa Clara County Woman of Achievement Award 1985; Recipient of first Juliette Gordon Low Award for Community Serv 1987; first black woman on Superior Court in Northern California 1988-; Distinguished Citizen Award, Exchange Club 1989. **BUSINESS ADDRESS:** Judge, Superior Court, 191 N First St, San Jose, CA 95113.

CORDOVA, RENALDO C.
Business executive. **PERSONAL:** Born Aug 28, 1947, Brooklyn. **EDUCATION:** NY Comm Coll. **CAREER:** Barnes, Cordova & Eley Ltd, vice pres 1966-; United Merchants & Mfgrs Inc, traffic clerk 1965-66. **ORGANIZATIONS:** Vp Minority Bus Council; co-chmn Mgmt Asst Prog; mem Nat Bus League; mem Council of Cncrnd Black Execs, Inc; mem Bed-Stuy Jaycees; invlvmnt career guidnc prog at pub sch. **HONORS/ACHIEVEMENTS:** 4 yrs nominee 1974 Black-Enterprise Mag Annual Achv Award. **MILITARY SERVICE:** AUS sgt 1967-68. **BUSINESS ADDRESS:** 246 Marion St, Brooklyn, NY 11233.

CORINALDI, AUSTIN
Retired hospital executive. **PERSONAL:** Born Mar 31, 1921, NYC; son of Oswald Corinaldi and Claris Corinaldi; married Dorothy; children: Dyhann, Greg. **EDUCATION:** Columbia Univ, MS, hosp admin, 1969; MPH, 1964; NYU, BA, 1949; Coll of City of NY, attended 1942. **CAREER:** US Coast & Goedetic Survey, topographical draftsman, 1941-43; Riverton Labs, NYC, lab tech, detailman 1945-55; New York City Bd of Educ, teacher, health educ, 1955-67; Public Health Sanitarian NYC, Dept of Health, 1950-69; Harlem Hosp Cntr, admin resident 1968-69, dep asst commr planning 1969-70, dep asst commr operations 1970, assoc exec dir 1970-74, acting exec dir 1974-77; Coler Mem Hosp, retired deputy exec dir, 1977-85. **ORGANIZATIONS:** Mem Am Coll of Hosp Admin; Am Hosp Assn; Am Pub Health Assn; The Royal Soc of Health, England, Fellow; Nat Assn Of Hlth Serv Execs; Black Caus of Harlem Hlth Wrkrs; Nat Environ Hlth Assn; Assn of the Alumni of the Columbia Univ Sch of Pub Hlth; NY Univ Alumni Assn; Smithsonian Assoc; mem NY NAACP; NY Urban League; YMCA of Gr NY, Harlem Br; pres Harlem Neighborhds Assn; Beta Lambda Sigma Hon Soc Biology. **MILITARY SERVICE:** USAF acting s/sgt 1943-46.

CORLETTE, EDITH
Attorney. **PERSONAL:** Born Oct 19, 1942, Oklahoma City, OK; daughter of Stephen Parker and Gwendolyn Parker. **EDUCATION:** Hampton Inst, BS 1964; NW Sch of Law, JD 1974; UCLA, MS 1975. **CAREER:** Self-employed, atty. **ORGANIZATIONS:** Mem Delta Sigma Theta Sor 1962; Alpha Kappa Mu Hon Soc 1963-64; Langston Law Clb 1974; SW Bar 1974; LA Co Bar 1975; Nat Conf of Black Lwyrs 1975; pres Women's Div of NBA; sec CA Assn of Black Lwyrs; past mem at large NBA; sec Black Women Lwyr of So CA 1975; Nat Bus Assn 1976; Beverly Hills Law Assn 1977; bd dir NAACP, Hollywood Br; bd dirs Proj HEAVY. **HONORS/ACHIEVEMENTS:** Woodrow Wilson Fellowship 1964; Outstanding Young Women of America 1966; NW Urban Fellow 1973-74. **BUSINESS ADDRESS:** PO Box 8692, Los Angeles, CA 90008-0692.

CORLEY-SAUNDERS, ANGELA ROSE
Government official. **PERSONAL:** Born Jun 09, 1947, Washington, DC; married John Howard. **EDUCATION:** Howard U, BA 1975. **CAREER:** The White House, spec asst 1977-77; USDA Ofc of the Asst Sec for Rural Dev, spec asst 1977-79; Equal Opportunity Specialists 1986-; USDA Farmers Home Admin mgmt analyst 1979-. **ORGANIZATIONS:** Mem Natl Council of Negro Women 1978-; bd mem Unity Church of Christianity 1984-85. **BUSINESS ADDRESS:** Management Analyst, US Dept of Agric, 14th & Indep Ave SW Rm 5511, Washington, DC 20250.

CORMIER, LAWRENCE J.
Business executive. **PERSONAL:** Born Sep 26, 1927, San Benito, TX; married Helen Jones; children: Patricia Watkins, Janet, Lawrence. **EDUCATION:** Pace Univ, 1965-72. **CAREER:** US Merchant Marine, 3rd officer 1950-55; Ebony Oil Corp, bd chmn, ceo 1955-; Cormier & Ebony Trucking Inc, bd chmn, ceo 1964-; The Inner-City Mgmt Co, ceo, bd chmn 1977-; Cormier Industries Inc, Jamaica, NY, ceo and bd chair. **ORGANIZATIONS:** Pres, charter mem, bd mem, Assoc of Minority Bus Enterprise NY Inc; bd mem, past vice pres Gr Jamaica C of C; past pres, bd mem Intl Kiwanis, Jamaica Club; pres Gr Jamaica Devel Corp; adv bd mem Queens Urban League; past pre, bd mem, charter mem United Black Men of Queens Cty Inc. **HONORS/ACHIEVEMENTS:** Bus & Comm Serv Awd Omega Psi Phi 1965; NY State Small Businessman of the Year US Small Bus Adm 1967; Spec Recog Awd NAACP 1968; Outstanding Serv Awd Jamaica C of C 1970; Business Man of the Year Jamaica C of C 1974; Delta Sigma Theta outstanding community serv award, 1974; Assn of Minority Enterprise serv award, 1979; NY Urban League community serv award, 1981; NY State Dept of Commerce outstanding leadership award, 1982; Queens Fedn of Churches outstanding leadership award, 1983; Natl Cancer Soc outstanding community serv award, 1984; Businessman of the Year, St Albans Cham of Commerce, 1985; Benjamin S Rosenthal Humanitar-

ian Award, B'nai B'rith, 1985; Regl Minority Mfr of the Yr Award, US Dept of Commerce, 1986; Natl Minority Mfr of the Yr Award, US Dept of Commerce, 1986; US Small Bus Admin outstanding bus achieve award, 1986. **MILITARY SERVICE:** US Merchant Marines. **BUSINESS ADDRESS:** Chief Exec Officer, Bd Chmn, Mont Blanc Limousine, Cormier Industries Inc, 107-35 Merrick Blvd, Jamaica, NY 11433.

CORMIER, RUFUS, JR.
Attorney. **PERSONAL:** Born Mar 02, 1948, Beaumont, TX; married Yvonne Clement; children: Michelle, Geoffrey. **EDUCATION:** So Meth Univ, BA 1970; Yale Univ, JD 1973. **CAREER:** Paul Weiss Rifkind Wharton & Carrison, attny 1973-74; US House of Reps Judiciary Comm, spec asst to counsel 1974; Baker & Botts, attny. **ORGANIZATIONS:** Mem Amer Bar Assoc, Houston Bar Assoc, Houston Lawyers Assoc. **HONORS/ACHIEVEMENTS:** Avella Winn Hay Achievement Awd 1970; One of Five Outstanding Young Texans selected by Texas Jaycees 1981. **BUSINESS ADDRESS:** Attorney, Baker & Botts, 3000 One Shell Plaza, Houston, TX 77002.

CORNELISON, CAROLE JANE
Government admin., financial admin. **PERSONAL:** Born Jan 25, 1946, Dyersburg, TN; married Timothy E Cornelison; children: Jeanne, Sara, Arjuna. **EDUCATION:** Upsala Coll, BA 1969; George Washington Univ, MA 1971; Cornell Univ, MA 1975. **CAREER:** Trenton State Coll, instr, asst dir afro-amer studies 1971-72; Univ of Cincinnati, instr of history 1975-78; Edgecliff Coll, instr afro-amer history 1975-76; Bond Hill Redevelopment corp, admin asst 1976-78;; Cincinnati Girls Club, exec dir 1978-79; Northern KY Univ, instr of history 1979; MA Comm Action Inc, admin coord 1980, exec dir 1980-81; Action for Boston Comm Dev, spec consult 1981; City of Cambridge MA, div head dept of human serv 1981-84; City of Lincoln Heights OH, tax commnr 1984; Cincinnati-Hamilton Co Comm Action Agency, grants mgr 1985-86; United Way/Comm Chest of Gr Cincinnati, consultant 1987. **ORGANIZATIONS:** Sec Assoc of Women Faculty Univ of CT 1977-78; faculty adv Womens Ctr Univ of CT 1977-78; bd mem Women Helping Women 1977-78; bd pres Bond Hill Child-Dev Ctr 1977-78; task force mem Police Comm Relations City of Cambridge 1984; sub-comm chair Regional Needs Assessment Survey 1985-87; sec Black Cultural Workshop Boosters OH. **HONORS/ACHIEVEMENTS:** Coretta Scott King Awd Amer Assoc Univ Women; Cornell First Year & Continuing Fellowships Cornell Univ Grad Study in History. **HOME ADDRESS:** 9314 Daly Rd, Cincinnati, OH 45231. **BUSINESS ADDRESS:** Development Dir, St John Social Service Ctr, 121 East 13th St, Cincinnati, OH 45210.

CORNELIUS, ROBERT NELSON, JR.
Judge. **PERSONAL:** Born Jul 13, 1928, Philadelphia, PA; married Dorothy Lewis; children: Robert III, Michael, Anthony, Jude. **EDUCATION:** Villanova Univ, AB; Univ of PA, JD; Temple Univ, post-grad bus admin & econ. **CAREER:** State of PA, dep atty gen 1956-58; Nix Rhodes & Nix, partner 1958-68; Common Pleas Court Philadelphia Cty, judge 1968-71; Supreme Court PA, justice 1972-. **ORGANIZATIONS:** Bd dirs USO 1969-; bd dirs Germantown Boys Club 1968-; mem Council Pres Assn La Salle Coll Omega Psi Phi 1971; adv bd La Salle Coll HS; bd consult Villanova Univ Sch of Law 1973-. **HONORS/ACHIEVEMENTS:** 1st PA Award; Guardian Civic League Achievement Award. **MILITARY SERVICE:** AUS 1953-55.

CORNELIUS, ULYSSES S., SR.
Clergyman. **PERSONAL:** Born Dec 12, 1913, Waskom, TX; married Willie Hicks; children: Ulysses Sidney, Jr. **EDUCATION:** Bishop Coll, BA 1947, MEd 1952, Hon DD 1975; Miami U, grad; VA U. **CAREER:** Mt Sinai Bapt Ch, Dallas, pastor, TX pastor; LA, pastor; Waskom,TX, instr pub schs; Interracial Bapt Inst, Dallas, instr; Bishop Coll, instr. **ORGANIZATIONS:** Vp Nat Bapt SS & Bapt Training Union-Congress USA, Inc; pres BM&E St SS & BTU Congress of TX; fin Sec-treas LK Williams Ministers Inst;mem Interdnmntnl Ministerial All of Dallas; mem trustee bd BM&E Conv of TX; mem bd dir Interracial Bapt Inst of Dallas; mem 32 deg Prince Hall Masons; past mem bd trustees Bishop Coll; past mem bd dir Black C of C of Dallas; mem bd dir TX Fed of Garden Clubs. **HONORS/ACHIEVEMENTS:** Recip "Big Boss" Ldrshp Award, YMCA; cert of Appreciation for Dedicated Ldrshp in Advancemnt of Bishop Coll 1969-75; Alumni Citation Award, Bishop Coll 1968; srv Award Bethlehem Bapt Ch, Bonham TX 1971; srv Award Mt Sinai Bapt Ch, Dallas 1973; srv Award NW Dist Bapt Assn 1974. **MILITARY SERVICE:** AUS t/sgt 1943-46. **BUSINESS ADDRESS:** 1106 Pemberton Hill Rd, Dallas, TX 75217.

CORNELIUS, WILLIAM MILTON
Educational administrator. **PERSONAL:** Born Dec 04, 1936, Hinds Co. **EDUCATION:** Tougaloo Coll, BA 1955-59; IN U, MA 1971-72; KS State U, PhD 1974-79. **CAREER:** Utica Jr Coll, dir of special serv 1969-; Wilkinson County Public Schools, instructor, asst princ 1965-69; Saints Jr Coll, instructor, dean 1962-65. **ORGANIZATIONS:** Mem Nat Geo Soc; mem So Historical Assn; mem So Sociological Soc; mem Academic of Art & Sciences; mem Nat Council of Social Studies; mem MI Educators Assn; mem Nat Tchrs Assn; mem Nat Assn of Geography Tchrs; mem Hinds Co Tchrs Assn; mem Nat Assn of Coll & Univ Prof; mem IN Univ Alumni; mem KS State Univ Alumni; mem Tougaloo Coll Alumni; mem Am Mus of Nat History; mem Nat Assn of Curriculum & Supervision; mem MS Assn of Educ Opportunity Prog Personnel; mem Southeastern Assn of Educ Opportunity Prog PersonnelO. **HONORS/ACHIEVEMENTS:** Dean's Honr List 1959; grant Merrill-Palmer Inst 1960; grant Wayne State Univ 1960-61; Most Cooperative Tchr Award 1963; summer grant Hampton Inst 1965; grantIN Univ 1967; grant Univ of Southwestern LA 1968; grant Norfolk State Coll 1969; grant Howard Univ 1970; Outstanding Educators of Am 1974; Faculty Devel Grant 1974-79. **BUSINESS ADDRESS:** Dir of Special Services, Utica Junior College, Utica Campus, Utica, MS 39175.

CORNELY, PAUL B.
Retired educator, physician. **PERSONAL:** Born Mar 09, 1906, Pointe a Pitre, Guadeloupe;son of Eleodore Cornely and Adrienne Mellon Cornely; married Mae Stewart; children: Paul B Jr. **EDUCATION:** Univ of MI, AB 1928, MD 1931, Dr PH 1934, DSc (Hon) 1968; Univ of Pacific, D Public Service (Hon) 1972. **CAREER:** Freedmen's Hosp Wash DC, med dir 1947-58; Dept Health Family Practice Howard U, prof & chmn 1955-73; Agency Intl Devel, Washington DC, consultant 1960-74; System Sciences Bethesda MD, sr med consultant 1971-82. **ORGANIZATIONS:** Pres Technical Assn Inc 1977; chmn Board of Dir Prof Exam Serv 1978-82; pres Phys Forum 1960-61; pres Community Group Health Found 1968-73; mem Pres Committee on Popl & American's Future 1970-72; pres John Carroll Society Wash DC 1971-73. **HONORS/ACHIEVEMENTS:** Pres American Public Health Assn 1971-72; fellow Amer Coll of Preventive Med fellow Amer Board of Preventive & Public Health; fellow (Hon) Amer Coll of Hospital Admin; Sedgwick Mem Awd Amer Public Health Assn 1972.

CORNISH, BETTY W.
Executive director. **PERSONAL:** Born Jul 10, 1936, New York City, NY; married Edward H Cornish. **EDUCATION:** Boston Univ, BFA (Cum Laude) 1958; Univ of Hartford, MEd 1962, MAEd 1980. **CAREER:** Hartford Neighborhood Ctrs, youth group leader 1959-63; Bloomfield Publ Schools, teacher 1958-68; Central CT State Coll, asst prof, art ed 1966-83; Gemini User Group Inc, exec dir 1983-. **ORGANIZATIONS:** Mem CT Ed Assoc 1960-74; coord Afro-Amer Studies Prog 1969-73; mem NAEA; pres & exec bd CT Art Ed Assoc 1975; mem Amer Assoc of Univ Prof 1976-; exec bd New England Art Ed Conf 1977-79; pres affirm action comm Central CT State Univ 1978-80; co-chair Central CT State Univ Pres Comm Race Relatations; mem Soc CT Craftsmen, Hartford Reading Is Fundamental Comm, Heart Found Art Exhibitions, Black Studies & Art & Art Ed; presentations to civic school & adult groups; chmn student-faculty comm Afro-Amer Studies Prog CCSC; mem Council Unitarian Soc of Hartford. **HONORS/ACHIEVEMENTS:** Delta Sigma Theta Scholarship Awd 1954-55; Boston Univ Full-Tuition Scholarship Awd 1954-58; Outstanding Art Ed in CT Awd 1979; implemented art ed maj CCSC; Black Alumni CCSV Serv Awd. **BUSINESS ADDRESS:** Executive Dir, Gemini User Group Inc, 151 Farmington Ave, Hartford, CT 06156.

CORNISH, JEANNETTE CARTER
Attorney. **PERSONAL:** Born Sep 17, 1946, Steelton, PA; daughter of Ellis Pollard Carter and Anna Stannard Carter; married Harry L Cornish, Dec 24, 1970; children: Lee Jason, Geoffrey Charles. **EDUCATION:** Howard Univ, BA 1968; Howard Univ Law Sch, JD 1971. **CAREER:** Office of Gen Counsel USDA, law clerk 1968-71; Newark-Essex Jt Law Reform Proj, attorney 1971-72; Equal Employment Opportunity Comm, attorney 1972-73; BASF Corp (formerly Inmont Corp), sr atty/asst sec 1974-. **ORGANIZATIONS:** Mem Amer Bar Assn; mem Natl Bar Assn; mem Amer Corp Counsel Assn; bd mem Paterson YWCA; bd mem Lenni-LenapeGirl Scout Council. **HONORS/ACHIEVEMENTS:** Scholarship Alpha Kappa Alpha Sor 1964-65; Scholarship Delta Sigma Theta Sor 1964-66. **BUSINESS ADDRESS:** Sr Attorney/Asst Secretary, BASF Corporation, 1255 Broad St, PO Box 6001, Clifton, NJ 07015.

CORNWALL, SHIRLEY M.
Dentist. **PERSONAL:** Born Dec 08, 1918, Panama, Panama;married Jerlene; children: Howard, Caral, Cedric, Rupert, Vicount, Francis. **EDUCATION:** BS 1946; MS 1947; DDS 1952. **CAREER:** Charlotte Nc, intern & residency 1952;DDS prvt practice 1955; real estate bus, 1960. **ORGANIZATIONS:** Mem N MS Med Dental Pharm & Nurses Soc; mem Kappa Alpha Psi Frat; St & Francis Cath Ch. **HONORS/ACHIEVEMENTS:** First black receive MA NC Coll Durham NC. **BUSINESS ADDRESS:** 125 W Johnson St, Greenwood, MS 38930.

CORNWELL, EDWARD EUGENE, III
Physician/surgeon. **PERSONAL:** Born Nov 30, 1956, Washington, DC. **EDUCATION:** Brown Univ, BA 1978; Howard Univ Coll of Medicine, MD 1982. **CAREER:** LA County USC Med Ctr, surgical residency 1982-; MD Inst for Emergency Medical Serv Systems Baltimore, trauma surgery fellowship 1987-. **ORGANIZATIONS:** Pres Howard Univ Coll of Medicine Class of 1982; mem Natl Medical Assoc 1982-. **HONORS/ACHIEVEMENTS:** Alpha Omega Alpha Medical Honor Soc 1982; Awds in Clinical Performance Howard Univ Coll of Medicine (internal medicine, ob/gyn, pediatrics, surgery) 1982.

CORNWELL, W. DON
Investment banker. **PERSONAL:** Born Jan 17, 1948, Cushing, OK; married E LaVerne Manning; children: Kievdi. **EDUCATION:** Harvard U, MBA 1971; Occidental Coll, AB 1969. **CAREER:** Corporate Finance, vp; Goldman, Sachs & Co, vp; Hartford Comm Capital Corp Hartford Nat Corp, mgr 1970; Essence Communications Inc, advr. **ORGANIZATIONS:** Vol Vol Urban Consult Grp Trustee Nat Urban League. **HONORS/ACHIEVEMENTS:** Nat Merit Achvmt Schlrshp 1965. **BUSINESS ADDRESS:** Vice President, Goldman, Sachs & Co, Investment Banking Div, 85 Broadway St, New York, NY 10004.

CORPREW, CHARLES SUMNER, JR.
Educator. **PERSONAL:** Born Feb 14, 1929, Norfolk, VA; married Bertha Delois Bryant; children: Jovandra Stacey Sanderlin, Charles Sumner III. **EDUCATION:** WV State Coll Inst WV, AB 1951; NY Univ, MA 1963; Kent State Univ Old Dominion Univ, postgraduate study. **CAREER:** Norfolk City School Bd, adv council vice chmn 1965; Norfolk City Schools, elem principal 1967-69; Educ Assn of Norfolk, pres 1969-70; Norfolk City Schools, asst prin in admin 1969-71, principal secondary 1971-. **ORGANIZATIONS:** Pres, Norfolk Teachers Assn Federal Credit Union 1978-; classroom tchrs state pres Norfolk City Sch 1960; eastern regional dir Natl Council of Urban Educ Assn NEA 1964-67; educ com chmn Chamber of Commerce, Norfolk 1969; keeper of records & seals Omega Psi Phi Fraternity, 1954-55; mem Phi Delta Kappa Educ Fraternity, 1970; music dept chmn First Baptist Church, Norfolk 1978-80. **HONORS/ACHIEVEMENTS:** Outstanding Contributions in Field of Educ Award, Omega Psi Phi Frat Norfolk VA Lambda Omega Chap 1971; Outstanding Contributions in Field of Educ Award, VA Educ Assn Minority Caucus 1977. **MILITARY SERVICE:** AUS maj 1951-69; Medal of Honor. **BUSINESS ADDRESS:** Principal Secondary, Norfolk City Schools, PO Box 1357, Norfolk, VA 23501.

CORRIN, MALCOLM L.
Association executive. **PERSONAL:** Born Jun 12, 1924, Sea Bright, NJ; widowed; children: Weldon, Lois, Linda. **EDUCATION:** Morehouse Coll, AB 1950; Univ PA, MBA 1953; Am Coll Of Life Underwriters, 1960; Stanford U, Grad Sch Bus Admn, 1972. **CAREER:** Bishop Coll bus mgr 1952-54; great lakes mutual life ins co agency dir 1954-56; CT gen life ins co estate & analyst ins spl 1966-67; Interracial Council For Bus Opportunity NJ Br exec dir natl pres 1974; rutgers grad sch bus adminstrn vis prof. **ORGANIZATIONS:** Mem E Orange Bd Educ 1972, Pres 1974; E Orange Fire Commr 1971-72; mem NAACP; Urban League. **HONORS/ACHIEVEMENTS:** Commendation, Pres Richard Nixon 1970. **MILITARY SERVICE:** 1st lt 1943-47. **BUSINESS ADDRESS:** President & CEO, Interracial Cncl for Bus Oppor, 800 2nd Avenue, Ste 307, New York, NY 10017.

CORRY, PATRICIA A.
Physician. **PERSONAL:** Born Mar 24, 1944, Shelby, NC. **EDUCATION:** Bennett Coll, BS 1965; Meharry Med Coll, MD 1970. **CAREER:** Cook Co Hosp, intern 1970-71;Univ Chicago & LoyolaUniv Med Ctr, psychiatry resd 1970-71; Middle TN Mental Hlth Inst, Psychiatrist. **ORGANIZATIONS:** Mem NAACP So; Poverty Law Ctr; PUSH. **HONORS/ACHIEVEMENTS:** Listed Who's Who in Am Coll's & U's 1963; recpt Outsdng Yng Women Am 1971; mem Alpha Kappa Mu Nat Hon Soc; Betta Kappa Chi Sci Hon Soc.

CORTADA, RAFAEL LEON
Educator. **PERSONAL:** Born Feb 12, 1934, New York, NY; married Selonie Head; children: Celia, Natalia, Rafael. **EDUCATION:** Fordham Coll, AB 1955; Columbia U, MA 1958; Fordham Coll, PhD 1967; Harvard Grad Sch Bus, cert 1974. **CAREER:** Metropolitan Community Coll, pres; Hostos Coll, vice-pres 1971-74; Medgar Evers Coll, dean 1970-71; Federal & City Coll, assoc prov 1968-70; Smith Coll, dir 1969-72; US Dept Of State, foreign serv 1966-69; Univ Of Daytona, asst prof 1964-66; New Rochelle High School, 1957-64, bd of governors 1964-66. **ORGANIZATIONS:** Mem Overseas Liaison Comm 1970; vice pres Wash Task Force On African Affrs 1969; Consult Media Sys Corp 1976; Nat Adv Comm Danforth Foun; comm E Harlem Experimental Coll 1971-75; adv KTCA TV Minneapolis 1976; accr visitor Middle States Assn; ed bd "Current Biblio on African Affrs" 1973. **HONORS/ACHIEVEMENTS:** Publ 88 articles & reviews In Caribbean, Afro-Amer, Latin Amer; history publ "Black Studies, An Urban & Comparative Curriculum" 1974. **MILITARY SERVICE:** AUS 1st lt 1955-57.

CORTEZ, JAYNE
Poet. **PERSONAL:** Born May 10, 1936, Arizona; married Melvin Edwards, 1975; children: Denardo Coleman. **CAREER:** Poet and lecturer. **HONORS/ACHIEVEMENTS:** Rockefeller Foundation grant, 1970; Creative Artists Public Service poetry award, New York State Council on the Arts, 1973, 1981; National Endowment for the Arts fellowship in creative writing, 1979-80, 1986; New York Foundation for the Arts award, 1987. **BUSINESS ADDRESS:** c/o Bola Press, PO Box 96, Village Station, New York, NY 10014.

CORTOR, ELDZIER
Painter, printmaker. **PERSONAL:** Born Jan 10, 1916, Richmond, VA. **EDUCATION:** Attended, Art Inst of Chicago, Inst of Design, Columbia Univ. **CAREER:** Taught at Centre D'Art, Port-au-Prince & Pratt Inst; various exhibitions, Art Inst of Chicago, Metro Museum of Art, Martha Jackson Gallery, Howard Univ, Carnegie Inst, Assoc Amer Artists, The Studio Museum of Harlem, Museum of Nat Cntr of Afro-Amer Artists Boston. **ORGANIZATIONS:** Mem Soc Amer Graphic Artists. **HONORS/ACHIEVEMENTS:** Carnegie Awd; Bertha Aberle Florsheim Awd, William H Bartels Awd; Amer Negro Exposition Awd; Rosenwald Fellowship 1944-45; Guggenheim Fellowship 1950. **BUSINESS ADDRESS:** 35 Montgomery St, New York, NY 10002.

COSBY, JAMES C.
Accountant. **PERSONAL:** Married Thersia; children: Felecia, James Jr, Kimberly. **EDUCATION:** Rutgers U, BA 1958; Seton Hall U, Intl Accts Bus Sch. **CAREER:** Dorchester Inc Milburn, NJ, acct supr. **ORGANIZATIONS:** Co-chrmn NOLA Non Partisan Civic Organ 1966; pres Oranges & Maplewood NAACP 1968; chmn NJ St NAACP; conf mem Frontiers Intl Pres; N J BrNAACP; pol action chmn NJ State Conf of NAACP; vice chmn & finance chmn Essec Co Youth & Rehab Commn; Polit Action Comm 1973-; com memNatl NAACP; Time & Place Com 1975-77; past vchmn bd dir Essex Co Youth & Rehabilitation Commn 1969-75; mem Larry Stalks Civic Assn; mem NJ Cork & Bottle Club; past chmn Finance Com; ECY; RC; mem Frontiers Internat; Who's Who in Black Am 1976-77; elected Dist Committeeman E Orange NJ Twice 1972-; mem E Orange 2nd Ward Dem; E Orange Jaycees. **HONORS/ACHIEVEMENTS:** Recipient of E Orange NJ Outst Citizen's Awd 1976; co-chmn NOLA; recipient Lorreta Miller Civic Assn Award; recipient The Pepermint Comm Awd 1975;recipient Cert of Appreciation from US Navy Recruiting Command 1975; recipient of Essex Co Econ Commn for dedicated serv 1974; recipient of NAACP Thalheimer Awd for outstdng prgm act 1973-77; recipient of Renee Sch Commn Serv Awd 1974; recipient of Lorretta Miller's Civic Assn Serv Awd 1972; recipient Essex-Hudson United Way's 1st Outstdng Comm Awd 1973; recipient of Cert of Appreciation Awd, Kilmer Job Corp 1966; Co-campaign, co-coord Assemblyman Eldridge Hawkins 1973; campaign mgr CoSurrogate 1972; United Way Comm Award 1973; cert of Appreciation, Job Corps Ctr 1962.

COSBY, WILLIAM HENRY
Entertainer. **PERSONAL:** Born Jul 12, 1937, Germantown, PA; married Camille Hanks; children: Erika, Erinn, Ennis, Ensa, Evin. **EDUCATION:** Temple Univ, BA; Univ of MA, MA, EdD. **CAREER:** First Black co-star in a dramatic series I Spy; star & producer of The Bill Cosby Show; made several movies & over 23 comedy & musical albums; commercials for Jello, Coke, Del Monte, Ford & other major firms; author of two books The Wit & Wisdom of Fat Albert, Bill Cosby's Personal Guide to Power Tennis; made first concert film Bill Cosby-Himself 1984; stars in series The Cosby Show. **ORGANIZATIONS:** Active in PUSH, NAACP, United Negro College Fund; bd dirs & natl chmn Sickle Cell Foundation. **HONORS/ACHIEVEMENTS:** 8 Grammy Awds; 4 Emmy Awds; NAACP Image Awd; author The Wit and the Wisdom of Fat Albert 1973, Bill Cosby's Personal Guide to Power Tennis, Fatherhood 1986. **MILITARY SERVICE:** USNR 1956-60. **BUSINESS ADDRESS:** Performer, The Brokaw Co, 9255 Sunset Blvd, Ste 706, Los Angeles, CA 90069.

COSE, ELLIS
Columnist. **PERSONAL:** Born Feb 20, 1951, Chicago, IL. **EDUCATION:** Univ of IL Chicago, CBA Psych 1972; George Washington Univ, MA Sci Tech & Publ Policy 1978. **CAREER:** Chicago Sun-Times, columnist/reporter 1970-77; Joint Center for Polit Studies Washington, sr fellow/dir energy policy studies 1977-79; Detroit Free Press, edit writer/columnist 1979-81; Natl Acad Scis, resident fellow 1981-82; USA Today, spec writer 1982-83; Inst Journalism Edn, pres 1983-. **ORGANIZATIONS:** Mem Natl Assn of Black Journalists; mem environ adv com Dept Energy 1978-79; mem Natl Urban league Energy Proj 1979-80. **HONORS/ACHIEVEMENTS:** Aughor, "Energy and Equity, Some Social Concerns" 1978; "Energy and the Urban Crises" 1978; named Outstanding Young Citizen of Chicago Jaycees 1977; recip 1stPlace Newswriting Award IL UPI 1973; Stick-o-Type Award Chicago Newsp Guild 1975; Best Polit Reporting Lincoln Univ Natl Unity Award 1975 & 1977.

COSHBURN, HENRY S., JR.
Business executive. **PERSONAL:** Born Mar 15, 1936, NYC, NY; married Veanna G Ferguson. **EDUCATION:** Univ of PA, BS 1957; Columbia Univ, MS 1964. **CAREER:** US Army Signal Corps, chem engr 1958-60; Yardney Elec Corp, sales engr 1960-63; Mobil Oil, sr engr 1964-68; Esso Eastern, mktg analyst 1968-71; Exxon Intl Co, acct exec 1973-82; First Natl Crude Oil, vice pres. **ORGANIZATIONS:** Mem Alpha Phi Alpha, Alpha Chi Sigma, Amer Inst of Engrs, Amer Electrochem Soc, ACS, Amer Soc Lub Engrs, Princeton Club; NY Admission Rep Univ PA; visiting prof mktg Southern Univ Bethune Cookman Coll, Wilberforce Univ, Miles Coll, Norfolk St Coll; instr ICBO Mktg mem Harlem Hosp Bd; pres Harlem Civ Imp Counc; vice pres Penn/Princeton Club NYC; bd dirs Univ of PA Alumni Assn; patents hardware greases. **HONORS/ACHIEVEMENTS:** Cert Recog Amer Inst Chem Engr NY Sect 1970; Cert Apprec Urban League 1971-74; Vol Serv Award ICBO 1971-74; Citation Univ PA 1974; Alumni Award of Merit Univ of PA. **BUSINESS ADDRESS:** Vice President, First Natl Crude Oil, 148 East Ave, Norwalk, CT 06851.

COSTEN, MELVA WILSON
Theological educator. **PERSONAL:** Born May 29, 1933, Due West, SC; daughter of John Theodore Wilson and Azzie Lee Ellis Wilson; married James Hutten Costen, May 24, 1989; children: James, Jr., Craig Lamont, Cheryl Costen Clay. **EDUCATION:** Harbison Jr Coll, Irmo SC, 1947-50; Johnson C Smith Univ, Charlotte NC, AB Educ 1950-52; Univ of North Carolina, Chapel Hill NC MAT Music 1961-64; Georgia State Univ, Atlanta GA, PhD Curriculm and Instruction/Music 1973-78. **CAREER:** Mecklenburg County School, Charlotte NC, elementary teacher, 1952-55; Edgecombe County, Rocky Mount Nashville NC, elementay teacher, 1956-57; Nash County, Nashville NC, elementary and music teacher 1959-65; Atlanta Public Schools Atlanta GA, intinerant music teacher 1965-73; Interdenominational Theological, Atlanta GA, Helmar Nielsen Professor of Worship and Music, 1973-. **ORGANIZATIONS:** Regional director, Natl Assn of Negro Musicians 1973-75; co-chair, choral div, District V Georgia Music Educators Assoc 1981-82; mem of bd Presbyterian Assn of Musicians 1982-86; chairperson, Presbyterian Church Hymnal Committee 1984-1990; mem of bd Liturgical Conference 1985-91; mem of bd Mid-Atlanta Unit, Cancer Society of America, 1985-87. **HONORS/ACHIEVEMENTS:** Conducted 500-voice elementary chorus, Music Educators Natl Conference 1970; Teacher of the Year, Slater School, Atlanta Ga, 1973; Teacher of the Year, Interdenominational Theological Center, 1975; Golden Dove Award, Kappa Omega Chapter, Alpha Kappa Alpha Sorority 1981; conducted 800-voice adult choir, Reuniting Assembly of Presbyterian Church 1983; Doctor of Humane Letters, Erskine Coll, Due West SC, 1987. **HOME ADDRESS:** 3360 Laren Lane, SW, Atlanta, GA 30311.

COSTON, BESSIE RUTH
Association executive. **PERSONAL:** Born Nov 29, 1916, Jackson, GA; daughter of Elbert Bivins (deceased) and Nannie J Harkness Bivins (deceased); married Floyd Thomas; children: Lynn Ruth Phillips. **EDUCATION:** Wilberforce U, BS 1939; OH State U, MA in Soc Adm 1941; Youngstown U, Grad Study; Westminister Coll, Grad Study. **CAREER:** Phyllis Wheatley YWCA Indianapolis, IN, dir older girls activities 1941-44; Neighbor House Columbus, OH, prog dir 1944-46; Bureau of Employment Sec Youngstown, OH, interviewer/cnslr/supr 1947-63; YWCA, prog dir 1963-68, asst exec dir 1968-70, exec dir 1970-74. **ORGANIZATIONS:** Commr Youngstown Metro Housing Bd 1974-78; mem Advisory Council Soc Serv 1972-74; mem/sec bd Doris Burdman Homes 1973-76; natl pres Iota Phi Lambda Sor Inc 1969-73, natl 1st vice 1968-69, natl 2nd vice 1966-68, northern regional dir 1954-58; pres/vp/sec/dean of pledges Alpha Nu Chap Iota Phi Lambda Sor Inc 1949-57; mem Acad Certified Social Workers 1972-77, 1989-; mem Natl Assn Social Workers 1972-77, 1989-; White House Conf Children Wash, DC 1970; White House Conf on Aging 1971; hon mem Gamma Phi Chap Delta Kappa Gamma; life mem NAACP; mem/former state convenor Natl Council of Negro Women; mem Youngstown Area Urban League; mem McGuffey Centre; mem St Andrew's AME Ch; mem American Assn of Retired Persons, 1985-; mem Natl Council of Senior Citizens 1985-; mem Advisory Bd, Retired Volunteer Serv, 1985-88. **HONORS/ACHIEVEMENTS:** Honorable Mention Intl Assn Personnel Employment Sec Chicago 1963; Achievement Award NatlBus & Prof Women 1971; Mayors Proclamation City of Youngstown 1973;Civic Award Jr Civic League 1970; Merit Award WKBN Radio 1963; Outstanding Serv Award McGuffey Centre 1963; Woman of the Yr Alpha Nu Chap Iota Phi Lambda 1963; Mother of the Yr W Fed YMCA 1963; This is Your Life Natl Council of Negro Women 1958.

COTHARN, PRESTON SIGMUNDE, SR.
Retired government official. **PERSONAL:** Born Jan 29, 1925, E St Louis, IL; son of Robert Provina Cotharn (deceased) and Lula Whitenhill Cotharn (deceased); married Berteal Whitehead, 1964 (deceased); children: Preston Jr, Cynthia, Titus, Christopher. **EDUCATION:** Lincoln U, BS 1946; Gov State U, MA 1973; DePaul U, MEd 1975; Univ Sarasota, EdD 1977; 9 acad degrees; law degree; hon DD Degree; ordained minister 1978. **CAREER:** Illinois Dept of Labor, Bureau of Employment Security, mgr, interstate benefits, exec IV, exec III, office mgr II, office mgr I, claims supervisor, adjudication supervisor, adjudicator, supervising claims examiner; IL Dept Labor-cons, free lance mgmt; Fuller Elem Sch, tchr; Grant Elem Sch, tchr; ISTSB HS Div; asst asst dep warden; Armour & Co, correction supr admin assst to night supt; Armour & Co, toured US & abroad. **ORGANIZATIONS:** Fisk Jubilee Singers with Mrs James A Myers. **HONORS/ACHIEVEMENTS:** Recipient voice tng, Dr O Anderson Fuller & Frank Laforge. **HOME ADDRESS:** 11601 S Aberdeen, Chicago, IL 60643.

COTHORN, MARGUERITE ESTERS
Retired social worker. **PERSONAL:** Born Dec 23, 1909, Albia, IA; divorced; children: John A. **EDUCATION:** Drake Univ, Des Moines IA, BA 1930; Drake Univ, MA 1932; Univ of IA School of Social Work, MSW 1954. **CAREER:** Polk Co Juvenile Ct, Des Moines, probation officer 1930; Baltimore Emergency Relief, caseworker 1933-41; Willkie Hse (Settlement & Rockford IL), dir 1941-52; VA Hosp Knoxville IA, caseworker (psych) 1954-56; Des Moines United Way, planning div 1956-65, dir of planning div 1965-73; 1965-73; United Way Central Ins, retired social worker ACSW. **ORGANIZATIONS:** Mem (ACSW) Natl Assn, Social Workers Charter; mem, Natl Conf Social Workers; Mem, NAACP, broadlawns med center psychiatric advisory com, 1975-; various offices, Delta Sigma Theta Sorority 1927-; camp vistor Amer Camping Assn, 1957-60; various capacities League of Women Voters, 1983-. **HONORS/ACHIEVEMENTS:** Plaque for leadership Black Comm 1973; Alice Whipple Award, Outstanding Serv in Health & Welfare S IA Central Federation of Labor (AFL-CIO); Key to City Mayor & Voter Bureau 1973; Distinguished alumni Drake Univ, 1974; Club Women's Comm Award PL Culture Club 1974; Distin-

guished serv IA Civil Rights Comm 1983; elected IA Women's Hall of Fame 1986. **HOME ADDRESS:** 1249 43rd St, Des Moines, IA 50311.

COTHRAN, TILMAN CHRISTOPHER
Educator. **PERSONAL:** Born Nov 17, 1918, Hope, AR; son of Thomas Cothran and Willie Cothran; married Gladys Williams, Aug 1940; children: Brenda Faye Bradley, Tilman Christopher. **EDUCATION:** Univ of AK Pine Bluff, BA 1939; Univ of IN, MA 1942; Univ of Chicago, PhD 1949. **CAREER:** Univ of AK Pine Bluff, dept & dean 1939-59; Dillard Univ, Dean of Social Science 1947-49; Phylon Altanta Univ, chair of Sociology & Educ of Phylon 1959-70; Govnrs St Univ Park Forest So IL, academic vice pres 1970-72; Western MI Univ, assoc dean, head of Social Sciences 1972-79; Western MI Univ, prof Sociology & Gerontology 1979-. **ORGANIZATIONS:** Mem of public com Amer Socioloy Society 2 Yrs; chrm-Dubois-Johnson-Frazier Amer Soc Society 1980-84; chmn Kalamazoo Co Comm On Aging 1983-; mem of Southcentral MI Area Agency On Aging 1982; mem of Program Committee Gerontological Soc of Amer 1984; mem of Univ MI Com to study health care in China and Russia 1983; Advisory Comm, State Office of Servs to the Aged; pres, Kalamazoo Branch NAACP, 1985-; Mem, MI State Office on Aging Advisory Comm, Exec Comm, Southcentral MI Commn on Aging. **HONORS/ACHIEVEMENTS:** Alpha Kappa Mu Honor Soc; Alpha Delta Honor Soc; Natl Honor Soc, Gerontology. **MILITARY SERVICE:** Committee to Study Integration in Army in Japan and Korea 1951. **HOME ADDRESS:** 1315 Greenwood Ave, Kalamazoo, MI 49007.

COTMAN, HENRY EARL
Physician. **PERSONAL:** Born Apr 13, 1943, Archer, FL; married Jacqueline Nickson. **EDUCATION:** FL A&M U, BA 1965; Univ FL; Harvard Peter Bent Brigham Hosp, externships; MD 1970. **CAREER:** Gulf Coast Oncology Center, pvt prac; Univ AZ Hlth Div Sci Ctr Div Radiation Oncology, asst prof 1975-77; Wm Beaumont Army Hosp Med Ctr Div Radiation Oncology, chf 1975; Univ of MN, resd 1971-74; Union Meml Hosp, med internship 1970-71; MI State U, asso clinical prof. **ORGANIZATIONS:** Mem Am Coll of Radiology; Am Soc of Therapeutic Radiology; Nat Med Assn; Ingham Co Med Soc; mem Alpha Phi Alpha Frat Inc; clinical flw Am Cancer Soc 1971-74; chf resd Radiation Oncology 1974. **HONORS/ACHIEVEMENTS:** One of the first blacks to gradUniv of FL Coll of Med; publ "The Usage of The Bipedal Lymphogram As A Guide During Laparotomy in Hodgkin's & Non-Hodgkin's Lymphomas" ACTA Radiologica; "Combination Radiotherapy & Surger in the Mgmt of Squamous Carcinoma of the Head & Neck" Radiology Soc meeting 1976. **MILITARY SERVICE:** Med Corp maj 1975. **BUSINESS ADDRESS:** Gulf Coast Oncology Center, 701 Sixth St South, St Petersburg, FL 33701.

COTMAN, IVAN LOUIS
Area administrator. **PERSONAL:** Born Apr 04, 1940, Detroit, MI; son of Louis Richard Cotman and Marguerite Caine; married Jeanetta Hawkins; children: Ivan Louis, Jr, Arthur Robert, Amir Charles. **EDUCATION:** KY State U, BA English, Soc Sci 1958-62; Atlanta U, MA Social Work 1962-64; Univ of MI, Schl Public Hlth Medical Care Org 1969-70; Univ Of Manchester (England), Cerifiticate in New Town Planning 1972; Wayne State Univ, EdD Curriculum & Admin 1975; Univ Oklahoma, Advanced Studies 1983. **CAREER:** Detroit Bd of Educ, schl social worker 1964-69; United Co Serv Detroit, agcy prog consul/assist budget dir 1969-72; New Detroit Inc, dir of employment 1972-73; MI Dept of Ed Disability Deter Serv, area admin 1973-79; MI Dept of Education, assoc superintendent 1979-. **ORGANIZATIONS:** Mem Acad of Certif Social Workers, Natl Assoc of Disablility Exams, Natl Assoc of Social Workers, Natl Rehab Assn, MI Civil Serv Oral Appraisal Bd, MI Occupational Info Statutory Comm; past natl vice pres Alpha Phi Alpha Frat, Inc; past bd mem United Neighborhood Ctr of Amer; life mem NAACP; adjunct prof Michigan State Univ; State Credit Union Supervisor Committee. **HONORS/ACHIEVEMENTS:** Resolution of Tribute MI Senate 1973; Dist Alumni KY State Univ 1975; Dist Citizen MI House of Rep 1977-80; Regional Commissioner's Citation Social Sec Adminstration 1979; Order of KY Colonels; 32 Degree Prince Hall Mason; Disting Alumni Awd KY State Univ, Natl Assoc for Equal Oppor in Higher Educ; cited for Leadership by US Sec of Educ; 6 week exec placement in Washington based Commn on Excellence; articles on Leadership published in MI Sch Bd Journal, Waterloo (Ontario) Press, Detroit News, Michigan Chronicle, Congressional Record; Board of Governors, Meadville Lombard Theology School (Univ of Chicago). **HOME ADDRESS:** 20141 McIntyre, Detroit, MI 48219. **BUSINESS ADDRESS:** Associate Supt Bureau Rehab, MI Dept Of Ed, P O Box 30010, Lansing, MI 48909.

COTTON, ALBERT E.
Director. **PERSONAL:** Born Oct 06, 1939; married Kathleen; children: Christopher, Eric B. **EDUCATION:** San Francisco State U, BA 1970; San Francisco State U, MBA 1977. **CAREER:** Chaklee Corp, dir benefits & compensation 1979-; Shaklee Corp, dir ind relations 1978-79; Shaklee Corp, personnel mgr 1975-78; Hunt Wesson Corp, personnel mgr 1974; City of Richmond CA, CETA dir 1972-74; Schlage Lock Corp, mfg supr 1964-71. **ORGANIZATIONS:** Bd of dir N CA Ind Relations Council 1974-; mem Am Soc of Personnel Adminstr 1974-; mem Am Compensation Assn 1979; Beta Gamma Sigma Nat Chap 1969. **HONORS/ACHIEVEMENTS:** Scholorship Award, No CA Ind Relations Council 1970. **BUSINESS ADDRESS:** Shaklee Corp, 444 Market St, San Francisco, CA.

COTTON, GARNER
Civil engineer. **PERSONAL:** Born Nov 10, 1923, Chicago, IL; son of Deleon Cotton and Pearl Little Cotton; divorced; children: Garner T, Atry S. **EDUCATION:** Lincoln Univ, Jefferson City MO, BS 1947; Drexel Inst, Philadelphia PA, Diploma 1951; Edison Techl, Seattle WA, Certificate 1959; Temple Univ, Philadelphia PA, Certificate 1965. **CAREER:** United Engineers, sr structural designer 1956-62; NY Shipbuilding, structural engineeer 1962-65; Allstate Engineering, structural designer 1965-67; School Dist of Philadelphia, structural engineer. **ORGANIZATIONS:** Owner, chief engineer G Cotton Engineering Assoc Inc 1965-; fac engineer Boeing Aircraft, Seattle WA 1958-60; construction supt Frederick Masiah Construction 1958-59; structural designer Gen Ind Engineers 1947-54; council pres Borough Lawnside, NJ 1961-76; counnty cmmr Borough of Lawnside, NJ 1966-74. **HONORS/ACHIEVEMENTS:** Citizen Award of the Year, New Jersey Soc of Professional Engineers 1977; Citizen Award, Lawnside Democratic Club 1970; Registered Professional Civil Engineer New Jersey; Registered Professional Planner New Jersey; Fellow, Amer Soc of Civil Engineers 1988. **HOME ADDRESS:** 505 N Warwick Rd, Lawnside, NJ 08045.

COTTRELL, COMER J.
Business executive. **PERSONAL:** Born Dec 07, 1931, Mobile, AL; married Isabell Pauloing; children: Renee, Comer III, Aaron. **EDUCATION:** Univ of Detroit, 1952. **CAREER:** Sears Roebuck, sales mgr, 1964-69; Pro-Line Corp, chmn, pres, 1970-. **ORGANIZATIONS:** Dir Republic Bank, Southwest Dallas Hosp Corp, Western Pacific Indust, Dallas Financial Corp, Pro-Ball Inc. **BUSINESS ADDRESS:** President, Pro-Line Corporation, 2121 Panoramic Circle, Dallas, TX 75212.

COTTROL, ROBERT J.
Educator. **PERSONAL:** Born Jan 18, 1949, New York, NY. **EDUCATION:** Yale Univ, BA 1971, PhD 1978; Georgetown Univ Law Ctr, JD 1984. **CAREER:** CT Coll, instructor 1974-77; Emory Univ, asst prof 1977-79; Georgetown Univ, lecturer 1979-84; Boston Coll Law School, asst prof of law 1984-87, assoc prof of law. **ORGANIZATIONS:** Consult GA Commn on the Humanities 1978-79; mem Amer Historical Assoc 1974-, Amer Soc for Legal History 1982-, Amer Bar Assoc 1985-; mem Law and SocietyAssoc 1985-. **HONORS/ACHIEVEMENTS:** Author The Afro Yankees, Providence's Black Community in the Antebellum Era publ by Greenwood Press 1982. **MILITARY SERVICE:** AUS (Reserve) capt 1971-81; USAFR capt 1981-87, major 1987-. **BUSINESS ADDRESS:** Assistant Professor of Law, Boston College Law School, 885 Centre St, Newton Centre, MA 02159.

COUCHE, ROBERT
Educational administrator. **PERSONAL:** Born Dec 18, 1918, Gainesville, GA; married Ruby Sherman. **EDUCATION:** GA State Coll, attended 1938-41; NYU, BS 1952; NYU, MA 1953; Queens Coll, professional cert in couns 1965; St John's U, attended 1967-69; NY State Secondary Sch, Pring Cert 1969. **CAREER:** Prospect Hts High Sch Brooklyn, principal 1973-79; Andrew Jackson High Sch Queens, asst principal 1969-73; Guidance Serv Big Sister's Educ Family Serv, dir counseling 1967-69; Out-of-Sch Youths Bd of Educ NYC, guidance counselor 1963-64; Newtown High Sch & Springfield Gardens High Sch, guidance counselor 1962-69; NYC, tchr 1952-62. **ORGANIZATIONS:** Pres Distributive Educ Assn 1958-62; mem Nat Assn of Secondary Sch Prin 7 yrs; mem High Sch Prin Assn New York City 6 yrs; mem numerous educ assns for prins & couns; co-founder Springfield Gardens Comm Day Care Center Springfield Gardens NY; founder & bd chmn Springfield Gardens St Albans Sr Citizens Center 1973-; various offices NAACP brs; mem various dem coms; bd mem & chmn exec com Allied Fed Savings & Loan Assn Jamaica NY; youth adv & bd mem Nat Conf of Christians & Jews; orgn mem & treas New Dimensions Day Care Center; mem St John's Univ Chpt; Phi Delta Kappa Frat. **HONORS/ACHIEVEMENTS:** Pub numerous educ articles 1961-68; various educ awards sororities clubs & assns; various comm serv awards frats & chs; Martin Luther King Jr Award, Wilmington DE Martin Luther King Jr Com; One-In-A-Million Award, Citizens of Queens & Nassau Co NY; Dedicated Serv Award, NY Assn of Black Educators; Brotherhood Award & Cert of Recognition, Nat Conf of Christians & Jews; Purple Heart Inf 1945. **MILITARY SERVICE:** Inf 1st lt 1941-46. **BUSINESS ADDRESS:** Bd of Educ, City of NY, Brooklyn, NY 11225.

COUCHE, RUBY S.
Educator. **PERSONAL:** Born Dec 10, 1919, Whigham, GA; married Robert Couche. **EDUCATION:** Savannah State Coll, BS 1941; Hunter Coll, MA 1952; Long Island Univ, Hofstra, Puerto Rico Univ, Plattsburg Univ, Pottsdam Univ, Adv Study. **CAREER:** Todd Grant High School, Darien GA, teacher 1941-43; New York City School Dist 28, teacher 1950-59, school comm coord 1959-68, asst principal 1968-71, dep to supt 1971-72, curriculum adm comm 1972-77 (retired); Western IL Univ, adjunct prof 1980. **ORGANIZATIONS:** Mem Assoc of Suprv & Curriculum Devel 1972-; mem chmn, 3rd vp, 2nd vp, concert chmn Jamaica Comm Concert Assoc; mem bd of dirs S Queens Choral Assoc; mem bd dirs Merrick-Queens Co Comm Ctr; mem Ed Comm Queens Reg Natl Conf Christians & Jews; mem Steering & Coord Comm, SE Queens Emancipation Proclamation Centennial Auth; mem Phi Delta Kappa, Beta Omicron Chapt, Jamaica Br NAACP, Tri-Comm Council, St Albans Comm Council, Abyssania Bapt Church, Protestant Teachers Assoc of NYC, School-Comm Coord Assoc, 103rd Police Precinct Youth Council, Urban League, Adm & Suprv Assoc NYC, Amer Women in Ed, Queensboro Teacher Assoc, Natl School Publ Rel Assoc; ldrshp conf Civil Rts; chtr mem Phi Delta Kappa, Beta Omicron Chapt; tour Madrid, Paris, London, Rone 1978 and 1986; study tour West Africa 1980; natl pres Phi Delta Kappa 1981-85; mem 1st Pres Ch;vp Laurelton Springfld Day Care Ctr; coord Human Rel Inst Natl Body. **HONORS/ACHIEVEMENTS:** Supreme 2nd Anti-Basileus Natl Acheivement Awd 1969-; listed in Who's Who Biog Record of School Dist Officials 1976; Nom for Supreme Basileus of Natl Sor of Phi Delta Kappa 1977-81; Nom for Who's Who Among Women; Participant IDEA Fellows Prog Kettering Found; NAACP Humanitarian Awd 1986.

COULON, BURNEL ELTON
Educator. **PERSONAL:** Born Jul 06, 1929, New Orleans, LA; married Syliva; children: Michele, Angela, Burnel II, Sylvia II. **EDUCATION:** Tuskegee Inst, BS 1953; NC A&T State U, MS 1960; Bulter U/Ball State U/IN U, grad work. **CAREER:** Indianapolis Public Schools, dean of students 1979-, chmn industrial arts 1976-79; Shortridge Press & Indianapolis Public Schools, instr & mgr 1964-76; Paramount Graphics, pres 1970; Louisville Public Schools, instructor graphic arts 1961-64; MS Valley State Univ, dir public relations 1953-60. **ORGANIZATIONS:** Bd of dirs MS State Negro Fair 1957-59; pres Indianapolis Fedn of Tchrs 1973-76; sec Indianapolis Chap Phi Delta Kappa 1978-79; sec Marion Co Graphic Arts Assn 1968-70; first v grand basileus Omega Psi Phi Frat 1978-79; grand basileus Omega Psi Phi Frat 1979-. **HONORS/ACHIEVEMENTS:** Honor grad, Tuskegee Inst 1953; Outstanding Grad Alumnus, NC A&T 1975; Omega Man of the yr, 10th Dist Omega Psi Phi Frat 1976; Cert of Merit, Mayor New Orleans 1980. **BUSINESS ADDRESS:** Omega Psi Phi Fraternitey, 2714 Georgia Ave, Washington, DC 20001.

COUNTEE, THOMAS HILAIRE, JR.
Retired attorney and state official, business executive. **PERSONAL:** Born Aug 07, 1939, Washington, DC; son of Thomas H. Countee, Sr. and Arrieanna C. Countee; divorced; children: Mekela IJ. **EDUCATION:** Amer Univ, Washington, DC, BA, 1963; Georgetown Univ Law Center, JD, 1967; Harvard Graduate School, MBA, 1971. **CAREER:** chief exec officer, 1978-88; MD, Natl Capital Park & Planning Commn, gen counsel, 1977-78; Office of Mat & Budget, legislative counsel; exec offce of pres, 1975-76; MODEDCO Inv Co, pres, 1971-75; Howard Univ, Washington, DC, prof, 1973; Fed City Coll, prof,1973; Poloroid Corp, Cambridge MA, asst general counsel, 1971; Roxbury Small Business Devel Center, Boston, consultant, 1970; Securities & Exchange Commn, Washington, DC, attorney, 1969. **ORGANIZATIONS:** mem, DC Bar; Practiced before US Dist Court, DC, US Court of Appeals for DC, and US Court of Mil Appeals; mem, bd of dir, Channel 50, 1977-, Chesapeake

Bay Found 1982-, New Life Inc 1972-, Black Student Fund 1982-; mem, Govt Council on Serv to the Handicapped 1982-; alumni recruiter, Phillip's Acad, 1979, Harvard Business School, 1971; mem, Kappa Alpha Psi. **HONORS/ACHIEVEMENTS:** Harvard Univ Scholarship, 1956-58; Harvard Business School Fellowship, 1969-71; Georgetown Law School, Lawyers Co-op Publishing Co Prizes; Published History of Black-Owned & Operated Finance Institutes, 1968. **HOME ADDRESS:** 2100 Washington Ave, #9C, Silver Spring, MD 20910.

COUNTS, GEORGE W.
Physician, educator. **PERSONAL:** Born Jun 14, 1935, Idabel, OK; married Claudette R; children: George IV, David, Philip. **EDUCATION:** Univ OK, BS 1957; Univ OK, MS 1960; Univ IA, MD 1965; OH State Univ Hosp, intern resd 1965-68; Infectious Diseases Univ WA, fellowship 1968-70. **CAREER:** Univ WA, asso prof of med 1975-; Harborview Med Ctr, chf div infectious diseases 1975-; Univ Miami Sch of Med, asst prof pathology 1972-75; Jackson Meml Hosp, dir clinical microbiology sect 1972-75; Jackson Meml Hosp, dir infection control dept 1972-75; Univ of Miami, asst prof med 1970-75. **ORGANIZATIONS:** Bd dir Assn for Practitioners in Infection Control 1977-80; Am Fed for Clinical Rsrch; licenses to practice in IA OH WA FL; fellow Infectious Deseases Soc of Am 1974; Nat Med Assn; NY Acad Sci; AAAS; Nat Med Flwsp 1961-65. **HONORS/ACHIEVEMENTS:** Leopold Schepp Found Schlrsp 1961-65; diplomate Am Bd of Internal Med 1970; flw Am Coll of Physicians 1971; Leinfelder Award,Univ IA 1965; mem Alpha Omega Alpha 1965; publ num jour & books. **BUSINESS ADDRESS:** Marborview Med Ctr, 325 9th Ave, Seattle, WA 98104.

COURTNEY, CASSANDRA HILL
Educational administrator. **PERSONAL:** Born Feb 08, 1949, Newport News, VA; daughter of Marion Alton Hill and Mary Stokes HIll; married Vernon Stanley Courtney, Sep l974; children: Aliya Diane. **EDUCATION:** Wilson Coll, AB (Cum Laude) 1971; Penn State Univ, MS 1974, PhD 1980. **CAREER:** Middlesex Co School Bd Saluda VA, dir federal projects 1974-76; Pennsylvania State Univ, academic Counselor 1979-81; Wilberforce Univ, social science div chairperson and asst prof psychology 1982-83, vice pres academic affairs 1983-l988, Wilberforce Univ, exec asst to the pres, l989. **ORGANIZATIONS:** Mem Academic Dean's Task Force of the Council of Independent Colls 1983-85; mem Adv Comm Campus Trends of the Amer Council on Educ 1985-; mem Amer Educ Rsch Assoc, Phi Delta Kappa, Amer Assoc for Higher Educ; mem Jack & Jill of Amer Inc, Cooperative Educ Assoc, Natl Assoc for Women Deans Administrators and Counselors, Alpha Kappa Alpha; pres, Springfield, OH Chapter of Links, Inc, l989. **HONORS/ACHIEVEMENTS:** Natl Achievement Scholar 1967-71; Phi Beta Kappa 1971-; Fellowship Natl Fellowships Fund 1973-74, 1977-80; Harvard Inst for Educ Mgmt, l989. **BUSINESS ADDRESS:** Exec Asst to the Pres, WilberforceUniv, Shorter Hall, Wilberforce, OH 45384.

COURTNEY, STEPHEN ALEXANDER
Senior engineer. **PERSONAL:** Born Nov 16, 1957, Philadelphia, PA; son of Archie Lee Courtney and Olga Viola Facey Squires Courtney; married Jennifer Williams Courtney, Jun 26, 1988. **EDUCATION:** Drexel Univ, BSEE 1980; American Univ, MBA 1987. **CAREER:** IBM Corp, customer engr 1979; E-Systems, elec engr 1980-82; Booz Allen & Hamilton, sr consultant 1982-85; Contel Corp, sr engr 1985-. **ORGANIZATIONS:** Career develop coord Black Data Processing Assoc 1985; convention coord Washington DC Black Data Processing Associates 1985; mem Black MBA Assoc 1987, Inst of Electrical and Electronic Engrs 1987. **HOME ADDRESS:** 6607 Ivy Hill Drive, McLean, VA 22101. **BUSINESS ADDRESS:** Senior Engineer, Contel Corp, 12015 Lee Jackson Hwy, Fairfax, VA 22033.

COUSIN, PHILIP R.
Clergyman. **PERSONAL:** Born Mar 26, 1933, Pittston, PA; married Joan; children: Philip Jr, Steven, David, Michael, Joseph. **EDUCATION:** Central State Univ; Boston Univ, ThM; Colgate Rochester Divin Sch, PhD Ministry. **CAREER:** Pastored churches in NC/VA/FL; Kittrell Coll, pres 1960-65; AME Church, bishop of AL; Edward Waters Coll, pres; AME Church, bishop 11th Episcopal Dist. **ORGANIZATIONS:** Pres bd governors Natl Council of Churches of Christ; chmn bd Edward Waters Coll; natl bd SCLC; chmn Human Relations Commn Durham 1968-69; chmn NC Voter Educ Proj 1968-; trustee Lincoln Hosp Durham 1966-72; trustee Fayetteville State Univ 1972-; chmn Polit Comm Durham Comm on Affairs of Black People 1966-; mem Durham Co Bd of Soc Serv 1970-; mem Durham Co Bd of Educ 1972-. **HONORS/ACHIEVEMENTS:** Kellogg Fellowship 1965; Martin Luther King Fellow in Black Ch Studies 1972; conducted Days of Dialogue Germany for AUS in Europe 1973; 1985 Honoree The Religion Award for achievements as pres of Natl Cncl of Churches, and for leadership as a bishop of the AME Church. **MILITARY SERVICE:** AUS 2nd Lt 1953. **BUSINESS ADDRESS:** Natl Cncl Chs of Christ USA, 475 Riverside Dr, New York, NY 10115.

COUSINS, ALTHEA L.
Educator. **PERSONAL:** Born Nov 05, 1932, New York, NY; married Carl M Cousins; children: Kimberly, Karen. **EDUCATION:** Fisk U, BA 1953; Columbia U, MA 1955; Temple U, MA 1957; Univ of PA Elementary Principal's Certificate 1963; Univ of PA, Comprehensive Principal's Certificate 1969; Temple U, post graduate program 1972-73; Temple U, Superindendents Certificate 1975; Walden U, doctoral program 1976-. **CAREER:** Div of Pupil Personnel & Counseling, School Dist of Philadelphia, dir 1974-; Childs Elementary School, prin 1972-73; Compers Elementary School, prin 1970-71; elementary school prin, admin asst to dist supt 1967-70; Wagner Jr High School, asst to prin 1966-67; Sartain Elementary School, counseling teacher 1957-66, teacher 1954-57; Barratt Jr High School, teacher 1953-54; Gideon Summer School, teacher 1960; headstart counselor summer 1966; Miller School, outreach counselor 1966; Friends Neighborhood Day Camp, supvr 1958 -59. **ORGANIZATIONS:** Mem Nat Assn of Pupil Personnel Adminstr; Nat Educ Assn; Am Personnel & Guidance Assn; Am Sch Counselors Assn; PA Sch Counselors Assn; Nat Assn of Coll Admissions Counselors; Philadelphia Assn of Sch Adminstr; Women in Educ 1974-; has served on numerous com councils; bd dir Main Line Day Care Center 1973-; exec bd Ithan Elem Sch 1969-71; mem Rotary Ann's Group 1973-; Golden Circle Women 32 degree Masons 1975; Mt Hebron Friends & Neighbors Comm Group 1973-; Women's Aux; Am Vet Med Assn; various alumni groups; Links, Inc; Delta Sigma Theta Sor; Zion Bapt Ch; Women's Aux; Alpha Phi Alpha Frat; League of Women Voters. **HONORS/ACHIEVEMENTS:** Recipient Philadelphia Sch Adminstr Assn Recognition Award; Chapel of the Four Chaplins Award; Philadelphia Home & Sch & Council Award; Dist Two Supt Recognition Award; article photograph Nat Assn of Pupil Personnel Adminstr Journal & PA Sch Counselors Assn Journal; author of num publs & articles. **BUSINESS ADDRESS:** 21 Parkway, Philadelphia, PA 19103.

COUSINS, JAMES R., JR.
City official. **PERSONAL:** Born Apr 29, 1906, Washington, DC; married Ethel Boatwright; children: James R. **EDUCATION:** Morgan State Coll, BS 1973. **CAREER:** Glenarden MD, contractual commn liaison advisor councilman 1974-; Town Council Bd, chmn 1973-74; Glenarden, mayor 1941-70; Glenarden, chief of police 1939-41. **ORGANIZATIONS:** Chmn Prince Georce Co Municipal Assn 1969; mem exec bd MD Mun League 1973; mem bd Visitors Bowie State Coll 1972; mem Pr George Co Adv Com on Aging 1974; chmn Deacon Bd First Bapt Ch Glenarden 1950-74; moderator Bapt Assn of So Md 1972-74; pres Glenarden Civic Assn 1939-41; chief Glenarden Fire Dept 1936-39; chmn of Incorp Com for Glenarden. **HONORS/ACHIEVEMENTS:** Trophy Outstanding Mayor for 1968; award Outstanding Service as Mayor 1941-70; award Glenarden Civic Assn, testimonial by citizens of Glenarden 1970. **BUSINESS ADDRESS:** 9171 Central Ave, Capitol Heights, MD 20027.

COUSINS, WILLIAM, JR.
Attorney, alderman, judge. **PERSONAL:** Born Oct 06, 1927, Swiftown, MS; son of William Cousins, Jr and Drusilla Harris Cousins; married Hiroko Ogawa, May 12, 1953; children: Cheryl, Noel, Yul, Gail. **EDUCATION:** Univ of IL, BA 1948; Harvard Univ, LLB 1951. **CAREER:** Chicago Title & Trust Co, atty 1953-57; Cook Co, asst state's atty 1957-61; Private Practice, law 1961-76; 8th Ward Chicago, alderman 1967-76; DePaul Law School, lecturer 1981-84; Circuit Ct Cook Co, judge 1976-. **ORGANIZATIONS:** Asst moderator United Church of Christ 1981; admitted to practice before IL, US Dist, Fed Ct of Appeals & US Supreme Ct; IL Supreme Ct appointee to exec comm IL Judicial Conf 1984-; mem Amer, Chicago, Natl, Cook Co Bar Assns; mem Delta Sigma Rho; mem Kappa Alpha Psi; former trustee Lincoln Memorial United Church; former pres Chatham Avalon Pk Comm Council; former vice pres Independent Voters IL; former bd mem PUSH; former mem Chicago Chapter NAACP; former bd mem Planned Parenthood Assn; Parkway Comm House; Ams Dem Action; Chairman, IL Judicial Council, 1987-88. **HONORS/ACHIEVEMENTS:** Edward N Wright Award Cook Co Bar Assn 1968; William R Ming Jr Civil Rights Award 1974; Outstanding Judge of Yr Award John Marshall Chapter Black Law Students Amer 1980; delegate Dem Natl Convention 1972; Outstanding Layman of Year Lincoln Mem Church 1958; author, A Judges View of Judicial Selection Plans, Illinois Bar Journal, 1987. **MILITARY SERVICE:** AUS lt 1951-53; lt col JAG (res) 1975-.

COVAN, DEFOREST W.
Actor. **PERSONAL:** Born Sep 09, 1917, Chicago. **CAREER:** Columbia Pictures TV & ABC-TV, movie, state & TV actor; Jina Productions Hollywood, asst prod 1972; K-CALB Productions, assoc prod 1971; Million Dollars Prod, asst prod 1939-42. **ORGANIZATIONS:** Mem Screen Actors Guild 1938; mem AFTRA 1973-; mem NAACP. **HONORS/ACHIEVEMENTS:** Award for production coop 1971; Comm Achievement Award 1974; Outstanding TV Award 1974; Performing Award. **MILITARY SERVICE:** AUS pvt 1942. **BUSINESS ADDRESS:** Lil Cumber Agency, 6515 Sunset Blvd, Ste 300 A, Los Angeles, CA 90028.

COVERDALE, HERBERT LINWOOD
Business executive, psychologist, educator. **PERSONAL:** Born Oct 09, 1940, Philadelphia, PA; married Cornelia G Gibson; children: Christina, Valerie Lin, Geoffrey, Eric, Gregory. **EDUCATION:** PA State U, BS 1962; Howard U, MS 1966; IL Inst of Techn, PhD 1970. **CAREER:** Health Servs Mgmt, E Oakland Family Health Center CA, admin 1980; CA State Univ Hayward, prof of Marketing & Mgmt 1980; Mills Coll Oakland, lecturer in psychology 1980; School of Business Admin, Univ of CA Berkeley, visiting assoc prof of Marketing 1978-80; Consumer Analysts Inc, pres, rsch dir; Coverdale-Glore Inc, vice pres; Roosevelt Univ, assoc prof; Chicago State Univ, asst prof 1970-74; Behavioral Systems Inc, res dir 1970-75; Dept of Mental Health, conselor 1971-; Soc Research Inc, psychologist 1969-70; IL Inst of Tech, asst prof 1969-70. **ORGANIZATIONS:** Mem Amer Psychol Assn; mem Am Marktg Assn; IL Psychol Assn; Pi Sigma Epsilon; Nat Assn of Black Prof; Beta Gamma Sigma Chicago Forum; past polemarch Kappa Alpha Psi (Delta Theta Chap) 1961; mem Hyde Park Business & Prof Assn; bd dir Youth for Christ Inc; bd dir Hyde Park Kenwood Commn Health Ctr; bd dir Natl Assn of Market Develprs Chicago Chpt; pres Natl Honor Soc in Psychology. **HONORS/ACHIEVEMENTS:** Psi Chi Research Award; publ "Prof of Yr Award"; 4 Bus Adv Grp RooseveltUniv 1976; "Pupil Size as a Predictor of Coupon Return Perf" 1698; "Consuming Black Images" 1973; "Salience of Perceived Dim of Corp Soc Resp a black consumer persp" 1975; "push expo '73 black consumer profile" 1974; "newspaper Readership Among Blacks in 16 Cities" 1974; "Black Cultural Value Dynamics".

COVIN, DAVID L.
Educator. **PERSONAL:** Born Oct 03, 1940, Chicago, IL; son of David Covin and Lela Clements Johnson; married Judy Bentinck Smith; children: Wendy, Holly. **EDUCATION:** U Univ of IL, BA, 1962; Colorado Univ, MA, 1966; Washington State Univ, PHD, 1970. **CAREER:** California State Univ, Sacramento, asst prof, Govt & Ethnic Studies, 1970-74, assoc dean, general studies, general studies, 1972-74, assoc prof, govt & ethnic studies, 1975-79, prof, govt & ethnic studies, 1979; Union Graduate School, adjunct prof 1979-; State of CA, consultant, 1979; California State Univ, Sacramento, dir, Pan African studies. **ORGANIZATIONS:** Contributing editor, Rumble, 1973-; commr, CA Educ Evaluation & Mgmt Commn 1977-81; Black Caucus Criminal Justice Brain Trust, 1977-; vice-chmn, Sacramento Area Black Caucus, 1978-83; consultant, Sacramento City United School Dist, 1980; co-chair, Sacramento Chapter of Natl Black Independent Political Party, 1981-85; political/educ chair, Sacramento Area Black Caucus, 1983-; educ chair, Black Comm Activist Comm, 1985-; mem, Sacramento Chapter, Natl Rainbow Coalition Org Comm; delegate, Natl Party Congress, Natl Black Independent Political Party; mem, The Natl Faculty, 1988-; acting chair, Black Science Resource Center, 1987-present; exec bd, Women's Civic Improvement Club, 1987-present; chair, Sacramento Area Black Caucus, 1988-present. **HONORS/ACHIEVEMENTS:** Community Serv Award, Sacramento Area Black Caucus, 1976; grant recipient, CA Council for Humanities Public Policy, 1977; Sacramento Community Serv Award, Sacramento Kwanza Comm, 1978; Man of the Year, Omega Psi Phi, 1982; Community Serv Award, All African People, 1986; novel, Brown Sky, 1987; Meritorious Performance Award, California State Univ, Sacramento, 1988; Short Story, The Walk, 1988; Article, "Towards A Pan African Vision of the Carribean," 1988. **BUSINESS ADDRESS:** Dir of Pan African Studies, California State University, 6000 J St, Sacramento, CA 95819.

COVINGTON, DOUGLAS
President. **PERSONAL:** Born Mar 07, 1935, Winston-Salem, NC; married Beatrice Mitchell; children: Anthony Douglas, Jeffrey Steven. **EDUCATION:** Central State Univ, BS

1957; OH State Univ, MA 1958, PhD 1966. **CAREER:** Montclair NJ Public Schools, deputy supt of schools 1972-74; Tuskegee Univ, vice pres development affairs 1974-77; Winston-Salem State Univ, chancellor 1977-84; Alabama A&M Univ, pres 1984-. **ORGANIZATIONS:** Bd dirs Council for Advancement & Support of Educ, Amer Assoc of State Colls & Univs; bd trustees Faulkner Univ; chmn HBCU Adv Comm US Dept of Interior; bd dirs Amer Heart Assoc, Huntsville Chamber of Commerce; state chmn Africatown Comm. **HONORS/ACHIEVEMENTS:** Disting Alumnus Awd OH State Univ; Disting Alumnus Awd Central State Univ; Academic Scholarship Jessie Smith Noyes Foundation. **BUSINESS ADDRESS:** President, Alabama A&MUniv, PO Box 285, Normal, AL 35762.

COVINGTON, H. DOUGLAS
Educator. **PERSONAL:** Born Mar 07, 1935, Winston-Salem, NC; married Beatrice Mitchell; children: Anthony Douglas, Jeffrey Steven. **EDUCATION:** Central State Univ Wilberforce OH, BS 1957; OH State Univ, MS 1958, PhD 1966. **CAREER:** Dayton OH Public Schools, psych; Gary IN Public Schools, supr testing & rsch; Saginaw MI, asst supt for curriculum; Montclair NJ, dep supt school; Tuskegee Inst, vice pres devel affairs; Winston-Salem NC State Univ, chancellor. **ORGANIZATIONS:** Adj prof, lecturer various univs, colls; bd dir ARC, NC Theater Arts; trustee Natl Council Econ Ed; mem NC Med Care Commiss; mem adv bd Office for Advancement of Public Negro Colls; mem adv com dept training & devel United Negro Coll Fund; vchairperson public serv area United Way Campaign; bd mem Winston-Salem C of C; dir Amer Assoc State Colls & Univ; bd dir Rotary. **HONORS/ACHIEVEMENTS:** Awd fro various orgs incl NAACP, Natl Council Negro Women, Alpha Phi Alpha, Phi Delta Kappa, Natl Council Exceptional Children, Saginaw Model Cities Policies. **BUSINESS ADDRESS:** President, Alabama A&M University, PO Box 285, Normal, AL 35762.

COVINGTON, JAMES ARTHUR
Clergyman, administrator. **PERSONAL:** Born Aug 04, 1927, Hernando, MS; married Mary Ella Blackwell. **EDUCATION:** MS Indsl Coll Holly Springs, BA 1950; Univ of OR, MA 1953; Pacific Sc of Religion Berkley CA, MTh 1957; Mount Hope Bible & Theol Sch Houston, Hon DMin 1979. **CAREER:** Bebee Tabernacle CME Ch Houston, reverend 1978-; Phillips Chapel CME Ch Tucson, pastor 1970-78; Phillips Meml CMECh Phoenix, pastor 1966-70; Phillips Temple CMECh San Diego, pastor 1962-66; AK Dist Christian ME Ch, presiding elder 1959-62. **ORGANIZATIONS:** Chmn bd of dirs Pima Co AZ CEO 1975-76; Thirty-three dgr mason, Prince Hall Affiliation 1957; organizer CMECh AK 1959. **HONORS/ACHIEVEMENTS:** Recipient Ford Fellowship Grant for Study in Urban Ministry, Univ of Chicago 1968-69. **BUSINESS ADDRESS:** Bebee Tabernacle CME Church, 822 W Dallas, Houston, TX 77019.

COVINGTON, JOHN RYLAND
Physician. **PERSONAL:** Born Mar 27, 1936, Philadelphia, PA; married Delores E; children: Deidra. **EDUCATION:** St Joseph Coll, BS 1964; Philadelphia Coll of Osteopathic Med, DO 1971. **CAREER:** Osteopathic phys pvt prac; analytical chemist rsrch; Covington Medical Group, pres. **ORGANIZATIONS:** Mem Am Osteopathic Assn; Ethics Com St of PA; Am Coll of Emerg Room Phys; Sigma Sigma Phi Nat Hon Osteopathic Soc; mem Omega & Psi Phi Frat; NAACP. **HONORS/ACHIEVEMENTS:** Grad in top ten percent of Med Sch Class; winner 3 of top 5 gradn awds; publ 2 sci papers. **MILITARY SERVICE:** AUS.

COVINGTON, M. STANLEY
Attorney. **PERSONAL:** Born Apr 25, 1937, Langhorne, PA; son of Marlow O Covington (deceased) and Madalyn Johnson Covington; married Laura Aline; children: Lisa, Eric (deceased), Scott. **EDUCATION:** Bloomsburg U, BS 1955-59; Rutgers U, 1960; Howard Univ School of Law, JD 1962-65. **CAREER:** NJ Dept of Labor, field/acting Refers 1965-66; Allstate Ins Co, trial attorney 1966-. **ORGANIZATIONS:** Alternate mem Governing Board, Dist Of Columbia Assign Claim Bureau 1984-; mem bd of Dir Alumni Assoc Bloomsburg Univ 1978-80; mem Natl Bar Assn 1972-; mem Amer Bar Assn, Washington 1972-; mem Bar Assn Dist of Columbia Br 1972-; mem Maryland Bar Assn 1985-, Montgomery Cnty Bar Assn; Fellowship of Christian Athletes 1981-. **HONORS/ACHIEVEMENTS:** Achievement award, Kiwanis Langhorne, PA 1955; Little All Amer Football End hon men by Asso Press 1957-58; elected to Neshaming High School Football Hall of Fame, Langhorne Pennsylvania 1987. **HOME ADDRESS:** 1508 Rainbow Dr, Silver Spring, MD 20904. **BUSINESS ADDRESS:** House Counsel, Allstate Ins Co, 6411 Ivy Lane SUite 312, Greenbelt, MD 20770.

COVINGTON, WILLA ALMA GREENE
Retired educator. **PERSONAL:** Born Nov 26, 1902, Los Angeles, CA; married Floyd C Covington Sr; children: Floyd C Jr. **EDUCATION:** Univ of So CA, BA 1920, MA 1925; UCLA, Teaching Credentials 1930. **CAREER:** LA Unified Sch Dist, teacher, varied grades and subjects 1925-65, retired principal. **ORGANIZATIONS:** Mem CA Teachers Assoc, Elem Sch Administrators, Natl Educ Assoc, CA Elem Sch Admin, Delta Sigma Theta, League of Allied Arts, NAACP, Urban League. **HONORS/ACHIEVEMENTS:** City of Los Angeles Proclamation "Floyd and Willa Covington Day" presented by Mayor Tom Bradley 1984.

COWAN, JAMES R.
Physician, business executive. **PERSONAL:** Born Oct 21, 1919, Washington, DC; married Juanita G; children: James Jr, Jay, Jill. **EDUCATION:** Howard U, BS 1939; Fisk U, MA 1940; Meharry Med Coll, MD 1944; Harlem Hosp, intern 1944-45; Freedmen's Hosp, res 1945-48; Howard U, flw 1948-50. **CAREER:** Blue Cross & Blue Shield of Grtr NY, sr vice pres 1976-; Hlth & Envir, asst sec of defense 1974-76; Ofc of the Asst Sec of Defense, consult 1974; NJ St Dept of Hlth, commr 1970-74; pvt prac 1953-70. **ORGANIZATIONS:** Mem Am Med Assn; Am Coll of Preventive Med; Essex Co Med Soc; Interns & Residents Assn; Howard U; Am Assn of Pub Hlth Phys; Am Assn of Univ Profs; Acad of Med of NJ; Acad of Med of Washington DC; Mental Hlth Assn of Essex Co; Assn of Mil Surg of US; Am Hosp Assn; Am Pub Hlth Sci; Nat Cancer Adv Bd; Interagy Drug Rev Task Force of White House Domestic Counc; Nat Commn on Arthridtis & Related Musculoskeletal Diseases; Armed ForcesMed & Policy Counc; Nat Counc on Intl Hlth; Strat Counc on Drug Abuse; Nat Adv Counc on Alcohol Abuse & Alchol; Nat Adv Mental Hlth Counc; Nat Adv Dental Rsch Counc; Nat Adv Allergy & Infect Diseases Counc; Nat Arthritis Metabolism & Digestive Diseases Adv Counc; Nat Adv Child Hlth & Human Devel Counc; Nat Adv Eye Counc; Nat Adv Gen Med Sci Counc; Nat Heart & Lung Adv Counc; Nat Adv Neurol Diseases & Stroke Counc; Nat AdvRsch Resrcs Counc; Sickle Cell Disease Adv CounF Hyperten Info & Educ Adv Com; pres Com on Mental Retardation. **MILITARY SERVICE:** AUS chief of surgery battalion surgeon 1950-53. **BUSINESS ADDRESS:** President, United Hosp Med Center, 15 S 9th St, Newark, NJ 07107.

COWAN, LARINE YVONNE
Civil rights educ administrator. **PERSONAL:** Born Mar 25, 1949, Kensett, AR; daughter of William Cowan and Ola Mae Cowan; children: Alexander Milton Omar Cowan, Christopher Alvin Lamar Cowan. **EDUCATION:** Univ of AR-Pine Bluff, BA 1971; Univ of AR-Little Rock, MSW 1973; Management and Training Develop Workshops, 1974-89. **CAREER:** City of Champaign Comm Relations Dept, dir 1974-79; IL State Council of OICA Inc, state coord/volunteer 1983-; Univ of IL Aff Act Nonac Ofc, equal oppor ofcr 1982-85; Univ of IL Urbana-Champaign 1985-, Affirmative Action Nonacademic Office, dir, currently. **ORGANIZATIONS:** Mem Amer Assoc of Univ Women, Black Women in the Middle West Project, IL Affirmative Action Officers Assoc, Natl Assoc for Female Execs, NAACP, Illini Union Bd, Amer Assoc for Affirmative Action, Women's Studies Adv Bd, Nonacademic Employee Council; bd dirs Family Serv of Champaign County; bd dirs YWCA; IL state coord Oppors Industrialization Ctrs of Amer; mem Blacks in Govt, Coll and Univ Personnel Assoc, Industrial Relations Rsch Assoc, Natl Urban League, Natl Women's Studies Assoc, Private Industry Council, State of IL Job Serv Employment Comm, State Univ Civil Serv System Seniority Comm, Southern Poverty Law Ctr & Klanwatch Project, Women's Business Council-Urbana Chamber of Commerce. **HONORS/ACHIEVEMENTS:** Outstanding Serv in Human & Civil Rights Champaign Human Relations Comm 1979; Proclamation-Special Achievements in Human Rights City of Champaign 1979; Proclamation-Outstanding Contributions in the Field of Human Rights Urbana Human Relations Comm 1979; Boss of the Year Awd Champaign-Urbana Jaycees; Outstanding Achievement in Volunteerism United Way 1985; co-author "Police Community Relations, A Process, Not a Product," The Police Chief's Magazine 1976; publication Police Community Relations, A Process, Not A Product, Police Community Relations, 2nd Edition, Paul F Cromwell Jr and George Keefer West Publishing Co 1977; co-author The Human Rights Ordinance for the City of Champaign, IL; United Way Gold Award, United Way of Champaign County 1989; Chancellor's Award of Appreciation for Outstanding Service, Chancellor Weir, UIUC 1988; Very Best Campaign at any State University Award, United Way of Champaign County 1988; Special Services Award, Brigadier General Joel McKean, Chanute Air Force Base 1988; Certificate of Appreciation for Outstanding Volunteer Service Benefiting our Community, United Way of Champaign County 1989. **BUSINESS ADDRESS:** Dir Affirmative Action, University of Illinois, 52 E Gregory, 136 Personnel Serv Bldg, Champaign, IL 61820.

COWANS, ALVIN JEFFREY
Certified Credit Union Executive. **PERSONAL:** Born Jun 15, 1955, Alexandria, VA; son of Willie L Cowans and Jessie M Cowans; married Shirley Mae Smith, Dec 18, 1976; children: Alvin Jeffrey II, Marcus Adrian. **EDUCATION:** Univ of Fl, BS 1977; Inst of Financial Educ, supervisory training cert 1979;graduate of Florida Credit Union Management Institute, graduate of the Certified Credit Union Executive Program. **CAREER:** US Pipe & Foundry, sales rep 1977-78; Pioneer Federal Savings & Loan, asst vice pres, office mgr, admin asst 1978-83; McCoy Federal Credit Union, sr vice pres 1983-85, pres 1986-. **ORGANIZATIONS:** Mem Central Florida Urban Bankers Assn; mem, Southwest Orlando Jaycees; mem, Credit Union Executive Society; mem and president Univ of Florida Lettermens Association; director, Orange County Florida Purchasing Review Committee. **HONORS/ACHIEVEMENTS:** Grad of the Chamber of Commerce Leadership Orlando Prog 1980; Outstanding Young Men in America 1981; Citizen of the Year, Chi Tau Chapter, Omega Psi Phi Fraternity. **BUSINESS ADDRESS:** President, McCoy Federal Credit Union, PO Box 593806, Orlando, FL 32859-3806.

COWARD, JASPER EARL
Marketing manager. **PERSONAL:** Born Nov 21, 1932, Kinston, NC; married Josephine Stuldivant; children: Renee, Natalie. **EDUCATION:** Howard U, BA 1960. **CAREER:** Joseph Schlitz Brewing Co, mgr spl markets/Dixie Div 1963-; Carling Brewing Co Atlanta, rep 1962-63; Johnson Pub Co Atlanta, mdse rep 1960-62. **ORGANIZATIONS:** Mem Nat Assn of Marketing Developers 1958-80; mem DAV; mem NAACP. **HONORS/ACHIEVEMENTS:** Recipient Good Conduct Medal/UN Serv/Korean Serv/Nat Defense Serv Awards. **MILITARY SERVICE:** USAF airman 2nd class 1953-56. **BUSINESS ADDRESS:** Joseph Schlitz Brewing Co, PO Box 614, Milwaukee, WI 53201.

COWDEN, MICHAEL E.
Educator. **PERSONAL:** Born Jul 17, 1951, Louisville. **EDUCATION:** Shoreline Commun Coll, AA 1971; Univ Washington Seattle, 2 yrs. **CAREER:** Louisville Public Schools, martial art instructor, chinese boxing 1975-; actor; poet; playwright.

COWELL, CATHERINE
Nutritionist. **PERSONAL:** Born Nov 13, 1921, Norfolk, VA. **EDUCATION:** Hampton Inst, BS 1945; Univ of CT, MS 1947; Univ of CT, grad asst in nutrition 1945-47. **CAREER:** Metabolism Clinic Mt Sinai Hosp NYC, lab techn 1947-49; pub health nutrionalist 1969; Bur Nutrition, acting dir 1971; NY Med Coll Flower Fifth Ave Hosp, asst clin instr preventave med pub health indsl & hygiene 1953-55; Albert Einstein Sch of Med Yeshiva Univ NYC, instr nutrition environmental med 1962-69; NY U, vis lectr; Montclair State Tchr; Coll Rep to NY Nutrition Council 1963-; Nutrition Bur New York City Dept of Health, dir. **ORGANIZATIONS:** Mem White House Conf on Food Nutrition & Health 1969; adv council Ch Human Ecology, Cornell Univ 1970-72; mem Manhattan Br; Nat Council Negro Women; fellow, Am Pub Health Assn; mem Am Home Econ Assn; NY State Home Econ Assn; chmn health & welfare section 1961-62; pres 1971-; mem St George Assn of New York City Health Dept; Royal Soc Health; mem Hampton Alumni Assn; Lambda Kappa Kappa Mu natl pres 1961-65; Order Eastern Star Club. **HONORS/ACHIEVEMENTS:** Recipient Nutritional Award, New York City Pub Health Assn 1960; JF Goodwin Scholarship, Reading PA; contrib articles to professional jours. **BUSINESS ADDRESS:** 93 Worth St, Room 714, New York, NY 10013.

COWELL, STANLEY A.
Business executive, musician. **PERSONAL:** Born May 05, 1941, Toledo, OH; married Vii Mclaughlin. **EDUCATION:** Oberlin Coll, BM 1962; Mozarteum Academy Salzburg Austria, atnd 1960-61; Univ of Wichita KS; Univ of So CA 1963-64; Univ of MI, MusM 1966. **CAREER:** Strata-east Records, pres; NY Jazz Rep Co Carnegie Hall, musical dir 1974; Am-

herst Coll, lectr black composition; Intl Festival of Music Shiraz Iran, panelist; Max Roach Abbey Lincoln, accomp. **ORGANIZATIONS:** Incorporater founding mem Collective Black Artists Inc; founder organizer musical dir Piano Choir 1971-; owner Stanco Pub Co affiliated with Am Fed of Musicians; has worked with such notable groups as max roach, sonny rollins, roland kirk, art blakey, miles davis, jimmy health, charles Tolliver; most recent recordings are Handscapes III MUSA-SOLO Piano Vol II. **BUSINESS ADDRESS:** New York, NY.

COWENS, ALFRED EDWARD, JR.
Professional athlete. **PERSONAL:** Born Oct 25, 1951, Los Angeles, CA; married Velma; children: Purvis, Dante, Trinetta. **CAREER:** Kansas City Royals, outfielder 1974-79; CA Angels, outfielder 1980; Detroit Tigers, outfielder 1980-81; Seatle Mariners, outfielder 1982-. **HONORS/ACHIEVEMENTS:** Named winner of the Old Spice "Big Stick Awd" on the syndicated "This Week in Baseball" prog; named Royals' Player of the Year 1977; runnerup to MN Rod Carew(388) in the AL Most Vauable Player voting 1977.

COX, ARTHUR JAMES, SR.
Social work educator. **PERSONAL:** Born Jun 15, 1943, Avon Park, FL; married Deloris Murray; children: Arthur Jr, Travis J, David I. **EDUCATION:** Howard Univ, AB 1965, MSW 1970; Columbia Univ, DSW 1978. **CAREER:** FL State Univ, asst prof 1975-78; East TN State Univ, chmn/assoc prof 1978-83; Southern IL Univ, dir & assoc prof 1983-86; Salem State Coll, dean & prof 1986-. **ORGANIZATIONS:** Adv panel mem CONTACT 1978-83; chmn Human Serv Goals Directions 2000 Program 1980-83; secty/treas Inst of Children Resources 1980-82; steering comm mem Southeast Child Welfare Training Resource Ctr Univ of TN Sch of Social Work 1981-82; treas Assoc of Baccalaureate Prog Dirs 1981-83; pres Natl Assoc ofSocial Workers TN Chap 1981-82; mem Publications Comm Cncl on Social Work Educ 1981-84; mem Alcohol Treatment Serv Adv Bd Jackson County Comm Mental Hlth Ctr Carbondale IL 1984-; mem editorial review bd Journal of Social Serv Rsch GWB Sch of Social Work Washington Univ St Louis 1985-88; mem Natl Assoc of Black Social Workers, Natl Assoc of Social Workers, Cncl on Social Work Educ, Natl Conf of Social Welfare; elected delegate TN Governor's State Conf on Families, White House Conf on Famili es Minneapolis. **HONORS/ACHIEVEMENTS:** NIMH Fellowship for Doctoral Study 1973-74; Teacher of the Year Lehman Coll of CUNY 1973, FSU Sch of Social Work 1977; Jaycees Man of the Year 1979; ACE Fellow 1979; TN Chap NASW Social Worker of the Year 1980; numerous papers presented, workshops, special lectures,TV appearances, chapters in books and articles published. **HOME ADDRESS:** 34 Carlton Road, Marblehead, MA 01945. **BUSINESS ADDRESS:** Dean School of Social Work, Salem State College, 352 Lafayette St, Salem, MA 01970.

COX, CORINE
Editor. **PERSONAL:** Born May 31, 1944, Mansfield, LA; married Doyl Cox; children: Dwayne E. **EDUCATION:** Texas Southern U, 1962-63; Univ Bus Coll, cert sec training 1964. **CAREER:** Society and Women's Ed Forward Times Pub Co, compositer supr newswriter soc ed 1964-. **ORGANIZATIONS:** Mem adv bd Ct Calanthe; Eta Phi Beta; Mt Rose Missionary Bapt Ch tchr Mission I; ch sec Prairie View A&M U. **HONORS/ACHIEVEMENTS:** Award media coverage 1974; outstanding Neophyte Awd 1974-75; woman of year awd at Ch. **BUSINESS ADDRESS:** 4411 Almeda Rd, Houston, TX 77004.

COX, DUBOIS V.
Investment banker. **PERSONAL:** Born Mar 24, 1950, St Louis, MO; son of Roland Cox and Christine Y Willis; divorced; children: Mercedes Nicole Cox. **EDUCATION:** Southern Illinois Univ, Edwardsville IL, BS 1973; Southeastern Univ, Washington DC, MS Study Intl Business, 1981; Johns Hopkins Univ, Washington DC, MS Study Intl Business, 1981. **CAREER:** Calvert Group, Washington DC, investor relations 1980-82; US Army Europe, West Germany, logistician 1982-86; Congressman W E Fauntroy, Washington DC, branch mgr, 1987-88. **ORGANIZATIONS:** Pres, bd of trustees Invest America Capital Fund 1988-; mem Natl Assn of Securities Professionals; mem Kappa Alpha Psi Fraternity; mem Urban League, Washington DC. **HONORS/ACHIEVEMENTS:** Author of several financial planning articles in community newpapers, professional conference materials and army publications while in Europe. **BUSINESS ADDRESS:** Vice President, WR Lazard & Co Incorporated, 655 15th Street, NW, Suite 300, Washington, DC 20005.

COX, EUOLA WILSON
Educator. **PERSONAL:** Born in Muskogee, OK; children: Daryl E, Vodra E Dorn. **EDUCATION:** Langston Univ OK, BA English; Univ of Albuquerque, Univ of NM, College of Santa Fe, MA Ed Admin; Univ of NM, additional training 1978. **CAREER:** Hoover Middle School, teacher 1970-71; Highland HS, teacher 1971-73; Univ of Albuquerque, part-time prof 1973 & 1975; Albuquerque HS, teacher 1973-75; Wilson Middle School, asst principal 1975-80; Eastern NM Univ, assoc prof emeritus 1980-. **ORGANIZATIONS:** Sponsored Y-Teen Group Albuquerque YWCA 1962-69; mem bd of dir South Braodway Oppty Ctr 1964-67; coord, organizer Black Voices Comm Choir 1965; initiated 1st Black Heritage Observance in Albuquerque Public Schools 1969; conducted Black History Seminars in Model Cities Neighborhood 1970-71; sponsor Youth Group NAACP 1972;Univ of NM Schl of Pharm Minority Recruitment Comm 1973-75; recruiter of Minority Youth NM Employment Sec Comm 1973-75; mem bd of trustees Bernalilillo Cty Mental Hlth Ctr 1974; consult Farmington Pub Schl Syst Initiation of Ethnic Studies Prog for the Syst 1974; recruited 25 minority students for SSandia Corp Pilot Prog 1974; recruiter Alb Pub Schls 1976; mem Albuqerque Urban Coaltion 1976; pres bd of dir Cntrl Cities Consult Coop 1976; David King's Political Action Comm NAACP 1976; co-chrprs United Negro Coll Fund Telethon 1978; title IX wkshp consultUniv of NM & Alb Pub Schls 1978-79; spsr ConcrndWomen for Chg ENMU Weusi Choir 1980-82; adv Blk Stdnt Union ENMU 1980-82; adv bd NM Eth Hrtg Tchr Training Proj 1981; Phi Delta Kappa; Delta Sigma Theta. **HONORS/ACHIEVEMENTS:** Multiple publ, lectures & papers incl "Multicultural Ed" TX Tech Jrnl of Ed 1982 Fall, Title I Reg III Workshop Eastern NM Univ "Barriers to Conferencing with Parents of Minority Students" 1982, Natl Black Family Conf "A Model for Community Involvement" 1983; assoc prof emeritus Eastern NM Univ 1985. **BUSINESS ADDRESS:** Associate Prof Emeritus, Eastern New Mexico University, Station 25, Portales, NM 88130.

COX, GEORGETTA MANNING
Educator. **PERSONAL:** Born Sep 16, 1947, Washington, DC; married Walter Bishop Cox Jr; children: Malakia Iman. **EDUCATION:** Hampton Inst, BA 1970; Howard Univ Coll of Dentistry, DDS 1976; Johns Hopkins Univ, MPH 1979. **CAREER:** Howard Univ Coll of Dentistry, prog coord 1977-78, asst prof 1979-86; assoc prof. **ORGANIZATIONS:** Presentor/mem Intl Assoc for Dental Rsch; mem Sigma Xi Rsch Soc, Amer Public Health Assoc; consultant United Planning Org Health Adv Comm 1982-; managing editor NDA Journal Natl Dental Assoc 1983-; vice pres 1984, pres 1985 Omicron Kappa Upsilon Natl Dental Honor Soc; vice pres Howard Univ Dental Alumna Assoc 1985. **HONORS/ACHIEVEMENTS:** President's Awd Natl Dental Assoc 1984; Outstanding Service Awd Natl Dental Assoc 1986; articles published "Pathological Effects of Sickle Cell Anemia onthe Pulp," Journal of Dent for Children 1984, "Oral Pain Experience in Sickle Cell Patients," Oral Surgery, Oral Medicine, Oral Pathology 1985; "The Psycho Social Aspects of Pregnant Adolescents, A Dental Perspective," Journal of Dentistry for Children 1986. **BUSINESS ADDRESS:** Associate Professor, HowardUniv Coll of Dentistry, 600 W St NW, Washington, DC 20059.

COX, HANNIBAL MACEO, JR.
Business executive. **PERSONAL:** Born Mar 21, 1923, Chicago, IL; married Margaret Robinson; children: Michael Wade, M Wesley, Michelle Harrington, Julienne Mallory. **EDUCATION:** TN State Univ, BS 1949; Univ of Chicago, MBA 1960; Geo Peabody Coll of Vanderbilt Univ, EdS 1970; Western CO Univ, PhD 1974. **CAREER:** Eastern Airlines, dir ground equipment 1972-79; Embry Riddle Aeronautical Univ Grad Sch, adjunct prof; US Air Force, officer (career) 1943-72; Eastern Airlines Inc, corp dir of affirmative action, corp dir equal oppor urban affairs. **ORGANIZATIONS:** Mem P-47 Fighter Pilots Assn; mem Negro Airmen Intl; mem bd of dirs Citizens Crime Comm Greater Miami, Greater Miami United, Bus Assistance Ctr; council mem Arts & Sciences Council of Dade Cty; life mem Kappa Alpha Psi Frat; mem Soc of Mfg Engrs; Soc of Automotive Engrs; P-40 Warhawk Pilots Assn; Arnold Air Soc; Air Force Assn; P-51 Mustang Pilots Assn; Natl Assn of Market Devel; Assn of Black Psychologists; Armed Serv Mutual Benefit Assn; BlackMBA Assn Univ of Chicago; Greater Miami C of C; Miami-Dade C of C; Dade Co Sports Auth; bd mem Priv Industry Cncl of South FL; Greater Miami Aviation Assn; mem bd trust Museum of Sci & Space Transit Planetarium; chmn United Negro Coll Fund So FL 1986-87 Telethon; mem Navy Legue of the US; life mem Order of the Daedalians; mem Arnold Air Soc. **HONORS/ACHIEVEMENTS:** Tuskegee Inst Alumni Awd of Excellence 1978; Outstanding Alumnus of the Yr Dept of Engrg TN State Univ 1980; Civic Achvmnt Award FL State Confs of NAACP branches 1981; Recogn of Excellence Greater Miami Urban League 1981; Harriet Tubman Award Natl Assn of Black Airline Employees; Recogn of Achievementin Aviation Atlanta NAACP 1982; Natl Achievement Award Natl Tuskegee Airmen 1982; East St Louis IL Proclaimed a Co Hannibal "Killer" Cox Day 1982; Statesman, Scholar, Humanitarian Award Black Awareness Cncl McGuire AFB 1983; Black Achievers Award Carver YMCA 1983; Outstanding Achievement Award Stockton StateColl New Jersey 1983; Dade Co Proclamation of Apprec for Outstanding Civic Serv 1984; Vietnam Veterans Leadership Conf Award of Excellence 1984; Col Hannibal "Killer" Cox Day proclaimed in Dade Co 1985; Outstanding Achvmnt Award Young Executives in Politics 1985; Air Force Commendation Medal with one oak leaf cluster; Meritorious Achvmnt Medal; Disting Unit Citation; Mediterranean Campaign Medal with six bronze stars; Amer Campaign Medal; WWII Victory Medal; KoreanServ Medal with four bronze stars; Republic of Korea Unit Citation; United Nations Serv Medal; Natl Defense Serv Medal with one bronze star. **MILITARY SERVICE:** USAF col 29 1/2 yrs; 21 medals & awds incl Legion of Merit; Disting Flying Cross w/two Oak Leaf Clusters; Bronze Star Medal; Air Medal w/15 Oak Leaf Clus. **BUSINESS ADDRESS:** Corp Dir Equal Oppor, Eastern Air Lines, Inc, Miami International Airport, Miami, FL 33148.

COX, JAMES ALPHONSO
Psychiatrist. **PERSONAL:** Born May 22, 1920, Luther, OK; married Maaedella Summers; children: James III, Dorothy. **EDUCATION:** Fisk U, BA 1941; Meharry Med Coll, MD 1944. **CAREER:** Self, psychiatrist. **ORGANIZATIONS:** Mem AMA; Am Psychiat Assn; asso prof of psychiatry Univ OK Hlth Sci Crt. **MILITARY SERVICE:** AUS Capt 1943-44, 1952-55. **HOME ADDRESS:** 3413 E Maxwell Dr, Oklahoma City, OK 73121-2247.

COX, JAMES L.
Business executive. **PERSONAL:** Born Dec 11, 1922, Birmingham, AL; married Marjorie; children: Adria, Chandra, James III. **EDUCATION:** Lincoln Univ, AB 1949; Atlanta Univ, MSW 1952. **CAREER:** Salvation Army, USO dir 1952-54, Forrest Neighborhood House, social group worker 1954; Malone Comm Center, exec dir 1955-62; Univ of NE Sch of Social Work, lecturer 1957-62; Community Welfare Council of Buffalo & Erie County, comm planning dir 1962-64; Catholic Univ of America, Natl Catholic Sch of Social Service, asst prof 1964-69; People's Comm Services of Metropolitan Detroit, pres. **ORGANIZATIONS:** mem, Natl Assn of Social Workers; NAACP; Natl Conf on Social Welfare; Natl Fed of Settlements & Neighborhood Centers; Acad of Certified Social Workers; mem, Alpha Phi Alpha Fraternity; Intl Assn of Lions Clubs. **HONORS/ACHIEVEMENTS:** WOMC Metro Media Radio Brotherhood Awd 1975; Cert of Honor Amer Red Cross of Lancaster Co 1962; Comm Headstart Inc of Catholic Social Serv 1975. **MILITARY SERVICE:** AUS 1943-45. **BUSINESS ADDRESS:** President, People's Comm Serv of Detroit, 412 W Grand Blvd, Detroit, MI 48216.

COX, JESSE L.
Newspaper company executive. **PERSONAL:** Born Jun 01, 1946, Bay Minette, AL; son of Jesse Cox Sr and Artensie Wesley Cox; married Mary Walker Cox; children: April, Anwar, Tasia. **EDUCATION:** AL A&M Univ, BS 1969; Mercy College, BS 1979. **CAREER:** Alexander's Dept Stores, mgr 1971-83; Buffy Merchandising Corp, general mgr, 1983-86. **ORGANIZATIONS:** Mem, Kappa Alpha Psi Fraternity, 1965-; consultant, Clitee Assocs, 1979-; Jamaican Amer Varieties, Lewis Security Corp, 1986-; Legislative advisory Comm, NY City Council 1985-. **HONORS/ACHIEVEMENTS:** Articles published on business & drugs Parkchester News 1985. **MILITARY SERVICE:** AUS E-4 2 years; Bronze Star. **BUSINESS ADDRESS:** Circulation Distribution Manager, 1 Gannett Drive, Gannett Weschester Rockland Newspapers, Bldg #1, White Plains, NY 10604.

COX, JOHN WESLEY
Assistant vice president-community affairs. **PERSONAL:** Born Aug 02, 1929, College Park, GA; married Marian E. May, Jul 03, 1960. **EDUCATION:** Morehouse College, Atlanta GA, BA, 1952; Atlanta University, Atlanta GA, MSW, 1957; Western Reserve University, Cleveland OH, 1961. **CAREER:** Butler Street YMCA, Atlanta GA, branch director, 1947-52, youth director, 1952, asst program director, 1952-54, program director, 1956-58, president, 1969-75; Goodric Bell Social Settlement, Cleveland OH, director, 1958-65; US De-

partment of Labor, manpower specialist, 1965-66, executive asst manpower administration, 1966-68; City of Atlanta, director youth council, 1968-69; self-employed consultant, 1975-78; Delta Air Lines, Inc, Atlanta, consultant, 1978-82, director of community affairs, 1982-83, asst vice pres of community affairs, 1983—. **ORGANIZATIONS:** NAACP, Urban League, Georgia Epilepsy Foundation, United Youth Adult Conference, Georgia Commission on Higher Education, Martin Luther King, Jr., Center for Nonviolent Social Change, Atlanta Mental Health Association. **HONORS/ACHIEVEMENTS:** Awards from National Association of Social Workers, United Youth Adult Conference, YMCA, Job Corps, City of Atlanta, City of Cleveland. **MILITARY SERVICE:** US Army, 1956.

COX, JOSEPH MASON ANDREW
Writer and poet. **PERSONAL:** Born Jul 12, 1930, Boston, MA; son of Hiram Cox and Edith Henderson Cox. **EDUCATION:** Columbia University, BA, 1949, LLB, 1952; World University, Hong Kong, APsD, 1972. **CAREER:** New York Post, New York NY, reporter and feature writer, 1958-60; Afro-Asian Purchasing Commission, New York NY, president, 1961-68; New York City Board of Education, Brooklyn NY, consultant, 1969-71; Manhattan Community College of the City University of New York, New York NY, lecturer, 1972-73; Medgar Evers College of the City University of New York, Brooklyn NY, asst prof of English, 1973-74; Cox & Hopewell Publishers, Inc, New York NY, president, 1974; poet and writer. **ORGANIZATIONS:** International Poetry Society, International Poets Shrine, United Poets Laureate International, World Literature Academy, Authors League of America, Poetry Society of America, Phylaxis Society, NAACP. **HONORS/ACHIEVEMENTS:** International Essay Award, Daniel S. Mead Agency, 1964; "Great Society" writer's award from President Lyndon B. Johnson, 1965; Master Poets Award, American Poet Fellowship Society, 1970; World Poets Award, World Poetry Fellowship Society, 1971; PEN grant, 1972; Humanitarian Award and Gold Medal for poetry from International Poets Shrine, both 1974; American Book Award nomination, 1979, for New and Selected Poems; "Statue of Victory" World Culture Prize from Accademia Italia, 1985; Gold Medal, American Biographical Association, 1987.

COX, KEVIN C.
State representative. **PERSONAL:** Born Dec 01, 1949, Oklahoma City, OK; daughter of Frank Cox and Martina Cox; married Carlise Ann Washington. **EDUCATION:** Florida A&M Univ, BS Polit Sci 1972; Univ of GA, M Public Admin 1974. **CAREER:** State of OK, field monitor 1974-77; Energy Conservation & Housing Foundation, minority business develop 1977-80; State of OK, state representative, 1980-. **ORGANIZATIONS:** Mem Natl Assoc of Black Elected Officials; bd of dirs Eastside YMCA; life mem Kappa Alpha Psi Frat Inc; life mem NAACP; mem bd dir Urban League; chmn Ins Comm. **HONORS/ACHIEVEMENTS:** Eastside YMCA Volunteer of the Year; Set Club Citizen of the Year; Jaycees Outstanding Young Man of the Year; Hon Alumnus Langston Univ. **HOME ADDRESS:** 5909 No Terry, Oklahoma City, OK 73111. **BUSINESS ADDRESS:** State Representative, State of Oklahoma, 537-A State Capitol, Oklahoma City, OK 73105.

COX, M. MAURICE
Beverage company executive. **PERSONAL:** Born Dec 20, 1951, Dover, NC; son of Earl E Cox and Nicy Chatmon Cox; married Earlene Hardie Cox, Jul 01, 1978; children: Michelle Hardie Cox. **EDUCATION:** Univ of North Carolina, Greensboro NC, BA Economics, 1974. **CAREER:** Greensboro News Co, Greensboro NC, reporter, 1973-74; Associated Builders & Contractors, Washington DC, editor, 1975-78, dir communications, 1979-81; Pepsi-Cola Co, Somers NJ, manager public relations, 1981-86, dir public affairs, 1987-. **ORGANIZATIONS:** Black Managers Assn, mem, 1986; White Plains Youth Council, mentor, 1988-.

COX, OTIS GRAHAM, JR.
Government official. **PERSONAL:** Born Oct 29, 1941, Winston-Salem, NC; married Wanda Woodlon; children: Wendi, Kevin, Keith. **EDUCATION:** Savannah State Coll GA, BSIA 1963; FBI Academy Quantico VA, law enforce cert 1969; Suffolk Univ Boston, MPA 1980. **CAREER:** Baltimore Co MD, sch teacher 1963-67; Westinghouse Elec Corp, engr writer 1967-69; FBI, special agent investigator 1969; FBI Boston, supr civil rights 1977; FBI Washington DC, adminstr pub 1979, special agent supr pub 1979-, asst section chief. **ORGANIZATIONS:** Mem Alpha Phi Alpha Frat 1960-80; mem Natl Police Assoc 1972-78; treas mem MA Assoc of Afro Amer Policemen 1976-78; mem Amer Soc for Public Admin 1979; mem NOBLE, Urban League, Black Exec Exchange Prog. **HONORS/ACHIEVEMENTS:** Toland Collier Meml Awd Savannah State Coll 1961; A A Leadership Awd Alpha Phi Frat Delta Eta 1963; Cert of Bravery MA Assn of Afro Am Policemen 1975; Cert of Accomplishment Assessment & Designs Inc 1975.

COX, ROBERT L.
Business executive. **PERSONAL:** Born Mar 14, 1933, Jonesboro, NC; married Audrey L Revis; children: Lorecia, Kenneth, Brian, Gerald. **EDUCATION:** Columbia U, 1973; Adelphi U, MBA 1972; Adelphi U, BA 1956. **CAREER:** National Westminster Bank USA, vp; Co of Nassau NY, dep sheriff; Franklin Natl Bank, admin asst; Equitable Life Assurance Soc of US, underwriter. **ORGANIZATIONS:** Assoc mem Natl Bankers Assn; dem candidate for public office 1959, 67; treas Great Neck March of Dimes; youth adv NAACP; pres regional dir Natl Credentials Com Emancipation Centennial Dinner Chmn 1957-64; adv com commr Nassau Co Com for Human Rights 1962-65; trustee exec comm pres sec to bd of trustees Adelphi Univ Alumni 1972-80; asst treas dir exec com vice pres LI YMCA 1971-80; mem NY Governor's Policy Advisory Comm LI Sound Crossing; chmn LI Chap American Diabetes Assn 1978-; mem Natl Council of YMCA's; mem, Urban Bankers Coalition; chmn, ADL "A World of Difference" Coalition 1989-; chmn, Town of North Hempstead Minority Affairs Council. **HONORS/ACHIEVEMENTS:** Hall of Fame Adelphi Univ Sch of Bus Admin; Man of the year YMCA; Small Business White House Conf; Friend of Westinghouse, George Westinghouse HS, Brooklyn 1988. **BUSINESS ADDRESS:** Vice President, National Westminster Bank USA, 97-77 Queens Blvd, Rego Park, NY 11374.

COX, RONNIE
Public relations manager. **PERSONAL:** Born Sep 05, 1952, New York, NY; married Anthony; children: Stacey, Anthony. **EDUCATION:** Pace Univ Bus Admin Marketing & Mgmt, attended 1978; certified in internatl marketing mgmt 1951. **CAREER:** Am Express Co, proj mgr 1980; Dudley-Anderson-Yutzy & Pub Relations Inc, account exec 1975-80; Bankers Truct Co, head teller 1971-74. **ORGANIZATIONS:** Chairperson Nat Task Force on Minorities Pub Relations Soc of Am 1979-80; chairperson Com on Minorities Pub Relations Soc of Am New York City 1979-80; black professional role model Spelman Coll Atlanta; visiting prof Urban League BEEP; guest lectr New Sch for Social Research; guest lectr Fashion Inst of Tech; pres Parent's Group Toddlers Park Day Care Cntr Westchester Community Opportunity Programs Inc 1974-76; co-chairperson Day Care Policy Council 1975-76; second vicepres bd of dir Westchester Community Opportunity Programs Inc 1976-79; mem Am Women in Radio & TV; mem Pub R Relations Soc of Am; mem Coalition Of 100 Black Women. **HONORS/ACHIEVEMENTS:** Guest on The hour-long consumer affairs prog "Let's Talk About It" WUSS-AM; guest on the "Gail Archer Show" WHBI-FM. **BUSINESS ADDRESS:** Am Express Co, 125 Broad St, New York, NY 10004.

COX, SANDRA HICKS
Attorney. **PERSONAL:** Born Apr 28, 1939, Baton Rouge, LA; daughter of Henry Beecher Hicks and Eleanor Victorine Frazier Hicks; married Ronald Virgil Cox; children: Michelle Louella, Damien Monroe. **EDUCATION:** Howard Univ, BA 1959; OH State Univ Coll of Law, JD 1962. **CAREER:** San Francisco Neighborhood Legal Assistance Foundation, chief domestic relations dept 1969-72; State of CA Public Utilities Commn, legal asst to public utilities commn 1972-73; Kaiser Foundation Health Plan Inc, counsel 1973-84; Kaiser Foundation/Kaiser Foundation Health Plan Inc Hosps, vice pres and regional cousnel 1984-; Dixon & White, Attorneys at Law & William C Dixon & Associates, Oakland CA, counsel, 1965-67; Donald P McCullum Esq, Oakland CA, counsel, 1965. **ORGANIZATIONS:** Mem OH State Bar 1963-, CA State Bar 1964-; mem Agency Relations Council United Way Inc 1985-86; chmn Memorial Scholarship Comm Altrusa of Pasadena 1986-87; mem bd of dirs Altrusa Club of Pasadena CA Inc 1986-87; mem Natl Bar Assoc. **HONORS/ACHIEVEMENTS:** Chmn By-Laws Comm 1986-87, Parliamentarian 1986-87 Delta Sigma Theta Sorority Inc; Black Women of Achievement Award, 1987; NAACP Legal Defense & Educational Fund Inc, 1987. **BUSINESS ADDRESS:** Vice President Regional Counsel, Kaiser Foundation Health Plan Inc, Walnut Center, 393 E Walnut St, Pasadena, CA 91188.

COX, TAYLOR H., SR.
Accountant, manager. **PERSONAL:** Born Feb 28, 1926, Clarksburg, WV; son of Wade Cox (deceased) and Matilda Cox (deceased); married Betty Leftridge (died 1947); children: Taylor Jr, Patricia Conner, Nancy Willis; married Edith Burroughs, 1964; children: Annette Austin, Lamont Seals. **EDUCATION:** WV Wesleyan Coll Buckhannon, BS Business Econ (Cum Laude) 1953; IN Univ Bloomington, MBA 1954. **CAREER:** Home Fed Savings & Loan Assoc, Detroit (only black owned & oper in state), general mgr 1954-59; Detroit Coca-Cola Bottling Co, asst to sales mgr (1st black mgr) 1959-64; Motown Records Detroit, dept head-artist mgmt 1964-72; Invictus Records Detroit, vice pres artist mgmt 1972-73; MI Bell Telephone Co, dist mgr minority econ devel. **ORGANIZATIONS:** Life mem Detroit Crime Comm NAACP 1955-; columnist MI Chronicle 1955-79; publ issues task force Urban League Detroit 1975-79; mem affirmative action comm United Comm Serv Detroit 1975-79; mem Natl Business League 1976-80; proj mgr New Detroit Inc 1978-79; exec bd mem Amer Bridge Assn 1979-80; mem Detroit Assn of Business Econ 1979-80. **HONORS/ACHIEVEMENTS:** Numerous Certificatess of Appreciation & Plaques NAACP, Urban League, New Detroit Inc, United Comm Serv 1955-79; listed Natl Top 50 List Amer Bridge Assn 1979-80. **MILITARY SERVICE:** AUS sgt 1944-46, 1948-49; Bronze Starr ETO. **BUSINESS ADDRESS:** District Manager, Michigan Bell Telephone Co, 444 Michigan Ave S #818, Detroit, MI 48226.

COX, WARREN E.
Attorney. **PERSONAL:** Born Apr 26, 1936, Brookhaven, MS; married Alpha D Whiting; children: Diethra Diane, Reggie Renee. **EDUCATION:** Alcorn A&M Coll, BSEd 1957; So IL U, MEd 1966; Univ of MS, JD 1969. **CAREER:** US Equel Employ Opp Commn, dist counsel; EEOC, sr investigator 1973; Holly Springs, staff atty 1969-72; Univ Law Sch, research asst 1966-69; Lincoln's Attendance Cntr, tchr band dir 1964-69; Gentry HS, tchr band dir 1957-64. **ORGANIZATIONS:** Mem NAACP; MS Dem Pary MS Bar Assn; Nat Bar Assn; Am Bar Assn; Magnolia Bar Assn; MS Lawyers Assn; Federal Bar Assn; Am Judicate Soc. **BUSINESS ADDRESS:** 203 Bldg W Capitol St, Jackson, MS 39201.

COX, WENDELL
Dentist, broadcasting executive. **PERSONAL:** Born Nov 07, 1914, Charleston, SC; married Iris; children: Wendell Haley, Iris Marie. **EDUCATION:** Talladega Coll, AB; Meharry Coll, DDS 1944; Fisk Univ & Boston U, grad courses. **CAREER:** PrivPrac Inkster, dentist 1946-; radio stations KWK St Louis WCHB-AM & wjzz-FM Detroit, vp. **ORGANIZATIONS:** Mem Am & Nat Dental Assns; mem Mayor's Com on Human Realtions; bd mem New Detroit Com; Detroit C of C; Detroit Inst of the Arts; Meharry Med Coll. **BUSINESS ADDRESS:** 32790 Henry Ruff Rd, Inkster, MI 48141.

COX-RAWLES, RANI
Educator. **PERSONAL:** Born Nov 09, 1927, Buffalo, NY; daughter of George Hale and Robuty G Hale; married Cornelius Milton. **EDUCATION:** Univ of Paris Sorbonne, BA, MA 1948-54; Univ of Buffalo, PhD 1965. **CAREER:** E HS, teacher 1957-70, improve prog 1970-79; Buffalo Bd of Ed, proj admin; Buffalo Vocational Tech Ctr, occupational spec 1979-. **ORGANIZATIONS:** Adv Future Teachers of Amer, Girls Charm Club Yearbook 1957-62; Aspire instr Proj Able 1964-66; commencement speaker Kleinhans 1970; serv Future Health Planning Career Council Syracuse 1974; dir CAC Youth Employement 1974; bd of dir Girls Scouts of Amer 1977-81; mem Black Educ Assn, Comm Adv Council, Notary Publ Officer, Natl Educ Assn, Sr Citizens Adv; community consultant to TV Channels 2, 7 & 29; YOP Buffalo Psych Ctr; mem Mayors Heritage Comm, Archit Historians Preserv Soc, Amer Museum of Natural History, Soc for Provention Cruelty to Children; educ comm Emmanuel Temple;mem VEA Comm for Erie Community Coll 1980-. **HONORS/ACHIEVEMENTS:** Outstanding Citizen Awd Bethel AME Church 1973; Woman of the Year Awd SUNY Buffalo Urban Ctr Div 1973; Yearbook Dedication for E HS 1974; Omicron Soc Awd 1974. **BUSINESS ADDRESS:** Occupation Specialist, Buffalo Board of Education, 820 Northampton St, Buffalo, NY 14211.

COXE, G. CALIMAN
Illustrator. **PERSONAL:** Born May 07, 1908, Carlisle, PA; widowed. **EDUCATION:** Univ Louisville, BS. **CAREER:** Ft Knox KY 1 man exhibit Louisville, retired illustrator 1968. **ORGANIZATIONS:** Founded Louisville Art Workshop 1966. **HONORS/ACHIEVEMENTS:** Many 1 man & major group exhibits. **MILITARY SERVICE:** USN.

COXE, WILLIAM HADDON
Retired architect, director. **PERSONAL:** Born Oct 12, 1920, Mebane, NC; married Laurice Young; children: Karen Lynn, William H Jr. **EDUCATION:** Attended, Johnson C Smith Univ; Howard Univ, BArch 1953; Univ of No CO, Landscape Arch, Natural Urban Sys. **CAREER:** George M Ewing Co Architects-Engrs Washington DC, priv industry 15 yrs, Philadelphia office 1953-66; US Post Office Dept, engrg & res div 1958-61; DC PublicSchs, architect facilities planner dir div of buildings & grounds (retired). **ORGANIZATIONS:** Mem Assn of Sch Bus Ofcls of MD & DC; Building Coe Adv Council of DC; Metro Sch Facilities Planners; mem All Comm Sch Planning Comm; Anthony Bowen Br YMCA DC. **HONORS/ACHIEVEMENTS:** 1st place medal Architectural Design Howard Univ 1953; represented Howard Univ in Intl Arch Design Competition San Palo Brazil 1952. **MILITARY SERVICE:** AUS WW II; Italian Campaign 1942-45.

COY, JOHN T.
Police officer. **PERSONAL:** Born Oct 05, 1939, Princeton, NJ; son of John I Coy (deceased) and Alice Jeanette Douglas Coy; married Faithe Suzanne Parago, Jan 31, 1959; children: Barrie A (deceased), Wendy D, David S, Dhana P, Dawn C. **EDUCATION:** Trenton State Coll, Ewing Township NJ, 1972-73; Mercer County Community Coll, West Windsor NJ, 1983-86; Atlanta Univ, Criminal Justice Institute, 1983-88. **CAREER:** Trenton Police Dept, Trenton NJ, patrolman, 1964-70, detective, 1970-78, sergeant, 1978-82, detective sergeant, 1982-. **ORGANIZATIONS:** Charter mem, past pres, Brother Officers Law Enforcement Society, 1968-; mem, Trenton Superior Officers Assn, 1978-; mem, Mayor's Advisory Committeee on Affirmative Action, 1981-; bd of dir, Carver Youth & Family Center, 1983-; mem, Roga Golf Club, 1983; mem delegate, Natl Black Police Assn, 1983-; pres, Carver Century Club, 1984-; information officer, New Jersey Council, Natl Black Police 1985-; mem, NAACP, 1985-; information officer, Northeast Region, Natl Black Police Assn, 1987-; mem bd of dir, Natl Black Police Assn 1987-. **HONORS/ACHIEVEMENTS:** Author of article on police/community relations in The Police Chief, 1974; author of Police Officer's Handbook for the Trenton Police Division 1980, 1986; Valor Award, Trenton Police Division, 1980; founder & current pres, Carver Century Club, 1984; founder & current editor, Vanguard ANJ Publication for Black Police Officers, 1984; superior office of the year, City of Trenton, 1985; founder & current editor, Northeast Regional News, Natl Black Police Assn 1985; superior officer of the year, City of Trenton, 1985; mem of the year, Natl Black Police Assn Northeast Region, 1986. **HOME ADDRESS:** 513 Eggerts Crossing Road, Trenton, NJ 08638.

COYLE, MARY DEE
Association executive. **PERSONAL:** Born Apr 06, 1916, Wichita Falls, TX; widowed; children: Doris, Paul, Luther, Larry, Charles. **EDUCATION:** Tex Thcr Coll Harrison Tchr Coll Eden Theol Sem. **CAREER:** Union Sarah Corp, dir contact worker; Community Corp Chap (LAW), con league for adequate wflr; Mo Natl wlfr Right Org, rep. **ORGANIZATIONS:** Mem NAACP; Foundation Area & Neighborhood Assn; Parents for Progress; Anna Malone Children Hm. **HONORS/ACHIEVEMENTS:** Mother of yr Chick-Finney awd 1973; community services awd 1974.

COZART, JOHN
Judge. **PERSONAL:** Born Aug 31, 1928, Birmingham, AL; married Powell L Hairston; children: Rhonda, Steven. **EDUCATION:** Howard Univ Wash DC, BS 1950; Wayne State Law School Detroit, JD 1955. **CAREER:** Wayne Cty Dept of Social Welfare, soc worker 1952-54; Cozart Real Estate Co, real estate broker 1955-; Common Pleas Ct Detroit, judge. **ORGANIZATIONS:** Founder Med Professional Bldg Complex 1967; mem Alpha Phi Alpha; trustee Greater New Mt Moriah Bapt Church. **BUSINESS ADDRESS:** Judge 36th District Court, Madison Center Building, 421 Madison Ave, Detroit, MI 48226.

CRABLE, DALLAS EUGENE
Government official, educator. **PERSONAL:** Born Mar 31, 1927, Brownsville, PA; married Galena Mae Woodson; children: Woodson Dillard. **EDUCATION:** Huchtinson Comm Jr Coll KS, AA 1971; Sterling Coll KS, BA 1975; Wichita State Univ KS, MEd 1978. **ORGANIZATIONS:** Mem KS Bd of Tax Appelas 1979-; perscnnel dir Krause Plow Corp Hutchison KS 1976-79; dir Title IV Upward Bound & Asso Coll Cntl KS 1974-76; counselorTitle IV Spcl Serv Hitchinson Jr Coll 1971-74; dir Shadduck Pk Comm Cntr 1969-71; mem Black Am; adv com Hutch Jr Coll; NAACP 1968-; mem Hutchinson Jr Coll Endowment Assn 1974; bd of dirs Hutchinson Hosp Corp 1976-; mem Hutchinson KS Planning Commn 1970-71; mem Hutchinson KS City Commn 1971-73; mem KS Dem Century Club 1980. **HONORS/ACHIEVEMENTS:** Who's who among am jr coll students Hutchinson Comm Jr Coll 1970. **MILITARY SERVICE:** USN E-6 1944-46 & 1950-68. **BUSINESS ADDRESS:** Kansas Board of Tax Appeals, State Office Bldg 1030- S, Topeka, KS 66612.

CRABLE, DEBORAH J.
Television producer, host. **PERSONAL:** Born Sep 03, 1957, Newport News, VA; daughter of Wilbur A Crable and Christine O Chambers Crable. **EDUCATION:** University of London, 1977; Univ of Maryland, BA Speech Communications, 1978. **CAREER:** JF Kennedy Center, admin asst, 1978-80; WINX Radio, new dir, 1980-81; WOL Radio, talk show host, 1981-82; WRC Radio, news reporter, 1982-85; WHMM-TV, TV host, 1983-85; America's Black Forum, news reporter, 1982-85; Ebony Jet Showcase, host, 1985-. **ORGANIZATIONS:** Mem, Chicago Foreign Relations Council; mem, AFTRA; mem, Omicron Delta Kappa; founding mem, Selective Focus, 1983; founding mem, The Arts Forum, 1986-; pres/founder, The Ovation Arts Council, 1987-; honorary mem, The Natl Epicureans, 1989. **HONORS/ACHIEVEMENTS:** Career Excellence Award, Natl Epicureans, 1989; Distinguished Service, Natl Assn Colored Women's Clubs; United Press Intl, Best News Cast Award, 1982; Community Service Award, Mt Vernon Mental Health Assn; Career Excellence Award, Omircon Delta Kappa; Nethula Journal, Publicist, An Anthology of Literature/Art, 1979-81; New Heights: A Leadership Summit for Youth, annual summer camp coordinator.

CRAFT, E. CARRIE
Nurse, educator. **PERSONAL:** Born Feb 16, 1928, Jeffersontown, KY. **EDUCATION:** Harlem Hosp Sch Nursing, RN 1952; Hunter Coll, BS 1959; Hunter Coll, MS 1962; attended workshops & seminars nursing; Univ of AL Birmingham, Post-Masters Cert as Nurse Educator in Oncology 1980-81. **CAREER:** New York City Dept Health, pub health nurse 1953-59; Misericordia Hosp Sch Nursing Bronx, 1959-60; Rutgers Univ, Newark NJ Coll Nursing, instr 1962-64; St Mary & Elizabeth Sch Nursing Louisville, instr 1965-66; Montifiori Hosp Bronx, summer staff nurse 1969; St Lukes Hosp NYC, supr 1971-72; Mt Holly Nursing Home Lou, summer part time staff nurse 1974-76; IN Univ School of Nursing, Southeast Campus, assoc prof 1966-71, 1972-80, 1981-. **ORGANIZATIONS:** Treas IN State Nurses Assn 1974, 1976-; mem Amer Nurses Assn; mem Nat League for Nurses; mem KY League for Nurses; bd, mem Clark Co Cancer Soc 1979-81; mem First Bapt Ch Jeffersontown, NAACP, Urban League; bd mem Louisville Lutheran Home 1983-; sec & mem bd of dirs Louisville Lutheran Home 1985-86; mem Southern IN Heart Assoc 1986-87; travelled to learn of health care facilities in Spain, Australia; chairperson, Scholarship comm, First Baptist Church of Jeffersontown. **HONORS/ACHIEVEMENTS:** Certificate 10 yrs serv 1977, 15 yrs 1982, 20 yrs 1987 IN Univ School of Nursing, Southeast Campus. **BUSINESS ADDRESS:** Associate Professor, INUniv Southeast Campus, 4201 Grantline Rd, New Albany, IN 47150.

CRAFT, SALLY-ANN ROBERTS (SALLY-ANN ROBERTS)
Journalist. **PERSONAL:** Born Feb 14, 1953, Chandler, AZ; married Willie Jerome. **EDUCATION:** Univ of So MS, BA 1976; Univ of So MS, MS 1977. **CAREER:** WWL-TV New Orleans, reporter 1977-; WDAM TV Sta Hattiesburg MS, weathercaster/Reporter 1977; WXXX Radio Sta Hattiesburg MS, radio announcer 1976. **ORGANIZATIONS:** Mem MS Press Women 1977; mem AFTRA; big sister Big Sisters of Greater New Orleans; program com mem St Mark's United Meth Ch. **HONORS/ACHIEVEMENTS:** 1st place Gen Reporting MS Press Women 1977; 2nd place Gen Reporting Nat Assn of Press Women 1977; gaines baston meml award AFTRA 1978; TV journalist of the year Physically Limited Assn for a More Constructive Environment (PLACE) 1979. **BUSINESS ADDRESS:** WWL-TV, 1024 N Rampart St, New Orleans, LA 70126.

CRAFT, THOMAS J., SR.
Biologist, educator, administrator. **PERSONAL:** Born Dec 27, 1924, Monticello, KY; son of Thomas Marion Craft and Wonnie Travis Craft; married Joan Ruth Hunter, Sep 04, 1948; children: Thomas J Jr, Yvonne Diane. **EDUCATION:** Central State Univ, BS 1948; Kent State Univ, MA 1950; OH State Univ, PhD 1963. **CAREER:** Central State Univ, Instructor 1950-51, asst prof 1951-59, assoc prof 1959-63, prof 1963-; Wright State Univ, adjunct prof 1973-79; FL Memorial Coll, program dir DOE energy grant 1980, natural sciences & math div dir 1981, institutional planning dir 1982, dean of faculty 1984-87. **ORGANIZATIONS:** Coordinator Amer Math Soc Miami Region of Blacks & Math 1984; mem Dade Co FL Educ Task Force of the Beacon Council 1984; mem Research Resources Council Natl Inst of Health 1973-76; CSU/NASA 14 CSU/NASA 1972-76; health science admin HEW NIH Div of Rsch Resources Bethesda MD 1977-79; NSF NIH OH State Dept of Health ad hoc consulting; mem chmn Rsch Resources (NIH) Group on Minority Biomedical Research 1976-; investigator Rsch Projects 1970-; chmn WSU/Med Sch Anatomy Faculty Search Comm 1976-; mem exec comm OH Acad of Sci 1975-77; fellow Ohio Academy of Science; mem Advisory Pannel, Educ Devel Center, Newton MA; fellow Amer Assn for the Advancement of Sci; consultant Natl Science Foundation, Ahmedebao, India, Hyderabao, India; Science consultant, Gujurat Univ 1967, Univ of Hyderabao 1968. **HONORS/ACHIEVEMENTS:** Tri-Beta Biological Honor Soc Sigma Pi Phi Boule; Soc of Sigma Xi; AAAS; OH State Univ, Citation for Achievement 1979. **MILITARY SERVICE:** USMCR corporal, 1943-46; company (recruit) Honor Man.

CRAIG, CLAUDE BURGESS
Elected government official. **PERSONAL:** Born Dec 17, 1946, Atlantic City, NJ; married Dawn; children: Tamikio, Claude II. **EDUCATION:** Hampton Inst, BS 1970. **CAREER:** Newark Bd of Ed, hearing officer; East Orange City Council, chmn. **HONORS/ACHIEVEMENTS:** Outstanding Young Man of Amer Jaycees 1980. **HOME ADDRESS:** 75 Prospect St #3A, East Orange, NJ 07017. **BUSINESS ADDRESS:** Chairman, East Orange City Council, 44 City Hall Plaza, East Orange, NJ 07019.

CRAIG, ELLEN WALKER
Retired mayor. **PERSONAL:** Born Jun 05, 1906, Franklin Co; married James H Craig (deceased); children: James P, Esterleen Moore. **EDUCATION:** Urbancrest & Columbus Public Schools. **CAREER:** Village of Urbancrest OH, 12 yr council member, mayor (retired). **ORGANIZATIONS:** Mem Manpower Adv Council; Mid OH Region Planning Commn; bd trustees United Comm Council; mem Franklin Ouncy Mayor Council; Black Women Leadership Council; OH Black Polit Assembly; Central OH Mayor's Council; State OH Mayor's Council; chmn of bd Manpower Advising Council; mem PIC; mem CETA; mem Urbancrest Civil Improvement Assn; Urbancrest Comm Recreation Bd; Black Women Leadership Council; 1st pres CMACAO's Federal Credit Union; dir Men's Chorus Union Bapt Church; sunday sch teacher Union Bapt Church. **HONORS/ACHIEVEMENTS:** Bapt Ch Humanity Awd Columbus Metro Ares Comm Action Orgn 1972; Outstanding Achievement Fedn Consumers Council 1974; Ellen Walker Craig Day OH Gov Gilligvan 1974; Humanitarian Awd OH Balck Polit Assembly 1974; Serv to Mankind Awd Grove City Sertoma Club 1975; Ellen Walker Craig Day the City of Springfield OH 1975; Merit Awd Affiliate Contractors Am Inc 1975; Mayor's Medal City of Columbus OH 1978 Tom Moody Mayor.

CRAIG, ELSON L.
Physician. **PERSONAL:** Born Nov 27, 1933; divorced; children: Joellyn, Carlton. **EDUCATION:** OH State U, BS 1955; OH State U, MS 1961; OH State U, MD 1966f. **CAREER:** Aff Coll of Medicine OH, opthalmologist, asst dean for students 1970-. **ORGANIZATIONS:** Mem Acad of Me of Columbus & Franklin Co; Am Assn of Ophthalmology; Am Med Assn; bd of dir OH Soc for the Prevention of Blindness 1977; Columbus Assn of Physicians & Dentists; OH State Med Assn; Nat Med Assn; Electron Mocroscope Soc of Am; mem Nu Sigma Nu; Simga XI; Soc of Heed Fellows; Alpha Omega Alpha Med Soc; Landacre Soc. **MILITARY SERVICE:** AUS 1st Lt 1956-58. **BUSINESS ADDRESS:** 456 Clinic Dr, Columbus, OH 43210.

CRAIG, EMMA JEANELLE PATTON
Educator. **PERSONAL:** Born Feb 11, 1942, Arcadia, LA. **EDUCATION:** Grambling State Coll, BS 1966; Univ of Scranton, MS 1976, post masters 1982, Grambling State Univ, 1977-79, 1982, LA Tech Univ, 1978, 1979. **CAREER:** Galveston TX Indus School Dist, teacher 1967-68; Richland Parish School Bd, teacher/dance inst 1966-68; Des Moines Indus School Dist, teacher 1968-70; Bloomsburg State Univ, asst dir of Center for Acad Devel & asst resident dean of student life 1974-76; RCA Serv Co Govt Serv, mgr of educ, voc training & data consultant, 1970-74 & 77-78; Grambling St Univ Lab School, teacher & HS coach (girls Varsity Basketball); Al Nellums & Assoc Inc, consultant 1978-79; Orleans Parish School Bd, teacher & chapter coordinator, 1979-82; St Charles Parish Public Schools, teacher 1982-84; Grambling State Univ, EEO officer & telecomm coordinator, 1984-86, telecommunications liaison officer 1986-. **ORGANIZATIONS:** Mem Alpha Kappa Alpha Sor; mem LA

Equal Oppor Assoc 1984-86; mem Assoc of Social and Behavioral Scientists Inc 1984-86; mem Energy Mgmt/Telecomm Surveillance and Security Systems Comm Grambling State Univ 1984-; managing editor Journal of Social & Behavioral Scis 1985-86; mem steering comm Cancer Prevention Awareness Grambling State Univ 1985-; mem Amer Assoc for Higher Educ 1986-; mem Adv Comm for Telecommunications Grambling State Univ 1986-; research & proposal writer RCA Serv Co Government Services 1971-74 & Bloomsburg State 1975-77. **HONORS/ACHIEVEMENTS:** Outstanding Award for Serv to Students, Orleans Parish LA 1982; Certificate of Achievement The LA State Dept of Educ 1981-83; Certificate of Achievement United States Dept of Labor; The North LA Consortium for Education Teacher Appraisal & The Improvement of Instructions 1978-79. **HOME ADDRESS:** 111 South Main St, PO Box 560, Grambling, LA 71245-0560.

CRAIG, FREDERICK A.
Oral surgeon. **PERSONAL:** Born Apr 28, 1933, Selma; married Leslie J Cyrusd. **EDUCATION:** Fisk U, BS 1954; MS 1958; Meharry Med Coll, DDS 1963. **CAREER:** Fisk U, instr 1956-58; US Post Office, 1958; Private Dental Prictice, 1966-67; Chicago Bd of Health, oral surgeon 1967-70; Private Practtce, oral surgeon; Daniel Hale Williams Neighborhood Health Center, dental dir. **ORGANIZATIONS:** Bd dirs Daniel Hale Williams Neighborhood Health Center; mem Dental Subcom Chicago Heart Assn; mem IL Soc Oral Surgery; Chicago Soc Oral Surgery; Am IL Chicago Dental Socs; Alpha Phi Alpha Frat. **MILITARY SERVICE:** AUS 1954-56. **BUSINESS ADDRESS:** 2011 E 75 St, Chicago, IL 60649.

CRAIG, RHONDA PATRICIA
Attorney. **PERSONAL:** Born Nov 27, 1953, Gary, IN; daughter of William Craig and Myrtle Glover; married Fulton Douglas Smith Jr, Jun 28, 1985; children: Andaiye Spencer, Fulton Douglass Smith. **EDUCATION:** Valparaiso Univ, BA 1975, Sch of Law JD 1978. **CAREER:** Wayne Co Neighborhood Legal Svcs, staff atty 1978-79; Legal Aide and Defender's Office, public defender 1979-80; Wayne Co Corp Counsel, asst corp counsel 1981; State of MI, administrative law judge 1982-. **ORGANIZATIONS:** Legal counsel Soc of Engrs & Applied Scientists 1982-; mem Wolverine Bar Assoc 1982-; Assoc of Black Judges of MI 1983-; mem bd of dirs Legal Aide & Defender's Assoc 1987. **HONORS/ACHIEVEMENTS:** Special Achievement Awd SEAS 1984. **BUSINESS ADDRESS:** Adminstration Law Judge, State of Michigan, 1200 Sixth St #540, Detroit, MI 48226.

CRAIG, RICHARD
Personnel administrator. **PERSONAL:** Born May 10, 1915, Springfield, OH; married Catherine Elise; children: Donald, Richard. **EDUCATION:** Univ of Toledo, BA 1940; Univ of MI, MA 1962. **CAREER:** Claflin Coll, coach & athletic dir 1940-42; Univ of Toledo, asst football coach 1943; Ft Valley State Coll, coach & athletic dir 1945-54; Jefferson Jr High School, Pontiac Bd of Educ, teacher 1954-62, prin 1962-68, Pontiac Bd of Educ, dir of personnel 1968-83 (retired). **ORGANIZATIONS:** Chmn Rules Com So Athletic conf 1952; mem NAACP; mem Omega Psi Phi; institutional rep BSA 1966; bd dirs ESCRU 1966-67; bd dirs Pontiac Boys Club 1968-75; bd dirs Pontiac Urban League 1969-72; mem Amer Assn of Sch Personnel Adminstrs 1979-; mem Diocesan Commn on Ministry 1980. **HONORS/ACHIEVEMENTS:** First Black Staying onUniv of Toledo Campus 1936-40; First Black from Univ of Toledo to play in All-Star Game 1940; Organizer Black HS State Track Meet in GA1950; Orgn First Black HS All-Star Football Game in GA 1952; helped 60 HS Grads receive Athletic Scholarships to Coll; Track Facility named "Richard Craig Track Facility" Pontiac Bd of Educ 1978; inducted Hall of Fame Univ of Toledo 1980; inducted into Fort Valley State Coll Hall of Fame as a coach 1982. **BUSINESS ADDRESS:** Dir of Personnel, Pontiac Bd of Educ, Sch Dist City of Pontiac, 350 Wide Track Dr E, Pontiac, MI 48058.

CRAIG, ROGER TIMOTHY
Professional athlete. **PERSONAL:** Born Jul 10, 1960, Preston, MS; married Vernessia; children: Damesha, Rometra, Rogdrick. **EDUCATION:** Attended, Nebraska Univ. **CAREER:** San Francisco 49ers, fullback 1983-. **ORGANIZATIONS:** Works with numerous charitable groups during offseason. **HONORS/ACHIEVEMENTS:** Played tailback & fullback for NE Cornhuskers; first player in NFL history to surpass 1,000 yds receiving and rushing in a single season; named to AP, UPI College and Pro Football Newsweekly; mem Super Stars competition on NBC; NFLPA's John Mackey Awd for leading League in receptions; Len Eshmont Awd given annually to most Courageous and Inspirational player; mem 1986 NFL Pro Bowl team. **BUSINESS ADDRESS:** San Francisco 49ers, 711 Nevada St, Redwood City, CA 94061.

CRAIG, STARLETT RUSSELL
Educational administrator. **PERSONAL:** Born Aug 17, 1947, Asheville, NC; daughter of Mr & Mrs Robert Russell; divorced; children: Kemi, Karma. **EDUCATION:** Spelman Coll, BA Sociology 1969; Bryn Mawr Grad School of Social Work & Social Rsch, MSS 1969-71. **CAREER:** Univ of NC Asheville, dir office for aging 1978-80; Western Carolina Univ, foreign student adv 1981-, asst to the vice chancellor for student devel 1981-. **ORGANIZATIONS:** Mem rsch comm NC Assoc of Women Deans, Counselors & Admin 1982-85; grad advisor Alpha Kappa Alpha Sor 1984-85; mem Natl Assn of Foreign Student Affairs; mem Jackson County Council on the Status of Women. **HONORS/ACHIEVEMENTS:** Field Scholar Spelman Coll 1965-69; Holt-Manley Wilburn Young Scholar Alumnus Awd 1965-67; Outstanding Young Women of Amer 1983; congressional intern, summer 1984. **HOME ADDRESS:** PO Box 2162, Cullowhee, NC 28723. **BUSINESS ADDRESS:** Asst to the Vice Chancellor, Western Carolina University, 460 HF Robinson Admin Bldg, Cullowhee, NC 28723.

CRAIG-RUDD, JOAN
Government administrator. **PERSONAL:** Born Oct 05, 1931, Flushing, NY; children: Carolyn Hopkins, Michael, Reginald. **EDUCATION:** Attended, Immanuel Lutheran Coll 1948-49, NC Central Univ 1949-50, US Army Logistics Mgmt Ctr 1969; Natl Contract Mgrs Assoc, seminars 1977-78. **CAREER:** US Air Force Brooklyn, expeditor 1958-64; US Army New York City, purchasing agent contract negotiator 1967-71; Otis Air Force Base, procurement specialist 1971-72; New York City Off Track Betting Corp, contract administrator, contracts compliance officer, mgr contracts 1975-. **ORGANIZATIONS:** Credit union loan commn Off Track Betting Corp 1976-; mem Natl Contract Mgrs Assoc 1976-81; OTBC rep New York City Prevailing Wage Council 1981-; OTBC Informal Hearing Officer 1983-; life mem NAACP 1985; peer counselor NY Chap Natl Multiple Sclerosis Soc 1985-. **HONORS/ACHIEVEMENTS:** Service Awd NY Multiple Sclerosis Society 1986. **HOME ADDRESS:** 168-42 127th Ave #2A, Rochdale Village, NY 11434. **BUSINESS ADDRESS:** Manager, New York City Off Track Betting Corp, 1501 Broadway, New York, NY 1003

CRAIGWELL, HADYN H.
Architect, engineer. **PERSONAL:** Born Jun 12, 1907, NYC; married Ruth. **EDUCATION:** Swiss Fed Polytech Zurich, 1932; Tech Univ Berlin, MS 1935. **CAREER:** Priv Pra arch-engr 1946-. **ORGANIZATIONS:** Mem NY State Soc Professional Engrs 1960; Ar Inst Architects 1960; Nat Tech Assn 1937; mem Grand Jury NY County 1947; arbitrator Ar Abritration Assn 1961; bd dirs Greater NY YMCA 1967-69; mem past pres Lions Intl 196 69; mem Aircraft Owners Pilot Assn. **MILITARY SERVICE:** Nat Guard 1937-39.

CRAMER, JOE J., JR.
Educator. **PERSONAL:** Born in Houston; children: 3. **EDUCATION:** TX So U, BB 1959; IN U, MBA 1960; IN U, DBA 1963. **CAREER:** TX Southern Univ, student ass 1955-57; Wilson & Cooker CPA's, staff accountant 1957-59; IN Univ, Bureau Business Research, asst accountant 1959-60; IN Graduate School of Business, teacher 1960-62; IN Warehouse Inc, accountant 1963; PA State Univ, asst prof 1963-66, assoc prof 1966-69; Arthur Andersen & Co, faculty resident 1968-69; PA State Univ, prof 1969-74; Arthur Andersen Facult Fellow, prof 1974-; PA State Univ, head dept accounting 1971; FL A&M Univ, visiting pro 1972; AICPA, consultant 1973; Financial Accounting Standards Bd, consultant 1974. **ORGANIZATIONS:** Mem Bata Gamma Sigma; Beta Alpha Psi; Alpha Kappa Psi; Alph Kappa Mu; Am InstCertified Pub Accuntants; Am Accounting Assn; Com Coordinate Am AccountingAssn; Adv Panel Nat Assn Accountants; Nat Const Com. **HONORS/ACHIEVEMENTS:** Presented many professional & tech Papers; student achievement awar Wall St Journal 1959; opportunity fellow John Hay Whitney Found 1959-60. **BUSINESS ADDRESS:** Sch of Accounting Univ of So CA, U Park, Los Angeles, CA 90007.

CRANFORD, SHARON HILL
Executive director. **PERSONAL:** Born Feb 08, 1946, Jaoquin, TX; daughter of Rev Garfield Hill (deceased) and Eulalia Hill; married Dr Evies O Cranford; children: Charlton F, Corey M. **EDUCATION:** TX Woman's Univ, BA 1966; Atlanta Univ, MA 1970; Kansas State Univ, PhD 1981. **CAREER:** TX State Dept of Human Resources, coord volunteer serv 1976-77; Jarvis Christian Coll, dir student union 1977-79; Residential Homes for Boys, dir 1983-84; Wichita State Univ, asst prof 1984-85; Cranford Adult Living-Learning Centers Inc, exec dir 1982-. **ORGANIZATIONS:** Corres sec The Links Inc 1985-87; public relations chair Alpha Kappa Alpha Sor Inc 1985-87; first vice pres City of Wichita Public Library Bd of Dirs 1985-; mem County Coalition for Mental Hlth 1986-; pres Residential Area Providers of Handicapped Serv 1986-; mem KS State Dept Social Serv Bd 1987-89; KS Para Transit Council 1987-; grad advisor Alpha Kappa Alpha Sor Inc 1987-; soprano/soloist Calvary Bapt Church and Choir 1984-. **HONORS/ACHIEVEMENTS:** Title XIX Doctoral Fellowship KS State Univ 1979-81; Service Commendations to Handicapped Elks Training Ctr 1984; Service to Youth Awd Natl Alliance of Business 1985; Public Serv Awd Omega Psi Phi Frat 1986; soprano/soloist Porgy and Bess 1st Natl Black History Soc 1987. **HOME ADDRESS:** 2420 N Dellrose, Wichita, KS 67220.

CRANSTON, MONROE G.
Clergyman, counselor. **PERSONAL:** Born Mar 18, 1915, NYC; married Catherine Thomas; children: Vivian, Beatrice, Priscilla. **CAREER:** St Joseph Ch, priest; Cnrtl Labor Council Job Placement Prog, counselor; Training Prog, coord 1969-72; Atlas Baby Carriage, shop steward 8 yrs; "Jewel Theatre" Movie House in Harlem, first black to manage. **ORGANIZATIONS:** Mem Exec Bd Local 76b 7 Trustee; trustee Black Trade Unoinist Leadership Com New York City Contrl Labor Council; worked with Adam C Powell organize Woolworth at125th St for Black Workers; mem Harlem Labor Union. **HONORS/ACHIEVEMENTS:** Recip awards for Counselorship 1958, 1959, 1961, 1965, from Labor Council AFL-CIO Cornell Univ Scho of Industrial Labor Relations 1966; recip plaque from Lodge for oustanding Serv Rendered 1974; candidate for Comm Sch Bd 1975.

CRAVENS, THIRKIELD ELLIS, JR.
Physician. **PERSONAL:** Born Feb 23, 1932, Chattanooga, TN; married Gloria Ellen Smith. **EDUCATION:** Clark Coll, BS 1948; Howard U, MD 1956; NY Univ Med Sch, postgrad 1960-61. **CAREER:** Homer G Phillips Hosp St Louis, intern 1956-57; Los Angeles, resident, opthalmology 1957-60; Los Angeles, opthalmology practice 1964-; Clinic Met State Hosp Norwalk CA, chief opthalmology 1964-68; Univ of CA at Irvine, attending physician 1966-68; Univ of So CA So Central Multi-Purpose Health Center Los Angeles,chief opthalmology-optomery serv 1967-; Morningside Hosp Los Angeles, chief opthalmology dept 1969-70, 1971-73; Dominguez Valley Hosp Compton, 1974-; Crenshaw Center Hosp Los Angeles, 1972-. **ORGANIZATIONS:** Dir Comprehensive Med Facilities Inc Los Angeles; dir adv bd Paramed Center Los Angeles; trustee Morningside Hosp; mem AMA; Nat Med Assn; Los Angeles Soc Opthalmology; treas Iner-Alumni Council United Negro Coll Fund Los Angeles 1970-71; bd educ bd dir Harbor View House San Pedro; Crenshaw YMCA LosAngeles; mem Urban League; Omega Psi Phi; Chi Delta Mu. **HONORS/ACHIEVEMENTS:** Recipient golden helmet award Baldwin Hills Youth Football Assn. **MILITARY SERVICE:** USAF 1961-64. **BUSINESS ADDRESS:** 3756 Santa Rosalia, Los Angeles, CA 90008.

CRAWFORD, BARBARA HOPKINS
Business executive. **PERSONAL:** Born Feb 04, Aurora, IL; divorced. **EDUCATION:** Drake U, 1942; Northwestern U, 1945; DePaulUniv Law Sch, 1964; Govs St U, BA 1974; Roosevelt U, grad study 1976. **CAREER:** Dollars & Sense Mag managing ed 1980-; Charles A Davis & Asso, vice pres 1977-79; Dearborn Real Estate Bd, acct exec 1974-77, exec dir 1973-74; Nat Ins Assn, asst dir 1968-73; law firm, exec sec 1947-68; Dollars & Sense Mag, asso editor 1977-79; Issues Unltd WGN-TV panelist 1977; Chicago Chap Nat Assn ofMedia Women, prs 1973-77, natl 1st vice pres 1977-81; NAMU, natl rec sec 1975-77. **ORGANIZATIONS:** Mem Women in Communicatiolns; co-chmn Minority Recruitment Prog 1973-76; dir Pro & Con Screening Bd 1975-; mem Chicago Urban League; NAACP; League of BlackWomen; Nat Hook-up of Black Women Inc; AFRICARE; Chicago Chap Media Woman of Yr; Natl Asso of Media Women 1977-78. **HONORS/ACHIEVEMENTS:** Nat Pres Plaque NAMW 1976; publ Articles Dollars & Sense Mag 1976; Image Bvuilder Awd, Operation PUSH; wrote, prod slide film Natl Ins Assn 1973; wrote, prod slide film Natl Conf of Christians & Jews 1977. **BUSINESS ADDRESS:** 840 E 87th St, Chicago, IL 60619.

CRAWFORD, BETTY MARILYN
Program analyst. **PERSONAL:** Born Sep 25, 1948, Philadelphia, PA; daughter of James

Crawford and Dolores Fuller Crawford. **EDUCATION:** DC Bible Institute 1985-87; Gayles Theological Seminary, DC 1988. **CAREER:** Univ of Pennsylvania, receptionist; Internal Revenue Service, temporary clerk/typist acctg dept, account maintenance clker; IRS Washington DC, computer systems analyst 1977-1983; IRS Wash DC program analyst 1983-. **ORGANIZATIONS:** Mem Assoc for the Improvement of Minorities-IRS 1972-; mem Guildfield Baptist Church, Wash DC 1983-; dir District Federation of Young People of DC & Vicinity 1987-; chairman Black Employment Program Managers-IRS 1988-. **HONORS/ACHIEVEMENTS:** Profiled in Black Enterprise magazine for career accomplishments 1987; honored as an outstanding Adopt-A-School Volunteer 1988; employee of the year Internal Revenue Service 1989. **BUSINESS ADDRESS:** Program Analyst, Internal Revenue Service, 1111 Constitution Ave NW, Rm 2210, Washington, DC 20024.

CRAWFORD, CARL M.
Educational administrator. **PERSONAL:** Born Nov 14, 1932, Tallahassee, FL; married Pearlie Wilson; children: LeVaughn Harrison. **EDUCATION:** FL A&M Univ Tallahassee, FL, BA 1954; Boston Univ MA, MEd 1965; Univ of Miami Sch of Educ Coral Gables, FL, EdD 1971. **CAREER:** Battery D 95th Anti-Aircraft Artillery Battalion, Mannheim Germany, exec officer 1954-56; Dillard Elementary School Grades 1-6, Ft Lauderdale FL, art teacher 1956-60, teacher grade 6 1960-61, teacher grade 5 1961-62, art teacher grades 1-6 1962-65; S FL School Desegregation Consult Center, School of Educ, Univ of Miami, asst consultant 1965-66, assoc consultant 1966-67; Art Center Title III ESEA Proj Broward Co Bd of Public Instr, coord/comm 1967-70; Psychology & Educ Dept, Miami-Dade Comm Coll S Campus, Miami FL, chmn 1970-73, chmn self-study steering comm 1972-73; N Campus Broward Comm Coll, dean 1974-75. **ORGANIZATIONS:** Nat & S Regnl Cncl on Black Am Affairs; Nat Assn of Black Sch Educators; Phi Delta Kappa; FL Assn of Comm Coll; Am Assn of Comm & Jr Coll; NAACP; The Urban League; consult The Annual Fest of the Arts Nat YMCA Week NW Branch YMCA Ft Lauderdale, FL 1963-66; consult The World of Work Conf Dept of Attendance & Equal Educ Oppor Palm Beach, FL 1966; speaker African Art Spring Fest in Music/Drama & Art Dillard Comp HS Ft Lauderdale, FL 1966; consult Pinellas Co Tchrs Assn Human Rel Cncl Conf on Integration of Sch Fac Chinsegut Hill Univ of S FL 1968; speaker African Art Cult Enrichment Series Allapattah Jr HS Miami, FL 1968; consult African Art for Intro to Afro-Am Studies Palm Beach Jr Coll Palm Beach, FL 1969; consult Miami Springs Jr HS Humanizing theFac & Stdnts 1971; chmn Curriculum Com on S Assn Visiting Com for Evaluation of St Thomas HS Ft Lauderdale, FL 1971; reactor Synergy in Med Serv sponsored by SAA at Dupont Plaza Hotel Miami, FL 1971; reactor WEB Du-Bois Lecture Series 1971. **HONORS/ACHIEVEMENTS:** Disting Serv Award for Prof Educ Broward Co Tchrs Assn 1967; Outstand Achievement & Serv in the Field of Educ Award Piney Grove 1st Bapt Ch 1971; Awardfor Appreciation Symbolic of Friends of Educ Mrs Susie H Womack Principal Sunland Park Elem Sch 1972; Cert of Recog for Serv as a Resource Bank Vlntr for Enriching the Classroom Exper of Stdnts in Broward Co Sch 1974-75; Appreciation for Outstand Ontrib in Fostering Better Comm Rel in Broward Co Award Broward Co Ofc of Comm Rel 1975; Outstand Educators of Am in Admin Published by a Div of Fuller & Dees Wash, DC 1975; Cert of Appreciation for Educ Achievement The Links Inc 1975; The Johnnie Ruth Clarke Award for Excell in Comm & Jr Coll Serv S Regnl Cncl on Black Am Affairs Richmond, VA 1982; Biography in "Black Pioneers of Broward Co" "A Legacy Revealed" published by The Links Inc The Ft Lauderdale Chap 1976. **MILITARY SERVICE:** AUS lt 1954-56. **BUSINESS ADDRESS:** Provost, Broward Comm Coll, 1000 Coconut Creek Blvd, Coconut Creek, FL 33066.

CRAWFORD, CHARLES L.
Government executive. **PERSONAL:** Born Apr 03, 1929, Fordwick, VA; married Marion Elizabeth Osborne; children: Charles Preston, Keith Warren, Cynthia Evette. **EDUCATION:** Howard U, BSCE 1956; Catholic Univ of Am, MSE 1964. **CAREER:** Bur of Design & Engineer Dept of Environmental Svcs, chief engineering div; Federal City Coll Sch of Engineering Washington DC, asso prof 1968-72; Dept of Highways & Traffic Bridge Design Div, structural engr 1961-65; various engineering posts. **ORGANIZATIONS:** Mem Am Soc of Civil Engrs; mem Am Public Works Assn; Nat Soc of Professional Engrs; pres Sousa Jr HS PTA 1973-74; mem Dupont Park Civic Assn; chrmn Public Works Com Far Northeast-Southeast Council 1974; pres Sousa Jr HS Comm Sch Bd 1975. **HONORS/ACHIEVEMENTS:** Author Naval Ship R&D Center Report #2532 "buckling of web-Stiffened sandwiched cylindrical shells" 1967; democratic at-large candidate for DC city Council 1974. **MILITARY SERVICE:** USAF Corpl 1947-51. **BUSINESS ADDRESS:** 415 12 St NW, Washington, DC 20004.

CRAWFORD, CRANFORD L., JR.
Business executive. **PERSONAL:** Born Jan 12, 1940, Marshall, TX; married Jennie Henry Crawford (deceased). **EDUCATION:** Tx So U, BA 1963. **CAREER:** REECO, sr clerk; ZionUniv Meth Church, black comm developer; Juvenile Ct, probation officer 1970-73; Prot Serv & Juvenile Prob, supr intake units 1973-76; Clark Cty Juvenile Ct Svcs, prog dir 1976-87, div supv detention 1987-. **ORGANIZATIONS:** Vp Las Vegas Br NAACP 1973-77; life mem Alpha Phi Alpha NV Chapt, Natl Assn of Black Soc Workers, Prince Hall Mason, Clark Cty Com on Christian Social Concerns, Westside Athletic Assn, Alpha Kappa Alpha; grand master Most Worshipful Prince Hall; mem MWPH Grand Lodge of NV, F&AM 1985-, Scottish Rite Masson 33 degree; hon past potentate, imperial adviser Ophir Temple #211; mem AEAONMS Inc. **HONORS/ACHIEVEMENTS:** Serv to Manking Awd 1973; Awd of Merit Las Vegas NAACP 1973; Afro Unity Festival Awd of Merit 1978,80; YMCA Serv Awds 1978,81,82; 100 Most Influential Black in NV 1980; Afro-Amer of the Year SOMBER 1982; Grand Marshall Dr ML King Jr Parade 1985; Serv Awd Sickle Cell Anemia Found of NV 1986. **BUSINESS ADDRESS:** Division Supervisor, Clk Co Juvenile Crt Serv, 3401 E Bonanza Rd, Las Vegas, NV 89191.

CRAWFORD, DEBORAH COLLINS
Educator. **PERSONAL:** Born Oct 06, 1947, San Antonio, TX; divorced; children: Candice Aundrea. **EDUCATION:** Prairie View A&M Coll, BS 1969; Our Lady of the Lake Univ, MEd, Admin Cert. **CAREER:** St Philips Coll, dance instr; Union Carbide, accts recv clk 1970; Valhalla Sch Dist, pe instr 1970-71; Summer Camp, White Plains, pe instr 1971; Alamo Community Coll Dist Office Mgmt Workshop, coord insvc, computer literacy instr 1987; City of San Antonio Human Resources, presenter "Why Man Creates"; San Antonio Ind School Dist, summer principal. **ORGANIZATIONS:** Mem AWRT; coord YWCA Seminar; lectr Our Lady of the Lake Univ Black Hist Wk Activity; Bus & Professional Womens Club; co-emcee Miss PV Pageant; res person NAACP State Conv; mem Links Inc; AKA Sor; Miss Black SA Pageant & Choreographer 1977; Ella Austin Comm Ctrs Bd; St Philips Coll Rest Mgmt Prog; Eastside Boys Club; Pine St & Ctr YWCA; Girl Scouts Publicity Com; NAACP publicity com; bd mem Yth Philharmonic; mem Black Expressions Art League; mem City Fine Arts Commission; mem TX State Teachers Assn 1978-; mem Dance Educators of Amer 1988-; mem Jack & Jill of Amer 1988. **HONORS/ACHIEVEMENTS:** Disting Public Serv Awd Prairie View A&M 1974; Awd for Cause of Human Dignity NAACP 1975; nom Outstanding Young Woman in Amer 1976; Serv Awd Sr Oppty Serv Ctr 1975-76; Model Comm Ldrs Awd Miss Black SA Bd 1976; Comm Serv Awd Walker-Ford Gospel Singers; mayoral appointment to Martin Luther King Jr memorial Commission for the City of San Antonio as Media Chairperson 1987; city council appointment to arts & cultural adv bd; citation from Mayor Cisneros & Councilman Webb, for Public Service 1989; dir Debbie's Darlings, Inc 1989. **BUSINESS ADDRESS:** Summer Principal, San Antonio Ind Schl Dist, 141 Lavaca, San Antonio, TX 78207.

CRAWFORD, DOCK D., JR.
Retired educator, musician. **PERSONAL:** Born Apr 06, 1899, Norcross, GA; married Josephine Marshall. **EDUCATION:** Columbia Univ Chicago Mus Coll; OH St Univ Marshall U; Morehouse Coll, BA 1934; WV U, MA 1952. **CAREER:** Wn Talbert Band Pantages Keith Orpheum Lowe and Fox Theatres, trombonist 1925-27; Carroll Dickerson Band Chicago; Lucky Milliner Bands NY; NYC, dir own band1931-32; AL State College, band dir 1935-39; Stratton High School, Beckley WV, band dir, music teacher 1939-58; Moton-Reeves School, Beckley WV, prin 1958-64; Count Basie, Lionel Hampton, Benny Goodman, Cootaie Williams, Bennie Carter, former students are band dirs, teachers, and musicians with big name bands. **ORGANIZATIONS:** Life mem v chrm Raleigh Co Salvation Army Adv Bd; 1967-; chmn Sr Citizen Council Bd Raleigh Co Community Action Assoc 1970-; trustee Central Bapt Ch; past pres Raleigh Co Retires Tchrs; past vice pres Raleigh Co Elem Prin Assn; mem Omega Psi Phi Frat. **HONORS/ACHIEVEMENTS:** Recipient outstanding achievement award Links Inc So WV 1975.

CRAWFORD, ELLA MAE
Educational administrator. **PERSONAL:** Born Sep 08, 1932, Coffeyville, KS; married Willie E Sr; children: Willie E. **EDUCATION:** WA State U, adminstrn internship for Vocational Educ 1979-80. **CAREER:** Tacoma Public School #10, occupational information asst & financial aid officer; LH Bates Vocational-Tech Inst, coordinator for disadvantaged 1968-71; Tacoma Urban Coalition, coordinator for secretarial improvement program 1968; City of Tacoma WA, supr res relocation for families & individuals 1960-68; Tacoma Housing Authority, relocation asst 1954-60. **ORGANIZATIONS:** Former mem Spl Educ Task Force (WA State -Spl Needs); former v-chmn WA State Developmental Disabilities Planning Council; former sec Pacific NW Regional Nat Housing & Redevel Ofcls (Puget Sound Chpt); mem WA State Financial Aid Adminstrs; Black Prog Educators for Tacoma Pub Schls; Title IX Sex Equity Adv Com; Educ for all Legislation (WA State DSHS Council); bd mem & chmn of Scholarship Com Tacoma Chap of NAACP 1968-; mem, former pres Tacoma Altrusa Club 1968; mem E B Wilson Civic Club Bethlehem Ch 1975; bd mem Pierce Co Personel Review Bd 1978-81; bd mem City of Tacoma Pub Utilities 1979-85; mem United Good Neighbors Planning Cncl 1967-79; mem UGN Budget Com 1967-79; sec Tacoma Model Cities bd 7 yrs; former mem Hilltop Improvement Council (Study Com for Poverty Prgm) OEO; mem Minority Concerns Task Force; Sat Morning Collective; Civic & Prog Assn; Employment Com for WA State Develpment Planning Council; liaison & 1st vice pres Tacoma Urban League Guild. **HONORS/ACHIEVEMENTS:** Citizen award OEO Poverty Prgm 1964; woman of yr Zeta Phi Beta Sorority (Acad) 1972; outstanding citizen award Tacoma Model Cities Exec Bd 1975; Appreciation Award; Title IX Chmn. **BUSINESS ADDRESS:** 1101 S Yakima Ave, Tacoma, WA 98405.

CRAWFORD, HAZLE R.
Housing management executive. **PERSONAL:** Born Jan 18, 1939, Winston-Salem, NC; married Eleanora Braxton; children: Leslie, Hazle, George, Gregory, Lynne. **EDUCATION:** Howard Univ, 1961-63; DC Tchrs Coll, 1963-65; Am Univ, 1967; Chicago St Univ, BA; NC Architectural & Training Univ, hon LLD 1975. **CAREER:** Crawford/Edgewood Manager's Inc Washington DC, natl housing mgmt exec, bd chmn, pres; Housing Mgmt US Dept Housing & Urban Devel, asst sec; HR Crawford Inc,, pres 1972-73; Kaufman & Broad Asset Mgmt Inc, vice pres 1971-73; Polinger-Crawford Corp, vice pres 1969-73; Polinger Co, 1968-69; Frederick W Berens Sales Inc, prop mgr 1966-68. **ORGANIZATIONS:** Mem Inst Real Estate Mgmt, Builders Owners & Mgrs Assn; Nat Assn Housing & Redevel Officials; Professional Property Mgrs Assn; Washington Bd Realtors; Natl Assn Real Estate Brokers; Washington Planning & Housing Assn; Natl Assn Home Builders; Resident Mgrs Assn; dir Bonabond Inc; Washington DC Adv Bd of Recreation; Anacostia Economic Devel Corp; Frederick Douglass Comm Center; Congress Heights Assn for Serv & Educ; Am Cancer Soc; Jr Citizens Corp Inc; bd mem NAACP; Kiwanis Club. **HONORS/ACHIEVEMENTS:** Numerous awards, honors, speciall achievements; JW Paletou; IREM Mgr of the Year 1973; Natl Real Estate Brokers & Omega Tau Rho Distinguished Serv Awards; Cherokee Indians Goodwill Award. **MILITARY SERVICE:** USAF sgt 1956-65. **BUSINESS ADDRESS:** Councilmember, Council of Distict of Columbia, 1350 Pennsylvania Ave N, Washington, DC 20004.

CRAWFORD, JACOB WENDELL
Dentist. **PERSONAL:** Born Oct 26, 1942, Bartleville, OK; married Barbara C; children: Brett, Jacy. **EDUCATION:** Univ of San Francisco, BS 1964; Meharry Med Coll, DDS 1969; Mt Zion Hosp, intership. **CAREER:** Pvt Practice, dentist. **ORGANIZATIONS:** Mem Kappa Alpha Psi; staff Mt Zion; bd dir John Hale Health Plan; chmn bd dr Drug Treatment Program; dental consult & Haight-asbury Free Ford Program; mem Century ClubUniv of San Francisco; Meharry Alumni Assn Omicron Kappa Upsilon Honor Dental Soc; Am Acad of Goldfoil Operations; Alpha Omega Frat; Am Soc of Dentistry for Cildren; Nat Dental Assn; sec of Golden State Dental Assn; bd dir Sickle Cell Anemia; Acad of Gen Gen Dentistry; Am Endodontic Soc. **HONORS/ACHIEVEMENTS:** Outstanding young man of am; nashville dental prize; am of endodontic awards. **BUSINESS ADDRESS:** 1342 Haight St, San Francisco, CA 94117.

CRAWFORD, JAMES WESLEY
Foundation executive. **PERSONAL:** Born Jun 05, 1942, Nashville, TN; son of Robert Crawford Jr and Bessie Harris Crawford; divorced; children: Conrad. **EDUCATION:** Philander Smith Coll, BA 1960-64; Eastern Montana Coll, 1967-68. **CAREER:** US Peace Corps Tanzania, volunteer 1964-66; Economic Opportunity Agency, Pulaski City AR, vista supv 1968-70; Action Region 6, Dallas TX, program officer 1970-73; The Pathfinder Fund, program operations dir Africa 1973-79, regional dir Africa/Middle East 1979-87, dir of spe-

cial projects 1987-. **ORGANIZATIONS:** Mem Alpha Phi Alpha 1962-, Assn of Black Found Execs 1974-, Natl Council for Intl Health, Amer Public Health Assn; consultant Harvard School of Public Health 1983-; mem NAACP. **BUSINESS ADDRESS:** Regional Dir, The Pathfinder Fund, 9 Galen St, Watertown, MA 02172.

CRAWFORD, JAYNE SUZANNE
Social service administrator. **PERSONAL:** Born May 11, 1958, Hartford, CT. **EDUCATION:** Lincoln Univ, BA 1980. **CAREER:** Inquirer Newspaper Grp, reporter 1980-82; Focus Magazine, assoc editor 1981-83; Crawford-Johnson Assoc, partner 1981-; Comm Renewal Team, indus organizer 1983-84, asst to the exec dir. **ORGANIZATIONS:** Co-chmn Young Executives 1983; bd of dirs Urban League of Greater Hartford 1982-85; pres Urban League Guild of Greater Hartford 1982-85; mem Leadership Greater Hartford Inc; exec chairperson New England Urban League Guild Network 1986-87. **HONORS/ACHIEVEMENTS:** Co-editor "Beyond Ourselves" Comm Renewal Team 1982. **BUSINESS ADDRESS:** Asst to Exec Dir, Comm Renewal Team, 3580 Main St, Hartford, CT 06120.

CRAWFORD, LAWRENCE DOUGLAS
Mayor, dentist. **PERSONAL:** Born Jun 13, 1949, Saginaw, MI; married Winnie Hill; children: Lawrence D Jr, Alan A. **EDUCATION:** Univ of MI, Pol Sci 1967-70; Univ of MI Dental School, DDS 1970-74. **CAREER:** LD Crawford DDS PC, dentist 1974-; Town of Saginaw, city councilman, mayor 1981-. **ORGANIZATIONS:** Mem Saginaw Cty Cental Soc, Saginaw Valley Dental Soc, MI State Dental Assoc, Natl Dental Assoc, Amer Dental Assoc, Mid-State Study Club; consult Univ of MI Dental Admiss Hattie M Strong Found; mem bd of dir 1st Ward Comm Ctr; commiss E Central MI Planning Commiss; pres RCA View Devel Corp; mem Frontier's Intl, Black Businessmen's Assoc of Saginaw, Alpha Phi Alpha Frat, East Side Lions Club, Bethel AME Church. **HONORS/ACHIEVEMENTS:** Natl Merit Semifinalist; Public Health Fellowship; 1967 Honor Awd; Frontier's Businessman of the Year Frontier's Intl Saginaw 1980; Family Members United Meritorious Serv Awd 1980; Professional Achievement Awd Zeta Phi Zeta Sor 1981; Outstanding Young Men of Amer 1981. **BUSINESS ADDRESS:** Mayor, Town of Saginaw, PO Box 1746, Saginaw, MI 48602.

CRAWFORD, MARGARET WARD
Elected official. **PERSONAL:** Born Apr 18, 1937, Pontiac, MI; married Samuel Kenneth Crawford Sr; children: Cheryl, Samuel Jr, Gary, Sara Elizabeth, Adrienne Irene. **EDUCATION:** Wayne State Univ, BS. **CAREER:** MI Dept of Social Svcs, social worker 1960-73; Free Lance Volunteer, counsellor, facilitator, political, social activist 1973-; Schrock Adult Care Homes, admin, asst to the dir 1980-; Lincoln Consult Schools, pres bd of ed. **ORGANIZATIONS:** Mem MI Assoc of School Bds 1974-; trustee Lincoln Schools Bd of Ed 1974-; mem Natl Assoc of School Bds 1975-; instr MI Dist Congress on Christian Ed 1979-; pres Lincoln Schools Bd of Ed 1981-; mem Sumpter Housing Rehab Council 1981-; bd of dir The Corner Health Ctr 1981-82; mem Legislative Comm 1982-84, Washtenaw Cty Black Elected Officials 1983-; designated friend The Corner Health Center 1983-; mem Sumpter Twp Political Action Comm 1984-; trustee, church clerk Mt Hermon Missionary Baptist Church 1984-; mem Resolutions Comm 1985-; ex-officio mem Sumpter Young Women's Assoc 1985-; mem Sumpter NAACP; various committees Gifted & Talented Spec Ed Child Advoc; mem delegate Washtenaw Cty School Officers Assoc. **HONORS/ACHIEVEMENTS:** Speaker & consult Students Rights, Spec Ed, School Boardsmanship, Youth Advocacy, State & Fed Legislation Impacting Youth, Womens Issues 1979-; Key Awd MI Assoc of School Bds 1984; Certif by Twp School Dist & Natl Black Child Devel Council. **HOME ADDRESS:** 49372 Arkona, Sumpter Twp, Belleville, MI 48111.

CRAWFORD, MARY GREER
Educator. **PERSONAL:** Born May 28, Marshall, TX; daughter of M Francis Greer and Lucy Clark Greer; divorced; children: Margaret, Cranford, Jr. **EDUCATION:** Wiley Coll, BA 1947; New Mexico Highland U, MA 1953; E Texas State Univ 1974, 1980; East TX Baptist Univ, 1985. **CAREER:** Wiley Coll, head dept bus 1947-70, prof/advisor dept office adm bus educ; prof 1947-. **ORGANIZATIONS:** Coord Div Social Sci & Bus 1967-69; chmn Dept Office Admin & Bus Educ 1970-71; adv 1972; mem Natl Alumni Assn Wiley Coll; sec Pi Omega Pi Natl Frat; Natl Council UNCF; sec chmn Const Commn Pre-Alumn Act Natl Educ Assn; sec Faculty Wiley Coll; mem TX Bus Educ Assn; mem TX Bus Educ Assoc; TX Cong Col, PTA, E TX Soc Cul Civ Educ Dev; asst Juris Conf Central Jur; TX & Gulf Coast Confs; asst sec Del Gen Conf UMC Charter; mem Natl Assn Negro Bus & Professional Women's Clubs Lctr; consult dir workshops in fields; mem Amer Assoc of Univ Profs, Region VIII TX Bus Educ Assoc, Pi Omega Pi Natl Business Teachers Honor Soc, Natl Business Educ Assoc, Mountain Plains Business Educ Assoc. **HONORS/ACHIEVEMENTS:** Woman of the Year Zeta Phi Beta Sor; Alumnus of the Year Pemberton HS Alumni Assoc; Outstanding Citizen of Marshall; Outstanding Educator of Amer, Leading Lady Business Civic and Politics of Marshall; elected/installed TX Black Women's Hall of Fame; Teacher of the Year Dist VIII TBEA; Piper Prof 1986; cited in TV productions as Teacher of Excellence; "Mrs MG Crawford Day" held at Wiley Coll. **HOME ADDRESS:** 808 Atkins Blvd, Marshall, TX 75670.

CRAWFORD, MURIEL C.
President. **EDUCATION:** Hampton Univ, BS 1956; Cuyahoga Comm Coll, refresher course architectural drawing 1978; Univ of WI Sch of Engrg & Science, attended 1979; Case Western Reserve Univ Weatherhead Sch of Mgmt, course in business planning 1986. **CAREER:** York Rd Jr HS, art instructor 1956-57; Cleveland Bd of Educ, art instructor 1957-69; Charles Eliot Jr HS, art dept chmn 1967-69; Self-employed, interior designer 1969-75; The Halle Bros Co, interior designer 1975-78; Edith Miller Interiors, interior design 1978-84; Management Office Design Inc, pres 1982-. **ORGANIZATIONS:** Professional mem holding various positions incl vice pres elect 1987 Amer Soc of Interior Designers; Interior Design Educ Tour England Amer Soc of Interior Designers 1978; designer Dining Room Hope House Amer Cancer Soc ASID Benefit 1979; vignette designer March of Dimes Gourmet Gala/ASID Benefit 1984; speaker Natl Endowment for the Arts Recog of Women in the Design Profession 1985; juror Natl Cncl for Interior Design Qualification Qualifying Exam for Interior Design Profession 3 yr appt 1986. **HONORS/ACHIEVEMENTS:** Amer Soc of Interior Designers Presidential Citation Ronald McDonald House 1979, Hope House Designer 1979, Personal Dedication to Ohio North Chap 1985; Natl Endowment for the Arts Women in the Design Profession recognition as Interior Designer 1985. **BUSINESS ADDRESS:** President, Management Office Design Inc, 16611 Chagrin-Lee Plaza, #202, Shaker Heights, OH 44120.

CRAWFORD, NATHANIEL, JR.
Clergyman. **PERSONAL:** Born Aug 22, 1951, Tarpon Springs, FL; married Helen Jones; children: Nathaniel III, Isaac Antonia, Erica Rachell. **EDUCATION:** St Leo Coll, BS 1974; Atlanta Univ, MSW 1976; Interdenominational Theol Ctr, MDiv 1980. **CAREER:** State of FL, youth counselor 1973-74; Pasco Co Manpower Svcs, job counselor 1975; Whitehead Boys Club, athletics dir 1976-78; Rockdale Co Boys Club, prog dir 1977-78; Stat of GA Youth Svcs, youth devel worker 1978-; USAF, chaplain 1980-. **ORGANIZATIONS:** Bd mem Faith Ctr 1979-80; Faith COGIC 1979-84. **MILITARY SERVICE:** USAF chaplain capt 7 yrs. **BUSINESS ADDRESS:** Chaplain, United States Air Force, 3201 ABG/HC, Eglin AFB, FL 23542.

CRAWFORD, RAYMON EDWARD
Educational administrator. **PERSONAL:** Born Jul 01, 1939, Charlotte, NC; married Albertha G. **EDUCATION:** NC A&T Univ, BS 1957-61; Hampton Inst, MS 1973; Central MI Univ, MS 1978; Atlanta Univ, EdD 1986. **CAREER:** US Army, Lt LTCOL 1962-83; Morehouse Coll, vice-pres 1983-. **ORGANIZATIONS:** Mem Natl Assn of Student Personnel Admin 1984; mem Southern Assn for College Student Affairs 1984; mem Natl Assn of Personnel Workers 1984; exec bd DeKalb NAACP 1983-85; vice-pres Nu Mu Chapter Alpha Phi Alpha 1983-85; convention chmn Natl Assn of Personnel Workers 1984-85; mem Southeastern Assn of Housing Officers 1984-. **HONORS/ACHIEVEMENTS:** Military Man of Year US Army 1982; Man of Year Nu Mu Chapter Alpha Phi Alpha Frat 1983; life mem DeKalb NAACP 1983. **MILITARY SERVICE:** Infantry lt col 1962-83; Joint Serv Medal Purple Heart Combat Infan Badge Bronze Star Army Comm Medal, Air Medal Para Badge Joint Chief of Staff Badge. **BUSINESS ADDRESS:** Vice Pres Student Affairs, Morehouse College, P O Box 47, Atlanta, GA 30314.

CRAWFORD, SAMUEL D.
Educator. **PERSONAL:** Born Nov 25, 1936, Dothan, AL; married Naomi Levert; children: Samuel D, Sabrina, Kitamba. **EDUCATION:** Tuskegee Inst, BS 1966; Univ NE, MS 1968. **CAREER:** Creighton Univ, assoc vice pres student personnel 1972; Tech Jr High School, prin 1971-72; Druid Hill School, prin 1970-71; New Careers Program, dir 1969-70; Franklin Elementary School, teacher 1968-69. **ORGANIZATIONS:** Mem Urban League; NATE; Phi Delta Kappa; Phi Beta Sigma; NAACP. **HONORS/ACHIEVEMENTS:** Co-author Black Language Reader 1973; citizens award Afro-am Culture Cntr 1972; hon adm citation Royal Navy NE Govs Ofc 1974; outstanding educ am award1974-75; black excelence journ award 1975; meritorious serv award Urban League 1975. **MILITARY SERVICE:** USAR 1959-61; pfc 1961-62. **BUSINESS ADDRESS:** 2500 California St, Omaha, NE 68178.

CRAWFORD, VANELLA ALISE
Social worker, mental health worker. **PERSONAL:** Born Nov 25, 1947, Washington, DC; daughter of James Vance Jackson, Jr and Dororthy S Raiford Patton; married William Alexander Crawford, Apr 1971 (divorced); children: Kahina B Crawford. **EDUCATION:** Fisk Univ, 1965-67; Federal City College, BA, 1973; Howard Univ, MSW, 1975; Washington School of Psychiarty, Certified, 1983. **CAREER:** Urban Professional Assoc, dir of outpatient service, 1975-79; Lt Joseph P Kennedy Institute, counselor, 1977-79; Howard Univ Hospital, psychiatric social worker, 1980-86; The Congress of Natl Black Churches Inc, project dir, 1986-. **ORGANIZATIONS:** Pres, The Vanella A Crawford Group Consultant, 1988-; Young People's Project 15-24 Clinic, 1985-88; Private Productions/Co-Owner, Psychological Resource Center, 1985-87; Consultant, The Congress Of Natl Black Churches, 1986; Georgetown Univ Chid Devel Dept, 1978; United Way of Amer, 1978; Trainer, DCPC, 1985; CNBC 1985; Natl Assn Of Black Social Workers, 1985; Natl Assn of Social Workers, 1979; DC Coalition of Social Work Health Care Providers; Dir of Christian Educ North Brentwood AME Zion Church 1982-85; Advisory Board, Amer Red Cross Adolescent Program, Executive Board Co-Chairperson, Duke Ellington School of the Performing Arts. **HONORS/ACHIEVEMENTS:** Alpha Delta Mu National WOrk Honor Society. **HOME ADDRESS:** 1109 Michigan Avenue, NE, Washington, DC 20017.

CRAWFORD, WILLIAM A.
State representative. **PERSONAL:** Born Jan 28, 1936, Indianapolis, IN; son of Kenneth C Crawford and Essie L Crouch Crawford; married Lennie M Crawford. **CAREER:** Postal clerk and community organizer; St John's Missionary Baptist Church, Indianapolis IN, youth coordinator, 1972-78; General Assembly, state representative, 1973-86; Marion County Clerk, administrative asst, 1978. **ORGANIZATIONS:** Mem, NAACP; mem, Urban League; mem, TransAfrica Southern Christian Leadership Conf; mem, Free South Africa Movement. **MILITARY SERVICE:** US Navy. **BUSINESS ADDRESS:** Indiana Black Legislative Caucus, State House, Room 4-2, Indianapolis, IN 46202. *

CRAWLEY, A. BRUCE
Business executive. **PERSONAL:** Born Mar 24, 1946, Philadelphia, PA. **EDUCATION:** St Josephs Coll, BS 1967; Charles Morris Price School of Advertising, Adv Cert 1973; Temple Univ, MJ 1983. **CAREER:** 1st Pennsylvania Bank Corp, br mgmt trainee 1967-69, commercial credit analyst 1969-79, sr officers asst/main office, commercial lending 1970-71, mktg officer 1971-73, asst vice pres br adv 1973-76, vp, dir of adv 1976-79, vp, dir of public & investor relations 1979-. **ORGANIZATIONS:** Vchmn, dir Urban League of Philadelphia; gen chmn Philadelphia United Negro Coll Fund Telethon; past pres, bd mem Natl Assoc of Urban Bankers; past pres, bd mem Natl Assoc of Urban Bankers; past pres Urban Bankers Assoc of DE Valley; dir Philadelphia Indust Devel Corp; mem Public Relations Soc of Amer, Natl Investor Relations Inst; mem corp adv comm Natl Assoc for Equal Oppty in Higher Ed; mem public relations adv comm Adoption Ctr of DE Valley; lay mem Fee Dispute comm Philadelphia Bar Assoc; mem Mktg Comm Exec Intl; mem Japan Karate Assoc, Philadelphia Karate Club, US Karate Team, 1977; campaign chmn Comm to Elect Madaline G Dunn City of Philadelphias 4th Councilmanic Dist; numerous speaking lecturing engagements. **HONORS/ACHIEVEMENTS:** Philadelphia Chap Public Relations Soc of Amer-Pepper Pot Awd Hon Mention 1982; Penny Awd Annual Report Competition Penn-Jer-Del Chap Bank Mktg Assoc 1982; Finalist Outstanding Young Leader of Philadelphia 1981; Outstanding Banker of the Year Urban Bankers Coalition 1976-78; Disting Alumnus Awd Charles Morris Price School of Advertising & Journalism 1977; Selected one of 77 People to Watch in 1977 Philaelphia Mag; Outstanding Serv to Spanish Merchants Assoc Awd 1976; Copywriting Awd Charles Morris Price School 1973; Advertising Media Selection Awd Charles Morris Price School 1973; Co Leadership Awd US Army Basic Training Exercises Ft Campbell KY 1968. **BUSINESS ADDRESS:** Vice President, Dir, 1st Pennsylvania Bank & Corp, Centre Sq Bldg, Philadelphia, PA 19101.

CRAWLEY, BETTYE JEAN See BROWN, BETTYE JEAN

CRAWLEY, DARLINE
Elected govt. official. **PERSONAL:** Born Sep 03, 1941, St Louis, MO; married Lou E Crawley. **EDUCATION:** Assoc Degree Human Services. **CAREER:** Real estate entrepreneur; City of Pagedale MO, alderwoman ward 3. **ORGANIZATIONS:** CORO grad; Women in Leadership; deaconess Fifth Baptist Church. **HOME ADDRESS:** 1835 Ferguson, Pagedale, MO 63133.

CRAWLEY, GEORGE CLAUDIUS
Government official. **PERSONAL:** Born Mar 19, 1934, Newport News, VA; married Cynthia Hewitt; children: Judith Crawley Johnson, Jason Claudius. **EDUCATION:** VA State Univ, BA 1956. **CAREER:** Southeastern Tidewater Oppor Project, exec dir 1966-73; City of Norfolk, div of social serv dir 1973-76, dept of human resources dir 1976-83, city mgrs office asst city mgr 1983-. **ORGANIZATIONS:** Dir Legal Serv Corp of VA, United Way of Tidewater, Athletic Foundation of Norfolk State Univ, Darden Sch of Business, Univ of VA Inst of Mgmt, Southeastern Tidewater Manpower Auth, Norfolk Investment Corp, STOP Organization; chmn Hampton Roads Alumni Group of Virginia State Univ; dir Virginia State Univ Alumni Adv Bd; dir Girls & Boys Club of Hampton Roads VA, St John AME Church. **HONORS/ACHIEVEMENTS:** Distinguished Serv Awd Tidewater Conf of Minority Public Administrators 1985; received numerous awds and citations for contributions from govtl, civic, social and religious organizations. **MILITARY SERVICE:** AUS lt 1957-58. **HOME ADDRESS:** 1466 Holly Point Rd, Norfolk, VA 23509. **BUSINESS ADDRESS:** Asst City Manager, City of Norfolk, City Hall Bldg, Norfolk, VA 23501.

CRAWLEY, OSCAR LEWIS
Personnel administrator. **PERSONAL:** Born May 19, 1942, Lafayette, AL; married Clemestine Clausell; children: Deitra Phernam, Oscar Lewis III. **EDUCATION:** AL State U, BS psychology 1963; Univ of S AL, graduate study. **CAREER:** Westpoint Pepperell Inc Fairfax Towel Operation, personnel dir 1975-; asst pers dir 1972; Marengo High Sch & Dixon Mills AL, tchr 1963-72. **ORGANIZATIONS:** Mem Alpha Phi Alpha Inc 1974; commr Goodwill Inds 1976; chmn bd of comr Lanett City Housing Auth 1978; dist committeeman George H Lanier Council of Boy Scouts 1975; chmn Indsl Com Chambers Co Mental Health 1978; chmn Aux Com Chambers Co Bd of Educ 1979; gov staff State of AL Gov George C Wallace 1977. **BUSINESS ADDRESS:** Boulevard St, PO Box 297, Fairfax, AL 36854.

CRAY, ROBERT
Musician. **PERSONAL:** Born in Columbus, GA. **CAREER:** Mem Robert Cray Band; released first album in 1980 most recent album (5th) Strong Persuader; appeared with Tina Turner for HBO Special; appeared at Chuck Berry's 60th Birthday Party. **HONORS/ACHIEVEMENTS:** Named Best R&B Artist by Rolling Stone's critics.

CRAYTON, JAMES EDWARD
Administrator. **PERSONAL:** Born Dec 18, 1943, Thomasville, AL. **EDUCATION:** AL State Univ, BS 1964; Atlanta Univ, MLS 1968; CA State Univ Long Beach, MA 1975; Claremont Grad Sch, PhD Educ/Higher Educ Admin 1980. **CAREER:** Milton FL Sch Dist, 1964-65; Cobb Co Bd of Educ Austell GA, 1965-67; Anaheim Pub Lib, 1968-70; LA Co Pub Lib, 1970-72; Pasadena City Coll, lib 1972-80, dir of occupational education 1980-, associate dean Community Skills Center. **ORGANIZATIONS:** Mem ALA 1970-; mem council CA Lib Assn 1974-, minority adv 1973-74; chmn Black Caucus Leg Comm 1972-; mem NAACP LA Urban League. **HONORS/ACHIEVEMENTS:** Publ "What Black Librarians Are Saying" 1972; art "Wilson Library Bulletin" Jan 1974; art "Film Library Quarterly" vol 7 1974; travel, Mexico, Europe, N Africa. **BUSINESS ADDRESS:** Associate Dean, Pasadena City Coll, Community Skills Center, Pasadena Area Community College District, 325 S Oak Knoll Ave, Pasadena, CA 91101.

CRAYTON, SAMUEL S.
Business executive. **PERSONAL:** Born Feb 15, 1916, Omaha, GA; married Elizabeth Adams; children: 11 Children. **EDUCATION:** Morris Brown Coll, atnd 1935; NY Univ 1938-39; Babson Coll 1942-43. **CAREER:** Asst to vp; gen mgr corp in Lowell MA 1941-50; SS Crayton & Sons, owner & mgr 1950-. **ORGANIZATIONS:** Past pres Merrimack Valley Br NAACP; bd mem Comm Devel Cit Adv Council; life mem NAACP; chmn; life mem; com Merrimack Valley Br NAACP; mem Gr Lowell Lions Club; mem Contractors Assn of Boston Recip; Community Teamwork, Inc, former chmn of bd; Lowell Human Relations Commission, former chmn; former mem, Lowell City Redevelopment Advisory Comm, Lowell Plan Advisory Bd, Census Advisory Comm, Human Services Bd, Greater Lowell Mental Health Assoc; Univ of Lowell, former parent & student coord for Talent Search Prog; International Institute, former mem bd of dir; mem of bd, Goodwill Industries Merr Valley Rehab Ctr, Board of Educ Found, Inc; Merrimack Valley Hsg Serv, treasurer. **HONORS/ACHIEVEMENTS:** Cert of commendation Gr Lowell Council of Chs 1964; founder originator Black News in Merrimack Valley Over WLLH Radia; cert of commendation Greater Lowell Mental Health Assn 1972; Univ of Lowell Beulah Pierce Memorial Award for outstanding service in the community, 1984. **HOME ADDRESS:** 673 School St, Lowell, MA 01851.

CREAM, ARNOLD (JERSEY JOE WALCOTT)
Retired sheriff, boxing commissioner. **PERSONAL:** Born Jan 31, 1914, Pennsauken, NJ; married Lydia; children: 6 Children. **CAREER:** Professional boxer since age 15 became World Heavyweight Champion 1951; defended title & retained it July 1952; lost title to Rocky Marciano Sept 1952; Camden Co, sheriff 1971-74; City of Camden, juvenile officer 1953-64, apptd asst dir of juvenile affairs 1964-68, apptd dir of comm relations 1968-71; State of NJ, boxing commissioner 1974-83 (retired). **BUSINESS ADDRESS:** State of New Jersey, Court House, Camden, NJ 08101.

CREARY, LUDLOW BARRINGTON
Physician. **PERSONAL:** Born Nov 17, 1930, Kingston, Jamaica;married Lou Jene. **EDUCATION:** Long Island U, BS 1956; Howard U, MD 1960. **CAREER:** Wayne Co Hosp Detroit, intern 1960-61; Ventura Co Hosp CA, resident family practice 1961-63; Los Angelas, practice med & specializing in family practice 1964-; W Adams Comm Hosp, chief med staff 1971-72; med Dr 1972-; Broadway Hosp, chief med 1969-72; Div Family Practice, physician in charge continuing educ interim chief; Charles R Drew Postgrad Med Sch; Martin Luther King Jr Hosp Los Angelas 1970-;Univ of CA at Los Angelas, asso prof; Am Bd Family Practice diplomat; am acad gen pratice, fellow. **ORGANIZATIONS:** Mem Am Acad Family Hysicians; mem CA Assn Del; Los Angeles Co Med Assn. **BUSINESS ADDRESS:** 11924 S Central, Los Angeles, CA 90059.

CREDITT, THELMA COBB
Nurse. **PERSONAL:** Born Jun 01, 1902, Baltimore, MD; widowed. **EDUCATION:** Cheyney Training Sch, 1919; Provident Hosp Sch of Nursing, 1922; Winston Salem Tchrs Coll, 1948-49; A&T Coll, 1950-52; DePaul U, 1959-62. **CAREER:** Provident Hosp, dir 1956; Lunsford Richardson Hosp, dir 1950; Kate Bitting Reynolds Hosp, dir 1948; Kate Betting Reynolds Hosp, supr 1946; Winston Salem, pvt duty 1932; Freedman's Hosp, supr 1926; Milwaukee, pvt duty 1924; Vis Nurses Assn 1923; Provident Hosp, supr 1923. **ORGANIZATIONS:** Colored Grad Nurses Assn 1926; Am Nurses Assn 1930; Provident Hosp Alumna 1940; edtrl staff 1st Dist Nurses Jour 1958; Am Soc for Dor of Vol Servs1967; Council for Dir of Hosp Vol; Nat Hlth Council Survey Vol Serv Taylor Homes; mem Epis Ch; Bishops Commn on Metro Afrs; Loop Coll Cert of Completion for Dir Vol Health Care; bd of hlth Model Citites Prgm; Chicago Lassiter Hlth Mgmt. **HONORS/ACHIEVEMENTS:** Pictured NC Nell Hunter Singers Nat Med Assn Jour 1969; requested to sing for Pres FD Roosevelt Chapel Hill; requested to sing for King & Queen of England White House; wrote dir shows for Nat Negro Hlth Wk; pulb poetry 1941; wrote dir Nurses Prayer & Hym 1959; wrote 8 lullabys 1964; employee of yr Chicago Hosp Council 1968; cert of Recog Chicago Hosp Council 1977. **BUSINESS ADDRESS:** 426 E 51st St, Chicago, IL 60615.

CREIGHTON-ZOLLAR, ANN
Educator. **PERSONAL:** Born Sep 16, 1946, Thomasville, AL; daughter of Thomas E Creighton and Jimmie A Gordon; divorced; children: James A, Nicai Q. **EDUCATION:** Univ of IL Chicago, BA 1973, MA 1976, PhD 1980. **CAREER:** Garfield Park Comprehensive Comm Health Center, program evaluator 1979-80; VA Commonwealth Univ, asst prof soc 1980-88, assoc professor, 1988-. **HONORS/ACHIEVEMENTS:** "A Member of the Family, Strategies For Black Family Continuity" Chicago Nelson Hall 1985; "The Contribution of Marriage to the Life Satisfaction of Black Adults" Jrnl of Marriage and the Family 1987. **BUSINESS ADDRESS:** Asst Professor of Sociology, Virginia CommonwealthUniv, VCU Dept of Soc/Ant, Box 2040, Richmond, VA 23284.

CRENNEL, ROMEO A.
Coach. **PERSONAL:** Born Jun 18, 1947, Lynchburg, VA; daughter of Joseph L Crennel, Jr and Mary Donigan Crennel; married Rosemary, Jan 07, 1967; children: Lisa, Tiffany, Kristin. **EDUCATION:** Western Kentucky Univ, BS Physical Educ, Master's degree 1970. **CAREER:** Western Kentucky Univ, physical educ instructor/coach 1971-74; Texas Tech Univ, defensive asst 1975-77; Univ of MS, defensive end coach 1978-79; Georgia Tech, defensive line coach 1980; New York Giants, special teams coach 1981-. **ORGANIZATIONS:** Mem Sigma Delta 1969-70; mem Amer Football Coaches Assoc. **HONORS/ACHIEVEMENTS:** Captain Western Kentucky Football Team 1969; mem Ohio VAlley All Conference Football Team 1969; mem NY Giants World and Super Bowl Champions 1987. **BUSINESS ADDRESS:** Assistant Coach, New York Giants, Giants Stadium, East Rutherford, NJ 07073.

CRENSHAW, REGINALD ANTHONY
City official. **PERSONAL:** Born Sep 29, 1956, Mobile, AL; married Portia LaVerne Johnson. **EDUCATION:** Morehouse Coll, BA Economics 1978; Univ of S AL, MPA Public Admin 1984. **CAREER:** Mattie T Blount HS, high school instructor 1978-79; SD Bishop State Jr Coll, rsch analyst & instructor 1980-; City of Prichard, councilman 1980-. **ORGANIZATIONS:** Mem of adv bd Commonwealth Natl Bank 1982-; bd of dirs Mobile Co Urban League 1983-; vice pres bd of dirs Deaborn St Comm Ctr 1984-. **HONORS/ACHIEVEMENTS:** Man of the Yr Awd Alpha Phi Alpha Frat 1980; UNCF Distinguished Leadership Awd 1982 & 1983; Mobilian of the Yr Awd Mobile Chap of Phi Beta Sigma Frat 1983; Comm Leadership Awd Ladies Auxiliary of Knights of Peter Claver #172 1984. **HOME ADDRESS:** 1021 Sample St, Prichard, AL 36610.

CRENSHAW, RONALD WILLIS
Attorney. **PERSONAL:** Born Jan 04, 1940, St Louis, MO; married Jo Ann D; children: Ronald Jr, Candace P. **EDUCATION:** Fist U, BA 1962; Univ of SD Sch of Med, grad; Univ of SD Coll of Law, JD 1971. **CAREER:** Ronald W Crenshaw & Asso PC, atty 1976-; State of MI, spl asst atty gen 1974-; Elliard Crenshaw & Strong, partner 1973-76; Zechman & Crenshaw, partner 1972-73; US Atty's Ofc, law clrk 1971; Fredrikson Byron & Colborn Law Ofcs, legal intern 1970; Univ of SD Sch of Med, resrch asst 1968; Dept of Aero-Space Med Mcdonnell Aircraft Corp, asso physiologist 1964-67; Dept of Biochemistry Cntrl Resrch Div Monsanto Co, resrch biochemist 1964; Dept of Radiophysics Sch of Med Wash Univ St Louis, resrch asst 1962-64. **ORGANIZATIONS:** Mem State Bar of MI; mem Wolverine Bar Assn; mem Fed Bar Assn; mem Am Bar Assn; mem num other Bar Assn; mem public adv com on jud cands Detroit Bar Assn; chmn of adm com Detroit Bar Assn 1978-79; vice pres bd of dirs Don Bosco Hall Juvenile Home; chmn Kappa Alpha Psi Frat; found & chmn Martin Luther King Jr Meml Scholar Found Univ of SD 1968-71; chmn Martin Luther King Jr Meml Day Activities 1968-70; mem Hon Code Rev Com Univ of SD 1969; memConstl Rules Com 1969-70; pres Vermillion Chap Phi Delta Phi Legal Frat; licensed State Cts of MI; Fed Dist Ct for the E Dist of MI; US Ct of Appeals 6th Cir. **HONORS/ACHIEVEMENTS:** Fellow awd Univ of SD 1967; pub articles "The Vagrancy Statute to be or not to be", " the purposeful inclusion of am indians" 1970-71; contestant Moot Ct 1969; Am Jurisprudence Awd Univ of SD 1970; gunderson seminar awd Univ of SD 1971.

CRENSHAW, WAVERLY DAVID, JR.
Attorney. **PERSONAL:** Born Dec 17, 1956, Nashville, TN; son of Waverly D Crenshaw, Sr and Corinne Smith Crenshaw. **EDUCATION:** Vanderbilt University, Nashville TN, BA, 1978, Doctor of Jurisprudence, 1981. **CAREER:** Chancery Court, Nashville TN, legal counsel to chancellors 1981-82; US District Judge John T Nixon, Nashville TN, law clerk 1982-84; Tennessee Attorney General, Nashville TN, asst attorney general 1984-87; Passino & Hildebrand, Nashville TN, attorney 1987-. **ORGANIZATIONS:** Mem, Panel for Selection of US Magistrate, 1984; pres, Napier-Looby Bar Assn 1986-87; bd mem, Nashville Bar Assn Young Lawyers Division, 1986; bd mem, Middle Tennessee, Amer Civil Liberties Union, 1986-88; bd mem, Nashville Urban League, 1986-; mem, Chancellor's Committee on Women & Minorities at Vanderbilt Univ, 1987-; bd mem, Tennessee Capital Case Resource Center, 1988-; chair mem committee, Nashville Bar Assn, 1989. **HONORS/**

ACHIEVEMENTS: Sylvan Gatchal Award, Vanderbilt Univ, 1978. **HOME ADDRESS:** 1044 Second Ave South, Nashville, TN 37210.

CREUZOT, PERCY P.
Assoc. executive. **PERSONAL:** Born May 28, 1924, New Orleans, LA; married Sallie Elizabeth Coleman; children: Percy P III, Angele C Williams, John C. **EDUCATION:** Hampton Univ, BS 1949. **CAREER:** Pyramid Life Ins Co, vice pres 1949-60; Percy P Creuzot Ins Agency, owner 1950-59; Free Lance Auto Sales, salesman 1961-63; Herff Jones Jewelry Co, salesman 1963-67; Texas Employment Commission, interviewer 1967-69; Frenchy's Po-Boy, Inc, president. **ORGANIZATIONS:** Mem TX Restaurant Assn 1977-; mem Natl Restaurant Assn 1978-; mem Private Industry Council, State of TX 1980-81; regent TX Southern Univ 1981-; civil service comm City of Houston, TX 1982-; adv bd Houston Restaurant Assn 1982-; bd of directors South Main Bank 1984-; mem Private Industry Council, State of TX 1980-81; dir MacGregor Park Natl Bank Feb-Jul 1984; mem bd of dir Greater Houston Convention & Visitors Council 1985. **HONORS/ACHIEVEMENTS:** Man of the Year Houston Forward Times 1976; Disting Comm Serv Awd TX Southern Univ 1977; Who's Who in the South and Southwest 1978; Outstanding Alumnus Hampton Univ 1982; Humanitarian Awd TX Southern Univ Maroon and Grey Club 1982; Top 100 Black Businesses Black Enterprise Magazine 1983-85; Disting Serv AwardTX Southern Univ for Superlative Accomplishments in Bus & Commerce, Retailing, Marketing, Franchising Aug 13, 1983. **MILITARY SERVICE:** USN carpenter 3rd class 1943-46. **BUSINESS ADDRESS:** President, Frenchy's Creole Fried Chicken, 6830 Mykawa Rd, Houston, TX 77033.

CREW, JOHN L., SR.
Educator, psychologist. **PERSONAL:** Born Nov 02, 1926, Westminister, SC; married Brooksie Wilks; children: John L. **EDUCATION:** Morgan St U, BS 1952; Morgan St U, post-grad 1952-53; Am U, grad stud 1953-54; NY U, MA 1955; Univ of MD, PhD 1968. **CAREER:** Baltimore Public Schools, supt 1976-, interim supt 1975-76, deputy supt & planning res & eval 1973-75; Plan Res & Eval, Baltimore Public Schools, acting assoc supt 1972-73, dir div of special serv 1969-72. **ORGANIZATIONS:** Prof educ & Assn &Dir of Res West Chester Coll 1968-69; st supv Res & Eval MD St Dept of Educ 1966-68; spec asst Educ Testing Balt City Pub Schl 1955-66; educ psychol Balt City Pub Sch 1960-65; psychometrist Balt City Pub Schl 1955-60; consultantships at Model Cit Agcy Econ Dev Prog MD St Dept of Educ Spec Educ Div of Archdiocese of Balt; instruct asst NDEA InstUniv of MD; res asstUniv of MD; mem Amer Psy Assn Amer Educ Res Assn; mem Er Per & Guid & Assn MD Schl Psy Assn; mem MD Acad of Sci; mem MD Per & Guid Assn; mem MD Assn of Meas & Eval in Guid; mem NatlCoun on Meas in Edn; mem Psi Chi Frat; mem MD Psy Assn Amer Assn of Schl Adm 1974-; mem Bd of Trustees; mem Samuel Ready Sch 1972-73; mem advcomm to the Sec of Personnel St of MD 1971-73; v chmn St Plan & Adv Counc on Develop Disabilities to sec of Health & Ment Hygiene; dir of Ment Retard 1970-73; mem Adv Counc on Ment Hygiene to Sec of Health & Commiss of Ment. **MILITARY SERVICE:** USN 1950-52; AUS res col 1950-. **BUSINESS ADDRESS:** 3 E 25th St, Baltimore, MD 21218.

CREW, SPENCER R.
Curator. **PERSONAL:** Born Jan 07, 1949, Poughkeepsie, NY; son of R Spencer Crew and Ada L Scott Crew; married Saundra Prioleau Crew, Jun 19, 1971; children: Alika L Crew, Adom S Crew. **EDUCATION:** Brown Univ, Providence RI, AB, 1967-71; Rutgers Univ, New Brunswick NJ, MA, 1971-73; Rutgers Univ, New Brunswick NJ, PhD, 1973-79. **CAREER:** Univ of MD Baltimore County, Catonsville MD, assistant professor, 1978-81; Smithsonian Institution, Natl Museum of Amer History, Washington DC, historian 1981-87; Natl Museum of Amer History, curator 1987-89. **ORGANIZATIONS:** Program chairperson, Oral History in the Mid-Atlantic Region, 1985-86; executive board member, Oral History in the Mid-Atlantic Region, 1986-90; mem Oral History Assn 1988-; 2nd vice pres African Amer Museums Assn, 1988-89; program co-chairperson, Oral History Assn 1988; commissioner (bd mem), Banneker-Douglass Museum, 1989-93; editorial board mem, Journal of Amer History, 1989-93; program chairperson, African Amer Museums Assn, 1989; senior youth group coordinator, St John Baptist Church, 1989. **HONORS/ACHIEVEMENTS:** Curator for exhibition "Field to Factory: Afro-American Migration 1915-1940"; author of booklet Field to Factory: Afro-American Migration 1915-1940, 1987; Osceola Award, Delta Sigma Theta Sorority, Inc 1988. **BUSINESS ADDRESS:** Curator, Natlional Museum of American History, Smithsonian Institution, Washington, DC 20560.

CREWS, DONALD
Author, illustrator. **PERSONAL:** Born Aug 30, 1930, Newark, NJ; son of Asa H Crews and Marshanna White Crews; married Ann Jonas Crews, Jan 28, 1964; children: Nina Melissa, Amy Marshanna. **EDUCATION:** Cooper Union, New York NY, certificate of completion for the Advancement of Science & Art, 1956-59. **CAREER:** Dance Magazine, New York NY, asst art director 1959-61; Will Burton Studios, New York NY, staff designer 1961-62; freelance designer for varoius employers; author and illustrator, 1979-. **HONORS/ACHIEVEMENTS:** Caldecott Honor Award for books Freight Train, 1979, and Truck, 1980, American Library Assn. **MILITARY SERVICE:** Army, pfc 1962-64.

CREWS, WILLIAM HUNTER
Clergyman. **PERSONAL:** Born Mar 18, 1932, Winston-salem, NC; married June; children: William H. **EDUCATION:** Virginia Union U; Newy York U, M Ed; Union Theological Sem of NY; George Coll Downers Grove IL. **CAREER:** YMCA Highland Park Branch Detroit, exec dir; Shiloh Bapt, pastor 1969-. **ORGANIZATIONS:** Mem bd dir Rotary Intnl Bapt & Pastors Council of Detoit; bd dir Mcih Mental Health Soc; assoc Prof YMCA Dir; Omega Psi Phi. **HONORS/ACHIEVEMENTS:** Outs comm ser award St of Mich 1973; comm ser award from First Bapt Ch 1970. **BUSINESS ADDRESS:** 557 Benton, Detroit, MI 48201.

CREWS, WILLIAM SYLVESTER
Business executive. **PERSONAL:** Born Mar 05, 1947, Advance, NC; married Patricia Edwards; children: David, Angela, William Jr. **EDUCATION:** Winston-salem State U, BA 1969. **CAREER:** Wachovia Bank & Trust, audit & control trainee 1969-70, asst local auditor 1970-73, retail credit analyst 1973-75, mgr 1975-, vice pres, bond opers. **ORGANIZATIONS:** Mem Bankersednl Soc Inc 1978; mem Nat Bankers Assn 1978; mem Omega Psi Phi Frat 1967; treas Nature Sci Ctr 1979. **BUSINESS ADDRESS:** Vice President, Wachovia Bank & Trust NA, PO Box 3099, Winston-Salem, NC 27102.

CRIBBS, JOE
Professional athlete. **PERSONAL:** Born Jan 05, 1958, Sulligent, AL. **EDUCATION:** Auburn Univ, attended. **CAREER:** Birmingham Stallions, running back. **HONORS/ACHIEVEMENTS:** 1st rushing championship title as a professional 1984; Consensus All-USFL The Sporting News, Pro Football Weekly & Coll & Prof Football Newsweekly; Named Pony's USFL Running Back of the Year League's Championship Game at Tampa Bay in July; 3 times named All-Pro in NFL & NFL Amer Football Conf Rookie of the Year 1980; Named All-Southeastern Conf & 2nd team All-Amer in jr & sr years at Auburn Univ; Twice named to Parade Mag Prep All-Amer Football Team.

CRIBBS, THEO, SR.
State legislator. **PERSONAL:** Born Mar 11, 1916, Sulligent, AL; son of Charlie Cribbs and Isabella Marchbank Cribbs; married Vera, Apr 30, 1948; children: Theo Jr, Tommie, Lois. **EDUCATION:** Lamar Co Training School, Vernon, AL. **CAREER:** Wichita KS, state rep dist #89 1972-; mem Public Health & Welfare Comm, Labor & Industry Comm, Insurance Comm; Interstate Cooperation Comm, ranking minority mem. **ORGANIZATIONS:** Mem Chapel AME Church, Noah Well Masonic Lodge #110, Wichita Urban League; treasurer Wichita A Phillip Randolph Institute; mem Wichita Natl Educ Assn Progressive Democratic Quorum, State Democratic Comm. **HONORS/ACHIEVEMENTS:** Outstanding Citizen Award 1978. **HOME ADDRESS:** 1551 N Minnesota, Wichita, KS 67214.

CRIBBS, WILLIAMS CHARLES
Public relations manager. **PERSONAL:** Born Oct 11, 1927, Linwood, IA; children: Carol A. **EDUCATION:** Univ of No IA, BA 1950; Des Moines Barber Coll, m barber 1957. **CAREER:** John Deere Waterloo Tractor Works, affirmative action coordinator 1976-; US Congressman & Ed Mezvinsky, adminstrv aide 1973-76; Davenport Civil Rights Commn 1st exec dir 1969-73. **ORGANIZATIONS:** Vp Cribbs & Cribbs Landscaping Co 1955-76; mail carrier US PO 1950-56; chmn comm devel com Davenport C of C 1968-73; exec Bd Intl Assn of Human Rights Agys 1969-73; Davenport Civil Serv Commn 1970-73; mem & pres Davenport Br NAACP 1940-; 1st black city councilman City of Galesburg IL 1968-70; first pres KBBG Radio Sta Waterloo IA 1976-79. **HONORS/ACHIEVEMENTS:** Citizen of the yar Cath Inter-racial Council 1968; distinguished serv award City of Davenport 1972; bill cribbs day City of Davenport 1973; man of the year award Black Students St Ambrose Coll 1973. **MILITARY SERVICE:** AUS agt 1946-48. **BUSINESS ADDRESS:** 400 Westfield Ave, Waterloo, IA 50701.

CRIDER, EDWARD S., III
Administrative law judge. **PERSONAL:** Born Feb 07, 1921, Kimball, WV; married Verdelle Vincson. **EDUCATION:** WV State Coll, BS 1941; advanced study, Columbia Univ, 1947-49; Brooklyn Law School, JD 1953; Modern Mgmt Tech Long Island Univ, Certificate, 1970. **CAREER:** Sr public health sanitarian 1947-67; part time practitioner of law 1955-; New York City Dept of Health, regional dir 1967-77; New York City Dept of Health, spl asst to dir pest control 1974-77; Dept of Health NY, admin law judge. **ORGANIZATIONS:** Pres, NY Chapter, WV Coll Alumni Assn 1975-; pres Brooklyn Alumni Chapter, Kappa Alpha Psi 1957-59; Y's Men; sec Westbury Branch NAACP; Urban League; YMCA; Kimball HS Alumni NY Chapter; NY State Trial Lawyers Assn; Nassau Co Bar Assn; NY State Sanitarians Conf; Fellow Food & Drug Law Inst NYU Law School 1959. **MILITARY SERVICE:** AUS 1st Lt 1941-45. **BUSINESS ADDRESS:** Dept of Health, 65 Worth St, New York, NY 10013.

CRIM, ALONZO A.
Educator. **PERSONAL:** Born Oct 01, 1928, Chicago, IL; son of George Crim and Hazel Howard Crim; married Gwendolyn Motley; children: Timothy, Susan, Sharon. **EDUCATION:** Roosevelt Coll, BA 1950; Univ of Chicago, MA 1958; Harvard Univ, EdD 1969. **CAREER:** Chicago Pub Schs, teacher 1954-63, supr 1968-69; Whittier Elem Sch, principal 1963-65; Adult Educ Ctr, 1965; Wendell Phillips HS, 1965-68; Compton Union HS, 1969-70; Compton Unified Sch Dist, 1970-73; Atlanta Pub Sch, 1973-88; GA State Univ, prof 1988. **ORGANIZATIONS:** Mem various offices and committees, Amer Assn Sch Admin; Natl Alliance Black Sch Superintendents; Natl Alliance Black Sch Educ; Harvard Grad Sch Educ; Jr Achievement Gr Atlanta; So Council Intl & Pub Affairs; Educ Prog Assn Amer; GA Council Economic Educ; Amer Cancer Soc; GA Assn Sch Superintendents; Atlanta YMCA; Natl EdD Prog Educ Leaders; Rotary Club; Atlanta Council for Intl Visitors; Atlanta Area Scout Council's Expo; Phi Beta Kappa; numerous publs in field; life mem NAACP; mem Amer Assn of Sch Administrators; mem Kappa Alpha Psi, Kappa Boule, Phi Delta Kappa. **HONORS/ACHIEVEMENTS:** Eleanor Roosevelt Key Awd Roosevelt Univ 1974; Vincent Conroy Awd Harvard Grad Sch 1970; Distingushed Educators Awd Teacher's Coll Columbia Univ 1980; Father of the Year Awd in Educ SE Region of the US 1981; Honor of the Yr Awd in Patriotism Military Order of World Wars 1981; Hon life mem IL Congress of Parents and Teachers 1982; One of North Amer 100 Top Execs The Executive Educator magazine 1984; Big Heart Awd GA Special Olympics 1985; The Golden Staff Awd GA State Univ; Volunteer of the Year YMCA of Metro Atlanta; Horace Mann Bond Cup Fort Valley Coll 1985; Abe Goldstein Human Relations Awd Anti-Defamation League 1985; Distinguished Public Relations Awd GA Chap of the Public Relations Soc of Amer 1986; hon DL degree Newberry Coll, hon doctor of public serv degree Gettysburg Coll, hon degree Georgetown Univ; hon degree Princeton Univ; hon degree Harvard Univ; hon degree Tuskege Univ; hon degree Columbia Univ. **MILITARY SERVICE:** USNR 1945-46. **BUSINESS ADDRESS:** Professor, Georgia State University, Department of Educational Administration, University Plaza, Atlanta, GA 30303.

CRIM, RODNEY
Financial service comany director. **PERSONAL:** Born Jun 29, 1957, Chicago, IL; son of Elisha Crim and Katie Brown Crim; married Yolande Inez Bruce Crim, Jul 26, 1980. **EDUCATION:** Univ of Minesota, Minneapolis, Minn, BSB Accouting 1975-80. **CAREER:** Pillsbury, Minneapolis MN, internal auditor, 1979-81; The Musicland Group, Minneapolis MN, financial analyst, 1981-82; IDS Financial Services, Minneapolis MN, general accounting supervisor 1982-83, human resources staffing associate 1983-84, manager of financial reporting 1984-87, assistant controller 1987-88, director controller 1988-89. **ORGANIZATIONS:** Pres, Alpha Phi Alpha, Minneapolis MN, 1977-78; teacher, Junior Achievement, 1984; Allocation Panel Mem United Way 1985; pres Natl Assn of Black Accounts, MN 1985-87; mem Leadership Minneapolis Program 1987; bd mem YMCA Board, Minneapolis MN, 1988-89. **HONORS/ACHIEVEMENTS:** Vita Tax Assistance, State Board of Accountancy 1983; mem of the year, Natl Assn of Black Accountants 1988.

CRINER, CLYDE
Educator, musician. **PERSONAL:** Born Dec 02, 1952, Albany, NY; son of Clyde Criner, Jr and Charlotte M Criner; married Alanna M Georgens, Jul 05, 1983. **EDUCATION:** Williams Coll, BA Psychology, 1975; New England Conservatory, MM (honors), 1977; Univ of MA at Amherst, EdD Urban Educ, 1978-81; Julliard School of Music, postdoctoral study, 1984-; private study in composition with Vivan Fine, 1985-. **CAREER:** Music dir, Western MA Upward Bound Program, 1978-81; lecturer in music, Williams Coll, Williamston, MA, 1983-84; adjunct prof, Coll of New Rochelle, NY, 1983-85; asst prof of music, Long Island Univ, Brooklyn, NY, 1984-; visiting prof of music, Bennington Coll, 1985; debut recording as solo artist, composer, New England, Vanguard Records, 1985; original works performed by Boys Choir of Harlem, Carnegie Recital Hall, New York, NY, 1985; world premier of commissioned work, The Black Swan, Merkin Concert Hall, New York, NY, 1986; visiting lecturer in music, Pace Univ, 1986-; recording artist with Alphonson Johnson, CBS Records, 1977, Archie Shepp, Blue Marge Records, 1980, Chico Freeman, Elektra/Musician Records, 1982, Sanford Ponder, Private Music, 1985, Geoffrey McCabe, Timeless Records, 1985, Craig Harris, JMT/Polygram, 1988, 1989, Avery Sharpe, Sunnyside Records, 1988, Anthony Davis, Gramavision/Polygram, 1989, Victor Bailey, Atlantic Records, 1989, Hannibal, Atlantic Records, 1989; pianist with Dewey Dedman, Woody Shaw, Reggie Workman, Max Roach, Art Blakey, Kevin Eubanks, Wynton Marsalis, Dizzy Gillespie, Wayne Shorter, Carlos Santana, Noel Pointer, Arthur Blythe, David Murray, James Newton, Marcus Miller, Omar Hakim, St Luke's Orchestra and Chorus with William H Curry conductor; recording artist, BMG/RCA Records, New York, New York, 1987-; composer, pianist, Behind the Sun, RCA/Novus Records, 1988, The Color of Dark, RCA/Novus Records, 1989. **ORGANIZATIONS:** Member, Natl Assn of Jazz Educ, 1979-, Black Music Assn, 1980-, Black Music Caucus, 1980-, Amer Jazz Alliance, 1980-. **HONORS/ACHIEVEMENTS:** Phi Kappa Music Honor Soc, 1977; Sack Theater Music Composition Award, 1978; composer, performer, documentary film on community coll sponsored by Exxon Corp, 1981; Natl Endowment of the Arts, 1983, 1985; 125 Alumni to Watch, Univ of Massachusetts, 1988. **HOME ADDRESS:** 233 E 96th St #4FE, New York, NY 10128. **BUSINESS ADDRESS:** Asst Professor of Music, Long Island University, University Plaza, Brooklyn, NY 11201.

CRINER-WOODS, JOYCE VERDELLO
Psychologist. **PERSONAL:** Born Jul 31, 1943, Hope, AR; married Willie E Woods; children: Stacy B. **EDUCATION:** Univ of Hawaii, BA 1969; Purdue Univ, MA 1972; Union Grad Sch, PhD 1980. **CAREER:** Purdue Univ, asst dean of women 1970; On Staff at several colleges; Private Practice, psychologist 1975-85. **ORGANIZATIONS:** Mem bd dir YWCA 1979; consulting psychologist to "New Horizons" television. **HONORS/ACHIEVEMENTS:** White House Fellow Finalist 1971; Black Entertainment TV Wash DC 1985; lecturer Christian Org 1979-. **BUSINESS ADDRESS:** Clinical Psychologist, 12937 Olivine Way, Silver Spring, MD 20904.

CRIPPENS, DAVID L.
Public television executive. **PERSONAL:** Born Sep 23, 1942, Jefferson City, TN; son of Nathaniel Crippens and Dorothy Crippens; married Eloise Crippens, Aug 04, 1968; children: Gerald. **EDUCATION:** Antioch College, Yellow Springs OH, BA, 1964; San Diego State University, San Diego CA, MA, 1968. **CAREER:** Free-lance writer/journalist, 1971-73; KCET, Channel 28, Los Angeles CA, director of educational services, 1973-77, vice pres, 1977—. **ORGANIZATIONS:** Eisenhower Foundation, California Federation of Employment & Disability, Black on Black Crime, Antioch College Board of Trustees. **HONORS/ACHIEVEMENTS:** Corp for Public Broadcasting fellowship, 1969; distinguished alumni, Graduate School of Social Work, San Diego State University, 1973; named one of Pittsburgh's most influential blacks, Pittsburgh Post Gazette, 1973; service to media award, San Diego chapter of NAACP, 1975; minority telecommunications award, National Association of Educational Broadcasters, 1978; commendation from California State Legislature for Voices of Our People, 1983; outstanding service award, Young Advocates, 1986; honored by National Association of Media Women, 1986.

CRISWELL, ARTHURINE DENTON
Administrator. **PERSONAL:** Born Jan 30, 1953, Memphis, TN; daughter of Arthur Denton and Celia Hambrick Denton; married Gordon Maxwell Criswell; children: Joshua Michael. **EDUCATION:** Park College, BA 1973; Univ of KS, MSW 1981. **CAREER:** KS Children's Serv League, social work intern 1979-80; KS Dept of Social & Rehab Svcs, grad intern 1980-81, program supervisor 1981-84, area mgr 1984-. **ORGANIZATIONS:** Mem Natl Assoc of Social Workers 1979-, Natl Assoc for Couples in Marriage Enrichment 1983-; bd mem Private Industry Council 1984-85. **HONORS/ACHIEVEMENTS:** Educational Stipend KS Dept of Social & Rehab Serv 1979-81. **HOME ADDRESS:** 2966 N 58th, Kansas City, KS 66104. **BUSINESS ADDRESS:** Kansas City Area Director, KS Dept of Social/Rehab Serv, PO Box 171248, Kansas City, KS 66117.

CRITE, ALLAN ROHAN
Consultant. **PERSONAL:** Born Mar 20, 1910, Plainfield, NJ. **EDUCATION:** Harvard U, BA 1968; Harvard U, cons. **CAREER:** Liturgical Art, lecturer; Rambusch Dec Co, writer; self-employed; artist 1950; Harard Univ Press, author; Boston Public Library, exam com. **ORGANIZATIONS:** Mem Archaeological Soc of Am; mem Harvard Alumni Assn; Alumni Assn of Boston Mus Sch; Harvard Club; Faculty Club of Harvart U; Mus of Fine Arts Boston ; Mus of Natural Hist of NY; Smithsonian Inst; consult Semitic Mus; lay ldr Episcopal Diocese of MA; adv bd Nat Ctr of Afro Am Artists Sect of Sch Bldg Named For Allan Crite. **HONORS/ACHIEVEMENTS:** Schlrsp Boston Mus Sch. **BUSINESS ADDRESS:** Ext Libr, Harvard Univ, Cambridge, MA 02138.

CROCKER, CLINTON C.
President. **PERSONAL:** Born Sep 07, 1928, Norfolk, VA; married Doris Hickson; children: Clinton Jr, Leah Kay, Roger, Ronald. **EDUCATION:** Westminister Choir Coll Princeton, NJ, BMus 1952; Kean Coll, Union, NJ, MA 1967. **CAREER:** Newark, NJ, public schl tchr 1955-67; Newark State Coll Union, NJ, adjunct prof 1959-67; Brookdale Comm Coll Lincroft, NJ, exec dean 1969-72; Univ Arts Serv Rutgers U, New Brunswick, NJ, dir 1972-84; 200th NJ State Legis "The Commermorative Session", dir 1983-84. **ORGANIZATIONS:** Consultant NY & NJ Arts Council 1975-; consultant William H Sword & Co Princeton, NJ 1979; mem Advisory Council, NJ State Museum 1978-;; mem brd of trstees, Intr Univ of Haiti 1982-; fdr & past pres NJ Haiti Partners of the Am 1977-83; dem candt NJ State Legisl 1977; co-chair Friends of the Arts Comm to Re-elect Gov Brenden Byrne 1977; fndr Hispanic Arts Inst Rutgers Univ 1975; curator Bamberger's/Hse Beautiful Mag Art Exhibit 1984; prdr Rutgers Univ Summer Festvl TV Special 1980; fndg mem & past pres NJ Sch of the Arts 1980; mem Intl Order of St John Knights of Malta. **HONORS/ACHIEVEMENTS:** Composer & lyrist Alma Mater Brookdale Com Coll 1971; NJ soc of Architects AIA NJ 1971; United Fund Monmouth Co NJ 1977; producer pres- elect Abe LincolnApper before NJ Legislature 1983; Outstanding Public Serv Award Brookdale Comm Coll 1972. **MILITARY SERVICE:** AUS E-4 1952-54. **HOME ADDRESS:** 120 Willshire Dr, Tinton Falls, NJ 07724. **BUSINESS ADDRESS:** President, CC Crocker & Co Inc, 120 Willshire Dr, Tinton Falls, NJ 07724.

CROCKER, CYRIL L.
Educator, physician. **PERSONAL:** Born Aug 21, 1918, New Orleans; married Anna Ruth Smith. **EDUCATION:** Talladega Coll, AB 1939; Howard U, MD 1950; Univ of CA, MPH 1968. **CAREER:** Natl Bureau of Standards Washington, chemist 1942-46; Obstetrics & Gyneology, Flint Goodridge Hospital New Orleans, dir 1955-56; Howard Univ, instructor 1956-62, asst prof 1962-68; Makerere Univ, lecturer 1968-69; Mulago Hospital, Kampala Uganda, E Africa, consultant 1968-69; Howard Univ, prof 1969-72; Family Planning Serv, Dept of Ob/Gyn Howard Univ, project dir 1970-76; Dept of Ob/Gyn Howard Univ, prof, chmn 1976-. **ORGANIZATIONS:** Mem Alpha Omega Alpha 1975; Kappa Pi Honor Soc; Am Coll of Obstetricians & Gynecologists Am Coll of Surgeons; Nat Med Assn; Med Soc of DC Medico-chirurgical Soc of DC; Am Assn of Planned Parenthood Physicans; HowardUniv Med Alumni AssnRecipient. **HONORS/ACHIEVEMENTS:** Distinguished serv award Chmn DC Met Interagency Council on Family Planning 1975. **MILITARY SERVICE:** USNR 1945-46. **BUSINESS ADDRESS:** Howard Univ Hosp, Georgia Ave NW, Washington, DC 20060.

CROCKETT, DELORES LORAINE
Government administration. **PERSONAL:** Born Jun 18, 1947, Daytona Beach, FL; divorced; children: Ayanna T. **EDUCATION:** Spelman Coll, BA Psych (Cum Laude) 1969; Altanta Univ, MA Guidance & Counseling 1972. **CAREER:** Minority Women's Employment Prog, proj dir 1974-77; Avon Products Inc, employment & commun suprv 1977-79; Natl Alliance of Bus, metro dir 1979; US Dept of Labor, reg dir. **ORGANIZATIONS:** Selected Leadership Atlanta 1977, Leadership GA 1978; bd of dir Big Brothers/Big Sisters 1985-; bd of trustees Leadership Atlanta 198-81; bd of dir Amer Red Cros 1982-; AH Task Force Natl Conf of Black Mayors 1985. **HONORS/ACHIEVEMENTS:** Listed in Outstanding Young People of Amer 1977; Woman of Achievement Business & Professional Women's Clubs Inc 1977,79; One of the Ten Outstanding Young People ofAtlanta 1979; Listed in Personalities of the South 1981; Citation for Outstanding Comm Serv Atlanta Women in Business 1984; Selected by Labor Dept as 1 of 2 reps to serve on Panel III studying Intl Training Prog to Eliminate Sex Imbalances in the Work Place Paris France 1983,84; Outstanding Alumnae Awd Spelman Coll Class of 1969 1984. **BUSINESS ADDRESS:** Regional Dir, Women's Bureau US Dept Labor, 1371 Peachtree NE Rm 323, Atlanta, GA 30367.

CROCKETT, EDWARD D., JR.
Physician. **PERSONAL:** Born Aug 26, 1937, Chattanooga, TN; married Mary Alice; children: 3 Children. **EDUCATION:** Amherst Coll, BA 1958; Howard Univ, MD 1962. **CAREER:** Howard Univ, asst prof, Private Practice, physician internal medicine & pulmonary diseases. **ORGANIZATIONS:** Mem Med Chirugical Soc DC; DC Thoracic Soc; DC Med Soc; asst chmn Undergrad Med Educ Dept Med Howard Univ 1973. **HONORS/ACHIEVEMENTS:** Fellow, Amer Coll Physicians, Amer Coll Chest Physicians. **MILITARY SERVICE:** USN 1967-69. **BUSINESS ADDRESS:** 1827 First St NW #A, Washington, DC 20001.

CROCKETT, GEORGE W., III
Judge. **PERSONAL:** Born Dec 23, 1938, Fairmont, WV; son of George William Crockett Jr and Emily Ethelene Jones Crockett; divorced; children: Enrique Raul. **EDUCATION:** Morehouse College Atlanta, GA, B.A. 1961; Wayne State University Detroit, MI, 1958-; Detroit College of Law Detroit, MI, J.D. 1964. **CAREER:** Recorders Court for the City of Detroit, judge; Defenders Office Detroit, dep Defender 1970-76; Wayne Co Neighborhood Legal Serv, supv atty 1967-70; asst corp counsel 1967; pvt practice 1965-66. **ORGANIZATIONS:** Mem ABA, NBA, MI State Bar, Wolverine Bar Assn, Assn of Black Judges of MI. **BUSINESS ADDRESS:** Judge, Recorder's Court for the City of Detroit, 1441 St Antoine, Detroit, MI 48226.

CROCKETT, GEORGE WILLIAM, JR.
Congressional representative. **PERSONAL:** Born Aug 10, 1909, Jacksonville, FL; married Harriette Clark MD; children: Elizabeth Ann Hicks, George W III, Ethelene Jones. **EDUCATION:** Morehouse Coll, AB 1931; Univ of MI Law School, JD 1934. **CAREER:** US Dept of Labor, 1st black lawyer 1939; Fair Labor Standards Act, sr atty, dept spec on employee lawsuits; Fair Employment Practices Comm, one of 1st hearing examiners 1943; Intl United Auto Workers Fair Employment Practices Dept, founder & dir 1944; United Auto Workers, admin asst to intl sec/treas, gen counsel 1946; Detroit Recorders Court, judge 1946-66, 1972-78; Goodman Crockett Eden Rob, sr partner; Detroit Recorders Court, presiding judge 1974; MI Court of Appeals, vstg judge; City of Detroit, acting corp counsel 1980; US House of Representatives, state rep 1980-. **ORGANIZATIONS:** Phi Beta Kappa; mem FL Bar, WV Bar, US Supreme Court Bar, MI Bar; founder & 1st chmn Judicial Council of Natl Bar Assoc; mem NAACP, Kappa Alpha Psi, Natl Conf of Black Lawyers Friends & Founders Comm, Hartford Baptist Church; elected to 97th, 98th, & 99th Congress; Comm on Foreign Affairs, Africa & Intl Operations Subcomm, Comm on Judiciary, Subcomm on Monopolies & Commercial Law & Immigration Refugees Intl Law; Select Comm on Aging, Housing & Consumer Interest Subcomm; mem Dem Study Group, Congressional Black Caucus, Congressional Hispanic Caucus (Hon); exec bd mem Congressional Arts Caucus; mem Congress Auto Caucus, Congress Caucus for Women's Issues, Northeast-Midwest Coalition, Environ Study Group, Arms Control & Foreign Policy Caucus. **HONORS/ACHIEVEMENTS:** First Black lawyer in the US Dept of Labor; Honorary LLD Morehouse Coll 1972, Shaw Coll 1973; apptd by President Reagan as Public Delegate to United Nations 1987. **BUSINESS ADDRESS:** U S Representative, 13th Congressional Dist, 8401 Woodward Ave, Detroit, MI 48202.

CROCKETT, GWENDOLYN B.
Attorney. **PERSONAL:** Born Apr 25, 1932, Monroe, LA; children: John, Jr, Donald. **EDUCATION:** So U, BA 1954; So Univ Law Sch, JD 1958. **CAREER:** So Univ Law Sch Baton Rouge, instr Law 1961-67; Legal Aid Soc Baton Rouge, dir 1967-72; US Dept Labor Wash 1972-73; US Consumer Product Safety Commn 1973-; Washington DC Louis A Martinette Legal Soc La, pvt prac & law ofc. **ORGANIZATIONS:** Nat Assn Black Women Law-

yers; General Counsel Blacks in Government; LA State Bar Assn; DC Bart Assn; Wash Bar Alpha Kappa Alpha Sorority. **HONORS/ACHIEVEMENTS:** Distinguish serv award Legal Aid Soc Baton Rouge 1972; Nat Client Council 1971; CPSC Chmn citation 1977. **BUSINESS ADDRESS:** President, Crockett & Johnson, PC, 2021 Brooks Dr, Ste C-2, Forestville, MD 20747.

CROCKETT, ULYSSES-ATUM
Educator, director. **PERSONAL:** Born Aug 17, 1938, Houston, TX; children: Gaeron Asari, Todd Anthony, Lori Nicole, Paris Atum. **EDUCATION:** Columbia Univ Sch of Law, LlM 1973; Univ CA, JD 1971; Univ CA, AB 1968. **CAREER:** Pace Univ Law School, assoc prof, presently; First Natl City Bank World Headquarters, intl tax law clerk 1972-73; Bank of Amer World Headquarters, intl tax law clerk 1971-72; CA Rural Legal Asst Prgm, legal rsch clerk 1966; Meltzer Aron & Lemon Advt, account exec trainee 1965. **ORGANIZATIONS:** Pres bd trstes chmn Atum Univ Inc 1977; Mgmt Systems Rsrch Ltd 1977; pres Mun Systems Analysts Ltd 1977; intl tax mgr bd chmn Intl Bus Scis Inc 1977; Am Soc of Intl Law 1971-77. **HONORS/ACHIEVEMENTS:** Publ "Law & Fin of Corp & Small Bus Enter" 1977; "Law & Econ of Mun Fin" 1976; articles Taxation of Int-on-Indebtedness in Corp Acquisitions; Fed Taxation of Corp Unifications a rev of legisl policy; fed taxation of nonresident aliens & fgn corps 1974. **BUSINESS ADDRESS:** Pace University, 78 N Broadway, White Plains, NY 10603.

CROFT, IRA T.
School adminstrator, mayor. **PERSONAL:** Born Feb 07, 1926, White Hall, AR; son of Rev Ed Croft and Effie Croft; married Dorothy Jean Croft, Feb 10, 1951; children: Sonya Faye Croft, Lisa Juanita Croft. **EDUCATION:** Shorter Coll, North Little Rock AR, BA Sociology, 1951; Fisk Univ, Nashville TN, Advanced Study in Sociology, 1951; Arkansas State Coll, Amer History Inst, Jonesboro AR, 1964; Oklahoma State Univ, Economic Inst, Stillwater OK, 1969. **CAREER:** West Memphis School Dist, West Memphis AR, teacher and admin, 1957-86; City of Edmonson, AR, mayor. **HOME ADDRESS:** 400 Harrison, PO Box 65, Edmonson, AR 72332.

CROFT, WARDELL C.
Insurance executive. **PERSONAL:** Born in Gadsden, AL; son of Thomas Croft and Minnie Croft; married Theora; children: Bobbie. **EDUCATION:** Attended, Stillman Coll, Alexander Inst, Univ MI Extension Div, Loma Flint MI. **CAREER:** Wright Mutual Ins Co, mgmt responsibility 1950-62, pres & bd chmn 1962-. **ORGANIZATIONS:** Vice chmn bd of dirs 1st Independence Natl Bank one of founders; mem bd of dirs Physician Drug Center, Detroit Renaissance, New Detroit Inc; mem bd of trustees Stillman Coll; bd mem & chair, Life Insurance Assoc of MI; chmn Detroit Inst of Commerce; vice chmn UNCF Exec Comm of MI. **HONORS/ACHIEVEMENTS:** MI Citizen of the Year MI Chronicle; "S" Award Stillman Coll; Citizen Award Phi Beta Sigma Fraternity; Silver Beaver Award Boy Scouts of Amer; CC Spaulding Award Natl Business League; Equal Opportunity in Higher Educ; Focas & Impact Oakland Univ. **MILITARY SERVICE:** AUS WW II 1st sgt. **BUSINESS ADDRESS:** President/Board Chairman, Wright Mutual Ins Co, 2995 E Grand Blvd, Detroit, MI 48202.

CROMARTIE, ERNEST W., II
Attorney. **PERSONAL:** Married Raynette White; children: Ernest W, Antionette. **EDUCATION:** MI State Univ, 1968; George Washington Natl Law Ctr, JD (Cum Laude) 1971. **CAREER:** Cureton & Cromartie, attorney 1974-76; EW Cromartie, II, attorney 1976-; City of Columbia Dist II, councilman. **ORGANIZATIONS:** Life mem NAACP; mem Optimist Club, East Columbia Jaycees, United Way Bd of Trustees, 32nd Degree Mason, Shriners, Midlands Elks, Townmen Club, Columbia Chamber of Commerce, Housing Comm of Greater Columbia Chamber of Comm, United Way Governing Bd, Kiwanis Club; mem Bishop Mem AME Church, past pres usher bd, sunday school teacher, mem bd of trustees, chmn of bldg fund, chmn Men's Day Activities; mem SC Bar Assoc, Richland Cty Bar Assoc, Amer Bar Assoc, SC Trial Lawyers Assoc, Amer Trial Lawyers Assoc; Admitted to practice in SC Supreme Court, US Dist Court, US Court of Appeals 4th Circuit. **HONORS/ACHIEVEMENTS:** Outstanding Young Man of Amer 1975; Appt by the Mayor to City of Columbia Zoning Bd of Adjustments & Appeals 1976-80, 1980-85; Attny of the Year 1979; Who's Who in South & Southwest 1980; chmn Eau Claire Task Force for Comm Ctr 1980-81; Outstanding Serv Awd SC Chap Natl Assoc of Real Estate Brokers; Living Legacy Awd Natl Council of Negro Women; Appt to SC Youth Serv Bd. **HOME ADDRESS:** 2213 Lorick Ave, Columbia, SC 29203.

CROMARTIE, EUGENE RUFUS
Military. **PERSONAL:** Born Oct 03, 1936, Wabasso, FL; son of Ulysses and Hannah; married Joyce Mims; children: Eugene II, Leonardo, Marcus, Eliseo. **EDUCATION:** FL A&M Univ, BS 1957; Univ of Dayton, MS 1968; US Army Command & Gen Staff Coll, 1970; Natl War Coll, 1977. **CAREER:** Assignments incl command MP Co, two MP battalions & a criminal invest reg covering 22 states; Univ of Dayton OH, asst prof of military sci; US Army Military Police Sch, staff/faculty mem; Command & Gen Staff Coll, staff/faculty mem; 82nd Airborne Div, provost marshal; Wash, DC, assignment ofcr/ofcr personnel directorate; USA-CIDC, spec asst to the commanding gen; US Army Criminal Invest Command Fort Meade, MD, commander first reg; US Army Europe & Seventh Army, dep provost marshal, provost marshal; US Army Military Community Mannheim, Germany; US Army Criminal Invest Command, spec asst to the commanding gen, commanding general. **ORGANIZATIONS:** Exec com Intl Assn of Chiefs of Police 1983-; mem Intl Fedn of Sr Police Officers 1981-; Natl Cncl Law Enforcement Explorer Boy Scouts of Amer 1983-; mem Alpha Phi Alpha Frat 1954-; mem Natl Org of Black Law Enforcement Exec 1984-; natl chmn Law Enforcement Exploring Comm Boy Scouts of Amer 1986-. **HONORS/ACHIEVEMENTS:** FAMU Meritorious Achievement Award 1982; State of FL Resolution Acknowledged as Outstanding Floridian recorded in State Archives 1982; City of Tallahassee & Leon Co declared May 1, 1982 as Brigadier Gen Eugene R Cromartie Day; Key to City of Tallahassee 1982; featured in Ebony Mag Army's Top Cop 1985; 1st inductee into FL A&M Univ ROTC Hall of Fame 1986; Awd FL A&M Centennial Medallion for Distinguished Serv 1987. **MILITARY SERVICE:** AUS Major Gen; served over 30 years; 2 Bronze Star Medals; 3 Meritorious Serv Medals; 2 Army Commendation Medals; Parachutist Badge. **BUSINESS ADDRESS:** Commanding General, US Army Criminal Invest Comm, 5611 Columbia Pike, Falls Church, VA 22041.

CROMBAUGH, HALLIE
Business executive. **PERSONAL:** Born Sep 09, 1949, Indianapolis, IN; married Dennis; children: Trenna, Kendra. **EDUCATION:** Porter Coll, 1974; IN Central Coll; St Mary of the Woods Coll. **CAREER:** Indy Today & Comm, dir, comm affairs, exec producer/host; WISH-TV, asst dir, comm Affairs; 1975-76; Coll/U Corp, auditor, gen accounting dept 1974-75; Am Fletcher Nat Bank, IBM & opr; IN Nat Bank, NCR opr. **ORGANIZATIONS:** Chmn by-laws com Nat Broadcast Assn Comm Affairs; bd dir Comm Servs Council of Greater Indpls; chmn Family Violence Task Force; chmn bd of Dirs Wishard Meml Hosp Midtown Comm Mental Hlth Ctr; adv bd Indianapolis Jr League; vchmn Queens Selection & Coronation Com Indianapolis 500 Festival Asso; bd dirs Indianapolis 500 Assn Inc; mem Gamma Phi Delta Intl Sor Inc; asso min St Paul AMECh; mem IN Conf of 4th Episcopal Dist; ordained deacon AME Ch;chmn adv bd Auntie Mames CDC. **HONORS/ACHIEVEMENTS:** Recpt & outsdng serv award United Award 1975-79; media yr award Marion Co Heart Assn 1975-76; outsdng serv award Indianapolis Pub Sch Operation Catch-up 1977; outsdng serv award Indianapolis Pre-sch Inc 1975-79; outsdng serv award Indy Trade Assn 1977; golden heart award Am Heart Assn 1979 outstanding mental health serv award 1978-79. **BUSINESS ADDRESS:** Community Affairs Dir, WISH-TV 8, PO Box 7088, Indianapolis, IN 46207.

CROMWELL, MARGARET M.
Administrator. **PERSONAL:** Born Jan 30, 1933, Bridgeport, CT; daughter of McKinley H Cromwell Sr and Margaret M Cromwell; married McKinley H; children: Marcelina Johnson, Mc Kinley, Jr, Jarrett. **EDUCATION:** Training on family planning in educ & admin, 1966; Training for instructional aide, 1967. **CAREER:** Screening & Educ Cnrt CT State Dept of Health, coordinator/Counselor sickle cell disease 1972-; CT of Social Work's Summer Inst Training, instructor, 1972; Family Planning/Neighborhood Health Servcs, dir 1968-72; Family Planning Center, coordinator 1966-68; Bridgeport bd educ, instr aide 1967-68. **ORGANIZATIONS:** Past mem Action for Bridgeport Community Devel; past mem Action for Bridgeport Community Devel; exec bd vice-chmn North End Neighborhood Action Coun; past vice pres YWCA; past chmn Cntr for Racial Justice YWCA; past mem bd of Comprehensive Health Planning; past mem Unite Community Services; past co-chmn ParentAdv Coun of Hall Neighborhood House Day Care Cntr; past chmn Dept Children Youth Serv Multi-Serv Cntr; Bridgeport Chap Child Guidance; pres Planned Parenthood Chap Com of Bridgeprot ; past co-chmn Police Community Relations for Urban Coalition; past mem Bridgeport Chap Heart Assn; mem Nat Coun of Negro Women; bd dirs ARC; Channel 8 Minority Adv Com New Haven CT; State Police Coun; NAACP; chmn Youth Outreach Prevention Program Hall Neighborhood House; bd dirs Hall Neighborhood House 1975-78; Gov Planning Com for Criminal Adminstrn Youth Crime & Delinquency sub-com; US Commn on Civil Rights; CT Adv Com; pres Community Awareness Progrma Sickle Cell Anemia; Urban Coalition; vp. **HONORS/ACHIEVEMENTS:** Recipient serv award Action for Bridgeport Community & Devel 1969; volunteer award Parent Adv Com Hall Neighborhood House 1970; serv award 1970; certificateof recognition for Community Serv 1972; serv award Urban Coalition 1972; community serv award 1972; numerous other civic & serv Awards. **BUSINESS ADDRESS:** ABCD Inc, 815 Pembroke St, Bridgeport, CT 06497.

CROPP, DWIGHT SHEFFERY
School administrator. **PERSONAL:** Born Aug 05, 1939, Washington, DC; married Linda Washington; children: Allison, Christopher. **EDUCATION:** Howard U, BA & MA 1965; Yale, Post Master's 1970. **CAREER:** DC Bd Edn, exec sec; DC Pub Schs, exec asst to supt 1971; DC City Coun, spl Asst Chmn 1971; DC Pub Schs, educ 1965; US Dept of State, research analyst 1964. **ORGANIZATIONS:** Mem Am Assn Sch Adminstrn; mem Urban League, US Office of Educ fello 1969; fellow Yale Urban 1970. **MILITARY SERVICE:** AUS first lt 1961-63. **BUSINESS ADDRESS:** 415 12 St NW, Washington, DC 20004.

CROSBY, EDWARD WARREN
Educational administrator. **PERSONAL:** Born Nov 04, 1932, Cleveland, OH; son of Fred D Crosby and Marion G Naylor Crosby; married Shirley Redding, Mar 17, 1956; children: Eduard Michael, Darryl M L, Elliot Malcolm. **EDUCATION:** Kent State Univ, BA 1957, MA 1959; Univ of KA, PhD 1965. **CAREER:** Educ Resources Inst Inc E St Louis, vice pres program devel 1968; Experiment in Higher Educ SIU, dir of educ 1966-69; Inst for African Amer Affairs Kent State Univ, dir 1969-76; Univ of WA, dir Black Studies Program 1976-78; Kent State Univ, assoc prof 1969-. **ORGANIZATIONS:** Resident consult Regional Council on Intl Educ; Faculty Inst on the Black World 1970-72; consult Peat Marwick Mitchell & Co 1971-72; pres NE OH Black Studies Consortium 1974; pres OH Consortium for Black Studies 1980-; mem African Heritage Studies Assn. **HONORS/ACHIEVEMENTS:** Hon Leadership Award Omicron Delta Kappa 1976; Hon mem Alpha Kappa Mu; publ "The Black Experience, "An Anthology" 1976; published "Chronology of Notable Dates in the History of Africans in the Am & Elsewhere" 1976; publ "The Educ of Black Folk, An Historical Perspective" The Western Journal of Black Studies 1977; publ "The African Experience in Community Devel" Two Vols 1980; Your History, A Chronology of Notable Events 1988. **MILITARY SERVICE:** SCARWAF corporal 1952-54. **BUSINESS ADDRESS:** Chmn Dept Pan-African Studies, Kent StateUniv, Rm 18, Center of Pan-African Culture, Kent, OH 44242.

CROSBY, FRED MCCLELLEN
Corporate chief executive officer. **PERSONAL:** Born May 17, 1928, Cleveland, OH; son of Fred Douglas Crosby and Marion Naylor Crosby; married Phendalyne' D Tazewell, Dec 23, 1958; children: Fred C, Esq, James R, Llionicia L. **CAREER:** Crosby Furniture Co Inc, pres, chief exec officer, 1964-. **ORGANIZATIONS:** Gov appointee bd trustees OH Fair Plan Advisory Bd 1971-74; exec Order of OH Commodores 1974; advisory bd council Workman's Comp 1974-81; vice-chmn natl bd Inroads 1977-80; pres OH Furnishing Assnc 1978-83; appointee of USA to Advisory Council SBA 1978-80; mayor appointee City of CLeveland Cable Comm 1984; gov appointee State Boxing Comm 1984-87; bd dir First Natl Bank Assn; bd dir First Interncity Bank Corp; bd dir United Black Fund; CBL Economic Devel Corp; the Buckeye Exec Club of State of OH; ex bd trustee Greater Cleveland Growth Assn; bd dir Auto Club, Ohio Retail Merchants Assn; Public TV; Surveyors Telecomm; bd of trustee Cleveland Cuyahoga Port Authority; chmn Minority Economic Dev Corp; chr bd of Glenvilla YMCA; bd trustee Forest City Hospital Found; Several others. **HONORS/ACHIEVEMENTS:** Citizens Award Bel Air Civic Club 1969; Family of Year Metro Club 1969; Businessman of Day WDOK Radio 1970; Family of Year Urban League of Cleveland 1971; Outstanding Civic Leadership YMCA 1971; Outstanding Leadership YMCA; Sustaining Mem Enrollment BSA 1972; Access Dept of Commerce Publication 1972; Black Enterprises 1973; 1,000 Successful Blacks The Ebony Success Library 1974; Sojourner Truth Collection Prince George Library 1974. **MILITARY SERVICE:** AUS s/sgt 1950-52.

BUSINESS ADDRESS: President, Crosby Furniture Co Inc, 12435 St Clair Ave, Cleveland, OH 44108.

CROSBY-LANGLEY, LORETTA
Agency administrator. **PERSONAL:** Born Sep 14, 1957, Clover, SC. **EDUCATION:** Lander Coll, BS Psychology 1979; Winthrop Coll, continuing educ. **CAREER:** SC Dept of Social Servs, generalist/analyst 1982-86; Richmond County Dept of Family & Children Servs, county eligibility consultant 1986; Emory Univ, personnel generalist 1986; Greenville News-Piedmont Co, exec sec 1986-87; SC Develop Disabilities Council, program information coordinator, 1987-. **ORGANIZATIONS:** Vice Pres/Pres Lambda Lambda Chapter, Alpha Kappa Alpha 1977/78; treasurer, Pamoja Club African-Amer; mem, Psych Club Greek Council Entertainment Council review Magazine staff; participant Poetry for the People Workshop, 1981. **HONORS/ACHIEVEMENTS:** First place poetry in Lander Coll Review Literary Magazine 1979; Published poetry in review, Scribblings, The Bears Tale, News & Views Magazine, The Naiad; Published commentary in News & Views Magazine. **HOME ADDRESS:** 206A Willowbrook Dr #A, Morganton, NC 28655.

CROSLAN, JOHN ARTHUR
Marketing research manager. **PERSONAL:** Born Aug 24, 1939, Henderson, NC; married Emogene Barnes; children: John Jr, Kimberly Rignald. **EDUCATION:** NC Central Univ, BS 1962, MBA 1963. **CAREER:** NC Dept of Revenue, revenue collector 1965-67; Operation Breakthrough Inc, accountant 1967-68, asst bus mgr 1968-69, exec dir 1969-72; State Dept of Human Resources, consultant 1972-74, dir grant mgmt 1974-76, spec asst to comm 1976-. **ORGANIZATIONS:** Pres Parent-Teacher Assn 1981; pres Neighbor Watch Club 1984; mem comm NAACP 1984. **HONORS/ACHIEVEMENTS:** Outstanding Leadership NC Central Univ 1962; Distinguished Serv Chamber of Commerce 1970; Outstanding Leadership Chamber of Commerce 1980. **MILITARY SERVICE:** AUS spec 5 2 yrs. **HOME ADDRESS:** 1908 King Charles Rd, Atlanta, GA 30331.

CROSS, AUSTIN DEVON
Management consultant. **PERSONAL:** Born Jun 08, 1928, Villa Ridge, IL; son of George A Cross and Ada M Cross; married Frances J Dedeaux. **EDUCATION:** Wilberforce Univ (OH), BA 1950; John Marshall Law Schl Attended 1954. **CAREER:** Amoco Oil Co, mrg-credit & cust serv 1969-71; Amoco Oil Co, coord-minority affairs 1971-74; Standard Oil Co (Ind), sr coord-merit emply 1974-76; Standard Oil Co (Ind), consultant-employee rel 1976-85; Amoco Corp, sr consultant human resource 1985-. **ORGANIZATIONS:** Bd dir Wilberforce Univ Alumni Assoc 1969-; mem NAACP, NUL; oper comm chmn Harbor Hse Condo Assoc 1977; finance chmn Frontier Intl, Inc 1984-; pres Wilberforce Univ Alumni Assoc 1986-; bd of trust Wilberforce Univ 1986. **HONORS/ACHIEVEMENTS:** Distinguished Alumni Awd Wilberforce Alumni Assoc; Distinguished Serv Awd So IL Reunion Council; Distinguished Serv Awd Natl Alliance of Businessmen; Distinguished Serv Awd Chicago Chamber of Commerce; Distinguished Alumni Awd NAFEO; Honorary Doctor of Humanities, Wilberforce Univ 1989. **MILITARY SERVICE:** AUS sgt major 1950-52; Honor Student-Leadership Schl AUS 1950. **BUSINESS ADDRESS:** Sr Consultant Human Resources, Amoco Corp, 200 E Randolph Dr MC-3603, Chicago, IL 60601.

CROSS, BETTY JEAN
Educational administrator. **PERSONAL:** Born May 30, 1946, Osceola, AR; children: Douglas, Darrell, Victoria. **EDUCATION:** Michael Reese Hospital, 1968. **CAREER:** Osceola Nursing Home, mgr 1968-72; Nassau Cty Youth Bd, prog monitor 1976-81; Nassau Cty Med Ctr, med 1981-; Hempstead Bd of Ed, treasurer. **ORGANIZATIONS:** Treas Hempstead School Bd 1978-; mem Natl School Bd Assn 1978-; mem bd of dir Black Caucus NSBA 1980-, DK Robins Day Care Ctr 1980; mem Bd of Christian Ed Faith BC, Black & Hispanic Voters League, Hempstead Republic Club. **HONORS/ACHIEVEMENTS:** Plaque & Cert NSBA Black Caucus 1982; Cert Hempstead School Admin 1983; Awd for Outstanding Serv Hempstead PTA Council 1984; Testamonial Citizens for a Better Hempstead 1984. **HOME ADDRESS:** 14 Frazier St, Hempstead, NY 11550. **BUSINESS ADDRESS:** Treasurer, Hempstead Board of Education, 185 Peninsula Blvd, Hempstead, NY 11550.

CROSS, HAMAN, JR.
Clergyman. **PERSONAL:** Born Jan 28, 1949, River Rouge, MI; son of Haman Cross, Sr. and Malettor Cross; married Roberta Annette; children: Haman III, Gilvonna Corine, Sharryl Lanise. **EDUCATION:** Nyack Coll, 1968; Highland Park Comm, Oakland Comm Coll, 1969-71; William Tyndale Coll, BRE 1975. **CAREER:** Det's Afro-Amer Mission Inc, admin 1971-82; Here's Life Black Amer, consult 1977-83; William Tyndale Coll, head varsity basketball coach 1973-79; Christian R&D, cons, instr 1982-; Rosedale Park Bapt Church, founder, sr pastor 1982-. **ORGANIZATIONS:** Bd of dir Joy of Jesus 1983, Victory Christian School 1984; consult Taylor Univ 1985, World Christian Center 1985, Cedine Bible Mission Inc 1986; bd of dir Childrens Center of Detroit 1986; consult Justice Fellowship 1987; bd of dir Cener for Black Church 1987; bd of direc, Black Amer Response to African Crisis; bd of direc, Carver Foreign Missions; bd of direc, Detroit Afro-Amer Mission. **HONORS/ACHIEVEMENTS:** MVP, Basketball Capt of Team William Tyndale 1969-73; Honorary Citizen of El Paso TX City of El Paso 1986; author of Dating and Courtship, Christian Res and Devel, God's Honor Roll of Faith, Christian Res and Devel, The Life of Moses, Christian Res and Devel; author of videos, "Tough Talk on Love, Sex and Dating," "Parent/Teen Rltnships," and "How to Reach and Disciple Black Men.". **HOME ADDRESS:** 14017 Robson, Detroit, MI 48227. **BUSINESS ADDRESS:** Sr Pastor, Rosedale Park Bapt, 14161 Vaughan, Detroit, MI 48223.

CROSS, JACK
City official. **PERSONAL:** Born Oct 07, 1926, Bessemer, AL; married Vergie Dlee Hooks; children: Deborah, Raymond, David. **EDUCATION:** IN Univ, 1946-47; John Carroll Univ, 1950-55. **CAREER:** Price Waterhouse and Co, public acct 1951-61; Own Firm, 1961-71; exec asst adminstr 1969-71; city treasurer 1971-; all Cleveland. **ORGANIZATIONS:** Nat Assn Accts; Nat Assn Blak Accts; Black Accts Soc OH; treas YMCA; Boy Scout & United Torch Dr; dist chmn USAAC 2 yrs. **BUSINESS ADDRESS:** City Hall, Rm 116, Cleveland, OH 44114.

CROSS, JUNE VICTORIA
Journalist. **PERSONAL:** Born Jan 05, 1954, New York, NY; daughter of James Cross and Norma Booth Storch. **EDUCATION:** Harvard/Radcliffe Coll, BA 1975. **CAREER:** The Boston Globe Boston, MA, corresp 1975-76; WGBH-TV (PBS) Boston, MA, asst dir 1976-78; WGBH-TV (PBS) Boston, MA, prodn mgr 1977-78; NacNeil/Lehrer NewsHour, reporter urban reg affairs 1978-80, reporter def & natl sec 1980-84, reporter politics 1984-85, producer/corresp 1985-, producer CBS News 1987-. **ORGANIZATIONS:** Judge Electron Journalism Awards Natl Urban Coal 1984; judge Electron Journalism Awards Robt F Kennedy Meml 1983; founding bd mem Harvard-Radcliff Black Alumni Assn NY (1980) & Washington (1983); mem TransAfrica 1979-; council on foreign relations Natl Press Club; mem Natl Acad of TV Arts & Sci; mem Nat'l Assoc of Black Journalists 1988-. **HONORS/ACHIEVEMENTS:** Emmy Award Outstanding Coverage of Breaking News Story (Grenada) natl Acad of TV Arts & Scis 1983; Journalism Fellowship Carnegie-Mellon Sch of Urban/Publ Affairs 1979; Emmy nominee Outstanding Series The 1985 Defense Debate 1986; Joan S Barone Awd for Outstanding Reporting Defense Debate. **BUSINESS ADDRESS:** Producer, CBS News, 524 W 57th St, New York, NY 10019.

CROSS, WILLIAM HOWARD
Clergyman. **PERSONAL:** Born Oct 19, 1946, Cincinnati, OH. **EDUCATION:** Univ Cinn, 2 yrs; St Gregory's Sem, Ph B; St Mary's Sem, MDiv. **CAREER:** Social Justice & New Testament Theol at McNicholas High Sch, tchr 1980; Guardian Angels Ch, asso pastor; Mt St Mary's Sem, student librn 1972-73; St Jame's Cath Sch Dayton OH, religious educ 1973-4; St Joseph Ch & Archdiocess of Cinn, assoc pastor; St Joseph Cath Sch, rel educ coord. **ORGANIZATIONS:** Mem Archdiocesan Soc Action Commin; 1st degree Knights of Columbus; mem Cinn W End Task Force; Nat Office Black Catholics; Nat Black Catholic Clergy Caucus. **BUSINESS ADDRESS:** 6531 Beechmont Ave, Cincinnati, OH 45230.

CROSS, WILLIAM R.
Business executive. **PERSONAL:** Born Aug 25, 1913, Louisville, KY; married Evelyn Elizabeth Lewis; children: Shirley Fortson, Bobbye Wilhite, Sharon (Hinkle). **CAREER:** Remodeling Cntrctr, self-empl 1962-; JTS Brown & Sons Distillery, waresmn, distiller, gen man 1935-62. **ORGANIZATIONS:** Mem Mayor's Adv Bd; mem, past chrmn Bardstown Bd of Ed; past master Masonic Ldg; deacon Bapt Ch; committeeman Nelson Co Fair Bd; mem Euclid Ldg #13 F&AM; Couples Soc Clb.

CROSSE, ST. GEORGE IDRIS BRYON
Attorney, clergyman. **PERSONAL:** Born Sep 16, 1939, St Georges; son of S Winston C Crosse and Iris E Crosse; married Delois Bowman; children: Karin Vanessa, Liris Jewel Christina. **EDUCATION:** Univ of MD Eastern Shore, BSc (Magna Cum Laude) 1964; Coppin State Coll, MEd 1975; Wesley Theol Seminary, MDiv 1980; Univ of Baltimore School of Law, JD 1970. **CAREER:** Calvary United Methodist Church, sr pastor 1975-78; Lewin United Methodist Church, sr pastor 1978-80; Crosse-Henson & Assoc, pres & CEO 1979-83; St Matthew's United Methodist Church, sr pastor 1980-; US Dept of Housing & Urban Devel, special advisor for minority affairs, regional manager of Maryland 1987-. **ORGANIZATIONS:** Staff atty MD Human Relations Comm; founder, pres Soc for the Advancement of Families Everywhere 1979-85, Baltimore Coalition Against Crime 1980; natl delegate Natl Republican Convention 1980; founder MD Coalition Against Crime 1981; elected mem MD State Central Comm 1982; ordained elder Baltimore Wash Conf of United Methodist Church 1982; Maryland Housing Policy Council 1987-; Regional Planning Council 1988-. **HONORS/ACHIEVEMENTS:** Alumni Scholarship Univ of MD 1964; Scholar of the Year Omega Psi Phi Frat 1964; Special Ambassador Nation of St Kitts-Nevis 1983; Outstanding Alumnus Univ of MD Eastern Shore 1984; Father of the Year, WEBB Charities 1988; Excellence in Minority Business, Minority Contractors of Maryland 1989. **MILITARY SERVICE:** AUS spec 4 clas 6 yrs; Marksman, Good Conduct Medal 1964. **HOME ADDRESS:** 3509 Kings Point Rd, Randallstown, MD 21133. **BUSINESS ADDRESS:** Regional Mgr of Maryland, US Dept of Housing & Urban Devel, 10 N Calvert St, Baltimore, MD 21401.

CROSSLEY, CHARLES R., II
Artist, educator, businessman. **PERSONAL:** Born Oct 11, 1938, McComb, MS; married Freddie L; children: Juan Derke, Charles R. **EDUCATION:** Coronado Sch Fine Arts, grad. **CAREER:** Studio Frame Gallery, owner; Studio 38, found 1971; E County Fair, Elcajon CA, art juries 1970. **ORGANIZATIONS:** The Fine Arts Cultural Grp 1970; mem San Diego Adult Ed, Spring Valley; mem C of C 1974. **HONORS/ACHIEVEMENTS:** 1st pl Ghetto Bowl Festival 1971; Artist of Yr Award, Fine Arts Culture Grp 1972. **MILITARY SERVICE:** USN 1956-58. **BUSINESS ADDRESS:** 711 S 38 St, San Diego, CA 92113.

CROSSLEY, FRANK ALPHONSO
Consulting engineer. **PERSONAL:** Born Feb 19, 1925, Chicago, IL; son of Joseph Buddie Crossley and Rosa Lee Brefford Crossley; married Elaine J Sherman, Nov 23, 1950; children: Desne Adrienne Crossley Murdoch. **EDUCATION:** IL Inst of Tech, BS ChE Dean's List 1945; IL Inst of Tech, MS PhD, MetE 1947, 1950. **CAREER:** TN A&I State U, prof dept head 1950-52; IIT Research Inst, sr scientist 1952-66; Lockheed Palo Alto Resch Lbtry, sr mem 1966-74; Lockheed Missiles & Space Co, dept mgr 1974-79; Lockheed Missiles & Space Co, cnltg engr 1979-86; Aerojet Propulsion Rsch Inst, rsch dir propulsion matls 1986-87; Gen Corp Aerojet Tech Systems, dir materials applications 1987-. **ORGANIZATIONS:** Chrmn Titanium comm The Metallurgical Soc -AIME 1974-75; mem matls Comm Am Inst of Aero & Astro 1979-81; mem Nat'l Materials Advsry Brd Ad Hoc Comm on Welding High Strength Structures 1972-74. **HONORS/ACHIEVEMENTS:** Patentee Transage Titanuim Alloys 1976; Flw Am Socty for Metals 1978-; articles 54 published in various technical jnls 1951-86; patents 7 issued 1957-83; prof serv Northern CA Coun of Black Prof Engrs 1978. **MILITARY SERVICE:** UNSR lt jg Victory Ribbon WW II Am Theater Asiatic-Pacific 1944-54. **BUSINESS ADDRESS:** Director, Materials Applications, Gen Corp Aerojet Tech Systems, PO Box 13222, 9935/2019A2, Sacramento, CA 95813.

CROSSLIN, EVELYN STOCKING
Physician. **PERSONAL:** Born Feb 28, 1919, Daytona Beach, FL; married Neill Orlanda; children: Marjorie C, Neill O. **EDUCATION:** Barber Scotia Coll, Concord NC, 1938; Fisk U, AB 1940; Meharry Med Coll, Nashville, MD 1944; Hahnemann Hosp, Scranton PA, intrnshp 1944. **CAREER:** Daytona Beach FL, md 1944-. **ORGANIZATIONS:** Mem FL Acad of Family Phys; mdm Volusian Co Med Soc; mem FL Acad of Med; mem Nat Med Assn; sec, mem Silver Leaf Charity Clb; mem Mary Mahoney Nrs Clb; mem Alpha Kappa Alpha Sor. **BUSINESS ADDRESS:** 714 Second Ave, Daytona Beach, FL 32014.

CROUCH, ANDRAE
Gospel singer/composer/musician. **PERSONAL:** Born Jul 01, 1942, Pacoima, CA. **CAREER:** Singing gospel since age of 12; youth dir Father's Church age of 15; has recorded over one dozen gospel albums; organizer/leader The Disciples gospel group 1968-. **HONORS/ACHIEVEMENTS:** Won 5 Grammys and numerous other awds & honors; Gold Record "Jesus is the Answer"; author "Through It All" 1974; composer numerous songs; named Soul Gospel Artist of 1975 and 1977 Billboard Magazine; Grammy Awd for Best Soul Gospel Performance 1984.

CROUCHETT, LAWRENCE PAUL
Executive director, historical society. **PERSONAL:** Born Mar 18, 1922, Beaumont, TX; married Lorraine Jacobs; children: Dennis P Handis, Diane L Saafir. **EDUCATION:** Tillotson Coll, AB 1949; Univ of CA-Berkeley, MA 1969, EdD 1973. **CAREER:** Diablo Valley Coll CA, history prof 1962-68, dean of sp prog 1968-83; Downey Place Publishing House Inc, pres/publisher 1983-88; Northern CA Center for Afro-American History and Life, Exec Dir, Oakland CA. **ORGANIZATIONS:** Mem Sigma Pi Phi Frat 1972-; contributing editor The Boule Journal Sigma Pi Phi 1980-; project dir Visions Toward Tomorrow, The History of the East Bay (CA) Afro-Amer Comm. **HONORS/ACHIEVEMENTS:** Danforth Fellow Univ of CA-Berkeley; William Byron Rumford, The Life and Public Service Career of a California Legislator 1984. **MILITARY SERVICE:** AUS corpl 1941-46; Good Conduct Medal, Two Bronze Stars. **BUSINESS ADDRESS:** President/Publisher, Downey Place Publishing House, PO Box 1352, El Cerrito, CA 94530.

CROUTHER, BETTY JEAN
Educator. **PERSONAL:** Born Mar 02, 1950, Carthage, MS; daughter of Lee M Crouther and Eugene Garner Crouther; divorced; children: Velsie Dione Pate. **EDUCATION:** Jackson State Univ, BS (Summa Cum Laude) 1972; Univ of MS, MFA 1975; Univ of MO Columbia, PhD 1985. **CAREER:** Lincoln Univ, asst prof of art 1978-80; Jackson State Univ, asst prof of art 1980-83; Univ of MS, asst prof of art & art history 1983-. **ORGANIZATIONS:** Mem Natl Art Educ Assn, Southeastern College Art Conf, MS Art Educ Assn; assoc Museum Associates Univ of MO Columbia; mem, Kappa Pi International Honorary Art Fraternity 1988-. **HONORS/ACHIEVEMENTS:** Juried exhibition "Images '84" The Mississippi Pavilion, Louisiana World Exposition New Orleans 1984; Superior Graduate Achievement Awd Univ of MO 1985; J Paul Getty Postdoctoral Fellowship Stanford Univ 1986; contributor exhibition catalogue "Dean Cornwell, Painter As Illustrator," Museum of Art and Archaeology Univ of MO-Columbia 1978; co-moderator with Dr Joanne V Hawks in enrichment program "Uniting Generations Together/The Search for Meaning," 1984; author of "Deciphering the Mississippi River Iconography of Frederick Oakes Sylvester," MUSE, vol20, pp 81-9, 1986; "Black American Art in the South Before 1900," Smithsonian Institution, 1988; reader for Jacob K Javit's Fellowship Fund, U S Department of Education 1989. **BUSINESS ADDRESS:** Asst Prof of Art & Art History, University of Mississippi, Art Dept, University, MS 38677.

CROUTHER, BETTY M.
Educator. **PERSONAL:** Born Jun 05, 1931, St Joseph, MO; married Melvin Jr; children: Lou-Ann. **EDUCATION:** Lincoln U, BA 1952; NY U, MA 1953. **CAREER:** Cleveland Bd of Educ, 5th grade enrichment teacher 1985; Moses Cleveland School, teacher 1963-77; Garfield School, Columbus OH, 1961-63; Blewett School, St Louis, 1956-61; AR Baptist Coll, Little Rock AR, 1954-56; Newport School, 1954; Stephens School, Asheville, 1953-54. **ORGANIZATIONS:** Chmn for vars comm,life mem-past pres Nat Assn Negro B&PW Clbs, Inc; past pres Nat Council Negro Women; mem Delta Sigma Theta; Nat Bus League;NOW Cuyahoga Co Coalition; Alpha Wives. **HONORS/ACHIEVEMENTS:** Who's Who in Am Women 1972-73; Woman of Yr, Bapt Ch 1972; Ollie C Porter Ldrshp Award 1973; Outstndng Elem Tchr of Am 1974; Cleveland Sr Clb Apprec Award 1976. **BUSINESS ADDRESS:** Moses Cleaveland Sch, 4092 E 146 St, Cleveland, OH 44128.

CROUTHER, MELVIN S., JR.
Executive director. **PERSONAL:** Born Nov 22, 1926, Little Rock, AR; married Betty Madison; children: Lou-Ann. **EDUCATION:** Lincoln Univ, BS; Warren Brown Sch Washington Univ, MSW 1960. **CAREER:** Cleveland Reg Ofc, reg dir 1962-66; Neighborhood Opportunity Cntr, assoc dir 1966-67, dir 1967-68; Cuyahoga Hills Boys Sch, dep supt 1968-71, supt 1971-74; Ohio Youth Commn Review Bd, chmn & chief Institutional Serv 1974-; Council for Econ Opportunities Greater Cleveland, exec dir 1979-; Cuyahoga County Dept Human Svcs, chief, intake Child Abuse & Neglect. **ORGANIZATIONS:** Pres Warrensville Kiwanis 1975; life mem NAACP; life mem Alpha Phi Alpha; mem Lee Rd Bapt Ch; Nat Assn Soc Wrkrs; Acad Certified Soc Wrkrs; mem Nat Comm Action Agency Exec Dirs Assn; mem OH Assn CAA; Lincoln Univ Alumni; Prince Hall Mason 32 degrees Knights Temp; Shriner; Eastern Star; OH Cts & Correction Assn; Nat Council Crime & Delinq; Police Athletic League. **HONORS/ACHIEVEMENTS:** Highest Drama Award LU 1951; developed 1st state subsidized home for delinquent youth 1964; selective serv sys 1971-74; Dist Serv Award Grand Jury Assn 1973; Spl Recognition Award Case Western Res Medicine-Law Acad 1973. **MILITARY SERVICE:** USMC 1945-46. **BUSINESS ADDRESS:** Chief Intake Child Abuse & Neg, Cuyahoga County Dept Human Serv, 1350 W 3rd St, Cleveland, OH 44113.

CROW, HIAWATHA MOORE
Educator, elected official. **PERSONAL:** Born Jul 19, 1907, Columbia, MO; daughter of Rev Curtis Leon Moore (deceased) and Rosie Elizabeth Johnson Moore (deceased); married James H Crow (deceased). **EDUCATION:** Lincoln Univ, Teachers Cert 1928; Culver-Stockton Coll, BS Ed 1960; Northeast MO State Univ, MA Elem School Admin 1966. **CAREER:** Douglass Jr HS, teacher eng & soc studies 1958-60; Monroe City Elem School, teacher, principal 1960-66; Monroe City HS, Jr HS, teacher lang arts 1966-73; Marion Cty In-Home Svc, coord 1979-83; Hannibal Sr Ctr, coord 1983-84; City Council Hannibal, councilwoman ward 6, re-elected April 7 1987 (4 yr term). **ORGANIZATIONS:** Historian, coord Restoration Proj 8th & Ctr St 1977-; sec asst to rsvp dir RSVP 1978-80; pres Hannibal Amer Assoc of Univ Women 1979-81; Marion-Ralls Area Retired Teachers Unit 1979-81; mem Univ of MO Extension Council 1980-; 6th ward councilwoman, mem of fin & sts comm Hannibal City Council 1983-88; chairman Political Action Comm Hannibal NAACP 1984-87; served on Sts & Alleys Commn 1983-89, adv bd Hannibal Industrial Council, Affirmative Action Ad Hoc Comm Fire Bd 1983-88; mem vice pres MO Div AAUW; president NEMO Re Dist 1986-88; mem of nominating committee South West Central Region American Assn of Univ Women 1987-89; bd mem appointed to bd of North East MO Area on Aging 1988; 6th Ward Councilwoman Hannibal City Council, Finance Committee, Bd of Public Works, Advisory Committee Chairman 1989. **HONORS/ACHIEVEMENTS:** Golden Cert of Recognition Missionary Baptist Convention of MO 1979; Citation for Untiring Serv to the Wellbeing of Retired Persons Natl Retired Teachers Assoc 1981; Recognition of Significant Serv a Named Gift to Amer Fellowships Amer Assoc of Univ Women 1981; 2nd Named Gift by MO State Div Amer Assn of Univ Women 1983-84; Spec Recognition of Women of Distinct by MO Div AAUW 1984; Plaque "Another Voting Woman" in apprec for outstanding serv as Regional Dir Coord by MO Women's Vote Project 1984; Cert of Merit The James T Brown President Award for Serv to the Community of Hannibal by Hannibal, MO Branch NAACP; 2nd Place in Recogn of Outstanding Public Serv Activity and Use of the Tools of Communication Resulting in Signif Contrib to the Community and Enhanced Publ Awareness of AAUW 1985; name honored Amer Assoc of Univ Women Educ Foundation 1985-86. **BUSINESS ADDRESS:** Councilwoman, City Hall, 4th & Broadway, Hannibal, MO 63401.

CROWDER, RANDOLPH CHANNING (SUGAR BEAR)
Professional athlete. **PERSONAL:** Born Nov 22, 1926, Little Rock, AR; married Betty Madison; children: Dacha. **EDUCATION:** Lincoln U, BS; Warren Brown Sch, MSW, Washington U, St Louis MO, Attend 1960; NY U, MEd; Indiana U, cand PhD 1985. **CAREER:** Council for Econ Opportunities Gr Cleveland, exec dir 1979-; OH Youth Commn & Review Bd, chmn; Institutional Svcs, asst chief 1974-; Cuyahoga-Hills Boys Sch, supt 1971-74, dep supt 1968-71; Opportunity Cntr, Cleveland, dir 1967-68, assoc dir 1966-67; Cleveland Reg Off, reg dir 1962-66. **ORGANIZATIONS:** Life mem NAACP; Alpha Phi Alpha; mem Lee Rd Bapt Ch; Nat Assn Soc Wrkrs; Acad Cert Soc Wrkrs; mem Nat Comm Action Agency Exec Dirs Assn; mem OH Assn CAA; Lincoln Univ Alumni; 32 deg Prince Hall Mason; Knights Temp; Shriner; Eastern Star; OH Cts & Correction Assn; pres Nat Cnc Crime & Delqncy; pres Warrensville Kiwanis 1975; Police Ath League; dev 1st st subsidized home for delqunt youth 1964. **HONORS/ACHIEVEMENTS:** Highest Drama Award, LU 1951; Dist Serv Award, Grand Jury Assn 1973; Spl Recog Award, Case Western Res, Med-Law Acad 1973; Sel Srv Sys 1971-74. **MILITARY SERVICE:** USMC 1945-46. **BUSINESS ADDRESS:** Tampa Bay Buccaneers, 1 Buccaneer Place, Tampa, FL 33607.

CROWE-UNDERWOOD, HOLLIS JONETTA
Physician. **PERSONAL:** Born Oct 29, 1957, Chicago, IL; married Paul Lester Underwood Jr MD. **EDUCATION:** Attended, Univ of MD College Park 1975-79; Howard Univ Coll of Medicine, MD 1983. **CAREER:** Mayo Graduate Sch of Medicine, resident internal medicine 1983-86, special clinical fellow 1986-87. **ORGANIZATIONS:** Mem Natl Medical Assoc 1983; co-founder Mayo Minority Fellows Assoc 1984; medical consultant Sweet Sensations Chocolate Co 1984-; assoc Amer Coll of Physicians 1985-; mem Alpha Kappa Alpha Sor Inc, Amer Tennis Assoc, Ebon Sisters Civic Org of Rochester. **HONORS/ACHIEVEMENTS:** Diplomate Natl Bd of Medical Examiners 1983, Amer Bd of Internal Medicine 1987. **BUSINESS ADDRESS:** Special Clinical Fellow, Mayo Graduate Sch of Medicine, Mayo Clinic, Rochester, MN 55904.

CROWELL, BERNARD G.
Educator/executive. **PERSONAL:** Born Nov 03, 1930, Chickasha, OK; married Virginia M; children: Bernard Jr, Christopher L. **EDUCATION:** Langston Univ, BS 1953; Univ of OR, MS 1958; OK State Univ, EdD 1970. **CAREER:** Langston Univ, exec asst to the pres 1970-75; dir of inst rsch 1973-75, inst rsch consortium 1973-75, dir interdiscip prog coord coll & univ 1973-74; dir for admissions & records 1973-75; TN State Univ, vice pres for academic affairs 1975-84, exec admin for intl affairs 1984-. **ORGANIZATIONS:** Mem President's Council TN State Univ 1975-; chmn Satisfactory Progress Comm TN State Univ 1985-; Faculty Athletics Rep TN State Univ 1986-; pres Optimist Club 1986-. **HONORS/ACHIEVEMENTS:** Boss of the Year TN State Univ Secretaries Assn 1977; Phi Beta Lambda Awd 1981; Disting Service Awd TN State Univ 1984; Resolution/Faculty Senate TN State Univ 1984. **HOME ADDRESS:** 861 Stirrup Dr, Nashville, TN 37221. **BUSINESS ADDRESS:** Exec Admin for Internl Afrs, Tennessee State University, 3500 John A Merritt Blvd, Nashville, TN 37203.

CROWELL-MOUSTAFA, JULIA J.
Educator, importer of Egyptian artifacts. **PERSONAL:** Born Oct 08, 1923, Philadelphia, PA; daughter of Rev James Lincoln Lewis and Josephine Gaines; married Moustafa Saad Moustafa, Oct 23, 1985. **EDUCATION:** Cheyney State Coll, BS; Univ of MD, MEd; Wayne State Univ, Specialist in Admin. **CAREER:** MI Educ Assn, professional; traveler, importer of Egyptian artifacts. **ORGANIZATIONS:** First black sec & pres, Area Six Assn Classroom Teachers, 1966, 1967; First black treasurer, president-elect, Region Six MEA, 1968-73; member, evaluating team, Natl Council for Accreditation of Teacher Educ, 1971-74; first woman elected to Clintondale Board of Educ, 1969-73; reg dir, Great Lakes Region Zeta Phi Beta Sorority Inc, 1974; Youth Serv Commn Clinton Township, 1974; sec, pres, Area D Council Urban Renewal; elder deacon, elder commr gen assembly, Peace United Presbyterian Church; admin comm implementing reorganization Detroit Presbyterian; member, MI Acad of Professional Educ; MEA-NEA-R; retired volunteer, Amer Cancer Soc WICS; bd of dir, Selective Serv Bd. **HONORS/ACHIEVEMENTS:** Teacher of the Year, 1969; Woman of Year, 1970; Beta Omicron Zeta Chap Zeta Phi Beta Sponsorship Awdar, 1972.

CRUISE, NKECHIELA **See BAT NAPHTALI, ASHIRAH SHOLOMIS**

CRUISE, WARREN MICHAEL
Attorney. **PERSONAL:** Born Jun 03, 1939, Baltimore, MD; divorced; children: Enid, Wesley. **EDUCATION:** Morgan St U, AB 1963; Howard Univ Law Sch, JD 1970. **CAREER:** Nat Ed Assn, legal cnsl 1985; Nghbrhd Legal Srv Prg, staff atty. **ORGANIZATIONS:** Vp, bd of dir NEA Credit Union; mem Retirement Bd, NEA Kappa Alpha Psi Frat; Phi Alpha; Delta Law Frat; NAACP; Nat Bar Assn; Conf of BlackLwyrs; Am Bar Assn. **HONORS/ACHIEVEMENTS:** MJ Naylor Meml Award; high acad achvmt in field of Philosophy. **BUSINESS ADDRESS:** 1201 16th St NW, Washington, DC 20036.

CRUM, ALBERT B.
Physician, psychiatrist. **PERSONAL:** Born Nov 17, 1931. **EDUCATION:** Univ of Redlands, CA, 1973; Harvard Med Sch, MD 1957; Columbia Univ Div, Bellevue Hosp, internshp 1957-58; Psychiatric Inst of Columbia Presb Med Ctr, NYC, residency. **CAREER:** Am Inst of Addictive Disorders, chief psychiat cons; Human Behavior Found, med dir; Human & Behavior Pub Co, gen ed. **ORGANIZATIONS:** Mem AMA; Kings Co Med Soc; Delta Alpha Honor Soc; NY St Med Soc; World Med Assn; Duke Hall Camp Harvard Med Soc chrmn; Harvard Clb of NYC; mem Acad of Med Studies, MENSA; Kappa Alpha Psi; bd dirUniv

of Redlands Sci Assoc Hon DSc, Redlands CA 1974. **HONORS/ACHIEVEMENTS:** Brooklyn Young Man of the Yr 1966; diplomat Nat Bd of Med Exam; diplomat Pan Am Med Assn. **MILITARY SERVICE:** USAF capt.

CRUMP, ARTHEL EUGENE
Elected official, attorney. **PERSONAL:** Born Oct 19, 1947, New York, NY; son of Watler E and Mary L; married Linda Rose Cooke; children: Kathryn Rose, Eric Eugene. **EDUCATION:** NE Wesleyan Univ, 1965-67; Univ of NE Lincoln, BA 1973; Univ of NE College of Law, JD 1976. **CAREER:** Legal Serv of Southeast NE, attorney 1976-82; Gov Robert Kerrey NE, legal counsel 1983-85; Dept of Justice, deputy atty general. **ORGANIZATIONS:** Mem NE State Bar Assn House of Delegates, Natl Assn of Atty Generals, Natl Gov's Assn, Educ Comm of the States; bd dirs Univ of NE Gymnastic Booster Club, Family Serv Assn of Lincoln, United Way of Lincoln & Lancaster Cos, Theater Arts for Youth, Malone Comm Ctr, Lincoln Comm Playhouse, Malone Headstart Program, Coalition of Landlords & Tenants; panel mem NE Arts Council; mem Touring Artists' Progs, Minority Arts Adv Comm, NAACP, NE Civil Liberties Union, Coalition of Black Men, Univ of NE Booster Club Womens' Athletics; bd of trust NE Wesleyan Univ; adv comm Lincoln Public Schools Gifted Children, Lancaster Co Child Care, NE Leg Sub-Comm Revision of Licensing Regulations for Child Care Insts, Lincoln Public Schools Multi-Cultural Educ; mem Lancaster Co ad hoc comm reorganization of cowelfare adv comms, Malone Area Citizens Council, Lincoln Public Schools Evaluation of Student Health Educ Project, State Dept of Public Welfare Comm to Review Daycare Center Licensing Standards. **HONORS/ACHIEVEMENTS:** Silver Key Award Law Student Div/Amer Bar Assn; NE Law College Scholarship; Kelso Morgan Scholarship; Council on Legal Educ Opportunity Stipend. **MILITARY SERVICE:** AUS sgt 1967-70; Natl Defense Medal; Good Conduct Medal; Armed Forces Expeditionary Medal. **BUSINESS ADDRESS:** Deputy Attorney General, Department of Justice, 2115 State Capitol, Lincoln, NE 68509.

CRUMP, NATHANIEL L., SR.
Engineer. **PERSONAL:** Born Jul 18, 1920, Little Rock, AR; married Ruby M Chappell; children: N Lloyd Jr. **EDUCATION:** Lincoln Univ, BS Chem 1948. **CAREER:** McDonnell Douglas Aerospace Co, space eng; Mercury, Gemini, Apollo, Sky Lab Shuttle Progs, unit chief 1962-; St Louis Child's Hosp, Cardiol Sec, res asst 1961-62; Hanley Ind, & Pyrotechnics & Explo Chem, proj eng 1959-61; Universal Match R & D Arma Div, lab asst, proj eng 1952-59; DuGood Micro-analytical Lab, St L, micro-analyst 1948-52. **ORGANIZATIONS:** Mem Am Chem Soc; mem Soc Aerospace Mtrls & Process Eng; Am Assn Contam Cont Kappa Alpha Psi Frat; bd mem Coalition for the Environ; vice pres St L Co Chap, Civitan Interntl Civic Org; srvd on 12 man adv com to Vice Pres Humphrey, "Youth Motivation" 1965-68; apptd to bd of Human Rel of Univ City, MO 1972-78. **HONORS/ACHIEVEMENTS:** Author papers on Organic Microanaly, Analytical Chem, Space Sys Contam Cont, Aircraft Hyd Sys Clean Cntrl. **MILITARY SERVICE:** Res 1942-43; Act Duty 1943-46. **BUSINESS ADDRESS:** Unit Chief, McDonnell-Douglas, PO Box 516, St Louis, MO 63166.

CRUMP, WILBERT S.
Business executive. **PERSONAL:** Born in Portsmouth, VA; married Phyllis Lorraine Archer; children: Deborah D, David P. **EDUCATION:** Howard Univ Wash DC, BA (Cum Laude) 1965. **CAREER:** Pfizer Inc NY, suprv professional placement 1971-73; CUNY LaGuardia Coll, adj lecturer 1972-75; Allied Signal Inc, mgr critical manpower admin 1973-76; Natl Urban League, lecturer, black exec exchange prog 1975-; Allied Signal Inc, dir eeo 1976-. **ORGANIZATIONS:** Mem Alpha Phi Alpha, NAACP, Edges Group Inc; various business/professional org. **HONORS/ACHIEVEMENTS:** Full Scholarship Howard Univ; Pres Cup for Outstanding DMG Grad Sr Howard Univ 1965; Black Achiever in Industry Awd 1976; pub article "Executive Accountability" 1988. **MILITARY SERVICE:** AUS capt 1965-70; Bronze Star Medal, Army Commendation Medal. **BUSINESS ADDRESS:** Business Exec, Allied Corp, Box 2245R, Morristown, NJ 07960.

CRUMP, WILLIAM L.
Educator. **PERSONAL:** Born Jul 21, 1920, Enid, OK; divorced; children: Debra C, Utley III, Lisa Kai, Jacquelyn Denise. **EDUCATION:** Lincoln U, BS 1942; Northwestern U, MA 1946; Northwestern U, PhD 1949. **CAREER:** School of Business & Public Management, Univ of Washington DC, dean; MD State Coll, prof, chmn business admin; TN A&I Univ Div of Business, prof, dir; KY St Coll Dept of Business, chmn; Central State Univ Div of Busubess, chmn; NASA, mgmt cons. **ORGANIZATIONS:** Bd chmn Urban Bus Educ Assn; bd mem DC Municipal Rsrch Bur; vice pres Intl Assn of Black Bus Educators; Kappa Alpha Psi; Delta Pi Epsilon; Pi Omega Pi; Phi Delta Kappa. **HONORS/ACHIEVEMENTS:** Ford Found Fellow INUniv 1960; Elder Watson Diggs Award Kapp Alpha Psi 1972; coauthor The Story of Kappa Alph Psi. **MILITARY SERVICE:** Armed forces 1942-45. **BUSINESS ADDRESS:** Univ of District of Columbia, 4200 Connecticut Ave, NW, Washington, DC 20008.

CRUMP-MCCOY, ROBBIE L.
Public relations director. **PERSONAL:** Born May 10, 1921, Aberdeen, MS. **EDUCATION:** Tucker's Business Coll; Rust Coll; Univ of Missouri, Ext; Lewis Business Coll; Wayne State Univ; Howard Univ, summer course Black Religion Writing. **CAREER:** Crump-McCoy & Assocs, public relations director. **ORGANIZATIONS:** Mem Natl Religion Newswriters Assc; Todd-Phillip Home for Boys; supervisor Payne-Pulliam Sch of Trade; life mem NAACP; press chmn Bapt Conv; mem Warren Ave Bapt Ch; Natl Bapt Staffer; mem, press dir Women's Aux Natl Baptist Convention USA Inc. **HONORS/ACHIEVEMENTS:** Recipient of 73 awards. **BUSINESS ADDRESS:** Public Relations Dir, Crump-McCoy & Assocs, PO Box 32352, Detroit, MI 48232.

CRUSE, CHARLES PLUMMER
Law enforcement. **PERSONAL:** Born Jan 12, 1914, Lexington, KY; married Mary Ann; children: Jackie, Ruth, Tommy, Chris. **EDUCATION:** Univ of KY, Counterfeiting 1946. **CAREER:** Lexington Police Dept, policeman 1942-57; City of Lexington, dep constable 1957-81, constable 1981-85. **BUSINESS ADDRESS:** Constable Dist 1, City of Lexington, 431 S Broadway Ste 122, Lexington, KY 40508.

CRUSE, HAROLD WRIGHT
Educator. **PERSONAL:** Born Mar 08, 1916, Petersburg, VA. **CAREER:** Prof emeritus, Univ of MI History/Afro-Amer Studies. **ORGANIZATIONS:** Corr mem European Acad of Arts, Sciences, & Humanities. **MILITARY SERVICE:** AUS quatermaster staff sgt 1941-45. **BUSINESS ADDRESS:** Professor Emeritus of History, Univ of MI, Dept of History, Univ of MI, Ann Arbor, MI 48109.

CRUTCHER, BETTY NEAL
Administrator/education. **PERSONAL:** Born Nov 21, 1949, Tuskegee, AL; married Ronald Andrew Crutcher; children: Sara Elizabeth Neal. **EDUCATION:** Tuskegee Inst, BS 1971; Univ of MI, MPH 1973. **CAREER:** Univ of NC at Greensboro, asst to the chancellor 1980-85; Guilford Coll, asst to the pres 1985-. **ORGANIZATIONS:** Bd dirs Humana Hospital 1981-85; bd dirs Altrusa Intl 1984-85; mem of arts and letters comm Delta Sigma Theta Sor 1972-; bd dirs Childen's Home Soc 1986-. **HONORS/ACHIEVEMENTS:** Outstanding Serv Natl Council for Negro Women 1974-79; Alumni Leadership Greensboro 1981-; Loaned Executive United Way 1984-85; Advocate for Black Teenage Mothers Junior League of Greensboro 1986-. **BUSINESS ADDRESS:** Asst to the President, Guilford College, 5800 W Friendly Ave, Greensboro, NC 27410.

CRUTCHER, EDWARD TORRENCE
Business executive. **PERSONAL:** Born Dec 02, 1920, Hot Springs, AR; married Ina M; children: R Marcelletta. **EDUCATION:** Friends U, BA 1950; Wichita St, post-grad 1950-51. **CAREER:** Dayton Urban Leag, exec dir 1973-; Model Cities Prog, adm 1969-72; Dayton Human Rel Spec, 1967-69; Dayton Urban Leag, hlth & wlfr dir 1965-67; Cuyahogan Co, probatn Off 1956-65; Cuyahoga Co Welfare Dept, casewrkr 1956. **ORGANIZATIONS:** Mem Dayton View, Optimist Clb. **HONORS/ACHIEVEMENTS:** Gov Award for Comm Action 1974; City Beaut Award, Dayton 1967; estbld Dayton Urban Leag Youth Form & Eco Dir Empl Dept; mem Dayton Hm Town Plan; writer, ed Black Nwspr. **MILITARY SERVICE:** AUS 1941-45.

CRUTCHER, RONALD ANDREW
Educator. **PERSONAL:** Born Feb 27, 1947, Cincinnati, OH; son of Andrew Crutcher and Burdella Crutcher; married Betty Joy Neal; children: Sara Elizabeth. **EDUCATION:** Miami Univ, BA, BM 1969 (Cum Laude); Yale Univ, MMA 1972; State Acad of Music (Frankfort W Germany), Diploma 1976; Yale Univ, DMA (with distinction) 1979. **CAREER:** Bonn (W Germany) School of Music, cello instructor 1976-79; Wittenberg Univ, asst prof 1977-79; UNC Greensboro, asst prof 1979-83, assoc coord of string area 1983-88. **ORGANIZATIONS:** Chmn Orchestra Greensboro Symphony Comm and Assoc Principal Cellist 1980-86; bd of dirs Greensboro Symphony Soc 1980-84; consultant NC Arts Council 1981-; bd dirs Amer Cello Comm Council 1982-88; founder and pres Carolina Cello Club 1983-88; mem Guilford Coll Bd of Visitors 1983-88; consultant Natl Endowment for the Arts 1986-; bd of dirs Greensboro Cerebral Palsy Assn 1986-; pres elect NC Amer String Teachers Assn 1986-88; bd of dirs, Eastern Music Festival 1988-; bd of dirs, United Arts Council of Greensboro 1988-. **HONORS/ACHIEVEMENTS:** Woodrow Wilson Fellow 1969; Phi Beta Kappa; Ford Foundation Fellowship 1969-72; Fulbright Fellow 1972-74; Outstanding Serv to Strings Awd NC Amer String Teachers Assoc 1983; Pi Kappa Lambda; Omicron Delta Kappa; Danforth Fellowship Nominee, Univ of Miami 1969. **HOME ADDRESS:** 1402 McDowell Dr, Greensboro, NC 27408. **BUSINESS ADDRESS:** Associate Vice Chancellor for Academic Affairs, University of North Carolina at Greensboro, 201 Mossman Building, Greensboro, NC 27408-5219.

CRUTCHFIELD, SUSAN ELLIS
Medical administration. **PERSONAL:** Born Jul 29, 1940, Charleston, WV; married Robert F Mitsch; children: Charles, Carleton, Christopher, Bobby Mitsch. **EDUCATION:** Univ of MN, BA 1960, BS 1960, MD 1963. **CAREER:** Lexington Clinic, physician private practice 1969-72; Prudential Ins Co, assoc med dir 1972-78, med dir 1978-80, vice-pres medical 1980-. **ORGANIZATIONS:** Bd of directors Amer Heart Assn Minneapolis Brnch; bd of directors Twin Cities Opportunities Industry Center 1982; faculty Bd of Life Ins Medical Directors 1985; chair bd of directors Univ of MN Med School Alumni Assn 1985-86. **HONORS/ACHIEVEMENTS:** Bd Certified in Family Practice 1978; Bd Certified in Insurance Medicine 1979/1985. **BUSINESS ADDRESS:** Vice President-Medical Serv, Prudential Ins Co of Amer, 3701 Wayzata Blvd, PO Box 1143, Minneapolis, MN 55440.

CRUTCHFIELD-BAKER, VERDENIA
Financial administrator. **PERSONAL:** Born Jul 27, 1958, Sylvester, GA; married Joe Thomas Baker. **EDUCATION:** FL State Univ, BS 1976-79, MSPA 1981-82. **CAREER:** Health and Rehabilitative Svcs, counselor; School Bd St Lucie Co, teacher 1980; Dept of Labor Employment Security, interviewer 1982; Broward Cty Budget Office, budget analyst. **ORGANIZATIONS:** Mem NAACP 1977-79; mem Delta Sigma Theta 1977-; mem Amer Soc of Public Admin 1981-; mem Natl Forum of Black Public Admin 1983-. **HONORS/ACHIEVEMENTS:** Service Awd Delta Sigma Theta 1981; Outstanding Young Women of America 1982; lst Black budget analyst Broward Cty Govt. **BUSINESS ADDRESS:** Budget Analyst, Broward County Budget Office, 115 S Andrews Ave, Fort Lauderdale, FL 33313.

CRUTHIRD, J. ROBERT LEE
Educator. **PERSONAL:** Born Dec 10, 1944, LeFlore Cty, MS; son of Harvie Cruthird and Mary Florence Black Cruthird; divorced; children: Robert Lee Jr. **EDUCATION:** Univ of IL, BA Sociology 1973, MA Sociology 1976; Chicago State Univ, 1982; Critical Thinking and Acculturation Inst Univ of Chicago, attended 1986; Univ of Wisconsin at Madison summer 1983. **CAREER:** IL Dept of Corrections, correctional counselor 1977-78; Kennedy-King Coll, dir institutional rsch 1982, asst prof of sociology 1978-; Mayor's Summer Youth Employment Prog City Colls of Chicago, site coord 1984-86; KKC, Title III basic skills develop 1985-86; City Colls of Chicago, academic support serv coord 1986-87; City Colls of Chicago, coord of coll advisement project 1987; City Colleges of Chicago Assoc. Prof. of Sociology 1987; Asst. Director MSYEP - CCC 1987-1989. **ORGANIZATIONS:** Mem Amer Sociological Assn; mem Assn for Institutional Rsch; mem Assn for the Study of the Life and History of Afro-American; consultant Educational Mgmt Assocs 1981-82; sponsor Phi Theta Kappa 1982-; life mem UIC Alumni Assoc; mem Natl Assoc for Develop Educ, Alpha Phi Alpha Frat Inc. **HONORS/ACHIEVEMENTS:** Fellowship Crime and Delinquency Rsch Training 1976; fellowship Natl Endowment for the Humanities 1983; visiting scholar Univ of WI 1983; Hall of Honors IL Phi Theta Kappa 1984, 1988, 1989; IL Phi Theta Kappa Hall of Honors 1986; "Black Rural-Urban Migration" ERIC 1984; "Remedial/Developmental In-

structions" ERIC 1987. **MILITARY SERVICE:** AUS specialist E4 2 yrs; Good Conduct medal Letter of Commendation 1967. **HOME ADDRESS:** 259 E. 107th Street, Chicago, IL 60628. **BUSINESS ADDRESS:** Asst Prof of Sociology, Kennedy-King College, 6800 S Wentworth Ave, Chicago, IL 60621.

CRUZ, EMILIO
Artist, poet. **PERSONAL:** Born Mar 15, 1938, New York, NY. **EDUCATION:** Marshall Professional School of Art Inst of Chicago, 1970-. **CAREER:** Ox-Bow, visiting artist 1973; Metro Educ Council of Arts, artist 1969; S Bronx Multi-Purpose Educ Serv, teacher 1967-68; Ramblerny School for Performing Arts 1967. **ORGANIZATIONS:** Mem Coll Art Assn; Am Assn of Univ Prof; IL Arts Cncl 1974-75; Nat Soc of Liter & Arts; lectr Univ of MO 1969; Cooper Union 1966; Washington Univ 1969; Webster Coll 1969; Lake Forest Coll 1972; Cornell Univ 1972; consult Coll Art Assn Meeting 1973; Coll of Dayton Art Inst 1974; Coll Art Assn Meeting 1974; Hawthorne Art Fest 1974; Sub Fine Arts Ctr 1974. **HONORS/ACHIEVEMENTS:** Num exhibits; awd Walter Gutman Found 1962; John Hay Whitney Flwsp 1964-65; Cintas Found Flwsp 1965-66; Nat Endowment for Arts 1970-71.

CRUZ, ILUMINADO ANGELES
Physician, associate professor. **PERSONAL:** Born Nov 20, 1936, Philippines; son of Dr Iluminado S Cruz Sr and Flora Angeles; married Aurora Bunda; children: Danny, Eliza, Loralei. **EDUCATION:** Univ of the Philippines, MD 1962. **CAREER:** Howard Univ Coll of Med, instr 1968-69, asst prof 1971-76, assoc prof 1977-. **ORGANIZATIONS:** Dir Hemodialysis Unit Howard Univ; fellow Amer Coll of Physicians; mem Amer Soc of Nephrology; Intl Soc of Nephrology; Natl Med Assn; Med Chirurogical Soc DC; DC Med Soc; Amer Heart Assn; Natl Capital Med Found. **BUSINESS ADDRESS:** Associate Professor, HowardUniv Coll of Medicine, 2041 Georgia Ave NW, Washington, DC 20060.

CRUZ, VIRGIL
Educator, clergyman. **PERSONAL:** Born Dec 21, 1929, New York, NY; married Margot Cruz-DeNijs; children: Miguel Newcomb, Isabel DeNijs. **EDUCATION:** Houghton Coll, BA Greek major 1953; Pittsburgh Seminary, MDiv 1956; Vrije Universiteit Amsterdam, Neth, PhD 1973. **CAREER:** Hebron United Presb Ch, 1956-60; Univ of Dubuque Seminary, prof of New Testament 1966-82; Western Theol Seminary, prof of Biblical studies 1982-. **ORGANIZATIONS:** Moderator Albany Presbtery 1959-60; chair Natl Comm for Ordination Examin 1979-80; mem Gen Assembly Cncl of Presby Ch 1984-; mem The Soc of Biblical Literature 1968-; mem The Soc for the Study of Black Religion 1975-; dir Presbyterians United for Biblical Concerns 1985-; dir Found for Educ & Rsch 1985-. **HONORS/ACHIEVEMENTS:** Purdy Scholarship Pittsburgh Seminary 1954; Lee Church Hist Award Pittsburgh Seminary 1956; Foreign Student Scholarship Vrije Univ 1960; Grant from German Govt for language study 1968; Higgins Fellowship (2 times); Presb Grad Fellowship 1972; author of "The Mark of the Beast, A Study of Charagma in the ApocalypseAmsterdam Acad Press 1973; numerous articles and book reviews. **BUSINESS ADDRESS:** Prof of Biblical Studies, Western Theological Seminary, 86 E 12th St, Holland, MI 49423.

CRUZAT, EDWARD PEDRO
Physician. **PERSONAL:** Born Apr 28, 1926, Chicago, IL; married Mildred Clemons; children: Severa, Edward II, Liza. **EDUCATION:** Univ of IL, AB 1947; Meharry Med Coll, MD 1952. **CAREER:** Univ of IL, clin asst, prof of surgery; Northwestern Univ, instr in surg; Edward P Cruzat & Assocs, private practice. **ORGANIZATIONS:** Mem Chicago Med Soc,; IL Surg Soc; Amer, Natl Medical Assocs, Cook Cty Med Soc; Am & Coll of Chest Phys; Am Coll of Surg; Intl Coll of Surg; Chic Surg Soc. **HONORS/ACHIEVEMENTS:** Cert Pan-Am Surg Soc Dr; Am Bd of Surg 1961. **MILITARY SERVICE:** USN lt 1955-57. **BUSINESS ADDRESS:** Edward P Cruzat & Assocs, 8501 Cottage Grove Ave, Chicago, IL 60619.

CRUZAT, GWENDOLYN S.
Professor. **EDUCATION:** Fisk Univ, BA Math 1951; Atlanta Univ, MSLS Lib Sci 1954; Wayne State Univ, PhD 1976. **CAREER:** Fisk Univ, ref-serials 1954-60; Harper Hosp Detroit, asst lib 1960-64; NY Pub Lib, ref lib 1962; Sch of med Lib Wayne State Univ, ref lib/assoc dir post-master's fellowship prog 1964-70; Univ of W Ontario, lectr 1970; Sch of Information and Library Studies Univ of MI, lectr/asst prof/assoc prof 1970-79; prof Information and Library Studies 1979-; Affirmative Action Office Lib of Congress, consult 1975; Natl Lib of Med Extramural Progs, rsch consult 1978; Grad Sch of Lib Studies Univ of HI, visiting assoc prof 1977; Sch of Lib & Info Studies Univ of MD, guest lectr 1978; Natl Lib of Med, mem bd of regents 1980-84. **ORGANIZATIONS:** Mem Med Lib Assn 1967-; consult to various com & assns 1968-; mem Amer Lib Assn 1971-; chair ALA Comm on Collective Bargaining 1976-79; ALA Comm on Accreditation 1984-86; chmn conf on librarianship Tri State Hosp Assembly 1968; workshop coord MI Health Sci Lib Conf 1973; mem MI Interorganizational Comfor Cont Lib Educ 1976-; mem Cont Lib Educ Network & Exchange 1976-; mem scholarship com Beta Phi Mu 1976; mem Health Care Lib Sect; steering comm Assn of Specialized & Coop Lib Agencies 1978-80; mem Invitational Conclave on Establishment of a Vol Cont Educ Recog System for Lib Infor Media Personnel 1978; mem Assn of Amer Lib Schs 1979-80; mem Amer Soc for Info Sci; mem Assn of Univ Profs; mem Metro Detroit Med Lib Group; mem Special Lib Assn, Amer Lib Assn, Assn of Coll & Rsch Libraries; mem exec comm Univ of MI Extension Serv 1975-; mem Univ of MI Long Range Planning Com; mem Adv Com for State Relations 1979-; mem Fisk Univ Alumni Club, Delta Sigma Theta Sor. **HONORS/ACHIEVEMENTS:** Atlanta Univ Alumnus in Residence, 1989; Univ of MI Cofaculty Rep to Big Ten Intercollegiate Conf 1981-; Gabriel Awd for Scholarship Fisk Univ; Beta Phi Mu; Distinguished Serv Awd of the Univ of MI 1977; Janet Doe lectr Med Lib Assn 1978-79; various rsch activities & funded grant proposals Lib Assn 1978-79; various rsch activities & funded grant proposals 1964-; num publs 1963-. **BUSINESS ADDRESS:** Professor of Information and Library Studies, Univ of Michigan, Sch of Information and Library Studies, Ann Arbor, MI 48109.

CRYER, LINKSTON T.
Dental surgeon. **PERSONAL:** Born Jul 10, 1933, Mt Hermon, LA; married Elizabeth. **EDUCATION:** Southern Univ, BS 1945; Meharry Medical Coll, DDS 1961; Dade County Research Clinic, post graduate studies in endodontics, oral surgery, minor tooth movement, periodontal surgery. **CAREER:** FL State Dental Health Dept, 1961-62; Variety Children's Hospital, staff 1966-; Private Practice, dental surgeon 1962-. **ORGANIZATIONS:** Dade County Dental Soc 1961-; pres South Dade Political Action League 1965-80; spres Richmond Enterprises Inc 1965-; vice pres Dunbar Medical Arts Inc 1971-; pres Iota Pi Lambda Chapter Alpha Phi Alpha 1972-; mem Dade County Dental Research Clinic 1980-, The Acad of General Dentistry 1980-; pres Dade County Dental Soc 1985-87; mem Amer & Natl Dental Assns, The Amer Inst of Hypnosis; life mem Alpha Phi Alpha. **HONORS/ACHIEVEMENTS:** Founder of Iota Pi Lambda Chapter of Alpha Phi Alpha. **MILITARY SERVICE:** AUS 1st lieutenant 1954-56. **BUSINESS ADDRESS:** 11350 Dunbar Dr, Miami, FL 33158.

C'SHIVA, OYA **See FORTUNE, GWENDOLINE Y.**

CUDJOE, SELWYN REGINALD
Educator. **PERSONAL:** Born Dec 01, 1943; son of Lionel and Carmen; married Gwendolyn Marie Long; children: Frances Louise, Kwamina. **EDUCATION:** Fordham Univ, BA 1969, MA 1972; Cornell Univ, PhD 1976. **CAREER:** Fordham Univ, instructor 1970-72; Ithaca Coll, adjunct asst prof 1973-75; Ohio Univ, assoc prof 1975-76; Harvard Univ, asst prof 1976-81; Wellesley Coll, assoc prof. **HONORS/ACHIEVEMENTS:** Resistance and Caribbean Literature Ohio Univ Press 1980; Movement of the People Calalouх Published 1983; A Just and Moral Society Calaloux Published 1984; VS Naipaul: A Materialist Reading, Univ of MA Press, 1988. **BUSINESS ADDRESS:** Associate Professor, Wellesley College, Black Studies, Wellesley, MA 02181.

CUFF, GEORGE WAYNE
Clergyman. **PERSONAL:** Born Sep 03, 1923, Chester, PA; son of Theodore Cuff and Lydia Cuff; married Mary Elizabeth; children: Henry Earl Tucker Jr, Selena Cuff Shockley. **EDUCATION:** Lincoln Univ PA, BA 1951; M Div Crozer Theol Sem, 1955. **CAREER:** Office of Finance & Field Serv, field rep; Bd of Global Ministries United Meth Ch, 1979-; Hillcrest Bellefonte United Methodist Church, Wilmington DE, pastor, 1975-79; Wilmington Dist Peninsula Conf, supt 1973-75; Dover Dist Peninsula Conf, supt 1969-73; NJ/DE/MD, pastor 1955-69; retired 1986. **ORGANIZATIONS:** Bd of trustees Wesley Coll Dover DE 1970-; bd of govs Wesley Theol Sem Wash DC 1973-; bd of dir Wilmington Good Will Industries 1973-79; gen bd mem Global Ministries United Methodist Church. **HONORS/ACHIEVEMENTS:** Plaque of Appreciation, Meth Action Program of Wilmington Dist 1975; Good Conduct Medal; WWII Medal; Sharp Shooters Medal. **MILITARY SERVICE:** USN third class petty officer 1943-46.

CUFFEE, JEFFREY TOWNSEND
Clergyman. **PERSONAL:** Born May 29, 1928, New York, NY; married Carol Marlene Hunt; children: Aaron, Paul, Carol, Elizabeth. **EDUCATION:** St Augustine's Coll, BA 1956; VA Theol Seminary, diploma 1959; Iona Coll Fordham U, MSW 1972. **CAREER:** NY Dept of Correctional Serv, rev; Fishkill Correctional Facility, sr 1974-; St Joseph's Home (Peeksill), CS supr 1971-74; Graham Home for Children, chaplain 1968-71; St Augustine's Ch, priest in charge 1964-68; St John's Ch, vicar 1960-64. **ORGANIZATIONS:** Vchmn Lower E Side Civil Rights Assn 1965-67; mem Lower E Side Neighborhood Assn 1965-68; mem planning bd #3 Borough of Manhattan 1966-68; mem of Region II bd Diocese of NY 1971-77; mem bd of trustees Cathedral St John the Divine 1973-79. **BUSINESS ADDRESS:** Box 307, Beacon, NY 12508.

CULBREATH, TONGILA M.
Broadcasting executive. **PERSONAL:** Born Jun 09, 1959, Atlanta, GA. **EDUCATION:** Univ of CO Boulder, BA 1981; Atlanta Univ, MBA 1987. **CAREER:** Educ Media Ctr, media tech 1977-81; H Harper's Design Studios, asst mgr 1981-82; Sandusky Broadcasting KNUS-AM, tech producer 1982-84; New City Comm WYAY-FM, acct exec 1984-. **ORGANIZATIONS:** Mem NBMBAA 1986-87, Atlanta Media Network, Atlanta Broadcast Advertisers Club. **HOME ADDRESS:** 452 McGill Place, Atlanta, GA 30312.

CULLERS, SAMUEL JAMES
Consulting firm chief executive. **PERSONAL:** Born in Chicago, IL; son of Samuel P. Cullers and Letitia Terry; married Geraldine Lewis, Jan 01, 1950; children: Samuel J, Jr, Mark E. **EDUCATION:** MIT, MCP 1952; Fisk Univ, BA, Sociology, 1950. **CAREER:** Deputy dir, Hartford Redevel Agency, Hartford, CT, 1952-58; chief of party, Litchfield, Whiting, Bowne & Assoc, New York, consultants to Ministry of Iterior, Thailand, 1958-60; city planning advisor, Ministry of Interior, govt of Thailand, Bangkok, 1960-61; dir, Chicago Community Renewal Program, 1961-63; dir, urban renewal study, Metropolitan Toronto Planning Bd, 1963-66; acting dir and chief ,urban planning, California Office of Planning, 1966-70; acting dir, office of planning and research, California governor's office, 1970-71; vice pres, environmental and urban planning, Engineering Science Inc, 1971-79; pres, Samuel J Cullers & Assoc, environmental planning and devel consultants, 1971-; lecturer, govt planning, Univ of California Davis, Golden Gate Univ; lecturer, Univ of California Los Angeles, Univ of Toronto, California State Univ Sacramento. **ORGANIZATIONS:** Council of State Planning Agencies, bd of dir 1968-69; Amer Planning Assn, 1st vice pres 1969-70; DHUD, urban fellowship advisory bd 1969-73; Sacramento Symphony Assn, bd of dir 1972-84; Sacramento Metro Chamber of Commerce, bd of dir 1974-78; Sacramento City-County Human Rights Comm, chmn 1975-79; Rotary Intl, mem 1976-; comm on transportation & land devel policy NRC 1977-79; Sacramento Area Comm and Trade Assn, bd of dir 1980-83; Sacramento Metro YMCA, chmn 1980-81; Washington Neighborhood Center, bd of dir 1980-; Sacramento Urban League, chmn, 1984-85; Alpha Phi Alpha. **HONORS/ACHIEVEMENTS:** Published, Zoning—A Tool for Renewal, Ontario Housing 1964; publ, An Expl of Planning Relationship to Integration ASPO 1967; contributor, Discoveries on the Civic Design Aspects of Toronto's City Hall Journal Royal Arch Inst of Canada 1965; MIT Graduate Scholarship, 1959-62; John Hay Whitney Fellowship, 1950-52; Fisk Univ Scholarship, 1948-50. **HOME ADDRESS:** 6409 S Land Park Dr, Sacramento, CA 95831.

CULLERS, VINCENT T.
Advertising executive. **PERSONAL:** Married Marian; children: Vincent Jr, Jeffery. **EDUCATION:** Art Inst of Chgo, attd; Am Academy of Art; Univ Chgo. **CAREER:** Am 1st Blk Advertising Agy, founder; Vince Cullers Advertising Inc, Chicago 1956-; Nat Agency of Record for Sears Roebuck and Co. **BUSINESS ADDRESS:** Vince Cullers Advertising Inc, 520 N Michigan Ave, Chicago, IL 60611.

CULPEPPER, BETTY M.
Librarian. **PERSONAL:** Born Jan 15, 1941, Lynchburg, VA; daughter of Roosevelt Culpepper and Louise Head Culpepper Witcher. **EDUCATION:** Howard Univ, BA 1963; Kent State Univ, MA 1966; Cath Univ, MS 1969; Howard Univ, MPA 1981. **CAREER:**

Washington DC Public Library, reader's adv 1964-67; Prince George's County Memorial Library, branch librarian 1967-72; Washingtoniana Div DC Public Library, chief 1972-77; Moorland-Spingarn Research Center Howard Univ, bibliographer/head of ref 1977-86; Moorland-Spingarn Research Center Howard Univ, asst chief librarian Technical Service & Automation 1986-. **ORGANIZATIONS:** Mem Amer Librarian Assn; mem Columbia Historical Soc; mem Afro-Amer Historical & Genl Soc; NAACP; Assn for Study of Afro-Amer Life & History; mem Washington Metro Area Caucus of Black Librarians; Alpha Kappa Alpha. **HONORS/ACHIEVEMENTS:** Awarded Scholarship Howard Univ; Fellow Kent State Univ; Scholarship MD Library Assn. **BUSINESS ADDRESS:** Assistant Chief Librarian, Technical Serv & Automation, Moorland-Spingarn Rsch Ctr, HowardUniv, 500 Howard Pl NW, Washington, DC 20059.

CULPEPPER, DELLIE L.
Traffic court director. **PERSONAL:** Born Mar 24, 1941, Talbotton, GA; daughter of Willie Culpepper and Daisy Culpepper. **EDUCATION:** Dimery's Business College, Atlanta, GA, ABA 1963; Atlanta Law School, Atlanta, GA, LLB 1979. **CAREER:** Southwest Council Atlanta Chamber of Commerce, member executive comm 1978; Traffic Court, Atlanta, GA, court administrator/director. **ORGANIZATIONS:** Member NAACP 1980; member Ida Prather YWCA 1980; vice president The Cruisers Fund Raising 1984; member Black Public Administrators 1984; member National Association of Trial Court Administrators 1984; member Atlanta Chapter COMPA 1985. **BUSINESS ADDRESS:** Director, City Court of Atlanta, 104 Trinity Ave SW, Atlanta, GA 30335.

CULPEPPER, LUCY NELL
Physician. **PERSONAL:** Born Jun 11, 1951, Awin, AL; married Joseph Williams. **EDUCATION:** AL A&M Univ, BS 1973; Meharry Medical Coll, MD 1977. **CAREER:** Martin Luther King Jr General Hosp, intern, resident 1977-80; NHSC, pediatrician medical dir 1980-82; Private Practice, pediatrician 1982-. **ORGANIZATIONS:** Mem Zeta Phi Beta Sor Inc 1972-; active staff mem DCH Regional Medical Ctr 1980-; mem Tuscaloosa Co Medical Soc 1982-, Medical Assoc of State of AL 1982-; youth dir First Baptist Church 1984-; mem West AL Pediatric Soc 1984-, West AL Medical Assoc 1985-, AL State Medical Assoc 1985-. **HONORS/ACHIEVEMENTS:** Outstanding Young Women of Amer 1983; Woman of the Year Christian Study Ctr of AL 1983; Who's Who in the South & Southwest 1984-85. **HOME ADDRESS:** 1315 Briarcliff, Northport, AL 35476. **BUSINESS ADDRESS:** 609-28th Ave, Tuscaloosa, AL 35401.

CULVER, RHONDA
Accountant. **PERSONAL:** Born Nov 18, 1960, Phoenix, AZ; son of Roscoe Culver and Rose Culver. **EDUCATION:** Arizona State Univ, BS 1981, MBA 1986. **CAREER:** Searle Consumer Products Div, asst cost accountant 1983-84; Garrett Airline Serv Div, sr accountant 1984-86, accounting supervisor 1986-. **ORGANIZATIONS:** Bd of dirs/treas Natl Assoc of Accountants Phoenix 1983-; mem Assoc of MBA Execs 1984, Mayor's Citizen Tax Fairness Commn 1986; comm chmn United Negro Coll Fund Phoenix 1986,87; finance comm Alpha Kappa Alpha Sor 1985-87; technical communications coord Focus Software Users Group. **HONORS/ACHIEVEMENTS:** Black Board of Directors Honoree Phoenix 1986; Outstanding Woman 1987. **HOME ADDRESS:** PO Box 27786, Tempe, AZ 85282. **BUSINESS ADDRESS:** Accounting Supervisor, Garrett Airline Service Div, PO Box 29003, Phoenix, AZ 85038.

CUMBER, VICTORIA LILLIAN
Columnist. **PERSONAL:** Born Feb 05, 1920, San Antonio, TX. **EDUCATION:** Phillips Bus Sch 1935-36; Metro Business Sch, attended 1936-38. **CAREER:** Sepia Hollywood Mag, pub 1941-45; Herald Attractions Agency, mgr 1949-55; Lil Cumber Attractions Agency, theatrical agent 1956-; SW Wave Newspaper, columnist 1967-86; Scoop Newspaper 1986-. **ORGANIZATIONS:** Mem Sec Comm Actions Com 1958-60; mem NAACP Hollywood Beverly Hills Br 1937-; co-organizer Beverly Hills Hollywood Image Awards 1967. **HONORS/ACHIEVEMENTS:** Placque Bus & Professional Women's Club 1967; Black Filmmakers Hall of Fame 1974; Who's Who of Amer Women 1977-78; Coorganized the first Commercial Casting Directors/Industry Awds saluting honorees who have been voted as an awardee by their peers 1982; So Calif Motion Picture Council 1987 honoree. **BUSINESS ADDRESS:** Lil Cumber Attractions, 6515 Sunset Blvd, Hollywood, CA 90028.

CUMBO, MARION WILLIAM
Musician. **PERSONAL:** Born Mar 01, 1899, New York, NY; married Clarissa Wilhelmina Burton, Nov 02, 1924 (deceased); children: William. **CAREER:** NY, violon cellist; Philadelphia Concert Orchestra, soloist 1934-35; Motion Picture Theatre, 1925-28; Ford Dabney's Orchestra, 1919; Negro String Quartet, 1919-27; Broadway Musicals Shuffle Along Chocolate Dandies, musician 1923-25; Kwamina, 1961; No Strings, 1962; Nat King Cole Tour, musician 1963; Royal Winnipeg Ballet, 1965; Triad Presentations Inc, co-founder 1970-80. **ORGANIZATIONS:** Mem Sym of the New World 1965-77; mem Sr Orch Local 802 1970-77. **HOME ADDRESS:** Parkview Nursing Home, 6585 Broadway, New York, NY 10471.

CUMBY, GEORGE
Professional football player. **PERSONAL:** Born Jul 05, 1956, LaRue, TX; married Audrey; children: Christopher George. **EDUCATION:** Univ of OK. **CAREER:** Green Bay Packers, professional football player (linebacker). **ORGANIZATIONS:** Mem of Packers' off-season speakers' bureau; speaks on behalf of Christian Fellowship of Athletes. **HONORS/ACHIEVEMENTS:** Coll, named to AP, UPI, Football Coaches, Football Writers, Walter Camp, Sporting News and Football News first team All-Americas as senior; played in 1980 Hula and Senior Bowls; profl, 70 unassisted tackles in 1984 and led Packer linebackers in assisted tackles with 23; Packers' third-ranking tackler in 1983 with 100 unassisted stops; led Packer defense in unassisted tackles in 1982 season; teams no 3 tackler in 1981 with 102 unassisted tackles.

CUMMINGS, ALBERT R.
Marketing manager. **PERSONAL:** Born Oct 27, 1940, Fort Scott, KS; son of Booker Cummings and Cleo Cummings; children: Simone, Albert Jr, Valerie. **EDUCATION:** KS State Coll of Pittsburg, BA Math 1962; WA Univ St Louis, MS Appl Math & Comp Sci 1971; Southern IL Univ Edwardsville, MBA 1974. **CAREER:** Defense Mapping Agency USAF; physical scientist 1962-69; Ralston Purina, oper rsch analyst 1969-75; Southern IL Univ, asst prof mgmt sci 1974-80; Anheuser-Busch, mgr sales & mktg analysis 1975-82; Brand Manager, King Cobra 1982-. **ORGANIZATIONS:** Dir Anheuser Busch Credit Union 1983-; mem Alpha Phi Alpha Frat 1961-. **MILITARY SERVICE:** AUS E-4 2 yrs. **HOME ADDRESS:** 1811 Oxford Ln, St Louis, MO 63136. **BUSINESS ADDRESS:** Senior Product Manager, Anheuser Busch Inc, One Busch Place, St Louis, MO 63118.

CUMMINGS, CARY, III
Medical doctor. **PERSONAL:** Born Jul 13, 1949, Monticello, FL; children: Lindsey. **EDUCATION:** SUNY Binghamton, BS 1972; Meharry Medical Coll, MD 1976. **CAREER:** Univ of Rochester, intern 1976-77; US Public Health Svcs, lt commander 1977-79; Harrisburg Hosp, residency; Hershey Emergency Medicine Prog, asst prof dept of internal medicine 1981-83; Memorial Sloan-Kettering of Cornell Univ, fellow in critical care medicine 1983-84; Harrisburg Hosp, asst prof dept of internal medicine 1984-86; Hershey Medical Ctr, asst prof emergency medicine & trauma 1985-86; Private Practice, physician. **ORGANIZATIONS:** Bd mem Amer Cancer Soc Dauphin Co 1985-, River Rescue Ambulance Serv 1985-; mem Dauphin Co Medical Soc 1985-, PA Medical Soc 1986-; bd mem Harrisburg Hospital LCO 1986-; adv bd mem Dauphin Co Dept of Drugs and Alcohol 1986-. **BUSINESS ADDRESS:** 1617 N Front St, Harrisburg, PA 17102.

CUMMINGS, CHARLES EDWARD
Physician. **PERSONAL:** Born Oct 02, 1931, Richmond, VA; married Mary Quash; children: Charles Jr, Kevin. **EDUCATION:** VA Union Univ, BS 1958; Howard Univ Sch of Medicine, MD 1962. **CAREER:** Charles E Cummings MD Ltd, president 1964-; 1540 Broadcasting Co, president 1977-. **ORGANIZATIONS:** Bd mem VA State Univ Foundation 1979-86, VA Heart Assoc 1985-86; mem Alpha Kappa Mu Honor Soc Beta Kappa Chi. **HONORS/ACHIEVEMENTS:** Gold Heart Awd Amer Heart Assoc 1980. **MILITARY SERVICE:** USAF staff sgt 1950-54; Korean Service Medal. **BUSINESS ADDRESS:** President, 1540 Broadcasting Co, 2809 North Ave, Richmond, VA 23222.

CUMMINGS, CIMENA MCCANE
Business executive. **PERSONAL:** Born Aug 17, 1945, Chicago, IL; divorced; children: De Janette, Ayanna M. **EDUCATION:** Loyola Univ Chgo, BS, AD 1970; Cosmopolitan C of C Free School of Bus Mgmt, IIT Chgo, 1975. **CAREER:** Ford Motor Co Chicago Assembly Plant, sr cost acct; US Universal, gen mgr; Zenith Radio Corp, programmer; Analized Data processing Concepts, data processing forms analyst; Teletype Corp Skokie IL, instr; TLC Co Inc, pres. **ORGANIZATIONS:** Mem, former officer Phi Chi Theta Women Professional Frat; bd of dir Loyola Alumni Assoc Chgo; officer Chicago C of C & Industry-Youth Motivation Speakers; mem Soc of Advancement of Mgmt; delegate White House Conf on Small bus 1980; mem Natl Assoc of Women Bus Owners; pres Woodlawn/Yancey Chicago Boys and Girls Clubs. **HONORS/ACHIEVEMENTS:** Outstanding Achievement Chicago Merit Employment Comm 1970-72; Dedicated Serv Natl Alliance of Bus 1973; Bus & Professional Person Bus & Ref Guide 1978; Bd Memof the Year Woodlawn/Yancey Units of Boys Club 1983; Chog Boys Club Outstanding Campaigner Awd 1983; Kizzy Scholarship Awd 1981. **BUSINESS ADDRESS:** President, T L C Company, Inc, 3801 S Sangamon St, Chicago, IL 60609.

CUMMINGS, DONNA LOUISE
Manager. **PERSONAL:** Born Jan 17, 1944, Cleveland, OH; divorced; children: Dahlia Loi. **EDUCATION:** Cleveland State U, BA Psych 1966-77; Baldwin-Wallace Coll, MBA Syst Mgmt 1979-81; Gestalt Inst of Cleveland, Ptgrde Certif Org & Syst Develp 1981-83. **CAREER:** TRW Inc, various admin pos 1963-74; TRW Inc, comm affairs assist 1974-75; TRW Inc, comm affairs rep 1975-77. **ORGANIZATIONS:** Consult Nbrghd Ctrs Assoc 1982-83; pres Karamu Hse 1981-83; chrmn Assoc of Black Found Exec 1978-79; chrmn Windermere Child Care Ctr 1976-79. **HONORS/ACHIEVEMENTS:** Outsdg Young Wmn of Am 1978; certif of merit YWCA 1977 & 1978; One of Cveland's 80 Most Interesting People Cleveland Magz 1980; Charles L Loeb Outstdng Young Urban League of Grtr Cleveland 1982. **BUSINESS ADDRESS:** Manager, TRW Inc, 23555 Euclid Ave, Cleveland, OH 44117.

CUMMINGS, E. EMERSON
Educator. **PERSONAL:** Born Jun 17, 1917, Winchester, MA. **EDUCATION:** Bates Coll, BS 1939; MA Inst Tech, grad studies; NH U, tchr. **CAREER:** Math & Science Dept, Old Orchard Beach, teacher, chmn; town clk; assessor; Police Force, sergeant; Assessment Review, bd chmn ; councilman 7th term; owned & operated Taxi & Bus business; Amusement Co, bookkeeper; MA Savings Bank, corporator; Salvation Army, bd dir. **ORGANIZATIONS:** Mem Lions Club; Am Leg; VFW; chmn Sch Bldg Commn. **MILITARY SERVICE:** 1st sgt. **BUSINESS ADDRESS:** 123 Portland Ave, Old Orchard Beach, ME 04064.

CUMMINGS, FRANCES MCARTHUR
Educator. **PERSONAL:** Born Feb 02, 1941, Lumberton, NC; married Jimmy Floyd Cummings; children: Isaiah T. **EDUCATION:** Livingstone Coll, BS Bus Ed 1961; NC Central Univ, MS Bus Ed 1974; Univ of NC at Greensboro, Bus & Office Voc Cert 1976. **CAREER:** NC Assoc of Classroom Teachers 1978-79; Southeast Reg Assoc of Classroom Teachers, pres 1980; Natl Ed Assoc, dir 1980-87; NC Assoc of Ed, pres 1983-84; Lumberton Sr HS, teacher. **ORGANIZATIONS:** Mem Mt Olive United Meth Church 1970-85; chartered mem Alpha Kappa Alpha 1974; mem Robeson Cty Dem Women 1979-85, NC Council on the Status of Women 1980-85; commiss Ed Commiss of the States Gov Appt 1983; bd of dir NC Ctr for Public Policy Rsch 1983-86. **HONORS/ACHIEVEMENTS:** The Order of the Long Leaf Pine Governor's Awd 1983; Gov's Public School Prog of Excellence Governor's Awd 1983; Outstanding Leader of Robeson Cty RobesonCty Black Caucus 1983; Par Excellence Serv Awd Gen Baptist Conv of NC 1984; Tar Heel of the Week News & Observer Raleigh 1984. **BUSINESS ADDRESS:** Lumberton Senior High School, 3901 Fayetteville Rd, Lumberton, NC 28358.

CUMMINGS, JAMES C., JR.
Business executive. **PERSONAL:** Born Sep 22, 1929, Indianapolis, IN; married Norma Lewis; children: Cynthia, James III, Cecilia, Ronald, Claudia. **EDUCATION:** IN Central U, BS 1962; IN U, grad work. **CAREER:** Urban Advance, pres; Oxford Devel Co, asst vice pres 1970-71; Bd For Fundamental Edn, dir of operations 1966-70; Village Mgmt Corp, proj mgr 1960-66. **ORGANIZATIONS:** Chmn Nat Black Rep Council, mem exec com Rep Nat Com; chmn IN Black Rep Council; exec asst chmn IN Rep State Com; del Rep Nat Conv Fdr 1976; pres IN Black Expo 1971-73; former vice-chmn Inst of Industrialized Bldg Oppty; mem Public Works IN; bd mem Zoning Appeals IN; former mem of bd IN NAACP. **HON-**

ORS/ACHIEVEMENTS: Disting Hoosier Award, Gov Edgar Whitcomb; Sagamore of the Wabash IN High Est Award, Gov Otis Bowen; Key to City of Indianapolis, Mayor William Hudnut. **MILITARY SERVICE:** AUS corpl 1951-53. **BUSINESS ADDRESS:** 155 W Market St, Indianapolis, IN 46204.

CUMMINGS, PAT MARIE
Author/illustrator of children's books. **PERSONAL:** Born Nov 09, 1958, Chicago, IL; daughter of Arthur Cummings and Christine Taylor Cummings. **EDUCATION:** Pratt Institute, Brooklyn NY, BFA, 1974. **CAREER:** Free-lance author/illustrator, 1974—. **ORGANIZATIONS:** Graphic Artists Guild, Society of Children's Book Writers, Children's Book Illustrators Group. **HONORS/ACHIEVEMENTS:** Coretta Scott King Award, 1983, for My Mama Needs Me; Black Women in Publishing Illustration Award, 1988.

CUMMINGS, ROBERT TERRELL
Professional athlete. **PERSONAL:** Born Mar 15, 1961, Chicago, IL; married Vonnie; children: Robert, Sean. **EDUCATION:** De Paul Univ. **CAREER:** Milwaukee Bucks, forward 1982-; pres Music Publishing & Production Co. **ORGANIZATIONS:** Ordained Pentecostal Minister/Evangelist; singer/songwriter; public speaker. **HONORS/ACHIEVEMENTS:** Named NBA'S Rookie-of-the-year 1982-83; ranked 10th in the League in both scoring (237) and rebounding (106). **BUSINESS ADDRESS:** Milwaukee Bucks, 901 N 4th St, Milwaukee, WI 53203.

CUMMINGS, ROBERTA SPIKES
Librarian. **PERSONAL:** Born May 01, 1944, Angie, LA; daughter of William H Collins and Wanda Coby Collins; children: 1. **EDUCATION:** Grambling State Univ, BS Speech & Drama 1960; Univ of SW LA Lafayette, 1968; LA State Univ Baton Rouge, MSLS Library Sci 1972; S Univ Baton Rouge, Media Broadcasting 1973-77; MS Computer Science 1987. **CAREER:** Lafayette Parish Sch Bd, librarian 1966-73; East Baton Rouge Parish Public Library, librarian 1973; US Army Reserve, personnel mgmt super 1975-81; Atty Genl's Office State of LA, consultant for the Huey P Long Library 1982; 321st MMC TAACOM, equipment authorization tech 1981-; S Univ Sch of Law, asst law librarian & head of acquisitions 1973-. **ORGANIZATIONS:** Mem of following organs Alpha Kappa Alpha 1964; Grambling State Univ Debate Team against Harvard Univ Debate Team 1965; Istrouma Chap of Scouters of Amer 1979; Spec Librarians Assn; Natl Bar Assn; Southeastern Chap Amer Assn of Law Librarians; Amer Assn of Law Libraries; Southwestern Librarians Assn Natl Educ Assn. **HONORS/ACHIEVEMENTS:** Best Supporting Actress Awd 1962; Alpha Theta Phi Honor Soc; published an article "Many Views" Natl Library Week 1971; co-authored "Black History & Culture" 1972; developed a media pkg "Past, Present, and Future of School Libraries" 1978. **MILITARY SERVICE:** AUS cw2; Army Achievement Medal; Army Prof Develop Ribbon Level 1; Army Serv Ribbon; Expert Badge. **BUSINESS ADDRESS:** Assistant Law Librarian, SoUniv Law Center, Law Library, Baton Rouge, LA 70813.

CUMMINGS, TERRY
Pro basketball player. **PERSONAL:** Born Mar 15, 1961, Chicago, IL; married Vonnie; children: Terry Jr. **EDUCATION:** Attended, DePaul Univ. **CAREER:** Church of God in Christ, ordained pentecostal minister; San Diego Clippers, forward. **HONORS/ACHIEVEMENTS:** Rookie of the Yr. **BUSINESS ADDRESS:** Milwaukee Bucks, 1001 N 4 St, Milwaukee, WI 53203.

CUMMINGS, THERESA FAITH
Director. **PERSONAL:** Born Feb 27, Springfield, IL; daughter of Nelson Mark Cummings and Mary Jeanette Irvine Cummings. **EDUCATION:** Winston-Salem State Teachers Coll, BS Educ; So IL Univ, MS Educ. **CAREER:** St Louis Public School System, teacher 1957-67; Multi-purpose Neighborhood Serv Center System of Springfield/Sangamon Co Comm Action Agency, proj dir 1967-69, exec dir 1969-85; Aband Mine Hands Reclam Cncl, asst dir 1987-. **ORGANIZATIONS:** Couns/guidance chairperson Human Devel Corp 1965-67; planner/cons Mr Achievers Summer Inst Banneker Dist St Louis Pub Sch 1966-67; mem League of Women Voters; mem Amer Assn Univ Women; mem Altrusa Intl; past exec bd Central IL Compr Health Planning Council; past vice chmn Springfield Sangamon Co Crime Prev Commn; mem Natl Council for Negro Women; past bd dir Natl Self Help Resource Ctr; bd dir Sangamon Co March of Dimes; past western regional dir Iola Phi Lambda Sor Inc; mem St Paul AME Ch; life mem NAACP; bd mem Midwest Women's Ctr; past mem Human Subject Com to SIU Sch of med; mem various other orgns; mem Ambulatory Surgical Treatment Ctr Licensing Bd; vice chair & chair Natl Woman Political Caucus; appointed to the Federal Reserve Consumer Adv Cncl; Greater Springfield Chamber of Commerce; Business & Professional Women's Club; Women In Govt; Women In Mgmt. **HONORS/ACHIEVEMENTS:** Citation Gr Lakes Regional Office of Economic Opportunity for Svc; citation Springfield Ministerial Alliance for Dedication & Devotion to Duty; cert for serv & contrib to Project Mainstream Together Inc; cert Consumer Credit Counseling Serv Bd of Dirs; cert Contrib to Comm Develop OH Chapter of NACD; runner-up plaque Lola M Parker Achievement Award; Medallion for Serv March of Dimes; Fellow SIU Sch of Med 1979; Woman of the Yr Zeta Phi Beta Sor 1982.

CUMMINGS, WILLIS NELSON
Dentist, athlete. **PERSONAL:** Born Jul 29, 1894, Galveston, TX; son of William Nelson Cummings (deceased) and Mary European Badger Cummings (deceased); married Blanche M Rudd Cummings, Nov 27, 1935. **EDUCATION:** Fisk Univ, AB 1916; Univ PA Dental School, DDS 1919. **CAREER:** Private Practice, dentist 1919-69. **ORGANIZATIONS:** Member, Allied Dental Council 1922-34, First Dist Dental Amer Dental Assn 1928-68, Alpha Phi Alpha Fraternity 1919, Alpha Gamma Lambda, Alpha Physical Cultural Club 1917-32; charter member Psi Chap 1920. **HONORS/ACHIEVEMENTS:** First black to run cross-country, Univ of PA 1916; first black scoring member of ICAAAA Cross-Country Championship Team, Univ of PA 1917; Third black awarded varsity "P" 1917; first black captain of varsity cross-country team, Ivy League & Big Ten Coll, Univ of PA 1918; first black, first runner to win the Jr & Sr Middle Atlantic-Amateur Athletic Union-Cross Country Championships 1918; first black elected member, Univ of PA Varsity Club 1920; first black elected Omicron Kappa Upsilon Dental Honor Soc 1919; first black in US awarded Fifty Year Captain's Pin, Univ of PA 1969; first black appointed by city of New York to be Dentist to Outpatient Dept, Harlem Hosp 1927; elected member Harlem Professional Hall of Fame 1977; first black dental alumnus to be honored by the Dental School of the Univ of PA; guest speaker, Alumni Faculty Sr Dinner. **MILITARY SERVICE:** AUS MR 1917-1919.

CUNDIFF, JOHN HOWARD
Dentist. **PERSONAL:** Born in Roanoke, VA; married Virginia Radcliffe (deceased); children: Daphne Renee, John Howard Jr. **EDUCATION:** WV State Coll, BS; Howard Univ, graduate student; Howard Univ School of Dentistry, DDS. **ORGANIZATIONS:** Mem, bd of mgrs Hunton Branch YMCA; former chmn Memorial Comm Omega Psi Phi Fraternity; former parliamentarian Omega Psi Phi Fraternity; former dist chmn Mohawk Dist BSA; mem, bd of dir Delta Dental Plan of Virginia. **HONORS/ACHIEVEMENTS:** VA Dentist of the Year Award 1976; Man of the Year Award, Omega Psi Phi Gamma Alpha Chapter 1976.

CUNNINGHAM, ARTHUR H.
Composer. **PERSONAL:** Born Nov 11, 1928, Piermont, NY. **EDUCATION:** Columbia Tch Coll, MA 1955-57; Fisk U, AB 1947-51; Juilliard Sch Music; Met Music Sch; studied with John Work & Teddy Wilson. **CAREER:** Composed; conducted; lectured; publ; perfromed; Cunningham Music Corp, owner. **ORGANIZATIONS:** Mem ACA; mem ASCAP; Am Music Center; recorded Desto Records; publ Theodore Presser Co. **HONORS/ACHIEVEMENTS:** ASCAP Award for Composition 1972; Nat Endowment for The Arts Grant 1974. **MILITARY SERVICE:** AUS spl serv 1953-55. **BUSINESS ADDRESS:** Box 614, Nyack, NY 10960.

CUNNINGHAM, BENNIE LEE
Professional athlete. **PERSONAL:** Born Dec 23, 1954, Laurens, SC. **EDUCATION:** Clemson Univ, BA Secondary Educ 1976. **CAREER:** Pittsburgh Steelers, tight end 1976-85. **HONORS/ACHIEVEMENTS:** Named as tight end on The Sporting News Coll All-Amer Team 1975; Played in AFC Championship Game following 1976,79,84 seasons; Played in NFL Championship Game following 1979 season. **BUSINESS ADDRESS:** Tight End, Pittsburgh Steelers, 300 Stadium Circle, Pittsburgh, PA 15212.

CUNNINGHAM, BLENNA A.
Business executive. **PERSONAL:** Born Dec 26, 1946, Chicago, IL. **EDUCATION:** Rutgers U-Stonier Grd Sch of Bankg, M 1982; Univ of AK, BS 1968. **CAREER:** Suburban Trust Bnk, bnch mgr 1974-76; United Nat'l Bnk, asst cashier 1976-79; United Nat'l Bnk, asst vice pres 1979-82; Retail Bnkg Div United Nat'l Bnk, vice pres 1982-83. **ORGANIZATIONS:** Brnh mgr First Nat'l Bnk Little Rock, AR 1972-74; venture analy MESBIC of AR 1970-72; dietn NY Hospt Syst 1968-70; brd of dir DC Husg Fin Agency 1985-; brd of dir DC Devel Corp 1982-; brd of trustee Capitol Hill Hosp 1982-84. **HONORS/ACHIEVEMENTS:** Consul Achieve Jr Achvmnt, Inc; Award of Merit Howard Univ Schl of Bus. **BUSINESS ADDRESS:** Senior Vice President, United Natl Bank, 1850 K St NW, Washington, DC 20006.

CUNNINGHAM, DAVID S., JR.
Elected official. **PERSONAL:** Born Jun 24, 1935, Chicago, IL; married Sylvia AC Krappel; children: David Srumier III, Leslie, Robyn, Amber. **EDUCATION:** Univ of Riverside, BA; Occidental Coll, MA 1970. **CAREER:** Cunningham Short Berryman & Assoc, Inc, consultants former partner; Los Angeles City Council, 1973-. **ORGANIZATIONS:** Chmn Grants Housing & Comm Develop; vice chmn Finance & Revenue Comm; mem Police Fire & Public Safety Comm; authored or co-authored many laws among which include the establish of the Mayor's Office of Small Business Assis; reduc of the minimum age fore firefighters from 21 to 18 yrs; pioneered the use of fed block grants for local govt use; created the city's dept of aging; created Vista Montoya Los Angeles' first subsidized condo project for low and median income families; initiated organ of the Mid-Town Chamber of Commerce and Pico-Union Chamber of Commerce; charter mem CA Minority Employ Council; mem Los Angeles Black Agenda; mem Bd of Interracial Council for Business Affairs; mem Urban League; bd of dirs Los Angeles Co Sanitation Dist No 1; chmn Natl Black United Fund; past pres CORO Alumni Assn; life mem Omega Psi Phi Frat Inc; life mem NAACP; life mem Natl Council of Negro Women; col in the CA Guard; former mem World Affairs Council; chmn LA Brotherhood Crusade 1971-72; S CA Assn of Govts Comm & Economic Develop Comm 1978-79; bd of dirs Natl League of Cities 1981-83. **HONORS/ACHIEVEMENTS:** Man of Tomorrow Omega Psi Phi 1973; Los Angeles Brotherhood Crusade 1973, 1976; Honorary Mayor of Baton Rouge LA 1974; Mid-City Chamber of Commerce 1974; DeltaSigma Theta 1982,83,84; Dept of the Navy 1984; Boy Scouts of Amer; S CA Fair Housing Congress 1984; Alex Haley Heritage Awd 1984. **BUSINESS ADDRESS:** Chairman, Natnl Black United Fund Inc, 2090 Seventh Ave Room 1020, New York, NY 10027.

CUNNINGHAM, E. BRICE
Attorney. **PERSONAL:** Born Feb 17, 1931, Buffalo, TX; son of Hattie Cunningham and Tessie (Roblow) Cunningham; married Rosie Nell (Portis) Cunningham, Mar 06, 1964; children: La Wanda Kay, Lednei, Michele, Elana. **EDUCATION:** Howard Univ Sch of Law, BA, LLB 1960. **CAREER:** E Brice Cunningham (Professional Corp), atty/pres; City of Dallas, muni ct judge 1971-72; City of Dallas, appeals judge. **ORGANIZATIONS:** Mem State Bar of TX 1960; State Bar Com on Coord with Other & Groups; mem State Bar Public Affairs Com; mem State Bar Sub-Com Grievance Com; Dallas Bar Assn; Special Cts Com; Fee Disputes Com Dallas Bar Assn; Courthouse Com; State Board Code of Criminal Pruc Study Com; Nat Bar Assn Inc; Am Judicature Soc; past vice chmn S Br of YMCA chap mem; legal Adv Most Worshipful Prince Hall Grand Lodge F&AM of TX; bd dirs Children's Aid Soc; Planning Commn Dallas 1973-76; Alpha Phi Alpha Frat; Paul Drayton Lodge No 9; Dale Consistory No 21; Elks; mem NAACP; atty metrop br Dallas NAACP; Hearing Ofcr Dallas 1974-76; Dallas City Planning Commn 1973-76. **HONORS/ACHIEVEMENTS:** Recip Award in Law Com of 100 1973; Award for Legal Services, Dallas TX NAACP 1977; Black Historical Achievement Award, Aldersgate United Methodist Church; Certificate of Merit, J L Turner Legal Assn; Certificate of Merit, Legislative Black Caucus of the State of Texas 1981. **MILITARY SERVICE:** AUS corpl 1948-54. **BUSINESS ADDRESS:** President, E Brice Cunningham Professional Corp, 777 S RL Thornton Freeway, Ste 121, Dallas, TX 75203.

CUNNINGHAM, ERSKINE
Financial credit manager. **PERSONAL:** Born Oct 03, 1955, Talladega, AL; son of Frank Cunningham and Dorothy Ragland Cunningham. **EDUCATION:** Northwood Inst Midland MI, BA 1977; Rosary Coll River Forst IL, MBA 1981. **CAREER:** Detroit Bank & Trust, asst branch mgr 1979; Ford Motor Credit Co, accounts rep 1979-84; Rowntree DeMet's Inc, financial credit mgr 1985-. **ORGANIZATIONS:** Mem Chicago Chap Natl Black MBA Assoc 1984-; mem Chicago Midwest Credit Manager's Assoc 1985-; election

comm Rosary Coll Grad Student Business AlumniAssoc 1985-86. **HONORS/ACHIEVEMENTS:** Outstanding Young Men in Amer 1984. **HOME ADDRESS:** 2801 S King Dr Apt 1901, Chicago, IL 60616. **BUSINESS ADDRESS:** Financial Credit Manager, Rowntree DeMet's Inc, 230 W Monroe Ste 2738, Chicago, IL 60606.

CUNNINGHAM, F. MALCOLM
Attorney. **PERSONAL:** Born Jan 27, 1927, Plant City, FL; married Nealia Brookins; children: Karren, Malcolm, Jr, Deneal, Mallorye. **EDUCATION:** FL A&M U, BA 1950; Howard Univ Sch of Law, LLD 1953. **CAREER:** Cunningham & Cunningham, senior partner 1953-. **ORGANIZATIONS:** Mem FL Bar Assn; Palm Beach Co Bar Assn; Am Trial Lawyers Assn; NBA; Am Arbitration Assn; Am Bar & Assn; Ethic & Circuit Ct Adv Com Palm Beach Co Bar Assn; co-organizer vchmn bd First Prudential Bank of West Palm Beach; vice-chrmn Planning Bd Riviera Beach 1961; elected to City Council 1962 re-elected 1964,66; Dem Candidate for House of Rep 1968; City Atty Riviera Beach FL 1971-73; pres Palm Beach Co Referral Bd & Kindergarten Inc (United Fund Agy) 1956-62; chrmn trustee bd Tabernacle Bapt Ch 1965-67; chmn Comm Action Council of Palm Beach Co 1967-68; past mem Gulf-stream Council BSA; Phi Beta Sigma; Vanguard Club; Elk; Mason; bd Palm Beach Co Chap AKC; legal adv local chap NAACP; dir Vis Nurses Assn. **HONORS/ACHIEVEMENTS:** Recipient Harriet T & Dorrah Merit Award FL Assn of Women's Club Inc 1963; citation for Comm Leadership State Voters League 1964; citation Omega Si Phi 1963; solid citizen Award Comm Round Table of W Palm Beach 1967; Comm Leadership Award City of Riviera Beach 1968; family of the year Tampa Urban League 1968. **BUSINESS ADDRESS:** 600 Rosemary Ave, West Palm Beach, FL 33401.

CUNNINGHAM, GLENN DALE
Law enforcement & elected official. **PERSONAL:** Born Sep 16, 1943, Jersey City, NJ. **EDUCATION:** Jersey City State Coll, BA cum laude 1974; Rutgers Sch of Criminal Justice, MA 27 credits. **CAREER:** Hudson Co NJ Bd of Chosen Freeholders, freeholder 1975-78; Jersey City State Coll, adjunct inst 1980-81; Housing Auth of Jersey City, housing & sec mgr 1982-84; Jersey City Police Dept, 1967- current rank capt, (on leave of absence while holding elective office). **ORGANIZATIONS:** Grad Natl Crime Prevnetion Inst 1976; mem Amer Acad for Prof Law Enforcement 1976-; mem Superior Officers Benevolent Assoc 1977; cert police inst NJ Police Training Comm 1977-; former exec bd mem NAACP 1978-80; bd of school estimates JC Bd of Educ 1981-82, 85-87; grad Security Mgmt & Admin Inst 1984; Jersey City Bank board of trustees. **HONORS/ACHIEVEMENTS:** Policeman of the Month Detectives Crime Clinic 1972; Outstanding Young Men of America Awd 1975; life fellow NJ Assn of Counties 1978; Muhamed Ali Awd Urban League of Hudson Co NJ 1980; Black Male Achievement Awd Tau Gamma Delta Sor Inc 1980; Alumnus Awd Jersey City State Coll 1982. **MILITARY SERVICE:** USMC nco 4 1/2 yrs; Honorable Discharge. **HOME ADDRESS:** 230 Bergen Ave, Jersey City, NJ 07305. **BUSINESS ADDRESS:** Council President, City of Jersey City NJ, 280 Grove St, Jersey City, NJ 07302.

CUNNINGHAM, JAMES J.
Educator. **PERSONAL:** Born Apr 19, 1938, Pittsburgh, PA; married Lois Vines; children: Lita Denise, James Jr. **EDUCATION:** BS, 1964; MA, 1967; EdS, 1969; DEd, 1971. **CAREER:** Elementary school teacher, 1964-66; Washington DC, counselor, prin 1966-68; Fed City Coll, Washington DC, 1968-71; Assoc Cont Res & Analysis Inc, Washington DC, consultant 1969; Fed City Coll, dir of admissions 1971; HEW/DE, Washington DC, consultant 1971; Moton Consortium on Adm & Financial Aid, co-dir 1971-72; TX Southern Univ, dean of students, prof of educ 1972-74; Mankato State Coll, Mankato MN, vice pres student servs, prof of educ 1974-; TX Southern Univ Houston, special asst to the pres 1986, prof of educ, vice pres institutional advancement. **ORGANIZATIONS:** Mem Natl Assn for Higher Edn; Personnel Guidance Assn; Assn of Coll Adm Counselors; DC Couns Assn; Elem Classroom Tchrs Assn; Natl Tchrs Assn; TX Personnel Serv Adminstrs; MN State Coll Student Assn; MN Student Serv Adminstrn; NAACP. **HONORS/ACHIEVEMENTS:** Listed Who's Who Among Student in Amer Univ & Colls 1962-63. **MILITARY SERVICE:** USAF A/1C 1955-59. **BUSINESS ADDRESS:** Vice Pres Institut Advancemnt, Texas Southern University, 3100 Cleburne St, Houston, TX 77004.

CUNNINGHAM, JOHN F.
Clergyman. **PERSONAL:** Born Oct 27, 1941, Homer, LA; married Alva Atkinson; children: Michael, Timothy. **EDUCATION:** Am Bapt Theol Sem Nashville, BA 1965. **CAREER:** Mt Enon Baptist Church, pastor; Mt Olive Bapt Ch Clarksville TN, former pastor, active leader 1964-; Bd Trustees Am Bapt Coll of Bible Nashville TN, mem; The So & Nat Bapt Conv USA Inc, a joint venture; Clarksville Bapt Extension Unit of Am Bapt Coll of Bible, registrar, treas, instr. **ORGANIZATIONS:** Pres Clarksville Br NAACP 1968-72; chmn Montegomery Co Voter's Council Affiliate of The TN Voter's Council; minority group chmn Clarksville Human Relations Commn 1969-71; mem Citizens Adv Task Force Clarksville; regional pres TN Bapt Educ Congress; mem The Educ Fund Com Lemoyne-Owen Coll Memphis; moderator Stones River Dist Assn 1969-72; mem Clarksville C of C; mem bd dir, treas TN Opportunity Program for Seasonal Farm Workers; mem bd dir Clarksville-Montgomery Co. **MILITARY SERVICE:** USO; AUS 1959-60. **BUSINESS ADDRESS:** Mt Enon Baptist Church, 1501 W Thrid, Dayton, OH 45407.

CUNNINGHAM, LOUIS ERNEST
Physician. **PERSONAL:** Born May 07, 1951, Jackson, TN. **EDUCATION:** Lane Coll, BS (Cum Laude) 1973; Meharry Medical Coll, MD (w/Honor) 1979. **CAREER:** Tulane Affiliated Hospitals, medical resident 1979-81; Hubbard Hosp of Meharry Medical Coll, medical resident 1981-82, chief resident/instructor 1982-83, asst prof of medicine 1983-85; Veterans Administration Hosp, staff physician 1983-85; Harlem Hospital Ctr, cardiology fellow 1985-. **ORGANIZATIONS:** Mem Natl Medical Assoc 1979, Natl Assoc of VA Physicians 1983, Amer Medical Assoc 1984, Amer Coll of Physicians 1984, Amer Heart Assoc 1984, TN Medical Soc 1984, Nashville Medical Soc 1984, Amer Coll of Cardiologists 1985. **HONORS/ACHIEVEMENTS:** Diplomate Amer Bd of Internal Medicine 1982; "Acute Lead Poisoning from the Betel Nut," w/T Worrel, J Leflore Journal of the Tennessee Medical Assoc Vol 78 No 8 1985.

CUNNINGHAM, MARGARET See DANNER, MARGARET ESSIE

CUNNINGHAM, PAUL RAYMOND GOLDWYN
Surgeon/educator. **PERSONAL:** Born Jul 28, 1949, Mandeville, Jamaica;son of Winston P Cunningham and Sylvia F Marsh Cunningham; married Sydney Keniston, Feb 14, 1987; children: Rachel, Lucinda. **EDUCATION:** University of the West Indies, Jamaica, MB, BS, 1966-72. **CAREER:** Joint Disease North General Hospital, New York NY, asst dir of surgery, 1979-81; Bertie Memorial Hosptial, Windsor NC, attending physician, 1981-84; East Carolina University, Greenville NC, asst professor of surgery, 1984—, preceptor for science track enhancement program, 1986—. **ORGANIZATIONS:** American Medical Association, National Medical Association, Southern Medical Association, Eastern Association for the Surgery of Trauma, Transplantation Society. **HONORS/ACHIEVEMENTS:** American College of Surgeons fellow, 1986. **BUSINESS ADDRESS:** East Carolina University, Department of Surgery, School of Medicine, Greenville, NC 27834.

CUNNINGHAM, RANDALL
Football player. **BUSINESS ADDRESS:** c/o The Philadelphia Eagles, Broad & Patsn, Philadelphia, PA 19148. *

CUNNINGHAM, RICHARD T.
Minister. **PERSONAL:** Born May 30, 1918, Dallas, TX; son of Edd Cunningham and Ida Henry Cunningham; married Jessie Jewel; children: R Theo Jr, Michaela, Carlotta, Carlette, Melanie. **EDUCATION:** Paul Quinn Coll, AB,, 1940; Dallas Thological Coll, MDiv. 1945; Mt Hope Bible Coll, D, Min, 1968. **CAREER:** Mt Hope Bible Coll Houston, fac mem pastor's tsch dirs 1974-; Christian ME Ch Houston, minister 1975-. **ORGANIZATIONS:** Trustee Phillips Sch of Theol Atlanta; mem Com on Episcopacy CME Ch; mem NAACP; mem Prince Hall Masonic Lodge; mem Harris Co Grand Jury Assn; trusteeTX Coll Tyler TX; chmn bd trustees Mt Hope Bible Coll Houston 1974; assoc editor The Christian Index Ofcl Orgn CME Ch; mem Adv comm to Mayor of Houston; mem TX Sheriff's Assoc; exec comm Ministers Conf at Prairie View Univ, TX Southern Univ Chaplaincy Prog; mem Interfaith Judicatory Forum Rice Univ; public relations consultant Houston Police Dept; trustee Houston Grad Sch of Theol.

CUNNINGHAM, SAMUEL LEWIS, JR.
Athlete. **PERSONAL:** Born Aug 15, 1950, Santa Barbara, CA. **CAREER:** Univ So CA, fullback; New England Patriots, all amUSDC 1974. **ORGANIZATIONS:** Team mvp Patriots 1974; Pro Bowl 1978. **BUSINESS ADDRESS:** New Eng Patroits, Schaefer Stad Rt 1, Foxboro, MA 02035.

CUNNINGHAM, VERENESSA SMALLS-BRANTLEY
Physician. **PERSONAL:** Born Aug 04, 1949, Charleston, SC; married Herman Cunningham. **EDUCATION:** Spelman Coll, BS 1971; Meharry Medical Coll, MD 1975. **CAREER:** Martland Hosp Newark NJ, resident 1975-76; Monmouth Medical Ctr Long Branch NJ, resident 1976-77, fellowship 1977-79; Perth Amboy General Hosp, dir of nurseries 1980-83; Private Practice, pediatrician 1983-85; Point Pleasant Hosp, dir of nursery 1985-86; Kaiser-Permanente, pediatrician/neonatologist. **ORGANIZATIONS:** Mem Amer Acad of Pediatrics 1983-85, Natl Assoc of Black Business & Professional Women 1985-, Atlanta Medical Soc 1987. **HONORS/ACHIEVEMENTS:** Achievement Awd Natl Council of Negro Women Inc North Shore Area 1985. **MILITARY SERVICE:** USAR capt 1 yr. **BUSINESS ADDRESS:** Pediatrician/Neonatologist, Kaiser-Permanente, 505 Fairburn Rd SW, Atlanta, GA 30331.

CUNNINGHAM, WILLIAM (PETE)
Business owner. **PERSONAL:** Born Nov 07, 1929, Union Co, NC; divorced. **EDUCATION:** Perry's Bus Coll, 1951; Johnson C Smith U, 1952-54; FL State Univ Extension, 1972. **CAREER:** NC Mutual Life Ins Co, debit mgr 1957-61; SE Bus Coll, instr 1969-70, vp, admin dean 1970-72; RSL, assoc dir of minority recruiting 1972-73; Hatchett & Cunningham Assoc, partner; Affordable Used Car, owner; NC House of Representatives, rep; HKL Inc, chief exec officer. **ORGANIZATIONS:** Mem Charlotte C of C; Charlotte BBB; mem Parkwood Inst CME Ch; YMCA; Retired Veterans Assn; Johnson C Smith Alumni Assn; CLU Civil Liberties Union; contributing mem United Negro Coll Fund; mem Voter Educ Proj; contributing mem Urban League. **MILITARY SERVICE:** USN 20 yrs active duty. **BUSINESS ADDRESS:** Chief Executive Officer, HKL Inc, 1915 I 85 North, Charlotte, NC 28216.

CUNNINGHAM, WILLIAM DEAN
Educator. **PERSONAL:** Born Aug 09, 1937, Kansas City, MO; divorced; children: Crystal. **EDUCATION:** Univ of KS, BA 1959; Univ of TX, MLS 1962, PhD 1972. **CAREER:** Federal Aviation Agency, chief library serv 1965-67; Topeka Public Library, head adult serv 1967-68; US Dept of Educ, program officer 1968-71; Howard Univ, dir univ libraries 1970-73; Univ of MD Coll of Library & Information Services, asst prof 1973-. **ORGANIZATIONS:** Mem Amer Library Assn 1970-, Assn for the Study of Afro-Amer Life and History 1974-; bd dirs Soul Journey Enterprises 1974-; mem Natl Black Heritage Council 1984-. **HONORS/ACHIEVEMENTS:** Citations from Dept of Education, FAA, ASALA; books "Blacks in Performing Arts", co-author "Black Guide to Washington". **MILITARY SERVICE:** USAF t/sgt 1954-60. **BUSINESS ADDRESS:** Assistant Professor, University of Maryland, Coll of Library & Info Serv, College Park, MD 20742.

CUNNINGHAM, WILLIAM E.
Physician. **PERSONAL:** Born Apr 06, 1920, Chicago, IL. **EDUCATION:** Northwestern Univ, 1942; Howard Univ Sch of Med, 1945. **CAREER:** Self-employed, physician; Michael Reese Hospital & Mercy, staff pos. **ORGANIZATIONS:** Mem Am Med Assn; mem IL St Med Soc; mem Chicago Med Soc; mem Nat Med Vet Soc; mem Military Surgeons of US; mem Med & Assn of Chicago; mem Med Assn Bldg Corp; past pres Med Assn Bldg Corp 1974,75. **MILITARY SERVICE:** USNG brig general retired. **BUSINESS ADDRESS:** 3233 S King Dr, Chicago, IL 60616.

CUNNINGHAM, WILLIAM L.
Government official. **PERSONAL:** Born Aug 28, 1939, Little Rock, AR; children: Karm Joy. **EDUCATION:** Univ of AR Pine Bluff, BS 1961; St Vincent Med Center Little Rock, Asso 1964; US Dept Of Agriculture Salt Lake City, Mgmt Cert 1967; Univ of Utah Salt Lake City, MA 1972. **CAREER:** State of UT Anti-dicrimination Div, investigator/concilator, pres; State of UT, lbr econmst 1970-72; Univ of Wash Med Center, lab supr 1968-70; US Dept of Agrl, agr engr 1966-68; Univ of UT Med Center, researcher 1965-66; Univ of AR Med Cen-

ter, biochemist 1964-65; US Dept of Agrl, field adv 1965-68; Wash Univ Med Center, med consult 1968-69; State Of UT, economist adv 1971-73. **ORGANIZATIONS:** Bd mem NAACP 1957-61; officer Elks 1965-68; bd mem Elks 1966-67. **HONORS/ACHIEVEMENTS:** Special service award USAF 1962; hon mem cert am Basketball Assn 1973; spl serv award, Elks 1975; exalted ruler award Elks 1977; outstanding citizen award Elks 1979. **MILITARY SERVICE:** USAF a/1c 1961-63. **BUSINESS ADDRESS:** Sr Investigator, Conciliator, State of Utah, 160 E 300 S, Salt Lake City, UT 84102.

CURETON, JOHN PORTER
Personnel manager. **PERSONAL:** Born Oct 04, 1936, Oxford, NC; married Carolyn Bethea; children: Tonya Yvette, John Porter. **EDUCATION:** Johnson C Smith Univ, BS Psychol 1960; Adelphia Univ, postgrad 1960-61; Univ of PA, attended 1962-63; Univ of Hartford, M Orgnl Behavior 1980. **CAREER:** NY State Dept Mental Hybiene, psychiat soc wrkr 1960-62; Inter-State Staffing Inc, mgmt consult 1962-66; Philco Ford Corp, sr employ rep 1966-68; Tanatex Div Sybron Corp, indus rela mgr 1968-73; US Postal Svcs, reg labor rela exec 1973-75; Heublein Inc Groc Products Grp, mgr empl rela 1975-78; US Tobacco Co, vice pres of personnel 1978-. **ORGANIZATIONS:** Mem Natl Assn of Market Developers; mem Employment Mgmt Assoc; mem Inst Rela & Rsch; mem Inst Collective Bargaining & Group Relations; mem Amer Soc Prsnl Admins; mem Amer Soc Training & Develop; mem NY Indus Rela Soc Inc; bd mem Voluntary Action Ctr; mem Ct UNCF Comm; mem Kappa Alpha Psi; mem Natl Urban League, NAACP. **BUSINESS ADDRESS:** Vice President of Personnel, US Tobacco Co, 100 W Putnam Ave, Greenwich, CT 06830.

CURETON, STEWART CLEVELAND
Clergyman, educational administrator. **PERSONAL:** Born Mar 24, 1930, Greenville, SC; married Claudette Hazel Chapman; children: Ruthye E Cooley, Stewart C Jr, Santee Charles, Samuel C. **EDUCATION:** Benedict Coll, AB, 1953; Starks School of Theology, BD 1956; Morris Coll, Dr of Divinity, 1982; Benedict Coll, Dir of Divinity 1983. **CAREER:** North Warren HS, instructor 1956-61; Beck HS, instructor 1965-82; Amer Baptist Theological Seminary, instructor 1961-85; SC Congress of Christian Education, instructor 1965-83. **ORGANIZATIONS:** Moderator Reedy River Baptist Assn 1972-76; state vice pres Natl Baptist Convention 1977-85; commissioner Human Relations 1978-84; state rep of E&M Baptist Convention of SC; honorary state vice pres NAACP 1982-83; member Urban League Board of Directors 1983; treasurer SHARE 1983-85. **HONORS/ACHIEVEMENTS:** Service Award Martin Webb Learning Center 1980; Outstanding Citizen Human Relations 1983; Outstanding Service Christian Action Council 1984; Outstanding Serv Awd South Carolina State House of Representatives 1986. **HOME ADDRESS:** 1103 White Horse Rd, Greenville, SC 29605.

CURLS, PHILLIP B.
Elected official. **PERSONAL:** Born Apr 02, 1942, Kansas City, MO; married Melba; children: Phillip II, Michael, Monica Joi, Louis Brandon. **EDUCATION:** Rockhurst Coll, BS, BA 1965; OH State Univ, Univ of KS, Chicago Univ, Add Studies. **CAREER:** Jackson Cty Circuit Court, asst clerk 1960-67; Oper Upgrade of Model Cities Prog, chief fin admin 1970-71; MO State Rep, rep 1972-83; MO State Senate 9th Dist, senator 1983-. **ORGANIZATIONS:** Sec, treas Curls, Curls & Assoc; past pres Freedom Inc; mem Appraisers Inst. **BUSINESS ADDRESS:** Senator, MO State Senate 9th Dist, State Capitol Building, Jefferson City, MO 65101.

CURRENT, GLOSTER BRYANT
Retired administrator, retired clergyman. **PERSONAL:** Born Apr 26, 1913, Indianapolis, IN; son of John T and Earsy P Current; married Rebecca Busch; children: Angela, Gloster Jr, John. **EDUCATION:** WV State, AB 1941; Wayne State Detroit, MI, MPA 1950; Rust Coll, Hon HHD 1977; Bethune Cookman Coll FL, Hon LLD 1977; attended Detroit Inst of Musical Art. **CAREER:** Detroit NAACP, exec sec 1941-46; New York NAACP, dir of branches 1946-77, administrator 1976-77; NAACP, dep to ex dir 1977-78; WestchesterUnited Methodist Ch, pastor 1979-83; Brooklyn, NY NAACP, deputy exec dir 1983-84; retired administrator/retired minister. **ORGANIZATIONS:** Mem Kappa Alpha Psi Frat 1939-; life mem NAACP 1957-; Band Leader Gloster Current's Orchestra 1930-39; asst pastor St Paul United Methodist Ch 1953-78; bd mem NY State Minority Comm Aging 1984-; bd mem Ft Schuyler House NY 1984-; bd mem Natl Caucus & Center on Black Aged 1983-; bd mem & vice pres United Methodist City Soc NY 1975-; pres, United Methodist City Society 1989-; bd mem, General Bd of Discipleship, United Methodist Church 1984, 1988-. **HONORS/ACHIEVEMENTS:** Delegate Gen and Jurisdictional Conferences United Meth Ch 1972, 1976, 1984; Living Legacy Award from Natl Caucus Black Aged 1979; Natl Parliamentarian-NANM Natl Assn Negro Musicians 1977-. **HOME ADDRESS:** 100-30-203rd St, Hollis, NY 11423.

CURRIE, EDDIE L.
Business executive, clergyman. **PERSONAL:** Born Sep 05, 1927, Brownsville, TN; married Mildred. **EDUCATION:** Lane Coll, BA 1954; San Francisco State; So Bapt Theol Sem, 1959; Memphis State U, BD 1974. **CAREER:** 1st Bapt Ch Brownsville;; pastor 1957-67; Christ Missionary Bapt Ch; Soul Rands Inc, vice pres 1970-72; Lowensteins Dept Store, buyer, mgr 1972-73; Ed Currie& Assos, pres. **ORGANIZATIONS:** Mem Memphis Bd Educ 1959-64; Memphis & Shelby County Neighborhood Youth Corps 1965-67; Nat Urban League 1967-69; Frontiers Intl Inc; Alpha Phi Alpha Frat; Nat Bus League; pres NAACP pres Haywood County Br 1960-65; Blk Econ Adv Com To Sml Bus Admst; Shelby County Dem Club; United Dem Com;W TN BM & E Assn; Memphis Educ Assn; TN Educ Assn; Nat Educ Assn mem Haywood County Civic & Welfare League 1959-67; Operation Freedom 1960-74. **HONORS/ACHIEVEMENTS:** Acad Dean's Award 1954; Statue Liberty Annual Award, Women For Legisslative Action 1962; Humanitarian Award, Ministers Philadelphia & Vicinity 1964. **MILITARY SERVICE:** AUS 1954-56. **BUSINESS ADDRESS:** 347 N Main, Memphis, TN 38103.

CURRY, CHARLES E.
Business executive. **PERSONAL:** Born Jan 22, 1934, Jackson, TN; married Beverly; children: Charles F, David E, Michael A. **EDUCATION:** Lane Coll Jackson TN, AB 1955; Emory Univ Atlanta GA, 1973; King Meml Coll, Hon Doctorate 1977. **CAREER:** Quaker Oats Co, mgr comm affairs. **ORGANIZATIONS:** Exec dir Youth Action 1969-70; deputy dir Youth Action 1968; area dir & westside Youth Action 1966-67; dir Chicago Youth Cntr Streetwork Prog 1965; Advisory Com Chicago ALL Of Business 1969-70; Chicago Catalyst 1967-72; Gtr Lawndale Consult Comm 1967-68; Mid-west Vice Pres Nat Urban Affairs Coun 1972-73; pres Urban Affairs Coun 1972-73; mem Public Affairs Coun Wash 1971-; mem Nat Assn Manuf; chairman Urban Affairs Com; exec con Chicago Urban Affaris Coun 1974; So Shore Valley Org 1969-; Mid-west Vice Pres Lane Coll Alumni Assn; Chicago Chap Pres Lane Coll Alumni Assnl; bd dir Chatam YMCA 1972; bd dir Urban Gateway 1973; bd of trustees Lane Coll 1977; adv bdUniv Of Chicago Metro Cntr 1972; Steering Com NAACP Legal & Defense Fund 1972. **HONORS/ACHIEVEMENTS:** Spec Alumni Award for outstand serv 1972-74; Lane Coll WGRT Good Guy Award 1973; a salute to Black bus & pronl Men Leag Of Black Women 1977; Achievement Award for youth serv Inspiration For Youth 1973; Beautiful People Award Chicago Urban League 1974. **BUSINESS ADDRESS:** Merchandise Mart Plaza, Chicago, IL 60654.

CURRY, CLARENCE F., JR.
Lecturer. **PERSONAL:** Born Aug 15, 1943, Hampton, VA; married Agnes A Mason; children: Clarence III, Candace. **EDUCATION:** Lafayette Coll, BS Met Eng 1965; Univ of Pittsburgh, MBA 1971; Carnegie Mellon U, MS IA 1973. **CAREER:** Univ of Pittsburgh, 1974-; Westinghouse Elec, engr; Univ of Pittsburgh School of Business, director Small Business Devel Center. **ORGANIZATIONS:** Panelist Amer Arbitration Assn; several consulting projects for 500 Firms; United Way; Minority Business Opportunity Comm. **HONORS/ACHIEVEMENTS:** Pennsylvania Minority Business Advocate SBA 1983. **BUSINESS ADDRESS:** Dir Small Business Devel Ctr, Graduate School of Business, Univ of Pittsburgh, 343 Mervis Hall, Pittsburgh, PA 15260.

CURRY, GEORGE E.
Reporter, author. **PERSONAL:** Born Feb 23, 1947, Tuscaloosa, AL; married Jacqueline. **EDUCATION:** Knoxville Coll, 1970; Harvard U; Yale U. **CAREER:** Sports Illus, rptr 1970-72; St Louis Post-dispatch, rptr 1972-; St Lou Is Assn of Black Journ, co-fndr. **ORGANIZATIONS:** Mem Soc of Pro Journalists Sigma Delta Chi; bd mem St Louis Journalism Review; spec corresp The NY Times; bd mem Metro St Louis Sickle Cell Anemia Assn; bd mem Knoxville Coll 1969-70. **HONORS/ACHIEVEMENTS:** Nom Pulitzer Prize; Who's Who Ammong Students In Amer Univ and Col 1969-70; appear on The Today Show 1969; United Negro Coll Funds Award for Leadership inthe Overall Improvement of a Pre-alumni Chap 1969; author,"Jake Gaither, Americas Most Famous Black Coach" Dodd Mead & Co 1977; listed Contemporary Authors; Comm Ldrs & Noteworthy Ams 1976-77. **BUSINESS ADDRESS:** C/O St Louis Post- Dispatch, 1133 Martin Luther King Dr, St Louis, MO 63101.

CURRY, GLADYS J. See WASHINGTON, GLADYS J.

CURRY, JERRY RALPH
Former army officer/assoc executive. **PERSONAL:** Born Sep 07, 1932, McKeesport, PA; children: Charlein, Jerry, Toni, Natasha. **EDUCATION:** Univ of NE, BA 1960; Command and General Staff Coll, 1967; Boston Univ, MS Internatl Relations 1970; Luther Rice Seminary, D Ministry 1978. **CAREER:** AUS War Coll, promoted from 2nd lt 1952 to brig gen Aug 1975; Vietnam, sr advisor 1970-71; AUS WA, ops rsch analyst ofc as asst v chief of staff 1971-72; 3rd Inf Div Germany, brig cmdr 1973; V Corps Frankfurt Germany, chief of staff 1975-76; 4th Inf Div Ft Carson, asst div comdg gen 1977-78; AUS Test & Eval Command Aberdeen Proving Ground MD, comdg gen 1978-79; Dept Defense, asst sec pub affairs 1979-; V Corps, chief of staff retired 1985; Natl Perspectives Inst, founder/pres 1984-; The Freedom Council, pres 1984-. **ORGANIZATIONS:** Bd of dirs Greenleaf Found 1979-; bd regents CBN Univ; mem Natl Eagle Scout Assoc, Intl Honor Soc History. **HONORS/ACHIEVEMENTS:** Disting Alumni Univ NE 1979; Washingtonian of Year 1982. **MILITARY SERVICE:** AUS commd 2nd lt 1952; Infantryman Badge; Parachutist Badge; Master Army Aviator Badge; Legion of Merit w/Oak Leaf Cluster; Bronze Star w/V Device; Silver Star; Cross of Gallantry w/Palm (Vietnam). **BUSINESS ADDRESS:** 3328 Upper Palace Green, Virginia Beach, VA 23452.

CURRY, LEVY HENRY
Personnel administrator. **PERSONAL:** Born Feb 03, 1949, Buffalo, NY; married Dianne. **EDUCATION:** Morehouse Coll, BA 1971; Atlanta Law Sch, JD 1975; FL Intl U, hon 1975. **CAREER:** Steak & Ale Restaurants Of Am, Dir of personl 1975-; Steak & Ale Restaurt, dir of affirmative 1975; Equal & Employment Opportunity Commn, legal research analyst 1974; Intl Harvester Co, sales mgr 1971-73; Colsolid Mfg Co, plant mgr 1971; Nat Urban League Beep Program, vis prof 197 7; Hospitality Industries Inc, bd of dir 1978. **ORGANIZATIONS:** Mem bd of dir Chain Restaurant Compensation Assn 1978; Morris Brown Coll Sch of Restaurant & Instrumental Mgmt 1977; mem Dallas Personnel Assn/Am Socof Personnel 1977; consult jr Achievement Project Bus 1979. **HONORS/ACHIEVEMENTS:** Mary C Miller Scholarship, Nat Urban League 1967; hon degree FL Intern AtUniv 1976. **HOME ADDRESS:** 636 Misty Glen, Dallas, TX 75232.

CURRY, MITCHELL L.
Clergyman, author, psychotherapist. **PERSONAL:** Born Feb 05, 1935, Augusta, GA; son of Walter M Curry and Ernestine Curry; married Carolyn D; children: Sonja M, Edwards, Reuben B, Rachel M, Michele L. **EDUCATION:** Morris Brown Coll Atlanta GA, BA 1960; Andover Newton Theol Sch Newton Ctr MA, MDiv 1964; Univ of Louisville, Lousville KY, MSSW 1972; Schl of Theol at Claremont CA, PhD 1979. **CAREER:** Natl Urban League-Western Reg, asst reg dir 1972-75; Lewis Metro Meth Ch LA, minister 1974-76; Florence Ar Presby Ch LA, minister 1976-80; LA Co Dept Mental Htlh, psychotherapist 1976-; Allen AME Ch San Bernadino, pastor 1985-; psychotherapist in private practice; Curry Temple AME Church, Los Angeles, pastor 1989. **ORGANIZATIONS:** Consult Natl Inst of Mntl Htlh 1972-79; flw Am Assoc of Pastoral Couns 1979; LCSW State of CA 1975; mem ACSW NASW 1974; mem brd of govr Natl Council of Ch 1980; mem Alpha Phi Alpha Frat 1959. **HONORS/ACHIEVEMENTS:** LHD Reed Christ Coll Angeles 1976; scholarship Grant Natl Inst of Mental Health 1970-72; scholarship Grant Lilly Found 1961; scholarship Grant Am Missionary Assoc 1960-64. **MILITARY SERVICE:** AUS 1954-56. **BUSINESS ADDRESS:** Psychotherapist, Crenshaw Counseling Service, 4306 Crenshaw Bl, Los Angeles, CA 90068.

CURRY, NORVELLE
Physician. **PERSONAL:** Born Apr 05, 1930, Memphis, TN; married Eleanor Alice Barnes; children: Debra L Bowen, Norvelle M, Michael S, Michele R. **EDUCATION:** LeMoyne Coll Memphis, BS 1951; NY Univ, MA 1954; Meharry Med Coll Nashville, MD 1955-59. **CAREER:** McKeesport Hosp PA, intern 1959-60; USN, gen med officer 1961-62; NAS N Is-

land & Imperial Beach CA, naval flight surgeon 1962-66; NRMC San Diego, urology res 1966-70; NRMC Camp Pendelton CA, chief/dept of urology 1970-71; NRMC San Diego, asst chmn/dept of urology 1972-77; Naval Regional Med Ctr Camp Pendelton CA, chief dept of urology 1977-. **ORGANIZATIONS:** Mem Soc of Govt Serv Urologists 1973; mem Assn Military Surgeons of US 1973; mem Amer Urology Assn 1973; mem Amer Fertility Soc 1974; mem Natl Med Assn and Amer Med Assn 1983; diplomate Amer Bd of Urology 1973; fellow Amer Coll of Surgeons 1974; consulting staff urology Univ Hosp San Diego. **MILITARY SERVICE:** USN capt 1961-; Natl Defense Medal.

CURRY, PHYLLIS JOAN
Government official. **PERSONAL:** Born Apr 05, 1929, Pittsburgh, PA; married Joseph. **EDUCATION:** Hunter Coll of the City of New York, BA; Columbia Univ Sch Of Social Work, MS Social Work 1969. **CAREER:** NY State Dept of Correction Serv, superintendnt 1977-; NY & State Dept Correction Serv, dep supt for progm 1977; NY State Dept of Correction Serv, regnl training coordinator 1972-77; NY State Div of Parole, parole ofcr/supr 1960-72; Dept of Social Serv, social worker 1955-60. **ORGANIZATIONS:** Mem Nat Council Crime & Delinquency 1979-; mem Am Correction Assn Spt & Wardens Assn 1979-; student/faculty adv com ColumbiaUniv Sch of Social Work 1967-69; mem ColumbiaUniv Sch of Social Work Alumni 1969-; mem Coalition of 100 Black Women 1977-; adv council Westchester Community Coll 1977-; adv com Dept Corr Servs-multi-yr Plan 1979-; mem Middle Atlantic States Correction Assn 1980. **BUSINESS ADDRESS:** 247 & Harris Rd, Bedford Hills, NY 10507.

CURRY, SADYE BEATRYCE
Educator, physician. **PERSONAL:** Born in Reidsville, NC; daughter of Charlie Will Curry and Limmmer Palmer Curry. **EDUCATION:** Johnson C Smith Univ, cum laude 1963; Howard Univ Coll of Med, 1967; Duke Univ Med Center, Internship 1967-68. **CAREER:** VA Hospital, Washington, DC, residency 1968-69; NIH Fellowship in Gastroenterlogy; Duke Univ, instructor in medicine 1969-72; Howard Univ, asst prof of medicine 1972-77; Howard Univ Svc, Washington DC General Hospital, asst chief medical officer 1973-74; Howard Univ Coll of Medicine, asst chief of medicine 1974-78, assoc prof of med, 1978-. **ORGANIZATIONS:** Mem Natl Med Assn; Am Med Assn; Medico-chirurgical Soc of DC; DC Med Soc; Nat Insts of Health-nat Inst of Arthritis Metabolic & Digestive Diseases Training Grants Com in Gastroenterolgy & Natrition 1972-73; mem Am Digestive Diseases Soc; mem Gastrointestinal Drug Adv Com FDA 1975-76; mem Alpha Kappa Alpha; Beta Kappa Chi; Alpha Kappa Mu; US Friendship Force ambassador to West Berlin, 1980; immediate past pres, Leonidas Berry Society for Digestive Diseases; mem, bd of trustees, Lake Land Or Property Owners Assn, Ladysmith VA. **HONORS/ACHIEVEMENTS:** Recipient student council faculty award for teaching excellence Howard Univ Coll of Med 1975; Kaiser-Permanente Award for Excellence in Teaching Howard Univ Coll of Med 1978. **BUSINESS ADDRESS:** Associate Professor of Medicine, Howard Univ Hospital, 2401 Georgia Ave, NW, Washington, DC 20060.

CURRY, WILLIAM THOMAS
Physician, surgeon. **PERSONAL:** Born Jan 04, 1943, Mineola, NY; married Katherine E Lum; children: William Jr, Christian. **EDUCATION:** NY Univ, BS 1964; Howard Univ, MD 1968. **CAREER:** George Wash Hosp, surgical intern 1968-69; The NY Hosp Cornell Med Ctr, surgical resident 1969-72, chief resident surgeon 1972-73; Cornell Univ Med Coll, asst prof; NY Hosp, attending surgeon. **ORGANIZATIONS:** Practicing gen & vascular surgery with emphasis on cancer; fellow surgery 1969-72; instr surgery 1972-76; clinical asst prof surgery Cornell Univ Med Coll 1976-; diplomate Amer Bd of Surgery 1974; fellow Amer Coll of Surgeons 1976; Kappa Alpha Psi Frat; Reveille Club of NY; mem bd dir Music for Westchester Symphony Orch; Mt Kisco Country Club. **MILITARY SERVICE:** AUSR med corps 1972. **BUSINESS ADDRESS:** New York Hospital, 342 E 67th St, New York, NY 10021.

CURSON, THEODORE
Musician. **PERSONAL:** Born Jun 03, 1935, Philadelphia, PA; married Marjorie; children: Charlene, Theodore II. **EDUCATION:** Granoff Mus Conservatory, 1952-53. **CAREER:** PBS TV Show "Jazz Set", Star 1972; NY U, Concerts; Antibes, Lugano, Warsaw, And Others, appearances, radio, tv, clubs, jazz festivals; Max Roach, Joe Jones, trumpeter; Jazz Festivals incl, Jazz Yatra in India, Pori Jazz Festival in Finland 1965-87, Camden Festival in England, Monterey in CA, Bled in Yugoslavia, Blue Note Jam Session NYC, Le Petit Opportun Paris, Juan Sebastian Club Caracas Venezuela; recording artist, jazz trumpeter & bandleader. **ORGANIZATIONS:** Mem Charles Mingus & Jazz Wrksp 1959-60; pres Nosruc Pub Co 1961-; mem Am Fedn Musicians. **HONORS/ACHIEVEMENTS:** Composer "Fliptop" 1977; "Typical Ted" 1977; new jazz artist Jazz Podium; Ted Curson & Co winner Down Beat Readers Poll 1978; LI Musicians Soc Awd 1970; albums, Snake Johnson, Ted Curson & Co, Canadian Concert 1985-86.

CURTIS, HARRY S.
Data processing manager. **PERSONAL:** Born Aug 26, 1934, Springfield, IL; married Syovia; children: Diana, Harry Jr, Eric, Christopher. **EDUCATION:** Attended Thornton Comm Coll of Chicago; Gov's State Univ, BA Public Admin. **CAREER:** DKV Estates, real estate salesman 1964-66; RR Retirement Bd, supervisory computer systems analyst. **ORGANIZATIONS:** Mem bd dirs Natl Caucus Black Sch Bd Mems 1970-; pres Bd of Educ Dist #147 1972-73, 1976-79, 1970-83; chief negotiator bd of edn; Vol Police Reserve Harvey 1975-; mem Scottish Rite Masonic Order AF & AM; mem Nobles of the Mystic Shrine; mem Federal Mgrs Assoc, Natl Sch Bd Assoc Federal Relations Network 1982-83. **HONORS/ACHIEVEMENTS:** Nominee Outstanding Supr Employee Fed Employee of Yr. **MILITARY SERVICE:** IL NG 1956-62. **BUSINESS ADDRESS:** Super Computer Sys Analyst, US Railroad Retirement Board, 844 North Rush St, Chicago, IL 60611.

CURTIS, ISSAC FISHER
Professional athlete. **PERSONAL:** Born Oct 20, 1950, Santa Ana, CA; married Diana; children: Kesha, Issac. **EDUCATION:** Attended, San Diego State. **CAREER:** Weingardner & Hammons Inc, natl sales mgr; Cincinnati Bengals, wide receiver 1973-. **ORGANIZATIONS:** Active in charities. **HONORS/ACHIEVEMENTS:** Led NFL in average pass rec yds 1975; Pro Bowl (4 times); All Amer San Diego State Coll; All Time record for Bengal recepts. **BUSINESS ADDRESS:** Cincinnati Bengals, 711 Clinton Springs, Cincinnati, OH 45229.

CURTIS, JAMES L.
Physician, educator. **PERSONAL:** Born Apr 27, 1922, Jeffersonville, GA; married Vivian A Rawls; children: Lawrence, Paul. **EDUCATION:** Albion Coll, AB 1943; Univ of MI, MD 1946. **CAREER:** State Univ of NY, instructor asst prof 1954-67; Cornell Univ Med Coll, assoc prof 1968-81; Columbia Univ Clinic, prof of psychiatry 1982-. **ORGANIZATIONS:** Mem Amer Psychiatric Assn; Amer Orthopsychiatric Assn; NY Acad Medicine; Amer Acad Psychoanalysis; AMA; Natl Med Assn. **HONORS/ACHIEVEMENTS:** Published book Blacks Medical School & Soc; many other publications. **MILITARY SERVICE:** USAF capt 1952-54. **BUSINESS ADDRESS:** Dir of Psychiatry, Harlem Hospital Center, 506 Lenox Ave, New York, NY 10037.

CURTIS, JOSEPH F., SR.
Clergyman. **PERSONAL:** Born May 02, 1916, Washington, DC; son of Joseph M Curtis(deceased) and Mary Matilda Kelly Curtis(deceased); married Cora L (deceased); children: Joseph, Jr, Wilson T, Mary S. **EDUCATION:** St Augustine Seminary, Postal Inst; St Josephs Seminary, Diaconate Training; DC Gen Hosp, Chaplains Training. **CAREER:** US Post Office, cleaner/carrier/ clerk, Washington DC, 1941-69; US Post Office, foreman operator, Washington DC 1969-71; Holy Comforter-St Cyprian Church, minister 1971-; DC Gen Hosp, Asst Catholic chaplin 1971-74; Hadley Mem Hosp, Catholic chaplain 1974-83; Archdiose of Washington. **ORGANIZATIONS:** Mem Greater Washington Catholic Chaplains Assn; Natl Alliance of Postal & Fed Employees; Knights of St John Holy Name Society; St Vincent de Paul Soc. **MILITARY SERVICE:** USMC cpl.

CURTIS, JOSEPHINE MONICA
Educator. **PERSONAL:** Born Dec 23, 1903, Cincinnati, OH; married Guy P; children: Guy P. **EDUCATION:** Normal Tchr Training Sch St Louis; Kroeger Conservatory of Music St Louis MO; Univ of Chicago, PhD Hist & English; Columbia Univ New York City Hon; St Marys CollSouth Bend, HHD 1967. **CAREER:** Vashon High School, St Louis MO, teacher History & English, dean of girls. **ORGANIZATIONS:** Bd mem AAUW; bd mem Michiana Arts & Sci Council; bd mem St Josephs Co Scholarship Fund; mem Alpha Kappa Alpha Sorority; mem Urban League Guild; mem St Pierre Ruffin Club; co-chmn St Joseph Co Concerned Women; organizer HT Burielgh Misic Assn 1933; commr S Bend Housing Authority; bd mem Nat Conf of Christians & Jews; pres City Council PTA; pres Womens Council on Human Relations; founder St Joseph Co Decent Literature Com. **HONORS/ACHIEVEMENTS:** Hering House Serv Award 1950; Woman Of The Year, Indianapolis Recorder 1951; Human Relations Award - YMCA 1954; Award For housing, United Ch Women 1955; Who's Who of American Women 1959; NCC J Brotherhood Award 1961; Prince Hall Grand Lodge Masons Award 1962; Supreme Service Award, Alpha Kappa Alpha 1968; Josephine Curtis Day, Proclaimed By Mayor Jerry Miller 1975; Open House in Honor, HT Burleigh Music Assn 1975; Urban League Comm Serv Award 1977.

CURTIS, JUANITA GWENDOLYN
Educator. **PERSONAL:** Born Feb 06, 1920, Chicago, IL; married Norvel W Sr. **EDUCATION:** Phoenix Coll, diploma 1939; AZ St Univ Tempe, BA 1940; AZ St Univ Tempe, MA 1944; AZ St Univ Tempe, EdD 1963. **CAREER:** Univ of Pacific, prof of educ 1964-; Univ of Washington Seattle, guest lecturer 1969; Berkely Unified School Dist, curriculum consultant 1963-64; Prairie View A&M Coll TX, prof 1950-54; Sam Huston Tillotson Coll, prof 1946, summers 1947-49; Phoenix School Dist #1, teacher 1941-63; Avondale Elementary School AZ, teacher 1940-41. **ORGANIZATIONS:** Soc studies & reading consult State of NV Dept of Educ 1972-75; num professional consult through the country; wrkshps cond for num Sch past 30 yrs; mem Emmanuel Bap Ch/Stockton Chap of Links Inc/Intl Reading Assn/ASCD/ALPHA Kappa Alpha/Delta Kappa Gamma/Phy Delta Kappa/NEA/RELATED Professional Orgn; eval bd mem Nat Counc for Accreditation of Coll of Tchr Educ 1974-78.

CURVIN, ROBERT
Educator. **PERSONAL:** Born Feb 23, 1934, Newark, NJ; married Patricia; children: Frank, Nicole. **EDUCATION:** Rutgers, BA 1960; Rutgers, MSW 1967; Princeton, PhD 1975. **CAREER:** CUNY Brooklyn Coll, assoc prof; Rutgers Univ, lecturer comm des spl 1968-74; League for Industrial Democracy, dir training Program 1965-66; Essex City Welfare Bd, supvr case work 1960-65. **ORGANIZATIONS:** Treas 21st Century Found 1977; trst Princeton Univ 1977; trst Channel 13 WNET 1977; natl v chmn CORE; chmn Newark Essex CORE 1962-63; mem Tri-state RegPlanning Commn 1977; Com for Resp Legis 1977; Wallace Eljabar Flowsp 1971-73; Ford Found Travel Study 1976-77. **MILITARY SERVICE:** AUS 1st lt 1953-57. **BUSINESS ADDRESS:** Bedford & Ave H, Brooklyn, NY 11210.

CURWOOD, SARAH T.
Educator. **PERSONAL:** Born Jan 23, 1916, Binghamton, NY; widowed; children: Sarah Emily, Stephen Thomas. **EDUCATION:** Cornell U, AB 1937; Boston U, MEd 1947; Radcliffe Grad Sch, PhD 1956. **CAREER:** Rhode Island Coll, prof Sociology emerita; Self-employed, consult lecturer 1967-; Dept Chmn, Knoxvl Coll, prof Sociology 1969-70, visiting prof 1971-72; RI Coll, prof Socoligy 1972-; Univ of New Hampshire, lecturer 1968-69; Antioch Coll, asst prof 1955-61; Harvard Graduate School of Educ, lecturer 1952-55; Mass Com on Children & Youth, cons. **ORGANIZATIONS:** Fellow Am Sociol Assn; Intl Sociol Assn; Adv Com Rochingham Co Coop Extension Svc; Southern Sociol Assn; Black Caucus of Sociologists; Rockingham Co Woodlotowners Assn; mem GSA Nat Vol 1926; Friends Nat Legislation 1967-70; Execcom New England Div of Am Friends Serv Com; mem Phi Beta Kappa;Pi Lambda Theta; trustee Gullford Coll Greensboro NC 1984; natl bd mem Amer Friends Serv Comm 1986; adv comm 4H Natural Resources 1984-. **HONORS/ACHIEVEMENTS:** Recipient ella cabot lyman award 1968; comm leadership award 1971; providence human relations commn 1962-64; listed whos who among am women; whos who in theeast & other biogragpical editions. **HOME ADDRESS:** Doowruc Farm RFD 1 Box 38, Barrington, NH 03825.

CUSHINGBERRY, GEORGE, JR.
Government official. **PERSONAL:** Born Jan 06, 1953, Detroit, MI; married Maria Hazel Drew; children: George III, Brandon Drew. **EDUCATION:** Wayne State Univ, BA 1974. **CAREER:** Southend News Wayne State U, editor, vice-chmn Assn of Black Students; State of MI, state rep. **ORGANIZATIONS:** Mem Student Faculty Counc Wayne State U; trust Afro-Am Mus of Det; mem Detroit Pub Sch Decentrlztn Com; dir Westside Citzns for Retarded; dir Kirwood Mental Hosp; life mem NAACP; mem Optimist of N Detroit, Jr ROTC; pres Amer Coal Co 1984; mem plng comm Mt Carmel Mercy Hosp 1978-. **HONORS/**

ACHIEVEMENTS: Superior Cadet Awd Cass Tech High 1971; Young Man of The Year Jaycees 1975; Comm Serv Awd EBONI Women 1975; Young Dem Awd 1st Cong Dist 1975; Together Bros & Sisters Comm Serv Awd 1975; Man of The Year MI Chronicle Newspaper 1977. **HOME ADDRESS:** 8625 Marygrove, Detroit, MI 48221.

CUSHMAN, VERA F.
Manager. **PERSONAL:** Born Jul 28, 1944, Dermott, AR; married John R; children: Christophe Stephen. **EDUCATION:** Grambling Coll, BS Educ 1966; Univ of NM, MA 1974; Univ of MN, MA Pub Adminstrn. **CAREER:** BIA Navajo Reservation, teacher 1966-68; EEO Women in Mgmt Minority Women, panelist/cons natl & local workshop leader 1968-; Bur of Indian Affairs-Navajo Reservation, educ spec 1969-71; SW Indian & Polytech Inst, instr 1971-76; Dept of Interior, eeo investigator 1973-76; Natl Council Negro Women, various offices 1973-; Kirtland AFB, discrimination complaints officer 1976-. **ORGANIZATIONS:** Bd mem Albuquerque Montessori Sch 1975-77; del State of MN; Houston Womens Conf 1977; mem Standards & Goals Com Criminal Justice Dept Dtate of MN 1977; locator NM & AZ Contribution of Black Women 1978-79; mem NAACP, NOW, MN WPC; organizer, charter mem, officer Black Comm Forum 1979; pres Nat Council of Negro Women Albuquerque Chap 1980-81; mem Gov Penitentiary MN Blue Ribbon Panel to Monitor Invest of Riot & Advise the Govt on Improvement 1980; organizedlocal ACTSO NAACP 1982; pres Albq Bus & Professional Women 1985-86; youth dir, mem bd of dir Algq NAACP 1986-87; dir Dist I New Mex Fed of Bus & Professional Women 1987-88. **HONORS/ACHIEVEMENTS:** Who's Who in Am Coll & Univ 1966; Natl Council Negro Women 1976; Outstanding Young Woman of Amer 1982; Disting Public Serv Awd State of NM highes honor state bestows on a citizen 1985; Outstanding NM Woman 1986; NM Women's Hall of Fame 1986; chair, bicentennial project Pub Book "Profiles in Leadership The Black Woman in Amer". **BUSINESS ADDRESS:** Discrimination Compalints Ofcr, Kirtland AFB, 1606 Air Base Wing, Albuquerque, NM 87117.

CUSTER-CHEN, JOHNNIE M.
Staff attorney/government. **PERSONAL:** Born Aug 26, 1948, Birmingham, AL; divorced; children: Christopher, Michael. **EDUCATION:** Howard Univ, BA 1971; Washington Univ, MEd 1972; Cleveland-Marshall College of Law, JD 1984. **CAREER:** St Louis OIC, dir of counseling 1974-75; State Comm Coll, career educ counselor 1975-77; Cuyahoga Comm Coll, coord cooperative educ 1980-85; Loop Coll, dir cooperative educ 1986; IL Dept of Children and Family Svcs, attorney 1987-. **ORGANIZATIONS:** Mem Amer, Chicago and IL State Bar Assocs; mem PUSH, Urban League, League of Black Women. **HONORS/ACHIEVEMENTS:** Chicago's Up & Coming Black Business & Professional Women Awd Dollars & Sense Magazine 1986. **HOME ADDRESS:** 2801 So King Dr, Chicago, IL 60616. **BUSINESS ADDRESS:** Staff Attorney, IL Dept of Child & Fmly Serv, 100 West Randolph Ste 6-200, Chicago, IL 60601.

CUSTIS, CLARENCE A.
Business executive. **PERSONAL:** Born Nov 09, Bridgeton, NJ; married Yvonne; children: Steven, Kim, Jon, Darren. **CAREER:** Mainline Sales & Serv Co, owner; Moores Super Stores Vineland NJ Br, truckdriver, salesman, asst mgr; farmer 1959-64. **ORGANIZATIONS:** Mem Fairfield Twnshp Bd of Educ 1967-75; Farmers Home Adminstrn Loan Adv Com 1971-74; Cumberland Co Fairfield Vol Fire Co 1959-; chief bd dirs Intl Self Help Hsng Asso 1967-69; vP Cumberland Regional bd of edn. **HONORS/ACHIEVEMENTS:** Recip cert of merit FHA 1967; honored by Fairfield bd of educ 1975; Devoted Serv & Leadership. **MILITARY SERVICE:** USAF 1955-59.

CUTLER, DONALD
Educator. **PERSONAL:** Born Oct 20, 1943, Tampa, FL; married Rosemary N. **EDUCATION:** Albany State Coll Albany GA, BS 1971; GA State U. **CAREER:** Dougherty County Public Schools, educator 1972; Goodwill Ind, Albany GA, dir work adj training 1971-72; WJIZ Radio, Albany GA, disc jockey 1969-70; WAYX Radio, Waycross GA, radio announcer 1965-66; Waycross Jour Herald, Waycross GA, news correspondent 1965-66; WALB-TV, Albany GA, sports announcer, weekend anchor 1973-77; Cougherty Co Albany, co commr bd of commrs 1978-. **ORGANIZATIONS:** Vpp Cong of Black Orgn Albany 1977-; org/spokesman Albany Black Caucas 1979-; mem NEA/GAE/DCAE/NAACP; Handicapped Employer of the Year SW; GA Easter Seal Soc 1976; elected mem Dougherty Co Dem Exec Commn elected 1st Black Commr Dougherty Co Commn; elected mem Exec Com SW GA APDC. **BUSINESS ADDRESS:** Pine Ave, PO Box 1827, Albany, GA 31701.

CUTLIFF, JOHN WILSON
Assistant public defender. **PERSONAL:** Born Dec 02, 1923, Shreveport, LA; divorced; children: Jennifer C. **EDUCATION:** So U, BA 1945; Lincoln U, LlB 1948; NY U, LlM 1961; Atlanta U, MSLS 1968. **CAREER:** Private practice, atty 1980-; NC Central U, assoc law libr, assoc prof 1973-; Media Serv & Fed City Coll, assoc dir, assoc prof 1968-73; Howard Sch of Law, assoc law libr 1965-67; SC State Coll Sch of Law, law libr 1948-65. **ORGANIZATIONS:** Mem Amer Bar Assn; Natl Bar Assn; Amer Assn of Law Libraries; SC Bar 1950; life mem NAACP; Kappa Alpha Psi; mem Unitarian Universalist Assn; Ford Fellow, NYU 1959-61. **BUSINESS ADDRESS:** Attorney at Law, PO Box 1097, Chester, SC 29706.

CUYJET, ALOYSIUS BAXTER
Physician. **PERSONAL:** Born May 20, 1947, Jersey City, NJ; married Denise; children: Trevor. **EDUCATION:** Brandeis U, BA 1968; NY U, MD 1972. **CAREER:** Amer Bd of Intl Med, diplomat; Harlem Hosp Ctr, cardiology flw 1975-77, intern & resd 1972-75; Columbia Univ Coll of Physicians & Surgeons, asst instr 1975-77; United Hospitals Medical Ctr, dir adult critical care medicine, assoc dir dept of medicine. **HONORS/ACHIEVEMENTS:** Fellow Amer Coll of Cardiology 1988. **BUSINESS ADDRESS:** Assoc Dir Dept of Medicine, United Hospitals Med Ctr, 15 South 9th St, Newark, NJ 07107.

CUYJET-JOHNSON, CYNTHIA K.
Corporate development manager. **PERSONAL:** Born May 16, 1948, Philadelphia, PA; daughter of C Jerome Cuyjet and Esther King Cuyjet; married Bradley A Johnson, Jul 01, 1989. **EDUCATION:** Marymount Coll BA 1970; Jersey City State Coll, MA 1974; NYU. **CAREER:** Marymount Coll, Tarrytown, NY, admissions counselor 1970-71; Prudential Insurance Co, adult educ instr 1971-72; Jersey City St Coll, asst admission dir 1972-76; Selection & Placement Manager, Supermarkets Gen Corp, mgr 1976-77; Avon Products Inc, supr mgmt devel 1977, corporate mgr mgmt devel & training 1978-80, div sales mgr 1980-84; Coca Cola USA, mgr mgmt trng. **ORGANIZATIONS:** Co-chairperson, Women in Business Comm Atlanta Business League; mem Atlanta Womens Network; mem Amer Soc for Training/Develop 1984-85; chair employment comm Coalition of 100 Black Women; exec bd mem Council of Concerned Black Executives 1976-80; exec bd mem NJ Assoc for Sickle Cell Anemia; mem Black Merit Academy E St Louis IL; mem Black Executive Exchange Program Natl Urban League; mem, Amer Soc Training & Devel; mem, Atlanta Women's Network, consultant to Inroads/Atlanta, Inroads/Chicago. **HONORS/ACHIEVEMENTS:** Women in Business/Industry Award NCNW 1981; participant White House Conf Women in Work Force 1983. **BUSINESS ADDRESS:** Pres, Cuyjet Mgmt Consultants, Inc, 680 N Lake Shore Dr, Suite ll2l, Chicago, IL 60611.

D

DABBS, HENRY ERVEN
Television producer, art director. **PERSONAL:** Born Oct 15, 1932, Clover, VA; son of Charles and Gertrude; married Loretta D Young; children: Lisa DeLane. **EDUCATION:** Pratt Inst, BFA 1955. **CAREER:** Berton Wink Inc, book designer 1958-62; USN John F Small Adv Agency, creative dir minority adv 1975-78; Henry Dabbs Prod Englishtown NJ, pres 1977; Cinema & Graphic Design Jersey City St Coll, instr 1977; wrote produced and directed "Joshua" a full length feature film shot on location in Charleston SC and Harlem NY 1979; Fitzgerald Sample NYC, art dir producer dancer 1963-. **ORGANIZATIONS:** Produced original 39 paintings of famous Afro-Amer in Amer history permanent collection Frederick Douglass Mus Smithsonian Inst Washington; mem NAACP; created History Fact Pack 1968; First Multi-Media, audio visual prog on Black American,. **HONORS/ACHIEVEMENTS:** Author "Afro-Amer History Highlights" 1968; screened "Joshua" at the Cannes Film Festival France along with Steven Spielberg's ET 1982; authored & published "Black Brass" Black generals & admirals in the Armed Forces of the US the first book of its kind ever published 1984; aurthor Black History section NY Times. **MILITARY SERVICE:** AUS 1955-58.

DABNEY, DAVID HODGES
Psychiatrist, lobbyist. **PERSONAL:** Born Aug 18, 1927, Washington, DC; divorced. **EDUCATION:** Univ of PA, BA 1949; Howard Med Sch, MD 1955. **CAREER:** Mass Participation Lobbyists Assn, legal psychiatrist/registered lobbyist (Cong); Forensic Psychiatry Res Consultants, consultant. **ORGANIZATIONS:** Mem Omega Psi Phi 1946-; expert witness in courts (DC & State, Fed & Military) 1957-; experience in mental homes & prisons since 1957; mem Amer Psychiatric Assn; AMA; Amer Correctional Assn; DC Medical Soc; Washington Psychiatric Soc; Medico-Chirurgical Soc; Natl Medical Assn; consultant Skidmore Owings & Merrill Chicago; pres Chance for a Child Inc; bd dir Tiber Island Condominium 1965-70; SW Comm Assy Health & Welfare Task Force 1965-70; mem Univ of Pennsylvania Alumni Fund-Raising & Secondary Educ Committees. **HONORS/ACHIEVEMENTS:** Natl winner, Elks Oratorical Contest, "The Negro and the Constitution," 1943; author of publication voted Best Paper on Rehabilitation at APA Convention 1963; congressional candidate 1972, 1974; cited by judges of US Dist Ct of Appeals DC in landmark cases (criminal responsibility).

DACOSTA, SANDRA TRIM
Director (performing arts). **PERSONAL:** Born Nov 07, 1948, New York, NY; married Claude. **EDUCATION:** New York City Coll, Assoc; Richmond Coll, BA 1974. **CAREER:** Columbia Records, dir artist devel (first black female dir) 1979; CBS Records, assoc dir press info 1978; Rogers & Cowan, East Coast mgr 1974; Polydor, asst mgr 1969-72. **ORGANIZATIONS:** Bd of dirs Nzingha 1978-; mem Black Music Assn 1979-; mem NAACP Black Achiever Harlem YMCA 1980.

DADE, MALCOLM G.
Clergyman. **PERSONAL:** Born Feb 27, 1903, New Bedford, MA; son of Issaih Dade and Margaret Dade; married Sonnie Jean; children: Malcolm, Jr, Duwain, Margaret, Julie. **EDUCATION:** Lincoln Univ, BA, Williston Acad, attended; Episcopal Theol School, attended; Wilberforce Univ, Hon DD. **CAREER:** Dioces of MI, St Augustine, St Clements, Church of the Resurrection, admin asst to Bishop Richard S Emrich; The Episcopal Church of St Cyprian, rector emeritus. **ORGANIZATIONS:** Admin bd Detroit House of Correction 1974; gov bd Goodwill Indust of Detroit; Red Cross; mem Presiding Bishops Bi-Racial Comm of Protestant Episcopal Church; founder Westside Human Relations Counc; mem Alpha Phi Alpha, Grand Chaplain Masonic Lodge F&AM, 33 deree Mason; conferred Hon Canon of Cathedral Church of St Paul 1961; hon mem Local 600 UAW; mem MI State Troops; delegate to MI Const Conv 1964. **HONORS/ACHIEVEMENTS:** Cert of Tribute MI State Leg 1967; Brotherhood Awd Bethel AME Church 1978; Disting Warrior Awd Detroit Urban League 1983; Hon JD Boston Univ.

DADE, MALCOLM G., JR.
Executive assistant. **PERSONAL:** Born May 07, 1931, New Bedford, MA; married Kitty L Wallingford; children: Sharon, Malcolm G III, Karen. **EDUCATION:** Macalester Coll St Paul MN, attended; Wayne State Univ, BA Pol Sci; Wayne State Univ School of Social Work, grad studies; Columbia Univ, Exec Mgmt Prog. **CAREER:** The Detroit Edison Co, vice pres community & govt affairs; Sen Philip A Hart, special asst 1973; Coleman A Young, Mayor, campaign dir 1973, interim office 1973-74; Atty Gen Frank Kelley, State MI, admin asst 1971-73, senate campaign 1972; Off Sch Decentralization, asst decentralization coord 1970-71; Dem Party, dep chmn 1969-70; Dem State Central Com, staff dir 1968-70; Mayor's Com Human Resources Devel, 1968-70; Comm Children & Youth, 1963-67; Dept Pub Welfare, 1956-63. **ORGANIZATIONS:** Am Dem Act; Am Civil Lib Union; Trade Union Leadership Council. **MILITARY SERVICE:** USAF s/sgt 1951-55. **BUSINESS ADDRESS:** Vice President, The Detroit Edison Co, 2000 Second Ave, Detroit, MI 48226.

DAGGS, LEROY W.
Attorney. **PERSONAL:** Born Aug 09, 1924, St Louis; married Harriet; children: LeRoy, III, Leslie. **EDUCATION:** Univ MI, AB 1947; Univ Detroit, LLB 1952. **CAREER:** Detroit, int rev agt 1950-55; Daggs Ins Agy, owner 1955-68; pract atty Detroit 1953-. **ORGANIZATIONS:** Mem State Bar Of MI 1953-; Am Bar Assn 1953-; Detroit Bar Assn 1955-; Wolverine Bar Assn 1955-, dir 1947 & 75; mem Half Million Dollar Round Table (NIA) 1957;

mem student legisUniv MI 1946 & 47; life mem Alpha Phi Alpha Frat; life mem NAACP. **HONORS/ACHIEVEMENTS:** Outstanding Athlete Univ MI 1946-47; Honor Man Company US Navy 1943; outstanding contrb support of bowling basketball & baseball teams Brewster Cntr 1960-63; Univ MI Track Team 1946-47. **MILITARY SERVICE:** USN 1c 1942-45. **BUSINESS ADDRESS:** 3116 David Stott Bldg, Detroit, MI.

DAILEY, QUINTIN TERRELL
Professional athlete. **PERSONAL:** Born Jan 22, 1961, Baltimore, MD. **EDUCATION:** San Fran, 1981. **CAREER:** Chicago Bulls, guard 1982-. **HONORS/ACHIEVEMENTS:** Named mem NBA First Team All-Rookie Squad 1982-83; owned best rookie scoring mark in 1978-79.

DAILEY, THELMA
Association executive. **PERSONAL:** Born in Baltimore; divorced. **EDUCATION:** BA, AAS. **CAREER:** Trade Union Women of African Heritage Inc, pres, founder. **ORGANIZATIONS:** Bd mem NCNW; mem Women's Forum Inc; coord Bronx Chap United Nations Assn; Multi-Ethnic Woman Workshop at Fashion Inst Tech; publs The Ethnic Woman Inc; coord Inst of Polit Educ of Black Women; mem IWY Tribune. **BUSINESS ADDRESS:** 13 Astor Pl, New York, NY 10003.

DAIS, LARRY
Educational administrator. **PERSONAL:** Born Nov 03, 1945, Columbia, SC; son of Wade Dais and Manie Dais; married Olga D; children: Landon, Larik. **EDUCATION:** Baruch Coll, BS 1974; Columbia Univ Graduate School of Business, MS 1976; Cornell NYSSILR, and Hofstra Univ School of Law, Certificate, 1986. **CAREER:** Grumman Engrgineering, admin 1964-68; State Univ of Farmingdale, admin 1968; Leadership Inst Hofstra Univ, asst dir 1968-69; Columbia Coll, Columbia Univ, dir 1969-80; Columbia Univ, dir, asst vice pres govt relations & dir of community affairs. **ORGANIZATIONS:** Pres Natl Council of Educational Opportunity Progs 1982-84; sr vice pres NY Urban League; vice pres Harlem YMCA. **HONORS/ACHIEVEMENTS:** Various awards from professional civic & comm groups nationwide. **MILITARY SERVICE:** AUS sgt E-5 1960-63. **BUSINESS ADDRESS:** Dir, ColumbiaUniv, 301 Low Library, New York, NY 10027.

DALE, CLAMMA CHURITA
Opera singer. **PERSONAL:** Born Jul 04, 1948, Chester, PA. **EDUCATION:** Settlement Mus Sch Phila; studied with Alice Howland/Hans Heinz/Corneilius Reed; Juilliard Sch Opera, Masters Deg. **CAREER:** Houston Opera Co, singer 1976; NY City Opera Co, 1975; performed with Bronx Opera Co/Brooklyn Opera Theatre/Met Opera's Mini-Met; Houston Grand Opera Co,revival 1976-77; Manhattan Theatre Club, completed successful engagement singing popular works by Ellington/Rodgers & Hart/others 1977; appeared in premiere ofLeonard Bernstein's Am Song Cycle "Songfest" 1977; clarinet player. **HONORS/ACHIEVEMENTS:** Cue Golden Apple as Best Broadway Actress for role of Bess in "Porgy & Bess" 1976; recipient 2 Naumburg Awards; recitals at Avery Fischer Hall & Lincoln Cntr. **BUSINESS ADDRESS:** c/o ICM Artists Ltd, 40 W 57th St, New York, NY 10019.

DALE, ROBERT J.
Advertising agency owner. **PERSONAL:** Born May 02, 1943, Chicago, IL; son of Charles McDearmon and Jessie M Dale; married Shirley J White, Jul 08, 1989; children: Kondo, Yusef, Kareem. **EDUCATION:** Arizona State Univ, Tempe AZ, BS Business, 1971; Stanford Univ, Stanford CA, MBA Business/Mktg, 1973. **CAREER:** Kaiser Broadcasting, Chicago IL, account exec, 1973-74; Field Spot Television Sales, Chicago IL, natl account exec, 1974-75; F J Dale & Assoc, Chicago IL, consultant, 1976-78; Small Business Admin, Chicago IL, mgmt consultant, 1978-79; Chicago State Univ, Chicago IL, asst prof, 1979-84; R J Dale Advertising, Chicago IL, pres, CEO, 1979-. **ORGANIZATIONS:** Mem, Amer Mktg Assn, 1977-, PUSH Intl Trade Bureau, 1984-, Natl Black United Front-Chicago, 1984-, Amer Assn of Advertising Agencies, 1986-; bd mem, NAACP-Chicago; co-chair, Chicago State Univ Coll of Business Hall of Fame Bd, 1987-; advisory bd mem, Black Public Relations Soc-Chicago, 1988-; bd mem, March of Dimes Birth Defects Found, 1989-. **HONORS/ACHIEVEMENTS:** Outstanding Black Businessman Award, Natl Black United Front, 1986; Pinnacle Award, Being Single Magazine, 1989. **MILITARY SERVICE:** US Air Force, E-3, 1962-66. **BUSINESS ADDRESS:** President & Chief Executive Officer, R J Dale Advertising Inc, 500 N Michigan Ave, Suite 2204, Chicago, IL 60611.

DALE, VIRGINIA MARIE
Administrator, educator. **PERSONAL:** Born Aug 08, 1925, Haskell, OK; married Luther William Dale; children: Kenneth Ray Gilmore, Jr, Pamela Kay (McClain), Anita Ray (Harris), Joey Luther Dale. **EDUCATION:** KS State U, BS 1967; KS State U, San Jose State, KC MO U, Grad study. **CAREER:** Dale's Acad, admin, teacher; teacher in public schools for over 20 yrs; social worker. **ORGANIZATIONS:** Order of Eastern Star; Zeta Phi Beta; Black Econ Union; avd bd Penn Valleycoll; Am Fed of Tchrs; United Trade Group; mem West Paseo Christian Ch; orgnr Bus & Prof Women's Assn of Gr KC; San Mateo Chap Jack & Jill. **HONORS/ACHIEVEMENTS:** Elected Outstanding Woman of Year (Small Bus). **BUSINESS ADDRESS:** 7304 Cleveland, Kansas City, MO.

DALEY, GUILBERT ALFRED
Educator. **PERSONAL:** Born Dec 31, 1923, Washington, DC; married Thelma Thomas. **EDUCATION:** Catholic Univ of Amer, BA 1949, MA 1952; Univ of NC, LDA 1968; So IL Univ, PhD 1978. **CAREER:** Shaw Univ, Raleigh NC, asst prof 1953-62; NC High School Drama Assoc, exec dir 1953-62; Intercollegiate Drama Assoc, exec dir 1956-60; IDA, pres 1960-62; The Crescent, natl editor 1978-79, 1981-; Coppin State Coll, prof & coord speech/theatre 1962-. **ORGANIZATIONS:** Mem AAUP; Amer Theatre Assn; Coll Language Assn; Speech Assn of Amer; mem treas Gr Baltimore Arts Council 1966-69, pres 1969-71; mem Phi Beta Sigma1947-; vice pres Baltimore Pan-Hellenic Council; pres Zeta Sigma Chap Phi Beta Sigma Frat Inc; pres Wm T Dorsey Educ Loan Fund 1984. **HONORS/ACHIEVEMENTS:** Carolina Playmakers Scholarship 1960; Teaching Fellow SIU Carbondale. **MILITARY SERVICE:** AAF 1944-46. **BUSINESS ADDRESS:** Coordinator Speech Theatre, Coppin State College, 2500 W North Ave, Baltimore, MD 21216.

DALEY, THELMA THOMAS
Educator. **PERSONAL:** Born Jun 17, Annapolis; married Guilbert A. **EDUCATION:** Bowie St Coll, BS; NY U, MA. **CAREER:** Raleigh & Baltimore County Bd of Educ, prof, counselor; NC Central, Western MD Coll, Univ of WI, Harvard Univ, visiting instructor. **ORGANIZATIONS:** Nat pres Am Sch Counselor Assn 1971-72; natl treas Delta Sigma Theat 1963-67, natl vice pres 1971-75; pres Am Personnel & Guidance Assn 1975-76; mem NAACP; Black Adoption Prog 1968-73; Nat Proj Chrwmn 1967-71. **HONORS/ACHIEVEMENTS:** MD Personnel & Guidance Achievemt Award 1972; Life Mem Award NAACP 1973; appointed Commn Educ Panel Scholars Career Educ 1972; natl pres Delta Sigma 1975-77. **BUSINESS ADDRESS:** Bd Educ, Towson, MD 21204.

DALFERES, EDWARD R., JR.
Medical researcher, educator. **PERSONAL:** Born Nov 04, 1931, New Orleans, LA; married Anita Y Bush; children: Edward Rene, Anthony Renard. **EDUCATION:** Xavier Univ, BS 1956. **CAREER:** St John Parish School Bd, science teacher 1956-57; Louisiana State Univ School of Medicine, med rsch 1957-75, instructor 1975-. **ORGANIZATIONS:** Mem LA Heart Assn; Amer Assn for Advancement of Sci; So Connective Tissue Soc; Soc of Complex Carbohydrates; in collaboration with others author of numerous publs. **MILITARY SERVICE:** AUS Med Corps 1950-52. **BUSINESS ADDRESS:** Instructor, LSU Sch of Medicine, 1542 Tulane Ave, New Orleans, LA 70112.

DALLEY, GEORGE ALBERT
Attorney. **PERSONAL:** Born Aug 25, 1941, Havana, Cuba;son of Cleveland Ernest Dalley and Constance Joyce Dalley; married Pearl Elizabeth Love, Aug 01, 1970; children: Jason Christopher, Benjamin Christian. **EDUCATION:** Columbus Coll, AB 1963; Columbua Univ School of Law, JD 1966; Columbia Univ Grad School & Business, MBA 1966. **CAREER:** Metropolition Agt Res Cntr, assis to the pres 1962-69; Stoock & Stroock & Lawan, assoc cousnel 1970-71; US Comm of the Judicaary, assis cousnel 1971-72; Congressman Charles Rangel, admin asst 1973-76; US Dept of State, deputy asst sec of state 1977-79; US Civil Aero Bd, mem 1980-82; Mondale for Pres, deputy camp mgr 1983-84; Cong Charles Rangel, coun and staff dir 1985-1989; senior vice pres Neill and company Inc 1989-. **ORGANIZATIONS:** Adjunct prof Am Univ Schl of Law 1981-; avat human rights Am Bar Assoc; Intl law comm Nat'l Bar Assoc Fed Bar Assoc 1976-; mem Transition for Mayer M Barry 1982-83; mem Comm Assoc 1975-; mem Trans NAACP Urban League 1974-; Crestwood Comm Assn 1986-; mem bd or dir Africare Transafrica DC Support Group; Georgetown Day School; consultant, United Nations Devel Program 1989-. **HONORS/ACHIEVEMENTS:** Published art Federal Drug Abuse Enforcement 1974; speeches Dem Corp Select Process 1976; various Mags 1977-82. **HOME ADDRESS:** 1706 Crestwood Dr, NW, Washington, DC 20011. **BUSINESS ADDRESS:** Senior Vice President, Neill and Company, 815 Connecticut Ave, NW, Washington, DC 20006.

DALTON, RAYMOND ANDREW
Educator. **PERSONAL:** Born Jan 15, 1942, Chicago, IL; married Alfonsa Vicente; children: Carlos, Julio, Solange. **EDUCATION:** IL State Univ, BS 1964, MS 1966; doctoral study Univ of San Francisco 1978; Purdue Univ, Doctoral candidate 1984-. **CAREER:** Antelope Valley High School, instructor 1965-67; Lake Hughes, instructor 1967; Drew Jr High School, instructor 1967-68; Univ of IL, asst dean, asst prof 1971-84. **ORGANIZATIONS:** Advsr Black Student Organ of Archt & Art 1972-75; co-clrm Art Comm 1972; consul Park Forest Pub Sch Black Art Workshop 1973; co-advsr Orgn of Intl Stud 1975; mem Prof Orgn Academic Affairs Admin Midwest; mem Natl Conf of Artists, Union of Black Artists, Coll Art Assn, Natl Art Educ Assn, Natl Conf of Art Admin; mem Assn of Collegiate Registrars & Counselors; Grad Asstshp IL State Univ 1964-65, Purdue Univ 1984-85; sab lv Univ of Puerto Rico 1977. **HONORS/ACHIEVEMENTS:** Edwards Medal IL State Speech Contest 1965.

DALY, FREDERICA Y.
Psychologist. **PERSONAL:** Born Feb 14, 1925, Washington, DC; daughter of Samuel P Young (deceased) and Geneva A Sharper Young (deceased); married Michael E, Mar 15, 1972. **EDUCATION:** Howard U, BS 1947, MS 1949; Cornell Univ PhD 1956. **CAREER:** Howard U, Instr 1950; Cornell U, teachg asst 1953-55; George Jr Republic, clincal psychology 1955-72; SUNY Empire State Coll, assoc prof 1972-80; UNM MentalHlth Prog, clinical Psychology 1980-81; Alcohol Prog VA Med Ctr, Coord 1981-88; State Commn on Statue of Women, volunteer, 1989. **ORGANIZATIONS:** Gov's task force mem State of NM 1984; bd mem Family Serv Agency 1958-60. **HONORS/ACHIEVEMENTS:** Grant Fellowship Cornell Univ 1954-55; Cora Smith Fellowship Cornell Univ 1953-54; "Perspectives on Native American Women's Racism & Sexism Experiences" paper in process.

DALY, MARIE MAYNARD
Biochemist. **PERSONAL:** Born Apr 16, 1921, New York, NY; married Vincent Clark. **EDUCATION:** Queens Coll, BS 1942; NY U, MS 1943; Columbia U, PhD 1947. **CAREER:** Albert Einstein Coll of Medicine, Yeshiva Univ, assoc prof, asst prof 1960-71; Columbia Univ, assoc 1955-59; The Rockefeller Inst, asst 1951-55, vis invst 1948-51; Howard Univ, instr 1947-78; Queens Coll, fellow, tutor 1942-44. **ORGANIZATIONS:** Am Chem Soc; fellow AAAS; mem bd of govs NY Acad of Sci 1974-76; Harvey Soc; Am Soc of Biol Chemists; fellow Council on Arteriosclerosis, Am Heart Assn; NAACP; Nat Assn of Negro Bus & Prof-Women; fellow Am Cancer Soc 1948-51; est investigator Am Heart Assn 1958-63; career scientist Health Rsrch Council of NY 1962-72.

DALY, RONALD EDWIN
Printing company executive. **PERSONAL:** Born Feb 23, 1947, Chicago, IL; son of Edwin W Daly and Ella McCreary Brown; married Delores, Jul 28, 1978; children: Dawn, Ronald Jr, Erin. **EDUCATION:** Governors State Univ, University Park IL, BA Business Admin, 1977; Loyola Univ, Chicago IL, MBA Finance, 1980. **CAREER:** R R Donnelley & Sons, Chicago IL, supvr, 1972-79, mgr, 1980-84, Cherry Hill NJ, gen mgr, 1984-87, Lancaster PA, gen mgr, 1987-88, Chicago IL, div dir, 1988-. **ORGANIZATIONS:** Mem, Urban League of Chicago, 1988-. **HONORS/ACHIEVEMENTS:** Black Achiever, YMCA, 1977. **BUSINESS ADDRESS:** Vice President & Division Director, Chicago Financial Printing Division, R R Donnelley & Sons Co, 350 E 22nd St, Chicago, IL 60616.

DAMES, KENNETH ALBERT
Consultant. **EDUCATION:** John Jay Coll of Criminal Justice, BA 1977; Grad School City Univ of NY, PhD 1983. **CAREER:** New York City Police Dept, police officer 1968-84; Bronx VA Hosp, clinical internship 1980-81; Newark Pre-School Council, consult mental health coord 1981-84; Leake & Watts Childs Home, consult treatment coord 1985; New Wave

Consultants, exec dir. **ORGANIZATIONS:** Rsch principal investigator The Relationship of Burnout to Personality and Demograpgic Traits of Nurses; mem Amer Psychological Assn; mem Amer Soc for Training and Develop; mem Assn of Black Psychologists; mem PhD Alumni Assn City Univ of NY; vice pres Greenburgh Black Parents Assn. **HONORS/ACHIEVEMENTS:** Fellow Amer Psychological Assn Fellowship; fellow Helena Rubenstein Found Fellowship; nominee Danforth Fellowship; comm serv awd John C Dearie NYS Assembly. **MILITARY SERVICE:** AUS sp/4 1963-65; Honorable Discharge.

DANCE, DARYL CUMBER
Educator. **PERSONAL:** Born Jan 17, 1938, Richmond, VA; daughter of Allen W Cumber and Veronica B Cumber; married Warren C Dance; children: Warren Jr, Allen, Daryl Lynn. **EDUCATION:** VA State Coll, AB 1957, MA 1963; Univ of VA, PhD 1971. **CAREER:** VA State Coll, asst prof of English 1962-72; VA Commonwealth Univ, asst prof of English 1972-78, assoc prof of English 1978-85; prof of English 1985; editorial advisor, Journal of West Indian Literature 1986-. **ORGANIZATIONS:** Danforth Assoc 1964-; adv editor Black Amer Lit Forum 1978-. **HONORS/ACHIEVEMENTS:** Author "Shuckin' & Jivin', Folklore from Contemporary Black Americans" 1978; various fellowships & grants; Folklore for Contemporary Jamaicans 1985; Fifty Caribbean Writers 1986; Long Gone The Mecklenburg Six & The Theme of Escape in Black Literature, 1987. **BUSINESS ADDRESS:** Prof of English, VA CommonwealthUniv, P O Box 2005, Richmond, VA 23287.

DANCY, WILLIAM F.
Minister. **PERSONAL:** Born Nov 06, 1924, Greenville, MS; married Darnell E Pruitt; children: Antonia M, Wm. **EDUCATION:** Roosevelt U; Central Bapt Sem; Robert Terrell Law Sch. **CAREER:** Allen Chapel Overland Pk, KS, minister, dist supt; Sr Citizens Home, admin; Mt Life, sales rep & election commr. **ORGANIZATIONS:** 3rd Degree Mason; life mem NAACP; real estate broker Chmn Oak Pk Soc Serv Orgn Hon Doctorate Edward Waters Coll, AME Sem. **MILITARY SERVICE:** USN store keeper 1943-45. **BUSINESS ADDRESS:** Metropolitan Life Insurance, 10890 Benson #305, Overland Park, KS 66210.

DANDRIDGE, BOB
Athlete. **PERSONAL:** Born Nov 15, 1947, Richmond, VA; married Barbara. **EDUCATION:** Norfolk State, 1969. **CAREER:** Washington Bullets, forward 1977-; Milwaukee Bucks, player 1969-77. **HONORS/ACHIEVEMENTS:** 29th on All-Time Scoring List with 15,248 points; NBA All Star Team 1973, 75, 76 & 79. **BUSINESS ADDRESS:** Washington Bullets, 1 Harry S Truman Dr, Landover, MD 20786.

DANDRIDGE, RAYMOND EMMETT
Athlete. **PERSONAL:** Born Aug 31, 1913, Richmond, VA; married Henrietta; children: Lawrence, Raymond, Jr, Delores. **CAREER:** Mexican League; Natl Negro Leagues, third baseman 14 seasons. **HONORS/ACHIEVEMENTS:** Most Valuable Player & Rookie of the Year 1950; mem Baseballs Hall of Fame 1987. **HOME ADDRESS:** PO Box 1139, Palm Beach, FL 32906.

DANDRIDGE, RITA BERNICE
Educator. **PERSONAL:** Born Sep 16, 1940, Richmond, VA. **EDUCATION:** VA Union Univ, BA 1961; Howard Univ, MA 1963, PhD 1970. **CAREER:** Morgan State U, asst prof English 1964-71; Univ of Toledo, asst prof English 1971-74; Norfolk State U, prof English 1974. **ORGANIZATIONS:** Subscriber Modern Language Assn, Coll Language Assn, Sage, Multi-ethnic Lit of US; mem Natl Women's Studies Assn, South Atlantic Modern Lang Assn. **HONORS/ACHIEVEMENTS:** Selected Articles, 1 "But Some of Us Are Brave", Eds Gloria T Hull & Others, Old Westbury, NY, The Feminist Press, 1982; 2 "Louise Meriwether", Dictionary of Literary Biography, Afro-Am Fiction Writers after 1955, Eds Thadious Davis & Trudier Harris, Detroit; Gale Research Co 1984 Vol 33, Pp 182-186; "Josephine Joyce Turpin, Richmond Writer," The Richmond Quarterly 9 Fall 1986 11-13; book "Ann Allen Shockley, An Annotated Primary and Secondary Bibliography," 1987 Greenwich Press Westport CT. **BUSINESS ADDRESS:** English Professor, Norfolk State Univ, 2401 Corprew Ave, Norfolk, VA 23504.

DANDY, CLARENCE L.
Clergyman, business executive. **PERSONAL:** Born Jan 07, 1939, St Petersburg; married Luagussie; children: Cynthia, Louis, Anthony, Jackie, Korbett. **EDUCATION:** Full Gospel Minister Intl of Dallas, DD; FL A&M U, 1959. **CAREER:** United Full Gospel Temple (3 Temples in NC), founder, pres; The Prayer Tower Raleigh, NC, dir. **ORGANIZATIONS:** Chmn bd dir Rev C Dandy Evangelistic Assn Raleigh. **HONORS/ACHIEVEMENTS:** Recipient 1st Prize Trophy, Evangelist of the Year, by United Full Gospel Temple 1974. **MILITARY SERVICE:** AUS pfc 1956. **BUSINESS ADDRESS:** 417 S Person St, Raleigh, NC.

DANDY, ROSCOE GREER
Government official, educator, scholar. **PERSONAL:** Born Dec 20, 1946, Los Angeles, CA; son of Roscoe C Dandy and Doris L Edwards Dandy; divorced. **EDUCATION:** California State Univ, BA 1970; Univ Southern California, MSW 1973; Univ of Pittsburgh, MPH 1974, MPA 1975, DrPH 1981; Harvard Univ, certificate 1981; Univ of Illinois, Urbana, IL, 1965-68; LaSalle Extension Univ, Chicago, IL, 1966-68. **CAREER:** California State Youth Authority, youth counselor 1971; Univ of Pittsburgh, instructor 1977-80; US Public Health Serv, lt commander, assoc dir out-patient clinic 1980-81; Central Michigan Univ, instructor 1981-; Veterans Administration, asst chief medical admin 1983-85, social worker 1985-; Colorado State Dept of Health, Denver, CO, health intern, 1974; Green Engineering Corp, health intern, 1975. **ORGANIZATIONS:** Consultant Jackson State Univ, Jackson, MS, 1977; mem Southern Christian Leadership Conf 1973-; mem, NAACP, 1987-; mem, Amer Public Health Assn, 1987-; advisory bd, Howard County Police Comm Relations, 1989-; mem, Joint Center for Political Studies, 1986-; mem, Brokings Inst, 1985; mem, Federation of Amer Scientists, 1988-. **HONORS/ACHIEVEMENTS:** Fellow Dr Martin Luther King Jr, Woodrow Wilson Foundation Princeton Univ 1971-73; Outstanding Unit Citation US Public Health Serv Scientist 1981; Drama Award, David Stan Jordan High School, Los Angeles, CA, 1964; author, Board and Care Homes in Los Angeles County, 1976. **MILITARY SERVICE:** USAF sgt 1965-68; USMC Reserves sgt 1 yr; Air Force/Vietnam Era Veteran Award. **BUSINESS ADDRESS:** Social Worker, Veterans Administration, VA Medical Ctr, Fort Howard, MD 21052.

DANFORTH, ROBERT L.
Director, association executive. **PERSONAL:** Born Apr 25, 1945, Aiken, SC; married Iris A. **EDUCATION:** Benedict Coll, 1967; Spgfld Coll, 1969. **CAREER:** Springfield Action Commn Inc, exec dir; Am Intl Coll, asst prof; City of Springfield, exec dir Intergroup Relations, asst dir; Dept of Welfare NY, social worker. **ORGANIZATIONS:** Mem Omega Psi Phi; bd dir Dumbar Comm; Trinity Nursery Sch; NAACP; Hampden Co Mental Health; mem New England Comm Action Dirs Assn; MA CAP Assn Outstanding Young Men of Am. **BUSINESS ADDRESS:** 721 State St, Springfield, MA 01109.

DANIEL, ALFRED IRWIN
Business administrator. **PERSONAL:** Born Aug 07, 1934, Plainfield, NJ; son of Leonard I Daniel and Emilie B Daniel; married Cornelia; children: Charisse, Kimberly, William. **EDUCATION:** Albright Coll, BS Biology/Chem 1957; Seton Hall Univ MBA Marketing/Industrial Relations 1972. **CAREER:** CIBA/Geigy Pharmaceuticals, sr pharmacologist 1957-69; Ortho Pharmaceuticals, rsch info super 1969-75; ER Squibb, clinical info scientist 1975-77; Stuart Pharmaceuticals Div ICI Americas, invest material coord 1977-88; Pharmaceutical Consultant, Daniel Associater, 1988-. **ORGANIZATIONS:** Bd Plainfield YMCA 1969-74; bd Plainfield Area United Way 1974; bd Village 2 Civic Assoc 1974-77; bd mem Northeast Area Partners 1979-85; bd mem Christina School Dist 1981-86; chair DE Human Relations Comm 1984-85; commissioner, De Human Relations Comm, 1979-. **MILITARY SERVICE:** AUS sp4 1957-65. **HOME ADDRESS:** 27 Cordele Rd/PO Box 7760, Newark, DE 19714.

DANIEL, DAVID L.
Administrator. **PERSONAL:** Born Jan 02, 1906, Columbia, TN; son of David Daniel (deceased) and Mahalah Loyd Daniel (deceased); married Mary Beatrice Evins, Aug 04, 1935. **EDUCATION:** Fisk Univ, BA Chem 1928; Univ of Chicago, MA 1954, additional courses in Social Serv Admin 1955-56. **CAREER:** Cook County Dept of Public Aid, dir, associated with this dept since 1938-; IL Dept of Public Aid, asst dir 1974-83. **ORGANIZATIONS:** Mem Natl Assn of Social Workers; Academy of Certified Social Workers; Amer Public Welfare Assn; IL Welfare Assn; Natl Conference on Social Welfare; bd mem, past pres Natl Assn of County Welfare Directors 1969-76; life mem Alpha Phi Alpha; mem Urban League; life mem NAACP; mem Amer Acad Political and Social Science; mem Mid America Congress on Aging; mem Chicago Dept on Aging and Disability; mem United Way I & R Committee; mem Exec Service Corps; mem Chicago Commons Bd; mem Youth Guidance Bd; mem Metro Chicago Coalition on Aging; bd mem, past pres City Club of Chicago 1949-. **HONORS/ACHIEVEMENTS:** Honors and Awards received from Xi Lambda Chapter Alpha Phi Alpha Fraternity, Greater Chicago Churchmen, City Club of Chicago (past pres), Fisk Univ, Joint Negro Appeal, United Way/Crusade of Mercy, Greater Chicago Amvets Post #1, and many others. **MILITARY SERVICE:** AUS 1943-46; graduated from The Infantry School; Military Police Detachment Commander; US Army Reserve Corps, Civil Affairs/Military Govt Officer, Captain retired 1961. **HOME ADDRESS:** 5839 S Michigan Ave, Chicago, IL 60637.

DANIEL, GRISELDA
Educator/administrator. **PERSONAL:** Born Feb 07, 1938, Battle Creek, MI; children: Cornell A, Gary L, Cheri A, Patrick H. **EDUCATION:** Western Michigan Univ, BS (Magna Cum Laude) 1973, MS Admin 1980. c x. **CAREER:** Borgess Hospital, surgical nurse 1958-66, Kalamazoo St Hospital, attendant nurse 1966-70; WMU Coll of Gen Studies, counselor/trainer 1970-73, dir Martin Luther King, Jr prog 1975-80, asst to vice pres acad affrs/dir spec prgms 1980-88, asst to dean of the Graduate Coll, currently. **ORGANIZATIONS:** WMU designer/devlpr Mentor Program 1980-81; WMU award Invaluable Contribution Upward Bound Program 1982. **HONORS/ACHIEVEMENTS:** Member NAACP, American Assn Univ Administrators, Natl Assn Female Executives, Natl Consortium for Black Prof Devel, received award from Delta Kappa Gamma for Outstanding Contribution to Field of Educ, 1981; Creative Programming Award, Continuing Educ Assn, 1989; Outstanding Leadership and Committment, the Martin Luther King Jr Program, 1989; Committment to Public Serv Award, Van Buren County Dept of Social Serv, 1989. **HOME ADDRESS:** 4281830th St, Paw Paw, MI 49079. **BUSINESS ADDRESS:** Asst to the Dean of the Graduate Coll, Western Michigan University, W Michigan Ave, Kalamazoo, MI 49008.

DANIEL, JACK L.
Educator. **PERSONAL:** Born Jun 09, 1942, Johnstown, PA; married Jerlean Colley; children: Omari, Marijata. **EDUCATION:** Univ of Pittsburgh, BS Psych 1963, MA Speech 1965, PhD Speech 1968. **CAREER:** Central MI Univ, asst prof 1967-68; Univ of Pittsburgh, chmn, assoc prof 1969-73; Univ of Pittsburgh, Coll of Arts & Sciences, assoc dean 1973-78; Stanford Univ, amer council of ed fellow 1974; Faculty of Arts & Sciences, assoc dean 1978-83. **ORGANIZATIONS:** Mem Speech Commun Assoc, Intl Commun Assoc, Soc for Intercultural Ed Training & Rsch; bd mem Red Cross Ed Ctrs. **HONORS/ACHIEVEMENTS:** Publ in Todays Speech, Jrnl of Communications, Speech Teacher, Black Scholar, Black Lines, Crisis. **BUSINESS ADDRESS:** Assistant Provost, Univ of Pittsburgh, Pittsburgh, PA 15260.

DANIEL, JAMES L.
Consultant. **PERSONAL:** Born Nov 16, 1945, Brunswick, GA; married Connie Kenney; children: Richard, James Jr, Tonya. **EDUCATION:** Tuskegee Inst, 1963-64; Brunswick Coll, AS BA 1976. **CAREER:** Sears Roebuck & Co, div mgr 1968-76; Brunswick City, city commr, 1972-76; Stripe-A-Lot/Precision Pavement Marking & Maintenance Co, owner 1986-; Southern Bell Telephone, acct exec 1978-80, serv consultant 1980-. **ORGANIZATIONS:** Pres, Founder Leaders of Amer Dem Soc, 1959; ex-officer, Brunswick Chamber of Commerce, 1972-76; bd dir, Am Help Am 1974-76. **HONORS/ACHIEVEMENTS:** Outstanding Serv, Christ Memorial Baptist Church, 1982; Brunswick City Comm, 1976, Frat Order of Police 1973. **MILITARY SERVICE:** USAF amn 1st cl 4 yrs; Expert Marksman Medal, Vietnam Serv Medal, Natl Defense Serv Medal, Pres, Unit Citation, Airforce Unit Commedation, 1964-68. **HOME ADDRESS:** 9795 Whitfield Ave, Savannah, GA 31406. **BUSINESS ADDRESS:** Service Consultant, Southern Bell Telephone, 6602 Abercorn, Savannah, GA 31405.

DANIEL, JESSICA HENDERSON
Psychologist. **PERSONAL:** Born Aug 02, 1944, San Antonio, TX; daughter of James Henderson and Geraldine Henderson; children: Margaret. **EDUCATION:** Fayetteville State

Coll, BS 1964; Univ of IL Urbana, MS 1967, PhD 1969; Harvard Medical School, Postdoctoral Clinical Fellow 1974-76. **CAREER:** Univ of IL, asst prof educ psych 1969-70; Univ of Oregon, asst prof dept of special educ 1970-72; Boston Coll, asst prof educ psych 1972-76; Harvard Medical Sch, instructor in psych 1976-; Children's Hosp, rsch assoc/psych 1972-; Judge Baker Children's Ctr, psychologist 1976-; Harvard Law School, Cambridge, MA, teaching fellow, 1989. **ORGANIZATIONS:** Mem vice chmn Bd of Registration of Psychologist, State of MA, 1984-; mem bd Brookline Arts Center 1985-; mem Tech Adv Comm Robert Wood Johnson Foundation 1986-; psychology consultant Public Schools Brookline, Cambridge MA; mem Charles St AME Church, Amer Psychological Assoc, MA Psychological Assoc; fellow Amer Orthopsychiatric Assoc; chmn, Bd of Registration of Psychologist (MA,) 1989. **HONORS/ACHIEVEMENTS:** Black Achiever Greater Boston YMCA 1984; President's Awd Boston Chap NAACP 1986; Distinguished Alumni Citation of Yr Natl Assoc for Equal Opportunity in Higher Educ 1986; Resource, Harvard Negotiation Project, Harvard Law School, 1989. **HOME ADDRESS:** P O Box 605, Brookline, MA 02146. **BUSINESS ADDRESS:** Senior Staff Psychologist, Judge Baker Children's Ctr, Children's Hospital, 295 Longwood Ave, Boston, MA 02115.

DANIEL, LEVI GARLAND
Business executive. **PERSONAL:** Born Jul 28, 1918, Halifax Co, VA; son of Charles Daniel and Cora Daniel; married Elizabeth Francis Barnhart; children: Ervin Stanley, Levi Melvin, William Tyrone, Enzy Raymond, Norma Faye, Carol Louginia, David Garland, George Darnell, Timothy Elisha, Karen L, Letisha. **CAREER:** United Mine Workers of America (UMWA), intl rep, coord; UMWA, Occup Health & Safety Dept, intl rep 1974; UMWA, dir of field service office 1974, pres Dist 29 1973, intl exec bd mem 1972-73, observer Dist 29 1972; Local Union 5955, rec sec 1953-72. **ORGANIZATIONS:** Bd Gulf Area Housing Assn; bd WV Coal Field Housing; mem NAACP.

DANIEL, MARY REED
Artist. **PERSONAL:** Born in E St Louis, IL; married William J Daniel Sr; children: William J Jr. **ORGANIZATIONS:** Mem, Artist Guild of Chicago, Artist League of the Midwest, S Side Comm Art Center; Old Town Triangle Art Center Surface Design Assn; Chicago Artists Coalition. **HONORS/ACHIEVEMENTS:** Listed Afro-Amer Artists Boston Publ Library; shows Earl Graves Publ Co Black Enterprise Mag NYC, Art Inst Sales & Rental Gallery Chgo, Milliken Rug Design Competition NYC, Galerie Triangle Wash DC, Lansburgh Ctr Wash DC, Evans-Tibbs Collection Wash DC A Montgomery Ward Gallery Chicago IL, Tweed Museum Duluth MN, Paramaribo Suriname South Amer; publ Black Dimensions in Contemporary Amer Art.

DANIEL, PHILLIP T. K.
Educational administrator. **PERSONAL:** Born Aug 08, 1947, Philadelphia, PA; married Dr Vesta Ann Henderson; children: Asegai, Thamret. **EDUCATION:** Cheyney Univ of PA, BS 1969; Univ of IL, MS 1970, DEd 1973. **CAREER:** Kent State Univ, asst prof 1973-74; Northern IL Univ, prof 1974-, asst dean grad school, prof 1984-. **ORGANIZATIONS:** Mem Kappa Delta Pi 1970-, Phi Delta Kappa 1971-, Assoc for the Study of Afro-Amer Life & History 1974-; mem bd of dir Childrens Found Inc 1976-; mem Amer Assoc for Higher Ed 1981-, Amer Teachers Assoc 1982-; treas Childrens Learning Ctr 1983-; mem bd of dir Childrens Home & Aid Soc of IL 1983-. **HONORS/ACHIEVEMENTS:** Pacesetter Awd IL State Board of Ed 1980-81; ACE Fellow Amer Council on Ed 1981-82; Outstanding Young Men of Amer, 1982; Who's Where Among Writers. **BUSINESS ADDRESS:** Asst Dean/Professor, Northern Illinois University, 205A Altgeld Hall, De Kalb, IL 60115.

DANIEL, SIMMIE CHILDREY
Business education teacher. **PERSONAL:** Born Feb 09, 1934, Shorter, AL; daughter of Luther J Childrey (deceased) and Ora M Childrey. **EDUCATION:** Alabama State Univ, BS, 1957; Indiana Univ, MS, 1967; St Louis Univ, Univ of Nevada, special student. **CAREER:** Albany State Coll, Albany GA, exec sec, 1957-60; St Louis Public Schools, St Louis MO, business teacher, 1963; El Reno Public Schools, El Reno OK, English teacher, 1963; Clark County School District, Las Vegas NV, 1964-. **ORGANIZATIONS:** Natl Business Educ Assn; Clark County Classroom Teachers Assn; Nevada State Educ Assn; Natl Vocational Educ Assn; Professional Coll Women Assn; Natl Sorority of Phi Delta Kappa Inc, 1973; Gamma Phi Delta Sorority, 1975. **BUSINESS ADDRESS:** Teacher, Eldorado High School, 1139 Linn Lane, Las Vegas, NV 89110.

DANIEL, WALTER C.
Educator. **PERSONAL:** Born May 12, 1922, Macon, GA; married LaUna Harris. **EDUCATION:** Johson C Smith Univ, BA 1941, MA 1959; Bowling Green State Univ, PhD 1962; Lincoln Univ of MO, LHD (Hon) 1972; Harvard Univ Grad School of Bus, Post Doct. **CAREER:** LA City Schools, teacher; NC Central Univ, asst prof English; St Augustines Coll, prof & head of English; Div of Humanities, NC A&T State Univ, prof, head of English, chmn div of humanities; NC A&T, dir 13 coll curr devel proj; Lincoln Univ of MO, pres; Univ of MO Columbia, prof of English. **ORGANIZATIONS:** Mem Comm on Inst N Central Assoc of Coll & School; past pres MO Conf of Coll Pres; mem bd trustees MO School of Religion; mem Coll Lang Assoc, Rotary Intl; mem bd trustees Columbia Publ Library; vice pres admin Gr Rivers Council Boy Scouts of Amer; sec Capital Funds Comm Presbyterian Church US; comm Columbia MO Housing Auth; dir Natl Archetecture Accrediting Assoc; mem natl adv Council for Career Ed, Phi Delta Kappa, Phi Kappa Phi, Kappa Delta PiHon Scholastic Soc. **HONORS/ACHIEVEMENTS:** Wisdom Awd of Honor Wisdom Soc 1970; Order of the Star of Africa Republic of Liberia 1972. **BUSINESS ADDRESS:** Professor of English, Univ of Missouri, 210 A Arts & Science Building, Columbia, MO 65211.

DANIEL, WILEY YOUNG
Attorney. **PERSONAL:** Born Sep 10, 1946, Louisville; married Ida Seymour; children: Jennifer, Stephanie, Nicole. **EDUCATION:** Howard Univ, BA 1968; Howard Univ Sch of Law, JD 1971. **CAREER:** Volunteer legal work; Dickinson Wright McKean Cudlip & Moon, attorney 1971-77; Gorsuch Kirgis Campbell Walker & Grover, attorney 1977-. **ORGANIZATIONS:** Mem/bd mem Natl Bar Assn, Co Bar Assn; vice pres CO Bar Assn; CO Supreme Ct Grievance Comm; Amer Bar Assn; Managing Ed Howard LLJ; mem Delta Theta Phi Law Frat, Alpha Phi Alpha Social Frat; Law Journal 1970-71; mem Detroit Coll of Law part-time faculty 1974-77; Univ of CO School of Law 1978-81; mem Iliff Sch of Theology. **HONORS/ACHIEVEMENTS:** 1986 Disting Serv Awd Sam Cary Bar Assoc, Colorado Assoc of Black Attorneys. **BUSINESS ADDRESS:** Attorney, Gorsuch Kirgis Campbell Walker, 1401 17th St #1100, Denver, CO 80202.

DANIEL-ALSTON, TRACY ANN See ALSTON, TRACEY DANIEL

DANIELS, A. RAIFORD
Financial executive. **PERSONAL:** Born Dec 13, 1944, Columbia, SC; son of Willie L Daniels and Alma Gordon Daniels. **EDUCATION:** Lincoln Univ, BA 1966; Columbia Univ NY, MBA 1973; postgraduate studies: Cornell, Stanford and Rutgers Univ and the Univ of CA (Berkely.). **CAREER:** Prudential Insurance Cty Newark, mgmt trainee group insurance 1966-67; Citibank, account officer, Natl Bank Group 1968-72; Corning Corp, NY, sr financial analyst, 1973-74; Bank of America, San Francisco, vice pres, N America Div, 1974-78; Prudential Insurance Co, vice pres, Capital Markets Groups, 1978-88; The Wilalm Group, managing principal and CEO. **ORGANIZATIONS:** Columbia Club; Lincoln Univ Alumni; Minority Interchange NY; The Amer Soc of CLU and ChFC; Naval Research Assoc; NAACP; YMCA, Natl Off Assn; Newark Chamber of Commerce. **HONORS/ACHIEVEMENTS:** Calder Fellow Calder Found NY 1972; licensed mortgage, real estate and insurance broker; registered investmnet advisor and general securities representative. **MILITARY SERVICE:** USNR Commander, 1966-. **BUSINESS ADDRESS:** Managing Principal, The Wicalm Group, Ltd, PO Box 1098 (Number Six Bleeker St), Newark, NJ 07101.

DANIELS, ALFRED CLAUDE WYNDER
Educator. **PERSONAL:** Born Mar 22, 1934, Philadelphia, PA; married Ginger Daniels; children: Carmen, David, Jerry. **EDUCATION:** AZ State U, BS 1965; Harvard Law School, JD 1975. **CAREER:** Harvard Law Sch, asst dean 1975-; NE HH Aerospace Design Co Inc, vice pres. **ORGANIZATIONS:** Mem Nat Assn of Black Mfr; pres Black Corp Pres of New England; mem Urban League; NAACP. **MILITARY SERVICE:** USAF maj 1952-72. **BUSINESS ADDRESS:** Harvard Law Sch, Cambridge, MA 02138.

DANIELS, ANTHONY HAWTHORNE
Clergyman. **PERSONAL:** Born Jun 09, 1950, Kingsport, TN. **EDUCATION:** Morristown Jr Coll, AA 1970; Knoxville Coll, BS 1972; Graham Bible Coll, ABE 1983. **CAREER:** Knoxville Comm Dev Agency, coord 1972; Boxing Rehabilitation Prog, founder & dir 1976; TN Valley Auth, energy advisor 1977; Bethel Baptist Church, asst pastor 1984; First Baptist Church, pastor 1985. **BUSINESS ADDRESS:** Pastor, First Baptist Church, Church & Third St, Barbourville, KY 40906.

DANIELS, CASANDRA
Financial administrator. **PERSONAL:** Born Mar 01, 1957, West Palm Beach, FL; divorced; children: Shariah M, Mahasin I. **EDUCATION:** Elizabeth-Seton Coll, AAS 1979; Southampton Coll Long Island Univ, BS 1983; W Averell Harriman Coll for Policy Analysis & Public Mgmt, MS 1985. **CAREER:** Chicago Title Ins Co, title examiner 1975-79; Bankers Trust Co, accountant 1979-81; Town of Southampton, aide to budget dir 1982; Neighborhood Work Project, asst to dir 1984; Vera Inst of Justice, housing planner/analyst. **ORGANIZATIONS:** Mem Natl Forum for Black Public Admin; mem Natl Assn for Female Execs; mem Amer Soc for Public Admin; statistical analysis Stage XVI Grad Apt Complex 1984; panel moderator Black Political Agenda 1984; panelist SUNY Stonybrook 1984; mem Delta Mu Delta; consultant Vera Inst of Justice 1984; comm mem Mgmt School Comm at SUNY 1984-85; comm mem Pres Task Force on Women's Safety at SUNY 1984-85. **HONORS/ACHIEVEMENTS:** Presidential Scholarships Southampton Coll LI Univ 1981-83; Grad Fellowship Alfred P Sloan Found 1983-84; Grad Fellowships in Public Policy & Mgmt W Averell Harriman Coll for Policy Analysis & Public Mgmt 1983-85. **HOME ADDRESS:** 41 Silverbrook Dr, Riverhead, NY 11901.

DANIELS, CECIL TYRONE
Educator. **PERSONAL:** Born Nov 23, 1941, Miami, FL; married Patricia Ann Robinson; children: Lee Ernest, Letitia Nicole, La Keitha Jonise. **EDUCATION:** Univ No CO, MA 1974; FL A&M U, BA Elem Ed, Social Studies, Drivers Ed 1964. **CAREER:** Dade County Public School System, prin, asst prin 1974-76, teacher 1965-73, human relations coord 1970. **ORGANIZATIONS:** Nat Alliance of Black Sch Educators; Dade Co Schs Adminstr Assn; Dade Co Guidance Assn; consultUniv of No CO 1975-76; FL A&M Alumni Assn;Univ of No CO Alumni Assn; vice pres Lions Club Intl 1977; Phi Delta Kappa; Big Bros Inc jack & jill of am inc. **HONORS/ACHIEVEMENTS:** Serv Award, WJ Bryan Elem PTA 1976; Serv Award, Fulford Elem PTA 1977; Serv Award, Cub Scouts 1977; nom Adminstr of the Year 1976-77; cert for runner-upAdminstr of the Year 1977; Fulford Comm Award 1976-77; Admin of the Year 1978; Ad Hoc Com Dade Co Sch Sys 1980. **MILITARY SERVICE:** College ROTC 1960-64. **BUSINESS ADDRESS:** 3125 NW 176 St, Opa-Locka, FL 33055.

DANIELS, CLARENCE A., JR.
Lodging & food service executive. **PERSONAL:** Born Jun 05, 1949, Marion, AR; married Monet Latham; children: Sonya Aliya, Clarence Anware. **EDUCATION:** Bowling Green State Univ, BS Educ 1971, MEd 1972; Howard Univ School of Law, JD 1978. **CAREER:** Children's Defense Fund, attorney, 1978-81; DC Public Schools Office of Supt, legislative counsel 1981-84; Marriott Corp, dir vendor relations, human resources 1985-86; Host Intl Inc, vice pres corp devel, 1986-. **ORGANIZATIONS:** Mayor's adv comm Educ of the Handicapped, 1980; bd of dir City Lights School for Emotionally Disturbed 1982; educ advisory comm, Natl Black Child Devel Inst1984; pres Concerned Black Men 1984; mem District of Columbia Court of Appeals, US Dist Court of the Dist of Columbia. **HONORS/ACHIEVEMENTS:** Bowling Green Univ, Distinguished Serv Award, 1971; Published, The Legal Implications of Minimum Competence Testing, 1978; Legal Trends of Family Law, 1979. **HOME ADDRESS:** 30608 Vista Sierra Dr, Malibu, CA 90265. **BUSINESS ADDRESS:** Vice President of Corp Dev, Host International Inc, 3402 Pico Blvd, Santa Monica, CA 90406.

DANIELS, CURTIS A.
Sales representative. **PERSONAL:** Born Apr 01, 1941, Italy, TX; married Cynthia A Epps. **EDUCATION:** Bishop Coll, BA 1973. **CAREER:** Fox & Jacobs, sales rep; Ingham Co Hosp, asst physical therapist 1961-62; Titche-Goettinger, buyer 1961-62. **ORGANIZATIONS:** Mem Fox & Jacobs' "Million Dollar Circle" 1975; lectr Bishop Coll; mem Omega Psi Phi, Mu Gamma Chpt. **HONORS/ACHIEVEMENTS:** Outstanding Airman, USAF. **MILITARY SERVICE:** USAF. **BUSINESS ADDRESS:** 2800 Surveyor Blvd, Carrollton, TX 75006.

DANIELS, DAVID HERBERT, JR.
Physician. **PERSONAL:** Born Sep 01, 1941, Little Rock, AR; married Doris; children: David, Dorothy, Doreen, Danny, Dora. **EDUCATION:** Philander Smith Coll, BS 1968; Univ AR Med Sch, MD 1967; Los Angeles Co Med Ctr 1967-68. **CAREER:** Cardiac Ctr Dir Cardiac Pulmonary Serv, physician cardiologist; Montclair & Chino Gen Hosp, physician. **ORGANIZATIONS:** Dir cardiac chmn Cardiac Surgery Com Dr's Hosp; mem Am Coll of Cardiology, Am Coll of Physician, Am Coll of Cert Physicians. **HONORS/ACHIEVEMENTS:** Listed Who's Who Am U'S & Colls 1972; mem Alpha Kappa Mu Nat Hon Soc 1962; Beta Kappa Phi Nat Schi Hon Sco 1962; cert flw Am Coll. **MILITARY SERVICE:** USAF maj 1968-74. **BUSINESS ADDRESS:** 1770 N Orange Grove, Pomona, CA.

DANIELS, ELIZABETH
Educator. **PERSONAL:** Born Sep 23, 1938, Sebastian, FL; daughter of Levi Daniels and Addie Blackshear Daniels; divorced; children: Jennifer. **EDUCATION:** TN State Univ, BS 1958; Howard Univ, MS 1962; Univ of CA, PhD 1968; Univ of Conn Sch of Dental Med, DMD 1977. **CAREER:** Lockheed Propulsion Co, proposal writer 1963-64; Pfizer Inc, medicinal chemist 1968-73; Private Practice, 1978-; Meharry Med Coll Sch of Dentistry, asst prof 1977-1985, asst dean academic affairs 1985-88; Department of Periodontics, assoc prof 1988-. **ORGANIZATIONS:** Natl Dental Assoc, mem 1978-; American Assoc of Dental Schools, mem 1978-; NAACP, mem 1981-; TN State Univ Natl Alumni Assoc, vice pres 1986-88. **HONORS/ACHIEVEMENTS:** NASA Fellowship at Univ of CA, 1964-68; Outstanding Young Women of America, 1969; Outstanding Men and Women of Science, 1970. **HOME ADDRESS:** 2933 Stanwyck Dr, Nashville, TN 37207.

DANIELS, GERALDINE L.
Government official. **PERSONAL:** Born Sep 09, Harlem, NY; married Eugene Ray Daniels II (deceased); children: Eugene R III. **EDUCATION:** CUNY Queens Coll, BA Polit Sci; Malcolm-King Harlem Coll, AA. **CAREER:** The New York State Legislature, former chairperson for standing comm on social svcs, presently chairperson for the steering comm; New York State Legislative Caucus, chairwoman. **ORGANIZATIONS:** Vice pres Inner City Broadcasting Corp; vice chair Harlem Urban Develop Corp; chairperson NY County Democratic Comm; treas Council of Black Elected Democrats of NYS; district leader Martin Luther King Jr Democratic Club in Central Harlem; life mem NAACP. **HONORS/ACHIEVEMENTS:** Sojourner Truth Awd Negro Business & Professional Women of New York; raised monies for preventive health care programs; "Mid-Day-Live" on NY City Cable Television. **BUSINESS ADDRESS:** Assemblywoman, New York State Legislature, 163 W 125th St, Room 919, New York, NY 10027.

DANIELS, GILL D. **See ROBINSON, GILL DONCELIA**

DANIELS, JEAN E.
Educator. **PERSONAL:** Born Dec 04, St Louis, MO; daughter of Chester Daniels and Ella M Daniels. **EDUCATION:** Univ of KS, BA 1964; Howard Univ, MSW 1966; UCLA, MPH 1973, DSW 1976. **CAREER:** Neuropsychiatric Ins UCLA, psych social worker; Sociology Dept CA State Univ, prof 1989-; Various Local Consultations. **ORGANIZATIONS:** Bd mem Am Lung Assn 1976-; chairperson Amer Public Health Assn, Social Work Sect 1984; Natl pgm comm Alpha Kappa Alpha Sor 1982-86; prog dev bd joint policy committee CA Council on Geriatrics and Gerontology; officer, Natl Women of Achievement, Los Angeles Chapter 1987-89. **HONORS/ACHIEVEMENTS:** Honored Educator Phi Delta Kappa LA 1977; Found Ford Fellowship 1975; American Lung Assn of Los Angeles County Serv Awd 1980; CSUN Faculty Dev Awd 1985; Top Ladies of Distinction, Inglewood Chapter Award 1989. **BUSINESS ADDRESS:** Professor, CA State University, 18111 Nordhoff St, Northridge, CA 91330.

DANIELS, JERRY FRANKLIN
State excise police officer (retired). **PERSONAL:** Born Dec 14, 1915, Indianapolis, IN; son of Jerry R Daniels (deceased) and Anna Gleason Franklin Daniels (deceased); married Jean M Watson, May 11, 1956; children: Charlotte Denise Huggins, Damon Anthony Daniels. **EDUCATION:** Indiana Univ, 1950-52. **CAREER:** County Clerk, Indianapolis IN, deupty, 1946-48; Mac Arthur Conservatory of Music, Indianapolis IN, instructor, 1948-50; Sec of State, Indianapolis IN, deputy, 1950-54; State of Indiana, Indianapolis IN, excise police, 1958-86. **HONORS/ACHIEVEMENTS:** One of the founding members of the Ink-Spots, 1930-36; author of a column for Indiana Harold, State Wide Newspaper on "Making Mine Music"; Sagamore of Wabash, Governor Robert Orr, 1988. **MILITARY SERVICE:** US Army, 43rd Seigneur Battalion, T/4, 1943-46, Line Chief, 5 Battle of Stars. **HOME ADDRESS:** 3632 N Guilford Ave, Indianapolis, IN 46205.

DANIELS, JESSE
Design engineer. **PERSONAL:** Born Oct 14, 1935, Montgomery, AL; son of David M Daniels and Prince C Baron; married Ella McCreary; children: Jessica, Kenneth, Eric, Adrienne, Diane and Carl. **EDUCATION:** AL State Univ, BS 1961; Graduate Credit, Auburn Univ, Emory Univ, Wake Forest Univ, Clemson Univ, GA Southern Coll. **CAREER:** Ford Motor Co, design engr. **ORGANIZATIONS:** Mem Engrg Soc of Detroit 1963-78, 1978-83; mem Kappa Alpha Psi Frat 1964-, Prince Hall Masons 1974-, Southeastern MI Acapella Chorus 1982-, Screen Actors Guild 1984-, NAACP 1985-. **HONORS/ACHIEVEMENTS:** 2 Natl TV Commercials Ford Motor Co 1984; 1986 Disting Alumnus AL State Univ 1986; Narrator, Ford College Recruitng Video. **HOME ADDRESS:** 11360 Auburn, Detroit, MI 48228. **BUSINESS ADDRESS:** Design Engineer, Ford Motor Co, B&CE Bldg Room 2019, PO Box 2053, Dearborn, MI 48121.

DANIELS, JOHN C.
University executive. **PERSONAL:** Born Apr 24, Macon, GA; married Bess; children: Leslie, John. **EDUCATION:** Cheshire Acad 1956; Villanova U, 1960; Nat Urban Fellow, Yale U, 1971; Occidental Coll, 1972. **CAREER:** Yale Univ, mgr Affirmative Action; West Haven High School, teacher 1961-65; EOC, dep dir 1965-67; NH Redevelopment Agency, proj dir 1967-69; Quinnipiac College, asst & pres Urban Affairs 1969-70; Joint Center Political Studies, special asst 1970-72. **ORGANIZATIONS:** Trustee Hannah Gray Home; bd dir YMCA; bd dir Dixwell Comm House; bd dir Urban League; bd mem Family Planning; NAACP; adv bd Highland Hts 1969-71; mem Prince Hall Masons; Alpha Phi Alpha; assoc fellow Trumbull Coll; fellow Calhoun Coll. **HONORS/ACHIEVEMENTS:** Recipient Outstanding Citizens Award 1969; listed Who's Who in Politics 1965; Who's Who in the East 1967. **BUSINESS ADDRESS:** 143 Elm St, New Haven, CT.

DANIELS, JORDAN, JR.
State supervisor. **PERSONAL:** Born Nov 26, 1923, Shreveport, LA; married Ellita. **EDUCATION:** Compton Coll, graduate; Political Sci, LA City Coll, 1 yr life underwriting training course; LUTC, ins laws & conts; Attended, Loyola Univ, Xavier Univ 1941-43; CLU Studies, 1 yr. **CAREER:** Insurance Exec, 25 yrs; Supreme Life Ins Co of Am, state supr; State & Assem blyman, admin asst 6 yrs; Greene's Travel Serv Inc, vp; Henry A Waxman Assemblyman, admin asst 1975; State of CA Dept of Commerce Office of Small Business, bd chmn 1983-86; LA County Commn for Public Social Svcs, commissioner. **ORGANIZATIONS:** Pres Lutheran Human Relations Assn, 1965-71; pres Proj Hope; mem Westside Comm Improvemt Assoc; Consolidated Comm Action Assn; del Lutheran HS Assn; "Men of Tommorow"; chmn bd of trustees St Paul Luth Ch; pres LA Mgmt Assn Black Ins Cos 1972-73; Psi Beta Sigma 25 yrs; class moderator "Staff Mgr's Training Sch" Univ of So CA 1972-73; mem Fairfax High Adv Council; mem McBride Sch; Handicap Adv Bd; mem W Hollywood Coord Council; vice chmn Hollywood Wilshire Scouts 1972-73; mem Baldwin Hills Dem Club; mem Dem Co Cent Com; rep Mini-convention KC 1974. **HONORS/ACHIEVEMENTS:** Aware of Merit Lutheran Businessmen's Assoc Long Beach CA 1968. **BUSINESS ADDRESS:** Commissioner, Commn for Public Social Serv, PO Box 781015, Los Angeles, CA 90016.

DANIELS, JOSEPH
Medical director. **PERSONAL:** Born Mar 18, 1931, Linden, NJ; children: Joan, Jean. **EDUCATION:** Lincoln Univ PA, BA (cum laude) 1953; Howard Univ Coll Med, MD 1957; Med Ctr Jersey City, Intrnshp 1957-58; Worcester City Hosp MA, Res Med 1958-59; Ancora Psych Hosp, Res Psych 1962-65. **CAREER:** NJ Psychiatric Hospital Ancora, attending psych 1965-66; Salem Out-Patient Clinic, Salem NJ, dir 1966-67; Mental Health Center, Wycksoff WI, dir 1967-70; In-patient Unit Mt Carmel Guild, dir 1970-71; NJ Coll of Medicine, chief out-patient 1971-77; Center Growth & Rcncltn Inc, med dir. **ORGANIZATIONS:** Clnl asso prof psych NJ Coll Med 1970-81; Cnsltnt psych E Orange Bd of Edctrs 1970-75, Newark Bd of Edctrs 1977-85, Victory Hse Inc 1970-77; bddirs Yth Devlp Inc 1968-73, Northside Addict Rehab Ctr 1969-71; bd trustees Nyack Coll Nyack, NY 1973-82; pres bd chmn Mnstry Of Recncltn, Inc 1981-85. **HONORS/ACHIEVEMENTS:** Beta Kappa Chi Natl Scntfc Hnry Scty 1953; Am Coll Stdnt Ldrs 1953; Outstndng Yng Men of Am 1967; Psychodynmcs & Psychopathlgy of Racism Publ 1969. **MILITARY SERVICE:** AUS Med Corp cptn 1959-62. **BUSINESS ADDRESS:** Medical Dir, Ctr Grwth & Recncltn, Inc, 498 William St, East Orange, NJ 07019.

DANIELS, LEGREE SYLVIA
Former government official. **PERSONAL:** Born Feb 29, 1920, Barnwell, SC; married Oscar Daniels; children: two stepdaughters. **EDUCATION:** Attended Temple University and Central Pennsylvania Business School. **CAREER:** Staff asst, former Senate Minority Leader Hugh Scott; PA State Tax Equalization Bd, Harrisburg PA, chairman, 1979-85; PA Bureau of Elections, Harrisburg PA, commissioner, 1985-86; PA Dept of State, Harrisburg PA, deputy secretary of commonwealth, 1986-87; US Dept of Education, Washington DC, assistant secretary for civil rights, 1987-89; member, Republican Natl Committee Executive committee. **ORGANIZATIONS:** Chairman, Natl Black Republican Council; chairman, Black Voters for Reagan/Bush; secretary, Republican State Committee of PA; director, PA Council of Republican Women; board member, Natl Endowment for Democracy; US Army Science Board; member of advisory board, US Commission on Civil Rights; Joint Center for Political Studies; board member, Young Women's Christian Association; PA Martin Luther King Commission; past matron, Order of the Eastern Star; Baptist Missionary Society. **HONORS/ACHIEVEMENTS:** DHL, Atlanta University, 1988. **HOME ADDRESS:** 1715 Glenside Dr, Harrisburg, PA 17109.

DANIELS, LINCOLN, SR.
Educational administrator. **PERSONAL:** Born Feb 17, 1932, Hickman, KY; married Robbie L Davis; children: Karen Lee, Lincoln, Jr, Terence Leon. **EDUCATION:** Philander Smith Coll, BA (cum laude) 1953; Wash U, MA 1969; Wash U, Doctoral Can. **CAREER:** St Louis Bd of Educ Div of Evaluation, divisional asst 1975-; St Louis Bd of Educ Div of Evaluation, research statistician 1973-75; St Louis Bd of Educ, elementary teacher 1964-69; Washington Univ, coordinator elementary educ summer 1971, master teacher summer 1970, clinical assoc 1967-70, supvr elementary educ 1970-73; St Louis Co Social Studies Implementation Project, master teacher 1966-69; Washington Univ, research adv sum 1970. **ORGANIZATIONS:** Treas St Louis City Counc Internatl Reading Assn 1976-77; chmn Block Unit #375 Natl Urban League Confederation of Block Units 1976-; vice pres Midwest RegionPhilander Smith Coll Natl Alumni Assn 1977-; pres-elect St Louis City Counc; Internatl Reading Assn 1977-78; participant St Louis formum on Fgn Policy co-sponsored by St Louis Counc on World Affaries & the US St Dept of State 1977; research asst St Louis Metro Soc Studies Cntr Wash Univ 1966-69; various activities Wash U; mem Comm Black Recruitment; comm Undergrad Ed; Pre-serv Tchr Educ Comm; Who's Who Among Students in Am Univ & Coll 1952-53; Kappa Delta Pi Educ Honort Soc 1969; pres Kappa Delta Pi St Louis 1970-71; historian-reprtr Kappa Delta Pi St Louis 1971-72; mem Phi Delta Kappa Ed Ldrshp Soc 1969-; Philander Smith Coll Alumni Chap 1966-68; past pres Metro-st Louis Philander Smith Coll Alumni Chpt; sec Metro-st Louis Philander Smith Coll Alumni Chptr 1970-. **MILITARY SERVICE:** AUS paratrooper para-medic 1953-55. **BUSINESS ADDRESS:** Instructional/Coordinator, St Louis Public Schools, 911 Locust St, St Louis, MO 63101.

DANIELS, MELVIN J.
Professional athlete, basketball talent scout, coach. **PERSONAL:** Born Jul 20, 1944, North Carolina; son of Maceo Daniels and Bernice Daniels; married Cecilia. **EDUCATION:** Attended, Burlington Jr Coll, Univ of NM. **CAREER:** American Basketball Assn, 1967-75; MN Muskies, forward 1967-68; IN Pacers, center 1968-74; Memphis Sounds, center 1974-75; NY Nets, center 1976-; Indiana State, asst basketball coach; IN Pacers, asst basketball coach/scout 1981-. **ORGANIZATIONS:** Began Amer Quarter Horse Farm Circle M Ranch, Sheridan IN breed train show Lady Bugs Moon and Dash for Cash bred stock since 1972, specializing in barrel racing and pole bending. **HONORS/ACHIEVEMENTS:** Named to ABA All League Team 1968-72; Rebound Leader 1967-71; Team Ctr All Star Game 1968-73; Most Valuable Player All Star Game 1971; Rookie of Yr 1968; Most Valuable Player, ABA 1968, 1971. **BUSINESS ADDRESS:** Indiana Pacers, Market Square Arena, Market St, Indianapolis, IN 46204.

DANIELS, PATRICIA ANN
Manager, city parking collections bureau. **PERSONAL:** Born Aug 06, Kaufman, TX; daughter of James H Alexander and Mary Elizabeth Barnett-Alexander; married Valjean Daniels, Dec 02, 1964; children: Barry M Alexander, Brette M Daniels. **EDUCATION:** Los Angeles Junior Coll of Business, Los Angeles CA, AA, 1964; Univ of San Francisco, San Francisco CA, BS, 1979. **CAREER:** City of Berkeley, Berkeley CA, supvr, 1968-81, mgr, 1981-. **ORGANIZATIONS:** Mem, Gamma Phi Delta Sorority, Volunteer Serv, 1971-; charter mem, Beta Sigma Chapter, 1971-; California Fedn of Business & Professional Women, 1983-; mem, membership, pres-elect, Diversity Task Force, Bay Valley Dist, 1983-; Natl Forum for Black Public Admin, 1986-; dir, Far Western Region, Gamma Phi Delta Sorority, 1989-. **HONORS/ACHIEVEMENTS:** Rose Pin Award, Gamma Phi Delta Sorority, Natl, 1976; Woman of the Year, Far Western Region, Gamma Phi Delta Sorority, 1979; Dedicated Serv, Beta Sigma, 1986; Outstanding Community Serv, Natl Forum for Black Public Admin, 1987; Woman of Achievement, California Fedn of Business & Professional Women, 1988; author of two leadership manuals, Gamma Phi Delta Sorority. **HOME ADDRESS:** 1810 Hillcrest Rd, San Pablo, CA 94806.

DANIELS, PETER F.
Educator. **PERSONAL:** Born Dec 05, 1928, Pine Bluff, AR; married Ruby; children: Peter Jr, Ronson, Darryl, Connie. **EDUCATION:** AR AM&N Coll, BS 1951; IN U, MSE 1965; State Coll AR; AR State U. **CAREER:** Linwood School Dist, supt 1969-; Vaster High School, prin 1956-69, instructor Biology & Science 1953-56; Sherrill Jr High School, instructor Biology; Joiner AR, teacher 1951. **ORGANIZATIONS:** Mem Nat Educ Assn; AR Educ Assn; Jefferson Co Educ Assn; Nat Alliance Black Sch Edn; AR Adminstrn Assn; AR Sch Bus Officials; AR Adv Bd, ESAA & Title I; adv bd AR Tech Asst Ctr; Jefferson Co Comprehensive Hlth Bd; Black Children Adoption Cncl; NAACP; Kappa Alpha Psi Frat; deacon,bd mem St Paul Missionary Bapt Ch. **BUSINESS ADDRESS:** PO Box 61, Moscow, AR.

DANIELS, REBECCA HAYWOOD
Educator. **PERSONAL:** Born Oct 10, 1943, Columbus Co, NC; married George Daniels; children: Geraldine Renee, Starlin Wynette. **EDUCATION:** Fayetteville State Univ, BS 1966. **CAREER:** Richard B Harrison, teacher 1966-67; S Lumberton Elem, teacher 1967-69; Acme-Delco Jr Sr High School, teacher 1970-. **ORGANIZATIONS:** Councilwoman 1975-77, mayor pro-tem 1975-, town clerk 1974 Town of Bolton; mem NC Assoc of Classroom Teachers, Bicentennial Comm, NC Ext Homemakers Assoc Inc, NEA, NCEA, PACE, Green Ghapel Missionary Baptist Church, VFW Aux Post 9003.

DANIELS, REGINALD SHIFFON
Seminarian. **PERSONAL:** Born Sep 06, 1963, Newport News, VA; son of Thomas Daniels and Bertha Mae Daniels. **EDUCATION:** Attended, Christopher Newport Coll 1981-82; Averett Coll, BA 1986; Virginia Union Univ Sch of Theology 1986-89. **CAREER:** Loyal Baptist Church, assoc minister 1983-86; 31st St Baptist Church, assoc minister 1986-87; Pilgrim Baptist Church, christian education dir 1987-88; Richmond Memorial Hospital, chaplain 1988; Eastern State Hospital, chaplain 1988. **ORGANIZATIONS:** Recruiter NAACP 1982-86; scoutmaster Boy Scouts of Amer 1984-86; missionary Intl Assoc of Ministers' Wives 1985; pres Baptist Student Union 1986-87; Peninsula Track Club 1981-85; Richmond Road Runners 1989. **HONORS/ACHIEVEMENTS:** Academic Scholarship Ebony Blazers 1981; Keesee Fellowship 1982-86; West Hampton Baptist Church Scholarship 1982-86; VA Baptist Assoc Scholarship 1982-86; Julian Hodgenson Scholarship 1986; Academic Scholarships Intl Assoc of Ministers Wives 1986, VA Union Univ Sch of Theol 1986; 31st St Baptist Church Scholarship 1987. **HOME ADDRESS:** PO Box 4778, Richmond, VA 23220.

DANIELS, RICHARD D.
Clergyman. **PERSONAL:** Born Jan 27, 1931, Micanopy, FL; married Doris B Bagley. **EDUCATION:** FAMU, BS 1958. **CAREER:** St Luke AME, Gainesvl, pastor 1958-59; Silver Spgs 1959-64; St Stephens AME, Leesburg, FL, 1964-71; Mt Zion AME, Ocala, 1971-72. **ORGANIZATIONS:** Del Gen Conf AME Ch 1972; mem NAACP; Masonic Lodge; Blood Bank Assn, Alachua Co; presiding elder AME Ch 1973-. **MILITARY SERVICE:** AUS, Korean Conflict, 1951-53.

DANIELS, RON D.
Associate executive. **PERSONAL:** Married Mary Jane; children: Malik, Sundiata, Jeannette. **EDUCATION:** Youngstown State, BA 1965; Univ NY, MA 1967; Union Grad Sch at Antioch, Candidate for Doctoral Degree in Pol Sci 1976. **CAREER:** Assoc Neighborhd Ctr, Hagstrom House, S Side Ctr, Camp Lexington, boys' prog dir, youth & young adult worker, camp counselor, camp prog dir 1961-64; Youngstown State Univ, educator 1967-69; Kent State Univ, instr African Affairs, educator 1971; Hiram Coll, OH, educator 1973, asst prof of Pol Sci & Pan-African Studies, 1974-77; curr pres, Institute for Community Organization and Development; Jesse Jackson for Pres Campaign, Southern Regional mgr, 1988; exec dir, Natl Rainbow Coalition, 1987; moderator and producer, "Ron Daniels Show," WYTV, Youngstown OH, 1968-87; founder and chairman, Freedom Inc., 1967-75, exec dir, 1969-74/. **ORGANIZATIONS:** Natl co-chairperson, Natl Black Independent Party, 1981—; Pres Nat Black Pol Assembly 1974-; candidate for Mayor 1977; founder Cadet Corps; asso exec NAACP; vice pres Kappa Alpha Psi; columnist; mem bd dir Buckeye Rev Newspaper; Econ Devel consult Intl Black Ministers' Conf, Tanzania; exec Cong African People; founding mem African Liberation Day Coord Com; convener OH delegation Nat Black Polit Conv, Gary, IN; pres OH Black Pol Assembly; Rep Nat Black Pol Assembly, elected pres 1974; co-minister Pol Empowerment, Nat Black Pol Assembly; training & proj eval consult Episcopal Ch Gen Conv Spec Prog; mem bd dir & chmn Educ Com Freedom Consumer Co-operative; coordinator Mid-West Regional Coalition; mem Council of Elders, Fedn of Pan-African Educ Insts; consult & lecturer Midwest Colleges; moderator Perspectives in Black; elder Marcus Garvey Sch; mem Urban League, Black Pol Assembly, Welfare Rights Orgn; founder Freedom Inc; adjunct prof & mem bd dir OH Inst of Practical Pol 1973; del No Am Reg Steering Conf, Sixth Pan-Africa Conf; Citizenship Education Fund, prog development, 1987; Help Us Make A Nation (HUMAN) Training Inst; Natl Economic Development and Law Center. **HONORS/ACHIEVEMENTS:** Psi Phi Community Service Award 1975; A Phillip Randolph Award 1968; Talk-In Award 1969; Comm Action Council Award 1969; Youngstown Urban League Serv Award 1971; AR Black Caucus Award 1973; Youngstown Black Pol Assembly Award 1973; Northside Old Timers' Cert Apprec 1973; Gov's Award for Com Action 1974; Mahoning Co Welfare Rights Orgn Award 1974; Assoc Neighborhood Centers Award 1974; Youngstown Black Polit Assembly-Freedom Inc Award 1974; Minority Affairs Dir's Award 1974; Model Cities Citizen Participation Orgn Award 1974;Omega Psi Phi community service award, 1979; McGuffey Center community service award, 1982; African Cultural Weekend Award for dedicated leadership, 1985; Inter-Faith Community Action Committee Award, 1986; Inter-Denominational Clergywomen's Alliance civic award, 1986; First Williams Publishing Co Pioneer Award fo outstanding contributions to civil rights in the media, 1988. **BUSINESS ADDRESS:** Natl Black Independent Pol Pty, 1628 Hillman, Youngstown, OH 44507.

DANIELS, RUBEN
Administrator. **PERSONAL:** Born Oct 17, 1917, Broken Bow, OK; married Elizabeth Chapman; children: Malik, Sundiata. **EDUCATION:** MI State U, 1957; Saginaw Val State Coll, Hon LlD/LittD 1974. **CAREER:** First Ward Community Center, exec dir 1965-; Saginaw Police Dept, patrolman & juvenile officer 1947-65; Gen Motors Corp, 1945-47, 1940-43; Grants Wholesale Groc, warehouseman 1939-40; Saginaw Dept of Recreation WPA, recreation leader 1936-39. **ORGANIZATIONS:** Past pres Saginaw Bd of Edn; adv com Social Studies Dept Delta Coll; trustee MI Natl Bank; chmn bd dir Saginaw Osteopathic Hosp; chmn CommunityAffairs Dept Cath Diocese; dir Saginaw Co Drug Treatment Ctr; mem Statewide Voc Task Force, MI Assn of Sch Bds; mem educ com MI Assn of Sch Bds; mem Human Relations Commn; exec bd OIC; mem Jefferson Meml Scholarship Fund; mem Local 699 Scholarship Fund; lay rep Jr League; mem Nat Alliance of Bus; chmn Law Enforcement Com, Human Relation Commn. **HONORS/ACHIEVEMENTS:** Citations Saginaw Polic Dept 1947-65; Lions Club Award 1963; NW Kiwanis Award 1966; Frontiersman of the Year, Frontiers Intl Saginaw Chap 1966; Achievement Award Saginaw Club Nat Assn of Negro Bus and Professional Womens Club Inc 1968; Layman of Year, Bethel AME Ch 1968; Distinguished Alumnus Saginaw High Sch 1972; Community Serv Award, Saginaw Chap Frontiers Intl 1979; Bob Alberts Award, C of C; Liberty Bell Award; Recognition Award, NAACP 1979; Regocnition Award, Youth Employment Serv; Kwame Nkruman Award, Black Honors Convocation. **MILITARY SERVICE:** USNR po 3rd class 1943-45. **BUSINESS ADDRESS:** 1410 N 12th St, Saginaw, MI 48601.

DANIELS, SIDNEY
Clergyman. **PERSONAL:** Born Jul 28, 1923, Trumbull Co, OH; married Emma Lee Bryant. **EDUCATION:** Youngstown Coll, BA 1945-49; Oberlin Theol Sem, 1949-50; Gammon Theol Sem, 1950-51; Howard Univ Sch Rel, BD 1951-53; John Hopkins Univ, 1970-72; MA 1976. **CAREER:** Civil Aero Bd, fed govt clerk 1950-52; Fairmont Hill Jr Sr HS, educator 1970-71; Samuel Gompers Jr HS, edcuator 1971-72; Emanuel C C Ch, minister 1958-; Equal Opportunity Officer. **ORGANIZATIONS:** IDBC; past pres Harlem Park Neighborhood Council Baltimore; chmn Empoyment Com Interdenomination Ministers' All; bd mem Baltimore Adv Council Voc Edn; bd mem founder Opportuniteis Industrialization Ctr Baltimore; pres Vol Pov War; volunteer work Crownsville Hosp Ctr; served TV & radio on educ & religious topics; established IOU Course given at Comm Coll Baltimore; First black chpln; Baltimore Fire Dept 1973. **MILITARY SERVICE:** AUS pvt 1943-44. **BUSINESS ADDRESS:** 1210 W Lanvale St, Baltimore, MD 21217.

DANIELS, WILLIAM ORLAN
Administrator. **PERSONAL:** Born Apr 26, 1944, Rendville, OH; married Lamerial Ann Garrison; children: Leslie Michelle. **EDUCATION:** Fisk U, BS. **CAREER:** New Eng Terr Dayco Printing Products Co, district mgr 1980; Dayton Urban League Inc, dir educ & employment; Dayton Urban League Inc, adminstr acting exec dir 1974-80; Montgomery Co Childrens Serv Bd, social worker 1972-74; Dayton Pub Sch Dist, tchr 1969-72; Dayton Pub SchESAA Adv Com, chmn 1976-77;Trotwood Madison Sch Dist CapitalUniv Without Walls, consult 1976 1978. **ORGANIZATIONS:** Mem Miami Valley Personnel Assn 1980-; mem Kappa Alpha Psi Frat Inc 1965-; mem Miami Valley Reg Planning Commn 1977-; commr City of Dayton Tennis Commn 1978-; founder Dayton Urban League Youth Forum 1974; founder Dayton Urban League Summer Employment Project 1976.

DANNER, MARGARET ESSIE (MARGARET CUNNINGHAM)
Poet. **PERSONAL:** Born Jan 12, 1915, Chicago, IL; daughter of Caleb Danner and Naomi Danner; married Cordell Strickland; children: Naomi; married Otto Cunningham. **EDUCATION:** Attended YMCA Coll, Chicago,IL, Roosevelt Univ, and Northwestern Univ; also studied under Karl Shapiro and Paul Engle. **CAREER:** Poetry magazine, Chicago, IL, editorial asst, 1951-55, asst editor, 1956-57; Wayne State Univ, Detroit, MI, poet in residence, 1961-62; touring poet, Baha'i Teaching Committee, 1964-66; Whitney fellow in Senegal, Africa, and Paris, France, 1966; Virginia Union Univ, Richmond, poet in residence, 1968-69; LeMoyne-Owen Coll, Memphis, TN, poet-in-residence, 1970-75; founder of Boone House (Center for the Arts), Detroit, MI, and of Nologonyu's, Chicago, IL. **ORGANIZATIONS:** Mem, Soc of Afro Amer Culture; Contemporary Artists; Natl Pen Women; Memphis Cable TV; Natl Council of Teachers of English; Poets in a Bottle; dir, Boone House; life mem, Chicago Southside Comm Art Center Nologonias. **HONORS/ACHIEVEMENTS:** Author of Impressions of African Art Forms, Broadside Press, 1960, To Flower: Poems, Counterpoise Series, 1963, Iron Lace, Poets Press, 1968, The Down of a Thistle, Country Beautiful, 1976; editor of anthologies Brass Horses, 1968, and Regroup, 1969; recorded, with Langson Hughes, Writers of the Revolution; John Hay Whitney Fellowship; Amer Writers Award; Harriet Tubman Award; Native Chicagoans Literary Award; Midwestern Writers Award; named Teacher of the Year, LeMoyen-Owen Coll, 1975. **HOME ADDRESS:** 626 East 102nd Pl, Chicago, IL 60628. *

DANSBY, JESSE L., JR.
Government official. **PERSONAL:** Born Aug 17, 1942, Bessemer, AL; son of Rev Jesse L Dansby, Sr and Ora L Martin; married Bette Joyce Ringstaff; children: Natasha Lynn, Mischa Anita. **EDUCATION:** TN State Univ, BS 1964; Univ of OK, MA 1973; Industrial College of the Armed Forces, Management Certificate 1975; Air Command and Staff Coll, Management Certificate 1977; Air Force Inst of Tech Intl Logistics, Management Certificate 1977. **CAREER:** Intl Logistics Ctr, dir Middle East & African program 1979-80; Defense Electronic Supply Ctr, dir of installation serv 1980-83; Kwang Ju Air Base South Korea, base commander 1983-84; HQ Air Force Logistics Command, dir of inquiries and govtl affairs office of inspector general 1984-. **ORGANIZATIONS:** Mem Omega Phi Phi 1962-; mem Greater Dayton Real Estate Investment Assoc 1980-; bd dirs Girl Scouts of Amer 1982-; mem Industrial Relation Assoc 1985-; mem Ancient Egyptian Arabic Order of the Mystic Shrine. **HONORS/ACHIEVEMENTS:** Outstanding Social Actions Officer USAF Europe 1974; Presidential Citation Khartoum Sudan 1979; author handbook on Equal Oppor USAF Europe 1973; co-author handbook "Human Relations in the Military" USAF Europe 1973; 33 Degree Mason 1988. **MILITARY SERVICE:** USAF lt col 1964-; Defense Meritorious Serv Medal; Efficiency Medal First Class (Govt of Sudan); Air Force Meritorious Serv Medal

w/Two Oak Leaf Clusters; Air Force Commendation Medal. **HOME ADDRESS:** 7221 Brandt Vista, Dayton, OH 45424. **BUSINESS ADDRESS:** Dir of Inq and Govtl Affairs, HQ Air Force Logistics Command, Office of Inspector General, HQ AFLC/IGQ, Wright Patterson AFB, OH 45433.

DANTLEY, ADRIAN
Professional athlete. **PERSONAL:** Born Feb 28, 1956, Hyattsville, MD; married DiNitri. **EDUCATION:** Univ of Notre Dame, Bus 1977. **CAREER:** Buffalo Braves, player 1976-77; IN Pacers, player 1977; LA Lakers, player 1977-79; UT Jazz, player; Detroit Pistons, player; Dallas Mavericks, player, 1989-. **HONORS/ACHIEVEMENTS:** Gold Medal Team US Olympic Basketball; Twice All-Amer; Rookie of the Yr 1976-77; Leading Scorer NBA 1980-81; NBA Comeback Player of the Year Awd 1983-84;Rookie of the Year 1977; mem NBA All Star Team 1980,81,82. **BUSINESS ADDRESS:** Dallas Mavericks, Reunion Arena, 777 Sports Place, Dallas, TX 75207. *

DANTZLER, HERMAN
Mayor. **PERSONAL:** Born Mar 20, 1937, Spartansburg, SC. **EDUCATION:** Tuskegee Inst, 1953-54; GE 1966. **CAREER:** State of OH Store Mgmt, 1943;Univ Cincinnati, 1973; Home Fed, 1974; City Lincoln Hghts OH, mayor 1975-; Club Ebony, mgr 1974-76; State OH, 1971-74; GE Co, stock clk 1966-71; Cincinnati Corcrete & Pipe Co, leadman 1958-66; City Lincoln Hghts OH, rec supr 1957-58; Lincoln Hghts, cnclmn. **ORGANIZATIONS:** Mem Lincoln Hghts Rec Commn; Hamilton Co Black Caucus; treas Lincoln Hghts; Dem Party; pres 4th Ward Dem Club; del Nat Black Polit Conv; alternate OH-KY-IN Reg Cncl Gov; mem Mayor's Assn OH; OH Muncpl League; The Am League; Shriner's; Optimist Intl Club; Mayor's Assn Hamilton Co; Mayor's Assn Mid-w Region; Masons; Comm Action Com. **MILITARY SERVICE:** AUS 1955-57. **BUSINESS ADDRESS:** 1201 Steffens Ave, Lincoln Heights, OH 45215.

DANZY, LEROY HENRY
Law enforcement. **PERSONAL:** Born May 22, 1929, Wayside, KS; son of Henry Danzy and Julia Danzy; married Velma Lee Ballard; children: Gwenevere, Gail, Leronna, Vance. **EDUCATION:** US Army School, Heavy Equip Maint 1955; IN Vocation Tech, Cert 1969. **CAREER:** Farmer, 1944-54; US Army, 1954-56; Wheelabrator, shop laborer 1963-65, milwright 1965-; MI Constable & Court Officers Assoc, vp, pres 1987-. **ORGANIZATIONS:** Constable Calvin Twp Cass Cty 1957-; deacon Chain Lake Baptist Church 1962-; steward & guide committeeman United Auto Workers Union 1964-72, 1972-79 Bargaining Committeeman; vice pres educ dir MI Constable & Court Off Assn 1970-; mem & sec Cassopolis Publ Sch Bd 1972-84; fair practice chmn United Auto Workers Union 1972-; pres Cassopolis Public Sch Bd 1984-86; vice pres Cassopolis Publ Schl Bd 1986-88. **HONORS/ACHIEVEMENTS:** Constable of the Year MI Constable & Court Off Lansing 1972. **MILITARY SERVICE:** AUS spec 3 1954-56. **HOME ADDRESS:** 17532 Williamsville St, Cassopolis, MI 49031.

DAPREMONT, DELMONT, JR.
Automobile dealer. **HONORS/ACHIEVEMENTS:** Named one of the top one hundred auto dealers by Black Enterprise in June, 1988. **BUSINESS ADDRESS:** Coastal Ford Inc, 7311 Airport Blvd, Mobile, AL 36608. *

DARBY, CASTILLA A., JR.
Physician. **PERSONAL:** Born Jul 17, 1946, Anniston, AL; children: Kimberlynne Michelle. **EDUCATION:** AL State Univ, BS 1968; VA Hosp Tuskegee Inst AL, Corrective Physical Therapy 1968-69; Schiff Scout Reservation Teng Ctr Mendham NJ, scout exec 1970; Meharry Medical Coll, MD 1978. **CAREER:** Woodson HS, biology instructor; Ford Greene Elem Sch Nashville, physical educ instructor 1969-70; Boy Scouts of Amer Middle TN Cncl, dist scout exec 1970-71; TN Valley Authority Nashville, clinical physician; Douglas Memorial Hospital Jefferson TX, medical dir 1980-83; Private Practice, physician; Lake CliffHospital Dallas TX, chief of staff. **ORGANIZATIONS:** Mem NAACP 1986, Meharry Medical Coll Alumni Assoc 1986-87, AMA, Natl Federation of Independent Business 1986-87; mem TX Federation of Sr Citizens 1987; life mem Kappa Alpha Psi Frat Inc; mem TX Medical Assoc. **HONORS/ACHIEVEMENTS:** AL State Univ Freshman Awd for Academic Excellence; tutor Anatomy & Physiology AL State Univ; Jessie S Noyles Scholarship Obstetrics & Gynecology 1978. **BUSINESS ADDRESS:** Chief of Staff, Lake Cliff Hospital, 1400 Martin L King Blvd, Dallas, TX 75215.

D'ARBY, TERENCE TRENT
Singer, recording artist. **HONORS/ACHIEVEMENTS:** Grammy Award for best male in R&B category, 1989. **BUSINESS ADDRESS:** c/o CBS Records Group, 51 W 52nd St, New York, NY 10019. *

DARDEN, CHARLES R.
Business executive. **PERSONAL:** Born Jul 06, 1911, Lauderdale Co, MS; married Gertrude Graham; children: Charles Jr, John Rodney, Ralph, Renee, Shelia, Mary Venona. **EDUCATION:** Jackson State Coll. **CAREER:** Darden's Florist & Gift Shop, mgr; Darden's Gen Ins Agy; Darden's Photo Service; tchr 1932-33; elementary principal 1933-37; Metal Arts Class & Jewelry, salesman 1942-49; Geo Spies Grad Supplies of Chgo, sales mgr 1949-59; Josten's Mfg Co MN, sales 1959-70. **ORGANIZATIONS:** Founder pres Meridian Negro Bus & Prof League 1946; pres Meridian Br NAACP 1956; pres MS State Conf of Branches NAACP 1955-60; mem Nat Bd NAACP 1957-; mem JFKennedy Nat Com of Constitutional Rights & Am Freedom 1960; mem IN-HOTEP Conv on Integration of Hospitals 1958-61; past steward now layleader St Paul United Meth Ch; mem bd dir OIC Meridian. **HONORS/ACHIEVEMENTS:** Recipient Methodist NAACP Award, New York City 1959; Man of the Year for Outstanding Courage & Leadership, Orange & Maplewood Branches NAACP NJ 1964; Outstanding Comm Leadership Award, Meridian Action Com 1973. **BUSINESS ADDRESS:** 1202 27 Ave, Meridian, MS 39301.

DARDEN, CHRISTINE MANN
Aerospace engineer. **PERSONAL:** Born Sep 10, 1942, Monroe, NC; married Walter L Darden, Jr; children: Jeanne Darden Riley, Janet Christine. **EDUCATION:** Hampton Inst, BS Math High Honors 1962; VA State Coll, MS Math 1967; George Washington Univ, DSc Mech Eng 1983. **CAREER:** Brunswick Co Sch, tchr 1962-63; Portsmouth City Sch VA, tchr 1964-65; VA State Coll, math instr 1966-67; NASA Langley Rsch Ctr, data analyst 1967-

73, aerospace eng. **ORGANIZATIONS:** Pres Hampton Roads Chpt, Natl Tech Assoc 1984-; assoc fellow Amer Inst of Aeronautics & Astronauts 1973-; elder Carver Mem Presbyterian Ch 1980-; mem Gamma Upsilon Omega Chap of AKA 1960-, Natl Langley Exchange Cncl 1979-; chmn boundaries comm Southern VA Presbyterian Church USA 1983-88. **HONORS/ACHIEVEMENTS:** 20 Year Alumnus Award, Hampton Inst 1982; Author or Co-author of over 28 Technical reports & articles; received Dr AT Weathers Tech Achievement Awd from Natl Tech Assoc 1985; recognized by Dollars & Sense Mag in its salute to 100 Top Black Bus & Professional Women 1986. **BUSINESS ADDRESS:** Aerospace Engineer, NASA, M S 411 Langley Res Ctr, Hampton, VA 23665.

DARDEN, GEORGE HARRY
Attorney. **PERSONAL:** Born Mar 14, 1934, Cadiz, KY; married Gwen Wright; children: George II, Tiffany, Betsy, Josette. **EDUCATION:** KY State Univ, BS 1955; Winner NY O or Oratoral contest 1952, KY State Dance Club "Oscar" 1954, Salivon P Chase College of Law, JO 1964. **CAREER:** Hamilton Cnty, OH, asst cnty prosecutor 1964-66; Cincinnati OH Hopkensvl, KY, priv pract 1964-69; Legal Serv Proj Ctr OH, chief attny 1967-68; Lincoln Hts, OH, city solicitor 1967-68; EEOC, Wash, DC, staff attny 1969-71, supiory 1973-73, chief legal consel div 1973-75; EE OC, rgnl attny 1975-. **ORGANIZATIONS:** Pres Double Dollar Co 1965-68; chrmn, legal comm Hopkinsville, KY =Naacp 1968-69; chrmn, legal redress comm Denver, CO 1984-. **HONORS/ACHIEVEMENTS:** Citations EEOC Houston Hearings 1972-73, Chief Judge, Cincinnati Muncpl Ct 1968, WCIN Radio Station 1968; Cincinnati Herald Paper 1968.

DARDEN, JOSEPH S., JR.
Educator. **PERSONAL:** Born Jul 25, 1925, Pleasantville, NJ; son of Joseph S Darden, and Blanche Paige Darden; children: Michele Irene Darden Burgess. **EDUCATION:** Lincoln Univ, AB 1948; NY Univ, MA 1952, EdD 1963. **CAREER:** Clark Coll, instructor Biological Science 1952-55; Albany State Coll, assoc, assoc prof Biology & Health Educ 1955-64, chmn science div 1959-60; Wagner Coll, visiting lecturer Health Educ 1966-88; Rutgers Univ, adjunct prof Sex Educ 1974,75; Montclair State Coll, 1975; Kean Coll of NJ, chair health & recreation dept 1979-84, prof & coordinator Health Educ 1964-. **ORGANIZATIONS:** Pres E Dist Assn AAHPERD 1974-75; vice pres & chmn Health Educ Div E Dist Assn AAHPERD 1971-72; vice pres Health Educ NJ Assn for HPER 1967; mem adv bd "Health Educ" AAHPERD 1973-76; editorial bd "The Journal of School Health" ASHA 1969-72; governing council Amer School Health Assn 1970-73; author, lecturer, workshop dir, radio & TV panelist in sex educ; bd dir Assn for Advisors of Health Educ 1975-78; founder NJ Health Educ Council 1967; dist representative 1979-82, pres 1975 EDA, AAPHERD; mem Natl Council on Family Relations; NJAHPERD; ASHA; AAHPERD, SIECUS, AASECT; Fellow ASHA; bd of trustees Planned Parenthood of Essec County 1985-. **HONORS/ACHIEVEMENTS:** Assoc Danforth Found Fellow 1958-59; Distinguisheded Serv, Amer School Health Assoc 1971; Hon Fellow Award, NJ Assoc for Health, Physical Educ & Recreation 1972; Honor Award NJ Health Educ Council 1975; Distinguished Leadership Award, NJ Assoc for Health, Physical Educ & Recrestion 1975; Distinguished Hon Award, East Distinguished Assoc AAHPER 1976; Distinguished Serv Award, Alpha Alpha Lambda Chapter Alpha Phi Alpha 1975; Alliance Honor Award AAHPERD 1985; Outstanding Coll/Univ Teacher of the Year Eastern Dist AAHPERD 1983; numerous articles published in state, regional & natl journals, Charles D Henry Award, AAHPERD, 1988. **MILITARY SERVICE:** AUS t/sgt 1944-46. **HOME ADDRESS:** 1416 Thelma Dr, Union, NJ 07083. **BUSINESS ADDRESS:** Kean Coll of New Jersey, Physical Educ, Recreation & Health Dept, Union, NJ 07083.

DARDEN, ORLANDO WILLIAM
Business executive. **PERSONAL:** Born Jun 02, 1930, Washington, DC; married Peggie Hamer; children: Orlando Jr, Michael. **EDUCATION:** Howard U, BA 1953. **CAREER:** Comm Fed Sav & Loan Assn of Washington, pres 1974-; mort bnkr; real est brkr. **ORGANIZATIONS:** Mem bd of teh PA Ave Devel Corp; Mayor's Econ Devel Com for DC; Adv Com of Pub Serv Commn of DC; mem DC Gambling Study Commn; Devel Sch Found; chmn bd CF Financial Corp; dir Dolphin & Evans Settlements, Inc; vice pres Urban Mgmt Serv Listed Mortgage Banker 1973. **HONORS/ACHIEVEMENTS:** Washington Real Estate Brokers Award, DC C of C. **MILITARY SERVICE:** USAF 1st lt 1953-55. **BUSINESS ADDRESS:** President, OWD Enterprises, Inc, 1511 K Street, NW #319, Washington, DC 20005.

DARDEN, THOMAS V.
Communications director. **PERSONAL:** Born Aug 28, 1950, Sandusky, OH; married Jolyn Burrucker; children: Todd V, Marisa T. **EDUCATION:** Univ of MI, BS 1972. **CAREER:** Cleveland Browns, defensive back 1972-81; Natl Football League, all pro probowler 1978-79. **ORGANIZATIONS:** Brd of dir Ronald McDonald House 1983-, Lexington Square Comm Cntr 197-. **BUSINESS ADDRESS:** Vice President Dir, Win Communications, WQAL Radio, 1621 Euclid Ave, Cleveland, OH 44115.

DARDEN, WILLIAM BOONE
Retired police chief. **PERSONAL:** Born Aug 16, 1925, Atlanta, GA; married Rose M Meyers, Jun 06, 1956; children: Darrell, William Jr, Kimberly. **EDUCATION:** Nova Univ FL, MA Criminal Justice 1977; SE Univ SC, MA Pub Adminstrn 1976; FL Intl U, BS Criminal Justice 1974; Palm Beach Jr Coll, Asso Arts 1971. **CAREER:** Retired 1983; Riviera Beach Police Dept, chief of police 1971-83; Migrant Leg Serv, chf investgtr 1971; ret Lt 1965; W Palm Beach Police Dept, lt patrol 1960; W Palm Beach Police Dept, sgt patrol 1956; W Palm Beach Police Dept, detect 1952; W Palm Beach Police Dept, walking patrolman 1948. **ORGANIZATIONS:** Chmn affirmative action Dem Parto of FL; mem Nat Dem Com-Nat Rules Com-dem Party; bd of dirs Nat Ofcrs of Black Law Enforcement Execs; mem Alpha Phi Alpha Frat; mem Lambda Alpha Epsilon; Am Crim Justice Assn; Sigma Pi Phi Frat. **HONORS/ACHIEVEMENTS:** Mem, Natl Tranportation Advisory Comm, presidential appointment by Pres Carter, 1978-81. **MILITARY SERVICE:** Milit Police World War II.

DARITY, EVANGELINE ROYALL
Retired educator. **PERSONAL:** Born Jun 16, 1927, Wilson, NC; daughter of Dock Moses Royall and Ossie Jenkins Royall; married William Alexander Darity, Dec 23, 1950; children: William Jr, Janiki Evangelia. **EDUCATION:** Barber-Scotia Coll Concord NC, BSc 1949; Smith Coll Northampton MA, MEd 1969; Univ MA Amherst, EdD 1975-78. **CAREER:** Smith Coll, asst to class dean 1968-75; Barber-Scotia Coll, vice pres student affairs 1978-80; Holyoke YWCA, exec dir 1980-81; Mt Holyoke Coll, assoc dean of studies 1981-88. **OR-**

GANIZATIONS: Mem Amer Assn for Counseling & Devel 1975; mem natl prog planning comm Natl Assn Women Deans Counselors Admin 1975-; trustee Barber-Scotia Coll 1979-; corp mem Comm Savings Bank 1981-; bd mem United Way Holyoke Granby & South Hadley 1981-; membership chair Amer Assn Univ Women CT Valley Br 1982, pres 1986-88. **HOME ADDRESS:** 105 Heatherstone Rd, Amherst, MA 01002.

DARITY, WILLIAM A.
Educator. **PERSONAL:** Born Jan 15, 1924, Flat Rock, NC; son of Aden Randall Darity and Elizabeth Smith Darity; married Evangeline Royall, Dec 23, 1950; children: William Jr, Janki Evangelia. **EDUCATION:** Shaw U, BS 1948; NC Central U, MSPH 1949; Univ of NC, PhD 1964. **CAREER:** Univ of MA, prof, 1965—, prof pub health and dean, Sch of Health Sci, 1973—; World Health Orgn, regional advisor, 1953-64, consultant, 1971-80; Peace Corps Training Programs, consult dir, 1962-67; Headstart Training Programs, consult lectr, 1965-67; Univ of NC, vis prof, 1973; external examiner, Univ of Ibadau, Nigeria, and Univ of West Indies, 1973-85; Natl Cancer Inst, dir and principal investigator, Res on Cancer and Smoking in Black Populations, 1986—. **ORGANIZATIONS:** Fellow Am Pub Health Assn; fellow Soc for Pub Health Educ Inc; fellow Am Sch Health Assn; mem Am Nat Council on Health Edn; mem Intl Union on Health Edn; Delta Omega; asso Danforth Found; mem bd dir Drug Abuse Council Inc 1972-; bd dir Planned Parenthood Fed of Am Inc 1967-73; bd dir SIECUS 1967-71; pres MA Assn for Mental Health 1967-69; pres Hampshire Public Health Assn 1967-70; bd of trustees, Univ of NC-Chapel Hil, 1985—; bd of Scientific Counselors, Natl Cancer Inst, 1986—; bd of dir, MA Water Resources Authority, 1989—; Phi Kappa Phi; Sigma Xi; mem & official of many other civic orgns. **HONORS/ACHIEVEMENTS:** Recipient Fellowship World Health Orgn; Hildrus Poindexter Public Health Service Award, BCHW/APHA, 1975; Distinguished Lecture/Chancellor's Medal, Univ of MA, 1989. **MILITARY SERVICE:** US Army, infantry, 1st lieutenant, 1943-47. **BUSINESS ADDRESS:** Professor of Public Health, University of Massachusetts, Arnold House, Amherst, MA 01003.

DARK, LAWRENCE JEROME
Government official. **PERSONAL:** Born Jan 18, 1953, Americus, GA; son of Charlie Dark and Frances Adrilla Harris Howard; married Okianer B Christian; children: Harrison Edward. **EDUCATION:** Denison Univ, BA 1976; Northwestern Univ, JD 1980. **CAREER:** Frostburg State Coll, asst to the pres 1979-82; Amer Bar Assn Council on Legal Educ Oppor, assoc dir 1982-85; Claflin Coll, dir corporate foundation relations and devel 1985-86; Amer Univ, adjunct faculty mem 1985; Claflin Coll, part-time faculty mem 1985-86; American Red Cross, corporate initiative assoc 1986-; Virginia Council on Human Rights, dir (appointed by Gov Gerald L Baliles as the first dir for this new state agency). **ORGANIZATIONS:** Natl advisory comm mem Natl Inst for Citizen Educ in the Law 1986-; mem Alpha Phi Alpha Fraternity Iota Upsilon Lambda Chapter; bd mem MD Humanities Council 1980-84, MD State Bd for Social Serv 1982-84; comm mem United Way 1988-; field service chair American Red Cross EOH 1988-; comm mem American Red Cross Volunteer Communications Campaign Advisory Comm, Policy Issues Comm 1989-; comm mem Amer Society of Public Admin 1989-. **HONORS/ACHIEVEMENTS:** Citation by Sec of the MD Dept of Human Resources for Serv on the State Bd for Social Serv 1984; Citation for Serv on the MD Humanities Council 1984; Natl Scholarship Serv and Fund for Negro Students Award; Woodrow Wilson Natl Fellowship 1985-86; Improved Fundraising Capabilites Program; United Negro Coll Fund Leadership Pin Award 1986; Council on Legal Educ Opportunity Scholarship; Natl Endowment for the Humanities Fellowship 1981; selected to attend American Red Cross Leadership Institute 1987, The Governor's Educational Program, Virginia Executive Institute 1988; selected to attend the 1989/1990 Leadership Metro Richmond Leadership Development Program 1989, Executive Leadership Institute of the National Forum for Black Public Administrators 1989. **BUSINESS ADDRESS:** Dir, Virginia Council on Human Rights, James Monroe Building, 17th Floor, 101 N 14th St, Richmond, VA 23219.

DARKE, CHARLES B.
Dentist, administrator. **PERSONAL:** Born Sep 22, 1937, Chicago, IL; son of Paul O Darke and Annie W Tennin Darke; children: Charles B Darke, II. **EDUCATION:** Wilson Jr Coll, AA 1960; Meharry Medical Coll, DDS 1964; Univ of California, Berkeley, MPH 1972. **CAREER:** qn Staff, Mt Zion Hospital, St Mary Hospital, San Francisco General Hospital; Dept of Labor Job Corp Region 9, dental consultant; Univ of California School of Med, asst clinical prof; Univ California School of Dentistry, lecturer; San Francisco General Hospital, dir dental serv; San Francisco General Hospital, asst admin, Satellite Health Centers; part time private practice, dentist. **ORGANIZATIONS:** State Bd of Dental Examiners California; dir Dental Ser San Francisco General Hospital div of outpatient & comm serv consult prepaid health plans; bd dirs CA Children's Lobby; field consultant Joint Commn on Accreditation of Hospitals. **MILITARY SERVICE:** USAF capt 1965-67. **BUSINESS ADDRESS:** 2175 Hayes St, San Francisco, CA 94117.

DARKES, LEROY WILLIAM
Electrical engineer. **PERSONAL:** Born Sep 26, 1924, Atlantic City, NJ; married Mamie Doris Simpson; children: William S, Leroy S, Lois L Bond, Matthew S. **EDUCATION:** Rutgers Univ, BS Elec Engr 1947, MS 1948. **CAREER:** Atlantic City Elec Co, elec engr 1948, distrib engr 1953, syst planning engr 1958, mgr Var Areas 1965-. **ORGANIZATIONS:** Mbr IEEE 1948-, Natl Soc of Professional Engineers 1955-, Atlantic Cty Bd of Ed 1969-87, Atlantic County Planning Bd 1972-89. **HONORS/ACHIEVEMENTS:** Licensed NJ Professional Engineer 1955-. **MILITARY SERVICE:** AUS pfc 1944-46. **BUSINESS ADDRESS:** Manager of Engineering Service, Atlantic City Electric Co, P O Box 1500, Pleasantville, NJ 08232.

DARKINS, DUANE ADRIAN
Clergyman. **PERSONAL:** Born Oct 31, 1934; married Betty Abbot; children: Duane Jr, Samuel. **EDUCATION:** Trinity Coll, DD; Coll & Sem Pillar of Fire, DSS; PhD; Moody's Inst, MDiv; Univ of Pittsburgh; Fuller Normal Indsl Coll; Pittsburgh Theol Sem; Univ of Pittsburgh, LLD. **CAREER:** Faith Tabncl Ch of God in Christ, pastor; Eastern Jurisdiction of PA, consecrated asst bishop; Walk in Day Camp, fdr dir; Proj Serv Unlimited, exec dir; Charles Harrison Mason Bible Coll, state vp; Commonwealth of PA, refree; Lichenstein & Bartiromo Law Firm, legal cons/adjunct; Controller Ofc City of Pittsburgh, chief auditor; Controller Ofc City of Pittsburgh, auditor; City of Pittsburgh, chief clerk; Nghbrhd Youth Corps, asst to coord. **ORGANIZATIONS:** Couns Outreach Approach Young Mens Christian Assn; chmn bd of dir; v chmn; treas; v sec; YMCA; chpln E End Jr Little League; chpln Silver Lake Comm Assn; chmn Citzns Of Polit Progress; preside City & Co Inauguration Afrs & Evenst; pres Psoriasis Found; chmn Mayor's Commn on Human Relat; past bd of dir mem NAACP; mem Homewood Brushton Renewal Council; trustee John J Kane Hosp; regstr Nat Ch of God in Christ; state vice pres Charles HarrisonBible Coll; regnl area dir Charles Harrison Mason Bible Coll; mem So Ldrshp Conf; pres Homewood Burshton Ministerian; bd of dir Race & Religion Council; pres fdr Penncostal Crusade Nationwide; fdr Outreach Radio Ministry Prgm; chpln Outreach Min Pennial Inst; pres Homewood Brushton Council of Chs; chpln mem Pittsburgh Hosp; chmn Ordination Bd of Nat FBH Ministers; chmn Invest Com Nat FBH Mins; supt Dist of & Ch of God in Christ; moderator Eastern Jurisdiction of PA; num political activities. **HONORS/ACHIEVEMENTS:** Awards Hand & Hand; Talke Mag; Best Dress Man of Yr; Pittsburgh Courier; E Liberty Gafield Annual Awards; Martin Luther King Jr; consult panelist lectr numevents workshops.

DARLING, LEROY (ROY WEST)
Director. **PERSONAL:** Born Jan 19, 1939, Tupelo, OK; married Mary Elizabeth Dewalt; children: Lisa Antoinette, Eliot Dewalt. **EDUCATION:** OK U, attended 1957. **CAREER:** KDIA Radio, dir of news & info 1979-; WPAT AM & FM New York, news & publ affairs dir 1975-78; Nat Black Network, natl news dir 1973-75; ABC Radio & TV NY, staff announcer 1971-73; WDIA Radio Memphis TN, dir 1970-71; WNJR Radio Newark NJ, news dir 1968-70; WLIB AM & FM Radio NY, anchor-reporter 1966-68; Music & News AFRS/TV Morocco & France, daily air shows 1959-65; WNAD Radio Norman OK, staff announcer 1957-58; Briod & Fields Inc, associate; Pub Relations firm. **ORGANIZATIONS:** Mem bd of dir Operation PUSH New Jersey Chap 1974-78; mem bd of dir 13th Step Study SAAR Ltd (Alcoholism Program) 1980. **HONORS/ACHIEVEMENTS:** 1st Black Dir of News & Pub Affairs, WDIA Radio Memphis 1970; several articles published. **BUSINESS ADDRESS:** KDIA Radio, Bay Bridge Toll Plaza Rd, Oakland, CA 94662.

DARLING, MARSHA JEAN
Educator. **PERSONAL:** Born Feb 01, 1947, New York, NY; daughter of Maurice C Darling and Martha T Tyson. **EDUCATION:** Imperial Coll of London, film studies 1970; Staten Island Coll CUNY, AA (honors) 1971; Vassar Coll, BA 1973; Newberry Library, Statistical Methodologies 1975; Duke Univ, MA 1975, PhD 1982. **CAREER:** Sickle Cell Anemia Testing Prog Albany, testing dir 1973; Ctr for the Study of Civil Rights and Race Relations Duke Univ, exec dir 1977-78; Blacksides Films Inc, film prod researcher 1979; Harvard Univ, teaching fellow 1978-79; Solomon Fuller Mental Health Inst, lecturer 1979; Hunter Coll, asst prof of women's studies, 1987; Wellesley Coll Dept Black Studies, asst prof 1979-88; Natl Black Women's Health Project, consultant, 1988; Natl Comm for Responsive Philanthropy, consultant, 1988-89. **ORGANIZATIONS:** Vice chairperson President's Natl Adv Council HEW 1975-76; rsch asst prog analyst Prog in Urban & Regional Develop Comparative Area Studies Prog 1975-76; adv bd Amer Historical Assn 1978-80; vol Black & Third World Women's Collective 1978-82; bd dirs MA Found for Humanities & Policy 1982-88; consultant Faculty & Curr Develop Northeastern Univ 1983; consultant Natl Endowment Humanities Office of Educ; Natl Women's Studies Assn 1982-85; Feminist Press Reprints Comm 1982-85; vol Black Achievers Linkage Prog YWCA-YMCA 1983-; vol Faculty Adv Comm Project Exploration 1983-88; Joint Harvard/MIT Women in Intl Develop Group 1983-. **HONORS/ACHIEVEMENTS:** Rsch Assoc WEB DuBois Rsch Inst Harvard 1982-83; recipient Gr Boston YWCA-YMCA Black Achiever's Awd 1983; Summer Seminar Fellow Natl Endowment for Humanities 1984; Pinanski Awd for Excellence in Teaching Wellesley Coll Distinguished Teaching Awd 1984; Postdoctoral Fellowship Rockefeller Found 1984-85; Fulbright Sr Scholars Award, India, 1988; Faculty Fellow, Smithsonian Inst, 1989; publications including,"Black Landownership" the Encyclopedia of S Culture 1989; "Critical Issues in the Integration of Women of Color Into the Liberal Arts Curriculum" presented at the Mellon Faculty Seminar 1982; dissertation, The Growth & Decline of the Afro-Amer Family Farm, Warren County, NC, 1910-1960, 1982; author, The Disinherited as Source: Rural Black Women's Memories, Michigan Quartely Review, 1987. **BUSINESS ADDRESS:** PO Box 25103, Georgetown Station, Washington, DC 20007.

DARNELL, EDWARD BUDDY
Airport management official. **PERSONAL:** Born Mar 04, 1930, Chicago, IL; son of Edward Darnell and Mary Darnell; married Gwendolyn Wilson, Aug 19, 1953; children: Glenn T, Gary L. **EDUCATION:** Detroit Inst of Tech, BAA, 1968; Wayne State Univ, MSW, 1971; Univ of MI, Specialist in Gerontology 1971. **ORGANIZATIONS:** Imperial first Ceremonial Master; Imperial Council Shriners 1988; grand recording sec United Supreme Council, 1977. **HONORS/ACHIEVEMENTS:** Legion of honor Prince Hall Shriners 1973; Scottish Rite Hall of Fame Prince Hall Scottish Rite 1984. **MILITARY SERVICE:** USMC sgt; Presidential Unit Citation 1953. **HOME ADDRESS:** 1301 Orleans #2211, Detroit, MI 48207.

DARNELL, EMMA IONE
City official. **PERSONAL:** Born Mar 01, 1937, Atlanta, GA. **EDUCATION:** Fisk U, BA; Columbia U, MA; Howard Sch of Law, JD. **CAREER:** Grant Review Bd for city of Atlanta, intergovt programs coordinator & chmn; Morris Brown Coll & Atlant U, asst prof of psychology & edn; US Equal Employ Oppor, served as legal investigator. **ORGANIZATIONS:** Mem Atlanta chpts; NAACP; YWCA. **BUSINESS ADDRESS:** Office of Mayor, 68 Mitchell St, Atlanta, GA 30303.

DARRELL, BETTY LOUISE
National minority business advocate. **PERSONAL:** Born Mar 16, 1934, Louisville, KY; daughter of Jerome McDonald and Cleoda Mason McDonald; married Neville T Darrell, Mar 16, 1984; children: Tasha Wiesing, Lew K Olive, Elayna R Olive, Anthony C Olive. **EDUCATION:** Univ of Louisville, Louisville KY, BA, 1955, attended 1955-56; Washburn Univ, Topeka KS, MA, 1969. **CAREER:** Bd of Educ, Louisville KY, teacher, 1955-56; Kansas Comm on Civil Rights, Topeka KS, educ specialist, 1968-69; Washburn Univ, Topeka KS, upward bound instructor, 1968-69, Natl Bd YWCA, New York NY, Racial Justice Assoc natl dir, 1970-78; Project Equality, New York NY, assoc natl dir, 1978-82; New York/New Jersey Minority Purchasing Council, New York NY, exec dir, 1982-84. **ORGANIZATIONS:** Mem, Delta Sigma Theta Sorority, 1954, English Speaking Union, 1964-66, British Amer Women's Assn, 1964-66, NAACP, 1970-74, Teaneck NJ Community Relation Advisory Comm, 1975-78, Ethnic Heritage Comm, Natl Educ Assn, 1975-77, Black Agency Exec, 1975-78; sec, Natl Minority Business Directory, 1985-89; nominating comm, Natl Minority Supplier Devel Council, 1987. **HONORS/ACHIEVEMENTS:** Anglo-Amer Award, British Amer Women's Org, 1966; Community Relations, Teaneck NJ Advisory Council, 1978; Affirmative Action/EEO Project Equality, 1982; Minority Vendor Coordinator's Award, New York/New Jersey Vendor Input Comm, 1985; Black Achievers in Industry, Harlem YMCA, 1986. **HOME ADDRESS:** Tonetta Lake Way Dr, Brewster, NY 10509.

DARRELL, LEWIS E.
Attorney. **PERSONAL:** Born Aug 12, 1932, St George, Bermuda;married Shirley Ann Bruce; children: Pamela, Valerye, Elizabeth. **EDUCATION:** Hampton Inst, BS 1955; Univ of OK College of Law, LlB 1961. **CAREER:** Pruce & Rougan, Attorneys, priv pract 1961-66; Legal Aid Soc of OK Cnty, exec dir 1966-70; Darrell, Bruce, Johnson and Simms Attorneys, priv pract 1970-74; Legal Aid Soc OK Cnty, asst oK atrny gnrl 1978-83. **BUSINESS ADDRESS:** Private Attorney, 3624 N Jordan, Oklahoma City, OK 73111.

DARTON, EDYTHE M.
Educator. **PERSONAL:** Born Nov 06, 1921, Ruffin, SC; children: 2 Children. **EDUCATION:** Claflin Coll, AB 1947; Atlanta U, MEd 1948; Central MO State U, specialist 1968. **CAREER:** Kansas City MO School Dist, elementary school dir; Meservey School, prin 1971-72; Mary Harmon Weeks School, admin cood, instructor 1968-71; Title I Program, reading asst 1965-68; primary teacher 1948-65; Avila Coll, instructor 1972-74. **ORGANIZATIONS:** Mem Assn for Supervision & Curriculum Evelop; Alpha Kappa Alpha; Kansas City Sch Adminstr AssnF Intnl Reading Assn; MO State Tchr Assn; NEA; Assnof Tchr Educators; Atlanta 19 Alumni Assn; Am Bus Women's Assn; Phi Delta Kappa; Nat Assn of Elem Prin; Central MO State Alumni Assn; mem Jack & Jill of Am; NAACP; Nat Council of Negro Women; Ward Parkway Country Club; Girl Scouts of Am; ARR; Carver Neighborhood Cntr Bd Phi Kappa Phi 1972. **HONORS/ACHIEVEMENTS:** Women of Yr, Am Woman's Assn 1972; Certificate of Award, E C Meservey PTA 1972. **BUSINESS ADDRESS:** 1211 Mc Gee, Kansas City, MO 64106.

DASH, HUGH M. H.
Financial administrator. **PERSONAL:** Born Feb 19, 1943, Brooklyn, NY; married Patricia Morris; children: Angela, Phillip. **EDUCATION:** Morehouse College, Business Admin 1969; Howard Univ, Executive Management 1974. **CAREER:** Citizens Trust Bank, commercial lending & credit officer 1972-72; Interracial Council for Business Opportunity, dep exec dir 1972-75; Southern Conf of Black Mayors, sr economic dev 1975-76; Enterprises Now, Inc, executive vice pres 1976-80; Prudential Health Care Plan, Inc, dir of admin & asst cont 1980-. **ORGANIZATIONS:** Member Leadership Atlanta 1978-; board member and president Atlanta Business League 1978-79, 1985; Georgia treasurer White House Conf on Small Businesses 1979-80. **HONORS/ACHIEVEMENTS:** Catalyst Interracial Council for Business Opportunity 1977. **MILITARY SERVICE:** AUS Sp4/E4; served 3 years. **HOME ADDRESS:** 1374 Dodson Drive SW, Atlanta, GA 30311. **BUSINESS ADDRESS:** Dir of Administration, Prudential Health Care Plan, 2849 Paces Ferry Road, Ste 400, Atlanta, GA 30339.

DASH, LEON DECOSTA, JR.
Reporter. **PERSONAL:** Born Mar 16, 1944, New Bedford, MA; son of Leon Dash and Ruth Dash; children: Darla, Destiny. **EDUCATION:** Howard Univ, BA 1968. **CAREER:** The Washington Post, reporter 1966-68; Kenya, Peace Corps tchr 1969-70; The Washington Post, reporter/Africa corresp/reporter investig desk 1971-. **HONORS/ACHIEVEMENTS:** Honorable mention, Robert F Kennedy Awd for outstng Coverage of Disadvantaged 1973; George Polk Award Overseas Press Club 1974; Balt-Wash Guild Award for Intl Reporting 1974; Capitol Press Club Intl Reporting Award 1984; First Place, General News Award, Natl Assn of Black Journalists, 1986; President's Award, Washington Independent Writers, 1989; co-author, Shame of Prisons, 1972; author, When Children Want Children, 1989. **BUSINESS ADDRESS:** Reporter Investigative Desk, The Washington Post, 1150 15th St NW, Washington, DC 20071.

DAUGHTRY, HERBERT DANIEL
Clergyman. **PERSONAL:** Born Jan 13, 1931, Savannah, GA; son of Alonzo Austin Daughtry and Emmie Cheatham Williams; married Karen Ann Smith, Apr 28, 1962; children: Leah, Sharon Chambers, Dawnique, Herbert Jr. **CAREER:** African Peoples Christian Org, pres 1982-; Natl Campaign Comm of Rev Jesse Jackson, special asst & confidant 1983-84; The House of the Lord Churches, natl presiding minister; Natl Black United Front, chairman, 1979-86, chairman emeritus, 1986-. **ORGANIZATIONS:** Bd of dir, vice chmn Bedford Stuyvesant Youth in Action 1968; vice chmn Operation Breadbasket 1969; co-chmn Ministers Against Narcotics 1969; founder Commission on African Solidarity 1977; founder, pres Coalition of Concerned Leaders & Citizens 1977; bd of dir Black United Fund NY 1980-; bd of dir United African American Churches of NYS, 1988-; bd of dir Natl Rainbow Coalition, 1985-; bd of dir Randolph Evans Memorial Scholarship Fund, 1978-. **HONORS/ACHIEVEMENTS:** Hon mem Malik Sigma Psi Fraternity; Doctor of Letters Seton Hall Univ 1980; author, Jesus Christ: African in Origin, Revolutionary and Redeeming in Action. **BUSINESS ADDRESS:** Natl Presiding Minister, The House of the Lord Churches, 415 Atlantic Ave, Brooklyn, NY 11217.

DAUPHIN, BOREL C.
Insurance company executive. **BUSINESS ADDRESS:** Williams-Progressive Life & Accident Insurance Co, 348 S Academy, Opelousas, LA 70570. *

DAUWAY, LOIS MCCULLOUGH
Church administrator. **PERSONAL:** Born Jul 30, 1948, Boston, MA; daughter of Eural Allen McCullough (deceased) and Pearl Kathleen Griffith McCullough. **EDUCATION:** Univ of MA, studies in Educational Admin; Manhattanville Coll, BA. **CAREER:** Career Oppor Prog MA State Dept of Educ, asst dir 1970-72; Project JESI Univ of MA, project site dir 1972-74; Natl Div General Bd of Global Ministries, black comm developer 1974-77; General Bd of Global Ministries United Methodist Ch, sec of mission personnel 1977-82; Natl Council of the Churches of Christ in the USA, asst general sec for justice and liberation. **ORGANIZATIONS:** Natl training staff Black Comm Developers Prog The United Methodist Church 1977-; bd of dirs Natl Black United Fund 1980-83; mem Natl Assoc of Female Execs 1986-; mem Black Women's Concerns Prog Initiative Area; women's caucus Black Methodists for Church Renewal, Natl Council of the Churches of Christ, Theology in the Amers; bd mem Women's Theol Ctr, Anna Howard Shaw Ctr Boston Univ Sch of Theology; guest lecturer New York Theological Seminary; Washington Office on Haiti. **HONORS/ACHIEVEMENTS:** Delegate UN End of the Decade for Women NGO Forum Nairobi Kenya; authored Women's Section of the Report of the Futures Task Force UMC; Intl BPDE Outstanding Leadership in Religious Educ 1977; Outstanding Young Women of Amer 1980. **BUSINESS ADDRESS:** Asst General Secretary, Natl Cncl Churches of Christ, Commn on Justice/Liberation, 475 Riverside Dr Rm 866, New York, NY 10115.

DAVALT, DOROTHY B.
Educator. **PERSONAL:** Born Dec 25, 1914, Jacksonville, FL; married Clarence J; children: Clarence J, Vincent P. **EDUCATION:** FL A&M U, BS 1949; Univ So FL, W FL, Univ Rochester, NY. **ORGANIZATIONS:** past pres, FL Educ Assn Escambia Bd Pub Inst, 1972-73; pres, Escambia Co Teachers FL Educ Assn; FL Women's Polit Caucus; W FL Women's Caucus 1968-74; mem NEA; NAACP; Natl Council Urban & State Educ Assns; Nat Dem Women's Conf 1966; FL Educ & Vocational Assns; FL Educ Assn Bd 1968-72; exec Com 1970-72; pres 1972-73; v chmn Escambia Co Dem exec com 1974-80; Gov's Conf Educ; State Political Action Com,; Keep FL Beautiful; Common Cause League Arts; Human Rights Com Escambia Educ Assn; Elks; Precinct Committeewmn; Pensacola Chamber of Commerce; Mt Zion Baptist Church. **HONORS/ACHIEVEMENTS:** COPE & NEA convs; effected merger black/white local teacher assn 1966-68; Gov's Commn Teacher Training Center, 1976; past pres, Pensacola Delta Sigma Theta. **BUSINESS ADDRESS:** 30 E Texas Dr, Pensacola, FL 32503.

DAVE, ALFONZO, JR.
Government official, real estate broker. **PERSONAL:** Born Apr 02, 1945, St Louis; son of Alfonzo Dave and Pearl Dave; children: Alfonzo III. **EDUCATION:** Univ of CO, BA, 1967, graduate study, Univ of CA. **CAREER:** Licensed real estate CA; Al Dave & Asso Realty, broker & owner; CA Employment Devel Dept, dist admin; alternate LA County Regional Admin, State Coordinator for Special Youth Project; previous assignments as mgr, asst mgr, staff instructor, case worker, job developer, employment interviewer. **ORGANIZATIONS:** LA City Private Indus Council, PIC Youth/Young Adult Comm, Central City Enterprise Zone Business Advisory Council; Project Genesis, LA Chamber of Commerce; S California Employment Round Table; LA Urban League's Youth Entrepreneur Program, LA Metro & Western LA Employer Advisory Comm through EDD; Intl Assn of Personnel in Employment Security, Weingart YMCA; Personnel & Industrial Relations Assoc Inc, Natl Conf of Christians & Jews; N Hollywood Chamber of Commerce; Community Rehabilitation Industries, Alpha Kappa Delta Natl Sociology Honor Soc, Alpha Phi Alpha. **HONORS/ACHIEVEMENTS:** Commendation LA Co Probation Dept 1975; N Hollywood Chamber of Commerce, 1977; Selected participant in 21st Annual Wilhelm Weinberg Seminar, Cornell Univ, 1979; Cash bonuses, State of CA Managerial Performance Appraisal Program, 1986, 1988; Certificate in Mgmt, Amer Mgmt Assn, 1974; Certificate in Mgmt, State Personnel Bd, 1970; Selected by US Conference of Mayors to make presentation on "Remediation in the Inner City," 1988; Commendation for completion/instruction of Masters of Executive Excellence through EDD, 1988. **BUSINESS ADDRESS:** District Administrator, Employment Development Dept, 1525 S Broadway, Rm 420, Los Angeles, CA 90015.

DAVENPORT, C. DENNIS
Attorney. **PERSONAL:** Born Dec 27, 1946, Lansing, MI; married Dr Roselle Wilson; children: Ronald, Charlene. **EDUCATION:** MI State Univ, BA 1969; MI State Univ, MA 1970; Univ of MI, JD 1972. **CAREER:** General Motors Corp, attorny 1972-; Natl Bar Assoc, mem 1973-; MI State Bar, mem 1973-; Wolverine Bar Assoc, mem 1973-. **ORGANIZATIONS:** Mbr NAACP; mem KAPPA Alpha PSI Frat. **BUSINESS ADDRESS:** Attorney, General Motors Corporation, 3044 West Grand Blvd, Detroit, MI 48202.

DAVENPORT, CALVIN A.
Educator. **PERSONAL:** Born Jan 15, 1928, Gloucester, VA; son of James Robert Davenport and Carrie Brooks Davenport; married Beverly Jean Wills; children: Dean Darnell, Lynn Angela. **EDUCATION:** VA State Coll, BS 1949; MI State Univ, MS 1950; MI State Univ, PhD 1963. **CAREER:** CA State Univ, prof microbiology 1969-; VA State Coll, prof microbiology 1963-69; MI State Univ, res asst 1957-62; Michigan Dept of Health, Div of Laboratories 1952-53, 1955-56; Letterman Army Hosp San Francisco, lab tech 1953-55. **ORGANIZATIONS:** Mem Coord Council for Health Sci Educ 1971-74; chmn 1974; mem Accreditation Team Wstrn Assn of Schs & Colls 1973-; Orange Co Long Beach Health Consortium 1973-83; chmn bd trustees 1974-75; Am Soc for Microbiology 1963-; CA State Employees Assn 1973-; Amer Public Health Assn 1968-; mem Beta Kappa Chi Natl Scientific Hon Soc 1948-; Kappa Alpha Psi Frat; Iota Sigma Lambda Hon Soc; coord Health Manpower Educ Proj CA Univ Fullerton 1974-75; consult Nat Inst of Health Washington 1973-; mem Sr Commn of the Western Assn of Sch & Coll 1976-79; mem evaluation panel in biophysics & biochemistry Natl Sci Found; reading comm Danforth Found 1977-80; sec Acad Assembly of the CA Univ & Coll Med Tech Programs 1978-79; mem Univ Minority Affiars Council 1981-85; consultant Delst Chem Co 1981-; Univ chairman Academic Affirmative Action Comm 1982-84; Univ dir of incentive grants prgm of the Natl Action Council for Minorities in Engineering 1983-84; dir Univ "Investment in People" prgm 1983-84; mem Univ AIDS education 1984-; Minority Biomed Rsch Support Advisory Comm, Gerontology Rsch Inst, Univ Inst for Health Educ & Training, Univ Health Professions Comm, Dept Long Range Planning Comm, Academic Assembly of the California State Universities and Colleges. **HONORS/ACHIEVEMENTS:** Babcock Fellow, Michigan State Univ 1950-51; awards in recogintion of outstanding contributions to the CA St Univ Fullerton Black Organization of Engineers and Scientists 1982, and from the CA St Univ Fullerton Affirmative Action Program 1983, 1984, 1985. **MILITARY SERVICE:** AUS pfc 1953-55. **BUSINESS ADDRESS:** Professor of Microbiology, California State University, Department of Biological Science, 800 N State College Blvd, Fullerton, CA 92634.

DAVENPORT, CHESTER C.
Government official. **PERSONAL:** Born Dec 13, 1940, Athens, GA; married Phyllis Hudson; children: Corey, Cece. **EDUCATION:** Univ GA Law Sch, LLB 1966; Morehouse Coll, 1963. **CAREER:** US Dept of Transp, sec for policy & intl affairs 1977; HUD/DOT Policy Planning Grp, ldr 1976; Hudson Leftwich & Davenport, lawyer 1973-76; RH Lapin & Co, vice pres gen cnsl 1971-73; Senator Alan Cranston, legislative asst 1969-71; Appelate Sect Tax Div Dept of Justice, atty 1966-69. **ORGANIZATIONS:** Mem GA Bar Assn; DC Bar Assn; US Cts of Appeals 2nd Circuit Bar; 7th Circuit Barf 9th Circuit Br; DC Ct of Appeals; pres Kappa Alpha Psi 1960-63; Hon prgm Appellate Sect Tax Div Dept of Justice Washington DC; statewide treas Seanator Alan Cranston's Campaign Com. **BUSINESS ADDRESS:** 400 7th St SW, Room 10228, Washington, DC 20950.

DAVENPORT, ERNEST H.
Certified public accountant, educational administrator. **PERSONAL:** Born Apr 12, 1917, Lima, OH; son of William E Davenport (deceased) and Emily Kennedy Davenport (deceased); married Lucille. **EDUCATION:** Morris Brown College, Atlanta, GA, BA 1940; Wayne State Univ Det, MI, 1948; State of MI, certified public accountant 1956. **CAREER:** US Armed Forces, officer 1941-46; Austin, Washington & Davenport, CPA's (Det MI), part-

ner 1956-71; Audit Div US Office of Econ Opportunity Washington DC, dir 1971-73; US General Accounting Office, Washington DC, asst dir 1973-82; Howard Univ, Washington DC, Center for Acct Educ, School of Business, dir. **ORGANIZATIONS:** Council mem Amer Inst of CPA's 1977-81; pres Mont Pr, Geo Chapter Assn of Govt Accountants 1978-79; pres Dist of Columbia Inst of CPA's 1980-81; pres Middle Atlantic State Acct Conf 1982-83. **HONORS/ACHIEVEMENTS:** Outstanding Alumnus Morris Brown Coll 1969; Achievement Award Natl Assn of Black Accountants 1975, M/PG Chapts Assn of Govt Accts 1976,78; Outstanding Serv Natl Assn of Minority CPA Firms 1980; Order of Kentucky Colonels 1985; Laurel Wreath Award Kappa Alpha Psi 1985. **MILITARY SERVICE:** AUS ltcol; Air Medal W/3 Oak Leaf Clusters 1945; Licensed Comm Pilot 1946. **HOME ADDRESS:** 8201 16th St #605, Silver Spring, MD 20910.

DAVENPORT, GREGORY MICHAEL
Educator. **PERSONAL:** Born Jan 14, 1949, Lansing, MI; married Cynthia; children: Theodore James. **EDUCATION:** Univ of MI, B 1970, M 1971, PhD 1973. **CAREER:** Indianapolis Teacher Corps, educ develop specialist & asst prof of educ 1973-74; Prairie View A&M Univ, dir of plng & devel 1974-75; MI State Univ, asst prof 1977-78; Northern MI Univ, asst dean 1983-86; Univ of Nebraska Medical Ctr, dir. **ORGANIZATIONS:** Mem Omega Psi Phi; chmn Minority Student Affairs Adv Comm UNMC 1986-; mem Natl Assoc of Minority Medical Educators 1986-; mem Assoc of Amer Medical Colls 1986-; exec bd NAACP of Omaha 1986-; mem Urban League 1986-.

DAVENPORT, HORACE ALEXANDER
Judge. **PERSONAL:** Born Feb 22, 1919, Newberry, SC; son of William Davenport and Julia Davenport; married Alice I Latney; children: Alice D Alexander, Beverly A, Horace Jr, Nina E. **EDUCATION:** Howard Univ, BA 1946; Univ of PA, MA 1947, LLB 1950. **CAREER:** Gerber, Davenport & Wilenzik, atty, Court of Common Pleas of 38th Judicial Dist of PA, judge. **ORGANIZATIONS:** Former dir Central Montgomery County Bd of Amer Red Cross; former dir GW Carver Comm County; former dir Central Montgomery County Council of Human Rel; former dir Norristown Comm Concerts; mem Vet of Foreign Wars; mem Historical Soc of Montgomery Cty; mem Norristown Branch NAACP; former mem Norristown Republican Club; former dir Norristown School Bd; dir Citizens Council of Montgomery Cty; former dir Norristown Art League; former dir Montgomery County TB & Health Assc; former Dir Montgomery Hospital; former area cpt Salvation Army; former Norristown Schl Bd Lay Rep to Area Voc-Tech Schl; pres PA School Bd Solicitors Assc 1972-73; dir Natl Schl Bds Assc 1969-76; former dir PA School Bd Solicitors Assc 1969, 1970, 1971; trustee Johnson C Smith Univ Charlotte NC; solicitor Cntrl Montgomery County Area Voc-Tech School 1968-76; solicitor Norristown Area School Dist 1966-76; solicitor Norristown Area School Authority 1966-76; solicitor Montgomery Cty Election Bd 1958-76; solicitor Montgomery County Tax Claim Bureau. **HONORS/ACHIEVEMENTS:** Recipient numerous community awards. **MILITARY SERVICE:** Corps Engr capt. **BUSINESS ADDRESS:** Judge, Ct of Common Pleas 38 Dist, Montgomery Cty Court House, Norristown, PA 19404.

DAVENPORT, J. LEE
Clergyman, social worker, counselor. **PERSONAL:** Born Oct 02, 1935, Mayo, FL; son of Jesse David Davenport and Fronie Bell (Hadley) Davenport; married Bernice M (Webb) Davenport, Dec 22, 1958; children: Valarie E (Davenport) Harris, Velina L Davenport, Otis Davenport, David Davenport. **EDUCATION:** Cameron Univ, Lawton OK, BA, 1970; Oklahoma Univ, Norman OK, MSW, 1975. **CAREER:** St John's Baptist Church, Lawton OK, sr pastor 1965-; Oklahoma Dept of Mental Health, Lawton OK, social worker 1970-85. **ORGANIZATIONS:** Worshipful Master Golden Gate Ldg 1961-63; NAACP; pres Lawton's Chpt; Comm Action bd mem 1965-68; Rotary mem; mem gov adv comm human rel; mem OK Planning Health Comm 1973-74; parole adv; Pastor St John's Baptist Ch; mem Natl Acad Soc Workers; Dean West dist cong Christ educ; disc leader youth disc group Natl Baptist conv Inc USA; 2nd vice pres OK State Conv 1974-78; bd mem Cameron Univ 1981-; state pres One Church, One Child Inc 1988-; bd mem United Way 1985-; pres Coalition for Minority Affairs 1984-. **HONORS/ACHIEVEMENTS:** Oustanding Leadership, NAACP 1986; Humanitarian Award, Alpha Kappa Alpha 1988; Developed Task Force with Justice Dept on Police-Community Relations 1986; Developed a Feed The Hungry Program for Homeless People 1987. **MILITARY SERVICE:** USAF 1953-58, A/1C, Oustanding Marksman Award 1954, GCM 1955. **BUSINESS ADDRESS:** Senior Pastor, St John's Baptist Church, 1501 Roosevelt St, Lawton, OK 73501.

DAVENPORT, JAMES H.
Physician. **PERSONAL:** Born Jan 22, Roper, NC; married Gertrude Thompson; children: James II, Michele, Keith. **EDUCATION:** NY U, AB 1948; NY Med Coll, MD 1952; Am Bd of Radiology, dipl 1957. **CAREER:** Faxton Hosp, dir radiation med 1975-; Queens Hosp Ctr, phys in charge radiation 1969-75; StateUniv NY at Stonybrook, asso prof clinical radiology 1972-; Cath Med Ctr, rad therapy consult 1972-75; Harlem Hosp, radiation therpst 1967-69; NY Med Coll, clinical instr radlgy 1958-60; Parkchester Gen Hosp, chf radiation therapy 1960-63; VA Hosp, asst chf radiology 1958-59. **ORGANIZATIONS:** Mem past master Prog Lodge #64; mem Oneida Co Med Soc; flw Centr NY Acad of Med; mem NAACP; Phi Beta Sigma Frat; Phi Delta Epsilon Med Frat; NYState Med Soc; NMA; Am Soc of Therapeutic Radiologist. **HONORS/ACHIEVEMENTS:** Publ NY State Jour of Med; Am Jour of Roentcenology Cancer; Am Jour of Observ & Gyn. **MILITARY SERVICE:** AUS 1942-43. **BUSINESS ADDRESS:** 1676 Sunset Ave, Utica, NY 13502.

DAVENPORT, LAWRENCE FRANKLIN
Educational administrator. **PERSONAL:** Born Oct 13, 1944, Lansing, MI; married Cecelia Jackson; children: Laurence, Anita, Anthony. **EDUCATION:** MI State Univ, BA 1966, MA 1968; Fairleigh Dickinson Univ, EdD 1975. **CAREER:** Tuskegee Inst, vice pres for develop 1972-74; San Diego Comm Coll Educ Cultural Complex, pres 1974-79; San Diego Comm Coll Dist, provost 1979-81; ACTION, assoc dir for domestic & anti-poverty opers 1981-82. **ORGANIZATIONS:** Comm Martin Luther King Jr Fed Holiday Comm 1985-86. **HONORS/ACHIEVEMENTS:** Outstanding Young Citizen of San Diego-San Diego Jaycees 1978. **BUSINESS ADDRESS:** Asst Sec Elem & Secon Educ, US Dept of Education, 400 Maryland Ave SW, Room 2189, Washington, DC 20202.

DAVENPORT, WILLIE D.
City government executive. **EDUCATION:** Southern Univ Baton Rouge, BS 1970, ME 1974. **CAREER:** East Baton Rouge Parish Schl System, tchr 1970; City of Baton Rouge LA, exec dir mayor-pres council of youth opport 1970-80; Southern Univ Baton Rouge,head track coach 1971-74; Independent Landman & Broker, 1979-; Army Natl Guard, hq comp commander 1981-; New Orleans East on Educ, independent consult 1981; New Orleans East, asst to dir mrkt 1981-82; State of LA Dept Health & Human Resources, dir of governors council on phys fitness & sports 1984-. **HONORS/ACHIEVEMENTS:** Olympic Games, 1964 Tokyo Semi-Finalist 110 Hurdles, 1968 Mexico City Gold Medal, 1972 Munich 4th Place, 1976 Montreal Bronze Medal Flag Bearer Closing Ceremonies, 1980 Lake Placid 12th Place Bobsled Team. **MILITARY SERVICE:** AUS 1962-65.

DAVID, ARTHUR LACURTISS
Educator. **PERSONAL:** Born Apr 13, 1938, Chicago, IL; son of Mr & Mrs Carey H David, Sr; married Martha Barham; children: Alexis, Sean. **EDUCATION:** Lane Coll, BA 1960; Phillips Sch of Theol, BD 1963; NE U, MA 1970; ITC, MDiv 1971; Middle TN State U, Arts D 1973. **CAREER:** Soc Sci Div Lane Coll, chmn; Lane Coll, prof of hist 1963-67 69-77; NE Wesleyan Univ, 1967-69; Motlow State Commn Coll, 1972-73; Lane Coll, dean. **ORGANIZATIONS:** Mem So Hist Assn; Am Hist Assn; Orgn of Am Historians; mem Pi Gamma Mu Sociol Sci, Hon Soc; Phi Alpha Theta Hist Hon Soc; Sigma Theta Epsilon Hon Soc for Clergymen; Kappa Kappa Psi Hon Band Frat; Alpha Phi Alpha Frat Inc. **HONORS/ACHIEVEMENTS:** Dissertation "The Involvement of the Black Man in the Teaching of Western Civilization a Study of Black Colleges & Univs" 1973. **BUSINESS ADDRESS:** Dean of the College, Lane College, 545 Lane Ave, Jackson, TN 38301.

DAVID, GEORGE F., III
Business executive. **PERSONAL:** Born Nov 06, 1923, Wilberforce, OH; son of George F David II and Olivette Poole David; divorced; children: George FIV, Lynn David Irby. **EDUCATION:** Wilberforce Univ, BS 1943; St Andrews Univ Scotland, 1946. **CAREER:** Gliden Co, chemist 1950-52; Oscar Mayer & Co, food technologist, plant mgr 1952-60; Sinai Kosher Sausage Co, plant supt 1960-62; Superior Meat Co, plant supt 1962-63; Superiors Brand Meats, mgr/asst operations mgr 1962-68; Parks Sausage Co, vice pres/dir 1968-88. **ORGANIZATIONS:** Bd mem USO-CENTRAL MD 1982-, Girls Scouts-Central MD 1984-; pres Hilltop Comm Orgn, Woodlawn MD 1974-76; bd mem Combined Health Agencies 1986-88. **HONORS/ACHIEVEMENTS:** Achievement Award Eastern Province Kappa Alpha Psi 1976 & 1980; Wm "Box" Harris Award 1986. **HOME ADDRESS:** 2110 Meadowview Dr, Baltimore, MD 21207.

DAVID, GERALDINE R.
Elected official. **PERSONAL:** Born Sep 15, 1938, Helena, AR; married Odell Davis Jr; children: Cheryl, Vivian, Odel III, Eva, Darin, Vivian L Ross, Eva Gammon. **EDUCATION:** Univ of Pine Bluff, attended; Rust Coll Holly Springs MS, attended; Phillips Cty Comm Coll, attended. **CAREER:** Elaine Jr HS, librarian asst 1967; Lake View Coop Assoc, bookkeeper 1970; Lake View Elem School, librarian asst 1974; City of Lake View, sec, treas 1978-. **ORGANIZATIONS:** Bd of dir Cty Ext Comm, Lake View Med Clinic 1980-, East AR Area on Aging 1980-. **HONORS/ACHIEVEMENTS:** Governors Office Volunteer Awd Governors Office 1980; Volunteer Tax Awd Federal Income Tax Office 1980; Tri-Cty Leadership 1980; Mid-Delta Comm Serv Volunteer Awd Comm Serv 1980; Phillips Cty Notary Sec of State Office. **HOME ADDRESS:** Rt 2 Box 350-A, Lexa, AR 72355. **BUSINESS ADDRESS:** Secretary, Treasurer, City of Lake View, Rt 1 Box 221-A, Helena, AR 72342.

DAVID, LAWRENCE T.
Chaplain. **PERSONAL:** Born Jan 14, 1930, Cheraw, SC; married Hilda Black; children: Kenneth, Marc, LaDonna, Chapelle. **EDUCATION:** Morris Coll, BA 1954; Gammon Theol Sem, BD 1958; Columbia Bible Coll Grad Sch, 1964-65. **CAREER:** AUS, chplan 1959-; St John's Bapt Ch Gainesville GA. **HONORS/ACHIEVEMENTS:** Awarded numerous ribbons medals citations including Bronze Star with four clusters; Vietnamese Presidential Citation; US Pres Unit Cit with two Oak Leaf Clusters; Viet Nam Cross of Gallantry. **MILITARY SERVICE:** AUS 1957-59 promoted to ltc 1974.

DAVIDSON, ALPHONZO LOWELL
Dentist. **PERSONAL:** Born Dec 12, 1941, Fredericksburg, VA; married Carolyn; children: Alphonzo Jr, Stephanie. **EDUCATION:** Howard U, BS 1964; Howard U, DDS 1968; Howard U, cert oral surgery 1973. **CAREER:** Dept of Oral Surgery Howard Univ, asst prof; Howard Univ Hospital, attending oral surgeon. **ORGANIZATIONS:** Asso staff mem Prince George Co Hosp; mem Am Soc Oral Surgery 1975; Assn Mil Surgeons 1970; DC Dental Soc; Am Dental Soc 1969; Robert T FreedmanDental Soc; Nat Dental Soc 1969; Chi Delta Mu Frat 1967; Assn of Interns & Residents of Freedmen's Hosp 1972; Dental Soc of Anesthesiology 1978; Oral Cancer Soc 1968-80; pres DC Oral Surgery Soc 1979-80; Omicron Kappa Upsilon Pi Pi Chap 1979-80; mem Sigma Phi Sigma Nat Physics Hon Soc; sec Robert T Freedman Dental Soc; mem Am Bd Oral Surgery 1976. **MILITARY SERVICE:** USAF capt 1968-70. **BUSINESS ADDRESS:** Landover Mall W, Office Ridge 308, Landover, MD 20785.

DAVIDSON, ARTHUR B.
Administrator. **PERSONAL:** Born Dec 05, 1929, Detroit; son of Arthur B and Idella; married Edith. **EDUCATION:** Detroit Inst Tech, BA 1964; Wayne State U, M Pub Adm 1970. **CAREER:** Human Resources Devel, area adminstrator 1964-68; Butzel Family Ctr Coordinate Serv, dir 1968-70; City Detroit, planning administrator 1970-81, oper & mgmt serv admin 1981-82, dir admin serv & weatherization 1982-88, assistant director, 1988-. **ORGANIZATIONS:** Mem planning exec 1972-; Nat Assn Housing & Redevelopment & Officials 1964-; New Detroit Inc 1970-; OmniCare Health Plan Bd of Trustees, Treasurer, Chmn of Finance, mem of Executive Committee. **HONORS/ACHIEVEMENTS:** Cert excellence Urban League 1965; cert recognition Greater Macedonia Bapt Ch 1965. **MILITARY SERVICE:** AUS 1951-53. **BUSINESS ADDRESS:** Assistant Director, City of Detroit, 5031 Grandy, Neighborhood Serv Dept, Detroit, MI 48211.

DAVIDSON, ARTHUR TURNER
Physician, attorney. **PERSONAL:** Born Jul 30, 1923; married Ezeria Jennie White; children: Arthur T Jr, Ronald W, Michael G, Kathie E. **EDUCATION:** Howard Univ Sch of Med, MD 1945; St John's Univ Sch of Law, JD 1974. **CAREER:** Downstate Med Ctr Brooklyn, asst clinical prof of surgery; Columbia Univ Coll of Physicians & Surgeons NY, asst clinical prof of surgery; Albert Einstein Coll of med Bronx, assoc clinical prof of surgery; Private Practice, physician. **ORGANIZATIONS:** Mem AMA; mem Natl Med Assn; mem

Amer Bar Assn. **HONORS/ACHIEVEMENTS:** Publ, "Mechanical Small Bowel Obstruction with Gangrene Presenting Narrowing of Pulse Pressure A New Diagnostic Sign" JNMA 56 393 1964; publ "Thymotropic Action of Vitamin A" Federation Proceedings of the Amer Soc of Experimental Biologists 1973; publ "Enhanced Lymphocytic Action on Breast Tumor" JNMA 66 472 1974. **MILITARY SERVICE:** AUS med corps capt 1951-53. **BUSINESS ADDRESS:** Arthur T Davidson Sr MD PC, 1378 President St, Brooklyn, NY 11213.

DAVIDSON, CHARLES ODELL
Physician. **PERSONAL:** Born Nov 12, 1935, Pine Bluff, AR; married Fredricka Cooper; children: Harryl, Darryl. **EDUCATION:** Howard Univ Med Sch, MD 1961; Homer G Phillips Hosp, Internship 1961-62; Homer G Phillips Hospital, Resident, Chief Resident, 1962-65. **CAREER:** The Methodist Hospital of Gary Inc Med Staff, pres 1980-81. **ORGANIZATIONS:** bd trustee, Methodist Hospital of Gary Inc; bd of dirs Gary Bd of Health, 1978-; chmn, Ob-Gyn Gary Merrillville Methodist Hosp; private practice, 1968-77; hosp comdr Malstrom AFB 1967-68; chmn OB-BYN Malstrom AFB 1966-68; supr Ob-Gyn Homer G Phillips St Louis 1965-66; sec-treas Gary Med Specialists Inc; chmn NW IN Planned Parenthood Med Adv Council; mem, Am Fertility Sox; Assn of Amer Gynecological Laparoscopists Diplomat Am; bd of Ob-Gyn 1967; Fellow, Am Coll Ob-Gyn, 1972. **MILITARY SERVICE:** USAF maj. **BUSINESS ADDRESS:** 2200 Grant St, Gary, IN 46404.

DAVIDSON, CHARLES ROBERT
Physician. **PERSONAL:** Born Jan 07, 1922, Lincolnton, NC; married Margaret L Roseboro; children: Margaret D Hayes, Wanda, Charles, Jr, Russell. **EDUCATION:** Johnon C Smith Univ Charlotte NC, BS 1941; BD 1945; Drew Univ Madison NJ, MA 1946; Howard Univ Med Sch Wash DC, MD 1952. **CAREER:** Pvt Practice Baltimore, physcn 1954; Rural Ch Allen Univ & Benedict Coll Columbia SC, tchr 1947-48; Rural Ch Dept Bishop Coll Marshall TX, tchr 1946-47. **MILITARY SERVICE:** AUS 2nd lt 1952-54. **BUSINESS ADDRESS:** 2034 W North Ave, Baltimore, MD 21217.

DAVIDSON, DONALD RAE
Business executive. **PERSONAL:** Born Jun 09, 1943, Indianapolis, IN; son of Fred Davidson and Frances Davidson; children: Renae, Donald Rae, Dawn, Ingrid. **EDUCATION:** Drake Univ, BA 1964. **CAREER:** RCA Corp Indianapolis, mgr material coordinator 1965-67; Solar Devel Corp Indianapolis, treas 1967-71; Davidson Hardy & Assocs Indianapolis, sec-treas 1966-68; Dahar Corp Indianapolis, pres 1968-74; FCH Serv Inc Chgo, asst vice pres 1971-73; First Natl Bank of Chgo/Nigeria Lagos, mgr 1973-74; IL Housing Devel Authority, housing devel production admin 1974-77; Salk Ward & Salk Chicago, vice pres 1977-78; Metro Finance Group Ltd Chicago, chmn 1978-; Metro Equities Corp Investment Bankers, pres. **ORGANIZATIONS:** Bd dirs Midwest Assoc for Sickle Cell Anemia; mem IL Mortgage Bankers Assn, Mortgage Bankers of Amer, Real Estate Securities & Syndication Inst; bd dirs IL Serv Fed Savings & Loan Assn, IL Development Finance Authority; bd dir Natl Assn of Securities Profls. **BUSINESS ADDRESS:** President, Metro Equities Corp, 220 S State St, #2014, Chicago, IL 60604.

DAVIDSON, EARNEST JEFFERSON
Sculptor, educator. **PERSONAL:** Born Aug 16, 1946, Little Rock, AR; son of Earnest Jefferson Davidson and Alice Sanders; children: Tamara S, Earnest III. **EDUCATION:** Philander Smith Coll, BA 1972; AR Art Center, MA 1969; Univ of AR at Little Rock, MA 1975; Syracuse Univ, MFA 1972; Univ of AR at Little Rock 1986. **CAREER:** Adventures in Ed Syracuse, NY, woodwork Spclst 1972; Lomax Hanna Jr Coll, teach arts & crafts 1978; Southeast Art & Sci Ctr, teach pottery 1984; AR Art Cntr, teach sculpture 1984; Univ of AR at Pine Bluff, assoc profsr 1972-, Standing Committee on Student Appeals (Adademic Evaluation), chmn. **ORGANIZATIONS:** Chrprsn Visual Arts Com Arts & Science Ctr 1985; rep for sw USA FESTAC 77 2nd Wld Black & African Festvl of Arts & Culture; sw rgnl coordntr Natl Conf of Artists 1974-76; Emergency School Aid Act Artist-In-Residence Selection Committee 1976-82; mem Intl Sculpture Assn, 1988-, Amer Foundrymen Soc, 1988-; potter consultant, SE Arkansas Arts & Science Center. **HONORS/ACHIEVEMENTS:** Under grad ad Omega Psi Phi Te 1985-87; Apprentice Qin the Arts Grant 1982; Gov Award Little Rock Arts & Crafts Fair 1974; Title III Grant Univ of AR at Little Rock 1975; Commissioned to create bronze statue of Martin Luther King, Northern Univ of IL at Dekalb 1985-86; Title III Grant Univ of AR at Little Rock 1986; Pine Bluff Business for the Arts Award 1988; One of three finalists for the Arkansas Vietnam Veterans Memorial 1987; Arkansas Art Registry; Commissioned to execute statue of Dr Martin Luther King Jr by the Student Assn of Northern Illinois Univ at Dekalb and the Northern Illinois Univ 1986. **BUSINESS ADDRESS:** Associate Professor, University of Arkansas at Pine Bluff, Fine Art Department, P O Box 53, Pine Bluff, AR 71601.

DAVIDSON, ELVYN VERONE
Surgeon. **PERSONAL:** Born Oct 06, 1923, New York, NY; son of John Davidson and Hattie Davidson; married Esther M Johnson, Jun 09, 1953 (deceased); children: Pamela D Branner, Evelyne M, Elvyn V II. **EDUCATION:** Lincoln Univ PA, AB 1949; Meharry Med Coll, MD 1953; NYU Post Graduate School Med, certificate in Surgery 1954. **CAREER:** Univ TE MRC&H Knoxville, instr in surgery 1959-70, asst prof of surgery 1970-; ET Bap Hosp Knoxville, chief of surgery 1974-75; The Amer Soc Abd Surgeon, fellow 1968; Knox County, Deputy Medical Examiner 1979-. **ORGANIZATIONS:** Mem AMA, NMA, KMA, VSMA, TMA, AHA, CSS, SMA, ACS; mem bd dir VIP Home Health Assn 1983; mem Century Club UMCA NAACP; past bas Omega Psi Frat; past grant knight, Knights of Columbus 1982-83; district deputy Knights of Columbis; mem bd of dir Columbus Home. **MILITARY SERVICE:** AUS tech sgt 1942-46; Purple Heart Combat Inf Award. **HOME ADDRESS:** 831 Biddle Hgts, Knoxville, TN 37914. **BUSINESS ADDRESS:** Dr Elvyn Verone Davidson, 2210 Martin Luther King Ave, Harry Pro Bldg, Knoxville, TN 37915.

DAVIDSON, EZRA C., JR.
Educator. **PERSONAL:** Born Oct 21, 1933, Water Valley, MS; son of Ezra C Davidson Sr; divorced; children: Pamela, Gwendolyn, Marc, Ezra K. **EDUCATION:** Morehouse Coll, BS 1954; Meharry Med Sch, MD 1958. **CAREER:** LA County Univ of So CA Med Ctr, 1970-80; Martin Luther King General Hospital, chief-of-serv 1971-; Univ of So CA School of Med, prof 1971-80; UCLA, prof 1979-; Drew Univ of Medicine and Science, prof, chmn dept ob/gyn 1971-. **ORGANIZATIONS:** Consult Natl Found March of Dimes 1970-77; mem bd of consult Intl Childbirth Educ Assn Inc 1973-80; mem Natl Med Adv Com Natl Found March of Dimes Inc 1972-77; mem bd dir Prof Staff Assn Found Martin Luther King Jr Gen Hosp 1972-; examiner Amer Bd of Ob/Gyn 1973-; mem Sec Adv Comm for Pop Affairs 1974-77; chmn Serv Task Force 1975-77; mem bd dir Natl Alliance for School Age Parents 1975-80; natl chmn sec Ob/Gyn Natl Med Assn 1975-77; sec Amer Coll of Ob/Gyn 1983-89; pres Assoc of Professors of Gyn and Ob 1987-88; pres Golden State Medical Assn 1989-90; pres-elect Amer Coll of Ob/Gyn 1989-90. **HONORS/ACHIEVEMENTS:** Fellow Am Coll of Ob-Gyn; fellow Am Coll of Surg; fellow LA Ob-Gyn Soc Inc; num lectures; num articles publ mem Alpha Omega Alpha Honor Soc; fellow Robert Woods Johnson Health Policy Inst of Med Washington, DC 1979-80. **MILITARY SERVICE:** USAF captain 1959-63. **BUSINESS ADDRESS:** Professor, Chairman Ob/Gyn, 12021 S Wilmington Ave, Los Angeles, CA 90059.

DAVIDSON, FRED, III
Appointed official & naval officer. **PERSONAL:** Born Oct 03, 1941, Indianapolis, IN; married Regina; children: LaShavon, Freddia. **EDUCATION:** Central State Univ, BA History & Pol Scis; Howard Univ Sch of Law, attended; Natl Univ, LHD (honorary). **CAREER:** US Treasury Dept, white house intern 1959-63; Fed Bureau of Investigation, US special police 1965-66; US Marine Corps, 1966-69; US Marine Corps Reserve, lt col 1969-; Ford Motor Co, zone mgr 1969-77; Xerox Corp, govt acct rep 1977-80; Metro Financial Group Ltd, vice pres 1980-81; Dept of the Navy, deputy asst sec of the Navy 1981-. **ORGANIZATIONS:** Master mason Waterford Lodge #13 F&AM; shriner Persian Temple #46 AEAONMS; Republican Presidential Task Force 1981-; mem US Senatorial Club, mem Amer Security Council; past dir Gr Indianapolis Housing Develop Corp 1978; mem Marine Corps Reserve Officers Assn. **MILITARY SERVICE:** Combat Action Ribbon; Natl Defense Medal; Naval Unit Citation; Vietnamese Campaign Medal; Vietnamese Civil Affairs Ribbon; Vietnamese Cross of Gallantry.

DAVIDSON, KERRY
Statewide academic officer. **PERSONAL:** Born May 01, 1935, Water Valley, MS; married Betty Vanover; children: Mary Jaures, Elizabeth Jeanette. **EDUCATION:** Morehouse Coll, attended; Univ of IA, M Pol Sci; Tulane Univ, PhD. **CAREER:** Southern Univ New Orleans, former chmn dept of history; Fisk Univ, former chmn; LA Bd of Regents, commr acad affairs. **HONORS/ACHIEVEMENTS:** Author of 20th Century Civilization; Danforth Grant. **BUSINESS ADDRESS:** Associate Commissioner, Louisianna Bd of Regents, 1 American Pl, Baton Rouge, LA 70816.

DAVIDSON, LURLEAN G.
Director. **PERSONAL:** Born May 03, 1931, West Point, GA; married Ogletree Davidson; children: Marzette, Jerome, John, Darlene, Mary. **EDUCATION:** Case Western Res; OH Univ. **CAREER:** Parent Resource Cntrs Cleveland Bd Edn, dir; Sol Victory Mutual Life Ins, 1958-60; medical sec 1951-52; various positions as auditor, intervwr, election clerk; tchrs; asst. **ORGANIZATIONS:** Mem & Parent Adv Bd YMCA; Precinct Committeewoman 1960-73; mem Glenville Area Coun Phyllis Wheatley Assn NAACP; Urban League; Jewish Council VariousPTA'S; life membership PTA 1965. **HONORS/ACHIEVEMENTS:** Outstanding serv award to the Comm 1961; outstanding soc award & certificate of merit NAACP 1962. **BUSINESS ADDRESS:** Geo W Carver Sch, 2201 E 49 St, Cleveland, OH.

DAVIDSON, RICK BERNARD
Banking executive. **PERSONAL:** Born Oct 06, 1951, Nashville, TN; son of Robert Davidson and Beula Jones Davidson; married Izola Putnam, Sep 22, 1979; children: Sandra Putnam, Robert Derrick. **EDUCATION:** Tennessee School of Banking, Nashville TN, diploma, 1979-80; ABA Commercial School of Lending (undergraduate & graduate), Univ of Oklahoma, diploma, 1981-83; Graduate School of Banking of the South, Louisiana State Univ, Baton Rouge LA, certificate, 1986-89; Tennessee Commercial Lending School, Nashville TN, certificate, 1988. **CAREER:** Third Natl Bank, Nashville TN, asst mgr, 1969-78; Commerce Union Bank, Nashville TN, mgr, 1978-80; Commerce Union Bank, Nashville TN, asst vice pres/comm lending officer, 1981-84; Nashville City Bank, Nashville TN, loan review specialist, 1984; Citizens Bank, Nashville TN, first vice pres, 1985-88, pres and CEO, 1988-. **ORGANIZATIONS:** Dir 1985-89, treasurer 1986-88, Bethlehem Center; pres, Middle Tennessee Chapter, Amer Inst of Banking, 1986-87; pres, Amer Inst of Banking, 1986-87; commr, Tennessee Collection Service Bd, 1987-; treasurer, Uptown Nashville, 1989-; dir, Project Pencil, 1989; Legislative Comm, 1989-. **HONORS/ACHIEVEMENTS:** Profiled in Nashvile Tennessean Newspaper, 1988, and in Nashville Banner Newspaper, 1989. **BUSINESS ADDRESS:** Pres and Chief Exec Officer, Citizens Savings Bank and Trust Co, 401 Charlotte Ave, Nashville, TN 37219.

DAVIDSON, ROBERT C., JR.
Company executive. **PERSONAL:** Born Oct 03, 1945, Memphis, TN; son of Robert C Davidson, Sr and Thelma Davidson; married Alice Faye Davidson, Jan 05, 1978; children: Robert C Davidson, III, John R Davidson, Julian L Davidson. **EDUCATION:** Morehouse Coll, BA, 1967; Graduate School of Business Univ of Chicago, MBA, 1969. **CAREER:** Cresap, McCormack & Paget, sr assoc consultant, 1969-72; Urban National Corp, vice pres, 1972-74; Avant Garde Enterprises, exec vice pres, 1974-75; R Davidson & Assoc, consultant, 1975-78; Surface Protection Ind, pres, 1978-. **ORGANIZATIONS:** Planning Commission, 1986-; bd of dir, Pasadena Art Workshop, 1986-. **HONORS/ACHIEVEMENTS:** Business listed as #21 in Black Enterprise's list of top 100 black firms, 1989.

DAVIES, EVERETT J.
Business manager. **PERSONAL:** Born Mar 16, 1945, Monrovia, Liberia;married Wendy Marcia; children: Rosetta, Quaimme, Aisha. **EDUCATION:** Shaw Univ, BA 1972; Columbia Univ, MBA 1972; Achievers Industry Awards, 1974. **CAREER:** Liberty Mutual Ins, claim analyst 1969-70; NY Tele Co, supvsr 1970-72; Merrill Lynch, sec Mgr 1972-80; Citicorp Capital Mkt, citicorp 1981-84. **ORGANIZATIONS:** Mbr YMCA 1974; sec Friendly Fortunes Assoc 1983. **HONORS/ACHIEVEMENTS:** Academic excell Shaw Univ 1968. **BUSINESS ADDRESS:** Manager, Citicorp-Cap Mkts, 111 Wall St, New York, NY 10048.

DAVIES, LAWRENCE A.
Elected official, clergyman. **PERSONAL:** Born Jul 07, 1930, Houston, TX; married Janice J Pryde; children: Lauren A, Karen M, Sharron L. **EDUCATION:** Prairie View A&M Coll, BS 1949; Howard Univ School of Religion, MDivinity 1957; Wesley Theological Seminary, M Sacred Theology 1961; Fredericksburg BibleInst & Sem, DD (Honorary) 1985. **CAREER:** Good Samaritan Baptist Church WA DC, pastor 1956-60; Shiloh Baptist Church WA

DC, asst pastor & religious ed dir 1960-62; City of Fredericksburg, 1st black city councilman 1966-76, 1st black mayor 1976-; Shiloh Baptist Church Fredricksburg VA, pastor 1962-. **ORGANIZATIONS:** Pres Fredericksburg Area Ministerial Assoc 1965-66, Fredericksburg Baptist Ministers Conf 1969-70, Rappahannock Citizen Corp 1968-, VA Assoc for Mental Health 1974-76; adv dir Perpetual Amer Bank 1975-; bd of dir Natl Conf of Black Mayors 1977-, Natl Kidney Found of VA 1984-86; pres VA Municipal League 1984-85, VA Conf of Black Mayors 1985-; founder Fredericksburg Area Sickle Cell Assoc; mem Fredericksburg Lions Club, Alpha Phi Alpha Frat, Prince Hall Masons, Governor's Commn on Transportation in the 21st Century 1986-; mem bd of visitors Mary Washington Coll 1986-. **HONORS/ACHIEVEMENTS:** Young Man of the Year Fredericksburg Jaycees 1966; Citizen of the Year Omega Psi Phi Frat 1966; Citizenship Awd Fredericksburg Area Chamber of Comm 1976; Man of the Year VFW #3103 1977; Outstanding Serv Awd Natl Assoc for Mental Health 1979; Humanitarian of the Year Awd Mt Bethel Baptist Assoc 1984. **BUSINESS ADDRESS:** Mayor, City of Fredericksburg, Fredericksburg, VA 22401.

DAVIES, MARVIN
Government assistant. **PERSONAL:** Born Feb 16, 1934, Hampton, FL; married Jean Miller; children: James, Roby, Valarie, Joi. **EDUCATION:** FL A&M Univ, BS Pol Sci 1959; De Paul Univ Coll of Law, Legal Studies 1960; Univ of FL, counseling studies 1963; Univ of GA, Housing Studies 1964; FL NewThought Inst, MsD Metaphysics 1974. **CAREER:** Lee Cnty Brd of Educ, tchr, scl studies 1960; State of FL, Social Worker 1962, emplyment cnslr 1963 FL A&M u, manpower coordntr 1964; FL NAACP, exec dir 1966. **ORGANIZATIONS:** Ownr/pres Dimension & Assoc 1972; pres Soul Delight Prod 1977 spcl asst office of th gov 1978; exec dir fL NAACP 1966-72; fndr chair FL Black AgendaCoalition 1979; fndr brd mem Natl Black Voters Assoc 1984; fndr pres FL Assoc Min Bus Owners 1978. **HONORS/ACHIEVEMENTS:** Alpha Kappa Mu 1958, Sigma Rho Sigma 1958, Kappa Delta Phi 1958, Alpha Phi Alpha 1958 FL A&M Univ; meritorious qachvmnt FL A&M Univ 1972. **MILITARY SERVICE:** AUS sgt 1st class 1953-56; NCO (Leadership & European Command Award 1954. **HOME ADDRESS:** 1018 Sunnyside Dr, Tallahassee, FL 32304. **BUSINESS ADDRESS:** Special Assistant, State of FL, Office Of The Governor, State Capital, Tallahassee, FL 32301.

DAVIS, ABRAHAM, JR.
Educator. **PERSONAL:** Born May 14, 1923, Beaufort, SC; married Modestine R; children: Silena R, Wilkins Garrett Jr. **EDUCATION:** Lancaster Sch of the Bible & Theol, diplomas in Bible & Theol 1949; H Oughton Coll, BA 1955; Temple U, MA 1956; Univ of IA, Penn State U, Western Reserve U, 1960; IN Univ Bloomington, PhD 1971. **CAREER:** Messiah Coll, Philadelphia PA, prof of comm 1978-, admin acad dean 1975-78; Asbury Coll, visiting prof 1973-74; Messiah Coll, Philadelphia PA, acting dean 1973-74; sabbatical lecturer & oral inter Afro-Amer Literature & Rhetoric 1972-73; Houghton Coll, assoc prof & prof of Speech 1967-72; IN Univ Bloomington, assoc teacher in public speaking 1965-67; Houghton Coll, instructor Speech & English Composition 1961-65; Greenville Co Negro Public Schools, co speech therpst 1958-61; SC State Coll for Neg, Orangeburg SC, speech therpst & instructor 1958-59. **ORGANIZATIONS:** Speaker & oral interpreter of Afro-Am lit & rhetoric various chs, comm groups, pub assemblies, faculty In Serv; mem & speaker Regional & Nat Professional Speech Comm Assn 1972; mem & spkr Nat Couc of Tchrs of Engl 1973; vis lectr "The Fundamentals of Oral & Written Communication" 1976; pub Doctoral Dissertation & Abstract "An Accelerated Spch Curriculum for Sel Educationally Disadvtd Negroes" Dissertation Abstracts Intl 1971; pub "Your God is too White"Jour of Am Sci Affiliation 1971; pub book review of "The Oratory of Negro Leaders 1900-196 for Ethnic & Minority Studies Newsletter of WI State" 1972; pub book review "Black Jargon in White Am" for Jour of Am Sci Affiliation 1973; pub article "Evangelicals Listen, Please Listen" Bridge 1976. **BUSINESS ADDRESS:** 1543 North College Ave, Harrisonburg, VA 22801.

DAVIS, ADRIANNE
Elected official. **PERSONAL:** Born Sep 06, 1945, Newark, NJ. **EDUCATION:** Montclair State Coll, MA 1967. **CAREER:** West Side HS Newark NJ, instr 1967-73; North Ward Ctr Inc Newark NJ, admin 1973-; Essex Cty New Jersey, freeholder at large. **ORGANIZATIONS:** Consult John Hay Whitney Found 1973-74; chrprsn Essex Cty Coll Personnel Comm 1979, Essex Vty Coll Bd of Trustees 1979-80; mem Essex Cty Bd of Freeholders 1982-, Budget Review Comm Essex Cty Bd of Freeholders 1983-, Essex Cty Econ Devel Corp 1983-. **HONORS/ACHIEVEMENTS:** Disting Serv Awd Theatre of Universal Images 1980; Apprec Awd Essex Cty Coll 1980; Citizens Apprec Awd Comm of Womens Concerns Essex Cty 1980; Dr Martin Luther King Recog Awd North Ward Ctr 1983. **BUSINESS ADDRESS:** Essex County, 465 High St #560A, Newark, NJ 07102.

DAVIS, ALFRED C., SR.
Commissioner, clergyman, administrator. **PERSONAL:** Born Mar 11, 1938, Vaiden, MS; married Mary L Mack; children: Alfred C Jr, Darlene, Frederick Jerome, Angel Aleeta. **EDUCATION:** NW Training Center OR State, 1968-69; Tacoma Vocational Tech, 1970; Trinity Hall Coll & Seminary York, PA, DD 1980. **CAREER:** New Jerusalem, asst pastor 1958-61; Altheimer Meml Ch, asst pastor 1961-64; Eastside Comm Church, pastor/founder 1964-; Multi Serv Center (Eastside) ODI, asst dir 1965; Eastside Comm Day Care Center, founder/adminstr 1972-; Tacoma Housing Authority, minister. **ORGANIZATIONS:** Pres & exec ofcr FORCE 1973-; founder majestic Aires Rehab Farm Yelm 1975-; past chmn bd of commr Tacoma Housing Authority 1977-; pres Tacoma Ministerial Alliance 1978-80; bd mem Natl Commn ERS Com of Nahro's 1979-; charter mem The Tacoma Club; mem NAACP; mem Tacoma Urban League; chmn of the Ministrial Alliance; evangelism & mem of the Adv Bd to the TMA Pres. **HONORS/ACHIEVEMENTS:** Service to Mankind Award Puget Sound Sertoma Club 1980; Dist Serv to Mankind Award BC-WA Dist NW Region Sertoma 1980; Key to City of Tacoma, WA from Mayor Mike Parker 1980. **MILITARY SERVICE:** USAF; Received Good Conduct Medal 1960. **BUSINESS ADDRESS:** Minister, Tacoma Housing Authority, 4420 Portland Ave, Tacoma, WA 98404.

DAVIS, ALGENITA SCOTT
Attorney. **PERSONAL:** Born Oct 01, 1950, Houston, TX; daughter of C B Scott and Althea Lewis Scott; married John W Davis III; children: Marthea, John IV. **EDUCATION:** Howard Univ, BBA 1971, JD 1974. **CAREER:** US Govt Printing Office, clerk-typist 1969-70,71; Howard Univ Dept of Residence Life, grad fellow 1971-74; US General Accounting Office, legal intern 1972; Shell Oil Co, tax serv mgr, tax compliance dept 1974-77, office of legislation & industry affairs mgr 1977-79, tax atty, tax compliance dept 1979; Burney Edwards Hall Hartsfield & Scott, partner 1975-78; Port of Houston Authority, counsel 1979-89; Texas Commerce Bancshares, vice pres, Community Affairs officer. **ORGANIZATIONS:** Mem State Bar of TX, US Tax Court, US Southern Dist Court & Fifth Circuit Court of Appeals, US Supreme Court, Interstate Comm Commn, Fed Maritime Commission; charter mem Natl Bar Inst; political action comm 1975-76, bd dir 1976-77, 1985-88, pres 1988-89 Houston Lawyers Assn; founding mem 1975, bd mem 1975-78, 1986-87, vchair 1983-84, parliamentarian 1986-87 Black Women Lawyers Assoc; Judicial Campaign Worker for Domestic Relations Court Candidate 1976; Judicial Candidates 1978, 1980, 1984, 1986; campaign cochair Congressional Candidate 1978; co-chair Speakers Bureau Houston Bar Assoc 1978-79; rep Single Mem Dist coalition for Houston Lawyers Assn 1979; sec 1984- NBA Invest Corp 1984-; fundraising chair Committee-to-re-Elect Judson Robinson Councilman-at-Large Position 5 1985; Natl Bar Assn vice pres 1988-89, sec 1983-84; NBA Women's Division vice pres 1987-89. **HONORS/ACHIEVEMENTS:** Distinguished Christian Serv Sloan Methodist Church 1977; Distinguished Comm Serv Trinity Methodist Church 1978; Natl Bar Assn Distinguished Serv Awd 1982; One of Houston's Most Influential Black Women Black Experience Magazine 1984; Houston Lawyers Assoc Serv Awd 1985, 1987, 1988; Human Enrichment of Life Program Inc Young Achievers Awd 1986. **BUSINESS ADDRESS:** Vice Pres and Community Affairs Officer, Texas Commerce Bancshares, Mail Satation 10TCB-S-45, PO Box 2558, Houston, TX 77252-2558.

DAVIS, ALICE R.
Retired educator. **PERSONAL:** Born Dec 25, 1904, Jetersville, VA; daughter of Mr. & Mrs. Elias Mullen. **EDUCATION:** Hampton Inst, BS 1929; Hampton Inst, MA 1946; Atlanta, IN & ND Universities, further studies. **CAREER:** Prof Emeritus 1977; Paine Coll, assoc prof 1944-; Boggs Acad, instructor, 1940-44; Madison Jr HS & Atkins HS, instructor. **ORGANIZATIONS:** Mem Natl Assn of Univ Women; Southeastern Coll Art Conf; AAUP; acting recording sec Natl Conf of Artists; Triangle Assn of Colleges Humanities Project; Womens Civic Club; GA Council on Human Relations; NEA; GTEA; past sec bd trustees Christ Presbyterian Church. **HONORS/ACHIEVEMENTS:** Recipient certificates of merit, Natl Conf of artists 1968-70; "Art & Music a humanistic approach to interdisciplinardy art studies"; introduction to the humanities" 1971-77; Woman of the Year, Natl Assn of Univ Women, 1989-90; Certificate of Merit-Art, Delta Sigma Theta, 1986.

DAVIS, ALONZO J.
Artist. **PERSONAL:** Born Feb 02, 1942, Tuskegee, AL. **EDUCATION:** Otis Art Inst, MFA 1973; BFA 1971; UCLA pgrad 1966; pepperdine coll, ba 1964. **CAREER:** CA State U, instr 1976-; UCLA, lectr 1973 Padasena City Coll, instr 1971; Mt San Antonio Coll, instr 1971-73; La Unified sch dist instr 1962-70; Watts Towers & Art Ctr, consult 1976-; LA Co Mus of Art, consult 1976; Contemporary Crafts Inc, consult 1968-70. **ORGANIZATIONS:** Exec dir Brockman Gallery Prodn 1973-; owner co-dir Brockman Gallery 1967-73; bd mem CA Confederation of Arts 1976-; bd mem Cultural News Serv 1977-; bd mem Comm Arts Devel Group 1976-77; bd mem Artists for Econ Action; editor Neworld Mag 1977; fndr Support The Arts 1976-; exhibits Transition Gallery1976; Bowrs Mus 1975; Just Midtown Gallery 1975; Pomona Pub Libr 1975; Otis Art Inst 1977; LA Muncpl Art Gallery 1977; Studio Mus of Harlem 1977; Craft& Folk Art Mus 1977; Fisher 1976; Mural & Grafiti Exh 1976; number others Grants NEA & 1973-77; Brockman Gallery 1976; Inner City Mural Grant 1974. **HONORS/ACHIEVEMENTS:** Publ "Black Artists of the New Generation" 1977; varying Dir of Contemporary Black Artists" 1975; "Afro Am Artists" 1973; Black Artist on Art" 1971; Wilson Libr Bull 1969. **BUSINESS ADDRESS:** Brockman Gallery, 4334 Degnan Blvd, Los Angeles, CA 90008.

DAVIS, ALVIN GLENN
Professional athlete. **PERSONAL:** Born Sep 09, 1960, Riverside, CA; son of William Davis and Mylie Davis; married Kim. **EDUCATION:** AZ State Univ, 1979-82. **CAREER:** Seattle Mariners, first baseman 1984-. **ORGANIZATIONS:** All-Pac 10 honors 3 time & All-Amer third team sr yr AZ State Univ 1982. **HONORS/ACHIEVEMENTS:** 1st Mariner to win a major Amer League Awd when he was named the league's Rookie of the Year; Mariners' All-Star rep in the All-Star Game at Candlestick Park in San Francisco. **BUSINESS ADDRESS:** Seattle Mariners, PO Box 4100, Seattle, WA 98104.

DAVIS, AMOS
Psychiatrist. **PERSONAL:** Born Apr 02, 1932, Statesboro, GA; married Beatrice Lacy; children: Amy Louise, Amos Anthony. **EDUCATION:** Meharry Med Coll, MD 1963; Fisk U, BA 1958; Bd Cert Psychiatry 1975. **CAREER:** Martin Luther Kind Co Hosp LA, staff psychiatrist; Private Prac; LA Co Dept of Mental Health, staff physician 1967-72; Metro State Hosp, residency training. **ORGANIZATIONS:** Mem Charles Drew Med Soc; Am Psychiatric Assn; So CA Psychiatric Soc; Charles Drew Scholarship Loan Fund Inc. **MILITARY SERVICE:** AUS 1955-57. **BUSINESS ADDRESS:** 11665 W Olympic Blvd, Ste 516, Los Angeles, CA 90064.

DAVIS, ANGELA LUCRETIA
Educational administrator. **PERSONAL:** Born Jun 11, 1942, Peoria, IL; married Theodore Davis, DDS; children: Jonathon Jay. **EDUCATION:** Southern IL Univ Carbondale, BS 1965; Southern IL Univ Edwardsville, MEd 1980; Southern IL Univ Carbondale PhD 1983, Clark Doctoral Scholor-dedicationto improvement of educ for women and minorities. **CAREER:** Chicago Public Schools, hs biology teacher, counselor 1965-79; Southern IL Univ Edwardsville, asst dir sci awareness proj 1980-81; Souther IL Univ Carbondale, grad asst/co-dir upward bound 1981-82; Elgin Comm Coll, dir affirmative action/minority affairs. **ORGANIZATIONS:** Mem Phi Delta Kappa Prof Ed Frat, IL Assoc for Counseling & Devel, IL Assoc for Non-White Concerns in Personnel & Guidance, Delta Sigma Theta Inc 1982-;Sec IL Com on Black Concerns in Higher Ed, Phi Kappa Phi Natl Hon Soc; State Co-ord AAW-CJC, Brd of Dir Centro de Informacion. **HONORS/ACHIEVEMENTS:** Grad Deans Fellowship SIU-C 1982-83; Clark Doctoral Scholar SIU-C 1983; Leaders for the 80's Inst for Leadership Devel 1985;Ace Fellowship finalist 1987; Citizen Ambassador Prgm to China 1987.

DAVIS, ANITA LOUISE
Administrator. **PERSONAL:** Born Oct 03, 1936, Williamsport, PA; married Morris S; children: Lynn M, Lyles Jeyious, Wayne D Lyles, Mark E Lyles. **EDUCATION:** Buffalo State Coll, 1954-55; Univ of ND Grand Forks AFB, 1968-69; Univ of NH Pease AFB, 1970-71; Univ of Buffalo 1971-72, 76; buffatlo state coll, 1977-079; Tallahasee Comm Coll & FSU 1980-. **CAREER:** Health & Rehab Servs Leon Start Center, adminstrv asst sec III 1979-. **ORGANIZATIONS:** Bd of dir African Am Cultural Center 1975-80; gen mgr Nifty Enterprises Inc 1978-79; asst dir & acting dir BUILDS Half-way House 1974-78; comm coordinator

BUILDS Half-way House 1974; bookkeeper & office mgr Black Devel Found 1971-73; treas & bd of dirs Black Devel Found; former 1st vice pres & com chmn CAO Head Start Overall Policy Council; mem Criminal Justice Com BUILD of Buffalo Inc; criminal justice chairperson NAACP; social dir AD Price & Perry Sr Citizens; coord Masten Dist Block Club Assn. **HONORS/ACHIEVEMENTS:** Recipint outstanding serv to sch & comm award PTA 1965; comm servs award Comm Relations Group of Portsmouth NH 1971; award for ch & comm work Great Lakes Missionary Bapt Assn 1973, 1978; comm serv/outstanding citizenship award Glen-main Block Club 1973-74; completion of leadership training sessions cert Niagara Comm Coll 1974; achievement of merit/outstanding performance award CAO Head Start-prog Overall Policy Council 1974; cert for Spl Serv Auburn NAACP 1976; outstanding membership award CAO Head Start Prog 1976; outstanding citizen award for comm serv Membership Com Lackawanna NAACP 1977; outstanding & dedicated serv award Juneteenth Com 1978; outstanding serv award NAACP Buffalo Chap 1978 bd of dirs presidents award African Am Cultural Center 1978; presidents award NY State Conf of NAACP Brs 1979; outstanding comm serv award Eriei Co Sherriff 1979; outstanding ch work award St PaulBapt Ch 1979. **BUSINESS ADDRESS:** Employment Specialist, Job Service of Florida, Dept of Labor, 1307 N Monroe, Tallahassee, FL 32304.

DAVIS, ARNOR S.
Educator. **PERSONAL:** Born Dec 19, 1919, Patterson, GA; children: 3 Children. **EDUCATION:** Savannah State Coll Savannah GA, BS; Sch of Religion Howard Univ Wash DC, BD; Religous Educ Sch of Religion Howard Univ Wash DC, MA. **CAREER:** Inst Relations DC Redevel Land Agency, Washington DC, asst area dir; Antioch Baptist Church, Washington DC, asst minister 1975; New Bethel Baptist Church, Washington DC, dir of religious educ 1960-75; Zion Baptist Church, Washington DC, asst minister 1950-52. **ORGANIZATIONS:** Bd dir local council of Chs; mem Housing Task Force Council of Chs; bd dir Hillcrest Childrens Center 1971-74; bd dir DC Citizens for Better Educ 1970-74; pres bd dir Nat Med Aso Found 1967-74; bd dir Lincoln-Westmoreland Non-Profit Housing Corp; mem Savannah State Alumni Assn DC Chap 1948-74; bd dir Mt Ethel Bapt Training Union 1969-74; mem Bapt Ministers Conf 1960-74; mem HowardUniv Alumni Assn; exec dir Second Precinct Clergymens Assn 1948-74; NAACP 1970-74. **HONORS/ACHIEVEMENTS:** Publs A Guide to Chs & Institutions in the Shaw & Urban Renewal Area 1974; Chs in Shaw 1970; A Guide SAC Area Chs Schs & Non-profit Sponsorships 1975. **MILITARY SERVICE:** AUS 1941-46.

DAVIS, ARRIE W.
State official. **PERSONAL:** Born Jul 21, 1940, Baltimore, MD; children: Joanne, Aria. **EDUCATION:** Morgan State Coll, BA 1963; New York Univ, MA 1966; Univ Baltimore, JD 1969. **CAREER:** Baltimore City Public Sch, former english instr, swimming coach 1964-69; Supreme Bench Baltimore, baliff 1968-69; State MD, asst atty gen counsel to div of correction; Baltimore City, asst state's attorney, prof of law 1970-71; Villa Julie Coll, asst prof; Commercial Law Morgan Coll Grad Sch, asst prof; Private Practioner; City of Baltimore, judge circuit court. **ORGANIZATIONS:** Baltimore City Bar Assn; MD State Bar Assn; Am Bar Assn; Nat Bar Assn; Monumental Bar Assn.

DAVIS, ARTHUR, III
City planner, lecturer, educator. **PERSONAL:** Born Nov 12, 1942, Sampson Co, NC; son of Bishop & Mrs Arthur Davis; divorced; children: Arthur Paris. **EDUCATION:** Morehouse Coll, BA 1965; Carnegie-Mellon Univ, MA 1966; Univ of Pittsburgh, MPA 1967. **CAREER:** A&T State Univ, lecturer 1967-68; City of Greensboro, sr planner 1969-; Guilford Coll, lecturer 1975-81; Various Agencies, consultant 1975-; A&T State Univ, asst prof of planning & design, consultant assoc; Carolina Evaluation Research Center, city, corporate, church planner 20 years. **ORGANIZATIONS:** Bd NC Fellows Bd 1971-; Natl Greene Sertoma pres & bd 1971; bd & pres Greensboro Interclub Council 1971; pres bd Greensboro Credit Union 1978, mem Gen Green Council 1980-; Gnl Greene Council BSA 1980-; bd chmn Greensboro Emp Comem 1978-82; Grimsley PTA bd 1982-86; bd sec Amer Planning Orgn 1981-85; United Arts Council Bd 1983-85; USOA Bd 1985-; Morehouse Coll Alumni Club; bd mem NC ASPA 1987-; sec, mem NC APA 1980-86. **HONORS/ACHIEVEMENTS:** Cmmty Serv Awd A&T 1974,1975;Univ S Jaycees, Amer Plng Assoc A&T St Univ 1975; Men of Achievement 1976; awd Greensboro YMCA 1978; comm serv Seaoma Intrnl 1981; numerous citations US Dept of Comm, President Leadership awd 1983; Sertoma International. **BUSINESS ADDRESS:** Senior Planner, City of Greensboro, Drawer W-2, Greensboro, NC 27402.

DAVIS, ARTHUR, JR.
Educator. **PERSONAL:** Born Apr 17, 1933, Bessemer, AL; married Loretta J; children: Arthur III, Deborah, Sarah. **EDUCATION:** AL A & M, BS 1955; Univ of IL, MA 1968; Univ of IL, PhD 1970. **CAREER:** Northeastern Univ, dir assoc prof of educ 1976-; KY State Univ, asst prof 1970-76; Univ of IL, asst dir 1966-70; Dept of the Air Force, Chanute Tech Training Center, civilian elec electron training instructor 1963-66; Aero-space Ground Equip Branch, civ aircraft & missle ground suppost equipment repairman tech 1961-63; Aerospace Equipment Branch, civ training instructor ground support 1959-61. **ORGANIZATIONS:** Pres Wrightway Ed Consutl LTD 1972-76; asst coord St Univ of NY 1970-73; consul Urbana Pub Schl 1966; consul Univ of IL Pal Prog; consul Dean of Stud on Loc Urban Commn Needs & Prob 1968-69; c Prgm sul adm of the Clerical Learner Prgm on Design Curr Dev & Eval9 1968-70; consul Rochester NY Model Cities Prog 1971; consul Parents Adv Com on Title I ESEA 1972; consul Univ of IL 1977; consul S IL Univ Coll of Educ 1977; mem Adm Oper & Comm; mem Univ Cabinet; mem Steering Comm on Ath; mem Black Recruit Adv Comm; mem Search Comm for Dean of Coll of Edn; mem Univ Cabinet; mem Task Force on Compensatory Edn; mem Adv Comm on the Arts. **HONORS/ACHIEVEMENTS:** Publ "Racial Crisis in Pub Educ a quest for social order " 1975; presently writing 2 books "the pedagogic of the african am studies" & "the educ of the Am Negro from Slavery to the Presnet" sev articles & ed 2 other books; num art publ. **MILITARY SERVICE:** AUS 1955-57. **BUSINESS ADDRESS:** Coll of Educ NortheasternUniv, 360 Huntington Ave, Boston, MA 02115.

DAVIS, ARTHUR D.
Musician, educator, psychologst. **PERSONAL:** Married Gladys; children: Kimaili, Mureithi. **EDUCATION:** Hunter Coll, BA Psych/Mus (Summa Cum Laude) 1973; City Coll, MA 1976; NY Univ, MA 1976; NY Univ, PhD (w/Distinction) 1982. **CAREER:** Internationally acclaimed composer, musician, educator, 1958-; Borough Manhattan Comm Coll, asst adjunct prof 1972-; Univ of Bridgeport, prof 1979-82; Head Start, consultant, psychologist 1981-82; NY Medical Coll, instr 1983-; Lincoln Medical & Mental Health Ctr, clinical psychologist 1982; Lakeside UFSD, psychologist 1985-86; Orange Coast Coll, faculty, 1987; Private Practice, 1986-; psychologist/assoc prof; prof CA State Univ, Fullerton, 1988-. **ORGANIZATIONS:** Mem Amer Soc of Authors Composers and Publishers 1976-; mem Amer Psychological Assn 1977-; mgr Little League Inc 1979-82; chmn cub pack Cub Scouts of Amer 1979-80; exec bd mem Local 802 Jazz Musicians Found 1984-; mem Orange County Psychological Assn 1989-; consultant to mental health svcs, consultant to music projects etc; in music gave first double bass concerts in many cities; producer Art Davis Quartet; numerous lectures workshops clinics both in psychology and music. **HONORS/ACHIEVEMENTS:** Named No 1 Bassist Downbeat Intl Critics Poll 1962; World's Foremost Double Bassist Dict of International Biogr 1969-; Phi Beta Kappa, Psi Chi Natl Honor Socs; Life Fellow Intercontinental Biographical Assoc 1974-; The Arthur Davis System For Double Bass 1976; Dr Art Davis Live 1984; mem Astronomical Soc of the Pacific 1980-, Assoc of Black Psychologists 1983-, New York Acad of Scis 1984-; Gold Note Jazz Award LION, Natl Black MBA Assn 1985; cited in NY Times as one of the world's top gourmet chefs; cited for music in Chap 9 of "Music; Black, White & Blue" 1972 Morrow Publ; music album: "Art Davis Quartet, Life" Soulnote 1443 1987. **BUSINESS ADDRESS:** ARKIMU, 3535 East Coast Hwy, Suite 50, Corona Del Mar, CA 92625.

DAVIS, ARTHUR PAUL
Educator. **PERSONAL:** Born Nov 21, 1904, Hampton, VA; married Clarice Winn (deceased); children: Arthur Paul Jr. **EDUCATION:** Columbia Univ, AB 1927, MA 1929, PhD 1942. **CAREER:** North Carolina Coll for Negroes, instructor 1927-28; VA Union Univ, prof 1929-44; Howard Univ, prof and univ prof emeritus 1944-. **ORGANIZATIONS:** Mem Omega Psi Phi 1924-, Sigma Pi Phi 1941-. **HONORS/ACHIEVEMENTS:** Literary Scholarship Coll Lang Assoc 1975; Disting Critic Awd Middle Atlantic Writers Assoc Inc 1982; Hon Litt D Howard Univ 1984. **BUSINESS ADDRESS:** Professor Emeritus, Howard University, Washington, DC 20059.

DAVIS, BARBARA D.
Corporate affirmative action officer. **EDUCATION:** St Joseph Calumet Coll, B Sociology, A Social Work; Certificates, Training Counselor IN Univ, Univ of WI Labor Studies, Recruitment and Training Inst. **CAREER:** Insland Steel Project, officer mgr 1976-77, recruiter-counselor 1977-78, asst project dir 1978-79, dir 1980; Gilbane Building Co, equal employment oppor officer 1982, corporate affirmative action specialist 1984-. **ORGANIZATIONS:** Mem IL Affirmative Action Officers Assoc; chairperson IAAOA Conf 1985; liaison Black Contractors United/Chicago Urban League; consultant World's Fair Plan on Affirmative Action; pres Women in Construction; consultant Intl Women Economic Develop Corp; mem IN Civil Rights Comm; vice pres Fair Share Organization; consultant Women's League State Affiliation NAACP. **HONORS/ACHIEVEMENTS:** Union Counselor Awd AFL-CIO Lake Co Central Labor Union and United Steel Workers of Amer Local 1010; Affirmative Action Officer of the Year Awd Black Contractors United; Dedicated Serv Awd Natl Council of Black Child Develop New York; Special Awd Black Contractors United 1985. **BUSINESS ADDRESS:** Corporate Affirm Action Ofcr, Gilbane Building Co, 200 West Madison, Ste 700, Chicago, IL 60666.

DAVIS, BELVA
Urban affairs specialist/program host. **PERSONAL:** Born Oct 13, 1933, Monroe, LA; married William Vince Moore; children: Steven Eugene, Darolyn Denise. **EDUCATION:** Oakland City College. **CAREER:** Sun Reporter Newspaper, San Francisco CA, womens ed, 1963-68; KPTX-TV, San Fancisco, anchor/program host, 1967-77; KQED-TV, San Francisco, anchor/reporter, 1977-81; KRON-TV, urban affairs specialist/program host. **ORGANIZATIONS:** Corporate bd mem Blue Shield of CA 1980-; board mem Mt Zion Hospital SF 1981-; awards committee SF Foundation 1982-; natl vice pres Amer Fed of TV &Radio Artist 1984-; board mem Womens Form N West; board member Howard Thurman Foundation; board mem Black Filmmakers Hall of Fame; mem Links Inc. **HONORS/ACHIEVEMENTS:** 5 Emmy's No Cal TV Academy; Natl Journalism Awd Natl Urban Coalition 1985; Natl Journalism Awd Ohio State Univ 1985; Community Service No Cal United Nations Assoc 1984. **BUSINESS ADDRESS:** KRON Channel 4, 1001 Van Ness Ave, San Francisco, CA 94109.

DAVIS, BENJAMIN O., JR.
Business executive. **PERSONAL:** Born Dec 18, 1912, Washington, DC; married Agatha Scott. **EDUCATION:** US Mil Acdmy, BS 1936. **CAREER:** USAF, retired lt gen; Cty of Cleveland, dir pub sfty 1970; Office of Civ Aviatn, dir; Dept Trans, sec 1970-71; Trans for Environ Sfty & Consmr Affrs, asst sec 1971-. **ORGANIZATIONS:** Mem Bd of Vstrs US Mil Acdmy 1970-73; mem bd dir Retired Officers Assn; bd trust Assn of Grads US Mil Acdmy 1971-74; Nat vice pres Nat Def Transp Assn 1972-74; chrmn Interagcy Com Transp Sec; chrmn Interagcy Com on Civ Avatn Sec 1971-74; chrmn Interagcy Exec Gr Mil; asst to Safty & Trfc; mem Ctzns Advsry Com to DC Bar; mem bd Pepperdine U; mem Nat Com for Educ Ctr Air Frc Acdmy Found; mem Hon Bd Trust; Nat Educ Inst. **HONORS/ACHIEVEMENTS:** Hon Degrees DMilSc WilberforceUniv 1948; DSc Morgan State Coll 1963; LLD Tuskegee Inst 1963; Mil decrtns Dist Ser Medal; 2 Oak Lf Clstrs; SilverStar; Dist Flyg Crs; Leg of Merit W/2 Oak Lf Clstrs; Air Medal W/5 Oak Lf Clstrs; Croix de Guerre w/Palm; Star of Africa; Rep China Cloud & Bnar Medal; 1 Oak Lf Clstr; Rep Korea Ordr Nat Sec Merit; 2nd Cls; many othrs. **MILITARY SERVICE:** AUS; USAF retired ltn gen.

DAVIS, BENNIE L.
Urologist. **PERSONAL:** Born Dec 07, 1927, Muskogee, OK; children: Benjamin, Duane. **EDUCATION:** Samuel Houston Coll, BS 1947; Howard U, MD 1952. **CAREER:** Homer G Philips Hosp St Louis, internship 1952-53; Terre Haute IN, gen practice 1953-54; Homer G Phillips Hosp, surgery resident 1953-55; urology resident 1954-58; Private Practice Indianapolis IN, urologist 1960-. **ORGANIZATIONS:** Mem Am Me Assn; Nat Med Assn; Alpha Phi Alpha Frat; Chi Delta Mu Scientific Frat; Sigma P Phi Frat; Am Urological Assn; instr in Urology IN Univ Med Cntr; mem Indianapolis C of C; Rotarty Club; C of C of the US; vice-pres Our Savior Luthern Ch; chm Div of Urology Meth Hosp Grad Med Ctr 1968-71; chm Urology Sec Natl Med Assn 1974. **HONORS/ACHIEVEMENTS:** Recipient of, Diplomate Am Bd of Urology 1961; fellow Am Coll of Surgeons 1963. **MILITARY SERVICE:** USAF urologist 1958-60. **BUSINESS ADDRESS:** 2615 N Capitol Ave, Indianapolis, IN 46208.

DAVIS, BETTYE J.
Appointed official. **PERSONAL:** Born May 17, 1938, Homer, LA; married Troy J Davis; children: Anthony B, Sonja D. **EDUCATION:** St Anthony Sch of Nursing, GN 1961; Grambling State Univ, BSW 1971. **CAREER:** YWCA San Bernardino, asst dir 1971-72; DFYS Anchorage, child care specialist 1975-80; AK Black Leadership Educ Prog, dir 1979-82; Anchorage Youth Serv Div of Family, soc worker 1980; Anchorage Div of Soc Svcs, foster care coord; elected official at large 1984-85; Anchorage Bd of Ed, vp; State of AK Div of Family & Youth Svcs, foster care coord, asu 1982-. **ORGANIZATIONS:** Pres Anchorage Chap of Delta Sigma Theta 1979-80, North to the Future BPW Club Inc 1978-79,83, AK Black Leadership Conf; treas AK Women's Lobby; bd of dir March of Dimes 1983-85; mem Blacks in Govt; chairperson AK Black Caucus; Anchorage Br NAACP; bd of dir Nat'l Black Caucus of Schl brd mems. **HONORS/ACHIEVEMENTS:** Woman of the Year AK Colored Womens Club 1981; Social Worker of the Year Natl Foster Parents Assn 1983; Child Care Worker of the Yr AK Foster Parent Assn 1983; Political Awareness Awd of the Year AK Black Caucus 1984; Outstanding Achievement Awd in Ed AK Colored Womens Club 1985; Outstanding Women in Ed Zeta Phi Beta 1985; Outstanding Serv Awd AK Black Caucus 1986; Outstanding Political Awareness Awd, AK Black Caucus 1986; Comm Serv Awd, AK Black Leadership 1986. **HOME ADDRESS:** 2240 Foxhall Dr, Anchorage, AK 99504. **BUSINESS ADDRESS:** Foster Care Coordinator, ASU, State of Alaska, Div of Family & Youth Serv, 400 Gamble Ste 201, Anchorage, AK 99501.

DAVIS, BILLY, JR.
Singer. **PERSONAL:** Born in St Louis, MO; married Marilyn; children: Steven. **CAREER:** Singer; original mem The Fifth Dimension 1965-75. **HONORS/ACHIEVEMENTS:** Recpt Grammy Award with Marilyn Mcoofor "You Don't Have To Be A Star" 1977. **BUSINESS ADDRESS:** 222 N Mayo Ave, #8, Compton, CA 90221.

DAVIS, BOB
Automobile dealer. **CAREER:** Allstar Chevrolet Inc, Elkridge MD, chief exec. **BUSINESS ADDRESS:** Allstar Chevrolet Inc, 5820 Washington Blvd, Elkridge, MD 21401. *

DAVIS, BOBBY
Association executive. **PERSONAL:** Born Jan 07, 1946, Lynchburg, VA; married Sandra Penn. **EDUCATION:** Norfolk State Coll, BS. **CAREER:** Natl Capitol Area Council BSA, exploring exec 1973-; Blue Ridge Mtn Council BSA, assoc dist exec 1971-73; Portsmouth Naval Yard, lifeguard 1969-70. **ORGANIZATIONS:** Chrm Activities Com Downtown Washington Jaycees; exec bd Big Brothers 1972; BSA; Omega Psi Phi; Norfolk State Coll Alumni Assn Mem DC Ach Bd Adv Com 1976-77; mem Martinsville Voter Registration Assn; NAACP. **HONORS/ACHIEVEMENTS:** Recipient BSA Achvmnt Trophy 1974; recipient Commn Ldrs & Noteworthy Am Awd. **BUSINESS ADDRESS:** Natl Cap Area Council BSA, 9190 Wisconsin Ave, Washington, DC 20014.

DAVIS, BRENDA LIGHTSEY-HENDRICKS
Educational administrator. **PERSONAL:** Born Dec 21, 1943, Fairfield, AL; married William R David, MD; children: Tonia D Kelly, William R Jr, Scott, Frank B, Joye Lynn. **EDUCATION:** Harlem Hospital School of Nursing, diploma 1964; Teachers College Columbia Univ, BS 1969, MEd 1972, EdD 1976. **CAREER:** Riverside Community College, dean occupational education. **ORGANIZATIONS:** Mem Natl League for Nurses 1975-; mem CA Comm Coll Administrators 1984-; mem Amer Vocational Educ Assoc 1984-; mem Diamond Bar Black Women's Assoc 1985-; mem Natl Black Nurses' Assoc 1985-; pres Inland Empire Black Nurses' Assoc 1986-; adv comm mem CA State Univ San Bernardino 1986; mem Black History Program Comm/DBBWA 1986-. **HONORS/ACHIEVEMENTS:** Training Grant New York State 1968-69; Minority Scholarship Teachers College Columbia 1970; Training Grant Natl Inst of Mental Health 1971-75. **HOME ADDRESS:** 2149 S Indian Creek Rd, Diamond Bar, CA 91765. **BUSINESS ADDRESS:** Dean Occupational Education, Riverside Community College, 4800 Magnolia Ave, Riverside, CA 92506.

DAVIS, BROWNIE W.
Insurance brokerage president. **PERSONAL:** Born Mar 13, 1933, Philadelphia, PA; divorced; children: Brenda, Bruce. **EDUCATION:** City Coll of NY, BA 1957; Life Underwriter Training Council, grad advanced underwriting & health ins. **CAREER:** VA Hosp Brooklyn, radioisotope tech; Farmingdale LI Unit, republic aviation supr; Williamsburgh Steel Prod Co, draftsman office mgr; Macy's Rego Park, mgr in charge of housewares; NY Life Ins Co, field underwriter; Guardian Life Ins Co of Amer, dist agency mgr; adjunct prof. Manhattan Communicty College 1986-; adjunct prof, LaGuardia Community College 1989; Brownie W Davis Agency Corp, pres. **ORGANIZATIONS:** Pres Queens Branch 1st Natl Assn of Life Underwriters; past mem NY Life Agent Adv Council 1973-74; adv bd mem Minority Bus Council; mem Queens Chamber of Commerce; bonding chmn vice pres Assn of Minority Bus Enterprises; pres Cedar Manor Co-op 1967-70; bd mem New York City Housing Auth, Symphony Orchestra; exec vice pres Natl Minority Bus Council. **HONORS/ACHIEVEMENTS:** Natl Quality Awd for Life-Health 1972-75; Centurion 1967-; Group Ins Leader 1973; Health Ins Leader 1967-75; Company Honor Roll over 100 consecutive months; Black Achiever in Industry 1974; speaker Co's Career Conf & Club Meetings also has made video tape training films for Co to help new underwriters; Leader Aetna Life & Casualty Reg; Leadership Award, York College 1989. **BUSINESS ADDRESS:** President, Brownie W Davis Agency Corp, P O Box 593, Lawrence, NY 11559.

DAVIS, CAROLYN ANN MCBRIDE
Senior compensation analyst, supervisor. **PERSONAL:** Born May 28, 1952, Mobile, AL; daughter of Samuel McBride and Janie Sole McBride; married Nolan Davis, Dec 17, 1977; children: Ashley Tamar, Nolan Jarod, Sean Thomas. **EDUCATION:** Wiley Coll, Marshall TX, BA Sociology, 1974; Kent State Univ, Kent OH, graduate program; Univ of South Alabama, Mobile AL, Masters of Public Admin, 1977. **CAREER:** Natchez Mental Health, Natchez MS, coord, therapist, 1978-79; Texas Dept of Human Serv, Houston TX, social worker, 1979-84; City of Houston, Personnel Dept, Houston TX, compensation specialist, 1984-88; Harris County Hospital District, Houston TX, sr compensation analyst, 1988-. **ORGANIZATIONS:** Mem, pres emeritus, Delta Sigma Theta Sorority, 1971-; founder, exec dir, Christian Debutante Soc of Amer, 1986-; treasurer, bd mem, Houston Youth Chorus, 1986-; Worthy Matron Eastern Star, Bells of Justice Chapter, 1987-; mem, Houston Compensation Assn, 1988-, The Assn of Human Resource Professionals, 1988-, Natl Forum for Black Public Admin, 1989-. **HONORS/ACHIEVEMENTS:** Graduate Assistantship, Kent State Univ, 1975; Graduate Assistantship, Univ of South Alabama, 1976-77; Vernita M Moore Award, Liberty Baptist Church, 1982, 1985; President/Founder, Ambiance Internal, Special Events & Theme Decorating Firm, 1987-. **BUSINESS ADDRESS:** Senior Compensation Analyst/Supervisor, Harris County Hospital Dist/Salary Admin, 726 Gillette St, 6th Floor, Admin Bldg, Houston, TX 77019.

DAVIS, CARRIE L. FILER
Educator. **PERSONAL:** Born Oct 19, 1924, Marianna, AR; married Wm Davis; children: Arthur, Norma, Helen, Gina. **EDUCATION:** Univ of AR, BA 1948; NE IL Univ, MA 1971; NW Univ, grad study; Univ of Sarasota, EdD 1982. **CAREER:** Robert Morton High School, educator 1948-55; Crest Finishing School, co-dir 1956-60; Englewood High School Chicago, counselor 1961-72; Chicago Bd of Educ, co-compiler of curriculum guide for drama, admin dist #19, instructional serv coord dist #27, administrator dist #19 1973-. **ORGANIZATIONS:** Mem Sigma Gamma Rho 1943-; campus coord Central Region 1972-74 dir 1974; grand epistoleus Sigma Gamma Rho Sor 1980-84; pres Roseland Comm Hosp Aux; chmn Calumet Dist United Charities Educ Comm; mem Good Citizenship Club Inc, Natl Scholarship Comm, Altgeld Urban Prog Ctr Educ Com; com chpsn Afro-Am Family Svcs; mem Quinn Chapel AME Church; mem Southshore YMCA; sub-com White House Conf for Youth; mem St Luke AME Ch; natl pres Natl Women of Achievement Inc; bd of trustees The Univ of Sarasota FL. **HONORS/ACHIEVEMENTS:** Citizenship Awd 1971; Woman of the Yr Grest Finishing Sch 1973; Outstanding Drama Coord 1978; Outstanding Admin 1979; Outstanding Serv to Comm Awd Sigma Gamma Rho Sor; Judge IL Speech Assn Awd; co-author "Curriculum Guide & Activities for Proficiency in Basic Skills" 1977; co-author "Curriculum Guide for Drama Classes" Chicago Bd of Educ; "Proficiency Skills Course" devised for Chicago Bd of Educ for high schools; recipient Governor of Arkansas Awd "Salute toExcellence for Native Arkansans," culminating the Arkansas Sesquicentennial 1986. **BUSINESS ADDRESS:** Administrator, Chicago Bd of Education, 9912 Ave H, Chicago, IL 60617.

DAVIS, CHARLES
City official. **PERSONAL:** Born Sep 04, 1944, Seattle; married Lonear W Heard; children: Charles II, Jenise A. **EDUCATION:** CA State Univ, BS 1972. **CAREER:** Hughes Aircraft Co Culver City CA, contract adm accountant 1966-73; City of Compton, clerk. **ORGANIZATIONS:** Mem Intl Inst Municipal Clerks 1973-; Amer Records Managemant Assn 1973-; Amer Management Assn Advisory bd Compton & Branch Salvation Army; exec bd YMCA; SE Area Planning Council. **HONORS/ACHIEVEMENTS:** Airforce Craftmanship Award Hughes Aircraft Co 1971; Community Serv Award Compton Model Cities 1974; Merit Award Inner City Challenge Inc 1974; council resolution of appreciation 1974-75; first black to receive "Certified Municipal Clerk" designation in the US, 1976. **MILITARY SERVICE:** USAF 1963-66. **BUSINESS ADDRESS:** City Clerk, City of Compton, 205 S Willowbrook, Compton, CA 90220.

DAVIS, CHARLES A.
Business executive. **PERSONAL:** Born Sep 29, 1922, Mobile, AL; son of Robert Davis and Clara Davis. **EDUCATION:** WV State Coll, 1943-44; Roosevelt Univ Chicago, Political Science 1950-53; Governors State Univ, Honorary Doctorate 1975. **CAREER:** Dir advertising, dir public relations, city ed, sportswriter, reporter, Chicago defender 1946-59; Jayson Bldg Assoc, general partner; The Phoenix Group, general partner; Adco Assoc, general partner; ADCO II, partner; Jayson Bldg Corp, pres; Natl Ins Assoc, exec dir; Charles A Davis & Assoc Inc, pres. **ORGANIZATIONS:** Pres Inner City Ind, chmn Inner City Foods Inc, dir Highland Comm Bank; sec Chicago Southside NAACP 1961-; dir Chicago Metro Area Bd, Natl Conf Christians & Jews; dir, United Way Chicago; dir, Great Books Found. **HONORS/ACHIEVEMENTS:** Citations, Contributor Minority Business Chicago Comm Human Relations 1974; Gold Oil Can Award Chicago Econ Devel Corp Chamber of Commerce; Spaulding Ins Award Natl Business League. **MILITARY SERVICE:** US Quartermaster Corps tech sgt 1943-46. **BUSINESS ADDRESS:** President, Charles A Davis & Assoc, 2400 S Michigan Ave, Chicago, IL 60616.

DAVIS, CHARLES ALEXANDER
Engineer, educator. **PERSONAL:** Born Aug 20, 1936, Petersburg, VA; married Clenetine Johnson; children: Lisa, Karen, Glen. **EDUCATION:** MI State Univ, BSEE 1959; Univ of MI, MSEE 1963; MI State Univ, PhD 1975; Univ of IL. **CAREER:** Univ of MI, rsch assoc, 1960-63; Bendix Corp, engr 1963-64; Ford Motor Co, engr 1964-67; Western MI Univ, prof, 1967-. **ORGANIZATIONS:** Pres, Douglass Comm Assn, 1979-80; commr, General Indus Safety Council 1978-; mem Kappa Alpha Phi, Delta Pi 1958-59; pres delegate Democratic Party 1978; mem Natl Soc of Professional Engr 1976-; mem IEEE, 1984-85. **HONORS/ACHIEVEMENTS:** Book Indus Electronics, 1973; engr, Registered Professional Engrs 1976-; engr honors Tau Beta Pi 1958, Eta Kappa Nu 1957. **HOME ADDRESS:** 816 Newgate Rd, Kalamazoo, MI 49007. **BUSINESS ADDRESS:** Professor of Engineering, Western MI Univ, Rm 3044 Kohrman Ave, Kalamazoo, MI 49007.

DAVIS, CHARLES TERRELL
Professional athlete. **PERSONAL:** Born Oct 05, 1958, Nashville, TN; married Toni. **EDUCATION:** Vanderbilt, BS 1981. **CAREER:** Wash Bullets, forward 1981-. **ORGANIZATIONS:** Held a free week-long clinic for children in his old neighbrhd in Nashville, TN for 2nd straight year. **HONORS/ACHIEVEMENTS:** Season high 14 points on four occasions; second leading scorer in Vanderbilt history. **BUSINESS ADDRESS:** Washington Bullets, 1 Harry S Truman Dr, Ste 510, Landover, MD 20785.

DAVIS, CHILI
Professional athlete. **PERSONAL:** Born Jan 17, 1960, Kingston, Jamaica. **CAREER:** San Francisco Giants, outfielder 1981-. **HONORS/ACHIEVEMENTS:** Cedar Rapids MVP 1978; Midwest League All-Star 1978; hit for the cycle at Bakersfield 1979; 6th in the Cal League in home runs (21) 1979; promoted to Double AShreveport 1980; led his squad in home runs & RBI'S for the 3rd straight season 1980; named to the Pacific Coast League All Star Team 1981; named to Baseball Digest's All-Rookie Squad 1982; tied for team lead in steals with 24; named to Topps and Baseball Digest's All Rookie Squads 1982; mem 1984 and 1986 All Star Teams; named NL Player of the week for June 9-15 1986. **BUSINESS ADDRESS:** San Francisco Giants, Candlestick Park, San Francisco, CA 94124.

DAVIS, CHRISTINE R.
Business executive. **PERSONAL:** Born in Nashville, TN; married Steve G Davis; children: Pamela E. **EDUCATION:** Fisk U; TN State U; Boston Business Coll; Catholic Univ of Am. **CAREER:** Washington Bureau Tuesday Publications Inc, dir; US Mem of Congress, admn Asst; Dem Nat Com, exec asst vice chrm, Com on Govt Operations House of & Representatives, staff dir. **ORGANIZATIONS:** Mem Links Inc; Girl Friends Inc; Nat Press Club; Nat Coun of Negro Women; Nat Coun of Women; Delta Sigma Theta Sorority. **HONORS/ACHIEVEMENTS:** Numurous awards from natl organizations, religous, ednl, political; civic & congressional. **BUSINESS ADDRESS:** 600 New Hampshire Ave NW, Ste 1150, Washington, DC.

DAVIS, CLARENCE
Government official. **PERSONAL:** Born Sep 25, 1942, Wilkes County, GA; married Barbara Jean Holder; children: Wayne C, Clarence R, Cherylle M, Dawn T. **EDUCATION:** Morgan State Univ, BA Pol Sci 1968, MS History, Soc Sci 1978. **CAREER:** MD Job Corps Ctr, asst dir 1972-75; Catonsville Comm Coll, coord of vet affairs 1975-79; Vietnam Vet Ctr, dir 1979-82; MD House of Delegates, delegate 45th leg dist. **ORGANIZATIONS:** Exec dir Hamilton Court Improvement Assoc 1968; suprv St Bernadine Comm Serv Ctr 1971-72; rsch asst Friends of Psychiatric Rsch 1972-75; bd mem Natl Assoc Sickle Cell Disease 1984-87; mem steering comm Natl Assoc Black Soc Wk 1984-86; command council mem Natl Assoc for Black Vets; chmn vet affairs Natl Caucus of Black State Leg. **MILITARY SERVICE:** USAF E-4 1960-64. **BUSINESS ADDRESS:** Delegate, Maryland House of Delegates, 323 House of Delegates Bldg, Annapolis, MD 21401.

DAVIS, CLARENCE A.
Accountant. **PERSONAL:** Born Nov 29, 1941, New York, NY; children: Todd. **EDUCATION:** Long Island Univ, BS Acct 1967. **CAREER:** Oppenheim, Appel, Dixon & Co, mgr 1976, partnership 1979, audit partner. **ORGANIZATIONS:** Chrmn Amer Inst CPA Minority Recruitment Equal Opport Comm 1977-83; appointed NY State Bd of Public Acct 1984-; appointed Amer Inst CPA Future IssuesComm 1984; fac mem LIU Brooklyn Ctr 1974-80; fac mem NY Inst of Finance 1973-79; fac mem Fnd for Acct Educ; mem NY State Soc of CPA; mem Amer Inst CPA; mem Natl Assc of Black Acct; mem 100 Black Men; mem Kappa Alpha Psi Frat; mem Acct for Public Interest; chrmn schl bd St Brigid's Elem Schl; track coach St Brigid's CYO Track Team 1976-; asst scoutmaster Boy Scout Troop 999 1981-; cubmaster Cub Scout Pack 999 1977-81. **HONORS/ACHIEVEMENTS:** Elected Archbishop Molloy HS Alumni Hall of Fame 1984; article written "Accounting & Auditing Careers" The Black Collegian Magazine 1982. **MILITARY SERVICE:** USMC corpl 1960-64; Hnrbl Discharge 1964. **BUSINESS ADDRESS:** CPA, Oppenheim, Appel, Dixon & Co, 101 Park Ave, New York, NY 10178.

DAVIS, CLIFTON D.
Actor, singer, songwriter. **PERSONAL:** Born Oct 04, 1945, Chicago, IL; married Ann; children: Noel, Holly. **EDUCATION:** Oakwood Coll AL, BA Theol; Attending, Andrews Univ Berrien Springs MI. **CAREER:** Star of "Two Gentlemen of Verona" a Broadway musical; "Clifton Davis-Melba Moore Show" variety show on ABC, host; films "Together For Days" 1973; "Lost In The Stars" 1974; plays Rev Reuben Gregory on TV series Amen; Loma Linda CA Univ Seventh-Day Adventist Church, assoc pastor. **ORGANIZATIONS:** Mem AEA; mem AFTRA; mem SAG. **HONORS/ACHIEVEMENTS:** Wrote gold record song "Never Can Say Goodbye"; Tony Award nomination for "Two Gentlemen of Verona" 1972; Theater World Award for "Do It Again"; Torch Award Am Heart Assn 1975. **BUSINESS ADDRESS:** President, Davis & Associates, PO Box 254, Berrien Springs, MI 49103.

DAVIS, CORNEAL A.
Former state representative. **PERSONAL:** Born Aug 28, 1900; married Elma Howell; children: Yvonne Maule. **EDUCATION:** Tougaloo Coll, 1914-17; Moody Bible Inst Chicago; John Marshall Sch of Law Chicago. **CAREER:** State of IL, 17 terms As State rep; Quinn Chapel AME Ch, asst mnstr oldest congregation established by Negro Am in Chgo. **ORGANIZATIONS:** Past pres Second Ward Dem Orgn; mem adv com Pub Aid; pub Health; Pub Welfarer; Pub Safety; ex officio mem ALL Commn in IL Gen Assembly; former chmn Com on Pub Aid; Pub Health; Pub Welfare & Pub Safety; chmn Businessmens Scholarship Fund Com for Tougaloo Coll; bd mem Ada S Mckinley Community Svc; Grand Chaplain of Prince Hall Grand Lodge Masons; past chaplain of George L Giles Post; Am Legion; past imperial potentate of Shriners; 33rd Degree Mason; mem Omega Psi Phi Frat; grand chaplain of Omega Psi Phi Frat; grant Traveling Dep IBPOBOW. **HONORS/ACHIEVEMENTS:** First black dean of IL House of Rep & Asst Majority Leader; first black to serve as Asst Minority Leader In & Dem Leadership; recip Prince Hall shriner ofyr 1954; chicago urban league award for passage of FEPC Legislation 1961; chicago NAACP award 1962; Sigma Omega excellence award 1963; citation from Bapt State Conv 1963; rep Gov Kerner at Vicksburg MS on 100th anniversary of battle of Vicksburg 1963; chmn Emancipation Proclamation Comn Commn in IL & established a Historymobile 1963; il mason of yr 1964; good am leadership award Chicago Com of 100 1965; am legion meritorioussvc award of merit State of IL 1965; civil war centennial award of merit State of IL 1965; selected by family of late adlai stevenson to deliver message & prayer in rotunda of capitol & Bldg IL 1965; award for serv to manking & FEPC achivements AFL-CIO 1966; master of ceremonies for First Annual Testimonial Dinner Honoring Dr George A Owens Chicago Tougalon Alumni Club 1967; award for protection & Enhancement of visual welfare IL Optometric Assn 1968; award for svs to sch community & State Tougaloo Coll Alumni 1968; cita. **MILITARY SERVICE:** WWI Vet.

DAVIS, CYPRIAN
Educator, clergyman. **PERSONAL:** Born Sep 09, 1930, Washington, DC; son of Clarence Davis and Evelyn Davis. **EDUCATION:** St Meinrad Coll, BA 1953; Catholic Univ of Amer, STL 1957; Univ of Louvain (Belgium), Licence in Hist Sci 1963, Doctorate in Hist Sci 1977. **CAREER:** St Meinrad Archabbey, archivist 1984-; Black Catholic Clergy Caucus, archivist 1984-; professor of Church History 1987. **HONORS/ACHIEVEMENTS:** Author of several articles, Black Catholic history, Black spirituality; author of textbook in Church History, "The Church A Living Heritage" "Black Spirituality, A Roman Catholic Perspective", Review and Expositor, "Black Catholics in Nineteenth-Century America", US Catholic Historian "Evangelization in the United States Since Vatican Council II" Catholic Evangelization Today A New Pentecost for the United States (Paulist Press, 1987); "The Holy See and American Blacks, A Forgotten Chapter in the History of the Amer Church", US Catholic Historian 7 157-181, 1988. **HOME ADDRESS:** St Meinrad Archabbey, St Meinrad, IN 47577.

DAVIS, DALE BROCKMAN
Educator. **PERSONAL:** Born Nov 11, 1945, Tuskegee, AL; children: Aiyana, Malik. **EDUCATION:** USC, BFA. **CAREER:** Brockman Gallery, co-founder 1967; Los Angeles City Schools, teacher 1969-. **ORGANIZATIONS:** Mem Natl Con of Artists; bd of dir Brockman Productions. **HONORS/ACHIEVEMENTS:** NEA 1973; Outstanding Community Serv 1983; Outstanding Alumni USC 1985. **BUSINESS ADDRESS:** Teacher, Los Angeles City Schools, PO Box 43608, Los Angeles, CA 90043.

DAVIS, DANNY K.
Executive director. **PERSONAL:** Born Sep 06, 1941, Parkdale, AR; son of H D Davis and Mazzie Davis; married Vera Garner; children: 2 Children. **EDUCATION:** AR AM&N Coll, BA 1961; Chicago State Univ, MS 1968; Union Grad School, PhD 1977. **CAREER:** US Postal Serv clerk 1961-62; Chicago Bd of Educ, tchr counselor 1962-69; Greater Lawndale Conservation Commn, exec dir 1969; Martin Luther King & Neighborhood Health Ctr Chicago, dir of training 1969-71; W Side Health Planning Org, manpower consult 1971-72; Miles Square Comm Health Ctr, special asst to pres 1976; W Side Health Planning Org, exec dir 1972-; 29th Ward City of Chicago, chmn comm on health, chmn comm on zoning, alderman 1979, 1983, 1987. **ORGANIZATIONS:** Lectr Malcolm X Coll 1972-74; freelance consult 1970-; organizing group W Side State Bank Chicago 1973-; pres Natl Assn of Comm Health Ctrs 1977; pres W Side Assn for Comm Action 1972-; mid-west rep Speaker of House Natl Assn of Neighborhood Health Ctrs; mem Amer Pub Health Assn; Lawndale People's Planning & Action Conf; commnr Chicago Health Systems Agency. **HONORS/ACHIEVEMENTS:** Achievement Awd Montford Pt Marine Assn 1972; Certificate of Merit Pres Task force on Youth Motivation 1970; featured on "He's A Black Man" Radio Series 1972-73; Comm Serv Awd United Concerned Parents 1973; Chicago Black Sociologists; Afro-Amer Patrolman's League; Austin Business Assoc; Circle Urban Ministries; Northwest Inst; Operation PUSH; Chicago Black United Communities; Best Alderman Awd IVI-IPO. **BUSINESS ADDRESS:** Alderman, 5730 W Division Street, Chicago, IL 60651.

DAVIS, DARWIN N.
Business executive. **PERSONAL:** Born Apr 10, 1932, Flint, MI; married Velmarie Broyles; children: Karen, Dana, Darwin Jr, Derek. **EDUCATION:** AR AM&N Coll, BS 1954; Wayne State Univ, ME 1960; Univ of MI, Additional Study; Ferris State Coll, Univ of AR, Hon Doctorate Degree. **CAREER:** Detroit Publ School System, math teacher 1956-66; Equitable Life Assurance Soc of US, agent 1966-69, dist mgr 1969-71, agency mgr 1971-74, vp, chief ofmanpower devel 1974-75, div agency vice pres 1975, reg vp, head of external affairs 1980-. **ORGANIZATIONS:** Bd mem Carnegie Mellon Univ; bd dir Boy Scouts of Amer; bd of regents Natl Fund for Med Ed; life mem Alpha Phi Alpha Frat; natl bd Coll Devel All Black Coll; life mem NAACP; mem Natl Urban League; bd of dir Natl Urban Coalition, Stamford Hosp & Girl Scouts. **HONORS/ACHIEVEMENTS:** Listed in Who's Who in Amer Coll & Univ 1954; Natl Builders Trophy 1970; Top 10 Mgrs of over 975 competing; Young Agency Mgr of the Year Natl Equitable Life 1972; Pres Trophy Equitable Life 1972,73. **MILITARY SERVICE:** AUS 1954-56. **BUSINESS ADDRESS:** Head of External Affairs, Equitable, 1285 Ave of the Americas, New York, NY 10019.

DAVIS, DIANE LYNN
Manager information support services, telecommunications. **PERSONAL:** Born Apr 11, 1954, Detroit, MI; daughter of V Davis and S Davis. **EDUCATION:** Wayne State Univ, Detroit MI, BS, 1981. **CAREER:** Lifams Investment, Detroit MI, consultant; Dow Chemical Co, Midland MI, programmer, analyst; Candid Logic, Hazel Park MI, programmer; General Motors Corp, Warren MI, software engineer; Electronic Data Systems, Detroit MI, system engineer mgr; Digital Equipment Corp, Novi MI, information support systems, telecommunication mgr; Mercy Coll of Detroit, instructor, 1987-. **ORGANIZATIONS:** Mem, Wayne State Univ Alumni Assn, 1981-; pres, Black Data Processing Assoc, 1984-; mem, CYTCIP Advisory Council, 1988-, Detroit Urban League, 1989-. **HONORS/ACHIEVEMENTS:** Member of the Year, Black Data Processing Assoc, 1987. **BUSINESS ADDRESS:** ISS/Telecommunications Manager, Digital Equipment Corp, 41451 W Eleven Mile Rd, Novi, MI 48050.

DAVIS, DONALD FRED
Educator, artist. **PERSONAL:** Born Jan 14, 1935, Baton Rouge, LA; son of Benjamin Davis and Annabelle Davis; married Anna Mae Eames; children: Anthony, Angela, Derek, Miriam, Michael. **EDUCATION:** Southern Univ, BA 1959, MEd 1966; AZ State Univ, PhD 1983. **CAREER:** Scotlandville High, art instr 1959-69; Istrouma High, art instr 1969-71; LSU Lab Schl art instr 1972-85. **ORGANIZATIONS:** Mbr Natl Art Ed Assoc mem LA Art Ed Assoc; mem Phi Delta Kappa mem gallery II, br, lA ; mem NAACP mem united methodist church. **HONORS/ACHIEVEMENTS:** Outstanding contrib to arts Links, Inc 1972; numerous art shows Baton Rouge, LA. **MILITARY SERVICE:** USN pn3 1952-56; Good Conduct, Korean Service, Natl Defense. **BUSINESS ADDRESS:** Instructor of Art, LSU Laboratory School, Dalrymple Dr, Baton Rouge, LA 70803.

DAVIS, DONALD W.
Attorney. **PERSONAL:** Born Feb 01, 1934, Oklahoma; married Marjorie D Williams; children: Lawrence, Wayne, Robert, Marjean. **EDUCATION:** Univ CO, BA; Univ WY. **CAREER:** US Dept of Interior; US Dept of Lbr; Mntn Sts Tel Co Denver; Priv Pract, atty. **ORGANIZATIONS:** Mem Nat Bar Assn Inc; The Nat Bar Fndtn; Crt Mdrnztn Com; gen Pract Sectn; am Bar Assn; Amer Judctr Soc; lwyr Refrl Com; mem Bnkng; Comrcl & Crdt Com OK Bar Assn; v-chrm JJ Bruce Law Soc; mem Masons; NAACP; bd dir Urbn Lgue; Ok Cty; coaltn of Civ Ldrshp; mem Fth; mem Bapt Ch. **MILITARY SERVICE:** USAF.

DAVIS, DONNA P.
Physician/family practice. **PERSONAL:** Born Oct 06, 1947, New York, NY; married Dr James W Hammel; children: Damien E Hammel, Grant A Hammel. **EDUCATION:** Cornell Univ, BA 1969; Meharry Medical Univ, MD 1973. **CAREER:** Heffner Medical Clinic, physician 1977-78; CIGNA Health Plan, physician 1978-87. **ORGANIZATIONS:** Mem AMA, CMA, AAFP, MADD; supporter NAPCA, Amer Cancer Soc, Amer Heart Assoc. **HONORS/ACHIEVEMENTS:** Community Serv Awd Alpha Kappa Alpha 1984; Who's Who in California 1987. **MILITARY SERVICE:** USN commander 10 yrs; First black female medical officer in US history 1975. **BUSINESS ADDRESS:** Physician/Family Practice, CIGNA Health Plan, 14501 Magnolia Ave, Westminster, CA 92683.

DAVIS, DORIS ANN
Public official. **PERSONAL:** Born Nov 05; divorced; children: John, Ricky. **EDUCA-**

TION: Attended, Chicago Tchrs Coll, MA Northwestern Univ, Howard Univ; Lawrence Univ Santa Barbara, PhD; UCLA, law student. **CAREER:** Chicago & LA, teacher; City of Compton, elected city clerk 1965, mayor 1973-77; Heritage Unlimited Inc, owner. **ORGANIZATIONS:** Mem bd dir Southern CA Cty Clks' Assn; mem CA Tchrs Assn, Southern CA Clrk's Assn, Intl Muncpl Clerk's Assn; mem Dem natl Policy Council; mem St CL Jnt Com for Revsn of Electn Laws; owner & fdr The Daisy Child Devel Ctrs; educ rscher SWRL; pres Davis Edgerton Assocs; adv bd Water Reclamation & Resource Recovery State of CA; bd dir Wlfr Infrmtn Serv; mem CA Museum of Sci & Industry; bd dir NAACP, Natl Urban League, Conf Negro Elected Officials, Phi Beta Kappa, Iota Lambda Phi, AKA Sor, PTA; del CA 1972 Dem Conv; mem Links Intl, League of Women Voters, Welfr Information Serv, Med-Dental & Pharmaceutical Aux; St CA Jnt Com Rvsn Elctn Code. **BUSINESS ADDRESS:** Heritage Unlimited Inc, 4206 E Rosecrans, Compton, CA 90221.

DAVIS, DUPREE DANIEL
Attorney. **PERSONAL:** Born Mar 18, 1908, Jackson, TN; married Cleo. **EDUCATION:** Morehouse Coll, AB 1930; TN State Univ, BS 1933; LaSalle Univ, LLB 1944; IA State Univ, JD 1944; Harvard Law Sch, post grad 1944-45; Washington Univ, grad work social work 1956. **CAREER:** TN Public Sch System, taught sch 12 yrs; St Clair Co IL, past 30 yrs atty asst state's atty; State of IL, spec asst atty gen; City E St Louis IL, city atty 14 yrs, corporation counselor. **ORGANIZATIONS:** Mem East St Louis Township Bd Auditors; hold license practice law IA, TN, IL; legal counsel NAACP hanford Washington area 1944-45. **BUSINESS ADDRESS:** City Attorney, E St Louis IL, 19 Collinsville Ave, East St Louis, IL 62201.

DAVIS, EARL W.
Retired association executive. **PERSONAL:** Born Nov 22, 1911, Ashland, KY; married Kathryn L Garrett; children: Earl Jr, Edward. **EDUCATION:** WV State Coll Inst. **CAREER:** Com on Political Educ AFL-CIO, minorities dir 1967-78; Intl Woodworker of Am CIO, asso dir of educ 1954-56; Operation Dixie CIO, organizer 1946-54; OH CIO Council, vice pres 1944-47; United & Transport Serv Employees, vice pres 1940-44. **ORGANIZATIONS:** Bd mem A Philip Randolph Inst 1973-; bd mem Richmond Urban League 1974-; life mem NAACP. **HONORS/ACHIEVEMENTS:** Cited by A Philip Randolph Inst for voter regstrtn work in Memphis & state of MS.

DAVIS, EDWARD
Salesman. **PERSONAL:** Born Aug 06, 1935, Germantown, TN; married Henrene Cannon Davis; children: Dara Dene, Debra Donne, Edward Jr. **EDUCATION:** TN State Univ Nashville, 1957. **CAREER:** Life Ins, salesman 1957; teacher 1960; Edward Davis & Co, ins & real estate broker 1964; TN Dist 33, state senator 1978-. **ORGANIZATIONS:** Mem Kappa Alpha Psi. **BUSINESS ADDRESS:** Senator, State of Tennessee, Dist 33, Memphis, TN 38106.

DAVIS, EDWARD
Business executive. **PERSONAL:** Born Feb 27, 1914, Shreveport, LA; son of Thomas Davis and Hester Davis; married Mary Agnes Miller. **EDUCATION:** Alexander Hamilton Inst of Bus, grad; Wayne State Univ, business courses; Cornell Univ School of Flabon, certificate. **CAREER:** Davis Motor Sales, pres 1945-55; Floyd Rice Inc (Ford dealer), vice pres, 1956-63; Ed Davis Inc, owner/pres, 1963-71; Detroit Transp, gen mgr 1971-73; Ed Davis Assoc, pres, currently. **ORGANIZATIONS:** Life honorary trustee Kalamazoo Coll 1984; vice pres Detroit Econ Club; bd dir exec com Better Bus Bureau; bd dirs Blue Cross-Blue Shield; bd dirs exec com C of C Metro Bd Detroit YMCA, bd trustees, Kalamazoo Coll; Natl Bd of Natl Conf Christians & Jews; Small Bus Adminst; bd of dirs Detroit SciCntr 1979; bd of dirs Meth Children Home 1980. **HONORS/ACHIEVEMENTS:** Outstanding Businessman of the Year Award, Small Business Admin, 1966; Natl Bus Man's Award 1964; MI Businessman of the Year Award 1967; Quality Dealer Award Time Mag 1969; First Black automobile dealer in US 1941-70; author autobiography "One Man's Way" 1979; Choice of the Year Award Detroit Public Library 1980. **BUSINESS ADDRESS:** Washington Blvd & State St, 3000 Book Building, Detroit, MI 48226.

DAVIS, EDWARD D.
Business executive. **PERSONAL:** Born Feb 01, 1904, Thomasville, GA; married Larone Taylor; children: Samuel Edward, Cynthia Marcia. **EDUCATION:** Paine Coll, BA 1928; Northwestern U, MA 1934; Columbia U, Post Grad Work 1939-40. **CAREER:** Tampa-ocala FL, hs principal 1929-42; real estate & merchandising bus 1942-55; Central Life Ins Co FL, sec 1955-64; pres 1964-. **ORGANIZATIONS:** Co-founder 1st Community Fed Sav & Loan Assn Faculty Ethune Cookman Coll FL A&M U; pres FL Voters League; founder, pres Marion Fed Cr Union; bd governors Tampa C of C; trustee Miles Coll Birmingham; Paine Coll Augusta; pres elect Nat Ins Assn; life mem NAACP; Paine Coll Nat Alumni Assn; pres Business & Professional Mens Club; Frontiers Am Kappa Alpha Psi; mem Christian ME Ch. **HONORS/ACHIEVEMENTS:** Who's Who Am Educ 1942; honored educ pioneering FL State Teaches Assn 1958; received citation Ocala Conrtibutions Civil & Human Relations 1958; outstanding acheivement voter registration FL Voters League 1963; outstanding service alumni assn & devotion ideals Paine College 1970; numerous other awards. **BUSINESS ADDRESS:** 1400 N Boulevard, Tampa, FL 33606.

DAVIS, EDWARD L.
Educator. **PERSONAL:** Born Dec 06, 1943, Union Bridge, MD; married Carol Johnson Davis; children: Tanya Lynn. **EDUCATION:** Morgan State Univ, BS 1965; OH Univ, MS 1967; Johns Hopkins Univ, MS 1973; NC State Univ, PhD 1977. **CAREER:** Morgan State Univ Math Dept, instr 1970-73; Univ of Cincinnati Coll of Business, asst prof 1976-80; Atlanta Univ Graduate School of Business, assoc prof 1980-83, chmn decision science dept 1983-. **ORGANIZATIONS:** Mem Operations Rsch Soc of Amer 1974-; mem Transport Rsch Bd 1980-; mem Alpha Phi Alpha Frat 1961-; task force mem Atlanta C of C 1982-; Operations Rsch Soc of Amer 1973-; Amer Inst for Decision Sci 1980-; Transp Rsch Bd 1980-. **HONORS/ACHIEVEMENTS:** MD Senatorial Fellowship 1961-65; Balt Colt Found Scholarship 1961-65; So Fellowship Found 1973-76; Volunteer of the Year City of Raleigh 1974; Eval of Engergy Conging Plans Urban Mass Transp Admin 1980; Decision Making of Bds of Dirs Urban Mass Transp Admin 1982; Joint Devel Analysis Dept of Transp 1983. **MILITARY SERVICE:** AUS 1st Lt 1967-69. **HOME ADDRESS:** 1424 Niskey Lake Tr, Atlanta, GA 30331. **BUSINESS ADDRESS:** Chmn Decision Sci Dept, Atlanta University, 223 Chestnut Street, SW, Atlanta, GA 30314.

DAVIS, ELAINE CARSLEY
Educator. **PERSONAL:** Born Apr 15, 1921, Baltimore, MD; daughter of Stanley Carsley (deceased) and Corinne Baker Carsley (deceased); married R Clarke Davis (deceased); children: R Clarke Jr, Lisa. **EDUCATION:** Coppin State Coll, BS 1942; Morgan State Coll, BS 1943; Univ of MD, LLB 1950; Johns Hopkins Univ, MEd 1955, PhD 1958 Phi Beta Kappa. **CAREER:** Baltimore City Public Schs, 1942-74; Morgan State Coll, instr 1959-73; Baltimore Jr Coll, instr 1963-68; Loyola Coll, instr 1963-66; Johns Hopkins Univ, instr 1964-, assoc prof dir of educ 1974-86. **ORGANIZATIONS:** Mem chmn bd of trustees of MD State Coll 1967-73; bd trustees Goucher Coll 1972-75; natl vice pres Pi Lambda Theta 1973-78; Delta Sigma Theta; bd trustees Morgan State Coll 1965-67; mem bd dir of the Rouse Co 1978-. **HONORS/ACHIEVEMENTS:** Elected to Law Review Staff Univ of MD 1948; Fellowships from Amer Assn of Univ Women 1957, John Hay Whitney 1957, George Peabody 1956-57; citations from Iota Phi Lambda 1972; Urban League 1947; Delta Sigma Theta; United Negro Coll Fund 1970; Distinguished Alumni of the Yr Natl Assn for Equal Opportunity Higher Educ 1982; Alumni Awd Coppin State Coll 1965.

DAVIS, ELBERTA COLEMAN
Librarian. **PERSONAL:** Born Mar 21, 1946, New Orleans, LA; daughter of Joseph Coleman and Elberta Plummer; children: Sean, Mark. **EDUCATION:** Memphis State Univ, BS Educ 1972; George Peabody Coll of Vanderbilt Univ, MLS 1975. **CAREER:** Memphis City Schools, librarian 1972-85; State Dept of Educ, evaluator 1985-88; Memphis City Schools, librarian 1988-. **ORGANIZATIONS:** National Education Assn; Alpha Kappa Alpha Sor Inc; Holy Rosary CC Outreach Program; St Peter Auxillary Exec Bd. **HOME ADDRESS:** 5859 Ridge Hill Dr, Memphis, TN 38115.

DAVIS, ELMER L., SR.
Educator. **PERSONAL:** Born Oct 31, 1926, Tulsa, OK; married Eddie Mae Hill. **EDUCATION:** Langston U, BA; Univ OK, MMe. **CAREER:** Separate School Music Bristow & Anadarko, supt 1950-57; Tulas Public Schools, teacher 1957-70; Vocal Music Tulsa Public Schools, supt. **ORGANIZATIONS:** Organizer founder conductor The Chorus of Angels; published composered G Shirmer Inc; Carl Fisher Inc; NY Assoc Minister of Music Paradise Bapt Ch; various offices coms numerous org. **HONORS/ACHIEVEMENTS:** Numerous appearances as conductor lecturer.

DAVIS, ERELLON BEN
Retired professional athlete. **PERSONAL:** Born Feb 19, 1912, Pensacola, FL; son of Ellis Davis and Bell Coker-Davis; married Ruby Nell Day-Davis, Apr 19, 1952. **EDUCATION:** Attended college 1935. **CAREER:** Golf instructor 54 years; Rackham Golf Course MI, head professional golfer. **ORGANIZATIONS:** Cotillian Club. **HONORS/ACHIEVEMENTS:** First black pro to play on governor's team, 1974; PGA MI Sectional Sr Champ, 1974; first black Golf Exec Sectional Officer, 1973; first black Head Golf Pro at a municipal course in US, 1968; five hole in ones; course record holder score of 59; course par 70; course rating by USGA 715; scholarship fund in his name, Oakland Univ, 1978; testimonial resolution, Common Council, 1986; proclamation, given by Detroit mayor Coleman Young, 1986; inductee, Black Hall of Fame, 1988. **HOME ADDRESS:** 1601 Robert Bradby Dr, Apt 413, Detroit, MI 48207.

DAVIS, ESTHER GREGG
Educational administrator. **PERSONAL:** Born Oct 16, 1934, Chicago, IL; married Fred A Cooper. **EDUCATION:** Hofstra U, BS 1966; Northwestern U, MA 1972; Northwestern U, PhD 1974. **CAREER:** VA Tech, visiting prof Educ 1979-; VA Commonwealth Univ, asst prof Educ 1976-; Blue Cross Assn, dir assessment centers 1974-75; Chicago Bd of Educ, teacher 1970-71; NY Bd of Educ, teacher 1966-67; Richmond Public Schools, ESEA Title I Project, consultant 1976-; Danforth Found, consultant 1976-77; Mgmt Center VA Commonwealth Univ, cons 1977-. **ORGANIZATIONS:** Mem Phi Delta Kappa 1973-; mem Am Mgmt Assn 1979; mem Mat Alliance of Black Sch Educators 1979. **HONORS/ACHIEVEMENTS:** "Intern Perception of Supervisory Support" ERIC 1974; "Classroom Mgmt" Kappa Delta Pi Record 1980-81; "Living Patterns of Urban Sch Adminstrs"; "Lewin's Force Field Theory a model for decision making". **BUSINESS ADDRESS:** VA Commonwealth Univ, Richmond, VA.

DAVIS, ETHELDRA S.
Educator. **PERSONAL:** Born May 11, 1931, Marianne, AR; children: Andrea. **EDUCATION:** Los Angeles City Coll, AA 1951; Los Angeles State Coll, BA 1954; Univ of AK, MA 1964. **CAREER:** Los Angeles Schools, teacher 1953-58; Anchorage Schools, teacher 1958-63, admin intern 1963-65, asst prin 1966, resource librarian; Project Head Start, dir 1966; HEW Region 10, field reader 1967-70; Western Region, OEO consultant 1967-70; Anchorage Borough School Youth, prin, presently; NAACP Anchorage Chapter, adv; TAJ Enterprises, owner. **ORGANIZATIONS:** AKA; NEA; ABEA; NAESP; APE; precinct chmn Dem 1959-61; pres Pan-Hellanic Coun of Clubs Anchorage 1960; dir Child Devel Cntr Anchorage Community Action Agy; tchr arts & crafts YMCA; Boothe Memorial Home for unwed Mothers; consult Volt & Co; mem Mayor's Adv Bd 1968; mem Parks & Recreation Bd; mem CampFire bd dir; founder of United League of Girls. **HONORS/ACHIEVEMENTS:** Woman of yr Northern Lights Club 1969; most outstanding in Educ 1970; Certificate of Merit Anchorage Post Ofc 1969; Honorable Award NAACP for being 1st black principal in Anchorage Sch. **BUSINESS ADDRESS:** Kennedy School, Pouch 300, Fort Richardson, AK.

DAVIS, EVELYN K.
Executive director. **PERSONAL:** Born Apr 20, 1921, Kansas City, KS; daughter of Louis Scott and Nettie Scott; widowed; children: Donna Jean Lewis-Moore, Robert Lee Lewis, Lawrence M III, Edward, James, Sherrie, Lester, Eddie Collien. **EDUCATION:** Area Comm Coll Ames IA, General Educ Certificate 1969; Drake Univ, Cert for Managerial 1969; Iowa State Univ, Cert for Family Environ Course 1969. **CAREER:** Helped organize Polk County Comm Action Cncl 1965; helped organize Urban Neighborhood Cncl 1970; helped organize Soul Village Learning Ctr 1970; organized initiate the Child Care Barrier Plng Cncl 1976; organized the Black Women's Polit Caucus 1977; organized the Ethnic Minority Women's Cncl 1978; Tiny Tot Child Care Inc, founder/dir 1966-. **ORGANIZATIONS:** Exec bd mem NAACP 1960-; bd mem Iowa Cncl for Children 1976-81; mem Red Cross Exec Comm; director's bd Right to Life Comm; mem Inner Urban Health Ctr Bd; chmn Gateway Oppor Bd; mem State Day Care Adv Bd; state chmn DCCDCA; mem NAEYC, DOVIA; mem Des Moines Child Care Cncl, Polk Co Health Serv Bd. **HONORS/ACHIEVEMENTS:** Dedi-

cation Letter from Pres Nixon 1970; Evelyn Davis Health Clinic; George Washington Carver Meritorious Awd Simpson Coll 1979; YWCA Achievement Awd 1983; Iowa Women's Hall of Fame 1983; Black Merit Acad Awd IN Univ; First Eleonor Robinson Awd Cncl of Intl Understanding 1986. **BUSINESS ADDRESS:** Executive Dir, Tiny Tot Child Care Inc, 1409 Clark St, Des Moines, IA 50314.

DAVIS, FRANCE ALBERT
Clergyman, educator. **PERSONAL:** Born Dec 05, 1946, Gough, GA; son of John Davis and Julia Davis; married Willene Witt; children: Carolyn Marie, Grace Elaine, France II. **EDUCATION:** Laney Coll, AA Arts and Humanities 1971; Merritt Coll, AA Afro-American Studies 1972; Univ of CA, BA Rhetoric 1972; Westminster Coll, BS Religion & Philosophy 1977; Univ of UT, MA Mass Comm 1978. **CAREER:** USAF, aircraft mechanic 1966-70; Univ of UT, instr 1972-76; Calvary Baptist Church, pastor 1973-. **ORGANIZATIONS:** Bd chmn UT Bd of Corr 1982-, bd mem 1975-; bd chmn UT Opportunities Industrialization Cntr 1974-; exec bd DIC/A; 1982 chmn Tribune Common Carrier Editorial Bd 1982; mem Albert Henry Educational Found 1976-; bd mem NAACP Salt Lake Branch 1975-77, 1985-; chmn Martin Luther King Jr Holiday Comm for Utah 1985-86; chmn Mignon Richmond Park Comm 1985-86. **HONORS/ACHIEVEMENTS:** Pres award Salt Lake NAACP 1975; serv award Beehive Elks 1975; torch bearer OIC/A 1979; OIC Torchbearer Awd 1979; civil rights worker Salt Lake NAACP 1984; Black Scholars Outstanding Image Maker 1986. **MILITARY SERVICE:** USAF staff sgt commendation award, Vietnam service award 1966-70. **BUSINESS ADDRESS:** Pastor, Calvary Baptist Church, 532 E 700 S, Salt Lake City, UT 84102.

DAVIS, FRANCIS D.
Dentist, educator. **PERSONAL:** Born Sep 01, 1923, Macon, GA; son of Dr Wanzie A Davis and Carro Appling-Davis; married Hattimarie; children: Robin, Francis. **EDUCATION:** Morehouse Coll, BS 1947; Howard U, DDS 1951. **CAREER:** Fairleigh Dickinson Univ Dental Sch, prof chmn dept oral diagnosis; Martland Hosp, oral surgeon; McQuire AFB, chief oral surgeon 1970; McQuire AFB, dir dental asst prgm 1970; Treatment Planning Preventive Dental Radiology, chmn & dept oral diagnosis. **ORGANIZATIONS:** Dir Minority Recruitment Prgm Consult NIH Black Health Providers Task Force 1977; pres Commonwealth Dental Soc 1977-79; bd trustee Nat Dental Assn 1974- 77; mem NDA Liaison Com Am Dental Assn 1974-77; mem bd trustees United Hospitals Med Center of Newark; mem Nat Dental Hon Soc OKU; mem Univ High Blood Pressure Detection Prog 1971-; mem Boul Frat. **HONORS/ACHIEVEMENTS:** Recpt Pres Award Nat Dental Assn 1975; USAF Commendation Medal 1965; Oak Leaf Cluster 1968; 2nd Oak Leaf Cluster; Pres Award Outstanding Serv Nat Dental Assn 1977; fellowship Am Coll Dentists. **MILITARY SERVICE:** USAF col (ret) 1953-73. **HOME ADDRESS:** 2 Woodhill Dr, Maplewood, NJ 07040.

DAVIS, FRANK
Law enforcement. **PERSONAL:** Born Mar 22, 1947, Claiborne Cty, MS; children: Tracy, Gary. **EDUCATION:** Alcorn State Univ, BS Physical Ed 1972; Southern Univ, Criminal Justice 1973. **CAREER:** US Army, 1966-68; Port Gibson MS, dep sheriff 1968-78; Claiborne Cty, civil defense dir 1978-79; Port Gibson Police Dept, asst chief of police 1978-79, sheriff 1980-. **ORGANIZATIONS:** Treas New Zion Lodge 1976; hon mem FBLA 1980; mem Kiwanis Club 1980; professional mem Amer Correctional Assoc 1983; mem, Mississippi Sheriff's Assn. **HONORS/ACHIEVEMENTS:** Civil Defense Council MS Civil Defense 1978; Cert of Merit Aide-de-Camp 1979; Outstanding Young Men of Amer OYM 1980; vice pres, Mississippi Sheriff's Assn 1988. **MILITARY SERVICE:** AUS E-6 1966-68. **BUSINESS ADDRESS:** Sheriff, Claiborne County, PO Box 427, Port Gibson, MS 39150.

DAVIS, FRANK ALLEN
Industrial sales engineer. **PERSONAL:** Born Nov 17, 1960, Washington, DC; married Elena L. **EDUCATION:** Bucknell Univ, BSEE 1982; Georgia State Univ, attending. **CAREER:** Westinghouse Control Div, div sales engr 1982-85; Westinghouse Industries Marketing, asst sales engr 1985-86, personnel consultant 1985-, industrial salesengr 1987-. **ORGANIZATIONS:** Mem Alpha Phi Omega 1984-, Natl Black MBA Assoc 1986-, Amer Mktg Assoc 1987-, Open Pit Mining Assoc 1987-. **HONORS/ACHIEVEMENTS:** William Randolph Hearst United State Senate Youth Scholar; winner Susan Thomas Hensinger prize; Hon Alpha Mu Alpha Natl Mktg. **HOME ADDRESS:** 6153 Brynwood Dr #7, Rockford, IL 61111. **BUSINESS ADDRESS:** Industrial Sales Engineer, Westinghouse Electric Corp, 90 Bagby Dr, Birmingham, AL 35259.

DAVIS, FRANK DEROCHER
Personnel consultant. **PERSONAL:** Born Jun 21, 1934, Quitman, GA; married Dr Carolyn Brown; children: Farita Denise, Alexria Siglinda, Frank Jr. **EDUCATION:** Tuskegee Inst, BS 1956; Florida A&M Univ, grad studies 1967. **CAREER:** W R Grace Chemical Co, human relations specialist 1968-71; General Electric Co, minority relations mgr 1971-74; Derocher Assocs Ltd, pres 1974-. **ORGANIZATIONS:** Bd of dirs Bridgeport Regional Narcotics 1976-81, Messiah Baptist Church 1976-86, Bridgeport Public Library 1982-86, Urban Action Grp Bridgeport 1984-86; vice pres The Minority Network 1983-86. **MILITARY SERVICE:** AUS lt col retired 22 yrs; Army Commendation Medal 1968, Meritorious Serv Medal 1984. **HOME ADDRESS:** 2013 Alabaster Dr, Silver Spring, MD 20904. **BUSINESS ADDRESS:** President, Derocher Assocs Ltd, PO Box 3714, Silver Spring, MD 20901.

DAVIS, FRED
Clergyman. **PERSONAL:** Born Oct 04, 1934, Chatham, VA; married Juanita; children: Michael, Karen, Donna, Phillip. **EDUCATION:** Rutgers Univ, BA 1967-72; Manhattan Bible Inst, Cert in Divinity 1972-74. **CAREER:** NAACP Urban League, life mem; Tri-County United Way, exec bd; PA State AFL-CIO Central Labor Council, exec bd; Harrisburg United Negro Coll Fund, exec comm; Shiloh Baptist Church, pastor; Amer Fed of State Cty & Municipal Employees, dir. **ORGANIZATIONS:** Staff rep Textile Workers of Amer 1971-72; dir AFSCME Dist Council 90 1974-. **HONORS/ACHIEVEMENTS:** Personnel dir NJ Health Ctr 1965-70; Rutgers Labor Ctr Spec Program 1963-64; Chosen 1 of 100 most influential young men in NJ to participate in comm actionprog at Rutgers Univ 1400 hours of spec ed & OJT 1963. **HOME ADDRESS:** #3 Crestview Drive, Willingboro, NJ 08046.

DAVIS, FREDERICK D.
Association executive. **PERSONAL:** Born Aug 06, 1935, Tulsa, OK; married Patricia; children: Grant Anthony, Frederick Douglass II, Mwindaace N Gai. **EDUCATION:** OK U. **ORGANIZATIONS:** Pres Tulsa Br NAACP; McDonnell Douglas Aircraft Corp 1956-; pres dir Tulsa Area United Way Bd of Dir; pub rel dir OK Prince Hall Free & Accepted Masons; UAW Constl & Cnvntn Deleg 1975-; past chm bd of trustees delegate dir of fair pracs UAW Local 1093; mem Paradise Bapt Ch 39 yrs; mem Coal Creek 88 Masonic Lodge; past pres vice pres Tulsa Econ Oppor Task Force; pres Tulsa Comm Recreation Cncl 1972-74; chm EOP Com McDonnell Douglas 1974-75; Police Comm Relations. **HONORS/ACHIEVEMENTS:** 1st Black Minority Developer (Major) in the St of OK.

DAVIS, GENE A.
Business executive. **PERSONAL:** Born Jun 29, 1939, Philadelphia, PA; married Jonna Bjorkefall; children: Peter, Philip. **EDUCATION:** Philadelphia Mus Sch of Art, adv design/undergrad 1958-60; New York City Coll, advertising copy 1964-65. **CAREER:** CBS Columbia Records, adv prod mgr 1966-68; Westinghouse Group W, mgr 1968-72; WNEW Radio NY, creative dir 1972-74; STOP TV Washington, mgr 1974-76; WMAQTV, mgr 1976-79; Corinthian Broadcasting Corp, vice pres/adv & Pub rel 1979-81; Essence Comm Inc, dir corp crea serv 1983-. **ORGANIZATIONS:** Mem Intl Radio/TV Soc 1978-; treas/sec Broadcasters Promotion Assn Inc 1978-79; BPA Awds (promo); MI State Awds 1974-77; Addy Awds Am Advertising Fed 1977-79. **HONORS/ACHIEVEMENTS:** TV Advt, US TV Commercial Awd 1978; Cable Marketing Awd 1981. **BUSINESS ADDRESS:** Director, Corp Creat Serv, Essence Comm Inc, 1500 Broadway, New York, NY 10036.

DAVIS, GEORGE B.
Educator, author. **PERSONAL:** Born Nov 29, 1939, Shepherdstown, WV; married Mary Cornelius, Aug 31, 1963; children: Pamela, George. **EDUCATION:** Colgate Univ, BA, 1961; Columbia Univ, MFA, 1971. **CAREER:** Washington Post, Washington, DC, staff writer, 1968-69; New York Times, New York, NY, deskman, 1969-70; Bronx Community Coll of the City Univ of New York, Bronx, NY, asst prof, 1974-78; Rutgers Univ, New Brunswick, NJ, asst prof, 1978-; freelance writer for various publications; Columbia Univ and Greenhaven Prison, teacher of writing workshops; Black Swan Communications (design and marketing firm for books, art objects, and creative leisure products), co-founder and pres. **ORGANIZATIONS:** Mem, Author's Guild; Grant New York Council on Arts; Natl Endowment for the Humanities; mem, Authors League of Amer. **HONORS/ACHIEVEMENTS:** Author of Coming Home, Random House, 1971, Love, Black Love, Doubleday, 1978, and (with Glegg Watson) Black Life in Corporate America: Swimming in the Mainstream, Doubleday, 1982; awards from New York State Council on the Arts, Amer the Beautiful Fund, and NEH. **MILITARY SERVICE:** US Air Force, 1961-68, became captain; received Air Medal. **BUSINESS ADDRESS:** Rutgers University, New Brunswick, NJ 08903. *

DAVIS, GLENDELL KIRK
Banking & finance officer. **PERSONAL:** Born in DeRidder, LA; daughter of Claudell Kirk and Ernestine, Simmons, Kirk; married Malcolm, Aug 30, 1969; children: Monica Katrese. **EDUCATION:** Univ of Hartford, MBA 1981; Rensselaer Polytechnic Inst, MS 1974; Southern Univ, BS (Magna Cum Laude) 1964. **CAREER:** Natl Science Foundation, teaching asst 1964; Southern Univ, Math prof 1964-65; General Electric Co, scientific programmer 1965-69; Travelers Insurance Co, dir 1969-. **ORGANIZATIONS:** Consultant Assoc for the Integration of Mgmt 1975, Natl Youth Motivation Task Force Alliance of Business 1978; v pres New England Telecomm Soc 1980; pres Travelers Toastmistress Club 1973-74; bd of dir, vice pres CT Opera Assoc; adivsory bd Economics & Business Dept St Josephs Coll 1984; mem Young Executives, NAACP, Alpha Kappa Alpha Sorority; vice pres & asst treasurer, CT Opera Assn. **HONORS/ACHIEVEMENTS:** Nom Woodrow Wilson Fellow 1964; hon soc Pi Mu Epsilon; hon soc Alpha Kappa Mu; Achievers Award 1980; IMPACT Award for Outstanding Performance in the Workplace 1985. **BUSINESS ADDRESS:** Dir, Travelers Insurance Company, One Tower Square IMN, Hartford, CT 06183.

DAVIS, GLORIA-JEANNE
Univ. affirmative action officer. **PERSONAL:** Born Feb 06, 1945, Gary, IN; married Wilbert Douglas Davis; children: Wilbert Douglas II, Rixie Hardin. **EDUCATION:** Eastern KY Univ, BBA 1970, MBA 1971; IL State Univ, PhD 1986. **CAREER:** Caterpillar Tractor Co, analyst/machine shop training 1974-78; Bloomington City Hall, financial advisor 1978-84; IL Central Coll, instructor/business dept 1986-; IL State Univ, univ affirmative action officer 1984-. **ORGANIZATIONS:** Mem Chancellor's Task Force IL State Univ 1985-86; mem Minority Coord Council IL State Univ 1985-; grad advisor Alpha Kappa Alpha Sor Inc 1986-. **HONORS/ACHIEVEMENTS:** Phi Delta Kappa Honor Soc 1984; Fellow Educ Policy Fellowship Prog 1985-86. **BUSINESS ADDRESS:** Affirmative Action Officer, Illinois State University, Hovey Hall Room 415, Normal, IL 61761.

DAVIS, GRADY D., SR.
Educator, clergyman. **PERSONAL:** Born in Pleasant Hill, NC; married Dorothy Hicks Davis; children: 5 Children. **EDUCATION:** Shaw Univ Raleigh, AB; Andover-Newton Theologcl Shl, BD; Boston U, PhD. **CAREER:** Philsophy & Religion at Univ, asst prof; Shaw Divinity School, dean; Oberlin Baptist Church, ministerr; East CA Univ, teacher; Fayetteville State Univ, prof Psychology; Union Baptist Church Durham, minister. **ORGANIZATIONS:** Mem Amer Psychlgcl Assn; NC Psychlgcl Assn; NEA; NC Assn Edctrs; Amer AssnUniv Profs; The Acdmy of Relgn & Mntl Hlth; mem Gov's Com JuvnlDelnqncy & Yth Crime 1962; mem NC Parole Comm; Phi Beta Sigma; NAACP; Cumberlnd Cnty Mntl Hlth Assn; asso mem Danfrth Fndrn 1973. **HONORS/ACHIEVEMENTS:** Listed Who's Who in Amer U's & Colls 1942. **MILITARY SERVICE:** AUS. **BUSINESS ADDRESS:** State of NC Parole Comm, 831 W Morgan St, Raleigh, NC 27603.

DAVIS, HAROLD MATTHEW
Business executive. **PERSONAL:** Born Mar 02, 1946, New York, NY. **EDUCATION:** Bronx Comm Coll, AA 1967; Wesleyon Univ Middleton, CT, BA 1969; Yale Univ Schl of Med, MD 1974; NYU-BELLEVUE Med Ctr, Intern/Res 1977. **CAREER:** Mobile Oil Corp, assist clinic div 1978; ITT Corp, assist med dir 1978-86; Prudential Insurance Co of America, vice pres employee health serv 1987-. **ORGANIZATIONS:** Atndng physcn NYU Medcl Cntr 1977-; admn comm NYU Medcl Schl 1977-; AMA; AOMA; dir Sponsors for Educational Opportunity 1965-, Assoc for Intergration of Mgmnt 1979-. **HONORS/ACHIEVEMENTS:** Watson Flw Thomas J Watson Flwshp 1969; lctur NY Acdmy of Med 1982; Black Achievers Award 1984; Charles Drew Award 1984; bd mem Campbell Inst of

Hlth and Fitness 1986-. **BUSINESS ADDRESS:** VP Emloyee Health Services, Prudential Insurance Co, 213 Washington St, Newark, NJ 07101.

DAVIS, HAROLD R.
Business executive. **PERSONAL:** Born Mar 25, 1926, High Point, NC; married Mauva Lane; children: Stpehen, Craig, Brenda, Peggy J Slaughter. **EDUCATION:** US Schl of Admnstrn, CLU, Amer Coll of Life Underwriters 1970; FLMI, Life Office Mgmnt Courses 1976. **CAREER:** NC Mutual Life Ins Co, vice pres field operations 1978-84, regnl agency dir 1973-77, asst agency dir 1969-72; dist mgr 1966-69. **ORGANIZATIONS:** Brd of dir Life Ins Mktg & Resch Assn 1982-84; vice pres Natl Ins Ass 1973-; mem Amer Soc of CLU 1970-; brd of dir Durham YMCA 1979-83. **MILITARY SERVICE:** USNA pfc 1945-46. **BUSINESS ADDRESS:** Vice Pres Marketing Services, N C Mutual Life Ins Co, Mutual Plaza, Durham, NC 27701.

DAVIS, HENRY E., JR.
Chief executive officer of business equipment dealership. **CAREER:** Highbeam Business Systems, Inc, East Orange, NJ, chief executive officer. **HONORS/ACHIEVEMENTS:** Davis's company achieved more than $6 million in sales in 1987. **BUSINESS ADDRESS:** Highbeam Business Systems Inc, 280 S Harrison, East Orange, NJ 07018. *

DAVIS, HERMAN E.
Business executive. **PERSONAL:** Born Mar 03, 1935, Carlton, AL; married Thelma; children: Millicent, Chiaka, Jennifer, Holly. **EDUCATION:** BEd 1962. **CAREER:** New Direction Budgeting & Financial Serv Cntr Inc, pres; Assn of Distributive Educ Coords, pres 1966; Dusable HS Chicago , tchr 1962-; Waddell & Reed Inc, rep 1964-. **ORGANIZATIONS:** Pres Bryn Mawr & West Area Council; bd mem South Shore Commn; chrmn Finance Com South Shore Commn; Keeper of Records & Seal, Sigma Omega Chap Omega Psi Phi. **HONORS/ACHIEVEMENTS:** Award of merit US Small Bus Adm & Cosmopolitan C of C 1968; sales champion award Waddell & Reed, Inc 1968; certificate of excellence Cosmopolitan C of C 1969-70. **MILITARY SERVICE:** AUS security agency sp2 1954-57. **BUSINESS ADDRESS:** 2051 E 75 St, Chicago, IL 60649.

DAVIS, HIRAM L.
Librarian. **PERSONAL:** Born Apr 10, 1943, St Joseph, MO; married Melind. **EDUCATION:** Valley CollMO, BS 1966; KS State Tchrs Coll, MLS 1969; Univ Mich, PhD Candidate 1972. **CAREER:** KC Pub Lib, ref lbrn 1967; Univ Kansas Lawrence, libr 1967-68; Muskingum Coll New Concord OH, head ref libr 1968-69; Kalamazoo & Valley Cmmnty Coll,dir lib serv 1969-70; Northwestern Univ Evanston IL, dir CIC lib sci doctoral prgm 1972-73; Univ Libs Univ OK, asso dir 1973 -. **ORGANIZATIONS:** Mem Am Lib Assn 1967; Am Soc for Information Sci 1972; Assn Coll & Research Libs 1970; Black Caucus AL 1973; OK Lib Assn 1973; ERIC/CEC Speaker Annual Conv 1968; mem Lib Dev Com OK Lib Assn 1974. **HONORS/ACHIEVEMENTS:** Awards Sigma Tau Delta 1966; Beta Phi Mu 1972; US Office Educ doctoral fellow 1970-72. **BUSINESS ADDRESS:** Univ OK, 401 W Brooks Rm 140, Norman, OK 73069.

DAVIS, HOWARD C.
Dental surgeon. **PERSONAL:** Born May 10, 1928, Washington, DC; married Lorethea; children: Lori, Howard, Jr. **EDUCATION:** Howard Univ, undergrad; Howard Univ Coll of Dentistry, DDS 1961. **CAREER:** Coll of Dentistry Howard Univ, instr Dept Oral Surgery 1961-62; Coll of Dentistry Howard Univ, asst prof Dept Oral Radiology 1962-65; self-employed, gen dental practice 1965-; Independence Fed Savings & Loan Assn Washington, vice pres. **HONORS/ACHIEVEMENTS:** Luther Halsey Gulick Award. **MILITARY SERVICE:** AUS sgt 1946-48; USAFR 2nd lt 1950-58. **BUSINESS ADDRESS:** 5505 5th St NW, Suite 200, Washington, DC 20011.

DAVIS, J. MASON, JR.
Attorney. **PERSONAL:** Born Jul 30, 1935, Birmingham, AL; son of J Mason Davis and Madeline Harris Davis; married June Carolyn Fox; children: Karen M, J Mason III. **EDUCATION:** Talladega Coll, AB 1956; State Univ of NY Law School, JD 1959. **CAREER:** Univ of AL, School of Law, adjunct prof of insurance and damages 1972-; Sirote and Permutt PC, attorney 1960-, sr partner; Protetive Industrial Insurance Co of AL Inc, chmn of the bd of dir, 1988-. **ORGANIZATIONS:** General counsel Natl Ins Assn 1962-77; exec comm mem AL Democratic Party 1970-; exec comm Birmingham Bar Assn 1974-77; sec Birmingham Bar Assn 1978-79; pres Natl Insurance Assn 1978-79; sec AL Democratic Party 1978-; chmn bd of dir Natl Ins Assn 1979-81; mem Alpha Phi Alpha Fraternity, Masons, Elks, NAACP, Sigma Pi Phi, Omicron Delta Kappa; chmn bd of trustees Talladega Coll 1981-88; pres Birmingham Bar Assoc 1985-86; vice chmn Birmingham Airport Authority. **HONORS/ACHIEVEMENTS:** Pres Citation Frontiers of Amer 1962; Man of the Yr Alpha Phi Alpha Fraternity 1973; Outstanding Serv Comm Serv Council 1973; Outdoor Recreation Achievement Award US Dept of Commerce 1975; AL Recreation Parks Soc Lay Award 1975; Outstanding Serv Univ of AL School of Law 1977; Exemplary Dedication to Higher Educ AL Assoc of Colls & Univs 1982. **BUSINESS ADDRESS:** Attorney, Sirote and Pe mutt, 2222 Arlington Ave, S, PO Box 55727, Birmingham, AL 35255.

DAVIS, JAMES
Banker. **CAREER:** State Mutual Federal Savings & Loan Assn, Jackson, MS, chief executive officer. **BUSINESS ADDRESS:** State Mutual Federal Savings & Loan Assn, 1072 Lynch, Jackson, MS 39203. *

DAVIS, JAMES A.
Business executive. **PERSONAL:** Born Nov 08, 1924, Philadelphia, PA; married Lorraine J; children: Michael, Keith. **EDUCATION:** Drexel U, BMech 1965; Howard U, Architecture 1953. **CAREER:** General Electric Co Urban Systems Program, program mgr; Philco-Ford Inc, project engr; Am Electronics Labs, sr engr; JaLords Inc, president; Sarah Potter Smith Com Devel Corp, consulting & mechanical & elec engr dir; licensed professional engr in Pennsylvania, Maryland, New York, New Jersey, Massachusetts, Delaware, Washington DC.. **ORGANIZATIONS:** Mem IEEE; NSPG; ASHRAE; mem NAACP; on the beam club Concept Therapy. **HONORS/ACHIEVEMENTS:** Achievement award Past Nat Pres Citation; scientific award Tech Design Philco Ford Inc; Invention Disclosure Cryogenic Starter. **MILITARY SERVICE:** USAF reserve captain 1952-65. **BUSINESS ADDRESS:** 2020 Chestnut St, Philadelphia, PA.

DAVIS, JAMES F.
Educational administrator. **PERSONAL:** Born Jan 29, 1943, Marion, SC; married Beverly A Hemmingway; children: Shean Askia, Donald Affonso. **EDUCATION:** Johnson C Smith Univ, BA 1964; Pepperdine Univ, MBA 1977. **CAREER:** EF Hutton & Co Inc, super 1968-71; SC Natl Bank, asst vice pres 1971-78; Rice Coll, faculty mem 1978-79; Benedict Coll, vice pres student affair 1979-. **ORGANIZATIONS:** Mem Columbia Chamber of Commerce 1979; mem US Army Assn 1979; mem Natl Assoc Coll Deans Registrars & Admissions Officers 1984; trustee mem Benedict Coll Fed Credit Union 1979-; mem Amer Assoc College Registrars & Admissions Officers; SCASAA; NASFAA; NAPW. **HONORS/ACHIEVEMENTS:** Outstanding Volunteer Worker Bibleway Child Develop Ctr 1984. **MILITARY SERVICE:** AUS private 1st class 9 months. **BUSINESS ADDRESS:** Dir Admssn Rcrds & Fin Aid, Benedict College, Harden & Blanding Sts, Columbia, SC 29204.

DAVIS, JAMES H.
Pediatrician. **PERSONAL:** Born Feb 09, 1941, Monti County, TN; children: Sarita, Ashley Layne. **EDUCATION:** TN State Univ, BS 1963; Middle TN State Univ, MS 1969; Indiana Univ Sch of Medicine, MD 1980. **CAREER:** Riverside Hospital, pediatrician. **ORGANIZATIONS:** Instructor Upward Bound Terre Haute IN/IN State Univ 1974-80; clinical instructor George Washington Univ 1983; diplomate Amer Assoc Pediatrics 1986-; dir Apnea Prevention/Monitoring 1986-; assoc neonatologist Riverside Hosp 1986-; consultant neonatologist 1986-. **HONORS/ACHIEVEMENTS:** Mem Alpha Kappa Mu Natl Honor Soc Educ, Beta Kappa Chi Science Honor Soc; Diplomate Neonatal/Prenatal Imaging 1983. **MILITARY SERVICE:** USAF ROTC cadet major 1958-61. **HOME ADDRESS:** 5259 Glencrag Way, Toledo, OH 43615.

DAVIS, JAMES HAROLD
Clergyman, educator. **PERSONAL:** Born Nov 02, 1932, Tulsa, OK; married Shirley Jean Tucker; children: James H Jr, Jeryl, Kim, Phillip, Byron, Robert, Geri, William. **EDUCATION:** Lincoln Univ, BMus 1961; OK Univ, MSW 1974; Trinity Bible Univ, DD 1974; Central Amer Univ, DMin 1982. **CAREER:** Langston Univ, vocal pedagogue 1964-66; County Supt of Schools, admin aide 1966-67; Logan County OK, NYC, counselor/asst dir 1967-71; Langston Univ, instructor, political science 1974-75, asst dir dorm life 1975; New Hope Baptist Church, pastor 1975-83; Langston OK School Bd, vice pres 1986; Ward #1 Langston OK, city councilman 1987; Central Amer Univ, Mt Bethel Baptist Church, vice-chancellor/pastor; city councilman, 1987-. **ORGANIZATIONS:** mem, Central Amer Univ Coll Approval Team, 1980-; pres, Congress St Mark Dist Congress Christian Educ, 1984-; lecturer, Natl Baptist Congress Christian Educ, 1972; police chaplain, Wichita P.D., 1979-83; Mayor's Comm, Wichita, 1980-83; charter mem, Sedgwick County Jail Ministry 1981-83; pres, Lions Intl Club of Langston; OK Historical Soc; bd of dir, Assn for Central Oklahoma Govt. **HONORS/ACHIEVEMENTS:** Mem, Smithsonian Inst 1972. **MILITARY SERVICE:** AUS Field Sgt served 3 yrs; 3rd Army Badge; 3 Star Campaign; Marksman. **HOME ADDRESS:** 522 NE Kansas St, Langston, OK 73050. **BUSINESS ADDRESS:** Vice Chancellor & Pastor, Central Amer Univ, Mt Bethel Baptist, PO # 547, Langston, OK 73050.

DAVIS, JAMES HAROLD
Engineer. **PERSONAL:** Born Jun 19, 1939, Southport, NC; married Mercell Price; children: Rhonda Yvette, Harriette, Jimmy. **EDUCATION:** Durham Tech Inst, Cert Mechanical Draft 1966; Cape Fear Tech Inst, Personnel Supvsn 1967; Drafting & Design Technology 1968; Rec Admin 1970; Southeastern Comm Coll, Bus Law 1974-75; Seneland Real Estate Sch, ICS Civil Engr Professional Real Estate Course 1978-79. **CAREER:** Carolina Power & Light Co, engr tech; Pfizer Inc, chem plant opr 1975-76; Brown & Root Constr Co, field piping engr 1972-75; Intl Terminal Ops, Stevedore foreman 1970-72; Sterns-Roger Corp, opr tech 1967-70; Babcock & Wilcox Co, draftsman 1966-67; AUS Corps of Engrs Philadelphia Dist, dragtender 1961-66; Rosemont Knitting Mach Philadelphia PA, knitting mach opr fixer 1960-61; NC Licensed Real Estate, broker. **ORGANIZATIONS:** Mem NC Employment Sec Commn 1974-78; mayor Pro-Tem City of Southport 1975-77; adlerman City of Southport 1971-79; chmn Southport Rec Commn 1971-75; v chmn Brunswick Co Planning Commn 1974-79; commr Columbus-Brunswick Co Housing Authority 1980; Southport Br NAACP; NC Minority Rep Conf; Mt CarmelAME Ch Habib Temple No 159; mem Am Soc of Safety Engrs NC Chpt. **HONORS/ACHIEVEMENTS:** Recip Stearns-Roger Corp Safety Award 1968-69; Who's Who in NC Award 1973; Outstand Young Mem of Am Award 1973; United Way Bronze Plaque Award 1980. **MILITARY SERVICE:** AUS pvt e-1 1958.

DAVIS, JAMES KEET
Utility administrator. **PERSONAL:** Born Apr 28, 1940, Florence, SC; son of James K Davis and Carrie Barnes Davis; married Glenda Gaither; children: James Keet III, Jacquelynn K. **EDUCATION:** Claflin Coll, BS Phys Sci Educ 1962; GA Inst of Tech, MS Urban Planning 1975; GA State Univ Exec Mgmt Sem, 1978; SEE Public Utilities Mgmt Course, 1982; Emory Univ Advance Mgmt Prog, 1984. **CAREER:** Oconee HS, coach/sci teacher 1963-64; Josten's Jewelry Co, salesman 1964-73; GA Power Co, employed 1972, vice pres corp relations 1982-. **ORGANIZATIONS:** Chmn Foxhead Develop Corp, Natl Conf of Black Mayors, So Christian Leadership Conf, Amer Assoc of Blacks in Energy, GA Assoc of Black Elected Officials, NAACP; mem, founder GA Assoc of Black Elected Officials Corp Roundtable; bd mem Butler St YMCA; Mayor's Task Force on Public Ed, Leadership Atlanta, Leadership Georgia; bd mem GA Dept of Human Resources; bd of trustees Gammon Theol Sem; chmn UNCF Telethon Atlanta 1986-89; mem 100 Black Men of Atlanta; bd mem Renaissance Capital Corp; bd mem Southeastern Electric Exchange; comm mem Edison Electric Inst Minority Bus Devel. **HONORS/ACHIEVEMENTS:** Citizenship Awd Omega Chap Men's Club 1976; Young Man of the Year Awd & Citizenship Awd 1976; GABEO Corp Roundtable Corp Leadership Awd; Atlanta Bus League Awd; numerous other awards. **BUSINESS ADDRESS:** Vice President, Georgia Power Company, PO Box 4545, Atlanta, GA 30302.

DAVIS, JAMES PARKER
Commissioner. **PERSONAL:** Born Jul 21, 1921, Memphis, TN; married Maurita Burnett; children: JeParker, Daphne, Lezlie. **EDUCATION:** LeMoyne Coll, BS 1943; Washburn U, LLB 1948. **CAREER:** Wyandotte Co, co commr 1973-, asst pros atty 1951-73; KS House, rep 1959-73; Multi-State Compact, asst minority dir 1969-71. **ORGANIZATIONS:** Chmn bd Omega Psi Phi 1975-76; mem Multi-State Compact 1971-73; gen counsel Cross Line Homes Inc; Bryant Manor Housing Proj; Royal Gardens Hsg Proj; Victory Hills Hsg Proj; past pres Chelsea Pz Homes Democracy Inc; mem NAACP; KS Bar Assn; Am Bar Assn. **HONORS/ACHIEVEMENTS:** Cert of recog Nat Bar Assn KS Econ Oppr Found 1976;

Meritorious Govtl Ldrsp OIC 1975. **MILITARY SERVICE:** AUS 1943-46. **BUSINESS ADDRESS:** 1314 N 5th, Kansas City, KS 66101.

DAVIS, JAMES W.
Research administrator. **PERSONAL:** Born Apr 08, 1926, Lexington, VA; married Rosetta; children: James G, Benita J. **EDUCATION:** W VA State Coll, BS 1951; Nashville YMCA Law Sch, JD 1972. **CAREER:** Meharry Med Coll, rsch admin asst prof genetics & molecular med dir of Sickle cell center school of graduate studies & rsch; Vanderbilt Univ, rsch assoc & lab mgr 1963-73; Case Western Reserve Cleveland OH, rsch tech rsch asst rsch supvr 1954-63. **ORGANIZATIONS:** mem, soc rsch admin; sec citizens realty & devel co Inc; pres, Nashville Univ; Urban League; deacon, 1st Bapt Ch; mem bd dir WDCN-TV Nashville; pres Eta Beta Sigma Chap Phi Beta Sigma 1973; dir 3rd Dist Frontiers Intl; chmn bd mgrs Bordeaux YMCA, 1972-73. **HONORS/ACHIEVEMENTS:** Man of yr Eta Beta Sigma 1972; frontiersman of yr Nashville Frontier Club 1972; special recognition, Nashville YMCA 1971; honored by WVOL Radio 1966. **BUSINESS ADDRESS:** Meharry Med Center, 1005 18th Ave N, Nashville, TN 37208.

DAVIS, JEAN M.
Physical therapist. **PERSONAL:** Born Dec 17, 1932, Natchitoches, LA; married Hayward Jr; children: Raynard T. **EDUCATION:** Howard Univ, BS 1953; Howard Univ Grad School, Zoology 1953-55; Univ of PA School of Phys Therapy, Cert PT 1956. **CAREER:** Howard Univ Hosp Dept Phys Med & Rehab, staff phys therapist to suprv physical therapist 1956-. **ORGANIZATIONS:** Mem Amer Phys Therapy Assoc 1956-; lecturer Howard Univ Med School 1975-80; speaker Career Day Progs in HS. **HONORS/ACHIEVEMENTS:** Appeared Network Continuing Med Ed NY 1976, video tape series & on cover Med TV Guide 1976; Cited in article Howard Univ Hosp Publ "Women" 1977; speaker Div of Orthopaedics Annual Continuing Ed Prog. **BUSINESS ADDRESS:** Supervisor, Physical Therapy, HowardUniv Hosp, Phys Med & Rehab Dept, 2041 GA Ave NW, Washington, DC 20060.

DAVIS, JEROME
Business executive. **PERSONAL:** Born Apr 27, 1950, Eufaula, AL; married Iriam Acevedo; children: Kamille. **EDUCATION:** Yale Univ Law Schl, JD 1976; Oxford Univ England, MA 1973; Princeton Univ, 1971. **CAREER:** Chemical Bank, v pres/team Ldr 1982-, v pres/calling oper 1980-82. **ORGANIZATIONS:** Trustee Princeton Univ 1978-83; mbr, brd of dir NY Civil Liberties Univ 198-82. **HONORS/ACHIEVEMENTS:** Harlem YMCA Youth Achievers 1983; New Business Award 1982. **BUSINESS ADDRESS:** Vice President, Chemical Bank, 277 Park Ave, New York, NY 10172.

DAVIS, JERRY, JR.
Business executive. **PERSONAL:** Born Jan 02, 1925, Terry, LA; married Gloria Jean Cotton; children: Robert, Amelia, Jerry Ann Frazier. **EDUCATION:** Approx 3 yrs coll during Army ser. **CAREER:** Unified Services Inc, pres 1971-; career soldier 1945-70. **ORGANIZATIONS:** Mem CC; Nat Bus League. **HONORS/ACHIEVEMENTS:** Bronze Star; Legion of Merit. **MILITARY SERVICE:** AUS lt col 1945-70. **BUSINESS ADDRESS:** 1101 17 St NW, #608, Washington, DC.

DAVIS, JOHN ALBERT
Educator. **PERSONAL:** Born Jan 06, 1935, La Grange, GA; married Judith Gail; children: Greg, Deanna, Keith. **EDUCATION:** UCLA, BA 1963, MA 1968, PhD 1971. **CAREER:** Office of Minority Affairs, Univ of Southern CA, 1972; UCLA, asst prof 1968; UCLA Berkely, visiting prof 1971; Social Action Training Center, dir of rsch 1965. **ORGANIZATIONS:** Mbr of brd Los Angeles Childrens Bureau 1983-, Milton F Williams Fund 1980-; pres Crenshaw Neighbors 1981-83. **HONORS/ACHIEVEMENTS:** Mbr Alpha Sigma Nu Soc Sci Hon Soc 1970; LA Times "Understanding Black & Chicano Groups" 1978; jrnl of negro history 1984. **MILITARY SERVICE:** AUS e-5 1959-61. **BUSINESS ADDRESS:** Assistant Professor & Chair, Loyola MarymountUniv, 7101 W 80th St, Department of Afro Am Studies, Los Angeles, CA 90045.

DAVIS, JOHN ALEXANDER
Civil rights activist. **PERSONAL:** Born Jun 02, 1960, Bronx, NY. **EDUCATION:** Columbia Univ NY, BA 1982; Attended, Rutgers Law Sch Newark. **CAREER:** Century Pacific Investment Corp, law clerk 1985; Cohn & Lifland, law clerk 1985-86; Integrity Life Insurance, paralegal 1986; NAACP, natl youth dir 1986-. **ORGANIZATIONS:** Trustee bd of governors DeWitt Clinton Alumni Org 1978-; natl bd mem NAACP Natl Bd of Dirs 1980-86; alumni officer Columbia Univ 1982-87. **HONORS/ACHIEVEMENTS:** Who's Who Among High School Students 1977; Roy Wilkins Scholarship NAACP 1978; One of Fifty Future Black Leaders Ebony Magazine 1982; Best Legal Brief Frederick Douglass Moot Ct Competition BALSA 1985; Who's Who Among Law Students 1986. **BUSINESS ADDRESS:** Dir Youth & College Div, NAACP, 4805 Mt Hope Drive, Baltimore, MD 21215.

DAVIS, JOHN AUBREY
Educator. **PERSONAL:** Born May 10, 1912, Washington, DC; son of John A Davis Sr and Gabrielle Beale Davis; married Mavis E Wormley, Sep 05, 1935; children: Dr John A Davis Jr, Smith W Davis. **EDUCATION:** Williams Coll, AB 1933; Univ of WI, AM 1934; Columbia Univ, PhD 1949. **CAREER:** Howard Univ, lectr 1935-36; Lincoln Univ, asst prof & prof of polit sci 1936-53; OH State Univ, vis lectr 1950-51; Ford Foundation fellow, 1950-51; Center for Adv Study in Behavioral Sci, fellow, 1969-70; City Coll of NY, assoc prof of olit sci 1953-61; City Coll & Grad Faculty CUNY, prof of polit sci & chmn, 1961-80, emeritus, 1980—. **ORGANIZATIONS:** Mem Faculty Fellowship Bd United Negro Coll Fund 1959-61; chf US Delegation World Conf of Black Writers Paris 1951; founder, exec dir, 1957-62, pres, 1962-66, Amer Soc of African Culture; bd of Editors Pres Studies Quarterly 1970-; bd dir Libr of US Presidential Papers 1966-70; mem adv com Dept Polit Sci Princeton Univ 1966-71; mem Seminar on Africa, 1967-71; Cncl on Foreign Rel 1964—; founding mem Black Acad of Arts & Letters 1969-72; vice pres, 1971-72, mem cncl & exec com Amer Pol Sci Assn 1957-59 & 1973; mem Natl Conf of Black Polit Sci 1972-75; bd trustees Williams Coll Williamstown, MA 1972-77; mem Cncl on Foreign Relations 1964-; founder/1st admin The New Negro Alliance 1933; dir Lincoln Univ Conf on Status of the Negro in a Fighting Democracy 1942; asst dir NY State Comm Against Discrim in Employment (1st in nation) 1942; dir of non-legal rsch for NAACP for Brown vs Topeka 1953-54; consult Gov of NY on adminstrn of a proposed law against discrim in employmnt on account of age 1956-57; life mem NAACP; Phi Beta Kappa; mem Democratic (Galbraith) adv comm 1959-60. **HONORS/ACHIEVEMENTS:** Chevalier, Republique Federale du Cameroun, 1964; Commandeur de l'Ordre National, Republique de Senegal, 1966; Recipient Pres Medal for Disting Educ Serv to City Coll, 1972; Faculty Fellow of the Fund for The Advancement of Educ The Ford Found 1950-51; LLD, Lincoln Univ, 1983, William College, 1989; numerous publications & articles including, "Southern Africa in Transition" JA Davis & JK Baker Eds 1966; "The Influence of Africans on American Culture" The Annals of the American Acad of Polit and Soc Sciences 1964; "The Administration of Fair Employment Practices in the United States" Univ of WI Madison 1951; Review of J Harvie Wilkinson III "From Brown to Bakke" Oxford Univ Press 1979 in Political Science Quarterly 1980. **BUSINESS ADDRESS:** Prof/Chmn Emeritus, The City College of CUNY, 138th & Convent Ave, New York, NY 10031.

DAVIS, JOHN W., III
City official & financial administrator. **PERSONAL:** Born Oct 29, 1958, Cincinnati, OH. **EDUCATION:** Georgetown Univ, BS 1980; Dun & Bradstreet, Financial Analy 1981; ICMA City Mgmt School; Harvard Univ; Indiana Univ, 1986. **CAREER:** Georgetown Univ, assoc prof 1979-80; City of Cincinnati, contract accountant 1980-82; Queen City Metro, computer programmer 1982-85; SORTA, superintendent of capital; City of Silverton, chief financial officer 1982-87. **ORGANIZATIONS:** Mem Natl Assoc of Accountants 1982-87, Municipal Fin Office Assoc 1982-87, NAACP 1983-87; notary public State of OH 1984-87; bd of trustee OKI 1984-85; mem Natl Budget Review Bd, Natl Cash Mgmt Comm; bd of trustees Cincinnati Branch NAACP. **HONORS/ACHIEVEMENTS:** Bachelor of the Year Ebony Mag 1983; Leader of the Future Ebony Mag 1983; Outstanding Young Person Under 30 Cincinnati Enquirer 1983; Hon Recruiter US Army 1984; Disting Budget Awd 1986. **HOME ADDRESS:** 6616 Coleridge, Silverton, OH 45236. **BUSINESS ADDRESS:** Chief Financial Officer, City of Silverton, 6860 Plainfield, Silverton, OH 45236.

DAVIS, JOHN WESLEY, SR.
Clergyman. **PERSONAL:** Born Aug 10, 1934, Laurel, MS; son of Willie Davis and Mary Alice Wright Davis; married Virgis Louise Sumlin, Jul 04, 1958 (deceased); children: John W Jr, Maurice Benard. **EDUCATION:** Jackson State Univ, BME 1960; America Bible Coll, BPhB 1962-63, MPhB 1965, DD 1968. **CAREER:** Campbell Coll, teacher 1960; Mt Olive D Congress, pres 1968-80; The Greater Antioch MB Church, pastor. **ORGANIZATIONS:** Trustee MI Coll Inst West Point 1975-85; mem Natl NAACP 1981-; mem SCLC 1981-; mem adv bd Judge Baker 1982; mem bd of dirs Natl Baptist Convention USA; pres New Educ State Convention; pres Dist Congress; vice pres, New Educational State Congress; parliametarian, Shiloh District Assn; past mem adv bd Governor of MS Ceta Prog; vice pres Mt Olive Dist Congress Alumni Assn; mem Ministerial Biracial Alliance; mem adv bd MS Cooperative Extension Serv; mem, Interdenominatinal Ministerial Alliance; mem, Youth Court Advisory Bd; mem, advisory bd, Salvation Army Domestic Violence Shelter. **HONORS/ACHIEVEMENTS:** Scholarship Jackson S Univ 1956-60; recording artist known nationally & internationally. **HOME ADDRESS:** 3401 Westlane Dr, Gautier, MS 39553.

DAVIS, JOHN WESTLEY
Real estate development manager. **PERSONAL:** Born Aug 13, 1933, Birmingham, AL; son of Richard L Davis (Deacon) and Gertrude Davis-Walker; married Shirley A Davis (Perry), Jan 02, 1955; children: Cheryle, Paul, Michael, Glenn, Tracy (deceased). **EDUCATION:** Allied Technical Coll, Chicago IL, attended, 1954-56; Chicago Technical Coll/ITT, Chicago IL, attended, 1957-59; Univ of Illinois at Chicago, Chicago IL, attended, 1963-64; Chicago Real Estate Inst Chicago Community Coll, degree, 1970. **CAREER:** AT&T Teletype Corp, Chicago IL, tool & die maker/designer, 1953-64; Oscar C Brown Real Estate Corp, Chicago IL, vice pres, 1963-66; City of Chicago, Dept of Planning, Chicago IL, supvr of rehabilitation, 1967-72; Dept of Housing & Urban Devel, Washington DC, dir of property disp, 1972-78; Cook County, Chicago IL, deputy accessor, 1981-84; Chicago Transit Authority, Chicago IL, Strategic Planning/Real Estate Devel, mgr, 1984-. **ORGANIZATIONS:** Vice pres, Chatham Lions Club, 1963-75; commr, Boy Scouts of Amer, 1965-70; mem, Illinois Assoc of Realtors, 1967-70; dir, bd mem, Natl Housing & Urban Rehabilitation Assn, 1967-72; volunteer, Chicago Uran League, 1970-74; chmn, Stony Island Church of Christ, 1977-; coord, task force, First Congressional Dist Housing Task Force, 1979-82; mem, Illinois Assn of Professional Planners, 1984-88, Amer Public Transit Assn, 1984-88; bd mem, Conf of Minorities in Transit Officials, 1984-. **HONORS/ACHIEVEMENTS:** Winner of the Public High School Oratorical Contest, Birmingham Public High School, 1950; Employee of the Year, Teletex Corp (AT&T), 1960; Certificate of Appreciation, Boy Scouts of Amer, 1971; Special Honors Achievement, Dept of Housing & Devel, 1974; Honoree for Comm Award, Bud Billiken, 1972; two publications on Public/Private Joint Devel, 1986, 1987. **MILITARY SERVICE:** US Army Ranger/Airborne, 1st Lt, 1950-53, Honorable Discharge, 1953. **BUSINESS ADDRESS:** Manager of Real Estate & Development, Chicago Transit Authority, PO Box 3555, Merchandise Mart Bldg, Suite 405, Chicago, IL 60654.

DAVIS, JOHNETTA GARNER
Educator. **PERSONAL:** Born Nov 01, 1939, Warrenton, VA. **EDUCATION:** DC Tchrs Coll, BS 1961; George Washington U, MA 1969; Howard U, PhD 1976. **CAREER:** Howard Univ, assoc dean, grad prof 1978-, assoc prof, prof 1972-78; Amer Speech & Hearing Assn, asst sec for prog dev 1971-72; Univ of Dist of Columbia, instructor 1969-71; Washington DC Public Schools, speech pathologist 1961-68. **ORGANIZATIONS:** Mem Am Speech & Hearing Assn 1961-; task force on intl grad educ Counc of Grad Schs in US 1978-; mem Assn of Black Grad Deans 1978-; bd of dir Stoddard Bapt Home 1976-; sunday sch tchr Mt Sinai Bapt Ch 1976-. **HONORS/ACHIEVEMENTS:** Outstanding faculty citation Students atUniv of DC 1971; Frederick Douglass Honor Soc HowardUniv Chap 1974; Outstanding Yng Women in Am 1976; flwshp US Office of Educ 1968. **BUSINESS ADDRESS:** 2400 4th St NW, Washington, DC 20059.

DAVIS, JOHNNY TERRELL
Professional athlete. **PERSONAL:** Born Oct 21, 1955, Detroit, MI; married Lezli; children: Reginald, Austin. **EDUCATION:** Dayton, 1977. **CAREER:** Cleveland Cavaliers, guard 1984-; Portland Trail Blazers, guard 1976-; Atlanta Hawks, guard 1982-; indiana Pacers, guard 1978-. **ORGANIZATIONS:** 1975 US Intercontinental Cup Team; Amer Pan Amer Games team that won the Gold Meadal; worked last summer in the Public Affairs Dept of WTBS-TV. **HONORS/ACHIEVEMENTS:** Ranked amoung NBA'S top ten in free throw percentage; led team in scoring with a career high 1,444 points; started at guard on the Blazers NBA Championship team; played on NBA Championship Team.

DAVIS, JOSEPH
Educator. **PERSONAL:** Born Oct 24, 1942, McKeesport, PA. **EDUCATION:** BS 1964.

CAREER: Oakland Univ, div assoc dir of admissions & scholarships 1971-, asst dir of admissions 1970-71, admissions adv 1969-70; Univ of Cincinnati, asst registrar 1967-69; Hughes Adult Educ, instructor 1965-67; Hughes Jr High School, coach 1964-66; Hughes High School, instr 1964-67. **ORGANIZATIONS:** Mem Assn of Coll Registrars & Admissions Officers 1967-; mem MI Assn of Coll Registrars & Admissions Officers 1969; mem Am Personnel & Guidance Assn 1972-; mem Mich Personnel & Guid Assn 1972-; mem Oakland Area Counselors Assn 1973-; mem Selection Com Nat Achievement Scholarship Prog for Outstanding Negro Students 1971-73; mem Assn of Non-White Concerns 1973-; mem MI Assn of Minority Student Affairs 1971-73; mem NAACP 1973-; mem adv bd Raise Aspiration for Youth & Adults 1974-; mem MI Alternative Educ Orgn 1975-. **BUSINESS ADDRESS:** 202 Wilson Hall, Oakland Univ, Rochester, MI 48063.

DAVIS, JOSEPH M.
Clergyman. **PERSONAL:** Born Aug 17, 1937, Macon, GA. **EDUCATION:** UUniv of Dayton, BS 1960; Catholic Univ, MA 1962. **CAREER:** The Marianists, regional supervisor (Africa); Natl Office for Black Catholics, former exec dir; St James Elementary School, Dayton, principal 1969-70; Chaminade High School, Dayton, asst principal/dean of studies 1968-69; St Patrick's Coll, Asaba, Nigeria, principal 1965-67. **ORGANIZATIONS:** Chmn, English Dept, St Patrick's Coll, Asaba, Nigeria, 1962-64; chmn, Midwest Assn of Principals, Nigeria, 1967; mem exec comm, Natl Assn of Principals, Nigeria, 1967; vice pres, acting pres, Natl Black Catholic Clergy Caucus, 1968-71. **HONORS/ACHIEVEMENTS:** Recipient, 6th Annual Brothers Newsletter Award, 1971; Unity Award, Black Catholic Conv 1973; participant, Intl Colloquy on Racism, Vatican, Rome 1972; Ebony Book on Successful Black Men & Women; nominee, Outstanding Young Men in Amer 1970. **HOME ADDRESS:** 655 Spadina Ave, Toronto, Ontario, Canada M5S 2H9.

DAVIS, JOSEPH SOLOMON
College administrator. **PERSONAL:** Born Apr 08, 1938, Macon, GA; married Sarah Frances Striggles; children: Joan Yvette, Oscar Wendall. **EDUCATION:** Tuskegee Inst, BS, MEd 1960-68. **CAREER:** Boggs Acad, teacher ind arts 196-65, guidance dir 1965-67; Stillman Coll, dir financial aid 1967-76, 1981-, dir counseling serv 1976-81, dir financial aid 1981-. **ORGANIZATIONS:** Mbr West Tuscaloosa Optimist Club 1980-. **HONORS/ACHIEVEMENTS:** Grad flwshp Southern Assoc of Secondary Schls 1967; Keyman Service, United Way Award; 1978; mem AL Comm on Higher Ed 1984. **HOME ADDRESS:** 2 Forest Brook, Northport, AL 35476. **BUSINESS ADDRESS:** Dir of Financial Aid, Stillman College, Stillman College, Tuscaloosa, AL 35403.

DAVIS, JOYCE
Manager. **PERSONAL:** Born Jan 07, New York, NY; divorced; children: Paula, Bruce, Valeria, Robert. **EDUCATION:** St Johns Univ, 1944; NY Bus School, 1946; Katherine Gibbs Women in Mgmt Prog, 1972. **CAREER:** St Philips Church, sec 11 yrs; Union Carbide Corp, non-exempt admin 1971-76; Union Carbide Corp Agr Prod Div, manager compensation & benefits 1976-. **ORGANIZATIONS:** Mem Gamma Phi Delta; past basileus Alpha Sigma Chap Gamma Phi Delta; mem Natl Sec Assoc, St Thomas Episcopal Church Bethel, St Philips Epis Church. **HONORS/ACHIEVEMENTS:** NY Black Achievement Awd Harlem Y 1974.

DAVIS, KATIE ELIZABETH
Educator. **PERSONAL:** Born Sep 11, 1936, Lumber City, GA; married Ernest Davis Jr; children: Theresa Lynn. **EDUCATION:** TN State Univ, BA 1957; TN State Univ, MA 1968; Univ IL, PhD 1974. **CAREER:** Norfolk State Univ, prof speech & English; teacher various public school since 1951. **ORGANIZATIONS:** Mem Nat Council Tchrs of Eng; Nat Educ Assn; Central States Speech Assn; communications consult mem NAACP; Alpha Kappa Alpha; Theta Alpha Pi; Pi Kappa Delta. **BUSINESS ADDRESS:** Professor, Norfolk State University, Speech Communication, 2401 Corprew Ave, Norfolk, VA 23504.

DAVIS, L. CLIFFORD
Attorney. **PERSONAL:** Born Oct 12, 1925, Wilton, AK; married Ethel R Weaver; children: Karen Renea, Avis Janeth. **EDUCATION:** Philander Smith Coll, BA 1945; Howard U, JD 1949. **CAREER:** Davis Sturns & Johns, atty 1949-. **ORGANIZATIONS:** Mem Omega Psi Phi Frat; trustee St Andrews United Methodist Church; past mem bd of Tarrant Cnty Unit Fund; Tarrant Cnty & Prec Worker's Council; charter revision com City of Fort Worth TX; adv coun of TX Legal Serv Corp. **MILITARY SERVICE:** AUS 1954-55. **BUSINESS ADDRESS:** 300 W Belknap, Fort Worth, TX 76112.

DAVIS, LARRY EARL
Psychologist. **PERSONAL:** Born May 11, 1946, Saginaw, MI; son of Kires and Clara. **EDUCATION:** Attended Delta Coll Bay City MI 1964-66; MI State Univ, BS Psychol 1968; Univ of MI, MSW 1973, MA Psychology 1975, PhD Social Work & Psychology 1977. **CAREER:** VISTA, New York City, volunteer, 1969-72; Washington Univ, asst prof social work & psychology. **ORGANIZATIONS:** Mem Assn Black Psychologists 1977-; mem Natl Assn of Black Social Workers 1977-; mem Natl Assn of Social Workers 1977-. **HONORS/ACHIEVEMENTS:** Published and co-published numerous articles, including "Racial Composition of Groups," Social Work MA, 1979; "Racial Balance, A Psychological Issue," Social Work With Groups, 1980; "Minority Content in Social Work Educ, A Question of Objectives," Journal of Educ for Social Work, 1983; co-author with Enola Proctor, Race, Gender and Class: Guidelines for Practice With Individuals, Families, and Group, Prentice-Hall, 1989. **BUSINESS ADDRESS:** Assoc Prof Social Work/Psychology, Washington University, St Louis, MO 63130.

DAVIS, LAVERNE GLORIA
Educator. **PERSONAL:** Born Sep 07, 1936, Greeneville, MS; divorced; children: Derek Rhodes. **EDUCATION:** Loyola U, MA 1972; Roosevelt U, BA 1965. **CAREER:** Barat Coll, Lake Forest IL, dir Upward Bound program 1972-; Mundelein Coll, instructor 1970-72;Univ of IL Chicago Cir, instructor 1969; Chicago Bd of Educ, instructor 1965-69; Barat Coll, instructor part-time 1966-70. **ORGANIZATIONS:** Mem asst sr choir dir First Congreg Ch; mem Comm Renewal Chorus 1971-; mem Hektoen Inst Women's Aux. **HONORS/ACHIEVEMENTS:** Recipient of award for excellence in training of teachers from Chicago Teachers Coll 1966.

DAVIS, LAWRENCE ARNETTE, JR.
Educator. **PERSONAL:** Born May 13, 1937, Pine Bluff, AR; married Ethel Louise Grant; children: Sonya, Lawrence III, Catherine. **EDUCATION:** AM&N Coll, BS 1958;Univ of AR, MS 1960; IA State U, PhD 1973. **CAREER:** Dept of Math & Physics, Univ of AR at Pine Bluff, chmn 1974-; NASA Research Project, Univ of AR, dir 1973-74; Engr Research Inst, IA State Univ, research asst 1971-73; IA State Univ, grad teaching asst 1969-71; NSF In-service Inst, AM&N Coll, dir 1967-68; NASA Office of Advanced Research & Techn summers 1964 1965; AM&N Coll, prof 1961-68; MS Valley State Coll, instructor 1960; Author of 3 papers or writings. **ORGANIZATIONS:** Mem Soc of Indsl & Applied Mathematicians; Math Assn of Am; Nat Assn of Mathematicians; AR Acad of Sci 1966-68; Am Assn for Advancement of Sci; Am Assn of Univ Prof; Am Assn of Physics Tchrs; Beta Kappi Chi; Alpha Kappa Mu. **BUSINESS ADDRESS:** Dept of Math & Physics, U of AR, Pine Bluff, AR 71601.

DAVIS, LELIA KASENIA
Admission counselor, mayor. **PERSONAL:** Born Nov 07, 1941, Taft, OK; daughter of Willie Smith and Canzaty Smith; married David Earl Davis, Nov 22; children: Mark, Kasandra, Starla (Smith) Phillips, Canraty, Derrick. **CAREER:** Amer Technical Inst, Muskogee OK, admission counselor, 1986-; City of Taft, Taft OK, mayor, 1973-. **ORGANIZATIONS:** Bd of dir, Eastern OKlahoma Devel Dist; pres, LeCon Org; chairwoman, Taft Parade Comm; advisory bd of dir, Dept of Corrections. **HONORS/ACHIEVEMENTS:** First Black Elected Female Mayor, 1973; Amer Ten Outstanding Young Women, 1974; Oklahoma Outstanding Young Woman Award, 1974; Muskogee League Hall of Fame.

DAVIS, LEODIS
Educator. **PERSONAL:** Born Sep 25, 1933, Stamps, AK; married N June Wilson; children: Melonie, Leon. **EDUCATION:** Victor Wilson Schl UMKC, BS Chem 1956; IA State Univ, MS Chem 1958, PhD Biochem 1960. **CAREER:** TN State Univ, asst prof chem 1961-62; Howard Univ Med Coll, asst prof biochem 1962-67, assoc prof biochem 1967-69; IA Univ, research assoc 1960-61, visit assoc prof 1969, assoc prof biochem 1969-76, prof of chem 1976-, chrmn of chem dept. **ORGANIZATIONS:** Full memsp Soc of Sigma XI 1960; HEW NIH Min Biomed Supp; biochem study sect Ad Hoc Consult1970-; chem comm on min affairs Amer Soc of Biolog 1973; Aging Rev Comm 1976-80; Natl Res Counc Rev of NSF Grad Fellow 1977-80. **HONORS/ACHIEVEMENTS:** One of ten med school fac mem in US awarded Lederle Med Fac Award 1967; Gen Elec Conf for Prof of Chem & Chem Eng 1973; bd of dir Univ of IA Credit Union 1986-. **BUSINESS ADDRESS:** Chairman, University of Iowa, Dept of Chemistry, Iowa City, IA 52242.

DAVIS, LEON
Business executive. **PERSONAL:** Born May 23, 1933, Chicago, IL; son of Henry Davis and Lillian Henry Davis; married Shirley Pickett, Oct 07, 1988; children: Leon Jr, Daryl, Terrence, Margo. **EDUCATION:** TN A&I Univ Nashville, 1951-1953; Crane Jr Coll Chicago, 1955; Wilson Jr Coll Chicago, 1956. **CAREER:** Congressman Abner J Mikva, exec asst 1969-71; Operation PUSH, natl exec dir 1971-72; Congressman Ralph H Metcalfe, exec asst 1972-73; The Peoples Gas Light and Coke Co, admin office of vice pres 1973-. **ORGANIZATIONS:** Chmn bd of govs IL State Coll and Univ 1973-; bd of higher educ State of IL 1977-; mem Chicago Bd of Educ 1980; Univ Civil Serv Merit Bd State of IL 1975-77; Community Serv & Continuing Educ Program State of IL 1977-79; bd mem Afro-Am Du Sable Museum 1977; Numerous Published Articles 1971- 76; Personal View Column Chicago Sun-Times 1979. **HONORS/ACHIEVEMENTS:** Chicago Sun-Times, Special Black History Month Section "The Political Legacy of Harold Washington" by Leon Davis 1988. **MILITARY SERVICE:** AUS pvt e-2 1953-55. **BUSINESS ADDRESS:** Superintendent, Peoples Gas Light & Coke Co, 122 S Michigan Ave, Chicago, IL 60603.

DAVIS, LEONARD HARRY
Manager. **PERSONAL:** Born Sep 03, 1927, Indianapolis, IN; married Erla Darling Robinson (deceased); children: Kevin L, Gail D, Janna L, Aaron L (dec), Barry C. **EDUCATION:** Univ of IL School of Fine & Applied Arts Champaign, BS, BA 1949-52. **CAREER:** Naval Ordinance Facility Indianapolis, asst art dir 1952-57; Indust Arts & Engrg Co San Diego, asst dir 1957-62; Cubic Corp, mgr tech publ graphic arts group. **ORGANIZATIONS:** Indus photographer Indus Art & Engrg Co San Diego 1957-62; past sec Kappa Alpha Psi Champaign 1949-52; pres Cubic Mgmt Assoc 1977-79; past pres San Diego Area Council 1980-81. **HONORS/ACHIEVEMENTS:** Numerous 1st through 3rd places for art exhibits 1948-65; Mem of the Year Cubic Mgmt Assoc 1979. **MILITARY SERVICE:** AUS corpl 1944-48. **BUSINESS ADDRESS:** Manager, Cubic Corp, 9333 Balboa Ave, San Diego, CA 92123.

DAVIS, LESTER E.
Engineer. **PERSONAL:** Born Aug 05, 1918, Tunica, MS; married Annie B Debro; children: Dorothy Wakefield. **EDUCATION:** KS State Univ, BS Arch Engrg 1950; Lincoln Univ, attended 1942 & 1946. **CAREER:** St of CA Dept of Transport, bridge engr 1953-75; Bay Area Rapid Transit Dist CA, supr engr structural/civil 1975- . **ORGANIZATIONS:** Mem Amer Soc of Civil Engrs; mem No CA Council of Black Prof Engrs; registered prof engr Civil Br State of CA; active in local church & civic organs; life mem Alpha Phi Alpha Frat; mem East Bay Structural Engrs Soc; mem Black Managers & Prof Assn at Bart. **MILITARY SERVICE:** USAF 1943-46. **BUSINESS ADDRESS:** Supr Engr Civil/Struct, Bay Area Rapid Transit DistCA, Metro-Center 2nd Floor, 101 8th St, Oakland, CA 94607.

DAVIS, LLOYD
Director. **PERSONAL:** Born May 04, 1928, Chicago; children: 3 Children. **EDUCATION:** DePaulUniv Chgo, PhB; LoyolaUniv Chgo, MSIR; Grad Fed Exec Inst; Westinghouse Mgmt Sch; US Civil Serv Mgmt Sch. **CAREER:** US Dept of Hsng & Urban Develop Wash DC, dir Ofc of Vol Compliance Ofc of Asst Sec for Fair Hsng & Equal Opp; Cath Interracial Council Archdiocese of Chgo, former dir; Intergroup Relations Ofcr Hsng & Home Finance Agency, former dir; Kennedy Adminstrn, spl asst to post master gen; Dixwell Renewal Proj New Haven CT, former dir; New Haven Redevel Agency, former asst dir; Westinghouse Elec Corp US Defense & Space Cntr Baltimore, former mgr sociol-Economic progs; Model Urban Neighborhood Demonstration Proj Baltimore MD, mgr; MLK Ctr Nonviolent Social Chng, vice pres for govt & intl affairs, exec dir fed holiday commission. **ORGANIZATIONS:** One founder Nat Cath Conf for Interracial Justice; pres Nat Assn of Intergroup Relations Ofcls; mem bd dirs Nat Assn of Human Rights Workers. **HONORS/ACHIEVEMENTS:** Scholarship Achievement Award; recip awards from City of Chicago

New Haven Baltimore; listed in num Who's Who Publs; Papers Presented to Dillard U. **MILITARY SERVICE:** AUS bat sgt maj. **BUSINESS ADDRESS:** Vice Presicent, Exec Dir, MLK Ctr/Nonviolent Social Chng, 449 Auburn Ave, Atlanta, GA 30312.

DAVIS, LOUIS GARLAND
Educator. **PERSONAL:** Born in Danville, VA. **EDUCATION:** Oberlin Coll Conservatory, 1948; New England Conservatory of Music, BMus 1951; Boston U, MMus 1955;Univ of Florence, 1951. **CAREER:** RI Jr Coll Warwick, asst prof Music & Italian 1968-; Moses Brown School, dir music 1961-68; Univ of RI, sum dir poverty prog 1968; Bryant Coll, instructor 1969-70; Phillips Academy & Bradford Jr Coll, instructor 1956-61; Newton Coll Sacred Heart, instructor 1955-56; Le Cercle Francais D'Amerique D'Ete L'Academic Internationale Nice, music dir 1965; Cincinnati Chamber Symphony Orchestra, soloist; Boston Univ Symphony Orchestra. **ORGANIZATIONS:** Mem Chopin Club; Nat Assn of Music Tchrs; Taft Museum; RISD Museum; bd trustees bass-baritone soloist Young Peoples Symphony Orch. **HONORS/ACHIEVEMENTS:** Hon doctorate Saengerfest HarvardUniv 1967. **BUSINESS ADDRESS:** RI Jr Coll, 400 E Ave, Warwick, RI.

DAVIS, LOWELL E.
Educational administrator. **PERSONAL:** Born Aug 01, 1931, Port Antonio, Jamaica;married Shirley Marie; children: Christian, Ian. **EDUCATION:** Howard Univ, BS 1958, MS 1960; Case Western Reserve Univ, PhD 1964. **CAREER:** Univ Hosp, post-doctoral fellow 1964-65; Case Western Reserve Univ, rsch assoc & instructor 1965-68, asst prof biol 1968-69; Syracuse Univ, assoc prof biol 1969-73, prof biol 1973-, assoc in academic affairs 1976-79, dean coll for human develop 1979-80; assoc vice chancellor, prof biol; campus dean, Univ of South Fl, St Petersburg campus. **ORGANIZATIONS:** Former bd mem Onondaga Cty Red Cross, Macy Rsch Grant Found, Partners of the Amer; seminars at various univs; reviewer rsch grant proposals, biol textbook manuscripts; assoc vice chancellor Syracuse Univ 1980-. **HONORS/ACHIEVEMENTS:** Received several public serv awds; publ over 50 scientific articles in intl jrnls, many chapts in books; received thousands of dollars for biological rsch 1964-76; US Citizen. **BUSINESS ADDRESS:** Campus Dean, Univ of South FL, 140-7th Ave S, St Petersburg, FL 33701.

DAVIS, LUTHER CHARLES
Dairy industry marketing consultant. **PERSONAL:** Born Sep 21, 1948, Key West, FL; married Sharon Ann Williams; children: Jason. **EDUCATION:** Cornell Univ, BA 1970. **CAREER:** Jewel Companies Inc, buyer 1977; Kraft Inc, Dairy Group, district sales mgr 1984; Mellin Ice Cream Co, vice pres 1985; Wisconsin Milk Marketing Bd, regional marketing mgr. **HOME ADDRESS:** 9713 Eustice Rd, Randallstown, MD 21133. **BUSINESS ADDRESS:** Regional Marketing Manager, Wisconsin Milk Marketing Bd, 4337 West Belt Line Hwy, Madison, WI 53711.

DAVIS, LYDIA JOANNA
Publishing executive. **PERSONAL:** Born May 04, 1958, Indiana; daughter of Henderson S and Ruth V. **EDUCATION:** Howard Univ, BA Broadcast Mgmt (Magna Cum Laude) 1980. **CAREER:** WRTV ABC Indianapolis IN, news reporter 1980-81; Johnson Publ Co, asst dir of public relations 1981-83; Ebony/Jet Celebrity Showcase, assoc producer; dir promotion 1983-85, vice president promotions 1985-. **ORGANIZATIONS:** Mem Quinn Chapel AME Church Chicago, IL; mem Executives Club of Chicago; mem League of Black Women; mem Women's Advertising Club of Chicago, mem Chicago Assn for Direct Mktg. **HONORS/ACHIEVEMENTS:** Cert of Merit Folio Magazine Circulation Direct Mail Awad for Johnson Publishing Co $50,000 Sweepstakes; CEBA Awd for Merit 1986. **BUSINESS ADDRESS:** Vice President of Promotion, Johnson Publishing Co, 820 South Michigan Ave, Chicago, IL 60605.

DAVIS, MAJOR
Administrator. **PERSONAL:** Born Nov 06, 1931, Hartsville, SC; married Elsie M Luck; children: Shynethia Catrice, Trent Damone. **EDUCATION:** Maricopa Tech Comm Coll, AA 1973; Phoenix Coll, AA 1975; AZ State Univ, BA 1979. **CAREER:** US Air Force, jet test flight engr 1951-72; Alpha Grand Lodge, grand master 1974-75; Miss Black AZ Pageant, dir 1971-; Miss Galaxy Intl Pageant, natl dir 1975-; Youth Together Inc, founder, bd chmn. **ORGANIZATIONS:** Public relations USAF Worlds Southern Hemisphere 1968; editor, publ Phoenix Chronicle Newspaper 1969; mem NAACP 1970-; editor, publ AZ News Mag 1973; mem Phoenix Advertising Club 1976, AZ Newspaper Assoc 1978, Phoenix Chamber of Comm 1978; Founder 1st private state sickle cell anemia found Phoenix. **HONORS/ACHIEVEMENTS:** 33rd Degree Mason Ivanhoe Grand Lodge AF&AM Denver 1964; Commander-In-Chief Jeremiah Consistory Denver 1965; Black & Gold Serv Awd Maricopa Tech Coll 1973; Key to the City Austin TX 1979, Las Vegas NV 1981. **MILITARY SERVICE:** USAF t/sgt 21 yrs; 15 Decorations. **BUSINESS ADDRESS:** Board Chairman, Youth Together Inc, 4310 W Verde Lane, Phoenix, AZ 85031.

DAVIS, MARIANNA WHITE
Educator. **PERSONAL:** Born Jan 08, 1929, Philadelphia, PA; daughter of Albert McNeil White and Laura Bowman White Frederick; widowed; children: Kenneth Renay. **EDUCATION:** SC State Univ, BA English 1949; NY Univ, MA English 1953; Boston Univ, DEd English 1966. **CAREER:** SC Pub Sch, tchr 1949-51, 1955-56; SC State Coll, asst prof 1956-64; Claflin Coll, prof 1966-69; Voorhees Coll, vis prof 1966-68; Boston Univ, vis prof 1967; Univ of TN, vis prof 1969; Benedict Coll, English prof & researcher 1969-82; Upward Bound Tufts Univ, instr; Benedict Coll English prof & rschr 1969-; Denmark Tech Coll, acting pres 1985-86; Davis & Assocs, pres 1980-. **ORGANIZATIONS:** Bd dir Natl Council of Teachers of English 1958-; Pi Lambda Theta Honor Assn 1965; professional examiner English Tests Educ Testing Serv 1971-73; co-founder & sec ABC Devel Corp 1972; mem SC Commn on Higher Educ 1973-76; pres SC Council of Teachers of English 1974-75; chmn Conf on Coll Composition & Comm 1975-76; exec comm ADE Modern Language Assn 1976-79; commr SC Educational TV 1980-; mem Public Broadcasting System Adv Bd 1981-; Francis Burns United Methodist Ch bd chm;Columbia Urban League bd mem 1981-82; Natl Council of Negro Women; YWCA; life mem NAACP; bd sec Columbia Urban League; Trinity United Methodist Ch; The Moles Inc; Black Women's Agenda; SC Council on Human Relations; coord Coalition for Concerns of Blacks in Post Secondary Educ in SC; mem Alpha Kappa Alpha Sor; mem Order of Eastern Star; chmn SC Intl Women's Yr Commission; founder VICOS Women's League for Comm Action; Babcock Center, Inc, pres; TISAWS, The Girlfriends, Inc; mem Civil Rights Comm Adv Bd 1985-; natl publicity chair, The Moles, 1988-90; bd of educ, S Carolina United Methodist Church, 1988-90. **HONORS/ACHIEVEMENTS:** SC State Coll Alumni Scholarship 1945-46; Crusade Scholar doctoral studies 1964-66; Outstanding Educator of Amer 1970-71; IMB-UNCF Fellowships post doctoral studies 1971 & 1974; Pi Lambda Theta Travel Scholarship for study in Soviet Union 1973; Outstanding Educ Award Kappa Alpha Psi Frat Athens GA 1974; Contrib to Educ Award SC Comm Affairs 1976; Educators Roundtable Awd 1976; Outstanding Cit Awd Omega Psi Phi Frat 1977; Emory O Jackson Journalism Awd 1978; Distinguished Research Award NAFEO 1980; Distinguished Faculty Awd Benedict Coll 1980; Distinguished Serv Award Columbia Urban League 1981; Distinguished Alumni Awd Boston Univ 1981; Distinguished Alumni Award SC State Coll 1981; Par Excellence Award in Educ Operation PUSH 1982; Outstanding Citizen Award, Cleveland, OH, 1984; Kappa Alpha Psi Univ of SC Outstanding Black Woman Award 1987; contributed papers to Boston Univ (Mugar Memorial Library), 1989; exec producer, "The Struggle Continues," black history teleconf on PBS; author of 14 books & many publ articles. **BUSINESS ADDRESS:** President, Davis & Associates, PO Box 3097, Columbia, SC 29230.

DAVIS, MARILYNN A.
Financial services company executive. **PERSONAL:** Born Oct 30, 1952, Little Rock, AR; daughter of James Edward Davis and Erma Lee Glasco Davis. **EDUCATION:** Smith College, BA, 1973; University of Michigan, MA, 1976; Washington University, St Louis MO, MA, 1980; Harvard Graduate School of Business Administration, MBA, 1982. **CAREER:** State Street Bank, Boston MA, senior credit analyst, 1981; General Motors Corp, Detroit MI, analyst, central office financial staff, 1982-83; General Motors Corp, New York NY, senior financial analyst, overseas borrowing section, 1984, senior financial analyst, financing, investment and financial planning section, 1984, asst to GM group vice president/chief economist, 1984-86; American Express Co, New York NY, vice president, risk financing, 1987—. **ORGANIZATIONS:** Member of board of trustees, Studio Museum in Harlem; chair of committee on residence, Bd of Counselors of Smith College; member of bd of directors, Queensboro Society for the Prevention of Cruelty to Children; member of management assistance committee, Greater NY Fund/United Way. **HONORS/ACHIEVEMENTS:** Named to 100 Top Black Business and Professional Women list, 1988; Black Achievers Award, Harlem YMCA, 1989. **BUSINESS ADDRESS:** Vice President, Risk Financing, American Express Company, World Financial Center, 200 Vesey St, New York, NY 10285-4845.

DAVIS, MARION HARRIS
Director. **PERSONAL:** Born Jul 27, 1938, Washington, DC; married Charles B; children: Alan Edward. **EDUCATION:** Univ of Pittsburgh, MPA Grad Sch of Pblc & Intrntl Affairs 1971; AmUniv Wash DC, Atnd 1966-70. **CAREER:** US Dept of Hsng & Urban Devel Area Ofc Detroit, deputy dir hsng mgmt div; Co Hsng Ofcr Fairfax VA, exec dir comm devel authority 1972; Deptof Urban Renewal & Economic Devel Rochester NY, dir of program planning 1971-72; Westinghouse Electric Corp, sr mgmt consult 1970-71; FHA Dept of Hsng& Urban Devel Wash DC, hsng prog spclst mgmt asst br div of low & mdrt incm hsng 1969-70; Ofc of the Sec Dept of Hsng & Urban Devel Wash DC, conf asst congr rltns ofcr 1967-69. **ORGANIZATIONS:** Mem Natg Assn of Hsn & Redevel Ofcls; Nat Inst of Real Estate Mgmt; Am Soc of Planning Ofcls. **HONORS/ACHIEVEMENTS:** Recip Carnegie Mid-Career Fellow Grad Sch of Pub & Internatl AffairsUniv of Pittsburgh 1970-71; travel study award $3,000 while attending grad sch Ford Found 1970-71. **BUSINESS ADDRESS:** US Dept of Housing & Urb Dev, 660 Woodward Ave, Detroit, MI 48226.

DAVIS, MARTIN
Brother. **EDUCATION:** Point Park Coll, BA Candidate. **CAREER:** St Augustine's Capuchin Franciscan Province, brother 1968-; St Brigid/St Benedict, brother The Moor Cath Parish 1970; Lwrncvll Hawks Bsktbll Team, organizer; Black Inner-City Parochial Schs, tchr. **ORGANIZATIONS:** Mem Nat Black Cath Clergy Caucus; Pttsbrgh Dance Council; solemn profession in Capuchin Franciscan Order 1964.

DAVIS, MARVIN COOLIDGE
Business executive. **PERSONAL:** Born Sep 18, 1924, Baltimore, MD; married Jeanne Parrott; children: Marjean Funn, Marvin P. **EDUCATION:** Morgan State U, BS 1948; Columbia U, MA 1957;Univ of MD; John Hopkins U; Loyola Coll; Coppin State Coll. **CAREER:** Community Coll of Baltimore, deputy vice pres for admin serv 1978-, dir of devel studies 1974-78; Baltimore City Public Schools, dir of personnel 1969-74, principal adult educ 1963-67, asst principal 1966-69, special asst 1964-66, placement counselor 1963-64, guidance counselor 1955-63, teacher 1948-55. **ORGANIZATIONS:** Mem Am Personnel Adminstr Assn 1969-75; mem Assn of Bus Officials 1978-; mem Phi Delta Kappa 1969-; mem Kappa Alpha Psi Frat 1944-; mem Prince HallMasons 1945-; mem NAACP 1948-; mem Urban League 1948-; mem Governor's Commn of Libr 1970-79; christian fellowship Madison Ave Presb Ch 1972. **HONORS/ACHIEVEMENTS:** Achievement Kappa Alpha Psi Frat 1964; achievement Madison Ave Presb Ch 1968; hall of fame Dunbar Sr HS 1969.

DAVIS, MARY-AGNES MILLER
Association executive. **PERSONAL:** Born in Montgomery, AL; daughter of George Miller and Mollie Miller; married Edward Davis. **EDUCATION:** Wayne State Univ, BA; Univ of Michigan, MSW. **CAREER:** Co-Ette Club Inc, founder natl dir; Metropolitan Detroit Teen Conf Coalition founder-director. **ORGANIZATIONS:** Pres Keep Detroit Beautiful Inc; bd dir Carmel Hall; Franklin-Wright Settlements; chmn Personnel Practices-Bylaws; League of Catholic Women; St Francis Home for Boys; Heartline Inc; Operation Understanding Brewster-Douglas Housing Project; mem Nominating Com Detroit Chap Amer Red Cross; Natl Council of US Women Inc; mem com Women's Assn of Detroit Symphony Orch; sec Edward Davis Assoc Inc; Detroit Area Chmn Meadowbrook Festival Com Oakland Univ; educ com Detroit Opera Assn; chmn ARC Central Region Recognition Ceremony 1980; Merrill Palmer Inst bd of dir; Natl Cncl of Women of the US, Inc; Ntl vice pres, prog chmn for USA; Catholic Youth Org bd of dir. **HONORS/ACHIEVEMENTS:** Heart of Gold Awd 1968; Hon Y Teen Awd (life) 1963; Leadership Awd United Negro Coll Fund 1967; Leadership Scholarship Awds Natl Conf of Christians & Jews; nominee Women of Conscience Awd Natl Council of Women of the US Inc 1979; Amer Bicentennial Inst Most Valued Amer Resource Awd 1976; Greater Detroit Chamber of Commerce Awd; City of Detroit Common Council Leadership Awd; One of Detroit's 12 Most Outstanding Women Awd by Detroit Bicentennial Commission; NCW Woman of Conscious Awd 1984 forLeadership Youth & the Community; One Hundred Most Distinguished Black Women In The USA 1988.

DAVIS, MATILDA LAVERNE
Physician. **PERSONAL:** Born Sep 23, 1926, Elizabeth, NJ; married Robert M Cunningham MD; children: Robert Davis Cunningham MD, Dellena M Cunningham PhD, William E Cunningham MD. **EDUCATION:** HowardUniv Wash DC, BS 1948; Howard U, MD 1951. **CAREER:** FAAFP Cunningham-Davis MD PA, dr 1971-; Karen Horney Horney Clinic, postdoctorate psychiatric 1967-71; Harlem Hosp NYC, intern 1951-52. **ORGANIZATIONS:** Mem AMA Present; alumni mem HowardUniv Med Sch Present; mem Nat Med Assn; life mem NAACP. **HONORS/ACHIEVEMENTS:** #1 women in the E in tennis 45 yrs & Older Tennis Players 1979; for substantial financial support HowardUniv 1974; charter fellow Am Ac of Family Phys 1974; physicians recognition award AMA 1980. **BUSINESS ADDRESS:** Physician, 230 W Jersey St, Ste 308, Elizabeth, NJ 07202.

DAVIS, MELVIN LLOYD
Construction company executive. **PERSONAL:** Born Mar 29, 1917, Richmond, VA; son of Thornton F Davis and Adelaide Turner Davis; married Helen Randolph Davis, May 22, 1939; children: Melvin Jr, Langston, Adelaide Flamer, Carolyn Harris, Wendell F, Kermit M, Nancy Elam, Anna Hudson, Leon V, Revell R, Deborah N Davis. **EDUCATION:** John Tyer Community Coll, 1948-49. **CAREER:** Thorton F Davis, laborer, 1931-35; Thornton J Davis Jr, painter, 1935-42; US Navy, painter, 1942-45; Davis & Myers Building Co, painter, 1945-60; Melvin L Davis General Contractor, owner, 1960-68; Davis Brothers Construction Co, pres, 1968-89. **ORGANIZATIONS:** Sunday school supt, Troop Providence Baptist Church, 1945-50;.

DAVIS, MELWOOD LEONARD
Research manufacturing company executive. **PERSONAL:** Born Dec 14, 1925, Youngstown, OH; son of Doyle Davis (deceased) and Annie Bell Davis (deceased); married Anne Norris, Dec 28; children: Adrienne Page Davis Dunning, Vikki Anne Davis. **EDUCATION:** A&T State U, BS 1950; Springfield Coll, MsEd 1975; Union Grad Sch, PhD 1978. **CAREER:** Multi-Devel Enterprises Inc, pres; Nat Bd of YMCA, dir Urban/Africa Affairs 1973-; YMCA asso gen exec 1969-73; arctic av YMCA, exec dir 1967-69; YMCA of Buffalo & Erie Co, asst exec dir 1958-67; Multi-Development Janitorial Supply Co, vice pres mktg. **ORGANIZATIONS:** Dir Youth Urban Serv 1970-73; consult YMCA Career Devel 1970, 72; bd dir NAACP 1973; mem Frontiers Intl 1976; bd dir Tri-Co Mental Hlth 1971; bd dir Sr Citz 1971; Assn Professional Dirs; convener Gov of PA Children & Youth Adv Com 1972; mem Rotary Club of Harrisburg; exec prod "Ride For 24" 1975. **HONORS/ACHIEVEMENTS:** Man of Yr Frontiers Internatl; award for excellence Race Rels 1976; Man of Yr Black Businessmen Assn; Silver Star 1945; A&T St Univ, Sports Hall of Fame; developed Community Urban Program, Harrisburg PA, Film, Ride for 24; led fund raiser for Harrisburg Community Hospital. **MILITARY SERVICE:** AUS corporal, 5 bronze, 1 silver star WWII. **BUSINESS ADDRESS:** Multi-Development Janitorial Supply Co, PO Box 2904, 596 Wareham Drive, Cincinnati, OH 14202.

DAVIS, MICHAEL JAMES
Judge of district court. **PERSONAL:** Born Jul 21, 1947, Cincinnati, OH; married Sara E Wahl; children: Michael, Alexander. **EDUCATION:** Macalester Coll St Paul MN, BA 1969; Univ of MN Law School, JD 1972. **CAREER:** Legal Rights Ctr Inc, lawyer 1975-78; Hennepin Co Public Defender's Office, Lawyer 1978-83; Hennepin Co Municipal Court, judge 1983-84; Hennepin Co Dist Ct, judge 1984-. **ORGANIZATIONS:** Mem MN Minority Lawyers Assoc, Hennepin Co Bar Assoc, MN State Bar Assoc, NAACP Minneapolis Branch; bd of dirs MN Lawyers Intl Human Rights, Try Us Meyerhoff Fund. **HONORS/ACHIEVEMENTS:** Attorney Commissioner Minneapolis Civil Rights Commn 1977-82; Adjunct Law Prof Univ of MN Law School 1982-. **BUSINESS ADDRESS:** Judge, 4th Judicial District, 1756-C Government Center, Minneapolis, MN 55487.

DAVIS, MILES DEWEY
Musician, composer. **PERSONAL:** Born May 25, 1926, Alton, IL; married Cicely Tyson. **EDUCATION:** Julliard Sch, attended 1945. **CAREER:** Played with Eddie Randall St Louis 1941-43, w/Charlie Parker, Coleman hawkins, then on tour with Eckstine's Band 1945-48; leader Band Royal Roost; appeared Paris Jazz Festival 1949, New York City 1950-51, Cafe Bohemia New York City 1957, NY Jazz Festival 1975, Carnegie Hall 1975; toured w/Jazz Inc 1952; composed soundtrack for "Jack Johnson" 1970; recs include Modern Idiom, Trumpet Stylists Cool & Quintet, Miles Ahead, Miles Davis Plus 19, Relaxin, Walkin, Cookin, Bags, Groove; collector's items Birth of the Cool, Round About Midnight, Miles & Monk at Newport, Live Evil, Miles Live at Fillmore, On the Corner, Sorcerery, Bitches Brew & many others. **HONORS/ACHIEVEMENTS:** Grammy Awds "Sketches of Spain", "Bitches Brew"; Downbeat Mag Hall of Fame. **BUSINESS ADDRESS:** c/o Columbia/CBS, 51 W 52nd St, New York, NY 10019.

DAVIS, MILT
College scout. **PERSONAL:** Born May 31, 1929; married Yvonne; children: Allison, Brian, Hilary. **EDUCATION:** UCLA; Undergrad degree, M Zoology, D Admin Educ. **CAREER:** Baltimore Colts, defensive back 1957-60; Baltimore Colts, scout 1967-76; Los Angeles City Coll, counselor and biology prof; Miami Dolphins, college scout. **MILITARY SERVICE:** AUS 1954-56.

DAVIS, MILTON
Chairman. **EDUCATION:** Morehouse Coll, Graduate; Washington Univ St Louis, Grad Study in Sociology and Economics. **CAREER:** South Shore Bank in Chicago, chairman 1983-. **ORGANIZATIONS:** Former chmn Chicago Chap Congress of Racial Equality.

DAVIS, MONIQUE DEON
State representative. **PERSONAL:** Born Aug 19, 1936, Chicago, IL; daughter of James McKay and Constance McKay; divorced; children: Robert A, Monique C Conway. **EDUCATION:** Chicago State Univ, BS 1967, MS 1975; Graduate Work, Univ of IL, DePaul Univ. **CAREER:** Chicago Bd of Educ, teacher 1967-86; City Colls of Chicago, teacher 1976-84; Chicago Bd of Educ, coord/administrator 1986-; General Assembly, state rep 1987-89. **ORGANIZATIONS:** Chmn Southside Chap IVI-IPO 1980-84; chmn Legislative Comm Chicago Area Alliance of Black School Educators 1981-83; coord Chicago Bd of Educ 1986-; bd mem Christian Bd Trinity United Church of Christ. **HONORS/ACHIEVEMENTS:** Teacher of the Year Award Gresham School 1978; Teacher Who Makes a Difference Center for New Schools; coord for election of Mayor Washington 1983, 1987; Excellent Legislator, Operation PUSH, 1989; Excellent Legislator, Dept of Aging, 1988. **BUSINESS ADDRESS:** State Representative, Chicago Bd of Educ/Serv Ctr, 9449 South Ashland Ave, Chicago, IL 60620.

DAVIS, MORRIS E.
Educator, attorney. **PERSONAL:** Born Aug 09, 1945, Wilmington, NC; married Janis Fox-Davis. **EDUCATION:** NC A&T State U, BS 1967;Univ IA Coll of Law, JD 1970;Univ CA Sch Pub Health, MPH 1973. **CAREER:** Dept Housing & Urban Devel San Francisco, atty-adv 1970-72; Inst Industrial Relations, Univ CA Berkeley, educ coordinator, editor 1974-75; Labor & Occupational Health Prog, Univ of CA, assoc dir 1975-; Journal of Black Health Perspectives, managing editor 1973-74; legal health cons, lecturer in health law, labor relations & med ethics 1972-. **ORGANIZATIONS:** IA Bar Assn; Nat Bar Assn; The Am Arbtrtn Assn; Am Pub Health Assn; Nat Health Lawyers Assn;Univ & Coll Labor Educ Assn; Am Soc Law & Med; memAmer Fed of Tchrs Summer Tchrs; fellowUniv CA (San Fran) Schl of Med 1974; fellowUniv CA (Berkeley) Schl Pub Hlth 1972-73; flwshpUniv IA Coll of Law 1967-70. **BUSINESS ADDRESS:** Inst of Industrial Ret, U of CA, Berkeley, CA 94720.

DAVIS, MYRTLE HILLIARD
Business executive. **PERSONAL:** Born Jun 13, 1926, Texarkana, AR; daughter of Arthur L Hilliard and Thelma Hacker Hilliard; divorced; children: Drew Hillard Davis. **EDUCATION:** Homer G Phillips Hosp, RN 1955; Univ of Cincinnati, MS 1977. **CAREER:** Harvard St Health Center Boston, MA, pres 1982-83; St Louis Comp Health Center, admin, 1969-82, pres 1983-. **ORGANIZATIONS:** Co-chair finance comm/bd dir St Louis Metro Urban League 1983-; chmn/personnel com/bd dir Tower Vill Geriatric Cntr 1984-; treas/bd dir MO Coalition Amb Care Cntrs 1984-; sec/bd dir, 1983-, chmn, bd of dirs, 1987-, Primary Care Cncl Greater St Louis; Spec Proj Comm St Louis Ambassadors 1985-; Top Ladies of Distinct St Louis Chap 1974-; pres, bd of dirs, Tower Village Nursing Care Center, 1987-; pres, chmn, Health/Medical Advisory Comm, St Louis Urban League, 1987-; vice pres, Gateway Chapter, Links Inc, 1989. **HONORS/ACHIEVEMENTS:** Cert of Apprec MO Senate; Disting Citizen St Louis Argus Newspaper; Disting Pub Serv Culinary Arts Club; Leadership/Publ Relations Order Eastern Star; Woman of Achievement, Suburban Journals/radio station KMOX, 1989. **BUSINESS ADDRESS:** President, St Louis Comp Health Center, 5471 Dr Martin Luther King Dr, St Louis, MO 63112.

DAVIS, MYRTLE V.
Nurse, educator. **PERSONAL:** Born Aug 23, 1930, Niles, OH; married Frank T Davis; children: Robin C. **EDUCATION:** St Elizabeth Hosp Sch of Nursing, Youngstown, OH, RN 1952; Youngstown State U, BS 1957; Kent State U, Kent, OH, MEd; TX Woman's U, MS 1980. **CAREER:** Youngstown State Univ, instructor 1976-; Choffin School Practical Nursing, Youngstown Bd of Educ, dir 1971-76; RN 1952-54; St Elizabeth Hospital, Youngstown OH, asst head nurse 1954-56, head nurse 1956-62; Choffin School of Practical Nursing, instructor 1963-71. **ORGANIZATIONS:** Mem Youngstown Supvr Personnel Assn; adv Bd St Elizabeth Hosp Sch Nursing; adv com Bd Licensed Pracitcal Nurse Assoc OH; Am Nurses' Assoc; DeltaSigma Theta; Youngstown chap Links Inc; Negro Bus & Prof Women's Club; life mem OH Voc Assoc; Am Voc Assoc; 3rd Baptist Ch. **HONORS/ACHIEVEMENTS:** Appointed first black dir Sch Practical Nursing, State of OH 1971.

DAVIS, N. JUNE (NORMA JUNE WILSON)
Educator. **PERSONAL:** Born May 01, 1940, Jacksonville, FL; married Leodis; children: Melonie, Leon. **EDUCATION:** Spelman Coll, BA 1961. **CAREER:** SNCC Atlanta, chmn 1960; IA City Parks & Rec Commn, vice chmn 1972-76; Admin Serv Dept Univ of IA, coord infor 1975-76, asst dir residence serv 1984-86, acting dir Affirmative Action 1985-86, asst to vice pres of finance 1986-. **ORGANIZATIONS:** Mem Ad Hoc Commn Racism IA City Sch Bd 1971-72; sec-treas Cedar Rapids Chap Links, Inc 1974-77. **BUSINESS ADDRESS:** Asst to VP-Finance, The University of Iowa, 101 Jessup Hall, Iowa City, IA 52242.

DAVIS, NATHAN T.
Educator. **PERSONAL:** Born Feb 15, 1937, KC, KS; married Ursula Broschke; children: Joyce Nathalie, Pierre Marc. **EDUCATION:** Univ KS, BME 1960; Wesleyan U, CT, PhD Ethnomusicology. **CAREER:** Club St Germain, Paris, prof debut with Kenny Clark 1963; Donald Byrd, Blue Note Club Paris, 1963; Chat Que Peche, Eric Dolphy, Paris, 1964; toured Europe with Art Blakly & New Jazz Messengers, 1965; Europe & Amer, recorded several albums as leader; total 10 LP's as leader; Belgium Radio-TV, staff compser. **ORGANIZATIONS:** Mem SACEM, Soc of Composers, Paris, France; co-chmn ed com Inst of Black Am Music; mem Afro-Am Bi-Cen Hall of Fame; est & created PhD degree prog in Ethnomusicology,Univ Pittsburgh; created Jazz Program atUniv Pittsburgh; created Jass Program Paris-Am Acad Paris. **MILITARY SERVICE:** AUS 298 army band, Berlin, 1960-62. **BUSINESS ADDRESS:** Professor, University of Pittsburgh, Music Department, 5th & Bellefield, Pittsburgh, PA 15260.

DAVIS, NIGEL S.
Banker. **PERSONAL:** Born Oct 01, 1955, Bastrop, LA; son of Charles Davis and Gladys Davis. **EDUCATION:** Grambling State Univ, Acct 1976. **CAREER:** Federal Reserve Bank of Kansas City, asst bank examiner 1977-82, bank examiner 1982-86, sr bank examiner 1986-. **ORGANIZATIONS:** Big Brothers of Amer. **HOME ADDRESS:** 11901 E 77 Terrace, Raytown, MO 64138. **BUSINESS ADDRESS:** Senior Bank Examiner, Federal Reserve Bank of KC, 925 Grand Ave, Kansas City, MO 64198.

DAVIS, NOEL GREGSON
Educator. **PERSONAL:** Born Oct 20, 1940; son of Oliver Davis and Evelyn Davis; married Daphne; children: Anika, Julian, Oliver, Sophia. **EDUCATION:** Harvard Coll, AB 1960; Univ of CA Berkeley, PhD 1968. **CAREER:** Antiqua Grammar School, St Johns Antigua WI, sr master 1960-61; Stanford Univ, acting asst prof 1966-68, asst prof 1968-75, assoc prof classics & comparative literature 1975-85, prof classics & comp lit 1985-. **ORGANIZATIONS:** Amer Philological Assn. **HONORS/ACHIEVEMENTS:** Latin Oration Harvard Commencement Exercises 1960; Arthur D Corey Travelling Fellow Harvard Univ 1961-62; Study Fellow Amer Council of Learned Societies 1970; Univ fellow Stanford Univ 1975-77; Internal Fellow Stanford Humanities Ctr 1983-84. **BUSINESS ADDRESS:** Professor, Stanford Univ, c/o Dept of Classics, Stanford, CA 94305.

DAVIS, NOLAN
Journalist, television and film producer, screenwriter, novelist. **PERSONAL:** Born Jul 23, 1942, Kansas City, MO; son of William L Davis and Francis Ann Davis; married Carol Lorraine Christian, Jul 20, 1963; children: Arian Valentinian, Pelia de Valoria. **EDUCATION:** Attended San Diego Evening Coll, 1964-65, Stanford Univ, Palo Alto, Calif, 1967-68. **CAREER:** San Diego Evening Tribune, San Diego, CA, staff writer, 1963-66; Economic Opportunities Commn of San Diego County, San Diego, dir of public relations, 1966-67; Newsweek magazine, New York, NY, staff correspondent, 1967-70; KNXT-TV, Hollywood, CA, producer, sr writer, 1970-71; KABC-TV, Hollywood, chief newswriter, 1971; SHARC Productions, Inc, Los Angeles, CA, partner, vice pres, beginning 1971; novelist, screenwriter, television and film producer, director. **ORGANIZATIONS:** Mem, Authors League of America, Writers Guild, Sigma Delta Chi. **HONORS/ACHIEVEMENTS:** Author of Six Black Horses, Putnam, 1971; author of O'Grady, Tarcher/Hawthorne, 1974; author of television script for series "Sanford and Son," NBC-TV, 1970, and for "Ironsides," Universal, 1974; author of television scripts "Storyline," ABC-TV, 1971, "The Jazz Show With Billy Eckstein," NBC-TV, 1972, "Further Than the Pulpit," NBC-TV, 1972; author of screenplays "Six Black Horses," "The Fighting 99th.". **MILITARY SERVICE:** US Navy, journalist, 1960-63. **HOME ADDRESS:** 3532 Sixth Ave, Los Angeles, CA 90018. *

DAVIS, NORMAN EMANUEL
Association executive. **PERSONAL:** Born Apr 06, 1941, Waycross, GA; married Mineola James Davis; children: Norman, Anthony, Corey V. **EDUCATION:** Tuskegee Inst, 1966. **CAREER:** Dial-A-Maid Inc, pres 1978-80; Migrant & Seasonal Farmworkers, exec dir 1980-; Young Volunteer in Action, dir. **ORGANIZATIONS:** Staff planner Planning Commiss; exec dir City of Tuskegee Migrant & Seasonally Employed Farmworkers; city recreation projects City of Tuskegee; mem F&A Mason 32nd Degree, Shriner, Tuskegee Jaycees, Electrolex Club, Elks Lodge, Intl Guild for Resource Devel, Amer Soc of Planning Officials, Amer Legion, Macon Cty Retardation & Rehab Exec Bd; adv bd Macon Cty Medicare & Medicaid; Talent Search Adv Bd; Macon Cty Mental Health Bd; Tuskegee Planning Commiss; Macon Cty Monumental & Historical Soc; Tuskegee-Macon Cty Youth Council; Omega Psi Phi; served 2 yrs as pres of Washington Publ Sch PTA; pres of City Wide PTA; elected 6 yrs to the Macon Co Bd of Edn; Model Cities soc planner for the City of Tuskegee 1969-78; dir & planner for Rec Dept. **HONORS/ACHIEVEMENTS:** Personalities of the South Awd; Legionnaire of the Year; Social Work Cert for Suprvs; State Mental Health Serv Awd; Youth Council Cert; Red Cross CampaignFund Raising Cert; Outstanding Achievement Awd City of Tuskegee; Jaycees Scotman Awd; Outstanding Achievement Awd Pro-Plan Intl; Jaycees Outstanding Business Awd Outstanding Young Man of the Year; Macon Cty Council Retardation & Rehab Appreciation Cert; Macon Cty 4-H Leadership Cert; Who's Who in Amer; designed, devel & implemented several community programs. **HOME ADDRESS:** 126 Marable Drive, Tuskegee, AL 36083. **BUSINESS ADDRESS:** Dir, Young Volunteer in Action, 214 North Main St, Tuskegee, AL 36083.

DAVIS, OLIVER CALVIN
Professional athlete. **PERSONAL:** Born Aug 29, 1954, Columbus, GA; married Deborah; children: Danielle. **EDUCATION:** TN State, Educ. **CAREER:** Cleveland, 1977-80; Cincinnati, 1981-82; Michigan, 1983-84; Oakland Invaders, cornerback 1984-. **HONORS/ACHIEVEMENTS:** Was team capt as jr & sr plus was team's MVP as sr; played in Senior Bowl.

DAVIS, OSSIE
Actor. **PERSONAL:** Born Dec 18, 1917, Cogdell, GA; married Ruby Dee; children: Nora, Guy, LaVerne. **EDUCATION:** Howard Univ, Class of 1939. **CAREER:** Actor Rose McClendon Players; dir Cotton Comes to Harlem, Kongi's Harvest, Black Girl, Gordons War, Countdown at Kusini; acted in The Defenders, The Sheriff, Night Gallery, The Scalphunters, The Cardinal, The Hill; stage roles Jeb, Wisteria Trees, Purlie Victorious; co-writer dir Today is Ours. **ORGANIZATIONS:** Mem Masons, NAACP, Grace Baptist Church; producer/co-host Ossie Davis/Ruby Dee Story Hour. **HONORS/ACHIEVEMENTS:** TV Emmy winning Teacher; author Purlie Victorious, Escape to Freedom, The Story of Young Frederick Douglass 1978, Langston 1982. **MILITARY SERVICE:** AUS med corp 1942-45. **BUSINESS ADDRESS:** The Artists Agency, 10000 Santa Monica Blvd, Los Angeles, CA 90067.

DAVIS, OSSIE B.
Clergyman. **PERSONAL:** Born May 14, 1922, Starkville, IL; married Ruby Lee Daniels; children: Ethel J, John A, Ossie C, Charles E, Willie J. **EDUCATION:** Rust Coll, AB 1948;Univ of IN, MA 1955; Gammon Theol Sem, post grad 1964; Candler Sch of Theology Emory U, BD 1968; Universal Bible Inst, MBS 1974. **CAREER:** Minister & ordained deacon 1952; elder 1954; various pastorates since 1950; Pickins Elem Sch, principal 1951-55; Gooddman Jr HS, principal 1955-59; Montgomery Training HS, principal 1959-62. **ORGANIZATIONS:** District sec Evangalism; district dir Youth Work; conf dir Evangelism; delegate 4th Family Life Conf; rep General Conf; part-time exec sec of Christian Edn, Methodist Ch; mem TN-MS Tchrs Assn; State PTA cchaplain; co-chrmn MS Freedom Dem Party; co-chrmn Nat Freedom Rider, SCLC; mem NAACP 1946-; delegate Nat Dem Conv; 32 deg Mason Comm organizer, housing counselor, Economic Opportunity Atlanta Inc; probation counselor Fulton Co Deliquency Treeatment Center; Atlanta Southside Comprehensive Health Center; alcoholic counselor Half Way House. **MILITARY SERVICE:** AUS 1941-47.

DAVIS, PATRICIA C.
Association executive. **PERSONAL:** Born Jul 25, 1943, Grand Rapids, MI; married Frederick Douglass; children: Grant Anthony, Frederick Douglass II, Mwindaace N' Gai. **EDUCATION:** Detroit Inst Of Commerce, 1969. **CAREER:** NAACP, exec sec; Amoco Production Co, adminsrv sec 1970-73; UAW Fai Practices & Anti-discrimination Dept, sec 1969-70; League Life Ins Co, stenog 1964-69; US Army Detroit Procurement Dist, clerk stenog 1963; Burroughs Corp, clerk typist 1962-63. **ORGANIZATIONS:** Lay mem Paradise Bapt Ch; Immaculate Conception Christian Bd Of Edn; asst sec OK St Conf of Branches NAACP; asst sec Tulsa Br NAACP; exec sec Tula Br (Naacp 1970-76.

DAVIS, PATRICIA STAUNTON
Economist. **PERSONAL:** Born Mar 29, 1945, Washington, DC; married James. **EDUCATION:** Howard U, BS 1966; Stanford U, MBA 1973; George Washington U, PhD 1977. **CAREER:** Fed Res Bd, econnomist; Booz, Allen & Hamilton, mgmt consult 1973-75; Urban Inst, programmer, sr prgmr mktg rep 1970-71; Progm Serv Corp, 1969-70; Serv Bur Corp, 1968-69; Hughes Aircraft Co, 1967-80; White House Fellows Prgm, spl asst sec labor 1967-68; Fed Res Bd, economist 1976-. **ORGANIZATIONS:** Mem Big Sisters Am; recpt shclrsp HowardUniv 1962-66; COGME Flwsp StanfordUniv 1971-73; White House Flwsp Prgm 1975-76. **BUSINESS ADDRESS:** 20th & Constitution Ave NW, Washington, DC 20551.

DAVIS, PRESTON AUGUSTUS
Management executive. **PERSONAL:** Born in Norfolk, VA; married Mary Pierson; children: Gwendolyn Dyess, Preston A Jr, Karen Heggs, June Kimbrugh. **EDUCATION:** WV State Coll, BS Bus Administration 1949; Command & Gen Staff Coll, MS Exec Mgmt 1965; George Washington Univ, MSA 1974; Post Graduate, Dartmouth and Harvard. **CAREER:** Fairmicco Industries, vp/gen mgr 1969-70; Morgan State Univ, vice pres for development 1970-71; US Dept of Agr, sr mgmt analyst 1971-78, spl asst to asst sec for adminstrn 1978-79; USDA Grad Sch & No VA Comm Coll, prof 1974-79; US Dept of Agr, dir small business affairs 1979-87; Kiwanis Intl, governor 1988-89; Davis & Davis Consultant Assoc 1989. **ORGANIZATIONS:** Bd dir & com chmn Agr Fed Credit Union 1976-; mem Masonic Lodge 1949-; mem Omega Psi Phi Frat 1948-; mem Phi Delta Kappa 1978-; gov Kiwanis Intl Capital dist (1st Black in So) 1988-89. **HONORS/ACHIEVEMENTS:** Disting Mil Grad WV State Coll 1949; Outstanding Achievement Award Salvation Army Wash, DC 1976; 1st Black Disting Gov in So Kiwanis Intl 1988-89;Cert of Merit for Outstanding Performance US Dept of Agr 1979; Publications, "Firepower Chinese Communist Army" & "Signatures of Soviet Nuclear Missle Systems"; NAFEO Distinguished Alumni Award; Small Business Administration's Award for Excellence. **MILITARY SERVICE:** RA Lt Col 1949-70; Bronze Star; Army Commendation Medal; Purple Heart; Army Meritorious Serv Award. **BUSINESS ADDRESS:** Consultant, Kiwanis International, 600 Sixth Pl SW, Washington, DC 20024.

DAVIS, RAOUL ANDR
Consultant. **PERSONAL:** Born Jul 04, 1931, Crewe, VA; married Waunetta; children: Tierney, Rianna, Raoul Jr. **EDUCATION:** Central State U, BS Psychology 1954; Columbia U, MA Personnel Psychology 1959; Grad Sch of Pub & Intl Affairs U, Urban League Fellow 1965-67. **CAREER:** Amityville Inst of small Bus Research & Devel, pres; Center for Life Planning & Career Devel, dir; Davis & Davis & Asso/Cons, pres & sr consult 1979; Suffolk Co Youth Bur Suffolk Col Govt Riverhead NY, dep Dir 1975-79; Manhasset Pub Sch Manhasset NY, com serv Dir 1971-74; Wyandanch Pub Sch NY, comm relations consult 1968-71; OIC Pittsburgh PA, exec dir 1967-68; Dept of Pub Safety Pittsburgh 1966-67; Urban League of Long Island, acting dir 1974-75; Gathering of Beautiful People, exec dir 1976. **ORGANIZATIONS:** Bd of dir Suffolk Comm Council 1969-71; bd of dir Urban & League of Ng Island 1975-79; bd of dir Nassau/Suffolk Health Systems Agency 1976-78. **HONORS/ACHIEVEMENTS:** Fellowships (Scholastic & Athletic) 1st Black to Attend Kiski Prep Schl 194950; urban league fellowUniv of Pittsburgh 1965-67; cert of Appreciation Wyandanch OEO Program Wyandanch Day Care Center 1977-78; plaque for Outstanding Serv Urban League of Long Island 1977. **MILITARY SERVICE:** AUS corpl 1954-56. **BUSINESS ADDRESS:** PO Box 774, Amityville, NY 11701.

DAVIS, REUBEN K.
Judge. **PERSONAL:** Born Jul 26, 1920, Columbus, MS; son of Reuben B Davis and Leola H Adkins; married Elizabeth Zangerle; children: Jennifer, Andrea, Mark. **EDUCATION:** VA State Coll, BA 1946; Boston Univ Law School, LLB 1949. **CAREER:** Hurst Davis & King, attorney 1955-66; City of Rochester, deputy corp consl 1966-68, comm of bldg 1968-72; Stewart & Bennett Inc, gen counsel 1972-74; Assoc Justice, Appellate div New York State Supreme Court, fourth Judicial Dept 1987-. **ORGANIZATIONS:** Trustee Meml AME Zion Church 1958-, Monroe Cty Bar Assoc 1966; chmn Monroe Cty Human Rel Comm 1966-69; Comm Savings Bank, trustee 1969-74; bd of dir YMCA 1976-; mem NY State & Monroe Cty Bar Assoc. **MILITARY SERVICE:** AUS 1st lt 1943-46. **BUSINESS ADDRESS:** Associate Justice, New York State Supreme Court, Appellate Div 4th Dept, Rm 225 Hall of Justice, Rochester, NY 14614.

DAVIS, RICHARD
Musician, composer. **PERSONAL:** Born Apr 15, 1930, Chicago, IL; married Patricia Jean Mulligan; children: Robert, Richard, Joshua; Persia. **EDUCATION:** Vandercook Coll Music Chicago, BME 1952. **CAREER:** Musician bass player freelance; Univ of WI Madison, prof bass & jazz studies; recordings include, "Philosophy of the Spiritual", "Epistrophy & Now's the Time", "Dealin", "With Understanding", "Muses for Richard Davis"; played with Chicago Civic Orch, Natl Orch Assn, Amer Symphony Orch, Orch of Amer, Igov Stravinsky, Gunther Schuller, Leonard Bernstein, Belgium Radio TV Orch, NY Philharmonic, bass prof Univ of WI, Intl Inst of DBL Bass; jazz groups, Ahmad Jamal, Gene Ammons, Thad Jones, Mel Lewis Orch, Kenny Dorham, Eric Dolphy, Charlie Ventura, Miles Davis, Bud Powell, John Tchas, various other groups; adjucator colls in US & France; WI Arts Bd, string bass player 1945-. **ORGANIZATIONS:** Mem NY Bass Choir 1969-; performed in TV specials w/Barbra Streisand "Like It Is", "Black Journal", NET; film soundtrack "Holy Mountain". **HONORS/ACHIEVEMENTS:** Downbeat Critics Poll Awd 1967-74; Downbeat Readers Poll Awd 1967-72; Outstanding Musician's Awd Vandercook Coll 1979; Outstanding Prof Awd Univ of WI Madison 1978-79; grantee Univ WI-WI Arts Board Natl Endowment Arts; ASCAP Awd 1976-79; compositions include, "Dealin", "Julie's Rag Doll", "Blues for Now"; performed at Newport & Monterey Jazz Festivals. **BUSINESS ADDRESS:** Professor Bass Player, Univ of WI, 4415 Humanities Bldg, Madison, WI 53706.

DAVIS, RICHARD
Attorney. **PERSONAL:** Born Sep 12, 1943, Miami, FL; married Doreen D; children: LaRonda R, Richard QuinRo. **EDUCATION:** Univ of AZ, BS Publ Admin (with Distinction) 1969, JD 1972. **CAREER:** Univ of AZ Coll of Law, lecturer 1973-; Chandle Tullar Udall & Redhair, assoc attny 1972-80, partner 1980-. **ORGANIZATIONS:** Mem Amer Bar Assoc 1972-, AZ Bar Assoc 1972-; bd of dir So AZ Legal Aid Soc 1975-, Tucson Urban League 1975-, Ododo Theatre 1975-; pres Tucson Urban League 1977-78; bd of dir Pima Cty Bar Assoc 1978-80, Amer Red Cross 1980-83, YMCA 1983-. **HONORS/ACHIEVEMENTS:** Woodrow Wilson Natl Fellowship 1969-72; commiss AZ Athletic Comm 1977-81; mem AZ Civil Rights Comm 1977-78; Distinguished Citizen Awd NAACP Tucson 1982. **MILITARY SERVICE:** US Air Force E-4 4 yrs. **HOME ADDRESS:** 5620 E So Wilshire, Tucson, AZ 85711. **BUSINESS ADDRESS:** Attorney, Chandler,Tullar,Udall,Redhair, 33 North Stone #1700, Tucson, AZ 85701.

DAVIS, RICHARD C.
Educator. **PERSONAL:** Born Sep 06, 1925, Los Angeles, CA; married Dolores Parks; children: Saundra, Marilyn, Jacqueline. **EDUCATION:** Geo Pepperdine Coll LA, BA 1952; Compton Coll, AA 1949. **CAREER:** Sacramento County, Office of Educ, Child Welfare & Attendance Servs, cons; Child Welfare & Attend, Compton Unified School Dist, supt 1970-74; Compton Union School Dist 1967-70; Compton Sr High School, vocational educ counselor 1966-67; Tubman High Schooll, continuing educ guidance counselor 1965-66; Ralph Bunche Jr High School, teacher 1957-65; Willowbrook Jr High School 1952-57; Los Angeles Conty Dept of Parks & Recreation, recreation dir 1948-52. **ORGANIZATIONS:** Pres elct CA Assn Suprvrs Chld Wlfr attended CTA; NEA; Compton Sec Ndry Tchrs Assn; CA Cont Educ Assn; Assn Compton Schls Adminstrators; mem many spec coms in professional capacity; mem LA Co Dist Attys AdvCouncil; cit adv com Reg Planning Commn; agcy exec Com Welfare Planning Council; chmnVandalism Prev Task Frc; chmn Feasibility Study YMCA; mem Del Amo Home Owners Assn; mem Comm Orgn to Study Student Behavior; PTA; bd dir Adv Concercened Cit for Neighborhood; pres Grant, UCa LA 1968. **HONORS/ACHIEVEMENTS:** Nat Jr Coll Track & Field Award; All Pacific Island Champ Football Award. **MILITARY SERVICE:** USMC corpl 1943-46. **BUSINESS ADDRESS:** 1623 E 118 St, Los Angeles, CA 90059.

DAVIS, RICHARD O.
Automobile dealer. **CAREER:** Davis Buik-Jeep Eagle, Inc, Battle Creek MI, chief exec officer. **BUSINESS ADDRESS:** Davis Buick-Jeep Eagle, Inc, 995 W Columbia Ave, Battle Creek, MI 49015. *

DAVIS, ROBERT E.
Business executive. **PERSONAL:** Born Aug 26, 1937, Indianapolis. **EDUCATION:** Assoc Degreee in Bus Mgmt 1963. **CAREER:** Fun & Travel Inc, pres; NAACP, youth advisor 1970-71; Addison YWCA, youth advisor 1965-67; Lawson's Dairy Store Cleveland, mgr 1963; Cleveland Public Library, purchsng clrk; Delta & Enterprise, talent booking agent 1967; Lorain Sound Recording Co, pub rel 1969; Jetay Music Publ Co, ow Ner 1970. **ORGANIZATIONS:** Mem Black Hist Inst; NAACP; mem Cleveland Bus League; Nat Assn of TV & Radio Announcers; treas Local 1054, Am Fed of State Co & Municipal Empl Oyees. **BUSINESS ADDRESS:** Box 20113, Cleveland, OH 44120.

DAVIS, ROBERT E.
Government official. **PERSONAL:** Born Nov 21, 1908, Kenensville, NC; married Bernice Shaw; children: Sandra Roberta. **EDUCATION:** Fayetteville State U, BS 1936. **CAREER:** State NC, rep 1978-80; David Bros Wholesale Grocers, co-owner 1940; City of Maxton, city councilman 1972-78; Robesou Co Bd of Edn, tchr 1930-43. **ORGANIZATIONS:** Master Masonic Lodge 86 Maxton 1950-54; illustrous potentate Ouda Temple 147 Shriner 1952-56. **BUSINESS ADDRESS:** Davis Bros Wholesale Grocers, Wilmington St, Maxton, NC 28364.

DAVIS, ROLAND HAYES
Administrator. **PERSONAL:** Born in Cleveland, OH; son of Sylvester S Davis Sr and Amaza Dewey Weaver Davis; divorced; children: Jeffrey, Leslie, Kurt. **EDUCATION:** Western Reserve Univ Cleveland OH, 1946; Hofstra Univ Hempstead NY, 1958; Long Island Univ, BA 1961; Adelphi Univ School of Social Work, MSW 1969. **CAREER:** Nassau Cty Dept of Soc Srvs, asst to deputy comm 1966-79; Hofstra Univ, coord of comm dev 1979-, Affirmative Action officer 1988-; Guardian Bank N A, dir 1975-. **ORGANIZATIONS:** Chmn bd dir Guardian Bank NA 1975-86; pres Assn of Minority Enterprises of NY Inc 1982-86; bd mem Hempstead Chamber of Comm; pres 100 Black Men of Nassau/Suffolk Inc 1980-86; dir Health & Welfare Council of Nassau Cty Inc 1983-; bd dir United Way of Long Island 1982-88; bd trustees Sci Museum of Long Island 1984-85; life mem Hempstead Branch NAACP; mem EDGES Group Inc; mem adv panel Project 2000 Long Island Assoc Commerce & Industry. **HONORS/ACHIEVEMENTS:** Unispan Award Hofstra Univ 1979; HUB Summer Career Awareness Prog 1980; Ldrshp Award LI Minority Bus Comm 1981; NYS Legislative Resolution Citation 1983; NOAH Prog Hofstra Univ 1984; Pres Recognition Award for Comm Srv 1984. **MILITARY SERVICE:** AUS 1st lt 1946-66. **BUSINESS ADDRESS:** Coordinator of Community Dev & Affirmative Action Officer, HofstraUniv, 1000 Fulton Ave, Hempstead, NY 11550.

DAVIS, RONALD P.
Corporate middle manager. **PERSONAL:** Born May 29, 1949, Montgomery, AL; son of William W Davis and Princess A Davis; married Tinny B Jones; children: Ronald Prince, Tracye Belinda. **EDUCATION:** Southern IL Univ, BS 1971; MS Coll, MBA 1975. **CAREER:** South Central Bell, sales mgr 1972-74, mgr emp/coord 1974-77, operations mgr I&M 1977-83; AT&T, district mgr/csso 1983-1987; district manager-training 1987-. **ORGANIZATIONS:** Pres Alpha Phi Alpha/Epsilon Lambda Chap 1977-79; bd mem Metropolitan YMCA 1979-83, Jackson MS Public Schools 1981-83, Hinds Co Human Resources Agency 1981-; mem Sigma Pi Phi Frat 1981-; pres Jackson MS Urban League 1983. **HONORS/ACHIEVEMENTS:** Service Appreciation Awd Jackson Professional Educators 1983. **HOME ADDRESS:** 5025 Oak Bluff Ct, Atlanta, GA 30360. **BUSINESS ADDRESS:** District Manager, AT&T, 240-2800 Century Pkwy, Atlanta, GA 30345.

DAVIS, RONALD W.
Business executive. **PERSONAL:** Born Sep 16, 1950, Camden, NJ; married Willabel; children: Ronald W II. **EDUCATION:** VA State U, BS 1968-72, MED 1973-75. **CAREER:** San Fran 49ers, football plyr 1972; St Louis Cardinals, football plyr 1972-76; United VA Bank, retail/Oper officer 1976-84; Metro Richmond Conven & Visitors Bureau, Deputy Executive Dir. **ORGANIZATIONS:** Pres of bd dir VA State Univ Found 1979-85; bd of dir Metropolitan Business League 1977-84; mem NFL Players Assn 1976-85; Guilfield Church Finance Bd 1985-89. **HONORS/ACHIEVEMENTS:** All Am NCAA Div II 1972; Man of the Yr Hlth Phys Ed & Recreation 1972; "Top 10 in Ricmond, "Richmond," Richmond Surroundings Mag; VA State Univ Sports Hall of Fame 1989. **BUSINESS ADDRESS:** Deputy Executive Director, Metro Richmond Convention and Visitors Bureau, Suite 309, Richmond, VA 23219.

DAVIS, ROSEMARY ORMOND
Consultant. **EDUCATION:** Lincoln Univ, BA 1969; Atlanta Univ, MA 1979; Univ of PA, DSc 1976. **CAREER:** Philadelphia Housing Authority, area dir social serv 1972-73; Temple Univ, interdisciplinary training dir 1974-76; EMC Institute, sr mgmt consultant 1976-78; RDA Consultants, pres 1978-. **ORGANIZATIONS:** Consultant to numerous organizations; mem Inst of Mgmt Consultant Firms, Amer Soc for Training Directors, Amer Mgmt Assoc, Philadelphia League of Women Voters; bd mem Citizen's Adv Comm on Health; mem Philadelphia Boosters Club; bd mem Martin Luther King Jr Ctr for Non-Violent Change. **HONORS/ACHIEVEMENTS:** Human Rights Awd City of Philadelphia 1978; Woman of the Year East Repertory Theatre Co 1978; The Fast Track Awd 1979; Leadership Awd The Black Women's Collective of America 1980; Networking Awd The Black Women's Collective of Amer 1981; Philadelphia Mayoral Citation for Economic Development 1984; 4 publications. **BUSINESS ADDRESS:** President, Rosemary Davis Associates, Inc, PO Box 42675, Philadelphia, PA 19101.

DAVIS, SAMMY, JR.
Singer, dancer, actor. **PERSONAL:** Born Dec 08, 1925, NYC, NY; married Altovise Gore; children: Tracey, Mark, Jeff. **CAREER:** Began career 1928 vaudeville Will Mastin Trio 1930-48; performed on Broadway "Mister Wonderful" 1956-57, "Golden Boy" 1964, "Sammy on Broadway" 1975; Films, "Porgy & Bess" 1959, "Ocean's Eleven" 1960, "Salt & Pepper", "Sweet Charity", "Save the Children", "Pepe", "Sargent's Three", "Johnny Cool", "Robin & Seven Hoods", "Sweet Charity", "A Man Called Adam" 1966, "One More Time"; TV appearances, Mod Squad, Laugh-In, Lucy Show, Sammy & Co numerous specials; Tropicana Hotel Las Vegas, vice pres. **ORGANIZATIONS:** Mem Friars Club; mem Amer Soc of Mag Photographers; mem Operation PUSH; mem United Negro Coll Fund. **HONORS/ACHIEVEMENTS:** Recipient of many major honors as performer & humanitarian; author of autobiography "Yes I Can" 1965. **MILITARY SERVICE:** AUS 1943-45. **BUSINESS ADDRESS:** c/o William Morris Agency, 1350 Ave of Americas, New York, NY 10019.

DAVIS, SAMMY, JR.
Educator, mayor. **PERSONAL:** Born Oct 02, 1930, Ferriday, LA; married Elizabeth A; children: Sammy III, Craig Fenton. **EDUCATION:** Grambling State Univ, BS 1954; Southern Univ Baton Rouge, MA 1967. **CAREER:** Teacher, Breauybridge LA 1954-57, Ferriday LA 1957; Concordia Parish, principal 1967-74 police juror; Concordia Parish Educ Assn, pres 1971-73. **ORGANIZATIONS:** Mem LEA-NEA; Kappa Alpha Psi; NAACP; Helping Hand; Police Jury Assn; Educ Comm of States; natl Assn of Counties; mem Corcordia Parish Civil League; Student Bar Assn; mem, Jamadi Temple #171 (A.E.A.O.N.M.E. Inc); mem, Louis R Price Consistory 32 Prince Hall. **HONORS/ACHIEVEMENTS:** Award for Outstanding Achievements in Politics; Special Award LEA-NEA. **MILITARY SERVICE:** AUS sgt 1951-53. **HOME ADDRESS:** P O Box 444, Ferriday, LA 71334.

DAVIS, SAMUEL RUEL
Professional athlete. **PERSONAL:** Born Jul 04, 1944, Ocilla, GA; married Gladys Seymour; children: Vanessa, Tami. **EDUCATION:** Allen U, BS 1967. **CAREER:** Pittsburgh Steelers, professional football player offensive team capt; Russ Contruction Co, sales consult 1974-75; Pittsburgh Courrier, sales rep 1973-74; Operation & Dig, adminstrv dir 1972-73; Operation Dig, dir edndir educ serv 1972-72; Westinghouse Electric, min recruiter 1970-71; Bidwell Cutural Cntr, rec dir 1968-69. **ORGANIZATIONS:** Mem Nat Football League Players Assn 1966; co-capt Pittsburgh Steelers 1972-74; NFL Championship Gamess 1974,75, 78 & 79; AFC Championship Game 1972,75, 76,78 & 79; mem YMCA.

DAVIS, SHIRLEY E.
Labor industrial relations manager. **PERSONAL:** Born Feb 23, 1935, New Haven, CT; married EL Davis Jr; children: Annette S Sands. **EDUCATION:** Attended Morgan State Coll Baltimore 1953-54; attended Quinnipiac Coll New Haven 1956-58; attended So CT State Coll. **CAREER:** US Postal Serv, distrib clerk/postal data systems tech 1958-; Natl Alliance of Postal & Federal Employees, natl secty. **ORGANIZATIONS:** Dist 8 pres NAPFE 1972-80; mem Natl Exec NAPFE Bd 1972-; bd of dirs Urban League of Greater New Haven 1974-80; commr Commn on Equal Oppor New Haven 1975-; vice chairperson Commn on Equal Oppor New Haven 1977-80. **HONORS/ACHIEVEMENTS:** First Black Female Career Employee New Haven PO 1958; First Female Pres NAPFE Local 811 New Haven 1969; First Female Pres NAPFE Dist 8 1972; First Female Natl Sec NAPFE 1980; One of the Highest Ranking Women US Labor Movement. **BUSINESS ADDRESS:** Natl Secretary, Nat All of Postal & Fed Employ, 1628 11th St NW, Washington, DC 20001.

DAVIS, STEPHEN SMITH
Educator. **PERSONAL:** Born Oct 24, 1910, Philadelphia; married Aileen Priscilla Harris; children: Stephen Harris. **EDUCATION:** Howard U, BS in Mech Engineering 1936; Harvard U, MS Mech 1947. **CAREER:** Howard Univ, faculty, mechanical engineering prof 1938, dept head 1962, dean School of Engineering & Architecture 1964-70; Natl Bureau Standards, mechanical engineer 1943-45; Naval Ordinance Lab, consultant 1953-63. **ORGANIZATIONS:** Mem Washington Acad Sci; Am Soc ME; AAAS; Am Soc Engineering Edn; DC Soc Professional Engrs mem Tau Beta Pi; Cosmos, WA. **HONORS/ACHIEVEMENTS:** Invented with patent Flexible Wing-tunnel Nozzle.

DAVIS, STEVE G.
Government employee. **PERSONAL:** Born in Birmingham, AL; married Christine Ray Davis; children: Pamela Elaine. **EDUCATION:** IL Inst TechUniv Chicago. **CAREER:** Morale & Wlfr Brnch, gen stf officer; Util Div, actg chf; Hum Rel Resrch Brnch, exec officer; Office of Asst Chf of Stf G1 Hdqrtrs Dept of Army; Prsnnl Ser Brnch, exec Officer; Equal & Rghts Brnch, chf; Mtvtn Brnch, chf; Prsnnl Serv Div Office of Depty ChF of Stf for Pr Snnl Hdqrtrs Dept of Army, chf. **ORGANIZATIONS:** Mem Bd Amer Red Cr WA DC; DistSer Medal US Pres. **HONORS/ACHIEVEMENTS:** Hon BS of Amer. **MILITARY SERVICE:** AUS col. **BUSINESS ADDRESS:** Pentagon, Washington, DC.

DAVIS, THOMAS J.
Business executive. **PERSONAL:** Born Apr 21, 1908, Memphis, TN; married Dahl Hollingsworth; children: Thomas L, Beryl J. **EDUCATION:** HS & Coll Equivalent. **CAREER:** Investigator 1934-38; columnist 1936-40; Statewide Political Org OH State Dem League, chmn 1936-44; city councilman 1938-40; advertising dir 1941-43; Tom Davis Agency, presbus & mktg consult 1958-. **ORGANIZATIONS:** Mem Greater Cleveland Growth Bd, NAMD, Detroit C of C, Cleveland Bus League, OH & MI Sales Rep for Amalgamated Publishers Inc, Amer Mktg Assoc, Randolph Wallace Kidney Found, NAACP, The Econ Club Detroit; Recess Club Detroit. **HONORS/ACHIEVEMENTS:** Thomas J Davis Roast; Prominent Detroit Bus Persons Called "Friends of Tom Davis"; Disting Contrib Awd OH

House of Rep; Disting Serv Awd NAACP; Disting Serv Awd NAMD; Disting Serv Awd MI State Hwy. **MILITARY SERVICE:** USCG Aux Flotilla comdr 9E-99. **BUSINESS ADDRESS:** President, Tom Davis Agency, 1940 E 6th St, Ste 721, Cleveland, OH 44114.

DAVIS, THOMAS JOSEPH
Educator. **PERSONAL:** Born Jan 06, 1946, New York City, NY; son of Otto J Davis and Alice R (McKenzie) Davis. **EDUCATION:** Ball State Univ, MA 1976; Columbia Univ, PhD 1974, MA 1968; Fordham Univ, AB 1967. **CAREER:** Southern Univ, instr 1968-69; Manhattanville Coll, dir afro-amer stud 1970-71; Earlham Coll, assoc/asst prof 1972-76; Natl Museum of Amer Hist, rsch assoc 1983-86; Howard Univ, prof/assoc prof 1977-87; State Univ of NY at Buffalo, prof 1987-. **ORGANIZATIONS:** Bd mem New York City Council Against Poverty 1964-67; consultant Natl Endowment for Humanities 1980, Educational Testing Serv 1979-, US Dept of Labor 1977-78; exec bd St Camillus Church 1983-86, Humboldt Journal of Soc Sci 1980-, Journal of Negro History 1974-. **HONORS/ACHIEVEMENTS:** Fellow Ford Found 1971, Herbert H Lehman 1969-71; Phi Beta Kappa 1967; Sigma Delta Chi 1976; Francis Cardinal Spellman Youth Award 1962; Newberry Library Fellow 1982; Smithsonian Inst Faculty Fellow 1983; Gustavas Myers Honorable Mention, Gustavas Myers Institute 1985; author, A Rumor of Revolt (New York: MacMillan/Free Press) 1985. **BUSINESS ADDRESS:** Professor, State University of NY, Dept AAS, Buffalo, NY 14260.

DAVIS, TWILUS
Clergyman. **EDUCATION:** Friendship Coll Rockhill SC, DD. **CAREER:** The Promiseland Bapt Church Caldwell St, N Memphis, pastor 1910 friendship baptist church buffalo, pastor 1929; promiseland baptist church buffalo, pastor; Erie Cnty Pen Old Folks Infirmary, fndr. **ORGANIZATIONS:** 1st Negro Poltcl Club Buffalo; 1st Minstrs Conf; 1st Dist Assn Buffalo Sp L & Achvmt Fndr 8th Grade Schl. **HONORS/ACHIEVEMENTS:** Hon plaque Cncl & Empire St Bapt Conv NYC; prsntd key city of memphis. **BUSINESS ADDRESS:** Promiseland Bapt Ch, 243 Mulberry, Buffalo, NY.

DAVIS, TYRONE THEOPHILUS
Assoc. executive. **PERSONAL:** Born Dec 10, 1948, Kansas City, KS; widowed; children: Monette M, Natalie R, Tyrena E. **EDUCATION:** Univ of Cincinnati, BBA 1970; Lexington Theological Seminary, M Divinity 1976. **CAREER:** Lexington-Fayette Co, exec dir 1972-74; Phillips Memorial CME Church, sr pastor 1972-76; Urban League of St Louis, accountant 1977-82; Parrish Temple CME Church, sr pastor 1976-79; Jamison Mem CME Church, sr pastor 1979-82; CME Church, admin coord 1982-86; Wesley CME Church, sr pastor 1986-. **ORGANIZATIONS:** Life mem Alpha Phi Alpha Frat 1968-; mem (former pres) Lexington Fayette Co 1973-76; treas KY Council of Churches 1974-76; former treas KY Conf of NAACP Chapts 1975-76; mem Natl Assoc of Black Accountants 1981-87; treas Beloit Branch NAACP 1986-; vice pres Beloit Comm Ministers Fellowship 1986-. **HONORS/ACHIEVEMENTS:** 110% Awd Merit Alpha Phi Alpha Frat 1976; Hon KY Col State of KY 1976; Achievement Outstanding Young Man in Amer 1983; GW Carver Awd Sigma Gamma Rho Sor 1984. **HOME ADDRESS:** 1762 Poole Court, Beloit, WI 53511. **BUSINESS ADDRESS:** Pastor, 1513 November Cir, #302, Silver Spring, MD 20904.

DAVIS, WALTER (SWEET D)
Professional athlete. **PERSONAL:** Born Sep 09, 1954, Pineville, NC; married Susan Hatter; children: Hillary Elyse, Jordan Elizabeth. **EDUCATION:** Univ of NC, attended 1973-77. **CAREER:** Phoenix Suns, guard 1977-. **HONORS/ACHIEVEMENTS:** Mem Gold Medal winning US Olympic Basketball Team Montreal 1976; Rookie of the Yr 1977-78; Pro Athlete of Yr Phoenix Press Box Assn 1979; 5 time mem Western Conf All Star Team; mem 37th NBA All Star Team. **BUSINESS ADDRESS:** Phoenix Suns, 2910 N Central Ave, Phoenix, AZ 85012.

DAVIS, WALTER G.
Labor executive. **PERSONAL:** Born Nov 26, 1920, New York, NY; married Doris E; children: Walter, Jr, Allison, Philip. **EDUCATION:** Columbia U, BS 1956; Attended Brooklyn Law School 2 Yrs. **CAREER:** United Transportation Serv Employees CIO, pres Local 290 1952-58; UTSE Nat Orgn, exec vice pres 1958-61; AFL CIO Civil Rights Dept, asst dir 1961-65; Fed EEO, dept & exec Dir 1965-66; AFL CIO, 1966; AFL CIO Labor Studies Center, asst sec bd trustees 1969; Comm Coll of the Air Force, mem adv commn 1973-. **ORGANIZATIONS:** Mem Adv Commn Comm Coll of the Air Force 1973; mem Labor Educ Adv Commn Cornell U,Univ of Houston, OH State U,Univ of Al; Panel of Experts ILO GenevaSwitzerland; mem bd of dir A Philip Randolph Inst Treas; Boy Scout Troup 175, Teaneck NJ 1963; mem Harlem Br NAACP; mem Jack N Jill of Am 1967. **HONORS/ACHIEVEMENTS:** Recipient A Philip Randolph Human Rights Award; Presidential Appointments, 1967; mem Nat Adv Council on Adult, Basic Educ Pres Johnson 1971; mem Nat Adv Council on Supplementary Centers & Svc, Pres Nixon 1975; mem Commn & on White House Fellows. **MILITARY SERVICE:** AUS WWII m/sgt. **BUSINESS ADDRESS:** 815 16 St NW, Washington, DC 20006.

DAVIS, WALTER J., JR.
Military officer. **PERSONAL:** Married Constance Surles; children: Sharon, Kimberly. **EDUCATION:** Naval Postgradute School, BS, MS, Aeronautical Engineering. **CAREER:** Commandant, Naval Dist Washington 1988-present; Naval Flag Officer, 1988; Special Asst to the Chief of Naval Operations, 1987; Commanding Officer of USS Ranger, 1985-87; Exec Asst to the Deputy Chief of Naval Operations, 1983; Commander, USS Sacramento, 1981; Asst Program Mgr, 1977. **HONORS/ACHIEVEMENTS:** Legion of Merit, Meritorious Serv Medal, Air Medal (ten awards); Navy Commendation Medal w/Combat "V"; Meritorious Unit Commendation, Battle "E" Ribbon, Navy Expeditionary Medal w/three Bronze Stars; Natl Defense Serv Medal, Armed Forces Expeditionary Medal with three Bronze Stars; Sea Serv Deployment Ribbon (two awards); Vietnamese Gallentry Cross with Bronze Star; Republic of Vietnam Meritorious Unit Citation; Vietnam Campaign Medal.

DAVIS, WANDA M.
Educational administrator. **PERSONAL:** Born Nov 09, 1952, Philadelphia, PA; daughter of Viola S Davis. **EDUCATION:** PA State Univ, BS 1974, MPA 1980, Doctorate ABD. **CAREER:** YWCA, program planning coordinator 1974-75; Lincoln Univ, residential dir 1975-78; PA State Univ, freshman counselor 1978-84, asst dean of students 1984-; interim dean of students, 1987-89. **ORGANIZATIONS:** NAFEO, mem 1980-; American Assoc of Higher Educ, mem 1980-; PA Coll Personnel Assoc 1980-; Phi Delta Kappa, vice pres, mem 1982-83; NAACP, Rorbert A Dave Found, 1989, AAUW. **HONORS/ACHIEVEMENTS:** CWENS, honorary candidate for academic standing 1972; Woodrow Wilson, fellow 1981. **HOME ADDRESS:** PO Box 10791, Calder Square, State College, PA 16805.

DAVIS, WARREN B.
Educator. **PERSONAL:** Born Sep 16, 1947, Gary, IN; son of Richard Davis and Armenta Davis; children: Kwame Inhatep; Ida Aisha. **EDUCATION:** Bowling Green State U, MA 1971, BA 1970; Defiance Coll, BA 1970; Developmental Educational Specialists, Appalachian State Univ 1984. **CAREER:** Bowling Green State U, assoc Dir student devel; Student Devel Prog, coord counseling serv 1973; Defiance Coll, instr Afro-am Hist II 1973; Student Devel Prog, counselor 1971-72; Neighborhood Youth Corps, supvr; Mid-town Coffee Hse, Gary Youth Activities, prog dir Trends in Afro-Am Thought, tchr 1969; USS Steel, laborer part time 1967-69; Coordinator University of Toledo Tutorial Services, Supervisor Career Planning Center; asst dir Academic Support Serv. **ORGANIZATIONS:** Mem Am Pers & Guid Assn 1971; Assn of Counselor Educ & Supvision 1971; Minority Educ Serv Assn of OH; Natl Assn for Developmental Education; Bd of directors Coalition for quality Integrated Education. **HONORS/ACHIEVEMENTS:** Recip Serv Award to Minority Students; BGSU 1974; serv BGSU 1977; Administrator of the Year BSU 1983.

DAVIS, WILEY M.
Educational administrator. **PERSONAL:** Born Dec 04, 1927, Meadowview, VA; son of William J Davis and Pearl Eva; married Mary Hargrove; children: Wiley Jr. **EDUCATION:** Swift Jr Coll, AA; St Augustines Coll, BA; Springfield Coll, MEd; Brigham Young Univ, EdD. **CAREER:** Meadowview Elementary School, teacher 1947; AUS, instructor 1952; Douglas HS, teacher 1953, principal 1956; St Augustine's Coll, dean of students 1960, admin asst to pres 1970, vice pres for admin 1973; vice pres for Student Affairs, 1974-. **ORGANIZATIONS:** Sec Elizabethton Principal Assoc; treas, pres Phi Beta Sigma; mem Raleigh, NC Community Action Council, Govt Comm on Employment of Handicapped, Phi Delta Kappa Hon Soc, NC Cemetery Commn; Hospice of Wayne County, Deacon, Martin St Baptist Church. **HONORS/ACHIEVEMENTS:** Honorary Mem St Augustines Coll Vet Club; Phi Beta Sigma Achievement Award. **MILITARY SERVICE:** AUS 1951-53. **BUSINESS ADDRESS:** VP Student Affairs/Special Project, St Augustine's College, Raleigh, NC 27611.

DAVIS, WILLIAM E., SR.
Architect, city & regional planner. **PERSONAL:** Born Dec 01, 1930, Camden, SC; son of Clarence Davis Sr and Margaret Davis; married Jacqueline Hawkins; children: William, Jr, Victor, Brian. **EDUCATION:** Howard Univ, BArch 1967; Columbia Univ, Pratt Inst of NY, MIT, grad studies; City & Regional Planning Pratt Inst, MS 1976. **CAREER:** US Treas Dept, 1958-66; RC Architects & Assocs, des & ofc mgr 1967-68; F&M Shaefer Corp Brooklyn, arch designer 1968-69; Brownsville Adv Planning Agency, planner 1969-70; Volmer Assocs NY, arch & planner 1971; City of Boston Model City Admin, chief phys planning 1972-75; Boston Model City, asst adminst 1975; US Dept of Housing & Urban Develop, loan specialist 1977-80; US Dept of Trans Urban Mass Trans Admin, comm planner 1980-87; program manager 1987-; Urban Consultants Inc, vice pres 1969-75; Onyx Consultants Inc, pres 1975-76; Massachusetts Dept of Public Works, Bureau of Transportation and Planning Development, regional planner 1976-. **ORGANIZATIONS:** Mem Conf MA Planning Dirs 1973-75; mem Amer Soc Planning Officials 1969-77; mem Natl Tech Assn 1968-75; org & acting chmn Black Planning Network of NY 1970; mem Comm Vol Assn for Educ Adv of our Children 1971; housing chmn Roxbury Neighborhood Devel Counc of Boston 1974; prog mgr SW Corridor Land Develop Coalition Proj in Boston 1971-75; Dedham MA town mem Title I Educ Adv Council 1975-76; exec committee Greater Manchester Branch NAACP; mem Greater Manchester Black Scholarship Fund 1987-; mem Martin Luther King Jr Speakers Bureau 1987-. **HONORS/ACHIEVEMENTS:** Martin L King Fellow 1969-71. **MILITARY SERVICE:** AUS 1955-57. **BUSINESS ADDRESS:** Program Manager, US Dept Trans/Urban Mass Admin, 55 Broadway Ste 904, Cambridge, MA 02142.

DAVIS, WILLIAM HAYES, SR.
Educational therapist. **PERSONAL:** Born Jun 13, 1947, Richmond, VA; married Ivy P West; children: William Jr. **EDUCATION:** Virginia State Univ, BA 1970; Virginia Commonwealth Univ, MEd 1983. **CAREER:** Gooehland Public Schools, teacher 1972-73; Commonwealth Psychiatric Ctr, ed therapist 1974-79; St Joseph's Villa, ed therapist 1979-81; Garfield Childs Memorial Fund, prog dir 1983-85; VA State Univ, sp educ coll instructor 1986-; Richmond Public Schools, clinical teacher 1981-. **ORGANIZATIONS:** Mem NAACP 1980-; guide right prog dir 1980-84, asst keeper of records 1984-85, Kappa Alpha Psi Inc Rich Alumni; co-owner Assessment Then Remediation 1986-. **HONORS/ACHIEVEMENTS:** Outstanding Leadership Guide Right Kappa Alpha Psi Rich Alumni 1982; Service to the Frat Ach Awd Kappa Alpha Psi Rich Alumni 1983; Inst for Educ Leadership Awd Rich Public Schs 1984-85. **MILITARY SERVICE:** ANG sp4 1970-76; Certificate of Training Achievement, Outstanding Performance of Duty 1970. **HOME ADDRESS:** 2500 Hawthrone Ave, Richmond, VA 23222.

DAVIS, WILLIAM L.
Association executive. **PERSONAL:** Born Dec 30, 1933, Hopewell, VA; married Glenice Claiborne; children: Kevin, Todd. **EDUCATION:** Morgan State Coll, AB 1955; Howard U, JD 1961. **CAREER:** United Planning Orgn, exec dir; UPO Washington DC, gen counsel 1970-73; Howard U, prof of law 1972; Neighborhood Legal Serv Prog Inc & Washington, acting exec dir 1969-70; NLSP, desp dir 1968-69; US Atty,asst 1965-68; US Dept of Justice DC, trial atty 1961-65; US Dept Navy, law clerk gen counsel 1960. **ORGANIZATIONS:** Mem Washington Bar Assn; Howard Law Sch Alumni Assn; mem bd of dir Independence Serv Corp; mem bd of dir Natl Children's Island Inc; mem Bd Dir UPO Enterprises Inc; mem bd dir UPO Comm Dev Corp Editor-in-chief; Howard Law Journal 1960-61; Class Pres 1960. **HONORS/ACHIEVEMENTS:** Bureau of Nat Affairs Award; Bancroft-whitney Co & Lawyer's Cooperative Publishing Co Award; Legal Writings 6 How L J 90 1960; 6 How L J 213, 1960; 7 HoW LJ 65, 1961. **BUSINESS ADDRESS:** 1021 14 St NW, Washington, DC 20005.

DAVIS, WILLIAM M., JR.
Educator. **PERSONAL:** Born Mar 06, 1929, New York City; married Shirley Humes; children: Michelle, Melanie. **EDUCATION:** BA, MA, PhD physchology 1971. **CAREER:**

Molloy College, assoc prof; Hofstra Univ, former asst prof; Health & Welfare Council of Nassau County, assoc dir rsch & devel 1972-, part-time, 1969-71 full-time; Economic Opportunity Commn of Nassau County, res dir 1965-68; New Opps at Hofstra Prog, dir counseling 1968-69; Rockville Centre Schools, consultant July 1977, May-June 1974; United Found of Long Island, 1973-74; North Shore Schools, 1972; Freeport High School, 1971-72; Economic Opportunity Commn of Nasau County, May-Oct 1971, Jan-June 1969. **ORGANIZATIONS:** Guest lectr Malverne HS Career Days 1970, 1974; Grand St Early Childhood Cntr 1974, 1975; Youth Bd 1973; Roslyn Jr HS 1972; Great Neck HS 1971; mem Malverne Sch Bd Adv Panel; panel mem Malverne Sch Bd & Better Educ Com parents night forum; exec bd mem Nassau Co Psychological Assn; past exec bd mem Nassau Co Psychological Assn Psychol Serv Inst; mem Am Psychological Assn; past mem Am Statistical Assn; Eastern Psychological Assn; Am Educ Res Assn; Intl Assn of Survey Statisticians. **MILITARY SERVICE:** AUS capt 1951-54. **BUSINESS ADDRESS:** Molloy College, Dept of Psychology, 1000 Hempstead Ave, Rockville Centre, NY 11570.

DAVIS, WILLIAM R.
Educator, physician. **PERSONAL:** Born Oct 04, 1934, Newport News, VA; children: 5 Children. **EDUCATION:** Hampton Inst, BS 1956; Med Coll of VA, MD 1964. **CAREER:** Fitzsimons Hosp, Denver, intern; Brooke Army Med Cntr, San Antonio, resident; Johns Hopkins Med Sch, instr pediatrics 1972; Baltimore, pvt prac Pediatrics 1969-;Univ of S CA, res fellow, aslergy Immunology 1985; HowardUniv Coll of Med, asst clincal prof pediatrics 1968-69; DeWitt Army Hosp, asst chief pediatrics 1967-68; Dept of Navy, res chemist 1956-60. **ORGANIZATIONS:** Mem Omega Psi Phi Frat; Chi Delta Mu Frat; hon Alumnus Johns Hopkins U; mem Beta Kappa Chi; hon Scienlike Soc;diplomate Nat Bd of Med Examiners; Am Bd of Pediatrics; fellow Am Acad of Pediatrics, NMA. **HONORS/ACHIEVEMENTS:** Recip Award for Metit Svc; Providtne Comp Health Cntr 1971. **MILITARY SERVICE:** AUS maj m c 1964-72. **BUSINESS ADDRESS:** LA Co USC Med Cntr, Hampton, VA.

DAVIS, WILLIAM R.
Educator. **PERSONAL:** Born Apr 28, 1921, Cincinnati, OH; son of William Davis and Florence Davis; married Gladys Hamilton; children: William R, Jr. **EDUCATION:** Univ of Cincinnati, BS 1950; OH State Univ, MA 1951; Northeastern IL Univ, MA 1969; Loyola Univ, doctoral candidate. **CAREER:** Cincinnati Public Recreation Commn, 1947-54; Chicago Public Schools, teacher, asst principal; Oldtown Chicago Boys Club, athletic dir & prog dir 1954-68; Loyola Univ of Chicago, dir Project Upward Bound, instructor, Curriculum and Instruction 1969-. **ORGANIZATIONS:** Pres Council for College Attend 1970-74; chmn Chicago Nat Coll Fair (NACAC) 1973-75 & 1978-80; mem bd dir IL Assn of Coll Admission Counselors 1974-76; pres I1L Assn for Non-White Concerns in Pers & Guidance 1977-78; pres IL Assn of Coll Admission Counselors 1981-82; mem Amer Sch Health Assn; Am Assn of Univ Profs; Nat Assn for Higher Edn; Nat Assn of Coll Admiss Counselors; Phi Epsilon Kappa; Phi Delta Kappa; Nat Upward Bound Steering Com 1970-72; Assn for Superv and Curriculum Dev; Am Assn for Counseling and Dev (APGA); midwest reg rep Assn for Non-White Concerns in Counseling and Dev; mem IL State Board of Educ Advisory Bd for Pupil Personnel Svcs. **HONORS/ACHIEVEMENTS:** Presidential Award Mid-Amer Assn of Educ Opportunity Program Personnel 1979; Presidential Awardd IL Assoc of Coll Admissions Counselors 1982; Presidential Citation Assoc for Multicultural Counseling & Devel 1984; Human Relations Award Natl Assn of Coll Admissions Counselors 1984; Hon Degree Doctor of Humanities Monrovia Coll Monrovia Liberia West Africa 1986. **MILITARY SERVICE:** AUS Corpl 1942-46; USAR 1st Lt 1950-64. **BUSINESS ADDRESS:** Dir Project Upward Bound, Loyola University, 6525 N Sheridan Rd, Chicago, IL 60626.

DAVIS, WILLIAM SELASSIE, JR.
Psychiatrist. **PERSONAL:** Born Aug 22, 1918, Baton Rouge, LA. **EDUCATION:** Dillard U, AB 1940; Howard U, MD 1944. **CAREER:** Faltlands Guidance Cntr Diocese of Brooklyn, med dir 1959-; Dept of Psychiatry Cath Med Cntr of Brooklyn & Queens Inc, dir 1971-79; Children's Cntr, chf psych 1949-53. **ORGANIZATIONS:** Life flw The Am Orthopsychiat Assn; life mem Brooklyn Psychiat Soc; life mem Am Psychiat Assn; NY Cncl for Child Psychiatry; World Fed for MentalHlth; Am Grp Psychotherapy Assn; Assn for the Advncmt of Psychotherapy; World Assn for Soc Psychiatry; Omega Psi Phi Frat. **HONORS/ACHIEVEMENTS:** Publ "Mental Hygiene" 1954; "Acta Paediatrica" 1957; "Topical Problems of Psychotherapy vol 5" 1965. **MILITARY SERVICE:** AUSMC 1st lt 1944-46; USAFMC capt 1953-55. **BUSINESS ADDRESS:** 142 Joralemon, Brooklyn, NY 11201.

DAVIS, WILLIE A.
Educator, coach. **PERSONAL:** Born Dec 10, 1948, Marks, MS; married Barbara M Landry. **EDUCATION:** Coahoma Jr Coll, AA; Jackson State U, MS 1967, BA; Western MI-Univ MI, MA 1974, MS 1970. **CAREER:** Neighborhood Youth Core, Jackson MS, summer counselor 1970; Jackson Public Schools, Mar-Jun teacher 1970; Albion Public Schools, Albion MI, teacher, coach Football/Track, summers 1973-74. **ORGANIZATIONS:** Pres NAACP Albion Branch; mem Albion Educ Assn; Educ Assoc; mem Twin Athletic Assn; mem HS Coaches Assn; mem Albion United Fund Bd; mem & pres Albion NAACP; mem US Jaycees; mem Big Brothers Am; mem SS Supt Tchr Behtl Bapt Ch; mem Phi Beta Sigma Frat Inc. **HONORS/ACHIEVEMENTS:** Honor student Quitman Co HS 1961-65; honor student Coahma Jr Coll 1965-67; honor student Jackson StateUniv 1967-1970; 1974 Nominee Educ Yr; Albion Distinguished Service Award nominee 1974; Albions Distinguished Serv Award 1975. **BUSINESS ADDRESS:** Albion Sr HS, 225 Watson St, Albion, MI 49224.

DAVIS, WILLIE D.
Business executive. **PERSONAL:** Born Jul 24, 1934, Lisbon, LA; married Ann; children: 2 Children. **EDUCATION:** Grambling Coll, BS 1956; Univ of Chicago, MBA. **CAREER:** City of Cleveland, tchr; Professional Athlete, Cleveland Browns 2 yrs, Green Bay Packers capt of def unit 10 yrs; Joseph Schlitz Brewing co, sales & pr 1964; WANA, owner; KACE-FM Radio WLUM-FM WAWA-AM Milwaukee, ceo; Willie Davis Distributing Co, owner/oper. **ORGANIZATIONS:** Mem bd dir Jos Schlitz Brewing Co; charter mem & dir Exec Savings & Loan Assn; color analyst KNBC Football Telecast; pub rel & promotion work Chrysler Corp; mem LA Co Spl Task Force; pres & dir LA Urban League; dir & bd mem W Adams Comm Hosp; chmn Central Div LA Explorers (BSA); mem Career Counseling Group; So CA Businessmen's Assn; adv bd Black Peace Officers Assn; Bicentennial Black Achievement Exhibit; Spl LA Co Study Commn; speaks on an average of once a week to hs civic or comm groups; toured Vietnam for State Dept 1966. **HONORS/ACHIEVEMENTS:** Selected to All-Pro teams for 6 yrs; Byron "Whizzer" White Awd; Hall of Fame of NAIA; Green Bay Packers Hall of Fame 1975; Man of Yr NAACP 1978; Part of 6 Div Championships/5World Championships; Black Enterprise Mag's list Top 100 Black Businesses. **MILITARY SERVICE:** AUS splst/5c 1956-58. **BUSINESS ADDRESS:** Willie Davis Dist Co, Inc, 1710 E 111 St, Los Angeles, CA 90059.

DAVIS, WILLIE J.
Attorney. **PERSONAL:** Born Sep 29, 1935, Ft Valley, GA; married Carolyn Scoggins; children: Kristen, Roland. **EDUCATION:** Morehouse Coll, BA 1956; New England School of Law, JD 1963. **CAREER:** MA Commiss Against Discrimination, field rep 1963; Commonwealth of MA, asst attny gen 1964-69; Dist of MA, asst US attny 1969-71, former US magistrate; Private practice, attny; Northeastern Univ, law enforcement instr. **ORGANIZATIONS:** Mem Amer Bar Assoc, Amer Judicature Soc, Alpha Phi Alpha; bd of trustees Advent School Boston. **HONORS/ACHIEVEMENTS:** Ten Outstanding Young Men Awd Boston Jr C of C 1971; Hon Deg JD New England School of Law 1972; Hon Deg DSc Lowell Tech Inst 1973. **MILITARY SERVICE:** AUS sp4 1958-60. **BUSINESS ADDRESS:** Law Enforcement Instructor, NortheasternUniv, 44 School St, Boston, MA 02108.

DAVIS, WILLIE JAMES
Lecturer. **PERSONAL:** Born May 14, 1940, Tyronza, AR; divorced; children: Rasul, Hasam. **EDUCATION:** George Washington Univ 1959; Herschel Rowland, Bass 1958; Lincoln Univ, Chem 1959-61; Art Davis, Bass 1962-67; George Andrea, Bass 1967-71; Julliard Schl of Music 1967-68; NY Univ, BS Music 1971, MA Music 1972; John Gilbert, Composition 1971-72; Alberto Socarras, Sofegeo 1980-. **CAREER:** Yardney Electric Co, electrochem engr 1961-63; luthier & free-lance musician arranger composer conductor contractor 1965-; Harlem Philharmonic Orchestra, contractor 1969-; Brooklyn Music Schl for Children, instr 1970-81; Youth Bd Inst of NY, music consult 1972; Bronx Comm Clge Music Dept, lecturer adjunct 1973-74; Rutgers Univ, instr bass lecturer music history 1977-81; Vassar Clge, lectuerer black music 1980-81. **HONORS/ACHIEVEMENTS:** DiscographyTV radio film awards, Freddie McCoy "Collard Greens" NY 1965 LP, Donald Williams "I Won the Race" & "Look Down the Road" Safaria Records 1971 45RPM, Jo Grinage "Mother's Love Song" Dakeeta Records 1971, Sun Ra "Pathways to Unknown Worlds" Impulse Records ASD 9298 LP, Carnegie Hall "Voice of America Broadcast" 1968, Count Basie Radio & TV 1974, "Folk Music Around the World" Tri Tone Records NY 1972, Lincoln Univ & Rolla Schl of Mines Orchestra LP 1960, Symphony of the New World "Anniversary Concert" NY 1966, Harlem Homecoming CBS TV 1974, Michael Olatunji NBC TV 1968, NY World's Fair Symphony Orchestra "Six Suites for the World's Fair" NBC TV & Film 1964, Les & Larry Elgart Radio Canton OH 1966, TV Wash DC 1966, Recording 1966, Miriam Makeba Recording Congo Algeria Tunis Rome TV & Film 1969, NY Univ Choir NBC TV 1973 Radio 1970, Sam Rivers "Shades" New York City 1970, Harlem Philharmonic Orchestra 1974, Joe Turner PabloRecords 1974, Leroy Jenkins "For Players Only" J00a 1010 NY 1975, Mort Lindsey Orchestra "Merv Griffin Show" NBC TV 1965-67, Dance Theatre of Harlem RecordingNY 1971, Charles Tolliver "Jazz Repertory Co" Carnegie Hall 1974. **BUSINESS ADDRESS:** 156 W 132nd St, New York, NY 10027.

DAVIS, WILLIS H.
Educational administrator. **PERSONAL:** Born Jun 30, 1937, Spartanburg, SC. **EDUCATION:** DePauwUniv Greencastle IN, BA 1959; Dayton Art Inst, studied ceramics 1964-65; MiamiUniv Oxford OH, MA 1967. **CAREER:** DePauw U, asst prof art 1971-; Coord of Black Studies 1971; Wright StateUniv Dayton OH, art instr 1969-71; ESEA Title & III Living Arts Cntr Dayton OH, art dir 1967-71; Dayton OH Pub Schs, tchr 1957-67;Black Hist & Cultural Workshops German Town OH, visiting artist & lectr series 1968; Bergamo Cntr1968 69 70; VISTA Prog; AuburnUniv AL 1969. **ORGANIZATIONS:** OH Scndry & Sr High Prins Assn Conf Cleveland 1970; Western Arts Assn NAEA Milwaukee 1970; Black Studies Inst MiamiUniv 1970; VA StateUniv Norfolk 1970;Univ of Cincinnati at Blue Ash Raymond Walters Br 1972; The HEW Inst in Afro-Am Studies Earlham Coll Richmond 1972; Living Arts Prog Dayton 1972; Archdiocese of Cincinnati Dayton Area Cath Schs 1972; PurdueUniv Lafayette IN 1972;Univ of MA 1972; Gov StateUniv Nat & Endowment for the Arts Prog 1972; Indianapolis Pub Schs Shortrigde HS IN Arts Council 1972; Lafayette Comm Cntr Summer Arts Prog IN Arts Council 1972; Work shown in group juried competitive exhibitions one-man shows priv collections permanent museum collections. **HONORS/ACHIEVEMENTS:** Publications Commns LaRevue Moderne Mag article Paris 1967; Mural Panorama on Black Hist Dayton Daily Newspaper 1968; Cover Design for Educ Booklet on Black Hist Geo A Pflaum Pub 1968; Calendar Illus for Nat Ofc for Black Cath Washington DC 1972; represented in book "Black Artists on Art" 1972 Black Artist Documentary "Color It Black" Channel 13 WLWI-TV Indianapolis 1972. **BUSINESS ADDRESS:** Central State University, Wilberforce, OH 45384.

DAVIS-MCFARLAND, E. ELISE
City official. **PERSONAL:** Born Oct 18, 1946, Greensboro, NC; married Arthur C McFarland; children: Kira Jihan. **EDUCATION:** Univ of NC, BA 1964-68; Univ of VA, MEd 1969-71; Univ of Pgh, PhD 1971-73; Harvard Univ, visiting scholars program 1975; Univ of WI, european studyprogram 1971. **CAREER:** VA State Univ, instructor dept of english 1971-73; Univ of Pgh, rsch asst dept of psychology 1973-76; Univ of Houston, asst prof dept of speech pathol 1976-79; Univ Affiliated Facilities Prog, asst dir 1978-79; CHEC Educ Oppor Ctr, dir 1979-82; Charleston Trident Chamber of Commerce, vice pres 1982-. **ORGANIZATIONS:** Commissioner SC Health & Human Services Finance Comm 1984-; sec SC Assoc of Elected and Appointed Women Officials 1984-; bd member Natl Rural Develop Finance Corp 1985-. **HONORS/ACHIEVEMENTS:** First Black Chamber of Commerce Vice Pres in SC 1982; nominations Outstanding Young Women of America 1982-83. **HOME ADDRESS:** 204 Grove St, Charleston, SC 29403. **BUSINESS ADDRESS:** Vice President-Public Affairs, Trident Chamber of Commerce, PO Box 975, Charleston, SC 29402.

DAVIS-WILLIAMS, PHYLLIS A.
Chief executive officer. **PERSONAL:** Born Apr 20, 1947, Philadelphia, PA; married Halton Wilbur Williams Jr. **EDUCATION:** Nazareth Coll, BA 1968; Wayne State U, mA 1972. **CAREER:** Barat Human Serv Detroit, exec dir 1978-; Planned Parenthood Fedn Great Lakes Region, asso regional dir 1976-78; State of MI Macomb Co vocational rehabsupr 1972-76; Wayne Co Projec Prescad, pub health consult 1970-72; State of MI Wayne Co, social worker 1968-70. **ORGANIZATIONS:** Bd of dir Accounting Aide Soc Detroit 1980; mem Nat Rehab Assn 1972-; mem Women's Economic Soc 1978-; mem Nat Com for Prevention of Child Abuse. **BUSINESS ADDRESS:** Barat Human Services, 5250 John R St, Detroit, MI 48202.

DAVISON, EDWARD L.
Attorney. **PERSONAL:** Born May 10, 1943, Akron, OH; son of Edward Davison and Marie Mapp; married Willa Rebecca Branham (deceased); children: Rebecca Marie, Christopher Larry. **EDUCATION:** Univ of Akron, Assoc Degree 1967, BS Natural Science 1973, JD 1977. **CAREER:** Westinghouse R&D, lab technician 1963-64; General Tire R&D, lab technician 1964-67; Babcock & Wilcox, perf engineer 1967-76; Babcock & Wilcox CRD, cont mgr 1976-89, sr cont mgr 1989-. **ORGANIZATIONS:** Atty Davison, Greene, Holloway & Walker 1978-83, Davison & Greene 1983-; treasurer United Council of Corvette Clubs 1983-, pres 1987-; vice pres planning & allocation Summit County United Way 1984-, treasurer 1987-. **HONORS/ACHIEVEMENTS:** Award of Merit Summit County United Way 1980; Outstanding Achievement Summit County Democratic Party 1978; United Council of Corvette Clubs, Outstanding Achievement 1986. **BUSINESS ADDRESS:** Attorney, 20 S Van Buren Ave, Barberton, OH 44203.

DAVISON, FREDERIC E.
Military official. **PERSONAL:** Born Sep 28, 1917, Washington, DC; married Jean E Brown; children: Jean M, Andrea S, Dayle A, Carla M. **EDUCATION:** Howard U, BS 1938; Geo Wash U, MS 1940; MA 1963. **CAREER:** Mil Dist of Wash AUS, comndg gen. **HONORS/ACHIEVEMENTS:** Distinguished alumnis Geo WashUniv 1971; distinguished alumnus HowardUniv 1973; hon degree LLD Estrn MIUniv 1974. **MILITARY SERVICE:** AUS maj gen 1941-74. **BUSINESS ADDRESS:** HQ US Army Military, District of Washington, Fort McNair, Washington, DC.

DAVY, GLORIA
Soprano. **PERSONAL:** Born Mar 29, 1936, Brooklyn, NY; divorced; children: Jean- Marc Penningsfeld. **EDUCATION:** Julliard School of Music, BS. **CAREER:** Little Orch Soc Town Hall, debut 1954; toured Italy, Germany, Sweden, Spain 1955-56; Nice Opera 1957; Vienna State Opera 1959; Convent Garden Opera Co 1958;guest performer La Scala in Milan, San Carlo, Naples, Teatro Communale, Bologna, Teatro Massimo, Palermo, Teatre Reggio, Parma; Deutsche Opera, Berlin, guest contract 1962-64; yearly tours of Italy, Germany, France, Switzerland. **HONORS/ACHIEVEMENTS:** Recipient, Marian Anderson Award 1951; Marian Anderson Special Award 1952; Award Music Educ League, New York City 1953; created integral work Karl Heinz Stockhausen's "Momente," Beethoven Hall, Bonn 1972; first performances Festival Hall London/Brussells Opera/Theatre De La Ville Paris/ Beethoven Halle-Brown 1973; created "Vortrag Uber Hu" Stockhausen Donauschingen Festival 1974; first performances London & Paris 1974; Wigmore Recital London 1983; Westminster Abbey performance for Royal Family 1983; Concert Gershwinconductor Giorgio Gaslini Orch 1985.

DAWKINS, DARRYL (DUNKS)
Professional athlete. **PERSONAL:** Born Jan 11, 1957, Orlando, FL. **EDUCATION:** Maynard Evans HS, 1975. **CAREER:** Philadelphia 76'ers,professional basketball player; NJ Nets,professional basketball player. **BUSINESS ADDRESS:** New Jersey Nets, Brendan Byrne Arena, East Rutherford, NJ 07073.

DAWKINS, JULIUS CALVIN
Professional athlete. **PERSONAL:** Born Jan 04, 1961, Monessen, PA. **EDUCATION:** Univ Of Pittsburgh. **HONORS/ACHIEVEMENTS:** Won 4 letters at Univ of Pittsburgh; first team AP All-Am.

DAWKINS, MICHAEL JAMES
Engineer. **PERSONAL:** Born Nov 11, 1953, Chicago, IL; son of Willie J. Dawkins and Willie M. Dawkins; married Cornelia A Long; children: Erika Michelle. **EDUCATION:** Univ of IL-Chicago, BS 1978, MS 1979. **CAREER:** Dow Chemical, rsch eng 1979-83; senior research eng 1983-86, project leader 1986-87; research leader 1987-. **ORGANIZATIONS:** Mem AIChE 1976-; adv bd Soc of Black Engrs LSU 1982-; chmn LSU SBE Adv Bd 1982-84; minority liason for Georgia Tech & LSU/Dow 1983-; contact Educ Enhancement/Dow 1984-86; NOBCCHE. **HONORS/ACHIEVEMENTS:** EIT Certification LA 1985. **MILITARY SERVICE:** AUS spl/5 3 yrs. **BUSINESS ADDRESS:** Research Leader, Dow Chemical Co, PO Box 150, Bldg 2513, Plaquemine, LA 70765.

DAWKINS, MILLER J.
Elected official. **PERSONAL:** Born Mar 10, 1925, Ocala, FL; married Nancy Sidney; children: Myron. **EDUCATION:** FL A&M Univ, 1953-55; FL Mem Coll, BS Social Sci 1969-71; Univ of North Colorado, MA Social Sci 1973-74. **CAREER:** Miami-Dade Comm Coll, chairperson contin ed dept 1977-78; Dade Cty Correctional Ctrs, dir of ed program 1977-82; Miami-Dade Comm Coll, coll prof/admin 1978-; City of Miami, city commiss 1981-. **ORGANIZATIONS:** Supvr Aircraft Serv Inc 1966-68; vocational counselor Youth Ind Inc 1966-68; admin officer Dade Cty Model City's Program 1969-71. **BUSINESS ADDRESS:** City Commissioner, City Hall, 3500 Pan American Dr, Miami, FL 33133.

DAWKINS, STAN BARRINGTON BANCROFT
Dentist. **PERSONAL:** Born Jul 11, 1933, Jamaica, WI. **EDUCATION:** City Coll of NY, BS 1959; NYUniv Coll of Dent, DDS & MSD 1963. **CAREER:** Self-employed, dentist; Bird S Coler Metropolitan Hospital, chief of prosthetics; Dept of Prosthetics NY Univ Coll of Dentistry, assoc prof. **ORGANIZATIONS:** Mem ADA; mem NE Gnathological Soc; Am Radiological Soc; art pub in NY State Journ; co-chair comm Encourage Blacks to Enter Med Prof; capt Cty Coll Track Team 1957-59; capt City Coll Soccer Team 1959. **HONORS/ACHIEVEMENTS:** Outstanding Athlete Award CCNY 1959; mem CCNY Hall of Fame 1974; disting serv medal good conduct medal USAF. **MILITARY SERVICE:** USAF sgt 1952-56. **BUSINESS ADDRESS:** 186 W 135 St, New York, NY 10030.

DAWSON, ANDRE
Professional athlete. **PERSONAL:** Born Jul 10, 1954, Miami, FL; married Vanessa Turner. **EDUCATION:** FL A&M Univ. **CAREER:** Montreal Expos, outfielder 1976-. **HONORS/ACHIEVEMENTS:** Four-time Gold Glove winner in center field; Natl League, The Sporting News, AP, UPI and Topps' Rookie-of-the-Year in 1977; five Gold Gloves (1981-85) for defensive excellence; three Silver Sluggers (1980-81 & 1983) for offensive superiority at his position; Expos' Player-of-the-Year in 1981 and shared the award withTim Raines in 1983; The Sporting News Natl League Player-of-the-Year 1981; twice runner-up in NL MVP balloting; three times voted as starting center fielder in the All-Star Game (1981-83); named Most Outstanding Major League Player by the NY Times in 1983 poll of all major leaguers (71% response); featured in a NatlFilm Board movie "A Cap for Steve" an adapt of a Morley Callaghan novel; 49 home runs 1987. **BUSINESS ADDRESS:** Chicago Cubs, 1060 West Addison St, Chicago, IL 60613.

DAWSON, B. W.
University president. **CAREER:** Selma Univ, Selma AL, acting president. **BUSINESS ADDRESS:** Selma University, Selma, AL 38701. *

DAWSON, CARRIE B.
Retired educator. **PERSONAL:** Born Apr 23, 1910, E St Louis, IL. **EDUCATION:** IL StateUniv Normal, dip 1930; LincolnUniv Jefferson City MO, BS 1942;Univ of IL Urbana, MS 1944;Univ of IL Urbanan, EdM 1957. **CAREER:** Gary IN Community Schools Copr, retired asst supt, dir developmental prog; Williams Elementary School, Gary IN, prin; Southern Univ LA, Univ of ME, IN Univ NW, visiting prof; E St Louis IL Bd of Educ, gen elementary supr, supr of art, teacher. **ORGANIZATIONS:** Mem NCATE; mem Danforth Found 4-Man Team for Study of St Louis Sch Systems; mem IRA's Com on Disabled Readers; mem US Commnr Com for Review Study; mem educ com Nat Urban League 1976-; work group supr practices Assn for Supervision Curr Development; bd of dir Urban League; NAACP; mem of numerousorn at Local E St Louis IL & Gary IN & state levels. **HONORS/ ACHIEVEMENTS:** Recipient More than 50 Plaques & Awards; recipient Keys to 2 Cities Presented by Mayors; elected Nat Educ Hon Soc; first black woman to Receive doctorate Uof IL Coll of Edn; first woman to serve as asst supt Gary IN Pub Sch; num pub articles on reading on curriculm Nat Professional Journs; $10,000 Carrie B Dawson Scholarship Edstablished Gary IN; E St Louis' Art Gallery named Marley Dawson Ball. **BUSINESS ADDRESS:** Devel Prog Gary School Corp, 620 E 10th Pl, Gary, IN 46402.

DAWSON, HORACE GREELEY, JR.
Government official. **PERSONAL:** Born Jan 30, 1926, Augusta, GA; married Lula M Cole; children: Horace G III, H Gregory. **EDUCATION:** LincilnUniv PA, AB 1949; Columbia U, AM 1950; StateUniv IA, PhD 1960. **CAREER:** NC Central Univ Durham, assoc prof & dir of public relations 1953-62; Uganda, cultural affairs officer 1962; Nigeria, public affairs officer 1964; Univ of Lagos Nigeria, visiting prof part-time 1966-67; Liberia, public affairs office 1967; USICA, sr seminary foreign policy 1970, cultural adv, dept asst dir 1971-77; Univ of MD, visiting prof part-time 1971-79, council on foreign relations 1976-; Intl Communication Agency, counselor public affairs 1977; Dept of State, ambassador extraordinary & Plenipotentiary Botswana 1979-83; Bd of Examiners of the Foreign Svc, 1983-85; US Information Agency, asst to the dir 1984-85, dir Office of Equal Employment Opportunity and Civil Rights 1985-. **ORGANIZATIONS:** Mem NAACP, American Legion, Alpha Phi Alpha Frat; mem sr bd of stewards Metropolitan AME Church. **HONORS/ACHIEVEMENTS:** Uperior honor award Fgn Serv (USICA) 1965; books New Dimensions in Higher Educ 1961; Handbook for High Sch Newspaper Adv 1961; numerous articles on comm in scholarly publs. **MILITARY SERVICE:** AUS staff sgt 1944-46. **BUSINESS ADDRESS:** Dir, US Information Agency, 301 4th Street, SW, Washington, DC 20657.

DAWSON, J. LIN
Professional athlete. **PERSONAL:** Born Jun 24, 1959, Norfolk, VA; married Margo E Bradford. **EDUCATION:** NC State Univ, 1977-81; Gordon-Conwell Seminary, 1983-. **CAREER:** Mt Sinai Temple Col, OH, assoc minister 1980-; Lin Dawson Ministries, dir 1981-; New England Patriots, chapel leader 1984-85, professional athlete 1981-. **ORGANIZATIONS:** Field rep Sports World Ministries Inc 1981-82; field rep Students Against Drunk Drivers Inc 1982-; consult Christian Promotions Inc 1985-; mem FCA 1977-81; Ichi Ban Dojo 1984-85; Natl Rifle Assn 1985. **HONORS/ACHIEVEMENTS:** Alternate to Pro Bowl 1985; Dick Christy Award 1980; ACC Champs 1979; Tangerine Bowl 1978; Peach Bowl 1977; Schacklford Award 1977; Track (MVP) 1977; Football (MVP) 1977; Human Relations Award Omega Si Phi 1977. **BUSINESS ADDRESS:** New England Patriots, Sullivan Stadium, Rt 1, Foxboro, MA 02035.

DAWSON, JESSE R.
Elected official. **PERSONAL:** Born Oct 15, 1921, Malakoff, TX; married Mary Freeman; children: Janice, Diane Wright, Jesse R, Jr, Michael W. **EDUCATION:** Dallas Police Academy, 1948; Texas A&M Univ, (Inservice Training School) 1962; IPMA - International Personnel Mgmnt Assoc LA, CA 1974. **CAREER:** Dallas Police Dept, all phases of police work 1948-76; Precinct 8 Dallas County, constable 1976-. **HONORS/ACHIEVEMENTS:** Committee of 100 Law Enforcement Award 1974; Recognition & Appreciation Arlington Park Community Learning Center 1982; Award in Law Enforcement Washington-Lincoln Alumni Assoc 1983; Football Sponsorship YMCA 1984. **MILITARY SERVICE:** AUS 1942-45. **BUSINESS ADDRESS:** Constable, Precinct 8, Dallas County, 414 So R L Thornton Frwy, Room 101, Dallas, TX 75203.

DAWSON, LEONARD ERVIN
Educator. **PERSONAL:** Born Feb 05, 1934, Augusta, GA; married Laura R; children: Michael, Randall, Lavinia, Stephanie. **EDUCATION:** George Washington Univ, ED 1973; Columbia Univ, MA 1960; Morris Brown Coll, BS 1954. **CAREER:** ULTRA Inc; Volt Tech Enter; US Office of Educ, Washington DC Public Schools, cons; Richmond Cty, Muscogee Cty, Harris Cty, GA Public Schools, teacher; Richmond Cty Public Schools, counselor; Paine Coll, dean; US Office of Educ, ed prog specialist; RR Moton Memorial Inst Inc, exec vice pres; United Negro Coll Fund, dir of spec proj. **ORGANIZATIONS:** Mem Phi Delta Kappa Hon Soc, Amer Personnel & Guidance Assoc, Amer Council on Ed, Assoc of Non-White Concerns, Amer Assoc of Univ Profs, Morris Brown Coll Natl Alumni Assoc, Alpha Phi Alpha, NAACP; fellow NDEA. **HONORS/ACHIEVEMENTS:** Disting Alumni Awd Morris Brown Coll. **MILITARY SERVICE:** AUS pfc 1956-58. **BUSINESS ADDRESS:** President, Voorhees College, Denmark, SC 29042.

DAWSON, LUMELL HERBERT
Government official. **PERSONAL:** Born Sep 05, 1934, Harrisburg, PA; married Jacquelyn Bourne; children: Angela Lynn, Jeffrey Bourne. **EDUCATION:** WV State Coll, BA 1961. **CAREER:** New York City Dept of Human Resources, supr caseworker 1962-65; Vocational Educ & Ext Bd, dir soc serv 1965-70; Nassau Co Comm Human Rights, dir 1970-. **ORGANIZATIONS:** Mem Omega Psi Phi Frat 1958-; voc adv bd mem State Univ of NY at Farmingdale 1979-85; voc adv bd mem Hempstead HS NY 1980-; chair fund raising comm Long

Island Coalition for Full Emply 1980-; recruiter WV State Coll 1980-; adv bd mem Leadership Training Inst 1982-; mem The EDGES Group 1985-; elected to session Christ First Presby Church Hempstead NY 1987. **HONORS/ACHIEVEMENTS:** Special Recognition Nassau Co Comm Human Rights 1983; Alumni Awd WV State Coll 1986; Outstanding Contrib & Support Operation Get Ahead 1986; Achievement Awd Natl Assoc of Counties 1986. **BUSINESS ADDRESS:** Dir of Job Dev Center, Nassau County Commission on, Human Rights, 320 Old Country Rd, Garden City, NY 11530.

DAWSON, MARTHA E.
Professor. **PERSONAL:** Born Jan 12, 1922, Richmond, VA; divorced; children: Greer Dawson Wilson, Martina M, James M. **EDUCATION:** VA State Coll, BS 1943; IN Univ, MS 1954, EdD 1956. **CAREER:** Richmond Public Schools, teacher, supr; Multi-Cultural Educ Center, dir; IN Univ, speaker, writer, cons, numerous publs in field; Hampton Inst, chmn dept of elementary educ 1960-70, vice pres for acad affairs. **ORGANIZATIONS:** Mem Delta Kappa Gamma Hon Soc 1971, Phi Delta Kappa 1975. **HONORS/ACHIEVEMENTS:** Who's Who Among Amer Women 1966; Who's Who in Amer 1967; Disting Tchr Hampton Inst 1967; Dictionary of Intl Biography 1968; Cert natl Council of Negro Women 1970; finalist Danforth Found Harbison Disting Tchr 1970; Outstanding Women of the 70's 1972; vstg scholar SoUniv 1974; paper World Conf on Multicultural Educ 1976. **BUSINESS ADDRESS:** VP for Academic Affairs, Hampton University, Hampton, VA 23668.

DAWSON, PETER EDWARD
Physician. **PERSONAL:** Born Nov 18, 1931, Plaquemine, LA; married Jean Lezama; children: Jonathan, Patricia. **EDUCATION:** Xavier U, BS 1954; Meharry Med Coll, 1962. **CAREER:** St Joseph Hosp, internship resd. **ORGANIZATIONS:** Charter mem Am Acad Family Physicians; asst dir So Infirmary; asso prof family med LSU Scho of Med; past pres Plaquemine Br; NAACP 1966-76;32nd degree Mason; chmn tst My Syremem BC; mem Alpha Phi Alpha Frat. **HONORS/ACHIEVEMENTS:** Physician Recognition Award 1969, 72, 75. **MILITARY SERVICE:** AUS sp 2 1954-57. **BUSINESS ADDRESS:** 1314 Meriam St, Plaquemine, LA 70764.

DAWSON, ROBERT EDWARD
Physician. **PERSONAL:** Born Feb 23, 1918, Rocky Mount, NC; son of William and Daisy; married Julia Davis; children: Dianne Elizabeth, Janice Elaine, Robert Edward, Melanie Lorraine. **EDUCATION:** Clark Coll, BS 1939; Meharry Med Coll, MD 1943. **CAREER:** Homer G Phillips Hosp St Louis, internship 1943-44, resident 1944-46; Lincoln Hosp Ophthalmology Dept, attending staff 1946-55; Duke Univ, preceptorship 1946; NC Central Univ Health Serv, consult ophthalmology 1950-64; 3310 Hosp Scott AFB, chief ophthalmology & otolaryngology 1955-57; Armed Forces Inst of Pathology, ophthalmic pathology 1956; Lincoln Hosp, chief ophthal & otolaryng 1959-76; NY Inst of Ophthalmology, 1962; NY Eye & Ear Infirmary, 1963; Watts Hosp, attend staff 1966; Duke Univ, clinical instr ophthalmology 1968; Durham Co Gen Hosp, attend staff 1976; DCGH, vice pres of staff 1976-77; Duke Univ, clin asst prof ophthalmology. **ORGANIZATIONS:** Fellow Amer Coll of Surgeons; deplomate Amer Bd of Ophthalmology; fellow Acad of Ophthalmology & Otolaryngology; Amer Assn of Ophthalmology; diplomate Pan Amer Natl Assn; Natl Med Assn; Chi Delta Mu Sci Frat; Soc of Eye Surgeons; Amer Med Assn; bd trustees Meharry Med Coll; exec com chmn Hosp & Health Affairs Comm; bd trustees Natl Med Assn; bd trustees NC Central Univ; chmn Faculty-trustee Relations Com NC Cent Univ; bd dirs Lincoln Comm Health Cntr; bd trustees Durham Acad 1969-72; NC adv comm on Med Asst; bd dir Natl Soc to Prevent Blindness; bd dir Amer Cancer Soc; adv bd NC State Commn for the Blind 1970-78; regional surgical dir Eye Bank Assn of Amer; bd dirs Better Health Found 1960-66; pres Sigma Pi Phi Frat; President's Comm on Employment of the Handicapped; bd dir Natl Soc to Pr event Blindness; St Joseph's AME Ch; NAACP; bd of visitors Clark Coll; mem Alpha Omega Alpha Hon Soc; pres AOA NMA. **HONORS/ACHIEVEMENTS:** Distinguished Service Award Natl Assn for Equal Opportunity in Higher Edn; Distinguished Service Award Clark Coll 1983; Recipient Physician of the Year Award 1969; Distinguished Service Award (Natl Med Assn) 1982; Publications, Journal of the Natl Med Assn "Equal Access to Health Care Delivery for Blacks, A Challenge for the NMA" Jan 1981; "Crisis in the Medical Arena, A Challenge for the Black Physician" Dec 1979; "Bedside Manner of a Computer" March 1980; "Federal Impact on Medical Care" June 1980. **MILITARY SERVICE:** USAF Major 1955-57. **BUSINESS ADDRESS:** 512 Simmons St, Durham, NC 27701.

DAWSON, SIDNEY L., JR.
Retired educational administrator. **PERSONAL:** Born Dec 27, 1920, Kansas City, MO; married Etta Mae Jacksson; children: Sandra Kaye, Sidney L III. **EDUCATION:** Univ of KA, BME 1948; Univ of AZ, MME 1956; Educ Admin Certificate, 1968. **CAREER:** Tucson Educ Assn, pres 1963-64; AZ Educ Assn, pres 1970-71; HS, principal, 1973-79; Catalina HS, asst principal for student activities 1979-84 (retired). **ORGANIZATIONS:** Phi Delta Kappa 1956; pres Rincon Rotary Intl, 1979-80; polemarch Alumni Chapters, Kappa Alpha Psi 1980-81; chairperson Tucson Police Advisory Comm 1983-. **HONORS/ACHIEVEMENTS:** Pusic Phi Mu Alpha 1948. **MILITARY SERVICE:** AUS t/sgt 1943-46; Honorable Discharge, 1946.

DAWSON, WARREN HOPE
Attorney. **PERSONAL:** Born Oct 17, 1939, Mulberry, FL; married Joan Delores; children: Wendy Hope. **EDUCATION:** FL A&M Univ, BA 1961; Howard Univ Sch of Law, JD 1966. **CAREER:** Self Employed, atty. **ORGANIZATIONS:** Pres FL Chap Nat Bar Assn 1979; Nat Bar Assn 1979; vice pres Tampa Chap Frontiers Internat; judicial admin selc & tenure FL Bar Assn 1980; standing com legal asst Am Bar Assn 1980; adv bd of dir Tampa Bay Buccaneers 1980; chmn Hillbro Co Civil Serv Bd. **HONORS/ACHIEVEMENTS:** Whitney M Young Meml Award Tampa Urban League 1979. **MILITARY SERVICE:** AUS co comdr 1961-63. **BUSINESS ADDRESS:** 3556 N 29th St, Tampa, FL 33605.

DAWSON, WILLIAM LEVI
Conductor, composer. **PERSONAL:** Born Sep 26, 1899, Anniston, AL; married Cecile D Nicholson. **EDUCATION:** Washburn Coll; Horner Inst Fine Arts Kansas City MO, MusB 1925; Am Conseervatory Mus Chicagl IL, M Composition 1927; Tuskegee Inst, MusD 1955; Eastman Sch Mus, postgrad. **CAREER:** Topeka Kansas City, mus dir 1921-25; Chicago Civic Symphony Orch, trombonist; Tuskegee Inst Sch Mus Tuskegee Choir, dir. **ORGANIZATIONS:** Led Tuskegee Choir at Radio City Mus Hall opening 1932-33; participant in NBC abc concert series; guest condr at numerous state festivals chorals groups in Spain under aspices of Dept State 1956; Nashville Symphony Orch 1966; Kansas City Philharmonic Orch 1966; Talladega Choir & Mobil Symphony Orch 1968; numeroustours; composer Negro Fold Symphony; Trio in A violin cello piano; Sonata in A violin & piano; Negro Work Song for Orch; Out In The Fields; Scherzo for Orch;numerous Negro folk song arrangements voices; Break, Break with orch. **HONORS/ACHIEVEMENTS:** Winner Chicago Daily News contest for Band Condrs 1929; & Redman Wanamaker contest for composition 1930-31; recipient Citation AwardUniv of PA Glee Club 1967;alumni achievement awardUniv of MO Kansas City 1963; AL Arts Hall of Fame 1975; award & citation Am Choral Director's Assn 1975; mem Phi Alpha Sinfonia. **BUSINESS ADDRESS:** Tuskegee Institute, PO Box 1052, Tuskegee, AL 36088.

DAY, BENJAMIN H.
Former mayor, educator. **PERSONAL:** Born Feb 15, 1925, Terre Haute, IN; married Lula; children: Laraine, Glynnis, Ingrid. **EDUCATION:** KA St Tchrs Coll Emporia KS, BS & MS. **CAREER:** City of Leavernworth KS, mayor 1972-75; Third Ave School & Muncie Grade School, prin 1970-80; KS Adult Authority, gov appointee 1980-. **ORGANIZATIONS:** Mem Phi Delta Kappa; Kiwanis Club; gov com on Crim Admnstrtn; hum resrce dev com KS Lgue of Muncipltiies; hum resrce dev com Legsltv Com Nat Lgue of Cties; mem Pent Ch; pstr Davis Temple Excelsior Springs MO; 1st vice pres Nat Sun Schl Assn Pent Assmblies of Wrld; chmn NW Dist Council 1976-80; edtr-inchf Apost Lght Lit Cincnti OH.

DAY, DANIEL EDGAR
Government official. **PERSONAL:** Born Dec 10, 1913, Montgomery, AL; married Sanone Nickerson; children: Sandra Ann, Gregory Alan. **EDUCATION:** Crane Jr Coll Chicago, attended 1932-33; Amer Univ, attended 1946, 1962, 1964; Univ of Chicago, attended 1958. **CAREER:** Robt S Abbott Pub Co Chicago, 1929-40; asst city editor, 1936-40; AUS, various ranks 1941-61; War Dept Washington, chief negro interest sect bureau public relations 1943-46; FL A&M Univ Tallahassee, prof military sci 1955-61; Natl Newspaper Pub Assn Washington, 1961-66; USDA, admin officer 1966, dept housing & urban devel Wash 1966-68, dep dir pub info div 1968-70, pub info officer 1970-84. **ORGANIZATIONS:** Mem Capital Press; Natl Press membership comm 1962-; mem Natl Assn of Govt Communicators; Pigskin Club. **MILITARY SERVICE:** US IL Nat'l Guard 1938-41; AUS 1941-61. **HOME ADDRESS:** 8212 Eastern Ave NW, Washington, DC 20012.

DAY, DONALD
Labor official. **PERSONAL:** Born Aug 01, 1936, Cleveland, OH; son of Orlie Day and Lillian Reeves Day; divorced; children: Deneen. **EDUCATION:** Kent Univ, BS, Govt Admin, 1962. **CAREER:** OH AFSCME & AFL-CIO, asst dir & reg lobbyist, 1971-; hospital career devel program center mgr, 1969-71; county probation officer, 1966-69; teacher, 1963-66; firefighter, 1962-63. **ORGANIZATIONS:** vice pres, OH AFL-CIO; mem, elected office & Jud Comp Comm for OH Serv Study Comm, 1973-74, Govt Advisory Comm to Intergovern Personnel Act, 1973-74; Found of OH Cit Unit Against Sickle Cell Disease, 1973-74; pres, OH Chapter of the Coalition of Black Trade Unionist; secretary, treasurer, Franklin County Chapter of the A Philip Randolph Inst; mem, bd of trust, Woman's Resource & Political Devel Center; bd of trust, Central OH Multiple Sclerosis Soc; Kappa Alpha Psi Frat; exec comm mem, Franklin County Democratic Party; Carter delegate, Democratic Natl Convention, 1976; mem exec comm, Central Ohio's United Negro Col Fund; Mem, OH Ethics Commn; pres, Columbus Center State Theatre. **HONORS/ACHIEVEMENTS:** Man of the Year Award, OH Chap of Public Personnel Assn, 1973. **MILITARY SERVICE:** USAR 1960-66. **BUSINESS ADDRESS:** Secretary-Treasurer, Ohio AFL-CIO, 271 East State Street, Columbus, OH 43215.

DAY, ERIC THERANDER
Law enforcement coordinator. **PERSONAL:** Born Dec 15, 1952, Mobile, AL; son of Joseph Day and Ruby James Day; married Valerie Jones, Mar 30, 1974; children: Eric Therander Jr, Joaquin Kyron. **EDUCATION:** Univ of South Alabama, Mobile AL, BA, 1977, MEd, 1979. **CAREER:** Mobile County Sheriff Dept, Mobile AL, asst dir work release, 1977-79, dir work release, 1979-80, asst warden, 1980-81, asst planning officer, 1981-84, dir victim witness program, 1984-85, deupty sheriff, 1985-87; US Attorney's Office, Mibile AL, Law Enforcement, Victim Witness, coord, 1987-. **ORGANIZATIONS:** Mem, Southern States Correctional Assn, 1975-, Lambda Alpha Epsilon, 1977-, Alpha Phi Sigma, 1977-, Alabama Peace Officer Assn, 1979-, Amer Correctional Assn, 1980-; vice pres, Fellowship of Christian Law Enforcement Officers, 1984-; bd mem, 2nd vice pres, Gulf Coast Federal Credit Union, 1985; chaplain, Southern Region Natl Black Police Assn, 1987; bd mem, Epilepsy Chapter of Mobile and Gulf Coast, 1988; mem, Mobile United, 1989. **HONORS/ACHIEVEMENTS:** Man of the Year, Alpha Phi Alpha Frat, 1977; Charter Mem, Omicron Delta Kappa, Univ of Southern Alabama, 1977; Highest Academic (Scholastic), Southwest Alabama Police Academy, 1983. **MILITARY SERVICE:** US Army, sergeant, 1972-74; Natl Defense Medal, 1972; Good Conduct Medal, 1974. **HOME ADDRESS:** 2800 Ramada Dr W, Mobile, AL 36693.

DAY, WILLIAM CHARLES, JR.
Business executive. **PERSONAL:** Born Sep 17, 1937, Houston, TX; married Evelyn Shaw; children: Margaret Ann, Stephen Brian. **EDUCATION:** TX So U, BA 1966. **CAREER:** First Harlem Securities Corp, exec Vp 1971-; Shearson Hammill Co Inc, account exec 1968-71; Armour Grocery Prods, sale rep 1967-68. **ORGANIZATIONS:** Chmn of bd First Harlem Mgmt Co; chmn of bd Colonial Quilting Co Inc; mem NY Stock Exchange. **BUSINESS ADDRESS:** First Harlem Sec Corp, 32 Broadway, New York, NY 10004.

DAYE, CHARLES EDWARD
Educator. **PERSONAL:** Born May 14, 1944, Durham, NC; son of Daye and Addie; married Norma S; children: Clarence L Hill III, Tammy V Hill. **EDUCATION:** NC Central Univ, BA high honors 1966; Columbia Univ, JD honors 1969. **CAREER:** UNC Chapel Hill School of Law, prof 1972-81; NCCU School of Law, visiting prof 1980-81; dean & prof 1981-85; UNC Chapel Hill School of Law, prof 1985-. **ORGANIZATIONS:** Law clerk Hon Harry Phillips 6th Cir 1969-70; assoc Covington & Burlington 1970-72; mem bd dirs In-Chu-Co Housing Devel Corp 1976-81; NC Assoc of Black Lawyers, pres 1976-78, exec sec 1979-; mem bars of, US Supreme Ct, NY, DC, NC; chmn Triangle Housing Devel Corp 1977-; vice pres Hayti Devel Corp 1984-; Bd dir United Way of Greater Durham 1984-; bd dirs & chair Minority Affairs Comm Law School Admission Council 1984-; mem Amer Bar Assn, NC State Bar, NC Bar Assn. **HONORS/ACHIEVEMENTS:** Lawyer of the Year NC Assn Black Lawyers 1980; Civic Award Durham Community Affairs Black People 1981; co-author

Casebook Housing & Comm Devel 1981; author articles in professional journals; Order of the Coif. **HOME ADDRESS:** 3400 Cambridge Rd, Durham, NC 27707. **BUSINESS ADDRESS:** Professor of Law, University of North Carolina, School of Law, Chapel Hill, NC 27514.

DAYE, DARREN TERRELL
Professional athlete. **PERSONAL:** Born Nov 30, 1960, Des Moines, IA. **EDUCATION:** UCLA, studied econ 1983. **CAREER:** Wash Bullets, forward-guard 1983. **HONORS/ACHIEVEMENTS:** Scored season high 16 Points; third team All-West Coast selection that year 1982-83. **BUSINESS ADDRESS:** Washington Bullets, 1 Harry S Truman Dr, Ste 1325, Landover, MD 20785.

DAYE, WALTER O.
Union executive. **PERSONAL:** Born Dec 28, 1918, Durham, NC; married Annette Latta; children: James W (dec), Gwendolyn, Cynthia. **EDUCATION:** Univ NC, summer instructor, 1959-62; Univ VA, certificate presented courses completed, 1963-64. **CAREER:** Local 176 Tobacco Workers Intl Union Liggett & Myers Inc, vp; Local 208 TWIU, pres 1958-68; Durham Central Labor Union, secretary treasurer 1961-; NC State ALF-CIO, vice pres 1971-; Tobacco Workers Intl Union, temporary staff rep 1971-74; ss teacher, 1946-. **ORGANIZATIONS:** Treasurer, Fourth Dist Comm Political Educ; dir, Durham Co Comm Political Educ, 1970-; co-chmn, Durham Comm Affairs Black People; action com Durham City Co Charter Com 1971-74; Durham's Human Relations Comm, 1970-75; social science teacher 1946-; deacon, Mt Calvary Baptist Church, 1948. **HONORS/ACHIEVEMENTS:** w/aid & assistance, helped bring job equality to people, Liggit & Myers Inc (effected the whole cigarette industry). **MILITARY SERVICE:** AUS sgt 1943-45.

DAYS, DREW SAUNDERS, III
Attorney. **PERSONAL:** Born Aug 29, 1941, Atlanta, GA; married Ann Ramsay Langdon; children: Alison Langdon, Elizabeth Jamerson. **EDUCATION:** Hamilton Coll; Yale Law Sch, LlB 1966. **CAREER:** US Dept of Justice, asst atty gen; NAACP Legal Defense & Educ & Educ Fund Inc, first asst counsel 1967-77; Temple Univ & Philadelphia, asso prof of Law 1973-75; Comayagua Honduras, peace corps volunteer 1967-69; Cotton Watt Jones King & Bowlus Chicago IL, law asso 1966-67; IL Civil Liberties Union, volunteer atty 1966-67; Agency for Internal Devel Honduras, consult program writer 1968-69; Rockefeller Commn to Latin Am, interpreter 1969. **ORGANIZATIONS:** Mem Congressional Black Caucus & Nat Conference on Educ for Blacks 1972; mem Com on Criminal Courts Law & Procedure Assn of the Bar of NY 1972-73 dir &pres Windham Child Care 1972-77; publ "Materials on Police Misconduct Litigation"; Reginald Heber Smith Lawyer Fellowship Program; co-editor "Federal Civil Rights Litigation", Practising Law Inst 1977. **BUSINESS ADDRESS:** YaleUniv, School of Law, Box 410 A, Yale Station, New Haven, CT 06520.

DAYS, MORGAN M.
Pastor. **PERSONAL:** Born May 30, 1891, Pine Level, AL; married Fannie. **EDUCATION:** Troy Bapt Acad, grad 1915; Cooke Acad, grad 1923; Colgate Univ, 1937. **CAREER:** Shiloh Bapt Ch, pastor 1937-77; Friendship Bapt Ch, pastor 1925-27; Friendship Bapt Ch, pastor 1918-25. **ORGANIZATIONS:** Vice Pres Nassau Cnty Coun of Churches; mem bd of dir Nassau Cnty Counc of Ch 20 Yrs; pres Intrracial Prot Min Assoc of Nassau Cnty; pres Bap Min Fellow of Queens Suffolk & Nassau Cntys; pres Interdenom Min Fellow of Cnty of Nassau Chmn, Human Rights Comm of Rockville Centre, NY 1963-75; Cit from Pres Harry S Truman Contrib to race relat in Nassau Cntry; cert of public serv Gov Rockefeller for 5 yrs in Civ Def in NY; "Rev Morgan M Days Park" village of Rockville Centre 1968. **HONORS/ACHIEVEMENTS:** Man of the year Bapt Min Fellow of ueens, Nassau & Suffolk Cntys 1967; AAF WW 1 chaplain 1917-18; AAF WW II chaplain. **BUSINESS ADDRESS:** 96 N Centre Ave, Rockville Centre, NY 11570.

DAYS, ROSETTA HILL
Education administrator. **PERSONAL:** Born in Gibsland, LA; married James Days; children: Yanise, Regiuel. **EDUCATION:** Grambling Coll, BS 1957;Univ MI, MS 1965. **CAREER:** Wilerson's Homesrv Inst, home economics lecturer 1957-60; Webster Parish Schools, teacher 1960-65, counselor 1965-67; Grambling Coll, chief counselor 1967, asst prof & acad counselor 1967-70, asst prof & dir, prof Rescue 1970-; LA & US Colleges, grants admin & Equal Opportunity Officer; Grambling State Univ, chmn Counseling & Testing Dept 1972-73; LA Assn Student Asst Progs, 1974-75. **ORGANIZATIONS:** Bd of dir SW Assn Stdnt Asst Progs 1974-75 V chmn LA State Adv Cncl on Mental Hlth; mem bd dir Nat Assn of Women in Criminal Justice; reg adv cncl Emergency Med Serv System; mem Amer Prsnnl gdnce Assn; Assn for Cnslr Ed & Suprvsn; Assn for non-white cncrns; Amer Coll Prsnnl Assn; LA Educ Assn; LA Assn for Msrmnt & Eval in Gdnce Aldrmn, Grambling, LA; sec-treas Legue of Womn Vtrs 1972; chap vP Mntl Hlth Assn 1973-74, pres 1974-75; Chap pres Delta Sigma Theta Inc 1971-73; sec Grambling C of C 1974-75; mem Nat Cncl of Negro Wmn; Bd Dir Lincoln Sickle Cell Assn1974-75; vP Lincoln Parish Blk Elcted Coordntg Com 1974-75. **HONORS/ACHIEVEMENTS:** Scroll of Honor Omega Psi Phi Frat 1973, 74; Lewis Temple CME Ch Womn's Day Citn 1972; mem Alpha Kappa Mu Nat Hon Soc. **BUSINESS ADDRESS:** Project Dir, Grambling State University, PO Drawer 8, Grambling, LA 71245.

D'BANANA, BEBE See MILLER, KENNETH BERNARD

DEAN, CLARA RUSSELL
Educational administrator. **PERSONAL:** Born Sep 11, 1927, Greenville, SC; married Miles Dean; children: Miles Jr, Angela, Jacquelynn, Barbara, Wanda, Patricia. **EDUCATION:** Essex County Coll, AAS 1968-70; Rutgers, BA Psychology 1970, MA Education 1972; Felician Coll, ASRN 1972; Jersey City State, nursing school 1973. **CAREER:** College Hosp Council, bd mem & chair affirm action 1975-79; CMDNJ, supv implimented dental clinic 1977; Essex Co, long range planning bd 1983-; Weequahic Multipurpose Center, dir/prin 1984-. **ORGANIZATIONS:** Mem 100 Black Woman 1982; life mem NAACP-NB; chairperson Three City Wide Health Fairs 1982-83-84; pres Clara Dean Civic Assoc 1976-; mem Bus & Prof Women 1978-; ed comm Greater Abyssinian Ch 1980-. **HONORS/ACHIEVEMENTS:** Achievement Awd PATCH-Newark 1981; Recogn Award Newark Br NAACP 1983; Recogn Award NJ State Commn for the Blind 1985. **BUSINESS ADDRESS:** Dir, Weequahic Multi Purpose Center, 146 Clinton Ave, Newark, NJ 07114.

DEAN, DANIEL R.
Business executive. **PERSONAL:** Born Jan 23, 1941, Atlantic City, NJ; son of Edward Dean and Cora L Harris Dean; married Edna Geraldine Jeter; children: Tracey, Kevin. **EDUCATION:** WV State Coll, BS in Business Admin 1963; Rutgers Univ, 1967-68; Pace Univ, 1976-77; Stonier Grad School of Banking, 1980-83. **CAREER:** Citicorp USA Inc Atlanta, relationship team mgr 1984-; Citibank, NA New York, NY, oper head 1978-84, oper mgr 1976-78, oper officer 1972-76. **ORGANIZATIONS:** Chmn bd of dir Frederick Douglas Liberation Library 1969-75; treas Somerset Cnty Comm Action Prog 1973-76; trustee Franklin Township Library Bd 1975-78; pres Superior Golf Assoc 1983-84; pres Southern Snow Seekers Ski Club 1985-88. **MILITARY SERVICE:** AUS 1st/lt 1963-65. **HOME ADDRESS:** 2501 Old Sewell Rd, Marietta, GA 30068. **BUSINESS ADDRESS:** President, D & E Floor Service Inc, 2501 Old Sewell Rd, Marietta, GA 30068.

DEAN, DIANE D.
Educator. **PERSONAL:** Born Aug 26, 1949, Detroit, MI. **EDUCATION:** Michigan State Univ, 1966-68; North Carolina A&T State Univ, BS 1971; Indiana Univ, MS 1973; Univ of California-Los Angeles, 1982-83; Stanford Univ, Summer Institute 1981. **CAREER:** Univ of Miami, area coordinator 1973-75; Occidental Coll, dir of housing 1975-78; Univ of Southern CA, asst dir of admissions, assistance & school relations 1978-80; Univ of CA-Los Angeles, asst dir of admissions 1980-81, assoc dir of admissions 1981-85; Leadership Education and Development (LEAD), dir of operations (consultant) 1983-85; Natl Action Council for Minorities in Engineering, dir incentive grants and scholarship programs 1985-. **ORGANIZATIONS:** Co-chair Region VI Natl Assn Student Personnel Admin 1985; co-facilitator mgmt CA Assn of College/Univ Housing Officers 1975-78; standing comm appointee Natl Assn of Coll Admissions Counselors 1979-86; apptd rep Graduate Mgmt Admissions Council 1981-85; mem Alpha Kappa Alpha; mem Black Womens Forum of Los Angeles 1980-, CA Museum of Afro-Amer Art 1984-, Studio Museum of Harlem 1985-, Council of Concerned Black Execs 1986; mem UCLA Alumni Assoc, North Carolina A&T Alumni Assoc, Urban League, NAACP and Corporate Woments Network. **HONORS/ACHIEVEMENTS:** Directory of Minority Personnel Associated with Admissions, Creator and Editor 1979-; Paddington Corp J&B Winners Circle Award 1984. **BUSINESS ADDRESS:** Dir, Incentive Grants Program, NACME, Inc, 3 West 35th St 3rd Floor, New York, NY 10001.

DEAN, FREDERICK RUDOLPH (MEAN FRED)
Professional athlete. **PERSONAL:** Born Feb 24, 1952, Arcadia, LA. **EDUCATION:** LA Tech. **CAREER:** San Diego Chargers, defensive end 1975-81; San Francisco 49ers, defensive end 1981-. **HONORS/ACHIEVEMENTS:** Pro Ftbl Wkly named Defensive Player Of Wk; named to All-NFC squad by Pro Ftbl Wkly & UPI; named To Pro Bowl for 4th time in last 5 yrs; only man to havewon NFLPA's Def Lineman-of-yr awd in both conf 1980 with San Diego AFC, 1981 with San Francisco NFC); All-Southland Conf linebacker all 4 yrs at LA Tech.

DEAN, JAMES EDWARD
Educator, social worker, officer. **PERSONAL:** Born Mar 14, 1944, Atlanta, GA; son of Steve Dean, Sr and Dorothy Cox Dean; married Vyvyan A Coleman; children: Sonya V, Monica A. **EDUCATION:** Clark Clge Atlanta GA, BA 1966; Fisk Univ Nashville TN, Grad 1967; Atlanta Univ, MSW 1968; Emory Univ Atlanta GA, Post Grad 1976. **CAREER:** Economic Opport Atlanta Inc, human resource 1965-66; Butler St YMCA Atlanta, human resource 1968; Atlanta Urban League Inc, human resource 1968; State of GA, gen assembly & trans 1969, 1982; Clark Coll, educ 1971; Natl Urban League Inc, human resource 1978; State of GA Dept of Transportation, dist EEO & training officer 1982-88, dist EEO review officer 1988-. **ORGANIZATIONS:** Atlanta Daily World Newspaper 1960-70; Atlanta Inquirer Newspaper 1962-68; vice pres Community Services Inc, Atlanta GA, 1982-89; sec/governing bd mem, Pine Acres Town & Country Club 1989; mem, Center for Study of Presidency, New York, 1988-89; mem, Amer Federation of Police. **HONORS/ACHIEVEMENTS:** Secr Men of Clark Clark Coll 1984-; former secr Eta Lambda Chaptr Alpha Phi Alpha 1969; Natl Urban League Fellowship; Atlanta Univ Multi-Purpose Schlrshp Award; Alpha Kappa Delta Soc Hnr Soc; Council of Religion & Intl Affairs Flwshp; Hnry Governor's Staff Appointment Admiral of GA Navy; Ldrshp GA Prog Flwshp; Hnry Gov Staff Appointment Lt Colonel Aide DeCamp Gov Staff; Outstanding Young Men of Atlanta Atlanta Jaycees; Souther Cntr for Interntl Studies, Atlanta Black/Jewish Coalition; Special Achievement Award, Dept of Transp State of GA 1988; A Study of Community Organizaton Techniques Utilized by Three Self-Help Projects in Securing Low-Income Involvement 1968. **HOME ADDRESS:** 87 Burbank Dr NW, Atlanta, GA 30314.

DEAN, VERNON
Professional athlete. **PERSONAL:** Born May 05, 1959. **EDUCATION:** San Diego St. **CAREER:** Washington Redskins, cornerback 1982-. **ORGANIZATIONS:** Present at "No Greater Love Party" held last Christmas for children whose fathers were killed in service to their country. **HONORS/ACHIEVEMENTS:** Named NFC Defensive Player of Week 1984; runner-up in ballotting for AP NFL Defensive Rookie of Yr; Ftbl Digest NFL Rookie of Yr scnd tm UPI All-NFC & 1st tm All-NFL Rookie Tm by Pro Ftbl Writers Asso.

DEAN, WALTER R., JR.
Educator. **PERSONAL:** Born Dec 12, 1934, Baltimore, MD. **EDUCATION:** Univ of MD, MSW 1969; Morgan State Coll, BA 1962. **CAREER:** Community Coll of Baltimore, asst prof; Social & Behavioral Sciences Dept & Asst Prof Comm Coll of Baltimore, coord human serv asst 1969-; Asso in Soc Res, Health & Welfare Council Baltimore 1968-69; St Club Worker Bur of Recreation, 1964-66; Afro-Amer Newspapers Baltimore, reporter 1962-64. **MILITARY SERVICE:** USAF a/1c.

DEAN, WILLIE B.
Association executive. **PERSONAL:** Born Mar 15, 1951, Potts Camp, MS; son of Eddie B Dean and Mattie Delyta Brown Dean; married Pamela Williamson Dean, Oct 25, 1985; children: Cedric Lamont, Jarrod Wilberforce, Matthew Alexander. **EDUCATION:** Memphis State Univ, Memphis TN, BS Education, 1974; Univ of Texas, Arlington TX, attending, 1977-. **CAREER:** Glenview YMCA, Memphis TN, program dir, 1974-75; McDonald YMCA, Ft Worth TX, exec dir, 1975-81; Mondanto YMCA, St Louis, MO, vice pres, exec dir, 1981-. **ORGANIZATIONS:** Mem, Jennings-North St Louis Kiwanis Club, 1981-89, pres, 1985; program chmn, 100 Black Men of Metro St Louis, 1983-89; mem, Omega Psi Phi Frat Inc, 1983-89. **HONORS/ACHIEVEMENTS:** Father of the Year, 100 Black Men of St Louis, 1985; Yes I Can Award, Metro Sentinel Newspaper, 1988. **BUSINESS AD-**

DRESS: Vice President, Urban Services, YMCA of Greater St Louis, 5555 Page Blvd, St Louis, MO 63112.

DEANDA, PETER
Actor. **PERSONAL:** Born Mar 10, 1938, Pittsburgh, PA; married Fatima; children: Allison, Peter. **EDUCATION:** Actors' Workshop. **CAREER:** Pittsburgh Playhouse, actor; Weslin Prodn, actor; Nasara Prodn Labor & Ind Com Beverly Hills, fndr. **ORGANIZATIONS:** Mem NAACP; mem AEA; Image Awards Com Publ Black Drama Anthology 1971; New Am Library; written articles for NY Times & other maj publs; prod OnBdwy, Off-bdwy & TV; films "Lady Liberty" 1971, "The New Centurions" & "Come Back Charleston Blue" 1972; TV "Cannon"; title role "Cutter", "Joe Forrester", & "Police Woman". **MILITARY SERVICE:** USAF 1955-59. **BUSINESS ADDRESS:** 3721 Weslin Ave, Sherman Oaks, CA 91403.

DEANE, MORGAN R.
Dentist. **PERSONAL:** Born Sep 17, 1922, Lawrenceville; married Lela W; children: Frances, Judith, Morgan Jr. **EDUCATION:** WV State Coll, BA 1949; Howard U, DDS 1953. **CAREER:** Cincinnati Health Dept, 1953-74; Health Serv Dir West End Health Center, Dental dir 1975; Dentist, Private Practice, 1953-. **ORGANIZATIONS:** OH Valley Dental & Soc; Cincinnati Dental Soc; OH State Dental Assn; Am Dental Assn; Am Soc Clinical Hypnosis. **HONORS/ACHIEVEMENTS:** Omega Psi Phi Frat; Westley Smith Lodge. **MILITARY SERVICE:** World War II active 3 yrs, inactive 8 yrs. **BUSINESS ADDRESS:** Physician, 1800 Linn St, Cincinnati, OH 45214.

DEANE, ROBERT ARMISTEAD
Physician. **PERSONAL:** Born Jul 05, 1919, Lawrenceville, VA; son of Robert Armistead Deane and Otelia Virginia Russell; married Miriam Thompson, Jun 24, 1942 (deceased); children: Sharon Deane, Linda Geneva Deane Gordon, Marjel Virginia Deane Thomas. **EDUCATION:** VA State Coll, BS 1940; Howard Univ, MD 1944. **CAREER:** Freedmen's Hospital Howard Univ, resident Ob/Gyn 1945-48; Walter Reed Army Medical Center Gynecology & Obstetrics Clinic, chief civilian out-patient physicians; Private Practice, gynecologist; medical examiner Ob/Gyn Walter Reed Army Medical Center, Washington DC 1963-. **ORGANIZATIONS:** Mem Amer Bd of Ob/Gyn 1959; Hon Science Soc Beta Kappa Chi 1939; mem Chi Delta Mu Fraternity 1941. **HONORS/ACHIEVEMENTS:** Article "Primary Carcinoma of the Vagina" Medical Assn of Washington DC Vol 30 No 7 co-authored with Chas M Cabaniss, MD 1961; article "From Physician to Inpatient at Howard Univ Hospital" Journal Natl Med Assn 1984. **MILITARY SERVICE:** AUS Reserve 2nd lieutenant 1940-44. **HOME ADDRESS:** 6505 14th St, NW #401, Washington, DC 20012. **BUSINESS ADDRESS:** Walter Reed Army Med Ctr, Gynecology & Obstetrics Clin, 3105 Georgia Ave NW, Washington, DC 20010.

DEARMAN, JOHN EDWARD
Judge. **PERSONAL:** Born Mar 28, 1931, Troy, TX; son of Melvin Dearman and Jessie Mae Banks-Evans; married Ina Patricia Flemming; children: Tracy, Kelly, Jonathan, Jason. **EDUCATION:** Wiley Coll, BA Social Studies 1950-54; Wayne State Law School, JD 1954-57; Univ of CA, Cert Labor Arbitrator 1973. **CAREER:** City of Detroit, social worker 1957-58; Private Practice, attorney 1957-59, 1961-77; State of CA, judge 1977-. **ORGANIZATIONS:** NAACP; dir Golden Gate Bridge Bd 1966-70; commissioner metropolitan Transportation Comm 1970-75; dir vice pres Family Serv Assoc of Amer 1968-72; pres of bd Family Serv Agency of SF 1968-72. **HONORS/ACHIEVEMENTS:** Judge of the Year SF Trial Lawyers Assoc 1984; Humanitarian Judge of the Year CA Trial Lawyers Assoc 1984. **HOME ADDRESS:** 217 Upper Terrace, San Francisco, CA 94112. **BUSINESS ADDRESS:** Judge, State of California, Room 435 - City Hall, San Francisco, CA 94102.

DEAUGUSTINO-TODD, LOYCE
Association executive. **PERSONAL:** Born Apr 03, 1928, Meridan, MS. **EDUCATION:** Wiley Coll Marshall TX, BA 1949; IN Univ Bloomington, 39 hrs toward MA 1960; numerous certs, various spec fields. **CAREER:** EF Young J Beauty Coll Meridian MS, dir vocational counselor 1953-57; TN A&I Univ Nashville, counselor 1957-59; Henderson Tutorial Prog LA, dir 1964-66; Henderson Teen Post #406, dir 1966-67; Second Bapt Childrens Ctr LA, asst suprv 1967-; CA State Youth Oppty Ctr Long Beach, consult counselor 1967-68; Youth Training & Employment Proj LA, counselor 1967-68; Venice Skill Ctr Venice CA, teacher, counselor 1968; CA State Employment LA, counselor 1968-70; CA State Devel Svc, job agent 1970-71, contractor compliance officer 1971-73; Office of Civil Rights, suprv equal oppty spec 1973-; retired fed investigator. **ORGANIZATIONS:** Consult WEMA 1971, Orange Cty Equal Oppty Employers Assoc 1971; consult speaker UCLA 1972, Natl Training Staff 1973; mem Natl Assoc media Women Inc BeverlyHills, Las Angelenas, Zeta Phi Beta, Alpha Chi Phi; 2nd vice pres NAACP Beverly Hills-Hollywood; mem, adv comm Status of Women Cty LA Cert Spec Secondary Teaching Credential; Fed Civil Serv Rating GS-12. **HONORS/ACHIEVEMENTS:** Outstanding Comm Participation Martin Luther King Scholarship; Citation City of LA 9th Dist Councilmanic Awd, Outstanding Comm Serv in the S Central & Watts area.

DEBAS, HAILE T.
Surgeon. **PERSONAL:** Born Feb 25, 1937, Asmara, Ethiopia;married Igancia Kim; children: Salem T, Meron T. **EDUCATION:** Univ of Coll of Addis Ababa Ethiopia, BS 1958; McGill Univ Montreal Canada, MD 1963; Ottawa Civic Hosp, Internship 1963-64; Vancouver Gen Hosp, Surgical Residency 1964-69. **CAREER:** Univ of British Columbia, rsch fellow 1969-70, asst prof of surgery 1971-72; Univ of CA Los Angeles & Wadsworth VA Med Ctr, rsch fellow 1972-74, prof of surgery 1980-85; Univ of British Columbia, assoc prof of surgery 1974-79; Univ of WA Seattle, prof of surgery, chief of surgery 1985-87; Univ of CA, professor & chmn surgery. **ORGANIZATIONS:** Fellow Royal Coll of Physicians & Surgeons of Canada 1969-, Royal Coll of Surgeons of Canada 1970-; fellow Amer Coll of Surgeons 1984-. **HONORS/ACHIEVEMENTS:** British Columbia Surgical Soc Essay Awd 1965; Med Rsch Council of Canada Fellowship 1972-74; William H Rorer Rsch Prize for Original Rsch So CA Soc ofGastroenterology 1973; Golden Scalpel Awd for Teaching Excellence Div of General Surgery UCLA School of Med 1981. **BUSINESS ADDRESS:** Professor, Chairman, Univ of CA at San Francisco, 2130 Fulton St, Dept of Surgery, San Francisco, CA 94117.

DEBERRY, LOIS MARIE
Educator, legislator. **PERSONAL:** Born May 05, 1945, Memphis, TN; divorced; children: Michael Boyer. **EDUCATION:** Lemoyne-Owen Coll Memphis. **CAREER:** TN House of Representatives, state representative 1972-80; Lemoyne Coll, instructor. **ORGANIZATIONS:** Pres Nat Caucus of Black Women; sec TN Black Caucus; commr TN Law Enforcement Planning Agy. **HONORS/ACHIEVEMENTS:** Tri-state woman of the year award Greyhound Corp 1972-73; social serv award Nat Orgn of LINKS 1975; outstanding woman in comm serv Epsilon Epsilon Chptof Alpha Kappa Alpha Sorority 1975; glorification of the image of black womanhood Nat Bapt Educ Bd 1975; outstanding woman in corrections award Shelby StateComm Coll 1979. **BUSINESS ADDRESS:** Legislative Plaza, Ste 17, Nashville, TN 37219.

DEBNAM, CHADWICK BASIL
Management marketing consultant. **PERSONAL:** Born May 10, 1950, Clayton, NC; son of Clarence Debnam and Madie Debnam; married Mauria Fletcher, May 01, 1979; children: Andrea Dione. **EDUCATION:** Pacific Univ, Forest Grove OR, BS Political Sci 1972; Portland State Univ, Post Grad Studies 1972-73. **CAREER:** Mary Acheson House, prog dir 1972-75; Urban Redevelopment Corp, mktg dir 1976-78; Three Sixty Degree Publishing, pres 1979-82; B Chadwick Ltd, pres 1982-. **ORGANIZATIONS:** Bd mem Multnomah Co Charter Review 1982-84; chmn Adv Steering Comm Inner NE YMCA 1983-85; mem Albina Lions Club 1983-; pres The Oregon Business League 1984-87; mem Amer Mktg Assoc 1986-87; chmn Black Republican Council of OR 1986-88. **HONORS/ACHIEVEMENTS:** Keynote speaker Annual Banquet Scottish Rites Masons 1984; Century Awd Portland Metro YMCA 1984-85; Businessman of Month MBE Torch Awd Amer Contractor Pub 1985; guest lecturer Camp Enterprise Downtown Rotary 1986. **BUSINESS ADDRESS:** President, B Chadwick Group Ltd, 3802 NE Union Suite 304, Portland, OR 97212.

DEBNAM, MARJORIE BOYD
Business/office manager. **PERSONAL:** Born Jun 17, 1930, Bristol, TN; married George C Debnam MD; children: Gwendolyn Debnam-Morgan, Marie G, Marjorie Lynette. **EDUCATION:** Fisk Univ, BA (Cum Laude) 1951; St Augustine Coll, NC Teacher Certification 1952; NC State Univ, attended 1983. **CAREER:** Wake Co Dept of Social Svcs, caseworker 1952-58; George C Debnam MD Family Practice Office, business/office mgr 1958-87. **ORGANIZATIONS:** Mem exec comm vice chair 1975, sec to Bd 1979-84 Wake C Hosp System; mem 1984, vice chair bd of trustees 1986 Morristown Coll; chmn Comm Serv Comm Holly Hill Hosp 1986; sgt at arms Auxiliary to the Natl Medical Assoc 1986,87; elected to Holly Hill Hosp Bd 1987; mem Alpha Theta Omega Chapt; memNAACP, Links, Chums. **HONORS/ACHIEVEMENTS:** Founders Awd Friends of Distinction Male Club 1969-86; Citizen of the Year Alpha Phi Alpha Frat 1980; NC Merit Mother NC Mothers Inc 1982; Woman of the YearYWCA Academy of Women 1983; Hon Doctorate for Comm Serv St Augustine's Coll 1984; United Negro Coll Fund Serv Awd 1984-86; Strengthening the Black Family Awd Raleigh Chap of Chums Inc 1985; Raleigh Housing Authority Citation 10 yrs Service; United Way Awd 1986; Citizens Awd Garner Rd YMCA 1986. **HOME ADDRESS:** 1615 East Davie St, Raleigh, NC 27610.

DEBRACY, WARREN
Attorney, educator. **PERSONAL:** Born Mar 28, 1942, Chicago, IL; son of Warren Jones, Sr and Amanda Eluira Jones; married Marilyn Ann Forger; children: Valerie, Justin, Catherine. **EDUCATION:** Loyola Univ Chicago, BS Soc Sci 1964; Rutgers Univ New Brunswick, NJ, MA Pol Sci 1966; Cornell Univ Ithaca, NY, JD Law 1971. **CAREER:** Rutgers Univ NJ, asst inst 1966; Loyola Univ Law Sch New Orleans, asst prof 1971-72; Univ of Detroit Law Sch, asst prof 1972-73; Univ of Toledo Law Sch, assoc prof 1973-79; Loyola Univ, New Orleans, LA, visiting prof, 1986; Valparoiso Univ, Valparoiso, IN, visiting prof, 1988-89. **ORGANIZATIONS:** Mem MI Democratic State Central Comm 1985-89; treas 2nd Cong Dist Dem Comm MI 1983-85, vice-chair 1979-81; mem, Rules Comm, Democratic Natl Convention, 1988; delegate, 1980 Democratic Natl Convention. **HONORS/ACHIEVEMENTS:** 1st yr moot court champion Cornell Law Sch 1969; best affimative debator Gennett Newpaper Tournament Rochester 1962; supplement to law, How Years and Social Change, 1978; Legality of Affirmative Action, Journal of Urban Law, 1974-75. **MILITARY SERVICE:** AUS 1st lt 1966-68; Vietnam Service Metal. **HOME ADDRESS:** 704 Linda Viota, Ann Arbor, MI 48103. **BUSINESS ADDRESS:** North Carolina Central, School of Law, Durham, NC 27707.

DEBRO, JOSEPH ROLLINS
Business executive. **PERSONAL:** Born Nov 27, 1928, Jackson, MS; married Anita English; children: Keith, Karl, Kraig. **EDUCATION:** Univ CA Berkeley, AB, MS 1953-59. **CAREER:** Model Cities, Oakland, CA, dir; Oakland Small Business Devel Cntr, dir; NASA, research scientist; Producers Cotton Oil Co, chem engr; Nat Asso Minority Contractors, exec dir. **ORGANIZATIONS:** Pres Reca Inc; pres Housing Assistance Council; pres JDA Consulting Group Inc; pres Gaylor Construction Co; chmn minority Bus Enterprise Task Force Inc; vice pres Trans Bay Engrs & Builders Sigma Xi; Alpha Phi Alpha; dem Ocrat; Bridge Who's Who in West; Who's Ho US; Who's Who Am; Who's Who Finance & Industry; Dictionary Intl Biography; Men Achievement; publicati On, More Than 25 Articles Scientific Bus Jounals. **BUSINESS ADDRESS:** World Trade Center, Ste 275 C, San Francisco, CA 94111.

DEBRO, JULIUS
Educator. **PERSONAL:** Born Sep 25, 1931, Jackson, MS; divorced; children: Blair, Renee. **EDUCATION:** Univ of San Francisco CA, BA Poly Sci 1953; Univ of San Fran Law Sch, 1957; San Jose State U, MA Sociology 1967; Univ of CA Berkeley, Doctorate of Crim 1975. **CAREER:** Inst of Crim Justice/Criminology Univ of MD College Pk MD, asst prof 1971-79; Joint Commn on Criminology/Criminal Justice Edn/Standards Wash DC, prin investgtr 1978-79; Dept of Public Admin, chrmn 1979-80; The Dept of Criminal Justice Atlanta U, chrmn 1979-, dir 1979-; Atlanta U, prof of criminology, chmn 1985-86 criminal justice/sociology, chmn criminal justice admin 1986-. **ORGANIZATIONS:** Dir Specl Oppor Prgm UC Berkeley 1968-70; bd mem Metropolitan Atlanta Crime Comm 1984-; mem Cncl of Higher Educ in Crim Just; mem Alpha Phi Alpha; mem Citizen's Review Bd Atlanta GA 1985-; mem Central Atlanta Progress Study Commn 1986-87, Atlanta Anti-Crime Bd 1987; chmn Metropolitan Atlanta Crime Commn 1987. **HONORS/ACHIEVEMENTS:** Fellow Nat Inst of Hlth 1969-70; fellow Ford Found 1971; Editorial Bd Crim Justice Review 1979-. **MILITARY SERVICE:** AUS col; Korean Victory Medal. **BUSINESS ADDRESS:** Professor of Criminology, Atlanta Univ, 740 Beckwith St SW, Atlanta, GA 30314.

DECATUR, ROBERT A.
Attorney, dean. **PERSONAL:** Born Mar 04, 1924, Chicago, IL; widowed; children: Randolph Stephen, Dawn Angela, Diane Elizabeth. **EDUCATION:** Univ of Akron-Williams Coll, AB 1943; Univ of Tokyo, 1945; Western Reserve, LLB 1951; Cleveland State, JD 1953. **CAREER:** Cuyahoga County Probate Court, comm 20 yrs; Cleveland State, prof 2 yrs; City of Cleveland, asst law dir 2 yrs; OH Paralegal Inst, dean 1975; Cleveland City Council, counsel 2 yrs; Howard Univ School of Law, prof. **ORGANIZATIONS:** Mem OH State Cuyahoga Cty, Cleveland Bar Assoc; bd trustees Cuyahoga Cty Bar Assoc; past pres John M Harlan Law Club; 1st pres Cath Lawyers Guild; 4th deg Knights of Columbus; chmn Bd for Cath Big Bros; mem bd ed Diocese of Cleveland; life mem NAACP; past pres Alpha Phi Alpha; owner DD Racing Stables; mem Phi Beta Kappa 1945; mem Intl Commiss on Human Rights; pres Decatur-Mobile Oil Co Richmond TX. **MILITARY SERVICE:** USAF 1943-46,51-52. **HOME ADDRESS:** 3074 Becket Rd, Cleveland, OH 44120.

DECLUE, ANITA
Educator. **PERSONAL:** Married Dr James; children: 2 Sons. **EDUCATION:** WA U, BS 1974. **CAREER:** Gov Serv, 1942-69; St Louis Public Schools, substitute teacher 1970-; Concordia Sem, delegate housing conf. **ORGANIZATIONS:** V chmn bd, mem League Women Voters; Human Resources.

DECOSTA, HERBERT ALEXANDER, JR.
Business executive. **PERSONAL:** Born Mar 17, 1923, Charleston; married Emily Spencer; children: Gail D. **EDUCATION:** IA State U, BS 1944. **CAREER:** Nat Adv Com for Aeronautics Langley Field, architectural Engr 1944-47; HA DeCosta Co Gen Contractors, vice pres 1948-60, pres 1960-, bd dirs 1969-75. **ORGANIZATIONS:** Nat Assn Minority Contractors 1974-75, 79-; bd dir Nat Assn Home Builders 1973-75; bd dir mem Home Builders Assn of Greater Charleston; active Boy Scouts of Am; bd visitors ‡C State C of C 1971-74; mgmt com Armed Forces YMCA 1972-75; bd dirs St John's Episcopal Mission Center 1965-75; sr warden St Mark's Episcopal Ch 1975, 80; Kiwanis Intl Charleston Chap Bd Dirs 1974-75; Charleston Area Community Relations Com 1970-75; Charleston Planning & Zoning Comm 1970-75; v chmn PA Comm Serv Inc Beaufort SC; mem SC State Bd for Tech & Comprehensive Edn; life mem NAACP; bd trustees Benedict Coll 1972-80; mem Sigma Ph Phi Frat 1978-; mem Bd of Architectural Review City of Charleston SC. **HONORS/ACHIEVEMENTS:** Man of yr Alpha Phi Alpha Frat 1970; silver beaver award Coastal Carolina Council Boy Scouts of Am 1972. **BUSINESS ADDRESS:** 93 Spring St, Charleston, SC 29403.

DECOSTA-WILLIS, MIRIAM
Educator. **PERSONAL:** Born Nov 01, 1934, Florence, AL; daughter of Frank A DeCosta and Beautine Hubertt DeCosta; married Russell B Sugarmon, Jr, Archie W Willis, Jr, Oct 20, 1972 (deceased); children: Tarik Sugarmon, Elena S Williamson, Erika S Echols, Monique A Sugarmon. **EDUCATION:** Wellesley Coll, BA 1956; Johns Hopkins Univ, MA 1960, PhD 1967. **CAREER:** Owen Coll, instructor 1960-66; Memphis State Univ, assoc prof of Spanish 1966-70; Howard Univ, assoc prof of Spanish 1970-74, prof of Spanish, chmn of FL dept, 1970-76; prof & chmn of dept 1974-76; LeMoyne-Owen Coll, prof, Romance Languages, prof of Spanish & dir of DuBois program, 1979-88. **ORGANIZATIONS:** Mem, Coll Language Assn; bd of dirs, MSU Center for Rsch on Women; founder Memphis Black Writers' Workshop 1980-; chair TN Humanities Council; bd Federation of State Humanities Councils; editorial bd Sage & Afro-Hispanic Review; life mem NAACP; chmn, Exec bd/mem, TN Humanities Council, 1981-87; chmn & founding mem, Memphis Black Writers' Workshop, 1980-. **HONORS/ACHIEVEMENTS:** Phi Beta Kappa 1956; Johns Hopkins Fellowship 1965; editor Blacks in Hispanic Literature Kennikat Pr 1977; articles in CLAJ, Journal of Negro History, Black World Negro History Bulletin, Revista Interamericana, Caribbean Quart; Sage Afro-Hispanic Review; Outstanding Faculty Mem of the Year, LeMoyne-Owen Coll, 1982; Homespun Images: An Anthology of Black Memphis Writers & Artists, 1988. **HOME ADDRESS:** 585 S Greer, #703, Memphis, TN 38111. **BUSINESS ADDRESS:** Visiting Commonwealth Prof of Spanish, Dept of Foreign Languages & Literature, Geogre Mason Univ, Fairfax, VA 22030.

DEE, MERRI
Newscaster, talk show host, announcer. **PERSONAL:** Born Oct 30, 1936, Chicago, IL; daughter of John Blouin; divorced; children: Toya Dorham. **EDUCATION:** St Xavier Coll, major in bus adm. **CAREER:** WBEE Radio, news hostess of talk-music prog women's ed 1966-72; WSDM-FM radio, hostess "The Merri Dee Show" 1968-69; Women's Ed & staff announcer; WSNS-TV, hostess ofTV talk show 1971-72; Cont Bank, spokesperson 1972-76; WGN-TV & WGN-Radio, news announ edit spokesperson 1972-76; Hillman's Foods, consumer adf 1974-75; Kraft Foods, nutrit spokesperson 1975-76 & 1979-80; WGN Broadcasting, newscaster/announcer. **ORGANIZATIONS:** Sec & exec bd mem Am Cancer Soc appearances at num Cancer soc-related events; charter trustee & dir Athletes for Better Edn; bd dir Mayors Open Land Project; per appear for Amer Cancer Soc, March of Dimes, Men Health Assoc, Chic Park Dist, Urban Leag, Chic Chamber of Comm Mayor Daley's Youth Found YWCA & YMCA, Chic Boys Clubs, univs, Chs, Schs; public speaker; general chmn United Negro Coll Fund; host of UNCF Telethon Chicago 10 yrs. **HONORS/ACHIEVEMENTS:** Chic Park Dist Recog Award 1974; Jr Citz Awards 1974; Woman of the Yr, PUSH Found Fam Award 1975; Woman of the Yr, Chic Ch Women's Fed 1975; Ten Best Dressed Women Award; perm mem Assn of Mannequins; Pioneer Award, Nat Assn of Women in Media 1975; recog award Buckingham Fountain Arts Fair 1975; Distinguished Citizen Award, Ebonari Found 1974; Communic of the Yr Am Cancer Soc 1973 & 79; Prof Serv Award, North IL Univ Journ Sch 1975; Humanitarian of the Year Awd Paul Hall Boys Club 1987; Outstanding Role Model Kellogg Corp; Black History Month Awds AT&T, Sabin Magnet Sch; Volunteer of the Year Awd Chicago Bd of Educ; Spirit of Love Awd Little City Foundation; Communicator of the Year Cosmopolitan Chamber of Commerce; Kizzy Scholarship Awd to Outstanding Women of Amer; Communications Award, Easter Seal Soc of Metropolitan Chicago, 1989; Black Heritage Award, Mahogany Found, 1989. **BUSINESS ADDRESS:** Newscaster/Announcer, WGN Broadcasting, 2501 W Bradley Pl, Chicago, IL 60618.

DEE, RUBY (RUBY ANN WALLACE)
Actress. **PERSONAL:** Born Oct 27, Cleveland, OH; married Ossie Davis; children: Nora, Guy, Laverne. **EDUCATION:** Hunter Coll, BA 1945; Amer Negro Theatre, apprentice 1941-44. **CAREER:** Actress appearing in numerousTV plays and motion pictures; Broadway productions, all Black cast of "Arsenic & Old Lace", "John Loves Mary", "Anna & Lucasta" 1946, "A Raisin in the Sun" 1959, "Purlie Victorious" 1961, "Boesman & Lena" 1971, "The Imaginary Invalid" 1971, "Wedding Band" 1972, role of Queen Gertrude "Hamlet" 1975; motion pictures, "The Jackie Robinson Story" 1950, "St Louis Blues" 1957, "A Raisin in the Sun" 1960, "Buck & the Preacher" 1971; collaborated with Jules Dassin & Julian Mayfield "Uptight", "Wedding Band" by Alice Childress 1973; 3 yrs with Ossie Davis & Ruby Dee Story Hour over Natl Black Network; editedan anthology of poems "Glow Child and Other Poems". **ORGANIZATIONS:** Mem NAACP, SCLC. **HONORS/ACHIEVEMENTS:** Obie Award 1971; Ann Martin Luther King Jr Award Operation PUSH 1972; Frederick Douglas Award NY Urban League 1970; Drama Desk Award 1974; author poetry Glowchild 1972, Take It from the Top. **BUSINESS ADDRESS:** The Artist Agency, 10000 Santa Monica Blvd, Los Angeles, CA 90067.

DEESE, MANUEL
City official. **PERSONAL:** Born Nov 08, 1941, Toomsboro, GA; married Jean Matthews; children: Eric, Byron. **EDUCATION:** Morgan State Univ, BA Pol Sci; Amer Univ School of Govt & Publ Admin, MPA. **CAREER:** Natl League of Cities DC, policy analyst 1969-71; City of Alexandria, asst to city mgr 1971-74; City of Richmond, asst city mgr admin 1974-77, asst citymgr operations 1977-79, city mgr 1979-. **ORGANIZATIONS:** Mem governing bd Amer Assoc for Public Admin; bd of dir Richmond Reg Criminal Justice Training Ctr; bd mem Intl City Mgmt Assn. **HONORS/ACHIEVEMENTS:** Alumnus of the Year Morgan State Univ 1981; Recipient of numerous awds for leadership in govt & civic affairs. **BUSINESS ADDRESS:** City Manager, City of Richmond, 900 E Broad St, Richmond, VA 23219.

DEGENESTE, HENRY IRVING
Law enforcement. **PERSONAL:** Born Aug 16, 1940, Newark, NJ. **EDUCATION:** Fairleigh Dickinson Univ, course work in math & elec engrg 1958-62; Rutgers Univ, certificate Criminal Justice Planning & Rsch 1975; Fed Bureau of Investigation, certificate Exec Management 1976; Columbia Univ, certificate Exec Management of Criminal Justice System 1976; Adelphi Univ, BA Business Admin (Cum Laude) 1976; Adelphia Univ, John Jay Cortege Grad course work towards MPA. **CAREER:** Edmond Assocs, draftsman 1962-65; Newark Public Schools, school teacher 1962-65; US Postal Serv, 1965-67; New York-New Jersey Law Enforcement, police officer 1967-74, police sgt 1974-76, police capt 1978-81, supt of police 1984-. **ORGANIZATIONS:** Pres Natl Org of Black Law Enforcement Execs 1982-83; mem Intl Assn of Chiefs of Police; mem New York State Assn of Chiefs of Police; bd mem Jersey City Chap NAACP; mem, Amer Mgmt Assn; bd mem New Jersey Special Olympics; guest lecturer in Crisis Mgmt at John Jay Coll & the Fed Emergency Mgmt Assn Headquarters; conducted seminars in Exec devel for minority police execs at Florida Intl Univ & Atlanta Univ; adj prof John Jay Coll Grad School; bd mem Boys Choir of Harlem; consultant on minority relations & recruitment to the New Scotland Yard/Metro Police London, England; treasurer, bd of dir, Hudson County Urban League of New Jersey; mem of exec comm, bd of dir, Newark, NJ, YMWCA; mem, bd of dirs, New Jersey Special Olympics. **HONORS/ACHIEVEMENTS:** 3 Police Commendation Awards; Meritorious Police Duty Medal; 2 Port Authority Exec Dirs Citations; Harlen "Y" Black Achievers in Indus Award; United Nations Peace Medal; Israeli Freedom Medal; Whitney M Young Jr Award, Hudson County Urban League. **BUSINESS ADDRESS:** Superintendent of Police, Port Authority of NY & NJ, 1 Path Plaza, Jersey City, NJ 07306.

DEGRAFFENREIDT, ANDREW
School administrator. **PERSONAL:** Born Mar 03, 1928, Kansas City, MO; married Eddie Pearl Black; children: Andrew, III, Fredi Grace, Carol. **EDUCATION:** Tougaloo Coll, MS, BS; PA State Univ, MS 1957; FL State Univ, 3 summer NSF program, 1966; FL Atlantic Univ, Univ Miami, certified supvr, admin. **CAREER:** Broward & Co School Syst, asst admin; Dillard HS Ft Lauderdale, FL, teacher; Everglades Jr HS, teacher chmn sci dept; Broward Co ITV Ctr, devel taught special prog, 1967-70. **ORGANIZATIONS:** Dir CTA; dir FEA; exec council mem FEA; chmn many educ cons; salary chmn BSAA; sch admin Piper HS; mem Ft Lauderdale City Comm Boy Scout Scoutmaster; nghbrhd scout commr; past mem, sub comm Broward Co Chrtr Commn; past bd mem United Way Broward Co; Girl Scout Council Broward Co; Family Serv Agency; Project on aging; chmn Gold Coast League Cities; past chmn NW Boys Club Adv Bd; past mem City Comm Serv & Facilities Bd; past mem Broward Co Health & Planning Council; mem Broward Co Planning Council & pres Brotherhood Org of Piney Grove Church.

DEHART, HENRY R.
Engineer. **PERSONAL:** Born Nov 11, 1931, Staten Island, NY; married Panzy Hawk; children: Henry, Linda. **EDUCATION:** Polytechnic Inst of NY, BCE 1958. **CAREER:** New York City Dept of Traffic, dir of hwy design. **ORGANIZATIONS:** Licensed professional engr NY; past warden, past dir SS; licensed lay reader St Gabriels PE Church; past pres Staten Island Br NAACP 1965; past commdr Amer Legion 1966; acolyte master St Gabriels Church. **HONORS/ACHIEVEMENTS:** Friend of Howard Adward NY Club, Howard Univ Alumni, 1975; past pres award, Staten Island Branch, NAACP, 1986; Bishop Cross Long Island Diocese, 1987; Meritorious Award for Community Serv 1987. **MILITARY SERVICE:** USAF 1952-56. **BUSINESS ADDRESS:** Dir of Highway Design, New York City Dept of Traffic, 28-11 Bridge Plaza N, Long Island City, NY 11101.

DEHART, PANZY H.
Social worker. **PERSONAL:** Born May 18, 1934, Cleveland County, NC; daughter of Henry Kilgore and Sallie Hawk Owens; married Henry Ross DeHart; children: Henry Jr, Linda. **EDUCATION:** Howard Univ, BA 1956, MSW 1958. **CAREER:** DC Dept of Welfare, child welfare social worker 1958-61; Veterans Administration, clinical social worker 1961-65; NY City Dept of Health, consultant 1968-70; Inwood House, supervisor 1966-68, 1970-72; NY Univ Medical Ctr, rehab social worker 1976-. **ORGANIZATIONS:** Pres Howard Univ Alumni Club of New York City 1970-74; mem bd of dir Parent Preparation Inc 1970-75; mem Queens Chap Jack & Jill of Amer Inc 1973-87; dir Jack & Jill Computer Assisted Lab 1985-87; mem Concerned Citizens of South Queens 1987. **HONORS/ACHIEVEMENTS:** Service Award Howard Univ Alumni Club 1972; Natl Achievement Award Lambda Kappa Mu Sor 1974; Service Award Jack & Jill of Amer Inc Queens Chap 1986. **HOME ADDRESS:** 110-06 214th St, Queens Village, NY 11429. **BUSINESS ADDRESS:** Social Worker, New YorkUniv Medical Ctr, 400 East 34th St, New York, NY 10016.

DEIZ, MERCEDES F.
Judge. **PERSONAL:** Born Dec 13, 1917, NYC, NY; married Carl H Deiz; children: Bill, Karen, Gilbert. **EDUCATION:** Northwestern Univ Sch of Law, JD 1959. **CAREER:**

Bonneville Power Admin Portland, law library asst 1949-53; Portland, legal sec 1954-59; General Practice Portland, trial lawyer 1960-67; OR Workmen's Comp Bd, hearing officer 1968-70; Multnomah Co, dist ct judge 1970-72; State of OR Multnomah Co Courthouse, circuit ct judge. **ORGANIZATIONS:** Mem Gov's Comm on Judicial Reform; mem OR State Bar Com on Pub Serv & Info; former chmn Minor Cts Com; lecturer Family Law Seminar; legal serv to 1967 legislature in OR; former sec-treas Multnomah Bar Assn; mem several bar assns; mem Amer Jud Soc; chmn Status Offenses Comm; mem Natl Council of Juvenile Ct Judges; chmn of com lectr juvenile & family law race relations rights of minorities Ct Sys serving bd dirs Lewis & Clark Coll; OR Museum of Sci & Industry; mem Golden Hrs Inc, CISCO; visiting fellow Woodrow Wilson Prog; dir Natl Assn of Women Judges; dir Assn of Family Conciliation Cts. **HONORS/ACHIEVEMENTS:** Woman of Accomplishment 1969; listed in Mothers Achvmt in Amer History 1776-1976; first Black elected to remunerative ofc in State of OR. **BUSINESS ADDRESS:** Circuit Court Judge, Multnomah County, 308 Multnomah Co Courthouse, Portland, OR 97204.

DEJARMON, ELVA PEGUES
Educator. **PERSONAL:** Born Feb 14, 1921, Hartsville, SC; daughter of Paul Pegues and Jessie Brailey Pegues; married LeMarquis, Jun 10, 1942; children: Michell Renee. **EDUCATION:** Wilberforce Univ, BS, 1941; Western Reserve Univ, MS, 1949; Natl Sci Inst, 1959; NYU, 1961-62; Univ NC, 1974; NCCU, Journalism, 1982-84. **CAREER:** Dunham Tech Community Coll, adult educ instructor; North Carolina Times, assoc editor, 1970-; Durham Tech Inst, coordinator, training program for disadvantaged, 1965-69; NC Central Univ, asst prof 1960-65; Cleveland Public Schools, teacher 1947-58; Editorial Rsch, 1942-45. **ORGANIZATIONS:** Mem NC Press Women; Am Dietetic Assn nutrition consult (RD); local & state nutrition councils; past pres Nat Barristers' Wives; Alpha Kappa Alpha; Dept of Social Serv 1971-74, mental health 1974-; Oper Breakthrough 1973-; stewardess AME Ch; Sch Adv Bd; NC Heart Assn; YMCA; NAACP; chmn Durham Co Commn Mental Health Cntr; chmn Nominating Com for Mid-Atlantic Reg; Rep to Natl Nominating Com; mem N Central Region Continuing Educ Com for Mental Health Serv-Substance Abuse-Mental Retardation; mem N Central Region Area Bd Chmn Area Dir Assn; neighborhood advisor Coordinating Council Sr Citizens; bd mem, Widowed Persons Services, 1988-90; Neighborhood Focus Bd, City of Durham, 1988-. **HONORS/ACHIEVEMENTS:** Hon Mid-Atlantic Region Conf, Alpha Kappa Alpha Inc, 1977; Volunteer of the Year Award, 1979; Certificate of Achievement, NC Central Univ, 1983; President's Volunteer Action Award, 1983; Leadership Award, Natl Council of Negro Women, Durham Sect, 1984; Contributions to AME Christian Recorder; Contributions of Black Women to Amer M Davis, YWCA, Women of Achievement Recognition, 1987; Several publications including cookbooks, brochures on Blacks in Durham, History of NCNW Durham Section; Golden Soror, Alpha Kappa Alpha Sorority Inc, 1988; YWCA Women of Achievement, 1988; Leadership Award, Alpha Kappa Alpha Sorority Inc, Alpha Zeta Omega Chapter, 1989; Recognition of Past Basilei, History of Alpha Zeta Omega Chapter, Alpha Kappa Alpha, 1989. **BUSINESS ADDRESS:** Adult Education Instructor, Dunham Tech Community College, 1637 Lawson St, Durham, NC 27701.

DEJOIE, C. C., JR.
Publishing executive. **PERSONAL:** Born Oct 25, 1914, New Orleans, LA; married Julia; children: Michael Charles. **EDUCATION:** Talladega Coll, BA 1937; Univ MI, MA 1938. **CAREER:** Louisiana Weekly, (only black newspaper in New Orleans) editor & business mgr 1938-69, pres & publisher 1969-. **ORGANIZATIONS:** Pres Nat Newspaper Pub Assn 1954-56; former treas & assn bd mem Amalgamated Pub Inc; bd dir Liberty Bank & Trust Co; former corporate owner of New Orleans Saints; dir Doley Securities; Orleans Parish Jury Commissioner. **BUSINESS ADDRESS:** President, The Louisiana Weekly, 616 Baronne St, New Orleans, LA 70113.

DEJOIE, CAROLYN BARNES MILANES
Educator. **PERSONAL:** Born in New Orleans, LA; daughter of Edward Franklin Barnes and Alice Milanes Barnes; children: Deirdre Jeanelle, Prudhomme III, Duan Kendall. **EDUCATION:** Universidad Nacional de Mexico, MA 1962; Univ of WI, MSW 1970; Union Grad Sch, PhD 1976; Xavier Univ of LA, BA. **CAREER:** Southern Univ, instructor 1962-63; VA State Coll, asst prof 1963-66; Univ of WI Ext, admin specialist 1967-68, asst to pres 1970-73; Univ of WI Madison, prof of human issues 1973-; Human Relations Counseling Serv, owner, dir 1980-; Sun and Shadows Publishing Co, owner 1987-. **ORGANIZATIONS:** Foreign language consult Travenol de Mexico Am British Cowdray Hosp Mex 1959-62; exec dir Centro Hispano-Americano Madison 1978-79; psychotherapist Private Practice 1980-; exec bd, NAACP, Madison WI 1987-; author, natl speaker, conference planner. **HONORS/ACHIEVEMENTS:** Fulbright US Gov't 1966; Achievemnt Against Odds WI Humanities Commn Smithsonian Inst Exhibit 1983; Outstanding Contrib to Soc Alpha Kappa Alpha 1984; Outstanding Contrib to Community WI Governor's Award 1984; Natl Assn Media Women Woman of the Year Award 1985; Natl Assn Negro Business & Professional Women Recognition of Serv Award 1986; Bd of Commissioners Genessee County MI Laudatory Resolution 1986; Golden Egg Award, Natl Assn Media Women 1987; Appreciation Award, city of New Orleans 1988; Unsung Heroine Award, NAACP-Madison WI 1988; publications, Students Speak Out: Racial Problems and What Students Can Do About Them; Wisconsin Minority Women's Perspectives on Women's Issues 1989. **HOME ADDRESS:** 5322 Fairway Dr, Madison, WI 53711. **BUSINESS ADDRESS:** Professor of Human Services, Univ of WI, 610 Langdon St, Room 320, Madison, WI 53703.

DEJONGH, JAMES LAURENCE
Educator. **PERSONAL:** Born Sep 23, 1942, St Thomas, Virgin Islands of the United States;son of Percy Leo deJongh and Mavis Elizabeth Bentlage deJongh. **EDUCATION:** Williams College, BA 1964; Yale Univ, MA 1967; New York Univ, PhD 1983. **CAREER:** Rutgers Univ Newark, instructor 1969-70; The City Coll of the City Univ of New York (CUNY), prof 1970-. **ORGANIZATIONS:** Mem The Dramatists Guild, Writers Guild of Amer East, Modern Language Assoc, Harlem Writers Guild, Zeta Psi Frat. **HONORS/ACHIEVEMENTS:** Fellow Center for Black Studies Univ of CA Santa Barbara 1981; Outstanding Achievement Awd The Black Action Council of the City Coll of New York 1982; Audelco Recognition Awd Outstanding Musical Creator 1984; Honorary Fellow Brookdale Ctr on Aging of Hunger Coll 1985; Natl Endowment for the Humanities Fellowship for College Teachers 1986; major plays and publications "Hail Hail the Gangs!" w/Carles Cleveland produced by NY Theatre Ensemble Inc 1976; "City Cool, A Ritual of Belonging," w/Carles Cleveland Random House 1978; "Do Lord Remember Me" Off-Broadway Premier Oct 10, 1982 produced by Wynn Handman The Amer Place Theater; "Play to Win, Jackie Robinson" w/Carles Cleveland Natl school tour 1984-86. **BUSINESS ADDRESS:** Professor of English, City College of the City Univ of New York, English Department, New York, NY 10031.

DEKNIGHT, AVEL
Artist. **PERSONAL:** Born 1933, New York. **EDUCATION:** Ecole des Beauz-Arts, Paris; Pratt Inst; Grand Chaumiere. **CAREER:** Contemporary Arts Mus, exhibits 1970; SF Mus Art, 1969; Minn Inst Arts; Whitney Mus, 1971; Acad Fine Arts; Larcada Gallery, 1968; num others; Metro Mus Art, collections; Wallcer Art Ctr. **HONORS/ACHIEVEMENTS:** Miles Coll recip Watercolor Soc 1967; Paton Prize, Nat Acad Sch of Fine Arts 1958, 67; Grumbacher Award Audubon Artist Soc 1964; Childe Hassam Fund Purchase, Am Acad of Arts & Letters 1960.

DELAIR, LOUIS, JR.
Foreign affairs officer. **PERSONAL:** Born Nov 01, 1947, New Orleans, LA; children: Louis III, Terrell Nicole. **EDUCATION:** So Univ of New Orleans, BA 1969; Xavier Univ of LA, MA 1977; IN Univ, Univ of VA, Loyola Univ School of Law, further study. **CAREER:** IN Univ, teaching asst 1969-70, counselor student leadership 1970; Urban League St Acad New Orleans, coord of student activities 1975; So Univ New Orleans, hs relations counselor 1975-80; US Dept of State, foreign affairs officer 1980-; Amer Embassy Jakarta Indonesia, vice consul. **ORGANIZATIONS:** Mem Amer Personnel & Guid Assoc 1975-80, Assoc for Non-White Concerns in Guidance 1975-80, Amer Bar Assoc Law Student Div 1978-80; pres Theta Beta Sigma Chap Phi Beta Sigma 1976-77; mem campus adv Alpha Phi Omega Serv Frat 1976-80; state dir Phi Beta Sigma Frat Inc LA 1978-79. **HONORS/ACHIEVEMENTS:** Listed in Who's Who Among Students in Amer Univ & Coll 1969, Outstanding Younng Men of Amer 1978; Natl Defense Medal USN; Outstanding Young Men of Amer 1978; Recognition for Outstanding Serv Phi Beta Sigma Frat Inc 1979; Professional Scuba Instr Natl Assoc of Scuba Diving Schools. **MILITARY SERVICE:** USNR lt commander 1970-80.

DELANEY, HAROLD
Association executive. **PERSONAL:** Born Aug 24, 1919, Philadelphia, PA; son of William Y D Delaney (deceased) and Henrietta Pinkney Delaney (deceased); married Geraldine East; children: Milton Y, Doyle O. **EDUCATION:** Howard Univ, BS 1941, MS 1943, PhD 1958. **CAREER:** Manhattan Project, Chicago IL, chemist 1943-45; North Carolina State A&T Coll, asst prof of chemistry 1945-48; Morgan State Coll, asst/assoc prof of chemistry 1948-67, dean & prof chem 1967-69; E I DuPont de Nemours, Chemist Summer 1966; SUNY Central Admin, vice chancellor/assoc provost 1969-72; Gen Admin Univ of NC, vice pres 1972-74; Manhattanville Coll, pres 1974-75; Natl Inst of Educ, asso dir 1976-77; Amer Assn of State Coll & Univ, exec vice pres 1977-86, emeritus 1987; Univ of Maryland System, special asst to the chancellor 1988-. **ORGANIZATIONS:** Chmn bd of dir Howard Thurman Educ Trust 1983-86; mem bd of dir Catalyst 1975-78; consult Middle States Assn of Sch & Coll 1974-76; mem bd of trustees Manhattanville Coll 1971-74; mem Am Chem Soc 1945-; fellow Am Inst of Chemists 1968-; mem MD Acad of Sci; mem bd of trust Paul Smith's Coll; bd of dir The Washington Center. **HONORS/ACHIEVEMENTS:** Distinguished Amer Found for Negro Affairs 1976; Sigma Pi Sigma Hon Soc of Physics; fellow Sigma Xi; Towson State Univ, LHD 1987. **HOME ADDRESS:** 1013 Cresthaven Dr, Silver Spring, MD 20903. **BUSINESS ADDRESS:** Executive Vice President, Amer Assn of State Coll & Univ, 1 Dupont Cir, Washington, DC 20036.

DELANEY, HOWARD C.
City official. **PERSONAL:** Born Sep 22, 1933, Lancaster County, NE; married Rosetta Johnson; children: Alvin Cooper, Dana E. **EDUCATION:** State of CO Cert Bd, "A" Wastewater Oper 1968, "A" Water Works 1969. **CAREER:** Construction, laborer 1951-66; Denver Sewage Disposal Dist # 1, suprv 1966-81; Longmont CO Wastewater Treatment Facility, supt 1981-. **ORGANIZATIONS:** Sec RMWPCA Personnel Adv Comm 1967-; mem WPCF Plant Oper Comm 1967-; mem Aurora Repeater Assoc 1977-. **HONORS/ACHIEVEMENTS:** 1st black supt of a major CO wastewater facility; 1st black mgr for City of Longmont 1981-. **BUSINESS ADDRESS:** Supt of Wastewtr Trtmnt Pl, City of Longmont, 1100 S Sherman St, Longmont, CO 80501.

DELANEY, JOHN PAUL
Newspaper senior editor. **PERSONAL:** Born Jan 13, 1933, Montgomery, AL; married Anita Jackson; children: John Paul III, David Allen. **EDUCATION:** Ohio State Univ, BA Journalism 1958. **CAREER:** Atlanta Daily World 1959-61; Atlanta Municipal Ct, probation officer 1961-63; Dayton, OH, Daily News 1963-67; Washington Star, reporter 1967-69; New York Times, corres, Washington Bureau 1969-74, Chicago bureau 1974-77, corres, asst natl editor 1977-80, deputy natl editor 1980-86, chief Madrid bureau 1987-89, senior editor. **ORGANIZATIONS:** Mem Robert F Kennedy Journalism Awards Comm 1973-75, chmn 1975; founding mem Natl Assn of Black Journalists; bd chmn Publicity Comm, Atlanta Br NAACP 1961-63. **HONORS/ACHIEVEMENTS:** Recipient, Scholarship, Ohio State Univ 1957. **MILITARY SERVICE:** AUS Corpl 1953-55. **BUSINESS ADDRESS:** Senior Editor, The New York Times, 229 W 43rd St, New York, NY 10036.

DELANEY, JUANITA BATTLE
Social worker. **PERSONAL:** Born Jan 04, 1921, Jacksonville, TX; children: Rachel. **EDUCATION:** TX Coll, BA 1943; TX Univ, MS 1955. **CAREER:** Brownsboro, sch tchr 1944-45; TX Welfare Dept, child welfare worker 1946-64; TX Dept Health E TX Chest Hosp, chief casework services;Univ of TX Tyler, dir med social servs 1980. **ORGANIZATIONS:** Mem Nat Assn Social Workers 1970; mem Acad Certified Social Workers 197; appointed Consult Social Work Services, Tuberculosis Div TX Health Dept 1973-; Coordntr Equal Employment Opportunity ETX Chest Hosp 1974 mem Delta Sigma Theta Sorority 1959-; pres local chap Delta Sigma Theta 1973-77. **HONORS/ACHIEVEMENTS:** Battle Family named Family of Month, Tyler 1971; Delaney family named Family Of Month, Tyler 1973. **BUSINESS ADDRESS:** PO Box 2003, Tyler, TX 75710.

DELANEY, WILLI
Government employee. **PERSONAL:** Born Mar 23, 1947, Washington, DC; divorced; children: Damon. **EDUCATION:** CathUniv of Am; Atlanta U. **CAREER:** Women's Bur, spl asst to dir; White House Pres Speechwriting Ofc; Carter Campaign for Pres, natl dir vol; City of Atlanta Ofc of Consumer Affairs, cnslr; Voter Educ Proj of Atlanta, rsrch asst. **ORGANIZATIONS:** Past mem WA Women's Forum 1977; mem Metro Dem Women's Club 1977; Nat Hook-up of Black Women Inc 1977. **BUSINESS ADDRESS:** US Department of Labor, Washington, DC 20210.

DELANY, HOLLY DIANE
Foundation executive. **PERSONAL:** Born Dec 05, 1957, New York, NY. **EDUCA-**

TION: Adelphi Univ Sch of Social Work, BSW (Summa Cum Laude) 1979; Univ of Chicago Sch of Social Serv Admin, AM 1981. **CAREER:** Family Focus/Family Resource Coalition Evanston/Chicago IL, special projects coord 1981-83; NY Comm Trust, prog officer 1983-. **ORGANIZATIONS:** Mem Assoc of Black Foundation Execs 1983-, Natl Assoc of Social Workers 1983-, NY Regional Assoc of Grantmakers 1983-; volunteer tutor Literacy Volunteers of Amer 1985-86; chairperson bd of dirs The Adolescent Pregnancy Care & Prevention Prog 1985-; mem bd of dirs The YWCA of Brooklyn 1986-, Ctr for Population Options 1986-. **HONORS/ACHIEVEMENTS:** Mem Delta Tau Honor Soc Adelphi Univ 1979; John Russwurm Black Scholar Awd Adelphi Univ 1979; Sol O Lichter Memorial Awd for Scholarship & Leadership 1981; co-authored "Working with Teen Parents — A Survey of Promising Approaches," 1983 Chicago; author of occasional paper at NY Community Trust on Criminal Justice 1986. **BUSINESS ADDRESS:** Program Officer, New York Community Trust, 415 Madison Avenue, New York, NY 10017.

DELANY, SAMUEL RAY
Author. **PERSONAL:** Born Apr 01, 1942, Harlem, NY; married Marilyn Hacker; children: Iva Alexander. **EDUCATION:** Attended, City College of NY. **CAREER:** Author, science fiction. **HONORS/ACHIEVEMENTS:** Hugo Awd; Nebula Awd. **BUSINESS ADDRESS:** Bantam Books, 666 5th Ave, Publicity Department, New York, NY 10103.

DELARUE, LOUIS C.
Clergyman. **PERSONAL:** Born Mar 24, 1939, Orange, TX; son of Garrett DeLarue and Ethel M DeLarue. **EDUCATION:** BS, 1974, Lamar Univ; St Joseph Seminary, 1 yr; St Thomas Univ, Houston, TX, MA, Theology; St Marys Sem, M Div; Catholic Univ America, 1 Yr. **CAREER:** St Mary's, asst pastor, 1st black priest ordained diocese Beaumont, TX 1975, 1st black diocesan asst pastor to serve a racial mixed parish, St Mary's, Port Arthur, TX; In-home parish serving the black community; 1st black pastor of native parish in the Beamont Diocese, 1986; Interfaith ministry & outstanding black clergyman in greater Orange community; Diocesan dir, Black Catholic Congress, 1987. **ORGANIZATIONS:** mem, Kiwanis Intl, 1989, TX Catholic Historical Soc, 1985-89, Natl Black Seminarian Assn, Natl Black Clergy Caucus, NAACP, Assn Pastoral Counseling; ecumenical dir, Diocese of Beaumont; mem, Ecumenical Dir of the TX Catholic Conf; spiritual dir, Parish Afro-Am Ecumenical Dance Group Henderson Sch of Dance; Diocesan Black Cattholic Commn; Greater Orange Ministerial Fellowship. **HONORS/ACHIEVEMENTS:** Outstanding Afro-Am Worship Award; Only black diocesan priest TX 1975; Outstanding Service Award, NAACP, 1987; Various other Honors/Awards. **MILITARY SERVICE:** USAF 4 Yrs. **BUSINESS ADDRESS:** Pastor, St Therese Church, 1409 North Sixth St, Orange, TX 77630.

DELAUDER, WILLIAM B.
College president. **CAREER:** Delaware State Coll, Dover De, president. **BUSINESS ADDRESS:** Delaware State College, Dover, DE 19910. *

DELCO, EXALTON ALFONSO, JR.
College educator. **PERSONAL:** Born Sep 04, 1929, Houston, TX; son of Exalton Delco and Pauline Delco; married Wilhelmina R; children: Deborah, Exalton III, Loretta, Cheryl. **EDUCATION:** Fisk Univ, BA 1949; Univ MI, MS 1950; Univ of TX, PHD 1962. **CAREER:** TX So Univ, instr 1950-55, asst prof 1957-60, rsch asst 1958-62; Huston-Tillotson Coll, assoc prof 1963-66; Prairie View A&M Coll, guest prof 1964;Huston-Tillotson Coll, head, biology dept, prof of biology 1966-69, vice pres for acad affairs 1967-85; Austin Co Coll, vice pres for acad affairs 1985-. **ORGANIZATIONS:** Fellow AAAS, Amer Inst of Biol Sci; vp, exec sec, mem of council Beta Kappa Chi Sci Honor Soc 1962-68; vp, pres Phi Delta Kappa 1969-72; mem Amer Fisheries Soc, Amer Soc of Ichthyologists & Herpetologists, Amer Soc of Limnology & Oceanography, Soc of Sigma Xi, NY Acad of Sci, TX Acad of Sci, Austin Housing Auth Commiss 1967-69; dist commiss Eagle Dist of Boy Scouts of Amer 1967-68; pres St Vincent de Paul Soc Holy Cross Church 1968; mem Travis Co Grand Jury Assoc, Comm Council of Austin & Travis Co 1968-70; mem 1968-71, pres 1982-85 Family Prac Residency Adv Comm of TX 1968-. **HONORS/ACHIEVEMENTS:** Stoye Prize Amer Soc of Ichthyologists & Herpetologists 1960; Danforth Assoc Huston-Tillotson Coll Campus 1966; Nominated Harbison Awd Danforth Found 1966; Piper Prof 1967; Natl Urban League Summer Fellow Allied Chem Co 1969; Outstanding Educator of Am. **MILITARY SERVICE:** Surgical tech in 46th MASH unit in Germany 1955-56; rank, SP3. **BUSINESS ADDRESS:** Vice President Acad Affairs, Austin Community College, PO Box 140526, Austin, TX 78714.

DELCO, WILHELMINA R.
State representative. **PERSONAL:** Born Jul 16, 1929, Chicago, IL; daughter of William P Fitzgerald and Juanita Heath Watson; married Dr Exalton A Delco, Jr, Aug 23, 1952; children: Deborah Diane Agbottah, Exalton A Delco III, Loretta Elmirle Edelen, Cheryl Pauline Delco. **EDUCATION:** Fisk Univ, BA 1950. **CAREER:** Prov Hosp, rec clerk; IL Bell Telephone, serv rep; Teachers State Assoc of TX, clerk; State of Texas, representative. **ORGANIZATIONS:** Sec, vchmn Citizens Adv Comm to Juv Ct; mem City of Austin Hum Relations Comm, Vol Soc Wkr, Travis Cty Welfare Dept; bd mem Volunteer Bur, Key Trnr; mem Well-Child Conf, Austin League of Women Voters; mem, sec 1972-74 Austin Ind School Dist; mem adv comm TX Employ Comm, TX Comm for Human & Publ Pol; del TX Assoc of School Bds 1973; mem bd trust, sec 1973-74 Aus Comm Coll; del TX Cath Conf 1972-; chmn, leg adv council, mem exec comm Southern Reg Ed; mem steering comm, exec comm Ed Comm of the States; vice chmn of State-Fed Assembly of the Natl Conf of State Legislatures; vchmn, bd of trustees Ed Testing Svc; cchmn Natl Black Caucus of State Legs; mem of commiss Standards of Southern Assoc of Colls & Schools; chrm bd of trustees ETS; chrm assembly on the legislature Natl Conf of State Leg; bd of trustees Southern Ed Found; chmn Higher Education Comm TX House of Reps, 1979. **HONORS/ACHIEVEMENTS:** Outstanding Woman Austin Amer Statesman, 1969; Serv Awd 1973 TX Congress of Parents & Teachers, 1973; Liberty Bell Awd Austin Jr Bar Assoc, 1969; Publ School SvcAwd Zeta Phi Beta, 1970; Publ Serv Merit Awd Omega Psi Phi, 1971; Apprec Awd Arthur DeWitty Awd 1971, NAACP 1972; Hon Mem Delta Kappa Gamma 1972; Coronat Med St Edwards Univ, 1972; Appreciation Award Blanton School, 1973; Serv Awd Sakarrah Temple, 1973; Serv Citation Optimist Club of E Austin, 1973; mem TX Women's Hall of Fame, 1986; Houston-Tillotson Coll, Austin, TX; Southwestern Univ, Georgetown, TX; Lee Coll, Baytown, TX; St Edwards Univ, Austin, TX; Wiley Coll, Marshall, TX. **BUSINESS ADDRESS:** State Representative, State of Texas, Capitol Bldg, Room 4130, Austin, TX 78769.

DELEON-JONES, FRANK A., JR.
Chief psychiatry. **PERSONAL:** Born May 06, 1937, Colon, Panama;married Silvia Cavallaro; children: Karen, Elizabeth. **EDUCATION:** Nat Inst of Panama, BS highest hon 1958;Univ of Rome, Italy, MD Surgery (summa cum laude) 1964; IL State Psychiatric Inst, Psychiatric Residency 1970. **CAREER:** VA Westside Hosp Chgo, chief of psychiatry; IL State Psychiatric Inst, asso dir research 1973-75, chief metabolic res units 1971-73, res asso 1970-71; Psychiatry Abraham Lincoln Sch of MedUniv of IL, asso prof; prac Psychoanalist; Chicago Inst for Psychoanalysis, grad. **ORGANIZATIONS:** Mem Am Psychiatric Assn; Am Assn for the Advancement of Sci; Am Psychoanalytic Assn; interested psycho pharmacology of depression, schizophrenia, drug addiction, other psychiatric disturbances. **HONORS/ACHIEVEMENTS:** Recip Ginsburg Fellow Troup for the Advancement of Psychiatry 1968-70. **BUSINESS ADDRESS:** Vets Adminstrn, Westside Hosp, Chicago, IL.

DELILLY, MAYO RALPH, III
Pediatrician. **PERSONAL:** Born Apr 03, 1953, Los Angeles, CA; son of Mayo R DeLilly Jr. MD and Irene Wood DeLilly; married Carol Covyeau DeLilly, Jun 28, 1986; children: Irene Rose, Lauren Marie. **EDUCATION:** Williams Coll, BA Biology 1974; Howard Univ Coll of Medicine, MD 1974-78. **CAREER:** Martin Luther King Genl Hosp, intern/resident 1978-81; Private Practice, pediatrician. **ORGANIZATIONS:** Mem LA Pediatric Soc 1981-, LA Co & CA Medical Assocs 1981-, Natl Medical Assoc 1981-; mem Big Brothers of Greater Los Angeles 1981-; medical advisor Sheenway Sch Los Angeles 1983-. **HONORS/ACHIEVEMENTS:** Academic Achievement Award Howard Univ Medical School 1976; Medical Alumni Award Howard Univ Medical School 1978; Outstanding Young Men of Amer 1981; mem Alpha Omega Alpha Honor Medical Society; fellow Amer Acad of Pediatrics 1984. **BUSINESS ADDRESS:** 1828 So Western Ave #22, Los Angeles, CA 90006.

DELK, FANNIE M.
Educator. **PERSONAL:** Born Dec 13, 1933, Lexington, MS; daughter of Theodore R Mitchell and Inez Mitchell; married Frank E Delk Jr; children: Gregory Kevin, Gerald Keith. **EDUCATION:** TN State Univ, AB English (with Distinction) 1956; Memphis State Univ, MEd English, Ed 1971; Univ of Chicago, Natl Endowment for the Humanities Fellow 1980; Ford Foundation Fellow, Univ of Mississippi, 1986-87. **CAREER:** FL School Memphis TN, teacher English 1956-57; Carver HS, teacher 1957-75; LeMoyne-Owen Coll, prof English 1975-. **ORGANIZATIONS:** Exec bd Alpha Kappa Alpha 1970-; consult Memphis City Schools 1973-; mem Reg Accrediting Teams, Southern Assoc Coll & Schools 1975-; lead volunteer teachert-task prog Memphis Volunteer Placement Prog 1975-; bd of dir Memphis Volunteer Placement Prog 1975-; act-so coord NAACP 1980-84; co-editor Homespun Images, An Anthology of Black Memphis Writers and Artists; pres Memphis Black Writers Workshop. **HONORS/ACHIEVEMENTS:** Humanities Scholar West TN Econ Council 1977; Publ "Toward Stabilization & Survival, The Rural Family in Transition" West TN Econ Council 1977; The Black Pearl Mag "Black Images" 1979, Southern Eye, Southern Mind, A Photographic Inquiry "The South, The Times, The Struggles" 1981; Fifty Yrs of Svc, A History of Beta Epsilon Omega Chap of Alpha Kappa Alpha 1985; AKA Woman of the Year 1982-82; MVP Volunteer of the Year 1982. **HOME ADDRESS:** 1556 S Wellington St, Memphis, TN 38106. **BUSINESS ADDRESS:** Professor, LeMoyne-Owen College, 807 Walker Ave, Memphis, TN 38126.

DELK, JAMES F., JR.
Automobile dealer. **CAREER:** Fairlane Ford Inc, Pottsville PA, chief exec officer. **BUSINESS ADDRESS:** Fairlane Ford Sales, Inc, N Claude A Lord Blvd & Mill Creek Ave, Pottsville, PA 17901. *

DELK, OLIVER RAHN
Educator. **PERSONAL:** Born Feb 04, 1948, Staten Island, NY. **EDUCATION:** Indiana Univ, BA Psychology 1974 honors graduate; GA State Univ, MS Criminal Justice 1976. **CAREER:** Sears, Roebuck & Co, asst mgr 1974-76; Southeast Branch YMCA Atlanta, comm prog dir 1976-77; Office of the Mayor Atlanta, tech assist specialist 1977-79; Morehouse Coll, dir of govt relations. **ORGANIZATIONS:** Mem Natl Assoc for Equal Oppor in Higher Educ 1985; pres Assoc for Fund-Raising Officers 1985; chmn Budget and Finance/Water/Waste Water Treatment Operators 1985; mem NAACP 1985; mem Omega Psi Phi Frat 1985; mem SCLC 1985. **HONORS/ACHIEVEMENTS:** Youth Services Awd WAOK Radio 1978; Outstanding Young Man of America awarded by US Jaycees 1979; Public Speaking Awd GA State Univ 1979; three career development program certificates from the YMCA; Outstanding Personalities of the South/Personalities of the South 1983. **BUSINESS ADDRESS:** Dir Governmental Relations, Morehouse College, 830 Westview Dr SW, Atlanta, GA 30314.

DELL, WILLIE J.
City official. **PERSONAL:** Born May 08, 1930, Weldon, NC; daughter of Emma A Grant; married Nathan Dell; children: Wayne, Arthur Jones. **EDUCATION:** St Augustines Coll, BA 1952; Richmond Professional Inst Coll William & Mary, MSW 1960. **CAREER:** Social Serv Bureau, social worker 1953-58; Med Coll VA, med social worker 1961-66; Richmond Public Health Dept, chief med soc worker 1966-68; VA Commonwealth Univ, asst prof 1968-74; JJ & W Assoc, exec dir; City of Richmond VA, mem city council; Richmond Comm Sr Ctr, exec dir 1976-; adjunct professor Univ of Richmond 1978-. **ORGANIZATIONS:** Pres Richmond Chap Natl Assoc Social Workers 1975; bd mem Commonwealth Psych; cur bd mem Richmond Chapter ARC & Fam & Children Svc, Natl League of Cities; mem VCU Grad School 1978-83, Richmond Comm Hosp 1976-83, Proj Jump St 1975-80; co-owner JJ&W Assoc Consultants, NAACP; sec North Side Civil Assn 1973-75; pres Black Ed Assoc 1973-75; sec St Augustines Chap 1973-75; mem Natl Assoc Black Soc Workers; past chmn Reg III NBC Leo; mem VA Council Soc Welfare Council Human Rel, Del Ver Women Clubs, Delta Sigma Theta; pres Natl Black Presbyterian Caucus; pres Richmond Chap Nat Causes Black Aged 1980-89; pres Adpts 1984-89; pres Richmond Urban Inst 1984-88; Bd Southern Regional Council; Diocese of Richmond, Haitian Commission. **HONORS/ACHIEVEMENTS:** Omega Citizen Year Award 1974; Govt Award Metro Bus League 1975; Delta's Civic & Polit Involvement Award 1975; Distinguished Serv Award St Augustine's Coll, 1982; Outstanding Woman Award in Govt YMCA 1982; Good Govt Award Eta Tau Chapter 1982; Outstanding Volunteer 1988, Powhatan Correctional Center. **HOME ADDRESS:** 2923 Hawthorne Ave, Richmond, VA 23222. **BUSINESS ADDRESS:** Executive Dir, Richmond Commun Sr Ctr, One Brenton St, Richmond, VA 23222.

DELLUMS, RONALD V.
Congressman. **PERSONAL:** Born Nov 24, 1935, Oakland, CA; married Leola Roscoe

Higgs; children: Brandy, Erik, Piper. **EDUCATION:** Oakland City Coll, AA 1958; San Francisco State Coll, BA 1960; Univ of CA, MSW 1962. **CAREER:** Berkeley CA City Council, mem 1967-71; US House of Representatives, mem of congress 1971-. **ORGANIZATIONS:** Chair House Comm on the District of Columbia; chair House Armed Serv Subcomm on Military Installations and Facilities; mem Defense Policy Panel, North Atlantic Assembly. **HONORS/ACHIEVEMENTS:** Author "Defense Sense, The Search for a Rational Military Policy," Cambridge MA, Ballinger Publishing Co 1983. **MILITARY SERVICE:** USMC 2 yrs.

DELOATCH, CLEVELAND M., SR.
Clergyman, educator. **PERSONAL:** Born Dec 17, 1925, Woodland, NC; married Launsie W; children: Veronica, Cleveland, Jr, Vickie. **EDUCATION:** Shaw U, BA 1965; Carolina U, E; VA State Coll, MEd 1975. **CAREER:** Halifax Co Pub Schs, tchr 1960-; Long's Chapel Bapt Ch, pastor; Jerusalem Bapt Ch; Shiloh Bapt Ch. **ORGANIZATIONS:** Mem Intl Clergyman's Assn; Halifax Co Tchr Assn; NC Educ Assn; Nat Educ Assn; Nat History Assn; NC Classroom Tchrs Assn 32 Degree Mason; ShawUniv Theol Frat; pres Scotland Neck Comm Assn; mem Halifax Co for People Council; NAACP; SCLC; NC Bapt Con; Tar River Union. **HONORS/ACHIEVEMENTS:** Outs leadership award ShawUniv 1963; Dr Humane letters Epsilon Intl U, East FL 1972. **MILITARY SERVICE:** USN coxswain 1943-46.

DELOATCH, EUGENE
University dean. **CAREER:** Morgan State University, School of Engineering, Baltimore, MD, dean. **BUSINESS ADDRESS:** Morgan State University, School of Engineering, Cold Spring and Hillen Roads, Baltimore, MD 21239. *

DELOATCH, MYRNA LOY
Association administrator. **PERSONAL:** Born Aug 25, 1938, Tarboro, NC; married Johnnie W Deloatch; children: Chris, Tamyra, Ivan. **EDUCATION:** Ag & Tech Univ, BS Home Econ 1962; Purude Univ, Spec Cert 1962. **CAREER:** Rural Ed Inst Chillan South Amer, teacher 1962-64; La Guardia House NY, dir of food serv 1964-65; Farmers Home Admin, home suprv 1965-68; Rich Square Training Ctr, home econ teacher 1968-76; Telamon Corp (formerly Migrant & Seasonal Farmworkers Assoc Inc) , employment training spec. **ORGANIZATIONS:** Mem, pres Ebonette Club 1971-; employment interviewer Employment Sec Commiss 1976-81; mem Tarboro Housing & Comm Devel Adv Bd 1979-84; mem Tarboro Arts Council 1981-; mem Tarboro City Sch Bd of Educ 1979-85. **HONORS/ACHIEVEMENTS:** Outstanding Citizenship East Tarboro Citizen League 1978; Past President Award Ebonette Club 1980; Meritorious Serv East Tarboro Citizens League 1981; spec Serv Awd Black Voices 1982; Meritorious Ser Awd East Tarboro Citizens League 1985. **HOME ADDRESS:** 901 Church St, Tarboro, NC 27886. **BUSINESS ADDRESS:** Employment Training Spec, Telamon Corporation, PO Box 970, Bethel, NC 27812.

DELPHIN, JACQUES MERCIER
Physician. **PERSONAL:** Born Apr 26, 1929, Cape Haitien; married Marlene M; children: Patrick, Barthold, Beverly, Miriam, Matthew, Janice. **EDUCATION:** Graduate of Secondary Studies, BS 1950;Univ of Haiti W Indies, med sch 1957. **CAREER:** St Cabrini Home W Park, NY, medical dir 1974-; St Francis Hosp Poughkeepsie, NY, attending phys 1968-; Ad Interim, commr of mental health 1973-74; Dutchess Co Dept of Mental Hygiene, psychiatric dir 1969-73; Hudson River Psychiatric Cntr, psychiatric dir 1966-69. **ORGANIZATIONS:** Past pres Mid-hudson Br of Psychiatric Assn 1972; Ffellow APA 1972; med license NY State 1967.

DEL PINO, JEROME KING
Clergyman. **PERSONAL:** Born Sep 12, 1946, Savannah, GA; married Kathleen Joy Peterson; children: Jerome Curtis; Emily Kathleen. **EDUCATION:** Gustavus Adolphus Coll, BA 1968; Boston Univ Sch of Theology, ThM (cum laude) 1971; Boston Univ Grad Sch, PhD 1980. **CAREER:** Union United Methodist Curch, Boston MA, asst pastor 1968-69; Emerson Coll, Boston MA, lecturer 1971-72; St Andrew's United Methodist Church, Worcester MA, co-pastor 1971-72; Greenwood Memorial United Methodist Church, Dorchester MA, pastor 1973-76; Wesley United Methodist Church, Springfield MA, pastor 1978-; Boston Univ School of Theology, visiting lecturer 1980-82; Luther/Northwestern Theological Seminary, St Paul MN, visiting lecturer 1984-85; Wesley United Methodist Church, pastor in charge. **ORGANIZATIONS:** Dir Gen Bd Higher Ed & Min UMC 1980-; Div of Ordained Min UMC 1980-; delegate Gen Conf UMC 1976, 1980, 1984; Northeast Jurisdictional Conf UMC 1976, 1980 1984; mem Am Soc of Ch Hist 1971-; pres Black Ecumenical Commn of MA 1983-85; mem advisory cncl Word & World Journ 1985-. **HONORS/ACHIEVEMENTS:** Rockefeller Fellowship Fund for Theo Ed Princeton 1971-73; N Am Black Doc Fellowship Fund for Theo Ed 1976-77; fellow Inst Reformation Research St Louis MO 1973; 1st Decade Alumni Achievemnt Award Gustavus Adolphus Coll St Peter MN 1978. **BUSINESS ADDRESS:** Pastor, Wesley United Meth Ch, 741 State St, Springfield, MA 01109.

DELPIT, JOSEPH A.
Business executive. **PERSONAL:** Born Jan 09, 1940, Baton Rouge; married Precious Robinson; children: Joseph, Jr, Thomas, Deirdre, Desiree, Derrick. **EDUCATION:** SoUniv Baton Rouge. **CAREER:** Chicken Shack's restaurants, owner operator 1959-; Gr Baton Rouge Devel Corp, investments In; Gen United Life Ins Co; sports Unlimited Inc, co-owner. **ORGANIZATIONS:** Mem bd dirs People's Savings & Loan Co, mem St Francis Xavier Cath Ch; Baranco Clark YMCA Bd Mgmt; bd dirs Baton Rouge Chap NAACP, past pres; mem City Parish Biracial Com; Cath Lay Congress; Op Upgrade Bd Dirs; Mental Health Soc Bd Mgmt; Capital Region Planning Commn; Mason; Shriner Hon mem John B Frazier Hon Soc 1974. **HONORS/ACHIEVEMENTS:** Outstanding Serv SoUniv Alumni Fed 1973; SoUniv Cntr for Bus & Economic Devel; Businessman of Yr 1973; listed Outstanding Young Men of Am 1972; LA EdnAssn Award 1971; Omega Psi Phi Frat In, Award for outstanging leadership in bus & civic comm serv 1971; SoUniv Am Women Soc for Outstanding Acad Support 1970; NAACP Nat Freedom Award 1970; Mckinley High Alumni Award outstanding serv to sch & comm 1968; Ofc of Economic Opp Sgtr Shriver Award dedicated serv to problem of poor in Am 1967; Baton Rouge Businessman of Yr Award, News Leader, 1961; Outstanding Serv Award, Baranco Clark YMCA 1960; first black councilman Baton Rouge; aptd by Nat Assn of Co Ofcls, chmn of Revenue Sharing Com & chmn of Civil Defense Com of LA Police Jury Assn.

DEMBER, JEAN WILKINS
Educator. **PERSONAL:** Born Jan 29, 1930, Brooklyn, NY; married Clarence Robert Dember; children: Clarence Jr, Judith, Regina, Lila Edwards, Theresa Brown, Zelie. **EDUCATION:** Lincoln Schl of Nurses, 1950; Manhattan Bus Inst, Cert Secr 1952; Empire State Clge Old Westb, Imcom BS Crim Justice 1983. **CAREER:** Black Histor Cultural Prog for Suffolk cty Jail, presentor designer 1978-83; NYS Delegation Black Political Assem, pres 1981-82; NYS Commission on Prisons & Genocide, org vol 1982-; Nassau Comm Clge Black Women Studies, adj prof 1983; Keep Encouraging Youth, consultant; Dember-Webb African Amer Heritage,curator 1975-. **ORGANIZATIONS:** Mem advocate NYS Human Srv Assc 1979-; mem State Youth Advocacy 1980-84; mem Catholic Interracial Council 1982-; fnd mem Tri Community Health Council1974-; fnd adv bd mem Natl Black Lay Cath Caucus 1970-; mem Evangelization Comm Natl Off for Black Catholics 1982-; mem Econ Opport Council of Suffolk 1982-84; designer White Racism Mental Health Comm SC Div Mental Health 1977-82; chairperson Long Island Day Care Serv 1986-87; mem NYS Commn Comm Mental Health Adv Comm; poet/lecturer African Amer History Hispanic/African Culture. **HONORS/ACHIEVEMENTS:** Who's Who in Black Amer; award Natl Off Black Cath Evangelization Award 1982; Who's Who in Amer Women Religion 1984; Martin L King Award Pilgrim State Human Rights Comm 1983; Citizen of Year Chi Rho Chprt Omega Psi Phi Frat Inc 1982; Amer the Beautiful grant for comm prog 1981; vol advocate for African Relief within Cath Church and broader comm mem Uganda Human Rights League 1982-83. **HOME ADDRESS:** 55 Court St, West Babylon, NY 11704.

DEMBY, JAMES E.
Electrical engineer. **PERSONAL:** Born Dec 24, 1936, Chesapeake, VA; married Mavis A Smith; children: James Jr, Ken, Len. **EDUCATION:** Tuskegee Inst, 1955-57; Howard U, BS 1961. **CAREER:** Norfolk Naval Shipyard, supervisory electrical engr 1973-; Norfolk Naval Shipyard, advancing positions 1961-. **ORGANIZATIONS:** Mem Naval Civilian Adminstrs Assn; Nat Assn of Naval Tech & Suprs vice pres United Civic League 1963-64; asst dist commr Tidewater Council BSA 1966- 73; mem Chesapeake Chap Nat Tots & Teens. **HONORS/ACHIEVEMENTS:** Superior Performance Award 1971; Beneficial Suggestion Award 1971; Certificate of Merit 1971; Scout Executive's Award 1970; Arrowhead Honor 1971; Scouter's Key1971; Order of the Arrow 1972.

DEMBY, WILLIAM E., JR.
Novelist, educator. **PERSONAL:** Born Dec 25, 1922, Pittsburgh, PA; son of William E Demby and Gertrude Lulu Hendrick; married Lucia Drudi; children: James Gabriel. **EDUCATION:** Fisk Univ, Nashville TN, BA, 1947. **CAREER:** College of Staten Island, prof of English, 1969-89. **HOME ADDRESS:** Box 363, corner Sag Harbor Tnpke & Deerfield Dr, Sag Harbor, NY 11963.

DEMERITTE, EDWIN T.
Insurance representative. **PERSONAL:** Born Jun 25, 1935, Miami, FL; son of Rev Arnold Demeritte (deceased) and Daisy M Yeare; married Edith W Dexter; children: Edwin Jr, Kathy Wynn, Deborah Renee, Dianne Marie. **EDUCATION:** FL A&M Univ, BS, MEdn; grad work guidance & counseling Barry Coll Miami; grad work admin & supr FL Atlantic Univ; Doc Prog Natl Educ D Prog Nova Univ. **CAREER:** N Dade Sr HS, teacher 1958-63, dept head 1963-65; Miami NW Sr HS, guidance counselor 1966-67; Miami NW Adult Educ Cent, instructor 1966-69; Miami Edison Sr HS, asst principal guid 1969-70; Hialeah Jr HS, Principal 1/2 of Quinmester Prog 1973; Metropolitan Ins Co, sales rep. **ORGANIZATIONS:** Part Natl Conf Chris & Jews on Violence & Youth 1969; part Natl Inst on Pol & Commun Rel 1970; part Natl Assn Secondary Sch Prin Annual Meeting 1971-73; consult So Reg Educ Bd; mem Million Dollar Round Table 1981-89. **HONORS/ACHIEVEMENTS:** Leaders Conf Qualifier Metropolitan Ins Co 1982, 1984; Metro Ins Co policies placed over 200 policy contacts 1983 Awd; 3 Metropolitan SE Territory Awds for Superior Sales Performance 1983; 1984 Qualifying Member of the Million Dollar Roundtable; Kiwanis Fellow in Guidance Counseling; Boy Scouting Awd Comm Serv Recog; Distinguished & Outstanding Personalities of the South Awd; Dade Co Sch Bd Awd for Commendable Contribution to Educ; pres conf Metropolitan Life 1988; Natl Sales Award NALU 1988; Natl Quality Awards NALU 1988. **BUSINESS ADDRESS:** Sales Rep, Metropolitan Insurance Co, 13780-A SW 56 St, Miami, FL 33175.

DEMILLE, DARCY (WILMA LITTLEJOHN JACKSON)
Journalist. **PERSONAL:** Born Dec 17, Chicago, IL; daughter of Rev R L Littlejohn and Soohia Shaw Littlejohn; married Gordon C Jackson; children: Carole Harris, Linda Luten, Shelley Bethay, Jill Jackson. **EDUCATION:** Univ of MI, BGS 1977; Michigan State U, Certificate 1977; Oakland U, Advanced Study 1975-78; Leadership Flint Training, Certificate 1988. **CAREER:** ANP, NPI, editor feature writer 1960-65; Sepia Mag, columnist 1963-82; Howard U, guest lecturer 1981; Jordan Coll, instructor 1982-83; Mott Commnty Coll, instructor 1982-85; The Flint Journal, columnist/feature writer 1982-85; Univ of MI, guest lecturer 1983-85; The Flint Journal, columnist feature writer 1982-89, "Dear Wilma" columnist 1986-89; Travel Consultant/Monarch Travel 1987-89; Medi-Rary Literary Service, Editorial Adviser 1987-89. **ORGANIZATIONS:** Creative consult Gail Mazaraki, Consult 1984-85; consult Manulife Ins Co 1981-82; consult Time Shares, Inc 1982-83; bd mem YWCA Public Affairs 1981-83, NAMW Inc Media Women 1975-85; founder Flint Chap NAMW Inc 1975-85; chartr mem The Links Inc, Flint Area Chptr 1980-85; Phi Delta Kappa Educ Frat 1983-85; mem, bd of dir MI League for Human Services, mem Public Affairs Comm; mem Top Ladies of Distinction, Grand Blanc Arts Guild Paint & Palette Art Group, Univ of MI Alumni Assn, Natl Assoc of Black Journalists; Leadership Flint, mem 1987-89; delegate, Intl Caribbean Conf, Women Aglow 1988. **HONORS/ACHIEVEMENTS:** Woman of Yr Media Women 1976-85; Darey DeMille Mag Award; Human Rel Award Mayor City of Flint 1982; "Special Tributes" State of MI 1978; Links Service Award 1984; NAMW Communications Award 1989; Honors Award/Community Service, Genesee Area Intermediate School District 1989; conducted: Writer's Workshops, Univ of MI-Flint 1984-89; creative writing seminars, Mott Community Coll 1987-89. **HOME ADDRESS:** 615 Lippincott Blvd, Flint, MI 48503. **BUSINESS ADDRESS:** The Flint Journal, 200 E 1st St, Flint, MI 48502.

DEMILLE, VALERIE CECILIA
Psychiatrist. **PERSONAL:** Born Jun 02, 1949, New York, NY. **EDUCATION:** North Carolina Central Univ, BS 1973, MS 1975; Meharry Medical Coll, MD 1977. **CAREER:** USAF Sheppard AFB, staff psychiatrist 1981-83; USAF Vandenberg AFB, chief of mental health serv 1983-84; Woodhull Hosp, staff psychiatrist 1985; NY Medical Coll/Lincoln Hospital, unit chief. **ORGANIZATIONS:** Mem Caolition of 100 Black Women 1986; chairperson of nominating comm metro chap Black Psychiatrist of Amer 1986. **MILITARY SER-**

VICE: USAF major 3 yrs. **BUSINESS ADDRESS:** Unit Chief, NY Medical Coll/Lincoln Hosp, 234 East 149th St, Bronx, NY 10452.

DEMONBREUN, THELMA M.
Registered nurse. **PERSONAL:** Born Jun 08, 1928, Chicago, IL; divorced; children: Gail Purnell Nutt, Kim Morris Purnell. **EDUCATION:** Thornton Comm Coll, AA 1972-74; Prairie State Coll 1981-82. **CAREER:** Ingalls Mem Hosp, staff nurse 1964-74; Harvey Headstart, nurse coord 1974-. **ORGANIZATIONS:** Chairperson Brownie Troop Adv Comm 1958-62; mem adv Comm Dist 205 1962-66; mem Bd of Educ Dist 147 1965-; founder United Citizen of Dist 147 1968-74; mem IL Assn of Sch Bd 1967-70; mem Natl Caucus of Black School Bd Members 1967-; student mem Student Adv Comm Thorton Comm Coll 1972-74; mem South Suburan Branch of the NAACP 1981-; campaign chmn Damon Rockett for Re-Election of City of Harvey Comm 1983. **HONORS/ACHIEVEMENTS:** First Black Woman Elected to the Bd of Educ Dist 147 South Suburban Leadership Coalition 1980; Appreciation of Support Harvey & US Jaycees 1980; Cert of Achievement completion of all requirements of academy prog AASA Natl Acad for School Execs 1980-83; presided over IL Sch Bd Joint Annual Conf 1983. **HOME ADDRESS:** 14730 Lincoln Ave, Harvey, IL 60426. **BUSINESS ADDRESS:** Registered Prof Nurse, Headstart Harvey, 15652 Homan Ave, Markham, IL 60426.

DEMONS, LEONA MARIE
Educational administrator. **PERSONAL:** Born Jan 05, 1928, Townsned, GA; divorced; children: Wynette Hammons, John, Chris, Donna Marie, Clinton Drummond. **EDUCATION:** Savannah State Coll, BS 1949; Atlanta Univ, MA 1962; NDEA Fellow Atlanta, Ga, 1963; Kansas State Univ, NDEA Fellow 1968-69. **CAREER:** Savannah State College, assist in publ relations 1950-52; Morehouse College, assist in placement 1963-65; Albany State College, counselor/dir of act 1965-69; Western Ill Univ, counselor 1970; Lincoln Land Comm Coll, counselor 1971-. **ORGANIZATIONS:** Human Development Facilitator 1974-84; NAACP; Urban League. **HONORS/ACHIEVEMENTS:** NDEA Fellow Dept of Health, Ed & Welfare 1963; NDEA Fellow Dept of Health, Ed & Welfare 1968; Qualified KS State (Consortium 1980) Univ (declined due to work obligations). **BUSINESS ADDRESS:** Counselor-Foreign Student Adv, Lincoln Land Comm College, PO Box 63, Springfield, IL 62708.

DEMPSEY, JOSEPH P.
Pastor, educational administrator. **PERSONAL:** Born Mar 08, 1930, Nashville, NC; son of Sidney H Dempsey (deceased) and Irene Alice Vick Dempsey (deceased); married Evelyntyne Humphrey, May 31, 1958; children: Denise P, Joseph T, Eric H, Kathy D. **EDUCATION:** Fayetteville State Univ, BS 1958; Shaw Div Sch, BD 1964; NC Cen Univ, MA 1971; Shaw Div Sch, MDiv 1972; Faith Evangelical Lutheran Seminary, Tacoma WA, DMin 1988. **CAREER:** Worthdale United Baptist Church Raleigh, NC, pastor; NC Cen Univ, instructor 1971-, assoc dir 1988-; pastor various locations since 1961; Elementary & High School, instructor; Pine Grove Baptist Church, Creedmoor NC, pastor 1986-87. **ORGANIZATIONS:** Mem Min Bd Wake Baptist Assn 1964; NC Personnel & Guid Assn; Am Personnel & Guid Assn; Exec Com, Wake Co Dem Party; bd dir NC General Baptist Con, bd dir YMCA 1967-; bd dir Comm Day Carde Center; mem Goals for Raleigh Educ Outreach; mem The Raleigh-Wake Martin Luther King Celebration Comm 1989. **HONORS/ACHIEVEMENTS:** Teacher of the Yr 1967; Raleigh, NC Christian Family of the Yr 1972; Outstanding Serv Award NC Central Univ 1973-74. **HOME ADDRESS:** 1409 E Martin St, Raleigh, NC 27610. **BUSINESS ADDRESS:** Assoc Dir, NCCU- Counseling Center, PO Box 19688, Durham, NC 27707.

DENDY, TOMETTA
Educator. **PERSONAL:** Born Nov 18, 1932, Ryland, AL; married Fred; children: Frederick, Theresa. **EDUCATION:** AL A&M Coll, BS (cum laude) 1952; Howard U, grad work 1953-54. **CAREER:** Catholic Univ School of Law, dir of admissions & financial aid 1975-, asst dir admissions 1973-75; US Coast Guard, admin asst 1960-65. **ORGANIZATIONS:** Am Assn of Higher Edn; u & rep Law Sch Admissions Council 1975-; freelance writer Alpha Kappa Alpha Sor; Cub Scout Ldr 1968-70. **HONORS/ACHIEVEMENTS:** Outstanding performance awards at USCG. **MILITARY SERVICE:** USCG. **BUSINESS ADDRESS:** Michigan Ave & Harewood Rd NE, Washington, DC 20064.

DENMARK, ROBERT RICHARD
Computer specialist. **PERSONAL:** Born Apr 01, 1930, Savannah, GA; son of Robert Denmark and Gladys Church Denmark; married Mamie E Sampson-Denmark, Aug 14, 1971; children: Gladys Denmark-Reed. **EDUCATION:** MTI Business Coll, Certificate Computer Science 1978; American River Coll, AA 1980; Univ of San Francisco, BS 1980-82. **CAREER:** Federal Aviation Admin, air traffic control 1969-71; Prudential Insurance Co of Amer, special agent 1971-74; Dept of Interior US Bureau of Reclamation, computer analyst/programmer 1974-84, adp contract administrator 1984-; US Dept of Interior Div of Data Processing, computer consultant, 1980-84; computer security officer, 1988-. **ORGANIZATIONS:** Chief rabban Ancient Arabic Order of Nobles of the Mystic Shrine of North and South Amer 1982-; pres Sphinx Club Alpha Phi Alpha Frat Inc 1985; cluster leader Sacramento Area Strategy Team Lutheran Church of Amer 1985-87; Zeta Beta Lambda Chap Alpha Phi Alpha, sec 1987, pres 1988; pres First English Lutheran Church Council 1987-; mem, NAACP, Black Data Processing Assn; mem exec bd Div of Aging; 32 Degree Mason of the Ancient Free & Accepted Masonic Congress. **HONORS/ACHIEVEMENTS:** Research project, Univ of San Francisco, A Study of the Potential of Office Automation, 1982; Outstanding Leadership Award Lutheran Church of Amer First English Lutheran Church 1982-84; Special Achievement Award US Dept of Interior 1985-86; Outstanding Serv Award Div of Data Processing Bureau of Reclamation 1987; Meritorious Serv, Zeta Beta Lambda Chapter, Alpha Phi Alpha Fraternity Inc, 1988; Outstanding Serv, Sacramento Area Lutheran Ministry, ELCA, 1988; Performance Award, US Bureau of Reclamation, Dept of the Interior, 1988. **MILITARY SERVICE:** USAF master sgt 20 yrs; Highest Awd The Air Force Commendation Medal 1969, Outstanding NCO of the Year 1963-64. **HOME ADDRESS:** 1043 Lake Glen Way, Sacramento, CA 95822. **BUSINESS ADDRESS:** ADP Contract Administrator, US Dept of Interior, Bureau of Reclamation, 2800 Cottage Way, Sacramento, CA 95825.

DENNARD, DARRYL W.
Broadcast journalist. **PERSONAL:** Born Sep 18, 1957, New York, NY; son of Glenn W Dennard and Eleanor Adamson Dennard; married Darlene Gray Dennard, Jul 13, 1979; children: Autumn Simone Dennard. **EDUCATION:** Fordham Univ, Bronx NY, summer 1985; State Univ Coll at Buffalo, Buffalo NY, BA Broadcasting, 1981. **CAREER:** US Customs Serv, Buffalo NY, import specialist trainee, 1977-79; WGR-TV, Buffalo NY, production asst, 1980-83; WGRZ-TV, Buffalo NY, news reporter, 1983-87; Johnson Publishing Co, Chicago IL, TV co-host, 1987-. **ORGANIZATIONS:** Mem, Natl Black Media Coalition, 1983-87; bd mem, Buffalo Urban League, 1985-87, SUNY Coll at Buffalo Alumni Assn, 1985-86; lecturer, SUNY Coll at Buffalo, 1987; community advisory bd, Community Dept, SUNY College at Buffalo, 1987. **HONORS/ACHIEVEMENTS:** Best Public Affairs Program, New York State Broadcasters, 1985; Best Newscast of the Year Award, United Press Intl, 1986; Black Leadership Award, 1490 Enterprises, 1986; Young Pioneer Award, Northern Region Black Political Caucus, 1986; Media Award, Buffalo Public Schools, 1987; Special Service Award, Seek/EOP SUNY Coll at Buffalo, 1988; Merit Award, United Negro Coll Fund, 1989. **BUSINESS ADDRESS:** Television Co-host, Ebony/Jet Showcase, Johnson Publishing Co, 820 S Michigan Ave, Chicago, IL 60605.

DENNARD, PRESTON JACKSON
Professional athlete. **PERSONAL:** Born Nov 28, 1955, Cordele, GA; married Jackie; children: Ryan, Ellan. **EDUCATION:** Univ of NM. **CAREER:** Los Angeles Rams, receiver 1978-83. **ORGANIZATIONS:** Worked with Spec Olym; 1984 Deaf Olym in Los Angeles. **HONORS/ACHIEVEMENTS:** Four letters at theUniv of NM; twice won All-WAC honors; pub a book of poetry; worked with his mother producing gospel Concerts; sung with a rhythm and blues group.

DENNARD, TURNER HARRISON
Physician. **PERSONAL:** Born Oct 12, 1913, Chicago, IL; son of Dr Ernest A Dennard (deceased) and Hattie O Dennard (deceased); married Elizabeth M Dennard, Sep 13, 1940; children: Charles Garrett Dennard (deceased). **EDUCATION:** Univ of MN, BS, 1937, MS, 1941; Howard Univ Coll of Med, MD, 1950. **CAREER:** Private Practice, physician 1960-; Freedman Hosp, 1957-59; Reynolds Hosp, 1952-57; resd 1951-52; Howard Univ Coll of Pharmacy, instr in pharmacy 1938-46; L Riehardson Meml Hosp, staff mem; Moses Cone Hosp; Wesley Long Comm Hosp. **ORGANIZATIONS:** Mem Greensboro Med Soc; Old N State Med Soc; Nat Med Assn bd dir Triad Sickle Cell Anemia Found. **HONORS/ACHIEVEMENTS:** First Black Eagle Scout In South 1929; Natl Honor Soc 1932. **MILITARY SERVICE:** USNR seaman 1934-38. **HOME ADDRESS:** 2009 Chelsea Ln, Greensboro, NC 27406.

DENNARD, WILLIE JAMES A., II
Psychologist. **PERSONAL:** Born Aug 25, 1935, Blitchton, FL; children: Richard. **EDUCATION:** FL A&M Univ, BS 1960, MEd 1967, MS 1978, DEd Nova Univ 1987. **CAREER:** State of FL Alcoholism Treatment Ctr, psychologist; FL Alcoholism Treatment Ctr, psychologist. **ORGANIZATIONS:** Mem Natl Educ Assoc 1960-, Natl Assoc of Social Workers 1973-, Assoc of Professional Alcoholism 1974-, Epsilon Delta Chi Frat 1975-, Soc for Psychologists in Addictive Behavior 1979-, Soc for Personality Assessment 1979-; mem Bledsoe Chap No 106 Holy Royal Arch Masons 1979-; mem Samuel C Nixon Cultural Ctr 1980-; sec NAACP; zoning bd City of Sebring Citizens Adv Task Force. **HONORS/ACHIEVEMENTS:** NDEA Grant Univ of FL 1966; mem Psi Chi Natl Honor Soc in Psychology 1978. **HOME ADDRESS:** 727 Tangerine Ave, Sebring, FL 33870. **BUSINESS ADDRESS:** Psychologist, State of Florida, FL Alcohol Trtmt Ctr, 100 W College Dr, Avon Park, FL 33825.

DENNERY, PHYLLIS ARMELLE
Physician. **PERSONAL:** Born Jun 05, 1958, Port-au-Prince, Haiti;married Gregory Lyman Mundy. **EDUCATION:** McGill Univ, BS; Howard Univ Coll of Medicine, MD. **CAREER:** Children's Hosp Natl Med Clinic, pediatric resident 1984-87; Rainbow Babies & Children Hosp, fellow in nednatology 1987; Children's Hosp Natl Med Ctr, pediatric sr resident. **ORGANIZATIONS:** Mem 1983-, pres 1983-84 Alpha Omega Alpha Med Hon Soc; mem Amer Medical Women's Assoc, Natl and Amer Medical Assocs. **HONORS/ACHIEVEMENTS:** Alma Wells Givens Awd Howard Univ 1982; Mordecai Wyatt Johnson Scholarship 1983; Michael Oliver Dumas Prize 1984; Amer Med Women's Assoc Awd 1984; Merck Manual Awd 1984; Dept of Anatomy Awd 1984; Godfrey C Burns Awd 1984. **BUSINESS ADDRESS:** Pediatric Senior Resident, Children's Hosp Natl Med Ctr, 111 Michigan Ave NW, Washington, DC 20010.

DENNING, BERNADINE NEWSOM
Educational administrator. **PERSONAL:** Born Aug 17, 1930, Detroit, MI; married Blaine; children: Blaine Jr. **EDUCATION:** MI State Normal EMU, BS 1951; Wayne State U, MA 1956, MA & 30 Spclst 1960, EdD 1970. **CAREER:** Detroit Public Sch, tchr 1951-62, cnslr 1962-70;Univ of MI, asst prof 1970-75; Title IV Civil Rights, dir 1975-77; Office of Revenue Sharing Dept of Treas, dir 1977-79; Detroit Public Sch, asst supt. **ORGANIZATIONS:** Trustee Central MIUniv 1980-; sec MI Atty Discipline Bd 1983-; chrmn MI Women's Commn 1980-; mem YWCA of USA Bd 1973-; vice chrmn Black United Fund 1984-; mem Black Family Devel Bd 1981-; sec Children's Aid Soc 1983-. **HONORS/ACHIEVEMENTS:** Emma V Kelly Award Daughters of IBPOE of W 1983; Disting Award US Coast Guard Acad 1982; Lifetime Achievemnt Award YWCA 1984; Negro Bus & Professnl Award 1978. **BUSINESS ADDRESS:** Assistant Superintendent, Detroit Public Sch, 5057 Woodward, Detroit, MI 48202.

DENNING, JOE WILLIAM
Elected official & banker. **PERSONAL:** Born Nov 30, 1945, Bowling Green, KY; married Arlene; children: Kita, Larecia. **EDUCATION:** KY State Police Acad, 1970; Western KY Univ. **CAREER:** Bowling Green Ind School District, member 1975-. **ORGANIZATIONS:** Mem BG Warren Co Chamber of Commerce; dir BG Warren Co Jaycees; mem Kiwanis Club 1984-85; trustee KY Chap Leukemia Soc 1983-; mem KY Job Training Coord Council 1983-. **BUSINESS ADDRESS:** Bowling Green I S D, P O Box 1020C, Bowling Green, KY 42101.

DENNIS, HUGO, JR.
Educator. **PERSONAL:** Born Aug 05, 1936, Tortola, VI; married Carmen Lydia Marrero; children: Tony, Hugh, Jancie, Reynaldo, Alex. **EDUCATION:** Hampton Inst, BS 1959;Univ of CT, 1968. **CAREER:** Central Labor Council of VI, pres 1976; St Thomas-St John Fedn of Teacher, pres 1967; VI Public Schools, math teacher 1960; VI Legislature, pres

1983-84; Virgin Islands Govt, acting commissioner of housing 1986-. **ORGANIZATIONS:** Del, 3rd Constl Conv of VI 1978; rep Study Tour of S Afr 1980. **BUSINESS ADDRESS:** Acting Commissioner Housing, Virgin Islands Government, P O Box 960, St Thomas, Virgin Islands of the United States 00801.

DENNIS, PHILIP H.
Physician. **PERSONAL:** Born Dec 01, 1925, St Louis, MO; son of Herman Dennis and Nellie H. Dennis; married Patricia; children: Pia Evene, Lisette Marie, Philip Herman, Michael Marion. **EDUCATION:** Attended, Lincoln Univ 1943-47, St Louis Univ 1951-53, Meharry Medical Coll 1953-57, Cook County Graduate School of Medicine, 1972, 1979, 1980, 1982, 1985, 1986, APA (CME), 1988. **CAREER:** City Hospital St Louis, internship 1957-58; Homer G. Phillips, Renard, & Cochran Hospitals, psychiatric resident, 1972, 1979, 1980, 1982, 1985, 1986; Southern IL Comm Coll, instructor 1971-74; SIU Edwardsville, counselor 1982-; Mental Health Ctr, dir 1980-. **ORGANIZATIONS:** Consultant in psychiatry, Illinois Retirement System, Southern Illinois Univ, Edwardsville; Family Serv Agency; mem Chamber of Commerce, Kiwanis, Amer Soc of Clinical Hypnosis. **HONORS/ACHIEVEMENTS:** NIMH Fellow 1958-59; Lovejoy Award; Golden Rule Award; Host for KATZ radio "Open Mike" 1968-81; Developer Pleasingly Soft Products 1982; Exhibitor one man art & sculpture show. **BUSINESS ADDRESS:** Neuropsychiatrist, 8787 State St, East St Louis, IL 62203.

DENNIS, RODNEY HOWARD
Psychiatrist. **PERSONAL:** Born Oct 03, 1936, Tampa, FL; son of Huerta W Dennis and Gussie Harris Dennis. **EDUCATION:** NY Univ Coll of Arts/Sci, BA 1958; Howard Univ Coll of Med, MD 1962; Kings County Hosp Brooklyn NY, Rotating Internship 1962-63; NY Sch of Psychiatry Brooklyn State Hosp, Psychiatric Res 1970-73. **CAREER:** Letterman Genl Hosp, general medical officer 1964-65; Univ of CA, LA Brentwood VA Hosp, psychiatric res 1965-67; Metropolitan State Hosp Norwalk CA, physician 1968-69; Kingsboro Psychiatric Center Brooklyn State Hosp, psychiatrist 1973-83; Woodhull Medical and Mental Health Center, consultation/liaison svcs, attending physician dept of psychiatry 1986-. **ORGANIZATIONS:** Mem Amer Psychiatric Assn; mem The Brooklyn Psychiatric Soc mem The NY Acad of Sci; mem NY Univ Alumni Assn; mem Assn of NY State Mental Hygiene Phys & Dentists; mem AAAS, Acad of Psychosomatic Medicine, Pi Lambda Phi Frat. **MILITARY SERVICE:** AUS capt medical corps 1962-65. **HOME ADDRESS:** 307 Decatur St, Brooklyn, NY 11233. **BUSINESS ADDRESS:** Attending Physician, Dept of Psychiatry, Consultation/Liaison Service, Medical Associates of Woodhull PC, 760 Broadway, Brooklyn, NY 11206.

DENNIS, RUTLEDGE M.
Educator. **PERSONAL:** Born Aug 16, 1939, Charleston, SC; son of David Dennis and Ora Porcher Dennis; married Sarah Bankhead; children: Tchaka, Imaro, Kimya, Zuri. **EDUCATION:** SC State Coll, BS 1965; WA State Univ, MA 1969, PhD 1975. **CAREER:** VA Commonwealth Univ, coord Afro-Am studies 1971-78, asso prof dept of Sociology 1978-; Assoc Chmn, Sociology Dept 1981-83. **ORGANIZATIONS:** Pres Assn of Black Sociologists 1981-83; mem Metropolitan Business League 1982-; pres Black Educ Assn 1974-75; editor to the sphinx Alpha Phi Alpha Frat 1983-84; mem of the vestry St Philip's Episcopal Ch 1983-; Commissioner Richard Redevelopment & Housing Authority 1979-81; mem NY Academy of Sciences, Am Sociologist Asst. **HONORS/ACHIEVEMENTS:** Sigma Xi Initiation Richmond Chapter Sigma Xi 1980; Reise-Melton Award VA Commonwealth Univ Cultural Award 1981; Boys Club Citizen Award Richmond Boys Club 1980; Distinguished Community Educ Award, Alpha Phi Alpha Frat 1985; Initiated into Omicron Delta Kappa 1986; The Politics of Annexation: Oligarchic Power in a Southern City (with John Moeser) 1982; Alpha Kappa Delta Founders' Address, Hampton Univ 1985. **MILITARY SERVICE:** AUS sp 4. **BUSINESS ADDRESS:** Associate Prof of Sociology, VA Commonwealth Univ, 312 N Shafer St, Richmond, VA 23284.

DENNIS, SHIRLEY M.
Government official. **PERSONAL:** Born Feb 26, 1938, Omaha, NE; married William D C Dennis; children: Pamela, Robin, Sherrie. **EDUCATION:** Cheyney State College, 1955-56; Real Estate Institute, 1959; American Institute of Planner, 1970; Temple Univ, AS 1985. **CAREER:** Tucker & Tucker, Philadelphia, sales & office mgr 1961-67; Redevelopment Authority, Philadelphia, equal opportunity specialist 1967-68; Urban League of Philadelphia, housing dir 1969-71; Housing Assn of Delaware Valley, managing dir 1971-79; Dept of Community Affairs, executive deputy secretary 1979-. **ORGANIZATIONS:** Member Philadelphia Tribune Charities 1978; co-chairperson Philadelphia Housing Task force 1978; chairperson PA Housing Finance Agency 1979-; executive bd member Council State Community Affairs 1980-; executive committee Natl State Housing Finance 1982-; member Coalition of 100 Black Women 1982; member Abington Memorial Hospital 1982; board member Philadelphia Martin Luther King, Jr Assn Inc 1985; board member NAACP Willow Grove Branch; exec bd mem PA State Conferenceof NAACP. **HONORS/ACHIEVEMENTS:** Redbook Magazine one of 12 outstanding women in Penna 1977; Black Journalist Award 1978; Public Service Award PA Federation of Business & Prof Women's Club 1980; Service Award NAACP 1980; Appreciation Award Carlisle OIC 1981; Community Serv Award Natl Assn of Negro Business & Prof Women 1981; Who's Who in American Politics, Who's Who 1983. **BUSINESS ADDRESS:** Secretary, Dept Of Community Affairs, Commonwealth of Penn, Room 317 Forum Bldg, Harrisburg, PA 17120.

DENNIS, WALTER DECOSTER
Pastor. **PERSONAL:** Born Aug 23, 1932, Washington, DC. **EDUCATION:** VA Coll, BA 1952; NY Univ, MA 1953; Gen Theo Sem, MDiv 1956; Interdeonom Theol Ctr, DD (Honorary). **CAREER:** Prot Episcopal Church, deacon 1956; St Philips Episcopal Church, curate 1956; Cathedral Church of St John the Divine, asst minister 1956-60; St Cyprians Church, vicar 1960-65; Amer Hist & Const Law Hampton Inst, adjunct, asst prof 1961-65; elected suffragan bishop 1979; CSJD Prog Admin, canon residentiary 1965-. **ORGANIZATIONS:** Mem Union of Black Epis, Guild of St Ives; corr sec, comm Clergy Deployment; mem The Standing Comm; mem Bishops Comm on Taxation; mem Comm on SocConcerns; fellow in res Univ of the South; mem Epis Church Natl Task Force on Hunger; adj prof Christ Ethics, Gen Theo Sem; convener Black Caucus, Epis Dio of NY Res & Publ Comm; bd mem Sex Info & Ed Council of US; bd mem Juvenile Justice Ctr, Epis Churchs Tchg Serv Ethics Vol 1975; bd of dir Manhattanville Comm Ctr Inc, Abort Repeal Assoc, Inst for the Study of Human Resources, Homosexual Comm Couns Ctr, Natl Org for the Reform of Marijuana Laws; lecturer The Div School, Univ of the South 1974-75; mem Christian Ed 1967-68; exam chaplin 1970-72; mem comm on Canons 1974-77. **HONORS/ACHIEVEMENTS:** Puerto Rican Neighborhood Awd 1958; Mex Amer Neighborhood 1960; Chap Publ "On the Battle Lines" 1962; arts publ in The Epis New Yorker, The Anglican Theol Rev, The St Lukes Jrnl of Theol. **BUSINESS ADDRESS:** Canon Residentiary CSJD, 1047 Amsterdam Ave, New York, NY 10025.

DENNISTON, DOROTHY L.
Educator. **PERSONAL:** Born Aug 10, 1944, Springfield, MA; daughter of Rev James H Hamer and Irma L (Washington) Hamer; divorced. **EDUCATION:** Northeastern Univ, BA 1967; Simmons College, MA 1975; Brown Univ, PhD 1983. **CAREER:** Hudson Settlement House NYC, psychiatric case-aide 1964-66; Secondary Schools, teacher of English 1967-71; Simmons Coll, asst to dir of admiss 1971-72, instr of English 1972-74, assoc dean 1974-76,79-80; Univ of TN, asst prof of English 1983-86; Brown Univ, vstg prof English 1987-88, asst prof 1988-. **ORGANIZATIONS:** Mem Nat Assoc Foreign Student Affairs 1972; mem Assoc for Study of Negro Life & History 1972-; mem Modern Lang Asso 1975- mem Alpha Kappa Alpha Soroity 1963-67; mem adv com for scholars-intership prog Martin L King Jr Cntr for Social Change 1976-; mem Natl Assoc of Interdiscipliny Ethnic Studies 1977-; mem standing comm on black studies Coll Lang Assoc 1983-; mem SE Lang Assoc 1984-; mem, Langston Hughes Center for the Arts 1988-; mem college bd, English Composition Test Committee 1984-87. **HONORS/ACHIEVEMENTS:** Omega Psi Phi Fraternity Scholarship Boston Chptr 1962; J Rosen Scholarship Award Boston Chptr NE Univ 1965; Fellow Natl Fellowship Fund 1976-79; award Outstanding Young Woman of Am 1977; authored Article " Paule Marshall" American Women Writers from Colonial Times to Present 1980; Dorothy Danforth Compton Fellowship Brown Univ Prov RI 1981-82; Univ Faculty Rsch Awd Univ of TN 1985; Faculty Rsch Awd Dept of English Univ of TN 1984; Fellowship Brown Univ 1986-87. **BUSINESS ADDRESS:** Assistant Professor of English, Brown University, Department of English, Box 1852, Providence, RI 02912.

DENSON, FRED L.
Attorney. **PERSONAL:** Born Jul 19, 1937, New Brighton, PA; married Catherine; children: Terry, Kelly, Kendra. **EDUCATION:** Rehsselaer Poly Inst, BChemE 1959; Georgetown U, JD 1966. **CAREER:** WOKR-TV ABC, host black dimensions 1972-; Urban League of Rochester, exec dir 1970-71; Eastman Kodak Co, atty 1967-70. **ORGANIZATIONS:** Bd mem NYS Pub Employ Relat Bd; exec dir Nat Patent Law Assn; dir Armarco Mktg; pres Genessee Region Home Care Assn; chmn adv counc NYS Div of Human Rights Am Bar Assn; Nat Bar Assn; Monroe Co Bar Assn; Nat Patent Law Assn; Am Arbitraton Assn. **HONORS/ACHIEVEMENTS:** Author, Know Your Town Justice Court; minority involv in the US Patent Sys; Rochester Comm Serv Awd 1974-76. **MILITARY SERVICE:** AUS 1st lt 1960-61. **BUSINESS ADDRESS:** 14 E Main St, PO Box 801, Webster, NY 14580.

DENT, ANTHONY L.
Business manager, scientist. **PERSONAL:** Born Apr 19, 1943, Indian Head, MD; divorced; children: Antonette, Robert, Christopher. **EDUCATION:** Morgan State Coll, BS 1966; Johns Hopkins Univ, PhD 1970. **CAREER:** Carnegie Mellon Univ, asso prof Chem Eng 1970-78; DuPont Co, rsch engr 1972; PQ Corp, sr chem, r&d assoc, r&d supervisor, mgr 1979-, principal scientist. **ORGANIZATIONS:** Mem Am Chem Soc; Am Inst Chem Engrs; Am Soc Engr Edn; co-chmn I & EC Annl Chem Engr Sympsm; CMU Fclty Snt 1971-75; sec treas pres elct pres dir Pitts Ctlys Soc 1972-81; chmn sch admsns com Wstrn PA Chap J Hpkns Univ 1972-75, pres Pitts Chap Almn Assn 1976-77; vice chmn 5th N Amer Mtng of Ctlys Soc 1977; Philadelphia Catalysis Club sec-treas, dir 1981-83, chmn elect 1989-90; pres Del Valley Chap of NOBCChE 1983-89, regional chmn 1989-; fellow Amer Inst Chemists 1986; Nat Rsrch Cncl Com; Idntfctn Adv Serv; rcrt wmn & min into engr grad level Sci & Engrs Min Bckgrnds. **HONORS/ACHIEVEMENTS:** Elctd Phi Lambda Upsln 1967, Sigma Xi 1968, Phi Beta Kappa 1969; Phi Kappa Phi Hon Soc 1972; nom Cml & Hnry Dryfs Tchr Schlr Grnt Carnegie- Mellon Univ 1974, 1975; Meritorious Service Award, NOBCChE 1988. **BUSINESS ADDRESS:** Manager, PQ Corporation, 280 Cedar Grove Rd, Conshohocken, PA 19428.

DENT, AUBREY O.
Psychiatrist. **PERSONAL:** Born May 07, 1934, Roanoke, VA; children: Gina, Judith, Lisa. **EDUCATION:** Howard Univ, BS 1958, MD 1968. **CAREER:** US Public Health Hospital San Francisco, med internship 1968-69; Mt Zion Hospital San Francisco, psychiatry resident 1969-72; Westside Methadone Clinic Westside Comm Mental Health Ctr, dir 1972-79; private practice, psychiatrist 1972-. **ORGANIZATIONS:** Mem Amer Psychiatric Assoc, Northern California Psychiatric Soc, Black Psychiatrists Northern California, Black Psychiatrists California, Black Psychiatrists of Amer, Natl Med Assn, San Francisco Med Soc, Omega Psi Phi; mem adv bd 1980-, chairperson 1984-85, Marin County Mental Health. **MILITARY SERVICE:** AUS Res maj.

DENT, CARL ASHLEY
Physician. **PERSONAL:** Born May 27, 1914, St Simon's Island, GA; son of Earnest Alton Dent and Josephine Lillian Green; married Lavetta; children: Cynthia, Patricia. **EDUCATION:** Pacific Union Coll, BS 1934; Loma Linda U, MD 1939. **CAREER:** Self Employed, physician Present; Med Staff Riverside Adventist Hosp, pres 1955-69; Riverside Adventist Hosp, med dir 1950-55; Los Angeles Co Gen Hosp, intern 1938-40; Seventh-day Adventist Health Services Nairobi Kenya, medical dir 1984-87. **ORGANIZATIONS:** Med Sect, & S Central Conf SDA Fellow, Am Soc Abdominal Surgeons. **HONORS/ACHIEVEMENTS:** Mem Soc Nuclear Med Refugee relief Q team leader, Intl Red Cross 1969. **BUSINESS ADDRESS:** 617 Nocturne Dr, Nashville, TN 37207.

DENT, PRESTON L.
Educator, psychologist. **PERSONAL:** Born Apr 30, 1939, Philadelphia, PA; son of William Dent and Alice Dent; married Imelda Velasco; children: David-Preston, Robyn Lynn. **EDUCATION:** PA State Univ, BS Psychology 1961; San Francisco State Univ, MA Psychology 1963; Univ of CA Santa Barbara, PhD Educ Psychology 1971. **CAREER:** San Francisco City Coll Dept of Psychology, graduate instructor, 1962-67; STIR Facility The Bunker-Ramo Corp, simulator flight control program operator, 1966-67; TRW Systems Inc Indus Relations Div, trainer, counselor, equal opportunity program office; Pierce Coll, psychology instructor 1967-72; Univ of CA Santa Barbara, asst to chancellor 1969-72; Coll of Letters Arts Science, dean, dir of devel & sponsored research; Univ of Southern CA, assoc prof higher educ 1972-86; The Dent-Glasser Corp, psychologist, pres. **ORGANIZATIONS:** mem, Intl Council of Psychology, Amer Psychology Assn, Omega Psi Phi, AAAS, Amer Assn of Univ

Admin, NAACP, United Nations Assoc, Sigma Xi; vice pres Golden State Minority Found; pres Keystone Health Serv Ltd; commr City of Los Angeles 1981-82; fellow Amer Council on Ed 1971-72; dir Los Angeles Child Guidance Clinic; mem The MacNeal-Schwendler Corp. **HONORS/ACHIEVEMENTS:** Outstanding Young Men of Amer Award, US Chamber of Commerce, 1970; Kappa Delta Pi Ed Hon, Phi Delta Kappa Ed Hon; Distinguished Serv Award from City of Los Angeles. **MILITARY SERVICE:** USAF 1st lieutenant 1963-66. **BUSINESS ADDRESS:** President, The Dent-Glasser Corp, 8514 S Broadway, Los Angeles, CA 90003.

DENT, RICHARD CALVIN
Professional athlete. **PERSONAL:** Born Dec 13, 1960, Atlanta, GA. **EDUCATION:** TN State, Commercial Arts. **CAREER:** Chicago Bears, defensive end 1983-. **HONORS/ACHIEVEMENTS:** Set TN State record with 39 career sacks; earned NFC Defensive Player of Week honors & game ball; Coll & Pro Ftbl Weekly's 1st team; All-NFC; AP second team;UPI 1st team; Super Bowl XX MVP; mem 1986 NFL Pro Bowl team. **BUSINESS ADDRESS:** Chicago Bears, Halas Hall, 250 N Washington Rd, Lake Forest, IL 60045.

DENT, THOMAS COVINGTON
Journalist, dramatist, free-lance writer. **PERSONAL:** Born Mar 20, 1932, New Orleans, MS; son of Albert Dent and Jessie Covington Dent. **EDUCATION:** Morehouse Coll, BA, 1952; Goddard Coll, MA, 1974. **CAREER:** Houston Informer, Houston TX, reporter, 1950-52; New York Age, New York City, reporter,1959; Assocn for the Advancement of Colored People (NAACP), New York City, public information worker for Legal Defense Fund, 1961-63; Free Southern Theater, New Orleans LA, assoc dir, 1966-70; Total Community Action, New Orleans,public relations officer, 1971-73; public lecturer; co-publisher of of On Guard for Freedom (political newspaper), 1960; co-founder of Umbra Workshop, New York City, 1962; co-publisher of Umbra (poetry magazine); co-founder of Callaloo (literary magazine), 1978; founder of Congo Square Writers Union, New Orleans, 1974;instructor at Mary Holmes College, 1968-70, University of New Orleans, 1979-81; free-lance writer and poetry reader. **ORGANIZATIONS:** Mem, Modern Language Assn; mem, African Literature Assn; exec dir, New Orleans Jazz and Heritage Found. **HONORS/ACHIEVEMENTS:** Whitney Young Fellow, 1973-74; author of Magnolia Street (poems), privately printed, 1976, reprinted, 1987; author of Blue Lights and River Songs: Poems, Lotus Press, 1982; author of one-act plays "Negro Study 34A," "Snapshot," "Ritual Murder"; co-author of one-act play "Song of Survival"; author of prose narrative "The Ghetto of Desire," CBS-TV, 1966. **MILITARY SERVICE:** US Army, 1957-59. **HOME ADDRESS:** Box 50584, New Orleans, LA 70150. *

DENTON, HERBERT H., JR.
Editor. **PERSONAL:** Born Jul 10, 1943, Muncie, IN. **EDUCATION:** Harvard Coll, BA (Cum Laude) 1965. **CAREER:** Washington Post, reporter 1963-73, MD editor 1973-76, city editor 1976-80, roving natl reporter 1980-81, White House correspondent 1982, Beirut bureau chief 1983-84, Canada bureau chief 1985-. **MILITARY SERVICE:** AUS 1966-68 Sp5; Vietnam; Bronze Star. **BUSINESS ADDRESS:** Canada Bureau Chief, Washington Post, One Yonge St, Toronto, Ontario, Canada M5E 1E5.

DENYE, BLAINE A.
Educator. **PERSONAL:** Born Jun 27, 1933, Chicago, IL; son of Julius DeNye and Gladys DeNye; married Doris L Thornton; children: Paul, Iva. **EDUCATION:** Roosevelt Univ, BA 1960; Chicago Teachers Coll, MEd 1964. **CAREER:** Teacher 1960-63; counselor 1963-69; Educ Program Planning, dir 1969-70; Model Cities Prog, dir 1969-73; Manley HS Chicago, principal 1973-86; District Ten, superintendent 1986-. **ORGANIZATIONS:** Chmn Diaconate Bd 1966; mem Trinity United Church Christ chmn exec council 1973-75; chmn Bldg Comm 1974-80; chmn Board Long Range Planning; mem Phi Delta Kappa; vice pres bd of dirs, Trinity; vice chmn, Trinity Community Housing Corp; vice chmn, Trinity Acres Housing Corp. **HONORS/ACHIEVEMENTS:** Phi Delta Kappa Educator of the Year; Ora Higgins Youth Foundation. **MILITARY SERVICE:** AUS 1st lt 1953-58. **BUSINESS ADDRESS:** District Superintendent, Chicago Public Schools Dist 10, 1830 South Keeler, Chicago, IL 60623.

DEPAUR, LEONARD
Director. **EDUCATION:** Juilliard Sch of Music Columbia U; Henry Cowell, Hall Johnson, Sergie Radamsky, pvt study; Pierre Monteux, spl study;; Lewis & Clark Coll, D Music. **CAREER:** Lincoln Cntr for the Performing Arts, dir of comm relations 1976-; Lincoln Cntr Internat, asso dir 1970-75; Cincinnati Symphony, guest conductor; Orch of Am; Miami Beach Sym; Buffalo Philharmonic; Sym of the New World, conductor 1971-73; conducted more then 2,300 performances 1947-68; Howard U, guest conductor & lctr;Univ of Rochester; Talladega Col; Olympia Coll;Univ of CA. **ORGANIZATIONS:** NY State Hist Assn; MENC Regional Conf; consult New York City Bd of Educ CHIP Prog; Westport Summer Music Prog; consult Cultural Develop for the Republic of Tunisia; co-chmn Am Com First World Festival of Negro Art Dakar Senegal; mem NAACP; ASCAP; Nat Assn for Am Composers & Conductors; Nat Acad of Telvision Arts & Sci; Soc of Black Composers; The Bohemians; Am Veterans Com; Aircraft Owners & Pilots Assn; Sigma Pi Phi Frat; various recordings ranging from Opera to Children's Educ Material. **HONORS/ACHIEVEMENTS:** Mayor's Award of Honor for Arts & Culture; award of meritUniv of PA Glee Club; covered & featured in the following time, newsweek, saturday review, Negro Digest, Opera News, Ebony, Jet, Musical America, Musical Courier, Diapason, Etude, Who's Who, Colliers, Pathfinder, Essence, Who's Who Among Black Am; Arranger; Conductor; Cons; num TV & Radio Prgms. **MILITARY SERVICE:** AUS cpt. **BUSINESS ADDRESS:** Lincoln Cntr Performing Arts, 140 W 65th St, New York, NY 10023.

DEPILLARS, MURRY NORMAN
Educator. **PERSONAL:** Born Dec 21, 1938, Chicago, IL; son of Mary Taylor; married Mary L. **EDUCATION:** JC Wilson Coll, AA Fine Arts 1966; Roosevelt Univ, BA Art Educ 1968, MA Urban Studies 1970; PA State Univ, PhD Art Educ 1976. **CAREER:** Mast Inst, Chicago comm on urban opportunity div of training 1968; Univ of IL Chicago, educ asst program asst dir 1968-71; numerous art exhibits throughout the US; VA Commonwealth Univ Richmond, dean school of art. **ORGANIZATIONS:** Bd of dir & illustrator 3rd World Press Chicago 1960-; bd of dir & art dir Kuumba Workshop Chicago 1969-; bd of dir & contributing ed Inst of Positive Educ Chicago 1970-; adv bd Journal of Negro Educ Washington 1973-; bd of dir N Amer Zone & co-chmn Upper So Region 2nd World Black & African Festival of Arts & Culture 1973-74; pres Natl Conf of Artists Richmond 1973-77; mem Intl Council of Fine Arts Deans 1976-; hmn of bd Natl Conf of Artists NY 1977; First Sino/Amer Conf on the Arts Taipei Taiwan 1980; arts commission Natl Assoc of State Univ & Land Grant Colls 1981-88; consultant Natl Endowment for the Humanities 1982-84; cons Corp of the Public Broadcasting & the Annenberg School of Communications 1983-; OH Eminent Scholars Program Panel OH Bd of Regents 1983-84; consult The O Paul Getty Trust 1984; Natl Endowment for the Arts Expansion Arts Program 1985-; Natl Jazz Serv Org 1985-; US Info Agency Acad Specialist to Malaysia 1985; Africobra 1985-; arts adv bd Coll Bd 1984-85; chmn, coordinator comm The Richmond Jazz Festival 1984-; art & architectural review bd Commonwealth of VA 1986-; 1976-. **HONORS/ACHIEVEMENTS:** Elizabeth Catlett Mora Award of Excellence Natl Conf of Artists 1977; Special Arts Awd & Art Educ Award Branches for the Arts 1980; Man of Excellence Plaque Ministry of Educ Republic of China 1980; Excellence in the Educ Preservation & Promotion of Jazz Richmond Jazz Soc 1981; Outstanding Admin Award Black Student Alliance 1982; Outstanding Achievement in the Arts Branches for the Arts 1982; Alumni Fellow Penn State Univ 1989. **MILITARY SERVICE:** AUS pfc 1962-63. **BUSINESS ADDRESS:** Dean, School of Arts, VA CommonwealthUniv, 901 W Franklin St, Richmond, VA 23284.

DEPREIST, JAMES ANDERSON
Orchestra music director and conductor. **PERSONAL:** Born Nov 21, 1936, Philadelphia, PA; son of James Henry DePreist and Ethel Anderson; married Ginette Grenier; children: Tracy Elisabeth, Jennifer Anne. **EDUCATION:** Univ of PA, BS 1958, MA 1961, LHD (hon) 1976; Philadelphia Conservatory of Music, student 1959-61; Laval Univ, DMus (hon) 1980; Univ Portland, DFA (hon) 1983; Pacific Univ, DFA (hon) 1985; St Mary's Coll, Doctor of Arts & Letters (hon) 1985; Lewis & Clark Coll, Doctor in Humanities (hon) 1986; Linfield Coll, DMus (hon) 1986; Willamette Univ, DFA (hon) 1987; Drexel Univ, DFA (hon) 1989. **CAREER:** State Dept, am specialist music 1962-63; NY Philharmonic, amer debut 1964; NY Philharmonic Orchestra, asst conductor to Leonard Bernstein 1965-66; Symphony of New World, prin guest conductor 1968-70; Rotterdam Philharmonic, european debut 1969; Natl Symphony Orchestra Washington, assoc conductor 1971-75, prin guest conductor 1975-76; L'Orchestre Symphonique de Que, mus dir 1976-83; Oregon Symphony, conductor 1980-. **ORGANIZATIONS:** Appeared with Philadelphia Orchestra 1972, Chicago Symphony 1973, Boston Symphony, Cleveland Orchestra 1974; conductor Amer premiere of Dvorak's First Symphony NY Philharmonic 1972; trustee Lewis & Clark Coll 1983-; composed ballet scores for, "Vision of America" 1960, "Tendrils" 1961, "A Sprig of Lilac" 1964; concert "Requiem" 1965; mem Sigma Pi Phi. **HONORS/ACHIEVEMENTS:** First Prize Gold Medal Dimitri Mitropoulos Intl Music Competition for Conductors 1964; Merit Citation City of Philadelphia 1969; grantee Martha Baird Rockefeller Fund for Music 1969; Medal of City of Que 1983. **BUSINESS ADDRESS:** Conductor, Oregon Symphony, 711 SW Alder #200, Portland, OR 97205.

DEPRIEST, OSCAR STANTON, III
Physician. **PERSONAL:** Born Apr 14, 1920, Chicago, IL; married Barbara Ann Downes; children: Oscar IV, Charles, Philip, Victoria, Stephanie. **EDUCATION:** Harvard Coll, AB 1950; Harvard Med Sch, MD 1954. **CAREER:** Physician, pvt pract; Columbia Hosp for Women, chief of surgery 1971-79. **HONORS/ACHIEVEMENTS:** Berlin Occupational Medal. **MILITARY SERVICE:** AUS maj 1956-65. **BUSINESS ADDRESS:** 2041 M L King Ave SE, Washington, DC 20020.

DEPTE, LARRY D.
Business executive. **PERSONAL:** Born Jun 08, 1950, Coatesville, PA. **EDUCATION:** Temple U, BS bus adminstrn 1972. **CAREER:** Philadelphia Intl Records, pres 1979-; Philadelphia Intl Records, vice pres finance & bus affairs 1975-76; Coopers & Lybrand, auditor 1972-75. **ORGANIZATIONS:** Mem Nat Assn of Black Accountants; com mem Rec Industry Assn of Am; mem Black Music Assn. **BUSINESS ADDRESS:** Philadelphia Intl Records, 309 S Broad St, Philadelphia, PA 19107.

DERR, GILBERT S.
Association executive. **PERSONAL:** Born Apr 22, 1917, Gastonia, NC; married Verrona Williams. **EDUCATION:** Hampton Inst, BS 1939; DePaul U, MA 1948;Univ of Sarasota, EdD 1976. **CAREER:** Socially Malajusted Children Chiacgo Bd of Edn, adminstr 1948-; Durham NC City Schs, tchr 1941-42, 46-47; Nat Youth Adm Forsyth, GA, tchr 1939-41; DePaul U, lectr. **ORGANIZATIONS:** Mem Kappa Delta Pi; Soc of Fellows DePaul U; IL Historical Soc; Delta Sigma Rho; Tau Kappa Alpha Forensic Soc DSable Heritage Com 1966; pres Central Southside Comm Workers 1968; bd trustees pres Henry Booth House 1968; vice pres IL Historical Soc 1970; IL Sesquicentennial Commn 1968. **HONORS/ACHIEVEMENTS:** Recip Omega Psi Phi Scholarship Award 1934; Phi Beta Sigma Award 1966; Hampton Script Award 1938; YMCA Award 1953; NAACP Award 1966; DePaulUniv Alumni Award 1972; IL Historical Soc Award 1969; sponser Gilbert & Verrona Derr Endowment providing black studies library, lectureship, & scholarship at DePaul U. **MILITARY SERVICE:** USN 1942-46. **BUSINESS ADDRESS:** 228 N La Salle St, Chicago, IL 60601.

DERRICOTTE, C. BRUCE
Business executive. **PERSONAL:** Born Jun 22, 1928, Fostoria, OH; married Toinette Webster; children: Anthony. **EDUCATION:** Defiance Coll, BS; MI U, EE 1955. **CAREER:** Systems Plng Div The Chase Manhattan Bank NA NYC, vice pres exec 1973-; Detroit Arsenal Centerline MI instrument engr 1955-60; IT&T NJ labs, product line mgr 1960-68; NY Dist & Control Data Corp, mgr 1968-73. **ORGANIZATIONS:** Mem Am Bankers Assn; Nat'l Planning Assn; Aircraft Owners & Pilots Assn; past mem Nat'l Exec Reserve 1966-68; VP's Task Force for Youth Motivation. **MILITARY SERVICE:** AUS corpl 1950-52. **BUSINESS ADDRESS:** Chase Manhattan Bank, N A 1 New York Plaza, New York, NY 10004.

DERRICOTTE, EUGENE ANDREW
Dentist. **PERSONAL:** Born Jun 14, 1926, Fostoria, OH; son of Clarence C Derricotte and Bessie M Anderson Derricotte; married Jeanne E Hagans; children: Robert. **EDUCATION:** Univ of MI, BS Pharmacy 1950, DDS 1958. **CAREER:** USAF, dental surgeon/chief dental surgeon various air force bases 1971-79; USAF Acad, command dental surgeon 1979-84; USAF Hosp Chanute AFB, dir dental serv 1984-85; Univ TX Health Sci Ctr at San Antonio, asst prof 1985-. **ORGANIZATIONS:** Mem Amer Dental Assn; mem Alpha Phi Alpha. **HONORS/ACHIEVEMENTS:** Bronze Star Medal; Meritorious Serv Medal; USAF Commendation Medal w/1 Oak Leaf Cluster; AUS Commendation Medal; Good Conduct Medal; WW II Victory Medal; NatlDef Serv Medal; USAF Longevity Serv Awd w/2

Oak Leaf Clusters; Vietnam Serv Medal w/2 Bronze Serv Stars; Republic of Vietnam Campaign Medal; Legion of Merit 1985. **MILITARY SERVICE:** Army Air Corps 1944-46; USAF 1962-85 Colonel (Ret). **HOME ADDRESS:** 3718 Morning Mist, San Antonio, TX 78230.

DESANDIES, KENNETH ANDRE
Physician. **PERSONAL:** Born Feb 16, 1948, New York, NY; son of Conrad DeSandies and Elsie DeSandies; married Karen Yvonne Grant; children: Kisha, Kanika. **EDUCATION:** Hampton Inst, BA 1969; Meharry Medical Coll, MD 1973. **CAREER:** Hurley Hosp, intern 1973-74; King's Co Hosp, resident ob/gyn 1974-78; Group Health Assoc, ob/gyn attending 1978-81; Private Practice, dir/owner 1981-. **ORGANIZATIONS:** Mem Amer Assoc of Gynecologic Laparoscopists 1980, Amer Fertility Soc 1980; fellow Amer Coll of Obstetrics & Gynecology 1981; mem National Medical Association 1980-89. **HONORS/ACHIEVEMENTS:** Bd Certified in Amer Coll of Ob/Gyn 1980; Physician Recognition Awd AMA 1983,86; AMA Physician Recognition Award 1989. **BUSINESS ADDRESS:** 4600 Duke St Ste-332, Alexandria, VA 22304.

DESASSURE, CHARLES
Educator. **PERSONAL:** Born Apr 19, 1961, Eutawville, SC; son of Moses DeSassure and Emma DeSassure. **EDUCATION:** Claflin College, BS 1984; Orangeburg-Calhoun Technical Coll, AS, 1989. **CAREER:** SC Dept of Youth Services, crt oper 1983; Orangeburg Sch Dist 3, compensatory/remedial educ teacher 1984-87; Mansfield Business Coll, computer instructor 1988-. **ORGANIZATIONS:** Mem Phi Beta Sigma, Phi Beta Lambda, NAACP; editor-in-chief Les Memoirs Claflin College Yearbook Staff 1982-83; former state pres SC Youth Conf NAACP 1982-84; mem South Carolina Business Educ Assn 1988-, Palmetto Personal Computer Club 1988-, NAACP Eutawville Branch; sec South Eutawville Democratic Party Precinct 1988-; mem South Carolina Young Democrats, Eutawville Lodge #402 of Free and Accepted Masons, St James Baptist Church, Eutawville SC. **HONORS/ACHIEVEMENTS:** Claflin Coll Creative Writing Awd Student Poetry 1981; Claflin Coll Male Student of the Year 1982, 83; Claflin Coll NAACP Presidential Awd 1983; American Legion Bronze Medal Dept of SC 1983; NAACP Natl Youth Achievement Awd NAACP Natl Office 1983; Outstanding Presidential Awd SC State Conference, Youth Div 1983; Omicron Alpha Beta Chap Phi Beta Lambda Outstanding Leadership Awd 1983; Outstanding Teacher of the Year Award, Mansfield Business College, Columbia SC 1989; poetry: Achieve, Black Future Magazine 1982, Setting Goals, Tomorrow's Business Leader Magazine, Vol 14, No3, p22, Washington DC 1983. **HOME ADDRESS:** Rt 1 Box 95, Eutawville, SC 29048. **BUSINESS ADDRESS:** Computer Instructor, Mansfield Business College, 2638 Two Notch Rd, Columbia, SC 29204.

DESHIELDS, HARRISON F., JR.
Educational administrator. **PERSONAL:** Born Jan 29, 1927, Philadelphia, PA; married Vivian Watts; children: Carla V, Harrison F III. **EDUCATION:** Wilber Force Univ, BA 1949; Columbia Univ, MA 1957. **CAREER:** AL A&M Univ, dean of students 1957-61; Volusia Cty Comm Coll, dean of instr 1961-63; Bethume-Cookman Coll, registrar, dir admiss 1963-76; AL State Univ, dean of admiss records 1976-80; Benedict Coll, dir of admiss records 1980-84; Fisk Univ, dir of admiss & records. **ORGANIZATIONS:** Mem Alpha Phi Alpha 1947-; former consult Alfred P Sloan Found 1965-69, Morton Inst of Admiss & Fin Aid 1965-76; 1st black mem Southern Reg of Coll 1967;past pres & admissions officer Natl Assoc of Coll Dean Registrar 1973-74. **HONORS/ACHIEVEMENTS:** James E Davis Admin of the Year Bethune-Cookman Coll 1967,75; Kappa Delta Pi Hon Soc; Phi Delta Kappa Hon Frat; Co-ed on handbook for Admissions & Fin Aid for United Negro Coll Fund 1969; Publ article in Naca Jrnl 1975. **HOME ADDRESS:** 4067 Malabar Rd, Montgomery, AL 36116. **BUSINESS ADDRESS:** Dir Admissions & Records, Fisk University, 17th Ave North, Nashville, TN 37203.

DESKINS, DONALD R., JR.
Educator. **PERSONAL:** Born May 10, 1932, Brooklyn, NY; married Lois Jackson; children: Sharon, Sheila, Sharlene. **EDUCATION:** Univ of MI, BA 1960, MS 1963, PhD 1970. **CAREER:** BOR US Dept of the Interior, supervisory recreation resource specialist 1964-68; Univ of MI, faculty counselor 1968-69, lecturer 1968-70, asst prof 1972-74, acting chmn 1974-75, chmn 1975-; Geography & Urban Regional Planning Prog, Univ of MI, assoc prof 1973. **ORGANIZATIONS:** Dir Commn on Geography & Afro-Am 1960-; Assn of Am Geographers; mem Commn on Geography & Afro-Am 1968-69; mem Task Force on Minority Research 1970-71; mem editorial bd Professional Geographer 1972-; councilor E Lakes Div 1973-76; chmn E Lakes Div 1975-; Assn of Am Geographers; mem Publ Com 1973-; memexec bd Assn of Social & Behavoiral Sci 1973-; mem GRE Advanced Geography Test Com 1974-; Educ Testing Svc; course dir ChautauguaType Short Courses 1973-76; Nat Sci Found; Am Assn for Advancement of Sci; mem Zoning bd of appeals City of Ann Arbor 1971-73; Assn of Am Geographers; Am Geog Soc; Assn of Social & Behavioral Sci; Population Assn of Am; Regional Sci Assn; Nat Council for Geog Edn; Am Assn for Advancement of Sci. **HONORS/ACHIEVEMENTS:** Sr honorsUniv of MI 1959; Fielding H Yost Honor Award 1959; Phi Kappa Phi Honor Soc 1962; Gamma Theta Upsilon 1966; Sigma XI 1974. **MILITARY SERVICE:** USMC 1953-57. **BUSINESS ADDRESS:** Dept of Geography, U ofMI, Ann Arbor, MI 48104.

DESOUZA, RONALD KENT
Educational administrator. **PERSONAL:** Born Jan 15, 1940, New York, NY; married Sharon Smith; children: Kelly, Ronald Jr. **EDUCATION:** Hunter Coll, City of New York, 1959; Morgan State Univ, BA, 1960-65, MS, 1965-66. **CAREER:** Balto Supreme Bench, probation ofcr 1966-68; Balto City Job Corps, cnslr 1968-69; Bowie State Coll, assoc dir Admissions, 1969-71; Coppin State Coll, dir of admissions, 1971-72, vice pres for admin, dir of admissions/records, 1972-74, vice pres, student affairs, 1974-82; vice pres, admin, 1982-, referee Natl Football League, 1980-. **ORGANIZATIONS:** Omega Psi Phi Fraternity, 1968-; team mem, Middle States Assn for Accreditation, 1978, 1981, 1987. **HONORS/ACHIEVEMENTS:** Church organist St Phillips Annapolis MD & Holy Nativity Balto MD 1962-74; Cert Appreciation US Army Recruiting 1970. **MILITARY SERVICE:** AUS major. **HOME ADDRESS:** 4732 Belle Forte Rd, Baltimore, MD 21208. **BUSINESS ADDRESS:** Vice President for Admin, Coppin State Coll, 2500 W North Ave, Baltimore, MD 21216.

DESSASO-GORDON, JANICE MARIE
Federal government official. **PERSONAL:** Born Apr 10, 1942, Washington, DC; daughter of John F Ford (deceased) and Marie E Sheppard; married Harold J Gordon, Aug 08, 1987; children: Eugene C, Michael A. **EDUCATION:** Univ of the District of Columbia, Washington DC, BA, 1977. **CAREER:** Various federal govt agencies, Washington DC, sec, 1960-70; US Dept of Commerce, Washington DC, program analyst, 1971-76, Minority Business Devel Agency, business devel specialist, currently. **ORGANIZATIONS:** Annual 30-hour dancer, Washington DC Special Olympics for Mentally Retarded-Dance Marathon, 1983-; exec vice pres, Holy Comforter-St Cyprian Community Action Group, 1988-; mem, Business & Professional Women's Assn, 1988-. **HONORS/ACHIEVEMENTS:** Outstanding Performance, US Dept of Commerce, 1973, 1979, 1984, 1986, 1988; Certificate of Appreciation, Natl Minority Supplier Devel Council, 1981; Outstanding Serv Award, Natl Minority Supplier Devel Council, 1985, 1987; Appreciation Award, Nevada Economic Devel Company, 1988. **BUSINESS ADDRESS:** Business Development Specialist, US Dept of Commerce/Minority Business Devel Agency, 14th & Constitution Ave NW, Room H-5096, Washington, DC 20230.

DESTINE, JEAN-LEON
Dancer, choreographer, teacher, lecturer. **PERSONAL:** Born Mar 26, 1928, St Marc, Haiti;daughter of Leon Destine Sr and Lucienne Destine; children: Gerard, Ernest, Carlo. **EDUCATION:** Lycee Petion Haiti, grad 1940-43; Howard University, Washington DC 1944; Columbia Univ, New York City 1945. **CAREER:** Haiti's 1st Troupe Nationale Folklorique, dir 1950; Destine Afro-Haitian Dance Co, dir 1951-; New Dance Group Studio NYC, teacher 20 yrs; Destine Dance Found, pres, choreographer, dancer, teacher, lecturer 1975-. **ORGANIZATIONS:** Mem Officier de l'Ordre Natl "Honneur et Merite' 1958. **HONORS/ACHIEVEMENTS:** Hon Cultural Attache Rep Haiti; appeared in 2 films; Award of Merit, Haitian-American Society 1970, 1975; Distinguished Visitor, Metropolitan Dade County FL 1986.

DESVERNEY-SINNETTE, ELINOR
Librarian. **PERSONAL:** Born Oct 08, 1925, New York, NY; daughter of James C DesVerney and Elinor Calloway DesVerney; married Dr Calvin H Sinnette, Nov 19, 1949; children: Caleen Sinnette Jennings, Darryle Sinnette Craig. **EDUCATION:** Hunter Coll of the City Univ of New York, AB, 1947; Pratt Inst School of Library Serv, MLS, 1959; Columbia Univ School of Library Serv, DLS, 1977. **CAREER:** The New York City Public Library, New York NY, librarian, 1947-54; New York City Bd of Educ, New York NY, school librarial, 1960-65; Inst of African Studies, Univ of Ibadan, Nigeria, lecturer, 1965-69; Ahmadu Bellow Univ, Zaria, Nigeria, lecturer, 1969-70; Moorland-Spingarn Research Center, Howard Univ, 1980-. **ORGANIZATIONS:** Life mem, The Oral History Assn, Oral History Middle Atlantic Region, mem, Black Caucus of the American Library Assn. **HONORS/ACHIEVEMENTS:** Distinguished Service Award, 92nd Infantry Div, World War II Assn, 1986; author of "Arthur Alfonso Schomburg, Black Bibliophile and Collector, A Biography," The New York Public Library and Wayne State Univ Press, Detroit MI, 1989. **HOME ADDRESS:** 1016 S Wayne St, Apt 409, Arlington, VA 22204.

DEVAUGHN, EDWARD RAYMOND
Attorney. **PERSONAL:** Born Oct 06, 1926, Cleveland, OH; married Anne Elizabeth Little. **EDUCATION:** Cleveland St U, BBA 1961; Cleveland Marshall Law Sch, JD 1966. **CAREER:** FCC, sr atty adv; Gen Elec Co, staff atty 1971-73; Midland-Ross Corp, sr atty 1967-71, tax acct 1963-67; Ford Motor Co, gen acct 1962-63. **ORGANIZATIONS:** Mem OH Bar 1966; mem Wash DC Fed & Amer Bar Assn; DC Bar Consumer Affairs Com; mem Natl Lawyers Club; mem Computer Lawyers Group; mem Natl Conf of Black Lawyers-Comm Task Force Fdr; chmn Consumer Prot Assn; v chmn Welfare Fed; mem Suicide Prev Ctr; Oppor Industrition Ctr; DC Ment Hlth Inst; SW Assem; participant DC Coal for Self-determ; bd mem chrpsn Waterside Tenants Counc Legal Com; chmn adv Comm on Pub Util to DC CityCounc; com chmn Stanton Park Neigh Assn; bd mem Wash Chap ADA including in "Us people of wash dc". **MILITARY SERVICE:** ASAF maj 1945-53. **BUSINESS ADDRESS:** 1954 M St NW, Washington, DC 20554.

DEVAUGHN-TIDLINE, DONNA MICHELLE
Health care management director. **PERSONAL:** Born Sep 20, 1954, Houston, TX; son of Canary DeVaughn and Louise Robinson DeVaughn; married Eric Tidline, Aug 27, 1988. **EDUCATION:** Southern Methodist Univ, BBA 1977. **CAREER:** Prudential Health Care Plan Inc, admin mgr claims 1983-84, dir of admin HMO 1984-86; Prudential Insurance Co Inc, assoc mgr acct 1980-83, dir of health care mgmt 1987-. **ORGANIZATIONS:** Mem Natl Assoc of Female Execs; volunteer Big Brothers/Big Sisters; mem Delta Sigma Theta. **BUSINESS ADDRESS:** Dir Health Care Mgmt, Prudential Insurance Co Inc, 845 Crossover Lane, Ste 220, Memphis, TN 38117.

DEVEREUEAWAX, JOHN L., III
Elected official. **PERSONAL:** Born Oct 19, 1953, Flowood, MS; children: Andre, John IV, Marie Janet. **EDUCATION:** Jackson State Univ, BA 1971-76. **CAREER:** CETA, mgr; Rockford Comm Assoc, exec dir 1981-; City of Rockford, alderman. **ORGANIZATIONS:** Mem NAACP; pres RKF Area MS Club 1980-; assoc mem Natl Council Negro Women 1984-. **HONORS/ACHIEVEMENTS:** Outstanding Young American 1984. **BUSINESS ADDRESS:** Alderman Ward 13, City of Rockford, 425 E State St, Rockford, IL 61104.

DEVONISH, LINDA DIANE
Accountant. **PERSONAL:** Born Jul 28, 1962, New York, NY. **EDUCATION:** Adelphi Univ, BBA 1984. **CAREER:** Melvyn Raphael CPA, acctg asst 1982-84; Arthur Young & Co, sr auditor 1984-87; Manufacturers Hanover Trust, financial analyst 1987-. **ORGANIZATIONS:** Income tax preparer Volunteer Inc Tax Asst IRS 1981-86; genl mem Natl Assoc of Black Accts 1984-. **HONORS/ACHIEVEMENTS:** Passed uniform CPA exam State Bd of Accountancy 1986. **BUSINESS ADDRESS:** Financial Analyst, Manufacturers Hanover Trust, 130 John St, New York, NY.

DEVORE, OPHELIA
Business executive. **PERSONAL:** Born in South Carolina; widowed. **EDUCATION:** NY U; New York City Coll; Vogue Sch of Modeling. **CAREER:** The Columbus Times, publisher; Ophelia DeVore Assos Inc NY, chmn bd, firm includes model agy, self-devel charm sch, cosmetic co & consult serv in marketing & pub relations. **ORGANIZATIONS:** Mem Am

Women in Radio & TV; Nat Assn of Market Developers; Nat Bus League; num other bus leagues.

DEVROUAX, PAUL S., JR.
Architect. **PERSONAL:** Born Oct 04, 1942, New Orleans, LA; son of Paul Devrouax Sr and Freddie Warner Devrouax; married Branda Stallworth, Sep 09, 1972; children: Lesley S. **EDUCATION:** Southern Univ, Baton Rouge LA, Bachelor of Architecture, 1968. **CAREER:** Nolan Norman & Nolan Architects, New Orleans LA, project architects, 1968-69; Urban Planners Inc, Arlington VA, dir of design, 1969-72; DiSilvestro Phelps & Phelps Architects, Miami FL, assoc & designer, 1972-73; Devrouax & Purnell, Architects-Planners PC, Washington DC, pres, 1973-. **ORGANIZATIONS:** Mem, Mayor's Comm for the Handicapped, Washington DC, 1976-79, The Amer Inst of Architects, 1980-; pres, The Natl Org of Minority Architects, 1980-81; bd mem, District of Columbia Chamber of Commerce, 1982-; mem, District of Columbia Architectural Review Panel, 1983-, The Amer Arbitration Assn, 1985-; chmn, AIA, Mid-Atlantic Region, 1986-87; sr dir, AIA, Washington Chapter, 1986; mem, District of Columbia Bicentennial Commn, 1987-92; bd of dir, Washington Project for the Arts, 1987-. **HONORS/ACHIEVEMENTS:** Recipient, Historic Preservation and Architectural Design Excellence, AIA, Washington Chapter, #4 Logan Circle, 1981; Recipient, Citation Award, AIA, Washington Chapter, The Iowa Complex, 1981; Recipient, Design Award, The Natl Org of Minority Architects Natl Award Program, Carter Beach House, 1984; Recipient, Professional Serv of the Year, Minority Enterprise Devel Community Award, Washington DC, 1986; Recipient, Architectural Serv Citation, Howard Univ, Washington DC, 1989; features spokesperson, Washington Urban League, Focus: "Design within an Urban Environment.". **MILITARY SERVICE:** US Army, sergeant, E-5, 1966-68. **BUSINESS ADDRESS:** President, Devrouax & Purnell, Architects-Planners PC, 717 D Street, NW, Washington, DC 20004.

DEWBERRY, MADELINA DENISE
Human resources professional. **PERSONAL:** Born Oct 18, 1958, Los Angeles, CA. **EDUCATION:** San Jose State Univ, attended 1981. **CAREER:** San Jose Unified School Dist, teacher 1980-81; Santa Clara Junvenile Hall, counselor 1981; Natl Medical Enterprises, personnel coord 1981-87; American Express, human resources specialist 1987-. **ORGANIZATIONS:** Vp 1986-87, natl affirmative action 1986-87, natl conf 1987-88 Intl Assoc for Personnel Women; co-chair United Christian Network 1986-; dir Planning Spirit Connections 1986-. **HONORS/ACHIEVEMENTS:** Outstanding Woman in Health Care YWCA 1986. **HOME ADDRESS:** 408 S Maine Ave, Compton, CA 90220.

DEWITT, FRANKLIN ROOSEVELT
Attorney. **PERSONAL:** Born May 25, 1936, Conway, SC; married Willa Waylis Johnson; children: Rosalyn Abrevaya, Sharolyn Renee. **EDUCATION:** South Carolina State Coll, BS Bus Admin 1962, LLB 1964; Georgia State Univ, Certificate Housing Mgmt 1973. **CAREER:** US Justice Dept, summer law clerk 1963; US Civil Serv Comm Washington DC, trial attny 1965-67; Atlantic Beach SC, town attny; Private practice, attny. **ORGANIZATIONS:** Municipal consult Glenarden MD 1965-67; mem Conway SC City Council 1969-84; delegate Natl Dem Party Conv in Miami Beach FL 1972; appt by gov of SC Spec Study Committed on Home Rule 1972; mem US Court of Appeals for Fourth Circuit, Washington DC Bar, US Supreme Court, mem SC State Bar Assoc, Amer Bar Assoc, Fed Bar Assoc; chmn, bd dir Horry-Georgetown Mental Health Clinic; life mem NAACP. **HONORS/ACHIEVEMENTS:** Usher of the Year Cherry Hill Baptist Church 1978; Who's Who in American Law 1st 2nd 3rd 4th 5th editions; Who's Who in Amer Politics 1983-84; Who's Who in Amer 1984-85, 1986-87; Who's Who in the World 1984-85. **MILITARY SERVICE:** USAF a/1c 1955-59, Active Reserve 1959-61; Good Conduct Ribbon USAF 1957. **BUSINESS ADDRESS:** Attorney, 510 Highway 378, Conway, SC 29526.

DEWITT, RUFUS B.
Educator. **PERSONAL:** Born Dec 01, 1915, Rossville, TN; married Mary Borders; children: Marilyn A, Beatrice Francine. **EDUCATION:** Columbia U, BA, MA, grad studies 1947. **CAREER:** Elementary school prin 1940-41; Montgomery Branch YMCA, exec dir 1948-55; Dearborn Street YMCA, dir 1955-63; SE Branch YMCA San Diego, dir; Adult Div Community Coll, San Diego Community Coll, vice pres. **ORGANIZATIONS:** Delegate from So area YMCA to Nat Coun YMCA 1949-54; mem So Area Nominating Com for nominating So area bd dir; mem Frontiers Intl 1969-63; mem United Supreme Coun, 33 Degree Masonry & Delegate; CA TB Assn; bd mem Local Draft Bd No 140-B CA 1970; adv to registrants 1973; pres San Diego Community Action Coun 1968; pres SE San Diego Community Theater; pers Zeta Sigma Lambda Chpt; Alpha Phi Alpha Scholarlastic Frat 1937-74; mem Pi Boule Sigma Pi Phi; Gulf Coast Savings & Loan Assn; sec 3 1/2 million dollar housing project; wrote 1st bldg prog for Model Cities funds. **HONORS/ACHIEVEMENTS:** Received Outst Vol Award 1973. **MILITARY SERVICE:** Served 1944-45. **BUSINESS ADDRESS:** 4033 Ruffin Rd, San Diego, CA.

D'HUE, ROBERT R., JR.
Artist, educator. **PERSONAL:** Born Jun 05, 1917, Cleveland, OH; divorced; children: Sandra, Gary. **EDUCATION:** Fine Arts, with honors 1954; Academie Royale Des Beaux Arts & Archt Liege, Belgium. **CAREER:** Artist, art instructor, art lecturer, art jurist, professional artist 1954-; voc counselor 1969-70. **ORGANIZATIONS:** Mem San Diego Water Color Soc, Religious Art Guild of San Diego Unitarian Church, works in punl collections, Ferrieres, Belgium, Firmalle-Haute, Belgium; Museum Des Beaux, Arts, Liege, Belgium; works in private collections Belgium, Luxemburg, Zaire, France, Spain, Monaco, Germany, Cyprus, US & Mexico. **HONORS/ACHIEVEMENTS:** Listed in Annuaire Des Beaux-Arts De Wallonie, Belgium 1960, Black Artist on Art US 1969. **MILITARY SERVICE:** AUS 1942-48.

DIALLO
Poet, editor. **PERSONAL:** Born Apr 23, 1947, Newport, RI; children: Charles, III. **EDUCATION:** Univ Washington, BA MA 1971. **CAREER:** Progress Mag, editor; Seattle U, instr; Educ Cultural Complex Sandiego Comm Colls, instr. **ORGANIZATIONS:** Founder chmn of bd Soul Inc; life mem Kappa Alpha Psi 1969. **HONORS/ACHIEVEMENTS:** This Is CJAII 1965; The Poet Diallo 1972; On My Mind, In My Heart 1975. **BUSINESS ADDRESS:** 2855 Tremont Pl, Denver, CO 80205.

DIAMOND, JOHN R.
Engineer. **PERSONAL:** Born Nov 29, 1905, Houston; married Nathalie Ritchie; children: John R Jr, Russell W. **EDUCATION:** Ford Trade Sch; Wayne State U. **CAREER:** Ford Motor Co, 1928-31, 1935-46; YMCA, 1932-35; Diamond Elec Co, owner 1946-. **ORGANIZATIONS:** Mem MI Soc Professional Eng; Intl Assn Electrical Inspectors; Nat Fire Protection Assn; Better Bus Bureau; Elec Examiners; Assoc Electricians Inc; mem Nacirema Club Inc; Non-Profit Housing Corp; minority Bus Mens Assoc.

DIAW, ROSEMARY K.
Educational administrator. **PERSONAL:** Born Mar 02, 1950, Guyana. **EDUCATION:** Kent State Univ, BS Sec Ed 1971, MA Romance Lang 1974, MEd 1975. **CAREER:** Kent State Univ, instr 1972, grad recruiter of minorities & women 1972-76, asst dir 1976-77; Cornell School of Indust & Labor Rel, cons, trainer 1979; SUNY Albany, dir affirm action 1977-80; Georgetown Univ Washington DC, spec asst to pres 1980-. **ORGANIZATIONS:** Senator SUNY Albany Faculty Senate 1980; mem SUNY Fair Employ Practices Comm 1979-; bd of dirs NE Reg Black & Hispanic Pol Caucus 1979-; bd of dir NAACP Albany Br 1978-, Labor Ed Advancement Prog; mem Delta Sigma Theta Sor Inc 1980; mem Gr WA DC Bd of Trade 1980-; chmn WA Metro Affirm Action 1983-85. **HONORS/ACHIEVEMENTS:** Dean's List & Omicron Delta Kappa Kent State Univ. **BUSINESS ADDRESS:** Special Assistant to President, GeorgetownUniv, 316 Kober-Cogan 3800 Reserv Rd, Washington, DC 20007.

DICK, GEORGE ALBERT
Manager of flight information. **PERSONAL:** Born Jan 31, 1940, Lloyds, St Thomas, Jamaica;son of Cleveland Drummond and Ruby Drummond; married Margaret Wesley, Aug 29, 1981; children: Pete Dick, Dave Dick, Charmaine Dick, Sharone Dick. **EDUCATION:** Bellevue School of Nursing, Kingston Jamaica, RMN, 1959-62. **CAREER:** Bellevue Hospital, Kingston, Jamaica, student nurse, 1959-62, staff nurse nurse 1962-67; Beverly Hills Hospital, Dallas, TX, staff nurse, supervisor, 1967-77, Southwest Airlines Co, Dallas, TX, ramp agent, 1977-79, flight information agent, 1979-83, flight information supvr, 1983-86. **ORGANIZATIONS:** Mem, Operations Comm Southwest Airlines, 1986-; pres, Third World Sports and Social Assn, 1974-76. **HOME ADDRESS:** 732 Havenwood, Dallas, TX 75232.

DICKENS, DORIS LEE (MRS. AUSTIN L. FICKLING)
Psychiatrist. **PERSONAL:** Born Oct 12, Roxboro, NC; married Judge Austin L Fickling (deceased). **EDUCATION:** VA Union Univ, BS Chemistry (magna cum laude) 1960; Howard Univ Coll of Med, MD 1966. **CAREER:** Howard Univ Coll of Medicine, faculty mem 1982-; St Elizabeths Hospital, dir mental health, prof for the deaf, psychiatrist 1973-. **ORGANIZATIONS:** Mem Amer Psych Assoc 1972-, WA Psychiatric Soc 1972-; bd dir Natl Health Care Found for the Deaf 1973-83; consult Natl Inst of Mental Health 1975-77; mem Mental Health & Deafness Assoc 1980-; faculty mem Howard Univ Coll of Med 1982-; policy adv counc Kendell School. **HONORS/ACHIEVEMENTS:** Hon (magna cum laude) VA Union Univ 1959; Beta Kappa Chi Hon Soc VA Union Univ 1959; Alpha Kappa Mu Hon Soc VA Union Univ 1959; Dept Awds Pediatrics Psychiatry & Neurology Howard Univ Coll of Med 1966; Superior Perf Awd St Eliz Hosp 1976; Dorothea Lynde Dix Awd St Elizabeths Hosp 1980; publ "How and When Psychiatry Can Help You" 1972, "You and Your Doctor" 1973; contrib author "Hearing and Hearing Impairment" 1979, "Counseling Deaf People, Research & Practice" 1985. **BUSINESS ADDRESS:** Psychiatrist, Dir, St Elizabeths Hospital, 2700 Martin Luther King Ave SE, Washington, DC 20032.

DICKENS, HELEN OCTAVIA
Physician, educator. **PERSONAL:** Born in Dayton, OH; daughter of Charles Dickens and Daisy Dickens; married Purvis Henderson MD (deceased); children: Jayne H Brown, Norman S Henderson. **EDUCATION:** Univ of IL, BS 1932; Univ of IL Coll of Med, MD 1934; Univ of PA Grad Sch of Med, MMSc 1945. **CAREER:** Mercy Douglass Hosp, dir dept of OB-GYN 1948-67; OB-GYN Med Coll of PA, asso clin prof 1954-65; Woman's Hosp Dept of OB, chief of serv 1956-64; Univ of PA Sch of Med, dir teen clinic 1969-, prof OB/GYN assoc dean. **ORGANIZATIONS:** Pres Pan Am Women's Alliance 1970-73; Coll of Physicians OB Soc of Phila; Philadelphia Cnty Med Soc; FACS 1950; FACOG 1953; AMA; NMA; AAMC; bd of dir Am Cancer Soc 1963, Children's Aid Soc 1968-, Nat Assn of Med Min Educators 1975-, Devereux Found 1979-. **HONORS/ACHIEVEMENTS:** Distinguished daughter of PA honored by Gov Woman FACS; 1st Negro Recipient 1971; The PA Gimbel Award 1970; Illini Achievement Award, Univ of IL 1982; Med Coll of PA Hon Doctor of Med Sci 1979; Univ of PA Hon Doct of Sci 1982. **HOME ADDRESS:** 2 Franklin Town Blvd, Philadelphia, PA 19103. **BUSINESS ADDRESS:** Prof OB/GYN Assoc Dean, U of PA Sch of Med, 3400 Spruce St, Philadelphia, PA 19104.

DICKENS, SAMUEL
Attorney. **PERSONAL:** Born Apr 05, 1926, Tallulah, LA. **EDUCATION:** BS 1957. **CAREER:** Juris doctor 1959. **ORGANIZATIONS:** LA St Bar Assn; Baton Rouge Bar Assn; Nat Bar Assn; Am Bar Assn. **MILITARY SERVICE:** USAF staff sgt 1947-54. **BUSINESS ADDRESS:** 8152 Scenic Hwy, Baton Rouge, LA 70807.

DICKERSON, ADOLPHUS SUMNER
Clergyman. **PERSONAL:** Born May 25, 1914, Greenville, GA; married Juanita B. **EDUCATION:** Clark Coll, AB; Gammon Theolo Sem, BD; Atlanta U, MA; BostonUniv Sch of Theol, STM; Clark Coll, DD. **CAREER:** United Meth Ch Asso, dir Coun of Ministreis; pastor; dist supt sem prof. **HONORS/ACHIEVEMENTS:** 1st black Dist Supt to serve in predom white conf in Un Meth Ch in GA; 1st black man to serve as pres of Chris Coun of Metro Atlanta; minister of year Omega Frat.

DICKERSON, BETTE JEANNE
Administrator. **PERSONAL:** Born May 21, 1951, Philadelphia, PA; daughter of Frank Clark Dickerson and Rosa Anthony Dickerson. **EDUCATION:** Morehead State Univ, BA 1972; Univ of Louisville, MEd 1975; Washington State Univ, PhD 1986. **CAREER:** Louisville/Jefferson Co Bd of Educ, teacher 1972-78; Washington State Univ, rsch asst 1978-81; Natl Urban League, intern/program dir 1981-82; WK Kellogg Foundation, program assoc 1982-86; Delta Sigma Theta Sor Inc, foundation dir 1986-. **ORGANIZATIONS:** Mem Amer Sociological Assn, Assn of Black Sociologists, Amer Soc of Assn Execs, Natl Assn of Female Execs; mem Delta Sigma Theta Sor Inc, Phi Kappa Phi Honor Soc; mem, Society for International Development; mem, National Black Alumni Assn; advisory bd, Private Eyes Inc; advisory bd, International Biographic Council. **HONORS/ACHIEVEMENTS:** Outstanding Young Women of Amer 1977; George Edmund Haynes Fellowship Natl Urban

League 1981; Comm Serv Award Washington Heights Comm Ministeries 1984; Women In Leadership, Junior League of Washington DC 1989.

DICKERSON, DENNIS CLARK
Educator. **PERSONAL:** Born Aug 12, 1949, McKeesport, PA; married Mary Anne Eubanks; children: Nicole, Valerie, Christina, Dennis Jr. **EDUCATION:** Lincoln Univ, BA 1971; Washington Univ, MA 1974, PhD 1978. **CAREER:** Forest Park Comm Coll, part-time instructor 1974; PA State Univ, part-time instructor 1975-76; Williams Coll, asst prof history 1976-83, assoc prof history 1983-85; Rhodes Coll, assoc prof history 1985-87; Carter Woodson Inst Univ of VA, visiting scholar 1987-88; Williams Coll, assoc prof history 1987-88, prof 1988-. **ORGANIZATIONS:** Pastor Payne AME Church Chatham NY 1980-85; mem IBPOEW; bicentennial comm African Meth Episcopal Church 1985-; itinerant elder AME Church; mem NAACP; pastor St Mark AME Church Mumford TN 1985-87; pres Memphis Chap Assoc for the Study of Afro-Amer Life and History inc 1986-87. **HONORS/ACHIEVEMENTS:** Fellowship Natl Endownment for the Humanities 1982; Moody Grant Lyndon B Johnson Found 1983; Grant-in-aid Amer Council of Learned Soc 1983-84; Fellowship Rockefeller Found 1983-84; articles in New Jersey History, Church History, Pennsylvania Heritage, New York State Journal of Medicine, Methodist History, Western PA Historical Magazine, AME Church Review; contributing author to Black Apostles at Home and Abroad, GK Hall 1982, Biographical Dictionary of Amer Labor Leaders, Greenwood Press 1984; Biographical Dictionary of Amer Social Welfare, Greenwood Press 1986; Life and Labor, SUNY Press 1986; author "Out of the Crucible, Black Steelworkers in Western Pennsylvania 1875-1980," Albany State Univ of NY Press 1986. **BUSINESS ADDRESS:** Professor of History, Williams College, Dept of History, Williamstown, MA 01267.

DICKERSON, ELLIS L., JR.
Certified public accountant. **PERSONAL:** Born Jul 27, 1934, Los Angeles, CA. **EDUCATION:** Univ So CA. **CAREER:** State of CA, corp examiner financial analyst 1961-69; Ellis Louis Dickerson Jr, owner; certified public accountant. **ORGANIZATIONS:** Mem Kappa Alpha Psi; various civic & prof soc. **MILITARY SERVICE:** USAF air weather service.

DICKERSON, ERIC
Professional athlete. **PERSONAL:** Born Sep 02, 1960, Sealy, TX. **EDUCATION:** Attended, Southern Methodist Univ. **CAREER:** L A Rams, running back 1983-. **ORGANIZATIONS:** NFL spokesperson for the anti-drug "Just Say No" campaign; natl chmn Natl Lung Assoc. **HONORS/ACHIEVEMENTS:** 1984 NFC Player of Yr by UPI, Football News, USA Today, Washington DC Touchdown Club, Atlanta Touchdown Club, Columbus Ohio Touchdown Club and Kansas City Comm of 101; NFL MVP 2 Yrs; Daniel F Reeves Mem Awd; won virtually all Rookie of Yr Hnrs & a flock of natl awds; mem 1987 NFL Pro Bowl team. **BUSINESS ADDRESS:** Los Angeles Rams, 2327 W Lincoln Ave, Anaheim, CA 92801.

DICKERSON, GLENDA J.
Educator. **PERSONAL:** Born Feb 09, 1945, Texas; children: Shani Anitra Yelode. **EDUCATION:** Howard U, BFA 1966; Adelphi U, MA 1969. **CAREER:** School of Arts, Western Univ, chmn dept of theatre; Black Amer Theatre, artistic dir 1969-71; Workshops, teacher 1970-74; Bureau of Ind Affairs, African Peoples Repertory Theatre San Francisco, conducted workshops 1973; Howard Univ, asst prof 1969-72; "The Unfinished Song", "El Hajj Malik", "Jesus Christ, Lawd Today", "The Torture of Mothers", "Jump at the Sun", dir; The Living Library Western U, dir; YELODE Inc, artistic dir. **HONORS/ACHIEVEMENTS:** Recipient Citation for special achievement in Am College Festival Mayor Washington 1970. **BUSINESS ADDRESS:** Sch of Arts, 35 & R StsNW, Washington, DC.

DICKERSON, JANET
Educator. **PERSONAL:** Born Feb 13, 1944, New York, NY; married J Paul Stephens; children: Jill Courtney, Karin Chase, Dawn Paulette. **EDUCATION:** The Western Coll for Women, BA 1965; Xavier Univ, MEd 1968; IN Univ, Univ of MI, Univ MO at Kansas City, further study; Univ of PA; doctoral candidate. **CAREER:** Cincinnati Public Schools, Ach Jr High School, English teacher 1965-68; Sawyer Bloom Jr High School, guidance counselor 1968-71; Univ of Cincinnati Educ Devel Prog, teacher, counselor 1971; Earlham Coll, Richmond, IN, dir supportive serv & asst prof 1971-76; Swarthmore Coll, assoc dean 1976-81, dean of the college 1981-. **ORGANIZATIONS:** Bd mem Pauline Trueblood Nursery Sch 1973-74; vice pres bd The Children's Sch 1974-75; mem bd of dir Children's Clncs of Chester & vicinity 1977-78; readerHWE proposals 1978-81; mem Swarthmore Home & Sch Assn Bd 1979-80; mem bd Client Security Fund of Commonwlth of PA 1983-; consult Davidson, Oberlin, Scripps; consult HERS/Brown Univ; consult Barnard Coll; consult Haverford Coll; consult Kalamazoo Coll. **HONORS/ACHIEVEMENTS:** Presented paper Assn of Social & Behavorial Scientists 1975. **BUSINESS ADDRESS:** Dean of the College, Swarthmore College, Swarthmore, PA 19081.

DICKERSON, LOWELL DWIGHT
Musician. **PERSONAL:** Born Dec 26, 1944, Los Angeles, CA; son of Charles E Dickerson and Ethel Hartie Dickerson. **EDUCATION:** CA State Univ, Los Angeles BA Music 1973; Boston Univ Berkley Coll of Music; private lessons from Ray Santisi & Margaret Chaloff; Univ of Southern California Masters in Music 1989. **CAREER:** Two albums "Sooner or Later" Discovery Record Label, "Windows" CA Three Record Label; performed with Gene Ammons, Conti Condoli, Junior Cook, Freddie Hubbard, Damita Jo, Sergio Mendes, Anita O'Day, Clark Terry, Joe Williams and many others; Los Angeles Musicians Union, piano musician. **ORGANIZATIONS:** Mem, P Kappa Lambda 1989. **HOME ADDRESS:** 3101Casitas St, Altadena, CA 91001.

DICKERSON, PAMELA ANN
Business executive, flight attendant. **PERSONAL:** Born Jan 14, 1953, New Orleans, LA; daughter of I W Dickerson and Catherine Grove Dickerson. **EDUCATION:** Southern Univ, New Orleans LA, BS, 1975; Loyola Univ, New Orleans LA, attended, 1979; Georgia State Univ, Atlanta GA, attended, 1984-85. **CAREER:** Delta Airlines, Atlanta GA, flight attendant, 1976-; X-ceptional Nail Inc, Atlanta GA, pres, CEO, 1987-. **ORGANIZATIONS:** Founder, pres, Natl Assn of Negro Business & Professional Women Inc, New Orleans Club, 1982-84; volunteer, Sickle Cell Anemia, 1982-83; past pres, mem, Natl Assn of Negro Business & Professional Women Inc, Decatur-Dekalb Club, 1984-; volunteer, Fund Raising Comm, Amer Cancer Soc, 1987-; volunteer, Democratic Natl Convention, 1988. **HONORS/ACHIEVEMENTS:** Appreciation Award, Natl Assn of Negro Business & Professional Women, New Orleans Club, 1982; Award of Excellence, Amer Cancer Soc, 1987; President's Award, Natl Assn of Negro Business & Professional Women, Decatur-Dekalb Club, 1988.

DICKERSON, WARNER LEE
Educator. **PERSONAL:** Born Jun 18, 1937, Brownsville, TN; married Arcola Leavell; children: Jarvis, Mechele. **EDUCATION:** TN State Univ, BS Math 1961; Memphis State Univ, MS Math 1969; Univ of Sarasota, EdD Voc Ed 1979. **CAREER:** Memphis City School, teacher 1961-64; State Tech Inc, teacher 1970-74, dept head devel studies 1974-76, ed admin 1976-78, dir of admin affairs 1978-81,dir 1981-84, Dept of Ed consultant 1984-86; superintendent 1986-. **ORGANIZATIONS:** Vp NAACP Memphis Br 1977-79; pres OIC Memphis Br 1977-, NAACP Memphis Br 1979-, Natl Assoc for the Advancement of Black Amers in Vocational Ed 1982-84. **HONORS/ACHIEVEMENTS:** Distinguished Teacher Awd State Tech Ins 1971. **BUSINESS ADDRESS:** State Dir, State Tech Inst, 5983 Macon Cove, Memphis, TN 38134.

DICKEY, CURTIS
Professional athlete. **PERSONAL:** Born Nov 27, 1956, Madisonville, TX; married Sheila; children: Courtney. **EDUCATION:** TX A&M. **CAREER:** Indianapolis Colts, running back. **ORGANIZATIONS:** Active in off-season boys' club work in Bryan, TX. **HONORS/ACHIEVEMENTS:** College, alltime leading rusher at TX A&M earning All-America honors; finished college career as second leading rusher in Southwestern Conf history; three-time NCAA indoor 60-yd dash champion; professional, ranked fifth in team history in rushing with 3,456 yds for five-yr career; voted by fans as the Colts' 1984 NFL/Miller Man of the Year; started all 16 games for the Colts in 1983; led the club in rushing and receiving yardage; ranked fifth in the AFC and 12th in the NFL in rushing; tied for second on the team with 21 catches for 228 yds making him team leader with 460 yds total offense; ranked as fifth-leading rusher in Colt's history with 3,456 yds on 791 carries; establ Colts rookie records in 1980 with 13 TDs.

DICKEY, ERMA COOK
Elected official, nurse. **PERSONAL:** Born Sep 03, 1929, Malakoff, TX; widowed; children: Carolyn Andrenia Barron, Audry Laverne. **EDUCATION:** Henderson Cty Jr Coll, LVN 1962-63; Navarro Coll, 1975; El Centro Coll 1975. **CAREER:** Henderson County Memorial Hosp, nurse 1962-65; Cedar Creek Nursing Home, charge nurse 1965-67; Maywood Manor Nursing Home, nurse 1968-78, 1st black nurses dir; Lakeland Med Ctr, license vocational nurse. **ORGANIZATIONS:** Youth counselor, Cedar Forks Baptist Church, 1970; counselor, Galilee Griggs mem Dist Youth Conf 1975-; nursing faculty Lakeland Med Ctr 1979-; mem city council City of Trinidad 1979-. **HONORS/ACHIEVEMENTS:** Mem East TX Council of Governments 1980-, Trinidad Chamber of Comm 1980; mayor protem City of Trinidad 1983-; appt mem State Task Force on Indigent Health Care 1984. **HOME ADDRESS:** 830 Pinoak, Trinidad, TX 75163.

DICKEY, LLOYD V.
Dentist. **EDUCATION:** Univ CAUniv of Pacific Dental Schs & Presidio of San Fran Army Base, post grad study Oral Surgery, Prosthetics, Radiology; San Fran State Coll, clinical psychology; Meharry Med Coll, DDS; TX Coll, BA. **CAREER:** Priv Prac, dentist 27 yrs; Life Sci, coll tchr; HS prin; tchr sci math; coach sports. **ORGANIZATIONS:** Pres organizer & founder Golden State Dental Assn; mem Bd Dirs San Fran Dental Care Found; Fillmore-Fell Girl's Home; WsternAdd Proj Area Com; pres N CA Chap Meharry Med Coll Alumni Assn; chmn coord Meharry Med Coll Wstrn Regional Mtng & Fund Raising Event; pres Parents Adv Com- pacific Heights Elem Sch; chmn Benj Franklin Jr HS Parents Adv Com for Implementing Fresno Plan; chmn Com to Build Schs in Wstrn Add; mem N CA Chap Nat Dental Assn; organizer pres Chater Chpt; N CA chmn state coord Meharry Alumni $88 Million Campaign Fund Drive; organizer Bay Area TX Coll Alumni Assn; mem Comm Ldrs of Am. **HONORS/ACHIEVEMENTS:** Recip Outstanding Alumnus Award Meharry Med & Moll TX Coll; comm serv Award Bay Area HowardUniv Alumni; author several outstanding scientific papers. **MILITARY SERVICE:** AUS captain WW II chief surgical tech; Korean War chief oral surgery & Prosthetics. **BUSINESS ADDRESS:** 1845 Fillmore St, San Francisco, CA 94115.

DICKINSON, GLORIA HARPER
Educational administrator. **PERSONAL:** Born Aug 05, 1947, New York, NY; daughter of Clifford Horace Harper and Martha Louis Sinton Harper; married Arthur Clinton Dickinson. **EDUCATION:** City Coll of NY, BA European Hist 1968; Howard Univ, MA African Studies 1970, PhD African Stud 1978. **CAREER:** Caden High School Camden NJ, geography/Social studies teacher 1970-71; English Dept Trenton State Coll, instructor 1971-73; Dept of African-Am Studies Trenton State Coll, chmn asst prof 1973-. **ORGANIZATIONS:** Editorial bd mem Journal of Negro History 1983-; mem NJ Committee on The Humanities 1984-; mem ASALH; mem ASA; mem AHSA; mem NCBS; mem NCNW; faculty advisor Zeta Sigma Chptr Alpha Kappa Alpha 1972-; contrib scholar NJ Women's Project 1984; proj dir TSC Summer Study Tours to Africa 1984-; mem NJ Historic Trust 1986-. **HONORS/ACHIEVEMENTS:** NEH summer fellowship for coll fac Univ of IA 1977, NY Univ School of Bus 1979, Univ of PA 1981, Princeton Univ 1984; Fac Mem of the Year Trenton State Coll 1984; Proj Dir NEH Summer Inst in African-Amer Culture Trenton State Coll 1987. **BUSINESS ADDRESS:** Chrmn African-American Stud, Trenton State Coll, CN 550 Hillwood Lakes, Trenton, NJ 08625.

DICKSON, DAVID W. D.
Retired educator. **PERSONAL:** Born Feb 16, 1919, Portland, ME; son of David A Dickson and Mary Daly Dickson; married Barbara, Feb 16, 1981; children: David, Deborah, Deirdre. **EDUCATION:** Bowdoin Coll, AB 1941; Harvard Univ, MA 1942, PhD 1949. **CAREER:** MI State, assoc prof, 1948-63; Northern MI Univ, prof & head of English Dept 1963-66; School of Arts & Science, Northern MI Univ Marquette, dean 1966-67, vice pres acad affairs 1967-68; Federal City Coll, Washington, provost, vice pres acad affairs, prof 1968-69, SUNY, Stony Brook, dean of continuing & devel educ, 1972-73, prof of engl 1969-73; Montclair State Coll NJ, pres 1973-84, distinguished prof 1984-88. **ORGANIZATIONS:** Consultant, Natl Found for the Humanities, 1969-71; Mott Found, 1973-74; bd of trustees, Montclair Art Museum; N Essex Devel & Action Council, Bowdoin Coll, Bloomfield Coll; mem, AAC Comm on Liberal Learning; Policy bd Project Change; mem, Phi Beta Kappa, Sigma Pi Phi, Omega

Psi Phi. **HONORS/ACHIEVEMENTS:** Rosenwald Fellow; Smith Mundt Fellow; MI State Univ, Distinguished Teaching Award; Distinguished Educ Award, Bowdoin; Hon LHD Bowdoin, 1975, Bloomfield, 1983, Montclair State College 1989. **MILITARY SERVICE:** SMAC 1st Lt.

DICKSON, ONIAS D., JR.
Minority rights advocate. **PERSONAL:** Born Jun 18, 1958, District of Columbia; children: Jennifer, O Timothy. **EDUCATION:** Hobart and William Smith, BA (w/Honors) 1981; Univ of Notre Dame, MA (w/Honors) 1983. **CAREER:** St Martins Parochial Sch, jr hs teacher 1983; American Greetings, biographical researcher 1984; Westat Rsch Corp, freelance investigator 1985; NAACP, natl rsch coord. **ORGANIZATIONS:** Staff writer Herald weekly newspaper Hobart & Wm Sm 1980,81; preime minister Third World Coalition Hobart & Wm Sm 1980; founder Hobart and William Smith Scuba Diving Assoc 1980-81; founder Black Grad Student Org Univ of Notre Dame 1981-83; chmn Govt Grad Student Org Univ of Notre Dame 1982-83; grad student govt rep Univ of Notre Dame 1983; mem Natl NAACP. **HONORS/ACHIEVEMENTS:** Teacher's Assistantship Hobart and Wm Smith 1980-81; Dorothy Danforth-Compton Grad Fellowship Awd 1981,82; Natl Conf of Black Political Scientist Grad Assistantship Awd 1982-83. **HOME ADDRESS:** 4805 Mt Hope Dr, Baltimore, MD 21215.

DICKSON, REGINALD D.
Business executive. **PERSONAL:** Born Apr 28, 1946, Oakland, TN; son of Louis Smith and Mildred Smith; married Illona White; children: Kia, Brandon, Rachel. **EDUCATION:** Univ of MO/Columbia, 1964-66; Harris Teachers Coll, Elementary Educ 1966-69; Washington Univ, Business Admin 1973-78; St Louis Univ, 1975-78. **CAREER:** St Louis Public Sch System, teacher 1969-73; INROADS, Inc, dir 1973-76, regional dir 1976-80, exec vice pres 1980-83, pres & ceo 1983-. **ORGANIZATIONS:** Co-chairman Salvation Army Tree of Lights St Louis 1977-78; area coord Boy Scouts of Amer 1978; mem Metro Develop Comm for Red Cross 1980; chairman exec comm Child Guidance Ctr 1982-83; bd of dirs First Amer Bank 1981-; bd of dirs Conf on Educ 1982-; mem Statewide Task Force on Educ 1984-; mem Urban League 1986-, Coro Foundation 1986-, Conference St Louis 1986-. **HONORS/ACHIEVEMENTS:** Participant Danforth Leadership Program St Louis 1978-79; Distinguished Serv Award INROADS Inc St Louis 1984; Distinguished Alumni Award Harris-Stowe State Coll 1985. **BUSINESS ADDRESS:** President/Chief Executive Ofcr, INROADS, Inc, 1221 Locust Ste 410, St Louis, MO 63103.

DIDDLEY, BO See MCDANIEL, ELIAS BATES

DIDLICK, WELLS S.
Retired educator. **PERSONAL:** Born Jun 16, 1925, Middletown, OH; son of Brack Didlick and Lena Didlick; married Beverly Chavis; children: four. **EDUCATION:** Miami Univ, BA 1952. **CAREER:** Campus Inter-Racial Club Miami Univ, pres 1950-51, pres student faculty council 1951-52; Woodlawn Planning Comm, comm 2 yrs; Woodlawn OH, councilman 8 yrs; Cincinnati Bd of Ed, retired teacher. **ORGANIZATIONS:** Mem NAACP; bd mem Zoning Bd of Appeals Village of Woodlawn 1979; appt Gov Task Force on Sch Discipline Cincinnati School Syst 1979; appt Indus Rel Comm Village of Woodlawn 1980, planning commission 1980. **MILITARY SERVICE:** USN seaman 1/c 1943-46.

DIGGS, ESTELLA B.
State legislator. **PERSONAL:** Born Apr 21, 1916, St Louis, MO; divorced; children: Edward A, Lawrence C, Joyce D. **EDUCATION:** NY Inst of Dietetics, grad; Pace Coll, attended; CCNY, attended; NY Univ, attended; Adult Continuing Ed Queens Coll, attended. **CAREER:** NY State, committee woman; real estate dealer; freelance writer for various publs; career counselor, catering bus, pres; State of NY, legislator, assemblywoman. **ORGANIZATIONS:** Neighborhood chmn Girl Scouts 15 yrs; org Rosary Soc St Augustines Roman Cath Church; chmn March of Dimes 15 yrs; founder & chmn Bronx Cit Comm; bdmem Comm Planning Bd #3, Forest House Day Care, Morrisania Pioneer Sr Citizens; charter mem Professional Women Bronx Chapt, Pride Inc; mem Natl Council of Negro Women, Catholic Interracial Council of the Bronx, Womans Grand Jury Assoc; org better housing comm; bd dir Halfway House for Women; exec mem Prison Rehab Bedford Hills Corr Inst. **HONORS/ACHIEVEMENTS:** Jackson Dem Club Hon Parade Marshall Afro-Amer Day Parade; numerous awds for fund raising BSA; Spec Salesmanship Awds Cushman Baker Co; Confidential Aidto Judge Donald J Sullivan Supreme Ct; Seagram Van Guard Soc Awd 1974; Ecumenical Awd Council of Churches New York City 1973. **BUSINESS ADDRESS:** Legislator, Assemblywoman, Legislative Office Bldg, Room 746, Bronx, NY 10456.

DIGGS, IRENE
Educator/anthropologist. **PERSONAL:** Born Apr 13, 1906, Monmouth, IL. **EDUCATION:** Monmouth Coll, Univ of MN, AB 1928; Atlanta Univ, MA 1933; Univ of Havana Cuba, Dr 1945. **CAREER:** Guest Professor, Bard Coll, Brooklyn Coll, Lincoln Univ, Univ of MD, Univ Coll, Univ of MD Sch of Nursing, Harvard Summer Sch of Arts & Scis & of Educ; Morgan State Univ, prof of anthropology & sociology 1947-76; Amer Anthropological Assn, visiting anthropologist 1964-72; Morgan State Univ, the library rsch & writing. **ORGANIZATIONS:** Fellow Amer Anthropological Assn; assoc in Current Anthropology; fellow Amer Assn for the Advancement of Sci; fellow Amer Assn of Physical Anthropologists; fellow Amer Assn of Applied Anthropology; fellow Evergreen House; mem NY Acad of Sci; mem Amer Assn of Univ Women; mem Intl African Inst; mem Natl Screening Comm Inst of Intl Education; mem Gov's Task Force on Corrections Probation & Parole; chwmn Comm on Correctional Decision Making Rsch & Training 1968; mem Professional Adv Comm of MD Assn for Mental Health; co-founder Phylon; founding mem Women's Comm Baltimore Museum of Art; sec Golden Jubilee Ball Comm Baltimore Museum of Art 1963-64; mem trustee comm Accessions & Deaccessions; mem women's comm Baltimore Museum of Art; mem prog comm Metro Baltimore Assn for Mntl Hlth 1967; mem vol adv comm Baltimore City Hosps 1968; mem The Women's Bd of the Peabody Inst; mem Amer Del of the Amer Anthrop Assn; mem Amer Del of the Amer Anthrop Assn 10 36th Congreso Internacional de Americanistas; mem Amer Del AAAS Tokyo 11th Pac Sci Congress. **HONORS/ACHIEVEMENTS:** Portrait of Irene Diggs in bronze & marble by Italian Sculptor Tina Dompe exhibited in Rome Florence Turin Paris; portraits (four) of Irene Diggs by Rivkah Rieger Jerusalem Israel; Roosevelt Fellow Inst for Intl Educ; Exchange Scholar resident in Montevideo Uruguay; Disting Alumni Awd 1964 Monmouth Coll; listed in Intl Directory of Anthropologists, Who Knows-and What, Amer Men of Sci-The Social and Behavioral Scis, Who's Who of Amer Women, Who's Who in Amer Educ, Leaders in Amer Scis, Natl Directory of Latin Americanists, Two Thousand Women of Achiev 1970; co-editor "Encyclopedia of the Negro" HW Wilson Co 1945;author of Black Chronology, From 4000 BC to the Abolition of the Slave Trade GK Hall Publ. **BUSINESS ADDRESS:** Professor of Anthropology, Morgan StateUniv, The Library Room 338, Baltimore, MD 21239.

DIGGS, ROY DALTON, JR.
Physician. **PERSONAL:** Born Mar 29, 1929, Detroit, MI; married Johnella Smith. **EDUCATION:** Wayne State Univ, 1946-48; Meharry Med School, MD 1953. **CAREER:** Hurley Hosp, intern 1953-54; KS City General Hospital #2, resd 1954-56; VA Hosp Buffalo NY, resd 1958-61; Lapeer St Home, surgeon 1961-63; Private practice, gen surgeon. **ORGANIZATIONS:** Diplomate Amer Bd of Surgery; fellow Amer Coll of Surgeons; mem Flint Acad of Surgery; fellow Amer Coll of Emergency Physicians; clinical assoc prof of surg MI State Coll of Human Med; mem AMA; life mem NAACP, Natl Urban League; bd dir Foss Ave Christian School; past bd mem Flint Urban League, Omega Psi Phi Frat. **HONORS/ACHIEVEMENTS:** Humanitarian Award Flint Human Relations Comm 1977. **MILITARY SERVICE:** USMC captain 1956-58. **BUSINESS ADDRESS:** General Surgeon, 4250 N Saginaw, Flint, MI 48505.

DIGGS, WILLIAM P.
Clergyman, educator. **PERSONAL:** Born Oct 19, 1926, Columbia, SC; married Clotilda J Daniels; children: Mary Lynne, William jr. **EDUCATION:** Friendship Jr Coll Rock Hill SC, 1943; Morehouse College, AB 1949; Atlanta U, MA 1951; Colgate-Rochester Div Sch, BD 1955; MDiv 1972. **CAREER:** Friendship Jr Coll, Rock Hill SC, instructor 1950-52; Friendship Jr Coll, instructor Sociology 1955-61; Galilee Baptist Church, York SC, pastor 1955-62; Second Baptist Church, Leroy NY, student pastor 1954-55; Benedict Coll, Columbia SC, asst prof Sociology 1964-74; Trinity Baptist Church, Florence SC & Morris Coll, Sumter SC, minister, asst prof Sociology. **ORGANIZATIONS:** Am Assn of Univ Prof; Alpha Kappa Delta Honorary Sociological Soc; pres Florence Br NAACP 1970-74; life mem NAACP; mem Community Relations Com Relations Florence, SC; chmn Community Action Agency Florence Co; mem Area Manpower Bd; mem Florence Co Bd of Health; mem trustee bd Friendship Jr Coll; mem trustee bd Morrisl Coll. **HONORS/ACHIEVEMENTS:** Valedictorian HS class; honorary DD Friendship Jr Coll 1973; Honorary LHD Morris Coll 1973; honored by Trinity Bapt Ch Florence; recognition of dedicated service ch & community 1969; honored Zeta Phi Beta Sorority Inc; Florence outstanding leadership civic econ comm involvement 1971; appeared in Personalities of the S 1972; citz of the yr Chi Iota Chap Omega Psi Phi Frat 1976; outst achvmt & serv Omega Psi Phi Frat 1976. **MILITARY SERVICE:** AUS t/5 1945-47. **BUSINESS ADDRESS:** 124 W Darlington St, Florence, SC 29501.

DIJI, AUGUSTINE EBUN
Psychiatrist. **PERSONAL:** Born Jun 27, 1932; son of James Sogo and Cecelia (Oyeloye) Sogo; married Celestine Gavor; children: Augustine, Angela. **EDUCATION:** Queen's Univ Belfast, BS 1958; Queen's Univ Belfast, MD 1961; Royal Victoria Hosp Belfast, intern 1962-63; Queen's Univ Belfast, resd 1963-67. **CAREER:** Ghana Med Sch, instr physiology 1967-69; Erie County Medical Center, special flwsp 1969-70; Erie Co Medical Ctr, 1971-; Buffalo General Hosp, staff 1971-; Part-time Pvt Practice, psychiatrist 1971-; State Univ NY at Buffalo, clinical asst prof 1975-; State Univ of NY at Buffalo, clinical asst prof 1975-; Geneva B Scruggs Comm Health Care Ctr Buffalo, consultant psychiatrist 1985-; Buffalo Psychiatric Ctr, psychiatrist II 1970-72, acting dept clin dir 1978-79, acting dir 1979, unit chief. **ORGANIZATIONS:** Mem British Med Assn 1963-76, Royal Coll of Physicians 1966-, Royal Coll of Psychiatrists 1966-, AMA 1970-, Amer Psychiat Assn 1970-, Natl Medical Assn 1971-, World Assn for Social Psychiatry 1976-; pres Medical & Dental Staff Buffalo Psychiat Center 1976-77; pres medical & dental staff Buffalo Psychiatric Center 1985-88. **HONORS/ACHIEVEMENTS:** Schlrsp Queen's Univ Belfast 1955-61; Milroy Medal Queen's Univ 1957; Hutchinson's Schlrsp Queen's Univ 1957-58; publ "Local Vasodilation Action of Carbon Dioxide on Blood Vessels of Hand" Queen's Univ 1959; "The Local Effects of Carbon Dioxide on Human Blood Vessels" Queen's Univ 1960; dissertation "A Survey of the Incidence of Mental Disorder in the Mentally Subnormal" 1965. **BUSINESS ADDRESS:** 1221 Kensington Ave, Buffalo, NY 14215.

DIKE, KENNETH ONWUKA
Educator. **PERSONAL:** Born Dec 17, 1917; married Ona; children: Chinwe, Chukwuemeka, Nneka, Ona, Obiora. **EDUCATION:** Leeds U, 1963; Columbia 1965; Princeton 1965; DLitt Boston U, 1962; Briminghon U, 1964; Ahmadu Bello U, 1965; Ibadan U, 1975;Univ Moscow, DSc 1963;Univ Durham, BA 1943;Univ Aberdeen, MA 1947; LLD 1961; London U, PhD 1950; LLD 1963; Northwestern U, LLD 1962. **CAREER:** Harvard Univ, prof History 1970-; Comm on African Studies, chmn 1972-, vice chancellor 1960-67, vice prin 1958-60; African Inst Social & Econ, sr rsch fellow 1952-54; Univ Coll Ibadan, lecturer History 1950-52. **ORGANIZATIONS:** Mem Ashby Comm Higher Educ in Nigeria 1957; chmn orgn com Interat Congress Africanists 1962; chmn Negerian Antiquited Commn 1954-67; flw Am Acad Arts & Sci; Royal Hist Soc; Kings Coll; Brit Hist Asn. **HONORS/ACHIEVEMENTS:** Author "Trade & Politics in the Niger Delta 1830-85" 1956; "A Hundred Years of British Rule in Nigeria" 1957; "The Origins of the Niger Mission" 1958. **BUSINESS ADDRESS:** HarvardUniv, Widener Lib, Cambridge, MA 02138.

DILDAY, JUDITH NELSON
Attorney. **PERSONAL:** Born Mar 28, 1943, Pittsburgh, PA; daughter of Frank Nelson and Alberta Nelson; married James S Dilday, Dec 1972; children: Ayana, Sekou, Zakia. **EDUCATION:** Univ of Pittsburgh, BA 1966; Millersville State Coll, Grad Credits in French; Boston Univ Sch of Law, JD 1974. **CAREER:** Pittsburgh Bd of Educ, French teacher 1966-70; Boston Model City, educ counselor 1970-71; Suffolk Co District Attorney, asst dist atty 1975; MBA Specialized Training/Advocacy Project, counsel 1977; Stern & Shapiro, attorney 1977-80; Office of the Solicitor US Dept of Interior, atty advisor 1980-81; Private Practice, counselor at law 1981-82; MA Bay Transportation Authority, asst general counsel 1982-. **ORGANIZATIONS:** Bd mem MA Black Lawyers Assn 1980-84; steering comm Lawyer's Comm Civil Rights 1980-; atty advisor US Dept of the Interior 1980-81; asst gen counsel MBTA 1982-; vice pres Psi Omega Chap Alpha Kappa Alpha 1984-86; bd of dirs Women's Bar Assn 1984-; delegate State Democratic Convention 1986; mem MA Bar Assn; treas Natl Bar Assn Region I; mem MA Black Women Attorneys, The League of Afro-Amer Women; first black pres elect, Women's Bar Assn; 1989; delegate State Democratic Convetion, 1987-89; sec of bd of dir, Daniel Marr Boy's Club. **HONORS/ACHIEVEMENTS:** First black female Assistant District Attorney Suffolk Co; Hearing Comm Mem Bd of Bar Overseers 1986-89; Adv Bd (gubernatorial apptmt) MA Comm Against Discrimination; Woman of the Year, Cambridge, YWCA, 1989. **HOME ADDRESS:** 9 Larchmont St, Boston, MA 02124.

BUSINESS ADDRESS: Asst General Counsel, MA Bay Transportation Auth, Transportation Bldg 10, Park Plaza, Boston, MA 02116.

DILDAY, WILLIAM HORACE, JR.
Business executive. **PERSONAL:** Born Sep 14, 1937, Boston, MA; son of William H Dilday and Alease Scott Dilday; married Maxine Carol Wiggins, Nov 06, 1966; children: Scott, Erika, Kenya. **EDUCATION:** Boston U, BS, BA 1960. **CAREER:** IBM, supv 1964-68; EG&G Roxbury, 1968-69; WHDH Inc, dir of personnel 1969-72; WLBT-TV, gen mgr; WJTV, exec vp, gen mgr. **ORGANIZATIONS:** Bd of dir NBC TV Affil Bd; bd of dir Nat Assn of Broadcasters; bd of dir Jackson-Hinds Comprehensive Health Center; bd of dir MS Mental Health Assn City of Jackson; past pres Jackson Urban League 1978-79; bd of dir Private Industry Council; bd of dir Congress Black Caucus' Comm Brain Trust; finance chairperson Boy Scouts of Amer, Seminole Dist, 1988-89; bd mem, Junior Achievement, 1988-89; bd mem, United Way, 1988-89. **HONORS/ACHIEVEMENTS:** 1st black gen mgr of a commercial TV station; 1st black elected to a TV network affiliate bd of dir; 1st black elected to Natl Assn of Broadcasters Bd of Dir. **MILITARY SERVICE:** USAR Sp4 1960-62. **BUSINESS ADDRESS:** Executive Vice Pres & General Mgr, WJTV, Box 8887, Jackson, MS 39204.

DILLARD, CECIL R.
Pharmacist. **PERSONAL:** Born Dec 28, 1906, Pontotoc, MS; married Alyce M Carter; children: Cecelia. **EDUCATION:** Okolona Jr Coll, instr coach 1933-43; Interlake Chem Corp, production foreman 1943-48; Thompson Med Supply, pharmacist 1949-50; Dillard Professional Pharmacy, owner paharmacist 1950-. **CAREER:** Dillard Professional Pharmacy, owner pharmacist 1950-; Thompson Med Supply, pharmacist 1949-50; Interlake Chem Corp, production foreman 1943-48; Okolona Jr Coll, instr coach 1933-43. **ORGANIZATIONS:** Mem past pres Chicago Pharmacist Assn 1962; mem past pres Nat Pharmaceutical Assn 1964; mem past pres IL Acad of Preceptors 1973; mem bd IL Pharmaceutical Assn; mem Am Pharmaceutical Assn; elected to membership Am Bd of Diplomates in Pharmacy; mem NAACP; Phi Beta Sigma. **HONORS/ACHIEVEMENTS:** Honored by Phi Beta Sigma & met C of C for work with bd of edn; founder chrmn bd CPA Scholarship Found. **BUSINESS ADDRESS:** Pharmacist, Dillard Prof Pharmacy, 67 E 43 St, Chicago, IL 60653.

DILLARD, JOEY L.
Retired educator. **PERSONAL:** Born Jun 26, 1924, Grand Saline, TX; son of M L Dillard and Thelma J Dillard; married Mary Lord; children: Kenneth Joseph. **EDUCATION:** So Methodist Univ, BA (Highest Hon) 1949, MA 1951; Univ of TX Austin, PhD 1956. **CAREER:** Quito Ecuador, fulbright lecturer 1958-59; Bujumbura Burundi, fulbright lecture 1967-68; Yaounde Cameroun, linguist with AID 1964-65; Inst of Caribbean Studies of Univ of PR Rio Piedras, rsch assoc 1961-75; Northwestern State Univ, assoc prof 1975-83; Northwestern State Univ Natchitoches LA, prof of english 1983-89. **ORGANIZATIONS:** Dir Urban Language Study Ctr for Applied Linguistics 1967; visiting lecturer Ferkauf Graduate School Yeshiva Univ 1968-73. **HONORS/ACHIEVEMENTS:** Alumnus Awd Phi Beta Kappa 1964; research grant Amer Philosophical Soc 1986-87; workshop grant Louisiana Endow for the Humanities 1987; Hendrix- Murphy Lecturer, Hendrix Coll, Conway AR, 1989. **MILITARY SERVICE:** USN yeoman 2nd cl 1942-45. **BUSINESS ADDRESS:** Northwestern State Univ, Dept of Language & Arts, Natchitoches, LA 71457.

DILLARD, JUNE WHITE
Attorney. **PERSONAL:** Born Sep 26, 1937, Youngstown, OH; divorced; children: Belinda Louise, Brian Martin, Stephen Jeffrey. **EDUCATION:** Univ of Chicago, AB 1958; Chicago Teachers Coll, MA 1964; Howard Univ Sch of Law, JD (Cum Laude) 1975. **CAREER:** Chicago Public Schools, teacher 1958-61; Office of Economic Oppor, field rep 1967-70; Securities & Exchange Commn, clerk 1975-76; Taylor & Overby, associate1978-80; JW Dilliar Esquire, attorney 1980-. **ORGANIZATIONS:** Treas Supt's Business & Industry Cncl; bd of dirs Prince George County Bar Assoc, Prince George County Fair Assoc, Prince George Arts Cncl, Voluntary Action Ctr Inc. **HONORS/ACHIEVEMENTS:** Top Ladies of Distinction; Cable TV Commnr; Service Awd Coalition on Black Affairs; Outstanding Contribution to Legal Comm Natl Bar Assoc; Disting Member Awd Natl Business League of Southern MD; Frederic Douglass Civic Achievement Awd MD Black Republican Cncl. **BUSINESS ADDRESS:** President, NBL of Southern MD Inc, 9200 Basil Court #209, Landover, MD 20785.

DILLARD, MARTIN GREGORY
Administrator physician. **PERSONAL:** Born Jul 07, 1935, Chicago, IL; son of Manny Martin Dillard and Evelyn Farmer Dillard; married Patricia Rachelle Cheek; children: Belinda, Brian, Stephen. **EDUCATION:** Univ of Chicago, BA 1956, BS 1957; Howard Univ Med Sch, MD 1965; Michael Reese Hosp Chicago, Internship/Red 1965-69, US Public Hlth Serv Fellowship 1969-70. **CAREER:** Howard Univ Hospital, assc prof of med 1974-; Howard Univ Coll of Med, asst prof of med 1970-74, admin, planning & exec com 1976-; asst dean/clinical affairs 1984-; Howard Univ Hosp, asst med dir; Howard Univ, prof of Med 1987-. **ORGANIZATIONS:** Asst chmn for educ Postgrad Dept of Med Howard Univ Hospital 1973-76; chief Hemodialysis Unit Howard Univ Hospital 1970-76; bd of dir Hlth Care Coalition Natl Capitol Area 1982-; govr advisory com Am Coll of Phys Wash DC 1980-. **HONORS/ACHIEVEMENTS:** Alpha Omega Alpha Honor Medical Society 1965; Natl Bd of Med Exmnr 1966; Am Bd of Intrl Med 1972; Am Bd of Intrnl Med Nephrology 1978. **MILITARY SERVICE:** AUS e-4. **BUSINESS ADDRESS:** Asst Medical Dir, HowardUniv Hosp, 2041 Georgia Ave N W, Washington, DC 20060.

DILLARD, MELVIN RUBIN
Insurance manager. **PERSONAL:** Born Feb 26, 1941, Kendleton, TX; son of Vellas Dillard and Ruby Lee Taylor Dillard; children: Melvin II, Melvia, Melvis. **EDUCATION:** Huston-Tillotson Coll, BA 1964; Prairie View A&M Univ, MA 1973; Life Underwriters Training Council, 1984. **CAREER:** Life Underwriter Training Council, moderator 1979-86; Natl Western Life, genl agent 1975-81, division mgr. **ORGANIZATIONS:** Mem TX Leaders Round Table 1970-87, Million Dollar Round Table 1977-87, Lone Star Leader 1983-87; natl committeeman, bd mem Houston Assoc Life Underwriters; natl pres Huston-Tillotson Alumni; bd mem TX Comm Corp, United Methodist Church Mission Bd and Pension Bd. **HONORS/ACHIEVEMENTS:** Articles published TX Assoc News Magazine 1979, Salesman Magazine 1980; Presidential Citation Natl Assoc for Equal Opportunity 1983; Doctorate Degree, Huston Tillotson College 1984. **BUSINESS ADDRESS:** Divisional Manager, Natl Western Life Insur, 2656 South Loop West, Ste 585, Houston, TX 77054.

DILLARD, SAMUEL DEWELL
Business executive. **PERSONAL:** Born Aug 12, 1913, Bolivar Co, MS; married Geneva E Lambert; children: Allen C, Edsel B, James E, Wanda F. **EDUCATION:** Tuskegee Inst, 1938; NC CentralUniv Sch of Bus Administrn;Univ of NC Sch of Bus Adminstrn. **CAREER:** Dillard's & Sons Inc & Dillard's Bar-B-Q House , pres 1945-. **ORGANIZATIONS:** Bd mem United Durham Inc; mem The Wildlife Assn; Doric Lodge #28; Durham C of C; Durham Bus & Professional Chain; NAACP; Nat Bus League. **HONORS/ACHIEVEMENTS:** Outstanding achievement in bus world Durham Bus & Professional Chain 1974. **BUSINESS ADDRESS:** President, Sam Dillard & Sons, 4910 Barbee Rd, Durham, NC 27713-1604.

DILLARD, THELMA DELORIS
Educator, elected official. **PERSONAL:** Born Jan 06, 1946, Macon, GA; divorced; children: Cartese. **EDUCATION:** Ft Valley State Coll, BS Business Ed 1966; GA Coll, Masters Special Educ 1975, Masters Bus Ed 1978. **CAREER:** Macon NAACP, sec 1965-; Ft Valley State Coll, teacher 1970; GA State NAACP, asst sec 1978, parliamentarian 1982; Area Planning & Devel Commiss, bd of dir 1980-; Democratic State Comm of GA, appointed mem 1983-; Central High, educator. **ORGANIZATIONS:** Mem Zeta Phi Beta 1965-; sec NAACP 1965-; mem GA Coalition of Black Women 1980-; chairperson Rules Comm Macon City Council 1980-; asst sec GA Assoc of Black Officials 1980-; vice chair 1983, chmn 1987-. Public Property Comm City of Macon. **HONORS/ACHIEVEMENTS:** 50 Most Influential Women NAACP Macon & Informer Mag 1981; Outstanding Woman of the Year NAACP 1983; 50 Most Influential Women GA Coalition of Black Women 1984; Several Comm Serv Awds from many orgs; mem Jack and Jill of America, 1988.

DILLIHAY, TANYA CLARKSON
Medical doctor psychiatry. **PERSONAL:** Born Aug 08, 1958, Columbia, SC; daughter of Zack C Clarkson and Rachel S Clarkson; married Otha R Dillihay Sr; children: Otha R II, Elliot Clarkson. **EDUCATION:** Spelman Coll, BS Biology 1979; Meharry Medical Coll, MD 1983. **CAREER:** Wm S Hall Psychiatric Inst, resident in training 1983-87. **ORGANIZATIONS:** Treas Afro-Amer Psychiatrists of SC 1986,87; chief resident of psycho-social rehabilitation WSHPI 1987; mem Ladson Pres Church Columbia SC. **HONORS/ACHIEVEMENTS:** "Suicide in Black Children" submitted to Psychiatric Forum 1987. **HOME ADDRESS:** 7812 Tradd St, Columbia, SC 29209.

DILLON, AUBREY
Educator. **PERSONAL:** Born Jan 25, 1938, Prentiss, MS. **EDUCATION:** Edinboro State Coll, BS 1961, MEd 1964. **CAREER:** Playground dir 1961-63; Erie, PA Sch Dist, teacher, guidance cnslr 1961-69; Erie Tech HS, tennis coach 1965-68; basic adult educ coord 1966-68; Edinboro State Coll, assoc dean of men 1969-. **ORGANIZATIONS:** PA State Educ Assn; dir Human Awareness Lab Edinboro 1965; YMCA asst boy's work dir 1964-66; supr student tchrs; chmn Black Studies Comm Edinboro 1969-72; PA Governor's Justice Commn mem; US SSS Registra; bd of Incorporators WQLN Educ TV; Erie ACT Comm Cntr Bd; Presque Isle Jaycees; Erie Human Rel Educ Com; Erie Urban Coalition; Kappa Delta Phi Natl Educ Frat; Alpha Phi Alpha Soc Frat; bd dir Meadville, PA Unity Cntr; NATO Comm Educ Com; Booker T Washington Comm Cntr Scoutmaster; Citiz Scholarship Found bd dir; Adelphi Univ Drug Inst particip; PA Black Conf on Higher Edn; musician; jazz dj Educ Radio WQLN Erie, PA; Inner-Frat Council Adv; Phi Delta Kappa Edinboro Univ of PA; Edinboro Univ Human Relations Comm; pres Phi Delta Kappa Beta Nu Chapter 1987-88. **HONORS/ACHIEVEMENTS:** Jaycee of the Month 1966; Runner-up Jaycee Man of the Yr 1967; Alpha Kappa Alpha Sor Sweetheart 1971. **BUSINESS ADDRESS:** Director of Retention Chairperson Dept of Academic Support Services, Edinboro State College, Edinboro, PA 16444.

DILLON, EVELYN HARDIN
Psychologist. **PERSONAL:** Born in Dallas, TX; widowed; children: Dianne Ridgley. **EDUCATION:** Fisk Univ, BA, MA 1958, Matriculation, Univ of Chicago, Denver Univ, Kansas Univ Univ of MO KC. **CAREER:** Bishop Coll Dallas, prof 1958-60; KC Public Schs, spl educ tchr 1960-65, sch psych 1965-69; KS Univ, rschr & evaluator 1970; KC MO Sch Dist, testcons & eval splst 1970-72; Tenured College Prof, assoc with Comm Colls of MO 1972-77; Private Practice, child psychology. **ORGANIZATIONS:** Organizer & dir Family Life Mental Health Ctr 1977-79; mem Amer Acad of Pol & Soc Sci; Natl Assn of Black Psy; Amer Assn of Univ Profs; Twin Citian Club; life mem NAACP; Fisk Univ Alumni Assn; mem Church of Christ.

DILLON, OWEN C.
Orthopedic surgeon. **PERSONAL:** Born Mar 31, 1934, Kingston, Jamaica;son of Noel Dillon and Clementina Dillon; married Pauline Y Titus; children: Denyse Sophia, Paul C. **EDUCATION:** Howard Univ, BS 1961; Howard Univ Med School, MD 1966. **CAREER:** Howard Univ Coll of Med, instr orthopaedics; several hosp staff appts & privileges, WA Hosp Ctr, WA VA Med Ctr, Providence Hosp; Private practice, orthopedic surgeon. **ORGANIZATIONS:** Mem DC Med Soc, Med Soc of DC Continuing Med Ed, Midico-Chirurgical Soc. **MILITARY SERVICE:** AUS maj 1969-71. **BUSINESS ADDRESS:** 3636 Georgia Ave NW, Ste 102, Washington, DC 20010-1699.

DILWORTH, MARY ELIZABETH
Educator. **PERSONAL:** Born Feb 07, 1950, New York, NY; daughter of Tom Dilworth and Martha L Williams Dilworth. **EDUCATION:** Howard Univ, BA 1972, MA 1974; Catholic Univ of America, EdD 1981. **CAREER:** Natl Advisory Council on Education Professions Development, education research analyst 1974-76; Natl Inst for Advanced Studies, sr program analyst 1978-82;Inst for the Study of Educational Policy, research assoc 1983-85; Howard Univ Hospital, coord education & training; ERIC Clearinghouse on Teacher Education, dir 1987-. **ORGANIZATIONS:** Mem Amer Educ Rsch Assoc; bd mem Natl Cnt on Rsch in Teacher Educ; mem Phi Delta Kappa; prog chair Natl Council of Negro Women; mem NAACP Task Force on Teacher Training and Assessment; mem Washington Urban League. **HONORS/ACHIEVEMENTS:** Frito Lay Black Woman Achiever Awd 1985; Mary McLeod Bethune Recognition Awd 1985; Howard Univ Urban Affairs Outstanding Community Serv Awd 1979, 85; author "Teachers' Totter, A Report on Teacher Certification Issues," 1984. **BUSINESS ADDRESS:** Director, Research and Information Services, American Assn of Colleges for Teacher Education, One Dupont Cir# 610, Washington, DC 20036.

DINES, GEORGE B.
Program management officer. **PERSONAL:** Born Feb 28, 1931, Washington, DC; married Dorothy L Baham; children: George Jr, Kedric, Christopher. **EDUCATION:** Howard Univ, Yale Univ, exchange student; Howard Univ, graduate studies; Harvard Univ, Graduate School of Business; various short courses, 1972-73. **CAREER:** Office for Sub-Saharan Africa/Office & for Intl Health OASH Dept of Health & Human Services, chief; Office Intl Health Office of the Asst Sec for Health DHEW, program mgmt officer; Div of Org Analysis & Devel Office of Org Devel Bureau of Comm Health Servs DHEW, dir; Div of Health Care Servs CHS DHEW, special asst to dir; Office of Program Evaluation Div of Health Care Servs DHEW, chief; Office of Health Affairs Office of Economic Opportunity, program coordinator; US Peace Corps Sierra Leone W Africa, assoc dir; US Peace Corps No Nigeria, dir; US Dept of Health & Human Servs, Assoc Admin, 1984-present. **ORGANIZATIONS:** mem, Amer Public Health Assn, Natl Assn for Comm Devel, Natl Assn of Neighborhood Health Centers, Amer Public Health Assn Intl Section; bd of dir, Boys & Girls Homes of Montgomery County MD; mem, AFRICARE, Blacks in Govt, Assn of Mil Surgeons of the US, Harvard Univ Business School Club of Washington, Natl Assn for Intl Health, Amer Assn for World Health, Natl Assn of Health Serv Execs, DHEW-OASH Exec Intern Program Review Comm, DHEW CHS Task Force on Data Systems for Neighborhood Health Centers, Health & Welfare Council, rep White House Conf on Food Nutrition & Health, CHS Healther Center Mgmt Work Group, CHS Task Force on Rural Health, NAACP, Pi Sigma Alpha, White House Task Force on Youth Opportunity, pres, bd of dirs, Woodlawn Cemetary Perpetual Care Assn; chmn, Comm Minority Relations Monitoring Comm; Commissioner, Housing Opportunities Commn, Montgomery County, 1986-present. **HONORS/ACHIEVEMENTS:** Published numerous health books & articles, 1961-77; recipient of Outstanding Student Award, Howard Univ Student Council 1953; Encyclopedia of Leading Negroes in the US, 1956; Special Citation Premier Govt of No Nigeria, 1962; Peace Corps Overseas Staff Dir, 1964; Certificate of Appreciation, Supt Kakuri Prison Kaduna, Nigeria, 1965; Honorary Citizen, State of AZ, 1975; Citation, St Phillips Coll, San Antonio, 1975; Admin Award for Excellence, DHHS, PHS, HRSA, 1987; Mem, US Saudi Arabia Joint Commission on Economic Cooperation Delegation, 1987, Advisory bd, Intl Conf on Emergency Health Care Devel, 1989. **BUSINESS ADDRESS:** Associate Administrator, Dept of Health and Human Services, HRSA, Rockville, MD 20857.

DINKINS, DAVID N.
Business executive. **PERSONAL:** Born Jul 10, 1927, Trenton, NJ; married Joyce Burrows; children: David Jr. **EDUCATION:** Howard Univ, BS 1950; Brooklyn Law School, Law 1956. **CAREER:** Dyett, Alexander, Dinkins, Patterson, Michael, Dinkins, Jones, attorney-partner 1956-1975; NY State Democratic Party, district leader 1967-; NY State Assembly, state assemblyman 1966; City of New York, pres bd of elections 1972-73, city clerk 1975-85, manhattan borough pres 1986-. **ORGANIZATIONS:** NY State Amer for Demacratic Action, bd of dir; Urban League, mem; 100 Black Men, bd of dir; March of Dimes, bd of dir; Assoc for a Better NY, bd of dir; Manhattan Women's Political Caucus, first male mem; NAACP, life mem; Black-Jewish Coalition, mem; Vera Institute of Justice, mem; Nova Anorca & NY State Urban Development Corp; Malcolm King Harlem Coll, bd of trustees; Marymount Manhattan Coll, pres advisory council; Assoc of the Bar of the Cityof NY, exec committee. **HONORS/ACHIEVEMENTS:** World Inst of Black Communications, pioneer of excellence 1986; NY Bd of Rabbie, righteous man awd 1986; Corrections Guardians Assoc, man of the year 1986; Federation of Negro Civil Service Org, distinguished serv awd 1986; Nat'l Assoc of Negro Bus and Prof Women's Clubs, man of the year awd. **BUSINESS ADDRESS:** Manhattan Borough President, City of New York, Municipal Building, Rm 2050, New York, NY 10007.

DISHER, SPENCER C., III
Investment banker. **PERSONAL:** Born Sep 30, 1957, Florence, SC; son of Spencer C Disher, Jr and Georgia G Montgomery. **EDUCATION:** Univ of WI-Madison, BSCE 1980; JL Kellogg GSM-Northwestern Univ, MBA 1986. **CAREER:** Mobil Oil Co, project engr 1980-84; Continental Bank, public fin assoc 1985-86; Citicorp Investment Bank, assoc 1986-87; BT Securities, NY, NY assoc 1987-88; Credit Natl, vice pres. **ORGANIZATIONS:** Mem Toastmasters 1984-86, Natl Black MBA Assoc 1985-; mem NAACP; founder Wisconsin Black Engrg Student Soc. **HONORS/ACHIEVEMENTS:** Chevron Fellowship 1985. **BUSINESS ADDRESS:** Vice Pres, Credit Natl, 520 Madison St, 34th Floor, New York, NY 10022.

DISMUKE, LEROY
Association executive. **PERSONAL:** Born Aug 18, 1937, Camden, AR; son of Roy Dismuke and Edna Mae Bragg; married Gladys M; children: Alan Roy. **EDUCATION:** Lane Coll, BA 1960; Eastern MI Univ, MA 1965; Eastern MI Univ, MA 1977. **CAREER:** Flint Educ Assn, 1966-69; United Teachers Flint Exec Bd, 1969-87. **ORGANIZATIONS:** Mem, Flint Educ Assn 1961-69; Professional Negotiation team mem, 1967-75; United Teachers Flint, 1969-87; MI Federation & Teachers, 1969-74; Amer Federation Teachers, 1969-74, represented many educ assn; GRIP; Black Caucus, Natl Educ Assn, 1970-74; representative to NEA 1971-87; chmn special educ dept, Flint Bd Educ; treasurer, NAACP 1983-87. **HONORS/ACHIEVEMENTS:** 10 & 15 yrs Serv Award, Big Brothers, 1967, 1972; Central Flint optimist award, 1985-86; Kappa Alpha Psi, 1985-86; Educator of the Year, Flint Council for Exceptional Children, 1989. **HOME ADDRESS:** 3834 Evergreen Parkway, Flint, MI 48503.

DIUGUID, LINCOLN I.
Science educator. **PERSONAL:** Born Feb 06, 1917, Lynchburg, VA; married Nancy Ruth Greenlee; children: David, Lewis, Renee, Vincent. **EDUCATION:** WV State Clge, BS Chem magna cum laude 1938; Cornell Univ, MS Chem 1939, PhD Chem 1945, Post Doctorate Organic Chem 1946-47. **CAREER:** AM&N Clge Pine Bluff AR, head chem dept 1939-43, prof chem 1939-43; Pine Bluff Arsenal, analytical chem 1942-43; Cornell Univ Ithaca NY, research asst organic chem 1945-46, research assc organic chem 1946-47; Du-Good Chem Lab St Louis MO, dir 1947-; AM&N Clge, consult in sci 1949-55; Stowe Tchrs Clge St Louis, prof of chem 1949-55; Harris Stowe State Clge, prof chem & chrmn phys sci dept 1955-82; Jewish Hosp, research assc 1959-61; Leukemia Guild of MO & IL, research dir 1961-63; Washington Univ St Louis, visiting prof of chem 1966-68; Harris Stowe State Coll, prof of Emieritus; Du-Good Chem Lab & Mfrs, president. **ORGANIZATIONS:** Sigma Xi; Amer Chem Soc; Natl Educ Assc; Phi Kappa Phi; Amer Assc of Univ Prof; MO State Tchrs Assc; Assc of Consult Chem & Chem Engrs Inc; Flw of Amer Inst of Chemists; Internat'l Leaders in Achievement 1987. **HONORS/ACHIEVEMENTS:** Publ "The Use of Amalgated Aluminum as a Catalyst in the Federal & Crafts Reaction, JACS 63", 1941, "LI Diuguid, Ref, In Organic Reactions Vol III 1946, Synthetic Organic Chemistry" 1953; "Benzothiazoles II Nuclear Chlorination in the Hertz Process" 1947, "Joint Symposium on Micro Chem & Pet Industry" 1949, "Synthesis of Long Straight Chain Dicarboxylic Acids via the Ketene Synthesis" 1952, "Methods for the Micro Detemination of Mixed Halogens & Amide Group" 1952, "Syntheiss of Large Carbon Ring Ketones" 1953, "Synthesis of Aliphatic Esters from the Reaction of Olefins & Formaldehyde Condensation" 1957, "Micro Determination of Sulfur in Organic Compounds by Perchloric Acid Digestion"; Man of Year Award Omega Psi Phi 1960; mem bd dir Leukemia Guild of MO & IL 1961-; vice pres Leukemia Guild of MO & IL 1963; Intl Bibliography Book of Hnrs 1984; Amer Men of Sicence; Chemical Who's Who, Who's Who in Amer Educ; Who's Who in the Midwest; Intl Biographies 1964 London; Communities Ldrs in the US; Who's Who in Finance & Industry Notable Amer 1978-79; recipient of Carver Civic Award 1979; recipient of Men of Achievement 1984; US Patenet 1985, Burning Efficiency Enhancement Method, Santonio Acid, Pgrizinoindole and Indole 85; 5,000 Outstanding Personalities of the World Distingushed Educators Award 1985. **BUSINESS ADDRESS:** President, Du-GOod Chem Labs & Mfrs, 1215 S Jefferson, St Louis, MO 63104.

DIXON, ARRINGTON LIGGINS
Business executive. **PERSONAL:** Born Dec 03, 1942, Washington, DC; children: Aimee, Drew. **EDUCATION:** Howard Univ, BA 1966; George Washington Univ, JD 1972. **CAREER:** Univ of Dist of Columbia, assoc prof 1967-74; Mgmt Info Systems, pres 1967-74; Council of the Dist of Columbia, chmn, mem 1975-82; The Brookings Inst, guest scholar 1983; Planning Rsch Corp, vice pres 1983-; Arrington Dixon & Assoc, inc, pres. **ORGANIZATIONS:** Bd mem Washington Ctr 1983-; advanced studies, adv comm The Brookings Inst 1983-; bd mem Greater SE Comm Hosp Found 1983-84, Anacostia Museum 1984-. **HONORS/ACHIEVEMENTS:** Congressional Appt US Air Force Acad 1963-65; Software, Statutes & Stare Decisis Howard Univ Law Jrnl 420 1967; Scholarship George Washington Univ Law 1969-72. **MILITARY SERVICE:** AUS Reserves maj 10 yrs. **HOME ADDRESS:** 1727 Massachusetts Ave NW, Washington, DC 20036.

DIXON, BENJAMIN
Educational administrator. **PERSONAL:** Born Apr 18, 1939, Hartford, CT; son of Cue Benjamin Dixon and Rose Carter Brown; married Carolyn Holmes; children: Kevin, Kyle, Kimberly. **EDUCATION:** Howard Univ, B Music Educ (Magna Cum Laude) 1962; Harvard Univ, MAT 1963; Univ of MA, EdD 1977. **CAREER:** Hartford CT Public Schools, teacher 1963-69; Westledge School West Simsburg CT, teacher/advisor 1969-71; Education/Instruction Inc Hartford CT, co-dir 1971-73; Bloomfield Public Schools CT, asst superintendent 1974-87; Capitol Region Educ Council Windsor CT, asst exec dir 1987-89; Capitol Region Educ Council, Windsor, CT, asst exec dir, 1987-89; The Travelers, Hartford, CT, dir Human Resouces, 1989. **ORGANIZATIONS:** Pres CT Assoc of Pupil Personnel Administrators 1983-84; mem bd of dir Univ MA Sch of Educ Alumni Assoc; sec bd of trustees Stowe School; mem CT State Adv Comm on Mastery Testing, Special Educ, Gifted/Talented; treas bd of dir Hartford Dist Catholic Family Services; governor's appointee CT Children's Trust Fund Council; mem bd of dir Educ/Instruction Inc; mem bd of trustees Metro AME Zion Church; mem, Amer Mgmt Assn, 1989; mem, Amer Soc of Personnel Admins, 1989. **HONORS/ACHIEVEMENTS:** Mem Pi Kappa Lambda Natl Honor Soc; Fellow in Exec Leadership Program Ford Foundation 1973-75; Educ Policy Fellow Inst for Educ Leadership 1983-84; Achievement/Service Award Bloomfield Concerned Black Parents for Quality Educ 1987; co-author "Stress and Burnout, A Primer for Special Educ & Special Services Personnel" 1981. **BUSINESS ADDRESS:** Dir, Human Resources, AMG-4NB, The Travelers, One Tower Squre, Hartford, CT 06183.

DIXON, BLANCHE V.
Educator. **PERSONAL:** Born in Philadelphia, PA; married Duvoille Dixon; children: Duvoille A, Carolyn, Douglas, Patricia, David, Charisse. **CAREER:** S Bronx Comm Progress Center, founder, bd mem 1964; Sch Dist 7, educ chmn 1965-70. **ORGANIZATIONS:** Mem Title I Com District 7; mem v chmn NY State Ruban & Com; mem former chmn Title Iii Com funded 3 million dollar South Bronx Supplementary educ cntr; past pres Parents Assn PS 29; JHS 38; IS145; first school bd re IS 151; founder bd mem Lucille Murray Child Devel Cntr NAACP; Urban League; mem Legislative Adv Council Assembleman Jose Serrano; founded United Black Educators. **HONORS/ACHIEVEMENTS:** Recipient 10 Plaques Outstanding Comm Service for edn, humanitarinism, headership, civic participation; cited Urban League; honored testimonial dinner outstanding leadership comm relations; recipient special citation parent leadership JHS 145; recipient S Bronx Comm Corp Founder Plaque.

DIXON, BRENDA JOYCE
Manager. **PERSONAL:** Born Jul 21, 1954, Houston, TX. **EDUCATION:** Univ of Houston, BS 1976. **CAREER:** K-Mart Apparel, asst apparel mgr 1977-78; K-Mart Apparel Corp, apparel mgr 1978-. **ORGANIZATIONS:** Advisor to the distrib educ program MB Smiley High School 1982-; speaker for annual employer/employee banquet for the Distributive Educ Program Smiley HS 1985; fashion show coord K-Mart Store #4080 1986; store reporter for K-Mart Store #4080 1986; mem Sigma Gamma Rho Sor; Reach to Recovery, volunteer visitor, American Cancer Society 1988, 1989. **BUSINESS ADDRESS:** Apparel Manager, K-Mart Apparel Corporation, 9929 Homestead Rd, Houston, TX 77016.

DIXON, ERNEST THOMAS, JR.
Clergyman. **PERSONAL:** Born Oct 13, 1922, San Antonio, TX; married Ernestin Clark; children: Sherryl D Clark, Ernest R, Muriel Jean. **EDUCATION:** Samuel Huston Coll Austin TX, BA (magna cum laude) 1943; Drew Theol Sem Madison NJ, STM 1945; Huston-Tillotson Coll Austin TX, DD 1962; Southwestern Coll Winfield KS, LHD 1973; BakerUniv Baldwin KS, LLD 1973; Westmar Coll Le Mars IA, LittD 1978; KS Wesleyan Salina, LHD 1980. **CAREER:** KS area United Meth Ch, bishop 1972-; Program Council UM Ch & Dayton OH, asst gen sec 1969-72; Philander Smith Coll Little Rock AR, pres 1965-69; Div of Local Ch Bd of Educ Meth Ch Nashville, staff mem 1952-64; W TX Conf Bd of Edn, exec sec 1951-52; Tuskegee Inst AL, dir rel extension serv 1945-51; Wallace Chapel AME Zion Ch Summit NJ & E Calvary Meth Ch Harlem NY, pastor & asst pastor 1943-45. **ORGANIZATIONS:** Bd of trustee KS Wesleyan Salina; BakerUniv Baldwin KS; Southwestern Coll Winfield KS; St Paul Sch of Theology KS City MO; So MethUniv Dallas; UnitedTheol Sem Dayton OH; Wesley Med Center Wichita KS; Lydia Patterson Inst El Paso TX; Mt Sequoyah Assembly Fayetteville AR; Gammon Theol Sem Atlanta GA; mem Alpha Phi Alpha Frat Inc. **BUSINESS ADDRESS:** 4201 W 15th, Topeka, KS 66604.

DIXON, GEORGE
Business executive. **PERSONAL:** Born Oct 19, 1933, New Haven, CT; married Carol Ina

Grant; children: Kirk Van, Eric George. **EDUCATION:** Arnold Coll, 1953; Univ of Bridgeport, BA 1959. **CAREER:** Green Bay Packers NFL, professional football player 1959; Montreal Alouettes & CFL, professional football player 1960-65; S Coorsh & Sons Ltd, advertising mgr 1962-64; Grant-Mann Litho, sales mgr 1964-67; Station CFCF TV, TV sportscaster 1968-70; Loyola Coll, head football coach 1969-74; Radio Station CJAD, football broadcaster 1975-; Montreal Express, football writer 1975-; George Dixon Promotions Ltd, pres 1967-. **ORGANIZATIONS:** Mem Football Reporters of Canada 1975-; consult Schenley Football Awards 1975-; consult & dir Cote De Neiges Black Comm Proj 1975-77; chmn Dr Charles H EsteBursary Comm, Union United Church 90th Anniv Comm, United Benevolent Soc; past pres Montreal Alouette Alumni Assn; mem Football Reporters of Canada; hon life mem Kiwanis Club of Montreal. **HONORS/ACHIEVEMENTS:** Natl Sportsmen Award, CFL, 1961-63; Jeff Russel Trophy, CFL, 1962; MVP, All Pro-League, 1962-63; Canadian Football Hall of Fame, CFL, 1974. **MILITARY SERVICE:** AUS pfc 1954-56. **BUSINESS ADDRESS:** Pres, George Dixon Promotions Ltd, 625 Pres Kennedy Blvd, Montreal, Quebec, Canada H3A 1K2.

DIXON, HANFORD
Professional athlete. **PERSONAL:** Born Dec 25, 1958, Mobile, AL. **EDUCATION:** Attended, Southern MS. **CAREER:** Cleveland Browns, cornerback 1981-. **ORGANIZATIONS:** Active in numerous local charitable organizations. **HONORS/ACHIEVEMENTS:** Regarded as best pure cornerback in draft by a number of scouting serv after outstanding sr season at Southern MS; All America by Sporting News and All-SouthIndependent selection 1981; NFL Defensive Player of Week Hon; 1st team All Rookie honors by Football Digest; mem 1987 NFL Pro Bowl team. **BUSINESS ADDRESS:** Cleveland Browns, Cleveland Stadium, Cleveland, OH 44114.

DIXON, HORTENSE
Administrator. **PERSONAL:** Born Jan 29, 1926, Houston, TX; married Thomas Jr. **EDUCATION:** TX Tech U, EdD 1970;Univ of MN, MS 1949f Prairie View State Coll, BS 1946. **CAREER:** City of Houston, exec assist 1975-; TX Southern Univ, dir, prof, and instruct 1952-74; Univ of WV, guest prof 1967; MI State Univ, guest consultant and lecturer 1966; Austin Public Schools, home couns 1951-52; Home Mang Resid Bishop Coll, dir 1949-51. **ORGANIZATIONS:** Bd Mem Cooperat Assess of Experiential Learning Natl Soc for Field Exper Edn; mem Amer Soc for Pub Admin; Amer Soc of Planning Offcls; Amer Home Econ Assoc; Natl Soc for Prog Instruct; Natl Assn of Home Econ Tchr Edustr; Amer Voc Asn; mem of panel of consult Dev Curriculum guides for Voc Home Econ 1953-56; natl advis bd FHA 1965-67; com named by Coll Pres in TX to Assist TX Coll in Plans for Redev 1966f Reg VI Coordin Confer of Minor Pub Adminst 1975; Alpha Kappa Alpha Sor; bd mem New Beginnings Inc; bd mem Houston Counc on Human Relat; United Fund; TX Assn of Dev Coll; Mayor's Telephone Reassur Prog; Houston Metro Minist; consult Commun-Based Hypertens Control Prgm Riverside Gen Hosp; advis counc KYOK Radio Stat; chrpsn Houston Urban Coalit; co-convener Houston Operation Big Vote 1976f bd mem San Jacinto Girl Scts 1975-76; Wisconsin Exch Prog Fellow 1965. **HONORS/ACHIEVEMENTS:** Instit Res Grant Carnegie Found 1964; several publ. **BUSINESS ADDRESS:** Mayor's Office City of Houston, PO Box 1562, Houston, TX 77001.

DIXON, IRMA MUSE
State representative. **PERSONAL:** Born Jul 18, 1952, New Orleans, LA; daughter of Joseph Muse Sr and Irma White Muse; married Reuben Dixon, Jun 26, 1976. **EDUCATION:** Univ of Houston, Houston TX, Certificate, 1974; Southern Univ of New Orleans, New Orleans LA, BA, 1976; Tulane Univ, New Orleans, MSW, 1979. **CAREER:** Dept of Devel, Kenner LA, dir, 1980; Office of Employment and Training, New Orleans LA, bureau chief, 1981-82; Dept of Recreation, New Orleans LA, dir, 1982-86; Dept of Culture, Recreation and Tourism, Baton Rouge LA, undersecretary, 1984-86; Dept of Property Mgmt, New Orleans LA, dir, 1987-88; House of Representatives, New Orleans LA, state representative, 1988-. **ORGANIZATIONS:** Mem, Natl Assn of Social Workers, 1980-, Smithsonian Assoc, 1984-, New Orleans Museum of Arts, 1984-, Amer Soc of Public Admin, 1984, Women Lobbying Network; consultant, Audubon Inst Aquarium (Bond Election), 1985, Orleans Parish School Board, New Orleans Public Schools (Bond Issue Election), 1986; mem, Urban League of Greater New Orleans, 1986-, Harvard Club of Louisiana, 1986-, Natl Order of Women Legislators, 1988. **HONORS/ACHIEVEMENTS:** Alumnas of the Year, Walter L Cohen Sr High School, 1984; Legislator of the Year Award, Alliance for Good Govt, 1988; Outstanding Serv Award, City of New Orleans-Mayor's Office, 1988; Leadership Award, Earhart-Tulane Corridor Assn Inc, 1989; Legislative Women's Award, Louisiana Conf of Elected Women, 1989. **BUSINESS ADDRESS:** State Representative, House of Representatives, 650 S Pierce St, 2nd Floor, New Orleans, LA 70119.

DIXON, ISAIAH, JR.
Business executive. **PERSONAL:** Born Dec 23, 1922, Baltimore; married Miriam Millard. **EDUCATION:** Howard U. **CAREER:** Gen Assembly MD, ins broker realtor delegate. **ORGANIZATIONS:** Mem Peoples Dem Orgn; NAACP; Kappa Alpha Psi Frat; del Dem Mini-Conv KC MO 1974; del Dem Natl Conv New York City 1976. **HONORS/ACHIEVEMENTS:** Cert of honor NAACP 1970; cert of merit Calverton Jr High Sch 1972; cert of Training & in mgmt Joint Ctr for Polit Studies. **MILITARY SERVICE:** AUS pfc.

DIXON, IVAN N.
Producer, director. **PERSONAL:** Born Apr 06, 1931, Harlem, NY; married Berlie Ray; children: Ivan, IV, N'Gai, Kimara, Nomathande. **EDUCATION:** NC Central U, BA 1954f Western Reserve U, grad studies; Karamu House; Am Theater Wing. **CAREER:** Duff Anderson "Nothing But a Man" (Movie), actor; Olly Winter "The Final War of Olly Winter" (CBS Playhouse); Kinchloe "Hogan's Heroes"; Asagai "Raisin In The Sun" Broadway & Movie; Bill Cosby Show, Room 222, Apple's Way, The Waltons and many others, director. **ORGANIZATIONS:** Mem Academy of Motion Picturs Arts & Sci; Director's Guild of Am; Screen Actor's Guild. **HONORS/ACHIEVEMENTS:** TV emmy nomination 1967; best black actor First World Black Arts Festival Dakar Africa 1966f best Dir image Award NAACP 1972; best prod Image Award NAACP 1974. **BUSINESS ADDRESS:** c/o Bokari Prod Inc, 3432 N Marengo Ave, Altadena, CA 91001.

DIXON, J. MELVIN
Engineer. **PERSONAL:** Born Mar 01, 1939, Orangeburg, SC; married Elma Ruth Sullivan; children: Derrick Lamont, Mark Christopher; Usna. **EDUCATION:** School of Visual Arts, BFA 1961; Natl Honor Soc; Derrick Dixon Graduated, USNA, 1986, Jet pilot. **CAREER:** Richard Avendon Studio NYC, asst mgr 1967-68; Hiro Studio, NYC, mgr 1968-69; Mel Dixon Studio, NYC, pres 1969-84; JMD Photo Arts, ownr; Database Originals, partner 1984-; Mel Dixon/Image Solutions, Inc, president 1986-; Human Factors Engineer, IBM, 1988. **ORGANIZATIONS:** Mem Amer Soc Magazine Photo 1971-85. **HONORS/ACHIEVEMENTS:** Clio Award Advertising Art Council 1978; Ceba Awards Advertising Council Black Advertising 1976-84; 6 "Photography for Everybody," TV series, 1988. **MILITARY SERVICE:** AUS pfc Inf S-2 Sec; Honorable Discharge Good Conduct 1962-64. **BUSINESS ADDRESS:** President, Image Solutions Inc, 1 Calam Ave, Ossining, NY 10562.

DIXON, JIMMY
Elected official. **PERSONAL:** Born Dec 09, 1943, Devereux, GA; divorced; children: Glenda, Thaddeus, Taranda. **EDUCATION:** GA Military, 1972, 1974, 1976; Univ of GA, 1975-78; GA Coll, 1976-81. **CAREER:** Central State Hospital, supr 1964-74; Sparta Parks & Recreation, dir 1975-79; Rheem Air Condition Div, storekeeper 1979-; Hancock Co Board of Ed, chmn 1978-. **ORGANIZATIONS:** Superintendent Jones Chapel AME Sunday School 1971-; mem Jones Chapel AME Steward Bd 1974-, GA School Bd Assoc 1975-, Stolkin Temple #22 1976-, Lebar Consistory #28 1976; GSBA Positions & Resolutions Comm 1979-; committee mem Democratic Party of GA 1982-85. **HONORS/ACHIEVEMENTS:** Appreciation Plaque Blackstone Shrine Club 1977. **HOME ADDRESS:** Rte 4 Box 175, Sparta, GA 31087.

DIXON, JOHN FREDERICK
Marketing manager. **PERSONAL:** Born Feb 19, 1949, Boston, MA. **EDUCATION:** Howard U, BA 1971; ColumbiaUniv Grad Bus Sch, MBA 1973; ColumbiaUniv Tchr's Coll, PhD Work 1980-. **CAREER:** Essence Communications Inc, marketing & research serv dir 1978-; Black Sports Magazine, marketing dir 1976-78; Standrad Brands Inc, asst prod mgr 1974-76; Xerox Corp, sales representative 1973-74; US Dept of Agriculture, agriculture marketing specialist 1971. **ORGANIZATIONS:** Consult Africa Mag 1976; consult Horn of Africa Mag 1977-78; mem Am Marketing Assn 1978-; mem Advertising Research Found 1978-; mem Media Research Dirs Assn 1979-; world mem Intl House 1971-; mem African-Am Inst 1973-; mem Alliance Francaise-French Inst 1975-78; mem NAACP 1979-. **HONORS/ACHIEVEMENTS:** Recipient educ fellowship Council on Grad Mgmt ColumbiaUniv 1971-73; co-founder Red-T Productions 1975-; co-inventor "Claim to Fame" Black History Game 1977; pub "Pony Goes After Young Blacks with 'follow the Leader' Tack" 1977; creator "Battle of New Orleans" 64-page fight Prog (Muhammad Ali vs Leon Spinks) 1978; established In-House Essential Media Ad Agency Essence Mag 1979-; distinguished serv award Harlem Teams for Self-Help 1979. **BUSINESS ADDRESS:** Essence Communications Inc, 1500 Broadway, New York, NY 10036.

DIXON, JOHN M.
Business executive. **PERSONAL:** Born Jan 25, 1938, Chicago, IL; divorced; children: Kwane Dubois. **EDUCATION:** Univ MT, BS 1959; New England Sch Law, JD 1966; Boston U, MBA 1976. **CAREER:** Sonesta NY, regional sales mgr 1968-70; Sheraton Mtr Inns, dir promotion 1970-73; Hyatt Regency O'Hare, exec asst mgr 1973; Burlingame CA, gen mgr 1973; Hyatt Regency, resident mgr 1974-; Hyatt Regency Cambridge, gen mgr 1975-. **MILITARY SERVICE:** AUS spec 1962-64. **BUSINESS ADDRESS:** 575 Memorial Dr, Cambridge, MA 02139.

DIXON, JULIAN C.
Legislator. **PERSONAL:** Born Aug 08, 1934, Washington, DC; married Betty Lee; children: Carey Gordon. **EDUCATION:** CA State Univ at LA, BS Polit Sci; Southwestern Univ, LLB 1967. **CAREER:** 10th Dist CA State Assembly, democratic assemblyman 1972-78; Democratic Rep 28th Dist of CA, congressman 1978-. **ORGANIZATIONS:** Chmn Congressional Black Caucus 1983-84; chmn 1984 Democratic Natl Convention Rules Comm; chmn House Comm on Standards of Official Conduct; house rep West Point Board of Supervisors; mem Appropriations Subcomm on Foreign Opers; principle author Congressional Black Caucus Budget Alternative; orig cosponsor Equal Rights Amendment; pres Congressional Black Caucus Foundation; chmn Appropriations Subcomm on the District of Columbia; chmn CA Assembly Democratic Caucus. **HONORS/ACHIEVEMENTS:** First Black mem in the history of Congress to chair an Appropriations Subcommittee; authored resolutions passed by the House that called for the awding of the Presidential Medal of Freedom to Dr Benjamin Mays and the declaration of Sept 1983 as "Sickle Cell Anemia Awareness Month". **BUSINESS ADDRESS:** Congressman, US House of Representatives, 2400 Rayburn HOB, Washington, DC 20515.

DIXON, LEON MARTIN
Medical director. **PERSONAL:** Born Nov 12, 1927, Brooklyn, NY; son of Leon M Dixon and Helen Moody Dixon; married Alfonso Baxter; children: Deborah, Carolyn Knight, Cynthia, Suzanne, Leon II. **EDUCATION:** Howard Univ, BS 1949, MD 1953. **CAREER:** Med/Cardiologa Colorad Un Sch of Med, instr 1963-65; US Walson Army Hosp, hosp cmdr 1973-77; Reynolds Metals Co, dir macmillian med ctr. **ORGANIZATIONS:** Cnsltn Disaster Plng Reynolds Metal 1977-, Cardiology Med First Army Area 1965-69; chrmn Pblc Hlth Prvntv Med Richmond Acad of Med 1980-81; mem Chesterfield Cnty Drug Abuse Advsr Com 1979-80. **HONORS/ACHIEVEMENTS:** Phys for Astronant Pgm Gemini Mercury NASA 1965-1969; articles pblchd Physiology of Heart Meningitis, Congenital Heart Disease, Chemotherapty of Tumors. **MILITARY SERVICE:** AUS col; Legion of Merit Two Oak Leaf Clusters 1969, 71, 77. **BUSINESS ADDRESS:** Dir MacMillan Med Ctr, Reynolds Metals Co, 1951 Reymet Rd, Richmond, VA 23234.

DIXON, LOUIS TENNYSON
Engineering manager. **PERSONAL:** Born Dec 13, 1941; son of Eitel V Dixon and Enid L Dixon; married Fvalarie Clunes (deceased); children: Michael. **EDUCATION:** Howard Univ, BS 1968; Johns Hopkins Univ, PhD 1973. **CAREER:** Ford Motor Co, principal rsch scientist/sr rsch scientist 1973-76, mgr chemistry dept 1976-78, principal staff engineer 1978-86, engineering associate, 1986-. **ORGANIZATIONS:** Mem Amer Chem Soc; Soc of Automotive Engrs; Soc of Manufacturing Engrs; vice pres Intl Club 1966-67; chmn People-To-People 1967-68; pres Phi Lambda Upsilon 1972-73. **HONORS/ACHIEVEMENTS:** Publications, "Infrared Studies of Isotope Effects for Hydrogen Absorption on Zinc Oxide" Journal of Amer Chem Soc 1972; "The Nature of Molecular Hydrogen Absorbed on Zinc Oxide" Journal of Physical Chem 1973; "Infrared Active Species of Hydrogen Absorbed by Alumina-Supported Platium" Journal of Catalysis 1975; "Hydrogen Absorption by Alumina-

Supported Supported Platinum" Journal of Catalysis 1975; "Foaming & Air Entrainment in Automatic Transmission Fluids" Soc of Auto Engr 1976; "Fuel Economy - Contributor of the Rear Axle Lubricant" Soc Auto Engr 1977. **BUSINESS ADDRESS:** Staff Materials Engrg Assoc, Ford Motor Company, Ste 200 Parklane Towers East, One Parklane Blvd, Dearborn, MI 48126.

DIXON, MELVIN W.
Educator. **PERSONAL:** Born May 29, 1950, Stamford, CT. **EDUCATION:** Wesleyan U, BA 1971; Brown U, MA 1973; Brown U, PhD 1975. **CAREER:** Queens Coll CUNY, assoc prof 1980-; Williams Coll, asst prof 1976-80; Fordham Univ, asst prof 1975-76. **ORGANIZATIONS:** Mem Poets & Writers Inc 1975-; mem Am Studies Assn 1975-; mem Modern Language Assn 1976-; contrib & editor CALLALOO Lit Journ 1978-; contrib editor ENCORE Mag 1980-. **HONORS/ACHIEVEMENTS:** Andr Istel Scholarship Alliance Franaise de New York 1973; French Govt Fellowship French Govt 1973; Richard Wright Award BLACK WORLD Mag 1974; Artist Fellowship in Poetry MA Arts & Humanities 1979. **BUSINESS ADDRESS:** Queens Coll, SUNY, Flushing, NY.

DIXON, RICH CALVIN
Professional athlete. **PERSONAL:** Born Aug 06, 1959, Roswell, NM. **EDUCATION:** California. **CAREER:** Oakland Invaders, leftback 1984-.

DIXON, RICHARD CLAY
Mayor. **CAREER:** Mayor of Dayton, OH. **BUSINESS ADDRESS:** PO Box 22, Dayton, OH 45401. *

DIXON, RICHARD NATHANIEL
Broker. **PERSONAL:** Born Apr 17, 1938, Westminster, MD; married Grayson Lee; children: Timothy A, Richard N. **EDUCATION:** Morgan State Coll, BS 1960; Morgan State Coll, MBA 1975. **CAREER:** Provident Hosp, hosp adm 1968-69; Morgan State U, asst prof sch of bus 1976-; Merrill Lynch, delegate/stock broker, asst vice pres. **ORGANIZATIONS:** Mem Bd of Educ 1970-78; pres former stdnt Robert M Sch 1970; sec MD Assn Bd of Educ 1973-74; chair of clinicl finding new ways to finance educ Natl Schl Boards Conv 1974; mem Morgan State Univ Found 1975-; pres and first black Cnty Sch Bd 1975-76; trustee Middle State Assoc of Colls & Schools; mem Budget & Audit Comm, House of Delegates, Maryland House of Pensions. **HONORS/ACHIEVEMENTS:** First black Bd of Educ; 1st blk pres of County Sch Bd Maryland; Future Black Leader in Baltimore, Baltimore Sunpapers 1979; selected top 5 of 50 new delegates 1984; selected to be among top 25 members, House of Delegates; Honorary Doctor of Laws, Western Maryland Coll. **MILITARY SERVICE:** AUS capt med serv corps 1960-68. **BUSINESS ADDRESS:** Merrill Lynch, 100 South Charles St, Baltimore, MD 21201.

DIXON, ROSCOE
State official. **PERSONAL:** Born Sep 20, 1949, Gilmore, AR; son of Roscoe Dixon, Sr; married Gloria Dobbins. **EDUCATION:** Savannah State Coll, 1971; Univ of Guan Juato, Spanish 1974; Memphis State Univ, BA Political Science 1975. **CAREER:** Congressman Harold Ford, south office dir 1975; insurance executive 1977-81; Black Merchants Assn, exec dir 1981-; State of TN, state representative. **ORGANIZATIONS:** Capt commander service battery 3-115 field artillery TN Army Natl Guard 1973-; bd mem Mid-South Regional Blood Ctr 1983-85; bd mem Dogwood Village; bd mem Memphis Health Center 1984-85; bd mem Operation PUSH Memphis 1975-. **MILITARY SERVICE:** AUS spec 5 2 yrs; Good Conduct Medal; Army Commendation. **HOME ADDRESS:** 3592 Huckleberry, Memphis, TN 38116. **BUSINESS ADDRESS:** State Representative, State of TN, #17 Legislative Plaza, Nashville, TN 37219.

DIXON, RUTH F.
Educator. **PERSONAL:** Born Sep 22, 1931, Camden, NJ; married George Dixon; children: Cheryl Yvette, Brian Duane. **EDUCATION:** BA 1953, MA 1965, EdD 1977. **CAREER:** Camden City Schools, elementary & secondary teacher 14 yrs, admin 3 yrs; NJ State Dept of Educ, supvr 2 yrs; Rutgers Univ, assoc prof of educ. **ORGANIZATIONS:** Ed consult State Coll 1965-71; mem State Assoc of Adult Ed 1965-; exec bd Black Peoples Unity Movement 1973-; exec bd of ed Oppty Fund Prog 1971-; mayors adv council 1974-; bd of ed Lay Comm 1972-; mem Kappa Delta Pi 1976; bd of trustees Camden Cty Coll 1984; mem council Camden Cty Private Indust 1983, Natl Assoc of Notaries 1984; bd of dir Soc of Ed & Scholars 1984, NJ Assoc of Black Ed 1978-, Our Lady of Lourdes Comm Adv Comm 1984, BPUM Child Devel Ctrs Adv Comm 1983, The World's Who's Who of Women 1981, Dir of Disting Amer in Ed & Comm Serv 1980. **HONORS/ACHIEVEMENTS:** BPUM-EDC Comm Awd 1973; Kappa Delta Pi; BPUM Spec Awd Outstanding Ed 1976; Soc for Ed & Schol Phi Delta Kappa Natl Honor Soc 1975; Pi Lambda Theta Natl Honor Soc 1975. **BUSINESS ADDRESS:** Associate Professor of Educ, RutgersUniv, 311 N Fifth St, Camden, NJ 08102.

DIXON, SHARON PRATT
Political activist. **PERSONAL:** Born Jan 30, 1944, Washington, DC; daughter of Carlisle E Pratt and Mildred Petticord; divorced; children: Aimee, Drew. **EDUCATION:** Howard Univ Falk Fellow, BA Political Science 1961-65; Harvard Univ Coop Scholarship, 1964; Howard Univ Law School, JD 1965-68. **CAREER:** Joint Center for Political Studies, house counsel 1970-71; Pratt & Queen PC, assoc 1971-76; Antioch School of Law, attny, prof 1972-76; Potomac Electric Power Co, assoc general counsel 1976-79, vice pres consumer affairs 1979-83, vice pres public policy 1983-. **ORGANIZATIONS:** Mem Amer Bar Assoc, Unified Bar of the DC, DC Womens Bar Assn; natl committeewoman DC Dem State Comm; vice chair DC Law Revision Comm 1977-83; treas Democratic Natl Comm. **HONORS/ACHIEVEMENTS:** Falk Fellow Outstanding Student Political Science Howard Univ 1962-65; Coop Scholarship Harvard Univ 1964; "Software Statues & Stare Decisis" Howard Univ Law Journal Vol 13 1967; Natl Political Science Hon Soc, Pi Sigma Alpha Howard Univ. **BUSINESS ADDRESS:** Dixon For Mayor, 1375 K Street, NW, 5th Floor, Washington, DC 20005.

DIXON, TOM L.
Educator. **PERSONAL:** Born Jan 29, 1932, Shreveport, LA; married Sarah Hunter; children: Abigail, Cleon. **EDUCATION:** Gramblins State U, BS 1959; Bradley U, MS 1968; Prairie View A&MUniv Northwestern State University, Advance Study. **CAREER:** Walnut Hill High School, teacher 1959; JS Clark Jr High, teacher 1960-61; Li'near High School; teacher 1961-71; Green Oaks High School, teacher 14 yrs; Caddo Parish School Bd, supr Vocational Educ. **ORGANIZATIONS:** Caddo Educ Assn; LA Educ Assn; Natl Educ Assn; chmn LA Indsl Arts Conf 1976; chmn Banquet LTAA 1975; Indsl Arts Curriculum Plng Com; Am Indsl Arts Assn; 1st blk pres North Shreveport Kiwanis Club 1973-74; pres Phi Beta Sigma Frat; bd dir YMCA. **HONORS/ACHIEVEMENTS:** Am Legion Indsl Arts Tchr Awrd Northwestern StateUniv 1968-69; Shreveport Times Edctr of Yr Awrd; outstndng serv prfsn & cmnty 1971; pres Kiwanis Club Awrd Outstndng Ldrshp. **MILITARY SERVICE:** AUS corpl 1953-55. **BUSINESS ADDRESS:** Caddo Parish School Board, PO Box 37000, Shreveport, LA 71103.

DIXON, WILLIAM R.
Musician, composer, educator. **PERSONAL:** Born Oct 05, 1925, Nantucket, MA; divorced; children: William Jr, Claudia Gayle, William II. **EDUCATION:** Hartnette Conservatory Music, diploma 1951. **CAREER:** UN Secretariat NYC, clk intl civil servant 1956-62; free lance musician composer NYC, 1962-67; Columbia Univ Teachers Coll, mem 1967-70; George Washington Univ, composer-in-residence 1967; Conservatory of Univ of the Streets NYC, dir 1967-68; OH State Univ, guest artist in residence 1967; Bennington Coll VT, mem faculty dept dance 1968-, chmn black music dept 1973-. **ORGANIZATIONS:** Vis prof Univ WI Madison 1971-72; lectr painting & music Mus Modern Art Verona Italy 1982; Found of UN Jazz Soc NYC; arch Jazz Composers' Guild for Performance of Contemporary Amer Black Music; organizer October Revolution a concert series; recs include Archie Shepp Bil Dixon Quartet 1962; Bill Dixon 7-Tette1963; The Bill Dixon Orchestra 1967; For Franz 1976; New Music Second Wave 1979; Bill Dixon in Italy 1980; considerations 1 and 2 Bill Dixon 1980, 82; Bill Dixon in the Labrinth 1983; paintings exhibited Ferrari Gallery Verona Italy 1982; exhibited paintings Multimedia Contemporary Art Gallery Brescia Italy 1982; mem Amer Fed of Musicians. **HONORS/ACHIEVEMENTS:** Duke Ellington Jazz Soc (Hon). **MILITARY SERVICE:** AUS 1944-46. **BUSINESS ADDRESS:** Chmn Dept of Black Music, Bennington Coll, Route 67A, Bennington, VT 05201.

DOANE, SAMUEL H.
Retired merchant. **PERSONAL:** Born Apr 21, 1917; married Ella Pearl Niskey; children: Raymond. **CAREER:** Delmarva Peninsula Farming, 1936-50; Penn RR, 1950-54; self-employed merchant, retired 1982. **ORGANIZATIONS:** Mem, bd of dir Somerset Cty Head Start 1974-75; mem Princess Anne Area C of C, Natl Fed Independent Bus, Alpha Phi Omega, MD Crime Investigating Comm, Comm Org for Progress Inc; bd of dirs Somerset Ct Head Start Policy Council; pres Somerset Ct Bd Ed Adv Council; mem Masonic Lodge, Elks, Men forProgress Inc; pres, scout master Boy Scouts; mgr Oaksville Eagles Baseball Club; mem MCEA Baseball Umpire; past master East Gate Lodge 65, Elks Lodge 194; bd mem Shore Up! Inc; pres Somerset Cty Br of NAACP 18 yrs; bd mem Somerset Cty Civic Assoc; founder, bd mem Somerset Cty Org for Progressive Enterprises; mem Bus Men Assoc Princess Anne; bd mem Somerset Cty Comm Action Prog, UMES bd mem of Sports Progs; bd mem Eastern Shore Baseball Hall ofFame Intereo. **HONORS/ACHIEVEMENTS:** Black Amer Leadership Awd Salisbury State Coll 1974; Awds & Certs from Head Start, Police Council 27, FIAM Lodge of Instr, Black Student Union of Salisbury State Coll, Miss Teen Pageant, Links Inc, MD State Conf Br of NAACP.

DOANES-BERGIN, SHARYN F.
Manager employee relations. **PERSONAL:** Born in Atlanta, GA; married Michael Bergin; children: Jennifer, Jessica. **EDUCATION:** Paine Coll, BA 1969; Atlanta Law Sch, JD 1978, ML 1979; Central MI Univ, MPA 1983. **CAREER:** Honeywell Information Systems, employee relations mgr 8 yrs; The New York Times Regional Newspaper Group Atlanta, employee relations mgr. **ORGANIZATIONS:** GA Exec Women 1980-87; vice pres Paine Coll Alumni 1982-87; vice pres Georgia Leukemia Soc 1984-87; trustee Paine Coll 1983-88, Odyssey 1985-. **HOME ADDRESS:** 6300 White Mill Road, Fairburn, GA 30213. **BUSINESS ADDRESS:** Manager Employee Relations, New York Times Newspaper, 3414 Peachtree St, Atlanta, GA 30326.

DOBBINS, ALBERT GREENE, III
Economic development consultant. **PERSONAL:** Born Jul 25, 1949, Detroit, MI; son of Albert Greene Dobbins and Barbara Williams Dobbins; divorced; children: Adia Ginneh. **EDUCATION:** Univ of MI, BSME 1971; VA Commonwealth Univ, MURP 1983; Harvard Univ, LOEB Fellow, 1989-90. **CAREER:** EI DuPont de Nemours & Co, process engineer 1972-77; City of Richmond VA, sr planner 1977-78; Neuair Inc, sr project engineer 1978-80; Philip Morris USA, rsch engineer 1980-81; Richmond Renaissance Inc, economic devel planner 1983-89. **ORGANIZATIONS:** Mem Amer Society of Mechanical Engineers 1972-81; mem Amer Planning Assn 1981-84; dir Greater Richmond Transit Co 1984-89; mem Natl Forum for Black Public Administrators 1984-86; dir Black History Museum and Cultural Center of Virginia Inc 1986-90; mem Richmond Jazz Society 1980-90; mem Concerned Black Men of Richmond VA Inc 1987-89. **HONORS/ACHIEVEMENTS:** Eagle Scout Boy Scouts of Amer 1963; Scholarship Awd Natl Merit 1967; Outstanding Student Amer Inst of Certified Planners 1983. **HOME ADDRESS:** 48 Trowbridge St, Cambridge, MA 02138.

DOBBINS, ALPHONDUS MILTON
Community worker. **PERSONAL:** Born Feb 17, 1924, Corsicana, TX; married LaVerta Pearl Love; children: Myrna D Ford, Blanche B, Alphondus M II, Cornelius L. **EDUCATION:** Bishops Coll, 1942; Southern Univ, 1945; Prairie View Univ, 1945; TN A&I Univ, BS 1946; St Louis Univ, Soc Work Workshops, 1948; Washington Univ, 1953; Millikin Univ, 1956. **CAREER:** Smith County School, voc agr teacher, 1946-48; Neighborhood House, boys work dir, 1948-53; A E Staley Mfg Co, process oper 1953-. **ORGANIZATIONS:** mem, Free & Accepted Masons, 1946-, NAACP 1948-, Antioch Missionary Bapt Church 1953-; driver Bloodmobiles 1953-; chmn of "Frontiers Comm House" 1968-; mem bd dir Amer Red Cross 1969-75, 1976-82, 1983-; chrmn Green Thumb Oper Amer Red Cross 1970-; planning comm Amer Red Cross 1976-79, 1980-81; Chmn, County Devel, 1977-79; Cty Dev Comm 1977-80; bd dir Boys Club of Amer 1977-; Comm Home Environmental Learning Proj 1977-; Public Relations Comm 1980-82, 1983-; adv Blue Book of Macon Cty 1983; Comm Health Serv 1981-82; Sr Citizens Adv Comm Secr of State IL 1983-; chmn African Famine Relief Campaign Northern Territory Amer Red Cross. **HONORS/ACHIEVEMENTS:** Work w/sr citizen's program, 1970-; life mem, IL PTA 1967; leadership bd dir, Amer Red Cross, 1969-75, 1976-82; Sertoma Breakfast & Noon Mankind Award 1975; Frontiers Distg Srv Award 1977; Univ of IL Coop Extention Serv for Comm Serv Helping Others 1978-80; In Recognition of Outstanding Efforts to Frontiers Intl Award Amer Bakeries 1979; IL, WI, IPBO Elks of W Civil Liberties 1979; Heart of IL Div Vol of the Year Award 1979; United Way Comm Civic Culture Award 1980-81; Macon Co Chapter Amer Red Cross Clara Barton

Award; Distinguished Serv Award Decatur Jaycees 1986; Outstanding Citizenship Awd Decatur Noon Kiwanis; Special Appreciation for Contribution & Sustaining Efforts Boys Club of Decatur 1986; Commemorative Medal of Honor Amer Biographical Inst 1986. **HOME ADDRESS:** 806 W King St, Decatur, IL 62522.

DOBBINS, LUCILLE R.
Financial administrator, govt. official. **PERSONAL:** Married George; children: Diane. **EDUCATION:** Roosevelt Univ, Acctg 1968; IL CPA Cert 1970. **CAREER:** Hyde Park Fed Savings & Loan, asst treas 1963-69; Blackman Kallick & Co, auditor 1969-73; Harris Trust & Savings Bank, vice pres 1974-84; City of Chicago Dept of Plng, 1st dep commissioner 1984-86; City of Chicago Mayor's Office, chief financial plng officer. **ORGANIZATIONS:** Mem Natl Soc of CPA's, Chicago Fin Exchange, IL Soc of CPA's; natl adv Black Career Women Inc, Natl Forum of Black Public Admin; mem Lambda Alpha Intl Hon Land Econ Soc, Chicago Econ Club. **BUSINESS ADDRESS:** Chief Financial Plng Officer, City of Chicago, Mayor's Office, 121 N LaSalle, Chicago, IL 60602.

DOBBS, GUY H.
Chairman/CEO. **PERSONAL:** Born 1927, Atlanta, GA; children: 2 children. **EDUCATION:** Goddard Coll, M Business Admin; Attended Howard Univ, Western Reserve Univ. **CAREER:** Xerox Corp, sr mgmt positions 1970-84; Dobbs Assocs Santa Monica, pres 1984-85; AAS Support Serv Los Angeles, sr partner 1985-; Medialink Intl Corp, chmn and chief exec officer 1985-. **ORGANIZATIONS:** Lecturer in data base systems UCLA Grad Sch of Library Sci; mem bd of dirs Behaviordyne Inc, Surface Protection Industries Inc, Atlanta Univ Rsch Inst; trustee Inst for the Future; mem bd of fellows Claremont Univ Grad Sch; mem LA County Productivity Adv Comm; mem 100 Black Men of Los Angeles; vice pres Corporate Allocations Comm United Way; mem bd of dirs Jazz Heritage Foundation, LA Brotherhood Crusade, Central City Comm Mental Hlth Ctr, Family Svgs & Loan Assoc; mem FL A&M Univ Business Roundtable, Statewide Bd MESA. **HONORS/ACHIEVEMENTS:** Los Angeles Basin Equal Opportunity League Awd 1981; NAACP ACTSO Awd 1981; Los Angeles Council of Black Engineers Awd for Engineering Achievement 1983; Golden Knight of Mgmt Natl Mgmt Assoc 1983; Awe Beverly Hills/Hollywood NAACP.

DOBBS, JOHN WESLEY
Educator. **PERSONAL:** Born Oct 08, 1931, Grenada, MS; married Mildred; children: Kiley, Kelly. **EDUCATION:** Wstrn MI U, BA 1954; Wayne St U, ME 1960; MI St U, PhD 1975. **CAREER:** Hempseatd Public Schools, supr of schools; MI Dept of Educ, asst supt; Detroit School System, teacher, counselor, asst prin, prin. **ORGANIZATIONS:** Staff lsn St Adv Cncl for Eql Educ Opp; lsn St Task Frc on Cnsl Guid; coord Task Frc on Out of Sch Out of Wrk Yth; rep MI Commn on Crmnl Jstc; ad com MI Hum Serv Ntwrk; mem AASA; NAACP; Urban Leag; Nat Allnc of Blck Sch Edc; ASCD; grad faculty Eastern MI Univ; bd dir Metro DetroitYouth Found. **HONORS/ACHIEVEMENTS:** Pres awd Nat Allnc of Blck Sch Educs; outst admin awd Dtrt Soc of Blck Educs; Resolution of Appreciation State of MI Concurrent House of Rep 1983; Outstanding Educ Leader & Humanitarian Awd Hempstead NY Bd of Educ 1986; Disting Educator in Support of Black Children Awd Leadership & Training Inst of Hempstead 1986; Mayor's Proclamation Outstanding Community Leader Village of Hempstead Long Island 1986. **MILITARY SERVICE:** AUS spec-5 1956-58. **BUSINESS ADDRESS:** Exec Dir Urban Ed Alliance, Eastern Michigan University, 34 Boone Hall, Ypsilanti, MI 48197.

DOBBS, MATTIWILDA
Opera, concert singer. **PERSONAL:** Born in Altanta, GA; married Bengt Janzen. **EDUCATION:** Spelman Coll, Atlanta, GA, BA (with honors) 1946; Tchrs Coll, Columbia, MA, 1948; studied voice under Mme Lotte Leham, New York City, 1946-50; Mannes Music Coll, 1948-49; Berkshire Music Festival, 1949; studied French music with Pierre Bernac, Paris, France, 1950-52. **CAREER:** Appeared with Dutch Opera Holland Festival, 1952; numerous recitals in Paris, Stockholm, Holland, and La Scala (Milan, Italy), 1953; concerts in Scandinavia, Austria, England, France, Italy, and Belgium; command performance, Covent Garden, London, 1954; concert tour, US, 1954; concert tour, Australia, 1955, 1959, 1972; concert tour, Israel, 1957, 1959; concert tour, USSR, 1959; concert tour, Hamburg State Opera, 1961-62; Amer operatic debut, San Francisco Opera, 1955; Metropolitan Opera debut, 1956; recitals in Philadelphia, PA, North Carolina, Florida, Alabama, Georgia, Louisiana, New York City, and the Midwest, 1972-75; performing voice prof, Univ of Texas, 1973-74. **ORGANIZATIONS:** Mem Metropolitan Opera Assn, Order of North Star Sweden 1954. **HONORS/ACHIEVEMENTS:** Recipient, second prize, Marian Anderson Award 1947; John Hay Whitney Fellow, Paris 1950; first prize, Intl Competition Music, Geneva Conservatory of Music 1951. **BUSINESS ADDRESS:** c/o Joanne Rile Mgmt, Box 27539, Philadelphia, PA 19118.

DOBSON, HELEN SUTTON
Educator. **PERSONAL:** Born Jan 06, 1926, Wheeling, WV; married Robert J Dobson; children: Robert, Leisa. **EDUCATION:** Bluefield State Coll, BS 1959; extra 15 hrs WV Univ Marshall Univ. **CAREER:** Beckley Jr HS, classroom teacher. **ORGANIZATIONS:** Announcer Trent & Durgan Funeral Home Prog; teacher Raleigh Co Bd of Educ; Delta Sigma Theta Sorority. **HONORS/ACHIEVEMENTS:** Serv Awd Bluefield State Coll; Honor Awd Sec of State A James Manehim; All Coll Achievement Soc NY; WWNR Radio Apprec Awd; 1st black women to sing atGov's Inauguration Gov John "Jay" Rockefeller; invited each year to sing at Dem Jefferson Jackson Day event; Citations from Sen Robt Byrd & Congressman Nick Rahall; Woman of the Year Awd McDowell Cty. **BUSINESS ADDRESS:** Beckley High School, South Kanawha St, Beckley, WV 25807.

DOBSON, WILLIAM DELAFAYETTE
Attorney. **PERSONAL:** Born Aug 13, 1924, Earlsboro, OK; married Ruth Elaine Jones; children: Rheanette Lee, Richard, Cynthia Napue, Debra O'Hara, Julie Alexander. **EDUCATION:** Tuskegee Inst, BA agr 1947;Univ of CA Davis, CA, MEd 1952; Hasting Coll of Law San Francisco, JD 1955. **CAREER:** Gen Practice of Law San Jose, atty 1978-; CA School Employees Assn San Jose, staff atty 1976-78; State Dept of Educ, Sacto CA, staff counsel 1972-75; San Joaquin Co, Stockton CA, juvenile court referee 1970-72; Gen Practice of Law, Stockton CA, atty 1959-71; Stockton Unified School Dist, school bd mem 1964-70, school teacher 1957-60; Haskell Public Schools, Haskell OK, veteran's agr teacher 1947-51. **ORGANIZATIONS:** Bd of dir Boy's Club of Stockton 1965-74; exec bd mem San Juan Bautista Child Devel Cntr 1976-80; chmn bd of dir Providence Bapt Ch San Fran CA 1955-57; pres Stockton Br NAACP 1959; exec bd Stockton Unified Sch Dist 1964-70; chmn Stockton Unified Sch Dist 1968-70; bd mem Stockton Br United Crusade 1968-72; exec bd mem Stockton Br NAACP 1958-74; exec bd boy Scouts 1965-74; exec bd Crippled Children's Soc 1965-74; exec bd Sr Serv Agency 1965-74. **HONORS/ACHIEVEMENTS:** Aw for outstndg contrib to Spornine Club & Comm 1963-69; commend Staockton Secondary Sch Adminstrn Assn 1970; hon life mem aw Stockton Elem Tchrs Assn 1970; global aw United Nations Fair 1970; aw for 6 yrs serv on Stockton bd of educ Stockton Tchrs Assn 1970; Spornine Men's Club Aw for outstndg serv to citz of Stockton 1970; NAACP aw for sincere efforts in the Betterment to Educ & Comm NAACP Stockton CA Br 1970; aw for valuable serv as mem of Stockton Bd of Educ Stockton Elem Adminstrn Assn 1970; aw for unselfish serv Black Tchrs Assn 1970; resol for outstndg serv to Educ & the Stockton Comm 1970; aw for outstndg serv rendered to the citiz of Stockton Esquire Social & Civic Club 1970; cert of apprec Stockton Br NAACP 1979. **MILITARY SERVICE:** AUS sgt 1942-46.

DOBY, ALLEN E.
Government administrator. **PERSONAL:** Born Jan 26, 1934, Mississippi; married LaFaye Ealy. **EDUCATION:** Calif State Univ Northridge, BS 1973, MPA program. **CAREER:** County of Los Angeles, district dir 1959-75; City of Compton, dir parks & rec 1975-80. **ORGANIZATIONS:** Member Calif Parks Rec Society 1961-; bd of directors Natl Recreation Parks Assoc 1971-; bd of directors NRPA Ethnic Minority Society 1971-; lecturer Calif Community College System 1973-75. **HONORS/ACHIEVEMENTS:** Administrator of Year Ethnic Minority Society 1977; Who's Who in Calif 14th edition 1983. **MILITARY SERVICE:** AUS Army E5 1955-57; Good Conduct & Service Medal. **BUSINESS ADDRESS:** Executive Dir Community Serv, City of Santa Ana, 20 Civic Center Plaza, Santa Ana, CA 92701.

DOBY, LAWRENCE EUGENE
Professional athlete. **PERSONAL:** Born Dec 03, 1924, Camden, SC; married Helyn Curvey; children: Chris, Leslie, Larry Jr, Kim, Susan. **EDUCATION:** Long Island U; NY U; VA Union U. **CAREER:** Cleveland Indians, played 1947-55; White Sox, 1955-59; Montreal Expos, coach 1971-73; Cleveland Indians, coach 1974; Montreal Expos, coach 1976; NJ Nets, dircomm relations. **ORGANIZATIONS:** Mem State Dept of Japan 1962; US Tour for Pres Council on Physical Fitness 1968. **HONORS/ACHIEVEMENTS:** 1st black in the Am League; played in 2 World Series 1948, 54; played in 6 consecutive All Star Games 1949-54; center fielder Baseball Writers Assn of Sporting News 1950; elected to Cleveland Hall of Fame 1955; Baseball Hall of Fame 1977; led the Am League in slugging 1952 Batted 542. **BUSINESS ADDRESS:** Dir of Community Affairs, N J Nets Basketball, Brendan Bynne Arena, East Rutherford, NJ 07073.

DOBYNES, ELIZABETH
Personnel advisor. **PERSONAL:** Born Dec 25, 1930, Marion, AL; married Lloyd Sr; children: Barbara, Lloyd Jr, Karl. **EDUCATION:** Miles Coll Birmingham AL, 1951-53; asst degree electronics pending. **CAREER:** Magnovox Co Fort Wayne IN, employee 21 yrs. **ORGANIZATIONS:** Ythadv & state bd rep IN NAACP 1965-; den leader Cub Scouts 1957-65; treas/coordinator Women's Aux NAACP 1978-; mem PUSH 1980; mem Ft Wayne Urban League 1980; publicity chairwomen Bapt Ministrial Alliance 1979-80; dir Bapt training union Faith Missionary Bapt Ch 1980; missionary tchr & choir mem Faith Missionary Bapt Ch 1980; vacation bible sch dir Faith Missionary Bapt Ch 1980; life mem NAACP Ft Wayne Chpt; public service PUSH Ft Wayne Chap 1975. **HONORS/ACHIEVEMENTS:** Delegate to natl conv NAACP 1967-. **BUSINESS ADDRESS:** NAACP, PO Box 296, Fort Wayne, IN 46802.

DOCKERY, RICHARD L.
Director. **PERSONAL:** Married Almeda D; children: Richard L Jr, Eric Richard, Erica Carmen. **EDUCATION:** Dillard U, BA 1950. **CAREER:** Spalding Bus Coll, instr 1946-59; Cedar Grv Theol Sem, instr 1950-51; City Rec Negroes, dir 1951-52; US Civil Serv, 1952-61; Kelly AFB, procurementdata spl 1961-68; Dockerys Paint Center, owner & mgr 1958-61. **ORGANIZATIONS:** Mem NAACP; Nat Found Fed Employees; TX Adv Com US Commn Civil Rights. **HONORS/ACHIEVEMENTS:** Community serv award KNOK Radio; plaque meritorious serv NAACP 1967; community serv awd Dallas Bock C of C 1975; appreciation award governors awd US Army ROTC Region 1975. **MILITARY SERVICE:** USN petty officer 2/c 1941-45. **BUSINESS ADDRESS:** Regional Dir, NAACP, 4805 Mt Hope Dr, Baltimore, MD 21215.

DOCKERY, ROBERT WYATT
Physician. **PERSONAL:** Born Dec 11, 1909, Charlotte, NC; son of Rev & Mrs Zonder Dockery; married Vera; children: Robert Jr, Glenna. **EDUCATION:** Johnson C Smith U, BS 1931; Meharry Med Coll, MD 1940; Harvard Med School Ch Boston City Hosp Univ Louisville, 1954-57. **CAREER:** Univ Louisville, clinical instr 1957-, assoc clinical prof 1985-; NC, tchr 1931-35; VA Hosp Louisville, ophthalmology consultant 1957-; VA KY, 1970-77. **ORGANIZATIONS:** Mem Louisville Acad Ophthalmology; pres 1969-70; Falls City Med Soc 1957; Jefferson Co Med Soc 1957; KY State Ophthal Soc 1957; AMA 1957; Nat Med Soc 1957; deacon bd tst Plymouth Congr Ch 1964-; mem Alpha Phi Alpha Frat; pres Alpha Lambda Chap Alpha Phi Alpha 1968-71; mem NAACP 1957; Urban League 1957; gov com KY Blind 1970-89; mem Pres Club Johnson C Smith Univ 1976-80, 1988. **MILITARY SERVICE:** USAF maj 1943-46. **BUSINESS ADDRESS:** 1918 W Broadway, Louisville, KY 40203.

DOCKETT, ALFRED B.
Business executive. **PERSONAL:** Born Jul 06, 1935, Thomasville, GA; married Erna Rodrigues; children: Alfred III, Michael H, Karen P. **EDUCATION:** IN Inst of Tech, BS 1957. **CAREER:** Wallace & Wallace Enterprises Inc, pres; Grumman Aerospace Corp, mgmt systems spec 1971-73; Gen Elec/RESD, prgm engr 1966-71; Boeing Co, systems test & mgmt systems engr 1961-66; AUS, intrn of Fire control & missel systems oper. **MILITARY SERVICE:** AUS 1958-61. **BUSINESS ADDRESS:** 200-33 Linden Blvd, St Albans, NY 11412.

DODD, BERNICE STEPHENS
Chief executive officer. **PERSONAL:** Born Mar 17, 1943, Phenix City, AL; married Dr William H; children: Charod Dante. **EDUCATION:** AL State Coll Montgomery, BS Educ 1963;Univ of ME at Omaha, MA 1973;Univ of NE at Lincoln, PhD 1978. **CAREER:**

Omaha Opportunity Industrialization Center, exec dir 1971-, dir of operations 1969, feeder supr 1967; Omaha Women's Job Corps, residential advisor 1965-67; Exec Dir Assoc of OIC/A, vice-convenor; Mid-Am Devel Corp, vice pres; Business Systems Devel Inc, pres. **ORGANIZATIONS:** Mem NAACP; mem Delta Sigma Theta Sor; bd of dir Nat Conf of Christians & Jews. **HONORS/ACHIEVEMENTS:** One of ten outstanding young Omahans C of C Omaha NE 1973; woman of the year in bus & prof Women's Pol Caucus Omaha 1974; Spearheaded Drive to Finance & Erect New OIC Training Ctr Omaha 1974-76; outstanding performance award Nat OIC 1976. **BUSINESS ADDRESS:** Omaha Opport Indus Cntr Inc, 2724 N 24th St, Omaha, NE 68110.

DODD, JAMES C.
Architect. **PERSONAL:** Born Jan 17, 1923, Texarkana, TX; married Constance M Curry; children: Florenda (Mitchell), James C Jr. **EDUCATION:** Univ of CA, BA 1952. **CAREER:** Dodd & Asso Architechts & Planners Sacramento, owner 1960-; Urban Construction Co Sacramento, owner 1972-; Barovette & Thomas, project architect 1956-61; State of CA Div of Architecture, designer 1953-56. **ORGANIZATIONS:** Past pres Central Valley Chap AIA 1969; mem bd dir CA Council AIA 1969, 73; vice pres Nat Orgn of Minority Architects 1972-73; mem Am Arbitration Assn; mem AIA; chmn bd governors CA Comm Colleges 1972-73; vice pres Sacrmento Br NAACP 1968-70; mem Coordinatin Council for Higher Educ 1968-70. **HONORS/ACHIEVEMENTS:** Recipient Masonry Honor Award for Architectural Design 1971; architectural achievement award NAACP 1972; merit award Central Valley Chap AIA 1974. **MILITARY SERVICE:** AUS 1st lt 1943-46. **BUSINESS ADDRESS:** James C Dodd & Assoc, 2710 X St, Ste 2, Sacramento, CA 95818.

DODDS, R. HARCOURT
Manufacturing officer. **PERSONAL:** Born Jan 11, 1938, New York, NY; married Barbara Anne Arrington; children: Julian A, Jason S, Sarah C. **EDUCATION:** Dartmouth Coll, BA (Magna Cum Laude) 1958; Yale Law School, LLB 1961. **CAREER:** Ministry of Justice Northern Nigeria, asst comm for native courts 1961-63; US Attny Office Southern Dist of NY, asst US attny 1963-66; Pfizer Inc, legal dept attny 1966-67; New York City Police Dept, dep police comm legal matters 1967-70; New York City Law Dept, exec asst corp counsel 1970-73; Ford Found, prog officer1973-82; Champion Intl Corp, dir corp responsibility prog 1982-. **ORGANIZATIONS:** Mem New Rochelle Council on the Arts 1980-; bd of governors New Rochelle Hosp Med Ctr 1983-; consult Clark Phipps Harris Clark 1983, Rockefeller Found 1983-84; independent drug expert Natl Basketball Assn & Natl Players Assn 1984-; vice pres CT Bar Found 1984-; mem NY State Commn on Crim Justice and Use of Force 1985-; mem Law Devel Commn Univ of Bridgeport Sch of Law 1985-; mem Community and Pub Issues Cncl; Conf Bd 1984-. **HONORS/ACHIEVEMENTS:** Trustee Dartmouth Coll 1973-83; overseer Amos Tuck School of Bus Admin 1974-80; mem Phi Beta Kappa. **MILITARY SERVICE:** NY NG pe5 3 mos. **HOME ADDRESS:** 61 Elk Ave, New Rochelle, NY 10804. **BUSINESS ADDRESS:** Dir of Corp Resp Prog, Champion International Corp, 1 Champion Plz, Stamford, CT 06921.

DODDY, REGINALD NATHANIEL
Systems engineer. **PERSONAL:** Born Jul 02, 1952, Cincinnati, OH; son of Nathan Doddy and Mildred Peek Doddy. **EDUCATION:** Northwestern Univ, BSEE 1975. **CAREER:** Eastman Kodak Co, mfg engineer 1975-77; Mead Corp, mfg engineer 1977-79; RCA Corp, assc mem stf engrg 1979-84; Cinncinnati Milacron, systems engineer 1984-. **ORGANIZATIONS:** Mem Inst of Elect & Elect Engr 1977-, Toastmasters Club 1976-77; tech dir RCA Minority Engrg Program 1980-83. **HONORS/ACHIEVEMENTS:** Nomination Outstanding Young Men of Am 1982-83; community serv Indianapolis Center for Leadership Devel 1982. **HOME ADDRESS:** 3595 Wilson Ave, Cincinnati, OH 45229. **BUSINESS ADDRESS:** Systems Engineer, Cincinnati Milacron, 4165 Half Acre Rd, Batavia, OH 45103.

DODSON, GRANVILLE M.
Business executive. **PERSONAL:** Born Jun 02, 1910, Ozark, AR; married Willie Idee. **EDUCATION:** BS 1947. **CAREER:** G M Dodson Construction Co Okla City & Dallas, gen contractor owner; Ideal Cabinet & Upholstery Shop, fdr oper 1939-41; Caston Lumber Co, foreman millwright 1941-43; instr vocational carpentry 1946-58. **ORGANIZATIONS:** Treas Minority Construction Inc mem treas okla city minority contractors assn; trustee central okla transp & parking auth 1967-; bd dir first State Bank & Trust Co 1966-. **HONORS/ACHIEVEMENTS:** Recipient Freedom Service Award NAACP Youth Council; outstanding leader award Okla City Set Club 1972; mayor's award for Civil Svc. **MILITARY SERVICE:** USAF flight chief. **BUSINESS ADDRESS:** 2901 NE Success, Oklahoma City, OK 73111.

DODSON, HOWARD, JR.
Business executive, educator. **PERSONAL:** Born Jun 01, 1939, Chester, PA; married Jualynne E White; children: Alyce Christine, David Primus Luta. **EDUCATION:** W Chester State Coll, BS 1961; UCLA, Additional Study 1964; Villanova Univ, MA 1964; UC Berkeley, ABF 1977. **CAREER:** Peace Corps, recruiter 1966-67, dir special recruiting 1967-68, training officer 1968; CA State Coll, assoc prof 1970; Shaw Univ, adjunct prof 1975; Emory Univ, lecturer 1976; Inst of the Black World, program dir 1973-74, exec dir 1974-79; Natl Endowment for the Humanities, asst to chmn 1980-82; The Schomburg Center for Rsch in Black Culture, chief 1984-. **ORGANIZATIONS:** Mem Alpha Phi Alpha 1959-64, SC Hist Soc, Peace Corps Vol 1964-66, Oakland Black Caucus 1969-73; consultant Natl Endowment for the Humanities 1979-80; chmn, ceo Black Theology Project 1982-84; mem bd of dir Inst of the Black World, Atlanta Assoc for Intl Ed; mem Ed Brain Trust Congressional Black Caucus, Atlanta Univ School of Soc Work, Natl Comm for Citizens in Ed, GA Assoc of Black Elected Officials, ESEA, Natl Credit Union Fed Ecuador; mem African Heritage Studies Assoc, Assoc for the Study of Afro-Amer History, So Hist Assoc; mem bd of overseers Lang Coll New Sch for Social Rsch; bd of dirs NCBS, AHSA, Caribbean Rsch Ctr. **HONORS/ACHIEVEMENTS:** PICCO Scholarship 1959-61; Grad Fellowship UC Berkeley 1969-73; Rsch Fellowship Inst of the Black World 1970-71; Editor-in-Chief Black World View 1977; Doctor of Humane Letters Widner Univ 1987. **BUSINESS ADDRESS:** Chief, Schomburg Center Rsch Black Culture, 515 Lenox Ave, New York, NY 10037.

DODSON, JUALYNNE E. (NEE WHITE)
Educational administrator. **PERSONAL:** Born Jan 04, 1942, Pensacola, FL; daughter of Benjamin White and Flora White; married Howard Dodson; children: Alyce Christine, David Primus Luta. **EDUCATION:** Univ of CA Berkeley, BA 1969, MA 1972, PhD 1984; Warren Deem Inst for Educ Mgmt Columbia Univ Sch of Business, attended 1985. **CAREER:** Atlanta Univ Sch of Social Work, instructor 1973-74, rsch project dir 1973-81, dir rsch ctr 1974-80, asst prof 1974-79, assoc prof 1979-82, chair Dept Child & Family Serv 1980-82; Black Theology Project, exec dir 1985-88; Union Theological Seminary, dean of seminary life 1982-87; visiting assoc prof, sociology dept, Hunter Coll, CUNY, 1987-88; sr research assoc, African & Africa-Amer Studies, Yale Univ, 1988-90. **ORGANIZATIONS:** Elected delegate Council on Social Work Educ 1979-82; presentor annual meetings Amer Acad of Religion 1981, 1983, 1984, 1987; Natl Council Convenor Feminist Theol Inst 1982-83; mem Soc for Scientific Study of Religion 1982, 1983, 1986; consult Natl Child Welfare Training Center Ann Arbor, MI 1983-85; chair/bd dirs Black Theol Project 1983-84; keynote speaker Natl Coalition 100 Black Women 1984; NY State Black & Puerto Rican Legislative Caucus Women's Conf 1985; NY State Affirmative Action Adv Council 1985-86; leader Black Church Studies & Student Caucus Retreat Colgate Rochester Divinity Sch spring & fall 1985; mem Soc of Amer Archivists 1986; sponsor, "I Have a Dream," 1988-89; scholar in residence, Irvington Abbott Unified School, 1989. **HONORS/ACHIEVEMENTS:** Research fellow for Applied Sociology Amer Sociological Assoc 1980; gubernatorial appointee White House Conf on Families 1980; Lucy Craft Laney Awd Black Presbyterians United UPCUSA 1982; Spivack Fellow Amer Sociological Assn 1983; adv bd Assoc of Black Women in Higher Educ 1985-88; Medal of Honor Outstanding Comm Serv One Church One Child Prog Indianapolis 1986; delegate Intl Conf "Ecumenical Sharing" Nanjing China 1986; bd of dirs New York Council for the Humanities 1986-90; author "A Sourcebook in Child Welfare," Natl Child Welfare Training Ctr Univ MI Ann Arbor 1982, "An Afrocentric Educational Manual" Univ TN Press Knoxville 1983. **BUSINESS ADDRESS:** 7 Fordham Hill, #8H, New York, NY 10468.

DODSON, VIVIAN M.
Government official. **PERSONAL:** Born Jan 22, 1934, Washington, DC; daughter of Brevard Mills and Maefield Wilson Mills; married Barke M Dodson, Dec 24, 1958; children: Tangie D, Kaphree A. **EDUCATION:** Washington Coll of Music, Washington DC, AA, 1956. **CAREER:** Prince Georges County Communications, Upper Marlboro MD, communications operator, 1973-89; Town of Capitol Heights, Capitol Heights MD, councilwoman, 1982-86, mayor, 1986-. **ORGANIZATIONS:** Mem, Girl Scouts of America, 1971-, Prince Georges Municipal Elective Women, 1982-; dir, Recreation for Capitol Heights, 1982-; bd mem, Prince Georges County Municipal League, 1983-; mem, Mothers On The Move, 1984-. **HOME ADDRESS:** 5635 Southern Ave, Capitol Heights, MD 20743.

DODSON, WILLIAM ALFRED, JR.
Government official. **PERSONAL:** Born Feb 09, 1950, Beckley, WV; son of William A Dodson Jr and Kira E Dodson; married Judythe Irene Taylor, Jul 27, 1975; children: Daymon. **EDUCATION:** Marshall Univ Huntington, WV, AB, Sociology, 1973; OH State Univ Columbus, OH, MA Public Admin, 1981. **CAREER:** Tri-state OIC Huntington, WV, instr 1972-73; ACF Ind Huntington, WV, instrl rel repr 1973-75; Office of Human Serv ODOD, field rep, 1975-77; Office of Appalachia ODOD, housing rep, 1977-82; WCVO-FM New Albany, OH, anchor 1980-; OH Dept of Dev, field rep/devel specialist, 1982-86; Columbus Metro Housing Authority, asst dir of housing programs; Columbus Metro Housing, MIS Mgr, 1988-89, mgmt analyst, 1989-. **ORGANIZATIONS:** Ethnic affairs dir, WCVO-FM, New Albany, OH, 1980-86; elder Rhema Christian Center, 1982-; program mgmt Grantmanship Center, 1982; economic devel financial Natl Devel Council, 1984; bd of dirs, Directions for Youth, 1986-; chmn, Neighborhood Services Advisory Council, Columbus, 1989-; vice pres, Programs, Directions for Youth, 1987. **HONORS/ACHIEVEMENTS:** Outstanding participant, Natl Alliance of Businessmen Jobs Campaign Huntington Metro, 1975; Natl Achievement Scholar, Natl Merit ETS, 1968; Certified Public Housing Mgr, 1987. **BUSINESS ADDRESS:** Asst Dir of Housing Programs, Columbus Metro Housing Auth, 30 E Broad St, Columbus, OH 43215.

DOGGETT, JOHN NELSON, JR.
Clergyman. **PERSONAL:** Born Apr 03, 1918, Philadelphia, PA; son of John Nelson Doggett and Winola Ballard Doggett; married Juanita Toley, Aug 03, 1975; children: Lorraine F, John III, William II, Kenneth Riddick. **EDUCATION:** Lincoln Univ, BA 1942; Union Theol Seminary, MDiv 1945; Saint Louis Univ, MEduc 1969, PhD 1971. **CAREER:** Union Memorial United Methodist Church, sr pastor 1964-76; Harris-Stowe State Coll, instructor in educ 1973-76; Metro Coll St Louis Univ, assoc prof 1976-78; UM Church St Louis Area, district supt 1976-82; Grace United Methodist Church, sr minister 1982-85; Cabanne United Methodist Church, minister 1985-(retired); Central Medical Ctr St Louis, chairman bd of dirs 1975-87 chr Emeritus 1987-; CMC Retirement Home, chmn bd of dirs 1985-. **ORGANIZATIONS:** Staff counselor Pastoral Counseling Inst St Louis 1968-; pres Chr Central Medical Ctr Complex St Louis 1973-; pres St Louis Branch NAACP 1973-80; mem Citizens Comm MO Dept of Corrections 1974-80; bd of dir United Way of Greater St Louis 1974-81; bd of dir Natl Council of Churches of Christ 1976-80; mem St Louis Ambassadors & RCGA 1980-; bd dir Amer Lung Assoc Eastern MO 1985-88, Family Planning Assoc MO 1986-88; mem Epilepsy Federation of Greater St Louis, Natl Family Planning & Reproductive Health Assoc Inc, ACLU; bd of dir Jefferson Memorial Chapel, UNA, 1986-88, Minister's Coalition; founder JN Doggett Scholarship Foundation; mem Lincoln Alumni Assoc, St Louis Conf on Educ; Confluence Natl Conf Christians and Jews. **HONORS/ACHIEVEMENTS:** Natl Chaplain's Awd Alpha Phi Alpha Fraternity 1973,79,86,87; Outstanding Alumni Awd St Louis Univ 1981; Martin Luther King Awd Alpha & Anheuser-Busch Project 1987; "Effect of Community School Achievement" St Louis Univ edition 1971; "Black Religious Experience" Gammon Theol Seminary Press GA 1973; Regional Hall of Fame Alpha Phi Alpha Fraternity 1988; Outstanding Service Award, Elijah Parish Lovejoy Society 1989. **MILITARY SERVICE:** USNG chaplain 1st lt 1946-50. **HOME ADDRESS:** 4466 West Pine Blvd #2C, St Louis, MO 63108. **BUSINESS ADDRESS:** President Med-West Consultants, 4615 Steinlage Avenue, St Louis, MO 63115.

DOIG, ELMO H.
Business executive. **PERSONAL:** Born Aug 14, 1927, Panama, Panama;son of Henry Doig; married Silvia; children: Elmo Jr, Yvette. **EDUCATION:** Am Sch, coll prep 1959; CCNY (Baruch) NYC, BBS & MBA 1969. **CAREER:** Manufacturers Hanover Trust Co, asst vp; Manufacturers Hanover Trust Co NYC, branch mgr 1964-; Flower Fifth Ave Hosp NYC, head payroll & accts payable dept 1963-64; Bezozi Corp, supr billing dept 1958-62; Ordnance Corps Panama, supr supply shop 1942-58. **ORGANIZATIONS:** Treas financial sec Bronx Lions Club Bronx NY 1971; financial com 100 Black Men Inc New York City 1975; treas Mt Kisco Village Condominium 1979. **HONORS/ACHIEVEMENTS:** Amer Sch Scholarship Chicago 1960; black achievers in industry Greater NY YMCA 1972; banking & finance Grodon Heights Comm City Tabernacle Church Seventh-day Adventist New York City 1978. **HOME ADDRESS:** 2411 SE Morningside Blvd, Port St Lucie, FL 34952.

DOLEY, HAROLD E., JR.
Business executive. **PERSONAL:** Born Mar 08, 1947, New Orleans, LA; married Helena Cobette; children: Harold III, Aaron. **EDUCATION:** Xavier U, BS; Attending, Harvard Univ. **CAREER:** Doley Properties, pres; So Univ New Orleans, instr; Bache Halsey Stuart Inc, acct exec; Howard Weil Labouisse & Friedrichs Inc, asst vice pres 1973-76; Minerals Mgmt Svcs, dir 1982-83; African Development Bank, exec dir 1983-85; Doley Securities Inc, pres/chmn. **ORGANIZATIONS:** Mem NY Stock Exchange; former treas bd mem Pub Broadcast Sys WYES-TV; Inter-racial Council for Bus & Opp; former natl bd mem Urban League of GreaterLeague of Greater New Orleans; former bd mem rep Nat Adv Com; Marine Cluster YMCA New Orleans; former bd mem OIC Adv Bd; Nat MESBIC Assn; Lloyds ofLondon; NY Futures; Alpha Alpha Boule; Bunch Club; NY Options Exchange; Atlanta Univ; LA Weekly Bd. **HONORS/ACHIEVEMENTS:** Guest spkr Nat Bankers Assn Nat Ins Assn 1973; 1 of Outstanding Stockbrokers by Shareholders Nat Real Estate Brokers; Harvard Mgmt Grad Sch of Bus;TV guest Today Show, Wall St Week, Good Morning Am, NY Times, Spotlight. **BUSINESS ADDRESS:** Chairman, Doley Secruities Inc, 616 Baronne St, New Orleans, LA 70113.

DOLPHIN, WOODROW B.
Business executive. **PERSONAL:** Born Nov 01, 1912, Boley, OK; married Edwina; children: Michele, Woodrow E, Karl. **EDUCATION:** Wayne State U, BSEE 1937; IL Inst of Tech, 1942-44; Malcolm X Coll, HHD 1970. **CAREER:** WB Dolphin & Assos, founder & owner; Chicago Nat Tech Assn, consult engrs 1970. **ORGANIZATIONS:** Mem Small Bus of Yr Cosmopolitan C of C 1976. **BUSINESS ADDRESS:** W B Dolphin & Associates, 6 North Michigan Ave, Chicago, IL 60606.

DOMINIC, IRWING
Human resources manager. **PERSONAL:** Born Aug 12, 1930, Spartanburg, SC; son of Jessie M (Hall) Hunt; married Catherine Virginia Chapman Dominic, Jun 14, 1956; children: Duane, Dwight, Denice, Deirdre, Deland, Damian. **EDUCATION:** Bellevue Coll, BA Sociology 1978; attended Univ of Nebraska-Omaha 1978-79, Creighton Univ Omaha 1979-80. **CAREER:** US Postal Serv, Omaha NE, mail handler, 1974-79, assoc training & devel specialist eas-14, 1979-80, training & devel spec eas-16, 1980-83, Cleveland manager training, 1983-86, Hicksville NY mgr employment and devel, 1986-88, Akron OH, mgr employment & training, 1988-. **ORGANIZATIONS:** Founding mem, Blacks in Govt Omaha NE Chapter, 1981-82; mem, Knights of Columbus, fourth degree 1980, Phoenix Rising Toastmasters, 1982, A-Plus, 1988; educ advisor, Natl Assn Postal Supvr, 1983, Phoenix Postal Supvr, 1983. **HONORS/ACHIEVEMENTS:** Superior Performance Award, US Postal Service, 1979; Managers Recognition Award for Superior Performance in Affirmative Action, 1982. **MILITARY SERVICE:** USAF radio operator and electronic analyst 26 years; Korean & Vietnam Serv, Sr Crew Mem Badge. **HOME ADDRESS:** 2489 Silver Springs Dr, Stow, OH 44224-1562.

DOMINO, ANTOINE (FATS DOMINO)
Musician. **PERSONAL:** Born Feb 26, 1928, New Orleans, LA; married Rosemary; children: 8 Children. **EDUCATION:** Self Taught Piano from 10 yrs old. **CAREER:** Semi-retired, Musician-performer; Toured Europe & Japan, 1970's; Chain of Drive-In Restaurants, owner-mgr 1969-70; Broadmoor Records, owner/rcrdng artist 1967; Toured Extensively Clubs-Concerts/Theaters, formed own group 1950-; New Orleans, performer in local clubs 1938-; Blue Note Chicago, appeared 1956; Antibes Jazz Festival, 1962; Village Gate NYC, 1966; Central Pk Mus Festival, 1968; Hollywood Bowl, 1969; Carnegie Hall, 1971; Madison Square Garden, 1972; MontreuxJazz Festival, 1973; Newport Jazz Festival, 1976; New Orleans Jazz & Heritage Festival, 1977. **HONORS/ACHIEVEMENTS:** Films Include; "Shake Rattle & Rock" 1956, "Jamboree" 1957, "The Big Beat" 1957; TV Appearacnes Include; Dick Clark's American Bandstand 1958, The Monkees Special 1969, Mike Douglas Show 1970, Amercian Bandstand's 23rd Birthday Special 1975; Capt & Tennille in New Orleans 1978; Recorded Soundtrack for "American Graffiti" 1973, "Return to Macon County" 1975, Miller Beer Commercial 1976; Hit Records Include "blueberry hill", "margie", "lady madonna"; Compositions Include "thefat man" (1st million dollar seller), "i'm walkin'", "ain't that a shame", "i'm in love again"; recordings include "fats domino Story" Vols I-IV United Artist, "Live at Montreux-Hello Josephine" Atlantic, "Fats" Warner Bros; recipient of 20 Gold Records; 4 time winner of Triple Crown Award Billboard Mag 1950's; Best R&B Personality of Yr Downbeat Mag Readers Poll 1956-57. **BUSINESS ADDRESS:** Associated Booking Corp, 1995 Broadway, New York, NY 10023.

DOMINO, FATS See DOMINO, ANTOINE

DONAHUE, WILLIAM T.
City official. **PERSONAL:** Born May 31, 1943, San Antonio, TX; married Monica Lechowick; children: Erin Michelle, Mark Pittman. **EDUCATION:** San Antonio Jr Coll. **CAREER:** Human Resources & Services, dir 1972-82; City of San Antonio, asst city mgr. **ORGANIZATIONS:** Volunteer US Peace Corps 1965-67; immediate past pres US Conf of City Human Svcs; Official Advisory Comm United Negro Coll Fund; life mem NAACP; co-chair 1980 UNCF Radiothon; delegate Pres Conf on Children & Youth; 1st Black Asst City Mgr City of San Antonio; bd of dir Natl Forum for Black Public Admin1982-; vice chair of the TX Emergency Serv Advisory Council; Commissioned as Admiral in TX Navy; D of Law from Univ TX at San Antonio; mem Internat'l City Manager's Assn; Recipient of Achievement Awd from South Central Region of AKA Sorority; mem TX City Mgrs Assn; Who's Who in Local Govt Mngmnt; Outstanding Texanby TX Legislative Black Caucus. **BUSINESS ADDRESS:** Assistant City Manager, City of San Antonio, PO Box 9066, San Antonio, TX 78285.

DONALD, ARNOLD WAYNE
Business director. **PERSONAL:** Born Dec 17, 1954, New Orleans, LA; son of Warren Joseph Donald Sr and Hilda Aline (Melancon) Donald; married Hazel Alethea (Roberts) Donald, May 18, 1974; children: Radiah Alethea, Alicia Aline. **EDUCATION:** Carleton Coll, Northfield MN, BA Economics, 1976; Washington Univ, St Louis MO, BS Mechanical Engineering, 1977; Univ of Chicago, Chicago IL, MBA Finance, 1980. **CAREER:** Monsanto, St Louis MO, sr mktg analyst, 1980-81, mktg research supvr, 1981-82, product supvr, 1982-83, Winnipeg, Canada, round-up product mgr, 1983, mktg mgr, 1983-86, St Louis MO, product dir, 1986, specialty crops dir, 1986-87, lawn & garden business dir, 1987-. **ORGANIZATIONS:** Mem, Canadian Agricultural Chemistry Assn, 1983-86, Natl Lawn & Garden Distributor Assn, 1988-; team captain, 1988-89, bd mem, 1989-92, Monsanto YMCA; participant, 1988-89, bd mem, 1989-92, Leadership St Louis; mem, Theater Project Co, 1989-91. **HONORS/ACHIEVEMENTS:** Class Salutatorian, St Augustine High School, 1972; Natl Achievement Scholar, Carleton Coll, 1972-76; Dave Okada Memorial Award, Carleton Coll, 1976. **BUSINESS ADDRESS:** Lawn and Garden Business Director, Monsanto Company, M2B, 800 N Lindbergh Blvd, St Louis, MO 63167.

DONALD, BERNICE BOUIE
Judge. **PERSONAL:** Born Sep 17, 1951, DeSoto County, MS; daughter of Mr & Mrs Perry Bowie; married W L Donald. **EDUCATION:** Memphis State Univ, BA Sociology 1974; Memphis State Univ Sch of Law, JD 1979; Natl Judicial Coll, Evidence Certificate 1984. **CAREER:** South Central Bell, clerk's mgr 1971-79; Memphis Area Legal Svc, attorney 1979-80; Shelby Co Govt Public Defenders Office, asst public defender 1980-82; General Sessions Court, judge 1982-88; US Bankruptcy Court 1988-. **ORGANIZATIONS:** Mem TN Bar Assoc; mem co-chair courts comm Memphis and Shelby County Bar Assoc; mem Ben F Jones Chap Natl Bar Assoc; mem Assoc of Women Attorneys; mem Natl Assoc of Women Judges 1983-; mem Amer Judges Assoc 1983-; chair General Sessions Judges Conference Educ 1987; bd of dirs Memphis State Univ Law Alumni; chair Comm on Excellence in Legal Educ; mem Zeta Phi Beta Sor, Alpha Eta Zeta Chapt; bd of dirs Shelby State Comm Coll, Criminal Justice Panel, Natl Conf of Negro Women, Business & Professional Women Clubs; assoc mem Natl Ctr for State Courts; mem JAD Div Amer Bar Assoc; mem Amer Trail Lawyers Assoc; mem Conference of Special Court Judges; numerous seminars, conferences, lectures and presentations. **HONORS/ACHIEVEMENTS:** 1st Black Female in US to serve on Bankruptcy Court; Elected First Black Female Judge in the history of the State of TN; Young Careerist Awd State of TN Raleigh Bureau of Professional Women; Woman of the Year Pentecostal Church of God in Christ; Martin Luther King Comm Serv Awd; Citizen of the Year Excelsior Chapter of Eastern Star; 1986 Comm Serv Awd Youth-Natl Conference of Christians and Jews; featured in Essence, Ebony, Jet and Memphis Magazine; participated on numerous TV shows to discuss legal and judicial issues; participated on numerous panels and forums dealing with legal process and the judiciary. **BUSINESS ADDRESS:** Judge US Bankruptcy Court, 969 Madison Ave, Suite 1207, Memphis, TN 38104.

DONALDSON, JAMES TERRELL
Professional athlete. **PERSONAL:** Born Aug 16, 1957, Meachem, England. **EDUCATION:** Wash State, 1979. **CAREER:** Los Angeles Clippers, center 1984-; Seattle Supersonics, 1980-83. **HONORS/ACHIEVEMENTS:** Was one of only two players on the Clippers to have played in all 82 games of the year; set a Clipper club record for highest field goal percetnage, hitting on596 of his shots; earned All Pacific-10 Second Team honors in his senior year at Wash State. **BUSINESS ADDRESS:** Los Angeles Clippers, 3939 S Figueroa St, Ste 1325, Los Angeles, CA 90037.

DONALDSON, JEFF R.
Artist, educator. **PERSONAL:** Born Dec 15, 1932, Pine Bluff, AR; son of Sidney Frank Donaldson and Clementine Richardson; divorced; children: Jameela K. **EDUCATION:** AR State Coll, BS Art 1954; Inst of Design of IL Inst of Tech, MS Art Educ 1963; Northwestern, PhD 1973. **CAREER:** Howard Univ, Coll of Fine Arts, assoc dean, artist; Internatl Festiv Com 2nd World Black & African Festiv of Arts & Cult, prof of art chmn of art dept vice pres 1975-77; USA Festac '77 Com, chmn/dir 1975-; Howard Univ Wash, dir of galleries of art 1970-76; part-time lectr art hist 1968-69; Northeastern IL State Coll Chgo, asst prof of art 1965-69; Chicago City Coll, asst prof of art 1964-66; John Marshall HS Chgo, chmn art dept 1959-65; Marshall HS, teacher 1958-59. **ORGANIZATIONS:** Mem of numerous bds & assns. **HONORS/ACHIEVEMENTS:** One of the creator of Chgo's orginal "Wall of Respect" 1967; recipient of several academic & professional awards; founding mem of Afri-Cobra Artists Guild 1968-. **BUSINESS ADDRESS:** Artist, HowardUniv, Coll of Fine Art, Washington, DC 20059.

DONALDSON, LEON MATTHEW
Educator. **PERSONAL:** Born Aug 16, 1933, Burton, SC; married Merita Worthy; children: Carter, TaJuania. **EDUCATION:** AL State U, BS 1963; So U, MS 1966; Rutgers U, EdD 1973; Auburn U; George Washington U; NC Centrl U. **CAREER:** Morgan State Univ, assoc prof; Corning Glass Works, chemical engineer 1970-71; TV McCoo High School, teacher 1963-70; Stauffer Chem Corp, chemist; IBM Corp, engineer. **ORGANIZATIONS:** Mem NAACP NEA; Nat Sci Tchrs Assn; Nat Cncl of Tchrs of Math; AL Educ Assn; SC Educ Assn; Civitan Internat; F & AM; Kappa Alpha Psi Frat Inc. **HONORS/ACHIEVEMENTS:** NSF fellow AL StateUniv NC Ctrl U; NSF fellow Southern U; EPDA fellows Rutgers U; num articles publ. **MILITARY SERVICE:** AUS sp5 1957-60. **BUSINESS ADDRESS:** Morgan StateUniv, Baltimore, MD 21212.

DONALDSON, RAY
Professional athlete. **PERSONAL:** Born May 18, 1958, Rome, GA; married Eileen. **EDUCATION:** Attended, Georgia. **CAREER:** Indianapolis Colts, center 1980-. **HONORS/ACHIEVEMENTS:** All-Amer honors from Sporting News, Associated Press, Newspaper Enterprise Assoc; played in East-West Shrine Game and the Senior Bowl 1980; Colts MVP 1985. **BUSINESS ADDRESS:** Indianapolis Colts, PO Box 535000, Indianapolis, IN 46250.

DONALDSON, RICHARD T.
Automotive executive. **PERSONAL:** Born Jul 02, 1935, St Petersburg, FL; married Charlie M Waller, Aug 02, 1955; children: Jewell, Kimiko, Lisa, Carol. **EDUCATION:** Tri-State Univ, Angola, IN, BAD, 1958-62; Emory Univ, Atlanta, GA, advanced mgmt, 1972. **CAREER:** General Motos Corp, supt mfg 1972; U.W. of Amer, production mgr, 1979; Chrysler, plant mgr, 1980, general plant mgr, 1983. **ORGANIZATIONS:** Engineering Soc Detroit, Mgmt Club, Allocation Comm Torch Drive/United Funds; Urban League, Big Brothers, Jr Achievement, NAACP, Trinity Baptist Church. **HONORS/ACHIEVEMENTS:** Distinguished Service Award Tri-State Univ, 1980. **MILITARY SERVICE:** Army paratrooper, Korean conflict.

DONAWA, MARIA ELENA
Physician/pathologist. **PERSONAL:** Born May 13, 1948, Detroit, MI; married John R Lupien. **EDUCATION:** Howard Univ Coll of Pharmacy, BS Pharmacy 1971; Howard Univ Coll of Medicine, MD 1976. **CAREER:** Marco Pharmacy, pharmacist 1971-72; Peoples Drug Stores Inc, registered pharmacist 1972-73; Howard Univ Hosp, resident 1976-80, chief

resident 1979-80; AbelLabs Inc, staff pathologist 1980; Food & Drug Admin Bureau of Medical Devices, special medical consultant 1981-83 to assoc dir for standards 1983-86; Food & Drug Administration Ctr for Devices & Radiological Health, asst dir for device safety & risk mgmt; Metro Laboratory, path dir 1982-83; Food & Drug Admin Intl Affairs Staff, health scientist admin essential drugs develop coord 1983; Assobiomedica Milan Italy, consultant on medical device. **ORGANIZATIONS:** Precinct chairperson Democratic Party 1978-79; bd of trustees 1979-86, chairperson quality control comm 1983-86, sec & mem exec comm 1985-86 District of Columbia General Hospital. **HONORS/ACHIEVEMENTS:** US Public Health Serv Achievement Awd 1983, Unit Commendation 1985, Serv Citation 1985, Unit Commendation 1986; network TV interview ABC News (World News Tonight) TSS, Tampons & FDA May 2, 1984 and June 21, 1982; selected media interviews; "The Case of Toxic Shock Syndrome," Knowledge Transfer Roundtable US Public Health Serv 1984 Report of Panel Presentations; articles "Toxic Shock Syndrome, Chronology of State & Federal Epidemiologic Studies and Regulatory Decision Making" with G Schmid, M Osterholm Public Health Reports Vol 99 No 4 1984. **HOME ADDRESS:** via Fonte di Fauno 22, Rome, Italy. **BUSINESS ADDRESS:** Consultant on Medical Device, Assobiomedica, via Accademia 33, Milan, Italy.

DONEGAN, CHARLES EDWARD
Attorney. **PERSONAL:** Born Apr 10, 1933, Chicago, IL; son of Arthur C Donegan, Jr and Odessa Arnold Donegan; married Patty L Harris; children: Carter Edward. **EDUCATION:** Wilson Jr Coll, AA 1953; Roosevelt, BSC 1954; Loyola, MSIR 1959; Howard, JD 1967; Columbia, LLM 1970. **CAREER:** US Commisson on Civil Rights; legal intern 1966; Poor Peoples Campaign, legal counsel 1968; SUNY At Buffalo, first asst prof of law 1970-73; Howard Univ, assoc prof of law 1973-77; OH State Univ, visiting assoc prof 1977-78; US EPA, asst reg counsel 1978-80; So Univ, prof of law 1980-84; CE Donegan & Assoc, atty at law; LA State Univ Law Sch, visiting prof 1981; Univ S Commission on Civil Rights, legal intern 1966; North Carolina Central Univ Law School, visiting prof 1988-89. **ORGANIZATIONS:** Labor arbitrator Steel Inds Postal AAA 1971-; cnsultant US Dept of Ag 1972; asst counsel NAACP Legal Defense Fund Inc 1967-69; hrng officer Various Govtl Agy 1975-; officer mem Am Natl Dist of Columbia Chicago Bar Assn 1968-; mem NAACP Urban League; Alpha Phi Alpha; Phi Alpha Delta; Phi Alpha Kappa; labor arbitrator FMCS 1985; counsultant Dist of Columbia Govt Dept of Public Works; mem, District of Columbia Consumer Claims Arbitration Bd 1987-90. **HONORS/ACHIEVEMENTS:** Most outstanding Prof So Univ Law Sch 1982; Ford Fellow Columbia Univ Law Sch 1972-73; NEH Fellow Afro Am Studies Yale Univ 1972-73; pub numerous Articals in Professional Journals 1966-85; contributor Dictionary of Am Negro Bio 1982. **HOME ADDRESS:** 4315 Argyle Terr N W, Washington, DC 20011. **BUSINESS ADDRESS:** Attorney, CE Donegan & Associates, 601 Indiana Ave, NW, Ste 900, Washington, DC 20004.

DONELAN, CLARENCE WARREN
Chief executive officer. **PERSONAL:** Born Aug 30, 1924, Boston, MA; married Phyllis Marie Roach; children: Richard Warren. **EDUCATION:** Bently Coll of Accounting & Finance, BA 1960-64; Northeastern U, Cert 1969-70; Fitchburg State Tchrs Coll, Cert 1974-76. **CAREER:** Opportunities Industrialization Centers (OIC), exec dir 1972-; OIC Boston, deputy exec dir 1969-72, dir operations 1968-69, dir admin 1967-68; Lawson Foundrys Inc, sr accountant 1964-66; Gen Wholesale Supply Co, asst office mgr 1963-64. **ORGANIZATIONS:** Bd mem Lower Roxbury Comm Corp 1966-80; exec com Exec Dirs Assn OIC 1976-80; bd mem Boston Pvt Indsl Council 1979-80; past master Widow Sons Lodge #3 AFAM 1947-52; mem NAACP 1950-80; mem Roxbury C of C 1972-80. **MILITARY SERVICE:** AUS staff sgt 1941-44. **BUSINESS ADDRESS:** Oppty Industrialization Center, 214 Dudley St, Roxbury, MA 02119.

DOOLEY, WALLACE TROY
Orthopaedic surgeon. **PERSONAL:** Born Jun 15, 1917, Conway, AR; married Orealia Clara Robinson; children: Wallace Jr, Orealia L. **EDUCATION:** KS U, AB 1939; KS U, MA 1941; Meharry Med Coll, MD 1947; Geo W Hubbard Hosp, internship 1947-48; Mercy Hosp, 1951-53; Children's Hosp, 1953-55. **CAREER:** Meharry Med Coll, prof div ortho surg 1968; Meharry Med Coll, asso & prof, head ortho surg 1965; Meharry Med Coll, asst prof ortho surg 1955;Riverside Hosp, Taborian Hosp, cons, ortho surg 1963; TN State U, team phys 1963; Meharry Med Coll, dir rehab med 1962; Geo W Hubbard Hsop, dir Crippled Children's Clinic 1955; Nat Med Assn, chmn Ortho Sec 1970-72; FF Boyd Med Soc, exec sec. **ORGANIZATIONS:** Vol State Med Assn; Am Cong of Rehab Med fdr Assn of Ortho chmn; chmn Research Com mem Adv Bd Assn Med Rehab Dir & Coords Inc 1975; Nashville Area C of C; mem, bd dir, chmn Health & Welfare Com Nashville Urban League 1968-73; Nashville Chap of Frontiers Internat; adv Meharry Chap & 19 Kappa Alpha Psi Frat Inc 1974; Nashville Ortho Soc; TN Orthos - Soc; Pride of TN Elks Lodge #1102 BPOE of W mem exec com Black Educators Council of Human Serv 1970; Manpower Devel & Training HEW 1968-71; dir coun of Comm Agency 1961-62; dir Nashville Br NAACP 1958-61; Outlook Nashville 1959-61; Goodwill Ind 1960-62; pres Comm Conf on Employment Oppor 1960-64; Gov Com on Emp of Physcally Handicapped 1965-67; President's Com on Employment of Physically Handicapped 1965-67; Nat Found for Infantile Paralysis March of Dimes 1959; chmn Div United Givers Fund 1961. **HONORS/ACHIEVEMENTS:** Men of Achvmt 1974; 2000 Men of Achvmt 1970; Personalities of the S; Dict of Intl Bed 1975-76; Royal Soc of Health (FRSH); "Outst Serv to Mankind" Plaque Meharry Med Coll 1972; "Outst Serv to Mankind" Plaque Kappa Alpha Frat 1974; Cert of Merit Distg Serv in Surg, Dict Intl Biog 1973; Cert of Aprrec, Outst Serv to Mankind, Frontiers Internat, Nashville Chap 1975; Cert of Outst Serv Assn Med Rehab Dir, Coord Inc 1975; Cert Merit, Dist Serv to Comm, Dict Intl Biog 1976. **BUSINESS ADDRESS:** Meharry Med Coll, 1005 18 Ave N, Nashville, TN 37208.

DOOMES, EARL
Educator. **PERSONAL:** Born Feb 08, 1943, Washington, LA; married Mazie Marie LeDeaux; children: Elizabeth Denise, Edward Earl, Elliot Doyle. **EDUCATION:** So Univ Baton Rouge, BS 1964; Univ of NE Lincoln, PhD 1969. **CAREER:** Northwestern Univ, post doctoral rsch 1968-69; Macalester Coll, asst prof 1969-74; FL State Univ, rsch assoc 1975-76; Macalester Coll, assoc prof 1974-77; Southern Univ Baton Rouge, assoc prof 1977-82, prof of chemistry 1982-. **ORGANIZATIONS:** Reviewer Petroleum Rsrch Fund Grant Prpsl 1970-80; cnsltnt Mnrty BiomedRsrch Sprt Pgm of the Natl Inst of Hlth 1979-86; Natl Sci Found Grants Pgm 1985. **HONORS/ACHIEVEMENTS:** Merck Sharpe & Dohme Univ of NE Lincoln 1968; Natl Sci Found TranieeshipUniv Of N 1967-68; Natl Sci Found Fclty Sci Flwhp FL State Univ 1975-76; rsrch grnts 8; pblshd artlcls 20. **BUSINESS ADDRESS:** Professor of Chemistry, SouthernUniv BR, P O Box 11513, SouthernUniv, Baton Rouge, LA 70813.

DORMAN, HATTIE L.
Management consultant, associate professor. **PERSONAL:** Born Jul 22, 1932, Cleveland, OH; daughter of James L Lawrence and Claire Correa Lenoir Lawrence; married James WL Dorman; children: Lydia Dorman, Lynda, James "Larry". **EDUCATION:** Attended, Fenn Coll 1950-58, DC Teacher's Coll 1959-64, Howard Univ, 1986-87 BA. **CAREER:** IRS, 1954-79; US Treasury, spl asst to deputy asst sec 1978-79; President's Task Force on Women Business Enterprise, mem 1978-79; Interagency Comm on Women's Business Enterprise US Small Business Admin, deputy dir 1979-83; US Small Business Admin Office of Comm and Govt Support, dir 1983-85; Dorman & Associates, management consultant 1985-. **ORGANIZATIONS:** Trainer Nation's Capital Girl Scout Cncl 1972-; mem Natl Assoc of Female Execs, Amer Assoc of Black Women Entrepreneurs, Black Career Women Inc, Sr Exec Assoc, Federal Exec Inst Alumni Assoc, Amer Polit Sci Assoc, Amer Sociological Assoc; life mem Natl Council of Negro Women; golden life mem Delta Sigma Theta Sor Inc; mem Natl Urban League; public speaker field of mgmt and business develop; articles Field of Small Business Develop. **HONORS/ACHIEVEMENTS:** Monetary Performance Awds IRS 1970-78; Mary McLeod Bethune Centennial Awd Natl Council of Negro Women; Monteary Performance Awds US Small Business Admin 1980, 1984, 1985; Boss of the Year Awd Amer Business Women's Assoc L'Enfant Chap 1981; other awds and citations from Delta Sigma Theta, PTA's, Amer Assoc of Black Women Entrepreneurs, Natl Assoc of Minority Women; "Survey of Support Patterns by Black Organizations for Black Political Appointees" Benjamin E Mays Monograph series Fall 1988 vol 1, No 2. **HOME ADDRESS:** 7801 13th St NW, Washington, DC 20012.

DORMAN, LINNEAUS C.
Scientist. **PERSONAL:** Born Jun 28, 1935, Orangeburg, SC; son of John A Dorman (deceased) and Georgia (Hammond) Dorman (deceased); married Phae Hubble; children: Evelyn S, John A. **EDUCATION:** Bradley Univ, BS 1952-56; IN Univ, PhD 1956-61. **CAREER:** No Regional Res Lab, chemist 1956-59; Dow Chem Co, rsch chemist 1960-68, rsch specialist 1968-76, sr rsch assoc 1976-83, assoc scientist 1983-. **ORGANIZATIONS:** Bd of dir Comerica Bk-Midland 1982-; midland sec counselor Am Chem Soc 1971-; chmn 1984,85 bd of fellows Saginaw Valley State Coll 1976-87, Natl Org of Black Chem & Chem Eng 1978-; pres Midland Rotary Clb 1982-83; chmn Midland Black Coalition 1973, 1977; bd of trustees Midland Found 1981-; United Negro College Fund; chmn Midland Area Campaign 1981-84; life mem NAACP; vice pres Midland Foundation 1988-. **HONORS/ACHIEVEMENTS:** Co-Recipient Bond Awrd Am Oil Chemst Soc 1960; inventor of the yr Dow Chem Central Rsch 1983; patentee in field; cnstribtr to Scientific Journals & Books; Honorary Doctor of Science, Saginaw Valley State Univ 1988. **BUSINESS ADDRESS:** Associate Scientist, Dow Chemical Co, 1702 Building, Midland, MI 48674.

DORN, ROOSEVELT F.
Judge, minister. **PERSONAL:** Born Oct 29, 1935, Checotah, OK; married Joyce Evelyn Glosson, 1965; children: Bryan Keith, Renee Felicia, Rochelle Francine. **EDUCATION:** Whittier Coll of Law, JSD 1969. **CAREER:** Los Angeles County, deputy sheriff/superior court bailiff, 1961-69; City of Los Angeles, asst city atty 1970-79; Inglewood Jud Dist CA, municipal ct judge 1979-80; Los Angeles County Superior Court, judge 1980-. **ORGANIZATIONS:** Founder, 1st pres Inglewood Dem Club 1977-79; mem NAACP, Urban League, LA Co Bar Assn, Langston Bar Assn, CA Black Lawyers Assn, Am Bar Assn, Lions Club; assoc minister Atherton Baptist Church Inglewood, CA; mem CA Judges Assoc, Natl Bar Assn, Los Angeles Trial Lawyers Assn, 100 Black Men of Los Angeles Inc. **HONORS/ACHIEVEMENTS:** Commendation for Outstanding Comm Serv, The Senate CA Legislature 1978; Commendation for Outstanding Serv CA State Assembly 1979; Commendation for Outstanding Achievement New Frontier Dem Club Inglewood Dem Club 1979; Outstanding Serv Awd in the field of Juvenile Justice Natl Sor of Phi Delta Kappa Inc Delta Kappa Chap 1983, John M Langston Bar Assoc 1983, Inglewood Democratic Club, Los Angeles Co Bd of Supervisors 1983, CA State Assembly 1983; Outstanding Contributions Support and Leadership for Youth Awd RDM Scholarship Fund Inc 1984, 1985; Meritorious Serv Youth Awd The Inglewood Teachers Assn 1986; Dedicated Service & Guidance Awd Inglewood High School Student Body; Natl Top Ladies of Distinction Humanitarian Award, 1987; Outstanding Service Award, Prairie View A&M Univ Alumni Assn, 1989. **MILITARY SERVICE:** USAF airman 1st class 1954-58. **BUSINESS ADDRESS:** Judge, Superior Court Los Angeles Cty, 110 Regent St, Inglewood, CA 90301.

DORSETT, KATIE GRAYS
Government official. **PERSONAL:** Born Jul 08, 1932, Shaw, MS; daughter of Willie and Elizabeth; married Warren G Dorsett; children: Valerie. **EDUCATION:** Alcorn State Univ, BS 1953; Indiana Univ at Bloomington, MS 1955; Univ of North Carolina at Greensboro, EdD 1975; State Univ of New York at Buffalo, attended 1981; Univ of Maryland at College Park, attended 1983. **CAREER:** School of Business & Economics North Carolina A&T St Univ, assoc prof 1955-1987; Greensboro City Council 1983-86; Guilford County Commission 1986-; Transportation Inst North Carolina A&T, rsch assoc 1983-87. **ORGANIZATIONS:** Bd mem, Guilford Tech Comm Coll 1978-; exec bd General Greene Council Boy Scouts 1980-; mem Greensboro Citizens Assn; life mem, NAACP; mem League of Women Voters; bd mem, Greensboro Natl Bank; bd mem, MDC Corporation. **HONORS/ACHIEVEMENTS:** 10 publications including "A Study of Levels of Job Satisfaction and Job Aspirations Among Black Clerical Employees in Greensboro & Guilford Co, North Carolina" 1976; Outstanding Civic Leader Greensboro Interclub Council 1978; TV Citizen of the Week WGHP TV 1978; One Comm Awd Feb One Soc 1982; Outstanding Citizen Award Negro Business & Prof Women 1983; Outstanding Comm Leader Mt Zion Baptist Church 1983; Leader of the Year Omega Psi Phi 1983; Woman of the Year Mt Zion AME Church 1984; "Training and Career Opportunities for Minorities and Women" Proceedings 1984; Sojourner Truth Award, Negro Business & Professional Women, 1985; Leadership Award, Negro Business & Professional Women, 1986; Distinguished Alumni, NAFEO, 1987; Leadership Award, Sigma Gamma Rho, 1987; Bennett College Comm Se rv, Bennett Coll, 1988; Silver Anniversary Serv Award, North Carolina Comm Coll, 1989; Woman of Year, NAACP, 1989. **HOME ADDRESS:** 1000 N English St, Greensboro, NC 27405.

DORSETT, TONY DREW
Professional athlete. **PERSONAL:** Born Apr 07, 1954, Alquippa, PA; married Julie; children: Shukura, Anthony Drew Jr. **EDUCATION:** Attended, Univ of Pgh. **CAREER:** Southwestern Drilling Mud Co of Midland TX, partner; Dallas Cowboys, running back 1977-.

ORGANIZATIONS: Mem Natl Easter Seals Sports Cncl; chmn Amer Heart Assn Jump-Rope-A-Thon 1980; promoted, United Way, United Negro College Fund, TX Dept of Hwys & Public Trans Seat Belt Prog, Dallas Civic Opera. HONORS/ACHIEVEMENTS: Heisman Trophy 1976; 1st player in NCAA history with 4-1000 yard seasons; Pro Bowl 1978-81-82-83; NFC Player of the Yr 1981; Best Dressed Man in Sports CustomTailors Guild NY 1981; holds numerous team records.

DORSEY, CAROLYN ANN
Educator. **PERSONAL:** Born Oct 08, Dayton, OH; daughter of James J Dorsey and Lorana M Webb Dorsey. **EDUCATION:** Kent State Univ, BS 1956, MEd 1961; Yale Univ, Danforth Fellow in Black Studies 1969-70; New York Univ, PhD 1976. **CAREER:** Cleveland Public Schools, teacher 1956-62; Tabora Girls Sch, Tanzania, E Africa, teacher 1962-64; Cleveland Job Corps Ctr, social studies dept chair & teacher 1965-67; Southern IL Univ Exper in Higher Educ Prog, curriculum spec & instructor 1967-69; Yale Univ Transitional Year Program, assoc dir & teacher, 1965-70; NY Univ Inst of Afro-Amer Affairs, jr fellow 1970-74; IN State Univ, asst prof of afro-amer studies 1976-77; Univ of MO, coord of Black studies & asst prof of higher educ 1977-81, coord of Black studies & assoc prof of higher educ 1981-85, assoc prof of higher educ 1985-, dir of graduate studies, 1986-. **ORGANIZATIONS:** Stephens Coll Bd of Curators; Amer Assn of Higher Educ, Natl Council for Black Studies; Phi Delta Kappa; Phi Lambda Theta; Assn for the Study of Afro-American Life & History; Alpha Kappa Alpha Sorority; mem of bias panel Amer Coll Testing Program Tests 1982- & The Psychological Corp Stanford Achievement Test, 7th & 8th editions. **HONORS/ACHIEVEMENTS:** Danforth Found Black Studies Fellowship yr spent at Yale Univ 1969-70; Southern Fellowship used for Dissertation Study at New York Univ 1973-74; Danforth Found Assoc 1980-86; resident participant in Summer Inst for Women in Higher Educ Admin, Bryn Mawr Coll, 1989. **BUSINESS ADDRESS:** Associate Professor, University of Missouri, 304 Hill Hall, Columbia, MO 65211.

DORSEY, CHARLES HENRY, JR.
Attorney. **PERSONAL:** Born May 18, 1930, Baltimore, MD; married Agnes; children: Kathleen, Andrea, Judith, Claire, Charles III, Leonard, Peter, Martin, Nicholas. **EDUCATION:** Epiphany Coll, 1947-48; Loyola Coll, 1949-57;Univ of IMD Law Sch, 1957-61. **CAREER:** US Post Office, clerk 1957-61; Human A Pressman Esq Baltimore, assoc 1961-62; George L Russell Jr, assoc 1962-63; Brown, Allen, Watts, Murphy & Russell Baltimore, assoc 1963-66; Brown & Allen, Dorsey & Josey Baltimore, parnter 1966-69; Baltimore City Solicitor, 1969; Legal Aid Bur, deputy dir 1969-74; Legal Aid Bur Inc, exec dir 1974-. **ORGANIZATIONS:** Mem adv commn Baltimore Dept of Social Serv 1967-69; mem bd dir Assoc Catholic Charities 1969-73; mem MD State Bar Assn; chmn 1971, sec 1972-74, vice pres 1984-85, pres elect 1985-86, pres 1986-87 Lawyer Referrral Serv Bar Assn of Baltimore; Monumental City Bar Assn; mem bd governors St Thomas More Soc Mem bd trustees Good Samaritan Hosp 1973; vice chmn Proj Advisory Group 1976-79; chmn Proj Advisory Group 1979; mem bd of trustees Western MD CollWestminister MD; mem MD Bar Foundation 1980; mem & bd dir Baltimore Legal Scholarship Fund; chmn judicial appointments MD State Bar Assn 1983-84. **HONORS/ACHIEVEMENTS:** Papal Order of Knights of St gregory; Man for all Seasons Awd St Thomas More Soc 1974; Alumni Laureate Awd Loyola Coll 1985; Community Serv Awd Monumental City Bar Assn 1986. **MILITARY SERVICE:** USAF 1951-56.

DORSEY, CLINTON GEORGE
Educator. **PERSONAL:** Born Oct 29, 1931, New York, NY. **EDUCATION:** Wilberforce Univ OH, BS Ed 1966; United Theol Sem Dayton OH, MDiv 1970; Wright State Univ Dayton OH, attended. **CAREER:** AME Church, United Church of Christ, 1962-68; Wright Patterson Air Force Base, Dayton OH, W OH Conf, United Methodist Church, pastor 1969-74; Sportsman Bar-B-Que Hut, proprietor; Troy High School, Troy OH, counselor 1975-. **ORGANIZATIONS:** Pres Clinton G Dorsey Assoc Motivational Human Devel; dist rep OH School Counselors Assoc 1971-76; consult Dem Nom US Rep Fourth Cong Dist OH 1976; bd mem Miami Cty Mental Assoc 1976; adv bd criminal justice comm Edison State Comm Coll 1979; APGA leg prog proj trainer Amer Personnel & Guidance Asn 1980. **MILITARY SERVICE:** USAF a1/c 1949-53. **BUSINESS ADDRESS:** Counselor, Troy High Schoo, 151 Staunton Rd, Troy, OH 45373.

DORSEY, EDMUND STANLEY
Broadcasting executive. **PERSONAL:** Born Aug 18, 1930, Washington, DC; married Louvenia; children: Michi, Toni, Karl, Edmunt Jr. **EDUCATION:** SeoulUniv Seoul, Korea, master of proficiency in lang; Kelo U, Tokyo, M degree polit sci. **CAREER:** WIND radio station Chicago, news dir 1964-; Westinghouse Broadcasting Netword Saigon, first black bureau chief 1966; WIND, head of minority training program; "Stars & Stripes", 1st black mng editor 1949; WWDC, 1st black White House broadcast corr; WOOK Radio Station, 1st black-TV news reporter in Wash; Malxolm X Coll, tchr, Broadcasting. **ORGANIZATIONS:** Mem Nat Overseas Capitol Press Clubs; bd dir YMCA Office. **MILITARY SERVICE:** AUS.

DORSEY, ELBERT
Attorney. **PERSONAL:** Born Oct 04, 1941, St Louis, MO; son of Velmer Dorsey and Juanita Jarrett Green; married Diane Elaine; children: Elbert Todd, Donielle Elaine, Daniel Christopher, Joseff Alexander. **EDUCATION:** Harris-Stowe State Coll, BA 1966; St Louis Univ School of Law, JD 1973. **CAREER:** St Louis Comm Coll Dist, asst librarian 1965-66; St Louis Bd of Educ, teacher 1966-70; St Louis Legal Aid Soc, law clerk 1971-72; Small Business Admin, loan officer/attorney 1973-74; Collier, Dorsey, & Edwards, attorney. **ORGANIZATIONS:** Historian Mound City Bar Assc; mem Judicial Conf Advy Com for the Eighth Circuit Ct of Appeals; chmn/bd of dir Yeatman/Union-Sarah Jnt Commn on Health; Polemarch St Louis Alumni Chptr Kappa Alpha Psi Frat; chmn/advsry bd St Louis Comprehensive Hlth Cntr Home Hlth Bd. **HONORS/ACHIEVEMENTS:** Ford Fellowship World Conf of Peace 1973; Humanitarian Award St Louis Alumni Chptr Kappa Alpha Psi 1985; Dedication Award Mound City Bar Assn of St Louis 1983. **BUSINESS ADDRESS:** Attorney, Collier, Dorsey & Edwards, 3330 Olive St, Suite 200, Ste 200, St Louis, MO 63103.

DORSEY, ERROL C.
City official. **PERSONAL:** Born Mar 27, 1945, Alexandria, LA; married Bernice Joseph; children: Monica, Judy, Erika. **EDUCATION:** La Coll, 1969-70; LA State Univ, 1970-72. **CAREER:** All State Ins Co, sales rep 1970-78; Wellans Dept Store, store mgr 1978-82; Peter Betts Lincoln, sales rep; Alexandria City Council, pres. **ORGANIZATIONS:** Mem VFW 1967-; mem Alexander City Council 1977-; assoc pastor Second Evergreen BC 180-85; pres Alexandria City Council 1982-85; 1st black mayor Alexandria 1984-. **HONORS/ACHIEVEMENTS:** Humanitarian Awd Natl Assoc of Univ Women 1978-79. **MILITARY SERVICE:** USMC sgt E-5 4 yrs; Purple Heart 1965. **BUSINESS ADDRESS:** President City Council, Alexandria City Council, 4441 Jackson St, Alexandria, LA 71301.

DORSEY, HAROLD AARON
Chief executive officer. **PERSONAL:** Born Jun 22, 1933, Louisville, KY; married Julia Anita Willis; children: Michelle, Harold II, Michael. **EDUCATION:** OH Univ Athens, BA Pol Sci 1965; OH State Univ Columbus, MA 1971. **CAREER:** Community Action Agency, asst dir 1965-69; Grad School OH State Dept Soc, rsch asst 1968-70; Community Action Agency, acting dir 1970; OH State Univ, teaching asst 1970-71; Mansfield OIC, exec dir 1971-. **ORGANIZATIONS:** Past pres Mansfield NAACP 1974; past chmn 9 Cty Manpower Adv Council 1975; bd of dir Mansfield Area C of C 1977-80; pres Natl Black Professional Assoc 1977-80. **HONORS/ACHIEVEMENTS:** Personality of the Week Local Newspaper-Mansfield News Jrnl; Businessman of Week Local Radio Staion; Ed Bd Gerontologist. **MILITARY SERVICE:** USAF a/1c. **BUSINESS ADDRESS:** Executive Dir, Mansfield OIC, 445 N Bowman St, Mansfield, OH 44903.

DORSEY, JOHN L.
Attorney. **PERSONAL:** Born Sep 24, 1935, New Orleans, LA; married Evelyn. **EDUCATION:** Dillard U, BA 1963; LoyolaUniv Law Sch, JD 1969. **CAREER:** New Orleans Legal Assistance Corp, atty 1968-70; Dorsey & Marks, New Orleans, atty 1970-; John L Dorsey, attorney at law. **ORGANIZATIONS:** Mem Nat Bar Assn; New Orleans Criminal Ct Bar Assn; Am Bar Assn; mem NAACP; New Orleans Urban League; Lower & Ninth Ward Neighborhood Council; Com on Alcholism & Drug Abuse for Greater New Orleans; All Conference Football 1961. **MILITARY SERVICE:** USAF a/1c 1955-59. **BUSINESS ADDRESS:** Attorney, Canal Place One, Ste 2300, New Orleans, LA 70130.

DORSEY, JOSEPH A.
Educational administrator. **PERSONAL:** Born Apr 19, 1932, Baltimore, MD; married Alma K Edmonds; children: Dwain Kevin, Kyle Joseph. **EDUCATION:** Springfield Coll, (cum laude) BS 1954-58; NY U, CAGS 1958-59; Northesastern U, MEd 1964-66; Boston U, DEd 1972-76;Univ of Lowell Dept of Health,prof, chmn 1976-; Boston State Coll & Phys Edn, asso prof, chmn 1968-76; Andover Sch System, tchr coach 1960-68; Wayne Co Gen Hosp Detroit, phys therapist 1959-60; Lawrence Gen Hosp, phys therapist 1960-66; Private Practice, phys therapist 1960-; Andover Bd Health & Sch System, consult pt 1977-78. **CAREER:** Bd of dir Andover ABC 1977-; com mem Merrimack Valley Health Council 1978-. **ORGANIZATIONS:** Coach of the Year MA Assn Gymnastic Coaches 1967-68; citations State Rep & State Sen 1968 & 1977; Andover Hall of Fame, Andover Sch System 1977; Fellow Am Coll of Sports Medicine 1979; Good Conduct Medal/UN Serv Medal/Korean Serv Medal W/3 Stars/Nat Defense Medal USMC. **MILITARY SERVICE:** USMC sgt 1951-54. **BUSINESS ADDRESS:** 1 Rolfe St, Lowell, MA 01854.

DORSEY, L. C.
Health center executive. **PERSONAL:** Born Dec 17, 1938, Tribbett, MS; daughter of Abraham Warren and Mary Davis; married Hildery Dorsey Sr, Feb 17, 1956 (divorced); children: Cynthia Dorsey Smith, Norma Dorsey, Anita Dorsey Ward, Michael Dorsey, Adriane Dorsey, Hildery Dorsey Jr. **EDUCATION:** Mary Holmes Coll, 1969-71; Worker Coll Tel Aviv Israel, 1970; State Univ of NY Stony Brook NY, MSW 1973, Howard Univ, DSW 1988. **CAREER:** Delta Ministry, asso dir 1977-; So Coalition on Jails & Prisons Inc, asso dir 1975; Washington Co Opportunities Inc, dir social serv 1974; No Bolivar Co Farm Coop, dir 1968-71; Operation Headstart, tchr 1966-68; Delta Health Center Inc, exec dir 1988-; Univ of Mississippi, research asst prof 1988; Memphis Health Center, asst to the Chief Health Officer 1986-88; Lutheran Social Services of Washington DC, Advocacy & Education, dir 1983-85. **ORGANIZATIONS:** Mem Pres Commn Nat Adv Comp on Econ Opportunity 1978-82; mem MS Conf of Social Welfare 1976-; pres Jackson chap NABSW 1976-78, 80-82; chmn polit action com, Stte NAACP 1979; mem New Bethel MB Ch choir 1975-80; writer, bd mem Jackson Adv 1978-80; poet, founding mem Black Women's Art Collective 1978-80; mem, Presidential Comm, Natl Advisory Council on Economic Opportunities, Washington DC 1978-80; mem, Governor's Commission on Children and Youth, Jackson MS 1980; mem, Governor's Task Force on Indigent Health Care, Jackson MS 1988-. **HONORS/ACHIEVEMENTS:** Meritorious Serv Awards Nat Med Assn, Women's Aux 1970; Woman of the Year New York City Utility Club 1971; Fellowship Black Women's Community Devel Found 1971, 1972; Fannie Lou Homer Award, Urban League of Jackson 1978; Fellow, MATCH Program, Natl Assn of Community Health Centers 1986-87; The Significance of Jealousy and Addictive Love in Acts of Homicide Among Black Women (Dissertation) 1987; Not In Our Names 1984; Cold Steel 1982; If Bars Could Talk 1980; Freedom Came to Mississippi 1978. **HOME ADDRESS:** P O Box 8, Shelby, MS 38774.

DORSEY, LEON D., SR.
Business executive. **PERSONAL:** Born Feb 10, 1909, Perry, TX; married Althea Fay Hutchings; children: Leon II, Robert. **EDUCATION:** Paul Quinn, 1931-32. **CAREER:** Dorsey-keatts Funeral Home Inc, owner pres; Independent Funeral Directors Assn, TX Pres Dorsey Funeral Benefit Assn, past chmn bd, past Fpres, past treas; TX Assn Life Ins & Offices, 1st vp. **ORGANIZATIONS:** Marlin City Councilman; finan sec Marlin Miss Bapt Ch; mem exec com Heart TX; Boy Scout Council. **HONORS/ACHIEVEMENTS:** Mortician Yr 1967; 33 deg Mason; Century mem Heart TX Boy Scouts 1973; Past Grand Joshua Heroines Jericho Princ Hall Affiliation 1970-73; v grand Joshua Heroins Jericho of Gen Conf Grand Cts PHA 1976-77; Silv Beaver Aw Scts 1976-77, 1974-75. **BUSINESS ADDRESS:** 907 Live Oak St, Marlin, TX.

DORTCH, THOMAS WESLEY, JR.
Business executive. **PERSONAL:** Born Apr 12, 1950, Toccoa, GA; married Undrea Jackson. **EDUCATION:** Ft Valley State Coll, BA; GA State U, masters. **CAREER:** US Senator Sam Nunn, admin aide; Dem Party of GA, asso dir; GA Dept Human Resources (ACCP Div), com devel cons; Atlanta & NAACP, job placement developer. **ORGANIZATIONS:** Mem Nat Assn Human Rights Workers; Nat Assn of Blk Soc Workers; Young People on the Go; NAACP; GA Assn Blk Elected Ofcl adv bd; EOA Vet Affairs; COMPA; chmn Polit Action Com, Young People on the Go; pres Nat Alumni FUSC; vice pres Council of Nat Alumni Assn. **HONORS/ACHIEVEMENTS:** Listed in Who's Who Among Coll & U; Outst Young Men in Am 1976-77; Personalities in the S 1976-77; Al Knox Award, FVSC 1972;

Ford Fellow; Sears & Roebuck Presidential Found Schlrshp; article "Atlant, The Black Mecca of the S", Ebony 1973. **BUSINESS ADDRESS:** 275 Peachtree St, Ste 930, Atlanta, GA 30303.

DOSS, EVAN, JR.
State official. **PERSONAL:** Born Jul 06, 1948, Lorman, Montserrat;married Emma Ruth Duffin; children: Evan III, Rashida Fayola. **EDUCATION:** Alcorn State U, BS 1970. **CAREER:** Claiborne Co, tax assessor & tax collector; Claiborne Co Sch System MS, Pt Gibson, MS, history tchr 1970-71. **ORGANIZATIONS:** Assessor Collector Assn; NAACP; Omega Psi Phi Frat. **HONORS/ACHIEVEMENTS:** Port Gibson MS Whitman "Grady" Mayo Scholarship Found Inc. **BUSINESS ADDRESS:** Tax Assessor & Collector, Claiborne County, PO Box 653, Port Gibson, MS 39150.

DOSS, LAROY SAMUEL
Business executive. **PERSONAL:** Born Oct 06, 1936, San Francisco, CA; married Mary Joyce Piper; children: Gwendolyn Marie. **EDUCATION:** St Marys Coll, 1955-59. **CAREER:** Crown Zellerback, warehouseman 1959-61; SF, playground dir 1961-63; Geary Ford, salesman 1963; Pittsburg Ford Inc, fleet mgr 1968-69, truck sales mgr 1969-71, used car mgr 1974, pres 1974-. **ORGANIZATIONS:** 2nd vp, bd dir St Marys Coll Alumni 1963-; Proj Inside/Out San Quentin Prison 1967-71; vice pres Optimist Club 1972-74; pres Pittsburgh C of C 1976-; bd dir E Contra Costa YMCA 1977-; dir Sr Citizens Home for Aging Bldg Fund 1977-, Black Political Assn 1975, Pittsburg Rotary Club 1975-, Pittsburg Business & Professional Assn; mem of bd of trustees St Marys Coll 1980-; pres Easter Seals Soc of Contra Costa Solano Cty 1983-84; bd of regents St Mary's Coll Moraga CA 1986-; chmn of the bd, Black Ford-Lincoln-Mercury Dealers Assn 1988. **HONORS/ACHIEVEMENTS:** All City Basketball 1955; All League Basketball 1958-59; Most Valuable Player 1959; #92 in 1977, #72 in 1978 Black Enterprise Magazine for Most Successful 100 Black Businesses in Amer. **BUSINESS ADDRESS:** President, Pittsburg Ford Inc, 2575 Railroad Ave, Pittsburg, CA 94565.

DOSS, LAWRENCE PAUL
Business executive. **PERSONAL:** Born Jun 16, 1927, Cleveland, OH; divorced; children: Paula, Lawrence, Lawry. **EDUCATION:** Nova Univ, Publ Admin attended; Ohio State Univ, 1947-49; Fenn Coll, 1949-51; Amer Univ 1954. **CAREER:** IRS, mgmt positions 1949-71; New Detroit Inc, pres 1970-77; Coopers & Lybrand, partner. **ORGANIZATIONS:** Mem Assoc of School Business Officials, Business Policy Review Council, Municipal Finance Officers Assoc; dir Amer Natural Resources, Hudson-Webber Found; bd mem Coleman A Young Found, Congressional Black Caucus Found, New Detroit Inc, Univ of Detroit; advisory mem Detroit Black United Fund; bd mem exec comm mem Detroit Econ Growth Corp; trustee Harper-Grace Hospital; vice chmn bd & exec comm Martin Luther King Jr Center; chmn comm devel comm Michigan Commiss on Jobs & Econ Devel; co-chmn Move Detroit Forward; spec consult Natl Council of Negro Women; chmn corp urban affairs comm & steering comm mem Natl Urban Coalition; pres Inner City Bus Improvement Forum 1967-71; chmn State of Michigan Neighborhood Educ Auth 1968-70. **MILITARY SERVICE:** USN 1 yr. **BUSINESS ADDRESS:** Partner, Coopers & Lybrand, 1800 M St NW, Washington, DC 20036.

DOTSON, BETTY LOU
Management consultant. **PERSONAL:** Born Jun 29, 1930, Chicago, IL; daughter of Heber T Dotson and Christine Price Dotson. **EDUCATION:** OH Wesleyan Univ, BA 1950; Lincoln Univ, JD 1954. **CAREER:** Dept of Urban Renewal, 1963; Cook Cty Dept of Public Welfare, caseworker-cons 1964-66; 1st Natl Bank of Chgo, legal serv trust dept 1966-68; US Dept of Agr Food & Nutrition Svc, dir civil rights 1970-75; Dept of Health & Human Services, Washington, DC, dir, office for civil rights, 1981-87; BLD & Associates, pres, currently. **ORGANIZATIONS:** Asst dir Equal Oppty Action 1975-78; asst to dir Equal Oppty USDA 1978-79; sr staff assoc Joint Ctr for Political Studies 1979-80; chief adjudicationsUSDA Equal Oppty Office 1980-81; bd dir Natl Capital YWCA 1981-84; mem Alpha Kappa Alpha; steeering comm Black Amers for Nixon/Agnew 1968. **HONORS/ACHIEVEMENTS:** Admin Asst Office of Pres elect Nixon 1969. **BUSINESS ADDRESS:** Pres, BLD & Associates, PO Box 2359, Washington, DC 20013.

DOTSON, PHILIP RANDOLPH
Educator. **PERSONAL:** Born Oct 10, 1948, Carthage, MS; son of Jim O R Dotson and Velma Ernest Dotson; married Judith Kerr Dotson, May 19, 1973; children: Philip T R, Tiffany M, Brian R. **EDUCATION:** Jackson State Univ, Jackson MS, BS Art Ed 1970; Univ of Mississippi, Oxford MS, MFA Painting 1972. **CAREER:** Memphis Jack & Jill Exhibition, curator, 1983-84; The Spirit of African Art in the South, Memphis State Univ, curator, 1983; LeMoyne-Owen Coll, chairman dept of art, 1972-87, chairman division of fine arts and humanities, 1988-. **ORGANIZATIONS:** Planning mem, Memphis in May Intl Fest, 1972-73; review mem, Tennessee Arts Commn, 1975-76; mem, Religious Comm Arts & the Amer Revolution, 1976, Chamber of Commerce; arts advisory bd, Mallory Knights Charitable Org, 1976-80; sponsor, Cotton Carnival Assoc, 1972-83; mem, Coll Art Assoc, 1978-80; bd mem, Artist in the Schools Program Arts Council; bd dir, Round Table of Memphis Museum Dir, 1982-; bd mem, Memphis Arts Council, 1986-; bd mem, Memphis Arts Festival, 1989-. **HONORS/ACHIEVEMENTS:** Honorable Mention, Natl Conference of Artists, 1969; Phi Kappa Phi, The Univ of MS, 1972; Art Work Permanent Collection in Nigeria Africa 1981, Permanent Collection Memphis Brooks Museum 1982; Video Tape in Collection State Dept of Archives; illustrations in three med books 1983; oil painting Anthropomorphic Psychosis, permanent collection, Memphis Brooks Museum of Art; co-edited Homespun Images: An Anthology of Black Memphis Writers and Artists. **HOME ADDRESS:** 1678 Newsum, Germantown, TN 38138.

DOTSON, WILLIAM S.
District manager. **PERSONAL:** Born Sep 29, 1911, Cave City, KY; married Alice Duncan; children: 2 Adopted Daughters. **EDUCATION:** KY State U, BS 1936. **CAREER:** Supreme Life Ins Co of Am, dist mgr. **ORGANIZATIONS:** Trustee Shiloh Bapt Ch; State treas NAACP 27 yrs; mem Omega Psi Phi Frat 40 yr man; past Nat pres KY StateUniv Alumni Assn; life paying mem NAACP; mem Lexington Life Underwriters Assn; Gen Agents & Mgrs Assn; mem bd dir United Way of Bluegrass; sec Lexington KY Urban Renewal; vice pres Lexington GAMA; LUTC Grad. **HONORS/ACHIEVEMENTS:** Recip Omega Man of Yr Psi Tau Chap 1975; 40 yr Plaque Omega Psi Phi Frat 1974. **BUSINESS ADDRESS:** 149 Dweest St, Lexington, KY 40508.

DOTSON-WILLIAMS, HENRIETTA
City official. **PERSONAL:** Born May 27, 1940, Valden, MS; daughter of Mr. and Mrs. Fred Perteete; married Michael J Williams; children: Angela L Holliman, Earl Dotson Jr, Dennis Dotson, Clifford Dotson. **EDUCATION:** IL Extsn Univ, Sec 1960. **CAREER:** IL Bell Telephone Co, operator to special eng clerk 1960-68; N IL Women's & Cntr, counsel 1974-; Sec of State, fclty serv clk; "Black Corner" Mntly TV Pgm, frmr moderator; Winnebago Co Bd Dist 12, supr 1972-, elected position. **ORGANIZATIONS:** Pres Winnebago Cty Bd of Hlth 1983-85, IL Assc of Bd of Hlth 1984-86. **HONORS/ACHIEVEMENTS:** Essence Mag Woman of the Month 1978; nominee for Woman of the Yr YWCA 1982 & 1986; Led an Effort to Retain Dr ML King's Birthday as a Legal Holiday for Winnebago County Employees, 800 People Attended Meeting. **HOME ADDRESS:** 1202 Kent St, Rockford, IL 61102.

DOTTIN, ROBERT PHILIP
Educator. **PERSONAL:** Born May 23, 1943, Trinidad, WI. **EDUCATION:** Univ of Toronto, BSC 1968, MSC 1970, PhD 1974; MIT, Post Doctoral 1974-76. **CAREER:** Univ of Copenhagen, visiting prof 1975; MIT, post doctoral 1974-76, John Hopkins Univ, asst prof 1976-82, assoc 1982-. **ORGANIZATIONS:** Mem Genetics Study Section; grantee Nat'l Inst Health 1984-; mem American Soc for Cell Biology; mem Nat'l Sci Foundation; American Heart Assoc; mem Amercian Soc for Human Genetics 1986; mem American Soc for Biological Chemists 1985. **HONORS/ACHIEVEMENTS:** Governors Generals of Canaada Medal 1968; Medical Research Council of Canada Fellowship 1974-76. **BUSINESS ADDRESS:** Johns Hopkins University, Dept of Biology, 3400 Charles St, Baltimore, MD 21218.

DOTTIN, ROGER ALLEN
Customer service manager. **PERSONAL:** Born Jul 13, 1945, Cambridge, MA; son of Reuben Dottin and Eunice Dottin; married Marilyn Ames, Apr 09, 1989. **EDUCATION:** Cambridge School of Business, Diploma 1963-65; Grahm Junior College, Honorary Associate. **CAREER:** Economic Opportunity Atlanta Inc, ctr dir 1970-73; City of Atlanta Comm Relations Commn, asst dir 1974-76; Metro Atlanta Rapid Transit Auth, sr comm relations spec 1976-84, mgr community relations 1984-86; Dallas Area Rapid Transit, mgr customer svcs. **ORGANIZATIONS:** Vice chair Sponsor-A-Family Project Atlanta 1983-87; mem Atlanta Public Schools Safety & Emergency Mgmt Adv-Council 1984-86; co-chair Atlanta Branch NAACP Afro-Academic Cultural Tech Scientific Olympics 1984-86; mem Conf of Minority Transportation Officials 1985-. **HONORS/ACHIEVEMENTS:** Outstanding Serv Awd John Harland Boys Club Atlanta 1982; Community Serv Awd NAACP Atlanta Branch 1984; Outstanding & Dedicated Serv to the NAACP Atlanta Branch 1986; YMCA Minority Achievers Program, Dallas YMCA 1988. **MILITARY SERVICE:** AUS E-2 1 1/2 yrs; Honorable Discharge. **BUSINESS ADDRESS:** Manager of Customer Services, Dallas Area Rapid Transit, 601 Pacific Ave Ste 300, Dallas, TX 75202.

DOUGHERTY, ROBERT I.
City commissioner. **PERSONAL:** Born Dec 27, 1908, Leavenworth, KS; married Orvaleen Hunt. **CAREER:** Leavenworth, policeman 1939-41; Lansing State Prison, 1942; Own Band, musician 15 yrs. **ORGANIZATIONS:** 1st black Deputy Sheriff Leavenworth 1966-72; elected city commr 1972-. **HONORS/ACHIEVEMENTS:** 1st Officer Leavenworth Co to capture bank robber 1970. **MILITARY SERVICE:** USN 1942-45. **BUSINESS ADDRESS:** City Hall, Leavenworth, KS.

DOUGHTY, GLENN MARTIN
Businessman, athlete. **PERSONAL:** Born Jan 30, 1951, Detroit, MI; married Janice Woods; children: Derek Jason, Nikeora Daniell. **EDUCATION:** Univ of MI, BS 1972. **CAREER:** WBAL-TV, sports analyst; Commercial Devel Co Shake & Bake Enterprises, pres & owner; Balt Colts, pro athlete; City of Baltimore, 5 yrs advt. **ORGANIZATIONS:** Mem coaches All-amer team Lubbock, TX 1972;coaches all-star Game Chicago 1972. **HONORS/ACHIEVEMENTS:** 3 yrs All Amer High Sch Freshman of the YrUniv of MI; All-big Ten Honors; broke records for avg yds per catch Colts 1973; ranked 2nd in NFL 1973; ranking6th All-time Receiving Yardage list for Colts.

DOUGLAS, AUBRY CARTER
Physician, orthopedic surgeon. **PERSONAL:** Born Feb 01, 1943, Onalaska, TX; son of Desso Douglas and Mary Douglas; married Janice Sanchez; children: Mary, Ronald, Anitra. **EDUCATION:** Fisk U, 1964; Meharry Med Coll, 1968. **CAREER:** Howard Univ, resident orthopaedics 1973-76; George Hubbard Hosp, resident gen surgery 1970-71; Fisk U, lab asst 1962-63. **ORGANIZATIONS:** Life scout BSA; mem Kappa Alpha Psi; Beta Kappa Chi; Harris & Co Med Soc; mem Houston Medical Forum. **MILITARY SERVICE:** AUS maj 1971-73. **BUSINESS ADDRESS:** 2000 Crawford St, Ste 860, Houston, TX 77002.

DOUGLAS, BOBBY EDDIE
Wrestling coach. **PERSONAL:** Born Mar 26, 1942, Bellaire, OH; son of Eddie Douglas and Belove Davis; married Jacqueline Davison, Aug 27, 1966; children: Bobby Frederick. **EDUCATION:** Oklahoma State Univ, Stillwater OK, BS, 1966; Arizona State Univ, Tempe AZ, MA, 1980. **CAREER:** Arizona State Univ, Tempe AZ, coach, 1974-. **ORGANIZATIONS:** Training Camps, dir, 1973-; USA Wrestling, exec comm, 1987-; NCAA (rules), mem, 1989-. **HONORS/ACHIEVEMENTS:** US Olympic Team (wrestling), 1964, team captain, 1968; author, Making of a Champion, 1973, Making of a Champion, Book II, 1975; video, Takedown, 1986; author, Takedown II, 1986; Hall of Fame, USA Wrestling, 1986; Coach of the Year, PAC 10, 1986-89; Coach of the Year, NCAA, 1988. **BUSINESS ADDRESS:** Head Wrestling Coach, Arizona State University, Athletic Department, Tempe, AZ 85287.

DOUGLAS, EDNA M.
Educator. **PERSONAL:** Born Jul 22, 1904, Little Rock, AR. **EDUCATION:** Univ of AR Pine Bluff, BA; Atlanta U,Univ of So CA Mills Coll Oakland, CA; Columbia U;Univ of AR; Philander Smith Coll. **CAREER:** Dunbar High School, Little Rock AR, teacher; Dunbar Jr Coll, teacher; Southwestern Jr High School, Grand Basileus of Sigma Gamma Rho Sorority, teacher; Natl Pan Hellenic Council, chmn. **ORGANIZATIONS:** Past mem bd trustees AM&N Coll; mem Classroom Tchr Assn; AR Tchr Assn; Nat Educ Assn; sponsor Student Christian Assn Dunbar Jr Coll Sec Little Rock Parks & Recreation Com 1952; bd dir ACHR Washington, DC 1952; panel mem Human Rights Day YWCA Radio broadcast 1953; 1st Negro bd dir, mem Greater Little Rock YWCA; chmn Com of Adminstrn Phyllis Wheatley Br YWCA; rep Florence Crittenton Bd of Little Rock, San Francisco 1954; vice

pres Little Rock Chap Nat Council of Negro Women 1953-53; Little Rock Com United Nations 1953-55. **HONORS/ACHIEVEMENTS:** Woman of Yr NCNW; Tchr of Yr Social Agency for Comm Participation; chmn Commun Devl Block & Grant S Little Rock 1976-77; Blanche Edwards Award Sigma Gamma Rho 1952; First Ford Found Fellowship offered to Little Rock Pub Sch System 1952-53; Comm Aprreciation Tea for Lengthy & meritorious serv Comm Center Bldg opened in her honor 1954; Residence Hall No 2, The Edna Douglas Hall named in her honor AM&N Coll 1958; mem African Study Tour Council for ChristianSocial Action United Ch of Christ 1961.

DOUGLAS, ELIZABETH ASCHE
Artist, educator. **PERSONAL:** Born Dec 22, 1930, Rochester, PA; daughter of Charles F Asche and Irma Edmonds Asche; married William R; children: Andrea, Vicki Gaddy, Nanette. **EDUCATION:** Carnegie Inst of Tech, BFA 1947-51; Univ of Pittsburgh, MA 1954-56; Univ of PA, 1979. **CAREER:** TX Coll, Tyler TX, asst prof 1955-58; Good Publshing Co, Ft Worth, TX , art dir 1958-61; Beaver (PA) Schls, Rochester (PA) Schls, tchr of Art 1962-66; Geneva Coll, Beaver Falls, PA, asst prof, assoc prof, prof, coord of humanities. **ORGANIZATIONS:** Prog chmn Brodhead Cultural Center 1977-78; sec-treas FATE (Foundations in Art, Theory & Educ) 1979-80; art comm Merrick Art Gallery Assoc 1980-; bd mem Christian Scholars Rev 1983-; chair Rochester Area Hum Rel Comm 1973-74; co-chr task force on jvnl delinq SW Regnl Plng Comm Governors Justice Comm 1976-78; mem Assoc for Integrative Studies 1985-; chmn Merrick Art Gallery Assoc Catalog Comm; mem Natl Conference of Artists 1980-; mem College Art Assn 1975-; bd mem Greater Beaver Valley Cultural Alliance 1989-; bd mem Northland Public Library Foundation 1989-. **HONORS/ACHIEVEMENTS:** Arts rev Christian Scholars Rev 1973-; achvmnt awd Beaver Valley Serv Club 1978; article publshd CIVA (Christians in Visual Arts) 1983; painting exhib awds various locations in country 1960-; article publ CIVA 1985; papers delivered annual meetings FATE Toronto 1984, Assoc Integrative Studies 1984, Hofstra Univ Conf Avant-Gard Lit/Art 1985; Scholar of the Year, Geneva College Faculty 1985; author/editor Catalogue of the Merrick Art Gallery 1988; article published Leonardo's Last Supper, Christian Scholar's Review 1988. **BUSINESS ADDRESS:** Coordinator of Humanities, Geneva Coll, Beaver Falls, PA 15010.

DOUGLAS, FLORENCE M.
Physician. **PERSONAL:** Born Mar 26, 1933; married Franklin E Mcfarlane; children: Valerie, Angela, Alychandra. **EDUCATION:** Hunter Coll NYC, BA 1955; HowardUniv Coll of Med, MD 1959. **CAREER:** Los Angeles Co Gen Hosp, intership 1959-60; Los Angeles Co Gen Hosp, residency gen psychiatry 1960-62; Montefiore Hosp NY, residency gen psychiatry 1972; Los Angeles Co Gen Hosp, residency gen psychiatry 1963; Los Angeless Co Gen Hosp, residency child psychiatry 1963-65; Los Angeles Co Gen Hosp Sch of Nursing, consult 1960-62; Los Angeles Co Juvenile Hall, consult 1960-62; Episcopal Ch Home for Children Pasadena, CA, consult 1963-67; Huntington Meml Hosp Pasadena, consult 1965-66; Los Angeles Co Mental Health Arcardia Sch System, consult 1965-67. **ORGANIZATIONS:** So CA Psychiat Soc; Am Med Assn; Los Angeles Co Med Assn; Am Psychiat Assn; Nat Med Assn; Am Assn for Adolescent Psychiat; Am & Orthopsychiatric Assn; CA Med Assn; Black Psychiat of So CA; Black Psychiat of Am; mem Mental Hlth Devel Commin, United Way; bd mem CA Dept of Rehab; former mem So CA Psychoanalytic Assn; Am Assn for Group Psychotheraphy; Coll of Psychol & Soc Studies bd mem Model Cities Child Care Center; Johnny Tillmon Child Devel Center lectr New Careerists; Inner City Students; Urban Corp Students; Mshauri Students; Medex Program; diplomate Am Bd of Psych & Neurology; bd certified Child & Adolescent Psychiatry; examiner Am Bd of Psychiatry & Neurology; prof of Psychiatry Charles R Drew post-grad med sch UCLA Med Cntr; physician M Edical Staff of Del Amo Hosp, Little Company of Mary Hosp, Torrance Meml Hosp; Fellow Am Acad of Child & Psychiatry. **HONORS/ACHIEVEMENTS:** Anna Bartsche Dunne Scholarship, HowardUniv Coll of Med 1956-58; listed in Who's Who in the West 1971. **BUSINESS ADDRESS:** 4305 Torrance Blvd, #205, Torrance, CA 90503.

DOUGLAS, FREDERICK WILLIAM
Physician. **PERSONAL:** Born Nov 08, 1913, Pittsburgh, PA; married Daisy Booker; children: Elaine, Alan. **EDUCATION:** Howard Med Sch, 1940; Provident Hosp, intern 1940-41; Freedman's Hosp, resident 1942. **CAREER:** Mountainside Hosp, Comm Hosp, Emeritus; Family Practice, physician 1946-. **ORGANIZATIONS:** Mem Howard Univ Med Alumni Assn, AMA, Natl Med Assn, Amer Acad Family Practice; mem NJ Mens Club, Montclair Chamber of Commerce; mem Golden Heritage NAACP; fellow Amer Acad Family Practice. **MILITARY SERVICE:** AUS mc capt 1942-46. **BUSINESS ADDRESS:** 160 Lincoln St, Montclair, NJ 07042.

DOUGLAS, HARRY E., III
Educator. **PERSONAL:** Born Nov 08, 1938; children: 2 children. **EDUCATION:** Univ of Denver, BA 1959; Univ of CA Los Angeles, MPA Personnel 1971; Univ of So CA, MPA Health Serv 1981, DPA Health Admin & Policy 1983. **CAREER:** Dept of Public Social Servs, proj dir, sr program asst, mgmt trainee, social worker 1960-68; Univ of Southern CA, training officer 1968; Martin Luther King/Charles R Drew Medical Center, personnel officer 1969-71, dir allied health training 1971-73; Cedars-Sinai Medical Center, dir manpower training & devel 1973-74; CA Reg Med Prog, prog dir HS/EP 1974-75; Howard Univ Coll of Allied Health Science, assoc dean, assoc prof 1975-83; Charles R Drew Postgrad Medical School, School of Allied Health, dean 1983-. **ORGANIZATIONS:** External cons/eval Norfolk State Univ; consult DHEW Div of Health Manpower; adv/cons Amer Soc of Allied Health Professions on Natl Data Gathering Proj;conducted zero based budget workshop Dept of Agr; health brain trust mem Cong Black Caucus; mgmt progs nursing personnel George Washington Univ; tech review comm CA Comm on Reg Medical Progs, CA State Dept of Ed; ad hoc adv comm Career Ed in Health Occupations; mem Amer Assoc of Comm & Jr Coll, School of Allied Health Study, Charles R Drew Postgrad Med School, San Francisco Personnel Dept, Natl Inst of Mental Helth, Orange Cty Personnel Dept, UCLA Proj for Allied Health Professions; bd dir DC Coalition on Health Advocates 1976-; treas, bd mem Natl Assoc of Allied Health 1977-; mem Dietetic Manpower Demand Study 1980-, Child-Find & Advocacy Adv Comm 1980-; chmn Amer Soc of Allied Prof 1980-, DC Adv Comm Magnet School for Health Careers 1982-; assoc coord Reg Leadership Ctr for Allied Health Ed 1982-; mem Amer Soc for Pub Admin, Amer Pub Health Assoc, Natl Soc of Allied Health. **HONORS/ACHIEVEMENTS:** Numerous presentations & publs incl, "The Declining Enrollment of Minority Group Members in Selected Allied Health Occupations" presentation 1980, "The Learniing Resource Ctr, A Mediating Structure for Reorganizing Allied Health Ed" presentation 1981, "A Systems Approach-Part II" workshop 1982, "Changing the Guard, A Methodology for Leadership in Transition" publ 1983; "Mobility in Health Career Ed" speech 1969; "The San Quentin Report" rsch 1971. **BUSINESS ADDRESS:** Dean, Charles R Drew Postgrad Med, School of Allied Health, 2113 S Orange Dr, Los Angeles, CA 90016.

DOUGLAS, HENLEY L.
Business executive. **PERSONAL:** Born Jan 29, 1929, Mexico, MO; divorced; children: 5 Children. **EDUCATION:** Lincoln U, BS 1950; IN U, atnd 1 Yr; Lockheed Mgmt Inst Santa Clara U, Cert of Completion 1968. **CAREER:** Product Assurance Ops & Control Lockheed Missiles & Space Co Inc, mngr 1968-; supr 1965-68; product assurance specialist 1963-65; qc engn 1962-63; Res Engr Asso, 1961-62; Chrysler Missile Co Detroit, qc engr 1958-61; Chem Engr Dept US Rubber Co, statistician 1955-57. **ORGANIZATIONS:** Mem Am Soc for QC 1955; Kappa Alpha Psi Frat 1947-50; Mason 1954-58; certified QC engr 1971, Am Soc for QC. **MILITARY SERVICE:** USAF s/sgt 1951-55. **BUSINESS ADDRESS:** Lockheed Miss & Space Co Inc, PO Box 504, Sunnyvale, CA 94088.

DOUGLAS, HERBERT P., JR.
Business executive. **PERSONAL:** Born Mar 09, 1922, Pittsburgh; married Rozell; children: Barbara Joy Ralston, Herbert III. **EDUCATION:** Xavier U, 1941-42;Univ of Pittsburgh, BS 1945-48;Univ of Pittsburgh, MEd 1950. **CAREER:** Nat Spl Markets, vice pres 1968-; Schieffelin & Co NYC, contial sales rep 1963-65; Nat Spl Markets Mgr, 1965-68; Pabst Brewing Co, sales rep dist mgr 1950-63; managed night business, fathers auto bus 1942-45; Nat Assn of Market Developers, vp. **ORGANIZATIONS:** Mem Track Com Internatl Olympians Track & Field Club; Optimist Club; Philadelphia Pioneer Club; NAACP; Nat Urban League; Omega Psi Phi Frat; Chris Atlete Club; Ebenezer Bapt Ch; Sales Exec Club. **HONORS/ACHIEVEMENTS:** Who's Who in Am, Marquis Chgo; Black Athletes Hall of Fame 1974; Beverage Ind Award Urban League Guild 1974; selected by Ebony success library as one of top 1000 Successful Blacks in US; played in Olympic Games 1948, currently last athlete from Pittsburgh to win a medal in Olympic Games.

DOUGLAS, JAMES MATTHEW
Educator. **PERSONAL:** Born Feb 11, 1944, Onalaska, TX; son of Desso D Douglas and Mary L Douglas; divorced; children: DeLicia. **EDUCATION:** TX Southern Univ, BA Math 1966, JD Law 1970; Stanford Univ, JSM Law 1971. **CAREER:** Singer Simulation Co, computer analyst 1966-72; TX Southern Univ Sch of Law, asst Prof 1971-72; Cleveland State Univ Sch of Law, asst Prof 1972-75; Syracuse Univ Sch of Law, assoc dean assoc prof 1975-80; Northeastern Univ Sch of Law, prof of law 1980-81; TX Southern Univ Sch of Law, dean & prof 1981-. **ORGANIZATIONS:** State Bar of TX; Houston Jr Bar Assc; Amer Bar Assc Chrmn of Educ Comm of Sci & Tech Section; bd dir Hiscock Legal Soc; fac adv to Natl Bd of Black Amer Law Students; bd of dirs Gulf Coast Legal Foundation; mem Natl Bar Assoc Comm on Legal Educ; mem editorial bd The Texas Lawyer; life mem Houston Chamber of Commerce; bd of dirs, Law School Admission Council; chmn, Minority Affairs Committee, Law Shool Admission Council. **HONORS/ACHIEVEMENTS:** Grad 1st in Law Schl Class; Most Outstanding 3rd Year Student; Winner of 10 Amer Jurisprudence Awards; mem of Sch Moot Court Team; Parlimentarian of Student Bar Assn; adv Alpha Phi Alpha Soc Frat; pres Sophomore Class; pres Student Body; pres Alpha Phi Alpha Soc Frat; publ "Some Ideas on the Computer and Law" TX Souther Univ Law Review 20 1971; work in prog "Cases & Materials on Contracts"; Outstanding Alumnus TX Southern Univ 1972. **HOME ADDRESS:** 5318 Calhoun Rd, Houston, TX 77021. **BUSINESS ADDRESS:** Dean, School of Law, TX SouthernUniv, 3100 Cleburne Ave, Houston, TX 77004.

DOUGLAS, JANICE GREEN
Physician. **PERSONAL:** Born 1944. **EDUCATION:** Meharry Medical School, Nashville, TN, MD; Vanderbilt University, National Institute of Health fellow in endocrinology, 1973. **CAREER:** National Institute of Health, senior staff fellow; Case Western Reserve University, Cleveland, OH, director of departments of Hypertension and Endocrinology. **BUSINESS ADDRESS:** Case Western Reserve University, 2040 Adelbert, Cleveland, OH 44106. *

DOUGLAS, JOE, JR.
Elected govt. official/fire chief. **PERSONAL:** Born Jun 09, 1928, Topeka, KS; married Nathalia Washington; children: Shelley Jolana Douglas Wilder. **EDUCATION:** Washburn Univ, 1948-49. **CAREER:** City of Topeka, firefighter 37 yrs, appointed fire chief Sept 1, 1983; USD #501, bd mem 1977-85. **ORGANIZATIONS:** Mem Topeka Council of Churches; 1st Conf Chairperson for KS East Conf Clomm on Religion and Race United Methodist Ch; bd of dir Boys Club of Amer 1971-73; chmn comm Adv Comm on Educ 1975-76; bd pres USD #501 1980-81 & 1983-84; bd of dir Boy Scouts of Amer; mem Mayor's Disaster Adv Cncl, Mayor's Task Force on Illiteracy, Sunset Optimists. **HONORS/ACHIEVEMENTS:** Dean United Methodist Youth Fellowship Inst 1971-73; Presidential Citation for Extraordinary Serv Boys Club of Amer 1972-73; Kansas Friends of Educ plaque winner; Annual Local Govt Official Category 1986. **MILITARY SERVICE:** AUS pfc 18 mos. **BUSINESS ADDRESS:** Fire Chief, City of Topeka, 324 SE Jefferson St, Topeka, KS 66607.

DOUGLAS, JOHN DANIEL
Elected official, educator. **PERSONAL:** Born Aug 18, 1945, Great Falls, SC; married Mildred Barber; children: Maurice. **EDUCATION:** Morris Coll, BS 1967; Winthrop Coll, MEduc 1976. **CAREER:** Chester Co Schools, teacher 1967-68; Carolina Comm Actions Inc, Head Start dir 1968-70; York Co Family Court, chief probation officer 1970-75; Charlotte-Mecklinburg School, teacher 1975-80; Rock Hill Sch Dist #3, teacher 1980-; York Co, councilman. **ORGANIZATIONS:** Pres Rock Hill NAACP 1976-81; pol action chmn Menzel Shiner 1980-; councilman York Co Dist #4 1980-; chmn Destinations Human Serv Trans 1982-; chmn Public Works York Co 1982-; financial sec Sterling Elk Lodge 1983-; bd of dirs South Carolina Assoc of Counties 1986; exec admin asst SC Assoc of Elks 1986. **HONORS/ACHIEVEMENTS:** Serv to Mankind Rock Hill NAACP 1979; Comm Serv Awd Elk-Sterling Lodge #344 Rock Hill 1980; Scroll of Honor Omega Psi Phi Frat 1983; Humanitarian Menzel Shiner 1984; Elk of the Year 1986; Man of the Year Rock Grove AME Zion Church 1986. **BUSINESS ADDRESS:** Councilman, York County, PO Box 11578, Rock Hill, SC 29731.

DOUGLAS, JOSEPH FRANCIS
Educator, engineer. **PERSONAL:** Born Oct 31, 1926, Indianapolis, IN; son of Louis J Douglas (deceased) and Marion Brabham D Burch (deceased); married Edna J Nichols, Apr

09, 1950; children: Marian E, Joseph Jr, Marie A, Barbara J. **EDUCATION:** Purdue Univ, BSEE 1948; Univ of MO, MSEE 1962. **CAREER:** Rural Electrification Admin, 1948-56; So Univ, 1956-64; Am Machine & Foundry Co, 1964-66; PA State Univ, engrg instr 1966-70, assoc prof 1970-87. **ORGANIZATIONS:** Mem IEEE 1949-, ASEE 1969-; reg professional engr 1954-; mem NAACP, Human Rel Adv Council, York-Adams Area Council, Boy Scouts of Amer, Comm Action Prog; mem bd of dir York Hosp PA 1982-. **HONORS/ACHIEVEMENTS:** The Role of the Engineering Teacher Conf Record Tucson 1972; Lindback Aarwd Distinguished Teaching 1972; contributor to a technical paper entitled Understanding Batteries, published by Volunteers In Technical Assistance (VITA), 1985. **MILITARY SERVICE:** AUS, Air Corps, aviation cadet 1944-45. **HOME ADDRESS:** RD #7 - Trout Run Road, York, PA 17402.

DOUGLAS, MAE ALICE
Business executive. **PERSONAL:** Born Dec 26, 1951, Rowland, NC. **EDUCATION:** University of NC at Greensboro, BA Sociology 1972. **CAREER:** Commission on the Status of Women, administrator 1973-74; CIBA-GEIGY Corp, eeo coordinator 1974-77, personnel manager 1978-, mgr human resources 1983-86, dir human resources 1987-. **ORGANIZATIONS:** Leadership Greensboro Chamber of Commerce 1979-80; planning division United Way 1980; professional review committee State Dept of Public Instruction 1981-82; Amer Soc for Personnel Admin 1978-; mem Women's Professional Forum 1985-. **HONORS/ACHIEVEMENTS:** Outstanding Young Women of America 1975; Outstanding Young Woman Greensboro Jaycettes 1978; Outstanding Woman in Business YWCA 1980. **BUSINESS ADDRESS:** Dir of Human Resources, CIBA GEIGY Corp, PO Box 18300, Greensboro, NC 27419.

DOUGLAS, MANSFIELD, III
Personnel officer. **PERSONAL:** Born Jun 28, 1930, Nashville, TN; married Barbara Jean Baker; children: Camella Renee, Reginald Mansfield, Karen Rochelle. **EDUCATION:** TN State U, grad. **CAREER:** Western Electric, personnel ofcr; prev experience in maintenance, accounting, purchasing. **ORGANIZATIONS:** Mem Exec Com Nashville Br NAACP 1962-66; pres Br NAACP 1966-68; pres Davidson Co Young Dem 1967; Vice Pres Exec Bd TN State Labor Council 1963-65; bd dirs S St Comm Cntr; TN Adv Com of US Commn on Rights. **HONORS/ACHIEVEMENTS:** Merit Serv Nashville Urban League 1972; Outstanding Recognition CWA Local 3870 1970. **MILITARY SERVICE:** AUS Korean Conflict. **BUSINESS ADDRESS:** 195 Polk Ave, Nashville, TN.

DOUGLAS, N. JOHN
Chairman. **EDUCATION:** Bates Coll, BS 1960; Howard Univ, MS 1962. **CAREER:** Castle & Cooke Inc, dir investor and public relations 1975-81; KSTS-TV, chairman. **BUSINESS ADDRESS:** Chairman, KSTS-TV, 2349 Bering Dr, San Jose, CA 95131.

DOUGLAS, SAMUEL HORACE
Educator. **PERSONAL:** Born May 10, 1928, Ardmore, OK; divorced; children: Carman Irving, Samuel, Emanuel. **EDUCATION:** Bishop Coll, BS 1950; OK State U, BS 1959; MS 1963; PhD 1967. **CAREER:** Praire View A&M Univ TX, asst prof Math 1959-63; dept chmn 1962-63; Grambling Coll LA, math prof 1967-; dept chmn 1967-. **ORGANIZATIONS:** MemPanel Spl & Problems Minority Groups; Am Math Soc; London Math Soc; Math Assn Am; consult Com Undergrad Prog Math dir summer & inservice InstsMath, NSF-GRAMBLING Coll 1968-71; vis lectr, vice-chmn, LA-MS sect, Math Assn Am Mem, Pi Mu Epsilon; Alpha Phi Alpha. **HONORS/ACHIEVEMENTS:** Distinguished Service Award, Pi Mu Epsilon 1970; fellow Sci Faculty 1963-67. **MILITARY SERVICE:** AUS 1943-46.

DOUGLAS, WALTER EDMOND
Association executive. **PERSONAL:** Born Aug 22, 1933, Hamlet, NC; married Retha Hughes; children: Petra, Walter Jr, Mark. **EDUCATION:** NC Cntrl Univ, BS Acctg 1954, MS Bus Admn 1955. **CAREER:** Intrnl Revenue Serv Data Cntr, brcnh chief 1968-69, asst chief sys div 1969-70, chief mgmt stf 1970-71, asst dir 1971-72; New Detroit, vice pres 1972-78, pres 1978-. **ORGANIZATIONS:** Pres part ownr DHT Tranp Inc 1979-; mem Fed Home Loan Bk of Indianapolis 1978-82, YWCA, Channel 56 (PBS), Hlth Alliance Plan, United Way; mem of Bd DetroitSymphony 1980-. **HONORS/ACHIEVEMENTS:** Grand Jury Invstgtns Pblsh by Detroit Clg of Law 1983; Liberty Bell Awrd Detroit Bar Assc 1975; Awrd from Pres Regan Exemplary Youth Dev Pgm 1984. **MILITARY SERVICE:** AUS. **HOME ADDRESS:** 20035 Lichfield, Detroit, MI 48221. **BUSINESS ADDRESS:** President, New Detroit, Inc, One Kennedy Sq, 719 Griswold, Detroit, MI 48226.

DOUGLAS, WILLARD H., JR.
Judge. **PERSONAL:** Born Feb 04, 1932, Amherst, VA; married Jane O Eggleston; children: Willard III, Wendelin Janna. **EDUCATION:** VA Union U, AB 1957; Howard Univ Sch of Law, JD 1960. **CAREER:** Juvenile & Domestic Relations Dist Ct Commonwealth of VA, chief judge 1974-; Asst Commonwealth Atty, 1969-74; Private Practice, 1965-69; US Commn on Civil Rights, staff atty 1962-65; US Copyright Office, staff atty 1961-62; Teamsters Union, admin asst bd of monitors 1960-61. **ORGANIZATIONS:** Mem Am Bar Assn; VA State Bar; VA State Bar Assn; Old Dominion Bar Assn; Richmond Criminal Law Assn; Richmond Trial Lawyers Assn; VA Trial Lawyers Assn, mem Kappa Alpha Psi Frat Bd Richmond Area Psychiatric Clinic; Richmond Epilepsy Found; Big Bros Ferrum Coll VA Wesleyan Coll; Lay Leader Wesley Memorial United Methodist Church; Asso Lay Leader VA Conf Bd of Laity & Richmond Dist Eastern Province; National Council of Juvenile & Family Ct Judges, bd mem 1986-89; United Methodist Church, Judicial Council, mem 1984-92. **HONORS/ACHIEVEMENTS:** Achievement Award, Richmond Alumni & Petersburg Alumni 1974; Man of Yr, Richmond Alumnae Delta Sigma Theta 1974. **MILITARY SERVICE:** USMC sgt 1951-54. **BUSINESS ADDRESS:** 2000 Mecklenburg St, Richmond, VA 23223.

DOUGLASS, ARTHUR E.
Educational administrator. **PERSONAL:** Born Apr 20, 1933, Camden, DE; married Rose Marie Stricklin; children: Daryl. **EDUCATION:** MD State Coll, BS 1957; TX A&M 1966; Tarleton State Univ, MA 1980. **CAREER:** US Air Force, officer 1957-76; Economic Opportunities Advancement Corp, program oper mgr 1976-82; TX State Tech Inst, coord contracts & grants 1982-. **ORGANIZATIONS:** Trustee, vice pres Marlin ISD 1979-. **MILITARY SERVICE:** USAF maj 20 yrs; Meritorious Serv Medal, Air Force Commendation with 3 Oak Leaf Clusters 1957-76. **HOME ADDRESS:** 400 Bennett, Marlin, TX 76661. **BUSINESS ADDRESS:** Coordinator-Contracts & Grants, TX State Tech Inst System, Waco, TX 76705.

DOUGLASS, JOHN H.
Educator. **PERSONAL:** Born Sep 04, 1933, Pittsburgh, PA; children: Steven, Helen, Pamela. **EDUCATION:** Univ Pittsburgh, BA, MA; San Diego State U; US Intl U; Walder U, doctoral candidate. **CAREER:** Univ CA San Diego, Lajolla CA, supvr Physical Educ; Univ CA San Diego, former asst chancellor 6 yrs; Dept of Pediatrics, Univ CA San Diego, School of Medicine, former staff reseach assoc 6 yrs; Analytical Chemistry Nuclear Fuel Lab, Gulf Gen Atomic, former supr 9 yrs; Univ of CA San Diego, former employment representative 1 yr; Univ of Pittsburgh Cardiac Research Group, Biochemistry Dept, former lab tech, grad sch public health 6 yrs; Mayor Wilson' S Manpower Planning Com, 1971-74. **ORGANIZATIONS:** Chpsnevaluation sub-com; other sub-com Appointments, council sponsor, adv council, nominating committee; pres Am Assn Health physical educ & recreation 1972; pres CA Assn Health physical educ & Recreation 1972; 1972, Pres Citizens United Racial Equality; 1974 pres Minority Involvement Com CAHPER; 1959, pres Alpha Phi Alph & Frat; 1973, pres Pop Warner Football Coach; 1973, pres Little League, Baseketball Coach; 1973, pres Little League Track Coach. **HONORS/ACHIEVEMENTS:** Varsity Letterman Club's Most Valuable PlayerUniv Pittsburgh 1961; varsity letterman Squash 1960; varsity letterman Tennis 1961; Sportsmanship Award, Pacific Coast Tennis Assn Championships 1969. **MILITARY SERVICE:** AUS corpl 1953-55. **BUSINESS ADDRESS:** Dept Physical Educ, C 017 Univ CA, San Diego, CA.

DOUGLASS, JOHN W.
State representative. **PERSONAL:** Born Mar 19, 1942, Princess Anne, MD; divorced. **EDUCATION:** Lincoln U, AB 1964; Johns Hopkins U, MA 1966. **CAREER:** Morgan State Coll, instr 1966-68; Mutual Funds, salesman 1967-68; RL Johnson Realty Co, 1967-; Baltimore City Council, clerk 1967-68; Baltimore City Planning Dept, consult 1970-71; MD House Delegates, mem 1971-, computer consultant. **ORGANIZATIONS:** Pres Businessmen's League of Baltimore 1968; Lincoln Univ Chap Amer Chem Soc 1964; Beta Kappa Chi; mem Assn Builders & Contractors 1968-70; Baltimore C of C 1968-70; Business Oppor Admin 1968; sec bd dirs Glenwood Country Club 1968; mem Mt Royal Dem Club 1968-70; New Dem Club 1968-; treasurer Eastside Dem Orgn 1968-71; mem New Dem Coalition 1969; Young Dem MD 1967-71; exec com Model Cities Prog 1968-69; Pres Alpha Phi Alpha Frat 1964; mem Adj Neighborhood Improvement Assn 1969-; mem Baptist Church Faculty Rsch Grant Morgan State Coll 1967. **HONORS/ACHIEVEMENTS:** Penn Senatorial Scholarship 1960; Rohm & Hass Fellow 1964; Gilman Fellow 1964; Amer Chem Soc Award 1964; Amer Legion Award 1956; Certificate of Achievement Morgan State Coll 1968, 1969; Norman E Gaskin's Prize 1964; Eastern LI Ward 1964. **BUSINESS ADDRESS:** MD House of Delegates, 323 Lowe Bldg, Annapolis, MD 21401.

DOUGLASS, LEWIS LLOYD
Judge. **PERSONAL:** Born Dec 12, 1930, Brooklyn, NY; son of Lloyd and Cornelia; married Doris Wildy; children: David, Lori. **EDUCATION:** Brooklyn Coll, BS 1953; St John's Law Sch LLB 1956. **CAREER:** Federal Prosecutor's Office, asst US atty 1961-65; Housing Redevelopment Agency, exec dept dir 1965-68; Housing Devel Orgn, general counsel 1968-71; Black Enterprise Magazine, exec vice pres 1971-75; NY State Prison System, exec deputy commr 1975-78; Supreme Court of NY, judge. **BUSINESS ADDRESS:** Judge, Supreme Court of NY, 360 Adams, Brooklyn, NY 11201.

DOUGLASS, MELVIN ISADORE
Educator, clergy. **PERSONAL:** Born Jul 21, 1948, Manhattan, NY; son of Isadore Douglass and Esther (Tripp) Douglass. **EDUCATION:** Vincinnes Univ, AS 1970; Tuskegee Inst, BS 1973; Morgan State Univ, MS 1975; New York Univ, MA 1977; Columbia Univ, EdM 1978, EdD 1981. **CAREER:** Public School 401-X, dean of students and teacher of fifth grade 1973-75; Amistad Child Day Care and Family Ctr, dir of sch age prog 1976-77; York Coll, coach of track and field 1980-81; Beck Memorial Day Care Ctr, dir of educ 1983-84; Dept of Juvenile Justice City of NY, chmn of Spofford juvenile ctr primary school dept 1984-85; Dept of Juvenile Justice City of NY, ombudsman Spofford juvenile ctr 1985-88; South Huntington School, Huntington Station NY, chmn 1988-; John Jay College, New York NY, adjunct prof 1988-. **ORGANIZATIONS:** Pres and founder Jamaica Track Club 1973-; mem bd of dirs Nu Omicron Chap of Omega Psi Phi Day Care Ctr 1984-; mem Prince Hall Masonry; pres bd of dirs NY City Transit Branch NAACP 1984-; co-chairperson Educ Comm NY State Conf of NAACP 1986-; chairperson Anti-Drug Comm Metro Cncl of NAACP Branches 1986-; mem Jamaica East/West Adolescent Pregnancy Prevention Consortium 1986-; basileus Nu Omicron Chap Omega Psi Phi Frat 1987-; mem bd of dirs, Queens Council on the Arts 1983-86; mem bd of dirs, Black Experimental Theatre 1982-; mem bd of dirs, The United Black Men of Queens County Inc 1986; mem, S Huntington Chmns' Assn, 1988-, Council of Admins & Supvrs, 1988-. **HONORS/ACHIEVEMENTS:** Grad Scholarship Columbia Univ 1978; Kappa Delta Pi Honor Soc in Educ inducted 1978; Service Awd NY City Transit Branch NAACP 1986; Citation for Comm Serv NYS Governor Mario Cuomo 1986; Citation Awd New York City Mayor Edward Koch 1986; Citation of Honor Queens Borough Pres Claire Shulman 1986; City Council Citation Award, New York City Councilman Archie Spigner 1988; Civil Rights Award, New York City Transit Branch NAACP 1988; Black Winners: A History of Spingarn Medalists 1984; Famous Black Men of Harvard 1988. **HOME ADDRESS:** 108-38 167th St, Jamaica, NY 11433.

DOUGLASS, MIKE REESE
Professional football player. **PERSONAL:** Born Mar 15, 1955, St Louis, MO. **EDUCATION:** Attended, San Diego State Univ. **CAREER:** San Diego Chargers, linebacker; Green Bay Packers, professional football player (linebacker). **HONORS/ACHIEVEMENTS:** College, posted 21 QB sacks as a junior; triple jumped 50 ft and 6 ft 8 in high jumper; shot put 59 ft; led the Green Bay defense in QB sacks in 1984 registering 9 for a total of 53 yds in losses; no 3 tackler on Kick Modzelewski's defensive platoon; made 68 solo tackles & contrib 15 assists; led Green Bay defense in unassisted tackles in three seasons - 127 in 1983; voted Packers' Most Valuable Defensive Player in 1983 & 1984 by Wisconsin's sports media; named to Sports Illustrated's All-Pro team three times 1981, 1982 & 1983. **BUSINESS ADDRESS:** Player, Green Bay Packers, 1265 Lombardi Ave, Green Bay, WI 54303.

DOUGLASS, ROBERT LEE
Senator. **PERSONAL:** Born Jun 23, 1928, Winnsboro, SC; married Bernice Viola Sales; children: Beverly, Ronald K, Eric L, Loren R. **EDUCATION:** Morgan State Coll, BS Math

1953; John Hopkins U, BS Elect Eng 1962; AmerUniv & Morgan State, M Deg Prog 1963, 65. **CAREER:** State of MD, sen; Baltimore Electron Assn, pres & fdr; City Counmn, 1967-74. **ORGANIZATIONS:** Mem State Econ Affairs Comm; chmn Ways & Means Sub-Comm; vchmn Educ Sub-Comm; Budget & Finan Comm; Urban Affairs Comm; mem Plng Commiss; pres Eastside Demo Ogn; co-formed Eastside Demo Ogn 1967; former advis & exec dir E Baltimore Commun Corp; former trustee Waters AME Ch; bd mem Balto Urban Coalit; Natl Bus Leag of Balti; Balti Chap of Boy Scts of Am; Model Urban Neighborhood Dev Corp; councm mem Paul Lawrence Commun Sch; Clifton Park Commun Sch; Johnston Sq CommunSch; mem Urban Serv Counc A Ctr; chmn MD Legislat Black Caucus 1976-77; elect deleg Demo Natl Convent 1972; elect mem 2nd dist State Central Comm 1970-74. **MILITARY SERVICE:** AUS 1st lt 1953-55. **BUSINESS ADDRESS:** 2503 E Preston St, Baltimore, MD 21213.

DOUTHIT, WILLIAM E.
Business executive. **PERSONAL:** Born Apr 02, 1925, Farrell, PA; married Dorothy; children: William, Jr, Char, Helen. **EDUCATION:** Dillard U, BA 1951;Univ of IL Inst of Labor & Industrial Relations, MA 1953. **CAREER:** Minneapolis Honeywell Co Aeronautical Div, supr 1962-64; Oklahoma City Urban League, exec dir 1959-62; Industrial Relations Dept St Louis Urban League, sec 1954-59; St Louis Urban League, exec dir. **MILITARY SERVICE:** AUS 1943-46. **BUSINESS ADDRESS:** 3701 Grandel Sq, St Louis, MO 63108.

DOVE, EVELYN FRANCYNE
Attorney. **PERSONAL:** Born Jan 04, 1954, Kinston, NC; daughter of William Dove and J Roberta Dove. **EDUCATION:** Univ of North Carolina, BA English 1975, JD 1978. **CAREER:** Legal Aid of Winston-Salem, NC, attorney 1978-80; City of Petersburg, VA, purchasing dir 1980-82; City of Gastonia, NC, city attorney 1982-84; NC Air Natl Guard, judge advocate 1983-84; City of Charlotte, assist city attorney; Positive Concepts Public Speaking, Charlotte Observer, copy editor. **ORGANIZATIONS:** Consultant SCLC 1981-82; dir Business Devel Center 1983-84; treasurer Gaston County Bar Assn 1983-84; member Black United Forum 1983-85; dir Boy's Club Board 1984; corresponding sec NC Assn of Black Lawyers 1984-85; member NC League of Municipalities 1984; Charlotte Business League Public Relations, chairperson; author, Sure As You're Born; Positive Concepts public speaking & public relations firm, owner. **HONORS/ACHIEVEMENTS:** NC Fellow Univ of North Carolina 1973-75; Member Order of the Valkyries-honor society 1974-75; Outstanding Women of America 1984; Leadership Charlotte UNCC/Chamber of Commerce-Chlt 1985. **MILITARY SERVICE:** NC Air Guard 1st Lt; served 1 1/2 years; Judge Advocate Gen Cert; Officer Medal 1984. **HOME ADDRESS:** 420 N Smith St, 2A, Charlotte, NC 28202.

DOVE, PEARLIE C.
Educator. **PERSONAL:** Born in Atlanta, GA; daughter of Dan Cecile Craft and Lizzie Dyer Craft; married Chaplain Jackson B Dove (deceased); children: Carol Ann Dove Horn. **EDUCATION:** Clark Coll, BA 1941; Atlanta Univ, MA 1943; Univ of CO, Ed Degree 1959. **CAREER:** Atlanta business & professional secretary, Phyllis Wheatley Branch, YMCA, 1943-45; Clark Coll, dir of student teaching, 1949-62, chmn, Dept of Educ, 1963-85, dist prof, 1975-86; Assoc Chair, Consolidation Steering Comm, Clark Atlanta Univ, 1988-89. **ORGANIZATIONS:** GA Stdnt Fin Comm, brd of dir 1981-87; Southern Asssoc of Coll & Schls, elem comm 1975-81; Amer Assoc Coll for Tchr Ed, bd of dir 1972-75; Assoc of Teacher Educators, natl exe comm 1970-73; Clark Coll, Amer Assoc of Univ Prof, pres 1978-80 1983-87; Atlanta Pan-Hellenic Cncl, pres 1960-64; Atlanta Alumnae Delta Sigma Theta Sor, pres 1962-63. **HONORS/ACHIEVEMENTS:** Distinguished mem, Assn of Teacher Educ, 1983; Chmn's Award, State Comm on the Life & History of Black Georgians, 1979; Serv Award, Atlanta Alumnae, Delta Sigma Theta Sorority, 1963; Woman of the Year in Educ, Iota Phi Lambda Sorority, 1962; Delta Torch Award, Delta Sigma Theta Sorority Inc, 1989; Distinguished Alumni Achievement Award, Clark Coll, 1989.

DOVE, RITA FRANCES
Educator, poet, writer. **PERSONAL:** Born Aug 28, 1952, Akron, OH; daughter of Ray A Dove and Elvira E (Hord) Dove; married Fred Viebahn; children: Aviva. **EDUCATION:** Miami Univ Oxford OH, BA 1970-73; Univ Tubingen West Germany, 1974-75; Univ of IA, MFA 1975-77. **CAREER:** Tuskegee Inst, writer in residence 1982; AZ State Univ, asst prof 1981-84, assoc prof 1984-87, full prof 1987-89; Univ of Virginia, full prof of English 1989-. **ORGANIZATIONS:** Ed bd mem Natl Forum The Phi Kappa Phi Journal 1984-; lit adv panel Natl Endowment for the Arts 1984-86; chair Poetry Grants Panel Natl Endowment for the Arts 1985; bd dir Assoc Writing Progs 1985-88; pres Assoc Writing Progs 1986-87; assoc ed Callaloo Journal of Afro-Amer Arts & Letters 1986-; advisory editor The Gettysburg Review 1987-, TriQuarterly 1988-; mem PEN Club Amer Ctr. **HONORS/ACHIEVEMENTS:** Presidential Scholar The Pres of the US of Amer 1970; Fulbright Scholar US Govt 1974-75; Literature Grant Natl Endowment for the Arts1978, 1989; Guggenheim Fellow Guggenheim Found 1983-84; Lavan Younger Poet Awd The Acad of Amer Poets 1986; Pulitzer Prize for Poetry Pulitzer Bd Columiba Univ 1987; General Electric Foundation Award for Younger Writers 1987; Ohio Governor's Award 1988; Honorary Doctor of Letters, Miami Univ 1988; Bellagio Residency, Rockefeller Foundation 1988; Andrew W Mellon Sr Fellowship, Natl Humanities Center, NC, 1988-89; Honorary Doctorate, Knox Coll, Illinois, 1989; collections of poems published: The Yellow House on the Corner, 1980, Museum, 1983, Thhomas & Beulah, 1986, Grace Notes, 1989; Collection of Short Stories published: Fifth Sunday, 1985. **BUSINESS ADDRESS:** Professor of English, University of Virginia, Dept of English, Wilson Hall, Charlottesville, VA 22903.

DOWDELL, DENNIS
Director. **PERSONAL:** Born Jul 29, 1919, Warren, OH; married Marjorie; children: Natalie, Dennis Jr, Gary A, Katherine E, Philip R. **EDUCATION:** Wilberforce U, BS 1943;Univ of MI, 1946-47; Wayne State U, MS 1950-52. **CAREER:** Urban Affairs Carrier Corp, dir; Urban Leag Offs, exec dir 1943-44, exec dir MI 1944-46, exec dir IN 1953-61; State of IN, assit commiss of corrections 1961-63; EEO Prog of USAF Contract Mgmt Dist, chf 1963-64; Beechwood Commun Ctr, exec dir 1948-53; EEO, cons; Urban Leag in Syracuse NY, exec dir; Yg Adult Grp & Urban Leag Guild, organz 1964-69; Urban Affairs Carrier Corp, dir. **ORGANIZATIONS:** Mem Educ Comm of Urban Leag of Onondaga Co; Syracuse Rotary Club; Cult Resour Counc; NAACP; past pres Men's Fellowshp & Trustee Bd of Bethany Bapt Ch; past mem Commun Advis Comm Urban Dev Corp; Debt Couns Serv; Crime Comm; lectr Police Commun Relat Workshops, Natl Counc of Negro Women 1966; Urban Leag of Onondaga Co Inc 1969; United Way camp 1974; Host & Prod of "News & Views-Black Perspect", (6th Anniversary Show) June 4, 1977. **BUSINESS ADDRESS:** PO Box 4800, Syracuse, NY 13221.

DOWDELL, DENNIS, JR.
Human resources administration. **PERSONAL:** Born Mar 08, 1945; son of Dennis Dowdell and Marjorie Dowdell; married Equinetta Cox, Aug 22, 1970; children: Malaika, Arianne, Cicely. **EDUCATION:** Central State Univ, Wilberforce OH, BS History/Political Science, LHD; Cleveland State Univ, Coll of Law, Cleveland OH, JD. **CAREER:** Cleveland Bd of Educ, Cleveland OH, teacher, 1968-71; Legal Serv Org of Indianapolis Inc, Indianapolis IN, staff atty, 1971-72; US Dept of Labor, Office of the Solicitor, Washington DC, Office of the Solicitor, trial atty, 1972-76, asst counsel, OSHA, 1976-78, co-counsel, Black Lung, 1978-80; Amer Can Company, Greenwich CT, Compliance Plans & Litigation, dir, 1980-84; Amer Natl Can, Greenwich CT, Performance Plastics Div, vice pres human resources, 1985-. **ORGANIZATIONS:** Mem, advisory bd of dir, The Maxima Corp, Washington DC; chmn, president's council, Central State Univ; vice pres, bd of dir, Aaron Davis Hall Performing Arts Theatre, City Coll of New York; bd of dir, Natl Urban League, Black Executive Exchange Program; mem, Natl Urban League, NAACP, Amer Bar Assn, Natl Bar Assn; treasurer, H&G of Westchester Inc; past natl pres, Central State Univ Natl Alumni Assn; exec leadership council, Omega Psi Phi Frat; school bd nominating comm, Town of New Castle (Chappaqua NY), 1986; school bd, Special Community Comm on Enrollment & Facilities Use, 1988-89. **HONORS/ACHIEVEMENTS:** Doctor of Humane Letters (Honoris Causa), Central State Univ, Wilberforce OH; "The Occupational Safety & Health Act of 1970", Practising Law Inst. **HOME ADDRESS:** 27 Hidden Hollow Ln, Millwood, NY 10546.

DOWDELL, KEVIN CRAWFORD
Management consultant. **PERSONAL:** Born Oct 09, 1961, Schenectady, NY. **EDUCATION:** Princeton Univ, BSE 1983; Wharton Business School, MBA 1985. **CAREER:** Strategic Planning Assocs, associate 1985-. **ORGANIZATIONS:** Mem Natl Black MBA Assoc; co-capt varsity tennis team Princeton 1982-83; pres Princeton Soc of Black Engrs 1982-83; vice chmn Whitney Young Conf at Wharton 1984-85. **HONORS/ACHIEVEMENTS:** Joseph Clifton Elgin Prize for Excellence in Engrg Princeton 1983; General Electric Co Engineering Fellow 1979-80; Johnson & Johnson Leadership Fellow at Wharton 1983-85. **BUSINESS ADDRESS:** Associate, Strategic Planning Associates, 2300 N St NW, Washington, DC 20037.

DOWDY, JAMES H.
Business executive. **PERSONAL:** Born Jun 03, 1932, New York, NY; son of Edward and Gertrude; married Elsia M; children: James Jr. **EDUCATION:** D&B Business School. **CAREER:** Limosine Serv; Real Estate firm; Vending Co; Contracting Co, 1962; East coast Devel Corp, pres, CEO; Harlem Commonwealth Council, exec dir; Commonwealth Holding Co, pres, CEO 1970-. **ORGANIZATIONS:** Past chmn Vanguard Natl Bank; bd of dir Freedom Natl Bank NYC; bd mem Harlem Interfaith Counseling Svc; mem Presidential Task Force, 100 Black Men; bd Cathedral Church of St John the Devine; former chmn Boys Choir of Harlem. **HONORS/ACHIEVEMENTS:** 1st Comm Serv Awd Gov of VI; Martin L King Awd. **BUSINESS ADDRESS:** President, Commonwealth Holding Co, Inc, 361 W 125 St, New York, NY 10027.

DOWDY, LEWIS C.
Chancellor. **PERSONAL:** Born Sep 01, 1917, Eastover, SC; married Elizabeth Smith; children: Lewis, Jr, Lemuel, Elizabeth. **EDUCATION:** Allen Univ, AB 1939; Indiana State Univ, MA 1949; Indiana Univ, EdD 1965; Indiana State Univ, LLD 1970; Univ of Maine, PdD 1975; Duke Univ, LLD 1977; Allen Univ, LittD 1964; Indiana Univ, LLD 1981. **CAREER:** Eastover SC, principal 1939-51; North Carolina A&T State Univ, teacher 1951-56, dean 1956-60; dean of instruction 1960-64, pres & chancellor 1964-80. **ORGANIZATIONS:** Mem Natl Assn of State Univ & Land-Grant Coll; Assn of Amer Coll; Amer Council on Educ; NC Assn of State Univ & Land-Grant Coll; mem Gov Council Aging; NC Atomic Energy Adv Comm 1968-73; Greensboro United Community Serv; C of C; YMCA. **HONORS/ACHIEVEMENTS:** Outstanding Alumnus Award, IN State Univ, 1967; City Greensboro Award, C of C, 1970; short-term study travel grant, Danforth Found, 1970-71.

DOWE, RALPH M.
Association executive. **PERSONAL:** Born Sep 20, 1942, Wilmington, NC. **EDUCATION:** St U, N C A&M 1968; INUniv Law Sch; NYU; Purdue U, 1974. **CAREER:** Wheeler Boys' Club, Indnpls Boys' Club Assn, exec dir 1973-; Wheeler Boys' Club, asst exec dir 1972; Southside Boys' Club, prgm dir 1971; Gorman Boys' Club, phys dir 1969; Hayes Taylor YMCA, gym asst. **ORGANIZATIONS:** Bd mem IN Scarsbrough Peace Games; mem Concerned Prof Assn; Boys Club Prof Assn; OH KY & IN Jr Ldrs; OKI Steering Comm; NA A&T StUniv Alumni Assn; Nat Assn Keystone Clubs Advisor; mem IN Ldrshp Ctr; PAL Club; Assn for Study Afro Am Hist; Prgmmr IN Boys Clubs 1972; Adult Advr Asn Keystone Clubs; zone chmn IN Boys Clubs Workrs Assn; 2nd vice pres OH KY & IN Jr Ldrs; consult INUniv Gen Asst Ctr; aided in rewriting Keystone Club Manual; line staff orientatioon & training faciliator Career Youth Workers IN. **HONORS/ACHIEVEMENTS:** Jefferson Award, Outst Com Serv 1980. **BUSINESS ADDRESS:** 2310 E 30 St, Indianapolis, IN.

DOWERY, MARY
Educator. **PERSONAL:** Born in Kentucky; divorced. **EDUCATION:** Knoxville Coll, 1950; Atlanta U, MSW 1952; Columbia U, 1963-64; NY U, 1965; Psychoanalytic Inst Training & Rsch, 1974-45; Tulane U, 1975; Union Grad Sch. **CAREER:** Ball State Univ, asst prof; Arch, 1971-74; Einstein Medical Coll; Comm Mental Coll; Comm Mental Health; Urban Renewal, Mobilization for Youth Inc; Residential Treatment for Adolescent Girls; CA Youth Authority; NY City Bd Educ; NY City, protestant cnc; Social Worker, 1953-65; Personnel By Dowery, founder & operator 1965-71; Black Greeting Card "Uhuru", orgnd pub 1968-71. **ORGANIZATIONS:** Mem Delta Sigma Theta; Assn of Personnel Agys NY City 1965-69; Am Mgmt Assn; NASW; Cncl on Social Wk Edn; 100 Black Women 1975-77; Leag Women Voters; NY Society for Sickle Cell Anemia; AU Alumni; Knoxville Coll Alumni Assn; bd mem United Day Care Ctr; Bethel Home for Boys; reviewer Nat Endowment ofHumanities; publ Greeting Card Mag 1970; partcp Mike Wallace Show 1964; publ Et Cetero Mag 1964; Black Enter 1970; Income Mag 1970; Daily News 1972; Bus Wk Peps 1969. **BUSINESS ADDRESS:** 710 N Mc Kinley Ave, Muncie, IN 47303.

DOWLING, MONROE DAVIS, JR.
Physician. **PERSONAL:** Born Feb 23, 1934, New York, NY; son of Monroe Dowling and Helen Johnson Dowling; married Judith Ann Prysbeck, Feb 02, 1978; children: Carla Dowling Brown, Monroe D III. **EDUCATION:** Harvard Univ, AB 1956; Howard Univ Coll of

Med, MD 1960. **CAREER:** Good Samaritan Hospital, 1989-; Bethesda Hospital, 1989-; Goldcrest Retirement Center, medical dir, 1987-89; Univ of Nebraska, asst prof of medicine, 1987-89; VA Hospital, Lincoln, Nebraska, consultant, 1977-89; St Elizabeth Comm Hlth Ctr, 1977-89; Bryan Meml Hosp, 1977-89; Lincoln Gen Hosp 1977-89; Meml Hosp Cancer & Allied Diseases, dir Out-Patient Hematology Clinic 1971-77, asst attending physician hematology serv 1971-77, clinical asst physician Dept Med 1968-71, sr clinical trainee 1967-68, clinical rsch trainee Dept Med 1966-67; Cornell Univ Med Coll, fellow med 1966-68, instr 1968-72, asst prof 1972-77; Henry Ford Hosp, resd 1961-61, 64-66; Univ CO Med Ctr, intern 1960-61; Sloan-Kettering Inst for Cancer Research, rsch fellow 1967-68, rsch assoc 1968-75, assoc 1975-77. **ORGANIZATIONS:** Mem Am Fedn for Clinical Rsch; AMA; Am Soc Clinical Oncology Inc; AAAS; Med Soc, State NY; Med Soc, Co NY; Natl Med Assn; Am Assn for Cancer Rsch; Nebraska Med Assn; Assn of Community Cancer Centers; Lancaster County Medical Assn; Muskingum County Medical Acad; Nebraska Cancer Control Program, chmn Tech Work Comm 1988; Nebraska Lymphoma Study Group. **MILITARY SERVICE:** USNR lt 1950-66; USN 1962-64. **BUSINESS ADDRESS:** Southeastern Ohio Cancer Center, Medical Arts Bldg, 1246 Ashland Ave, Suite 105, Zanesville, OH 43701.

DOWNER, LUTHER HENRY
Physician. **PERSONAL:** Born Dec 13, 1913, Athens, GA; married Dorothy B. **EDUCATION:** Morehouse Coll Atlanta, BS 1938; Atlanta U, MS 1940; HowardUniv Wash DC, MD 1949. **CAREER:** Evansville State Hosp, physician-dir of cont care unit 1975-; Physician, pvt prac 1952-75. **ORGANIZATIONS:** Mem AMA; mem IN State Med Soc; mem Vanderbugh Co Med Soc; mem Nat Med Assn; mem Am Acad of Family Prac. **HONORS/ACHIEVEMENTS:** Fellow Am Acad of Family Prac 1979. **HOME ADDRESS:** 2 Woodmere Ln, Evansville, IN 47715.

DOWNES, DWIGHT
Elected government official. **PERSONAL:** Born Apr 26, 1944, Detroit, MI; son of Mr & Mrs Milton Downes; married Deadra Ann; children: Damany. **EDUCATION:** Ferris State Coll, ASS Bus Admin 1966; MI Lutheran Coll, BA Bus Admin 1969; Univ of Detroit, Master Bus Admin. **CAREER:** Highland Park Community College, adult educ instructor, 1969-70; Chrysler Corp, admin trainee/indus relations representative, 1969-71, labor relations representative, 1971-72, labor relations personnel representative, 1972-74, safety admin, 1974-76; Allen Indus Inc, mgr of personnel & labor relations, 1976-79; Highland Park School District, job placement counselor, 1980-84; Stroh Brewery Co, indus relations-personnel specialist, 1984-85; Mains Enterprises, 1985-89; Wayne County Intermediate School District, part-time mgr/placement specialist, 1980-; City of Highland Park, council pres pro tem, currently. **ORGANIZATIONS:** Bd of dirs, Highland Park Caucus Club; bd of dirs, Chrysler Corp; mem, Lions Club; Highland Park Men's Forum. **BUSINESS ADDRESS:** Council President Pro Tem, City of Highland Park, 30 Gerald, Highland Park, MI 48203.

DOWNEY, AURELIA RICHIE
Educator, company executive. **PERSONAL:** Born Apr 17, 1917, McKenny, VA; daughter of Philip James Lundy and Aurelie Peterson Lundy; married Nathaniel Downey (deceased) (deceased); children: Rev W Temple Richie, Gloria McCoy Boston, Willistine A Betts. **EDUCATION:** VA State, BS 1939; So Baptist Theological Seminary, MA 1969. **CAREER:** Nannie Helen Burroughs School Inc, Washington DC, pres; Christian Worship Women's Auxiliary, Program Natl Baptist Convention, instructor 1968-71; Religious Educ Huntington WV, teacher 1940-51. **ORGANIZATIONS:** Exec bd mem Assn of Independent Schools of Greater Washington DC; mem, Business & Professional Women's League Washington DC; mem Church Women United; mem Women's Dept Program Natl Baptist Convention 1966-; sec/treasurer, Nannie Helen Burroughs Scholarship Fund, Inc, 1978-; treasurer, N Amer Baptist Women's Union, 1987-; World Council of Churches, Churches in Solidarity With Women, 1988-. **HONORS/ACHIEVEMENTS:** Recip Marshall A Talley Award 1972-73; honorary doctor of humanities award Am Bible Coll 1971; honorary legion of honor award Chapel of 4 Chaplains 1971; serv award Program Natl Baptist Convention 1974; Doctor Humane Letters, VA Seminary & Coll, 1984; Doctor of Humanities, Amer Divinity School, New York, NY, 1972, addressee for Women's Day, 1970.

DOWNING, ALVIN JOSEPH
Businessman, musical educator. **PERSONAL:** Born Jul 19, 1916, Jacksonville, FL; son of Ernest Downing, Sr and Mary Washington Downing; married Edna Bernice Gause, Dec 20, 1944; children: Dierdre Marie Parks, Evelyn Jean Hamilton, Alvinette Yvonne McCleave. **EDUCATION:** AL State Montgomery, AL, 1934-35; FL A&M Tallahassee, FL, Mus B 1935-39; Cath Univ Washington, DC, MM Music 1957 & 61; UCLA Los Angeles, CA, 1979. **CAREER:** Gibbs H Sch St Pete, FL, instr/music 1939-41; Gibbs Jr Coll St Pete, FL, instr/music 1961-65; St Pete Jr Coll Clearwater Campus, instr/music 1965-83; Sharps & Flats Music Ent, pres 1973-74. **ORGANIZATIONS:** Pres/ownr Al Downing Music Entpr, Inc 1970-; pres/leader All Stars Jazz Group 1961-; pres Allegro Music Soc 1973-80; pres Al Downing's FL Jazz Assoc 1981-85; 1st Black Comm St Petersburg Housing Authority 1966-77. **HONORS/ACHIEVEMENTS:** Organist Bethel Bapt/Trinity Presby Church 1966-84; minister of music Bethel AME Church St Pete, FL 1985; 1st black mem St Pete Philharmonic Orchestra 1963; produced oper enjoyment Lockbourne AFB OH 1947; Martin Luther King, Jr Drum Major for Justice Award Southern Christian Leadership Conference 1984; Outstanding Service Award St of St Petersburg FL 1981; composed music & lyrics to "Tuskegee Airman" national song of Tuskegee Airman Inc. **MILITARY SERVICE:** USAF maj, 20 yrs; Bronze Star 1950. **HOME ADDRESS:** 2121 25th St S, St Petersburg, FL 33712.

DOWNING, JOHN WILLIAM, JR.
Educator, physician. **PERSONAL:** Born Mar 13, 1936, Phoebus, VA; married Bessie; children: Kevin, Kimberlynn. **EDUCATION:** Morehouse Coll, BS 1957; Meharry Med Coll, MD 1961. **CAREER:** Cincinnati Children's Medical Center, fellow, pediatric cardiology 1967-70; Univ of Cincinnati, instructor Pediatrics 1969-70; Howard Univ, asst prof 1970-74, assoc prof 1974-80, prof 1980-. **ORGANIZATIONS:** Dir Pediatric Cardiac Clinic Howard Univ Hosp; consult DC Gen Hosp; chmn prof ed comm Amer Heart Assoc Nations Capital Affiliate; mem DC Med Soc; mem Amer Heart Assoc 1974-; ch cncl Third St Ch of God 1974-; bd dir Amer Heart Assoc Nations Capital Affiliate; diplomate Amer Bd Pediatrics; flw Am Coll Cardiology. **HONORS/ACHIEVEMENTS:** Several publ in med lit. **MILITARY SERVICE:** AUS MC capt 1964-67. **BUSINESS ADDRESS:** Professor, HowardUniv, 2041 Georgia Ave NW, Washington, DC 20060.

DOWNING, STEPHEN
Professional athlete. **PERSONAL:** Born May 28, 1950, Indianapolis; married Doris. **EDUCATION:** IN U, BS 1973; IUPUI, MS Counseling & Guidance 1978. **CAREER:** IN U, adminstrator asst to athletic dir 1978-; Boston Celtics, former bskbll prof. **ORGANIZATIONS:** Active childrens summer groups; first draft Boston 1973. **HONORS/ACHIEVEMENTS:** MVP Big Ten; Converse All-Amer Team; NCAA 3rd place team; HS All-Amer. **BUSINESS ADDRESS:** 1 Boston Pl, Boston, MA.

DOYLE, ERIE R.
Business executive. **PERSONAL:** Born Jul 26, 1917, Porter, OK. **EDUCATION:** Parsons Jr College, AA 1940. **CAREER:** Civilian Conversation Corp, leader 1940-41; Civil Service Comm, clerk 1947-49; US Postal Service, clerk 1950-70; Natl Alliance of Postal & Fed Employees,dir labor rel 1972-. **ORGANIZATIONS:** Treasurer Natl Alliance Political Action Fund 1985; member NAACP 1985; member Cancer Foundation 1985; member Metropolitan Police Boys & Girls Club 1985. **HONORS/ACHIEVEMENTS:** Outstanding Accomp Awd US Postal Service 1941; Superior Performance Awd US Postal Service 1963/76/84. **MILITARY SERVICE:** AUS corporal 1942-46; USAF staff sgt 1957-70; Good Conduct 3 Battle Stars. **HOME ADDRESS:** 1509 Elkwood Lane, Beaver Heights, MD 20743.

DOYLE, HENRY EMAN
Judge. **PERSONAL:** Born Mar 15, 1910, Austin, TX; married Vendya Middleton. **EDUCATION:** Samuel Huston Coll Austin, TX, AB 1933; TX SoUniv Law Sch Houston, TX, JD 1950. **CAREER:** First Court of Civil Appeals of TX, asso justice 1978-; Atty, self-employed 1946-76; Samuel Huston Coll, instr 1946-48; Prairie View A&M Coll, mgr subsistence dept 1942-45; Austin Pub Sch, head math dept 1933-41. **ORGANIZATIONS:** Mem Am Bar Assn; mem TX Bar Assn; mem Houston Bar Assn; Houston Lawyers Assn; Am Judges Assn. **BUSINESS ADDRESS:** 914 Preston Ave, Houston, TX 77002.

DOZIER, MORRIS, SR.
Retired insurance executive. **PERSONAL:** Born Nov 30, 1921, Americus, GA; married Mary Lois Strawn; children: Morris Jr, Yolonda Maria. **EDUCATION:** College level GED, 1953; KS State Univ, 1963; Brown Mackie Business Coll, 1965. **CAREER:** Civilian Conservation Clerk, admin clerk 1941-42; US Army, sr clerk typist 1942-44, command sgt major 1944-51, military personnel off 1951-62; US Govt Ft Riley, independent contractor 1967-78; Universal Insurance Service, owner/operator 1965-; Geary Co, comm 1973-85. **ORGANIZATIONS:** Pres PTA Westwood Elem Sch 1966; vice-pres Kawanis South, Jct City 1970; chmn Advisory Comm Sickle Cell Anemia Educ & Screening Prog 1975-; lay leaderChurch of Our Savior United Methodist 1980-; Geary County Senior Citizens Board of Directors, chmn 1988-; treasurer, Hunger Commission, Kansas East Conference, United Methodist Church 1985-. **HONORS/ACHIEVEMENTS:** Comm Medal 1957, 1st Oak Leaf Cluster 1962 US Army; Disting Citizen of the Yr Awd Omega Psi Phi Frat 1979; Plaque of Recognition for Outstanding Serv of State JTPA Prog Honorable John Carlin Gov State of KS 1983. **MILITARY SERVICE:** AUS chief warrant officer w3 20 yrs; Good Conduct Medal, Natl Defense Medal, Asiatic Pacific Medal, Philippine Liberation Medal 1943-45; Army Occupation Medals, Japan 1945, Italy 1946. **HOME ADDRESS:** 1701 W 17th St, Junction City, KS 66441.

DOZIER, RICHARD K.
Architect. **PERSONAL:** Born Jan 18, 1939, Buffalo, NY. **EDUCATION:** LA Tech Coll, AA 1962; Yale Sch of Arachitecture, BA 1969; Yale Sch of Architecture, MA 1970;Univ of MI, doctoral candidate 1974. **CAREER:** Historic Preservation Architect Tuskagee Inst AL, prv prac; The Architects Office New Haven, CT, pvt prac; Tuskegee Inst, chmn dept of architecture 1976-79; Yale U, prof of architecture 1970-76;Univ of MI, counselor; architect with various firms; History of Afro-Am Architects & Arachitecture, tchng & proflspeciliza-tion; So Ctr for Afro-Am Architecture Tuskegee, dir. **ORGANIZATIONS:** Mem Am Inst of Architects; Nat Orgn of Minority Architects. **HONORS/ACHIEVEMENTS:** Recip honor award Yale 1970; ldrshp award Yale 1969; rsrch fellow Graham Found 1970; Nat Endowment of the Arts Award 1974-; CT Found for the Arts. **MILITARY SERVICE:** USN radarman E-5 1956-60.

DOZIER, TILLMAN
Manager. **PERSONAL:** Born Oct 23, 1936, New Haven, MI; married Margie; children: Daria, Mark. **EDUCATION:** Wayne State U, BE 1958, MEd Psychol 1962;Univ of MI, Doctoral Candid Educ 1962-65. **CAREER:** Dearborn Eng Plant, ind relat mgr 1976-; Detroit Bd of Edn, tchr 1958-64; Ford Motor Co, statist analys 1964-66; Autolite-Ford Parts Div, ind relat analys 1966-68; Personnel & Organz Staff, classific analys 1968-69, ind relat rsrch analys 1969-70, personell plg mgr 1974-76; Metal Stamping Div, labor relat rep 1970; Pub Relat Staff, educ affairs prgm coordin 1970-72; Ind & Chem Prod Div, assist ind relat mgr 1974. **ORGANIZATIONS:** Former mem Detroit Bus & Ind Forum; life mem NAACP; mem be of trustees Detroit Inst of Commerc 1972; mem bd of dir United Commun serv 1976; trustee Stewart Vernon Chap AME Zion Ch 1969; mem Kappa Alpha Psi Frat. **BUSINESS ADDRESS:** Industrial Relations Manager, Ford Motor Company, 300 Renaissance Center, P O Box 43343, Detroit, MI 48167.

DRAKE, DANIEL D.
Educational administrator. **PERSONAL:** Born Oct 29, 1931, Memphis, TN; son of James Louis Drake, Sr and Bertha Steverson Calhoune; married Adrienne Carol Moore; children: Daniel, Adriana, Darian. **EDUCATION:** Miami Univ, BS Ed 1955; Cleveland State Univ, M Ed 1971; Univ of Akron, Ed D 1979. **CAREER:** Cleveland Public Schools, teacher 1955-68, principal 1968-73; Cleveland State Univ, adjunct prof 1971-85; Cleveland Public Schools, principal 1973-85; Sioux Falls Public Schools, asst supt 1985-89; Milwaukee Public Schools, community superintendent 1989-. **ORGANIZATIONS:** Area 5H coord Phi Delta Kappa Educ Frat 1984-85; pres Metro Cleveland All of Black Schl Educators 1980-85; exec v pres Cleveland Cncl of Admnstr & Supvr 1983-85; pres Phi Delta Kappa Educ Frat 1977-78; brd of dir Neighborhood Cntrs Assoc 1985-86; pres bd of dir Kathryn R Tyler Neighborhood Cntr 1983-85; chmn, bd of dir Carroll Inst; chmn of adv bd of dir Community Devel in Sioux Falls SD; vice chmn, bd of dir Amer Indian Serv Inc; mem Zoological Soc; bd dir Great Plains Zoo. **HONORS/ACHIEVEMENTS:** PDK Dist Serv Awd Phi Delta Kappa Professional Ed Frat 1981; Outstanding Scholastic Achievement 1980; S D Shankland Scholarship Amer Assoc of School Admin 1979; Toward Educational Excellence in an Urban JHS NASSP Bulletin Vol 60 No 401 Sept 1976; six other articles various journals 1977-84. **HOME ADDRESS:** 1200 O'Tonka Trail, Sioux Falls, SD 57103.

DRAKE, GEORGE BARR
Engineer. **PERSONAL:** Born Jun 15, 1938, Castalian Springs, TN; married Shirley Marie Harris; children: Francho Alandez, Cortez Demarco. **EDUCATION:** TN State U, BS Mech Eng 1959; Carnegie Mellon U, Exec Prog 1976. **CAREER:** Gen Motors Corp, rsrch mgr engineering lab Chev Div, mgr spec prod dept, sr proj engr; AUS Tank & Automotive Command, design eng; TN State U, electl maint engr; Little Basin Co Marina, pres; New Haven MI, mayor 1971-. **ORGANIZATIONS:** Mem bd of dir Macomb Co Child aid & Fam Serv 1965-71; mem advis bd Psychiatric Ctr of MI Hosp 1976-. **HONORS/ACHIEVEMENTS:** Spec award; art pub in "Automotive Ind" & " Prod Eng" Trade Mags; fellowship Carnegie MellonUniv Exec Prog GM. **MILITARY SERVICE:** AUS. **BUSINESS ADDRESS:** 30003 Van Dyke, Warren, MI 48090.

DRAKE, JOHN GIBBS ST. CLAIR, JR.
Educator. **PERSONAL:** Born Jan 02, 1911, Suffolk, VA; married Dr Elizabeth Johns; children: Karl, Sandra Elizabeth Drake Meyer. **EDUCATION:** Hampton Inst, BS 1931;Univ of Chicago, MA 1947;Univ of Chicago, Ph D 1954; Roosevelt Univ, LLD 1976. **CAREER:** Dillard Univ New Orleans, faculty 1935-36, 1941; Roosevelt Univ Chicago, faculty 1946-69; Univ of Ghana, W Africa (on leave from Roosevelt), visiting prof 1958-61. **ORGANIZATIONS:** Consultant Ford Found 1956-57; Peace Corp; tchr training staff for Africa Summers 1961, 1962, 1964; exec brd Amer Soc for Africa Culture 1960-68; mem AmerNegro Ldrshp Conf on Africa 1960-68. **HONORS/ACHIEVEMENTS:** Dubois-Johnson-Frazier Award for schlrshp & tchng, Amer Sociological Assoc 1973. **BUSINESS ADDRESS:** Prof Emeritus, Anthropology, Stanford University, Dept Of Anthropology, Stanford, CA 94305.

DRAKE, PAULINE LILIE
Elected city official. **PERSONAL:** Born Jul 20, 1926, Cliffwood, NJ; daughter of Gabriel Robinson and Daisy Robinson; married Howard William Drake; children: Sidney Howard. **EDUCATION:** NY Univ, 1945-46; Brookdale Comm Coll NJ, 1984-85. **CAREER:** Providence Baptist Church Cliffwood, church clerk 1957-65, youth choir dir 1960-72; Order of Eastern Star AF&AM, worthy matron 1958-60, Monmouth cty dep 1960-71; Order of Sunbeam Youth Dept OES AF&AM, deputy 1972-82. **ORGANIZATIONS:** Pres Matawan Hadassah NJ 1979-81; cert chmn Southern NJ Reg of Hadassah 1981-85; pres Monmouth Cty VFW Aux NJ 1980-81; publicity chmn State of NJ Ladies Aux VFW 1981-82, 1988-89; jr girls unit chmn NJ Ladies Aux VFW 1982-83; safety chmn NJ Ladies Aux VFW 1983-84; voice of democracy & youth activity chmn Ladies Aux VFW 1984-85; safety chmn 1986-87, guard 1986-87, conductress 1987-88 Dept of NJ Ladies Aux VFW; transfer and takedown chmn, Southern NJ Region of Hadassah 1987-1990; chaplain 1988; jr vice pres, NJ Ladies Aux VFW 1988-1990, rehabilitation chmn 1988-89. **HONORS/ACHIEVEMENTS:** Woman of the Yr Matawan Hadassah 1979; Citation Bayshore Recreation & Economic Develop 1979; Presidential Awd Natl Hadassah 1981; NJ Publicity 1st Place Natl VFWA Kansas 1982; NJ Jr Girls Unit 2nd Place Natl VFW Kansas 1984; NJ Safety Cert Natl VFW KS 1984; 15 Yr Pin Keyport Aux to VFW NJ 1985; NJ Publicity 1st place Natl VFWA 1988. **HOME ADDRESS:** 85 Kennedy Ave, Cliffwood, NJ 07721.

DRAKES, MURIEL B.
State official. **PERSONAL:** Born Nov 25, 1935, Bronx, NY; daughter of Alphonso Drakes and Frances Drakes. **EDUCATION:** DE State Coll, BS 1958; Columbia Teacher Coll, MA 1963. **CAREER:** NY State Environmental Conservation, dir of EEO, 1987-; NY State Office Gen Serv, dir promotion & pub affairs 1976-; Dept Commerce & Ind, dep commr 1974-75; Manpower Devel Commerce Labor Ind Corp, asst vice pres 1972-74; Comm Corp, asso dir prgm 1969-72; Bedford Stuyvesant Comm Corp, dir, educ explt prgm 1965-69; Famingdale Pub Sch, tchr 1958-65; NY City Childrens Aid Soc, vis lctr 1957-60; NY Sch Social Rsch, visiting guest spkr 1968; Dahomey W Africa, visiting guest lecturer 1971; NY State Lottery Public Rels, consult 1976. **ORGANIZATIONS:** Mem Delta Sigma Theta Sor; NEA; vice pres Brooklyn Kings Co Judiciary Sect Comm Bldg; mem C of C Brooklyn Managerial Club; Intl Ind Mktg Club; Albany Women's Press Club; pres Eleanor Roosevelt Educ Action Prgm. **HONORS/ACHIEVEMENTS:** Natl Black Public Admins, 1984 Woman of the Year, Albany, YWCA,; 1987 Outstanding Leadership by Albany Capital Dist Ethnic Heritage Orgs (28,) 1987; Willoughy Walk Tenants Cncl Recpt; distgd citz award Concord Bapt Ch; Outstanding Leadership Civic Assn Jersey City 1974; outsdg effort & Achvmt Inter Ethnic Civic Assn 1975; achvmt excellence Black Photographers Assn 1974; Brooklyn Distinguished Council Negro Women 1975; author "1965 Proposal of Bedford Stuyvesant Comm Corp on the Homework Study Prgm". **BUSINESS ADDRESS:** NY State, Environmental Conservation, 50 Wolf Rd, Albany, NY 12233.

DRAPER, EDGAR DANIEL
Educator. **PERSONAL:** Born Aug 29, 1921, Maryland; married Emma J Williams; children: Marie E, Yvonne T, Edgar D. **EDUCATION:** Howard U, BA 1943; NY U, MPA 1948, PhD 1966. **CAREER:** TX Southern Univ, dir & instructor 1948-49; Tubman Coll, pres 1949-51; Baltimore Housing Authority, asst mgr 1951-52; Morgan State Coll of Business, mgr & asst pres 1952-60; Conference African Resources NY Univ, asst dir 1960-61; African-Amer Trade Devel Assn, exec sec 1961-62; UN Inst Public Admin, deputy chief 1962-63; Governor Nelson Rockefeller, program asst 1963-66; Borough Manhattan Comm Coll, assoc dean, dean of college & faculty, 1967-70, pres 1970-84 (retired). **ORGANIZATIONS:** Bd mem Met Chap Amer Assoc Pub Adm; NY Plan; Natl Conference Christs Jews 1970-; Council Higher Educ Inst 1972-; Prof Training Com & Mem Com; BSA; Natl African Studies; Natl Ed Assoc; Comparative Ed Soc; Am Assoc Comm & Jr Coll; Assoc Assist Negro Businesses; Urban Leag; Gov Libr Com; Interstate Compact Ed; Joint Legislative Com; Host Radio WNYC-AM The Open Door 1973-74; chmn 4th Round Table Conference Perspectives Pub Adm Sudan; NY St Gov Com Manpower 1966. **HONORS/ACHIEVEMENTS:** Founders Day Award NY U. **MILITARY SERVICE:** AUS 1946-47.

DRAPER, EVERETT T., JR.
Educator. **PERSONAL:** Born Jan 23, 1939, Lochapoka, AL; son of Everett T Draper Sr and Susie W Draper; married Emma Jeanette Smith; children: Evangeline Hope. **EDUCATION:** Miles College, Birmingham, AL, BA 1960; North Adams State, MA, MEd 1969; Advanced Studies, Yale Univ, Fairfield Univ. **CAREER:** Housatomic Regional HS, mathematics teacher 1963-69; Harcourt Brace Jovanovich Inc, asst editor, Math 1969-1971; American Book Co, exec editor, Math & Sci 1971-78; LaGuardia Cmmty Coll, adjunct prof of Math 1974-85; Holf Rinehart and Winston, Publishers, sr editor Math 1979-86; Prentice-Hall, Inc, exec edit Math 1986-. **ORGANIZATIONS:** Mem Natl Cncl of Teachers of Mathematics, Natl Cncl of Supervisors of Mathematics, ASCD; NABSE; mem Mathematics Assoc of Amer; chmn Computer Task Force of Presbytery of Palisades 1984-. **HONORS/ACHIEVEMENTS:** Service Awd United Negro Coll Fund (NYC) 1973-74; first black teacher at Housatonic Reg HS; first black Math Editor at Harcourt Brace 1969, American Book Co 1971, and first black to be named as Math Dept head in publishing industry 1986. **BUSINESS ADDRESS:** Executive Editor Mathmatics, Prentice Hall Allyn & Bacon, Englewood Cliffs, NJ 07632.

DRAPER, FRANCES MURPHY
Newspaper executive. **PERSONAL:** Born Dec 18, 1947, Baltimore, MD; daughter of James E Wood Sr and Frances L Murphy; married Andre Reginald Draper; children: Kevin E Peck, Andre D, Andrea J. **EDUCATION:** Morgan State Univ, BA 1969; The Johns Hopkins Univ, MEd 1973; Univ of Baltimore, Graduate Certificate in Mgmt 1979, MBA 1981. **CAREER:** Baltimore City Public Schools, teacher 1969-73; New Jersey Afro-Amer, mgr 1973-76; Merrill Lynch Pierce Fenner & Smith, acct exec 1976-78; Morgan State Univ, asst vice pres develop 1978-83; Afro-Amer Newspapers, pres 1986-. **ORGANIZATIONS:** Mem Delta Sigma Theta Sor Inc 1968-; dir Afro-Amer Newspapers 1976-; dir Exec Women's Network 1983-85; pres Baltimore City Chapter Jack and Jill Inc 1985-87; vice chair, City of Baltimore's Literacy Foundation 1988-. **BUSINESS ADDRESS:** President, Afro-American Newpapers, 628 No Eutaw St, Baltimore, MD 21201.

DRAPER, FREDERICK WEBSTER
Educator. **PERSONAL:** Born Jul 10, 1945, St Louis, MO; married Carrie Todd; children: Fred W II, Angela. **EDUCATION:** IN State Univ, BS 1968, MS PE 1969, MS Pers Admin 1972, EdD 1976. **CAREER:** Project Upswing IN, asst dir 1969; GED Prog for Office of Economic Opportunity, supvr 1972-73; asst physical educ & head crosscountry coach 1969-, dir of ed programs; School of HPER IN State Univ, dir educ opportunity programs, prof. **ORGANIZATIONS:** Chmn Black Freshmen Orientation Prog IN State Univ 197-74; internship with vice pres IN State Univ for Student Affairs 1972-73; bd vice pres IN State Black Expo; bd dir Hyte Comm Ctr; bd of dir & treas IN Airport; faculty adv Kappa Alpha Psi; mem City Human Rel Comm, School Human Rel Comm, Boy Scout Troup Leader; pres Hulman Reg Airport; bd of dir, mem Civil Rights Commiss; chmn of bd IN Black Expo. **HONORS/ACHIEVEMENTS:** Outstanding Black Faculty Awd IN State Univ 1972-73; One of Nations Most Eligible Bachelors Ebony Mag 1969; Dean's List 1968; vice pres Alumni Club; All-conf intrack every year as an undergrad. **BUSINESS ADDRESS:** Director, Professor, School of HPER, Indiana StateUniv, Terre Haute, IN 47808.

DRAWOH, PHIL See VENABLE, HOWARD PHILLIP

DREHER, LUCILLE G.
Association executive. **PERSONAL:** Born Jun 24, 1910, Greenville, SC; married Rev Frederick D. **EDUCATION:** Claflin Coll. **CAREER:** Youth Village Center, founder & pres, 1959-66; Youth Village Family Day Care, dir, 1966-76; Bronx, local mayor 1975. **ORGANIZATIONS:** NAACP; Natl Council of Negro Women; NY City Planning Bd #3; Mayor's Vol Action Comm; Bronx Frontier Morrisania Educational. **HONORS/ACHIEVEMENTS:** Scholarship Comm Award, JFK Library Award for Minorities; Natl Council of Negro Women Community Achievement Award. **BUSINESS ADDRESS:** Youth Village Center, 1181 Boston Rd, Bronx, NY 10456.

DRENNEN, GORDON
Auditor. **PERSONAL:** Born Jul 15, 1947, Atlanta, GA; son of Gordon D Drennen Sr and Eliza Harris; married Diane Hatcher; children: Kimberly. **EDUCATION:** Fort Valley State Coll, BS 1970; TX Southern Univ, MBA 1971. **CAREER:** Wolf & Co CPA's, staff accountant 1971-73, sr accountant 1973-78; Tarica & Co CPA's, supervisor 1978-80, mgr 1980-. **ORGANIZATIONS:** Dir Amer Civil Liberties Union of GA 1986-; finance chmn Ft Valley State Coll Alumni Assn 1986-; mem GA State Soc of CPA's; mem/consultant Natl Assn of Comm Health Ctrs, GA Assn for Primary Health Care Inc; mem Kappa Alpha Psi Frat. **BUSINESS ADDRESS:** Manager, Tarica & Co CPA's, 3340 Peachtree Rd Ste 1560, Atlanta, GA 30026.

DREW, LARRY C.
Professional athlete. **PERSONAL:** Born Apr 01, 1958, Kansas City, MO. **EDUCATION:** Univ of MO, 1980. **CAREER:** Detroit Pistons, 1980-81; Kansas City Kings, 1982-. **ORGANIZATIONS:** Bd mem KC K's Red Cross; tchr Bsktbl Camps in KS & MO. **HONORS/ACHIEVEMENTS:** All Big 8 Honorable Mention; holds all time record for appearances (117) starts (114) consecutive starts (104) career assists (443) game assists (12) & career field goals (557); 1st round draft pick Detroit Pistons 1980; ranked 9th in NBA in assists 1984-85; led team in assists, 2nd in scoring Kansas City Kings 1984-85; 14 double assist scoring games 1984-85.

DREW, STEPHEN RICHARD
Attorney. **PERSONAL:** Born May 25, 1949, Detroit, MI; son of Richard T Drew and Gwendolyn M Drew; married Clarice Smith, Apr 22, 1989; children: Richard, Stephen, Anthony. **EDUCATION:** Univ of MI, BA 1971; Univ of MI Law School, JD 1974. **CAREER:** Williams Klukowski Drew & Fotieo, assoc 1974-77, partner 1977-87. **ORGANIZATIONS:** Chairperson City of Grand Rapids Comm Relations Commn 1984-85; consultant special investigator Saginaw Police Dept 1985-86; mem Sigma Pi Phi 1985-; judicial merit selection panel mem US Court of Appeals 6th Circuit 1986-; legal redress comm NAACP Grand Rapids Chapter 1987; trustee Grand Rapids Bar Assn 1987; mem Amer Bar Assn, Natl Bar Assn, MI Trail Lawyers Assn, Amer Trial Lawyers Assn; fellow State Bar of Michigan; pres, Floyd Skinner Bar Assn. **HONORS/ACHIEVEMENTS:** Chief trial attorney in various civil rights cases in MI area, Federal and State Courts 1978-; Outstanding Volunteer Award NAACP Grand Rapids Chapter 1982; Patriotic Serv Award Sec to the US Treasury 1986; Grand Rapids Giant Award Justice. **HOME ADDRESS:** 4224 Lamdale Ct, Grand Rapids, MI 49506. **BUSINESS ADDRESS:** Partner, Williams Klukowski Drew Fotieo, 934 Scribner NW, Grand Rapids, MI 49504.

DREW, THELMA LUCILLE
Government official. **PERSONAL:** Born May 06, Flushing, NY; married Archer S Drew, Jr; children: Richard Michael, Kenneth Edward, Joanne Michelle, Sheryln Liane, Kimberly Terese. **EDUCATION:** Queens Coll, NY, Engish 1946-49; Amer Inst of Banking, Mgmnt 1968-72; Empire State Coll, NY, Pub Admin 1978-80; Hofstra Univ Hempstead, NY, Cert inMuseum Studies 1983-85. **CAREER:** NY Tele Co, bus off rep 1949-58; Smithtown Town-

shp, town rec ldr (1st black) 1965-69; Natl Bank of N Amer, baner/mgmnt 1969-73; Suffolk Co Dept ofSoc Svcs, socl welfare examiner 1973-77; Suffolk Cnty Human Rights Comm, sr investgtr 1977-82. **ORGANIZATIONS:** Mbr, NYS Div of Human Rights Cncl 1983-; brd of dir Long Isl Affirmative Act Plan 1980-, Victims Inf Bureau 1980-, Inst of Labor/Mgmnt Studies 1979-;founding mem 100 Black Women of LI 1980-; mem Natl Assn of Female Exec 1982-, Natl Assn of Consumer Prot 1982-; prs/Chrprsn Suffolk Cnty Black Hist Assoc 1982-; pres Sec & fndng mem Long Island Minoritycoalition 1982-; org mem Womens Equal Oppty Cncl 1980-, Womens Equal Rights Congress 1980-82; pres & orgn mem NAACP Smithtown Branch 1966-82. **HONORS/ACHIEVEMENTS:** Womens Equal Rights comm Woman of the Year 1984; comm serv awd Natl Cncl Oppty Cncl/LI 1983; Community Serv Awd Natl Assoc of Cnties/LIAAO 1983; ldrshp Awd Natl Cncl Christ & Jews/LI 1982; comm serv Human Rights Comm/Suffolk Cnty 1981; candidate for pres recog Award for vlnt Rsm/Suffolk 1984. **BUSINESS ADDRESS:** Sr Consumer Affrs Investig, Suffolk County Govt, Dept of Consumer Protection, Bldg 340 County Center, Hauppauge, NY 11787.

DREW, WELDON
Educator. **PERSONAL:** Born Apr 22, 1935, Silsbee, TX; married Gloria Marie McIntosh. **EDUCATION:** Fisk U, BS 1957; TX So U, MS 1973. **CAREER:** New Mexico State U, head basketball coach 1975-; Houston Indep Sch District, tchr/coach 1957-75. **ORGANIZATIONS:** Mem & sponsor KAY 1956-; mem NAACP 1957-; mem NABC 1975-80. **HONORS/ACHIEVEMENTS:** TX & HS Coach of the Yr, Houston-austin 1974-75; Houston HS Coach of the Yr 1974-75; Natl Achvmt Award, NABC 1974-75; Coca-Cola Award, Houston 1974-75. **BUSINESS ADDRESS:** New Mexico State University, Box 3145, Las Cruces, NM 88003.

DREW-PEEPLES, BRENDA
Attorney. **PERSONAL:** Born Feb 28, 1947, Fresno, CA; daughter of Jesse Drew and Gladys Drew; married Horace Peeples, May 20, 1989; children: Cranford Thomas, Vanessa Leigh. **EDUCATION:** Des Moines Area Comm Coll, AA 1973; Drake Univ, BS Business Admin 1975; Univ of IA Coll of Law, JD 1978. **CAREER:** Iowa Cty Atty's Office, legal intern 1978; Aetna Life & Casualty Ins of Des Moines, claim rep 1979; Legal Serv Corp of IA, attorney 1979-81; Polk Co Attorney's Office, asst co atty 1981-83; Davenport Civil Rights Comm, director/attorney. **ORGANIZATIONS:** Mem Iowa State Bar Assn 1980-; moderator Davenport Comm Forum 1985; Quad Cities Vision for the Future; LULAC CLub; NAACP; SLCL; Poor People's Campaign Steering Committee; East Side Advisory Board; National Youth Sports Advisory Board; Quad Cities Merit Employment Council; Women's Encouragement Board; Davenport Civil Service Commission; Iowa Association of Human Rights Agencies; Intl Assn of Official Human Rights Agencies; Natl Assn of Human Rights Workers; Greater Quad Cities Telecommunications Corporation Board; Maternal Health Center Board; Scott County Bar Assn. **BUSINESS ADDRESS:** Director-Attorney, Davenport Civil Rights Commission, 226 W 4th St, Davenport, IA 52801.

DREWRY, CECELIA HODGES
Educator. **PERSONAL:** Born in New York, NY; married Henry N. **EDUCATION:** Hunter Coll, AB 1945; Columbia U, AM 1948; ShakespeareUniv of Birmingham, England, Cert 1949; Northwestern U, PhD 1967;Univ of Ghana, Cert 1969. **CAREER:** Princeton Univ, asst dean, asst prof; Haverford Coll, visiting prof of english 1977; Teachers Coll Columbia Univ, visiting instructor 1968; African & Afro-Amer Studies Prog, chairperson 1969-70; Rutgers Univ, assoc prof 1962-70; High School of Performing Arts NY, teacher 1952-59; Talladega Coll, instrutor 1945-47; Penthouse Dance & Drama Theatre NY, dir of speech 1948-52; Princeton High School, teacher 1959-61; various theatre appearances. **ORGANIZATIONS:** Mem AAVP; AAUW, MLA, SCA; trustee Cedar Crest Coll PA; mem Carnegie Found for Advmt of Tching; NAACP; Nat Council of Negro Women; Princeton Assn of Hum Rights. **HONORS/ACHIEVEMENTS:** Award for excellence in oral interpretation of literature NorthwesternUniv Sch of Speech; Alpha Psi Omega Hon Soc; Danforth Assn; Honoree Phi Delta Kappa. **BUSINESS ADDRESS:** Princeton University, 408 W College, Princeton, NJ 08540.

DREWRY, HENRY NATHANIEL
Educator. **PERSONAL:** Born Feb 08, 1924, Topeka, KS; son of Leonard E Drewry and Bessie Boyd Drewry; divorced. **EDUCATION:** Talladega Coll, AB 1948; Teachers Coll, Columbia Univ, MA 1949. **CAREER:** A&T Coll, Greensboro, NC, instructor, 1949-51; Social Security Admin, clains asst, 1952-54; Princeton NJ High School teacher, 1954-60; Princeton High School, History Dept Chmn, 1960-68; Princeton Univ, dir of Teacher Prep & Placement, lecturer, prof, 1968-89; Andrew Mellon Found, program assoc, 1989-. **ORGANIZATIONS:** NJ Historical Comm 1977-; mem, bd trustees Talladega Coll 1965-, Groton School, 1977-; mem, NY Historical Soc, 1986-, Council for Basic Educ, 1975-. **HONORS/ACHIEVEMENTS:** Fellowship, John Hays Fellos Prof, 1964; Distinguished Teacher Award, Harvard Univ, 1964; Oustanding alumnus UNCF, NJ State Org 1978. **MILITARY SERVICE:** USAAF corpl. **BUSINESS ADDRESS:** Program Associate, Andrew W Mellon Found, 140 E 62nd St, New York, NY 10021.

DREXLER, CLYDE
Professional athlete. **PERSONAL:** Born Jun 22, 1962, New Orleans, LA. **EDUCATION:** Univ of Houston, grad 1983. **CAREER:** Portland Trail Blazers, forward 1983-. **HONORS/ACHIEVEMENTS:** Newcomer of the Year in the Southwest Conf 1981; Houstons MVP as a sophomore; Jr season named Southwest Conf Player of the Year; Won 1st team All-Amer honors on the US Basketball Writers Assoc team; mem 36th NBA All Star Team. **BUSINESS ADDRESS:** Portland Trail Blazers, 700 NE Multnomah St, Portland, OR 97232.

DREYFUSS, JOEL P.
Writer, freelance TV producer. **PERSONAL:** Born Sep 17, 1945, Port-au-Prince, Haiti. **EDUCATION:** City Coll, BS. **CAREER:** Wash Post, reptr 1973-76; NY Post, rptr 1971-73; AP, reptr 1969-71. **HONORS/ACHIEVEMENTS:** Urban journalism fellow U, Chicago 1973. **BUSINESS ADDRESS:** 359 Jersey St, San Francisco, CA 94114.

DRIESSEN, HENRY, JR.
Elected government official. **PERSONAL:** Born Sep 28, 1927, Hilton Head Isl, SC; married Phoebe; children: Leon, Ann J, Bernard. **EDUCATION:** Savannah State Coll, BA 1957. **CAREER:** Driessen Groc & Serv Station & Bottle Shop, Merchant 1958; Town of Hilton Head, councilman. **ORGANIZATIONS:** Teacher Screven Ct HS 1957-58; area dir Bank of Beaufort; dir Palmetto Electric Coop Inc; past vice pres Hilton Head Island med Clinic; past master Happy Home Lodge #125; past pres Hilton Head Elem School PTA; past pres McCracken HS; past dir Hilton Head Island Chamber of Commerce. **HONORS/ACHIEVEMENTS:** Islander of the Month Hilton Head Island Chamber of Commerce. **MILITARY SERVICE:** AUS corpl 2 yrs. **BUSINESS ADDRESS:** Councilman, Town of Hilton Head, Box 593 Hwy 278, Hilton Head Island, SC 29928.

DRIGGRISS, DAPHNE BERNICE SUTHERLAND
Educational administrator. **PERSONAL:** Born in New York, NY; married Harvey Driggriss Sr (deceased); children: Harvey William Jr. **EDUCATION:** NY Univ, 1939-41-44; Queens Coll-City Univ of NY, 1949-50; Adelphi Coll-univ, BS 1963; Adelphi Univ, MA 1971; Pace Univ, certif & MS 1973. **CAREER:** Public Schl #136 Queens, NY, asst prncpl 1970; Public Schl #116 Queens, NY, asst prncpl 1974-78; Public Schl #35 Queens, NY, asst prncpl 1976-77; Public Schl #132 Queens, NY, prncpl 1978-. **ORGANIZATIONS:** Dist 29 treas Cncl of Spvrs & Admnstrs 1976-; New York City Elem Sch Prins Assn 1979-; NAACP-JAMAICA, NY 1950; Beta Omicron Chpts of natl sor of Phi Delta Kappa Inc 1966-; basileus Natl Sor of Phi Delta Kappa Inc Beta Omicron Chpts 1975-77, exec advsr 1977-79; natl coorinator internatl proj Nat Sor PhiDK Inc 1981-, constitution chrpsn Eastern Region 1984-. **HONORS/ACHIEVEMENTS:** Asst Prncpl Achvmnt Awd PTA PS #116 Queens, NY 1977. **BUSINESS ADDRESS:** Principal, Public Schl 132 Queens, 132-15 218 St, Springfield Gardens, New York, NY 11413.

DRIMMER, MELVIN
Professor. **PERSONAL:** Born Nov 02, 1934, New York; married Lillian Baehmer; children: Alan Stessin, Barbara. **EDUCATION:** City Coll NY, BA 1956; Oxford U, post grad summer 1957;Univ Rochester, PhD 1965; Sch Oriental & African Studies,Univ London, postdoctoral fellow 1966-67; Dubois Inst Harvard, post doctoral fellow 1981-84. **CAREER:** Hunter Coll, lecturer 1960-63; Spelman Coll, Atlanta Univ Center, asst prof, chmn History dept 1963-72; NY Univ, visiting prof summers 1965-66, visiting assoc prof summer 1968; Amer Instns Colgate Univ, A Lindsey O'Connor, visiting prof 1969-70; Cleveland State Univ, prof, dept chmn 1972-. **ORGANIZATIONS:** Exec dir Am Forum for Intl Study; dir 34 summer insts in Africa & Caribbean 1968-; dir Nat Def Educ Act Insts in Black Hist, Spelman Coll 1966,68; consult Ford Found Aspen Conf 1970; Yale Danforth Prgm 1970; John Jay Coll 1970; A Philip Randolph Inst 1970-72; bd dirs Path Equal Housing Prgm, Cleveland; mem Am Hist Assn; Assn for Study Negro Life & History; Phi Beta Kappa. **HONORS/ACHIEVEMENTS:** Recip fld summer grants 1964, 65; AtlantaUniv research grant 1966; Ford Humanities grant, ColgateUniv 1969-70; author articles; "Black History" Doubleday 1968;Issues in Black History 1987. **BUSINESS ADDRESS:** Prof & Chairman History, Cleveland State University, Cleveland, OH 44115.

DRISKELL, CLAUDE EVANS
Dentist. **PERSONAL:** Born Jan 13, 1926, Chicago, IL; son of James Driskell and Elizabeth Driskell; married Naomi; children: Yvette. **EDUCATION:** Roosevelt Univ, BS 1950; Univ of IL Coll of Dentistry, DDS 1954. **CAREER:** Lincoln Dental Soc, editor 1966-; Natl Dental Assn, dir publicity 1968-76; Natl Dental Assn Journal, asst editor; Private Practice, dentist. **ORGANIZATIONS:** Omega Psi Phi Fraternity 1948-77; fellow Acad General Dentistry 1973; mem Amer Dental Assn, Chicago Dental Soc; vice pres Jackson Park Assn; adjunct prof Minority Students in Pre-Dental Program Chicago State Univ; mem Dean's Com for Black Students Univ IL Coll Dentistry; life mem Chicago Inst Art, Roosevelt Univ, Univ IL; mem Amer School Health Assn, Intercontinental Bio Assn; adjunct off-campus prof for pre-dental students for Chicago State Univ, IL Inst of Technology 1986-87. **HONORS/ACHIEVEMENTS:** Editorial Award Natl Dental Assn 1968, 1972; publications "The History of the Negro in Dentistry" 1968; "The Influence of the Halogen Elements Upon the Hydrocarbon & their effect on General Anesthesia" 1970; "The Chicago Black Dental Profs 1850-1983"; Lincoln Dental Soc 1972, 1975; Fellowship Acad General Dentistry, 1973. **MILITARY SERVICE:** AUS 1944-46; European-African-Middle E Campaign Medal; Asiatic-Pacific Campaign Medal. **BUSINESS ADDRESS:** 11139 S Halsted, Chicago, IL 60628.

DRISKELL, DAVID C.
Artist, educator. **PERSONAL:** Born Jun 07, 1931, Eatonton, GA. **EDUCATION:** Howard Univ, AB 1955; Cath Univ, MFA 1962; Ricksbureau Kunsthistoriches Den Haag, Holland 1964. **CAREER:** Talladega Coll, assoc prof 1955-62; Howard Univ, assoc prof 1962-66; Fisk Univ, prof & chmn dept of art 1966-76; Univ Ife Nigeria, visiting prof 1970; Univ of MD, chmn dept of art 1978-83; Amistad Research Center, curator Aaron Douglas collection 1977-; Univ of MD, prof of art 1977-. **ORGANIZATIONS:** Mem Coll Art Assn Amer; SE Mus Conf; Amer Assn Mus; Amer Fedn Arts; bd dirs Barnett Aden Gallery; bd dirs Mus African Art & Frederick Douglass Inst Negro Arts & Hist; bd trustees Amer Fedn Arts; Tougaloo Coll Art Mus. **HONORS/ACHIEVEMENTS:** Who's Who in Amer Art 1959-70; Who's Who in SE 1963-70; Who's Who Amer 1973; Afro-Amer Artist 1973; Pubns, monograms, catalogs, film cons,; Purchase Awards Birmingham Mus Art 1972; Tougaloo Coll Gallery 1973; num art awards, scholarships, fellowships & grants; foreign study & travel.

DRISSEN, DAN
Professional athlete. **PERSONAL:** Born Jul 29, 1951, Hilton Head, SC; married Bonnie; children: Dominique, Devon. **EDUCATION:** Riley HS Bluffton, SC. **CAREER:** Cincinnati Reds, infielder 1973-84; Montreal Expos, infielder 1984-. **HONORS/ACHIEVEMENTS:** Let the NL in 1980 with 93 bases-on-balls; first designated hitter ever used by the NL in World Series play; played in three League Championship and two World Series; finished third in Natl League rookie-of-the-year balloting.

DRIVER, ELWOOD T.
Business executive. **PERSONAL:** Born Aug 20, 1921, Trenton, NJ; married Shirley Martin. **EDUCATION:** NJ State Coll, BS 1942; NY U, MA 1946. **CAREER:** Natl Aeromatic & Space Admin, dir aircraft mgmt office 1986-; Elwood T Driver & Assoc Inc, pres 1981-86; Nat Transp Safety Bd US Govt, vchmn 1978-; Nat Hwy & Traffic Safety Adminstrn, Dept of Transp, US Govt, acting asso adminstr for rule making 1977-78, Dir Office of Crash Avoidance; Minuteman Div Autonetics NAm Aviator USAF, system safety mgr 1962-67. **ORGANIZATIONS:** Past pres bd dir System Safety Soc 1968-70; mem bd dir Professional Safety Engr, State CA 1970-; mem Am Soc Safety Engr; pres Tuskogee Airman E Coast Chap Dist Flying Cross 1943. **HONORS/ACHIEVEMENTS:** Air Medal with Clusters 1943; Commendation Medal 1962; Cert of Achvmt N AmAviation 1965; Spl Achvmt Award US Govt

1970. **MILITARY SERVICE:** USAF maj 1942-62. **BUSINESS ADDRESS:** Dir Aircraft Mgmt Office, Natl Aeromatic & Space Admin, Washington, DC 20591.

DRIVER, JOHNIE M.
Analyst. **PERSONAL:** Born May 08, 1933, Centerville, AL; married Odessa Wright; children: Dwaine Stuart. **EDUCATION:** Univ of IL, BS Elec Eng 1961, MS Elec Eng 1963. **CAREER:** Sperry UT Co Salt Lake City, UT, proj engr 1963-66; Jet Propulsion Lab Mission Analysis Div, mem tech staff 1966-. **ORGANIZATIONS:** Pres Salt Lake City NAACP 1965-66; mem UT State Civil Rights Comm 1965; treas Pasadena, CA NAACP; mem/deacon Metropolitan Baptist Church. **HONORS/ACHIEVEMENTS:** 1st Black to address Joint Session UT State Legislature 1965. **MILITARY SERVICE:** USAF s/sgt 1950-58. **BUSINESS ADDRESS:** Member Technical Staff, Jet Propulsion Laboratory, 4800 Oak Grove Drive, Pasadena, CA 91103.

DRIVER, LOUIE M., JR.
Clergyman. **PERSONAL:** Born Mar 18, 1924, LA; son of Louie and Myrtle; married Lillian Stovall; children: Louie III, Lamar; Brenda. **EDUCATION:** Harbor Coll, Certificate 1950; Emmanual Bible Inst, Graduated 1956; Blue Mountain Coll, Psychology Certificate 1963; LTI Biola, Graduated 1975; Univ of Lavern, BA religion 1985; LA Ecumenical Center for Black Church Studies, BA 1985; Graduated 1988 Fuller Theological Seminary MA, 1988; LA Edumenical Center for Black Church Studies. **CAREER:** Saints Home Church of God in Christ, pastor; Grace Chapel Church, Pendleton OR, pastor. **ORGANIZATIONS:** Supt Sunday School Local/Dist; pres Young People Willing Workers, Local, Dist, State; appointed bd dir CH Mason Bible Coll 1977; chmn Bd Elders CA SW; Dist #4 supt CA SW Jurisdiction; mem Exec Bd CA SW Cogic; mem Chas H Mason Theological School, So CA Ext; chapel Chamber of Commerce, Pendleton OR; mem Natl COGIC Pastors Grievance Com; mem Newton St Police Ministers Council Clergy, Los Angeles County Sheriff's Dept Central Jail. **HONORS/ACHIEVEMENTS:** Recipient outstanding pastor of yr CA SW Jurisdiction Religious Workers Guild; hon DD Trinity Hall Coll 1975. **BUSINESS ADDRESS:** Church of God in Christ, Saints Home Ch, 1460 E 20 St, Los Angeles, CA 90011.

DRIVER, RICHARD SONNY, JR.
Editor, publisher. **PERSONAL:** Born Aug 16, 1926, Philadelphia, PA; son of Richard E Driver Sr and Helen Driver. **CAREER:** Free-lance advertising & public relations; Scoop USA, Newspaper editor publisher & owner. **ORGANIZATIONS:** Mem NAACP; consultant, mem United Black Business Assn 1987-89. **HONORS/ACHIEVEMENTS:** Distinguished Award 1962; Publisher of Scoop USA Newspaper since 1960; Citation Jazz at Home Club of Amer 1971; Advertising Award Lancaster Ave Business Assn 1973; City of Philadelphia Citation, City of Philadelphia 1978; Four Chaplains Legion of Honor Award, Chapel of Four Chaplains 1989. **MILITARY SERVICE:** AUS 1944-46. **HOME ADDRESS:** 1220 N Broad St, Philadelphia, PA 19121. **BUSINESS ADDRESS:** Publisher, Scoop USA, 1220 N Broad St, Box 1111, Philadelphia, PA 19121.

DRIVER, ROGERS W.
Business executive. **PERSONAL:** Born Jun 14, 1921, Elkton, TN; son of Rogers and Louetta; married Mackie L Baker; children: John R, William B. **EDUCATION:** Univ of HI, 1944; TN State Univ, BS 1948; TN Univ, Post Graduate 1969; Am Baptist Theological Seminary, BTH 1987. **CAREER:** Triangle Chem Co, sales rep 1948-66; Pearl Vocational School, instructor 1951-52; General Spec Co, owner mgr 1952-66; Triangle Chem Co, special sales consultant 1966-74, sales mgr 1974, buyer HBA 1978, part time, semi-retired, 1989. **ORGANIZATIONS:** Past vice pres Nashville Assoc Black Salesmen 1971; mem Natl Assoc Market Devel 1972-, Natl Business League; pres Middle TN Business Assoc; mem NAACP, Nashville Model Cities Cit Coordinating Comm, Economic Devel Comm, TN State Univ Alumni Assoc, Urban League, Chamber of Commerce; mem Amer Vocational Assoc 1976; charter mem NAABAVE 1977; mem Nashville Job Service Employer Comm State of TN 1973-; mem Inter-Faith Assoc; exec comm mem Nashville Area Rep Lee Chapel AME 1984; minister Lee Chapel AME 1986, ordained elder, AME Church, 1989. **HONORS/ACHIEVEMENTS:** Minority Business Serv Award Frito-Lay Inc 1966; Special Award Business TN State Univ 1968; Outstanding Cit Award WVOL Radio 1953; Cit Month Award Emmas Florist 1962; JC Napier Award Middle TN Business Assoc 1974; Fisk Univ Award 100% Right Comm 1974; appt Hon Sgt-at-Arms of TN House of Rep 1974; Commissioned Hon Dep Sheriff for Davidson Co TN 1975; commissioned to serve as mem TN Advisory Council for Vocational Ed 1975-; Sales Training Course Best Pitchbook Award 1979, inducted in Vintagers Club, TSU 1988, (40 years.). **BUSINESS ADDRESS:** Sales Manager & Buyer, Triangle Chemical Co, 1720 Charlotte Ave, Nashville, TN 37203.

DRUMMOND, DAVID L., SR.
Clergyman. **PERSONAL:** Born Jan 30, 1918, Hastings, FL; married Evangeline Griffith; children: David, Jr, Reginald, Cheryl, Jonathan. **EDUCATION:** Howard U, 1952; Temple Univ Theol Seminary, STB. **CAREER:** Sunday Dept, dist supt 1948-53; COGIC, field sec 1953-62; Youth Dept Commonwealth PA, state pres 1970-71; E Diocese, gen supt 1963-70; COGIC Inc, chmn housing & registration 1970-71; City of David Ch & Enterprises, pastor & adminstr; COGIC Inc, vp. **ORGANIZATIONS:** Mem Pastors Fellowship Conf COGIC 1963-70; many other offices Ch God Christ Intnatl Mem Human Relation Dept; Maoyrs spl com asst bd educ 1973. **HONORS/ACHIEVEMENTS:** Hon DD Am Bible Coll; serv award State Youth Dept 1961-67; pastor yr WDAS radio; leading agent award Bankers Life & Casualty Co 1968; Citation Chapel4 Chaplin. **MILITARY SERVICE:** USN seam 2/c 1943. **BUSINESS ADDRESS:** 6035 Ogontz Ave, Philadelphia, PA 19141.

DRUMMOND, THORNTON B., JR.
Police lieutenant. **PERSONAL:** Born Jul 03, 1927, Newport; married Estelle Gaines; children: Donald Thornton, Victoria Pauline, Nancy Ann. **EDUCATION:** BS 1970;Univ RI, MA 1975; Salve Regina Coll, class orator; Babson Coll, Adminstrn Certificate 1968; Bryant Coll, 1966. **CAREER:** Police Dept, dir community relations 1968-72; Newport Police Dept Newport, lit of police day watch & commander; Newport Neighborhood Youth, counselor 1966-69. **ORGANIZATIONS:** Chmn bd dir Dr Martin Luther King Ctr Newport 1969-73; Frat Order of Police Commissioned Police Officers Assn; bd dir Afro-Bus Leaders Enterprise 1968-73; grand master Prince Hall Mason State of RI 1975 mason 33 Deg; bd dir Child & Family Service Newport 1975; bd dir Newport Hosp Newport 1970-; NAACP; Urban League; State of RI budget panel & special Allocation Com United Ways; Mt Zion AME Ch formerly pastors steward, steward & bd trustee. **HONORS/ACHIEVEMENTS:** Boating, golf, horses State Award Sheriff Dept; E Stars Award service to community; testimonial dinner Martin Luther King Center Cultural Art Com 1973; awards from Police Depts outstanding contribution to police & community; Martin Luther King Center & Ch 20 yrs serv to community; resolution Newport; Masonic Awards service & nomination highs degree 33 service community & masonry. **MILITARY SERVICE:** 728 Mil Police Batallion corpl 1950-53. **BUSINESS ADDRESS:** Marlborough St, Newport, RI.

DRUMMOND, WILLIAM JOE
Educator, freelance journalist. **PERSONAL:** Born Sep 29, 1944, Oakland, CA; son of Jack Martin Drummond, Sr and Mary Louise Tompkins Drummond; divorced; children: Tammerlin, Sean. **EDUCATION:** Univ of CA, BA 1965; Columbia Univ Grad School of Journalism, MS 1966. **CAREER:** Courier-Journal, Louisville, KY, staff writer 1966-67; Los Angeles Times, staff writer 1967-79; Natl Public Radio, correspondent 1979-83; School of Journalism, UC Berkeley, prof 1983-, assoc dean 1989-. **ORGANIZATIONS:** Spcl correspondent Natl Public Radio 1983. **HONORS/ACHIEVEMENTS:** Edwin Hood Awd for dist foreign corr 1983; Natl Press Club Found Awd 1980; Chancellor's Dist Lecturer, UC Berkeley 1983; Sidney Hillman Prize, Sidney Hillman Foundation NY 1986. **BUSINESS ADDRESS:** Prof of Journalism & Assoc Dean, Uni of Califorrnia, Berkeley, School of Journalism, Berkeley, CA 94720.

DRUNGO, ELBERT, JR.
Professional athlete. **PERSONAL:** Born Apr 30, 1943, Columbus, MS; married Deborah Louise Mcmichael; children: Martha O'Brian Ctr. **EDUCATION:** TN State U, AB 1971. **CAREER:** Davidson Co, dep sheriff 1979-; Buffalo Bills, professional football player 1978-79; Houston Oilers, professional football player 1969-77; Martha O'Brian Ctr, wks w/under priv children (off season); Kaleidoscope Mag Nashvlle, co-pub. **HONORS/ACHIEVEMENTS:** Capt hs team 1961-63; all conf 1963; most improved player Award 1967; TN Royal Crown 1968; Pittsburgh Courier All Am Team; Ebony All Am Team; professional ballplayer of week five times; outstndg offensive lineman Houston Oilers 1971; Walter S Davis Award TN StateUniv 1978. **BUSINESS ADDRESS:** 506 2nd Ave N, Nashville, TN 37201.

DRYDEN, CHARLES WALTER
Military officer & business executive. **PERSONAL:** Born Sep 16, 1920, New York, NY; married Marymal Morgan; children: Charles Jr, Keith, Eric. **EDUCATION:** City College of New York, 1937-40; Hofstra College, BA Pol Sci 1955; Columbia University, MA Public Law & Govt 1957. **CAREER:** Pepsi-Cola Co, mgr special markets dept 1964-68; Presbyterian Eco Development Corp, exec dir 1968-70; Martins, exec asst of president 1972-73; Lockheed-Georgia Co, professional personnel administrator 1975-83, training services officer 1983-. **ORGANIZATIONS:** Councilman Matawan, NJ 1965-66; president Atlanta Chapter Tuskegee Airman 1983-86; member Military Academies Selection Committee, 5th Congressional District 1983-; member NAACP Urban League. **MILITARY SERVICE:** USAF lieut colonel 21 yrs; Air Medal, Air Force Commendation Medal w/6 Oak Lef Clusters 1941-62. **HOME ADDRESS:** 1273 Oakcrest Dr SW, Atlanta, GA 30311.

DUAL, PETER ALFRED
Educator. **PERSONAL:** Born Jan 27, 1946, Alexandria, LA; married Toni Irene; children: Nikki Averlee, Peter Aaron, Tony Ahmaad, Alfred Michael. **EDUCATION:** Lake Michigan Coll, AA 1966; Western MI Univ, BS 1969, MA 1971; MI State Univ, PhD 1973; Univ of TX, MPH 1975. **CAREER:** Asst Prof Univ of TX 1973-75; assoc dir African-American Studies 1973-75; Univ of MI, asst prof health behavior, director, Center for Prof Ed of Pub Health Professionals, asst prof of health behavior 1975-80; Eastern MI Univ, dean coll health/human services, prof of health admin, 1980-82; San Diego State Univ, dean coll health/human svcs, prof of public health 1982-. **ORGANIZATIONS:** Mem Amer Assoc of Higher Educ 1980-, Amer Public Health Assoc 1981-; sr consultant to Panama Project Hope 1985; tech consultant Zimbabwe USAID 1986; disting guest lecturer Chinese Med Assoc ROC 1986; lecture presentation in Health/Nursing Beijing PRC 1986; mem Alpha Pi Boule Chap Sigma Pi Phi Frat 1986-; Phi Beta Delta Honor Society for Intl Scholars; American Public Health Assoc 1971; mem bd of dir for Joint-Health Policy, Scripts Research Foundation/Institute SDSU 1988-. **HONORS/ACHIEVEMENTS:** Natl Public Health Fellowship Univ of TX 1974-75; publications in natl journals in health/human serv 1974-82; Citation Chinese Medical Assoc Republic of China 1986; Martin Luther King/Rosa Parks Vstg Prof Univ MI 1987-88; Confucius Awd Ministry of Education Republic of China; Lecturer Citation Beijing & Health Bureau; first black academic dean in history of Eastern MI Univ 1980; first black academic dean in history of San Diego State Univ 1983; Distinguished Alumnus Award, Lake MI Coll 1986; first black and now M.D. to deliver keynote address, Chinese Medical Assn 1987; Distinguished Alumnus Award, Coll of Ed, MI State Univ 1988. **BUSINESS ADDRESS:** Dean Coll of Hlth/Human Serv, San Diego StateUniv, Hepner Hall 124, San Diego, CA 92182.

DUBE, THOMAS M. T.
Educator. **PERSONAL:** Born Dec 25, 1938, Essexvale, Zimbabwe;married Ruth; children: Cengubuqotho, Thina. **EDUCATION:** Univ of Lesotho, BA 1958;Univ of So Africa, UED 1960; CW Post Coll of Long Island U, MS 1963;Univ of Chgo, MA 1972; MI State U, MA 1974; Uof Rochester, EdD 1969; Cooley Law Sch, JD Candidate. **CAREER:** Western MI Univ, asst prof Social Science; Geneva Coll PA, asst prof; Rochester NY, pre-school teacher; Ministry of African Educ, Rodesia Africa, high school teacher, elementary school teacher. **ORGANIZATIONS:** Mem Rhodesian African Tchrs Assn; vol activities in Black Comm Rochester, Pittsburg, Kalamazoo; mem Assn of African Studies in Am; founder mem Jairos-Jiri Inst for Physically-Handicapped; founder, mem, asst prin Mpopoma African Comm HS. **BUSINESS ADDRESS:** 337 Moore Hall, Kalamazoo, MI 49001.

DUBENION, ELBERT
Talent scout. **PERSONAL:** Born Feb 16, 1933, Griffin, GA; married Marilyn Earl; children: Debra Lynn, Carolyn Ann, Susan Marie, Lisa Renee. **EDUCATION:** Bluffton Coll Bluffton, OH, BS 1959. **CAREER:** Columbus Recreation Dept, 1960-67; OH Malleable Co Columbus, attendance dir 1963-64; Buffalo Bills, professional player 1960-68, college scout. **HONORS/ACHIEVEMENTS:** Voted MVP 3 times for Buffalo; All-AFL; mem Bills Silver Anniversary All-Time team. **MILITARY SERVICE:** AUS spec serv pfc 1953-55. **BUSINESS ADDRESS:** College Scout, Buffalo Bills Inc, One Bills Drive, Orchard Park, NY 14127.

DUBOIS, ASA STEPHEN
Administrator. **PERSONAL:** Born Feb 07, 1929, Rochester, NY; married Evangeline

Davis; children: Asalyn, Karen Elizabeth. **EDUCATION:** Howard Univ, BS 1952; City Univ of NY, MSW 1961; NYU Grad Sch of Public Admin, DPA 1981. **CAREER:** NY State Dept of Mental Hygiene NY, dir of social work 1966-67; Div of Mental Health NY, assoc mental hygiene prog analyst 1967-68; Div of Mental Health Albany NY, chief mental hygiene prog analyst 1968-; Natl Inst of Mental Health Washington, consult 1971-; State Univ of NY, asst clinical prof of social work 1972-; Gowanda Psychiatric Ctr, exec dir. **ORGANIZATIONS:** Mem Amer Soc for Public Adminstrs; Assn of Mental Health Adminstr; Amer Pub Health Assn; Assn of Black Social Workers; Natl Assn of Social Workers;Acad of Certified Social Workers; former br exec bd mem NAACP; former bd mem Hunter Coll Sch of Social Work Alumni Assn; mem Harlem Health Council. **HONORS/ACHIEVEMENTS:** Who's Who in the E; Cit Serv Awd 1973; mem NY State Negotiating Team NY State Office of Employee Relations 1973; mem Task Force to Review the Structure & Orgn of NY State Dept of Mental Hygiene 1969; Task Force on Greater Comm Involvement & Cit Participation in Dept of Mental Hygiene Progs 1972-73. **BUSINESS ADDRESS:** Chief Mental Hygiene Prog Dir, Gowanda Psychiatric Center, Helmuth, NY 14079.

DU BOIS, DAVID GRAHAM
Journalist, editor, writer, social activist. **PERSONAL:** Born Sep 1925, Seattle, WA; son of William Edward Burghardt and Shirley Graham Du Bois; divorced. **EDUCATION:** Attended Oberlin Conservatory of Music, 1942-43, New York School of Social Work, Columbia Univ, Peking Univ; Hunter Coll, New York City, BA, 1950, New York Univ, MA, 1972. **CAREER:** First Natl City Bank of New York, New York City, clerk-typist, 1950-59; Arab Observer, Cairo, Egypt, editor/reporter, 1960-72; news editor, Egyptian Gazette; reporter and editor, Middle East News and Features Agency; announcer and program writer, Radio Cairo; in public relations for Ghana govt, Cairo, 1965-66; official spokesperson, Black Panther Party; editor-in-chief of Black Panther Intercommunal News Service; editor of Black Panther, 1973—; lecturer, School of Criminology, Univ of California, Berkeley, and Cairo Univ. **ORGANIZATIONS:** Mem, Black Panther Party. **HONORS/ACHIEVEMENTS:** Author of And Bid Him Sing (novel), Ramparts, 1975. **MILITARY SERVICE:** US Army Air Force, Infantry, second lieutenant, 1942-46. **BUSINESS ADDRESS:** c/o Ramparts Press, PO Box 50128, Palo Alto, CA 94303. *

DU BOIS, NELSON S. D'ANDREA, JR.
Business executive. **PERSONAL:** Born Apr 24, 1930, Darlington, SC; married Evelyn M Andrews; children: Natasha Lynne. **EDUCATION:** Howard U, BS 1954; Howard U, MS 1955;Univ of CA Berkeley & Los Angeles, PhD 1965. **CAREER:** The Chase Manhattan Bank NA NYC, vice pres systems planning div 1977-; RCA Corp, dir 1974-77; NBC, dir 1970-74; TRW Systems, proj mgr 1966- 70;Univ of CA, statistician 1963-66; CA State Dept of Public Health, statistician 1960-63; Howard U, instr 1954-56; US Dept of HEW, consult 1968-70; Systems Develop Corp, consult 1966;Univ of So CA Coll of Med, consult 1964-66. **ORGANIZATIONS:** Bd dir Profitable Information by Design through Phased Planning & Control Users Assn Inc 1975-77; bd dir Profit Oriented Systmes Planning Prgms Inc 1975-77; bd dir Student Transfer Educ Prgm 1977-; mem New York City Computer Adv Com 1977-; mem Inst of Mathematical Statistics 1958; Am Statistical Assn1958; Am Physic Soc 1953; pres Kappa Alpha Psi 1957-58; Sigma Pi Sigma 1953; vice pres Cotswold Assn Inc 1976-77; pres Cotswold Assn Inc 1977-; sec Cotswold Asn 1974f pres Pi Mu Epsilon 1953-54. **HONORS/ACHIEVEMENTS:** Who's Who in the US; Men of Achievement 1975; Who's Who in the East; Who's Who in the West; Am Men of Science. **BUSINESS ADDRESS:** Chase Manhattan Bank, Na One Chase Manhattan Plaza, New York, NY 10015.

DUBOSE, CLARENCE R.
Attorney, business executive. **PERSONAL:** Born Oct 29, 1943, Selma; married Charlotte Miller Sherman. **EDUCATION:** Knoxville Coll, BA 1965; NYU Sch of Law, JD 1973; MUP; CityUniv of NY, 1969. **CAREER:** The Chase Manhattan Bank, atty vp; Fed Home Loan Bank NY & Wash, exec dir of cntr for exec 1971-72; The R and Corp NY & CA research consult 1971; Office of Mayor of NYC, dir of planning 1970-71. **ORGANIZATIONS:** Mem Nat Study Comm on Urban Cntrs; Nat Conference of Black Lawyers; Am Soc of Planning Officials; Am Inst of Planners; Nat Housing Rehab Assn; Am Banking Assn; mem Am Mgmt Assn; Nat Comm Against Discrimination in Housing; bd dir Nat Black Exec Assn. **BUSINESS ADDRESS:** Duco Ind/DuBose & Co, 3438 Norwood Blvd, Birmingham, AL 35234.

DUBOSE, CULLEN LANIER
Director. **PERSONAL:** Born Jul 05, 1935, Moss Point, MS; married Helena Joyce; children: Cheri, Cullen, Freddie. **EDUCATION:** Tougaloo Coll, 1954-56; Tri State Coll, BS 1958. **CAREER:** State of MI, bridge design engr 1958-70; State of MI Housing Devel Authority, civil Engr 1970; dir rehab 1971-72; dir construction 1972- 73; dir mgmt& marketing 1974-. **ORGANIZATIONS:** Mem Tri State Coll Alumni Club; West Side Action Center; Lansing Civic Center Bd; Omega Psi Phi Frat Inc; NAACP; dir housing com; mem Big Bro of Lansing; Model Cities Policy Bd; past pres Gov Milligens Task Force for Operation Break Through 1970-71. **HONORS/ACHIEVEMENTS:** Omega Psi Phi Citizens Award 1966; NAACP Citizen Award 1967. **MILITARY SERVICE:** Mil serv 1957-58.

DUBOSE, OTELIA
Government official. **PERSONAL:** Born Sep 16, 1949, Winter Haven, FL; daughter of Willie J DuBose; divorced. **EDUCATION:** Florida A&M Univ, Tallahassee FL, BS, 1968; New York Univ, New York NY, MA, 1971; Cornell Univ, Ithaca NY, MRP, 1981, PhD, 1984. **CAREER:** Community Mental Health Center, West Palm Beach FL, coord (community program), 1974-78; Coconut Grove Health Center, Miami FL, consultant, 1975-85; City of Riviera Beach, Riviera Beach FL, economic devel, 1985-87, asst to the city mgr, 1987-88, city mgr, 1988-; DeBose & Assoc Inc, pres, 1987-. **ORGANIZATIONS:** Delta Sigma Theta Sorority Inc, 1975-; mem, Urban League of Palm Beach County, 1985-, NAACP, 1985-; steering comm, Gold Coast California Credit Union, 1987-; mem, Democratic Exec Club, 1988-. **HONORS/ACHIEVEMENTS:** Community Serv, Florida A&M Univ Alumni, 1978; American Planning Assn Speaker, 1981, 1987, 1989; co-author, The Urban Agenda, 1981; Outstanding Young Women of Amer, 1985.

DU BOSE, ROBERT EARL, JR.
Clergyman. **PERSONAL:** Born Oct 09, 1927, Birmingham, AL; married Angela Grace Edwards; children: Robert III, Audrice, Gerald, Lucy, Angela. **EDUCATION:** St Augustine's Coll Raleigh, NC, BA/BS 1950; Seabury-Western Theol Sem Evanston, IL, LTh 1953; St Augustine's Coll, Hon DCL 1979. **CAREER:** Historic St Thomas' Episcopal & Ch, rector 1977-; House of Prayer Epis Ch Phila, PA, rector 1966-76; St Barnabas Epis Ch Phila, PA, asso rector 1964-66; St Cyprian's Epis Ch Phila, PA, vicar 1962-64; Historic St Thomas' Epis Ch Phila, PA, curate 1961-62; Ch of the Good Shepherd Montgomery, AL, vicar 1956-61; St Andrew's Tuskegee, AL, vicar 1953-56; Gen Conv of the Epis Ch, spl rep 1970. **ORGANIZATIONS:** Mem Commn on Finance of Property Epis Diocese of PA 1974-; mem Bishop's Task Force on Housing Epis Diocese of PA 1979-; active Qparticipant Bus Protest& Sit Ins With Dr M L King Montgomery AL 1956-61; active participant Selective Patronage Prog with Dr Leon Sullivan 1961-64; one of the founders Opport Indsl & Cntrs of Am & Intl 1964 & 67. **HONORS/ACHIEVEMENTS:** Key Award Opport Indsl Cntr Phila, PA 1969; Nat Distinguished Serv Award Alpha Phi Alpha Frat 1970; Outstanding Serv Award Greater W Oak Ln Coordinating Council 1970-71; Service Award The Sch Dist of Philadelphia Wagner Hr HS 1974. **BUSINESS ADDRESS:** Historic Saint Thomas' Episcap, Fifty Second & Parrish Sts, Philadelphia, PA 19139.

DUCKSWORTH, MARILYN JACOBY
Publicity manager. **PERSONAL:** Born in Stamford, CT. **EDUCATION:** Tufts Univ, BA (cum laude) 1978, MA English 1979; Tufts Univ in London England 1976-77. **CAREER:** Doubleday & Co Inc, publicity asst 1979-80, assoc publicist 1980-82, sr publicist 1982-83, mgr of publicity 1983-85; GP Putnam's Sons, mgr of publicity 1985, dir of publicity 1985-87; GP Putnam's Sons & The Putnam & Grosset Group, exec dir of publicity 1987-. **ORGANIZATIONS:** Mem (hon) College Language Assn 1978-; certified teacher of secondary educ rec'd certification from Tufts in 1978; mem Publisher's Publicity Assoc 1979-, The Women's Media Group 1986-. **HONORS/ACHIEVEMENTS:** Scholastic Achievement Awd Black Educators of Stamford 1974; Natl Honor Soc Hon Soc of Secondary Schools 1974; Dean's List Tufts Univ (every semester) 1974-78; Langston Hughes Literary Awd Tufts Univ 1978; 1st Black Mgr of Publicity at Doubleday & Co Inc 1983-85; First Black exec dir of publicity at GP Putnam's Sons. **BUSINESS ADDRESS:** Exec Dir of Publicity, GP Putnam's Sons, The Putnam & Grosset Group, 200 Madison Ave, New York, NY 10016.

DUDLEY, ALBERT LEROY
Hospital administrator. **PERSONAL:** Born Dec 11, 1952, Nashville, TN; married Nancy Elizabeth Edmond; children: Albert II. **EDUCATION:** Andrews Univ, 1970; Oakwood Coll, BA 1974; OH State Univ, MBA 1976. **CAREER:** US Fed Power Commn, field auditor 1973; S Central Conf of Seventh-day Adventists, spl asst 1974; Kettering Med Center, internal auditor 1976-78, vice pres 1978-. **ORGANIZATIONS:** Vp & bd chmn Contemporary Bus Servs of Dayton, OH 1979; vice pres Kettering Med Center Fed Credit Union 1979, pres & bd chmn 1980-82; mem Amer Coll ofHosp Adminstr 1978-; mem Natl Alliance of Bus Youth Mot Task Force 1979-; mem US Jaycees Greater Dayton Chap 1980-; vice pres So OH Youth Fedn AlleghenyW Conf 1980; Communication Dir Ethan Temple SDA Ch 1980-; bd pres Adolescent Substance Abuse Prog Dayton, OH 1982-84. **HONORS/ACHIEVEMENTS:** Full grad fellowship OH State Univ 1974-76; Outstanding Young Man in Amer US Jaycees 1979; nominated Who's Who Midwest 1980-81. **BUSINESS ADDRESS:** 3535 Southern Blvd, Kettering, OH 45429.

DUDLEY, CALMEZE HENIKE, JR.
Physician. **PERSONAL:** Born Sep 03, 1947, Detroit, MI; married Grenae D Dudley PhD; children: Brandon, Rachel. **EDUCATION:** Wayne State Univ, BA 1973; Meharry Medical Coll, MD 1980. **CAREER:** Blue Cross/Blue Shield of MI, internal auditor 1973-76; Mt Carmel Mercy Hosp, psychiatric consultant 1985-87; Sinai Hosp of Detroit, psychiatric resident 1982-85, dir day hospital 1985-. **ORGANIZATIONS:** Bd of dirs Metro Detroit Youth Foundation 1982-84, United Community Serv 1984-; psychiatric consultant Monarch Medical Inc 1985-; mem task force govt legislation MI Psychiatric Soc 1985-; medical/psychiatric dir Doctors Hosp 1986-; medical dir Health Mgmt Systems 1987-. **HONORS/ACHIEVEMENTS:** Sinai Annual Scientific Paper Awd Sinai Hosp of Detroit 1982; multiple ongoing public serv presentations on psychiatric issues. **MILITARY SERVICE:** AUS sgt E-5 1969-71; numerous citations, awds in Pentagon Counterintelligence Force. **HOME ADDRESS:** 22367 Chatsford Circuit, Southfield, MI 48034. **BUSINESS ADDRESS:** Dir Sinai Day Hospital, Sinai Hospital of Detroit, 6001 W Outer Dr #421, Detroit, MI 48235.

DUDLEY, CHARLES EDWARD
Executive officer, clergyman. **PERSONAL:** Born Feb 01, 1927, South Bend, IN; son of Joseph Dudley Sr and Julia (Talley) Dudley; married Etta Mae Maycock, Dec 28, 1947; children: Bonita Andrea, Charles Edward II, Albert Leroy Sr. **EDUCATION:** Oakwood Coll, attended 1947; Emmanuel Mission Coll, attended 1945; Baptist Theol Seminary, LLD 1969; Union Baptist Seminary, Birmingham AL, Doctor of Divinity; Oakwood College, Huntsville AL, Bachelor of Arts in Religion. **CAREER:** S Central Conference of 7th Day Adventists, pres 1962-; Pastor, TN, AL, LA, TX; South Central Conference of Seventh-day Adventists, Nashville TN, pastor 1947-54. **ORGANIZATIONS:** Pres S Central Conf Housing Inc; pres S Central Conf Assn; pres S Central Conf SDA; mem Sunbelt Hosp Systems Inc 1979; mem Review & Herald Publ Bd Hagertown MD 1980; S Coll Madison Hosp; Oakwood Coll; Regional Voice Pub Adventist Media Ctr; chmn, South Central Housing Boards Inc; chmn, NAD Black Caucus of Seventh-day Adventist; dir, N A Regional Voice Publication. **HONORS/ACHIEVEMENTS:** Pi Lambda Sigma Awd 1964; DD London Inst 1975; Merit of Honor OC Natl Alumni Assn 1977; Breath of Life Awd 1984. **BUSINESS ADDRESS:** President, S Ctrl Conf of 7th Day Adv, 715 Youngs Ln, Nashville, TN 37207.

DUDLEY, CRAYTON T.
Clergyman. **PERSONAL:** Born Feb 23, 1928, Atlanta; married Allegra Lewis; children: Angus Clement, Karen Yvette. **EDUCATION:** Clark Coll Atlanta, AB 1950; Gammon Theol Sem Atlanta, BD 1961; MDiv 1973;Univ Pitts, MLS 1965; AtlantaUniv Am U, Grad Study. **CAREER:** Interdenom Theol Ctr Atlanta, asst lib 1961-64; Rel & Phil Enoch Pratt Free Lib Baltimore, subj splst 1965-68; Coppin State Coll Baltimore, asso dir lib 1968-72; asso prof philos 1972-74; TN St U, collections dev librn 1976; St James Epis Ch Baltimore, worker priest 1968-72; St James, asst priest 1972-74; Montrose Training Sch for Girls State MD, chpln 1968-72; Holy Trinity Epis Ch Nashville, rector. **ORGANIZATIONS:** Life mem Phi Beta Sigma Frat; mem NAACP; Boy Scouts Am 1972-74; bd mem Grace Eaton Day Ctr 1974; v-chmn Urban Min Diocese of TN 1977; mem counc chpln mem Am Library Assn; Am Theol Library Assn; historiographer Diocese MD 1972-74. **HONORS/ACHIEVEMENTS:** Outstndg educators of Am 1971; Who's Who in Lib & Sci. **MILITARY SERVICE:** AUS sgt 1945-46, 1950-53, 1956-62.

DUDLEY, EDWARD R.
Supreme court justice. **PERSONAL:** Born Mar 11, 1911, S Boston, VA; married Rae; chil-

dren: Edward R Dudley Jr. **EDUCATION:** St John's Law Sch, LLB 1941; Johnson C Smith U, BS 1932. **CAREER:** US Ambassador to Liberia 1948-53; Dom Rel Ct NYC, judge 1955-60; NY Co, boro pres 1960-65; MY State Sup Ct, justice 1965-retirement. **ORGANIZATIONS:** Asst spec couns NAACP 1943-45, 47-48; asst att gen NY 1942. **HONORS/ACHIEVEMENTS:** Recipient of Honorary LLD's from several universities includingUniv of Liberia, Morgan State Coll, Johnson C Smith U.

DUDLEY, GODFREY D.
Attorney. **PERSONAL:** Born Mar 14, 1944, Newborn, AL. **EDUCATION:** Tuskegee Inst, BS 1967; Tuskegee toUniv MI, exchange student 1966; Howard U, JD 1970. **CAREER:** Tuskegee Inst Community Educ Prog, teacher coordinator 1965; Birmingham Dist Office, equal employment officer 1970; Labor Adv Nat Labor Relations Bd, atty 1970-; DC Office NLRB to Atlanta Regional Office, field atty 1972; instr for new attys & field examiners 1975 & 79; Nat Labor Relations Bd, dep asst gen counsel 1979-. **ORGANIZATIONS:** DC Bar Assn; Bar Assn DC; Am Bar Assn; Nat Bar Assn; AL Bar Asn; Phi Alpha Delta Law Frat NAACP; Urban League. **HONORS/ACHIEVEMENTS:** Certificates commendations Gen Counsel NLRB 1973 & 74; quality work performance awards 1973, 74, 78 & 79. **BUSINESS ADDRESS:** 1717 Pennsylvania Avenue NW, Washington, DC.

DUDLEY, HERMAN T.
Government official. **PERSONAL:** Born Apr 04, 1924, Richmond, KY; married Ruth. **EDUCATION:** BS 1956. **CAREER:** Detroit Engr Office Bur Archtl, dir 24 years. **ORGANIZATIONS:** Registered Archt State MI. **MILITARY SERVICE:** USMC corpl 1943-46. **BUSINESS ADDRESS:** 9th Fl Cadillac Tower, Detroit, MI 48226.

DUDLEY, THELMA
Educator. **PERSONAL:** Born Mar 05, 1923, Columbia, SC. **EDUCATION:** Albany State Coll, BA 1944; Rollins Coll, MAT 1970. **CAREER:** Advanced Instnl Devel, coord; Valencia Comm Coll, teacher 1970-; Jones High School, teacher 1946-70; Douglass High School, teacher 1944-46; Elbert Co, teacher 1941. **ORGANIZATIONS:** Mem NAACP; FL Assn of Comm Colls; Beta Xi chap Nat & Sor of Phi Delta Kappa; Corinthian Sect Nat Cncl of Negro Women; FL Cncl of Chs gov bd Nat Cncl of Chs; vice pres Women's Missionary Cncl Christian Meth Epis Ch. **BUSINESS ADDRESS:** PO Box 3028, Orlando, FL 32802.

DUDLEY-SMITH, CAROLYN J.
Educator. **PERSONAL:** Born Jul 21, 1946, Bessemer, AL; married Aubrey E Smith. **EDUCATION:** Stillman Coll, BA 1968; Howard Univ, MA 1975. **CAREER:** DC Public Schools, teacher 1969-72, job coord 1972-79, consultant 1980-, counselor 1979-. **ORGANIZATIONS:** Chairperson Title IX/Sex Equity Adv Bd; mem Delta Sigma Theta Sor, Amer Assoc Counsel Develop, Amer School Counselors Assoc. **HONORS/ACHIEVEMENTS:** Author Sex Equity Curriculum Guide published in ERIC 1984; Educational Fellow Inst for Educ Leadership 1985. **BUSINESS ADDRESS:** Counselor, DC Public Schools, 55th & Eads Sts NE, Washington, DC 20019.

DUERSON, DAVE CALVIN
Professional athlete. **PERSONAL:** Born Nov 28, 1960, Muncie, IN; married Alicia; children: Chase Anthony, Tregg Russell. **EDUCATION:** Notre Dame, BA 1983. **CAREER:** Chciago Bears, safety 1983-. **ORGANIZATIONS:** Formed Damco Corp, a drug & alcohol awareness camp for youngsters; involved in Brian Piccolo Cancer Res Fund & Red Cloud Ath Fund. **HONORS/ACHIEVEMENTS:** Led special teams with 11 tackles 1984; 4 time All American at Notre Dame; ND Capt and MVP 1982; mem NFL Pro Bowl teams 1986,87. **BUSINESS ADDRESS:** Chicago Bears, Halas Hall, Ste 400, Lake Forest, IL 60045.

DUFF, JOHN THOMAS
Dentist. **PERSONAL:** Born Feb 19, 1903, Nashville, TN; son of Thomas Duff and Ida Duff; married Wattie T Cole; children: John Jr, Robert, Beatrice. **EDUCATION:** Meharry Med Coll, DDS 1930. **CAREER:** Private Practice, dentist (retired). **ORGANIZATIONS:** Mem Nat Dental Assn; Pelican State Dental Soc; New Orleans Dental Soc; elder Emeritus Berean Presb Ch. **HONORS/ACHIEVEMENTS:** Serv Award New Orleans Dental Soc 1964; President's Award Meharry Medical Coll 1980; President's Award Meharry Medical Coll 1985.

DUFFOO, FRANTZ MICHEL
Nephrologist. **PERSONAL:** Born Mar 05, 1954, Port-au-Prince, Haiti;son of Franck Duffoo and Leonie Narcisse Duffoo; married Marcia Sylvester; children: Brian Anthony Duffoo. **EDUCATION:** City Coll of NY, BS, 1977; Meharry Medical Coll, MD, 1979; diplomate, Internal Medicine Amer Bd of Internal Medicine, 1984; diplomate, subspecialty of nephrology Amer Bd of Internal Medicine 1986. **CAREER:** Brookdale Hospital Medical Center, resident in internal medicine, 1979-82; Montefiore Medical Center, clinical fellow, 1982-83, research fellow, 1983-84; Woodhull Medical and Mental Health Center, attending physician/consultant nephrology, 1984-; instructor in medicine, 1985-88, asst prof of medicine, 1988-, SUNY Health Science Center at Brooklyn. **ORGANIZATIONS:** Mem, New York Acad of Sciences 1981-, Amer Coll of Physicians 1985-, Amer Soc of Nephrology 1985-, Intl Soc of Nephrology 1985-, New York Soc of Nephrology; charter mem, Amer Soc of Hypertension 1986-; charter mem, Intl Soc on Hypertension in Blacks. **HONORS/ACHIEVEMENTS:** Physician's Recognition Award, Amer Medical Assn, 1982, 1988; mem, The Editorial Research Bd, The Physician and Sportsmedicine, 1982; abstract selected for presentation, New York Soc of Nephrology, 1984. **HOME ADDRESS:** 1245 Park Ave #2A, New York, NY 10128.

DUFFY, EUGENE JONES
Administrative officer. **PERSONAL:** Born Aug 25, 1954, Columbus, OH; married Norrene Johnson. **EDUCATION:** Attended, Univ of Ibadan Nigeria; Morehouse Coll, BA 1976. **CAREER:** Dept Parks Recreation & Cultural Affairs, deputy commissioner; Office of Contract Compliance, director; Office of the Mayor, deputy chief admin officer. **ORGANIZATIONS:** Mem Natl League of Cities, Natl Conf of Black Public Administrators; trustee Morehouse Coll; mem YMCA; pres Atlanta Univ Ctr Student Council. **HONORS/ACHIEVEMENTS:** Listing Outstanding Young Men in Amer; Charles E Merrill Foreign Study Scholar Univ of Ibadan. **BUSINESS ADDRESS:** Deputy Chief Admin Officer, City of Atlanta, Office of Mayor, 68 Mitchell St SW, Atlanta, GA 30335.

DUGAS, HENRY C.
Physician. **PERSONAL:** Born Feb 10, 1917, Augusta, GA; married June Gordon; children: Denise, Henry. **EDUCATION:** Johnson C Smith Univ, BS 1937; Howard Univ, MD 1947. **CAREER:** Private practice, physician. **ORGANIZATIONS:** Mem Alpha Phi Alpha, Natl Med Assoc. **MILITARY SERVICE:** AUS capt, mc 1953-54. **BUSINESS ADDRESS:** 3737 N Kingshighway, St Louis, MO 63115.

DUGGER, EDWARD, III
Business executive. **PERSONAL:** Born Apr 14, 1949, Dayton, OH; son of Edward Dugger and Wertha Dugger; married Elizabeth Harris; children: Cyrus Edward, Langston Reid, Chloe D'Jenne. **EDUCATION:** Harvard Coll, AB (cum laude) 1971; Princeton U, MPA 1973. **CAREER:** Irwin Mgmt Co Inc, mgr real estate div 1973-74; UNC Ventures Inc, pres chief exec officer 1974-. **ORGANIZATIONS:** Dir UNC Ventures Inc 1977; founding dir Museum of Fine Arts Council 1981; mem Greater Boston YMCA 1981; mem indust adv bd Gov Office of Economic Devel 1985; dir United Way of MA Bay. **HONORS/ACHIEVEMENTS:** Natl Achievement Scholar Natl Merit Scholarship Found 1967-71; summer research Award Inst of Politics JF Kennedy Sch of Govt Harvard Univ 1970. **BUSINESS ADDRESS:** President & CEO, UNC Ventures, Inc, 711 Atlantic Avenue, Boston, MA 02111.

DUHART, HAROLD B.
Project manager. **PERSONAL:** Born Dec 15, 1938, Macon, GA; married Margaret Roberts; children: Bobby, Lori. **EDUCATION:** NC Agr & Tech U, BS 1963; GA Inst of Tech, advance study. **CAREER:** US Environmental Protection Agy, NC State Project Mgr 1970-; Dept HUD, engineering municipal project mgr 1968-70; US Army Corps of Engrs, space facilities design Engr 1964-68; City of Durham NC, engineering redevelopment officer 1964-65. **ORGANIZATIONS:** Pres Duhart Bros Enterprises of Macon, GA 1974-; mem Federal Water Pollution Control Assn; mem Equal Oppty Com EPA; asso mem ASCE; mem PTA; mem Task force on Minority Bus for EPA prgms; YMCA; SW Atlanta Comm Assn; mem SABFO. **HONORS/ACHIEVEMENTS:** Recipient membership champaign Award YMCA; spl achvmt Award EPA 1973; personalities of the south. **MILITARY SERVICE:** AUS, NATO 1961-63. **BUSINESS ADDRESS:** 345 Courtland St NE, Atlanta, GA 30302.

DUKE, GEORGE M. (DAWILLI GONGA)
Recording artist. **PERSONAL:** Born Jan 12, 1946, San Rafael, CA; married Corine Ann Salanga; children: Rashid Amon, John Lee Shiffer. **EDUCATION:** San Fran Conservatory of Music, MusB 1967; San Fran State Coll, MA 1970. **CAREER:** George Duke Band, Epic Records, leader 1977-; Billy Cobham-George Duke Band, Atlantic, co-leader 1976-77; Julian Cannonball Adderly, Capital & Fantasy, keyboardist/composer/arranger 1971-72; Frank Zappa, Warner Bros, keyboardist 1970-72, 1973-76; Jean-Luc Ponty, United Artists, pianist 1969-70; MPS/BASF Records, recartist (solo) 1973-76; Epic Records, solo recording artist 1976-. **ORGANIZATIONS:** Pres/fdr/mem Mycenae Music Publ Co 1968-; pres/fdr George Duke Enterprises Inc 1976-; consult Contemporary Keyboard Mag 1977-; mem NAACP 1979-; mem BMA 1979-. **HONORS/ACHIEVEMENTS:** Gold Record "Reach For It", RIAA 1978; Gold Record "Dukey Stick", RIAA 1979; Hit Record Awards, ASCAP 1979-80; A Taste of Honey "Twice As Sweet", Capital Records/G Duke Prod 1980.

DUKE, LESLIE DOWLING, SR.
Physician. **PERSONAL:** Born Mar 21, 1924, Washington, DC; married Dolores Douglass; children: Leslie Jr, Lori. **EDUCATION:** Howard U, BS 1950; Howard U, MD 1957. **CAREER:** Walter Reed Gen Hosp, phy 1962-77; Ft Meade, med ofcr 1959-62. **MILITARY SERVICE:** AUS sgt 1943-46. **BUSINESS ADDRESS:** 5223 S Dakota Ave, NE, Washington, DC 20011.

DUKES, CONSTANCE T.
Automobile dealer. **CAREER:** R. L. Dukes Oldsmobile Inc, Chicago IL, chief exec officer. **BUSINESS ADDRESS:** R. L. Dukes Oldsmobile, Inc, 7801 S State St, Chicago, IL 60619. *

DUKES, HAZEL N.
Director. **PERSONAL:** Born Mar 17, 1932, Montgomery, AL; divorced. **EDUCATION:** AL State Tchr Coll, AA 1950; Adelphi U, advance master prgm AdelphiUniv Grad 1978. **CAREER:** New York City Off-Track Betting Corp, exec dir of Logistic Services. **ORGANIZATIONS:** Mem bd of dir Town of N Hempstead Urban Renewal 1974-76; mem NASSAU Co Bd Consumer Affairs 1973-76; dir NY State Br NAACP 1975; NY State & Adv Counc 1976; pres New York City Off-Trac Betting; NAACP; bd of dir Econ Opport Commin of Nassau Co; adv bd NY State; bd of dir Westbury Negro Bus & ProflWomen's Club; sec Counc of Black Elected Dem of NY State; mem Dem Nat Com. **HONORS/ACHIEVEMENTS:** Social Action Award Delta Sigma Theta Sor Inc 1976; Sojurner Truth Award Nat Asssn of Negro Bus & Professional Women's Clubs Inc 1977; Comm Serv Award New York City OIC 1976; Appointed by Pres Carter to Nat Council on Economic Opportunity 1978; Long Island Media Women Humanitarian Award 1979; Guardian "Person of the Year" 1979; Catholic Interracial Council of New York John Lafarge Mem Award for Interracial Justice 1980; women of the yr Franklin Nat Bank 1974. **BUSINESS ADDRESS:** NY State NAACP, 1560 BroadwaySte 405, New York, NY 10036.

DUKES, JEROME ERWIN
Educational administrator. **PERSONAL:** Born Sep 09, 1938, Albany, NY. **EDUCATION:** Pennsylvania State Univ, Univ Park PA, BA 1961; State Univ of NY at Albany, MA 1971. **CAREER:** The Psychological Corp, life skills educator 1975; Capital Dist Educ Opportunity Center, Troy NY, coordinator of student personnel serv 1975-; State Univ of NY at Albany, lecturer Afro-Amer studies 1969-75; Mont Pleasant High School, Schenectady NY, teacher 1965-69; Southern Univ, Baton Rouge LA, instructor 1963-64; Rensselaer Polytechnic Inst, visiting lecturer Afro-Amer studies 1970-; Siena Coll, visiting lecturer English; NY Dept of Educ Coll Proficiency Div, consultant 1970-73. **ORGANIZATIONS:** Bd of dir Brewington S Stinney Scholarship Comm 1969-; bd of dir Albany Arbor Hill Interracial Council Inc 1978-; bd of dir NY State Council on the Arts 1979-. **HONORS/ACHIEVEMENTS:** Scholarship Award, C L Hughes Memorial Scholarship Fund, 1960; English Hon Award, Sigma Tau Delta Eng Hon Soc, 1960; Achievement Award, Alpha Phi Alpha Frat, Pennsylvania State Univ, 1961. **BUSINESS ADDRESS:** Student Personnel Serv Coord, Educational Opportunity Center, 145 Congress, Troy, NY 12180.

DUKES, OFIELD
Business executive. **PERSONAL:** Born Aug 08, 1932, Rutledge, AL. **EDUCATION:** Wayne State Univ, BA 1958. **CAREER:** WCHB Radio, news dir 1958-61; Michigan Chronicle, asst editor, advert mgr 1961-64; Information Pres Com on Equal Employment Opportunity & Plans for Progress,dep dir 1964-65; White House Conf to Fulfill These Rights, deputy dir publicaffairs, 1965-69; Vice Pres Hubert H Humphrey, asst 1966-69; Ofield Dukes & Assos Inc, pres 1969-; Howard Univ, instructor, 1972-. **ORGANIZATIONS:** mem, Public Relations Soc Amer; Natl Press Club; Washington chapter, Am Red Cross; bd mem, Jr Citizens Corps; vice pres, PRSA 1980; bd mem, Martin Luther King Center for Soc Change. **HONORS/ACHIEVEMENTS:** Outstanding faculty Award, Howard Univ School of Communication 1978; Washington Post, one of top six PR firms in DC 1971; Silver Anvil Award Public Relations Soc Amer 1974; Frederick Douglass Award Howard Univ School Communications 1974; male decision maker, Natl Assn Media Women 1971. **MILITARY SERVICE:** AUS 1952-54. **BUSINESS ADDRESS:** President, Ofield Dukes & Associates, 1426 Carrollsburg , SW, Washington, DC 20024.

DUKES, RONALD
Executive search consultant. **PERSONAL:** Born Dec 27, 1942, Neelyville, MO; married Albertine A Elliott; children: Barry Girard. **EDUCATION:** Lincoln Univ MO, BS 1964. **CAREER:** Continental Can Co, training supervisor 1969-71; Emerson Electric Co, sr corporate recruiter 1971-74; Amer Motors Corp, corporate dir of recruiting & mgmt develop 1974-78; Booz Allen & Hamilton, associate 1978-80; Heidrick & Struggles Inc, partner/mem bd of dirs 1980-. **ORGANIZATIONS:** Mem Phi Beta Sigma Fraternity; mem bd of dirs Chicago Youth Ctrs. **MILITARY SERVICE:** AUS capt 1966-69; Commendation Medal, Combat Badge 1967. **HOME ADDRESS:** 1105 Alden Ln, Buffalo Grove, IL 60089. **BUSINESS ADDRESS:** Partner/Mem Bd of Directors, Heidrick & Struggles Inc, 125 So Wacker Dr, Chicago, IL 60606.

DUKES, WALTER LUCUIS
Foundation president, attorney. **PERSONAL:** Born Jun 23, 1933, Youngstown, OH. **EDUCATION:** Seton Hall Univ, BS Economics 1953; NY Univ, MBA 1956; NY Law Schl, LLB 1959; NY Law Schl, Dr of Law 1968; Hunter Coll, MVP 1981. **CAREER:** Vista Travel Serv, vice pres 1963-67; US Labor Dept, atrny 1967-69; Civil Disorder, analysis comm 1969-70; Kennedy Develmnt Fdn Inc, pres 1970-. **ORGANIZATIONS:** Mbr Natl Mktg Club 1970-; mem NACCP 1951-; mem Urban Planners 1980-; vice pres Natl Org of Boys Scouts 1960-; mem Amer Bar Assoc 1961-; mem MI Bar Assoc 1968-; vice pres Boy's of Yester Year 1975-. **HONORS/ACHIEVEMENTS:** Dir Natl Youth Dir NAACP 1953-54; charter Life Underwriters Philly PA CLU; Athletic of the Year US Writers Guild 1953; vice pres Alliance Franchise 1975-84. **BUSINESS ADDRESS:** President, King-Kennedy Devl Fnd, 310 Greenwich St, New York, NY 10013.

DULIN, ROBERT O., JR.
Clergyman. **PERSONAL:** Born Mar 24, 1941, Lawrence, KS; married C Hawice Allen; children: Shannon E, Robert O, III. **EDUCATION:** Anderson Coll, BA 1963; Central Bapt Theol Sem, BD 1967. **CAREER:** 3rd St Ch God, asso minister 1964-66; 1st Ch God, pastor 1967-69; Nat Bd Christian Edn, asso sec 1969-74; Meth Ch of God, sr minister. **ORGANIZATIONS:** Life mem NAACP 1979. **HONORS/ACHIEVEMENTS:** Outstanding Young Men of Am 1973; Alumni Achievement Award Central Bapt Theol Sem 1974.

DUMAS, FLOYD E.
Clergyman. **PERSONAL:** Born Jan 27, 1926, Muskogee; son of Will and Ada; married Grace Lorene Provo; children: Floyd Earl II, Milton, Toya Diana. **EDUCATION:** Langston U, BA 1953; OK Sch of Religion, BTh 1954; Univ of Northern CO, additional study. **CAREER:** OK Employment Dept Tulsa, employment councellor 1953-55; Univ of OK Hospital, record libarian 1950-53; Gary & Human Relation Commn, field cons; New Hope Baptist Church Okla City, dir of religious ed; Mt Zion Baptist Church, Bethel Baptist Church, Galilee Baptist Church, pastor 1967-. **ORGANIZATIONS:** Sec Northern IN Baptist District Assn; sec Interdenominational Ministerial Alliance; pres Med-Town LCEOC Community Action Coun; life mem NAACP; pres Baptist Minister Conf of Gary & vicinity; presently pastor Met Baptist Church Gary IN. **MILITARY SERVICE:** USN 1943-47. **HOME ADDRESS:** 459 W 20 Pl, Gary, IN 46407. **BUSINESS ADDRESS:** Pastor, 1920 Broadway Metropolitan Baptist Church, Gary, IN 46407.

DUMMETT, CLIFTON ORRIN
Dental educator. **PERSONAL:** Born May 20, 1919, Georgetown, Guyana;married Lois Maxine Doyle. **EDUCATION:** Roosevelt U, BS 1941; Northwestern U, DDS 1941,MSD 1942; Julius Rosenwald Fund FellowUniv of MI, MPH 1947. **CAREER:** Meharry Medical Coll, prof, chmn dept periodontics oral diagnosis, chmn dental & admin com 1942-47; School of Dentistry, dean 1947-49; VA Hospital, Tuskegee AL, chief dental serv 1946-65; VA Research Hospital Chicago, 1965-66; Health Center Dir, Watts Health Center, dir 1966-68; School of Dentistry, Univ of Southern CA Los Angeles, prof, chmn dept comm dentistry, assoc dean extramural affairs 1968-. **ORGANIZATIONS:** Diplomate Am Bd Periodontology; mem Am Bd Oral Med; fellow AASS; mem Am Pub Health Assn; Am Coll Dentists; Intl Coll Dentists; hon mem Am Dental Assn; mem AK Dental Soc; Intl Assn for Dental Research pres 1969-70; Nat Dental Assn; Assn Mil Surgeons of US; Am Acad Dental Med; Acad Perioldontology; mem Air Force Assn; Sigma Xi Delta Omega; Sigma Pi Phi; Alpha Phi Alpha. **HONORS/ACHIEVEMENTS:** Recipient Award Nat Dental Assn 1952. **MILITARY SERVICE:** USAF 1955-57. **BUSINESS ADDRESS:** 925 W 34, Los Angeles, CA 90007.

DUMMETT, JOCELYN ANGELA
Pediatrician. **PERSONAL:** Born Sep 15, 1956, Leicster, England;daughter of Kenneth Dummett and Sheila Waterman Dummett. **EDUCATION:** Howard Univ College of Medicine, MD 1980. **CAREER:** Downstate Medical Ctr, clinical instructor 1983-85; LBJ School Health Program, preceptor 1985-; Health Science Ctr at Brooklyn, asst clinical prof 1985-; Javican Pediatric Assocs, co-founder 1985-87. **ORGANIZATIONS:** Fellow Amer Acad of Pediatrics 1982-, Brooklyn Pediatric Soc 1983-; mem Natl Medical Assoc 1983-; recording sec Provident Clinical Soc 1984-; medical secty Hanson Place SDA Church 1986. **HOME ADDRESS:** 98 Rutland Rd, Brooklyn, NY 11225. **BUSINESS ADDRESS:** Physician, 450 Clarkson Ave, Box 49, Brooklyn, NY 11203.

DUMPSON, JAMES R.
Social work educator, consultant. **PERSONAL:** Born Apr 05, 1910, Philadelphia, PA; son of James T Dumpson (deceased) and Edythe Francis Smith Dumpson (deceased). **EDUCATION:** State Teachers Coll, BS 1932; New School for Social Rsch, AB 1947; Univ of PA School of Social Work 1937-38, 1944, 1947; Fordham Univ School of Social Serv 1942-44, New School for Social Rsch, MA 1950; Univ of DACCA, PhD 1955; Hon LLD, Tuskegee Inst, Fordham Univ, St Peters Coll, Howard Univ, City Univ NY. **CAREER:** New York City Dept of Welfare, 1st dep commn 1957-59; New York City Dept of Welfare, commn 1959-65; Hunter Coll School of Social Work CUNY, prof assoc dean 1965-67; Fordham Univ Grad School of Soc Svcs, dean, prof 1967-74, prof Chair in Family and Child Welfare 1989-; NYC, commn of social serv & admin of human resources 1974-76; NY Comm Trust, vice pres 1976-. **ORGANIZATIONS:** Dir Bur of Child Welfare NYC, consult New York City Welfare Council; cons, supvr Childrens Aid Soc of NYC; supvr Philadelphia Dept of Public Asst; teacher, public school Oxford PA; mem Gov Carey's Task Force on Human Resources; UN adv Chief of Training Soc Welfare to Gov of Pakistan; consult Pakistan to Asia Found; chmn Mayor Lindsay Anti-Poverty Council & Anti-Poverty Oper Bd; mem bd Dept Juv Justice NYC, chmn Mayors Task Force on Foster Care; mem pres Kennedy's Commn on Narcotics & Drug Abuses; mem Pres Johnson's Commn on Alcoholism; pres Federation of Protestant Welfare Agencies 1987-; chair US Committee Intl Council on Social Welfare 1987-; chair Black Leadership Commn on AIDS 1989-; mem Governor's Advisory Council on AIDS 1989-. **BUSINESS ADDRESS:** Senior Consultant, NY Comm Trust, 415 Madison Ave, New York, NY 10017.

DUNBAR, ANNE CYNTHIA
Director. **PERSONAL:** Born Sep 24, 1938, New York City, NY; divorced; children: Christopher. **EDUCATION:** Borough of Manhattan Comm Coll, AA 1967; Brooklyn Coll, BA 1975, MS 1977; Columbia Univ School of Public & Intl Affairs, Cert 1985. **CAREER:** Citi-Bank/Canal St Training Ctr, asst to master 1968-69; 1st Venture Corp of NY, asst to vice pres 1969-70; Hunter Coll SEEK Fin Aid Prog, dir 1970-76; NYS Dept of Correctional Svcs, dir comm rel 1976-. **ORGANIZATIONS:** Mem Am Personnel & Guidance Assn; founder pres Break Thru in Art; pres NAACP Parkchester Br; adv mem NY City Busmn Coun for employment of ex-offender; educ sponsor Coalition of 100 Black Women; mem bd of dir Bronx Boys Clubs; mem NY State Catholic Conf Criminal Justice Advisory Com; mem Comm SchBd #12; chairperson Special Programs for Handicapped of Comm Sch Bd #12 1977-; mem Brooklyn Coll Alumni Assn; Borough of Manhattan Comm Coll Alumni Assn; Bronx Council on the Arts; Women's City Club of NY; consult Dept HEW Natl Inst of Health Sickle Blood Disease Prog 1977-79; volunteer Women's Div GovOffice 1969-71; chmn bd NY Urban League 1983-; trustee Bronx Museum 1981-. **HONORS/ACHIEVEMENTS:** Citation for Comm Coordination & Devel Northside Center for Child Devel 1972; "Ambassador of Love" Val-to-me Productions 1974; Citation of Achievement Eastern NY Correctional Facility Jaycees 1974; Citation for Activities in Penal Reform Gamblers Anonymous Greenhaven Prison Chap 1974; Certificate of Appreciation Eastern NY Correctional Facility 1975; Claire Joseph King Meml Citation 1975; Each One Teach One Comm Serv Award Harlem Professional & John Hunter Meml Camp Fund1975; founder of Ford-Whitfield-Young Scholarship Fund Hunter Coll CUNY 1975; Outstanding Serv Award Eastern Br NAACP 1975; honoree for Intl Women's Yr Nat Council of Negro Women Inc Flatbush Section 1975; Citation for Distinguished Services to Handicapped Children; Community Service Award Schaefer Brewry Co 1978; Citizen of the Year Award Bronx Boys Clubs 1979f Humanitarian Award Parkchester Cardiac Diagnostic Med Cntr 1979; Leadership Awd City Council of NY 1983; Disting Community Serv Council of Churches of NY; Commun Serv Awd Consolidated Edison of NY; Congressional Citation Rep Mario Biaggi 1978. **HOME ADDRESS:** 1940 E Tremont Ave, Parkchester, NY 10462.

DUNBAR, HARRY B.
Educational administrator. **PERSONAL:** Born May 10, 1925, Mineola, NY; married Cora Charlene Whitlow; children: Nona. **EDUCATION:** NY Univ BS, MA, Ph D 1949,51,61. **CAREER:** Rust Coll, Holly Spts MS, instructor 1949-50; Dunbar Jr Coll, Little Rock AR, instructor 1950-54; New York City Public Schools, teacher 1954-60; Nanuet High School, Nanuet NY, dept chmn 1960-65; New York City Community Coll, Brooklyn NY, prof, dean 1965-83; Bergen Community Coll, Paramus NJ, dean of evening div 1983-. **ORGANIZATIONS:** Free-lance consultant to small business, specializing in travel & hospitality ind; cochr elec comm Alpha Phi Alpha Frat, Inc, Chgo, IL 1980-; ed chrmn Nyack Branch NAACP, Nyack, NY 1980-; dir United Way of Rockland County 1970-74; trustee Nyack Hosptl, Nyack, NY 1968-74; bd of visitors Rockland Psychiatric Center 1986. **HONORS/ACHIEVEMENTS:** Fulbright Award US Govt 1957; John Hay Whitney flw J H Whitney Fdn 1959. **MILITARY SERVICE:** AUS staff sgt 1944-46; Asiatic Pacif Campaign Medal, WW II Victory Medal, EAME Campaign Medal, Good Conduct Medal 1944-46. **HOME ADDRESS:** 281 Rose Rd, West Nyack, NY 10994. **BUSINESS ADDRESS:** Dean of Evening Division, Bergen Comm College, 400 Paramus Rd, Paramus, NJ 07652.

DUNBAR, JOSEPH C.
Educator. **PERSONAL:** Born Aug 27, 1944, Vicksburg, MS; son of J C Dunbar Sr and Henrienne (Watkins) Dunbar; married Agnes Estorge, Jun 01, 0967; children: Andrea, Erica. **EDUCATION:** Alcorn Coll, Lorman MS, BS, 1963; Texas Southern, Houston TX, MS, 1966; Wayne State Univ, Detroit MI, PhD, 1970. **CAREER:** Texas Southern, Houston TX, instructor, 1966-67; Sinai Hospital of Detroit, Detroit MI, research assoc, 1970-78; Wayne State Univ, Detroit MI, prof, 1972-. **HONORS/ACHIEVEMENTS:** Author of 80 assorted publications. **BUSINESS ADDRESS:** Professor, Wayne State University, 540 E Canfield, Dept of Physiology, Detroit, MI 48201.

DUNBAR, MARJORIE HENDERSON
Educator. **PERSONAL:** Born Jun 22, 1932, New York City, NY; married Haines Dunbar. **EDUCATION:** CCNY, BA 1955; Teacher Coll, Columbia Univ, MA 1956; Fordham Univ, Professional Diploma 1973, EdD 1974. **CAREER:** New York City Schools, teacher 1957-67, principal; CCNY Black Studies Dept, adj prof; CES CCNY Admin Bldg, principal. **ORGANIZATIONS:** Dir State & Fed Prog in Dist 6M; assoc asst prof Supr of Grad Students, School of Educ CCNY; consultant Affirmative Action Prog; mem NY State Parent Adv Council; dir Black Prog Planning & Devel CCNY Educ; chmn NY State NAACP Conf of Br & New York City Branch; exec dir NY Assn of Black Educ; vice pres Vocational Guidance & Workshop Ctr; bd dir Harlem Neighborhood Assoc; bd dir HANA, Comm League of W 159th St, Ctr for Health Educ; mem Forham Doctorate Assn of Urban Educ Kappa Delta Pi 1956, Comm League of W 1968, Concilio Hispano Pro Ed 1969, Vocational Guidance Ctr 1969, NY State Admin of Compensatory Educ 1972, Paraprofessionals of Dist 6 1972, Natl Black Science Org 1974, Phi Delta Kappa 1974; served in various capacities as asst to comm

supt of Dist 9 Bronx NYC; lectures & participates in educ conf. **BUSINESS ADDRESS:** Principal, CES 126X, CCNY Admin Bldg, Convent Ave, 166th St, Bronx, NY 10031.

DUNCAN, ALICE GENEVA
Community service worker. **PERSONAL:** Born Mar 09, 1917, Chicago, IL; daughter of John Hurley South and Charlotte Harris South; married Clinton Wesley Duncan, Jul 13, 1945; children: Clifton John Black, Khesha Renee Duncan. **CAREER:** Helping Hand Baptist Church, Hannibal MO, treasurer, 1976—; Division of Family Services, Foster Home Care, 1972-82; Women in Community Services, job corp screener. **ORGANIZATIONS:** Secretary, NAACP, Hannibal MO branch, 1969—, life member, member of executive board; member of board, Douglass Community Center; treasurer, Northeast Area Resource Council; secretary-treasurer, Citizens for a New and Better City Government. **HONORS/ACHIEVEMENTS:** NAACP Unsung Heroine, 1985, 1986; NAACP Family of the Year, Hannibal MO branch, 1989. **HOME ADDRESS:** 2012 West Gordon St, Hannibal, MO 63401.

DUNCAN, CALVIN L.
Manager. **PERSONAL:** Born Dec 31, 1925, Greenville, NC; married Lillian M; children: Carol Ann, Richard E. **EDUCATION:** Franklin & Marshall Coll Pol Sci & Bus Adminisrn, 1954;Univ Louisville So Police Inst, Graduate 1957. **CAREER:** Sperry New Hollan, mgr 1977; Bur of Police Lancaster PA, retired cpt 1951-76. **ORGANIZATIONS:** Mem Nat Assn Blk Law & Exec 1974; exec bd Governors Commn on crime & Del 1967; stf instr PA State Police Acad 1968-75; bd of dir Millersville State Coll Youth Adv 1979; bd of Dir Private Ind Council 1980; bd of dir Urban League Lanc Co. **HONORS/ACHIEVEMENTS:** Five battle stars. **MILITARY SERVICE:** AUS sgt 1942-46. **BUSINESS ADDRESS:** Sperry New Hollan Frnklin & Ro, New Holland, PA 17557.

DUNCAN, CHARLES TIGNOR
Attorney. **PERSONAL:** Born Oct 31, 1924, Washington, DC; son of Todd Duncan and Gladys Jackson Duncan; widowed; children: Charles Todd. **EDUCATION:** Dartmouth Coll, BA (cum laude) 1947; Harvard Law Sch, JD 1950. **CAREER:** Reeves Robinson & Duncan, partner 1953-60; US Atty for DC, princ asst 1961-65; US Equal Employment Oppor Commn, general counsel 1965-66; Epstein Freidman Duncan & Medalie, partner 1970-74; Howard Univ Sch of Law, dean prof law 1974-78; Peabody Lambert & Meyers Washington, partner 1978-82; Reid & Priest Washington, partner 1982-. **ORGANIZATIONS:** Mem NY Bar 1951, DC Bar 1953, MD Bar 1955, US Supreme Ct Bar 1954, US Seventh Circuit Ct of Appeals Bar 1962; bd of dirs of Nat Bank of Wash 1973-79, Procter & Gamble Co 1982-88, Eastman Kodak Co 1978-, TRW Inc 1984-; mem DC Labor Rels 1973-75; chmn DC Judic Nomin Commin 1975-80; mem Dartmouth Coll Alumni Counc 1975-78; bd of dir NAACP, Wash Urban Leag, Nat Com Agst Discrim in Housing; NAACP Legal Def Fund; mem ABA Nat Bar Assn Wash Bar Assn & Dist of Colum Bar, pres 1973-74; Phi Beta Kappa, Alpha Phi Alpha; Sigma Pi Phi; Delta Theta Phi, Mason; act partic prepar & present of Sch Desegregation cases 1953-55; FAA Lic instr rated comm pilot; mem Burning Tree Club. **HONORS/ACHIEVEMENTS:** Hon LLD Dartmouth Coll 1986. **MILITARY SERVICE:** USNR ensign 1944-46. **BUSINESS ADDRESS:** Partner, Reid & Priest, 1111 19th St NW, Ste 1100, Washington, DC 20036.

DUNCAN, DAVID EDWARD
Educator. **PERSONAL:** Born Jun 22, 1926, Augusta, GA; married Dolores Tillman; children: Dana M, David E. **EDUCATION:** Paine Coll Augusta GA, BA 1951; Augusta Coll, (1st blk stdnt) 1965; San Francisco State U, MBA 1970, CPA 1980. **CAREER:** Augusta Coll School of Business Administration, asst admin, asst prof 1974; Paine Coll, asst to pres 1972-74; Wells Fargo Bank, systems officer, accountant 1966-72; Coll Bowl Inc, pres 1962-66; EI Dupont & Co, chemist 1953-62. **ORGANIZATIONS:** Mem Am Accounting Assn 1972; mem GA Assn of Accounting Instr 1972; mem GA Soc of CPA 1980; bd of dir United Way 1972-76; bd of dir ARA 1972; vpYMCA-Met bd of dir 1976. **HONORS/ACHIEVEMENTS:** Deans list Augusta Coll 1977. **MILITARY SERVICE:** USN petty ofc 3/c 1944-46. **BUSINESS ADDRESS:** 2500 Walton Way, Augusta, GA 30904.

DUNCAN, GENEVA
Director. **PERSONAL:** Born Aug 21, 1935, Cleveland; married Dave L Sr; children: Jolette, Dave, Jr, Brenda, Darnell, Darlynn, Kevin. **EDUCATION:** Feen Coll; Cleveland State U. **CAREER:** Ministerial Day Care Assn, dir social serv. **ORGANIZATIONS:** Mem Dem Exec Com; bd Dirs; Crest Found; bd HADC; mem Cuyahoga County Welfare Dept; Fedn for Comm & Plng; Comm Christmas Bureau; dir Pub Relations; Mt Nebo Bapt Ch; Mem Hough Area Council Glenville Area Council; Hough Area Devel Corp; Crest Found. **BUSINESS ADDRESS:** 2521 E 61 St, Cleveland, OH 44104.

DUNCAN, JOAN A.
Government official. **PERSONAL:** Born Sep 08, 1939, Butte, MT; daughter of Dr Walter E Duncan and Alyce M Driver Duncan. **EDUCATION:** Syracuse Univ, 1957-58; Carroll Coll, 1958-67. **CAREER:** Carroll Coll, ast dean of women 1961-67; RDMC Comm Action Agncy, dir Foster Grandparent Prog 1969-75; MT Dept Labor & Indstry, chief Women's Bureau 1975-81; City of Helena, city commr 1982-86; Montana Legislature, 1983-87; Helena Food Share Inc, exec dir, currently. **ORGANIZATIONS:** Dir Helena Area Econ Dvlmnt Inc 1985-, Rocky Dvlmnt Cncl Inc 1982-, United Way 1973-; writer prodcr host Leg 1979 TV Prog 1979, Women's Window R Dio 52 Stationss 1981, 51% 1976-81, Guardian of the Culch TV Prog 1982-; mem Last Chance Press Club 1976, MT Dem Party 1980, Lewis & Clark Health Brd 1983-86; Lewis & Clark County Tax Appeals Bd; Montana Communities Found. **BUSINESS ADDRESS:** Exec Dir, Helena Food Share Inc, PO Box 943, Helena, MT 59624.

DUNCAN, JOHN C., JR.
Attorney. **PERSONAL:** Born Jun 05, 1942, Philadelphia, PA; son of Major John C Duncan Sr (deceased) and Yvonne A Jackson Duncan; married Elizabeth Delores Tunsford Duncan, May 28, 1989. **EDUCATION:** DePauw Univ, BA 1964; Univ of MI, MS, MA 1965-66; Stanford Univ, PhD 1971; Yale Law Schl, JD 1976; Southeastern Univ, MBPA 1985. **CAREER:** Iraklion AS, Crete, Greece Staff Judge & Advocate 1978-79; Tactical Air Command, Chief Civil Law 1979-81; Hurlburt Field, FL, Staff Judge Advocate 1981-82; AF JAG Career Mgmnt, chief Military Manpower & Analysis (JAG) 1982-84; legal advisor to the Asst to the Secretary of Defense (Intelligence Oversight); Deputy Judge Advocate, United Nations Command, US Forces in Korea. **ORGANIZATIONS:** Life mem Alpha Phi Alpha 1968; admnstr Fed Govnmt 1969-; prof various Univer 1976-; cnslr Marriage Family & Child 1976-; ODO 1976, Amer Assoc of Marriage & Family Therapists 1976; Inter Amer Bar Assoc 1983; ABA, FBA, NBA. **HONORS/ACHIEVEMENTS:** Rector Scholar DePauw Univ 1960-64; Graduate w/distinction DePauw Univ, Leopold Schepp Found schlrshp 1965-66; schlrshp Stanford Univ 1967; flwshp Richardson Dilworth Fellow Yale 1974-76; Outstanding New Teacher Award, Southeastern Univ 1985. **MILITARY SERVICE:** USAF col,1969-; Meritorious Service medal (4), Air Medal (2); Defense Meritorious Service Medal. **HOME ADDRESS:** c/o Haynes, PO Box 502, Philadelphia, PA 19105. **BUSINESS ADDRESS:** Deputy Judge Advocate, HQ UNC/USFK JAJ, APO San Francisco, CA 96301.

DUNCAN, LOUIS DAVIDSON, JR.
Physician. **PERSONAL:** Born Oct 26, 1932, Lancaster, SC; son of Louis and Minnie. **EDUCATION:** Howard U, BS 1954; Howard Univ Sch of Med, MD 1958. **CAREER:** Private Practice, physician 1960. **ORGANIZATIONS:** Mem Med Surgical Soc DC Inc; mem Nat Med Assn Mem Mt Airy Baptist Church; Phi Beta Kappa. **BUSINESS ADDRESS:** 1105 Buchanan St, Washington, DC 20011.

DUNCAN, LYNDA J.
City official. **EDUCATION:** Motlow State Comm Coll, AS 1984. **CAREER:** Ray Belue & Assocs, model/actress 1974-77; Univ of TN, contract coord 1978-81; City of Tullahoma, court clerk 1982-86; WKQD FM/AM, mktg consultant/copywriter 1986-. **ORGANIZATIONS:** Mem Circle Player, Atlanta 1974-76; fund raiser Comm Action Guild 1977-79; coord youth activities Mt Zion Baptist Church 1977-79; sponsor Black History Club Tullahoma HS 1978-79; treasurer Bd of Dir Tullahoma Day Care Center 1979-81; chairperson C&D Stamps Scholarship Fund 1982-86; bd of dirs TENCO Developments Inc 1986-. **HONORS/ACHIEVEMENTS:** Appeared as principal character in numerous natlly distrib commercials; has appeared as a model in Ebony-Essence-GQ-Madamoiselle 1974-79. **BUSINESS ADDRESS:** Mktg Consultant/Copywriter, WKQD FM/AM, Westside Dr, Tullahoma, TN 37388.

DUNCAN, MALACHI, JR.
Manager. **PERSONAL:** Born Dec 12, 1937, Colp, IL; married Elsie M Davenport; children: Angela, Ronald, Cynthia. **EDUCATION:** Univ of MI 1976; So ILUniv 1960; Blackhawk Coll 1965. **CAREER:** John Deere Waterloo Tractor Wks, mgr fdry proc control 1974; John Deere Dubuque, engr analyst 1969-74; John Deere & Co, mat rsrch 1963-69. **ORGANIZATIONS:** Mem Am Found Soc; Basic Cncpts Com; 80-E Rsrch instr Cast Metal Inst; radiation safety training TX Nuclear Div Ramsey Engrng; bd mem KUNI-FM Radio; jr achvmt adv v chmn Waterloo Human Rights; mem NAACP; parent adv com Waterloo Jr HS; tchr Sunday Schl Publ "Practical Hot Melt Adhesive Control" 1976. **HONORS/ACHIEVEMENTS:** Outstng min achvmt mgmt & bus 1975. **MILITARY SERVICE:** AUS sp/4 1961-63. **BUSINESS ADDRESS:** Box 270, Waterloo, IA 50704.

DUNCAN, MARVIN E.
Educator, resources center director. **PERSONAL:** Born Nov 23, 1939, Greenville, NC; son of Leroy Duncan (deceased); married Sandra Fields Duncan, Mar 25, 1981; children: Crystal Lynn, Catayah Angelia. **EDUCATION:** North Carolina Coll, Durham NC, BA Math, 1962, MA Educ, 1963; Univ of Virginia, Charlottesville VA, attended, 1969-70; Michigan State Univ, E Lansing MI, PhD Inst Devel/Educ Psychology, 1972. **CAREER:** North Carolina Central Univ, asst dir, Learning Resources Center, 1963-70, dir, Learning Resources Center, 1972-, prof of educ, currently. **ORGANIZATIONS:** Evaluation consultant, Ohio State Univ, 1971; test consultant, Stanford Research Inst, Menlo Park CA; chmn, Durham Chamber of Commerce Leadership Devel Comm, 1981; planning consultant, North Carolina Schools & Colleges; mem, bd of dir, Edgemont Community Center, Durham NC, 1986-87; bd mem, Child Care Food & Nutrition Network Inc, 1986-87; mem, North Carolina Mental Health Assn 1986-87, Alpha Phi Alpha Frat, Assn for Educ Communication Technology, North Carolina Assn of Educ. **HONORS/ACHIEVEMENTS:** Outstanding Research Award, North Carolina Central Univ, 1988; Distinguished Serv Award, North Carolina Central Univ, 1988; author of 17 publications in the field of educ.

DUNCAN, ROBERT M.
Attorney. **PERSONAL:** Born Aug 24, 1927, Urbana, OH; married Shirley A Duncan; children: Linn, Vincent, Tracy. **EDUCATION:** Ohio State University, BS, 1948, JD, 1952. **CAREER:** General law practice, Columbus OH, 1954-57; State of Ohio, assistant attorney general, 1957-59; Bureau of Workmen's Compensation, attorney examiner, 1959-60; City of Columbus OH, asst city attorney, 1960-63; chief, workmen's compensation section, 1963-65; attorney general of Ohio, chief counsel, 1965-66; Franklin County Municipal Court, judge, 1966-69; Supreme Court of Ohio, justice, 1969-71; US Court of Military Appeals, judge, 1971-74, chief judge, 1974; US District Court for the Southern District of Ohio, Columbus OH, judge, 1974-85; Jones, Day, Reavis & Pogue, Columbus OH, partner, 1985—. **ORGANIZATIONS:** American Bar Assn; Ohio State Bar Assn; Columbus Bar Assn; Columbus Bar Foundation; Federal Bar Assn; Sixth Circuit Judicial Conference; judicial panel member, Center for Public Resources; Natl Center for State Courts; past president, Ohio State University College of Law Alumni Assn; exec committee member, Natl Council of Ohio State University College of Law; US Court of Military Appeals Court Committee; Phi Delta Phi; Kappa Alpha Psi; Sigma Pi Phi. **HONORS/ACHIEVEMENTS:** Franklin Univ Law School Liberty Bell Award, 1969; Ohio State Univ Alumni Centennial Award, 1970; Columbus Urban League Equal Opportunity Award, 1978; Alpha Kappa Alpha Humanitarian Award, 1980; Omega Psi Phi Fraternity Citizen of the Year, 1984; Columbus Education Assn Martin Luther King Award, 1984; Ohio Bar Medal for unusuallly meritorious service, 1985; Ohio State Univ Ralph Davenport Mershon Award, 1986; ACLU Award, 1986; Christopher Columbus Achievement Award, 1986; HDL, Ohio State Univ, Central State Univ, Wilberforce Univ, and Ohio Northen Univ. **MILITARY SERVICE:** US Army, 1952-54. **BUSINESS ADDRESS:** Jones Day Reavis & Pogue, 41 South High St, 19th Floor, Columbus, OH 43215.

DUNCAN, ROBERT TODD
Concert singer, actor. **PERSONAL:** Born Feb 12, 1903, Danville, KY; married Gladys. **EDUCATION:** Butler U, GA 1925; Columbia U, MA 1930; Howard U, Mus D 1930; OH Cent State U, Mus D; Valparaiso U, Doc of Humane Letters. **CAREER:** 2000 cncrt rctls in 56 countries 1940-65; Original Porgy in Geo Gershwins "Porgy & Bess"; "Cabin in the Sky", performer 1940; "The Sun Never Sets", performer 1936; "Lost in The Stars", performer 1950; "Synocopation", performer 1940; "Unchained", performer 1955; "Pagliacci", perform-

er; "Carmen", performer 1945; Louisville Municipal Coll, tchr English & Music 1925-30; Howard U, tchr 1931-35; prof of voice & head of dept of pub sch music 1930-45; presently voice instr & coach Wash. **ORGANIZATIONS:** Mem NAG White House Concert for Franklin D Roosevelt 1935. **HONORS/ACHIEVEMENTS:** Medal of Honor Haiti 1945; Donaldson Awrd & NY Drama Critics Awrd for "Lost in The Stars" 1950; recorded "Porgy & Bess". **BUSINESS ADDRESS:** 4130 16 St NW, Washington, DC 20011.

DUNCAN, RUBY
Association executive. **PERSONAL:** Born Jun 07, 1932, Tallulah, LA; married Roy Duncan; children: Ivy, David, Ronnie, Georgia, Kenny, Sondra, Roy. **CAREER:** Clark Co Welfare Rights Organ, past pres; Oper Life Comm Devel Corp NV Health Care Corp, chairwoman & exec dir. **ORGANIZATIONS:** Black Pol Conv 1972; World Conf for Peace Conv 1973; Intl Women's Yr 1975; speaker rep Poor Women for Full Emp 1976; speaker rep Poor Women for Full Emp 1976; speaker rep Natl Dem Platform Comm 1976; bd dir Pathfinder Chartered; Clark Co Reg Counc; NV State adv counc Voc-Tech Educ; bd dir Econ Opport Bd; So NV Human Rel; bd dir Clark Co Legal Svc; SW Equal Oppor Officers Assn; CETA Consortia Adv Counc; mem NAACP, Tchrs Corps, Gov's Leg Commn on Status of People, Clark Co Democratic Ctr Comm, Citizens Housing Adv Counc, Hlth Sys Agency Natl Legal Aid Def Assn; bd dir Natl Hlth Law Proj; mem Natl Org of Women, Natl Free Clinic Counc, Food Rsch & Action Ctr, Western Assn of Neighborhood Hlth Ctr. **HONORS/ACHIEVEMENTS:** First among women making the most significant cont McCall's Mag 1971; Afro-Amer of the Yr 1974. **BUSINESS ADDRESS:** Chwm Exec Dir, Operation Life Comm Dev Corp, 600 W Owens, Las Vegas, NV 89106.

DUNCAN, STEPHAN W.
Journalist. **PERSONAL:** Born Feb 02, 1924, St Louis, MO; married Sheila Shields; children: Stephan W. **EDUCATION:** Univ of Illinois, BS 1950; Rutgers Univ Urban Studies Ctr, Urban Fellow 1962-63; Columbia Univ Grad School of Journalism; Interracial Reporting Fellow 1968-69; Drew Univ School of Theology, Madison, NJ, Master of Theological Studies, 1987-89. **CAREER:** St Louis Argus, 1952-56; Baltimore AFRO-Amer, reporter 1956-57, city editor 1957-58; Afro Amer Newspapers, NJ editor 1958-62; New York World Telegram, asst Brooklyn editor; 1963-66; Region I Office of Econ Opportunity, civil rights officer 1966-68; NY Daily News, asst news editor; New York Daily News, New York, NY, Regional Editor, 1973-83; New York Daily News, New York, NY, assistant news editor, 1983-87. **ORGANIZATIONS:** Mem Alpha Phi Alpha Frat; Sigma Delta Chi; assoc in journalism, Columbia Univ Grad School of Journalism; adjunct prof of journalism Brooklyn Coll 1973-75, and 1987-; bd dir Adult School of Montclair NJ 1982-, Urban League of Essex Cty 1961-63, Newark Branch NAACP 1961-63; bd dir, Montclair Sr Housing Corp, 1983-; associate member, National Association of Black Journalists 1987-. **HONORS/ACHIEVEMENTS:** Certificate, Natl Conf of Christians and Jews 1961; Certificate of Appreciation Natl Assn of Business and Professional Women's Clubs 1961; news reporting award Mound City Press Club St Louis MO 1956. **MILITARY SERVICE:** AUS tech 5th grade; Four Battle Stars European Theatre of Oper 1943-46.

DUNCAN, VERDELL
Elected government official, personnel administrator. **PERSONAL:** Born May 09, 1946, Arkadelphia, AR; children: Constanc Regina, Cameron Chad, Jacobi Edwin. **EDUCATION:** Henderson State Univ, BSE 1964-68; Eastern MI Univ, MA 1972-74, MA 1974-76. **CAREER:** Greater Flint OIC, dr of training 1972-73; City of Flint, flint police officer 1973-77; City of Flint Retirement, trustee of retirement bd 1977-79; CON-CAM Publishing Corp, owner; City of Flint Hurley Med Ctr, 1st ward councilman asst personnel dir. **ORGANIZATIONS:** Mem Urban League; mem Natl Assoc for the Advance of Colored People; council liason City of Flint Human Relations Comm; mem MI Assn of Hospital PersonnelDirs; bd mem Partner In Progress; sec MI Assoc of Affirmative Action Off; pres/owner Twin & Assoc 1983-; mem Omega Psi Phi Frat; coord Hurley Medical Ctr Employee Assistance Prog; consultant pre-retirement, substance abuse, employee development; chief stockholder PHASE. **HONORS/ACHIEVEMENTS:** Educ scholarships WP Sturges Grant 1964-68. **MILITARY SERVICE:** AUS spec 4 1969-71; Combat Medical Badge; Natl Defense Medal. **HOME ADDRESS:** 6906 Daryll Dr, Flint, MI 48505. **BUSINESS ADDRESS:** Councilmember, City of Flint-Hurley Med Ctr, 1101 S Saginaw, One Hurley Plaza, Flint, MI 48502.

DUNCANSON, PATRICIA A.
Executive administrator. **PERSONAL:** Born Nov 27, 1944, Greenville, SC; married Lionel Alexander Duncanson I; children: Derrick Brian, Lionel Alexander II. **EDUCATION:** Brooklyn Coll, 1964-65; New York Univ Business School, 1977-78; Iona Coll, 1979-80. **CAREER:** Bedford Stuyvesant Youth in Action, Inc, officer manager 1965-76; New York City Health Dept, investigator 1965-67; Self employed, interior decorator 1970-77; Duncanson Elec Co, pres/CEO 1977-. **ORGANIZATIONS:** Amer Woman's Economic Develop Corp; Westchester Minority Contractors Assn; Women Business Owners of NY; Assn of Business and Professional Women in construction; Natl Elec Contractors Assn; chairperson Governor's Advisory Council for Minority Business Enterprise; mem NYS Advisory Bd on Public Work. **HONORS/ACHIEVEMENTS:** Awards of Recognition Westchester Minority Contractors Assn 1981; Harlem YWCA 1982; The Wives of Club 50 1983; Gamma Chapter Lambda Kappa Mu Sorority Inc/Natl Assoc for Negro Women 1983; NYS Dept of Environmental Conservation 1984; Interracial Council for Business Oppor Inc 1984; US Dept of Commerce-Minority Business Devel Agency 1984; State of NY Legislature of Erie Co 1984; City of Buffalo-Common Council 1984; Natl Coalition of 100 Black Women 1984; Coalition of 100 Black Women of Long Island 1985; Office of the Lt Gov Alfred B Del Bello 1985. **BUSINESS ADDRESS:** President, Duncanson Electric Co, 5 Court Square, Long Island City, NY 11101.

DUNCOMBE, C. BETH
Attorney. **PERSONAL:** Born Apr 26, 1948, Detroit, MI; married Joseph Nuttell Brown. **EDUCATION:** Univ of Michigan, BA 1970, MA 1971; Georgetown Univ Law Center, JD 1974. **CAREER:** Ed Change Tem Univ of Michigan, asst project dir 1970-71; Fed Trade Commission, law clerk 1972-73; Dickinson, Wright, Moon, Van Dusen & Freeman, partner 1981-. **ORGANIZATIONS:** Pres Nu Chapter Delta Sigma Theta Sorority 1968; dir, natl bd Black Amer Law Students Assoc 1973-74; co-chairperson Michigan State Bar Convention 1974-75; bd of dir Michigan Chapter Natl Conference of Black Lawyers 1975-76; mem, City of Detroit Civil Serv Comm 1979-82; mem Senator Donald Riegle's Fed Judicial Merit Selection Comm 1980; pres Wolverine Bar Assoc 1980; bd of dir Detroit Symphony Orchestra; mem MI State Bd of Law Examiners 1979-; bd of dir Keep Detroit Beautiful Inc 1978; pres Detroit Chapter Links Inc 1986-88. **BUSINESS ADDRESS:** Attorney, Dickinson, Wright, Moon,, Van Dusen & Freeman, Detroit, MI 48226.

DUNGEE, MARGARET R.
Teacher. **PERSONAL:** Born in Richmond; married Winfred A; children: Veronica Dungee Abrams. **EDUCATION:** VA Union U, BA 1962; VA Commonwealth U, MA 1971; Howard U; Univ of VA. **CAREER:** Fairmount School, teacher 1962-69; John B Caly School, 1969-70; Southampton, resource teacher 1971-72; Westhampton, diagnostic prescriptive teacher 1972-74; Richmond Public Schools, human relations adv specialist 1974-; Thirteen Acres Residential School, special educ 1981-86; Richmond Public Schools Clark Springs, teacher 1986-87. **ORGANIZATIONS:** Pres & vice pres PTA Fairmont Elem School 1959-61; pres Richmond Educ Assn 1973-74, Delta Sigma Theta; vol McGuire Hosp; advanced gift chmn VA Fund Renewal Conv Am Bapt Ch & Progressive Nat Bapt. **HONORS/ACHIEVEMENTS:** Who's Who Am Coll 1962; Who's Who VA 1974-75; 10 yr trophy PTA Serv 1969. **BUSINESS ADDRESS:** Teacher, Richmond Public Schools, 1100 Dance St, Richmond, VA 23220.

DUNGIE, RUTH SPIGNER
Personnel professional. **PERSONAL:** Born Nov 26, New York, NY; daughter of William M Spigner and Fannie Walker Spigner; married Elias; children: Christopher David. **EDUCATION:** College of New Rochelle, BA 1975; New School for Social Research, MA 1980. **CAREER:** IBM, personnel prog admin 1981-83, corporate litigation mgr 1983-85, eo prog administrator 1985-86, personnel rsch survey administrator 1987-. **ORGANIZATIONS:** Chap sec Alpha Kappa Alpha Sor; mem Natl Coalition of 100 Black Women, Natl Black MBA Assoc, NAACP; Westchester Personnel Mgmt Assoc (mem,) 1989; Amer Soc for Personnel Admin (mem,) 1989. **HONORS/ACHIEVEMENTS:** Who's Who in Professional & Exec Women 1987. **HOME ADDRESS:** 205 Langdon Ave, Mount Vernon, NY 10553.

DUNGY, CLAIBOURNE I.
Physician, educator. **PERSONAL:** Born Oct 29, 1938, Chicago, IL; married Madgetta T; children: Kathryn, Camille. **EDUCATION:** Eastern IL Univ, BS 1962; Univ of IL, MD 1967; Johns Hopkins Univ, MPH 1971. **CAREER:** Univ of CO; 1971-75; CA State Univ Long Beach, adjunct prof 1975-; Univ of CA, Irvine Medical Center, chief of division 1976-80, 1985-; CA State Univ at Long Beach, pres 1975-. **ORGANIZATIONS:** Reg dir Region XIII AAP Head Start Prog 1976-; mem CA State Child Hlth Bd 1976-; consult Brookhaven Natl Labs Marshall Islands 1982-; bd mem Urban League Orange Cty Chap 1982-; consult KOCE TV. **HONORS/ACHIEVEMENTS:** Distg alumnus Eastern IL Univ 1979. **MILITARY SERVICE:** AUS 1956-58; Hnrbl Dschrg.

DUNGY, MADGETTA THORNTON
Assoc. executive. **PERSONAL:** Born in Lynchburg, VA; married Claibourne I Dungy, MD; children: Kathryn, Camille. **EDUCATION:** Cornell College, Iowa, BA Political Science (1st Black Female graduate) 1964; University of Colorado, Boulder, MA Education 1974. **CAREER:** Chicago Urban Renewal Commission, field rep 1964; Chicago School Board, high school teacher-counselor 1964-67; University of Utah, admission counselor 1967-68; Stanford University, financial aids officer 1968-70; Girl Scout Council, dir of field services 1979-86, counselor/coord summer bridge prog; Univ of CA-Irvine, student affairs officer. **ORGANIZATIONS:** Mem Natl Assoc of Student Personnel Adminis 1973-; former board member League of Women Voters 1975-79, Orange Cty Visiting Nurses Assn 1976-81; citizens advisory council KOCE TV 1983; advisory board council for the Gifted & Talented 1978-; charter mem Orange Cty Chapter Jack & Jill of America 1980; Arts Comm Chmn Orange Cty Chapter The Links Inc 1982-; former vice president Orange Cty Chapter Delta Sigma Theta 1976-; CA Assoc for Counseling & Development 1975-; Directors of Volunteers in Agencies 1979-86. **HONORS/ACHIEVEMENTS:** Rsch asst to Lagos Nigeria-Stanford U/U of Lagos Nigeria 1970; What Counselors Need to Know about Health Professions Awareness magazine 1974; Meeting the Health Care Crisis Amer Assoc of Higher Education 1975; Concepts in Volunteerism cableTV program 1981. **BUSINESS ADDRESS:** Student Affairs Officer, University of CA Irvine, Special Services, Trailer Complex 901, Irvine, CA 92717.

DUNHAM, CLARENCE E.
Communications consultant. **PERSONAL:** Born Aug 29, 1934, Syracuse; children: Tracey, Joi, Audrey. **EDUCATION:** Syracuse U, 1953; AUS Comm Tech Teletype Sch, 1959. **CAREER:** Western Elec Co Inc, 1953-69; NY Telephone Co, communications cons. **ORGANIZATIONS:** Past coun mem Syracuse Nghbrhd Hlth Ctr; bd dir Dunbar Ctr scl serv & fclty; pres Grand St Boys; adv Jr Achievement Orgn 1972-73; Co Legislator1973; Onondaga Co Legislator Respresenting 23rd Legislative Dist; bd dir PEACE Inc 1974; bd dir WCNY TV 1974; adv bd Bishop Foery Found 1974; bd dir Onondaga Neighborhood Leg Serv 1975; bd dir Metro Syracuse Bus Ind Educ Council 1975; exec com Northern Region Black Pol Caucus. **HONORS/ACHIEVEMENTS:** Citation from Jr Achievement 1972; 1st runner-up in YMCA Black Achievement Award 1973; YMCA Black Achievement Award 1975. **MILITARY SERVICE:** AUS 1957-59. **BUSINESS ADDRESS:** 321 Montgomery St, Syracuse, NY 13202.

DUNHAM, JOHN L.
Business executive. **PERSONAL:** Born Mar 04, 1939, Charleston, WV; married Gloria. **EDUCATION:** Wilson Jr Coll; Roosevelt U;Univ of Washington; Am Sav & Loan Inst; IBM Sch. **CAREER:** US League of Sav Assn, exec; Systems Programmers Soc, co-founder; Skylite Enterprises Inc, fndr & pres. **ORGANIZATIONS:** Mem Black Exec of Chicago; Cosmopolitan Chap of Commerce; Nat Bus League; bd mem Systems Programmers Soc; bd mem Bio-med Careers; Sno-Gopher Ski Club mem; author of "Someday I'M Going to Be Somebody"; speaker at num coll sav & loan bd & related groups; made several TV appearances & in several magazines. **HONORS/ACHIEVEMENTS:** Listed in Who's Who.

DUNHAM, KATHERINE (KAYE DUNN)
Dancer, actress, writer. **PERSONAL:** Born Jun 22, 1910, Joliet, IL; daughter of Albert Millard Dunham and Annette Poindexter Dunham; married John Thomas Pratt, Jul 10, 1941; children: Marie Christine. **EDUCATION:** Attended Joliet Township Jr Coll; Univ of Chicago, PhB; Northwestern Univ, PhD; MacMurray Coll, Jacksonville, IL, LhD, 1972; Atlanta Univ, PhDL, 1977. **CAREER:** Director and teacher of own schools of dance, theater, and cultural arts in Chicago, New York, Haiti, Stockholm, and Paris, beginning in 1931; profes-

sional dancer, beginning in 1934; choreographer for theater, opera, motion pictures, and television; lecturer, beginning in 1937; Southern Illinois Univ, cultural counselor and director of Performing Arts Training Center at East St Louis campus, beginning in 1967, univ prof at Edwardsville campus, beginning in 1968. **ORGANIZATIONS:** Mem bd of gov, Amer Guild of Music Artists, 1943-49; Amer Guild of Variety Artists; Amer Federation of Radio Artists; Amer Soc of Composers, Authors, & Publishers; Screen Actors & Publishers; Screen Actors Guild; Actors' Equity; The Authors Guild Inc; Black Academy of Arts & Letters; Black Filmmakers Hall of Fame; Sigma Epsilon Honary Women's Sci Frat; Royal Soc of Anthropology, London; Amer Council on Arts in Educ; Advocates for the Arts; adv dance panel, Illinois Arts Council; Arts Worth/Intercultural Com; Certificate Com for Doctoral Program, Union Graduate School; Dance Scope; and numerous others. **HONORS/ACHIEVEMENTS:** Hatian Legion of Honor and Merit Chevalier, 1950, Commander, 1958, Grand Officer, 1968; named honorary citizen of Port Au Prince, Haiti, 1957; Laureate and Mem, Lincoln Academy, IL, 1968; awarded Key To East St Louis, IL, 1968; Professional Achievement Award, Univ of Chicago; Dance Magazine Award, 1969; Eight Lively Arts Award, 1969; Certificate of Merit, Improved Benevolent and Protective Order of Elks of the World, 1969; Southern Illinois Univ Distinguished Service Award, 1969; St Louis Argus Award, 1970; East St Louis Monitor Award, 1970; Katherine Dunham Day Award, Detroit, 1970; Certificate of Merit, Intl Who's Who in Poetry, 1970-71; Dance Div Heritage Award, Amer Assoc of Health, Physical Educ, and Recreation, 1971; Amer Dance Guild Annual Award, 1975; author of Katherine Dunham's Journey to Accompong, Holt, 1946 (reprinted, Greenwood Press, 1972), A Touch of Innocence, Harcourt, 1959 (reprinted, Books for Libraries, 1980), Island Possessed, Doubleday, 1969, Kasamance: A Fantasy, Third Press, 1974; co-author of play "Ode to Taylor Jones," 1967-68; choreographer for "Aida," Metro Opera, 1963. **BUSINESS ADDRESS:** Performing Arts Training Center, Southern Illinois Univ, 532 N 10th St, East St Louis, IL 62201. *

DUNHAM, ROBERT
Restaurateur. **PERSONAL:** Born 1932, Kannapolis, NC. **CAREER:** McDonald's Franchise Harlem, pres (3rd most successful of 2,800 outlets in US); NY Waldorf-Astoria Hotel, worked as salad man. **MILITARY SERVICE:** USAF. **BUSINESS ADDRESS:** 215 W 125 St, New York, NY 10027.

DUNIGAN, MAYME O.
Retired social planner. **PERSONAL:** Born Oct 04, 1921, Darling, MS; daughter of George Simmons and Corrie Simmons; married Charles Dunigan; children: 5 children. **EDUCATION:** Lincoln Univ, attended; Wayne State Univ, attended; Merrill Palmer Inst, Certified Home Mgmt; Wayne State Univ, BS. **CAREER:** MO Publ School, teacher 2 yrs; Mayors Comm for Human Resources Devel City of Detroit, home mgmt adv 1965-70; Mayors Comm for Human Resources Devel, social planner 1970-76; Neighborhood Service Dept - City of Detroit, counselor. **ORGANIZATIONS:** Founding mem 1st Independence Bank Detroit; mem Womens Guild of 1st Independence Bank; sec Lincoln Univ Alumni Assoc Detroit Chapter 1965-67,1970-72; pres 1972-74, chmn 1973-79 Natl Adv Council Lincoln Univ Alumni Assoc; mem bd of trustees Gr Macedonia Bapt Church 1978; chmn Budget Comm 1978-79, Scholarship Comm 1978-79, Crime & Justice Task Force, Womens Conf of Concerns 1975-78; mem Equal Justice Council; pres United for Total Comm for Deaf Met Detroit;mem bd trustees Children Hosp of MI; mem Mayors Task Force on Hunger & Malnutrition 1972-75, Interim Comm Nutrition Prog 1973, Womens Conf of Concerns, Greater Macedonia Bapt Church; appt to mem MI State Mental Health Adv Council on Deafness; mem Unity of Hands Deaf Chorale Bd of Dir. **HONORS/ACHIEVEMENTS:** Cited by NAACP for Achievement in Membership Drive 1972; Recommended MI Chronicle Mother of the Year 1974; nominated for "Heart of Gold" 1984.

DUNLAP, ESTELLE CECILIA DIGGS
Retired educator, mathematician. **PERSONAL:** Born Sep 26, 1912, Washington, DC; daughter of John F Diggs (deceased) and Mary F Chasley Diggs (deceased); married Lee Alfred; children: Gladys C Carpenti, Dolly A Sparkman. **EDUCATION:** DC Teachers Coll, BS 1937; Howard Univ, MS 1940; Catholic Univ of America, post grad 1941. **CAREER:** Garnet-Patterson Junior High Schol, instr & head of math dept 1941-56; MacFarland Junior High School; math sci instr 1956-72; DC Teachers Coll, visiting lecturer of math 1963-64. **ORGANIZATIONS:** Mem Natl Council of Teachers of Math; mem Amer Assn for the Advncmnt of Sci; vice pres Benjamin Banneker Math Club; mem Natl Ed Assn; mem Amer Math Soc; mem Natl Defense Preparedness Assn; mem Soc for Ind and Applied Math; recording sec NW Boundary Civic Assn; mem Smithsonian Resident Assn; founding mem Natl Historical Soc; sponsor Boys & Girls Clubs of Metropolitan Police; treas Petworth Block Club; charter mem WN Performing Arts Soc; Amer Assn of Univ Women; Howard Univ Alumni Assn; Natl Urban League; adv bd Amer Security Council; life fellow Intnl Biographical Assn; advisory bd Am Biographical Rsch Inst; Metropolitan Opera Guild; Amer Film Inst; US Olympic Soc; Natl Assn of Negro Musicians; Amer Assn of Retired Persons; Brunswick Bowling Clubhouse; Natl Council of Sr Citizens; DC Republican Club; Republic an Presidential Task Force. **HONORS/ACHIEVEMENTS:** Fellowship Natl Sci Foundation; Diploma of Honor Intl Inst of Comm Svcs; Certificate of Appreciation Superior Ct of DC; Certificate of Merit Editorial/Adv Bd of Dictionary of Intl Biography London; Cultural Doctorate World Univ; Personality of the Yr Awd World Culture Prize Italian Academia 1984; Honorary Doctorate Intl Univ Foundation 1985; Exec Life Rep World Inst of Achievement; Bronze Medal Awd Albert Einstein Intl Acad Foundation 1986.

DUNMORE, CHARLOTTE J.
Educator. **PERSONAL:** Born Nov 16, 1926, Philadelphia, PA. **EDUCATION:** Univ of PA, BS 1949; Columbia Univ, MSSW 1954; Brandeis Univ Florence Heller School, PhD 1968. **CAREER:** School of Social Work, Univ of Pittsburgh, prof 1977; Simmons Coll, School of Social Work, assoc prof 1967-77; Episcopal Comm Serv of Philadelphia, social worker 1962-64; Boston Children's Serv Assn, supvr, adoption dept, 1957-62; Mental Health Center, consultant 1974; Natl Inst of Health, consultant 1975. **ORGANIZATIONS:** Bd mem New England Med Center Accreditation commn Council for Social Work Educ 1976-79; review panel Council for Intl Exchange of Scholars 1976-; bd mem Nat Conf of Social Welfare NIMH Fellowship 1964-67; bibliography Black Am Council on Social Work Educ 1970. **HONORS/ACHIEVEMENTS:** Career Scientist Devel Award, Natl Inst of Mental Health, 1972-77; Black Children publ R & E Rsch Assn, 1976. **BUSINESS ADDRESS:** Univ of Pittsburgh, Pittsburgh, PA 15260.

DUNMORE, LAWRENCE A., JR.
Physician. **PERSONAL:** Born May 17, 1923, Georgetown, SC; married Gloria Parker; children: Gwendolyn, Jacquelyn, Lawrence, III. **EDUCATION:** SC State Coll, BS; Howard U, MD; Johns Hopkins U, MPH 1970. **CAREER:** DC Gen Hospital DC Govt Sec Standard Investments & Standard Ltd Partnership, exec dir. **ORGANIZATIONS:** Mem Health Adv Planning Comm; adv bd Shaw Health Ctr; Health Priorities Subcomm; DC Govt Adv Bd Phys Asst Sch of Allied Health Howard Univ. **HONORS/ACHIEVEMENTS:** Distinguished Pub Serv Award, Govt DC 1973; Outstanding Performance Award Dept Human Resources DC 1974. **MILITARY SERVICE:** AUS.

DUNN, BRUCE ERIC
Business executive. **PERSONAL:** Born Jul 23, 1959, Brooklyn, NY. **EDUCATION:** Ohio University, BS Communications, Associate of Philosophy 1976-81. **CAREER:** WOUB-TV, producer/director 1977-80; TPC Communications, associate dir 1981; WKID-TVS1, producer/director 1982, production manager 1983-84; WSCV-TVS1 operations manager 1985-; Asst Producer ABC Sports 1987; vice pres One World Entertainment 1987. **ORGANIZATIONS:** Police Benevolent Assn 1982-85. **HONORS/ACHIEVEMENTS:** Floridas Directors Gil Chapter music video award 1984; ABC Sports Olympic Committee for 1984 Summer Olympics Certificate of Recognition. **BUSINESS ADDRESS:** Assistant Producer, ABC Sports New York, 1330 Avenue of the Americas, New York, NY 10019.

DUNN, GEORGE WILLIAM
Judge. **PERSONAL:** Born May 16, 1930, New York, NY; son of George William Dunn, Sr and Helena Isabelle Stephenson; married Maria Teresa Gomez Orozco; children: Leslie Sharon, Darryl Clifford, Nicole Stephanie, Gregory Pascal. **EDUCATION:** OH State Univ, BSE 1956, MA 1958; Univ of Southern CA, JD 1965. **CAREER:** Legal Aid Found, 1966-67; Private Practice, atty at law 1967-78; Long Beach Municipal Ct, judge 1979-. **ORGANIZATIONS:** Dir Intl City Bank Long Beach 1984-; prof CA State Univ Long Beach 1974-; Rotary Club; Judge, Superior Court Los Angeles, assigned, 1988-. **HONORS/ACHIEVEMENTS:** Moot Ct Honors USC 1963-65; Justice Lassigned Ct of Appeal State CA 1980, 1985; prof, CA Judicial Coll, 1981-. **BUSINESS ADDRESS:** Judge Long Beach Municipal Court, 415 W Ocean Blvd, Long Beach, CA 90802.

DUNN, JAMES EARL
Educator. **PERSONAL:** Born Apr 07, 1955, Tunica, MS; son of Robert Dunn and Helen Dunn; married Dorothy Mae Collier. **EDUCATION:** Northwest Jr Coll, 1975; Ft Gordon GA Comm Sch, diploma 1978; Ft Sill Field Artillery Sch, diploma 1981; Delta State Univ, BS 1978, MA 1983. **CAREER:** Tunica Jr HS, school teacher 1978-; County of Tunica, co supvr. **ORGANIZATIONS:** Mem Natl Guard Assn 1978; mem NAACP 1980; mem Tunica Co PTA 1983; mem MS Assn of Supervisors 1984; mem 1984, bd of dir, 1989, Delta Council; treas Tunica Educ Assn 1983-; bd of dirs, North Delta Planning and Development District 1987. **HONORS/ACHIEVEMENTS:** US Jaycees 1981; Man of the Yr United Voters of Tunica-Tunica Co 1983; Mem of Democratic Executive Committee state of Mississippi, 1988. **MILITARY SERVICE:** ANG Captain 1986. **HOME ADDRESS:** PO Box 1463, Tunica, MS 38676.

DUNN, KAYE See DUNHAM, KATHERINE

DUNN, LILLIAN JOYCE
Educator elected official. **PERSONAL:** Born Aug 09, 1938, Robbins, IL; daughter of Douglas Ivory Daniels and Margie Moore Wesley; married Timothy T Barker, Aug 07, 1988; children: Darrin Douglas Dunn. **EDUCATION:** St Augustine's Coll, BA (Phi Delta Kappa Hon Soc) 1960; Chicago State Univ, MS 1976; completed endorsement program in Urban School Admin/Super 1977. **CAREER:** Mission Union Aid Soc, sec 1956-85; Chicago Bd of Educ, teacher/English & French 1960-76, guidance counselor; Simeon Vocational High School, guidance dept, 1976-89; Chicago Board of Educ, chairperson, 1986-89. **ORGANIZATIONS:** Certified Vocational Evaluation Specialist; Commission on Certification of Work Adjustment & Voc Evaluation Specialist; mem Phi Delta Kappa Prof Educ Fraternity; pres Chicago State Univ/ St Augustine's Coll Alumni Assoc; Alpha Kappa Alpha Sorority; sec Posen Robbins School Bd 1983-85; sec Robbins Ambulance Fund Comm 1984-85; Pride of Robbins Temple #915 Elks IBPOE of W; dtr ruler, Pride of Tobbins Temple #915, 1988-. **HONORS/ACHIEVEMENTS:** Past Grand Daughter Ruler Elks 1974; Teacher's Award Certificate Suburban Fed Credit Union 1977; One of the First Women on School Bd Dist 143 1/2; First Woman Sec 1983; work to form Robbins Park Dist, 1989. **HOME ADDRESS:** 13735 S Trumbull St, Robbins, IL 60472. **BUSINESS ADDRESS:** Guidance Counselor, Simeon Voc HS, 8235 S Vincennes Ave, Chicago, IL 60620.

DUNN, MARVIN
Psychologist, educator. **PERSONAL:** Born Jun 27, 1940, Deland, FL; married Linda Irene Lacy; children: Wanda, Fredrick, Kimberly, Jafari, Dierdre. **EDUCATION:** Morehouse Coll, BA 1961; Roosevelt U, MA 1966;Univ of TND phd 1972. **CAREER:** Miami, psychologist 1970-71; Cultural & Human Interaction Center, dir, founder 1973-; FL Intl Univ, assoc prof 1972-; Acad for Comm Educ, dir. **ORGANIZATIONS:** Mem Nat Assn of Black Phychologists; Dade Co Psychol Assn; vice pres Dade Co Mental Hlth Assn; vice pres Dademonroe Dist Mental Hlth D; treas FL State Assn of Dist Mental Hlth Bd 1975-76; bd of dir Dade Co Found for Emotionally Disturbed Youth 1975; bd of dir Ctr for Dialogue; mem bd of dir Transition Inc 1976-; pres of bd Driver Imprvmt Prgm 1976-; mem FL Cncl for Comm Mental Hlth; commr 11th Judicial Circuit Nom Commn 1977; pres bd & Human Inter-action Potential Inc; consult HEW/OCD Ford Found Early Admission to Coll Scholarship. **HONORS/ACHIEVEMENTS:** Award KAY SE Reg 1957; acad schlrshp 1969-61; achiever of yr award Achievers of Grtr Miami Inc 1977. **MILITARY SERVICE:** USN lt 1962-67. **BUSINESS ADDRESS:** Dir, Academy for Community Educ, 39 Zamora Ave, Coral Gables, FL 33134.

DUNN, ROSS
Business executive. **PERSONAL:** Married Rosa Lee; children: Martin De Rosseau, Rosephanye Tolandra, Kennedy Fitzgerald, Wilfred Julian. **EDUCATION:** AL State Univ, BS, MAdmin Supervision. **CAREER:** Dunbar Elem School Pine Mtn GA, teacher 1 yr; Whitesville GA, Johnson Elem School, teacher 9 yrs; Laney Elem School Waverly Hall GA, teacher 1 yrs; Dunbar Elem School, West Point GA, Johnson Elem School, school principal 3 yrs; Macon Cty School Syst, asst supt 1 yr; Muscogee Cty School Dist GA, adminasst 2 yrs; West Point Pepperell, personnel asst personnel rel dept 1974-. **ORGANIZATIONS:** Mem Natl

Ed Assoc, Muscogee Cty Assoc, GA ED Assoc, AL Ed Assoc, Textile Ind; pres Chambers Cty Valley Br NAACP; dir, pres Huguley Water Syst,dir Drew Rec Ctr, Goodwill Ind, AL Health Syst Agency Gadsden AL; mem Chattahoochee Valley Area Assoc for Retarded Children; bd mem Chambers Cty Pensions & Security LaFayette AL; mem Jr Achievement Lanett AL, Amer Red Cross West Point GA, Gov Staff Montgomery AL; mem exec bd George H Lanier Council BSA, West Point GA; co-chmn Chambers Co Child Abuse; mem Valley C of C, Valley Chap AL State Univ Alumni; mem bd trustees AL State Univ Montgomery AL;org Chambers Cty Valley Br NAACP leading br in AL; org Chambers Cty Voter Reg responsible for 75 per cent of black registered voters. **HONORS/ACHIEVEMENTS:** Responsible for revamping the elections for the Chambers Cty Comm & Chambers Cty Bd of Ed 1976; filed a class action desegregation Civil Action #1439 against Harris Cty GA Bd of Ed 1969; filed a desegregation Civil Action #844 with Natl Ed Assoc against Chambers Cty Bd of Ed 1975; 1st black to run for publ office in Chambers Cty Dem Comm; Outstanding Serv Boy Scouts 1968; Outstanding 4-H Leader 1969; Man of the Year 1970,71; Essie Handy Awd 1971; Admin Spirit Awd 1972; NAACP Cit Awd 1973; Dem Club of AL Awd 1974; listed in Who's Who Among Black Amer 1975; Pres Awd NAACP 1975; NAACP, 100 Membership Awd 1976-79; listed in Men of Achievement 1977, Personalities of the South 1979; BSA Silver Beaver Awd 1978, BSA Dist Awd of Merit 1977. **BUSINESS ADDRESS:** Personnel Assistant, West Point Pepperell, Personnel Relations Dept, Box 71, West Point, GA 31833.

DUNN, W. PAUL
Senior project engineer. **PERSONAL:** Born Oct 02, 1938, Fort Worth, TX; son of Willie Dunn and Lillian Dunn; married Alnita Frances Rettig; children: Sheri, Brian. **EDUCATION:** Univ of TX Austin, BS Civil Engr 1962; CA State Univ Los Angeles, MS Civil Engr 1969; CA State Univ Dominguez Hills, MBA Business Admin 1976. **CAREER:** Rocketdyne, research engr 1962-66; TRW Systems Group, mem tech staff 1966-71; Northrop Corp, mgr of engr 1971-77; The Aerospace Corp, sr engr spec 1977-. **ORGANIZATIONS:** Consult Hi-shear Corp 1970; adv bd mem CA State Univ Los Angeles Minority Engr Prog 1983-. **HONORS/ACHIEVEMENTS:** Public Service Award, Vice Pres US 1966; Manned Space Awareness Award NASA 1968; Award of Rec TRW Systems Group 1969; Special Achievement Award Sickle Cell Anemia Assn of TX 1979; Robert H Herndon Black Image Award 1985. **HOME ADDRESS:** 5625 Glenford St, Los Angeles, CA 90008.

DUNN, WILLIAM L.
Educator. **PERSONAL:** Born Feb 11, 1919, Birmingham; married Greta L; children: Darryl, Michael. **EDUCATION:** AL A&M Univ, BS 1947; KS State Coll, MS 1953; FL State Univ, graduate study, 1974. **CAREER:** St John's Ben Franklin School, principal, 1962-65; Bethune-Cookman Coll, assoc prof. **ORGANIZATIONS:** mem, Business & Professional Assn 1967-74; asst mgr, Magic Market, 1972-73; mem, MO Assn for Social Welfare 1967; vice pres, Democratic Club, 1962-65; mem, FL Hist Assn, 1967-74; FL College Teachers Hist, 1967-74; Bethune-Cookman Coll Faculty; regional local dir, Assn African-Amer Life & Hist; pres, FL Coll Teacher History Assn, 1974-75; pres, Bethune-Cookman Coll Faculty Assn, 1975-76; pres The Volusia Co Branch Assn for The Study of Afro-Am Life & Hist Inc 1973-77; pres Volusia Co Bd of Realtors 1975-77; bd mem the Halifahouse Dir; treas NAACP 1975-77; vis the 2nd Black World & African Arts Festival in Lagos Niger Feb 1977; mem Masonic Order 1954-74; Boy Scouts Am 1961-65. **HONORS/ACHIEVEMENTS:** Winner St Thomas Amateur Tournament 1964; plaque United Negro Coll Fund NAACP 1973. **MILITARY SERVICE:** AUS 1943-46. **BUSINESS ADDRESS:** Bethune Cookman Coll, Daytona Beach, FL 32014.

DUNNAVILLE, CLARENCE M., JR.
Attorney. **PERSONAL:** Born Aug 09, 1933, Roanoke, VA; married Norine Gunter; children: Christopher, Peter, Andrew. **EDUCATION:** Morgan State Univ, BA (High Honors) 1954; St Johns Univ NY, LLB (Honors) 1957. **CAREER:** IRS, spl atty 1957-61; So Dist NY, asst US Atty 1961-65; W Electric Co, atty 1965-70; Lawyers Com Civil Rights Under Law Jackson MS, vol atty 1966 (on leave from W Electric); NY Interracial Council for Bus Oppor, exec dir 1970-71 (on leave from W Electric); Western Electric Co, atty; American Telephone & Telegraph, atty. **ORGANIZATIONS:** Chmn Fed Bar Council's Civil Rights Com 1967-69; co-fdr Council of Concerned Black Exec 1968; co-fdr Assn for Integration in Mgmt 1969; fdr NJ Wkshops in Bus Oppor 1979; co-fndr/dir The Black Book Club Inc. **HONORS/ACHIEVEMENTS:** Black Achiever in Ind Awd Harlem YMCA 1980; Pres Second Mile Awd Morgan State Univ 1954. **BUSINESS ADDRESS:** Attorney, American Teleph & Telegr Co, 5 Woodhollow Rd, Parsippany, NJ 07054.

DUNNIGAN, JERRY
Educator, artist. **PERSONAL:** Born Jul 28, 1941, Cleveland; married Roberta; children: James, Jerome, Jeffrey. **EDUCATION:** Dayton Art InstUniv Dayton, BS 1965; Kent State U, MA 1970. **CAREER:** Linden Center, instructor 1964-65; Akron Art Inst, art instructor 1969-70; E Tech High School Black Acculturation Prog, instructor Black Art 1970-71; Nathan Hale Jr High School, dept chmn. **ORGANIZATIONS:** Mem Nat Conf Artists; numerous exhibitions Com Chmn OH; Div World Festival Black Art 1975. **HONORS/ACHIEVEMENTS:** Scholarships Columbus Coll Art & Design 1960-63;Univ Dayton 1963-65; Martha Holden Jennings Found Tchr Leadership Award 1973. **BUSINESS ADDRESS:** 3588 East Blvd, Cleveland, OH 44105.

DUNNING, ROOSEVELT
Deputy commissioner. **PERSONAL:** Born Jul 01, 1924, Norfolk, VA; married Mabel Washington. **EDUCATION:** Seton Hall U, BA 1958; Brooklyn Law Sch, JD 1958; Tchrs Coll, MA 1970. **CAREER:** NY City Police Dept, deputy commr; private practice of law; NY City Police Dept, heads commn affairs youth serv unit 1973-, law enfrcmnt 1948-69. **ORGANIZATIONS:** Consult Govt & Pvt Agys; lectr civic, acad, govt grps; broadcasts on WBLS FM & WNBC AM; appears rglrly on various TV shows; mem NAACP; Urban League; chrtrmem Nat orgn of Black Law Enfrcmnt Exec; Guardians Assn; Nat Cncl Christians & Jews; bd mem 100 Black Men; Brooklyn Law Sch & CollUniv Alumni Assn; Macon B Allen Bar Assn Grp. **HONORS/ACHIEVEMENTS:** Num awards. **MILITARY SERVICE:** AUS 1943-46. **BUSINESS ADDRESS:** 1 Police Plaza, New York, NY 10038.

DUNSON, CARRIE LEE
Educational administrator. **PERSONAL:** Born Apr 19, 1946, Kansas City, MO; daughter of Walter Dunson and Roberta Dunson; divorced; children: Anthony, Darren Harris. **EDUCATION:** Lincoln Univ, Jefferson City MO, BS Psychology 1974; Central MO State Univ Warrensburg, MS Corrections 1975, Educ Spec 1976; Univ of MO at Kansas City, PhD 1990. **CAREER:** USMC, Kansas City MO, mail clerk supvr, 1967; Washington DC Police Dept, supvr documents, 1971; MO Div of Ins, Jefferson City, sec, test examiner 1973; Central MO State Univ Warrensburg, instructor criminal justice 1975, asst prof indus security 1978, dir of equal employment 1978-. **ORGANIZATIONS:** Sponsor Sigma Gamma Rho Sorority 1975; mem Assn of Black Collegiates 1975, Amer Soc Indus Sec 1978, Order of Eastern Star KS Chapter 1973; Commn on Human Rights, MO Commn on Human Rights, 1976; mem, co-chmn, Commn of MO Affirmative Action Assn, 1979; Assn of Black Women in Higher Educ, 1980. **HONORS/ACHIEVEMENTS:** Honorary Mention in Scholarship, Ford Found 1971; Outstanding Young Women of Amer, Montgomery AL 1978; Certificate of Appreciaiton Jericho Rd Award MLK 1979-80. **BUSINESS ADDRESS:** Dir of Equal Employment, Central MO StateUniv, Affirmative Action, Warrensburg, MO 64093.

DUNSTON, ALFRED G.
Clergyman. **PERSONAL:** Born Jun 25, 1915, Coinjock, NC; divorced; children: Carol J Goodrich, Aingred G James, Dr Armayne G. **EDUCATION:** Livingstone Coll, 1938; Hood Theol Sem; Drew U; Allen U, DD; Liberia Coll, Monrovia, Liberia, DCL. **CAREER:** African Methodist Episcopal Zion Ch, bishop; Mother AME Zion, NYC, 1963-64; Big Wesley AME Zion, Phila, 1952-63; Logan Temple AME Zion, Knoxville, 1948-52; Wallace Chapel AME Zion, Summit, NJ, 1946-48; Price Mem AME Zion, Atlantic City, 1941-43; Wallace Temple, Bayonne 1939-41; St John AME Zion,NC 1937-38; Mt Sinai AME Zion, NC, 1936-37. **ORGANIZATIONS:** Tchr Inst for Black Ministries; narrator TV documentaries, "Run From Race" & "The Rising New Africa"; author "Black Man in the Old Testament and Its World" 1974; mem Philadelphia Human Relations Commn 1963; partic Selective Patronage Prgm 1960-63; co-founder OIC 1963; fdr, princ 92nd Inf Div Arty Illiteracy Sch 1943. **HONORS/ACHIEVEMENTS:** Citation for Meritorious Service 92nd Inf Div 1945; 2 Battle Stars. **MILITARY SERVICE:** AUS chaplain (capt) 1943-46. **BUSINESS ADDRESS:** AME Zion Church, Presidential Commons, A521 City LIne & Presidentail, Philadelphia, PA 19131.

DUNSTON, LEONARD G.
Government official. **PERSONAL:** Born Aug 02, 1940, New Bern, NC; son of Henry Dunston and Dorothy Dunston; married Gladys E Sapp; children: Kioka, Kwame. **EDUCATION:** Livingstone Coll, BA Sociology 1963, BA Secondary Educ 1963; Hunter Coll, M Admin 1976. **CAREER:** NY City Youth Bd, supervising street club worker 1966-76; New York City Mayor's Office of Serv Coord, regional coord 1976-78; NC Div of Youth Svcs, prog develop specialist 1978-83; NY State Div for Youth, dir 1983-. **ORGANIZATIONS:** Co-conference chmn Natl Assoc of Black Social Workers 1986-; mem Natl Black Child Development Institute; mem Blacks in Government; mem Amer Corrections Assoc 1986, Child Welfare League of Amer Inc 1986, Natl Assoc of Blacks in Criminal Justice 1986-, Amer Heart Assoc Minority Involvement and Educ Comm 1986. **HONORS/ACHIEVEMENTS:** Recipient of 21 various awds since 1986. **MILITARY SERVICE:** AUS special 4th class 2 yrs; Good Conduct Medal. **BUSINESS ADDRESS:** Dir, NY State Division for Youth, 84 Holland Ave, Albany, NY 12208.

DUNSTON, VICTOR
Dentist. **PERSONAL:** Born May 02, 1926, Atlantic City, NJ; son of Walter Rufus Dunston and Florence Lomax Dunston; married Lonnetta Gumbs, May 04, 1963 (divorced); children: Walter, Phillip; married Ruth Montiero; children: Victor, Mark. **EDUCATION:** Temple Univ Dental Sch, DDS 1952. **CAREER:** Private Practice, dentist 1953-89. **ORGANIZATIONS:** Mem, ADA; New Era Dental Soc; bd mem Fellowship House 1961-63; Lower Merion Human Relations Council 1968-72; mem bd of dir Berean Savings & Loan Assn 1977-89. **MILITARY SERVICE:** USN elctrcns mate 3 class 1945-46.

DUNSTON, WALTER T.
Dentist. **PERSONAL:** Born Jun 03, 1935, Williamsport, PA; children: Walter Jr, Michelle, Connie, Mark. **EDUCATION:** Lycoming Coll, BS 1956; Temple Univ Dental School, DDS 1960. **CAREER:** Dental Serv Inst of PA Hospital, chief 1968-; Temple Univ Dental School, instructor 1965-67; Univ of PA Dental School, instructor 1967-; Private Practice, dentist. **ORGANIZATIONS:** Mem bd trustees Lycoming Coll; mem Amer Dental Assoc, Natl Dental Assoc, PA State Dental Assoc; Fellow of Royal Sci of Health London England; mem New Era Dental School of Philadelphia; pres E Coast Investment Corp; apptd commanding officer Naval Reserve Dental Co 4-1; emm Naval Reserve Assoc, Philadelphia Cty Dental Soc. **MILITARY SERVICE:** USN Dental Corps 28 yrs.

DUPER, MARK
Professional athlete. **PERSONAL:** Born Jan 25, 1959, Pineville, LA; children: Mark II. **EDUCATION:** Attended, Northwestern St. **CAREER:** Miami Dolphins, wide receiver 1982-. **HONORS/ACHIEVEMENTS:** First team All-AFC Choice by UPI 1984; rated as number one receiver in AFC and number two in NFL by Sportsgrams computer rating system; mem NFL Pro Bowl Game 1983,84,87. **BUSINESS ADDRESS:** Miami Dolphins, 4770 Biscayne Blvd, Ste 1440, Miami, FL 33137.

DUPLESSIS, HARRY Y.
Association administrator. **PERSONAL:** Born Sep 21, 1915, Philadelphia; married Lillian Brown. **EDUCATION:** Temple U, BSC 1939; Wayne St U, 1950; AUS Command & Staff Coll, Grad 1966. **CAREER:** Recorders Ct Probation Dept, probation Off 1948-72, deputy dir 1985. **ORGANIZATIONS:** Mem Nat Assn Ct Admin 1974; Nat Cncl of Crime & Delinquency 1974; MI St Probation & Parole Assn 1974; adv bd Salvation Army 1972-74; mem Mayor's Commn on Alcoholism; adv bd Detroit-Wayne Co; LEAA 1974. **MILITARY SERVICE:** AUS lt col 1968. **BUSINESS ADDRESS:** 1441 St Antione St, Detroit, MI 48226.

DUPRE, EMILO JOSEPH
Court clerk. **PERSONAL:** Born Apr 26, 1945, New Orleans, LA; married Bernardine Porche; children: Monica Jeanne. **EDUCATION:** Xavier Univ, BA 1972; Univ of New Orleans, all courses comp toward MSUS in Urban Studies completing thesis. **CAREER:** Prudential Ins Co, agent 1967-69; New Orleans Plan, couns 1972-73; Consult Plng Assoc Inc, pres 1977; Magistrate Ct, clerk 1973-. **ORGANIZATIONS:** Mem Orleans Parish Dem Exec Comm 1972-76; mem LA State Dem Ctrl Comm 1976-; treas sec Reg Plng Commn 1975-; Manpower Adv Plng Council 1976-; Claver Fed Credit Union 1976-; bd mem Comm

Organ for Urban Polit (COUP) one of founding mem 1969, bd mem 1969-72, vice pres 1972-74, pres 1974-; mem Urban League 1970-; bd mem YDA 1971-; mem Xavier Univ Alumni Assn 1972-; NARC 1975; Alpha Phi Alpha Frat 1975; ASPO 1976; pres CCS 1977-; treas Cox Cable of New Orleans 1982-; vice pres New Orleans Jazz & Heritage Found 1983-. **HONORS/ACHIEVEMENTS:** Fellow Inst of Politics 1974; Who's Who in Amer Politics 1977; Merit Awd New Orleans 1975, 1977; YDA Awd 1974-77. **BUSINESS ADDRESS:** Clerk of the Court, Magistrate Ct, 2700 Tulane Ave, New Orleans, LA 70119.

DUPREE, BILLY JOE
Professional athlete. **PERSONAL:** Born Mar 07, 1950, Monroe, LA; married Marsha; children: Shon, Christopher. **EDUCATION:** MI State U. **CAREER:** Dallas Cowboys, professional football player tight end 1973-; Business Concrete Work Co, owner Present; NFC Championship, starting tight end 1973, 1975, 1977 & 78;NFL Championship, played in 1975, 1977 & 78; Pro Bowl, 1976-78. **HONORS/ACHIEVEMENTS:** Named All-Big Ten; Finalist Brian Piccolo YMCA Humanitarian Award 1979.

DUPREE, DAVID
Sportswriter. **PERSONAL:** Born May 31, 1946, Seattle, WA; married Gail; children: Bubba (Jondavid). **EDUCATION:** Univ WA, BA 1969. **CAREER:** WA Post, sportswrtr 1971-; Wall St Jour, stf wrtr 1969-71; Seattle Post-Intelligencer, sportswrtr 1968-69. **ORGANIZATIONS:** Mem Professional Basketball Writers Assn of Am; Baseball Writers Assn; Football Writers Assn; Track & Field Fedn; Nat Urban League 1968. **BUSINESS ADDRESS:** 1150 15th St NW, Washington, DC 20005.

DUPREE, DAVID H.
Attorney. **PERSONAL:** Born Aug 18, 1959, Knoxville, TN; son of Eloise E Dupree. **EDUCATION:** Howard Univ Sch of Business & Public Admin, BBA 1981; Howard Univ Sch of Law, JD 1984. **CAREER:** Howard Univ Academic Computing Svcs, student rsch asst 1978-84, systems analyst 1985-87; Self-Employed, rsch methodologist 1979-; Law Offices of David Dupree, attorney 1985-. **ORGANIZATIONS:** Mem Computer Law Assn 1985, DC Computer Law Forum 1985, PA Bar Assn 1985, PA Supreme Ct Bur 1985; mem Amer Judicature Soc 1986, DC Bar Assn 1986, Tax Court of the US 1986, Amer Bar Assn 1986, DC Court of Appeals 1986-; bd mem Achievement Scholarship Program 1986-. **HONORS/ACHIEVEMENTS:** Special Serv Awd Howard Univ Comp & Info System Soc 1982; Meritorious Serv Awd Howard Univ Academic Computing 1984; co-author, Affect of Parent Practices on Reading Achievement 1983; Does Rosen Still Live, An Analysis of Gift Tax Income Exclusion on Non-income Producing Property 1984. **BUSINESS ADDRESS:** Attorney, 6722 3rd St NW, Ste 103, Washington, DC 20012.

DUPREE, MARCUS JACKSON
Professional athlete. **PERSONAL:** Born May 22, 1964, Philadelphia, MS. **EDUCATION:** Oklahoma. **CAREER:** Portland Breakers, running back 1984-; New Jersey. **ORGANIZATIONS:** Was the subject of the book "The Courting of Marcus Dupree" a chronicle of his experiences during the recruiting wars. **HONORS/ACHIEVEMENTS:** Scored Breakers first Superdome touchdown on his first pro carry from one yard out; rushed 96 yards on 13 carries and a touchdown; sel All-Big 8 and second team All-Amer as a freshman at theUniv of OK in 1982; named Off Newcomer of the Year same season by both wire services; named Freshman Player of te Year by Football News; first rookie to lead OK in rushing, totaling 905 yards on 129 carries which was also second best for a freshman in Big 8 history; rec some Heisman votes as a freshman.

DUPREE, SHERRY SHERROD
Librarian, educator. **PERSONAL:** Born Nov 25, 1946, Raleigh, NC; daughter of Matthew Sherrod and Elouise (Heartley) Sherrod; married Herbert Clarence DuPree, Jan 11, 1975; children: Amil, Andre, Andrew. **EDUCATION:** NC Central Univ, BS Voc Home Economics 1968, MA Educ Media 1969; Univ of MI, AMLS Academic Librarian 1974, EdS Instructional Tech 1978. **CAREER:** Eastern MI Univ, visiting prof educ media 1974; Ann Arbor Public Schools, media specialist 1970-76; Univ of FL, assoc ref librarian 1977-83; Santa Fe Comm Coll, reference librarian 1983-; Inst of Black Culture, Univ of Florida, Gainesville, FL, project dir, 1982-. **ORGANIZATIONS:** Mem Zeta Phi Beta Sor Inc 1967-, NAACP 1977-, Alachua Library League 1977-; pres Univ of FL Library Assn 1981-82; mem Amer Library Assn, Assn of Coll & Rsch Libraries FL Chapt, Black FOCUS, Williams Temple Church of God in Christ. **HONORS/ACHIEVEMENTS:** Proctor & Gamble Awd for Outstanding Student in Home Economics NC Central Univ 1968; Graduate Fellowship NC Central Univ 1968-69; Governor's Award, Outstanding Florida Citizen, State of Florida, 1986; Travel Grant, Natl Endowment for the Humanities, 1986; Visiting Research Fellowship, Smithsonian Inst, 1987; Travel Grant, Southern Regional Educ Bd, 1988; books/articles published including DuPree Sherry & Jenkins Hertha "Library Media Ctr & Classroom Displays" Media Spectrum 1976; "Mini-Course in Library Skills" Univ of FL 1983; "WhatYou Always Wanted to Know About the Card Catalog But Was Afraid to Ask" 3rd edition revised Displays for Schs Inc 1987; editor, Biographical Dictionary of African-Amer Holiness Pentecostals: 1880-1990, 1989. **BUSINESS ADDRESS:** Reference Librarian, Santa Fe Comm College, 3000 NW 83rd St, Library P-105, Gainesville, FL 32602.

DURALL, DOLIS, JR.
Director. **PERSONAL:** Born Nov 13, 1943, Morgan City, LA. **EDUCATION:** Immaculate Conception Sem, BA 1965, ordained roman cath priest 1969. **CAREER:** Housing Authority, Kansas City MO, exec dir; City of Kansas City, human relations dept 1970-73; VA Hospital, chaplain; Annunciation Church, assoc pastor 1969-70; Park Coll, prt-time instructor 1971-76. **ORGANIZATIONS:** Mem, Adv Commn on Human Rel City of Kansas City MO 1979-; pres bd dir Carver Neighborhd Cntr 1971-73; Black Action Training Cntr Inc 1971-72; Nat Black Catholic Clergy Caucus 1968-74; prt-time asso pastor St Therese Ch 1972-74; mem Nat Assn Human Rights Wrkrs 1971-; Nat Assn of Housing & Redevel Officials 1973-; vice pres consult Blue Hills Homes Corp; mem Family & Children Serv of Kansas City MO 1972-78; Human Res Corp 1973-78; sec treas Exec Security &Consult Srv Inc 1978-79; priv invstgtr. **HONORS/ACHIEVEMENTS:** 1st Black Catholic Priest ordained for diocese of Kansas City-St Joseph 1969; designer of comm srv unit that recd recognition in Nat Journal of Housing; Certified Pub Housing Mngr; drafted firearms policy adopted by Local Police Dept; consult Personal Skill Devel Hum Rel Training Police Comm Rel. **BUSINESS ADDRESS:** 1016 Locust, Kansas City, MO 64106.

DURAND, WINSLEY, JR.
Consultant. **PERSONAL:** Born Jul 29, 1941, Bunkie, LA; son of Mr & Mrs Winsley Durand, Sr; married Sonya Marie; children: Winsley III, Janay. **EDUCATION:** Southern Univ, BS 1968; Bradley Univ, 1974; USL, 1963; Univ of IL, MBA 1987. **CAREER:** Western Engr, SALES, Special Assignment employee relations 1973, sales devel engr 1971-72, Acct coordinator 1970-71; Caterpillar Tractor Co, Equal Employment Coordinator 1977-, relations rep mgr 1974-, application engr 1970, jr sales devel engr 1968-70; Mgr Technical Recruiting 1987-; Caterpillar Inc, Peoria IL, annual quality improvement coordinator, 1988. **ORGANIZATIONS:** Civil Rights Movement 1960-65; chmn shop talk auto-mech Tire Rubber & Steel Co 1976; mem So Coll Placement Assn; SW Coll Placement Assn; chmn pres Carver Comm Ctr 1972-77; bd mem Tri Co Labor Educ & Indus Counsel 1977; chmn Voter Reg Drive 1976; pres Peoria Black Political Assembly 1974-75; pres; greater Peoria Big Brother/Big Sister, 1982; bd advisory, Greater Peoria Foundation, 1986; bd mem, Peoria Public Library, 1987. **HONORS/ACHIEVEMENTS:** Outstanding Newmanite for Leadership 1963; Outstanding Marine of Year Award 1965; outstanding marine award, outstanding leadership in civilian work Marines 1969; Dress Blue & Leather Neck Award 1965. **MILITARY SERVICE:** USM sgt. **BUSINESS ADDRESS:** Mgr Technical Recruiting, Caterpillar Inc, 100 NE Adams St, Peoria, IL 61629.

DURANT, CELESTE MILLICENT
Writer. **PERSONAL:** Born Apr 23, 1947, New York, NY. **EDUCATION:** Columbia Journalism, MSJ 1970; Grinnell Coll, AB Hist 1968. **CAREER:** LA Times, staff writer 1972-; Dayton Journal Herald, staff writer 1970-72; Life Mag, publicity asst 1968-70; freelance writer. **HONORS/ACHIEVEMENTS:** Recip LA Press Club Award 1974; OH Newspaper Women's Feature Writing Award 1971. **HOME ADDRESS:** 1916 N Hoover St, Los Angeles, CA 90027.

DURANT, NAOMI C.
Clergyman. **PERSONAL:** Born Jun 23, 1938, Baltimore, MD; married Albert; children: George, Victoria, Rodney, Hope. **EDUCATION:** Baltimore Coll of the Bible, DD 1970. **CAREER:** New Refuge Deliverance Holiness Church Inc, bishop founder 1967-; 4 Churches in Baltimore & Wash Area, overseer bishop; Radio Stations WEBB WSID WUST, gospeldisc jockey 1968-73. **ORGANIZATIONS:** Mem Advocates of Bltmr 1971; Ada Chap #1 Order of Eastern Star. **HONORS/ACHIEVEMENTS:** Recipient hon BTH degree MD Bible Coll 1972. **BUSINESS ADDRESS:** 1225 E Eager St, Baltimore, MD 21208.

DURANT, THOMAS JAMES, JR.
College professor. **PERSONAL:** Born Apr 09, 1941, Mansfield, LA; son of Thomas Durant and Lena Durant; married Mary C Peyton; children: Thomas III, Timothee, Tyrone. **EDUCATION:** Grambling State Univ, BS 1963; Tuskegee Inst, MS 1966; Univ of WI-Madison, PhD 1973. **CAREER:** US Peace Corps St Lucia Project, agric extension 1963-65; Tuskegee Inst, rsch assoc 1966-68; Virginia State Univ, assoc prof 1972-73; Louisiana State Univ, assoc prof of sociology 1973-. **ORGANIZATIONS:** International Rsch Ghana West Africa/USAID 1978; Rural Devel Rsch Sierra Leone West Africa/USAID 1983, 84, 86; mem NAACP, Amer Sociological Assoc, Southern Sociological Soc, Rural Southwestern Mid-South and Southern Societies. **HONORS/ACHIEVEMENTS:** Phi Beta Sigma Frat Inc Omicron Beta Sigma 1961-; Gamma Sigma Delta Honor Soc LA State Univ 1979-86; guest editor Sociological Spectrum Sociology Journal 1984; Omicron Delta Kappa Leadership Soc LSU Chap 1986. **BUSINESS ADDRESS:** Assoc Prof of Sociology, Louisiana State University, Dept of Sociology, Baton Rouge, LA 70803.

DURANT-PAIGE, BEVERLY
Public relations director. **PERSONAL:** Born Nov 07, 1954, New York, NY; daughter of Wesley Durant and Eunice Fuller; divorced; children: Desiree Spirit. **EDUCATION:** Hunter Coll, New York NY, BA, 1974. **CAREER:** CBS Records, New York NY, mgr publicity, 1978; Howard Bloom Public Relations, New York NY, sr account exec, 1983; PAIGE ONE Public Relations, New York NY, pres/CEO, 1985. **ORGANIZATIONS:** Mem, Public Relations Soc of New York; mem, Council of Negro Women, 1989-90; life mem, NAACP. **HONORS/ACHIEVEMENTS:** The Lillian Award, Delta Sigma Theta, 1988; Award of Appreciation, New York City Police Dept, 1989.

DURDEN, EARNEL
Coach. **PERSONAL:** Born Jan 24, 1937, Los Angeles; married June Pecot; children: Mike, Kevin, Allan. **EDUCATION:** OR State U, BS 1959; CA StateUniv Long Beach, MA 1969; CA State Bd of Edn, Life Diploma. **CAREER:** Hustn Oilers, off bckfld 1972-73; LA Rams, off bckfld 1971-72; UCLA, off bckfld coach 1969-71; Vrsty Lg Bch CA State U, hd fresh coach asst dfnsv bckfld coach 1968-69; Compton Coll, dfnsv bckfld coach 1966-68; Compton HS, bckfld coach wrstlng coach 1963-66; Jr HS, tchr coach entrprs 1960-63; LA Co Pks & Rec, dir 1959-60; Spl Sprt Prg for Yng Men, spl asst dir & orgnzr; San Diego Chargers, offensive backfield coach. **HONORS/ACHIEVEMENTS:** Recip 1st black Joe Coll OR State 1956-57; 1st black coach UCLA; 1st black football coach CA StateUniv Lg Bch; 1st black cch LA Rams; 1st black coach Hstn Oilers; 1st team Pcfc Coast Conf 1956-57; All Am 1956; selected to Hula Bowl 1958; played in Rose Bowl Game 1957; drftd Green Bay 1959; tied for lngst contns serv for 7 seasons on Charger Staff. **BUSINESS ADDRESS:** Coach/Entrepreneur, San Diego Chargers, PO Box 20666, San Diego, CA 92120.

DUREN, EMMA THOMPSON
Educator. **PERSONAL:** Born Jun 28, 1925, Macon, GA; married Edward Lee Duren Sr; children: Edward Lee Jr, Timothy Leon. **EDUCATION:** Winston-Salem Teachers Coll, BS Educ 1958; Woman's Coll Univ of NC, MEd 1964; Univ of Minnesota, additional studies. **CAREER:** Winston-Salem City Schools, teacher 1958-76; Winston-Salem State Univ, coord of intermediate educ, prof of educ 1976-. **ORGANIZATIONS:** Mem NEA, NCAE, ASCD, IRA; mem bd of advisors Student NC Assoc of Educ; pres WSSU-NCAE; coord Intermediate Educ WSSU; mem Alpha Kappa Mu, NAACP, YWCA, NCNW; sec Carolina Conference CME Church; mem bd of dirs Experiment of Self-Reliance. **HONORS/ACHIEVEMENTS:** Teacher of the Year 1975, Reynolds Scholarship Awd 1975 Winston-Salem/Forsyth Sch; one of first women on Judicial Court of the CME Church 1978-86; Excellencein Teaching Awd WSSU 1980. **HOME ADDRESS:** 3740 Spaulding Dr, Winston-Salem, NC 27105. **BUSINESS ADDRESS:** Coord-Intermediate Educ, Winston-Salem StateUniv, PO Box 13207, Winston-Salem, NC 27105.

DURGAN, ANDREW JAMES
Clergyman. **PERSONAL:** Born Aug 26, 1922, Wyco, WV; married Theresa Mae Hannah;

children: Andrea Mae Larkin, Andrew James Jr, Bethelia McCormick, Victor P, Lillian Wopara, Carl C; Michael L. **EDUCATION:** Bluefield State Coll, attended; Hilltop Seminar, attended. **CAREER:** Raleigh Cty Mines, coal miner 1940-43; Trent & Durgan Funeral Home, funeral dir 1951-; Raleigh Cty Schools, school bus driver 1961-68; Liberty Baptist Church, minister 1974-. **ORGANIZATIONS:** Mem Mens Civic League 1960-70, NAACP 1965; post commander VFW 1969-74; exec mem Cty Govt of Raleigh Co 1974; pres Black Ministerial Alliance 1984. **HONORS/ACHIEVEMENTS:** Civic Citation 20 Yrs Publ Serv WWWR Radio Station; Hon DD Faith Coll Birmingham AL 1980; WV Ambassador of Christian Serv WV Sec of the State 1983. **MILITARY SERVICE:** AUS corpl 1943-45; Hon Discharge, Good Conduct Medal, 4 Battle Stars. **HOME ADDRESS:** 407 Beauregard St, Charleston, WV 25301.

DURHAM, BARBEE WILLIAM
Chemist. **PERSONAL:** Born Oct 13, 1910, Aurora, IL; married Mary Elizabeth Spivey; children: Dianne Elizabeth, Sheila Gay, William Charles. **EDUCATION:** BS 1934. **CAREER:** The Reagent Lab OH State U, pharmctcl chem mgr 1937-. **ORGANIZATIONS:** Exec sec Columbus NAACP 1951-66; exec bd Task Force on Govt & Comm Concrns of 2nd Bapt Ch; Godman Guild & Nghbrhd Hs;Univ Community Assn; OH Cvl Srv Emplys Assn; adv com OH Cvl Rghts Commn; bdgt hrng pnl Untd Way. **HONORS/ACHIEVEMENTS:** Citations Columbus Ldrshp Conf 1974; Model Cities Columbus 1973; st martin de porres award Cath Intrrcl Com Columbus 1967; several publs in field NAACP. **BUSINESS ADDRESS:** 193 Mc Pherson Chem Lab, 140 W 18 Ave, Columbus, OH 43210.

DURHAM, CAREY WINSTON
Physician. **PERSONAL:** Born Dec 04, 1897, Orange Cnty; widowed; children: Rodger. **EDUCATION:** Uof NC, MD 1923; George Wash U, MD 1927. **CAREER:** Esso Standard Oil Co, physician 1932-70; Central Carolina Hosp, intern & surgn asst 1928-29, tchr of obstret 1928-29; Emerson Cnty Hosp, intern 1927-28; L Richardson Hosp, tchr of obstet 1932-33. **HONORS/ACHIEVEMENTS:** Gold label pin NC Med Soc 1978; 50 yr pin Masons 3rd Degr. **MILITARY SERVICE:** AUS 1st lt 1927, med exam 1934-45. **BUSINESS ADDRESS:** 209 Ridgeway Dr, Greensboro, NC 27403.

DURHAM, EDDIE L., SR.
Government official. **PERSONAL:** Born Mar 17, 1946, Newellton, LA; son of Rev Albert E Durham and Annie B Emerson Durham; married Fannie Henderson, Dec 14, 1966; children: Eddie Jr, Robert. **EDUCATION:** Southern Univ, Baton Rouge LA, BA English, 1968; Harvard Univ, Cambridge MA, attended, 1967; Univ of Utah, Salt Lake City Ut, MS Admin, 1974. **CAREER:** Stauffer Chemical Co, Dayton NJ, mgmt trainee, 1969-70; Agway Chemical Co, Yardville NJ, asst plant mgr, 1970-71; New Jersey Dept of Labor, Trenton NJ, claims reviewer, 1971-72, personnel asst, 1972-74, chief of admin, 1974-76, admin dir, 1976-. **ORGANIZATIONS:** Mem, Political Action Comm of Willingboro, 1975-82; pres, Amer Soc for Public Admin (New Jersey), 1976-77; dir, First Peoples Bank of New Jersey, 1977-82; mem, Willingboro Township Council, 1977-82; dir, Saints' Memorial Community Church, 1979-; mem, Blacks in Govt, 1984-, Forum for Black Public Admin, 1986-; dir, Better Day Care Center, 1986-. **HONORS/ACHIEVEMENTS:** Service Award, Saints' Memorial Community Church, 1983, 1984; Service Award, Cathedral of Love, 1989. **BUSINESS ADDRESS:** Administrative Director, New Jersey Department of State, 820 Bear Tavern Rd, 3rd Floor, CN 300, Trenton, NJ 08625.

DURHAM, JOSEPH THOMAS
Educational administrator. **PERSONAL:** Born Nov 26, 1923, Raleigh, NC; son of Watt Durham and Serena Durham; married Alice Spruill; children: LaDonna D Stamper, LaVerne. **EDUCATION:** Morgan State Coll, AB (honors) 1948; Temple Univ, EdM 1949; Columbia Univ, EdD 1963. **CAREER:** New Lincoln School, teacher 1956-58; Southern Univ, prof 1958-60; Coppin State Coll, chmn educ 1960-63; Albany State Coll, dean & prof 1963-65; Coppin State Coll, dean of college 1965-68; IL State Univ, assoc dean educ 1968-72; Howard Univ, dean of school of educ 1972-75; Coppin State Coll Baltimore, dean of educ 1975-76; MD State Bd for Higher Educ, dir inst approval; Comm Coll of Baltimore, pres. **ORGANIZATIONS:** Mem Phi Delta Kappa; mem Alpha Phi Alpha; visiting prof Univ of New Hampshire 1966. **HONORS/ACHIEVEMENTS:** Fellow General Educ Bd 1953-54; Fellow Danforth Found 1975; "The Story of Civil Rights as Seen by the Black Church" DC Cook Publishing Co 1971; Commissioner Montgomery Co Human Relations 1983-86; Presidential Leadership Medallion, Univ of Texas, 1989. **MILITARY SERVICE:** USAF sgt 3 yrs; Good Conduct Medal; Philippine Liberation Medal; Pacific Theater Medal. **HOME ADDRESS:** 13102 Morningside Lane, Silver Spring, MD 20904. **BUSINESS ADDRESS:** President, Comm Coll of Baltimore, 600 E Lombard St, Baltimore, MD 21202.

DURHAM, LEON
Professional athlete. **PERSONAL:** Born Jul 31, 1957, Cincinnati, OH; married Angela; children: Loren. **CAREER:** Chicago Cubs, first base 1980-. **ORGANIZATIONS:** Donated $25,500 to Chicago Public HS Athletic Prog. **HONORS/ACHIEVEMENTS:** Chicago Chapter of the Baseball Writers Assc of Amer when he received the Ken Hubbs Memorial Award; All-Star Game; Amer Assc Rookie of the Year 1 979; All-Star honors that season; TX League All-Star team in 1978. **BUSINESS ADDRESS:** Chicago Cubs, 1060 W Addison St, Chicago, IL 60613.

DURHAM, WILLIAM R.
Government manager. **PERSONAL:** Born Feb 05, 1945, Woodruff, SC; married Carol Almeda Pearson; children: Kenyatta. **EDUCATION:** South Carolina State Coll, BS 1967; Howard Univ, MBA 1978. **CAREER:** Federal Power Commn, accountant 1969-79; JIMLA Inc, pres 1982-85; Fed Energy Regulatory Commn, section mgr 1980-. **ORGANIZATIONS:** Past pres 1981-84, bd of dirs Resources Fed Credit Union 1981-; pres Washington DC Chap Natl Black MBA Assoc 1982-84; bd of dirs Natl Black MBA Assoc 1982-83; mem Kappa Alpha Psi Frat, NAACP, Transafrica, Natl Rainbow Coalition, Millwood Waterford Civic Assoc, Blacks in Govt; leader Quality Circle, Federal Energy Regulator Commn. **HONORS/ACHIEVEMENTS:** Meritorious Service and Outstanding Leadership Awds MBA Assoc 1981,83. **MILITARY SERVICE:** AUS capt 2 yrs active 6 yrs reserve; Bronze Star, Army Commendation Medals for Meritorious Serv in Vietnam 1968-69. **BUSINESS ADDRESS:** Section Manager, Federal Energy Reg Commn, 825 North Capitol St, Washington, DC 20426.

DURLEY, ALEXANDER
Educator. **PERSONAL:** Born Dec 18, 1912, Pittsburg, TX; married Wylma Brooks; children: Desiree, Patricia. **EDUCATION:** TX Coll, AB 1935; Atlanta U, MA 1942;Univ of TX, Further Study;Univ of Houston, Further Study. **CAREER:** TX Coll, asst coach 1935-42, head coach 1942-49; TX Southern Univ, head coach athletic dir 1949-65; Houston Oilers, Cincinnati Bengals, Kansas City Chiefs, football scout 1965-69; Prairie View A&M Coll, head coach, athletic dir, instructor of Math 1969-71; Prof United Leadership League Inc, dir of youth prog project PULL 1973-. **ORGANIZATIONS:** Chmn mem exec com NAIA 1962-64; mem compliance com pres SWAC 1957-64; mem Phi Beta Sigma Frat; Houston Bus & Prof Men's Club; Big Brother Orgn; YMCA; $100 Per Year Club; TX Coll Alumni Assn; Football Coaches Assn; TX Coll Assn of Tchr & Am Math Soc. **HONORS/ACHIEVEMENTS:** Elected dir of athletics Nat Coll Assn Hall of Fame 1973; AB Magne Cum Laude; Phi Delta Psi Honorary Soc of TX Coll; TSU Athl Hall of Fame UMl; named to panel to select SWAC Football Player of Week 1977.

DURO, AKIN See CHANDLER, DANA C., JR.

DUSTER, BENJAMIN C.
Business executive. **PERSONAL:** Born Mar 15, 1927, Chicago; married Murrell Higgins; children: 5 Children. **EDUCATION:** DePaul U, JD 1954; Grad Sch BusUniv Chgo, MBA Exec Program 1968. **CAREER:** Pvt Practice, atty 1955-68, Atty 1979-; GH Walker & Co, stockbroker 1968-71; Chicago Comm Ventures Inc, pres chief exec 1971-79; Williams Rux Hill Whitefield Ltd, spec counsel finance invest 1979-. **ORGANIZATIONS:** Chmn IL Commn on Human Realtions 1971-73; vice pres bd trustees Allendale Sch for Boys 1968-; gen counsel Chatham Village Assn1957-. **MILITARY SERVICE:** AUS pfc 1951-53. **BUSINESS ADDRESS:** 733 N La Salle St, Chicago, IL 60610.

DUSTER, DONALD LEON
Business executive. **PERSONAL:** Born Feb 10, 1932, Chicago, IL; son of Benjamin and Alfreda; married Maxine Porter; children: Michelle, David, Daniel. **EDUCATION:** Univ IL, BS 1953; DePaul U, MBA 1977. **CAREER:** IL Dept of Bus & Econ Devel, dir 1977-79; Commonwealth Edison Co, exec 1962-87; Chicago Commons Assoc, asst exec dir. **ORGANIZATIONS:** Bd mem Chicago Commons Assn; bd mem Latino Inst; bd mem USS Africa Leader Exchange Prgm; mem Com on Foreign & Domestic Affairs; exec comm Adlai Stevenson Center Univ Chicago; mem Economic Club of Chicago; mem Investment Analyst Soc of Chicago. **HONORS/ACHIEVEMENTS:** Outstanding achievemet award Nat Fed of Settlements 1976; appointed mem Gov Thompsons Cabinet 1977. **MILITARY SERVICE:** Lt exec officer. **BUSINESS ADDRESS:** Assistant Executive Dir, Chicago Commons Assoc, 915 N Wolcott, Chicago, IL 60622.

DUSTER, TROY
Educator. **PERSONAL:** Born Jul 11, 1936, Chicago, IL; son of Benjamin Cecil Duster and Alfreda M Barnett; divorced. **EDUCATION:** Northwestern Univ, BS 1957; Univ of CA, MA 1959; Northwestern Univ, PhD 1962. **CAREER:** Rose Monograph Series Amer Soc Assoc, assoc editor 1974; Comtemporary Sociology, assoc editor 1974-76; Univ of CA, dir inst for study of social change 1976, prof; Univ of CA at Berkeley, chmn Dept of Sociology 1985-89. **ORGANIZATIONS:** Mem Assembly of Behavioral & Social Sci Natl Rsch Council Wash 1973, Comm on Clinical Eval of Narcotic Antagonists, Natl Acad of Sci 1973; dir Natl Inst of Mental Health Training Grant 1971; assoc ed The Amer Sociologist 1968-70; rsch sociologist Univ of CA 1966-71, Stockholm Univ 1966-67, Corona CA 1964-66; vstg assoc prof Univ of British Columbia 1969; asst prof Univ of CA 1963-66; lecturer NW Univ 1962. **HONORS/ACHIEVEMENTS:** Guggenheim Fellowship London School of Econ 1971; various publ incl The Legis of Morality 1970, Aims & Control of the U's 1972, Some Conditions of Sustained Participation in Governance 1974; co-author Patterns of Minority Rel 1965; contrib to anthologies, Amer Sociologist 1976, Issues in the Classification of Children 1975, Social Policy & Sociology 1975, Sanctions for Evil 1971, Changing Perspectives in Mental Illness 1969, The Encyc of Ed 1971, Crime in Amer Soc 1971, The Liberal Univ Under Attack 1971, Amer Behavioral Scientist 1968, The State of Univ 1970, Social Psychiatry 1968, Our Childrens Burden 1968, Rsch Reports in Sociology 1963; co-ed with Karen Garrett "Cultural Perspectives on Biological Knowledge" 1984. **BUSINESS ADDRESS:** Professor, Univ of California, Dept of Sociology, Berkeley, CA 94720.

DYAS, PATRICIA ANN
Fire inspector. **PERSONAL:** Born Dec 06, 1952, Shreveport, LA; daughter of Henry Jefferson and Martile Jefferson; children: Patrick, Matthew. **EDUCATION:** Southern University, BS, 1976; University of Alabama-Tuskegee, degree, 1976. **CAREER:** Shreveport Fire Dept, Shreveport LA, firefighter, emergency medical technician and fire inspector, 1981—; licensed realtor. **ORGANIZATIONS:** Red Cross Safety Board; board member, YWCA; Greater Shreveport Optimists Club; Shreveport Black Chamber of Commerce. **HONORS/ACHIEVEMENTS:** Outstanding Young Firefighter, Shreveport, 1987; Outstanding community service award, 1987-88; Outstanding Woman of the Year, Zeta Phi Beta, 1987; Distinguished Black Female award, Traveleers Coalition, 1988; St Abraham Baptist Church Outstanding young Christian woman, 1988. **MILITARY SERVICE:** US Marine Corps, LCaptain, 1978-80. **HOME ADDRESS:** 2526 Hopewell St, Shreveport, LA 71104. **BUSINESS ADDRESS:** Bureau of Fire Prevention, PO Box 1143, Shreveport, LA 71163.

DYCE, BARBARA
Biochemist, educator. **PERSONAL:** Born Feb 17, Chicago, IL; daughter of Webster Thompson and Carolyn Goin; divorced; children: Sigidi Abdullah. **EDUCATION:** Loyola Univ, attended; Evansville Coll, attended; Univ of IL, attended; Univ of Chicago, attended; Univ of IL Med School, attended; Univ of So CA School of Med, MSc 1971. **CAREER:** Central Adult HS, instr; Trade Tech Comm Coll, instr; Univ of So CA Med School, asst prof of pharmacology; Crenshaw Adult School, adult basic educ instructor; Radioimmunoassay Lab of So CA, pres, tech dir. **ORGANIZATIONS:** Mem AAAS; founder, past pres Feminine Touch Inc; mem Urban League, NAACP, Alpha Kappa Alpha Sor, Top Ladies of Distinction Inglewood Branch; bd of dir Crenshaw Adult School, Concerned Citizens Comm. **HONORS/ACHIEVEMENTS:** Numerous papers published in scientific journals; Top Ladies of Distinction Inglewood CA.

DYE, CLINTON ELWORTH, JR.
Administrator. **PERSONAL:** Born Apr 09, 1942, Atlanta, GA; married Myrtice Willis; children: Clinton E III, Trevin Gerard. **EDUCATION:** Morehouse Clge, AB 1965; Atlanta

Univ Schl of Soc Work, MSW 1969; Atlanta Univ Schls of Soc Work and Bus Admin, PhD and MBA 1983-. **CAREER:** Economic Oppor Atlanta, dir drug recov prog 1971-73; Atlanta Regl Comm, coord drug and alcohol plng 1973-76; Atlanta Urban League Inc, dir comm srv 1976-79, deputy exec dir 1979-. **ORGANIZATIONS:** Mem Governor's Adv Coun on Mental Hlth 1975-76, Bd of Visitors Grady Mem Hosp 1983-, Ldrshp Atlanta 1971-; v chrmn bd mem Metro Atlanta Pvt Industry Owner 1983-; bd mem North Cntrl GA Health System Agcy 1981-84, Regl Dev Council 1979-83. **HONORS/ACHIEVEMENTS:** Listed Who's Who Among Black Amer, Who's Who Among Human Srv Prof, Outstanding Young Men of Amer, Men of Ach. **HOME ADDRESS:** 2807 Landrum Dr SW, Atlanta, GA 30311. **BUSINESS ADDRESS:** Deputy Executive Dir, Atlanta Urban League, Inc, 75 Piedmont Ave NE, Ste 310, Atlanta, GA 30303.

DYE, LUTHER V.
Judge. **PERSONAL:** Born Sep 26, 1933, Winston-Salem; son of Luther William Dye and Mattie Harpe Dye; married Doris; children: Barry, Bryan, Lisa, Blake. **EDUCATION:** Brooklyn Law Sch, LLB 1960; State Univ, BS NC A&T 1955. **CAREER:** Chicago Title Ins Co, title officer 1958-69; Demov Morris Levin & Shein, assoc atty 1969-73; NY Life Ins Co, assoc counsel office of gen counsel 1974-86; private law practice 1986-88; Civil Court of City of New York, judge, 1988-. **ORGANIZATIONS:** Mem Macon B Allen Black Bar Assn; NY State Bar Assn; exec mem Real Property Law Sect; Queens Co Bar Assn; mem Real Property Com Civil Rights Com & Admissions Com; Grievance Com; mem Local Draft Bd Selective Serv Sys; Brooklyn Law Sch Alumni Assn; former trustee Housing Devel Corp of Council of Churches. **HONORS/ACHIEVEMENTS:** Admitted to US Supreme Court & US Dist Court, elected to Civil Court 1988. **BUSINESS ADDRESS:** Judge, Civil Court of City of New York, Office of Court Administrator of State of New York, 120-55 Queens Blvd, Kew Gardens, NY 11424.

DYER, CHARLES AUSTEN
Computer manager. **PERSONAL:** Born Jul 24, 1936, St Ann's Bay, Jamaica;married Edwina Weston; children: Christopher E, Adam L. **EDUCATION:** Pratt Inst, Bachelor Indust Design 1957; Yeshiva Univ, MS 1962; CUNY, PhD 1980. **CAREER:** Digital Equip Corp, computers educ, artificial intelligence. **ORGANIZATIONS:** Bd mem Danny Sloan Dance Co. **HONORS/ACHIEVEMENTS:** Author of Preparing for Computer Assisted Instruction 1972; Teaching Aid patented 1973; Articles & papers on artificial intelligence & computer-assisted instruction 1980-. **MILITARY SERVICE:** AUS Infantry captain 9 yrs. **HOME ADDRESS:** 203 Grove St, Framingham, MA 01701. **BUSINESS ADDRESS:** Artificial Intelligence Consultant, Digital Equipment Corp, 5 Burlington Woods Dr, Burlington, MA 01803.

DYER, JOE, JR.
Business executive. **PERSONAL:** Born Sep 24, 1934, Bogalusa, LA; married Doris; children: Monica, Kimberly, Karen, Joseph III. **EDUCATION:** Grambling Coll, BA. **CAREER:** KNXT Comm Rels, dir 1965-; Sickle Cell in LA, 1st telethon co-prodcd; United High Blood Pressure Found, co-fndr; Black TV Commn, org; Avalon Carver Comm Ctr, 1st maj & fundraiser coord; Native Am Awareness Wk Resltn LA City Cncl, asst coord; LA, mayor. **ORGANIZATIONS:** Pres Sickle Cell Disease Rsrch Found; High Blood Pressure Found; exec bd mem KNXT Sugar Ray Robinson Yth Found; pub rels adv Watts Summer Festival;Fstvl in Black; LA Brthrhd Crsd; IMPACT; S Central Area Improv Cncl; bd mem Alchlsm Cncl Grtr LA; corp bd mem Untd Way Region 5; bd mem Avalon-Carver Comm Ctr; Protstnt Comm Serv; adv bd mem SW Coll; bd mem Willing Wrkrs for Mentally Retarded; planning com mem Chinese New Year's Celebr; bd mem Oper PUSH; LA Chap Media Women; LA Urban League; Untd Hgh Bld Pressr Found; Sickle Cell Dss Rsrch Found; Willing Wrkrs for Mentlly Retrdd; Dept Sr Citz; Sch Vol Prgm; Kutania People San Brnrdn; Nat Assn Jr Coll; Alpha Chi Pi Omega Sor; Nat Acad Motion Pictrs & TV; Teen Posts Inc; Comm Btfl Pgnt Com; Annl Fstvl Black Com; Lions; Rotaries; Kiwanis. **HONORS/ACHIEVEMENTS:** Winner Nat Abe Lincoln Award; citaion City Human Rels Commn; award Nat Assn Media Women. **MILITARY SERVICE:** USAF. **BUSINESS ADDRESS:** KNXT, 6121 Sunset Blvd, Los Angeles, CA 90028.

DYER-GOODE, PAMELA THERESA
Family practitioner, gynecologist. **PERSONAL:** Born Oct 07, 1950, Philadelphia, PA; children: Lisa, Shonn, ERica, Brian. **EDUCATION:** Cheyney State Coll, BS Biology, BS Chemistry 1971; Temple Univ Med Sch, MD 1977; Medical Coll of PA, internship 1977-78; Hanaemann Med Coll & Hosp, residency 1978-80; Temple Univ, attended (recent advances in medicine) 1985; Miami Univ, Internal Med Review. **CAREER:** Planned Parenthood, physician/ambulatory 1978-80; Gruiffree Med Ctr, physician/ambulatory care 1980-82; Broad St Hosp, ambulatory care physician 1982-84; SEPTA, industrial medicine & claims specialist 1986; Private Family Practice, 1986. **ORGANIZATIONS:** Mem Natl Organization of Women, Coalition of 100 Black Women, Natl Medical Assoc, PA Medical Soc, Amer Medical Assoc, Friends of the Pennsylvania BalletCo, Natl Med Assoc. **HONORS/ACHIEVEMENTS:** Distinguished Alumna Awd Cheyney State Coll 1986; Outstanding Alumna St Maria Goretti High School 1986; Philadelphia New Observer "Women on the Move" editorial presentation. **HOME ADDRESS:** 305 Pembree Cir, Bala-Cynwyd, PA 19004.

DYKES, DEWITT S., JR.
Educator. **PERSONAL:** Born Jan 02, 1938, Chattanooga, TN; son of Rev De Witt S Dykes, Sr and Violet T Anderson; married Marie Draper; children: Laura Marie Christine. **EDUCATION:** Fisk Univ, BA (Summa Cum Laude) 1960; Univ of MI, MA 1961, PhD candidate 1961-65. **CAREER:** MI State Univ, instructor Amer Thought & Language 1965-69; Oakland Univ, asst prof of history 1969-73; Oakland Univ, dean's asst for affirmative action 1975-78, coordinator Afro-Amer studies 1975-83; Univ of SC School of Public Health, consultant 1977; Oakland Univ, assoc prof of History 1973-. **ORGANIZATIONS:** African Heritage Studies Assn 1970; life mem Assn for the Study of Afro-Amer Life & History; charter mem Afro-Amer Historical & Genealogical Soc 1978; Alpha Phi Alpha Fraternity; bd of editors Detroit in Perspective, A Journal of Regional History 1978-84; vice chmn Historic Designation Advisory Bd City of Detroit 1980-82, chmn 1982-84; book review editor Journal of the Afro-Amer Historical & Genealogical Soc 1981-85; pres The Fred Hart Williams Genealogical Soc 1980-86; bd of trustees Historical Soc of MI 1983-; summer fellowship Natl Endowment for the Humanities 1985; pres Michigan Black History Network 1986-; bd of trustees, Historical Soc of MI, 1983-89; pres, MI Black History Network, 1986-88. **HONORS/ACHIEVEMENTS:** Published "Mary McLeod Bethune"; "Ida Gray Nelson Rollins DDS" Profiles of the Negro in Amer Dentistry 1979; "Augusta Savage;" "Jerome Cavanagh & Roman Gribbs;" "Amer Blacks as Perpetual Victims, An Historical Overview" Victimization of the Weak 1982; "The Black Population in MI, Growth, Distribution & Public Office, 1800-1983" Ethnic Groups in MI Vol 2 1983; Phi Beta Kappa, Honorary Fraternity, 1969; "The Search for Community: MI Soc and Educ, 1945-80" in MI: Visions of our Past, 1989. **BUSINESS ADDRESS:** Associate Professor of History, Oakland University, Dept of History, 378 O'Dowd Hall, Rochester, MI 48309-4401.

DYKES, DEWITT SANFORD
Architect. **PERSONAL:** Born Aug 16, 1903, Gadsden, AL; married Violet; children: Reida B Gardner, De Witt, Jr. **EDUCATION:** Clark Coll, AB 1930; Gammon Sem, BD 1931; Boston U, STM 1932; Rust Coll, DD 1971. **CAREER:** DeWitt S Dykes & Asso, architect 1970-; Research & Study, 1968-69; United Methodist Ch, natl div of missions 1956-68, minister 1932-54. **ORGANIZATIONS:** Mem Comm Design Center; mem AIA; mem NAACP; YMCA; Beck Cultural Center; mem bd Elec Exam & Review City of Knoxville TN; Alpha Phi Alpha; trustee Morristown Coll.

DYKES, MARIE DRAPER
Educational administrator, nurse. **PERSONAL:** Born Oct 13, 1942, Detroit, MI; daughter of William Cotrell Draper and Hattie Nlathan Draper Hall; married DeWitt Sanford; children: Laura Marie Christine. **EDUCATION:** Wayne State Univ Detroit, BS 1964; Univ of CA San Francisco, MS 1967; Univ of MI Ann Arbor, PhD 1978. **CAREER:** Detroit General Hospital, staff nurse 1966; Coll of Nursing Wayne State Univ Detroit, assoc prof 1967-, asst dean acad admin 1971-77; Univ of WI Oshkosh, rsch asst 1976-77; Wayne State Univ, assoc provost for acad programs 1977-. **ORGANIZATIONS:** Mem ANA 1964-; mem-at-large EACT Sec MNA 1969-70; mem Natl Black Nurses Assoc 1971-; treas Lambda Chap Sigma Theta Tau 1973-75; mem Sigma Gamma Rho Sor, NAACP; consultant evaluator, N Central Assn of Schools & Colls, 1982-; bd mem, Detroit Metropolitan Coordinating Comm, 1988. **HONORS/ACHIEVEMENTS:** Helen Newberry Joy Scholarship Wayne State Univ 1960-64; David D Henry Award Wayne State Univ 1964; Sigma Theta Tau Natl Honor Soc Nursing Wayne State Univ 1964; Mortar Bd Wayne State Univ 1964. **BUSINESS ADDRESS:** Associate Provost, Wayne State Univ, Acad Programs, 5050 Cass, Detroit, MI 48202.

DYKES, ROLAND A.
Business executive. **PERSONAL:** Married Elizabeth Smith; children: 7 Children. **EDUCATION:** Morristown Coll. **CAREER:** Dykes Masonry Const Works, owner 1967-. **ORGANIZATIONS:** Exec sec, E TN Devel Dist; mem, Commn on Equilable Salaries for United Meth Holston Conf; chmn bd dirs, Progressive Bus Leagues; pres, Cocke CoNAACP; asst Rablow, Alma Temple No 71; mem, Star & of East Loade #3352; Mason;cerf lay speaker, mem, Bd of Laiety, Morristown Dist; co-chmn, Newport Planning Commn; chmn adminstrv bd, Trustee, Woodlawn United Meth Ch; mem, Cocke Co Welfare Adv Bd; mem bd dirs, Coke Co Boys Clb of Am; bd dirs, Cocke Co Sr Cits; mem, Newport Kiwanis Clb. **HONORS/ACHIEVEMENTS:** Apptd hon Mayor, Newport, TN.

DYMALLY, LYNN V.
Elected official. **PERSONAL:** Born Sep 08, 1958, Los Angeles, CA. **EDUCATION:** Univ of CA San Diego, BA Comm, Sociology 1979; Univ of Redlands, MA Bus Mgmt 1987; Whittier Coll School of Law, 1988. **CAREER:** Network Data Processing, vice pres 1979-80; Drew Postgrad Med School Prog of Intl Health & Devel, admin analyst 1980-81; KBRT Radio, bus mgr 1981-85; Compton Unified School Dist, bd of trustee. **ORGANIZATIONS:** Spec asst CA State Museum of Sci/Summer Break & Indust 1973-78; analyst, consult Aid to Needy Children Mother's Anonymous Inc CA State Social Serv Prog 1979-; mem CA League of Women Voter 1983-; staff Youth for Christ 1983-; statewide co-chmn CA Rainbow Youth Coalition Jackson for Pres 1984. **HONORS/ACHIEVEMENTS:** Co-instr The Presidential Classroom 1985. **BUSINESS ADDRESS:** Board of Trustees, Compton Unified School Dist, 604 S Tamarind Ave, Compton, CA 90220.

DYMALLY, MERVYN M.
Congressman. **PERSONAL:** Born May 12, 1926, Cedros, Trinidad and Tobago;son of Hamid Dymally and Andreid Richardson; married Alice M Gueno; children: Mark, Lynn. **EDUCATION:** Lincoln Univ, 1946; California State Univ, BA 1954, MA 1969; US Intl Univ San Diego, PhD Human Behav 1978; Univ of W Los Angeles, LLD (hon); Lincoln Law Univ Sacramento, JD (hon) 1975; CA Coll of Law Los Angeles, LLD 1976; City Univ of Los Angeles, LLD 1976; Shaw Univ, HLD 1981. **CAREER:** Los Angeles, teacher exceptional children, 1955-61; Univ of CA, Davis, Irvine, Whittier Coll, Pomona Coll, Claremont Grad School, lecturer; Golden Gate Univ, adj prof; State of CA, coord, disaster office, 1961-62; State Assembly, mem 1963-67; State Senate, mem 1967-75; State of CA, lt gov 1975-79; Mervyn M Dymally Co Inc, pres, 1979-80; State of CA 31st Dist, congressman 1981-. **ORGANIZATIONS:** Chmn Caribbean Amer Rsch Inst; bd mem Joint Center of Political Studies, chmn 31st Congressional Dist Adv Commiss; pres Rsch Inst for Space Sci & Tech; task force on Missing in Action US House of Reps; mem, CA Dem State Central Comm, Arab Amer Affairs Council, Jewish Labor Comm, Japanese Amer Citizens League, Chinese Amer Assoc, Korean Amer Political Assoc, Mexican-Amer Political Assn, Asian Democratic Caucus, Urban League, Amer Civil Liberties Union, NAACP, Wash DC Commiss on Crime Prevention, Amer Assn of Univ Professors, Amer Assn for the Advancement of Sci, Amer Political Sci Assn, Amer Acad of Political Science, Amer Acad of Political and Social Science, Kappa Alpha Psi Frat. **HONORS/ACHIEVEMENTS:** Hon Soc Phi Kappa Phi; Recip Solomon Carter Fuller Award Black Psychiatrist of Amer 1975; Adam Clayton Powell Award Congressional Black Caucus 1975; Chaconia Medal Class 1 Order of Trinity for Pub Serv Govt of Trinidad & Tobago 1975. **BUSINESS ADDRESS:** Congressman, US House of Representatives, 1717 Longworth House Ofc Bldg, Washington, DC 20515.

DYSON, RONNIE
Singer, recording artist. **PERSONAL:** Born 1950, Washington, DC. **CAREER:** Broadway Play Hari, singer; Avery Fischer Hall Mill Run Theatre appeared in tribute to Duke Ellington 1976. **ORGANIZATIONS:** Appearances; talk shows; recording artist, "The More You Do It", "If You Let Me Make Love to You", "We Can Make It Last Forever", "One Man Band", "Why Can't I Touch You"; sang title song for movie, "Fortune In Men's Eyes"; command perf, Princess Margaret;TV appearances, Merv Griffen Show; Soul, 1974; Black Journal, 1975; film, "Putney Swope" 1969. **MILITARY SERVICE:** AEA mem.

DYSON, WILLIAM RILEY
State representative, educator. **PERSONAL:** Born Jul 12, 1940, Waycross, GA; son of Ed-

ward Dyson and Lorene Dyson; divorced; children: Sonia, Wilfred, Erick, Michael. **EDUCATION:** Morris Coll, BA 1962; So CT St Coll, MA 1976, 6th Year Certificate 1982. **CAREER:** New Haven CT, tchr; Douglas GA, tchr Blackshear GA, tchr; CT General Assembly, state rep. **ORGANIZATIONS:** Leadership, Dev Prog; Ford Found 1969-70; alderman, Bd of Aldermen, New Haven 1976; St Rep; CT Gen Assem 1977-89. **BUSINESS ADDRESS:** State Representative, Connecticut General Assembly, State Capital, Hartford, CT 06106.

E

EADES, VINCENT W.
Marketing executive. **PERSONAL:** Born Feb 19, 1956, Alexandria, VA; son of Lester Vincent Eades and Nerissia (Pierce) Eades; married Dorri Eades (Scott), Dec 27, 1980; children: Birttany Joy Eades. **EDUCATION:** Trenton State Coll, Ewing NJ, BS, 1981; Kansas Univ, Lawrence KS, Exec Devel Program, 1987. **CAREER:** FMC Corp, Princeton NJ, personnel asst, 1977-80; ITT Corp, New York NY, sales representative, 1980-82; CISS-Toys, New York NY, product mgr, 1982-84; Hallmark Cards, Kansas City MO, product mgr, 1984-86, sr product mgr, 1986-87, gen mgr, 1987-. **ORGANIZATIONS:** Mem, Strategic Planning Alliance, 1985-, Hallpac Political Action Comm, 1985-, Amer Mktg Assn, 1986-, Natl Assn of Market Developers, 1987-, Kansas City Consensus, 1988-. **BUSINESS ADDRESS:** General Manager, Developing Businesses, Hallmark Cards Inc, 2501 McGee Trafficway, Mail Drop 128, Kansas City, MO 64108.

EADY, MARY E.
Educational administrator. **PERSONAL:** Born in Waterbury, CT; married Eugene H Eady; children: Mary Vienassa, Alan, Larry, Barry, Audrey, John, Carol. **EDUCATION:** Bridgeport Hospital, lpn 1967; Housatonic Comm Coll, AS Drug & Alc Couns 1977; Sacred Heart Univ, BS Psychology 1977; Southern CT State Coll, MACouns 1978. **CAREER:** St Joseph's Manor, ward charge nurse 1967-74; Greater Baptist Methadone Ctr, staff nurse 1974-75; Dinan Mem Ctr, ward charge nurse 1975-76; Greater Baptist Mental Health Ctr, counselor 1976-78; Housatonic Comm Coll, proj dir spec serv 1979-. **ORGANIZATIONS:** Mem Professional Staff Assoc Housatonic Comm Coll 1979-, Comm Counselor Assoc 1980-; volunteer counselor St George's Church Mental Health Social Group 1980-;pres Housatonic Comm Coll Alumni Assoc 1982-; volunteer School Volunteer Assoc City of Baptist 1983-; mem New England Assoc of Ed Opport Prog. **HONORS/ACHIEVEMENTS:** Community Awareness Program on Sicle Cell Anemia 1969-73; NAACP Police & Community Relations Comm 1973; Univ of Bridgeport Oper Open Doors Program 1975; Chairperson Bridgeport Sr Citizens Activities Week 1976; NAACP Political Action Comm; Univ of Bridgeport's Ed Spec Team; North End Ed Comm, Citizens Non-partisan Register & Vote Comm; Bridgeport Bar Assoc Support to Improve Correctional Serv Comm; North End Neighborhood Council; NAACP Voter Reg Comm. **BUSINESS ADDRESS:** Project Dir Spec Serv, Housatonic Community Coll, 510 Barnum Ave, Bridgeport, CT 06608.

EAGAN, EMMA LOUISE
Dental hygienist. **PERSONAL:** Born Oct 12, 1928, Cartersville, GA; married Dr John D; children: 3 Children. **EDUCATION:** Spelman Coll, BA 1948; Meharry Med Coll, diploma 1953. **CAREER:** Working for Husband, orthodontist hygienist; Dr Earl Renfroe Chgo, hygienist; GA Sch Sys, sch tchr 3 yrs. **ORGANIZATIONS:** Mem Delta Sigma Theta Sor; AAVW; Jack n' Jill of Am; Dental Wives Orgn meharry alumni assn; vol worker MI cancer fund; mem moles sunday Sch TchrOrgn; Spellman Coll Alumni Club; League of Women Voters; Nat Dental Hyg Assn; mem Dental Hygiene Hon. **HONORS/ACHIEVEMENTS:** Recip scholarship achievement Medal Arts Award Meharry Coll; cover girl natl write-up on dental hygiene Jet Mag 1958; honored achievements by Spelman AlumniClub Civic & Professional 1960; mem dental hygiene hon soc Sigma Phi Alpha 1962. **BUSINESS ADDRESS:** 1130 Woodward Ave, Detroit, MI.

EAGLE, ARNOLD ELLIOTT
Company executive. **PERSONAL:** Born Jul 07, 1941, Brooklyn; son of Porter Eagle and Gwendolyn Eagle; divorced; children: Todd. **EDUCATION:** VA State Coll, BS 1964; VA State Univ, BS 1964; NY Univ, MA, 1975. **CAREER:** Mfrs Hanover Trust, personnel interviewer 1966-69; Colgate-Palmolive Co, employment mgr 1969-73; Bristol-Myers International, dir human resources, finance & headquarters admin. **ORGANIZATIONS:** Mem Black Retail Action Group 1974-; Am Mgmt Assn 1974-; Am Council of Intl Personnel 1975-; mem Employment Managers Assoc 1975-; mem bd dir Amer Council on Intl Personnel; vp, bd dir Amer Council on Intl Personnel 1982, pres 1987-; mem bd dir Omega Psi Phi Federal Credit Union 1986; mem, Employee Relocation Council, 1988-. **HONORS/ACHIEVEMENTS:** Omega Citizen of the Yer 1976; Basileus Omega Psi Phi Fraternity Iota Xi Chapter; Mem Business & Industrial Comm Omega Psi Phi; Omega Man of the Year 1983. **MILITARY SERVICE:** AUS 1st lt 1964-66. **BUSINESS ADDRESS:** Dir Personnel Administration, Bristol-Myers International, 345 Park Ave, New York, NY 10154.

EAGLESON, HALSON VASHON
Educator. **PERSONAL:** Born Mar 14, 1903, Bloomington, IN; married Helen Burroughs; children: William F, Juanita (Galle). **EDUCATION:** IM(U, AB 1931; PhD 1939. **CAREER:** Morehouse Coll, teacher Math & Physics 1924-47; Howard Univ, faculty 1947-; prof Physics & Acoustics 1947-; chmn dept Physics & Astronomy 1969-71; Univ of MD, visiting prof 1967-73. **ORGANIZATIONS:** Mem Philos Soc Washington; Am Assn Physics Tchrs; Acoustical Soc Am; bd dir proposed Washington Planetarium & Space Center; gen educ bd fellow 1930, 38; grantee NSF 1968-70; mem Alpha Phi Alpha; Alpha Phi Omega; chmn advancement com Anacostia Dist Nat Capital Area Council BSA 1970-72; asst councilcommr Anacostia Dist Nat Capital Area Council 1972-; dem; bapt. **HONORS/ACHIEVEMENTS:** Recipient silver beaver award BSA.

EALEY, ADOLPHUS
Art gallery director. **PERSONAL:** Born Feb 22, 1941, Atlanta, GA. **EDUCATION:** Howard Univ DC, BA 1963; Academie de La Grande Chaumiere Paris France, 1964; Univ of WI, Assc 1968; NYU, MA 1970. **CAREER:** Howard Univ, humanist in res 1979; Mc Donalds Corp Chicago IL, art consult 1982; Martin Luther King Ctr Atlanta GA, art consult 1985; Smithsonian Inst Wash DC, fine art consult 1985; Ealey, Mitchell # And Assc, dir 1985; Heritage Heirlooms Inc, dir pres 1985; Barnett Aden Gallery, dir 1985. **ORGANIZATIONS:** Pres Afro Amer Historical Arts Soc 1976-83; dir Afro Amer Historical and Cultural Museum 1978; pres Heritage Noir Inc 1983; dir Adolphus Ealey Inc 1983; mem Afro Amer Museum Assc 1985, Natl Conf of Artist 1985, NAACP 1985, Urban League. **HONORS/ACHIEVEMENTS:** Hnr sp archive Historical Arts Award Assc 1981; spec ach Natl Conf of Artist 1981, Amer Psychological Soc 1982, Natl Museum Assc 1983, United Way ofAmer 1985. **HOME ADDRESS:** 2825 31st Pl NE, Washington, DC 20018.

EALEY, MARK E.
Social worker. **PERSONAL:** Born Jun 13, 1926, Oklahoma City, OK; married Ruth Keenan; children: Michael K, Marquetta E, Roger K. **EDUCATION:** Howard U, BS 1950; Howard U, MSW 1952. **CAREER:** Clinical social worker; Pvt Practice, psychotherapy;Univ of the Pacific, chrmn black studies dept 1969-;Univ of CA Berkeley, instr 1960-69; CA Dept of Corrections, social worker 1953-60; San Diego Co Public Welfare Dept, social worker 1952-53. **ORGANIZATIONS:** Mem Nat Assn of Social Workers 1952; CA Probations Parole & Correctional Assn 1955-72; Nat Council on Crime & Delinquency; Nat Council on Social Work Edn; Am Assn ofUniv Profs; Inst on Race Culture & Human Dignity; adv council Comm Affairs Dept of KTVU-TV; Center for African & African-American Studies; mem NAACP 1946-; consult Solano Co CA Probation Office 1971; consult Vallejo Unified Sch Dist 1973; fdr & exec bd mem Nat Council for Black Studies 1975-; dirUniv Travel Tour Courses to W & E Africa 1973, 75, 77, 79 & 81; principal speaker Symposium for By Area Correctonal Workers Oakland 1957. **HONORS/ACHIEVEMENTS:** Recipient richard welling fellowship HowardUniv 1951; faculty fellowshipUniv of CA 1966-67; outstanding professional in human serv Am Acad of Human Serv 1974. **MILITARY SERVICE:** USN steward 3/c 1944-46. **BUSINESS ADDRESS:** 333 Maryland St, Vallejo, CA 94590.

EALY, MARY NEWCOMB
Educator, financial planner. **PERSONAL:** Born Aug 26, 1948, Charleston, MO; daughter of Gussie E Newcomb and Susie M Williams Newcomb; married Willie R Ealy, Jun 17, 1978; children: Lisa Denise. **EDUCATION:** Lake MI Coll, AA 1968; Western MI Univ, BS 1972. **CAREER:** Benton Harbor Area School, dept head, unit coordinator social studies 1973, sec 1970-71; Fox's Jewelry, edt mgr 1969-70; Shifren & Willens Jewelry, office coordinator 1969; Jordan Coll Berrien Campus, adjunct prof 1987-. **ORGANIZATIONS:** Mem Exec Comm MEA 1976-77; mem Andrews Unit Chpter; mem Phi Delta Kappa 1976; pres Essence of Blackness 1974-; mem NAACP; del MI & Natl Educ Assn Rep Assembly 1974-; mem NEA Offical Black Caucus 1974-; advisor Excelsior Chapter of Natl Jr Hon Soc 1975-; reviewer MI State Dept of Educ 1975-; researcher School Curr & Educ Leadership; mem Delta Sigma Theta Sorority Inc, BH-SJ Alumnae Chapter 1983-; first vice pres Benton Harbor-St Joseph Alumnae Chapter, Delta Sigma Theta 1987-89; coordinator Close-up Found 1985-. **HONORS/ACHIEVEMENTS:** Outstanding Teacher Award, MI Dept of Educ 1976; Certificate of Merit, MI Dept of Educ 1976; Nunn-Williams Family History 1986; Teacher of the Year, Benton Harbor High School 1987. **BUSINESS ADDRESS:** President, F&E Enterprises, PO Box 1163, Benton Harbor, MI 49022.

EARL, ARCHIE WILLIAM, SR.
Educator. **PERSONAL:** Born Nov 28, 1946, Suffolk, VA; married Doristine Gause; children: Karen, Archie Jr, Keisha. **EDUCATION:** Norfolk State Univ, BS 1971; Hampton Univ, MA 1976; Coll of William & Mary, EdD 1986. **CAREER:** Hampton Univ, statistics instructor 1983; Coll of William & Mary, grad asst 1983-85; Family Inns of Amer, night auditor 1985-86; City Colleges of Chicago, math lecturer 1986; Saudi Arabian Govt, Dammam Saudi Arabia, Math instructor 1987; Christopher Newport College, Newport News VA, asst prof of Math 1987-. **ORGANIZATIONS:** Deacon/treasurer Mt Pleasant Baptist Church 1983-; mem Assoc for the Study of Higher Educ 1986-, Mathematical Assn of Amer 1988-, Amer Mathematical Soc 1988-. **HONORS/ACHIEVEMENTS:** Co-author "A Preliminary Planning Study for a New College," College of Wm & Mary 1983; author "The Budget Information Systems of Selected Colleges & Universities in the State of VA as Described and Perceived by Budget Managers," College of Wm & Mary 1986; Using Mathematics to Determine Effectiveness of Information System, MAA Section Mtg presenter 1989, Using Time Series Multiple Discriminant Analysis to Predict Bank Failures, Christopher Newport College, Math dept presenter 1989. **BUSINESS ADDRESS:** Assistant Professor of Mathematics, Christopher Newport College, Newport News, VA 23606.

EARLES, RENE MARTIN
Physician. **PERSONAL:** Born Oct 31, 1940, New Orleans, LA; married Eve Evans; children: Robert, Andrea. **EDUCATION:** Howard U, BS 1963; Howard Univ Coll of Med, MD 1967. **CAREER:** Self Employed, dermatologist; Rush Med Ctr, resid 1972-75; Univ WA, preceptorship 1970-72; resident surgery 1968-70; Kemo Health Ctr Chicago IL, chief dermatologist. **ORGANIZATIONS:** Chmn Div of Dermatology Mt Sinai Med Ctr Chicago IL; attending dermatology Ruch Med Center Chicago IL; bd dir Region Four IL; Am Cancer Soc; past pres HowardUniv Alumni Assn of Chicago; frat life mem Kappa Alpha Psi; mem Sigma Pi Phi; mem Chicagoans; mem Saracens. **MILITARY SERVICE:** USN LCDR 1970-72. **BUSINESS ADDRESS:** 2600 S Michigan Ave, Ste 204, Chicago, IL 60616.

EARLEY, CHARITY EDNA
Corporate executive. **PERSONAL:** Born Dec 05, 1918, Kittrell, NC; daughter of Rev & Mrs E A Adams; married Stanley A Earley Jr; children: Stanley III, Judith E. **EDUCATION:** Wilberforce Univ, BA 1938; OH State Univ, MA 1946; Univ of Zurich Switzerland, attended 1950-52. **CAREER:** TN Univ, dean of student services 1948; GA State Coll, dean of student serv 1949; Dayton Power & Light Co, dir. **ORGANIZATIONS:** Mem chmn Dayton Metro Housing Authority 1964-79; bd of gov Amer Natl Red Cross 1972-78; bd of dir Dayton Power & Light Co 1979-; bd of dir Dayton Opera Co 1964-74; bd of trustees Sinclair Comm Coll Dayton OH 1977-; bd of dir Dayton Area Chap ARC; United Way. **HONORS/ACHIEVEMENTS:** Top Ten Women of the Miami Valley Dayton Daily News 1965; Outstanding Citizen Serv to Public Affairs Miami Valley Chapter of Amer Soc for Public Admin 1978; inductee OH Women's Hall of Fame 1979; Black Women Against the Odds by Smithsonian Inst; Senior Citizens, Golden Watch Award, 1987; One Women's Army, History Military, 1989; OH State Senate, service to community, 1989. **MILITARY SERVICE:** AUS WAC lt col 1942-46.

EARLEY, STANLEY ARMSTEAD, JR.
Physician. **PERSONAL:** Born Feb 12, 1919, Wellsville, OH; married Charity Edna Adams; children: Stanley III, Judith Edna. **EDUCATION:** OH State Univ, BA 1941; La-

fayette Coll Easton PA, German 1942; Univ of Zurich, MD 1951. **CAREER:** Bordeaux, intern ob-gyn; Jungian Inst; Kanton Hospital, intern pathology & pediatrics; Miami Valley Hosp, chief family prac 1973-; Dayton Pub Schs, schoolphysician 1955-; Private Practice, physician. **ORGANIZATIONS:** Mem Amer Arbitration Assn; Montg Co med Soc; OH State Med Soc; AMA; past pres Gem City Med Soc; Natl Med Soc; chmn Child Guidance Ctr 1976; bd Drug & Alcohol; bd mem Dayton Art Inst; Dayton Philharmonic Orch Soc; life mem past bd mem NAACP; 2nd vice pres Comm Health & Welfare Cncl; past bd mem Hlth Planning Cncl; past pres Dayton Area Cncl Serv; chtr mem Westmont Chap Optimist Intl & Dayton Racquet Club; mem Sigma Pi Phi Boule'; Alpha Phi Alpha Frat; YMCA; May Co Commr & Comm Citz; moderator State Health & Welfare Regional Meeting; bd mem Dayton Com Boys Club; Alfred Adler Inst Dayton; Mont Co Soc & Cancer Ctr; mem Med Adv Com Planned Parenthood. **MILITARY SERVICE:** USAF tech sgt 3 1/2 yrs. **BUSINESS ADDRESS:** School Physician, Dayton Bd of Educ, 3921 W 3rd St, Dayton, OH 45418.

EARLS, JULIAN MANLY
Scientist. **PERSONAL:** Born Nov 22, 1942, Portsmouth, VA; son of James Earls and Ida Earls; married Zenobia N Gregory; children: Julian Jr, Gregory. **EDUCATION:** Norfolk State Coll, BS 1964; Univ of Rochester, MS 1965; Univ of MI, MPH 1972, DrPH 1973; Harvard Univ Grad School of Bus, PMD Admin 1979. **CAREER:** Cuyahoga Comm Coll, adj math 1966-; NASA, physicist 1965-67; US Nuclear Regulatory Agency, radiation specialist 1967-68; NASA, physicist 1968-; Cleveland State Univ, adj prof 1973-; Capital Univ, adj prof 1984-; NASA Health Safety & Security Div, chief 1983-88, Office of Health Services, dir 1988-. **ORGANIZATIONS:** Mem Mayors Council for CETA Funded Program Cleveland 1980-; health phys consultant 1970-; natl pres Natl Tech Assn Inc 1976-77; pres, org Cleveland Chapter NTA Inc 1974-76; mem Amer Health Phys Soc Publ Inform Comm 1966-73, Amer Nuclear Soc 1966-, US Nuclear Reg Comm Radiation Emerg Team 1971-, Environ Pollution Cont Bd NASA 1970-; exec safety bd NASA 1972-; vstg comm Case Western Res 1975-; bd of overseers Case Western Res 1977-; chmn Cleveland Bdof Ed Occup Wk Exp Adv Bd 1975-77; mem OH Environ Manpower Symp Strgn Comm 1974-, Natl Urban League Black Exec Exchange Prog 1973-; chmn Norfolk State Coll Alumni Assoc 1971-72, Kappa Alpha Psi Frat Inc 1965-; bd of dir Oppty Ind Ctr Inc, Natl Black Coll Alumni Hall of Fame 1986-; bd of trustees Inner City Protestant Par 1974-76, Cuyahoga Community Coll 1987-. **HONORS/ACHIEVEMENTS:** Disting Alumnus Awd Norfolk State Coll 1974; Resol by state of OH House of Rep for serv to community 1974; US Atomic Energy Fellow 1964; NASA Fellow 1971; OIC Serv Awd 1974; EO Awd & Med NASA 1974; Fed Exec Bd Cert of Merit 1973; Natl Urban League Awd for BEEP 1973-74; Beta Kappa Chi Sci Hon Soc; Alpha Kappa Mu Honor; resolution passed by Cleveland City Council for Serv to Community 1978; Tech Achievement Awd Soc of Black Mfgs Engrs & Tech 1978; Disting Serv Awd Cleveland Jaycees; Disting Serv Awd Natl Tech Assoc 1981; Humanitarian Awd Wittenberg Univ 1983; Disting Serv Awd Natl Assoc of Black Accountants 1984; Nat'l Black College Alumni Hall of Fame 1986; Natl Urban League Black College Graduate of Distinction 1987; Technical Achievement Award, Natl Technical Assn 1987. **BUSINESS ADDRESS:** Dir, Office of Health Services, 21000 Brookpark Rd, Cleveland, OH 44135.

EARLY, PAUL DAVID
Military executive. **PERSONAL:** Born Sep 10, 1963, Pittsburgh, PA; married Marilyn Ruth Bronough; children: Micah, Paul, Marcus. **EDUCATION:** Attended, Central TX Coll, KS State Univ. **CAREER:** Voices of Truth Gospel Group, manager; Echo Co 4th MSB, staff sgt; Victory Records, owner. **ORGANIZATIONS:** Economic develop chmn NAACP Manhattan KS; layman Fellowship Temple COGC; master mason KAW BLUE Prince Hall Lodge #107; coach Fort Riley Boxing Team. **HONORS/ACHIEVEMENTS:** Certificate of Appreciation, Special Olympics, 1987-88. **MILITARY SERVICE:** AUS staff sgt 5 yrs; Arcom, Army Achievement Medal, Good Conduct Medal; Primary Leadership Development. **HOME ADDRESS:** 3132 Shady Trail, Tyler, TX 75702. **BUSINESS ADDRESS:** Proprietor, Victory Records, PO Box 1154, Junction City, KS 66441.

EARLY, ROBERT S.
Business executive. **PERSONAL:** Born Nov 10, 1935, New York, NY; son of Robert S Jr and Rose C; married Jane; children: David, Matthew; married Elizabeth Graham, Jun 07, 1986. **EDUCATION:** Univ of Hartford, BS 1957; Morgan State Coll, 1953-56. **CAREER:** Columbia Univ, vice pres of human resources, 1978-; Champion Intl Corp, dir of personnel 1974-78; dir of admin 1974; Speakman Co, dir of personnel & industria relations 1972-74; Colt Indus, mgr personnel & public affairs 1968-72; RCA Global Comm, personnel admin 1958-68; Paper Tech Found Western Michigan Univ, rep; AMA, instr 1969-70; DE Comm Coll, comp coll instr. **ORGANIZATIONS:** Chmn of bd, Intercommunity Camp, Westport, CT; bd of dirs, Higher Educ Retirement Community Assn; vice chmn, Planned Parenthood of New York City, 1987-. **MILITARY SERVICE:** AUS 1954-56. **BUSINESS ADDRESS:** Vice Pres, Human Resources, Columbia Univ, 311 Dodge, New York, NY 10027.

EARLY, S. ALLEN, III
Attorney. **PERSONAL:** Born Oct 27, 1946, Waco, TX; married Pamela Middlebrooks. **EDUCATION:** Olvt Coll, BA 1968; Yale Law Sch, JD 1971. **CAREER:** Jdg H Tyler Jr So Dist NY, law clrk 1971-72; DC US Atty's Ofc, asst US atty 1972-75; Wilmer Cutler Pickering, asso atty 1975-. **ORGANIZATIONS:** Mem bd edtrs Yale Law Jrnl 1970-71.

EARLY, SYBIL THERESA
Business executive. **PERSONAL:** Born Aug 25, 1952, Staunton, VA. **EDUCATION:** Bradley Univ, M Bus Admin 1972; Fashion Inst, commun 1974. **CAREER:** United Airlines, flight attendant; Winston Network TDI Inc, manager, account exec. **HONORS/ACHIEVEMENTS:** Outstanding Sales Performance Winston Network 1981; Outstanding Sales Performance 1982; Salesperson of the Year Winston Network 1983; Assoc Mem of the Year Awd for Amer Health & Beauty Aids Inst; Salesperson of the Year Winston Network 1986. **BUSINESS ADDRESS:** Account Executive, Winston Network/TDI Inc, 211 E Ontario, Chicago, IL 60611.

EARLY, VIOLET THERESA
Executive. **PERSONAL:** Born Sep 24, 1924, New Orleans, LA; daughter of William Thompson Sr (deceased) and Alphonsine Harris Thompson (deceased); married Sylvester Early, Jul 25, 1945 (deceased). **EDUCATION:** YMCA School of Commerce, diploma 1945; Agric Mech & Normal Coll, BS 1964; Henderson State Univ, MS Ed 1977. **CAREER:** Univ of AR at Pine Bluff, asst registrar 1961-85, foreign student advisor 1965-83, registrar/dir of admissions 1985-. **ORGANIZATIONS:** Mem AR AACRAO 1960-; mem Amer Assoc Registrars Admission Officers 1960-; adv Alpha Rho Chapter AKA Sor 1960-71; adv Alpha Kappa Mu Honor Soc 1970-; mem Phi Delta Kappa Frat 1977-; sec Pine Bluff Boys Club 1981-83; mem Kappa Delta Pi Educ Frat 1983-; sec Amer Red Cross Chapter 1985-; sec Phi Delta Kappa Educational Frat 1985-; mem Phi Beta Lampda Business Frat; lecturer St Peter Catholic Church; vice chmn, Economics Opportunity Commission 1975-88. **HONORS/ACHIEVEMENTS:** This is Your Life Plaque Univ of AR PB 1983; Alpha Kappa Mu Plaque (service) 1982-84; Alumni Serv Awd AM&N/UAPB Alumni Assoc; Plaque Kappan of Month Phi Delta Kappa 1986; Hall of Fame, Leadership Pine Bluff 1988; Appreciation Award, Royal Knight Society 1988. **HOME ADDRESS:** 706 W 14th St, Pine Bluff, AR 71601. **BUSINESS ADDRESS:** Registrar/Dir of Admissions, University of AR at Pine Bluff, University Drive North, Pine Bluff, AR 71601.

EASLER, MICHAEL ANTHONY
Professional athlete. **PERSONAL:** Born Nov 29, 1950, Cleveland, OH; married Brenda Jackson; children: Misty, Shandi, Khyla. **EDUCATION:** Attended, Cleveland State Univ. **CAREER:** Houston Oilers, 1973-75; CA Angels, 1976; Pittsburgh Pirates, 1977; Pittsburgh Pirates, 1979-83; Boston Red Sox, outfielder 1984; New York Yankees, player 1986; Philadelphia Phillies, player 1986-. **HONORS/ACHIEVEMENTS:** Selected as BoSox Club's Man of the Year for contrib to team & cooperation in comm endeavors; selected 1980 recipient Pirate's Roberto Clemente Award; mem All Star Team 1981.

EASLEY, EDDIE V.
Educator. **PERSONAL:** Born Nov 16, 1928, Lynchburg, VA; son of George Easley and Berta Easley; married Ruth Burton; children: Jacqueline, Michael, Todd. **EDUCATION:** VA State Univ, BS 1948; IA State Univ, MS 1951, PhD 1957. **CAREER:** Drake Univ, chrmn prof 1957-65, 1966-84; Univ of WI Milwaukee, prof 1965-66; Kimberly Clark Corp, mrkt spec 1969-70; Wake Forest Univ, prof of bus, 1984-. **ORGANIZATIONS:** Mrkt consultant Corps Hospital Govt United Way 1957-; NAACP 1985; Alpha Phi Alpha Fraternity 1948-; Bd of Zoning Adj 1971-73; Sigma Pi Phi 1985. **HONORS/ACHIEVEMENTS:** Outstanding Teacher Award Drake Univ 1968; Outstanding Educ of Amer. **MILITARY SERVICE:** AUS sp 3 1954-56; Honorable discharge 1956. **BUSINESS ADDRESS:** Professor of Business, Wake ForestUniv, Box 7285 Reynolda Station, Winston-Salem, NC 27109.

EASLEY, JACQUELINE RUTH
Business executive. **PERSONAL:** Born Oct 21, 1957, Ames, IA; daughter of Dr Eddie V Easley and Ruth Burton Easley; married Odell McGhee; children: Carey Lucia. **EDUCATION:** Carleton Coll, BA 1980. **CAREER:** Amer Republic Ins Co, personnel assoc 1980, asst vice pres 1984-. **ORGANIZATIONS:** Mem Admin Mgmt Soc 1982-, Des Moines Public Schools Career Adv Council 1983-; bd of dir YWCA of Des Moines 1983-, pres 1987; United Way of Central IA 1984-; mem Minority Ed Braintrust 1985-. **HONORS/ACHIEVEMENTS:** Woman of Achievement YWCA of Des Moines 1984; Des Moines Register - "Up & Coming Business Leader" 1986. **BUSINESS ADDRESS:** Asst Vice Pres Prsnl & Education, Amer Republic Ins Co, 601 Keo Way, Des Moines, IA 50334.

EASLEY, KENNY
Professional athlete. **PERSONAL:** Born Jan 15, 1959, Chesapeake, VA; married Gail. **EDUCATION:** UCLA, Pol Sci. **CAREER:** Seattle Seahawks, defensive back 1981. **ORGANIZATIONS:** Vlntr work United Way & United Cerebral Palsy. **HONORS/ACHIEVEMENTS:** 1984 NFL Def Plyr of the Year (AP, Pro Football Weekly, Kansas City 101 Club); NFL Alumni Assoc Def Back of the Year; First-team All-NFL (Pro Football Weekly, Sports Ill, NFL Films, Sporting News, AP, Pro Football Weekly, NEA,FOOTBALL Digest, College & Pro Football Newsweekly, Seagram Sports Award); First-team All-AFC (Pro Football Weekly, UPI); Seahawks Most Val Plyr; AFC-NFC Pro Bowl selection; AFC Def Co-Captn; AFC Def Plyr of Week Nine; Pro Football Weekly Def Plyr of week; 1981 AFC Def Rookie of Yr; First-team All-Rookie; First-team All-NFL, All-AFC; AFC Pro Bowl squad; Seahawks Most Val Plyr; 1983 First-teamAll-AFC; AFC Def Plyr of the Yr 1st plyr in Prac-10 history named all-conference four yrs; holds UCLA career interception record with 19; Most Val Plyr in both Hula Bowl & Japan Bowl; ABC-TV Def Plyr of the Game 3 times in career 1978 & 1979. **BUSINESS ADDRESS:** Seattle Seahawks, 23017 SE 41st Ct, Issaquah, WA 98027.

EASLEY, PAUL HOWARD, SR.
Minister. **PERSONAL:** Born Sep 07, 1930, Charleston, WV; married Sarita (deceased); children: Paul Jr, Verita Green, David Allen. **EDUCATION:** WV State Coll, BS 1956; Gammon Theological Seminary, BD 1959; Iliff Sch of Theology, MTS 1972; Interdenominational Theological Seminary, MD 1974. **CAREER:** Fairmont Trinity Methodist Church, pastor 1959-61; Roncevert-White Sulpher Charge, pastor 1961; US Army, chaplain 1961-80; Clark College, chaplain 1980-. **ORGANIZATIONS:** Mem Military Chaplains Assn 1962-, Amer Correctional Chaplains 1964-; Correctional Chaplains Assn 1964-, Clinical Pastoral Assn 1977-, Natl Campus Ministers Assn 1980-; charter president Optimist Intl 1984-. **HONORS/ACHIEVEMENTS:** Correctional Chaplain of Year 1974; Year Book Dedication of the Year Clark College 1981; Hall of Fame ROTC WV State College 1986. **MILITARY SERVICE:** AUS colonel 23 yrs; Legion of Merit, Bronze Star (2), Meritorious Serv Medal, Army Commendation (2). **BUSINESS ADDRESS:** Campus Minister, Clark College, 240 James P Brawley Dr, Atlanta, GA 30314.

EASTER, HEZEKIAH H.
State official. **PERSONAL:** Born Oct 16, 1921, Suffolk, VA; son of Hezekiah Easter and Jamie Woodruff Easter; married Ruth D Lowe; children: Gregory Paul, Michael Curtis, Scott Anthony. **EDUCATION:** Attended, Juilliard School of Music, Metro Music School, NY S Industrial and Labor Relations School, Cornell Univ. **CAREER:** Nyack Village, trustee 1965, 1967, 1969; Metro Area Apprentice Training, supvr 1968-72; Rockland Co Legislature, 1969-89; NY State Dept of Labor, job training specialist 1972-84, public work wage investigator 1984-. **ORGANIZATIONS:** Past mem Rockland Acacia Lodge #59; trustee Pilgrim Baptist Church; life mem Nyack brance NAACP; mem Nyack Rotary 1965-77; sec bd vis Letchworth Village 1969, 1974; advisory council BSA Rockland City Council 1965; past pres Hudson Valley Regional Council 1981-82; mem Nyack Hospital Corp 1966; pres Mt Moor Cemetery Assn; mem, bd of dirs Welfare League/Letchworth Village. **HONORS/ACHIEVEMENTS:** Distinguished Serv Award, RC Council of BSA 1962; Citizen of the Year VFW 1967; Rep of the Year, Orangetown Rep Club 1973; Serv Award, Nyack Village Bd 1971; 1st Black elected to public office Rockland Co; Dr Martin Luther King Brotherhood Award, Human Rights Com LVDC 1975; Capitals of the Age of Enlightment Award AFSCI

1976. **MILITARY SERVICE:** AUS corpl 1942-45. **BUSINESS ADDRESS:** Job Training Specialist, Public Work Wage Investigator, 30 Glenn St, White Plains, NY 10603.

EASTER, RUFUS BENJAMIN, JR.
Educational administrator. **PERSONAL:** Born Oct 05, 1928, Hampton, VA; married Evelyn Wills. **EDUCATION:** NYUniv Hampton Inst; Temple U; Piano Tech Schs. **CAREER:** Hampton Inst, admin 1950; VA State School for the Deaf & Blind, curr developer, consultant to supt 1954; Hampton Assn of Arts & Humanities, founder, exec dir 1967; WVEC, consultant comm affairs radio & TV stations 1970. **ORGANIZATIONS:** Bd dirs Assn Coll &Univ Concert Mgrs; Peninsula Symphony Orch; Peninsula Comm Theatre; mem of Asso Council Arts; Assn State & Local Hist; Assn Preservation VA Antiquities; mem Bachelor Benedict Club. **HONORS/ACHIEVEMENTS:** Man of yr award Penisula Vol Serv Bur for works of arts & humainities 1969.

EASTERLING, ROSANNA AVONNA
Assistant supervisor. **PERSONAL:** Born Oct 03, 1957, Chesterfield, SC. **EDUCATION:** Chesterfield Marlboro Coll, AA 1977; Francis Marien Coll, BS 1983. **CAREER:** Carolina Health Care, office mgr 1983-84; Health Care Mgmt Inc, asst admin 1984-86; DeKalb Genl Hosp, asst supervisor 1986-. **ORGANIZATIONS:** Mem SC Heart Assoc, Intl Student Org, Foreign Student Adv Asst, Boys Club of Amer. **HONORS/ACHIEVEMENTS:** Outstanding Young Women of Amer.

EASTMAN, ELEANOR CORINNA
Scientist. **PERSONAL:** Born Mar 24, New York, NY; divorced; children: Elizabeth Ann. **EDUCATION:** Hunter Coll, AB 1946; Brooklyn Coll, Grad School 1952. **CAREER:** Dept of Health, chem lab 1949; Dept of Public Works NY, chemist; Dept of General Services Lab, chief of physical testing div. **ORGANIZATIONS:** Exec vice pres Moore Water & Energy Consult Corp; sec, treas Natl Tech Assoc; exec bd, pres Chap 24, bd of del Civil Serv Tech Guild; bd of deacons Riverside Ch 1980-86; lay couns Riverside Church 1977; 5th vice pres 1970, 1st vice pres 1972 Riverside Ch Bus & Professional Womens Club. **HONORS/ACHIEVEMENTS:** Publ Rapid Colorimetric Determination of Formaldehyde in Toxoids, Jrnl of Amer Pharm Assoc 1951. **BUSINESS ADDRESS:** Chief of Physical Testing Div, Dept of Public Works, 480 Canal St, New York, NY 10013.

EASTMOND, JOAN MARCELLA
Educator. **PERSONAL:** Born May 10, 1940, Brooklyn, NY; daughter of Evans E Eastmond and Lerta Taylor-Eastmond; children: Brian S Malone. **EDUCATION:** West Virginia State Coll, Institute WV, BS Home Economics, 1963; Cornell Univ, Ithaca NY, summer instructor Afro Amer Studies, Certificate, 1969; Lincoln Univ, Lincoln Univ PA, Master of Human Services, 1988; Union of Experimental Colleges/Univ, Cincinnati OH, PhD, 1988. **CAREER:** New York City Bd of Educ, Brooklyn NY, teacher, 1963-70; State Educ Opportunity Center, Brooklyn NY, instructor; Afram Assoc, Harlem NY, asst to pres, 1971-78; Bedford Study Restoration Corp, Brooklyn NY, dir youth employment, 1978-85; Fort Green Sr Citizens Council, Brooklyn NY, dir youth workers, 1985-; Lincoln Univ, Lincoln Univ PA, adjunct prof, field study coord, 1988-. **ORGANIZATIONS:** Pres, Soc Unlimited, 1964-; chmn, Cotilion Found Comm, Natl Assn of Business Professional Women's Clubs, 1980-; mem, Fund Raising Comm, New York Council UNCF, 1980-84; chmn, Teens Found Comm, Jack & Jill of Amer, 1983-88; bd mem, Afram Assoc, 1987-, Health Watch, 1988-. **HONORS/ACHIEVEMENTS:** Crisco Award, Home Economic Dept WVSC, 1963; Trophy, Lil' Sisters Soc Unlimited, 1966; Essence Women, January 1971; Afrikan Liberation Day Bibliography (15pp), 1973; Devel Activities (12pp), 1973; Citation, Natl Council of Black Child Devel, 1974; Citation, Greater New York Council, Exploring Div, 1981; Certificate, 88 Princinct Council, 1987. **HOME ADDRESS:** 342 Macon St, Brooklyn, NY 11233.

EASTON, RICHARD JAMES
Business executive. **PERSONAL:** Born Jul 30, 1934, Chicago, IL; married Iris A Walker; children: Michael, Danitra, Richard Jr, Shawn, Ricarda, Erika. **EDUCATION:** Chicago State U, BS 1962. **CAREER:** Munic Credit Unoin of NYC, controller; NY State Spl Dep Controllers Ofc, chief analyst 1976-77; Recruitment & Training Prgm, dir 1970-75; Bedford & Stuyvesant Restoration Corp, mgr 1967-70; NYC, tchr 1963-67. **ORGANIZATIONS:** Mem Assn of Accountants; Nat Bus Tchrs Assn; mem Alpha Phi Alpha. **MILITARY SERVICE:** USN 1952-55. **BUSINESS ADDRESS:** 156 Williams St, New York, NY 10038.

EATMAN, BRENDA ALENE
Clergyperson in training. **PERSONAL:** Born Sep 17, 1957, Cleveland, OH. **EDUCATION:** Northwestern Univ Medill Sch of Journalism, BSJ 1979, MSJ 1980; Univ of Chicago Divinity School, MRS 1983. **CAREER:** Chicago Reporter, investigative political reporter 1978-80; Calmar Communications, public relations acct exec 1980-86; Chicago Magazine, rsch intern 1983; Medical Coll of Virginia Hospitals, chaplain resident 1986-87. **ORGANIZATIONS:** Mem Assoc for Clinical Pastoral Educ 1985-; student ministry intern Congregational Church of Park Manor 1986; In-Care for Ordination with Chicago Metr Assoc of the United Church of Christ 1986-88. **HONORS/ACHIEVEMENTS:** Benjamin E Mays Fellow for Ministry Princeton NJ 1984,85; Outstanding Young Woman of Amer 1985. **BUSINESS ADDRESS:** Chaplain, Medical Coll of VA Hospitals, MCV Station, Box 664, Richmond, VA 23298.

EATMAN, JANICE A.
Counselor, program facilitator. **PERSONAL:** Born Mar 03, 1959, Cleveland, OH. **EDUCATION:** Northwestern Univ, BS Communications 1981; Cleveland State Univ, Post Grad Work 1983-. **CAREER:** Welfare Rights Organization, community relations specialist 1984; Ohio Works, recruiter 1985; Vocational Guidance Servs, employment & training specialist 1985-88; Case Western Reserve Univ, Intervention Asst, 1987; HE Davis Intermediate School, coordinator of youth resource center, 1989-. **ORGANIZATIONS:** Mem Northwestern Alumni Assoc Cleveland Chapter 1981-; public relations consultant Group Dynamics Inc 1982-83; volunteer UNCF 1983-; mem Messengers of Joy Gospel Ensemble 1984-; planning comm Martin Luther King Jr Day Celebration 1984-85; mem Urban League of Greater Cleveland Fund Develop Comm 1984-85; grad advisor Alpha Kappa Alpha Sor Inc 1985-88 (2 terms); publicity co-chair Ways & Mean Comm AKA Program Years 1985, 1986; mem Northwestern Black Alumni Assoc 1986-; presenter, Carver Connection Adopt-A-School Program, 1987-88; presenter, Career Days Cleveland Public Schools, 1987-88. **HONORS/ACHIEVEMENTS:** Volunteer Serv Award HARAMBEE Serv to Black Families 1983; guest panelist Salute to Excellence Scholarship Program 1986; appointed by the headmaster to the Search Committee for the new Director of Upper School, Hawken School 1987; guest panelist, Minority Recruitment Forum, Hawken School, 1987; volunteer award, Cleveland Public Schools, Carver Connection Adopt-A-School, 1988; Workshop presenter, Pittsburgh Civic Garden Center, 1988. **BUSINESS ADDRESS:** On-Site Coordinator Youth Resource Center, Harry E Davis Intermediate School, 10700 Churchill Ave, Cleveland, OH 44106.

EATON, DAVID HILLIARD
Clergyman. **PERSONAL:** Born Dec 30, 1932, Washington, DC; married Dolores Pike; children: Claudia. **EDUCATION:** Howard Univ, BA; Boston Univ, M Sch of Theol 1959; Attended, Oxford Univ. **CAREER:** 2nd Unitarian Church, asst minister 1956-57; 1st Parish Church, Lincoln MA, asst minister, 1957-59; 1st Methodist Church, Pacoima, founder/pastor, 1959-60; Howard Univ, men's counsel, 1960-61, registrar 1961-63, methodist chaplin 1963-65; Opp Indus Ctr, exec dir 1965-68; Fed City Coll, assoc dean comm educ 1968, asst prof educ & dean student serv 1968-69; All Souls Unitarian Church, sr minister 1969-. **ORGANIZATIONS:** District of Columbia Bd of Educ at-large mem 1981-, chmn educ programs comm 1985-; bd of trustees, vice chair Metropolitan Washington YMCA; bd of trustees United Planning Org; mem, corp adv comm, Natl Assn for Equal Opportunity in Higher Educ; bd of dirs, Fair Housing Council; adv comm Independent Living for the Handicapped; bd of trustees Africare; chmn Project Area Comm Concerned Ministers; adv comm Howard Univ Sch of Religion; mem All Souls CHANGE Housing Corp Washington; bd of dirs DC Music Ctr, Columbia Heights Youth Club; hon advisory council FLOC; bd of dirs, Central Amer Refugee Center; hon adv council, New Arts Theatre; community advisory council, WETA TV 26. **HONORS/ACHIEVEMENTS:** YMCA Civic Award, 1969; Capital Press Club Award, Outstanding Comm Programming 1970; Natl Acad of TV Arts & Sci Emmy 1971; White House Conf of Children & Youth 1971; Citizen of Yr Natl Assn of Soc Workers 1977; co-founder, San Fernando Valley Fair Housing Conf; Man of the Yr Award, 1983 Shiloh Baptist Church Washington DC; Clarence R Skinner Award for Best Sermon on Social Issues "Racism Is Alive and Well" Unitarian Universalist Assn, 1986; Honorary Doctor of Sacred Theology degree Starr King Sch of Theology CA 1986. **MILITARY SERVICE:** AUS 1st lt 1954-56. **BUSINESS ADDRESS:** Minister, All Souls Unitarian Ch, 16th & Harvard Sts NW, Washington, DC 20009.

EATON, JAMES A.
Educator. **PERSONAL:** Born Dec 26, 1921, Portsmouth, VA; divorced; children: Christopher, Carl, Leeverest. **EDUCATION:** VA State Coll, AB 1943; Howard U, BD 1946; Boston U, MA 1952; Columbia U, EdD 1959. **CAREER:** Elizabeth City State Univ, prof 1959-63; Tuskegee Inst, acting chaplain 1955-56; War on Poverty Program Savannah, program dir 1965-67; Graduate Studies Savannah State Coll and Armstrong State Coll, assoc dean. **ORGANIZATIONS:** Mem Am AssnUniv Admistr; Am Assn Academic Deans; Am Personnel and Guidance Anns; Phi Delta Kappa Frat; Kappa Delta Pi; mem NAACP; Midway Congregational Ch; Chatham County Mental Health Assn; GA Interfaith Assn. **HONORS/ACHIEVEMENTS:** Outstanding Educator Am 1973, 74-75. **MILITARY SERVICE:** AUS capt 1951-55; AUS reserve maj 1955-65. **BUSINESS ADDRESS:** Savannah State Coll, Savannah, GA 31404.

EATON, JAMES NATHANIEL, SR.
Professor of history, director of black archives, research center & museum. **PERSONAL:** Born Sep 14, 1930, Richmond, VA; son of Rev John Jasper Eaton and Mrs Sarah Elizabeth Eaton; married Leathea Denesa Owen Eaton, Jul 29, 1985; children: Jacqueline Eaton-Thomas, Sabrina Elizabeth, James N Jr, Robert H, Samuel Kenyata. **EDUCATION:** Fisk Univ, Nashville TN, BA, 1952, MA, 1953; Duke Univ, Durham NC, 1962-63, 1964-66; Florida State Univ, Tallahassee FL, 1969-70. **CAREER:** Miles Coll, Birmingham AL, history instructor, 1953-55; Richmond Police Dept, Richmond VA, patrolman, 1956-57; Hanover School for Boys, Hanover VA, asst principal, 1957-58; Florida A&M Univ, Tallahassee FL, prof of history, 1958-; Black Archives, Tallahassee, FL, dir, 1975-. **ORGANIZATIONS:** Life mem, NAACP, Kappa Alpha Psi Frat; bd mem, Natl Historical Publications & Records Bd, 1978-81; fellow, Intl Initiative for Creative Communication, 1979-83; bd mem, Florida Museum Assn, 1984-; mem, African Amer Museums Assn, 1984-. **HONORS/ACHIEVEMENTS:** Danforth Scholar, Danforth Found, 1964-66; Certification in Archives Admin, American Univ, 1976; FSU/Rockerfeller Scholar, Florida State Univ, 1983; FAMU Centennial Medallion, Florida A&M Univ, 1988; James N Eaton Appreciation Day, 1988; cited in over 50 leading magazines and publications; published numerous articles; featured in "Take a Trip Through Black History," Tallahassee Democrat. **BUSINESS ADDRESS:** Director, Black Archives Research Center & Museum, Florida A&M University, Tallahassee, FL 32307.

EATON, LELA M. Z.
Educator. **PERSONAL:** Born Dec 30, 1946, Granville Co, NC. **EDUCATION:** Johnson C Smith U, AB 1968; Columbia U, MS 1971;Univ NC Tchr Kittrell Coll, PhD 1973. **CAREER:** "Daily Advance", columnist 1970-71; S Granville High School, teacher 1968-70; "W Harlem Spokesman", editor 1971. **ORGANIZATIONS:** Mem Nat Council Tchrs English; Assn Journalism; Granville Improvement & Assn; Nat Council Coll Newspaper Advisors; mem Belton Creek Bapt Ch. **HONORS/ACHIEVEMENTS:** English William Brewer Award 1968; fellowship Knight Newspaper Found 1971; alumni fellowUniv NC 1974-75; (cum laude) SmithUniv 1968. **BUSINESS ADDRESS:** Kittrell Coll, Kittrell, NC 27544.

EATON, MINETTA GAYLOR
Educator. **PERSONAL:** Born Oct 01, 1912, Whitakers, NC; married James W; children: Jeanne Phillips, Faye Yvonne. **EDUCATION:** Morgan State U, BA 1936; NY U, MA 1942; NYUniv Chicago U, additional study tour of Europe. **CAREER:** Raleigh City Schools NC, prin 1959-73, teacher 1944-59; Spaulding High School NC, teacher, librarian 1938-44; Brick School NC, teacher 1936-38. **ORGANIZATIONS:** State 2nd vice pres mem exec bd NC Adminstrv Women in Edn; mem NC Nat Council of Adminstrv Women in Edn; co-chairperson membership com State Dist & Raleigh-Wake Unit of NC Retired Personnel; mem NC Assn of Educators; Nat Educ Assn; Nat Elementary Prins Assn; bd dir Downtown Housing Improvement Corp 1974-77; bd dir Research Triangle Lung Assn; bd dir Wake Co Mental Health Assn; NC bd dir Mental Health Assn; adv council Inner City Statellite Mental Health Center; State Steering Com; chairperson com for state's 1975 fall forum NC Council of Women's Orgn Inc; mem Nat Council of Negro Women; Com ofAdminsrrn & Mgmt YWCA; Am Assn of Univ Women; Alpha Kappa Alpha Sorrity Inc; Women in Action for Prevention of Violence & Its Causes; Task Force of S Central Comm; RSVP Adv Council Bd 1975-77;

Wake Co Black Dem Cauces; NAACP; Raleigh-Wake Cit Assn; Dem Women of Wake Co; mem Alphabettes of Raleigh; Prestige Club; First Bapt Ch; Notable Ams of Era. **HONORS/ACHIEVEMENTS:** Appointed state co-chairperson of Women in Action for Prevention of Violence's State Chapter Meeting; appointed to Nat Publicity Com of Moles Inc; appointedTo Mid-Altantic Regional Nominating Com of Alpha Kappa Alpha Sorority; listed in Bicentennial Edition of Comm Leaders & Noteworthy Ams; several awards AlphaTheta Omega Chap of Alpha Kappa Alpha Sorority 1975f honored by Alpha Kappa Alpha Sorority Inc Ilpah Thega Omega Chpt; cert Nat Caucus of Black Aged Inc 1974-75; honored by Radio Station WPTF NC comm leader of am award 1969; listed in Outstanding Personalities of the S.

EATON, PATRICIA FRANCES
Foundation representative. **PERSONAL:** Born Jun 21, 1944, Washington, DC; children: David Howard. **EDUCATION:** Palmer Mem Inst, Coll Prep, 1959-62; TX Southern Univ, BA Engl 1967; Univ of CA San Diego, African Studies 1967. **CAREER:** Lesotho Southern Africa, Peace Corps Vol 1967-70; DC Public Schools, teacher 1970-71; DC Dept Human Res, comm relations officer 1971-74; Africare Inc, Comm dir 1974-77; Black Women's Comm Devel Fund, exec dir 1977-79; Overseas Educ Fund, dir for Africa 1979-80; US Peace Corps & USAID Africa, consult 1980-84; African Devel Found, fnd rep. **ORGANIZATIONS:** Mem bd dir DC Clothing for Kids Inc 1972-, 2nd Genesis Drug Rehab 1980-; life mem Africare 1980-. **HOME ADDRESS:** 4418.Eastern Ave NW, Washington, DC 20018. **BUSINESS ADDRESS:** Foundation Representative, African Dev Fnd, 1724 Massachusetts Ave NW, Ste 200, Washington, DC 20036.

EATON, THELMA LUCILE
Educator. **PERSONAL:** Born Dec 17, 1928, New Orleans, LA; married William; children: Maurice, Allison. **EDUCATION:** Fisk U, BA 1949; Xavier U, 1950-51; NY U, 1952;Univ of Sthrn CA, MSW 1965;Univ of Sthrn CA, DSW 1973. **CAREER:** Whittier Coll, assoc prof 1969-; USC Mini-CollUniv of Sthrn CA, admin off soc wk prog; Dept of Social Serv, staff dev offcr and training & supvis; Suicide Prevent Center, psychiat soc worker; Orleans Parish Sch Bd, tchr nursery sch and elem sch. **ORGANIZATIONS:** Amer Assn ofUniv Prof; State Leason Comm on Human Serv; Natl Assn of Soc Work; Geront Soc; Soc for the Stud of Social Prob; Counc on Social Work Edn; Natl Counc of Negro Women; advis bd Rio Hondo United Way; USC Geront Center Serv to Black Aged; Natl Caucus of Black Aged; Grtr LA Commun ActionAgency; bd of dir YWCA; Foster Grdparent Prog; Retired Sr Vol Prog; Rio Hondo Vol Center; pres Awar Women of CA; mem CA Demo State Central Comm LA Co Central Comm; Alpha Kappa Delta; CA State Commiss. **HONORS/ACHIEVEMENTS:** Outstanding Edutr of Amer 1974; Notable Am Award 1976-77; apptd Success to the Ltd Govr of CA; recip Key to Whittier Coll 1976. **BUSINESS ADDRESS:** Whittier Coll, Whittier, CA 90019.

EATON, TYRONE
Advertising executive. **PERSONAL:** Born Feb 22, 1943, New York, NY; married Rhonda Wrenn; children: Tyrone Jr, Felicia, Andre, Mark, Joi, Stevie. **EDUCATION:** Brooklyn Comm Coll, AS 1965; State Univ of NY, BS 1979. **CAREER:** NY City Off-Track Betting Corp, mktg specialist 1973-80; Warner Amex Cable Comm Co, mktg/sales supr 1980-82; Eaton & Wrenn Mktg Co, pres 1986-; Eaton & Assoc Mktg Comm Inc, pres/ceo 1982-. **ORGANIZATIONS:** Ordained minister Missionary Bapt Assoc NY 1979; pastor White Plains Missionary Bapt Church 1979-80; pastor First Bapt Church of Mt Auburn 1983-85; mem Amer Mktg Assoc 1986, World African Chamber of Commerce 1987, Master Mason Prince Hall. **HONORS/ACHIEVEMENTS:** Business Writer Dayton Defender Newspaper 1986. **HOME ADDRESS:** 1572 Earlham Dr, Dayton, OH 45406.

EAVES, A. REGINALD
Commission vice chairman. **PERSONAL:** Born Mar 29, 1935, Jacksonville, FL. **EDUCATION:** Morehouse Coll, BA 1956; New England Law School, LLB 1966, JD 1970; Boston Univ, attended. **CAREER:** City Boston School, guidance couns, teacher; Roxbury Youth Train & Emp Ctr, exec dir 1963-66; So End Neighborhood Action Prog Inc, exec dir 1966-69;Mayors Office of Human Rights Boston, admin 1969-72; Penal Inst Suffolk Cty & Boston, commiss 1972-74; Boston Univ School of Med, lecturer 1973-74; Commonweath MA, admin asst sent pres; Atlanta Univ, exec asst mayor 1974-; Dept of Publ Safety, commissioner 1974-78; Morehouse Sch of Medicine, lecturer 1983-; Fulton County Govt, commissioner 1979-. **ORGANIZATIONS:** Trustee, bd mem Fulton Cty Bd Health, Natl Assoc Urban Crim Justice Plnng Dir, Amer Dem Action, Advent School, Natl Young Men & Womens Devel Corp, New Breed Teachers, Assoc for Protection Span Spkng; life mem NAACP, Anti-Defamation League; life mem NAACP; mem Natl Org of Black Law Enforcement Execs, NOBLE, IACP, SCLC, Operation PUSH; trustee Fulton County Library; chmn Economic Oppor of Atlanta; chmn GA Assoc of Black Elected Officials; vice pres Natl Assoc of Black County Officials. **HONORS/ACHIEVEMENTS:** One of Ten Outstanding Young Men of Boston 1970; Outstanding Young Men of Amer 1970; Citation of Merit Graham Jr Coll 1971; Wall St Jrnl Stud AchievementAwd 1956; "Y's" Men Young Man of of the Year Awd 1974; over 350 awards and certificates. **MILITARY SERVICE:** AUS E-4 1957-59. **BUSINESS ADDRESS:** Commissioner, Dept of Public Safety, 165 Central Ave SW, Room 208, Atlanta, GA 30303.

EBERHARDT, CLIFFORD
Educational administrator. **PERSONAL:** Born Sep 19, 1947, Chattanooga, TN; married Tanya; children: Kenya. **EDUCATION:** TN State Univ, BS Pol Sci 1980, MPA 1982. **CAREER:** Luvphonse Corp, dir 1979-82; Neighborhood Housing Serv, rsch consultant 1980; Nashville Urban League, statistician 1981; Pensacola Voice Newspaper, columnist 1983-; Pensacola Jr Coll, asst dept head 1982-. **ORGANIZATIONS:** Consultant Southeastern Educ Assistance Ctr; mem State Adv Comm; mem Amer Soc for Public Administrators; mem FL Adult Educ Assn 1985; co-researcher on a Grant for the Southern Educ Found on Black Leadership in Nashville; conducted a prog evaluation of the Foster Care Review Bd of Davidson Co Juvenile Court TN. **HONORS/ACHIEVEMENTS:** Rsch Fellowship Housing Urban Development 1981; co-researcher Southern Educ Found 1981; Top Graduate in graduating class of 1982. **BUSINESS ADDRESS:** Acting Dean of Continuing Educ, Pensacola Junior College, 1000 College Blvd, Pensacola, FL 32504.

EBO, ANTONA
Religious councilor. **PERSONAL:** Born Apr 10, 1924, Bloomington, IL; daughter of Daniel Ebo (deceased) and Louise Teal Ebo (deceased). **EDUCATION:** St Louis Univ, St Louis MO, BS Medical Records Admin, 1962, MHA Hospital Exec Devel, 1970; Aquinas Inst of Theology, Dubuque IA; MTh Health Care Ministry, 1978. **CAREER:** St Claire Hospital, Baraboo WI, exec dir, 1967-71; St Marys Hospital Medical Center, Madison WI, asst exec dir, 1970-74; Catholic Health Assn, Madison WI, exec dir, 1974-76; St Marys Hospital Medical Center, Madison WI, chaplain, 1978-81; Univ of Mississippi Medical Center, Jackson MS, chaplain, 1981-87; Franciscan Sisters of Mary, St Louis MO, councilor, 1987-. **ORGANIZATIONS:** Mem, first group of sisters participating in "March on Selma"-St Louis Archdiocese, 1965, St Louis Archdiocesan Human Rights Comm, 1965-67; mem, pres, bd of dir, Natl Black Sisters' Conf, 1968-; mem, vice chairperson, Madison Urban League Bd of Dirs, 1972-76, Madison Housing Authority Commr, 1974-76; vice chairperson, Wisconsin Health Facilities Authority, 1976; mem, Natl Assn of Catholic Chaplains, 1979-, Comm on Catholic Health Care Ministry, 1987-88, Leasership Conf of Women Religious, 1987-, SSM Health Care System Bd of Dirs, 1987-, Leadership Conf of Women Religious Task Force on Women's Concerns, 1989-. **HONORS/ACHIEVEMENTS:** Featured in Catfish & Crystal, Doubleday, Garden City NY, Ernest Kirschten, 1965; Ebony Magazine, "Speaking of People," 1967; Liguori Magazine, "Negro Nun," 1969; Certificate of Commendation, Madison Urban League, Madison WI, 1976; Certificate of Commendation, Governor Patrick Lucey, Wisconsin Health Facilities Authority, 1976; Elected Delegate, Jackson MS Archdiocese, Natl Black Catholic Congress, 1987; Pioneer Healers, Health Care, Stepsis & Liptak, 1989. **BUSINESS ADDRESS:** Councilor, Franciscan Sisters of Mary, 1100 Bellevue Ave, St Louis, MO 63117.

ECCLES, PETER WILSON
Business executive. **PERSONAL:** Born Jan 31, 1936, Lawrence Long Island, NY; son of Wilson Eccles and Mable Eccles; married Achla Chib; children: Peter Rahul, Radika Elisabeth. **EDUCATION:** Dartmouth, BA magna cum laude 1958; Univ of Cambridge, Trinity Hall, Eng, fulbright 1959; Harvard Law Sch, JD cum laude 1963. **CAREER:** World Bank, atty 1963-65; Cleary Gottlieb Steen & Hamilton Law Firm, assoc 1965-69; Goldman Sachs & Co, vice pres 1969-74; Ultrafin Internat, vp, mgr corp fin 1974-77; Citibank, vice pres, dir, 1977-86; Prudential Bache Capital Funding, dir, investment banking, 1987-. **ORGANIZATIONS:** Bd of dir Citizens Com for Children 1967-74; mem exec com, trustees Found for Child Devel 1973-77; mem Econ Club of NY 1979-; charter mem Exec Leadership Council 1986-; mem bd of visitors Rockefeller Center of Social Sci at Dartmouth 1986-. **HONORS/ACHIEVEMENTS:** Phi Beta Kappa, Dartmouth Coll 1958; Fulbright Scholar, Cambridge Univ, England, 1959; various publs 1959-79. **BUSINESS ADDRESS:** Dir, Prudential Bache Capital Funding, 199 Water St, 19th Fl, New York, NY 10292.

ECHOLS, ALVIN E.
Attorney. **PERSONAL:** Born Dec 05, 1930, Philadelphia; married Gwendolyn G; children: Donna, Alison. **EDUCATION:** VA Unoin U, BS 1955; Howard U, LLB 1957. **CAREER:** North City Congress, exec dir 1963-; Priv Law Prac, 1957-63. **ORGANIZATIONS:** Commr Hum Rel Comm 1969-; mem PA chap of Nat Council on Crime & Delinquency 1971-75; Health & Welfare Council 1974-; mem Friends of Free Library 1972-75; Comm Ldrshp Seminar Program 1962-. **HONORS/ACHIEVEMENTS:** Distinguished merit citation Nat Conf of Christiand & Jews 1967; achievement award Industrialization Cntr 1966; ceretificat of appreciation Personnel Dept Philadelphia Med Coll PA 1972-; Grtr Philadelphia Partnership 1974-. **BUSINESS ADDRESS:** 1428 N Broad St, Philadelphia, PA 19121.

ECHOLS, CLARENCE LEROY, JR.
Personnel administration. **PERSONAL:** Born Aug 04, 1947, Chicago, IL; married Frances E Dougan; children: Andrea, Roger, Juanita, Jason. **EDUCATION:** Knox Coll, BA Biol 1965-69; Chicago State Univ, Grad Work 1971-74. **CAREER:** Proviso East HS, sci teacher 1969-75; Lockport East HS, sci teacher 1975-77; Curtiss Candy Co, personnel suprv 1977-80; Durkee Foods, suprv personnel& safety 1980-. **ORGANIZATIONS:** Mem IL & Amer Fed of Teachers 1970-77, Natl Assoc of School Bds 1978-, IL School Bd Assoc 1978-; vice pres 1985-, mem bd of ed Valley View School Dist #365U 1978-; commiss Bolingbrook Police & Fire Commiss 1981-84; mem Alpha Phi Alpha. **HONORS/ACHIEVEMENTS:** Outstanding Young Man Bolingbrook Chap Jaycees 1981. **BUSINESS ADDRESS:** Supervisor Personnel & Safety, Durkee Foods Div SCM, BO Vox 796, Joliet, IL 60434.

ECHOLS, DAVID LORIMER
Government official. **PERSONAL:** Born Oct 30, 1937, Buffalo, NY; married Eleanor Poole; children: Byron, Brent, Tanya, Robert. **EDUCATION:** Attended, Inst for Man & Sci; Univ of Buffalo, BA Polit Sci; Gibralter Inst, cert mgmt productivity; Canisius Coll, sr mgmt. **CAREER:** NY State Civil Service Comm US Post Office, consult 1956-69; City of Buffalo, component mgr model cities agency 1971-72, asst dir model cities agency 1972-73, dir demonstration proj 1973-75, coord state & fed aide 1975-78, commr human resources 1978-84, exec dir Buffalo municipal housing auth 1984-. **ORGANIZATIONS:** Sec United Way of Buffalo & Erie Co 1983-84; chmn Youth Com State Employment & Training Co 1979-; chmn Mayor's Complete Count Com 1980 Census; bd mem Ctr City Restoration Corp Buffalo 1979-; bd mem Council of Ch Buffalo 1980-; bd mem YMCA of Buffalo & Erie Co; mem Alpha Phi Alpha Frat Rho Lambda Chapt. **HONORS/ACHIEVEMENTS:** Citizen Participation Structure Awd Model cities Agency 1972; Awd for Outstanding Serv Spanish Speaking Comm 1973; Awd for Service to Youth YMCA of Buffalo & Erie Co 1976-78; Awd for Serv to the Comm United Way of Buffalo & Erie Co 1980; Pres Recognition Awd for Comm Serv 1984; Outstanding NCO-Oper Swift Strike III USAF 1963. **BUSINESS ADDRESS:** Executive Dir, Buffalo Municipal Housing Auth, 1701 City Hall, Buffalo, NY 14202.

ECHOLS, IVOR TATUM
Educator. **PERSONAL:** Born Dec 28, 1919, Oklahoma City, OK; daughter of Israel E Tatum and Katie Bingley Tatum; married Sylvester J Echols; children: Kalu Wilcox, Kim A. **EDUCATION:** Univ of KS, AB 1942; Univ of NE, One Year Grad 1945; Columbia Univ, MSSW 1952; Univ of Southern CA, DSW 1968. **CAREER:** Amer Red Cross Chicago, caseworker 1945-46; Neighborhood Clubs Okla City, exec dir 1949-51; Merrill Palmer Inst, faculty 1951-70; Univ of CT, asst dean & prof 1970-. **ORGANIZATIONS:** Teacher Public Schools Geary OK 1943-45, Holderville OK 1942-43; consult Public Schls Columbus OH 1964-66; Scott Paper Co Chester PA; natl chair minority affairs Natl Assn Soc Wrks 1977-79; secr and bd United Neighborhood Ctrs of Amer 1974-; past pres and bd Hartford Neighborhood Ctrs 1976; Ct Natual Gas Fnd Hartford CT 1984-85; CT State Historical Commission 1984-86, 1987-. **HONORS/ACHIEVEMENTS:** Sojourner Truth Award Natl Business and Prof Women 1969; Fellowships NIMH 1961, Natl Urban League 1951, Amer Red Cross; Soc Worker of Year CT 1978; publ Paper Journal of Amer Dietetics 1970; civic Achievement Ebonics Award USC 1984; CT Exhibit - Black Women of CT-State Humanities

Council; Outstanding Women of Decade United Nations Assn CT, 1987; Citation, Mayor Perry-City of Hartford, 1989; Woman of Year, CT Coalition of 100 Black Women 1989. **HOME ADDRESS:** 51 Chestnut Dr, Windsor, CT 06095. **BUSINESS ADDRESS:** Assistant Dean and Professor, Univ of CT, 1800 Asylum Ave, Hartford Campus West, Hartford, CT 06117.

ECHOLS, JAMES ALBERT
Public relations consultant, marketing. **PERSONAL:** Born Sep 14, 1950, Memphis, TN; son of Joseph Echols, Jr and Vellar C McCraven Echols; married Dorothy Mae Mithcell, Jun 08, 1978; children: Justin Fitzgerald Echols. **EDUCATION:** Central State Univ Edmond OK, BA, 1981. **CAREER:** Office of the Governor, state affirmative action office 1979-; Nigh for gov Campaign, adminstarn asst minority affairs 1978; Reserve Life Insurance Co, ins agt 1977-78; AUS, sr race relations instr 1976-77; E & C Trades LTD, pres & chmn of bd 1980; Honor Enterprises Inc, chairman of the board; US Army Reserve, career counselor, 1986-. **ORGANIZATIONS:** Mem Urban League of OK City 1977; mem NAACP 1978; vice pres OK Human Relations Assn 1978; mem, Veterans of Foreign Wars; mem, Economic Development Task Force, OK City Urban League. **HONORS/ACHIEVEMENTS:** Commendation medal Bronze Star AUS 1971; vietnamese gallantary cross Rep of Vietman 1972; 2nd AUS commendations (oakleaf cluster) AUS 1977; mem for excellent scholarship Phi Eta Sigma 1978; US Army Recruiting & Retention Non-Commissioned Officers Advanced Course, 1989. **MILITARY SERVICE:** US Army, sgt 1st class, 1969-. **BUSINESS ADDRESS:** Chairman of the Board of Directors, Honor Enterprises Inc, 2405 NW 39th Expressway, Suite 200-C, Oklahoma City, OK 73112.

ECKSTINE, BILLY See ECKSTINE, WILLIAM CLARENCE

ECKSTINE, WILLIAM CLARENCE (BILLY ECKSTINE)
Singer. **PERSONAL:** Born Jul 08, 1914, Pittsburgh, PA. **EDUCATION:** Attended, Howard Univ. **CAREER:** Night club singer & emcee in Buffalo, Detroit, Chicago at Club de Lisa; vocalist Earl Hines Band 1939; night club soloist 1943; organized Bop Music Band w/ Budd Johnson 1944; trombone player orch leader-ballad singer of popular mus 1948-; appearance include Mill Run Theatre Niles IL 1973; recorded w/band under Natl Records; recs include "Everything I Have Is Yours", "Prisoner of Love", "I Apologize", "My Way", "Jelly Jelly", "For the Love of Ivy", "The Best Thing", "If SheWalked Into My Life", "The Soul Sessions" vol 6 in NY 1972; presently rec w/Enterprise Records; appeared Desert Inn, Birdland, Caesar's Palace, Maisonette; TV "Sanford & Son", "Saturday Night Live", performed at Woldtrap 1976. **HONORS/ACHIEVEMENTS:** Esquire New Star Awd 1946; Down Beat Poll Winner 1948-52; Metronome Poll Winner 1949-54; voted #1 Crooner 1950.

ECTON, VIRGIL E.
National campaign director. **PERSONAL:** Born Jul 07, 1940, Paris, KY; married Harriette Morgan-Ecton; children: Brian Keith. **EDUCATION:** IN U, BS 1962; Xavier U, MEd 1966; Professional Institute of the American Management Assoc, 1974-75, 1976-77, 1981-82. **CAREER:** United Negro Coll Fund Inc, natl campaign dir; OH Civil Rights Comm, asst dir 1969-70; Scioto Village HS, asst princ 1968-69; Juvenile Diagnostic Cntr, asst princ 1966-69; Cincinnati Bd Edn, tchr 1963-66; UNCF, Eastern Reg Supv 1975; Depty Natl Campaign Dir 1976; Natl Campaign Dir 1977;Deputy Execu Dir 1979; Curr Execu Vice Pres & Chief Operating off United Negro Coll Fund- Oct 1982. **ORGANIZATIONS:** Bd dir Trade Pasport Corp 1972-; adv council OH Civil Rights Comm 1970-; allocations panel United Torch 1974; Cit League; Candidates Com 1973-; Youth Motivation Task Force 1972-; finance com OH Episcopal Diocese 1973-; mem Episcopal Ch 1973-; Cleveland Growth Assn 1970; Xavier Alumni Assn 1966-; Kappa Alpha Psi Frat 1960-; Urban League; NAACP;mem; Natl Society of Fund Raising Executives; certification brd; brd of directors; execu comm;advisory brd, urban league of New York, SIgma Pi Phi, Emmanual Episcopal Church; NY Chamber of Comm and Industry Execu Brd & Steering Commitee, Natl Philanthrop Day. **HONORS/ACHIEVEMENTS:** Outstanding Young Men Am 1973; merit serv award Nat Alliance Businessmen 1973; Who's Who Among Black Americans 1974-75; Natl Alliance of Bus Men-Merit ServAwd 1972-74; Blacks in Mgmt Comm Serv Awd 1975; Natl Tech Assoc Serv Awd 1974; UNCF Leadership Awrd 1978. **BUSINESS ADDRESS:** Executive Vice Pres & COO, United Negro College Fund, Inc, 500 E 62nd St, New York, NY 10021.

EDDINGS, CYNTHIA
Communications manager. **PERSONAL:** Born in Seattle, WA. **EDUCATION:** Sorbonne Paris France, French language 1973; CA State Univ at San Jose, BA 1974. **CAREER:** Essence Mag, assoc editor 1976-77; Fairchild Publications, reporter 1977-79; CBS News, researcher for documentaries including 60 Minutes 1979-82, business & economic news researcher evening news 1982-83; American Express Co, producer/host corporate video programs. **HONORS/ACHIEVEMENTS:** College grant Amer Newspaper Publisher Assoc 1972-73. **BUSINESS ADDRESS:** Communications Manager, American Express Co, Employee Communications, 125 Broad St 19th Fl, New York, NY 10004.

EDDINGTON, HERBERT HOOVER
Doctor of chiropractic. **PERSONAL:** Born Oct 25, 1929, Warren, OH; married Norma Woods; children: Susan, Herb Kenton F. **EDUCATION:** Wichita U, 1949-52; KS State Chiropractic Coll, 1953-57. **CAREER:** David C Treen, mem of congress; Boeing Co, toowl & prodn planner; Bell Aerospace Co, personnel rep. **ORGANIZATIONS:** Mem Chropractic Assn of LA; bd mem Amalgamated Builder & Contractor of LA 1977; Kappa Alpha Psi Frat; NAACP; past vice pres CROWN; vice pres Gentilly EDevel Anns; chmn Minority Div Rep Party of LA. **HONORS/ACHIEVEMENTS:** State cen commiteeman Rep Pary of LA; attneded 1972 & 1976 natl conv. **MILITARY SERVICE:** AUS sgt 1950-52. **BUSINESS ADDRESS:** 2001 Canal St, New Orleans, LA 70112.

EDDLEMAN, WILLIAM THOMAS
Retired clergyman. **PERSONAL:** Born Jan 01, 1900, Salisbury, NC; son of William J Eddleman and Emma Ingram Eddleman; married Lela Young, Nov 05, 1929; children: Loretta E Gordon, Myrtress G. **EDUCATION:** Emmanuel Lutheran Coll, BD 1925; Temple Univ, Graduate Study 1929. **CAREER:** Birmingham City Jail, minister to inmates 1948-53; Birmingham Ministerial Assn, mem 1970-; Lutheran Ministers' Assn, counselor circuit 9 1965-67; Mo Synod Pilgrim Luther, minister Lutheran Church 1925-71; Pilgrim Lutheran Church, retired Lutheran minister Mo Synod. **HONORS/ACHIEVEMENTS:** Honorary degree Payne Coll Birmingham AL 1968. **HOME ADDRESS:** 6304 South 3rd Ct, Birmingham, AL 35212.

EDDY, EDWARD A.
Educator. **PERSONAL:** Born Feb 27, 1938, Kansas City, KS; married Joyce B Carter; children: Darrell, Duane, Aaron. **EDUCATION:** Pittsburg State Univ, BS 1962; Univ of KS, MA 1966; KS State Univ, PhD 1981. **CAREER:** Pub Schls KCK, instr 1962-69; Univ of KS, instr 1969-73; Rockhurst, dir spec prog 1973-77; Rockhurst Clge, dean 1977-84; Chicago State Univ, dean; Chevy Chase Nursing Ctr, administrator. **ORGANIZATIONS:** OE regl steering comm TRIO Prog 1973-75; field reader OE Title III Proposals 1982-83; consult educ MLK Jr Hosp KCMO 1975-77; AACD mem Amer Assc Cnslng Dir 1985; natl youth conv staff Church of God 1985; guest soloist Oper PUSH Chicago 1985; mem Higher Educ Commn COG 1986-88. **HONORS/ACHIEVEMENTS:** Key to City Kansas City KS 1984; Who's Who Among Kansans; fnd dir Black Ethos Performing Arts Troupe 1971. **BUSINESS ADDRESS:** Administrator, Chevy Chase Nursing Ctr, 3400 So Indiana, Chicago, IL 60616.

EDELIN, KENNETH C.
Physician. **PERSONAL:** Born Mar 31, 1939, Washington, DC; married Barbara; children: Kenneth Edelin Jr, Kimberley, Corinne, Joseph. **EDUCATION:** Columbia U, BA 1961; Meharry Med Coll, MD 1967; Boston City Hosp, residency ob/gyn 1971-74, chief resident 1973. **CAREER:** Obs/Gyn BostonUniv Sch of Med, chmn, prof ob/gyn 1979-, gyn-in-chief 1979-, dir ob/gyn 1979-, assoc prof 1974-, assist prof oby/Gyn 1976; Boston City Hosp, chf resid ob/gyn 1973-74; Ambulatory Care Boston City Hosp, coord 1974-, instructr ob-gyn 1974-, assoc dir ob-gyn 1974-. **ORGANIZATIONS:** Mem bd of trustees Fuller Metnal Health Center; mem bd of trustees Planned Parenthood Leago of MA; mem bd of trustees NARAL; physic advis Planned Parenthood Leag of Amer; proj dir Boston Sickle Cell Center; mem Amer Assn of Gynecol Laparoscopists; sponsor MA Civ Lib Union; chmn New England Comm NAACP Legal Defense Fund; bd dir NAACP, LDF Inc; pres bd Roxbury Comprehensive Comm Health Center Inc. **HONORS/ACHIEVEMENTS:** Dean's List Meharry Med Coll 1963-67; ColumbiaUniv 1960-61. **MILITARY SERVICE:** USAF capt 1968-71; Commendation Medal USAF 1971; Commendation Medal Army 1971. **BUSINESS ADDRESS:** Chairman, Professor, BostonUniv, 720 Harrison, Dept Ob/Gyn, School of Medicine, Boston, MA 02118.

EDELIN, KENTON TERRELL
Professional athlete. **PERSONAL:** Born May 24, 1962, Alexandria, VA. **EDUCATION:** Virginia. **CAREER:** Indiana Pacers, forward 1984-. **HONORS/ACHIEVEMENTS:** Named CBS Player of the Game in VA 53-51 overtime win over AR March 18th scoring 8 points. **BUSINESS ADDRESS:** Indiana Pacers, 300 E Market St Market Sq Arena, Indianapolis, IN 46204.

EDELIN, RAMONA HOAGE
Business executive. **EDUCATION:** Attended Harvard Univ, 1966; Fisk Univ, BA (Magna Cum Laude), 1967; Univ of East Anglia, Norwich, England, MA, 1969; Boston Univ, PhD. **CAREER:** Univ of Maryland, European Div, lecturer in logic, 1970-71; Northeastern Univ, Boston, MA, acting chairperson of Afro-Amer Studies Prog, asst to dean of students, 1972-74, chairperson of Afro-Amer Studies, beginning in 1974; Emerson Coll, instructor in philosophy, 1974-75; Brandeis Univ, visiting prof of Afro-Amer Studies, 1974-75; Natl Urban Coaliton, Washington, DC, exec asst to pres, 1977-79, dir of operations, 1979-81, vice pres of operations, 1981-82, vice pres of prog and policy, beginning in 1982, became chief exec officer. **ORGANIZATIONS:** Mem, DC Humanities Council; bd of dir, Boston Black Repertory Co, The Bridge Inc, 1st World Foundation, Assoc for Better Living, WINNERS Inc; bd of elders, African Heritage Inst; chairperson, comm on goals, Boston Fisk Univ Alumnae Club, Delta Sigma Theta; breakfast comm, Martin Luther King Jr; adv comm, Mattapan Serv Proj; mem, Women in Politics, Amer Philosophical Assoc; comm on blacks, Amer Philosophical Assoc; co-founder, Boston Area Black Studies Consortium; mem, Center for African and African-Amer Studies, Atlanta Univ; mem comm, Afro-Amer Studies Faculty; chairperson, Comm to Review the Campus Police; comm W of the AAUP; chairperson, Liberal Arts Dept; search comm, Chief Acad Officer of Northeastern Univ; adv comm, Black Recruitment; appointee, Blue Ribbon Comm; consult, Affirm Action, Northeastern Univ, Engl Dept Remedial Courses and Afro-Amer Emphasis Courses Northeastern Univ, Freedom House Inst on Schools & Educ, Human Serv Major Northeastern Univ, Newport Rhode Island Pub School System Teacher Training Prog in Black Studies, Wellesley Center for Rsch on Women. **HONORS/ACHIEVEMENTS:** Sarah McKim Maloney Award, 1964; Gold Key Honor Soc, 1965; Outstanding Young Women of Amer, 1975; Roxbury Action Prog Distinguished Service Award, 1975; Phi Beta Kappa, 1967; listed in Who's Who Among Students in Amer Univ and Coll, 1966; "Women to Watch," Ebony magazine, 1982; 1986 YWCA Academy of Women Achievers, 1987; named one of the 100 Most Influential Black Americans; author of numerous publications, including Revolutionary Aspects of Acquiring Skills, Atlanta Univ, Role of the African Woman Since Slavery, Culture Bearer, 1975, Women at Work, 1978; appeared on television and radio stations, including WGBH-TV, WSBK-TV, WBZ-TV, WRKO Radio, WILD Radio. **BUSINESS ADDRESS:** National Urban Coalition, 1120 "G" St NW, suite 900, Washington, DC 20005. *

EDELMAN, MARIAN WRIGHT
Association executive. **PERSONAL:** Born Jun 06, 1939, Bennettsville, SC; daughter of Arthur N Wright and Maggie L Wright; married Peter Benjamin; children: Joshua Robert, Jonah Martin, Ezra Benjamin. **EDUCATION:** Spelman Coll, BA 1960; Yale Law School, LLB 1963; Univ of Geneva Switzerland 1958-59. **CAREER:** NAACP Legal Defense & Educ Fund, staff atty 1963-64, dir 1964-68; Washington Rsch Project of Southern Center for Public Policy, partner; Center for Law & Educ Harvard Univ, dir 1971-73; Children's Defense Fund, pres 1973-. **ORGANIZATIONS:** Mem DC, MS, Commonwealth of MA, BA Assocs; mem bd of trustees Martin Luther King Memorial Center; mem adv council M L King Memorial Library; mem Council M Foreign Relations; mem Aetna Life & Casualty Found; mem Yale Univ Corp; chair, bd of trustees Spelman Coll; mem bd of dir March of Dimes. **HONORS/ACHIEVEMENTS:** Merrill Scholarship, Univ of Paris & Geneva 1958-59; John Hay Whitney Fellow, Yale Law School 1960-61; Mademoiselle Magazine Award 1 of 4 Most Exciting Young Women of Amer 1965; Honorary Fellow, Univ of PA Law School 1969; Louise Waterman Wise Award 1970; Black Enterprise Professional of the Year Award 1980; Hon MA Yale Univ; Hon LLD Smith Coll; Lesley Coll; Lowell Tech Inst; Univ of Bo Maine; Wiliams Coll; Colby Coll; Coll of New Rochelle; Sworthmore Coll; SUNY; Leadership Award, Natl Women's Political Caucus 1980; Black Womens Forum Award 1980; Medal Columbia Teachers Coll 1984, Bernard Coll; Eliot Award, Amer Public Health Assoc; Hubert Hum-

phrey Civil Rights Award, Leadership Council on Civil Rights; John W Gardner Leadership Award of Ind Sector; Public Service Achievement Award Common Cause, MacArthur prize fellow 1985; A Philip Randolph Award, Natl Urban Coalition 1987; The William P Dawson Award, Congressional Black Caucus 1987; "Families in Peril": An Agenda for Social Change, Harvard University Press 1987. **BUSINESS ADDRESS:** Dir, Childrens Defense Fund, 122 C St, NW, Washington, DC 20001.

EDGAR, JACQUELINE L.
Automobile dealer. **PERSONAL:** Born Nov 27, 1948, Lafayette, LA; daughter of Anthony LeBlanc and Effie Mathews LeBlanc; married Allen Luke Edgar, Apr 20, 1968 (divorced); children: Rachael Marie, Allen Jr. **EDUCATION:** Christian Univ, General Motors Automotive Management, Dallas TX, 1980. **CAREER:** J P Thibodeaux Inc, New Iberia LA, sales, 1977-81; Broussard Pontiac-Buick-GMC, Abbeville LA, sales, 1981-83; Edgar Chevrolet Inc, Jeanerette LA, presd, 1983-86; Edgar Ford Inc, Breaux Bridge LA, pres 1989-. **HONORS/ACHIEVEMENTS:** Regional Minority Business Firm of the Year Award, 1985; Automotive Excellence for Essence Communication, 1988.

EDGERSON, BOOKER
Business executive. **PERSONAL:** Born Jul 05, 1939, Baxter, AR; married Patricia Denson; children: Cory, Vicki. **EDUCATION:** Wstrn IL U, 1962. **CAREER:** Erie Comm Coll, dir of affirm actn tchr comm rels; NY Tele, sprts cons; Denver Bronco, scout plyr; NBC TV, SPOTER; Buffalo Bills, plyr; All Rookie Team, 1962; All Pro, 1968-69. **ORGANIZATIONS:** N Flmr Bus; BSA; Ltl Leag; Ftbl Leag; Bsbl Leag; YMCA; Jewish Cntr. **MILITARY SERVICE:** NG pvt 1962-66.

EDGERTON, ART JOSEPH
Administrator. **PERSONAL:** Born Jan 27, 1928, Philadelphia, PA; married Della W; children: Edward. **EDUCATION:** St Joseph Coll, BS 1950; Frodham Coll, MS 1952. **CAREER:** Univ of Toledo, asst dir for affirmative action/human resources devel 1969-; Community Affairs, produced prog 1968-75, field representative bd of comm relat 1968-69; WTOL-TV, night newsman, editor 1965-68; WTTOL Radio, music dir, disc jockey, announcer 1958-65; Goodwill Inudst, public relations 1956-57. **ORGANIZATIONS:** Consult WCWA Radio 1973-; consult WGTE-FM Pub Radio 1976-; Radio & TV News Dir Assn 1966-; pres comm on Employment of the Handicapped; bd mem Toledo Chap Am Red Cross; Yth Adv Com oth the Toledo Bd of Comm Realat; bd mem Goodwill Indust; chmn Radio Reading Serv Com Blind & Physically Handicapped Am Fed of Musicians; state pres OH Citizen's Com for Spcl Educ 1971; served on gov com Employmetn of the Handicapped; mem Com to Implement the Devel Disabilties Service & Facilities Construction Act of 1970, 1971-74; exec mem Economic Opprty Planning Assn of Grtr Toledo Inc; mem Manpower Com; served Pub Relations Educ & Del Agency Com; mem Educ Com of the OH Civil Rights Commn; bd mem Bd of Comm Relations; mem Educ Com; mem Sigma Delta Chi; former bd mem Toledo Soc for the Handicapped; past chmn Black Am Law Students Assn; chmn Handicapped Avd Com. **HONORS/ACHIEVEMENTS:** Handicapped worker of the yr Toledo Lucas Co 1966; handicapped am of the yr State of OH & USA 1967; OH Super Hall of Fame 1970; reg winn Baldwin-Librace Found Contest 1980. **BUSINESS ADDRESS:** U of Toledo, 2801 Bancroft St, Toledo, OH 43606.

EDGHILL, JOHN W.
Business executive. **PERSONAL:** Born Apr 19, 1906; married Noelle Irma Burgan; children: Jaqueline, John. **EDUCATION:** Coll of the City of NY, BS 1931; HowardUniv Med Coll, MD 1934. **CAREER:** Pvt Practice, physician; Sydenham Hosp NY, asso vis urologist 1970; NY Med Coll, asst clinical prof urology 1970; Met & Flower Fifth Av, asso visurologist 1964; Harlem Hosp NY, asso vis urologist 1958; Bronx VA Hosp, sr resident urology 1956. **ORGANIZATIONS:** Mem HowardUniv Med Assn; NY Med Coll Urological Soc; pres Chesterfield Bridge Club 1973; pres Cavalier Men's Club 1979; mem St Phillips Prot Episc Ch. **HONORS/ACHIEVEMENTS:** Combat med badge AUS 1947; S G Specialist Urology NY State Compensation (Workmen's) bd 1956; fellow Am Coll of Surgeons 1956. **MILITARY SERVICE:** Aus capt MC 1943-47. **BUSINESS ADDRESS:** 245 Park Ave, New York, NY 10017.

EDLEY, CHRISTOPHER F., JR.
Educator. **PERSONAL:** Born Jan 13, 1953, Boston, MA; son of Christopher Edley Sr and Zaida Coles Edley; married Tana Pesso, Sep 23, 1983; children: Christopher Edley III. **EDUCATION:** Swartmore Coll, Swartmore PA, BA, 1973; Harvard Law School, Cambride MA, JD, 1978; Harvard Kennedy School, Cambridge MA, MPP, 1978. **CAREER:** White House Domestic Policy Staff, Washington DC, asst dir, 1978-80; US Govt, Secretary of Housing, Education & Welfare, Washington DC, special asst, 1980; Harvard Law School, Cambridge MA, prof, 1981-; Washington Post, Washington DC, part-time editorial page staff, 1982-84; Dukakis for President, Boston MA, natl issues dir, 1987-88. **ORGANIZATIONS:** Bd of managers, Swarthmore Coll, 1980-; bd of dir, Amer Council on Germany, 1981-84; founding trustee, Working Assets Money fund, 1982-84; steering comm, Boston Lawyers Comm for Civil Rights, 1984-87; mem, Comm on Policy for Racial Justice, 1984-; consultant, Joint Center for Political Studies, 1988-; bd of dir, Center for Social Welfare Policy & Law, 1989-; mem, Amer Bar Assn, Natl Bar Assn. **BUSINESS ADDRESS:** Professor, Harvard Law School, 1525 Massachusetts Ave, Cambridge, MA 02138.

EDLEY, CHRISTOPHER F., SR.
Attorney. **PERSONAL:** Born Jan 01, 1928, Charleston, WV; married Zaida Coles; children: Christopher F Jr, Judith Coles. **EDUCATION:** Howard Univ, AB 1949; Harvard Law Sch, LLB 1953; Rust Coll, Hon LLD 1975. **CAREER:** Office of Lewis Tanner Moore, law clerk 1953-54; City of Phila, asst dist atty 1954-56; Moore Lightfoot & Edley, atty partner 1956-60, 1960-61; US Commn on Civil Rights, chief admin justice div 1960; Fed Housing & Home Finance Region 3, reg counsel 1961-63; The Ford Found, prog officer govt & law 1963-73; United Negro Coll Fund, pres & ceo 1973-. **ORGANIZATIONS:** Corporate bd American Airlines 1977, The Boweny Savings Bank 1980-, The Great Atlantic & Pacific Tea Co 1981-; mem Amer, Natl, NY Bar Assns; numerous civic activities; comm & social affiliations. **HONORS/ACHIEVEMENTS:** Natl Scholarship Harvard Law Sch 1949; John Hay Whitney Fellow 1950; Howard Univ Alumni Awd 1959; Cert of Appreciation US Commn on Civil Rights 1960; Sigma Pi Phi 1961; Disting Serv Awd Philadelphia Commn on Human Relations 1966; Humanitarian Father of Yr Awd 1974; Outstanding Achievement Awd Ohio State Univ 1977. **MILITARY SERVICE:** AUS sgt 1946-47, 1950-51. **BUSINESS ADDRESS:** President/Chief Executive Ofcr, United Negro Coll Fund, 500 E 62 St, New York, NY 10021.

EDMOND, PAUL EDWARD
Corporate industrial relations manager. **PERSONAL:** Born May 29, 1944, Shreveport, LA; son of Clarence Lee Edmond and Juanita Brown Allen; divorced; children: Neeve E Samuels, Doran, Oran. **EDUCATION:** Southern Univ, Baton Rouge LA, BS, 1968; Indiana Univ, Bloomington IN, MS, 1973; Univ of Michigan, Ann Arbor MI, 1976. **CAREER:** State of Indiana, Ft Wayne IN, hospital admin, 1969-71; Lincoln Natl Insurance, Ft Wayne IN, personnel mgr, 1971-76; Miller Brewing Co, Milwaukee WI, corporate industrial relations mgr, 1976-. **ORGANIZATIONS:** Amer Soc Personnel Assn, 1973-; Industrial Relations Mgr Assn, 1979-; Personnel/Labor Relations Assn, 1980-; bd mem, OIC of Amer, 1986-; chairperson, United Way Allocation Comm, 1986-; comm mem, Milwaukee Urban League, Long Range Planning, 1987-; mem, Grambling Univ Accreditation Comm, 1987-; bd mem, Milwaukee Desegregation Comm, 1988-; mem, State of Wisconsin Educ Council, 1988-. **HONORS/ACHIEVEMENTS:** Outstanding Young Men, Ft Wayne Jaycees, 1973; Professional Achiever, Natl Career Center, 1974; Black Achiever, New York YMCA, 1983; President's Award, Miller Brewing, 1984. **MILITARY SERVICE:** US Army, 1st lt, 1968-70. **HOME ADDRESS:** 3612 N Sherman Blvd, Milwaukee, WI 53216.

EDMONDS, CAMPBELL RAY
Elected official. **PERSONAL:** Born Jun 09, 1930, Hopewell, VA; married Louise Smith. **EDUCATION:** VA State Univ Trade Sch, 1954; VSU Bus & Mgmt, 1956; Chase Inc Cost/Analysis, 1961. **CAREER:** Traffic Bd Hopewell, co-chair 1966-76; Blue Ribbon Crime Task Force, chmn 1981; City Council, councilman 1982; Hopewell VA, vice-mayor 1984. **ORGANIZATIONS:** Adjuant gen Albert Mills Post #1387 VFW 1975; bd of dirs C of C 1977-; mem Home Builder's Assn 1980; commr Veterans Affairs of VA 1981; bd mem Hopewell/Prince George Chamber of Commerce; mem bd of dirs Prince George County Heritage Fair; mem Hopewell Voters League; trustee bd 1964-, mem Friendship Baptist Church; aide to VA State Assoc Pres of IBPOE of W. **HONORS/ACHIEVEMENTS:** Outstanding Serv Sunlight Eld Lodge Hopewell 1969; Achievement Awd VA State Assn (Elks) Health Dept 1982; Comm Serv Hopewell Action Council (SCLC) 1985; Certificate of Merit City of Hopewell 1986; Outstanding Citizenship Awd United Fund 1987. **MILITARY SERVICE:** AUS E-5 1951-53; Korean Conflict. **HOME ADDRESS:** 1105 Winston Churchill Dr, Hopewell, VA 23860. **BUSINESS ADDRESS:** Vice Mayor, City of Hopewell, Municipal Bldg, Hopewell, VA 23860.

EDMONDS, HELEN G.
Educator. **PERSONAL:** Born Dec 03, 1911, Lawrenceville, VA. **EDUCATION:** Morgan St Coll, AB History 1933; OH St U, MA History 1938, PhD History 1946;Univ of Heidelberg, post-doctoral res in modern European hist 1954-55;NC Central U, Durham, dist prof of Hist 1941-, grad prof of Hist 1948-64. **CAREER:** Graduate School of Arts & Sciences, dean 1964-71. **ORGANIZATIONS:** Chmn, Dept of Hist & Soc Sci 1963-64; Mem, Am Historical Assn; Assn for Study of Negro Life & Hist; NEA; So Historical Assn; numerous other professional orgns; one of three mems, Interim-Com in Charge of Admin of NCCU 1966-67; mem, Peace Corps (ACTION) Nat Adv Cncl; served US Govt as Ldr-splst of Var Intrnatl Ed Prog; US Alternate Del to UN Gen Assembly 1970. **HONORS/ACHIEVEMENTS:** Author, numerous articles; author "Black Faces in High Places" 1971; recip of numorous hon, awards, flwshps & grants.

EDMONDS, JOSEPHINE E.
Educator. **PERSONAL:** Born Oct 05, 1921, Cambridge, MA; daughter of Alexander M Mapp (deceased) and Zylpha O Johnson (deceased); married Howard L Edmonds; children: Joel V Bolden Jr. **EDUCATION:** NY City Coll, attended; Amer Art School, attended; Springfield Coll, attended; Univ of Hartford, attended. **CAREER:** YWCA, art instructor 1965-69; Johnson Publishing, stringer 1957-86; Afro-Amer Cultural Ctr, Amer Intl Coll, art coordinator 1969-81. **ORGANIZATIONS:** Mem 1962-, council mem 1966-68 Springfield Art League 1962-; mem Springfield Library & Museum Assn, Studion Museum in Harlem 1974-, Natl Conf Artists 1973-; co-founder Afro-Art Alliance 1968; mem Urban League; cultural comm Springfield Bicentennial Comm 1973; mem NAACP, Springfield Chap Girl Friends 1958-; natl vice pres Girl Friends Inc 1979-80; trustees comm Springfield Museum of Fine Arts, George Walter Vincent Smith Museum 1980-; corporator Springfield Library & Museum Assoc 1982-; mayoral appt to Springfield Arts Lottery Commn 1986-. **HONORS/ACHIEVEMENTS:** Honor Willia Hardgrow Mental Health Clinic 1974; honored by Alumni Assoc of Amer Intl Coll 1977; Received Exchange Club of Springfields "Golden Deed Award, 1983; Proclaimed by Mayor June 3 1983 "Josephine Edmonds Day" in Springfield MA; Honored by PRIDE a Black Student Org of Amer Intl Coll.

EDMONDS, NORMAN DOUGLAS
Business executive. **PERSONAL:** Born Sep 16, 1938, Suffield, CT; divorced; children: Jeremy, Suzanne, Andrea. **EDUCATION:** Univ of CT, BS 1960. **CAREER:** Travelers Ins Co, dir mktg 1961-79; Phoenix Mutual Life Ins Co, vice pres 1979-. **ORGANIZATIONS:** Chmn founder CT Savings and Loan Assn 1968-; mem Greater Hartford Chamber of Commerce 1972-; bd of Selectmen chmn Town of Tollaud CT 1976-78. **HONORS/ACHIEVEMENTS:** Mem New England Championship Soccer Team 1959; All New England Soccer Team 1959-60; First Black Corporate Officer Travelers Ins Co 1967; distinguished serv award Greater Hartford Jaycees 1971; First Black Chief Elected Official in St of CT 1976. **MILITARY SERVICE:** Air Natl Guard airman 1961-67. **BUSINESS ADDRESS:** Vice President, Phoenix Mutual Life Ins Co, One American Row, Hartford, CT 06115.

EDMONDS, THOMAS NATHANIEL
Educator. **PERSONAL:** Born Jun 14, 1936, Suffield, CT; married Joyce Carole Burr; children: Thomas Jr, Allyn, Russell, James. **EDUCATION:** Stanford U, MBA 1972. **CAREER:** Northwestern Univ School of Law, assoc dean 1975-, dean 1974-75, asst dean, dir 1972-74; Stanford Univ Graduate School of Business, asst dir 1969-72; Lockheed Missisles & Space Co, experimental engineer, planner 1961-69. **ORGANIZATIONS:** Mem, Law Sch Admsn Cncl 1972-; Prelaw Com 1974-77; Ad Hoc Com on Fin Aid 1975-77; Nat Assn for Law Plcmnt 1974-; Am Assn of Coll Regs & Admsns Ofcrs 1973-; Com on Professional Schs 1975-76. **HONORS/ACHIEVEMENTS:** Publ financing grad & grad professional sch Educ 1976; 1st non atty black asso dean maj natl law sch; cert of apprec Oppty Indslzn Ctr W 1970; herberthoover flwshp 1969-70; benkendorf flwshp 1971-72; partic world educ tour 1971. **MILITARY SERVICE:** USN 2nd class petty ofcr 1956-60. **BUSINESS ADDRESS:** 357 E Children Ave, Chicago, IL 60611.

EDMONDSON, WILLIAM R., JR.
Physician. **PERSONAL:** Born Jul 10, 1926, Raleigh, NC; divorced; children: Brenda, Shar-

on. **EDUCATION:** Shaw U, BS 1944; Howard U, MD 1949; Harlem Hosp, internship 1949-50; Homer G Phillips Hosp, residency 1950-51; VA Hosp Brooklyn, NY, residency 1953-54; HarvardUniv Med Sch, post grad study 1960; DukeUniv Med Center, 1967; Johns Hopkins Med Inst, 1975. **CAREER:** Pvt Practice, physician 1954-; Rutgers U, student health serv 1972-; Odyssey House, staff physician 1968-73. **ORGANIZATIONS:** Mem Com on Narcotics Study Essex Co Med Soc; NJ State Med Soc; AMA; NMA; Acad of Med of NJ; Kappa Pi Medical Honor Soc 1949; NJ Public Health Assn; asso attending physician Hospital Center Orange, NJ; staff E Orange General Hosp; adv & consulting staff Essex Co Sanatorium 1965-; mem Urban League of Essex Co; chrmn M Edical Com United Negro College Fund of NJ; NAACP; Am Civil Liberties Union; YMCA; Alpha Phi Alpha; HowardUniv Alumni Assn; ShawU Alumni Assn Co-author "Pulmonary Alveolar Proteinosis" Annals & Internal Med 1960. **MILITARY SERVICE:** USAF capt 1951-53. **BUSINESS ADDRESS:** 109 S Munn Ave, East Orange, NJ 07018.

EDMONSON, BERNIE L.
Elected official. **PERSONAL:** Born May 09, 1918, Wallace, ID; married Lena Mae Fitchett; children: Bernie Jr, Joyce Fleming, Debra. **EDUCATION:** Jersey City State Coll, voc educ 1971; Rutgers Univ, certified 1974-79; Essex County Coll, 1976; Edison State Coll 1979. **CAREER:** Troop 9 Boy Scouts of Amer, scoutmaster 1959-61; Union Baptist Church, trustee 1962-76; East Orange Housing Auth, comm 1971-75; E Orange 1st Ward Democratic County Comm, chmn 1973-82; City of East Orange, councilman. **ORGANIZATIONS:** Supt 1963-67, chmn 1963-70, dir 1965-68 Union Baptist Church; NBC/LEO 1976-; admin E Orange Bd of Educ 1979-; chief examiner GED testing 1983-. **HONORS/ACHIEVEMENTS:** Plaque Trustee-United Way of Essex and West Hudson 1973-82; NAACP 1980-; VFW Post 7923 1981-. **MILITARY SERVICE:** USN elec mate 3 yrs; European Theatre Victory Medal 1943-45; crewmember of USS Mason (DE529) only line ship with predom Black crew. **BUSINESS ADDRESS:** Councilmember, City of East Orange, 44 City Hall Plaza, East Orange, NJ 07019.

EDMUNDS, WALTER RICHARD
Oral and maxillofacial surgeon. **PERSONAL:** Born Mar 25, 1928, Philadelphia, PA; son of McKinley and Waltha. **EDUCATION:** PA State Univ, BS; Howard Univ Coll of Dentistry, DDS; Univ of PA Grad School of Med, attended. **CAREER:** PA Hospital oral surgeon; Univ of PA School of Dental Med, assoc prof oral pathology; Jefferson Med Coll Thomas Jefferson Univ, clinical asst prof of otolaryngology; Private practice, oral & maxillofacial surgeon. **ORGANIZATIONS:** Mem bd Eagleville Hosp; fellow Amer Coll of Oral & Maxillofacial Surgeons, Soc Hill Club, Amer Bd of Oral Surgeons, Alpha Phi Alpha, Sigma Pi Phi, Chi Delta Mu; bd mem Philadelphia Cty Dental Soc. **MILITARY SERVICE:** AUS lt.

EDNEY, STEVE
Organization executive. **PERSONAL:** Born Jan 10, 1917, Anderson, SC; son of Steve Edney and Lena Jenkins; married Alberta Palmer, Jul 11, 1971; children: Henry. **CAREER:** Pan Pacific Fisheres Terminal Island, CA filling machine operator; United Cannery & Industrial Workers, business agent, vice pres, pres; United Industrial Workers of SIU, natl dir, 1989-; Seafarers Intl Union, vice pres, 1989-. **ORGANIZATIONS:** Vice pres, Los Angeles County Fedn of Labor, 1989-, California Fedn of Labor, 1989-; mem, Harbor Area Re-Devel Comm, 1989-, Welfare Planning Comm, 1989-, NAACP, 1989-; chmn, Fish-Canners United Industrial Workers Pension & Welfare, 1989-, La Victoria-United Industrial Workers Trust Fund, 1989-, Caribe Tuna-United Industrial Workers Pension Fund, 1989-. **HONORS/ACHIEVEMENTS:** Founder, Fish-Canners-Cannery Workers Union Welfare Trust, 1953; Man of the Year Award, Maritime Trades Dept, 1971, 1977; wrote booklet on the History of the Cannery Workers on Terminal Island. **BUSINESS ADDRESS:** Natl Dir, United Indus Workers of the Seafarers Intl Union of N America, 510 N Broad Ave, Wilmington, CA 90744.

EDWARDS, A. WILSON
City official. **PERSONAL:** Born Feb 19, 1908, Frankfort, KY. **EDUCATION:** Univ Louisville, cert police adminstrn; Intl Police Sch, cert in police scis; City of Louisville, cert in foreign svc, US Fgn Serv Inst Dir, pub Safety;Spl Serv Bureau of Louisille Police Dept, organized & commanded 1963; Nat Bureau of Investigation Liberia, organized & was head of, 1965; LouisvillePolice Force, police officer, patrolman, detective, sergeant, Lt Comm, parks sec & asst dir of safety 1935-66; late Pres Wm V S Tubman of Liberia, chief of security 1958-60. **CAREER:** Adv to Col Tran Minh Cong, chief of police Danang City, S Vietnam 1966-68; security officer for 1957 inauguration of Pres Dwight D Eisenhower & 1965 inauguration of Pres Lyndon B Johnson; security officer for first meeting of Orgn of African States.

EDWARDS, AL E.
Government official. **PERSONAL:** Born Mar 19, 1937, Houston, TX; married Lana Kay Cloth; children: Albert Ely II, Jason Kiamba, Alana Catherine Raquel. **EDUCATION:** TX So Univ, BS 1966; Tuskeegee Inst, 1965; Belize Univ, Hon D 1977. **CAREER:** Gen Foods Corp, acct mgr 1958-80; Al Edwards Real Estate, broker 1968-; Al Edwards Publ Relations Advt, pres 1968-; NAACP, publ relations 1976-78; State of TX, state rep 1978-. **ORGANIZATIONS:** Mem Houston Bus & Professional Men; mem Dean of Pledges Alpha Phi Alpha; founder, pres of bd Houston Team Tennis Assoc 1976-78; founder TX Emancipation Cultural Assoc; chmn Jesse Jackson for President Campaign TX 1984; chmn TX Senatorial Dist 13 Convention 1984; mem Dem Natl Comm 1984; natl vchmn Mondale for Pres Campaign 1984. **HONORS/ACHIEVEMENTS:** Authored House Bill 1015 Emancipation Day, TX Legal State Holiday 1979; Outstanding Serv in 66th Leg, TX Railroad Passenger Assoc 1980; Carried leg to Save So Rail Passenger Serv 1980; Al Edwards Freedom Heritage Park Dedicated in San Antonio, TX Emancipation Comm 1980. **BUSINESS ADDRESS:** Representative, State of Texas, PO Box 3910, Austin, TX 78769.

EDWARDS, ALFRED L.
Educator. **PERSONAL:** Born Aug 09, 1920, Key West, FL; married Willie Mae Lewis; children: Beryl L, Alfred L Jr. **EDUCATION:** Livingstone Coll Salisbury NC, BS 1948; Univ of MI, MA 1949; Univ of IA, PhD 1957. **CAREER:** So Univ, instr 1949-54; MI St U, asst prof 1957-62; US Dept of Agri, deputy asst sec 1963-74; Grad Sch Business Univ of MI, prof & dir of Rsch 1974-. **ORGANIZATIONS:** Dir Scrty Bank Corp 1980; Cnslnt Rockefeller Fndtn 1976-80; Cnslnt Andrew Brimmer & Co 1975-77; Bd of Trstees Wstrn MI-Univ 1980; Dir Legal Aid & Dfndrs Assn 1980-83; bd of dir for, Regal Plastics, Inc, MI Minority Tech Council, Inst for Amer Business, Consortium for Grad Study in Business. **HONORS/ACHIEVEMENTS:** Ford Found Fellow; Danforth Fellow. **MILITARY SERVICE:** AUS sgt 1943-46; Good Conduct Medal. **HOME ADDRESS:** 2448 Adare Cir, Ann Arbor, MI 48104. **BUSINESS ADDRESS:** Professor of Business Admin, Univ of Michigan, Grad Sch of Bus Adm, Ann Arbor, MI 48109.

EDWARDS, ARTHUR JAMES
Dentist. **PERSONAL:** Born Oct 30, 1902, Talbotton, GA; married Dr Vera Clement Edwards. **EDUCATION:** Ohio State Univ, DDS 1929. **CAREER:** Shoemaker Health Ctr, clinician 1929-32; Volunteer at Shoemaker Ctr and Public Dental Serv Soc (Emeritus Bd Mem), committees, clinician, consultant, supervisor, educator 1932-84; Private Practitioner, dental practice 1929-. **ORGANIZATIONS:** Mem YMCA 1930-; bd mem, supporter, subscriber United Appeal, Health Fed, Community Action & Change Orgs 1930-; mem Zion Baptist Church, Kappa Alpha Psi, Sigma Pi Phi; life mem NAACP 1935-, Amer Dental Assoc, OH Dental Assoc, OH Valley Dental Assoc, OH State & Natl Dental Assoc; mem Chicago Dental Soc; mem Amer Endodontic Soc 1976-; mem ODA, ADA. **HONORS/ACHIEVEMENTS:** Mem Intl Coll of Dentists; Kappa Alpha Psi 50 Yrs Serv Awd; Zion Baptist Church 50 Yr Awd; Cincinnati Dental Soc 50 Yr Serv Awd; mem Natl Skeet/Trap Shooting Assoc over 100 trophies & awds 1949-; mem & honoree Amistad Black History Assoc 1987. **HOME ADDRESS:** 231 Clinton Springs Ave, Cincinnati, OH 45217.

EDWARDS, AUDREY MARIE
Editor. **PERSONAL:** Born Apr 21, 1947, Tacoma, WA; married Benjamin Williams. **EDUCATION:** Univ of WA, BA 1969; Columbia Univ, MA 1974. **CAREER:** Fairchild Publication, promotion news editor 1977-79; Black Enterprise Mag, assoc editor 1978-79; Family Circle Mag, sr editor 1979-81; NY Univ, adjunct prof 1982-; Essence Mag, editor 1981-. **ORGANIZATIONS:** Regional dir Natl Assoc of Black Journalists 1981-83; prog chair New York Assn of Black Journalists 1983-. **HONORS/ACHIEVEMENTS:** Unity Awd in Media Lincoln Univ 1985. **HOME ADDRESS:** 45 Plaza St, Brooklyn, NY 11217.

EDWARDS, BESSIE REGINA
Meeting and conference planner. **PERSONAL:** Born Mar 14, 1942, Gates County, NC. **EDUCATION:** Brooklyn Coll, Special Bacculaurate Degree Program 1975-79; New School of Social Rsch, BA/MA 1979-81. **CAREER:** Opportunity Industrialization, counselor/teacher 1975-80; Manhattan Cable TV, affirmative action officer 1980-86; Paragon Cable, mgr training and develop. **ORGANIZATIONS:** Bd mem NY Chap Coalition 100 Black Women 1983-; sec Minorities in Cable 1984-; sec Women in Cable 1984-; bd mem EDGES; mem Women's City Club; mem, Brooklyn Chamber of Commerce 1989-90; adjunct lecturer, Borough Manhattan Community College 1988-90. **HONORS/ACHIEVEMENTS:** Cable Careers of the 80's modules in mass communications 1984; Black Achiever selected by Time Inc The Parent Co 1987. **HOME ADDRESS:** 195 Willoughby Ave, Suite 1006, Brooklyn, NY 11205.

EDWARDS, CECILE HOOVER
Educational administrator. **PERSONAL:** Born Oct 20, 1926, East St Louis, IL; married Gerald Alonzo; children: Gerald Alonzo Jr, Adrienne Annette, Hazel Ruth. **EDUCATION:** Tuskegee Inst, BS 1946; IA State U, 1946; Tuskegee Inst, MS 1947; IA State U, PhD 1950. **CAREER:** Research Awards, proj dir 1951-; White House Conf Panel on Community Nutrition, chmn 1969; Carver Found Tuskegee Inst, asst prof & rsch assoc 1950-56; Tuskegee Inst, head dept of foods & nutrition 1952-56; NC A&T State Univ, prof of nutrition & rsch dept home economics 1956-71,chmn dept of home economics 1968-71; Howard Univ, chmn, prof of nutrition dept of home economics 1971-74; School of Continuing Educ Howard Univ, dean 1974-87, prof 1971-. **ORGANIZATIONS:** 150 scientific & professional publs in major professional jrnls 1949-; pres Southeastern Conf of Teachers of Foods & Nutrition 1971; mem adv com to dir Nat Inst of Health 1972-75; mem Expert Com on Nitrates Nitrites & Nitrasamines 1975-79; consultUniv of Khartoum Sudan Ford Found 1978; proj dir Training Prog for Residents of Public Housing 1982; chmn Natl Conf on Black Youth Unemployment 1983; prog project dir Nutrition, Other Factors & The Outcomes of Pregnancy 1985-. **HONORS/ACHIEVEMENTS:** Award for Outstanding Achievement Nat Council of Negro Women 1963; Citation for Outstanding Contributions to Edn, City of E St Louis 1964; Award for Achievement in Sci, NC A&T StateUniv 1964; Scroll of Hon, Outstanding Achievement in Nutrition & Research The Links Inc 1970; Home Economics Centennial Alumni Award, IA StateUniv 1971; Alumni Achievement Award IA StateUniv 1972; Alumni Merit Award Tuskegee Inst 1974; Citation from House of Reps State of IL for Devotion to Eliminating Poverty 1980; Awd for Outstanding Unit in Academic Affairs Div Howard Univ 1982; Proclamation by Gov of State of IL April 5 1984 as Dr Cecile Hoover Edwards Day in witness of her contribution, her professional recognition nationally and internationally and the sharing of her expertise with communities around the world including East St Louis IL; one of 25 contemporary Tuskegeans honored at Biennial Convention of Alumni Assoc 1984. **BUSINESS ADDRESS:** Professor, Howard University, 2400 6th St NW, Washington, DC 20059.

EDWARDS, CLAYBON JEROME
Mortician. **PERSONAL:** Born Jul 15, 1929, Peach County, GA; married Mary Nevel; children: Deneise. **EDUCATION:** Morris Brown Coll, grad; Worsham Coll; Ft Valley State NW. **CAREER:** Edwards Fun Home, mgr; Sup Life Ins Co, home off rep, reg supr, insptr, dist mgr cons, 1st vice pres GA Funer Serv Prctnrs Assn. **ORGANIZATIONS:** Past vice pres Upsilon Nu Delta Morticians Frat; past & mem bd of dir Wabash YMCA; mem, past pres Alpha Phi Alpha Frat Inc; past mem bd of dir Peach Co UCF; sec GFSPA; mem bd of GA Area Plng & Dev Com; treas Citzshp Educ Com mem, Trinity Bapt Ch; mem trustee bd Trinity Bapt Ch; mem C of C Peach Co; mem trustee bd Morris Brown Coll; mem State Bd Dept of Human Rescs; mem NAACP Honored Mort of the Yr 1974; first black elect ofcl City Councmn of GA; Mayor protem, Ft Valley; chmn Police Com. **BUSINESS ADDRESS:** PO Box 310, Fort Valley, GA 31030.

EDWARDS, DAVID C.
Attorney. **PERSONAL:** Born Jan 29, 1948, Morristown, NJ; married Elaine Feliz; children: Dephann, Madera. **EDUCATION:** Bakersfield Coll, AA 1968; Stanford U, AB 1970; Rutgers Law Sch, JD 1973. **CAREER:** Priv Practice, atty. **ORGANIZATIONS:** Mem NJ Bar Assn; NJ State Chmn, Nat Conf of Black Lawyers, served in elected offices, Alderman 5th Ward 1972; Councilman 2nd Ward 1973; pres City Council 1974. **BUSINESS ADDRESS:** 55 Elm St, Morristown, NJ.

EDWARDS, DAVID H., JR.
Judge. **PERSONAL:** Born Jul 25, 1922, Norfolk, VA; married Sheilah H Gordon; children: Suzanne, Robert. **EDUCATION:** CCNY, BA 1943; NY School of Law, LLB 1948; NY Univ Grad School of Law, LLM 1953. **CAREER:** Private practice, attny 1949-65; NY State Supreme Ct, law sec 1965-72; NY State Senate, couns; Civil Ct of NYC, judge 1972-79; NY State Supreme Ct, justice 1979-. **ORGANIZATIONS:** Bd dir NY Cty Lawyers Assoc 1962; bd of dir Harlem Laweyrs Assoc; sec bd of judges Civil Ct of New York City 1974-78; mem NAACP, Mayors Comm of New York City 1959; chmn Local Draft Bd US Selective Serv 1968. **MILITARY SERVICE:** AUS sgt 92nd Inf Div 1943-46; Three Battle Stars; Battalion Citation. **BUSINESS ADDRESS:** Justice, NY State Supreme Court, 60 Centre St, New York, NY 10007.

EDWARDS, DENNIS, JR.
Judge. **PERSONAL:** Born Aug 19, 1922, New York City, NY; married Dorothy Fairclough; children: Lynne Mosley, Denise Young. **EDUCATION:** NY Univ, BA 1941; Harvard Law Sch, JD 1944. **CAREER:** NY State Supreme Court, law clerk 1948-65; Criminal Court New York City & State Court of Claims, judge 1965-. **ORGANIZATIONS:** Dir NY Co Lawyers Assn 1961-65; Harlem Lawyers Assn 1952; mem Amer Judicature Soc, Amer Bar Assn; dir Speedwell Soc for Children; mem Omega Frat, Elks, Masons, NAACP, Urban League, YMCA. **BUSINESS ADDRESS:** Judge, State Court of Claims, 111 Centre St, New York, NY 10013.

EDWARDS, DENNIS CALVIN
Professional athlete. **PERSONAL:** Born Oct 06, 1959, Stockton, CA. **EDUCATION:** USC. **CAREER:** Los Angeles Express, 1983-; Denver Gold, nose tackle 1984-. **HONORS/ACHIEVEMENTS:** Two-time first team All Pac-10 choice in 1980 & 1981 at USC; named 3rd team All-am as jr & sr; honorable mention All-Am by AP & the Sporting News; twice voted to UPI All-Coast team; played in 1982 East-West Shrine Game; mem of 2 natl championship & Rose Bowl title teams at USC.

EDWARDS, DENNIS L.
Plant manager, automobile manufacturer. **PERSONAL:** Born Aug 29, 1941, Indianapolis, IN; son of Rollin H Edwards and Ella Stange Edwards; married Judith Johnson Edwards, Jun 15, 1966; children: Camille, Dennis L Jr, Tiffany. **EDUCATION:** Parsons Coll, Fairfield IA, BA, 1964; Central Michigan Univ, Mt Pleasant MI, MA, 1976. **CAREER:** St Louis Hawks, basketball player, 1964-71; Chrysler Corp, St Louis MO, gen supt, 1978, Detroit MI, gen supt, 1981-, operations mgr, 1982, production mgr, 1983, production mgr, 1985, plant mgr, 1985. **ORGANIZATIONS:** Bd of dir, Goodwill Industries, 1986-, Wayne County Attention Center, 1986-. **HONORS/ACHIEVEMENTS:** All American Basketball Player, Parsons Coll, 1963,1964; selected to Participate in Pan-American Games, South America, 1963. **BUSINESS ADDRESS:** Plant Manager, Chrysler Motors-Jefferson Assembly Plant, 12200 East Jefferson Ave, Detroit, MI 48215.

EDWARDS, DONALD O.
Electrical engineer. **PERSONAL:** Born Apr 17, 1931, Mount Olive, NC; married Bernice Bullock; children: Derick, Keith, Cheryl. **EDUCATION:** AA 1955; BS 1965. **CAREER:** GE Missile & Space Div, electrical subsystem engr 19 yrs; MIT Draper Labs, resident engr. **ORGANIZATIONS:** Mem Alpha Phi Alpha Zeta Omicron Lambda Chpt. **HONORS/ACHIEVEMENTS:** USAF Craftsman Award 1968. **MILITARY SERVICE:** USAF s/sgt 1949-52. **BUSINESS ADDRESS:** 3198 Chestnut St, Philadelphia, PA 19104.

EDWARDS, DONALD PHILIP
Attorney. **PERSONAL:** Born Aug 27, 1947, Buffalo, NY; son of Robert D Edwards and Lorraine V Jarrett Edwards; married Jo Roberson. **EDUCATION:** Morehouse Coll, BA (Cum Laude) 1969; Boston Univ School of Law, JD 1973. **CAREER:** NAACP Legal Defense Fund, fellow 1973-76; Thomas Kennedy Sampson & Edwards PC, partner 1974-. **ORGANIZATIONS:** Chmn of bd Hillside Intl Truth Ctr 1980-83; bd of adv Atlanta Legal Aid Soc 1981-85; bd mem Atlanta Volunteer Lawyers Inc 1983-84; vice pres Northern District Litigation Fund 1984-85; bd mem Natl Bar Assoc 1984,85; pres Gate City Bar Assoc 1984; bd mem Fulton Cnty Dept of Family and Children Services 1986; dir Nat'l Bar Assn Region XI 1986-87; vice pres, Christian Council of Metro Atlanta 1987-89; bd mem, American Cancer Society, Atlanta Unit 1988-89. **HONORS/ACHIEVEMENTS:** Service Awd Coll Park Voters League 1981; Civil Rights Awd Gate City Bar Assoc 1983; Lawyer of the Year DeKalb Cty NAACP 1984; Top 100 Atlantans under 40 Atlanta Mag 1984; Leadership Atlanta 1985. **HOME ADDRESS:** 954 Willis Mill Rd SW, Atlanta, GA 30311. **BUSINESS ADDRESS:** Attorney, Thomas Kennedy Sampson Edwards Slayton PC, 55 Marietta St, Suite 1600, Atlanta, GA 30303.

EDWARDS, DOROTHY WRIGHT
Educator. **PERSONAL:** Born Jan 13, 1914, Jacksonville, FL; married Oscar J Edwards (deceased); children: Oscar J Jr. **EDUCATION:** FL A&M Univ, BS 1935; NY Univ. MA 1952; Additional Study, Hampton Inst, Miami Univ, Columbia Univ. **CAREER:** Physical educ instructor, 1935-40; BTW, business instructor 1940; Miami Housing Authority, cashier-booker 1940-41; Dorsey Jr-Sr High, sec, phys instructor 1941-47, dean of girls 1947-55; Miami Northwestern Sr High, asst prin of guidance 1955-70; Miami Spgs, asst prin of guidance 1970-71; Edward Waters Coll, dean of women 1971-72; Proj Upward Bound, counselor 1972-76; FL Memorial Coll, counselor for women 1976-78; Miami Northwestern Sr High School, jr coll assistance prog adv 1978-retired. **ORGANIZATIONS:** Bd dir OIC; bd dir Dade Mt Zion Fed Credit Union, Amer Assn of Univ Women, Council of Intl Visitors; life mem YWCA, Alpha Kappa Alpha Sor; mem Kappa Delta Pi; fin sec 100 Women for FL Meml Coll; church clerk Mt Zion Baptist Church; Docent at Jackson Meml Hosp Alamo; bd dir Family Health Center Inc. **HONORS/ACHIEVEMENTS:** Who's Who in Amer Educ 1961-63; Personalities of the South; Outstanding Serv to Youth Phi Delta Kappa; Star Tchr Miami NW Sr HS 1966-67; Certificate ofAppreciation YWCA 1975; Alpha Phi Alpha Frat Beta Beta Lambda Chap 1984 Outstanding Citizen Awd 1984. **BUSINESS ADDRESS:** Jr Coll Assis Prog Adv, Miami Northwestern Sr HS, 7007 NW 12 Ave, Miami, FL 33150.

EDWARDS, EDDIE
Professional athlete. **PERSONAL:** Born Apr 26, 1954, Sumter, SC; married Vivian Ruth; children: Diedre. **EDUCATION:** Miami FL. **CAREER:** Cincinnati Bengals, defensive end 1977-. **HONORS/ACHIEVEMENTS:** Cincinnati's 1st Ranked NFL Defense 1983; All-Am atUniv of Miami, FL. **BUSINESS ADDRESS:** Cincinnati Bengals, 111 North 21st St, Fort Pierce, FL 34950.

EDWARDS, MS. ELLA RAINO See ELLARAINO

EDWARDS, ESTHER GORDY
Record, film company executive. **PERSONAL:** Born Apr 25, Oconee, GA; married George H; children: Robert Bullock. **EDUCATION:** Attended, Howard U, Wayne State U. **CAREER:** Gordy Printing Co Detroit, co-owner genl mgr 1947-59; Motown Record Corp Detroit, sr vice pres sec dir 1959-; Motown Industries Hollywood, CA & Detroit, corporate sec, sr vice pres 1973-. **ORGANIZATIONS:** Detroit Recorders Ct Jury Commn 1960-62; chmn 1961-62; chmn of bd Am Devel Corp; exec dir Gordy Found 1968-; founder, chmn African-Am Heritage Assn 1976-; chmn Wayne Co Dem Women's Com 1956; MI del-at-large Dem Nat Conv 1960; interim asst dep auditor gen MI 1960; bd of dir Bank of the Commonwealth 1973-79; Booker T Washington Bus Assn; HowardUniv Alumni Assn vice pres Metro Detroit Conv & Visitors Bur; mem Wayne State Fund; adv bd sch of mgmtU of MI; Alpha Kappa Alpha. **BUSINESS ADDRESS:** Motown Industries, 2648 W Grand Blvd, Detroit, MI 48208.

EDWARDS, EUNICE L.
Director. **PERSONAL:** Born in Newport News, VA. **EDUCATION:** Hampton Inst, BS; Fisk Univ, MA. **CAREER:** Hampton Institute, various positions; Bluefield State Coll, admin asst 1935-57; Fisk Univ, admin asst to pres 1957-66, dir of financial aids 1966-84, dir personnel serv 1984-. **ORGANIZATIONS:** Mem Fin Aid to Students 1966-76; TN State Adv Council on Vocational Ed 1973-75, Amer Council Ed 1973-77; numerous workshops; mem num offices, commiss TN Assoc Student Aid Admin; pres So Assoc Student Fin Aid Admin; comm v Amer Coll Personnel Assoc; pres Natl Assoc Student Financial Aids Admin;comm Meed Assessment Procedures; mem bd of trustees Coll Entrance Exam Bd; mem TN Tuition Grant Prog; bd of trustees NASFAA; mem Coll Scholarship Serv Council 1983-86; mem Chairman's Advisory Cncl United Student Aid Funds 1986-; mem Regional Review Comm of Harry S Truman Schlrshp Committee 1986-. **HONORS/ACHIEVEMENTS:** Outstanding Admin Awd TN Assoc Student Fin Aid Admin 1972; Key to City Birmingham 1972; Woman of the Year State TN 1972. **BUSINESS ADDRESS:** Dir, FiskUniv, Personnel Services, Nashville, TN 37203.

EDWARDS, GEORGE R.
Broadcasting executive. **PERSONAL:** Born Feb 01, 1938, New York, NY; son of John Edwards and Olga Edwards; divorced; children: Lisa, Veronica, George Drew. **EDUCATION:** City Coll of New York, BA English 1955-59. **CAREER:** British Airways NY, sales mgr 1959-63; Pepsi-Cola Brooklyn NY, gen sales mgr 1964-65; Pepsi-Cola Bronx, gen mgr 1968-70; Venture Mktg Co Heublein Inc, vice pres mktg; Heublein Spirits Div, vice pres, group mktg dir 1974-78; Hartford Graduate Center, visitig prof mktg 1975-78; Natl Black Network, pres/coo. **ORGANIZATIONS:** Chmn mktg comm Greater Hartford Arts Council 1976-78. **BUSINESS ADDRESS:** President/COO, Natl Black Network, 10 Columbus Circle, New York, NY 10019.

EDWARDS, GILBERT FRANKLIN
Sociologist, educator. **PERSONAL:** Born Jun 02, 1915, Charleston, SC; son of Gilbert Franklin and Bertha Allan; married Peggy Jarvis Park; children: Donalee Marie. **EDUCATION:** Fisk Univ, AB 1936; Univ of Chicago, PhD 1952. **CAREER:** Fessender Acad FL, teacher social studies 1937-39; Howard Univ, faculty mem 1941-; sociology prof 1960-; Washington Univ St Louis, visiting teacher 1954, Harvard 1967, 68; consultant in field. **ORGANIZATIONS:** Public mem Natl Capital Planning Comm 1965-71; mem Pop Assn Amer Sociological Assn; alumni mem Phi Beta Kappa. **HONORS/ACHIEVEMENTS:** Author "The Negro Professional Class" 1959; editor E Franklin Frazier on Race Relations 1968.

EDWARDS, GROVER LEWIS, SR.
Construction consultant/educ. admin. **PERSONAL:** Born Feb 21, 1944, Henrico, NC; married Lucy Priscilla Moody; children: Reggie Lamont, Telsha Nicole, Kelsey Daneen, Grover Lewis Jr. **EDUCATION:** Elizabeth City State Univ, Associate 1965; Shaw Univ, Bachelors 1976. **CAREER:** RCA Training Prog, electronics instructor 1969-73, supervisor of instructors 1973-79; Edwards & Assocs Building Contractors, owner/pres 1979; Norfax Real Estate Corp, pres 1983-; Northampton Co Sch Bd, chairman. **ORGANIZATIONS:** Mem past youth adv NAACP 1969; mem past pres Gaston Religious Civic Organ 1971; pres Northampton Housing Assistance Prog 1972; mem NC Home Builders Assn 1980; Northampton Co Sch Bd mem 1972-, chmn 1984-; mem Prince Hall Masonic Lodge 1975-; mem bd of dirs NC Sch Bd 1984-. **HONORS/ACHIEVEMENTS:** Serv Awd Northampton HS West 1980; Serv Awd Athlete Assoc Tri-City Chums 1981; Outstanding Business Awd Northampton Co NAACP 1985. **MILITARY SERVICE:** USN E4 1965-69; Natl Defense Awd. **BUSINESS ADDRESS:** Chairman, Northampton Co School Bd, Star Route Box 52A, Henrico, NC 27842.

EDWARDS, HARRY
Educator. **PERSONAL:** Born Nov 22, 1942, St Louis, MO; married Sandra Y Boze; children: Tazamisha Heshima Imara, Fatima Malene Imara, Changa Demany Imara. **EDUCATION:** San Jose State, BA 1964; Cornell U, MA 1966, PhD 1972. **CAREER:** San Jose State, instructor Sociology 1966-68; Univ of Santa Clara, instructor Sociology 1967-68; Univ of CA Berkeley, asst prof Sociology 1970-77, assoc prof Sociology, prof Sociology. **ORGANIZATIONS:** Contributed editorials to Los Angeles Times, NY Times, San Francisco Examiner, Oakland Tribune, Chicago Sun-Times, Black Scholar, East St Louis Monitor, Milwaukee Courier, Newsday, Los Angeles Hearld Examiner, Sports Illustrated, Sports & Athletes & Inside Sports; served as consultant with producers of sports relatedprograms on NBC, CBS, ABC and PBS TV networks; sports commentary for Natl Public Radio via satellite to Washington DC; interview/commentary prog on KPFA-Radio Berkeley CA; consulted/appeared on camera for BBC TV (British), CBC TV (Candaian) West German TV for CBS' "60 Minutes", CNN's "Sports Focus", NBC's "Nightly News", ABC's "Sportsbeat" and "Nightline", PBS's "James Michner's World", Turner Sports Nework ESPN "Sports Forum" and numerous local & relgional TV productions focusing on issues relating to sports & society; participated in lecture & consulting fair at Natl Sports Inst Oslo Norway, Natl Sports Inst Moscow USSR; consultant San Francisco 49ers and Golden State Warriors. **HONORS/ACHIEVEMENTS:** NAACP Educ Incentive Scholarship CA State Univ 1960; Athletic

Scholarship CA State Univ 1960; Woodrow Wilson Fellowship 1964; Man of Yr Awd San Francisco Sun Reporter 1968; Russwurm Awd Natl Newspaper Publishers Assoc 1968; fellowship Cornell Univ 1968; Dist Scholar in Res fall 1980 OR State Univ; Hon Doctorate Columbia Coll 1981; Miller Scholar in Res fall 1982 Univ of IL Champaign/Urbana Charleston Gazette; Dist Scholar in Res spring 1983 Norwegian Coll of Physical Educ & Sports Oslow Norway; Dist Schlr Spring 1984Univ of Charleston; Dist Visiting Scholar fall 1984 IN St Univ. **BUSINESS ADDRESS:** Professor of Sociology, Univ of CA/Berkeley, 410 Barrows Hall, Berkeley, CA 94720.

EDWARDS, HARRY T.
Judge, educator, attorney. **PERSONAL:** Born Nov 03, 1940, New York, NY; son of George H Edwards and Arline Lyle; children: Brent, Michelle. **EDUCATION:** Cornell Univ, BS 1962; MI Law Sch, JD 1965. **CAREER:** Atty with Seyfarth, Shaw Fairweather & Geraldson, Chicago 1965-70; prof Univ Michigan Law School 1970-75, 1977-80; Harvard Univ Law School, prof 1975-77; Amtrak, bd dir 1977-80, chmn bd 1979-80; US Ct of Appeals Wash DC, judge 1980-. **ORGANIZATIONS:** Amer Law Institute; Amer Bar Assn; Amer Academy of Arts & Sciences; Amer Judicature Society; Exec Committee Order of the Coif. **HONORS/ACHIEVEMENTS:** Co-author "Labor Relations Law in the Pub Sector, 1985, "The Lawyer as a Negotiator" 1977, "Collective Bargaining & Labor Arbitration" 1979, "Higher Educ & the Law" 1980; author of more than 50 scholarly articles; Honorary Doctor of Law degress from Williams Coll; Univ of Detroit; St Lawrence Univ; Whitney North Seymour Medal, Amer Arbitration Assn 1988; Society of Amer Law Teachers Award for distinguished contributions to teaching and the public service 1982. **BUSINESS ADDRESS:** Judge, US Court of Appeals, US Courthouse/Dist of Columbia, Third & Constitution Ave NW, Washington, DC 20001.

EDWARDS, HORACE BURTON
Business executive. **PERSONAL:** Born May 20, 1925, Tuscaloosa, AL; divorced; children: Adrienne, Paul, David, Michael. **EDUCATION:** Marquette Univ, BS Naval Sci, Mech Engr 1947, 1948; Iona Coll, MBA 1972; TX Southern Univ, LHD (Hon) 1982; Stillman Coll, LLD (Hon) 1984. **CAREER:** Atlantic Richfield Co, controller mktg 1968-72, mgr fin & ops analysis 1973-76, mgr planning & control transp div 1976-79; ARCO Transp Co, vice pres planning & control 1978-80; ARCO Pipe Line Co, pres, ceo, chmn of bd. **ORGANIZATIONS:** Trustee Leadership Independence 1984-85, KS Chamber of Commerce Leadership KS 1985-86; dir, pres Independence Ind 1985; mem Assoc of Oil Pipe Lines Exec Comm, Amer Petrol Inst & Central Comm on Pipe Line Transp; pres of bd of dir Jr Achievement of Montgomery Cty Independence KS; mem bd of dir KS Chamber of Commerce & Industry, Independence Community Coll Endowment Bd; trustee Inst of Logopedics Whchita KS, KS Independent Coll Fund, KS Council on Economic Educ, TX Southern Univ Bus School Found; mem Natl Bar Assoc Advisory Comm to its Energy & Environ Law Sect; mem bd of dir Amer Assoc of Blacks in Energy; participant Natl Urban League's Black Exec Exchange Program; mem NAACP, FL A&M School fo Business, Industry's Ctr for Entrepreneurial Devel Roundtable. **HONORS/ACHIEVEMENTS:** Marquette Univ Disting Engrg Alumnus Awd 1984. **MILITARY SERVICE:** USN lt jg 1943-48. **BUSINESS ADDRESS:** President, Chmn of the Board, ARCO Pipeline, 200 Arco Bldg, Independence, KS 67301.

EDWARDS, JAMES TERRELL
Professional athlete. **PERSONAL:** Born Nov 22, 1955, Seattle, WA. **EDUCATION:** Univ of WA, 1973-77. **CAREER:** Phoenix Suns, center 1983-; Cleveland Cavaliers, 1981-83; Indiana Pacers, 1978-81; Los Angeles Lakers, 1977. **BUSINESS ADDRESS:** Phoenix Suns, P O Box 1369, Ste 510, Phoenix, AZ 85001.

EDWARDS, JOHN L.
Educator. **PERSONAL:** Born Oct 18, 1930, Muncie, IN; married Mavis J Jones; children: John, Robert. **EDUCATION:** AZ State U, EdD 1965; AZ State U, MA 1959; Ball State U, BS 1953. **CAREER:** AZ State Univ, Exten & Prof Coll, asst dean 1973, assoc prof 1969-75, asst prof 1966-69, instructor 1964-66, faculty assoc 1963-64, grad asst 1962-63; Julian Elementary School Phoenix, teacher 1955-62. **ORGANIZATIONS:** Mem Intnl Reading Assn 1963; NEA 1956; AZ Educ Assn; Am Assn ofUniv Prof 1964; Phi Delta Kappa 1966; Kappa Delta Pi 1962; has written many articles in his field, faculty Adv Kappa Alpha Psi, AZ StateUniv 1962-72 & 1975; bd mem Southwestern Coop End Lab; bd dir Jane Wayland Child Guidance Cntr 1969-75; mem AZ Right to Read Commn 1971; Phoenix Citizens Bond Com 1975; past chmn AZ Educ Assn Instructional & Professional Develop Com; bd dir Assn for Higher Educ 1964; Desert Area reading council 1966. **HONORS/ACHIEVEMENTS:** Outstanding Achievement, Western Provincial Alumni Award, Kappa Alpha Psi 1962; Phoenix Alumni Award, Kappa Alpha Psi 1965, 1963, & 1960; award for OutstandingAchievement Adult Basic Educ Inst 1970; Dictionary of Intnl Biography 1973; Personalities of the W & Mid W. **BUSINESS ADDRESS:** U Ex Acad Serv Bldg Rm 110, AZ State Univ, Tempe, AZ 85281.

EDWARDS, JOHN LOYD, III
Educator. **PERSONAL:** Born Feb 18, 1948, Nashville, TN; children: Adrian Joel, Nikita Michelle, Derek Traimain. **EDUCATION:** TN State Univ, attended 1966-68; Univ of TN at Chattanooga, BFA 1980. **CAREER:** Chattanooga Northstar Newspaper, writer/director advertising 1981-83; Mary Walker Foundation, exec dir 1983-. **ORGANIZATIONS:** Public relations United States Jaycees 1981-; pres Visual Media Productions 1985-; mem Assoc for the Study of Afro-Amer Life & History 1985-; vice pres Lakeside PTA 1986-. **HONORS/ACHIEVEMENTS:** Outstanding Comm Achievement for Vietnam Era Veteran City of Chattanooga 1979; Public Relations Dir of the Yr TN Jaycees 1983-84; Honorary Life Member United States Jaycees 1987. **MILITARY SERVICE:** AUS sgt 2 yrs; Bronze Star, Army Commendation Medal, Purple Heart, Vietnam Serv Cross, Combat Infantry Badge 1968-70. **BUSINESS ADDRESS:** Executive Dir, Mary Walker Foundation, 3031 Wilcox Blvd, Chattanooga, TN 37411.

EDWARDS, JOHN W., JR.
Physician. **PERSONAL:** Born Apr 09, 1933, Ferndale, MI; son of John W Edwards, Sr, MD (deceased) and Josephine Wood Edwards (deceased); married Ella Marie Law; children: Joella Marie, John W III. **EDUCATION:** Univ of MI, Ann Arbor, BS, 1954; Wayne State Univ, graduate studies, 1954-56; Howard Univ Coll of Medicine, MD, 1960. **CAREER:** Walter Reed Gen Hospital, internship, 1960-61, surgical resident, 1962-63, urological resident, 1963-66; Straub Clinic Inc, urologist, 1970-74, chief div of surgery, 1973; private practice, urologist, 1974-; asst chief dept of surgery, Queen's Medical Center, 1977-79; chief dept of clinical serv, active staff, Kapiolani Women's & Children's Medical Center, 1981-83; active staff, Kuakini Hospital; consulting staff, Rehabilitation Hospital of the Pacific; consultant in urology, Tripler Army Medical Center; John Burns School of Medicine, Univ of HI, assoc clinical prof; chief of surgery, Queen's Medical Center, 1989-90. **ORGANIZATIONS:** Certified, Amer Bd of Urology; fellow, Amer Coll of Surgeons; mem, Amer Urological Assn, Western Section Amer Urological Assn, Pan Pacific Surgical Assn, HI Urological Assn, Amer Medical Assn, Honolulu County Medical Soc, HI Medical Assn, South West Oncology Group, Natl Medical Assn, Alpha Phi Alpha, Chi Delta Mu, Waialae Country Club; life mem, NAACP; fellow, Amer Coll of Surgeons; commr, chmn, City and County of Honolulu Liquor Commn, 1987-89; governor from Hawaii, Amer Coll of Surgeons, 1987-90; pres, Western Section Amer Urological Assn, 1989-90. **HONORS/ACHIEVEMENTS:** Alpha Omega Alpha Honor Medical Soc, 1959; co-author, "Anuria Secondary to Bilateral Ureteropelvic Fungus Balls," Urology, 1980; Howard Gray Award, Urology Section Natl Medical Assn, 1988. **MILITARY SERVICE:** USAF capt 1959-63; AUS lt col 1963-70; Bronze Star. **BUSINESS ADDRESS:** Assoc Clinical Professor, Univ of HI, John Burns Sch of Medicine, 1319 Punahou St Ste 1160, Honolulu, HI 96826.

EDWARDS, JOHN WILSON
Director. **PERSONAL:** Born Feb 17, 1942, Durham County, NC; married Eloise Freeman; children: Brian, Robin. **EDUCATION:** Durham Coll, 1961; NC Fund, Comm Action Tech Training Prgm, 1965. **CAREER:** State Econ Opp Office NC, dir Present; Institutional Devel Soul City Co, mgr; Alumni Affairs Durham Coll, dir; Voter Educ Proj Atlanta, area coord; NC Voter & Educ Prgm Durham, organizer; Operation Breakthrough Inc Durham, leadership devel coord 1966-67; Winston-salem Boys Club, dir 1965-66; NAACP Durham, field sec-at-large 1962-65; NAACP Youth Workers, field supr, student 1961-62; NAACP, student field worker 1960-61. **ORGANIZATIONS:** Mem Soul City Found Inc; UOCI Fed Credit Union; Durham Con on Affairs of Black People; Durham Opp Found Inc; Durham Coll; Durham Bus & Professional Chain; NC Voter Educ Proj Inc; NC Fed of Child Care Ctrs ; Econ Devel Corp; Durham Coll Alumni Assn pres Pan African Early Educ Ctr; Lincoln Comm Health Ctr; past-chmn adv United Black Officers of Urham, NC consumer credit counseling serv of Wake Co Union Bapt Ct; mem Sr Usher Bd; mem Bd of Trustees. **BUSINESS ADDRESS:** PO Box 27687, Raleigh, NC 27611.

EDWARDS, KENNETH J.
Business executive. **PERSONAL:** Born Apr 05, 1947, Beaumont, TX; married Gloria J Holmes; children: Melissa R, Kenitha J, Kenneth J. **EDUCATION:** Lamar U, BS 1970. **CAREER:** John Deere Co, div sales mgr 1979-, serv mgr consumer prod 1977-79, div serv mgr 1976-77, terrtry mgr 1973-76, sales prom supr 1972-73, serv rep 1971-72; US Govt, reliablty engr 1970-71. **BUSINESS ADDRESS:** John Deere & Company, 1400 13th St, East Moline, IL 61244.

EDWARDS, LEO DEREK
Composer, music educator. **PERSONAL:** Born Jan 31, 1937, Cincinnati. **EDUCATION:** Mannes Coll of Music, BS 1966; CtyUniv NY, MA 1969. **CAREER:** Shumiatcher School Music, chmn theory dept 1965-; Mannes Coll Music, faculty 1968-; CityUniv NY, faculty 1969-75. **ORGANIZATIONS:** Soc Black Composers; Phi Mu Alpha Sinfonia (profl music frat); Music Tchrs Nat Assn. **HONORS/ACHIEVEMENTS:** Phi Mu Alpha composition contest winner 1960; Joseph Dillon Award Pedagogy 1966; music tchrs Nat Assn Award 1975. **BUSINESS ADDRESS:** The Mannes College of Music, 150 W 85th, New York, NY 10024.

EDWARDS, LONNIE
Physician. **EDUCATION:** Morehouse College, attended 1945; Howard Univ Sch of Medicine, MD 1948; Provident Hosp, internship 1948-49, residency genl surgery 1949-52; Mt Sinai Hosp, residency 1952-53; Roosevelt Univ, MPA 1974; Nova Univ, MPA 1977. **CAREER:** Private Practice, genl surgery 1955-70, family practice 1960; Fantus Health Ctr, assoc med dir 1970-71, dir 1970-71; Cook Co Hospital, dir division of ambulatory serv 1971-73, assoc med dir 1974-83; Fantus Health Ctr, dir employee health serv hospital based coord home health care prog 1974-83; Roosevelt Univ, public admin prog; Abraham Lincoln Sch of Medicine, former clinical asst prof of family prac; Chicago Medical Sch, clinical asst prof dept of family 1974-; Chicago Dept of Health, commissioner. **ORGANIZATIONS:** Medical staff Cook Co Hospital Dept of Surgery; mem Scientific Comm Exec Med Staff Cook Co Hosp; mem Medical Audit & Utilization Comm CCH; chmn Outpatient Medical Audit Comm Cook Co Hosp; mem Quality Assurance Comm CCH; mem House of Delegates Amer Hosp Assn; mem Health Serv Develop Grants Study Sect Dept of Health Educ & Welfare; past chmn Governing Council Assembly of Ambulatory & Home Care Serv Amer Hosp Assn; mem Natl Assn of Neighborhood Health Ctrs; mem Prairie State Med Soc; mem Amer Med Assn; mem IL State Med Soc; mem Chicago Med Soc; mem Industrial Med Assn; mem Central States Soc of Industrial Medicine & Surgery; mem amer Assn for the Advancement of Sci; mem Assn of Admin of Ambulatory Svcs; mem Amer Acad of Family Physicians; mem Natl Medical Assn; mem Cook Co Physicians Assn; mem Amer Public Health Assn; mem Amer Hospital Assn. **HONORS/ACHIEVEMENTS:** Numerous papers presented to various professional orgns and publications including, Ambulatory Care in a Large Urban Hospital Governors State Univ Seminar March 1978; Oral Cavity Evaluation-A Part of Prenatal Care IL Medical Journal Lonnie C Edwards MD Pedro A Poma MD et al Feb 1979 Vol 155 No 2; Selection of an Organizational Model for Maximizing the Effectiveness of Coordination of the Components of Outpatient Services 1977. **MILITARY SERVICE:** AUS Med Corp capt genl surgeon 1953-55. **BUSINESS ADDRESS:** Commissioner of Health, City of Chicago, 50 W Washington St, Chicago, IL 60602.

EDWARDS, LUTHER HOWARD
Elected official. **PERSONAL:** Born Jan 06, 1954, Butler, AL; son of Lee J Edwards Sr and Alma Jackson Edwards; married Geraldine Palmer. **EDUCATION:** Livingston Univ, BS 1972, ME 1976. **CAREER:** James River, Accounting; Town of Lisman, councilman & vice-mayor. **ORGANIZATIONS:** Pres Afro-Amer Soc; vice pres Owen Love Business Assn; mem Student Govt Assn; Collegiate Civilian; mem Men's Housing Council; mem Intramural Sports Assn; mem Yearbook Staff; mem Host & Hostess Comm; mem Phi Mu Alpha Sinfonia Frat; sec Lisman Vol Fire Dept 1980-; sec Pleasant Hill Lodge #950 1980-; sec Edwards Pride Royal Arch Masons 1982-. **MILITARY SERVICE:** AUSR E-6 10 yrs; Army Commendation Medal. **HOME ADDRESS:** PO Box 110, Lisman, AL 36912.

EDWARDS, MATTIE SMITH
Educator. **PERSONAL:** Born Apr 16, 1931, Roxboro, NC; married E Zeno MD; children:

Zenia Colette, Tanise Indra. **EDUCATION:** Elizabeth City StUniv NC, BS 1949; NC Cntrl U, MaA 1953; Duke U, EdD 1970. **CAREER:** Tanise Indra Asso, Springfield Coll MA, prof of educ 1969-; Cleveland Co Schools NC, gen supt 1965-69, reading coord 1965-69; Newbold School at Fayetteville State Univ, supr, teacher 1953-58. **ORGANIZATIONS:** Adv Commn Educ Personnel for St of MA 1978-; chairprsn, Springfield Coll Tchr Educ Dept 1973-76; bd of trustees Bay Path Jr Coll MA 1974; mem Kappa Delta Pi Intrntl Reading Assn; bd of dir Assn of Supr & Curriculum Dev; Dunbar Comm Cntr, Springfield MA 1977-; mem Urban League of Springfield; NAACP, Civil Lib. **HONORS/ACHIEVEMENTS:** Links Inc Award of Appreciation, Elizabeth City StUniv 1980.

EDWARDS, MILES STANLEY
Educator. **PERSONAL:** Born Mar 21, 1951, Fort Wayne, IN; son of William Howard Edwards, Sr (deceased) and Wanda Woods Edwards (deceased). **EDUCATION:** Ball State Univ, BS 1970-73; IN Univ, MS in Ed 1977-78; Ohio State Univ, GE Fellow 1980; Ball State Univ, admin cert 1981-83; Univ of Akron, PhD candidate 1987-. **CAREER:** Ft Wayne Community Schools, special ed teacher 1973-75; DeKalb GA County School Dist, math teacher 1975-76; Ft Wayne Community Schools, teacher of special education 1973-75; DeKalb, GA County School Dist, math teacher 1975-76; Operation Breadbasket Learning Acad, teacher 1985-; coordinator of instruction; Ft Wayne Community Schools, competency resource teacher 1976-87, resource teacher 1988-. **ORGANIZATIONS:** Natl Alliance of Black School Educators, mem 1983; Ministerial Alliance Scholarship Found, board mem 1983-86; Ft Wayne Alliance of Black School Educators, IN State Black Expo, board mem 1982; Homework Hotline, TV host of educational program 1982-85; The Natl Alliance of Black School Educators, mem 1983; Min board mem at large 1983-; Alpha Phi Alpha, corresponding secretary 1984-86; Phi Delta Kappa, mem 1985; IN State Education Assoc, board of minority affairs; Ministerial Alliance Scholarship Foundation, board mem 1983-; Ft Wayne Alliance of Black School Educators, board mem at large 1983-; Alpha Phi Alpha, corresp sec 1984-86; Natl Education Assoc-Delegate, mem 1985-86; Assoc of Teacher Educators, mem 1986; MLK Montessori School, board of directors 1986-; Phi Delta Kappa, mem 1985; IN State Education Assoc, minority affairs committee 1985-86; Natl Education Assoc, mem 1985-; International Reading Assoc, dist rep, 1986; Assoc of Teacher Educators, mem 1986; mem, 1986-, vice pres, 1989, MLK Montessori School, board of directors; MLK Living Memorial, Inc, board mem 1986-; mem Urban League, mem NAACP; mem Internatl Reading Assoc Local, State, & Natl 1973; Assn of Children & Adults with LD 1983; Reg field coord Project Alpha 1987; life mem Alpha Phi Alpha; Assn of Black Communicators 1982-85; exec bd Old Fort YMCA; pres Panhellenic Coun 1974-75; Ft Wayne Miss Blk Am Pagent Com Coord of Judges; vice pres Ft Wayne Polit Blk Assembly; mem Arlington Church of God, Akron OH; pres Indiana Black Expo-Ft Wayne Chapter 1988. **HONORS/ACHIEVEMENTS:** General Electric Co, Foundation Fellowship Award 1980; US Jaycees, "Outstanding Young Men of America" 1984.

EDWARDS, OSCAR LEE
Management consultant, media representative. **PERSONAL:** Born Dec 08, 1953, Long Beach, CA; son of Lewis Allen Edwards and Susie Belle Edwards; married Sharon Renee White (divorced); children: Oscar Jr, Ivan Lewis. **EDUCATION:** UCLA, BA 1978, MBA 1981. **CAREER:** Crenshaw YMCA, program dir 1977-79; Edwards Enterprises, pres 1978-81; Czand Assocs, vice pres of admin 1981-84; Pacific Serv Inc, project mgr 1984-85; Central News WAVE Publs, dir of mktg 1985-87; Edwards Assoc, pres 1987—; TMG/SER, Inc, pres 1987—; Triaxial Mgmt Service, mem of bd of dir, 1989—. **ORGANIZATIONS:** Bank credit analyst Bank of Amer 1980; rsch asst Mayor Bradley's Africa Task Force 1981-82; chmn bd of mgrs Crenshaw YMCA 1983-84; pres LA Chapter Natl Black MBA Assoc 1985-86; bd of dirs UCLA Black Alumni Assoc 1986—; adv bd Drew Health Educ Project 1986—; program comm UCLA Mgmt Alumni Assoc 1987—; certified NFL Contract Advisor 1987—; bd of advisors, So CA chapter, United Negro College Fund, 1989—; prog comm, Amer Marketing Assn, 1984-85; Assn of Mgmt Consultants, 1984. **HONORS/ACHIEVEMENTS:** 1977 Football All-Amer, UCLA; MBA of the Year NBMBAA Los Angeles 1985; MBA of the Year Natl Black MBA Assn, 1986; Very Special Professional, Congressman Augustus Hawkins 1986; Hon Race Dir Comm City of LA Marathon 1986, 1987; producer of Outreach Videos, 1986, 1988-89. **BUSINESS ADDRESS:** President, Edwards Associates, PO Box 43216, Los Angeles, CA 90043.

EDWARDS, PRESTON JOSEPH
Business executive. **PERSONAL:** Born Jul 03, 1943, New Orleans, LA; married Rosa; children: Preston Jr, Scott. **EDUCATION:** Atlanta U, MBA 1966; Dillard U, BA 1965. **CAREER:** The Black Collegian Mag, pub 1970-; Interracial Cncl for Bus Opp vice pres 1976-77; Great Atlantic & Pacific Tea Co, reg mgr 1975-76; So U, Baton Rouge, asst prof 1969-71; 1st Nat City Bank, asst cashier 1966-69. **ORGANIZATIONS:** Bd mem Jr Achvmt; adv bd Nat Alliance of Bus; pres Journal Inc; publ NSBE Journal , Jrnl of the Natl Tech Assoc, NAMEPA Jrnl; bd dir Council on Career Devel for Minorities; bd trust Finingstone Coll, adv bd Zavier Prep HS. **HONORS/ACHIEVEMENTS:** Hon Degree Doctor of Human Letters Feningstone Coll. **BUSINESS ADDRESS:** Publisher, The Black Collegian Magazine, 1240 S Broad St, New Orleans, LA 70125.

EDWARDS, ROBERT
Educator. **PERSONAL:** Born Jan 30, 1939, Slocombe, AL; married Barbara J Spalding; children: Randel Keith, Robert Corey. **EDUCATION:** Bethune-Cookman Coll, BS 1965; City Coll of NY, MS 1973. **CAREER:** Youth Training Acad, dir 1969; Progress Assn for Economic Devel, dir 1972; Opportunity Indus Center, branch mgr 1974; Dade County Public Schools, prin. **ORGANIZATIONS:** Exec council Assn for Study of Afro-Amer Life & History 1971; bd dir Lexia Sch for Young Adults 1974; bd dir OURS Inc 1974; mem Urban League, NAACP, Natl Alliance of Black Sch Educators, Kappa Alpha Psi, Bethune-Cookman Coll Alumni Assn, Assn for Study of Afro-Amer Life & History. **HONORS/ACHIEVEMENTS:** Disting Alumni Awd Bethune-Cookman Coll; OIC NY Supreme Dedication Awd for Altruistic Serv to the Educ of Youth; Awds from Alpha Phi Alpha, alpha Kappa Alpha, City of Miami, OIC NY Disting Serv Awd. **MILITARY SERVICE:** AUS 1961-63. **BUSINESS ADDRESS:** Principal, Dade Co Public Schools, 1801 N W 60th St, Miami, FL 33142.

EDWARDS, ROBERT ERSKINE
Educator. **PERSONAL:** Born Nov 07, 1904, Crawfordville, GA; married Louise E Davis; children: Sanford E. **EDUCATION:** Morehouse Coll, AB; Oberlin Grad Sch of Theol, BD. **CAREER:** Hancock Co High Schools, teacher retired 1985. **ORGANIZATIONS:** Mem Bd of Educ Hancock Co; cnslr Hancock & Greene Co; moderator Second Shiloh Assn 1960-; pres Second Shiloh & Sunday Sch Conv 1950-; mem Compass Lodge #160 F&AM, Prince Hall; chmn Heart Fund Dr. **HONORS/ACHIEVEMENTS:** Tchr of Yr, Hancock Co 1955; Distinguished Serv to Educ in GA, Ft Valley St Coll 1968; Unselfish Serv & Leadership, Second Shiloh Assn 1972.

EDWARDS, ROBERT VALENTINO
Educator. **PERSONAL:** Born Dec 15, 1940, Baltimore, MD; son of Robert F Edwards and Laura (Jackson) Edwards; married Anne Lindsay. **EDUCATION:** Johns Hopkins Univ, AB Math 1962, MS Chem Engrg 1964, PhD Chem Engrg 1968. **CAREER:** Case Western Reserve Univ, asst prof 1970-73, assoc prof 1973-79, full prof 1979-; chmn chem engrg dept 1984-. **HONORS/ACHIEVEMENTS:** Over 100 scientific papers and talks 1968-85; received more than $1,000,000 in rsch grants 1968-85. **BUSINESS ADDRESS:** Chmn Chemical Engineering, Case Western ReserveUniv, Smith Bldg, Cleveland, OH 44106.

EDWARDS, RONALD ALFRED
Business executive. **PERSONAL:** Born Jan 10, 1939, Kansas City, MO; children: Brian. **EDUCATION:** Univ of Syracuse, Cert in Comm Org 1965. **CAREER:** Nrthrn States Power Co, customer Bus Off 1970-72, coord Envrnmntl Affrs 1972-74, mgr Comm Affrs 1975-78, asst to pres Systms Oprtn 1977-79, asstto vice pres Corp Affairs 1980-83, asst to exec vice pres 1983-84. **ORGANIZATIONS:** V chm Minneapolis Civil Rghts Comm 1968-71; treas Minneapolis Urban League 1972-77; mem Minneapolis Civil Rghts Comm 1978-83, chair 1979-83; pres Minneapolis Urban Leag 1978-; 1st v chair Phyllis Wheatley Comm Ctr 1984-; mem Minneapolis Afrmtv Act Comm 1971; pres Northside Stlmnt Serv 1976-79; bd mem Phyllis Wheatley Comm Ctr 1981-; mem MN St Human Rights Bd 1977-79; mem Jr Chamber of Comm 1972-74; mem Hennepin Co Sntncng Task Force 1977; mem MN Affirmative Act Oversite Comm 1971-. **HONORS/ACHIEVEMENTS:** Otstndng civic serv awd Minneapolis Urban League 1971; comm serv awd Black Women Untd 1979; otstndng civic MN Afrmtv Action Assoc 1983; otstndng vol UntdWay of Minneapolis 1982; otstndng vol WTCN TV 1979; otstndng citzen City of Minneapolis 1978; otstndng civic Minneapolis Urban League Sr Prog 1979; exec prod & host Radio Prog Urban Views/KMOJ Radio Mpls; author Numerous News Stories. **BUSINESS ADDRESS:** Assistant to President, Northern States Power Co, 414 Nicollet Mall, Minneapolis, MN 55401.

EDWARDS, RONDLE E.
Educator. **PERSONAL:** Born Jul 19, 1934, Richmond, VA; son of Alfred M Edwards and Irene Taylor Edwards; married Gloria Twitty; children: Cassandra L, Lanee D Washington, Ronda D. **EDUCATION:** Virginia Union Univ, AB; Virginia State Univ, MA; Ohio Univ, PhD; Ohio State Univ, Columbia Univ, Post-doctoral Study. **CAREER:** Richmond Public Schools, asst supt for gen admr and pupil personnel 1972-75, asst supt for support serv 1975-76; E Cleveland City Schools, superintendent 1976-84; Portsmouth Public Schools, superintendent 1984-87; Virginia Dept of Educ, asst state supt 1987-. **ORGANIZATIONS:** Mem Cleveland East Rotary Club; mem exec bd and trustee Amer Red Cross Greater Cleveland Chapter; trustee Cleveland Scholarship Fund; mem Northern Ohio Lung Assoc, United Negro College Fund; bd of trustees adv bd Western Reserve Historical Soc; mem Phi Delta Kappa Professional Frat, Amer Assoc of School Personnel Administrators, Amer Assoc of School Administrators, Ohio Sch Bds Assoc, Manpower Planning and Develop of Cleveland; consultant Educational Testing Svcs; chmn Cuyahoga County Special Educ Service Ctr; adv comm John Carroll Univ Dept of Educ Ohio Adv Council for Vocational Educ; mem Amer Vocational Educ Legislative Study Team; expert witness before US House of Representatives Comm on Educ and Labor. **HONORS/ACHIEVEMENTS:** Awd for Excellence in Public Educ Delta Sigma Theta Sor; Outstanding Achievement Awd Kappa Alpha Psi Frat, Phi Delta Kappa; Man of the Year Cleveland Club of the Natl Assoc of Negro Business and Professional Women's Clubs; Exec Educator's Recognition One of North America's Top 100 Educators; Ohio Univ Alumni Medal of Merit for Notable Accomplishments in Educ Admin 1986; authored 4 books; numerous presentations. **BUSINESS ADDRESS:** Asst State Superintendent for Public Instruction, Virginia Department of Education, PO Box 6 Q, Monroe Building, Richmond, VA 23216.

EDWARDS, RUPERT L.
Physician. **PERSONAL:** Born Jul 05, 1929, New Amsterdam, Guyana;son of Robert and Edith; married Billie Jean; children: Robert Charles, Geoffrey Taylor. **EDUCATION:** Roosevelt U, 1953-55; IN Univ Sch of Med, 1959. **CAREER:** Wayne St U, instr 1964-65, clinical asst prof 1965-72, assoc prof 1972-; Edwards & Singal, PC, pres 1978-; chairman, Dept of Medicine and Family Practice, Samaritan Health Center, Detroit. **ORGANIZATIONS:** Chief of staff Hutzel Hosp, Detroit 1975-76; mem Detroit Med Ctr Adv Comm 1975-78; life mem NAACP; mem Detroit Athletic Club 1980; mem Detroit Econ Club 1983-; founder-pres Ministerial Phys Hlth Alliance. **BUSINESS ADDRESS:** 4727 St Antoine, Detroit, MI 48201.

EDWARDS, RUTH MCCALLA
Attorney. **PERSONAL:** Born Apr 23, 1949, Cleveland, OH; married Michael M Edwards; children: Ashaunda, Alanna, Kamala. **EDUCATION:** Hiram Coll, BA 1971; Univ of Cincinnati Coll of Law, JD 1974. **CAREER:** Legal Aid Soc of Cincinnati, atty & office mgr 1974-77; Private Law Practice, atty 1977-79; Hamilton County Public Defender Comm, atty 1979; Univ of Cincinnati, atty, prog coord, paralegal prog 1979-. **ORGANIZATIONS:** Admitted OH State Bar 1974; admitted Fed Bar So Dist of OH 1974; mem bd trustees Cincinnati Tech Coll 1977-; mem Amer, Cincinnati Bar Assns; mem & past pres Black Lawyers Assn of Cincinnati; past bd mem Legal Aid Soc of Cincinnati; bd mem & officer Winton Hills Med & Halth Ctr; bd mem & past officer Comprehensive Comm Child Care; bd mem Cincinnati Tech Coll; mem Alpha Kappa Alpha Sor; arbitrator Better Business Bureau Arbitration Prog; mem Assn of Comm Coll Trustees; sec Central Region Minority Affairs Assembly of the Assn of Comm Coll Trustees; mem Amer Assn for Paralegal Education Inc; chairperson bd trustees Cincinnati Tech Coll 1983-84; past bd mem, officer Winton Hills Med & Health Ctr; arbitrator Amer Arbitration Assoc; chair Central Region Minority Affairs Comm of the Assoc of Community Coll Trustees. **HONORS/ACHIEVEMENTS:** Hon Degree of Tech Letters Cincinnati Tech Coll 1985; YMCA Black Achievers Awd 1985. **BUSINESS ADDRESS:** Program Coordinator, Univ of Cincinnati, Paralegal Program, Cincinnati, OH 45221.

EDWARDS, SHIRLEY HEARD
Elected official. **PERSONAL:** Born Oct 23, 1949, Doddsville, MS; married Thomas E Edwards; children: Darron, Thomas Jr, Cheryl. **EDUCATION:** MS Valley State Univ, BS

1983. **CAREER:** Fannie Humer Day Care, sec bookkeeper 1969-79; Sunflower/Humphrey Co Progress, career counselor 1979-83; Sunflower Co Schools, school attendance officer 1983-; City of Ruleville, alderwoman. **ORGANIZATIONS:** Apt mgr Quick Construction 1972-. **HONORS/ACHIEVEMENTS:** Comm Serv Awd NAACP Sunflower Co 1983. **HOME ADDRESS:** 113 Vernice Ave, Ruleville, MS 38771.

EDWARDS, SOLOMON
Educator. **PERSONAL:** Born Apr 02, 1932, Indianapolis, IN; married Claudia; children: Gregory D, Risa M. **EDUCATION:** IN Univ, BS 1954, MS 1969, EdD 1984. **CAREER:** Arts Festival, coord 1956; IN Public Schools, teacher; Purdue Univ, assoc faculty 1971-79. **ORGANIZATIONS:** Mem Omega Psi Phi, NAACP, Phi Delta Kappa IN Univ. **HONORS/ACHIEVEMENTS:** Writers Conf Poetry Awd 1953; dir New York City Dramatic Readers 1957-58; poems published 1959-77; author of "What's Your Reading Attitude?" 1979; "This Day Father" 1979; Discussion moderator Intl Reading Assn Natl Convention 1979; educational game "Freedom & Martin Luther King" 1980.

EDWARDS, SYLVIA
Attorney. **PERSONAL:** Born May 09, 1947, Lackawanna, NY. **EDUCATION:** State Univ Coll at Buffalo, BS 1969; Howard Univ Sch of Law Washington, JD 1973. **CAREER:** Employment Sect Dept of Justice, trial atty 1973-76; Office of Spl Litigation Dept of Justice Washington DC, sr trial atty; Council of the DC, legislative counsel 1977-79; DC Law Revision Commn, sr atty 1979-. **ORGANIZATIONS:** Mem Adv Commn on Codification Wash DC 1977-79; legislative consult Com on Pub Serv & Consumer Affairs Council of DC 1979; mem NY Bar 1974; mem PA Bar 1974; mem Natl Assn of Black Women Atty 1978. **HONORS/ACHIEVEMENTS:** Spl Achievement Awd Howard Univ Sch of Law 1972; Intl Moot Ct Awd Howard Univ Sch of Law 1973; Spl Achievement Awd Dept of Justice Wash DC 1975; Resolution of Spl Achievement Council of DC 1979. **BUSINESS ADDRESS:** Sr Attorney, DC Law Revision Commn, 1411 K St NW, Ste 1000, Washington, DC 20005.

EDWARDS, THEODORE THOMAS
Retired government official. **PERSONAL:** Born Sep 08, 1917, Bridgeport, CT; married Vivian Blackmon (died 1987). **EDUCATION:** Quinnipac Coll, Newhaven CT, AA 1941; New York U, BS 1946; Columbia U, MSW 1947; Univ of Chicago, grad work 1957-59; US Public Health Hospital Lexington KY, 1956. **CAREER:** Goldwater Hospital NY, med social worker 1947-48; NJ Parole Bd, parole officer 1949-55; US Probation-US Parole Commn, retired probation officer 1955-77. **ORGANIZATIONS:** Youth wrkr, NY Youth Bd 1947; mem, Nat Cncl on Crime & Del 1955-80; mem, Federal Probation Off Assn 1956-80; co-founder, Narcotic Treatment Center 1956; mem, Middle Atlantic St Conf of Correction 1956-80; mem, Rotary International, Paterson NJ 1975-77; mem, Amer Correction Assn 1975-80; life mem Fed Prob Off Assn 1977. **HONORS/ACHIEVEMENTS:** 1st Black Federal Probation Officer, Newark NJ 1955; subject of "The Probation Officer;, Newark Sunday News 1957; Certificate Of App, Newark Boys Club 1969; 1st Black Fed Probation Dir, Paterson NJ 1975-77; 4 Battle Stars; Crox De Geurre; co-founder 1st Private Narcotic Treatment Center Newark NJ 1957. **MILITARY SERVICE:** AUS 1942-45; AUS tch sgt 1942-45.

EDWARDS, THEODORE UNALDO
Government official. **PERSONAL:** Born Sep 18, 1934, New York, NY; married Dr Ione L D Edwards; children: Donna M O'Bannon, Esq. **EDUCATION:** St Peter's College, BS 1955; Rutgers Univ, MSW 1962; BARO Clinic, Certificate 1967. **CAREER:** US Court/Justice Dept, probation officer 1962-69; Harlem Child Guidance Clinic, clinical dir 1969-78; Comm Serv Soc of NY, exec dir 1973-76; Coll of New Rochelle NY, adj prof 1979-; City of New Rochelle Dept of Human Svcs, deputy commissioner 1977-. **ORGANIZATIONS:** Bd mem Catholic Big Brothers of NY 1975-; commissioner Office of Black Ministry Archdiocese of NY 1977-; bd mem Salvation Army of New Rochelle 1985-; exec bd NAACP 1985-; mem Omega (Omicron Iota Chapt). **HONORS/ACHIEVEMENTS:** Community Serv Awd College of New Rochelle NY 1983-85; Spike Harris Serv Awd NY Counselors 1985; publication "Why Bartering," "Budget Time," both 1981 The Voice Magazine; "The City of New Rochelle Senior Population," 1986; Columnist for Tomorrow Newspaper, Westchester NY. **MILITARY SERVICE:** AUS sgt 2 yrs. **BUSINESS ADDRESS:** Deputy Commissioner, City of New Rochelle, Dept of Human Services, City Hall, New Rochelle, NY 10801.

EDWARDS, THOMAS OLIVER
Educational administrator,psychologist. **PERSONAL:** Born Jan 04, 1943, Vanceboro, NC; son of Calvin Edwards and Blanche Edwards; married Loretta McFadden; children: Tomia, Kuturi, Loretta, Tiffany, Calvin. **EDUCATION:** CCNY, BA 1965; NY Univ, MA 1968; CUNY, MPh 1980, PhD 1981. **CAREER:** Peace Corps Costa Rica, volunteer 1965-67; Alexander Burger Jr High School, teacher 1967-71; Medgar Evers Coll instructor/lecturer 1971-81, asst professor 1981-84, assoc professor 1984-,assoc dean of admin 1986-88, acting chmn, Social Science Division 1988-89. **ORGANIZATIONS:** Baseball coach Rochdale Village Little League 1979-; consultant Urban Strategies Inc 1980-; consultant Hale House for the Promotion of Human Potential 1983; board of dir mem Medgar Evers Coll Child Care Ctr 1983-; adjunct professor Coll of New Rochelle 1984-85. **HONORS/ACHIEVEMENTS:** Pamela Galiber Memorial Scholarship CUNY Grad Div 1977; Communication Skills in the Inner City, Effects of Race & Dialect on Decoding New England Ed Rsch Org Annual Best Papers Monograph 1983; co-organizer of International African-American Cultural & Research Assn; organizer of Annual Conference Focusing on the Black Male, Medgar Evers Coll/CUNY. **HOME ADDRESS:** 178-07 137th Ave, Springfield Garden, NY 11434. **BUSINESS ADDRESS:** Associate Professor of Psych, Medgar Evers Coll/CUNY, 1150 Carroll St, Brooklyn, NY 11225.

EDWARDS, VERBA L.
Auto executive. **PERSONAL:** Born Jul 15, 1950, Boligee, AL; married Roberta L; children: Keith, Christopher, Raquel. **EDUCATION:** Alcorn State Univ, BS Bus Admin 1973; Central MI Univ, MA Personnel Admin 1977. **CAREER:** General Motors Corp Chevy Truck Assembly Plant, coord equal employment oppor, general supervisor mfg, supervisor industrial relations, supervisor hourly personnel admin 1973-81; General Motors Corp Chevrolet Central Office, divisional salaried personnel admin 1981-83; General Motors Corp Saginaw Div, asst dir of personnel 1984-. **ORGANIZATIONS:** Mem Omega Psi Phi Frat, The Natl Alliance of Business Coll/Industry Relations Div, Natl Assoc for Equal Oppor in Higher Educ. **HONORS/ACHIEVEMENTS:** Outstanding Young Men of Amer; Who's Who in Black Corporate America. **HOME ADDRESS:** 1623 Brentwood Dr, Troy, MI 48098.

EDWARDS-ASCHOFF, PATRICIA JOANN
Director performing arts. **PERSONAL:** Born Feb 23, 1940, Louisville, MS; married Peter Richard Aschoff. **EDUCATION:** Chadron State Coll, BS 1972; Univ of No IA, MA 1974. **CAREER:** Dr William J Walker Chicago, dental asst 1963-70; Black Hawk Co, juvenile probation officer 1974-77; Univ of Northern IA, dir ethnic minorities cultural & educ center 1977, human relations instructor 1979-80, special prog asst, div of continuing educ & special progs; Domestic Violence Project Inc, exec dir. **ORGANIZATIONS:** Former bd chmn Minority Alcoholism Action Prog 1976-78; mem Professional & Sci Council 1977; training consult Jesse Cosby Neighborhood Ctr Parent Groups 1978; exec bd mem Family & Children's Council 1978; bd mem/treas Wesley Found 1978; mem Antioch Baptist Church Waterloo IA; bd mem Friends of KHKE/KUNI Pub Radio 1979; mem Alpha Chi #1736 ESA Intl Sorority Oxford MS. **HONORS/ACHIEVEMENTS:** Special Achievement Awd Educ Oppor Prog 1973-74; Outstanding Young Women in Amer 1974; Professional Serv Awd Juvenile Ct Serv 1977; Certificate of Appreciation Kiwanis Club of Oxford MS.

EFFORT, EDMUND D.
Dentist. **PERSONAL:** Born Jun 20, 1949, Chicago, IL; son of Exzene Effort and Beverley Effort; married Elaine Leaphart; children: Edmundson David, April Elaine. **EDUCATION:** Univ of IL, BS 1972; Univ of MI, DDS 1977; US Dental Inst, 1986-89. **CAREER:** Private practice, dentist. **ORGANIZATIONS:** Mem Alpha Phi Alpha, 1969-89; mem Amer Dental Assoc 1977-89, NAACP 1981-89, Urban League 1981-89, PA Dental Assoc 1981-89; bd dir Lemington Home for the Aged 1984; mem Lions 1985, Elks 1986; bd dir United Cerebral Palsy 1987, Connely Trade School 1987, Eva P Mitchell Residense 1987, Urban Youth Action 1986-87; coaco of little league baseball, Boys Club 1989. **HONORS/ACHIEVEMENTS:** Three articles written for Talk Magazine 1985; Black Achievers News in Print Magazine 1984; PA Air Commendation Medal PA ANG 1986; Community Serv Award Upward Bound Proj 1987; Good Samaritan Award, American Red Cross 1988. **MILITARY SERVICE:** PA Air Natl Guard maj 10 yrs; Air Commendation Medal 1986; General Stewart Medal 1985; Chief of Dental Serv, 171st PaANG. **BUSINESS ADDRESS:** Dentist, Gateway Towers Ste 215, Pittsburgh, PA 15222.

EGGLESTON, NEVERETT, JR.
President. **PERSONAL:** Born in Richmond, VA; married Jean Deloris; children: Neverett A III, Jayne. **EDUCATION:** AT&T Univ, BS 1955. **CAREER:** Mainstream Inc, pres; Golden Skillet, principal; Silas Lee and Assocs, principal; Eggleston Auto Serv Ctr, president and ceo 1979-; Eggleston's Motel, president and ceo 1960-. **ORGANIZATIONS:** Bd mem Natl Business League 1970-; chmn of bd Minority Supplier Develop Inc 1978-, E and R Janitorial Serv Inc 1978-; bd of mgmt Radiantherm Inc; mem bd of dirs Jefferson Sheraton Hotel; mem adv bd Womensbank; mem Richmond Chamber of Commerce, VA Chamber of Commerce; vice pres Capital Area Innkeepers Assoc; bd of dirs, pres Metro Business League; bd of dirs Richmond Urban League; mem bd of dirs Richmond Comm Action Program; mem bd of dirs Amer Red Cross; chmn People League of Voters; mem bd of dirs Greater Richmond Transit Co; mem of various bds and comms United Givers Fund. **HONORS/ACHIEVEMENTS:** Spoke Awd and Spark Plug Awd Junior Chamber of Commerce; Businessman of the Year Awd Metro Business League; Martin Luther King Comm Learning Week Business Recognition 1982.

EICHELBERGER, BRENDA
Executive director. **PERSONAL:** Born Oct 21, 1939, Washington, DC. **EDUCATION:** Govs St U, extens grad work in women's std 1976-; Chicago St U, MsS 1973; Eng and Bus Edn, BS; DC Tchrs Coll, 1963. **CAREER:** Natl Coll of Educ, m equiv school admin and supvr; Natl Allian of Black Feminists, div exec dir; Chicago Public School System, teacher, librarian, counselor 1967-77; Muscatine Community School Dist, teacher 1966-67; Washington DC Public School System, teacher 1964-65. **ORGANIZATIONS:** Found and exec dir, Natl Allian of Black Feminists 1976-; bd mem, Pro and Con Screening Bd 1976-; bd mem, Chicagoland Women's Fed Credit Union 1976-; found, Black Womens's Cntr 1976-; bd mem, treas, Chicago Consort of Women in Educ Prog 1976; fdr, Chrwmn, Chicago Chap Natl Black Feminist Org 1974-76; bd mem, Citz Comm on the Media 1975-76; adv bd mem, Blue Gargoyle Grp Hm for Girls 1975; sec, Dist Ten Tchr Cncl 1974-75. **HONORS/ACHIEVEMENTS:** Writer of artic 1977; Bicent Excell Award, for Black Womanhood, Elite Soc of Amer 1976; Outstndng Elem Sch & Tchr Award, Fuller & Dees 1975; Internatl Yr of the Woman Award, Love Memorial Mission Bapt Ch 1975; Outstndng Yg Woman of Am Award, Fuller & Dees 1975. **BUSINESS ADDRESS:** 202 S State St, Ste 1024, Chicago, IL 60604.

EICHELBERGER, WILLIAM L.
Educator. **PERSONAL:** Born Feb 07, 1922, Salisbury, NC; married Mary D Clapp. **EDUCATION:** Lincoln U, AB 1959; Princeton Theol Sem, MDiv 1962, MTheol 1963; NY Theol Sem, MST 1968. **CAREER:** Christian Soc Ethics, Louisville Presby Theological Seminary, assoc prof; Rutgers Univ & Newark Coll of Engineering, protestant chaplin 1967-72; NY Theological Seminary, visiting lecturer Theology & Ethics 1968-70; Newark Coll of Engineering, educ consultant 1968-69, instructor Contemp Literature & Expostry Writing 1968-72; Univ Coll, instructor Political Science dept 1971-72; Laconia Comm Presbytery Church, pastor 1965-67; Southern Univ Baton Rouge, campus pastor 1963-65; various positions as chaplin & instructional seminars; Author, Reality in Black & White; contributed to various periodicals; soc Ethics & Theology, lecturer; consultant in comm devel & soc change. **ORGANIZATIONS:** Mem KY Commn on Hum Rights 1975; mem Soc for Study of Blk Rel; Assn for Study of Afro-Am Life & Hist; Am Civ Lib Union; NAACP; Urban Leag; PUSH;pres bd dir Louisville Oppor Indstrlztn Ctrs Inc 1943-46, 48-58. **HONORS/ACHIEVEMENTS:** Dist alumni awd Lincoln U; elec to roll of hon Ministries to Blacks in Hghr Edn.

EIKERENKOETTER, FREDERICK J., II (REV. IKE)
Clergyman. **PERSONAL:** Born Jun 01, 1935, Ridgeland, SC; married Eula Mae Dent; children: Xavier Frederick, III. **EDUCATION:** Am Bible Coll, BTh 1956; DSci of Living Inst 1971; PhD 1969. **CAREER:** United Christian Evangelistic Assn, found, pres 1962-; United Ch Sci of Living Inst, 1969-; Rev Ike Found, 1973-; Dept Psychiatry, Harvard Med Sch, preacher, vis lectr 1973; Univ AL, 1975; Atlanta Univ Cntr, 1975; Rice U, 1977. **ORGANIZATIONS:** Fdr, Sci of Living Philosophy Church & Inst; life-time mem, NAACP. **HONORS/ACHIEVEMENTS:** Recip, World Serv Award For Outstnd Contributions to Mankind, Prince Hall Masons 1975. **MILITARY SERVICE:** USAF chapl sect 1956-58. **BUSINESS ADDRESS:** 4140 Broadway, New York, NY 10033.

EILAND, RAY MAURICE
Business executive. **PERSONAL:** Born Jul 08, 1932, Memphis, TN; married Doris V Williams; children: David M, Kathleen J, Karen V, Elaine, Lori. **EDUCATION:** DrakeUniv Des Moines, BS Educ 1956. **CAREER:** The Pillsbury Co, vice pres urban affairs 1978-, vice pres affirmative Act 1975-78, dir affirmative action 1973-75; Minneapolis Defense Contract-Admin Srv, chief off of contracts comp 1970-73; Control Data Corp, Minneapolis, pers admin 1968-70; Fed Aviation Admin, St Louis, pers mgr 1967-68; Jefferson Barracks, E St Louis & St Louis, altern dep equal empl 1965-67; Jefferson Barracks, St Louis, corrective therapist 1957-65. **ORGANIZATIONS:** Mem, Minneapolis Mental Hlth Assn 1985; mem, Minneapolis Mayr's Handicapped Com 1979; mem, Minnepaolis Personnel Mgr Assn 1985; mem, Minneapolis Urban Coalition AAP Task Force 1985; exec, Hay PTA Bd 1985; bd mem, NAACP 1970-80; bd mem MACI 1974; bd mem MN & Affirm Act Assn 1975-80; pers, commr Minnepapolis Civil Serv Commn, Minneapolis 1977-81. **HONORS/ACHIEVEMENTS:** Athl Schlrshp, DrakeUniv 1950; Hall of Fame, DrakeUniv 1972; Comm Award, NAACP 1975; Community Rec Award, Northside Minneapolis 1976; WCCO Radio Good Neighbor Award, Minneapolis 1976. **BUSINESS ADDRESS:** 608 2nd Ave S, Minneapolis, MN 55402.

EKECHI, FELIX K.
Educator. **PERSONAL:** Born Oct 30, 1934, Owerri, Nigeria;son of Egekeze Ekechi; married Regina; children: Kemakolam, Chidi, Okechukwu, Chinyere. **EDUCATION:** Holy Ghost Coll Umuahia Nigeria, Gd 2 Tchrs Cert 1955; Univ of MN, BA 1963; KS State Univ MA, 1965; Univ of WI Madison PhD 1969. **CAREER:** St Dominicks Sch Afara-mbieri, Nigeria, hdmstr 1955-58; Mt St Marys Coll Azaraegbelu, Owerri, tutor 1959-60; Alcon A&M Coll Lorman, MS, inst 1964-65; Univ of Port Harcourt, visiting prof 1983; Kent State Univ, asst/assoc prof 1969-. **ORGANIZATIONS:** Grad asst KS State Univ 1964-65; grad teaching asst Univ of WI-Madison 1965-69; mem Am Br Bicentennial Comm, Kent, OH 1976-77; pres Black Faculty & Staff Assoc Kent State Univ 1974; coord African Studies Prog Kent State Univ 1985; mem African Studies Assn, Amer Historical Assn. **HONORS/ACHIEVEMENTS:** IGBO Oral Hist Proj Lily Endwmnt 1975; Am Masns & Educ in Nigeria the Am Philosophical Soc 1979-83; Books, Masonry Enterprises & Rivalry in Igboland (London), 1971 Owerri in Transition, Owerri, Nigeria 1984; Tradition and Transformation in Eastern Nigeria, Owerri and its Hinterland, Kent State Univ Press, 1989; numerous articles and reviews in scholarly journals; Summer Seminar for School Teachers, Natl Endowment for the Humanities 1989. **BUSINESS ADDRESS:** Professor, Kent State Univ, Dept of History, Kent, OH 44242.

EL-AMIN, SA'AD (JEROYD X. GREENE)
Attorney. **PERSONAL:** Born Feb 10, 1940, Manhattan, NY; married Carolyn Adams; children: Je Royd W III, Nicole, Anissa. **EDUCATION:** Univ Sthrn CA, BA 1965; Yale U, JD 1969, MA 1969. **CAREER:** World Commun of Islam in the W, natl bus mang 1975-76; Greene and Poindexter, Inc, sr law prtnr 1971-75; Howard U, assit prof of law 1973-74; Sheffield & Greene, assoc in law firm 1969-71. **ORGANIZATIONS:** Amer Bar Assn; Natl Bar Assn; Natl Donfer of Black Lawy; Old Dominion Bar Assn; VA St Bar; VA Trial Lawy Assn; Richmond Criminal Bar Assn; Natl Assn of Criminal Def Lawy bar of the US Sup Ct 1973; fellow, The Urban Cntr Columbia U; Natl Consult & Lectr Cncl on Legal Ed 1974-75; pres, Advis Comm for Amer Muslims Propagat; Fin Assist Fund; mem Iman Consult Bd, Hon Elijah Muhammad Mosque #2. **HONORS/ACHIEVEMENTS:** Lawy of the Yr, Natl Confer of Black Lawy 1974. **BUSINESS ADDRESS:** 312 W Grace St, Richmond, VA 23220.

EL-KATI, MAHHMOUD (MILTON WILLIAMS)
Educator. **PERSONAL:** Born Oct 30, 1936, Savannah, GA; children: Erick, Stokley, Kamali. **EDUCATION:** Univ of Ghana, 1969; Univ of Wisconsin, 1964-65; Wilberforce Univ, BA 1960. **CAREER:** MacAlester Coll Antioch-Minneapolis Coll, instr; lecturer, writer & community activist. **ORGANIZATIONS:** Currently working with black prison inmates regarding educ programs; affiliated with several prison inst since 1966; volunteer, Urban League; NAACP; SNCC; CORE; Creative Ed; dir, The Way Community Center 1967-71. **HONORS/ACHIEVEMENTS:** Page 1 Award, Twin Cities Newspaper Guild 1968; Urban League Award 1969; EROS U-of-the-Streets, Merritt Coll 1969; Recognition Award, Univ of MN; Stillwater Black Inmate Pop 1974. **BUSINESS ADDRESS:** 1600 N Snelling Ave, St Paul, MN 55105.

EL-TOURE, ASKIA MUHAMMAD ABU BAKR (ROLLAND SNELLINGS)
Poet, educator. **PERSONAL:** Born Oct 13, 1938, Raleigh, NC; son of Clifford R Snellings and Nancy Bullock Snellings; married Dona Humphrey, Jun 1966 (divorced); children: Tariq Abdullah bin Toure; married Helen Morton Hobbs, 1970; children: Jamil Abdus-Salam bin Toure; married Agila. **EDUCATION:** Art Students League of New York, 1960-62. **CAREER:** Poet, essayist, artist, editor, educator; lecturer in African history, black studies, and creative writing at colleges and universities. **ORGANIZATIONS:** Literary fellow, Rockefeller Foundation and Omega Psi Phi. **HONORS/ACHIEVEMENTS:** Modern Poetry Association award, 1952; Columbia University Creative Writing Grant, 1969. **HOME ADDRESS:** 50 W 90th St, New York, NY 10025. *

ELAM, DOROTHY R.
Educator. **PERSONAL:** Born Jul 23, 1904, Philadelphia, PA; divorced; children: 2 Children. **EDUCATION:** Glassboro State Coll, BS 1956; Univ of Rutgers, attended; Glassboro, pursued MA. **CAREER:** Adult Evening Class Black Studies, teacher; Camden City Bd of Educ, worked on rsch progs; Berlin Township Schools, retired 1964, 37 years of teaching. **ORGANIZATIONS:** Wrote scripts for closed circuit Glassboro Bd Educ Harriet Tubman Dr G W Carver; served as NJ State Rep Assn of Negro Life & Hist; guest spkr ch schPTA Negro History; assisted in writing radio progs celeb of Negro Hist Week; edited published poetry book "A Slice of Black Living" 1970, 1971 added color sound filmstrip w/record & cassette; aptd exec bd Assn of Study of Negro Life & History 1972; organized Camden Co Intercultural Council 1947; rsch producedrecord album The Hist Interpretations of Negro Spirituals & Lift Every Voice & Sing; founder/dir Conlam Enterprises. **HONORS/ACHIEVEMENTS:** Woman of Yr Local Eta Chapt; Cert of Merit NJ Organ of Teachers; Cert of Appreciation Mt Zion AME Ch of Albion 1966; among first of two blacks to receive Disting Alumnus Awd Outstanding Achievement & Serv in Prof Comm & Fellowman Glassboro State Coll; Plaque NJ State Fed of Colored Women's Club Inc; Plaque Assn of Business a Professional Woman of Camden and Vicinity.

ELAM, HARRY JUSTIN
Associate justice. **PERSONAL:** Born Apr 29, 1922, Boston, MA; son of Robert Elam and Blanche Elam; married Barbara Clarke; children: Patricia, Harry Jr, Keith, Jocelyn. **EDUCATION:** Attended, VA State Coll 1940-42; Boston Univ Coll of Liberal Arts, AB 1946-48; Boston Univ Law School, LLB 1951. **CAREER:** Gov's Council MA, exec sec 1960-62; Office of Atty General MA, asst atty general 1964-66; Boston Municipal Ct, assoc justice 1971, chief justice 1978; MA Superior Ct, assoc justice 1983-. **ORGANIZATIONS:** Chmn bd dir Roxbury Multi Serv Center 1967-70; chmn bd of dir The Advent School 1973-77; chmn bd of dir The Elma Lewis School of Fine Arts 1974-78; chmn Com on EEO & Affirmative Action Trial Ct MA 1978-; mem MA Judicial Council 1978-; pres MA Black Judges Conf 1979-. **HONORS/ACHIEVEMENTS:** Civil Rights Award Boston NAACP 1968; Comm Serv Award Freedom House 1969; Outstanding Citizen Award Roxbury Multi Serv Center 1974; Citizen of the Yr Omega Psi Phi Frat 1978; Distinguished Public Serv Boston Univ Law School Alumni 1979; Outstanding Public Serv MA Assn of Afro-Amer Police 1979. **MILITARY SERVICE:** USAF sgt 1942-46. **BUSINESS ADDRESS:** Associate Justice, MA Superior Ct, Suffolk Co Ct House, Boston, MA 02108.

ELAM, HARRY PENOY
Physician, educator. **PERSONAL:** Born Jul 31, 1919, Little Rock, AR; married Sallyann; children: Regina, Bernadette, Joanne, Susanne, Bernard, Christopher. **EDUCATION:** Loyola Univ, BS 1949, MD 1953; Cook Cty Hosp, internship 1953-54, resd 1954-56, rsch fellow pediatric neurology 1957-59. **CAREER:** Cook County Hospital, attending physician 1956,61, The Children's Neurology Serv Children's Div, assoc dir 1956, assoc dir 1957; St Vincent's Orphanage, attending staff 1957; Mercy Hospital, jr attending staff 1957; Stritch School of Medicine Loyola Univ, asst clinical prof 1957, instructor 1956-58; Mental Health Clinic, Dept of Mental Health, medical dir 1962; Univ of Ibadon Nigeria, sr lecturer 1962; Stritch School of Medicine Loyola Univ, asst prof 1965, assoc clinical prof 1967; Mile Sq Health Center, medical dir 1967; Rush-Presbytery-St Lukes Medical Center, assoc clinical prof 1971; Rush Coll of Medicine, prof of pediatrics, assoc prof preventive medicine 1971-. **ORGANIZATIONS:** Mem med adv bd Good Samaritan School of Mentally Retarded Children 1963-65; mem Handicapped Childrens Council, Chicago Met Interagy Comm, Dept of MentalHlth 1967; professional adv bd United Cerebral Palsy of Gtr Chicago 1966-; mem Amer Acad of Pediatrics, Amer Acad of Cerebral Palsy 1970, Amer Soc of Adlerian Psych, Chicago Pediatric Soc, Alpha Omega Alpha Hon Med Soc 1971, Inst of Med of Chicago 1975. **BUSINESS ADDRESS:** Coordinator, Presbyterian St Lukes MC, 1753 W Congress Pkwy, Chicago, IL 60612.

ELAM, HATTIE BRISCOE
Attorney. **PERSONAL:** Born Nov 13, 1916, Shreveport, LA; married William M. **EDUCATION:** Wiley Coll, BA 1937; Prairie View Coll, MS 1951; St Mary's Law Schl, LLB 1956, JD. **CAREER:** Pvt Prac, atty 1956-; Kelly Air Base, clk, typist 1952-56; Briscoe Bea Uty Sal, beauty opr 1941-45; Booker Wash & Schl, tchr 1937-41. **ORGANIZATIONS:** Mem, past pres Delta Sigma Theta Sor 1937-; mem NACP 1945-; mem TX St Bar Assn 1956-; mem Am Bar Assn 1956-; mem Nat Assn of Def Lawyers 1964-; mem Nat Assn of Black Women Attys 1975-. **HONORS/ACHIEVEMENTS:** Hist Achvmt Award, Smart Set Soc Clb 1960; Civic Achvmt Award; Royal Dukes & his Ct 1962; supr achvmt in law Delta Sigma Theta Sor 1975; model comm ldr Miss Black San Antonio Bd 1975; Community Ldrs & Noteworthy Am Award; Ed Bd of Am Biographical Inst 1976-77; Who's Who in TX 1968; World's Who's Who of Women 1973. **BUSINESS ADDRESS:** 1416 E Commerce St, San Antonio, TX 78205.

ELAM, LLOYD C.
Educator, physician. **PERSONAL:** Born Oct 27, 1928, Little Rock, AR; married Clara Carpenter; children: Gloria, Laurie. **EDUCATION:** Roosevelt Univ, BS 1950; Univ of WA, MD 1957. **CAREER:** Univ of IL Hosp, internship 1957-58; Univ of Chicago, residency 1958-61; Univ of Chicago & Billing Hosp, instr of psychiatry 1961; GW Hubbard Hosp, dept of psychiatry 1961-63; Meharry Medical Coll, prof 1963-68, interin dean sch of medicine 1966-68, president 1968-. **ORGANIZATIONS:** Mem Natl Adv Cncl, John F Kennedy Ctr for Rsch Educ & Human Devel; bd trustees Fisk Univ; bd dir Kraft Inc Glenview IL, Merck & Co Rahway NJ, So Central Bell, Nashville Area C of C; mem bd trustees TN Dept of Mental Health & Retardation, CATV. **HONORS/ACHIEVEMENTS:** Religious Heritage of Amer Bus & Professional Leader of Yr Awd in Field of Medicine 1950-52; Hon Degrees DL Harvard Univ 1974, DSc St Lawrence Univ 1974,DHL Roosevelt Univ 1974; Eleanor Roosevelt Key Roosevelt Univ; Citizen of Year Omega Psi Phi. **BUSINESS ADDRESS:** President, Meharry Medical Coll, 1005 18th Ave N, Nashville, TN 37208.

ELCOCK, CLAUDIUS ADOLPHUS RUFUS
Physician. **PERSONAL:** Born Jan 07, 1923; married Annie Bactowar; children: Julia, Claudia. **EDUCATION:** Lincoln Univ, AB 1954; Howard Univ School of Med, MD 1959. **CAREER:** Mercy Douglass Hosp, med rsd, chief med officer 1960-70, med consult 1973; Presbyterian Hosp, staff mem 1973-77. **ORGANIZATIONS:** Chmn URC; treas Symposium 1943-50; mem Utilization Rev Comm, Quality Assurance Comm, Proj Outreach Comm; nurses adv comm Presb Hosp 1977; mem AMA, PMS, PCMS, PSIM, NMA, MSEP; elder Reeve Meml Presb Church; mem Home & School Assoc of Neighborhood School in Philadelphia 1964-69. **HONORS/ACHIEVEMENTS:** Chapel of Four Chaplains 1975. **BUSINESS ADDRESS:** 400 S 57th St, Philadelphia, PA 19143.

ELDER, ALMORA KENNEDY
Educator. **PERSONAL:** Born Jul 04, 1920, Rusk, CO; married Lamar; children: Ferria, Patricia, Wilbert, Barbara, Lamar Jr, Lacetta. **EDUCATION:** Bishop Coll, BS 1947, MA 1956; Prairie View A&M Coll, Attend; Stephen F Austin, 1976; E TX St Commerce TX, Attend. **CAREER:** Easton, TX, former mayor; Taturn IS Div, estb 1st home making ed dept 1938-39, coach girls bsktbl. **ORGANIZATIONS:** Pres, Taturn Girls Clb Sec 1948-58; mem, Sigma Gamma Rhoc; sec, Eastern Star Chap 1599; life Mem, FSFA; life mem, NEA; life mem CTA; mem, Longview Local Unit TAIR; E TX Cncl of Soc Studies; Aging Com Bapt Honiney Pirtee Kilgore. **HONORS/ACHIEVEMENTS:** Nat Ednr Award of World Books; Kingergarten Cert of Hon, SFA.

ELDER, GERALDINE H.
Government official. **PERSONAL:** Born Sep 13, 1937, Chicago, IL. **EDUCATION:** Morris Brown Atlanta, Attended 1955-57; LoyolaUniv Chicago, Attended 1958-59; EmoryUniv Atlanta, Attended 1968-69. **CAREER:** City of Atlanta, commr of parks & rec

1985, dir of comm affairs 1976-77, sec to vice-mayor; Ofc of Mayor City of Atlanta, chief of staff 1977-79, mayor'sexc sec 1974-76; Jackson Patterson Pks & Franklin, legal sec 1970-73; Emory Comm Legal Serv Cntr, ofc mgr 1967-70; Pope Ballard Uriell Kennedy Shepard &Foul, legal sec 1964-65. **ORGANIZATIONS:** Bd mem, Atlanta Conv & Visitors Bur; bd mem, Opp Ind Cntr; fund com chmn, Am Cancer Soc Fulton Co; mem Alpha Kappa Alpha Sorority. **HONORS/ACHIEVEMENTS:** Nominated for Outstndng Young Women of Am. **BUSINESS ADDRESS:** Commr of Parks & Recreation, City of Atlanta 260 Central Ave, Atlanta, GA 30303.

ELDER, LEE See ELDER, ROBERT LEE

ELDER, LONNE, III
Film writer, producer, playwright. **PERSONAL:** Born Dec 26, 1931, Americus, GA; son of Lonne Elder, Jr and Quincy Elder; married Betty Gross, 1963 (divorced 1967); children: David DuBois; married Judith Ann Johnson, Feb 14, 1969; children: Christian, Loni. **EDUCATION:** Attended Rutgers Univ; attended Yale Univ School of Drama, 1965-67. **CAREER:** Joined Harlem Writers Guild after AUS serv; actor in Broadway production of "A Raisin in The Sun," 1959, and "Days of Absence," 1965; screenwriter of films "Sounder," 1972, "Melinda," 1972, and "Bustin' Loose," 1981; author of plays "Ceremonies in Dark Old Men," 1965, and "Charles on East Fourth Street," 1967; writer for television series "NYPD" and "McCloud"; Negro Ensemble Company, New York, NY, dir of playwrights div, 1967-69; recorded "Reading Poetry to Jazz," RCA; produced own films at Yale School of Drama, Audio Visual Center. **ORGANIZATIONS:** Mem, Black Academy of Arts and Letters; mem, Harlem Writers Guild; mem, Black Artists Alliance. **HONORS/ACHIEVEMENTS:** Stanley Drama Award in playwriting, 1965, Pulitzer Prize nomination, 1969, Outer Drama Critics Circle Award, 1970, Vernon Rice Drama Desk Award, 1970, Stella Holt Memorial Playwrights Award, 1970, Los Angeles Drama Critics Award, 1970, and Christopher Award, 1975, all for play "Ceremonies in Dark Old Men"; John Hay Whitney fellowship, Yale Univ School of Drama, 1965-66; also received other scholarships; Academy Award nomination for best screenplay based on material from another medium, from Academy of Motion Picture Arts and Sciences, Christopher Award, Atlanta Film Festival Silver Award, and Image Award, all 1972, all for "Sounder," which was also nominated for an Academy Award for best picture. *

ELDER, ROBERT LEE (LEE ELDER)
Professional golfer. **PERSONAL:** Born Jul 14, 1934, Dallas, TX; married Rose Harper. **EDUCATION:** PGA Training Sch, 1967-75. **CAREER:** AUS, capt, golf team 1959-61; Lee Elder Enterprises, Inc, dir. **ORGANIZATIONS:** Lee Elder Schlrshp Found; Lee Elder Celebrity Pro-Am Golf Classic 1970; founder, Lee Elder Summer Youth Golf Dev Prog %Bd dir Police Boys Clb; Mason; mem natl adv bd, Goodwill Ind; bd dir, Met Wash Police-Boys Clb; life mem, NAACP; dir, PGA Episcopalian; Touchdown Clb, Washington DC; Professional Golfers Assn of Am Ranked on All Time Money Winners List 1968-. **HONORS/ACHIEVEMENTS:** First black to qualify for Ryder Cup Golf Team 1979; first black am to prtcpt in multiracial sprts, S Africa; first black to prtcpt in Dunlop Masters, England; May 3 declared Lee Elder Day, Washington DC; received Key to City of Washington 1974; Most Outstndng Ath on a Nat Basis from DC Met Area 1974; received Key to City, Pensacola FL 1975; Charles Bartlett Award, Golf Writers Am 1977; Herman A English Humanitarian Award, City of LA 1977; AG Gaston Award, Nat Bus League 1978; Wash Hall of Stars 1979; Sr PGA Tour winner of the Suntree Classic 1984; Hilton Head Invitational 1984; Champions of Golf 1985; Merrill-Lynch Seniors 1985; Digital Seniors 1985; Citizens Bank Seniors 1985; The Commemorative 1986; Foreign Championships incl Coca-Cola Grand Slam Japan 1984, Jamaica PGA Championship Kingston, Jamaica 1984, Coca-Cola Grand Slam Japan 1986. **MILITARY SERVICE:** AUS 1959-61. **BUSINESS ADDRESS:** Dir, Lee Elder Enterprises, 1725 K St NW, Ste 1112, Washington, DC 20006.

ELDERS, M. JOYCELYN
Educator. **PERSONAL:** Born Aug 13, 1933, Schaal, AR; daughter of Curtis L Jones and Haller Reed Jones; married Oliver B Elders; children: Eric D, Kevin M. **EDUCATION:** Philander Smith Coll, BA 1952; Brooke Army Med Ctr, RPT 1956; Univ of AR Med Sch, MD 1960, MS Biochem 1967. **CAREER:** US Army, 1st lt 1953-56; Univ of MN Hosp, intern-pediatrics 1960-61; Univ of AR Med Ctr, resident pediatrics 1961-63, chief res/peds 1963-64, rsch fellow in pediatrics 1964-67, asst prof pediatrics 1967-71, assoc prof peds 1971-76, prof pediatrics 1976-; Arkansas Dept of Health, dir 1987-. **ORGANIZATIONS:** Amer Assn for Adv of Sci; Soc for Pediatric Rsch; Acad of Pediatric; Cnrl AR Acad of Pediatrics; Amer Diabetes Assn; Lawson Wilkins Endocrine Soc; Amer Fed of Clinical Rsch; AR Diabetes Assn; The Endocrine Soc; assoc mem FEBS Amer Phys Soc; Amer Bd of Pediatrics 1965; bd mem N Little Rock Workman's Comp Comm 1975-79; AR Sci & Tech Comm 1975-76; Human Growth Found 1974-78; chmn membership comm Lawson Wilkins End Soc 1976; Human Embryologoy & Devel Study Sect 1976-80; Natl Adv Food & Drug Comm 1977-80; pres Sigma Xi 1977-78; Natl Pituitary Agency 1977-80; bd of dir Natl Bank of AR 1979; Maternal & Child Hlth Rsch Comm HHS, NIH 1981-; Editorial Bd Journal of Ped 1981-; sec AR Sci & Tech Comm 1983-; bd mem Noside YMCA 1973-84; 113 publications including "Disorders of Carbohydrate Metabolism" 1984 Disorders of Adrenal Metabolism 1984; Growth Hormone Effects on B- and T-cell Function", Effect of EGF on Gastrointestinal Mucosal Proliferation" 1984. **HONORS/ACHIEVEMENTS:** Alumni Academic Scholarship Philander Smith Coll 1949-52; Alpha Kappa Mu Natl Honor Soc 1951; BS Magna Cum Laude Philander Smith Coll 1952; USPHS Postdoctoral Rsch Fellow 1964; USPHS Career Develop Awd 1967-72; Alpha Omega Alpha 1972; AKA's Distinguished Women in Amer 1973; Woman of the Year, Arkansas Democrat 1989. **MILITARY SERVICE:** AUS 1st lt 1953-56. **BUSINESS ADDRESS:** Prof Pediatrics/Endocrinology, Univ of AR for Med Sciences, Dept of Peds/4301 West Markham, Little Rock, AR 72205.

ELDRIDGE, JAMES L., JR.
Business executive. **PERSONAL:** Born Jun 11, 1948, Winston-Salem, NC. **EDUCATION:** Highland Pk Coll, AA 1969; Wayne St U, BA 1971;Univ of MI, grad study. **CAREER:** Calumet Res Asso, IN U, instr; Blue Cross of MI, admin res; Cook Co Hosp, admin extern. **ORGANIZATIONS:** Mem, Nat Assn of Hlth Serv Execs; Wayne StUniv Alumni Assn; blood donor prog, Cook Co Hosp. **HONORS/ACHIEVEMENTS:** Recip Bd of Gov Schlrshp, Wayne StUniv 1970; Opportunity Awards Flwshp,Univ of MI 1971-73; Outstndng Srv Award. **BUSINESS ADDRESS:** 3400 Broadway, Gary, IN.

ELEAZER, GEORGE ROBERT, JR.
Psychologist. **PERSONAL:** Born Oct 16, 1956, E Patchogue, NY; married Cynthia; children: Toshalina, George III. **EDUCATION:** The Choate School, attended 1974; Tufts Univ, BS 1978; Hofstra Univ, MA 1978, PhD 1984. **CAREER:** Freeport Public Schs, intern psychologist 1980-81; United Cerebral Palsy of Suffolk, intern psychologist 1981-82; Westbury Public Schs, psychologist 1982-84;William Floyd Public Schs, psychologist 1984; Middle Island Sch, psychologist. **ORGANIZATIONS:** Pres of the bd Bellport Local Action Ctr 1980-81; mem South Country School Bd 1982-; adv bd Brookhaven Memorial Hosp 1984-; bd of dirs Bellport Rotary 1985-86. **HONORS/ACHIEVEMENTS:** Amer Legion Academic S Country Schs Awd 1970; David Bohn Mem Sch S Country Schs 1970; Daniel Hale William Tufts Univ 1978; Phi Delta Kappa Suffolk 1985. **HOME ADDRESS:** 57 New Jersey Ave, Bellport, NY 11713.

ELIAS, HOMER
Professional athlete. **PERSONAL:** Born May 01, 1955. **EDUCATION:** TN State, attended. **CAREER:** Detroit Lions, guard 1978-. **HONORS/ACHIEVEMENTS:** All-Amer at tackle Atlanta Daily World 1977.

ELKINS, VIRGIL LYNN
Educator. **PERSONAL:** Born Oct 18, 1925, Sarasota, FL; married Argaree; children: Virgil, Sylvia, Kathryn, Angela, Michael. **EDUCATION:** FL A&M U, BS 1946, MS 1959. **CAREER:** Univ of FL, area prog specialist 1965-, extens dist agent 1961-65, extens agent 1949-61, chair, agr 1948-49; FL School for Boys, teacher 1946-48. **ORGANIZATIONS:** Nat bd of dir, Comm Devel & Soc 1974-76; So Agr Econ Assn; sec, treas, Epsilon Sigma Phi Frat 1976-77; state pres, FL A&MUniv Alumni Assn 1974-;FL Commin on Aging; SER Clb; Kappa Alpha Phi Frat; bd of dir, Bethel AME Ch; Funders, Inc; Tallahassee Citizens Savings Clb; supt, Sun Sch; Rural Devel Goodwill Clb; pres FL A&MUniv Agr Assn; Am Assn ofUniv Prof. **HONORS/ACHIEVEMENTS:** Kappa Man of the Yr Award 1975; SER Clb Annual Award 1976; Leon Co Alumni Chap Award 1974; FL A&M Alumni Award 1971. **BUSINESS ADDRESS:** Box A-48, FL A&M Univ, Tallahassee, FL 32307.

ELLARAINO (MS. ELLA RAINO EDWARDS)
Actress. **PERSONAL:** Born Oct 07, 1938, Kilgore, TX; daughter of John Raino and Lola Raino; divorced; children: Bernard Otis Wright. **EDUCATION:** Los Angeles Metropolitan Coll, AA. **CAREER:** TV, "White Shadow", "Police Story", "Sanford & Son", "The Memory of Eva Ryker"; Films, "New York New York", "Big Time", "Mr Ricco"; Stage, "The Crucible" "The Jean London Show", "The Terraced Apartment"; numerous television, motion picture, stage & commercial credits; "Happy Days," asst assoc producer, 1979-82; "The New Odd Couple," assoc producer, 1982-83. **ORGANIZATIONS:** Founding & charter mem financial sec Kwanza Found Award; OH Close Sch for Boys 1972-74. **HONORS/ACHIEVEMENTS:** Community Serv Award, Alpha Gamma Omega Chapter, Alpha Kappa Alpha Award; Certificate of Commendation, City of Los Angeles; Certificate of Recognition, Jenesse Center.

ELLER, CARL L.
Health services executive. **PERSONAL:** Born Jan 25, 1942, Winston-Salem, NC; son of Clarence and Ernestine; married Mahogany Jaclynne (Fasnacht) Eller, Jan 21, 1979; children: Cinder, Regis, Holiday. **EDUCATION:** Univ of MN, Educ 1960-63, Certificate C D Counselor 1982; Metropolitan St Coll, Inst of Chemical Dependency, 1983-. **CAREER:** MN Vikings, defensive end 1964-78; Seattle SeaHawks, professional football player 1979-80; Viking Personnel, employee consultant 1982; Natl Football League, health consultant; Natl Inst of Sports & Hmnts, founder & dir 1981-; US Athletes Assoc, founder & exec dir 1983-; Triumph Life Center, pres. **ORGANIZATIONS:** Mem SAG/AFTRA Actors Talent Assn 1969-; Fellowhsip of Christian Athletes; bd mem MN Council on Chemical Dependency 1982-, MN Inst of Black Chemical Abuse 1982-; pres NFL Alumni MN Chapter 1982-85; Citizens Advisory Council, State of MN 1984-; bd mem Univ of MN 1984-, Youth Rescue Fund 1983-; Srants comm chair 1983-86; Chemical Dependency Div; State Dept of Health Human Serv; Mayors Task Force on Chemical Dependency 1985-; contributing editor Alcoholism & Addiction Magazine 1985-. **HONORS/ACHIEVEMENTS:** Author "Beating the Odds" 1985; nominee Pro-Football Hall of Fame 1985; producer "My 5th Super Bowl" Educ Film 1984; all-pro-football Natl Football League 1969-75; MVP lineman Defense, Natl Football League 1969-71; All American, Univ of Minnesota 1962-63; All Pro, Natl Football League 1969-75; George Halas Award, Best Defensive Lineman 1969; NFLPA Defensive Player of the Year 1971; Key Man Award, Miltipleclerosis Society 1977; Special Task Force Prevention of Chemical Abuse, The White House 1982; Hubert H Humphrey, Minnesota Labor Award 1982; Good Neighbor Award, WCCO Radio 1984. **MILITARY SERVICE:** Natl Guard private 1965-71. **BUSINESS ADDRESS:** President, Triumph Life Center, 3735 Lakeland Ave N, Suite 230, Minneapolis, MN 55422.

ELLERBY, WILLIAM MITCHELL, SR.
Elected official. **PERSONAL:** Born Sep 19, 1946, Manning, SC; married Sarah Croker; children: Mitchell Jr, Andre, Clifford. **EDUCATION:** Benedict Coll Columbia SC, AB 1971. **CAREER:** Sears Roebuck, div mgr 1971-73; Jackson Cty Headstart, admin asst 1973-74; Chevron USA Refinery, refinery oper 1974; State of MS, rep 1984-. **ORGANIZATIONS:** Mem Methodist Church, Omega Psi Phi; bd of dir Jackson Cty Area Chamber of Commerce; life mem VFW, Amer Legion, Elks, Evening Lions Club; vice pres Moss Point-Boxing Assoc; pres Eastside Voting Precinct; cty democratic exec comm, former commiss Jackson Cty Port Authority. **HONORS/ACHIEVEMENTS:** Host Awareness 1985 WHKS Moss Point. **MILITARY SERVICE:** AUS helicopter main sp4 E-4 1966-68; Vietnam Campaign Medals 1967-68. **BUSINESS ADDRESS:** Representative, State of Mississippi, PO Box 216, Moss Point, MS 39563.

ELLIGAN, IRVIN, JR.
Clergyman. **PERSONAL:** Born Nov 24, 1915, Chattanooga, TN; son of Irvin Elligan, Sr and Annie C Simmons E McDonald; married Florence Coston; children: Rachel Clark, Irvin III. **EDUCATION:** Knoxville Coll, BS 1938; Pittsburgh-Xenia Sem, MDiv 1944; Stillman Coll, DD 1965; Union Theological Seminary of VA, postgrad 1966-67; Presbyterian Institute on Industrial telation, 1968; Columbia Theological Seminary, attended 1972; Urban Training Center, Certificate in Org Devel, 1972, 1976. **CAREER:** Camden Acad, teacher 1939-41; pastorates in VA & TN, 1944-66; Knoxville Coll, bible instructor 1952; Presbyterian Church of US, assoc sec of church & soc bd of christian educ 1963-67; Lakeview Presbyterian St Petersburg, assoc pastor 1967-70; Columbia Theological Seminary, vis instructor 1972; New Covenant Presbyterian Church Miami, pastor; Assoc Prof of Pastoral Ministries; Dir of Field

Educ; SFL Center for Theological Studies. **ORGANIZATIONS:** Moderator of Synod of FL PCUS 1974-; Stillman Coll, FL Council Churches, FL Christian Migrant Ministry; vice chmn Dade Co Comm Relations; moderator Everglades Presbyterian PCUS 1980; Synod of FL Mission Council; Presbyterian US Minority Mission Council; bd mem Presbyterian Found; chmn of Racial/Ethnic Task Force Presbyterian Div of Natl Mission; Bd Trustees Presbyterian Church (USA) Foundation; bd Christian Community Service Agency of Miami; Greater Miami Religious Leaders Coalition; Miami Urban Coalition; Synod C Transition Com; Chmn Black Presbyterian Project of Tropical FL; Program Committee Greater Miami Urban Coalition, 1986-. **HONORS/ACHIEVEMENTS:** 1st Black Moderator Hanover Presbyterian VA 1963; Silver Beaver Award BSA; Outstanding Citizen Award Richmond VA 1962; Key to the City of St Petersburg FL 1970; Black Presbyterian Leadership Caucus Serv Honors 1973; Citizen of the Yr Award Omega Psi Phi Miami 1979; Honors certificates by Metro-Dade County and City of Miami, FL Natl Peace Seekers Award, So Presbyterian Peace Fellowship, 1981.

ELLINGTON, BRENDA ANDREA
Advertising executive. **PERSONAL:** Born May 13, 1960, Los Angeles, CA. **EDUCATION:** Stanford Univ, BA Economics 1982; Stanford Graduate School of Business, MBA 1986. **CAREER:** EF Hutton, stockholders apprentice 1982; Merrill Lynch, marketing intern 1982; Home Box Office, business analyst 1982-84; Salomon Bros, rsch analyst 1985; Leo Burnett Co, asst acct exec 1986-. **ORGANIZATIONS:** Co-pres Black Business Soc Stanford Univ 1981-82; project chair Los Angeles Jr Chamber of Commerce 1984; mem Stanford Grad Sch of Business Alumni Assn 1986-; mem Natl Black MBA Assn Chicago, League of Black Women. **HONORS/ACHIEVEMENTS:** Outstanding Serv Award City of Los Angeles 1980; COGME Fellow 1984; Stanford Graduate School of Business Fellowship 1984-86. **BUSINESS ADDRESS:** Account Executive, Leo Burnett Co, Prudential Plaza, Chicago, IL 60601.

ELLINGTON, MERCEDES
Performer. **PERSONAL:** Born in New York, NY. **EDUCATION:** Juilliard Sch of Music, BS 1960. **CAREER:** June Taylor Dancers Jackie Gleason Show, dancer 1963-70; Sophisticated Ladies, featured performed 1980-83; Balletap America/USA, co-artistic dir 1983-85; choreographer, Blues in the Night 1984,85, Juba 1985,86; asst choreographer for broadway productions of, No No Nanette, Hellzapoppin, Oh Kay, Happy New Year, The Grand Tour, Sophisticated Ladies, The Night That Made America Famous; Danc Ellington, artistic dir 1985-. **ORGANIZATIONS:** Mem Actors Equity Council AEA 1984-85; teacher Steps 74 (tap dance); lecturer/demonstrator; local bd AFTRA. **BUSINESS ADDRESS:** Artistic Dir, Danc Ellington, 1500 Broadway Ste 2013, New York, NY 10036.

ELLIOTT, ANTHONY DANIEL, III
Concert cellist, educator. **PERSONAL:** Born Sep 03, 1948, Rome, NY; married Paula Sokol. **EDUCATION:** IN University School of Music, Performer's Certificate 1969, BMusic 1970. **CAREER:** Aspen Chamber Symphony, principal cello 1970; Toronto Symphony Orchestra, section cello 1970-73; University of MN, instructor 1973-76; Minnesota Orchestra, assoc principal cello 1973-78; MacAlester College, instructor 1974-76; Vancouver Symphony Orchestra, principal cello 1978-82; Marrowstone Music Fesitval, asst music director; Western MI University, assoc prof of cello 1983-, music dir of univ symphony orchestra. **HONORS/ACHIEVEMENTS:** CBC Toronto Orch; CO Philharmonic; Indianapolis Philharmonic; Utica Symphony; Aspen Festival; Vancouver Symphony; Debut Recital-Town Hall; St Lawrence Centrefor Perf Arts, Toronto CAN 1973; recital appearances in US & CAN; featuring & sponsoring compositions by Black composers; supv, Inner-city Mus Proj, St Paul 1974; string clinician; chamber & ensamble perf; Kraus Meml Prize, INUniv 1968; semi-finalist, CBC Radio CAN Talent Festival 1973; listed in Who's Who in Music 1975; World Primiere Performance of Concerto for Cello & Orch, Primous Fountain with Stanislav Skrowaczewski & MN Orch 1977; First Black Musician to Maintain Prin Position in Maj Orchestra; only Am Semi-Finalist, Concours Cassado Florence Italy 1979. **BUSINESS ADDRESS:** Music Dir, Western Michigan University, School of Music, Kalamazoo, MI 49008.

ELLIOTT, FRANK GEORGE
Physician. **PERSONAL:** Born Aug 23, 1913, Portsmouth, VA; son of Frank G Elliott, II, MD and Laura Carr Elliott; married Edith Barham; children: Lynne Rosenwald, Alice Smith, Francine Campbell. **EDUCATION:** Lincoln Univ PA, AB 1935; Howard Univ School of Medicine, MD 1940; Freedman's Hospital, Washington DC, rotating internship, 1941. **CAREER:** US Public Health Serv, Oklahoma State Health Dept, 1942-44; family practice, Bridgeport CT, 1945-67; sr physician emergency dept, Bridgeport Hospital, 1967-78; family practice, primary care, Bridgeport CT, 1978-80; disability claim reviewer, Town of Stratford CT, 1980; emergency physician, Danbury Hospital, 1980-; Univ of Bridgeport School of Nursing, teacher, emergency and trauma medicine; Housatonic Community Coll, Bridgeport CT, teacher, EMT courses; Town of Stratford, teacher, EMT courses. **ORGANIZATIONS:** Charter mem, Amer Coll of Emergency Physicians 1968; bd of dir, medical advisory comm, CT Blue Cross-Blue Shield; dir & devel, First Methodone Drug Clinic Bridgeport 1973; pres, SW CT EMS Advisory Council 1978-80; chmn, CT State Leg Comm for Emergency Medical Services 1979-80; bd of dir, Bridgeport Area Found 1974-; fellow bd of dir, Peoples Savings Bank 1976; past pres, Bridgeport Medical Soc, Bridgeport Acad of Family Practice; Fairfield County Medical Soc; Amer Acad of Family Practice; World Medical Assn; Governor's Task Force on Drug Addiction; past pres bd dir, Family Serv Soc of Bridgeport; Governor's Task Force on Venereal Disease; State Advisory Comm on EMS; chmn, State Planning Comm on EMS; Bridgeport Hospital, Devel Comm, Pharmacy and Dietary Comm, Patient Care Comm, Trauma Comm; State of Connecticut House of Delegates from the Fairfield County Medical Soc. **BUSINESS ADDRESS:** 1475 Barnum Ave, Bridgeport, CT 06610.

ELLIOTT, IRVIN WESLEY
Educator. **PERSONAL:** Born Oct 21, 1925, Newton, KS; son of Irvin Elliott and Leota Jordan Elliott; married Joan Curl, Aug 27, 1952; children: Derek, Karen. **EDUCATION:** Univ of KS, BS 1947, MS 1949, PhD 1952; Harvard Univ, Univ of Copenhagen, postdoctoral. **CAREER:** Fisk Univ, prof of chem 1958; Howard Univ, visiting prof 1965-66; Ford Motor Co, visiting scientist 1964; FL A&M Coll, assoc prof 1952-57; Southern Univ, instr 1949-50; Wellesley College, Wellesley MA, visiting prof 1984-85. **ORGANIZATIONS:** Cons, Coll Chem, Amer Chem Soc; chmn, Nashville Section of Amer Chem Soc 1970; bd dir, Nat Adv Bd, CEMREL Inst 1968-74; exec com, Southern Conf of Grad Sch 1971-74; Grad Record Exam Bd 1974-; mem, Amer Chem Soc; Chem Soc of London; Intl Soc of Heterocyclic Chem; AAAS; Omicron Delta Kappa; Sigma Xi; Beta Kappa Chi; NSF Faculty Fellowship 1957-58. **HONORS/ACHIEVEMENTS:** Syntheses of Isoquinoline Alkaloids; author, Dibenzopyrrocoline Alkaloids, published in The Akaloids Academic Press, 1987. **BUSINESS ADDRESS:** Dept of Chem, Fisk Univ, Nashville, TN 37208.

ELLIOTT, J. RUSSELL
Mechanical engineer. **PERSONAL:** Born in Chicago, IL; son of J Russell Elliott and Blanche Smith Elliott; married Sharon Lomax. **EDUCATION:** Chicago Tech Coll, BSME 1968; Northwestern Univ, MBA 1975. **CAREER:** Johnson & Johnson Co, mech engr, suprv 1966-75; engineering mgr, Baby Products Co, 1975-80; Ortho Pharmaceutical Div of Johnson & Johnson, dir indus engrg 1980-85; Johnson & Johnson Baby Prod Co, engr mgr 1975-80, natl mgr package engrg 1986-. **ORGANIZATIONS:** Bd trustees Chicago Opportunity Industrialization Center 1973-75; bd trustees Sigma Phi Delta Engr & Fraternity 1967-69; adv hs youth group Good Shephard Church 1969-73; bd of deacons Good Shephard Congregational Church 1969-75; mem Chicago Urban League 1967-75; mem Alpha Phi Alpha; adv Soc of Black Engineers at Princeton Univ. **HONORS/ACHIEVEMENTS:** Certificate of Merit Chicago Assn of Commerce & Indus 1973-75. **BUSINESS ADDRESS:** Manager Package Engineering, J & J Baby Products Co, Div of Johnson & Johnson, 199 Grandview Road, Skillman, NJ 08558.

ELLIOTT, JOY
Journalist. **PERSONAL:** Born in St Ann, Jamaica. **EDUCATION:** Univ of the West Indies at Mona, BS; Univ of Poitiers Inst de Touraine, diplomas in French; Univ of Paris New Sch for Social Rsch, MA. **CAREER:** Associated Press, reporter 1970-72; Reuters News Serv, correspondent 1972-. **ORGANIZATIONS:** Mem, Natl Assn of Black Journalists; Intl Assn for Mass Communication Rsch; Coalition of 100 Black Women; mem Soc of Professional Journalists, NY Sponsoring Comm, NAACP Legal Defense Fund; interim bd of dirs NY Chap Univ West Indies Guild of Gradmakers; bd mem Carib News newspaper NY. **HONORS/ACHIEVEMENTS:** First black woman journalist, Associated Press 1970-72. **BUSINESS ADDRESS:** Correspondent, Reuters News, 1700 Broadway, New York, NY 10019.

ELLIOTT, WILLIAM DAVID
Actor, producer, director. **PERSONAL:** Born Jun 04, 1934, Baltimore, MD; children: David, Damon. **EDUCATION:** Self-employed, actor, prod, dir; Elliott Studio Prod, Hollywood, pres. **HONORS/ACHIEVEMENTS:** Films "Change of Habit" 1969; "Where Does It Hurt" 1972; "Coffy" 1973; "Superdude" 1975;TV "Bridget Loves Bernie"; "That's My Mama"; "Adam 12"; "Ironside" "Police Story" "Celebrity & Sweepstakes" "Rookies" drums, vocals, 12 Yr Musician In San Francisco, Baltimore, New York, & Los Angeles; recip of many awards andplaques from various orgns; Key to City of Newark 1973; Key to City of Baltimore 1974; honored, "Bill Elliott Day" in Baltimore 1974. **MILITARY SERVICE:** USN radarman seaman. **HOME ADDRESS:** 806 N Elm, Beverly Hills, CA.

ELLIS, ALLAN D.
Professional football player. **PERSONAL:** Born Aug 19, 1951, Los Angeles; married Jackie. **EDUCATION:** UCLA, BA 1973. **CAREER:** Chi Bears, def back 1973-. **ORGANIZATIONS:** Affil, Red Cloud & Boys Clb; mem, Easter Seals-Westside Hlth Org; %Mem, Better Boys & Found. **HONORS/ACHIEVEMENTS:** Freshman yr, capt ftbl team, soph, rookie of yr, sr, Outstndng Sr, outstndng sr, outstndng def player, UCLA; %Capt varsity squad, Pro Bowl Player 1978. **BUSINESS ADDRESS:** c/o Chicago Bears, PO Box 204, Lake Forest, IL 60045.

ELLIS, BENJAMIN F., JR.
City official. **PERSONAL:** Born Sep 17, 1939, Philadelphia, PA; son of Benjamine H Ellis and Tinner F Ellis; married Sylvia Ann Simmons; children: Letitia A, Wendy S, Benjamin III, Melanie R. **EDUCATION:** Temple Univ, Assn in Electronics 1967, BS Business Admin (cum laude) 1974. **CAREER:** Naval Air Eng Ctr, Philadelphia proj adm 1966-73; Penn Mutual Life Insurance Co, bldg supt 1973-76, bldg mgr 1976-79, asst vice pres 1979-81; 2nd vice pres 1981-88; City of Philadelphia, commr of public property, 1988-. **ORGANIZATIONS:** Corp Financial Comm mem BOMA Intl 1974-; dir BOMA Philadelphia 1978-; mem Toastmasters Intl 1967-73; dir Citizens Coalition for Energy Efficiency 1983-; dir, Philadelphia Center for Older People 1981-; allocations comm United Way of Se PA 1978-. **HONORS/ACHIEVEMENTS:** Outstanding apprentice of yr Naval Air Engr Ctr 1965; 1st Black Vice Pres Penn Mutual Life Insurance Co 1979. **MILITARY SERVICE:** USN 3rd class petty officer 2 yrs. **HOME ADDRESS:** 6702 Wayne Ave, Philadelphia, PA 19119. **BUSINESS ADDRESS:** City of Philadelphia, Commissioner of Public Property, Municipal Services Bld, Rm 1020, Philadelphia, PA 19102.

ELLIS, CALVIN H., III
Educator. **PERSONAL:** Born Jun 09, 1941, Whitesboro, NJ. **EDUCATION:** Glassboro St Coll, BA 1970, MA 1972. **CAREER:** Atlantic Human Res, training officer 1968-69; Glassboro State Coll, Univ Year for Action, dir 1969-. **ORGANIZATIONS:** Pres, bd trustees, Atlantic Human Res 1975; mem Nat Assn for Comm Dev 1975; Glassboro St Coll Com on Human & Res 1975. **BUSINESS ADDRESS:** UYr for Action, Glassboro State Coll, Glassboro, NJ.

ELLIS, DALE TERRELL
Professional athlete. **PERSONAL:** Born Aug 06, 1960, Marietta, GA. **EDUCATION:** Tenn, 1983. **CAREER:** Dallas Mavericks, forward 1983-. **HONORS/ACHIEVEMENTS:** Set an NBA record; went to the NCAA tourney; shared the '82 SEC title with KY; three times voted All SEC; twice conf player of the year; two-time All-Amer. **BUSINESS ADDRESS:** Dallas Mavericks, Reunion Arena, 777 Sports St, Dallas, TX 75207.

ELLIS, DOUGLAS, JR.
Public administration executive. **PERSONAL:** Born Jul 09, 1947, Chicago, IL; son of Douglas Ellis Sr and Dorothy Mae Rummage Ellis; married Anthony Marcus, Chad Dominick (divorced). **EDUCATION:** Univ of Illinois, Chicago IL, BS, 1976; Roosevelt Univ, Chicago IL, MS, 1979. **CAREER:** Chicago Police Dept, Chicago IL, sergeant, 1972-86; City-Wide Colleges, Chicago IL, instructor, 1984-86; City of Chicago, Bureau of Parking, Chicago IL, dir, 1986-. **ORGANIZATIONS:** Certified instructor, Chicago Police Academy, 1976-78; mem, Illinois CPA Soc, 1985-; bd of advisor delegate, Inst of Municipal Parking Congress, 1986-; membership dir, Natl Assn of Black Accountants, 1987-88. **HONORS/ACHIEVEMENTS:** Dept Commendation, Chicago Police Dept, 1981. **MILITARY SERVICE:** US Marine Corps Reserves, E7 Gunnery Sergeant, 1964-68 active duty, 1974- reserve

duty; Vietnam Combat Ribbons (various), 1966-67. **BUSINESS ADDRESS:** Director, City of Chicago, Department of Public Works, Bureau of Parking Mgmt, 510 N Peshtigo Court, Floor 3B, Chicago, IL 60611-4321.

ELLIS, DUKE ELLINGTON
Educator, psychologist. **PERSONAL:** Born Jul 02, 1933, Georgetown, IL; married Rebecca Ford; children: Wendell C, Eric M, Stephanie A, George E. **EDUCATION:** Anderson Coll, BS 1951-56; St Francis Coll, MS 1961-63;Univ of Cincinnati, PhD 1969-72. **CAREER:** School of Professional Psychology, Wright State Univ, Dayton OH, asst dean of std affairs & admin 1978-; Behavioral Science Applications Inc, Cincinnati OH, pres 1976-; Cincinnati, freelance orgn consultant 1972-76; Urban League, Dayton OH, dir of educ 1964-69. **ORGANIZATIONS:** Dir, Kiwanis Br YMCA Ft Wayne 1959-64; mem, Am Psychol Assn 1978-; mem Miami Valley Psychol Assn 1978-; mem, Assn of Black Psychologists 1978-; mem, Miami Valley Psychol Assn 1978-. **HONORS/ACHIEVEMENTS:** Recipt, Good Conduct Medal, AUS 1959; Martin Luther King Flwshp 1969; Danforth Flwshp 1969; listed, "Personalities of W & MW 1971. **MILITARY SERVICE:** AUS pfc 1957-59. **BUSINESS ADDRESS:** Wright State Univ, Dayton, OH 45435.

ELLIS, EDWARD V.
Educator. **PERSONAL:** Born Feb 09, 1924, Louisburg, NC; married Elizabeth Gill; children: Ednetta K, Bruce E, Gary D. **EDUCATION:** Shaw U, BS 1949; NC Coll, MSPH 1950;Univ of NC, PhD 1964. **CAREER:** Raleigh Public Schools, Wake County Health Dept, health educ, 1950-51; NC Coll, instructor 1951-52; Washingtom DC TB Assn, assoc health educ 1952-55; IN State Coll, faculty mem, school comm & health educ workshop 1963; PA Dept of Health, consultant 1955-63, sect chief 1955-63; PA State Univ, faculty mem 1964-65; Div of Public Health Educ, dir 1964-67; Univ of MN, asst prof 1967-69; PA State Univ, special asst to pres 1970-71, center head 1971-72, acting div dir 1972-74, assoc prof, assoc dean 1969-82; Univ of Maryland Eastern Shore, vice chancellor for acad affairs 1983-. **ORGANIZATIONS:** Numerous Consulting Positions; mem, Various Off; coms, Am Adult Ed Assn; Am AssnUniv Profs; Am Pub Hlth Assn; Prog Dev Bd; Soc Pub Hlth Ed; NatUniv Extension Assn; Soc Pub Hlth Ed; Coalition of Nat Hlth Ed Orgs; PA Pub Hlth; Cntrl PA Hlth Cncl; Centre Comm Hlth Cncl; Comm on Higher Ed; Adv Com, PA & Dept Publ Hlth; PA Com for Nat Hlth Security; Nat Black Alliance; mem, Vrious Off; Coms, Am Cancer Soc; Cnslng Svc, Inc,of Centre Co; Family Plng Cncl of Cntrl PA, Inc; Family Serv Assn of Am; Human Rel Commn; PA Lung Assn. **HONORS/ACHIEVEMENTS:** NumerousUniv affiliations, Spkng engagements, publs in field. **MILITARY SERVICE:** USN 1943-46. **BUSINESS ADDRESS:** Vice Chancellor for Acad Afrs, Univ of Maryland Eastern Shore, Princess Anne, MD 21853.

ELLIS, EFFIE O'NEAL
Physician, administrator. **PERSONAL:** Born Jun 15, 1913, Pulaski Co, GA; married James Solomon; children: Mrs Daniel Comegys. **EDUCATION:** Spelman Coll, AB 1933; Atlanta U, MA 1935;Univ IL, MD 1950. **CAREER:** Am Med Assn, spl asst to exec vice pres hlth serv 1970-; Provident Hosp, Baltimore, dir med ed 1954-56; S of OH, regl dir maternal & child hlth 1960-65; US Children's Bureau, regl med dir 1965-67; US Dept of HEW, regl commr for soc rehab 1965-70;Univ IL Hosp, served residency in peds; John Hopkins Hosp, ped Cardiology. **ORGANIZATIONS:** Mem, Am Pub Hlth Assn; Am Pub Welfare Assn; Am Asn on Mental Deficiency; Am Assn for Maternal & Child Hlth; liason for, Med Assn with Nat Med Assn & Women's Med Assn; mem, Alpha Gamma Phi; Delta Sigma Theta. **BUSINESS ADDRESS:** Health Consultant, 300 N State St #4605, Chicago, IL 60610.

ELLIS, ELIZABETH G.
Librarian. **PERSONAL:** Born Nov 06, Raleigh, NC; married Dr Edward V; children: Ednetta, Bruce, Gary. **EDUCATION:** NC Central U, BA 1947, BSLS 1949, MSLS 1962. **CAREER:** PA St U, head, undergrad libs 1969-; DrexelUniv Grad Sch Lib Sci, adj prof 1965-67; PA St Lib, lib 1956-67, lib 1947-56, univ sen 1975-76. **ORGANIZATIONS:** Chrmnshps & Offs, ALA; PA Lib Assn; mem, Assn Univ Women; League Women Voters; Am Assn Pub Admin Pubs, Lectures. **HONORS/ACHIEVEMENTS:** Librarian Yr, NC Lib Assn. **BUSINESS ADDRESS:** W106 Pattee Library, University Park, PA 16802.

ELLIS, ELWARD DWAYNE
Clergyman, chief executive officer. **PERSONAL:** Born Dec 17, 1948, Newark, NJ; son of Elward Ellis and Dorothy Mae Ward Ellis; married E Dawn Swaby Ellis, Oct 09, 1982; children: Dwayne Jonathan Oni Ellis. **EDUCATION:** Shaw Univ, AB History 1966-70; Gordon-Conwell Theological Seminary, MDiv 1970-74; Andover Newton Theological School, 1973; Harvard Divinity Sch, 1974. **CAREER:** Emmanuel Gospel Center, staff 1971-73; Christian Growth Center, staff 1973-74; Norfolk State Univ, UCCM chaplain 1974-79; Bank St Mem Baptist Church, asst to pastor 1975-79; Friendship Comm Church, minister 1979-80; Inter-Varsity Christian Fellowship, dir of black campus ministry 1980-87; Destiny Movement Inc, pres 1988-. **ORGANIZATIONS:** Mem Optimal Intl 1977; Tidewater Metro Bapt Ministers' Conf Educ Comm 1978-79; chmn Annual Youth Appreciation Week Sunrise Optimist Club 1978-79; adv bd mem Norfolk Public Schools Adv Comm on Spec Educ 1978-79; co-dir "Washington '80" Natl Conf on Ministry in Urban America 1979-80; bd mem Tidewater Big Brothers 1979-80; mem Natl Black Evangelicals Assn 1979-; mem Natl Black Pastor's Conf 1981-; bd mem Justice Fellowship Inc 1984-; bd mem, vice chmn Evangelicals for Social Action 1984-; bd mem Norfolk Comm for the Improve of Educ; mem local committee Georgia Inter-Varsity Christian Fellowship 1986-; bd mem Voice of Calvary Ministry 1988. **HONORS/ACHIEVEMENTS:** VA Baptist Training Union & Sunday School Congress Citation for Outstanding Contributions to Christian Educ; Mt Zion Baptist Church of Norfolk Citation for Yeoman Serv in Campus Ministry 1979; Comm of Christian Students Norfolk State Coll Citation for Outstanding Dedication to Coll Campus Ministry 1979; Bank St Memorial Baptist Church Citation Appreciation for Pastoral Service 1979; The Groove Phi Groove Social Fellowship Spartan Chap The Fellowship and Humanitarian Awd Norfolk State Univ 1978; Executive Dir Destiny '87 Intl Conf on Mission 1987; Silver Anniversary Citation, Natl Black Evangelical Assn 1988; Centennial Award, Gordon-Conwell Theological Seminary 1989. **HOME ADDRESS:** 6280 Phillips Corner Rd, Lithonia, GA 30058. **BUSINESS ADDRESS:** President, Destiny Movement Inc, 2227 Godby Rd, Suite 216, College Park, GA 30349.

ELLIS, ERNEST W. (AKBAR KHAN)
Business executive. **PERSONAL:** Born Dec 04, 1940, New York City, NY; son of Edmund and Mabel; divorced; children: Anthony, Darius Kenyatta, Edmund Kip. **EDUCATION:** Hartman Inst of Criminology, BS 1963; Am Inst of Banking, Advanced Degree 1977; Inst for Far Eastern Affairs, Cert 1981. **CAREER:** United Nations, reporter-general assembly 1962-64; Harmelin Agency, adm asst Ins 1964-66; Prudential, cnslnt ins 1966-69; State Dept CIA, 1967-70; intelligence off; Chase, 2nd vice pres 1970-. **ORGANIZATIONS:** Asst treas Western Hem Life Ins Co 1982-; chief exec off & pres Galactic Intl Ltd 1982-; contributing edtr Assets Protection Mag 1976-; visiting prof Wagner Coll 1976; visiting prof Upsala Coll 1981; v chmn Area Policy Bd 7 New York City 1979-81. **HONORS/ACHIEVEMENTS:** Clifford Brown Mem Music Award New York City 1976; Outstanding Citizen Award, Chase Bank New York City 1972; cert of merit The Assembly St of NY 1981; New Star Vibist Sound of Music 1970. **HOME ADDRESS:** 140-55 Burden Crescent, Briarwood, NY 11435. **BUSINESS ADDRESS:** Second Vice President, Chase Manhattan Bank, 80 Pine St, New York, NY 10081.

ELLIS, FREDERIC L.
Retired business executive. **PERSONAL:** Born Jun 16, 1915, Pensacola, FL; widowed; children: Roberta Jones-Booker, Ettamaria Ellis. **EDUCATION:** Morehouse Coll, AB 1938. **CAREER:** NC Mutual-Birmingham, dist mgr 1955; NC Mutual-Los Angeles, dist mgr 1963, Retired 1977. **ORGANIZATIONS:** Trustee Second Baptist Church, Men of Tomorrow, Kappa Alpha Psi Frat, NAACP. **HONORS/ACHIEVEMENTS:** AUS T/3 sgt 1942-46. **HOME ADDRESS:** 4323 Don Arellanes, Los Angeles, CA 90008.

ELLIS, GEORGE WASHINGTON
Educator. **PERSONAL:** Born Jan 01, 1925, Arcadia, FL; son of George Edward Ellis and Gussie Staley Ellis; married Alvalia G Jones; children: George, Ruth, Cheryl, Jean. **EDUCATION:** Ind Ed, Florida A&M Univ, BS 1947; Univ of Pittsburgh, EdM 1954; Columbia U, post grad studies 1961; Univ of Pittsburgh, Attend 1956-60; Univ of FL, Attend 1966-71; Univ of Miami, Attend 1969; FL Atlantic Univ, Attend 1969-70; FL Int Univ, Attend 1975-80; Dade Jr Coll, Attend 1974-77. **CAREER:** Alcorn A&M Coll, tchr, coach 1947-48; FL Memorial Coll, tchr 1948, 1969-70; Carver HS, assist prin & coach 1948-50; Bayview-Bonifay, prin 1950-53; Shadeville HS, prin 1953-56; Richardson HS, prin 1953-56; Monitor HS, prin 1956-57; Westside HS, prin 1960-62; Williston Voc HS, 1962-63; Center HS Waycross, 1963-67; Dade County Schools, asst principal, principal 1967-87; Southern Region, pres. **ORGANIZATIONS:** Pres, Alpha Eta Chapter, Phi Beta Sigma Frat 1946-; pres, Rho Sigma Chap 1970-72; v dir, St of FL 1973-74; dir, FL 1974; v dir, Sthrn Reg 1974-75, dir 1975-77; pres Miami Chap Kappa Delta Pi 1977-78; mem, Orange Blossom Classic Comm 1973-89; vp, Miami Chap FL A&M Alumni 1977-79; pres, Miami Chpt & FAMU Alumni 1980; FL St Chaplain, FL A&M Alumni 1979-80; offcr, NAACP 1972-75; mem, Affirm Act Comm, Minist & Laymen Assn of Miami; chmn, Metro Dade Co Mayor's Advis Bd for Animals; tchr Sun Sch, Church of the Open Door; dir so reg Third World Assembly Inc. **HONORS/ACHIEVEMENTS:** Outstanding Principal, Center HS; FL Sigma Man of the Yr 1972, 1977; Phi Beta Sigma's Natl Ed Award; Regl Dir Award, Phi Beta Sigma 1977; fl st treas, Phi Beta Sigma 1977-80; Black Liberation Award 1978, 1981, 1983; Public Health Trust of Dade Co 1984; Presidential Award Natl Alumni FAMU 1984; Goodwill Indust Awards 1982, 1983; Commendation Award Metro Dade Co FL 1978, 1987; Certificate of Appreciation City of Miami FL 1978, 1979, 1984; Martin Luther King Brotherhood Awd 1983, 1984, 1986. **BUSINESS ADDRESS:** Pres Outstanding Sigmas, Southern Region, 1055 NW 52nd St, Miami, FL 33127.

ELLIS, GERRY
Professional athlete. **PERSONAL:** Born Nov 12, 1957, Columbia, MO. **EDUCATION:** Ft Scott KS Jr Coll, attended; Univ of MO, attended. **CAREER:** Green Bay Packers, fullback 1980-. **HONORS/ACHIEVEMENTS:** Packers total offense leader (1359 yards) & set a team record for receptions by a running back (65); Green Bays leading rusher with 860 yards in 196 attempts. **BUSINESS ADDRESS:** Green Bay Packers, 1265 Lombardi Ave, Green Bay, WI 54307.

ELLIS, JOHNELL A.
Engineer. **PERSONAL:** Born Sep 28, 1945, New Orleans; married Audrey Baker; children: Kimberly, Sonja. **EDUCATION:** CA St U, BS Engr 1968; Univ of So CA, MBA 1972. **CAREER:** Getty Oil Co, staff eng 1985; Rockwell Intnl, fin analyst 1974; Dart Ind, acquisitions spec 1972-74; TRW Sys, Redondo Bch, admin asst 1969-72; Bunker-ramo & Westlake, engr 1968; Bambini Stores, Beverly Hills, acct; CA St U, instr. **ORGANIZATIONS:** Mem, Soc of Petro Engr; Inst of Elec & Electronic Engr; mem, Kappa Alpha Psi; Tau Beta Pi; Eta Kappa Nu. **HONORS/ACHIEVEMENTS:** Award of Appreciation, Improvement Act Com. **BUSINESS ADDRESS:** 3810 Wilshire Blvd, Ste 410, Los Angeles, CA 90010.

ELLIS, JOSEPH LOUIS
Retired travel agent. **PERSONAL:** Born Jul 07, 1916, St Louis, MO; married Evelyn Bernice Mann. **EDUCATION:** QM Officer Cand School, 2nd Lt 1943; Butler Univ, 1955-57. **CAREER:** US Gen Acct, auditor 1947-74; ID Herald Newspaper, photographer PR 1954-60; Twilight Travel Serv, travel agent 1971-80. **ORGANIZATIONS:** Owner 1st Black Certified Travel Agency in ID 1971-80; life mem, NAACP 1983; bd mem Indianapolis Chapter NAACP 1982-85; 33 Degree mason Prince Hall Masonic Ldg Scottish Rite & Shrine. **HONORS/ACHIEVEMENTS:** Mason of Yr Prince Hall Grand Ldg of IN 1973; comm in chief of Yr IN Scottish Rite 1975. **MILITARY SERVICE:** QMC 2nd lt 1944. **HOME ADDRESS:** 502 W 42nd St, Indianapolis, IN 46208.

ELLIS, KENNETH A.
Professional football player. **PERSONAL:** Born Sep 27, 1947, Woodbine, GA; married Joyce Heatly; children: Trent, Kebba. **EDUCATION:** So U, BPE 1970. **CAREER:** LA Rams, professional ftbl plyr 1979-; Detroit Lions, ftbl plyr 1979; Cleveland Browns, ftbl plyr 1977-79; Miami Dolphins, ftbl plyr 1976-77; Green Bay Packers, ftbl plyr 1970-75. **ORGANIZATIONS:** Mem, Baton Rouge Police Comm Rel Grp AIA 1970. **HONORS/ACHIEVEMENTS:** All-Pro 1972-73; Pro Bowl 1973-74; All Rookie Team 1970; led punt returns, NFL 1972; ;Afl-nFl Championship Game 1970; NFL Championship Game 1970, 1973-74, 1976; named cornerback on Sporting News NFC All Star Team 1973; NFC Championship Game 1979. **BUSINESS ADDRESS:** C/o Los Angeles Rams, 2327 Lincoln Ave, Anaheim, CA 92801.

ELLIS, LEANDER THEODORE
Psychiatrist. **PERSONAL:** Born May 30, 1929, Summerland, MS; married Gettie Thigpen; children: Leonard, Lawrence, Laura, Lowell. **EDUCATION:** Hampton Inst, BS 1950; Howard Univ, MD 1954. **CAREER:** Philadelphia General Hosp, psychiatric residency 1957-60, staff psychiatrist 1960-67; Philadelphia Psychiatric Ctr, attending staff 1962-; Woodhaven Southeastern State Sch & Hosp, staff psychiatrist 1975-77; Private Practice, general psychiatry 1960-. **ORGANIZATIONS:** Diplomat Amer Bd of Psychiatry and Neurology; psychiatric consultant North Central & Comprehensive MH/MR 1981,82; psychiatric consultant Sleighton School 1981-. **HONORS/ACHIEVEMENTS:** Publication "Stress, A Non-Specific Factor in Emotionality," Journal of Orthomolecular Psychiatry Vol 6 No 4 1977. **MILITARY SERVICE:** USNR lt medical corps 3 yrs. **HOME ADDRESS:** 100 So Swarthmore Ave, Swarthmore, PA 19081. **BUSINESS ADDRESS:** 2746 Belmont Ave, Philadelphia, PA 19131.

ELLIS, MARILYN POPE
Educator. **PERSONAL:** Born Jun 24, 1938, Newark, NJ; daughter of James Albert Pope and Gladys Hillman Pope; children: Kristina Pope. **EDUCATION:** CA State Univ Hayward, BA 1969; Univ CA-Berkeley, MA 1972. **CAREER:** Peralta Community Coll, prof History 1973-76; Skyline Coll, prof History 1973-. **HONORS/ACHIEVEMENTS:** Third World Artist in the US 1983-84; Crossroads Africa & Parsons African Artists School of Design Ivory Coast & Craftspeople 1984. **HOME ADDRESS:** 67 Werner Ave, Daly City, CA 94014. **BUSINESS ADDRESS:** Professor of History, Skyline College, 3300 College Dr, San Bruno, CA 94060.

ELLIS, O. HERBERT
Educator. **PERSONAL:** Born Mar 23, 1916, Chandler, OK; married Virginia Wilson; children: O Herbert Jr, Jeffrey W. **EDUCATION:** Langston U, AB, AM, MPH 1940;Univ of Mi, Attend 1949. **CAREER:** TB & Health Soc, Detroit MI, sr health educ 1950-56; Michigan Health Council, vice chmn 1954-56; Wayne Co Inter-Agency Council, chmn 1955; Ann Arbor Public Schools, teacher 1985; Washtenaw County TB & Health Assn, pres 1959-61. **ORGANIZATIONS:** Mem, Wash Co Comm-Mental Hlth Bd 1966-; chmn, Wash Co Bd of Commr 1970; mem, Wash Co Bd of Commr 1959-; pres Sr Cit Guild 1974-75; mem, AnnArbor Rotary Clb 1964-; United Meth Ch 1956-. **HONORS/ACHIEVEMENTS:** Recip, Ann Arbor Tchr of Yr Award 1969; 1st Black to serve as chair of Washtenaw Co Bd of Commr; v-chmn, chmn of bd, & various com, Wash Co Bd of Commr; selected as one of five pers to plan altern HS in Ann Arbor 1971. **BUSINESS ADDRESS:** Co Bldg, Main at Huron, Ann Arbor, MI 48103.

ELLIS, P. J.
Clergyman. **PERSONAL:** Born Sep 13, 1911, Alabama; widowed. **CAREER:** Morning Missionary Bapt Ch, minister 1985. **ORGANIZATIONS:** Pres, Bapt Ministers Conf of LA & So CA 1959-62, 1956-; moderator, LA Dist Assn 1959-68; bd dir 28th St YMCA 1957-; life mem, NAACP; parliamentarian, CA St Bapt Conv; mem, Nat Bapt Conv USA, Inc.

ELLIS, RAY
Professional football player. **PERSONAL:** Born Apr 27, 1959, Canton, OH. **EDUCATION:** Attended OH State Univ. **CAREER:** Philadelphia Eagles, safety 1981-. **BUSINESS ADDRESS:** Safety, Philadelphia Eagles, Philadelphia Veterans Stadium, Broad St & Pattison Ave, Philadelphia, PA 19148.

ELLIS, RODNEY
Elected official. **PERSONAL:** Born Apr 07, 1954, Houston, TX. **EDUCATION:** TX Southern Univ, BA 1975; Univ of TX, MPA 1977; London School of Econ, Univ of TX, JD 1979. **CAREER:** Lt Governor of TX, admin asst 1976-80; Chief Justice 3rd Court of Appeals, briefing attny 1980-81; TX Railroad Commiss, legal counsel 1981-; US Congress, admin asst 1981-83. **ORGANIZATIONS:** Chmn Committee on Econ Redevel; mem City's Charter Revision Comm, Flooding Mgmt Comm, State Bar of TX, Natl Bar Assoc, Amer Leadership Forum, TX Lyceum. **HONORS/ACHIEVEMENTS:** Des Porres Scholarship 1972-73; Athletic Scholarship 1973-75; Lyndon B Johnson School of Public Affairs Fellowship 1975-77; Earl Warren Legal Training Fellowship 1977-79. **BUSINESS ADDRESS:** City Councilmember, City of Houston, PO Box 1562, Houston, TX 77251.

ELLIS, TELLIS B., III
Physician. **PERSONAL:** Born Dec 15, 1943, Jackson, MS; married Patricia Ward; children: Tellis IV. **EDUCATION:** Jackson State Univ, BS 1965; Meharry Medical Coll, MD 1970. **CAREER:** Meharry Medical Coll, straight medical internship 1970-71, internal medicine residency 1971-74; Univ Medical Ctr, cardiology fellowship 1975-77; Private Practice, physician. **ORGANIZATIONS:** Mem Jackson Medical Soc, Natl Medical Assoc, Assoc of Black Cardiologists, Kappa Alpha Psi Frat. **HONORS/ACHIEVEMENTS:** Board Certification in Internal Medicine, Cardiovascular Disease. **BUSINESS ADDRESS:** 440 E Woodrow Wilson Ste 302, Jackson, MS 39216.

ELLIS, WADE
Consulting mathematician. **PERSONAL:** Born Jun 09, 1909, Chandler, OK; married Agatha Hampton; children: William W, Wade Jr. **EDUCATION:** Wilberforce Univ, BS chem & math 1928; Univ of NM, MS math 1938; Univ of MI, PhD math 1944. **CAREER:** Ft Valley St Clg GA, instr math 1938; Fisk Univ Nashville TN, instr math 1938-40; Univ MI, spec instr math 1943-45; MA Inst of Tech, staff mem radiation lab 1945; Air Force Rsch Lab Cambridge MA, mathematician 1946-48; Boston U, lecturer on math 1946-48; Oberlin Clg Oberlin OH, prof math 1948-67; FL A&M Univ Tallahassee, visiting prof of math 1950; Universidad Nacional de Ingenieria Lima Peru, visiting prof math 1964; Univ of MI, prof math, assoc dean grad school; Univ of MD Eastern Shore, vice chancellor for academics affairs 1979-80; Marygrove Coll Detroit, pres 1980-81; VA State Univ, eminent scholar 1983-84; consulting mathematician. **ORGANIZATIONS:** Math Assoc of Amer Vstg Lecturer 1955-62, 1967-77; consult Ministry of Ed & Rel Govt of Greece 1960; vice pres Oberlin Home Def Ent 1960-70; mem, v chair Oberlin City Council 1961-67; consult Ministry of Pub Ed Govt of Peru 1961-67; treas BLScott Masonry & Const Co 1963-69; mem Sch Math Study Grp Writing Panels Stanford Univ 1963-64; chair OH Sect Math Assoc of Amer 1963-64; mem bd of trustees & sci adv Inst on Man and Science 1964-; bd of gov Math Assoc of Amer 1964-67; bd of adv School Math Study Group 1964-67; consult Problems of BAsic Sci Ed Ford Found Mexico City Office 1965-66; bd mem & vice pres Coll Plcmnt Serv 1969-80. **HONORS/ACHIEVEMENTS:** Dr, Humane Letters (hnry degree) Marygrove Clg Detroit 1980; Comendador enas Palmas Magisteriales del Peru (natl decoration) Govt of Peru Lima 1964; Phi Beta KappaUniv Of MI (Schlrlshp in Gen); Sigma Xi,Univ of MI (Schlrshp in Sci); Pi Mu Epsilon,Univ of SD (Schlrshp Math); Kappa Mu Epsilon,Univ of NM (Schlrshp Math); Sword & Shield WilberforceUniv (Schlrshp in Gen); Comendador en la Orden de Las Palmas Magisteriales del Peru decoration Govt of Peru; Doctor ofHumane Letters Marygrove Clg. **MILITARY SERVICE:** UAS Inf Res 2nd lt 1928-38. **HOME ADDRESS:** 1141 Chestnut Rd, Ann Arbor, MI 48104. **BUSINESS ADDRESS:** Consulting Mathematician, (Independent), 1141 Chestnut Rd, Ann Arbor, MI 48104.

ELLIS, WILLIAM REUBEN
Attorney, editor, publisher. **PERSONAL:** Born Jul 23, 1917, Griffin, GA; married Rosemary Johnson, Rev. **EDUCATION:** Univ of Cincinnati Law Sch, grad 1950; Wilberforce Univ, attended; Ohio State Univ, attended. **CAREER:** Atty-at-law, 1985; The Reporter, editor & publisher 1985. **ORGANIZATIONS:** Found, pres, Akron Metro Opps Indstrlztn Cntr; former pres, Springfield OH Chpt, NAACP; served on Legal Redress-Com; assisted in Brown v bd ofEd; past pres, Springfield Hsng Devel; pres, Steel Records; past Grand High Priest; past Grand Thice Illustrous Master; past Grand Lectr; grand atty, Knight of Pythias; former supt, Sun Sch; 17 Yrs mem, AME Ch; mem, Akron Barristers Clb; chrtr mem, sec, Nat Bus League of Akron; mem adv bd, WAkron YMCA; mem, Nat Nwsprs Pub Assn; cand, Judge of Common Pleas CT of Mahoning Co 1966. **HONORS/ACHIEVEMENTS:** Sr Citizens & Model Cities Cit Prtcptn; recip, Achievement Award, OH Black Polit Assem; NAACP, Achievement Award; 2nd pl, St of OH Safety & Slogan; cited by Red Cross; March of Dimes; United Fund. **MILITARY SERVICE:** AUS air-inspector 99th fighter squadron. **BUSINESS ADDRESS:** 82 E Mill St, Akron, OH 44308.

ELLIS, ZACHARY L.
Industrial executive. **CAREER:** Ellis Enterprises, Kenner LA, chief exec. **BUSINESS ADDRESS:** Ellis Enterprises, 2241 Piedmont St, Kenner, LA 70062. *

ELLISON, DAVID LEE
City administrator. **PERSONAL:** Born Oct 11, 1955, Houston, TX; son of L T Ellison Sr and Alma Shelton Ellison; married Lethia Fanuiel Ellison, Oct 04, 1977; children: Dayna Leigh, Lyndsay Dalethia, Drew Leslye, Landon David Oran. **EDUCATION:** North TX State Univ, BS, Secondary Educ, 1980; Univ of North TX, MA, Public Admin, 1988. **CAREER:** City of Denton, TX, urban planner, 1980-83, sr planner,1983-87, asst to the city mgr, 1987-89; City of Mankato, MN, asst city mgr, 1989. **ORGANIZATIONS:** mem, Natl Forum of Black Public Admin, Amer Planning Assn/Planning & Black Com Div, Amer Soc of Public Admin/Conf of Minority Public Admin, Intl City Mgmt Assoc; Natl Trust for Historic Preservation; pres, North TX Chapter of Conf of Minority Public Admin, 1988; exec dir, City of Mankato & Blue Earth County Housing & Redevelopment Authorities, 1989-; Minnesota City Mgmt Assn. **HONORS/ACHIEVEMENTS:** Distinguished Serv Historical Preservation at the Cty Level TX Historical Comm, 1981. **BUSINESS ADDRESS:** Asst City Mgr/Community Development Dir, City of Mankato, 202 East Jackson, PO Box 3368, Mankato, MN 56001.

ELLISON, HENRY S.
Physician. **PERSONAL:** Born Oct 11, 1923, Greensboro, NC; married Etna Harris; children: Pamela, Henry Jr. **EDUCATION:** A&T Coll, BS (magna cum laude) 1943; Howard U, MD 1952; Freedman's Hosp, Intership Residency 1952-58. **CAREER:** Self-employed Youngstown, OH, physician 1958-. **ORGANIZATIONS:** Pres Mahoning Co Mental Health Bd; chmn bd Youngstown Area & Devel Corp; past pres Youngstown Humane Soc; past mem bd Goodwill Industries; trusteesMarch of Dimes; mem Adult Mental Health Bd. **MILITARY SERVICE:** USAF pfc 1946-47. **BUSINESS ADDRESS:** 1350 Fifth Ave, Ste 400, Youngstown, OH 44504.

ELLISON, NOLEN M.
Educator. **PERSONAL:** Born Jan 26, 1941, Kansas City, KS; married Carole; children: Marc, Steven. **EDUCATION:** Kansas U, BS 1963; Hampton Inst, MA 1966; MI State U, PhD 1971. **CAREER:** Cuyahoga Community Coll Dist, chancellor; Seattle Central Community Coll Washington, pres 1972-74; Metropolitan Jr Coll Dist, Kansas City MO, asst chancellor 1971-72; MI State Univ, East Lansing MI, asst pres 1970-71; Kellogg Found Project, MI State Univ, admin intern; Urban Affairs MI State Univ, assoc dir center 1968-70. **ORGANIZATIONS:** Mem Carnegie Council on Policy Studies in Higher Educ New York City 1973-; bd of overseers Morehouse Med Prog 1975; advisory bd ERIC Clearinghouse Jr Coll UCLA 1973-; bd dir Am Assn Community & Jr Colleges Assn; Governing BoardsUniv & Coll; pres adv com 1974-; exec bd N Central Assoc of Coll & Schs1977; Phi Delta Kappa mem 1968-. **HONORS/ACHIEVEMENTS:** Recipient Nat Jaycees Award; Ten Outstanding Young Men of America 1974. **BUSINESS ADDRESS:** President, Cuyahoga Community College, 700 Carnegie Ave, Cleveland, OH 44115.

ELLISON, PAULINE ALLEN
Federal personnel administrator, business executive. **PERSONAL:** Born in Iron Gate, VA; married Oscar Ellison Jr; children: Oscar III, Michele, Karla. **EDUCATION:** Amer Univ, M in Pub Admin; attended Howard Univ, Georgetown Univ, Fed Exec Inst. **CAREER:** No VA Chap Jack & Jill of Amer, fdr pres 1963-69; Dept of Housing & Comm Develop, dir of personnel DC redevel land agency; Links Inc, natl prog dir 1970-74; Arling Chap Links Inc, vice pres; admin, cons, natl pres 1974-78; Drs Johnson & Ellison Ltd, consultant. **ORGANIZATIONS:** Chmn membership bd of dir Fed Exec Inst Alumni Assn 1972-76; mem bd of dirs Natl Conf of Christians and Jews 1978-87 chmn Ethics Comm and chmn Outreach Comm; sec bd of dir Burgundy Farm Country Day Sch; mem drafting comm Black Econ Summit Meeting; chmn Personnel Policy Com Burgundy Farm Country Day Sch; pres Girls 4-H Club; pres Debating & Literary Club; pres Sr Class; youth leader Baptist Young Peoples Union & Bapt Training Union; mem Amer Soc of Public Admin; Natl Assn of Housing & Redcevel Ofcls; Natl Assn of Suggestion Sys; life mem NAACP; vice pres Arlington Comm TV 1986-87; pres Inter Serv Club Cncl 1986-87; pres Northern VA Chap Minority Political Women 1986-87; adv comm Arlington Hospital, Northern VA Junior League. **HONORS/ACHIEVEMENTS:** Beta Kappa Chi Natl Honor Sci Soc 1949; 1st Black Woman Employee Relat & Mgmt Splst Housing & Urban Devel 1965; 1st Black Woman Dir of Personnel for Fed Agency 1968; Outstanding Grp Performance Awd 1972; Outstanding Perfmc Awd Personnel Admin 1972-76; Disting Achvmt Awd Fed Exec Inst 1974; DistingYouth Serv Awd 1974; Disting Serv Awd Fed Exec Inst 1974; Outstanding Serv Awd Mayor of Washington 1975; Key to City of Roanoke 1975; Seal to City ofWashington 1976; 100 Most Influential

Blacks Ebony Mag 1976-78; Disting Serv Awd Mayor of Washington 1976; Hon Degree Dr of Humanities Wilberforce Univ 1976; commendation Pres of US 1977; Disting Leadership Awd The Links Inc 1978; Leadership Awd Alpha Phi Alpha Frat 1978; listed in Who's Who Among Black Amers 1978; Hon Dr of Humane Letters Livingstone Coll 1979; elected Pi Alpha Alpha Hon Soc Amer Univ; One of Eight Civil Rights Leaders to Advise Pres of US; winner State Oratorical Contest; Readers Digest Awd; Danforth Found Awd; numerous scholastic & civic awds; Jack and Jill Awd for Outstanding Serv 1981; apptd commissioner Arlington Civil Serv Commn 1983-87; Woman of the Yr Arlington 1986. **BUSINESS ADDRESS:** Consultant, Drs Johnson & Ellison Ltd, 2767 Annandale Rd, Falls Church, VA 22042.

ELLISON, RALPH WALDO
Author, educator. **PERSONAL:** Born Mar 01, 1914, Oklahoma City, OK; son of Lewis Alfred Ellison and Ida Millsap Ellison; married Fanny Mcconnell, 1946. **EDUCATION:** Attended Tuskegee Inst, 1933-36. **CAREER:** Writer, 1937—; New York Univ, Albert Schweitzer prof in humanities, 1970-79, prof emer, 1979—; Rutgers Univ, New Brunswick, NJ, visiting prof of writing and comp lit, 1962-64; Bard Coll, Annandale-on-Hudson, NY, teacher of literature, 1958-61; Univ Chicago, Alexander White Prof, 1961; lectr at numerous univs & colls thoughout the world. **ORGANIZATIONS:** Natl Council on the Arts, 1965-67; Carnegie Commission on Educational TV, 1966-67; Amer Academy of Arts and Sciences, 1964—; Amer Academy and Inst of Arts and Letters, 1975—; editorial bd, Am Scholar; Century Assn; trustee: natl advisory coun, Hampshire Coll, 1966—, John F Kennedy Center for Performing Arts, 1967-77, Educational Broadcasting Corp, 1968-79, New School for Social Res, 1969-83, Bennington Coll, 1970-75, Museum of City of New York, 1970-86, Natl Portrait Gall Commission, 1972-74, bd advisors, Ossabaw Island Proj, 1972-83, bd of visitors, Wake Forest Univ, 1972-85, Colonial Williamsburg Found, 1971-84. **HONORS/ACHIEVEMENTS:** Author of Invisible Man (novel), Random House, 1952, Shadow and Act (essays), Random House, 1964, and Going to the Territory (essays), Random House, 1986; contributor of short stories and essays to various literary journals and magaziness, beginning in 1939; Natl Book Award, 1953, Natl Newspaper Publishers' Russwurm Award, 1953, New York Herald Tribune Poll's "most distinguished work in last 20 yrs," 1965, all for Invisible Man; Medal of Freedom award, Pres Lyndon B Johnson, 1969; Chevalier de l'Ordre des Artes et Lettres Award, France, 1970; dedication of Ralph Ellison Library, Oklahoma City, OK, 1975; National Medal of Arts, US Pres and Congress, 1985; honorary degrees: Tuskegee Inst, PhD, 1963; Rutgers Univ, LittD, 1966; Univ of Mich, LittD, 1967; Grinnell Coll, LHD, 1967; Williams Coll, LittD, 1970; Ad elphi Univ, LHD, 1971; Long Island Univ, LittD , 1971; Coll of William and Mary, LHD, 1972; Wake Forest Univ, D of Letters, 1974; Univ of Maryland, LHD, 1974; Harvard Univ, D of Letters, 1974; Bard Coll, 1978; Wesleyan Univ, D of Letters, 1980; Brown Univ, D of Letters, 1980. **MILITARY SERVICE:** US Merchant Marine, 1943-45. **BUSINESS ADDRESS:** c/o William Morris Agency, 1350 Avenue of the Americas, New York, NY 10019. *

ELLISON, ROBERT A.
Attorney. **PERSONAL:** Born Jan 21, 1915, Winnsboro, SC; children: Robert, Charles. **EDUCATION:** NY City Coll, Ab 1941; Brooklyn Law School, JD 1952. **CAREER:** NY City Police Dept, detective 1942-61; NY City, private practice, atty 1961-65; Bronx School Dist, teacher 1963-65, prinicpal 1965; Dept of Public Safety VI, asst commr 1965-67; Dept of Law VI, asst atty general 1967-69; Police Science & Business Law Coll VI, instructor 1968-82; Dept of Public Safety VI, commr 1969-71, private practice, atty 1971-78; CA State Univ, instructor 1982-. **ORGANIZATIONS:** Past chmn VI Parole Bd; past commiss VI Publ Serv Commiss; past pres VI Bar Assoc; asst attny gen VI Dept of Law; chief Criminal/Family Law Div; mem Amer Arbitration Assoc, Intl Assoc Chiefs Police, Natl Bar Assoc, Rotary Intl; chmn, parole bd VI Publ Serv Commiss; mem VI Bar Assoc. **BUSINESS ADDRESS:** Instructor, California StateUniv, School of Bus Admin, 1250 Bellflower Blvd, Long Beach, CA 90840.

ELLISON, SANDRA LAVERNE
Higher education administrator. **PERSONAL:** Born in New Brighton, PA; married Marshall H Ellison; children: Marshall J. **EDUCATION:** Hampton Univ, BA 1969; Rutgers Grad Sch of Educ, MEd 1971. **CAREER:** Indiana Univ-Purdue Univ, academic counselor 1980-83, dir of minority affairs develop 1983-86. **ORGANIZATIONS:** Steering comm IN Coalition of Blacks in Higher Educ 1984-86; steering comm Allen Co Dr Martin Luther King Living Memorial 1985-86. **HONORS/ACHIEVEMENTS:** Outstanding Young Women in Amer 1976, 80; Circle Awd IN Coalition of Blacks in Higher Educ 1986.

ELLOIS, EDWARD R., JR.
Educator. **PERSONAL:** Born May 03, 1922, Ventress, LA; married Evelyn Reese; children: Joseph Bernard. **EDUCATION:** Seattle U, BS;Univ of IL, MA;Univ of OK, Doctorate. **CAREER:** St Francisville Elementary School LA, prin; Southern Univ Baton Rouge, assoc prof Educ, coordinator elementary student teacher; Coll Educ Southern Univ Baton Rouge LA, prof Educ & assoc dean; Workshops in LA, TX & OK, cons; Southern Methodist Univ Dallas, speaker; Arlington State Coll TX, dir student teaching conf seminars & workshops; SW Center for Human Relations Studies Consultative Center Coll of Continuing Educ, Univ of OK, Norman OK, grad asst. **ORGANIZATIONS:** Asst dir EPDA Inst in English; Alpha Kappa Delta; Kappa Phi Kappa; Phi Delta Kappa; Pi Gammu Mu; Psi Chi; Kappa Alpha Psi Frat; Am Assn Coll for Tchr Edn; Am Asn ofUniv Profs; LA Educ Assn; sec Council of Academic Deans SoUniv Baton Rouge; Kiwani Interant N Baton Rouge Early Rises Club; second vice pres Kappa Phi Kappa Nat Professional Frat in Educ for Men; Outstanding Educators of Am 1971; Intl & Biography of Educators; Leaders in Black Am; mem Holy Name Soc Immaculate Conception Ch; mem Knights of Peter Claver; St Agnes Council #12 Baton Rouge; vice pres Confraternity of Christian Doctrine Immaculate Conception Parish; Bishop's Adv Council; The Diocese of Baton Rouge LA; mem Lay Council; Diocesan Social Responsibility Bd. **MILITARY SERVICE:** AUS 1st sgt 1942-46. **BUSINESS ADDRESS:** PO Box 9634, Baton Rouge, LA 70813.

ELMORE, JOYCE A.
Nurse, educator. **PERSONAL:** Born Dec 18, 1937, Newton Falls, OH; married Andres Almonte; children: Nezhla Sanderson Almonte. **EDUCATION:** Howard U, 1955-56; Freedmen's Hosp Sch of Nursing, Diploma 1958; Santa Monica City Coll, 1959-60; CathUniv of Am, BSN 1962; CathUniv of Am, MSN 1965; CathUniv of Am, PhD 1974. **CAREER:** Coll of Nursing, Chicago State Univ, dean; Amer Nurses Assn Dept of Nursing & Educ, dir; DHHS Office of Family Planning, dir of training 1978-. **ORGANIZATIONS:** Mem ANA; NLN; HowardUniv Alumni Assn; Freedmen's Hosp Scho of Nursing Alumni Assn Inc; CathUniv Sch of Nursing Alumni Assn; Assn for Educ Communications & Technology; past pres Nurses' Exam Bd of DC; mem Commd Officers Assn; mem Mckendree United Meth Ch; pres, Elmore Enterprises Inc 1984-; bd chair Pearl Investors Inc 1986-87; pres, bd chair Pearl Enterprises Inc 1986-87. **HONORS/ACHIEVEMENTS:** Author of various professional articles & publications; recipient of many scholarships for higher edn; "Miss & Mecca Temple No 10"; "Miss Capitol Classic"; Comm Serv Award 1973; Who's Who in Government 1973; Chief Nurse Badge USAFR 1978; Commendation Medal USPHS Commd Corps 1980. **MILITARY SERVICE:** USAFR flight nurse capt-maj 1971-78; USPHS Commd Corps capt, nurse dir 0-6 1986-. **BUSINESS ADDRESS:** Dir of Training, DHHS/PHS Office of Fam Plng, 200 Independence AVe SW, Room 736-E, Washington, DC 20201.

ELZY, AMANDA BELLE
Educator. **PERSONAL:** Born in Pontotoc, MS. **EDUCATION:** Rust Coll, AB 1938; IN U, MS 1953;Univ MS, 1968-69. **CAREER:** Leflore Co Sch, asst supt 1968-, supr 1938-68. **ORGANIZATIONS:** Mem Ford Found Ldrsp Flws Prgm; Talent Serach Prgm; Early Childhood EducUniv TX; mem MS Assn of Edcrs; Nat Cncl of Newgro Women; Am Assn of SchAdminstr; Leflore & Co Tchr Assn; MS Library Assn; State Federated Clubs - Zeta Phi Beta - Sor; Assn of Supr & Curriculum Devel. **HONORS/ACHIEVEMENTS:** Amanda Elzy Sch named in hon Leflore Co Sch Bd of Educ 1959; Zeta Woman Of Yr Gamma Gamma Zeta Chap Zeta Phi Beta 1967; Outst Educator of Am 1970; Cert Achbmnt Am Assn of Sch Adminstr 1970; HHD Rust Coll 1973; Distinguished Educator of the Year Phi Delta Kappa 1979; Outstanding Community Service Award MS Valley StateUniv 1979. **BUSINESS ADDRESS:** Leflore Co Sch DES Bldg, Hwy 82 By Ps, Greenwood, MS 38930.

EMANUEL, JAMES ANDREW
Professor. **PERSONAL:** Born Jun 15, 1921, Alliance, NE; son of Alfred A.Emanuel and Cora Ann Mance Emanuel; married Mattie Etha Johnson, 1950 (divorced 1974); children: James A., Jr (deceased). **EDUCATION:** Howard Univ, Washington DC, AB, 1950; Northwestern Univ, MA, 1953; Columbia Univ, PhD, 1962. **CAREER:** US War Dept, Office of Inspector General, Washington DC, confidential secretary to asst inspector general of the Army, 1942-44; Army and Air Force Induction Station, Chicago IL, chief of pre-induction section (as civilian), 1950-53; YWCA Business School, New York City, teacher of English and commercial subjects, 1954-56; City Coll of the City Univ of NY, instructor, 1957-62, asst prof, 1962-70, assoc prof, 1970-73, prof of English, 1973—. **ORGANIZATIONS:** Mem, Fulbright Alumni Assn. **HONORS/ACHIEVEMENTS:** John Hay Whitney Found Opportunity fellowship, 1952-54; Eugene F. Saxon Memorial Trust fellowship, 1964-65; author of Langston Hughes (essays), Twayne, 1967; author of The Treehouse and Other Poems, Broadside Press, 1968; author ofA Chisel in the Dark: Poems, Selected and New, Lotus Press, 1980; author of A Poet's Mind, Regents Publishing, 1983; author of The Broken Bowl: New and Uncollected Poems, Lotus Press, 1983; works have been published in many anthologies and periodicals. **MILITARY SERVICE:** US Army, Infantry, staff sergeant, 1944-46; received Army Commendation Medal. **HOME ADDRESS:** 340 East 90th St, 3B, New York, NY 10028. **BUSINESS ADDRESS:** Department of English, City College of the City University of New York, Convent Ave at 138th St, New York, NY 10031. *

EMBREE, JAMES ARLINGTON
Educator. **PERSONAL:** Born Jan 18, 1934, New York City, NY; son of James Embree and Sylvia Embree; married Judith Aasum; children: Karen Secrest, Paul, Leslie Carmichael, Bruce. **EDUCATION:** San Jose State Univ, BA 1960; Sacto State Univ, MA 1984. **CAREER:** Alameda Co Probation, probation officer 1960-62; CA Youth Authority, parole agent 1962-72, sup/adm 1967-74, superintendent 1976-84. **ORGANIZATIONS:** Regional vice pres 1978-80, chair planning & scope 1983-84 CA Probation Parole & Correc Assn; mem San Jose Univ Varsity Basketball Team 1957-60; vol Downs Meml Ch Counseling Prog 1961-64; mem Assn Black Correctional Workers CA 1971-; mem human serv adv comm Amer River Jr Coll 1978-. **HONORS/ACHIEVEMENTS:** Presidential Unit Citation USMC; Credential Jr Coll Lifetime CA Dept of Educ 1978; In Appreciation-Senate Resolution #16 CA Legislature 1980. **MILITARY SERVICE:** USMC sgt 1st class 1952-56. **HOME ADDRESS:** #1 Downriver Court, Sacramento, CA 95831.

EMBRY, WAYNE
Vice president/general manager. **PERSONAL:** Born in Springfield, OH; married Terri; children: Debbi, Jill, Wayne Jr. **EDUCATION:** Miami Univ Oxford OH, BS Educ. **CAREER:** Cincinnati Royals, professional basketball player 1958-66; Boston Celtics, professional basketball player 1966-68; Milwaukee Bucks, professional basketball player 1968-69, vice pres and genl mgr, vice pres and consultant 1977-85; Indiana Pacers, vice pres and basketball consultant 1985-86; Cleveland Cavaliers, vice pres and genlmgr of basketball opers. **HONORS/ACHIEVEMENTS:** Mem ABU-USA Olympic Basketball Player Selection Comm for US Olympic Team; mem Miami Univ Hall of Fame; first black named to a top front-office position in the NBA and one of the first in professional sports.

EMEKA, MAURIS L. P.
Busniess executive. **PERSONAL:** Born Apr 04, 1941, Fargo, AR; married Sunday A Bacon; children: Amon, Gabriel, Justin. **EDUCATION:** Univ of KS, BA 1961;Univ of WA, MBA 1970. **CAREER:** Bike Master Inc, Pres; Bicycle Store, owner; Black Econ Union Kansas City, asst dir; Black Econ Reserach Cntr NY, asst dir. **HONORS/ACHIEVEMENTS:** Author of book and articles on Black & Banks. **MILITARY SERVICE:** USAF capt 1962-67. **BUSINESS ADDRESS:** 11 Bennett Rd, Englewood, NJ 07631.

EMMANUEL, TSEGAI
Educational administrator. **PERSONAL:** Born Mar 27, 1940; married Karen; children: Sarah, Ribka. **EDUCATION:** OK State Univ, BS 1968, MBA 1970; Univ of MO, PhD 1978. **CAREER:** Amer Assembly of Collegiate Schools of Business, chairman/committe on equal opportunities for minorities 1986-87; Southwest Business Admin Assoc, vice pres 1986-87, president 1987-88; Grambling St Univ, dean coll of business; professor of management. **ORGANIZATIONS:** Mem nominating committee AACSB 1984, mem articles & bylaws committee 1985-88; Southwest Federation of Administrative Disciplines; Southwest Business Administration Association; Secretary of State Commission on Corporations, State of Louisiana; The Louisiana Council of Black Economic Development; Academy of Management; Society of International Development; Amer Assn of Uinv Prof; Amer Productions and Inventory Control Society; Natl Economic Assn. **HONORS/ACHIEVEMENTS:** Mem NAACP 1986; mem Lions Club 1986. **HOME ADDRESS:** 708 Hundred Oaks Drive, Rus-

ton, LA 71270. **BUSINESS ADDRESS:** Dean, College of Business, Grambling State University, PO Box 848, Grambling, LA 71245.

EMMONS, RAYFORD E.
Clergyman. **PERSONAL:** Born Jun 25, 1948, Philadelphia, PA. **EDUCATION:** St Charles Seminary, BA 1970; Interdenom Theol, attended. **CAREER:** Field work experience in parochial schools, hospitals, comm & parish church activities; Atlanta Univ, asst Catholic chaplain 1972; St Patrics Church Norristown, asst pastor 1974-; Most Blessed Sanament Church, asst pastor 1978-80; St Elizabeth Church Philadelphia, asst pastor 1980-. **ORGANIZATIONS:** Mem natl Black Seminarians Assoc 1970-73, Natl Black Catholic Clergy Caucus 1974-; affiliate Natl Black Catholic Lay Caucus. **HONORS/ACHIEVEMENTS:** Several appearances on local & natlTV progs; speaker at civic & religious group affairs; featured in local newspapers; formerly involved in prison, hospital& youth work; 1st black priest ordained for Archdiocese of Philadelphia 1974. **BUSINESS ADDRESS:** St Elizabeth Church, Philadelphia, PA 19143.

EMORY, EMERSON
Physician, psychiatrist. **PERSONAL:** Born Jan 29, 1925, Dallas, TX; son of Corry Bates Emory and Louise Linthecum Emory; married Peggy Lillian Herald; children: Sharon, Karon Bailey, Emerson Jr. **EDUCATION:** Prairie View A&M Univ TX, 1940-42; Lincoln Univ PA, BA (Cum Laude) 1948; Meharry Medical Coll TN, MD 1952; Univ of TX Sch of Public Health, 1983-84. **CAREER:** VA Hospitals Dallas and McKinney, staff physician 1957-60; Terrell State Hosp Terrell, TX, staff psychiatrist 1969-71; Federal Correct Institution Seagoville, TX, chief psychiatric serv 1971-72; Private Practice, physician/psychiatrist. **ORGANIZATIONS:** Volunteer physician to Viet Nam Agency for Intl Development 1966; founder/past pres Natl Naval Officers Assn 1972; pres Dallas Council USO 1972; candidate for TX State Legislative 1974; candidate for Mayor of Dallas 1975-77; founder/past pres WA/Lincoln Alumni Assn 1976; administrator Forest Ave Comm Hosp Dallas 1983-84; founder/pres Clarence H. Harris Fraternal Order of Elks, Inc. 1987-; mem Prometheaus, Inc. 1945-. **HONORS/ACHIEVEMENTS:** Fellow in Psychiatry Univ of TX Southwest Med Sch Dallas 1966-69; Outstanding Alumni Award Lincoln Univ PA 1968; Humanitarian Award Amer Med Assn 1966; Appreciation Award State Dept (Agency for Intl Development) 1966; Publisher/Editor "Freedom's Journal" 1979-. **MILITARY SERVICE:** AUS Corporal served 3 yrs; USNR Captain 30 yrs; ETO-AP-Philippine Liberation WWII Victory Medal; Armed Forces Reserve Medal with 2 Hour Glass Devices. **HOME ADDRESS:** 4931 W Mockingbird Ln, Dallas, TX 75209. **BUSINESS ADDRESS:** Psychiatrist, 2606 Martin L King Blvd, Dallas, TX 75215.

EMRIT, RONALD C.
Mechanical engineer, educator. **PERSONAL:** Born Jun 26, 1945, Port-of-Spain, Trinidad and Tobago;married Karen Smith; children: Lisa, Tanya, Ronald. **EDUCATION:** Howard U, BS 1970; Univ of Bridgeport, MS 1973. **CAREER:** Boston State Coll, instructor 1976; Stone & Webster Engineering Corp, piping engineer, mechanical engineer 1973-; MD State Health Dept, student tech asst 1969; United Illuminating Co, asst engineer 1970-73. **ORGANIZATIONS:** Mem ASME; mem Alpha Phi Omega; West Haven Jaycees 1970-73; vice pres Caribbean Assn of HowardUniv 1968-69. **HONORS/ACHIEVEMENTS:** Author publ "Availability of Turbine Parts" 1973; mgr musical arranger Modern Sounds Steelband. **BUSINESS ADDRESS:** 245 Summer St, Boston, MA 02107.

ENGLAND, RODNEY WAYNE
Physician. **PERSONAL:** Born Jun 24, 1932, Mounds, IL; son of Lois England and Katie England; married Patricia R Shipp; children: Rodney, Michael, Stephen, John, Sarah. **EDUCATION:** Univ of Illinois, BS 1954, MD 1956. **CAREER:** Univ of Minnesota, clinical assoc prof internal medicine 1978-; Private practice, physician 1962-. **ORGANIZATIONS:** Diplomate Amer Bd of Internal Medicine 1964; bd of dirs Health East Corp. **MILITARY SERVICE:** USAF captain 1957-59. **BUSINESS ADDRESS:** 17 W Exchange, St Paul, MN 55102.

ENGLISH, ALEX
Professional athlete. **PERSONAL:** Born Jan 05, 1954, Columbia, SC. **CAREER:** Milwaukee Bucks NBA, forward 1976-78; IN Pacers, forward 1978-80; Denver Nuggets, forward 1980-. **HONORS/ACHIEVEMENTS:** Player NBA All-Star Game 1982,83. **BUSINESS ADDRESS:** Basketball Player, Denver Nuggets, PO Box 4286, Denver, CO 80204.

ENGLISH, CLARENCE R.
City official. **PERSONAL:** Born Sep 11, 1915, Morrilton, AR; son of William English and Lydia Pledger English; married Alpha Talley, Jun 16, 1934; children: Dorothy Brown, Clarence II, Loretta Choate, Joseph, James, Carol Hall, Paul. **EDUCATION:** Black Mayor's Workshops. **CAREER:** 3M Co, Little Rock AR, mechanic (retired), 1955-80; City of Menifee, mayor, 1979-. **ORGANIZATIONS:** Bd mem, West Central Planning, Bible School teacher, Church of Christ, chaplin, NAACP, 1960's; pres, PTA, 1960's; mem, Black Mayors Assn, 1980's; exec comm, HR Municipal League, 1980-89. **HONORS/ACHIEVEMENTS:** Grants received for City Parks, City Hall, Municipal Water Works, Streets; Certificate of Appreciation, 1955; Outstanding Community Ser, 1966; Distinguished Leadership, City of Menifee, 1986. **HOME ADDRESS:** 1 Talley Dr, Box 8, Menifee, AR 72107.

ENGLISH, KENNETH
Government official. **PERSONAL:** Born Jul 29, 1947, Waycross, GA; children: Crystal Denise, Constance MaryAlice, Kenneth II. **EDUCATION:** Morehouse Coll Atlanta; GA StateUniv Atlanta. **CAREER:** US Dept of Labor, regional rep region IV 1978-. **ORGANIZATIONS:** Pres United Rubber Workers Union Local 887 1969-78; vP GA State AFL-CIO 1972-78; mem Atlanta & Assn of Fed Exec 1978-; mem Indsl Relation Research Assn 1979-; mem of bd So Labor History Assn 1979-; bd of Dir & personnel com Urban League Albany Chap 1970-78; del 1974 Mini-Conv of the Nat Dem Party 1974; sec State Charter Commn GA Dem Party 1974-75; chmn 2nd cong dist Affirmative Action Com GA Dem Party 1975-77; mem GA State Employment & TngCounsel 1975-77; sec Albany-Dougherty Com NAACP Branch 1976-78; mem Dougherty Co Dem Com 1976-78; mem A Philip Randolph Inst Albany Chap 1976-; chmn Auditing Com GA Dem Party 1977-7 8; chmn personnel com Albany Urban League 1977-78; mem GA State Crime Commn 1977-78; mem Nat & Honor Soc Alpha Lambda Delta GSU 1979; mem Select Com on Revision of GA State Const 1979; vice pres Labor Studies Student Assn GSU 1979-. **HONORS/ACHIEVEMENTS:** Nominated for Who's Who in Am Nat Jaycees 1976. **BUSINESS ADDRESS:** Region IV US Dept of Labor, Room 624, 1371 Peachtree St NE, Atlanta, GA 30309.

ENGLISH, MARION S.
Retired business executive. **PERSONAL:** Born Jul 23, 1912, Jacksonville, FL; married Johnnye P Mitchell; children: Joyce A. **EDUCATION:** NY U, MA; Talladega Coll, BA. **CAREER:** Consolidated Edison Co, consultant 1978-, personnel mgr 1972-75; Public Affairs Westchester Div, ret asst 1972-78; vice pres Public Affairs Westchester Div Consolidated Edison Co of NY Inc 1972-; Urban Affairs, gen, mrg, former mgr 1969-72; NY State Narcotic Addiction Control Commn, comm relations specialist 1968-69; Civil Rights Compliance & EEO, special asst to commnr on aging in charge 1966-68-; Youth Serv Co Exec Westchester Co, special asst 1962-66; Urban League of Westchester Inc, exec dir 1956-62; Urban League of Greater Boston, exec dir 1954-56; YWCA, Mt Vernon NY, Harrisburg PA, Brooklyn NY, executive 1939-49. **ORGANIZATIONS:** Mem Rotary Club to White Plains; NY C of C; Westchester Clubmen & Found; mem Rotary Club; Zeta Boule Sigma Pi Phi Frat; asso trustee St Agnes Hosp White Plains NY 1980-88. **HONORS/ACHIEVEMENTS:** Recip Achievement, Annual NY Esquire 1953; White Plains Beautician Achievement Award 1962; bd dirs of the Urban League of Westchester Special Citation; Outstanding Achievements in Field of Human Rights for bldg a stronger Westchester Urban League 1963; Westchester Co Special Serv Award 1966; publications pamphlet "What is Your Comm Doing for its Youth? A Primer for Comm Action"; res paper "The Naure & Extent of the Purchase of Cough Medicines for its Alcoholic & Codeine Kicks", the youth of Westchester; Civil Rights Guidelines for the Adminstrn on Aging HEW. **HOME ADDRESS:** 20 Perry Ave, White Plains, NY 10603.

ENGLISH, PERRY T., JR.
Publisher. **PERSONAL:** Born Aug 12, 1933, Blounstown, FL; son of Perry English, Sr; divorced; children: Sharilynn, Lori Laverne. **EDUCATION:** Central State Univ, BS 1956; Faculte de Med Univ de Paris, MD 1965. **CAREER:** Sainte Antoine Hosp, house phys 1965-71; Friendship Med Center LTD, asst to exec dir 1974-75, admin 1975-; St Lukes Family Health Ctr Inc, pres 1977; Englewood Med Ctr Inc, pres 1978-; Beverly Hills Convalescent Ctr Inc, pres; Cook Co, phys assoc; Lopere Publishing Co Inc, pres. **ORGANIZATIONS:** Amer Public Health Assn; treas Chicago Investment Corp; vice pres Lake Vista Cntr Inc; pres Lop re Devel Corp; treas Am Leasing Corp; sec LET Devel Corp; pres Lop re Intl Inc; treas Madison Mgmt Corp; pres Lorgen Investment & Devel Corp; medl Grp Mang Assn; exec dir AESULAPIUS Soc appt by Gov of State of IL to the "IL Commission on Economic Development" mem Health Comm; Chicago Assoc of Commerce and Ind; mem Chicago Counc of Foreign Affairs; treasurer, The Consortium. **HONORS/ACHIEVEMENTS:** Award from 3rd Ward Democratic Party for Dedicated Serv to programs that benefit the less fortunate 1976. **MILITARY SERVICE:** Pfc 1953-55. **HOME ADDRESS:** 8045 South Calumet Ave, Chicago, IL 60619.

ENGLISH, RICHARD A.
Educator. **PERSONAL:** Born Aug 29, 1936, Winter Park, FL; married Ireita G W. **EDUCATION:** Talladega Coll, AB 1958; Univ of MI, MA 1959, MSW 1964, PhD 1970. **CAREER:** Flint Urban League, vocational youth serv dir, 1959-61, acting dir 1961-62; Neighborhood Serv Org Detroit, soc group worker 1963-66; Wayne State Univ, lectr 1965-67; Univ of MI, lecturer 1967-70, asst prof 1970-72; Univ of MI School of Soc Work, asst dean 1971-74; Univ of MI, assoc prof of social work, assoc vice pres for acad affairs 1974-; Univ of TX at Austin, RL Southerland prof; Howard Univ, dean school of social work 1985-. **ORGANIZATIONS:** Mem, Council on Social Work Educ; Natl Assn of Soc Workers; Natl Assn of Black Social Workers; Am Soc Assn; chmn 1977 Annual Program Meeting Council on Social Work Edn; mem Coun on Soc Work Educ Reaccrdtn Teams for Graduate School of Social Work 1973-; elec & mem House of Dels Coun on Soc Work Educ 1974-77; Annual Program Planning Comm Council on Social Work Educ 1975-78; elec pres Coun on Soc Work Educ 1981-84; Prgm Com of the Sem on Social Work Educ & Human Settlements; Intl Assn of School of Soc Work; vol Operation Crossroads Africa Ghana; mem, bd Amer Civil Liberties Union; mem adv panel Refugee Policy Group; mem Spaulding for Children. **HONORS/ACHIEVEMENTS:** Summer fellowship, Univ of Oslo Norway, 1956; Woodrow Wilson Fellow, Univ of MI 1958-59; co-ed Human Serv Org; Beyond Pathology rsch & theoretical Perspectives on Black Families; Distinguished Serv Award, Natl Assn of Black Social Workers 1983; Certificate of Appreciation Council on Social Work 1984; Distinguished Alumni Award, 1985. **BUSINESS ADDRESS:** Dean, Howard University, School of Social Work, Washington, DC 20059.

ENGLISH, WHITTIE
President. **PERSONAL:** Born Aug 03, 1917, New York, NY; married Lavinia Anderson, Apr 22, 1989; children: Bonita, Joanne. **EDUCATION:** Bergen Coll, attended 1936-38. **CAREER:** English Enterprises, pres. **ORGANIZATIONS:** Pres English Realty Assoc Inc 1955-, Ebony Builders 1955-, Empire Mortgage Co 1957-80, English Construction 1957-; mem NY State Black Republican Council 1985-; mem NAACP, Urban League; pres NJ State 369 Vets Assn. **MILITARY SERVICE:** Signal Corps transferred to Air Corps lst Lt 5 yrs. **BUSINESS ADDRESS:** CEO, English Enterprises, 248 Forest Ave, Englewood, NJ 07631.

ENGLISH, WILLIAM E.
Business executive. **PERSONAL:** Born May 18, 1934, Marianna, AR; married Shirley J; children: Ramona, Cheryl. **EDUCATION:** Lincoln U;Univ MN. **CAREER:** Control Data Corp; 3m, dist sales rep; Sabathani Comm Ctr, exec dir; US Bur of Prisons Justice Dept Pers Minnea Urban League, parole ofcr. **ORGANIZATIONS:** Mem adv bd Mankato State Coll; mem Urban Coalit; Met Cncl Criminal Justice; adv com past chmn Minneapolis Model Cities Prgm. **HONORS/ACHIEVEMENTS:** Midwest rgnl vice pres Nat Urban League's Pres Cncl; recp outst grad award Lovejoy HS 1964.

ENGS, ROBERT FRANCIS
Educator. **PERSONAL:** Born Nov 10, 1943, Colorado Springs, CO; son of Robert Engs and Myrtle Coger Engs; married Jean Oliver; children: Robert N. **EDUCATION:** Princeton U, AB (cum laude) 1965; Yale U, PhD History 1972. **CAREER:** UUniv of PA, assoc prof history 1979-; Univ of PA, asst prof history 1972-79; Princeton U, instr history 1970-72; NJ Black History Inst NJ Dept of Educ,dir 1969-72; Coll of William & Mary, commonwealth visiting prof 1984-85. **ORGANIZATIONS:** Faculty mem/cons Nat Humanities Faculty 1972-80; adv Nat Humanities Center 1978-80; mem Orgn of Am Historians 1975-; mem Am

Hist Assn 1975; mem Assn for Study of Afro-Am Life History 1975; chmn Presidents Forum Univ of PA 1985-87. **HONORS/ACHIEVEMENTS:** Short Term Am Grantee, US Dept of State 1971; William Penn Fellow, Moton Cntr for Ind Studies 1976-77; Freedom's First Generation, Univ of PA Press 1979; N&H Summer Fellowship, Natl Endowment of the Humanities 1980; Guggenheim Fellow 1982-83; Lindback Award for Excellence in Teaching, Univ of Pennsylvania 1988. **BUSINESS ADDRESS:** Associate Professor, University of PA, 207 College Hall, Philadelphia, PA 19104.

ENNIX, COYNESS LOYAL, JR.
Physician, educator. **PERSONAL:** Born Feb 12, 1942, Nashville, TN; married Katharine; children: Nicole, Kristina. **EDUCATION:** Fisk U, BS 1963; Meharry Med Coll, MD 1967. **CAREER:** Baylor Coll Med, asst prof surgery; Baylor Coll Med, postdoctoral fellow 1976-77; Cleveland Clinic Educ Found, fellow 1974-76; Cardiovascular Disease Baylor Coll Med, researcher; Methodist Hospital, staff surg; Inst Rehab & Rsch St Joseph Hos; VA Hosp; St Lukes Hosp. **ORGANIZATIONS:** Mem Amer Coll Surg; Michael E DeBakey Intl Cardiovascular Soc; Houston Med Forum; Harris Co Med Soc; TX Med Assn; Houston Acad Med; AMA; Amer Trauma Soc; Houston Surg Soc; Pan Pacific Surg Assn; Denton A Cooley Cariovascular Surgery Soc; dipl Amer Bd of Surgery; diplomate Amer Bd of Thoracic Surgery; Amer Heart Assn. **HONORS/ACHIEVEMENTS:** Most Outstanding Fellow Cardiovascular Surgery, Cleveland Clinic Educ Found 1976. **MILITARY SERVICE:** USN 1969-71. **BUSINESS ADDRESS:** 3300 Webster St, Ste 304, Oakland, CA 94609.

EPHRAIM, CHARLESWORTH W.
Educator. **PERSONAL:** Born Oct 14, 1942; married Brenda Harris. **EDUCATION:** USAF Tech Sch, radio operations honors 1964; USAF Instr Training Sch, 1964; StateUniv of NY, BA honors purchase valedictorian 1973; Yale U, MA, MPhil, PhD 1979; Nat Fellow Ford Found, 1973-78. **CAREER:** US Air Force, tech instructor, sgt, radio op US & overseas 1964-68; Bankers Trust Co NY, supr 1968-73; State Univ of NY Coll at Purchase Yale U, instructor; SUNY Empire State Coll & Mercy Coll, faculty dept of philosophy. **ORGANIZATIONS:** Mem Com for Vets Affairs; mem NY Metropolitan Assoc for Developmental Education; mem Amer Philosophical Assn; mem NAACP; mem Urban League; founder Free Community School of Mt Vernon 1980. **HONORS/ACHIEVEMENTS:** Completed USAF morse-code course in half time; first person in USAF hist to receive 24 GPM while in training, Keesler AFB MS 1964; grad coll in 2 1/2 yrs; rsch being done in Philosophy of the Black Experience; Awarded, Summer Rsch Grant, NY African Amer Inst to study, The Logic of Black Protest, 1988. **MILITARY SERVICE:** USAF sgt 1964-68.

EPPERSON, DAVID E.
Administrator. **PERSONAL:** Born Mar 14, 1935, Pittsburgh, PA; son of Robert Epperson and Bessie Lee Tibbs; married Cecelia Trower; children: Sharon, Lia. **EDUCATION:** Univ of Pittsburgh, BA 1961; Univ of Pittsburgh, MSW 1964; Univ of Pittsburgh, MA 1970; Univ of Pittsburgh, PhD 1975; Univ of the Bosporous & Chinese Univ, attended. **CAREER:** School of Social Work Univ of Pittsburgh, dean & prof 1972-; Dept of Political Sci Univ of Pittsburgh, Univ fellow in Urban Affairs, consultant 1969-72; Comm Action Pittsburgh Inc, exec dir 1967-69; deputy 1965-67; equal opportunities program univ of Pittsburgh, coordinator 1964-65. **ORGANIZATIONS:** Trustee, Natl Urban League & Natl Center for Social Policy & Practice; chairman, Urban League of Pittsburgh; vice chairman, Urban Redevelopment Authority of Pittsburgh & YMCA of Pittsburgh; chairman, YMCA of USA/Africa; particapated in Educational & Social Welfare Study Missions To Africa, Asia, Latin America & Western Europe. **MILITARY SERVICE:** USAF staff sgt 1954-58. **BUSINESS ADDRESS:** 2117 Cathedral of Learning, Pittsburgh, PA 15260.

EPPS, A. GLENN
Government employee, attorney. **PERSONAL:** Born Jul 12, 1929, Marshall, TX; divorced; children: David, Lawrence. **EDUCATION:** Univ of MI, BA 1950;Univ of WI, JD 1956. **CAREER:** MI Employment Sec Commn (MESC), hearing referee 1976-; atty priv prac. **ORGANIZATIONS:** Legal redress chmn Flint Br; Am Civil Libs Union 1960-68; legal redress chmn Flint Br; NAACP 1959-68; asst pros Genesee Co MI 1959-62; past memexec bd Nat Lawyers Guild; Flint Chap Nat Lawyers Guild; mem State Bar of MI; was involved in many civil rights cases in city of Flint. **HONORS/ACHIEVEMENTS:** Recip NAACP Meritorious Award, legal action in pursuit of fair housing; atty for J Merrill Spencer vs Flint Memorial Cemetary, causing integration of cemetaries in MI. **MILITARY SERVICE:** AUS sgt 1951-53. **BUSINESS ADDRESS:** 2501 N Saginaw St, Flint, MI 48503.

EPPS, ANNA CHERRIE
Educational administrator. **PERSONAL:** Born Jul 08, 1930, New Orleans, LA; daughter of Ernest Cherrie, Sr, MD and Anna Johnson Cherrie; married Joseph M Epps, MD, Nov 23, 1968; children: Joseph M Epps, Jr, MD, Grace Epps-Puglisi, PhD (stepchildren). **EDUCATION:** Howard Univ, BS 1951; Loyola Univ, MS 1959; Howard Univ, PhD 1966. **CAREER:** NIH Clinical Center, blood bank special 1959;Howard Univ School of Medicine, program dir & asst prof of microbiology 1960-69. Tulane Univ School of Medicine, USPHS faculty fellow, 1969, asst prof of medicine, assoc prof of medicine 1971-75, prof, medical dir, 1975-80; asst dean, 1980-86, assoc dean, 1986-, dir, medical rep, student academic support serv. **ORGANIZATIONS:** Prog asst br 1971-75; LA Bd of Health Social & Rehab Serv 1972; bd of regents emeritus, Georgetown Univ 1975-; bd trustees Children's Hospital 1978-79; mem Natl Adv Research Resources Council 1978-; chairperson AAMC GSA/MAS 1979-; mem bd of dir United Federal Savings & Loan Assn 1984-; Louisiana State Health Bd & Human Serv exec dept 1985-; mem Amer Assn of Blood Banks, Amer Assn of Univ Profs, Albertus Magnos Guild, WA Helminthol Soc, Amer Soc of Bacteriologists, Sigma Xi, Amer Soc of Tropical Medical & Hygiene, Musser Burch Soc, Amer Soc of Med Technologists, Amer Soc of Clinical Pathologists; mem Natl Adv Allied Health Professions Council, NIH, Bureau of Health Professions, Educ & Manpower Training Div of Health Manpower. **HONORS/ACHIEVEMENTS:** Award for Meritorious Research Interstate Postgraduate Medical Assn of N Amer 1966; publications "Fetoprotein Immunoglobulin," "Hepatitis Induced Antigen in Patients with Liver Disease in the New Orleans Area"; 72nd Annual Meeting Amer Gastroenterological Assn 1972; assoc editor "Medical Educ, Responses to a Challenge"; Merit Scroll, Natl Medical Assn, 1980; author, MEDREP at Tulane, 1984; Distinguished Serv Award, Natl Assn of Medical Minority Educ, 1988. **BUSINESS ADDRESS:** Assoc Dean, Offices of Student Serv & Prof of Medicine, Tulane Univ Sch of Medicine, MEDREP Tulane Med Center, 1430 Tulane Ave, Rm M-055, New Orleans, LA 70112.

EPPS, C. ROY
Association executive. **PERSONAL:** Born Jun 06, 1941, Bronx, NY; son of Clarence Epps and Alice Epps; married Cheryl Wall; children: Leah, Roy III, Leslye Renee, Camara Rose. **EDUCATION:** Wilberforce U, BS 1963; Rutgers U, MS 1970; MA Inst of Tech, Fellowship 1981-82. **CAREER:** Civic/Urban League of Greater New Brunswick, comm social worker 1967-68, asst dir 68-70, pres 1974-, exec dir/pres 1970-. **ORGANIZATIONS:** Rsch chem Colgate-palmolive Rsch & Devel 1966-67; vice chm New Brunswick Tomorrow 1975-; chm/hsng com New Brunswick Dev Corp 1976-; Former Pres/ mem New Brunswick Bd of Ed 1976-85; mem Middlesex County Private Industry Council 1983-; mem Governor's Adv Council 1984-; mem Black Issues Conf 1984-, NJ Minority Business Enterprise Commn 1984-, New Brunswick Minority Business Enterprise Commn 1985-. **HONORS/ACHIEVEMENTS:** Pres awd Natl Council of Urban League Exec 1978-80; pres awd Eastern Reg Council of Urban League Exec 1977-81; comm fellows prog MA Inst of Tech 1981-82. **MILITARY SERVICE:** AUS pfc 2 yrs. **BUSINESS ADDRESS:** President, Civic League of Greater New Brunswick, 47-49 Throop Ave, New Brunswick, NJ 08901.

EPPS, CHARLES HARRY, JR.
Physician. **PERSONAL:** Born Jul 24, 1930, Baltimore, MD; son of Charles Epps and Marjorie Epps; married Roselyn Payne; children: Charles Harry III, Kenneth Carter, Roselyn Elizabeth, Howard Robert. **EDUCATION:** Howard Univ, BS 1951, MD 1955. **CAREER:** Howard Univ, prof & chf div orthopaedic surg; Johns Hopkins Hosp, assoc prof orthopaedic surg; Howard Univ Orthopaedic Residency Training Prog, prog dir; ABOS, diplom 1964; Orthopaedic Surg, residency review comm 1971-; ABOS, examiner 1974-; Amer Bd of Orthotics & Prosthet, examiner 1970-. **ORGANIZATIONS:** Comm to study med devices food & drug admin 1972-; bd survey Residency Review Comm AMA 1974-; mem, pres Amer Orthopaedic Assoc 1976-83; Gov Health Legisl & Vet Affairs Comm; Amer Acad of Orthop Surg 1976; mem Kappa Alpha Psi Frat Bd of Trustees; Sidwell Friends Sch Wash DC; life mem NAACP; bd of dir Boys Club of Metro Police; gov American Coll of Surgeon 1982-88; mem, Ethical and Judical Council AMA 1982-87; mem, ABOS, 1977-83. **MILITARY SERVICE:** USAR capt med corps 1956-61; active duty 1961-62; inactive reserv 1962-65. **BUSINESS ADDRESS:** Dean, College of Medicine, Howard University, Seeley G Mudd Building 510, 520 W Street NW, Washington, DC 20059.

EPPS, CONSTANCE ARNETTRES
Dentist. **PERSONAL:** Born Feb 08, 1950, Portchester, NY; married Charles Ray Epps; children: Charles R II, Menika Elyse. **EDUCATION:** Bennett Coll, BS 1971; Howard Univ, DDS 1979. **CAREER:** Blood Rsch Inst Harvard Univ, coagulation technician 1971-72; US Govt Torrejon Air Base Madrid, teacher 1973-74; St Elizabeth Hospital, dental officer 1979-80; NC Dept of Human Resources, public health dentist 1980-86; Guilford Co Health Dept, public health dentist 1986-. **ORGANIZATIONS:** Mem ADA, NDA, Acad of General Dentistry, NC Dental Assoc 1979; mem Old North State & Guilford County dental Assocs 1984-; adjunct faculty Univ of NC Chapel Hill 1986-; treas NC Public Health Assoc (Dental) 1986; choir dir First United Baptist Church; mem High Point Org for Political Educ, Delta Sigma Theta, Guilford Co Headstart Adv Commn; chairman dental section, NC Public Health Assn, 1988-; trustee, First United Baptist Church, 1988-. **HONORS/ACHIEVEMENTS:** Dr Raymond L Hayes Scholarship Awd Howard Univ Dental Sch 1979. **BUSINESS ADDRESS:** Public Health Dentist, Guilford County Hlth Dept, 300 East Northwood St, Greensboro, NC 27401.

EPPS, DOLZIE C. B.
Educator. **PERSONAL:** Born Jan 01, 1907, Shreveport, LA. **EDUCATION:** DillardUniv (New Orleans U), 1929; Wiley Coll Marshall TX, AB 1945; ColumbiaUniv New York, MA 1950. **CAREER:** Caddo Parish School System, teacher Health & Physical Educ 1935-73; NAACP/Louisiana State Univ School of Medicine, bd of dir 1976-. **ORGANIZATIONS:** Mem Institutional Review Com on Human Experimentation Shreveport LA; bd of dir Caddo-Bossier Ct Observers 1976-; first vice pres Family Counseling & Children Serv 1976-; bd of dir Shreveport Negro C of C 1976-; bd of dir Phi Delta Kappa Sorority (Beta Alpha Chpt) 1976-. **HONORS/ACHIEVEMENTS:** Community Serv Award, Nat Council of Negro Women 1976; Ann Brewster Community Serv, NAACP 1978; Vacation Bible Sch Award, Galilee Bapt Ch 1979; Branch Serv Award, NAACP 1980. **BUSINESS ADDRESS:** 1859 Milam St, Shreveport, LA 71103.

EPPS, EDGAR G.
Educator. **PERSONAL:** Born Aug 30, 1929, Little Rock, AR; son of Clifford Epps and Odelle Epps; married Marilyn Miller; children: Carolyn, Raymond. **EDUCATION:** Talladega Coll, AB 1951; Atlanta Univ, MA 1955; WA State Univ, PhD 1959. **CAREER:** TN State Univ, asst, assoc prof 1958-61; FL A&M Univ, prof 1961-64; Univ of MI, rsch assoc, assoc prof 1964-67; Tuskegee Inst, assoc dir Carver Rsch Found, chmn div of soc sci, prof sociology 1967-70; Univ of Chicago, Marshall Field IV prof of Urban Educ 1970-. **ORGANIZATIONS:** Visiting prof Harvard Univ 1969; faculty mem Salzburg Seminar in Amer Studies Salzburg Austria 1975; mem bd of ed Chicago 1974-80; ed of books, "Black Students in White Schools" 1972, "Race Relations, Current Perspectives" 1973, "Cultural Pluralism" 1974. **HONORS/ACHIEVEMENTS:** Co-author "Black Consciousness, Identity & Achievement" 1975. **BUSINESS ADDRESS:** Marshall Field IV Professor, Univ of Chicago, 5835 S Kimbark Ave, Chicago, IL 60637.

EPPS, GEORGE ALLEN, JR.
Company executive. **PERSONAL:** Born Jul 03, 1940, Fallas, OK; son of George Allen Epps Sr and George Ellen Doak-Epps; married Linda Edwards, May 26, 1979; children: Gregory Allen, Michael Conrad. **EDUCATION:** Kansas City Junior Coll, Kansas City KS, 1957-58; Rockhurst Coll, Kansas City MO, 1968-71. **CAREER:** Bendix Manufacturing Co, electronic technician, 1962-65; Southwestern Bell, Kansas City MO, lineman, 1965-68, facility engineer, 1968-71, installation supvr, 1971-76, St Louis MO, plant mechanization supvr, 1976-79, dist mgr-I&M, 1979-85, dist mgr, admin serv, 1985-; Gundacker Realty, sales, 1985-. **HONORS/ACHIEVEMENTS:** Black Achiver in Indus, Southern Christian Leadership Conf, 1976; Optimist of the Year, Optimist Intl, 1987. **MILITARY SERVICE:** US Navy, E3, 1958-61.

EPPS, NAOMI NEWBY
Educator. **PERSONAL:** Born Sep 10, 1909, Elizabeth City, NC; widowed. **EDUCATION:** Agr & TechUniv Greensboro, BS 1935; Hunter Coll NYC, 1938. **CAREER:** Paterson NJ Bd of Educ, commr of educ, educator, supt of pubic schools 1961-74; Newark NJ Public Schools, educator 195-61; New York City Public Schools, educator 1945-50; Hope Day

Nursery NYC, dir 1938-45; Edgecombe County NC Public Schools, educator 1932-35. **ORGANIZATIONS:** Consult Dept of Educ Distar Program 1971; mini grant Div of Curriculum & Instr NJ 1971-72; human relations chmn Paterson Educ Assn/Bd of Educ 1973; life matron Woman's Home & Fgn Missionary Soc 1960; del 11th World Meth Con London 1966; dir of missionary edn; AME Zion Ch Woman's Home & Missionary 1967; state rep Natl Caucason Black Aged; bd mem NCBA Natl Adv Cncl on Elderly Abuse State of NJ; mem Operation Outreach; participation in NJ programs for the aged; mem OIC Bd; bd mem and founder Passaic Co Girls Club. **HONORS/ACHIEVEMENTS:** Outstanding Community Serv, YMCA 75th Anniversary Award 1976; Professional Adv Vol, Retired Sr Vol Program 1977; Outstanding Citizen Award, Passaic Co Bd of Freeholders 1978; Outstanding Performance Award, Dept Human Resources Paterson NJ 1979; Spl Serv Award, First Degree Neophyte Grand Lodge Antiqurus Araanus Ordo Rosa Rubeal et Aureae Crucis 1971; Soror of the Yr Award, Lambda Kappa Mu Sorority Inc 1976; Outstanding Serv Award, Mayor's Adv Councils On EmploymentTraining Aging & Handicapped, 1976; Spl Serv Award, Sec of Bergen-Passaic Co Health Systems Agency 1977; Nat Recognition Award Representing State Of NJ, ForumIII Fed Nat Mortgage Assn Conf on Housing for Ret 1978; Comm Serv Award, Nat Caucus on the Black Aged Jackson MS 1979; Honors received from Mother AME Zion Church of NY 1982, African Methodist Episcopal Zion Church 1982, Reach Out WCBS TV 1982, State Dept of NJ Dept of Comm Affairs 1982, US Representative Robert A Roe, NJ State Assoc Civil Liberties Dept, US Senate Special Comm 1983, Passaic Co Comm Coll 1983, House of Representatives 1983. **BUSINESS ADDRESS:** Educator, Bd of Education, 33 Church St, Paterson, NJ 07505.

EPPS, PHILLIP
Professional athlete. **PERSONAL:** Born Nov 11, 1958, Atlanta, TX; married Ceca Renee; children: Rachel Renee. **EDUCATION:** TX Christian Univ, BS Criminal Justice. **CAREER:** Green Bay Packers, wide receiver 1982-. **HONORS/ACHIEVEMENTS:** Rookie of the Year 1982; 9th ranking punt returner in Natl Football Conf; #6 punt returner in the NFC with a 90 yard average for 36 runbacks 1983; During 1982's off-season he starred in another sport-track-running the 5th fastest 60 yard dash ever (607 seconds) in a meet at OK City while competing for TX Christianin his final year of collegiate eligibility. **BUSINESS ADDRESS:** Green Bay Packers, 1265 Lombardi Ave, Green Bay, WI 54307.

EPPS, ROSELYN PAYNE
Physician, pediatrician. **PERSONAL:** Born Dec 11, Little Rock, AR; daughter of Dr William K Payne Sr and Mattie E Beverly Payne; married Dr Charles H Epps Jr; children: Dr Charles H III, Kenneth C, Roselyn E, Howard R. **EDUCATION:** Howard Univ, BS 1951, MD (w/Honors) 1955; Johns Hopkins Univ, MPH 1973; Amer Univ, MA 1981. **CAREER:** Private Practice, sickle cell rsch 1960-61; DC Govt, med officer, dir to mental retardation clinic, c&y project, infant & pre-school, maternal & child health, clinical programs, act commr of public health 1961-80; Howard Univ Coll of Med, prof of pediatrics/dir child devel center, 1981-88; rsch assoc, Natl Insts of Healthm 1989-. **ORGANIZATIONS:** Consultant US Dept of Health & Human Serv 1965-; bd of dirs Washington Performing Arts 1971-; consultant PSI Inc to Govt of Liberia 1984, United Nations Fund for Population Activities 1984; sec Natl Bd Girls Clubs of Amer 1988-; pres bd of dirs Hosp for Sick Children 1986-; exec bd Natl Assembly of VOL Agencies 1986-. **HONORS/ACHIEVEMENTS:** Distinguished Public Serv Award District of Columbia Govt 1981; Recognition Resolution & Day Council of the District of Columbia 1983. **HOME ADDRESS:** 1775 North Portal Dr NW, Washington, DC 20012. **BUSINESS ADDRESS:** Natl Cancer Institute, DCPC, Smoking, Tobacco & Cancer Program, Natl Insts of Health EPN-320, 9000 Rockville Pike, Bethesda, MD 20897.

EPTING, MARION
Artist. **PERSONAL:** Born in Forrest, MS. **EDUCATION:** Los Angeles City Coll, grad; Otis Art Inst LA Co, MFA 1969. **CAREER:** Otis Art Inst, rep permanent collections ;Univ CA; San Jose State Coll; Denison U; Seattle Art Mus; pvt collections of Bernie Casey, Dorothy Chandler, Claude Booker, Ruth Stoehr, James Bates. **HONORS/ACHIEVEMENTS:** Recipient num awards; 1st San Diego Nat Invitional Print Exhibition; Otpotsdam Prints; Northwest Printmakers; Del Mar; Portland Art Mus. **MILITARY SERVICE:** USN. **BUSINESS ADDRESS:** Dept of Art, CA StateUniv, Chico, CA 95926.

ERNST, REGINALD H.
Physician. **PERSONAL:** Born Aug 04, 1928, Detroit, MI; son of Clifford Ernst and Edna Ernst; children: Linda, Michael, Janis, Steven. **EDUCATION:** Univ of MI, BS 1950; Wayne State Univ, MD 1957; Wayne County General Hospital internal medicine 1957-61. **CAREER:** Wayne State Univ, asst prof of medicine 1962-87; Boulevard Gen Hospital, chief of medicine 1963-74; Detroit Medical Society, pres 1970-71; Southwest Detroit Hospital, chief of medicine 1976-77; Harper Hospital, physician. **ORGANIZATIONS:** Chmn Scholarship Black Graduates Univ of MI 1979-80; mem Natl Med Assn 1961-87, NAACP 1961-87, Amer Soc of Internal Med 1962-87, Amer Coll of Physicians 1964-87, Detroit Inst of Art 1965-87. **MILITARY SERVICE:** AUS sgt 1951-53. **BUSINESS ADDRESS:** 18241 W McNichols, Detroit, MI 48219.

ERSKINE, KENNETH F.
Educational administrator. **PERSONAL:** Born in New York, NY; married Maria; children: Clarke S Lewis F. **EDUCATION:** City Coll NY Convent Ave Campus, BS 1950; Columbia Univ Sch of Soc Wk, MSW 1952; variety of certs & advanced practice credits from various insts, schools & colls 1956-85. **CAREER:** Vets Adm Psych Out Patient Clinic Bk; psych soc wkr M H Clinic supv 1955-62; Col Univ Sch of Soc Work, asst prof Field Inst 1962-69; Vol in Serv to Amer Col Univ, consult trainer 1964-65; Columbi Univ Sch of Soc Work, asst dir of field work 1969-74; Col Univ C P & S Affil Harlem Hosp, asst dir for social work in Psychiatry; Edupsych Assocs, cons. **ORGANIZATIONS:** Partner Edu Psych Assoc 1962-; mbr, mem Bod Natl Assn of Social Workers; mem Assoc of Black Social Workers; mem Acad of Certified Social Workers; vice pres BOD Manhattan Cntry Sch 1974-; mem BOD Spence Chapin Serv for Children & Families 1974-; mem sec vice pres H & G Alum Man Chap 1970-; officer 4-D-O Coop 1983-. **HONORS/ACHIEVEMENTS:** NY State certified social worker NYS Dept of Ed 1972-. **MILITARY SERVICE:** USAAF OCS cadet/pfc 3 Yrs. **BUSINESS ADDRESS:** Consultant, Edupsych Assocs, 224 RSD, New York, NY 10025.

ERVIN, DEBORAH GREEN
Educational administrator. **PERSONAL:** Born Apr 04, 1956, Greenville, SC; daughter of David Green and Annie Green; married Larry Don Ervin (divorced); children: Sean Deon, Elanda Deliece. **EDUCATION:** Berea Coll, BA 1977; Clemson Univ, MEd 1986. **CAREER:** Clemson Child Develop Ctr, head teacher 1978-81; Clemson Univ, admissions counselor 1981-86, asst dir admissions 1986; Winthrop Coll, asst dir admissions. **ORGANIZATIONS:** Mem Carolina's Assoc of Collegiate Registrars and Admissions Officers 1981-, sec 1989-90; mem Southern Assoc of College Admissions Officers, Home Economics Adv Comm D W Daniel HS, Clemson Univ Day Care Comm, Clemson Univ Coll of Educ Faculty Selection Comm. **BUSINESS ADDRESS:** Asst Dir of Admissions, Winthrop College, 505 Eden Terrace, Rock Hill, SC 29733.

ERVIN, HAZEL ARNETT
Educator. **PERSONAL:** Born Dec 19, 1948, Washington, GA; daughter of Harrison M Arnett and Gladys Anthony Arnett; divorced; children: Kevin, Erica. **EDUCATION:** Guilford Coll, AB 1980; North Carolina A&T State Univ, MA 1985. **CAREER:** Nite Line Report, reporter 1982-85; Reidsville Jr HS, English teacher 1980-81; Hancock Co Sch, English/Journalism teacher 1981-82; Montgomery Co Schools, English teacher 1983-85; Shaw Univ, instructor of English 1985-. **ORGANIZATIONS:** Mem Langston Hughes Review Soc 1985-, Black Scholar 1985-, Natl Geographic 1985-, Obsidian II 1986-, Callalou 1987-; sec Faculty Senate Shaw Univ 1986-88; assoc mem, Smithsonian Institute 1988. **HONORS/ACHIEVEMENTS:** Review of works by Langston Hughes 1981, When Harlem Was in Vogue 1982, Rainbow Roun Mah Shoulder 1984, All God's Children Need Traveling Shoes 1986, Fatherhood 1987; over 20 feature stories for now defunct Nite-Line Report Greensboro NC 1982-85; founder Enrichment Camp for Black Youth which focuses on black heritage through literature and song 1982; United Negro College Fund's Educ Grant to pursue PhD in English 1987-88; summer internship as copy editor of American Quarterly 1989, Smithsonian Institute; one of many compilers for Callaloo's bibliography on works by African-Americans published in 1988; interview with author Ann Petry scheduled for publication 1989. **HOME ADDRESS:** 1330-301 Park Glen Dr, Raleigh, NC 27610.

ERVIN, JOHN B.
Educator. **PERSONAL:** Born Jul 20, 1916, Birmingham, AL; son of James Ervin and Ruby Browder Ervin; married Jane Minter; children: Jacquelyn. **EDUCATION:** Kent State U, BS 1938; Columbia Univ Teachers Coll, MA 1946, EdD 1950; Kent State U, LlD 1969 honorary degree. **CAREER:** Danforth Found, vice pres retired; School Continuing Educ & Summer Sch, dean 1968-77; Washington U, asso dean 1965-68; Harris Teachers Coll St Louis, dean instr 1962-65; Harris Teachers Coll St Louis, prof educ 1954-62; Stowe Teachers Coll St Louis, dir student teaching, chmn educ dept 1949-54; OH Public Schs, tchr 1935-49. **ORGANIZATIONS:** Pres 1975, sec 1973-75 Natl Univ Extension Assn; bd visitors Univ Pittsburgh 1974-78; Phi Delta Kappa; Assn Higher Edn; bd mem Danforth Found, St Louis Children's Hosp 1973-77; St Louis Art Mus 1969-75; United Way Greater St Louis; Regional Commerce Growth Assn 1974-76; South Side Day Nursery; life mem NAACP; life mem Alpha Phi Alpha; visiting com Continuing Educ Harvard U; Nat Advisory Council on Extension & Continuing Educ; St Louis Area Council Boy Scouts Am; Adult Educ Council. **HONORS/ACHIEVEMENTS:** Distinguished Alumni Award, Kent State Univ 1969; distinguished community leadership award, St Louis Frontiers Club 1968; outstanding achievement teacher educ Kent State Univ 1960; deans scholar, Teachers Coll Columbia Univ 1946-47; doctor of laws Kent State Univ/Kent, Ohio l969; doctor of laws Maryville Coll/St Louis, MO l987; doctor of Humanities Washington University/St. Louis, MO l989.

ERVIN, LEROY, JR.
Educational administration. **PERSONAL:** Born Aug 14, 1936, Ft Benning, GA; married Erin; children: Brett, Adara, Nia. **EDUCATION:** Wayne State Univ, BS Ed 1962; Case Western Reserve Univ, MS Public Mgmt 1970; Univ Of Akron, PhD Counseling 1975. **CAREER:** Cleveland Bd of Ed, teacher 1962-66; City of Cleveland, admin 1966-70; Oberlin Coll, asst ed dean 1970-76. **ORGANIZATIONS:** Mem Amer Ed Rsch Assoc 1979-; bd of dir Athens Youth Org 1980; univ chmn Heart Fund 1982; bd of dir Morton Theatre Corp 1982-84; mem Amer CollPersonnel Assoc, Assoc for Counselor Ed & Suprv, Natl Alliance of Black School Ed. **HONORS/ACHIEVEMENTS:** Fellowship HUD Case Western Reserve Univ 1969-70; Publ articles in psych reports, ed & psych measurements, ed & psych rsch, coll bd review 1979-85; fellowship Harvard Univ Inst of Ed Mgmt 1980. **MILITARY SERVICE:** AUS s/sgt 4 yrs. **BUSINESS ADDRESS:** Asst Vice Pres for Academic Affairs, University of Georgia, 208 Old College, Athens, GA 30602.

ERVING, JULIUS WINFIELD (DR. J)
Professional athlete. **PERSONAL:** Born Feb 22, 1950, Roosevelt, NY; married Turquoise; children: 4 children. **EDUCATION:** MA Univ, deg 1972. **CAREER:** Appeared in film "The Fish That Saved Pittsburgh" 1979; Philadelphia 76ers, player 1976-. **HONORS/ACHIEVEMENTS:** Rookie of the Yr 1972; Lupus Found Awd; NBA All Star Game 1977-80; MVP ABA 3 times, NBA 1980-81; Father Flanagan Awd in Omaha for serv to young people; on Dec 20th 1983 vs Seattle scored his 25,000 career point & became the only 9th player in NBA-ABA history to reach to lofty scoring plateau; twice winner of Seagrams Seven Crown of Sports Awd as the most productive player in the NBA. **BUSINESS ADDRESS:** Philadelphia 76ers, Veterans Stadium, Broad & Patterson Sts, Philadelphia, PA 19141.

ERWIN, CLAUDE F., SR.
Educator. **PERSONAL:** Born May 06, 1906, Morganton, NC; married Ruby Forney; children: Claude F, Jr. **EDUCATION:** Johnson C U, BS 1931. **CAREER:** Teacher, retired; Gamewell-Collettsville High School, 1965-71; Freedmon High School, 1937-65; McAlphine High School, 1932-37; Lenoir City, councilman, mayor pro-tem 1974-75. **ORGANIZATIONS:** Mem Humanities Com Calwell Co; v chmn Lenoir Nurse Day Care; trustee steward St Paul AME Ch; 2nd v chmn Dem Party of Caldwell Co. **HONORS/ACHIEVEMENTS:** Layman of yr 1969; distinguished serv award Prince Hall Grand Lodge 1971.

ERWIN, JAMES OTIS
Clergyman, educator. **PERSONAL:** Born Apr 28, 1922, Marion, NC; married Adeline Comer; children: Jo Nina Marie (abram), Janet Ann (Hall), Judith Kathryn. **EDUCATION:** Johnson C Smith U, BA 1943; Garrett Theol Sem, MDiv 1946; Iliff Sch Theology, MRE 1953, STM 1979; Rust Coll, LLD 1971; WV Wesleyan U, LLD 1972. **CAREER:** United Methodist Church, ordained to ministry 1946; Morristown Coll TN, chaplain, instructor 1946-48; Wiley Coll TX, pres 1970-72, chmn dept religion, philosophy, chaplain 1948-53; Lincoln Univ MO, asst prof 1953-66; Wesley Found Univ of IA, founder 1966-67; Philander Smith Coll AR, dean of students, chaplain 1967-70; Wesley United Methodist Church, pastor 1968-70; St James United Methodist Church Chicago, pastor 1972-76. **ORGANIZA-**

TIONS: Mem Douglas-Cherokee Ofc Econ Opportunity 1970-72; dist supt The United Meth Ch; mem Cherokee Guidance Center Morristown 1970-72; vice-chmn Little Rock BSA 1968-70; mem Intl Platform Assn; Alpha Phi Omega; Phi Beta Sigma. **HONORS/ACHIEVEMENTS:** Contrib articles to professional jours. **BUSINESS ADDRESS:** 77 W Washington St, Ste 1806, Chicago, IL 60602.

ERWIN, RICHARD C.
Attorney. **PERSONAL:** Born Aug 23, 1923, Marion, NC; married Demerice Whitley; children: Aurelia, Richard. **EDUCATION:** Johnson C Smith U, BA 1947; Howard U, LLB 1951. **CAREER:** Erwin & Beaty, partner 1951-. **ORGANIZATIONS:** Mem Found Com; Office Wachovia Bank & Trust Co; pres Forsyth Co Bar Assn; mem State Bd Edn; pres Urban Coalition; chmn Bennett Coll; mem NC Penal Study Commn; mem United Meth Ch Divinity Sch Duke U. **HONORS/ACHIEVEMENTS:** Man of yr Kappa Alpha Frat 1965-66; Silver Cup Urban Coalition 1974; Gen Asembly NC 1975. **MILITARY SERVICE:** 1st sgt 1943-46. **BUSINESS ADDRESS:** 1223 Wachovia Bldg, Winston-Salem, NC 27101.

ESCO, FRED, JR.
Elected official. **PERSONAL:** Born Sep 13, 1954, Canton, MS; son of Fred Lee Esco and Ida M Hudson Esco; married Freda Noel, Kristi Marie Jones, Aug 07, 1982. **EDUCATION:** MS Valley State Univ, BS 1978; Life Underwriter Trainer Council, Jackson MS. **CAREER:** Esco's Insurance Agency, owner & pres 1979; City of Canton, alderman ward 1979-81 1981-85, 1985-89, 1989-93. **ORGANIZATIONS:** 32 Degree Mason Prince Hall Affiliation 1979-85; mem Elk Club of Canton 1979-85; mem Natl Business League 1979-85; vice pres NAACP of Canton 1983-84; secretary/treasurer Optimist Club of Canton 1984-85. **HONORS/ACHIEVEMENTS:** Outstanding Sales Achievement Costal State Life Ins Co 1977. **BUSINESS ADDRESS:** Alderman Ward 5, City of Canton, City Hall, Canton, MS 39046.

ESCOTT, SUNDRA ERMA
Elected official. **PERSONAL:** Born Feb 21, 1954, Birmingham, AL; married David Russell. **EDUCATION:** AL State Univ, BS 1977, Secondary Educ Certificate 1977; Faith Coll Birmingham, Hon Doc Pol Sci 1984; Troy State Univ, MBA 1986. **CAREER:** Governor State of AL, admin asst 1976-80; self-employed Fashion Boutique 1976-80; Financial Assoc Inc, pres owner 1979-; AL Williams Marketing Firm, srvice pres 1980-; State of AL, state rep. **ORGANIZATIONS:** Bd of dirs Sickle Cell Birmingham 1980; sec AL Legislative Black Caucus 1980; state legislature AL House Rep 1980-86; mem Banking AL House of Rep 1982;co-chair local govt AL House of Reps 1982; co-chair political action comm Delta Sigma Theta Sor 1984; bd of dirs YWCA Birmingham Office 1984; bd of dirs Positive Maturity United Way Agency 1984. **HONORS/ACHIEVEMENTS:** Bd of Trustees Israel Methodist Church 1980; Who's Who Outstanding Women-Outstanding Women of AL 1980,1982, 1983, 1984; President's Council AL Williams Marketing Firm 1984 & 1985. **HOME ADDRESS:** 1500 Hibernian St, Birmingham, AL 35214.

ESKRIDGE, JOHN CLARENCE
Educator, minister. **PERSONAL:** Born Jun 06, 1943, Pittsburgh, PA. **EDUCATION:** DuquesneUniv Pittsburgh, BA 1966, MA 1971; Missionaries of New Truth IL, hon DD 1971; Pacific SoUniv CA, PhD Philosophy 1978. **CAREER:** Comm Coll, assoc prof Philosophy 1974-; Carlow Coll, dir turial instructor 1973-74; Comm Coll Allegheny County, philosophy faculty 1969-80; "Le Sacre Corps" Dance Co, artistic dir 1969-79; Pittsburgh Child Guidance Clinic, program dir, creative recreational arts program 1969-70; Comm Coll Allegheny County Campus, dir black studies 1969-71, coll speakers bureau 1978-80; First Baptist Church Pittsburgh, bd of deacons 1970-73; Pittsburgh High School of Creative & Performing Arts, adv bd 1979-80. **ORGANIZATIONS:** Mem Soc for Phenomenology & Existential Philosophy 1967-80; mem Am Philos Assn 1969-80; founding chmn Hermeneutic Circle 1977-80; bd dirs Inst For Collective Behavior & Memory. **HONORS/ACHIEVEMENTS:** NDEA study fellowship DuquesneUniv 1967-70; faculty spl serv award Comm Coll Allegheny Co Student Union 1978; Directory of Am Scholars 7th Edit 1978;Intl Who's Who in Educ 2nd Edit 1979. **BUSINESS ADDRESS:** Chairman, Comm Coll of Allegheny Cty, Dept of Phil & Foreign Lang, 808 Ridge Ave, Pittsburgh, PA 15212.

ESOGBUE, AUGUSTINE O.
Educator, engineer. **PERSONAL:** Born Dec 25, 1940, Kaduna, Nigeria. **EDUCATION:** Univ of CA LA, BS 1964; Columbia U, MS 1965; Univ of So CA LA, PhD 1968. **CAREER:** Com of Minority Career Advisors; Industrial & Systems Engineering, School of Health Systems, GA Inst of Technology Atlanta, prof; Morehouse Coll Atlanta, adjunct prof of community med; Atlanta Univ GA, adjuct prof of mathematical science; Operations Rsch & Mem Systems Rsch Center, Case Western Reserve Univ Cleveland, asst prof 1968-72; Engineering & Med, Univ of Southern CA, rsch assoc 1965-68; Water Resources Rsch Center, Univ of CA Los Angeles, devel engr 1966-67; Univ Assoc Inc & Environmental Dynamics, consultant 1968-72; GA Inst of Technology, chmn 1975, prof. **ORGANIZATIONS:** Mem several panels of the Nat Rsrch Counc, Nat Acad of Sci Engring; councillor, chmn ORSA; vis lctr Operations Rsrch & Mgmt Sci; adv editor Intl Jour on Fuzzy Sets & Systems; asso editor ORSA Hlth Applications Tech; mem US Subcom Intl Ctr on Systems & Cybernetics; mem Beverly Hills Rotary Club; faculty adv GA Tech Soc of Black Engrs 1976-; exec bd mem Environment Adv Group Atlanta Reg Commission 1980-; bd dir Atlanta Council of Black Professional Engrs 1981-. **HONORS/ACHIEVEMENTS:** Sigma Xi Fellow AAAS; num sci publ in various tch journals; biographical listings in Comm Leaders of Am; Dictionary of Intl Biography; Intl Inst of Comm Svc; Who's Who In Computer Rsrc Edn; Who's Who in Consulting; Am Men & Women of Sci 1975-76; listed in Who's Who in Amer 1982, Who's Who in the World 1984. **BUSINESS ADDRESS:** Professor, GA Inst of Tech, Sch of Indsl & Sys Engineering, Atlanta, GA 30332.

ESPREE, ALLEN JAMES
Educator. **PERSONAL:** Born May 04, 1941, Lake Charles, LA; married Clara G; children: Glenn Aldric, Gary Allen, Bernice Jeanine. **EDUCATION:** Univ of NE, BS Business 1970; Command & Gen Staff Coll, Master Military Science 1979; Univ of MO, Master Public Admin 1980. **CAREER:** RCPAC Enlisted Personnel Directorate, deputy dir 1980-83; Bishop Coll, prof of military science. **ORGANIZATIONS:** Consultant A&C Carpet Co 1984-85; superintendent Sunda6y Sch Faith Comm Lutheran Church 1984-85; mem Military Affairs Comm Dallas Chamber of Commerce 1984-85; mem/policy council Dallas Head Start Prog 1985. **HONORS/ACHIEVEMENTS:** Eagle Scout Calcasieu Area Council Lake Charles LA 1957-58. **MILITARY SERVICE:** AUS lt col 23 yrs; Bronze Star; Purple Heart; Army Commendation; Vietnam Service CIB. **BUSINESS ADDRESS:** Professor of Military Science, Bishop College, 3837 Simpson Stuart Rd, Dallas, TX 75241.

ESPY, MICHAEL
Congressman. **EDUCATION:** Attended, Howard Univ Washington DC, CA Univ of Santa Clara Law School. **CAREER:** Law Practice Yazoo City, attorney; Central MS Legal Servs, manager; State Secretary's Office, dir public lands and elections div 1980-84; State Attorney General's Office, chief of consumer protection div 1984-85; State of MS, congressman.

ESQUERRE, JEAN ROLAND
Aerospace consultant. **PERSONAL:** Born Dec 28, 1923, Yonkers, NY; son of Jean B Esquerre and Marie Bates Esquerre; married Maria Elisabet Edman; children: Johanna Maria, Malin Elisabet. **EDUCATION:** Coll of City of NY; NYU; Republic Aviation Corps Staff Engr School; Gruman Aerospace Corp, Training & Devel Ctr; Empire State College SUNY. **CAREER:** Opportunity Devel Dept Grumman Aeorspace Corp, asst to corp pres, dir 1969-89; price analyst 1969; Lunar Modular #4, engr supr, test dir, cognizant engr 1963-69; Republic Aviation Corp, principal designer 1953-63; NY Transit Authority, mechanical engr draftsman 1952-53; Specialty Assembling & Packing Co, draftsman 1949-52. **ORGANIZATIONS:** Mem, Soc of Automotive Engr; ETA Chapter Alpha Phi Alpha Fraternity, mem 1949-, pres 1951; pres, Planned United Devel Task Force for Huntington; pres & instructor, Grumman Martial Arts Club; mem, Huntington Branch NAACP; Labor & Ind Comm 1949-, chmn 1970; chmn, Sub-Comm for feasibility of Minority Enterprise Small Business Invest Corp; vice chmn, Nathan Hall Dist BSA; pres, Urban League of Long Island; bd dir, Grumman Aerospace Corps, Grumman Ecosystem Corp; bd dir, YMCA; mem, Family Serv Assn; mem, Girl Scouts of Suffolk Co; pres, N Atlantic Karate Assn, 1976; CCNY Varsity Club, 1952; CCNY Boxing Alumni Club, 1948; sec, LI Branch NY Karate Assn, 1961-; mem, Huntington Township Comm on Human Relations, 1961-; Huntington Freedom Ctr, 1963-; former mem Citizens Advisory Comm on Capital Budget for Huntington; former mem, Planned United Devel Task Force for Huntington; Huntington C I C Human Devel Comm. **MILITARY SERVICE:** USAAF sgt WW II. **HOME ADDRESS:** 193 Broadway, Greenlawn, NY 11740.

ESQUIVEL, ARGELIA VELEZ
Educator. **PERSONAL:** Born Nov 23, 1936, Havana, Cuba;married Dr Ricardo R; children: Raul P Rodriguez, Argelia M Rodriguez. **EDUCATION:** Univ of Havana Cuba, BS BA 1954; Sch of Sci,Univ of Havana, DSc, Mathematics 1960; Math InstUniv of wi, NSF Post Grad 1965; TX Chris U, Poast Post Grad 1967-68; SW Ctr for Adv Studies Dallas, Post Grad 1968. **CAREER:** Bishop Coll, dir, coord Educ Prof Devel Act-Teachers Training Devel 1970-73, prof & dept head Math Science 1968-, instructor Modern Math NSF In-Serv Inst for Secondary School Teachers 1964-68, lecturer NSF Summer Program Advanced High School Students of Math 1964; TX Coll, asst prof Math, chmn of dept 1962-64; Marianao Inst, Havana Cuba, instrutor to asst prof of Math & Physics 1957-61; Bishop Coll, dir, coord Coop Coll School of Science-Natl Science Found Math Proj for Jr High School Teachers 1972-74; Univ of Houston-Bishop Coll Coop Doc Program in Math Educ Houston, assoc dir 1973-74. **ORGANIZATIONS:** Mem Am Assn for the Advancement of Sci DC Am Mathe Soc Providence; Nat Coun of Tchrs of Mathe DC TX Academy of Sci Austin; Mathe Assn of Am DC; dir NSF Minority Inst Sci Improvement Proj 1976-78; dir NSF Pre-coll Tchr Develop Math Proj 1977-78; mem com on Affirmative Acton of the Conf Bd of Math Sci; Am Assn ofUniv Profs DC; m Assn ofUniv Women DC; Young Women Christ Assn Dallas; Cuban Cath Assn Dallas; Mem bd dirs Dallas Br Am Assn ofUniv Women 1973-; chmn Intl Rel Com of am assn ofUniv Women 1973-; speaker Annual Conv of Nat Coun of Tchr of Math NC Sec Nov 1972. **HONORS/ACHIEVEMENTS:** Recip natl sci found fellow summer 1965; computer assisted instr fellow for Coll &Univ Profs 1967-68; bishop coll liason rep to the & Am Assn ofUniv Women 1970-72; The World Who's Who of Women 1974; outstanding educator of am 1971; am men & women of Sci 1972; Who's Who of Am Women 1973. **BUSINESS ADDRESS:** 3837 Simpson Stuart Rd, Dallas, TX 75241.

ESSIET, EVALEEN JOHNSON
Educator, nurse. **PERSONAL:** Born Jun 21, 1933, Roxboro, NC; children: Aja, Bodie. **EDUCATION:** Montefiore Hosp Schl of Nurs, DIPLOMA 1955;Univ of Pgh BS Nursing 1965;Univ of Pgh MSW 1971;Univ of Pgh PhD Higher Ed 1983. **CAREER:** George Washington Univ Hospital, Washington DC, staff nurse psy 1955-58; Allegheny County Health Dept, supvr of public health nurses 1958-1963; Monefine Hospital School of Nursing, nursing fac 1963-66; Homewd/Bruston Center, St Francis Hospital CMHC, dir 1968-1969; Clinic Hempsted Hospital CMHC, dir of out-patient 1971-73; Comm Coll of Allegheny County, prof of nursing 1973-. **ORGANIZATIONS:** Pres/cons E Johnson Essiet Corp 1983-84; elder Presby Church USA 1985-; mbr/publ chr Chi Sta Phi Nursg Sorrority 1981-85. **HONORS/ACHIEVEMENTS:** Interpation of Nursg 1983; Prog (BS) Curric (Nat'l Study Pub) 1983; Poems publ Am Poetry Assoc 1981-84; Book Rev of Nursg for NLN 1980; Int'l Book ofHnr 1983. **MILITARY SERVICE:** USAFR capt 1962-68; Flight Nrs Wings From Schl of Aerospa Med 1963. **HOME ADDRESS:** 827 Bell Ave, North Braddock, PA 15104. **BUSINESS ADDRESS:** Prof of Nursing, Comm Coll of AC, 1850 Old Chairton Rd, Rt 885, West Mifflin, PA 15122.

ESTEP, ROGER D.
Educator. **PERSONAL:** Born Mar 02, 1930, Clarksville, MD; married Romaine V Cook; children: Frederic. **EDUCATION:** MD State Coll, BS 1951; PA State Univ, MS 1957; Tuskegee Inst, DVM 1962. **CAREER:** PA State Univ, instructor 1957-58; Tuskegee Inst, DVM 1958-62; Howard Univ, rsch & vet instr 1962-67, vet & asst prof of physiology 1967-70, exec asst to vice pres Health Affairs 1970-71, exec asst to pres 1971; NIH, dir div of rsch 1971-72; Howard Univ, vice pres 1972-. **ORGANIZATIONS:** Chmn publicity comm Amer Assn for Lab Animal Sci 1967; vice pres Natl Capital Area Br Amer Assn for Lab Animal Sci 1964-65, pres 1965-66; bd dir Amer Assn for Lab Animal Sci 1967, exec com 1967-; mem com on rsch Howard Univ 1963-69; chmn Com on Rsch Howard Univ 1969-70; asst gen chmn publicuty sub-com chmn Intl Com on Lab Animals 1969; mem sub-com Natl Acad of Sci 1962-63; mem Intergovtl Ad Hoc Com 1966-67; mem Amer Assn for the Accreditation of Lab Animal Care; mem Natl Adv Allergy & Infectious Diseases Council; pres elect, pres Amer Assn for Lab Animal Sci 1970, 1971; mem Long Term Radiation Effects Adv Com of Pub Health Svc; mem bd dir Natl Soc of Fund Raisers; mem Amer Vet Med Assn; DC Vet Med Assn; Amer Assn for Lab Animal Sci; assoc mem Amer Coll of Lab Animal Sci num papers. **HONORS/ACHIEVEMENTS:** Sch of Veterinary Medicine of Tuskegee Inst The Alumni Recognition Awd 1970; Tuskegee Inst Alumni Merit Awd 1980; NAFEO Distinguished Alumni of the Year Citation 1980; Tuskegee Veterinary Medical Alumni Assn Distinguished

Alumni Awd 1981; Univ of MD Eastern Shore Hall of Fame for Distinguished Alumni 1986. **MILITARY SERVICE:** USAF staff sgt 1951-55. **BUSINESS ADDRESS:** VP for Dev &Univ Rels, HowardUniv, 2400 6th St NW, Room 405, Washington, DC 20059.

ESTERS, GEORGE EDWARD
Educator. **PERSONAL:** Born May 30, 1941, Bowling Green, KY; married Bettie Jean; children: Delmer. **EDUCATION:** AR AM&N Pine Bluff, Hist 1964; Western KYUniv Bowling Green, MPS 1978; Western KYUniv Bowling Green, 1980. **CAREER:** Bowling Green City School Bd, dir of adult educ 1979-, coord of adult learning center, counselor & supr WIN 1972-73, teacher jr high 1971, teacher & high school coach 1964-70,. **ORGANIZATIONS:** Mem KEA-nEA-aGEA; charter KY Comm Educ Assn; mem KACE bd chmn Big Brothers & Sisters 1975-78; adv bd mem Bowling Green Bus Coll 1977;chmn of personnel com Head Start 1979. **HONORS/ACHIEVEMENTS:** Outstanding alumni achievement S Central Provincial KY 1977; outstanding young men of am US Jaycees-Montgomery AL 1978; outstanding citizen Human Rights Commn Bowling Green KY 1979; outstanding leadership AWARE Bowling Green KY 1980. **BUSINESS ADDRESS:** Bowling Green City Sch Sys, 224 E 12th St, Bowling Green, KY 42101.

ESTES, ELAINE
Librarian. **PERSONAL:** Born Nov 24, 1931, Springfield, MO; daughter of James M Graham and Zelma M Smith Graham; married John M Jr. **EDUCATION:** Drake Univ, BS 1953, Teaching Certificate 1956; Univ of IL, MS 1960. **CAREER:** Public Library of Des Moines, dir of library system 1956-. **ORGANIZATIONS:** Mem past pres IA Library Assn, past pres Des Moines Metro Library Assn, Amer Library Assn; bd mem IA Soc for Preservation of Historic Landmarks; bd trustees Des Moines Art Ctr; past bd mem Des Moines Comm Playhouse; past adv council Dept on Adult Ed; past bd adv Natl Trust for Historic Preservation; past mem Mayors Sister City Comm; bd mem Des Moines Civic Ctr; mem Polk Cty Historical Soc; past state vice pres Questers Inc; mem bd Terrace Hill Soc, Gov Comm for Restoration of Govs Mansion; past pres DM Chap Links Inc; past basilius Kappa Alpha Beta Phi Mu Hon Libr Scholastic Soc; chairperson City of Des Moines Historic Dist Commn; mem State of IA Natl Reg Nominations Review Comm; mem adv council Iowa Dept of Cultural Affairs; Rotary 1987-; Natl Commn on the Future of Drake Univ, Task Force on Libraries and Learning Resources 1987-88. **HONORS/ACHIEVEMENTS:** Des Moines Leadership Awd 1975; Distinguished Alumni Awd Drake Univ 1979; Outstanding Contribution to the Quality of the Built Environment, De Moines Architects Council Community Reward 1981; Award of Merit for Historical Preservation, Iowa State Historical Soc 1984. **BUSINESS ADDRESS:** Dir Library System, Public Library of Des Moines, 100 Locust, Des Moines, IA 50308.

ESTES, JOHN M., JR.
Mortician/proprietor. **PERSONAL:** Born Dec 06, 1928, Joplin, MO; married Elaine Graham. **EDUCATION:** Univ if IA, 1946-48; Drake Comm Coll, 1950,51,53; KS City Coll of Mortuary Sci, 1952; Chicago Resorative Art, Post Grad Work 1952. **CAREER:** Estes & Son Funeral Home, owner. **ORGANIZATIONS:** Bd mem BSA, Rep Party, Kappa Alpha Psi, NAACP, March of Dimes, Des Moines School Bd, United Comm Svc, Greater Des Moines United Way, Comm Action Council, Gr Oppty Bd, C of C, Gr United Way, Comm Survey Inc, Simpson Coll Trustee, Des Moines Public Housing Authority, Wilkie House Inc, Des Moines Symphony, Tiny Tots Inc, IA Civil Liberties. **HONORS/ACHIEVEMENTS:** Black Athlete Awd 25 yrs; Des Mones Human Rights Comm Recognition; 3 awds March of Dimes Natl Found; Univ of IA Alumni Assoc Awd; IA Employment Security Comm Awd; Des Moines Adult Ed Council Awd; Polk Cty Rep Party Awd; KSO Great Cty Awd; Des Moines Publ School Awd; Little All Amer League Awd; Natl Black Merit Acad Awd. **BUSINESS ADDRESS:** Mortician/Proprietor, Estes & Son Funeral Home, 1216 Forest Ave, Des Moines, IA 50314.

ESTES, SIDNEY HARRISON
Educational administrator. **PERSONAL:** Born Jan 18, 1932, Atlanta, GA; married Barbara Ann Brown; children: Sidmel, Edward, Cheryl, Chris. **EDUCATION:** Lincoln U, BA 1953; Atlanta U, MA 1959; IN U, EdD 1967. **CAREER:** Instructl Planning & Devel, Atlanta Public Schools, asst supt; Doctor Prog in Educ Admin, Atlanta Univ, dir 1971-73, exec dir educ & improv proj 1969-71, assoc dir educ improv proj; Atlanta Public Schools, Ralph Robinson Elementary, prin 1963-68, Slater Elementary, teacher 1957-63; Amer Assn of School Admin; Phi Delta Kappa Prof Frat; Natl Soc for the Study of Educ; Assn for Supvrs and Curriculum Devel, Alpha Phi Alpha Soc Frat BSA, exec Bd. **ORGANIZATIONS:** Mem Camp of Congressmn Andrew J Young 1972; mem Class Leadershp Atlanta 1975-76; mem advis bd Atlanta Counc for Children's TV. **HONORS/ACHIEVEMENTS:** Silver beaver award BSA 1973; publ "The Plight of Black Parents" 1972; " Instruction-inner City where it's really at" 1975; contribut co-auth booklet "Impact of Decentralization on & Curriculum" 1975. **MILITARY SERVICE:** AUS milit intellig aerial photointerpret 1953-55. **BUSINESS ADDRESS:** 2930 Forrest Hill Dr SW, Atlanta, GA 30315.

ESTES, SIMON LAMONT
Opera singer. **PERSONAL:** Born Feb 02, 1938, Centerville, IA. **EDUCATION:** Univ IA. **ORGANIZATIONS:** Mem U's Old Gold Singers; Deutsche Opera in Berlin, auditioned for; mem L-Beck & Hamburg Opera Companies. **HONORS/ACHIEVEMENTS:** Successes Include Moscow's First Intl Tchaikovsky Vocal & Competition; San Fran Opera; Am Opera Soc NY; San Sebastian Festival Spain; performed all four of the hoffman roles in Offenbach's "Tales of Hoffman", "Macbeth's Banquo", "The Magic Flute", "The Marriage of Figaro"; received scholarship to Juilliard Sch of Music, grant from Martha Bard Rockefeller Found; Tchaikovsky Medal; 1985 Honoree The Fine Arts Award for career achievements as world-class operatic bass-abritone, for pioneering appearances at the Bayreuth Festival, and for acclaimed performances as Porgy in the Metropolitan Opera's first production of Porgy and Bess. **BUSINESS ADDRESS:** Columbia Artist Mgmt, Inc, c/o Laurence Tucker, 165 West 57th St, New York, NY 10019.

ESTILL, ANN H. M.
Educator, coloratura soprano. **PERSONAL:** Born in Washington, DC; daughter of Dr Don V Estill and T Christine Smith-Estill. **EDUCATION:** Western MI Univ, BMusic; Columbia Univ Teachers Coll, MA; professional diploma; New York Univ, DA Voice Performance. **CAREER:** Kalamazoo Jr Symphony, performed violin four years; JCSC, researched & developed three courses in African & Afro-Amer Classical music; Jersey City State Coll, assoc prof music. **ORGANIZATIONS:** Numerous recitals in NYC, Washington, Atlanta, WLIB Radio NYC, NBC TV; WOR-TV Joe Franklin Show 1980; St Barthlomew's Church Chorus NYC performed over 60 Oratorios; Bernstein Mass, Kennedy Center; Scott Joplan's Treemonisha, Wolf Trap Farm for Performing Arts Vienna VA; Washington Choral Arts Chamber Choir; Protege Mm Luisa Fraceshi; Amer Inst of Music Studies Graz Austria; Sigma Alpha Iota Professional Hon Frat for Women in Music; Phi Delta Kappa Educ; Hon Kappa Phi Methodist Women. **HONORS/ACHIEVEMENTS:** European debut 1983-84 Rome Festival Orchestra 'La Regina della Notte Mozart's Il Flauto Magico; dissertation, "The Contributions of Selected Afro-Amer Women Classical Singers 1850-1955"; guest appearance, "Talent Hunters," Channel 10 Fairfax VA, 1988; Amahl in Gian-Carlo Menotti's Amahl and the Night Visitors, Essex County NJ Opera Co, 1988-89. **BUSINESS ADDRESS:** Associate Professor Music, Jersey City State Coll, Dept of Music, 2039 Kennedy Blvd, Jersey City, NJ 07305.

ETHEREDGE, JAMES W.
Government administration. **PERSONAL:** Born Jun 06, 1941, Leesville, SC; married Vanetta Bing; children: Lorna V, William Craig. **EDUCATION:** SC State Coll, BS 1963; IN State Univ, Soc 1966; Winthrop Coll, Pol Sci 1973; Univ of SC, MPA 1973. **CAREER:** City of Rock Hill, social prog spec 1969-70; Winthrop Coll, part time instr 1973-79; City of Rock Hill, dir of admin serv 1971-80; City of Charleston, dir of admin serv 1980-. **ORGANIZATIONS:** Mem SC City & Cty Mgmt Assoc, SC Municipal Assoc, Amer Soc for Public Admin, Omega Psi Phi Frat, Charleston United Way Agency, Charleston Bus & Professional Assoc. **BUSINESS ADDRESS:** Dir Dept of Admin Serv, City of Charleston, PO Box 304, Charleston, SC 29402.

ETHRIDGE, JOHN E.
Contractor. **CAREER:** J E Ethridge Construction Inc, Fresno CA, chief exec. **BUSINESS ADDRESS:** J E Ethridge Construction Inc, 5270 E Pine Ave, Fresno, CA 93727. *

ETHRIDGE, ROBERT WYLIE
Educational administrator. **PERSONAL:** Born Nov 12, 1940, Monroe, MI; son of Claude Ethridge, Sr and Hazel Johnson Ethridge; married Elizabeth Sneed; children: Stephan, Tracy, Michael. **EDUCATION:** Western MI Univ, AB 1962, AM 1970; Univ of MI Ann Arbor, PhD 1979. **CAREER:** Detroit Public Schools, teacher 1962-69; Western MI Univ, area coordinator housing 1969-72, admin asst to pres 1972-79, sec bd of trustees 1979-81; coordinator, Equal Opportunity Programs, Emory Univ 1981; Emory Univ, asst vice pres 1982-, adjunct asst prof, 1982-. **ORGANIZATIONS:** Mem CUPA, NACUBO 1981-, NAACP 1981-; 2nd vice pres 1981-82, 1st vice pres 1982-84 Amer Assoc for Affirmative Action; bd mem Natl Assault on Illiteracy Program 1983-; financial subcomm United Way 1984-; pres Amer Assoc for Affirmative Action 1984-88; bd mem Atlantic Contract Compliance Assn; mem Leadership Conference on Civil rights; United Way-Health Services Council 1984-; United Way-Admissions Panel 1984-; AAAA Natl Conf Planner 1982-84; mem Natl Inst for Employment Equity 1986-; chairman of the bd, Amer Contract Compliance Assoc, 1987-89; pres, Onyx Society of Western Michigan Univ, 1989-91. **HONORS/ACHIEVEMENTS:** Achievement Award Northern Province KAY 1961-62; Community Bldg Award Black Monitor 1985; Citation for Public Service-Kalamazoo 1979; GA Public Relations Assn 1985; 2nd annual Civil and Human Rights Award-Intl, 1988; Proclamation State of Michigan House of Representatives, 1988; Assn of Official Human Rights Agencies. **BUSINESS ADDRESS:** Assistant Vice President, EmoryUniv, 101 Administration Bldg, Atlanta, GA 30322.

ETHRIDGE, SAMUEL B.
Retired associate director. **PERSONAL:** Born Dec 22, 1923, Brewton, AL; married Cordia Baylr; children: Samuel David, Sherman George, Camille LaVerne, Steven Edsel. **EDUCATION:** Stillman Jr Coll; Howard Univ, AB 1948; Univ of Cincinnati, MEd 1957. **CAREER:** Mobile Public Schools, teacher, principal, supvr 1948-58; March of Dimes, assis dir Intergroup Rel 1958-61; United Negro Coll Found, sau reg sec 1962-64; Nat'l Ed Assoc, dir of Civil Rights Exec Asso 1964-84; Natl Ed Assoc, retired (asst to dir). **ORGANIZATIONS:** Nat sec Reading Is Fund 1970-89; mem of bd Martin Luther King Jr Center for Soc Change 1975-89; mem of bd Shillman Coll 1979-85. **HONORS/ACHIEVEMENTS:** Cit Am Teachers Assn 1966; cit Ft Worth UNCF 1969, AL State Teacher 1969, MS State Teacher 1972; Hum Rel awd NEA also NC Ed Assoc 1984; Ed Serv awd Nat Urban League 1984. **MILITARY SERVICE:** USNA T/5 1943-46. **HOME ADDRESS:** 1602 Allison St, NW, Washington, DC 20011.

EUBANKS, DAYNA C.
Radio & TV journalist. **PERSONAL:** Born Jun 07, 1957, Wichita, KS. **EDUCATION:** Univ of KS Lawrence, BS Journalism 1979. **CAREER:** KAKE-TV Wichita KS, psa actress 1975; KJHK Radio News Univ of KS, reporter vice pres Mondale trip 1977; KJHK Radio Univ of KS, newscaster, news editor 1977-78; Audio-Reader Univ of KS, newscaster, broadcaster/reader 1977-78; WREN-AM Topeka KS, legislative reporter 1978; WIBW-TV-AM-FM Topeka KS, newscaster, reporter, photographer, weekend news anchor,TV & radio 1978-79; KOOL-TV Phoenix AZ, weekend news anchor, gen assignment reporter 1979-81; WXYZ-TV ABC Detroit MI, weekendnews anchor, field anchor, Good Afternoon Detroit, gen assignment reporter 1981-. **ORGANIZATIONS:** Mem Amer Women in Radio & TV, Natl Assoc of TV Arts & Sci, Natl Assoc of Black Journalists, Sigma Delta Chi, Women in Commun, SAG, Amer Fed of TV & Radio Artists, Delta Sigma Theta; lifetime mem NAACP; co-chair & co-org Detroit Black-Jewish Leaders Forum; volunteer teacher & counselor "Who Said I Can't" Program; natl convention chairperson, natl exec bd mem IAWS 1979; advisor Judicial Bd GSP-Corbin Hall, Acad Success for KU Students; ku rep to the IAWS Natl Conv; rep Assoc of Univ Residence Halls. **HONORS/ACHIEVEMENTS:** Apprec Awd NAACP for Generosity to People & Community; Apprec Awd Black History Week 82nd Flying Training Wing Williams AFB 1981; Awd for Contribs to Broadcasting Hartford Mem Baptist Church; Outstanding Achievement in Commun Alpha Kappa Alpha 1981; Awd for Outstanding Achievement as an Anchorwoman JournalistPublic-Minded Citizen & Patron of the Arts 1982; Outstanding Woman in Broacast News Amer Women in Radio & TV 1982; Golden Heritage Awd for Outstanding Achievment in Commun Little Rock Missionary Baptist Church; Robert L Powell Lecturer NAACP Oakland Univ; Outstanding Minority in Industry YMCA 1984; Detroit Emmy Awd Nominee Behind the Best 1985; Ebony Mag Thirty Future Black Leaders 1985; Selected one of 1985 Outstanding Young Women of Amer.

EUBANKS, EUGENE E.
Educator. **PERSONAL:** Born Jun 06, 1939, Meadville, PA; married Audrey J Hunter; children: Brian K, Regina A. **EDUCATION:** Edinboro St U, BA 1963; John Carroll U, MA

1970; MI St U, PhD 1972. **CAREER:** Sch of EdUniv of MO, dean 1974-;Univ of DE, prof of educ admin 1972-74; Cleveland Pub Schs, tchr & admnstr 1963-70. **ORGANIZATIONS:** Consult Cleveland Found; consult KC Pub Schs; consult MO St Dept Edn; consult NAACP Sch Desegregation Suit in Cleveland OH; Nat Allinc Blk Sch Edctrs; Natl Conf Profs Educ Admin; Phi Delta Kappa; Am Assn of Univ Profs; NAACP; PUSH; Urban League; pres, AACTE, 1988; mem, Natl Policy Bd of Educ Admin, 1988. **HONORS/ACHIEVEMENTS:** Articles published: A Study of Teacher Perception of Essential Teacher Attributes, 1974; Big-City Desegregation since Detroit, 1975; Rev Jesee L Jackson & PUSH Program for Excellence in Big-City Schools, 1977. **MILITARY SERVICE:** USAF Sec Serv 1956-60. **BUSINESS ADDRESS:** Dean School of Education, University of Missouri-KC, 5100 Rockhill Rd, Kansas City, MO 64110.

EUBANKS, JOHN BUNYAN
Educator. **PERSONAL:** Born Feb 28, 1913, Clinton, LA; children: Judith, John Jr, David. **EDUCATION:** Howard U, Th B 1935, AB 1936; AM 1938; Univ Chicago, PhD 1947; Northwestern U; Univ MO 1977. **CAREER:** Howard U, prof; Jackson State Coll, 1955-60; Laos & Iraq, comm devel offcr 1953-55; Jarvis Coll, 1949-53; Morris Brown & Coll, prof 1946-49; YMCA, sec 1937-41; Rust Coll, consult 1966, 1975; Am Cncl on Educ, evaluator 1977. **ORGANIZATIONS:** Mem Am Acad of Rel; Amer Anthrop Assn; Soc for Science Study of Rel; soc for Applied Anthrop; council on Rel & Pub Educ; Comm Devel soc of Am; council on Anthrop & Educ; soc for Hlth & Human Values Schlr Univ Chicago; gen educ bd fellow; Harvard Inst fellow; EPDA inst Grantee. **HONORS/ACHIEVEMENTS:** Fellowship (Comparative Rel.) General Ed Board 1943-44. **BUSINESS ADDRESS:** Prof History of Religions, Howard University, Divinity School, 1240 Randolph St NE, Washington, DC 20017.

EUBANKS, RACHEL AMELIA
Educator, musician, composer. **PERSONAL:** Born in San Jose, CA; daughter of Joseph Eubanks and Elizabeth Amelia Gant; divorced. **EDUCATION:** Univ of CA Berkeley, BA 1945; Columbia Univ NY, MA 1947; Pacific Western Univ, DMA 1980; Fontabl, France, Eastman Schl of Music, UCLA, USC, additional studies. **CAREER:** Wilberforce Univ, chmn Music Dept 1949-50; Albany State Coll, hd of Music Dept 1947; Eubanks Conser of Music, pres, founder, 1951. **ORGANIZATIONS:** Southeast Sym Assoc; LA County Art Mus; comm Afro-American Museum 1984-; vice pres, bd dir Inglewood Philharmonic Orchestra Crenshaw Chamber of Commerce; mem, Natl Guild of Piano Teachers 1959-, Intl Congress on Women in Music 1984-, Musicians Union, Local 47, 1951-, Music Educators Conference, Music Teacher's Natl Assn, Natl Assn of Negro Musicians 1949-. **HONORS/ACHIEVEMENTS:** Mosenthal flwhp Columbia Univ 1946; musicianship: Vols I II and Tapes, Symphonic Requiem Oratorio, Trio, & others; Alpha Mu Honor Society, Univ of CA Berkley 1946; Composition Award, Natl Assn Negro Musicians 1948; Symphonic Requiem, Korean Philharmonic, Los Angeles 1982; three songs, Res Musica, Baltimore 1985. **BUSINESS ADDRESS:** President, Eubanks Consult of Music, 4928 Crenshaw, Los Angeles, CA 90043.

EUBANKS, ROBERT A.
Engineer, educator. **PERSONAL:** Born Jun 03, 1926, Chicago; married Helaine. **EDUCATION:** BS 1950; MS 1951; IL Inst of Tech Chicago IL, PhD 1953. **CAREER:** Univ of IL, prof 1965-; IIT Rsch Inst, science adv 1960-65; Borg-Warner Corp, scientist 1956-60; Amer Machine & Foundry Co, rsch engineer 1955-56; Bulova R&D Labs, sr rsch engineer 1954-55; IL Inst of Technology, asst prof 1950-54. **ORGANIZATIONS:** Geo a miller vis profUniv of IL 1964-65; vis distngd profUniv of DE 1973-74; fellow Am Acad of Mech; Am Assn ofUniv Profs; Am Math Soc; Am Socof Civil EngrS; registered Structural Engr IL; trst Unitarian-Universalist Ch; dir Civil Engineering Publ Serv Prog; exec bd Urban Leag; Soc of SigmaXi; Sigma Pi Sigma; fac mem Chi Epsilon. **MILITARY SERVICE:** AUS chief warrant off 1942-46. **BUSINESS ADDRESS:** 3129 Civil Engineering Bldg, U of IL, Urbana, IL 61801.

EUELL, JULIAN THOMAS
Museum director. **PERSONAL:** Born May 23, 1929, New York, NY; married Barbara J Tiggs; children: Julian, Juliette, Dana, Denise, Simeon, Miles. **EDUCATION:** NY U, BS 1969; Geo Wash U, Dctl Cnadt. **CAREER:** Oakland Museum, dir; Smthsn Inst, asst sec pub serv 1972-, prgm mgr 1970-72, consult 1968-70; Arts Prgm & Adolscnt Serv Einstein Coll of Med, dir 1967-70; Whitney Mus of Am Art, consult 1966-67; Nat Found on Arts & Hmnties, consult 1966; NY City Antipvty Com, prgm consult 1966; HARYOU-ACT, dir of arts & cult 1962-66; Prof Mus, 1959-62; Essex Co Yth House, couns 1956-69. **ORGANIZATIONS:** Mem Fgn Std Serv Coun; mem Am Mus Ntrl Hist; Nat Hstcl Soc; Nat Trust for Hstcl Presrvtn; Nat Soc of Lit & Arts; Am Assn of Mus; InternatCounc of Mus; Am Fed of Muscns. **HONORS/ACHIEVEMENTS:** Martin Luther King Schlshp; Biogphy "The Ency of Jazz" 1960; publ "Art & Comm Mntl Hlth" The Pscyh Rev. **MILITARY SERVICE:** AUS 1946-48. **BUSINESS ADDRESS:** Dir, Oakland Museum, 1000 Oak St, Oakland, CA 94607.

EUGERE, EDWARD J.
Pharmacologist, educator. **PERSONAL:** Born May 26, 1930, New Orleans; married Yolanda Rousseve; children: Edward, Jan, Gail, Lisa. **EDUCATION:** Xavier U, BS 1951; Wayne State U, MS 1953;Univ CT, PhD 1956; Baylor Coll Med, Postdoctoral Study Myocardial Biology 1973. **CAREER:** Numerous Companies, pharmacist 1951-57; Wayne State Univ, grad teacher asst 1951-53; Univ of CT, 1953-56; Highland Park Jr Coll, lecturer; Detroit Inst of Technology, asst prof 1956-57; TX Southern Univ, prof 1957-; School of Pharmacy, dean 1968-70. **ORGANIZATIONS:** Mem numerous offices coms Harris County Pharm Assn; pres Houston Pharm Assn; Am Heart Assn; Lone Star State Pharm Assn; pres Houston Area Chi DeltaMu Professional Frat; Am Assn Coll Pharmacy; Am TX Pharm Assns; Houston Pharmacologists; Sigma Xi Soc; Rho Chi Pharmacy Honor Soc; pres 1977; bd Educ Diocess Galveston-houston 1974-77; pres Grand Jury Assn Houston-harris County; pres Cath Interracial Council Houston; Gulf Coast Area Child Devel Ctr Inc; Am Assn of Colls of Pharmacy Chi. **HONORS/ACHIEVEMENTS:** Consult natl inst of health adv group serv certificate Nat Inst Health HEW 1973; leadership award Houston Pharm Assn 1971; guidance and leadership award Sr Class TX SoUniv 1968; Fesler Research awardUniv CT 1954-56; travel award Detroit Inst Tech 1957; faculty deve award TX SoUniv 1973; researcher Fungal Fungal Toxins Pharmacology. **BUSINESS ADDRESS:** Texas So Univ Sch Pharmacy, 3201 Wheeler Ave, Houston, TX 77004.

EURE, DEXTER D., SR.
Business executive. **PERSONAL:** Born Nov 20, 1923, Suffolk, VA; son of Luke Eure and Sarah Eure; married Marjorie A; children: Dexter Jr, David, Philip. **EDUCATION:** WV State Coll, BSME 1946. **CAREER:** PRAC Associates, vice pres 1960-61; Bradlee Div Stop & Shop, advertising product mgr; Boston Globe, asst to circulation mgr 1963-68, asst to editor 1968-70, dir of comm relations 1972-88 (retired). **ORGANIZATIONS:** First act dir Boston Comm Media Comm; mem Public Affairs Council Greater Boston Chamber of Commerce; mem Boston Globe Foundation; former member at large United Way of MA Bay; mem Congressional Black Caucus Comm Braintrust Comm; advisory com Crisis magazine NAACP; panelist Nieman Found for Journalism Harvard Univ Media Racism. **HONORS/ACHIEVEMENTS:** First undergraduate elected to Omega Psi Phi Fraternity Supreme Council; Distinguished Serv Award Union United Methodist Church 1984; President's Award for Meritorious Serv to the Greater Boston Comm NAACP 1986; MA Black Legislative Caucus Eight Annual Award for energizing the black community to make positive and political changes 1986; Dean Dexter Roast & scholarship Benefit by Boston Assn of Black Journalists, 1988. **MILITARY SERVICE:** AUS sgt 1st class 1948-50. **BUSINESS ADDRESS:** Dir of Comm Relations, The Boston Globe, 135 Morissey Blvd, Boston, MA 02107.

EURE, HERMAN EDWARD
Ecological animal parasitologist, educat. **PERSONAL:** Born Jan 07, 1947, Corapeake, NC; married Barbara Ann Collins; children: Lauren Angela, Jared Anthony. **EDUCATION:** MD St Coll, BS 1969; Wake Forest U, PhD 1974. **CAREER:** Wake Forest U, asso prof biology 1974-. **ORGANIZATIONS:** Mem British Soc Parasitology; mem Inst of EcologyUniv of GA; mem Sigma Xi; mem NAACP; mem Alpha Phi Alpha Frat Inc. **HONORS/ACHIEVEMENTS:** Ford Found fellow Ford Found; NSF fellow NSF; oustnd alumnus ND St Coll 1980; listed Who's Who in Am Coll &Univ MSC 1968-69; mem Beta Kappa Chi NatHon Soc; man of the yr awd MD St Coll 1968; first black to receive PhD Wake Forest U; first full-time black fac mem Wake Forest U; first black tenured Wake Forest U. **BUSINESS ADDRESS:** Box 7325, Reynolda Station, Winston-Salem, NC 27109.

EVAIGE, WANDA JO
Educator, mayor. **PERSONAL:** Born Jul 09, 1935, Frederick, OK; daughter of Sam Evaige and Lenora Oliver-Evaige (deceased). **EDUCATION:** Huston-Tillotson Coll, BA 1955; Univ of OK, current. **CAREER:** AME Church Rep, gov bd dir NCC USA 1973-76; Boyd Alumni Assn, natl pres 1973-75; Tillman Co Classroom Teachers, pres 1973; NEA, congressional contact 1983; City of Frederick, vice-mayor 1986, mayor, 1987-; Frederick Economic Dev Authority, vice chmn 1987; Frederick Public Schools, music specialist. **ORGANIZATIONS:** Pres TUO Chap Alpha Kappa Alpha Sor 1969-76; pres Frederick classroom Teachers 1973-74/1979-81; city council mem Ward III Frederick OK 1st woman elected 1983; legislative comm OK Municipal League 1984; lobbyist OK Educ Assn 1978-86; mem, Oklahoma Constitution & Revision Commission, State of Oklahoma 1988-. **HONORS/ACHIEVEMENTS:** Teacher of the Year Frederick Teacher/Frederick OK 1st Black 1981; Teacher of the Year Tillman Co Teachers 1st Black 1981; 1st Black & 1st female mayor in the 85 Year History of City of Frederick 1987-89. **HOME ADDRESS:** 400 S 3rd St, Frederick, OK 73542.

EVANS, ADA B.
Former mayor, educator. **PERSONAL:** Born Jun 09, 1932, Langley, SC; married Ray Allen; children: Cheri, Rachelle. **EDUCATION:** Benedict Coll, BS (magna cum laude) 1955. **CAREER:** Park County Schools, teacher 1966-; IDS Marketing & Life Insurance, registered representative, Aiken County Schools, teacher 1955-60. **ORGANIZATIONS:** Mem CO Educ Assn NEA; CO Commn on Status of Women 1974-77; mem NAACP; Southeastern CO Health Systems Agy; Pikes Peaks Are as Council of Govt. **BUSINESS ADDRESS:** 500 Front St, Fairplay, CO 80440.

EVANS, ALICIA
Public relations director. **PERSONAL:** Born May 28, 1960, Brooklyn, NY; daughter of Simon Levan Evans and Magnolia Ballard Evans. **EDUCATION:** Hofstra Univ, Hempstead NY, BA Communictions, 1982; New York Univ, New York NY, Business Mgmt Certificate, 1984. **CAREER.** Fortunoff's (upscale retail outlet), Westbury NY, promotional sales asst, 1977-84; CBS News, New York NY, program transcriber, 1981; Lockhart & Pettus Advertising Agency, New York NY, account exec, 1982-87; All Ways Natural Hair Care, Brooklyn NY, dir public relations, 1987-. **ORGANIZATIONS:** Mem, Natl Assn for Female Exec, 1988, Public Relations Soc of Amer, 1988. **HONORS/ACHIEVEMENTS:** News & Feature Editor, "The Satellite," Hofstra Univ, 1981, 1982; pruducer/copywriter, Con Edison, NY Utility Co (radio commercial), 1984; copywriter (brochure), Minority & Women's Div, New York Chamber of Commerce, 1984; producer/copywriter, Dark & Lovely Hair Care [illegible]ducts (radio commercial), 1987; senior editor, "Homecoming," Army ROTC Publicati[illegible] 87; African-American Achievement Award for Outstanding Serv & Commitmen[illegible]usiness Community, New York Million Dollar Boys Club, 1988. **HOME ADDRESS:** 4 First Ave, Westbury, NY 11590.

EVANS, AMOS JAMES
Association executive. **PERSONAL:** Born May 11, 1922, Rayne, LA; married Carolyn S; children: Winnfred, Adrian J, Wendell P, Donald R. **EDUCATION:** Lasalle Bus Coll 1946. **CAREER:** Port Arthur Br NAACP TX, pres 1972-80; Gulf Oil Corp, operator no 1 1946-80; Ch Sch, couns 1964-80; 7th St Br YMCA, pres 1973-77. **HONORS/ACHIEVEMENTS:** Recipient serv award & membership 7th Br YMCA 1970; outstanding serv to youth award St Paul United Meth Ch 1971; comm serv award Negro BPW Port Arthur TX 1976; meritorious award Port Arthur Br NAACP 1977; cong comm award Golden Gate Civic ZOB Sorority Man 1977. **MILITARY SERVICE:** USN petty officer 1944-46. **BUSINESS ADDRESS:** Port Arthur Branch NAACP, PO Box 1583, Port Arthur, TX 77640.

EVANS, ARTHUR L.
Educator. **PERSONAL:** Born Jul 26, 1931, Macon, GA; married Hattie Fears; children: Ivan Hugh. **EDUCATION:** Morehouse Coll, AB 1953; Columbia Univ, MA 1957; Univ of Miami, PhD 1972; Union Theological Seminary School of Social Music, attended. **CAREER:** Ballard-Hudson High School Macon, 1953-54; Miami Northwestern Sr High School, 1957-69; Miami-Dade Jr Coll, prof of humanities 1967-69; Hialeah-Miami Lakes Sr High School, chmn, choral dir 1970-72; SC State Coll Orangeburg, dir of concert choir, chmn dept of visual & performing arts. **ORGANIZATIONS:** Chmn humanities, music ed, dir Men's Glee Club Concert Choir; chmn Fine Arts Lyceum Comm 1973; conductor Coll Concert Choir 1974-75; mem Kappa Delta, Phi Mu Alpha Sinfonia, Natl Mus Eds Conf, The Amer

Choral Dir Assoc, SC Music Ed Assoc, Phi Beta Sigma. **HONORS/ACHIEVEMENTS:** Ed Awd Phi Beta Sigma 1972; Outstanding Achievement Awd Phi Beta Sigma 1987. **MILITARY SERVICE:** AUS pfc 1954-56. **BUSINESS ADDRESS:** Chmn Visual & Performing Arts, South Carolina State Coll, PO Box 1917, Orangeburg, SC 29117.

EVANS, BILLY J.
Educator, researcher. **PERSONAL:** Born Aug 18, 1942, Macon, GA; married Adye Bel; children: William, Carole, Jesse. **EDUCATION:** Morehouse Coll, BS (summa cum laude) 1963; Univ of Chicago, PhD 1968. **CAREER:** Univ of Manitoba, post-doctoral fellow dept of physics 1968-69; Howard Univ, asst prof chemistry 1969-70; Univ of MI, asst prof 1970-73, assoc prof dept geol & mineral 1973-75; Natl Bureau of Standards Alloy Physics Section, consultant 1971-; BASF Wyandotte, consult 1976-78; Univ of MI, assoc prof chem 1975-79, prof of chem 1979. **ORGANIZATIONS:** Rsch assoc Univ of Chicago; mem Amer Phys Soc; Amer Chemical Soc; Mineral Soc of Amer; Canadian Mineral Assn; Amer Geophysical Union; Minorities of the Amer Geophysical Union; Early Admission to Coll. **HONORS/ACHIEVEMENTS:** Merrill Scholar Morehouse Coll 1959-63; Phi Beta Kappa; Woodrow Wilson Fellow 1963-; Natl Rsch Council of CAN Postdoctoral Fellow Univ of Manitoba 1968-69; Alfred P Sloan Rsch Fellow 1972-75; Humboldt Sr Fellow 1977-78; Danforth Assoc 1977-83; guest prof Univ Marburg W Germany; Faculty Rsch Participant/Consultant US Geological Survey. **BUSINESS ADDRESS:** Prof of Chemistry, Univ of MI, Dept of Chemistry, Ann Arbor, MI 48106.

EVANS, CAROLE YVONNE MIMS
Attorney. **PERSONAL:** Born Oct 01, 1951, Hendersonville, NC; daughter of Evans King Mims and Mary Louise Valentine Mims; married Michael Duaine Evans, Sep 05, 1981; children: Tracey Renee Evans, Michael Thomas Evans, Karen Michelle Evans. **EDUCATION:** Wellesley Coll, BA 1973; Duke Univ Sch of Law, JD 1976. **CAREER:** Chambers Stein Ferguson & Becton, attorney 1976-88; Children's Law Center, 1989-. **ORGANIZATIONS:** Bd of dirs Charlotte Assn YWCA 1978-80; bd of dirs Planned Parenthood Charlotte Affiliate 1979-80; bd of dirs Charlotte Mecklenburg Urban League Org 1979-81; Charlotte Speech & Hearing Center 1983-89; NC Bar Assn Bd of Governors 1986-89; mem of bd Bio-Ethics Resources Group 1988-; mem of bd Leadership Charlotte 1988-. **BUSINESS ADDRESS:** Children's Law Center, 725 E. Trade Street, Suite 200, Charlotte, NC 28202.

EVANS, CASWELL ALVES, JR.
Dentist. **PERSONAL:** Born Apr 09, 1943, New York City, NY; married Arlene Grosvenor. **EDUCATION:** Franklin & Marshall Coll, AB 1965; Columbia Univ, DDS 1970; Univ MI, MPH 1972. **CAREER:** Seattle King Co Headstart Prog; Univ Chicago Hosp, intern 1970-71; Health Co Inc Soul City NC, chief dental serv dir rsch & eval 1973-75; Univ of NCSch Dentistry & Sch Pub Health, asst prof lecturer 1973-75; King Co Dept Pub Health, dir co health serv div. **ORGANIZATIONS:** Mem Amer Public Health Assn, Amer Assn of Pub Hlth Dentist, King Co Hlth Planning Council; clinical asst prof Sch Dentistry & Sch Pub Hlth Univ WA; chmn Hlth Serv Adv Comm. **HONORS/ACHIEVEMENTS:** Numerous grants and publ.

EVANS, CHARLOTTE A.
Business executive. **PERSONAL:** Born in Providence, RI. **EDUCATION:** NY Inst of Credit. **CAREER:** First Nat City Bank, switchboard operator, platform customer rep, official asst, asst mgr 1954-. **ORGANIZATIONS:** Mem Nat assn of Bank Women Inc; Urban Banders Coalition; former bd mem Hamilton Center Day Care Inc; former mem Manhattanville Comm & Center Inc; former mem Scitarnard Players of Providence RI; mem Black Achievers YMCA; original mem Am Negro Theatre of NY; honorary mem Iota Phi Lambda Sorority; vice pres Corr sec NY Rinkeydinks Inc. **HONORS/ACHIEVEMENTS:** Recipient 1970 luncheon Award Iota Phi Lambda Sorority 1971; one of first black achievers 1968; first black women officer of any bank in NY. **BUSINESS ADDRESS:** 125 St at Old Broadway, New York, NY 10027.

EVANS, CLAY
Clergyman. **PERSONAL:** Born Jun 23, 1925, Tennessee; married Liutha Mae; children: Diane, Michael, Ralph, Claudette, Faith. **EDUCATION:** No Bapt Theol Sem, attended; Univ Chicago School of Div, attended; AR Bapt Coll, DD. **CAREER:** Bapt Ministers Conf, pres 1964-66; WCFL-AM Radio & TV, ministry; Fellowship Bapt Church, pastor 1950-. **ORGANIZATIONS:** Chmn Emer Oper PUSH.

EVANS, CRECY ANN
Educator. **PERSONAL:** Born Apr 17, 1915, Benton, LA; married John W; children: Christine A Bates. **EDUCATION:** Wiley Coll, BA 1945; Bishop Coll, EdM 1952; Northeast State U, Addl Study; LA Tech U;Univ of CA Berkeley. **CAREER:** Retired public school admin; elementary school, prin 1934-45; jr & sr high school, asst prin 1945-74; Caddo Parish School Bd, Basileius Sigma Gamma Rho, 1966-74; Esquirett Soc Club, pres. **ORGANIZATIONS:** Life mem PTA NEA; LEA Sponsors Drop-n Serv for Harmony House Nursing Home; mem Scott A Lewis Chap 22 Order of Eastern Star; chair person Scholarship Com; warder amarantha YMCA; Comm Action Club; mem sec Rosa of Sharon No 149; various other activieties. **HONORS/ACHIEVEMENTS:** Trophy outstanding serv Sigma Gamma Rho 1967; sigma of yr 1972; trophy sigma of yr SW Reg 1972; adv of yr Undergrad Chap Sigma Gamma Rho 1974; trophy for serv rendered Valencia Jr HS 1974; develop functional program in Guidance & Reading for Slow Learners Disadvantages Youth.

EVANS, DAVID LAWRENCE
Educator. **PERSONAL:** Born Dec 27, 1939, Wabash, AR; married Mercedes L Sherrod; children: Daniel, Christine. **EDUCATION:** TN State Univ, BS 1962; Princeton Univ, MS Engrg 1966. **CAREER:** Boeing Com, electrical engineer 1962-64; Lockheed, electrical engineer 1964; Princeton Univ, teaching asst 1964-66; IBM Corp, electrical engineer 1966-70; Harvard Univ, admin officer, asst dean 1970-. **ORGANIZATIONS:** Mem bd trustees St Georges Sch; mem Gov Bd Princeton Grad Alum Assn; mem Inst of Elec & Electronic Engrs, Amer Audlgy Soc; mem Natl Assn ofColl Admiss Couns; mem Alpha Phi Alpha Frat; Harvard Club of Boston; mem Assn of Black Princeton Alumni; Princeton Alumni Assn of New England; select com Natl Merit Corp; prd film Unique Afr Rebels of Surinam 1975; Natl Sci Found Traineeship 1965-66. **HONORS/ACHIEVEMENTS:** Outstanding Young Men of Amer 1971; TN State Univ Alum of the Yr 1972; publ "Making It as a Black at Harvard/Radcliffe" NY Times 1976; "On Criticism of Black Student" Ebony 1977; "School Merit Pay System Gone Awry" LA Times 1984; "An Appeal to Black Alumni" Newsweek 1984.

EVANS, DONNA BROWDER
Educational administrator. **PERSONAL:** Born in Columbus, OH; children: Jocelyn Michelle Brown-Smith. **EDUCATION:** OH State Univ, BSc 1958, MS 1964, PhD 1970. **CAREER:** Univ of Cincinnati, asst prof 1969-73; Univ of Maine, prof/grad dean 1973-83; Skidmore Coll, prof/chair dept of educ 1983-. **ORGANIZATIONS:** Mem Alpha Kappa Alpha Sor Albany Chapt; mem Coalition of 100 Black Women Albany 1984-; mem Amer Assoc of Univ Women Saratoga Springs 1984-; mem Links Inc Albany Chap 1984-; bd of dirs Assoc Black Educators/Profs 1985-87; bd of dirs Soroptomist Intl 1985-87; bd dir Lake George Opera Festival; bd dir Task Force Against Domestic Violence Saratoga Spngs. **HONORS/ACHIEVEMENTS:** Reviewer Brooks Cole Publishing Co 1980-; editorial bd Journal of Reality Therapy 1984-; publications "Success Oriented Schools in Action" 1981, "A Conversation with William Glasser" 1982, "Opening Doors to the Future Through Education" 1984, "Reality Therapy, A Model for Physicians Managing Alcoholic Patients" 1984. **BUSINESS ADDRESS:** Prof & Chair Dept of Educ, Skidmore College, North Broadway, Saratoga Springs, NY 12966.

EVANS, DORSEY
Attorney. **PERSONAL:** Born Dec 07, 1930, Kansas City, KS; married Ruth Wilson; children: Dorsey Delwin, Velma, Elizabeth, Gary C. **EDUCATION:** Univ of KS, B 1952; Howard Univ, JD 1958. **CAREER:** Howard Univ, legal aid soc; Turner Memorial AME Church, cons; Local Funeral Home, cons; Pride Econ Devel Inc, cons; Storage Co, cons; Westinghouse ElectCorp, cons; Congressman Walter E Fauntroy's Camp Comm, former treasurer 1972-; Delco Settlement Co, pres; Delwin Realty Co, pres; Private practice,attny; Howard Univ, legal counsel. **ORGANIZATIONS:** Mem Natl, Wash DC, Amer, Bar Assocs; mem Amer Judicature Soc, Amer Arbitration Assoc, Supreme Ct US, Supreme & State Ct KS; mem, adv comm Superior Ct Rules Civil Procedure DC; mem Info Ctr for Handicapped Children, Turner Mem Meth Church; former vp, pres Homemaker Svc; past pres Young Dem Clubs, Woodridge Civic Assoc, Young Adult Club; past vice pres Fed Civic Assoc; past chmn 12 Precinct Police Crime Council. **HONORS/ACHIEVEMENTS:** Outstanding Trial Counsel Chief Judge Bazelon. **MILITARY SERVICE:** AUS 1953-55. **BUSINESS ADDRESS:** Attorney, HowardUniv, 1301 Pennsylvania Ave, N W, Washington, DC 20004.

EVANS, EDGAR E.
Educator. **PERSONAL:** Born Jan 20, 1908, Pittsview, AL; married Zelia V Stephens. **EDUCATION:** Fisk Univ, AB 1930; Univ of MI, MA 1948. **CAREER:** Apopka FL, Winter Garden, Starke, Siluria AL, Waynesboro VA, principal 1931-48; AL State Univ, prof 1949-72; Royal Soc of Health, ret fellow 1965-. **ORGANIZATIONS:** Mem The Pres Club; life mem Phi Delta Kappa, Phi Beta Sigma Frat, Amer Soc for the Study of Ed, Amer Acad of Pol Sci, Amer Sociol Assoc; dep Shaaban Temple 103; trustee St John AME Church; mem So Pride Elks Lodge 431; 3rd vice pres 9th Episcopal Dist AME Church; life mem NAACP, 33 Deg Mason. **HONORS/ACHIEVEMENTS:** Plaque Shaaban Temple 103; Certs of Apprec Library of Humn Resources of the Amer Bicentennial Inst, Cty Dist Attny 15th Jud Circuit, Ret Sr Vol Prog of the US of Amer, Dexter Ave Bapt Church, Cleveland Ave YMCA; Man of the Year Awd St John AME Church 1977; Personalities of Amer 1985; The Amer PublicHealth Assoc pays Tribute to Edgar E Evans 1986; Phi Beta Sibma Man of the Year 1987. **MILITARY SERVICE:** Corpl 1942-45.

EVANS, EDWARD BUTRAM
Educator. **PERSONAL:** Born May 07, 1894, Kansas City, MO; married Conzelta Riles. **EDUCATION:** Jones State U, DVM 1918; Jones State U, DSC 1958. **CAREER:** Emeritus Prairie View A&M Univ, pres 1918-67; School of Veterinary Medicine Tudyu Inst AL, leave of absence to establish 1945. **ORGANIZATIONS:** Mem City Counsel Prairie View 1970-75; TX Tuberculosis Assn; Prairie View Retires Tchrs Assn & Recip. **HONORS/ACHIEVEMENTS:** IA state u Alumni award 1960. **MILITARY SERVICE:** AUS 2nd lt 1918. **BUSINESS ADDRESS:** A&M University, Ofc Prairie View, Prairie View, TX.

EVANS, EDWARD CLARK
Journalist. **PERSONAL:** Born Dec 27, 1955, Detroit, MI; married Doreen Mercia DeCohen; children: Allyson Joy. **EDUCATION:** Eastern Washington Univ, 1974-76; CA State Univ Los Angeles, BA 1977-80. **CAREER:** CA Behavior Ctr, media consultant 1977-; KHJ-AM, public affairs asst 1980-81; KRTH-FM Los Angeles, public affairs dir 1981-83; KHJ-TV, public affairs/editorial mgr 1983-85; KGFJ-AM, account exec 1985-87; KJLH-FM Los Angeles, account exec 1987-. **ORGANIZATIONS:** Mem Black Journalist Assoc of S Calif 1983-85; mem Natl Broadcast Editorial Assn 1983-85; mem Los Angeles NAACP 1983-85; mem Natl Broadcast Assn forComm Affairs 1983-85; mem Los Angeles Jr Chamber of Commerce 1984-85; mem Natl Assoc of Market Developers 1984-85; mem Urban League, Southern CA Media Network 1985-87; vice pres/bd of dirs Young Saints Scholarship Foundation Inc. **HONORS/ACHIEVEMENTS:** President Phi Eta Psi Frat Theta Chap 1975-76. **BUSINESS ADDRESS:** Account Executive, KJLH Radio, 3847 Crenshaw Blvd, Los Angeles, CA 90008.

EVANS, ELEANOR JUANITA
Educator. **PERSONAL:** Born Nov 08, 1944, Annapolis, MD. **EDUCATION:** San Diego State Coll, BA 1967; San Diego State U, MS 1974;Univ of So CA, Predoctorate 1974. **CAREER:** San Diego Unified Schools, teacher 1968-; Office of Urban Affairs Community Relationa Div, human relations team 1976-77; Johnson Elementary School, teacher,sub prin 1974-76; Teacher Corps Proj, Dept of HEW, Washington DC, team leader 1971-72; School of Educ, San Diego State Univ, Cert perf evaluation com Teachers & Admin, adjunct prof; San Diego State Coll, educ consultant, Operation Stimulation 1965-67. **ORGANIZATIONS:** Mem CA Assn Afro-Am Educ Rep San Diego 1969; Nat Assn Afro-Am Edn; NEA; mem Nat Cncl of Negro Women 1969-; educ liason 1970-71; mem Pub Rels Com Black Action Council; Organized Statewide Conf Congress of Racial Equality 1969, pres 1965-66; bd of dir San Diego Urban League 1971-; dist rep 79th Assembly Co Cntr Com 1972-78; mem Delta Sigma Theta. **HONORS/ACHIEVEMENTS:** Author Black Dialect & its Implementation at the Elem Level for Teaching Reading; listed Whos Who of Women 1972-74; listed Whos Who of Black Am 1975-76; cert of achvmt San Diego Urban Leugue 1976.

EVANS, EVA L.
Educator. **PERSONAL:** Born Jan 14, 1935, Memphis; married Howard. **EDUCATION:**

Wayne State U, BA; MI State U, MA;Univ of MI, Study. **CAREER:** Lansing School Dist, dir of elementary; Detroit Public Schools, teacher; Lansing Public Schools, teacher. **ORGANIZATIONS:** Mem Delta Kappa Gamma; Nat Soc Women Educators; Phi Delta Kappa; Educ Res Fraternal Group; Assn of Childhood Edn; Am Assn of Sch Adminstrs; bd dirLansing Br NAACP; chmn Educ Com NAACP 1970; bd Lansing United Negro Coll Fund; Capitol Area Rail Council; past mem Adv Com Lansing Comm Coll Great Lakes Regional Dir; Alpha Kappa Alpha; charter mem Lansing-e Lansing Chap Links Inc. **HONORS/ACHIEVEMENTS:** Outstanding Great Lakes Soror 1970. **BUSINESS ADDRESS:** 519 N Kalamazoo, Lansing, MI.

EVANS, GREGORY JAMES
Recreation director. **PERSONAL:** Born Feb 15, 1954, Chicago, IL; son of Johnnie and Willie. **EDUCATION:** Wilbur Wright Jr Coll, AA 1975; Southern IL Univ, BA Phil 1977; Southern IL Univ, MS Health Ed 1979. **CAREER:** Amer Cancer Soc, public ed, coord 1980-82; Oak Park YMCA, phys ed instr 1982-84; Amer Cancer Soc, publ ed dir 1982; Health & Sports Productions, dir 1982-84; Randolph Tower Fitness Ctr, mgr 1983-84; Village of Oak Park, manager adult educ 1986-; Special Event Entertainment Group 1989. **ORGANIZATIONS:** Free lance amateur photography; black belt karate Ahn's Tae Kwon Do Assoc 1978; ice hockey coach volunteer Oak Park Hockey Assoc 1980-81; gen mem IL Interagency Council on Smoking & Disease 1980-83; vice pres IL Soc of Publ Health Ed 1981-82; mem Oak Park Area Jaycees 1984-; general mem IL Park & Recreation Assoc 1984-; Amer Assn of Physical, Health & Recreation 1989. **HONORS/ACHIEVEMENTS:** Natl Publ Ed Ctr Amer Cancer Soc 1980; Basic Fitness Cert Oak Park YMCA 1981; Semi-Pro Football Champs Cook Cty Cowboys 1981; Publ Coach & Athlete Playing Tall with Pylons 1981; Articles & Rsch Innovative Factors on Player Performance Preparation & Conditioning Factors 1981; 10 days training Natl Ctr for Comm Educ 1986; Cultural Arts Awd Jack & Jill Assoc of Amer West Suburban Chap 1986; Revenue Source Mgmt School 1988; Natl Youth Sport Coach Assn 1987; Amer Coaches Effectiveness Program 1985. **HOME ADDRESS:** 246 W Washington, Oak Park, IL 60302. **BUSINESS ADDRESS:** Village of Oak Park, 1 Village Hall Plz, Oak Park, IL 60302.

EVANS, GWENDOLYN
Business executive. **PERSONAL:** Born in North Carolina; daughter of James L Evans and Filmadge Whriley. **EDUCATION:** Essex Coll of Business, Certificate 1965; Rutgers Univ, BS 1973; New School Soc Res, Post Graduate Work 1975-77. **CAREER:** Prudential Insurance Co, various admin, technical & clerical assigments, 1962-74; College Relations, assoc mgr 1974-75; Equal Opportunity specialist 1975-76; assoc mgr corporate personnel admin 1976; mrg field serv personnel 1976-78; Prudential Insurance Co, exec. **ORGANIZATIONS:** Dir serv personnel Prudential Insurance CO 1978-, dir field office planning 1982-; instructor Coll in Co Prud Essex County Coll 1973-75; mem Hampton Inst Cluster Proggram VA 1975-77; charter mem Educ Center Youth Newark; exec comm, bd mem Natl Comm Prevention of Child Abuse New Jersey Chapter 1983-; mem Amer Soc of Devel New Jersey Chapter 1984-85. **HONORS/ACHIEVEMENTS:** Certificate of Appreciation, Amer Soc Training Devel 1984; YWCA Black Achiever Award, Newark NJ 1981. **BUSINESS ADDRESS:** Executive, Prudential Insurance Co, 745 Broad St, Broad St, Newark, NJ 07101.

EVANS, HELEN W.
Director. **PERSONAL:** Born Aug 05, 1905, Tazwell, VA; widowed; children: John R. **EDUCATION:** VA State Coll, 1927; OH State U, BS 1948. **CAREER:** OH Dept Welfare, fld rep & revwr 1939-52; Treas of States Office, asst prsnl dir 1952-60; OH State Auditors Office, examiner 1958-62; Dept Industrial Relations OH, dep dir 1962-70; OH Dept of Indsl Rel, dir 1975; OH Rep Council, exec sec 1952-. **ORGANIZATIONS:** Mem OH Rep Party 1938-. **HONORS/ACHIEVEMENTS:** Whos Who am Politics 1973. **BUSINESS ADDRESS:** 2323 W 5th Ave, Columbus, OH 43216.

EVANS, HERBERT B.
Attorney. **PERSONAL:** Born Dec 02, 1919, Kansas City, MO; married Audrey. **EDUCATION:** St JohnsUniv Sch of Law, JD 1950. **CAREER:** Inified Ct System of St of NY, chief adminstrv judge 1979-; NY St Supremem Ct, justice appelate div 1977; NY St Supreme Ct, justice 1972-; New York City CivilCt, judge 1966-72; New York City Housing & Redevel Agy, commr 1963-66; NYC, councilman 1960-63; Nat Urban Leag, gen counsel 1961-63; NY St, Commr of Parole 1958-59; NY St, asst counsel gov 1955-58. **ORGANIZATIONS:** Founder Freedom Nat Bank of NY; chmn Harlem Urbn Devel Corp; mem bd One Hundred Black Men Inc. **HONORS/ACHIEVEMENTS:** Philomonic Council Key for Schlshp; hon LLD St John'sUniv 1980. **MILITARY SERVICE:** AUS ret major.

EVANS, JACK
College president. **CAREER:** Southwestern Christian Coll, Terrell TX, pres. **BUSINESS ADDRESS:** Southwestern Christian College, Terrell, TX 75160. *

EVANS, JAMES CARMICHAEL
Government official. **PERSONAL:** Born Jul 01, 1900, Gallatin, TN; married Roselline; children: James Carmichael, Rose E. **EDUCATION:** Roger Williams U, AB 1921; MA Inst Tech, BS 1925, MS 1926; VA State Coll, LLD 1955; Central State Coll, 1956; Argl & Tech Coll NC, LHD 1961. **CAREER:** Miami FL, elec eng cnstr 1926-68; Booker T Wash HS Miami, tchr 1927; Trade & Tech Div WV State Coll, prof tech industries dir 1928-37, admnstrv asst to pres 1937-42; Sec War, asst civilian aide 1943-47, civilian aide 1947-48; Sec Def, adv 1947-49, asst 1947, couns Ellor mil & cvln affrs 1964-70; Howard U, adj prof elec engr 1946-70; Afro-Am Life Ins Co, vice pres 1954-; Indsl Bank Washington, dir; Council Nat Def War Mnpwr Com Wash, 1941-43. **ORGANIZATIONS:** Mem Nat Inst Sci; Am Inst Elec Engr; IRE; Am Assn Univ Profs; Nat Educ Assn; Nat Tech Assn, Exec Sec, 1932-57; mem Tau Beta Pi; EpsilonPi Tau; Sigma Pi Phi; Alpha Kappa Mu; Alpha Phi Alpha; Bapt; Adelphian; Miami Club; Musolit; trustee FL Meml Coll Miami; regent Marymount Coll VA. **HONORS/ACHIEVEMENTS:** Cosmos Washington recipient Harmon award in Sci Research in Electronics 1926; Dorie Miller Meml Fnd Award 1953; career serv award Nat Civil Serv League 1959; Sec Def Meritorius Civillian Serv Medal 1970; Patent Holder for Utilization of Exhaust Gases to Prevent Icing on Aircraft.

EVANS, JOE B.
Mayor pro tem. **PERSONAL:** Born Dec 26, 1929, Fair Bluff, NC; son of Henr P Evans, Sr. and Cora Barden Evans; married Carrie E; children: Debra, Rocky, Anthony, Natalie. **CAREER:** Addis Cates Co Inc; Fair Bluff City, mayor protem. **ORGANIZATIONS:** Mem Fair Bluff Sch Adv Council 1967-; Evans Subdivision Fair Bluff; Columbus Co Civic League; NAACP; City Councilman 1970-; past master Oak Grove Lodge 775 1971-72; Dorothy Patron Pleasant Plain Chapter 275 1969-; dir United Carolina Bank; dir Telephone and Data Systems; vice pres Inter Government Commn; bd of director Carver Community Center. **HONORS/ACHIEVEMENTS:** United Masonic Com of Columbus Co twenty-fourth dist award 1972. **MILITARY SERVICE:** US Army, Sargeant, 1951-56. **BUSINESS ADDRESS:** Mayor Pro Tem, City of Fair Bluff, Barden St, Fair Bluff, NC 28439.

EVANS, LEE
Professional athlete. **PERSONAL:** Born Feb 25, 1947, Madera, CA. **CAREER:** Nigerian Natl Team, phys fitness couns, coach 1975-80; professional athlete 1973-. **ORGANIZATIONS:** Mem Olympic Track Team 1968,72. **HONORS/ACHIEVEMENTS:** Won 2 Olympic Gold Medals Mexico 1968; won AAU 440 yrd 1966,67,69,69,70; won 400m gold medal Pan-Amer Games 1967; achieved world 400m dash & 1600m relay records Olympics 1968; won AAU 450 1968,72; won AAU 400m 1972.

EVANS, LEON, JR.
Manager. **PERSONAL:** Born Jan 08, 1953, Union Springs, AL; son of Leon Evans, Sr. and Ruth Evans; married Nyle Denise Hallback; children: Andrea Lactrice, Carlos LaRoy. **EDUCATION:** Tuskegee Univ, BS 1977; Samford Univ, MBA 1985. **CAREER:** New England Bankcard Assoc, mgr trainee 1973-75; John Hancock Ins Co, life underwriter 1977-80; Blue Cross/Blue Shield of AL, consultant/mgr 1980-. **ORGANIZATIONS:** Team leader Big Brothers/Big Sisters Fund Drive 1985; vice pres Groove Phi Groove Graduate Chapter 1985; consultant Junior Achievement of Birmingham 1985-86; certified instructor Ren Advanced Office Controls 1986; mem NBMBA 1986-87; fellow Life Office Mgmt Assn 1987. **HONORS/ACHIEVEMENTS:** Awd for Outstanding Leadership Junior Achievement 1986. **BUSINESS ADDRESS:** Manager Quality Assurance, Blue Cross/Blue Shield of AL, 450 River Chase Pkwy East, Birmingham, AL 35298.

EVANS, LEON EDWARD, JR.
Business executive. **PERSONAL:** Born Dec 28, 1942, Chicago, IL; married Doris J Davis; children: Aaron Gerard, Sheila Rene. **EDUCATION:** Wilson Jr Coll, Park Coll, attended. **CAREER:** Continental IL Natl Bank of Chicago, bookkeeping clk 1963-67; Independence Bank of Chicago, asst cashier 1967-69; Exchange Natl Bank of Chicago, asst cashier 1969-70; Gateway Natl Bank of Chicago, vice pres cashier 1970-72; Douglass State Bank, vice pres cashier 1972-75; Comm Bank of NE, pres/ceo 1975-. **ORGANIZATIONS:** Mem Creighton Omaha Regional Health Care Corp, Gr Omaha C of C; bd sec Jr Achievement; mem Metro Tech Comm Coll Found; vice chmn Metro Utilities Dist; mem Natl Conf of Christians & Jews; mem Omaha Comm Found, Omaha Public Sch Found; treas Omaha Telecasters; chmn of bd United Way of the Midlands; pres's council Creighton Univ; mem Frontiers Intl, Omaha Rotary Club. **BUSINESS ADDRESS:** President, Comm Bank of NE, PO Box 4070, 5180 Ames, Omaha, NE 68104.

EVANS, LEROY W.
Attorney. **PERSONAL:** Born Dec 15, 1946, Houston; married Robbie Moore; children: Anana Salisha. **EDUCATION:** Boalt Hall Sch of Law Berkeley, JD 1972;Univ of Houston, BA 1969. **CAREER:** Small Farm Devel Corp, admin dir 1979-; Consortium for the Devel of the Rural So East, exec dir 1977-79; Emergency Land Fund, att, gen, couns 1974-; Shearman & Steal, asso 1972-74. **ORGANIZATIONS:** Asst sec, treas, bd mem Riverfront Enterprises Inc; mem Nat Conf of Black Lawyers; mem LABA; bd mem So E YMCA; mem Dekalb Co Young Dem; memDekalb Co NAACP; CA Bar Assn; NY Bar Assn; mem Practicing Law Inst. **HONORS/ACHIEVEMENTS:** Recipient EE Worthing Scholarship 1965; Sigma Iota Epsilon; Martin Luther King Fellowship 1969; Distinguished Military Graduate 1969. **BUSINESS ADDRESS:** 836 Beecher St SW, Atlanta, GA 30310.

EVANS, LILLIE R.
Realtor. **PERSONAL:** Born Mar 23, 1913, Chattanooga, TN; married William D; children: William D III. **EDUCATION:** TN A&I State Coll Nashville, 1931-32; UCLA, 1962-63. **ORGANIZATIONS:** Mem Consolidated Realty Bd 1956; second vp, dir Consolidated Realty Bd 1962-64; charter mem Los Angeles Club of Nat-Assn of Negro Bus & Professional Women'sClub Inc 1960-; couns W Coast real estate; AME Zion Ch; initiator Comm Swimming Pool Proj 1970-71. **HONORS/ACHIEVEMENTS:** First black woman realtor; first black LA Bd of Realtors 1962; first black dir LA Bd of Realtors 1971-73; recipient Outstanding Contributions in Field of Bus Award, Nat Assn of Negro Bus & Professional Women's Club 1963; Key to City of Chattanooga 1972. **BUSINESS ADDRESS:** Lillie R Evans Realtor, 7315 S Normandie, Los Angeles, CA 90044.

EVANS, LORENZO J.
Clergyman, educator. **PERSONAL:** Born Feb 21, 1909, Marion, AL; married Dr Louise B; children: Mrs Eddie Greffus, Stacy, M Evans. **EDUCATION:** Clark Coll, AB; Atlanta U, MA; Gammon Theol Sem, BD. **CAREER:** Disciples of Christ Indianapolis, natl dir of christian educ 1947-; Second Christian Church Muskogee, pastor 1941-42; YMCA Atlanta, sec 1945-47; US Army, chaplain 1942-45; Christian Educ Nation Christian Missionary Conv, dir 1947-60; UCMS & DHM, dir field prog, dir minority groups 1966-74. **ORGANIZATIONS:** Mem Leadership Com, Nat Council of Ch NY 1948-54. **HONORS/ACHIEVEMENTS:** Hon DD TX ChristianUniv 1974. **MILITARY SERVICE:** AUS capt 1942-45.

EVANS, MARI (E. REED)
Educator, writer. **PERSONAL:** Born Jul 19, 1923, Toledo, OH; divorced; children: William Evan, Derek Reed. **EDUCATION:** Attended Univ of Toledo. **CAREER:** Indiana Univ—Purdue Univ at Indianapolis, instr in black literature and writer-in-residence, 1969-70; Indiana Univ at Bloomington, asst prof of black literature and writer-in-residence, 1970-78; Northwestern Univ, visiting asst prof, 1972-73; Purdue Univ, West Lafayette, IN, visiting asst prof, 1978-80; Washington Univ, St Louis, visiting asst prof, 1980; Cornell Univ, visiting asst prof, 1981-85; State Univ of New York—Albany, assoc prof, 1985—. **ORGANIZATIONS:** Consultant, Discovery Grant Program, Natl Endowment for the Arts, 1969-70; consultant in ethnic studies, Bobbs-Merrill Co, 1970-73; chmn lit adv panel, Indiana State Arts Commission, 1976-77; chmn, Statewide Committee for Penal Reform; mem bd mgmt, Fall Creek Pkwy YMCA, 1975-81; bd dirs, 1st World Found; mem, Indiana Corrections Code Commis-

sion; mem, African Heritage Studies Assn; mem, Authors Guild; mem, Authors League of Amer. **HONORS/ACHIEVEMENTS:** Producer, director, and writer for television program "The Black Experience," WTTV, Indianapolis, 1968-73; author of poetry volumes Where Is All the Music, P. Breman, 1968, I Am A Black Woman, Morrow, 1970, and Night Star, Center for African Amer Studies, 1980; author of books for juveniles, including J.D., Doubleday, 1973, I Look at Me, Third World Press, 1974, Singing Black, Reed Visuals, 1976, and Jim Flying High, Doubleday, 1979; playwright of "River of My Song," 1977, and "Eyes" (musical), 1979; editor of Black Women Writers, 1950-1980: A Critical Evaluation, Doubleday-Anchor, 1984; contributor of poetry to textbooks, anthologies, and periodicals; John Hay Whitney fellow, 1965-66; Woodrow Wilson Foundation Grantee, 1968; Indiana Univ Writers Conference Award, 1970; 1st Annual Poetry Award, Black Academy of Arts and Letters, 1970; MacDowell Fellow, 1975; Copeland Fellow, Amherst Coll, 1980; Natl Endowment for the Arts Grantee, 1981-82; also author of Boo chie (play), 1979, Portrait of a Man, 1979, The Way They Make Beriani, and Glide and Sons (musical); L.H.D., Marian Coll, 1975. *

EVANS, MARY ADETTA
Educator. **PERSONAL:** Born Jun 13, 1909, Coldwater, VA; married Warren A; children: James W, Warren, David. **EDUCATION:** VA State Coll, BS 1948; Columbia U, MA 1958. **CAREER:** King & Queen, teacher of public schools 1931-39; Nottoway Training School, 1941-48; Baker Elementary School, 1948-50; Albert V Norrell Elementary School, 1950-74. **ORGANIZATIONS:** Bldg rep VA Tchrs Assn; mem Richmond Tchrs; NEA; Richmond Retired Tchrs; VA Nat Retired Tchrs Assns; Richmond Nat AssnsUniv Women; past pres, sec, Nat Council Negro Women; past supt jr dept Rapahannock River Southside Bapt Assn; vice pres Area C Woman's Aux; Bapt Gen Conv of VA; 1st vice pres Bapt Woman's Aux, Rappahannock River Southside Assn; mem Delver Woman's Club; YWCA; Crusade for Voters; vA Museum Fine Arts; Jr Red Corss sponsor 1972-73; mem Alpha Kappa Alpha Sor; chap pres, sec exec bd VA Minister's Wives Assn; mem Bapt Ch.

EVANS, MELVIN H.
Physician. **PERSONAL:** Born Aug 07, 1917, Christiansted, Virgin Islands of the United States;married Mary Phyllis Anderson; children: Melvin Jr, Robert, William, Cornelius. **EDUCATION:** Howard U, BS magna cum laude 1940; HowardUniv Coll of Med, MD 1944;Univ of CA Berkeley, MPH 1967. **CAREER:** US Virgin Islands 96th Cong, mem of cong 1979-; self-employed physician; pvt practice medicine 1967-69; vI, commr of health 1959-67; USPHS, sr asst surgeon 1948-50; chief municipal physician 1951-59; Frederiksted Mun Hosp, physician-in-charge 1945-48, 1950-51. **ORGANIZATIONS:** Charter mem Assn of Am Public Health Physicians; past pres VI Med Soc; past chrmn US VI Bd of Medical Examiners; Fellow Am Coll of Physicians; mem AMA; NMA; Pan American Med Assn; APHA; past vice chrmn Southern Governors Assn 1972-73; chrmn 1973-74; mem AMA Council on Environmental, Occupational & Public Health; chrmn bd trustees Coll of VI 1962-69; charter mem Rotary Club of St Croix. **HONORS/ACHIEVEMENTS:** First elected Governor, US VI 1971-; Mason Hon DHL, Morgan State Coll 1971; Hon LLD, HowardUniv 1972; trustee's award, Fairleigh DickensonUniv 1972. **MILITARY SERVICE:** AUS 2nd lt reserve 1942-43. **BUSINESS ADDRESS:** Government House, Charlotte Amalie, St Thomas, Virgin Islands of the United States 00801.

EVANS, MILTON L.
Chief executive officer/president. **PERSONAL:** Born Oct 09, 1936, Snowhill, NC; son of Herbert Evans, Jr. and Lola Vines Evans; married Alice Corella Brown; children: Milton Jr, Alan, Glenn, Warren, Kenneth. **EDUCATION:** Shaw Univ, BS Chem 1960; Tuskegee Inst, MS Chem 1964. **CAREER:** General Electric, r&d mktg mgmt 1964-73, section mgr compacts 1974-78, section mgr strategic planning, general specialty elastomers 1980-82; High Tech Services Inc, pres/CEO. **ORGANIZATIONS:** Dir Siena Coll Business Council, Outreach Inc, Schenectady Private Industry Council, NY Head Injury Assn. **HONORS/ACHIEVEMENTS:** Gold and Silver Medallions GE Inventors Awds. **BUSINESS ADDRESS:** President, High Technology Services Inc, 250 Jordan Rd, Ste 210, Troy, NY 12180.

EVANS, MYRA LYNN
Business executive. **PERSONAL:** Born Jun 10, 1959, Cleveland, OH. **EDUCATION:** Yale Univ, BA Chem 1981. **CAREER:** Standard Oil of OH, asst chem engr 1977-79, asst chemist 1980; Columbia Presbyterian, biomedical rsch asst 1979; Goldman Sachs & Co, financial analyst 1981-83; Gelato Modo Inc, pres. **ORGANIZATIONS:** Financial Analyst Assn; Chem Engr Soc at Yale; mem Yale Club; mem Laurel Alumni Assn; mem/treas Black Church at Yale. **HONORS/ACHIEVEMENTS:** Outstanding Young Women of Amer; Business Awd Natl Assoc of Negro Bus & Prof Women; Youth Awd Avon Natl Black Leadership Round Table; Natl AchievementSemifinalist; Who's Who Among Amer High School Students; Laurel School Disting Alumnae Awd Miller Brewing Calendar 1985. **BUSINESS ADDRESS:** President, Gelato Modo, Inc, 464 Columbus Ave, New York, NY 10024.

EVANS, PATRICIA P.
Educator. **PERSONAL:** Born in Topeka, KS; daughter of C Kermit Phelps and Lucille Mallory Phelps; married Langston Phelps, Kimberly Dawn, Kristina Ann (divorced). **EDUCATION:** Avila Coll, Kansas City MO, BS Chemistry, 1961; Columbia Univ, New York NY, currently pursuing MS Educ. **CAREER:** St Mary's Hospital, Kansas City MO, medical technologist, 1962-68; Univ of Illinois Medical Center, Chicago IL, clinical teaching asst, asst supvr hematology, 1968-71; Mount Sinai Hospital, New York NY, asst supvr abnormal hematology, 1971-72; Veterans Admin Hospital, Mdison WI, medical technologist, 1974-75; St Mary's Hospital Madison WI, medical technologist, 1977-81; Univ Hospital & Clinics, Madison WI, project specialist oncology research 1982-86. **ORGANIZATIONS:** Mem, Amer Soc for Medical Technologists, 1961-89, Amer Assn of Blood Banks, 1962-89, Amer Soc of Clinical Pathologists, 1962-89, Amer Assn for Advancement of Science, 1968-89; co-chair, Membership Comm, Wisconsin Soc for Medical Technologists, 1972-89; past corresponding sec, membership chair, Madison Area Soc for Medical Technologists, 1977-89; PTA bd mem, chairperson, Shorewood Hills Elementary School, 1978-86; chairperson, bd mem, Jack & Jill of Amer Inc, 1979-84; Cub Scout Den Mother, Cub Scouts of Amer, 1979-83; Girl Scout leader, Girl Scouts of Amer, 1982-88; parent mem, Boy Scouts of Amer, 1983-89; bd mem, West High School PTSO 1989-90. **HONORS/ACHIEVEMENTS:** Faith Dravis Award, Wisconsin Soc for Medical Technologists, 1989; Omricon Sigma Recognition, Wisconsin Soc for Medical Technologists, 1989. **BUSINESS ADDRESS:** Associate Lecturer, University of Wisconsin-Madison Campus, 1300 University Ave-Medical Science Center, Madison, WI 53706.

EVANS, PHILLIP L.
Industrial relations company executive. **PERSONAL:** Born Mar 18, 1937, Cincinnati, OH; son of Eddie Evans and Mildred Thompson Evans; married Constance Beckham, Jun 27, 1959; children: Phillip L Jr, Damon A. **EDUCATION:** Univ of Cincinnati, Cincinnati OH, BA, 1959, MA, 1963. **CAREER:** Cincinnati Public Schools, Cincinnati OH, work/study coord, 1962-68; RCA Corp, Indianapolit IN, industrial relations mgr, 1968-76; Miller Brewing Co, Milwaukee WI, Industrial Relations-Breweries, corporate mgr, 1976-. **ORGANIZATIONS:** Amer Soc of Personnel Admin; bd mem, Milwaukee Area Technical Coll. **HONORS/ACHIEVEMENTS:** Black Achievement Award, Harlem YMCA, 1987; Silver Ring Merit Award, Philip Morris Corp, 1988. **BUSINESS ADDRESS:** Corporate Manager, Industrial Relations-Breweries, Miller Brewing Company, 3939 W Highland Blvd, Milwaukee, WI 53208.

EVANS, ROBERT WARREN
Educator. **PERSONAL:** Born Sep 29, 1927, Marysville, OH; married Elizabeth Barnett; children: Robert Jr, Leonard. **EDUCATION:** OH St U, BS 1950; Kent St U, PhD, ME 1966 & 73. **CAREER:** OH Dept of Educ, asst supt for public instruction 1980-; KEDS DAC Kent State Univ, dir 1976-80; Cleveland Heights School, dir of secondary educ 1974-76; Hartford Jr High School, prin 1969-74, asst prin 1968-69; Canton Public Schools, teacher, coach 1953-68; Union Graduate School, adjunct prof 1979-80. **ORGANIZATIONS:** Mem Omega Psi Phi; mem Phi Delta Kappa; mem AASA NABSE; mem KSU Alumni Bd; pres Keastones; pres OH Allums Blk Sch Edn; consult ed OEA Urban Afrs Com 1971-72. **HONORS/ACHIEVEMENTS:** Bowman flwshp in educ admin Kent StUniv 1972; outst edctr Canton Frontiers of Am 1974; blk achvmnt in educ awd Canton Blk Comm Orgn 1977; Charles A Glatt meml awd OEA Commn on Hum Relat 1980; ldrshp in educ awd Phi Delta Kappa Kent St Chap 1980. **MILITARY SERVICE:** AUS corpl 1946-48.

EVANS, RUTHANA WILSON
Educator. **PERSONAL:** Born Mar 26, 1932, Roxie, MS; daughter of James Wilson (deceased) and Lueberta Wilson (deceased); married Lit Parker Evans Jr, Mar 22, 1957; children: Cedric Glenn, Valerie Denise. **EDUCATION:** Tougaloo Coll, BS 1955; Univ of IL, Post-grad 1965; NC Coll, 1967; Delta State Coll, MS 1971; Delta State Univ, MS Psychometrist 1977, AAA Counseling 1981; pursuing a degree in administration. **CAREER:** Shaw School, elem teacher 1955-57; Nailor Elem School, teacher, curriculum chmn 1957-60, teacher, librarian 1960-62, librarian 1963-64; Preschool Story Hour, librarian 1964-66; Bolivar County Dist 4; library supvr 1965-67; Ed TV Jackson, curriculum resources teacher 1968-70; Parks & Pearman Elem Schools, librarian 1968-70, org elem school libr prog 1969; Greenville Elem School, consult 1970; MS Head Start, educ dir 1970-79; Bolivar County Dist 4 Schools Titles I, counselor 1979-; Bolivar County Headstart, psychometrist 1985-; Bolivar Schls, psychometrist; Cleveland Schools testing coord 1986-. **ORGANIZATIONS:** Consult Indianola Preschool Activities 1971; org inventory, classification systems Head Start 1970; mem PTA 1955, MS Personnel & Guid Assoc, MS Library Assoc; job trainer Neighborhood Youth Corps Cleveland 1969; trainer manpower prog STEP 1970-, CETA 1977; sec Negro's Citizens Comm Cleveland 1957-61; active BSA; mem Baptist Training Union Cleveland 1972-, Negro Voters League; treas E Side HS Band Booster 1972; treas 1971, pres 1973 Athena Soc Club; sec Womens Club 1970; mem Natl Council Black Child Devel 1975-78; MS Counselors Assoc; Nat'l Educ Assoc; mem, sec, St Paul Baptist Church. **HONORS/ACHIEVEMENTS:** First runner-up to Miss Tougaloo Coll, 1955. **HOME ADDRESS:** 816 Cross St, Cleveland, MS 38732. **BUSINESS ADDRESS:** Counselor-Test Coordinator, Bolivar Cty Dist 4, 305 Merritt Dr, Cleveland, MS 38732.

EVANS, SAMUEL LONDON
Educational administrator. **PERSONAL:** Born Nov 11, 1902, Leon County, FL; married Edna Hoye; children: Retha EB Kelly. **EDUCATION:** Columbia Univ, attended 1948; NY Univ, integrated concepts science philosophy & educ 1951-53; Combs Coll, MusD (Hon) 1968. **CAREER:** US Div of Physical Fitness, coordinator 1941-45; Philadelphia Chamber Orchestra, impressario 1961-71; S London Publishing Co, publisher; PA State AthleticComm, secretary; Bicentennial Corp, exec vice pres 1971-; AFNA Natl Educ and Rsch Fund, pres/chairman of the board. **ORGANIZATIONS:** Comm member in celebration of the US Constitution 200 year anniversary; Columbia Univ World Study Tour 1948; concept and founder African American Hall of Fame Sculpture Garden 1984; founder, pres, natl chmn Amer Found for Negro Affairs 1968-; mem Mayors Comm on Municipal Svc; bd dir Amer Trauma Soc, Amer Heart Assoc; bd dir, prodn gen mgr Philadelphia Coffee Concerts Com; mem Natl Trust for Historic Preservation, Amer Pub Health Assoc. **HONORS/ACHIEVEMENTS:** Philadelphia Academy of Science Awd sculptured bronze bust by Zenos Frudakis 1981; Sister Clara Muhammad School Annual Education Awd 1983; Philadelphia Miniversity Citizens Awd 1985; USN Awd for Extraordinary Leadership 1976; Charles R Drew Awd 1978; Black Expo Awd 1972; Serv Awd 3rd World 76' Inc 1972; Achievement AwdPhiladelphia Cotillion Soc 1972; Community Serv Awd Philadelphia Oppty Indust Ctrs 1972; Achievement Awd NAACP Reg II 1972; author "The AFNA Plan, A Projection for the Year 200 and Now in Medicine, Law, Business & Commerce, Science Tech" 1974, "Nothing to Fear", "Second Phase of Democracy An Amer Manifesto". **BUSINESS ADDRESS:** President, American Foundation for Negro Affairs, 117 S 17th St, Suite 1200, Philadelphia, PA 19103-5025.

EVANS, SLAYTON ALVIN, JR.
Educator. **PERSONAL:** Born May 17, 1943, Chicago, IL; son of Slayton A Evans Sr and Corine M Thompson; married Timmie A Johnson, Jul 15, 1967; children: Slayton A Evans III, Amy R Evans. **EDUCATION:** Tougaloo Coll, BS Chemistry 1965; Case Western Reserve Univ, PhD Chemistry 1970; Univ of Texas at Arlinton, postdoctoral fellow, 1970-71; Univ of Notre Dame, post doctoral fellow 1971-72; Illinois Institute of Technology, 1965-66. **CAREER:** Univ of NC, prof of Chemistry 1974-; Dartmouth Coll, research instr 1972-73. **ORGANIZATIONS:** Mem Am Chem Soc 1968; Soc of Sigma Xi; New York Academy of Sciences, Alpha Xi Sigma. **HONORS/ACHIEVEMENTS:** Kenan Research Leave, Univ of NC 1984-85; Fulbright 1984-85; NATO Grant for Collaborative Research, NATO 1987-89; over sixty scientific publications in organic chemistry; Chmn of NIH BI-4 Study Section, Participant in ICPC in Tallinn SSR, USSR 1989. **BUSINESS ADDRESS:** The Univ of North Carolina, Department of Chemistry, CB 3290, Chapel Hill, NC 27514-3290.

EVANS, SPOFFORD L.
Educator. **PERSONAL:** Born Jan 31, 1919, Lancaster, SC; married Betty Jackson; children: Brenda, Janice, Sigredda, Dwight Spencer, Mordecai Lewis. **EDUCATION:** Friendship Jr Coll; Johnson C Smith U, AB; Temple U; NC Coll, MA; NC Coll, SC State Coll, Atlanta U,Univ of SC,, grad study. **CAREER:** Black Rock Baptist Church of Chester SC,

pastor; Friendship Jr Coll, pres 1973-. **ORGANIZATIONS:** Mem Mayor's Comm Rel Com of Rock Hill SC; mem Rock Hill Chap ARC; mem Phi Beta Sigma; Lancaster Consistory (32 Deg Masonic Order); Shrine Temple; SC Educ Assn; Dept of Secondary Sch Principals (State & Nat); Purity Masonic Lodge 42. **HONORS/ACHIEVEMENTS:** Author of various articles & book "Marriage & the Family", publ by Vantage Press of NY; Listed Personalities of the South 1971, 1974; Outstanding Americans 1975; Honorary DD, Friendship Jr Coll. **BUSINESS ADDRESS:** PO Box 10750, Rock Hill, SC 29730.

EVANS, STICKS
Musician. **PERSONAL:** Born Feb 05, 1923, Greenville, NC. **EDUCATION:** BM, MEd 1971. **CAREER:** Professional percussionist, played TV shows; Steve Allen, Ed Sullivan, Lonnie Sattin, NBC Today Show, Sammy Davis Jr, Teddy Wilson's Trio for CBS, Jack Parr; conductors as, Jasha Fishberg, Hugh Ross, Eubie Black, John Mortly, Gunther Schuller, many others; recorded with in pop field, Tony Bennett, Andy Williams, Frankie Laine, Enzio Stuarti, Lou Perez, many others; recorded with in rock & gospel field, Lenny Welch, Neil Sadaka, The Platters, Dian & the Belmonts, Frankie Avolon, many others; recorded with in jazz field, John Lewis Orchestra USA, James Moody, Kai Windig, Charlie Mingus,. **MILITARY SERVICE:** USN 3 yrs; AUS 3 yrs.

EVANS, THERMAN E.
Physician, health director. **PERSONAL:** Born Aug 20, 1944, Henderson, NC; son of Irvin Evans Sr and Constine Evans; married Bernetta Jones, Jul 30, 1966; children: Thomas E Evans Jr, Clayton Evans. **EDUCATION:** Howard Univ, BA 1966, MD 1971. **CAREER:** Operation PUSH, natl health dir; East of the River Health Ctr Washington, phys; CT General Ins Co, 2nd vice pres/corp med dir; CIGNA, asst med dir 1979-83, corp med dir 1983-87, vice pres/corp med dir 1987-. **ORGANIZATIONS:** Natl bd of dirs Operation PUSH 1983, review & adv comm for various agencies of Fed Govt; pres Washington DC Bd of Educ; clinical faculty Howard Univ; pres Operation PUSH, Philadelphia Chapter 1983-86; bd of dirs Southeastern PA Wellness Council 1987-88, Philadelphia Health Mgmt Corp 1988-. **HONORS/ACHIEVEMENTS:** Visiting Regent's Scholar-Lecturer at the Univ of CA; published over 25 articles on various health related subjects in journals & magazines; guest expert on numerous natl & local radio and TV health oriented progs; Alumnae of the Year, Howard Univ Alumnae Assn, Philadelphia Chapter 1988; Stress and the College Student, The Black Collegian Magazine 1989; Being Black in America is Hazardous to Your Health, Journal of the Natl Medical Assn 1989. **BUSINESS ADDRESS:** Vice President & Corporate Medical Dir, CIGNA Corporation, One Logan Square, Philadelphia, PA 19103-6930.

EVANS, THOMAS
Clergyman. **PERSONAL:** Born Aug 11, 1925, Ramer, AL; married Irene Parks; children: Tommie, Deborah. **EDUCATION:** AL U, Wayne State U, BS Edn, MEd 1953, 1971; Selma U, studied; Theiol & Bible Moody Bible Inst. **CAREER:** Ch of Our Father Bapt, minister 1957-; Barbour Jr HS Detroit Bd Edn, reading coord; Christ Educ Galilee Dist Conv, minister 1946-51. **ORGANIZATIONS:** Mem Wayne & Co Reading Assn; past pres Dexter-Joy Home Improvement Assn; mem NAACP; mem 11th Percent Police Comm Relation Council. **MILITARY SERVICE:** WW II 1943-46; Korean War 1950-52. **BUSINESS ADDRESS:** 5333 E Seven Mile Rd, Detroit, MI 48234.

EVANS, THOMAS ARCHIE
Oral dental marketing & research. **PERSONAL:** Born Aug 31, 1928, Philadelphia, PA; married Constance Elizabeth Swain; children: Karen, Elizabeth, Thomas, Anthony. **EDUCATION:** Shaw Univ, BS 1950; Temple Univ, DDS 1958; Columbia Grad School of Bus, 1980. **CAREER:** Lawside NJ & Philadelphia, practice gen dentistry 1958-69; Warner-Lambert Co, dir professional relations 1972-81; Clinical Resources Inc, pres 1981-. **ORGANIZATIONS:** Mem Amer Med Writers Assoc, Intl Assoc for Dental Rsch, Natl & Amer Dental Assoc, Tri-County NJ So Dental Soc; vp, explorer adv Troop 45 Comm BSA; bd dir Camden Cty Council on Econ Oppty, Camden Cty Legal Serv Comm; adv comm Expanding Horizons, Prexel Inst; bd of dirs Morris Cty United Way1979, Rsch Officers Assoc, Omega Psi Phi. **MILITARY SERVICE:** AUS served with chem corps 1951-53. **BUSINESS ADDRESS:** President, Clinical Resources Inc, 95 7th ave, Newark, NJ 07104.

EVANS, VERNON D.
Auditor, accountant. **PERSONAL:** Born Mar 07, 1950, Ft Worth, TX; son of Rev Dellie Evans and Thelma Evans; married Viola Ruth Cross (divorced); children: Victor, Vinikka, Vernessa. **EDUCATION:** N TX State U, BBA, MBA 1972; Cert Public Accountant, 1973; Cert Mgmt Accountant, 1980; Cert Internal Auditor, 1985; Cert Fraud Examiner, 1989. **CAREER:** Dallas/Fort Worth Intl Airport Bd, dir of internal audit, 1986—; Fort Worth Independent Schol Dist, chief internal auditor, 1982-86; Ernst & Whinney, audit mgr and supr, 1972-82; Evans McAfee & Co, mnging partner 1976-78; Ernst & ErnstCPAs, staff accountant, sr accountant, 1972-76. **ORGANIZATIONS:** So Regional Dir, 1987-90, Inst of Internal Auditors; Mem Nat Assn Accountants 1974-80; state dir, TX Soc of CPA's, 1988-90; vice pres, 1979-81, pres 1981-83, Nat Assn of Black Accountants; Assn of Govt Accountants; Govt Finance Officerts Assn; Natl Forum of Black Public Administrators; accounting dept advisory bd, North TX State Univ; chair, United Way Allocation Com III 1979-80; chmn McDonald YMCA 1980; treas Metro Economical Devel Corp, 1980; bd of dir, Ft Worth Black Chamber of Commerce; bd of dir, Day Care Assn. **HONORS/ACHIEVEMENTS:** Outstanding Achievement Award, Sickle Cell Anemia Assn of TX 1979; Outstanding Achievement Award, Nat Assn of Black Accountants 1979, 1987; Greek Image Award, Pan-Hellenic Coun, 1983; Henry A Meadows Volunteer of the Year Award, YMCA-MFW, 1983; outstanding service awards, McDonald YMCA, 1985, United Negro Coll Fund, 1986; Chi Rho Award, YMCA-MFW, 1988; F M Miller Award, McDonald YMCA, 1989. **BUSINESS ADDRESS:** Director of Internal Audit, Dallas/Ft Worth International Airport Board, PO Drawer DFW, Dallas/Fort Worth Airport, TX 75261.

EVANS, VINCE CALVIN
Professional athlete. **PERSONAL:** Born Jun 14, 1955, Greensboro, NC; married Chyla. **EDUCATION:** Univ of Southern CA, Speech Comm Major. **CAREER:** Chicago Blitz, quarterback 1977-; Denver Gold, quarterback 1984-. **HONORS/ACHIEVEMENTS:** MVP at LACC his only year there; MVP of 1977 Rose Bowl; won Southern Cal's Teschke Awrd in 1976 as team's most inspirational player; co-capt in 1976.

EVANS, W. RONALD
Business executive. **PERSONAL:** Born Jul 22, 1938, Buffalo, NY; children: Mark T, John H. **EDUCATION:** Attended Howard Univ 1957-62. **CAREER:** AAA Bus Svcs, accnt tax consult bus adv1962-72; Prog Prop, pres 1962-77; Small Bus Dev Ctrof United Plan Organ, chief loan dev splst 1964-65; Natl Bus League, bus fran analyst & dir of fiscal opers 1967-69; Mainstream Comp Serv Inc, vice pres mktng 1969-70; Small Bus Admin, gen bus & indus splst 1970-72; ITT Wash Relations, mgr pub affs 1972-74; Prog Entrpse Ltd, pres 1972-83; Congrsnl Bud Office; inform officer 1975-76; Booker T Wash Fnd, consult 1977-83; Progressive Prop Realty Corp, pres 1977-83; NBL, vice chair 1981-83; US Dept of Energy, staff asst 1983-84; Atlantic Group Inc, vp; US Dept of Energy, pres appointee as spec asst to the admin econ reg admin 1982-. **ORGANIZATIONS:** Past bd mem DC C of C 1968-78; pres & chmn of bd DC C of C 1972-73; mem Natl Assn of Real Estate Brokers 1973-; bd & sec Natl Bus League 1974-81; mem Natl Soc of Real Estate Appraisers 1975-78; pres Wash Real Estate Brokers Assn 1976-77; mem Natl Black Republican Council 1980-; mem Natl Auctioneers Assn 1981-. **HONORS/ACHIEVEMENTS:** 1974 Thomas W Parks Disting Serv Aws DC C of C.

EVANS, WEBB
Association executive. **PERSONAL:** Born Nov 20, 1913, Greensboro, AL; married Cora Golightly. **EDUCATION:** TN State Coll, 1936-37; Cortez Peters Bus Sch, 1943. **CAREER:** House of Saunders Chgo, mgr 1974-; Evans Food Mart Chgo, owner 1949-74; Wells Consumers Coop Inc Chgo, mrg 1945-47. **ORGANIZATIONS:** Pres United Am Progress Assn 1961-; treas Forrestville Civic Improve League 1963-74; treas Fellowship Bapt Dist Assn1971-73; pres Layman Dept Prog Bapt State Convention of IL 1966-68; bd of dir Southside Comm Com for Juv Delinq Prevention 1949-65; bd dir Cosmop C of C 1961-65; pres 41st & 42nd Wells St Block Club; trustee Cathedral Bapt Ch 1964-. **HONORS/ACHIEVEMENTS:** Recipient Top Male Volunteer Award, Vol Bur of Met Chicago 1961; award Outstanding Serv to Civil Rights Movement, Christian Religious Builders 1964; Civil Progress Award, Inter-Denom Min Civ League of IL 1964; Citizen of Week, WBEE Radio 1969; Hon Citizen of State of TN, Gov Frank Clement, 1966; citation, United Am Prog Assn 1972. **BUSINESS ADDRESS:** 523 E 79 St, Chicago, IL 60619.

EVANS, WILLIAM C.
Clergyman. **PERSONAL:** Born Nov 03, 1899, Winchester, KY; son of William and Anna; married Emma Lee Evans. **EDUCATION:** Metro Bible Coll; VA Theological Seminary & Coll, DD. **CAREER:** South Hempstead Baptist Church, pastor 1940-. **ORGANIZATIONS:** Chmn Evangelistic Bd E Baptist Assn; bd mem Empire State Conf; bd dir E Baptist Assn; bd mem Educ Center; mem Ministers Conf NY City; mem Natl Baptist Convention US Inc; bd mem Urban Renewal; mem Evangelistic Bd Natl Baptist Convention; life mem NAACP;, New Home Lodge 1123 IBPOE Elks; street named in behalf; mem Republican Presidential Task Force 1981-, United States Senatorial Club 1983-. **HONORS/ACHIEVEMENTS:** Commendation Gov NA Rockefeller; Unispan Awd Hofstra Univ; Commendation President Ronald Reagan; Commendation Governor M Coumo. **BUSINESS ADDRESS:** Pastor, South Hempstead Baptist Church, 81 Maple Ave, Hempstead, NY 11550.

EVANS, WILLIAM CLAYTON
Attorney. **PERSONAL:** Born Apr 20, 1944, Louisville; married Hallie A Coleman; children: Alecia Marlene, Angela Christine. **EDUCATION:** Wilberforce U, BA 1967;Univ KY, JD 1971. **CAREER:** Disbility Eterminations Div of Human Resources Dept State of KY, dir; Pvt Practice, atty 1972-79; NY Stock Exchange, tranfer clerk 1966-67; Comm ActionLexington Fayette Co, comm worker 1968; Nat Bankers Assn, 1969-70; Housing Dept Lexington Fayette Co Human Rights Commn, legal aid 1970-71; Econ Dev, 1971-72; Regional Heber Smith Comm Lawyer Prog, law clerk 1971-72; Private Practice, atty. **ORGANIZATIONS:** Mem KY Am Nat Bar Assns all 1971-; mem NAACP. **BUSINESS ADDRESS:** Disability Determination, PO Box 1000, Louisville, KY 40602.

EVANS, WILLIAM D., JR.
Professional athlete. **PERSONAL:** Born Mar 30, 1899, Louisville, KY; married Lillie Ragland; children: William D III. **EDUCATION:** Livingstone Coll Saulsbury NC, 1916-19; Municipal Coll Louisville, Special Courses 1931-32. **CAREER:** Louisville White Sox, professional baseball 1915-19; Gilkerson Chicago Union Giants, professional baseball 1921-24; Am Giants, professional baseball 1924; Homestead Grays Pittsburgh, 1930-34; Brooklyn Giants, ctr fld 1928-29; Cinncinati Tigers, mgr 1934; Central News, writer 1965-69; F&Am Masonic Lodge Louisville, 1920-40; N Am Aviation 1st Black, radar insp 1951-67; Louisville News & LA Spotlight, sports wirter 1961; NAACP, bd of promise 1909. **ORGANIZATIONS:** Mem NAACP 1918; original mem Urban League 1921; original mem & chmn AME. **HONORS/ACHIEVEMENTS:** AME zion ch award Gov of KY Mayor of Louisville; lousiville flood dir of recreation 1937; auxiliary fireman top secret depts frugal converstaion award NAA 1953-67; recipient 1974; thomas w parks distinguished serv award DC C Of C.

EVANS, WILLIAM E.
Educational administrator. **PERSONAL:** Born Nov 28, 1931, Mebane, NC; son of Mozelle Evans; married Gloria Battle, May 05, 1952; children: Sandra Evans Holland, William, Jr, David Franklin. **EDUCATION:** Hampton Inst, BS, 1954; Southern Connecticut State Coll, MS, 1961; Bridgeport Univ, sixth year certificate, 1964; Southern Connecticut State Coll, further study; Yale Univ, Drug Educ, 1970-71; Univ of Connecticut, PhD, 1985. **CAREER:** Laurel Ledge School, Beacon Falls CT, teacher, 1957-58; Barnard School, Waterbury CT, teacher, 1958; elementary physical educ instructor, 1958-59; Wilby High School, Waterbury CT, physical educ instructor, 1958-67; Project Upward Bound, Univ of Hartford, reading instructor, 1966-67, curriculum coord & reading instructor, 1967-68, asst project dir, 1968-72; Community Action Agency, Waterbury, 1967; Waterbury School System, supvr health & physical educ, biology teacher, 1967-72; Waterbury Public Schools, drug coord, 1971; Mattatuck Community Coll, Waterbury, 1971-72; Waterbury Dept of Educ, dir educ grants, 1972-; Waterbury Tercentennial Inc, student coord. **ORGANIZATIONS:** Waterbury Teachers Assn; Connecticut Educ Assn; NEA exec bd & past pres; NAACP; bd dir YMCA; bd dir Jr Achievement; first dist marshall Omega Psi Phi Frat; corporator Waterbury Savngs Bank; Spel Projects Com United Councl & Fund; bd of incorporators Boy's Club of Amer; School Admin of Waterbury. **HONORS/ACHIEVEMENTS:** Hampton Alumni Fellowship 1967; Outstanding Alumnus Award, Hampton Inst, 1974; Univ of CT Foundation Fellowship 1984. **MILITARY SERVICE:** AUS 2nd lt 1954-56, 1st lt 1956-; honorable discharge 1957. **HOME ADDRESS:** 154 Chicory Dr, Wolcott, CT 06716.

EVANS-DODD, THEORA ANITA
Educator, administrator. **PERSONAL:** Born Sep 11, 1945, Chicago, IL; daughter of Theodore Evans and Lucille Jackson Evans; divorced; children: Victor Cortez, Theodore Artez, Kimberly Toirelle, Karetha Anita. **EDUCATION:** Loyola Univ, Chicago IL, BS, 1976, MSW, 1978; Univ of Illinois, Chicago IL, MPH, 1987. **CAREER:** Univ of Chicago Hospitals, Chicago IL, project dir, 1980-81; Merrill, Lynch, Pierce, Fenner & Smith, Chicago IL, account exec, 1981-89; Rush Presbyterian St Luke's Medical Center, Adolescent Family Center, Chicago IL, unit coordinator/faculty, 1984-86; Northeastern Illinois Univ, Chicago IL, visiting lecturer, 1985-87; Illinois MCH Coalition, Springfield IL, exec dir, 1987-; Univ of Iowa, Iowa City IA, clinical asst prof, 1988-. **ORGANIZATIONS:** Mem, Chicago Chapter, Natl Assn of Black Social Workers, 1976-; vice pres, Iowa State Bd, Natl Assn of Social Workers, 1980-89; mem, Natl Urban League, NAACP; sec, Chicago Loop Bd, YWCA, 1982-86; mem, soror, Alpha Kappa Alpha Sorority, 1983-; comm mem, Chicago Plan Advisory Commn, 1985-86; mem, Women Health Exec Network, 1986-, Amer Public Health Assn, 1986-; consultant, Natl Healthy Mothers, Healthy Babies, 1988; bd mem, Mayor's Youth Employment Program, 1989-. **HONORS/ACHIEVEMENTS:** Fellowship Award, Loyola Univ of Chicago, 1976; Merit & Achievement Award, Chicago Bd of Educ, 1978. **BUSINESS ADDRESS:** Clinical Asst Prof/Dir of Field Education, University of Iowa, School of Social Work, 308 North Hall, Iowa City, IA 52242.

EVANS-MCNEILL, ELONA ANITA
Consultant. **PERSONAL:** Born Nov 22, 1945, Washington, DC; daughter of Julius Wilherspoon Evans and Angelisa Stewart Evans; divorced. **EDUCATION:** Howard Univ, attended 1963-64; Graduate School US Agricultural Dept, attended 1965-66; Amer Univ, attended 1969-72. **CAREER:** Community Govt Relations, consultant 1983-85; Washington Healthcare Man Corp, comm/govt relations consultant 1981-86; Washington Hospital Center, ambulator services ombudsperson 1986-. **ORGANIZATIONS:** Mem Ward One Democrats 1978-; mem vice chair Bd of Trustee Public Defender Serv 1979-85; vice chair/past chair Adv Neighborhood Comm 1979-86; mediator Citizens Complaint Ctr 1979-; bd mem My Sister's Place Shelter for Battered Women 1980-82; bd mem Calvary Shelter for Women 1982-83; mem DC Democratic State Comm 1984-88; mem Student Non-Violent Coord Comm; Red Cross volunteer Washington Hosp Ctr psychiatric ward; mem DC Women's Political Caucus 1979; past pres & past treas Natl Steering Comm; mem, Natl Real Estate Educators Assn; mem, Natl Assn of Real Estate License Law Officials, 1988-91; commissioner, DC Real Estate Commission, 1988-91. **HONORS/ACHIEVEMENTS:** Gettysburg Symposium Rep "Panorama"; Amer Univ Repres 1970 Gettysburg Symposium; recipient Scholastic Excellence Awards Amer Univ 1970-71; recipient Outstanding Comm Volunteer Award Black Policemen's Assn 1980. **HOME ADDRESS:** 3055 16th St NW, Washington, DC 20009.

EVE, ARTHUR O.
Elected govt. official. **PERSONAL:** Born 1933, New York, NY; married Lee Constance Bowles; children: Arthur Jr, Leecia Roberta, Eric Vincent, Martin King, Malcolm X. **EDUCATION:** Erie Comm Coll, Associate; WV State Coll, BSS. **CAREER:** NY State Assembly, assemblyman 1966-. **ORGANIZATIONS:** Estab First School Health Demon Project; chmn NY State Black & Puerto Rican Leg Caucus 1975,76; 1st black to win a major party's primary for Mayor 1977; Deputy Speaker of the Assembly 1979; founded the Black Develop Found and the Black Business Development Corp; formed the Minority Coalition. **MILITARY SERVICE:** AUS 1953-55. **BUSINESS ADDRESS:** Assembly Member District 141, New York State Assembly, 1373 Fillmore Ave 2nd Fl, Buffalo, NY 14211.

EVE, CHRISTINA M.
Educator. **PERSONAL:** Born Mar 18, 1917, Gainesville, FL. **EDUCATION:** ShawUniv Raleigh NC, AB 1940; NYU, MA 1958;Univ Miami, Postgrad. **CAREER:** Treasure Island Elementary School, Miami Beach FL, prin; Dade Co, dist reading teacher, owner-operator, public steno serv, 1st black prin, white school; 1969; Egelloc Civic & Soc Club, founder. **ORGANIZATIONS:** Mem Sigma Gamma Rho; anti basileus AAUW; Meth Ch; FL Adminstrv & Supr Assn; Assn Supr & Curric Dev; Dade Co Sch Adminstrs Assn; FL prins FL Elem Sch; Dept Elem Sch Prins Citizen of Day Local Radio Sta 1969. **HONORS/ACHIEVEMENTS:** Outstanding serv awards Egolloc Club & Sigma Gamma Rho 1970; awardUniv Miami TTT Proj 1971; award dept elem prins dedicated serv 1973. **BUSINESS ADDRESS:** 7540 E Treasure Dr, Miami Beach, FL 33141.

EVEGE, WALTER L., JR.
Educator. **PERSONAL:** Born Jan 13, 1943, Jackson, MS; son of Walter L Evege Sr and Cletora Carter Evege (deceased); married Dorthy Ruffin Evege, Mar 01, 1974; children: Daryl, Dietrich, Daphine. **EDUCATION:** Tougallo Coll, Tougaloo MS, BS, 1964; Atlanta Univ, Atlanta GA, MBA (one semester), 1969. **CAREER:** Jackson Public Schools, Jackson MS, math teacher, 1964-66; Tougaloo Coll, Tougaloo MS, dir financial aids, 1966-69; The Univ of Akron, Akron OH, asst dir, 1970-80; Community Action Agency, Akron OH, assoc dir, 1980-82; Allstate Insurance Co, Akron OH, sales agent, 1982-87; The Univ of Akron, Akron OH, acting dir, 1987-. **ORGANIZATIONS:** Bd Dir, Alpha Phi Alpha Homes Inc, 1974-85; advisory bd, Cuyahoga Street Area Block Club, 1983-; mem, Music Boosters, Copley-Fairlawn Schools, 1987-, chmn, Levey Comm, 1988-, The Ohio Consortium of Blacks in Higher Educ, 1989-. **HONORS/ACHIEVEMENTS:** Outstanding Young Men of Amer, Natl Jaycees, 1978; Youth Motivational Task, Akron Jaycees, 1979; Top New Sales Agent, Allstate Insurance Co, 1983; Service Award, Alpha Phi Alpha Frat (Eta Tau Lambda), 1980; Black History Brochure, Univ of Akron, 1988; Students at Risk Workshops, 1988-89; Volunteer Ser, Crosby Elementary School, 1989. **BUSINESS ADDRESS:** Acting Director, Black Cultural Center, University of Akron, 202 E Hall, Akron, OH 44325-1801.

EVERETT, BENJAMIN A.
Physician. **PERSONAL:** Born Aug 01, 1933, Columbia, SC; married Barbara; children: Lauren. **EDUCATION:** Univ MI, BS 1954; Meharry Med Coll, MD 1958. **CAREER:** MLK Hosp, intrnst 1973-; Watlis Hlth Found, 1985; Charles Drew Post Grad Sch, asst prof 1968-70; USN Dispensary, chf, pro srv 1968-70; Long Bch City Hlth Dept, asst hlth ofcr, chf 1963-64. **ORGANIZATIONS:** Mem Nat Med Assn; Am Coll Phys; Am Coll Chest Phys; diplomate Am Bd Intrnal Med; flw Am Coll Chest Phys. **MILITARY SERVICE:** USNR cmdr 1968-70. **BUSINESS ADDRESS:** 2051 E 103rd St, Los Angeles, CA 90002.

EVERETT, DAVID LEON, II
Clergyman. **PERSONAL:** Born Sep 19, 1922, Giddings, TX; married Doris Naomi Raymond. **EDUCATION:** Samuel Huston Coll, AB 1943; Gammon Theol Sem, BD 1946;Univ Oslo, Grad Sch Cert 1955; Union Inter-bapt, MTh 1962; Prairie A&M U, MEd 1974; Union Bapt Theol Sem, DDiv 1958; Union-inter-bapt, DLaws 1964. **CAREER:** Bethesda Bapt & Ch, minister 1947-50; Ebenezzar Bapt Ch, 1949-50; Mt Zion Missionary Bapt Ch, 1950-57; Jerusalem Missionary Bapt Ch, 1957-. **ORGANIZATIONS:** Bd educ Houston Indpndnt Sch Dist 1969-; exec dir Conf Minority Concerns; Shriner 32 Deg; pres bd trustees Houston Comm Coll Sys; mem Omega Psi Phi Frat; Ministers Assn; Nat Geographic Soc; assn for Study Afr-am Life & History; newspaper columnist, poet, author, awards; frontiersmen, Nat Council Negro Women; Cinco De Mayo 1972; Huston-tillotson Alumni 1972; Distinguished Distinguished Alumnus Prairie View 1974. **HONORS/ACHIEVEMENTS:** Citizen of yr 1973; citation KYOK Radio Homestead Bank; plaque forgive inc 1974; comm serv award progressive amateur & Bosing assn 1973. **BUSINESS ADDRESS:** Resident Pastoral Minister, Jerusalem Missionary Bapt Ch, 2201 Tuam Ave, Houston, TX 77004.

EVERETT, J. RICHARD
Attorney. **PERSONAL:** Born Oct 02, 1936, Montezuma, GA; married Bernice Knowings; children: Jocelyn, Jeannenn. **EDUCATION:** Morehouse Coll, BS 1960; St John's Univ Law Sch, LLB 1967; Patent Offices Patent Academy, US 1968. **CAREER:** Food & Drug Admin, analytical chemist 1961-66; Food & Legal Officer, 1966-77; Eastman Kodak Co, admin asst, 1974-76; US Patent Office, patent exam, 1967-69, patent attorney, 1969-79, sr attorney, 1980-. **ORGANIZATIONS:** Mem Am Bar Assn; NY State Bar; Monroe Co Bar Assn; Rochester Patent Law Assn; Nat Bar Assn; Nat Patent Law Assn Volunteer Atty Monroe Co Bar Assn; Legal Assistance Corp; Rochester Bus Oppor Corp & Urban League Panel; mem NY State Public Employees Bd; co-dir Patent Awareness Program; former pres of bd Urban League of Rochester; former v chmn United Comm Chest; mem bd Banker's Trust. **MILITARY SERVICE:** USN e-5 1954-57. **BUSINESS ADDRESS:** 343 State St, Rochester, NY 14650.

EVERETT, PERCIVAL L.
Dentist. **PERSONAL:** Born Aug 01, 1933, Columbia, SC; married Dorothy L; children: Percival II, Vivian. **EDUCATION:** Allen Univ, BS 1955; Meharry Med Coll, DDS 1962. **CAREER:** State Park Health Center Columbia, stf dntst 1962-68; Self Employed, dentst. **ORGANIZATIONS:** Am Dental Assn; SC Dental Assn; Central Dist Dental Soc; Congaree Med Dental & Phar Soc; Palmetto Med Dental & Pharm Soc City of Columbia bd of Health; Greater Columbia C of C; Civilian Military Liason Com mem trustee Capital City Devel Found; SC Commn on Human Affairs; United Way Agency Relations bd; SC C of C; Alpha Phi Alpha Frat. **HONORS/ACHIEVEMENTS:** Whos Who in Am SE 1969. **MILITARY SERVICE:** AUS spec first class 1956-58. **BUSINESS ADDRESS:** 2124 Washington St, Columbia, SC 29204.

EVERETT, RALPH B.
Attorney. **PERSONAL:** Born Jun 23, 1951, Orangeburg, SC; son of Francis G S Everett Jr and Alethia Hilton Everett; married Gwendolyn Harris, Jun 22, 1974; children: Jason G. **EDUCATION:** Morehouse Coll, BA 1973; Duke Univ Law School, JD 1976. **CAREER:** NC Dept of Justice, assoc attorney general 1976; NC Dept of Labor, admin asst for legal affairs 1976-77; Senator Fritz Hollings, spec asst 1977-78, legislative asst 1978-83; US Senate, comm on commerce, sci & transportation, attny, democratic chief counsel, staff dir 1983-86; US Senate, comm on sci & transportation chief counsel and staff dir 1987-. **ORGANIZATIONS:** Mem NC & DC Bars; admitted to US Dist Court for DC; US Court of Appeals for DC Court; US Tax Court; US Court of Claims; US Supreme Court; mem Amer Bar Assoc, Alpha Phi Alpha; mem, Alumni Board of Visitors, Duke Univ Law School. **HONORS/ACHIEVEMENTS:** Phi Beta Kappa; Phi Alpha Theta Intl Hon Soc in History. **HOME ADDRESS:** 1937 Shiver Dr, Alexandria, VA 22307. **BUSINESS ADDRESS:** Chief Counsel/Staff Dir, US Senate, Comm on Commerce Sci & Trans, Washington, DC 20510.

EVERS, JAMES CHARLES
Mayor. **PERSONAL:** Born Sep 11, 1922, Decatur, MS; divorced; children: Pat, Carolyn, Eunice, Sheila, Charlene. **EDUCATION:** Alcorn State U, BS 1951. **CAREER:** Fayette MS, mayor 1969-; MS State Senate, cand 1975; MS, cand Gov 1971; US House Reps, candidate 1968; MS NAACP, field secy 1963-69; Medgar Evers Fund, pres founder 1969-. **ORGANIZATIONS:** Mem Dem Nat Com; adv bd Black Enterprise Mag; exec com MS Municipal Assn; bd dirs SW MS Planning & Devel Dist; Govs Manpower Conf 1974-; NAACP Recipient Nine Hon Degrees Humanities; Social Sci; Philosophy Jurisprudence. **HONORS/ACHIEVEMENTS:** EVERS Author 1970; man of yr award NAACP 1969; MS Lectr Colls Univs Sociology & Humanities 1964-. **MILITARY SERVICE:** AUS sgt maj 1946. **BUSINESS ADDRESS:** President, Medgar Evers Funds Inc, PO Box 158, Fayette, MS 39069.

EVERS, MYRLIE
Civil rights leader, author. **CAREER:** Claremont Coll CA, asst dir educ opportunity 1967-. **ORGANIZATIONS:** Active in NAACP. **HONORS/ACHIEVEMENTS:** Author "For Us the Living" 1967. **BUSINESS ADDRESS:** c/o NAACP, 1072 W Lynch St, Jackson, MS.

EWELL, RAYMOND W.
Legislator. **PERSONAL:** Born Dec 29, 1928, Chicago, IL; married Joyce Marie; children: David, Marc, Raymond. **EDUCATION:** Univ IL, BA 1949;Univ IL, MA 1950;Univ Chgo, LLB 1954. **CAREER:** IL Gen Assembly 29th Dist, legislator 1966-; Chgo, practicing atty; Chgo, tchr pub shcs. **ORGANIZATIONS:** Mem Cook Co Bar Asn; mem bd Chicago Conf to Fulfill These Rights; Fed Pub & Defender Program; mem NAACP; YMCA. **BUSINESS ADDRESS:** 9415 S State St, Chicago, IL 60619.

EWERS, JAMES BENJAMIN, JR.
Educator. **PERSONAL:** Born Sep 29, 1948, Winston-Salem, NC; married Bonita Maria Taylor; children: Christopher. **EDUCATION:** Johnson C Smith Univ, BA 1970; Catholic Univ of Amer, MA 1971; Univ of MA, EdD 1980. **CAREER:** Washington DC Public Schools, teacher 1971-75; Stockton State Coll, asst dir of admissions 1976-1978; Univ of MD Eastern Shore, dir of admin & registrar 1978-84; Livingstone Coll, vice pres for student affairs 1984-. **ORGANIZATIONS:** Mem Ntl Assoc of Personnel Wkrs 1985-; mem Phi Kappa Phi 1983-; mem Amer Assoc for Counseling Devel 1982-; mem Ntl Assoc of Foreign Student Affairs 1981-; mem NAACP 1983-; mem Alpha Phi Alpha 1967-; mem Salisbury/Rowan Human Rel Cncl 1985-. **HONORS/ACHIEVEMENTS:** Using Alumni to Recruit Students Black Issues In Higher Educ 1986; Who's Who In The East 1985; Who's Who Among

Human Services Professionals 1986. **BUSINESS ADDRESS:** VP for Student Affairs, Livingstone College, Dodge Hall, Salisbury, NC 28144.

EWING, BARBARA LEE
Educator. **PERSONAL:** Born May 26, 1945, Sequin, TX; married Sgt Richard T. **EDUCATION:** TX Luth Coll, BA 1967; SW TX St U, MEd 1974. **CAREER:** Houston Indep Sch Dist, tchr. **ORGANIZATIONS:** Pres Sequin HS PTA; sec Comm Counc of So Cen TX; bd chmn Zenobian Child Plcmnt Ctr; vice pres Sequin Classroom Tchrs; mem Sequin City Counc 1972-76; Sequin C of C 1972-74; Delta Kappa Gamma; NEA; TSTA; NAACP; leg com TX Municipal Leag. **HONORS/ACHIEVEMENTS:** 1st blk ever elected to Sequin City Counc; 1st woman ever elected to counc; Am Outst Yng Wmn 1977. **BUSINESS ADDRESS:** 815 Lamar, Seguin, TX 78155.

EWING, JOHN R.
Musician. **PERSONAL:** Born Jan 19, 1917, Topeka, KS; married Vivian. **CAREER:** Disneyland Teddy Buckner Band, trombonist; Lucy Show with Lucille Ball, 1970-74; Sinah Washington, Sam Cooke, Nancy Wilson, Diane Ross, & Others, recorded with; Cab Calloway Band, 1946; Jimmie Luncford, 1943-45; Earl Hinesband, 1938-41.

EWING, MAMIE HANS
Government administrator. **PERSONAL:** Born Aug 15, 1939, Houston, TX; married Robert; children: Steve, Perry. **EDUCATION:** Univ of TX Austin, BA 1960; Prairie View A&M U, MEd 1974. **CAREER:** TX Dept of Human Resources, regl admnstr 1978-; TX Dept of Human Resources, fld liason ofcr 1977-78; TX Dept of Human Resources, dir Civil Rights 1975-77; TX Dept of Human Resources, dir & EEO 1973-75; Austin Neighborhood Youth Corps, div exec dir 1972-73; TX Dept of Human Resources, supr Child Welfare div 1969-71. **ORGANIZATIONS:** Bd dir Tarrant Co United Way 1979-80; mem Nat Assn of Social Workers; mem Assn of Black Social Workers; mem Alpha Kappa Alpha Sorroity; mem Jack & Jill; mem MAACP. **HONORS/ACHIEVEMENTS:** Recipient meritorious serv award Travis Co Child Welfare bd 1971; trailbazer of the yr award Bus & Professional Womens Assn of Tarrant Co 1979; achievement award Assn of Black Social Workers 1979.

EWING, PATRICK
Professional athlete. **PERSONAL:** Born Aug 05, 1962, Kingston, Jamaica. **EDUCATION:** Georgetown Univ, BA 1985. **CAREER:** New York Knickerbockers, center. **ORGANIZATIONS:** Lead US Bsktbl Team to Gold in Olympics 1984; New York City Bd of Educ "Drop Out Prevention Pgm" 1985; Leading All-Time Rebounder & Shot Blker in Georgetown History; NCAA Most Valuable Player 1984; Big East Conf Co-Player of the Year 1984-85. **HONORS/ACHIEVEMENTS:** Mem US Olympic Gold Medal winning team 1984; NBA first draft choice 1985; NAISMITH 1985; Kodak Awd 1985; Rupp Trophy 1985; 3 time All-Amer Bsktball Select 1983-84; UPI and AP First Team All American; named "Met Life" Knick of the Year; mem 36th NBA All Star Team. **BUSINESS ADDRESS:** New York Knickerbockers, Madison Square Garden Center, 4 Pennsylvania Plaza, New York, NY 10001.

EWING, RUSS
Reporter. **PERSONAL:** Born Dec 28, 1933, Chicago, IL; married Ruth. **EDUCATION:** Northwestern Univ, BA 1968. **CAREER:** Professional musician; WMAQ-TV, radio desk editor radio news writerTV reporter 1968-; NBC News Channel 5 Chicago, investigative reporter. **HONORS/ACHIEVEMENTS:** Jacob Scher Awd 1969; Amer Bar Assn Gavel Awd; United Press Intl Enterprise Reporting Awd; Emmy 1974; YMCA Excellence Black Achiever. **MILITARY SERVICE:** USN radioman 2nd class. **BUSINESS ADDRESS:** Reporter, NBC News Merchandise Mart, 222 Merchandise Mart Plaza, Chicago, IL 60654.

EWING, WILLIAM JAMES
Attorney. **PERSONAL:** Born Sep 10, 1936, New York. **EDUCATION:** Seton Hall Law Sch, LLB 1963. **CAREER:** Essex County Prosecutors Office, atty; CBS Aspen Systems Corp, legal cmptrs corp exec. **ORGANIZATIONS:** Mem NJ State Am Nat Bar Assns; Concerned Legal Asso of NJ; reg dir Young Lawyers Sect Nat Bar Assn; mem Attys for Montclair; NAACP; exec bd Montclair Urban Coalition. **HONORS/ACHIEVEMENTS:** Outstndg Man Of Yr 1973. **BUSINESS ADDRESS:** 363 Bloomfield Ave, Montclair, NJ.

EXUM, THURMAN MCCOY
Business executive. **PERSONAL:** Born Mar 29, 1947, Seven Springs, NC; married Wanda R Edwards; children: Thurman Jr, Jermaine. **EDUCATION:** A&T State Univ, BS Auto Tech 1965-69; CO State Univ, 1983-84; NIASE, Auto Service Excellence ID#23880-3862 1985, MS Indust Ed 1986. **CAREER:** Buick Div GM, dist ser mgr 1971-78; GM Training Ctr, instructor 1978-79; Pat Mullery Buick, dir of service 1979; No VA Comm Coll, instructor/auto 1980-81; Metro Auto Emission Serv Inc, pres 1981-. **ORGANIZATIONS:** Consultant Natl Home Study Council 1981-82; consultant NJ Comm Coll 1981; consultant Texaco Oil Co 1981; vice pres Council Auto Apprent Coord 1982-83; consultant CO State Univ 1983-84; coord Natl Auto Dev Assoc 1983; mem MD Quality Assurance Moratorium 1984; consultant DC Dept Transportation 1981-; consultant St of VA 1982-; mem No Amer Emissions Control Conf 1982-; coord St of MD Vehicle Admin 1984-. **HONORS/ACHIEVEMENTS:** Instr Certification Dept State Police VA 1981; Cert of Achievement MD State/EPA 1983; "Making It" article Black Enterprise Magazine 1984; dev course curric DC and State of MD for emissions train current use. **HOME ADDRESS:** 1818 Sharpe Road, Greensboro, NC 27406. **BUSINESS ADDRESS:** President, Metro Auto Emmissions Serv Inc, 8861 Walker Mill Rd, Capitol Heights, MD 20743.

EZELL, WILLIAM ALEXANDER
Veterinarian. **PERSONAL:** Born Nov 18, 1924, Kansas City, MO; married Ina; children: William, Ruth, Wayman, Paul. **EDUCATION:** KS State Coll, Univ of NE, DVM, 1946. **CAREER:** Inkster Animal Hosp, owner, 1950; Detroit Health Dept, sr veterinary inst, 1948-50; Tuskegee Coll Veterinary Med, head dept, Physiology, 1947. **ORGANIZATIONS:** Past Secretary, pres, Bd of Educ, 1954-75; Inkster Lib Commn, 1957-75; Life mem, past pres Alpha Phi Alpha Fraternity, 1966-; exec bd, Wayne County School Bd Assn, 1967-73; mem/past pres SE MI Vet Med Assn 1972-; Vet Alumni Council MI State Univ, 1973-77; bd of dir, MI Humane Soc United Found/African Am Art Gallery; Lay Reader Episcopal Church Diocese MI; mem Am Veternary Med Assn/Am Animal Hosp; Assn/MI Vet Med Assn-found Soc of Detroit Inst of Arts; life mem NAACP; Apptd MI bd of vet Examiners Gov Milliken 1980; Reso-

lution of Recognition, State of MI House of Legislature 1972; Recognized Am Heritage Rsch Assn Lib of Human Resources 1975; dist mem Editorial bd. **HONORS/ACHIEVEMENTS:** Dr Wm Ezell Educ Day City of Inkster, 1976; Certificate of Appreciation, William Milliken, 1976; Special Tribute State Sen David Plawecki 12th Dist 1976; Outstanding Community Serv Award SE MI Veterinary Med Assn, 1977; Published articles in Veterinary Journal. **MILITARY SERVICE:** AUS 1944-45. **BUSINESS ADDRESS:** 28438 Michigan Ave, Inkster, MI 48141.

EZIEMEFE, GODSLOVE AJENAVI
Coal transfer company executive. **PERSONAL:** Born Dec 10, 1955, Ilue-Ologbo, Nigeria;son of Felix and Margaret; married Carolyn Fay Brown; children: Edita, Nicole, Ajenavi. **EDUCATION:** Maritime Coll SUNY, B Engrg 1979; Univ of New Orleans, MBA 1981. **CAREER:** Electro-Coal, asst mgr of maint 1981-85; Ace Enterprises, consultant/proprietor 1985-87; Electro-Coal Transfer, mgr of maint 1985-88; International Marine Terminal, mgr of maintenance & engineering 1988-. **ORGANIZATIONS:** Mem Amer Inst of Plant Engrs 1986-; mem Assoc of Nigerian Profls 1986-; mem New Orleans Anti-Aparthied Coalition 1986-. **HOME ADDRESS:** 2028 Sugarloaf Dr, Harvey, LA 70058.

F

FABRE, EDWIN G.
Attorney. **PERSONAL:** Born Mar 13, 1945, Brooklyn, NY. **EDUCATION:** City Coll of NY, BA 1968;Univ of MI Law Sch, JD 1971; Wayne StateUniv Law Sch, LLM 1974. **CAREER:** International Union USW, asst gen counsel. **ORGANIZATIONS:** Mem Nat Bar Assn; chmn of labor Law Section; State Bar of MI mem Labor Section; Am Bar Assn; mem Labor Section. **BUSINESS ADDRESS:** Right, Fabne, Reed & Whitfield, 531 Ford Building, Detroit, MI 48226.

FABRICE See SIMON, FABRICE JULE

FADULU, SUNDAY O.
Educator. **PERSONAL:** Born Nov 11, 1940, Ibadan, Nigeria;married Jacqueline F; children: Sunday Jr, Tony. **EDUCATION:** OK, BS, MS, & PhD 1969. **CAREER:** TX Southern Univ, asst prof 1972-; Univ of OK School of Medicine, res assoc Hematology 1970-71; Univ of Ife Nigeria, rsch drug unit 1969-70; Univ of Nigeria, lecturer pharmaceutical microbiology 1969-70. **ORGANIZATIONS:** Mem Sigma Xe 1968; Beta Beta Beta Biol Hon Soc 1973; Med Mycological Soc of Ams 1974; Intl Soc for Hum & Animal Mycology 1975; mem Friends of Youth Houston TX 1975; Nat Inst of Sci Beta Kappa Chi; mem Nat Geog Soc 1973; Smithsonian Inst Recip Fac Res Grant Urban Resources Cntr Sickle Cell Research; Minority Biomedical Res Nat Inst of Health. **BUSINESS ADDRESS:** Biol Dept TX So Univ, 3201 Wheeler Ave, Houston, TX 77004.

FAGAN, HAROLD LEONARD
Business executive. **PERSONAL:** Born Jul 09, 1920, Oklahoma City, OK; married Salli E; children: James, Elizabeth. **EDUCATION:** Life Underwriters Training Coun, 1954; Layers Sch, 1970; Limra Mgmt Sch, 1970; Limra Agency Officers Sch, 1973. **CAREER:** Atlanta Life Ins Co, asst vice pres area dir; Post Tribune Newspaper, pres & publisher 1963-72. **ORGANIZATIONS:** Bishop Coll bd of mgmt 1973-74; Dallas Urban League 1974-75; YMCA Park S 1970-74. **HONORS/ACHIEVEMENTS:** Man of yr award; president club Seven Times. **BUSINESS ADDRESS:** 2606 Forest Ave, Ste 206, Dallas, TX.

FAGBAYI, MUTIU OLUTOYIN
Business research analyst. **PERSONAL:** Born Jan 09, 1953, Lagos, Nigeria;married Patricia Ann Russell; children: Jumoke, Yinka. **EDUCATION:** Univ of Dayton, BChE (Cum Laude) 1976; Penn State Univ, MSChE 1978. **CAREER:** Eastman Kodak Co, rsch scientist 1978-85; sr business rsch analyst 1985-. **ORGANIZATIONS:** Mem Webster Rotary Club 1982-; sec Webster Rotary Club 1983-84; pres Rochester Chap Natl Org for the Professional Advancement of Black Chemists and Chem Engrs 1983-; bd of trustees Webster Montessori Sch 1984-86; mem exec bd NOBCChE 1986-; mem Tau Beta Pi Engrg Natl Honor Soc; admin NOBCCHE Long-Range Strategic Plan 1987-92. **HONORS/ACHIEVEMENTS:** United Way Volunteer Service Excellence Awd NOBCChE 1986 (presented to Rochester Chap for its Adopt-a-School Science Prog). **HOME ADDRESS:** 15 Old Westfall Rd, Rochester, NY 14625. **BUSINESS ADDRESS:** Sr Business Rsch Analyst, Eastman Kodak, 343 State St, Rochester, NY 14650.

FAGIN, DARRYL HALL
Management official. **PERSONAL:** Born May 18, 1942, Washington, DC; married Susan; children: Elizabeth Peggy, Adam Vincent. **EDUCATION:** Olivet Coll, BA 1968; GWU Nat Law Cntr, JD 1971. **CAREER:** US Treas Dept of Treas, asst; US House of Reps, leg asst subcom On employ oppt 1978-79; Equal Employ Oppt Commn, law clk 1977-78; Am Security Bank, legal rsrchr for asso counsel 1975-77; Judge Sorrell,Superior Ct DC, law clk 1974-75; Indsl Bank of WA, loan ofcr & asst cshr 1973-74; Black Students Union Olivet Coll, chrtr pres 1968. **ORGANIZATIONS:** Mem Lawyers Com DC Arts Commn 1971; mem Pub Protection Com Met Bd of Trade 1976. **HONORS/ACHIEVEMENTS:** Legal fellowship award; Reginal Huber Smith community law fellowship Washington DC 1971. **BUSINESS ADDRESS:** Dept of the Treas, 15th & PA Ave NW, Washington, DC 20220.

FAILS, MADINE HESTER
Executive director. **PERSONAL:** Born Jun 12, 1953, Sharon, PA; married Harold Vernon. **EDUCATION:** Slippery Rock State Coll Political Sci, BA 1975. **CAREER:** Shenango Valley Urban League, exec dir 1979-; Shenango Valley Urban League, educ dir 1975-79; PA Dept of Comm Affairs, stud admin intern 1974. **ORGANIZATIONS:** Bd of dir Shenango Valley C of C; adv com Mercer Co Consortium Svcs; pres of bd Shenango Valley Primary Hlth Care Cntr. **HONORS/ACHIEVEMENTS:** Who's Who Among Studs in Am Coll &Univ Slippery Rock State Coll 1974; outstdg young women in Am 1975; comm serv award Mercer Co Frontiers Club Intl 1976.

FAIR, FRANK T.
Minister. **PERSONAL:** Born Oct 19, 1929, Clinton, SC; son of Leo Fair (deceased) and Vetda Thomas (Fair) Bell (deceased); married Thelma Belton, Dec 22, 1956; children: Frank Thomas II, Tamera Lee, Donna Machelle Conn, Selwyn Tyrelle. **EDUCATION:** Benedict Coll, 1950; Crozer Sem, M Div 1955; Gammon Sem, STM 1959; Eastern Baptist Seminary Philadelphia, DMin 1979. **CAREER:** New Hope Bapt Church, pastor 1961-; Farrow-Croft Mental Hosp, chaplin 1959-61; JJ Starks Schl of Theol, tchr 1957-61; Benedict Ext Serv for Min, tchr 1957-61; Royal Bapt Church, pstr 1955-61; SC Area Trade Sch, chaplin & teacher 1951-52; Gethsemane Assn of Natl Bapt Conv Inc, ordained to minister; Am Bapt Conv, min 1961-; Montco OIC, exec dir. **ORGANIZATIONS:** Deputy dir of Montgomery Cnty Oppor Indsl Ctr Inc 1973-80; exec dir Montgomery County Oppor Indsl Cntr 1980-; past pres Norristown Area Coun of Churches 1970-72; mem bd of dir Dept of Pub Assist 1971-; lay adv Cent Montgomery Tech Schl 1972; mem Norristown Area Schl & Discipline Comm 1973-, Norristown Area Manpower Coun 1974-, Masons; chairperson bd of dirs Selective Service System #107 1982-89; chairperson Interdenominational Clergy Energy Council 1985-; bd of dirs Habitat for Humanities, Norristown PA 1988-. **HONORS/ACHIEVEMENTS:** Author "Orita for Black Youth" 1977. **BUSINESS ADDRESS:** Executive Dir, Montco OIC, Arch & E Basin Sts, Norristown, PA 19401.

FAIR, RONALD L.
Author. **PERSONAL:** Born Oct 27, 1932, Chicago, IL; married Neva June Keres; children: Rodney D, Glen A. **EDUCATION:** Attended Stenotype School 1953-55. **CAREER:** Chicago Courts, court reporter 1955-66; Encyclopedia Britt, writer 1967; Columbia Coll Chicago, instructor 1967-68; Northwestern Univ, instructor 1968; Wesleyan Univ, visit fellow 1969-70; writer/poet. **HONORS/ACHIEVEMENTS:** Author of, "Many Thousand Gone, An American Fable" 1965; "Hog Butcher" 1975; "World of Nothing, Two Novellas" 1970; "We Can't Breathe" 1972; "Excerpts" 1975; "Rufus" 1977; Selected Periodical Publications, "Excerpts from Voices, The Afro-Americans" Black American Literature Forum 13 1979; "Fellow Writers Comment on Clarence Major's Work A Review of All-Night Visitors" Black American Literature Forum 1979; "The Domestic" Black American Literature Forum 1980; "The Walk" Callaloo 1980.

FAIR, TALMADGE W.
Association executive. **PERSONAL:** Born Jan 15, 1939, Winston-Salem, NC. **EDUCATION:** Johnson C Smith Univ, BA Sociology 1961; Atlanta Univ School of Social Work, MSW 1963. **CAREER:** Urban league of Greater Miami Inc, assoc dir 1963, pres & ceo 1964-. **ORGANIZATIONS:** Pres Miami Varsity Club 1978-; mem Miami Citizens Against Crime Exec Comm 190-; pres Comm Blacks in Org Labor 1981-; mem FL Reg Coord Council for Vocational Ed 1984-88, Beacon Council Organizational Task Force 1985. **HONORS/ACHIEVEMENTS:** Outstanding Dedicated Serv Troop 40 Boy Scouts of Amer 1984; Appreciation Awd Martin Luther King Dev Corp 1984; Gratitude Valuable Contrib Econ Oppty Family Health Ctr 1984; Appreciation Awd Progressive Firefighters Assoc 1985.

FAIRFAX, ROGER ANTHONY
Administrator. **PERSONAL:** Born Mar 05, 1951, Washington, DC; married Charlene; children: Roger Jr, Virginia, Christopher, Justin. **EDUCATION:** Econ Harvard U, BA 1975. **CAREER:** Urban League of Pittsburgh Inc, dep exec dir; Ofc of Allegheny Co Cmnr Pittsburgh, exec asst 1976-78; The Sanctuary Inc Cambridge MA, asso dir 1975-76; HarvardUniv Cambridge, spl proj asst 1974-75; PBA Drug Abuse Ctr Inc Pittsburgh, dir rsrch & evaluation 1971-73. **ORGANIZATIONS:** Bd mem PBA Drug Abuse Cntr 1978-; bd mem Bus & Job Devel Corp 1979-; bd mem Penn Group Health Plan 1979-; chmn of the bd Black Cath Ministries & Laymens Council 1979-; treas Kay & Shadyside Boys Clubs 1979-; chmn Finance Com Ozanam Cultural Cntr 1979-. **HONORS/ACHIEVEMENTS:** Fifty Young Black "Leaders of the Future" Ebony Mag 1978; Excellence in the Field of Human Serv Allegheny Co Young Black Rep 1978; outstanding achievement award Talk Mag 1978; outstanding Young Men of Am US Jaycees 1980. **BUSINESS ADDRESS:** Urban League of Pittsburgh Inc, 200 Ross St, Pittsburgh, PA 15219.

FAIRLEY, RICHARD L.
Government official. **PERSONAL:** Born Jul 16, 1933, Washington, DC; son of Richmond and Gladys; married Charlestine Dawson, Mar 25, 1989; children: Ricki Louise, Sharon Rene. **EDUCATION:** Dartmouth Coll, BA 1956; Stanford U, MA 1969;Univ Massachusetts, EdD 1974. **CAREER:** Office Ed, regional dir 1965-67, broad chief 1967-69, assoc commr 1969-80; Dept Ed, depty assist scty 1980-82, dir inst spt 1982-84, dir mgt serv, dir higher educ prog 1987-. **ORGANIZATIONS:** Ed prog splt USO E/Dept Defense 1961-65; tchr DC Public Schls 1955-61; ed comm Natl Urban League 1968-84; mem Maryland Advisory Comm 1970; US Civil Rghts Comm; mem Kappa Alpha Phi 1975-. **HONORS/ACHIEVEMENTS:** USOE flw 1976; superior serv awd USOE 1968; Bill Cosby awd Univ MA 1982; Doctor of Humane Letters Rust College 1988; Doctor of Humane Letters St. Pauls College 1989. **MILITARY SERVICE:** USAR capt 13. **BUSINESS ADDRESS:** Dir Higher Education Prog, US Dept Education, 400 Maryland Ave SW, Washington, DC 20202.

FAIRLEY, WILMA
Educator. **PERSONAL:** Born Apr 25, 1933, District of Columbia; children: Ricki, Sharon. **EDUCATION:** Stanford U, BA 1970; DC Tchrs Coll, 1956. **CAREER:** Montgomery County Public Schools, EEO officer 1973-; Human Relations, dir 1971-; Human Relations Training, coord 1970-71; language arts teacher, specialist 1969-70; Vario School System, teacher 1960-69; Tots & Teens Inc, past second vice pres. **ORGANIZATIONS:** Nat Alliance of Black Sch Educators; Am Assn of Sch Adminstr; Delta Sigma Theta Sor; Phi Delta Kappa Sor; Pi Lambda Theta Hon Eductrs Sor; Nat Urban Leag; Nat Counc of Negro Women; Takoma Park-silver Spring Comm Found; past bd dir YMCA; past bd mem Nat Girl Scouts; Nat Assn of Human Rights Workers; Elem Prin Assn Led Discussion on Human Relat Training for Eductrs at Nat Conf of Christians & Jews 1977; Exec Report in The Advertiser 1976. **HONORS/ACHIEVEMENTS:** "Back to Basics & Multiculturalism are not Mutually Exclusive" NEA Human Rights Conf; "Creative Solutions to Staff Reduction" AASA; woman of year Montgomery Co 1979; Design & Implemented Multiethnic Convention for Educators & Cnsltnt-Sexism; Presented Paper on Making Integration Work at AASA Conf 1976. **BUSINESS ADDRESS:** 850 Hudgerford Dr, Rockville, MD 20850.

FAIRMAN, JIMMY W.
Corrections superintendent. **PERSONAL:** Born May 20, 1948, Cleveland, MS; married Jeanne Arthur Hester; children: Bridgette, Darrin, Victor. **EDUCATION:** Coahoma Jr Coll, AA 1967; Hardin-Simmons Univ, BS 1970; Chicago State Univ, MS 1975. **CAREER:** Chicago DART Work Release, counselor 1971-72, center supvr 1972-77; IL Dept of Corr Work Release, dep supt 1977-79; Stateville Correct Center, asst supt 1979; Pontiac Correct Center, warden 1979-82; Joliet Correct Center, warden 1982-. **ORGANIZATIONS:** Mem IL Correct Assn 1979-; mem Amer Correct Assn 1980-; mem Natl Assn Blacks in Criminal Justice 1976-. **HOME ADDRESS:** RR 3 Caton Farm Rd, Lockport, IL 60441.

FAIRMAN, JOHN ABBREY
Health care executive. **PERSONAL:** Born Jun 28, 1949, Cleveland, MS; son of Rev Jimmy W Fairman and Luberta Holmes Fairman; divorced; children: Antonio, Tanzala, BeVona, Johnny Abbrey, Quentin Sherrod. **EDUCATION:** Hardin-Simmons Univ, Abilene TX, BS, 1972; Trinity Univ, San Antonio TX, MHA, 1974; Univ of Houston, Houston TX, Certificate, 1975-77. **CAREER:** Hendrick mem Hosp, Abilene TX, business office clerk, 1970-72; Bexar County Hosp, San Antonio TX, purchasing clerk, 1972-73; Nveces County Hosp, Corpus Christi TX, admin resident, 1973-74; Harris County Hosp Dist, Houston TX, asst admin, 1974-76, dep chief admin, 1976-87; Denver Health & Hospitals, Denver CO, mgr/CEO, 1987-. **ORGANIZATIONS:** Bd mem, Hospital Shared Services; bd mem, Harris County Health Facility Dev Board; bd mem, Gulf Coast Hospital Finance Authority Bd; apointee, Grand Jury; babinet mem, Mayor's Cabinet, city of Denver; mem, Greater Denver Chamber of Commerce; mem, Colorado Hospital Assn; mem, Amer Hospital Assn; mem, Natl Assn of Public Hospitals; mem, Natl Assn of Health Services Executives. **BUSINESS ADDRESS:** Manager/CEO, Denver Department of Health and Hospitals, 777 Bannock Street, Denver, CO 80204.

FAISON, HELEN SMITH
Educator. **PERSONAL:** Born Jul 13, 1924, Pittsburgh, PA; married George. **EDUCATION:** Univ Pgh, AB 1946, MEd 1955, PhD 1975. **CAREER:** Pittsburgh Public Schools, asst supt; Allegheny County, bd asst, social caseworker, teacher, girls adv, activites dir, conselor, vice prin, prin. **ORGANIZATIONS:** Mem Nat Cncl Negro Women; past bd mem YWCA; mem Pi Lambda Theta; Admin Women in Edn; Am AssnUniv Women; past chmn State Implementation; past mem bd TstUniv Pittsburgh; Educ TV Sta WQED; Negro Educ Emergency Drive; mem Harriet Tubman Guild Inc. **HONORS/ACHIEVEMENTS:** Bapt Temple Ch Recpt courier top hat award; educator yr award Guardians; Helping Women Advance Professionally AASA/FORD Found 1977; Supt Work Conf ColumbiaUniv 1971. **BUSINESS ADDRESS:** Deputy Supt School Management, Pittsburgh Public Schools, 341 S Bellefield Ave, Pittsburgh, PA 15213.

FAISON, JOHN W.
Business executive. **PERSONAL:** Born May 24, 1908, Northampton Co, NC; married Emily Daniels; children: Linda D Gaither. **EDUCATION:** Freelinghuysen Mortuary, 1932. **CAREER:** Faison's Funeral Home, founder, dir 1960-. **ORGANIZATIONS:** Mem IBPOE of W 1934; (Elk) Masonic Order 1946; pres Northampton Co NAACP 1947-69; Northampton Co Commr 1970-; mem Mt Zion Bapt Ch; deacon of Mt Zion 1958-; treas Mt Zion Ch 1946-; grand auditor Elk Order 1960-70; Masonic Order of NC 1972. **HONORS/ACHIEVEMENTS:** NAACP for work beyond call of duty with register voter dr 1972; Elk Grand Lodge, Grand Exalted Ruler's Honors 1974.

FAISON, THURMAN LAWRENCE
Clergyman. **PERSONAL:** Born Feb 17, 1938, Texarkana, TX; married Dolores Banks; children: Susan, Rebecca, Paul, Elizabeth, Steven, Mark, Deanna. **EDUCATION:** E Pentec Bible Coll, diploma 1963; N Central Bible Coll MN, BA 1972; Natl Coll of Educ, MS Adult Educ 1981. **CAREER:** Emmanuel Assembly of God, minister 1965-68; USN, agent 1967-78; Southside Tabernacle, minister 1968-71; Liberty Natl Life, life ins 1971-72; Chicago Drug Rehab Prog, exec dir Chicago teen challenge 1974-76; Christian Comm of Chicagoland, dir of ministries 1976-; Christian Communications of Chicagoland, charitable gift consul. **ORGANIZATIONS:** Leadership counc mem Evangel Bible Translators Annaheim CA 1978-. **HONORS/ACHIEVEMENTS:** Articles pub "Climate of Change" Pentcostal Evangel 1970; "Concerned with Spiritual Values" Pentecostal Evangel 1972; "What About Our Cities" Pentecostal Evangel 1972; "The Black and the Church" Campus Ambassadors 1974; Outstanding Serv to Christian Educ Evangel Coll 1970; Excellence in Communicating the Christian Gospel through TV Outreach Ministries Chicago 1979. **MILITARY SERVICE:** USAF A/2c 1956-60. **BUSINESS ADDRESS:** Charitable Gift Consultant, Christian Comm of Chicagoland, 20 N Walker Dr, Chicago, IL 60606.

FAKHRID-DEEN, NASHID ABDULLAH
Educator. **PERSONAL:** Born Feb 24, 1949, Monticello, AR; son of N T Thompson and Mary Thompson; married Pauline Rashidah Williamson; children: Jashed, Ayesha, Yasmeen. **EDUCATION:** Grand Valley State Univ, BA 1978; Western MI Univ, grad work 1978-79; Univ of Baltimore, School of Law, JD 1984-88. **CAREER:** Nation of Islam, minister 1975-79; Grand Valley State Univ, asst dir of talent search 1980-83, asst dir of admissions 1979-83; Bowie State Univ, coordinator of recruitment. **ORGANIZATIONS:** General business mgr Nation of Islam 1972-76; mem bd dirs Climbing Tree School 1977-78; mem bd dirs Family Services Outreach 1982-83; mem Mid-America Assn of Educ Oppor Program Personnel; Exec Council Black Law Students, Univ of Baltimore; Admissions/Retention Committee; Moot Court Board, 1986-88; Developer/presentator of CARE (motivational workshop), Baltimore/Washington Metro Area; pres, Black Law Students Assn, Univ of Baltimore School of Law 1987-88. **HONORS/ACHIEVEMENTS:** Outstanding Community Service World Community of Islam 1981, 1982; Grand Valley St Univ, Outstanding Service Talent Search Prgm 1983; Office of Admissions, Outstanding Service Award 1983; Outstanding Community Service, 1980-82; Charles Hamilton Houston Award, Univ of Baltimore Black Law Students Assn 1988. **MILITARY SERVICE:** USAF E-4 Sgt 3 1/2 years. **HOME ADDRESS:** 2233 Aberdeen Dr, Crofton, MD 21114.

FALANA, LOLA
Singer. **PERSONAL:** Born Sep 11, 1943, Camden, NJ. **CAREER:** Dancing jobs on the East Coast; recorded for Frank Sinatra's Reprise Label & Motown Records; Sammy Davis Jr's broadway musical Golden Boy, dancer; ABC TV, 2 specials; appeared in several films; Las Vegas, singer. **HONORS/ACHIEVEMENTS:** She has smashed nearly every Las Vegas nightclub attendance & box office record & is recognized as the First Lady of Las Vegas; author of a book. **BUSINESS ADDRESS:** LaFalana Enterprise, 3422 Happy Ln, Las Vegas, NV 89120.

FALKNER, BOBBIE E.
Automobile dealer. **CAREER:** Falkner Enterprises Inc., Harvey, IL, chief executive. **BUSINESS ADDRESS:** Chief Executive, Falkner Enterprises Inc, P O Box 1634, Harvey, IL 60426. *

FANAKA, JAMAA
Writer, producer, director. **PERSONAL:** Born Sep 06, 1942, Jackson, MS; son of Robert L Gordon and Beatrice Gordon; children: Tracey L, Michael, Katina A, Twyla M. **EDUCATION:** Compton Jr Coll, AA 1971; UCLA, BA (summa cum laude) 1973; UCLA, MFA 1978. **CAREER:** Jamaa Fanaka Prodns Inc, writer/producer/dir (motion pictures) "Penitentiary", "Penitentiary II", "Penitentiary III," "Emma Mae", "Welcome Home Brother Charles" 1974; IBM Corp, customer engr 1968-70; Bethlehem Steel, engineering clk 1964-68. **ORGANIZATIONS:** Pres Black Filmmakers Alliance 1975-79; mem Big Brothers of Am 1980. **HONORS/ACHIEVEMENTS:** Ford Found Grant, Ford Found 1972; Rockefeller Grant, Rockefeller Found 1973; UCLA Chancellor's Grant, UCLA 1973; Am Film Inst Grant, Am Film Inst 1976. **MILITARY SERVICE:** USAF a/1c 1960-64. **BUSINESS ADDRESS:** MGM Studios, Culver City, CA 90230.

FANCHER, EVELYN PITTS
Librarian. **PERSONAL:** Born Jul 12, 1924, Marion, AL; married Charles B; children: Charles, Jr, Mark, Adrienne. **EDUCATION:** AL State Univ, BS 1946; AL Univ, MSLS 1961; Peadody/Vanderbilt Univ, EdS 1969; Peadbody/Vanderbilt Univ, PhD 1975. **CAREER:** Central High, librarian, 1959-62; AL A&M Univ, librarian 1958; TN State Univ, librarian, 1962-75, prof library Sci, 1975, dir libr 1976-. **ORGANIZATIONS:** Lib consult (USAID) Swaziland, Africa 1982; pres TN Lbr Assoc 1984-85; brd mrb TN Advy Cncl Lbrs 1983-89; Girl Scout brd dir Comberland Vly 1980-84; SE Lbry Assoc 1985; Am Lbry Assoc 1987; Mdl TN Lbry Assoc 1987; TN Higher Educ Committee Library Tech Council. **HONORS/ACHIEVEMENTS:** "Educational Technology A Black Perspective" Eric 1984; "Edtg Ethric Minorities" Negro Ed Rev XXV 1974; "College Adm Practices & the Negro Student" Begro Ed Rev XXII 1971; "Merger of TN State Univ & the Univ of TN Libraries" TN Librarian Vol 32 Witner 180. **BUSINESS ADDRESS:** Dir of Libraries, TN State Univ, 3500 Merritt Blvd, Nashville, TN 37203.

FARLEY, WILLIAM HORACE, JR.
Government official. **PERSONAL:** Born Feb 20, 1950, Skowheegan, ME; son of William H Farley, Sr and Laura C Farley; married Gale Foster Farley, Nov 27, 1982; children: William Foster Farley. **EDUCATION:** Yale Univ, BA (cum laude) 1972; Oxford Univ England, Hons BA 1974; Yale Law School; JD 1977. **CAREER:** McDermott, Will & Emery, atty (partner) 1977-86; City of Chicago, First Asst Corp Counsel 1987-89; Chicago Transit Authority, Gen Counsel 1989-. **ORGANIZATIONS:** Bd of Dir, Constitutional Rights Foundation 1985-. **HONORS/ACHIEVEMENTS:** Rhodes Scholarship 1972; contributing author, Architect and Engineer Liability: Claims Against Design Professionals, by John Wiley & Sons 1987. **HOME ADDRESS:** 3200 North Lake Shore, #2811, Chicago, IL 60603. **BUSINESS ADDRESS:** General Attorney, Chicago Transit Authority, 429A Merchandise Mart Plaza, Chicago, IL 60654.

FARLOUGH, H. EUGENE, JR.
Clergyman. **PERSONAL:** Born Jan 04, 1938, New Orleans, LA; married Arlyce Vivianne Johnson; children: Chris-Darnell Eugene, Milynn Leroyce. **EDUCATION:** CA State Poly Coll, BS Soc Sci 1960; San Francisco Theol Sem, MDiv 1965; San Francisco Theol Sem, DMin 1975. **CAREER:** Sojourner Truth United Presb Ch Richmond CA, organizing pastor 1972-; Center for Urban-Black Studies Berkeley CA, asso dir 1970-72; Faith Presb Ch Oakland CA, pastor 1963-70; San Francisco Theol Sem San Anselmo CA, adjunct Prof, counselor 1975-. **ORGANIZATIONS:** Vp E Bay Interdenominaational Ministerial Alliance Oakland CA 1966; chmn bd Richmond Discovery Center (Drug Abuse) 1976; commr Contra Costa Co Human Serv Adv Com 1979-. **HONORS/ACHIEVEMENTS:** All-Am Gymnastic Team, CA State Polytechnic Coll 1959; Who's Who Among Coll &Univ Students, CA State Poly Coll 1960; Father of the Year, Minority Adoption Com Oakland CA 1975; First Black Moderator, San Francisco Presbytery 1979. **MILITARY SERVICE:** AUS 2nd lt 1960-61. **BUSINESS ADDRESS:** 2621 Shane Dr, Richmond, CA 94806.

FARMER, BRUCE ALBERT
Business executive. **PERSONAL:** Born Mar 25, 1957, Rochester, PA. **EDUCATION:** Univ of Pittsburgh, 1975-79; St Vincent Coll, BA 1980; Temple Univ, attended 1982-83. **CAREER:** Marriot Inn, bus coord 1979; Hill Refrigeration, prod schedular 1980-81; William H Rorer, mgr 1981-86; Stadium Enterprises, vice pres 1986-; Transitions Inc,asst program dir 1986-. **ORGANIZATIONS:** Bd mem Amer Forestry Environ 1981; pres consult PA Minorities About Change 1981,82,83,84; reporter/editor Philadelphia Org Devel 1982; pres Cultural Awareness Comm 1983-84; bd mem Montgomery Zoning Commiss 1984-85; mem NAACP, Alpha Phi Alpha, GABT, UNCF. **HONORS/ACHIEVEMENTS:** Pres Rochester HS 1972-75; vice pres Alpha Phi Alpha 1978; Brother of the Year Alpha Phi Alpha 1978; Man of the Year Montgomery Cty Comm on Human Rights 1982. **HOME ADDRESS:** 754 Tennyson Dr, Warminster, PA 18974.

FARMER, CLARENCE
Business executive. **PERSONAL:** Born Jun 19, 1915, Rochester, PA; married Marjorie Nichols; children: Clarence Jr, Franklin. **EDUCATION:** Geneva Coll, AB 1936. **CAREER:** Commn on Human Rel, chmn 1969-; Commn on Human Rel, exec dir 1967-69; Philadelphia Police Adv Bd, exec sec 1965-67. **ORGANIZATIONS:** Chmn fndr Grtr Philadelphia Enter Devel Corp; pres First Loan Co & Farmer Press Inc; exec com Philadelphia Urban Coalition Inc; bd dir Wissahickon Boys' Club; bd dir Founders' Club; bd dir St Joseph's Coll Acad of Food Mkg; bd dir Nat Bonding Serv Found; bd dir Grtr Philadelphia C of C; United-Fund; World Affairs Coun of Phila; Philadelphia Housing Devel Corp; Options for Women Inc; Philadelphia Civic Ballet Co; Cape May Tennis Club; mem Grace Epis Ch; Fellow Commn; NAACP; Urban Leag of Phila; Nat Assn of Intergroup Rel Off; STEM Inc; Philadelphia Adv Coun on Naval Affairs; Geneva Coll Alumni Assn; Alpha Phi Alpha Frat; Benjamin Lodge F & A M; chmn City Employees' Cancer Crusade 1969; v chmn City Employees' Unted Fund Campaign 1969, 71, 72. **HONORS/ACHIEVEMENTS:** Recip North City Congress Awd 1965; Bat Ministers Conf 1965; Travelers' Club Awd 1967; Gardian Civic Leag Awd 1967; Legion of Cornelius 1967; Geneva Coll Distng Serv Awd 1969; Vare Jr High Sch Awd 1969; Philadelphia Barr Assn Achmnt Awd 1969; Coun of Clergy Awd 1972; 100000 Pennsylvanians Awd for Comm Serv 1972; Cardinal's Commn on Human Rel Awd 1972; Alpha Phi Alpha Distng Serv Awd 1971; Richard Allen Awd; Mother Bethel AME Ch 1974; USAAF 1943-45. **MILITARY SERVICE:** USAAF 1943-45. **BUSINESS ADDRESS:** 601 City Hall Annex, Philadelphia, PA 19107.

FARMER, FOREST J.
Automotive executive. **PERSONAL:** Born Jan 15, 1941, Zanesville, OH; married Rosalyn; children: Forest, Jr, Chris. **EDUCATION:** Purdue Univ, Lafayette, IN, BS, 1962. **CAREER:** Chrysler Motors Corp, Detroit MI, Jefferson Assembly Plant plant mgr, 1981, Newark DE assembly plant mgr, 1983, Sterling Heights MI plant mgr, 1984, dir, advance mfg planning, 1986-87, Highland Park MI gen plant mgr, 1987-88; Acustar, Inc, Troy, MI, pres, 1989-. **BUSINESS ADDRESS:** President, Acustar, Inc, 1850 Research Dr, Troy, MI 48083.

FARMER, FRANCESTA ELIZABETH
Government official. **PERSONAL:** Born Oct 28, 1949, Ft Bragg, NC; children: Niambi. **EDUCATION:** Radcliffe Coll, BA 1971; Harvard Law Sch, JD 1974. **CAREER:** Office of Interagency Coordination Equal Employment Opportunity Commn, dir; Ofc for Civil Rights Dept of HEW, dir of intergovernmental affairs 1977-78; Ofc of Sen Edward W Brooke, legislative asst 1975-77; Simpson Thatcher & Bartlett NY, law asso 1974-75; Harvard Radcliffe Afro-Am Cultural Center, dir 1968-69; Newsweek Mag, intern 1970. **ORGANIZATIONS:** Bd of dir Nat Bar Assn 1978-79; mem Nat Conf of Black Lawyers; founder & mem Black Senate Staff Group 1976-78; pres Harvard BALSA 1972-73; bd of dirGirls Clubs of Greater Wash 1978; bd of dir Arts Media Serv 1979-; commnr exec com DC Dommn on Arts & Humanities 1979-. **HONORS/ACHIEVEMENTS:** Nat Achievement Scholar, Nat Merit Found 1967-71; Summer Thesis Award, Kennedy Inst of Politics; Articles on Bakker Case, Change Mag/Nat Urban League Mag. **BUSINESS ADDRESS:** Equal Employ Oppor Comm, 2401 E St NW Rm 4208, Washington, DC 20506.

FARMER, HAROLD E.
Physician, educator. **PERSONAL:** Born Feb 19, 1904, Philadelphia, PA; married Agnes Cherington Speck; children: Carol Cherington Hoskins, Diana Deirdre, Alexander Kenneth Coleman. **EDUCATION:** Univ of PA, AB 1928, MD 1932; Harvard Med Sch, internal med 1938-39; Univ of PA, grad sch med 1951-52; Univ of PA Hosp, resident 1952-55; MA Gen-Hosp, internal med. **CAREER:** Mercy Hosp, intern 1932-33; Mercy Hosp, chief resident 1933-34, staff appointments 1934-51; Henry Pipps Inst Univ of PA, 1934-38; Univ of PA, instr 1955-70; Bryn Mawr Hosp, instr 1955-; PA Hosp, instr internal med 1970-72; Bryn Mawr Hosp, attending physician emeritus 1984; Univ of PA Med Sch, instr. **ORGANIZATIONS:** Sec bd dir Main Line Sch Night Assn; bd dir Family Serv Main Line Neighborhood; vice pres Bd of Health. **HONORS/ACHIEVEMENTS:** Article "Daniel Hale Williams, His Life & Times" 1939; "Revival of Classical Learning, Potent Force" in Negro Prog Journ of Negro Educ 1940; first issue "TheBryn Mawr Hospital Bulletin" assoc editor and continuous contributor in every issue since inauguration. **MILITARY SERVICE:** AUS Cpt. **BUSINESS ADDRESS:** 315 W Wayne Ave, Wayne, PA 19087.

FARMER, JAMES
Educator. **PERSONAL:** Born Jan 21, 1920, Marshall, TX; married Lula Peterson (dec) (deceased); children: Tami, Abbey. **EDUCATION:** Wiley Coll, BS 1938; Howard Univ, BD 1941; Morgan State Coll, HHD 1964. **CAREER:** NAACP, program dir 1959-60; Congress of Racial Equality, founder 1942, natl dir 1961-66; Health Education & Welfare, asst sec 1969-70; Coalition of Amer Public Employees, exec dir 1977-82; Mary Washington Coll, prof of history. **ORGANIZATIONS:** Chmn of the bd Fund for an Open Society 1974-; mem adv bd ACLU 1984-. **HONORS/ACHIEVEMENTS:** Numerous awards including Omega Psi Phi Awd 1961,63; First Citizen Awd Queens Region Hadassah 1969; American Humanist Awd 1976; Author of "Freedom When?" 1966, "Lay Bare the Heart" 1985; many other articles and essays. **HOME ADDRESS:** Route 3 Box 1305, Fredericksburg, VA 22401. **BUSINESS ADDRESS:** Professor of History, Mary Washington College, 1301 College Ave, Fredericksburg, VA 22401.

FARMER, LARRY CLINTON
Educator. **PERSONAL:** Born Jan 31, 1951, Denver, CO. **EDUCATION:** UCLA, BS 1969-73. **CAREER:** UCLA, asst basketball coach 1973-80, head basketball coach 1980-83. **HONORS/ACHIEVEMENTS:** All American UPI, honorable mention 1973; Best in Histroy Basketball Record,.

FARMER, ROBERT CLARENCE
Physician. **PERSONAL:** Born Jan 01, 1941, Rochester, PA; son of Francis A Farmer Sr and Ora Juanita Farmer; married Linda Kay Hill; children: Saundra, Robert, James, Wendy. **EDUCATION:** Howard Univ, BS 1963, MD 1967. **CAREER:** Univ of Pittsburgh, instructor pediatric radiology 1973-74; Howard Univ, asst prof radiology 1974-75, asst prof pediatrics 1974-77; St Anthony Hosp, dir radiology 1977-81; Fayette Co Hospital, dir radiology 1978-83; Ft Stewart Hospital, dir radiology 1980-81; Connellsville State General Hosp, dir radiology 1982-85; Highlands Hospital & Health Ctr, dir radiology 1985-. **ORGANIZATIONS:** Life mem NAACP 1953-; life mem Alpha Phi Alpha Frat; mem Radiology Soc of North Amer 1973-, Natl Medical Assn 1977-, Amer College of Radiology 1978-; mem Amer Cancer Soc 1983-, Bd of Health 1984-; bd dirs Amer Lung Assn 1985-; bd of dirs Comm Housing Resource Bd of Fayette Cty PA; mem FROGS Club of Pittsburgh; pres Fayette County NAACP 1989-; treasurer Gateway Medical Society NMA 1988-. **HONORS/ACHIEVEMENTS:** Publications "Carcinoma of the Breast; A Clinical Study," NMA Journal 1969; "Immunological Responses in Infantile Cortical Hyperostosis," Pediatric Rsch Vol 10 1976; "Immunological Studies in Caffey's Cortical Hyperostosis," Pediatrics 1977; Black Achiever of SW Pennsylvania 11th dist Debora Grand Chapter OES 1988. **MILITARY SERVICE:** AUS capt 1966-68. **BUSINESS ADDRESS:** Dir of Radiology, Highlands Hospital & Hlth Cntr, 401 East Murphy Ave, Connellsville, PA 15469.

FARMER, WILLIE SIDNEY, SR.
Educator. **PERSONAL:** Born Dec 22, 1930, Meridian, MS. **EDUCATION:** Jackson State U, BS 1954;Univ of So MS, MEd 1972;Univ of CO, EdS 1973;Univ of CO, EdD 1976. **CAREER:** MS State Univ, dir of special student servs 1977-, asst prof Educ Leadership 1977-; Jackson State Univ, coord of veterans affairs 1973-77; Univ of CO, intern dean 1973; Gulfport Cty Sch, band dir & social studies teacher 1955-66; Utica Jr Coll, head of music & band dir 1954-55; Picayune Public School, asst prin & band dir 1953-54. **ORGANIZATIONS:** Mem Phi Delta Kappa 1972-; reviewer for journal, So Coll Personnel Assn 1977-; mem Nat Assn

of Student Personnel Adminstrn 1977-; mem Am Coll Personnel Assn 1978-; mem SE Assn of Educ Oppor Prog Personnel 1978-; mem NAACP 1960-; deputy commissioner King Hiriam Grand Lodge 1972-; faculty adv Omega Psi Phi Frat 1977-. **HONORS/ACHIEVEMENTS:** 15 yrs Volunteer Serv Award, VA Hosps 1956-71; 32nd degree Mason, King Hiriam Grand Lodge of MS 1970-; Man of the Yr Award, Omega Psi Phi Frat 1973; recipient of Outstanding Bandsman & Good Conduct Medal 1949. **MILITARY SERVICE:** AUS sgt 3 yrs. **BUSINESS ADDRESS:** Asst Dir/Admissions, MS StateUniv, Drawer E L, Starkville, MS 39762.

FARR, HERMAN
Clergyman. **PERSONAL:** Married Bruetta Dupre; children: 4 Children. **EDUCATION:** Detroit Bible Coll. **CAREER:** Clien Air Bacteria Service, proprieter; Ford Motor Co, former employee; Lien Chemical Co, former salesman; Oak Hill Bapt Ch Chmn of Equal Employment Com, presently pastor; Interdenominational Ministerial Alliance, corresponding sec; Mt Herman Bapt & District Assn, treas; Bapt Ministers Fellowship, pres; Shreveport Chap of NAACP, publicity chmn 1-74; NAACP, exec sec 1968-71. **ORGANIZATIONS:** Mem YMCA; coordinator Weekly Radio Broadcast for Ministerial Alliance. **HONORS/ACHIEVEMENTS:** Comm service award AKA Sorority during 41st Central Regional Conf 1973; appreciation award NAACP 1972; certificate of appreciation for service Kiwanis Club 1973; comm service award Negro C of C 1973. **BUSINESS ADDRESS:** 190o Milan St, Shreveport, LA 71103.

FARR, LLEWELLYN GOLDSTONE
State official. **PERSONAL:** Born Sep 06, 1928, Kingston, Jamaica;married Edna Rogers; children: Siobhan. **EDUCATION:** St Georgeas Coll Jamaica, diploma 1946; Brooklyn Coll, BS 1959; CityUniv NY, postgrad 1959-64. **CAREER:** NY State Labor Dept, economist 1960-62, sr economist 1962-68; NY State Commerce Dept NYC, asso economist 1968-69. **ORGANIZATIONS:** Asso bus consult 1969-70; dir Job Incentive Bur 1970-; exec sec NY State Job Incentive Bd 1970-; bd dir Bushwick Hylan Comm Center, Brooklyn 1967; pres Local 1473 Am Fedn State Co & Municipal Employees 1966-68; mem Am Statis Assn; mem Am Econ Assn NAACP; Grand Central Athletic Club NYC. **MILITARY SERVICE:** AUS 1951-53. **BUSINESS ADDRESS:** 230 Park Ave, New York, NY 10017.

FARR, MELVIN
Business executive. **PERSONAL:** Born Nov 03, 1944, Beaumont, TX; married Mae R Forbes; children: Mell Jr, Michael A, Monet A. **EDUCATION:** UCLA, 1963-67; Univ of Detroit, BS 1969-70. **CAREER:** Detroit Lions, professional football player 1967-73; Mel Farr Ford Inc, pres 1975-; Flint, MI 7-Up franchise, co-owner (1st 100% Black-owned major soft drinkfranchise). **ORGANIZATIONS:** Bd mem March of Dimes 1973-79; bd mem St Francis Home for Boys 1978-; chairman of bd Black Ford & Lincoln Dealer Assn 1982-84. **HONORS/ACHIEVEMENTS:** All-American Football UCLA 1965-66; All Pro Nat Football League Detroit Lions 1967-68. **BUSINESS ADDRESS:** President, Mel Farr Ford, Inc, 24750 Greenfield Rd, Oak Park, MI 48237.

FARRAKHAN, LOUIS
Clergyman. **PERSONAL:** Born May 11, 1933, New York, NY; married Betsy; children: 9 children. **EDUCATION:** Winston-Salem Teachers Coll. **BUSINESS ADDRESS:** Minister, Nation of Islam, 734 West 79th St, Chicago, IL 60620.

FARRELL, ODESSA WRIGHT
Educator. **PERSONAL:** Born Oct 26, 1908, Kansas City, MO. **EDUCATION:** Stowe Tchrs Coll, grad; IA U, IMA; PA; Washington; St Louis U. **CAREER:** Dunbar Elementary School, teacher; Vashon High School; Hadley Technical High School. **ORGANIZATIONS:** Dept head Sumner HS; lectr State Coll CA, Hayward; presently asst dir Audiovisual Serv Curriculum Svcs; St Louis Pub Schs Bd Educ Del & Govs Conf Educ 1966, 1968; mem Planning Com 1970; White House Conf St Louis 1972; pres Bd trustees Ferrier-Harris Home Aged; del Gen Conf AME Ch; officer mem Exec Bd Fifth Episcopal Dist Lay Orgn AME Ch; mem bd control MO Council Social Studies; sec trustee bd St James AME Ch; rep participant educ confs & meetings chmn Legislative Research Com; mem bd dir Council Press Women's Nat Orgns; mem Welfare Com MO State Tchrs Assn; mem exec bd Greater St Louis Council Social Studies; treas St Louis Div CTA MO State Tchrs Assn; sec bd dir Heritage House Redevel Corp; appointed Govs Com Children & Youth; appointed Commrs Com authorized MO State Bd Edn; mem St Louis Brs Am-AssnUniv Women; pres bd of control Aid to Victims of Crime Inc; vice pres Ret Sch Employees of St Louis; mem Hist Assn of Greater St Louis; Nat AssnUniv Women.

FARRELL, ROBERT C.
Government official. **PERSONAL:** Born Oct 01, 1936, Natchez, MS. **EDUCATION:** UCLA, BA 1961. **CAREER:** CA Eagle Newspaper, reporter; Los Angeles Sentinel Newspaper, reporter; Jet Magazine, correspondent; Star Review News in Watts, publisher. **ORGANIZATIONS:** Dep to city councilman Billy C Mills 1963-71; adminstrv coordinator for S Los Angeles on Mayor Bradley's & staff 1969 73; Los Angeles City Councilman 8th Dist 1974-; mem Sigma Delta Chi; Radio & TV News Assn of So CA; Pub Relations Soc of Am NAACP Legal Defense & Educ Fund; NAACP; UCLA Alumni Assn; Urban League. **MILITARY SERVICE:** USN 1954-59. **BUSINESS ADDRESS:** City Hall Rm 236, 200 N Spring St, Los Angeles, CA 90012.

FARRELL, SAMUEL D.
Business executive. **PERSONAL:** Born Oct 07, 1941, New York, NY; children: Samuel Jr, Ronette. **EDUCATION:** DNR Assoc, chmn & CEO. **CAREER:** Pres Alumni Varsity Assc 1982-83; mem bd dir CCNY Alumni Assc Dem. **BUSINESS ADDRESS:** Chairman & Chief Exec Officer, DNR Assoc, 3333 Broadway, D32c, New York, NY 10031.

FARRELL-DONALDSON, MARIE D.
Government official. **PERSONAL:** Born Aug 10, 1947, Detroit, MI; daughter of Herman Morgan and Lorine Morgan; married Dr Clinton L Donaldson; children: Piper Farrell, Christia. **EDUCATION:** Wayne State Univ, BS 1969; Harvard Univ John F Kennedy Sch of Govt, Certificate 1982. **CAREER:** MD Farrell, CPA, owner 1973-75; City of Detroit, auditor general 1975-84, ombudsman 1984-. **ORGANIZATIONS:** Bd mem Natl Council of Govt Accts 1979-82; pres Natl Council of Alcoholism 1979-85; treas MI Metro Girl Scouts 1984-; treas United Comm Serv 1986-; bd of dir MI Assoc of CPA's 1986-; pres Women's Economic Club 1987-88. **HONORS/ACHIEVEMENTS:** First black female CPA State of MI 1972; Michiganian of the Year Detroit News 1982; Outstanding Young Working Woman Glamour Magazine 1985; Outstanding Alumni Wayne State Univ 1985. **HOME ADDRESS:** 6353 W Outer Dr, Detroit, MI 48235. **BUSINESS ADDRESS:** Government Official, City of Detroit, 114 City-County Bldg, Detroit, MI 48226.

FARRINGTON, THOMAS ALEX
Business executive. **PERSONAL:** Born Nov 12, 1943, Chapel Hill, NC; married Juarez Harrell; children: Christopher, Trevor, Tomeeka. **EDUCATION:** NC A&T State Univ, BS 1966; Northeastern Univ Grad School, attended. **CAREER:** RCA Corp, 1966-69; IOCS Inc, president 1969-. **ORGANIZATIONS:** Bd dirs Boston Private Industry Council; mem Air Traffic Control Assocl; bd dirs Greater Boston Chamber of Commerce, Armed Forces Communications & Electronics Assoc. **HONORS/ACHIEVEMENTS:** Minority Contractor of the Year Dept of Transportation 1984; Natl Minority Serv Industry Firm of the Year US Dept of Commerce 1986. **BUSINESS ADDRESS:** President, Input Output Computer Service, 400 Trotten Pond Road, Waltham, MA 02254.

FARRIS, JEROME
Judge. **PERSONAL:** Born Mar 04, 1930, Birmingham, AL; son of Willie Joe Farris and Elizabeth Farris; married Jean Shy; children: Juli Elizabeth, Janelle Marie. **EDUCATION:** Morehouse Coll, BS 1951; Atlanta Univ, MSW 1955; Univ of WA, JD 1958. **CAREER:** Weyer Roderick Schroeter & Sterne, assoc 1958-59; Weyer Schroeter Sterne & Farris, partner 1959-61; Schroeter & Farris, partner 1961-63; Schroeter Farris Bangs & Horowitz, partner 1963-65; Farris Bangs & Horowitz, partner 1965-69; WA State Court of Appeals, judge 1969-79; US Court of Appeals 9th Circuit, circuit judge 1979-. **ORGANIZATIONS:** Pres WA State Jr Chamber of Commerce 1965-66; trustee Pacific NW Ballet 1978-83; chmn ABA Appellate Judges' Conf 1982-83; chmn State Fed Judicial Councilof WA 1983-87; adv bd Natl Ctr for State Courts Appellate Justice Project 1978-81; mem Univ of WA Law Sch Found 1978-84; adv bd Tyee Bd of Adv 1984-; Regent Univ of WA 1985-. **HONORS/ACHIEVEMENTS:** Clayton Frost Awd Jaycees 1966; Honorary LLD Morehouse Coll 1978; Order of Coif Univ of WA Law School. **MILITARY SERVICE:** AUS Signal Corps 1952-53. **BUSINESS ADDRESS:** Circuit Judge, U S Court of Appeals 9th Cir, 1010 Fifth Ave US Courthouse, Seattle, WA 98104.

FARRIS, VERA KING
Educational administration. **PERSONAL:** Born Jul 18, 1940, Atlantic City, NJ; widowed; children: King. **EDUCATION:** Tuskegee Inst, BA Biol 1959 (magna cum laude); Univ of MA, MS Zool 1962, PhD Zool, Parasitology 1965; Univ of MI, Post Doctoral Fellowship 1965-68. **CAREER:** Oak Ridge Natl Lab, rsch asst 1958-59; Univ of MA, rsch asst 1963-64; Univ of MI, rsch assoc 1965-66, instr 1967-68; SUNY Stony Brook, lecturer biol1968-71, asst prof 1970-72, assoc prof 1972-73, asst to vice pres acad affairs 1969-70, dir inst on innovative teaching & counseling 1968-73; SUNY Brockport, prof biol sci 1973-80, various admin positions 1973-80; Kean Coll of NJ, vice pres acad affairs 1980-83, prof biol sci 1980-83; Stockton State Coll, prof biol sci 1983-, pres 1983-. **ORGANIZATIONS:** Mem AAAS Comm of Young Scientists 1970-71; bd mem Children's TV Workshop 1979-, George W Carver Rsch Found 1979-; mem SUNY Bd of Trustees Spec Task Force 1979-82, Acad Vice Pres Council of NJ 1981-83, Elizabethtown Gas Co 1983-, Martin L King Jr Commemorative Commiss of NJ 1984-, Atlantic City Med Ctr Bd of Governors 1984-, Amer Assoc of State Coll & Univ Comm on Undergrad Ed 1984-; bd mem Mellon Bd 1984; regional bd mem American Cancer Soc, NJ Citizens for Better Schools, NJ Student Assistance Bd, Dept of Higher Educ, Atlantic City Mecical Ctr Bd of Governors, Public Broadcasting Authority, South Jersey Develop Council, The Middle States Assn of Colls and Schools; adv bd NJ Licensure and Approval; bd mem The Vail-Deane School; bd of trustees State Univ of NY. **HONORS/ACHIEVEMENTS:** Sigma Xi 1962, Alpha Kappa Mu 1958, Beta Kappa Chi 1958; Cert of Recog & Apprec Kiwanis Club 1976; Kappa Delta Pi 1982; NAACP Awd 1984; Kappa Alpha Psi Awd for Achievement in Higher Ed 1984; Pres Citation in Recog of Exemplary Experience that Honor Your Inst 1984; Who's Who in Amer 1984; Atlantic City Mag "People to Watch" Awd 1984; 26 awds in teaching including Awd for Highest Teacher Eval at SUNY Stony Brook, Outstanding Teaching Awd SUNY; Alumni Assoc Awd for Excellence in Teaching SUNY Brockport; Meritorious Serv Awd Brockport Students; 1st Woman Coll Pres of NJ Univ of Coalition on Women's Ed & NJ Coll;Danforth Associate; Natl Defense Scholarship; Natl Black Women's Conference Awd for Outstanding Achievement in Higher Educ; Kappa Alpha Psi Awd for Achievement in Higher Educ; Disting Comm Serv Awd Anti-Defamation League Atlantic City; Humanitarian Awd Chapel of 4 Chaplains Philadelphia; Univ of the State of NY Disting Serv Awd; Black History Awd for Outstanding Accomplishments in Educ; People to Watch Awd Atlantic City Magazine; Unified Black Student Soc Awd. **BUSINESS ADDRESS:** President, Stockton State College, Jimmy Leeds Rd, Pomona, NJ 08240.

FARROW, HAROLD FRANK
Dentist. **PERSONAL:** Born May 10, 1936, Pensacola, FL; married Virginia; children: Heather, Vance. **EDUCATION:** TN State U, BS 1959; Howard U, DDS 1970. **CAREER:** Dentist pvt prac 1972-; Wayne Co Hlth Dept, proj prescad 1971-72; Children's Hosp, Detroit, staff mem 1970-71. **ORGANIZATIONS:** Sec Wolverine Dental Soc 1974; pres Wolverine Dental Soc 1976; Wolverine Dental Soc 1977; mem ADA; MDA; DDDA; NDA; Chi Delta Mu Frat 1970; 32nd degree Mason Unity Lodge #28 1974; noble Marracci Temple #13 Mystic Shrine 1974; life mem NAACP 1976; tst New Prospect Bapt Ch 1977; pres's club HowardUniv 1977; recpt N15 Metabolism Edsel Ford Inst 1964. **HONORS/ACHIEVEMENTS:** Achvmt hon award Wolverine Dental Soc 1974. **MILITARY SERVICE:** AUS 1960-62. **BUSINESS ADDRESS:** President, 334 Livernois, Ferndale, MI 48220.

FARROW, SALLIE A.
Attorney. **PERSONAL:** Born Dec 31, 1942, Plainfield, NJ; daughter of James R Rivera and Sallie Mitchell Rivera; divorced; children: Richard H Staton Jr. **EDUCATION:** Denver Univ, Denver CO, BA (with Honors), 1974; Univ of Nebraska, Lincoln NE, JD, 1976. **CAREER:** Mutual of Omaha, Omaha NE, asst gen counsel, 1977-87; New York Life Insurance Co, New York NY, assoc counsel, 1987-. **ORGANIZATIONS:** Mem, Kappa Delta Pi, 1973-; cousultant, ACE Counselor SBA, Omaha, 1980-85; panelist, US Office of Educ, Washington DC, 1981; chairperson, Boys Scouts of Amer, Omaha, 1982; organizer, adviser, Metro Science and Engineering Fair Inc, 1982-87; moot court judge, Creighton Univ, 1983-87; consultant, Omaha Public Schools, Career Awareness, 1983-87; dir, Girls Club of Omaha, 1985-87; editor, bar-journal, Natl Bar Assn, 1986-; comm mem, Omaha Bar Assn, 1986-87.

HONORS/ACHIEVEMENTS: Natl Bar Assn Memoirs and Legal Journal, 1986, 1988; Outstanding Achievement, Girls Club of Omaha, 1987. **BUSINESS ADDRESS:** Associate Counsel, New York Life Insurance Company, 51 Madison Ave, Room 10SB, New York, NY 10010.

FARROW, WILLIE LEWIS
Military officer, pilot. **PERSONAL:** Born Nov 26, 1941, Wetumpka, AL; married Oneita Boyd; children: Stephen Michael. **EDUCATION:** Knoxville Coll, BS 1965; Central MI Univ, MA 1979. **CAREER:** Dover AFB, squadron training mgr 1974-75, operations exec officer 1975-76, aircraft maint officer 1976-77, pilot resource mgr 1977-79, wing flying training mgr 1979-81; Lt Col C-5 pilot/air operations staff officer; Budget/Financial Advisor. **ORGANIZATIONS:** Mem Omega Psi Phi Frat; master mason Prince Hall; mem Sigma Iota Epsilon Hon Mgmt Frat; mem Chi Gamma Iota Hon Mgmt Frat. **HONORS/ACHIEVEMENTS:** Recipient Distinguished Flying Cross USAF 1967; USAF Meritorious Serv Medal; USAF Commendation Medal; USAF Air Medal; featured Ebony Magazine 1979. **BUSINESS ADDRESS:** Lieutenant Colonel, 3rd Military Airlift Squadron, Dover AFB, Dover, DE 19901.

FATTAH, FALAKA
Company executive. **PERSONAL:** Born Dec 28, 1931, Philadelphia, PA; married David; children: Stefan, Robin, Kenneth, Chaka, Nasser, David. **EDUCATION:** Course Whitern New School Mse, Course Completed 1949; Fleischers Art School, Course Completed 1949; Temple Univ, English for Writers, Course Completed 1953; Junt Eucniny School, Course Completed, 1956. **CAREER:** Philadelphia Bulletin Tribune Afro-Amer Newspaper Pittsburgh Courier, journalist, 1952-68; UMOJA Magazine, editor 1968-; Arthur A Little Assoc Ofc Jrvl Jstc, consultant 1982-83; Eisenhower Found, Control Data, consultant, 1982-83; Hse UMOJA Boystown, chief executive officer. **ORGANIZATIONS:** Exctr comm Urban Affair Partnership, 1983-; bd dir exec Com Eisenhower Foun 1983-; brd dir Mayonb Comm Wmn; comm Mayor's Drug Alcohol Comm 1982-83; sec, Natl Center Neighborhood Enterprise, 1982-; life mem, Historical Soc PA 1983-; vice chmn, Philadelphia Youth Counseling Ctr 1983-. **HONORS/ACHIEVEMENTS:** Reduction of Gang Deaths in Philadelphia via vol; coordinator of "IV Gang War in 1974 Campaign". **HOME ADDRESS:** 5625 Master St, Philadelphia, PA 19131.

FAUCETT, BARBARA J.
Educational administrator. **PERSONAL:** Married Michael; children: Cynthia Mock, James Mock. **EDUCATION:** Univ Of WI Milwaukee, BS Soc Welfr 1968;Univ Of WI Milwaukee, MS Ed 1973. **CAREER:** Univ Of WI Milwaukee, acad adv relts 1971-72, dir fld exp hmn relts 1972-76, asst dean of ed 1976-79, depy asst chnlr 1979-80, dir prsl. **ORGANIZATIONS:** Mem desegregation team Champaign IL Univ of WI Milwaukee 1980-81; const EEO Nat'l Nat'l Coll of Ed 1975-76f coll ed const on persl City of Milwaukee & Cty of Milwaukee 1977-79; mem & past prest WI chapter IPMA 1979-; mem TEMPO 1981-; bd mem Big Brothers, Big Sisters Inc Milwaukee WI 1989. **HONORS/ACHIEVEMENTS:** Board of Directors, Penfield Childrens Center 1986-89; Phi Kappa Phi 1985-; Academic Staff Outstanding Performance Award, Univ of WI 1989; report: Assesment of Affirmative Action in the City of Milwaukee 1988. **HOME ADDRESS:** 7837 N Boyd Way, Milwaukee, WI 53217. **BUSINESS ADDRESS:** Dir of Personnel, U of WI Milwaukee, P O Box 413, Milwaukee, WI 53201.

FAULCON, CLARENCE AUGUSTUS, II
Educator. **PERSONAL:** Born Aug 08, 1928, Philadelphia, PA; son of Leroy and Addie; married Jacqueline Beach; children: David Clarence. **EDUCATION:** Lincoln U, 1946-48; Univ PA, BMus Ed 1950; Univ PA, MMus Ed 1952; Philadelphia Conservatory of Music, MusD in Musicolgy 1962-. **CAREER:** Chairperson Sulzberger Jr Hi (Phila), music teacher, chairperson 1951-63; Cazenovia Coll (Cazenovia, NY), asst prof, chairperson 1963-68; Morgan State Univ (Balt), prof, chairperson 1968-79; Morgan State Univ, prof 1979-. **ORGANIZATIONS:** Mstr tchr Middle Atlantic States 1967; consult Edl Testing Serv 1974; const Westminister Chr Coll 1974; consult Off of Adolect Preg 1978-80; consult Nat'l Inst Adoles 1984; cond Philadelphia Concert Orchta 1952-55; cond 111th Regimtl Combat Tm PA NG 1952; first faclty pnl Nat'l Assoc of Jr Coll Conf 1965; MD state rep Nat'l Adult Cont Ed Project Go (MENC) 1970; delegate, Intl Biographical Centre Arts & Communication Congresses, 1981-. **HONORS/ACHIEVEMENTS:** Morgan State Univ Promethan Soc Faculty Award, 1983; Intl Biographical Cong Medal of Cong, Budapest, Hungary, 1985; "A Need for Definition and Identefication" State Asso Jr Col 1965 Conf NY State, Reprt NY 1968; "Two Year College Pace Setrs for Music" The Schl Music News 1977-79; First Post Doctl Rant (Morgan Penn Project) 1977-79; Afro Amer Music in Health Promotion Disease Prevention and Therapy, Montreal, Canada, Conf Natl Medical Assn 1984; recital accompanist & artist accompanist in various countries, 1982-88. **HOME ADDRESS:** 617 Ridgeview Rd, Runnymede, Hockessin, DE 19707. **BUSINESS ADDRESS:** Prof of Music, Morgan State Univ, Baltimore, MD 21239.

FAULDING, CHARLES
Union official. **PERSONAL:** Born Feb 26, 1916, Fredericksburg, VA; married Lorraine Hocker; children: George, Edward. **EDUCATION:** Cornell Sch of Labor & Empire State Coll, 1970. **CAREER:** United Motormen's Div of TWU, shop steward 1948, vice chmn 1951, chmn 1965; Transport Workers Union Local 100; vice pres & Intl vice pres 1969, full time organizer, recording sec 1974, sec treas 1979. **ORGANIZATIONS:** Pres BMT Surface Operators Club Inc; regl vice pres Union Label & Serv Trade Dept State of NY; pres emeritus Black Trade Unionists Ldrshp Com of New York City Labor Council; adv council Empire State Coll; bd mem NY Urban League; bd mem New York City Central Labor Rehab Council; bd mem Health Care Inst Inc Occupational Safety & Health Office. **HONORS/ACHIEVEMENTS:** A Philip Randolph Institute & Black Trade Unionists Leadership Comm; Guy R Brewer United Democratic Club, Inc NY City Central Labor Council, AFL-CIO; Arthritis Foundation.

FAULDING, JULIETTE J.
Financial advisor. **PERSONAL:** Born Aug 02, 1952, Jackson, MS; daughter of Luella B Tapo and Vannette Johnson. **EDUCATION:** Tougaloo Coll, BA 1974; Columbia Univ, MBA 1976. **CAREER:** Mobil Oil Corp, banking analyst 1976-77, financial analyst 1977-79, short term investor 1979-81, sr financial analyst 1981-88, financial advisor 1989-. **ORGANIZATIONS:** Comm mem Boy Scout Troop 75 1982-87; assoc advisor Explorer Post 75 Queens NY 1982-87; participant Black Exec Exchange Prog; mem Black MBA Assoc. **HONORS/ACHIEVEMENTS:** Distinguished Grad Awd NAFEO 1984. **HOME ADDRESS:** 230-36 130th Ave, Laurelton, NY 11413. **BUSINESS ADDRESS:** Financial Advisor, Mobil Oil Corporation, 150 E 42nd St, New York, NY 10017.

FAULK, ESTELLE A.
Educator. **PERSONAL:** Born in Chicago, IL; divorced; children: Lalita, Gina. **EDUCATION:** Chicago State Univ, BE; DePaul Univ, MA; Univ of IL Chicago, PhD; DePaul Univ, Roosevelt Univ & Chicago State Univ, addl study. **CAREER:** Malcolm X Coll, instructor part-time; Gladstone School, principal. **ORGANIZATIONS:** Mem Samuel B Stratton Assn; Chicago Prin Assn; Natl Assn of Elem Sch Prin; Natl Assn of Supervision & Curriculum Develop; Natl Alliance of Black Sch Educators; Phi Delta Kappa; Amer Assn of Sch Admins; Near West Side Council Chicago; imm past pres Chicago Area Alliance Black Sch Educators; pres DePaul Univ Education Alumni Bd. **HONORS/ACHIEVEMENTS:** Commendation Awd Univ of IL Coll of Educ 1984; Outstanding Leadership Chicago Area Alliance of Black Sch Educators 1983. **BUSINESS ADDRESS:** Principal, Gladstone Sch, 1231 S Damen Ave, Chicago, IL 60608.

FAULKNER, GEANIE (JEANNE FAULKNER)
Performer, professional singer. **PERSONAL:** Born in Washington, DC; daughter of Ernest Faulkner and Mildred James Faulkner; children: David Michel Dabney. **EDUCATION:** Catholic Univ, BM 1963, MM 1964. **CAREER:** New Jersey Symphony, singer 1971; New York City Opera/Opera Theatre, singer 1972-78; Alvin Ailey Dance Theatre, singer 1973; Brooklyn Philharmonia Orchestra, singer 1976, 1979-82; New York Jazz Rep Orchestra, singer 1976, 1979, 1982; Harlem Opera Soc, principal singer 1969-; NY City Rep Opera Theatre, singer 1986; New York Foundation for the Arts, artist-in-residence; Harlem Cultural Council, pres; producer, Amer Black Festival, Palermo Italy, 1985-; Harlem Week in Madris Spain, 1989. **ORGANIZATIONS:** Vice pres 1984-85, mem/trustee 1971-pres Schomburg Corp; producer/dir Dancemobile Project 1971-; mem Whitney Museum 1977-84 (1st black mem); pres Harlem Performance Ctr 1978-; mem Bellevue Hospital Art Advisory Bd 1978-84; music consultant Arts/Humanities Project Teacher Corps Hunter Coll 1979-81; mem vice pres Fine Arts Federation; cultural consultant NY State Council on the Arts 1985-, New York City Dept of Cultural Affairs 1985, 1987. **HONORS/ACHIEVEMENTS:** Critical Reviews, New York Times, New York Post, Village Voice, Chicago Daily News, Boston Globe, Houston Post, San Francisco Chronical, Amsterdam News, Am News, High Fidelity/Musica America, Music Journal, Newsweek, Opera News, Porter Andrew "Music of Three Seasons". **HOME ADDRESS:** 317 W 98th St, Apt 6BR, New York, NY 10025. **BUSINESS ADDRESS:** President, Harlem Cultural Council, 226 Lenox Ave, New York, NY 10027.

FAULKNER, JEANNE See FAULKNER, GEANIE

FAULKNER, MARQUETTA LARNEITA
Physician. **PERSONAL:** Born Mar 04, 1953, Houston, TX; married Roosevelt; children: Terrance. **EDUCATION:** TX Southern Univ, BS 1977; Meharry Medical Coll, MD 1981. **CAREER:** Hubbard Hosp, intern 1981-82, resident 1982-84; St Dominic's Hosp, assoc staff; Jackson-Hinds Comp Health, chair quality assurances. **ORGANIZATIONS:** Mem Amer Coll of Physicians, Natl Medical Assoc, Jackson Medical Soc, Zeta Phi Beta Sor. **HONORS/ACHIEVEMENTS:** Bd Certified Amer Bd of Internal Medicine 1985; Fellowship Long Island Jewish Medical Ctr 1987; Licensure TN and MS. **BUSINESS ADDRESS:** Physician, Jackson Hinds Comp Hlth Ctr, 4433 Medgar Evers Blvd, Jackson, MI 39203.

FAUNTLEROY, JOHN DOUGLASS, SR.
Judge. **PERSONAL:** Born Sep 06, 1920, Washington, DC; son of Frederick Fauntleroy and Esther Fauntleroy; married Phyllis Gibbs; children: John, Jr, Phylicia, Jacqueline, Frederick. **EDUCATION:** Robert H Terrell Law School, LLB 1941; Amer Univ, BS 1953; Georgetown Univ, 1954; Natl Coll for Juvenile Justice Univ of Nevada, 1969; Natl Coll for the State Judiciary Univ of Nevada, 1971, 1972, 1974, 1980. **CAREER:** Office of Chief of Staff, supply clerk 1941-42; Office of Dependency Benefits Newark NJ, adjudicator, reviewer, sr adjudicator, supv of adjudicators, instr 1942-46; private practice, atty 1947-67; Juvenile Court of the Dist of Columbia, assoc judge 1967-71; Superior Court of the Dist of Columbia, assoc judge 1971-83, retired 1983, appointed presiding judge tax div 1979-82, sr judge 1983-85; US Dist Court, special asst to the mayor for corrections 1986-87, special asst to monitor consent decrees and other litigation, 1987-. **ORGANIZATIONS:** Mem Bar Assn of DC, Dist of Columbia Bar Assn, Washington Bar Assn, Amer Bar Assn, Natl Bar Assn; subs trust Marion P Shadd Scholarship Fund for Needy Female Grads McKinley Tech HS 1956-; mem Judicial Conf of Dist of Columbia Circuit 1960-67, 1982, 1983; mem, bd of dir Capitol View Devel Corp 1967-, Armstrong Alumni 1970-, Info Center for Handicapped Children 1971-; info prog officer US Naval Acad 1975-; mem visiting comm School of Social Work Howard Univ 1976-86; mem adv bd Georgetown Univ Child Devel Center 1978-; coord Dist of Columbia 1979-; pres Natl Naval Officers Assn 1980-82; mem genetics adv panel Georgetown Hosp, George Washington Hospital, Howard Univ Hospital, Children's Hosp 1980-; chmn Navy Recruiting Command 1982-84. **HONORS/ACHIEVEMENTS:** Outstanding Serv Awd Armstrong High School 1981; Plaque Outstanding Serv as Pres Natl Naval Officers Assn 1980-82; Recognition of Exemplary & Distinguished Serv Cardoza HS 1983; Certificate of Appreciation Dist of Columbia Bar Assn for Unselfish Serv to Superior Court 1983; Testimonial Dinner Armstrong Alumnie Assn 1983; Proclamation by the Mayor of Dist of Columbia proclaiming June 27, 1983 as John D Fauntleroy Day; Meritorious Serv Awd Amer Vets Comm, Faithful & Devoted Serv Duke Ellington Jazz Soc; Distinguished Public Serv Awd US Navy 1983; Distinguished Alumnus Amer Univ 1984; Outstanding Serv as Chmn Washington Recruiting Dist US Navy 1984; Meritorious Serv as Presiding Judge Tax Div by Chief Judge Superior Court of the Dist of Columbia 1986. **MILITARY SERVICE:** AUS t/sgt 1943-45; USNR comdr 1973-. **BUSINESS ADDRESS:** Judge, Superior Ct, 500 Indiana Ave, Washington, DC 20001.

FAUNTROY, WALTER E.
Congressman. **PERSONAL:** Born Feb 06, 1933, Washington, DC; married Dorothy Simms; children: Marvin Keith. **EDUCATION:** VA Union Univ, BA cum laude 1955; Yale Univ Divinity Schl, BD 1958. **CAREER:** New Bethel Bapt Church, pastor 1959; Wash Bureau of Southern Christian Ldrshp Conf, dir coord of Selma To Montgomery March 1965; DC City Council, 1st appointed vice chrmn 1967-69; Poor People's Campaign, natl dir 1969; House of Representatives, DC delegate 1971-. **ORGANIZATIONS:** Pres Natl Black Ldrshp Roundtable; chrmn bd dir Southern Christian Ldrshp Conf; vice pres Govt Affairs MLK Jr Cntr for Soc Change; natl dir 20th AnivMarch on Wash for Jobs Peace & Freedom

1983. **HONORS/ACHIEVEMENTS:** Hubert H Humprey Humanitarian Award Natl Urban Coalition 1984; hnry degrees, Georgetown Univ Law Schl, Yale Univ, VA Union Univ. **BUSINESS ADDRESS:** District Columbia Rep, US House of Representative, 2135 Rayburn House Ofc Bldg, Washington, DC 20515.

FAUST, NAOMI FLOWE
Educator/author/poet. **PERSONAL:** Born in Salisbury, NC; daughter of Christopher Leroy Flowe and Ada Luella Graham Flowe; married Roy Malcolm Faust. **EDUCATION:** Bennett Coll, AB; Univ of MI-Ann Arbor, MA; New York Univ, PhD. **CAREER:** Public School System Gaffney SC, elem teacher; Atkins High School Winston-Salem NC, english teacher; Bennett Coll & Southern Univ Scotlandville LA, instr of English; Morgan State Univ Baltimore MD, prof of English; Greensboro Public Schools & New York City Public Schools, teacher; Queens Coll of CUNY, prof of English/Educ. **ORGANIZATIONS:** Mem Amer Assoc of Univ Profs, Natl Council of Teachers of English, Natl Women's Book Assoc, World Poetry Soc Intercontinental, NY Poetry Forum, NAACP. **HONORS/ACHIEVEMENTS:** Publications "Speaking in Verse," a book of poems 1974; "Discipline and the Classroom Teacher," 1977; "All Beautiful Things," poems 1983; also contributes poetry to magazines and newspapers and gives poetry readings; named Teacher-Author by Teacher-Writer 1979; Certificate of Merit Cooper Hill Writers Conf; Certificate of Merit Poems by Blacks; Honored by Long Island Natl Assoc of Univ Women for High Achievement; poetry book "And I Travel by Rhythms and Words" to be published 1990. **HOME ADDRESS:** 112-01 175th St, Jamaica, NY 11433.

FAVORS, KATHRYNE TAYLOR
Educator, publisher. **PERSONAL:** Born Jun 29, 1924, Omaha, NE; married Dr John Samuel Favors; children: Kathryne Thearis Favors-Reinholm, John Samuel Jr. **CAREER:** Del Paso Heights School Dist, dir educ serv 1981-; Jonka Enter, co-owner present; Grizzly Peak & Hillside Schs, prin 1975-80; Berkeley Unified School Dist, dir human relations 1964-75; Berkeley CA, elem tchr 1959-63; Omaha Pub Schs, elem tchr 1946-59. **ORGANIZATIONS:** Mem Delta Sigma Theta Sor, CA Task Force for Integrated Edn; vice pres Nat Black Writers Consortium; mem Pres Nat Adv Com on Sickle Cell Anemia, Mt Zion Bapt Ch, Kappa Gamma Delta, NAACP, Nat Coun Negro Women, Nat Educ Assn, CA Educ Assn, Assn of CA Sch Administr, YMCA, Jack & Jill Orgn, Coll BouncersOrgn; life mem NE & CA PTA; mem ASCO, NAPSE, CAPSE, CA Assn of Gifted; natl consult Educ for African Amers, Egyptology. **HONORS/ACHIEVEMENTS:** Mem serv award Urban League; woman of yr Sun Rptr SF Newspaper 1958; admin of yr Alameda CO 1969; outst achvmt award NE; most outst lectrUniv of NE Deseg Inst 1971; awards Cons/Letctr/Sem Ldr; num books & articles "Before The Bus Ride"/"John Q Adams & The Amistad"/"White Am Who Cared"/"Exercise & Nutrition Guide", "K-12 Reading & Lang Aid Prog"; book "Master Plan for the Black Church". **BUSINESS ADDRESS:** Dir Educational Serv, Jonka Enterprises, Del Paso Heights School Dist, Sacramento, CA 95838.

FAW, BARBARA ANN
Educational administrator. **PERSONAL:** Born Jul 27, 1936, Cullen, VA; married Joseph A. **EDUCATION:** Morgan StateUniv Baltimore, BA 1965; HowardUniv Wash DC, MA 1966. **CAREER:** Community Coll of Baltimore, dean of coll 1977-, dean of student activities 1973-77, admin asst to pres 1971-73, chmn dept of business administration 1970-71, prof business administration 1965-71; coordinator & sponsor small business inst 1967-70, chairwoman Conf "Know your Rights" 1973. **ORGANIZATIONS:** Mem Natl Econs Assoc, Sales & Marketing Assn, Amer Assn of Univ Prof, W Arlington Community Org, Mayor's Vol Cadre on Educ, Task Force for Role Scope & Commitment; co-author Study of Unemployment & the Inner City Baltimore Dept of C of C Wash DC 1967-68; mem Natl Council on Black Amer Affairs of the Amer Assoc of Community & Jr Colls 1985-; presidential search comm Comm Coll of Baltimore 1985-86; panelist Conf on Women's Career Paths Univ of Baltimore 1986; bd of review comm Middle States 1987-. **HONORS/ACHIEVEMENTS:** Outstanding Educator of Am 1975; Senate of MD Resolution As First Chancellor ofCommunity College of Baltimore 1986; The City Council of Baltimore Resolution As the Chancellor of Community Coll of Baltimore 1986. **BUSINESS ADDRESS:** Dean, Community College of Baltimore, 2901 Liberty Heights Ave, Baltimore, MD 21215.

FAX, ELTON C.
Author, artist, lecturer. **PERSONAL:** Born Oct 09, 1909, Baltimore, MD; son of Mark Estelle and Willie Estelle; widowed; children: 2 children. **EDUCATION:** Syarcuse Univ, BFA 1931; Rockefeller Found Study & Research Center Bellagio, Italy, scholar-in-residence 1976. **CAREER:** Claflin Coll, teacher 1935-36; A&T Coll, teacher 1935-36; New York City Harlem Art Center, 1936-40; free lance since 1940; illustrated children's books 1943-. **ORGANIZATIONS:** Mem PEN Am Center; Author's Guild of Amer; partic in Intl Writers' Conf on World Peace Sofia, Bulgaria Bharati Cent Celebration, India 1982. **HONORS/ACHIEVEMENTS:** Recip Coretta Scott King Award 1970; Louis E Seley MACAL Award for best oil painting 1971; author pub & distrib of portfolio of 10 prints from original Fax-Drawings 1969; honored by Arena Players 1972; Key Women of Amer 1974; author of "HASHAR" impressions of life in Soviet Central Asia Progress Publ Moscow USSR1980; author of "ELYUCHIN" impressions of Soviet Transcaucasia Moscow USSR 1984 Progress Publ; writer in residence Langston Hughes Library Queens NY 1987 grant from NY State Council on the Arts; "Soviet People as I Knew Them" (illust by author) Progress Publ Moscow 1988. **BUSINESS ADDRESS:** Box 2188, Astoria Station, Long Island City, NY 11102.

FAY, TONI G.
Communications director. **PERSONAL:** Born Apr 25, 1947, New York, NY; daughter of George and Allie. **EDUCATION:** Duquesne Univ, BA 1968; Univ of Pittsburgh, MSW 1972, MEd 1973. **CAREER:** New York City Dept of Social Svcs, caseworker 1968-70; Time Inc, dir community relations; Dir Planning & Devel Natl Cncl of Negro Women 1977-81; Exec VP, D Parke Gibson Assoc 1981-82, dir, Pittsburgh Drug Abuse Ctr Inc 1972-74; chief, Governors Cncl on Drug & Alcohol Abuse 1974-77. **ORGANIZATIONS:** Bd mem New York City Private Industry Council, Bethune Museum and Archives for Black Women's History Washington, DC; mem Greater NY Fund/United Way Comm Agency Dev Comm; mem Alpha Kappa Alpha Sor; Vice Pres National Coalition of 100 Black Women; bd of dirs, Girl Scout Council of Greater NY, Federation of Protestant Welfare Agencies. **HONORS/ACHIEVEMENTS:** Dollars & Sense-100 Black Women in Business 1986; YWCA of America Twin Award, 1987. **BUSINESS ADDRESS:** Director, Community Relations, Time Inc, Time-Life Building, Rockefeller Center, New York, NY 10020.

FAZANDE, HILLIARD C., II
Attorney. **PERSONAL:** Born Nov 11, 1943, New Orleans; married Ida Payne; children: Keith, Tyrone, Michael, Sloane, Hilliard, III. **EDUCATION:** XavierUniv of LA, BS 1965; Howard U, 1970. **CAREER:** Cotton Jones Fazande & Dennis, atty 1971-; Reginald Heber Smith Fellow, New Orleans, 1970-71. **ORGANIZATIONS:** Pres Louis A Martinet Legal Soc, New Orleans; mem Nat Conf of Black Lawyers; mem Nat Bar Assn; recip LA Bar Assn. **HONORS/ACHIEVEMENTS:** Civil Rights Award HowardUniv 1970; Outstanding Achievement State Louis A Martinet Soc.

FEARING, JOHN T.
Business executive. **PERSONAL:** Born Oct 21, 1916, NYC; son of John and Ada; married Clara Neblett; children: Susan, Marilyn. **EDUCATION:** Coll of the City of NY, 1939-40;Univ of Bridgeport, 1968-69. **CAREER:** Exmet Corp, admin research & devel 1949-; Edison Tech, Mt Vernon, 1950-53; New York City Transit System, post office clerk, motorman 1940; FO Reconcilliation MRA & Harlem Chris Youth Council, 1930. **ORGANIZATIONS:** Active NAACP; CORE Cath Inter-racial Council; chmn bd Norwalk Museum Zoo 1973-; chmn Proj Intergroup 1974-; bd Norwalk Drug Abuse Commn 1970. **HONORS/ACHIEVEMENTS:** Recipient Honor Man Great Lakes Naval Training Center 1941. **MILITARY SERVICE:** USN seaman 1/c 1946.

FEARN-BANKS, KATHLEEN
Publicist, educator. **PERSONAL:** Born Nov 21, 1941, Chattanooga, TN; daughter of Dr James E Fearn and Dr Kayle M Fearn; divorced. **EDUCATION:** Wayne State Univ, BA, Journalism, 1964; UCLA, MS, Journalism, 1965. **CAREER:** NBC Publicity Dept, mgr, media relations, 1969-present; KNXT-TV News LA, newswriter, producer, 1968-69; Los Angeles Ctn Coll, instructor, Journalism, English, Creative Writing, 1965-; Los Angeles Times, Feature Writer, 1968. **ORGANIZATIONS:** Mem, Writers Guild Amer; mem, Publishers Guild; Public Relations Comm Acad of TV & Sciences; mem, Metro Opera Guild; bd of dir, vice pres, Founding Neighbors of Watts; mem, Delta Sigma Theta Sorority, Theta Sigma Phi Journalism Fraternity; bd advisor, Cambridge Plays, Los Angeles. **HONORS/ACHIEVEMENTS:** CA Sun Magazine writers Award, UCLA 1965; Will Rogers Fellowship, UCLA, 1964-65; Numerous freelance Magazine articles; 3 Textbooks, The Story of Western Man, co-authored w/David Burleigh. **BUSINESS ADDRESS:** Publicity Representative, NBC-TV Network, 3000 W Alameda, Burbank, CA 91523.

FEDDOES, SADIE C.
Business executive. **PERSONAL:** Born in St Vincent, West Indies. **EDUCATION:** Pace Univ NY, BA, Business. **CAREER:** Citibank, asst vice pres, community and govt relations officer, 1955-; New York Amsterdam News, columnist, 1972-; "Face the Women," cable television show, alternate guest panelist. **ORGANIZATIONS:** Chairperson of the bd, Billie Holiday Theater of Bedford Stuyvesant Restoration Corp; bd mem, Bedford Stuyvesant Restoration Corp, Brooklyn Economic Devel Corp, Kings County Overall Econ Devel Program Comm, Overall Economic Devel Program for Brooklyn; mem, Coalition of 100 Black Women, Natl Women in Communications, New York Women in Communications, Caribbean Cable TV Co; served, 1984-85 New York Regional Panel of the President's Commn on White House Fellowships. **HONORS/ACHIEVEMENTS:** Outstanding Performance Award, First Natl City Bank, 1970; Community Serv Award, Brooklyn Club of Natl Assn of Negro Business & Professional Womens Clubs; Journal Award, Brooklyn Chapter Natl Assn of Key Women; The Intl Womens Year Award, Natl Council of Negro Women, Anemia, Journalism Award from Bethany United Meth Church 1973; Journal Award, Empire State Fed of Womens Clubs; Distinguished Citizen Award, Boy Scouts of Amer; Woman of the Year, Bd of Mgr Brooklyn Home for Aged People, 1982; Woman of the Year, Brooklyn Branch NAACP, 1984; recognized as one of 60 outstanding mem, New York Women in Communications, 1984; citation, 25 years with Citibank, presented by borough pres Howard Golden on behalf of the people of Brooklyn; 30 years with Citibank, entered in Congressional record by Congressman Edolphus Towns; awards, Salvation Army, Amer Red Cross, New York State Black and Puerto Rican Legislative Caucus, Natl Urban League, Lions Intl, Natl Conf of Christians and Jews, Coalition of 100 Black Women, Navy Yard Boys and Girls Club, Church Women United of Brooklyn; television appearances, NBC's "Today Show," WPIX-TV's "Black Pride". **BUSINESS ADDRESS:** Asst Vice Pres, Community and Govt Relations Officer, Citibank, 885 Flatbush Ave, Brooklyn, NY 11226.

FEELINGS, MURIEL GREY
Writer and teacher. **PERSONAL:** Born Jul 31, 1938, Philadelphia, PA; married Thomas Feelings, Feb 18, 1969 (divorced 1974); children: Zamani, Kamili. **EDUCATION:** Philadelphia Museum School of Art, Philadelphia, PA, 1957-60; California State Univ, Los Angeles, BA, 1963. **CAREER:** Writer; elementary and secondary school teacher in Philadelphia, PA, New York, NY, Kampala, Uganda, and Guyana; works in a museum in Philadelphia. **ORGANIZATIONS:** Columbian Design Soc. **HONORS/ACHIEVEMENTS:** Author of Zamani Goes to Market, Seabury, 1970, Moja Means One, Dial, 1971, Jambo Means Hello, Dial, 1974; Moja Means One and Jamba Means Hello were Amer Library Assn Notables; Moja Means One was runner-up for Caldecott Medal, 1972, and was cited by the Brooklyn Arts Books for Children, 1973; Jambo Means Hello was nominated for Amer Book Award, 1982. **BUSINESS ADDRESS:** Dial Books, 2 Park Ave, New York, NY 10016. *

FEELINGS, THOMAS
Artist. **PERSONAL:** Born May 19, 1933, Brooklyn, NY; married Muriel Grey; children: Zamani, Kamili. **EDUCATION:** George Westinghouse Voc Schl, High Schl Dimp 1948-51; Cartoonist & Illist Sch, 1951-53; Schl Visval Arts, 1958-61. **CAREER:** Ghana Govt Publshg Hse Ministy of Ed, tchr consult 1964-66; Guyana (SA) Minstry of Ed, tchr consult 1971-74; Self Empld, Freelance Illust. **HONORS/ACHIEVEMENTS:** 2 caldecott Hnr Bk Moja Means One - Jambo Means Hello 1972-74; otsdg alum awd Sch Vsl Arts 1974; Boston Globe Horn Bk awd Jambo Means Hello 1973; AmBk awd nomtn Jambo Means Hello 1981; Coretta Scott King awd Something On My Mind/NEA Visl Arts Flwshp Grant 1982. **MILITARY SERVICE:** USAF airmen 1st class 1953-57; Good Conduct Mdl 1953-57. **BUSINESS ADDRESS:** Artist, 31 West 31 St, New York, NY 10001.

FEEMSTER, JOHN ARTHUR
Physician. **PERSONAL:** Born Sep 09, 1939, Winston-Salem, NC. **EDUCATION:** Knox Coll, BS 1959; Meharry Med Coll, MD; Am Coll Surgeons, physician self flw 1977; Am Coll Angiology; Thorocic-Cardiovascular Surgery, bd cert 1975 wayne state u, resd 1974-75; bd cert gen surgery 1971; u mN, gen surg resd 1970. **CAREER:** Kirwood Gen Hosp, chf dept

surg. **ORGANIZATIONS:** Mem Nat Med Soc; Am Coll Emergency Physicians; v pres Detroit Med Soc; mem Detroit Surg Soc; Detroit Surg Assn; mem Omega Psi Phi Frat; Alpha Omega Alpha Hon Med Soc; NAACP; Founders Soc Detroit Ints Arts. **HONORS/ACHIEVEMENTS:** Founders Soc Detroit Symphony Orch Young Investigator's Award, Am Coll Cardiology 1969; Outsdng Young Men Am 1970; Intl Who's Who 1969; flwsp, Oakridge Inst Nuclear Studies. **MILITARY SERVICE:** AUS mc col 1970-72. **BUSINESS ADDRESS:** 1054 Fisher Bldg, Detroit, MI 48203.

FEGGANS, EDWARD L.
Business executive. **PERSONAL:** Born Mar 05, 1919, Atlantic City, NJ; son of Edward L and Ethel M; married Ozra Young, Feb 25, 1950; children: James E Kearney, Helen A Thobani. **EDUCATION:** Howard U, Suffolk U, Sterling Inst, Syracuse U, LaSalle Extension U, attended. **CAREER:** 1st Nat Bank of Boston, clerk; Indus Bank of Washington, teller, asst auditor; USPO, railway mail clk; Herf Jones Co, jewelry salesman; Kaplan & Crawford Dodge & Plymouth, asst sales mgr; Small Bus Devel Cntr, bus cons; DC Pub Schs in Bus Mgmt, coordinator; Small Bus Guidance & Devel Cntr, asst dir; Howard U; Office of Minority Bus Enterprise, US Dept Commerce, comm relations specialist; Washington Area Contractors Assn, exec dir; Ed Feggans Oldsmobile Inc, pres, owner; Washington Tech Inst, instr. **ORGANIZATIONS:** Mem various bds, coms, offices, DC C of C; Downtown Progress; Nat Bus League; DC Met Area Transp Fed; Greater Washington Bus Center; Small Bus Adminstrn; DC Minimum Wage & Indsl Safety Bd; Automotive Trade Assn; VOICE; DC Fedn of Musicians, Local 161-710; DC Chap Nat Red Cross; Hemisphere Nat Bank Adv Bd; Fed City Coll Bd Councillors; Mayor's Adv Com; City Council Spl Adv Commn on Indusl & Commercial Devel; Sales & Marketing Execs of Washington; Davis Meml Goodwill Industries; mem Gateway Comm Assn; Neptune Yacht Club; Seafarers Yacht Club; Mecca Temple #10; Simon Commandry Knights of Templar; Prince Hall Chap Royal Arch Mason; Prudence Lodge #27 F & AM; Kiwanis Internat, Capitol Hill Club; Pi Sigma Epsilon Frat; mem Washington DC Consumer Arbitration Board, 3rd term 1987-. **MILITARY SERVICE:** AUS 1941-45. **HOME ADDRESS:** 2504 S Dakota Ave NE, Washington, DC 20018.

FELDER, LORETTA KAY
Dentist. **PERSONAL:** Born Apr 19, 1956, Sumter, SC; daughter of Rev & Mrs Daniel DeLeon Felder Sr. **EDUCATION:** Old Dominion Univ, BS 1978; Howard Univ, DDS 1982. **CAREER:** US Public Health Svcs, lt 1982-85; Ruskin Migrant Health Care Inc Hillsborough Co FL, dentist 1982-84; Midlands Primary Health Care Inc, dental dir 1984-87; private practice 1988-. **ORGANIZATIONS:** Consultant/mem SC Richland Co Governors Primary Health Task Force 1984; mem Natl Dental Assn, 1985-87; bd of dirs YWCA of Sumter Area 1986-88; mem Natl Council of Negro Women, NAACP; bd of dirs Big Brothers/Big Sisters Inc of Greater Columbia; mem SC Dental Assoc, American Dental Assoc. **BUSINESS ADDRESS:** Dentist, 2009 Greene Street, Suite 112, Columbia, SC 29205.

FELDER, THOMAS E.
Chief executive. **CAREER:** Victory Savings Bank, Columbia, SC, chief exec. **BUSINESS ADDRESS:** Victory Savings Bank, 1545 Sumter St, Columbia, SC 29201. *

FELDER, TYREE PRESTON, II
Educational administrator. **PERSONAL:** Born Oct 06, 1927, Mound Bayou, MS; son of B Ottowiess Felder; married Muriel Diggs; children: Gladys Washington, Frankie O, Deborah Schorlemmer, Marva Carter, Muriel T Rogers. **EDUCATION:** Tuskegee Univ, BS Comind 1948; VA Cmmnwlth Univ, MS Bus 1970. **CAREER:** Univ S Army, quartermaster 1948-68; VA Cmmnwlth Univ, EEO manager 1970-. **HONORS/ACHIEVEMENTS:** Board mem VA Div Amer Cancer Soc 1982-, Richmond Div 1981-; board mem Adult Dev Cntr for Handicapped 1972-; Citizen of the Year Omega Psi Phi (Phi Phi Chapt) 1981; Public Educ Awd VA Div ASC 1983; Outstanding Serv (treasurer) Amer Assoc for Affirm Action 1976-78; Presidents' Promotional Service Awd AAAA 1980. **MILITARY SERVICE:** AUS quartermaster 1st Lt 1948-68; Bronze Star 1968. **BUSINESS ADDRESS:** EEO Manager, Virginia CommonwealthUniv, 901 W Franklin St, Richmond, VA 23284.

FELDER-HOEHNE, FELICIA HARRIS (FELICIA HARRIS HOEHNE)
Educator, librarian. **PERSONAL:** Born in Knoxville, TN; daughter of Geraldine Ivey; married Paul Arthur Hoehne, Jan 02, 1980. **EDUCATION:** Knoxville Coll, BS, Atlanta Univ, MSLS 1966; Univ of TN, 1978. **CAREER:** SCLS, sec 1958; Knoxville Coll, asst to dir of public relations 1963-65; Knoxville Coll, circulation libr 1966-69; Knoxville Coll Admin Office, admin asst; Athens, GA secondary schools, teacher; McMinn County Schools, teacher of English; Univ of TN, prof/reference librarian 1969-. **ORGANIZATIONS:** Knoxville Roundtable, Natl Conf Christians & Jews 1971-; mem Publ Rels Comm TN Libr Assoc, SE Libr Assoc, E TN Libr Assoc, Intl Womens Yr Decard, NAACP, YWCA, YMCA, Knoxville Planned Parenthood, Knoxville Coll Alumni Assoc; mem Knoxville Black Official Coalition 1976-79; Interdenominational Concert Choir 1970-80; adv bd Beck Cultural Exchange Ctr 1976-; mem Knoxville Nativity Pageant Choir 1975-, Payne Adv Bapt Church Choir; mem & mem bd of dirs Knoxville Comm Chorus; pres Spring Place Neighborhood Assoc 1980-; mem religious task force 1982 World's Fair; bd of dirs UT Federal Credit Union 1984-89; charter mem Natl Museum of Women in the Arts 1985-; mem hon comm Diva Foundation 1987-88; dir of public relations, Concerned Assn of Residents East; mem, Tennessee Valley Energy Coalition; mem, Kiwanis Club of Knoxville. **HONORS/ACHIEVEMENTS:** Outstanding Contributions in Educ Library Serv & Community Affairs, Jack & Jill of Amer Inc, 1976; Religious Serv Awd NCCJ 1976; Apprec Plaque Interdenominational Concert Choir 1976; Outstanding Serv Plaque Knoxville-Knox Cty Libr Bd Tst 1977; Chancellor's Citation Extraordinary Comm Serv 1978; Publ "Doubt I You-Nevermore" Natl Poetry Press 1975, "Parents Without Partners, The Single-Parent Family" a Bibliography 1978, "A Selected List of Guides to Current Ed Free & Inexpensive Matls" 1978, "A Selected List of Sources on Student Fin Aid/Asst" 1978,83, "A Brief Historial Sketch of Payne Ave Baptist Church 1930(?)-83"; Outstanding Young Woman of Amer 1967; Citizen of the Year Awd Order of the Eastern Star Prince Hall Masons 1979; Public Serv Awd Univ of TN Natl Alumni Assoc 1984. **HOME ADDRESS:** 5413 Spring Place Cir NE, Knoxville, TN 37924-2174. **BUSINESS ADDRESS:** Professor/Reference Librarian, Univ of Tennessee at Knoxville, 1015 Volunteer Blvd, Knoxville, TN 37996-1000.

FELICIANA, JERRYE BROWN
Educational administration. **PERSONAL:** Born Aug 20, 1951, Bethesda, MD; daughter of James D Brown and Katie G McNair Brown; married Albert Feliciana; children: Wayne, Jaison, Kyanna. **EDUCATION:** George Washington Univ, BA 1974; Trinity Coll, MA 1976. **CAREER:** Georgetown Univ, asst dir upward bound 1977-78; US Dept of Agr, consultant 1981; Trinity Coll, asst dir for minority affairs 1983-84; Trinity Coll, dir upward bound 1978-. **ORGANIZATIONS:** Chairwoman DC Consolidation for Ed serv 1983-; mem of exec bd Mid-Eastern Assoc of Educ Oppty Prog 1983-. **HOME ADDRESS:** 5200 Vienna Dr, Clinton, MD 20735. **BUSINESS ADDRESS:** Dir Upward Bound, Trinity College, 125 Michigan Ave NE, Washington, DC 20017.

FELIX, DUDLEY E.
Educator. **EDUCATION:** London Univ, London England; Royal Faculty of Physicians and Surgeons, Scotland; Howard Univ, Washington DC; Univ of Pennsylvania Medical and Dental Colleges; Philadelphia General Hospital. **CAREER:** Univ of Pennsylvania Gen Hospital, Otorhinolaryngology and Temporo-Mandibular Joint Clinic, resident and attending physician; Philadelphia Gen Hospital, Dept of Oral/Internal Medicine, resident; Howard Univ, clinical instr oral and maxillofacial surgery, 1969-73; Howard Univ, Div of District of Columbia Gen Hospital, dir of senior students, 1974; Meharry Medical Coll, faculty mem school of dentistry, dir of didactic program in oral diagnosis and oral medicine, head of section on oral medicine. **ORGANIZATIONS:** Attending consultant, Hubbard Hospital; lecturer and attending consultant, Dept of Pediatric Medicine, Meharry Medical Coll; guest lecturer and attending consultant, Tennessee State Univ; fellow Royal Soc of Health, United Kingdom; Amer Acad of General Dental Surgery 1979; diplomate Amer Specialty Bd of Oral Medicine 1981; mem Intl Acad of Preventive Medicine 1982; fellow Intl Acad of Medical Preventics 1983; mem Amer Cancer Soc; mem Amer Soc of Regional Anesthesia; mem Intl Assn for Pain Study; mem Amer Assn for Pain Study; mem Intl Soc for Advanced Educ; co-chmn faculty eval comm 1987, mem grievance comm 1987, faculty rep of faculty senate 1988, mem faculty council 1988, mem curriculum comm 1988, Meharry Medical Coll; mem Amer Assn for the Study of Headache. **HONORS/ACHIEVEMENTS:** Academic Fellowship, Amer Acad of Oral Medicine; Outstanding Teacher Award, Howard Univ and Meharry Medical Coll; Outstanding and Dedicated Serv Award of Oral/Maxillofacial Surgery, Howard Univ; Clinical Prof of the Year, Meharry Medical Coll; Expertise in Medical Lectures, Meharry Medical Coll; guest of Dr Siaka Stevens, president of Sierra Leone, 1983; guest lecturer in West Africa, Canada and USA; publications include "Oral Symptoms as a Chief Sign of Acute Monoblastic Leukemia, Report of Case," JADA, 1986; Instructor of the Year, Meharry Medical Coll, 1988. **BUSINESS ADDRESS:** Head, Section on Oral Medicine, Meharry Medical College, 1005 D B Todd Blvd, Nashville, TN 37208.

FELKER, JOSEPH B.
Clergyman. **PERSONAL:** Born Nov 25, 1926, Chicago, IL; married Ruthie Crockrom; children: Cordelia, Jacquelyn. **EDUCATION:** Univ Chgo, CBI 1953; IL Barber Coll, MA 1952; No Bapt Theol Sem, BTH 1956; McKenney Theol Sem. **CAREER:** Mt Carmel Baptist Church, pastor 1957-; Vet Barber Shop, pres 1957-. **ORGANIZATIONS:** Moderator Grtr New Era Dist Assn of Chicago 1968-; treas JH Jackson Lib; mem NAACP; The Urban League; treas MI Towers S; chmn of moderators, Bapt Gen State Conv 1973-. **HONORS/ACHIEVEMENTS:** CBI Cert of Achvmt 1971; Outsdng Ldrsp as Moderator, Chs, Grtr New Era Dist Assn 1973; Most Outsdng & Prog Moderator Yr, Midwestern Bapt Layman Flwsp Inc 1974; Civic & Rel Work Hon, Fgn Mission Bd of MB Conv 1976; cert of recg, Gen State Conv IL 25 Yrs of Denominational Christian Serv 1977. **MILITARY SERVICE:** USN petty ofcr 3rd class. **BUSINESS ADDRESS:** 2978 S Wabash Ave, Chicago, IL 60616.

FELTON, ANN SHIREY
Educator. **PERSONAL:** Born Sep 14, 1941, Baltimore, MD; married Maceo N Felton; children: Joy T, Travis A. **EDUCATION:** Morgan State Coll, AB 1963; Howard Univ Sch of Social Work, MSW 1968. **CAREER:** Onondaga Co Health Dept, social worker 1968-70; SUNY Coop Coll Ctr, academic & vocational advisor 1970-72; Dunbar Ctr, social work super 1972-74; Onondaga Comm Coll, assoc prof. **ORGANIZATIONS:** Mem Assoc of Black Social Workers 1970-; past pres Syracuse Section Natl Council of Negro Women 1970-; past pres Alpha Kappa Alpha local chap 1972-; consultant Consortium for Children's Services 1973-; owner AMF Enterprises 1980-; mem Assoc of Black Women in Higher Educ 1981-; bd of dirs Urban League of Onondaga Co 1984-. **HONORS/ACHIEVEMENTS:** Comm Serv Awd Bd of Trustees Onondaga Comm Coll; Comm Serv Awd Syracuse and Onondaga Co NAACP; Comm Serv Awd Syracuse Alpha Kappa Alpha. **HOME ADDRESS:** 5203 Duane Drive, Fayetteville, NY 13066. **BUSINESS ADDRESS:** Associate Professor, Onondaga Community College, Onondaga Hill, Syracuse, NY 13215.

FELTON, JAMES A.
Association executive. **PERSONAL:** Born Jul 06, 1919, Hertford, NC; married Annie Mary Vaughan; children: Maria, James, Sharon, Keith, Michele, Camilla. **EDUCATION:** Elizabeth City State Univ, BS 1946; NC Cntrl Univ, MA Admin Sprvsn of Educ 1954; Attended, Hampton Inst, Howard Univ, E Carolina Univ, A&T State Univ. **CAREER:** Faith Mission Rich Sq NC, pastor/rector; NC, tchr prin pub schs 1947-67; Peoples Prog on Poverty, dir 1967-68; Pres Commn on Rural Poverty, mem 1968;Family Training Ctr, family couns legal & acute problems Migrant & Seasonal Farmworkers Assn 1973-83; retired 1983. **ORGANIZATIONS:** Bd dirs Mid-East Regional Economic Develop Commn 1972-; bd dirs NC Family Life Council 1970-; mem Assembly of Hertford Co; exec bd mem NAACP; Perfect Ashler Lodge No 63; CS Brown Consistory; spearheaded low-income housing prog in Black Belt E NC black purchased hsng before price rise 1967; wrote proposal for Family Training Prog gave birth to only Family Training Ctr in US 1968; founder/pres CS Brown Restoration Assoc 1984. **HONORS/ACHIEVEMENTS:** Published book "Fruits of Enduring Faith" 1965; NAACP Awd Hertford Co Chapt; Meritorious Serv to Humanity 1967; Five Yr PPOP Awd Meritorious Serv to low income families; rcd FDA Spl Merit Awd MSFA Training Ctr Rich Sq NC; named to serve on NC Family Life Council's Legislative Liaison Com to NC Gen Assembly; NC Family Life Cncl Dist Awd & Bowl for serv to NC families 1985; headed Statewide Migrant Ministries for Gnl Baptist St Conv 1987; founded C,S Brown Cult Arts Cntr & Museum exec dir/curator 1986-87. **MILITARY SERVICE:** USMC 1943-45. **BUSINESS ADDRESS:** Family Counselor, Family Training Ctr, Box 395, Rich Square, NC 27896.

FELTON, JAMES A.
Educator, administration. **PERSONAL:** Born Jun 20, 1945, New York, NY. **EDUCATION:** Tufts, MA 1969; Bradley, BA 1967. **CAREER:** Univ MA, dir financial aid;Univ MA, asst dir financial aid; Metro Mus Art NYC, intern treasury dept; One Yrs Tour Europe, Germany, Africa, Egypt, Nigeria, Mali; MA Assn Coll Minority Adminstrs;Howard U, Phi Mu Alpha Sinfonia, Foreian Affairs & Scholar. **BUSINESS ADDRESS:** U MA at Boston, Boston Harbor Campus, Boston, MA 02125.

FELTON, JAMES EDWARD, JR.
Business executive. **PERSONAL:** Born Dec 01, 1932, New York, NY; married Elizabeth Madison; children: Robin Felton Leadbetter, James E III, Cynthia, Corey. **EDUCATION:** Robert Louis Stevenson Inst & the NY School of Tech, 1956; Rutgers University, courses in the principles of supervision 1974. **CAREER:** General Service Administration grade level of WC-l0, 1957-72; United States Post Office, 1972-77; United Custodial Serv Armed Forces, 2 years; Ebon Serv Intl Inc, sr vp. **ORGANIZATIONS:** Founder United Custodial Service 1969; founder EBON Services Intl 1973; member Bldg Service Contractors Assoc Intl, Essex County Private Industry Council, Human & Civil Rights Assoc of NJ; vice president and Chairman of the Bd EBON Service Intl 1985; mem Bethany Baptist Ch Newark, NJ; co-founder NJ United Minority Business Brain Trust. **HONORS/ACHIEVEMENTS:** Dedicated services award Young Man's Christian Assn 1983; appreciation award Area 9 Essex County Special Olympics 1983; certificate of appreciation Muslums United for Social and Political Change Award 1984; advocacy award Nwk Minority Business Development Center 1984. **MILITARY SERVICE:** AUS pvt first class 2 yrs; Honorable Discharge 1955. **BUSINESS ADDRESS:** Senior Vice President, Ebon Services Intl Inc, Newark International Airport, Terminal "B", Newark, NJ 07114.

FELTON, OTIS LEVERNA
Bank official. **PERSONAL:** Born Jun 08, 1946, Monroe, LA; divorced; children: Lawrence Dwayne, Chloe Queana. **EDUCATION:** Southern Univ, BS 1968; Natl Univ, MS 1976; Grossmont Coll, Special Courses in Real Estate. **CAREER:** Security Pacific Bank, branch exam off 1970-75; San Diego Trust & Svgs Bank, asst mgr 1975-77; Gibraltar Svgs, vice pres & mgr. **ORGANIZATIONS:** Pst bd mem East Co Bd United Way 1980-82; charter mem treas San Diego Urban Bankers 1980-82; mem Los Angeles Urban Bankers 1985; past mem & pres Rotary Intl. **MILITARY SERVICE:** AUS E-5 spec; Bronze Star; Army Commendation Medal; Commendation Medal w/Oak Leaf Cluster; Vietnam Serv Medal; Good Conduct Medal. **BUSINESS ADDRESS:** Vice President & Manager, Gibraltar S&L, 3245 Wilshire Blvd, Beverly Hills, CA 90010.

FELTON, ZORA BELLE
Museum educator. **PERSONAL:** Born Jun 22, 1930, Allentown, PA; daughter of James William Martin and Josephine Elizabeth Cobbs Martin; married Edward P Felton, Jr, Jul 12, 1975; children: Erica Booker, Eric, Edward (stepchildren). **EDUCATION:** Moravian Coll, Bethlehem PA, BA, 1952; Howard Univ, Washington DC, MEd, 1980. **CAREER:** Sleighton Farm School for Girls, Media PA, field counselor, 1952; Dayton YWCA, Dayton OH, dir teenage dept, 1952-58; Southeast Neighborhood House, Washington DC, dir educ and group work, 1958-67; Anacostia Museum, Washington DC, chief educ dept, 1967. **ORGANIZATIONS:** Sec, Washington DC Chapter, African-Amer Museum Educ, African Amer Museums Assn, 1985-89; mem, Phi Delta Kappa, Museum Educators' Roundtable; bd mem, Washington DC Council for the Social Studies, 1986-89; mem, Natl Black Child Devel Inst; bd mem, Natl History Day Bd (Washington DC); mem, Mayor's Blue Ribbon Comm for the Promotion of the Arts and Economic Devel, 1986-88, Delta Sigma Theta Sorority; sec, Ethel James Williams Scholarship Fund Inc, 1986-90. **HONORS/ACHIEVEMENTS:** Outstanding Graduating Sr Award, Moravian Coll, 1952; Recipient, First Annual Raymond S Haupert Humanitarian Award, Moravian Coll, 1970; author of A Walk Through 'Old' Anacostia, 1975, as well as numerous articles, museum educ materials and learning packages; America's Top 100 Black Business and Professional Women, 1988; Certificate of Appreciation for service to museums of this country, Inst of Museum Services, 1988; Certificate of Appreciation for service to the Ethel James Williams Scholarship Fund, 1989. **BUSINESS ADDRESS:** Chief, Education Department, Anacostia Museum-Smithsonian Institution, 1901 Fort Place, SE, Washington, DC 20012.

FELTUS, JAMES, JR.
Minister. **PERSONAL:** Born Apr 16, 1921, Gloster, MS; son of James Feltus, Sr and Lilly Packnett Feltus; married Hazel Luter; children: Erasmus, Gerald, Joan, Eunice, Michaell, James III, Elliott, Percy. **EDUCATION:** Xavier Univ, EdM, PhB 1946; Campbell Coll, BD 1954, DD 1955; New Orleans Bapt Theol Sem, MRE 1973. **CAREER:** British Honduras, dist supt dist 8 1953-65, overseer 1955; Orleans Parish Sch Bd, substitute teacher 1954-74; First Church of God in Christ, pastor 28 yrs; The Churches of God in Christ (United) in US London & Jamaica, founder 1974; Jurisdiction #2 Church of God in Christ, bishop. **ORGANIZATIONS:** Pres, Interdenominational Ministerial Alliance, 1987-; mem, District Attorney's Committee Against Drugs, 1988-89. **HONORS/ACHIEVEMENTS:** Certificate of Merit Outstanding Serv & Key to City Mayor of New Orleans 1971; Silver Anniversary Serv Awd Radio Station WYLD 1971; Honorary Civil Sheriff of Orleans Parish by Paul Valteau, 1983; Civil Sheriff Deputy by Paul Valteau; Colonel of the Staff to Gov Edwin Edwards of the State of Louisiana, 1987; Certificate of Appreciation for Contribuiton to the City of New Orleans, Awarded by Mayor S Bartholomew, 1987, Awarded by Mayor Moreal, 1983; Long career of performing good works that daily benefit the City of New Orleans, adopted by the City Council of New Orleans, 1986; Commended and cited by City Council for contribution to community and leadership exhibited, 1987; proclaimed as Bishop James Feltus Jr's Day in New Orleans; adopted by Mayor S Bartholomew and City Council of New Orleans, 1987. **BUSINESS ADDRESS:** Bishop, Churches of God in Christ United, 2453 Josephine St, New Orleans, LA 70112.

FENTRESS, ROBERT H.
Publishing executive. **PERSONAL:** Born Oct 24, 1921, Brownsville, TN; married Alice; children: Robert, Barbara. **EDUCATION:** TN State U, attnd. **CAREER:** Johnson Pub Co Inc Chgo, vp, circulation dir; company pub 4 Mags, Ebony, Jet, Black Stars, Ebony, Jr; started with co as circulation rep 1950-53; asst circulation mgr 1954-57; circulation mgr 1958; v pres 1968. **BUSINESS ADDRESS:** 820 S Michigan Ave, Chicago, IL 60605.

FENTRESS, SHIRLEY B.
Corporate officer. **PERSONAL:** Born Nov 16, 1937, Bolivar, TN; married Ernest Fentress; children: Sherral Fentress Sain. **EDUCATION:** TN State Univ, 1955-57; Cortez Business Coll, 1968. **CAREER:** Frank Thrifty Grocery, owner 1980-81; Frank Thrifty Liquor Corp, owner 1981-84; City Colleges of Chicago, dir of payroll. **ORGANIZATIONS:** Sec New Philadelphia Baptist Courtesy Comm 1972; co-chmn 1st Union Baptist Church Pastor Anniv 1985, Chairperson Pastors Anniv 1986-87; capt 1st Union Baptist Church Anniversary 1985; Coordinator Crusade of Mercy City Coll of Chicago 1986-87. **HONORS/ACHIEVEMENTS:** Woman of the Week WBEE Radio Station Chicago 1974; Citation of Merit WAIT 820 Radio Station Chicago 1974; Great Gal Awd WJPC Radio Station Chicago 1974. **HOME ADDRESS:** 308 Hickory, Glenwood, IL 60425. **BUSINESS ADDRESS:** Dir Payroll Records, City Colleges Of Chicago, 30 E Lake St, Chicago, IL 60601.

FERDINAND, KEITH C.
Cardiologist. **PERSONAL:** Born Dec 05, 1950, New Orleans, LA; son of Vallery Ferdinand Jr and Inola Copelin Ferdinand; married Daphne Pajeaud Ferdinand, Feb 16, 1973; children: Kamau, Rashida, Aminisha, Jua. **EDUCATION:** Telluride Scholar, Cornell University, 1968-69; University of New Orleans, BA, 1972; Howard University College of Medicine, MD, 1976. **CAREER:** US Public Health Hospital, New Orleans LA, intern, 1976-77; LSU Medical Center, New Orleans LA, internal medicine resident, 1977-79, cardiology fellow, 1979-80; Howard University Hospital, Washington DC, cardiology fellow, 1981; Flint Goodridge Hospital, New Orleans LA, chief of cardiology, 1981-85; Medical Associates, New Orleans LA, private practice, 1981-83; Xavier University of New Orleans LA, visiting professor, 1981-82, associate professor, 1982—; Health Corp, New Orleans LA, consultant, 1982-85; Heartbeat Life Center, New Orleans LA, private practice, 1983—; LA State Univ Medical Center, New Orleans LA, clinical instructor, 1986—; United Medical Center, New Orleans LA, chief of cardiology, 1985—, chief of medical staff, 1987-88. **ORGANIZATIONS:** Board member, 1987—, editor of newsletter, 1988—, Assn of Black Cardiologists; fellow, American College of Cardiology; board member, American Lung Assn of LA, 1987—; vice-president, LA Medical Assn, 1988-; American Heart Assn; Trilateral Committee to End Violence in the Black Community; board member, Greater New Orleans Mental Health Assn, 1985-87; board member, Urban League of Greater New Orleans, 1984; Alpha Omega Alpha; board member of several community service groups. **HONORS/ACHIEVEMENTS:** First Place, Unity Awards in Media, Lincoln Univ of MO, 1982; Outstanding Service Award, LP Nurses of LA, 1983; Black Man of the Year, New Orleans Assn of Black Social Workers, 1985; distinguished service award, Greater Liberty BC, 1987; Frederick Douglass Award, Natl Assn of Negro Business and Professional Womens Club of New Orleans, 1988. **BUSINESS ADDRESS:** Heartbeats Life Center, 1201 Poland Ave, New Orleans, LA 70117.

FEREBEE, CLAUDE T., SR.
Retired dentist. **PERSONAL:** Born Apr 08, 1901, Norfolk, VA; son of Charles Ferebee and Nanny Ferebee; married Hazel Jones; children: Claude T (deceased). **EDUCATION:** Wilberforce U, BS 1923; Columbia U, DDS 1929. **CAREER:** Dentist, pvt prac; Howard U, faculty of Dentistry 1929-36; Washington DC, pvt prac 1936-41; AUS, Dental Reserve Corps 1932; RT Freeman Dental Soc Wash DC, past pres; Dental Reserve Corps 428th Inf Reserve Ft Howard MD, active duty training 1932-40; 366th Inf Regt Ft Devens MD, extended active duty 1940. **ORGANIZATIONS:** Mem Nat Dental Assn; Am Dental Assn; Odontochirurgical Soc Philadelphia; Am Acad of Dental Med; Am Endodontic Soc; past pres N Harlem Dental Soc; Omikron Kappa Upsilon Dental Honorary Frat Columbia Univ Chpt; Alpha Phi Alpha Frat; NAACP; Luth Ch; Lectr & Clinician Dental Orgns. **HONORS/ACHIEVEMENTS:** Bronze Star Medal with Citation from SW Pacific Theater of Operations 1945; Robert T Freeman Dental Soc Award Gold Plaque; N Harlem Dental Soc Award; Bronze Plaque; The OKU. **MILITARY SERVICE:** AUS maj 1932-45.

FERERE, GERARD ALPHONSE
Educator. **PERSONAL:** Born Jul 21, 1930, Cap Haitian, Haiti;married Nancy; children: Magali, Rachel. **EDUCATION:** Naval Acad of Venezuela, Ensign 1953; Villanova Univ, MA 1967; Univ of PA, PhD 1974. **CAREER:** Haitian Navy, naval officer 1953-58; Haiti, language teacher 1958-63; St Joseph's Univ, prof 1964-. **ORGANIZATIONS:** Translator interpreter SELF 1964-; pres Coalition for Haitian Concerns 1982-. **HOME ADDRESS:** 215 Red Barn Rd, Willow Grove, PA 19090. **BUSINESS ADDRESS:** Professor of Languages, St Joseph'sUniv, City Ave at 54th St, City Line at 54 St, Philadelphia, PA 19131.

FERGERSON, MIRIAM N. (NEE WATSON)
Arts education consultant. **PERSONAL:** Born Sep 15, 1941, Homestead, PA; married Cecil Fergerson; children: Melanie, John, Kinte. **EDUCATION:** VA State Univ, BA French/Ed 1964; Azusa Pacific Univ, MA Marriage, Family & Child Counseling 1975. **CAREER:** CA Superior Court Conciliation Court, family counselor 1977-78; Youth Training Sch, youth counselor 1978-83; SanMar Group Homes, substance abuse social worker, 1983-; Art Educ Consultant Servs, founder/admin, 1974-. **ORGANIZATIONS:** Youth counselor Missionary Dept Messiah Bapt Church 1982-86; mem bd Christian Educ Messiah Bapt Church 1983-; bd chmn Friends Wm Grant Still Arts Ctr1983-; vice pres arts/culture 10th Councilmanic Dist Women's Steering Comm 1984-85; consultant Dr Chas R Drew Historical Exhibit Drew Medical Sch 1984-85; researcher City Watts, Watts Towers Art Ctr 1984-85; mem CA for Drug Free Youth 1984; Rev Jesse Jackson for Pres 1984; vice pres Parent Adv Cncl Fairfax High 1984-85; editor/consultant Watts Towers Jazz Festival Publ 1986; liason 10th Dist Arts Adv Council 1986-87; mem Friends of Geneva Cox for City Council; pres Trinity Mission Circle Messiah Church. **HONORS/ACHIEVEMENTS:** TV Documentary Watts Festival Recounted Univ Jenkins Production 1980; Community Counseling Serv Awd Westminster Presbyterian Church, 1984-85; West Angeles Christian Acad Outstanding Volunteer Serv Awd 1986; Natl Conf of Artists Outstanding Serv Awd 1987; article Golden State Life Ins Travel & Art magazine 1978. **HOME ADDRESS:** 1417 So Ogden Dr, Los Angeles, CA 90019.

FERGUSON, ANDREW L.
Chief executive. **CAREER:** Auburn Ford/Lincoln-Mercury, Inc, Auburn, AL, chief executive, 1985-. **BUSINESS ADDRESS:** Auburn Ford/Lincoln-Mercury, Inc, 615 Ophelia Rd, Auburn, AL 36830. *

FERGUSON, CECIL (DUKE)
Graphic artist. **PERSONAL:** Born Mar 13, 1931, Chicago, IL; married Irene; children: Mark. **EDUCATION:** Art Inst of Chgo; Inst of Design, IL Inst of Tech; Am Academy of Art. **CAREER:** Ebony Mag, asst art dir; "The Ebony Success Library", designer; Johnson Publ, promotional illustrations & layouts. **BUSINESS ADDRESS:** 820 S Michigan Ave, Chicago, IL 60605.

FERGUSON, EDWARD A., JR.
Financial administrator. **PERSONAL:** Born Jul 21, 1942, New York, NY; son of Edward A Ferguson Sr and Oletha Higgs Ferguson; married Cynhia Henderson; children: Edward III, Candace, Derek. **EDUCATION:** Iona Coll, BBA 1965; St John's Univ, MBA 1974; New York Univ, Post Grad 1975-78. **CAREER:** Citi Bank, offcl asst 1965-70; Bankers Trust Co,

asst mgr 1970; Bedford Stuyvesant Rest Corp, dir of admin serv 1970-74; Xerox Corp, 1974-78, mgr br control New York City 1978-80; Xerox Corp Rochester NY, mgr sales commn admin, serv consult 1980-84; Xerox Corp Columbus, support mgr dist ops 1984-85; Xerox Corp Akron OH, dist mgr customer serv 1985-88; Xerox Corp, district bus mgr 1988-. **ORGANIZATIONS:** Biographer Who's Who in America Finance & Industry 1983-; dir Catholic Youth Orgzn-Roch, NY 1980-84, Berkshire Farm & Youth Serv 1976-; biographer Who's Who in Amer Midwest 1987. **MILITARY SERVICE:** AUS lt col 22 yrs, Army Achvmnt, Army Accomodation, Good Conduct, Natl Def Medal; over seas ribbon, army reserve medal, NYS joyr medal. **BUSINESS ADDRESS:** District Business Manager, Xerox Corp, 471 E Broad Street, Columbus, OH 43215.

FERGUSON, GEORGE A.
Educator. **PERSONAL:** Born May 25, 1923, Washington, DC; married Francesca C; children: 5 children. **EDUCATION:** BS 1947; MS 1948; PhD 1965. **CAREER:** Clark Coll, chmn dept of physics 1950-53; US Naval Research Lab, research scientist 1954-75; Howard Univ, prof 1967-. **ORGANIZATIONS:** Mem Amer Inst Physics; Amer Physical Soc; Amer Nuclear Soc; Wash Philosophical Soc; Amer Soc for Engr Edn; AAAS; mem Joint Bd Sci Educ 1960-; Sigma Pi Sigma 1957-; Administrative Judge US Nucl Reg Comm 1973-. **HONORS/ACHIEVEMENTS:** AEC Fellow 1948-50; Thomas Edison Fellow 1964-65. **MILITARY SERVICE:** AUS 1943-46. **BUSINESS ADDRESS:** Professor, Howard University, School of Engineering, Washington, DC 20059.

FERGUSON, IDELL
Corporation executive, real estate broke. **PERSONAL:** Born Oct 20, Montgomery, AL; married Dennis E (divorced); children: Ronald, Mary, Dennis. **EDUCATION:** Actual Business Coll MI, attended; Hammal-Actual Bus Coll AL, attended; Univ of Akron OH, Real Estate Courses; Certificate, Hammel-Actual Business Coll Akron, OH, Certicate, Akron Univ,; Mount Union Coll, Alliance, OH 1977-78, 1980-81. **CAREER:** Russell Realty Co, sec salesperson, legal sec, mgr; certified appraiser 1959-; Advance Realty, owner, broker 1960-65; Corp Advance Realty, 1961-66; Natl Assoc Real Estate Brokers Inc, instructor, real estate classes 1965-71; pre-kindergarten teacher 1965; Idell Ferguson Realty, owner, broker 1965-; FHA, appraiser 1969-72; notary public 18 yrs; Lawyers Title Insurance Corp, title plant mgr 1975-; License Real Estate Broker Akron, OH 1960-87. **ORGANIZATIONS:** Coordinator Jesse Jackson for Pres Comm Summit County 1984; mem OH Assoc RE Brokers Inc, Columbus Assoc RE Brokers 1963-65; 1st sec, pres 1969-71, org 1965 Akron Assoc RE Brokers; chairperson State Conv 1966, State Bd 1965-71; mem Women's Council Akron Area Bd Realtors 1968-, Human Relations Comm Akron Bd Realtors 1970-; bd mem Fair Housing Contact Serv 1965-67; housing comm Urban League 1961-63; bd mem Akron NAACP 1961-62; den mother BSA 1961-62; mem OH Civil Rights Comm 1961-65, YMCA, YWCA, Young Business & Professional Womens Club, Akron Business & Professional Womens League, Akron Club Natl Assoc Negro Business & Professional Womens Clubs Inc, Centenary United Methodist Church, NEFCO 1976-, Womens Council of Realtors of the Natl Assoc of Realtors; bd mem United Church Women Columbus 1963-64, Akron 1964-67; headed program Negro History 1968-69; org, sponsored Akron Young Adult Club Natl Assoc Negro Business & Professional Womens Clubs Inc 1971; dist gov NANBPW 1972-74; org Wesley Serv Guild 1953; bd mem Fair Housing Contact Serv 1979; co-chairperson, admin bd Centenary United Methodist Church 1979. **HONORS/ACHIEVEMENTS:** Listed in OH State Newspaper; Achievement Award 1970; Recog Award 1972; Leadership Citation 1973; Safari Excellence 1974; Outstanding Serv Award for Leadership & Serv in Re-Org the Akron Assoc of RE Brokers OH Assoc of RE Brokers; Outstanding Serv to Natl Assoc of Negro Business & Professional Women's Club Kent Area Chap Links Inc 1980; Award Realtist Pioneer Natl Assoc of RE Brokers Inc Akron Assoc 1982.

FERGUSON, JOHNNIE NATHANIEL
Retail banking officer. **PERSONAL:** Born Jan 17, 1943, Washington, DC; son of James H Ferguson and Viola Cooper; married Delphine David, Oct 31, 1964; children: Michelle D. **EDUCATION:** Univ of the Dist of Columbia, AAS 1973. **CAREER:** FBI, fingerprint tech 1967; Riggs Natl Bank, programmer 1977, data processing supervisor 1979, banking officer. **ORGANIZATIONS:** Pres Orr Elem School PTA 1976-84; mem Washington DC Assn of Urban Bankers 1977-83; pres Riggs Natl Bank Club 1979; treas DC Congress of Parents & Teachers 1982-84; treas Adv Neighborhood Comm 6C 1982-; mem DC Federation of Farmers & Consumers Markets 1983-; treasurer Kiwanis Club of Eastern Branch 1988-; 1st v pres D C Congress of PTA 1989-. **HONORS/ACHIEVEMENTS:** Cert of appreciation Amer Cancer Society 1980; cert of appreciation DC Advisory Council on Vocational Educ 1980; cert of awd Benjamin G Orr Elem Sch 1980-84; honorary life member National Congress of Parents & Teachers 1987-; life member D C Congress of PTA 1986. **MILITARY SERVICE:** AUS sgt E5 3 yrs; Army Commendation Medal; Good Conduct Medal. **BUSINESS ADDRESS:** Retail Banking Officer, Riggs National Bank of Washington, Universal Office, 1875 Connecticut Ave NW, Washington, DC 20009.

FERGUSON, LLOYD N.
Educator. **PERSONAL:** Born Feb 09, 1918, Oakland, CA; son of Noel Swithin Ferguson and Gwendolyn Louise Johnson Ferguson; married Charlotte Welch; children: Lloyd Jr, Stephen Bruce, Lisa Annette. **EDUCATION:** Univ of CA Berkeley, BS 1940, PhD 1943. **CAREER:** Univ of CA Berkeley, research asst Natl Defense Proj 1941-44; A&T Coll Greensboro NC, asst prof 1944-45; Howard Univ faculty mem head chem dept 1958-65; Natl Bureau of Standards Wash DC, chemist 1950; Naval Ordinance Lab White Oak MD, chemist 1951; Univ of OR Eugene, visiting prof 1958, 1960, 1963,visiting prof Univ of Nairobi, Kenya 1971-72; CA State Univ Los Angeles, prof chmn chem dept 1968-71; Dept of Agr Pasadena CA, chemist 1967; Univ of HI, MARC visiting scientist 1982; CSU at Los Angeles, emeritus prof 1986-. **ORGANIZATIONS:** Mem Amer Chem Soc; mem Amer Assc of Univ Prof; mem Sigma Xi; mem Phi Kappa Phi Natl Honor Soc; mem Fellow Amer Assc for Adv of Science; mem Fellow Chem Soc of London; chrmn Southern CA Sect Amer Chem Soc 1983; chmn Div Chem Educ Amer Chem Soc 1980; mem chem examination comm, graduate record examination; mem Bd of Scientific Counselors for Natl Inst of Environmental & Health Sci 1979-83; mem US Natl Sea Grant Review Panel 1978-81, 1982-84; mem US Natl Comm to Intl Union of Pure & Applied Chem 1973-76; mem at large Natl Acad of Sciences Natl Research Council Div of Chem 1970-73; mem Natl Cancer Inst Chemotherapy Adv Comm 1972-75; mem Medicinal & Organic Chem Review Comm Natl Inst of Health 1966-70; mem Adv Comm on Research in Physical & Biological Sciences Food & Drug Admin 1966-70; mem Adv Bd Petro Research Fund Amer Chem Soc 1966-70; mem Admin Comm of Natl Flwshp Fund Atlanta GA chrmn Educ Comm Southern CA Sect Amer Chem Soc 1979-80, 1968-89, alternate cnslr 1969-72. **HONORS/ACHIEVEMENTS:** CA State Univ & Coll Trustees Outstanding Prof Award 1981; Natl Org of Black Chem & Chem Engrs Outstanding Tchng Award 1979; Amer Chem Soc Award In Chem Educ 1978; Amer Fnd Negro Affairs Distg Amer Medallion 1976; Outstanding Prof Award CA State Univ Los Angeles 1974; Manu Chem Assc Award for Excel in Teaching 1974; Oakland Museum Assc Award 1973; honoray DSc Howard Univ 1970, & Coe Clge IA 1979; Guggenheim Fellowship 1953-54 Cytochem Dept Carlsberg Lab Copenhagen Denmark; Natl Sci Fnd Fac Fellowship 1961-62 Swiss Fed Inst of Tech Zurich Switzerland; Amer Chem Soc ACS Tour Speaker Plaque 1974; feature July/August 1971 issue "Chemisty", "Lloyd N Ferguson - Traveling Salesman for Chemical Education"; feature in "The Post" Oakland CA local newspaper June 1973; cited in "Careers in Chemistry, Opportunit ies for Minorities" Amer Chem Soc Career Guide 1976. **HOME ADDRESS:** 4477 Wilshire Blvd #208, Los Angeles, CA 90010. **BUSINESS ADDRESS:** Emeritus Professor, CSU at Los Angeles, 4221 Cloverdale Ave, Los Angeles, CA 90008.

FERGUSON, MAYNARD W.
Band leader, trumpet player, musician. **PERSONAL:** Born May 04, 1928, Montreal, Quebec, Canada;married Floralu; children: Kim, Corby, Lisa, Bentley, Wilder. **CAREER:** Dorsey & Kenton, Birdland Dreamband, 1955-66; formed own touring 13-piece orch 1957-65; formed sextette 1965; Maynard Ferguson Music Inc, owner; formed High Voltage 1986, 7 piece electric fusion band. **HONORS/ACHIEVEMENTS:** Awds in Downbeat Jazz poll, Playboy Jazz poll, various other jazz awds; Grammy nomination for "Gonna Fly Now" from Rocky movie in 1977. **BUSINESS ADDRESS:** Maynard Ferguson Music, PO Box 716, Ojai, CA 93023.

FERGUSON, RENEE
Journalist. **PERSONAL:** Born Aug 22, 1949, Oklahoma City, OK. **EDUCATION:** IN Univ, BA 1971; IN Univ, MA 1972. **CAREER:** Indianapolis News, news reporter 1971-72; WLWI-TV Indpls, news reporter 1972-76; WBBM-TV Chgo, news reporter 1976-82; CBS News, news reporter 1982-. **ORGANIZATIONS:** Bd of dir The Assoc for Children 1975-78; bd mem Big Sisters of Amer/Indianapolis 1975-78; mem Kappa Alpha Sor. **HONORS/ACHIEVEMENTS:** Ed Writer of the Year Awd Natl Ed Assoc IN 1977; Assoc Press Newswriters Awd Assoc Press 1977; 4 Time Emmy Awd Winner Chicago Chap Natl Acad of TV Arts & Sci 1978-80. **BUSINESS ADDRESS:** CBS News, 524 W 57th, New York, NY 10019.

FERGUSON, ROBERT LEE, SR. (FERGIE)
Consultant in aero-systems management, counseling, psychology. **PERSONAL:** Born Feb 18, 1932, Rascon San Luis, Mexico;son of Booker T Ferguson and Corrilea (Jackson) Ferguson; married Ruby Evelyn Brewer Ferguson, Nov 01, 1953 (deceased); children: Robert Jr, Duane. **EDUCATION:** Bakersfield Coll, attended 1950-51; Southwestern Coll, AA 1969; Naval Postgraduate Sch, BA 1973; Univ of N CO, MA 1975; Pacific Western Univ Los Angeles CA, PhD 1986. **CAREER:** USN Hawaii, captain's steward 1951-52; Heavy Attack Squadron, aircraft maintenance chief; USN, adv in human/minority relations psychology counseling 1967-77; NAS Miramar CA, asst dept head aircraft maintenance 1973-75; USS Enterprise, asst dept head aircraft maintenance 1975-78; NAS Lemoore CA, officer in charge aircraft maintenance 1978-80; Fighter Squadron 124, dept head aircraft maintenance 1980; Rail Company, sr logistics analyst; systems acquisition mgmt cons. **ORGANIZATIONS:** Mem Fleet Res Assn 1963-65; mgr Parkview Little League Chula Vista CA 1969-77; mem VFW 1974-; mem Naval Aviation Tailhook Assn 1972-; alumni Univ of N CO 1975-; mem Natl Naval Officer Assn 1977-; mem San Diego Museum of Art; corresp chmn African Arts Comm. **HONORS/ACHIEVEMENTS:** Good Conduct Medal 1956 1967 1973 1980; Secnav Medal 1967 1971; Air Medal 1971; Navy Commendation 1980. **MILITARY SERVICE:** USN comdr 30 yrs served; Naval Gallantry Cross; Vietnam Service; Korea. **HOME ADDRESS:** 604 Marlposa Cir, Chula Vista, CA 92011.

FERGUSON, ROSETTA
State representative. **PERSONAL:** Born Jul 01, 1920, Florence, MS; children: 4 Children. **EDUCATION:** Detroit Inst of Tech. **CAREER:** 20th District, Detroit, MI, former state rep; Loyalty Investigation Comm, mem staff mgr real estate firm. **ORGANIZATIONS:** Mem Dem State Central; exec bd & precinct Delegate for 10 Yrs; recording sec 13th Congressional District; mem Wayne Co Dem Rep Human Relations Coun on Civil Rights; Gray Lady for Red Cross; cub scout den mother ofr 3 yrs; mem PTA; NAACP,; TULC; Women's Pub Affairs Com of 1000 Inc; orgn Youth Civic Eagles; founder & finan Sec Peoples Community Civil League; mem Missionary Soc of Peoples Bapt Ch; mem MI Right to Life Com & People Taking Action Against Abortion Com; numerous other civic orgn; Ch sponser of Pub Act 127 of 1966 Fair Textbook Law. **HONORS/ACHIEVEMENTS:** Featured in Ebony Mag as one of the Black Women Leaders in State of MI; "Alpha Kappa Alpha Sorority's Heritage Series #1, Black Women in Politics"; tribute of honor for "Far-sighted vision & dedication to the full maturity of the human family; MI House of Rep 1970.

FERGUSON, ST. JULIAN
Educator. **PERSONAL:** Born Apr 13, 1935, South Carolina; son of Alonzo and Irene; married Albertha Simmons; children: Darian, Gerald, Bernard. **EDUCATION:** SC State, BS 1957; Loyola Univ, MEd 1971. **CAREER:** Lower N Youth Ctr, music dir; Tilden Tech HS, inst music tchr 1965-69; Madison Elem, tchr 1969-71; Chicago Bd of Educ, tchr early remediation 1971; Bryn Mawr Elem Sch, teacher 1971-. **ORGANIZATIONS:** Mem NEA, IL Tchr Assn, Chicago Fed of Musicians Local 10208, Operation PUSH; professional piano & trumpet player. **MILITARY SERVICE:** USMC pfc 1953-57. **HOME ADDRESS:** 9956 S Union Ave, Chicago, IL 60621.

FERGUSON, SHELLIE ALVIN
Corporate officer. **PERSONAL:** Born Oct 04, 1943, Waterbury, CT; married Mavis H; children: Damon G, Charmain D. **EDUCATION:** Univ of CT, BS 1965, MS 1970. **CAREER:** Town of Watertown-Secondary, bus instr 1965-69; New Oppty for Waterbury & Pvt Practice, bus cons, ec devel consult 1968-77; Chase Brass & Copper Co, personnel mgr 1969-71; Mattatuck Comm Coll, acctg prof 1971-73; FIP Corp, dir 1979-; IBM Seminars, lectr, natl & reg; lectr on small bus, computerization real estate fin & others, various colls; FIP Corp, vp, treas 1973-, sr vice pres treas. **ORGANIZATIONS:** Mem NAACP 1970-. **HONORS/ACHIEVEMENTS:** Daisy Lord Meml Awd Wilby High School Waterbury Ct 1961; Teacher of the Year Awd Town of Watetown Bus Div 1969; Publ numerous articles on computerization fin & etc Hartford Courant, CT Bus Jrnl, Natl Computer Mag 1978-; Hon Student Univ of CT All-Conf Basketball Player HS & Coll. **BUSINESS ADDRESS:** Sr Vice-President, Treasurer, FIP Corp, McKee Pl, Cheshire, CT 06410.

FERGUSON, SHERMAN E.
Educator, musician. **PERSONAL:** Born Oct 31, 1944, Philadelphia. **EDUCATION:** Berklee Coll of Music. **CAREER:** Professional Musician, appearing on TV & making numerous recordings 14 yrs; Catalyst, member music group; Percussion, teacher. **BUSINESS ADDRESS:** PO Box 15593, Philadelphia, PA 19131.

FERGUSON, WILKIE DEMERITTE, JR.
Judge. **PERSONAL:** Born May 11, 1939, Miami, FL; daughter of Wilkie Sr and Inee; married Betty J Tucker; children: Tawnicia, Wilkie III. **EDUCATION:** Florida A&M Univ, BS 1960; Howard Univ, JD 1968. **CAREER:** McCrary Ferguson & Lee, partner 1970-73; Judge Industrial Claims, admin law judge 1973-77; Circuit Court, judge 1977-81; Court of Appeal, judge 1981-. **ORGANIZATIONS:** Mem Amer & Natl Bar Assocs 1970-; bd chmn JESCA 1972-80, Florida Memorial Coll 1982-, United Way of Dade Co FL 1986-; mem Supreme Court Comm Jury Instructions for Civil Cases 1986-. **HONORS/ACHIEVEMENTS:** SE Region Brother of the Year Alpha Phi Alpha Frat 1982; Leadership Awd United Negro Coll Fund 1984; Community Leadership United Way of Dade Co 1985; Thurgood Marshall Awd for Judicial Gallantry Black Lawyers Assoc Miami 1986. **MILITARY SERVICE:** AUS Airborne Infantry captain; Honorable Discharge 1968. **BUSINESS ADDRESS:** Judge Dist Court of Appeal, State of Florida, 2001 SW 117th Ave, Miami, FL 33175.

FERNANDEZ, JOHN PETER
Manager. **PERSONAL:** Born Oct 22, 1941, Boston, MA; divorced; children: Michele, Eleni, Sevgi. **EDUCATION:** Harvard U, (magna cum laude) Government AB 1969;Univ of CA, Berkeley, sociology MA 1971;Univ of CA Socio Berkeley, PhD 1973. **CAREER:** Bell of PA, div mgr customer serv 1978-; AT&T Basking Rioge NJ, mgr mgmt educ & devel 1975-78; Yale U, asst prof 1974-75; AT&T NYC, personnel supr-rsrch 1973-74; YMCA Dorchester MA, prog dir 1965-69. **ORGANIZATIONS:** Mem Am Socio Assn 1973-; mem Council of Concerned Black Exec 1975-. **HONORS/ACHIEVEMENTS:** Outst sophomore Govt Major NortheasternUniv 1967; special careers fellowship,Univ of CA Berkeley 1969-73. **MILITARY SERVICE:** USN elec tech E-5 1960-64. **BUSINESS ADDRESS:** Bell of Pennsylvania, 15 E Montgomery Ave, Pittsburgh, PA 15212.

FERNANDEZ, LYNNE ANN
Physician. **PERSONAL:** Born Apr 21, 1957, New York, NY. **EDUCATION:** Cornell Univ, BS 1978; Howard Univ Coll of Medicine, MD 1984. **CAREER:** New York Medical Coll, chief resident rehabilitation medicine, attending physician 1987-. **ORGANIZATIONS:** Black Agriculturalist Cornell Univ; student advisor Cornell Univ; mem La Asociacion Del Canbe Cornell Univ; NYS School of Agriculture Comm for Minority Policies. **HONORS/ACHIEVEMENTS:** Deans List Cornell Univ; papers presented "Intraoperative Spinal Cord Monitoring" at the Amer Soc for Clinical Evoked Potential 1986; "Electrodiagnosis of Carpal Tunnel Syndrome" at the NY Acad of Medicine 1986. **BUSINESS ADDRESS:** Chief Resident Rehab Medicine, New York Medical College, Metropolitan Hospital, New York, NY.

FERNANDEZ, OCTAVIO ANTONIO
Professional athlete. **PERSONAL:** Born Aug 06, 1962, San Pedro de Macoris, Dominican Republic;married Clara; children: Joel. **CAREER:** Toronto Blue Jays, player 1980-. **HONORS/ACHIEVEMENTS:** Named the All Star SS for the Carolina League 1981; named IL's All-Star SS 1982; R Howard Webster Awd as Syracuse's MVP 1982, 83; named team's Rookie of the Year by Toronto Chap of BBWAA 1984; led AL shortstops in assists 1985; Labatt's "Blue" Player of the Month June 1986; named to Sporting News and UPI's Amer League All Star Team and Assoc Press Major League All-Star team; Gold Glove winner; mem All Star Team 1985, 1986. **BUSINESS ADDRESS:** Toronto Blue Jays, Box 7777, Adelaide St, Toronto, Ontario, Canada M5C 2K7.

FERREBEE, THOMAS G.
Police officer. **PERSONAL:** Born Jan 24, 1937, Detroit; married Irma; children: Gregory G, Debra L, Angela M. **EDUCATION:** IA State U, BS 1960; Eastern MI U, MA 1963. **CAREER:** Detroit Police Dept, cmdr Recruiting Div; Ford Motor Co; Hamtramck HS, tchr; Chrysler Corp. **ORGANIZATIONS:** Bd trustees personnel com Childrens Hosp of MI; Cntr for Criminal Justice & Minority Employment in Law Enforcement; consultant Minority Police Recruiting;mem Optimist Club of Detroit; area activity chmn BSA; MI Pub Personnel Assn; mem Concerned Polic Ofc for Equal Justice. **BUSINESS ADDRESS:** 8045 Second Ave, Detroit, MI 48202.

FERRELL, ROSIE E.
Business executive. **PERSONAL:** Born May 26, 1915, Clarksdale, MS; married Charlie; children: Henry, Joyce, Wilma, Lois, Joseph, Rose, Nathaniel. **EDUCATION:** Delta Comm Coll, AA 1974; Saginaw Val State Coll, BA. **CAREER:** Saginaw, city directory enumberator 1946-71; Field Enterprises Inc, sales rep 1964-66; Saginaw, sch census taker city & state 1965-67; Saginaw Gen Hosp, ward clk 1967; Comm Action Comm, comm aide 1967-69; Dept Model Cities, team capt; Saginaw Multi-Purpose Serv Ctr, information referral splst 1971-76; OurImage Inc, fdr, pres 1976-. **ORGANIZATIONS:** Bd Saginaw Co Social Serv Club 1974-75; Greater Williams Temple Ch of God in Christ 1934-; personal evangelist 1963; NAACP 1935-; chairlady ch membership drive 1965-75; bd mem CAC 1967; worked in drives for United Fund, March of Dimes, Cancer, Sickle Cell; chairlady Muscular Dyst 1961-75; bd mem, coordntr E Side MD Drive 1974-75; v pres Police Comm Relations 1973-76; chairlady Human Resources League Women Voters 1974-75; pres Saginaw City Council PTA 1975-76. **HONORS/ACHIEVEMENTS:** Comm Serv Award Professional & Bus Women 1972; Woman of Yr Zeta Omega Phi Beto Sor Inc 1975; hnr dinner Greater Williams Temple Ch of God in Christ 1975; firehelmet MD 1964; Sailors Regional Award Week 1964; Child Evangelism Tchrs Cert 1963; Am Legion Post 500 Humanitarian Award 1975; treas 8th Dist Co Rep Com; candidate for Saginaw City Council (first black woman to run) 1975-77. **BUSINESS ADDRESS:** 220 N 7 St, Saginaw, MI 48607.

FEW, TERRY LEE
Engineer. **PERSONAL:** Born Mar 12, 1948, Dayton, OH; divorced; children: Kynda R, Raena R. **EDUCATION:** OH State Univ, BSAAE 1966-71; Univ of Cincinnati, MS (fluids) 1972-74. **CAREER:** Fan Rev/Prel Dsgn/Test Facilities, prog engr 1971-72; Test Facilities Engr, test facilities engr 1973-76; Aero Thermo Comb Dsgn, combus dsgn eng 1976-78; Mech Simulator Devel, dsgn engr 1978-80; Adv Fan & Compr Dsgn, mngr compr dsgn 1981-83; Adv Exhaust Syst Dsgn, mngr Augmehto dsgn 1983-. **ORGANIZATIONS:** Vice pres South Hill Enterp 1981-. **HONORS/ACHIEVEMENTS:** Pre license NSPE 1975-. **BUSINESS ADDRESS:** Manager GE37 Augmenter Design, General Electric, Cincinnati, OH 45215.

FEWELL, RICHARD
English instructor. **PERSONAL:** Born Feb 02, 1937, Rock Hill, SC; son of Thomas Fewell (deceased) and Laura Steele Fewell (deceased); married Geraldine Whitted; children: Renee Lorraine, Richard Gerald. **EDUCATION:** Univ of Bridgeport, BA (Magna Cum Laude) 1976, MA 1980. **CAREER:** US Postal Service, mail classification & requirements/postal services; Univ of Bridgeport, part-time English instructor. **ORGANIZATIONS:** Pres 1975-76, mem 1975-, Alpha Sigma Lambda; bd mem NAACP 1976-; mem Frank Silvera Writer's Workshop (Harlem) 1978-; freelance writer Fairfield County Advocate, contributing editor Connecticut Update 1982-83; bd of dirs Bridgeport Arts Council 1982-; comm mem Action for Bridgeport Comm Develop 1984-; founding mem New Bridge Ensemble 1986-; editor Natl Alliance of Postal & Federal Employees Newsletter/Local 808. **HONORS/ACHIEVEMENTS:** Bert & Katya Gilden Memorial Short Story Awd 1975; 1st prize article in Writer's Digest Creative Writing Contest 1977; Literature Awd Connecticut Commn on the Arts 1984; published in The Black Scholar, The Greenfield Review, Callaloo, Obsidian, The Anthology of Magazine Verse & Yearbook of Amer Poetry, The South Carolina Review, Okike (Nigeria) others; author "Blackberries in a Taiwanese Mirror"; Heritage Award/Arts & Humanities, Alpha Kappa Alpha Sorority 1987; actor with Dot Playhouse, played role of "Rev Sykes" in To Kill a Mockingbird 1988; poetry readings (own work) with Chapel Arts Circus/New Haven, CT 1988-89; excerpts from unpublished novel/published in Mwendo (Iowa), Obsidian (NC) & Beanfeast (CT). **MILITARY SERVICE:** USAF 1955-61. **HOME ADDRESS:** 89A Yaremich Dr, Bridgeport, CT 06606.

FIELDER, FRED CHARLES
Educator. **PERSONAL:** Born Jun 16, 1933, Hattisburg, MS; son of Ben Fielder and Quinnie Fielder; married Vivian Johnson; children: Fred Charles, Jr. **EDUCATION:** Tougaloo Coll, BS 1956; Meharry Med Coll, DDS 1960; Hubbard Hosp, intern 1960-61; Univ of MI, MS in Oper Dent 1964; MIT, post grad 1966. **CAREER:** Meharry Med Coll Dept of Oper Dent, instr 1961-63, asst prof 1964-66, assoc prof 1967-74; Meharry Med Coll Schl of Dent, asst dean 1968-; Meharry Med Coll Dent Clinic, supt 1971; Meharry Med Coll Dept Oper Dent, prof/chmn 1974-; Meharry Medical Coll, Nashville, TN, exec assoc dean 1989. **ORGANIZATIONS:** Operative Dentistry of Amer Assoc of Dent Schls; comm mem Manpower & Aux of Amer Assn of Dent Schs 1969-70; councl Intl Assn of Dent Res 1969-73; consul NC St Bd of Dent Exam 1970; vice pres Capital City Dent Soc 1972-74, pres 1974-76; vice pres Omicron-Omicron Chap of Omicron Kappa Upsilon Honor Dent Soc 1970-72, past pres 1972-74; past pres Kappa Sigma Pi Honor Soc 1961-62; past zone vice pres Pan TN Dent Assn 1968-75, state vice pres 1979; clinical consult for commn Dent Accred of Amer Dental Assn 1979-; consult the Quarterly Journal of the Natl Dental Assn. **HONORS/ACHIEVEMENTS:** Most Outstanding Soph Dent Student Meharry Med Coll 1958; Chi Delta Mu Awards 1958; Meth Scholarship Award; Mosby Schol Bk Award; Caulk Prize 1959; MethShol Award High Sch Aver for 3 years 1959; number 1 ranking student 1960; honor student 1960; Acad of Dent Med Award 1960; Acad of Gold Foil Award 1960; Donley H Turpin Mem Award 1960; Mizzy Award in Crown & Bridge 1960; Pan TN Dent Assn Award 1960; Jos Frank Dent Award 1960; Mosby Book Award 1960; Caulk Prize 1960; Nashville Dent Supply Prize 1960; Snyder Dent Prize 1960; Alpha Omega Award 1960; Fellow United Health Found 1963; dean's list Tougaloo Coll 1953-55; Magna cum Laude 1956; pres of class 1952-56; Valedictorian Royal St HS 1952; Recog & plaque one of 100 most valuable employees, Meharry Med Coll 1975; Dedication Recip Merharrian yearbook 1964; Recogn & plaque Growth & Devel Meharry Coll 1971; Outstanding Faculty of the Year Natl Alumni Assn 1988. **BUSINESS ADDRESS:** Professor/Chairman, Meharry Med College, 1005 D B Todd Blvd, Dept Oper Dent, Nashville, TN 37208.

FIELDING, HERBERT ULYSSES
State legislator. **PERSONAL:** Born Jul 06, 1923, Charleston, SC; son of Julius P L Fielding and Sadie E Gaillard Fielding; married Thelma Erenne Stent; children: Julius PL II, Herbert Stent, Frederick Augustus. **EDUCATION:** WV State Coll, BS 1948. **CAREER:** SC House of Representatives, rep 1971-74, 1983-84; SC State Senate, senator, 1985—; Fielding Home for Funerals, vice president, funeral director. **ORGANIZATIONS:** Former member, SC Comm Vocational Rehabilitation; Trident Chamber of Commerce; USC Budget Bd; Bd McClennan Banks Hosp; SC Human Affairs Comm; SC Coastal Counc, 1987—; chair, Charleston County Senate Delegatin, 1989; pres Robert Gould Shaw Boys Club; Univ of SC Budget Bd; bd, McClennan Banks Hosp; Trident Council on Alcoholism; Omega Psi Phi Frat; founder & past co chmn Charleston County Political Action Comm. **HONORS/ACHIEVEMENTS:** First recipient Chas Business & Professional Mens Assn Man of Year Awd 1966; 1st Black elected to SC House since Reconstruction 1970; Silver Beaver Awd Boy Scouts of Amer 1971; Mu Alpha Chap Man of Year Awd 1972; SC Legislative Black Caucus Awd 1975; Harvey Gantt Triumph Award, 1985; Citizens Comm of Charleston County Award, 1985; Outstanding Legislator Award, 1987; Royal Arch Masons Award, 1988; SC Farm Cooperatives Award, 1988. **MILITARY SERVICE:** US Army in American & European Theaters, 1943-46; 500th QM Co. **BUSINESS ADDRESS:** Suite 610, Gressette Senate Office Building, PO Box 142, Columbia, SC 29202.

FIELDS, A. LEO
Administrator. **PERSONAL:** Born Jul 20, 1947, New York, NY; married Jennie Lanz. **EDUCATION:** VA State Coll, BS 1970; NY State U, MA 1975. **CAREER:** Univ of IA, assoc dir Dept of Special Support Serv 1976-, acting dir 1975-76; SUNY, coun Transitional Year Program 1972-75; IBM Corp, assoc engineer 1970-72. **ORGANIZATIONS:** Mem Soc for Intercultural Educ Training & Research; mem NAACP; mem IA chap Mid-Am Assn Educ Opp Prgm; life mem Alpha Phi Alpha Frat;Univ of IA Student Study Group. **HONORS/ACHIEVEMENTS:** Publications, "From Student Devel Theory to Student Serv Programming Is It Really A Quantum Leap? An Equal Access to Post-Secondary Educ Perspective"Univ of IA 1979; "Peer Counseling an academic & experiential intercultural communication focus", unpub manuscrpt, u of IA 1979. **BUSINESS ADDRESS:** Associate Dir, University of Iowa, Special Support Service, 310 Calvin Hall, Iowa City, IA 52241.

FIELDS, ALVA DOTSON
Educational administrator. **PERSONAL:** Born May 29, 1929, Athens, TN; daughter of Walter E Dotson and Estella V Vaught Dotson; married James Henry Fields III; children: Gordon, James, Sherri. **EDUCATION:** Knoxville Coll TN, AB (cum laude) 1958; Univ

of TN, MSSW 1966, additional work. **CAREER:** Chattanooga State Tech Comm Coll, dept head 1978-, coordinator of minority affairs, counselor; Florence AL City Sch, sch social worker 1976-78; Univ of N AL, instr 1976-78; TN Dept of Human Services, dir (1st black in TN) 1973-75, asst dir 1968-73, caseworker/field supr 1958-68. **ORGANIZATIONS:** Curriculum consultant on ethnic content Univ of N AL UMk-m,; panelist TN Governor's Conf on Families 1980; Title XX Regional Adv Com 1979-82; Comm Serv of Greater Chattanooga Inc 1979-82; bd mem Metro Council of Comm Serv 1980-91; mem bd Chattanooga Area Urban League Inc, Family & Childrens Serv Inc, Presbyterian Homes of Chattanooga, VENTURE, Friends of Black Children; chmn Consortium on Adolescent Pregnancy, Venture Task Force on Adolescent Pregnancy; mem Governors Task Force on Healthy Children, Infant Mortality Sub-Committee; mem TN Child Welfare Serv Comm; pres TN Conf on Social Welfare 1984, Delta Sigma Theta; vice pres, Chatt Links, Inc, 1989-91; advisory bd, Univ of Chattanooga SE Institute for Educ in theatre, 1989-; TN Conf on Social Welfare; Natl Assn of Social Workers. **HONORS/ACHIEVEMENTS:** Nominated Social Worker of the Year, Muscle Shoals NASW 1974; Big Brothers-Big Sisters Internat, Chattanooga Chapter 1975; TN NASW Social Worker of the Year 1984; Delta Sigma Theta Hall of Fame for Outstanding Community Serv 1985; recognized by Knoxville Links Inc as one of Knoxville's Black Achievers 1986. **BUSINESS ADDRESS:** Coordinator of Minority Affairs/Counselor, Chattanooga State Tech Community Coll, 4501 Amnicola Hwy, Chattanooga, TN 37406.

FIELDS, ARLONDA M.
Financial analyst. **PERSONAL:** Born Aug 28, 1963, Cleveland, OH. **EDUCATION:** Fisk Univ, BS 1985; Amer Inst of Banking. **CAREER:** Natl City Bank, teller 1983; First Tennessee, installment loan clerk 1984; First Amer Corp, banking assoc trainee 1985-86; First Amer Memphis, financial analyst 1986-. **ORGANIZATIONS:** Mem Big Brothers/Big Sisters of Memphis, Memphis Jaycees, Alpha Kappa Alpha Sor Inc; bd dir Community & Govt Affairs. **HONORS/ACHIEVEMENTS:** UNCF Scholarship 1982-85. **BUSINESS ADDRESS:** Financial Analyst, First American Bank-Memphis, 4894 Poplar, Memphis, TN 38118.

FIELDS, DEXTER L.
Psychiatrist, educator. **PERSONAL:** Born Oct 12, 1944, Detroit, MI; married Margaret L Betts. **EDUCATION:** Wayne State U, BA 1967; Wayne StateUniv Coll of Med, MD 1972. **CAREER:** Operation Hope Comm Mental Hlth Ctr, internal medicine resident, consult psychiatrist 1976-77, 80; Detroit Bd of Edn, consult 1979-; Recorder's Ct Psychiatric Clinic, consult 1980-; Kirwood Gen Hosp & Hutzel Hosp, staff physician; Kirwood Mental Hlth Ctr, consult psychiatrist 1976-80; NE Guidance Substance Abuse Ctr, consult psychiatrist 1974-76; Boston City Hosp, psychiatric resident 1972-73; Detroit Psychiatric Inst, psychiatric resident 1973-75; clinical fellow in Psychiatry Harvard Coll 1972-74. **ORGANIZATIONS:** Mem Black Psychiatrists Forum of Boston 1972-73; Black Psychiatrists of Am 1973; Solomon Fuller fellow 1974. **BUSINESS ADDRESS:** 17117 W 9 Mile Rd, Ste 1221, Southfield, MI 48075.

FIELDS, EARL GRAYSON
Government official. **PERSONAL:** Born Jun 18, 1935, Brooklyn, NY; son of Ralph Allen Fields and Queena Rachel Grayson Fields; married Pauline Hay; children: Cheryl, Mark, Leslie. **EDUCATION:** CCNY, BA 1968. **CAREER:** US Bureau of Customs, customs inspector 1963-68; US Dept of HUD, multi family/coll housing rep 1968-72, model city rep 1972-74, program mgr 1974-78; US Dept of HUD, Santa Ana CA, manager 1978-. **ORGANIZATIONS:** Vice chmn Orange County Urban League 1981-82; treasurer/co chmn Bowers Museum Black Cultural Council 1982-; mem Orange County Master Chorale 1983-; policy bd mem, Los Angeles Federal Executive Board 1988-. **HONORS/ACHIEVEMENTS:** Cert Assoc of Minority Real Estate Devel 1980; Integrity Knowledge Serv Inland Empire Mortgage Bankers Assn 1981; Volunteer Awd United Way of Orange Cty 1982; Patriotic Serv US Dept of Treasury 1984. **BUSINESS ADDRESS:** Manager, Dept of Housing & Urban Devel, 34 Civic Center Plaza, Santa Ana, CA 92712.

FIELDS, EDWARD E.
Minister. **PERSONAL:** Born Jun 24, 1918, Kirkwood, MO; married Marshan; children: Marshan, Edward. **EDUCATION:** Lincoln Univ, BS 1940; KS State Teachers Coll, MS 1947; Univ of Kansas City, Univ of MO, NYU; Univ of KS, DEd 1959. **CAREER:** Indus arts teacher, 1945; Lincoln High School & RT Coles Vocational High School, coordinator of Co-op Occupational Educ 1946-47; MO Public School, elementary principal, 1947-56; Coll of St Teresa, instructor, 1959-65; Central Jr High School, principal, 1962-71; Dept Career & Continued Educ, dir 1971-72; Div Urban Edn, asst supt 1972-74; assoc supt instr, 1974-75; School Dist of Kansas City, act supt 1975-78; ret school dist 1979; 5th Dist NW MO Annual Conf AME Church, minister. **ORGANIZATIONS:** Mem, MO State Teachers Assn; bd dir, Kansas City Teachers Credit Union; natl, state local Elementary Principal Assns; past chmn Kansas City Teachers Ins Com; life mem NEA; mem Phi Delta Kappa; Natl Assn for Supervision & Curriculum Devel; MO Assn for Supervision & Curriculum Devel; Natl & State Assn of Secondary Sch Prin; Intl Reading Assn; Intl Indus Arts & Voc Educ Assn; Am Assn of Sch Adminstr; exec bd Kansas City School Admin Assn mem Natl Alliance of Black Educators; Conf of Minority Public Admins; mem KCMO-TV Minority Relations Bd. **HONORS/ACHIEVEMENTS:** Lecturer; Various Citations for contributions as educator and contributions to BSA; Ordained Am Meth Episcopal Minister. **MILITARY SERVICE:** USN.

FIELDS, IKE See FIELDS, WILLIAM I., JR.

FIELDS, INEZ C.
Attorney. **PERSONAL:** Born Mar 13, Hampton, VA; married F C Scott; children: Fred G Scott. **EDUCATION:** BostonUniv Law Sch, LlD 1921. **CAREER:** Atty. **ORGANIZATIONS:** Life mem NAACP; hon mem Hampton Woman's Serv League; mem Am Assn ofUniv Women; Catherine Fields Lit Club; Women's Forum; Old Dominion Bar Assn; VA State Bar; Mt Olive Tent Lodge; Third Bapt Ch; Harry T Burleigh Comm Chorus. **HONORS/ACHIEVEMENTS:** Recip plaque King St Comm Cntr in apprec of outstanding comm svc; mem 25 yrs Delta Sigma Theta Sor; plaque significant comm svc.

FIELDS, KENNETH HENRY
Professional athlete. **PERSONAL:** Born Feb 09, 1962, Iowa City, IA. **EDUCATION:** UCLA, BA 1984. **CAREER:** Milwaukee Bucks, forward 1984-. **HONORS/ACHIEVEMENTS:** One of the most successful players in history of UCLA; finished his four year career for the Bruins ranked 6th among school's all-time scoring leaders behind Lew Alcindor; started 1st 16 games of his freshman season at UCLA; finished the season as 4th highest scorer with a 101 pgg mark; led the Bruins in field goal percentage.

FIELDS, KIM
Actress. **PERSONAL:** Born May 12, 1969, New York, NY. **EDUCATION:** Attending, Pepperdine Univ. **CAREER:** Recorded, Dear Michael, He Loves Me He Loves Me Not; starred in several Los Angeles stage productions incl Fight the Good Fight; ABC series Baby I'm Back, actress; NMC series The Facts of Life, actress "Tootie" 5 1/2 yrs. **ORGANIZATIONS:** Mem West Angeles Church of God in Christ. **HONORS/ACHIEVEMENTS:** Recipient 2 yrs "Youth In Film Awd" Best Actress; NAACP Image Awd 1985 Best Actress; 1987 Justice Dept Role Model of the Year Awd. **BUSINESS ADDRESS:** Natl Broadcasting Co, 3000 W Alameda Ave, Burbank, CA 91523.

FIELDS, M. JOAN
Association executive. **PERSONAL:** Born Jul 15, 1934, New Middletown, OH; married Stanley; children: Veta Gabrielle, Scott Grant. **EDUCATION:** Cntrl State Coll, BS 1952-56; Wayne State Univ, 1967-69. **CAREER:** Neighborhood Serv Organ Relocation Prog, dir 1969-; Grabo Corp, cons, trainer; Detroit Hsng Commn Social Serv Prog 1973-74; MSW, Comm Social Work Sequence,. **ORGANIZATIONS:** Mem Program Planning Com, Detroit YWCA 1966-67; mem Urban Alliance of Metro Detroit 1968-69; Assn of Black Social Workers 1969-; field instr, grad & undergrad students from 6 diff U, in social work 1970-; mem bd dirs Professional Skills Alliance 1971-; Nat Pub Relations Council 1974; NAHRO 1974; mem bd dirs Don Bosco Home for Boys 1974-; mem bd Neighborhood Institutional Agency Council 1974-. **HONORS/ACHIEVEMENTS:** Recip Outstanding Comm Serv Award, FAAYM, 1967. **BUSINESS ADDRESS:** 909 Woodland, Detroit, MI 48211.

FIELDS, NATHANIEL
Government official. **PERSONAL:** Born May 03, 1949, Albany, GA. **EDUCATION:** Blftn Coll Blftn OH, BA Econ & Soc 1971; J HpknsUniv Sch of Adv Intrnt Studs, MA Intrnl Rltns 1975. **CAREER:** White Hs Ofc of Sci & Tech Plcy, sr plcy anlyst 1978; Hs Fgn Afrs Com Subcom on Afrc US Cngrs, staff assoc 1978; Dept of St, intrnt econ agency for intrnt devel 1976-78; Wrld Bank, econ rsrch anlyst 1975-76; Govt of Bstwn, consult 1975; Devel Altrntvs Inc, econ rsrch anlyst 1974-75; Gdyr Tire & Rbr Co, indsl engr. **ORGANIZATIONS:** Dir afro-am cntr asst ftbl coach Blftn Coll OH 1971-73; mem Soc for Intl Evel 1975; chmn bd Dnms Inc Wash DC 1979; bd of dir OARS Fnd Wash DC 1979; mem US Del Untd Nats Conf on Sci & Tech Vienna Austria 1979. **HONORS/ACHIEVEMENTS:** Blck Almn Awd Blftn Coll 1973; Outst Yng Men in Am 1979; various artcls pub.

FIELDS, RICHARD A.
Superintendent. **PERSONAL:** Born Apr 18, 1950, Washington, DC; married Sylvia Crisp; children: Kirstyn, Richard. **EDUCATION:** Hampton Inst, BA 1971; Duke Univ Sch of Medicine, MD 1975. **CAREER:** Duke Univ, resident in psychiatry 1975-78; Comm Mental Health Activity AUS, chief 1978-79; Dept of Psychiatry & Neurology AUS, chief 1979-80; Neuse Mental Health Ctr, dir 1980-82; GA Regional Hospital of Atlanta, superintendent 1982-. **ORGANIZATIONS:** Vice chair Council of Natl Affairs 1982-; pres Black Psychiatrists of Amer 1984-; bd of trustees GA Psychiatric Assoc 1986-; pres GA Chap Amer Assoc of Admin Psychiatrists 1987-. **MILITARY SERVICE:** AUS capt 2 yrs; Army Commendation Medal 1980. **BUSINESS ADDRESS:** Superintendent, Dept of Human Resources, 3073 Panthersville Rd, Decatur, GA 30037.

FIELDS, SAMUEL BENNIE
Business executive. **PERSONAL:** Born Dec 24, 1925, St Louis, MO; married Helen Lucille Brown; children: Sharon Hall. **EDUCATION:** St Louis Music & Arts Univ, BA Music Instrumental 1949; Weaver School of Real Estate, Diploma 1950; Mensh School of Real Estate, Cert 1970. **CAREER:** Model Cities Commiss DC, planning chmn 1969-75; New Model Cities Housing Devel Corp, pres, chmn 1971-73; DC Devel Co, vice pres 1974-77; DC Government, comm1976-; Sam Fields & Assoc, pres. **ORGANIZATIONS:** Planning chmn Shaw Project Committee DC 1975-79; chmn of bd Neighborhood Devel Ctr UPO #1 1975-77; mem East Central Civic Assoc DC. **MILITARY SERVICE:** USN musician 3/c 1944-46; Amer Theatre Med & Pres Commendations 1946. **BUSINESS ADDRESS:** President, Sam Fields & Associates, 1351 R St NW, Washington, DC 20005.

FIELDS, SAVOYNNE MORGAN
Education administrator, counselor. **PERSONAL:** Born May 26, 1950, Rocky Mount, NC; daughter of Charlie Morgan and Hazel C Brown Morgan; divorced. **EDUCATION:** North Carolina A&T State Univ, BS Psych 1972, MS Guidance 1979. **CAREER:** Public Library High Point North Carolina, library asst III 1975-79; Louisiana State Univ Eunice, counselor, coord 1979-82; Lousiana State Univ at Eunice, counselor & minority recruiter, 1982-88; Lousiana State Univ at Eunice, recruiter/career placement coord, 1988-. **ORGANIZATIONS:** LASAP 1979-, LAHSRP 1982-; coord LSUE's Black History Activities 1982-; founding mem LADE 1982-; mem NAUW 1983-; mem ACPA 1984-, AACD 1984; mem NAUW Historian 1986-; mem & past recording & corresponding sec, Chat-A-While, Inc. **HONORS/ACHIEVEMENTS:** 1st Black Recruiter Louisiana State Univ at Eunice 1982-; Matron of the Year Little Zion Baptist Church 1984; Little Zion BC Matrons President's Awd 1985; LADE Developmental Educ of LSUE 1986; recognized by Chat-A-While Club as Outstanding Educator, 1987; selected as Outstanding Developmental Educ at LSUE by LADE 1988; selected NAUW Woman of the Year, 1988. **BUSINESS ADDRESS:** Recruiter/Career Placement Coord, Louisiana State Univ at Eunice, Career and Placement Center, PO Box 1129, Eunice, LA 70535.

FIELDS, STANLEY
Insurance agent. **PERSONAL:** Born Sep 12, 1930, Detroit; married Mamie Joan Grant; children: Beta Gabrielle, Scott Grant. **EDUCATION:** Wayne State U, BA 1956, MA 1960. **CAREER:** Detroit Bd Edn, art instr 1956-; EIT, liaison person 1974; Mayor's Com for Human Resources Devel, project FAST 1967; Am Mutual Life Ins Co, insagt 1972-; Alexander Hamilton Life Ins Co, agt, registered rep 1970-74; Multivest Inestment Co, rep 1974-75; N Am Life & Casualty Co, agt 1975; World Wide Cycling Assn, Detroit area, dir 1974-75; independent auctioneer 1974-; direct sales, distributorship & world trade 1970-; subcontractor, hardwood floors 1942-75. **ORGANIZATIONS:** Consult Model Cities Educ Component 1972-; bd dirs Uplift-Harper House 1970-71; Metro Distributors 1972-; bd dirs

Detroit Pub Schs Art Tchrs Club 1972-73; vp, bd dirs Wayne StateUniv Art Educ Alumni 1973-74; treas 1st Nighter 1970-; mem Friends of Belle Isle 1974-; Chequemates 1970-73; The Set Inc 1955-75;Motor City Yacht Club 1974-; charter mem Family Motor Coach Assn, Detroit chpt, 1974-; judge Detroit Edison MI Chronicle Lighting Contest 1972, Block Club Beautification Contest 1975. **HONORS/ACHIEVEMENTS:** Mem X-Country Team, Wayne, 1948; lectr 1969, 70Univ Detroit; individual reord holder, Champion X-Country Run, Detroit Pub Schs 1974. **MILITARY SERVICE:** AUS 1952-54. **BUSINESS ADDRESS:** 10235 W Mc Nichols Rd, Detroit, MI 48221.

FIELDS, VICTOR HUGO
Chemist. **PERSONAL:** Born Jul 11, 1907, Milwaukee, WI; divorced; children: Victor Hugo. **EDUCATION:** Fisk U, BA 1931, MA 1935; Marquette U, PhD 1944. **CAREER:** Fisk U, instr 1935-41, asst prof 1941-57; Kelmer Labs, Milwaukee, consult 1944-46; FL A&M Coll, prof, dept chmn 1947-49; Hampton Inst, prof, chemistry, dept chmn natl sci & math 1949-, dir div sci & math, chem dept chmn 1967-73. **ORGANIZATIONS:** Mem VA Acad Sci; AAAS; Nat Inst Sci; mem Beta Kappa Chi; Omega Psi Phi; Ch of Christ; Bachelor Benedict Club, Hampton.

FIELDS, WILLIAM I., JR. (IKE FIELDS)
Nonprofit executive. **PERSONAL:** Born May 04, 1944, Frankfort, KY; son of William I Fields, Sr and Anna Catherine Fields; married Faye Ford, Mar 29, 1974. **EDUCATION:** Kentucky State Coll, Frankfort KY, BS, 1966 Univ of Louisville, Louisville, KY, MS 1971. **CAREER:** Community Action Commn, Cincinnati, OH, coordinator field service, 1971-72; Community Council, Cincinnati, OH, planning assoc, 1972-74; Community Chest, Cincinnati, OH, assoc dir planning, 1974-77; United Community Planning Corp, Boston, MA, assoc exec vice pres, 1978-81; ATE Mgmt, Ridayh, Saudi Arabia, dir admin/personnel, 1981-83; United Way of America, Washington, DC, vice pres/dir, 1983-. **ORGANIZATIONS:** Vice pres, Health Planning Council of Greater Boston, 1979-81; mem, Natl Forum Black Public Admin, 1984-86; mem, Big Brothers of Greater Washington, 1985-86; mem, Org for New Equality, 1985-. **HONORS/ACHIEVEMENTS:** Outstanding Young Men in America, US Jaycees, 1980. **MILITARY SERVICE:** US Army, Specialist IV, 1967-69. **BUSINESS ADDRESS:** Vice Pres, United Way of America, 701 N Fairfax St, Alexandria, VA 22314.

FIERCE, HUGHLYN F.
Bank executive. **PERSONAL:** Born in New York, NY; married Jewel; children: Holly, Heather, Brooke. **EDUCATION:** Morgan State Coll, BA econ; NY U, MBA finance. **CAREER:** Chase Manhattan Bank, NYC, vice pres & commercial loan officer, joined bank in 1963; Freedom Nat Bank of NY, pres 1974-77; Chase Manhattan Bank, vp. **ORGANIZATIONS:** Mem Minority Equity Capital Co Inc. **BUSINESS ADDRESS:** Chase Manhattan Bank, 1 Chase Manhattan Plaza, New York, NY 10015.

FIERCE, MILFRED C.
Educator. **PERSONAL:** Born Jul 06, 1937, Brooklyn. **EDUCATION:** Wagner Coll, BA, MS; Columbia U, MA, MPhil, PhD. **CAREER:** Vassar Coll, dir Black Studies 1969-71; Hunter Coll, prof. **ORGANIZATIONS:** Apptd exec dir Assn of Black Found Exec Inc 1976; apptd NY St Coll Proficiency Exam Com in African & Afro-Am History, fall 1976; apptd research dir Study Commn on US Policy toward South Africa 1979; mem African-Am Tchrs Assn; African Heritage Studies Assn; Assn for Study of Afro- Amer Life & History; mem Am Historical Assn; Orgn of Am Historians. **HONORS/ACHIEVEMENTS:** So Hist Assn recipient, NDEA 1965; EPDA 1969; delegate Intl Congress of Africanists 1973; recipient Natl Endowment for the Humanities Fellowship, CityUniv of NY, 1976. **MILITARY SERVICE:** AUS 1960-63. **BUSINESS ADDRESS:** 695 Park Ave, New York, NY.

FIGARO, MARK O.
Clergyman. **PERSONAL:** Born Apr 25, 1921, Lafayette, LA; son of John W Figaro and Marie Rita Jacquet Figaro. **EDUCATION:** St Augustine's Sem; Bay St Louis, MS; St Mary's Sem Techny, IL, Loyola Univ of Chicago, Univ of So CA, Undergraduate & grad studies; Cath Univ of Am, MA 1954. **CAREER:** Notre Dame de Perpetruel Secours Ch, St Martinville, LA, asso pastor 1949-52; St Benedict the Moor Ch, Duson, LA, pastor 1952; St Augustine's Sem, Bay St Louis, MS, tchr 1954-57; Christ the King Ch, Jackson, MS, pastor 1957-62; Verbum Dei HS, LA, tchr 1962-66; Regina Coeli HS, Compton, CA, 1962-66; St Joseph Ch, Broussard, LA, pastor, 1966-69; Notre Dame de Perpetuel Secours Ch, St Martinville, LA, pastor 1969-73; Diocese of Lafayette, LA, episcopal vicar for black Caths; St Anthony Church Lafayette, pastor 1980-82; Holy Cross Church, pastor 1982-86; Holy Ghost Church, pastor 1986-. **ORGANIZATIONS:** Mem or consult of dioceasan bds & comm; consultor to bishop; one of priests adv to the Nat Conf of Cath Bishops, Com on Priestly Life & Ministry; mem com of NOBC that presented paper to Bishops Synod on the Evangelization of Blacks 1974.

FIGURES, MICHAEL
State legislator. **PERSONAL:** Born Oct 13, 1947; married Vivian Davis; children: Akil, Davis. **EDUCATION:** Degree from Stillman College; law degree from Univ of Alabama. **CAREER:** Alabama House of Representatives, Montgomery AL, state senator, District 33. **HONORS/ACHIEVEMENTS:** Delegate to Democratic Natl Convention, 1980. **BUSINESS ADDRESS:** House of Representatives, State Capitol, Montgomery, AL 36130. *

FIGURES, THOMAS H.
Attorney. **PERSONAL:** Born Aug 06, 1944, Mobile, AL; son of Coleman Figures and Augusta Figures; married Janice; children: Thomas Anthony. **EDUCATION:** Bishop State Jr Coll, Assoc in Science 1964; AL State Univ, Bachelor of Science 1966; IN Univ, MBA 1968; Univ of IL, Juris Doctor 1971. **CAREER:** Exxon Corp, atrny & asst sec 1971-75; Westchester Cty, NY, asst dist atrny 1975-76; Mobile Cnty AL, asst dist Atrny 1976-78; Southern Dist of AL,asst US attrny 1978-85; Figures, Ludgood and Figures, partner 1985-87; Thomas H. Figures, attorney at law 1987; municipal judge 1988-; referee, Mobile County Circuit Court 1988-89. **ORGANIZATIONS:** State Bars AL & NY, Fdrl Bars, US Supreme Ct US Court of Appeals, US Dist Court, Bar Assns AL State Bar, Natl Bar Assn Mobile Cnty AL V chrmn Mobile Cnty Dem Conf 1976-78, 1989-; Mobile Comm Action, Inc 1976-80; grad Leadership Mobile 1978; SCLA; NAACP; Omega Psi Phi; Natl Assn of Bond Attorneys 1985-. **HONORS/ACHIEVEMENTS:** Outstanding Young Men of Amer 1973; Community Ldrs & Noteworthy Americans 1977; Outstanding Comm Serv Awd 1977; Christian Comm Award 1984. **HOME ADDRESS:** 6120 Palomino Dr N, Mobile, AL 36693. **BUSINESS ADDRESS:** 212 S Lawrence St, Mobile, AL 36602.

FILER, KELVIN DEAN
Attorney. **PERSONAL:** Born Nov 25, 1955, Los Angeles, CA; son of Maxcy Filer and Blondell Filer; married Felicia Marie Johns; children: Brynne Ashley. **EDUCATION:** Univ of CA Santa Cruz, BA 1977; Univ of CA Berkeley, JD 1980. **CAREER:** Deputy state public defender 1980-82; private practice, atty 1982-; Compton Unified Sch Dist, Bd of Trustees, mem. **ORGANIZATIONS:** Compton Chamber of Comm, 1st vice pres; mem bd of dirs Compton Chamber of Commerce 1983-; mem South Central Bar Assn; Compton Branch of the NAACP, life mem; Compton Athletic Foundation, founder/bd of dir; member of, CA Attorneys for Criminal Justice, CA State Bar, American Bar Assn, Natl Bar Assn, CA Assn of Black Lawyers; Pres, Compton Chamber of Commerce 1988-89. **HONORS/ACHIEVEMENTS:** Successfully argued case before CA Supreme Court resulting in a unanimous opinion (People vs Taylor 1982 31 Cal 3d 483). **BUSINESS ADDRESS:** Member Board of Trustees, Compton Unified Sch Dist, 363 W Compton Blvd, Compton, CA 90220.

FINCH, GREGORY MARTIN
Attorney. **PERSONAL:** Born Sep 14, 1951, Madera, CA; married Valerie Michelle Beecher; children: Damon, Megan, Christopher. **EDUCATION:** Univ of CA, BA Soc/Art 1974; McGeorge School of Law, JD 1979. **ORGANIZATIONS:** Delegate State Bar Convention 1983; vice pres Wiley Manuel Law Assoc 1983; Active 20/30 Club # 1; recording sec 1985, bd of dir 1987, 2nd Vice Pres 1987; sec Natomas Planning Advisory Council; chmn Small Business Advocacy Comm, Sacramento Chamber of Commerce. **HONORS/ACHIEVEMENTS:** Rookie of the Year Active 20/30 Chapter # 1 1985. **MILITARY SERVICE:** USAF Reserve staff sgt 6 years. **HOME ADDRESS:** 690 Pelican Court, Sacramento, CA 95815.

FINCH, JANET M.
Educator. **PERSONAL:** Born Jun 04, 1950, Nashville, TN; daughter of James W Mitchell and Helen Ardis Mitchell; married Harold William Finch; children: Harold, Toria. **EDUCATION:** TN State Univ, BA Math 1972, MA Educ 1977; Vanderbilt Univ, EdD 1985. **CAREER:** Nashville State Tech, educ specialist 1977-80, project dir 1980-81, dept head develop studies 1981-85, asst dean 1981-; Middle TN State Univ, ACE fellow; Motlow State Community College, Tullahoma TN, dean of academic affairs 1988-. **ORGANIZATIONS:** Sec Temple Child Care Develop Center 1984-85; pres Parent Teacher Fellowship 1985-86; youth choir dir/pianist 15th Ave Baptist Church 1985-; mem, Youth Committee YWCA. **HONORS/ACHIEVEMENTS:** Minority Scholarship Vanderbilt Univ 1981; Outstanding Young Woman of Amer 1981, 1982; Leader of the 80's Fund for Improving Post Secondary Educ 1984; ACE Fellowship Amer Council on Educ 1986-87; selected to participate in exec leadership institute-sponsored by League for Innovation 1989. **HOME ADDRESS:** 221 Rising Sun Terrace, Old Hickory, TN 37138.

FINCH, RAYMOND LAWRENCE
Judge. **PERSONAL:** Born Oct 04, 1940, Christiansted, St Croix, Virgin Islands of the United States;married Lenore Luana Hendricks; children: Fay Allison, Mark, Jennifer. **EDUCATION:** Howard U, BA 1962; HowardUniv Sch of Law, LlB 1965. **CAREER:** Territorial Ct of the VI, judge 1977-; Municipal Ct VI, judge 1976-77; Hodge Sheen Finch & Ross, partner (law firm) 1971-75; Hodge & Sheen, law clerk 1969-70; Municipal Ct VI, law clerk 1965-66. **ORGANIZATIONS:** Mem Am Bar Assn/Nat Bar Assn/Am Judges Assn/Judicial Ethics Com of Am Bar Assn; mem bd dirs Boy Scouts of Am, St Croix 1976-; bd dirs Boys Club, St Croix 1975-. **HONORS/ACHIEVEMENTS:** Marquis Who's Who in Am 1978-79; Personalities of the South Award 1978-79; recipient Army Commendation Medal/Nat Defense Service Medal/Viet Nam Service Medal/Viet Nam Campaign Medal w/60 Device/ Bronze Star Medal/Two Overseas Bars. **MILITARY SERVICE:** AUS cpt 1966-69. **BUSINESS ADDRESS:** Judge, Territorial Court of the VI, Toro Bldg Est Golden Rock, Christiansted, St Croix, Virgin Islands of the United States 00820.

FINCH, WILLIAM H.
Educator. **PERSONAL:** Born Apr 10, 1924, Columbus, OH; married June Johnson; children: Lisa, Tina. **EDUCATION:** OH State U, BS 1947; DePaul U, MA 1953; Nova Univ, EdD 1983. **CAREER:** Chicago Bd of Educ, teacher 1947-58, master teacher 1958-59, asst prin 1959-65, prin 1965-71, presently dist supt; Loyola Univ, asst dir Upward Bound Project 1966-69; Chicago State Univ, instr 1969-71; Chicago Public Schools, asst supt for curriculum. **ORGANIZATIONS:** Pres St Edmunds Church Credit Union 1972-; treas Men St Edmund's Church; mem Alpha Phi Alpha; bd dir S Central Community Svcs; pres Dist Supt Assn1981-86; mem Phi Delta Kappa, Chicago Area Alliance of Black School Educators, Samuel Stratton Assoc, Chicago Principals Assoc, Amer School Health Assn, Amer Assoc of School Admins, Assoc of Supv and Currciulum Devel. **HONORS/ACHIEVEMENTS:** Resolution Reocognition mayor & City Council; Hon Life Mem IL Congress of Parents & Teachers; Outstanding Contrib Awd Chatham Avalon Park Community Council; Medal of Merit Community Relations Council of Brainerd; Serv Awd District 20 Educ Council; Serv Awd Dist 17 Educ Council; Educ Awd PUSH; Appreciation Awd 6th Police Dist Appreciation Awd Englewood Community Serv Center; Community Serv Awd Women's Auxiliary Southtown YMCA; Educ Awd Englewood Community Org. **BUSINESS ADDRESS:** Assistant Superintendent, Chicago Public Schools, 1819 W Pershing, Chicago, IL 60609.

FINLAYSON, WILLIAM E.
Physician. **PERSONAL:** Born Sep 01, 1924, Manitee, FL; married Edith; children: Reginald, James. **EDUCATION:** Morehouse Coll, BS 1948; Meharry Med Coll, MD 1953, intern resd 1953-57;Univ MN, resd 1957-58. **CAREER:** Physician, Self-employed. **ORGANIZATIONS:** Mem Milwaukee Med Soc; House Del WI Med Soc; past pres Milwaukee GYN Soc; mem St Joseph's Hosp; Mt Sinai Med Ctr; tchr Milwaukee Med Complex; mem-Deaconess Hosp; Cream City Med Soc; Am Coll Surgery; flw Am Coll OB-GYN; Med Coll WI; bd dirs, chmn N Milwaukee State Bank; bd dirs Southeastern WI Health System Agency; past pres Alpha Phi Alpha; Frontiers Int; life mem NAACP; mem Urban League; We-Milwaukeeans; past pres YMCA local br; mem Grtr Gailee Bapt Ch. **MILITARY SERVICE:** AUS 1st lt 1943-46. **BUSINESS ADDRESS:** 2003 W Capitol Dr, Milwaukee, WI 53206.

FINLEY, BETTY M.
Educator. **PERSONAL:** Born Aug 03, 1941, Edison, GA; married Isaac T Finley, Jr; chil-

dren: Michael. **EDUCATION:** Tuskegee Inst, BS 1962; Framingham State Coll, MEd 1977; Simmons Coll Boston, MA 1986. **CAREER:** East St Louis School Bd, english teacher 1967-68; Pemberton Township School Bd NJ, english teacher 1968-70; Dept of Public Welfare Div of Child Guardianship Boston, social worker 1970-72; Metropolitan Educ Training Dover MA, coord of minority students 1973-74; Dover Sherbon School Bd, teacher 1974-. **ORGANIZATIONS:** Comm mem appt to Headmaster's Adv Comm 1981-82; mem Natl Council Teachers of English 1984-87; organizor Operation Foodbasket 1984; bd mem Children's Literature Foundation 1987-88. **HONORS/ACHIEVEMENTS:** Apptd mem Evaluation Team of New England Assoc of Schools & Colls 1982,86; Ellen Raskin Fellow Simmons Coll 1985. **HOME ADDRESS:** 4 Temi Rd, Holliston, MA 01746.

FINLEY, MORRIS
Business executive. **PERSONAL:** Born Jun 11, 1939, Atlanta, GA. **EDUCATION:** Clark Coll Atlanta, attended 1958. **CAREER:** Diamond Printing Co, exec pres; So Rural Action Atlanta, dir; City of Atlanta, councilman 5th Dist; Circle Corporation Inc, vice pres. **ORGANIZATIONS:** Spl coordntr Christian Leadership Conf; past bd mem Metro Atlanta Summit Leadership Congress; bd mem United Youth & Adult Conf; Atlanta DeKalb Corp; E Atlanta DeKalb YMCA; past bd mem Operation Breadbasket; vice chmn DeKalb Co Comm Relations Commn; mem Dem Party Co Exec Com; Baptist Tabernacle Ch; comm organizer Metro Atlanta Mental Health Assn; NAACP; Natl & Atlanta Bus League; Atlanta Coalition Current Comm Affairs; Atlanta Urban League; Natl Assn Market Developers; past co-capt YMCA; Amer Acad Polit & Social Sci. **HONORS/ACHIEVEMENTS:** Outstanding Men in S; Outstanding Blacks Amer; Outstanding Comm Serv to Youth DeKalb Co 1972; Pub Serv Awd YMCA 1973; Coach of Yr YMCA 1972; Omega Psi Phi Frat Scroll Honor; Outstanding Councilman of the Yr Bronner Bros 1978. **MILITARY SERVICE:** AUS spc 4th class 1959-61.

FINLEY, SKIP
Broadcasting executive. **PERSONAL:** Born Jul 23, 1948, Ann Arbor, MI; son of Eweu W. Finley and Mildred V. Johnson Finley; married Karen M. Woolard, May 06, 1971; children: Kharma Isis, R. Kristin. **EDUCATION:** Northeastern University, Boston MA, 1966-71. **CAREER:** Skifin Gallery, Boston MA, owner, 1970-71; WHDH-TV, Boston MA, floor director, 1971; WSBK-TV, Boston MA, floor manager, asst director, producer, 1971-72; WRKO-Radio, Boston MA, account executive, 1972-73; Humphrey, Browning, MacDougall Advertising, Boston MA, account manager, 1973-74; Sheridan Broadcasting Corp, sales manager for WAMO AM/FM, 1974-75, general manager for WAMO AM/FM, 1975-76, vice-president/general manager for SBC Radio Division, 1976-77, vice-president, corporate office, 1976-82, eastern sales manager, 1977-79, executive vice-president/general manager, 1979-81, president, 1981-82; Albimar Omaha Ltd Partnership/Albimar Management Inc, Boston MA, president and general partner, 1982—. **ORGANIZATIONS:** Chairman of broadcast advisory board, United Press International; National Thespian Society; trustee on board of overseers, Vineyard Open Land Foundation; Martha's Vineyard Rod and Gun Club. **HONORS/ACHIEVEMENTS:** Excellence in Media Award, Natl Assn of Media Women, 1981; Communicator of the Year Award, Washington Area Media Organization, 1982; author of numerous articles on media related subjects. **BUSINESS ADDRESS:** President, Albimar Communications, 60 State St, Suite 550, Boston, MA 02109.

FINN, JOHN WILLIAM
University administrator. **PERSONAL:** Born Apr 30, 1942, Lexington, KY; married Joan Washington; children: Jarell Wendell, Janelle Wynice. **EDUCATION:** BS 1966; MBA 1971; taking courses toward PhD in higher educ. **CAREER:** Gary IN Schools, teacher, coach, recreation leader 1967-69; Anderson Boys Club, activity dir 1968-69; Univ of MI, asst dir of housing 1969-71, assoc dir housing 1977-. **ORGANIZATIONS:** Mem MI Housing & Food Serv Officers; MI Coll Personnel Assn; Natl Assn of Student Personnel Admins; Assn of Coll & Univ Housing Ofcls; Amer Assn for Higher Educ; Amer Assn of Jr Coll; mem United Fund; Boys Club of Amer; NAACP; Kappa Alpha Psi Frat Inc; pres Ann Arbor Sportsmen; Black Faculty & Staff Assn. **HONORS/ACHIEVEMENTS:** All City-All State Football 1968-69; Outstanding Young Men of Amer; First Black in Admin pos in Housing Office Univ of MI. **BUSINESS ADDRESS:** Associate Dir of Housing, Univ of MI, 1011 Student Act Bldg, Ann Arbor, MI 48109.

FINN, ROBERT GREEN
Engineer. **PERSONAL:** Born Jan 24, 1941, Lexington, KY; married Mary E Johson; children: Leatrice, Lezelle, Lechrista. **EDUCATION:** Morehead State U, BS 1963. **CAREER:** IBM, spl engrng request coord. **ORGANIZATIONS:** Councilman 2nd Dist; past pres PTA; vice pres NAACP; Mason; Shriner; Jaycee; mem exec bd Blue Grass Boy Scouts; mem exec council Morehead Alumnus; mem Nat Honor Soc 1959. **HONORS/ACHIEVEMENTS:** Mem Nat Honor Soc 1959; DAR Award 1959. **BUSINESS ADDRESS:** IBM 740, New Circle Rd, Lexington, KY.

FINNEY, ERNEST A., JR.
Circuit court judge. **PERSONAL:** Born Mar 23, 1931, Smithfield, VA; married Frances Davenport; children: Ernest III, Lynn, Jerry. **EDUCATION:** Claflin Coll, BA (cum Laude) 1952; SC State Coll School of Law, JD 1954; Natl Coll State Judiciary Reno NV, Grad 1977; New York Univ Sch of Law, srappellate judges seminar 1985. **CAREER:** Sumter County Courthouse 3rd Judicial Circuit of SC, resident judge 1976-; South Carolina Supreme Ct, assoc justice 1985-. **ORGANIZATIONS:** Chmn of bd Buena Vista Devel Corp; mem Amer, SC, Natl, Sumter Cty Bar Assocs; mem Amer Judicature Soc, Black Lawyers Caucus of SC, Southeastern Lawyers Assoc, Judicial Conf of US 4th Circuit, SC Sentencing Guidlines Commiss, Prison Overcrowding Task Force; mem NAACP, Alpha Phi Alpha, Univ of SC Bd ofVisitors, United Meth Church Gen Council on Fin & Admin Legal Responsibilities Comm; chrmn of bd of trustees Claflin Coll. **HONORS/ACHIEVEMENTS:** City of Sumter Disting Serv 1970; SC Council for Human Rights 1972; SC State Coll Alumnus Awd 1973; ACLU Civil Libertarian of the Year 1973; Omega Psi Phi Citizen of the Year 1973; Bedford-Styvesant NY Jaycee Awd 1974; Claflin Coll Politic & Alumni Awd 1974; SC Council Human Rights James M Dabbs Awd 1974; Selected to rep SC at Amer Bar Assoc Criminal Code Revision Conf San Diego 1975; Wateree Comm Action Inc Serv 1975; SC NAACP Native Son 1976; Delta Sigma Leadership Serv 1976; Emmanuel Meth Church Serv of Mankind Awd 1977; HHD (Hon) Claflin Coll 1977; Natl Assoc for Equal Oppt in Higher Ed 1986; Distinguished Alumni of the Year Awd from Claflin Coll, SC State Coll; Alpha Phi Alpha Awd of Achievement 1986. **BUSINESS ADDRESS:** Associate Justice, South Carolina Supreme Court, PO Drawer 1309, Sumter, SC 29151.

FINNEY, ESSEX EUGENE, JR.
Government official. **PERSONAL:** Born May 16, 1937, Michaux, VA; son of Eugene Finney and Etta Finney; married Rosa Ellen Bradley; children: Essex E III, Karen Finney Shelton. **EDUCATION:** VA Polytechnic Inst, BS (w/Honors) 1959; PA State Univ, MS 1960; MI State Univ, PhD 1963. **CAREER:** Rocky Mt Arsenal Denver CO, branch chief 1963-65; Agricultural Rsch Serv USDA, rsch scientist 1965-77; Agricultural Mktg Rsch Inst, inst chmn 1972-75; Beltsville Agricultural Res Ctr, asst dir 1977-83, assoc dir 1983-87; North Atlantic Area Associate Director, 1987-. **ORGANIZATIONS:** Councilman Town of Glenarden MD 1975; sr policy analyst Office of the Science Advisor to the Pres 1980-81; bd of dirs Prince George's Chamber of Commerce 1983-; pres Beltsville Org of Professional Employees of the US Dept of Agriculture 1984-85. **HONORS/ACHIEVEMENTS:** CRC Press Handbook of Transportation & Mktg in Agriculture 1981; Fellow Amer Soc of Agricultural Engrs 1983; Awd for Administration Gamma Sigma Delta Univ MD 1985; Outstanding Engrg Alumni Awd Penn State Univ 1985. **MILITARY SERVICE:** US Army, Transportation Corps Captain, 1963-65. **HOME ADDRESS:** 11206 Chantilly Lane, Mitchellville, MD 20716. **BUSINESS ADDRESS:** Associate Director, North Atlantic Area, Agricultural Research Service, US Dept Agriculture, 600 E Mermaid Lane, Philadelphia, PA 19118.

FINNEY, JOHN H.
Executive director. **PERSONAL:** Born Oct 31, 1938, Savannah. **EDUCATION:** Savannah State Coll, BS sociology 1967; Atlanta U, MA 1972. **CAREER:** Econ Opp for Savannah-Chatham Co Area Inc, exec dir; Outreach Serv EDA for Savannah, dir 1970-72; Atlanta Southside Health Cntr, supr comm orgn 1973; Neighborhood Youth Corps, US Dept of Labor, Savannah, coun, dir 1967-69. **ORGANIZATIONS:** Mem Alha Kappa Delta Nat Honor Soc; exec bd Westside Health Cntr; mem United Comm Serv Health Coun; chmn Savannah Sickle Cell Prog; Armstrong Savannah State Social Work Adv Bd; W Broad St YMCA; chmn Vets Com; NAACP; bd mem Coastal Area Planning Health Coun; exec bd United Way of Savannah. **HONORS/ACHIEVEMENTS:** Pub master thesis, "The Human Ecology of Savannah, GA a spatial analysis of residential segregation, 1940-1970"; 1973 edition of "personalities of The S";Chatham Co Cardiovascular Coun, Stroke, 1974; Soldier of Month, Ft Stewart, 1964; Soldier of Month, Ft Sheridan, 1964. **BUSINESS ADDRESS:** 21 W Park Ave, Savannah, GA 31405.

FINNEY, LEON D., JR.
President/executive director. **PERSONAL:** Born Jul 07, 1938, Louise, MS; married Sharon; children: Kristin, Leon III. **EDUCATION:** Roosevelt U, BA 1964; Nova U, PhD 1978; Goddard Coll, MS 1974. **CAREER:** Univ Chicago, faculty lctr, fld instr 1970-; TWO/WCDC, exec dir, pres 1969-; Fisk U, vis lctr 1970-71; Luth Sch Theol, vis prof 1968-70; LA State U, cons; The Woodlawn Organization, president/exec director. **ORGANIZATIONS:** Mem Chicago United; v chmn, bd dirs Guaranty Bank & Trust Co; mem Chicago Assn of Commerce & Ind; mem Black IL Legislative Lobby 1976-; Chicago Urban League 1970-. **HONORS/ACHIEVEMENTS:** One of four black Ams invited to Israel to study Israeli-Arab Rels, Israeli govt 1973; Affirmative Action Merit Award, Breadbasket Commercial Assn 1973; PACE Award, Pervis Staples 1973; Outst Alumni Award, Hyde Park HS 1972; Dstgsd Educator Award 1972; cert of merit Central StateUniv Alumni Assn 1971; 10 Most Outst Yng Men of 1970; Jr C of C 1970; Ford Found Grant 1970. **MILITARY SERVICE:** USMC 1959-63. **BUSINESS ADDRESS:** President/Exec Dir, The Woodlawn Organization, 6040 S Harper Ave, Chicago, IL 60637.

FINNEY, MICHAEL ANTHONY
Accountant. **PERSONAL:** Born Oct 02, 1956, Flint, MI; married Gina Michelle Mickels. **EDUCATION:** Saginaw Valley State Coll, BBA 1979; Central MI Univ, MA Candidate. **CAREER:** Deloitte Haskins & Sells CPA, admin asst 1978-79; J C Penney Co, merchandise mgr 1979-81; Saginaw Valley State Coll, admin rep 1981-84; City of Saginaw,asst city mgr. **ORGANIZATIONS:** Bd of dirs Big Brothers/Big Sisters of Saginaw Inc 1982-83; bd of dirs Saginaw Valley State Coll Alumni Assn 1981-; mem Saginaw Jaycees 1984-, Intl City Mgrs Assoc, MI City Mgrs Assoc. **HONORS/ACHIEVEMENTS:** President-Student Govt Saginaw Valley State Coll 1978-79; Outstanding Young Men in Amer US Jaycees 1979; State Dir of MI Phi Beta Sigma Frat 1979-80; Outstanding Achievement in Black Affairs SVSC Black Student Assn 1983. **BUSINESS ADDRESS:** Assistant Manager, City of Saginaw, 1315 S Washington, Saginaw, MI 48601.

FINNIE, ROGERS L., SR.
Football player. **PERSONAL:** Born Nov 06, 1945, Winder, GA; married Debbie; children: Shannon Monique, Rogers Lewis Jr. **EDUCATION:** FL A&M U, 1964-69. **CAREER:** NY Jets, played offensive tackle, guard, defensive end & tight end 1968-72; St Louis Cardinals, 1973-. **ORGANIZATIONS:** Works with various youth orgn; mem NFLPA. **HONORS/ACHIEVEMENTS:** Named Pittsburg All-Am 1968; Defensive Lineman of Yr, Ebony All-Am, Defensive Lineman; received game balls, NY Jets 1969 & 1971; trophy for best offensive line in the NFL for fewer quarterback sacks.

FISCHER, WILLIAM S.
Musician. **PERSONAL:** Born Mar 05, 1935, Shelby, MS; son of R A and Willye; married Dolores; children: Darius, Marc, Bryan, Paul. **EDUCATION:** Xavier Univ, BS; CO Coll, MA; Univ Vienna, attended Akademie Fur Musik und Darstellende. **CAREER:** Xavier Univ, assoc prof 1962-66; Newport Coll & Cardiff Coll, lecturer 1966; NY Public Sch, 1967-75; NY, publisher 1967-; Atlantic Records, music dir 1968-70, arranger conductor 1965-, record producer 1973-74; Arcana Records, owner 1971-. **ORGANIZATIONS:** Mem Amer Soc Composers Authors & Publishers 1964; mem MENC 1964, Amer Federation Musicians 1953; exec dir Soc Black Composers 1971-; mem Edgar Stern Family Fund Commn 1963-65; grants, Akademischer Austausdienst W Germany 1964; mem NY Council on the Arts 1971, Natl Endowment Arts 1971. **HONORS/ACHIEVEMENTS:** Fulbright Grant 1965-66; Austrian Govt Grant 1965. **MILITARY SERVICE:** USMC 1956-57.

FISHER, ADA L.
Attorney, educator. **PERSONAL:** Born Feb 08, 1924, Chickasha, OK; married Warren W Fisher; children: Charlene, Bruce T. **EDUCATION:** Langston U, BA;Univ of OK, JD; OK State U, MA further study. **CAREER:** General Practice, Oklahoma City OK, atty 1952-57; Langston Univ, chmn & prof of Social Science 1957-. **ORGANIZATIONS:** Assn of Am Historians; Nat Assn of Social Scientests; OK Bar Assn; OK Ed Assn; Nat Ed Assn; Alpha Kappa Alpha Sor; Urban League; NAACP; mem adv coun, Black History, ref book for Okla City sch 1972; mem adv com on civil rights for OK Regents for Higher Ed 1974-75; NAACP

Nat Youth Coun 1949; Okla City Urban League 1948; Nat Conf of Ch of God in Christ 1969; Am Civil Liberties Union; United Nations Orgn 1973. **HONORS/ACHIEVEMENTS:** First black to seek admission toUniv of OK; plaintiff in case Sipuel vs OK, 322 US 631 (1948) which led to admission of blacks to previously all-white coll & univ in OK; achievement awards in civil & human rights. **BUSINESS ADDRESS:** Dept of Social Science, Langston Univ, Langston, OK 73050.

FISHER, ALMA Z.
Fisher, librarian. **PERSONAL:** Born Dec 22, 1945, Learned, MI; married Eugene. **EDUCATION:** Tougaloo Coll, BA english 1967; Rosary Coll, MALS 1970. **CAREER:** Utica Jr Coll, librn 1972-; Chicago Pub Libr Sysd librn 1970-72; chgo pub sch sys, tchr 1967-69. **ORGANIZATIONS:** Mem Am Libr Assn; mem MI Libr Assn; mem MI Tchrs Assm; mem Black Caucus ALA; mem Urban Leag; mem NAACP; mem Utica Jr Coll Alumni Assn. **HONORS/ACHIEVEMENTS:** Recip Assn of Coll & Res Librs Mellon intnshp Jan 1975; recip IL St Libr Sch Schlshp 1969. **BUSINESS ADDRESS:** Utica Jr Coll, Utica, MS 39175.

FISHER, CARL ANTHONY
Clergyman. **PERSONAL:** Born Nov 24, 1945, Pascagoula, MS; son of Peter W Fisher (deceased) and Evelyn Grant Fisher. **EDUCATION:** Epiphany Coll, Newburgh, NY, AA 1964; St Joseph's, Washington, DC, BA 1967; Oblate Coll, Washington DC, MTheology; Amer Univ, Washington, DC, MSPR 1974; Loyola Univ, New Orleans, LA, Licentiate 1974; Princeton Univ, Prin, NJ, Cert 1976. **CAREER:** Litton Ind, conslr emp rep 1971; Chevron Oil, mgt training spec 1972; Soc of St Joseph, dir, dept of vocations 1973-82; Josephite Harvest M Azine, assoc editor 1973-82; San Pedro Pastoral Region of the Archdiocese of Los Angeles, roman catholic bishop. **ORGANIZATIONS:** Natl chaplain J Cath Daughters of the Americas 1981-; mem Public Rel Soc of Amer; former pastor Oldest Black Catholic Church in the US 1982-87; mem Bd of Regents Loyola-Marymount Univ Los Angeles CA; mem bd of trustees Mt St Mary Coll Los Angeles. **HONORS/ACHIEVEMENTS:** Disting Serv Awd United Negro Coll Fund 1973; Cath Comm Scholar of the Yr Cath Comm Found of US 1974; Natl Comm Serv Awd Phi Beta Sigma 1977; named first Black Catholic Bishop in Western US by Pope John Paul on Dec 19, 1986; Doctor of Divinity Degree, The Dominican School of Philosophy & Theology, Graduate Theo. Union Berkeley CA 1988. **MILITARY SERVICE:** USN Chaplain Corp 1st Bk Catholic Chaplain in US Navy 1968-71. **BUSINESS ADDRESS:** Archdiocese of Los Angeles, 3555 St Pancratius Place, Lakewood, CA 90712.

FISHER, E. CARLETON
College professor. **PERSONAL:** Born Nov 03, 1934, St Louis, MO; children: Victor, Bruce, Vernon. **EDUCATION:** Howard Univ, BS, MS 1956-57; American Univ; Morgan State Univ, EdD 1986. **CAREER:** Univ of Chicago, numerical analyst 1957-66; IBM, personnel mgr 1966-72; Univ of MD, exec asst to chancellor for affirmative action 1973-77; Notre Dame, exec dir minorities in engr 1977-78. **ORGANIZATIONS:** Kappa Alpha Psi, mem 1952-; American Guild of Organists, mem 1970-; MD Assoc of Affirmative Action Officers, president/founder 1975-77, 1983-85; Prudential Ins, director, college relations 1978-80; Affirmative Action, prof of mathematics asst to pres 1981-. **HONORS/ACHIEVEMENTS:** Morgan State Univ, goldseker fellow 1983-85. **BUSINESS ADDRESS:** Professor, Anne Arundel Community College, 101 College Parkway, Arnold, MD 21012.

FISHER, EDITH MAUREEN
Librarian, educator. **PERSONAL:** Born Jul 29, 1944, Houston, TX; daughter of Freeman Fisher and Ruby Jase. **EDUCATION:** University of Illinois, Urbana IL, MLS, 1972; Queens College of the City University of NY, certificate of ethnicity and librarianship, 1975; University of Pittsburgh, PhD program, 1987—. **CAREER:** University of California, San Diego, La Jolla CA, ethnic studies collection development librarian, 1972—, adjunct lecturer, 1974—; University of Pittsburgh, Pittsburgh PA, reference librarian, 1987-88; University of California, Los Angeles, lecturer, 1989. **ORGANIZATIONS:** American Library Assn; Assn of College and Research Libraries; Black Caucus of the American Library Assn; Multi-Ethnic Literature of the US; National Assn of Ethnic Studies; CA Librarians Black Caucus; CA Library Assn; University of CA Black Faculty and Staff Assn; CA Ethnic Services Task Force; National Youth Sports Program Advisory Board. **HONORS/ACHIEVEMENTS:** Carnegie fellowship, 1971; PhD fellowship, 1987; Provost fellowship, Univ of CA, San Diego, 1987; Provost Stipend, Univ of Pittsburgh, 1988; author of numerous articles. **BUSINESS ADDRESS:** 656 Crest Dr, Encinitas, CA 92024.

FISHER, EDWARD G.
Surgeon. **PERSONAL:** Born Apr 22, 1932; son of Guy O D Fisher and Elisa Howell Fisher Dawes; married Judy Ann; children: Yvonne, Ronald. **EDUCATION:** Brooklyn Coll, BS 1956; Howard U, MD 1961. **CAREER:** HU, med offcr 1966-68; Operating Rm Com Hadley Hosp, chmn; Hadley Memorial Hosp, active attending; Howard Univ Hosp; Freedmens Hosp, instr 1966-68; Greater SE Comm and Washington Adventist Hospitals, staff privileges; Inst of Urban Living Washington DC, medical dir. **ORGANIZATIONS:** Mem Med Care Evaluation Com; presently surgeon in private practice; mem DC Med Soc; mem DC Medico-chirurgical Soc; mem Nat Med Assn; former mem AMA & Interns & Residents Assn of Freedmens Hosp; mem Nat Assn of Interns & Residents; mem Political Action Com; life mem Urban League Honor Medical Soc 1961; Diplomate Am Bd of Surgery; Joint Conf Hadley Hosp; president Medical Staff Hadley Memorial Hosp; mem bd of trustees Hadley Memorial Hospital. **HONORS/ACHIEVEMENTS:** Author of numerous publications; co-author w/wife, Human Sexuality - Christian Perspective 1984. **BUSINESS ADDRESS:** Edward G Fisher MD PC, Hadley Medical Office Building Suite 302A, 4603 Martin Luther King Jr Ave SW, Washington, DC 20032.

FISHER, GAIL
Actress. **PERSONAL:** Born Aug 18, Orange, NJ; children: Samara L Levy, Jole Levy. **EDUCATION:** Am Acad of Drmtc Arts; Lncln Cntr Rprtry Thtr. **CAREER:** Prmnt Studios, actress; TV Series, actress mannix; NY Stage, A Rasin in the Sun, The Rock Cried Out, Susan Slept Here; Love Am Style, gst star; Room 222, gst star; My Three Sons, gst star; Fantasy Island, gst star; General Hospital, gst star; Hotel, gst star; He's The Mayor, gst star. **HONORS/ACHIEVEMENTS:** Recip Image Awd 1969; Emmy Awd 1969; 1st blck actrs to rcv Emmy in TV Hist; Gldn Glb Awd 1970; Gldn Glb Awd 1972; only black female recipient of Duse Awd Lee Strasberg Actors Studio Awd. **BUSINESS ADDRESS:** 8668 Burton Way, Los Angeles, CA 90048.

FISHER, GEORGE CARVER
Accountant. **PERSONAL:** Born Dec 12, 1939, Texarkana, AR; son of Thomas Fisher (deceased) and Naomi Johnson Fisher; married Annie Kate Carter; children: Anthony Karl. **EDUCATION:** Univ of AR Pine Bluff, BS 1969; Univ of AR Fayetteville, MBA 1974. **CAREER:** Arkansas Best Corp, accountant 1969-73, supv carrier acctg 1973-84, dir carrier acctg 1984-. **ORGANIZATIONS:** Treas EO Trent Consistory #223 1973-79; dir Arkansas Best Federal Credit Union 1983-; chmn Fort Smith Civil Serv Commn 1983-; mem Amer Inst of CPA's; vice pres Fort Smith Girls Club; mem Sparks Reg Medical Ctr Adv Trustee; treas Sunnymede Elem PTA; CPA Arkansas; mem NAACP; life mem Kappa Alpha Psi; past master Widow's Son Lodge #3; bd of dir, Leadership Fort Smith 1989-92; bd of dir, United Way of Fort Smith 1988-91. **HONORS/ACHIEVEMENTS:** Distinguished Service Arthritis Foundation 1986. **MILITARY SERVICE:** USN storekeeper second class petty officer 1957-60. **HOME ADDRESS:** 2007 North 48th Circle, Fort Smith, AR 72904. **BUSINESS ADDRESS:** Dir Carrier Accounting, Arkansas Best Corporation, 1000 South 21st St, Fort Smith, AR 72902.

FISHER, JOSEPH
Union officer. **PERSONAL:** Born Feb 07, 1933, Lawnside, NJ; son of Horace J Fisher and Vera Ann Arthur Fisher; married Barbara Bryant, Apr 1952; children: Joseph Jr, Darlene Still, Barbara Arthur, James Fisher. **EDUCATION:** Temple Univ, Philadelphia PA, BS, 1955. **CAREER:** Liberty Knitting Mills, Philadelphia PA, office manager 1956-58; Intl Ladies Garment Workers Union, Philadelphia PA, vice pres, 1958-. **ORGANIZATIONS:** Mem, PA Advisory Committee, US Civil Rights Commission; bd mem, PA Job Training Coordinating Council; bd mem, Philadelphia Urban Coalition. **BUSINESS ADDRESS:** Vice Pres, Regional Director, International Ladies Garment Workers Union, 35 South 4th Street, Philadelphia, PA 19106.

FISHER, JUDITH DANELLE
Physician/psychiatric consultant. **PERSONAL:** Born Feb 17, 1951, Sanford, NC. **EDUCATION:** Howard Univ, Coll of Liberal Arts BS 1974, Coll of Medicine MD 1975. **CAREER:** Howard Univ Hosp, resident psychiatry 1975-77; Hahnemann Medical Coll, resident psychiatry 1977-78; Hahnemann Med Coll, fellowship 1978-79; CMHC Hahnemann, medical dir 1979-80; Hahnemann Hosp Phila, asst dir in-pt unit, psych unit 1980-81; CamCare Health Corp, psych actg med dir 1981-83; Eagleville Hosp, dir womens in-pt unit 1983-84; Wake Co MHC, staff psychiatrist 1984-85; NC Disability Determination Svcs, psychiatric consultant 1985-. **ORGANIZATIONS:** Part time private practice Psychiatry 1980-; general mem Amer Psychiatric Assoc 1981-; bd of dirs Women in Transition Philadelphia 1982-84; mem Smithsonian Assocs 1984-, Natl Assoc of Disability Examiners 1985-, Amer Film Inst 1986-, State NC Employees Assoc 1986-. **HONORS/ACHIEVEMENTS:** NIMH Minority Fellowship Amer Psychiatric Assoc 1976-78; Certificate of Recognition Alpha Kappa Alpha Sor Raleigh 1985; Assoc mem Livingstone Coll AlumniAssoc 1985-. **HOME ADDRESS:** PO Box 822, 836 Boykin Ave, Sanford, NC 27330. **BUSINESS ADDRESS:** Psychiatric Consultant, NC Disab Deter Div of SS Admin, 1110 Navaho Dr, Raleigh, NC 27602.

FISHER, LLOYD B.
Attorney. **PERSONAL:** Born Jan 13, 1942, Marthaville, LA; married Shirley T Little; children: Jawara M J. **EDUCATION:** Purdue U, BS; ValparaisoUniv Sch of Law, JD 1973. **CAREER:** Lloyd B Fisher Atty at Law, atty 1979-; Lake Co Government, pub defender 1977-79; City of Gary, asst city atty 1973-76; B002 Allen & Hamiltol, consult 1969-70; Gary & Opportunities Industrialization Center, vice pres bd of dirs, 1975-. **ORGANIZATIONS:** Mem TMLA 1979-80; asst to chmn Criminal Law Sect Nat Bar Assn 1980; Basileus Omega ; mem TMLA 1979-80; asst to chmn Criminal Law Sect Nat Bar Assn 1980; Basileus Omega Psi Phi Frat Alpha Chi Chap Gary IN 1974-76; mem Am Bar Assn 1974-; mem Nat Bar Assn 1974-; pres Lake Co Opportunities Devel Found Inc 1975-; mem Bar Assn of the 7th Fed Cir; mem IN State Bar Assn; pub relations chmn of pack Com Pack 23 Of 23 of Cub Scouts of Am Gary; bd mem Thurgood Marshall Law Assn; mem NAACP 1976-; bd mem Purdue Club of Club of Lake Co 1976-. **HONORS/ACHIEVEMENTS:** Cert of appreciation Tolleston Comm Council 1977; cert of Appreciation NAACP 1977; dedicated serv award Gary Opportunities Industrialtization Center 1980. **MILITARY SERVICE:** AUS 1st lt 1966-68. **BUSINESS ADDRESS:** Attorney, Lloyd B Fisher Atty-at-Law, 504 Broadway, Ste 506, Gary, IN 46403.

FISHER, MATTIE COOK See COOK, MATTIE

FISHER, RICHARD LAYMON
Clergyman. **PERSONAL:** Born Sep 28, 1934, Evanston, IL; married Joan Spratley; children: Susan Elizabeth, Richard Jr. **EDUCATION:** Boston Univ, BS 1956, STB 1959; Livingstone, DD 1977; Univ Chicago, Advanced Studies. **CAREER:** Washington Metro AME Zion, pastor 1972-; Martin Temple, pastor 1961-72; Campbell Chapel, pastor 1959-61; Inst for Black & Ministries, trustee; Clinton Jr Coll, trustee; Livingstone Coll, trustee; AME Zion Church, bishop 1984-. **ORGANIZATIONS:** Mem, Black Consultant Educ Theological Seminary; bd chmn, Protestant Chaplancy Homer G Phillips Hospital; past mem bd, Curators Univ, MO; bd pres exec com Urban League; St Louis Bd of Educ Citizens Task Force; chmn Minister Support Group for Sch Tax Levy; Kappa Alpha Psi; bd of United Way; bd mem St Louis Regional Commerce & Growth Assn Hon DD Clinton Coll 1972; Eden Sem guest lecturer Eden Sem Webster Coll; Fist U; mem World Council of Churches, Natl Council of Churches; gov bd, mem Counsultation of Methodist Bishops. **HONORS/ACHIEVEMENTS:** Articles Star of Zion, Missionary Seer. **BUSINESS ADDRESS:** Bishop, AME Zion Church, 607 N Grand Ave, St Louis, MO 63103.

FISHER, ROBERT F.
City official. **PERSONAL:** Born Nov 22, 1936, Canton, OH; married Mary Rose Whitehurst; children: Rod, Myra, Craig. **EDUCATION:** Kent State U, 1961; Akron U, Govt Seminar 1969-70; Kent State U, Grad Courses. **CAREER:** Canton, dir pub serv 1973; Budget & Projects Canton, dir 1965-73; State Pection & Supervision of Pub Office; Income Tax & Accountant; Canton Water Dept, commercial accountant. **ORGANIZATIONS:** Mem Goodwill Bd of Trustees; OH Housing Develop Bd; Hosp Bureau Bd; NEFCO; Frontiers Club Intnl; Canton Negro Oldtimers Athltc Assn; Walsh Coll Adv Bd; Stark Wayne Manpower Consortium; sec Stark Council of Govt. **HONORS/ACHIEVEMENTS:** Outstanding young man of Yr Jr C of C 1971. **BUSINESS ADDRESS:** 218 Cleveland Ave SW, Canton, OH 44702.

FISHER, RUBIN IVAN
Corporate officer. **PERSONAL:** Born Sep 25, 1948, Baltimore, MD. **EDUCATION:** Univ of CT, BA 1971. **CAREER:** Travelers Ins Co, asst dir personnel; adminstr Personnel 1977-78; employment couns 1974-77; Aetna Life & Casualty Ins Co, supr field controllers dept1972-74. **ORGANIZATIONS:** Mem Am Soc for prsnl Adminstrn; mem Reserve Officer Assn of Am; mem Urban League; mem NAACP; accredited personnel specialist designation Am Soc for Personnel Adminstrn-accreditation Inst 1978. **MILITARY SERVICE:** AUS capt 1971-72. **BUSINESS ADDRESS:** Assistant Dir, The Travelers, One Tower Square, Hartford, CT 06183.

FISHER, SHELLEY MARIE
Educator. **PERSONAL:** Born Jul 02, 1942, Gary, IN; married Alfred J Fisher; children: Tiffiny, Eric. **EDUCATION:** Indiana Univ, BA 1964, MA 1969. **CAREER:** Gary Comm School Corp, educator 1964-. **ORGANIZATIONS:** Bd of dirs Self-Marketing Inc 1981-84; franchiser Natl Employment Transmittal Inc 1981-84; natl sec Natl Tots and Teens Inc 1981-85; 3rd vice pres Drifting Dunes Girl Scout Council 1986-; exec bd Gary Educators for Christ 1987; mem Affiliate Educ Assistance Council Inc 1987; owner/director Best Score SAT Scholarship Coll Career Info 1987; mem Alpha Kappa Alpha Inc. **HONORS/ACHIEVEMENTS:** Reading Fellowship Indiana ST Univ 1976; Short fiction published in Indiana Univ/Literary magazine 1979; authored "Resume Writing Slanting Skills in New Direction," 1981. **HOME ADDRESS:** 1700 Taft St, Gary, IN 46404. **BUSINESS ADDRESS:** Teacher, Gary Community School Corp, PO Box 156, Gary, IN 46402.

FISHER, WALTER
Educator. **PERSONAL:** Born Aug 19, 1916, Baltimore, MD. **EDUCATION:** Howard Univ, AB (Magna Cum Laude) 1936, AM 1937; Univ of PA, Doctoral Studies 1941-42,46-48. **CAREER:** VA Union Univ, instructor History (summers) 1937-39; Howard Univ, instructor History 1937-38; DE State Coll, instructor Social Science 1938-51; Morgan State Univ, dir library 1966-75, prof History 1949-81, emeritus prof History 1981-. **ORGANIZATIONS:** Dir of prog Annual Meetings Assoc for Study of Negro Life & History 1966-70; exec council Assoc for Study of Afro-Amer Life & History 1969-84; consult Dept of Ed Baltimore City & Cty, Anne Arundel Cty, State of MD; coord Penn-Morgan Consortium Lecture Series Univ of PA 1969; co-adv, coord Natl Endowment for the Humanities Afro-Amer Studies Post-Doctoral Fellowship Prog, Johns Hopkins Univ, Morgan State Coll 1970-73; coord Danforth Found, Post-Doctoral Fellowship, Black Studies, Morgan State Coll 1970-71; coord, editor Morgan State Course Guides in Afro-Amer Studies 1970-71; mem Morgan State Performing Arts Series, Bicentennial Comm, Task Force on Student Life; sec MD Council for Publ Broadcasting; bd dir MD Conf of Social Concern; bd trustees Baltimore Walters Art Gallery 1972-84 & The Peale Museum 1967-84; cit comm on Black History, Peale Mus; assoc fellow Ctr for African & Afro-Amer Studies; adv council Natl Archives of US 1975-81; vp, bd dir MD Libr Class & Auto Proj 1972-74; mem bd dir Baltimore Heritage 1983-, Historic Baltimore Soc 1984-; bd trust Friends of Enoch Pratt Free Libr 1981-. **MILITARY SERVICE:** AUS capt 1942-46, 1951-53.

FITCH, CLARENCE E.
Educator. **PERSONAL:** Born Dec 10, 1929, Cleveland; married Norma Nee Walker; children: Stephen, Cheryl, Melanie. **EDUCATION:** Case Western Reserve U, BA, MA 1955-57; Northeastern Univ Boston MA, EdD 1983. **CAREER:** Patrick Henry Jr High School, teacher 1955-60; Glenville Sr High, counselor 1960-66; Franklin D Roosevelt Jr High School, teacher 1966-70; Congressman Louis Stokes, 21st Congressional Dist, admin asst 1970-74; Continuing Dn Dyke Coll Cleveland, dean; Case Western Reserve Univ, Cuyahoga Comm Coll, Cleveland State Univ, lecturer; Coll of Wooster; Miami Univ; Bluffton Coll; Venture Assoc Mgmt Cons, pres 1985-. **ORGANIZATIONS:** Mem NAACP Urban League; cntr for Human Serv; vice pres Ludlow Comm Assn Pres; chmn Cleve Area Councils Membership Drive 1970-72; St James AME Ch; Am Soc Public Asminstr; mem Am AssnUniv Prof; mem Nat Cooperative Educ Assn Assn Participant March for Jobs & Freedom 1963; leader Cleve Delegation; Meredith March Against Fear 1966; Coordinator Delegates 1972; Nat Black Polit Assembly 3 Nat Dem Conv. **HONORS/ACHIEVEMENTS:** Outstanding Advocate of Minority Bus in OH Declaration of SBA 1986. **MILITARY SERVICE:** AUS sgt combat engrs 1951-53.

FITCH, HARRISON ARNOLD
Attorney. **PERSONAL:** Born Jul 04, 1943, Elizabeth, NJ; married Ruth Mckinney; children: Harrison A, Jr, Robin L. **EDUCATION:** Columbia Coll, AB 1965; Columbia U, LLB 1968. **CAREER:** Boston Legal Assistance Project, atty 1968-69; Boston Univ Sch Law, lectr 1969-; Goodwin Procter & Hoar Trustee Boston Five Cents Savs Bank, atty. **ORGANIZATIONS:** Mem Babson & Coll; dir Boston Legal Aid Soc Steering Com Lawyers Com for Civil Rights Under Law; dir MA Law Reform Inst; Boston Legal Assistance Proj;mem Governor's Ad Hoc Adv Com on Judicial Appointments 1972. **BUSINESS ADDRESS:** Goodwin Procter & hoar, 28 State St, Boston, MA.

FITTS, LEROY
Pastor & educator. **PERSONAL:** Born Jul 06, 1944, Norlina, NC; son of Johnnie Fitts and Louise Fitts; married Alice Louise Alston; children: Timothy, Dietrich, Angelique, Leticia. **EDUCATION:** Shaw Univ, BA 1967; Southeastern Bapt Theo Sem, M Div 1970; VA Sem, D Div 1975; Princeton Univ, (NEH Inst) 1984; Baltimore Hebrew University, MA 1985. **CAREER:** First Bapt Ch of Jacksonville, NC, pastor 1968-72; First Bapt, Baltimore, MD, pastor 1972-; Comm Coll of Baltimore, adjunct prof 1978-80; VA Sem & Coll, pres 1981. **ORGANIZATIONS:** Editor Loft Carey Baptist Convention 1975-; brd of mgrs VA Sem & Coll 1980; mem NAACP, Assoc for the Study of Negro Hist 1978-; bd of mgrs, St. Marys Seminary & University. **HONORS/ACHIEVEMENTS:** Author, Lott Carey First Black Msnry to Africa 1978, A History of Black Baptists 1985; article "The Church in the South & Social Issues", Faith & Mission vol II, No I, Fall 1984. **HOME ADDRESS:** 3912 The Alameda, Baltimore, MD 21218. **BUSINESS ADDRESS:** Adj Prof Black Church Hist, St Marys Seminary &Univ, First Baptist Church, 525 N Caroline St, Baltimore, MD 21205.

FITTZ, SENGA NENGUDI (SUE IRONS)
Artist. **PERSONAL:** Born Sep 18, 1943, Chicago, IL; daughter of Samuel Irons and Elois Jackson Irons; married Ellioutt; children: Sanza, Oji. **EDUCATION:** CA State Univ at LA, BA 1966; Waseda Univ Tokyo, Japan, Foreign Studies Prog 1966-67; CA State Univ at LA, MA 1971. **CAREER:** Pasadena Art Museum, art inst 1969-71; Childrens Art Carnival NYC, art instructor 1971-74; Watts Towers Art Center LA, art inst 1965, 1978; Comm Artists Program LA, program coord 1982-88. **ORGANIZATIONS:** Mem curatorial comm perf art The Woman's Bldg, LA 1984-85. **HONORS/ACHIEVEMENTS:** Dance scholarship Orchesis Cal State Univ at LA 1964; CAPS Grant Sculpture Creative Artists Public Serv Prog 1972; co-creator of "Double Think" Natl Public Radio Limited Arts Series 1984-85; creator & independent radio producer for "Mouth to Mouth Conversations on Being" 1988-; "Art as a Verb" Group Travelling Exhibit 1988-89; "Coast to Coast," Group Travelling Exhibit, A Women of Color Artists Box and Books Exhibit 1988-92.

FITZGERALD, CARRIE EUGENIA
Educator/gerontologist. **PERSONAL:** Born Mar 28, 1929, Atlantic City, NJ; daughter of Littleton Bowser and Carrie E Bowser; divorced; children: Cheryl Lynne Bowser, Michelle Anne Bowser Bailey. **EDUCATION:** Atlantic Comm Coll, AA 1972; Rutgers Univ, BA 1974; Temple Univ, MSW 1976, EdD 1984. **CAREER:** Mercy-Douglas Human Serv Inc, educational consultant 1976-80; Health Care Inst Inc, educ consultant 1980-82; Temple Univ African History Dept, instructor/consultant 1982-86; Glassboro State Coll, prof/instructor 1983-. **ORGANIZATIONS:** Mem NAACP, Urban League, Natl Council/Black Aged, Natl Assoc of Social Workers; bd dirs Amer Foundation for Negro Affairs; mem Alumni Assoc Temple Univ, Rutgers Univ. **HONORS/ACHIEVEMENTS:** "Planning and Developing In Service Training for Nursing Home Employees," Master's Thesis Temple Univ 1976; "The Perceptions of Nursing Home Aides and Supervisors Concerning Job Responsibilities and Training Programs for Entry Level Employees," Doctoral Dissertation Temple Univ 1984, "Nursing Special Project Grant, A Training Proposal for Nusing Home Aides," US Dept of Health and Human Serv 1987. **HOME ADDRESS:** PO Box 362, Camden, NJ 08102. **BUSINESS ADDRESS:** Professor, Glassboro State College, Glassboro, NJ 08109.

FITZGERALD, CHARLOTTE DIANE
Educator. **PERSONAL:** Born May 16, 1949, Altavista, VA. **EDUCATION:** Hampton Inst, BA (magna cum laude) 1970; Univ of VA, MA 1973, PhD 1978; Univ of NC, MSPH 1981. **CAREER:** US Bureau of Census, statistician 1970-71; Christopher Newport Coll, asst prof 1973-75 & 1977-78; Livingstone Coll, asst prof 1978-80; Randolph-Macon Coll, assoc prof & chair 1982-. **ORGANIZATIONS:** Mem VA Sociological Assn 1983-; mem of bd Hanover Adult Care Inc 1984-; co-youth dir NAACP 1984-; adv bd Hanover County Gifted and Talented Students; bd mem Barksdale Theater. **HONORS/ACHIEVEMENTS:** Fellow Phelp-Stokes Organ 1971-73; Outstanding Young Woman in Amer 1973; Fellow Amer Sociological Assn 1975-78; Thomas Branch Awd for Excellence in Teaching Randolph-Macon Coll 1983; Thomas Branch Awd for Excellence in Teaching Randolph Macon Coll 1987; residency Virginia Ctr for the Humanities 1987. **HOME ADDRESS:** 601 Henry St, Ashland, VA 23005.

FITZGERALD, ELLA
Jazz singer, entertainer. **PERSONAL:** Born Apr 25, 1918, Newport News, VA; divorced; children: Ray. **CAREER:** Chick Webb Orch, singer 1934-39; US/Japan/Europe, tours with Jazz at the Philharmonic 1948-57; Decca Records, recording artist 1936-55; Verve Records, recording artist; Pablo Records, recording artist; motion picture appearance in Pete Kelly's Blues; night club appearances at, Sahara Hotel, Caesar's Palace, Fairmont Hotel, Ronnie Scott's Club; TV appearances with Frank Sinatra, on All Star Swing Festival 1972; concert with Boston Pops 1972; concert appearances with over 40 symphony orchestras throughout the US. **ORGANIZATIONS:** Recordings inlcude, At Duke's Place 1966, Best 1967, Clap Hands 1961, Cote d'Azur (with Duke Ellington) 1967, Ella, Ella Fitzgerald in Hamburg 1965, Mack the Knife, Ella in Berlin 1960, Sunshine of Your Live, Things Ain't What They Used to Be, Tribute to Porter 1965, Whisper Not 1966, Watch What Happens 1972; Take Love Easy 1975, Ella in London 1975, Montreaux Ella. **HONORS/ACHIEVEMENTS:** Recip 8 Grammy Awards; numerous popularity awards from Downbeat Magazine, Metronome Mag; JAY Award Poll; named number 1 female singer 16th Intl Jazz CriticsPoll 1968; Amer Music Award 1978; Recip Kennedy Center Honor 1979; Grammy Award as Best Female Jazz Vocalist 1981, 1984; Natl Medal of the Arts presented atthe White House, Washington DC 1987. **BUSINESS ADDRESS:** c/o Norman Granz, 451 No Canon Dr, Beverly Hills, CA 90210.

FITZGERALD, HERBERT H.
Detective. **PERSONAL:** Born Jul 17, 1928, Trenton, NJ; divorced; children: Darrel A, Denise A. **EDUCATION:** HowardUniv Rider Coll, Bus Adminstrn & Police Adminstrn 1974. **CAREER:** Detective Mercer Co, prosecutor; Trenton NJ Police Dept, officer & detective. **ORGANIZATIONS:** Mem Co Detectives Assn of NJ Inc; pres Bro Officers Law Enforcement Soc; NJ Narcotic & Enforcement Officers Asn; Intl Narcotic Enforcement Officers Assn; mem Alpha Phi Alpha Zeta Iota Lambda Chpt; NAACP; Trenton Housing Authority Commr 1971; bd mem Model Cities Policy Com 1972; Mercer Co Alcoholism Program 1972; master mason King David Lodge # 15 F & AM Trenton NJ 32nd Degree Mason Ophir Consistory 48, trenton Nj; adv bd mem Union Indsl Home for Boys Trenton NJ; Frontiers Intl Bd of Gov Police Athletic League. **HONORS/ACHIEVEMENTS:** Many certificates of commendation for meritorious serv Trenton Police Dept; Drew Pearson Cultural Achievement Award. **MILITARY SERVICE:** USN. **BUSINESS ADDRESS:** Mercer Co Court House, Office of Co Prosecutor, Trenton, NJ 08607.

FITZGERALD, HOWARD DAVID
Government official. **PERSONAL:** Born Sep 24, 1938, Trenton, NJ; son of Charles and Mollie; divorced; children: Howard D Jr, Wayne. **EDUCATION:** Antioch Univ, BA Human Serv 1976, MA Admin & Suprv 1978. **CAREER:** NJ Dept of Ed, migrant coord 1970-; Middlesex Cty Schools, dir of CETA proj 1980; NJ Dept of Ed, coord of prog mgmt 1982; Trenton City Council, councilmember-at-large. **ORGANIZATIONS:** Chmn comm ed Trenton School Bd 1979; mem bd of ed Trenton School Bd 1979-82; mem Trenton Housing Auth 1982-; bd of dir Henry Austin Health Ctr 1982-; chmn Carver YMCA 1982-; pres We Inc 1983-85. **HONORS/ACHIEVEMENTS:** Outstanding Bd mem Trenton School Bd 1980; Ed Excellence Afrikan Peoples Movement 1980; Up & Coming Politican Candlehight Sports Club 1981; Recognition World Hungry Prince Haile Salassie II 1984. **MILITARY SERVICE:** AUS squad leader 1957-59. **BUSINESS ADDRESS:** Councilmember-at-Large, Trenton City Council, 225 N Warren St, Trenton, NJ 08618.

FITZGERALD, ROOSEVELT
Educator. **PERSONAL:** Born Apr 04, 1941, Natchez, MS; divorced; children: Benito, Marco. **EDUCATION:** Jackson State Coll, BA Hon Grad 1963;Univ of Notre Dame, MA 1968; Hearst Fellowship, 1968;Univ Fellowship, 1969;Univ of Notre Dame, PhD, ABD.

CAREER: Univ of NV, dir ethnic studies prog; Clark County School Dist, human relations specialist; Greenwood MS, high school consultant Nellis Air Force Base Race Relations Commn, teacher; Multi-cultural Awareness Workshop Univ of NV Las Vegas, dir 1973; Natl Conf of Christians & Jews; Police Acad; Public School Systems; Church Groups, lectr. **ORGANIZATIONS:** Mem Western Historical Assn, NAACP, Western Social Sci Assoc, Natl Social Sci Assoc, Notre Dame Alumni Assoc, Jackson State Univ Alumni Assoc, NV Historical Soc. **HONORS/ACHIEVEMENTS:** Nat Task Force listed Who's Who in Am Colleges & Univ 1961-62, 1962-63; Who's Who in Am Coll & Univ 1962-63; Experienced Tchr Fellowship recipient Notre Dame 1967; Who's Who in Teaching 1970; have published scholarly articles in professional journals on black social, political and economic history; feature columnistfor black newspaper The Sentinel, Las Vegas; presented numerous papers at professional conferences. **BUSINESS ADDRESS:** Dir of Ethnic Studies, University of NV-Las Vegas, 4505 S Maryland Pkwy, Las Vegas, NV 89154.

FITZGERALD, ROY LEE
Council member. **PERSONAL:** Born Jun 15, 1911, Hiram, GA; son of Joe Fitzgerald; married Ezma Barnwell; children: Eugene, Helene, Katherine Martin, Josie MartinMargared Zachery Donald (deceased). **CAREER:** Minister, council member; vice mayor; Roylins, supervisor. **HONORS/ACHIEVEMENTS:** Outstanding Performance Awards from Post Office, Coca Cola & Bd of Educ. **HOME ADDRESS:** 117 Ragsdale St, Hiram, GA 30141.

FITZGERALD, WILLIAM B.
Chief executive. **CAREER:** Independence Federal Savings Bank, Washington, DC, chief exec. **BUSINESS ADDRESS:** Independence Federal Savings Bank, 1229 Connecticut Ave, NW, Washington, DC 20036. *

FITZHUGH, HOWARD NAYLOR
Marketing/corporate relations consultant. **PERSONAL:** Born Oct 31, 1909, Washington, DC; married Thelma Evelyn Hare; children: H Naylor Jr, Richard H, J. Idorenyin Jamar. **EDUCATION:** Harvard Univ, BS 1930, MBA 1933; Columbia Univ, post grad studies 1939-41; Amer Univ, post grad studies 1959-61; VA State Coll, LLD 1971. **CAREER:** Howard Univ, asst prof of marketing 1934-65, organizer, Small Business Ctr, 1964, chair, adv comm of Howard Univ Bus Sch,1965-72; Pepsi-Cola Co, vice pres, 1965-74; Amer Mktg Assn, vice pres pub policies & issues div 1970-71; Pepsi-Cola, proj consult 1974-; US Bur of the Census, expert consult Minority Statistics Prgm 1975-81. **ORGANIZATIONS:** Mem, Amer Mktg Assn Census Adv Comm, 1972-75; specl adv to pres, Natl Bus League, 1970-; past exec dir/past pres, Natl Assn of Market Developers, 1967-68 & 1976-77; mem, Operations Council, Jr Achievement of Greater NY, 1973-; sr adv, Bd of Christian Educ, 1974-76; volunteer coordinator, Advertising Coun, Amer Red Cross Natl Avt Prgm, 1969-71; mem, advisory comm, Columbia Univ School of Business, 1970-72; chair, visiting comm, Harvard Business School Black Alumni Assn, 1977-78, chair emeritus, 1978-; bd chair, Fedn of Corp Professionals, 1982. **HONORS/ACHIEVEMENTS:** Author of a number of articles & booklets in marketing/mgmt & minority business enterprises; author/developer, Pepsi/DECA Learn & Earn High School Project, 1972-; author/director, Learning and Doing Business Proj, 70,001 Ltd, 1982; DECA Hon Life Mem, 1977; "Tribute to Fitz" given at 1st Annual Booker T Washington Dinner, 1975; named Dean of Black Business, Black Entertainer Mag, 1974; listed in Who's Who in Amer;named Newsmaker of the 60s, Advertising Age, 1969; H Naylor Fitzhugh Annual Award of Relevance created by Natl Black MBA Assn, 1979; Top Natl Award, Industry-Educ Assn, 1984; named Man of the Year, Excel Mag, 1986; Harvard Business School distinguished serv award, 1987; LLD, Howard Univ, 1987; Pioneer Award, Natl Assault on Illiteracy Prog, 1988; DHL, Livingston Coll, 1988.

FITZPATRICK, ALBERT E.
Business administrator/journalist. **PERSONAL:** Born Dec 30, 1928, Elyria, OH; son of Ben Fitzpatrick and Mary Fitzpatrick; married Derien Lucas; children: Sharon, Karyle, Albert II. **EDUCATION:** Kent State Univ, BA Journalism, Sociology 1956. **CAREER:** Akron Beacon Journal, rptr asst news edtr, news edtr, City edtr, mng & exec edtr 1956-84; Knight-Ridder, dir of Minrty Affrs 1985; asst vp, minority affairs, 1987-. **ORGANIZATIONS:** Chmn of bd Wesl Ey Temple AME Church 1965-84; pres Buckeye Chptr, Sigma Delta Chi 1971; assoc prof Medill Sch of Journalism NW Univ 1979-80; pres AkronPress Club 1981-83; pres Natl Assoc of Black Journalists 1985-87; chmn minorities bd mem Amer Cancer Soc, Boy Scouts, Cntr on Economics Educ; chrmn UNCF advisory bd, 1989. **HONORS/ACHIEVEMENTS:** Outstanding Alumnus Award Kent State Univ (Journalism) 1973; Editor of Year-Freedom Journal Cuyahoga Comm Coll, Cleveland 1978; John S Knight Award Sigma Del Ta Chi, Akron, OH 1980; Frederick Douglass Award Lifetime Achievement Natl Assn Black Jounalists 1984. **MILITARY SERVICE:** AUS sgt 2 yrs, USAAF stf sgr 4 yrs, Sharpshooters Medal 1946. **BUSINESS ADDRESS:** Assistant Director of Minority Affairs, Knight-Ridder Inc, One Herald Plaza, Miami, FL 33132.

FITZPATRICK, EDWARD B.
Chief executive. **CAREER:** Puget Sound Chrysler-Plymouth, Inc, Renton, WA, chief executive, 1986-. **BUSINESS ADDRESS:** Puget Sound Chrysler-Plymouth, Inc, 585 ranier, S, Renton, WA 98055. *

FITZPATRICK, JULIA C.
Association executive. **PERSONAL:** Born May 11, Macon, GA; married Wm J; children: Lorraine, Thomas, Tisha L Thomas. **EDUCATION:** Tuskegee Inst Tusekgee AL, did not finish; B'Ham Bapt Bible Coll B'Ham AL, Hon Dr Hmnts Degree. **CAREER:** Macon GA, former schl tchr; Nat'l Grd Chptr OES, nat'l grnd matron 1952-. **ORGANIZATIONS:** Life mem Nat'l Council Negro Wmn Inc; life mem Gamma Phi Delta Sorority Inc; life mem Wmns Aux Nat'l Bpt Conv USA; Golden Heritage life mem NAACP Million Dlr Medln Club brd mem Todd Philip Bpt Boys Hme 1979-; life mem Nat'l Assn Colored Wmn's Clubs Inc; Wmns Conf Conc Present; vice pres Fed Eastern Stars World Inc; imperial commandress Imperial Grand Court Daughters of Isis; 1st vice pres 400 Study Club (Civic & Charitable). **HONORS/ACHIEVEMENTS:** Elks Wmn Yr Emma V Kelly Tpl #650 1973; Hmtrn yr awd Gamma Phi Delta Sor, Inc 1978-81; appr awd NAACP 1983-84; otsdng ldrshp awd Cindrella Civic& Ed Club L1980-82; comm serv awd Florence Ames Tpl #740 IBPOE of W 1981. **HOME ADDRESS:** 1901 Boston Blvd, Detroit, MI 48206. **BUSINESS ADDRESS:** Natl Grand Matron, Natl Grd Chptr Ord E Star, 5040 Joy Rd, Detroit, MI 48204.

FITZPATRICK, WILLIAM J.
Fraternal leader. **PERSONAL:** Born Jan 20, 1889, Fitzpatrick, AL; married Dr Julia C; children: Lorraine, Dollie. **EDUCATION:** Tuskegee Inst, Grad; Union Bapt Sem, Hon DD; Miller U, Hon LLD. **ORGANIZATIONS:** Most Powerful Sovereign Grand Comdr Nat Supreme Council Ancient & Accepted Scottish Rite Masons 1948-; previously Nat Dep & Nat Grand Sec Gen; fndr of Nat Masonic Charity Relief Dept & Nat Educ Dept; mem Fdn of Masons of the World. **BUSINESS ADDRESS:** 5040 Joy Rd, Detroit, MI 48204.

FLACK, HARLEY EUGENE
Educator. **PERSONAL:** Born Feb 12, 1943, Zanesville, OH; married Mignon Scott; children: Harley E II, Christophere Farrar. **EDUCATION:** OH State Univ, BS Phys Therapy 1965; Kent State Univ, MS Rehab Counsel 1968; State Univ of NY Buffalo, PhD Counselor Ed 1971. **CAREER:** School of Health Related Prof Sunyab, asst dean 1971-74; Family Life Ctr, counselor 1982-; Coll of Allied Health Sci Howard Univ, dean, professor 1974-. **ORGANIZATIONS:** Phys therapist Highland View Hosp 1965-67, Western Reserve Convalescent Home 1967-68; lecturer Counseling Psych Dept Rehab 1969-71; co-chair Health Brain Trust Congressional Black 1979-81; volunteer care giver Omega Hospice & St Agnes Homes 1981-84; pres Natl Soc of Allied Health 1986-88; coord first natl conf Black Perspectives in Biomedical Ethics. **HONORS/ACHIEVEMENTS:** 20 Piano Choir Compositions 1968-; dir St John Baptist Youth Choir 1979-84; "Giant Steps" book on sons relationship with father dying of cancer 1982; pianistmartin Luther King Baptist Church Columbia 1984-. **BUSINESS ADDRESS:** Dean, Professor Allied Health, HowardUniv, 6th & Byrant St NW, Washington, DC 20059.

FLACK, ROBERTA
Singer, recording star. **PERSONAL:** Born Feb 10, 1940, Asheville, NC. **EDUCATION:** Howard U, BA Piano & Voice. **CAREER:** Atlanta Records, discovered by Les McCann; Small Clubs, folk singer; accompanist for operatic school; piano teacher; nationally famous singer & recording star. **ORGANIZATIONS:** Mem Sigma Delta Chi; trustee Atlanta U; mem Delta Sigma Theta. **HONORS/ACHIEVEMENTS:** Numerous records include "The First Time Ever I Saw Your Face", "Chapter Two", "Quiet Fire", "Feel Like Makin' Love"; Owner 2 music publishing firms; named topfemale vocalist Downbeat Mag 1971-73; Grammy Award 1972; gold record 1972; Robert Flack Human Kindness Day Honors Wash DC 1972; Grammy Award Best Popular Female Vocal "Killing Me Softly With His Song" 1973; composer with Jesse Jackson & Joel Dorn "Go Up Moses"; performed Montreux, Schaefer, Newport, Hampton, Cincinnati Jazz Festivals; performed Shelley's Manne Hole Philharmonic. **BUSINESS ADDRESS:** Singer, Recording Star, Magic Lady, Inc, One West 72nd St, New York, NY 10023.

FLAGG, E. ALMA W.
Educator, consultant. **PERSONAL:** Born Sep 16, 1918, City Point, VA; daughter of Hannibal G Williams (deceased) and Caroline Moody Williams (deceased); married J Thomas Flagg; children: Dr Thomas L, Luisa Flagg Foley. **EDUCATION:** Newark State Coll, BS 1940; Montclair State Coll, MA 1943; Columbia U, EdD 1955; Newark State Coll, LittD 1968. **CAREER:** Washington, grade teacher 1941-43; Elem Sch, grade tchr 1943-57, remedial reading tchr 1957-63, vice principal 1963-64, prin 1964-67; Newark State Coll, adjunct instr in English 1964; Sch Bd of Educ Newark, asst supt 1967-83; Newark State Coll, Rutgers Univ, adjunct instructor 1982-; Educ Consultant, 1983-. **ORGANIZATIONS:** Mem NCTM; NCTE; NSSE; Am Assn of Sch Adminstr; American Assn of University Women; Assn for Supervision & Curriculum Develop; Dir YMWCA 1964-73; mem Alpha Kappa Alpha; Soroptimist Intl of Newark; Urban League of Essex Co; NAACP; educ chair Project Pride 1980-; mem Governor's Comm on Children's Serv Plng 1983-87; vice pres, Newark Youth Art Exhibition Inc 1988-; mem Kappa Delta Pi Honor Society in Education 1954-; pres League of Women Voters of Newark 1982-84. **HONORS/ACHIEVEMENTS:** Distinguished Serv to Educ NSC Alumni 1966; Citizenship Awd Weequahic Comm Council 1967; Hon Degree of Litt D Newark State Coll 1968; Roster of Superior Merit East Side HS Alumni 1969; Disting Serv Awd Cosmopolitan 1970; Adam Clayton Powell Educ Awd NJ Alliance of Black Sch Educators 1981; E Alma Flagg Scholarship Fund establ 1984; E Alma Flagg School Newark dedicated 1985; Sojourner Truth Awd Negro Business and Professional Women 1985; ESHS Disting Alumni Awd 75th Anniversary 1986; Educ Law Ctr Awd 1986; Distinguished Alumna Awd Teachers Coll Columbia Univ 1986; published: Lines and Colors (poetry) 1979, Feelings, Lines, Colors (poetry) 1980, Twenty More With Thought and Feeling 1981. **HOME ADDRESS:** 44 Stengel Ave, Newark, NJ 07112.

FLAGG, J. THOMAS
Educator. **PERSONAL:** Born Jul 10, 1917, Hawkinsville, GA; married E Alma Williams, Jun 24, 1942; children: Dr Thomas L, Luisa Flagg Foley. **EDUCATION:** AB 1940; AM 1942; Rutgers U, EdD 1964. **CAREER:** Englewood NJ, tchr 1942-52; Newark, 1952-71; elm tchr; jr high sci tchr; dept chmn; v prin; summer sch prin; first black dir secondary educ 1967-71; Neighborhood Youth & Corps, dir first in nation 1964-65; Newark's Anti Poverty Program, educ dir 1966; Newark's Pre-sch Council, exec dir 1966-67; S Side Project Newark Bd Edn, coordntr 1963-64; Montclair Newark Tchr Corps Program, coordntr 1969-71; Montclair State Coll, prof of ed 1971-84; Montclair State Coll, prof emeritus. **ORGANIZATIONS:** Mem NAASP; AASA; ASCD; PDK; AAUP; life mem NAACP, Alpha Phi Alpha; charter mem Athletic Hall Fame Montclair State Coll; trustee Boys Clubs Newark Frontiers Intl; consultant Natl Science Found. **HONORS/ACHIEVEMENTS:** Frontiers Man of Yr 1965; Distinguished Alumnus Awd Montclair State Coll 1967; Bronze Shield Boy's Club Amer; three NSF Grants 1959-61; bd dir Urban League & Essc Co; Friendly Fuld Neighborhood House; S Ward Unit Boys Clubs; 25 yr Serv Awd Boys Club of Amer; Distinguished Alumnus Awd Barringer HS 1972; J Thomas Flagg Awd for Excellence during student teaching 1985; Resolutions NJ Senate & NJ Assembly 1984. **MILITARY SERVICE:** AUS sgt 1943-46; Normandy Invasion 3 Battle Stars. **BUSINESS ADDRESS:** Professor Emeritus, Montclair State College, Upper Montclair, NJ 07043.

FLAGG, JOSEPH H.
Mayor. **PERSONAL:** Born Jun 17, 1914, Tennile, GA; married Eloise Wilson. **EDUCATION:** Savannah State Coll, BS 1940; SC State Coll, Masters 1959; Tuskegee Inst, Six Yr Cert 1970. **CAREER:** Sylvania GA, mayor pro tem; Screven Co Sylvania, vo ag tchr 1946-74; Walton Co Monroe, vo ag tchr 1942-46; Royal Jr High/Tennile HS, sci tchr 1939-42. **ORGANIZATIONS:** Mem GA Assn of Educs/NEA 1939-74; mem Screven Co Assn of Educs 1946-74; mem GA Vo Asso Screven Co FR Bureau 1946-74; mem Boy Scout orgn 1950-68; mem Masonic Lodge #39 1956-70. **HONORS/ACHIEVEMENTS:** Sel Tchr of Yr Screven Co Tchrs Assn 1964-65; Sr Warden Masonic Lodge #39 1960-70; award of apprct GA

Vo Ag Educ Serv 1941-74; award of apprct East Seal & Boy Scouts of Am 1960-74; award of apprct Mil Sel Serv 1970-76.

FLAKE, FLOYD H.
Clergyman, congressman. **PERSONAL:** Born Jan 30, 1945, Los Angeles, CA; son of Robert Booker Flake Sr and Rosie Lee Johnson-Flake; married Margaret Elaine McCollins; children: Aliya, Nailah, Rasheed, Hasan. **EDUCATION:** Wilberforce Univ, BA 1967. **CAREER:** Miami Valley Child Develop Ctrs, social worker 1967-68; Bethel AME Ch, pastor 1968-70; Xerox Corp, marketing analyst 1969-70; Sec Presb Ch, pastor 1971-73; Lincoln Univ, assoc dean students 1973; Martin Luther King Jr Afro Amer Ctr Boston Univ, univ chaplain marsh chapel & dir 1973-76; Mt Zion AME Ch, pastor 1974-75; Allen Sr Citizen Complex, developer; The Allen Christian School, founder; US House of Representatives, congressman 1986-; Allen AME Ch Jamaica NY, pastor 1976-. **ORGANIZATIONS:** Life mem NAACP; ordained minister African Methodist Episcopal Church; life mem SCLC. **HONORS/ACHIEVEMENTS:** Alfred P Sloan Scholarship Northeastern Univ 1974; Outstanding Admin Lincoln Univ 1972; Richard Allen Fellowship Payne Theol Sem 1967-68; Gilbert Jones Philos Scholarship Wilberforce Univ 1964-66; Ebony's Religion Award; Ebony magazine Black Achievement Award in Religion 1986; Doctor of Humanities Degree, Wilberforce Univ 1987; Doctor of Human Letters, Morris Brown College 1989; Doctor of Divinity, Monrovia College 1984. **BUSINESS ADDRESS:** Congressman, US House of Representatives, 1427 Longworth, House Office Building, Washington, DC 20515.

FLAKE, NANCY ALINE
Small business development executive. **PERSONAL:** Born Jul 23, 1956, Detroit, MI; daughter of Thomas M Flake and Margaret E Flake. **EDUCATION:** Howard Univ, BBA acct 1977; DePaul Univ, MS taxation 1981. **CAREER:** Arthur Andersen & Co, sr tax accountant 1977-80; Laventhol & Horwath, tax accountant supv 1980-81; Coopers & Lybrand, tax accountant mgr 1981-84; Howard Univ, assoc prof of taxation; Howard Univ Small Business Dev Ctr, dir 1984-; Small Business Magazine TV Series, exec producer 1987-. **ORGANIZATIONS:** Advisor Jr Achievement 1979-86; natl conf treas Natl Black MBA Assoc 1983; pres Natl Assoc of Black Accountants 1984-85; bd mem Natl Assoc of Negro Business & Professional Womens Clubs Inc Economic Development Corp 1984-87; bd mem DC Chamber of Commerce 1987-; chairwoman Business Comm DC Chamber of Commerce 1986-87; council mem Mayor Barry's Coord Council Self Sufficiency 1985-, chair Alternatives to Welfare Committee 1989-; comr DC Commiss for Women 1987-90; mem National Assn of Black Accountants. **HONORS/ACHIEVEMENTS:** Cert Publ Accountant 1979-; Minority Bus Advocate of the Year 1987, US Small Bus Admin WA DC 1987; Outstanding Business Leader Bus Exchange Network WA DC 1986; Certificate of Appreciation Amer Assoc of Comm Serv Awd Grad Sch of Business & Public Admin 1987; Delta Sigma Pi Frat 1988-; Executive Producer, Small Business Magazine Television Series 1989. **BUSINESS ADDRESS:** Dir, HowardUniv Small Bus Dev, 2600 6th St NW, PO Box 748, Washington, DC 20059.

FLAKES, LARRY JOSEPH
Consulting civil engineer. **PERSONAL:** Born Jan 27, 1947, Birmingham, AL; son of John Wesley Flakes and Lunlene Patton Flakes. **EDUCATION:** Howard U, BSCE 1969. **CAREER:** DC Hwy Dept Bridge & Traffic Div, engr aide 1965; Water Operations Div, 1968; Wash DC Met Area Govts Dept Sanitary Engr System Planning Div, urban career mgmt intern & urban career student trainee 1967; Lockheed Ga Co Marietta, assoc aircraft engr 1969-70; City of Atlanta, certified position #16, traffic engineer I 1970-71; AL Power Co, electric power transmission & distribution constr contract admin engineer 1972-74; So Ry Co, civil engineer 1974-, property tax engineer 1976-81; Atlanta Area Tech Sch, part-time evening inst 1978-82; Norfolk Southern Corp, proj engr mw&s dept, 1981-89; self-employed consulting engineer, currently. **ORGANIZATIONS:** Certified in open competition position #16 Traffic Engineer I City of Atlanta GA 1970-71; reg professional engineer, State of GA 1981; registered professional civil engineer, State of Alabama, 1983; mem Amer Soc Civil Engineering, 1969-; Natl Bapt Convention USA; mem Amer Railway Engineering Assn, 1983-; Natl Soc of Professional Engineers, 1986; NAACP. **HONORS/ACHIEVEMENTS:** Scholarship to atttend Tuskegee Inst, United Negro Coll Fund, 1964; Tuition Scholarship, School of Engineering & Architecture, Howard Univ, 1964-65; Deans List Howard Univ Washington 1967, 1969; Natl Awd ASCE NY 1967; ASCE Awd Natl Student Chap for being editor of "Tel Star" Student Civil Engrs Newsletter; articles written for Tel Star "The Master Builder" origins of civil engrg 1967; ASCE, MD, DC area univs conf & lecture on peaceful uses of nuclear energy and tour of Goddard Space Flight Ctr activities report 1967; Certificate Traffic Eng Inst NW Univ 1970; Cert Mun Adm & Supv Univ GA 1971; Cert Dept of Defense Multi-Protection Design of Structures 1974; Cert Business Law Mktg 1978. **MILITARY SERVICE:** USAF ROTC cadet 1964-66. **BUSINESS ADDRESS:** Consulting Engineer, PO Box 87522, College Park, GA 30337-0522.

FLAMER, JOHN H., JR.
Educator. **PERSONAL:** Born Oct 13, 1938, Phila; married Mary E Holder; children: Crystal, Dawn, Melanie, Tedd, Todd, Tamiko, Timothy, John, III, Christopher. **EDUCATION:** So IL U, BS 1964; MS 1975. **CAREER:** Job Corps SIU, teacher, coach 1965; IL Youth, prin 1967; Business Affairs SIU, asst to vice pres 1968; Affirmative Action Minority Affairs SIU, asst to pres 1969-; Consult EEO US Civil Svc; Assn Health Recreation & Physical Educ; Alpha Phi Alpha; Natl Affirmative Action Officers, pres 1973; Ethnic Adv Com. **ORGANIZATIONS:** Mem State IL; bd Mem Madison St Clair County Urban League; pres Metro Sickle Cell Anemia; Employment Adv Com Inland Steel; vice pres IL Track & Field Coaches Assn Treas Nat Black Alliance for Grad & Professional Edn.

FLANAGAN, ROBERT B., SR.
Association executive. **PERSONAL:** Born Jan 02, 1929, Atlanta, GA; son of Thomas J Flanagan, Sr and Willie Maude Bales Flanagan; married Ressie J; children: Robert Jr, Shree, Tracy. **EDUCATION:** Morehouse Coll, AB; NY Univ, safety prog org course; NW Univ, traffic mgmt course; Columbus Coll, police comm rel course; Atlanta GA, urban crisis ctr race relations course. **CAREER:** NAACP, exec sec Atlanta Br 2 yrs 1967; pres GA conf 1978; field dir natl staff 1968; mem natl bd of dirs 1985; dir field operations Voter Education Project Atlanta GA 1980-84. **ORGANIZATIONS:** Black/Jewish Coalition 1979-87. **HONORS/ACHIEVEMENTS:** Thalheimer State Conf Awd Outstanding Prog Activities Natl NAACP 1973-75 1979; cited by Chief Fulton Co Registrar for voter registration efforts; commendation for leadership and serv as a resource person Pres of GA Assn of Police Comm Rel Officers; cited for work done for rural blacks in GA GA Coun on Human Rel; commended by Chief of Staff USAF for work done a mem of Spec Study Gr Pentagon. **MILITARY SERVICE:** USAF ret maj. **HOME ADDRESS:** 937 Redbud Ln SW, Atlanta, GA 30311.

FLANAGAN, T. EARL, JR.
Dentist. **PERSONAL:** Born Jan 20, 1937, Baltimore, MD; son of Thomas E Flanagan Sr and Marjorie B Flanagan; married LaVerne; children: Thomas III, Shelley, Brian. **EDUCATION:** Howard Univ, BS 1959, DDS 1966; St Elizabeth Hosp, intern 1966-67; Howard Univ Hosp, resd 1974-75. **CAREER:** St Elizabeths Hosp, instr intern prog, chief dental officer 1969-; Private Practice, dentist 1966-. **ORGANIZATIONS:** Mem Natl Dental Assn, Amer Dental Assn, Acad of Gen Dentists, Amer Dental Soc of Anesthesiology, Amer Assn of Hosp Dentists State chmn 1977, RT Freeman Dental Soc, MD Dental Soc of Anesthesiology; life mem NAACP 1976; life mem Urban League 1969-; mem Kappa Alpha Psi, Chi Delta Mu; fellow Amer Dental Soc of Anesthesiology. **MILITARY SERVICE:** AUS 1st lt 1959-62. **BUSINESS ADDRESS:** 905 Sheridan St, Hyattsville, MD 20783.

FLATEAU, JOHN
Executive director. **PERSONAL:** Born Feb 24, 1950, Brooklyn; married Lorraine Witherspoon. **EDUCATION:** Washington Sq Coll NY U, BA 1972; Baruch Coll, Masters Adm Baruch 1977; US Office of Edn, Pub Serv Educ Fellowship 1975-76. **CAREER:** NYS Commn on Hlth Educ & Illness Prevntn, prin resrch analist; Adult Educ Dist Council 37 AF-SCME & Hunter Coll CUNY, tchr 1968-74; Program Adminstrn BED-STUY Summer Program, supr 1968-72; NY State Assblymn Albet Vann NY State Legislature, past adminstrv asst; Black & Puerto Rican Caucus Inc of the NY State Legltr, exec dir 1977-78; Nat Black Lay Cath Caucus, past youth chmns natl office black caths, bd dir, Harlem Youth Devel Ctr, past comm wckr 1976; Bedford Stuyvesant Pastoral Planning Program, v pres; Bed-stuyvesant Laymen's Convocation pres past. **ORGANIZATIONS:** Mem Urban Voter Educ Assn; mem Comm Educ Task Force; founding mem Vanguard & Indepdt Dem Assn Inc 56th AD; mem Kings Co Dem Com 1972-; Del NY Judicial Conv 2nd District 1972-; mem NAACP Brooklyn Br; mem Alumni Assos NYU/Baruch Coll; mem MLK Jr Alumn Assn; pres JARM Research Assos Ltd 1979-; political action chmn Convention Planner Black Agenda Conv Brooklyn NY 1980; mem Black United Front NY Met Chpt; mem Macon-macdonough-lewis-stuyvesant Block Assn; former mem 592 Prospect Pl Tenants Assn Recipient. **HONORS/ACHIEVEMENTS:** Life membership award Vannguard Civic Assn; listed Dictionary of Intl Biography 1978; listed Comm Leaders & Noteworthy Am 1978; listed outstanding young men of am 1979. **BUSINESS ADDRESS:** C/O Assemblyman Albert Vann, 1360 Fulton St Room 519, Brooklyn, NY 11216.

FLATTS, BARBARA ANN
Attorney. **PERSONAL:** Born Sep 27, 1951, New York, NY; married Robert L Peoples; children: Albert Paul Peoples, Amy Christina Peoples. **EDUCATION:** Hampton Inst, BA 1972; AmUniv Wash Coll of Law, JD 1974. **CAREER:** Office of Corp Counsel DC Govt, asst corp counsel 1976-80; US Dept of labor Benefits Rev Bd, atty-advsor 1975-76; Laorer's Dist & Council Wash DC, law clk 1973-74; US Dept of Justice Environmental Enforcement Section Land & Natural Resources Div, trial atty 1980; New York City Housing Auth Contracts Real Estate & Fin div, atty 1984; State of NY Employment Security Bureau, asst atty gen 1986-. **ORGANIZATIONS:** Bd of dir Girl Scout Council of the Nation's Capital 1977-; bd of dir Wash Urban League 1977-80; mem Juvenile Justice Adv Com DC 1979-80; mem Alpha Kappa Alpha Sor; mem Washington bar Assn; mem past sec Kappa Beta Phi Legal Assn 1976; exec com bd of dir Council on Legal Educ Opportunity 1973-75; pres AmUniv Chap Black Am Law Student Assn 1974; mem Am Bar Ssn 1975-; mem Alpha Kappa Alpha, Epsilon Pi Omega; connection comm coord Alpha Kappa Alpha. **HONORS/ACHIEVEMENTS:** Selected on of the outstanding young women of am 1979. **BUSINESS ADDRESS:** Assistant Attorney General, NY State Department of Law, One Main St, Fulton Landing, Brooklyn, NY 11201.

FLEARY, GEORGE MCQUINN
Judge. **PERSONAL:** Born Sep 06, 1922, Brooklyn, NY. **EDUCATION:** CCNY, BS 1948; Brooklyn Law Sch, LlB 1951. **CAREER:** City of NY, judge civil ct. **ORGANIZATIONS:** Vp NY State NAACP; bd chmn Brooklyn Urban League 1974-77; pres comus club inc hole in one Clariview Golf Course 1975. **MILITARY SERVICE:** USAF 1st lt Wwii capt orean war. **BUSINESS ADDRESS:** 141 Livingston St, Brooklyn, NY 11201.

FLEMING, ALICIA DELAMOTHE
Personnel administrator. **PERSONAL:** Born in New York, NY; married John A Fleming. **EDUCATION:** NY Univ, BS 1972, MS 1980. **CAREER:** NY Univ Med Ctr, office mgr admin 1966-79; Booz Allen & Hamilton, mgr non-exempt personnel 1979-81; Time Inc, employment counselor 1981-85; Non-Exempt Recruiting & Develpmnt, manager 1985-. **ORGANIZATIONS:** Mem EDGES 1985; mem Women in Human Resources Mgmt 1983. **HOME ADDRESS:** 392 Central Park West, Apt 8T, New York, NY 10025.

FLEMING, ARTHUR WALLACE
Cardiothoracic surgeon. **PERSONAL:** Born Oct 01, 1935, Johnson City, TN; daughter of Smith George Fleming, Sr (deceased) and Vivian Cecile Richardson Flemming; married Dolores Caffey; children: Arthur Jr, Robyn, Jon, Mark, Robert, Bernadette, Erik. **EDUCATION:** IL State Normal Univ, attended 1953-54; Wayne State Univ, BA 1961; Univ of MI Medical Sch, MD 1965. **CAREER:** Detroit Inst of Cancer Rsch, rsch asst 1958-61; Walter Reed Army Medical Ctr, thoracic/cardiovascular surg serv staff 1972-83; Walter Reed Army Inst of Rsch, dept of surgery staff 1974-76, div of experimental surgery chief 1976-77, dir dept of surgery 1977-83; Uniformed Serv Univ of the Health Scis, assoc prof of surgery 1978-83; King-Drew Medical Ctr, dir trauma ctr 1983-, prog dir genl surg 1983-; Charles R Drew Univ of Medicine & Science, professor & chairman, Dept of urgery, 1983-; MLK General Hospital, chief of surgery, 1983. **ORGANIZATIONS:** Mem Los Angeles County Trauma Directors Cmte 1984-; mem bd of dirs Amer Coll of Surgeons So CA Chap 1986-; pres Soc of Black Academic Surgeons 1986-. **HONORS/ACHIEVEMENTS:** Gold Medal paper Forum on Progress in Surgery Southeastern Surgical Congress 1977; The Surgeon General's "A" prefix Highest Military Medical Professional Attainment 1981; The Legion of Merit Investigative projects in combat casualty care pioneering of autologous blood transfusions US Army 1983. **MILITARY SERVICE:** AUS col 17 1/2 yrs; Meritorious Serv Awd USAF 1984. **BUSINESS ADDRESS:** Chief of Surgery, King/Drew Medical Center, 12021 So Wilmington Ave, Los Angeles, CA 90059.

FLEMING, BRUCE E.
Educator. **PERSONAL:** Born Jul 17, 1921, Richmond, VA; married Ruth Lewis; children: Jacqueline, Bruce Jr, Shelia, Gregory. **EDUCATION:** VA St Coll, BS 1942; NY U, MA 1948; IN U, spec 1967; NY U, EdD 1969. **CAREER:** US Dept of Educ, educ program offi-

cer 1974-80; HQ Dept Army, dir instrnl tech 1973-74; Pentagon, EEO officer 1971-73; US Army, educ program officer 1970-71; Ft Lee, EEO offocer 1967-70, educ A-V spec 1954-63; Camp Pickett, 1950-54; NY Univ, consultant 1970-72; IN Univ, assoc prof 1963-65; Washington High School, prin 1949-50; Lucille Hunter School, teacher 1948-49; Walker-Grant High School, 1942-43; VA State Univ, vol counselor career planning & placement office; Intl Educ Serv Inst, vice pres for African Affairs. **ORGANIZATIONS:** Life mem NAACP; Phi Beta Sigma; past v reg dir Eastern Reg Phi Beta Sigma; educ coord VA St Conf NAACP; past mem NEA; mem Nat Urban Leag; past chmn Dist Advancement Com BSA; exec com Petersburg Improvement Assn. **HONORS/ACHIEVEMENTS:** Recpt soc action serv awd Phi Beta Sigma Frat 1956; listed Who's Who in Am Educ 1965-66; sev awd human rel Kappa Delta Pi Hon Soc in Educ 1968; educ serv awd Phi Beta Sigma Frat 1974; tchg flw NYUniv 1961; grad asst A-V Cntr INUniv 1966; recipient OH State Univ Serv Awd 1978; recipient Commanding General Ft Lee VA Public Serv Awd 1986. **MILITARY SERVICE:** AUSR lt col 30 yrs.

FLEMING, CAROLYN
Editor. **PERSONAL:** Born Jan 11, 1946, Orange, NJ; married Ronald Howard; children: Ronald H. **EDUCATION:** Drake Coll of Business, 1965; Virginia Union Univ, 1966. **CAREER:** Fine Print News, editor; Testing Dept VA Union U1966; Astara Inc Mystery Sch 1976; The Rosicurican Order AMORC. **ORGANIZATIONS:** Dir Fashion Show Blacks Arts Festival 1970; dir Art & Show Black Arts Festival 1970. **BUSINESS ADDRESS:** Editor, Fine Print News, PO Box 57, Ellicott Station, Buffalo, NY 14205.

FLEMING, CHARLES WALTER
Judge. **PERSONAL:** Born Apr 20, 1928, Cleveland, OH; married Norma; children: Reginald, Patrice, Charles, Gerald, Carlos. **EDUCATION:** Kent State Univ, BA, 1951; Cleveland Marshall Law LLB, 1955; Cleveland Marshall Law, JD 1968; Cleveland State Univ, DL, 1969. **CAREER:** Internal Revenue Serv, Intl Revenue, 1954-56; Cuyp County OH, asst rector, 1961-69; OH Attorney General, special asst, 1969-75; Cleveland Municipal Court Judge, 1976. **ORGANIZATIONS:** Pres, John Harlan Law Club, 1971-75; chmn, Criminal Law Section, NBA 1973; bd of dir, NBA 1973; immediate past pres & admin judge, 1982-83; bd of dirs, Natl Assn of Criminal Lawyers, 1970-74; honorary past impl por El Hasa Temp #28; chmn elect, Judicial Council NBA; bd of trustees, Oldo Municipal County Judges. **HONORS/ACHIEVEMENTS:** Outstanding past pres, John Harlan Law; supreme judicial serv, OH Supreme Court cong achive US Congress; 330 mason Prince Holl Eureka #52. **MILITARY SERVICE:** AUS 1947; Honorable Discharge. **BUSINESS ADDRESS:** Judge, Cleveland Municipal Court, 1200 Ontario St, Court Room 14C, Cleveland, OH 44113.

FLEMING, ELLIS T.
Business executive. **PERSONAL:** Born Mar 26, 1933, Baltimore, MD; son of Lewis Fleming and Lavanna (Moore) Fleming; married Subenia Mae Pettie, Jun 14, 1953. **EDUCATION:** Brooklyn Coll, Graduated Industrial Relations 1957; attended CCNY 1958-59; LaSalle Law Correspondence Course, 1963. **CAREER:** NY Proc Dist, adminstr dir of military personnel prog 1957-62; Haryou-Act, asst exec dir of programs 1963-66; New Breed Ent (1st largest Black clothing mfg in USA), part-owner 1966-70; ETF Assoc Bus Cons, pres; Org & Program Consultants, Bed Stuy Lawyers Assoc, Gov Nelson Rockefeller, White House 1972-73, Jackie Robinson Mgmt Corp 1972; ETF Financial Services, president; Consultant, exec dir Natl Bankers Assoc, CUNY Hostos Coll, Bd of Educ Health/Physical Educ Dept, Spanish Amer Merchants Assoc; Congressman Edolphus Towns 11th CD New York, special assistant; ETF Financial Serv, pres, currently. **ORGANIZATIONS:** Co-founder & orig exec dir of Marcus Garvey Health Facility 1975-78; consult to Congr E Towns 11th CD (BK) 1984; ex-dir E Flatbush (EF) Ed Proj; chr EF Comm Corp; founder/pres Comm of EF Presidents; EF Urban Planning Study 1978-79; mem Operation Breadbasket; mem Congr Black Caucus Roundtable; co-founder EF Church AV Merch Assn; mem Fed of Block Assn; contrib writer Consequences of Powerlessness Youth in the Ghetto; consult clothing mfg & retailers; lectr to bus comm Planning Bd of Regional Planning Assn for NY, NJ, CT; Pres Staff on programs for Black Americans; gen adv to Natl Youth Movement; adv Opportunity Ind Centers NY; field coord Brooklyn Boro Pres 1985. **HONORS/ACHIEVEMENTS:** Writer/contributor "Consequences of Powerlessness" authored by Dr Kenneth Clark; author "The Great Deluge"; Man of the Year Awd Alphas Cas of Brooklyn 1978. **MILITARY SERVICE:** Korean Conflict 1950-52.

FLEMING, G. JAMES
Retired educator. **PERSONAL:** Born Feb 15, 1904, St Croix, Virgin Islands of the United States;son of Alexander and Ernestine; married Hazel L Hampton. **EDUCATION:** Univ of WI, BA 1931; Univ of PA, AM 1944, PhD 1948. **CAREER:** Journal & Guide, news editor 1931-33; Amsterdam News, news editor 1935-37, exec editor 1952-54; The Amer Dilemma, staff mem 1937-40; Philadelphia Tribune, mgng ed 1939-41; President's Comm Fair Employ Pract, examiner 1941-45; Amer Friends Serv Comm, sec race relations 1945-50; WLIB Radio, news dir 1952-54; Morgan State Univ, prof 1954-74, retired; mem, bd of dir Good Samaritan Hospital of Maryland. **ORGANIZATIONS:** Lecturer to various universities and other organizations; chmn Bd of Regents Morgan State Univ 1976-80; life mem NAACP; mem Hampton Alumni Assn; WI Alumni Assn; former bd mem Florence Crittenton Svc; past-pres MD Assn Pub Adm; former mem Civil Serv Comm. **HONORS/ACHIEVEMENTS:** Author "Who's Who in Colored Amer" 1951; Supervising ed "Who's Who in the United Nations" 1952; Author "All Negro Ticket in Baltimore" 1960; "Why Baltimore Failed to Elect A Black Mayor" 1972; Phi Beta Kappa Univ of Wisconsin; Doctor of Human Letters, Hon, Univ of Maryland.

FLEMING, JOHN EMORY
Museum director. **PERSONAL:** Born Aug 03, 1944, Morganton, NC; son of James E Fleming and Mary E Fleming; married Barbara Durr; children: Tuliza, Diara. **EDUCATION:** Berea Coll, BA 1966;Univ of KY, 1966-67; Howard U, MA, PhD 1970-74. **CAREER:** KY Civil Rights Commn, educ specialist 1966-67; Peace Corps, visual aids special 1967-69; USCR Commn, program officer 1970-71; Inst for the Study of Educ Policy, sr fellow 1974-80; Natl Afro-American Museum, dir 1980-. **ORGANIZATIONS:** Mem NAACP 1974-87; bd Assoc Study of Afro-Amer Life and History 1978-87; bd Journal of Negro History 1982-87; vice pres bd Art for Comm Expression 1984-87; panel Columbus Foundation 1986-87; v pres Ohio Museums Assoc 1989-90. **HONORS/ACHIEVEMENTS:** "The Lenghtening Shadow of Slavery," Howard Univ Press 1976; "The Case for Affirmative Action for Blacks in Higher Education," Howard Univ Press 1978. **BUSINESS ADDRESS:** Museum Dir, Natl Afro-American Museum, Box 578, Wilberforce, OH 45384.

FLEMING, JUANITA W.
Educator. **PERSONAL:** Born in Lincolnton, NC; daughter of Joseph Wilson and Bertha Wilson; married William Fleming; children: Billy, Bobby. **EDUCATION:** BS, 1957; MA, 1959, PhD, 1969. **CAREER:** DC Genl Hosp, head nurse 1957-58; DC Bur of PH, PH nurse 1959-60; Freedman's Hosp Sch of Nursing, instr 1962-65; Howard Univ Dept of Ped, PH nursing consult 1965-66; Univ KY Coll of Nursing, prof nursing assoc dean dir grad studies, assoc vice chancellor academic affairs and prof of nursing. **ORGANIZATIONS:** Mem Sigma Theta Tau, Amer Nurses Assn Secr 1986-89; mem Council Nurse Rschers 1976-79; exec comm MCH Council 1982-85; inducted Amer Acad of Nursing 1975, governing council 1982-84. **HONORS/ACHIEVEMENTS:** Omicron Delta Honr Frat 1983; Women Achievement Awd YWCA 1984; Outstanding Woman Frankfort Lexington Links Inc 1976; ANA Comm Nursing Rsch 1976-80; Fellow Admin Amer Council Educ 1977-78; Outstanding Alumni Awd Hampton Inst 1977; Outstanding Educ Awd KY League for Nursing 1978; Cert of Need and Licensure Bd 1980-84; KY Health Servcs Adv Council appointed by Gov of KY 1979-83, reappointed 1983-85; Maternal Child Health Rsch Grants Review Comm appointed by Sec HEW 1979-84; Great Tchr Awd Alumni Assn Univ of KY 1973; Mary Roberts Fellow 1963, Pre-Doctoral Fellowship 1967-69; Alpha Kappa Mu Hon Soc; Hall of Fame Hampton Univ 1987; Marion McKenna Leadership Award Delta Psi Chapter Sigma Theta Tau, 1988. **BUSINESS ADDRESS:** Professor, Univ of Kentucky, Medical Center, Lexington, KY 40506.

FLEMING, JUNE H.
Administrator. **PERSONAL:** Born in Little Rock, AR; daughter of Herman Dwellingham and Ethel Dwellingham; married Roscoe L; children: Ethel, Roscoe. **EDUCATION:** Talladega Coll, BA 1953; Drexel U, MLS 1954; Stanford U, Cert 1974. **CAREER:** Brooklyn Public Library, branch librarian 1954-55; Little Rock School Syst, librn 1955-56; Phil Smith Coll, assoc prof 1960-66; Palo Alto Calif, dir librn 1967-81; Palo Alto Calif, asst city mgr. **ORGANIZATIONS:** Asst city mgr Palo Alto CA 1981; adv bd YWCA 1983-; Soroptimsit Club 1980-82; mem Peninsula Links 1986-, Delta Sigma Theta, Rotary 1988-. **HOME ADDRESS:** 27975 Roble Blanco, Los Altos Hills, CA 94022. **BUSINESS ADDRESS:** Assistant City Manager, Palo Alto Calif, 250 Hamilton Ave, Palo Alto, CA 94303.

FLEMING, MELVIN J.
Business executive. **PERSONAL:** Born Jun 10, 1926, Webster Groves, MO; married Dorothy Adams; children: Barbara, Mel Jr, Kenneth. **EDUCATION:** Lincoln U, BA 1949; UCLA, grad training 1963-64; USC, 1964-65. **CAREER:** Martin Lutehr King Hosp Los Angeles CA, hosp admin 1973-; Martin Luther King Hosp, asso hosp admin 1970-73; asst hosp admin 1969-70; Dept of Pub Soc Soc Services Los Angeles CA, head prog asst 1967-69; Charles R Drew Postgrad Med Sch Los Angeles, lecturer 1970-; UCLA, preceptor 1972-; USC, preceptor 1972-. **ORGANIZATIONS:** Mem Model Neighborhood Exec Com 1974; LincolnUniv Los Agneles Alumni Chap 1956-; LincolnUniv Jeff City MO Alumni Century Club. **HONORS/ACHIEVEMENTS:** Received Achievement Award CA Legislature 1974; man of yr los angeles given by Watts Community 1974; outstanding cit awards from Watts Labor Community Action Com LA Model Neighborhood Prog & LincolnUniv LA Alumni Chap 1974. **BUSINESS ADDRESS:** 12021 S Wilmington, Los Angeles, CA 90059.

FLEMING, PATRICIA STUBBS
Government official. **PERSONAL:** Born Mar 17, 1937, Philadelphia, PA; daughter of Dr Fredrick D Stubbs and Marion Turner Stubbs; divorced; children: Douglass, Craig, Harold. **EDUCATION:** Vassar Coll, BA 1957, graduate studies; Univ of PA; Cranbrook Acad of Fine Arts; NY Univ. **CAREER:** Legislative asst to Representative Augustus Hawkins 1971-73, Representative Shirley Chisholm 1973-75, Representative Andrew Young, Committee on Rules, US House of Representatives 1975-77; special asst to Secretary of Health, Educ & Welfare 1977-79; deputy asst sec for Legislation, US Dept of Educ 1980-81; admin asst to Representative Ted Weiss (D-NY) 1983-86; professional staff mem, Subcommittee on Human Resources and Inter-governmental Relations, US House of Representatives 1986-. **ORGANIZATIONS:** Bd mem Minority Legisl Educ Prgm; bd mem United Black Fund; bd mem Black Student Fund, TransAfrica, Maryland Council on Latin America, Natl Center for Therapeutic Riding. **HONORS/ACHIEVEMENTS:** Educ Policy Fellows Program 1971-72; speeches, panels, related to educ for disadvantaged or minority persons, the AIDS epidemic; articles on same topics in a variety of Publ. **BUSINESS ADDRESS:** Professional Staff Mbr, US House of Representatives, Subcomm on Intergovtl Relations, B372 Rayburn Bldg, Washington, DC 20515.

FLEMING, QUINCE D., SR.
Educational administrator. **PERSONAL:** Born Dec 07, 1915, Mt Hope, WV; married Vivian; children: Quince D. **EDUCATION:** Tuskegee Inst, BS 1939; PA State;Univ of WI at River Fall. **CAREER:** Jefferson County Bd of Educ, admin 1967-72, teacher 1940-67. **ORGANIZATIONS:** Pres Charles Town City Council; pres Jefferson Co Parks & Recreation; mem Jeff Co Bd of Edn. **HONORS/ACHIEVEMENTS:** Achievement award NAACP; serv award Selective Serv USA; 5-10-15 & 20 Yrs Agr Serv Future Farmers of Am.

FLEMING, RAYMOND RICHARD
Educator. **PERSONAL:** Born Feb 27, 1945, Cleveland, OH; son of Theodore Robert Fleming and Ethel Dorsey Fleming; married Nancy Runge, Nov 15, 1969; children: John, Peter, Stephen. **EDUCATION:** Univ of Notre Dame, IN, BA, 1967; Univ of Florence, Italy, 1967-68; Harvard Univ, Cambridge MA, 1968-69, PhD, 1976. **CAREER:** Univ of Notre Dame, Notre Dame IN, instructor, 1969-72; Univ of CA, San Diego CA, asst prof, 1973-80; Miami Univ, Oxford OH, assoc prof of Italian and asst dean of graduate school, 1980-, assoc dean of graduate school, 1985-87; PA stateUniv, Univ Park PA, prof of com lit and Italian. **ORGANIZATIONS:** Dante Society of Amer, Amer Council of Learned Societies. **HONORS/ACHIEVEMENTS:** Ford Foundation Fellowships, 1966, 1972; Fulbright Grant to Florence Italy, 1967; Woodrow Wilson Fellowship to Harvard Univ, 1968; Ingram-Merrill Poetry Award, 1971; Alexander Von Humboldt Fellowship to Germany, 1978; author of Ice and Honey (book), 1979; American Philosophical Society Research Grant, 1982; author of Diplomatic Relations (book), 1982; author of Keats, Leopardi, and Holderlin (book), 1987; Natl Endowment for the Humanities Grant, 1989. **BUSINESS ADDRESS:** Professor of Comparative Literature and Italian, Pennsylvania State University, 433 N Burrowes Building, University Park, PA 16802.

FLEMING, STANLEY LOUIS
Dentist, educator. **PERSONAL:** Born Oct 21, 1933, Johnson City, TN; married Gayle;

children: Stanley II, Ron, Lovie, Tanya, Shawn. **EDUCATION:** Wayne State U, 1955-58; HowardUniv Coll of Dentistry, DDS 1958-62; Georgetown U, MS 1969-72. **CAREER:** Private Practice, dentist 1974-; NC Memroial Hositalp, staff 1974-; School of Dentistry Univ NC, asst prof 1974; Howard Univ Coll of Dentistry, 1972-74; Private Practice, 1963-74; Coll of Medicine Georgetown Univ, post doc fellow 1969-72; Howard Univ Coll of Dentistry, asst prof 1967-69; Dental Health Clinic, staff 1963-67; Coll of Dentistry Howard Univ, instructor 1962-66. **ORGANIZATIONS:** Pres Old N State Dental Soc; Nat Dental Assn; pres Durham Acad of Med; Durham-orange Dental Soc; NC Dental Soc; Am Dental Assn; Acad of Gen Dentistry; Am Assn ofUniv Prof; mem Chi Delta Mu Frat; Omega Psi Phi Frat; UNC Golf Assn chm NC; Old N State Dental Soc Prgm Com; Old N State Dental Soc Memsp Com; mem Study Com on Dental Auxs & Labs Old N State Dental Soc; Admissions ComUniv NC Sch Dentistry; Bio Tract Coord & ComUniv NC Sch of Dentistry; Adv Com On Minority AffairsUniv NC Sch Of Dentistry; Med & Comm Prgm Com of Am Heart Assn NC Affiliate; mem Durham C of C 1979-; mem bd Custom Molders Inc; mem bd Cardinal Savs & Loans Inc vP Old N State Dental Soc 1977-78; pres Old N State Dental Soc 1978-; pres Durham Acad of Med 1977-; Citation DC Dental Soc as chmn of Childrens Dental Hlth Com 1973-74. **HONORS/ACHIEVEMENTS:** Cert Dentsply Ceramics 1974; comm serv award Sigma Gamma Rho Sor 1973; 100% Right Club 1973; cert Analgesia NYUniv 1969; post grad tumors of Oral Cavity 1963-64; Cit HowardUniv Coll of Dentistry meritorious serv 1962; Publ "Natriuretic Responce to a Salt Load in Normal & Hypertensive Wistar Rats" 1974; "Effect of Stabilization on Retention of Vitreaus Carbon Implants" Am Assn of Dental Resrch 1977; Bibliographies Marquis Whos Who in S & SW 1973-75; Personalities of the S 1973-75; Library of Human Resources of the Am Bicentennial Rsrch Inst 1973; Men of Achvmt The Intl Whos Who of Men 1975; dentist of the yr award Old N State Dental Soc 1979. **MILITARY SERVICE:** USAF staff sgt 1951-55. **BUSINESS ADDRESS:** Medical Dental Park Ste 100, 601 Fayetteville St, Durham, NC 27701.

FLEMING, VERN HENRY
Professional athlete. **PERSONAL:** Born Feb 02, 1962, Long Island City, NY; married Michelle Clarke; children: Vern Jr. **EDUCATION:** Georgia, 1984. **CAREER:** Indiana Pacers, guard 1984-. **ORGANIZATIONS:** US Olympic gold medal winning basketball team. **HONORS/ACHIEVEMENTS:** Coaches Kodak All-Amer team for 1983-84; unanimous selection for AP & UPI first team All-SEC; All-Amer honors along with MVP of SEC tourney and All-TournamentSelection; mem of the US Select Team. **BUSINESS ADDRESS:** Indiana Pacers, 300 E Market St, Market Square Arena, Indianapolis, IN 46204.

FLEMING, VERNON CORNELIOUS
Manager. **PERSONAL:** Born Dec 19, 1952, Louisa County, VA; son of William E Fleming and Helen J Fleming; married Vanessa Doris Seaberry; children: Chanell A, Charmaine A. **EDUCATION:** Hampton Univ, BA 1974; College of William & Mary, MBA 1980; US Army Command & General Staff Coll, diploma 1987. **CAREER:** US Army (Coll of Wm & Mary), asst prof of military sci 1980-83; US Army Reserves, instructor 1985-; Procter & Gamble, purchasing manager 1983-. **ORGANIZATIONS:** Chmn bd of dirs Williamsburg Head Start 1982-83; mem Reserve Officers Assoc 1983-, Black Mgr Work Group 1983-; Kappa Alpha Psi Frat; co-chmn prog cmte Natl Black MBA Assoc; Reserve Officers Assoc; district chrmn Boy Scouts of America; treasurer, Kappa Alpha Psi fraternity. **HONORS/ACHIEVEMENTS:** Service Awd Peninsula League of Youth 1982; Officer of the Year Cincinnati Chap Kappa Alpha Psi 1985; Polemarch's Awd Cincinnati Chap Kappa Alpha Psi 1987. **MILITARY SERVICE:** AUS Air Defense Artillery major 9 yrs active 6 yrs reserve; Army Commendation Medal w/3 Oak Leaf Clusters, Army Achievement Medal w/One Oak Leaf Cluster, Overseas Ribbon, Natl Defense Ribbon, Parachutist Badge, Army Serv Ribbon. **HOME ADDRESS:** 2435 Montana Ave, Cincinnati, OH 45211. **BUSINESS ADDRESS:** Purchasing Manager, Procter & Gamble Company, Two Procter & Gamble Plaza, Cincinnati, OH 45202.

FLEMING, WELDON G., JR.
Business executive. **PERSONAL:** Born Jul 28, 1944, Jamaica, NY; married Yolanda Elzie; children: Yana Shani. **EDUCATION:** OH State U, BSC 1962-66; Pace U, MBA Hon 1973-75, DPS Hon 1975-83. **CAREER:** RCA Corp, mgr planning 1970-75; Citibank, avp 1975-77; Am Security Corp/A S Bank, svp/div head 1977-83; Nordheimer Bros Co, chief exec officer 1983-86; The Maxima Corp, pres. **ORGANIZATIONS:** Dir The Maxima Corp 1978-; mem Robert Morris Assoc 1976-83; mem DC Mayors Committee on Econ Devl 1980-85; ltc DC Army Nat Guard 1978-85; mem Reserve Officers Association 1970-; mem Airplane Owners & Pilots Association 1981-. **HONORS/ACHIEVEMENTS:** Mem Delta Mu Delta 1975; commercial pilot rotary wing & fixed wing (FAA) 1972. **MILITARY SERVICE:** AUS ltc; m army aviator Bronze Star; Purple Heart 1966-70; NY National Guard 1970-77, captain; Army Commendation, Army Achievement. **BUSINESS ADDRESS:** President, The Maxima Corporation, 2101 E Jefferson St, Rockville, MD 20852.

FLEMMING, LILLIAN BROCK
Elected official. **PERSONAL:** Born Jul 27, 1949, Greenville, SC; married Rev Johnandad M Flemming; children: Davit, Johnandad II, Emanuel. **EDUCATION:** Furman Univ, BA 1971, MEd 1975. **CAREER:** Greenville City Council Citizen Advisory, chmn 1979, 1980; Southside HS, math teacher 1971-; Greenville City Council, vice mayor pro tem, councilmem 1981-85. **ORGANIZATIONS:** State & natl delegation Natl Educ Assoc 1976,77,78,79; vice pres Greenville Cty Educ Assoc 1978-79; pres Greenville Cty Educ Assoc 1979-80; bd of dir Sunbelt Human Advancement Resource Ent 1981-; bd dir Sr Action Ctr; del Dem Natl Conv San Francisco CA 1984. **HONORS/ACHIEVEMENTS:** Comm Serv Client Council of Western Carolina 1981; Woman of the Year Client Council of Western Carolina 1982; Human Relations Greenville Cty Educ Assoc 1984; Outstanding Comm Serv Epsilon Iota Zeta Chap Sor 1984; Teacher of the Year for Southside HS 1974; Outstanding Young Woman of Amer 1976; Outstanding Secondary Ed of Amer 1972. **BUSINESS ADDRESS:** Mayor ProTem, City of Greenville, PO Box 2207, Greenville, SC 29602.

FLETCHER, ARTHUR ALLEN
Administrator. **PERSONAL:** Born Dec 22, 1924, Phoenix, AZ; married Bernyce; children: Phyllis, Sylvia, Arthur J, Paul, Phillip, Joan. **EDUCATION:** Washburn U, BA 1950; KS State U, Postgrad Courses; San Fran State Coll. **CAREER:** President Richard M Nixons Domestic Cncl Cabinet Com, chmn; Nat Urban League, exec dir 1972-73; UN Gen Assmbly, US & altrnt del; US Dept of Labor, asst sec for wage & labor 1969-71; State Of WA, cand for election as Lt Gov 1968; WA, spl asst to Gov 1969. **ORGANIZATIONS:** Mem Of numerous professional & civic groups. **HONORS/ACHIEVEMENTS:** Recipient of numerous awards.

FLETCHER, HOWARD R.
Government employee. **PERSONAL:** Born Dec 24, 1924, Washington, DC; married Eva Irene; children: Carolyn, Howard Jr. **EDUCATION:** Howard Univ, BS 1949, additional studies 1949-50. **CAREER:** Bureau of the Census Washington DC, computer mgmt 1951-80; United Nations, computer tech adv 1980-81; Washington DC, data processing consult 1981-82; Mt Vernon Coll Washington DC, comp sci faculty 1983; Towson State Univ, computer sci faculty 1984; MCES Univ of MD Coll Park, comp & info syst officer 1984-. **ORGANIZATIONS:** Mem, sr warden 1975, vestryperson 1971-73, 1983-85, convenor convocation 10 1971-73, lay reader 1970-80, Transfiguration Episcopal Church; past pres DC Chap of the Prometheans Inc 1972-73; mem Kappa Alpha Psi Polemarch 1975-76; mem ACM, Amer Natl Stardards Inst, ANSI SIG on Programming Langs. **HONORS/ACHIEVEMENTS:** US Dept of Commerce Silver Medal Awd for Computer Programming Tech 1967; Episcopal Wash Diocesan Review Bd 1972-75; Kappa Alpha Psi Eastern Province Achievement Awd 1974. **MILITARY SERVICE:** AUS 1943-46. **BUSINESS ADDRESS:** Computer & Info Syst Officer, MCES Comp & Info Systems, University of MD, College Park, MD 20742.

FLETCHER, JAMES ANDREW
Executive. **PERSONAL:** Born May 08, 1945, Tulsa, OK; son of Howard Bruce Fletcher and Edna Katherine Fletcher; married Karen Kite; children: Howard Bruce, Jamie Katherine, Lancelot Lansing. **EDUCATION:** MIT, BS 1967; Fairleigh Dickinson Univ, MS (Cum Laude) 1973; Harvard Grad Sch of Business Admin, MBA (w/High Distinction) 1972. **CAREER:** GE Systems, simulation engr 1967-68; General Rsch Corp, systems analyst 1969; IBM Corp, mktg rep 1972-73, financial prog administrator 1974-76, lab controller 1976-78, financial program mgr 1979-81, planning consolidation mgr 1981-83, pricing mgr IPD 1983, dir of plans & controls 1983-85; Unisys Corp, staff vice pres pricing & business analysis 1985-89, vice pres of Finance, Communications Line of Business Marketing Division 1989-. **ORGANIZATIONS:** Mem Amer Friends Serv Comm 1980-; mem Friends Comm for Natl Legislation; mem NAACP, White House Fellows Assoc. **HONORS/ACHIEVEMENTS:** George F Baker Scholar Harvard Grad Sch of Business Admin 1972; White House Fellow 1973-74; mem AFSC South Africa Trip Delegation 1979, mem, FWCC South Africa Trip Delegation, 1989; author "A Quaker Speaks from the Black Experience, The Life and Collected Works of Barrington Dunbar,"1980; co-author Friends Face the World 1987; elected mem of Harvard Business School Century Club; exec asst to deputy dir Office of Management & Budget. **BUSINESS ADDRESS:** Vice President of Finance, Communications LOB Marketing Division, Unisys Corporation, 2200 Renaissance Blvd Suite #400, King of Prussia, PA 19406.

FLETCHER, JAMES C., JR.
Government official. **PERSONAL:** Born May 20, 1934, Bowie, MD; son of James C Fletcher and Margruitte Helen Shelton-Fletcher; married Vernelle A Hammett Fletcher, Mar 18, 1954; children: Anthony (deceased), Carol Anderson, Andrea Fletcher. **EDUCATION:** Attended Howard Univ, Washington DC. **CAREER:** Fed Govt (retired), Washington DC, computer analyst; City of Glenarden, Glenarden MD, councilman, 1974-83, mayor, 1985-. **ORGANIZATIONS:** Bd of dir, Prince Georges Municipal Assn, 1986-88, pres, 1988-89; bd of dir, Maryland Municipal League, 1987-. **MILITARY SERVICE:** US Air Force, Airman 1st class, 1953-57. **BUSINESS ADDRESS:** Mayor, Town of Glenarden, 8600 Glenarden Pkwy, Municipal Building, Glenarden, MD 20706.

FLETCHER, LOUISA ADALINE
Retired government official. **PERSONAL:** Born Jan 03, 1919, Independence, KS; daughter of Charles L Wesley and Anna T Wilson Wesley; married Allen T Fletcher, Mar 24, 1938 (deceased); children: Jerold V Fletcher. **EDUCATION:** Amer Technical Society, Chicago IL, Certificate, Business Admin, 1938; several management training certificates, 1970-72. **CAREER:** US Navy Dept, Bremerton WA, clerk typist, 1944-45; Campbell Grocery Store, Bonner Spring KS, clerk, 1945-52; US Treasury, Kansas City MO, graphotype operator, 1952-53; Dept of Health, Education, and Welfare, Social Security Administration,Kansas City MO, clerk typist, 1954-65, reviewer, 1965-67, computer claims clerk supervisor, 1965-75; manager, Fletcher's Rentals, 1970-; mem, Kansas Public Employees, Relation Board, 1977-85. **ORGANIZATIONS:** Pres, NAACP KS State Conference, 1974-; Natl Assn of Retired Federal Employees, 1977-; NAACP Natl board of dir, 1979-; Natl Comm to preserve Social Security and Medicare, 1988-; pres, PTA Bonner Springs KS School, 1940-42. **HONORS/ACHIEVEMENTS:** Outstanding Performance, SSA, 1964-67; NAACP outstanding service Award, 1964, 1977, 1984; NAACP App Service Award, 1976, 1986, 1989; Louisa A Fletcher Day, Kansas City KS, 1978; Mother of the Year, Church Award, 1979, 1986; Gov First MLK Award, 1985; Plaque, Special Leader for Community, Bonner Springs, 1986; author of articles for Kansas City Call & Globe papers, 1987-1988; Speeches printedfor Tabor Coll, 1987-88.

FLETCHER, ROBERT E.
Photographer, film maker, writer, educator. **PERSONAL:** Born Dec 12, 1938, Detroit, MI; son of Robert Fletcher and Rose Lillian Fletcher; children: Kabenga. **EDUCATION:** Fisk Univ, attended 1956-59; Wayne State Univ, BA 1961; Natl Educ TV Film Training Sch, attended 1970; Comm Film Workshop Council TV News Cinematography Prog 1971; Natl Acad of TV Arts & Sci/Third World Cinema Prod Inc 1976-77. **CAREER:** No Student Movement Harlem, field organizer 1963-64; SNCC Jackson MS, Selma AL Atlanta GA, photographer field coord editorial & air dir 1964-68; freelance photographer journalist & film maker 1968-; Brooklyn Coll, adj prof dept of film studies 1975-76; "Vote for Your Life", prod/dir 1977; "Weatherization, What's It all About?"; Video & TV Prod, summer 1977; WPIX-TV, bi-weekly talk show; "A Nation in View", co-producer. **ORGANIZATIONS:** Mem Intl Photographers of the Motion Picture Indus; chmn bd dir Rod Rodgers Dance Co 1973-; photographs pub in Ebony, Essence, Black Enterprises, Tuesday, Life, Redbook, NY Mag; author of publ in MS. **HONORS/ACHIEVEMENTS:** Cinematographer dir "A Luta Continva" 1971; documentary film on liberation struggle in Mozambique "O Povo Organizado" 1975; panelist "Voices of the Civil Rights Movement" Smithsonian Inst 1980.

FLETCHER, TYRONE P.
Educational administrator. **PERSONAL:** Born Mar 05, 1939, River Jct, FL; married Doris M McRae; children: Michael, Jeffrey, Carol, Kim. **EDUCATION:** FL A&M U, BS 1957-61; Central MI U, MPA 1976. **CAREER:** US Army Command & Gen Staff Coll, instructor 1975-79; US Army ROTC, Ft Valley State Coll, pms 1979-83, dir of recruitment 1983-. **OR-**

GANIZATIONS: State coord Assault on Illiteracy Pgm 1984; advisory bd mem Columbus GA Times Newspaper 1984; Alpha Phi Alpha 1959; Sigma Pi Phi 1984. **HONORS/ACHIEVEMENTS:** Roy Wilkins Meritorious Award NAACP 1980; Who's Who in GA 1973; Outstanding Young Men of Am 1972. **MILITARY SERVICE:** AUS lt col; Silver Star; Bronze Star; Legion of Merit; Meritorious Serv Medal 1961-83. **HOME ADDRESS:** 2420 Courtland Ave, Columbus, GA 31907. **BUSINESS ADDRESS:** Dir of Recruitment, Fort Valley State College, PO Box 4203 FUSC Fort Valley, Fort Valley, GA 31030.

FLETCHER, WINONA LEE
Educator. **PERSONAL:** Born Nov 25, 1926, Hamlet, NC; daughter of Henry F Lee and Sarah Lowdnes Lee; married Joseph G Fletcher, Mar 28, 1952; children: Betty Ann Fletcher. **EDUCATION:** Johnson C Smith Univ, Charlotte NC, AB, 1947; Univ of Iowa, Iowa City, MA, 1951; Indiana Univ, Bloomington PhD, 1968; attended 5 Univ in West Africa, Toga, Dahomey, Ghana, Nigeria, 1974. **CAREER:** Delwatts Radio/Electronics Inst, Winston-Salem NC, sec/teacher, 1947-51; Kentucky State Univ, Frankfort, prof/area coordinator, 1951-78; Lincoln Univ, Jefferson City MO, dir/costumer instructor, summers 1952-60; Indiana Univ, Bloomingtn, prof theatre & afro-amer studies, 1978-, asoc dean coll of arts and sciences, 1981-84. **ORGANIZATIONS:** Costumer, Michiana Summer Theatre, summer 1956; dir of cultural affairs, Upward Bound, KY St. Univ, 1966-67; adjudicator, Amer Coll Theatre Festival, 1973-; mem, KY Arts Commission, 1976-79; consultant, John F Kennedy Center, 1978-; natl pres, Univ/Coll Theatre Assoc, 1979-80, mem, Natl Commission on Theatre Educ, 1980-85, American Theatre Association; US Natl Commission for UNESCO, 1981-85; coordinator, Kennedy Center Black College Project, 1981-84; advisory bd mem, 1st Intl Women Playwrights Conference, 1987-88. **HONORS/ACHIEVEMENTS:** Elected to Coll of Fellows, Amer Theatre Assn, 1979; co-author, Offshoots: The H F Lee Family Book, 1979; Graduate Natl Service Award, Alpha Kappa Alpha, 1980; US Delegate to 5th World Congress on Drama, 1981; Distinguished Alumna, Johnson C Smith Univ, 1986; Elected to Natl Theatre Conference, NTC,New York City, 1988. **HOME ADDRESS:** Campus View House, Apt 705, Bloomington, IN 47408. **BUSINESS ADDRESS:** Dept of Theatre/Drama, Indiana University, Theatre Building, Bloomington, IN 47405.

FLEURANT, GERDES
Educator. **PERSONAL:** Born Jul 07, 1939, Port-au-Prince, Haiti;son of Pradel Fleurant and Fanie Fleurant; married Florienne Saintil; children: Herve, Maimouna. **EDUCATION:** Univ of Haiti, BA Soc Sci 1964; New England Conservatory of Music, BMus Organ 1968; Northeastern Univ, MA Sociology 1971; Tufts Univ, MMus Composition 1980, PhD Caribbean Culture and Music 1987. **CAREER:** Ecole Ste Trinite Haiti, dir of gen music 1959-64; Coll St Pierre Haite, social studies teacher 1962-64; Brockton Schools, gen music teacher 1968-70; Brandeis Univ, lecturer in black music 1973-74; Assumption Coll, vstg lecturer in sociology 1976-77; Wellesley Coll, vstg lecturer in black music 1985-; Salem State Coll, assoc prof of sociology 1971-89; prof of sociology 1989-; dir of african amer studies. **ORGANIZATIONS:** Consult City of Boston Bilingual/Bicultural Phase II 1976, RI Black Heritage Soc Desegregation Program 1980-81; bd mem Advocacy for Comm Changes 1980-83; mem editorial bd New England Jrnl of Black Studies 1982-; bd mem Cambridge Haitian Amer Assoc 1984-85; mem Cambridge Nuclear Studies Peace Comm 1984-85; pres Natl Council for Black Studies NE Reg 1984-86; consultant Humanities Inst Belmont MA 1987; Patriotic Coumbite of Haitian Diaspora (pres) 1987-89. **HONORS/ACHIEVEMENTS:** Article "Class Conflict in Haiti" in Ethnic Conflict & Power 1973; Disting Serv Salem State Coll 1980, 1985; Professional Devel Grant Salem State Coll 1981, 1985; Article "Ethnomusicology of the Rada Rite of Haiti" Perfiles Tufts Univ 1984; Introductory Readings in African American Culture (ed) Ginn Press 1988. **HOME ADDRESS:** 222 Putnam St, Cambridge, MA 02139. **BUSINESS ADDRESS:** Prof, Dir, Salem State College, African American Studies, 352 Lafayette St, Salem, MA 01970.

FLEWELLEN, ICABOD
Business executive. **PERSONAL:** Born Jul 06, 1916, Williamson, WV. **EDUCATION:** Cuyahoga Comm Coll, Associate Degree 1974. **CAREER:** African & Afro-Amer History & Black Studies, researcher 1943-84; Comm Develop Block Grant, dir 1983-84; Afro-Amer Cultural & Historical Soc Museum & Rsch Library, founder/dir 1953-. **ORGANIZATIONS:** Multiple exhibits including two-day exhibit for City of Cleveland Mayor's Comm on Aging 1975; lecture & slide exhibit at Cleveland's Main Public Library on Alexander S Pushkin & Alexander Dumas Pere; 30 day exhibit at Karamu House "Early Black Church in Cleveland and Its Music" 1980; mem Natl Museum of Afro-Amer Culture & History appointed by Gov John J Gilligan 1972. **HONORS/ACHIEVEMENTS:** Cert of Appreciation City of Cleveland 1973; grant recipient Natl Endowment for the Humanities 1980; Carter G Woodson Awd of Distinction 1980; Cert of Recognition City of Cleveland 1980; Thomas Jefferson Awd WJKW TV and the Amer Inst of Public Serv 1980; Comm Awd OH Conf of the United Church of Christ 1980; Comm Awd Cleveland Chap of the WV State Coll Alumni; Comm Awd Cuyahoga Bd of Comm 1980. **MILITARY SERVICE:** Quartermaster 1942. **BUSINESS ADDRESS:** Dir, Afro-Amer Cul & Histor Soc Mus, 1765 Crawford Road, Cleveland, OH 44106.

FLIPPEN, FRANCES MORTON
Association executive. **PERSONAL:** Born in Point Pleasant, WV; daughter of Edward L Morton and Mary J Morton; married John; children: J Bryan. **EDUCATION:** WV St Coll, BS business admin; NYU, MA; NYUniv & WV U, post-grad. **CAREER:** Delta Sigma Theta Inc, dep dir, management consltant; Nat Council of Negro Women Inc, program specialist; US Dept of Labor, WICS liaison job corps; Shady HS, counselor; Stratton HS, teacher. **ORGANIZATIONS:** Mem Am Personnel & Guid Assn; NEA; NBEA; former vice pres prgm devel chmn Am Assn ofUniv Women; Raleigh Co Educ Assn; Am Assn of United Nations; Nat Congress of PTA; life mem NAACP; bd dir YWCA; Am Leg Aux Post 70; life mem former regl dir Midwest Delta Sigma Theta; life mem Nat Coun of Negro Women; mem Links Inc, Eastern Area Treasurer; mem Raleigh Co Assn of Mental Hlth; Raleigh Co Assn of Arts & Hum; Maids & Matrons Soc Study Club; former bd of religious educ Ebenezer Bapt Ch; Alpha Delta Sigma Honorary Society, mem Women's Committee, Washington Performing Arts Society; mem, Women's Committee for the Natl Symphony; bd of dirs Boys and Girls Clubs of America, Washington DC. **HONORS/ACHIEVEMENTS:** Spec recogn awd vol Comm Welfare Coun & WICS Job Corps.

FLIPPEN, GREG
Mayor. **PERSONAL:** Born Jul 02, 1950, Shaw, MS. **EDUCATION:** Valley State U, 2 yrs; Delta State U, Grad 1972. **CAREER:** Shaw MS, mayor; Internal Revenue, 2 1/2 yrs; Bolivar Co Neighborhood Youth Core, counselor; Chenault Chevrolet Co, car salesman. **ORGANIZATIONS:** Fellow Inst of Politics. **BUSINESS ADDRESS:** 106 Mose Ave, Shaw, MS 38773.

FLOOD, SHEARLENE DAVIS
Educational administrator. **PERSONAL:** Born May 13, 1938, Jefferson Co, AL; married Ralph; children: Angela Harris, Clinton Harris Jr. **EDUCATION:** Elem Educ & Music AL State U, BS 1958; FellowUniv of AL Guidance Inst, EDPA 1968-69; Educ Adminstr & Higher EducUniv of AL Tuscaloosa, EdD 1 976. **CAREER:** Jefferson State Jr Coll, dir of counseling, career lab, special serv 1969-; Birmingham Public School System, instructor of Speech Art & Music 1963-68; Jefferson County Public School System, instructor of English & Music 1960-63; Opelika Public School System, instructor of Music 1958-60. **ORGANIZATIONS:** Mem Am Assn of Comm & Jr Coll; Council on Black Am Affairs; exec mem Student Personnel Div AL Jr & Comm Coll Assn; mem AL Personnel & GuidanceAssn; mem Advisor Nat Assn of Mental Health; comm devel office City of Birmingham; supr of Comm serv JECCO Comm Serv. **HONORS/ACHIEVEMENTS:** Citizens award of Merit in Field of Psychological Services; Booker T Washington Business Coll Beta Psi accounting honor soc 1971; outstanding faculty mem Jefferson State & Jr Coll; service award Jefferson State Jr Coll 1980. **BUSINESS ADDRESS:** Jefferson State Junior College, 2601 Carson Rd, Birmingham, AL 35215.

FLORENCE, JOHNNY C.
Expo vice chairman, transportation director. **PERSONAL:** Born Jun 09, 1930, Birmingham, AL; son of Johnnie Florence and Eugenia Franklin Florence; married Lillie M Florence Dowdell, Aug 27, 1949; children: Cynthia Ann Patton, Byron Richie, June Levern Kennedy, Robert Daryln, Cedric Jon. **EDUCATION:** Drake Univ, Des Moines IA, 1948; Temple Univ, Philadelphia PA, 1949-51; Indiana Univ NW, East Chicago IN, court management, 1952. **CAREER:** Inland Steel Co, East Chicago IN, machinist, 1951-76; Lake County Court, Crown Point IN, probation off, 1968-71; City of East Chicago, IN, recreation dir, 1971-83, transit dir, 1983-. **ORGANIZATIONS:** Vice pres, Conference of Minority Transportation Conference; vice chairman, Indiana Black Expo; NAACP Voters Registration Drive; Indiana State Minority Education Bd. **HONORS/ACHIEVEMENTS:** Indiana Black Expo Award, 1976, 1982, 1984; NAACP Award, 1984. **BUSINESS ADDRESS:** Director, East Chicago Public Transit, 5400 Cline Ave, East Chicago, IN 46312.

FLORENCE, VIRGINIA PROCTOR POWELL
Librarian. **PERSONAL:** Born Oct 01, 1897, Wilkinsburg, PA; daughter of Socrates Edward Powell and Caroline Elizabeth Proctor Powell; married Charles Wilbur Florence, Jul 18, 1931 (deceased). **EDUCATION:** Oberlin College, BA, 1919; Pittsburgh Carnegie Library School, librarianship degree, 1923. **CAREER:** New York Public Library, New York NY, assistant librarian, 1923-27; Seward Park High School, Brooklyn NY, librarian, 1927-31; Cardozo High School, Washington DC, librarian, 1938-45; Maggie L Walker Senior High School, Richmond VA, librarian, 1950-65. **HONORS/ACHIEVEMENTS:** First African-American woman to complete a professional education program in librarianship; Outstanding professional service award, University of Pittsburgh Library School, 1981. **HOME ADDRESS:** Westport Convalescent Center, 7300 Forest Ave, Richmond, VA 23226.

FLOURNOY, VALERIE ROSE
Author, editorial consultant. **PERSONAL:** Born Apr 17, 1952, Camden, NJ; daughter of Payton I Flournoy Sr and Ivie Mae Buchanan Flournoy; divorced. **EDUCATION:** William Smith Coll, Geneva NY, BA History 1974. **CAREER:** The Dial Books for Young Readers, asst editor 1977-79; Silhouette Books/Pocket Books, sr editor 1979-82; The Berkley Publishing Group/Second Chance at Love, consulting editor 1982-83; Vis A Vis Publishing Co 1985-. **ORGANIZATIONS:** Mem Black Women in Publishing. **HONORS/ACHIEVEMENTS:** ALA Notable Book American Library Assoc Chicago 1985; Christopher Award The Christophers Inc 1985; Coretta Scott King Award for Illustrations ALA/Chicago 1985 all awards for The Patchwork Quilt; First recipient Ezra Jack Keats New Writer Award 1986 sponsored by Ezra Jack Keats Found and The NY Public Library; books published "The Twins Strike Back" The Dial Press 1980; "The Best Time of Day" Random House 1978; "The Patchwork Quilt" The Dial Press/Dutton 1985. **BUSINESS ADDRESS:** Vis A Vis Publishing, 505 Arch St, Palmyra, NJ 08065.

FLOWERS, LOMA KAYE
Psychiatist. **PERSONAL:** Born Feb 27, 1944, Chardon, OH; daughter of Dr George W Brown and Elsie Kaye Brown; married Edgar Flowers Jr; children: George, Brandon. **EDUCATION:** OBK, Sr in Absentia 1964; Western Reserve Univ, AB hons in Biology 1965; Case Western Reserve Univ, MD 1968. **CAREER:** San Francisco Gen Hosp, internship 1968-69; Stanford Univ Med Center, residency in psychiatry 1969-72; E Palo Alto Comm Health Ctr, dir of mental health 1971-73; VA Hospital San Francisco, chief mental hygiene clinic 1973-77; Various Schools Health Business Org, consultant 1970-; Delaney & Flowers Dream Center, dir1983-; Univ of CA, assoc clinical prof of psychiatry; Host, BET Cable TV, "Dr Flowers on Call" 1985-86; private practice of Psychiatry, 1977-. **ORGANIZATIONS:** Vice pres 1983-85, chmn of bd of dirs Assn for the Study of Dreams 1984-85; AMA; Amer Psychiatric Assn; Negro Business & Professional Women's Assn; NAACP, Black Psychiatrists of America. **HONORS/ACHIEVEMENTS:** Motar Bd 1963; Francis Hobart Herrick Prize 1964; Phi Beta Kappa 1964; Magna cum laude 1965; Medical School Faculty Awd for Rsch 1968; author, "The Morning After: A Pragmatists Approach to Dreams," Psychiatric Journal, Univ of Ottawa, 1988; author, "Psychotherapy Black & White," Journal of Natl Medical Assn, 1972. **BUSINESS ADDRESS:** Delaney & Flowers Dream Center, 337 Spruce St, San Francisco, CA 94118.

FLOWERS, RALPH L.
Attorney. **PERSONAL:** Born Jan 23, 1936, Palatka, FL. **EDUCATION:** FL A&M U, BS 1957, EdM 1968, JD 1968. **CAREER:** Private Law Practice; City of Fort Pierce, former judge, prosecutor 1972-73; Riviera Beach, prosecutor ad litem 1971-73; Lincoln Pk Acad, band dir 1959-65; atty 1968. **ORGANIZATIONS:** Bd dir & legal adv Indian Rvr Invstmnt Corp Pioneer Investment Capital Corp; bd dir FL Rural Legal Serv; chmn Judicial Council FL Chap Nat Bar Assn; Exalted Ruler Pride of St Lucie Lodge IBPOE of W 1970; mem Alpha Phi Alpha; Am Bar Assn; FL Assn of Trial Lawyers; mem St. **HONORS/ACHIEVEMENTS:** St Lucie Co C of C Flowers for the living award Radio Station WIRA 1973; pub safety award St Lucie Co Safety Council 1974; Alpha Phi Alpha man of the year 1976. **MILITARY SERVICE:** AUS 1st lt 1957-59. **BUSINESS ADDRESS:** Sunrise Theatre Bldg, Fort Pierce, FL 33450.

FLOWERS, RUNETTE (RUNETTE FLOWERS WILLIAMS)
Physician. **PERSONAL:** Born Apr 02, 1945, Donaldsonville, GA; married W Alphonso. **EDUCATION:** Dillard Univ New Orleans, BA Biology 1967; Tuskegee Inst, MS 1969; Meharry Med Coll Nashville, MD 1973. **CAREER:** Dekalb Grady Clinic, staff pdtrcn 1976-; Dept of Preventive Medicine EmoryUniv & Sch of Med, asst prof 1976-; Emory U, residency 1973-76; Edwood-parent-child Ctr, consult 1977-; Sch of Nursing GA Bapt Hosp, lectr 1978-79; Nurse Practritioner Program Emory, preceptor 1978-79. **ORGANIZATIONS:** Mem Health Systems Agency GA 1980; mem Greater Atlanta Pediatric Assn 1978-; mem Delta Sigma Theta Sorority/Beta Kappa Chi Sci Honor Soc. **HONORS/ACHIEVEMENTS:** Most Outstanding Student in Pediatrics Meharry Med Coll 1973; Grace M James Award in Pediatrics Meharry Med Coll 1973. **BUSINESS ADDRESS:** Emory Univ Sch of Med, Atlanta, GA.

FLOWERS, W. HAROLD, JR.
Attorney. **PERSONAL:** Born Mar 22, 1946, Chicago, IL; son of W Harold Flowers Sr; married Pamela Mays. **EDUCATION:** Univ of CO, BA 1967, Law School JD 1971. **CAREER:** Adams County, deputy district attorney; Private Practice, 1979-. **ORGANIZATIONS:** Bd of dirs KGMU Radio Station 1981-84; bd of dirs CO Criminal Defense Bar 1982-83; regional dir Natl Bar Assoc 1984-85, bd of governors 1985-; exec bd Boy Scouts of Amer 1983-; pres elect 1986, pres 1987 Sam Cary Bar Assoc; mem Comm Corrections Bd 1984-; bd of governors, Colo Trial Lawyers Assn, 1988-; mem, Judicial Nominating Comm 1988-. **BUSINESS ADDRESS:** 2260 Baseline Rd Ste 201, Boulder, CO 80302.

FLOWERS, WILLIAM KNOX, JR.
Physician. **PERSONAL:** Born Sep 22, 1916, Sulphur Springs, TX; married Annette L. **EDUCATION:** Wiley Coll, 1934-38; Meharry Med Coll 1938-42. **CAREER:** Self-Employed, physician. **ORGANIZATIONS:** CV Roman Med Soc; Nat Dallas So Clinical Soc; Dallas Co Med Soc; TX Med Assn; mem Omega Psi Phi Frat; mem Alpha Epislon Boule & Sigma; mem Pi Phi; mem Fellow Am Acad Family Practice AMA Physician City Well Child Conf 1960; Planned Parenthood 1967; Martin Luther King Comm Hlth Crt; mem Dallas Hlth Mus Com; adv Bd Sr Citz; N TX Hlth Planning Commn; Big Bros Inc; pres Trumans Hlth Commn; mem Am Acad Family Physicians. **HONORS/ACHIEVEMENTS:** Recpt Dallas Co United Fund Campaign award 1965; Dallas Big Bros 20 Yr; serv award 1969; Alpha Phi Alpha Frat citzsp award; CV Roman med aux recg award. **MILITARY SERVICE:** AUSR mc lt. **BUSINESS ADDRESS:** 2701 Grand Ave, Dallas, TX 75215.

FLOYD, DEAN ALLEN
Physician. **PERSONAL:** Born Mar 10, 1951, Loris, SC; son of Mr & Mrs Stephen J Floyd Sr; married Gail Payton; children: Anissa Deanne, Dean Allen II, Allycia Summer. **EDUCATION:** Clemson Univ, BS 1972; Medical Univ of SC, MD 1976; Richmond Memorial Hospital, residency 1977-80. **CAREER:** Family Health Centers, Inc, medical dir 1980-85; Private Practice, 1985-. **ORGANIZATIONS:** Medical consultant SC State Health & Human Services 1985-. **BUSINESS ADDRESS:** 2601 Millwood Ave, Suite H, Columbia, SC 29205.

FLOYD, ERIC BARRY
Professional athlete. **PERSONAL:** Born Mar 06, 1960, Gastonia, NC. **EDUCATION:** Georgetown, Political Science, Public Admin, 1982. **CAREER:** NJ Nets, guard; Golden State Warriors, guard 1983-. **ORGANIZATIONS:** Mem black student Alliance Club. **HONORS/ACHIEVEMENTS:** Georgetown's All-Time leading scorer; MVP, NCAA West Region Tourney.

FLOYD, JAMES T.
Association executive. **PERSONAL:** Married Dr Barbara Floyd; children: James T Jr, Norman V, Kimberly V, Javonda A. **EDUCATION:** Allen Univ, BS 1957; Tuskegee Univ, MS 1965. **CAREER:** Sanders HS, teacher 1957-58, head football coach 1960-64; Beck HS, chmn sci dept 1965-69; Union Carbide Corp, process engr 1969-72; WR Grace & Co, process engr 1972-75, quality assurance mgr 1976-82, group leader process engrg; Phi Beta Sigma Frat, natl president. **ORGANIZATIONS:** Vice chmn Greenville Co Crime Commn; advisor J L Mann School System. **HONORS/ACHIEVEMENTS:** Community Leaders & Noteworthy Americans 1979-80; Who's Who in the South and Southeast 1980-81; selected to Ebony's 100 Most Influential Blacks in Amer 1985, 86. **MILITARY SERVICE:** AUS 2 yrs. **HOME ADDRESS:** 106 Brandon Way, Simpsonville, SC 29681.

FLOYD, JEREMIAH
Association executive. **PERSONAL:** Born Jan 08, 1932, Laurens, SC; son of Willie J. Floyd and Clara Floyd; married Clara Brown; children: Camille, Edgar. **EDUCATION:** Allen U, BS 1956; Northwestern U, MA 1960, PhD 1973. **CAREER:** Evanston Public Sch, princpl 1970-73; Nat Sch Bd Assn, dir urban & minority rel 1973-76, asst exec dir 1976-78, assoc exec dir 1978-. **ORGANIZATIONS:** Vp NorthwesternUniv Alumni Educ 1973-76; pres NU Chap Phi Delta Kappa 1972-74; mem bd of dir United Way Evanston 1971-76; vice chmn, Montgomery Community Services Partnership 1986-; mem, Montgomery Coll Gen Educ Advisory Comm 1988-; mem, State Advisory Comm on Adult Educ and Community Service 1986-88. **HONORS/ACHIEVEMENTS:** NSF fellowship Nat Sci Found NorthwesternUniv 1959-62; IDEA fellow Rockford Coll 1969; pres Wilmette Sch Dist 39 Bd of Educ 1976; mem Montgomery Cnty Bd of Educ MD 1984; vice pres Montgomery Cnty Bd of Educ MD 1985-86. **MILITARY SERVICE:** USAF m sgt; Nat Defense Medal; Good Conduct Medal 1955. **HOME ADDRESS:** 5909 Aberdeen Rd, Bethesda, MD 20817. **BUSINESS ADDRESS:** Associate Executive Dir, Nat'l Schl Brds Assoc, 1680 Duke St, Alexandria, VA 22314.

FLOYD, MARQUETTE L.
Judge. **PERSONAL:** Born Oct 14, 1928, Winnsboro, SC; married Helen. **EDUCATION:** NYU, BS 1958; Brooklyn Law Sch, LLB 1960. **CAREER:** Suffolk Co, dist court judge; Pvt Prac NY, atty; Ronek Park Civic Aassn, pres. **ORGANIZATIONS:** Pres N Amityville Rep Club; dir chmn ACE Cntr; OEO; dir Legal Aid Soc; dir Sunrise Psychia Clinic; dir & Key Amityville Youth Orgn; sec Eta Theta Lambda Chpt; Alpha Phi Alpha Frat Inc; mem Suffolk Co Bar Assn; NY State Bar Assn; Dist Ct bd of Judges Suffold Co; Dist Ct bd of Judges of Nassau &Suffolk Co. **HONORS/ACHIEVEMENTS:** Recip outstanding serv award Hollywood Bapt Ch 1971; justice of yr award LI Guardians 1972; man of yr award Co Line Guild of Business & Professional Women 1970; churchman of yr 1975. **MILITARY SERVICE:** USAF t/sgt 1948-54. **BUSINESS ADDRESS:** Suffolk District Court, 1000 Veterans Memorial Highway, Hauppauge, NY 11787.

FLOYD, OTIS L., JR.
University president. **CAREER:** Tennessee State University, Nashville, TN, president. **BUSINESS ADDRESS:** Tennessee State University, Nashville, TN. *

FLOYD, SAMUEL A., JR.
Scholar. **PERSONAL:** Born Feb 01, 1937, Tallahassee, FL; son of Samuel Floyd and Theora Floyd; married Barbara; children: Wanda, Cecilia, Samuel III. **EDUCATION:** Florida A&M Univ, BS 1957; Southern IL Univ, MME 1965, PhD 1969. **CAREER:** Smith-Brown HS, dir instrumental music 1957-62; Florida A&M Univ, asst dir bands 1962-64; Southern IL Univ, instructor, assoc prof 1968-78; Fisk Univ, prof 1978-83; Columbia Coll Chicago, dir ctr for black music rsch 1983-. **ORGANIZATIONS:** Mem College Music Soc 1970-87, Sonneck Soc 1980-87, Amer Musicological Soc 1986-87. **HONORS/ACHIEVEMENTS:** Publs "Black Music in the United States," Kraus Publications 1983; "Black Music Biography," Kraus Publications 1987; Distinguished Service Awd Natl Assoc of Negro Musicians 1986. **BUSINESS ADDRESS:** Dir, Columbia College, Center for Black Music Rsch, Chicago, IL 60605.

FLOYD, VERNON CLINTON
Broadcast executive, engineer & electronics instructor. **PERSONAL:** Born Nov 20, 1927, Chickasaw Terrace, AL; son of Nathan D Floyd and Ora A Ellis Floyd; married Vonghett Otis Floyd; children: Marjorie A, Victor C. **EDUCATION:** Dunbar Trade School, Chicago IL, 1945-46; Industrial Training Inst, Chicago IL, 1945-46; Tuskegee Inst, Tuskegee Inst AL, 1948-52. **CAREER:** Station WMOZ, Mobile AL, chief engineer, 1953-65; Carver Technical Trade School, Mobile AL, electronics instructor, 1966-68; Community Educ Program, Hattiesburg MS, 1988; Circuit Broadcasting Co, Hattiesburg MS, founder/owner, 1969-; Electrical Contractor, Hattiesburg MS, 1972-; WORV-AM/WJMG-FM. **ORGANIZATIONS:** Advancement chmn, Boy Scouts of Amer, 1971-73; mem, BOAZ Lodge #4, 1980-; electrical bd mem, City of Hattiesburg, 1981-83. **HONORS/ACHIEVEMENTS:** Pioneered & developed station WORV-AM, 1969; One of 10 Most Outstanding Men, Hattiesburg Ministerial Group, 1971; designed, built & made total technical instillation, WJMG-FM, 1982. **MILITARY SERVICE:** One-hundred fifty-ninth Artillery Batt, T5, 1946-48. **BUSINESS ADDRESS:** President, General Manager & Chief Engineer, Circuit Broadcasting Company of Hattiesburg, 1204 Graveline St, Hattiesburg, MS 39401.

FLOYD, VIRCHER B.
Educator. **PERSONAL:** Born Apr 03, 1928. **EDUCATION:** Earlham Coll, BA 1952; Earlham Coll, MA 1954; Univ of Pittsburgh, MSW 1962. **CAREER:** Sewickley Community Center, exec dir 1956-60; Pittsburgh Regional Office of Pennsylvania Dept of Public Welfare, state social worker 1961-63; Rural Community Devel Unit, Tlaxcala Mexico, AFSC 1963-65; Townsend Community Center, Richmond IN, dir 1965-68; Urban Programs, Peace Corps, Bogota Colombia, staff dir 1968-70; Career Serv Office, Earlham Coll, asst prof, dir 1970-75. **ORGANIZATIONS:** Vice pres, Allegheny Co Fedn of Settlements; natl bd mem, Amer Friends Serv Comm 1972-75; dir, Foster Parents Plans, Colombia. **HONORS/ACHIEVEMENTS:** Author of several publications. **MILITARY SERVICE:** AUS 1954-56.

FLOYD, WINSTON CORDELL
Physician. **PERSONAL:** Born Nov 13, 1948, Edgefield, SC; married Francena Pinckney. **EDUCATION:** Tuskegee Inst, BS 1969; MD 1973; Cook Co Hosp, intern 1973-74; Meharry Med Coll, resd 1974-77. **CAREER:** Pvt Prac, internal med; Anderson Meml Hosp, attending staff; Meharry Med Coll, instr internal med 1976-77. **ORGANIZATIONS:** Dipl Nat Bd of Med Exmnrs 1974; Am Bd of Internal Med 1977; mem AMA; mem Alpha Phi Alpha Frat. **BUSINESS ADDRESS:** 1007 Ella St, Anderson, SC 29621.

FLUELLEN, JOEL M.
Actor. **PERSONAL:** Born Dec 01, Monroe, LA. **EDUCATION:** Studied acting under Morris Carnovsky, Hume Cronyn, Charles Laughton, Mme Ouspenskaya. **CAREER:** Started in motion pictures as extra; Worked on Broadway stage,LA Theater; appeared in many TV shows:FBI, Ispy, Gidget, Tarzan, Laramie, The Invaders, Dr BenCasey, The Iron Horse, The Rd West Wild Wild West, Breaking Point, Death Valley Days, Slattery's People, Dick Van Dyke Show, Ramar of the Jungle, The Great Adventure, Alfred Hitchcock Presents, The Christmas Story, Miss Jane Pittman, Marcus Welby, Columbo; Motion Pictures: The Chase, Good Neighbor Sam, He Rides Tall, Porgy & Bess, Imitation of Life, The Decks Ran Red, Friendly Persuasion, Raisin in the Sun, Run Silent Run Deep, Sitting Bull, The Burning Cross. **ORGANIZATIONS:** Mem NAACP Performers Charity Club; Organized The First Meaningful Theater for Black Actors in LA Negro Art Theater 1950; mem SAG/AEA; Worked NAACP Performers Charity Club. **HONORS/ACHIEVEMENTS:** Black filmmakers award 1975. **BUSINESS ADDRESS:** C/O Paul Kohner, 9619 Sunset Blvd, Los Angeles, CA 90069.

FLUKER, PHILLIP A.
Retired association executive. **PERSONAL:** Born Nov 10, 1920, Birmingham; son of Ernest Herman Fluker and Eunice Alberta Stanford Fluker; married Jeanette Robinson; children: Billy Ray, Samuel Fuston Andrew, Douglas Allen, Winfred, Willie Ernest, Tracy Lynn, Phyllis Gale Christian, Eunice Patricia Hicks, Barbara James. **ORGANIZATIONS:** Tchr Sunday school supt adult sunday sch chmn usher bd 1st Bapt Ch Harlan; chmn com Boy Scout Troop 104; pres Rosenwal HS PTA 1963; pres Harlan Parent Tchr League 1964; adv NAACP Youth Coun 1965-68; mem bd dir Harlan Co Comm Action Agency; chmn Planning for NAACP State Conf 1967; delegate to Ofc of Interior for Stte of KY; rep Southeastern KY to Negro Leadership Conf; pres Harlan Soc lites Soc Club 1976; pres Harlan Chap NAACP 1973-77; pres Willing Workers 1974; mem First Bapt Ch of Harlan KY; pres Harlan Chapt Rosenwald Heritage Orgn; bd dirs Rosenwald Harlanite's Inc; chmn Housing Com for Harlan Co Fair Housing Affirmative Action Com; bd trustees & chmn of usher bd First Baptist Ch Harlan KY; mem Gov Breathitt Adv Commn Hon Order of KY Col; vice pres Rosenwald Heritage Organ Harlan; chmn of Scholarship for Preservation of Rosenwald Heritage; chmn Scholarship for the London Dist Missionary and Educ Assn; treas for COAP Inc Christian Outreach w/Appalachian People; bd of dir, Harlan County Community Action Agency.

FOARD, FREDERICK CARTER
Pharmaceutical industry executive. **PERSONAL:** Born Mar 10, 1945, Philadelphia, PA; daughter of Howard A Foard and Adele C Foard; married Ione Fraser; children: Nicole, Justin. **EDUCATION:** Lincoln Univ of PA, BA 1967; Capital Univ Columbus, MBA 1976. **CAREER:** HRB-Singer Div Singer Co, behavioral scientist 1967-69; Schering Labs/Schering-Plough, mkt rsch analyst 1969-71; Bristol Labs/Bristol-Myers Co, sr mkt rsch 1971-73; Warren-Teed Pharm/Rohm & Haas Co, mgr mkt rsch 1973-74, product mgr 1974-77; Smith Kline & French Labs/Smith Kline Beckman Corp, sr product mgr 1977-83, product dir 1983-86, dir mktg comms 1986-88, vice pres, Diuretic Products 1988-. **ORGANIZATIONS:** Ofcr & various comm chairmanships Omega Psi Phi Frat 1963-; mem Amer Mgmt Assoc 1977-, Pharmaceutical Adv Council 1986-; mem Fund Raising co-chmn Natl Black MBA Assoc 1983-; corp mktg rep Pharmaceutical Manufacturer's Assoc 1986-. **HONORS/ACHIEVEMENTS:** CEBA World Communications 1980; Legion of Honor Chapel of Four Chaplains 1981. **BUSINESS ADDRESS:** Vice Pres, Diuretic Products, Smith Kline & French Lab, 1500 Spring Garden St, Philadelphia, PA 19101.

FOGGIE, CHARLES H.
Retired bishop. **PERSONAL:** Born Aug 04, 1912, Sumter, SC; son of James L Foggie and Mamie Foggie; married Madeline Sharpe; children: Charlene Marietta. **EDUCATION:** AB, AM, STB, STM, DD LLD. **CAREER:** Third Dist, bishop; AME Zion Church, pres bd of bishops. **ORGANIZATIONS:** served AME Zion Ch; pres NAACP; pres Housing Auth City of Pitts; Pittsburgh FellowshipUniv of Pittsburgh; SW Asso Mayors Comm on Resources World Council of Chs; Nat Council of Chs; Consult Ch Union; Black Concerns WCC-sEC bd of Bishops AME Zion Ch; sec bd trustees Livingstone Coll; World Bank Sponsor; chmn N Am Sec Worship Com of World Meth Council; mem Prog Com World Meth Council; Western PA Black Political Assembly; Leadership Conf on Civil Rights; chrmn Home Missions Bd AME Zion Church. **HONORS/ACHIEVEMENTS:** Recip Martin Luther King Award, Pittsburgh Courier Award, evangelism AME Zion Award, Home Mission Award AME Zion Ch; Humanitarian Awd AME Church; First Annual Serv Awd NAACP Pgh Branch; Congressional Record Citation Fifty Years in the Pastoral Ministry; Awd for Natl Black Org Bishop Foggie Pres of Bd of Bishops AME Zion Church. **BUSINESS ADDRESS:** Bishop AME Zion Church, 1200 Windermere Dr, Pittsburgh, PA 15218.

FOGGS, EDWARD L.
Clergyman. **PERSONAL:** Born Jul 11, 1934, Kansas City, KS; son of Eddie Foggs and Inez Lewis-Foggs; married Joyce; children: Lynette, Iris, Edward Elliot, Joy, Alycia. **EDUCATION:** Anderson Coll & Ball State U, AB 1958; Anderson Sch of Theol & Christian Theol Sem. **CAREER:** Exec Council of Church of God, assoc exec sec 1975-88, exec sec/CEO 1988-; Afro-Am Studies Anderson Coll, adj faculty 1968-; Urban Mnstrs Bd Of Ch Ext & Home Missions of Ch of God, dir 1970-75; Sherman St Ch of God Anderson IN, pastor 1959-69; Anderson Univ, adjunct faculty 1968-82. **ORGANIZATIONS:** Past pres & past vice pres Inspirational Youth Convention of Nat Assn of Ch of God 1964-72; mem Family Serv of Madison Co 1964-66; chmn IN Gen Assembly of Ch of God 1967-68; pres Urban League of Madison Co 1969-71; bd mem Nat Conf of Black Churchmen 1971-72; mem Operation PUSH 1974-75; alternate bd mem Urban Training Center for Christian Mission 1974-75; mem Am Mgmt Assn 1976-; mem Balck Exec in Denominations Related Orgn & Communions 1977-78; mem Nat Religious Adv Council of Nat Urban League 1978-; Conv Speaker/Conf & Leader/Consult Ch Work; mem Planning Conf for Sixth World Conf of Ch of God in Nairobi Kenya E Africa 1978; Contrib to Nat Ch Publ Building Bridges to Racial Understanding 1967; key speaker 5th World Conf of Ch of God in Oaxlepec Mexico 1971; bd mem Community Hospital of Madison County 1988-, United Way of Madison County 1989-, Inner City Foundation for Excellence in Education, Los Angeles CA 1988-; mem Anderson Area Chamber of Commerce 1988-, Martin Luther King Jr Memorial Committee 1987-88; convener 1991 World Conference of the Church of God, Wiesbaden, West Germany. **HONORS/ACHIEVEMENTS:** Co-authored Study Guide Andrew Billingsleys Book "Black Families & the Struggle for Survival" 1974; Honorary Degree, Doctor of Divinity, Anderson Univ, Anderson IN 1984. **BUSINESS ADDRESS:** Executive Secretary/CEO, Exec Cuncil of Church of God, 1303 W 5th St, PO Box 2420, Anderson, IN 46011.

FOGGS, JOYCE D.
Educator. **PERSONAL:** Born Feb 13, 1930, Indianapolis, IN; daughter of Wilbur Stone (deceased) and Marry Elizabeth Stone (deceased); married Edward L, 1955; children: Lynette, Iris, Edward Elliot, Joy, Alycia. **EDUCATION:** Anderson Coll, BS 1954; Ball State Univ, MA 1967, Adm License 1978. **CAREER:** Park Place School Anderson IN, teacher grade 6 1970-; Hazelwood School Anderson IN, teacher grade 3 1963-70; Westvale School Anderson IN, teacher grade 4 1959-60; Dunbar Elementary School Kansas City KS, teacher grade 4 1954-55; Anderson Community School Corporation, asst principal, Robinson Elementary School, 1988-89. **ORGANIZATIONS:** 1st Black mem Madison Co Delta Kappa Gamma Honor Soc for Women in Educ 1973-; mem Kappa Delta Pi 1973-; 1st Black mem Madison Co Am Assn of Univ Women 1959-65; Nat Spiritual Life Dir Women of the Church of God; mem exec bd Women of the Church of God 1978-; commr Gruenwald Home Historic Preservation 1977; vp bd of trustees Anderson-Anderson Stoney Creek Lib bd 1967-; bd mem, Urban League of Madison County, 1982-; commissioner, Anderson Housing Authority, 1984-; bd mem, Community Hospital Foundation, 1988-. **HONORS/ACHIEVEMENTS:** Contributor Religious Devotional Books; Contributor to National Church Publication "Building Bridges to Racial Understanding".

FOLK, FRANK STEWART
Physician. **PERSONAL:** Born Oct 02, 1932, Varnville, SC; divorced; children: 3 children. **EDUCATION:** Hampton Inst, 1954; Brooklyn Coll, BS, 1957; Howard U, MD, 1961. **CAREER:** Freedman Hosp, New York, NY, res gen surgery, 1962-66, medical officer, 1969-70; Howard Univ, Washington DC, res gen surgery, 1962-66, inst in surgery, 1969, res fellow, 1969-70; US Public Health Service, Staten Island NY, asst resident, 1964-65, chief resident, 1967-68; DC Gen Hosp, Washington DC, chief resident, 1965-66, medical officer, 1969-70; St Barnabas Hosp, Bronx NY, asst resident, 1966-67, assoc atnd, 1970—, assoc dir of surgery, 1980-82; IBM, Brooklyn NY, med dir 1971-75; Downstate Med Coll, Brooklyn NY, asst instr 1973-76, clinical instr, 1976-86; Hosp for Joint Diseases Med Ctr, New York NY, asst atnd, 1973-79; Brooklyn Jewish Hosp, Brooklyn NY, asst atnd surgeon, 1973-81; NY State Athletic Commission, New York NY, asst med dir, 1980—, acting med dir 1986; NY Med Coll, asst prof of surgery 1987; Health/Hospital Corp, dir. **ORGANIZATIONS:** Cert Nat bd of med Examrs 1966; NY State Med bd 1967; Am bd of Surgery 1977; Am Coll of Cardiology; candidate Am Coll of Surgeons; mem Nat Med Assn; NY Cardiological Soc; Assn for Acad Surgery; Manhattan Cntrl Med Soc; Provident Clinical Soc of Brooklyn; AMA; founding mem, Amer Trauma Soc; Bronx Co Med Soc; Howard U Med Alumni Assn; Empire State Med Soc; NY State Med Soc; mem Unity Dem Club; asst former State Senotor Basil Paterson 1970; bd dir NY City Hlth Hosp Corp Legislative Med & Prof Capital; bd Dir Charles A Drew Hlth Clinic 1974-; Goldberg-paterson Election Fin Com 1970; chmn Reg 1 Nat Med Assn 1971-74; v chmn United Dem Mens Club 1971-75; mem exec Com of Unity Dem Club 1972-; exec bd of Provident Clinical Soc 1971-; Kings Co Hosp comm bd for Mr Thomas R Fortune 1971-74; Num Other Orgns NG 1962-66. **MILITARY SERVICE:** DC Natl Guard, 115th Med Bn, 1962-66, OIC Troop and Med Clinic, 1964-66; NY State Natl Guard, 42nd Infantry Div, div surgeon, colonel, 1973—.

FOLKS, LESLIE SCOTT
Record company executive. **PERSONAL:** Born Dec 04, 1955, New York, NY. **EDUCATION:** Purdue Univ West Lafayette IN, BA 1977. **CAREER:** CBS Records, NY minority intern trainee 1976-77, IN college rep 1976-77, Detroit MI field sales merchandiser 1978-80, NY asst dir of product mgmt 1980-85; Electra Records NY, dir a&r 1985-. **ORGANIZATIONS:** Mem Black Music Assoc. **HONORS/ACHIEVEMENTS:** YMCA Black Achiever in Industry Awd 1984; involved in Gold or Platinum projects by, Luther Vandross, Anita Baker, Starpoint, Sade, The Clash, Midnight Star, Isley Brothers, Eddy Grant. **HOME ADDRESS:** 204 Park Place #3, Brooklyn, NY 11238. **BUSINESS ADDRESS:** Director/Artist/Repetoire, Electra Records, 75 Rockefeller Plaza 21st FL, New York, NY 10019.

FOMUFOD, ANTOINE KOFI
Physician, educator. **PERSONAL:** Born Oct 16, 1940, Mankon, Cameroon;married Angelina Hirku; children: Antoine, Ngwabi, Nina H. **EDUCATION:** Univ of Ibadan Nigeria, MD 1967, Residency in Pediatrics 1968-70; Johns Hopkins Univ Sch of Med, Fellowship in Pediatrics 1970-73; Johns Hopkins Univ Sch of Hygiene, MPH 1974. **CAREER:** Howard Univ, asst prof of pediatrics 1974-78, assoc prof of pediatrics 1978-, dir, neonatology, 1986-. **ORGANIZATIONS:** Mem DC Med Soc 1975-; mem Am Acad of Pediatrics 1975-; mem Johns Hopkins Med-Surgical Soc 1974-; sec to bd Asoc of African Physicians in North Amer 1980-; mem Sect on Perinatal & Neonatal Pediatrics Am Acad of Pediatrics; Affil Fellow Franklin Square Hosp 1971-73; med staff Hosp for Sick Children 1975-; mem Southern Medical Assoc 1985-, Amer Assoc for the Advancement of Sci 1985-, Southern Perinatal Assoc 1985-, World Congress of Martial Arts 1986-. **HONORS/ACHIEVEMENTS:** Merit Award Howard Univ Med Student Council 1981; Outstanding Physician Residents Dept of Pediatrics Howard Univ Hosp 1982; Over 35 papers published in medical journals as of Dec 1986. **BUSINESS ADDRESS:** Assoc Prof Ped/Dir of Neonatol, Howard University, 2041 Georgia Ave NW, Washington, DC 20060.

FONROSE, HAROLD ANTHONY
Physician. **PERSONAL:** Born Aug 31, 1925, Brooklyn, NY; married Mary Elizabeth; children: Wayne, Mark, Drew, Ward. **EDUCATION:** Adelphi U, BA 1952; Cornell U, MS 1954; Howard U, MD 1958. **CAREER:** A Holly Patterson Home, med dir 1970; internist 1962-; A Holly Patterson Home, consult 1962-70; Am Bd Internal Med, diplomate 1968; Mt Sinai med Faculty Elmhurst Campus, attending staff physician. **ORGANIZATIONS:** Past bd dir Vanguard Nat Bank 1972-76; mem NY State & Nassau Co Med Soc; Sigma Pi Phi Frat; Alpha Sigma Boule; Alphi Phi Alpha Frat; Fellow Am Coll of Physicians 1977; Am Coll of Geriatrics 1971. **HONORS/ACHIEVEMENTS:** Publ "Digitalis Withdrawal in Aged" Journal of Geriatrics; "Role of Med Dir in Skilled Nursing Facility". **BUSINESS ADDRESS:** Physician, Mt Sinai Medical Faculty, Old Cedar Swamp Rd, Jericho, NY 11753.

FONTENO, MYRTLE C.
Business executive. **PERSONAL:** Born Mar 09, 1927, Mocksville, NC; married John Fonteno. **EDUCATION:** Knoxville Coll; Howard U, Grad Study; Maryville Coll, sum sch; John C Smith U; Williams Bay. **CAREER:** Better Tours & Travel Houston, owner 1962-; TX So U, instr basic educ 1967; YWCA Houston, adult program dir 1956-60; Knox Comm Cntr, asst dir 1953-55; Radcliffe Presb Ch Atlanta, dir of Christian Educ 1948-53. **ORGANIZATIONS:** Bd mem YWCA 1974; mem United Fund Budget Panel 1972-74; Crisis Hotline Bd 1973; vice pres Traveler's Aid Soc 1973-74; mem Delta Sigma Theta; ARC Serv to Military Families Com 1974; Am Soc of Travel Agents 1972-74; planning bd White House ConF on Aging 1971; Post Convention Bd 1972; Nat Recruiter YWCA 1970-74. **HONORS/ACHIEVEMENTS:** Outstanding AchievementUniv of Houstin Alpha Kappa Alpha 1969; woman of yr Iota Phi Lambda 1972; appreciation award United Negro Coll Fund 1973; outstanding Comm achievements Gamma Phi Delta 1974; Fred D Patterson Award outstanding contributions in Black Comm 1974. **BUSINESS ADDRESS:** 2215 Cleburne Ave, Houston, TX.

FONTENOT, LOUIS K.
Retired judge. **PERSONAL:** Born Sep 19, 1918, Alexandria, LA; married Dorothy B Williams. **EDUCATION:** Leland Coll, BS 1940; John Marshall Law Sch, LLB JD 1949. **CAREER:** Will Co, asso circuit judge 1978-; Kankakee Co, asso circuit judge 1971-78; Kankakee Co, first asst State's Att 1967-71; Joliet, gen practice of law 1955-67; Will Co, asst State's atty 1955-67; Police Training Inst Div ofUniv ExtensionUniv of IL, lecturer 1955-67; Chicago Loop Firm of Fontenot Power Dixon & Burton, gen practice of law 1950-55; HS math tchr & basketball coach 1939-42. **ORGANIZATIONS:** Mem Cook Co Bar, Will Co Bar, Kankakee Co Bar, Am Bar & Nat Bar Assn; Nat Judicial Coun; IL State Atty Assn; Natl & Intl Assn of Probate Judges;Am Judicature Soc; IL Judges Assn; admitted to prac in Fed Courts including US Tax Court & US Supreme Ct Washington; IL State Invstgtr; legal cncl & adj of VFW post; legal cncl & mem Brown's Chapel Ch; legal cncl of Caterpillar Tractor Credit Un & Joliet PO Credit Un; pres NAACP Ottawa-Streetor Br; chmn Legal Aid Com of Will Co Bar Assn; bd govs Joliet Br YMCA; mem Will Co adv bd; Joliet Mayors Commn of Flood Cntrl; Judicial Rules Com Kankakee Co Bar Assn; Coll Fnd Bd Kankakee Commn Coll. **HONORS/ACHIEVEMENTS:** Bronze Star Medal with 3 battle stars; several Campaign Ribbons. **MILITARY SERVICE:** AUS Air Corps 1942-46.

FONTENOT-JAMERSON, BERLINDA
Community relations manager. **PERSONAL:** Born Jul 05, 1947, San Fernando, CA; daughter of Leroy Fontenot and Velma Kyle Fontenot; married Michael Jamerson, Jun 16, 1984. **EDUCATION:** Los Angeles CA Trade Technological Coll, AA, 1972; CA State Univ, Los Angeles, BA, 1978; Pepperdine Univ, Los Angeles CA, MBA, 1984. **CAREER:** Southern CA Gas Co Los Angeles CA, sr prof recruiter, consumer affairs mgr, 1984-87, community relations mgr, 1987-. **ORGANIZATIONS:** Natl board mem, Amer Assn of Blacks

in Energy; bd mem, Women of Color, 1987-; bd mem, Careers for Older Americans, 1987-; bd mem, Museum of African Amer Art, 1988-; vice pres, administration, DATACOM, 1988-; committee chair, NAACP-LDF Black Women of Achievement, 1989. **HONORS/ACHIEVEMENTS:** Leadership Award, YWCA, 1985; Gold Award, United Way, 1986; Black Women of Achievement Merit Award, NAACP-LDF, 1986; Merit Award, Amer Assn Blacks in Energy, 1986, 1988; Certificate of Support, LA Urban League, 1988. **BUSINESS ADDRESS:** Community Relations Manager, Southern California Gas Company, 810 S Flower Street, Mail Loc 110D, Los Angeles, CA 90017.

FONVIELLE, WILLIAM HAROLD
Director. **PERSONAL:** Born Dec 18, 1943, Chicago, IL; son of William Fonvielle (deceased) and Elizabeth Brown Fonvielle; divorced; children: Michelle R, Deanne V. **EDUCATION:** Shimer Coll, AB (with honors) 1963; Northwestern Univ, Doctoral work in Philosophy 1963-64; Yale Sch of Org & Mgmt, MPPM 1981. **CAREER:** J Walter Thompson Co, media buyer 1966-68; Vince Cullers Adv Inc, media dir 1968-70; Communicon Inc, pres 1970-75; State of IL, dir motion picture/TV prodn/publ info ofcr 1975-77; Denver Reg Cncl of Govts, dir publ affairs 1977-79; Goodmeasure Inc, vp/dir consulting 1981-86; The Forum Corp, dir of rsch and develop 1987-. **ORGANIZATIONS:** Accred comm Colorado Publ Relations Soc of Amer 1978-80; founder Cncl of City & Co Communicators 1978-79; dir Lovespace Inc 1972-75; dir The Apartment Store Inc 1968-70; elec trustee Vill of Carol Stream, IL 1973-77; trustee Garrett-Evang Theol Seminary 1974-76; dir Northeastern IL Planning Commn 1973-77; dir Homes of Private Enterprise 1973-77; chmn MA Product Develop Corp 1986-; mem MENSA 1987-; founding mem Greater Boston Chapter of the International Customer Service Assn 1987-; Organization Development Network 1988-. **HONORS/ACHIEVEMENTS:** CLIOs (w/F Grant) for Best Copy Writing US Radio; Best Public Service Commercial, Special Citation 1975; SCLC MLK Jr Award Chicago Suburban Chap 1977; Natl Finalist White House Fellowship Competition 1977; Distinguished Alumni Award Shimer Coll 1975; author "From Manager to Innovator, Using Information to become an Idea Entrepreneur" AMS 1988. **HOME ADDRESS:** 17 Lucia Rd, Marblehead, MA 01945. **BUSINESS ADDRESS:** Dir of Rsch and Develop, The Forum Corporation, One Exchange Place, Boston, MA 02109.

FOOTE, LEONARD HOBSON BUCHANON
Physician. **PERSONAL:** Born Apr 11, 1898, Cockeysville, MD; married Rosa Hilda Jones; children: Cynthia Yvonne Jones, Harold Carlton Jones. **EDUCATION:** HowardUniv Wash DC, BS 1922; HowardUniv Wash DC, MD 1925. **CAREER:** Private Practice Tallahasee, physician 1926-; prof of materia medica-drugs & solutions for nurses 1929-52; FL A&MUniv & Hosp, radiologist 1929-51; SurgicalDiseases for Nurses at the U, prof 1927-51; FL A&MUniv Hosp, med dir & admin 1926-49; Student Health, physician & dir 1926-48; John A Andrew Clncl Soc, srgcl supr 1930-48, supr/pres 1932-35. **ORGANIZATIONS:** Pres FL Med Dental Pharm Assn 1935-37; trustee bd Natl Med Assn 1941; mem Awards Natl Med Assn; sec Med Staff FL A&MUniv Hosp 1940-53; asst sec Natl Med Assn 1949-55; pres So Eastern Med Soc 1954-56; held numerous offices & membrshps in various orgs; mem Tallahassee Civic League 10 yrs; bd mem Sr Citizens Plng 1973-74; served as chmn on numerous com for various orgs. **HONORS/ACHIEVEMENTS:** Cert of Appreciation Pres of US 1943; Alumni Award Bd of Trusteed of HowardUniv 1951; Appreciation Award FL A&MUniv 1962; numerous awards & certificates ofappreciation from various groups. **BUSINESS ADDRESS:** 1747 S Adams, Tallahassee, FL 32301.

FOOTE, YVONNE
Educational administrator. **PERSONAL:** Born Dec 24, 1949, Philadelphia, PA; daughter of Lorenzo Alleyne and Alma Alleyne; married Nathaniel A Foote; children: Omar Y. **CAREER:** DE Valley Reg Planning Comm, cost accountant 1975-81; Thomas & Muller Co Inc, bookkeeper 1982-84; Laborers Dist Council Legal Fund, secretary/bookkeeper 1984-; Lawnside Bd of Edn, vp. **BUSINESS ADDRESS:** Vice President, Lawnside Board of Education, 326 Charleston Avenue, Lawnside, NJ 08045.

FORBES, CALVIN
Professor. **PERSONAL:** Born May 06, 1945, Newark, NJ; son of Jacob Forbes and Mary Short Forbes. **EDUCATION:** New School For Social Research; Rutgers University; Brown University, MFA, 1978. **CAREER:** Emerson College, Boston, MA, assistant prof of English, 1969-73; Tufts Univ, Medford, MA, asst prof of English, 1973-74, 1975-77; Howard Univ, Washington, DC, writer in residence; Washington College, Chestertown, MD, asst prof of creative writing, 1988-89; Fulbright lecturer in Denmark, France, and England, 1974-75; guest lecturer at the Univ of West Indies, 1982-83. **ORGANIZATIONS:** Modern Language Assn, College Language Assn. **HONORS/ACHIEVEMENTS:** Author of Blue Monday, Wesleyan Univ Press, 1974; From the Book of Shine, Burning Deck Press, 1979; Natl Endowment for the Arts fellowship, 1982-83; DC Commission on the Arts fellowship, 1984; New Jersey State Council on the Arts fellowship. **BUSINESS ADDRESS:** 73 Arsdale Ter, East Orange, NJ. *

FORBES, GEORGE L.
Attorney. **PERSONAL:** Born Apr 04, 1931, Memphis, TN; son of Cleveland Forbes and Elnora Forbes; married Mary Fleming; children: Helen, Mildred, Lauren. **EDUCATION:** Manassas, 1949; Baldwin-Wallace Univ, 1957; Cleveland Marshall Law Sch, JD 1962. **CAREER:** City of Cleveland, teacher 1958-62, housing insp 1959-63; radio talk show host 1972-75; council majority leader 1972-73; Cuyahoga Co Dem Party, co-chmn 1972-78; Cleveland City Council 1964-, pres 1973-; Forbes Forbes & Teamor, attorney. **ORGANIZATIONS:** Mem Nat Assn Def Lawyers; Cuyahoga, Ohio & Cleveland Bar Assns; Gtr Cleveland Growth Corp & Assn; Council for Econ Opportunity; Legal Aid Soc; NAACP, Urban League; John Harlan Law Club; Greater Cleveland Safety Council; Natioanl League of Cities. **HONORS/ACHIEVEMENTS:** Citation of Merit 1967; Humanitarian of Year 1968; Man of Year 1969; Outstanding Political & Civic Efforts 1971; citizen participation 1973; Ohio Assn Commodores 1973; Distinguished Merit Awd 1976; Ohio Gov Awd 1977; Police Athletic League Outstanding Service Award 1978; Black Affairs Council Outstanding Community Leadership, 1983; Black Professional of the Year, 1987. **MILITARY SERVICE:** USMC corpl 1951-53. **BUSINESS ADDRESS:** City Council President, Forbes, Forbes & Teamor, 1300 Rockefeller Building, 614 Superior Ave, NW, Cleveland, OH 44113.

FORD, AILEEN W.
Teacher. **PERSONAL:** Born Apr 28, 1934, Shelby, NC; married Charles; children: Valerie Journeane, Regina Antoinette. **EDUCATION:** Fayetteville State U, BS 1954; Howard U, Western Carolina U, Appalachian U,Univ of NC at Charlotte, further study. **CAREER:** Shelby Public Schools, teacher & reading teacher. **ORGANIZATIONS:** Pres local chap NCAE; dist dir NCAE; district pres NCACT; pres Gastonia Chap Delta; organizer & sec Cleveland Co Civic League; active in YMCA; Girl Scouts; youth adv in ch; as tchr served on many com & commn; mem Delta Sigma Theta Sorority; NC Assn of Ed; NC Assn of Classroom Tchr; Nat Ed Assn; Am Assn of Univ Women; Intl Reading Assn; bd dir Cleveland Co Orgn Drug Abuse Prevention 1974; bd of dir Cleveland Co Comm Concert Assn; mem Shelby Human Relations Cncl; pres PTA Shelby Jr HS 1974; treas Shelby Negro Woman's Club; pres Audacian Club 1974; mem NAACP; Nat Coun Negro Women; sunday sch tchr & mem Mount Calvary Bapt Ch. **HONORS/ACHIEVEMENTS:** Listed in Who's Who in Am Coll & Univ 1953; Who's Who Am Student & Leaders; outstanding ed in NC 1973. **BUSINESS ADDRESS:** James Love Sch, 925 James Love Rd, Shelby, NC 28150.

FORD, ALBERT S.
Dentist. **PERSONAL:** Born Jan 23, 1929, Elizabeth, NJ; married Mary Victoria Burkett; children: Albert S Jr MD, Stephen D MD, Teresa D JD. **EDUCATION:** Attended, WV St Coll, Seton Hall Univ; Meharry Med Coll, DDS 1958. **CAREER:** Newark Comm Health Serv Group Dent Serv, dir. **ORGANIZATIONS:** Bd of mgmt Meharry Med Coll; mem ADA; mem vice pres Commonwealth Dent Soc; mem Intl Assoc of Begg Study Groups; mem Amer Endodontic Soc; mem Acad of Gen Dentistry; bd mem NJ State Bd of Dental Examiners NE Regional Bd of Dental Examiners 1979; past pres NAACP; mem exec bd Urban League; vicepres Sr Cit Housing Corp; mem adv bd First Natl Bank of Central Jersey; mem Sigma Pi Phi Mu Boule; mem Omega Psi Phi; past mem NJ State Bd of Dental Examiners; past vice pres assoc prof & chmn Treatment Planning Fairleigh Dickinson Univ Sch of Dentistry. **HONORS/ACHIEVEMENTS:** Fellow Amer College of Dentists; Fellow Royal Soc of Health; Diplomat Natl Bd of Dent Examiners; John Dewey Hon Soc 1952. **MILITARY SERVICE:** NG capt 1968-70. **BUSINESS ADDRESS:** 1001 Chestnut St, Roselle, NJ 07203.

FORD, ANTOINETTE
Company executive. **PERSONAL:** Born Dec 14, 1941, Philadelphia; married Melvin W Ford. **EDUCATION:** Laval Univ Quebec, attended 1960; Chestnut Hill Coll, BS 1963; Am U, MS 1966; Stanford Univ, attended 1967. **CAREER:** Natl Oceanographic Data Center, oceanographer 1966-69; Ogden Corp, oceanographer 1969-71; White House fellow 1971-72; Inst Serv of Edn, devel dir 1972-73; TELSPAN Intl Inc, pres. **ORGANIZATIONS:** Mem, DC City Council 1973-75; exec vice pres B & C Assn Inc; Harvard Univ Fellow Inst of Politics 1975; mem numerous professional & business orgs; bd dirs, several orgs; NSF fellow 1967; mem Pres Clemency Bd 1975. **HONORS/ACHIEVEMENTS:** Outstanding Serv Award, Presidential Classroom 1972; Most Successful Under-30 Woman, New Woman Magazine 1971. **BUSINESS ADDRESS:** President, TELSPAN International Inc, 2909 Park Dr SE, Washington, DC 20020.

FORD, AUSBRA
Educator. **PERSONAL:** Born Feb 28, 1935, Chicago, IL; son of Thomas Ford and Carrie Ford; married Thelma Wakefield; children: Rangi, Maji. **EDUCATION:** Ray Vogue Art School, 1956-77; Chicago Art Inst, BAE 1959-64, MFA 1964-66. **CAREER:** Chicago Public School, art instructor 1964-66; Gary Public School, art instructor 1966-68; Southern Univ Baton Rouge, LA, asst prof Art 1968-69; Chicago State Univ, prof of Art 1969-. **ORGANIZATIONS:** Mem Natl Conf of Artists 1975-; chmn Visual Artists Roundtable 1983-. **HONORS/ACHIEVEMENTS:** Young scholars fellowship Natl Endowment of Humanities 1971-72; Intl Studies Award Black Studies Dept Chicago State Univ 1973; Creative Serv Award Kemetic Inst of Chicago 1985. **MILITARY SERVICE:** USAAF a/bc 1954-56. **BUSINESS ADDRESS:** Professor of Art, Chicago State Univ, 95th at King Dr, Chicago, IL 60628.

FORD, BOWLES C.
Business executive. **PERSONAL:** Born Oct 03, 1911, Columbus, OH; married Edwina R Westmoreland; children: Bowles C. **EDUCATION:** AB 1933. **CAREER:** Standard Oil of OH Cleveland, 1933-36; Guaventy Life Ins Co, exec vp; Atlanta Life Ins Co; Acme Ins Agency, pres 1950-75. **ORGANIZATIONS:** Div head United Comm Appeal; ARC; bd mem YMCA; div head March Dimes; chmn Chatham Co Savannah Metro Planning Commn. **HONORS/ACHIEVEMENTS:** Outstanding & Dedicated Serv Award, Past Masters Council of Savannah; Prince Hall Masons; Citation for Excellance in Educ by Am Cancer Soc; various plaques & cert. **BUSINESS ADDRESS:** 460 W Broad St, Savannah, GA.

FORD, CHARLES
Educator, elected official. **PERSONAL:** Born Jun 05, 1936, Patterson, LA; son of Charles Ford, Sr (deceased) and Maxie Columbus Reels; married Doris Jefferies; children: Bryan, Gwendolyn, Monica. **EDUCATION:** Dillard Univ, BA 1960; Univ of AZ, MEd 1966; Atlanta Univ, DEd 1976. **CAREER:** Model Cities Program Tucson AZ, ed spec 1970; City of Tucson, city countil mem 1979-; Pima Comm Coll, instr 1977-79; Tucson Unified School Dist, educator, school admin 1970-74, 1976-. **ORGANIZATIONS:** Systems analysis for public schools Tucson Unified School Dist 1970; bd of dir Awarenss House, A Drug Free Community 1972; ford fellowship Washington DC Politics & Ed 1975; seminars Northern AZ Univ, Taft Inst of Govt 1981, Harvard Univ, Kennedy School of Govt 1982; bd mem Amer Cancer Soc 1984; co chair Harvard Black Faculty & Admin Org 1989. **HONORS/ACHIEVEMENTS:** Outstanding Admin of Schools Channel 6 TV 1973; Pre-Doctoral Ford Fellowship Atlanta Univ 1974; Lugman Awd of Outstanding Comm Serv 1982; Community Serv Awd Tucson Urban League. **MILITARY SERVICE:** AUS pfc 1956-58; Expert Rifleman, Good Conduct, Soldier of the Month 1956-58. **HOME ADDRESS:** 86 Hillside Rd, Watertown, MA 02172. **BUSINESS ADDRESS:** Assoc Dir, John F Kennedy School of Govt, Harvard Univ, 79 JFK St, Rm 109, Cambridge, MA 02138.

FORD, CHARLES T. See FORDE, CHRISTOPHER THEOPHILUS

FORD, CLAUDETTE FRANKLIN
Equal employment specialist. **PERSONAL:** Born May 05, 1942, Washington, GA; married Louis Allan. **EDUCATION:** Howard U, BA 1964; Am U, grad study 1967-69. **CAREER:** Office of Women's Bus Enterprise-Small Bus Adminstrn, bus prog analyst 1979-; Outreach Subcom of Pres Carter's Interaby Com on Women's Bus Enterprise, staff dir; exec ed proj dir a woman owned bus 5 yrs; Wash off of midwest based woman-owned mktg & pub

rel firm, mgr early 60's; Delta Sigma ThetaNat Pub Serv Sor, asst; Am Savs & Loan Leag Inc, information spl; Wash Off Kaiser Assn Advt, dir; EEOC; equal opp spl. **ORGANIZATIONS:** Fndr The Oracle Set Book Club; mem bd of dirs Nat Coor Coun on Drug Abuse Information; ass dir pub affairs & vol servs corp for pub broadcasting; natl 2nd vice pres Delta Sigma Theta Sor; mem Nat Bd YWCA; asst dir for comm affairs Corp for Pub Broadcastingf coor adv coun of 100 major natl orgns; vice pres Nat Capital Area YWCA; mem Nat Coun of Negro Women; mem NAACP; mem bd of dirs Wash Halfway Home for Women. **HONORS/ACHIEVEMENTS:** Listed Oustnd Young Woman of Am 1970; Who's Who of Am Women 1971-72. **BUSINESS ADDRESS:** Small Business Administration, Washington, DC 20416.

FORD, DARNELL GLENN
Professional athlete. **PERSONAL:** Born May 19, 1952, Los Angeles, CA; married Patricia Sneed; children: Danny Jr, Kimberly. **EDUCATION:** SW CC in CA; Mesa CC in AZ. **CAREER:** MN Twins, 1975-78; CA Angels 1979-81; Baltimore Orioles, outfielder 1982-84. **HONORS/ACHIEVEMENTS:** Earned Twins "Rookie Of The Year" Award by vote of Twin Cities BBWAA; named to the Topps major league rookie team outfield. **MILITARY SERVICE:** AUS. **BUSINESS ADDRESS:** Baltimore Orioles, Memorial Stadium, Baltimore, MD 21218.

FORD, DAVID LEON, JR.
Educator. **PERSONAL:** Born Sep 25, 1944, Fort Worth, TX; son of David Leon Ford and Vernita V Williams; married Joan Sessoms; children: David III. **EDUCATION:** IA State Univ, BS 1967; Univ of WI Madison, MS 1969, PhD 1972. **CAREER:** Purdue Univ, asst prof of mgmt 1972-75; Yale School of Org & Mgmt, visiting assoc prof 1980-81; Univ of TX at Dallas, prof or org behavior. **ORGANIZATIONS:** Pres DL Ford & Assoc Mgmt Consult 1977-, Assn Social & Behavioral Scientists 1978-79; mem Leadership Dallas Alumni Assoc 1978-, Leadership Dallas Adv Council 1978-80; bd of dir Greater Dallas Housing Oppty Ctr 1978-80; budget comm United Way of Metro Dallas 1979; dir Pro Line Corp 1981-; chmn, bd of dir NTL Inst for Applied Behavioral Sci 1985-. **HONORS/ACHIEVEMENTS:** 1st Black Engrg Co-op Student LTV Aerospace Corp 1962-67; Leadership Awd KNOK AM-FM Radio 1966; Outstanding Young Alumnus IA State Univ 1977; Scholarship Achievement Assoc of Social & Behavioral Scientists 1983; Distinguished Service Citation, Univ of Wisconsin-Madison, 1988. **MILITARY SERVICE:** AUS Reserve capt 1967-76. **HOME ADDRESS:** 10011 Silver Creek Rd, Dallas, TX 75243. **BUSINESS ADDRESS:** Professor of Org Behavior, Univ of Texas At Dallas, Box 688, Richardson, TX 75080.

FORD, DEBORAH LEE
School board member. **PERSONAL:** Born Sep 22, 1945, Decatur, IL; married David Franklin Ford; children: Alisa, Bryan, Laquitta. **EDUCATION:** Millikin Univ, Music; Richland Comm Coll, Business. **CAREER:** AE Staley Mfg Co, messenger & office pool sec (1st black in office) 1964; Day Care Licensed Family Svc, suprv, owned, operated 1972-78; US Dept of Commerce, reserve crew leader 1980; Decatur School Dist 61, noon suprv 1983, school board mem; bd mem Mental Health Assoc of Macon Co Inc 1985; bd mem Family Serv 1985. **ORGANIZATIONS:** Dist sec Title I 1980; dist chairperson Title I 1981,82; task force mem Comm Strategic Planning Group 1984; asst leader pre-school prog Dove Inc 1984; dir Wedding Coord 1984. **HONORS/ACHIEVEMENTS:** Cert of Appreciation for Meritorious Asst in Conduct of the 1970 Census US Dept of Commerce Bureau of the Census; Awd of Recognition Title I 1982; Awd of Appreciation Volunteer in Decatur Public School 1982; Who's Who Among Black Amers 1985. **HOME ADDRESS:** 846 S Webster St, Decatur, IL 62521.

FORD, DONALD A.
Assistant director. **PERSONAL:** Born May 15, 1928, Philadelphia, PA; married Christina K; children: Donald A, Douglas E, Christel A. **EDUCATION:** Shaw U, BA 1950; Am Intl Coll, attending. **CAREER:** Westfield State Coll, asst dir of student union; Urban Educ Adv for Third World, Westfield State Coll, asst dir 1971-74. **ORGANIZATIONS:** Bd dir MA Heart Assn Western Chap 1971-73; mem Assn of Coll Unions Intl 1971-; mem Assn of Prof Adminstrn 1973-; Ch decon St John's Congreational Ch 1964-; mem St John's Congreational Ch Choir; chmn Affirmative Action Com, Westfield State Coll 1975; mem Kappa Alpha Psi Frat 1946-; mem Admission Com Westfield State Coll. **HONORS/ACHIEVEMENTS:** Recipeient Air Force Commendation Award; 2nd Oak Leaf Cluster 1970. **MILITARY SERVICE:** USAF smsgt 1950-71. **BUSINESS ADDRESS:** Western Ave, Westfield, MA 01085.

FORD, EVERN D.
Elected official. **PERSONAL:** Born Apr 28, 1952, Salem, NJ. **EDUCATION:** Goldey Beacom Jr Coll, AA Business 1970-73. **CAREER:** Salem Co School Bd Assoc, vice-pres 1982-84; Mannington Twp Bd of Educ, president 1984-86. **ORGANIZATIONS:** Asst dir NJ Conf Young Peoples Div/AME Church 1983-85; legislature chmn Dist #3 NJ School Bds Assoc 1984-86; pres Salem Co School Bds Assoc 1985-86; chmn adv bd to Salem Co Vocational Techn Schls; mem of Co of Assn Leaders of NJ School Bds Assn. **HOME ADDRESS:** RR #2 Box 375, Woodstown, NJ 08098. **BUSINESS ADDRESS:** E I DuPont, Jackson Laboratory, Wilmington, DE 19898.

FORD, FRED, JR.
Musician/composer/arranger. **PERSONAL:** Born Feb 14, 1930, Memphis, TN; son of Fred Ford and Nancy Jane Taylor; divorced; children: Joseph Vallier, Jessica Ann Thomas, Jamil A, Jamal A, Idrees A, Jacob A. **EDUCATION:** Studied Music under Eddie Pete Ware 1943-45. **CAREER:** Elks Club Band, clarinet player 1945-46; Royal American Shows, clarinet baritone sax 1949-50; Duke/Peacok Records Houston TX, clarinet, sax 1950-54; Fred Ford's Beale St USA, orchestra founder/dir 1977-79; Fred Ford/Honeymoon Garner Trio, leader 1970-. **ORGANIZATIONS:** Co-producer Beale St Music Festival 1977,78; producer Sybil Shepherd album Vanilla 1978; chosen as poster subject TN Homecoming "86" 1985; producer album Bear Water-Beale St Scene Fred Ford/Honeymoon Garner Trio 1985. **HONORS/ACHIEVEMENTS:** Honored for preserving Memphis Music Heritage 1985; declared Colonel of State of TN Gov Lamar Alexander 1985; acknowledgment of Honor Pres & Mrs Ronald Reagan 1985; resolutions City, County, Mayor, State Legislature, Congressman of 8th District 1985. **MILITARY SERVICE:** AUS Band corpl 1st class 1955-57. **HOME ADDRESS:** 1591 Sunset, Memphis, TN 38108.

FORD, GARY L.
Attorney. **PERSONAL:** Born Dec 18, 1944, Detroit. **EDUCATION:** OH State U, BA 1966; JD 1969. **CAREER:** Willkie Farr & Gallagher, prev senior atty; Stauffer Chem Co. **ORGANIZATIONS:** Mem Counc NY Law Assos; Westchester-Fairfield Corp Couns Assn; founder Consortium Met Black Attys; OH StateUniv Law Sch Ad Hoc Open Housing Com. **BUSINESS ADDRESS:** Counsel, Stauffer Chemical Company, Nyala Farm Rd, Westport, CT 06881.

FORD, HAROLD E.
Congressman. **PERSONAL:** Born May 20, 1945, Memphis, TN; married Dorothy Bowles; children: Harold, Jake, Sir Isaac. **EDUCATION:** John Gupton Coll, AA 1968; TN State Univ, BS 1967; Howard Univ, MBA. **CAREER:** TN House of Representatives, mem 1970-74; US House of Representatives, congressman. **ORGANIZATIONS:** Mem 94th-100th Congress from 9th TN Dist; mem Ways and Means Comm; Select Comm Aging; mem natl adv bd St Jude Children's Rsch Hosp; mem Dem Steering & Policy Comm, Subcommittee on Oversight; chmn Subcomm on Public Asst & Unemployment Compensation, Dem Whip representing the states of TN, LA, MS during the 99th Congress; bd mem Metro Memphis YMCA, Alpha Phi Alpha. **HONORS/ACHIEVEMENTS:** Named Outstanding Young Man of the Year Memphis Jaycees 1976; Outstanding Young Man of the Year TN Jaycees 1977; Named Child Advocate of the Year Child WelfareLeague of Amer 1987. **BUSINESS ADDRESS:** Congressman, U S House of Representatives, 2305 Rayburn House Office Bldg, Washington, DC 20515.

FORD, HILDA EILEEN
Business executive. **PERSONAL:** Born Apr 19, 1924, New York City, NY. **EDUCATION:** Brooklyn Coll; Coll of St Rose. **CAREER:** City of Baltimore, dir peronnel; NY St Off of Employee Rels, chf negotiator; NY St Dept of Civil Serv, asst div dir; Youth Opprt Ctr, dir. **BUSINESS ADDRESS:** 111 N Calvert St, Baltimore, MD 21202.

FORD, JAMES W.
Government official. **PERSONAL:** Born Feb 03, 1922, Florida; married Catherine Britton; children: Daniel J, Cynthia A. **EDUCATION:** FL A&M Univ, BS 1943; TN Agr & Indust Univ, MS 1948; KS State Univ, MS 1949; WA State Univ, Postgrad 1950; KS State Univ, 1951; Boston Univ, 1959-60; Univ of Pittsburgh, 1965. **CAREER:** Ft Valley State Coll, head dept animal sci 1949-51; Alcorn A&M Coll, assoc prof 1951-52, head dept animal husbandry; AID State Dept Libya, N Africa, ext spec 1952-59; Ministry of Agr Eastern Nigeria, livestock adv spec 1960-62; Food & Agr Office Washington, asst to food & agri, acting dep food & agr officer, natl livestock adv, tech adv to agr dir of Brazil 1965; NE Brazil Mission, agr officer 1965, reg agi adv 1965-69; AID Missions Ghana, Accra, food & agr officer 1970-75; State Dept AID, agr devel consult 1975-; State Dept AID Consultant, 1975-. **ORGANIZATIONS:** Mem Omega Psi Phi, Mason. **HONORS/ACHIEVEMENTS:** Aid Study Grantee Johns Hopkins School Advanced Intl Studies 1969-70. **MILITARY SERVICE:** AUS 1942-46.

FORD, JAMES W.
Physician, minister, politician, funeral director. **EDUCATION:** TN State Univ, BS Zoology; Attened, Amer Baptist Theol Seminary, Columbia Univ Coll of Surgeons, Union Theological Seminary, NY Law Sch, Memphis State. **CAREER:** Harlem Hosp, residency & internship ophthalmology; NJ Ford & Sons Funeral Home, funeral dir; Fellowship Baptist Ch, pastor; private practice, ophthalmologist; Dist 6 City of Memphis, councilman. **BUSINESS ADDRESS:** Councilmember, 655 E Raines Rd, Memphis, TN 38109.

FORD, JOHN NEWTON
Government official. **PERSONAL:** Born May 03, 1942, Memphis, TN; married Maxine Foster; children: Kemba Nyja, Sean, Autumn Leigh, Michelle. **EDUCATION:** TN State U, BA 1964; Memphis State U, MA 1978. **CAREER:** Memphis, TN, city cnclmn 1971-79; TN Genl Assembly, TN state senator 1974-; TN State Senate, state senator, speaker pro tempore 1987-. **ORGANIZATIONS:** Chrmn Senate Genl Welfare, Hlth & Human Resources Committee; mem Finance, Ways & Means Committee; pres NJ Ford & Sons Funeral Parlors; pres Ford & Assoc; life mem NAACP; mem Nat League of Cities; mem Nat Black Caucus; bd mem Regnl Sickle Cell Anemia Cncl; mem State and Local Govt Comm. **HONORS/ACHIEVEMENTS:** Outstand Citizens Award Mallory Knights Chariatable 1974; Outstand Accomplishment Civil Liberty League 1975; Community Achievemnt Lutheran Baptist Ch 1976;Disting Grad Memphis StateUniv 1978. **HOME ADDRESS:** 3655 Summershade Cove, Memphis, TN 38116. **BUSINESS ADDRESS:** State Senator, TN State Senate, 12 S Parkway W, Memphis, TN 38109.

FORD, JOHNNY L.
Mayor. **PERSONAL:** Born Aug 23, 1942, Tuskegee, AL; married Frances Baldwin Rainer; children: Johnny, Christopher Ashley. **EDUCATION:** Knoxville Coll, BA 1964; Natl Exec Inst, postgrad 1965; Auburn Univ, MA 1977. **CAREER:** Multi-Man Dist, exec Bronx 1967-68; Sen Robt Kennedy, polit campaign strategist 1968; Tuskegee Model Cities Program, exec coord 1969-70; Atty Fred Gray, campaign mgr 1970; Multi Racial Corp, asst dir 1970-72; US Justice Dept Montgomery, state supr comm rel serv 1971-72; City of Tuskegee, mayor. **ORGANIZATIONS:** Chmn AL Conf of Black Mayors; v chmn Natl Comm for Two Party Syst; mem Tuskegee Airmen Intl; Silver Trowel Lodge #10 F & AM; Gov Manpower Ancillary Com; Environmental Com; Tourism Council; Law Enforcement; NAACP; Kappa Alpha Psi; exec com AL League of Municipalities; mem Governor's Job Training Partnership Act Commission, Governor's Tourism Council; appointed by Pres Reagan to serve as mem of Presidential Adv Comm on Federalsim and the White House Interfov Affairs Comm on Trade; appointed by former AL Gov George Wallace as the 1st black to serve on AL Foreign Trade Relations Commiss. **HONORS/ACHIEVEMENTS:** Top Campaigner Award BSA 1967; Young Man of the Year Women's Reserve 1967; Youngest Multi-Dist Exec in Nation BSA 1967; Outstanding Young Man of Amer; Has been awarded the key to more than 100 Amer and foreign cities. **BUSINESS ADDRESS:** Mayor, City of Tuskegee, City Hall, 214 N Main St, Tuskegee, AL 36083.

FORD, JUDITH DONNA
Judge. **PERSONAL:** Born Aug 30, 1935, Eureka, CA. **EDUCATION:** Univ of CA at Berkeley, BS 1957; Boal T Hall Law Sch, JD 1974. **CAREER:** Petty Andrews Tufts & Jackson, assoc atty 1974-79; Consumer Fraud Crime Div SF Dist Atty's Office, dir 1977-79; Fed Trade Comm, dir 1980-82; Oakland-Piedmont-Emeryville Jud Dist, judge 1983-. **ORGANIZATIONS:** CA Judges Assn; Alameda Co Trauma Review Comm; US Magistrate Merit

Selection Comm; San Francisco Bar Assn Lawyer Referral Serv Comm 1976; NSF SoftwareAuditing Wkshp 1976; Comm for Admin of Justice 1976-79; delegate from San Fran Bar Assn Lawyer Refrl Serv Comm 1976; chair E Oakland Planned Prnthd Adv Comm 1977-80; spkr Bank Admin Inst 1977; spkr EDP Audit Cntrls Wkshp 1977; spkr CPA Soc 1977; various TV & Radio appearances; spoke to comm groupson consult fraud 1977-79; spkr Joint meeting of IIA and EDPA 1978; dir Planned Prnthd 1978-80; chair Blk Women Lawyers, N CA Finance Comm 1979-80; San Fran Lawyers Comm Urban Affairs 1979-80; chair SF Bar Assn Comm Legal Ed Comm 1979-80; bd mem Consumer Union 1979-82; ref St Bar Ct 1979-82; cnclr Law Cntr Bd of Cnclrs 1979-83; radio & TV spkr on Fed Trade Comm 1980-82; SF Bar Assoc Judiciary Comm 1981-82; Chas Houston Bar Assoc 1974-; CA Assoc of Black Lawyers 1978-; bd mem Peralta Serv Corp 1983-. **BUSINESS ADDRESS:** Judge Municipal Court, Oakland-Piedmont Emeryville, 661 Washington St, Oakland, CA 94607.

FORD, KENNETH A.
Association engineering administrator. **PERSONAL:** Born Aug 10, 1949, Washington, DC; married Shirley Payne; children: Travelle. **EDUCATION:** Howard U, BSCE 1972, MCE 1977. **CAREER:** Limbach Co, project engr 1972-75; Potomac Elec Power Co, envirnmntl engr 1975-77; Parametric Inc, pgm dir 1977-82; WA Suburban Sanitary Commission, planning mgr 1982-84; Nat Assn of Home Builders, mgr of civil engring. **ORGANIZATIONS:** Mem Nat Society of Professnl Engr 1977-; advisory bd mem Utility Location & Coord Cncl 1984-; mem Building Seismic Safety Cncl 1984; bd of dir BlackSci Inc 1984-85; mem Amer Soc of Civil Engrs. **HONORS/ACHIEVEMENTS:** Who's Who Among Stdnts in Am Coll &Univ 1972. **HOME ADDRESS:** 11303 Sherrington Ct, Upper Marlboro, MD 20772. **BUSINESS ADDRESS:** Manager of Civil Engineering, Nat Assn of Home Builders, 15th & M Sts NW, Washington, DC 20008.

FORD, LUTHER L.
Educator. **PERSONAL:** Born Dec 03, 1931, Florence, SC; married Dr Willie B Ford. **EDUCATION:** Grambling State U, BS 1961;Univ IA, MA 1964;Univ NE, EdD 1974. **CAREER:** Carthage AR, 1962-63; Tallulah LA, teacher 1963-65; Davenport IA, special educ teacher 1965-66; Evaluation Vocational Rehabilitation, Oakdale IA, teacher 1966-67; Univ of NE, visiting prof 1971; Grambling State Univ, prof 1967-. **ORGANIZATIONS:** Mem Black Educators Council Human Serv; mem Assn for the Study of Afro-Am Life History Inc; Kappa Delta Pi Honor Educ Soc; life mem Phi Delta Kappa; mem Disabled Am Vet; bd of dirs Black Analysis Inc NY 1977; Nat Soc for Study of Edn; LA Educ Assn; LA Philosophy Edn; LA Educ Research Assn; life mem Omega Psi Phi; Ford Found Fellowship 1973-74; TTT Fellowship 1971-73; Doctorate Fellowship Black Analysis Inc 1972-74; trch stipend 1973-74; Danforth Assoc Prof 1976-84; mem NAACP, natl Soc for the Study of Educ, Important Black Man 1987; life mem Grambling Alumni. **MILITARY SERVICE:** AUS army airborne sgt 1951-58. **BUSINESS ADDRESS:** Professor, Grambling StateUniv, PO Box 644, Grambling, LA 71245.

FORD, MARCELLA WOODS
Educator. **PERSONAL:** Born in Athens, GA; married Jesse W Ford (deceased). **EDUCATION:** Shaw Univ, AB; Amer Bapt Sem, MA; Shaw Univ, Doctor of Humane Letters Degree 1982. **CAREER:** Mather School, teacher; Shaw Univ, asst profl, dir; Oakland CA, dir of release time classes; Berkeley Unified School Dist, teacher; Berkeley Adult Ed, teacher 1962-64;Black History. **ORGANIZATIONS:** Mem Ch Women United; pres Bus & Professional Women, No CA Amer Bapt Church; pres, sponsor Interfaith Intercultural Fellowship of E Bay; pres Amer Bapt Women Oakland Area Assoc; mem, bd of dir Intertribal Friendship House; mem Budget United Crusade Panel & Speakers Bur; resource person Human Rel & Afro-Amer History, Oakland Publ School 1969-; History Docent of Oakland Museum; mem dedication comm Oakland Museum; mem Amer Bapt Church of the W Campus Ministry Stud Found; life mem Natl Council of Negro Women; mem steering comm Shaw Univ Alumni 1968-69; dir Rel Ed Beth Eden Bapt Church; mem Alpha Nu Omega Chap Alpha Kappa Alpha Sor, Amer Assoc of Univ Women, YWCA; co-org E Bay Negro Hist Soc; mem Oakland Museum Assoc; life mem Assoc for the Study of Afro, Amer Life & History; mem CA Retired Teachers; life mem NAACP, Natl Retired Teachers Assoc. **HONORS/ACHIEVEMENTS:** Num articles publ Woman of the Year Eden Bapt Church, Marcella Ford Circle of Women's Soc of McGee Ave Bapt Church 1959,69; featured in "Faces Around the Bay" The Post Newspaper 1970; Woman of the Year Comm Serv Amer Assoc of Univ Women; appt by Gov mem Allensworth State Historical Park Adv Comm 1969; mem Historic Landmarks Preservation Bd appt by Mayor & City Council 1973; Leadership Awd Far Western Reg Conf of AKA Sor 1976; Dedication of Allensworth State Hist Park Comm Serv Awds & Rose Bushs planted by Alpha Nu Ome Chap AKA & Marcella Ford Cir 1976; Christian Womanhood Awd Shaw Divinity School Raleigh NC 1976; Recog & MW Ford Scholarship Shaw Univ, Beth Eden Bapt Church 1977; Oakland Piedmont Chap AAUW Scholarship Honor of Mem M Ford 1977; Comm Serv Awd by Cultural & Ethnic Affairs Guild Oakland Museum 1977; Pre-Kwanza Awd Assoc Africans & African Amer Oakland; Natl Sojourner Truth Awd by the Natl Assoc of Negro Bus & Professional Womens Clubs Inc, East Bay Area Club 1981; Woman of Achievement Women Helping Women Awd Soroptimist Intl of Oakland 1982; Resolution of Honor, California Legislature Assembly, 1989; Letter of Commendation, Lionel J Wilson, mayor of Oakland, 1989; Plaque for 20 years of service, Advisory Comm for the Restoration of Colonel Allensworth State Historic Park, 1989.

FORD, MARION GEORGE, JR.
Dental surgeon, business executive. **PERSONAL:** Born Aug 22, 1937, Houston; divorced; children: Inge, Erika, Marion, III. **EDUCATION:** Univ TX, BS (magna cum laude) 1958;Univ TX Dental Br, DDS (magna cum laude) 1962;Univ Bonn Germany, Fulbright Scholar. **CAREER:** Cty Houston, hydro-engr 1953-62;Univ TX Dental Br, german-french translr 1958-62; UTDB, rsrchr 1959-62; Cty Houston & Am Red Cross, aquatics dir 1955-62; Pvt Pract, dens peridontal surg; Ford Intl Ent Inc, pres. **ORGANIZATIONS:** Mem Am Dental Assn; Charles A George Dental Soc; assoc mem ILA872; dir NE Bank 1970-72; dir Franklin Ben 1971-72; dir Min Affairs Farnklin Bank 1972-75; chf oral surgery Lockwood Hosp 1968-70; sec Lockwood Professional Grp; Dep Minister Dental Hlth Tanzania E Africa 1972; secy NE Houston Sch Bd 1968-; mem Mayor's Police Commn 1968-69; mem NAACP; Urban League. **HONORS/ACHIEVEMENTS:** All state swimmer 1951-54; football all city 1954; most outstndg chem stud 1954; Who's Who S & SW; developer Denture Acrylic Resin & Shade Guide 1962. **BUSINESS ADDRESS:** 4315 Lockwood Dr, 3215 Sherman, Houston, TX 77026.

FORD, NANCY HOWARD
Educational administrator. **PERSONAL:** Born Jul 29, 1942, Wilmington, DE; children: Sergio Howard, Charis. **EDUCATION:** Central State Univ, BS 1964; Univ of DE, MEd 1972. **CAREER:** CT State Welfare Dept, welfare home economist 1968; Seattle Public Schools, teacher-home arts 1968-70; Wilmington Public Schools, teacher corps intl 1970-72;Cheyney State Coll assoc dean res life 1972-76; Dept of Public Instruction DE, state specialist 1977-. **ORGANIZATIONS:** US Peace Corps volunteer US Peace Corps in Brazil 1964-66; misc vol w/various comm organizations 1970-71; vol teacher DE Adolescent Program, Inc 1971. **HONORS/ACHIEVEMENTS:** Natl Honor Soc Wilmington HS 1960; second highest ranking student in home econ Central State Univ 1964; cert of recognition US Peace Corps Service from the White House 1966. **BUSINESS ADDRESS:** State Specialist, Dept of Public Instruction, Townsend Building, Dover, DE 19901.

FORD, PHIL ALLAN
Professional athlete. **PERSONAL:** Born Feb 09, 1956, Rocky Mount, NC. **EDUCATION:** Univ of NC Chapel Hill, BS 1978. **CAREER:** Kansas City Kings, guard 1978-82; New Jersey Nets, 1982; Milwaukee Bucks, 1982-83; Houston Rockets, 1983-. **ORGANIZATIONS:** Mem 1976 US Olympic Gold Medal team. **HONORS/ACHIEVEMENTS:** Won Rookie of Year honors first team All-Rookie & second team All-NBA.

FORD, PRONTY L.
Government employee. **PERSONAL:** Born Apr 06, 1921, Pittsburgh; married Ramona Goods; children: Larry W, Ramona M, Prondolyon E. **EDUCATION:** Schenley Evening Sch, 1940. **CAREER:** Prondolyon E Allegheny Co, treas, asst paymaster; 5th Ward Pittsburgh, 5th Ward Dem chmn mem 25th Dist; re-elected Demo Chmn 1974; re-elected constable 1973; parole & sponsor 1943-73; elected 1st Child Dist Atty Hill City Youth Municipality 1939; elected Model Cities commr area 4 1967; Hill City, special police officer assigned 1944-67; DPW Pitt in charge NYC, chief clerk 1965-69. **ORGANIZATIONS:** Mem Century Club Male Social Club 35 yrs; pres, social chmn; mem Ebenzer Bapt Ch. **BUSINESS ADDRESS:** 2220 Wylie Ave, Pittsburgh, PA 15219.

FORD, RICHARD D.
Administrator. **PERSONAL:** Born Mar 22, 1935, Birmingham, AL; married Nancy Thompson; children: Robin, Richard T. **EDUCATION:** Miles Coll Birmingham, BA 1959; Johnson C Smith Theological Sem Charlotte, BD 1962; State Univ of NY at Buffalo, MSW 1969. **CAREER:** Westminster Comm House, dir of comm serv & christian educ 1963-66; School of Social Welfare, State Univ of NY, asst prof 1969-70, dir of admissions 1970-72; CA State Univ School of Social Work, dean 1972-. **ORGANIZATIONS:** Pres BUILD of Buffalo NY 1970-72; pres United Presby Health Educ & Welfare Assn 1975-76; mem Council on Soc Work Educ 1972-; mem Natl Assn of Black Soc Workers; mem Natl Conf of Deans of Soc Work 1972-; mem Fresno Co Planning Commn 1978-; mem Steering Comm for Region IX Child Welfare Trng; mem West Side Planning Group Fresno. **BUSINESS ADDRESS:** Dean, School of Social Work, CA StateUniv of Fresno, Fresno, CA 93740.

FORD, ROBERT See IFORD, ROBERT

FORD, ROBERT BENJAMIN
Librarian. **PERSONAL:** Born Nov 27, 1935, Miami, FL; married Seretta J Pertilla; children: Lisa, Maria. **EDUCATION:** Bethune-Cookman Coll, BA Speech Drama 1955; NY Univ Sch of Educ NYC, MA 1958; Pratt Inst Lib Sch, MLS 1959. **CAREER:** Bunche Park Elementary School, Opa Locka FL, teacher 1955-56; Dade County Public Schools Miami, librarian 1961-67; Engrg Socs Library NYC, monograph & serials cataloger 1967-68; Queensborough Community Coll Library NYC, serials & periodicals librarian 1968-70; Medgar Evers Coll Brooklyn, chief librarian 1975-. **ORGANIZATIONS:** Tchr Adult Basic Educ Prog Dade Co Pub Schs 1965-67; refer librarian N Bellmore Pub Library N Bellmore NY 1969-72; sub tchr HS Equivalency Prog Urban Ctr NY 1970-73; treas Library Assn City Univ of NY 1971-73; sec Council of Chief Librarians City Univ of NY 1974-75; bd dir Coll & Univ Libraries Sect NY Library Assn 1979-81; treas/vp NY Black Librarians Caucus 1975-80. **HONORS/ACHIEVEMENTS:** "Title IIA-A Bargain at the Price, A Symposium" Journ of Acad Librarianship 1979; "Help for the Decision Maker, A Decision-Process Model" The Bookmark 1979. **MILITARY SERVICE:** AUS pfc 1959-61. **BUSINESS ADDRESS:** Chief Librarian, Medgar Evers Coll, 1150 Carroll St, Brooklyn, NY 11225.

FORD, ROBERT BLACKMAN
Dentist. **PERSONAL:** Born Nov 22, 1924, Montgomery, AL; married Katherine Brosby; children: Teri, Wendy, Sondra. **EDUCATION:** Morehouse Coll, BS 1948; Howard U, DDS 1952; Veteran's Hosp Tuskegee, additional study 1952-53; 300 hrs post grad study. **CAREER:** Pvt practice. **ORGANIZATIONS:** Mem Am Dental Assn; OH State Dental Assn; Dayton Dental Assn coun; 1970-73; Buckeye State Dental Soc, treas; Academy of General Dentistry; elected to Jefferson Twp Bd of Edn; past pres 1968-72; bd of mgmt YMCA; bd mem Community Research Inc; mem Kappa Alpha Psi. **HONORS/ACHIEVEMENTS:** First Black in OH appointed to the State Dentl Bd 1974. **MILITARY SERVICE:** USMC 1944-46. **BUSINESS ADDRESS:** 3807 W Third St, Dayton, OH 45417.

FORD, ROBERT CALVIN
Professional athlete. **PERSONAL:** Married Janice Buck; children: Robert II; Jason. **EDUCATION:** Univ of Houston, 1970-74; Western IL Univ, MA Educ 1975. **CAREER:** Western IL Univ, asst coach 1974-75; New Mexico St Univ, asst coach 1976-79; Oregon St Univ, asst coach 1980-81; MS St Univ, coach of offensive ends 1982-84; Houston Gamblers, coach of receivers.

FORD, SARAH ANN
Educator. **PERSONAL:** Born Aug 29, 1951, Gary, IN. **EDUCATION:** Ball State Univ, BS 1973, MA 1974; Keller Grad Sch of Mgmt, MBA 1986. **CAREER:** Marquette Univ, dir multi-cul ctr 1974-78; Univ of WI Extension, arts consultant 1978-84; Univ of WI, business consultant 1984-; US Army Reserves/Guard, drill sgt/1st lt 1975-; Colorlines Magazine, publisher 1980-; Rowland Financial GR, security agent 1980-82; Small Business Develop Ctr, business counselor/instructor. **ORGANIZATIONS:** Mem Delta Sigma Theta Sor 1970-; Talk show host WISN TV "Look In" 1975-82; pres/performer Heritage Chorale 1984-; sec Council on Minority/Small Bus 1987-; pres Colorlines Foundation for Arts and Culture Inc 1986-. **HONORS/ACHIEVEMENTS:** Most Interesting People in Milwaulee-Milwaukee

magazine 1983; Awd of Excellence Colorlines Magazine Milwaukee Art Comm 1983; Outstanding Serv Awd Milwaukee ArtMuseum 1984. **MILITARY SERVICE:** NG 1st lt 6 yrs. **BUSINESS ADDRESS:** Business Counselor/Instruct, Small Business Devel Ctr, UWM 929 No 6th St, Milwaukee, WI 53203.

FORD, VIRGINIA
Retired educator. **PERSONAL:** Born Jul 03, 1914, Toledo, OH; daughter of Russell Ford (deceased) and Marie Ford Robinson (deceased). **EDUCATION:** Univ of MI Ann Arbor, PH Cert 1938-42; Catholic Univ of Am Washington DC, BSNE 1950, MSN 1960, PhD 1967. **CAREER:** US Public Health Serv H Huachuca Mission to Liberia, public hlth advisor 1941-46; Am Nat Red Cross/Korea/Japan, staff asst 1948-50; UN World Hlth Organ/India/Taiwan, public hlth advisor 1955-59; US Veteran's Admin Chicago, asso chief 1966-67; DePaul Univ Chicago, asso prof 1967-74; Chicago State U, dean & prof emeritus 1974-77. **ORGANIZATIONS:** Bd of dir Infant Welfare Society Chicago 1969-78. **HONORS/ACHIEVEMENTS:** Inactive Delta Sigma Theta 1938; Sigma Tau; pre-doctoral research fellow Nat Inst of Hlth (NIMH) 1960-65; service league Univ of Chicago 1983-. **MILITARY SERVICE:** US Public Hlth Serv maj 1945-46, 1950-55; Am Campaign Medal; European-African Middle Eastern Campaign Medal; WW II Victory Medal 1963; US Public Health Service, Bronze Medal 1963. **HOME ADDRESS:** 5530 S Shore Dr, Apt 14B, Chicago, IL 60637.

FORD, WALLACE L., II
Executive director. **PERSONAL:** Born Jan 13, 1950, New York, NY. **EDUCATION:** Dartmouth, grad; Harvard Law Sch, rec'd law degree. **CAREER:** WDCR radio, disc jockey; NY State Supreme Court, law secty; NY State Assembly Committee on Banking, counsel; Amistad DOT Venture Capital Inc, exec vice pres & genl counsel; NY State Dept of Commerce Div of Minority Business Develop, deputy commissioner; State of NY Mortgage Agency, exec officer & ceo; Drexel Burnham Lambert, Inc, 1st vp. **ORGANIZATIONS:** Former pres Dartmouth Afro-Amer Society; former pres of the Harlem Lawyers Assoc; former vice pres New York City Chap of Dartmouth College Alumni Assn; mem Dartmouth Alumni Council; mem Dartmouth Black Alumni Assn; Malcolm King Coll, bd of trustees; Nat'l Assoc of Securities Professionals, mem; NY Urban League (Harlem Branch), bd of dir. **HONORS/ACHIEVEMENTS:** Listed Ebony Magazine One Hundred Leaders of the Future 1978; listed Time Magazine Fifty Faces of the Future 1979; speaker Dartmouth Bicentennial Commencement Exercises 1970; Nat'l Housing Conference annual awd 1984. **BUSINESS ADDRESS:** 1st Vice President, Drexel Burnham Lambert, Inc, 60 Broad St, New York, NY 10004.

FORD, WILLIAM L., JR.
Vice president. **PERSONAL:** Born Jul 31, 1941, Kayford, WV; married Eleanor Holmes; children: Karen, Valerie. **EDUCATION:** Russell Sage Evening Coll, 1961-66; State Univ of Albany NY, 1967-68. **CAREER:** Mayfair Inc Albany, ofc mgr 1968-70; WROW-WTEN Albany, chief acct 1970-71; WROW Radio Albany, bus mgr 1971; WKBW-TV & Radio Buffalo, bus mgr 1971-76; WFSB-TV Hartford, vice pres bus & admin affairs 1976-78; Post-Newsweek Stations MI Inc WDIV, vp, sta mgr 1978-83; Cellular Telecommunications, vice pres 1984-. **ORGANIZATIONS:** Bd of dir Better Bus Bur of Met Detroit 1979-, Jr Achievement of Southeastern MI, 1979-, Broadcast Fin Mgmt Assoc 1979-; commiss Detroit Black UnitedFund 1979-; bd of gov Detroit Chap Natl Acad of TV Arts & Sci 1980-; bd of dir MI Assoc of Broadcasters 1980-. **BUSINESS ADDRESS:** Vice President, Cellular Telecommunications, 550 Lafayette Blvd, Detroit, MI 48231.

FORD, WILLIAM R.
Economic consultant. **PERSONAL:** Born Dec 19, 1933, Highland Park, MI; children: Eric, Natalie, Todd. **EDUCATION:** BS, MA 1959. **CAREER:** St Sch for Delinquent Boys St Dept Soc Welfare Lansing, tchr curriculum corr 1957-63; Szt Bd Edn, consult spl prgms 1963-64; MI Cath Conf Lansing, dir training 1964-66; MI Econ Opp Off, exec dir 1966-69; MI Employment Security Commn Detroit, dir 1969-71; USAID Mission to Lagos Nigeria US Agency for Intl Devel, mission dir 1971-76; Delta Oil Nigeria, econ cons. **ORGANIZATIONS:** Mem Gov's Manpower Commn MI 1968-71; Intl Assn Personnel in Employment Security 1968-71; bd mem Assn St Employment Serv Dirs 1969-71; Sch Holding Power Commn St Dept Educ 1966-71; bd mem MI Easter Seal Soc 1969-71; Metro Detroit Area Comm Chest 1969-71; St Adv Bd Voc Educ 1967-71; bd mem Detroit Urban Leag 1969-71; Nat Assn Comm Devel 1966-70; Detroit Urban Coalition 1968-71. **HONORS/ACHIEVEMENTS:** Recip spl commendation Gov George Romney 1967; awd Golden St Mutual Life Ins Co 1969; Joint House-Senate Res MI St 1970; young man of yr Detroit 1970; Elder Watson Diggs awd Kappa Alpha Psi Frat 1972; Comm Ldrs & Noteworth Am 1975. **BUSINESS ADDRESS:** PO Box 3606, Lagos, Nigeria.

FORDE, CHRISTOPHER THEOPHILUS (CHARLES T. FORD)
Writer, businessman. **PERSONAL:** Born Mar 08, 1907; married Lucille Eaton. **EDUCATION:** Columbia Newspaper Inst Home Corres Course in Journalism, cert; Special Course in Watchmaking Gyroscope Constr, completed. **CAREER:** Tuxedo-Mint Records, founder & managing dir; Playfare Records Corp, org/pres/treas; Bus Dynamics Corp, consult skilled tech & div organizer 1971-79; HO Boehme Instrument Corp, consult skilled tech 1969-70; Tuxedo Records/Mint Records, organizing dir 1951; Big Nickle Records, organizing mgr 1950-52; Reeves Instrument Corp, consult skilled tech 1950-69; Ford Mus Pub Co, songwriter & organizer 1948; Watchcraft Co Watchcraft Inc, master watchmaker 1944; G Marchand & Co, master watchmaker 1943; Le Mare Watch Co, master watchmaker 1942; New Life Watch Co,. **BUSINESS ADDRESS:** Tuxedo Mint Records, 132 Nassau St, New York, NY 10038.

FORDE, FRASER PHILIP, JR.
Business executive. **PERSONAL:** Born Nov 24, 1943, Tuskegee, AL; son of Fraser Philip Forde Sr and Joyce Nourse Forde; married LaVerne; children: Tracey, Fraser III, Erika. **EDUCATION:** Hofstra Univ, BBA 1965; Pace Univ, MBA candidate 1980. **CAREER:** Morgan Guaranty Trust Co, asst vice pres 1987-, asst treas 1973-87; asst officer personnel rep 1971-73; Money Transfer Dept, asst group head 1970-71; Bank & Operations Dept, educ trainee 1969-70; Dun & Bradstreet Inc, credit analyst 1967-69. **ORGANIZATIONS:** Treasurer, Milford Civic Assn of Central Islip Inc 1980-; delegate, Central Islip School District Budget Advisory Comm 1981-. **HONORS/ACHIEVEMENTS:** Award Outstanding Trainee; Basic Training; Scout Dog Training; CIB O/S Bar; Vietnam Serv Award; Vietnamese Serv Award; Black Achievers In Industry, YMCA of Greater NY, Harlem Branch 1974. **MILITARY SERVICE:** AUS sp/4 1965-67. **BUSINESS ADDRESS:** Assistant Vice President, Morgan County Trust Co, 23 Wall St, New York, NY 10015.

FORDE, JAMES ALBERT
Director health services. **PERSONAL:** Born Jan 23, 1927, Brooklyn, NY; divorced; children: Janice Ross, Jacqueline Sullivan. **EDUCATION:** Brooklyn Coll, BA English 1949; CCNY, MPA 1955; NY State Univ, Doctoral Courses 1955-60; Ithaca Coll, Nursing Home Admin 1975. **CAREER:** Office of Program Planning & Coord NY State Dept of Mental Hygiene, assoc commiss 1971-74; Willowbrook Devel Ctr, acting dir 1974-75; Mid-Hudson Reg Dept of Mental Hygiene, reg dir 1975-76; Health Care Agency Cty of San Diego, dep admin 1976-79; San Diego Cty Dept of Health Svcs, dir 1979-86; SD Urban League, exec dir. **ORGANIZATIONS:** Dir Bureau of Mgmt Serv Dept of Mental Hygiene 1963-67; dir Bureau of Budget Serv 1967-68; asst commiss NY State Dept of Mental Hygiene Local Serv Div 1968-71; mem Amer Public Health Assoc, CA Black Health Network, State of CA Hypertension Adv Council; consultant Federal Office of Health Affairs 1973; mem Willowbrook Review Panel 1975-78; bd mem CD Reg Center for Devlopmentelly Disabled 1979-86. **HONORS/ACHIEVEMENTS:** JCC Disting Serv Awd 1963; Paper Unified Serv A Shift from Who to How "The Bulletin 1973; Aid Awd for Med 1980; NAACP Awd for Health 1981; Statewide Black Health Individual Achievement Awd 1982. **MILITARY SERVICE:** AUS sgt 2 yrs. **BUSINESS ADDRESS:** Executive Dir, San Diego Urban League, 4261 Martin Luther King Way, San Diego, CA 92102.

FORDHAM, MONROE
Educator. **PERSONAL:** Born Oct 11, 1939, Parrott, GA; married Freddie; children: Cynthia, Barry, Pamela. **EDUCATION:** Emporia St U, BS 1957; Emporia St U, MS 1962; SUNY, PhD 1973. **CAREER:** Buffalo St Coll, History teacher; Wichita St U, coordinator of black studies; Wichita Pub Schl, Social Studies teacher; Buffalo State Coll, Chairman History Department 1970-. **ORGANIZATIONS:** Pres Afro-Amer History Assn of Niagara Frontier. **HONORS/ACHIEVEMENTS:** Appointed NY St Bi-centennial Comm Author "Major Themes in Northern Black Religious Thought 1800-1860", numerous art on Afro-Amer History; Ed Afro-amer in NY Life & Hist; an interdisciplinary journal; African American Presence in NYS History, Editor 1989. **BUSINESS ADDRESS:** Chairman, Dept of History, Buffalo State College, 1300 Elmwood, Buffalo, NY 14222.

FOREE, JACK CLIFFORD
Business owner. **PERSONAL:** Born Mar 29, 1935, New Castle, KY; son of Jesse Foree and Etta Foree; married Daisy Spencer; children: Julia Foree Burton, Stacey, Etta. **EDUCATION:** KY State Univ, BA 1959; Catherine Spalding Univ, BA 1966; Indiana Univ, MA 1971. **ORGANIZATIONS:** Pres Breakfast Optimist; mem Jefferson Co Educators Assoc, KY Educators Assoc, Natl Educators Assoc, Natl Building Contractors Assoc, Natl Assoc of Math Educators, State Assoc of Math & Science Educators; chmn of KY and TN Sunday School Assocs 1972-85. **HONORS/ACHIEVEMENTS:** Kentucky Colonel. **MILITARY SERVICE:** AUS Sgt E7 2 yrs. **BUSINESS ADDRESS:** President, Franklin Square W, 206 Old Harrods Creek Rd, Louisville, KY 40223.

FOREMAN, CHRISTOPHER H.
Attorney. **PERSONAL:** Born Sep 01, 1925, New Iberia, LA. **EDUCATION:** Univ of Cincinnati, BA high hon 1950;Univ of Cincinnati, MA;Univ of MD, LLB 1957. **CAREER:** Atty pvt prac; Dept of EconomicsUniv of Cincinnati, asst; US Ordnance Corps, first lt; Ordnance Training Command, Ordnance & Sch Aberdeen Proving Ground, instr; Hon Emory H Niles, law clerk 1956-57. **ORGANIZATIONS:** Phi Beta Kappa; Order of Coif; Am Judicature Soc; mem Law Firm, Callegary, Bracken, Callegary 1957-60; asst Gen Counsel, Dept HEW 1961-62; mem St Thomas Moore Soc 1957-; former gen counsel BACMONILA Inc.

FOREMAN, DOYLE
Sculptor, educator. **PERSONAL:** Born Jun 17, 1933, Ardmore, OK; married Selma J; children: Doyle, Jr, Maia. **EDUCATION:** CA Coll of Arts & Crafts, BA 1960. **CAREER:** Oakland Recreation Dept, arts & crafts specialist 1957-60, landscape, gardening & land mgmt 1961-65; Univ of CA, Coll V Santa Cruz, assoc prof of art & sculptor 1968-; CA Coll of Arts & Crafts, 1969; Yardbird Publishing Corp, art editor, art dir, bd dir 1971-. **ORGANIZATIONS:** Mem Santa Cruz Co Art Commn 1972-74; mem City of Santa Cruz Bicentennial Com 1975; com chmn to organize New Perspectives in Black Art, Kaiser Center Gallery Oakland 1968. **MILITARY SERVICE:** AUS 1953-55. **BUSINESS ADDRESS:** Coll V Univ of CA, Santa Cruz, CA.

FOREMAN, GEORGE
Minister, former professional boxer. **PERSONAL:** Born Jan 22, 1948, Marshall, TX; married Mary; children: Micki, Leola. **CAREER:** Former professional boxer; started boxing career while on Job Corps training program at Grants Pass, OR conservation camp; won Corps Diamond Belt Tournament; enteredGolden Gloves competition 1967; lost by split decision, won a berth on US Olympics Squad; turned professional 1969 after winning 19 of out 22 amateur bouts in 2 years; Church of the Lord Jesus Christ, pastor/preacher/proprietor. **HONORS/ACHIEVEMENTS:** Won Heavyweight Olympic Gold Medal Mexico City 1968; Won 37 straight professional wins when entered ring against Joe Frazier for World's Heavyweight Championship which he won Jan 22, 1973; Boxer of the Year World Boxing Assn 1974.

FOREMAN, JOE CORNELIUS, JR.
Government official. **PERSONAL:** Born Nov 20, 1943, Birmingham, AL; married Roslyn Elizabeth Scruggs. **EDUCATION:** StateUniv Coll of NY at Buffalo, BS 1973; Canisius Coll, pursuing MS. **CAREER:** Erie County Sheriff's Dept, supt 1977-; Canisius Coll, Buffalo NY, dir of security 1975-77; United Way of Buffalo & Erie County, assoc staff dir 1975; FUILD Org, Buffalo NY, skill & work evaluator 1974. **ORGANIZATIONS:** Chmn polit action com AFRO-AM Police Assn Buffalo 1979; mem Erie Co Speakers Bur on Child Abuse; mem Rho Lambda Chpt, Alpha Phi Alpha Frat. **HONORS/ACHIEVEMENTS:** Black Achievers Award in Govt; 1490 Enterprises Buffalo NY 1978; Unit Citation USAF 1963; Law Enforcement Officer of the Yr Award, Eri Co Bar Assn 1980. **MILITARY SERVICE:** USAF E-4 1961-67. **BUSINESS ADDRESS:** 10 Delaware Ave, Buffalo, NY 14202.

FOREMAN, S. BEATRICE
Retired teacher, educational administrator. **PERSONAL:** Born Sep 23, 1917, Garysburg, NC; daughter of Douglas Ransom and Susie Ransom; married James W Foreman. **EDUCATION:** Hampton Inst, BS 1939; Western Reserve Univ, MS 1956. **CAREER:** Murfreesboro TN, public sch teacher 1939-41; Cleveland OH, public sch teacher 1942-61; Stamford CT, public sch teacher 1961-82, bd of educ member. **ORGANIZATIONS:** Past pres Westchester Co Chap Delta Sigma Theta Sor; mem League of Women Voters; mem Retired Teachers Assn; mem Democratic Womens Club; mem Hampton Alumnae Assn; mem Urban League; mem Yerwood Ctr; mem The Girlfriends Inc; mem Interfaith Council of Stamford; mem Catholic Interracial Council; mem St Bridgets RC Church; mem Heart Fund Chmn; mem Amer Red Cross Bloodmobile Aide; mem Fairfield Co Alumnae Chap Delta Sigma Theta Sor Inc; 1st vice pres New Neighborhoods Inc 1969-; bd of trustees first black female Stamford Hosp 1972-83; 1st vice pres NAACP 1979-84; CT Justice Comm 1981-82; pres Business/Educ Alliance 1988-89; Bd of Educ 1st black female 1981-; bd of dirs Wright Tech Sch 1981-; Mayor's Comm on Drugs & Alcohol. **HONORS/ACHIEVEMENTS:** Serv awd Interfaith Council 1972; educ awd Stamford Black Educators 1978, Westhill HS 1978, Stamford Educ Assn Outstanding 1978; Outstanding Educ Stamford Educ Assn 1978; top vote getter city primary & regular election 1981 & 1984; serv awd CT Justice Comm 1982; outstanding educator CT State Ministers Wives & Widows Assn outstanding educator 1983; serv awd Stamford Hosp 1984; outstanding sor awd Fairfield Co Alumnae Chap Delta Sigma Theta Sor Inc 1984; comm serv awd Yerwood Womens Club 1984; Ed Awd NAACP 1985; Citizen of Year 1987; Senior Employment Service Award 1989. **BUSINESS ADDRESS:** Board of Education, Stamford School Dist, 195 Hillandale Ave, Stamford, CT 06902.

FORNAY, ALFRED R., JR.
Editor, author. **PERSONAL:** Born Jun 08, Cincinnati, OH; son of Alfred Fornay Sr and Margaret Fornay. **EDUCATION:** Wilfred Acad of Beauty & Hair Design, 1966; CityUniv City Coll of NY, AAS 1968; StateUniv of NY/Fashion Inst of Tech, AAS 1971. **CAREER:** Fashion Fair Cosmetics, beauty/training dir 1973-78; Revlon, Inc, polished ambers creative dir 1978-80; Elan Mag, elan bty editor 1980-82; Ebony Mag, beauty & fashion editor 1982-85; EM Magazine, editor 1985-1988; Essence Mag, assoc beauty editor 1972-73; Clairol Inc, asst ethnic mktng mgr 1971-72; American Visions Magazine, fashion & beauty contributing writer 1989-; Johnson Publishing Co Inc, Fashion Fair Div, beauty consultant 1988-. **ORGANIZATIONS:** Mem Nat Assn of Black Journalists/NY Chptr 1984; mem Nat Beauty Culturist League 1983; friend/former bd mem Boys Choir of Harlem. **HONORS/ACHIEVEMENTS:** Alumni of the Yr Award Fashion Inst of Tech 1976, Mortimer C Ritter Award 1976; judge Miss World Beauty Pageant London, Eng 1982; contributor McGraw Hill Book Co Encyclopedia of Black Am 1981; BBW articles 1984; Awd in Excellence Black Women in Publishing NY 1986; Beauty Book: Fornay's Guide to Skin & Makeup for Women of Color, Simon & Schuster Publishers 1989. **BUSINESS ADDRESS:** PO Box 1321, Grand Central Station, New York, NY 10163.

FORNEY, MARY JANE
Social service administrator. **PERSONAL:** Born May 23, 1949, Galesburg, IL; children: James LaMour. **EDUCATION:** Sangamon State Univ, BA Child Family Comm Serv 1977, Grad Student Soc Serv Admin. **CAREER:** Springfield & Sangamon Co Comm Action, admin asst 1968-74; IL Dept of Children & Family Svcs, child welfare worker & soc serv planner 1974-78; Family Serv Ctr of Sangamon Co, dir of child care svcs. **ORGANIZATIONS:** Council mem Head Start Policy Council 1974-76; mem Natl Assn for the Educ of Young Children vice pres 1981-83; chmn Mother's March-March of Dimes 1984 &1985; mem Natl Assn Black Social Worker 1974-; sec Streetside Boosters Neighborhood Adv Bd of Dirs 1976-; comm mem Springfield Reg Adv Bd Dept Children & Family Serv 1981-; spec projs chmn Delta Sigma Theta Inc 1983-; adv bd Chr Sangamon Cty Dept of Public Aid 1985-; mem DPA Adv Bd 1982-; vice pres exec bd March of Dimes. **HONORS/ACHIEVEMENTS:** Founders Day Awd St John AME Church 1979; Social Worker of Yr Natl Assn of Black Soc Workers 1979; Vol Awd Amer Lung Assn 1981; Hall of Fame Awd Springfield-Sangamon Co Comm Action 1981; Outstanding Young Woman-Outstanding Young Women of Amer 1982; Mother's March Chairperson March of Dimes Awd 1985; YWCA Woman of the Year Awd; March of Dimes 5 Year Service Awd 1987. **HOME ADDRESS:** 2033 Randall Ct, Springfield, IL 62703. **BUSINESS ADDRESS:** Dir of Child Care Serv, Family Ser Ctr Sangamon County, 1308 S 7th St, Springfield, IL 62703.

FORREST, ALVANE M.
Retired educator. **PERSONAL:** Born Jun 25, 1916, Ofahoma, MS; daughter of Edward Merchant and Libby Merchant; married David C; children: David Jr, Paula. **EDUCATION:** Rust Coll, BA 1940; Fisk Univ, 1963; Rollins Coll; Educ Degree, 1983. **CAREER:** Elementary School teacher, 1946-89 (retired). **ORGANIZATIONS:** Orange Co Bd Public Inst Classroom Teachers Assn; Florida United Serv Assn; Nat Educ Assn; life mem NEA; pres Orlando Chapter; Jack & Jill Amer Inc, 1963-64; pres BeLe Co Lon Literary Social Club 1969-72; pres, Orlando Chapter of Girl Friends Inc; pres, Kappa Delta Pi Honor Soc; Kappa Delta Pi Honor Soc; Basileus, AKA Sorority. **HONORS/ACHIEVEMENTS:** Outstanding Elementary Teacher Amer, 1972; Certificate of Recognition, Ebenezer United Methodist Church; Citation, Florida Educ Assn bd dir, 1972-74; Certificate of Appreciation, Serv Field Educ 1975; Orange Co CTA; Picture appeared on the front page of the major newspaper (a first for blacks); Interviewed and appeared on TV following a reception given by the supt and school bd. **HOME ADDRESS:** 2410 Monte Carlo Trail, Orlando, FL 32805.

FORREST, LEON RICHARD
Educator. **PERSONAL:** Born Jan 08, 1937, Chicago, IL; son of Leon and Adeline; married Marianne Duncan. **EDUCATION:** Wilson Jr Coll, attended 1955-56; Roosevelt Univ, attended 1957-58; Univ of Chicago, attended 1958-60 1962-64. **CAREER:** Woodlawn Observer, managing editor 1967-69; Muhammed Speaks, assoc dir 1969-71, managing editor 1971-73; Northwestern Univ, prof Afro-Amer Studies 1973-. **ORGANIZATIONS:** Mem The Authors Guild Inc 1974-; awds pres Soc of Midland Authors 1981; pres Soc of Midland Authors 1981; lectr Yale-Rochester-Wesleyan 1974-89; librettist for opera commissioned IN Univ Sch of Music 1980. **HONORS/ACHIEVEMENTS:** Sandburg Medallion Chicago Pub Library 1984; author of 3 novels & a play; Society of Midland Authors Award for Fiction; Friends of Literature; Du Sable Museum Award for Fiction; Mayor Harold Washington proclaims April 14, 1985 as "Leon Forrest Day" in Chicago. **MILITARY SERVICE:** AUS spec 4 1960-62. **BUSINESS ADDRESS:** Prof African-Amer Studies, NorthwesternUniv, 633 Clark, Evanston, IL 60201.

FORREST-CARTER, AUDREY FAYE
Educator. **PERSONAL:** Born Apr 01, 1956, Greenwood, SC; daughter of Willie Forrest Sr and Ruth B Forrest; married Ewing Carter Jr, Sep 06, 1986; children: Channing Kamille Carter. **EDUCATION:** Bennett Coll, BA 1978; NC A&T State Univ, MA 1979. **CAREER:** A&T State Univ, teaching asst 1978-79; Winston-Salem State Univ, instructor 1979-84; Miami Univ, doctoral assoc 1984-88. **ORGANIZATIONS:** Mem Delta Sigma Theta, comm on graduate women Miami Univ 1984-85; mem grad comm English dept Miami Univ 1984-85; mem rsch team computers & composition Miami Univ 1985. **HONORS/ACHIEVEMENTS:** Publ poem Worn Out 1982; DAP Awd Miami Univ 1984-88; Faculty Develop Grant Winston-Salem State Univ 1984-88; Silver Poet Awd World of Poetry 1986; Board of Governor's Grant, Univ of North Carolina at Chapel Hill, 1988-89, 1989-90. **HOME ADDRESS:** 714 S Locust St, Oxford, OH 45056.

FORSTALL, KWEKU DWAYNE
Attorney. **PERSONAL:** Born Apr 20, 1960, New Orleans, LA; married Adrienne Vinson. **EDUCATION:** Wesleyan Univ, BA 1982; New York Univ, JD 1985. **CAREER:** Atlanta Legal Aid Soc Inc, attorney 1985-. **ORGANIZATIONS:** Mem Atlanta Bar Assoc 1986, Decatur Bar Assoc 1987, Gate City Bar Assoc 1987. **HONORS/ACHIEVEMENTS:** Chadbourne Prize Wesleyan Univ 1979; Comm Serv Awd NY Univ Black Amer Law Student Assoc 1985. **HOME ADDRESS:** 1108 To-Lani Farm Rd, Stone Mountain, GA 30083. **BUSINESS ADDRESS:** Attorney, Atlanta Legal Aid Society Inc, 231 W Ponce DeLeon Ave, Decatur, GA 30030.

FORSTER, CECIL R.
Psychologist. **PERSONAL:** Born Apr 21, 1911, Brooklyn, NY; married Evelyn P Lattimore; children: Cecil Jr, Sandra. **EDUCATION:** NY U, BS 1936, MA 1938, PhD 1955. **CAREER:** VA Hosp, Brooklyn, chief counseling psychologist 1951-64; Neighborhood Youth Corps/US Dept Labor, regional dir 1965-66; Bureau of Work Pgms/US Dept of Labor, spec asst to admin 1966-67; Dept of Psychiatry/NY Med Coll, dir rehab serv 1967-69; Dept Psychiatry/NY Medical Coll, asst prof 1967; NY StateBd for Psychology, mem 1971-78; Psychology Dept Baruch Coll, adj asso prof 1971; New York City Police Dept, sr psychological consult 1980-; Private Practice. **ORGANIZATIONS:** Chrmn Committee for Public Higher Educ 1983-; pres NY State Psychological Assn 1975-76. **HONORS/ACHIEVEMENTS:** Distinguished Serv Award Assoc of Black Psychologists 1984; Honorary Surgeon, New York City Police Dept, 1981; Distinguished Serv Award NY Society of Clinical Psychologists 1979. **MILITARY SERVICE:** USCGR chief boatswain mate 1942-45. **BUSINESS ADDRESS:** 862 E 21st St, Brooklyn, NY 11210.

FORSTER, CECIL R., JR.
Business executive. **PERSONAL:** Born Nov 11, 1943, New York. **EDUCATION:** Middlebury Coll, BA1964; St John's U, JD 1967. **CAREER:** Westinghouse Broadcasting Co Inc, vice pres 1974-; WINS Radio, gen mgr 1977-; Counsel PepsiCola Met Bottling Co Inc, vice pres sec 1971-74. **ORGANIZATIONS:** Mem Irving Trust Co 1967-68; mem bd dir Westinghouse Broadcasting Co Inc; bd dir EG Bowman Co Inc; bd dir Howard Meml Schlrsp Fund; bd tst AFTRA Pension & Welfare Fund; Equal Oppt Cons; bd of governors Intl Radio & TV Soc; mem Advisory Com; mem Black Exec Exch Program; mem Nat Urban League; mem 100 Black Men; mem Am Bar Assn. **MILITARY SERVICE:** USMC capt 1968-71. **BUSINESS ADDRESS:** 90 Park Ave, New York, NY 10016.

FORT, EDWARD B.
Education administrator. **PERSONAL:** Born in Detroit, MI; married Lessie; children: Clarke, Lezlie. **EDUCATION:** Wayne State Univ, Bachelors 1954, Masters 1958; Univ of CA Berkeley, Doctorate 1964. **CAREER:** Detroit MI Public Schools, curriculum coord 1964-67; Inkster MI Public Schools, supt 1967-71; Sacramento CA City Schools, supt, dep supt 1971-74; Univ of WI Ctr System, chancellor 1974-81; NC A&T State Univ, chancellor 1981-. **ORGANIZATIONS:** Vstg prof of ed admin Univ of MI Ann Arbor 1965-66; adj prof urban ed Univ of MI Dearborn 1968-71; vstg prof MI State Univ 1974; bd of adv Fund for Improvement of Post Sec Ed 1979-81; bd of ed adv Phi Delta Kappan 1980-84; pres commiss NCAA 1984-86; bd of dir Natl Assoc for Equal Oppty in Higher Ed 1984-; mem Greensboro NC Chamber of Commerce Exec Bd. **HONORS/ACHIEVEMENTS:** Press Awd Ed Press Assoc of Amer 1969; Chosen Symposium Participant Dept of Sociology Univ of Pretoria S African 1977; Eighty for the 80's Milwaukee Jrnl Awd 1979; Who's Who in Amer Natl Chap 1980-84. **MILITARY SERVICE:** AUS corpl 2 yrs; Good Conduct Medal 1955-56. **BUSINESS ADDRESS:** Chancellor, North Carolina A&T StUniv, Admin Bldg, Greensboro, NC 27411.

FORT, JANE
Educational administrator. **PERSONAL:** Born Aug 27, 1938, Nashville, TN; daughter of William Fort and Geraldine Fort; divorced; children: Sekou Fort Morrison. **EDUCATION:** Fisk Univ, BA (cum laude) 1958; Univ of Mass, MS 1960, PhD 1962. **CAREER:** City of New York, JOIN, dir of research, psychologist, 1964; City Coll, William Alans White Inst, New York City, research assoc, 1965; Harvard Univ Grad School of Educ, research assoc, 1965-69; Newton MA Schools, Reading Program, consultant/psychologist, 1974-75; Brookline Public Schools (BEEP), Brookline MA, consultant and sr research assoc, 1977-81; Roxbury Comm Coll, Roxbury, MA, staff assoc, program developer, 1979-81; Univ of California-Davis, lecturer, researcher, 1981-83; Clark College, program Manager for evaluation/dir, 1984-87; Morehouse School of Medicine, Dept of Comm Health and Preventive Medicine 1987-. **ORGANIZATIONS:** Mem numerous bds of dirs; lecture, seminar, conference coordinator/chair; mem alumni clubs; mem Alpha Kappa Alpha Sorority; mem Assn of Black Psychologists; mem Amer Psychological Assn. **HONORS/ACHIEVEMENTS:** Ford Foundation Fisk Univ early entrant 1958; Who's Who Awards 1958-78; Outstanding Young Women 1966-74; Founder Award, Assn of Black Psychologist 1987. **HOME ADDRESS:** P O Box 4384, Atlanta, GA 30302. **BUSINESS ADDRESS:** Assistant Professor, Department of Community Health & Preventive Medicine, Morehouse School of Medicine, 720 Westview Drive SW, Atlanta, GA 30310.

FORT, WILLIAM H.
Attorney. **PERSONAL:** Born Jul 18, 1915, Tuscumbia, AL; married Ruth Wilson; children: Gailmarie, W Howard Jr. **EDUCATION:** OH State Univ, BS 1940, JD 1946; Univ of KS, undergrad work; Univ of WA, post grad work. **CAREER:** OH Bell Telephone, former dir; Goodyear Tire & Rubber Co, dir; Private Practice, attorney 1947-. **ORGANIZATIONS:** Exec bd N Central Assn Commn on Higher Educ; mem Akron OH & Amer Bar Assn; past chmn Akron Planning Comm; mem Amer Judicature Soc, Natl Council Juvenile

Judges, Akron Barristers Club, Akron Law Library Assn; mem bd trustees Akron Area Council BSA; vice chmn bd trustees chmn Amer Red Cross; past pres Akron Area C of C; mem Akron Gen Hosp; chmn Univ Akron 1974-77; bd dir First Natl Bank of Akron; chmn Akron City Planning Comm; pres Akron Urban League; mem exec com bd of trustees Akron Reg Devel Bd; mem exec com bd of trustees Goals for Greater Akron; mem bd of trustees Natl Alliance of Bus Men; bd trustees Akron Child Guidance Ctr; life mem NAACP; pres Frontiers Intl; knight commr Republic of Liberia; pres Bluecoats Inc 1983-; chmnBoys & Girls Clubs of Summit Co OH 1983-84; bd of govs Amer Natl Red Cross 1981-. **HONORS/ACHIEVEMENTS:** Peter Bommarito Awd 1969; pres Frontiers Intl Hon D of Laws Central State Univ 1969; Silver Beaver Awd BSA 1971. **BUSINESS ADDRESS:** Attorney, 40 East Mill St, Akron, OH 44308.

FORTE, JOHNIE, JR.
Retired army officier, educational administrator. **PERSONAL:** Born Dec 20, 1936, New Boston, TX; son of Johnie and Sadie; married Dolores Bowles Johnson; children: Mitchell C Johnson, Shermaine L Johnson, Denise M. **EDUCATION:** Prairie View A&M Univ, BA 1956; Auburn Univ, MA 1976. **CAREER:** AUS, Commd 2nd Lt 1956; advanced through grades to Brig Gen; Dept Army, personnel mgmt officer, dir personnel and insp gen W Germany; Dept Army Washington, dir personnel plans and systems; 8th Infantry Div, asst div commander; Wiesbaden Germany, military community commander; 32nd Army Air Defense Command US Army Europe, dep commanding gen; US Army ODCSPER, brigadier general; asst supt, General Services, Fairfax County, VA Public Schools. **ORGANIZATIONS:** Mem Assn US Army Vice Pres Chap 1977-78; mem Rock's Professional Org; Phi Delta Kappa. **HONORS/ACHIEVEMENTS:** Accelerated promotions to lt col, col & brigadier gen based on performance of duties. **MILITARY SERVICE:** AUS; Decorated Legion of Merit; Defense Superior Serv Medal; Army Meritorious Serv Medal; Army Commendation Medal; Air Force Commendation Medal. **BUSINESS ADDRESS:** General Service Spt Center, Fairfax County Public Schools, 6800B Industrial Rd, Springfield, VA 22153.

FORTE, MINNIE T.
Educator. **PERSONAL:** Born Feb 12, 1916, Goldsboro, NC; children: William, Lonnie, Minnie Mae. **EDUCATION:** Fayetteville State U, BS 1939; NC Central U, MA 1951; NC Central U, PhD 1960; Duke U, additional study;Univ of NC. **CAREER:** Durham City Sch Sys, tchr 1944-60; Fayetteville State U, 1960-62; Shaw U, 1962-65; Operation Breakthrough Cntr for Children, dir 1965-66; St AugustinesColl, asso prof coordinator Early Childhood Educ 1966-. **ORGANIZATIONS:** Chmn bd of Christian Edn, White Rock Bapt Ch; vice pres New Hoep Bapt Assn; life mem Nat Educ Assn; adv student NEA-nCAE 1966-; spl asst Early Childhood Educ 1974; coordinator Early Childhood Educ 1970; aptd by Nat Council for Accreditation of Tchr Educ to evaluate undergrad & grad elem educ progof St Francis Coll Fort Wayne IN 1975; aptd by NC Bd Educ to evaluate elem educ prog of Fayetteville StateUniv 1975. **HONORS/ACHIEVEMENTS:** Tuition scholarship,Univ of Pittsburgh; study in England summer 1970; study grant Phelps-Stokes Fund, St Augustines Coll, 4 countries in W Africa.

FORTIER, THEODORE T.
Dentist. **PERSONAL:** Born Aug 15, 1926, San Diego, CA. **EDUCATION:** UCLA,Univ of PA, attended; HowardUniv Coll of Educ of Dentistry, DDS 1957. **CAREER:** Los Angeles, dentist pvt practice; Continuing Dental Educ USC Sch of Dentistry, instr 1968. **ORGANIZATIONS:** Staff mem LA Co/USC Med Cntr-Compt on PTA Sch Dentist 1959-61; pres Angel City Dental Soc 1968-69; vice pres Dental Found of CA 1971; mem bd dir Los Angeles Dental Soc; mem Acad of Gen Dentistry; delegate to house of delegates of CA Dental Assn; chief of Denatl Dept of Hollywood Presb Med Cntr 1972-74; mem vice pres Kiwanis Club of Angeles Mesa; gen chmn Fund-raising Dr for Crenshaw YMCA 1975; mem Omicron Kappa Upsilon. **HONORS/ACHIEVEMENTS:** Dental Honor Soc; recipient US Pub Health Fellowship for study of dental disease unique ot social isolated segment of eastern US population; Surgical Technician. **MILITARY SERVICE:** AUS corpl T/5. **BUSINESS ADDRESS:** Dentist, 3701 Stocker #408, Los Angeles, CA 90008.

FORTSON, ELNORA AGNES
Poet. **PERSONAL:** Born May 07, 1943, Pittsburgh, PA; married Walter Lamar; children: Akilah, Ayanna, Anika. **EDUCATION:** Grace Martin Bus Sch, Cert of Com 1961;Univ of Pittsburgh Deliverance Bible Inst, 1977-81. **CAREER:** Univ of Pgh, Sch of Social Work, secy 1961-62; Westinghouse Elec Corp, capital stk clerk 1962-77; Fuller Ins Agency, data maintenance & acctg 1983-; ACT II Jewelry, Inc, jewelry advisor 1984-; PRAISE Poetry Wkshp, founder inst. **ORGANIZATIONS:** Mem Intl Platform Assoc 1980; mem Chicago Intl Black Writer's 1976; publicity dir Homewood Poetry Forum 1973-75; publicity dir Greater Pgh Christian Temple 1980-; publicity dir Temple Christian Acad 1981-; mem Kuntu Writer's Wkshp 1980-; instructor PRAISE Poetry Wrkshp 1984-. **HONORS/ACHIEVEMENTS:** Danae Award & Pub Clover Intl Poetry Cont 1974; Poet of the Yr Homewood Poetry Forum 1975; literary fellowship PA Cncl on the Arts 1981; fellowship poems, "Jesus Walks the Waters of My Soul"" 1981; Who's Who in the Bicentennial Era 1976; poetry anthology "Love from Black Women to Black Men 1976; poetry anthology"Ridin' On a Good Wind" 1975; published "Pre-Natal/Post-Natal" Essence Mag 1977. **BUSINESS ADDRESS:** Instructor, PRAISE Poetry Wkshp, White Westinghouse Inc, 930 Ft Duquesne Blvd, Pittsburgh, PA 15230.

FORTSON, HENRY DAVID, JR.
Dentist. **PERSONAL:** Born Sep 11, 1946, Haines City, FL; son of Henry Fortson and Nancy Fortson; married Wilnita Yvette Varner; children: Henry D III, Dennis Gregory, William Christopher. **EDUCATION:** Daytona Beach Jr Coll, AA 1966; Knoxville Coll, BS 1968; Meharry Medical Coll, DDS 1984. **CAREER:** Holston Army Ammunition Plant, chemist; Private Practice, dentist. **ORGANIZATIONS:** Shriner 32 degree 1976; mem Omega Psi Phi Frat 1967-, NAACP 1985-, Thomasville Dental Study Group 1986, GA Dental Soc 1986, Mason; mem Thomasville Thomas Co Comm Club; mem Bd of Recreation in Thomasville. **BUSINESS ADDRESS:** Dentist, 1205 East Jackson St, Thomasville, GA 31792.

FORTUNE, ALVIN V.
Educator. **PERSONAL:** Born Mar 13, 1935, Bronx, NY; married Carol; children: Scott, Mark, Alvin, Erik, Matthew, Justin. **EDUCATION:** CO StateUniv 1960; Boston U;Univ of MD; grad sch Antioch. **CAREER:** Newton High School MA, teacher, coach 1960-69; Fairmont Heights High School, Prince Georges County MD, prin 1969-71; Edw Devotion School MA, asst prin 1971; John School, prin. **ORGANIZATIONS:** Houston Oiler Prof Football Club 1960; mem Nat Alliance of Black Sch Ed 1973-74; Am Assn of Sch Personnel Admin 1973-74; Human Relations Commn 1965-67; Omega Psi Phi Frat; pres New England Day Camping Assn 1974-75. **HONORS/ACHIEVEMENTS:** Outstanding Young Man of Am 1970; Outstanding Achievement Award, Omega Psi Phi Frat 1961. **MILITARY SERVICE:** USAF 1952-56. **BUSINESS ADDRESS:** Brookline Public Schools, 333 Washington St, Brookline, MA 02146.

FORTUNE, GWENDOLINE Y. (OYA C'SHIVA)
Educator, writer. **PERSONAL:** Born in Houston, TX; daughter of W Hermon Young and Mittie McCain Young (deceased); divorced; children: Frederic, Phillip, Roger. **EDUCATION:** JC Smith Univ, BS 1948; SC State Coll, MS 1951; Roosevelt Univ, MPh 1972; Nova Univ, EdD 1979. **CAREER:** Chicago Public Schools, teacher 1954-66; Dist 68 Skokie IL, team coord 1964-70; Oakton Comm Coll, prof ethnic studies coord 1970-84; Consultant "Discovery", dir 1984-. **ORGANIZATIONS:** Exec bd IL Council for Black Studies 1980-83; exec comm IL Consultation on Ethnicity in Educ 1980-84. **HONORS/ACHIEVEMENTS:** Intl Black Writers Conference First Place Non-Fiction 1986; 2 articles Black Family Magazine 1986; non-fiction second place, International Black Writers Conference 1987; poetry reading, Chicago Cultural Center 1988; poem "Tom Cats" Korone, 1988; other poems published in InnerQuest & Prairie St Companion.

FOSTER, ALVIN GARFIELD
Veterinarian. **PERSONAL:** Born Apr 07, 1934, Preston, MD; married Gertrude Dallis; children: Alvin Garfield, Kerwin, Kelsie. **EDUCATION:** MD State Coll, BS 1956; Tuskegee Inst DVM 1960; WA State U, MS 1967; PhD 1969. **CAREER:** US Dept of Agr, Meat Inspec Div Spokane, vet meat insp 1963-64; WA State U, NIH postdoctoral fellow 1965-69; Merck Inst for Therapeutic Research Rahway NJ, sr micro-biologist 1969-; Merck & Co Inc Rsch, dir animal sci. **ORGANIZATIONS:** Mem Am Vet Med Assn, Alpha Kappa Mu, Phi Zeta, Sigma Xi, Alpha Phi Alpha, Monmouth County Men's Club. **HONORS/ACHIEVEMENTS:** Black Achiever in Industry YMCA of NY 1974. **MILITARY SERVICE:** USAF capt 1960-62. **HOME ADDRESS:** 27 Old Mill Rd, Tinton Falls, NJ 07724.

FOSTER, ANDREW D.
Business executive. **PERSONAL:** Born Jul 06, 1919, Indianapolis, IN; married Pearl Burwell; children: Annetta, Patricia, Andrew Jr, Jacqueline Terry. **CAREER:** Foster Hotels, pres 1955-, org 1948; Andrew D Foster Trucking Co, operator 1944-58. **ORGANIZATIONS:** Charter org Midwest Nat Bank 1973; org Indianapolis Chap Nat Bus League 1966; co-chmn, life mem NAACP 1969, bd dirs 1972; bd dirs Indianapolis Urban League 1973; bd dirs Martin Center Sickle Cell Anemia 1973; bd, mem Nat Alliance of Bus Men 1973; pres Indy Trade Assn 1975; co-chmn Marion Co Health & Hosp Corp 1976; past pres Indianapolis chap Nat Bus League 1966-73; bd dirs Indianapolis Bus Devel Found 1970; past vice pres Gtr Indianapolis Progress Com 1970-74; past mem, bd dirs Marion Co Health & Hosp Corp 1973-76; past mem, bd dirs United Way 1973-76; past mem Small Bus Adminstrn Adv Council 1973-74; mem Nationwide Hotel Assn 1965. **BUSINESS ADDRESS:** President, Foster Hotels, Inc, 2358 N Kenwood Ave, Indianapolis, IN 46208.

FOSTER, CLYDE
Business executive. **PERSONAL:** Born Nov 21, 1931; married Dorothy M Harri; children: Anitra, Edith, Clydis, Byron, Carla. **EDUCATION:** AL A&M U, BS 1954. **CAREER:** Marshall Space Flight Cntr, chief, EEO for Civil Serv Employees 1972, instr training courses; AL A&M U, dir Computer Sci Dept, est Data Processing Lab & undegrad degree prog in Computer Sci, first in State of AL Educ Sys of Higher Learning 1968-70; Marshall Space Flight Cntr, mathematician, instr Computation Lab 1960; Army Ballistic Missile Agency, Redstone Arsenal, 1957; Dallas Co Sch Sys, Selma, AL, sci tchr. **ORGANIZATIONS:** Petitioned Probate Judge, gained rejuvenation of Triana, AL 1964; aptd mayor; helped est first rural water sys in Madison Co; instituted first black-managed fee-free recreation river-front land in TN Valley; est Triana Indus Devel Co (promotes indus for employment of disadvantaged minorities); helped organize Data Processing Asso Inc 1970; fdr, pres Triana Indus Inc, first industry to locate in Town of Triana; provided scndry, post-scndry students with edl & occupational opps; dev proposal to est first adult educ prog for sharecroppers 1967; developed proposal for hard-core head-of-household famales to be taught skills in elec soldering, schematic reading, electronic components 1972; aptd to AL Commn of Higher Educ By Gov Geo Wallace 1974. **HONORS/ACHIEVEMENTS:** Recip awards for conscientious performance from following MSFC/NASA 1968; NASA apollo achvmnt award & MSFC award of achvmnt 1969; NASA fifteen Yr Serv Award 1970; Alpha Kappa Sor Dedicated Pub Serv & Outstanding Leadership Award 1971; Omega Psi Phi Frat Merit Serv Award 1971; Delta Sigma Theta Sor Appreciation& Serv Rendered 1972; TARCOG Appreciation for Outstanding Contribution Toward Grown & Devel 1972; MSFC Commen of Achvmnt Award 1972; Citizens of Triana Comm Outstanding & Dedicated Serv Award 1972; AL A&MUniv Distinguish Serv Award 1973; African Meth Epis Ch, Burningham, Comm Serv Award, 1973; Omega Psi Phi Frat Seventh Dist Man of Yr Award 1974. **MILITARY SERVICE:** AUS pfc 1954-56.

FOSTER, DEBORAH VALRIE
Consultant/broker. **PERSONAL:** Born Oct 05, 1955, Beaumont, TX; daughter of Hardy Valrie and Leona E Collins Valrie; married Willie J Foster Jr; children: Janell, Jaulik, Jasmin. **EDUCATION:** Univ of TX at Austin, BSci 1978; College for Financial Planning, Denver CO, CFP, 1988. **CAREER:** Sanger-Harris Dallas, asst buyer 1977-80; Gordon's Jewelers Dallas, asst store mgr 1980-82; Deb's Designs, co-owner/mgr 1982-83; DV Foster Consultant/Broker, owner/general mgr 1983-88; Merrill Lynch, Arlington TX, financial consultant/CFP, 1989-. **ORGANIZATIONS:** Finance comm mem, CBCL Business Resource Group, 1986; consultant/preparer, Tax R' Us, 1986; mem, Speaker's Bank, AWED, 1986-; mem, NAACP, 1986-, Lancaster Chamber of Commerce 1986; mem, Duncanville Chamber of Commerce, 1989; mem, AWED, 1989-. **HONORS/ACHIEVEMENTS:** Certificate of Participation, Risk Management Workshop, Dallas Independent School Dist, 1986; Certified Financial Planner, 1988. **BUSINESS ADDRESS:** Financial Consultant/CFP, Merrill Lynch, 2221 E Lamar Blvd, Suite 800, Arlington, TX 76006-0457.

FOSTER, DELORES JACKSON
Educational administrator. **PERSONAL:** Born Jan 24, 1938, Halltown, WV; daughter of Daniel David Jackson and Mary Frances Taylor; married James H; children: Mark Darnell Bailey, James Jr, Arthur. **EDUCATION:** Shepherd Coll, BA 1960; Jersey City State Coll,

MA 1974. **CAREER:** Page-Jackson HS, teacher 1960-61; Dickinson HS, teacher 1961-71, teacher coord 1971-73, guidance counselor 1973-84, acting vice principal 1982-83, vice principal 1985-, acting principal 1986, guidance counselor, vice principal 1987. **ORGANIZATIONS:** Corresponding sec Black Educators United 1975; 1st vice pres Coll Women Inc 1979-81; pres Coll Women Inc 1981-83; vchmn cong Park Ave Christ Church Disciples of Christ 1982-84; pres Central Atlantic Conf of United Church of Christ 1984-87; mem Empowerment for Change; leadership training United Church of Christ 1979; adv bd Upward Bound Project St Peter's Coll Kersey City NJ 1975-79; workshop leader NJ Alliance of Black Ed conf 1983; elected lay del 15th Gen Synod OCC Ames IA 1985; lay delegate 16th Gen Synod Cleveland OH 1987; mem of St Mark's AME Church 1988; asst dir bd of Christian Ed. **HONORS/ACHIEVEMENTS:** Co-author Book Integrating the Classroom with the World of Work 1980; Honored as a lay woman in the United Church of Christ at 15th Gen Synod in Ames IA 1985. **HOME ADDRESS:** 89 Hawthorne Avenue, East Orange, NJ 07018. **BUSINESS ADDRESS:** Vice Principal, Jersey City Bd of Educ/Synder H S, 239 Bergen Ave, Jersey City, NJ 07305.

FOSTER, DOUGLAS LEROY
Psychiatrist. **PERSONAL:** Born Mar 03, 1931, New York, NY; children: 2 sons, 1 daughter. **EDUCATION:** City Coll of NY, BS 1953; Meharry School of Med, MD 1957. **CAREER:** St Margaret Hospital, internship 1957-58; Fellow of the Menninger School of Psychiatry, 1961-64; Topeka VA Hospital, residency 1961-64; Jackson Park Hospital, chmn dept of psychiatry 1971-79; Bismarck Hospital, consulting psychiatrist 1983-; St Lawrence Hosp, consulting psychiatrist 1985-; Saginaw Comm Hospital, consulting psychiatrist 1985-; Saginaw private practice, psychiatrist 1986-. **ORGANIZATIONS:** Mem pres Jackson Park Hospital; pres tech advisory comm Dept of Public Health St of IL; mem bd dir pres Foster & Assn Clinic Ltd Sub Abuse Treat Center Inc; pres Comprhnsv res & Dev 1977-78; mem bd dir Sub Dupage Co Hlth Sys Agcy 1976-77; me dir Safari Train & Hum serv Inc; mem dir Impact Clnc; chmn Tech Adv Comm; mem Dept of Public Health; chmn St of IL Task Force on Training Edn; Meharry Med Sch Alumni Assn; mem IL Psy Soc; IN St Med Assn; Lake Co Med Assn; AMA; Am Assn of Univ Prof; Amer Assn for the Advancement of Science; Natl Med Assn; Chicago Med Soc; Gov Com for Revsn of Mental Health Codes 1975-77. **HONORS/ACHIEVEMENTS:** Fellow APA; Menninger Found Alumni Assn Award 1961; black excellency award Countee Cullen School 1973; Award for Dist Comm Psychiatrist & General Mental Health Serv. **MILITARY SERVICE:** USNR lt commander 1957; USNR staff psychiatrist; US Naval Hospital 1964-66. **BUSINESS ADDRESS:** Medical Director, Activcare Health Centers, 5444 State Street, Saginaw, MI 48603.

FOSTER, E. C.
Educator. **PERSONAL:** Born Jan 04, 1939, Canton, MS; married Velvelyn Blackwell; children: Garnet A, Sunyetta M. **EDUCATION:** Jackson State Univ, BS 1964; Carnegie-Mellon Univ, MA 1967, DA 1970. **CAREER:** Natchez Public School, teacher 1964-65; Brushton Inner City Project, community organizer 1965-66; Pittsburgh Public Schools, teacher 1967-68; Jackson MS City Council, pres 1985-; Jackson State Univ, prof of history 1969-. **ORGANIZATIONS:** Pres Faculty Senate (JSU) 1974-79; bd mem Farish St YMCA 1976-79; assoc editor Journal of Negro History 1978-; pres Assn of Soc & Behav Scientists 1982; legislative comm chmn Local PTA 1984; city councilman Jackson MS 1985-. **HONORS/ACHIEVEMENTS:** Jackson State Univ Alumni Service Awd 1985; Man of the Year Awd Omega Psi Phi 1985; NAEFO Presidential Citation Awd 1986; Dr Martin Luther King Service Awd JSU/SGA 1986; author of approx 30 publications 1969-85. **MILITARY SERVICE:** AUS Specialist 4 1961-63; Good Conduct Medal 1963. **BUSINESS ADDRESS:** Assoc Grad Dean, Jackson StateUniv, Jackson, MS 39217.

FOSTER, EDWARD, SR.
Manager. **PERSONAL:** Born Sep 27, 1945, Maplesville, AL; son of Mamie Foster; married Jacqulyn E Grant; children: Edward, Forrest Cedric. **EDUCATION:** Selma Univ, AS 1967; AL A&M Univ, BS 1971. **CAREER:** Xerox Corp, prod supv 1972-82; GTE Corp, sr quality supv 1983-86; NCR Corp, prod mgr 1986-. **ORGANIZATIONS:** Pres AL A&M ALumni Assoc 1981-82; vice pres Rochester Chap AL A&M Alumni Assoc 1982-83; mem Amer Mgmt Assoc 1984, Amer Soc Quality Control 1985; 32 degree Lodge 107 Masonic Temple 1985; mem Surface Mount Tech 1986. **HONORS/ACHIEVEMENTS:** Outstanding Work in Higher Ed NAFEO 1983. **HOME ADDRESS:** 314 Lancelot Dr, Clemson, SC 29631.

FOSTER, FRANCES HELEN
Actress. **PERSONAL:** Born Jun 11, 1924, Yonkers, NY; married Morton Goldsen; children: Terrell R, Bernette Ford, Lisa Yarboro, Russell M. **EDUCATION:** Amer Theatre Wing, BA 1949-52. **CAREER:** World Theatre Festival London, actress 1969; Munich Olympics play, actress 1972; Australia 1977; Negro Ensemble Co, actress. **ORGANIZATIONS:** Mem Screen Actors Guild 1952; councillor Actors Equity Assn 1953-67; founding mem Negro Ensemble Co 1967; artist in residence City Coll of NY 1973-77; mem Amer Fed of Radio & TV Artists; founding mem Black Women in Theatre 1982. **HONORS/ACHIEVEMENTS:** Audelco Best Actress Do Lord Remember Me 1978; Audelco Best Dir Hospice 1983; appeared in 25 NEC productions, more than 100 TV shows, films, soap operas; 1985 Obie for Sustained Excellence of Performance. **BUSINESS ADDRESS:** Actress-Director, 146 E 49th #7B, New York, NY 10017.

FOSTER, FRANCES SMITH
Educator. **PERSONAL:** Born Feb 08, 1944, Dayton, OH; married Warren R Foster; children: Lisa Ramirez, Krishna, Quinton. **EDUCATION:** Miami Univ, BS 1964; Univ of South CA, MA 1971; Univ of CA, PhD 1976. **CAREER:** Cincinnati Public Schools, teacher 1964-66; Detroit Public Schools, teacher 1966-68; San Fernando Valley State Coll, instructor 1970-71; San Diego State Univ, asst dean 1976-79, prof 1971-. **ORGANIZATIONS:** Mem Humanities Adv counc KPBS, San Diego State Univ Career Plan & Placemt Ctr Adv Comm; mem NAACP, Coll Lang Assoc, Mod Lang Assoc, Philological Assoc of the Pac Coast; mem West Coast Women's Historical Assn; NEH Rsch Fellowship; CSU Faculty Rsch Fellowship; mem Phi Beta Kappa, Phi Kappa Pi, Althenoi Phi Kappa Delta, Alpha Kappa Alpha, Children's Literature Assoc, MELUS. **HONORS/ACHIEVEMENTS:** Ford Found Fellowship; San Diego Fellowship; Gen Motors Scholar; articles publ "Changing Concepts of the Black Woman", "Charles Wright, Black Black Humorist", "The Black & White Masks of Franz Fanon & Ralph Ellison", "Witnessing Slavery, The Develop of the Ante-Bellum Slave Narrative" Greenwood Press 1979; "VoicesUnheard Stories Untold, Teaching Women's Literature from a Regional Perspective"; SDSU Outstanding Faculty Awd; numerous articles and reviews on Afro-Amer literature. **BUSINESS ADDRESS:** Professor, San Diego StateUniv, Dept of English & Comparative, San Diego, CA 92182.

FOSTER, FRANK B., III
Musician, educator. **PERSONAL:** Born Sep 23, 1928, Cincinnati, OH; married Cecilia Jones; children: Anthony, Donald, Frank IV, Jardis. **EDUCATION:** Central State Coll, 1946-49. **CAREER:** Musician, composer, arranger with Count Basie Orchestra 1953-64; professional musician performing with many well-known artists Wilberforce Collegians Band, saxophonist, composer-arranger 1946-49; professional musician performing with many well known artists 1949-51; musician, composer, arranger with Count Basie Orchestra 1953-64; freelance composer, arranger, performer & instructor 1964-71; New York City Public Schools, music consultant 1971-72; Music Dept Rutgers Univ, Livingston Coll, asst prof; arranger Frank Sinatra's "LA is my Lady" album and video. **ORGANIZATIONS:** Mem ASCAP; AGAC; conductor, mem Collective Black Artists; mem bd dirs Instr Young Musicians Clinic of Jazz Interactions Inc; instr Jazzmobile Wkshp, Ensemb Jazzmobile Inc; hon mem Hartford Jazz Soc; hon mem Jazz at Home Club, Phila; mem Am Fed of Mus 802. **HONORS/ACHIEVEMENTS:** Auth of innumerable published compositions and albums; currently performing with own 23-pc band in US & abroad; author of saxophone exercise book & stage band arrngmnts; recip of many awards & citations including Outstanding Contribution to Jazz Award 1971; Nat Endowment for the Arts grant for Jazz/Folk/Ethnic Composition Fellowships; monetary recognition by Popular Awards Panel of ASCAP for past nine yrs. **MILITARY SERVICE:** AUS pfc 1951-53. **BUSINESS ADDRESS:** Musical Dir, Count Basie Orchestra, PO Box 262, Selden, NY 11784.

FOSTER, GEORGE ARTHUR
Professional athlete. **PERSONAL:** Born Jan 01, 1948, Tuscaloosa, AL. **CAREER:** San Fran Giants, outfldr 1969-71; Cinncinnati Reds, outfielder 1971-81; NY Metss, outfielder 1982-. **ORGANIZATIONS:** Runs George Foster Hme disadv children Upper Dayton OH. **HONORS/ACHIEVEMENTS:** 48th plyr major leag history reach 300 homer plateau nbm 300 off Pete Falcone 1984; voted Most Valuable Plyr All-Star Game 1976; Holds World Series record most putouts by leftfieldewr one game; major league record most hme righhnd batter 1977; Led Nat'l Leag runs batted three stright yrs (121 in 1976) (149 in 1977; and (120 in 1978); Most Valbl Plyr Nat'l Leag Basbl Wrtrs Assoc 1977; selected Nat'l Leag Plyr Yr by the Sporting News 1976-77; Led Leag Hmewith 52 1977; led Leag with 40 hme runs 1977; Silver Slugger Tm; Led Mets 12 game Winning RBI 1983; Nat'l Leag Plyr of Week for May 2-8; Hit Two Grd Slams Seven Day Perd Aug 14 And Aug 20; Leag All-Star 1968; unanimous sel CA Leag All-Starr Tm 1969.

FOSTER, GLADYS M.
Retired attorney. **PERSONAL:** Born Jul 12, 1927, Brooklyn, NY; divorced. **EDUCATION:** Barnard Coll Columbia Univ, AB 1949; Columbia Law Sch, JD 1953. **CAREER:** Workmen's Compensation & Unemployment Ins Appeal Bd, attorney, NY State Div of Human Rights, sr attorney. **ORGANIZATIONS:** Mem Brooklyn Bar Assn; Brooklyn Women's Bar Assn; mem Vocational Adv on Law for Barnard Coll; mem NAACP; mem Barnard Coll Alumni By-Laws Com; mem Crown Heights Assn; past vice pres Natl Assn of Coll Women.

FOSTER, GLORIA
Actress. **PERSONAL:** Born in Chicago, IL; married Clarence Williams III. **EDUCATION:** IL St U; Art Inst of Chgo's Goodman Meml Theater, grad;Univ of Chicago Ct of Theatre;Univ of MA Amherst, mEd 1978. **CAREER:** Yerma, Yerma, broadway actress; A Hand is on the Gate, broadway actress; Clytemnestra, Agamemnon, off-broadway; Mme Ranyevskaya, The Cherry Orchard; Mother Courage/Mother Courage & Her Childred/Volumnia/Coriolmus; Sister Sonji; Black Visions; Titania & Hippolyta A Midsummer Night's Dream; Poetry & Fold Music of Am Negroes; Medea, Medea; In Whtie Am; Daughter of Indra A Dream Play, stock or touring; Andromache, The Trojan Womena; Ruth, A Raisin in the Sun; Man & Boy, motion pictures; The Angel Levine; The Comedians; Nothing But A Man; The Cool World; To All My Friends on Shore, TV spl. **ORGANIZATIONS:** Mem Actors Equity Assn; Schreen Actors Guild; Am Fed of Radio & TV Artist; Acad of Motion Pictur Aarts & Sci; Am Film Instr; life mem NAACP. **HONORS/ACHIEVEMENTS:** Village Voice & Off-Broadway OBIE awd best perf In White Am 1963-64;Drama Desk Vernon Rice awd 1963-64; Theatre World Awd promising per of the 1965-66 season; Village Voice Off-Broadway OBIE Awd 1965-66; outst contrib in field of arts Alpha Kappa Alpha Awd 1966; AUDELCO Black Theatre Awd Agamemnon 1977; memForensics Soc; 1st place Women's oratory ILS T Oratorical Contest; elected IL StUniv 1st Sweetheart of the Campus. **BUSINESS ADDRESS:** c/o Albert L Shedler CPA, 225 W 34th St, New York, NY 10001.

FOSTER, HENRY WENDELL
Physician. **PERSONAL:** Born Sep 08, 1933, Pine Bluff, AR; son of Henry W Foster and Ivie Hill Watson; married St Clair Anderson; children: Myrna, Wendell. **EDUCATION:** Mrhs Coll, BS 1954; UAR, MD 1958; Rcvng Hosp Dtrt, Intern 1959; Mldn Hosp, Res 1962; Malden Hospital, residency, surgery 1962; George W Hubbard Hospital, residency, OB-GYN 1962-65. **CAREER:** Hbbrd Hosp Nshvl, phys 1962-65; Tskg Inst AL, ob/gyn chf 1965-; JA Andrew Meml Hosp, chf ob & gyn 1965-; Mhry Med Coll Nashville, prof, chmn dept ob/gyn 1973-; Macon Co Hosp Tskg, on staff; VA Hosp Tskg, consult staff. **ORGANIZATIONS:** Mem pres Macon Co Med Soc 1970; AMA; Nat Med Assn; Nat Acad Sci Inst Med; dip Am Bd Ob/Gyn. **HONORS/ACHIEVEMENTS:** Fellow Am Coll Ob & Gyn; Alpha Omega Alpha. **MILITARY SERVICE:** USAF capt 1959-61. **BUSINESS ADDRESS:** Chairman Ob/Gyn Department, Meharry Medical College, 1005 Todd Blvd, Nashville, TN 37208.

FOSTER, JAMES H.
Educator, association executive. **PERSONAL:** Born Jul 20, 1931, Roanoke, AL; married Sallye Maryland Burton; children: James H. **EDUCATION:** Bethune Cookman Coll, BS 1957; Atla U, MA 1963. **CAREER:** Duval Teachers United, Jacksonville FL, asst exec dir 1974-; The Boeing Co, supvr industrial relations 1973-74; Titusville High School, counselor 1964-72; Frederick Douglas High School , prin 1962-63; Wedowee High School, head coach 1961-62; Randolph Co Training School, head coach 1959-61; Woodville Elementary School, prin 1957-59; FL Theater, mgr 1968-69; Sears Roebuck & CO, part-time sales person; General Electric Co & Bendix Corp, summer employment 1967-71. **ORGANIZATIONS:** Mem Titusville Negro Civic & Voters League 1964-67; exec bd dir & employment offcr Classroom Tchrs Assn; Human Rel Com 1969-72; NAACP 1957-; A Phillip Randolph Inst 1973-4; Nat Urban League 1971-; exec bd Titusville Centennial Inc 1966; bd dir YMCA 1969-73; bd dir Brevard Co United Way 1969-74; chrpsn Titusville Hum Rel Commn 1973-74; pres United Black Front, Brevard Co 1972-74. **HONORS/ACHIEVEMENTS:** Tchr of Yr Titusville Jr C of C 1965; ldrshp award United Black Front, Brevard Co 1973. **MILITARY SER-**

VICE: AUS sgt 1st class 1950-53. **BUSINESS ADDRESS:** 103k La Salle St, Jacksonville, FL 32207.

FOSTER, JAMES H.
Clergyman. **PERSONAL:** Born Apr 29, 1938, Valdosta, GA; children: James II. **EDUCATION:** Morris Brown Coll, BA 1960; United Theol Sem, MDiv 1973, STM Cand; Vanderbilt Univ, Doctoral Study. **CAREER:** Migrant Ministry MA Council of Church, chaplain 1962-63; Albany State Coll, dean of chapel 1962-66; Alcorn Coll, chaplain 1966-67; Valdosta City School, dirof soc svc, vstg teacher 1967-69; St James AME Church Pittsburg, asst to pastor 1969-71; Christian Assoc of Metro Erie, assoc dir 1970-72; Wilberforce Univ, chaplain 1972-. **ORGANIZATIONS:** Mem Adv Council, Conf Comm, IN Newman Found, Black Consciousness Comm in Theol Ed, Ministries to Blacks in Higher Ed, Amer Philosophical Assoc; inst rep Comm for Higher Ed Religion Studies; bd mem OIC 1974-77, ARC, Comm Hosp Found 1974-75; mem Optimist Club; chaplain staff Greene Mem Hosp Xenia OH 1979-; consult Oper PUSH 1972-73. **BUSINESS ADDRESS:** Chaplain, WilberforceUniv, Wilberforce, OH 45384.

FOSTER, JAMES HADLEI
Educator, clergyman. **PERSONAL:** Born Apr 29, 1938, Valdosta, GA; son of Rev Arthur Foster, Sr and Willie Mae Wright Foster; married Delores Jackson, Sep 25, 1982; children: Mark Darnell, Arthur. **EDUCATION:** Morris Brown Coll, Atlanta GA, BA, 1960; Pittsburgh (PA) Theological Sem, 1969-70; United Theological Sem, Dayton OH, MDIV, 1973; Vanderbilt Univ, NashvilleTN, DMIN, 1981. **CAREER:** Massachusetts Council of Churches, Boston MA, dept pastoral serv, 1962-63; Albany State College, Albany GA, dean of the chapel/instr, 1962-66; Alcorn State Univ, Lorman MS, chaplain/asst prof, 1966-68; Christian Assoc of Metro Erie, Erie PA, assoc dir, 1970-73; Wilberforce Univ, Wilberforce OH, chaplain/assoc prof, 1973-80; Dartmouth Coll, Hanover NH, assoc chaplain/lecturer, 1980-84; A Better Chance, Boston MA, Northern New England regional dir, 1980-82; Mercy Coll, Dobbs Ferry NY, prof of religion, 1984-. **ORGANIZATIONS:** Mem, Optimist Club, 1975-; assoc pastor, St Mark's AME Church, East Orange NJ, 1985-; mem, Community Relations Commission, NJ Council of Churches, 1985-88; mem, Special Task Force, E Orange Bd of Education, 1985-86; pres, Jersey Chapter, Morris Brown Coll Alumni Assn, 1988-. **HONORS/ACHIEVEMENTS:** LHD Union Coll, 1971. **HOME ADDRESS:** 89 Hawthorne Avenue, East Orange, NJ 07018.

FOSTER, JAMES L.
Attorney. **PERSONAL:** Born Aug 30, 1943, Memphis, TN. **EDUCATION:** Johnson C Smith U, BA Econ 1967;Univ of MD Law Sch, Juris Doc 1970. **CAREER:** Legal Aid Bureau, atty 1970-73; Foster, Moore & Hill, PA, atty & pres 1974-. **ORGANIZATIONS:** Mem Am Bar Assn; mem MD Bar Assn, & Nat Bar Assn; mem Am Arbitration Assn. **MILITARY SERVICE:** Served as an advisor to registrants for selective svc.

FOSTER, JANICE MARTIN
Attorney. **PERSONAL:** Born Jun 14, 1946, New Orleans; married John P. **EDUCATION:** Chestnut Hill Coll, AB 1967; Tulane Law Sch, JD 1970. **CAREER:** Jones Walker Waechter Poitevent Carrere & Denegre Law Firm, atty. **ORGANIZATIONS:** Mem New Orleans, LA & Am Bar Assn; bd dir New Orleans Legal Aid Corp. **BUSINESS ADDRESS:** 225 Baroone St & Floor, New Orleans, LA 70112.

FOSTER, LADORIS J.
Business executive. **PERSONAL:** Born Oct 31, 1933, St Louis, MO. **CAREER:** Johnson Pub Co Inc, Chgo, personnel dir 1972-, rec, sec, admnstrv Asst 1957-72. **ORGANIZATIONS:** Bd mem So Side Comm Art Cntr; adv bd Amtrak; mem Women's Div Chicago Econ Devel Corp. **BUSINESS ADDRESS:** 820 S Michigan Ave, Chicago, IL 60605.

FOSTER, LLOYD L.
Scientist. **PERSONAL:** Born Jul 03, 1930, Austin, TX; married Leatrice Norman; children: Lloyd Jr, Lionel Laird, Lyle Lerone. **EDUCATION:** Huston-Tillotson Coll, BS 1951; Incarnate World Coll, MS 1966; Baylor Sch of Medicine, Cert in Physiology with Modern Instrumentation 1967. **CAREER:** Brooks, AFB, medical tech 1963-64, research chemist 1963-; biologist 1964-70, research chemist 1970-74, educ tech 1974-76; Sch of Aerospace Medicine, Brooks AFB, research chemist. **ORGANIZATIONS:** Biology instructor St Philip's Coll 1966-; Nat Assn for Equal Opportunity in Higher Educ 1977-; Am Chemical Society 1974-. **HONORS/ACHIEVEMENTS:** Academic Achievemnt Huston-Tillotson Coll 1974; Alumni Chap Award Nat Assn of Black Coll 1976. **BUSINESS ADDRESS:** Research Chemist, Sch of Aerospace Medicine, Brooks AFB, San Antonio, TX 78235.

FOSTER, LUTHER H.
Retired executive. **PERSONAL:** Born Mar 21, 1913, Petersburg, VA; son of Luther H Foster Sr (deceased) and Daisy Poole Foster (deceased); married Vera Chandler; children: Adrienne F Williams, Hilton. **EDUCATION:** Virginia State Coll, BS, 1932; Hampton Inst, BS, 1934; Harvard Univ, MBA, 1936; Univ of Chicago, PhD, 1951. **CAREER:** Howard Univ, budget officer, 1936-40; Tuskegee Inst, business mgr, 1941-53, pres, 1953-81; Moton Memorial Inst, chmn & CEO, 1981-87; Tuskegee Univ, pres Emeritus, 1981-. **ORGANIZATIONS:** Dir retired Sears, Roebuck & Co; trustee Acad for Educ Devel; dir United Negro Coll Fund; gov, Joint Center for Political Studies. **HONORS/ACHIEVEMENTS:** Hon degrees, Adams State Coll 1957, The Univ of Liberia 1958, Virginia State Coll, 1959, The Univ of Michigan 1967, Colby Coll, 1971, Loyola Univ of Chicago, 1970, Northeastern Univ, 1974, The Univ of Alabama, 1978, Tuskegee Inst, 1981, Howard Univ, 1983, Winston-Salem State Univ, 1983, Univ of the South, 1984, Hampton Univ, Lincoln Univ, 1985; Alumni Award Hampton Inst, 1974; mem, Alabama Acad of Honor, 1974; Alumni Award, Harvard Business School, 1988; Alumni Medal, University of Chicago 1986.

FOSTER, MILDRED THOMAS
Educational administrator. **PERSONAL:** Born Nov 20, 1927, Pottsville, PA; married Rufus Herbert Jr; children: Vincente Leon, Kathy Maree. **EDUCATION:** SC State Coll, BS 1949; UN U, MS 1959; Clemson U, EdS 1974. **CAREER:** Cherokee County School Dist No 1, elementary prin 1969-; Spartanburg Union & Cherokee County School Districts, head start staff trainer 1969; Cherokee County Head Start, dir 1967-68; Cherokee County School Dist No 1, first grade teacher 1954-67; Spartanburg City Schools SC, first grade teacher 1949-54. **ORGANIZATIONS:** Mem Nat Assn of Elem Sch Adminstr; past sec-treas SC Assn of Elem Sch Prin 1975-76; mem SC Assn of Sch Adminstr 1975-76; mem United Teaching-Prof; Basileus, Lambda Rho Omega Alpha Kappa Alpha Sor 1952-80; mem chmn Cherokee Co Mental Health Assn 1975-80; bd mem Cherokee Co Comm on Alcohol & Drug Abuse 1975-80; bd mem Cherokee Co United Way 1977-80; sec Limestone Coll Bd of Assos; mem SC State Library Bd 1977-81; Ford Found Sci, Bank St Coll 1965. **HONORS/ACHIEVEMENTS:** Pub Article on Head Start in Palmetto Educ Assn Journal 1966; habilitation service award Hablttn Serv Cherokee Co Mentally Retarded 1977; elected woman ofthe year Spartanburg Chap Of Links Inc 1979. **BUSINESS ADDRESS:** Cherokee Co Sch Dist No 1, PO Box 460, Gaffney, SC 29340.

FOSTER, PEARL D.
Physician. **PERSONAL:** Born Oct 23, 1922, New York City, NY; married Charles Hunt, MD; children: Joanne, Patrice. **EDUCATION:** Queens Coll, BS 1943; Howard Univ Med Sch, MD 1948; CW Post 1985 M.P.A. **CAREER:** Ft Monmouth, chem tstr 1943; New York City Health Dept, jr bacteriologist 1943; SAM Lab, employee 1943-44; Freedman's Hosp, 1949-50; Harlem Hosp, resd 1950-53; Private Practice, physician 1953-. **ORGANIZATIONS:** Attending physician internal med Harlem Hosp 1963-; physician Harlem Hosp Ctr 1964; chf ward Harlem Hosp 1963-68; mem Harlem Hosp Ctr Med Bd 1970; asst med Columbia Univ 1968-69; instr Columbia Univ 1972-73; asso Columbia Univ 1972-73; physician in charge United Nations Intl Sch 1961-70; bd trustees UN Intl Sch 1961-64; chmn 1974, vice chmn 1970-74, adv com Home Health Agency 1975-; cont med educ com Hillcrest Gen Hosp 1975; physician in charge Jamaica Day Nursery 1955-81; med consult Div of Soc Hygiene mem Manhattan & Queens Co PSRO; 1st vice pres Amer Coll Quality Assurance Utilization Review; bd certified Amer Bd Quality Assurance & Utilization Review; mem Med Bd Hillcrest Gen Hosp 1973-86; adv com Home Hlth Homemaker Serv 1976-88; mem NMA, AMA, Queens Med Assn Queens Clinical Soc, ; Assn of Former Interns & Resd of Freedman's Hosp; NY Acad of Sci; NY Heart Soc; Amer Pub Hlth Assn; Black Caucus of Harlem Health Workers; mem Exec Bd Howard Univ Med Alumni Assn; mem Med Bd St Joseph 1986-; mem Bd of Professional Med Conduct 1988-. **HONORS/ACHIEVEMENTS:** Distinguished Alumni Awd Queens Coll 1983; publ "Chemotherapy in Neoplastic Diseases"; "Biochem Changes in Neoplastic Diseases"; "Hepatitis in the Drug Addict"; "Hlth & Manpower Devel Corp"; mem Kappa Pi; Cit Alumnae Assn 1958; mem White House Conf on Youth 1970-75; Kappa Pi 1947, Pi Alpha Alpha 1980.

FOSTER, RAUNELL H.
Investigator. **PERSONAL:** Born Feb 25, 1938, Deport, TX; married Hubert. **EDUCATION:** NMUniv Portales NM, BAE 1961; MAUniv of Pacific Stockton CA, 1977. **CAREER:** CA Youth Authority, EEO investigator 1977; Karl Holton School, Stockton CA, teacher 1971-77; Kadena Educ Center, Kadena Air Force Base, Okinawa, dir 1969-71; San Joaquin Dept of Public Asst, Stockton CA, social work supvr 1963-68, social serv worker 1961-63; Blackshear High School, Lamesa TX, teacher 1961. **ORGANIZATIONS:** Mem Phi Delta Kappa AssnUniv of Pacific 1976-; exec bd mem Nat Assn of Blacks In Crim Jus 1975-79; state pres CA Assn of Black Corr Workers 1974-79; sec/dir bd of Christian educ St Matthew CME Ch 1971-; pres Positive Educ Opportunities/Lasting Equality 1973-74; sec A Philip Randolph Inst Stockton CA 1973-75. **HONORS/ACHIEVEMENTS:** Outstanding serv award Communtiy & Family Bapt Women's Orgn 1979; achievements community serv CA Assembly Res CA State Assembly 1978; James E Stratten award Corrections & Comm Serv CA Assn Blk Corr & Wkrs 1978; outstanding comm serv award Bapt Ministerial Union 1977; outstanding com serv award CA Black League of Voters Inc 1980. **BUSINESS ADDRESS:** CA Youth Authority, 4241 Williamsbourgh Dr, Sacramento, CA 95823.

FOSTER, ROBERT DAVIS
Investigator. **PERSONAL:** Born Sep 02, 1929, Brenham, TX; children: Carol Ann, Robert Jr, Michael L. **EDUCATION:** Univ of San Francisco, BS 1974; MA. **CAREER:** Ambrose Park, recreation dir/park supervisor 1968-69; Oakland Public Sch, dir JROTC 1969-74; Chuska Sch Bureau of Indian Affairs, pupil personnel dir 1975-78; Contra Costa Co Medical Ctr, psychologist 1978-79; Equal Employment Oppor Commn, investigator. **ORGANIZATIONS:** Mem bd dirs Concerted Serv 1982-85. **MILITARY SERVICE:** AUS MSG E-8; Bronze Star, Air Medal, Purple Heart. **HOME ADDRESS:** 146 Clearland Dr, Pittsburg, CA 94565. **BUSINESS ADDRESS:** Investigator, Equal Employ Oppor Commn, 1333 Broadway, Wells Fargo Bldg Ste 430, Oakland, CA 94612.

FOSTER, ROBERT LEON
Executive officer. **PERSONAL:** Born Mar 11, 1939, Atlanta, GA; married Ethel Doris Bolden. **EDUCATION:** Morris Brown Coll, BA 1961. **CAREER:** Center for Disease Control HEW, asst exec officer 1978-, asst to dir 1975-78, EEO officer 1972-75. **ORGANIZATIONS:** Mem Phi Beta Sigma Frat; mem NAACP. **HONORS/ACHIEVEMENTS:** Recipient MBC Athletic Hall of Fame. **MILITARY SERVICE:** AUS prc 1962-64. **BUSINESS ADDRESS:** Center for Disease Contrl Dept, 1600 Clifton Rd N E, Atlanta, GA 30333.

FOSTER, RODERICK ALLAN
Professional athlete. **PERSONAL:** Born Oct 10, 1960, New Britian, CT. **EDUCATION:** UCLA. **CAREER:** Phoenix Suns, guard 1983. **HONORS/ACHIEVEMENTS:** Selected second team All-Am and first team All PAC-10; second team Freshman All-Am by Bsktbl Weekly. **BUSINESS ADDRESS:** Phoenix Suns, P O Box 1369, 777 Sports St, Phoenix, AZ 85001.

FOSTER, ROSEBUD LIGHTBOURN
Educational administrator. **PERSONAL:** Born Nov 13, 1934, Miami, FL; married Harris E; children: Harris Emilio II, Sheila Rosebud, Byron Edward, Lorna Lightbourn. **EDUCATION:** Fisk Univ, Chem & Pre-Nursing 1951-53; Meharry Med Coll Nashville, BSN 1956; Wayne State Univ, MS Nursing Ed 1960; Univ of Miami, EdD Higher Ed Admin 1976; Bryn Mawr Coll, Cert Post Grad Residency Inst 1981. **CAREER:** Detroit General Hospital, head nurse 1956-58, 1969-72; Henry Ford Hospital School of Nursing, Detroit MI, instructor 1960-62; Providence Hospital, Southfield MI, asst dir 1962-65; Kirkwood General Hospital, dir of nursing 1967-69; Holy Cross Hospital, asst admin 1960-72; Olivia & Bancroft Extended Care Facilities, consultant 1969-72; Univ of Miami, prof of nursing 1972-73; School of Health & Social Svc, assoc dean 1973-77, dean 1977-78; FL Intl Univ, vice provost Bay Vista Campus, prof 1978-. **ORGANIZATIONS:** Bd mem, exec bd sec Fair Havens Nursing and Retirement Center 1974; bd mem & exec bd officer Health Systems Agency of Southern FL 1976; mem Amer Public Health Assn 1976; mem Public Health Trust of Dade Cty Citizens Adv

Council 1977; mem comm serv comm Delta Sigma Theta 1977; mem Health Educ & Quality of Life Comm N Miami 1980; bd of dir mem Young Men's Christian Assn of Greater Miami, accred visitor Southern Assn of Colleges & Schools 1980; proj mem Nursing Curriculum Proj Kellogg Fdn Southern Region Educ Bd 1981; bd mem New Horizons Community Mental Health Center 1981; mem Mayor's Econ Task Force of N Miami 1981; bd of dir mem Ruth Foreman Theatre 1981; bd of dir mem N Dade Chamber of Commerce 1982; mem N Miami Chamber of Commerce 1982; chairperson Delta Sigma Theta Task Force on Econ Devel of Blk Community 1983; adv bd mem Health Planning Council of Dade & Monroe Counties 1983; dir Culture Fest 1983; mem Art Music, Drama N Dade Proj 1983; bd mem Concerned Citizens of NE Dade Inc 1983; mem Amer Public Health Assn 1983; adv council mem Delta Intl The African Diaspora Natl Planning Comm & Adv Council 1984; comm events grant panel Metro Dade County Council Arts & Sci 1984; bd dir United Home Care Serv. **HONORS/ACHIEVEMENTS:** JC Holman Microbiology Awd, Meharry Med Coll School of Nursing, 1955; Recognition of Outstanding Serv Certificate, Meharry Med Coll; Pres Awd for 25 Yrs of Outstanding Serv to Mankind, 1956-81; Outstanding Nurse Alumni Awd, Coll of Med Dentistry Nursing, Meharry Coll, 1972; Certificate of Appreciation, Health Syst Agency of S Florida, 1979; Certificate of Appreciation for Outstanding Contrib Towards the Devel of Nursing Educ, Amer Hosp of Miami Inc, 1980; Certificate of Appreciation, Lutheran Serv for the Elderly, 1982; Outstanding Professional Achievement Awd, Miami Alumnae Chap, Delta Sigma Theta, 1983; Person of the Year Awd, N Miami Chamber of Commerce, 1984; Public Serv Awd, Outstanding Professional Achievement; Outstanding Women 12 honors 1986; Miami Ballet Soc; Amer Council on Educ; Florida Statewide Coordinator for Women Exec in Higher Educ; North Dade Chamber of Commerce Outstanding Person for Quarter 1987. **BUSINESS ADDRESS:** Vice Provost, Professor, Florida IntlUniv, Tamiami Trail, Miami, FL 33199.

FOSTER, ROY
Professional athlete. **PERSONAL:** Born May 24, 1960, Los Angeles, CA; married Karen; children: Roy Jr. **EDUCATION:** Attended, Southern Cal. **CAREER:** Miami Dolphins, player 1982-. **HONORS/ACHIEVEMENTS:** All-Amer UPI, Football Writers, Football Coaches Assoc, Sporting News; played in Hula Bowl, Olympia Gold Bowl; UPI First-team All-AFC; mem Pro Bowl teams 1986,87. **BUSINESS ADDRESS:** Miami Dolphins, 2269 NW 199 StBlvd, Ste 1440, Opa-Locka, FL 33056.

FOSTER, V. ALYCE
Business executive. **PERSONAL:** Born Feb 06, 1909, Weston, TX. **EDUCATION:** Bishop Coll, BS 1963. **CAREER:** HC Foster Real Estate & Ins Agency & Mortgage Loan Correspondent Golden State Mututal Life Ins Co Los Angeles, owner. **ORGANIZATIONS:** Mem Greater Dallas Bd of Realtors; mem Local State & Nat Assn of Real Est Brokers Inc; past pres & charter mem So Dallas Bus & Professional Women's Club; natl awards chmn Nat Assn of Negro Bus & Professional Women's Clubs Inc; past dir Planned Parenthood of Dallas; adv bd Bishop Coll; life mem YMCA; mem Nat Council of Women of US; Delta Sigma Theta; chmn of trustees St John Bapt Ch; treas & v chmn Highland Village Charitable Found.

FOSTER, WILLIAM K.
Business executive. **PERSONAL:** Born Jun 10, 1933, Pittsburgh, PA; married Dolores J Porter; children: Kimberly Anne, William K. **EDUCATION:** DuquesneUniv Pittsburgh, BA 1963;Univ of WI-MADISON Grad Sch of Banking, 1977;Univ Of WI-MADISON Post Grad Sch of Banking, 1978. **CAREER:** Franklin Fed Savings & Loan Assn, vice pres 1979-; New & World Nat Bank, pres/CEO 1977-79; Pittsburgh Nat Bank, comm banking off 1967-77; Natl Biscuit Co, sales rep 1963-67. **ORGANIZATIONS:** Treas Homewood-Brushton Medical Cntr 1975-76; bd mem Governor's Council on Small Bus 1977; treas Program to Aide Citizens Enterprise 1978-. **HONORS/ACHIEVEMENTS:** Athlete of the year Pittsburgh Optimist Club 1948; airman of the month USAF 1955; good conduct Nationl Service USAF 1956. **MILITARY SERVICE:** USAF air 1st class 1952-56. **BUSINESS ADDRESS:** Marktg/Business Dev Officer, Seaway Natl Bank, 645 East 87th St, Chicago, IL 60619.

FOSTER, WILLIAM PATRICK
Educator, band director. **PERSONAL:** Born Aug 25, 1919, Kansas City, KS; son of Frederick Foster and Venetia Highwarden; married Mary Ann Duncan, Aug 08, 1939; children: William Patrick Jr, Anthony Frederick. **EDUCATION:** Univ of KS, BMus 1937-41; Wayne State U, MA 1947-50; Columbia U, EdD 1953-55. **CAREER:** Lincoln High Sch, dir of bands 1941-43; Ft Valley State Coll, dir of music 1943-44; Tuskegee Inst, dir of bands & orchestra 1944-46; FL A&M Univ, dir of bands 1946-; G Leblanc Corp, advisory bd 1966-; Intl Music Festivals, advisory bd 1970-; McDonald's All Am HS Band, dir 1980-; FL A&M Univ, dir of bands. **ORGANIZATIONS:** Pres Coll Band Dir Nat Assn 1981-83; bd of dir Am Bandmasters Assn 1977-79; pres FL Music Educators Assn 1977-79; bd of dirs, Rotary Club of Tallahassee, 1989-91; bd of dirs, John Philip Sousa Found, 1989-. **HONORS/ACHIEVEMENTS:** Fellowship Genl Educ Bd 1953-55; joint resolution FL House & Senate 1977; Distinguished Serv Award Univ of KS 1973; Distinguished Serv Award Kappa Kappa Psi 1972; Celebrity Roast, Florida A&M Univ Booster Club, 1987; Tallahassee Natl Achievement Award, Easter Seal Soc, 1988; Distinguished Alumni Award, Wayne State Univ, 1988; one million dollar endowed chair named in honor, Florida A&M Univ, 1988; composer of four marches for band, 1987. **BUSINESS ADDRESS:** Dir of Bands & Chmn of the Music Dept, Florida A&M Univ, 1635 Martin Luther King Jr Blvd, Tallahassee, FL 32307.

FOULKS, CARL ALVIN
Physician. **PERSONAL:** Born Jun 10, 1947, Greensboro, NC; married Deborah Casandra Smith; children: Carl Jr, Dion, Cory. **EDUCATION:** Howard Univ Coll of Pharmacy Washington DC, RPh; Howard Univ Medical School, MD. **CAREER:** Providence Hospital, chief resident; Cumberland County Medical Clinic, dir; Private Practice, physician. **BUSINESS ADDRESS:** 407 Owen Dr, Fayetteville, NC 28304.

FOULKS-FOSTER, IVADALE MARIE
Elected official. **PERSONAL:** Born Mar 30, 1922, Sidney, IL; daughter of Warren T Foulks and Edwarda C Martin; married Wardell Foster (deceased); children: Wardella Marie Rouse, Christina Jo. **EDUCATION:** Danville Area Comm Coll, BS Elem Educ 1966. **CAREER:** Laura Lee Fellowship House, jr activities super 1958-66; City of Danville Recreation Dept at Lincoln Park, recreation dir 1968-73; Vermilion Co Health Dept, homemaker/home health aide 1970-73; Sch Dist #118, teachers aide 1973-74; Herb Crawford Multi Agency Inc, sr citizens dir & asst dir 1974-78; East Central IL Area on Aging, reaching out to the elderly trainee 1976-77; East Central IL Area Agency, sr citizen employment spec 1981-82; Vermilion Co, co bd member Dist 8 1980-89, chmn 1988-89. **ORGANIZATIONS:** Past pres present sec Bradley-Maberry Amer Legion Aux 736 1962-; past sec present bd mem Pioneer Ctr for Substance Abuse 1973-; sec Neighborhood House Inc 1975-; precinct comm woman Precinct 26 1978-; pres of Sr Citizens Adv Group Neighborhood House Inc 1980-90; vice pres Vermilion County Council American Legion Auxiliary 1987-88, pres 1988-89. **HONORS/ACHIEVEMENTS:** Most Outstanding Church Pianist, Faithful Worker & Pianist-30 yrs Allen Chapel AME Church Union Missionary Baptist Church 1976 & 1984; Honorary Banquet for Letter Writers to the Editorial Page Editor of the Danville Commercial News 1979 & 1980; 10 Most Outstanding Leaders of Danville, Danville Commercial News Series & Pictures 1981; Outstanding Comm Contributions Danville Branch NAACP 1981; One of 3 of Danville's Outstanding Women nominated by readers and sel by comm of Danville Commercial News 1964; First Black woman elected to serve on the Vermilion Co Bd; re-elected in 1982 for 2 yrs; re-elected in 1984 for 4 yrs; Chaplain of the Vermilion Co Bd in 1981-89. **HOME ADDRESS:** 516 Anderson St, Danville, IL 61832.

FOUNTAIN, VENOAL M., SR.
Chief executive. **CAREER:** Le Font Electronics Corporation, Bridgeport, CT, chief executive, 1983-. **BUSINESS ADDRESS:** Le Font Electronics Corp, Ten Island Brook Ave, Bridgeport, CT 06606. *

FOUNTAIN, WILLIAM STANLEY
Educator. **PERSONAL:** Born Aug 12, 1920, Milford, DE; married Alfredia. **EDUCATION:** BS; BA. **CAREER:** State Dept of Public Instruction, teacher; City of Milford, vice mayor 10 years. **ORGANIZATIONS:** Pres Tri-State Elks, MD, DE, DC. **HONORS/ACHIEVEMENTS:** 1st black v mayor State of DE.

FOUSHEE, GERALDINE GEORGE
Executive secretary. **PERSONAL:** Born Aug 14, 1947, Newark, NJ; daughter of Clarence George; married Joseph E Foushee; children: Chere Michele, Kyle Edward. **EDUCATION:** Essex County Coll, AS (Magna Cum Laude) 1976; Seton Hall Univ, Certificate of Business Mgmt 1977; Rutgers Univ, Certificate of Business Mgmt 1977, BA (Magna Cum Laude) 1981; Jackson State Univ, Jackson, MS, Criminal Justice Admin Certificate 1988; Atlanta Univ, Atlanta, GA, Criminal Justice Certificate 1987. **CAREER:** Essex County Coll, tech asst/admin asst/acting coord of the learning resource ctr 1968-79; Hartford Insurance Group, field claims investigator/adjustor 1979-81; Newark Police Dept, police officer 1981-84; Office of the Sheriff of Essex County, detective/fugitive warrant squad 1984-86; City of Newark Alcoholic Beverage Control, exec sec 1986-. **ORGANIZATIONS:** Mem Lehigh Ave Block Assoc 1969-, Sharpe James Civic Assoc 1975-, New Jersey Notary Public Commn 1980-, North NJ Women in Police 1981-, Bronze Shields Inc 1981-, Natl Black Police Assoc 1981-, Fraternal Order of Police 1981-, Rutgers Univ Alumni 1981-, Intl Assoc of Women Police 1982-, Baton's Inc 1984-; chmn membership comm Essex Co Coll Alumni Assoc 1985-; adv mem DYFS Home Placement Adv Comm 1986-; treas Safety Officers Coalition Newark 1986-; mem NJ Council of Negro Women 1986-, NJ Chap Natl Police Officers Assoc of Amer 1987-; bd of dir, League of Women Voters 1988-; bd of dir, Dayton Community Corp 1988-. **HONORS/ACHIEVEMENTS:** Outstanding Police Awd Bronze Shields Inc 1981; Merit Awd State of NJ Police Training Commn 1981; Police Officer of the Month FOP Lodge #12 1982; Comm Serv Awd Lions Club of Hillside NJ 1984; Police Officer of the Year Central Ward Comm 1984; Law Enforcement Awd Mayor Sharpe James City of Newark 1986; Sheriff's Officer of the Month Essex County Sheriff's Dept 1986; Achievement Awd Bronze Shields Inc 1987; Comm Serv Awd Natl Cncl Negro Women 1987; Achievement Awd Baton's Inc 1987; Natl Police Officers Assn 1988. **HOME ADDRESS:** 150 Lehigh Ave, Newark, NJ 07112.

FOUTZ, SAMUEL THEODORE
Attorney. **PERSONAL:** Born May 03, 1945, Beaumont, TX; son of Freddie James Foutz and Mamie Foutz; married DeVonne Desmerries Draughn; children: Dietra Michelle, Fredrick William. **EDUCATION:** Lamar State Coll of Tech, BS 1967; Howard Univ Sch of Law, JD 1972. **CAREER:** Dallas Legal Serv Found, Inc, atty 1972-74, chief cnsl 1974-76, exec dir 1976-77; Private Law Practice, atty & counselor at law 1978-. **ORGANIZATIONS:** Law clerk Dept of HEW, Office of Gen Coun 1971; Nat Bar Assn 1972-; J L Turner Legal Soc 1972-; Delta Theta Phi Legal Frat 1967-. **HONORS/ACHIEVEMENTS:** Am Jurisprudence Acad Award-property 1972; smith fellow Reginald Heber Smith Fellowship Fdn Inc 1972-75; Personalities of the South 1974; Outstanding Young Men of Am Fuller & Dees 1976. **MILITARY SERVICE:** AUS specialist 5 (E-5) 1967-69; NDSM; VCM; VSM; GCMDL; SPS (M-14); 2 O/S Bars 1967-69. **BUSINESS ADDRESS:** Attorney, Private Practice, 351 W Jefferson Blvd #604, Dallas, TX 75208.

FOWLER, JAMES DANIEL, JR.
Business executive. **PERSONAL:** Born Apr 24, 1944, Washington, DC; son of James D Fowler and Romay Lucas Fowler; married Linda Marie Raiford, May 25, 1968; children: Scott, Kimberly. **EDUCATION:** Howard Univ, Washington DC, 1962-63; US Military Acad, West Point NY, BS, 1967; Rochester Inst Tech, Rochester NY, MBA, 1975. **CAREER:** Xerox Corp, Rochester NY, coord of graduate relations, 1971-74, mgr personnel admin, 1974-75; DP Parker & Assoc Inc, Wellesley MA, sr consul, 1975-76; ITT World Headquarters, New York NY, mgr of staffing, 1976-78; ITT Aetna, Denver CO, vice pres dir of admin 1978; ITT Consumer Financial Corp, Minneapolis MN, sr vice pres dir of admin 1978-84, sr vice pres dir admin & mktg, 1984-87; exec vice pres dir of admin & mktg, 1987-. **ORGANIZATIONS:** Trustee US Military Acad West Point 1978-86, 1987-; mem Assn of MBA Execs; mem Amer Mgmt Assn; mem natl Consumer Finance Assn; mem Twin Cities Personnel Assn; nominating comm US Military Acad West Point; charter mem, mem of Educational Development Committee. **HONORS/ACHIEVEMENTS:** Black Achiever Awd, ITT, 1979. **MILITARY SERVICE:** US Army, capt, 1967-71; Bronze Star w/Oak Leaf Cluster; Army Comm Medal with 2 Oak Leaf Clusters. **BUSINESS ADDRESS:** Exec Vice Pres Dir Admin & Mktg, ITT Consumer Financial Corp, 400 S County Road, Ste 800, Minneapolis, MN 55440.

FOWLER, JOHN D.
Educator. **PERSONAL:** Born Mar 22, 1931, Clinton, NC; son of John D. Fowler and Sallie L. Howard Fowler; married Wilma J. Butler Fowler, Apr 22, 1984; children: Ronald M. Fowler, Valerie D. Fowler Wall, Chirstopher E. Fowler. **EDUCATION:** Winston-Salem Central Univ, honor student 1954; State Univ New Paltz, MA 1974; Northeastern Univ, additional educ studies; NC Central Univ; Univ Of VT. **CAREER:** Mt Pleasant Elementary School,

principal 1955-58; CE Perry High School, teacher 1958-63; W Pender School, 1963-64; Dunbar Elementary School, 1964-65; Hudson City School Dist, asst principal, AV coor 1965-; City School Dist, Rochester NY, vice principal, 1985-. **ORGANIZATIONS:** Mem NY State Reg Plan Assoc; bd of dirs Columbia County Extension Serv; mem Omega Psi Phi Fraternity Inc; life mem NEA; NAACP; former mem Hudson Jr Chamber of Commerce Vice Pres Kiwanis of Greater Hudson; chmn Const By-Laws Com Van Rennselear Div Kiwanis Intl; former chmn 4-H Club Program Com Columbia County; past pres John L Edwards School PTA; City Councilman, 1980-85; County Supervisor, 1985; Lt Governor, Kiwanis International, 1981-82; mem bd of dir, Anthony L Jordan Health Center. **HONORS/ACHIEVEMENTS:** Alumni scholarship Winston-Salem Central Univ 1950; High School Valedictorian of CE Perry School, 1950; 1st black chosen from Columbia County to represent Northeast Synod; chairperson of many committees whiile on city council in Hudson Ny, 1980-85; Administrator of the Year, PTO of #6 School, 1988-89. **HOME ADDRESS:** 247 Maplewood Avenue, Rochester, NY 14613.

FOWLER, LEON, JR.
Dentist. **PERSONAL:** Born Apr 28, 1943, Fayetteville, NC; children: Roderic Lloyd, Lauren Onell. **EDUCATION:** Hampton Inst, BA 1965; HowardUniv Coll of Dentistry, DDS 1969. **CAREER:** Winston Salem, Dentist; HowardUniv Coll of Dent, instr 1969-70. **ORGANIZATIONS:** Mem Am Dental Asso; Natl Dent Asso; Old North St Dent Soc; Am Professional Pract Asso; NC Acad of & Gen Dent; NC Dent Soc; second Dist Dent Soc; Forsyth Cnty Dent Soc; Intl Analgesia Soc; Southeastern Analgesia Soc; Twin Cty Dent Soc; Am Fed of Phys & Dent; mem Better Bus Bur; Forsyth Cnty Econ Dev Corp 1974-75; YMCA 1970-75; bd of dir Salvation Army Boys Club 1974-. **HONORS/ACHIEVEMENTS:** Listed in the directory Dist Amer 1981. **BUSINESS ADDRESS:** 3035 Patterson Ave, Winston-Salem, NC 27105.

FOWLER, QUEEN DUNLAP
Educational administrator. **PERSONAL:** Born in St Louis, MO; children: Darnell Keith. **EDUCATION:** Harris Teachers Coll, BA 1960; St Louis Univ, MEd 1965, PhD 1974, Admin & Superintendency 1977-79. **CAREER:** WA Univ St Louis MO, lecturer & instructor 1975-79, coord field studies 1977-78, asst dir of adm coord of rec & pub rel 1969-79; School Dist of Wellston-Wellston MO, superintendent 1979-84; Pupil Personnel Svcs, exec dir. **ORGANIZATIONS:** Urban League of Metropolitan St Louis 1965-; bd of dir exec bd Girl Scouts Greater St Louis 1978-; bd of dir United Way of Greater St Louis 1979-; natl prog plan comm Amer Assn of School Admin 1982-83; natl adv bd Amer Psych Assoc 1982-86; bd of curators Lincoln Univ Jefferson City MO 1983-87; vice pres Bd of Dirs Metro YWCA 1984-; bd of dirs Natl Assoc of Christians & Jews 1984-88; exec bd Alpha Pi Chi Business & Professional Sor 1984-; regional dir & bd of dirs Delta Sigma Theta Sor Inc 1986-. **HONORS/ACHIEVEMENTS:** Outstanding Contributions in the Field of Psychology King Fanon Comm Mental Health Awd 1980; Volunteer Serv Girl Scout Council of Greater St Louis 1982; Alpha Phi Alpha Outstanding Educator Awd 1982; Disting Leadership United Negro Coll Fund St Louis MO 1983; Comm Serv City of Wellston MO 1983; Disting AlumniHarris-Stowe State Coll St Louis 1983. **BUSINESS ADDRESS:** Executive Dir, Pupil Personnel Services, 5031 Potomac, St Louis, MO 63139.

FOWLER, THADDEUS POSTELLE, JR.
Retired educational administrator. **PERSONAL:** Born in Nevlandville, TX; married Clarice Verdell Gillespie; children: Robert L. **EDUCATION:** TX Coll, BA 1934; McMurry Coll, MEd 1959. **CAREER:** Booker T Washington HS Greenville TX, teacher/coach 1938-41; Loraine Colored School, coach 1943-49, principal/coach 1949-53; Booker T Washington HS Sweetwater TX, principal/coach 1953-63; DW Wallace HS Colorado City TX, principal/coach 1963-66; Colorado City TX Schools, home school coord & liaison 1966-81; cattle rancher. **ORGANIZATIONS:** Mem TX & Southwestern Cattle Raisers Assn 1948-; coach Loraine TX School's Girls Track Team 1949-52; life mem; Natl Ed Assoc 1954-55; life mem TX State Teachers Assoc 1956; mem CO City TX Lions Club 1965-, Mitchell Cty TX Historical Commiss 1966-; reg participant NEA Year of the Non-Conference 1966-67; mem TX Farm Bureau 1967-, Legislation Committee Home School Coord of TX 1968-72, 174-80; reg participant Council for Exceptional Children Convention NY 1968; pres Mitchell Cty Univ Amer Cancer Soc 1970-72, 1978-80; mem House of Delegates Dist XVIII TX State Teachers Assoc 1979, Bd of Trustees TX Coll 1980-; life mem TX Retired Teachers Assn 1981-; mem Permian Historical Soc 1981-; sec CO City TX Lions Club 1982-; pres Mitchell Cty Retired Teachers Assn 1982-84; chmn legislation comm Mitchell Cty Retired Teachers Assn 1984-. **HONORS/ACHIEVEMENTS:** Listed in Personalities of the South 1971-72; Layman Awd Northwest TX Conf Christian Methodist Episcopal Church 1972; Article Mitchell Ctys Negro Heritage 1977; Appreciation Cert Amer Cancer Soc 1978; Service Cert Boy Scouts of Amer. **BUSINESS ADDRESS:** PO Box 249, Loraine, TX 79532.

FOWLER, WILLIAM E., JR.
Chief judge. **PERSONAL:** Born Nov 04, 1921, Akron, OH; married Norma June; children: Claude, John, Diane. **EDUCATION:** Fordham Law Sch, AB LLB. **CAREER:** US Nat Transp Safety Bd, chief adminstrv law judge; Bd Appeals & Review, US cvl serv comm 1966-69; US Dept Labor, trial exam 1964-66; US Dept Justice, spl asst att gen 1961-64; State OH, asst att gen 1959-61; Akron OH, city prosecutor 1956-59. **ORGANIZATIONS:** Pres Federal Adminstrn Law Judges Conference 1974-75; DC Mental Health Assn 1972-74; mem Federal Bar Assn; toastmasters Club 1970-75; dir Fed Bar Assn1972-74; Housing Opportunities Council 1970-74; Amer Bar Assn; Nat Bar Assn; Wash Bar Assn. **HONORS/ACHIEVEMENTS:** 1st black pres Judges Conference; chief judge Natl Transp Saf Bd USN 1942-45. **BUSINESS ADDRESS:** Chief Judge, Natl Transp Saf Board, 800 Independence, SW, Washington, DC 20594.

FOWLKES, DORETHA P.
Real estate administrator. **PERSONAL:** Born Apr 02, 1944, Meherrin, VA; children: Tracey. **EDUCATION:** VA Commonwealth Univ, J Sargeant Reynolds, no degree 1965-82. **CAREER:** RL Williams, sales assoc office mgr 1975-79; Robinson Harris, sales assoc 1979-81; Fowlkes & Ricks, broker pres 1981-. **ORGANIZATIONS:** Pres Ebony Ladies 1975-77; pres Richmond Bd of Realtists 1981-84; bd mem N Richmond YMCA 1983; bd mem Zoning Appeals Bd 1984; bd mem Metro Bus League 1985; pres VA Assoc Realtist 1985-. **HONORS/ACHIEVEMENTS:** Business of Year Metro Business League 1982; Bussiness Assoc of Year Amer Business Women 1984; business person Youth NAACP 1984. **BUSINESS ADDRESS:** President, Fowlkes & Ricks, Inc, 2519 Chamberlayne Ave, Richmond, VA 23222.

FOWLKES, NANCY P.
Social worker. **PERSONAL:** Born Aug 26, Athens, GA; married Vester Guy Fowlkes (deceased); children: Wendy Denise. **EDUCATION:** Bennett Coll for Women, AB 1946; Syracuse Univ, MA 1952; Smith Coll School for Social Work, MSW 1963; Pace Univ, MPA 1983. **CAREER:** Bennett Coll, dir of publ relations 1946-47, 1949-50; VA Ed Bulletin, asst editor 1950-52; Comm Serv Soc NYC, asst ofc mgr 1952-55; W Cty Dept Soc Svc, social caseworker, asst suprv div childrens serv 1959-67; Adoption Svc, suprv 1967-74; Homefinding, suprv 1974-. **ORGANIZATIONS:** Mem Urban League of W 1960-; bd mem Family Serv of W 1961-71; pres Regency Bridge Club 1963-65; mem Acad of Cert Soc Workers 1964-; pres W Chap Jack & Jill of Amer Inc 1965-67; vice pres Regency Bridge Club 1965-67; sec, treas Eastern Reg Jack & Jill of Amer Inc 1967-71; treas United Meth Women 1969-72; chmn, admin bd, pres Womens Soc Christian Serv 1970-72; adv council Adult Ed Ctr White Plains Publ School 1970-; 1st vice pres E View Jr HS PTA 1970-71; mem Intl Platform Assoc 1971; pres Inter Faith Council of White Plains 1971-74; pres United Meth Women 1972-75; lay speaker Trinity United Meth Church 1972-; trustee Trinity United Meth Church 1973-; trustee 1982-, pres 1983- NY Conf United Meth Church; bd of trust NY Conf United Meth Church 1982-; trust 1982, pres 1983- NY Conf United Meth Church. **HONORS/ACHIEVEMENTS:** Schaefer Awd for Distinguished Comm Serv 1963; Recog Plaque Jack & Jill of Amer Inc 1976. **BUSINESS ADDRESS:** Supervisor, Homefinding, 112 E Post Rd, White Plains, NY 10601.

FOWLKES, NELSON J.
Health care marketing executive. **PERSONAL:** Born Dec 26, 1934, Chattanooga, TN; son of Edward B Fowlkes, Sr and Dorothy F Johnson (deceased); married Peggy Jackson, Sep 25, 1957; children: Errol A, Janet Fowlkes-Allen, Nelson Joseph. **EDUCATION:** Central State Univ, BS Chem 1957; Univ of TN, MS Biochem 1970; Pacific Lutheran Univ, attended 1971-74; Consortium of CA Univ & Colls, MPA 1982. **CAREER:** Letterman Army Med Ctr, chief clinical chem 1974-75; MI Biomed Lab, admin asst 1976-78; St Agnes Med Ctr, lab manager 1978-80, planning asst 1980-82, asst dir planning 1982-84, dir rsch & planning 1984-86, dir corporate relations 1986-. **ORGANIZATIONS:** Mem Business Adv Council School of Business 1980-89; treas Alumni Trust Council FSU 1984-89; pres Twentieth Century Golf Club 1985-88; exec dir, Harrison Bryant Kearney Boulevard Plaza, Inc; vice chairman Valley Small Business Devel Corp. **HONORS/ACHIEVEMENTS:** "Corporate Health Risk Mgmt: An Employer's Journal of Health Care Newest Tool to Reduce Health Care Costs" Marketing, March, 1989. **MILITARY SERVICE:** AUS Medical Service Corps ltc 20 yrs; 1st Oak Leaf Cluster to Army Commendation Medal. **BUSINESS ADDRESS:** Director, Corporate Relations, St Agnes Medical Center, 1303 E Herndon Ave, Fresno, CA 93710.

FOX, EVERETT V.
Hospital executive. **PERSONAL:** Born Jun 16, 1915, Richmond, VA. **EDUCATION:** Hampton Inst, BS 1937;Univ of Chgo, MBA 1960; Doctorate Pub Adminstrn NY U, adv study 1972; Grad Prog in Hosp Adminstrn. **CAREER:** NYUniv Med Cntr, clinical asst prof - Preventive Medicine Hosp Adminstrn; NYUniv Hosp, v p, adminstr 1974-; NYUniv Med Cntr, affiliation adminstr 1965-74; Kate Bitting Reynolds Mem Hosp, med serv inves & adminstr 1948-65; Winston Salem, accnt priv prac 1946-48; So Life Ins Co, supvr auditor 1932-41. **ORGANIZATIONS:** First natl pres Nat Assn of Health Serv - Execs; mem Com on Provision of Health Serv Am Hosp Assn; presUniv of Chicago Alumni Assn, mem Am Coll of Hosp Adminstrs; consult Clinical Res Cntr Com Nat Inst of Health HEW; mem Nat Assn Health Serv Execs. **HONORS/ACHIEVEMENTS:** Mem CIAA Conf Basketball Champions Hampton Inst 1936; honor man USN 1941; award of honor Am Hosp Assn Spec Com on Provision of Hlth Serv 1971; Clyde Reynolds Health Exec award Nat Assn of Health Serv Execs 1975; exec of year Nat Assn of Health Serv Exec; mem health team on two week tour of sovietunion observing health progs in four Soviet Union cities. **MILITARY SERVICE:** USN 1941-43. **BUSINESS ADDRESS:** 550 1 Ave, New York, NY 10016.

FOX, JEANNE JONES
Educator. **PERSONAL:** Born Aug 17, 1929, Chicago; married Richard K Jr; children: Jeanne A, Jane E, Helen K. **EDUCATION:** Rosary College, 1947-49; Roosevelt College , 1949-50;Univ MN, BS 1961; Fgn Serv Inst, lang training 1965-68. **CAREER:** Buchanan Elementary School, teacher 1961-62; Washington DC Public Schools, substitute teacher 1962; Petworth Public Library, supvr, library asst 1962-64; US Information Agency, foreign serv & limited reserve officer 1964-65; Radnor Elementary School, teacher 1970-71; Mark Battle Assos Mgmt Cons, sr assoc 1971-73; Joint Center for Political Studies, assoc dir research 1973-. **ORGANIZATIONS:** Mem Urban Mass Transit Adv Panel for The Congress of the US; office tech Assessment 1974; bd mem Meridian Ho Intl 1973; mem, unit leader League WomenVoters 1956-60; mem Pi Lambda Theta Hon Educ Assn; bd dirs Am Sch of Madrid; sec, scholarship chmn Madrid Spain 1968-70; am chmn Spanish Red Cross Drive Madrid 1969; mem Scholarship Com Am Women's Club Madrid 1965-66.

FOX, RICHARD K., JR.
Retired US ambassador. **PERSONAL:** Born Oct 22, 1925, Cincinnati, OH; son of Richard K Fox Sr and Kathryn Lynch Fox; married Jeanne Jones; children: Jeanne Fox Alston, Jane, Helen. **EDUCATION:** Indiana Univ, AB, 1950; Indiana Univ Grad School, Grad Degree, 1950. **CAREER:** Urban Leagues St Louis, St Paul, 1950-56; MN Comm Against Discrimination St Paul, asst dir 1956-61; Dept of State, spec asst to dep asst sec for personnel 1961-63, spec asst to dep under sec for admin 1963-65; US Embassy Madrid, counselor for admin affairs 1965-70; Bur Ed Cultural Affairs, dep asst sec 1973-74; Dept of State, dep dir personnel 1974-76; Sr Semnr in Frgn Policy, mem 1976-77; US Ambassador to Trinidad & Tobago 1977-79; Dept of State, dep inspector gen 1979-83; Meridian House Intl, vp, exec dir visitor prog serv 1983-. **ORGANIZATIONS:** Bd mem, past pres Luth Human Relations Assoc Amer, 1971-76; v chmn Dist Columbia Bd Higher Ed 1972-76; mem, bd of trustees Concordia Sem in ExileSt Louis 1975-77; bd of trustees Univ of DC 1976-77; chmn, bd of dir Wheat Ridge Found Chicago 1979-; pres Amer Foreign Serv Protective Assoc WA 1979-; mem Pres Adv Counc Valparaiso Univ 1979-. **HONORS/ACHIEVEMENTS:** Alpha Kappa Delta Hon Soc Indiana Univ, 1950; Superior Honor Awd Dept of State, 1964,83; Meritorious Honor Awd Embassy Madrid, 1970; Doctor of Laws, Valparaiso Univ, 1983. **MILITARY SERVICE:** USN 1944-46. **BUSINESS ADDRESS:** Senior Vice President and Director, Visitor Program Service, Meridian House Intl, 1624 Crescent Place NW, Washington, DC 20009.

FOX, THEODORE B.
Educator. **PERSONAL:** Born Oct 25, 1912, Jacksonville, AL; married Agnes M Watley; children: Sydney Long, June Davis, Barbara Todd, Sandra Sudduth. **EDUCATION:** Selma

U, student 1929-30; Gen Mtrs Inst, 1935-36; AL State U, cert 1954; Allen Elec Co Sch, 1950; AL A&M U, 1956. **CAREER:** Anniston Army Depot, supvr 1940-46; Anniston Area Vocational Tech, vocational instructor 1946-80; Anniston City Bd of Educ, instructor; First Baptist Church Jacksonville, assoc pastor 1978-; Jackson City Council, mayor-pro-tempore. **ORGANIZATIONS:** Pres Anniston Area Bapt Mins Conf; supt Sunday Sch 1936-72; deacon Bapt Church 1936-77; pres Snowcreek Bapt SS & BTU Congress; scoutmaster 1941-72; pres Jacksonville Civic League 1951; mem AL Educ Assn Nat Assn; mem Jacksonville City Council 1968-; pres Educ Assn of Anniston 1970-71; notary pub;bd dirs Jacksonville Day Care Cntr; Calhoun Co Red Cross; BSA; mem NAACP; Masonic Lodge; mem AL Democratic Conference, East AL Planning Commn. **HONORS/ACHIEVEMENTS:** Recipient Silver Beaver Boy Scout Award 1962; distinguished serv award AL Vocational Assn; outstanding serv award AL NAACP; listed in Who's Who in S &SW 1973-74; Personalities of the S 1973-74, 75. **BUSINESS ADDRESS:** Mayor Pro Tem, Jacksonville City Council, Jacksonville City Hall, 310 Church St SE, Jacksonville, AL 36265.

FOX, THOMAS E., JR.
Attorney. **PERSONAL:** Born Jul 22, 1963, Brooklyn, NY; son of Thomas Fox and Juanita Aquart. **EDUCATION:** Jackson State Univ, Jackson MS, BA, 1988; Harvard Law School, Cambridge MA, JD, 1988. **CAREER:** Natl City Board of Correction, New York NY, asst to counsel, 1985; Harvard Prison Legal Assistance Project, Cambridge MA, student attorney, 1986; Brown & Wood Law Firm, New York NY, summer associate, 1987; Honorable Clifford Scott Green, Philadelphia PA, law clerk, 1988-89; White & Case Law Firm, New York, associate, 1989-. **ORGANIZATIONS:** Mem, Natl Conference of Black Lawyers, 1987-; former pres/chairman, Natl Black Law Students Assn, 1987-88; mem, New York State Bar, 1989-. **HONORS/ACHIEVEMENTS:** Allan Locke Scholar, Educational Foundation of Phi Beta Sigma, 1984; Rhodes Scholar Finalist, State of Mississippi, 1984; Agnes Fellow, NAACP, 1985-86; EarlWarren Fellow, Legal Defense Fund, NAACP, 1985-88. **HOME ADDRESS:** 2101 Chestnut St, #1525, Philadelphia, PA 19103.

FOX, WILLIAM K.
Association executive. **PERSONAL:** Born Sep 25, 1917, Beloit, WI; married Reubans Staltz; children: William, Jr, Katherine. **EDUCATION:** TN, A&I U, BS 1940;Univ Chicago, BD 1943; Butler U, MS; Christian Theol Sem, 1963; Tougaloo Coll, DD 1973. **CAREER:** UCMS, field work war serv 1943; Chicago, asst pastor 1940-43; Religion Ext SCCI Edwards MS, dir 1943-47; TN A & I, dean men, coll chpln, prof history 1947-50; Gay-Les Ch Nashville, pastor 1947-50; Centomucl Ch St Louis, pastor 1950-60; Ch Federation Indpls, dir spec studies 1961-65; NJ Council Chs E Orange, asst to gen sec 1965-69; Tri-City Citizens Econ Union Newark, exec dir 1969-70; Summit Ch Dayton, pastor 1970-72; Gen Office ChristianCh Disciples Christ, asst to gen minister & pres. **ORGANIZATIONS:** Editor Christian Plea 1953-57; asso editor Christian Evangelist 1957-60; interm dir ch planning Ch Fed Indianapolis 1962; Lilly-Endowment Ch Planning Fellow 1961-63; lectr black history Montelar State Coll NJ 1969; mem Panel Urban Ch & Consult Bd Ch Ext Indianapolis 1969-72; adj faculty Urban Ch United Theol Sem Dayton 1971-72; v pres, pres Alumni Council Christian Theol Sem Indianapolis 1974-. **HONORS/ACHIEVEMENTS:** Mem Phi Beta Sigma Frat 1939; Phi Bota Tu Scholastic Hon Soc 1943; Honor Soc CTS 1964; 1969 man of year award Frontiers Intl Club; man of yr Oranges & Maplewood Frontiers Intl Club NJ; first black disciple to receive full fellowship; pres of several local natl regional ch groups 1948-. **BUSINESS ADDRESS:** Box 1986, Indianapolis, IN 46206.

FOXALL, MARTHA JEAN
Nurse, educator. **PERSONAL:** Born Mar 17, 1931, Omaha, NE; married Pitmon. **EDUCATION:** Bryan Mem Hosp Sch of Nursing, RN 1952;Univ of NE Omaha, BSN 1954; MA 1961;Univ of NE Med Cntr, MSN 1976;Univ Of NE Lincoln NE PhD 1979. **CAREER:** Univ of NE Med Cntr Coll of Nursing Omaha, asso prof 1980-; Div of Nurs Midland & Luth Coll Fremont NE, assoc dir 1975-80; Immanuel Med Cntr OmahaNE, asso dir of nursing educ 1968-75; Immanuel Med Cntr Omaha NE, teaching faculty maternity nursing 1953-68. **ORGANIZATIONS:** Lect "Aging & Sexuality" Midland Lutheran Coll 1979-80; chmn CEU com NE League for Nursing 1979-80; research proj dirUniv of NE Med Cntr 1979; memchairperson Com on Mental Health Delta Sigma Theta Sorority 1980; diabetic screening Omaha Area Ch 1978; immunization prog Midland Luth Coll 1977. **HONORS/ACHIEVEMENTS:** Selected to represent US Great Plains Nursing Leaders People to People 1980; faculty reviewer Student Research ForumUniv of NE Med Cntr 1979; mem Sigma Theta Tau; Nat Hon; Soc of Nursing 1979; certification of spl rec NE Nurse's Assn Comm on Nursing Educ 1979; research grantUniv of NE 1978. **BUSINESS ADDRESS:** Associate Professor, University of Nebraska, Medical Center, 4111 Dewey Ave, Omaha, NE 68105.

FOXX, REDD
Comedian. **PERSONAL:** Born Dec 09, 1922, St Louis, MO; children: Debraca. **CAREER:** Began in clubs in NY & Baltimore 1940's; teamed up with Slappy White on black vaudeville circuit for 4 yrs; combined LA nightclub work & sign painting until1955 when he recorded "Laff of the Party", performed 35 more party records for Dooto Records, recorded 14 more party LP's for Loma/Reprise Records; guest appearances on Today Show, Johnny Carson, Merv Griffin, Steve Allen, Mike Douglas, Flip Wilson; specials include "A Time for Laughter"; Soul NBC 1968; film "Cotton Comes to Harlem" 1970; appeared Carnegie Hall 1975; film "Norman is That You?" 1976; top club attraction Las Vegas; star of Redd Foxx Show 1977, Sanford & Son 1972-77,80-81; The Redd Fox Show ABC 1984-85. **HONORS/ACHIEVEMENTS:** Publ "The Redd Foxx Encyclopedia of Black Humor" 1977. **BUSINESS ADDRESS:** c/o ABC-TV, 1330 Ave of Americas, New York, NY 10019.

FOYE-EBERHARDT, LADYE ANTOINETTE
Social worker. **PERSONAL:** Born Aug 15, 1943, Birmingham, AL; daughter of John D Eberhardt and Mary Jean Foye Eberhardt. **EDUCATION:** The Univ of Akron, BA Sociology/Social Work 1976, BA Psychology 1978. **CAREER:** The Univ of Akron, proctor-tutor 1972-78; Cuyahoga Valley Psychiatric Hosp, vocational rehab volunteer 1979-80; Dept of Human Svcs, friendly visitor volunteer 1980-, social worker II 1980-; Akron Dept of Human Services Mgmt, EPSDT, Healthcheck, Children's Medical, social worker 1983-89. **HONORS/ACHIEVEMENTS:** Volunteer Services Award, Dept of Human Services 1980-89. **HOME ADDRESS:** 1359 Orrin St, Akron, OH 44320.

FRANCE, ERWIN A.
Business executive. **PERSONAL:** Born Oct 26, 1938, StLouis, MO; divorced; children: Mark Joseph, Eric Stephen. **EDUCATION:** George Williams College, BS 1959; Loyola Univ, MA 1965; Union Graduate School, PhD 1975. **CAREER:** Mayor Richard J Daley Chicago, admin asst; Model Cities/Chicago Comm on Urban Opportunity, exec dir; Chicago Network of Youth Opportunity Center, dir; IL State Employment Serv in Metro Chicago, deputy dir; Chicago Comm on Youth Welfare, asst exec dir; Chicago Housing Authority, interim exec dir; George Williams Coll, Loyola, Roosevelt & Chicago State Univs, adjunct prof; Erwin A France & Assocs, president. **ORGANIZATIONS:** Mem US delegation United Nations Conf on the Prevention of Crime & Treatment of Delinquents Sweden 1963; mem US delegation studying the development of industrialized housing and new towns in several european countries 1978; leader first delegation of Amer youth permitted to tour People's Republic of China 1973; chmn Section on the Child Intl Conf on Social Welfare Israel 1978; commr Chicago Planning Comm; chmn Housing Task Force; mem Natl Task Force on Perinatal Health Care; life mem Alpha Phi Alpha Fraternity Inc; natl officer Sigma Pi Phi Frat; mem mgmt comm YMCA Camp Pinewood; former chmn bd trustees Congregational Church of Park Manor; mem US Dept of Housing & Urban Develop Secty's Task Force on the Natl Center for Housing Mgmt; dir Project Alpha; Mayor's Lakefront Study Comm; mem Joint Negro Appeal; chap chmn March of Dimes Birth Defects Found; chmn DuSable Museum of Afri-Amer Hist; mem Chicago Arch Asst Ctr; mem Chicago Theological Seminary; mem Sigma Pi Phi, TRUST Inc, Roosevelt Univ, George Williams Coll, Seaway Natl Bank, YMCA, S Side Develop Task Force. **HONORS/ACHIEVEMENTS:** The Ebony Success Library; Outstanding Negroes in Chicago; Affirmative Action Achievement Citation Operation Breadbasket; Excellence Award Operation PUSH; Alumni Achievement Awards Loyola Univ of Chicago, Geo Williams Coll; Man of the Yr 1982 March of Dimes Birth Defects Foundation. **BUSINESS ADDRESS:** President, Erwin A France And Associates, 1 N LaSalle Dr, Suite 2417, Chicago, IL 60602.

FRANCE, FEDERICK DOUG, JR.
Real estate investor, business executive. **PERSONAL:** Born Apr 26, 1953, Dayton, OH; son of Fred France, Sr and Waldine M France, Sr; married Lawrene Susan Hind, May 14, 1988; children: Kristin Renee, Jason Kenneth, Kari Lynn. **EDUCATION:** Ohio State Univ, elem educ major 1971-75. **CAREER:** Professional football player, Los Angeles Rams, Houston Oilers; real estate agent; actor. **ORGANIZATIONS:** Marathon runner; stain glass artist. **HONORS/ACHIEVEMENTS:** Hon mention All-Am Tight End Time Mag; 2nd team NEA; 1st team All-Bag Ten AP; Sporting News NFC All-Stars 1978; Pro Bowl 1977-78; NFC Championship Game 1975, 1976, 1978, 1979; Superbowl XIV 1980. **BUSINESS ADDRESS:** President, A Plus Office Products, 10 Hughes A105, Irvine, CA 92718.

FRANCIS, CHARLES S. L.
Government administrator. **PERSONAL:** Born Sep 13, 1943, Kingston, Jamaica;married Wilma Smith; children: Charles, II, Michael, Erica. **EDUCATION:** CA State U, BS 1970; MCRP 1977. **CAREER:** Fresno Model Cities Program, project devel splst one year; CA State U, part time; Office Admin Mgmt City Fresno, presently admin analyst. **ORGANIZATIONS:** Regional chmn Nat& Assn Planners 1972-75; full mem Am Soc Planning Ofcls 1972-; Mem Central Valley YMCA Board dir 1973-; coordntr State Fed Liason Black Polit Council 1975-; chm Lincoln Elem Sch PTA; mem Affirmative Action Com Fresno Co Bd Edn; pres Alpha Phi Alpha Frat Lota Nu Lambda Chap 1973-75. **HONORS/ACHIEVEMENTS:** Who's Who Am Coll &Univ 1970; Asso Students service & leadership award 1970. **MILITARY SERVICE:** USN 2nd class petty ofcr 1960-64. **BUSINESS ADDRESS:** 2326 Fresno St, City Hall, Fresno, CA 93706.

FRANCIS, CHERYL MARGARET
Association executive. **PERSONAL:** Born Sep 07, 1949, New Orleans; married F Daniel Cantrell. **EDUCATION:** Loyola U, BS 1971;Univ of Chicago, PhD 1975. **CAREER:** Contracting Corp of Amer Educ Admin & Conselors, dir 1979-; Coll of Urban Science, Univ of IL, prof; Natl Com for Cits in Educ, midwest staff; Midwest Admin Center, Univ of Chicago, rsch asst; Supt of Schools, Skokie IL, admin asst 1974; Niles Township Demographic Study, consultant 1974; MW Admin Center, rsch asst 1971-74, dir students serv 1972-73; Upward Bound Proj New Orleans, program dir 1968-70; Headstart, recruiter 1970; Scope Program, teacher 1970. **ORGANIZATIONS:** Bd sec bd dirs Chicago Opps Indsiztn Ctr Inc; Nat Aliance Black Sch Educs; mem Chicago Focus; Am Assn Sch Adminstrs; League Black Women; S Shore Commn; mem Assn for Supervision & Curric; adv panel Nat Inst for Educ Women's Aux for Mary Bartelme Home for Girls; mem Am Educ Research Assn Ford Flwshp Urban Adminstrs 1971; Nat Flwshps Fund Fellow 1974 1974. **HONORS/ACHIEVEMENTS:** Louis J Twomney award Humanitarian Concern 1971; Cardinal Key Hon Soc.

FRANCIS, DAVID ALBERT (PANAMA)
Professional jazz musician. **CAREER:** Studio musician 1952-73; Cab Calloway, band member 1946-52; Lucky Millinder, band member 1940-46; Billy Hicks Sizzling Six, band member 1938-39; Panama Francisand His Savoy Sultans, member/leader 1937-. **HONORS/ACHIEVEMENTS:** Grammy Nominee for Album of the Year in Jazz 1982; "Grooving" (Stash Records) 1982; "The Savoy Sultans Vol I" (Classic Rec) 1980; "Getting in the Groove" (Classic Rec) 1980; Voted The Band of the Year NY Jazz Club 1980; Voted Best Recording of the Year France & England 1980.

FRANCIS, E. ARACELIS
Educator, social worker. **PERSONAL:** Born Dec 02, 1939, St Thomas, Virgin Islands of the United States;daughter of Amadeo I Francis (deceased) and Ethanie Maria Smith Francis. **EDUCATION:** Inter-am U, BA Magna Cum Laude 1960; Univ of Chgo, Sch of SS Admin, MA 1964; Columbia U, Sch of Soc Wrk, DSW 1979. **CAREER:** Adelphi U, Sch of Soc Wrk, asst prof 1971-75; Dept of Social Welfare, exec dir 1975-80; US Dept of Hlth & Human Svcs, h h fellow 1980-81; Univ of MD, Sch of Social Wrk & CP, asst prof 1982-85; Council on Social Work Education, dir minority fellowship prog 1986-. **ORGANIZATIONS:** Mem Amer Public Welfare Assoc 1962-, Acad of Cert Soc Wrkrs 1965-; vice chrmn State Manpower Serv Cncl 1976-80; bd of dir League of Women Voters VI 1977-80, Caribbean Studies Assoc 1981-; pres NASW VI Chap 1978-80; chrmn Comm on Minority Groups, Cncl on Soc Work Ed 1982-85; chrmn Comm on Inquiry NASW Metro DC Chap 1984-86; chairperson Planning Comm NASW 1987 Minority Issues Conference. **HONORS/ACHIEVEMENTS:** Magna Cum Laude Inter Am Univ 1960; NIMH Schlrshp Columbia U, Sch of Social Work 1967-69, CWS Schlrshp 1969-70; HHS Fellow US Dept of Hlth & Human Serv 1980-81; Ed Black Task Force Report, author "Foreign Labor in the US VI". **HOME ADDRESS:** 901 6th St SW, Apt 907, Washington, DC 20024. **BUSINESS ADDRESS:** Director, Minority Fellowship Programs, Council on Social Work Education, 1744 "R" St NW, Washington, DC 20009.

FRANCIS, EDITH V.
Educational administrator. **PERSONAL:** Born Jul 25, 1925, New York, NY; daughter of Mr and Mrs James A Audain; married Dr Gilbert H Francis; children: Deborah Ann Scott MD, Dwayne H, Francis. **EDUCATION:** Hunter Coll, BA, MA Childhood Ed, MS Guidance; NY Univ, EdD Admin. **CAREER:** Ed Dept Media Cntr-Audio Visual Proj Ph I Student Tchr Imp, adj prof 1959-61; St Tchg, instr suprv 1962-63; Elem Schl, tchr 1963-66; Student Tchg Prog, critic tchr 1963-66; Jr/Sr HS, suprv 1967-68; Campus Schls, asst dir 1968-69; Hunter Coll Elem Sch, princ 1968-69; NY City Bd of Ed, consult 1969-70; Except Gifted Chldrn Proj at PS, coord 1970-71; Princeton Reg Schls, princ 1970-76, act spt of schls 1976-77; Hunter Col Dept of Curr & Tchg; adj prof 1971-72; US Dept of HEW, consult 1973-; Ed Testing Serv, tech asst consult 1975-; Ewing Twnshp Pub Schls, supt of schls 1977-87; prof, practitioner/scholar, Teachers Coll, Columbia Univ, New York City. **ORGANIZATIONS:** Pres Princeton Reg Admin Assoc 1974-75; chairperson of ed comm Princeton Bicentennial Comm 1974-77; bd of dir Public Library 1976-77; Witherspoon Devel Corp 1976-82; legislative comm NJ & Amer Assoc of School Admin 1977-; bd of dir YWCA Trenton NJ, 1977-; bd of dir Training School for Boys & Girls 1978-80; intl pres Grand Basileus of Zeta Phi Beta 1980-86; bd of examiners NJ Ed Dept, 1980-; bd of examiners NJ Ed Dept 1980-; bd mem & trustee Natl Assault on Illiteracy 1982-86; bd of dir Helene Fuld Hosp 1982-86; governors task force Trenton NJ 1982-86; bd of dir Natl Merit Scholarship Corp 1982-; Comm on Future Financing of Rutgers State Univ of NJ 1983-88; mem Natl Assoc of Suprv & Curriculum Devel, Natl Council of Admin Women in Ed, NJ Council of Admin Women in Ed, CUNY BLack Professor s & Admin Women in Ed, Amer Assoc of School Admin, Amer Assoc of Univ Prof, Zeta Phi Beta Bd of Dirs, Schoolmasters of NJ, NJ Assoc of School Admin, NJ Ed Assoc, NJ Council of Ed, Phi Delta Kappa. **HONORS/ACHIEVEMENTS:** Hon PhD Humanity of Art Amer Bible Univ 1969; Intl Women's Achvmnt Awd Global News Synd 1970; Woman of the Year, Zeta of the Year 1971; Hon PhD Arts Phil World Univ 1973; NAACP Awd 1978; Honor Awds NJ Dept of Ed, Rider Col, Ewing Cmmty & NJ State Fed Colored Womens Club 1979; Prof Dev Awd Mercer Cty CC 1980; Outstndg Woman Awd NAACP 1980; Awd Trenton St Coll 1980; One of Most Infuential Black Amer, Commendation by Hamilton Twp Mayor, Mansfield M Finney Achvmnt Awd, Ed Awd Gamma Rho Sigma 1981-1984; Black Media Inc citation 1982; Ntl Black Monitor Hall of Fame Awd 1982; NAACP Life Membership Awd 1982; Alpha Kappa Alpha Awd for dedicated service 1982; Friends of United Negro College Fund Awd for Outstanding Ldrshp & Commitment to Furthering Higher Education 1982; Natl Cncl of Women of the US Inc Woman of Conscience Awd 1982; many speaking engagements including Rider Coll, Mercer Cty Com Col, Trenton St Coll, Leadership Conf, Cleveland OH; three publications "Booker T Washington, Temporizer & Compromiser," "Educating Gifted Children," "Gifted Children As We See Them.". **HOME ADDRESS:** 875 Bear Tavern Rd, Trenton, NJ 08628.

FRANCIS, GILBERT H.
Education program specialist. **PERSONAL:** Born May 27, 1930, Brooklyn, NY; married Dr Edith V Audain; children: Dr Deborah Scott Martin, Dwayne H. **EDUCATION:** Mercer Co NJ, licensed substitute teacher; NJ State Civil Serv Commn, Exec Training Inst; Social Security Admin, Oral Communicational Course. **CAREER:** US Dept of Health Educ and Welfare Office of Civil Rights, asst chief elem and secondary educ branch 1967-73; NJ Div of Civil Rights Dept of Law & Public Safety, dir of civil rights 1973-74; Supermarkets Genl Corp, dir equal employ oppor 1974-76; Comprehensive Compliance Svcs, consultant/pres 1976-; NJ State Dept of Educ, educ prog specialist. **ORGANIZATIONS:** Lecturer Niagara Univ, Hunter Coll, Trenton STate Coll, Lehman Coll, Sweet Briar Coll; mem EDGES Group; natl comm co-chairperson Assault on Illiteracy Prog; bd of dirs, chairperson higher educ prog NJ Conf of Branches NAACP; mem Natl Alliance of Black Sch Educators; life mem NAACP; mem Lions Intl, Frontiers Intl; mem legal comm Intl Assoc of Official Human Rights Agencies; mem Natl Assoc of Human Rights Workers, Comm of One Hundred; comm affairsadvisor Hunter Coll Campus Schools NYC; mem Phi Beta Sigma Frat Inc. **HONORS/ACHIEVEMENTS:** NJ Div on Civil Rights Serv Awd; Natl Pan-Hellenic Council Disting Serv Awd; Man of the Year Awd Phi Beta Sigma Frat Inc; Zeta Phi Beta Sor DistingServ Awd; Hon Doctorates World Univ L'Universite Libre, Benedict Coll; Man of the Year Awd Zeta Phi Beta Sor Inc Central NJ; Awds for Serv from the states of MI, OK, TN; Man of the Year Awd Phi Beta Sigma Frat Inc; Citation Who's Who in Govt; Key to the City of Newark NJ; Dr Alvin J McNeil Outstanding Serv Awd Phi Beta Sigma Frat Inc. **MILITARY SERVICE:** AUS corpl 2 yrs; Army Service Medal,. **HOME ADDRESS:** 875 Bear Tavern Rd, Trenton, NJ 08628.

FRANCIS, HENRY MINTON
Government employee. **PERSONAL:** Born Dec 23, 1922, Washington, DC; married Doris E; children: Marsha Jones, H. **EDUCATION:** USMA, BS 1944;Univ of Syracuse, MBA 1960. **CAREER:** Hwrd U, dept of plng; HUD Wash, spec asst to sec; Ofc of Pstmstr Gen, dpty for plns; AVCO Prntng & Publ Div Bstn, vice pres gen mgr; The Rchmnd Organ NY, exec dir vp. **ORGANIZATIONS:** Mem bd dir exec com NAACP; Lgl Def Educ Fund Inc; Jzmbl NY; Crsps Atcks Chldrn's Cntr Bstn; adv bd Prnt Chld Fnd; Boone Yng Assoc; dir at lrg Prntng Ind of New Engl; Beta Gamma Sigma tST ASSN oF US MLTRY ACAD GRAD; ASSN oF SYRCS ARMY CMPTRLRS; URBAN LEAG; Sigma Pi Phi. **MILITARY SERVICE:** RA ofcr 1944-65. **BUSINESS ADDRESS:** Howard University, Department of Planning, Washington, DC 20001.

FRANCIS, JAMES L.
Assistant city manager. **PERSONAL:** Born Dec 30, 1943, Cincinnati, OH; son of James L Francis and Marjorie L Murphy Caliman; married Melanie Hall Francis, Aug 06, 1966; children: Renee L Francis, Darryl L Francis. **EDUCATION:** Ohio Univ, Athens, BA, 1965; Howard Univ, Washington DC, graduate studies, 1966-67; Central Michigan Univ, Mt Pleasant, MPA, 1978. **CAREER:** Govt Employees Insurance Co, Washington DC, claims examiner; City of Dayton, OH, asst to executive dir, supt, div of property management, dir dept of public works, asst city manager. **ORGANIZATIONS:** Mem, Alpha Pi Phi Fraternity, 1963-; mem, Westmont Optimist Club, 1984-; mem, Intl City Managers Assn, 1985-89; mem, Sigma Pi Phi Fraternity, 1986-; bd mem, Natl Forum Black Public Admin, 1987-90. **HONORS/ACHIEVEMENTS:** Readers Digest Foundation, Sister City Technical Assistance Program to Monrovia, Liberia, 1986; Certificate of Merit, Louisville KY, Board of Aldermen, 1988. **BUSINESS ADDRESS:** Assistant City Manager, City of Dayton, 101 West Third Street, City Managers Office, Dayton, OH 45401.

FRANCIS, JOSEPH A.
Clergyman. **PERSONAL:** Born Sep 30, 1923, Lafayette, LA. **EDUCATION:** Catholic Univ Amer, BA, MA; Xavier Univ New Orleans, postgrad; Loyola Univ; Mt St Mary's Coll. **CAREER:** Ordained priest Roman Catholic Ch 1950; St Augustine's Sem, instr & asst dean of stdnts 1951-52; Holy Rosary Inst, asst dir 1952-60; Immaculate Heart of Mary Parish, adminstr 1960; Holy Cross Parish Austin, adminstr 1960-61; Pius X HS, instr 1961-62; Verbum Dei HS Watts CA, fdr & 1st prin 1962-67; Western Province of Soc of the Divine Word, provincial superior 1967-73; Sthrn Province of Soc of the Divine Word Bay St Louis, provicial superior 1973-. **ORGANIZATIONS:** Pres bd mem Conf of Major Superiors of Men in the USA; bd mem Nat Cath Conf of Interracial Justice; Proj Equality; adv bd Nat Ofc for Blk Cath;bd trustees Divine Word Coll Epworth IA; Cath Theol UnionUniv Chgo; mem Bd consult Diocese of Nathchez-Jackson; mem AD HOC Com NCCB on Priestly Ministry Formation; mem Blk Priests Caucus; trustee Immac Concept Sem Mahwah, NJ; bd overseers Harvard Div Sch. **BUSINESS ADDRESS:** 139 Glenwood Ave, East Orange, NJ 07017.

FRANCIS, LIVINGSTON S.
Executive director, chief executive officer, educator. **PERSONAL:** Born Dec 02, 1929, Brooklyn, NY; son of James R Francis and Ethel Price-Francis; married Helen Owensby; children: Brian, Ronald, Gary. **EDUCATION:** Adelpha Univ, Garden City NY, BS, MSW; Columbia Univ, New York NY, Management Certificate. **CAREER:** NYC Parks, Recreation & Cultural Affairs, New York NY, asst to commissioner, 1960-69; Community Council of Greater New York, NY, assoc executive dir, 1970-77; YMCA of Greater NY-Harlem Branch, New York NY, executive dir, 1977-80; Greater New York Fund/United Way, New York NY, deputy executive dir, 1980-86; Livingston S Francis Assoc, pres, Roosevelt NY,1986-; Assoc Black Charities, New York NY, executive dir, 1988-; NY State Univ at Farmingdale, assoc adjunct prof, 1974-76; Adelphi Univ, Garden City NY, adjunct prof, 1976-80; Fordham Univ, New York NY, adjunct prof, 1980-. **ORGANIZATIONS:** Vice chairman, North General Hospital; chairman, Ombudsman Review Board; Reveille Club; Omega Psi Phi. **BUSINESS ADDRESS:** Executive Director, Associated Black Charities, 105 East 22nd Street, New York, NY 10010.

FRANCIS, NORMAN C.
Educator. **ORGANIZATIONS:** Chmn bd Coll Entrance Examination Bd 1976-. **BUSINESS ADDRESS:** President, XavierUniv, New Orleans, LA.

FRANCIS, RAY WILLIAM, JR.
Labor union administrator. **PERSONAL:** Born Jan 22, 1927, New Orleans, LA; son of Ray William Francis, Sr and Ida M Johnson Francis; married Doris A Gill, Mar 20, 1949; children: Ray III, Gerald, Glenn, Robin. **EDUCATION:** Chicago Univ, Chicago, IL, 1961; Labor Educ. **CAREER:** USWA, Chicago, IL, mng editor, 1961-62, grievance com, 1963-65; AFL-CIO, Washington, DC, field representative, 1965-80, asst dir, 1980-86, dir, 1986-. **ORGANIZATIONS:** Mem, Intl Labor Press Assn, 1963-65; pres, Du Sable Alumni Club, 1966-78; exec bd mem, South Shore Comm, 1974; pres, South Shore Little League, 1978-80 vice pres & chmn, Jeffery-Yates Neighbor. **HONORS/ACHIEVEMENTS:** Achievement award, Du Sable Alumni, 1977; A Philip Randolph, Award Muskegan County, 1984, Indiana State A.P.R.I., 1984, Chicago Chapter, 1985, Scott County,Iowa, 1985. **MILITARY SERVICE:** Infantry/Quartermaster, Platoon Sgt, E.T.O., Good Conduct, Infantryman awards. **HOME ADDRESS:** 8010 S Clyde Ave, Chicago, IL 60617.

FRANCIS, RICHARD L.
Physician. **PERSONAL:** Born Oct 10, 1919, Millerton, NY; son of Champ Carter Francis and Irene Virginia Harris; married De Wreathe Valores Green (deceased); children: DeWreathe V, Irene D. **EDUCATION:** Howard Univ, BS 1941; Howard Univ Med School, MD 1944; Sydenham Hosp NY, Internship 1945; VA Hosp Tuskegee AL, Psych Residency 1947-49; Harlem Valley Psych Ctr Wingdale NY, Psych Residency 1955-57; Vanderbilt Clinic Columbia Presbyterian Med Ctr, Psych Residency 1958-59; NY State Psych Inst, Post Grad Psych & Neurology 1960; Syracuse Univ, Advanced Mgmt Training or Admin in Public Health Facilities 1970-71. **CAREER:** NY City Farm Colony Staten Island, resident physician 1945-47; VA Hosp Tuskegee AL, neuropsychiatrist 1947-53; Harlem Valley Psychiatric Ctr Wingdale NY, sr physician 1955; Harlem Valley Psychiatric Ctr, supvr psychiatrist 1955-61; Sunmount Devel Ctr, chief of med svcs; Sunmount Devel Center, Tupper Lake, NY, dir 1968-81; Sunmount Devel Center, Tupper Lake, NY, chief of Medical Services 1981-88. **ORGANIZATIONS:** 1st black asst dir and first black dir NY State Dept of Mental Hygiene Facility, asst dir Harlem Valley Psych Ctr 1961-67, dir Sunmount Devel Ctr 1968-81; sec Mid-Hudson Dist Branch Amer Psych Assoc 1963-67; mem advisory comm North Cty Comm Coll 1968-77; chmn ethics comm Amer Assoc on Mental Deficiency 1971-72; chmn, Narcotic Guidance Council of Tupper Lake NY 1971-76; 1st vice pres Rotary Tupper Lake NY 1973; mem Natl Med Assoc, Amer Assoc of Psych Admin, NY State Med Soc Franklin Cty Med Soc. **HONORS/ACHIEVEMENTS:** Publ "Further Studies in EKG Changes in Old Age" 1947; NY State Qualified Psychiatrist 1959; Cert by Amer Bd of Psych & Neurology in Psych 1970; Licensed Nursing Home Admin 1971; Community Leaders of Amer Awd 1973. **MILITARY SERVICE:** AUS Med Corp capt 1953-55; Natl Defense Serv Med, Army Occupation Med Germany. **HOME ADDRESS:** South Little Wolf Rd, PO Box 1046, Tupper Lake, NY 12986.

FRANCIS, YVETTE FAY
Pediatrician/medical director. **PERSONAL:** Married Olvin McBarnette; children: 6 children. **EDUCATION:** Hunter Coll, BA 1945; Columbia Univ, MA 1946; Yale Univ, MD 1950. **CAREER:** Downstate Univ Med Sch Brooklyn, former instr; NY Hosp Cornell Univ Med Sch; Windham Children's Serv, dir med svc; Jamaica Hosp, attending physician; George & Robert Carter Comm Helath Cntr, dir pediatrics; HEP Program Dist 4 New York City Bd Edn, med dir; St Albans Cntr for Youth & Child Svcs, med dir private practice 1955-83; Sickle Cell Center for Research, med dir. **ORGANIZATIONS:** Amer Med Assn; Natl Med Assn; Queens Cnty Med Soc; Queens Clinical Soc; Amer Bd Pediatrics; Amer Med Women's Assn; sec Found for Rsch & Educ in Sickle Cell Disease; mem Health, Educ & Welfare Adv Comm on Sickle Cell Diseases; NY State Adv Comm on Sickle Cell Disease; mem the Prospective PaymentAssessment Commn of Congress of the US. **HONORS/ACHIEVEMENTS:** Phi Beta Kappa 1945; Alpha Kappa Alpha Sorority 1945. **HOME ADDRESS:** 5413 Graywing Ct, Columbia, MD 21045.

FRANCISCO, ANTHONY M.
City official. **PERSONAL:** Born Jun 30, 1960, Nashville, TN; son of Anceo Francisco and Maurine Francisco; married Kimberly Statum-Francisco, Oct 03, 1987; children: Alexandria Morgan Francisco. **EDUCATION:** Univ of Oklahoma, Norman, OK, BA, 1978-81; 1981; Univ of Texas/Austin, Austin, TX, SPPS, 1981; Syracuse Univ, Syracuse, NY, MPA, 1983.

CAREER: Syracuse Housing Authority, Syracuse, NY, admin aide, 1983; City of Kansas City, MO, mgmt intern, 1983-84; City of Oklahoma City, ok, mgmt/budget analyst, 1984-86; financial enterprise budget officer, 1986-88, dir of street maintenance, 1988-. **ORGANIZATIONS:** Mem, Christian Church (DOC), 1962-; local sec/treasurer, Kappa Alpha Psi Fraternity, 1979-; mem, Intl City Mgmt Assn, 1983-88; mem, Ambassadors' Concert Choir, 1985-; local pres, Natl Forum for Black Public Admin, 1987-.

FRANCISCO, JOSEPH SALVADORE, JR.
Educator, physical chemist. **PERSONAL:** Born Mar 26, 1955, New Orleans, LA; son of Joseph Salvadore Francisco, Sr and Lucinda Baker. **EDUCATION:** Univ of TX at Austin, Austin, TX, BS (Honors), 1977; Massachusetts Inst of Tech, Cambridge, MA, PhD, 1983. **CAREER:** Univ of Sydney, Sydney, Australia, visiting lecturer, 1981; Cambridge Univ, Cambridge, England, research fellow, 1983-85; MA Inst of Tech, Cambridge, MA, provost post doctoral fellow, 1985-86; Wayne State Univ, Detroit, MI, asst prof of chemistry, 1986-. **ORGANIZATIONS:** Faculty advisor, NSU, Nobcche Student Chapter, 1986-; volunteer, Inst Research Appreticeship for Minority High School Students, 1987-; mem, MIT Corp Visiting Comm, 1987-; mem, NASA HBCU Research Panel, 1987-; consultant, Inst for Defense Analysis, 1988-; mem, Amer Physical Soc; mem, AAAS; mem, Natl Org of Black Chemists and Chemical Engineers. **HONORS/ACHIEVEMENTS:** Robert Welch Undergraduate Research Fellow Univ of TX, 1973-76; Jr Fellow, Univ of TX, 1977; HEW Fellow, MIT, 1978-81; Wayne State Faculty Award, Wayne State Univ, 1986; Presential Young Investigator Award, Natl Science Found, 1988; co-author of book, Chemical Kinetics and Dynamics, 1989. **BUSINESS ADDRESS:** Asst Prof of Chemistry, Wayne State Univ, Dept of Chemistry, Rm 33, Detroit, MI 48202.

FRANCISCO, MARCIA MADORA
Information systems consultant. **PERSONAL:** Born Aug 14, 1958, Washington, DC. **EDUCATION:** Univ of MD, BS 1980; Pennsylvania State Univ, MBA 1986. **CAREER:** Sperry Corp, systems analyst 1980-86; Touche Ross, mgmt consultant 1986-. **ORGANIZATIONS:** Mem Amer Mktg Assoc 1980-85; instructor Capital Area Intermediate Unit 1982-85; mem recording sec Delta Sigma Theta Sor 1982-; leader Girl Scouts of Amer 1983-86; mem Data Processing Mgmt Assoc 1987-; network comm mem Natl Black MBA Assoc 1987-; mem Urban League Student-Mentor Program. **HONORS/ACHIEVEMENTS:** Outstanding Young Women of Amer 1985; Outstanding Achievement Dept of Public Welfare Information Systems 1985. **HOME ADDRESS:** 10713 Hampton Mill Terrace, #210, Rockville, MD 20852.

FRANCOIS, EMMANUEL SATURNIN
Surgeon. **PERSONAL:** Born Dec 23, 1938, Pórt-au-Prince, Haiti;son of Saturnin F Ceau and Fausta Lauren Ceau; married Edda Gibbs, Jun 19, 1965; children: Randolph Emmanuel, Herve Daniel, Chantal Claire. **EDUCATION:** Coll St Louis De Gonzague, 1958;Univ of Haiti, 1964; Harlem Hosp Ctr Columbia U, resd 1966-72. **CAREER:** Pvt Prac, surgeon 1973-; Provident Hosp, 1972-73. **ORGANIZATIONS:** Mem Baltimore Cty Med Soc; Med-Chi Soc of MD; AMA; Nat Med Assn; Assn of Haitian Physician Abroad; mem Am Assn for Automotive Med; Trauma Soc; Smithsonian Inst. **MILITARY SERVICE:** AUS maj 1969-71. **BUSINESS ADDRESS:** 1235 E Monument St, Ste 200, Baltimore, MD 21202.

FRANCOIS, TERRY A.
Judge. **PERSONAL:** Born Aug 28, 1921, New Orleans, LA; married Marion L; children: Wade, Gary, Brian, Eric, Carol. **EDUCATION:** Xavier U, New Orleans, BA 1940; Atlanta U, MA 1942; Hastings Coll of Law,Univ of CA, JD 1949. **CAREER:** San Fran FEP Commn, mem 1957-59; City & Cntry of San Fran, mem, bd of supr 1964-78; City Coll of San Fran, lecturer political sci 1967- 75; San Fran Municipal Ct, judge, pro-tem 1982-. **ORGANIZATIONS:** Mem Panel of Arbitrators, AmArbitration Assn; former pres Charles Houston Bar Assn; former pres Multi Culture Inst; mem bd of dir San Fran Legal Aid Soc 1950; pres San Fran NAACP 1959-63; mem bd of dir San Fran Urban League 1950; mem natl bd Catholic Conf for Interracial Justice 1950. **HONORS/ACHIEVEMENTS:** Author Readers Digest article, "A Black Man Looks at Black Racism" 1969; Acting Mayor of San Fran on numerous occasions; 1st Black to Serve on Cnty Bd of Supr in State of CA 1964. **MILITARY SERVICE:** USMC platoon sgt 1942-45; 51st Defense Battalion; one of 1st black to ever serve in USMC. **BUSINESS ADDRESS:** Attorney, Francois & Francois Attorneys, 870 Market St, Ste 608, San Francisco, CA 94102.

FRANCOIS, THEODORE VICTOR
Clinical psychologist/psychoanalyst/clergyman. **PERSONAL:** Born Sep 10, 1938, Brooklyn, NY; son of Theodore V Francois, Sr and Sylvia A Froix Francois. **EDUCATION:** Manhattan Coll, BS 1960; Fordham Univ, MA 1968; Woodstock Coll, MDiv 1970; NY Univ, MA 1975, PhD 1977; NY Univ, post-doctoral certificate in psychoanalysis 1985. **CAREER:** St Francis Acad, guidance counselor 1967-70; NY Univ Med Ctr, intern clinical psych 1973-75; Charity RC Church, assoc pastor 1974; NY Univ Med Ctr, intern rsch psych 1975-76; Coll of Med Downstate Med Ctr SUNY, clinical instr psych 1978-83, clinical asst prof of psych 1983-; Kings Cty Hosp Ctr, sr psych 1978-83, chief psych, psych dir of training 1983-; field supervisor in clinical psychology at Yeshiva Univ 1983- and Pace Univ 1986-; dir of psych serv Kings Cty Hosp Ctr 1988-. **ORGANIZATIONS:** Consult NY Jesuit Provincial 1971-73; co-dir Assoc Black Cath Women of Harlem 1973-75; treas, bd of trust 1974-, mem adv bd of dir 1976-, Dwayne Braithwaite School; consult Natl Black Sisters Conf 1976, Black SJ Caucus; mem of, Natl Assoc Black Psych 1977, Amer Psychological Assoc 1977-, NY Assoc of Black Psychologists 1977-, NY Soc of Clinical Psychologists 1985- NY State Psychological Assoc 1986-, NYU Psychoanalytic Soc 1985-. **HONORS/ACHIEVEMENTS:** NSF Awd Chem 1958-59; Natl Inst Mental Health Traineeship Clinical Psych 1970-73; NYU Philip J Zlatchin Awd in clinical psychology 1978. **HOME ADDRESS:** 507 Macon St, Brooklyn, NY 11223.

FRANK, RICHARD L.
Educator. **PERSONAL:** Born Aug 12, 1931, Utica, NY; divorced; children: 6. **EDUCATION:** Police Sch, 1953; Spl FBI, 1955; Spl Police Training Sch by Chief Gossin, 1960; Spl Police Training Sch by Chief Picola, 1960. **CAREER:** Utica Police Dept, patrolman 1953-55, acting detective 1955-56; NYC, private investigator 1956-57, patrolman 1957-61; Private Business, operator 1961-70; Neighborhood Youth Corps, asst dir; Utica Coll, asst to dean 1970-72, asst dean students 1972-; Utica Coll, acting dean 1974. **ORGANIZATIONS:** Organized chmn Negroes United Comm Devel; developed program innercity youth, dir bd Utica Bus Opportunity Corp; Hiring Hall; Utica Comm Action; chmn Housing Com; candidate City Councilman; mem Mayor's Adv Bd Hosuing; Cancer Soc; Coop Extension Agency Oneida Co Extraordinary Courage & Resourcefulness. **HONORS/ACHIEVEMENTS:** Courage devotion to duty; outstanding athlete. **BUSINESS ADDRESS:** Utica Coll of Syracuse, Burrstone Rd, Utica, NY 13501.

FRANKLIN, ALLEN D.
Educator. **PERSONAL:** Born May 25, 1945, Berkeley, CA. **EDUCATION:** Merritt Coll, AA 1966; San Francisco State U, BA 1969;Univ CA Berkeley, MBA 1971; PhD 1974. **CAREER:** CA State Univ, Hayward School of Business & Economics, pres, assoc dean & asst; Graduate School of Business Administration, Univ of CA Berkeley, instructor 1973-74; Planning Dept City of Hayward, consultant 1973-; Far West Lab, consultant 1972-73; Math & Computing Dept, Lawrence Berkeley Lab, math programmer 1969-71. **ORGANIZATIONS:** Mem Caucus of Black Economists/Nat Econ Assn 1971-; bd dir Minority Bus Assistance Student Develop Found 1974-; institutional Mangmt sci 1972-75; Assn for computing Mach 1972-; adminstrv adv Vol Inc Tax Asst Prog 1973. **HONORS/ACHIEVEMENTS:** Outstanding young man am 1975; cert appreciation The Exchange Club Oakland 1975; cert of hon Bus Majors Assn CA StateUniv Hayward 1974. **MILITARY SERVICE:** USNR petty officer 3c 1967-69. **BUSINESS ADDRESS:** Sch of Bus & Econ, CA State Univ, Hayward, CA.

FRANKLIN, ARETHA
Entertainer. **PERSONAL:** Born Mar 25, 1942, Memphis, TN; children: Clarence, Edward, Teddy, Kecalf. **CAREER:** Renowned vocalist & recording artist; named "Queen of Soul" by fans; recorded first single for Chess Records 1954; recorded with Columbia Records 1961; produced such albums as, The Electrifying Aretha Franklin, Laughing on the Outside, Runnin' Out of Fools, Unforgettable; appeared at Newport Jazz Festival, Lower OH Jazz Festival; recorded first two million-seller albums with Atlantic Records 1967 I Never Loved a Man & Aretha Arrives; other albums include, Lady Soul, Aretha Now, Aretha in Paris, The Tender, The Moving, The Swinging, Live at Filmore West, Young, Gifted & Black, Amazing Grace, Jump To It, I Knew You Were Waiting (For Me); appeared in movie "The Blues Bros" 1980. **HONORS/ACHIEVEMENTS:** Record "Respect" won 10 Grammies; 14 Golden Single Records; 7 Gold Albums; opened Natl Dem Conv with soul version of "The Star Spangled Banner"; named Top Female Vocalist 1967; Number One Female Singer 1968; Radio Artists Best Female Vocalist 1974; Hall of Fame Music Awd; Ebony Mag Black Music Poll 1975; Special Citation SCLC for support of various civil rights & activities; toured US & Europe including command performance for the Queen of England and Prince Charles of Wales & his wife Lady Diana; 1989 Grammy Award for best soul gospel female for "One Lord, One Faith, One Baptism.". **BUSINESS ADDRESS:** c/o Rev Cecil Franklin, 16919 Stansbury, Detroit, MI 48235. *

FRANKLIN, BENJAMIN
Engineer. **PERSONAL:** Born Jan 12, 1934, Pilot Point, TX; son of L T Franklin and Gasie Lee; married Mary Kathryn Bryson; children: Keven Dwayne, Karen Bennett, Benjamin II, Ouida Kathryn. **EDUCATION:** Univ of WA, BArch 1969; Prairie View A&M Univ, BArchEng 1957-. **CAREER:** The Boeing Co, payloads sr engr 1977-; research engr 1957-71; Seattle Opportunities & Insdl Cntr, dir of programs 1971-74; Seattle Opportunities Indsl Center, program mgr 1968-70; Consult Mt Baker Rehab Housing Program. **ORGANIZATIONS:** Life mem Univ of WA Alumni; bd mem Masonic Lodge Martin Luther King Jr Lodge #65; bd mem Randolph Carter Indsl Wkshp; mem Rainier Kawanis; mem Seattle Mental Health; bd mem NW Cncl of Blk Professional Engrs; asso mem Am Inst of Arch; mem Preparedness; connectional bd mem, chaplain, African Methodist Episcopal Church; bd vice pres Primm Tabernacle AME Church; mem Am Defense Preparedness Assn; Boeing advisor to the Jr Achievement Program, 1988, 1989. **HONORS/ACHIEVEMENTS:** Employee Award, 1980, Div Employee of the Quarter, 1985, Group Employee of the Month, 1985, Group Employee of the Year, 1986 & 1988, The Boeing Co, Seattle; lead engr 757-200 Airplane Prog Reuton WA The Boeing Co 1979-; achievement award AME Ch Denton TX 1977; man of the year award Primm Tabernacle AME & Ch Seattle 1966; Seattle Scout award 1972; pride in excell award The Boeing Co Seattle 1969; artist award Prairie View A&M Univ 1956-57. **MILITARY SERVICE:** ROTC Prairie View A&M Univ, 2 yrs.

FRANKLIN, BENJAMIN EDWARD
Federal judge. **PERSONAL:** Born Sep 05, 1922, Mobile, AL; son of Dr and Mrs J A Franklin; married Pauline B Brooks (deceased); children: Alicmarie, Benjamin Jr. **EDUCATION:** XavierUniv of New Orleans, PhB 1947;Univ of Detroit Sch of Law, LLB 1952. **CAREER:** Dist of KS us bankruptcy judge 1976-; bd of pub util of Kansas city, KS atty 1969-76; KS, us atty 1968-69; asst us atty 1961-68; Wyandotte Cnty, asst cnty couns 1957-61; Pvt Pract, atty 1954-61. **ORGANIZATIONS:** Mem bd of dir Am Woodmen Life Ins Co; C of C Kansas City KS 1973-76; unit Fund of KC; KCK Bar Asso; Nat Bar Asso; fed Bar Asso; KS Bar Asso; KS Trial Lawyers Asso; Nat Dist Atty Asso 1963-69; mem Alpha Phi Alpha Frat; Sigma Pi Phi Frat, NAACP; Urban League; Amer Bar Assn. **HONORS/ACHIEVEMENTS:** John Marshall award Dept of Justice 1968; award of excellence KCK Bar Asso 1969; B'Nai B'Rith award Beth Horon Lodge 1969; C Francis Stradford award of Nat Bar Asso 1969. **MILITARY SERVICE:** AUS corpl 1943-46. **BUSINESS ADDRESS:** Chief Judge, United States Bankruptcy Court, District of Kansas, U S Court House, Kansas City, KS 66101.

FRANKLIN, BYRON PAUL
Professional athlete. **PERSONAL:** Born Sep 04, 1958, Florence, AL; married Gail; children: Aston. **EDUCATION:** Auburn. **CAREER:** Buffalo Bills, prof ath.

FRANKLIN, CLARENCE FREDERICK
Manufacturing manager. **PERSONAL:** Born Jan 30, 1945, Knoxville, TN; son of Clarence David Shell and Geraldine Franklin Waller; divorced; children: Carissa Racquel. **EDUCATION:** Tuskegee Inst, attended 1962-63; Univ of TN, attended 1963-64; Cooper Inst, BS Bus Mgmt 1978. **CAREER:** Union Carbide Corp, machinist 1968-79; Martin Marietta Inc, foreman. **ORGANIZATIONS:** VFW 1962; alumni assoc Tuskegee Inst; Optimist Club of Mechanicsville. **HONORS/ACHIEVEMENTS:** Honor Student Campbell High 1962; Honor Student, Cooper Institute 1975-78. **MILITARY SERVICE:** AUS spec 4th class 2 yrs; Vietnam Serv Medals. **HOME ADDRESS:** 1227 Pickett Ave, Knoxville, TN 37921.

FRANKLIN, CLYDE
Electrical engineer. **PERSONAL:** Born May 23, 1929, Rosser, TX; married Ora Lee; chil-

dren: Gary, Lesli. **EDUCATION:** Prairie View A&M Coll, BA 1951; Seattle U, BSEE 1960. **CAREER:** USAF Armarillo TX, technical instr 1952-57; Boeing Airplane Co Seattle WA, engr sr design splst 1957-; NW Council of Black Professional Engr, past pres & founder 1972-73. **ORGANIZATIONS:** Mem WA State Soc of Professional Engr; mem NAACP 1951-. **HONORS/ACHIEVEMENTS:** Engr of month Boeing Airplane Co Jan 1975. **BUSINESS ADDRESS:** Boeing Airplain Co, Renton, WA.

FRANKLIN, COSTELLA M.
Nurse. **PERSONAL:** Born Mar 14, 1932, Durham, NC; divorced; children: Saadia Ardisa, Kevin Leonard, Michale Bernard. **EDUCATION:** Hampton Sch of Nursing, Grad 1953;Univ of CA. **CAREER:** Coronary Care Meml Hosp Long Beach, asst chg nurse 1968-71; Daniel Freeman Hosp, asst head nurse 1960-65; Childrens Hosp LA, asst head nurs 1956-60; Childrens Hosp WA, chg nurse 1955-56; Blue Angels Charity Club Inc, fdr orgnzr 1st pres. **ORGANIZATIONS:** Life mem contrb supp co-owner Blue Angels Sch for Except Children 1968-; chrpsn Banneker Alumni Parent Assn for Developmentally Disabled Adults 1977; mem CA Professional Nurses Assn; CA Counc for the Ratarded; Nat Assn for Retarded Childredn; SW Assn for Retarded Childred; Except Childrens Found Women's Aux; Except Adult Parent Guild; Grtr Carson-Compton Parent Grp; Parent Advocate for Human Civil Legal Rights of the Retarded CA Protection Advocacy Agy. **HONORS/ACHIEVEMENTS:** Distinguished cit award 1977; Who's Who Among Black Am 1976; angel of yr award 1972; cit award for outstand achvmt in comm 1971; merit award Lon Beach Meml Hosp Quality control 1969; CA state senate award Senator James Wedworth 1968; Lane Bryant Vol Citzns Comm Award 1967; LA Press Club Award 1962; Sweetheart of the Yr New Decade 1980; Proclamation from the City of Compton 1980; first vice pres Cultural Affairs Assn of West Indian Am Peoples 1980-81.

FRANKLIN, CURTIS U., JR.
Psychiatrist. **PERSONAL:** Born Oct 30, 1929, Commerce, TX; married Rose Marie Henry; children: Curtis, III, Vicki, Lisa, William, Valerie, Rose Marie, Jr. **EDUCATION:** Prairie View A&M Coll, 2 yrs; Fisk U, AB 1949; HowardUniv Coll of Me D, MD 1953. **CAREER:** Pvt Prac, psychiatry 1967-; Psychiatric Receiving Cntr KC, residency in psychiatry 1964-67; The Doctor's Clinicl KC, practiced internal med 1960-64; Homer G Phillips Hosp, internship residency. **ORGANIZATIONS:** Psychiatric consult to Swope Parkway Health Cntr; Catholic Family & Comm Svc; Vocational Rehabilitation; Social Security Adminstration; asst clinical profUniv of MO-kC Med Sch; diplomate of Am Bd of Psychiatry & Neurology; fellow Am Psychiatric Assn; AMA; Nat Med Assn; MO Med Assn; Jackson Co Med Soc; KC Med Soc; Alpha Phi Alpha. **MILITARY SERVICE:** USAR med corp capt 1955-58. **BUSINESS ADDRESS:** 4301 Main Ste 14, Kansas City, MO 64111.

FRANKLIN, DAVID M.
Attorney, business executive. **PERSONAL:** Born Apr 27, 1943, Atlanta, GA; married Shirley; children: Kai, Cabral, Kali. **EDUCATION:** Morehouse College, BA 1964; Amer Univ Law School, JD 1968. **CAREER:** David M Franklin & Assoc, pres 1975-; Patterson Parks & Franklin, part 1972-75; Warner Bros Films & Records Inc, exec prod; Roberta Flack, Richard Pryor, CIcely Tyson, Loretta McKee, Howard Kenney, Julian Bond, UNAmb, Andrew Young, Mayor Maynard Jackson & Louis Gossett Jr, mgr invst couns. **ORGANIZATIONS:** Consultant, Natl Urban Coalition; Cooperative Assistance Fund; Rockefeller Bros Fund; Ford Found; Field Found; Natl Minority Contractors Conf, 1969-73; Natl Urban Coalition, 1968-70; mem, Amer Bar Assn; Washington DC Bar Assn; Phi Alpha Delta Frat; bd of dir, 20th Century Fund; bd of dir, Emergency Black Land Found; bd of dir, Penn Ctr; bd of dir, Garland Foods; bd of dir, WSOK Radio. **HONORS/ACHIEVEMENTS:** Selected black professional, Black Enterprise Magazine, 1977. **BUSINESS ADDRESS:** President, David M Franklin & Assoc, 401 West Peachtree St, Suite 1505, Atlanta, GA 30308-3228.

FRANKLIN, DOLORES MERCEDES
Dentist/administrator. **PERSONAL:** Born in Washington, DC; daughter of Charles Franklin and Madeline DeLoach Franklin. **EDUCATION:** Barnard Coll, AB 1970; Columbia Univ Sch of Pub Health, MPH 1974; Harvard Sch of Dental Medicine, DMD 1974. **CAREER:** NJ Dental Group, dir dental serv 1974-75; NY Coll of Dentistry, asst dean for student affairs 1975-79; Cook-Waite Labs Sub of Sterling Drug Inc, dental dir 1979-80; Job Corps US Dept of Labor, gen dental consult 1981-82, principal dental consult 1982-85; Columbia Univ, NY Univ, NJ Coll of Dentistry, adj asst prof; DC Commn of Public Health dental coordinator 1985-. **ORGANIZATIONS:** Consult dental headstart Dept HEW 1974-77; consult quality assurance proj Amer Dental Assn; pub health serv 1977; consult Colgate Palmolive Co 1974-76; bd trustees Natl Urban League 1977-80; bd dir/sec Barnard Bus & Professional Women Inc 1977-78; dental adv comm Dept HHS Bureau of Health Care Delivery & Assistance 1986; dental section council, Amer Public Health Assn, 1987-90; consultant, Dept DHHS Year 2000 Oral Health Objectives of the Nation. **HONORS/ACHIEVEMENTS:** Kizzy Award for Image & Achievement Womafest Chicago 1979; Voted one of the 50 Leaders of the Future Editors of Ebony 1978; Dr Milleken Award Best Paper in the Field of Dental Health Harvard Univ 1974; Author/Editor of professional publications including one book Author of Articles; 1st Black Woman Grad Harvard Sch of Dental Med; keynote speaker Equal Oppty Day Dinner Hartford Urban League & United Way 1978; woman and 1st Black Dean NYU Coll of Dentistry;Dept HHS Secty's Outstanding Comm Health Promotion Awd 1986. **BUSINESS ADDRESS:** Dental Coordinator, DC Commission of Public Health, 1660 L St, NW, Suite 802, Washington, DC 20036.

FRANKLIN, EUGENE T., JR.
Association executive. **PERSONAL:** Born Jun 08, 1945, Detroit; married Beverkly King. **EDUCATION:** KY State Coll, BA 1972;Univ Louisville, MEd EPDA Grad 1972. **CAREER:** KY State U, dir Title III project for tchr educ instr 1972-74; Detroit Urban League, dir educ svcs. **ORGANIZATIONS:** Mem Nat Educ Assn; KY Center for Bio-Psychosynthesis; Assn Tchr Educators; Am Inst Econ Research; Detroits Coalition Peaceful Integration; Com Desegregation; former mem Frankfort-Franklin Co Commn Human Rights. **HONORS/ACHIEVEMENTS:** First black houseparents researchers KYC Child Welfare Research Found; responsible research that led to formation KY Sickle Cell Anemia Found 1971; recip grad flwshpUniv Louisville; butzel scholarship Detroit Urban League 1970; deans list KY State U. **MILITARY SERVICE:** AUSR 1966-72. **BUSINESS ADDRESS:** 208 Mack Ave, Detroit, MI.

FRANKLIN, FLOYD
Attorney, educator. **PERSONAL:** Born Dec 26, 1929, Hot Springs; married Myrtle Christy. **EDUCATION:** KY State Coll, BA 1953; CA State Coll, MA 1957; San Fernando Vly Coll, JD 1969. **CAREER:** CA Community Coll, instructor in law. **ORGANIZATIONS:** ABA; CA State Bar Assoc; Langston Law Club; CA Parole Assoc NAACP; bd of dir Legal Aid Found; mem Omega Psi Phi Frat; cosmo Golf Club; pres KY State Club LA Chap 1965-71. **HONORS/ACHIEVEMENTS:** Man yr Omega Psi Phi 1966; supporter yr Urban League & YMCA. **MILITARY SERVICE:** AUS pfc 1950-52. **BUSINESS ADDRESS:** 5140 Crenshaw Blvd, Los Angeles, CA 90043.

FRANKLIN, GRANT L.
Physician. **PERSONAL:** Born Jun 21, 1918, Paul's Valley, OK; married Rita Bruckschlogl; children: Monique, Julie, Grant Jr, Dr Carol Susan. **EDUCATION:** Langston Univ, BS 1941; Atlanta Univ, MS 1947; Meharry Medical College, MD 1951. **CAREER:** Hubbard Hosp, intern 1951-52; Cleveland Veterans Admin and Case Western Reserve Univ Hosps, genl surgical residency 1952-56; Polyclinic Hosp, chief of surgery; Woman's Hosp, chief of surgery; Case Western Reserve Medical Sch, sr clinical instructor of surgery; Cleveland Wade Veterans Admin Hosp, surgical consultant; Private Practice, surgeon; Huron Road Hosp, assoc chief of surgery. **ORGANIZATIONS:** Cert by Amer Bd of Surgery 1957; mem Amer College of Surgeons 1959-, Cleveland Acad of Medicine, Cleveland Surgical Soc, Pan Amer Surgical Soc, Soc of Abdominal Surgeons, Amer Medical Assoc, Ohio Medical Assoc, Cleveland and Natl Medical Assocs, Natl Alumni Assoc of Meharry Medical Coll; mem surgical staffs Lutheran Medical Ctr, St Vincent's Medical Ctr, St Luke's Hosp; mem adv bd Cleveland Foundation; bd of trustees Summer Music Experience; life mem NAACP; mem PUSH. **HONORS/ACHIEVEMENTS:** Honored as Physician of the Year Polyclinic Hosp Reunion; honors extended from Ohio 21st Dist US Congressman Louis Stokes, Cuyahoga Co Commissioners Office, Virgil Brown, and City of Cleveland Council President George Forbes; as trustee of Forest City Hosp was co-presenter of one and one-half million dollars to Eliza Bryant Ctr which is thought to be the largest contribution from one black charitable instution to another in the city and perhaps the nation 1984. **MILITARY SERVICE:** USAF 1st lt 4 yrs. **HOME ADDRESS:** 2599 North Park Blvd, Cleveland Heights, OH 44106. **BUSINESS ADDRESS:** Assoc Dir of Surgery, Huron Road Hospital, 10900 Carnegie Ave, Cleveland, OH 44106.

FRANKLIN, HAROLD A.
Educator. **PERSONAL:** Married Lilla M Sherman. **EDUCATION:** AL State U, AB; Auburn U, MA TuftsUniv Bradeis U, Further Study. **CAREER:** AL State Univ, teacher 1965; Tuskegee Inst, 1965-68; NC A&T Univ, instructor, visiting prof 1969, 1970; AL Serv Center for Black Elected Officials, dir 1969-70; Talladega Coll, asst prof 1968-, counselor, outreach specialist. **ORGANIZATIONS:** Pres NAACP; mem E AL Planning Commn; Talladega County Overall Econ Commn; Black Coalition Talladega; AL Dem Conf Boy Scouts Am; Citizen's Conf on Pub Affairs; AL Hist Commn Bd Advisors; AL League for Adv of Edn; mem bd treas Star Zion AME Zion Ch; bd advisors Community Life Inst ; mem AL Crt Higher Edn; AL Council Human Relations. **HONORS/ACHIEVEMENTS:** Sigma Rho Sigma Honor Soc; community leadership & serv award; Herbert Lehman scholarship. **MILITARY SERVICE:** USAF 1951-58. **BUSINESS ADDRESS:** Counselor/Outreach Specialist, Talladega College, 627 W Battle St, Sylacauga, AL 35160.

FRANKLIN, HERMAN
Educational administrator. **PERSONAL:** Born May 01, 1935, Mayslick, KY; son of Arthur and Margaret; married LaRaeu Ingram; children: Stephen LaMonte. **EDUCATION:** KY State Univ, BS 1960; Tuskegee Univ, MS 1964; Ohio State Univ, PhD 1973. **CAREER:** AL Cooperative Extension Serv, asst co agent 1963-64; Tuskegee Inst, dir adult ed res project 1964-66; AL State Office of Economic Oppor, dir AL techasst corp 1966-70; City of Tuskegee AL, ex dir model cities 1970-71; Office of Minority Affairs, admin assoc 1971-73; TN State Univ, asst prof ext cont educ 1973-74; Tuskegee Inst, dean of students 1974-77; Southern Assoc of Colleges & Schools, consultant 1976-81; Gene Carter and Assoc, consultant/evaluator 1981-83; Middle States Assn of Colleges & Schools, consultant 1981-; US Dept of Educ consultant 1982-83; Univ of MD, vice pres for student affairs. **ORGANIZATIONS:** Charter mem bd of dirs Chair Pub Comm Optimist Intl; mem Lions Intl 1968-70; mem vice chair of bd JJ Ashburn Jr Youth Center 1970-73; chair of comm to reactivate the Chamber of Commerce of Tuskegee 1970, 1974-77; bd of dir-exec bd-vice pres of Chamber of Comm LIons Intl 1975-77, 1976; presenter Student Services Inst 1979-80; presenter Natl Assoc for Equal Oppor in Higher Educ 1979-80; mem of exec bd Boy Scouts of America 1984-. **HONORS/ACHIEVEMENTS:** Graduate Fellowship Tuskegee Inst 1962-63; grad assistantship OH State Univ 1971-73; Patriotic Civilian Awd Tuskegee Inst ROTC 1976; century mem Boy Scouts of Amer 1976, 1977; Outstanding Serv Awd Lower Shore Assoc of Counseling & Develop 1983-84. **MILITARY SERVICE:** AUS E-4 2 yrs. **HOME ADDRESS:** Rte 1 Box 154-A, Pittsville, MD 21850. **BUSINESS ADDRESS:** Vice Pres/Student Affrs, Univ of Maryland Eastern Shore, Backbone Rd Ext, Princess Anne, MD 21853.

FRANKLIN, J. E.
Writer. **PERSONAL:** Born Aug 10, 1937, Houston, TX; daughter of Robert Franklin and Mathie Randle Franklin; children: Olff, Malika. **EDUCATION:** Univ of TX, Austin, TX, BA, 1960; Union Theological Seminary, 1972-73. **CAREER:** City Univ of New York, New York, NY lecturer, 1969-75; Skidmore Coll, Saratoga Springs, NY, dir, 1979-80; Brown Univ, Providence, RI, resident playwright, 1983-89. **ORGANIZATIONS:** Mem, Dramatists Guild, 1971-. **HONORS/ACHIEVEMENTS:** Drama Desk Award, The Drama Desk, 1971; author of Black Girl (play and film,) 1971; author The Prodigal Sister, 1974; Dramatic Arts Award, Howard Univ, 1974; NEA Award, Natl Endowment, for the Arts, 1979; Rockefeller Award, Rockefeller Found, 1980; Writers Guild Award, Writers Guild of Amer, E, 1981; author of Where Dewdrops of Mercy Shine Bright, 1983; author of Borderline Fool, 1988; author of Christchild, 1989. **BUSINESS ADDRESS:** Ms J E Franklin, c/o Victoria Lucas Associates, 888 Seventh Ave, Suite 401, New York, NY 10019.

FRANKLIN, JOHN HOPE
Educator. **PERSONAL:** Born Jan 02, 1915, Rentiesville, OK; son of Buck C Franklin and Mollie Franklin; married Aurelia E Whittington; children: John Whittington. **EDUCATION:** Fisk Univ, AB 1935; Harvard Univ, AM 1936, PhD 1941. **CAREER:** Fisk Univ, hist instr 1936-37; St Augustine's Coll, hist prof 1939-43; NC Coll at Durham, hist prof 1943-47; Howard Univ, hist prof 1947-56; Brooklyn Coll, chmn dept hist 1956-64; Cambridge Univ, Pitt Prof Amer Hist 1962-63; Univ Chicago, prof Amer hist 1964-82; Duke Univ, James B Duke profhist 1982-85, emeritus 1985-. **ORGANIZATIONS:** Mem editorial bd Amer Scholar 1972-76; bd dirs Salzburg Seminar Mus Sci and Industry 1968-80; trustee Chicago

Symphony 1976-80; chmn bd trustees Fisk Univ 1968-74; mem Amer Hist Assn (pres 1978-79); So Hist Assn (pres 1970-71); Orgn Amer Historians (pres 1974-75); Assn for Study Negro Life and History; Amer Studies Assn (past pres); Amer Philos Soc; AAUP; Phi Beta Kappa (senate 1966-, pres 1973-76); Phi Alpha Theta. **HONORS/ACHIEVEMENTS:** Guggenheim Fellow 1950-51, 1973-74; "From Slavery to Freedom, A History of Negro Americans" 6th edition 1987; "Militant South" 1956; "Reconstruction After the Civil War" 1961; "The Emancipation Proclamation" 1963; "A Southern Odyssey" 1976; "Racial Equality in America" 1976; Jefferson Medal 1983; George Washington Williams, A Biography 1985; Clarence Holte Literary Prize 1986; Bunn Award 1987; Haskins Lecturer, ACLS; Cleanth Brooks Medal, fellowship of Southern Writers, 1989; honorary degrees at many universities. **BUSINESS ADDRESS:** History Professor, DukeUniv, Dept of History, Durham, NC 27706.

FRANKLIN, MARTHA LOIS
Senior programmer analyst. **PERSONAL:** Born Nov 14, 1956, Nacogdoches, TX; daughter of William Sanders, Jr and Ida Smith Sanders; divorced. **EDUCATION:** Prairie View A&M Univ, Prairie View, TX, BS, 1980;Amer Inst of Banking, Houston, TX, 1986-87. **CAREER:** Texaco USA, Houston, TX, programmer analyst, 1980-83; Gulf Oil Corp, Houston, TX, sr business analyst, 1983-85; City of Houston, Houston, TX, sr programmer analyst, 1985-86; TX Commerce Bank, Houston, TX, sr programmer analyst, Software Design, Houston, TX, vice pres, 1989-; Pennzoil Co, Houston, TX, sr system analyst, 1988-. **ORGANIZATIONS:** Mem, Ski Jammers, 1985-89; pres, Black Data Processing Assoc, Houston TX, 1985-89; mem, Houston Educ Assn for Reading and Training, 1987-89; mem, Alpha Kappa Alpha, Omicron Tau Omega, 1987-89; mem, Prairie View A&M Alumni, 1988-89; mem, Toastmasters, 1989; vice pres, Software Design, 1989. **HONORS/ACHIEVEMENTS:** Natl Outstanding Sr, 1975. **HOME ADDRESS:** 9822 Paddock Pk, Houston, TX 77002.

FRANKLIN, MILTON B., JR.
Government employee. **PERSONAL:** Born Aug 22, 1950, Cleveland, OH; married Anita Lowe; children: Carla Annette, Milton B. **EDUCATION:** Cuyahoga Comm Coll, Grad. **CAREER:** VA Regional Ofc, vets benefits counselor. **ORGANIZATIONS:** Pres Cleveland Regional Ofc VA Employees Assn 1973-75; chmn Youth Adv Com 1971-72; mem Karamu House Theatre Cleveland OH 1969-73; mgmt Adv Jr Achievement Glenville area Prog 1972-74; vice pres Am Fedn of Govt Employees Local 2823 VA Regional Ofc Cleveland 1975. **HONORS/ACHIEVEMENTS:** Ten outstanding young cit award Cleveland Joycees for Cleveland Area 1973-; award for outstanding community service VA Cleveland 1973; outstanding performance award VA Regional Office Cleveland 1979. **BUSINESS ADDRESS:** 1240 E Ninth St, Cleveland, OH 44199.

FRANKLIN, OLIVER ST. CLAIR, JR.
Public official, publisher. **PERSONAL:** Born Oct 30, 1945, Washington, DC; son of Rev Oliver St Clair Franklin, Sr; married Patricia E Mikols, Jul 07, 1977; children: Julien K Franklin. **EDUCATION:** Lincoln Univ, Lincoln Univ PA, BA, 1966; Edinburgh Univ, Edinburgh Scotland, diploma, 1967; Balliol Coll, Oxford Univ, England, Wilson Fellow, 1967-70. **CAREER:** Univ of Pennsylvania, Annenberg Center, Philadelphia PA, director, 1972-77; independent film producer & critic, 1977-84; City of Philadelphia, PA, deputy city representative, 1987-89; independent publisher, 1989-. **ORGANIZATIONS:** Pres, Oxford & Cambridge Society, 1985-; bd mem, Opera Company of Philadelphia, 1985-; bd mem, Afro-Amer Historical & Cultural Museum, 1985-; dir, Citizens for the Arts, 1985-; bd mem, Institute of Contemporary Art, 1986-; vice pres, Intl Protocol Assn, 1987-; bd of advisors, First Commercial Bank of Philadelphia, 1989-; mem, The Franklin Inn, 1989. **HONORS/ACHIEVEMENTS:** Volunteer of the Year, Volunteer Action Council, 1988; Distinguished Alumni, Natl Assn for Equal Opportunity in Higher Education, 1989. **HOME ADDRESS:** 525 South 41st Street, Philadelphia, PA 19104. **BUSINESS ADDRESS:** President, St Clair, Franklin & Company, The Fidelity Bld, Suite 2600, 123 South Broad St, Philadelphia, PA 19109.

FRANKLIN, PERCY
Manager. **PERSONAL:** Born Jan 01, 1926, Freeport, IL; married Georgette Davis. **EDUCATION:** Western IL U, BS 1950; DePaul, Bus 1961. **CAREER:** MBE Purchasing Motorola Inc, mgr training 1967-; Falstaff Brewing Co, sales 1962-67; Gallo Wines Inc, sales 1960-62; Liggett & Meyers Tobacco Co, sales 1957-60; Chicago Defender Newspaper, sales 1957-60; Chicago Bd of Edn, pub instr 1950-57; Johnson Products Co, sales mgr 1967-70; Motorola Inc, sales mgr 1970-. **ORGANIZATIONS:** Dir athletics prog Catholic Youth Orgn 1950-59; dir athletics prog Mayor Daley Youth Found 1959-74. **BUSINESS ADDRESS:** Motorola, Inc, 1301 E Algonquin Rd, Schaumburg, IL 60196.

FRANKLIN, RENTY BENJAMIN
Scientist, educator. **PERSONAL:** Born Sep 02, 1945, Birmingham, AL; married Gloria J Howard; children: LaTania, Omari. **EDUCATION:** Morehouse Coll, BS 1966; Atlanta Univ, MS 1967; Howard Univ, PhD 1972; Harvard Sch of Medicine, Porter Found Rsch Fellow 1974. **CAREER:** NSF, med educ prog grant reviewer; Morehouse Coll, consultant admission com; Atlanta Univ Center, pre-baccalaureate; Robert Wood Johnson Found, cons; St Augustine's Coll, instructor 1967-69; Howard Univ Coll of Medicine, asst prof 1972-77; Univ of MD Dental School, assoc prof. **ORGANIZATIONS:** Mem Sigma Xi Soc; Amer Physiology Soc; AAAS; NY Acad of Scis. **HONORS/ACHIEVEMENTS:** Outstanding Faculty Rsch Awd Howard Univ Coll of Med 1976; Porter Found Fellowship Awd 1974; author of over 30 sci articles & abstracts. **BUSINESS ADDRESS:** Associate Professor, Univ of MD Dental School, 520 W Lombard St, Baltimore, MD 21201.

FRANKLIN, ROBERT MICHAEL
Educator. **PERSONAL:** Born Feb 22, 1954, Chicago, IL; married Dr Cheryl Diane Goffney. **EDUCATION:** Morehouse Coll/Univ of Durham, England, BA 1975; Harvard Univ Divinity School, MDiv 1978; Univ of Chicago, PhD 1985. **CAREER:** St Paul Church of God In Christ, Chgo, asst pastor 1978-84; St Bernard's Hosp Chgo, prot chaplain 1979-81; Prairie St Coll, Chicago Hts, instr in Psych 1981; Univ of Chgo, instr in Rel & Psych, field ed dir 1981-83; Colgate Rochester Divinty School, dean/prof of Black Church Studies. **ORGANIZATIONS:** Harvard Divinty School, assoc dir/Ministerial Studies 1984-85, lecturer in Ministry 1985-87. **HONORS/ACHIEVEMENTS:** Mem American Acad of Religion, Soc for the Scientific Study of Rel; Assoc for the Sociology of Rel, Soc for the Study of Black Rel; Black Doctoral Fellowship FTE 1978-=80; BE Mays Fellowship FTE 1975-78; Phi Beta Kappa Morehouse Coll 1975; Publications, Union Seminary Qtrly Review 1986, The Iliff Review 1985, Criterion 1984. **BUSINESS ADDRESS:** Dean/Prof of Black Church Std, Colgate Rochester Divinity Sch, Bexley Hall/Crozer Theol Sem, 1100 S Goodman St, Rochester, NY 14620.

FRANKLIN, ROBERT VERNON, JR.
Judge. **PERSONAL:** Born Jan 06, 1926, Toledo, OH; married Kathryn Harris; children: Jeffery, Gary. **EDUCATION:** Morehouse, BA (Cum Laude) 1947; Univ of Toledo, JD 1950; Natl Coll of State Trial Judges, attended; Traffic Inst Northwestern, Univ of Denver, Fordham, attended. **CAREER:** Private practice, attny 1950-60; Toledo OH, prosecuting attny 1953-59, 2nd asst law dir 1959-60; Toledo Mun Ct, judge 1960-69; Lucas Cty Common Please Ct, admin judge 1973-75, judge 1969-. **ORGANIZATIONS:** Mem exec comm OH Common Pleas Judges Assoc; mem Toledo Bar Assoc, Natl Bar Assoc, Lucas Cty Bar Assoc, OH Bar Assoc, Bd of Mgrs, IN Ave YMCA; vice pres Boys Club of Toledo; past pres OH State Conf NAACP, Toledo NAACP; bd of trustees Morehouse Coll, Defiance Coll, Toledo Auto Club, YMCA, Toledo Zoological Soc, St Lukes Hosp; emeritus publ mem Assoc of the US Foreign Svc, Torch Club; pres Scholarship Fund Inc; mem 3rd Babtist Church. **HONORS/ACHIEVEMENTS:** Outstanding Superior & Excellent Judicial Svc, Supreme Ct of State of OH 1972,73,74,75,76; Phi Beta Kappa, Phi Kappa Phi Natl Honor Socs; The Univ of Toledo Gold "T" Awd 1981; 1st BALSA Awd for Excellency in the Field of Law 1983. **MILITARY SERVICE:** AUS 1st sgt 1950-52. **BUSINESS ADDRESS:** Judge, Lucas Cty Common Pleas Court, Lucas Co Courthouse, Toledo, OH 43624.

FRANKLIN, SHIRLEY CLARKE
Government official. **PERSONAL:** Born May 10, 1945, Philadelphia, PA; daughter of Eugene H. Clarke and Ruth Lyons White; divorced; children: Kai Ayanna, Cabral Holsey, Kali Jamilla. **EDUCATION:** Howard Univ, Washington DC, BA, 1968; Univ of Pennsylvania, Philadelphia PA, MA, 1969. **CAREER:** US Dept of Labor, Washington DC, contract officer, 1966-68; Talladega College, Talladega AL, instructor, 1969-71; City of Atlanta, Atlanta GA, director/commissioner of cultural affairs, 1978-81, chief administrative officer, 1982—. **ORGANIZATIONS:** NAACP, National Urban Coalition, Georgia Council for the Arts. **HONORS/ACHIEVEMENTS:** Distinguished alumni award, National Association for Equal Opportunity in Higher Education, 1983; leadership award, Atlanta chapter of NAACP, 1987; Abercrombie Lamp of Learning Award, Abercrombie Scholarship Fund, 1988. **BUSINESS ADDRESS:** City of Atlanta, 55 Trinity St, Atlanta, GA 30335.

FRANKLIN, THOMAS E.
Educator. **PERSONAL:** Born Jan 17, 1947, Youngstown, OH; married Mary Ann Harris; children: Kim, Kelly, Dina, Chadd. **EDUCATION:** Youngstowns State U, BS 1970; Youngstown State U, MS 1977. **CAREER:** W Fed St YMCA, bd dir 1970-71; Youngstown State Univ, asst football coach 1971-73, counselor of black studies 1971-; Kaiser Aluminum Chemical, Corp Spokane WA, industrial relations representative. **ORGANIZATIONS:** Area consultant for Far W Lab of Educ Research & Devel of San Francisco; mem Omega Psi Phi Frat 1967; mem Minority Educ Serv Assn of OH 1975; mem Assn of Coll Unoins Intl 1974; Youngstown StateUniv Grid Vets Assn; rep of Holi-dar Travel Inc; advisor African-Am Student Unoin Youngstown State 1972-. **HONORS/ACHIEVEMENTS:** Outstanding young mem of Am 1971; all sports award Youngstown StateUniv 1970; natl pub relations com Psi Phi Frat 1973-74. **HOME ADDRESS:** 814 W Woodway Ave, Spokane, WA 99218.

FRANKLIN, WAYNE L.
Area manager. **PERSONAL:** Born Jun 07, 1955, Topeka, KS; son of Earl L Franklin and Barbara W Walker Franklin; married Ethel M Peppers, Sep 12, 1981; children: Wayne Michael Franklin, James Nathaniel Franklin. **EDUCATION:** KS State Univ, Manhattan, KS, BS Political Science, 1978. **CAREER:** Kansas State Univ, Manhattan, KS, financial aid counselor, 1976-78; Southwestern Bell Telephone Co, Kansas City, KS, asst mgr-residence serv center, 1978-81; Southwestern Bell Telephone Co, Salina, Abilene & McPherson, KS, mgr-comm relations, 1981-83; Southwestern Bell Telephone Co, Topeka, KS, area mgr, of constituency relations, 1983-. **ORGANIZATIONS:** Past mem, Shawnee County Advocacy on Aging, 1984-88; past pres, Sunset Optimist Club of Topeka, 1984-85; past bd mem, Topeka Jr Achievement, 1984-85; mem, Topeka Chapter NAACP, 1984-; bd mem, Topeka Metropolitan Transit Authority, 1985-; pastor/founder, St Paul Church of God in Christ, 1985-; past bd mem, Private Industry Council-JPTA, 1986-88; mem/past chmn, Mayor's Literacy Commn, 1986-; bd chmn, KS Found for Partnerships in Educ, 1988-89; Lt Governor, KS Optimist Org, 1988-89. **HONORS/ACHIEVEMENTS:** Appreciation of Serv Award, Salina, KS, 1983. **HOME ADDRESS:** 2621 SW Duncan Ct, Topeka, KS 66614. **BUSINESS ADDRESS:** Public Relations Mgr, Southwestern Bell Telephone Co, 823 Quincy, Rm 106, Topeka, KS 66614.

FRANKLIN, WILLIAM B.
Financial consultant. **PERSONAL:** Born May 02, 1948, Brooklyn, NY; married Barbara J Burton; children: Gerald R, Alyce M. **EDUCATION:** New York City Comm Coll, AAS Acct 1971. **CAREER:** Bache & Co Inc, supvr 1966-71; Daniels & Bell Inc, operatios mgr 1971-75; WB Franklin & Assoc, owner 1975-80; Davis/Franklin Planning Group, vice pres 1980-83; Franklin Planning Group, pres 1983-. **ORGANIZATIONS:** Mem NAACP 1975-; council mem South Belma9ür 1982-; mem Intl Assoc of Financial Planners 1982-; bd of dir Monmouth County Black United Fund 1983, Monmouth County Check-Mate Inc Comm Action Agency 1984; pres Kiwanis Club of Belmar 1984; arbitrator, New York Stock Exchange, 1988. **HONORS/ACHIEVEMENTS:** Professional Achievement Award from The Central Jersey Club of NANB & PW Clubs Inc 1985; Outstanding Pres Award Belmar Kiwanis Club 1984; Professional Award for Business Excellence natl Assn of Negro Business and Professional Women's Club of Central NJ.

FRANKS, EVERLEE GORDON
Physician. **PERSONAL:** Born May 11, 1931, Washington; married Ruby H; children: Everlee G Jr, Philip W, Karen J. **EDUCATION:** Howard Univ Coll of Pharmacy, BS 1953; Howard Univ Coll of Medicine, MD 1961. **CAREER:** Private Practice, physician. **ORGANIZATIONS:** Treas 1980-84 Natl Medical Assoc 1965-; vice pres Medico Chirargical Soc of DC 1965-; mem DC Medical Soc 1965-; mem Amer Soc of Internal Medicine 1968-; mem Gordon's Corner Citizens Assoc 1970-; mem Chi Delta Mu Frat grand pres 1984-86. **MILITARY SERVICE:** AUS Sp3 2 yrs. **BUSINESS ADDRESS:** 3230 Pennsylvania Ave SE, #204, Washington, DC 20020.

FRANKS, JULIUS, JR.
Dentist. **PERSONAL:** Born Sep 05, 1922, Macon, GA; son of Julius Franks and Nellie Mae

Solomon Franks; children: Daryl, Cheryl, Bobby, Beverly A Funnye, Fredrick. **EDUCATION:** Univ of MI, BS 1947, DDS 1951. **ORGANIZATIONS:** Exec comm, vp, pres 1951-87; mem Kent County Dental Soc 1951-87; mem MI and Amer Dental Assocs 1951-87; trustee Western MI Univ 1964-82; dir Blvd Memorial Medical Ctr 1974-84; dir United Way Kent County 1987-90. **HONORS/ACHIEVEMENTS:** MI Hall of Honor Univ of MI 1983; Trustee Emeritus Western MI Univ 1983. **HOME ADDRESS:** 1919 Meadow Field NE, Grand Rapids, MI 49505. **BUSINESS ADDRESS:** Dentist, 26 Sheldon SE Ste 506, Grand Rapids, MI 49503.

FRASER, ALVARDO M.
Physician. **PERSONAL:** Born Feb 08, 1922, New York City, NY. **EDUCATION:** Long Island U, BS 1949; NY U, AB 1954; Meharry Med Coll, MD 1959. **CAREER:** CK Post (Alcholica Treatment Cntr) ATC at Centra Islip NY, dir 1979-; Sch Med StateUniv NY, asst prof clinical psychiratry; Mercy Hosp, former asst clinical atdg. **ORGANIZATIONS:** Mem Prince Hall Masonic Lodge. **MILITARY SERVICE:** USAAF 1943-46. **BUSINESS ADDRESS:** 9 Centre St, Hempstead, NY 11550.

FRASER, EARL W., JR.
Business executive. **PERSONAL:** Born Dec 17, 1947, New York, NY; married Alexis L Flint; children: Shawn, Justin. **EDUCATION:** Syracuse Univ, BA Econ 1970; Syracuse Univ Maxwell School, MPA 1970-72. **CAREER:** Syracuse Univ, instr econ 1970-72; Emotionally Disturbed Children Inst for Commun Devel Syracuse, counselor 1973; Syracuse Coop Coll Ctr, asst prof econ 1973; Urban League of Onondaga Cty Syracuse, dir econ devel & employ 1973-74; Shenango Valley Urban League Inc, exec dir 1975-79; Urban League of Gr New Haven Inc, pres. **ORGANIZATIONS:** Spec consult Chrysler Corp New Process Gear Syracuse 1973-74; exec dir 1977-80, 2nd vice pres Eastern Reg Counc of Pres; contrib mem Amer Acad of Polit & Soc Sci 1978-; mem Sharon PA Kiwanis Club 1975-79; mem CT Proj to Increase Mastery of Math 1978-; mem United Way of Greater New Haven Priorities Task Force on Adv & Comm Serv 1979-; assoc fellow Jonathan Edwards Coll Yale Univ 1984-; pres The Grad Club 1979; pres adv counc Quinnipiac Coll; mem Black Tie Soc at Yale; private ind council, bd mem exec comm Govs Comm on Employment of Handicapped; mem New Haven Poverty Commiss; bd mem Foster Grandparents; mayors task force on Ed; editorialist WELI; bd mem School Volunteers; mem S Central Reg Council on Ed for Employment, State Civil Rights Coord Comm; pres, adv bd New Hampshire Coll; mem Natl Council Urban League Exec; pres 1981, adv comm Eli Whitney Reg Tech Vocational School; conn proj Increase Mastery of Math; mem panel New Haven Housing Auth Grievance Panel; mem New Haven Public Schools Dem Ed Task Force. **BUSINESS ADDRESS:** President, Urban League of Gr New Haven, 1184 Chapel St, New Haven, CT 06511.

FRASER, JEAN ETHEL
Educator, artist. **PERSONAL:** Born Aug 20, 1923, New York, NY. **EDUCATION:** The Cooper Union (for advancement of sci & art) NYC, Cert of Grad 1954; Pratt Inst Brooklyn, BFA 1970; Baruch Coll NY, MS. **CAREER:** HS Art & Design, asst art chairperson 1965-; L Rattner Co Advertising & Public Relations NYC, art dir 1958-65; Richards Parents & Murray Ad Agency NYC, artist researcher 1954-58; Alex Wittman Paintings NYC, artist 1950-54; Navy Dept Brooklyn Navy Yard NYC, apprentice engineer, draftsman 1942-45. **ORGANIZATIONS:** Consult & art instr Harlem Parents Com 1966-67; consult & art instr Cooper Union Green Camp Summer Prog 1968-69; alumni council Cooper Union Alumni Council 1973-79; mem NYCATA & NYABE 1970-; faculty adv prod dir HS Art & Design Black Students Drama Group 1974-77; art show judge NAACP NYC/Jamaica Br 1978-79. **HONORS/ACHIEVEMENTS:** Illustrator "Bare Tissue of Her Soul" by Rochelle Folder Edition New York City 1972; group faculty show HS Art & Design at Greenwich Savs Bank 1976-78. **BUSINESS ADDRESS:** 1075 Second Ave, New York, NY 10022.

FRASER, LEON ALLISON
Physician. **PERSONAL:** Born Nov 15, 1921, Winchester, TN; son of Phil E Fraser (deceased) and Dora L Seward Fraser (deceased); married Elizabeth Louise Smith; children: Leon Jr, Keith. **EDUCATION:** Fisk Univ, BA 1948; Howard Univ Sch of Medicine, MD 1952. **CAREER:** Homer G Phillips Hosp St Louis, intern 1952-53, resident 1953-56; NJ State Dept of Health, public health physician 1958-72; dir chronic diseases 1972-75; Trenton NJ Public Schools, medical dir 1982-; Private Practice, internal medicine 1956-. **ORGANIZATIONS:** Mem Mercer Medical Ctr Hospital Staff 1956-, Mercer Co and NJ Medical Socs 1958-, Natl medical Assoc 1965-, Amer Public Health Assoc 1970-; mem Harvard-Radcliffe Parent's Assoc 1971-; mem Grand Boule Sigma Pi Phi Frat 1986-; life mem NAACP, Kappa Alpha Psi; trust Father's Assoc Lawrenceville Prep School 1972-75. **HONORS/ACHIEVEMENTS:** Alumni Achievement Awd Kappa Alpha Psi 1968; published article "Huntington's Chorea, Case Study," 1966; singles tennis champion Mercer County Med Soc 1982. **MILITARY SERVICE:** USN SK 1c 3 yrs. **BUSINESS ADDRESS:** Physician, 671 Pennington Ave, Trenton, NJ 08618.

FRASER, RHONDA BEVERLY
Physical therapist. **PERSONAL:** Born Jul 14, 1960, Watertown, NY; children: Franklin. **EDUCATION:** Howard Univ, BS 1982; Columbia Univ Teacher's Coll, MA 1986. **CAREER:** Perry Point VA Hospital, physical therapist 1982; Manhattan VA Hospital, physical therapist 1982-83; Private Practice, physical therapist; Columbia Univ/Harlem Hospital, sr physical therapist 1983-86. **ORGANIZATIONS:** Mem Alpha Kappa Alpha Sor Inc 1978-, Amer Physical Therapy Assoc 1979-, APTA Private Practice & Comm Health Section 1986-; mem CHARM. **HOME ADDRESS:** 436 Cokesbury Road, Port Deposit, MD 21904.

FRASER, RODGER ALVIN
Physician. **PERSONAL:** Born Feb 14, 1944, Kingston, Jamaica;married Lesley Crosson. **EDUCATION:** Tuskegee Inst, BS 1969; Howard Univ Sch of Medicine, MD 1974. **CAREER:** Hubbard Hosp, residency ob/gyn 1978; Private Practice, ob/gyn. **ORGANIZATIONS:** Fellow Cook County Hospital 1978-79; mem Amer, Natl Medical Assocs; jr fellow Amer Coll of Obstetrics & Gynecology; mem Royal Coll of Ob/Gyn. **HONORS/ACHIEVEMENTS:** Publication "Changes in the Umbilical Cord in Normal & Pre-Eclamptic Pregnancy," Medical News 1975. **MILITARY SERVICE:** USAF Sgt 2 yrs. **BUSINESS ADDRESS:** 377 Roseville Ave, Newark, NJ 07107.

FRASIER, LEROY B.
Retired business executive. **PERSONAL:** Born Mar 06, 1910, Camden, SC; son of Joseph and Rebecca; divorced; children: Leroy, Ralph. **EDUCATION:** SC State Coll, BS 1931. **CAREER:** NC Mutual, retired vice pres agency dir. **ORGANIZATIONS:** Past vice pres Natl Ins Assn; mem NC Humanities Council; mem Durham Co Social Serv Bd; past vice pres Durham United Fund; past vice pres NC Symphony; trust Elizabeth City State Univ; NC United Way; chmn Durham Co Social Serv Bd; chmn trustee Elizabeth City State Univ; life mem NAACP; life mem Alpha Phi Alpha; mem Sigma Pi Phi Fraternity. **HONORS/ACHIEVEMENTS:** Man of the Yr Durham Business Chain 1956; Alumnus of Yr SC State 1975. **HOME ADDRESS:** 715 Massey Ave, Durham, NC 27701.

FRASIER, MARY MACK
Educator. **PERSONAL:** Born May 17, 1938, Orangeburg, SC; married Richard; children: Deirdre Richelle, Mariel Renee. **EDUCATION:** SC State Coll, BS 1958; SC State Coll, MEd 1971;Univ of CT, PhD 1974. **CAREER:** Univ of GA, assoc prof dept of educ, psychology, co-coordinator programs for the gifted 1974-; SC State Coll, dir special serv for disadvantaged students in insts of higher educ 1971-72; Wilkinson High School, Orangeburg SC, instructor Choral Music 1958-71. **ORGANIZATIONS:** Pres GA Fedn-Council for Exceptional Children 1977-78; exec bd Nat Assn for Gifted Children 1977-81; bd of govs The Assn for the Gifted 1978-80; memPi Lambda Theta 1973; mem Delta Sigma Theta Sorority Athens Alumnae Chap 1974-; mem Phi Delta Kappa 1979-. **HONORS/ACHIEVEMENTS:** Ford Found Early Entrant Scholar FiskUniv 1954-55; Who's Who in Am Coll andUniv SC State Coll 1958; Ford Found Advanced Study FellowshipUniv of CT 1972-74;articles pub in "The Gifted Child Quarterly and Exceptional Children"; chap in book "New Voices in Counseling the Gifted" Kendall-Hunt 1979. **BUSINESS ADDRESS:** 325 Aderhold, Athens, GA 30602.

FRASIER, RALPH KENNEDY
Business executive. **PERSONAL:** Born Sep 16, 1938, Winston-Salem, NC; son of Leroy B Frasier and Katheryn Kennedy Frasier; married Jeannine Marie Quick-Frasier; children: Karen Denise Frasier-Money, Gail S Frasier Griffin, Ralph K Jr, Keith L, Marie K, Rochelle D. **EDUCATION:** Univ of NC, 1958; NC Central Univ, BS Commerce 1962; NC Central Univ Schl of Law, JD magna cum laude 1965. **CAREER:** Huntington Natl Bank of Northeast Ohio, Cleveland, OH, vice pres & asst sec, 1983-84; Union Capital Mgmt Corp, Cleveland OH, vice pres & asst sec, 1983-87; Huntington Mortgage Co, dir & sec, 1976-; Huntington Leading Co, dir to sec 1977-; The Huntington Investment Mgmt Co, dir and sec 1978-; Huntington Natl Life Insurance Co, dir & sec, 1980-; Huntington Bancshares Inc, vice pres 1976-86, sec 1981-; Huntington Co, dir and sec 1981-; Seventeen Corp, dir & sec 1981-; The Huntington State Bank, dir and sec 1981-; Huntington Bancshares Financial Corp, dir and sec 1982-; Huntington Natl Bank, Columbus, OH, vice pres & general counsel, 1975-76, sr vice pres, general counsel & sec, 1981-83, exec vice pres, general counsel, sec & cashier, 1983-. **ORGANIZATIONS:** Admitted to bar NC 1965-, OH 1976-; mem, Assn of Bank Holding Cos Lawyers' Comm, 1981-; mem, Amer Soc of Corporate Secs Inc, 1981-; dir, Central Ohio Chap of Amer Corporate Counsel Assn Inc, 1984-; dir, Inroads/Columbus OH Inc, 1985-; dir, Columbus Urban League Inc, 1987-; Ohio Bd of Regents, mem, 1987-96, acad affairs comm, 1987-; advisory comm, Ohio Black Expo, 1988; trustee, Riverside Methodist Hospital Found Inc, Columbus, OH, 1989-; dir, Community Mutual Insurance Co, Cincinnati, OH, 1989-. **MILITARY SERVICE:** US Army, 1958-60; US Army Reserves, 1960-64; Hon Discharge, 1964. **BUSINESS ADDRESS:** Exec Vice Pres/Genl Counsel, Huntington Natl Bank, 41 S High St, PO Box 1558, Columbus, OH 43287.

FRAZER, EVA LOUISE
Physician. **PERSONAL:** Born Jun 30, 1957, St Louis, MO; daughter of Charles Rivers Frazer, Jr and Louise Richardson Forrest; married Steven Craig Roberts, Nov 24, 1984; children: Steven Craig Roberts II. **EDUCATION:** Univ of Missouri, Kansas City MO, BA, MD, 1981; Mayo Grad School of Medicine, Rochester MN, internship, residency 1981-84. **CAREER:** St Mary's Health Center, St Louis MO, physician, 1984-. **ORGANIZATIONS:** Mem, Natl Medical Assn, 1984-; Univ of Missouri, Board of Curators, 1984-. **HONORS/ACHIEVEMENTS:** Kaiser Merit Award; Univ of Missouri Alumni Award, 1985. **BUSINESS ADDRESS:** St Mary's Health Center, 6420 Clayton Road, St Louis, MS 63117.

FRAZIER, ADOLPHUS CORNELIOUS
Educational administrator. **PERSONAL:** Born in Jacksonville, FL; married Mary Charlene; children: Pamela, Eric. **EDUCATION:** FL A&M Univ, BS 1968; Columbia Univ, MA 1975. **CAREER:** Denver Broncos Football Team, prof athlete 1960-64; Lookout Mtn School for Boys Denver CO, principal supvr 1964-67; York Coll of CUNY, professor, 1969-;, dir financial aid. **ORGANIZATIONS:** Mem NAACP, Coalition on Higher Ed 1979; bd of dir Community Bd 12 1979-, Rochdale Village Inc 1981, Jamaica Arts Ctr 1982. **HONORS/ACHIEVEMENTS:** Delegate Queens Cty Judicial Convention 1976-84; Sports Hall of Fame FL A&M Univ 1979; Campaign Aide Pres Carter 1980; Community Serv Awd S Ozone Park Women Assoc 1981; elected District Leader 32nd Assembly Dist Queens County NYC. **MILITARY SERVICE:** AUS pfc 18 months. **HOME ADDRESS:** 172-40 133 Avenue, Jamaica, NY 11434.

FRAZIER, AUDREY LEE
Business executive. **PERSONAL:** Born Sep 04, 1927, Charleston, WV; married Edward Paul; children: Dwayne Lewis, Paul Vincent. **EDUCATION:** WV State Coll, 1945-47. **CAREER:** Audrey Frazier Inc, pres; Key Creations Inc(mfg), vp/gen mgr 1972-73; Audrey Frazier Enterprises Inc (Mfg), pres 1969-71; Pearlgreen-S&T Supply Co (Hardward & Co), office mgr 1965-69. **ORGANIZATIONS:** Chairperson women's com Nat Assn Black Mfrs 1978-80; chairperson-com on communications Economic Rights Calition 1979-80; co-chairperson State of NY WhiteHouse Conf on Small Bus 1980; asst sec Minority Caucus-White House Conf on Small Bus 1980; del from State of NY Small Bus Unity Com 1980. **HONORS/ACHIEVEMENTS:** Woman of the year The Harlem Mothers Assn 1970; woman of the year Utility Club Inc 1970; outstanding services Women's Com Nat Assn of Black Mfrs 1979; woman of the year NABM 1979. **BUSINESS ADDRESS:** 671 West 162nd St, New York, NY 10032.

FRAZIER, CHARLES DOUGLAS
Educator, coach. **PERSONAL:** Born Aug 12, 1939, Houston, TX; married Betty Alridge. **EDUCATION:** TX So U, BS 1964; TX So U, MS 1975. **CAREER:** TX Christian U, receivers coach 1976-;Univ of Tulsa, receivers coach 1976; Rice U, receivers coach 1975; Houston

Oilers & New Eng Patriots, prof football player 1962-70. **ORGANIZATIONS:** Mem Football Coaching Assn; mem Hiram Clark Civic Club. **HONORS/ACHIEVEMENTS:** Mem Record-Setting US 400-meter Relay Team 1962; mem AFL All-Star Team AFL 1966; mem Helms NAIA Hall of Fame for Track & Field LA 1969. **BUSINESS ADDRESS:** TX ChristianUniv, Dept of Athletics, Fort Worth, TX 76129.

FRAZIER, CLIFFORD B.
Broker, consultant. **EDUCATION:** Langston Univ, Modesto Jr Coll, Grant Tech Coll, Sacramento State, CA Davis State Coll, attended. **CAREER:** CB Frazier Realty, real estate broker & consultant 1953-. **ORGANIZATIONS:** Consul No CA Bapt Conv, United Christian Ctrs Greater Sacramento, Shiloh Arms Housing Proj, UCC Proj Devel Corp Housing Prog; mem Comm Welfare Council Sacramento, United Crusade Sacramento, Del Paso Robla Neighborhood Council, United Christian Ctrs; vice pres Cit Adv Comm; Shiloh Baptist Ch; commnr Ann Land Bertha Herschel Comm; former mem DPH C of C; past chrprsn DPH PAC 3 yrs; life mem NAACP; mem N Sacramento Rotary; chrprsn Comm Svcs. **MILITARY SERVICE:** USAF WW II 1946; Korean War. **BUSINESS ADDRESS:** PO Box 38499, Sacramento, CA 95838-0499.

FRAZIER, DAN E., SR.
Elected official & clergyman. **PERSONAL:** Born Dec 23, 1949, Ypsilanti, MI; son of Horace Frazier and Mattie Frazier; married Evelyn Westbrook; children: Dennis, Sharron, Evelyn, Daniel Jr. **EDUCATION:** Linfield Coll; LaVerne Univ; Portland State Univ. **CAREER:** NY Life Insurance Co, field underwriter 1976-78; Dorite Gen Contractor, owner-oper 1978-80; Carter Memorial Church, assoc pastor 1981-84; Abundant Life Ministries, pastor/founder 1984-; City of San Bernardino, city councilman. **ORGANIZATIONS:** Bd mem San Bernardino Redevelop Agency 1983-; mem NAACP San Bernardino; corporate bd mem San Bernardino Comm Hosp; political affairs chair Inland Empire Interdenominational Ministrial Alliance. **HONORS/ACHIEVEMENTS:** Million Dollar Round Table Club NY Life Insurance Co; brought first to city San Bernardino Comm based police station 1983; comm achiever A Phillip RandolphInst San Bernardino Chapt; chosen Most Influential Metropolitan Precinct Reporter Black in the Inland Empire 1984. **BUSINESS ADDRESS:** City Councilman, City of San Bernardino, 300 North D St, San Bernardino, CA 92418.

FRAZIER, EUFAULA SMITH
Executive director. **PERSONAL:** Born Oct 16, 1924, Dodge County, GA; married Arthur Lee; children: Maurice, Noland, Edwin, Michelle. **EDUCATION:** FL Intl U, BS 1977. **CAREER:** Tenant Educ Assn of Miami, exec dir; comm orgnzr 1967-77; Little Nook Beauty Parlor, owner 1956-67; Atlanta Life Ins Co, underwriter 1951-53. **ORGANIZATIONS:** Dir FL Tenant's Orgn; co-author FL Tenant's Bill of Right; mem Model Cities Task Force 1971-; consult S FL Hlth Task Force 1973-; mem consult Nat Welafare Rights Orgn 1969-; exec com mem Metro-Dade Co Dem Com 1974; co-host Dem Nat Conv 1972; mem People's Coalition 1972-; plng advr Counc for Countinuing educ for Women 1971-74f mem Brownsville CAA 1964-74; mem facilitator Radical Relat Inst 1973-74; dir Tenant Educ Info Ctr 1974; comm orgnzr Family Hlth Ctr 1969-72; mem NAACP 1972-77; Legal Serv of Miami 1974-77; Mental Hlth 1975-77; alternate Nat Dem Party Conv 1976. **HONORS/ACHIEVEMENTS:** Women of yr Miami Time Newspaper 1974; woman of yr Achiever Civil Club 1976. **BUSINESS ADDRESS:** Executive Dir, Magic City Develop Assn Inc, 4300 NW 12th Ave, Miami, FL 33142.

FRAZIER, JIMMY LEON
Physician. **PERSONAL:** Born Aug 29, 1939, Beaumont, TX; son of E L Frazier and Thelma Cooper Frazier; married Shirley Jolley; children: Andrea, Daveed, Keith. **EDUCATION:** TX So Univ, BS 1960; Meharry Med Coll, MD 1967. **CAREER:** Beaumont TX, teacher 1960-63; NASA, engr 1964; Family Practice, physician 1971-; Wright State Univ Sch of med, admissions com 1977-8l. **ORGANIZATIONS:** Mem Alpha Phi Alpha, Amer Acad of Family Prac, natl Med Assn, AMA, OH State Med Assn, Shriners-Prince Hall Mason; selectman Dayton OH Montgomery Co Med Assn; Gem City Med Soc; diplomate Amer Bd of Family Practice; fellow Amer Acad of Family Physicians; mem Dayton Racquet Club; mem NAACP. **MILITARY SERVICE:** AUS maj 1969-71. **BUSINESS ADDRESS:** 1401 Salem Ave, Dayton, OH 45406.

FRAZIER, JOE
Businessman, professional boxer. **PERSONAL:** Born Jan 17, 1944, Beaufort, SC; married Florence; children: Marvis, Weatta, Jo-Netta, Natasha, Jacqui, Hector, Marcus. **CAREER:** Professional Boxer 1958-; Heavyweight Champion NY MA IL ME 1968; World Boxing Assn Heavyweight Champion 1970-73; winner fight with Mohammad Ali 1971; mem rock-blues group Knockouts; Smokin Joe's Corner, owner; Joe Frazier & Sons Limousine Serv Phila, owner/pres 1974-; Joe Frazier's Gymnasium Phila, owner/mgr/trainer 1974-; mgr prizefighter Marvis Frazier. **HONORS/ACHIEVEMENTS:** Olympic Gold Medal 1964. **BUSINESS ADDRESS:** c/o Lynne & Reilly Agency, 6290 Sunset Blvd, Ste 326, Los Angeles, CA 90028.

FRAZIER, JOSEPH NORRIS
Police inspector. **PERSONAL:** Born Jul 05, 1925, New York, NY; married Dolores Woodard. **EDUCATION:** Atlantic Comm Coll, AA; Stockton Coll, BA. **CAREER:** Atlantic City Police Dept, inspector of police 1975-; promoted to capt 1974; promoted to sgt 1970; patrolman 1954. **ORGANIZATIONS:** Mem NAACP; Sigma Chi Chi Frat; Police Benevolent Assn; Nat Conf of Police Profls; NOBLE. **HONORS/ACHIEVEMENTS:** William Sahl Meml Award in Law Enforcement 1973. **MILITARY SERVICE:** USCG seaman 1st class 1942-46. **BUSINESS ADDRESS:** South Carolina & Arctic Avs, Atlantic City, NJ 08401.

FRAZIER, JULIE A.
Chemical engineering assistant. **PERSONAL:** Born Dec 09, 1962, Cleveland, OH; daughter of Mrs Gerald N Frazier. **EDUCATION:** Tuskegee Univ, BS 1986. **CAREER:** Sherwin Williams Technical Lab, lab technician 1984-85; AT&T Bell Labs, Atlanta, GA, chemical engineering asst 1987-89. **ORGANIZATIONS:** Mem Amer Inst of Chemical Engrs 1985-86; volunteer Greater Cleveland Literacy Coalition 1986-87; mem Assault on Illiteracy Program 1986-87. **HONORS/ACHIEVEMENTS:** Chemical Engineering Honor Society Tuskegee Univ 1985-86. **HOME ADDRESS:** 114 Brook Ridge, Doraville, GA 30340.

FRAZIER, LEE RENE
Health services administrator. **PERSONAL:** Born Aug 31, 1946, Washington, DC; son of Charles Frazier and Doretha Frazier; married Deborah Ann Lombard; children: Michelle, Bridgette, Adrienne, Yvette. **EDUCATION:** Delgado Coll, SBA 1969; Loyola Univ, BS 1972; Amer Acad of Orthopedic Surgeons, REMT 1974; Tulane Univ, MPH/MHA 1974. **CAREER:** Charity Hospital, exec dir 1974; Harlem Hospital Ctr, exec dir 1977; South St Seaport, vice pres 1979; Natl Medical Enterprises, vice pres corporate develop 1984; New Orleans General Hospital, administrator/owner 1980-; The Bryton Group, vice pres; Provident Medical Ctr, pres & ceo; visiting professor, Roosevelt Univ. **ORGANIZATIONS:** Consultant J Aron Charitable Foundation; bd mem/treas Natl Assoc of Health Serv Execs; bd mem YMCA; elected to Louisiana State House of Representatives 1981. **HONORS/ACHIEVEMENTS:** Legislator of the Year Metro Press Club 1984. **MILITARY SERVICE:** AUS 2nd lt ROTC unit 4 yrs; Honorable Discharge.

FRAZIER, LEON
Educator. **PERSONAL:** Born May 16, 1932, Orangeburg, SC; married Irlene Janet Sharperson; children: Angela, Chris, Celeste. **EDUCATION:** SC State Coll, BS 1954; SC State Coll, Grad Study 1955;Univ of OK, Grad Study 1967; AL A&M U, MS 1969; OK State U, DEd 1970. **CAREER:** AL A&M Univ, vice pres adademic affairs, dir 1971-73, assoc prof, asst dean of grad studies 1971-73; US Army Missile School Redstone Arsenal, educational specialist 1968-69, training admin 1961-68, instructor 1958-61; US Air Force Electronics Training Center, Keesler Air Force Base MS, training instructor 1956-58; Aiken County Public Schools SC, teacher 1954-56; State of AL, licensed psychologist. **ORGANIZATIONS:** Mem AAAS; Am Psychological Assn; Nat Educ Assn; Nat Rehab Assn; Nat Assn of Coll Deans Registrars & Admissions com Chmn; Coun of Academic Deans of the So States; Phi Delta Kappa Intl Educ Frat; AL Educ Assn; AL Psychological Assn; Madison Co Mental Health Bd Professional adv com; dir Huntsville-Madison Co Community Action Com; vice pres Madison Co Mental Health Assn; mem Madison Co Community Coun of Orgn; trustee Huntsville Art League & Museum Assn; mem Madison Co Democratic exec com; Nat Assn for the Advancement of Colored People; state dir of public relations Ch of God in Christ; trustee deacon & dir of finance Gov's Dr Ch of God in Christ. **HONORS/ACHIEVEMENTS:** Listed in Am Men & Women of Science; Community Leaders & Noteworthy Am; Leaders of Black Am; Dictionary of Intl Biography; Personalities of the S; Who's Who in The Chrs of God in Christ Intl Edition; recipient of numerous community serv awards. **MILITARY SERVICE:** Army. **BUSINESS ADDRESS:** Alabama A&M Univ, Normal, AL 35762.

FRAZIER, LESLIE CALVIN
Professional athlete. **PERSONAL:** Born Apr 03, 1959, Columbus, MS; married Gale. **EDUCATION:** Alcorn State, BA. **CAREER:** Chicago Bears, cornerback 1981. **ORGANIZATIONS:** Involved in Red Cloud Athletic Fund; Fellowship of Christian Athletes; Lake Forest C of C; Brian Piccolo Cancer Research Fund. **HONORS/ACHIEVEMENTS:** Kodak All-Am; most valuable defensive back for Alcorn State in 1980; also MVP on baseball team. **BUSINESS ADDRESS:** Chicago Bears, Halas Hall, 250 N Washington Rd, Lake Forest, IL 60045.

FRAZIER, LEVI, JR.
Artistic director. **PERSONAL:** Born Jul 03, 1951, Memphis, TN; married Deborah Glass. **EDUCATION:** Southwestern at Memphis, BA 1973; Memphis State U, MA 1975. **CAREER:** Blues City Cultural Center Memphis, artistic dir; State Tech Inst at Memphis, instructor 1979-, audio-visual coordinator 1976-79, scriptwriter (Audio-visual) 1976; WTTW TV-Station Chicago, local coordinator, producer 1974-75; WREC Radio Station Memphis, news reporter 1972-74. **ORGANIZATIONS:** Mem Am Vocational Assn 1976-; mem TN Vocational Assn 1976-; mem Am Tech Educ Assn 1976-; mem AFTRA; Mem Adv Panel TN Arts Commn. **HONORS/ACHIEVEMENTS:** Recipient most outstanding sophomore Omicron Delta Kappa (Southwestern) 1971; listed "Black Playwrights 1823-1977" Annotated Bibliography (Bowker Co) 1977; wrote & produced Play "Down on Beale" Richard Alled Center for Culture & Art 1979; Colored People & Contributions (Poetry) Good People of Gomorrah 1979.

FRAZIER, RAMONA YANCEY
Business executive. **PERSONAL:** Born Jun 27, 1941, Boston, MA; daughter of Raymond E Yancey Sr and Gladys E Springer Yancey; divorced; children: Pamela Rae Frazier. **EDUCATION:** Howard Univ, 1959-60; Simmons Coll, 1961-62; Pace Univ, BA 1984. **CAREER:** Brown Bros Harriman & Co, employment mgr 1969-73; Anchor Savings Bank, dir of personnel 1973-74; Boston Univ, personnel officer 1974-77; Raytheon Co, eeo mgr 1977; Anchor Savings Bank, asst vice pres personnel officer 1977-79; GAF Corp, dir eeo 1979-84; FW Woolworth Co, dir of personnel 1984-87, corporate mgr 1987-. **ORGANIZATIONS:** Pres The EDGES Group Inc; mem Friend of the Mayor's Commiss on the Status of Women NYC, Human Resources System Profls; mem Delta Sigma Theta. **HONORS/ACHIEVEMENTS:** Black Achiever in Industry Harlem YMCA 1973-78; Mary McLeod Bethune Recognition Award, National Council of Negro Women 1989. **BUSINESS ADDRESS:** Corporate Manager-Human Resources, FW Woolworth Co, 233 Broadway #2766, New York, NY 10279.

FRAZIER, RANTA A.
Business executive. **PERSONAL:** Born Nov 02, 1915, Marlboro County, SC; married Grace Lee Booker; children: Barbara, Brenda, Bonita. **CAREER:** Society Hill, councilman 1969-74; Grocery Store, owner operator. **ORGANIZATIONS:** Mem Citizens Club of Darlington County; Royal Arch Masons Assn; mem Pee Dee Masonic Lodge #56; Cub Scout leader. **HONORS/ACHIEVEMENTS:** 1st Black councilman in Darlington Co.

FRAZIER, RAY JERRELL
Street commissioner. **PERSONAL:** Born Jun 27, 1943, Lake Providence, LA. **EDUCATION:** Grambling Univ, attended. **CAREER:** KLPL Radio, announcer; Town of Lake Providence, councilman 1974-; Town of Lake Providence, SoUniv St commr. **ORGANIZATIONS:** MW Prince Hall Grand Lodge F & AM of LA Sunrise Lodge #109; mem NAACP. **BUSINESS ADDRESS:** St Commissioner, Town of Lake Providence, PO Box 625, Lake Providence, LA 71254.

FRAZIER, REGINA JOLLINETTE
Director of pharmacy. **PERSONAL:** Born Sep 30, 1943, Miami, FL; married Ronald E Frazier; children: Ron II, Robert Christopher, Rozalynn Suzanne. **EDUCATION:** Howard Univ, BS Pharmacy 1966; Univ of Miami, MBA 1983. **CAREER:** Comm Drug Store Inc Miami, pharmacy intern 1966; Peoples Drug Stores Inc Washington, pharmacy intern 1967-68, staff pharmacist 1968-69; Natl Assoc of Retired Tchrs & Amer Assoc of Retired Persons Drug Serv Washington, staff pharmacist 1969-70; Economic Oppor Prog, volunteer coord 1970; Univ of Miami Hosps & Clinics, sr pharmacists 1970-73, dir of pharmacy 1973-. **ORGANIZATIONS:** Natl parliamentarian Assoc of Black Hospital Pharmacists; mem Amer Soc of Hosp Pharmacists, Natl Pharmaceutical Assoc, Pharmacy Adv Comm Shared Purchasing Prog The Hosp Consortium Inc, FL Pharmaceutical Assoc; mem adv comm FL/GA Cancer Info Svcs; mem Women's Chamber of Commerce of So FL Inc, The Miami Forum; mem Metro Dade County Zoning Appeals Bd 1977-; pres The Links Foundation Inc; mem League of Women Voters, Amer Assoc of Univ Women; bd ofdirs United Negro Coll Fund, Natl Coalition of Black Voter Participation; mem Alpha Kappa Alpha Sor Inc Gamma Zeta Omega Chapt; mem The Carats Inc, Zonta Intl Greater Miami I Club. **HONORS/ACHIEVEMENTS:** Devoted Serv Awd The Links Inc 1980; Comm Headliner Awd Women in Communication 1984; Trail Blazer Awd Women's Comm of 100 1984; Salute to Leadership Awd Agricultural Investment Fund Inc 1986.

FRAZIER, REGINALD LEE
Attorney. **PERSONAL:** Born Feb 27, 1934, Smithfield, NC; married Levonia P. **EDUCATION:** NC Coll NC Central Law Sch, AB LLB. **ORGANIZATIONS:** Mem Am Bar Asso; Nat Bar Asso; Am Judicature Soc; NC Trial Lawyers; Gen Coun SCLC; Gen Coun Nat Vet Frat; mem New Bern Civil Rights Asso; Elks Zeno Lodge; trustee AME Zion Church USM. **BUSINESS ADDRESS:** 1044 Broad St, P O Drawer 430, New Bern, NC.

FRAZIER, WALT
Professional basketball player. **PERSONAL:** Born Mar 29, 1945, Atlanta, GA. **EDUCATION:** So IL U, Student. **CAREER:** NY Knickerbockers, basketball player 1967-. **HONORS/ACHIEVEMENTS:** Named to Nat Basketball Assn All-Denfensive Squad for 8 consecutive yrs. **BUSINESS ADDRESS:** c/o Madison Square Garden, 4 Pennsylvania Plaza, New York, NY 10001.

FRAZIER, WILLIAM JAMES
Physician. **PERSONAL:** Born Aug 20, 1942, Gary, IN; married Veronica; children: Kevin, Monica, Nicole. **EDUCATION:** Fisk U, 1964; INUniv Sch Med, 1968; BaylorUniv Med Ctr 1968-70; Barnes Hosp WA U, 1972-75. **CAREER:** Self, physician. **ORGANIZATIONS:** Mem AMA; Dallas Co Med Soc; Am Coll Surgeon; diplomate Am Bd Urology; mem Am Coll Emergency Physicians; mem CV Roman Med Soc; Nat Med Assn. **HONORS/ACHIEVEMENTS:** Publ "Use of Phenylephrine in the Detection of the Opening Snap of Mitral Stenosis" Am Heart Jour 1969; "Early Manipulation & Torsion of the Testicle" JourUrology 1975; bronze star for Meritorious Serv. **MILITARY SERVICE:** USAF maj 1970-72. **BUSINESS ADDRESS:** 3600 Gaston, Dallas, TX 75246.

FRAZIER, WYNETTA ARTRICIA
Governor's assistant. **PERSONAL:** Born Jul 21, 1942, Mounds, IL; married Sterling R; children: Renee, Tommie, Clifford. **EDUCATION:** Governors St U, BS & MA 1975;Univ of IL, CDA. **CAREER:** Gov for Health Affairs, asst; Hlth Serv Adminstr, sr health planner; Comp Health Planning Sub Area, exec dir; Lloyd Ferguson Health Center, asst adminstr; Health Occupations, dir; Nat Asso Health Serv Exec, vice pres. **ORGANIZATIONS:** Mem Steering Com AM PUB HEALTH ASSO; NAT ASSO oF NEIGHBRHD HEALTH CTRS; pRES AUXILIARY COOK CNTY HOSP; pRES KOZMINSKI SCH PTA; vICE pres Sch-Com Hyde Park Kenwood Community Conf; mem Independent voters of IL; chmn Health Com; mem Leag of Black Women; bd mem Afro Am Fam & Community Service; mem Chicago Forum. **HONORS/ACHIEVEMENTS:** Ten outstanding young people Award Chicago Jaycees; grant Chas Gavin Scholarshp Found; Clinic Awards Chicago Med Soc 1972-74f citizen of the wk WJPC & WAIT radio stations. **BUSINESS ADDRESS:** 160 N La Salle St, Chicago, IL 60601.

FREDD, CHESTER ARTHUR
Educational administration. **PERSONAL:** Born in Hale Cty, AL; married Hattie Beatrice Long; children: 3 children. **EDUCATION:** AL State Univ Montgomery AL, BS Sec Ed; Fisk Univ Nashville TN, summer study; AL State Univ Montgomery, MEd Suprv; State Univ of Buffalo, Doctoral Study in Ed Admin; Selma Univ Selma AL, Litt D. **CAREER:** Jr High Schools (2), principal; Morgan Cty training School Hartselle AL, principal; Hale Cty Training School Greensboro AL, principal; AL Sunday School & Baptist Training Union Congress, instr; CA Fredd State Tech Coll Tuscaloosa AL, pres, president emeritus. **ORGANIZATIONS:** Pres AL Assoc of Secondary School Principals, AL Leadership Study Council, AL State Teachers Assoc; minister Greater Fourteenth St Bapt Church; mem, bd of dir Benjamin Barnes Br YMCA; dean Sunday School & Baptist Training Union Congress; mem, bd of dir W AL Planning & Devel Council; charter mem, bd of trustees Selma Univ; mem Greensboro Zoning Bd; statistician AL State Baptist Convention; life mem Natl Ed Assoc; mem AL Ed Assoc, AL Leadership Study Council, Assoc for Suprv & Curriculum Devel; retired life mem CA Fredd State Teachers Assoc; mem Amer Vocational Assoc, Masonic Lodge Prince Hall Affil, Omega Psi Phi; mem Hale Co Bd of Educ, West AL Mental Health Bd; chmn Hale Co Democratic Conference. **HONORS/ACHIEVEMENTS:** Recipient of Centennial Anniversary Awd AL State Univ 1974; Recipient of Centennial Anniv Awd AL A&M Univ 1975; Tuscaloosa State Tech Coll was named CA Fredd State Tech Coll in honor of CA Fredd Sr its 1st pres. **BUSINESS ADDRESS:** President Emeritus, CA Fredd St Tech Coll, 3401 Thirty Second Ave, Tuscaloosa, AL 35401.

FREDERICKS, LEROY OWEN
Retired school board member. **PERSONAL:** Born May 17, 1924, New York, NY; married Betty; children: Carol Nicholson, Roy Bolus. **EDUCATION:** Brooklyn Coll, BA 1976. **CAREER:** Metropolitan Trans Auth, clerk 1956-77; US Postal Service, super 1980; Comm School Dist 14, school bd mem (retired). **ORGANIZATIONS:** Mem Crispus Attucks 1966; mem Comm Bd #1 1978; mem 369 Vet Assoc Inc. **HONORS/ACHIEVEMENTS:** Brooklyn Coll Dean's Honor List 1975-76. **MILITARY SERVICE:** USMC pfc 1st class 1943-46.

FREDRICK, EARL E., JR.
Physician. **PERSONAL:** Born Aug 13, 1929, Chicago, IL; son of Earl Eugene Fredrick Sr and Lucille Ray Fredrick; married Barbara Cartman, Mar 21, 1987; children: Earl E III, Erica E. **EDUCATION:** Univ of IL, BS 1951; Howard Univ, MD 1958. **CAREER:** Univ of Chicago Food Research Inst, 1953; IL Dept of Public Health, bacteriologist 1953-55; Freedmans Hospital, med lab teacher 1956-58; Cook County Hospital, rotating internship 1958-59; residency 1959-61; VA Research Hospital, fellowship 1961-62; Fredrick Ashley Clinic, physician internal medicine & hematology; Anchor Organization for Health Maintenance, physician internal medicine 1974-, Anchor-Park Forest Office, clinical dir 1982-85. **ORGANIZATIONS:** Chicago IL State Medical Soc; Natl Medical Assn; Cook County Physicians Assn; Clinical Assn Internal Medicine Chicago Medical School 1963-73; bd mem Chicago Found for MedCare 1977; bd of trustees Chicago Medical Soc 1977; mem Amer Coll of Physicians; attending Physician Cook County Hospital chmn Dept of Med 1974-76; pres of med staff St Francis Hospital 1978-79; chmn of bd Washington Park YMCA 1977-; consultation staff Roseland Community Hospital; Provident Hospital; Louise Burg Hospital; vice chmn, bd of trustees Chicago Medical Society 1983-85. **HONORS/ACHIEVEMENTS:** Glucose 6-Phosphate Dehydrogenage Deficiency, A Review J, Natl Medical Assn 1962. **MILITARY SERVICE:** AUS 1951-53. **BUSINESS ADDRESS:** 10830 S Halsted St, Chicago, IL 60628.

FREE, WORLD B.
Professional athlete. **PERSONAL:** Born Dec 09, 1953, Atlanta, GA. **EDUCATION:** Guilford, 1976. **CAREER:** Philadelphia 76er's, guard 1975-; Los Angeles Clippers, guard 1978-; Golden State Warriors, guard 1980-; Cleveland Cavaliers, guard 1982-. **HONORS/ACHIEVEMENTS:** Voted MVP by teammates; 4 Plyr of Week Noms; consideration for Plyr of Month Award; starting lineup for West in the 1980 All-Star Game in Landover; named Clippers MVP & earned 2nd team All-NBA hnrs; led NBA in free throw attempts (865) and free throws made (654); helped the Sixers into the Finals of the NBA Playoffs. **BUSINESS ADDRESS:** Philadelphis 76ers, PO Box 25040, Philadelphia, PA 19147.

FREELAND, ROBERT LENWARD, JR.
Business executive, recorder. **PERSONAL:** Born May 05, 1939, Gary, IN; married Carolyn J Woolridge; children: Robin, Brandon. **EDUCATION:** IN Inst of Real Estate, Cert 1962; IN Univ; Calumet College, Whiting IN, 1980, 1981. **CAREER:** IN state rep 1973-74; Black Horsemen Liquor Stores, owner 1969-81; Four Roses Distillers Co, mktg rep 1968-71; Len Pollak Buick, salesman 1966-68; Mobil Oil Corp, sales engr 1963-66; Devaney Realtors, salesman 1961-63; city of Gary Common Council, city councilman 1975-79, vice pres 1976, pres 1977-79; city of Gary, police commr 1979-83; Calumet Township Trustee, Gary IN, chief deputy trustee 1988. **ORGANIZATIONS:** NAACP; Urban League; Frontiers Intl; bd mem Northwest Indiana Regional Plan Commission 1975-78. **HONORS/ACHIEVEMENTS:** Recip Legis award NAACP 1973; recog award Precinct Orgn 1973; distinction award IN Div Assn for Study of Afro-Am Life & Hist 1973; Lake Co concerned cit recog award 1973; merit serv award Club Carpetbaggers 1972; patriotic serv award 1964; special recog & commend IN Dept of Civil Defense 1961; friendship award Frat Order of Police 1973; first black from Gary elected state rep; first black to serve on House Ways & Means Com; elected del to First Nat Black Assem 1972; elected del to Dem State Convention 4 Times; served on state dem platform com twice; Black History Commemorative Service, WTLC 105FM, Indianapolis IN 1988. **BUSINESS ADDRESS:** Lake County Recorder, Lake County Government Center, 2293 N Main St, Recorder's Office, Crown Point, IN 46307.

FREELAND, RUSSELL L.
Consultant. **PERSONAL:** Born Jul 13, 1929, Lawrenceburg, IN; son of John H. Freeland and Hulda M. Earley Freeland (deceased); married Joan M; children: Deborah, Mark, Douglas. **EDUCATION:** DePauw Univ, BA 1951; Butler Univ, MS 1960. **CAREER:** Intl Harvester Co, mgr mfg oper, 1980-82; Intl Harvester, general plants mgr, 1982-83; Intl Harvester, dir, renew operations, 1983; Intl Harvester, director tech admin, 1983-86; retired, 1986; navistar, consultant, 1987-; Engine Operations Intl Harvester, plant mgr 1978-80; Intl Harvester Co, mgr direct labor syst 1978; Indianapolis Plant Intl Harvester Co, mgr mfg operations 1977-78; Indianapolis Plant Intl Harvester Co, mgr production operations 1976-77; Indianapolis Plant Intl Harvester Co, mgr indus engineering 1974-76. **ORGANIZATIONS:** Mem, Amer Inst of Indus Engrs, 1974-82; host TV talk show "Opportunity Knocks" WFBM-TV 1971-76; mem bd of visitors DePauw Univ 1979-85; mem Allocations Comm United Way Metro Chicago 1979-80. **HONORS/ACHIEVEMENTS:** Silver Anniversary Team, Indiana High School Basketball 1972; Silver Anniversary Team All-Amer, Natl Assn of Basketball Coaches 1976; Civic Award, Intl Harvester, 1976; DePauw Univ, All Sports Hall of Fame, 1989. **MILITARY SERVICE:** USAF s/sgt 1951-55. **HOME ADDRESS:** 1569 Vest St, Naperville, IL 60563.

FREEMAN, ALBERT CORNELIUS, JR.
Actor. **PERSONAL:** Born Mar 21, San Antonio, TX; married Sevara E Clemon. **EDUCATION:** LA City Coll, student 1957; Amherst Univ, MA. **CAREER:** Actor in various theatres in US 1960-; appeared in, "The Long Dream" 1960, "Kicks & Co" 1961, "Tiger Tiger Burning Bright" 1962, "The Living Premise" 1963, "Trumpets of the Lord" 1963, "Blues for Mister Charlie" 1964, "Conversations at Midnight" 1964, "The Slave" 1964, "Dutchman" 1965, "Measure for Measure" 1966, "Camino Real" 1968, "The Dozens" 1969, "Look to the Lilies" 1970, "Are You Now Or Have You Ever Been" 1972, "Medea" 1973, "The Poison Tree" 1973, "The Great Macdaddy" 1974; movies incl, "Torpedo Run" 1958, "Dutchman" 1967, "Finian's Rainbow" 1968, "The Detective" 1968, "Castle Keep" 1969, "The Lost Man" 1969, "My Sweet Charlie" 1970; actor. **HONORS/ACHIEVEMENTS:** Recipient Russwurm Award; Recipient Golden Gate Award; Recipient Emmy Award 1979. **MILITARY SERVICE:** USAF.

FREEMAN, CHARLES E.
Educator. **PERSONAL:** Born Apr 10, 1915, Patterson, LA; married Ruby Edwards; children: Charles III, Cheryl, Stanley. **EDUCATION:** Wiley Coll, BS 1938; City Coll of NY; Columbia U; TX Christian U; OK State U; TX Southern U; Lamar U, Grad Study. **CAREER:** Gulf Oil, merchant seaman 1938-42; NYC, self-employed 1947-50, 1952-56; Port Arthur Independent School Dist, sec teacher Chemistry 1959-77; Charles Freeman & Assoc Real Estate & Insurance Brokerage, pres. **ORGANIZATIONS:** Mem NEA, TSTA, TCTA; licensed Real Estate Broker; licensed ins agt; Omega Psi Phi Frat; former state rep & local pres; finance chmn Beauchamp Dist; BSA; 1st black elected to Port of Port Arthur Navigation Dist 1969 Reelected 1971,73 Served As vice pres 1973-75; Waterways membership Com of C of C; present local chmn United Negro Coll Fund; city co & state govt com & specially panels All Am City Team etc; mem NAACP. **HONORS/ACHIEVEMENTS:** Awarded Silver

Beaver 1969; Omega man of yr 1960; man of yr 1973-74; Golden Gate Social & Civic Club for pub service; cited for leadership 1974 as vice pres PortCommn; listed in Nat Roster of Black Elected Officials 1974, 75; Notable Ams 1976-77; Personalities of the S 1976-77; awards 40 yr serv placque Omega at 57th Grand Conclave 1976; cited Xi Upsilon Chap 1977; distg serv UNCF 1974. **MILITARY SERVICE:** AUS WWII & Korea. **BUSINESS ADDRESS:** Port Arthur Independent Sch Di, Port Arthur, TX.

FREEMAN, CHARLES ELDRIDGE
Circuit judge, attorney. **PERSONAL:** Born Dec 12, 1933, Richmond, VA; son of William Isaac Freeman and Jeanette Winston Freeman; married Mary Lee Voelker; children: Kevin. **EDUCATION:** VA Union Univ Richmond VA, BA 1954; John Marshall Law Schl Chicago IL, JD 1962. **CAREER:** Cook Cty Dept of Public Aid, prop & ins consult 1959-64; Office of Atty Gen Of IL, asst atty gen 1964; State's Attorneys Office, asst state's atty 1964; Bd of Election Commissioners, asst atty 1964-65; IL Industrial Comm, arbitrator 1965-73; IL Commerce Comm, commissioner 1973-76; Circuit Court Cook Cty, elected 1976; First Dist IL Appellate Court, elected term for 1986-96. **ORGANIZATIONS:** Bd dir Conf to Fulfill These Rights; vice pres Englewood Businessmen & Civic League; mem Cook Cty Bar Assc; bd dir Ralph H Metcalfe Youth Fnd; Third Ward Dem HQ; mem Phi Beta Sigma Frat; bd dir Garfield Park Comm Growth Cntr Inc; bd dir Southern Shores Yacht Club 1982-; mem, Chicago Bar Association, Illinois Judge Association, Judical Council of Illinois, American Judge Association. **HONORS/ACHIEVEMENTS:** Hnrd by Harold Washington Mayor City of Chicago to admin oath of office during swearing in ceremonies 1983. **MILITARY SERVICE:** AUS sp/3 1956-58. **BUSINESS ADDRESS:** Justice Appellate Court, State of IL, Daley Center 28-109, Chicago, IL 60602.

FREEMAN, DAVID CALVIN, SR.
Funeral director. **PERSONAL:** Born Oct 17, 1942, Colerain, NC; married Mabel Butts; children: David, Jr, Demetria, Monique,. **EDUCATION:** Elizabeth City State Univ, BS 1966; Hampton Univ, 1970. **CAREER:** Pasquotank Co Schl System, Teacher 1966-70; Elizabeth City Pub Schl Sys,TeacherAsst Principal 1970-79; Walson Funeral Home, Owner/Operator 1980-. **ORGANIZATIONS:** State & Natl Funeral Dir & Embalmers Assoc, Board of Dir of Skills, Inc 1980-85;Northeastern NC Schoolmasters CLub, President 1982; NAACP, 1968; Christian Aid,1982; Corner Stone Missionary Baptist Church, Deacon 1976;Omega Psi Phi, 1983; Eastern Star Lodge; United Supreme Council; SJ Prince Hall, Golden Leaf Lodge1985. **HONORS/ACHIEVEMENTS:** AWD for Expertise in the field of Business 1982; Outstanding Alumni Awd, Business 1984; Presidential Citation by the Natl Assoc for Eq Opp in Higher Educ, |(*%,Awd for Appreciation in Recognition of Continued Dedication & Service to Education. **HOME ADDRESS:** 507 Shepard St, Elizabeth City, NC 27909. **BUSINESS ADDRESS:** 504 South Road St, Elizabeth City, NC 27909.

FREEMAN, EDWARD ANDERSON
Clergyman. **PERSONAL:** Born Jun 11, 1914, Atlanta, GA; married Ruth; children: Edward Jr, Constance, William. **EDUCATION:** Clark Coll, Ab 1939; Central Bapt Sem, BD 1949; Central Sem, ThM 1950, ThD 1953. **CAREER:** NAACP Kansas City, chaplain 1949-54; Argonne Post Amer Legion, chaplain 1947-55; Interracial Interdenom Ministerial Alliance, 1955; CCSA, pres 1957-58; Austell Publ School, teacher, principal; First Bapt Church, pastor. **ORGANIZATIONS:** Mem City Planning Commiss 1954-; chmn City Planning Commiss KC 1968-; pres Missionary Bapt State Conv KS 1957-82, Natl Sunday School & Bapt Training Union Congress 1968-83; pastor 1st Bapt Church 1946-; vice pres Baptist World Alliance 1980-85; life mem NAACP; bd mem Oper PUSH; mem Study Comm Ch Doctrines& Coop Bodies World Bapt Alliance; bd mem Natl Council Churches, Natl Bapt Conv USA Inc. **HONORS/ACHIEVEMENTS:** Man of the Year Womans C of C Wyandotte Cty 1950; Natl Bapt Conv India 1955; Law Day Awd 1973; Outstanding Alumnus Awd Central Bapt Sem 1972; publ "Epoch of Negro Bapt & the Foreign Mission Bd" Central Sem Press 1953; "The Eighth Century Prophets" Sunday School Publ Bd 1960, "Bapt Jubilee Advance" 1964, "Bapt Rels with Other Christians" 1974; Doctor of Divinity, OK School of Religion, 1978, Central Baptist Seminary, 1987. **MILITARY SERVICE:** AUS maj 1941-46; Bronze Stars. **BUSINESS ADDRESS:** Pastor, First Baptist Church, 500 Nebraska Ave, Kansas City, KS 66101.

FREEMAN, EDWARD C.
Attorney. **PERSONAL:** Born in Beta, NC; widowed; children: Mrs. **EDUCATION:** Knoxville Coll, AB; TX SoUniv Sch of Law, LLB JD; HowardUniv Sch of Law, attnd legal sem;Univ of MI Sch of Law;Univ of TN Law Sch; HarvardUniv Sch of Law. **CAREER:** Pvt Prac, atty couns 1951-; social worker 18 yrs; TN Valley Auth, mail clerk. **ORGANIZATIONS:** Dir Nat Yth & Adm; dir Social Welfare for Mil Manhattan Dist; mem Nat Bar Assn; mem TN & TX Bar; licensed to prac before all State Cts Fed Ct & Supreme Ct of US; v chmn Knox Co Tax Equal Bd; Knox Co Dem Primary Bd; deL Dem Nat Conv 1976; mem steering com election of Jimmy Carter; mem TN Voters Coun; charter mem Soc Workers of Am; charter mem Magnolia Fed Savings & Loan Assn; former scout master; mem Sect of Am Bar Assn on Continuing Legal Edn; mem Am Bar Assn; Knoxville Bar & TN Bar Assn; exec bd NAACP; Omega Psi Phi Frat; Elks & Mason; exec com Dem Party; Mount Zion BaptCh; hon trst Juvenile Ct for Knox Co TN. **BUSINESS ADDRESS:** 2528 Mc Calla Ave, Knoxville, TN 37914.

FREEMAN, EVELYN
Educator. **PERSONAL:** Born Feb 16, 1940, Marksville, LA. **EDUCATION:** Western Washington, BA Educ 1962;Univ of WA, 5th yr; Seattle U;Univ of CA Los Angeles, MA 1973. **CAREER:** Issaquah Public School, prin 1974-; Adams School, prin 1974; Long Beach, gifted program 1970-73; Leschi Seattle, established non-graded approach to reading & math 1966-70. **ORGANIZATIONS:** Mem ESPA; NAACP; mem FIGHT Rochester, NY; foudn mem Nat Council of Negro Women Seattle; treas Seattle chap 1968f sec Los Angeles chpt. **BUSINESS ADDRESS:** Sunny Hills, Box L, Issaquah, WA.

FREEMAN, FRANKIE M.
Attorney. **PERSONAL:** Born Nov 24, 1916, Danville, VA; married Shelby; children: Shelbe Freeman Bullock. **EDUCATION:** Howard U, LLB 1947; Hampton Inst, 1933-36. **CAREER:** US Treas Dept, clerk 1942-44; Office of Price Admin, statistician 1944-45; Coll of the Fingerlakes, instr business law 1947-49; attorney at law, 1949-56; Freeman Whitfield Montgomery Staples and White, partner/attorney. **ORGANIZATIONS:** Mem US Commn on Civil Rights; assoc gen counsel St Louis Housing & Land Clearance Authorities; mem Amer, Natl, Mound City Bar Assns; Lawyers' Assn of St Louis; Natl Assn of Housing & Redevelopment Officials; Natl Housing Conf; League of Women Voters; former pres Delta Sigma Theta Sor; bd dir Natl Council of Negro Women; bd mem St Louis Branch NAACP, United Way of St Louis; mem bd of trustees Howard Univ, Laclede Sch of Law; 1st vice pres Natl Council on the Aging; bd mem St Louis Region Natl Conf of Christians and Jews, The Amer Red Cross, St Louis Bi-State Chapt, St Louis Urban League, Gateway Chap of Links Inc; mem trustee bd Washington Tabernacle Baptist Church. **HONORS/ACHIEVEMENTS:** Recipient of numerous honors including Outstanding Citizen Award Mound City Press Club 1953; Women of Achievement Award Natl Council of Negro Women 1956, 1965; Woman of Achievement Awd in Public Affairs St Louis Globe Democrat; Outstanding Alumni Awd for Distinguished Career Hampton Inst; Outstanding Alumni Awd Howard Univ; Outstanding Achievement Awds Omega Psi Phi Frat, Iota Phi Lambda Sor, Links Inc; Mary Church Terrell Awd Delta Sigma Theta Sor; Hon DL Degree Univ of MO 1975; honored by Dollars and Sense Magazine as one of America's Top 100 Women 1985; Hon DHL Harris-Stowe Coll 1986. **BUSINESS ADDRESS:** Attorney at Law, 3920 Lindell Blvd, St Louis, MO 63112.

FREEMAN, HAROLD P.
Director of surgery. **PERSONAL:** Born Mar 02, 1933, Washington, DC; son of Clyde and Lucille; married Artholian C; children: Harold Paul, Neale Palmer. **EDUCATION:** Catholic Univ of Amer , AB 1954; Howard Med School, MD 1958. **CAREER:** Howard Univ Hosp, intern 1958-59, resd gen surgery 1959-64; Sloane Kettering Cancer Ctr, resd 1964-67; Columbia Univ, assoc prof clinical surgery 1974; Columbia Presbyterian Hosp, assoc attending surgeon 1974; Columbia Univ, assoc prof clinical surgery; Harlem Hosp Ctr, attending surgeon 1974-, dir of surgery; prof of clinical surgery Columbia Univ 1988-. **ORGANIZATIONS:** Mem Soc of Surgical Oncology 1975-; bd of dir Amer Cancer Soc 1978-; medical dir Breast Examination Ctr of Harlem 1979; chmn Natl Adv Comm on Cancer in the Socio-Economically Disadvantaged Amer Cancer Soc 1986-88; Exec Council of Soc of Surgical Oncology 1987; Governor of Amer Coll Surgeons 1988; natl pres Amer Cancer Soc 1988-89; elected to Alpha Omega Alpha (honorary medical soc) 1989. **HONORS/ACHIEVEMENTS:** Harris Awd for Outstanding Gentlemen Cath Univ 1954; Prize in Psychaitry Howard Univ 1958; Daniel Hal Williams Awd Outstanding Achievement as Chief Resident Howard Univ Hosp 1964; Natl Boys Singles Tennis Champion Amer Tennis Assoc 1948. **BUSINESS ADDRESS:** Dir of Surgery, Harlem Hospital Center, 135th & Lenox Ave, New York, NY 10037.

FREEMAN, JAMES JASPER
Clergyman. **PERSONAL:** Born Sep 08, 1907, Bertie Co, NC; married Mary C Taylor; children: 5 children. **EDUCATION:** Shaw Univ, AB 1937, BD 1938, LHD 1965; Virginia Theol Sem, DD 1944; New York Univ, MDiv MA 1962. **CAREER:** Brown's Chapel Baptist Church Clinton, pastor 1934-39; New Mt Zion Bapt Ch, pastor 1935-39; Lawson Chapel Baptist Church Person Co, pastor 1938-39; First Bapt Church, pastor 1939-49; Norfolk State Coll, teacher evening coll 1960-73; Roanoke Inst Unit of Shaw Univ, dean teacher 1952-58; teacher 1960-; Queen St Baptist Church, pastor 1949-88. **ORGANIZATIONS:** Mem bd trustees Shaw Univ; Comm for Improvement of Educ; life mem NAACP; sec Lott Carey Baptist Foreign Mission Conv 1954-88; past pres Hampton Inst Ministers Conf; sec Hampton Inst Ministers Conf. **HONORS/ACHIEVEMENTS:** Service Awd Shaw Univ 1973. **BUSINESS ADDRESS:** Pastor, Queen St Baptist Church, 413 E Brambleton Ave, Norfolk, VA 23510.

FREEMAN, KENNETH D.
Accountant. **PERSONAL:** Born Dec 08, 1912, Oakland, CA; married Amelia Anna Tyler; children: Kenneth M, Donald T, Lionel W, Shirley A. **EDUCATION:** Attended, Merritt Bus Sch, Lincoln Law Sch, Univ of CA Extension, US Treasury Dept of Accounting Courses 1932-42. **CAREER:** Ken Freeman's Californiana, orchestra leader 1931-36; IRS, dep collector 1942-51; Self-employed, public accountant 1952-. **ORGANIZATIONS:** Mem Gov Adv Commn on Children & Youth 1964-65; mem bd of dirs CA State Central Comm Exec Bd 1964-70; exec bd mem CA State Dem Central Com 1964-70; mem Alameda Co Instn Commn 1966-70; mem Alameda Co Assessment Appeals Bd 1970-74; mem Alameda Co Commn for Prevention of Juvenile Delinquents 1972-73; former diocese social justice commn Hanna Boys Ctr Sonoma Co 1972-78; pres E Bay Chap Soc of CA Accountants; mem Natl Assoc of Black Accountants Inc. **BUSINESS ADDRESS:** Public Accountant, 1452 70th Ave, Oakland, CA 94621.

FREEMAN, KERLIN, JR.
Educator. **PERSONAL:** Born Sep 24, 1930, Chelsea, MA; married E Juanita Maybin; children: Leslie R, Beverly Oubre, Alan K. **EDUCATION:** Metro State Coll Denver Co, BA Elem Ed 1975; Lesley Coll Cambridge MA, MA Computers in Ed 1985. **CAREER:** NAACP, human relationa com 1976-, pres 1977-; Xi Pi Chapter Omega Psi Phi, recorder 1977-; Colorado Springs Dist #11, elementary school teacher. **ORGANIZATIONS:** Chmn human rel comm City of CO Springs 1983-85; chmn minority caucus CO Ed Assoc 1982-; mem NEA, CEA, CSTA, United Teaching Professional CO Football Officials Assoc, Black Ed Dist 11; del Dem Natl Conv 1976; mem Intl Assoc Approved Basketball Officials 1973-. **HONORS/ACHIEVEMENTS:** Listed in Who's Who in Amer Politics 1977; voted 1 of 10 Most Influential Blacks in CO Springs. **MILITARY SERVICE:** USAF msgt 1950-71; Non-Commd Officer of the Year USAF-ADC 1970; Meritorious Serv Medal AF 1971. **BUSINESS ADDRESS:** Teacher, Colorado Springs Sch Dist 11, 890 N Walnut St, Colorado Springs, CO 80905.

FREEMAN, LELABELLE CHRISTINE
Physician. **PERSONAL:** Born Oct 27, 1923, Chicago, IL; daughter of Henry C Freeman and Ella Washington Freeman; children: Christine Robinson, James E Robinson Jr. **EDUCATION:** Spelman College, BA 1944; Howard Univ Medical School, MD 1949. **CAREER:** Private Practice Cleveland, pediatrician 1953-79; Health Resources Cleveland, pediatrician 1975-77; Maternity and Infant Care Project Cleveland, pediatric consultant 1983-86; Cuyahoga Co Bd of Health Cleveland, pediatrician 1977-87; Case Western Reserve Sch of Medicine Cleveland, demonstrator of pediatrics 1954-86, clinical instructor of pediatrics 1986-. **ORGANIZATIONS:** Asst pediatrician Univ Hospitals of Cleveland Dept of Pediatrics 1954-; charter mem Northern OH Pediatric Soc 1954-; clinical physician Metropolitan General Hosp Cleveland 1954-; mem NY Acad of Science 1979-81; council on scientific affairs, ad hoc comm, prepubescent sports American Medical Assoc 1985-86; "Reviewing the Past to Prepare for the Future" seminar at Shaw High School topic "The Health of Afro-Americans" 1987. **HONORS/ACHIEVEMENTS:** Service Awd PTA and Retarded Students of Cuyahoga Co; Univ Hospital of Cleveland CHAIR "25 Years of Service" from 1954-79; 6 publications including "Studies in Sickle Cell Anemia, Effect of Age (Maturation) on incidence of

the Sickling Phenomenon," Pediatrics Vol 14 No 3 p 109-214. **HOME ADDRESS:** 16306 Aldersyde, Shaker Heights, OH 44120.

FREEMAN, MCKINLEY HOWARD, SR.
Elected official. **PERSONAL:** Born Aug 27, 1920, Detroit, MI; married Virginia Burgen; children: McKinley Jr, William Randall. **EDUCATION:** Lawrence Tech, diesel engr 1938-40; Slade-Gragg, upholstry school 1946-47. **CAREER:** US Postal Service, special delivery messenger 1940-42; Great Lakes Ins Co, agent 1945-47; Wyatt & McCullars, real estate sales 1955-58; Dept of Transportation, driver-instructor 1948-78. **ORGANIZATIONS:** AL-#181 post commander 1947-48; consultant Econo Group Travel 1978-; VFW #5315 1982-; vice president Democratic Party Newaygo County 1984-; exec board Democratic Party 9th district 1985-; life mem NAACP, VFW 1986-; Newaygo Cnty Planning Commissioner 1985; State Central Democratic Comm 9th Dist 1987-; co-chmn Newaygo Cnty Sesquicentannial Committee 1986-87; exec committee, Newaygo County Democratic Party 1988; special deputy sheriff, Newaygo County 1989-. **HONORS/ACHIEVEMENTS:** Certificate Special Award for Political Action from VFW 1984; selected as sr citizen of 9th dist democratic party to attend Jefferson, Jackson dinner 1985. **MILITARY SERVICE:** USMC 1st sgt 1942-45. **HOME ADDRESS:** 406 Pierce Rd, Brohman, MI 49312.

FREEMAN, NANCY CECILE
Executive administrator. **PERSONAL:** Born Sep 09, 1944, Monroe, LA. **EDUCATION:** Tougaloo Coll, BA Sociology 1968; Boston Univ, MSSS Social Work 1970. **CAREER:** Comprehensive Mental Health Ctr of Tacoma, mgr youth serv system 1974-78; City of Seattle, mgr youth employment 1978-81, dir div of youth serv 1981-82; King Cty Govt, asst to dir exec admin 1982-84; Seattle-King Cty Dept of Public Health, central dist admin. **ORGANIZATIONS:** Instr Boston Univ New Careers Prog 1972; bd mem Allied Arts 1977-78; affiliate instr Univ of Washington School of Social Work 1981; bd mem Metro Center YMCA 1983-84; mayoral appt Bd of Central Area Publ Devel Authority 1984-. **BUSINESS ADDRESS:** Central District Administrator, Seattle-King Cty Public Hlth, 1500 Public Safety Bldg, Seattle, WA 98104.

FREEMAN, NELSON R.
Educator. **PERSONAL:** Born Dec 30, 1924, Lake Wales, FL; married Willie Mae Freeman; children: Pickens A Patterson Jr, Albert B Patterson. **EDUCATION:** Savannah State Coll, BS Bus Admin 1948; Columbia Univ, MA Guidance & Student Personnel 1956. **CAREER:** Savannah State Coll, veterans counselor 1948-53, acting dean of men 1953-54, dean of men 1954-56, personnel dir 1956-65, dean of students 1965-72, placement dir 1972-76, acting dean of students 1976-81, placement dir 1981-84, retired acting vice pres for student affairs & placement dir 1984-86. **ORGANIZATIONS:** Chatham Co Bd of Registrars 1973-77; Helpline Vol Counselor 1976-78; Tax Equalization Bd of Chatham Co 1978; Southern Coll Personnel Assn; Natl Assn of Personnel Workers; Natl Assn of Student Personnel Admin; Southern Coll Placement Assn, GA College Placement Assn; GA College Personnel Assn; GA Assn for Counselor Education and Supervision; Alpha Phi Alpha Frat; Eureka Lodge of Free and Accepted Masons; Butler Presby Church; former mem of Bd of Management; May St YMCA; former mem of Bd of Dir Family Counseling Center of Savannah; former mem Minority Employ Oppor Comm; former comm Savannah Adult Softball League; Southern Assoc for Coll Student Affairs; mem Frogs Inc, Wolves Club, Mules Club, Savannah Guardsmen Inc; bd of dir Rape Crisis Center; volunteer, Victim's Witness, District Attorn ey's Office 1987-. **HONORS/ACHIEVEMENTS:** Kappa Delta Pi Honor Soc 1956; Chap Pres Regional Leadership Awd; Alpha Phi Alpha Frat Inc 1962; Man of the Year Awd Beta Phi Lambda Chap Alpha Phi Alpha Frat Inc 1963; Nelson R Freeman Honor Soc Wayne Co Training Sch Jesup GA 1965, Alumni Leadership Awd 1965; Natl Urban League Fellowship with Chas Pfizer & Co 1966; Alpha Phi Omega Serv Frat 1966; self-study consultant and served on visiting comm for the Southern Assn of Colleges and Schools; Wayne County Training School Alumni Leadership Awd Jesup GA 1965. **MILITARY SERVICE:** USNR personnel yeoman-in-charge, legal yeoman; 1943-46. **HOME ADDRESS:** 626 W 45th St, PO Box 22092, Savannah, GA 31405. **BUSINESS ADDRESS:** Acting Vice Pres for Student Affairs, Savannah State College, State College Branch, Savannah, GA 31404.

FREEMAN, NORMAN E., SR.
Automobile dealer. **PERSONAL:** Born Nov 06, 1950, Chase City, VA; son of Arthur C Freeman and Jennie Wood Freeman; married Mary Terrell, Nov 02, 1974; children: Angela D, Nicole M, Norman E Jr. **EDUCATION:** Virginia State Univ, Petersburg, VA, BS, 1974. **CAREER:** Chevrolet Metal Fabricating, Flint, MI, asst buyer, 1973, production foreman, 1974; Buick Motor Div, Washington, DC, dist serv mgr, 1977-83; Buick Motor Div, Boston, MA, mgr of zone serv operations, 1983-85; Buick Motor Div, Flint, MI, field serv eng, 1985; Freeman Motors Inc, Hopkinsville, KY, pres, 1986-. **ORGANIZATIONS:** Mem, Natl Automobile Dealers Assn, 1986-; mem, Kentucky Automobile Dealers Assn, 1986-; mem bd of dir, Hopkinsville Christian County Chamber of Commerce, 1987-; mem, Economic Devel Comm, Hopkinsville Human Relations Commn, 1987-; mem, Virginia Street Baptist Church, 1987-; chmn Nominations Comm, Pennyroyal Arts Council, 1987-89; mem, Leadership Hopkinsville Alumni, 1988-; mem, Leadership Kentucky Alumni, 1988-. **HONORS/ACHIEVEMENTS:** Winner of Duffy's Duel, Buick Motor Div, 1980-82; Dist Serv Mgr of Year, Buick, Pittsburgh, 1981. **MILITARY SERVICE:** US Army, lst lieutenant, 1974-77, numerous letters of commendation. **BUSINESS ADDRESS:** Freeman Motors Inc, 512 S Clay St, Hopkinsville, KY 42240.

FREEMAN, PAUL D.
Symphony orchestra conductor. **PERSONAL:** Born Jan 02, 1936, Richmond, VA; son of Mr & Mrs L H Freeman; married Cornelia Perry; children: Douglas Cornelia. **EDUCATION:** Eastman School of Music, BMus 1956, MMus 1957, PhD Theory 1963; Hochschule Fur Musik Berlin, additional studies; Orchestral & Operatic Conducting with Prof Ewald Lindemann 1957-59; L'Ecole Monteux with Pierre Monteux; Amer Symphony Orchestra League Workshop with Dr Richard Lert. **CAREER:** Hochstein Music School, Rochester NY, dir 1960-66; Opera Theatre of Rochester, music dir 1961-66; San Francisco Community Music Ctr, dir 1966-68; San Francisco Little Symphony, music dir 1967-68; Dallas Symphony Orchestra, former assoc conductor 1968-70; Detroit Symphony, conductor-in-residence 1970-79; Saginaw Symphony, music dir; Helsinki Philharmonic Orch, principal guest conductor; Columbia Black Composers Series, artistic dir; numerous guest appearances in the US, England, Germany, Denmark, Norway, Sweden, Poland, Italy, Finland/Yugoslavia; numerous recordings; Chicago Sinfonietta, music dir, conductor 1987-; Victoria, BC, Canada Symphony, conductor 1979-88; music dir emeritus Victoria Symphony Orchestra, 1988-. **HONORS/ACHIEVEMENTS:** Winner, Dimitri Mitropolous Intl Conductors Competition, 1967; Special Spoleto Awd to conduct Tristan und Isolde, 1968 Festival of Two Worlds; Distinguished Alumni Citation, Univ of Rochester, 1975; Distinguished Citation Award, United Negro Coll Fund; Koussevitzky Intl Recording Award, 1974; included in Time magazine's Top Five Classical Records Listing, 1974; nominated for Ebony Arts Award, 1989. **BUSINESS ADDRESS:** Music Director, Chicago Sinfonietta, 7900 W Division, River Forest, IL 60305.

FREEMAN, PRESTON GARRISON
Educational administrator. **PERSONAL:** Born Apr 12, 1933, Washington, DC; married Jean Marie Hall; children: Jacqueline, Michelle, Nicole, Monica. **EDUCATION:** Morgan State Coll, BS 1955; George Washington Univ, MA 1961; Catholic Univ of Amer, PhD 1974. **CAREER:** Washington DC Public Schools, asst supt 1975-, asst supt 1972-74, exec asst 1969-72, dir 1966-69, counselor 1963-66, teacher 1955-63. **ORGANIZATIONS:** Mem, Amer Assn of School Admins; mem Assn for Supvr & Curriculum Devel; mem Phi Delta Kapp; mem Kappa Alpha Psi Fraternity; vice chmn Health & Welfare Council 1965-70; vice chmn Prince Georges Comm Action Com 1967-70; mem Child Day Care Assn 1968-70; Council of the Great Cities Fellow 1970-71; Exec Internship. **MILITARY SERVICE:** AASA Arlington, VA 1973-74. **BUSINESS ADDRESS:** DC Pub Sch 3rd Douglas Sts N E, Washington, DC 20002.

FREEMAN, ROBERT LEE
Clergyman, educator. **PERSONAL:** Married Clara Bellamy; children: Zallis, Roberta, Ollie, Juanita, Robertiera, Robert, Jr. **EDUCATION:** Morehouse Coll, AS; Atlanta Univ, MA; Daniel Payne Coll, HonDD. **CAREER:** Elberton County Schools, prin 1940-41; Toccoa High School, prin 1942-46; McCoy Hill Elementary School Americus, teacher 1946-57; Staley High School Americus, asst prin 1957-71; Theol School Albany, instructor 1971-73; School Am Baptist Seminary Nashville, Albany extension; Bethesda Baptist Church, reverned. **ORGANIZATIONS:** Past pres Americus Area Ministerial Assn; pres NAACP Americus Br; mem Masonic Lodge Americus; vice pres Americus & Sumter Co Improvement Assn; Elberton GA Shiloh Bapt Ch Townsville; Friendship Bapt Ch Toccoa; Bethesda Bapt Ch Americus. **HONORS/ACHIEVEMENTS:** Tchr of yr for Americus Unit of GA Tchrs & Educ Assn 1968-69.

FREEMAN, ROBERT TURNER, JR.
Management consultant. **PERSONAL:** Born Apr 25, 1918, New York, NY; son of Robert Freeman Sr and Eva Freeman; married Mary Frances Jones; children: Veronica Coleman, Robert Turner III. **EDUCATION:** Lincoln Univ, BA 1941; NY Univ Grad Sch, student 1941-42. **CAREER:** WPB, statistician 1942-45; United Mut Life Ins Co, vice pres actuary 1945-55; Ghana Ins Co Ltd, founder mng dir 1955-62; Ghana Genl Ins Co Ltd, 1959-62; Providence Ins Co Liberia, consult actuary 1958-59; Gr Nigeria Ins Co Ltd Lagos, dir founder 1960-63; Ghana State Ins Corp Accra, mng dir 1962-65; Nigerian Broadcasting Corp Lagos, 1964-65; Peace Corps, assoc dir for mgmt 1965-66; USA, consult minority affairs 1966-68; Freeman Cole & Assocs Inc, pres 1966-68; Bur Africa AID, dir office capital devel & finance 1968-71; Govt Ethiopia, ins adviser 1971-73; Consumers United Ins Co, pres chmn of the bd 1973-83; Freeman Intl Insurance Co, pres & chmn of the bd 1974-. **ORGANIZATIONS:** Mem Lafayette Fed Credit Union 1966-; trustee Solebury Sch PA; mem NAACP Task Force on Africa; trustee Lincoln Univ PA; dir & 1st vice pres Girl Scouts of the Nations Capitol; dir Children's Hosp; dir Richardson Bellows & Henry; trustee Phelps Stokes Fund; mem Lincoln Univ Alumni Assn; mem Alpha Phi Alpha; Rotarian; pres chmn of bd Freeman Intl Ins Co; mem Mayor's Fire Adv Comm DC, Mayor's Intl Trade & Investment Comm; mem Economic Develop Comm Conf of Black Mayors; dir Riggs Natl Bank; trustee Davis Memorial Goodwill Indust 1982-84. **HONORS/ACHIEVEMENTS:** Distinguished Alumni Awd NAFCO 1986; Hon LLD Lincoln Univ PA 1987; Bob Freeman Clinic Bldg, State Insurance Corp of Ghana 1987. **BUSINESS ADDRESS:** President/Chairman of Board, Freeman Intl Insurance Co, 1140 Connecticut Ave NW #609, Washington, DC 20036.

FREEMAN, RONALD J.
Attorney. **PERSONAL:** Born Aug 17, 1947, Winslow, NJ; married Adrenee Glover. **EDUCATION:** Rutgers Law Sch, JD 1972; Lincoln U, BA 1969. **CAREER:** Freeman Zeller & Bryant, atty; Legal Assistance, comm legal serv phil 1973; Camden Reg Legal Serv Inc, legal counsel 1972-73; Glassboro State Coll, adj 1973; NJ Dept Law & Pub Safety & Div Civil Rights in coop Rutgers Law Sch Clinic Prog, senior field representative aide 1972; NJ Dept Law & Public Safety Div on Civil Rights in coop Rutgers StateUniv Sch Law Clinical Prog, 1971; Rutgers StateUniv Coll Cntr, staff asst 1970. **ORGANIZATIONS:** Bar of the Supreme Ct PA 1973; Bar of the US District Ct E Dist PA 1973; Bar ot the US Ct Appeals Third Ciruit 1974; Bar of the Spuremem Ct NJ 1974; Bar of the US District Ct District NJ 1974; PA Bar Assn; Amer Bar Assn; Nat Bar Assn; Phil Bar Assn; Nat Conf Black Lawyers; Phi Alpha Delta; NJ Bar Assn. **BUSINESS ADDRESS:** 309 Market St, Camden, NJ 08102.

FREEMAN, RUBY E.
Registered nurse. **PERSONAL:** Born Apr 10, 1921, Port Arthur, TX; married Charles; children: Charles, III, Cheryl, Stanley. **EDUCATION:** Harlem Sch Nursing, RN 1942; NY U, BS 1945; Lamar U, Post Bacclaureate & Graduate Study. **CAREER:** Pt Arthur Ind Sch Dist, sch nurse Registered Profl; Port Arthur Indp Sch Dist, resourcer; Lincoln Hosp, med supr 1945-47; Grasslands Hosp, head nurse 1951-56; Nursing Co-Ed Post, explorer advisor. **ORGANIZATIONS:** Youth adv Jack & Jill Am Inc Nat Educ Assn; Texas State Tchrs Assn; Texas Classroom Tchrs Assn; NAACP; Delta Sigma Theta Inc; C of C; Links Top Ladies Dinstinction Inc; Three Rivers Council BSA; Ladies Aux Knights of Peter Claver; adv com Manpower Devel Training Act; numerous Mayoral & chamber commerce com; membership com Comm Concert Assn 5 yrs; mem Port Arthur Little Theatre; adv bd TX Artists & Museum 1975-; Port Arthur Hist Soc; namedto Port Arthur's Citizen's Adv Com; charged with formulating recommendations for spending $132 million fed comm devel funds for 1st of 4-yr city project; 1 of 40 Texans appointed to serv on Adv Council of TX Employment Commn 1975-; mem St John Cath Ch; Delta Sigma Theta. **HONORS/ACHIEVEMENTS:** Awarded Cert Apprec Women in Comm Serv 1969; Outstanding Comm Leader Delta 1973; cited by Am Black Outreach 1st black wsoman in TX 1970-74; served 2 yrs TX Employment Commn; listed Personalities of the S 1976-77; World Who's Who of Women 1976; Comm Ldrs & Noteworthy Ams 1976-77; show; among first group black women to appear Woman's World annual. **BUSINESS ADDRESS:** 401 W 12 St, Port Arthur, TX 77640.

FREEMAN, RUGES R.
Educator. **PERSONAL:** Born Feb 25, 1917, St Louis, MO; son of Ruges R Freeman and Willie Barr Freeman; married Maxine Carter; children: Wilatrel. **EDUCATION:** So IL Univ, BE 1935; Univ IL, MA 1936; Washington Univ, PhD 1972; Attended, Stowe Tchrs Coll, Univ Chicago, St Louis Univ. **CAREER:** Dunbar HS, tchr 1936-38; Chicago Relief Admin, caseworker 1938-40; Vashon HS, tchr 1940-47, boys counselor & admin asst 1947-50; Dunbar Elem, asst/prin 1950-51; Carver Elem, Dumas Elem, Cote Brilliante Elem, principal 1951-64; Sumner HS, asst prin 1964-68, principal 1968; Beaumont HS, principal 1965-66; Harrison Elem, principal 1968-73; Teacher Corps, asst dir 1977-79, dir 1979-82; Secondary Student Teaching So IL Univ, assoc prof & coord 1973-76, prof 1982, emeritus 1983. **ORGANIZATIONS:** Bd dir United Church Men 1972-; vice pres Social Health Assn Gr St Louis 1972-; dir tchr corps Prog Dev Splst 1977-79; mem Dean's Adv Council 1978-81; bd dir Nursery Found 1978-81; mem SW IL Supt Conf 1978-; mem 1979-81, chmn 1981-82 Presidential Scholars; dir Tchr Corps 1979-82; mem Natl Soc Study Educ, Amer Educ Rsch Assn, Natl Educ Assn, Assn Supervision & Curriculum Devel, Phi Delta Kappa, Alpha Phi Alpha, Gaylords, Gnashers; St James AME Ch. **MILITARY SERVICE:** AUS 1944.

FREEMAN, THEODORE H., JR.
Business executive. **PERSONAL:** Born Nov 18, 1950, Auburn, NY; married Carrie E Burnett; children: Bonita Deanna, Theodore H III, Nyree Yolanda. **EDUCATION:** Villanova Univ, BA 1972; SUNY Brockport Grad School, 1976-77. **CAREER:** Haverford Comm Ctr Philadelphia, asst dir 1971-73; Booker T Washington Comm Ctr Auburn NY, exec dir 1973; Urban League of Rochester NY, dir of youth programming 1974-78; City of Rochester NY, exec consult 1977; Eastern Reg Council of Urban League Exec, exec comm mem 1978-; CETA Planning Council of JerseyCity, v chmn 1979-; Urban League of Hudson Co Inc, pres, chief exec officer 1978-. **ORGANIZATIONS:** Bd mem Central NY Reg Planning Bd 1972-73; arbitrator & mediator Amer Arbitration Assoc 1975-; exec dir Awd for Outstanding Serv Urban League of Rochester 1976; assoc prof St Peters Coll Jersey City 1979-. **HONORS/ACHIEVEMENTS:** Publ "Youth Programming-Comprehensive Look at Youth Svc" 1977; Outstanding Young Men of Amer US Jaycees 1977; Comm Serv Awd NAACP, Jaycees Chap 1979; Bobby Jackson Civic Assoc Serv Awd Jersey City 1979. **BUSINESS ADDRESS:** President, Urban League of Hudson Co Inc, 779 Belmont Ave, Jersey City, NJ 07306.

FREEMAN, THOMAS F.
Clergyman, educator. **PERSONAL:** Born Jun 27, 1920, Richmond, VA; children: Thomas, Jr, Carter, Carlotta. **EDUCATION:** Univ of Nigeria, Lagos;Univ of Ghana, Ghana E Africa; VA Union U, BA 1939; Andover Newton Theol Sch, BD 1942;Univ of Chicago, PhD 1948; Howard U, further study; Boston U, further study;Univ of Vienna, Austria, further study; African U. **CAREER:** Weekend Coll, dean; TX Southern Univ, dir continuing educ; Model Cities Training Ctr TSU, dir 1970-74; Coll of Arts & Sci TSU, asst dean 1968-70, dept head Philosophy 1950-67; Carmel Baptist Church, minister 1944-50; VA Union Univ, prof Practical Theology 1944-49; Monumental Baptist Church Chicago, assoc minister 1942-44; Pleasant St Baptist Church, Westerly RI, minister 1940-44; Concord Baptist Church, Boston MA, asst minister 1939-40; Mt Horem Baptist Church; Rice Univ, visiting prof. **ORGANIZATIONS:** Pres Alpha Kappa Mu Nat Honor Soc 1962-66; alumni dir Alpha Kappa Mu Nat Honor Soc 1966; bd dir Andover Newton Alumni Assn; bd dir Assn of Churches; mem NAACP; mem Boy Scouts; Urban League. **HONORS/ACHIEVEMENTS:** Recip Clarke Scholarship VA UnionUniv 1939; turner fellowship Andover Newton 1939-42; fellowshipUniv of C 1942-46;Univ DivintyUniv Faculty Mem of Yr 1950-51; TSU-PI CC Award TSU 1974; book Choices of The Pew 1963; Am Press co-author "From Separation to Special Designation" 1975.

FREEMAN, WALTER EUGENE
Manufacturing manager. **PERSONAL:** Born Apr 28, 1928, West Hartford, CT; son of Walter J Freeman and Clara Taylor Freeman; married Shirley Davis, Nov 01, 1952; children: Walter E Jr, Brian M. **EDUCATION:** Virginia State Coll, BS 1950. **CAREER:** Pratt & Whitney Aircraft Co, supv metalurgical test 1962-70, supv metrology 1970-77, asst chief nondestructive test 1977-83, chief purchase matl insp 1983-. **ORGANIZATIONS:** Mem Alpha Phi Alpha Frat 1946-; sec bd of dirs CT Savings & Loan Assoc 1968-79; mem Windsor Human Relations Commn 1976-80; dir Womens League Day Care Ctr 1977-; mem Sigma Pi Phi Frat 1982-; natl mem chmn Amer Soc for Metals 1984-86. **HONORS/ACHIEVEMENTS:** Black and Hispanic Achievers Awd Hartford CT YMCA 1981; Fund Raiser Awd Beta Sigma Lambda Chap Alpha Phi Alpha 1985. **MILITARY SERVICE:** AUS Chem Corp corpl 2 yrs. **HOME ADDRESS:** 68 Hope Circle, Windsor, CT 06095. **BUSINESS ADDRESS:** Chief Purchased Matls Inspec, Pratt & Whitney Aircraft, 400 Main St, East Hartford, CT 06108.

FREEMAN, WILLIAM M.
Educator, clergyman. **PERSONAL:** Born Jan 08, 1926, Nashville, NC; son of Fred Freeman and Roberta Freeman; married Arletha Greene (deceased); children: Robin, William III, Robert. **EDUCATION:** DE State Coll, BS 1949; Shaw Univ, BD 1958, MDiv 1970; NC Central Univ, MS 1960; Luther Rice Sem, DMin 1977. **CAREER:** Lillington NC, asst vocational agr teacher; Fuquay-Varnia HS, guidance counselor; Fuquay Varnia Elementary School, principal; Fuquay Springs Consolidated HS, principal 1973-75; Wake Co Public Schools NC, dir fed program; Wake Co School Raleigh NC, asst supt 1975-77; Nash Co Sch Nashville NC, asst supt for personnel 1977-83; Congressman Ike Andrews 4th Congressional Dist, staff asst; The Fuquay-Varina Indepednent NC, columnist "The Other Side of Fuquay"; North Carolina General Assembly, House of Representatives Dist 62; AME Zion Church, staff writer for Sunday school publ bd, dist supt presiding elder 1981-. **ORGANIZATIONS:** Mem Phi Delta Kappa; Fuquay-Varina Town Commr 1st Black 1973; Mayor Pro Tem 1st Black 1979-; bd dir Chamber of Commerce; NEA; NC Assn of Educators; mem Omega Psi Phi; Mason; Elk. **HONORS/ACHIEVEMENTS:** Outstanding Serv & Achievement Award in Educ & Govt in 6th Dist Omega Psi Phi; Human Rellations Award Wake Co & NCAE Dist 11; Outstanding Dedication Wake Co; NCAE First Newsletter Editor "The Teachers Pet" 1973; 1st place among Newsletters in the state published by local NCAE Units in 1976; Outstanding Contributor to Fuquay-Varina HS & Comm; School Advisory Council Bd Dir Wake Co Opportunities Inc 1975; Citizen of Yr Fuquay-Varina 1973; Omega Man of Yr 1975-76; Honored as one of top ten grads from Delaware State Coll decade of 1940-49 honored in 1983; inducted into Delaware State Athletic Hall of Fame for Football, Boxing and Wrestling 1985. **MILITARY SERVICE:** USMCR sgt E-5 1953-64. **HOME ADDRESS:** 502 Burton St, Fuquay-Varina, NC 27526.

FREEMAN-LINDSAY, DIANE
Educational administrator. **PERSONAL:** Born in Springfield, MA; divorced; children: Uraca Jorge, Joaquin Arturo, Javier Akin. **EDUCATION:** Central CT State Univ, BA Anthropology 1970; Univ of CT, MSW Casework 1977; Wellesley Coll, Cert Mgmt 1983. **CAREER:** Univ of Hartford, social work consul 1977, dir sociological & multicultural studies prog 1977-78, asst dir for admin 1978-80; Hartford Bd of Educ, therapist special educ 1980-81; Trinity Coll, asst dir career counseling 1981-84; Greater Hartford Comm Coll, dir special svcs/ASTRA. **ORGANIZATIONS:** Instructor New Hampshire Coll CT campus 1979-82; instructor Eastern CT State Univ 1981; instructor Greater Hartford Comm Coll 1985; adv Students of Color Trinity Coll 1984-85; vice pres New England Minority Women Admin in Higher Ed 1984-86.

FREEMONT, JAMES MCKINLEY
Physician. **PERSONAL:** Born Dec 02, 1942, Monroe, LA; married Erma Turner; children: James Jr, Joi Michelle, Jonathan Marcus. **EDUCATION:** Southern Univ, BS 1966; Emory Univ Sch of Med, MD 1973. **CAREER:** Health First (HMO), sec/treas 1980-82; Southwest Comm Hosp, chief, dept ob/gyn 1985-86. **ORGANIZATIONS:** Mem Omega Psi Phi Frat 1962-; med dir Women Health Ctr 1980-; pres Atlanta Chap Southern Alumni Assoc 1983-; bd mem United Comm Corp 1985-. **HONORS/ACHIEVEMENTS:** Outstanding Alumni NAFEO 1986. **MILITARY SERVICE:** AUS sgt 1966-68. **BUSINESS ADDRESS:** 777 Cleveland Ave, Atlanta, GA 30315.

FREGIA, DARRELL LEON
Administrator. **PERSONAL:** Born Sep 08, 1949, San Francisco, CA; married Deborah Brooks; children: Marque, Akil Fregia. **EDUCATION:** City Coll of San Francisco, AA Gen Educ 1967-69; Stanford U, BA Soc 1970-72;Univ of Wash, MHA 1975-77. **CAREER:** Group Hlth Coop of Puget Sound Central Hosp & Med Center, asst hosp adminstr 1979-; Group Hlth Coop Fed Way Med Center, adminstr 1978-79; Group Hlth Coop Eastside Hosp & Med Ctr, adminstr 1977-78; VA Hosp Seattle, adminstr, intern 1976; San Mateo Co Probation Dept Redwood City CA, adult probationofficer 1973-75. **ORGANIZATIONS:** Mem StanfordUniv Buck Club 1972-; mem StanfordUniv Alumni Assn 1972-; cons/analyst Pioneer Mgmt Inc Seattle 1978-; life mem Alpha Phi Alpha Frat Inc 1977; mem Seattle Comm Coll Curriculum Task Force 1978; sec bd of dirs Ctr for Addiction Servs Seattle 1978-; vice pres bd of dir Paul Robeson Theatre Prod 1980. **HONORS/ACHIEVEMENTS:** Recip player of the yr award San Francisco HS AAA Bsktbll 1967; buck club athletic scholorship StanfordUniv Bsktbll 1970-72; scholarships grad sch Vice Pres for Hlth AffairsUniv of Wash 1975-77; traineeship US Dept of Pub Hlth 1975-77; outst young man of Am award US Jaycees 1979. **BUSINESS ADDRESS:** Central Hosp & Med Center, 201 16th Ave E, Seattle, WA 98112.

FREGIA, PAUL DOUGLAS
Manager. **PERSONAL:** Born Jul 25, 1958, Beaumont, TX. **EDUCATION:** Lamar Univ, BSEE 1981. **CAREER:** Container Corp of Amer, super quality assurance 1984, general supervisor 1984, sr system specialist 1984-85, financial analyst 1986. **ORGANIZATIONS:** Alumni committee Natl Soc of Amer 1979-86; workshop worker Ascension to Manhood 1985-86; consultant Junior Achievement 1986. **HONORS/ACHIEVEMENTS:** Chap founder & president Natl Soc of Black Engineers 1979; GEM Grad Engineering Scholarship 1981; listed in Who's Who Among Students in America 1981; Outstanding Young Men of America 1984. **BUSINESS ADDRESS:** Financial Analyst, Container Corporation of Amer, 2 N LaSalle St, Chicago, IL 60602.

FRELOW, ROBERT DEAN
Educator. **PERSONAL:** Born Aug 01, 1932, Seminole, OK; divorced; children: Robert, Fred, Michael. **EDUCATION:** San Francisco State Coll, BA 1954; San Francisco State Univ, MA 1964; Univ of CA-Berkeley, PhD 1970. **CAREER:** Oakland Unified Schools, teacher 1960-66; Berkeley Unified Schools, asst to supt 1966-70; Greenburgh Dist 7, asst supt 1970-74, supt 1974-. **ORGANIZATIONS:** Mem Amer Assoc of Sch Admin 1970-; adjunct assoc prof Pace Univ 1973-; bd of dirs Westchester Arts Council 1982-87, Amer Red Cross 1985-86. **HONORS/ACHIEVEMENTS:** Omega Citizen of the Yr Beta Alpha Chap Omega Psi Phi 1984; Proclamation Robert D Frelow Day Westchester Bd of Legislators 1985. **MILITARY SERVICE:** USAF capt 3 yrs. **HOME ADDRESS:** 25A Hillside Terr, White Plains, NY 10601. **BUSINESS ADDRESS:** Superintendent of Schools, Greenburgh Central Sch Dist 7, 475 West Hartsdale Ave, Hartsdale, NY 10503.

FRENCH, GEORGE WESLEY
Educator. **PERSONAL:** Born Nov 28, 1928, Philadelphia, PA; married Elene Johnson; children: Andrea Natasha, Geofrrey Wesley. **EDUCATION:** Temple U, BS Ed, MS Ed, EDD Ed 1970. **CAREER:** School Dist of Philadelphia, dir, prin, teacher 1952-; Penn-Susquehanna School Dist, consultant 1969; Pennsauken School Dist, 1969; Fordham Univ, 1975; Kent State Univ, 1975; Dayton School Dist, 1975; McGraw-Hill Pub Soc Stud Text, 1975-77; PA State Dept of Educ, 1970-77; Beaver Coll, 1971; Fels Inst of Govt, 1976. **ORGANIZATIONS:** Mem Anti/Defamation Leag 1970-71; mem PA St Dem Com 1970-76; Am Acad of Political Sciences; Am Hist Soc; Asso for Curr Devel & Supervsn; Assn for Black Leadership in Ed; pres Black Ed Forum; mem Law Ed & Part Adv Bd; Nat Hist Soc; Black Pol Forum; Nat Coun for the Soc Studies; Orgn of Hist; PA conf for Black Basic Ed; pres Bd of Alice Rouse Donaldson Self-help Ctr; mem Big Broth Assn; pres Christian Sts Men's Club; pres Bd Florence Crittenton Serv; sec Bd of Germantown Stevens Acad; mem exec bd Northwest NAACP; mem Soc of PA; Unit Way Review Com. **HONORS/ACHIEVEMENTS:** Black Educ Forum Award 1970-71; OV Catto Elks Award; Educator of the Yr 1974; citation of honor Christian St YMCA 1968; Gov Award for outst leadership in Ed 1974. **MILITARY SERVICE:** USNA corpl 1946-47. **BUSINESS ADDRESS:** Rm 330 21st Parkway, Philadelphia, PA 19103.

FRENCH, JAMES J.
Editor, publisher. **PERSONAL:** Born Oct 07, 1926, Kansas City, KS; married Olivia Jackson; children: James, Jr, Nanette Maria, Simona Alison. **EDUCATION:** KS Tech Coll, 1949; San Francisco State Coll. **CAREER:** The Chronicle, editor & publ. **ORGANIZATIONS:** Bd mem SC Counc Human Right; SC Task Force Adminstrv Justice; life mem NAACP; vice pres Ctr Preservation & Cultural Black Arts. **HONORS/ACHIEVEMENTS:** NNPA Award Best Columnist 1973; Presidential Unit Citation; Bronze Star Vietnam Combat Journalist. **MILITARY SERVICE:** USN chief journalist 1951-71. **BUSINESS ADDRESS:** PO Box 2548, Charleston, SC 29403.

FRENCH, JOSEPH HENRY
Physician, educator. **PERSONAL:** Born Jul 03, 1928, Toledo, OH; married Marilyn E

Doss; children: Lenore, Joseph, Lisa, John. **EDUCATION:** OSU, AB 1950, MD (cum laude) 1954. **CAREER:** Johns Hopkins Hospital School of Medicine, fellow 1960-61; Univ of CO School of Medicine, asst prof 1961-64; Albert Einstein Coll of Medicine, 1964-79; Dept of Pediatrics, Norwalk Hospital, chmn 1979-80; Clinical Serv Inst for Basic Rsch in Developmental Disabilities, dep dir 1980-; Rose F Kennedy Center for Child's Evaluation, asst dean dir; Albert Einstein Coll of Medicine, asst prof, prof Pediatric Neurology. **ORGANIZATIONS:** Chmn Pediatric Neurology Sect; co-editor Intl Reviews of Child Neurology 1982-; exec comm Intl Child Neurology Assn 1980-84; pres Tri-State Child Neurology Soc 1982-83; peripheral & central nervous system drugs adv comm Food & Drug Admin 1980-84; exec comm Child Neurology Soc 1977-79; Kappa Alpha Psi 1947; Phi Beta Kappa 1950; Alpha Omega Alpha 1954; Alpha Epsilon Delta 1950; Phi Delta Upsilon 1950; Sigma Pi Phi 1984. **MILITARY SERVICE:** AUS t/5. **BUSINESS ADDRESS:** 1050 Forest Hill Rd, Staten Island, NY 10314.

FRENCH, MARYANN
Journalist. **PERSONAL:** Born Aug 12, 1952, Washington, DC. **EDUCATION:** Attended, Boston Univ 1969-70, Johns Hopkins Univ 1979; Johns Hopkins Sch of Advanced Intl Studies, MA 1982. **CAREER:** Black Women's Comm Develop Found, dir of program admin 1977-78; The Washington Post, researcher 1981-82; Time Magazine, reporter/researcher 1982-84; The Louisville Courier Journal, reporter 1984-86; St Petersburg Times, Washington corres 1986-. **ORGANIZATIONS:** Mem Louisville Assoc of Black Communicators 1984-86, Natl Assoc of Black Journalists 1984-, Washington Assoc of Black Journalists 1986-. **HONORS/ACHIEVEMENTS:** Fellowship Modern Media (Poynter) Inst 1982; Metro Louisville Sigma Delta Chi Awd for continuing coverage of the artificial heart experiment 1984. **BUSINESS ADDRESS:** Washington Correspondent, St Petersburg (FL) Times, 1414 22nd St NW, Washington, DC 20037.

FRENCH, ROBERT P.
Salesman. **PERSONAL:** Born Jan 28, 1919, Rankin, PA; married Jeanette Foster. **EDUCATION:** M Litt, AB 1954. **CAREER:** Point Park Coll, former part-time instr sociology; PA State U, part-time inst sociology, cont educ prgm; Seagram Dist Co, salesman (retired). **ORGANIZATIONS:** Bd mem Youth Devel Ctr of W PA; former pres Counc Braddock Hills Boro; mem exec bd Local #131 AFL-CIO 16 yrs; mem bd dir Braddock General Hosp for past 4 yrs; mem trustee bd Mt Olive Baptist Church. **MILITARY SERVICE:** AUS capt.

FRESH, EDITH MCCULLOUGH
Educator. **PERSONAL:** Born Sep 23, 1942, Quincy, FL; married Frederick Anthony Fresh; children: Kevin W, Bradford, Carla, Eric. **EDUCATION:** IN Univ, AB 1960-70; Univ of MI, MSW 1970-72; Gestalt Inst of Cleveland, Diploma 1976-77; GA State Univ, Doctoral grad student Clinical Psych 1985-. **CAREER:** Project Headline Detroit MI, dir outpatient treatment 1972-73; Public Tech Inc, human resources spec 1973-77; FL A&M Univ FL, asst prof 1977-83; EM Fresh & Assoc FL, sr assoc 1977-83; Morehouse School of Med, clinical social worker. **ORGANIZATIONS:** Mem Acad of Cert Social Workers 1976-, Natl Assoc of Social Workers 1976-; reg coord Natl Hook-Up of Black Women 1980-84; clinical mem Amer Assoc ofMarriage & Family Therapists 1980-; site visitor for the Commission on the Accreditation for Marriage and Therapy Educ 1982-; visiting staff Gestalt Inst of Cleveland 1981-; bd mem Mental Health Dist Bd II-B Leon Cty, FL 1982-83; mem Amer Assn of Univ Women 1983-. **HONORS/ACHIEVEMENTS:** Rep Gwen Cherry Memorial Awd for Outstanding Contrib for Women's Rights in the State of Florida Southern Reg Journalists Assoc 1980; Woman of the Year Zeta Phi Beta 1982; Outstanding Young Women of Amer 1979. **BUSINESS ADDRESS:** Clinical Social Worker, Morehouse School of Medicine, 720 Westview Dr SW, Atlanta, GA 30310.

FRIES, SHARON LAVONNE
University administrator. **PERSONAL:** Born Jul 26, 1959, Chattahoochee, GA. **EDUCATION:** Univ of MD-College Park, BS 1981; The OH State Univ, MA 1983. **CAREER:** The OH State Univ, asst dir Morrill Tower 1981-82, student develop grad asst 1982-83; Towson State Univ, area coord 1983-85; Univ of MD, asst to vice pres for student affairs, chancellor 1985-. **ORGANIZATIONS:** Mem Amer Coll and Personnel Associate 1981-; mem rsch bd ACPA 1985; directorate of comm IX assessment for student devel ACPA 1986; membership chair/assoc staff rep Black Fac/Staff Assoc; mem St James AME Church; mem Media and Editorial Bd ACPA; rep multicultural affairs comm ACPA; mem Amer Assoc of Affirmative Action Officers; mem Black Women's Council The Univ of MD-College Park; consultations Univ of MD Campus Programs and Off Campus Presentations. **HONORS/ACHIEVEMENTS:** New Presenters Awd MACUHO 1985; Human Relations Serv Awd State of MD 1986; Associate Staff Outstanding Contibution Award, Univ of MD, 1988; mem of Omicron Delta Kappa 1989; Outstanding Service Award, Black Faculty and Staff 1986-88. **BUSINESS ADDRESS:** Assistant to the Vice President for Student Affairs, University of Maryland College Park, 2108 Mitchell Building, College Park, MD 20742.

FRINK, JOHN SPENCER
Insurance company executive. **PERSONAL:** Born Sep 07, 1930, Fernandina Beach, FL; married Emmie Mae Williams; children: Bruce Romell, Jaques Rummel. **EDUCATION:** Bethune Cookman Coll, BS 1955. **CAREER:** Atlanta Life Insurance Co, agent, 1955-58, dist mgr 1958-70, asst vice pres area dir 1970-77, vice pres dir of agencies 1977-83, vice pres dir of agency devel 1984-. **ORGANIZATIONS:** chapter pres, Omega Psi Phi Fraternity, 1960-71; vice pres agency section; bd of dirs, Natl Insurance Assn, 1982-83. **HONORS/ACHIEVEMENTS:** John S Frink Day City of Daytona Beach 1982; Distinguished Alumni Citation NAFEO 1983; Agency Officer of the Year Natl Ins Assn, 1983. **MILITARY SERVICE:** AUS sgt 1st class 1950-53; NCOIC, Crypto Ctr, FECOM 1951-52. **HOME ADDRESS:** 1201 Sunset Circle, Daytona Beach, FL 32017.

FRINK, RONALD MURICE
Professional engineer. **PERSONAL:** Born Dec 23, 1959, Whiteville, NC. **EDUCATION:** NC State Univ, BS Civil Engrg 1984. **CAREER:** NC Dept of Transportation, bridge design engr 1984-. **ORGANIZATIONS:** Chairmanship Alpha Phi Alpha Frat Inc 1980-; mem Amer Soc of Civil Engrs 1984-. **HONORS/ACHIEVEMENTS:** New Era Assoc Scholarship 1983. **BUSINESS ADDRESS:** Bridge Design Engineer, NC Dept of Transportation, 41 Oberlin Rd, Raleigh, NC 27607.

FRISON, LEE A.
Business manager, financial administrator. **PERSONAL:** Born Jun 09, 1941, LaFayette County, MS; married Luxie M Greene; children: Jacqueline M, Lee A. **EDUCATION:** MS Valley State U, BS 1963;Univ of Omaha, Bus Mgmt Cert 1968; Harvard U, Educ Mgmt Cert 1974; Jackson State U, completed course work MBA 1979. **CAREER:** MS Valley State Univ, business mgr 1977-; Jackson State Univ, asst to vice pres for fiscal affairs 1962-77; MDTA Center, MS Valley State Univ, bookkeeper 1966-77; Coahoma Jr Coll, business mgr 1967-69; Beta Alph Chapter of Omega Phi Psi Frat, keeper of finances 1973-77. **ORGANIZATIONS:** Mem Panel for S Assn of Coll & Sch Accreditation Team 1978; grand treas MW Stringer Grand Lodge 1973-. **HONORS/ACHIEVEMENTS:** Serv award Jackson StateUniv 1977; Good Conduct Medal AUS. **MILITARY SERVICE:** AUS E-5 1963-66. **BUSINESS ADDRESS:** P O Box 1177, Itta Bena, MS 38941.

FRITZ, JAMES B.
Executive director. **PERSONAL:** Born May 22, 1927, Wash, PA; married Mary G; children: Pam, Kelly, Christina. **EDUCATION:** Wayne State U, 1954; Worsham Coll Mortuary Sci, BS 1961. **CAREER:** Fritz Funeral Home, mortician funeral dir. **ORGANIZATIONS:** Mem MI Selected Morticians Assn; Nat Funeral Dir & Morticians Assn; Epsilon Nu Delta Mortuary Frat; chmn Selective Serv Local Bd 98; vice pres MOORS Bus &Professional Men's Club; bd dir Family Serv of Detroit & Wayne Co; sec treas Kirwood Mental Hlth Ctr; trustee Peoples Comm Ch; life mem NAACP; mem SherwoodForest Assn. **MILITARY SERVICE:** AUS supply sgt 1950-52. **BUSINESS ADDRESS:** 246 E Ferry St, Detroit, MI 48202.

FRITZ, MOSES KELLY
Executive director. **PERSONAL:** Born Jul 06, 1904, Uniontown, AL; married Johnnie M. **EDUCATION:** Eckels Coll Mortuary Sci, 1925. **CAREER:** Fritz Funeral Home, propr Operator. **ORGANIZATIONS:** Mem Nat Funeral Dir & Morticians Assn; MI Selected Morticians Assn; MI Funeral Dir & Nat Funeral Dir Assn; mem Adv bd Selective Serv Local Bd 92; vice-chmn bd mgmt Northern Br YMCA; chmn Camping Com Detroit Area Counc Camp Fire Girls; treas Housing Found of MI; mem 13th Congressional Dist Dem Orgn; mem-at-large Detroit DistArea Counc BSA; counc mem Intl Inst; mem Elks; Masonic Order Narracci Temple Shrine #13; Wolverine Consistory #6; 33rd Degree Mason; Omega Psi Phi Frat; Cathedral Ch of St Paul (Episcopalian); vice pres Concord Co-op Townhouses; mem Jolly Old-Timers & Amles Club of Detroit.

FROE, DREYFUS WALTER
Agency director. **PERSONAL:** Born Feb 18, 1914, Bluefield, WV; widowed; children: Dreyfus L II, Dana A. **EDUCATION:** WV State Coll, BSA 1933; WV U, MS 1944; Marshall U, Adv Study 1948; Boston U, Adv Study 1965. **CAREER:** Bluefield State Coll, tchr & coach 1936-45; Mercer Cnty Sch, tchr & admin 1945-59; US Dept of State, diplomatic serv 1959-69; Mercer Cnty EOC, exec dir 1969-85. **ORGANIZATIONS:** Asst dir Flanner House; Masons; state dir ed Elks-Civitane 1965-75; sir archon Sigma Phi Pi Frat; basalus Omega Psi Phi. **HONORS/ACHIEVEMENTS:** Layman of the Yr United Meth Ch WN Conf 1980; Outstand Citizen Mountain State Bar Assn 1980; Outstand Leadership NAACP Mercer Cnty Bar 1981; Football Hall of Fame WV State Coll 1983. **HOME ADDRESS:** 314 Belcher, Bluefield, WV 24701.

FROE, OTIS DAVID
Research administrator. **PERSONAL:** Born Dec 24, 1912, Bluefield, WV; married Otyce Brown; children: Lynne Pamela. **EDUCATION:** Bluefield State Coll, BS Math 1935; Univ of MI, MS Stat 1940;Univ of Chgo, PhD Meas 1947. **CAREER:** Morristown Coll, dean 1940-47; Central State U, dean 1947-50; Morgan State U, dir inst res 1950-76; Research Svcs, Inc, dir, research svcs. **ORGANIZATIONS:** Pres Nat Media Assoc 1957-76; pres MD State Personnel & Guid Assoc; bd of dir Balto Symphony Orc 1975-77; Phi Delta Kappa Prof Edn; Alpha Phi Alpha Soc Frat; Promethean Kappa Tau Hon Soc. **HONORS/ACHIEVEMENTS:** Research fellow Southern Reg Educ Bd; books & articles Re Human Behavior. **MILITARY SERVICE:** AAF. **HOME ADDRESS:** 2301 Ivy Ave, Baltimore, MD 21214. **BUSINESS ADDRESS:** Director, Research Services, Research Services, Inc, 2301 Ivy Ave, Morgan State Univ, Baltimore, MD 21214.

FROHMAN, ROLAND H.
Dentist. **PERSONAL:** Born Aug 18, 1928, Detroit; married Alice F Hibbett; children: Roland, Jr, Shelley, Jill. **EDUCATION:** Wayne State U, AB 1951; Howard U, DDS 1955. **CAREER:** Denstistry, prvt prac 1961-; Dr Robert L Moseley, assoc 1957-61; Harper Hosp Detroit, on staff 1968-. **ORGANIZATIONS:** Mem Am Dental Assn; Wolverine Dental Assn; MI State Dental Assn; Detroit Dist Dental Assn; mem Tot's & Teen's Orgn. **HONORS/ACHIEVEMENTS:** Redip Cert of Recognition by Mayor of Detroit for serv in Mayors Youth Employment Prgm 1968. **MILITARY SERVICE:** AUS capt 1955-57. **BUSINESS ADDRESS:** 13026 W Mc Nichols, Detroit, MI 48235.

FROST, HUGH A.
Association executive. **PERSONAL:** Born Sep 29, 1926, Youngstown, OH; married Daisy Lillian; children: Hugh L, Gary L, Neal, & Lynette C. **EDUCATION:** Bluffton Coll, BS Social Sci 1951; W Reserve U, Grad Sch Applied Social Sci 1959-61; Westminster Coll, MA Educ Psychology 1966-67;Univ of Dayton; Youngstown U; Geo Williams Coll; McGee Brokerage Firm. **CAREER:** Younstown State U, asst to pres 1968-; McGuffey Ctr Inc, exec dir 1956-68; Westlake Playground Assn, playground dir 1947-50; Findlay YMCA, instr physical activities 1950; Bradfield Ctr, vol physical dir 1950; Spring St YMCA, boys work sec 1951-52; Deccamen Co, sec treas 1951-55; West Fed St YMCA, boys work prgm sec 1952-54; Am Motors, part-time car slsmn 1952-55; Senate Ave YMCA, mem sec 1955; Chevrolet, part-time car slsmn 1956-57; Real Estate, slsmn 1960-65; Jackson Realty, br mgr 1961-63; Head Consult Agy, 1962-; Lctr, area colls 1965-. **ORGANIZATIONS:** Vp OH Affirmative Action Ofcrs Assn; bd trustees Youngstown Rotary Club; bd trustees Comm Chest Corp; bd trustees Assn Nghbrhd Ctrs; bd trustees Exec Com Mahoning Co; pres McGuffey Ctr Inc; adv bd Nat Plng Assn for Planners; vice pres Youngstown Boys Clubs of Am; bd trustees Fresh Air Camp; mahoning Co Draft Bd #80; alumni pres adv com bd trustees Bluffton Coll; adv com Youngstown Soc for Blind past bd dirs; adv com Youngstown Hearing & Speech Ctr; mem NAACP; Mahoning Co Cits Adv Com on Comm Devel. **HONORS/ACHIEVEMENTS:** Recip recog for serv rendered as chmn Christmas Shopping Tour Youngstown Jr C of C 1958; man of yr award Youngstown Jr C pf C 1961-62; cert appreciation Hubbard Rotary Club 1962; spl cit judge prosecutor & jurors for outst ldrshp as jury forman of session of Mahoning Co Grand Jury 1963; Educ Award OH Assn of Beauticians 1966; comm ldr award Troop 18 Boy

Scouts 1967-68; award for comm involvement & serv Rotary Club 1969; outst alumnus award Bluffton Coll 1970; urban family of yr Youngstown C of C 1971; civic award for serv to co & comm Alpha Kappa Psi 1972; meritorious serv award OH Counc for Vocation Educ 1972; outst civic award Buckeye Elks 1972; cert of appreciation valuable serv contributed to nation & Selec Serv Sys in Admin of Military Selec Serv Act of 1967, Pres of US 1973; Younstown StateUniv Student Gov Serv Award outst serv 1974. **MILITARY SERVICE:** USAAF cpl. **BUSINESS ADDRESS:** 410 Wick Ave, Youngstown, OH 44555.

FROST, OLIVIA PLEASANTS
Educator. **PERSONAL:** Born in Asbury Pk, NJ; divorced; children: Carolyn Olivia, James W, Charles S Jr. **EDUCATION:** Hunter Coll, BA; Columbia Univ, MA 1951; NY Univ, Dept of Human Relation s, Sch of Educ, PhD 1972. **CAREER:** Haryou-Contributor to Youth in the Ghetto, rsch assoc 1963-66; NY Urban League, rsch dir 1965-66; Haryou-ACT, rsch assoc 1969-70; New York City Youth Bd Comm Council of NY, rsch assoc; Columbia Univ, Malcolm King Harlem Coll, Ext MARC Demonstration Proj on Adolescent Minority Females, rsch consultant 1971-75; CUNY, assoc prof 1972-77; Central SEEK, dir prog devel; licensed real estate broker; College of New Rochelle, prof. **ORGANIZATIONS:** Mem Natl Assn Social Workers, Afro-Amer Historical & Genealogical Soc Inc; mem Assn Black Social Workers; dir comm study Harlem A Neglected Investment Oppor; mem NAACP, NY Urban League; trustee Schomburg Corp. **HONORS/ACHIEVEMENTS:** Warburg Fellowship, Dept of Human Relations, Sch of Educ, NYU, 1968; grant for doctoral dissertation, Dept of Labor, Washington DC; founder, Assn of Black Women in Higher Educ.

FROST, WILLIAM HENRY
Mayor. **PERSONAL:** Born Apr 17, 1930, Maysville, NC; son of Philanders Frost and Gracie Parle Perry; married Ari Mae Jones, Jun 20, 1951; children: Warren, Leddia Frost Chapman, Aletha, Elroy. **CAREER:** US Civil Service, Camp Lejeune NC, warehouseman, 1955-65, chauffeur, 1965-68, radio dispatcher, 1968-77, bus driver, 1977-85; Town of Maysville, NC, aldermaan, 1972-85, mayor, 1985-. **ORGANIZATIONS:** Warehouseman, Civil Serv, chauffeur, 1965-68, radio dispatch, 1968-77, bus driver, 1977-85. **HONORS/ACHIEVEMENTS:** Three Civil Serv Awards for Outstanding work, 1981, 1983-84. **MILITARY SERVICE:** US Army, Cpl, 1950-55, Good Conduct Medal. **HOME ADDRESS:** PO Box 191, Maysville, NC 28555.

FROST, WILSON
City official, attorney. **PERSONAL:** Married Gloria Shepard; children: Jacqueline, Baldridge, Rhey Orme. **EDUCATION:** Fisk U, BA 1950; Chicago Kent Coll of Law, JD 1958; DePaulUniv & Lawyers Inst. **CAREER:** Frost Sherard Howse & Coleman, atty 1958-73; Meyer & Frost, 1973-; Postal Transportation Svc, clerk 1950-52; Provident Hosp, acct statistician 1952. **ORGANIZATIONS:** IL Youth Commn Very active in city govt; mem Originial Forty Club; Kappa Alpha Psi Frat; Phi Alpha Delta Legal Frat; IBPOE Lodge #43; com NAACP; Legal Redress Com; com Chicago Varsity Club; Cook Co Bar Assn; IL Bar Assn; Chicago Fisk Club; Chicago Kent Coll of Alumni Assn; Chicago Idlewilders Club;Original Chicago Idlewilders & Lions Internat; past legal adv & vice pres City Club of Chicago; past mem IL Probation & Parole Assn; mem Epsicopal Ch; elected Alderman 21st Ward 1967; acting Dem Ward Com 34th Ward 1970; committeeman 1972; alderman 34th Ward 1971; pres Protem City Counc 1973; floor ldr Com Chmn on France; delegate ot Nat Dem Conv 2nd Congressional Dist 1972. **MILITARY SERVICE:** AUS Signal Corps. **BUSINESS ADDRESS:** 123 W Madison St, Chicago, IL 60602.

FRY, LOUIS EDWIN, JR.
Architect, business executive. **PERSONAL:** Born Sep 11, 1928, Prairie View, TX; married Genelle Wiley; children: Jonisa, Oliver, Louis Edwin III, Vicki Lynn Wilson, Alexa Genelle Hawkins. **EDUCATION:** Howard Univ, BA Sociology 1947; Harvard Univ, BArch 1953; Fullbright Fellowship, Tech Hogeschool, Delft, Holland, 1954-55; Harvard Univ, MA Urban Design 1962. **CAREER:** Various Arch firm in the Wash DC, draftsman to project mgr 1955-60; Fry & Welch Architect, jr partner 1960-72, pres 1972-. **ORGANIZATIONS:** Fellow Am Inst of Architects 1973; founding mem Nat Organ of Minority Architects; mem Am Inst of Architects Committee on Design 1984; mem Overseers Committee to visit The Grad Sch of Design, Harvard Univ 1984-; mem DC Redevel Land Agency (RLA) Architectural Review Panel, Wash DC 1974-; mem Am Arbitration Assns Panel of Arbitrators 1983-. **HONORS/ACHIEVEMENTS:** Fellow Am Inst of Architects 1973; Fullbright Fellowship to study City Planning in The Netherlands 1954; Cert of Appreciation for serv as pres of The DC Architectural Regis Bd 1982; Cert of Award outstanding professional serv rendered to The Morgan Comm Sch Bd, Wash DC 1981. **BUSINESS ADDRESS:** President, Fry & Welch Architect, 7600 Georgia Ave, NW, Ste 401, Washington, DC 20012.

FRY, SIMON See AGURS, DONALD STEELE

FRYAR, IRVING
Professional athlete. **PERSONAL:** Born Sep 28, 1962, Mount Holly, NJ; married Jacqueline; children: Londen. **EDUCATION:** Attended, Nebraska. **CAREER:** New England Patriots, wide receiver 1984-. **HONORS/ACHIEVEMENTS:** Played in East-West Shrine game; Japan Bowl All Star game; first player selected in the 1984 NFL draft; named AP All-Pro 2nd team; College and Pro Football Newsweekly All-Pro 2nd team; took part in NBC Superteams competition; mem Pro Bowl team 1986. **BUSINESS ADDRESS:** New England Patriots, Schaefer Stadium Route 1, Foxboro, MA 02035.

FRYE, CHARLES ANTHONY
Educational administrator, editor. **PERSONAL:** Born Mar 18, 1946, Washington, DC; divorced; children: Odeyo J, Sekou C, Anthony F, Lia M. **EDUCATION:** Howard Univ, BA 1968, MA 1970; Univ of Pgh, PhD 1976. **CAREER:** DC Public Library, librarian 1968-69; DC Public Schools, teacher 1969-70; Afro-Amer Studies Howard Univ, asst prof 1970-77; Interdisciplinary Studies Fayetteville State Univ, dir 1977-78; Hampshire College, assoc dean of students/assoc prof of educ. **ORGANIZATIONS:** Consul Institute for Serv to Educ Wash 1974-77; chair/journal editor Natl Council for Black Studies New England 1980-82; chair/journal editor 5 College Black Studies Exec Comm 1983-85; mem Assoc for Supervision & Curriculum Dev 1977-; bd mem Natl Council for Black Studies; reviewer Journal of Negro History 1982-. **HONORS/ACHIEVEMENTS:** Adv Study Fellowship Ford Found 1972-73; The Impact of Black Studies on Three UnivsUniv Press of Amer 1976 and 1979; Towards a Philosophy of Black Studies R&E Rsch Assocs 1978; Level Three A Black Philosophy ReaderUniv Press of Amer 1980; Values in Conflict Blacks and the Am Ambivalence Toward Violence UPA 1980. **BUSINESS ADDRESS:** Associate Dean of Students, Hampshire College, Enfield House, Amherst, MA 01002.

FRYE, HENRY E.
Associate justice. **PERSONAL:** Born Aug 01, 1932, Richmond Co, NC; son of Walter Frye and Pearl Frye; married Shirely Taylor; children: Henry E, Harlan E. **EDUCATION:** A&T State U, BS 1953;Univ of NC Law Sch, JD 1959; SyracuseUniv Law Sch, summer 1958. **CAREER:** US Att NC, asst 1963-65; NCC Univ Law Sch, 1965-67; Frye & Johnson atty; NC house of rep, mem; NC Senate, mem; Supreme Court of NC, assoc justice 1983-. **ORGANIZATIONS:** Mem Greensboro Bar Assn; Am Bar Assn; NC Bar Assn; Black Lawyers Assn; Am Judicature Soc; life mem Nat Bar Assn; mem Kappa Alpha Psi Frat; formermem sec bd mgmt Hayes Taylor YMCA; deacon of Providence Bapt Ch; life mem NAACP. **HONORS/ACHIEVEMENTS:** Elected one of Guilford Co 6 rep in NC House 1968; 1st black in this century to NC House; received honorary Doctorate Degree Shaw Univ 1971; alumni excellence award A&T StateUniv 1972. **MILITARY SERVICE:** USAF capt 2 Yrs; USAFR. **BUSINESS ADDRESS:** Associate Justice, North Carolina Supreme Court, PO Box 1841, Raleigh, NC 27602.

FRYE, NADINE GRACE
Nurse, educator. **PERSONAL:** Born in Greensburg, PA; daughter of Charles Frye and Virgie Middles Frye Grasty. **EDUCATION:** Univ of Pittsburgh, BSN 1947, M Lit 1951, PhD, 1987. **CAREER:** Western Psych Inst & Clinic, Pgh PA, staff nurse/head nurse 1948-50; Detroit Dept of Hlth, Detroit MI, public hlth nurse 1951-53; Northville State Hosp (Nrsg Educ Dept), instructor/dir 1953-56; Lafayette Clinic, Detroit MI, dir nrsg educ 1956-57; Wayne State U, Detroit MI, instructor of nrsg 1957-59; Mercywood Hosp, Ann Arbor MI, dir nrsg educ 1959-61; Univ of MI Sch of Nrsng, asst prof/dir of nrsng 1961- 66; Western Psych Inst & Clinic, Pgh PA, assoc dir of cmh/mr nursing 1969-73;Univ of Pgh PA Sch of Nrsng, clinical/asst prof of nrsng 1969-. **ORGANIZATIONS:** Bd of dir 3 Rivers Youth Pgh PA 1971-77; consult St Agnes Catholic Sch Pgh PA 1971-73; consult Univ of S MS Sch of Nrsg 1976; consultUniv of Pgh Sch of Nrsg1980-81; mem Am Nurses Assn 1947-; mem Alpha Kappa Alpha 1944-; mem Pgh Club Nat Assn Negro Bus & Professional Women 1973-84; mem, Advisory Community Youth Ministry, Pittsburgh, PA, 1988-. **HONORS/ACHIEVEMENTS:** Monetary Award Kappa Alpha Psi, Pgh PA 1943; Robert L Vann Mem Schlrshp 1943; Alumni Award Univ of Pgh 1980; elected parish cncl Calvary Episcopal Ch 1980; chrmn Calvary Episcopal Ch Mission Commn 1984-86; Alumni Serv Awd Univ of Pittsburgh 1986; mem, Intl Sigma Theta Tau Honorary Nursing Sorority, 1988-. **BUSINESS ADDRESS:** Clinical Asst Prof of Nursing, Univ of Pittsburgh, Sch of Nursing, Victoria Hall Bldg, 3500 Victoria St, Pittsburgh, PA 15261.

FRYE, REGINALD STANLEY
Construction company president. **PERSONAL:** Born May 18, 1936, Yakima, WA; son of Virgil O Frye and Elise Garrett; married Mikki Goree, Jun 24, 1956; children: Gregory, Martin, Trana. **EDUCATION:** Los Angeles Community Coll, Los Angeles CA, 1955-56. **CAREER:** V O Frye Manufacturing, Seattle WA, salesman, 1959-64; Washington Natural Gas, Seattle WA, salesman, 1964-72; 3A Industries Inc, Seattle WA, pres, 1972-. **ORGANIZATIONS:** Pres, Central Contractors Assn, 1976-85; vice-chair, State of Washington OMWBE Advisory Bd, 1983-87. **HONORS/ACHIEVEMENTS:** Martin Luther King Jr Humanitarian Award, The Medium Newspaper, 1974; Community Service Award, United Inner City Devel Found, 1974, 1976; Special Recognition, Port of Seattle, 1983; Special Recognition, Natl Assn of Minority Contractors, 1983. **BUSINESS ADDRESS:** Chief Executive Officer, 3A Industries Inc, PO Box 14029, Seattle, WA 98114.

FRYE, ROBERT EDWARD
Government official. **PERSONAL:** Born Oct 11, 1936, Washington, DC; son of James E Frye and Alberta Edwards Frye; married Rotha Isabel Holbert, May 30, 1987; children: Robert Jr, Amanda. **EDUCATION:** Howard Univ, BSc 1958; Amer Univ, MPA 1970; Fed Exec Inst, 1975. **CAREER:** US Army Map Svc, cartographer 1958-65; Wolf R&D Corp, project mgr 1965-69; Natl Bureau of Standards, computer syst analyst 1969-73; US Consumer Prod Safety Com, div dir 1973-; Natl School Bd Assoc, consult 1985-. **ORGANIZATIONS:** Founding mem Reston Black Focus 1969-; mem Kappa Alpha Psi, Fire Reporting Com NFPA 1972-; mem at large Fairfax Cty School Bd 1978-85; mem Natl Caucus of Black School Bd Mems 1979-85; vice pres DA Frye Real Estate Inc 1979-85; mem finance comm VA School Bds Assoc 1982-85; mem Fairfax County Committee of 100 1985-. **HONORS/ACHIEVEMENTS:** Community Serv Awd Urban League Nova Chap 1982; Commun Serv Awd Natl Council of Negro Women 1985; CPSC EEO Achievement Awd 1986; CPSC Chairman's Award, US Consumer Product Safety Commission 1988. **MILITARY SERVICE:** AUS lt 1959-61.

FRYE, WILLIAM SINCLAIR
Government official. **PERSONAL:** Born Sep 08, 1924, Montclair, NJ; married Helen. **EDUCATION:** US Army Command & Gen Staff Coll, 1970; Rutgers U, 1972. **CAREER:** US Postal Serv Montclair NJ, postmaster; US Postal Serv Montvale NJ; postmaster 1977; rutherford NJ postal serv, officer in charge 1976; US Postal Serv Verona NJ, branch mgr 1964. **ORGANIZATIONS:** Asst div comdr 50th Armored Div 1977; comdr State Area Command 1978; mem NAACP;Urban League;Nat Guard Assn;Assn of the AUS Lions Club. **HONORS/ACHIEVEMENTS:** Nominated for ARCOM Comdr, Major Gen 1980; Meritorious Serv Medal; Army Commendation Medal. **MILITARY SERVICE:** AUS brig gen 35 Yr. **BUSINESS ADDRESS:** US Postal Serv, 125 Glen Ridge Ave, Montclair, NJ 07042.

FRYSON, SIM E.
Chief executive. **CAREER:** Sim Fryson Buick-Saab Inc, Smyrna, GA, chief executive, 1985-; Sim Fryson Pontiac-Oldsmobile-GMC Truck, Inc, Fulton, NY, chief executive. **BUSINESS ADDRESS:** Sim Fryson Pontiac-Oldsmobile-GMC Truck, Inc, Fulton, NY. *

FUDGE, ANN MARIE
Marketing manager. **PERSONAL:** Born in Washington, DC; married Richard Fudge Sr; children: Richard Jr, Kevin. **EDUCATION:** Simmons Coll, BA (honors) 1973; Harvard Bus Sch, MBA 1977. **CAREER:** Genl Elec, manpower specialist 1973-75; General Mills, marketing asst 1977-78, asst prod mgr 1978-80, prod mgr 1980-83, marketing dir 1983-. **ORGANIZATIONS:** Natl Black MBA Assn 1981-; Jr League 1981-. **HONORS/**

ACHIEVEMENTS: COGME Fellow 1975-76; YWCA Leadership Awd 1979. **BUSINESS ADDRESS:** Marketing Dir, General Mills, Inc, PO Box 1113, Minneapolis, MN 55440.

FUENTES, RIGOBERTO (TITO FUENTES)
Baseball player. **PERSONAL:** Born Jan 04, 1944, Havana, Cuba;married Carmen Ramirez; children: Jerry, Dion, Tito, Sophia, Souja, Cliuch, Patrick, Barbara. **CAREER:** San Diego Padres, 1974-; San Francisco Giants; Giants farm sys, 1962-65. **HONORS/ACHIEVEMENTS:** Most Popular Player in Decatur IL 1963; All Star Second Base in Lakeland, FL 1962; broke J Robinson record for less err in a season; broke Mazerowski recordfor fielding percentage; broke Jackie Robinson & Bill Mazerowski Fielding Record 1973. **BUSINESS ADDRESS:** San Diego, PO Box 2000, San Diego, CA 92120.

FUENTES, TITO See FUENTES, RIGOBERTO

FUGET, CHARLES ROBERT
Educational administrator. **PERSONAL:** Born Dec 15, 1929, Rochester, PA; son of Clinton H Fuget and Mary Harris Fuget; married Enid Deane; children: Craig D. **EDUCATION:** Geneva Coll, BS, 1951; PA State Univ, MS 1953, PhD 1956. **CAREER:** State Univ of NY, Coll at Buffalo, prof, chem, 1963-64; Geneva Coll, Beaver Falls PA, chmn, prof of physics 1964-71; Inndiana Univ of PA, assoc dean, School of arts/science, 1971-76, dean, coll natl sci/math 1977-84, acting vice pres, student Univ affairs, 1984-85; Coll Natl sci/math 1985-88; PA Dept of Educ, Harrisburg, PA, 1988-. **ORGANIZATIONS:** Consult AUS Ballistic Rsch Labs, Aberdeen, MD 1968, 1969; rsch chemist, Callery Chem Co Callery, PA 1957-63; rsch chemist, Esso Rsch & Engineering, Linden, NJ 1955-56; bd of dir IN Rotary Club 1982-88; IN Hosp Corp 1978-83; bd of governors, General Bd of Higher Educ & Ministry, 1980-88; chmn, PA Commn for United Ministries in Higher Educ 1978-80; vice pres, Univ Senate of the United Methodist Church, 1989-92. **HONORS/ACHIEVEMENTS:** Distinguished Serv Award, Alumni Assn, Geneva Coll, 1976; Distinguished Serv Award, Upper Beaver Valley Jaycees 1969; Indiana Univ of Pennsylvania, Pres' Medal of Distinction, 1988; LHD, Hahnemann Univ, 1988. **BUSINESS ADDRESS:** Deputy Secretary & Commissioner for Higher Educ, Dept of Educ, Commonwealth of Pennsylvania, 333 Market St, Harrisburg, PA 17126-0333.

FUGET, HENRY EUGENE
Bank president. **PERSONAL:** Born Aug 08, 1925, Rochester, PA; married Gladys Mae Smith; children: Sonja L. **EDUCATION:** Univ of Pittsburgh, BA 1966, MA 1967. **CAREER:** Upper Fifth Ave Office Mellon Bank, NA, manager 1972-79; Gulf Office, Mellon Bank, NA, avp & manager 1979-82; Mellon Bank, NA, avp & asst mngr 1982-85;New World Natl Bank, president. **ORGANIZATIONS:** Sickle Cell Soc, Inc,, treasurer 1983-; Three Rivers Rotary Club, Pgh, mem; Central Baptist Church, Pgh, deacon. **MILITARY SERVICE:** AUS mst sgt 20 years. **BUSINESS ADDRESS:** President, New World Natl Bank, 6393 Penn Ave, Pittsburgh, PA 15206.

FUHR, SAMUEL E.
Educator. **PERSONAL:** Born Aug 23, 1918, Oklahoma Co, OK. **EDUCATION:** Langston U, BS 1939; OK State U, MSc 1952; grad student 1960-61. **CAREER:** Rosenwald High School, Henryetta OK, teacher 1939-41; Dunbar High School, Hennessey OK, 1941-43; Okmulgee OK, 1943-48; OK State Univ, State Supr Institutional Farm Training 1948-51; USOM Iran, agr & educ specialist 1953-57, vocational educ adv 1957-58, dep chief educ adv 1958-59; USAID Nigeria, dep chief educ div 1961-64, chief educ div 1964-68; Africa Bur AID, dep chief educ div 1968; Africa Bur, prin educ officer 1969-70; US Aid Uganda, chief educ officer 1970-73; Africa Bur A10, educ officer 1973-74. **ORGANIZATIONS:** Mem Nat Educ Assn; OK Tchr Assn; mem Am Rifleman Assn; Am Legion; Alpha Phi Alpha; Phi Kappa Phi. **HONORS/ACHIEVEMENTS:** Commendation Award. **MILITARY SERVICE:** USOM 1956; USAID 1963; AUS 1956.

FULLER, ALMYRA OVETA
Research scientist, professor. **PERSONAL:** Born Aug 31, 1955, Mebone, NC; daughter of Herbert R Fuller and Deborah Evelyn Woods Fuller; married Jerry Caldwell, Jun 16, 1984; children: Brian Randolph Caldwell. **EDUCATION:** Univ of North Carolina, Chapel Hill, BA, 1977, PhD, 1983; Univ of Chicago, IL, postdoctoral Study, 1983-88. **CAREER:** Univ of Chicago, IL, research asst, 1980-81, instructor & fellow, 1984-85, research associate, 1987-88; Univ of MI, Ann Arbor, asst prof, 1988-. **ORGANIZATIONS:** Alpha Kappa Alpha, Basileus of Alumni Chapter, 1976-; Natl Technical Assn, co-founder of research triangle 1980-; UNC-CH Summer Apprentice Research Program, asst dir, 1981-82; Sigma Xi Research Society, mem, 1983-; Amer Assn for the Advancement of Science, mem, 1984-; Amer Society of Microbiology, mem, 1984-; DeVeras Inc, consultant, 1987-89; Advisory Committee to Fellows Programs, Lineberger Cancer Research Center, 1989-; Ad Hoc Reviewer, Louisiana bd of regents, 1989. **HONORS/ACHIEVEMENTS:** NTA Service Award, Research Triangle Chapter of NTA, 1983; author of scientific publications, 1983-89; Anna Fuller Fund Postdoc Award, 1983-84; Thornton Professional Achievement Award Chicago chap, NTA, 1984; NIH Postdoctoral Research Award, Nat Inst of Science, 1984-86; Postdoctoral Research Award, Ford Foundation, 1986-87. **BUSINESS ADDRESS:** Assistant Professor, University of Michigan Medical Center, 6736 Medical Science Bldg II, Ann Arbor, MI 48109-0620.

FULLER, CHARLES
Author. **PERSONAL:** Born Mar 05, 1939, Philadelphia, PA; married Miriam A Nesbitt; children: Charles, David. **EDUCATION:** LaSalle Univ & Villanova Univ, Hon PhD Fine Arts. **CAREER:** "The Brownsville Raid," author prod by Negro Ensemble Co 1976; "The Sky is Gray", screenwriter prod for TV 1980; "Zooman & the Sign", author Negro Ensemble Co 1980; freelance writer playwright; "A Soldier's Play", Negro Ensemble Co 1981. **HONORS/ACHIEVEMENTS:** CAPS Fellowship in Playwriting Creative Artist in Pub Serv 1975; Rockefeller Grant in Playwriting Rockefeller Found 1976-77; Natl Endowment Fellowship in Playwriting Natl Endowment of Arts 1976-77; John Simon Guggenheim Fellow in Playwriting John Simon Guggenheim Found 1977-78; Obie Awd Best Playwright 1981; Theatre Club Awd Best Play; Pulitzer Prize for Drama 1982; NY Critics Best Amer Play Awd 1982; Outer Circle Critics Awd Best Play 1982; Anselco Awds Best Playwright & Best Play 1981 & 1982; Hazelett Awd PA Council on the Arts Distinguished Artist. **MILITARY SERVICE:** AUS 1st lt 1959-62; Good Conduct Medal. **BUSINESS ADDRESS:** Wm Morris Agency, 1350 Ave of the Americas, New York, NY 10019.

FULLER, CURTIS D.
Musician, composer, arranger. **PERSONAL:** Born Dec 15, 1934, Detroit, MI; married Judith Patterson; children: Ronald, Darryl, Gerald, Dellaney, Wellington. **EDUCATION:** Detroit Inst of ArtsUniv of Detroit; Wayne State U, BA; Bronx Comm Coll, mus theory; Henry St Settlement Inst, jazzmobile prog under Billy Taylor. **CAREER:** Dizzy Gillispie Orch; Lester Young; James Moody; Quincy Jones Orch; Art Blakey "Jazz Messengers" Count Basie Orch; John Coltrane, recorded with & many others; LITU Long Island, NY, counselor & Instr. **ORGANIZATIONS:** Mem Local 802 Musicians Union; mem Broadcast Music Inc for writers For 17 yrs. **HONORS/ACHIEVEMENTS:** Downbeat Award; Pittsburg Courier Award; recorded World Award Shaefer Beer Award, recorded musical Cabin In Sky by Vernon Duke with the NY Phil Strings & Brass on ABC Paramount; performed at NY Radio City Jam Session 1973; performed at Tribute to Charlie Parker 1975; performed at Newport Jazz Fest; compositions include "Smokin", "Jacque's Groove", "Sop City", "People Places & Things", recordings include "Crankin", "Smokin", "Kwanza", "Love & Understanding" & "A Caddy for daddy". **MILITARY SERVICE:** AUS band. **BUSINESS ADDRESS:** 1864 7 Ave #52, New York, NY 10026.

FULLER, DEWEY C.
Executive director. **PERSONAL:** Born Apr 04, 1934, Alabama; married Inez. **EDUCATION:** Univ of Cincinnati, BA 1946; MI U, Certificate of Labor & Ind Relations 1966;Univ of Cincinnati, grad work. **CAREER:** Urban League of Greater Cincinnati, dir 1973-, asst dir 1968-73, dir econ 1964-66; Hamilton Co Welfare Dept, case worker 1960-64; US Postal, clk 1950-60. **ORGANIZATIONS:** Nat Urban League Leadership Group - Process Tng;Univ of Cincinnati Human Relations Seminar in Interpersonal Skills; Red Cross Comm Orgn Workshop; Nat UrbanLeague Conf Tech in Problem Solving; Comm Chest Methods Change Seminar; mem Kappa Alpha Psi Frat; bd trustees PREP; JET; sec OH Valley Council of Urban Lg; Cincinnati Manpower Planning Council; bd trustees Funds for Self-interprise; mem Madisonville Kiwanis Club; Wesley Smith Lodge; Prince Hall Mason; OHAdv Council on Voc Edn. **MILITARY SERVICE:** Sgt 1943-46. **BUSINESS ADDRESS:** 2400 Reading Rd, Cincinnati, OH 45202.

FULLER, DORIS JEAN
Manager. **PERSONAL:** Born May 26, 1945, Houston County, GA; daughter of Sim C Fuller Jr and Bertha Clark Fuller. **EDUCATION:** Morris Brown Coll, BS 1966; GA State Univ, MEd 1975; Univ San Francisco, NSF Inst 1969. **CAREER:** Atlanta Bd of Educ, teacher 1966-78; Southern Bell, asst mgr 1978-. **ORGANIZATIONS:** 2nd vice pres Atl Alumnae Chap DST Sor 1977-79; pres 1979, 1983, 1986, educ vice pres Magic Toastmasters TI 1978, 1984, 1987; nominating comm chairperson Southern Region DST Sor Inc 1978-80; mem Southern Bell Speaker's Bureau 1980-; state youth leadership coord Dist 14 TI 1981; recording sec MBC Natl Alumni Assoc 1984-88; pres Atl Chap MBC Alumni Assoc 1985-87; co-chairperson Mens & Womens Unity Day Beulah Bapt Church 1985; NAACP 1988-; vice pres, MBC National Alumni Assn 1988-. **HONORS/ACHIEVEMENTS:** President's Awd Toastmasters Intl 1980; Outstanding Corporate Alumni NAFEO Washington DC 1983; Presidential Citation MBC Alumni Assoc Atl Chap 1985; Outstanding Alumni MBC Student Govt Assoc 1985; Southern Bell Speakers Bureau Achievement Awd 1986; Alumna of the Year, MBC National Alumni Assn 1989; Count On Me, Employee Recognition Program of Southern Bell 1989; Southern Bell Best-of-the-Best Winner (a company-wide Speakers Bureau competition) 1988. **HOME ADDRESS:** 2190 Star Mist Dr SW, Atlanta, GA 30311. **BUSINESS ADDRESS:** Assistant Manager, Southern Bell, 27L63 SBC, 675 W Peachtree St NE, Atlanta, GA 30375.

FULLER, JACK LEWIS
Designer. **PERSONAL:** Born Dec 30, 1945, Toombs County, GA; son of Mell Fuller and Elvera Gillis Fuller. **EDUCATION:** Parsons School of Design, BFA 1965. **CAREER:** Kasper for Joan Leslie, asst designer; Elliott Bass, Upper Crust Sportswear, Nuance Dresses, designer; Leslie Fay Inc, designer; Jardine Ltd, designer; Bleyle-By Jack Fuller, designer. **ORGANIZATIONS:** Consultant on Harlem Public Schools, New York City Bd of Educ. **HONORS/ACHIEVEMENTS:** Key to City of Cincinnati 1975-76; Pres' Awd, Univ of Cincinnati 1976; Rising Stars Fashion Show, Press Week, Plaza Hotel 1975; Urban League Designer of the Year 1975. **BUSINESS ADDRESS:** Designer, Jack Fuller, Ltd, 100 W 15, New York, NY 10011.

FULLER, JAMES J.
Educational administrator. **PERSONAL:** Born Nov 01, 1946, Eutawville, SC; married Ruth Smothers; children: Julian, Mark. **EDUCATION:** Morgan State U, AB 1972; Howard U, currently pursuing Master Divinity. **CAREER:** Univ of MD, dir campus activities 1974-, asst dir minority recruitment 1972-74, Baltimore Co; Prudential Life Insurance Co Baltimore, special agent 1970-72; New Shiloh Baptist Church Baltimore, licensed minister 1974. **ORGANIZATIONS:** Adv Franklin Sq Boys Clubs Am 1968; Prince Hall Free & Accepted Masons 1973;Univ MD Black Caucus Faculty & Staff 1972; Sons of Prophet, New Shiloh Bapt Ch1974; Assn Coll Unions Intl 1974; Am Assn Collegiate Registrars & Officers Admissions 1972; Urban Leagues Educ adv bd 1972. **HONORS/ACHIEVEMENTS:** Man of Yr Prudential Life Ins 1971; Richard H Hunt meml Fund Resolution 1975; Sons of Prophet Cert; 1975; AUS Good Conduct Medal 1968; Am Legion Serv Award 1963. **MILITARY SERVICE:** AUS splst 4 1966-68. **BUSINESS ADDRESS:** 5401 Wilkens Ave, Baltimore, MD 21228.

FULLER, NORVELL RICARDO
Industrial minerals company executive. **PERSONAL:** Born Apr 08, 1953, St Petersburg, FL; children: Nicole Rasheda, Duane. **EDUCATION:** Howard Univ, BS 1976; many company management & skills courses. **CAREER:** Cargill Inc, resin chemist/sales rep 1976-81; K&N International (Importers), vice pres; Pfizer Inc, western mineral sales rep 1981-. **ORGANIZATIONS:** Mem Federation opf Coatings Technology 1979-, Adhesive & Sealants Council 1981-; mem United Way, SLLC, Transafrica & World Visions, Howard Univ Alumni, Socof Plastic Inst, Cultured Marble Inst, So CA Coatinas Soc, Mile Swimmers Club, Ski Club. **HONORS/ACHIEVEMENTS:** Leader in Western Region Sales for 4 years Pfizer Inc 1982-86; ordained minister Universal Triumph, The Dominion of God 1983. **HOME ADDRESS:** 1800 N New Hampshire Ave #230, Los Angeles, CA 90027-4249. **BUSINESS ADDRESS:** Sales Representative, Pfizer Inc, 2800 Ayers Ave, Los Angeles, CA 90023.

FULLER, THOMAS S.
Appointed government official. **PERSONAL:** Born Oct 18, 1934, Abbeville, SC; children: Hazel Jenkins, Toni. **EDUCATION:** Allen Univ, BPsy; Roosevelt Univ, MPA. **CAREER:** Amer Hosp Assoc, dir div of comm relations 1969-74; State of IL Equal Employment Oppor Office, dir 1975-77; Cook Co Sheriff, asst 1977-78; Metro Sanitary Dist of Gr Chicago, comm. **ORGANIZATIONS:** Mem Amer Public Works Assoc; bd mem Comm & Economic Develop Assoc Cook Co; mem NAACP; mem Operation PUSH Chicago Urban League. **HONORS/ACHIEVEMENTS:** Adjunct professorship Chicago State Univ. **MILITARY SERVICE:** AUS 2 yrs. **BUSINESS ADDRESS:** Commissioner, Metro Sanitary Dist of Chicago, 100 E Erie St, Chicago, IL 60611.

FULLILOVE, PAUL A., SR.
Clergyman. **PERSONAL:** Born Oct 17, 1916, St Louis, MO; married Josephine; children: Paul A, Jr, Jo Ethel. **EDUCATION:** Gordon Coll, BTh 1946. **CAREER:** Union Bapt Ch New Bedford, pastor 1946-50; Third Bapt Ch Springfield, MA, pastor 1950-; Wesson Memorial Hosp, chaplain; Hampden Co House of Correction; Am Intl Coll; Bay State Medical Center, chaplain; Third Baptist Church, minister. **ORGANIZATIONS:** Headed Martin Luther King Fund Dr 1969; pres United Bapt Conv of MA & RI; treas New England Bapt Missionary Conv; bd dir Child & Family Serv; bd dirWesson Memorial Hosp; bd dir Na Bapt Conv USA Inc; mem Rotary Internat; Area Leader Foreign Mission Bd of NBC Inc; headed Bombed Ch Drive forNBC & Inc 1965; pres Pastors' Council 1964-72; pres Jr Hawaiians Soc Club 1935-85. **HONORS/ACHIEVEMENTS:** Honorary DD Am Intl Coll 1968; 10 yrs Service Award, New England Bapt Conv; 25 yrs Service Award Am Bapt Ch of MA 1971; Hon DD Gordon Coll1981; bd dir Gordon Coll 1985-86; Outstanding Citizens Leg Black Caucus Boston 1985; Man of the Year Springfield Harambee Com 1986; Christians & Jews Awd1985. **BUSINESS ADDRESS:** Minister, Third Baptist Church, 149 Walnut St, Springfield, MA 01105.

FULLWOOD, HARLOW, JR.
Food service company executive. **PERSONAL:** Born Jan 26, 1941, Asheville, NC; son of Mr & Mrs Harlow Fullwood Sr (deceased); married Elnora Bassett; children: Paquita Tara, Harlow III. **EDUCATION:** Comm Coll of Baltimore, AA 1973; VA Union Univ, BA 1977; Baltimore Police Academy, 1964; Kentucky Fried Chicken Training Center, 1984. **CAREER:** Baltimore City Police Dept, police recruiter 1964-86; El Pa Ha Foods Inc, pres 1986-; Fullwood Foods Inc (featuring Kentucky Fried Chicken restaurants), pres, 1984; Penn-North Foods Inc (featuring Kentucky Fried Chicken restaurants), pres, 1988-. **ORGANIZATIONS:** Bd of trustees Concord Baptist Church; trustee bd VA Union Univ; dir Baltimore Delta Alumni Foundation Inc; bd Assoc Black Charities; mem Baltimore County Chamber of Commerce; Advisory Board, Greater Baltimore Committee; Maryland Educational Opportunity Ctr; Arena Players, Inc Honorary Life Member; The Natl Congress of Parents & Teachers; bd of dirs, Signal 13 Found Inc; Presidents' Roundtable; bd of dirs, Hub Inc; bd of dirs, Baltimore Symphony Orchestra; life mem, Alpha Phi Alpha Fraternity; Paul Harris Fellow, Rotary Found of Rotary Intl; Golder Heritage Life Mem, NAACP. **HONORS/ACHIEVEMENTS:** The Evening Sun Policeman of the Year Awd 1979; J C Penney Golden Rule Awd 1983; The Jefferson Awd 1983; Man of the Year The Natl Assoc of Negro Business & Professional Women's Clubs Inc 1983; Baltimore's Best Awd 1984; Kentucky Fried Chicken Five Star Awd 1985; Kentucky Fried Chicken White Glove & 2 SC Awd 1985; Governor's Citation 1986; Mayor's Citation 1986; Meritorius Service Award, The United Negro College Fund,1983;The Natl Alliance of Business Commendation, 1984; Optimist International, 1979; Community Service Award 1983; The Vanguard Justice Society, Inc, Police Officer of the Year 1984;Helen O Gattie Memorial AwdContinental Societies, Inc, 1985; VA Union Univ FIrst Distinguished Leader Awd 1982; Afro-American Newspaper Award, 1973; VUU Alumnus of the Year, 1979; Distinguished Service Award, Baltimore City Police Dept 1986; Kentucky Fried Chicken Million Dollar Award, 1987 & 1988; Minority Business Advocate of the Year - State of Maryland, US Small Business Admin, 1989; Outstanding Leadership & Service to the Business Community & Education Award, Bowie State Univ, 1989; Community Service Award, Inst for Amer Business, 1989. **HOME ADDRESS:** 13 Country Mill Ct, Catonsville, MD 21228. **BUSINESS ADDRESS:** President, Fullwood Foods, Inc, 2542 W Franklin St, Baltimore, MD 21223.

FULTON, DONALD LEE
Educator. **PERSONAL:** Born Apr 23, 1935, St Louis, MO; married Ida Harris; children: Christina M, Donald Jr, Janalynn, Jeanine. **EDUCATION:** LincolnUniv Jefferson City, MO, BS educ 1959;Univ of MO Columbia, MS educ 1969. **CAREER:** Federal Programs, Sikeston Public Schools R-VI, admin dir 1969-; ABE State of MO, state supervisor 1969; Sikeston R-VI Schools, elementary, secondary & asst prin 1964-69; Lincoln Elementary, Sikeston R-VI Schools, teacher 1963-64; Lincoln Jr High, Sikeston R-VI Schools, teacher 1961-63; John Pershing School, State of MO, teacher 1959-61. **ORGANIZATIONS:** Dir fiscal officer Missourians Men's Club Inc 1965; pres chmn Delta Area Econ Comm; Headstart 1969-74; mayor city cnclmn City of Sikeston, MO 1969-75; pres vice pres Phi Delta Kappa Educ Frat 1978-79. **HONORS/ACHIEVEMENTS:** Man of the Year Omega Psi Phi Frat Inc Eta Chap 1969; Scouters Key Boy Scouts of Am Sikeston 1969; Order of Merit Boy Scouts of Am Sikeston 1971; Appreciation Plaque DAEOC bd of dir Portageville, MO 1974. **MILITARY SERVICE:** USN s/r 2. **BUSINESS ADDRESS:** 1002 Virginia St, Sikeston, MO 63801.

FULTON, ROBERT HENRY
Company executive. **PERSONAL:** Born Nov 15, 1926, Philadelphia, PA; son of David Fulton (deceased) and Carlotta Nixon (deceased); married Kathryn Lawson Brown, Aug 29, 1987; children: Eleanor Price, Vincent, Anthony, Darlene Brown, MarcellaDoreen Brown. **EDUCATION:** Cornell Univ School of Indus & L/R, liberal arts 1974. **CAREER:** Transport Workers Union Local Local 100, vice pres 1979-81; Transport Workers Union Local 100, staff rep 1963-79. **ORGANIZATIONS:** Vp Rochdale Village Recreation & Org 1974-80; commr Boy Scouts of Am New York City So Dist 1975-80; chmn of training BSA/EXPLORER Div Career & Educ 1976-80; exec bd mem Black Trade Unionist Leadership Com 1974-78. **HONORS/ACHIEVEMENTS:** BSA Merit of Honor, Boy Scouts of Am queens 1976; George Meany Scouting Award, AFL/CIO Washington, DC 1978; RVRO Man of the Year Award Rochdale Village Rec Orgn Queens 1979; St George Assn Chapter II NYCTS, publicity dir, Public Relation Award, 1981; Rochdale Village Spring Festival, Mr Spirit of Rochdale, 1982; The Labor Merit Award, 1988; NY City Transit Authority, recognition for 41 yrs of loyal service, 1988; The Silver Beaver Award, Boy Scouts of Amer, 1981; United Negro Coll Fund, Distinguished Leadership Award, 1984, Meritorious Service Award, 1985. **MILITARY SERVICE:** AAC sgt 1945-46. **HOME ADDRESS:** 100-5 Bellamy Loop 5E, Bronx, NY 10475. **BUSINESS ADDRESS:** Vice President, Transport Workers Union, 80 West End Ave, Rm 604, New York, NY 10023.

FUNDERBURG, I. OWEN
Business executive. **PERSONAL:** Born Aug 21, 1924, Monticello, GA; married Clara C; children: I Owen Jr, Ilon Edward, Douglas. **EDUCATION:** Morehouse Coll, BA 1947; Rutgers Univ Grad Sch of Banking, grad 1959; Univ of MI, attended 1947-48. **CAREER:** Mechanics & Farmer's Bank Durham, NC, teller; Gateway Natl Bank St Louis, exec vp/ceo 1966-74; Citizens Trust Bank Atlanta, GA, pres 1974-. **BUSINESS ADDRESS:** President, Citizens Trust Bank, 75 Piedmont Ave NE, Atlanta, GA 30303.

FUNDERBURK, WILLIAM WATSON
Physician. **PERSONAL:** Born Aug 26, 1931, South Carolina; married Marilyn; children: William, Julie, Christina. **EDUCATION:** Johnson C Smith U, BS 1952; Howard U, MD 1956. **CAREER:** DC Cancer Soc, 1967-74; Howard Univ, assoc dean student affairs 1970-72; Howard Univ, assoc prof surgery 1971-77; Ctr for Ambulatory Surgery, med dir 1977-84; Self Employed, physician. **ORGANIZATIONS:** Mem AOA 1956-87, NMA 1956-, Med Chi Soc 1956-. **BUSINESS ADDRESS:** 1145 19th St NW, Ste 203, Washington, DC 20036.

FUNN, CARLTON A., SR.
Educator. **PERSONAL:** Born Jan 29, 1932, Alexandria, VA; married Joan Berry; children: Carlton Jr, Tracye, Marc. **EDUCATION:** Storer Coll Harpers Ferry WV, BA 1953; VA State Coll Petersburg VA, MEd 1972. **CAREER:** Fairfax County Public School Syst, teacher, minority relations cons; VA School System, teacher 25 yrs; Washington DC Public School Syst, teacher 3 yrs; The History & Culture of Minorities, dir cultural educ prog. **ORGANIZATIONS:** mem, Natl Educ Assn, VA Educ Assn, Fairfax Educ Assn, WA Urban League, NAACP, Alexandria Bicentennial Comm, PTA 1974, Alexandria Dem Committeeman 1967-69; trustee Alfred St Bapt Church 1967-68; bd mem Alexandria Human Relations Council 1973-; vice pres Alexandria Coun on Human Relations, 1972-73, Alexandria Chamber of Commerce, 1967-68; vice pres, Hopkins House Assn, 1972. **HONORS/ACHIEVEMENTS:** Human/Civil Awd VA Ed Assoc, VA Min Caucus 1976; Human Relat Awd Fairfax VA Ed Assoc 1976; Citizen of the Year Awd No VA Psi Nu Chap Omega Psi Phi Frat Inc 1976; Carter G Woodson Awd Natl Ed Assoc 1976; Apprec Awd Fairfax Ed Assoc Black Caucus 1977; Citizen of the Year Awd Recog Comm of 3rd Dist Omega Psi Phi Frat Inc 1977; Storer Coll Serv Awds, Certs, Scholarship; Robert F Kennedy Scroll Cincinnati Teachers 1972; Cert of Apprec Hopkins House Assoc 1973; Amer Coll Student Leaders Awd 1953; Natl Defense Serv Medal Good Conduct Medal & Marksman Badge AUS; Human Relations Exhibit 1979; History & Culture of Minorities Exhibit, Natl Shown 169 Times 1980; Natl Trends Awd Arlington VA Chap of the Links Inc 1979; NAACP Awd of Appreciation The Alexandria VA Br 1979; Cert of Apprec Natl Assoc of Human Rights Workers 1979; Omega Man of the Year Omega Psi Phi Frat Inc 1979; Meritorious Serv Awds 3rd Dist Omega Psi Phi Frat Inc 1979-80; DOD sponsored showing at Pentagon Bldg 1975; State Dept Rec Assoc sponsored exhibit 1975; Natl Capitol Parks sponsored 15 day showing 1975; taught 10 week course in Black Hist/Human Relat to civ & mil personnel at Vint Hill Farms Mil Post Warrenton VA 1974. **MILITARY SERVICE:** AUS pfc 1953-55.

FUNN, COURTNEY HARRIS
University library administrator. **PERSONAL:** Born Nov 30, 1941; daughter of Jerry L Harris (deceased) and Evelyn B Harris (deceased); divorced; children: LaMarr T Funn. **EDUCATION:** Fisk Univ, Nashville, TN, BA, 1963; Columbia Univ, New York, NY, MA, 1967; Univ of Maryland, College Pk, MD, MLS, 1971; Study Tour, Western Europe, 1965. **CAREER:** Baltimore Public Schools, Baltimore, MD, music resource teacher (K-6), 1963-66; Columbia Univ, New York, NY, asst to music librarian, 1965-67; Bowie State Univ, Bowie, MD, asst prof of music, 1967-, dir of library, 1969-; Provident Hospital, Baltimore MD, art specialist, 1968-69. **ORGANIZATIONS:** Vice chmn, Prince George's County Human Relation Commn, 1985-; chmn, Library Technical Comm, Metropolitan Washington Council of Govt, 1985-86; Natl Forum for Black Publication Admin (NFBPA), 1987-; chmn, Educ Comm St Margaret's Parish Council, 1987-; Mem of Elderly Abuse Oversight Comm, 1988; Mem of District of Columbia Library Assn, (DCLA), 1988; County Executive's Policy Comm, 1988; Mem of White House Conf on Libraries Task Force, 1988; County Facilities Naming Comm, 1988; Exec Comm, Board of Directors, Amer Red Cross, 1988; County Executive's Policy Comm, 1988; chair, State Coll of Library Directors, 1986. **HONORS/ACHIEVEMENTS:** Woman of the Year, Fisk Univ, 1962-63; author of Beyond the Work Week: Some Creative Uses of Leisure Time, The Crab, 1974; author of Acronyms: Alphabet Soup, The Crab-Maryland Library Assn, 1975; author of A Guide to Libraries of the Maryland State Colleges, 1975; Presidential Citation for Outstanding Services BSC, 1977; Alpha Kappa Alpha Sorority, Beta Phi Mu Honor Society. **BUSINESS ADDRESS:** Bowie State Univ, Thurgood Marshall Library, 14000 Jericho Pk Rd, Bowie, MD 20715.

FURMAN, JAMES B.
Educator. **PERSONAL:** Born Jan 23, 1937, Louisville, KY. **EDUCATION:** Univ of Louisville, B Music Educ 1958, M Music 1965; Brandeis Univ & Harvard Univ, PhD studies. **CAREER:** Public School System Louisville KY, teacher 1959-60; Mamaroneck NY Public School System, music teacher 1964-65; Choral director, arranger, pianist; published "Four Little Foxes" a choral suite; "Go Tell It On the Mountain", "Some Glorious Day" & "An Oratorio"; Western CT State Coll, Danbury, prof of music; Western CT State Univ, prof of music 1965-. **ORGANIZATIONS:** Mem ASCAP, Amer Assn of Univ Profs, Phi Mu Alpha, Phi Delta Kappa, Afro-Amer Music Oppor Assn, CT Composers Inc, Amer Fed of Teachers; choral dir BBC Documentary film on the Life of Charles Ives 1966; conductor debut at NY City Town Hall 1967; music dir, pianist, TV & radio appearances throughout the USA, Central Amer, Europe & the Orient; composer-pianist, TV & radio appearances throughout the USA. **HONORS/ACHIEVEMENTS:** Top Music Student Omicron Delta Kappa Award 1958; Award of Merit Natl Fed of Music Clubs 1965-77 & Parade of Amer Music 1967; published "Hehlehlooyuh", "Come Thou Long Expected Jesus" & "The Quiet Life"; 1st place in composition Louisville Philharmonic Society's Student Musicians Competition 1953; 1st place composition competition Brookline Library Music Composition Competition 1964; Composer music publ by Oxford Univ Press, Music 70-80, Hinshaw, Dorn, & Sam Fox. **MILITARY SERVICE:** AUS Pfc 1960-62; music dir Ft Devens MA 1960-62; conductor 1st place in 1st Army of the All Army Entertainment Contest 1961; music dir, pianist World Touring Army Show "Rolling Along of 1961" 1961-62. **BUSINESS ADDRESS:** Professor of Music, Western CT State College, 181 White St, Danbury, CT 06810.

FUSE, BOBBY LEANDREW, JR.
Educator. **PERSONAL:** Born Feb 17, 1952, Americus, GA; married Angela Michelle Lamar. **EDUCATION:** Morehouse Coll, BA 1974; Michigan State Univ, MA 1975. **CAREER:** College of Urban Develop, grad asst to the dean 1974-75; Martin Luther King Jr Ctr, dir youth component 1974-76; Fulton County Democratic Party, exec dir 1977-78; Atlanta Bd of Educ Frederick Douglass HS, teacher 1976-. **ORGANIZATIONS:** Jr deacon Friendship Bapt Church-Americus 1970-; advisor Douglass HS Student Govt 1977-85; bd of trustees Martin Luther King Jr Ctr for Nonviolent Social Change Inc; youth cncl advisor NAACP; mem St John Lodge #17 F&AM, Holy Royal Arch Lodge #4 Americus, Natl Educ Assoc, Natl Assoc of Secondary School Principals, Assoc for Supervision and Curriculum Develop; mem State Comm Life Hist of Black Georgians; mem MI State Univ Alumni Assoc, Morehouse CollAlumni Assoc. **HONORS/ACHIEVEMENTS:** John Wesley Dobbs Scholar Prince Hall Masons of Georgia 1970; Georgia Bapt Conv 1970-74; Scholarship Alberta Williams King Fund 1977; Century Club Butler St YMCA 1981; faculty member Martin Luther King Ctr Institute of Non-violence 1987. **HOME ADDRESS:** 1379 Westboro Dr, Atlanta, GA 30310. **BUSINESS ADDRESS:** Teacher, Atlanta Public Schools, Frederick Douglass HS, 225 Hightower Rd NW, Atlanta, GA 30310.

FUTRELL, MARY HATWOOD
Educator. **PERSONAL:** Born May 24, 1940, Altavista, VA; daughter of Josephine Austin; married Donald Futrell. **EDUCATION:** Virginia State Univ, BA; George Washington Univ, MA; Maryland Univ, Univ of VA Polytechnical Inst & State Univ, Graduate Work. **CAREER:** Alexandria's George Washington HS, headed bus ed dept; Ed Assoc of Alexandria, pres 1973-75; NEA VA Ed Assoc, pres 1976-78; NEA, bd dir 1978, sec-treas 1980, pres 1980-89. **ORGANIZATIONS:** Bd advisors Esquire Register 1985; mem Task Force on Teaching Carnegie Forum on Educ and the Economy 1985; mem Natl Comm on the Role and Future of State Colls and Univs; mem editorial bd ProEducation magazine; mem Educ Adv Council Metropolitan Life Insurance Co; bd trustees Joint Council on Economic Educ; mem NEA's Special Comm on Attacks on Public Educ; co-convener 20th Anniversary Celebration of the Historic March on Washington led by Dr Martin Luther King; mem Select Comm on the Educ of Black Youth; mem US Natl Comm for the United Nations Educ Scientific and Cultural Organization; mem exec comm World Confederation of Organizations of the Teaching Profession. **HONORS/ACHIEVEMENTS:** Human Relation Awd (2) Natl Conference of Christians and Jews 1976, 1986; Outstanding Black Business and Professional Person Ebony Magazine 1984; One of the Country's 100 Top Women The Ladies Home Journal 1984; One of 12 Women of the Year Ms Magazine 1985; One of the Most Influential Blacks in Amer Ebony Magazine 1985, 86; Anne and Leon Schull Awd Americans for Democratic Action 1986; Honorary Doctorates George Washington Univ, VA State Univ, Spelman Coll; Certificate of Appreciation United Nations Assoc/Capital Area Div; named to Academy of Women Achievers Young Women's Christian Assoc; NAACP President's Award; Honorary Doctorates: Adrian Coll; Central CT State Univ; Eastern Michigan Univ; Lynchburg Coll; N Carolina Central Univ; Univ of Lowell; Xavier Univ. **BUSINESS ADDRESS:** President, Natl Education Assoc, 1201 16th St NW, Washington, DC 20036.

FYKES, LEROY MATTHEWS, JR.
Educator, attorney. **PERSONAL:** Born Oct 23, 1945, Indianapolis, IN. **EDUCATION:** Univ of So CA, BS 1967; Harvard U, MBA 1974; UCLA, JD 1972; NYU, LlM 1976. **CAREER:** Seton HallUniv Law Ctr, asst prof; Pfizer Inc, atty 1972-75; Nat Black MBA Assn, dir, bd chmn, bd sec 1974-; NYCTI Assn Inc, dir 1975-; Am Arbtrn Assn, arbtrn panel. **ORGANIZATIONS:** Mem NY Bar Trustee, bd sec Studio Mus in Harlem 1973; mem 100 Black Men Inc of NYC. **BUSINESS ADDRESS:** 1111 Raymond Blvd, Newark, NJ 07102.

G

GABBIN, ALEXANDER LEE
Educator. **PERSONAL:** Born Sep 06, 1945, Baltimore, MD; son of John and Dorothy; married Joanne Veal; children: Jessea Nayo. **EDUCATION:** Baltimore City Coll, HS 1963; Howard U, BA 1967;Univ of Chicago, MBA 1970; Temple Univ, PhD 1986. **CAREER:** Tech Constr Co, asst to pres 1968-70; Touche Ross & Co, staff auditor 1970-72; Chicago Urban League, dep exec dir 1972-74; Price Waterhouse & Co, auditor 1974-75; Lincoln Univ, assoc prof 1975-85; James Madison Univ, 1986-. **ORGANIZATIONS:** Mem IL Soc of CPA'S 1978; mem Chicago Urban League, Kappa Alpha Psi, PA Soc of CPA's, Amer Accounting Assoc, Amer Inst of Cert Public Accountants. **HONORS/ACHIEVEMENTS:** Who's Who Among Coll Students Howard Univ 1967; Grad Fellowship Humble Oil & Refining Co 1968-69; Builder's Award Third World Press 1978; Accounting Educators Award Nat Assn of Minority CPA Firms 1979; Lindback Disting Teaching Awd 1982, School of Accounting Outstanding Teacher 1986, 1988. **BUSINESS ADDRESS:** Assistant Professor, James MadisonUniv, Harrisonburg, VA 22807.

GABBIN, JOANNE VEAL
Educator. **PERSONAL:** Born Feb 02, 1946, Baltimore, MD; daughter of Joseph Veal and Jessie Smallwood Veal; married Alexander L Gabbin, Jul 02, 1967; children: Jessea Nayo. **EDUCATION:** Morgan State Univ, Baltimore MD, BA, 1967; Univ of Chicago, Chicago IL, MA, 1970, PhD, 1980. **CAREER:** Catalyst for Youth Inc, Chciago IL, prog dir, instructor, 1973-75; Lincoln Univ, University PA, asst prof of English, 1977-82, assoc prof of English, 1982-85; James Madison Univ, Harrisonburg VA, assoc prof of English, 1985-86, dir, Honors Program, 1986-. **ORGANIZATIONS:** Editor of BCOHE Journal, Black Conf on Higher Educ; mem, Langston Hughes Soc, Zora Neale Hurston Soc; assoc editor, Middle Atlantic Writer Assn Inc, the MAWA Journal; mem, Coll Language Assn; chair, Student Emergency Fund, First Baptist Church, 1989-. **HONORS/ACHIEVEMENTS:** Outstanding Achievement Award, Black Conf on Higher Educ, 1982; Distinguished Teaching Award, The Christian R & Mary F Lindback Found, 1983; Creative Scholarship Award, Coll Language Assn, 1986; Women of Color Award, James Madison Uni, 1988; Honorary Mem, Golden Key Natl Honor Soc, 1988; Chairperson, Toni Morrison & The Supernatural, panel at the Middle Atlantic Writers Assn, 1988; Speaker, Creating a Masterpiece, Freshman Convocation James Madison Univ, 1988; publications: Sonia Sanchez: A Soft Reflection of Strength, The Zora Neal Hurston Forum, 1987; A Laying on of Hands: Black Women Writers Exploring the Roots of their Folk & Cultural Tradition; Walk Together Children: Color and the Cultural Legacy of Sterling A Brown, 1988. **BUSINESS ADDRESS:** Professor of English, Dir of the Honors Program, James Madison University, Hillcrest, Harrisonburg, VA 22807.

GABRIEL, BENJAMIN MOSES
Business executive. **PERSONAL:** Born Sep 17, 1931, Brooklyn, NY; married Rebecca; children: Shirley Ann, Janice, Brenda, Benjamin Jr. **EDUCATION:** Cornell U, 1931; Empire State U, BS. **CAREER:** New York City Transit Authority, supt 1976, contract compliance officer 1973, mgr training ctr 1971, supr 1968, rr porter 1957. **ORGANIZATIONS:** Mem 100 Black Men; trustee Luth Hosp 1976-; bd dir Brooklyn TB & Lung Assn 1975-; chmn Labor & Industry, ENY NAACP, 1976-; v chmn, bd dir Asso Transit Guild; training coord, Asso Transit 1971-; candidate, dist leader 40th AD Dem Party 1976; campaign mgr Local Sch Bd Elections 1973, 75. **HONORS/ACHIEVEMENTS:** Doswell Meml Award, Asso Transit Guild 1977; Comm Serv & Transit Accomplishments, Elite Benevolent Soc 1975; Comm Serv Award, Grace Bapt Ch 1974. **MILITARY SERVICE:** USAF 1949-53. **BUSINESS ADDRESS:** NYCTA 370 Jay St, Brooklyn, NY 11201.

GACHETTE, LOUISE FOSTON
Funeral home executive. **PERSONAL:** Born Apr 17, 1911, Clarksville, TN. **EDUCATION:** A&M Coll, 1938 Huntsville, AL; Gupton & Jones Sch, mortuary; Nashville, Eckels Coll, embalming degree, mortuary tech. **CAREER:** Public School Huntsville AL, teacher 1938-42; Foston Funeral Home, mgr & owner. **ORGANIZATIONS:** Mem Natl Embalmers & Funeral Dir Assn; Middle Tennessee Embalmers & Funeral Dir; Tennessee State Funeral Dir & Moriticians Assn Inc; Natl Business & Professional Women, Nashville TN; Cosmopolitan Art & Study Club; mem Women Interested in Community Affairs, Clarksville TN; mem Clarksville Montgomery Co C of C; mem Adv Comm of the Mayor of Clarksville; mem Montgomery Co Citizens Adv Comm; mem United Charities Bd, Clarksville TN; mem Gov's Adv Comm, State of Tennessee; mem Memorial Hospital Auxiliary; bd dir USO; sec United Givers Fund Campaign; co-chmn Cerebral Palsy Fund; bd dir Clarksville High School; mem United Church Women. **HONORS/ACHIEVEMENTS:** "Miss A&M College," Huntsville AL, 1937; Woman of the Year Award, Funeral Dir & Morticians 1972; trustee, stewardess, former clerk & treas for 25 years, Wesley Chapel CME Church. **BUSINESS ADDRESS:** President, Foston Funeral Home, 816 Franklin St, Clarksville, TN 37040.

GADSDEN, EUGENE HINSON
Judge. **PERSONAL:** Born Feb 04, 1912, Savannah, GA; married Ida Jenkins; children: Greer Larned, Geoffrey E. **EDUCATION:** Savannah State Coll GA, AB 1934; LincolnUniv Oxford, PA, BS 1937; NC CentralUniv Law Sch Durham, LlB 1953. **CAREER:** Eastern Jud Circuit of GA, judge superior ct 1979-; GA State Bd of workmen's Comp, admin law judge 1974-79; Self Employed, atty 1953-74; Housing Authority of Savannah, asst mgr 1941-50; Lee Co Bd of Educ Sanford, NC, sci tchr 1937-39. **ORGANIZATIONS:** Dir (Sec) Toomer Realty Co Inc 1966-; dir Carver State Bank 1971-; pres Legal Aid Soc of Savannah 1966-74; dir So Regional Council Inc 1970; chmn ofbd Westside Comprehensive Health Cntr 1972. **HONORS/ACHIEVEMENTS:** RR Wright Award of Excellence Savannah State Coll 1973; Citizen of the yr Mu Phi Chap Omega Psi Phi Frat. **BUSINESS ADDRESS:** Chatham Co Courthouse, Room 20, Savannah, GA 31401.

GADSDEN, NATHANIEL J., JR.
Educational administrator. **PERSONAL:** Born Oct 03, 1950, Harrisburg, PA; son of Nathaniel Gadsden and Rosetta Robinson Gadsden; married Carol L, Aug 03, 19; children: David L, Nathaniel J III. **EDUCATION:** West Chester Univ, BS 1973, grad sch 31 credits; Columbia Pacific Univ, MA 1984; NJ Bible Inst; Hershey Med Center, clinical pastoral education; Harrisburg Hospital Clinical Pastoral Educ; Columbia Pacific Univ PhD 1986. **CAREER:** WCU, resident hall dir 1973-77; Child Abuse Hotline, case worker 1977-80; PA Dept of Education, equity coord 1980-; planner for alternative sentencing of PA, 1985-; HelpHouse Inc., Harrisburg, PA, counselor 1989. **ORGANIZATIONS:** Bd of dirs Multi-Disciplinary Team Dauphin Co Children & Youth; bd of dirs Multi-Disciplinary Team PA Dept of Children & Youth; bd mem Comm Home Care Services Inc; pres Central PA Black Social Workers 1982-84; dir The Writers Wordshop 1978-; host WMSP-FM radio 1979-; host WHP TV Channel 21 1982-; bd of dirs Metro Arts 1982-; bd of dirs Susquhanna Arts Council 1982; black advisory bd WITF-TV; bus assoc Central PA Guidance Associate 1984-; columnist The City News Harrisburg PA weekly 1984-; mem Intl Org of Journalists; Harrisburg dir of PA Black United Fund; bd dir Children's Playroom Inc; minister Community Chapel Church of God in Christ, Harrisburg, PA. **HONORS/ACHIEVEMENTS:** Mem Natl Alliance of Third World Journalists 1980-; interviewed Yasser Arafat, Prime Minister Maurice Bishop of Grenada; named Comm Worker of Yr by conference on Black Basic Educ; Harrisburg Chap of Frontiers Intl; published poet and writer. **HOME ADDRESS:** 2209 N 2nd St, Harrisburg, PA 17110.

GADSON, ROSETTA E.
Educator. **PERSONAL:** Born Apr 02, 1938, Chicago; divorced; children: Anthony Paul, Craig Daryl. **EDUCATION:** Wayne State U, BA. **CAREER:** WTVS-TV, dir public relations & promotion, past asst dir of Devel; Natl Bank of Detroit, service representative; Michigan Consolidated Gas Co, customer service representative; Wayne State Univ Coll of pre-School Educ, sec & part-time teacher. **ORGANIZATIONS:** Mem Nat Assn of Media Women; Women in Communications; Nat Assn of Market Developers; Black Communicators Assn; pending applications; Am Women in Radio &TV; Women's Advertising Club; Pub Relations Soc of Am; mem Women's Com United Negro Coll Fund; NAACP Freedom Fund Dinner; Black Causes Assn; Media mem Dept of Pub Information City of Detroit; past pres Midland Elem Sch PTA; adv coun Highland Park HS. **HONORS/ACHIEVEMENTS:** Speaker Award Booker T Washington Bus Assn 1974; DAR Honor Student Recipient, Northwestern HS grad; Today's Woman by Marie Teasley MI Chronicle 1972. **BUSINESS ADDRESS:** 7441 2 Blvd, Detroit, MI 48202.

GAFFNEY, FLOYD
Educator. **PERSONAL:** Born Jun 11, 1930, Cleveland, OH; married Yvonne; children: Michelle, Antione, Brett, Monique. **EDUCATION:** Adelphi Univ, BA 1959, MA 1962; Carnegie Inst of Tech, PhD 1966. **CAREER:** Gilpin Players Karamu House, actor 1945-49; Pearl Primus African Dance Co, dancer 1950-51; Jerome School of Dancing, teaching asst 1960-62; Adelphi Univ, instr of dance 1961; Waltann School of Creative Arts, teacher of dance & drama 1961; Clark Coll, asst prof, Speech 1961-63; William Balls Amer Conservatory Theatre, guest artist 1965; Univ of Pittsburgh, guest dance instructor 1966; OH Univ, asst prof in theatre 1966-69; FL A&M Univ, dir of fine arts project upward bound 1968; Univ of CA Santa Barbara, assc prof drama 1969-71, co-chmn of Black Studies dept. **ORGANIZATIONS:** Mem UCSD Dept of Drama Grad 1978-, Undergrad 1979-; mem UCSD Black Fac & Staff Assc 1979-; mem Intercampus Cultural Exch Comm 1979-81; mem Third Clge Fac Comm UCSD 1980-; chmn Contemporary Black Arts Prog UCSD 1981-; mem Performing

Arts Sub-Comm 1972-; mem Fac Mentor Prog UCSD 1982; mem Pres Chair Search Comm UCSD 1982; mem San Diego Div of Acad Senate UCSD; bd dir Free Southern Theatre 1963-65; mem Amer Soc for Theatre Research 1966-69; mem Natl Humanities Fac 1974-75; bd dir Combined Arts & Educ Council of San Diego Cty 1982-; mem Amer Theatre Assc Black Theatre Prog 1966; artistic dir Southern CA Black Repertory Theatre Inc San Diego 1980-83; mem Confederation For The Arts 1983-; mem Steering Comm State & Local Partnership of San Diego Cty 1982-; bd dir Educ Cultural Complex Theatre 1981-; bd mem Horton Plaza Theatre Fnd 1983-84; panel mem Natl Research Council for Minority Flwshp 1984-87; mem Phi Lambda Rho Frat 1958; mem Amer Theatre Assc 1966-85; mem Amer Assc of Univ Prof. **HONORS/ACHIEVEMENTS:** Andrew Mellon Fellowship Drama 1964-65; OH Univ Bd Trustees Grant 1968; Fac Senate Grant Univ of CA Santa Barbara 1970; Ford Fnd Grant 1970; Faculty Sen Grant Univ of CA 1971-73; US Info Srv Cultural Exch Prof to Brazil 1972; Natl Humanities Fac 1974-75; grant Univ of CA Creative Arts Inst Grant 1974; Outstanding Educ of Amer Award; special proj grant Natl Endowment for the Arts 1977; Fulbright Scholar to Brazil 1979; Instr Improvement Grant 1979-81, 1984; participant Intl Congress of Black Communication Univ of Narirobi Kenya 1981; moderator Realism To Ritual, Form & Style in Black Theatre ATA Black Theatre Prog Panel 1982; Spotlight Award Combo & Act, Best Dir of Year "Trials & Tribulations Of Staggerlee Booker T Brown" 1982; Black Achievement Award for Drama Action Interprises Inc, 1980, 1984; Chancellor's Assocs, Merit Award; Outstanding Community Serv, Univ of California, San Diego, 1983; Natl Endowment for the Arts; US-Japan Alliance Best Director of Drama, 1986; NAACP Creative Arts Awards, 1986. **MILITARY SERVICE:** AUS 3rd class petty ofc 1951-65. **BUSINESS ADDRESS:** Professor of Drama/Chairman, Univ of CA San Diego, Contemporary Black Arts D-009, PO Box 109, La Jolla, CA 92093.

GAFFNEY, JOHN W.
Chief executive officer. **PERSONAL:** Born Aug 27, 1930, Idabel, OK; married Doreatha. **EDUCATION:** Langston U, BS 1954; OK City U, MBA 1966. **CAREER:** Comm Hlth Proj Inc, proj dir 1972-; OK State U, personnel mgr 1970-72; Langston U, bus mgr 1954-70; OK Assn Coll &Univ Bus Ofcrs, past pres; Cntrl Assn Coll &Univ Bus & Ofcrs; Nat Assn Coll &Univ Bus Ofcrs; Cn?Rl Assn Coll &Univ Personnel Ofcrs; Soc for Advncmt of Mngmt; Am Puib Hlth Assn; OK Nat Assn of Comm Hlth Pub Hlth Assn; So Assn of Comm Hlth Ctrs. **ORGANIZATIONS:** Past mem Bd of Educ Guthrie, OK; past mem sec Logan Co Hlth Ctr; chmn, trustee bd, ch treas Claver; vol Sr Citizens Day Care Prog 1978; sponsor Jr Red Cross 1979-; extensive world traveler & speaker, Bapt Ch; mem bd of dir Vix Nurses Assn; past pres Ambulatory Hlth Care Consortium; past presLangston Fed Cancer Soc for Serv on Bd 1975-76; 1st Black Woman In TX to host KJAC TV Black Outreach Show 1970-74.

GAFFNEY, MARY LOUISE
Health services. **PERSONAL:** Born Jul 30, Beaufort, SC. **EDUCATION:** VA Union Univ, BS 1966; George Washington Univ, Grad Study. **CAREER:** Adv Neighborhood Commn, Commr, 1976-; Mather School Alumni, natl pres 1978-; Benedict Coll, trustee 1978-; VA Union Univ, financial sec 1984-; George Washington Univ Hospital, radiation safety tech. **ORGANIZATIONS:** mem, Soc of Nuclear Med, 1983, Delta Sigma Theta Sorority Inc, Washington Inter-Alumni Council, Benedict Coll Alumni, Far-Northeast Civic Assn, Sr Choir, Bowling League-New Bethel Baptist Church, Amer Public Health Assn. **HONORS/ACHIEVEMENTS:** Basic Radiation Univ of VA 1980; St Law Georgetown Univ; Employee of the Week George Washington Univ Medical Center 1985; Publ "Isolation & Partial Characterization of the Most Immunologically Reactive Antigen From Mycobacterium Tuberculosis H37Ra Culture Filtrate". **BUSINESS ADDRESS:** Radiation Safety Technologist, George WashingtonUniv Hosp, 2300 K St, NW #201, Washington, DC 20037.

GAFFNEY, THOMAS DANIEL
Government official. **PERSONAL:** Born Jun 19, 1933, Laredo, TX. **CAREER:** San Antonio ISD School Bd, vice pres; US Govt, 23 yrs. **ORGANIZATIONS:** Mem AFRES; San Antonio Museum Assn;Ruth Taylor Theater; mem NAACP; 433 TAW/EEOC; 2851 ABGP/WELFARE Fund; LCL Adv Council; Ex Com UNCF; pres PovertyAgency Bd; vice pres sch bd 1973-77; mem San Antonio Rive Com; mem Black Unity Coordination Council; life mem BT Washingotn PTA; mem AFA; ACLU; Nat Caucus of Black - School Bd; mem NCOA. **MILITARY SERVICE:** USAF 4 yrs. **BUSINESS ADDRESS:** 141 Lavaca, San Antonio, TX.

GAILLARD, BERNARD
Attorney. **PERSONAL:** Born Mar 27, 1944, Charleston, SC; married Joyce Anita Williams; children: Lisa, Khari. **EDUCATION:** Columbia Univ, Cert 1966; SC State Coll, AB 1967; EmoryUniv Sch of Law, JD 1970. **CAREER:** So Regional Council, legis asst 1968; OEO, law clerk to regional counsel 1969; ICC, atty adv 1970, dir small bus assistance office 1977, assoc dir compl and consumer asst 1984-. **ORGANIZATIONS:** ICC rep vol serv to WA lawyers com for civil rights under the law 1972-75; mem ABA; mem SC, Natl, DC Bar Assns; mem Fed Senior Exec Science 1981;mem Com on Equal Employment in the Surface Transportation Indus 1972; ICC rep Minority Bus Oppor Com 1975-; pres Student Govt Assn 1966-67; pres Interfraternity Council 1966-67. **HONORS/ACHIEVEMENTS:** Sigma Rho Sigma Hon Soc Sci Frat; Who's Who Among Students in Amer Univs & Colls 1966-67. **BUSINESS ADDRESS:** Associate Dir, ICC, 12th & Constitution Ave NW, Washington, DC 20423.

GAILLARD, RALPH C., SR.
Tobacco company executive. **PERSONAL:** Born Dec 24, 1943, Chicago, IL; son of Julius F Gaillard Jr and Adele Chilton Gaillard; married Mary Washington, Dec 31, 1964; children: Ralph Jr, Sean, Nicolle, Courtney. **EDUCATION:** Chicago City Jr Coll, Chicago IL, attended, 1962-64. **CAREER:** R J Reynolds Tobacco USA, Los Angeles CA, asst div mgr, 1969-71, div mgr, 1971-78, San Francisco CA, chain acct mgr, 1978-81, Winston-Salem NC, sales vending/military mgr, 1981-84, natl military sales mgr, 1984-88, dir military sales, 1988-. **ORGANIZATIONS:** Pres, Southern California Candy & Tobacco Table, 1977; bd mem, Amer Logistics Assn, 1984-89, convention chmn, 1987, pres, 1988-89; mem, Diocese of Charlotte NC, Bd of Educ, 1984-85, pres, 1985; mem, North Carolina Dept of Public Instruction's Mktg Advisory Comm, 1988-. **BUSINESS ADDRESS:** Director-Military Sales, R J Reynolds Tobacco USA, 401 N Main St, Plaza 13th Floor, Winston-Salem, NC 27102.

GAINER, ANDREW A.
Business executive. **PERSONAL:** Born Jul 28, 1919, Gracevill, FL; son of Ally Gainer and Bessie Gainer; married Ruth Gainer; children: Patricia, Kim, Janet. **EDUCATION:** Attended one room grad sch Tallavast, FL; Booker High School, Sarasota FL, Graduated 1939; Tuskegee Institute 1938. **CAREER:** NY Gas Maintenance Co Inc, pres 1950-; Gain-robin Assn, pres 1977; AUCOA Contractors of Am, exec vice pres 1965; US Navy, aviation metalsmith 1st class 1944. **ORGANIZATIONS:** Bd mem COM 1975; mem 100 Black Men Inc 1978; bd & mem Comm Bd #9 1980; bd mem, Uptown Chamber of Commerce 1989. **HONORS/ACHIEVEMENTS:** Good Conduct Medal USN; Pacific Area Ww I Ribbon; Unsung Hero Award Ballantine 1965; Bus Award Nat Assn of Negro Bus & Professional Women's Club 1969. **MILITARY SERVICE:** USN Aviation Metalsmith 1st class 1942-45, Good Conduct, Asian Pacific. **BUSINESS ADDRESS:** Heating Specialistenance Co In, New York Gas Maintenance Co Inc, 309 W 116th St, New York, NY 10026.

GAINER, FRANK EDWARD
Coordinator. **PERSONAL:** Born Jun 18, 1938, Waynesboro, GA; son of Walter Gainer and Edith Gainer; married Alice M Ingram; children: Edward, Ervin, Todd. **EDUCATION:** Morehouse Coll, BS 1960; Tuskegee Inst, MS 1962; IA State Univ, MS 1964, PhD 1967. **CAREER:** Antibiotic Analytical & Quality Control, mgr 1978; Eli Lilly & Co, sec treasurer; JCG&M. **ORGANIZATIONS:** Asso chmn Amer Chem Soc 1975; chancellor Amer Chem Soc 1977; Sigma Xi; Beta Kappa Chi Hon Sci Soc; NAACP; Urban League; sec Mary Riggs Neighborhood Ctr 1976, treas 1977, bd of dir 1975-; published science journal. **BUSINESS ADDRESS:** Lilly Corporate Center, Eli Lilly & Company, Indianapolis, IN 46285.

GAINER, JOHN F.
Educator, musician, singer, composer, arranger, choral conductor. **PERSONAL:** Born Aug 08, 1954, East Orange, NJ; son of Benjamin Franklin Gainer and Stella Wynn Gainer. **EDUCATION:** AZ State Univ, BA 1980. **CAREER:** Various church and comm choirs, dir/musician 1968-; AZ State Univ Gospel Choir, founder/dir 1975-80; Lane Comm Coll, music instructor 1984-85; Univ of OR, adjunct faculty 1983-. **ORGANIZATIONS:** Mem Amer Soc of Composers Authors and Publishers 1972-; minister Church of God in Christ Inc 1979-; mem OR/Lane County Rainbow Coalition 1983-; precient comm person Central Democratic Comm 1984-; mem Edwin Hawkins Music & Arts Seminar 1984-; mem Lane Regional Arts Council 1985-; mem/chapter rep Gospel Music Workshop of Amer 1986-; mem Amer Inst of Architecture Students 1986-. **HONORS/ACHIEVEMENTS:** First black gospel artist to perform at the Hult Center for the Performing Arts 1983; invited to teach original compositions in the New Song Seminar at the Natl Convention of the Gospel Music Workshop of Amer Inc held in Atlanta GA 1984, New York NY 1985, Miami FL 1986; Honorary DD Church of God 1986; inspirational sounds one of 4 gospel choirs nationwide which performed at the great american gospel gala at Alice Tully Hall of the reknown Lincoln Center for the performing arts, 1987. **HOME ADDRESS:** 610 Palomino Drive, Eugene, OR 97401.

GAINER, RUBY JACKSON
Educator. **PERSONAL:** Born Mar 09, Buena Vista, GA; married Herbert Gainer; children: James, Ruby, Cecil. **EDUCATION:** AL State Univ, attended 1939; Atlanta Univ, MA 1953; Selma Univ, Hon HHD 1970; B'ham Bapt Coll, LLD; Daniel Payne Coll, Dr of Humane Letters; COState Christian Coll, PhD; Faith Coll B'ham AL, LLD 1976; Bishop Coll Dallas, Dr of Humane Letters 1977. **CAREER:** Jefferson County School System, teacher 12 years; Santa Rosa Public School System, teacher 1 year; Escambia County Public School System, teacher English, guidance counselor 49 years; William J Woodham High School, admin dean (retired). **ORGANIZATIONS:** Pres Escambia Classroom Tchr; pres FL State Classroom Tchr; vice pres FL State CTA; vice pres Assn of Classroom Tchr NEA; exec com ACT-NEA; mem Natl Ed Assn; FL Ed Assn; FUSA; Escambia Ed Assn; Amer Assn of Univ Women; League of Women Voters; life mem NAACP; pres City Assn of Federatred Clubs Pensacola; pres Past Grand Daughter Rulers Council of FL; pres Delta Iota Omega Chap of Alpha Kappa Alpha Sor; NACW; Mary McCleod Bethune Fed Club; cand reg dir S Atlanta Region Alpha Kappa Alpha Sor; basileus Delta Iota Omega Chap Alpha Kappa Alpha; mem NW Chap Phi Delta Kappa; mem Escambia Co Dem Com exec bd AL StateUniv Natl Alumni Assn; vice pres FL Assn of Women's Clubs; mem New Idea Art & Study Club; Human Relations Coun; City Fed of Clubs; chmn Escambia Ed Human Relations Com; dir of ed Orange Blossom Temple of Daughters of Elks; mem State Daughter Rules Coun; pres FL Assn of Women's Clubs;pres AL State Alumni Assn Pensacola Chapt; deputy supvsr Election Club; life mem Natl Cncl of Negro Women, Natl Assoc of Colored Women's Clubs. **HONORS/ACHIEVEMENTS:** Shriners Woman of Yr 1946; Zeta Woman of Yr 1947; Zeta's Finer Womanhood Awd; Tchr of Yr 1965; Mother of Yr 1966; Band Mother of Yr 1966; Cit of Yr 1967; Leader of Yr 1968; Outstanding AKA Sor 1969 1973; Outstanding Ed of Yr 1970; Regional Achievement Awd 1970; Most Aggressive Black Woman 1973; Humanitarian of Yr 1974; voted Pensacola's Top Lady of the Yr; nom Dau Isis of the Yr Comm Serv; elected Com Woman Dem Com; Lady of the Decade Awd Top Teens; Comm Serv Awd 5 Flag Fiesta 1980; runner-up Top Lady of Yr Natl Top Ladies of Distinction Inc 1980; Serv Awd FL Assn of Women's Clubs; Biographical Hall of Fame; Woman of the Yr 1984; Harriet Dorrah Federated Awd; WEAR Making a Difference Awd Channel 3 1984; AL State Univ Alumni of the Year 1986; IBA Fellow.

GAINES, ADRIANE THERESA
Communications. **PERSONAL:** Born Aug 27, 1947, Mt Vernon, NY; daughter of James McCoy and Dorothy McCoy. **EDUCATION:** Fordham Univ, BA cum laude 1978. **CAREER:** Marine Midland Bank, sec & safekeeping deputy 1965-68; State Natl Bank of El Paso, investment & sec deputy 1968-71; Rochester Inst of Tech, asst info specialist 1971-72; Culinary Inst of Amer, asst librarian 1972-73; Unity Broadcasting Network, dir of corp admin 1973-82, corporate vice pres NBN Broadcasting, Inc 1982-. **ORGANIZATIONS:** Co-founder bd mem The World Inst of Black Comm 1978-; acting gen mgr Katz AM/WZEN FM Radio 1982; comm bd of dir Coalition of 100 Black Women, 1984-85; mem Women in Cable 1985; mem Natl Acad of TV Arts & Sciences 1982-; mem Adv Women in Radio & TV 1982-; mem Bronx Co Borough President's Club 1984-; bd of trustees Apollo Theater Hall of Fame 1986-. **HONORS/ACHIEVEMENTS:** Media Woman of the Year Natl Assn of Media Women 1985; co-exec producer Ceba Awards 1978-. **BUSINESS ADDRESS:** Corporate Vice President, NBN Broadcasting Inc, 10 Columbus Circle, 10th Floor, New York, NY 10019-1285.

GAINES, CLARENCE E.
Educator. **PERSONAL:** Born in Paducah, KY; married Clara Berry; children: Lisa Gaines McDonald, Clarence E. **EDUCATION:** Morgan State Coll Baltimore, BS; ColumbiaUniv NYC, MA. **CAREER:** Winston-Salem State Univ, athletic dir; Winston-Salem State Univ

Parochial School, coordinator. **ORGANIZATIONS:** Mem AAHPER; NEA; NC Assn for Hlth Physical Educ & Recreation; Nat Assn for Bsktbll Coaches; Nat Assn for Collegiate Dir of Athletics; dist chmn Nat Assn of Intercollegiate Athletics (NAIA) 1966-72; bd of mgmt Patterson Ave YMCA 1968-71; pres Central Intercollegiate Athletic Assn (CIAA) 1972-74; chmn AAHPER Publ Com 1972-74; pres CIAA Bsktbll Coaches Assn 1972-76; coordinator Modern Concepts of Hlth Fitness & Leisure for Senior Citizens Winston-Salem State U; mem Forsyth Co Heart Assn; mem US Olympic Com; bd of mgmt Winston-Salem Boys Club; mem Bsktbll Games Com of the US CollegiateSports Counc; bd of dir Winston-Salem Found. **HONORS/ACHIEVEMENTS:** Football coach of the yr CIAA 1948; bsktbll coach of the yr CIAA 1957, 61, 63, 70, & 75; bsktbll Coach of the yr NCAA 1967; halls of fame NAIA Helms 1968; family of the yr award Winston-Salem Urban League 1973; sports hall of fame Morgan State Coll 1973; honor award NC AAHEPR 1974; hall of fame CIAA 1975;outst coach award NAIA Dist 26 1975-78; nominated for NC Sports Hall of Fame 1978; CIAA Tournament Outst Coach Award. **BUSINESS ADDRESS:** Station A, Winston-Salem, NC 27102.

GAINES, CLARENCE L.
Judge. **PERSONAL:** Born Mar 09, 1914, Dallas, TX; married Pearl; children: Pearl, Delaney, Clarence III, George. **EDUCATION:** Western Reserve U, BBA 1950; Cleveland Marshall Law Sch, LLB 1955. **CAREER:** City Council, elected 1963, 65; City of Cleveland, dir of Hlth & Welfare 1966-68; Gaines Rogers Horton & Forbes, sr partner; Cleveland Municipal Ct, judge. **ORGANIZATIONS:** Mem Coun on Human Relations; NAACP; Boy Scouts; Urban League; Welfare Fedn; Alcoholic Control Ctr; and others. **MILITARY SERVICE:** WW II officer. **BUSINESS ADDRESS:** Cleveland Municipal Court, 1200 Ontario St, Cleveland, OH 44113.

GAINES, DORA BELLE
Former mayor. **PERSONAL:** Born May 05, 1927, Ecorse, MI; married John Hamberth Jr; children: Gayrelle Boyer, Timothy Marlow, Cynthia Harrison, Douglas, Lynette Banks, Vance LaShay, Lana Wilkerson, Jeffery Marlow, Kurt Vaughn. **EDUCATION:** Wayne State Univ, 1972-73. **CAREER:** Ecorse MI, mayor 1st black woman elected 1975-77; City of Ecorse, elected councilwoman 1972; numerous office jobs 1945-54. **ORGANIZATIONS:** Precinct del Dem Party 1955-56; treas PTA of Bunche 1958-59; mem NAACP 1965-; Dau Silver Star Temple 1972; life mem, First Baptist Church; mem, Natl Black Women Political Leadership Council 1975-76. **HONORS/ACHIEVEMENTS:** Hon Mayor WSBC Woman's Aux 1976; Hon Mayor Mt Zion Missionary Baptist Church, 1976; Hon Mayor Detroit Chapter of Spelman Alumnae 1976.

GAINES, EDYTHE J.
Educator, government official. **PERSONAL:** Born Sep 06, 1922, Asheville, NC; married Albert; children: 2 sons. **EDUCATION:** Hunter Coll, AB 1944; NY Univ, MA 1947; Harvard Univ, EdD 1969; Montclair State, LLD 1977. **CAREER:** NY City Public Schools, teacher 1945-67; Hartford Coll for Women, prin, asst prin; NY School Dist #12, comm supr 1967-71; Learning Coop, dir 1971-73; New York City Public Schools, exec dir educ planning & support 1973-75; Hartford CT, supt of schools 1975-78; Gr Hartford Consortium for Higher Educ, consultant to bd of govs 1978-79; State of CT, Public Utilities Control Authority, commr 1979-. **ORGANIZATIONS:** Corporator Mt Sinai Hosp, Hartford Hosp and The Inst for Living; bd of dir Hartford Hosp; dir CT Natl Bank & Hartford Natl Corp; bd of dir Kaman Corp; bd of dirs Hartford Stage Co; bd of dirs CT Opera Assn; chair Comm on Ministry Episcopal Diocese of CT; mem Gov's Task Force on South African Investment Divestiture Policy; dir Old State House Assoc. **HONORS/ACHIEVEMENTS:** Honoree CT Black Women Achievement Against the Odds; Recipient of numerous honors & awds including the Family of Man Medallion Awd for Excellence in Education. **BUSINESS ADDRESS:** Commr Public Util Control, State of CT, One Central Park Plaza, New Britain, CT 06051.

GAINES, ERNEST J.
Author. **PERSONAL:** Born Jan 15, 1933, Oscar, LA. **EDUCATION:** Attended Vallejo Jr Coll; attended San Francisco State Coll; Denison Univ, DLitt (hon). **CAREER:** Univ Southwestern LA Dept of English, prof and resident writer; author. **HONORS/ACHIEVEMENTS:** Recip Gold Medal Commonwealth Club of CA 1972, 1984; LA Libr Assn Award 1972; Black Acad Arts and Letters Award 1972; Award for Excellence of Achievement in field of lit San Francisco Arts Comm 1983; Author of books, "Catherine Carmier" 1966; "Of Love and Dust" 1968; "Bloodline" 1968; "The Autobiography of Miss Jane Pittman" 1971; "A Long Day in November" 1971; "In My Father's House" 1978; "A Gathering of Old Men" 1983. **BUSINESS ADDRESS:** Professor/Resident Writer, Univ Southwestern LA, Dept of English, Lafayette, LA 70503.

GAINES, HERSCHEL DAVIS
Educational administrator. **PERSONAL:** Born Oct 07, 1942, Parkin, AR; married Wilbert Gaines; children: Jacquelyn LaRue, Michelle LaRue, Genee La Rue. **EDUCATION:** Univ of AR at Pine Bluff, BA 1962; AR State Univ, MS 1979. **CAREER:** Phelix High School, english teacher 1962-69; Marion Sr High School, english teacher 1969-71; McArthur Middle School, chmn english dept 1971-81; Jonesboro High School, asst prin 1981-. **ORGANIZATIONS:** Bd dirs Jonesboro Classroom Tchrs Assn 1972-; bd dir AR Educ Assn 1976-79; mem affiliate relations com NEA 1977-79; basileus anti-basileus & grammateus Kappa Nu Omega Alpha Kappa Alpha Sor 1976-80; corr sec Alpha Delta Kappa 1979-; apptd by Gov Bill Clinton to Employment Sec Div Adv Coun 1981; nom com Crowley's Ridge Girl Scout Council 1981-83; educ comm Crowley's Ridge Girl Scouts 1981-83; bd dir United Way of Greater Jonesboro 1985-86; Advisory Cncl Upward Bound of AR State Univ 1980-; pres AR State Univ Faculty Women's Club 1985-87. **HONORS/ACHIEVEMENTS:** Educ Awd Alpha Kappa Alpha Sor Jonesboro AR & AR Council of AKA 1976 & 1978; Outstanding Young Educator Awd Jaycees of Jonesboro 1977; Who's Who in S Central Region of Alpha Kappa Alpha 1978; Silver Soror-Alpha Kappa Alpha 1985. **BUSINESS ADDRESS:** Assistant Principal, Jonesboro HS, Jonesboro, AR 72401.

GAINES, JAUNELL WALLACE
Business executive. **PERSONAL:** Born Jan 21, 1942, Ft Smith, AR; married Izetta L; children: Christopher, Kandi. **EDUCATION:** DrakeUniv Des Moines IA, 1965. **CAREER:** Hampton Bus Forms Inc, prs chief exec off 1969-73; Ford Motor Co, finan analyst controller's staff 1973-74; Nat Urban Leag, lect; Nat Black Manufacturers Assn, orgn com; US Govt Small Bus Adminstrn, lectr; General Elec Co, dist mgr. **ORGANIZATIONS:** Mem Nat Black Mfr Assn; Bus Fedn of Am; mem Gainescheck Nat Bicentennial Proj; exec com BSA; mem Boys Club of Am; deacon in Bapt Ch; instr Young Adults Ch Sch. **HONORS/ACHIEVEMENTS:** Publ of first black bus & professional directory in VA; honored by C of C Memphis TN; outstnd jr off USAF 1966-68; first black mfr of computer forms in Am; selected for Ford Motor Co select mgmt training prog. **MILITARY SERVICE:** USAF capt 1965-69. **BUSINESS ADDRESS:** PO Box 25761, Oklahoma City, OK 73125.

GAINES, LESLIE DORAN (BUBBA)
Performer. **PERSONAL:** Born Feb 12, 1912, Waynesboro, GA. **CAREER:** USO, entertainer AUS 1951-71; Three Dukes Internat, Aristocrats of Dancing, original mem 1932-41. **ORGANIZATIONS:** Mem NY Assn of Musicians; founding mem Copasetics 1950-80. **HONORS/ACHIEVEMENTS:** Recip 5 Battle Stars. **MILITARY SERVICE:** AUS corpl 1942-45.

GAINES, MANYLES B., JR.
Educational administrator. **PERSONAL:** Born Dec 31, 1938, Tulsa, OK; married Geraldine White; children: Michelle, Melissa. **EDUCATION:** Langston U, BA 1962;Univ of Tulsa, 1968; Northeastern State U, MEd 1969; Oklahoma State U, Adm Cert 1973. **CAREER:** Tulsa Public Schools, Tulsa OK, elementary classroom teacher 1965-70, asst elementary school prin 1970-72, elementary school prin 1972-82, dir headstart program 1975, admin school comm rel specialist. **ORGANIZATIONS:** Pres Tulsa Assn of Elem Sch Princpl 1982-83; pres NAESP Conv, New Orleans LA 1984; pres OK Alliance of Black Sch Educators 1984-; pres LUAA Midwestern Reg 1976-; pres Alpha Tau Lambda Chap Alpha Phi Alpha Frat Inc 1973-84; chrmn of bd Hutcherson Branch Family YMCA, Tulsa OK 1982-. **HONORS/ACHIEVEMENTS:** Published tutorial handbook for Tulsa Public Sch, Tulsa OK 1982; Disting Achievement Award LangstonUniv OK 1982, Disting Alumni Award 1984; Dedicated Serv Award LangstonUniv Alumni Assn 1984. **MILITARY SERVICE:** AUS spclst 4th class 1962-64. **BUSINESS ADDRESS:** Administrator-Sch/Comm Rel, Tulsa Public Schools, 3027 S New Haven, Tulsa, OK 74147.

GAINES, OSCAR CORNELL
Physician. **PERSONAL:** Born May 21, 1954, Memphis, TN; divorced. **EDUCATION:** Lambuth Coll, BS 1976; Meharry Medical Coll, MD 1982. **CAREER:** US Army, capt/physician 1983-87. **ORGANIZATIONS:** Mem Prince Hall Mason Lodge 1986, Alpha Phi Alpha. **MILITARY SERVICE:** AUS capt 3 yrs. **HOME ADDRESS:** 1616 Moss Creek Rd, Waycross, GA 31501. **BUSINESS ADDRESS:** Physician, Martin Army Hospital, Emergency Room, Fort Benning, GA 31905.

GAINES, PAUL LAURENCE, SR.
Educator; government official. **PERSONAL:** Born Apr 20, 1932, Newport, RI; son of Albert P Gaines Sr and Pauline P Jackson Gaines; married Jo Eva Johnson, Jul 18, 1959; children: Jena, Patricia Scholer, Paulajo, Paul Jr. **EDUCATION:** Xavier Univ of LA, BEd 1951-55; Bridgewater State Coll, MEd in Cnslng 1966-68. **CAREER:** Newport RI Public Sch, sch tchr 1959-68; Newport RI Rogers HS, bsktbll coach 1959-68; Newport RI Youth Corps, cnslr 1960-66; Bridgewater State Coll MA, admin 1968-; Bridgewater State Grad Sch, coll prof 1970-; Bridgewater State Coll, asst to pres 1983-. **ORGANIZATIONS:** Bd of dir Newport Cnty Regnl YMCA; bd of dir RI Minority Caucus; trustee Bank of Newport RI; corp mem Newport RI Hosp; mem Newport Branch NAACP; mem Newport Lions Club; mem Cncl #256 Knights of Columbus; bd of dirs Aquidneck Banking Center (Newport, RI) 1988-; Urban League of Rhode Island 1986-; Commissioner, Rhode Island Ethics Commission 1987-;. **HONORS/ACHIEVEMENTS:** 1st Black Sch Committeeman Newport RI Sch 1969-72; 1st Black City Cnclmn Newport City Cncl 1977-81; 1st Black Mayor Newport RI 1981-83; Citizen of The YrOmega Psi Phi Frat (Sigma Nu Chpt) 1981; recipient George T Downing Award RI 1982; elected to RI Constitutional Convention 1985-86; RI Adv Comm to the US Commn on Civil Rights 1985-87. **MILITARY SERVICE:** AUS 82nd recon div sp 3 1955-57. **HOME ADDRESS:** 227 Eustis Ave, Newport, RI 02840. **BUSINESS ADDRESS:** Assistant to the President, Bridgewater State Coll, Harrington Hall, Bridgewater, MA 02325.

GAINES, RAY D.
Surgeon, educator. **PERSONAL:** Born Aug 04, 1932, Minneapolis; married Frances Hunter. **EDUCATION:** Creighton U, BS 1954, MD 1958; Wayne Co Gen Hosp, internship 1958-59; Santa Cruz Co Hosp CA, gen practice residency 1959-60; Wayne Co Gen Hosp, residency in surgery 1960-64. **CAREER:** St Joseph Hospital, assoc chief emergency serv 1975-78; Douglas Co Hospital NE, chief surg serv 1974-76; VA Medical Center, Omaha NE, assoc chief surg serv; Creighton Univ, asst prof 1973-; Public Health Serv Bureau of Health Manpower, consultant 1967-70; Amer Coll of Surgeons, fellow 1966; Amer Bd of Surgery, diplomate 1965; Univ of MI Center, clinical instructor 1965-73; Wayne County General Hospital, staff 1964-73; staff appts at several hospitals. **ORGANIZATIONS:** Mem Nat Med Assn; Omaha-Douglas Co Med Sch; NE Med Soc; bd dirs Dougals/Sarpy Div Am Cancer Soc 1975-; fellow Southwestern Surgical Congress; mem adv co Med/Am Counc BSA 1975-76; mem Am Burn Assn; mem CreightonUniv Surg Soc; med offcr Gen Daniel James Ct Squad CAP 1976-77; mem Assn of VA Surgns; Assn for Acad Surgery; Omaha Midwest Clinical Soc; u Assn for Emer Medicine; Detroit Surgical Assn; mem Kappa Alpha Psi; Phi Beta Pi; lifemem NAACP; bd dir NE Heart Assn; mem Joslyn Art Mus; mem Ak Sar Ben Guest Examiner,; Am Bd of Surgery Omaha 1974. **BUSINESS ADDRESS:** Dept of Surg, 601 N 30 St, Omaha, NE 68131.

GAINES, RICHARD KENDALL
Business owner. **PERSONAL:** Born Apr 11, 1947, St Louis, MO; son of Mr & Mrs Richard Harris; married Anne-Marie Clarke; children: Kimberly, Yvette. **EDUCATION:** Coe Coll, BA Sociology 1969; St Louis Univ, Grad School. **CAREER:** City of Des Moines, deputy dir concentrated employ prog 1969-70; St Louis Bd of Educ, dir of comm educ 1970-73; St Louis Univ, dir of upward bound 1973-76; Urban League of Metropolitan St Louis, dir of educ 1976-77; Richard K Gaines & Assocs; Daniel & Henry Insurance Brokers, vice pres. **ORGANIZATIONS:** Mem Jaycees St Louis 1972-75; mem Amer Personnel & Guidance Assn 1973-76; past pres YMCA Men's Club City North 1980-81; mem Natl Assn of Life Underwriters 1977-; registered rep Natl Assn of Security Dealers 1977-; mem Independent Ins Agents of MO 1984-; mem St Louis Bd of Educ 1983-89; bd of dir YMCA; past pres St Louis Bd of Educ 1987-88; bd mem St Louis Black Repertory Company 1989-; bd mem Royal Order of Vagabonds, Inc 1986-. **HONORS/ACHIEVEMENTS:** Awards salesman-mgr General American Life; presenter Natl Comm Schools Conf 1972; Sales Awd Lincoln Natl Life Ins

1977-. **BUSINESS ADDRESS:** Richard K Gaines & Assoc, 100 N Jefferson, St Louis, MO 63103.

GAINES, SAMUEL STONE
Business executive. **PERSONAL:** Born Jan 25, 1938, Fort Pierce, FL; married Theressa Ann Dillard; children: Andre, Arnold, Alwyn. **EDUCATION:** Talladega Coll, BA 1960; McAllister Sch of Embalming, 1961. **CAREER:** FL Mortician Assn, pres 1979-81; Epsilon Nu Delta Mortuary Frat, natl pres 1982-84; Nat Funeral Dir & Morticians, natl vice pres 1984-85, pres- elect 1985-, natl pres 1986; St Lucie Co Sch Bd, vice-chairman 14yrs. **ORGANIZATIONS:** Treas Omicron Tau Chap Omega; secy Sunrise Consult #202; treas FL Mortician Assn; mem St Lucic Cnty Sch Bd 1972-; life mem Omega Psi Phi Frat; goldenhertigage mem NAACP; Grand Inspector General of the 33rd degree of the Ancient & Accepted Scottish Rite of Free Masonry for the Southern Jurisdiction. **HONORS/ACHIEVEMENTS:** Community Serv Award Club Entre Nous, Ft Pierce 1980; Ft Pierce Chap of Links 1981; FL Mortician Assn 1982; Man of The Yr Alpha Gamma Chap Epsilon Nu Delta 1983. **BUSINESS ADDRESS:** 317 N 7th St, Fort Pierce, FL 34950.

GAINES, SEDALIA MITCHELL
Educator. **PERSONAL:** Born Mar 31, Houston, TX; daughter of William Mitchell and Sarah Mitchell; children: William Anthony Jr, Sandra R Lopes. **EDUCATION:** Tillotson Coll, BS 1939; Temple U, MEd 1947; Intl Sch of Travel, Cert Travel Agent; UNC Greensboro, Cert Early Childhood Training. **CAREER:** Fessenden Acad, tchr 1940; FL A&M Coll, dir nursery school 1947; School Dist Phila, chmn home econ 1952; HEW, head start tchr trainer 1968; UNC Greensboro School Dist Phila, supvr day care 1966-80; Philadelphia School Dist, retired supvr day care. **ORGANIZATIONS:** Mem Assoc Supervision & Curriculum Devel; mem Haven United Methodist Church; mem Delaware Valley Assoc for Educ Young Child; basileus Beta Delta Zeta Chap, Zeta Phi Beta; pres Philadelphia Council, Natl Council of Negro Women; life mem NAACP Natl Council of Negro Women, Phi Beta; mem bd dir Red Cross; mem NAEYC; mem bd dir ARC; mem of bd Theological Educ Consortium. **HONORS/ACHIEVEMENTS:** Ranking student Tillotson Coll; honoree Assn Natl Black Child Devel; Career Woman of the Yr Afro Amer Newspaper; Service Award March of Dimes; Berean Recognition Awd; Four Chaplins Awd; Admin Women in Educ Awd. **HOME ADDRESS:** 2131 W Master St, Philadelphia, PA 19121.

GAINES, SYLVESTER, JR.
Port director. **PERSONAL:** Born May 13, 1921, Thomson, GA; married Edith Thomas. **EDUCATION:** LaSalle Coll, 2 Yr Study; Nat Training Ctr, US Customs Training Prgm 1972; Baltimore, Labor-Mgmt Seminar 1974. **CAREER:** Customs at Alexandria VA, port dir 1973-; US Customs Insp, 1958-73; Customs Port Patrol Officer, 1957-58; Custom Files, supr 1956-57; US Customs, cargo handler 1955-56; Railway Mailclerk 1952-54; Naval Aviation Supply Depot Philadelphia, property & supply clerk 1948-52; Postal Clerk, 1947-48. **ORGANIZATIONS:** Co-chmn of capitol funds com Freeway Golf Club Turnersville, NJ; mem Optimist Club of Alexandria; mem Arlington Divots Golf Club; mem Eastern Golfers Assn 1955-; mem Intl Golfers Assn; chmn Entertainment Com Fairview Golf Club 1958-63; chmn Entertainment Com Douglas Golf Club 1966-70; chmn Keystone Open Golf Tournament Douglas Golf Club 1969-70. **HONORS/ACHIEVEMENTS:** Letter of commendation from CO 1944; letter of commendation from CO 5th Engineer Spl Brigade 1944. **MILITARY SERVICE:** AUS sgt 1943-46. **BUSINESS ADDRESS:** GSA Bldg, C/o Port Dir Franklin & Union, Alexandria, VA 22314.

GAINES, THURSTON LENWOOD, JR.
Physician. **PERSONAL:** Born Mar 20, 1922, Freeport, NY; son of Thurston L Gaines and Albertha Robinson Gaines; married Jacqueline Kelly; children: Beverly Doreen Gaines Harvey, Terrell Lance, William Wesley. **EDUCATION:** Howard U, 1941-43; NY Univ, BA 1948; Meharry Med Coll, MD 1953. **CAREER:** Hempstead, NY, private practice of surgery 1959-76; South Nassau Comm Hosp, Oceanside, NY, dir prof educ & training 1964-69; Mercy Hosp, Rockville Centre, NY, dir surgical educ 1969-74; Western Mass Hosp, Westfield, MA, chief of prof serv 1977-78; Soldiers Home in Holyoke, med dir 1979-88. **ORGANIZATIONS:** Assoc attending surgeon Nassau County Med Ctr, East Meadow, Long Island, NY 1959-77; mem Kiwanis Club of Hempstead, NY 1963-67; deputy county med examiner Nassau County, Long Island, NY 1964-77; pres Hempstead Community Chest, Hempstead, NY 1965; bd of trustees Catholic Hosp Assn, St Louis, MO 1973-76; asst clinical prof of surgery State Univ of NY at Stonybrook Med Sch 1976-77; diplomate, Amer Bd of Quality Assurance Utilization Review Physicians; fellow, Amer Coll of Utilization Review Physicians. **HONORS/ACHIEVEMENTS:** Diplomate Amer Bd of Surgery 1963-; fellow Amer Coll of Surgeons 1965-; fellow Intl Coll of Surgeons 1976-. **MILITARY SERVICE:** USAAF 1st lt fighter pilot instructor pilot; 332nd Fighter Group Air Medal; 2 Oak Leaf Clusters; Purple Heart 1943-47.

GAINES, VICTOR PRYOR
University administrator. **PERSONAL:** Born Jul 25, 1939, Staunton, VA; children: Victor P II, Johnathan. **EDUCATION:** KY State Univ, BA 1960; Univ of KY, MA 1969, EdS 1977, EdD 1981. **CAREER:** Univ of KY, dir of special student programs 1972-74, employee counselor 1974-, employee counselor/acting dir equal oppor 1977-80, acting vice chancellor minority affairs 1984-85, exec dir for minority resource develop and employee counselor 1985-. **ORGANIZATIONS:** Mem bd dirs Lexington Urban League; mem Phi Delta Kappa; bd mem Univ of KY Credit Union 1982-; corporate mem Amer Assoc for Equity & Excellence in Higher Educ 1986-. **HONORS/ACHIEVEMENTS:** Article published "Career Counseling as Experienced by Practicing Black Ophthalmologists," Natl Medical Assoc 1980. **BUSINESS ADDRESS:** Exec Dir Minority Resource Dev, Univ of KY, Rm 207 Administration Bldg, Lexington, KY 40506.

GAINEY, LEONARD DENNIS, II
Association executive. **PERSONAL:** Born Aug 23, 1927, Jacksonville, FL; married Carolyn Higgs; children: Leonard III, Derek, Kassandra. **EDUCATION:** Morehouse Coll, BA 1949. **CAREER:** US Post Office Dept Ft Lauderdale FL, carrier 1953-66; Gaineys Bus Affairs, owner 1953-66; Econ Oppty Coord Group Inc, dep dir, comptroller 1966-73; Stae of FL Ed Dept, fiscal officer 1973-76; Urban League of Broward Cty, pres, ceo 1976-81; Ken Thurston & Assoc Inc, bd mem 1979-80; The Omega Group Inc, mgr mgmt consult br office. **ORGANIZATIONS:** Pres Ivory Mizell Republ Club; treas FL Black Republ Council; bd mem exec comm Broward Cty Republ Party; mem Omega Psi Phi 1957; mem Ed Comm Ft Lauderdale Broward C of C 1980, Human Affairs Council Natl Council Christians & Jews 1980; chmn Broward Cty Human Relations Adv. **HONORS/ACHIEVEMENTS:** Omega Man of the Year Omega Psi Phi Frat; Citation Broward Cty Human Relations Div 1979. **MILITARY SERVICE:** AUS corpl 1950-52. **BUSINESS ADDRESS:** Manager, Mgmt Consult Br Off, The Omega Group Inc, 25 SE 2nd Ave Ste 1014, Miami, FL 33131.

GAITAN, FERNANDO J., JR.
Judge. **PERSONAL:** Born Aug 22, 1948, Kansas City, KS. **EDUCATION:** Pittsburgh State Univ, BS 1970; Univ of MO Kansas City, JD 1974. **CAREER:** Bureau of Prisons; US Justice Dept; Public Defender; Legal Aid Soc; Southwestern Bell Telephone Co, attny 1974-80; Sixteenth Judicial Circuit Jackson Cty Courthouse, circuit court judge. **ORGANIZATIONS:** Mem MO Bar Assoc, Kansas City Bar Assoc, Jackson Cty Bar Assoc, Amer Bar Assoc, Natl Bar Assoc, State & Natl Judicial Conf, St Lukes Hosp, De La Salle Ed Ctr, Ozanam Home for Boys, NAACP, Volunteers in Corrections, Natl Conf of Christians & Jews. **BUSINESS ADDRESS:** Circuit Court Judge, Jackson County Courthouse, 415 E 12th, Kansas City, MO 64106.

GAITHER, ALONZO S.
Retired educator. **PERSONAL:** Born Apr 11, 1903; married Sadie Robinson. **EDUCATION:** Knoxville Coll, AB 1927; Ohio State U, MA 1937; Knoxville Coll, Hon LLD 1962. **CAREER:** Henderson Inst Henderson, NC, coach 1927-35; St Paul Jr Coll Lawrenceville VA, 1935-37; FL A&M U, asst coach 1937-44, hd coach, prof, Athl dir 1945-69, athl dir, prof 1970-73. **ORGANIZATIONS:** Trustee Am Ftbll Coaches Assn Fellowship of Christ Athletics; mem FL Bd Pardons & Parole Qualifications Com 1974; elder Trinity United Presb Ch; memUrban League; NAACP; v ch ARC; mem Local Assn Charities; mem Sunrioe Optimist Club; Phi Beta Sigma; Sigma Phi Phi Frat. **HONORS/ACHIEVEMENTS:** College coach of the yr Am Ftbll Coaches Assn 1961; Helmo Hall of Fame NAIA Bethune Medallion 1973; FL Hall Fame & TN Hall of Fame; elected to Nat Ftbll Found Hall of Fame Jan 1975; TN Distinguished Am Award 1972.

GAITHER, CORNELIUS E.
Dentist. **PERSONAL:** Born Feb 28, 1928, Philadelphia, PA; son of Cornelius Hopson Gaither and Edith Albertha Robinson Gaither; married Anna Louise Whittaker Gaither; children: Cornelius, Carmen, Carol, John, Reginald. **EDUCATION:** Meharry Med Coll, DDS 1953; Lincoln Univ, AB 1949. **CAREER:** USAF, dentist 1957-. **ORGANIZATIONS:** Mem So NJ Dental Soc; NJ Dental Soc; Am Dental Assn; Nat Dental Assn; Am Coll of Grad Dentistry; Philadelphia Co Dental Soc; New Era Dental Soc;Chi Delta Mu Med Dental Pharm Frat; Am Dental Soc of Anesthesia; Aerospace Med Assn; S Jersey Med Dental Assn; Acad of Grad Dentist; Chester-Delaware Co Dental Soc; Am Assn of Hosp Dentist; mem DE Valley Reg Med Plng Bd 1968-73; bd dir Beckett New Town HMO 1974; area coord Operation Drug Alert1970; bd dir Am Cancer Soc 1970-74; Gloucester Co Vis Nurse Assn 1968-; adv bd Gloucester Co Bd of Hlth; mem Gloucester Co TB & Hlth Assn 1960-68; Hlth Assn 1970-; bd dir Gloucester Co Children's Shelter 1968-74; pres Kiwanis Intl 1960-74; mem Adv Bd of Wilmington; DE Bd of Educ 1960-74; Christ Presb Ch 1970-72; United Fund Bd Dir 1964-65; sec Salvation Army 1960-; mem Alpha Phi Alpha Frat. **MILITARY SERVICE:** USAF 1954-57; USAFR lt col 1957-. **BUSINESS ADDRESS:** 128 Kings Hwy, Swedesboro, NJ 08085.

GAITHER, DOROTHY B.
Physician. **PERSONAL:** Born May 27, 1941, St Louis, MO; daughter of Alexander D Gaither and Dorothy Gaither; married Marion A Randolph; children: Alexander, Michele. **EDUCATION:** Knoxville Coll, BS 1964; Howard U, MD 1970. **CAREER:** Howard Univ Hosp, intern resident 1970-75, instructor 1975; private practice 1975-, ob gyn; Women's Medical Ctr, medical dir 1985-87; Aunandale Women's Center 1988-. **ORGANIZATIONS:** Treasurer Amer Medical Women's Assn 1983-85 sec 1983-87, pres 1985-86; Branch I Arlington Links; sec Northern Virginia Chap Coalition of 100 Black Women 1984-85; mem Natl Medical Assn DC Medical Society, Medical Chirugical Society, Alpha Kappa Alpha Sor; fellow Amer College Ob/Gyn; mem Physicians Serv Commn Blue Cross/Blue Shield; mem Girlfriends Inc, Jack & Jill of Amer Inc, Carats Inc, Just Us; mem Medical School Admissions Commn Howard Univ 1983-85, Impaired Physicians Commn DC Medical Soc 1983-85. **HONORS/ACHIEVEMENTS:** Articles published in Natl Medical Assn Journal 1968, 1972, 1973. **HOME ADDRESS:** 9411 Mt Vernon Cir, Alexandria, VA 22309. **BUSINESS ADDRESS:** 3230 Pennsylvania Ave SE, Washington, DC 20020.

GAITHER, EDMUND B.
Association executive, artist. **PERSONAL:** Born Oct 06, 1944, Great Falls, SC. **EDUCATION:** Morehouse Coll, BA 1966; Brown U, MA 1968. **CAREER:** Museum of Fine Arts, spl cons; Museum Nat Cntr of Afro-Am Artists, dir/curator; Elma Lewis Sch of Fine Arts; Spelman Coll, lectr; Boston U, asst prof; Harvard Coll, lectr; NY U, vis critic; Wellesley Coll, lectr; Nat Endowment of the Arts NY State Council on Art & Hum, panelist; Lectures Widely;Piedmont Art Festival Atlanta, judg E 1975; Indpndnc Art Fest Jamaica WI, judge 1971; Afro-Am Artists Musm of Fine Arts, chief organizer. **ORGANIZATIONS:** Mem Nat Conf of Artists. **HONORS/ACHIEVEMENTS:** Insight award Am Assn of Museums RAP 1975; Who's Who in Am Art 1973. **BUSINESS ADDRESS:** 122 Elm Hill Ave, Boston, MA 02121.

GAITHER, RICHARD A.
Attorney. **PERSONAL:** Born Oct 28, 1939, Washington, DC; son of John Gaither and Miriam Gaither; married Deanna Dixon; children: Jamala, Marisa. **EDUCATION:** Univ of Dayton, BS Chemistry 1962; Univ of Balimore, JD 1970; New York Univ, LLM Trade Regulation 1981. **CAREER:** AUS, officer 1963-65; FDA, research chemist 1963 & 1965-67; US Patent & Trademark Office, patent examiner 1967-72; Lever Brothers Co, atty 1972-74; Hoffmann La Roche Inc, asst gen counsel. **ORGANIZATIONS:** mem Natl Bar Assn 1970-; mem Amer Bar Assn 1970-; mem Natl Patent Law Assn 1970-. **HONORS/ACHIEVEMENTS:** Black Achiever Newark, NJ YMCA 1980. **MILITARY SERVICE:** AUS 1st lt 1963-65; numerous letters of commendation. **BUSINESS ADDRESS:** Assistant General Counsel, Hoffmann La Roche Inc, 340 Kingsland St, Nutley, NJ 07110.

GAITHER, THOMAS W.
Educator. **PERSONAL:** Born Nov 12, 1938, Great Falls, SC. **EDUCATION:** Claflin Coll, BS 1960; Atlanta U, MS 1964;Univ IA, PhD 1968. **CAREER:** Cong of Racial Equality CORE, field sec 1960-62; Iowa City, forester 1968; Slippery Rock State Coll, assoc prof

1968-. **ORGANIZATIONS:** Mem Botanical Soc Am; mem Mycological Soc Am; Am Assn for the Advancement & Sci; mem Soc Sigma Xi. **HONORS/ACHIEVEMENTS:** Woutstanding young mem Am Alpha Kappa Mu Nat Scholastic Hon Soc 1972; Outstanding Educators Am 1975; Who's Who in Am 1974. **BUSINESS ADDRESS:** Dept Biology, Slippery Rock State Coll, Slippery Rock, PA 16057.

GALAMISON, MILTON A.
Clergyman. **PERSONAL:** Born Jan 25, 1923, Philadelphia, PA. **EDUCATION:** Lincoln U, BA 1945, DDiv 1961; LincolnUniv Sch of Theol, BDiv 1947; Princeton Theol Sem, MTheol 1949. **CAREER:** Siloam Presb Ch, pastor 1949-. **ORGANIZATIONS:** Chmn of bd of dir Opport Industlzn Ctr of NY Inc; appt bd of trustees Princeton Theol Sem; chmn bd of dir Bedrod-Throop Housing & Devel Fund Inc. **BUSINESS ADDRESS:** Siloam Presbyterian Church, 260 Jefferson Ave, Brooklyn, NY 11218.

GALBREATH, TONY (MR. EVERYTHING)
Professional athlete. **PERSONAL:** Born Jan 29, 1954, Fulton, MO. **EDUCATION:** MO U. **CAREER:** New Orleans Saints, professional football player; MVP Saints, pro athlete. **BUSINESS ADDRESS:** New Orleans Saints, 6928 Saints Dr, Metairie, LA 70003.

GALES, JAMES
Government official. **PERSONAL:** Born May 18, 1922, Jefferson Co; married Lucinda Perkins; children: Blanche, AC, Robert, Frank, Mary Ellen, Ronnie, Angela P. **EDUCATION:** Jefferson Co Training Sch; Alcorn A&M Coll, Cert 1949. **CAREER:** Town of Fayette, mayor pro tem city councilman 1969-; Internatl Paper Co, safety dept 1949. **ORGANIZATIONS:** Bd of dirs Adams Jefferson Franklin Caliborne Comm 1969; bd of dirs Unity Action Agency ARC 1973-; bd of dirs Medgar Evers Comprehensive Health Clinc 1970; bd dir Indl Park for City & Co 1969-. **HONORS/ACHIEVEMENTS:** Faithful worker award NAACP Jefferson Co Chap 1967; faithful worker award AJFC Comm Action Agency 1979; faithful worker award ARC Atlanta GA Chap 1979. **MILITARY SERVICE:** AUS sgt. **BUSINESS ADDRESS:** City Hall, PO Box 98, Fayette, MS 39069.

GALIBER, JOSEPH L.
State senator. **PERSONAL:** Born Oct 26, 1924, New York, NY; son of Joseph F and Ethel; married Emma E Shade; children: Pamela Susan, Ruby Dianne Wint. **EDUCATION:** City of NY Coll, BS 1950; NY Law Sch, JD 1962. **CAREER:** Youth Counsel Bur Bronx Co Dist Atty Ofc, counselor & borough dir 1950-63; Riverside Hosp NYC, drug abuse counselor recreation dir 1953-59; JOIN, execdir 1963-65; Fed Ofc of Econ Oppty, inspector 1966-68; private practice, atty 1965-; NY State, senator 1969-. **ORGANIZATIONS:** Chmn Bronx Co Dem Com 1966-79; del & asst majority leader NY State Constl Conv 1967; del Dem Nat Conv 1968; vice chmn NY State Dem Com 1975; mem St Augustine Presby Ch; life mem NAACP; mem Alumni Assn of CCNY, S Bronx Urban League, SE Bronx Nghbrhd Cntrs; mem policy adv council State Legistlative Inst Baruch Coll. **HONORS/ACHIEVEMENTS:** Numberous Awards for Pub Serv; Five Battle Stars AUS 1943-45. **MILITARY SERVICE:** AUS staff sgt 1943-45. **BUSINESS ADDRESS:** State Senator, New York State Senate, The Capitol, Albany, NY 12247.

GALL, LENORE ROSALIE
Educational administrator. **PERSONAL:** Born Aug 09, 1943, Brooklyn, NY; daughter of Olive R Weeks-Bryant. **EDUCATION:** New York Univ, AAS 1970; New York Univ Tisch School of Business & Public Admin, BS 1973, Training and Development Certificate 1975; New York Univ SEHNAP, MA Counselor Educ 1977; Teachers Coll, Columbia Univ, EdM 1988; Ed D 1988. **CAREER:** Ford Foundation, various positions 1967-76; New York Univ Grad School of Business, deputy dir 1976-79; Pace Univ Lubin School of Business, dir of career develop 1979-82; Yale Univ School of Organization and Mgmt, dir of career devel 1982-85; Brooklyn Coll CUNY, asst to the assoc provost 1985-88; asst to the provost 1988-;. **ORGANIZATIONS:** Chairperson bd of dirs Langston Hughes Comm Library 1975-79, 1982-89; first vice pres, awards comm chairperson, Dollars for Scholars 1976-; dir Placement Secretarial Devel Workshops, College Placement Serv 1978-81; lecturer LaGuardia Comm Coll CUNY 1981-; program chairperson New Haven Chamber of Commerce 1984; mem bd of dirs Assn of Black Women in Higher Educ Inc 1985, pres-elect 1989; mem Amer Assn of Univ Women 1985; Natl Assn of Univ Women mem 1986, first vice pres 1988; mem Amer Assn of Univ Administrators 1986; mem Natl Assn of Women Deans, Administrators and Counselors; Natl Urban League; first vice pres Natl Council of Negro Women North Queens Section 1987-. **HONORS/ACHIEVEMENTS:** Mem Educational Honorary Organization Kappa Delta Pi 1986; mem Phi Delta Kappa Columbia Univ Chap 1986; grant/scholarship Jewish Foundation for the Education of Women 1986/87. **BUSINESS ADDRESS:** Asst to Provost, Brooklyn College/CUNY, Bedford Ave & Avenue H, Brooklyn, NY 11210.

GALLAGER, MIKE JOHN
Radio station executive. **PERSONAL:** Born Jan 19, 1945, Toledo, OH; married Mary. **EDUCATION:** John Carroll Univ, bus 1967. **CAREER:** Reams Broadcasting Corp, sr vice pres 1977-80; WABQ, Inc, pres 1980-87. **ORGANIZATIONS:** Mem Alpha Kappa Psi 1968-. **MILITARY SERVICE:** USA capt 6 yrs. **BUSINESS ADDRESS:** President, WABQ Inc, 8000 Euclid Ave, Cleveland, OH 44103.

GALLAGHER, ABISOLA HELEN
Educator. **PERSONAL:** Born Oct 13, 1950, Chicago, IL; daughter of Leroy Gallagher and Lulla M Jointer. **EDUCATION:** Northeastern Illinois Univ, BA (w/Honors) 1972; Univ WI-Whitewater, MS 1974; Rutgers Univ, EdD 1983. **CAREER:** Univ of Wisconsin System Central Admin, educ admin intern 1974-75; Univ of Winconsin-Parkside, counselor-prog coord 1975-78; Douglass Coll Rutgers Univ, asst dean student life 1981-85; Unlimited Potential, management consultant 1985-87; Rutgers Coll/Rutgers Univ, residence dir 1978-81, asst dean office of academic serv 1987-. **ORGANIZATIONS:** Vice pres 1983-87, pres 1989-, Assn of Black Psychologists New Jersey Chap 1983-87; exec bd mem Coalition of 100 Black Women New Jersey 1985; mem Assn of Black Psychologists 1985-87, Amer Psychological Assn 1987, New Jersey Psychological Assn 1987. **HONORS/ACHIEVEMENTS:** Martin L King Scholarship 1979-80, 1980-81 Rutgers Univ; Outstanding Young Women in Amer 1982,84; Outstanding Service Awd Kappa Alpha Psi Frat 1984; Distinguished Serv Awd Paul Robeson Cultural Ctr Rutgers Univ 1985; publication "Black Women in Group Psychotherapy," Women in Groups Springer Press 1986. **HOME ADDRESS:** 111 Livingston Ave, New Brunswick, NJ 08901. **BUSINESS ADDRESS:** Asst Dean Office of Acad Serv, Rutgers Coll/RutgersUniv, 103 Millerdoler Hall, New Brunswick, NJ 08903.

GALLON, DENNIS P.
Educator. **PERSONAL:** Born in Monticello, FL. **EDUCATION:** Edward Waters Coll, BS 1964; Indiana Univ Bloomington, MS 1969; Univ of FL, PhD 1975. **CAREER:** Florida Cmmty Coll, professor 1972-1979, business mngr 1979-81, dean of vocational ed 1981-84; dean of instruction 1984-85. **ORGANIZATIONS:** Mem Amer Socfor Training & Development; mem Jax Chamber of Comm; mem FL Assn of Cmmty Colleges. **HONORS/ACHIEVEMENTS:** Mem Jax Urban League; past chairman Jax Cmmty Relations Commission; Kappa Alpha Psi. **BUSINESS ADDRESS:** Dean, Liberal Arts & Science, Florida Community College, 501 W State St, Jacksonville, FL 32202.

GALLOT, RICHARD JOSEPH
Elected official. **PERSONAL:** Born Jan 31, 1936, Swords, LA; son of Freddie Gallot and Loretta Gallot; married Mildred Bernice Gauthier; children: Daphne, Loretta, Richard Jr. **EDUCATION:** Tyler Barber Coll, Barber Degree 1961; Grambling State Univ, BS Acct 1975. **CAREER:** Gallo's Barbershop, barber 1961; Gallo's Grocer & Liquor & Serv, owner 1969; Town of Grambling, mayor 1981. **ORGANIZATIONS:** Pres Grambling Chamber of Com 1967; dir Grambling Fed Credit Union 1973, Parish Council-St Benedict Church 1975; mem Lion's Club 1983. **HONORS/ACHIEVEMENTS:** Businessman of Year Business Dept Grambling State Univ, 1981; Outstanding Black in LA Teal Enterprise 1982; Appointed to Governor's Com Community Devel 1985. **MILITARY SERVICE:** AUS Spec 4 1958-62. **HOME ADDRESS:** 111 Richmond Dr, Grambling, LA 71245. **BUSINESS ADDRESS:** Gallot's Enterprise, 102 South Grand Ave, Grambling, LA 71245.

GALLWEY, SYDNEY H.
Educator. **PERSONAL:** Born Nov 17, 1921, Winnipeg, Manitoba, Canada;son of Sidney and Rebecca; married Lucy Newman; children: Steven Lindsay, James Charles. **EDUCATION:** Howard U, BA 1950; Cornell U, Perm Cert Soc Stud 1960-61. **CAREER:** City Sch, tchr 1964-66, tchr 1969-70; SVC Brockport, tchr 1970-74; City Sch, tchr 1975-76; Rochester City Schools, tutor & instructor, 1980-87; Urban League, bus educ inst, academic instructor 1982-88. **ORGANIZATIONS:** Dir state branches NYS Assoc for Study Afro Am Life & History 1970; Urban League of Roch 1980-85; lecturer workshops Urban League 1980-85. **HONORS/ACHIEVEMENTS:** Outstanding serv Urban League, Roch NY 1983-84; Research, Publications, History of Black Family in Western New York, 1961-. **MILITARY SERVICE:** US Army s/sgt 1940-45.

GALVIN, EMMA CORINNE
Educator. **PERSONAL:** Born May 02, 1909, Richmond, VA; married Alx Galvin MD. **EDUCATION:** Shaw U, BA 1924;Univ PA, MA; Cornell U, PhD 1943. **CAREER:** Ithaca Coll, retired prof; Ithaca School Dist, academic counsultant; Southside Center, teacher; Tompkins Co Med Aux, lecturer, writer past pres. **ORGANIZATIONS:** Mem Ntnl Com Amer AssnUniv Wmn; past pres Pi Lambda Theta & Phi Gamma Delta; mem Alpha Kappa Alpha; mem Citzns Adv Com Envrn Qulty St NY; del Ntnl Conv Lgue Wmn Vtrs; chrprsn Tompkins Cnty Comm Chst; past pres Ithaca PTA; mem Ithaca B & P W Club; bd chmn Sthside Comm Ctr; orgnzr Ithaca Wmn's Comm Bldg. **HONORS/ACHIEVEMENTS:** Comm serv award Black Mem of Ithaca 1974; achvmnt comm for a better Am bk pub Eisenhower Admn; womn of yr ShawUniv 1924; wmn of yr Ithca B & PW 1959. **BUSINESS ADDRESS:** 122 Ashland Pl, #16M, Brooklyn, NY 11201.

GAMBLE, JANET HELEN
Minority specialist. **PERSONAL:** Born May 05, 1917, Dallas, TX; married Toby. **EDUCATION:** Biggers Bus Coll; Oakland Merritt Bus Coll;Univ of AK. **CAREER:** AK Dept Labor, minority splst Present, supr 1944-47; Oakland Naval Supply Depot, minority splst; Alameda Cty Outpatient Dept, minority splst; Ofc of Milo H Fritz MD, minority splst. **ORGANIZATIONS:** Deaconess Shiloh Bapt Ch 1952-; pres Anchorage Union & Missionary Soc 1971; chmn bd dir Opportunities Indsl Ctr 1974-76; past vice pres Eye-Ear- nose Throat Found; exec bd AK NAACP; immediate past pres Ch Women United Intl; dir fdr Minority Outreach Employment Svc; OES Order of Eastern Star. **HONORS/ACHIEVEMENTS:** Hon mem Mothers Christian Fellowship Club; Most Outst in Religion 1974 & 77; P Worthy Matron Alpha Guide #8; Anchorage Br Bestowed Dr of Letters; Grand Dep Worthy Matron of United Grand Chap CA & AK. **BUSINESS ADDRESS:** 940 La Touche, Anchorage, AK 99503.

GAMBLE, KENNETH
Business executive, musician, record pro. **PERSONAL:** Born Aug 11, 1943, Philadelphia; married Dione La Rue. **CAREER:** Kenny Gamble & Romeos, lead vocal; Gamble Huff Prods, 1968-; Gamble Huff & Bell Prods, 1969-. **ORGANIZATIONS:** Pres/Chmn Philadelphia Intl Records Asso Music Inc; mem BMI; mem AFM; mem NARM; mem NATRA; mem RIAA. **HONORS/ACHIEVEMENTS:** Decade award Top 100 Black Enterprises Record World 1973; prodr of yr NATRA 1968-69; top pub award BMI; songwriter of yr BMI; producer of num gold albums For The Love of Money/Love Train/When Will I See You Again; Many Spl Achievements. **BUSINESS ADDRESS:** Chairman, Philadelphia Intnatl Records, 309 S Broad St, Philadelphia, PA 19107.

GAMBLE, KENNETH L.
City official. **PERSONAL:** Born Apr 24, 1941, Marshall, MO; son of Rev Ira J Gamble (deceased) and Elizabeth L Gamble (deceased); married Shiela M Greene, Apr 19, 1969; children: Jerry L Swain, Andrew J Swain, Kendra L E Gamble. **EDUCATION:** Morgan State Coll, Baltimore MD, attended, 1959-62; Youngstown State Univ, Youngstown OH, BA, 1971; Univ of Akron, Akron OH, MA Urban Studies, 1975. **CAREER:** Univ of Akron, Center for Urban Studies, Akron OH, research asst, 1972-73; Trans Century Corp, Washington DC, consultant, Public Housing, 1973; Canton Urban League, Canton OH, assoc dir, Housing & Community Serv, 1973-77; Toledo NHS, Toledo OH, exec dir, 1977-80; City of Saginaw, Saginaw MI, dir, Dept of Neighborhood Serv, 1980-. **HONORS/ACHIEVEMENTS:** Dean's List, Youngstown State Univ, 1969-71; Dean's List, Univ of Akron, 1972-73; HUD Fellowship Recipient, 1972-73. **MILITARY SERVICE:** US Air Force, staff sergeant, 1962-65. **BUSINESS ADDRESS:** Director, Department of Neighborhood Services, City of Saginaw, 1315 S Washington, Room 207, Saginaw, MI 48601.

GAMBLE, OSCAR CHARLES

Professional athlete. **PERSONAL:** Born Dec 20, 1949, Ramer, AL. **CAREER:** NY Yankees, outfldr 1979, 1976; San Diego Padres, outfldr 1978; Chicago White Sox, outfldr 1977, 1969; Cleveland Indians, outfldr 1973-75; Philadelphia Phillies, outfldr 1970-72. **HONORS/ACHIEVEMENTS:** Played in Championship & World Series 1976. **BUSINESS ADDRESS:** NY Yankees, Yankee Stadium, Bronx, NY 10451.

GAMBLE, ROBERT LEWIS

Elected official. **PERSONAL:** Born Apr 27, 1947, Carroll County, GA; married Lucy Ann Dixon; children: Venus Marie, Athenia Marie. **EDUCATION:** Carver HS, 1966; USMC, data processing 1967. **CAREER:** USMC, printing press oper 1966; United Parcel Service, feeder driver 1970; City of Whitesburg, mayor. **ORGANIZATIONS:** Chmn Carroll County Pre-health Clinic 1981; vice-chmn Carroll County Vocational Sch 1984. **MILITARY SERVICE:** USMC sgt 3 yrs; two Purple Hearts Vietnam Service Medal Natl Defense Good Conduct Medal. **BUSINESS ADDRESS:** Mayor, City of Whitesburg, PO Box 151, Whitesburg, GA 30185.

GAMBLE, WILBERT

Educator. **PERSONAL:** Born Jun 19, 1932, Greenville, AL; married Zeferene Tucker; children: Priscilla Ann. **EDUCATION:** Wayne State Univ, BS (first in class) 1955, PhD 1960. **CAREER:** OR State Univ, asst prof 1962-67; Johnson Res Found Univ PA, visiting prof 1967-76; Univ Sci & Tech Kumasi Dhana, Fulbright prof 1971-72; Natl Inst Health, visit res worker 1976-77, 1983-84; OR State Univ, prof of biochemistry 1977-. **HONORS/ACHIEVEMENTS:** NIH Postdoctoral Fellow Cornell Univ 1960-62; Danforth Assoc Danforth Found 1969-; mem Phi Lambda Upsilon Hon Soc 1957; mem Sigma Chi Honor Soc 1960; mem Amer Soc of Bio Chemists; Lehn & Fink Medal for Advancement of Pharm Sci 1955; NIH Predoctoral Fellowship 1959; NIH Postdoctoral Fellowship 1960 & 1968. **BUSINESS ADDRESS:** Prof of Biochemistry, Oregon StateUniv, Biochemistry & Biophysics, Corvallis, OR 97331.

GAMBLE, WILLIAM F.

Purchasing manager. **PERSONAL:** Born Jan 03, 1950, West Palm Beach, FL; married Jacqueline A Butler; children: Kayla, Cameron, Tabitha, Chimere, William Jr. **EDUCATION:** FL A&M Univ, BS, 1971; State Univ of NY, Albany, MA, Public Admin, 1976. **CAREER:** Comm Affairs NY State, grants admin 1975-76; John Bryant's & Assocs, deputy dir 1976-77; Broward Co Govt, special project consultant,1977-80, Cuyahoga Co Govt Mgmt & Bud, asst dir 1980-82; Cleveland City School Dist, dir purchasing. **ORGANIZATIONS:** Consultant HIP House 1976-77; consultant Cuyahoga Co Govt 1982; bd of dirs Peoples & Cultures 1981-83; mem Conf of Minority Public Admin, 1977-; Amer Soc of Public Admin 1977-; mem Intl City Mgmt Assn, 1977-. **HONORS/ACHIEVEMENTS:** Housing Urban Devel State Univ of NY, 1976-77; Natl Urban Fellow Natl Urban Fellows Inc, NY, 1980-81; Outstanding Young Amer, US Jaycees 1981. **BUSINESS ADDRESS:** Dir Purchasing, Cleveland School District, 1380 E 6th St, Cleveland, OH 44114.

GAMMON, REGINALD ADOLPHUS

Educator. **PERSONAL:** Born Mar 31, 1921, Philadelphia, PA; married Janice Goldberger. **EDUCATION:** Philadelphis Museum Coll of Art, 1949; Temple Univ, Stella Elkins Tyler School of Fine Art, 1950-51. **CAREER:** Freelance artist; prof, Western MI Univ; Poverty Programs, part-time teacher; US Post Office, advertising artist; WMU, exhibition space gallery; NC Central Univ, exhibition 1977; Acts of Art Gallery, exhibit 1973, 1974; NY Cultural Center, exhibit blacks, 1973; Dnauss Western MI Univ, exhibit floors windows & flks 1947; Knauss Hall Western MI Univ, photo exhibit 1972; Detroit Inst of Art, jazz/Art 1971; Eastern MI Univ, black artist exhibition still gallery; Western MI Univ, faculty exhibition; Studio Museum in Harlem, exhibition sale; M Jackson Gallery, exhibition sale; SI Museum Coalition 70, exhibit. **ORGANIZATIONS:** mem, City of Kalamazoo Arts Comm. **HONORS/ACHIEVEMENTS:** Mentioned in Art News, The Spiral Group, Tuesday Magazine, Cue, The Art Gallery, The Evening News, Staten Island Sunday Advance, Sunday News, New York Amsterdam News; mentioned in various other newspapers, books and periodicals; Michigan Council for the Arts Creative Artists Grant, 1983; Creative Artist Grant, Arts Fund of Kalamazoo Co, 1988. **MILITARY SERVICE:** USNR 3rd cl shipfitter 1944-46. **BUSINESS ADDRESS:** Western MichiganUniv, 208 Moore Hall, WMU Coll of Gen Studies, Kalamazoo, MI 49008.

GANDY, ROLAND A., JR.

Physician, educator. **PERSONAL:** Born Dec 10, 1924, Philadelphia, PA; son of Roland A Gandy and Louise L Humbert; married Yvonne M McGoodwin; children: Roland A Gandy III, Robyn A Gandy. **EDUCATION:** Lincoln Univ PA, BA 1947; Temple Univ Med Sch, MD 1951. **CAREER:** Priv practice, physician Present; Med Coll of Ohio, assoc clinical prof 1975; Mercy Hosp Toledo, dir of surgical educ 1972; Med Coll of Ohio, clinical prof of surgery 1980-. **ORGANIZATIONS:** Pres Lucas Co Med Soc 1973; mem OH State Med Bd 1974; pres OH Chap Amer Coll Surgeons 1979; pres OH State Med Bd 1980; team physician Univ of Toledo 1968-. **MILITARY SERVICE:** USN lt 1945-46.

GANEY, JAMES HOBSON

Dentist. **PERSONAL:** Born Apr 29, 1944, Plainfield, NJ; married Peggy; children: Jayme, Christopher. **EDUCATION:** Howard Univ Coll Pharm, BS 1969; NJ Coll Dentistry, DMD 1974. **CAREER:** Dental Practice, dentist. **ORGANIZATIONS:** Registered pharmacist Wash DC, NJ; licensed dentist NJ; mem Amer Pharm Assn, NJ Pharm Assn, Natl Pharm Assn; Amer Dental Assn; NJ Dental Assn; Natl Dental Assn, Acad of Gen Dentistry, Union Co Dental Soc, Plainfield Dental Soc, Commonwealth Dental Soc; faculty mem Farleigh Dickinson Univ Dental Sch 1979; mem Health Profls Educ Adv Counc for State of NJ 1979; mem bd dir Planfield Camp Crusade; mem NAACP, Psi Omega Dental Frat; Chi Delta Mu Frat. **HONORS/ACHIEVEMENTS:** Cert of Merit Howard Univ Coll Pharm. **BUSINESS ADDRESS:** 108 E 7th St, Plainfield, NJ 07061.

GANNAWAY, NANCY HARRISON

Dentist. **PERSONAL:** Born Oct 20, 1929, Trinity, NC; married Robert; children: Renee, Susan. **EDUCATION:** Shaw U, BS 1950; Howard U, DDS 1954; St Elizabeth Hosp Wash DC, intrnshp 1954-55. **CAREER:** Dentist, self-employed. **ORGANIZATIONS:** Mem Acad Gnrl Dntstry; Twin City Dntl Soc 1971; treas 1969; Old N State Dental Soc; NC Dntl & Soc; Am Dntl Assoc Urbn League Guild; Delta SigmaTheta Sor; sec Altrusa Ind; v pres bd dir YWCA 1973-75.

GANT, RAYMOND LEROY

Educational administrator. **PERSONAL:** Born Jul 07, 1961, Paw Paw, MI. **EDUCATION:** Ferris State Coll, BBA. **CAREER:** Ferris State Coll, budget analyst 1984-86, dir minority affairs 1986. **ORGANIZATIONS:** Ferris State Coll, mem, alumni bd of dir, minority student scholarship selection committee; Phi Beta Sigma. **HONORS/ACHIEVEMENTS:** Phi Beta Sigma, recipient of Distinguished Service Key Awd. **BUSINESS ADDRESS:** Dir of Minority Affairs, Ferris State College, Rankin Center, Big Rapids, MI 49307.

GANT, WANDA ADELE

Government manager. **PERSONAL:** Born Oct 04, 1949, Washington, DC; daughter of Monore E Banks and Adela M Banks; divorced; children: Richard W Gant V. **EDUCATION:** Central St Univ Wilberforce OH, BS 1971; Southeastern Univ Washington DC MBPA 1982. **CAREER:** General Services Admin, equal opportunity specialist 1971-78; US Dept Labor, equal opportunity specialist 1978-84; US Info Agency, fed women's prog mgr 1984-. **ORGANIZATIONS:** Member, Outstanding Young Women of America, 1981; Natl Council Negro Women, 1983-; Alpha Kappa Alpha 1983; Federal Women's Interagency Bd 1984; DC-Dakar Sister Cities Friendship Council 1985-; Amer Assn of Univ Women 1986; Business & Prof Women 1986. **HONORS/ACHIEVEMENTS:** Superior Performance of Duty 1971; Outstanding Young Women of Amer 1983. **BUSINESS ADDRESS:** International Visitors Exchange Specialist, United States Information Agency, 301 4th St SW, Rm 266, Washington, DC 20547.

GANTT, GLORIA

Research scientist. **PERSONAL:** Born May 23, 1945, Charleston, SC. **EDUCATION:** Hampton Inst Hampton, VA, BA bio (cum laude) 1965f MedUniv of SC Charleston, MS 1972. **CAREER:** Dept of Neurochem Medicine, Univ of SC Charleston, rsch scientist 1978-; Dept of Med & Dept of Basic Clinical Immunology & Microbiology, rsch scientist 1974-78; Burke High School Charleston, teacher 1969-70; US Naval Research Lab, Washington DC, tech lib 1965-69. **ORGANIZATIONS:** Mem Am Soc of Microbiology; mem Choraliers Music Club Charleston; mem Hampton Alumni Assn Charleston; mem YWCA; mem Morris St Bapt Ch Charleston; mem Alpha Kappa Alpha 1963-. **HONORS/ACHIEVEMENTS:** Pub sci paper on Immunologic Responses Assoc with Thoracic Duct Lymphocytes.

GANTT, HARVEY BERNARD

Architect. **PERSONAL:** Born Jan 14, 1943, Charleston, SC. **EDUCATION:** Clemson Univ, BArch 1965; MIT, MA 1970. **CAREER:** Univ NC Chapel Hill, lecturer 1970-72; Clemson Univ, visiting critic 1972-73; City of Charlotte, mayor pro tem 1981-83, mayor 1983-87; Gantt, Huberman Assocs, architect. **ORGANIZATIONS:** Mem Charlotte City Council, AIA, Amer Planning Assoc, Charlotte Chap NAACP, NC Design Found. **HONORS/ACHIEVEMENTS:** Citizen of the Year Charlotte Chap NAACP 1975,84. **HOME ADDRESS:** 517 N Poplar St, Charlotte, NC 28202. *

GANTT, WALTER N.

Retired educator. **PERSONAL:** Born May 29, 1921; son of Walter Gantt and Gladys E Gantt. **EDUCATION:** Coppin State Coll, BS 1942; NY Univ, MA 1949; Univ MD, EdD 1968. **CAREER:** Baltimore MD, prin & tchr 1942-68; Univ of MD, assoc prof 1968-78; Comm Coll of Baltimore, personnel admin 1978-85; Peace Corps Honduras 1985-87, retired 1987. **ORGANIZATIONS:** Coord Urban Tchr Educ Ctr 1969-70; asst chmn Dept Early Childhood Elem Educ 1971-74; mem Proj Aware; Cit Black History Exhibits; Phi Delta Kappa; chmn Career & Occupational Devel Com; mem Assn Supervision & Curriculum Devel; AAUP; NCSS. **HONORS/ACHIEVEMENTS:** Circulus Scholarum Coppin State Coll; Serv Awd Phi Delta Kappa Univ MD 1975. **MILITARY SERVICE:** USAF 1942-46.

GARBEY, BARBARO

Professional athlete. **PERSONAL:** Born Dec 04, 1956, Santiago, Cuba. **CAREER:** Detroit Tigers, outfielder 1984. **HONORS/ACHIEVEMENTS:** Names Tiger Rookie-of-the-Year by Detroit Sportsbroadcasters Assoc 1984; Names to Southern League All-Star Team 1982. **BUSINESS ADDRESS:** Detroit Tigers, 2121 Trumbull Ave, Detroit, MI 48216.

GARCIA, KWAME N.

Elected official. **PERSONAL:** Born Apr 04, 1946, St Croix, Virgin Islands of the United States;married Grete James; children: Kenny, Sharifa, Khalfani, Gustavo. **EDUCATION:** Coll of the Virgin Islands, AA 1967; NY Univ, BS 1969; Univ of MA, MBA 1973. **CAREER:** VI Bd of Ed, elected mem 1978-; Coll of the Virgin Islands, asst dir coop ext serv 1979-. **ORGANIZATIONS:** Mem Natl School Bd Assoc 1978-; mem bd of trustees VI Public TV Syst 1982-84, Coll of the Virgin Islands 1982-84. **HONORS/ACHIEVEMENTS:** "Learning About the VI Tax System" Coop Ext Serv Coll of the VI. **HOME ADDRESS:** PO Box 4141, Christiansted, St Croix, Virgin Islands of the United States 00820. **BUSINESS ADDRESS:** Asst Dir Coop Ext Serv, College of the Virgin Islands, PO Box L, Kingshill, St Croix, Virgin Islands of the United States 00850.

GARCIA, WILLIAM BURRES

Educator, educational administrator. **PERSONAL:** Born Jul 16, 1940, Dallas, TX. **EDUCATION:** Prairie View A&M Univ, music courses 1958-61; N TX State Univ, BMus 1962, MMus Ed 1965; Univ of IA, PhD 1973; Howard Univ, NEH Fellow 1973-74; Carnegie-Mellon Univ, College Mgmt Prog 1984. **CAREER:** Philander Smith Coll, instructor of music 1963-64; Langston Univ, asst prof of music 1965-69; Miles Coll, assoc prof of music 1974-77; Talladega Coll, acting academic vice pres 1982-83, prof of music 1977-, chmn of music dept 1977-, chmn of humanities div 1981-85; Selma Univ, acad dean 1986-. **ORGANIZATIONS:** Mem Phi Mu Alpha Sinfonia 1965; bd Div of Higher Educ Disciples of Christ 1978-81; bd Talladega Arts Council 1981-; life mem Amer Choral Dirs Assn; mem Amer Choral Found; mem Amer Musicological Soc; mem Coll Music Soc; mem Intl Heinrich Schutz Soc; mem Natl Assn of Teachers of Singing; mem Thomas Music Study Club of Natl Assn of Negro Musicians. **HONORS/ACHIEVEMENTS:** Doctoral Fellowship Grants S Fellowships Fund Inc 1969-73; Ford Found Fellowship Grant for Dissertations in Ethnic Studies 1971-72; Outstanding Educators ofAmer 1975; Who's Who in the South & Southwest 1978-79; publications & lectures including article, "Church Music by Black Comp?osers, A Bibliography of Choral Works" Black Perspective in Music 1974; lecture, "John Wesley Work, Choral Composer" Ethnic Music Workshop Coll of Fine Arts 1974; lecture "John Wesley Work, Black Amer Composer" Afro-Amer Music Workshop Ctr for African & Afro-Amer Studies

Atlanta Univ 1975; paper, "African Elements in Afro-Amer Music" Anniston Museum of Natl History AL 1982. **HOME ADDRESS:** PO Box 913, Selma, AL 36702. **BUSINESS ADDRESS:** Academic Dean, Selma University, 1501 Lapsley St, Selma, AL 36701.

GARDINER, GEORGE L.
Educational administrator. **PERSONAL:** Born May 03, 1933, Cambridge, MA; married Reida B Dykes; children: Jesse B, Veronica ?, Lynne, George DeWitt. **EDUCATION:** FiskUniv Nashville, AB 1963;Univ of Chicago, MA 1967, CAS 1969. **CAREER:** Oakland Univ, Rochester MI, prof, dean of library science 1972-; Univ of MI School of Library Science, Ann Arbor MI, visiting prof 1975; Central State Univ, Wilberforce OH, dir of library 1970-72; IL State Univ, Normal IL, refrence librarian 1967-70; Am Lib Assn Chicago, asst to exec sec lib admin div 1967. **ORGANIZATIONS:** Mem Am Lib Assn 1967-; mem Am Soc for Infor Sci 1979-; mem Nat Lib Assn 1978-; elctd bd mem Normal Pub Lib Normal IL 1968-70; Afro-Am HistComm IL of C of Supt of Pub Instr 1969-70; Bd Black Coll Program Pontiac MI 1974-; chmn bd MI Lib Consortium 1978-79; chm N MI Council of StateLib Dir 1979-80. **HONORS/ACHIEVEMENTS:** Publ A Bibliography of the Pub Writings of Charles S Johnson 1960; 1st prize Nat Essay Contest Am Missionary Assn 1961; lavern noyes scholUniv co Chicago 1963-67; publ The Spirit of Fisk 1866-76, 1968, The Empirical Study of Ref, 1969, Bibliography Section in Role & Contributions of Am Negroes in History of US & IL 1970; Computer Asstd Indexing in Central StateUniv Lib 1975. **MILITARY SERVICE:** AUS corpl 1953-55. **BUSINESS ADDRESS:** Oakland University University, Rochester, MI 48063.

GARDNER, BETTYE J.
Educator. **PERSONAL:** Born in Vicksburg, MS. **EDUCATION:** Howard Univ, BA 1962, MA 1964; George Washington Univ, PhD 1974. **CAREER:** Howard Univ, instructor 1964-69; Social Sys Intervention Inc, sr rsch assoc 1969; Washington DC Bd of Educ, consultant 1969; Black History Calvert Ct MD, consultant; Washington Technical Inst, asst prof 1969-71; Coppin State Coll, asst prof, dean of arts & sciences & prof of history 1981-. **ORGANIZATIONS:** Mem NAACP, Org of Amer Historians, Assoc of Black Women Historians, Assoc for the Study of Afro-Amer Life & History; mem AAUP, Natl Educ Assn; moton fellow Moton Inst for Independent Study 1978-79; Danforth Assoc 1980; editorial bd Journal of Negro History; exec counc Asso for the Study of Afro-Amer Life & Hist; So Hist Assoc; MD Comm on Afro-Amer & Indian Hist & Culture; publ numerous articles. **BUSINESS ADDRESS:** Dean of Arts Sci/Prof History, Coppin St Coll, 2500 W North Ave, Baltimore, MD 21216.

GARDNER, CEDRIC BOYER
Attorney. **PERSONAL:** Born Jul 22, 1946, San Antonio, TX; son of Tommie L Gardner and Willie Mae Sanders Espree; married Sylvia Irene Breckenridge, May 07, 1972; children: Zayani Aisha, Bilal Amin, Cedric Ahmed, Saida Ujima. **EDUCATION:** CA State Univ Los Angeles, BA 1975; Univ of KS, JD 1983. **CAREER:** Urban League of Wichita, assoc dir 1977-80; Shawnee County Dist Attorney, asst dist attorney 1983-84; Univ of KS, training Mgr 1984-85; KS Dept of Health & Environ, attorney 1985-. **ORGANIZATIONS:** Mem Douglas County NAACP 1978-81, Urban League of Wichita 1980-87; mem Douglas Co Amateur Radio Club 1984-87; mem, Douglas County Assn of Retarded Citizens. **HONORS/ACHIEVEMENTS:** Outstanding Service Wichita NAACP both 1980. **MILITARY SERVICE:** USAF airman 1st class 4 yrs; Outstanding Airman of the Year 1966. **BUSINESS ADDRESS:** Special Asst Attorney General, KS Dept of Health/Environ, 900 Jackson, Topeka, KS 66612.

GARDNER, EDWARD G.
President. **PERSONAL:** Born Feb 15, 1925, Chicago, IL; married Betty Ann; children: Gary, Guy, Tracy, Terri. **EDUCATION:** Chicago Teachers College, BA; Univ of Chicago, Masters. **CAREER:** E G Gardner Beauty Products Co, owner; Chicago School System, elem school asst prin 1945-64; Soft Sheen Products, president. **HONORS/ACHIEVEMENTS:** Soft Sheen Prods listed in Black Enterprise Mag in top 10 of 100 Top Black Businesses in the US. **MILITARY SERVICE:** S/sgt. **BUSINESS ADDRESS:** President, Soft Sheen Products Inc, 1000 E 87th St, Chicago, IL 60619.

GARDNER, FRANK W.
Educational administrator. **PERSONAL:** Born Jun 12, 1923, Chicago; married Elaine St Avide; children: Craig M, Glenn P, Susan M. **EDUCATION:** Chicago Tchrs Coll, BA 1948; DePaul U, MEd 1953;Univ of Chicago, Grad Student 1958; Northwestern U, PhD 1975. **CAREER:** Chicago Public Schools, teacher 1948-54; Betsy Ross Elementary School Chicago, asst prin 1955-65; Ray Elementary School Chicago, prin 1965-68; Bd Of Examiners, Chicago Public Schools, asst sec 1968; Loyola Univ of Chicago, lecturer. **ORGANIZATIONS:** Dir wrtng Title III Proposal for Establ of Indep Lrng Cntr for Ray Elem Sch; mem Sch Study Comm of the Archdiocese of Chicago 1970-71; mem Chicago Urban League; mem Phi Delta Kappa; mem Am Assn Sch Personnel Adminstrn; chmn St Clotilde Elem Sch Bd 1966-69; bd dir Faulkner Sch Chicago 1971-72. **MILITARY SERVICE:** WWII s/Sgt 1943-46. **BUSINESS ADDRESS:** 228 N La Salle St, Chicago, IL 60601.

GARDNER, JACKIE RANDOLPH
Physician. **PERSONAL:** Born Apr 07, 1930, Tampa, FL; children: Adrian Randolph, Pia JoAnna. **EDUCATION:** Fisk Univ, BA (departmental hon) 1948; Univ of MI, Grad Sch Public Health 1949-50; Meharry Med Coll, MD 1955. **CAREER:** Mercy Hosp Buffalo, internship 1955-56; Sydenham Hosp NY, residency 1958; Kingsbrook Med Ctr Brooklyn, residency 1958-59; Private Practice, physician gen med & fam practice Brooklyn 1961-. **ORGANIZATIONS:** Chmn The Source (civic group) Brooklyn NY 1980; mem Alpha Phi Alpha Frat. **MILITARY SERVICE:** USN lt (sr gr) 1956-58. **BUSINESS ADDRESS:** 678 St Marks Ave, Brooklyn, NY 11216.

GARDNER, LAMAURICE H.
Educator, psychologist, psychoanalyst. **PERSONAL:** Born Feb 13, 1936, Morehead, MS; son of William Gardner and Ida Gardner; married Dolores Mallare; children: LaMaurice, Jr, Erika, Victorio, Crystal. **EDUCATION:** Univ Detroit, PhB 1958;Univ Detroit, MA 1960; Loyola U, PhD 1964; Detroit Psychoanalytic Inst, post doctoral educ 1966-70. **CAREER:** Sina Hosp Detroit, chief & psychologist & admin asst 1964-68; Childrens Center Wayne Co, dir 1968-74; Wayne State U, part time faculty 1964-74; Met Hosp, consult 1964-66; VA Hosp Allen Pk, consult 1973-; Clinical Psychology, pvt practice 1966-; Comm Psychology Wayne StateUniv Detroit; prof idr; Psychoanalysis & Psychotherapy, pvt practice 1966-; consultant, Detroit Osteopathic Hospital 1987-. **ORGANIZATIONS:** Mem v chmn Detroit-wayne Co Comm Mental Health Serv Bd 1966-68; Com Children & Youth 1972; mem bd dir Wayne Co Chap MI Soc Mental Health 1966-68;Kappa Alpha Psi; MI Assn Emotionally Disturbed Children, bd dir 1970; TechAdv Research Com State of MI Dept of Mental Health 1979; council agency dirs United Comm Serv Detroit 1971-74; mem bd dir Detroit Urban League 1972; mem bd of dir Mid Western US Div Am Bd of Professional Psychology 1976-; Am Psychol Assn; Am Acad Psychoanalysis MI Psychol Assn; Detroit Psychoanalytic Soc; Com Ethnocentricity among Psychiatrists Am Psychiat Assn; Council Nat Register of Health Serv Providers in Psychology. **HONORS/ACHIEVEMENTS:** Who's Who Midwest; Comm Leaders Am; Natl Social Dir; 2000 Men Achievement, Intl Directory of Distinguished Psychotherapists; published books & articles scientific journals; Psi Chi Honor Soc Psychology; diplomate Am Bd Prof Psychology. **BUSINESS ADDRESS:** Private Practice, 22250 Providence Dr., Southfield, MI 48075.

GARDNER, SAMUEL C.
Judge. **PERSONAL:** Born Nov 27, 1931, Detroit, MI; divorced. **EDUCATION:** Wayne St U, BS 1958; Wayne State U, M Educ in guidance & counseling 1960; Wayne StateUniv Sch of Law, JD 1965. **CAREER:** Frank Murphy Hall of Justice, chief judge of the recorder's ct 1977-, judge of the recorder's ct 1973-77; Bell & Gardner, atty 1972-73; Free Legal Aid Clinic Wayne State U, supervising atty 1969-72; Gragg & Gardner PC, atty 1969-72; NAACP, legal counsel 1968; Wayne State Univ Law Sch legal research instr 1966-68; Dingell Hylton & Zemmol, atty 1966-69; Lawyers Comm for Civil Rights Under Law, staff atty 1966; Hertzberg Jacob & Weingarten, atty 1965-66; Detroit Bd of Educ Craft Elem Sch, sci tchr 1958-65. **ORGANIZATIONS:** Mem Detroit Bar Assn; mem MI State Bar; mem Nat Bar Assn; treas bd mem Nat Bar Found; past pres Wolverine Bar Assn 1970-71; mem Am Arbitration Bd; chmn MI State Bar Grievance Bd, bd mem Legal Aid & Defender; mem Am Civil Liberties Union; tech & com Ct Procedures State of MI; mem spl commnReview Article Vi the Jud Article of the Const of MI, detroit Bd of Educ 1970; referee Civil Rights Comm; mem Wayne Co Jail Adv Comm Sr Class Rep Student Bd of Govs Wayne StateUniv Sch of Law; Staff Writer, The Wayne Adv Law Sch Jour; Sr Ed, Wayne StateUniv Law Review. **HONORS/ACHIEVEMENTS:** Bronze Award for Achievement Wayne StateUniv Law Sch 1965; Article Pub "Constl Law Right of Non-mem of a Race to Raise Systematic Exclusion that Race in Jury Selection" Wayne State Law Review Vol Ii 1965. **BUSINESS ADDRESS:** The Recorder's Court, Frank Murphy Hall of Justice, Detroit, MI 48226.

GARDNER, WARREN E., JR.
Business executive. **PERSONAL:** Born May 23, 1922, NYC, NY; married Oveta Kellogg; children: Douglas. **EDUCATION:** Hampton Inst, BS 1947; Syracuse Univ, MS 1949. **CAREER:** Baltimore Afro-Amer, newspaper reporter 1949; Our World Mag, writer editor 1950-55; New York City Pub Works Dept, 1956-58; WNEW Radio, newswriter prod 1959; Pitney Bowes Inc, writer editor 1959-60; New York City Human Rights Commn, dir pub relations 1960-62; Mobilization for Youth Inc NYC, asst to admin dir 1962-66; Office of Mayor NYC, asst press sec 1966; Gov of NY, asst press sec 1966-73; Fed Energy Ofc NYC, pub affairs officer 1974; New York City Parks Recreation & Cultural Affairs Admin, asst admin 1974-75; Gen Serv Admin, bus & pub affairs 1975-. **ORGANIZATIONS:** Mem Pub Relations Soc of Amer; mem 100 Black Men Inc. **HONORS/ACHIEVEMENTS:** Listed in Who's Who in the East. **MILITARY SERVICE:** Naval corres WW II. **BUSINESS ADDRESS:** Bus & Pub Afrs Dir, Genl Serv Administration, 26 Fed Plaza, New York, NY 10007.

GARIBALDI, ANTOINE MICHAEL
Educator. **PERSONAL:** Born Sep 26, 1950, New Orleans, LA; son of Augustin Garibaldi and Marie Brule' Garibaldi. **EDUCATION:** Howard Univ, BA (Magna Cum Laude) 1973; Univ of Minnesota, PhD 1976. **CAREER:** Holy Comforter-St Cyprian DC, elem teacher 1972-73; Univ of Minnesota Coll of Educ, rsch asst 1973-75; St Paul Urban League St Acad, principal 1975-77; Natl Inst of Educ, rsch admin 1977-82; Xavier Univ of Louisiana, chmn, assoc prof of educ. **ORGANIZATIONS:** Mem Amer Psychological Assn, Amer Educ Rsch Assn, Assn of Black Psychologists, Phi Delta Kappa, Phi Kappa Phi; pres Univ of Minnesota Black Studies Psychological Assn 1974-75; mem US Army Sci Bd 1979-83; lecturer Howard Univ School of Educ 1981; assoc editor Amer Educ Rsch Journal 1982-84; consultant US Dept of Educ 1983-85; mem New Orleans Library Bd 1984-93; Journal of Negro Education board; co-chmn, Mayor's Foundation for Educ, 1987-; co-chmn educ comm, Urban League of Greater New Orleans, 1984-. **HONORS/ACHIEVEMENTS:** Outstanding Young Man of Amer 1977; editor Black Coll & Univ, Challenges for the Future 1984; Serv Awards Univ of Minnesota, Archdiocese of Minneapolis-St Paul, Black Student Psychological Assn, Food & Drug Admin; articles published in Journal of Educ Psychology, Urban Review, Journal of Negro Educ, Journal of Rsch in Sci Teaching; author of 3 books & 5 book chap; author of The Decline of Teacher Production in Louisiana (1976-83) & Attitudes Toward the Profession, 1986; author of Southern Education Foundation monograph 1986; Researcher of the Year, Univ of New Orleans, Phi Delta Kappa, 1989; Outstanding Book Award American Educ Studies Assn for Black Colleges & Universities, 1985; author of Educating Black Male Youth, A Moral and Civic Imperative, 1988; editor of Teacher Recruitment & Retention (With a Special Focus on Minority Teachers), Natl Educ Assn, 1989. **BUSINESS ADDRESS:** Chmn, Assoc Prof of Ed, XavierUniv of Louisiana, Campus PO Box 59A, New Orleans, LA 70125.

GARLAND, HAZEL BARBARA
Columnist-consultant. **PERSONAL:** Born Jan 28, 1913, Burnette, IN; married Percy A. **EDUCATION:** Univ of Pittsburgh, 1952-53. **CAREER:** Retired, 1977; New Pittsburgh Courier, editor in chief 1974-77, city editor 1972-74; Pittsburgh Courier, women's editor 1965-72, entrtnmnt-tv- radio editor 1955-65, feature editor 1954-55, asso magazine editor 1952-54, asst woman's editor 1947-52, gen assgnmnt reporter 1946-47, part-time reporter 1944-46, stringer1943-44. **ORGANIZATIONS:** Pres gateway chap Am Women in Radio-TV 1968-70; pres Pittsburgh Chap Girl Friends Inc 1969-71; vice pres Pittsburgh Comm Found 1975-77. **HONORS/ACHIEVEMENTS:** Nat hon mem Iota Phi-Lambda Sor Wash DC 1969; natl sojourner truth award Bus & Professional Women 1974; editor of the yr award Nat Newspaper Pub Assn 1974; natl headliner award Women in Comm Inc Tulsa OK 1975. **BUSINESS ADDRESS:** 315 E Carson St, Pittsburgh, PA 15219.

GARLAND, PHYLLIS T.
Music critic. **PERSONAL:** Born Oct 27, 1935, McKeesport, PA. **EDUCATION:** Northwestern Univ, BS Journalism. **CAREER:** Pittsburgh Courier, journalist, writer, feature ed 1958-65; Ebony Mag, asst, assoc contrib ed 1965-77; NY, editor 1969-71; State Univ of NY

Coll at New Paltz, asst prof, acting chmn dept of black studies 1971-73; Columbia Univ Grad School of Journalism, asst prof 1973-79, assoc prof 1979-. **ORGANIZATIONS:** Mem Delta Sigma Theta, Commin on Arts & Letters; jazz adv panel Natl Endowment for the Arts; adv bd Columbia Jrnl Review; contrib ed Stereo Review Mag 1977-. **HONORS/ACHIEVEMENTS:** Golden Quill Awd Outstanding Feature Writer 1962; Headliner Awd Outstanding Women in Country in Field of Communications Theta Sigma Phi 1971; Now Women in commun Awd NY Chap of Publ Rel Soc of Amer 1974; author "The Sound of Soul, The Story of Black Music"; author 2 books, contrib of art to books & mags. **BUSINESS ADDRESS:** Associate Professor, ColumbiaUniv, Grad School of Journalism, New York, NY 10027.

GARNER, CHARLES
Musician, educator. **PERSONAL:** Born Jul 27, 1931, Toledo, OH; married Judith Marie Bonner; children: Kevin, Darchelle. **EDUCATION:** Cleveland Inst of Mus, BMus 1953; Boston U, AM 1957; Yale U, adv stud. **CAREER:** Southern Connecticut State Univ, composer, arranger, prof of music; Hartt Sch of Music, Univ of Hartford, instr 1961-65; East & Midwest, numerous piano & ensemble recitals. **ORGANIZATIONS:** Pres NE Commercial Mus Serv Co; mem Am Assn of Prof; mem Phi Delta Kappa; Kappa Gamma Psi; Kappa Alpha Psi; Am Soc of Composers Authors & Pub. **HONORS/ACHIEVEMENTS:** Recipient Am Fedn of Mus; Mu Phi Epsilon Scholarship 1948; Friends of Mus Award 1949; 1st place OH Mus Tchr Auditions; Ranney Scholarship of Cleveland 1949-52; Charles H Ditson Award of Yale Univ 1968; Frances Osbourn Kellogg prize in counterpoint Yale Univ 1969. **MILITARY SERVICE:** AUS radio operator 1953-55. **HOME ADDRESS:** 190 Corbin Rd, Hamden, CT 06517.

GARNER, EDWARD, JR.
Attorney. **PERSONAL:** Born Dec 04, 1942, Skippers, VA; married Betty J; children: Erica P, Edward P, Elizabeth P. **EDUCATION:** NC A&T State Univ, BS (Cum Laude) 1967; Squadron Office School USAF 1972; Univ of NC Law School Chapel Hill, JD 1975; Air Command & Staff Coll, 1983. **CAREER:** Akzo Amer Inc, corp attny 1976-85; NC Dept of Crime Control & Public Safety, asst sec. **ORGANIZATIONS:** Mem NC Bar, Amer Bar Assn, Air Force Assn, NC Assn of Black Laywers, Aircraft Owners & Pilots Assn, Negro Airmen Intl Inc, Assn of Trial Lawyers of Amer, NC Acad of Trial Lawyers, US Air Force Reserve/NC Air Natl Guard; former chmn of bd of dir Asheville-Buncombe Comm Relations Counc; mem of bd YMI Cultural Ctr Inc; mem Asheville City Personnel Commiss; Govs adv commiss Military Affairs. **MILITARY SERVICE:** USAF pilot 1968-73; Disting Flying Cross; Flew C-123 Transport, B-52 Bomber & C-130 Transport; 2 yrs combat duty in Southeast Asia. **BUSINESS ADDRESS:** Assistant Secretary, NC Dept Crime Cntrl/Pub Safety, P O Box 27687, Raleigh, NC 27611.

GARNER, GRAYCE SCOTT
Educator. **PERSONAL:** Born Apr 27, 1922, Cambridge, MA; son of Athelohnsend Garner and Ruby Blackman Garner; married Rawle W Garner, Jun 24, 1961. **EDUCATION:** Cambridge Hosp, RN 1944; Simmons Coll, attended 1944-45; Boston Univ, BS Nursing 1954, MS 1956; Columbia Univ, EdD 1963; Boston Univ, post doctoral 1970; Univ RI, post doctoral 1982-83. **CAREER:** Boston Univ, prof, nursing, faculty mem, 1959-77; Univ of RI, prof of nursing, 1977-85; Univ of MA, prof of nursing & coordinator med health; Prof, Univ of MA, Coll of Nursing, 1985-present. **ORGANIZATIONS:** Consult Boston & Worcester St Hosp, Bedford & Brocton VA Hosp, Boston City Hosp; mem Amer Nurses Assn 1977; past bd of dir MA Nurses Assn; mem MA Assn Mental Health; mem Alpha Kappa Alpha Sor. **HONORS/ACHIEVEMENTS:** Merit Awd Mental Health Careers Prog 1974; Navy Merit Awd 1975; Merit Awd Consumer Educ Prog Barbados WI 1975; 1st Black Faculty mem; 1st Black Full Prof; 1st Black Coord of Prog Univ of RI Coll of Nursing; NIMH Rsch Awd; Prog Dir of a 5 yr NIMH grant for grad students in Mental Health Nursing; Several State URI Awds for Devel Grad Program Nursing. **MILITARY SERVICE:** USAF nurse corps 1st lt 1946-51. **BUSINESS ADDRESS:** Prof of Nursing, Univ of Massachusetts, Harbor Campus, Boston, MA 02125.

GARNER, JOHN W.
Academic relations manager. **PERSONAL:** Born Dec 29, 1924, Franklin, TN; married Leslie Olga Abernathy; children: Reginald J, Paul L. **EDUCATION:** Fisk U, BA Chem 1950, MS 1952; IL Inst of Tech MS Physical Chem 1955. **CAREER:** Percy L Julian Labs, chemist 1952-53; IL Inst of Tech Res Inst, res chemist 1954-66; 3m Co Dental Prod Lab, sr res chemist 1966-70; 3m Co Med Prods Div, sr clinical res coord 1974-75; 3m Health Care Grp, academic reltns mgr 1976-85; Riker Labs Int'l/ 3M Co, mgr licensing adm1985-. **ORGANIZATIONS:** Bd of trustees FiskUniv 1977-; bd of dir Big Bros/Sis of Greater St Paul 1975-87; ind adv bd Biomed Eng Dept TulaneUniv 1979-; human rel adv comm 3m Co 1978-86; life Mem Alpha Phi Alpha Frat Inc 1976-; mem Omicron Boule Sigma Pi Phi Frat Inc 1979-; MN Metro Golf League 1980; mem Am Chem Soc AAMI Natl Tech Asso 1985; mem Blk Chem Eng Urban League, NAACP, vice pres Sterling Club 1985; bd of dir City Walk Condo Assoc 1985-87; mem licensing exec soc/ USA-Canada. **HONORS/ACHIEVEMENTS:** Distiguished Black Clg Alumnus Awd FiskUniv (NAFEO) 1983; Christian Father of Yr Awd Trinity United Ch Chicago IL 1966; Natl Life Mbrshp Prog Awd Alpha Phi Alpha Frat Inc 1978; "Think Higher" Awd 3m Health Care Grp 1972; Whos Who Among Blk Americans 1980-81. **MILITARY SERVICE:** AUS staff sgt (field commissioned) 1943-46; 4 Bronze Battle Stars, 2 Invasion Arrow Heads, Europe, Purple Heart 1943-46. **HOME ADDRESS:** 66 East 9th St #2105, St Paul, MN 55101. **BUSINESS ADDRESS:** Licensing Administration, 3M Health Care Group, 3M Center 225-15-07, St Paul, MN 55144.

GARNER, JUNE B.
Columnist. **PERSONAL:** Born Jul 19, 1923, Detroit, MI; daughter of Simpson Malone and Vela Malone; married Warren C Garner; children: Sylvia Mustonen. **EDUCATION:** Detroit Public Schools; Wayne State Univ, 2 yrs. **CAREER:** Detroit News, retired columnist; Michigan Chronicle, classified adv mgr 1974-. **ORGANIZATIONS:** Founder Let's Read Summer School, A Free Reading Prog for Children 1980; Computer Programming. **HONORS/ACHIEVEMENTS:** Best columnist Natl Assn of Newspaper Published 1967, 1968; Best Columnist Detroit Press Club 1972, 1973. **HOME ADDRESS:** 14400 Hess Rd, PO Box D, Holly, MI 48442.

GARNER, LA FORREST DEAN
Educational administrator. **PERSONAL:** Born Aug 20, 1933, Muskogee, OK; son of Sanford Garner and Fannie Garner; married Alfreida Thomas; children: Deana Y, Thomas L, Sanford E. **EDUCATION:** IN Univ School of Dentistry, DDS 1957, MSD 1959, Certificate, Orthodontics, 1961. **CAREER:** IN Univ School of Dentistry, assoc prof 1967-70; VA Hosp Dental Div, consultant 1979-; James Whitcomb Riley Hospital, orthodontic coordinator, 1979-; IN Univ School of Dentistry, prof & chmn 1970-. **ORGANIZATIONS:** Bd of dir, Visiting Nurses Assn, Indianapolis, 1973-77, Boys Clubs, 1976; Chmn, Council on Rsch, Amer Assn of Orthodontists, 1976-77; mem, Boule, 1978-; bd of dir, Park Tudor School, Indianapolis IN 1980-; Life Mem, NAACP, 1980-; Chmn, United Way Ancillary Serv 1984-85; pres Amer Assn for Dental Rsch, 1984-85; bd of dir, Indianapolis Zoo, 1987-, bd of dir, Fall Creek Parkway YMCA, 1989. **HONORS/ACHIEVEMENTS:** Natl pres Omicron Kappa Upsilon Natl Dental Scholastic 1974-75; local pres Omicron Kappa Upsilon Local Chapter, 1974-75; fellow of Amer Coll of Dentist 1974; bd of dir Amer Cleft Palate Educ Found 1975-79; mem Sigma Xi 1976. **BUSINESS ADDRESS:** Assoc Dean, Indiana Univ, 1121 W Michigan St, Indianapolis, IN 46202.

GARNER, LON L.
Mortician, politician. **PERSONAL:** Born Jul 17, 1927, San Augustine Co, TX; married Vonzella Jones; children: David, Conchita, Alex. **EDUCATION:** Three Yrs Coll. **CAREER:** Percy Garner & Son, mortician; San Augustine, city alderman serving 3rd 2 yrs term 1969-; Alberta King Day Care Center, dir 1974; San Augustine Fed Credit Union, dir 1972-. **ORGANIZATIONS:** Patron McPhearson Lodge Order Eastern Star 150 San Augustine 1967; mem NFDA 1953; mem Masonic Lodge 1948-; Order Knight Pythian 1947; srvd chmn bd mem Am Red Cross Dr & Chap 1964-; 1st black mem San Augustine C of C; chmn deacon bd True Vine Bapt Ch 1969. **HONORS/ACHIEVEMENTS:** 1st black elected official & 1st elected official San Augustine Co; cert award C of C 1972; outstndng ambul serv only black firm to ever offer serv State TX 1969; 1st credit union soley controled by black San Augustine Fed Credit Union. **BUSINESS ADDRESS:** Manager, Percy Garner & Son Mortuary, 304 Ironosa Rd, PO Box 491, San Augustine, TX 75972.

GARNER, MARY E.
Psychologist. **PERSONAL:** Born in Paterson, NJ; children: Floyd, Jr, Steven. **EDUCATION:** William Paterson Coll, BA Psych 1973; Fairleigh Dickinson Univ, MA Clinical Psych 1976; CUNY, PhD 1983. **CAREER:** Passaic City Community, prof psych 1983; Fairleigh Dickinson Univ, prof psych summers 1982-84; William Paterson Coll, prof psych 1982-; Paterson Dept Human Resources, spec asst to dir 1982-83, dir 1983-. **ORGANIZATIONS:** Mem & past pres preakness Hospital Bd of Mgrs 1982-84; chairwoman Riverview Towers Tenants Assoc 1973-; mem Coalition for Public Accountability 1982-; mem Zonta Intl (Paterson Area Club) 1983-; mem Black Business & Professional Assoc 1983-; mem NJ Amer Psychological Assoc. **HONORS/ACHIEVEMENTS:** Community serv Social & Economic Change for All Inc 1983, Modern Beautician's Assoc 1983, Black History Month Committee 1984 & 1985; Pres Awd Preakness Hosp Bd Mgrs 1984. **HOME ADDRESS:** 85 Presidential Blvd 15C, Paterson, NJ 07522. **BUSINESS ADDRESS:** Dir, Paterson Dept Human Resources, City Hall, 155 Market St 2nd Floor, Paterson, NJ 07505.

GARNER, MELVIN C.
Attorney. **PERSONAL:** Born Feb 09, 1941, Philadelphia, PA; son of George Garner and Frieda Garner; married R Patricia Grant. **EDUCATION:** Drexel Univ, BS 1964; NY Univ, MS 1968; Brooklyn Law School, JD 1973. **CAREER:** IBM Poughkeepsie NY, jr engr 1964-66; CBS Labs Stamford CT, engr 1966-69; Sequential Inf Sys Dobbs Ferry NY, proj engr 1969-70; Bell Telephone Labs Holmdel NY, mem patent staff 1970-73; Brumbaugh Graves Donohue & Raymond, attny 1973-82; Darby & Darby, attny 1982-. **ORGANIZATIONS:** Mem ABA, NY Patent Trademark & Copyright Law Assoc, Natl Patent Law Assoc, Eta Kappa Nu (Hon Elect Engrs Soc), Brooklyn Law Review. **BUSINESS ADDRESS:** Attorney, Darby & Darby, 805 Third Ave, 27 FLOOR, New York, NY 10022.

GARNER, NATHAN WARREN
Business executive. **PERSONAL:** Born Dec 25, 1944, Detroit, MI; married Indira S Licht Garner; children: Mark C, Erica D, Vincent C, Warren C. **EDUCATION:** Wayne State Univ, BS 1966; Wayne State Univ Grad School of Ed, MS Ed 1971; Columbia Univ Grad School of Bus, MBA 1975; Stanford Grad Sch of Bus Fin Mgt Prog 1984. **CAREER:** Scholastic Inc, dir mktg 1969-78; Time Distrib Serv Inc, dir of mktg 1978-80; US Dept of Edn, spec asst to sec of educ 1980-81; Time-Life Films Inc, vice pres 1981-82; Preview Subs TV Inc, pres 1982-83; Manhattan Cable TV Inc, vice pres; Paragon Cable TV Manhattan, president. **ORGANIZATIONS:** Adv FL A&M Univ Entrepreneurial Devel Ctr 1983-85; mem Cable TV Admin & Mktg Soc 19083-85; mem Assoc for a Better NY 1984-85; bd of dirs East Mid Manhattan Chamber of Comm 1984-85; chmn Natl Assoc of Minorities in Cable 1987-88; steering comm 21st Century Fund Cncl of 100 Black Republicans; mem Friends of Alvin Ailey Dance Theatre, Alumni Assoc; pres Exec Exchange Program; adv group Columbia Univ Business School Telecommunications Policy Rsch and Information Studies Program. **HONORS/ACHIEVEMENTS:** Black Achievers Harlem YMCA of Greater NY 1983; Andrew Heiskell Awd Time Inc 1986; Excellence in Communications East Manhattan Chamber of Commerce 1987. **MILITARY SERVICE:** AUS spec 5th class 2 yrs. **BUSINESS ADDRESS:** President, Paragon Cable TV Manhattan, 5120 Broadway, New York, NY 10034.

GARNER, THOMAS L.
Executive director. **PERSONAL:** Born Sep 13, 1930, Cincinnati, OH; married Joann Calmeise; children: Stuart, Geoffrey. **EDUCATION:** Cincinnati U, BSE 1952, Grad Work 1975; MI State, Grad Work; OH State, Grad Work. **CAREER:** Cincinnati Human Relations Comm, exec dir; Model Cities Bd, chair; Better Housing Leag, neighborhood coor 1966-68; Southwestern Reg Council on Alcoholism, assoc dir. **ORGANIZATIONS:** Mem Central Psy Clinic; YMCA; mem Cinti Firearms Comm; Nat Asso Human Rights Workers; Intl Asso Official Human Rights Agencies; Housing Opportunities Made Equal Bd; bd mem Cinti Public Dental Assn; bd mem Union Coll Univ Without Walls; bd mem Seven Hills Schs; founder Prog Unlmtd; mem Comm Ctr Bd. **MILITARY SERVICE:** USAF reserve 1948-68. **BUSINESS ADDRESS:** Associate Dir, SW Reg Cncl on Alcoholism, 830 Main St, Ste 1205, Cincinnati, OH 45202.

GARNES, WILLIAM A.
Dentist. **PERSONAL:** Born Jul 06, 1924, New York; married Yvonne Ponce; children: Barbara, Valerie, William. **EDUCATION:** BA 1951; DDS 1955. **CAREER:** Priv Prac,

dentist; New York City Dept of Health, dentist Present; Guggenheim Dental Clinic NY, supvr. **ORGANIZATIONS:** Mem Local Sch Bd #9 Bronx NY 1961-63; Am Dental Assn; NY State Dental Assn; First Dist Dental Soc NY. **MILITARY SERVICE:** USN, AOM 3/C 1944-46; USAF capt 1955-57.

GARNETT, BERNARD E.
Reporter. **PERSONAL:** Born Nov 18, 1940, Washington, DC; children: Cyprian, Malik. **EDUCATION:** Newspaper Inst of Amer, New York, Cert 1966; Howard Univ, Washington DC. **CAREER:** The Wall St Journal, reporter; Race Relations Information Ctr Nashville, staffwriter audio feed dir 1969-72; Jet Magazine Washington Bureau, assoc editor 1967-69; Washington Afro-Amer, reporter 1965-67. **ORGANIZATIONS:** Past mem Black Perspective 1968; past mem regional coordinator Nat Assn of Black Media Workers 1970. **BUSINESS ADDRESS:** 55 Marietta St NW, Ste 1515, Atlanta, GA 30303.

GARNETT, MARION WINSTON
Judge. **PERSONAL:** Born Feb 18, 1919, Jeffersonville, IN; married Juanita Oretta Nogest; children: Marion F, Galda Irma McCants. **EDUCATION:** Univ of Chicago, Bachelor Philosophy 1947, JD 1950; State of IL, admitted to bar 1950; US Court of Appeals 7th Circuit, admitted to bar 1967; US Supreme Court, admitted to bar 1965. **CAREER:** Wilson & Garnett, partner at law, 1950-52; Hunter, Wilson & Garnett, partner at law 1952-61; Rogers, Strayhorn, Harth, Wilson & Garnett, partner at law 1961-68; Rogers, Garnett, Harth, Vital & Stroger, partner at law, 1968-74; Circuit Court of Cook County, supreme circuit judge. **ORGANIZATIONS:** Exec bd mem, Judicial Council of NBA 1980-; chmn elect, IL Judicial Council 1983-84; chrmn IL Judicial Council 1984-85; grand counselor, Omega Psi Phi Fraternity Inc, 1964-70, first vice grand basileus 1970-73, grand basileus 1973-76. **HONORS/ACHIEVEMENTS:** Keys to city, Birmingham AL, El Paso & Houston TX, Las Cruces, NM, Miami, FL, New Orleans LA, Oklahoma City OK; honorary citizen, New Orleans; Ebony list of 100 most influential Blacks 1974-76; Certificate of Merit Los Angeles; MI House of Rep 339; Commodore Port of Jeffersonville IN;. **MILITARY SERVICE:** USN qmc/2 1942-45. **BUSINESS ADDRESS:** Supervising Circuit Judge, Circuit Court of Cook County, 2301 Daley Center, Chicago, IL 60602.

GARNETT, RONALD LEON
Attorney. **PERSONAL:** Born May 27, 1945, Louisville, KY. **EDUCATION:** Central State U, BS 1967; Columbia U, JD 1971. **CAREER:** US Atty's Office, asst US atty 1974-77; Am Express Co, atty 1973-74; Winthrop Stimpson Putnam & Robts, Atty 1972-73; US Dist Judge Robert McGee, law clk 1971-72. **ORGANIZATIONS:** Mem Am Bar Assn 1973-; NY State Bar Assn 1973; mem NY Co Lawyers Assn 1973-; mem Kappa Alpha Psi Inc 1964-. **BUSINESS ADDRESS:** 1 Stamford Forum, Stamford, CT 06904.

GARNETTE, BOOKER THOMAS
Dentist. **PERSONAL:** Born Apr 28, 1930, Norfolk, VA; married Meanor Wilson; children: Barbetta Jones, Donna Y, Carla R Bufford. **EDUCATION:** Howard Univ, BS 1951, DDS 1955. **CAREER:** Norfolk Gen Hosp, 1st black dentist; St Vincent DePaul Hosp, 1st black dentist; Norfolk Comm, staff; VA Tidewater Dental Assoc, comm on dental health; VA Dental Assoc, alt house of del; Private practice, dentist 1957-. **ORGANIZATIONS:** Past basileus Lambda Omega Chap Omega Psi Phi 1970-72; mem Tidewater Dental Assoc, Amer Dental Assoc, John McGriff Dental Soc, Old Dominion Dental Soc,Campbell Lodge #67 F&A Masons Prince Hall, Tux Club, Bachelor Benedict Club; past 3rd dist rep Omega Psi Phi; mem housing auth Omega Psi Phi, Natl Soc Acttion Comm, Natl Publ Rel Comm; life mem Omega Psi Phi; chmn Natl Recommendations Committee Omega Psi Phi. **HONORS/ACHIEVEMENTS:** Disting Omega Man Awd Pi Gamma Chap 1977; Omega Man of the Year Lambda Omega Chap Omega Psi Phi 1977; 3rd Dist Omega Man of the Year Omega Psi Phi 1977; 25 Yr Cert Omega Psi Phi. **MILITARY SERVICE:** USNR comrd 1955-75; 1st black naval officer from Norfolk VA; Naval Reserve medal USNR. **BUSINESS ADDRESS:** 2412 E VA Beach Blvd, Norfolk, VA 23504.

GARR, RALPH ALLEN
Professional athlete. **PERSONAL:** Born Dec 12, 1945, Monroe, LA; married Ruby Mack; children: Shonte, Ralph Jr, Rae, Kisha. **EDUCATION:** Grambling, BS. **CAREER:** CA Angels, professional athlete 1979-; Chicago White Sox, professional athlete 1976-79; Atlanta Braves, professional athlete 1970-75. **HONORS/ACHIEVEMENTS:** Led NL in Balt Aver 1974; NL All-Star 1974.

GARRAWAY, MICHAEL OLIVER
Educator. **PERSONAL:** Born Apr 29, 1934; married Annie Marie Watkins; children: Levi Alexander, Isla Pearl, Doris Lorraine. **CAREER:** McGill Univ Montreal, teaching asst 1959-60, rsch asst 1960-62; Univ of CA Berkeley, rsch asst 1962-66, post doc 1966-68; OH State Univ, asst prof 1968-71, assoc prof 1971-78, prof plant pathology 1978-. **ORGANIZATIONS:** Mem Can Phytopath Soc 1961, Amer Phytopath Soc 1963, Amer Inst for Biol Sci 1964; life mem AAAS 1967; mem OH Acad of Sci 1969; pres Gamma Sigma Delta OH Chap 1977-78; mem Mycological Soc of Amer 1980; consult mildew induced defacement of organic coatings Paint Rsch Inc. **HONORS/ACHIEVEMENTS:** Author, Fungal Nutrition and Physiology, J Wiley & Sons Inc, 1984; Gamma Sigma Delta, Ohio Chapter, Award of Merit for Research 1989. **BUSINESS ADDRESS:** Professor of Plant Pathology, Ohio StateUniv, 201 Kothman Hall, 2021 Coffey Rd, Columbus, OH 43210.

GARRETT, ALINE M.
Educator. **PERSONAL:** Born Aug 28, 1944, Martinville, LA. **EDUCATION:** Univ SW LA, BA 1966; Oberlin OH, AM 1968;Univ MA, PhD 1971. **CAREER:** Univ of Southwestern LA Lafayette, assoc prof Psychology 1971; Univ of MA Amherst, grad res asst; Summer School Faculty USL, teacher 1970 & 1969; Psychometrist Lafayette Parish Schools, summer 1967; Project Head Start, Lafayette LA, teacher 1966. **ORGANIZATIONS:** Mem Am Psychol Assn; mem Nat Assn Black Psychol; mem Soc for Research in Child Devel; mem Psi Chi; mem SE Psychol Assn; mem LA Psychol Assn; mem bd dir Nat Council Black Child Devel; mem com on Acad Affairs & Standards 1972; mem Faculty Senate 1973-; mem Grad Faculty 1971-; mem Equal Employment Opportunity Com 1972; mem council on tchr educ coll educ USL 1974-; mem adv bd SGA-USL Child Care Cntr; mem adv bd Cath Soc Serv 1973; mem Health Adv Bd of Tri-Parish Progress Inc 1974; candidate St Martin Parish Sch Bd 1974; mem Agency Parent Council of SMILE Inc USL Rep 1974; mem byappointment Mayor Willis Soc & Economic Com St Martinville 1974; mem bd dir Lafayette Chap Epilepsy Found; mem Alpha Lambda Delta. **HONORS/ACHIEVEMENTS:** Faculty advisor Nat Honor Soc; inclusion in the 9th edit Who's Who of Am Women 1975-76; outstanding black citizen award So Consumers Educ Found Field of Educ 1975; research grant to do family res HEW Office Child Devel 1974-75; SEPA Visting Women Program 1974-. **BUSINESS ADDRESS:** Psychology Dept PO Box 3131 US, Lafayette, LA 70501.

GARRETT, CAIN, JR.
Retired lieutenant commander. **PERSONAL:** Born May 11, 1942, Kilgore, TX. **EDUCATION:** Univ CO Boulder, BSEE 1968; Naval Post Grad Sch Monterey, MSEE 1973; Naval Post Grad Sch Monterey, elec engr deg 1974. **CAREER:** Electral engr 1974; communications officer 1968-70; operators dept head 1970-72; lieut comdr flag secretary. **ORGANIZATIONS:** Mem IEEEE; Big Brothers Steerign Com Boulder 1964-68. **HONORS/ACHIEVEMENTS:** Commendation medal US Chess Fedn Navy; navy achievement medal Vietnam; good conduct medal; 4 unit awards Vietnam Sea of Japan S China Seeas Operations; spirit of honor award Kawinas 1968; meritorious serv meda USN 1980. **MILITARY SERVICE:** USN lcdrl 1959. **BUSINESS ADDRESS:** COMCRUDESGRU 5 FPO, San Francisco, CA 96601.

GARRETT, CALVIN LAVELLE
Professional athlete. **PERSONAL:** Born Jul 11, 1956; married Deborah; children: Yolanda. **EDUCATION:** Austin Peay; Oral Roberts, 1980. **CAREER:** Los Angeles Lakers, guard/forward. **HONORS/ACHIEVEMENTS:** Started 35 games with Rockets as a Rookie; career-scoring high of 22 points in his 16th games as a pro vs Seattle; most memorial game as a rookie came in final game of the Championship Series vs Boston; started 5 games in his second season all at forward. **BUSINESS ADDRESS:** Los Angeles Lakers, P O Box 10, Ste 510, Inglewood, CA 90306.

GARRETT, CHERYL ANN
Political official, educator. **PERSONAL:** Born Aug 31, 1946, Bethel Springs, TN; married Larry Eugene Garrett; children: Larry Eugene II, David Conrad, Cheryl Lynn. **EDUCATION:** Grambling Univ, BS 1969. **CAREER:** Memphis Park Commiss, community ctr dir 1970-72; Central State Hosp, coord adj therapy 1972-74; Memphis City Schools, sub teacher 1974-; CJH Resources Inc, pres 1983-; Natl Black Republican Council, southern reg vp; Fixit Home Repair, administrative assist 1985. **ORGANIZATIONS:** Commiss Shelby Cty Civil Serv Bd 1979-; v chmn TN Commiss on Status of Women 1980; state president TN Republican Assembly 1980-; treas South Shelby Republican Club 1982-. **HONORS/ACHIEVEMENTS:** Merit Awd Shelby Cty Republican Party 1979; Key to City Chattanooga TN 1981; Family Awd Shelby Cty Republican Party 1983; State Coord Black Vote Div Regan/Bush 1984 Campaign 1984. **BUSINESS ADDRESS:** Southern Regional Vice Pres, Natl Black Republican Council, 1188 Minna Pl, Memphis, TN 38104.

GARRETT, E. WYMAN
Obstetrician, gynecologist. **PERSONAL:** Born May 25, 1933, Newark. **EDUCATION:** Morgan State Coll Balto MD, BS 1955; HowardUniv Coll of Med, MD 1961. **CAREER:** Newark Mini-Surgi-Site, owner & med dir; Freemdmen's Hosp Wash DC, internship 1961-62; Harlem Hosp NYC, res OB/GYN 1yr; Newark City Hosp, res 2yr; OB/GYN NJ Coll of Med & Denistry, Asso prof. **ORGANIZATIONS:** Mem Newark Bd of Ed 1967-70; All-Am Basketball Morgan State; Beta Kappa Chi; Nat Scientific Soc; Alpha Kappa Mv; orgn dir Drive to Increase Black & Puerto Rican Enrllmnt in NJ Coll of Med & Denistry; Organization of Black Professional & Bus Women. **HONORS/ACHIEVEMENTS:** Nat hon soc Morgan State; Man of Yr Award 1972. **MILITARY SERVICE:** AUS 1st lt chemical corps 1955-57.

GARRETT, GUY THOMAS, JR.
Business executive. **PERSONAL:** Born Jun 07, 1932, Peekskill, NY; married Constance; children: Lynn, Guy III. **EDUCATION:** Howard Univ, BA 1954; grad study CCNY; Harvard Business Sch, attended advanced mgmt prog. **CAREER:** Household Finance, 1957-62; New York City Bd of Educ, 1962-63; Long Island Lighting Co, 1963-73; The New York Times Co, vice pres personnel. **ORGANIZATIONS:** Mem bd dir Newspaper Personnel Relation Assoc; mem bd dir Natl Assoc Corporate & Prof Recruiters; mem Amer Soc for Personnel Admin; past dir NY Personnel Mgmt Assn; mgmt asst com Grtr NY Fund; past dir Family Serv Assn; past trustee Good Samaritan Hosp; past mem Regional Health Council of LI; bd of dirs NY March of Dimes. **MILITARY SERVICE:** AUS 1st lt 1955-57. **BUSINESS ADDRESS:** Vice Pres Personnel, The New York Times Co, 229 W 43rd St, New York, NY 10036.

GARRETT, JOYCE F.
Associate director. **PERSONAL:** Born Aug 16, 1931, Detroit, MI; daughter of Thomas A Finley and Mary F Fleming; divorced. **EDUCATION:** Smith Coll, AB 1953; Wayne State Univ, 1959, 1974, MA 1966; Foreign Serv Inst, 1962. **CAREER:** City of Detroit, director, personnel; Joyce F Garrett & Assoc, pres; Dept of Public Information, dir 1978-; Detroit News, columnist 1978; Mayor Coleman A Young, inaugural coor 1977-78, exec asst to campaign dir 1977; Detroit Bicentennial, exec dir 1974-; Wayne County Office of Human Relations, dir 1969-74; MI Civil Rights Comm, dir 1967-69; Oakland Community Coll, pers admin 1965-67; Mayor's Youth Employment Project Detroit, job devel placement specialist 1964-65; Wayne County Civil Serv Comm, personnel tech II 1963-64, personnel tech 1956-61; Dept of State Washington DC & Caracas, Venezuela, for serv ofc 1962; Wayne County Com Coll, educ 1969-72. **ORGANIZATIONS:** Mem Intl Personnel Mgmt Assn; life mem NAACP; bd dir Smith Coll Alumnae Assn 1971-73; pres Neighborhood Serv Org 1974-76; mem Founders Soc Detroit Inst of Arts; mem Detroit Historical Soc; mem Centy Club Democratic Party of MI; mem Steering Comm Coleman Young for Mayor; exec com mem Metropolitan Fund; bd mem, Museum of African Amer History; mem, Economic Club of Detroit; life mem, NAACP; Natl Council of Negro Women; Music Hall Center, Executive and Program Committees. **HONORS/ACHIEVEMENTS:** Spirit of Detroit Award 1974; Women of Wayne Headliner 1972; L'Ordre Nat du Merite 1978.

GARRETT, LEROY
Broadcasting executive. **PERSONAL:** Born Nov 26, 1913, Talladega; married Viola; children: Arnold Lee. **CAREER:** Integ Broadcasting Inc WEUP Radio, owner/mgr. **ORGANIZATIONS:** Bd of dirs AL A&M Univ; mem C of C Washington, DC; mem C of C Huntsville, AL; mem Better Business Bur.

GARRETT, LOUIS HENRY
Company executive. **PERSONAL:** Born Jul 07, 1960, Monroe, LA; son of Mattie M Garrett. **EDUCATION:** US Air Force Non-Commissioned Officers Acad, attended 1982; LA Tech Univ, graduated Cum Laude 1983; Moody Bible Institute, certificates of completion in Christian Education, 1987. **CAREER:** Visions of Louisiana Infinite Beauty Art Exhibition a 25th Anniversary Showcase of the Miss Louisiana Pageant, chmn and originator 1987-88; Miss Louisiana Pageant Inc, dir of advertising; first vice pres, Leadership Division, Monroe Chamber of Commerce. **ORGANIZATIONS:** Mem Baptist Student Union Fall Quarter Retreat 1983; chmn 1986 Northeast LA Special Olympics Raffle Ticket Sales; mem 1986 Monroe Jaycees Christmas Shopping Tour for Needy Children; mem Natl Assoc of Miss Amer State Pageants 1986-87; first black mem Louisiana Pageant Bd of Dirs 1986-87; mem Monroe Jaycees 1986-87; chmn 1987 Jaycees Winter Project; mem Phi Beta Sigma Frat Inc; mem LA Jaycee Fall Bd Meeting LA Action Legislature; life mem Young Democrats of Amer; pres, Ouachita Parish Head Start Policy Council, 1988-89; treasurer, Little Flower Academy PTO, 1988-; Friendly Brothers Kiwanis of Monroe, Publicity Chairman, Scholarship Fundraiser, 1988-; Ouachita Parish Election Commissioner, 1988-; Urban League of Greater New Orleans, 1987-. **HONORS/ACHIEVEMENTS:** Mem Sigma Tau Delta Honor Soc in English 1981-83; Phi Alpha Theta Honor Soc in History 1982-83; Chairman and Program Host, 1989 Youth Gospel Choir Highlights; Natl Bd of Advisors, Amer Biographical Institute, 1989. **MILITARY SERVICE:** USAF Reserves 1979-87; Outstanding Non-Commissioned Officer of the Quarter, Commanders Awd 1985, Air Force Longevity Serv 1982, Air Force Achievement Medal 1985; US Army Reserves, certificate of Outstanding Military Performance 1988 at Fort Benning Georgia Infantry Training Center, 1987-. **HOME ADDRESS:** 1605 Booth St, Monroe, LA 71201-8210. **BUSINESS ADDRESS:** First Vice Pres, Leadership Div, Monroe Chamber of Commerce, 1605 Booth St, Monroe, LA 71201.

GARRETT, MELVIN ALBOY
Marketing manager. **PERSONAL:** Born Jun 01, 1936, Montclair, NJ; married Maryann Harris. **EDUCATION:** Upsala Coll E Orange NJ, 1956-64. **CAREER:** United Airlines, mktng mgr; Becker Constrn Co, accountant 1964-65; United Airlines, ticker agt sales rep account exec mktng mgr 1965-; Eisle King Libaire Stout & Co NYSE, asst to mgr 1957-60; Halevy H Simons Architect, pub relations opns coordinator 1962-63; Nat State Bank Newark, banking clk 1963. **ORGANIZATIONS:** Dist co committeeman Montclair NJ Essex Cty Dem 1965; NAACP; Urban League; United Airlines Black Employees Assn; The Black Professional Orgn; mem Alpha Kappa Psi Frat. **HONORS/ACHIEVEMENTS:** Interliner of the year 1977 The Detroit Interline Club 1977; mem of hon Detroit Interline Club 1978; ambassador of good will Detroit-Windsor Interline Club Inc; salesman of the year award United Airlines; community serv award United Airlines; leaderhip award United Airlines; black achiever award NY Harlem YMCA 1980; soldier-of-the-month; good conduct medal AUS 1962. **MILITARY SERVICE:** AUS sp/4 1960-62. **BUSINESS ADDRESS:** 1221 Ave of the Americas, New York, NY 10020.

GARRETT, NAOMI M.
Educator. **PERSONAL:** Born Aug 24, 1906, Columbia, SC. **EDUCATION:** Benedict Coll, AB 1927; Atlanta U, MA 1937; Columbia U, PhD 1954. **CAREER:** High School SC Baltimore, instructor, 1927-41; Project Haiti, US govt English teacher, 1942-44; WV State Coll, prof modern foreign languages, 1947-72; chmn 1958-71; WV State Coll, foreign student adv 1954-72; Denison Univ, Univ prof 1972-74; Univ of Charleston WV, visiting prof 1980; Denison Univ Granville OH, visiting prof, 1974-79. **ORGANIZATIONS:** Medm CLA; MLA; ACTFL; LASA; League Women Voters. **HONORS/ACHIEVEMENTS:** Rosenwald fellow, 1944-45; Columbia Univ, fellow 1946-47; Ford fellow 1951-52; Fulbright fellow Paris 1958-59; contributing editor, HLAS; author "Renaissance of Haitian Poetry"; reviews, articles professional jours AAUW.

GARRETT, NATHAN TAYLOR
Business executive. **PERSONAL:** Born Aug 08, 1931, Tarboro, NC; married Wanda June Jones; children: Andrea Mausi, Devron, Nathan Jr. **EDUCATION:** Yale Univ, AB Psych 1952; Wayne State Univ, post grad in Acct & Bus 1960; NC Central Schl of Law, JD 1986. **CAREER:** Richard H Austin & Co Detroit, acct 1958-62; Nathan T Garrett, CPA Durham, proprietor 1962-75; NC Fund Durham, deputy dir 1964-67; Fnd for Comm Dev Durham, fndr exec dir 1967-72; Garrett, Sullivan, Davenport, Bowie & Grant. **ORGANIZATIONS:** Bd chair of audit comm exec comm NC Mutual Life Ins Co Durham 1977-; bd exec comm Mech & Farmers Bank Durham 1965-78; chrmn investment comm chair Cooperative Asst Fund NY 1970-; bd exec comm Opport Funding Corp DC 1970-77; bd vice chr of Acad Affairs Comm Duke Univ 1978-; corp mem Triangle Research Inst Fnd 1980-; bd treas Scarboro Nursery Schl 1963-; chrmn of People Panel NC 2000 Commission of the Future 1983;NC State Board of CPA Examiners 1986. **HONORS/ACHIEVEMENTS:** Serv as pres Natl Assc of Minority CPA Firms 1978; srv as elect official 25 Civic Grps in Durham & State of NC 1975. **MILITARY SERVICE:** AUS corpl 1952-54. **BUSINESS ADDRESS:** Chairman & Founder, Garrett,Sullivan,Davenport, Box 1029, Durham, NC 27702.

GARRETT, PAUL C.
Attorney, city official. **PERSONAL:** Born Feb 08, 1946, Charlottesville, VA; son of Dr Marshall T Garrett and Pauline H Garrett; married Louise Lawson; children: Matthew L. **EDUCATION:** Brown Univ, AB 1968; Univ of VA Sch of Law, JD 1971. **CAREER:** USAF, asst staff judge advocate 1972-76; City of Charlottesville VA, asst city atty 1976-80; Charlottesville Circuit Court, clerk 1981-. **MILITARY SERVICE:** USAF capt 1972-76; USAFR major 1976-. **HOME ADDRESS:** 2242 Banbury St, Charlottesville, VA 22901. **BUSINESS ADDRESS:** Clerk of the Court, Charlottesville Circuit Ct, 315 East High St, Charlottesville, VA 22901.

GARRETT, ROMEO BENJAMIN
Retired educator. **PERSONAL:** Born Feb 02, 1910, Natchez, MS; widowed. **EDUCATION:** Dillard U, AB 1932; Bradley U, MA 1947; New York U, PhD 1963. **CAREER:** Bradley U, prof Sociology 1947-76; Bradley U, retired prof emeritus. **ORGANIZATIONS:** Vice pres NAACP 1980-85. **HONORS/ACHIEVEMENTS:** Arno pres Published Famous First Facts About Negroes 1972; assoc publishers Published The Presidents & The Negro 1982. **MILITARY SERVICE:** USAAF sgt. **HOME ADDRESS:** 431 W Fifth St, Peoria, IL 61605. **BUSINESS ADDRESS:** BradleyUniv, Peoria, IL 61606.

GARRETT, RUBY GRANT
Business executive. **PERSONAL:** Born May 13, 1941, Covington, GA; married William H; children: Victoria, Laran. **EDUCATION:** Carver Voc Sch of Practical Nursing, LPN 1960; Atlanta Coll of Art, BFA 1971; GA State U, Masters Pgm 1971-73. **CAREER:** Ruby G Graphics Design, owner 1969-72; Eric Hill & Assoc Planning, art dir design consult 1971-72; G Designs Inc Adv & PR, pres owner 1972-79; Garrett Comm, pres 1979-. **ORGANIZATIONS:** Pres NAMD Atlanta Chapter 1982-83; bd mem Enterprise Atlanta 1983-85; comm chmn NAMD Atlanta Chapter 1983-87; bd & comm chm Atlanta Bus League 1983-87; consult speakerUniv of GA Extension Serv 1984; consult Atlanta Jr Coll 1984. **HONORS/ACHIEVEMENTS:** Recognition The Collaborative Inc 1974; recognition Broadcast Enterprise Nat Inc 1984; President Award Nat Assoc of Market Developers ATC Chptr 1984. **HOME ADDRESS:** 2121 Beecher Rd SW, Atlanta, GA 30311. **BUSINESS ADDRESS:** President, Garrett Communications, PO Box 53, Atlanta, GA 30301.

GARRETT, THADDEUS, JR.
Educator, clergyman, businessman. **PERSONAL:** Born May 18, 1948, Akron, OH. **EDUCATION:** Univ of Akron, BA; George Washington Univ, grad sch of pub adminis; Howard Univ, grad sch of religion; Allen Univ, DD; ordained African Meth; Wilberforce Univ, DD; Livingstone Coll, DD. **CAREER:** Wesley Temple African Methodist Zion Church, Akron OH, Episcopal Zion minister & assoc pastor; Vice President George Bush, asst at White House 1981-83; Garrett & Co, pres 1983-. **ORGANIZATIONS:** Aide former Rep Nat'l Chmn Ray C Bliss 1968; former asst to congresswoman Shirley Chisholm 1970-74; mem St Bd of Educ OH 1972-80; vice chmn US Consumer Prod Safety Commn 1976-77; former asst to vice pres of US Nelson Reckefeller 1976-77; OH Civil Rights Commn, commr 1980; former asst Congressman Wm HAyres; spl asst US House Educ & Labor Comm; tchr Akron Buchtel HS & Govt Seminar Univ of Akron; mem US Office of Educ Adv Council on Higher Educ; natl chmn YMCA Youth-In-Govt Prog; vice chmn Akron's Hum Rel Com; mem exec bd March of Dimes; OH Lung Assn; YMCA Youth-In-Govt Prog; Martin Luther King Scholarship Fund; OH Rep Council; NAACP; UMCA; steering comm Natl Black Rep Council; Bd of Trustees, Howard Univ, Kent State Univ; Bd of Directors First Bank Cleveland, OH. **BUSINESS ADDRESS:** President, Garrett & Company, 1630 Connecticut Ave NW, Ste 202, Washington, DC 20009.

GARRETT-BROWN, FANNIE E.
Retired educator. **PERSONAL:** Born Aug 21, 1924, Jackson, MS; daughter of Edward P Garrett and Bessie Willing Garrett; married William H Brown; children: William E, Kevin C, Mary Devra McMullen. **EDUCATION:** St Mary's Infirmary, Nursing Diploma 1946; Holy Names College, BS Nursing Ed 1969; San Francisco State Univ, MS Health Sci 1972; Nova Univ, Ed Doctorate 1978. **CAREER:** St Mary's Infirmary operating rm surgical nurse 1946-47; St Mary's Hosp, med/surgical staff nurse 1947-48; Providence Hosp, med/surgical staff nurse 1948-49; Joel E Lewis MD, office nurse 1950-51; Providence Hospital, desk charge nurse 1952-54, nursery staff nurse 1955-62; Kaiser-Permanente Hosp, pediatric clinic staff nurse 1962; Providence Hospital-Peralta Hospital-Sam Merritt Hospital, private duty nurse 1963-67; Richmond Unified Schools, school public health nurse 1969-72; City Coll of San Francisco, nursing instructor & superviser inservice health educ 1972-78. **ORGANIZATIONS:** Nursing adv bd mem Holy Names Coll 1978-; nursing adv bd mem City Coll of San Francisco 1979-; guest lecturer City College, Diablo Valley Community Coll, San Francisco State Univ 1979-83; exec bd mem Family Aid to Catholic Educ 1980; former bd mem Mercy Retirement & Skill Nursing Facility 1984; mem Oakland Bd of Realtors 1984; mem Registered Nurses Alumni Assn Holy Names Coll; mem Amer Public Health Assn; mem CA Teachers Assn; mem Amer Assn Univ Women; program vice pres Oakland/Piedmont Amer Assn Univ Women. **HONORS/ACHIEVEMENTS:** Traineeship HEW 1969-70; Improving the Applicant Selection Process of the Nursing Prog at City Coll of San Francisco, a doctoral dissertation 1978; publication "Juvenile Prostitution, A Nursing Perspective" Journal of Psychiatric Nursing & Mental Health Serv 1980; Distinquished Alumni Award, Natl Assn for Equal Opportunity in Higher Educ 1989; "Leadership America" Participant, Foundation for Women Resources 1989. **HOME ADDRESS:** 4433 Arcadia Ave, Oakland, CA 94602.

GARRISON, ESTHER F.
Secretary. **PERSONAL:** Born Jul 16, 1922, Ocilla, GA; divorced. **EDUCATION:** Savannah State Coll, attended. **CAREER:** Sub tchr; sec real estate firms ins firms; AUS; Intl Longshoreman's Assn Local #1414, sec. **ORGANIZATIONS:** Mem Chatham-Savannah Bd Educ 1964-; vice pres & tempore life mem NAACP sec local Br; mem Zion Bapt Ch. **HONORS/ACHIEVEMENTS:** First black woman elected Bd educ S of Mason-Dixon Line; outstanding serv to commn Adult Educ Program 1965; woman of yr Savannah State Coll Chap NAACP 1966; award Prince Hall Mason & Eastern Stars 1975; hon tribute to a black woman Mutual Benevolent Soc 1974; first woman hon in history of 98 yr olf Soc; richard r wright award Svannah State Coll 1974. **BUSINESS ADDRESS:** 221 NE Lathrope Ave, PO Box 1262, Savannah, GA 31402.

GARRISON, JEWELL K.
Educator. **PERSONAL:** Born Nov 06, 1946, Dayton, OH; children: Brandon. **EDUCATION:** Central State Univ, BA social work 1969; Atlanta Univ Grad Sch of Social Work, MSW 1972. **CAREER:** Montgomery Co Juvenile Court, probation counselor 1969-70; Cath Social Serv, sch social worker 1970-71; Atlanta Pub Sch System, sch social worker 1971-72; Montgomery Co Children Serv Bd, dir of staff devel 1972-77; Wright State Univ Dayton, asst prof 1977-84, assoc prof/practicum coord 1984-. **ORGANIZATIONS:** Sec 1976-78, pres 1977-80 Dayton Chap Natl Assn of Black Social Workers; 1st vice pres OH State Natl Assn of Black Social Workers 1978-81; bd dir Urban League Dayton 1977-; bd dirs Dayton Citizen Child Adv Inc 1978-82; citizen child review bd Montgomery Co Juvenile Ct 1979-83; Urban Minority Alcoholism Outreach Comm 1980-84; chair Natl Educ Comm-Natl Assn of Black Social Workers 1982-; bd of dirs Daybreak Runaway Shelter 1983-85; bd dir Choice Inc; bd chair Dayton Urban League 1985-88; mem Rural Council on Human Services 1986-87; Montgomery County Mental Health Bd 1987-; Natl Urban League Bd of Trustees 1988-; vice pres, bd of dirs, Community Connections Inc, 1988-; exec comm, New Future Bd of Dirs, 1988-; bd mem, Dayton Area Council on Youth, 1988-. **HONORS/ACHIEVEMENTS:** Cert of Recognition Who's Who Among Coll & Univ 1968-69; Cert of Recognition Who's Who Among Young Women in Amer 1979-80, 1983-84; Natl Inst of Mental Health trainee Atlanta Univ Grad Sch of Soc Work; Alpha Kappa Delta Awd Natl Sociological Hon Soc Alpha Chapt; Leadership Dayton 1986; The Altursa Soc 1986-. **BUSINESS ADDRESS:** Associate Prof/Practicum Coord, Wright StateUniv, E 480 Millett Hall, Dayton, OH 45435.

GARRISON, ROBERT E., JR.
Physician. **PERSONAL:** Born Apr 11, 1923, Columbus, OH; son of Robert Garrison and Mamie Lambert Garrison; married Ruby Doyle; children: Paul M Duffy, Peggy G Drew, Judy G Rodgers, Robert D. **EDUCATION:** Ohio State Univ, BSc Pharmacy 1948, MD 1957. **CAREER:** Hackley Hosp, chief of staff 1986; Muskegon Comm Coll, chmn of bd of trustees 1981-85, bd of trustees 1972-. **ORGANIZATIONS:** Bd mem Michigan Consolidated Gas Co 1979-86; bd of trustees, 1st vice pres Assoc of Comm Coll 1981; exec comm New Muskegon 1982-; Exec Comm Bd of Dir 1982-; Pres Assoc of Comm Coll Trustees 1985-86; bd dir First of Amer Bank 1985-89; vice pres New Muskegon Corp 1986-88; bd mem Muskegon County Comm Found 1988-; bd mem Muskegon Economic Growth Alliance 1988-. **HONORS/ACHIEVEMENTS:** Outstanding Citizen Award, United Way of Muskegon County 1987; Johnathan Walker Award, Urban League of Greater Muskegon 1988. **MILITARY SERVICE:** USAF 99th Fighter Squad 1st lt 2 yrs. **HOME ADDRESS:** 1913 Crestwood Ln, Muskegon, MI 49441.

GARRISON, ZINA
Professional tennis player. **PERSONAL:** Born Nov 16, 1963, Houston, TX. **EDUCATION:** Attended Ross Sterling High School. **CAREER:** Professional Tennis Player. **HONORS/ACHIEVEMENTS:** Female Amateur Athelte of the Yr US Olympic Committee 1981; ITF Junior of the Year Awd for 1981, won both the Wimbledon and US Open Junior titles; Zina Garrison Day in Washington DC Jan 6, 1982; was First Black Female to be ranked No 1 in Texas region; won European Indoor title in Zurich 1984. **BUSINESS ADDRESS:** c/o Andrew P Moran, 5625 Milart St, Houston, TX 77021.

GARRISON-CORBIN, PATRICIA ANN
Business executive, management consultant. **PERSONAL:** Born Jun 18, 1947, Louisville, KY; married Dr James D Corbin. **EDUCATION:** Western KY Univ, BS 1969; Univ of Louisville, MS Urban Studies & Comm Devel 1970-71; MIT, MS Mgmt 1979. **CAREER:** MIT, asst to vice pres 1974-78, dir of personnel serv 1979-80; South FL State Hosp, dir human resources 1980-82; State of FL Amer Mgmt Corp, vice pres 1980-82; Greater Philadelphia First Corp, dep exec dir & treas 1982-; Drexel Burnham Lambert Inc, vice pres municipal finance. **ORGANIZATIONS:** 1st dep city mgt City of Philadelphia 1982-84; dep exec dir Greater Philadelphia First Corp 1984-; bd of dir Natl Assoc for Black Public Admin; vice pres PACoalition of 100 Black Women. **HONORS/ACHIEVEMENTS:** 1st Black Female Sloan Fellow MIT 1979; Urban Ed Fellow Louisville Bd of Ed 1971. **BUSINESS ADDRESS:** President, P G Corbin & Company, Inc, 1411 Walnut St, Suite 1225, Philadelphia, PA 19103.

GARRITY, MONIQUE P.
Educator. **PERSONAL:** Born Mar 26, 1941; divorced. **EDUCATION:** Marygrove Coll, BA 1963; Boston Coll, PhD 1970. **CAREER:** Univ of MA, assoc prof; Wellesley Coll, asst prof 1970-71; Univ of MA, asst assoc prof 1968; Econ Research Unit, instructor; OECD Paris, cons; Metro Area Planning Council Boston , state analyst 1965. **ORGANIZATIONS:** Rengl chmn Caucus of Blk Econ 1971-72; dir Blk Econ Resrch Ctr; Am Scholar Coun; Fulbright Hayes Sr Lectureship AveUniv of Dakar 1974-75; consult Guinea-Bissau 1978; Senegal 1979. **HONORS/ACHIEVEMENTS:** Resrch grant to haiti YaleUniv 1972-73. **BUSINESS ADDRESS:** University of Massachusetts, Dept of Econ, Boston, MA 02125.

GARROTT, HOMER L.
Judge. **PERSONAL:** Born Apr 25, 1914, Los Angeles, CA; married Bertha Tabor. **EDUCATION:** SouthwesternUniv Sch of Law, LLB 1958. **CAREER:** Municipal Ct Compton Judicial Dist, judge 1973-; Municipal Ct Los Angeles Judicial Dist, commr 1968-73; Juveniel Ct Los Angeles Co, referee 1967-68; Los Angeles Co, deputy pub defender 1964-67. **ORGANIZATIONS:** Bd of dir SouthwesternUniv 1978-. **MILITARY SERVICE:** AUS spec 1936-39. **BUSINESS ADDRESS:** Compton Judicial District, 200 West Compton Blvd, Compton, CA 90220.

GARTRELL, LUTHER R.
Engineer. **PERSONAL:** Born Aug 20, 1940, Washington, GA. **EDUCATION:** NC A&T St U, BSEE 1964; Old Dominion U, MEEE. **CAREER:** NASA Langley Res Cntr, res engr. **ORGANIZATIONS:** Mem NAACP; IEEE; AIAA; VA Acad of Sci NASA publ. **HONORS/ACHIEVEMENTS:** Spec achievement award NASA. **BUSINESS ADDRESS:** Electronics Engineer, NASA, Langley Station, Hampton, VA 23665.

GARVIN, JONATHAN
Electrician. **PERSONAL:** Born Apr 26, 1932, Jasper County; married Elizabeth Horton; children: Tony Millard, Earl Bernard. **EDUCATION:** Savannah State, attneded 1951. **CAREER:** Private Practice, electrician. **ORGANIZATIONS:** Chmn Dem Party Jasper County; Band Booster Club; Athletic Club; biracial com Sch Bd Mason; mem choir leader Padgbett Br Bapt Ch; VEP; comm leader. **MILITARY SERVICE:** USMC 2 yrs.

GARVIN, MILDRED BARRY
Administrator. **PERSONAL:** Born Nov 29, 1929, Chicago, IL; married Ralph Garvin; children: Patricia Barry, Jacquelyn Barry, Ralph Jr, Derrick, Corey. **EDUCATION:** Attended, Univ of IL, Chicago, Paterson State Teachers' Coll, Paterson NJ. **CAREER:** Rutgers Univ, Urban Studies Center, rsch assoc 1963-71, rsch assoc office of Nwk studies 1971-72; Mayor's Policy & Devel Office, deputy dir review & planning 1972-75; Rutgers Graduate School of Public admin, program coordinator, 1975-. **ORGANIZATIONS:** Exec bd mem, NAACP Orange & Maplewood Chapter; assemblywoman NJ Gehn Assembly Dist 27 Essex 1977; mem Amer Soc for Public Admin; mem Steering Comm NJ State Dem Party; chmn Assembly Educ Comm; vice chmn Assembly Higher Educ & Regulated Professions Comm; co-chmn, Joint Comm on Public Schools; chair Women's Legislative Democratic Caucus; chmn Natl Conf of State Legislators Educ & Labor Comm; state coord legislator Natl Black Caucus of State Legislators; mem NJ Historical Comm; mem YWCA Youth Advisory Bd; mem NJ State Legislative Black Caucus; mem Natl Black Caucus of Local Elected Officials; mem, Essex Co Vocational School Bd Long Range Planning Comm; mem Coalition of 100 Black Women. **HONORS/ACHIEVEMENTS:** First Black to serve on East Orange Bd of Educ; Woman of the Year, Civic Action League of E Orange 1970; co-author "A Revised Policy Concerning Newark's Pequannock Watershed" Rutgers Office of Newark Studies 1971-72; Award for Excellence in Educ Operation PUSH 1979. **BUSINESS ADDRESS:** Program Coordinator, Rutgers Graduate School of Public Admin, 134 Evergreen Place, East Orange, NJ 07018.

GARY, ALONZO G., JR.
Business executive. **PERSONAL:** Born Sep 10, 1928, Tampa, FL; divorced; children: Madonna, Taihita, Ineko. **EDUCATION:** Florida Avia Coll, 1948; LIAMA Agncy Officer's Sch, 1971 NIA Inst in Agncy Mngmt, 1959. **CAREER:** Central Life Ins Co of FL, agency dir 1964-74; dist mgr 1957-64. **ORGANIZATIONS:** Past vice pres Nat Ins Assn; seven times chrmn Consult Com Nat Ins Assn; Nat Ins Week Com; special awards com Nat Serv Weeks Com; past pres LakelandChap NAACP. **HONORS/ACHIEVEMENTS:** Spec citizenship award City of Lakeland 1964; mgr of year 1958, 1959, 1963. **MILITARY SERVICE:** USAF. **BUSINESS ADDRESS:** PO Box 3286, Tampa, FL 33601.

GARY, LAWRENCE EDWARD
Educator. **PERSONAL:** Born May 26, 1939, Union Spring, AL; son of Ed Gary (deceased) and Henrietta Mays Gary; married Dr Robenia Baker, Aug 08, 1969; children: Lisa Che, Lawrence Charles Andre, Jason Edward. **EDUCATION:** Tuskegee Inst, BS 1963;Univ of MI, MPA 1964, MSW 1967, PhD 1970. **CAREER:** MI Econ Opportunity Prog, staff asst 1964;Univ of MI, lecturer & asst prof 1968-71; Howard U, asst to vice pres for academic affairs 1971-72, dir prof 1972-; Inst Urban Affairs & Rsch, dir & prof of social work & urban studies. **ORGANIZATIONS:** Mem action bd Am Public Hlth Assoc 1973-74; bd of dir DC Inst of Mental Hygiene 1976-84; editorial bd Journal of Social Work 1977-81; Hlth Brain Trust Black Congressional Caucus 1977-87; publications bd Cncl on Social Work Educ 1982-87; consulting editor Jrnl of Social Work 1985-; social welfare adv bd Natl Urban League 1985-; bd of mgmt, Howard Univ Press 1987-; mem Youth Advisory Bd, Lilly Endowment, Inc. Indianapolis, IN 1987-; bd mem, Child Welfare Inst, Atlanta, GA 1988-; editorial bd, Journal of Teaching in Social Work 1987-; Bd of Trustees, St Paul AME Church, Washington, DC 1984-; mem of Advisory Bd, DC Commn on Public Health 1984-87. **HONORS/ACHIEVEMENTS:** Distinguished Alumni Award Nat Assoc for Equal Opportunity in Higher Educ 1979; Eminent Scholar VA StateUniv 1982; outstanding publication Nat Assoc of Black Social Workers 1983; Labor of Love Award Nat Head Start Assoc 1984; Eminent Scholar Norfolk State Univ 1986; The Henry & Lucy Moses Disting Vstg Prof Hunter Coll NY 1986-87; elected delegate, Council on Social Work Educ 1988-89; Founder's Medallion Natl Assn of Social Workers 1988; Distinguished Alumni Award Natl Assn For Equal Opportunity in Higher Educ 1988; publications, Black Men 198l, Mental Health: A Challenge to Black Community 1978; mem of Alpha Phi Alpha Fraternity, Inc. **BUSINESS ADDRESS:** Director, Professor, Inst Urban Afrs/Rsrch, Howard Univ, 2900 Van Ness St NW, Washington, DC 20009.

GARY, MELVIN L.
Psychologist. **PERSONAL:** Born Apr 12, 1938, Brownsville, PA; son of Joseph Gary and Marie Hood; married Juneau Mahan; children: Joseph Tyler. **EDUCATION:** Haverford Coll, AB 1961; OH State U, MA 1964; OH State U, PhD 1967. **CAREER:** Ctr for Voc & Tech Educ OH State Univ, res assoc 1965; OH State Univ, res assoc 1967; Temple Univ, asst prof psych & ed psych 1968; Livingston Coll, assoc dean of students 1971; Rutgers Univ, assoc for academic prog devel 1975, dean of academic affairs & assoc dean of coll 1977, assoc prof of psych. **ORGANIZATIONS:** Mem Am Assn for Advancement of Science, Am Assn of Univ Profs, Am Psychological Assn, Assn of Black Psychologists, Soc for Psych Study of Social Issues, Amer Assoc of Higher Educ, NJ Black Issues Convention. **HONORS/ACHIEVEMENTS:** Hon men Woodrow Fellowship 1961; Society of Sigma Xi 1968; fellow Am Council on Educ Fellow UCLA 1974. **BUSINESS ADDRESS:** Assoc Professor of Psychology, RutgersUniv, Psychology Dept, New Brunswick, NJ 08903.

GASKILL, ROBERT CLARENCE
Brigadier general (retired). **PERSONAL:** Born Apr 12, 1931, Yonkers, NY; married Erotida Maria Ponce; children: Robert Clarence, Vivienne Renee, Juli Ann Gaskill Henderson, Cheryl Lynn Gaskill Foster. **EDUCATION:** Howard Univ, BA (Cum Laude) 1952; George Washington Univ, MBA 1960. **CAREER:** US Army, commd 2nd lt 1952 advanced through the grades to major general 1977; served in Korea, Vietnam, Europe; Letterkenny Army Depot Chambersburg PA, comdr 1974-75; 1st Support Brigade Kaiserlautern Germany, comdg general 1975-76; 21st Support Command, comdg general 1976-77; Army War Coll Carlisle Barracks PA,dep comdt 1977-78; Def Logistics Agency Cameron Sta VA, dep dir 1978-81 (retired). **ORGANIZATIONS:** Instructor accounting Univ VA Ft Lee 1962; disting commander Boy Scouts Amer W Ger 1975-77; founding mem Woodbridge HS Choral Boosters Club 1979-; consultant, assoc professional lecturer business and public admin No VA Comm Coll Woodbridge 1981-; instructor acctg lectr in field; chmn Ft Belvoir Retiree Cncl; mem citizen adv comm Consortium Continuing Higher Educ in No VA; bd dirs Army Quartermaster Found; elder, deacon Covenant Presbyterian Ch; mem Assoc US Army, Amer Def Preparedness Assoc, Amer Mgmt Assoc, NAACP, Omega Psi Phi. **HONORS/ACHIEVEMENTS:** Decorated DSM, Legion of Merit, Meritorious Service Medal w/Oak Leaf Cluster, Army Commendation Medal w/Oak Leaf Cluster; Honor Medal 1st Class (Republic ofVietnam); author of essays and book reports in field. **MILITARY SERVICE:** AUS.

GASKIN, JEANINE
Human resource representative. **PERSONAL:** Born Dec 11, 1945, Detroit; married Harry Thomas Gaskinn III. **EDUCATION:** Univ MI, BA 1971. **CAREER:** Harper-Grace Hosp, hum rsrc rep 1976; Detroit Mem Hosp, persnl asst 1971-74; Detrt Bd of Edn, tchr 1970-71; Detrt News, persnl asst 1966-69. **ORGANIZATIONS:** Mem UWAA 1972-;Univ MI Alum Assn 1971-; Ed Com Coleman Yng Sentrl Conf Com; Secy Blenheim Forest Comm Counc 1973-; mem NW Orgzn Dtrt 1973-; mem Am Prsnl Guid Assn; mem Nat Empl Couns Assn; mem Assn for Non-white Concerns in Persnl & Guid; mem of Fdrs Soc Det Inst of Arts; mem Nat Hist Soc 1975. **HONORS/ACHIEVEMENTS:** Nat Hon Soc Award 1964; Citznshp Award 1964; Schlrshp Award 1964; Archdiocesan Dev Fund Wrtng Award 1964; listed Who's Who of Wmn 1977; Comm Ldrs & Noteworthy Am Award 1976-77. **BUSINESS ADDRESS:** Director, Employment Services, Mt Carmel Mercy Hospital, 6071 W Outer Dr, Detroit, MI 48235.

GASKIN, LEONARD O.
Musician, composer, educator. **PERSONAL:** Born Aug 25, 1920, Brooklyn; married Mary; children: Leonard, Jr, Poppy. **CAREER:** Prince George's Co Pub Sch, supr of art; bassist musician & composer; one of 52d St musicians instrumental in creating modern jazz; appeared with Charlie Parker, Dizzy Gillespie, Billie Holliday & Thelonious Mon during 40's; bassist for Lena Horne, Ella Fitzgerald, Erroll Garner, Stan Getz, Miles Davis, Eddie Condon & Louis Armstrong; presently conducting jazz wrkshps and lectrng on hist of jazz wrkng to-

wards acad accept of jazz as an art form. **ORGANIZATIONS:** Pres Jazz Heritage Soc; mem Intl Soc of Bassists; mem Am Fed of Musicians; mem Intl Art of Jazz.

GASKIN, LEROY
Educator, artist. **PERSONAL:** Born Jun 05, 1924, Norfolk, VA; son of Rosa Edwards Osborne; married Nina Mildred Locke, Dec 25, 1953; children: Edwin Leroy. **EDUCATION:** Hampton Inst Hampton VA, BS magna cum laude 1950; Columbia Univ NY, MA 1955, tchrs clge prof diploma 1961; PA State Univ Univ Park PA, Doctor Educ 1972. **CAREER:** Prince George's Cty Pub Schl MD, art instr 1950-67, supr tchr for students of area clges & univ 1954-74; Letcher's Art Ctr Wash DC, comm art instr 1956-59; Prince George's Cty Pub Schl, helping tchr of sec art 1967-70, supr of art K-12 1976-89. **ORGANIZATIONS:** Spec consult educ Natl Collection of Fine Arts Smithsonian Inst Wash DC 1970-71; eval for summer inst in Art History for hs art tchrs Univ of MD Clge Park MD 1973; eval for Museum & Community Conf for MD Art Educ Assc Baltimore Museum MD 1970; vice pres The Assc for the Presentation of the Arts Inc Wash DC 1968-70; pres of DC Art Assc Wash DC 1976-78; pres of MD Art Educ Assc North Englewood MD 1982-84; deacon, Vermont Ave Baptist Church 1959-89. **HONORS/ACHIEVEMENTS:** Museum & Art Tchr Research Prog Natl Gallery of Art & GW Univ 1966; Art Educ Citation Eastern Arts Assc Kutztown PA 1962; Citation Outstanding Contribution Art Educ Smith-Mason Gallery of Art Wash DC 1971; Community Art Award Assc Preservation & Presentation of Art Inc Wash DC 1977; Natl Art Educ Assc Outstanding Contribution to Art Educ Award State MD Atlanta GA 1980; Natl Art Educ Assc Div of Supr & Admin Outstanding Art Educ Award Eastern Region, Dallas, TX, 1985. **MILITARY SERVICE:** USN petty officer 2nd class. **HOME ADDRESS:** 1601 Woodhill Ct, North Englewood, MD 20785. **BUSINESS ADDRESS:** Supervisor of Art K-12, Prince George's Cty Pub Sch, William Paca Instructional Services Ctr, Landover, MD 20785.

GASKINS, LOUISE ELIZABETH
Educator. **PERSONAL:** Born Jun 02, 1930, Raleigh, NC; daughter of Joseph B F Cutchin (deceased) and Claytae V Hall Watson (deceased); children: Pamela, Donna Gaskins-Wetherbee, Eric. **EDUCATION:** NCCU, BS 1951; Fitchburg State, MEd 1972. **CAREER:** Atkins HS, teacher 1951-54; AEC Germ, teacher 1957-58; Germany, teacher 1959; WA State, teacher 1960-61; Ligon HS, teacher 1961-62; Army Educ Ctgr Germany, teacher 1964; Ayer HS, teacher math 1965-72; Ayer Jr HS, guid counselor 1972-75, acting princ 1975-76, princ 1976-; Ayer Public Schools, Administrator/Principal 1965-. **ORGANIZATIONS:** Mem Ayer's Tchr Assn 1965-; mem NEA 1965-; mem MA Teachers Assn 1965-; past faculty rep Professional Assn 1966-70; past advr Afro-Amer Culture Club 1967-74; mem N Central MA Guid Assn 1968-; mem MA Sch Couns Assn 1968-; past mem Adm Selec Team 1970-73; past mem Professional Negot Team 1970-75; past chmn Supt Sel Com 1971-72; past mem bd dir Adven House 1973-75; mem MA Jr H Midl Sch Prin Assn 1975-; state del NEA Conv 1975-; dir MA NEA 1976-; mem Natl Sec Sch Prin Assn; mem New Eng Assn of Black Educators; Black Polit Task Force; MA Dept of Educ Study Com for Jr High/Middle Sch; MADept of Educ Evaluation Strategy Group for Handicapped Students; vice pres Montachusett Rgn NAACP 1977-78. **HONORS/ACHIEVEMENTS:** Natl Sci Found Grant 1967; Human and Civil Rights Award, Massachusetts Teachers Assn, 1988. **BUSINESS ADDRESS:** Principal, Ayer Jr High School, Washington St, Ayer, MA 01432.

GASPARD, PATRICE T.
Pediatrician. **PERSONAL:** Born Jun 30, 1954, New Orleans, LA; son of Mr & Mrs O Gaspard Jr; married LeRoy Maxwell Graham MD; children: Arianne Marie, Leroy M III. **EDUCATION:** Tulane Univ, BS 1976; Tulane Univ Sch of Medicine, MD 1980. **CAREER:** Fitzsimmons Army Medical Ctr, pediatric residency; Ft Knox KY, chief of inpatient svcs; Fitzsimons Army Medical Ctr, fellow in adolescent medicine; Chief, Adolescence Med Clinic, FAMC. **ORGANIZATIONS:** Certified Amer Bd of Pediatrics 1984; mem Amer Acad of Pediatrics; mem American Medical Association, mem National Medical Association, mem Society for Adolescent Medicine. **HONORS/ACHIEVEMENTS:** First black elected to Alpha Omega Alpha Honor Medical Soc at Tulane Univ. **MILITARY SERVICE:** AUS 1980-; Army Commendation Medal, 1st Oak Leaf Cluster.

GASTON, ARNETT W.
Clinical Psychologist. **PERSONAL:** Born Apr 01, 1938, New York, NY; married Sandra; children: Robyn, Brett. **EDUCATION:** AA 1970; BA magna cum laude 1971; MA 1975, MPh 1977; CityUniv of NY, PhD 1981. **CAREER:** Dept of Correction Prince George's Co MD, dir; Mayor's Crisis Task Force, exec asst commr; Minimum Standards, bd of rev; NY State Standards & Goals for Criminal Justice Plng Com Honolulu Symphony Orchestra 1957; composer author musician conductor; Prison Suicide, recognized as authority; John Jay Coll of Criminal Justice, prof of psychology & forensic studies; New York City Dept of Corrections, former 1st dep commr, commanding officer training acad, clinical psychologist. **ORGANIZATIONS:** Mem 100 Black Men; Nat Assn of Black Psychologists; Nat Assn of Black in Criminal Justice; Am Psychol Assn; Am Correctional Assn. **HONORS/ACHIEVEMENTS:** Num awards professional & pub svc; num articles publ; cited in Am Med Assn Journ; advanced through ranks faster than any man in hist of depart; youngest dep Warden; youngest dep commr. **MILITARY SERVICE:** USAF 1956-59. **BUSINESS ADDRESS:** Clinical Psychologist, New York City Dept of Corr, 100 Centre St, New York, NY 10013.

GASTON, ARTHUR G., SR.
Business executive. **PERSONAL:** Born Jul 04, 1892, Demopolis, AL; married Minnie; children: Arthur G Jr. **EDUCATION:** Graduated Tuggles Inst Birmingham. **CAREER:** TN Coal, Iron and Steel Co; Booker T Washington Burial Soc (later Booker T Washington Ins Co), partner; owner and bd chmn, AG Gaston Home for Senior Citizens; New Grace Hill Cemeteries Inc; Zion Memorial Gardens; Vulcan Realty & Investment Corp; Gaston Gardens I & II; Smith & Gaston Funeral Directors Inc;Citizen Fed Savings Bank; Booker T Washington Broadcasting Co (WENN Radio FM and WAGG-AM). **ORGANIZATIONS:** Founder A G Gaston Boys' Club affil club to Boys' Clubs of America; contrib to scholarships and loans for law students. **HONORS/ACHIEVEMENTS:** Received over 10 honorary degrees; received hundreds of certificates and awards for service to community and country. **MILITARY SERVICE:** AUS. **BUSINESS ADDRESS:** 1728 3 Ave, Birmingham, AL 35203.

GASTON, CLARENCE EDWIN
Professional athlete. **PERSONAL:** Born Mar 17, 1944, San Antonio, TX; married Denise; children: Adrian, Carly. **CAREER:** Atlanta Braves, 1967; San Diego Padres, 1969-74; Atlanta Braves, outfielder/pinch-hitter 1975-77; Pittsburgh Pirates, 1978; Atlanta Braves, 1978; Inter-Amer League, 1979-80; Atlanta Braves, hitting instructor 1981; Toronto Blue Jays, batting coach. **HONORS/ACHIEVEMENTS:** All-Star Season 1970; rep San Diego in All-Star Game at Cincinnati 1970. **BUSINESS ADDRESS:** Coach, Toronto Blue Jays, Box 7777, Adelaide St PO, Toronto, Ontario, Canada M5C 2K7.

GASTON, LINDA SAULSBY
Professional association executive director. **PERSONAL:** Born Jun 15, 1947, San Francisco, CA; daughter of Harvey Harris and Arvis Dixon Harris; married James Gaston, Sep 27, 1985; children: Loren Saulsby, Leslie Saulsby. **EDUCATION:** City Coll of San Francisco, San Francisco CA, AA; State Univ of New York, Albany NY, BA. **CAREER:** Linda Saulsby Mgmt Consulting, Oakland CA, owner; Coopers & Lybrand, Washington DC, Tucson AZ, dir of admin & personnel, 1983-86; Natl Assn of Black Accountants, Washington DC, exec dir, 1986-. **ORGANIZATIONS:** Mem, bd of dir, YWCA, Oakland CA, Tucson AZ, 1981-83, 1985-86; mem, Howard Univ School of Business Advisory Bd, 1987-; pres, Longmead Crossing Homeowners Assn, 1988-; mem, Natl Community Associations Inst, 1988-, Price Waterhouse & Co Minority Recruiting Task Force, 1989-. **HONORS/ACHIEVEMENTS:** President's Membership Council Award, Greater Washington DC Bd of Trade, 1985; articles published: Spectrum (Journal of Natl Assn of Black Accountants), 1987, 1988. **BUSINESS ADDRESS:** Executive Director, Natl Associaiton of Black Accountants, 300 I Street NE, Suite 107, Washington, DC 20002.

GASTON, MACK CHARLES
Military chief executive officer. **PERSONAL:** Born Jul 17, 1940, Dalton, GA; son of John Gaston (deceased) and Felicia Gilliard Gaston; married Lillian Bonds, Aug 15, 1965; children: Sonja Marie. **EDUCATION:** Tuskegee Inst, BS Electronics 1964; US Naval War College, grad level cert 1977; US Industrial Coll of Armed Forces, diploma 1983; Marymount Coll, MBA1984. **CAREER:** USN, electronic officer/combat information officer USS Buck 1965-67, engrg officer USS O'Brien 1967-69, material officer/squad engr destroyer sqd five staff1969-71, personal aide/admin asst navy dir r&d test & eval office of cno 1971-73, exec officer USS Conyngham 1974-76, commanding officer USS Cochrane 1977-79; branch head jr off assignment Navy mil pers cmd 1979-81, commanding officer USS Cone 1981-82, head surface warfare tra branch office of cno 1983-84; US Navy, dir equal oppor div; commanding officer battle cruiser USS Josephus Daniels (CG 27) 1986-88; chief of naval operations strategic studies group (CNO Fellow) 1988-89; surface warfare manpower and training dir 1989-. **ORGANIZATIONS:** Jr Deacon & Sunday Sch Tchr Hopewell Baptist Ch 1953-64; Couns & Career Planner Natl Naval Off Assn Washington DC 1977-; Sunday Sch Tchr Greater Zion Bapt Church 1981-85. **HONORS/ACHIEVEMENTS:** Meritorious Serv Medal; Navy Commendation Medal (two awards one with Combat "V"); Navy Achievement Medal; Natl Defense Serv Medal; Vietnamese Gallantry Cross; Vietnamese Serv Medal with 6 Campaign Stars; Republic of Vietnam Campaign Medal; Sea Serv Ribbon; Humanitarian Ribbon. **MILITARY SERVICE:** USN capt 24 yrs. **HOME ADDRESS:** 42 Polk Ct, Newport, RI 02840. **BUSINESS ADDRESS:** Dir Surface Warfare Manpower and Training, Deputy Chief of Naval Operations for Surface Warfare, Office of the CNO, The Pentagon, Washington, DC 20350-2000.

GASTON, MARILYN HUGHES
Physician, educator. **PERSONAL:** Born Jan 31, 1939, Cincinnati, OH; daughter of Myron Hughes and Dorothy Hughes; married Alonzo; children: Amy, Damon. **EDUCATION:** Miami Univ, AB 1960; Univ of Cincinnati, MD 1964. **CAREER:** Philadelphia Gen Hospital, intern 1965; Childrens Hospital Medical Center, resdent 1967; Community Pediatrics, assoc prof 1968-70; Childrens Hospital Medical Center, asst dir 1968, assoc prof pediatrics 1972-; Cincinnati Comprehensive Sickle Cell Center, dir 1972-; Lincoln Heights Health Center, medical dir 1973-; Howard Univ, asst clinical prof of pediatrics; NIH Sickle Cell Disease Branch Natl Heart Lung & Blood Inst, deputy branch chief; US Piblic Health Serv, captain commissioned corps. **ORGANIZATIONS:** Mem Amer Acad Pediatrics, United Black Faculty Assn, Amer Public Health Assn; medical advisory bd State Crippled Childrens Serv; bd of trustees Childrens Health Assn, Pi Kappa Epsilon 1964; medical dir Commissioned Corps US Public health Serv, NMA. **HONORS/ACHIEVEMENTS:** Outstanding Young Woman of Amer 1973; Outstanding Black Women Cincinnati 1974; City's Young Leader Health 1974; Harriet Tubman Woman of the Year 1976; Commendation Medal Public Health Serv Dept of Health & Human Serv; Health Center names Buford-Gaston; Outstanding Service Medal, Univ of Cincinnati; Distinguished Alumnae Award; NIH Directors Award; Marilyn Hughes Gaston Day, City of Cincinnati OH; Gaston H et al-Proph Penicillin in Sickle Cell Anemia, New England Journal 1986; Special Presentation on Capitol Hill 1989. **BUSINESS ADDRESS:** Deputy Branch Chief, NIH Rockville Pike, Sickle Cell Disease Br, Natl Heart Lung & Blood Inst, Bethesda, MD 20814.

GASTON, MINNIE L.
Educational administrator. **PERSONAL:** Born Apr 03, 1909, Burkville, AL; married A G Gaston. **EDUCATION:** Tuskegee Inst, BS 1938; New York U; Gregg Coll. **CAREER:** Cedartown GA School System, teacher; Minnee Cosmetics, pres; Lowndes County School System, prin; Booker T Washington Insurance Co, first vice pres 1939; Booker T Washington Jr Coll of Business, pres, dir 1943-. **ORGANIZATIONS:** Mem Muscular Dystrophy Assoc of Am 1974-82; exec in residence AuburnUniv 1982; dist lecturer Tuskegee Inst 1983; mem dean's advisory cncl Sch of Bus ALState U; mem adv cnclUniv of AL at Birmingham; mem AL Women's Commission; mem Alpha Kappa Alpha; mem Natl Cncl of Negro Women; exec bd Coalition of 100 Black Women; treas Assoc of Independent Coll and Sch; mem Home Economics State (AL) Adv Comm; trustee St John African Methodist Episcopal Church; mem Birmingham Debate '88 Adv Bd, Jefferson Co Child Develop Council. **HONORS/ACHIEVEMENTS:** EDHE Award AL Assoc of Coll &Univ 1980; appreciation cert AL NAACP Youth Cncl & Coll 1982; Rust Coll Shield Rust Coll 1983; spec awd SCORE 1984; outstanding achievements Jefferson Cty Historical Commission 1984; honorary mem in AAS Livingston U; Alumni Merit Award Tuskegee Inst; Cert of Merit Natl Alumni Assoc Booker T Washington Jr Coll of Business; Great Black Alabamian AL Conf of Black Mayors 1985; Presidential Citation Natl Assoc for Equal Oppor in Higher Educ 1985; Cert of Appreciation Fort Valley State Coll 1985; Meritorious Serv Awd United Negro Coll Fund 1986; Appreciation Awd United Handicap Industries of Amer 1986. **BUSINESS ADDRESS:** President, Dir, BT Washington Jr Coll of Bus, 1527 Fifth Ave N, Birmingham, AL 35203.

GATES, AUDREY CASTINE
Educator. **PERSONAL:** Born Dec 09, 1937, Napoleonville, LA; married George M; children: George M, Geoffrey L. **EDUCATION:** Dillard U, BA 1958; LA Stae U, addtl trng;Univ of New Orleans; Am Mgmt Assn; Dominican Coll. **CAREER:** Mayor's Ofc of Consumer Afrs, asst dir 1972-; Cntrl City Edon Oppty Corp, training & tech asst adv 1971-72; Urban League of Grtr New Orleans, coord 1970-71; Nghbrhd Yth Corps, couns 1969-70; Orleans Parish Sch Sys, tchr 1959-68. **ORGANIZATIONS:** Consumer Adv Bd; mem LA Consumers League; mem Counc of Consumer Orgn; Am Counc of Consumer Intersts; New Orleans Consumer Task Force; Mater Dolorosa Sch PTA; metro area Com Ldrshp Forum 1971; Govs Milk Study Com; US Consumer Prod Safety Adv Bd; State Dept of Educ Consumer Educ Task Force; adv bdOrleans Parish 4-H Clubs. **BUSINESS ADDRESS:** 1 W12 City Hall, New Orleans, LA 70112.

GATES, CLIFFORD E., JR.
Business executive. **PERSONAL:** Born Nov 15, 1946; married Jacqui; children: Angela, Cliff III. **EDUCATION:** Central State Univ, BS 1968; MI State Univ, grad courses in Industrial Mgmt 1971-72; Harvard Univ, MBA Exec Dev Prog 1974. **CAREER:** Pittsburgh Bd of Edn, tchr 1968-69; Westinghouse Elec Corp Bettis Atomic Power Lab, personnel rep/benefits admin 1968-71; General Foods Corp Battle Creek, MI, personnel spec/sr personnel spec 1971-73; General Foods Corp Corp Hdqtrs NY, assoc mgr equal opp/urban affairs 1971-73; Xerox Corp, asst mgr empl relations/mgr empl relations/mgr group mktg & field operations/mgr empl rel/ombudsman 1973-77; Executex Inc Mgmt Consulting Firm, pres 1977-78; Revlon Inc NY, corp vice pres 1978-. **ORGANIZATIONS:** Mem adv bd Black Exec Exchange Prog Natl Urban League; bd dir Negro Ensemble Co; chmn Business Adv Cncl Central State Univ. **HONORS/ACHIEVEMENTS:** Citation for Outstanding Achievement Natl Alliance of Businessmen; Xerox Special Merit Award for Outstanding Perf; Outstanding Young Men of America 1981. **BUSINESS ADDRESS:** Corporate Vice President, Revlon Inc, New York, NY.

GATES, CLIFTON W.
Business executive. **PERSONAL:** Born Aug 13, 1923, Moscow, AR; married Harriet; children: Mark, Lisa. **CAREER:** CW Gates Realty, pres 1959-; Gateway Natl Bank, chrmn 1964-; Lismark Distributing, pres 1975-. **ORGANIZATIONS:** Bd of dirs Municipal Opera, Cardinal Glennon Hosp for Children, Blue Cross, Boy Scouts of Amer, Boys Town of MO, Convention and Visitors Bureau, President's Cncl of St Louis Univ, Gateway Natl Bank, Local Develop Co, St Louis Comprehensive Health Ctr, Civic Entrepreneurs; chmn St Louis Housing Authority;past police commissioner St Louis. **HONORS/ACHIEVEMENTS:** Management Awd City of Hope Beta Gamma Sigma Univ of MO Chapt; St Louis Argus Public Service Awd; listed in Who's Who in Finance and Industry, Who's Who in the World, Who's Who in the Midwest. **MILITARY SERVICE:** AUS 1943-45. **HOME ADDRESS:** 5249 Lindell Blvd, St Louis, MO 63108. **BUSINESS ADDRESS:** President, Lismark Distributing Co, 1350 S Kingshighway Blvd, St Louis, MO 63110.

GATES, HENRY LOUIS, JR.
Educator. **PERSONAL:** Born Sep 16, 1950, Keyser, WV; son of Henry-Louis Gates, Sr and Pauline Augusta Coleman Gates; married Sharon Lynn Adams, Sep 01, 1979; children: Maude Augusta, Elizabeth Helen-Claire. **EDUCATION:** Yale Univ, BA (summa cum laude), 1973; Clare Coll, Cambridge, England, MA, 1974, PhD, 1979. **CAREER:** Time, London Bureau, London, England, staff correspondant, 1973-75; Amer Cyanamid Co, Wayne, NJ, public relations representative, 1975; Yale Univ, New Haven, CT, lecturer in English, 1976-79, asst prof of English, 1979-84, assoc prof of English, 1984-85; Cornell Univ, Ithaca, NY, prof of English, 1985-, WEB Du Bois Prof of Literature, 1988-, dir Black Periodical Fiction project, 1989-. **ORGANIZATIONS:** Pres, Afro-Amer Acad; mem, African Literature Assn, Modern Language Assn of Amer, Union of African Writers, Coll Language Assn, Phi Beta Kappa; mem bd of dir, Black Amer Literature Forum, Critical Inquiry, Cultural Critique, Diacritics, PMLA, Proteus, Studies in Amer Fiction; advisory editor, Contributions to African and Afro-Amer Studies, Critical Studies on Black Life and Culture. **HONORS/ACHIEVEMENTS:** Carnegie Found fellowship for Africa, 1970-71; Phelps fellowship, Yale Univ, 1970-71; Mellon fellowship, Yale Univ, 1973-75, 1983-; A Whitney Griswold fellowship, Yale Univ, 1980; Natl Endowment for the Humanities grants, 1980-84, 1981-82; Rockefeller Found fellowship, 1980-81; MacArthur Prize fellowship, MacArthur Found, 1981-86; Whitney Humanities Center fellowship, 1982-84; Afro-Amer Cultural Center Faculty Prize, 1983; Ford Found grant, 1984-85; Zora Neale Hurston Soc Award for Creative Scholarship, 1986; Honorable Mention, John Hope Franklin Prize, Amer Studies Assn, 1988; Amer Book Award, 1989; Anisfield Book Award for Race Relations, 1989; Candle Award, Morehouse Coll, 1989; author, Figures in Black: Words, Signs, and the Racial Self, 1987, The Signifying Monkey: Towards a Theory of Afro-Amer Literary Criticism, 1988; editor, Our Nig, 1983, Black Literature and Literary Theory, 1984, "Race," Writing, and Difference, 1986, The Classic Slave Narratives, 1987; series editor, The Schomburg Library of Nineteenth-Century Black Women Writers, 1988; co-compiler, Wole Soyinka: A Bibliography of Primary and Secondary Sources, 1986; contributor of articles and reviews to periodicals and journals. **BUSINESS ADDRESS:** Dept of English, Cornell Univ, Rockefeller Hall, Ithaca, NY 14853.

GATES, JACQUELYN KNIGHT
Corporate manager. **PERSONAL:** Born Jul 12, 1951, Brooklyn, NY; married Clifford E Gates, Jr; children: Antoinette, Anthony, Jacquelyn Tiffany. **EDUCATION:** Attended Univ of IL Champainge/Urbana; Brooklyn Coll, BA 1973; New School for Social Rsch, MA. **CAREER:** Agency for Child Develop NY, family counselor 1973-76; NY State Supreme Ct, sec to supreme ct justice 1976-77; JC Penny Corp Headquarters, employment placement rep 1977-79; Revlon Inc, personnel admins/recruiter 1979-81; Paramount Pictures Corp, mgr indust relations NY,NY, 1981-82; Pepsi Cola Co, mgr of professional placement 1982-83; Pepsi-Co Inc Purchase, NY, mgr of corp relations 1983-; private practice, personnel, public affairs cons. **ORGANIZATIONS:** Natl dir resource devel, chair bus women's council Natl Assn of Negro & Bus & Professional Women Club 1985-; 3rd vice pres bd of dir Brooklyn Boro Bd New York Urban League 1978-; mem NAACP; visiting prof Black Exec Exchange Program Natl Urban League; consult Youth Motivation Task Force Natl Alliance of Business; mem Business Adv Council Central State Univ, EDGES Group, Black Retail Action Group. **HONORS/ACHIEVEMENTS:** Comm Leader of Amer 1980; Natl Youth Achvmnt Award NANBPWC 1980; Achvmnt Award Alpha Cosmetologists of Brooklyn 1979; Outstanding Young Woman 1979; Student Achvmnt Award Brooklyn Young Adults NANBPW 1965; Black Achiever in Industry Harlem YMCA 1984; Sojourner Truth Award East New York Club of Brooklyn NANBPW 1984; 100 Young Women of Primise in 21st Century Good Housekeeping Mag 1985; Top 100 Black Bus & Professional Women in Amer Dollars & Sense Mag 1986; Bus Awd KingsCounty Club NANBPWC Inc 1986; Young Achiever Awd Natl Council of Women of USA 1986. **HOME ADDRESS:** 5473 N University Dr Rur Box 197, LauderHill, FL 33351.

GATES, NINA JANE
Health care manager. **PERSONAL:** Born Jul 27, 1947, Beckley, WV; married Charles W Gates Sr; children: Charles Jr, Stephanie Lee-Ann. **EDUCATION:** Applachian Regional Hosp Sch of Nursing, Nursing diploma 1968; Central State Univ, BS 1978; Central MI Univ, MA 1983. **CAREER:** Dayton Sch of Practical Nursing, instructor 1975-78; Good Samaritan Hosp & Health Ctr, continusing educ coord 1978-80, supervisor 1980-86, asst dir clinics 1986-. **ORGANIZATIONS:** Mem Montgomery County Joint Voc Adv Bd 1978-; safety serv instructor Amer Red Cross 1978-; leader Buckeye Girl Scouts 1983-; regional recording sec Iota phi Lambda Sor Inc 1985-; financial sec Jack & Jill of Amer Inc 1986-; mem Ambulatory Nurses Assoc 1986-; mem Delta Sigma Theta Sor Dayton AlumnaeChapt. **HONORS/ACHIEVEMENTS:** Outstanding Young Women of Amer 1983. **HOME ADDRESS:** 5250 Big Bend Dr, Dayton, OH 45427.

GATES, OTIS A., III
Business executive. **PERSONAL:** Born Feb 26, 1935, Chattanooga, TN; married Barbara L; children: George, Theresa, Todd, Khari. **EDUCATION:** Harvard Coll, AB; Harvard Grad Sch of Bus Admin, MBA. **CAREER:** Kaufman & Boad Homes Inc, asst to gen mgr 1963-64; MI Blue Shield, mgr computer systems & opers 1964-66; Zayre Corp, mgr computer systems devel 1966-68; Arthur Andersen & Co, mgr 1969-76, partner 1976-. **ORGANIZATIONS:** Youth servc com MA Bay United Way Fund 1974-; bd of trustees Univ Hospital 1983-; bd of dirs Jobs for Youth; bd dirs Danforth Museum. **MILITARY SERVICE:** USAF capt retired reserve. **BUSINESS ADDRESS:** Arthur Andersen & Co, 100 Federal, Boston, MA 02110.

GATES, PAUL EDWARD
Oral and maxillofacial surgeon. **PERSONAL:** Born Aug 16, 1945, Keyser, WV; son of Henry Louis Gates Sr and Pauline Coleman Gates; divorced; children: Eboni, Jennifer. **EDUCATION:** Potomac State Jr Coll, AA 1964; WV U, BA 1966 WVUniv Sch of Dentistry, DDS 1970; NYUniv Sch of Dentistry, 1971; Harlem Hosp Ctr, Resd 1970-73. **CAREER:** Fairleigh Dickinson Dental School, oral surgeon 1973, asst clinical prof 1973-76, dir minority affairs 1979-86, prof 1986, asst vice pres acad admin 1986-87; acting dean Coll of Dental Medical 1988-89; asst to pres for health planning and policy 1988-89. **ORGANIZATIONS:** Mem ADA Student 1966-70, 73-77; Xi Psi Phi Frat; WVUniv Alumni Assn; student Am Dental Assn; mem Passaic Co Dental Soc 1973-77; NJ Dept Dentistry 1973-77; bd dir INCAA 1973-74; NJ Dental Soc 1973; Am Bd Oral Surgery Diplomate 1975; Am Soc Oral Surgery 1977; Am Soc Dental Anesthesiology; Am Assn Hosp Dentistry 1977; NJ Soc Dental Anesthesia; Harlem Hosp Soc Oral Surgery; attdg oral surgeon St Joseph's Hosp; NJ Dept Dentistry 1973-77; bd dir INCAA 1973-74; co-chmn Hlth & Nutrition Com Paterson Headstart; vice pres Southside Multiservice Ctr Paterson Task Force; editor Jour Passaic Co Dental Soc; exec com Southside Multiservice Ctr Paterson Task Force; chief of oral & maxillofacial surg & assoc chmn Dept of Dent St Joseph's Hosp & Med Ctr; bd trustees St Joseph's Hops & Med Ctr 1984-87; Natl Dental Assn Commonwealth Dental Society. **HONORS/ACHIEVEMENTS:** Outstanding Young Men of Amer 1970,81; OKU Natl Dental Honor Soc 1980; Amer Council on Educ Fellow 1984-85; publ "Meningitis as a Result of Post Extraction Infection Report of a Case" Jrnl Oral Surgery 1972; publ" Visceral Kaposis's Sarcoma presenting with Gingival Lesions" Oral Surgery Oral Med & Oral Pathology 1980, "Oral Lesions in Crohn's Disease, Report of a Case" NY State Dental Jrnl, "The Dental Cartridge-Its Contents & Clinical Implications" DMD 1980, "Calcium Nutrition & the Aging Process, A Review" Jrnl of Gerodontology 1985, "The Dental Cartridge It's Contents & Clinical Implications" DMD 1985; "Minority Recruitment and Retention at FDU" Journal Natl Dental Assn 1988; Fellow Amer Coll of Dentist 1989. **BUSINESS ADDRESS:** Asst Vice Pres Acad Admin, Fairleigh DickinsonUniv, 110 Fuller Pl, Hackensack, NJ 07601.

GATES, THOMAS MICHAEL
Educator. **PERSONAL:** Born Jan 09, 1943, St Louis, MO; married Doris Atwater; children: Steven A, Genice Arnold. **EDUCATION:** Howard Univ, BFA 1970; CA State Univ Sacramento, MA 1972. **CAREER:** Economic Opportunity Council, instructor, drama workshop 1971-72; CA State Univ, dir, black theatre program 1972-; CA State Univ, Sacramento, assoc prof, theatre, prof theatre. **ORGANIZATIONS:** Mem Amer Theatre Assoc, CA Black Staff & Faculty Assoc, Sacramento Kwanza Comm; guest dir Black Arts/West Theatre Seattle WA 1975; actor Film "South by Northwest" 1975; dir "The River Nigger"1976; dir five black-one-act plays 1979; directed/produced 40 one-act plays and 17 full length plays at CA State Univ-Sacramento. **HONORS/ACHIEVEMENTS:** Natl Finalist and Awd of Excellence Amer Coll Theatre Festival 1973; Proclamation by Mayor City of Sacramento 1973; Resolution by State Senate; Joint Resolution CA State Assembly & Senate 1985; production "The Sty of the Blind Pig" first black production to be performed in the JFK Ctr for Performing Arts. **MILITARY SERVICE:** USAF E-4 4 years. **BUSINESS ADDRESS:** Professor-Theatre Arts, CA State University, 6000 J St, Sacramento, CA 95819.

GATEWOOD, ALGIE C.
Educational administrator. **PERSONAL:** Born Dec 17, 1951, Wadesboro, NC; son of Haywood J Gatewood and Bessie M Gatewood; married Elaine Thornton, Oct 1973; children: Wendolyn Charmaine, Andrea Marzina, Algie Carver Jr. **EDUCATION:** Livingstone Coll, BA Social Science/History 1973; Appalachian State Univ, MA Higher Educ/Coll Admin 1977; NC State, Certificate in Guidance & Counseling 1982; Univ of NC, Doctoral Studies, 1988. **CAREER:** Anson Tech, community serv 1974-80, dir of inst research, dir of human resources devel & project dir for community serv 1980-; dean of students. **ORGANIZATIONS:** Mem Phi Beta Sigma Fraternity 1971-; field reader US Office of Educ 1980-82; task force mem State Dept of Com Coll 1983-84; trustee Ebenezer Baptist Church 198-; vice pres Professional Videa Serv Inc 1985-. **HOME ADDRESS:** Route 2 Box 161, Peachland, NC 28133.

GATEWOOD, LUCIAN B.
Government official. **PERSONAL:** Born Jun 25, 1945. **EDUCATION:** Univ WI, PhD 1977; MA 1969; Kent State U, BA 1967. **CAREER:** Dept of Employment & Training Adminstrn, spl asst; Ernest G Green, spl asst; Empl & Training US Dept Labor, asst sec; AEC, jr trne; Unoin Carbide Corp Mining & Metals Div, sr trne;Univ WI, rsrch asst; Kent State

U, coord instr black studies; Labor & Human Resources OH State U, asst prof. **ORGANIZATIONS:** Mem Indsl Rels Rsrch Assn. **HONORS/ACHIEVEMENTS:** Publ "Uncle Tome in the Exec Suite" 1976; "The Black Aratisan in the US" 1890-1930; "The Rev of Black Polit Economy" 1974; "Factfinding in Tchr Disputes the WI experience" monthly labor rev 1974; dissertation grant manpower adminstrn US dept labor; advanced oppor flwsp u WI; rsrch asstspUniv WI; listed Who's Who in Am Coll's & U's 1967; blue key NHS; mem Omicron Delta Kappa Nat Ldrsp Frat; natl polit sci hon Pi Sigma Alpha. **BUSINESS ADDRESS:** Office of Asst Sec of Employ &, 200 Constitution Ave NW, Washington, DC 20210.

GATEWOOD, WALLACE LAVELL
Educator, economist. **PERSONAL:** Born May 31, 1946, West Bend, KY; son of Cecil Gatewood and Minnie Lucas Gatewood; married Sharon JM Oliver, Sep 29, 1985; children: Eboni, Shannon, Ashley. **EDUCATION:** Berea Coll, Berea KY, BS 1968; Oberlin Coll, Oberlin OH, Post-Baccalaureate Certificate 1969; Washington Univ St Louis, MBA 1971; Univ of IL Champaign-Urbana, PhD Labor & Industrial Relations 1975. **CAREER:** W L Gatewood & Assoc Consulting Firm, pres 1979-; FMCS, labor arbitrator 1980; independent certified financial planner 1980-; Florida A&M Univ Tallahassee, asst prof economics 1974; Florida State Univ Tallahassee, asst prof mgmt labor relations 1974-77; Morgan State Univ Baltimore, assoc prof business & economics 1977-79; Univ of Baltimore, assoc prof mgmt & labor 1980-82; Baruch Coll NYC, asst prof 1982-84; Coppin State Coll Baltimore, assoc prof mgmt science 1984-86; Morgan State Univ, prof business admin & mgmt 1986-, chair 1988-; Long & Foster Real Estate Inc, real estate agent 1987-89; Century 21 Associated Inc, real estate agent 1989-. **ORGANIZATIONS:** Mem Amer Soc for Productivity Improvement; Amer Soc of Training & Devel; Industrial Relations Research Assn; Natl Black MBA Assn; Natl Economics Assn; mem employment advisory comm Baltimore Urban League 1968-; mem NAACP Baltimore 1980; mem Academy of Mgmt, Assn of Human Resources Mgmt & Organizational Behavior; exec bd, pres Maryland Chapter AHRMOB; mem Baltimore Mktg Assn; coord NAACP Lecture Series 1981-82; mem Howard County Commission for Women 1981-84; coord Mgmt Science Serv Coppin State Coll 1984-86; sec Patapsco Valley Regional Council Episcopalian Diocese 1987-88; mem dir Center for Financial Success 1986-. **HONORS/ACHIEVEMENTS:** Scholarship Berea Coll 1964-68; Post-Baccalaureate Fellowship, Oberlin Coll 1968-69; Consortium Fellowship, Washington Univ 1969-71; Fellowship, Univ of Illinois 1971-73; Research Intern, Congressional Budget Office 1978; Faculty Fellow, Social Security Admin 1979; Man of the Year, Soc for Advancement of Mgmt MSU 1980; Advisor of the Year Univ of Baltimore 1981. **HOME ADDRESS:** 4206 Hanwell Rd, Randallstown, MD 21133.

GATHE, JOSEPH C
Physician. **PERSONAL:** Born Dec 15, 1929, Scott, LA; married Marion; children: Joseph Jr, Jeffrey, Joy, Julia, Jillian. **EDUCATION:** Xavier U, New Orleans, BS 1949; St Louis U, MD 1953. **CAREER:** Riverside Surgical Clinic, owner 1960-. **ORGANIZATIONS:** Treas Pan-texas Mortgage 1970-75; mem State Bd Educ 1972-80; advisory comUniv Savings 1982-; pres Aid to Culturally Deprived Children. **HONORS/ACHIEVEMENTS:** Outstanding citizenship award Urban League 1949. **MILITARY SERVICE:** USAF capt 1954-56. **BUSINESS ADDRESS:** Surgeon, 2914 Blodgett, Houston, TX 77004.

GATLIN, ELISSA L.
Educational administrator. **PERSONAL:** Born Aug 10, 1948, Gary, IN. **EDUCATION:** W MI Univ Kalamazoo, BS Speech Pathology 1970; MI State Univ E Lansing, MA Speech Pathology 1970, PhD Speech Pathology. **CAREER:** MI School for the Blind Lansing, speech & language therapist & pre-school language consultant 1971-73; Provincial Hosp & Surgi-Clinic Lansing, paraprofessional, counselor 1973-76; MI State Univ E Lansing, teaching asst dept of audiology & speech science 1973-76; NE State Univ, Tahlequah OK, asst prof of special educ & clinic coord 1976-80; MI State Univ, adjunct asst prof dept of aud & speech science 1980-; Coll of Osteo Medicine, MI State Univ, dir of admissions 1980-85; Western Michigan Univ, dir Center for Human Services 1985. **ORGANIZATIONS:** Mem Amer Speech Hearing & Lang Assn; mem Amer Assn for Couns & Dev; mem Natl Assn of Med Min Educators, NAACP, Delta Sigma Theta Sor Inc, oral appraisal bd MI Dept of Civil Serv; bds dir Greater Kalamazoo YWCA, Kalamazoo Center for Independent Living, Red Cross; exec comm Southern Tier Chap of the March of Dimes; mem Kalamazoo County Children and Youth Servs Coordinating Council-Chair Adolescent Pregnancy and Parenthood Comm; mem Amer Pub Health Assn; mem Amer Soc of Allied Health Professions; mem Nat'l Soc of Allied Health Professions; mem Nat'l Rehabilitation Assn. **HONORS/ACHIEVEMENTS:** Who's Who Among Students in Amer Colls & Univs W MI Univ Kalamazoo 1970; Outstanding Yount Woman in Amer Awd OK 1978; mem Delta Kappa Gamma Hon Soc of Women Educators Tahlequah OK 1978; Who's Who in the SW OK 1979; Who's Who in the Midwest 1981; Who's Who Among Black Americans 1981. **BUSINESS ADDRESS:** Director, Ctr for Human Servs, Western MichiganUniv, Henry Hall, Kalamazoo, MI 49008.

GATSON, WILINA IONE
Administrative assistant. **PERSONAL:** Born Apr 17, 1925, Galveston, TX; daughter of Willie Lee Garner (deceased) and Ina Ivory Sibley Garner; divorced; children: Natalie, Kenneth. **EDUCATION:** Sch of Voca NursUniv of TX Med Br, 1954; TX So U, 1955-57; NursUniv of TX Med Br, BS 1960. **CAREER:** Moody State Sch for Cerebral Palsied CholdUniv of TX Med Branch, first black nursing supr 1965-; John Sealy Hosp, LVN on psychiatry; St Mary's Hosp US Pub Health Hosp asst night sup; Galveston Coll & UTMB Sch of Nurs guest lecturer. **ORGANIZATIONS:** Mem NAACP-TNA; ANA; Nat Coun Negro Women Inc; held various off in Delta Signa Theta Sor Inc; Ladies Aux Amer Leg; UTMB Alumni Assn; Versatile Dames;Civil Liberty; Sickle Cell Anemia Found; Jack & Jill of Amer Inc; mem First Union Baot Courts of Calanthes Ch; served on many bds in comm & state during past 20 years coms in Delta on local & regnl levels. **HONORS/ACHIEVEMENTS:** First black to grad from UTMB Deg Nurs Sch 1960; first black to serve as Off in UT Nurs Alumni Assn 1961-62; rec outstndg student of year award from UTMB in 1958; has been honored on various occas by local groups & chs for comm serv; first black to receive Distinguished Alumnus Awd UTMB School of Nursing & Alumni Assn in 99 years 1989. **BUSINESS ADDRESS:** Adm Asst, St Mary's Hospital, 404 St Mary's Blvd, Galveston, TX 77550.

GAUFF, JOSEPH F., JR.
Educator. **PERSONAL:** Born Apr 20, 1939, Helena, MT; son of Joseph F Gauff Sr; divorced; children: Lisa M, Denise A, Nathan A, Rebecca R. **EDUCATION:** Univ of Washington, BA Business 1971, MBA 1973, PhD 1979. **CAREER:** Western Washington St Univ, asst prof of mktg 1977; Univ of Denver, asst prof of mkts 1977-80; General Telephone & Electronics, mktg rsch specialist & forecasting 1980-82; Grambling State Univ, prof of mktg 1982-83; California State Univ-Fresno, prof of mktg 1983-86; Florida A&M Univ, prof of mktg 1986-. **ORGANIZATIONS:** Supervisor King County Juvenile Court 1969-77; mem Natl Chap AAS 1974-; partner Business Insight Consulting 1979, 1980; bd of dir mem United Way Denver 1979; bd of dir mem Fresno Madera Counties Chap Red Cross 1984, 1986. **HONORS/ACHIEVEMENTS:** Publications, "Consumer Aspects of Marketing in a Small Health Maintenance Organization," Univ of WA 1979; Hewlett-Packard BASIC, Bellwether Press 1986; "Health Care Marketing," Health Marketing Quarterly Vol 3 No 4 1986; "A Prospectus for a Conceptualization of Preventive Health Behavior Theory," Health Marketing Quarterly Vol 3 No 4 1986. **HOME ADDRESS:** 220-8 Belmont Rd, Tallahassee, FL 32301. **BUSINESS ADDRESS:** Professor of Marketing, Florida A&M University, School of Business & Industry, Tallahassee, FL 32307.

GAULT, MARIAN HOLNESS
Educator. **PERSONAL:** Born Oct 01, 1934, Panama, Panama;children: Taisia Marie, Daryl Justin. **EDUCATION:** St Agnes Med Ctr, Nursing 1952-55; Villanova Univ, 1962; Glassboro Coll, BA Health Ed 1971, MA Ed 1978;; Drexel Univ Philadelphia, Mgmt Cert 1980. **CAREER:** West Park Hosp, admin suprv 1963-64; Roxborough School of Nursing, nurse ed 1965; SUNY Downstate Med Ctr, teaching, rsch nurse 1966-67; Washington Mem Hosp, dir nursing 1972-78; Einstein Med Ctr, asst dir nursing admin 1979-81; NJ State Dept of Ed, cons, ed of health. **ORGANIZATIONS:** Consult urban ed State Dept Ed 1968; chairperson comm for action NJ Soc Nursing Admin 1978; natl consult jona listing Palpack Entr 1978; seminars, conf, workshops Palpack Entr; bd mem Utopia Youth Mission; mem Natl Assoc Female Exec, Amer Nurses Assoc, Natl League Nursing. **HONORS/ACHIEVEMENTS:** Letter of Commendation for Public Serv US Senator William Cahill 1969; Distinguished Alumnae St Agnes Med Ctr Class, 1955, 1980. **HOME ADDRESS:** 11 Yale Road, Atco, NJ 08004. **BUSINESS ADDRESS:** Consultant, Educator, Health, New Jersey Dept of Education, 225 West State St, Trenton, NJ 08625.

GAULT, WILLIE JAMES
Professional athlete. **PERSONAL:** Born Sep 05, 1960, Griffin, GA; son of James Gault Jr and Willie Mae Roberts; married Dainnese Mathis, Jun 11, 1983; children: Shakari Denise. **EDUCATION:** Univ of TN Knoxville, Mktg 1979-83. **CAREER:** US Olympic Team, track & field 1980; US Natl Team, track & field 1980-83; Chicago Bears, wide receiver pro football; Winter Olympics Bobsleigh, 1988; Los Angeles Raiders, pro athlete. **ORGANIZATIONS:** Chmn ministry Lay Witnesses for Christ 1983-; public speaker for schools & churches, Lou Garett commercial 1983; Distonia Commercial 1985; Fair Housing Commerical City of Chicago; pres Gault's Retail Store (men/ladies); natl spokesperson for AIDS and diabetes associations. **HONORS/ACHIEVEMENTS:** 1st man in history of NCAA to win both 60 yards & 60 yard hurdles 1982; MVP Univ of TN Track & Football Team 1983; Athlete of the Year in the Southeastern Conf 1983; NFL All Rookie Team Football Chicago Bears 1983; world record in 4x100 relay track & field 1983; world record 4x110 hurdlers track & field 1982. **HOME ADDRESS:** 6760 W 86th Pl, #5, Los Angeles, CA 90045.

GAVIN, JAMES RAPHAEL, III
Physician. **PERSONAL:** Born Nov 23, 1945, Mobile, AL; son of James R Gavin, II and Bessie S Gavin; married Dr Annie Ruth Jackson Gavin, Jun 19, 1971; children: Raphael Hakkim, Lamar Kenyon. **EDUCATION:** Livingstone Coll, BS (Magna Cum Laude) 1966; Emory Univ, PhD 1970; Duke Univ Medical School, MD 1975. **CAREER:** Natl Insts of Health, staff assoc 1971-73; Duke Univ Hospital, pathologist 1975-76; US Public Health Service, commander 2 1/2 yrs active, 11 1/2 yrs reserves; Washington Univ School of Medicine, assoc prof medicine 1979-86; Univ of OK Med Center, prof of medicine 1986-, chief diabetes sect 1987-; OUHSC, OK City, William K Warren prof of Diabetes Studies, 1989-. **ORGANIZATIONS:** Life mem Alpha Phi Alpha 1963-; consultant Eli Lilly/Upjohn/Pfizer 1979-, Robert Wood Johnson Found 1982-; bd sec King-Fanon Mental Health Center 1983-85; bd of dirs Amer Diabetes Assn 1983-87; mem Sigma Pi Phi 1985-; bd of dirs Alpha Educ Foundation 1986-; mem Alpha Omega Alpha; editorial bd Amer J Physiology 1982-; natl program dir & sr program consultant, Robert Wood Johnson Foundation, 1987-; trustee, OK State Student Loan Authority, 1989-94. **HONORS/ACHIEVEMENTS:** Clincial Teacher of the Year Barnes Hosp Dept Med 1981-82; Wm Alexander Leadership Award Epsilon Lambda Alpha Phi Alpha 1982; St Louis Sentinel Special Achiever St Louis Sentinel 1982; Distinguished Alumnus of HBI NAFEO 1987; Editoral Board, Amer Journal of Medical Sciences, 1989-. **BUSINESS ADDRESS:** Professor of Medicine, Univ of Oklahoma Med Ctr, 941 Stanton Young Blvd, 302 BSEB, Oklahoma City, OK 73190.

GAVIN, L. KATHERINE
Educational administrator. **PERSONAL:** Born in Chicago Heights, IL. **EDUCATION:** Chicago State U, BA 1952; Columbia U, MA 1963; Nova U, EdD 1976. **CAREER:** Prairie State Coll, dir peronalized learning program 1970-, dir child devel progran 1968; Lincoln School, Chicago Heights School Dist #170, prin 1966; Chicago Heights School Dist #170, dean of students, classroom instructor. **ORGANIZATIONS:** Helped found IL Assn of Personalized Learning Programs 1974; mem exec com conducts many workshops/Presenter at many confs/eg SESS-IAPLP-NCTE; mem S Suburban Chicgo Chap of Links Inc; chariperson bd of dirs Dr Chrles E Gavin Meml Found; mem NAACP PUSH. **HONORS/ACHIEVEMENTS:** Outstanding citizens award PUSH; outstanding civic and serv to youth S Suburb Chicago Chap of Links Inc; scholarship image award Fred Hampton Found; lifetime hon ALUMNI Assn Gov State U; mem Hall of Fame Bloom Township High Sch 1980; recognition award outstanding serv Prairie State Coll. **BUSINESS ADDRESS:** 202 S Halsted St, Chicago Heights, IL 60411.

GAY, BENJAMIN
Clergyman, educator. **PERSONAL:** Born Oct 22, 1916, Valdosta, GA; married Johnnie Morgan. **EDUCATION:** Morris Brown Coll, AB; Turner Theol Sem, BD. **CAREER:** AME Mem, minister. **ORGANIZATIONS:** Tau Beta Chap Phi Beta Sigma Frat 1974; NAACP; treas GA Ann Conf; bd tsts Morrison Brown Coll; past mem Gen Bd of African Meth Epis Ch; natl secAlumni Assn of Turner Theol Sem. **HONORS/ACHIEVEMENTS:** Ldrsp recog Civil Rights Movement; religious achvmt award Nat Alumni Assn; outsdng pastor of yr Morris Brown Coll 1975; award of the GA Ann Conf forComm Serv; Ann Founder's Day Speaker 1977; dr of humane letters degree AME Ch 1977. **BUSINESS ADDRESS:** PO Box 1151, Savannah, GA 31401.

GAY, BIRDIE SPIVEY
Media specialist. **PERSONAL:** Born Mar 13, 1918, Atlanta; married Howard Donald.

EDUCATION: Morris Brown Coll, Grad 1939; AtlantaUniv Sch of Library Svc, 1962. **CAREER:** Brooks County, tchr 1939-41; Eatonton, GA, 1941-42; Moutlrie, GA, tchr, librn 1942-45; ER Carter Elem Sch Atlanta, 1946-59; librn & media spec 1959-. **ORGANIZATIONS:** Mem Atlanta GA Assn & Educators; NEA; GA Am Library Assn; mem Com on Adminstrn YWCA; solicitor Cancer Drive, Easter, Retarded Children, Muscular Dystrophy; mem NAACP; UNCF; Morris Brown Alumni Assn; Eta Sigma chpt, Sigma Gamma Rho Sor Beta Phi Mu intl library sci Hon Frat 1961. **HONORS/ACHIEVEMENTS:** Tchr of yr ER Carter Sch 1960-61; outstanding serv plaque Sigma Gamma Rho Sor 1970. **BUSINESS ADDRESS:** E R Carter Sch, 80 Ashby St NW, Atlanta, GA 30314.

GAY, EDDIE C.
Chemical engineer. **PERSONAL:** Born May 13, 1940, Starkville, MS; married Sylvia J; children: Steven E, Richard C. **EDUCATION:** BS 1962; DSc 1967. **CAREER:** Argonne Nat Lab Battery Prog; mgr 1975; Argonne Natl Lab Battery Prgm, grp ldr 1941-75; Lithium-chalcogen Cell Devel Argonne Nat Lab, problem ldr 1969-71; Lithium & Chalcogen Cell Devel Argonne Nat Lab, asst engr 1968-69. **ORGANIZATIONS:** Mem Electrochemical Soc; Am Inst Chem Engr; sigma xi; pres Nat Orgn Professional Advancement Black Chemists & Chem Engr; mem Faith United Protestant Ch. **HONORS/ACHIEVEMENTS:** faith United Protestant Ch schlorship Rosalie Tilles Scholarship; resident res Thesis Award Argonne Nat Lab; dist military Student Grad. **MILITARY SERVICE:** AUS capt 1967-68. **BUSINESS ADDRESS:** Chem Engineering Div, 9700 S Cass, Argonne, IL 60439.

GAY, HELEN PARKER
City official. **PERSONAL:** Born Mar 14, 1920, Rocky Mount, NC; daughter of Mr & Mrs Frank L Parker, Sr; children: Leslie. **EDUCATION:** Scotia Coll, Barber; NC State Coll. **CAREER:** Employment Security Com of NC, interviewer II 37 years; Rocky Mount City Council, council mem; re-elected council member for 4 years, 1987. **ORGANIZATIONS:** Reg IV chairperson Natl OIC Bd 1984-89; 2nd vice pres NC Elected Municipal Officer 1989; bd mem Fountain Correctional School for Women 1984-85; bd mem Private Ind Council 1984-89; bd chairperson Rocky Mount OIC 1984-85; 1st Black female elected to Rocky Mount City Cncl; chairperson Trustee Bd Mt Pizgah Presbyterian Ch Rocky Mount, NC; first black female elected mayor pro tem Rocky Mount City Council 1985; vice chair NC League of Municipal Comm and Economic Devel Comm; chairman 1989. **HONORS/ACHIEVEMENTS:** 1st place Merit Awd Emp Sec Com of NC 1950; 2nd place Merit Awd Emp Sec Com of NC 1960; 1st Black elected as president of the NC Chap Intl Assn of Personnel im Employment Sec 1972-73; chosen as one of Sigma Gamma Rho Sor Inc Outstanding Women of the 20th Century, Honorary mem of Sigma Gamma Rho Sor Inc 1986; mem Rocky Mount Moles Inc 1988; honorary life mem Presbyterian Women Rocky Mt 1989. **HOME ADDRESS:** 1629 Kings Circle, Rocky Mount, NC 27801.

GAY, JAMES F.
Attorney at law, business executive. **PERSONAL:** Born Dec 09, 1942, Norfolk, VA; married Marlynn Miller; children: James F Jr. **EDUCATION:** Norfolk State Coll, BS Chem 1965; Univ of VA Law School, JD 1968. **CAREER:** Allied Chem Corp, legal adv 1968; Natl Business League, asst to pres 1969; Tidewater Area Business League, past pres; Coastal Pharmaceutical Co Inc, pres 1970-77; Energy Dynamics Inc, pres; Legal Center of Gay & Simmons, sr partner; Aqua Dynamics, pres. **ORGANIZATIONS:** Mem Natl Bar Assn, Natl Platform Soc, VA State Bar, Amer Judicature Soc, Amer Bar Assn, Twin City-Bar Assn, Old Dom Bar Assn; gen council, bd mem Natl Business League; mem Natl Soc for Prevention of Cruelty to Animals, Planned Parenthood, Cancer Assn, Norfolk Comm for Imp of Educ, JCC, Alpha Phi Alpha. **HONORS/ACHIEVEMENTS:** Phi Beta Lambda Business Leadership Awd. **BUSINESS ADDRESS:** President, Aqua Dynamics, 1317 E Brambleton Ave, Norfolk, VA 23504.

GAY, MILTON F., JR.
Priest, urban planner. **PERSONAL:** Born Jan 23, 1942, Norfolk, VA; married Joelena Wells Gay; children: Millen Annette, Milton, III. **EDUCATION:** Norfolk State Coll, BS 1963; Episcopal Div School Cambridge, MDiv 1967; Howard Univ Washington DC, MUS 1971; Publ Policy Training Inst Wash DC, Certof Completion 1972-73; Amer Univ Wash DC, MPA 1982. **CAREER:** YMCA Monrovia Liberia, world serv worker 1963-64; Norfolk State Coll, lecturer 1967-68; Grace Episcopal Church Norfolk, asst rctr 1967-69; St Monica Episcopal Chapel Wash DC, vicar 1969-71; Analy of Group Behavior Howard Univ, grad asst 1970-71; Morgan State Coll, lecturer 1970-71; Yale Univ Drug DependencyInst, training staff 1971; DC Mental Health Assoc Wash, exec dir 1971-72; Mayor of Washington DC, spec asst 1972-73; Dept Human Resources Wash, 1973-81; Commiss of Publ Health, spec assst 1981-82; DC Mental Health Admin, gen asst admin. **ORGANIZATIONS:** Pres VA NAACP Youth & Coll 1969-71; bd of dir NW Gardens Ballroom 1970-73, Visitors Serv Ctr 1972; founder Drug Info Inst Wash DC 1971; mem Downtown Jaycees 1971-; founder Ch & Corr Group DC 1972; bd dir Council Chs Greater Wash, chmn Task Force on Health Rehab & Differing Sexual Life Styles 1972-; mem Budget Comm DC Health & Welfare Council 1973-; reg III rep Natl Black Caucus on Alcoholism 1974-; bd dirs Mission of Comm Concern 1975-; treas Mary M Bethune Inst 1975-; interim rector St Timothy's Episcopal Church 1976; civilian replace chaplain, Andrews Air Force Base 1977; interim rector St Christopher's Episcopal Church 1977; chmn Prince George Co MD Nursing Home Adv Comm 1978-80; keeper of fin Omega Psi Phi Gamma Pi Chap 1979-80; mem Jack & Jill ofAmer Fathers Club, Prince George Cty MD 1979-; dr of chiropractic humanities Sherman Coll Spartanburg 1981; mem Childrens Intl Summer Vlgs Inc 1981-;active in various drug prog, black ecumenical training & counseling; mem Omega Psi Phi; bd dir Midtown Montessori School; bd dir E Harris Med Student Fund. **HONORS/ACHIEVEMENTS:** Listed in Who's Who in Amer Univ & Coll 1962; Salmon-Wheaton Prize 1966,67; Amer Bible Soc Awd 1967; Natl Inst Mental Health Fellow 1971; Pi Lambda Sigma Honor Soc Awd Human Relations Daniel Payne Coll Birmingham 1971; AL A&M Univ Citation for Serv & Counel, Inst on Drug Dependence 1971; listed in Who's Who in Religion III; Ploughman & Fisherman Club of Prince George MD; Public Serv Awd Natl Assoc of Black Chiropractics. **HOME ADDRESS:** 9709 Dorval Ave, Upper Marlboro, MD 20772.

GAY, WILLIAM
Professional football player. **PERSONAL:** Born May 28, 1955; married Gwen; children: Ruben, Lauren. **EDUCATION:** Attended San Diego City Coll; Southern Cal. **CAREER:** Detroit Lions, defensive end 1978-. **ORGANIZATIONS:** Volunteer comm work for Detroit Mayor Coleman Young; past mem celeb comm for the Sarnia/Lambton Centre for Children and Youth in Sarnia, Ontario. **HONORS/ACHIEVEMENTS:** Coll, as a Trojan led SC in minutes played in final two seasons; caught 26 passes in a run-oriented defense; profl, during 1984 perf 52 tackles and 23 assisted tackles in 16 starts.

GAYLE, ADDISON, JR.
Educator, author, poet. **PERSONAL:** Born Jun 02, 1932, Newport News, VA; married Rosalie Norwood. **EDUCATION:** City Coll, BA Jonas Salk Scholarship 1965; Univ CA, MA 1966. **CAREER:** Doubleday & Random House, consulting minority writers; Black Lines Magazine, editorial staff; Third World Press, editorial adv; The NY Times, book reviewer 1968-70; City Coll of NY, lecturer 1969; Univ of WA, visiting prof 1971; Livingston Coll, asst prof 1971-72; Baruch Coll, prof. **ORGANIZATIONS:** Mem Author's Guild; PEN; comm mem Black Arts & Cultural Festival; mem Baruch Coll Affirmative Action Com; Univ Faculty Senate; Chancellor's Com on Prisons & theUniv Devel of Resource Ctr, Search Comm for Ctr Dir; mem Grad Ctr Com on programs in english. **HONORS/ACHIEVEMENTS:** Publs, "Black Expression" 1969, "The Black Situation" 1970, "The Black Aesthetic" 1971, "Bondage Freedom & Beyond" 1971, "Oak & Ivy, A Biography of Paul Laurence Dunbar" 1971, "The Black Poet at War" 1972, "The Way of the New World" 1975, "Wayward Child, A Personal Odyssy" 1977, "Richard Wright, Ordeal of a Native Son" 1980. **MILITARY SERVICE:** USAF. **BUSINESS ADDRESS:** Professor, Baruch College, 17 Lexington Ave, New York, NY 10010.

GAYLE, HELENE D.
Epidemiologist. **EDUCATION:** Barnard College, New York, NY, BS, 1976; University of Pennsylvania, Philadelphia, PA, MD; Johns Hopkins University, Baltimore, MD, masters degree. **CAREER:** CDC Epidemic Intelligence Service, staff member, 1984-86; Centers for Disease Control, Atlanta, GA, staff member, 1986-. **BUSINESS ADDRESS:** Centers fro Disease Control, Mailstop G-29, 1600 Clifton Road, Atlanta, GA 30333. *

GAYLE, IRVING CHARLES
Assistant secretary & treasurer. **PERSONAL:** Born Dec 29, 1920, New Orleans, LA; married Shirley Washington; children: Kim Gayle, James. **EDUCATION:** Leland Coll, AB 1942; Dillard U, 1938-39; Army Adminstrn Sch. **CAREER:** Gertrude Geddes Willis Life Ins Co, asst sec & treas 1955; Liberty Loan & Investment Co, mgr 1950-55; US PO 1946-50; Gayle's Music & Book Store Inc, pres 1973; Lady Bronze Cosmetics Inc, dir; Central City Econ Opportunity Corp, dir; New Orleans-sickle Cell Anemia Found, dir. **ORGANIZATIONS:** Sec Nat Ins Assn 1971; pres New Orleans Ins Exec Council 1974-76; sec Nat Bapt Laymen's Movement 1963-67; C of C New Orleans Area. **HONORS/ACHIEVEMENTS:** Serv Award New Orleans Ins Exec Council 1976; serv award Nat Ins Assn 1975. **MILITARY SERVICE:** AUS msgt 1943-45. **BUSINESS ADDRESS:** 2128 Jackson Ave, New Orleans, LA 70113R.

GAYLE, LUCILLE JORDAN
Retired educational administrator. **PERSONAL:** Born Jun 10, 1920, Leegate, TN; daughter of James Henry Jordan and Ella Brewer Jordan; married Robert E Gayle, Jun 15, 1950. **EDUCATION:** Lincoln Univ, Jefferson City MO, BS Early Childhood Educ, 1942; Teachers Coll, Columbia Univ, New York NY, MA Early Childhood Educ, 1949, Professional Diploma in Guidance, 1954; Digby Coll, London, England, 1957-69; Amer UGWU, Howard Univ, Washington DC; Washington School of Psychology, New York. **CAREER:** Agee School, Dalton MO, teacher, 1942-43; Washington School, teacher, 1943-48; Lowell School, Alton IL, teacher, 1947-48; Attucks School, Kansas City MO, teacher, 1948-54; Grimke School, Washington DC, teacher, 1954-63; Administrative, Washington DC, asst dir guidance dept, 1963-76 (retired). **ORGANIZATIONS:** Awards coord, Amer Bridge Assn, 1962-; prog planner, scholarship, Northal Portal Civic Assn, 1964-; mem, NAACP, 1970-, Urban League, 1970-, Natl Council of Negro Women, 1980-; vice pres, Chums Inc, 1984-88; poll worker, Washington DC Bd of Election; mem, Minority Political Women's Assn, 1986-, Black Women's Agenda, 1988-89. **HONORS/ACHIEVEMENTS:** Publisher/Owner, Agnes Myer Fellowship, Washington Post, 1969; Delegate to White House Conf for Children, 1970; Distinguished Alumni Award, Lincoln Univ, Jefferson City MO, 1974; Commr for the Aging, District of Columbia Mayor Marion Barry, 1988. **HOME ADDRESS:** 8339 E Beach Drive NW, Washington, DC 20012.

GAYLE-THOMPSON, DELORES J.
Physician. **PERSONAL:** Born Feb 28, 1938, Portland, Jamaica;daughter of Lucilda R Gayle; married Amos F Thompson; children: Colin, Allison. **EDUCATION:** Howard Univ, Coll of Liberal Arts BS 1963, Coll of Medicine MD 1967; Columbia Univ School of Public Health, MPH 1984. **CAREER:** Freedmen's Hospital Washington, intern 1967-68; Harlem Hospital, resident in pediatrics 1968-70, physician pediatric clinic 1970-83, assoc dir 1983-. **ORGANIZATIONS:** Instructor in pediatrics College of Physicians & Surgeons Columbia Univ 1979-; mem Natl Medical Assn 1979-, Ambulatory Pediatric Assn 1979-, Amer Public Health Assn 1982-. **HONORS/ACHIEVEMENTS:** Citation Howard Univ Century Club 1986; Citation & Membership Howard Univ President's Club 1986; Civic Awd Friends of East Portland Jamaica West Indies 1986. **BUSINESS ADDRESS:** Assoc Dir Ambulatory Pediatric, Harlem Hospital Center, 506 Lenox Ave, New York, NY 10037.

GAYLES, ANNE RICHARDSON
Educator. **PERSONAL:** Born Jun 04, 1923, Marshallville, GA; daughter of Franklin J Gayles and Marian R Gayles. **EDUCATION:** Fort Valley State Coll, BS 1943; Columbia Univ, MA 1949, Prof Diploma, 1953; IN Univ, EdD 1961. **CAREER:** Stillman Coll, dir student teaching 1952-54; Albany State Coll, 1954-57; FL A&M Univ, dir student teaching 1957-62, head dept of secondary educ 1962-82, prof of secondary educ 1982-; Fort Valley State Coll 1949-52; Instructor, Social Sciences; Rust Coll Associate Prof of Social Sciences; Arkansas Baptist Coll Head Dept of Sociology 1950-51. **ORGANIZATIONS:** 1st vice pres Assoc of Social & Behavioral Serv 1961-62; mem of exec comm Soc of Prof Educ 1969-70; mem served on committees Amer Assoc in Teacher Educ Coll 1970-80; comm on master teacher Assoc of Teacher Educators 1982-85; mem Delta Sigam Theta, Pi Lambda Theta, Phi Delta Kappa, Kappa Delta Pi, Alpha Kappa Mu, Pi Gamma Mu Honor Societies; Natl Republican Party Presidential Task Force; State of Florida Governors Commemorative Celebration Comm on Dr Martin Luther King, Jr; Governor's Bd of Independent Coll & Univ (State of FL); Governor's Comm on Quality Educ; Urban League; Republican Party of Florida. **HONORS/ACHIEVEMENTS:** Published 59 articles; author of two books, co-author of one book; author of three monographs, co-author of one monograph; 5 rsch studies; 5 bibliographies; dissertation editer, writer, reader. Nominated for Exec Committee of Assoc of Teacher Educ, Florida A&M Uninv, Teacher of the Year, 1989. **HOME ADDRESS:** 609 Howard

Ave, Tallahassee, FL 32310. **BUSINESS ADDRESS:** Professor of Secondary Educ, Florida A&M University, Tallahassee, FL 32307.

GAYLES, FRANKLIN JOHNSON
Government official & educational administrator. **PERSONAL:** Born in Marshallville, GA; son of Franklin Johnson Gayles Sr and Marian Richardson Gayles; married Ruth Teele; children: Michael Perry. **EDUCATION:** Univ of Illinois, AB 1939-42, AM 1946-47; New York Univ PhD (highest honors) 1960. **CAREER:** Virginia Union Univ, prof pol sci, div dir, academic dean 1948-80; City of Richmond, treasurer. **ORGANIZATIONS:** Mem Treasurers' Assoc of Virginia, Assoc of Constitutional Officers of Virginia; life mem Alpha Phi Alpha, Sigma Pi Phi, Crusade of Voters, NAACP; Serves on Bd of Friends of Housing Opportunities Made Equal. **HONORS/ACHIEVEMENTS:** Founders Day Awd from New York Univ, 1976; Civic Awd from Alpha Phi Alpha, 1983; Civic Awd from Delta Sigma Theta, 1983. **MILITARY SERVICE:** USN 1942-46. **BUSINESS ADDRESS:** Treasurer, City of Richmond, 900 East Broad St, Richmond, VA 23219.

GAYLES, JOSEPH NATHAN WEBSTER, JR.
Educator, administrator, scientist. **PERSONAL:** Born Aug 07, 1937, Birmingham, AL; son of Joseph N Gayles Sr and Earnestine Williams-Gayles; children: Jonathan, Monica. **EDUCATION:** Dillard Univ, AB (Summa Cum Laude) 1958; Brown Univ, PhD 1963; Dillard Univ, LLD (honorary) 1983. **CAREER:** Bur of the Census, demographic stat 1957-58; Brown Univ, rsch assoc 1958-62; OR State Univ, post doc rsch assoc, asst prof; Morehouse Coll, WoodrowWilson tchg assoc 1963-66; IBM, staff sci & proj dir 1966-69; Morehouse Coll, prof (tenured) 1969-77, assoc prof chem 1969-71; Morehouse School of Med, assoc prog dir 1975-77; Morehouse Med Ed Prog, prog dir 1972-75; Morehouse Coll, health professions adv 1971-77; Talladega Coll, pres 1977-83; Jon-Mon & Assoc, pres 1983-; Morehouse School of Med, vice pres 1983-; research professor of medicine, 1983-. **ORGANIZATIONS:** Bd tests Morehouse Coll 1973-77; bd dir Positive Futures Inc; consult Whitney Found, Ford Found, Woodrow Wilson Found; bd tests Woodrow Wilson Found; consult Natl Inst of Health & DHHS; bd of visitors MIT; mem Alpha Phi Alpha, Amer Chem Soc, Amer Physical Soc, Phi Beta Kappa, Sigma Xi, BXC, AAAS, Amer Assoc of Pol & Soc Sci, GA Conservancy, Sigma Pi Phi; nat assn of fund raising executives. **HONORS/ACHIEVEMENTS:** Andover Full Support Scholarship Phillips Acad 1953; Exchange Cup Scholar 1954; Brawley Writing Awd 1955; Davage Awd; Brown Univ Fellow; Summer European Travel Fellowship 1965; Amer Men of Sci 1967-; Rhom & Haas Fellow; Woodrow Wilson Teaching Fellow; Drefus Teacher Scholarship; Powers Travel Fellow 1975; Teacher of the Year Morehouse Coll 1976; Disting Alumnus Awd Dillard 1977; Omega Psi Phi Ed Achievement Awd; Comm Serv Awd Elks; listed in Who's Who in Amer 1979; Ed Achievement Awd, Emancipation Day Comm Birmingham 1980; Kiwanis Talladega; Morehouse School of Medicine Award, Trustees, 1985. **HOME ADDRESS:** 1515 Austin Rd SW, Atlanta, GA 30331.

GAYLES, LINDSEY, JR.
City government official. **PERSONAL:** Born Jul 06, 1953, Memphis, TN; son of Lindsey Gayles Sr and Ella Woods; married Shirley Ann Baines, Feb 17, 0983; children: Chanel Shanta. **EDUCATION:** Univ of Illinois, Urbana IL, Bachelor's of Urban Planning, 1976; Roosevelt Univ, Chicago IL, attending. **CAREER:** City of Chicago, Chicago IL, sr research asst, 1977-83, city planner, 1983-84, admin asst, 1984-85, Office of Mayor, city council liaison, 1985-; Gayles & Associates Inc, pres, 1986-. **ORGANIZATIONS:** Bd of dir, chmn program comm, Demmicco Youth Serv Inc, 1988-. **HONORS/ACHIEVEMENTS:** Publications: The Cabrini-Green High Impact Program Final Report, City of Chicago, Dept of Planning, 1979; Municipal Security Report: 71st Street Study, City of Chicago, Dept of Planning, 1981; Tournament Coord, Mayor Harold Washington's Holiday (boys and girls) High School Basketball Tournament, 1983-85; Chmn of Mayor Harold Washington's Host Comm for the World Conf of Mayors, 1986; Distinguished Serv Award, Chicago Coalition of Urban Professionals, 1986. **BUSINESS ADDRESS:** Lindsey Gayles Jr, City Council Liaison, Office of the Mayor, City of Chicago, 121d N LaSalle, Room 1111, Chicago, IL 60602.

GAYLORD, ELLIHUE, SR.
Pastor. **PERSONAL:** Born Aug 15, 1922, Center Ridge, AR; married Aurelia; children: Carolyn Riane, Ellihue Jr, Ronald Wayne. **EDUCATION:** AM&N Coll Pine Bluff AR, BS 1950. **CAREER:** Starlight Baptist Church, pastor 1964-; Farmers Home Admin, asst co supervisor 1965-79, county supervisor 1979-80; Columbia Baptist District Congress, pres. **ORGANIZATIONS:** Mem Omega Psi Phi Frat 1970-; bd mem AR Black Caucus 1978-; AR Farm Land Develop Co 1980-; bd mem Columbia Bapt Dist Assoc 1984-; state pres NAACP 1984-; bd mem Natl NAACP 1985-; bd mem Urban League of AR 1985-. **HONORS/ACHIEVEMENTS:** Outstanding Service Urban League of AR, Senator Donald Pryor, El Dorado, Governor of AR. **MILITARY SERVICE:** AUS pfc 2 yrs. **HOME ADDRESS:** 71 Timberlane Dr, Magnolia, AR 71753.

GAYMON, NICHOLAS EDWARD
Librarian. **PERSONAL:** Born Apr 08, 1928, Pinewood, SC; son of Rufus and Viola; married Marjorie J Sinkfield; children: Renwick, Dara, Warren, Debra. **EDUCATION:** Morehouse Coll, AB 1956; Atlanta Univ, MSLS 1959; FL State Univ, AMD 1973, PhD 1975. **CAREER:** Lockheed Aircraft Corp, structural assemblyman 1953-59; Atlanta Univ, acquisitions librarian 1959-65, circulation librarian 1965; Dillard Univ, head librarian 1965-69; FL State Univ, adj instr 1974; FL A&M Univ, dir of libraries 1969-. **ORGANIZATIONS:** Mem FL Library Assn; mem SE Library Assn, Amer Library Assn; participant Lawrence Livermore Lab 1977; mem So Assn Visiting Com of Coll & Sch 1971-; mem SE Library Network 1978-; exec bd Dist Adv Counc for Leon Co Sch Bd 1978-; mem Black Caucus of Amer Library Assn; vice pres 1890 Land Grant Colls 1979-. **HONORS/ACHIEVEMENTS:** Ford Found Grant 1967. **MILITARY SERVICE:** AUS corpl 1951-53. **BUSINESS ADDRESS:** Dir of Libraries, FL A&MUniv, PO Box 78, Tallahassee, FL 32307.

GAYNOR, FLORENCE S.
Retired executive director. **PERSONAL:** Born Oct 29, 1920, Jersey City, NJ; daughter of Oscar Small (deceased) and Pearl Fields (deceased); divorced; children: Brenda, W Michael, Matthew. **EDUCATION:** New York Univ, BS 1964, MA 1966;Univ of Oslo, Norway, 8 Credits 1965; Harvard Graduate School of Business; USC, "The Other Chinas; UCLA, 4 credits. **CAREER:** Sydenham Hosp, exec dir 1971-72; Univ Medicine & Dentistry of NJ, exec dir 1972-76; Meharry Medical Coll, dir hosp & health serv 1976-79; West Phil Community Mental Health Consortium, retired exec dir 1980-84; YMCA, part-time; Univ Medicine & Denistry of NJ, dir hosp & health serv. **ORGANIZATIONS:** Pres Natl Assoc Health Care Exec 1973; bd mem Family Planning Assoc 1982-84; bd mem Philcop Public Interest Law Center Phil Bar Assoc 1983-84; Treasurer Forum Exec Women 1983-84; fellow Amer Coll of Hospital & Health Care Admin; mem Amer Public Health Asson; treasurer, Forum of Executive Women 1983-84. **HONORS/ACHIEVEMENTS:** Leadership Award Natl Council Negro Women 1972; Woman of the year Masons New York City 1973; 100 prominent blacks Ebony Books 1973. **HOME ADDRESS:** 4962 S Tupelo Turnpike, Wilmington, DE 19808.

GAYTON, GARY D.
Attorney. **PERSONAL:** Born Feb 25, 1933, Seattle. **EDUCATION:** Univ of WA, BA 1955; Gonzaga U, JD 1962. **CAREER:** Stern, Gayton, Neubauer & Brucker, att PS 1965; Western Dist Wash, asst US att 1962-65. **ORGANIZATIONS:** Mem Am Bar Assn; Am Trial Lawyers Assn; King Co Bar Assn; Wash State Bar Assn; Nat Bar Assn; bd mem Universal Security Life Ins Co; Past SeattlePark Comm; mem Seattle Repertory Bd; past mem Seattle Ethics & Fair Camp Comm; mem Seattle King Co Bicentennial Comm; mem bd Salvation Army; mem bd of NW Civic Cultural & Char Orgns; past bd mem NAACP; mem bd inst of black am Music Inc. **MILITARY SERVICE:** AUS 1955-57. **BUSINESS ADDRESS:** Deputy Administrator, Urban Mass Transportation Adm, 400 Seventh St SW, Washington, DC 20590.

GEARY, CLARENCE BUTLER
Psychiatrist. **PERSONAL:** Born Aug 01, 1912, Steelton, PA; son of Robert Geary and Annie Adams Geary; married Harriet Williams; children: Steven Craig. **EDUCATION:** Howard Univ Wash DC, BS 1937, MD 1944; Provident Hosp Chgo, Intern in Gen Med 1945-46. **CAREER:** Cook Cty School of Nursing, instr 1948-53; Cook Cty Hosp, staff psychiatrist 1949-59; Mercy Hosp Clinic, clinic psych 1949-51; Chicago Police Dept, consult psych 1954-61; Chicago Municipal Court, staff psych 1959-63; Cook Cty Hosp, staff psych 1963-78, dir dept of psych 1970-72, dir liaison div 1973-78; Chicago Coll of Osteopathic Med, clinical prof psych 1978; Private practice, psych 1949-. **ORGANIZATIONS:** Mem Natl Med Assoc 1950-65, AMA 1951-, Amer Psych Assoc 1951-80; diplomate Amer Bd of Psych & Neurology 1951; mem Natl Assoc of Fed Disability 1969-73; life mem Amer Psych Assoc 1980-, NAACP; mem Urban League, Druids Mens Club of Chgo; emeritus mem AMA & affiliates 1982; mem Pres Club Howard Univ. **HONORS/ACHIEVEMENTS:** 10 Yrs Recog Awd Howard Univ Coll of Med 1972-84; Physicians Recog Awd AMA 1974-77, 1979-82; Physicians Serv Awd Cook Cty Hosp Chicago 1975; Physicians Recog Awd AMA, APA 1982-85. **MILITARY SERVICE:** AUS MAC 2nd lt 1942-44. **BUSINESS ADDRESS:** 1137 E 50th St, Chicago, IL 60615.

GECAU, KIMANI J.
Educator. **PERSONAL:** Born Jul 17, 1947. **EDUCATION:** Univ of East Africa, BA 1969; McMaster Univ, MA 1970; State Univ of New York, PhD 1975. **CAREER:** McMaster Univ, teaching asst 1969-70; SUNY Buffalo, teaching asst 1970-72; State Univ Coll Buffalo, instructor 1970-71; Geneseo, instructor 1972-75; Univ of Nairobi, lecturer 1975-. **BUSINESS ADDRESS:** Lecturer, Dept of Literature, Univ of Nairobi, Box 30197, Nairobi, Kenya.

GEE, AL (ALBERT GERMANY)
Disc jockey, director. **PERSONAL:** Born Oct 23, 1942, Leeds, AL; married Jessica Khan; children: Mark, Shawn. **EDUCATION:** Univ of Pittsburgh Geo Heide Sch of Announcing, 1964. **CAREER:** WLIB NY, prgm dir 1973; WLIB NY, 1973; WPIX, 1972; WWRL, 1968-72; Washington Radio, U968; WZUM Pittsburgh, 1966-68; WAMO, 1964-66; Syndicated Radio Show Rap & Rythm; Radio Station ZDK, co-owner; NATRA Natl Assn of radio & TV Announcers, exec dir 1976-77; St Johns Antiqua Professional Black Announcers of NY, West Indies pres. **BUSINESS ADDRESS:** 801 2nd Ave, New York, NY.

GEE, WILLIAM ROWLAND, JR.
Engineer. **PERSONAL:** Born Oct 04, 1940, Washington, DC; son of W Rowland Gee and Marietta Brittain Gee; married Sadie H Phillips; children: Moira G Travis, Morris B, Cathy D Porter, Julia E, W Rowland III. **EDUCATION:** Howard U, BSME (cum laude) 1962; Oak Ridge Sch of Reactor Tech, Nuclear Eng 1963; Stanford U, MS Applied Mech 1971; Loyola Coll Baltimore MBA 1981. **CAREER:** US Atomic Energy Commn, project engr 1962-66; GE Breeder Reactor Devel, engr 1966-73; Potomac Electric Power Co, mgr nuclear engineering 1975-77, mgr generating engineering 1981-89, vice pres generating engineering and construction 1989-. **HOME ADDRESS:** 405 S Harrison Rd, Sterling, VA 22170. **BUSINESS ADDRESS:** Vice President - Generating Engineering & Construction, Potomac Electric Power Co, 1900 Pennsylvania Ave N W, Washington, DC 20068.

GEIGER, DAVID NATHANIEL
Business executive, veterinarian. **PERSONAL:** Born Jan 10, 1933, Jacksonville, FL; married Barbara J Holloway; children: Sharon L, Stacey L, Shelly L, David N. **EDUCATION:** FL A&M U, BS 1954; Tuskegee Inst, DVM 1958. **CAREER:** Pacific-coast Bank, chmn of bd & pres; Geiger Hosps Inc, dir 1963-80; Pacific Coast Bank, chmn of bd 1977-80. **ORGANIZATIONS:** Mem Alpha Phi Alpha 1952; mem NAACP 1956; mem AVMA CVMA & SACVAMA 1963. **MILITARY SERVICE:** USAF capt 1958-60. **BUSINESS ADDRESS:** Pacific Coast Bank, 4871 Logan Ave, San Diego, CA 92113.

GELLINEAU, VICTOR MARCEL, JR.
Marketing manager. **PERSONAL:** Born Nov 03, 1942, New York, NY; son of Victor M Gellineau and Marcella Gonzalez Gellineau; married Carole Joy Johnston, Jun 05, 1965; children: Victor M III, Maria M, Carmen E. **EDUCATION:** Howard Univ, BA 1967; Baruch Coll of Business & Public Admin, MBA 1974. **CAREER:** Burlington Industries, salesman 1967-69; Lever Bros, asst prod mgr 1969-71; Amer Home Products, product mgr 1971-73; Zebra Assoc, vice pres dir of acct mgmt 1973-76; Heublein Inc, mktg mgr 1976-83; Ponderosa Inc, dir mktg 1983-85; General Foods Corp, sr product mgr 1985-89; Carol Joy Creations Inc, president. **ORGANIZATIONS:** Mem Amer Mgmt Assn 1970-; visiting prof Natl Urban League Beep Prog 1974-; bd mem pres Artists Collective 1978-83; student advisor Junior Achievement 1978-83; mem Natl Black MBA Assn 1983-; facilitator Inroads. **HONORS/ACHIEVEMENTS:** Black Achiever Awd Hartford YMCA 1980. **HOME ADDRESS:** 10 Kilian Dr, Danbury, CT 06811. **BUSINESS ADDRESS:** Carole Joy Creations, Inc, 39-B Mill Plain Road, Suite 130, Danbury, CT 06811.

GENTRY, ALBERT NEWMAN, III
Real estate developer. **PERSONAL:** Born Jun 25, 1956, Cincinnati, OH; married Mary Lea Powell. **EDUCATION:** Williams Coll, BA 1978; Harvard Business Sch, MBA 1982. **CAREER:** Chemical Bank, asst loan officer 1978-80; Aetna Realty Investors Inc, asst real estate investment officer 1982-85; John Hancock Equity Real Estate, asst realestate investment officer 1985-86; Future Develop Co Inc, principal. **ORGANIZATIONS:** Bd of trustees Natl Urban League 1982-; bd of dirs Urban League of Eastern MA 1986-; bd of advisors Boys & Girls Club of Boston Roxbury Clubhouse 1986-; student liason Harvard Black Alumni 1987. **HONORS/ACHIEVEMENTS:** 30 Leaders Under 30 Years of Age Ebony magazine 1985.

GENTRY, ATRON A.
Educator. **PERSONAL:** Born in El Centro, CA. **EDUCATION:** Pasadena City Clge, AA 1958; CA State Polytechnic Clge, 1959; CA State Univ at Los Angeles, BA 1966; Univ of MA, EdD 1970. **CAREER:** Apple Creek State Inst OH, asst supr 1975-76; Cleveland State Hosp OH, supr 1976-78; Hull Clge of Higher Educ Hull England, visiting prof 1981; Univof MA, prof of educ;Visiting Profess in Beijing Tchrs Coll 1986. **ORGANIZATIONS:** Assc dean Schl of Educ Univ of MA 1971-72, 1972-75, dir of the Center for Urban Educ 1968-71; staff mem 1984 Olympic Games L A Olympic Org Comm 1984; Kentucky Colonel 1974; mem Phi Delta Kappa 1971;Dir of Boston Scndry Schls Project, a collaborative prgm between Univ of Mass at Amherst & Boston Secondary Schls. **HONORS/ACHIEVEMENTS:** Citizen of the Year Omega Psi Frat 1967; Urban Srv Award Ofc of Econ Apport US Govt 1966; Urban Educ The Hope Factor Philadelphia Sounder 1972; The Politics of Urban Educ for the 80'S Natl Assc of Sec Schl Principals 1980; Dedication & Service, Boston Secondary School Project 1987; The Dr. Carter G. Woodson Memoriay Uplift Award Tau Iota Chapter,Omega Psi Fraternity 1988. **MILITARY SERVICE:** AUS sgt 1954-56. **BUSINESS ADDRESS:** Professor of Educ, School of Educ, Univ of MA, Amherst, MA 01002.

GENTRY, DENNIS CALVIN
Professional athlete. **PERSONAL:** Born Feb 10, 1959, Lubbock, TX. **EDUCATION:** Baylor, BS 1982. **CAREER:** Chicago Bears, running back 1982-. **HONORS/ACHIEVEMENTS:** Was 3rd on team in KOR's with 130 yards includ 186 average. **BUSINESS ADDRESS:** Chicago Bears, Halas Hall, Ste 400, Lake Forest, IL 60045.

GENTRY, LAMAR DUANE
Government official. **PERSONAL:** Born Dec 19, 1946, Chicago, IL; children: Mark J, LaMar P, Carlos D. **EDUCATION:** So IL Univ, BA 1970; Univ of IL, JD 1979. **CAREER:** Gov Ofc IL, model cities specialist 1970-72, dir model cities 1972-74, dir prog planning & devel 1974-75; Capital Devel Bd IL, regional sch dist analyst 1975-76; City of E St Louis IL, commr comm develop 1981, acting comptroller 1983, dep mayor dir of adminis 1979-. **ORGANIZATIONS:** Bd dir E St Louis Comm Develop Credit Union; bd dir Boy's Club Springfield IN 1973-75; bd dir Springfield Urban League 1973-75; pres Kappa Alpha PsiSpringfield Alumni 1974-76. **BUSINESS ADDRESS:** Deputy Mayor/Dir of Adminis, City of East St Louis, #7 Collinsville Ave, East St Louis, IL 62201.

GENTRY, NOLDEN I.
Attorney. **PERSONAL:** Born Aug 30, 1937, Rockford, IL; son of Nolden L Gentry and Omega Gentry; married Barbara Lewis, Apr 24, 1965; children: Adrienne, Natalie, Brian. **EDUCATION:** Univ of IA, BS 1960; IA Coll of Law, JD 1964. **CAREER:** Brick, Seckington, Bowers, Swartz & Gentry, PC; FBI, spl agt; IA Atty Gen, asst; Urban Affairs Dept Grtr Des Moines C of C, mgr 1968-69; Des Moines City Atty, spl asst. **ORGANIZATIONS:** Former Bd mem Des Moinse Indep Comm Sch Bd; bd mem Greater Des Moines Comm Found Drake Relays Com; bd mem Valley Nat Bank; bd mem Iowa Resources, Inc; bd mem Delta Dental Plan of IA. **BUSINESS ADDRESS:** 550-39th St, Suite 200, Des Moines, IA 50312.

GEORGE, ALLEN
Attorney. **PERSONAL:** Born Oct 13, 1935, New York, NY; married Valerie Daring; children: Gerald, Kenneth, Johnathan. **EDUCATION:** NYH Univ, BS 1964; NY Univ Graduate School of Business, 1965-68; Howard Univ, 1973; Cleveland State Univ, LLM 1980. **CAREER:** Pittman George & Copeland Co LPA, pvt practice 1978; Standard Oil Co, atty 1973-77; Lucas, & Tucker & Co, tax accountant 1969-70; IRS revenue agt 1966-69; Bur of Credit Unions, credit union Examiner 1965-66. **ORGANIZATIONS:** Treas Phi Alpha Delta Law Fraternity 1972-73; Nat Bar Assn; Am Bar Assn; OH Bar Assn; Bar Assn Of Greater Cleveland; Cleveland Lawyers Assn; Cuyahoga Co Bar Assn Bd; mem Glenville YMCA 1976; bd mem Catholic Interracial Council; mem Caribbean Comm Cultural Club; mem Knights of Columbus. **HONORS/ACHIEVEMENTS:** Cleveland State Univ Coll of Law 1975-76; published The Tax Treatment of The-cost of Class C Stock Purchases by Farmers' Coop 1971. **MILITARY SERVICE:** USAF a/1c 1956-59. **HOME ADDRESS:** 2933 Southington Rd, Shaker Heights, OH 44120.

GEORGE, CARRIE LEIGH
Retired educator, minister. **PERSONAL:** Born Sep 28, 1915, Winder, GA; daughter of Elijah Leigh and Olian O Leigh; widowed; children: Faith O, Donald T. **EDUCATION:** Clark Coll, (Salutatorian, Cum Laude) AB 1936; Atlanta Univ, MA 1937; Gammon Theological Seminary, MDiv 1954; NYU, EdS 1961; Atlanta Univ, PhD 1970; Famous Writers Sch New Haven CT, Certificate 1976; Burton Coll & Seminary, EdRD (Hon) 1960; OH State Univ, 1943; Hartford Seminary Found, 1956-57; Garrett-Northwestern Univ, 1960; Gregg Coll Chicago, Certificate, 1944. **CAREER:** Clark Coll; assoc prof, math & business educ, 1938-48; Atlanta Public School System, supply teacher, 1948-55; Gammon-interdenominational Theological Center, assoc prof, religious educ & dir of field exp 1955-64; Archer High School, head math dept, 1956-57; US Dept of Labor, admin asst to Atlanta Concentrated Employee Program Monitor 1967-68; Economic Systems Corp Poland ME, cur dev spclst & sr cnslr 1968; Cross Keys H S, math tchr 1968-70; GA St U, dir of official pub 1970-71; GA State Univ, sr counselor & asst prof of curriculum & instr 1971-80, rsch/asst prof, 1980-86. Georgia State Univ (retired, 1986). **ORGANIZATIONS:** Consultant Educ Dept, Atlanta Job Corp Center, 1980-83; consultant, Center Personnel Morehouse Coll 1981; teaching staff Brown HS Atlanta 1981; Bishop Coll, 1978; Workshops for Teachers of Elementary Math, M Agnes Jones Elementary School & Margaret Fain Elementary Sch 1981; Workshops for Student Personnel Workers & Vocation & Career HS Teachers Lawson Comm Coll Bir AL 1982; Workshops for Freshmn on "Study Habits & Skills" Morehouse Coll 1983; Workshop in Leadership Training Baptist Convention Annually; pres Friendship Uplifters 1977-79; pres Atlanta Chptr of Natl Assn of Baptist Women Ministers 1984-; Interdenomination Assoc of Ministers Wives & Widows (Dean of Educ Dept 1980-82); pastor George Mem Baptist Church of Faith 1981-. **HONORS/ACHIEVEMENTS:** Elected Honorary Fellow of Anglo-Amer Acad Cambridge England 1980; appt hon mem of Editorial Adv Bd of Amer Biographic Inst "In Recognition of Noteworthy Accomplishments, Superior Ability & Outstanding Serv to Comm, State & Nation" 1971-75-81; recd GA St Univ Women of Excellence Awd for Spiritual Devel, 1983; Received the Atlanta Chapter of Frontiers Club of Amer Community Serv Award 1983; mem, GA St Univ Speakers Bureau 1984; Writings "Some Properties of Algebraic Invariants", "Conselor As Person Philosophical, Theoretical & Practical Orientations", Leadership in Action", "Who Are The Development Studies Students?", "What is Counseling", "Alternative Schools in Public Educ in GA", (co-authored); "A Study Skills Workshop Manual", "An Ecumenical Communion Serv for Christian Women", Leadership Training Series "Parlimentary Usage", "Communicating Our Faith", "Christ in You-The Hope of Glory", "The Art of Worship"; "From the Pen of the Shepherdess" contributing ed, the Herald; columnist for Atlanta Daily World Newspaper. **HOME ADDRESS:** 1652 Detroit Ave N W, Atlanta, GA 30314.

GEORGE, CLAUDE C.
Educational administrator. **PERSONAL:** Born Nov 22, 1922, Atlanta, GA; married Dr Herma Hightower-George; children: Collette Scott, Yvette, Valeria Hightower, Kimerly Hightower. **EDUCATION:** Tuskegee Inst, BS Ed 1948; NY Univ, MA Ed 1949; Atlanta Univ, EdS 1972, EdD 1981. **CAREER:** Atlanta Public Schools, dir, student desegregation 1973-77, dir, alternative ed 1978-83, dir, intl exchange, dir, job placement. **ORGANIZATIONS:** Mem Kappa Alpha Psi Frat 1977-85, Atlanta Univ Alumni Assoc 1977-85, CL Harper Mem Fund 1977-85; commiss Atlanta Clean City Commiss 1977-85; chairperson Senate Selection Comm of the Congress Bundstay Youth Exchange; mem Japan-Amer Soc of GA. **HONORS/ACHIEVEMENTS:** Jewish Ed Alliance Achievement Awd NY 1949; Outstanding Personalities of the South Awd 1969; 1972 Creative & Successful Personalities of the World 1972; Tuskegee Hall of Fame Tuskegee Inst 1975. **MILITARY SERVICE:** AUS tech sgt 2 yrs 8 mo; Good Conduct, European Theater Operation Awd 1943-45. **BUSINESS ADDRESS:** Dir Job Placement, Atlanta Public Schools, 551 Houston St NE, Atlanta, GA 30312.

GEORGE, EDWARD
Business executive. **PERSONAL:** Married Cutie Bell; children: 5. **EDUCATION:** Attnd Coll 1 1/2 Yrs. **CAREER:** Pres & bus agent, Amalgamated Transit Union 1970-72. **ORGANIZATIONS:** Bd mem Legal Aid Soc San Joaguin Co 1969-73; dir Southeast Comm Assn 1972-73; bd mem A Phillip Randolph Institute 1972-73; bd mem KUOP FM Radio StationUniv of Pacific Stockton CA; pres NAACP Stockton; Bd Mem Cit Adv Com San Joaquin Co Planning Assn; adv bd San Joaquin Co Manpower Prog; adv bd mem Child Health Disability Prevention Prog San Joaquin Co. **HONORS/ACHIEVEMENTS:** Achievement award in comm involvement SE Comm Cntr 1971; Cert of App Rec Comm Action Coun; bd dir 1973; service rendered during 1973 Stockton Boy & Girl Drill Team. **BUSINESS ADDRESS:** 805 E Webor Ave, Stockton, CA.

GEORGE, GARY RAYMOND
Elected government official. **PERSONAL:** Born Mar 08, 1954, Milwaukee, WI; married Mary Cook; children: Alexander Raymond Jr, Daniel McLean. **EDUCATION:** Univ of Wisconsin Madison, BBA Accounting 1976; Univ of Michigan Ann Arbor, JD 1979. **CAREER:** Arthur Young & Co, tax atty 1979-80; self-employed, atty 1982-; State of Wisconsin, senator 6th dist 1981-. **ORGANIZATIONS:** Co-chair Joint Audit Comm 1981-85; mem Uniform State Laws Comm 1981, Ed Block Grant Adv Comm 1981, Ed Comm Bd 1981, Sexual Assault & Child Abuse Study Comm; chmn Park West Redevel Task Force 1981; mem Milwaukee Cty Zoo Bd 1981, Neighborhood Improvement Devel Corp 1982; bd of trustees, mem Family Hosp Inc & Family Hosp Nursing Home Inc 1983; chmn Joint Finance Comm Ed Subcommittee 1983; mem Comm Devel Finance Auth 1983, Alcohol & Drug Abuse Study Comm 1983, State Supported Programs Adv Comm 1983, Mayor's Anti-Gang Initiative Task Force 1984; co-chmn Joint Finance Comm 1985; mem Performing Arts Ctr Bd of Dir 1985; mem WI State Bar, Democratic Party of WI, Natl Caucus of State Legislators, Council on State Govts, Milwaukee Forum, Natl Black Caucus of State Legislators, NAACP, WI Special Olympics. **BUSINESS ADDRESS:** Senator Dist 6, Wisconsin State Senate, South State Capitol, PO Box 7882 # 119, Madison, WI 53702.

GEORGE, LAURA W.
Educational administrator. **PERSONAL:** Born in Wetumpka, AL; married Rev Robert L George; children: Ralph, Willie, Linda, Renee. **EDUCATION:** Case-western Res U; Ursuline Coll. **CAREER:** Hurd's Day Care Center, initiated 1974; Werner Day Care 1969; Club of AL, pres; Fedn of Controlled Child Care Centers of AL. **ORGANIZATIONS:** Mem Glenville of Gtr Cleveland Nghbrhd & Ctr Assn 1965-71; mem (Al Assn of Women's Club Coop; AL Conf on Child Care; Nat Assn for Educ of Young Children; So Assn for Children-under Six; AL Assn for Children; PTA; Sunday Schl Tchr; Tri Comm-citizens; Elmore Co Civic & Improvement League ; Gtr Montgomery Urban-league; NAACP. **HONORS/ACHIEVEMENTS:** Boy Scouts of Am Award 1958; Am Red Cross Vol Serv 1964; CEO 1969; honored for Initiating 1st Black Non Profit Day-care Ctr in Elmore Co Elmore Co Civic Leagtue 1974; Pres Club of AL 1977. **BUSINESS ADDRESS:** Rt 3 Box 392, Wetumpka, AL 36092.

GEORGE, THEODORE ROOSEVELT, JR.
Physician. **PERSONAL:** Born Dec 27, 1934, Cincinnati, OH; son of Theodore R George, MD and Christine Tatum George; married Jeanne Sharpe; children: Theodore III, Blair. **EDUCATION:** Howard Univ, BS, 1952-56, MD, 1956-60; Freedman's Hosp, intern, 1960-61, resident, 1963-67. **CAREER:** DC Gen Hosp, Howard Univ Hosp, WA Hosp Ctr, physician; Howard Univ Coll Med, clinical instr; DC Gen Hosp, sr med officer; Theodore R George Jr MD, physician. **ORGANIZATIONS:** Mem Natl Med Assn, Med Soc DC, Chi Delta Mu Med Soc, Former Interns & Resd of Freedmen's Hosp, Amer Assn of Gynecologic Laparoscopists, Alpha Phi Alpha Frat, WA Gyn Soc, Medico-Chirurgical Soc, Pan Am Med Assn, Urban League, Jr Citizens Corps, NAACP, Police Boy's Club, Cincinnati Club; MD Medical License 1960; DC Med License 1965; Cert Amer Bd Ob & Gyn 1969; chmn Pro Tem St Paul AME Church Trustee Bd; mem, Daniel Hale Williams Reading Club, 1972-; mem, Southern Medical Assn, 1980-. **HONORS/ACHIEVEMENTS:** Natl Competitive Scholarship, 1952-56; Rep Aviation Awd 1954; Dean's list 1952-56; Dean's Cup 1955; Pres's Cup 1956; AFROTC Awd 1956; Outstanding Male Grad Student Council 1956; Grad Cum Laude 1956; Natl Medical Assn Scholarship 1957; Psychiatric Awd 1960; Natl Medical Assn Awd 1967; AMA Physicians Recognition Awd, 1972; Amer Acad of Family Physicians Awd 1974; Howard Univ Med Alumni Assn Awd 1974; Amer Cancer Soc Cert of Merit 1975; Natl Fraternal

Order of Police 1976; publ "Delivery in Elderly Primagravida Following Myomectomy" 1964; "Vascular Systems Recovery of Red Blood Cells from the Peritonial Cavity" 1965; "Concomittant Use of Stomaseptin & Metronidazole in the Treatment of Trichomonas Vaginalis Complicated by Moniliasis" 1966; "Pelvic Exenteration" 1967; "The Changing Role of Cesarean Section" 1969. **MILITARY SERVICE:** USAF capt 1961-63; Commendation Medal. **BUSINESS ADDRESS:** Physician, Theodore R George Jr MD, 5505 5th St, Ste 200, Washington, DC 20011.

GEORGE, ZELMA WATSON
Lecturer, writer, consultant. **PERSONAL:** Born Dec 08, 1903, Hearne, TX. **EDUCATION:** NYU, PhD, 1954; Western Reserve Univ, 1947-48; NYU, MA 1943; Am Conservatory of Music, 1925-27; Northwestern Univ, 1924-26; Univ of Chicago, PhB 1924; Chicago Business Coll, 1921; wid lecturer, writer, Consult 1974. **CAREER:** Cleveland Job Corps Center for Women, exec dir 1966-74; Danforth Found, Lectr & Consult 1964-66; W Colston Leigh Inc Agy, Lectr Consult 1961-64; XV Gen Assembly of Nations, us del 1960; World Tour, lectr 1959; Western Reserve U, instr 1958; opera singer 1949-55; professional vol 1944-49; The Rockefeller Found, research fellow 1942-44; Avalon Comm Center, founder exec dir 1937-42; TN State U, adminstrn dean of women 1932-37; Juvenile CT Chicago, probation officer 1925-32; Asso Charities IL, case worker 1924-25; UNA/USA, dir 1971; Nat Bd World Federalists 1959-66. **ORGANIZATIONS:** Exec bd Amer Soc African Culture, 1959-71; bd dir, Corp for Public Broadcasting 1971-72; bd mem, Natl Scholarship Serv & Fund for Negro & Students 1957-62; Natl Conf of Christians & Jews 1950-54; ARC 1948-49; Met YWCA Bd 1956-60; Council on Human Relations 1954-68; Council on World Affairs Bd 1961-64; Girl Scout Bd 1945-52; League of Women Voters 1946-50; Spl Youth Com Cleveland Occupational Planning Council 1958-62; US Com Intl Peace Acad 1971-74; Pres Com 1960 White House Conf on Children & Youth; Defense Adv Co on Women in-the Serv 1954-57; Nat Conf on Comm's Responsibility For Devel of Minority Potential 1958; Nat Minority Youth Tng/Incentive 1957; Ethnic Heritage Studies Devel Program Exec Comm, 1974; World Future Soc 1971; Cleveland Intl Youth Leaders Exchange Prog 1956-69; Am Assn Univ Women 1948; Antioch Baptist Church, Alpha Kappa Alpha, Urban League, NAACP; Links Inc; Natl Council of Negro Women, Amer Mgmt Assn. **HONORS/ACHIEVEMENTS:** Phillis Wheatley Assn recip honary LHD Cleveland StateUniv 1974; LHD Baldwin Wallace Coll 1961; LHD Heidelberg Coll 1961; alumnus of yr NYU 1973;Univ of chicago 1969; honorary mem delta kappa gamma Soc; Phi Delta Gama; Fedn of Women's Clubs; phi delta kappa sorority; dag hammerskjold award 1961; dahlberg Peace Award 1969; centennial citation Wilson Coll 1969; TX Centennial Fair 1968; Zelma George Day 1968; exhibit in Ft Concho Preservation & mus Outstanding Texan 1974; honary vice pres World & Federalists USA 1974; Bicentennial Girl Scout Calendar 1976; Kent StateUniv Semicentennial Award 1961 & 1963; keynote Speaker First StudentIntl Security Council Mtg 1969; Ban the Bomb Conf Accra Ghana 1962; People Power Award 1974; Outstanding Cit Award 1974; Role of Honor Emancipation Centennial Celebration Chicago 1963; Mary-bethune Gold Medallion 1973; humanitarian Award 1972; numerous plaques; spl Tribute Donated to zelma George Incentive Fund 1975; Gov Award 1973; Nat Council of Jewish Women 1974; numerous other Awards.

GERALD, ARTHUR THOMAS, JR.
Educational admin. **PERSONAL:** Born Oct 13, 1947, Boston, MA; married Henrietta; children: Arthur Michael. **EDUCATION:** Lincoln Univ, 1965-67; Berkshire Christian Coll, AB Theology 1967-70; Gordon-Conwell Seminary, Masters Degree 1970-72. **CAREER:** Sales State Coll, advisor to afro-american soc 1972-73, dir of minority affairs 1973-81; assoc dean, academic affairs. **ORGANIZATIONS:** Associate minister 12th Baptist Church 1972-. **HOME ADDRESS:** 31 Holyoke St, Lynn, MA 01905. **BUSINESS ADDRESS:** Assoc Dean & Academic Affairs, Salem State College, 352 Lafayette St, Salem, MA 01970.

GERALD, GILBERTO RUBEN
Health services administrator. **PERSONAL:** Born Nov 27, 1950, Panama, Panama;son of Dr Alfred Nelson Gerald and Dorothy Whiteman Gerald. **EDUCATION:** Pratt Inst, Brooklyn, NY, BArch, 1974. **CAREER:** Georgetown Univ Hospital Office of Planning, Washington, DC, project mgr, 1975-77; Perkins and Will, Washington, DC, designer draftsman, 1977-79; Hennigson Durham and Richardson, Alexandria, VA, project architect, 1979-81; Hellmuth Obata and Kassabaum, Washington, DC, project architect, 1981-82; Arthur Cotton Moore and Assoc Inc, Washington, DC, sr staff architect, 1982-83; Natl Coalition of Black Lesbians and Gays, Washington, DC, exec dir, 1983-86; Natl AIDS Network, Washington, DC, dir of minority affairs, 1986-89; Minority AIDS Project, Los Angeles, CA, exec dir, 1989-. **ORGANIZATIONS:** Mem, bd of dir, Metropolitan Community Church of Washington, 1979-81, Shaw Project Area Comm, Washington, DC, 1979-82, Natl Coalition of Black Lesbians and Gays, 1980-83, 1987-, Human Rights Campaign Fund, 1981-84, Gay Rights Natl Lobby, 1985, Americans for Democratic Action, 1986, Natl Minority AIDS Council, 1987; pres, Downtown Shaw Neighborhood Assn, 1980-81, DC Coalition of Black Gays, 1982-83; mem, District of Columbia Comprehensive Plan Downtown Comm, 1984, AIDS Advisory Comm for evaluation of grant proposals, US Conf of Mayors, 1985, Steering Comm, Natl March on Washington for Lesbian and Gay Rights, 1987. **HONORS/ACHIEVEMENTS:** Dr Frank Kameny Award, 1983; Certificate of Appreciation, Govt of the District of Columbia, 1984; Special Achievement Award, Intl Assn of Black and White Men Together, 1984; Certificate of Appreciation, DC Coalition of Black Gay Men and Women, 1985; Gene Frey Award, Whitman-Walker Clinic, 1987; named one of the Advocate 500 important individuals of the gay and lesbian community, Advocate, 1988; Bayard Rustin Award, Natl Black Lesbian and Gay Leadership Conf; author, "With My Head Held Up High," In the Life: A Black Gay Anthology, 1986, "What Can We Learn from the Gay Community's Response to the AIDS Crisis?" Journal of the Natl Medical Assn, 1989; welcoming speech, Natl Conf on AIDS in the Black Community, Natl Coalition of Black Lesbians and Gays, Washington, DC, 1986; moderator, AIDS in the Black Community workshop panel, Joint Center for Political Studies, Fifth Natl Policy Inst, Washington, DC, 1988; speaker, participant in panel presentations, contributor to publications, 1979-. **BUSINESS ADDRESS:** Exec Dir, Minority AIDS Project, 5159 W Jefferson, Los Angeles, CA 90019.

GERALD, MELVIN DOUGLAS
Family physician. **PERSONAL:** Born Jul 17, 1942, Cerro Gordo, NC; son of Paul Grerald, Sr (deceased) and Mattie Vann Gerald (deceased); married Lenora Graham; children: Sonja, Melvin Jr. **EDUCATION:** Morehouse Coll Atlanta, BS 1964; Howard Univ, MD 1970; Johns Hopkins Univ School of Public Health, MPH 1974. **CAREER:** Shaw Comm Health Center, med dir 1973-75; Howard Univ, asst prof 1974-, dir family practice 1976-78; Gerald Family Care Assn, physician 1978-. **ORGANIZATIONS:** Bd of dirs MD State Cancer Soc 1979-. **BUSINESS ADDRESS:** President & Medical Director, Gerald Family Care Asso, PC, 1160 Varnum Street, NE, Suite 117, Washington, DC 20017.

GERALD, PERRY
Professional athlete. **PERSONAL:** Born Oct 30, 1960, Savannah, GA. **CAREER:** Atlanta Braves, left fielder 1984. **HONORS/ACHIEVEMENTS:** Nat League Player of the Week, Hit 400 With A Homer & 6 RBIS; Braves Bill Lucas Minor League Player of the Yr 1982; helped lead AAA Richmond to its 1st IL Pennant in 15 yrs 1982; won Western Carolinas League Batting Championship with a 333 averg 1979; named Most Community Minded Richmond Brave 1983. **BUSINESS ADDRESS:** Atlanta Braves, PO Box 4064, Atlanta, GA 30302.

GERALD, WILLIAM
Clergyman. **PERSONAL:** Born Dec 15, 1918, Irwin County, GA; married Fannie M; children: Edmond, Clarence, Frank, Raymond. **EDUCATION:** Eastern Amer Univ, DD 1980; Howard Univ; Cortez Peters Bus Clge. **CAREER:** Bible Way Church Wash DC, secr to presiding bishop 1948-69; Bible Way Church World Wide Inc, rec secr 1962-83; Lighthouse Church over WANN Annapolis, radio minister 1965-; "Spread A Little Sunshine" channel 9, sub TV host 1969-83. **ORGANIZATIONS:** Clerk typist acct JE Hanger Inc 1978-84; radio minister Lighthouse Apostolic Church Bible Way 1965-; sub TV host "Spread A Little Sunshine" channel 9 Wash DC 1970-83; corr rec secr Bible Way Church World Wide 1962-83; secr to presiding Bishop Smallwood E Williams 1948-69. **HONORS/ACHIEVEMENTS:** Books publ, "Coping With & Overcoming Today's Problems" 1977, "Divine Basics And Concepts" 1983, "The Golden Years" 1984; co-authored other books of prominence; musician & songwriter. **HOME ADDRESS:** 701 Glenwood St, Annapolis, MD 21401.

GERAN, JOSEPH, JR.
Designer, educator. **PERSONAL:** Born Nov 23, 1945, San Francisco, CA; son of Joseph Geran Sr; married divorced (divorced); children: Paige K. **EDUCATION:** City Coll of San Francisco, AA 1963-66; CA State Univ at San Francisco, BA 1967-70; CA Coll of Arts and Crafts, MFA 1970-72; Univ of RI, 1985-87. **CAREER:** CA State Univ at San Francisco, lecturer 1969-70; CA Coll of Arts and Crafts, asst prof 1970-74; RI Sch of Design, dean of students 1974-77; Comm Coll of RI, instructor 1980-82; Jewelry Inst Providence, RI, instructor 1986-88; Geran Enterprises, designer/modelmaker. **ORGANIZATIONS:** Bd of dir RI Black Heritage Soc 1979-82; mem Black Artists of Rhode Island (BARI), 1985-. **HONORS/ACHIEVEMENTS:** Illinois Sculpture Award, Illinois State Univ 1972; commissioned by the State of Rhode Island to sculpt the bust of Dr Martin Luther King, Jr (bronze), 1986; The Jazz Trumpet (bronze) funded by Black Artists of Rhode Island, 1989; Bird of Hope (bronze)included in the permanent collection of the Smithsonian Inst, Washington, DC, 1973. **BUSINESS ADDRESS:** Geran Enterprises, 19 Academy Ave, Providence, RI 02908.

GERMAN, ANN LOUISE
Association executive. **PERSONAL:** Born in Kingston, Jamaica;children: Dawn, Artist, Jr, Jann. **EDUCATION:** London C of C, Commercial Educ Certificate; Shorthand Inst London England, Certificates Pitman's; Bishop Coll Marshall TX, BS; TX State Tchrs, Life Certificate; So MethUniv Dallas, 1960; Am Inst Life Ins Co's. **CAREER:** Dallas Girl Scout Council; asst office mgr; St Anthony Cath Schl, tchr; SW Region NAACP; NAACP, fld Drctr at Lrg NAACP 1971. **ORGANIZATIONS:** Bd mem Dallas Deanery of Catholic Women; Women's Dialogue UCCIJ; UCCIJ Chmn Cath Interracial Council; bd mem Sr Citizens Neighborhood Council Land MarkDevel Corp; chmn WRR Negotiation Com Dallas-fortworth Coalition for Free Flow Information; Dallas Negro C of c; Alpha Kappa Alpha Sorority; interior decorating; gormet-cooking; sewing. **HONORS/ACHIEVEMENTS:** Alumni Citation Award; outstanding-achievement & srvc which reflects honor on Bishop Coll Bishop Coll 1970; citizen of the day, recognition outstanding community & srvc KBOX Radio Station; outstanding community involvement Dallas Interdenom. **BUSINESS ADDRESS:** 2600 Flora St, Room 100, Dallas, TX 75215.

GERMANY, ALBERT See GEE, AL

GERMANY, SYLVIA MARIE ARMSTRONG
College administrator. **PERSONAL:** Born Jan 10, 1950, New Orleans, LA; married Plenty Morgan Germany, Jr; children: Jobyna Joidella, Adam Nathan. **EDUCATION:** Southern Univ in New Orleans, BS 1980. **CAREER:** Orleans Parish Sch Bd, adm exec sec 1977-80; Pre-Employment Program, business instructor 1980-81; Sidney N Collier Vo-Tech, business instructor 1981-85; Oakwood Coll, personnel assistant 1985-. **ORGANIZATIONS:** Mem LA Vo-Tech Assoc 1981-85; mem Amer Soc for Personnel Administrators 1985-. **BUSINESS ADDRESS:** Personnel Administrator, Oakwood College, Personnel Office, Oakwood Rd, Huntsville, AL 35896.

GERVIN, GEORGE (ICEMAN)
Professional athlete. **PERSONAL:** Born Apr 27, 1952, Detroit, MI; married Joyce; children: George Jr, Jared, Tia Monique. **EDUCATION:** Eastern MI, attended 1973. **CAREER:** San Antonio Spurs, basketball player; Chicago Bulls, basketball player. **HONORS/ACHIEVEMENTS:** NBA All Star Game 1977, 1979, 1980; NBA Scoring Champ; All Star 8 times; League's Leading Scorer 4 times; 10th on the all-time points list with 23,746; All-Star Game MVP 1980; Seagram's Crown 1978, 1979. **BUSINESS ADDRESS:** Chicago Bulls, One Magnificent Mile, 980 North Michigan Ave, Chicago, IL 60611.

GEYER, EDWARD B., JR.
Rector. **PERSONAL:** Born Aug 23, 1929, New York City; married Laura E Williams; children: Edward Blaine, III, Ruth Anne. **EDUCATION:** Wash Sq Coll,aB NYU; STB Magna Cum Laude Div Sch Episcopal Ch Phila; Schl Educ NYU, post grad Work. **CAREER:** St Peter's, NYC, curate 1958-60; St Luke's, New Haven CT, rector 1960-68; St Peter's, Bennington VT 1968-72; Good Shepherd, Hartford CT 1972; Provincial Synod, Del 1974; Greater Hartford Council of Chrs, Vice Pres 1973-78; Capitol Region Conf of Ch 1978-79; Martin Luther King Jr Housing Devel Hartford, Pres 1974. **ORGANIZATIONS:** Mem Exec Council Diocese of Vermont 1970-72; New England Provincial Synod 1971-72; New Eng Prvncl Synod Cncl 1973; Com On State Of Ch 1975; Comm on Ministry 1971-72; Ch Diocesan Liturgical Comm 1971-72; mem Bd trsts Philadelphia Div Sch 1968-73; Gen Theol Sem 1970; vice pres Bennington Cncl Of Chrs 1969-72; mem Bennington Hsng Auth 1970-72; mem bd Bennington-rutland Opp Cncl 1968-72; treas BROC 1971-72; mem bd Phoenix House 1971-72;

Bennington Ministerial Assoc 1968-72; Exec Council Diocese of Conn 1965-68; Dept of Christ Educ 1965-68; bd of Dirs New Haven Comm Council 1964-68 ; mem Educ Comm 1964-68; Chaplain New Haven State Jail 1966-68; mem Clergyman's Adv Com CT Planned Parenthood 1965-68; mem Urban Task Force New Haven C of C 1968; bd Re Ctr for Mental Retatdation 1965-68; Children's Ctr Hamden, Ct 1967-68; mem Steering Comm of the NH Young Mother's Prgm 1965-68; Civil Serv Cmmssnr New Haven 1698; mem Christ Ch Cathedral Cathedral Chap Hartford 1968-73; fld Wrk Supr Gen Theol Sem 1958-60 . **BUSINESS ADDRESS:** 155 Wyllys St, Hartford, CT 06106.

GHENT, HENRI HERMANN
Writer, art/music critic, exhibition director. **PERSONAL:** Born Jun 23, 1926, Birmingham, AL; son of Reuben Gantt and Jennie Gantt. **EDUCATION:** New England Conservatory, Boston MA, 1951; Museum School of Fine Arts, Boston, 1952; Longy School of Music, Cambridge MA, 1953; Univ of Paris, France, 1960. **CAREER:** Cultural news editor, Elegant magazine, New York City, 1964-68; asst dir, Inst of Arts & Sci Brooklyn, 1968-69; dir, Comm Gallery, Brooklyn Museum, 1968-72; New York correspondent, Le Monde de la Musique, Paris; Danser Magazine, Paris. **ORGANIZATIONS:** Consultant, Natl Endowment for the Arts, Washington DC, 1973-74; chief juror, Dayton Art Inst All-Ohio Painting Sculpture Biennial, 1972; chief juror, Grad Students Art & Design, Pratt Inst, Brooklyn NY, 1972; contributed significant articles on visual & performing arts to Le Monde de la Musique Paris, New York Times, Los Angeles Times, Cleveland Plain Dealer, Art Intl (Lugano, Switzerland), Artforum (New York), Art in Amer (New York), Boston Globe, Village Voice (New York). **HONORS/ACHIEVEMENTS:** Hon degree humanities, Allen Univ, Columbia SC, 1966; Art Critics Award, Natl Endowment for the Arts, Washington DC, 1973-74; Ford Found Travel & Study Fellowship, 1974-75; Samuel H Kress Found Award in Arts Research; Martha Baird Rockefeller Fellowship in Music, 1957-58; Achievement in the Arts Award, NAACP, 1973. **MILITARY SERVICE:** AUS tech/5th 1945-46; Good Conduct; Good Marksmanship 1946. **HOME ADDRESS:** 310 E 75th St, 1st Fl, New York, NY 10021.

GHOLSON, GENERAL JAMES
Educator. **PERSONAL:** Born Oct 15, 1944, Norfolk, VA; children: Christopher James. **EDUCATION:** MI State U, BM 1966; Cath U, MM 1970; Cath U, DMA 1975. **CAREER:** Memphis State Univ, instructor, asst prof, assoc prof of Clarinet 1972; Catholic Univ, Washington DC, grad asst 1970-72; US Navy Band, Washington DC, section clarinetist & solist 1966-70; Memphis Woodwind Quintet, 1972; Opera Memphis, solo clarinet 1972; Memphis Symphony, solo clarinet 1975. **ORGANIZATIONS:** Faculty adv Kappa Alpha Psi; "Problem Solving in the Clarinet— Studio" Woodwind World 1979; videos "How to Make All West" Jamus 1985, "Kards in the Key of Kroepsch" Jamus 1986, "How to Make All Region a Breeze" Jamus 1986. **BUSINESS ADDRESS:** Associate Professor, Memphis StateUniv, Central & Patterson, Memphis, TN 38152.

GHOLSTON, BETTY J.
Educational administrator. **PERSONAL:** Born Feb 01, 1942, Wagram, NC; married Willie Gunter; children: Lisa Regina, Betty Cornelia, Saranarda, Willie G Jr. **EDUCATION:** NC Central Univ, BS Commerce 1959-63; NC A&T State Univ, MS Adminis 1977-79; Univ of NC, further study 1978. **CAREER:** Richmond Cty School, media specialist 1968; Cameron Morrison School, media specialist 1968-77; Cameron Morrison Youth Ctr, project dir/media specialist 1977-83; Richmond Cty Schools, job placement coordinator 1984; NC Dept of Correction, dir of fed proj/educ spec. **ORGANIZATIONS:** Vice pres Cameron Morrison NCAE 1982-83; bd of directors Black Elected Municipal Officials 1983-84; Mayor Pro Tem Wagram Bd of Commissioners 1974-; rep NC Council of Govt-Region N 1982-. **HONORS/ACHIEVEMENTS:** Founder of Wagram Brnch Library 1975; Teacher of the Year NC Dept of Youth Services 1977; listed in Who's Who Among Amer Women 1981-82. **BUSINESS ADDRESS:** Dir of Fed Proj/Educ Spec, NC Dept of Correction, Cameron Morrison Youth Ctr, Hoffman, NC 28347.

GIBBES, EMILY V.
Educator. **PERSONAL:** Born Aug 14, 1915, New York, NY; daughter of George Gibbes and Genevieve Gibbes. **EDUCATION:** Hunter Coll, BA (Cum Laude) 1937; NY Univ, MA (Cum Laude) 1951; NY School of Social Work, attended 1952; Attended, Alliance Francaise Paris. **CAREER:** NY City Council, confidential sec to minority leader, 1941-49; Religious Educ United Presbyterian Church, field dir 1949-57; United Presbyterian Women, general dir educ program 1957-68; Church Educ Africa, consultant 1968-72; Natl Council of Churches, assoc general sec for educ & ministry; NY Theological Seminary, dean of religious educ 1980-. **ORGANIZATIONS:** Conducted study seminars for Church Women to Latin Amer Africa Asia 1953, 1968; consultant in religious education to the Natl Churches Cameroon West Africa, Kenya 1969-72; pres Religious Educ Assoc 1975-78. **HONORS/ACHIEVEMENTS:** Kappa Delta Pi Hon Soc 1950; author of numerous articles study guides training models curricula for church women; Distinguished Alumnae Award School of Educ NY Univ 1978; Church Woman of the Year Award Religious Heritage Assn 1979; Alumnae Hall of Fame Hunter Coll 1981; DHL Mary Holmes Coll 1983. **BUSINESS ADDRESS:** Dean of Religious Education, NY Theological Seminary, 5 West 29th St, New York, NY 10001.

GIBBONS, JOHN
Law enforcement. **PERSONAL:** Born Aug 20, 1956, Newark, NJ; married Shelby Hall. **EDUCATION:** Amer Intl Coll, BA 1978, MA 1979. **CAREER:** Hampden Co House of Corrections, correctional counselor 1978-79; MA State Police, detective. **ORGANIZATIONS:** Elder Martin Luther King Comm Church 1981-; bd mem Springfield Urban League 1981-; chmn of membership Omega Psi Phi Frat Inc 1984-; vice pres of bd of dir Amer Intl Coll 1984-85. **HONORS/ACHIEVEMENTS:** Beyond the Call of Duty Elks Club Northampton 1982; Outstanding Young Man Outstanding Young Men of Amer 1982; Pres Cup Amer Intl Coll 1978; Pol Sci Academic Awd Amer Intl Coll 1978. **HOME ADDRESS:** 228 Navajo Rd, Springfield, MA 01109.

GIBBONS, WALTER E.
Electrical engineer. **PERSONAL:** Born May 28, 1952, New York, NY; son of Eustace Gibbons and Iris Balfour Gibbons; married Celeste M Hanson, Jun 05, 1976; children: Adam, Melanie. **EDUCATION:** Massachusetts Inst of Technology, SB, EE 1974, SM, EE 1975; Stanford Univ, MS Mgmt 1986. **CAREER:** Bell Lab, Holmdel NJ, mem of technical Staff 1973-76; Bell Lab, Naperville IL, mem of technical staff 1976-79, Bell Laboratories, supvr 1979-1986; AT&T Bell Lab, Dept Head 1986-. **ORGANIZATIONS:** Member, IEEE 1987-. **HONORS/ACHIEVEMENTS:** Natl Achievement Scholar MIT 1969-73; published article "Traffic Service Position System No 1 Remote-Trunking Arrangement Hardware & Software Implementation", The Bell-System Technical Journal vol 58 no 6, 1979; Stanford Sloan Fellow 1985-86. **BUSINESS ADDRESS:** Department Head, AT&T Bell Laboratories, 1200 East Warrenville Rd, Naperville, IL 60566.

GIBBS, ALMA G.
Educator. **PERSONAL:** Born Jul 24, 1914, Dendron, VA. **EDUCATION:** BS 1946; Univ MI & VA State Coll, Grad Study. **CAREER:** Surey HS, head dept Home Econ 1974; Surey HS, entire teaching career of 29 yrs. **ORGANIZATIONS:** Mem VA Tchrs Assn; past pres Surey Co Ed Assn; VHET; AHEA; AVA; AAUW; Black Caucus; vice president Surryprince Geo Chap VA State Coll Alumni; memPTA; pres LP Jackson Alumni; Ch Trustee & Clk; VA Lung Assn Southside Reg; bd dor Bicentennial Com; Girl Scouts VA Mun League. **HONORS/ACHIEVEMENTS:** Recipient, Women for Political Action Award, 1970; S Side TB Assn Award, 1970; Recogntion for Outstanding Work w/Youth Bd of VA Lung Assn, 1975; State Coll Alumnae Award 1971.

GIBBS, JEWELLE TAYLOR
Educator. **PERSONAL:** Born Nov 04, 1933, Stratford, CT; daughter of Rev Julian A Taylor and Margaret P Morris Taylor; married James Lowell Gibbs Jr; children: Geoffrey Taylor, Lowell Dabney. **EDUCATION:** Radcliffe Coll, AB (Cum Laude) 1951-55, Certificate in Business Admin 1958-59; Univ of California, MSW 1970, MA Psychology 1976, PhD Psychology 1980. **CAREER:** US Labor Dept Washington, jr mgmt asst 1955-56; Pillsbury Co, Minneapolis MN, market research analyst 1959-61; Stanford Univ, psychology social worker 1970-74, 1978-79; Univ of CA Berkeley, prof 1979-. **ORGANIZATIONS:** Clinical psychology private practice consulting 1983-; consultant Carnegie Corp 1983-; bd of regents Univ of Santa Clara 1980-85; bd of dir Amer Orthopsychiatric Assoc 1985-88; mem task force on special populations Pres Commission on Mental Health WA 1976-78; mem ed bd Amer Journal of Orthopsychiatry 1980-84; mem bd of publs Natl Assoc of Social Workers 1980-82; adv bd FL Mental Health Inst Univ of South FL at Tampa FL 1985-88; Advisory Board, Natl Center for Children in Poverty, 1987-90. **HONORS/ACHIEVEMENTS:** NIMH Pre-Doctoral Fellowship, Univ of CA 1979-80; John Hay Whitney Opportunity Fellowship, Radcliffe Coll 1958-59; fellow Bunting Inst Radcliffe Coll 1985; authornum professional papers, chapters on adolescent psychopathology, minority mental health & brief treatment; McCormick Award, Amer Assn of Suicidology, 1987; editor, Young, Black and Male in Amer: An Endangered Species, 1988; co-author, Children of Color, co-author with Larke N Huang PhD, 1989. **BUSINESS ADDRESS:** Associate Professor, University of California, School of Social Welfare, 120 Haviland Hall, Berkeley, CA 94720.

GIBBS, KAREN PATRICIA
Financial futures analyst. **PERSONAL:** Born May 09, 1952, Boston, MA. **EDUCATION:** Roosevelt Univ Chicago, BSBA 1976; Univ of Chicago Grad Sch of Business, MBA 1978. **CAREER:** Cont Commodity Serv Inc, intrest rate specialist 1978-82; Harris Trust & Savings Bank, gvt securities rep 1982-83; Dean Witter Reynolds, hedgng & trading strategist 1983-85, sr financial futures analyst 1985-. **ORGANIZATIONS:** Sec bd of dirs Henry Booth House 1981-85; bd of dirs Chicago Lung Assoc 1983-; pres Dorchester Condo Assoc 1984-; sec Chicago Chap Natl Black MBA Assoc 1985-86; mem Natl Assoc of Security Professionals. **HONORS/ACHIEVEMENTS:** Quoted frequently in NY Times and Wall St Journal; articles published in CBOT's Financial Exchange; recently selected by pres of Dean Witter's Capital Mkts Group for Natl Ad Campaign to recruit minority employees. **HOME ADDRESS:** 5012 So Dorchester, Chicago, IL 60615. **BUSINESS ADDRESS:** Asst Vice Pres Financial Futures, Dean Witter Reynolds, 150 So Wacker Dr, Chicago, IL 60606.

GIBBS, MARLA
Actress. **PERSONAL:** Born Jun 14, Chicago, IL; children: Angela, Jordan Jr, Dorian. **EDUCATION:** Cortez Peters Bus Coll, attended 1952. **CAREER:** Tandem Prods, "The Jeffersons", actress 1974-; Marla Gibbs Enterprises, pres 1978-; Marla's Memory Lanes, restaurant owner; Hormar Inc, vice pres; TV show "227", starring role. **ORGANIZATIONS:** Treas UGMAA Found; mem Sci of Mind Church; travel consult United Air Lines 1965-75. **HONORS/ACHIEVEMENTS:** Awd Natl Acad Arts & Scis 1976; Awd Miss Black Culture Pageant 1977; Awd United Negro Coll Fund 1977; Appreciation Awd LA Sch Dist 1978; Awd WomenInvolved 1979; Awd Watts Reperatory Co 1980; Tribute to the Black Woman Awd WISE 1979; The Image Awd NAACP 1979-80-81-82-83; Comm Serv Awd Crenshaw HS1980; Awd Paul Robeson Players 1980; Awd CA State Assembly 1980; Emmy nominee 1981,82,83,84,85. **BUSINESS ADDRESS:** Hormar Inc, 7085 Hollywood Blvd, Ste 731, Los Angeles, CA 90028.

GIBBS, SANDRA E.
Educator. **PERSONAL:** Born Aug 16, 1942, Chicago, IL. **EDUCATION:** N Coll Pine Bluff AR, AB, AM English 1964;Univ of IL Urbana IL, AM English 1971, PhD English 1974. **CAREER:** Little Rock AR Public Schools, high school english teacher 1964-70; Univ of IL, teacher of fresh rhtrc 1970-71; Natl Cncl Teacher English, dir of min affairs spec proj 1973-. **ORGANIZATIONS:** Con AR Dept Educ Little Rock AR 1969; mem adv bd Prime Time Sch of TV 1975; consult HEW Wmn's Proj Bndct Coll 1978-80; prop rvwr Nat Endwmnt for the Humt 1979; mem Delta Sigma Theta Sor; mem Alpha Kappa Mu Hon Soc. **HONORS/ACHIEVEMENTS:** Tchrs of Engl Flwshp 1971; 4yr Schlr Crst Co 1960-64; 2 NDEA Flwshp 1966-67; pub chap Engl & Min Grps in Engl in the 80's; Consultant Editor for "Tapping Potential, English and Language Arts for the Black Learner," 1984 Natl Council of Teachers of English; Distinguished Alumni Citation, Natl Assn for Equal Opportunity in Higher Education 1986. **BUSINESS ADDRESS:** Dir, Natl Cncl of Tchrs of English, 1111 Kenyon Rd, Urbana, IL 61801.

GIBBS, VERNON D. G.
Editor. **PERSONAL:** Born Jan 14, 1951, Kingston, Jamaica. **EDUCATION:** Columbia Univ, BA 1974; Columbia Univ Journalism School. **CAREER:** Blues, Arista Records NY, dir rhythm 1977; began writing for rock mag, expanded into Essence magazine & other publications; contrib editor, freelancer. **ORGANIZATIONS:** Mem Common Cause. **BUSINESS ADDRESS:** Box 621, Cathedral St, New York, NY 10025.

GIBBS, WARMOTH T.
Retired educator. **PERSONAL:** Born Apr 05, 1892, Baldwin, LA; married Marece Jones; children: Marece Elizabeth, Warmoth T. **EDUCATION:** Wiley Coll Marshall, AB 1912;

Harvard Coll Cambridge MA, AB 1917; Harvard U, Ed M 1925; Wiley Coll Marshall TX, LlD 1956; Agr & Coll Greensboro NC, LlD 1962. **CAREER:** NC A&T State Univ, past pres 1965; NC Tech State Univ, various levels from teacher to pres 1926-65; real estate operator 1966; Piedmont Devel Corp, chmn of bd; Shepargib Foods Corp, chmn of bd; Boston Urban League; Burger King Franchise exec sec. **ORGANIZATIONS:** Mem Nat Assn of Collegiate Deans & Registrars 1929-55; mem Am Assn for Study of Negro Life & Hist 1930-60; mem (Military com) Nat StateUniv & Land Grant 1959-65 author "MW Dagas & Wiley Coll" 1937; author "Hist of NC Agr & Tech Coll" 1965. **MILITARY SERVICE:** AUS 2nd lt 1917-19. **BUSINESS ADDRESS:** NC A&T State Univ, Greensboro, NC 27411.

GIBSON, ALBERT (THE MAD GIBSON)
Performer. **PERSONAL:** Born Jun 19, 1918, Atlanta, GA; married Mildred Josephine Pollard. **CAREER:** Gibson's Generation Gap, performer mad 1975-78; Jazz Dance Theater Mexico & Africa, Choreographer 1968-69; Moke & Poke, dance team 1961-65; Miller & Gibson Show "Hi-lights", dancer & choreographer 1957-60; "Peckin" 3 Chocolateers, choreographer; Olsen & Johnson Hells Ap Poppin, dancer 1927-30; Gibson Family Chocalate Box Review, dancer 1922-27. **ORGANIZATIONS:** Ex-shriner Mason; mem Negro Actors Guild; mem Copasetics Social Club. **HONORS/ACHIEVEMENTS:** Swam Across Hong Kong Bay 1933; Gold Coin Haillie Sallasie 1969; Nat Endowment for the Arts Grant for Variety Show 1978. **MILITARY SERVICE:** AUS pvt 1943-44.

GIBSON, ALTHEA
Professional tennis player, golfer. **PERSONAL:** Born Aug 25, 1927, Silver, SC. **EDUCATION:** FL A&M Coll, BS 1953. **CAREER:** US Europe & S Amer, amateur tennis player 1941-58; Lincoln Univ, asst instructor Dept Health & Physical Educ 1953-55; appeared in movie The Horse Soldiers 1958; professional tennis tour w/Harlem Globetrotters 1959; Ward Baking Co, comm relations rep 1959; Ladies Professional Gold Assn, prof golfer 1963; apptd to NY State Recreation Council 1964; Essex Co Park Commn Newark, staff mem 1970, recreation supr 1970-71, dir tennis programs; Valley View Racquet Club Northvale, professional tennis player 1972; City of East Orange, recreation mgr 1980-83; NJ State Athletic Control Board; NJ Governor's Council on Physical Fitness and Sports, special consultant, 1988-. **ORGANIZATIONS:** Mem Alpha Kappa Alpha. **HONORS/ACHIEVEMENTS:** Named to Lawn Tennis Hall of Fame & Tennis Museum 1971; Won World Professional Tennis Championship 1960; Woman Athlete of the Year AP Poll 1957-58; SC Athletic Hall of Fame 1983; author "I Always Wanted to be Somebody" 1958; Monmouth Coll, Honorary DPA degree 1980; FL Sports Hall of Fame 1984; UNC Wilmington, Honorary Littd Degree, 1987.

GIBSON, BENJAMIN F.
Judge. **PERSONAL:** Born Jul 13, 1931, Safford, AL; married Lucille Nelson; children: Charlotte, Linda, Gerald, Gail, Carol, Laura. **EDUCATION:** Wayne State Univ, BS 1955; Detroit Coll of Law, JD (with distinction) 1960. **CAREER:** City of Detroit, acct 1955-56; Detroit Edison Co, acct 1956-61; State of MI, asst atty gen 1961-63; Ingham County MI, asst pros atty 1963-64; Lansing MI, pvt practice law 1964-; US Dist Ct Western Dist Grand Rapids MI, judge 1979-. **ORGANIZATIONS:** Hearing officer East Lansing; bd dirs Lansing Jr Achivement, Greater Lansing Legal Aid Bur; mem Amer Trial Lawyers Assn, Amer Bar Assn, Ingham County Bar Ass; grievance bd hearing panel State Bar MI 1971; mem Sigma Pi Phi, Rotary. **BUSINESS ADDRESS:** Judge, Michigan Western District, 616 Federal Bldg, 110 Michigan St NW, Grand Rapids, MI 49503.

GIBSON, DONALD B.
University educator. **PERSONAL:** Born Jul 02, 1933, Kansas City, MO; son of Oscar J Gibson and Florine Myers Gibson; married Jo Anne Ivory, Dec 14, 1963; children: David, Douglas. **EDUCATION:** Univ of Kansas City, Kansas City MO, BA, 1955, MA, 1957; Brown Univ, Providence RI, PhD, 1962. **CAREER:** Brown Univ, Providence RI, instructor, 1960-61; Wayne State Univ, Detroit MI, asst prof, 1961-67; Univ of Connecticut, Storrs CT, assoc prof, 1967-69, prof, 1969-74; Rutgers Univ, New Brunswick NJ, distinguished prof, 1974-. **ORGANIZATIONS:** Mem, Coll Language Assn, Modern Language Assn 1964-; editorial bd, Black Amer Literature Forum, 1972-; consultant, Educ Testing Serv, 1976-; mem, Natl Council of Teachers of English, 1987-. **HONORS/ACHIEVEMENTS:** Postdoctoral Fulbright, Fulbright Hayes Comm, 1964-66; Study Grant, Natl Endowment for the Humanities, 1970; Research Grant, Amer Council of Learned Socities, 1970; author, The Fiction of Stephen Crane, 1968; editor, Five Black Writers, 1970; editor, Twentieth-Century Interpretations of Modern Black Poets, 1973; author, The Politics of Literary Expression: A Study of Major Black Writers, 1981; author, The Red Bridge of Courage: Redefining The Hero, 1988. **BUSINESS ADDRESS:** Professor of English, Rutgers University, Department of English, Murray Hall CN5054, New Brunswick, NJ 08903.

GIBSON, EDWARD LEWIS
Physician. **PERSONAL:** Born Jun 06, 1932, Chicago, IL; married Nannette; children: Joan, Edward Jr, Paula. **EDUCATION:** Roosevelt UL, BS 1953; HowardUniv Coll Med, MD 1957. **CAREER:** Columbia U, physician, self; asst prof anesthesiology, coll physicians & surgeons; Bellevue Med Ctr, Vis Flw 1962-64; Columbia-presbyn Med & Ctr, asst resd 1958-62; Michael Reese Hosp, intern 1957-58; Princeton Med Ctr, dir anesthesiology 1967-74; Robert R Moton Meml Inst Inc, Tst. **ORGANIZATIONS:** Mem AMA; Am Soc Anesthesiologists. **HONORS/ACHIEVEMENTS:** USAF capt 1958-62. **MILITARY SERVICE:** USAF capt 1958-62. **BUSINESS ADDRESS:** 47 Locust Ln, Princeton, NJ 08540.

GIBSON, ELVIS EDWARD
Chief fair housing enforcement. **PERSONAL:** Born Jul 15, 1937, Calvert, TX; married Sylvia M; children: Patricia Elaine. **EDUCATION:** Park Coll, BA Social Work (Cum Laude) 1973. **CAREER:** Martin Luther King Hosp, bd of dir 1970-; pres KCMO Black United Fund 1976-; Natl Black United Fund, bd of dir 1978-; Charlie Parker Acad of the Arts, chmn 1980-; Black Historical/Genealogy, vice pres 1980-; US Dept of HUD, chief fair housing enforcement. **ORGANIZATIONS:** Chmn OIC Opportunities Industrialization Ct 1974; bd of dir Black Archives of Mid-Amer 1975; radio commentator "Health" KWKI FM radio 1975; chmn Forum for Social Expression Inc 1980; quasi judicial officer Kansas City MO Neighborhood Justice Court; social engr/consultant to private groups. **HONORS/ACHIEVEMENTS:** Jefferson Awd Taft Broadcasting Corp 1986; Disting Comm Serv Awd. **MILITARY SERVICE:** USAF staff sgt 1955-58. **HOME ADDRESS:** 3338 Benton Blvd, Kansas City, MO 64128.

GIBSON, ERNEST ROBINSON
Clergyman. **PERSONAL:** Born Aug 08, 1920, Washington, DC; married Etta; children: Ernest Jr, Dolores, Mark, Bessie Mae, Virginia, Frederick. **EDUCATION:** Howard U, BA 1963; HowardUniv Schl of Religion, BD cum laude 1966. **CAREER:** Counc of Chs of Grtr Washington, exec dir 1975; Counc of Chs of Grtr Washington, acting exec dir 1975; Inner City Ministry Counc of Chs of Grtr Washington, dir 1967-75; Neighbrhd Yth Corps Prgm, dir 1966-67; 1st Rising Mt Zion Bat Ch, pastor 1952; Naval Gun Factory, journeyman Molder 1941-56. **ORGANIZATIONS:** Mem bd of dir Model Inner City Comm Orgn 1966-70; Proj Find, chmn 1966-67; Bapt Com on Wider Coop, chmn 1968-70; 1st Rising Mt Zion Bapt Ch Housing Corp, pres 1969; DC Adv Counc for Vocational-edn, chmn 1971-73; Interfaith Assn in Theol Edn, chmn bd of dir 1970; bd mem Redevel Land Agency 1976. **MILITARY SERVICE:** Armed Servs 1945-46. **BUSINESS ADDRESS:** 1239 Vermont Ave NW, Washington, DC 20005.

GIBSON, GREGORY A.
Mortgage banking executive. **PERSONAL:** Born Oct 15, 1948, Los Angeles, CA; married Shelly Rae Walthall; children: Katrina, Gregory Jr, Nicole. **EDUCATION:** Attended, Los Angeles City Coll 1966-67, Portland State College 1975-78, Northwestern Univ; School of Mortgage Banking, Graduate 1982-85. **CAREER:** AMFAC Mortgage Corp, field representative 1977-80; General Electric Mortgage, asst vice pres loan servicing 1980-85; MeraBank, vice pres loan admin 1986-. **ORGANIZATIONS:** Mem OR Mortgage Bankers Assoc 1979-84; loan servicing comm Mortgage Banker Assoc 1985-; mem Phoenix Black Bd of Dirs Project 1987. **HONORS/ACHIEVEMENTS:** Outstanding Mgmt Awd 1983; General Electric Mortgage Corp 1984. **MILITARY SERVICE:** AUS sgt E5 2 yrs; two Army Commendation Medals for Heroism, Bronze Star Vietnam 1967-69. **BUSINESS ADDRESS:** Vice Pres Loan Administration, MeraBank, 20002 No 19th Ave, Phoenix, AZ 85027.

GIBSON, HARRIS, JR.
Cardio-thoracic surgeon. **PERSONAL:** Born Nov 19, 1936, Mobile, AL; son of Harris Gibson Sr and Maude Richardson Gibson; married Marva A Boone; children: Michael, Michelle. **EDUCATION:** AL State Univ, BS 1956; Northwestern Univ, MS 1957; Meharry Medical Coll, MD 1961. **CAREER:** USPHS Hosp NY, internship 1961-62; USPHS Hosp Boston, surgery residency 1962-66; USPHS, asst chief surgery 8 yrs; Boston City Hosp Boston Univ, thoracic surg residency 1966-68; Cardio-Thoracic Assocs Inc, surgeon 1969-; Winchester Hosp, chief thoracic surgery; Boston Univ Medical Sch, asst clinical prof surgery. **ORGANIZATIONS:** Pres New England Medical Soc of NMA 1981-82; pres Middlesex East District Medical Soc of AMA 1983-84; mem Amer Medical Assoc, Soc of Thoracic Surgery. **HONORS/ACHIEVEMENTS:** Mem Alpha Omega Alpha; Fellow Amer Coll of Surgeons, Amer Coll of Chest Physicians; mem Signa Xi. **BUSINESS ADDRESS:** Asst Clinical Prof of Surgery, BostonUniv Medical School, 101 George P Hassett Dr, Medford, MA 02155.

GIBSON, HARRY H. C.
Attorney, company chief executive. **PERSONAL:** Born Oct 08, 1913, Atlanta, GA; son of Truman K Gibson, Sr (deceased) and Alberta A Dickerson Gibson; married Mildred C Mickey (deceased), Oct 14, 1939 (deceased); children: Edward L Gibson, MD. **EDUCATION:** Univ of Illinois, BA, 1933, JD, 1935. **CAREER:** Supreme Life Insurance Co of Amer, sr vice pres/general counsel, 1955-; Bd of global ministries United Methodist Church, present; Chicago Burr Oak Cemetery, pres, 1970-; N IL Conf, Dist Supt, Joint Com on Educ & Cultivation, asst general sec 1970-71; bd of Trustees Gammon Theological Seminary. **ORGANIZATIONS:** Natl Bar of Assn; Amer Bar Assn; IL State Bar Assn; Chicago Bar Assn; Bar Assn of the Seventh Federal Circuit; Amer Judicature Society; Amer Cemetery Assn; Sigma Pi Phi Fraternity; Kappa Alpha Psi Fraternity; Royal Coterie of Snakes; Druids Club; NAACP, Chicago Urban League; United Negro Coll Fund; Exec Club of Chicago; Chicago Assn of Commerce and Industry. **HONORS/ACHIEVEMENTS:** Hon DD Philander Smith 1968; Ill State Bar Assn, senior counselor; Chicago Bar Assn, Honoarary Mem; Certificate for dedication and outstanding service to the legal profession for more than 50 years; Univ of IL Coll of law, senior alumnus; Chicago Land Clearance Commission Award, for able and faithful service as a commissioner IL State Bar Assn, privileged member. **BUSINESS ADDRESS:** Senior Vice President, Supreme Life Ins Co of America, 3501 South King Drive, Chicago, IL 60616.

GIBSON, JAMES O.
Equal opportunity company executive. **PERSONAL:** Born Apr 01, 1934, Atlanta, GA; son of Calvin Harrison Gibson Sr and Julia Richardson Gibson; married Flora Kathryn Defrantz, Jul 18, 1964; children: Tanya Mechelle, Julia Louis, Carl Oliver. **EDUCATION:** Duquesne Univ, Pittsburgh PA, AB, 1956; Atlanta Univ, Atlanta GA, attended, 1959-60; Temple Univ, Philadelphia PA, attended, 1960-61. **CAREER:** The Potomac Inst, Washington DC, exec assoc, 1966-79; Harambee House Hotel Corp, Washington DC, CEO, 1975-78; Univ of Southern California, Washington Public Affairs Center, adjunct faculty, 1979-81; Govt of District of Columbia, Planning & Devel, asst city admin, 1979-82; The Eugene & Agenes E Meyer Found, Washington DC, pres, 1983-85; The Rockefeller Found, New York NY, program dir, 1986-. **ORGANIZATIONS:** Mem, bd of dir, Assn of Black Found Exec; mem, assoc of the council, Council on Found; mem, visiting comm, Graduate School of Design, Harvard Univ; mem, bd of dir, Kaiser Permanente Community Health Plan of Mid-Atlantic States; consultant, Natl Planning Found, US Conf of Mayors, White House Conf on Civil Rights; mem, bd of governors, Corcoran Gallery of Art, 1968-72; exec comm mem, Federal City Council, 1971-75; founding mem, Cultural Alliance of Greater Washington, 1977; panel on the underclass, Amer Agenda, 1988. **MILITARY SERVICE:** US Army, sp7, 1956-59; Honorable Discharge, 1959; mem, US Le Clerc Team, 1957-58.

GIBSON, JOHN A.
Law enforcement, government official. **PERSONAL:** Born in Philadelphia, PA; married Eleanor Simmons; children: Sean Edward. **EDUCATION:** Camden City Coll, AS 1979; Glassboro State Coll, BA 1981; Eastern Baptist, MA 1984; Temple Univ Philadelphia PA, PhD candidate. **CAREER:** Rutgers Univ, mgr 1964-75; Lawnside Police Dept, police lt 1975-; Borough of Somerdale, NJ, councilman, chief of police, 1987-. **ORGANIZATIONS:** Deacon Calvery Baptist Church; minister, Calvary Batist Church, Chester, PA, 1987-. **MILITARY SERVICE:** AUS Reserves Commission Ofcr. **HOME ADDRESS:** 200 Gloucester Ave, Somerdale, NJ 08083. **BUSINESS ADDRESS:** Chief of Police, Somerdale Borough, 105 Kennedy Blvd, Somerdale, NJ 08083.

GIBSON, JOHN THOMAS
Educator. **PERSONAL:** Born Sep 19, 1948, Montgomery, AL; married Mayme Voncile

Pierce; children: John Thomas Jr, Jerard Trenton, Justin Tarrance, Shayla Voncile. **EDUCATION:** Tuskegee Inst, BS EdM (fellowship winner) Disting Military Grad 1971; Univ of CO Boulder, EdS, PhD (fellowship winner) 1973; Harvard Univ, cert in mgmt 1982. **CAREER:** Tuskegee Inst, instructor of physical educ 1971-72; Smiley Jr High School Denver, admin asst 1971-73; AL State Univ, dir of lab experiences 1973-75, coord of fed rels 1975-76, coord 1976-83, exec asst to pres 1983-86, vice pres of business and finance 1986. **ORGANIZATIONS:** Chmn Affirmative Action Comm Mont Elmore & Autauga Co 1976-; bd mem Bellingrath Exec Council 1976-; treas mem bd of trustees First Congregational Ch1977-; vice polemarch & polemarch Montgomery Alumni Chap Kappa Alpha Psi Inc 1978-; sec IBPOE The Elks Southern Pride #431 1978; Shaaban Temple #103, 330 Mason, Optimist Int'l. **HONORS/ACHIEVEMENTS:** Outstanding Educator of Amer 1975; Outstanding Young Men of Amer 1976-77; Men of Achievement Intl 1978; listed in Who's Who in the South and Southwest 1979;publs, Public School Finance; 30 publs subj of educ finance & admin FA; Men of Achivement Int'l 1980; Phi Delta Kappa, outstanding education leader 1981. **MILITARY SERVICE:** Capt 1970-78. **BUSINESS ADDRESS:** VP Business and Finance, AL A&MUniv, PO Box 369, Normal, AL 35762.

GIBSON, JOHNNIE M. M.
Business executive. **PERSONAL:** Born Mar 01, 1949, Caryville, FL; daughter of Alphonso Maldon and Rosie Maldon; divorced; children: Tiffany Michele. **EDUCATION:** Chipola Junior College, FL, AA Nursing 1968; Albany State College, GA, BS Health Physical Education 1971; Georgia State University, GA, Med 1976. **CAREER:** Marianna HS, FL, high school teacher 1971-72; Albany, GA Police Dept, policewoman 1972-76; FBI, FL, special agent 1976-79; FBI, Washington, special agent 1979-82; FBI, White Collar Crime Div, supervisory special agent 1981-82; Office of Congressional and Public Affairs, supervisory special agent 1982-87; Criminal Investigative Division FBI-Detroit, supervisory special agent, 1988. **ORGANIZATIONS:** Member NOBLE 1981-; member Capital Press Club 1982-; guest lecturer Historical Black Colleges-Universities 1982-; visiting lecturer Urban League Black Executive Exchange Program 1982-; FBI spokeswoman FBI Public Affairs Office 1982-; member IAWP 1984; member-at-large Natl Assoc of Media Women 1985-. **HONORS/ACHIEVEMENTS:** Several letters of commendation from Dir of FBI, 1978, 1980, 1981, 1989; Key to City of Louisville, KY, 1982; Honorary Kentucky Colonel, City of Louisville, 1982; Community Service Award, United Black Fund, Greater Natl Chapter, 1984; Law Enforcement Pioneer Award, North State Law Enforcement Officers Association, 1988; Outstanding Support of Men & Women of the Air Force, The Air Force District of Washington, DC; CBS movie, Johnnie Mae Gibson: FBI, 1986. **BUSINESS ADDRESS:** Supervisory Special Agent, Federal Bureau of Investigation, 477 Michigan Avenue, 26th floor, Detroit, MI 48226.

GIBSON, KENNETH ALLEN
Mayor. **PERSONAL:** Born May 15, 1932, Enterprise, AL; married Muriel Cooke; children: Cheryl, JoAnn, Joyce. **EDUCATION:** Newark Coll, BS Engrg 1960. **CAREER:** NJ Hwy Dept, engr 1950-60; Newark Housing Auth, chief engr 1960-66; City of Newark, chief structgural engr 1966-70; City of Newark, mayor 1970-. **ORGANIZATIONS:** Past pres US Conf of Mayors 1976-77; bd dirs Newark Urban Coalition; co-chmn Bus & Indusl Coord Council; bd dirs Newark YMCA-YWCA; mem Amer Soc CE; Frontiers Intl. **HONORS/ACHIEVEMENTS:** Jaycee's Man of the Yr Newark 1964. **MILITARY SERVICE:** CE, AUS 1956-58.

GIBSON, MAURICE
Claims representative. **PERSONAL:** Born Feb 27, 1960, Fayetteville, NC; married Dale Monica Brace. **EDUCATION:** American Intl Coll, BS 1982, MBA 1987. **CAREER:** Hartford Insurance Group, acct assoc 1983-, claims rep 1985-. **ORGANIZATIONS:** Mem Alpha Phi Alpha Frat Inc 1981-; pres Alpha Kappa Chap 1982; mem NAACP Springfield 1985-. **HONORS/ACHIEVEMENTS:** Special Achievement Awd PRIDE Amer Intl 1982. **HOME ADDRESS:** 15 Leatherleaf Dr, Springfield, MA 01109.

GIBSON, MIKE ANTHONY
Professional athlete. **PERSONAL:** Born Oct 27, 1960, Williamsburg Cnty, SC. **EDUCATION:** SC Spartanburg, Phys Ed Mjr 1982. **CAREER:** Washington Bullets, forward center 1982-. **HONORS/ACHIEVEMENTS:** Opted to play in Philippines & Contntl Bsktbl Assn 1982-83; led SC Spartanburg to NAIA Dist 6 title; first team NAIA All-Am sr season as SC Spartanburgwon the NAIA Tournmnt; named tourney's MVP. **BUSINESS ADDRESS:** Washington Bullets, One Harry S Truman Dr, 777 Sports St, Landover, MD 20785.

GIBSON, MILDRED M.
Interior decorator. **PERSONAL:** Born in New York, NY; married Harry HC. **EDUCATION:** Northwestern U; Roosevelt U; Lasalle-extension U. **CAREER:** Mildred M Gibson Interiors, interior designer 1977; Lois RLowe Women's Div UNCF, chmn 1974-78; United Negro Coll Fund, natl bd; Friends of New Provident Hosp 1976. **ORGANIZATIONS:** Former mem bd of dir Chicago Lying in hosp; mem Girl Friends Nat Orgn; mem Northeasterners Nat Orgn; life mem Womens Scholarship Assn of RooseveltU. **BUSINESS ADDRESS:** 601 E 32nd St, Chicago, IL 60616.

GIBSON, PAUL, JR.
Business executive. **PERSONAL:** Born Aug 05, 1927, New York, NY; married Marcia A Johnson. **EDUCATION:** City Coll NY, BA 1953; NYUniv Sch of Law, JD 1952. **CAREER:** Am Airlines, vice pres gen mgr; City of NY, dep mayor for planning; New York City Bd Educ, educ; Fleary Gibson & Thompson, atty 1954; New York City Housing Auth, comm coord 1955-59; New York City Council, leg couns 1966; NY St Sup Ct, law sec 1969; Am Airlines, dir urban affairs 1969; Urban & Environ Affairs, asst vice pres 1971. **ORGANIZATIONS:** Gen couns NY St NAACP 1962-69; housing chmn NAACP; pres Jamaica NY NAACP; chmn bd dir Jamaica NAACP Day Care Ctr Inc; dir Nat Aerospace Educ Assn; vice pres Jamaica C of C; mem Urban & Reg Affairs Com US C of C; mem Urban Affairs Com Nat Assn Mfgrs; mem corp adv com Nat Urban Coalition; mem bd dir Flagship Intl Inc; pres City Counc 1966-69; chmn Pragmetic Ind NYC; chrmn Intl Trav Ind Exec Com & St John's Epis Ch; mem Queens Co Bar Assn; mem bd trst Niagara U; mem NY St Bar. **MILITARY SERVICE:** AUS 1946-47.

GIBSON, RALPH MILTON
Educator. **PERSONAL:** Born Oct 05, 1923, Cleveland, OH; son of Milton Gibson and Audrey Gibson; married Rose Cleland Campbell; children: Ralph Jr, John Samuel. **EDUCATION:** Univ of MI, BS 1945, MS 1947, PhD 1959. **CAREER:** Cleveland Ohio Child Guidance Clinic, chief psychologist 1947-51; Univ of MI Med Sch, asst prof 1962-65, assoc prof 1965-70, prof 1970-, asst dean 1976-83, prof of psychology. **ORGANIZATIONS:** Assoc staff mem, Wayne Co Gen Hosp 1963-73; State of MI Comm Cert of Psychologists 1963-65; mem Rotary Club 1965-70; bd dir United Fund 1966-68; mem, 1966-74, pres, 1973-74, bd of trustees, Greenhills School; vice chmn bd in control Intrcoll Att, Univ of Michigan, 1969-74, 1986-87; mem, Natl Advisory Council on Child Health & Human Development, Natl Inst of Health, 1987-91. **HONORS/ACHIEVEMENTS:** 1st black full prof, Univ of Michigan Med School, US Public Health Service, 1952-53; Wade H McCree Jr Distinguished Faculty Award, Univ of Michigan Alumni, 1987; Outstanding Achievement in past 50 years, Rackham Graduate School, Univ of Michigan, 1988. **HOME ADDRESS:** 321 Riverview Dr, Ann Arbor, MI 48104. **BUSINESS ADDRESS:** Prof of Psychology, Univ of MI Medical Schl, 1924 Taubman Hlth Care Ctr, Ann Arbor, MI 48109.

GIBSON, REGINALD WALKER
Judge. **PERSONAL:** Born Jul 31, 1927, Lynchburg, VA; children: Reginald S Jr. **EDUCATION:** Virginia Union Univ, BS 1952; Howard Univ School of Law, LLB 1956; Univ Pennsylvania, Wharton School of Finance 1952-53. **CAREER:** Dept of Treasury, internal revenue agent 1957-61; Tax Div Dept of Justice, trial attorney 1961-71; Intl Harvester Co, sr attorney 1971-76, general atty 1976-82; US Claims Court, federal judge. **ORGANIZATIONS:** Mem Amer Bar Assn; mem District of Columbia Bar Assn; mem Federal Bar Assn; mem Illinois Bar Assn; mem Natl Bar Assn; mem Claims Court Bar Assn; mem J Edgar Murdock Amer Inn of Court Taxation. **HONORS/ACHIEVEMENTS:** US Attorney General's Certificate of Award 1969; Distinguished Alumni of the Year Howard Univ Law School 1984; Wall Street Journal Award, Ranking student in Business Admin 1952; Amer Jurisprudence Award, Excellence in Taxation and Trusts 1956; US Atty General's Certificate of Award 1969; Special Commendation for Outstanding Service in Tax Division, US Department of Justice 1970; Alumni of the Year Howard Univ School of Law 1984. **MILITARY SERVICE:** AUS corpl, 1946-47. **BUSINESS ADDRESS:** Federal Judge, US Claims Court, 717 Madison Place NW, Washington, DC 20005.

GIBSON, ROBERT
Professional baseball coach. **PERSONAL:** Born Nov 09, 1935, Omaha, NE. **EDUCATION:** Attended Creighton Univ. **CAREER:** St Louis Cardinals, player 1959-75; NY Mets, coach 1981-82; Atlanta Braves, coach 1982-; St Louis Cardinals, announcer. **HONORS/ACHIEVEMENTS:** Player World Series 1964,67-68; Recip Cy Young Award Natl League 1968,70; named Most Valuable Player Natl League 1968; named to Baseball Hall of Fame 1981; mem Natl League All Star team 8 times. **BUSINESS ADDRESS:** Announcer, St Louis Cardinals, 250 Stadium Plaza, St Louis, MO 63102.

GIBSON, SARAH L.
Educator, consultant. **PERSONAL:** Born May 08, 1927, Princeton, KY; daughter of Earl N Gray, Sr and Fiercie E Edmonds Gray; children: Piper E Fakir, Kyle C. **EDUCATION:** Wayne Univ, BS 1948; Wayne State Univ, MEd, PhD 1972. **CAREER:** Bureau of Social Aid, social worker 1949-53; Pontiac School System, teacher 1955-60; Detroit Public School, teacher 1960-68, school admin 1968-84; GECS, educ consultant 1974-. **ORGANIZATIONS:** Mem ASCD, NAACP, MAMSE 1963; assoc prof Univ of Detroit 1965-67; mem & consultant Trade Leadership Council 1967-; sec Metropolitan Detroit Assoc of Black Admin 1969-72; consulting nurse Harper Hospital 1969-72; consultant Marygrove Coll 1970-71. **HOME ADDRESS:** 2139 Bryanston Crescent, Detroit, MI 48207.

GIBSON, TRUMAN K., JR.
Attorney, corporation executive. **PERSONAL:** Born Jan 22, 1912, Atlanta; married Isabelle Carson. **EDUCATION:** Univ of Chicago, PhB 1932; JD 1935. **CAREER:** Chicago, atty 1935-40; War Dept, asst to civilian aide to sec of War 1940-43, acting civilian aide 1943, civilian aide 1943-45; Chicago, atty 1946-. **ORGANIZATIONS:** Mem firm Gibson & Gibson; gen counsel Tuesday Publs Inc; dir mem exec com Supreme Life Ins Co; dir Parkway Hotel Mgmt Inc; apptd mem Pres's AdvCom on Universal Mil Training 1946; Pres's Com on Morals Character Devel & Religion in Armed Serv 1948;former mem sec Chicago Land Clearance Commn; mem Kappa Alpha Psi; Sigma Pi Phi. **HONORS/ACHIEVEMENTS:** Awarded medal of merit Sec of War Stimson 1945. **BUSINESS ADDRESS:** 471 E 31 St, Chicago, IL 60616.

GIBSON, WARREN ARNOLD
Attorney. **PERSONAL:** Born Jul 16, 1941, Gary, IN. **EDUCATION:** IN U, BS 1965; INUniv 1972; In U, cume laude 1973. **CAREER:** Dow Chem Co, atty; Exxon Corp, emp Rel Rep 1967-70; Montgomery Wards, supr 1966-67. **ORGANIZATIONS:** Mem Am Bar Assn; Nat Bar Assn; MI Bar Assn; Midland Bar Assn. **HONORS/ACHIEVEMENTS:** Mem Alpha Phi Alpha; bd of dir Midland Jr Achvmt 1976-78; Urban League Black Exec Exchange Prgm. **BUSINESS ADDRESS:** c/o The Dow Chemical Co, 400 Westbelt South, Houston, TX 77210.

GIBSON, WILLIAM HOWARD, JR.
Dentist. **PERSONAL:** Born Jan 28, 1941, Memphis, TN. **EDUCATION:** Lincoln U, BS 1961; KS State U, MS 1962; Howard U, DDS 1968. **CAREER:** Yeatman Hlth Ctr, dentist 1969-77; Metro Med WUniv Park Med Grp, partner. **ORGANIZATIONS:** Mem Am Dental Assn; Nat Dental Assn; MO Dental Assn; Midwestern States Dental Assn; Grtr St Louis Dental Soc; Mound City Dental Soc; Acad of Gen Dentistry; mem LincolnUniv Alumni Assn; HowardUniv Alumni Assn; Royal Vagabonds; Rotary Internat; bd dirUniv City MO Club; Chi Delta Mu Frat 1967; Ford Found Flw 1961; pres Alpha Phi Chap 1961; mem Phi Delta Kappa 1962. **BUSINESS ADDRESS:** 7165 Delmar, University City, MO 63130.

GIBSON, WILLIAM M.
Clergyman. **PERSONAL:** Born Sep 11, 1934, Hackensack, NJ; son of James Gibson and Evelyn Scott Gibson; married Jean J Scott Gibson, May 02, 1989; children: Monica, Wayne, Wesley, Caycee, Jerrell Johnson (step Children). **EDUCATION:** Rutgers, BA 1956; Boston Univ Law, JD 1959; Boston Coll, MSW 1966; Harvard Business School, AMP Certificate 1973; Valordictorian MDiv Virginia Magna Cum Laude 1989. **CAREER:** US Dept of Justice, asst US Atty 1961-64; Boston Univ Law, dir law & poverty project 1966-70; Boston Univ

School Afro Amer Studies, Assoc Prof 1968-71; Office Economic Opportunity, regional counsel 1970-72; FTC, regional dir 1972-78; Fuller Mental Health Center, supt area dir; Richmond, VA Metro Dist OIC, deputy district manager; St Paul's Baptist Church, minister of educ and singles. **ORGANIZATIONS:** Mem Natl Assoc Social Work 1966; mem Academy Certified Social Worker 1968; mem MA Bar Assoc 1984; Sharon Fish and Game Club. **HONORS/ACHIEVEMENTS:** 10 Outstanding Young Men Award Boston Jr CC 1968; Community Serv Award Roxbury YMCA 1969; Outstanding Performance Award FTC 1972; Outstanding Govt Serv Award NAACP Boston 1975; Outstanding Serv Award Salvation Army 1980; Samuel Horace Theological Award, VA Union School of Theology, 1989. **MILITARY SERVICE:** USAF Medical Corps staff sargent 1959-64. **HOME ADDRESS:** PO Box 6102, Richmond, VA 23222.

GIDNEY, CALVIN L.
Dentist. **PERSONAL:** Born Dec 22, 1930, Mt Airy, NC; married Willa Broome; children: Calvin, III, Craig, Evan. **EDUCATION:** Fisk U, AB 1952; Meharry Med Coll, DDS 1959. **CAREER:** Doctor of Dental Surgery, priv prac present. **ORGANIZATIONS:** Mem Omega Psi Phi; mem FiskUniv Alumni Assn; trustee Sheridan School. **HONORS/ACHIEVEMENTS:** Alumni of yr FiskUniv Washington Club 1971. **MILITARY SERVICE:** AUS 1953-55. **BUSINESS ADDRESS:** 511 Kennedy St NW, Washington, DC 20011.

GIFFORD, BERNARD R.
Scholar. **PERSONAL:** Born May 18, 1943, Brooklyn, NY; married Ursula M Jean; children: Antoinette, Bernard. **EDUCATION:** Long Island U, BS 1965;Univ of Rochester Med Sch, MS 1968;Univ of Rochester Med Sch, PhD 1972. **CAREER:** Russell Sage Found, resident scholar 1977-; New York City Public School System, dep chancellor & chief of business affairs office 1973-77; New York City Rand Inst, pres 1972-73. **ORGANIZATIONS:** Mem Adv Com John F Kennedy Inst of Politics HarvardUniv 1973-; bd of visitors City Coll of NY 1973-; bd of trustees NYUniv 1975-; mem acad adv com US Naval Acad 1979-; consult CA Supreme Ct 1978-79; consult Asst Sec for Com Planning & Devel Dept of Housing & Urban Devel 1979; consult Nat Acad of Pub Adminstrn 1979-80; consult Nat Inst of Educ 1980-; bd of Dir NY Urban Coalition 1973-; bd of trustees German Marshall Fund of US 1973-; mem edit bdUrban Affairs Quarterly 1973-; bd of edit advs NY Affairs 1978-; edit bd NY Educ Quarterly 1978-; edit bd Policy Analysis 1978-; apptd adj prof Pub Adminstrn ColumbiaUniv 1975-77; apptd adj lectr Pub Policy John F Kennedy Sch of Govt HarvardUniv 1977-78; apptd adj & visiting prof Dept of Urban Studies & Planning Hunter Coll/CityUniv of NY/MA Inst of Tech present; US Atomic Energy Comm Fellow in Nuclear Sci 1965-71. **HONORS/ACHIEVEMENTS:** Mem Phi Beta Kapp; numerous presentations & papers; co-author "Revenue Sharing & the Planning Process" 1974; author "The Urbanization of Poverty a PreliminaryInvestigation of Shifts in the Distribution of the Poverty Population by Race Residence & Family Structure" 1980; numerous other publications.

GIGGER, HELEN C.
Attorney. **PERSONAL:** Born Dec 24, 1944, Houston, TX; married Nathan J Gigger. **EDUCATION:** TX South U, BA Pol Sci 1965; TX So U, JD 1968. **CAREER:** State of OK, OK crime comm, legal coun, planner; Dean of Law Sch, res asst; Houston Leg Found, legal intern; Okla City & Co Comm Act Prog Inc, prog analyst. **ORGANIZATIONS:** Mem Am Nat & OK Bar Assns; sec JJ & Bruce Law Soc; mem Amer Judiccature Soc; EEOC off Okla Crime Comm; mem Nat Spa Courts Plan Org; lect Crim Just OK City U; mem YWCA; Urban League; League of Women Voters Georgia Brown's Demo Women's Club; OK Black Pol Cau; past pres Delta Sigma Theta Sor Inc; sec Local & State NAACP; elected Nat Scholarship & Standards Com 4 yr term; policy making com Delta Sigma Theta Inc 1975. **HONORS/ACHIEVEMENTS:** Grad with Hons in 1961, 1965 & at top of Law Class in 1968; re chrprsn of Reg VI NAACP Conf 1974; who's Who Among Am Women; Parli; Nat Delta Conv 1973; Delta Cen Reg Parli 1974; mem of Greater Cleves CME Ch; Ch Prog Chrprsn. **BUSINESS ADDRESS:** 3033 N Walnut, Oklahoma City, OK 73105.

GIGGER, NATHANIEL JAY
Attorney. **PERSONAL:** Born Jan 01, 1944, Elmore City, OK; son of Ernest Gigger and Katie Wyatt Gigger; married Helen Coleman Gigger, Oct 25, 1968; children: Nikolle Janelle. **EDUCATION:** Langston Univ, Langston OK, BA, 1963; Texas Southern Univ, Houston TX, JD, 1967. **CAREER:** State of Oklahoma, Oklahoma City OK, asst state atty gen, 1970-79, deputy atty, Dept of Human Resources, 1979; Derryberry, Duncan & Nance Law Firm, Oklahoma City OK, mem, 1979-82; Self-Employed, Oklahoma City OK, atty, 1982-. **ORGANIZATIONS:** Mem, Prince Hall of Masons, 1967-; vice pres, State Conf of Branches NAACP, 1972-77; state legal chmn, Intl Benevolent Protective Order of Elks, 1975-80; mem, Mayor's Comm for Business Devel, 1976-79; exec bd mem, Community Action Agency, 1976-81; mem, Assn of Black Trial Lawyers, 1982-; bd mem, Oklahoma Business & Devel Council, 1984-86; mem, Northeast Oklahoma City Chamber of Commerce, 1987-, J J Bruce Law Soc. **HONORS/ACHIEVEMENTS:** Roscoe Dunjee Humanitarian Award, Oklahoma NAACP, 1975; Personalities of South Award, Amer Biographical Inst, 1976-77; Outstanding Citizenship Award, Alpha Phi Alpha Frat, 1976; Outstanding Citizen Award, Oklahoma City Set Club, 1981; Outstanding Lawyer Award, NAACP Youth Council, 1986. **BUSINESS ADDRESS:** Attorney at Law, 732 Northeast 36th St, Oklahoma City, OK 73105.

GILBERT, ALBERT C.
Business executive. **PERSONAL:** Born Oct 19, 1924, Carlisle, PA; married Iris Boswell; children: Walda Ann, Albert, Charles. **EDUCATION:** Morgan State Coll, BS 1950. **CAREER:** Continental Can Co, joined in 1950 hourly employee became financial sec then pres of union, supr 1958, supt 1964, first black mgr 1969-. **ORGANIZATIONS:** Vice chmn Fibre Box Assn; sch bd mem E Cleveland Sch 1971-; mem Natl Black Sch Bd; Natl Safety Council; mem Citizens League Greater Cleveland; mem El Hasa Masonic Shrine 32 degree mason; mem Cleveland C of C; OH Mfgr Assn; former Scout Master; bd dirs Rainey Inst of Music; spec sales rep Continental Group; dir East Cleveland Kiwanis. **HONORS/ACHIEVEMENTS:** Morgan State Coll Hall of Fame Outstanding Football Player & Wrestler 1974. **MILITARY SERVICE:** AUS WW II sgt; awarded 4 Bronze Stars. **BUSINESS ADDRESS:** Manager, Continental Can Co, 14800 Emery Ave, Cleveland, OH 44135.

GILBERT, CHRISTOPHER
Psychologist. **PERSONAL:** Born Aug 01, 1949, Birmingham, AL. **EDUCATION:** Univ of MI, BA 1972; Clark Univ, MA 1975, PhD 1987. **CAREER:** Judge Baker Guidance Ctr, psychologist 1979-84; Univ of MA Med Sch, psychologist 1979-84; Cambridge Family & Childrens Svcs, psychologist 1983-85; Univ of Pgh English Dept, vstg poet 1986. **ORGANIZATIONS:** Bd of dirs Elm Park Center for Early Educ 1980-84, Worcester Chap Civil Liberties Union of MA 1983-85, Worcester Children's Friend 1983-86. **HONORS/ACHIEVEMENTS:** MA Artists Foundation Fellowship 1981; Walt Whitman Awd Acad of Amer Poets 1983; NEA Fellowship Poetry 1986; Robert Frost Awd 1986. **BUSINESS ADDRESS:** PO Box 371 West Side Station, Worcester, MA 01602.

GILBERT, ELDRIDGE H. E.
Clergyman. **PERSONAL:** Born Oct 27, 1912, New Orleans, LA; married Annie Lee Wilson; children: Eldridge HE Jr. **EDUCATION:** Amer Bapt Theol Sem Nashville, BTh 1944; Rockford Sch Grad Beloit Coll WI, BA 1947; Attended, Virginia Union Univ; Rockford Coll, Hon Doctorate of Humane Letters. **CAREER:** Rock Valley Jr Coll, tchr the negro in amer history; Rock River Meth Conf Lake Geneva, counselor/tchr; Rock River Bapt Assn Lake Springs, counselor/tchr/pastor; Rockford & Vicinity Bapt Assoc, teacher; Pilgrim Bapt Ch, pastor. **ORGANIZATIONS:** Past pres & sec Ministerial Assn; religious counselor Rockford Coll; past pres Greater Rockford Clergy; past pres Rockford Ministers Fellowship; pub paper "Survey Analysis of Rockford" 1947; pub epilogue "That We Should Know So Little of Men"; guest speaker World Council of Chs Europe 1953; visitor 15 African& Near E Countries 1969; visitor Haiti Missions 1973; mem World Council of Churches; alternate delegate ABC Vancouver BC; bd mem ABC; Comm on Church Unity 4 yrs; Professional Standards Causes of Great Rivers Region 4 yrs. **HONORS/ACHIEVEMENTS:** Citation for Min & Comm Serv Plaque Balthasar 32 Lodge 1974; Citation Natl Council of Negro Women 1975; ordained 4 ministers for pastorate; mem EcumenicalInst Study Confs of the Ministry Salamanca Spain 1977; Citation Winnebago Cty OIC 1975 1977-78; Natl Registry of Prominent Amers 1976-77; Who's Who in IL;Stewardship Awd Protestant Welfare Assn; Alumni of the Yr Awd Beloit Coll. **BUSINESS ADDRESS:** Pastor, Pilgrim Bapt Church, 1703 S Central Ave, Rockford, IL 61102.

GILBERT, FRED D., JR.
Educational administrator. **PERSONAL:** Born Dec 02, 1947, New Orleans, LA. **EDUCATION:** Dillard Univ, BA Business Admin 1970; Loyola Univ, MEd Educ Admin 1972; IA State Univ Higher Educ, PhD 1978. **CAREER:** Upward Bound Project, admin asst, 1971-73; Upward Bound & Special Serv Proj Xavier Univ, dir 1973-75; IA State Univ, rsch asst 1975-76, univ married housing area adv 1976-77, dir, asst prof 1978-; IA State Univ Coll of Ed, asst dean. **ORGANIZATIONS:** mem, Mid-Amer Assn of Educ Opportunity Program Pers, Natl Assn of Student Personnel Admin, Amer Assoc of Univ Admin, Phi Delta Kappa, The Soc of Ethnic & Spec Studies; bd of dir IA Comprehensive Manpower Serv Grant for $248,000 for High School Disadvantaged Students Dept of HEW 1978-80. **HONORS/ACHIEVEMENTS:** Outstanding Young Men of Amer US Jaycees 1979; Book Review of Black Coll in Amer Publishing in Educ Studies 1979; A Study of Power & Authority unpublished PhD Dissertation 1978. **BUSINESS ADDRESS:** Asst Dean, IA State Univ, Coll of Educ, N002 Quadrangle, Ames, IA 50011.

GILBERT, HERMAN CROMWELL
Public service executive, author. **PERSONAL:** Born Feb 23, 1923, Marianna, AR; married Ivy McAlpine; children: Dorthea Gilbert Lassister, Vincent Newton. **EDUCATION:** LaSalle Extension Univ, Corres Law, 1943; Parkway Comm House Chicago, Creative Writing 1952; IBM Educ Cntr, Acct Machines & Computers 1973. **CAREER:** Packinghouse Wrkrs Union AFL-CIO, asst educ adv 1955-57; Westside Booster Newspaper Chicago, managing edit 1959-60; Citizens Newspapers Chicago, managing edit 1964-66; IL Bureau of Employment Sec, data proc dir 1970-73, asst admin 1973-81; Path Press Inc, exec vice pres. **ORGANIZATIONS:** Vice chrmn Assembly of Black State Exec 1973-77; chrmn Automated Systems Comm Interstate Conf 1974-75; bd mem International Black Writers Conference 1975-; chief of staff Cong Gus Savage 2nd IL 1981-82; exec vp/edit dir Path Press Inc 1982-; mem Society of Midland Authors 1983-; spec adv Cong Gus Savage 2nd IL 1984-. **HONORS/ACHIEVEMENTS:** Novel publ, "The Uncertain Sound" 1969, "The Negotiations" 1983; Congressional Comm Rep William Clay 1st MO 1984; Cert of Spec Cong Rec Rep Mickey Leland 18th TX 1984; "Sharp Blades in Tender Grass" will be produced in 1987; "This Needs Saying" in progress; "The Campaign" in progress. **MILITARY SERVICE:** AAC staff sgt 1943-46; Unit Citation 1944; Good Conduct Medal 1945. **HOME ADDRESS:** 11539 S Justine St, Chicago, IL 60643. **BUSINESS ADDRESS:** Executive Vice President and Editorial Director, Path Press Inc, 53 W Jackson Blvd, Suite 1040, Chicago, IL 60604.

GILBERT, JEAN P.
Educator. **PERSONAL:** Born Aug 06, 1928, Mcdonald, PA. **EDUCATION:** Univ of Buffalo, Ed D 1962;Univ of Buffalo, Ed M 1955; Bluefield St Coll, BS 1947. **CAREER:** Brooklyn Coll, counselor, educator 1964-; Univ of IL, counselor, educator 1962-63; Hampton Inst, dir of testing 1957-60; AL A&M Coll, counselor, lecturer 1956-57 ; SC State Coll, counselor, educator 1964-65; Cons, Amer Airlines; Basic Sys; Exxon. **ORGANIZATIONS:** Mem bd dir DST Telecommunications Inc; Delta Sigma Theta; Pi Lambda Theta; Kappa Delta Pi; Amer Psychlgcl Assn; Amer Persnnl & Guidnc Assn; Ntnl Voc Guidnc Assn; Assn Non-White Concrns; Psychmtrc Dir Educ Prog Eval & Resrch JPG Consltnts Inc; author "Counseling Black Inner City Children in Groups"; con JOB'S Prog; Mdl Cities; Comm Dev Grps; bd grdns bd dir New York City Prtstnt; mem GS Cncl of Grtr NY; mem Bd Gov NY St Prsnl & GuidncAssn Ford Fndtn Grnt 1974. **HONORS/ACHIEVEMENTS:** Women of Achvmnt Award 1966; John Hay Whitney Fndtn Grnt 1960; James Fndtn Grant 1957; outstndng Edtrs of Amer 1974; hon (cum laude) Bluefield St Coll1947. **BUSINESS ADDRESS:** Brklyn Coll Sch of Ed, Bedford Ave H, Brooklyn, NY.

GILBERT, RICHARD LANNEAR
Engineer. **PERSONAL:** Born Dec 26, 1921, Indianapolis, IN; married Margaret; children: 4 children. **EDUCATION:** Lain Drafting Coll, attended; Purdue Univ Lafayette IN, attended; Franklin Univ Columbus OH, attended; Youngstown Univ OH, attended; Bowling Green State, attended, OH State Univ Columbus, attended; OH Univ Zanesville, attended. **CAREER:** US Naval Air Station Port Columbus, engr tech 1951-54; Erdman Anthony & Hosley Consult Engrs Columbus, engr tech 1954-55; Photronix Inc Aerial Photogrammetric & Consult Engrs Columbus OH, consult engr 1956-60; OH State Hwy Dept Div Design & Const Columbus, engr tech 1960-61; Lordstown Military Reservation Warren OH, engr 1961-62; Muskingum Area Tech Inst Zanesville OH, instr, chmn engr dept 1969-82; Inertial Guidance & Calibration Group, civil engr 1962-. **ORGANIZATIONS:** Assisted housing problem Urban League, Warren OH 1960-62; comm mem Minority Housing, Citizens Advisory Comm, Zoning Bd of Appeals, Amer Cancer Soc; bd of dirs Zanesville Comm Center 1962-; exec bd mem Muskingum Cty Action Program 1962-; pres Muskingum-Athens/Morgan &

WA County NAACP 1962-; mem advisory bd OH Univ Zanesville, OH Black Political Assy, Admission Counselors & Officials 1962-; hon mem Black Caucus of OH 1962-; chmn Muskingum Cty Branch NAACP; tech advisor Coalition of Concerned Citizens; mem Near East Side Area Council & Urban League 1955-75, Muskingum County Drug Council; pres NAACP; lecturer OH Univ Zanesville; develtech Muskingum Area Tech Ins 1969-70; instructor, various special classes on enginerring; coordinator MBE, WBE SE OH; council mem Zanesville Cty 1982-84; mem BEDO. **BUSINESS ADDRESS:** City Councilperson, City of Zanesville, 401 Market St, Zanesville, OH 43701.

GILCHRIEST, LORENZO
Educator. **PERSONAL:** Born Mar 21, 1938, Thomasville, GA; married Judith Graffman; children: Lorenzo David, Lorena. **EDUCATION:** Newark State Coll, BS 1962; Pratt Inst, MS 1967; Maryland Inst Coll of Art, MFA 1975. **CAREER:** Asst prof art dept; Morgan State U, guest artist print workshop summer 1977; Baltimore Msm of Art, art tchr adult prgm 1973-74; Cornell U, guest prof 1972-73; Sen Robert Kennedy Proj Bedford Stuyvesant Youth in Action, asst dir 1965-67. **ORGANIZATIONS:** Mem Am Radio Relay League; Gen Class Amateur Radio Lisc 1976/Advanced Class Amateur Radio Lisc 1980. **HONORS/ACHIEVEMENTS:** Samuel Kress Award 1971; Who's Who in Am Art 1976; afro am slide depository Samuel Kress Found 1971; Fellow Internatl Artists Seminar 1962; prot-g- of Elaine Dekooning 1963. **MILITARY SERVICE:** AUS 1956-57. **BUSINESS ADDRESS:** Assist Prof of Art Dept, Towson State University, Towson, MD 21204.

GILCHRIST, CARLTON CHESTER
Government official. **PERSONAL:** Born May 25, 1935, Brackenridge, PA; children: Jeffery Carlton, Scott Richard. **CAREER:** Cleveland Browns, professional football player 1954; played in CAN 1954-61 with Sarnia, Kitchner, Hamilton, Sask, Toronto, Buffalo 1962-64, Denver 1965, 67, Miami 1966; C Gilchrist Lighting Co CAN, founder, pres 1957-61; Mayd Serv Ltd CAN Denver Carlton Ests Devel Inc PA, founder 1965; Black Pride Intl Inc Los Angeles, pres; Peace Corps, spl asst to Regl dirs; Denver Cts, vet probation ofcr 1965-69; Denver Police Dept, hon lt 1967-68; Prodn Inc Denver, exec vp. **HONORS/ACHIEVEMENTS:** Rep Named Player of the Yr Buffalo Bills 1962; Hall of Fame Buffalo Bills 1971. **BUSINESS ADDRESS:** PO Box 69797, Los Angeles, CA 90069.

GILCHRIST, ROBERTSON
Elected govt. official/const. owner. **PERSONAL:** Born Aug 24, 1926, Parksville, SC; married Evelyn Landise Searles; children: Gezetta. **EDUCATION:** Mims HS, diploma 1945. **CAREER:** Owner construction co; councilmember. **ORGANIZATIONS:** Co-owner operator of restaurant known as Lan's Deli; mem Co Council; mem NAACP; mem Masonic Lodge. **HONORS/ACHIEVEMENTS:** Public Serv & Private Business Awd Comm on Black History 1980; Appreciation Serv & Leadership Awd 4-H Club 1983. **MILITARY SERVICE:** AUS corpl 18 months. **HOME ADDRESS:** PO Box 84, Parksville, SC 29844. **BUSINESS ADDRESS:** Councilmember, Drawer H, McCormick, SC 29835.

GILCREAST, CONWAY, SR.
Elected government official. **PERSONAL:** Born Feb 01, 1924, West Helena, AR; married Willie Mae Hamner; children: Helen, Conway Jr, Connie, Quiency, Harold, Betty, Carolyn, LaDon, Bre nda, Cleopatra. **EDUCATION:** AR Baptist Coll, AA 1951; Phelander Smith Coll, BA 1959. **CAREER:** Dansby Elementary School, principal 1956-59; Dora E Perkins Elementary School, teacher 1963-68; MM Tate Elementary School, teacher 1968-72; PLM&D Congress, teacher 1966-; City of West Helena, alderman. **ORGANIZATIONS:** Voter registration City of Helena 1978; election judge School Elections state & natl 1948-; pastor Baptist churches 1951-. **HONORS/ACHIEVEMENTS:** Political advisor Political Org for Equal Rights 1979; alderman City of W Helena 1980; political advisor PLM&D, Inc 1981; Teacher of the Year PLM&D Congress 1984. **MILITARY SERVICE:** AUS t/5 2 1/2 yrs; Good Conduct ATO ETO Marksman Hon Discharge 1943-46. **HOME ADDRESS:** 513 W Park, West Helena, AR 72390.

GILES, ALTHEA B.
Advertising executive. **PERSONAL:** Born Mar 10, 1926, East Orange, NJ; daughter of Russell Banks and Beatrice Smith-Banks; married William R Giles, Jun 15, 1947; children: William R, Sharon Giles-Alexander, Kevin E. **EDUCATION:** Kean Coll, Union NJ, BS, 1951. **CAREER:** East Orange Board of Educ, teacher, 1952-82; EPC Intl Inc, East Orange NJ, vice pres, 1983-, pres, currently. **ORGANIZATIONS:** Consultant, Selig Assoc Inc; pres, Extra Personal Care Inc; consultant, Nancy Wilson Cosmetics; sec, Enterprising Twenty Inc; Arts & Culture Comm, Coalition 100 Black Women; NAACP; Natl Urban League; United Negro Coll Fund; Specialty Advertising Intl Inc. **HONORS/ACHIEVEMENTS:** Community Serv Award, East Orange Mayor Hatcher; Black Heritage Award, City of East Orange; Meritorious Serv Award, United Negro Coll Fund; Outstanding Volunteer Award, United Negro Coll Fund; Citiation, Newark Municipal Council, Newark NJ. **HOME ADDRESS:** 43 Edgemont Rd, West Orange, NJ 07052. **BUSINESS ADDRESS:** Vice President, EPC International Inc, 141 S Harrison St, PO Box 880, East Orange, NJ 07018.

GILES, CHARLES WINSTON
Personnel administrator. **PERSONAL:** Born Jan 19, 1942, Brooklyn, NY; married Lillian; children: Kelvin, Kenneth, Karen, Winston. **EDUCATION:** Morgan State U, BA 1965. **CAREER:** EEO Carborundum Co, mgr 1970-; United Way of Niagara, asst dir 1969-70; Niagara Comm Action Prog, dep dir 1967-69; Niagara Co Soc Serv Dept , case worker 1965-67. **ORGANIZATIONS:** Mem Nat Alliance of Busmen; local dir Nat Conf of Christian & Jews 1975-; Life mem NAACP; dir United Way of Niagara 1970-; past chmn Niagara Falls Commn on Human Rights 1973-75; dir past-pres Family & Childrens Serv 1971-; past dir Red Cross Niagara Comm Ctr Girls Club CORE Tract II. **HONORS/ACHIEVEMENTS:** Top Hat Man of the Week 1976; vol of the yr Comm Ctr 1976; black achvr awd Tract II 1976. **BUSINESS ADDRESS:** Carborundum Co, 3rd St, Niagara Falls, NY 14302.

GILES, JAMES T.
Federal judge. **EDUCATION:** Amherst Coll, BA 1964; Yale Univ, LLB 1967. **CAREER:** Pepper Hamilton & Scheetz, assoc 1968-79; US Dist Ct Philadelphia PA, judge 1979-. **ORGANIZATIONS:** Mem Natl Labor Relations Bd Philadelphia 1967-68; mem Fed Bar Assn, Philadelphia Bar Assn. **BUSINESS ADDRESS:** Judge, US Dist Court Philadelphia, Federal Judiciary, 601 Market St, Philadelphia, PA 19106.

GILES, JIMMIE, JR.
Professional athlete. **PERSONAL:** Born Nov 08, 1954, Greenville, MS; married Vivian; children: Jimmie, Jonathan, Candace. **EDUCATION:** Alcorn State Univ, degree Business Admin. **CAREER:** Houston Oilers, professional football player 1977; Tampa Bay Buccaneers, professional football player 1978-. **ORGANIZATIONS:** Mem Lions Club. **HONORS/ACHIEVEMENTS:** First team All-NJC Newark Star Ledger 1979; hon ment All-Pro Sports Illus 1979; named second team All-NFC by UPI 1979; mem 1986 NFL Pro Bowl Team. **BUSINESS ADDRESS:** Tampa Bay Buccaneers, One Buccaneer Place, Tampa, FL 33607.

GILES, WALDRON H.
Corporate officer. **PERSONAL:** Born Feb 17, 1932, Jersey City, NJ; married Marjorie C Mayner; children: Wayne Howard, Gregory Howard. **EDUCATION:** Rutger Univ New Brunswick NJ, BS 1954; NY Univ Bronx, MS 1962; NY Univ Bronx, PhD 1963. **CAREER:** GE Phil, prog gen mgr 1977-, sect mgr 1972, supr engr 1969; Bristol-Myers Prod Div, grp ldr 1963; NY Univ Chem Engring, resch asst 1962; Giljo Inc, pres 1969. **ORGANIZATIONS:** Mem Nat Air Pltion Cntrl Tech Adv 1972; elder Laffeyette Presb Ch 1963; pres Concrnd Black Parents-Mainline 1969; bd of dirs Mt Pleasant Wayne PA Civic Assn 1972. **HONORS/ACHIEVEMENTS:** Rec Good Conduct Medal AUS 1957; Black Achvrs in Ind Harlem Br YMCA 1970; Black Men of Sci Franklin Inst 1974; Nelson P Jackson Awd Nat Space Club 1978; grp achv awd Ames Resch Cnt 1980. **MILITARY SERVICE:** AUS sp 4 served 3 yrs.

GILES, WILLIAM R.
Business executive. **PERSONAL:** Born Nov 12, 1925, South Carolina; son of Bennie Giles and Mattie Giles; married Althea; children: William Jr, Kevin, Sharon. **EDUCATION:** Benedict Coll. **CAREER:** East Orange Genl Hosp, bd of trustees; Cannolene Company,Nancy Wilson Cosmetics, exec vice pres; Evening of Elegance, sponsor; United Negro Coll Fund, major fund raiser; New Hope Bapt Church, chmn bldg fund; 100 Black Men of NJ, pres; Benedict Coll, bd of trustees; EPC Intl Inc, East Orange NJ, founder and chairman. **ORGANIZATIONS:** Chmn, Selig Assoc, Extra Personal Care Inc, Giles Co Inc, Wm R Giles & Co Inc; developer, City Natl Bank; bd of dir, E Orange PAL; joint enterprise Trusteeship Corp; bd dir, E Orange Gen Hosp; mem, Kiwanis Club, Premium Mktg Assoc, Natl Urban League, Greater Newark Chamber of Commerce, Advtsg Spec Inst, E Orange Chamber of Commerce; bd of dir Enterprising Twenty Inc; mem NAACP, Spec Advtsg Assoc Intl, United Negro Coll Fund; assoc mem, Amer Health & Beauty Aid Inst, Spec Advtsg Assoc of Greater NY; exec vice pres, OIC's of Amer. **HONORS/ACHIEVEMENTS:** Meritorious Serv Awd, United Negro Coll Fund; Appreciation Awd, Howard Univ Sch of Law; Humanitarian Awd, City of East Orange NJ; Outstanding Awd for the Develop of Minority Youth, Seventh Day Adventist Church; Appreciation Awd, Police Dept, City of East Orange; Honorary Citizen, City of New Orleans; Achievement Awd, Natl Coalition of Black Meeting Planners; Comm Serv Awd, Natl Council of Negro Women; Dedicated Serv in Educ Business & Politics Awd, Mayor John Hatcher; Family Enterprise Awd, Urban League of Essex Co; Black Heritage Awd, City of East Orange; Special Recognition Awd, Minority Interchange Inc; Outstanding Minority Business Awd, Natl Minority Business Council; DHL, Benedict Coll, Columbia SC. **MILITARY SERVICE:** AUS. **BUSINESS ADDRESS:** Chairman, EPC International Inc, 141 S Harrison St, PO Box 880, East Orange, NJ 07018.

GILES, WILLIE ANTHONY, JR.
Educational administrator. **PERSONAL:** Born Mar 08, 1941, Conway, AR; married Carolyn Joan Williams; children: Dwayne, Keenon, Dana. **EDUCATION:** AR AM&N Coll, BS 1964; Univ of MI, MA Educ Specialist 1967; Univ of MO Kansas City, Educ Specialist 1986-. **CAREER:** KS City MO School Dist, assoc supt 1986-, dir of desegregations monitoring 1985-86, dir of secondary educ 1981-85, dir of admin servs 1978-81; NE High KS City MO School Syst, principal 1976-78; Paseo High KS City MO School Syst, principal 1971-75; Humboldt High KS City MO School Syst, principal 1969-70; KS City MO School Syst, teacher, 1968-69; Detroit MI School Syst, teacher 1964-67. **ORGANIZATIONS:** Bd mem Whatsoever Cir Comm House present; bd mem Urban Serv KS City MO present; bd mem Paseo Daycare Serv present; trustee sec Paseo Baptist Church present; mem Citizens Crusade Against Crime present; mem Phi Delta Kappa present; Personnel Outstanding Serv Social Sec Admin 1971; Comm Outstanding Serv NE Comm Council 1978. **HONORS/ACHIEVEMENTS:** Boss of the Year Award Business & Professional Women Starlight Chapter KS City MO 1978; Outstanding Educator Award, Alpha Phi Alpha Fraternity 1980. **BUSINESS ADDRESS:** Associate Superintendent, Kansas City School District, 37 Paseo, Rm 309, Kansas City, MO 64109.

GILFORD, ROTEA J.
Appointed government official. **PERSONAL:** Born Nov 20, 1927, Willis, TX; married Judith Ellen; children: Stephen J, Judy Marie, Chance M. **EDUCATION:** City Coll of San Francisco, AA 1944; SF State Coll, 1954. **CAREER:** San Francisco Police Dept, inspector of police 1960-78; San Francisco Mayors Office, dep mayor for criminal justice. **ORGANIZATIONS:** Mem Kappa Alpha Psi 1948-, Black Leadership Forum 1970-, Natl Assoc Criminal Justice Planners 1978-, Natl Black Public Admin. **MILITARY SERVICE:** AUS tech 5th grade 1946-47. **BUSINESS ADDRESS:** Deputy Mayor, City of San Francisco, City Hall Room 159, San Francisco, CA 94102.

GILKES, CHERYL TOWNSEND
Minister, educator. **PERSONAL:** Born Nov 02, 1947, Boston, MA. **EDUCATION:** Northeastern Univ, BA 1970, MA 1973, PhD 1979. **CAREER:** Harvard Univ the Divinity Sch, research assoc, visiting lecturer 1981-82; faculty fellow Bunting Inst, & Radcliffe Coll; Union Baptist Church, assoc minister 1982-; Boston Univ, asst prof of sociology 1978-. **ORGANIZATIONS:** Sec Cambridge Civic Unity Comm 1978-; asst dean Congress of Christian Education United Baptist Convention of MA, RI, NH 1986-; mem Amer Sociological Assoc, Assoc of Black Sociologist, Delta Sigma Theta 1983-. **HONORS/ACHIEVEMENTS:** Eastern Sociological Society, I Peter Gellmon awrd 1986. **BUSINESS ADDRESS:** Asst Prof of Sociology, Boston University, Dept of Sociology, 96-100 Cummington St, Boston, MA 02215.

GILKEY, WILLIAM C.
Educational administrator, government official. **PERSONAL:** Born Jul 03, 1932, Macon, MS; married Juanita P. **EDUCATION:** IN State U, BS 1958; IN U, MS 1965; IN U, EdS 1974. **CAREER:** Clay Middle School, S Bend IN, prin 1979-; Human Resources & Eco-

nomic Devel, City of S Bend, dir 1976-78; Memorial High School, vice prin 1969-76; Lasalle High School, asst prin 1968-69; Central High School, teacher, coach 1958-68. **ORGANIZATIONS:** Pres Bldrs Untd Inc; bd dir Blds Untd Inc; bd dir Batteast Constrn Co Inc; bd of mgrs YMCA; Phi Delta Kappa; Polemarch Kappa Alpha Psi 1963-67;Lions Club; exec bd Untd Way; Untd Way Plann Com; Urban League; NAACP; NASSP; NAHRO; regional exec bd NAHRO; IN Manpower Devel Coun; Am Soc of Plann Offcls. **HONORS/ACHIEVEMENTS:** Track Coack of Yr 1967; I-Men's Disting Awd 1973; Am Coll Student Ldrs 1953; All-European Football 1956; 1st black dept adminstr S Bend 1976; capt football baseball IN State U. **MILITARY SERVICE:** AUS sp 3 1955-56. **BUSINESS ADDRESS:** 52900 Lily Rd, South Bend, IN 46637.

GILL, GERALD ROBERT
Educator. **PERSONAL:** Born Nov 18, 1948, New Rochelle, NY; divorced; children: Ayanna E. **EDUCATION:** Lafayette Coll, AB 1966-70; Howard Univ, MA 1974, PhD 1985. **CAREER:** City School Dist, New Rochelle NY, social studies teacher 1970-72; Inst for the Study of Educ Policy, research asst 1976-78, research fellow 1978-79; Tufts Univ, lecturer, instructor 1980-85. **ORGANIZATIONS:** Consult NAACP 1979; consult Ohio Hist Society 1980-85; mem Organ of Am Historians; mem Am Hist Assoc; mem Southern Hist Assoc; mem Assoc for the Study of Afro-American Life and History; mem Natl Assoc for the Advancement of Colored People. **HONORS/ACHIEVEMENTS:** Co-author The Case for Affirmative Action for Blacks in Higher Ed 1978; author Meanness Mania 1980; author The Rightward Drift in Amer in the State of Black America Natl Urban League 1981. **BUSINESS ADDRESS:** Lecturer, TuftsUniv, TuftsUniv, Medford, MA 02155.

GILL, ROBERT LEWIS
Educator. **PERSONAL:** Born Dec 26, 1912, Winnsboro, SC; married Rubye Cordelia; children: Walter, Roberta. **EDUCATION:** Livingstone Coll, AB 1933;Univ of MI, MA 1937;Univ of MI, PhD 1942;Univ of MD Law Sch, 1951-53. **CAREER:** Morgan State Univ, prof 1945-; Lincoln Univ, teacher 1940-42; Atlanta Univ, teacher 1946; TX Southern Univ, teacher 1948; Univ of DE, teacher 1965; Univ of MA, teacher 1968-69; Univ of MD, teacher 1967-73; State Univ of NY, teacher 1973-74; Univ of MD Far E Div (Japan, Okinawa, Vietnam, Thailand, Taiwan & Korea), teacher 1970-71. **ORGANIZATIONS:** Mem Charter Commn Baltimore City 1963-64; Airport Zoning Bd of Appls 1964-72; splst civil rights educ comm relat US Ofc of Educ 1967-68; dir WilliamRobertson Coe Found 1958-59; exec bd Baltimore Br NAACP 1954-68; Life mem NAACP; bd dir ACLU 1950-70; bd dir Hlth & Wlfr Coun 1958-68; bd dir Untd Nat Assn of MD 1964-70; bd dir Big Bros Inc 1965-73; exec bd Baltimore Urban League 1952-60; bd dir Prisioners Aid Assn of MD 1956-72; author 2book & 95 publ artcls on race & relat & pub law; pres Assn of Soc & Behvrl Sci 1962-63. **HONORS/ACHIEVEMENTS:** Pres hon awd ASBS 1973; Disting Achvmt Awd 1961; spl hon awd ASBS 1975; Life mem Omega Psi Phi Frat; 40 yr Serv Plaque 1970; Disting Alumni Awd 1961. **MILITARY SERVICE:** USAF 1st lt 1942-45; MD NG maj 1946-48. **BUSINESS ADDRESS:** Morgan StateUniv, Baltimore, MD 21239.

GILL, ROSA UNDERWOOD
Accountant. **PERSONAL:** Born May 14, 1944, Wake Co, NC; married Jimmie; children: Angie Rosharon, Natalie Denise. **EDUCATION:** ShawUniv Raleigh NC, BS Math 1968; NC CentralUniv Durham, attended 1978-79; NC StateUniv Raleigh, attended 1979-80. **CAREER:** Wake Co Bd of Elections, 1st black female chrpsn present; State Govt Raleigh NC, acct I 1980-; Wake Co Raleigh NC, mat instr 1971-80; Johnson Co Smithfield NC, math instr 1968-70; Nationwide Ins Raleigh NC, acctg clerk 1965-68. **ORGANIZATIONS:** Adv Inter-sch Coun 1978-79; adv Student Coun 1975-80; girl scout ldr Girl Scouts of Am 1974-78; trnd girl scout ldr 1976-78; sec Dem Party Wake Co1974-78; dem 1st black female vice chmn Dem Party Wake Co 1978. **BUSINESS ADDRESS:** Wake Co Bd of Elections, 136 Salisbury St, Raleigh, NC 27603.

GILL, SAMUEL A.
Bass violinist. **PERSONAL:** Born Nov 30, 1932, Brooklyn, NY; son of Everton Gill and Clarendon Gill; divorced. **EDUCATION:** Juilliard School of Music; Manhattan School of Music; BA in Music; MD in Music Educ, 1960; Univ of Colorado, D Music, 1989. **CAREER:** Denver Symphony Orchestra, bass violin; career includes jazz and symphony work; played with Max Roach; Coleman Hawkins; J J Johnson; Harry Belafonte Singers; Randy Weston Trio Master Mason Mt Evans Lodge; 32 Degree Mason Mountain & Plains Consis. **HONORS/ACHIEVEMENTS:** Shriner Syrian Temple Sym Social Award Tilden High 1950; Scholar to Julliard School of Music 1950; Scholar to Manhattan School of Music 1955; Win of Down Beat Int Crit Award 1955; among first of race to be engaged by major symphony 1960. **BUSINESS ADDRESS:** Denver Symphony Soc, 1615 California St, Denver, CO 80202.

GILL, TROY D.
Physician. **PERSONAL:** Born Aug 07, 1937, Chicago, IL; son of Troy Gill and Mary Gill; divorced; children: Eunice, Donald, Mary, Omari. **EDUCATION:** Dillard Univ, BA 1959; Howard Univ Coll of Medicine, MD 1963. **CAREER:** Little Company of Mary Hospital Illinois, med intern 1963-64; Maricopa Cty Gen Hospital Arizonia, ped res 1964-65; Good Samaritan Hospital Arizonia, chief ped res 1965-66; Univ of Utah Medical Center, adult & child psych fellow 1968-72; Rubicon Intl, phys, public speaker, business owner; Utah State hospital, clinical dir of youth center. **ORGANIZATIONS:** Bd governors Salt Lake Area Chamber of Commerce 1975-78; bd mem Natl Alliance of Business 1977-80; mem Intl Platform Assn 1984-; mem World Medical Assn 1984-; chmn mem Utah State Bd of Mental Health 1976-83; mem Univ of Utah Coll of Nursing Adv Bd 1978-; mental health consultant US Job Corp Clearfield Utah 1972-73; staff mem & consultant Raleigh Hills Hospital 1972-82; mem Utah Medical Assn 1988-; mem Amer Scoiety for Training & Development 1988-. **HONORS/ACHIEVEMENTS:** Black history instr Westminster Coll 1970-74; black history workshop West HS 1970-71; author of chap on creativity in The Management Team, Royal Publ 1984; mem Salt Lake Exec Assn 1972-76; state comm mem White House Conf of Children 1970. **MILITARY SERVICE:** USN lt comm 1966-68. **HOME ADDRESS:** 2024 La Tour Cir, Salt Lake City, UT 84121. **BUSINESS ADDRESS:** Clinical Director - Youth Center, Utah State Hospital, Provo, UT 84118.

GILLAM, ISAAC THOMAS, IV
Business executive. **PERSONAL:** Born Feb 23, 1932, Little Rock, AR; married Norma Jean Hughes; children: Michael, Teri Forte, Traci, Kelli. **EDUCATION:** Howard Univ, BA 1948-53; TN A&I State Univ, 1957-61. **CAREER:** Dryden Flight Research Cntr NASA, prog mgr Delta 1968-73, prog mgr small veh and int pros 1973-76, dir Shuttle opers 1976-79, deputy dir 1977-78, dir 1978-81; NASA HQ, special asst 1981-82, asst asso admin 1982-84, asst admin 1984-. **ORGANIZATIONS:** Mem Air Force Assoc 1977-82; fellow Am Astronautical Society 1978-; asso fellow Am Inst Aeronautics and Astronautics 1978-; mem Am Mgmt Assoc 1978-84; mem Am Def Prepareoness Assoc 1979-; mem Natl Space Club, Alpha Phi Alpha, NAACP. **HONORS/ACHIEVEMENTS:** NASA Dist Serv Medal NASA DSM 1976; NASA Exceptional Serv Medal NASA ESM 1982-83; Tau Beta Pi Howard Univ; AIAA Space Commerce Awd 1985; NASA Equal OpporMedal 1985; Alumni Achievement Awd Howard Univ; Dist Prof Eng Sci Prairie View A&M; Comm Awd Natl Assoc of Media Women. **MILITARY SERVICE:** USAF captain 1953-63. **BUSINESS ADDRESS:** Assistant Administrator, NASA, 600 Independence Ave SW, Washington, DC 20546.

GILLESPIE, AVON E.
Educator. **PERSONAL:** Born Apr 12, 1938, Los Angeles. **EDUCATION:** IN State U, BS 1960; Memphis State U, MA 1968. **CAREER:** Schulte High School, teacher 1960-64; Mclean Jr High School, 1964-65; Unitarian Ch Evanston, dir mus 1966-72; Evanston Township High School, teacher 1965-71; Mus Center of N Shore, 1970-71; Barat Coll, guest lecturer 1971-72; Latin School Chicago, teacher 1971-72; Antioch Coll, visiting lecturer 1973-74; Cap Univ, asst prof 1972-. **ORGANIZATIONS:** Bd mem Am Orff Schulwerk Assn 1973-75; mem MENC; Am Choral Dirs Assn; Phi Mu Alpha Sinfonia; bd mem Culture & Worship Com Nat Ofc Black Cath ; numerous appear, lecs, dems, wrkshps for US Sch Dists orgns, grps, convs, confs. **BUSINESS ADDRESS:** Capital Univ Conservatory Music, Columbus, OH 43209.

GILLESPIE, DIZZY **See GILLESPIE, JOHN BIRKS**

GILLESPIE, JOHN BIRKS (DIZZY GILLESPIE)
Musician. **PERSONAL:** Born Oct 21, 1917, Cheraw, SC; married Lorraine Willis. **EDUCATION:** Larinsburg Inst, grad; Rutgers Univ, DMusic (Hon) 1970. **CAREER:** Toured with Teddy Hill band 1937-39, Earl Hines, Bill Eckstine others 1930-44; band leader 1946-50; combo 1950-56; rep US Dept State on culture tour to Iran Pakistan Lebanon Turkey Greece Syria SA Yugoslavia 1956-58; led quintet 1958-; toured Argentina 1961; appearances at Juan-les-Pains (France) Festival, Jazz Workshop San Fran, Monterey Jazz Festival 1962; Musical Life of Charlie Parker 1974; White House Performance 1978; Newport & Montreux Jazz Festivals; numerous toursTV appearances night club dates festivals; numerous recs including At Village Vanguard "My Way"; jazz trumpet player 1930-. **ORGANIZATIONS:** Mem ASCAP, Baha'i Faith, Masons; conductor/composer/co-fndr The Bop Movement; records "Greatest Jazz Concert Ever", "Oscar Peterson & Dizzy Gillespie", "Havin' A Good Time in Paris" (Pablo Label). **HONORS/ACHIEVEMENTS:** Tribute to Dizzy Gillespie Avery Fischer Hall 1975; first prize in soundtrack Berlin Film Festival 1962; Jazzmobile's Paul Robeson Awd; Grammy with Oscar Peterson 1976; Grammy Awds 1975 1980; Jazz-Master's Awd; Jazzmobile guest speaker Joint Session SC Legis 1976; numerous awds Downbeat Mag; Musician of the Yr Inst of High Fidelity 1975; appeared Radio City Music Hall 1976, Carnegie Hall 1975, City Ctr 1976; author autobiography "To Be, or NotTo Bop" 1979; 1989 SpecialGrammy Award. **BUSINESS ADDRESS:** Care Assoc Booking Corp, 1995 Broadway Ste 501, New York, NY 10023. *

GILLESPIE, MARCIA A.
Editor. **PERSONAL:** Born Jul 10, 1944, Rockville Centre, NY. **EDUCATION:** Amer Studies, Lake Forest Coll, BA 1966. **CAREER:** Communications consultant, writer 1980-; Essence magazine, editor-in-chief 1971-80; Time-Life Books, Time Inc, New York, div 1966-70. **ORGANIZATIONS:** Lect & speak; mem Nat Assn Media Women; mem Nat Coun Negro Women. **HONORS/ACHIEVEMENTS:** Outstdg alumni awd Lake Forest Coll 1973; Who's Who Am Women 1974-75; Matrix Awd NY Women in Communications 1978; named One of the Fifty Faces for Amer Future Time Mag 1979; March of Dimes Awd as One of Ten Outstanding Women in Mag Publ 1982. **BUSINESS ADDRESS:** Communications Consultant, 1500 Broadway, New York, NY 10036.

GILLESPIE, RENA HARRELL
Educational consultant. **PERSONAL:** Born Oct 26, 1949, Starkville, MS; widowed. **EDUCATION:** MS State Univ, BS 1972, PhD 1981; Univ of Cincinnati, ME 1974. **CAREER:** Cincinnati Public Schools, resident counselor 1972-74; MS Univ for Women, minority student counselor 1974-78; MS State Univ, residence hall dir 1979-82; Univ of NC at Chapel Hill, assoc dir health careers prog 1983-86; Self-Employed, educational consultant. **ORGANIZATIONS:** Mem United Methodist Local Bd of Ministries 1975-; mem Southern College Personnel Assoc 1979-; mem Amer Personnel & Guidance Assoc 1980-; mem Assoc ofCollege Student Personnel 1980-; mem Natl Minority Health Affairs 1984-; volunteer Outreach Counselor Economic Oppor Atlanta Project Delay, Teenage Pregnancy Prevention Prog 1987-; volunteer Helpline Counselor GA Council on Child Abuse 1987-. **HONORS/ACHIEVEMENTS:** Minority Doctoral Fellowship MS Univ for Women 1978-81; Outstanding Young Woman of Amer 1984. **BUSINESS ADDRESS:** Educational Consultant, Educational Solutions Inc, 2007 Candice, Atlanta, GA 30316.

GILLESPIE, TOM P., JR.
Chief executive. **CAREER:** Gillespie Ford, Inc, Gary, IN, chief executive, 1980-. **BUSINESS ADDRESS:** Gillespie Ford, Inc, 3333 Grant St, Gary, IN 46408. *

GILLESPIE, WILLIAM G.
Clergyman, educator. **PERSONAL:** Born May 12, 1931, Knoxville, TN; married Martha Cox; children: Vendetta Lambert, William, Harry. **EDUCATION:** Knoxville Coll, BS 1952; Johnson C Smith, BD 1955; Tarkio Coll, DD 1969; Eden Sem, STM & D Min 1970; Univ of MO, LLD 1987. **CAREER:** Davie St Presb Ch Raleigh, pastor 1955-56; Linwood Coll St Chas, asst prof 1971-73; Eden Sem Webster Groves MO, lectr 1972-74; Maryville Coll St Louis, lectr 1972-74; Cote Brilliante Presby Ch, pastor 1956-. **ORGANIZATIONS:** Pres bd of trustees Johnson C Smith Sem Atlanta 1976-; pres bd of regents Harris-Stowe State Coll St Louis 1978-; bd of trustees Interdenom Theol Ctr Atlanta 1979-; pres bd of dirs Mathews-Dickey Boys Club St Louis 1970-; bd mem Family & Children's Serv St Louis 1978-; bd mem United Way of Gr St Louis 1980. **HONORS/ACHIEVEMENTS:** Citizen of the Yr Awd Sigma Gamma Rho Sor 1975; Disting Citizen Awd Mathews-Dickey Boys Club 1977; Disting Serv Awd St Louis Argus Newspaper 1979; Martin L King Jr Humanitarian Awd St Louis

Alliance Against Racial Repression 1980. **BUSINESS ADDRESS:** Pastor, Cote Brilliante Presby Ch, 4673 Labadie Ave, St Louis, MO 63115.

GILLETTE, FRANKIE JACOBS
Association executive. **PERSONAL:** Born Apr 01, 1925, Norfolk, VA; daughter of Frank Jacobs and Natalie Taylor; married Maxwell Claude Gillette. **EDUCATION:** Hampton Inst, BS 1946; Howard Univ, MSW 1948. **CAREER:** Ada S McKinley Comm House Chicago, supr 1950-53; Sophie Wright Settlement Detroit, program dir 1953-64; Concerted Serv Proj, dir 1964-65; Univ of California Soc Welfare Ex, program coord 1965-68; US Comm Serv Admin, spec program coord 1968-81; G & G Enterprises, pres; Natl Assn Negro Business and Professional Women's Clubs Inc, pres 1983-87. **ORGANIZATIONS:** Dir Time Savings & Loan Assn 1980-; vice pres San Francisco Handicapped Access Appeals Bd 1982-87; chairperson, bd of dirs NANBPWC Inc 1983-87; commissioner San Francisco Human Rights Commn 1988-; vice pres Urban Economic Devel Corp, San Francisco 1987-. **HONORS/ACHIEVEMENTS:** Alumnus of the Year Hampton Inst 1966; Sojourner Truth NANBPWC Inc 1980; publications The Organizer; The Governor NANBPWC Inc 1978 & 1981; "Women Who Make It Happen" Frito-Lay and Natl Council of Negro Women 1987. **BUSINESS ADDRESS:** President, G&G Enterprises, 85 Cleary Court #4, San Francisco, CA 94109.

GILLETTE, LYRA STEPHANIE
Physician. **PERSONAL:** Born Mar 01, 1930; children: 1 daughter. **EDUCATION:** Barnard Coll, AB 1960; Howard U, MD 1964; Columbia U, MPH 1968. **CAREER:** Harlem Hosp, vstg clincn & consult 1969; Univ Vienna, guest physician 1969; US PUSH, dep chief ob/gyn 1970; Martin Luther King Jr Hop, dir ambulatory serv ob/gyn 1971; Watts Health Found, chief ob/gyn; Univ So CA, assoc clinical prof ob/gyn 1986; Los Angeles County Dept Health Svcs, md specialist. **ORGANIZATIONS:** Chmn Pub Hlth Com Am Med Women's Assn 1977; consult ob-gyn Device Panel FDA 1976; dip Nat Bd Med Exmnrs 1965; Am Bd OB-GYN 1972; flw Am Coll OB-GYN 1974; Los Angeles OB-GYN Soc 1973; Am Pub Hlth Assn 1971; mem Assn Pub Hlth OB-GYN 1974. **HONORS/ACHIEVEMENTS:** PHS grant 1968; AMA Physician Rec Awd 1969; publ "Mgmt of Adenomatous Hyperplasia" OB World 1977. **MILITARY SERVICE:** USAF Med Corps maj 1980-83. **BUSINESS ADDRESS:** Physician Specialist, LA County, 1522 East 102 Street, Los Angeles, CA 90002.

GILLIAM, ARLEEN FAIN
Association administrator. **PERSONAL:** Born Jan 02, 1949, Huntington, WV; daughter of Cicero Fain and Lorraine Fain; married Reginald E Gilliam Jr. **EDUCATION:** MA Inst of Tech, MBA 1976; Skidmore Clge, BS 1970. **CAREER:** Congressional Budget Office, budget analyst 1976-77; Asst Secr of Labor US Dept of Labor, exec asst 1977-81; AFL CIO Fed Natl Intl Labor Unions, asst dir dept soc sec 1981-84, director of budget and planning 1984-. **ORGANIZATIONS:** Reston Chapter of Links 1977-87; MIT Sloan Club Bd of Governors. **HONORS/ACHIEVEMENTS:** Distg srv award US Dept of Labor 1979. **BUSINESS ADDRESS:** Dir Budget Planning, AFL CIO, 815 16th St, Washington, DC 20006.

GILLIAM, DOROTHY BUTLER
Editor. **PERSONAL:** Born in Memphis, TN; married Sam; children: Stephanie, Melissa, Leah. **EDUCATION:** Sch of Jour, Grad 1961; Lincoln U, BA. **CAREER:** WA Post, clmnst 1979-, asst ed 1979; Panorama WTTG/TV, brdcstr 1967-72; WA Post, rptr 1961-66. **ORGANIZATIONS:** Lctr AmUniv & HowardUniv 1967-68, wrtr 1967-72; vice pres Inst for Jour Edn. **HONORS/ACHIEVEMENTS:** Publ "Paul Robeson All Am" 1976; grant African-Am Inst 1961; Anne O'Hare McCormick award NY Nwspr Wmn's Club; jour of yr Capital Press Clubs 1967; emmyaward for Panorama; outst alumni LincolnUniv 1973. **BUSINESS ADDRESS:** 1150 15th St NW, Washington, DC 20071.

GILLIAM, DU-BOIS LAYFELT
Government official. **PERSONAL:** Born Oct 29, 1951, Omaha, NE; married Paula Lyles; children: DuBois L. **EDUCATION:** Univ of NE at Omaha, BS Urban Studies 1971;Univ of NE at Omaha, bS Econ 1975. **CAREER:** State of NE, dir govnr's spl grants 1979-; City of Coun Bluffs IA, human rel dir 1976-79; First Nat Bank of Omaha, gen off mgr 1970-71; Omaha Nat Bank, gen off mgr 1970. **ORGANIZATIONS:** Chmn Douglas Co Young Repub Party 1978-79; state cen com State of NE Young Repub 1979-; labor chmn State of NE Repub Party 1979-; mem Govtl AffairsCom 1978-; mem Omaha JCs 1978-; mem govtl affairs com Omaha C of C 1979-. **HONORS/ACHIEVEMENTS:** Team mem natl fedn of young repub man of the yr awd Douglas Co Young Repub 1979; outstndg contrbtr awd Youth NAACP 1979. **BUSINESS ADDRESS:** 501 Lincoln Bldg, Lincoln, NE 68508.

GILLIAM, EARL B.
Federal judge. **PERSONAL:** Born Aug 17, 1931, Clovis, NM; married Barbara Jean; children: Earl Kenneth, Derrick James. **EDUCATION:** CA State Univ, BA 1953; Hastings Coll of Law, JD 1957. **CAREER:** San Diego CA, dep dist atty 1957-62; San Diego Mcpl Ct, judge 1963-74; Superior Ct CA San Diego Cty, judge 1975-80; US Dist Ct CA, judge 1980-. **BUSINESS ADDRESS:** Judge, California District Court, 940 Front St, Courtroom 6, San Diego, CA 92189.

GILLIAM, FRANK DELANO
Business executive. **PERSONAL:** Born in Steubenville, OH; married Velma; children: Frank Jr, Gayle, Michelle. **EDUCATION:** Attended, Iowa State Univ. **CAREER:** Winnipeg and Vancouver Canadian Football League, pro football player; Iowa State, asst coach 1966-70; Minnesota Vikings, scouting dir, dir of player personnel 1975-.

GILLIAM, HERMAN ARTHUR, JR.
Business executive. **PERSONAL:** Born Mar 06, 1943, Nashville, TN. **EDUCATION:** Yale University, BA 1963; University of Michigan, MBA 1967. **CAREER:** Universal Life Insurance Company, vice president 1967-74; US Congressional Office, administrative asst 1974-75;Gilliam COmmunications, Inc; Pres 1977- . **ORGANIZATIONS:** Dir Memphis Area Broadcasters Assn 1985; board of trustees Lemoyne-Owen College 1985; Brd of Dir, Memphis Area Chamber of Commere 1987; Memphis Black Business Assoc 1987; Leadership Memphis 1987. **HONORS/ACHIEVEMENTS:** Ten Outstanding Young Men of America US Jaycees 1976; Human Rights Award Coalition of Benevolent Youth. **BUSINESS ADDRESS:** President, Gilliam Communications Inc, 363 So Second St, 363 S 2nd St, Memphis, TN 38103.

GILLIAM, JAMES H., JR.
Corporation lawyer. **PERSONAL:** Born Apr 21, 1945, Baltimore, MD; married Randilyn Woodruff; children: Alexis Randilyn, Leslie Brooke. **EDUCATION:** Morgan State Univ, BA, 1967; Columbia Univ, JD, 1970. **CAREER:** Paul, Weiss, Rifkind, Wharton & Garrison, New York, NY, associate, 1970-73; Richards, Layton & Finger, Wilmington, DE, associate, 1973-76; State of Delaware, Dept. of Community Affairs and Economic Devel, cabinet sec, 1977-79; Beneficial Corp, Wilmington, DE, vice pres legal, 1979-81, sr vice pres legal, 1982-85, sr vice pres, gen counsel, 1986-, sec, 1987-. **ORGANIZATIONS:** Amer Bar Assn, Natl Bar Assn, Sigma Pi Phi, Kappa Alpha Psi. **HONORS/ACHIEVEMENTS:** Trustee, bd dirs, Medical Center of Delaware, Howard Hughes Medical Inst. **HOME ADDRESS:** Dr James H Gilliam, Jr, 109 Weldin Park Dr, Wilmington, DE 19803. **BUSINESS ADDRESS:** Dr James H Gilliam, Jr, Beneficial Corp, P O Box 911, Wilmington, DE 19899.

GILLIAM, JAMES H., SR.
Business executive. **PERSONAL:** Born Aug 06, 1920, Baltimore, MD; married Louise Hayley; children: James Jr, Patrice. **EDUCATION:** Morgan State Coll, AB Sociology 1948; Howard Univ Schl of Soc Work, MSW 1950; Yale Univ Summer Schl of Alcohol Studies. **CAREER:** Greater Wilmington Dev Council Inc, dir neighborhood & housing srv 1965-67; Greater Wilmington Housing Corp, exec dir 1967-70; Leon N Weiner & Assc Inc, vice pres 1970-71; Family Court of the State of DE, admin dir of treatment srvs, 1971-72; Leon N Weiner & Assc Inc, vice pres 1972-74; New Castle Cty Dev ofComm Dev & Housing, dir 1974-. **ORGANIZATIONS:** Dir Natl Assc of Housing & Redev Officials 1978-; dir Middle Atlantic Reg Council Natl Assc of Housing & Redev Officials 1976-; dir United Way of DE; dir Medical Cntr DE 1971-; dir Childrens Bureau of DE 1980-; dir New Castle Economic Dev Corp 1981-; bd dirs Urban Coalition of Metro Wilmington; mem NAACP; bd dirs Natl Housing Conf; bd dirs United Way of DE; task force mem Housing for Sr Citizens State of DE; judicial review comm Family Court of DE; adv panel men YWCA; mem Bd on Prof Responsibility, Supreme Court of Delaware; mem, Sigma Pi Phi Fraternity. **HONORS/ACHIEVEMENTS:** Distg Delawarean Award State DE 1982; Social Worker of the Year Natl Assc of Social Workers DE Chap 1969; Alumni Award Howard Univ Schl of Soc Work 1952; publns, "The Program Formulation Process of the Maryland Tuberculosis Assn During the Period 1946-1948" Masters Thesis Howard Univ 1950; "The Role of theArea Office in Harlem Park" paper Residential Rehabilitation 1956 Sch of Architecture Univ of MN; NAHRO Natl Ambassador Awd 1985; Regional Ambassador Awd MARC/NAHRO 1985; BPA Achievers Awd for Significant Contribs in Govt 1985; State Ambassador Awd DE NAHRO 1985; Honorary Doctorate, Business Admin Goldey Beacom Coll 1989; Order of the First State, State of DE, Gov P.S. DuPont 1982. **MILITARY SERVICE:** AUS capt; Bronze Star 1945. **HOME ADDRESS:** 1803 Fairfax Blvd, Wilmington, DE 19803. **BUSINESS ADDRESS:** Dir, New Castle Cty Dept Comm, 800 French St, Wilmington, DE 19801.

GILLIAM, JOHN RALLY
Athlete. **PERSONAL:** Born Aug 07, 1945, Greenwood, SC; married Fannie Pearl Harley; children: Vadrien, Teryn, John. **EDUCATION:** SC State Coll, BS 1967. **CAREER:** Atlanta Falcons, professional football player 1976-; MN Vikings, professional football player 1972-75; J Gilliam Inc, owner 1976-; St Louis Cardinals, professional football player 1969-71; New Orleans Saints, professional football player 1967-68. **ORGANIZATIONS:** Mem Atlanta Bus League; Atlanta C of c; bd of dir, vice pres Merchants' Assn Omni Inter; bd of idr Grayy's Boys Home; 1st Black owned & operated bus in downtown Atlanta; sponsor Pony League Football Team; coach Little League Baseball; sw YMCA; chmn NAACP Night in Las Vegas Benefit; toured army bases USO Japan, Korea, Seoul, Hawaii, DMZ zone, Alaska, Philipines, Tokyo. **HONORS/ACHIEVEMENTS:** Man of the Yr SC State Coll 1976; tied world record 100 yrd dash 1965; cited in Jet visiting hosp youths 100% Wrong Club 1964-66; undergrad professional 1973; Pittsburg Courier All-Star Team 1966; outstanding citations Hardin Elem; Celebrity Golf Classic Columbus, OH; J Gilliam Day Atlanta 1976; cited Atlanta Sch Bd 1971-77; judge Special Olympics Atlanta & Cola, SC; MVP Offensive MN Vikings 1972; awarded 10 team balls for outstanding games MVP-SC State 1965-67; All-Pro1973-75; part 4 all-star games; 5th active all-time receiver; model Ebony mag; MVP Pumpkin Classic 1965. **BUSINESS ADDRESS:** 305 Omni Internatl, Atlanta, GA 30303.

GILLIAM, MARVIN L.
Educator. **PERSONAL:** Born Aug 14, 1941, Cairo, IL; married Cora L Pearson; children: Marlin, Daryl. **EDUCATION:** Drake U, BA 1964;Univ ND, post grad 1966. **CAREER:** Gary Income Maintenace Experiment, IN Univ, business personnel officer 1970-74; Des Moines Chamber of Commerce, economic advisor 1969-70; Northwestern Bell Telephone Co, lineman 1963-64; Project 70,001 DECA, IN Univ NW, prog mgr. **ORGANIZATIONS:** Mem Distributive Educ Clubs Am DECA; mem Kappa Alpha Psi Frat; mem Toastmasters Inter; Inat D Lettermen's Club DrakeUniv Hon Cubmaster BSA Gary 1974-75;supt sunday sch Galilee Bapt Ch Gary 1973-; Sunday sch supt 1975; IN Midwestern Bapt Laymen's Assn; Capt DrakeUniv Varsity Track Team 1963. **HONORS/ACHIEVEMENTS:** Varsity Letterman Track 1961-63; MO Valley Conf Long Jump Champion 1961-63; Triple Jump Champ 1963. **MILITARY SERVICE:** USAF capt 1964-69. **BUSINESS ADDRESS:** 3400 Broadway, Gary, IN 46408.

GILLIAM, REGINALD EARL, JR.
Attorney, educator. **PERSONAL:** Born Dec 29, 1944, New York, NY; married Arleen Fain. **EDUCATION:** Lincoln Univ PA, AB (cum laude) 1965; Harvard Law Schl, JD 1968. **CAREER:** Williams Clge, asst dean lecturer law poli sci 1972-75; US Senator John Glenn, legislative Counsel 1975-80; US Interstate Commerce Comm, v chrmn 1980-83; George Wash Univ, dist visiting prof 1983-85; NY State Dept of Transportation, assistant comm for rail and freight policy, dir freight div 1986-. **ORGANIZATIONS:** Trustee Williams Clge 1979-84; mem NAACP, Omega Psi Phi Frat, Transafrica, Adirondack Mountain Club. **HONORS/ACHIEVEMENTS:** Book New Reality of Natl Black Politics 1985, Black Political Dev 1975; award dist srv Amer Short Line Railroad Assc 1982; award distg srv Minority Trucker Transportation Dev Corp 1980. **HOME ADDRESS:** 2413 Black Cap Ln, Reston, VA 22091.

GILLIAM, ROBERT M., SR.
Attorney. **PERSONAL:** Born Jul 12, 1926, Cleveland, OH; married Elva Ann Hickerson; children: Georgia, Robert, Jr. **EDUCATION:** Bus Ad BS 1950; LlB 1958; JD 1961. **CAREER:** Legal Aid Soc of Cleveland, atty 1968-; Civ Dir, 1971-73; Sen Staff, atty 1973-; Priv Prac, 1958-61; City of Cleve, asst law dir 1961-68. **ORGANIZATIONS:** Mem Cleveland Bar Assn; Ohio Bar Assn; Cleveland Lawyers Assn; John Harlen Law Club; NAACP; Urban League; NLADA; Kappa Alpha Psi Frat; P Omega P; Hon Bus Frat; bd dir Margie Home

for Retarded Adults; bd dir Brdwy YMCA 1945-46. **BUSINESS ADDRESS:** 1223 W 6th St, Cleveland, OH 44113.

GILLIAM, SAM, JR.
Painter, educator, artist. **PERSONAL:** Born Nov 30, 1933, Tupelo, MS. **EDUCATION:** Univ Louisville, BA, MA 1961. **CAREER:** Whitney Mus Annual, painter, educator, artist 1970; Corcoran Gallery, 1969; Embassies, WA Gallery of Modern Art, art 1967; Martin Luther King Memorial, exhibition mus of modern art 1969; Harlem, exhibited studio mus 1969; 1st World Festival of Negro Arts, 1966; Inst of Contemporary Art, 1965; Venice Biennale, Italy, 1970; Art Inst of Chicago, 1970; WA Gallery of Modern Art, 1964; Pacy Gallery, NY, 1972; Maison de la Culture Rennes France, 1973; Phoenix Gallery, San Francisco, 1974; Philadelphia Museum of Art, 1975; Galerie Darthea Speyer Paris, 1976; Dart Gallery Chicago, 1977. **HONORS/ACHIEVEMENTS:** Norman Walt Harris prize, others. **BUSINESS ADDRESS:** 1752 Lamont St NW, Washington, DC 20010.

GILLIAM, SHARON
Director. **PERSONAL:** Married Russell Gilliam. **EDUCATION:** Attended, Mundelein College. **CAREER:** City of Chicago, model cities prog, grant coord/asst budget dir budget & mgmt office; Dept of Consumer Svcs, commissioner; Office of Budget & Resource Washington DC, dir district office, budget officer dept of housing and comm develop; City of Chicago Office of Budget and Mgmt, dir. **BUSINESS ADDRESS:** Budget Dir, City of Chicago, Office of Budget & Management, City Hall Room 604, 121 N LaSalle St, Chicago, IL 60602.

GILLIAMS, TYRONE
Business executive. **PERSONAL:** Born Mar 08, 1941, Camden, NJ; married Rosalind Louise Lee; children: Tyrone Jr, Haile, Tesemma. **CAREER:** Careers Inc, pres 1970-; Forrest Ballard Assn, coun 1969-70; Camden Bd of Edn, tchr guidance 1964-69; Fortunes 500, minority recruitment for 100 spl co listed by. **ORGANIZATIONS:** Elected mem Camden Bd Edn; mem bd dir UAME Credit & Housing Corp; chmn Camden City Mayor's Trans Com; chmn Camden Co Mental Hlth Assn United Way Fund Drive; mem bd dir Mental Hlth Assn Camden Co; Camden Educ Assn; part NJEA ldrshp conf; sponsored drug sem 4h Club of Am; rep Black Educ Conf; Camden Educ Assn; mem Personnel Com Camden Co Mental Hlth Assn; Camden City Mayor's Ad Hoc Com; NAACP; part Nat Urban League Ann Conv; BPUM-eDC bd dir; mem exec bd Kappa Alpha Psi. **BUSINESS ADDRESS:** Ste 604 Commerce Bldg, Camden, NJ 08103.

GILLIARD, JOSEPH WADUS
Educator. **PERSONAL:** Born Nov 23, 1914, Taylor, SC; son of Jocephus Gilliard and Anna Durant; married Bertha Holder; children: Bernard O, Brenda Lee Gilliard Johnson. **EDUCATION:** Hampton Inst, BS 1941, MA 1952. **CAREER:** Hampton Inst, faculty, 1941-, asst prof art, 1949-71, asst prof art, 1971-75, prof of art, 1975-; Ceramic Natl Syracuse Museum Fine Arts Richmond Museum Fine Arts, ceramic art exhibit. **ORGANIZATIONS:** Amer Indus Arts Assn; Amer Assn Univ Profs Institutional Rep Dist Comm Peninsula Council, BSA; trustee, Zion Baptist Church, Hampton, VA; Amer Ceramic Society Emeritus. **HONORS/ACHIEVEMENTS:** Recipient Merit Award, 2nd Biennial Showing of Chesapeake Craftsmen Norfolk Mus 1954; Meritoriouis Award Pininsula Jaycees 1958; Walter R Brown Award, Gamma Ita Chapter Alpha Phi Alpha; Outstanding Achievement Award, Gamma Epsilon Chapter Omega Psi Phi 1964; Silver Beaver Award, BSA 1966; Outstanding Achievement Award, Alpha Delta Mu Honor Soc Hampton Inst, 1965-66; Christian R Mary L Lindback Award Distinguished Teaching, 1975; Art of Public Serv, Presidential Citation, Hampton Univ, 1989; art exhibited at Hampton Univ Museum, 1987; art and Invention exhibited, Hampton Univ Museum, 1988. **MILITARY SERVICE:** USN, Metal Smith 1st class, 1942-45. **HOME ADDRESS:** 108 W Cty St, Hampton, VA 23363.

GILLIS, THERESA MCKINZY
County official. **PERSONAL:** Born Sep 16, 1945, Fort Meade, FL; daughter of Arthur McKinzy and Dezola Williams McKinzy; married Eugene Talmadge Gillis, Dec 23, 1973; children: Reginald, Jarett, Jeraemy. **EDUCATION:** Talladega Coll, BA, 1967. **CAREER:** Broward Employment and Training Administration, counselor, manager SYEP dir, 1976-82; Broward County Community Development Division, citizen participation coordinator, 1982-84, asst dir, 1984-86, director, 1986-89. **ORGANIZATIONS:** SSO'SMem past officer, Delta Sigma Theta Sorority, 1968-; of bd, FL Community Development Assn, 1984-; mem, Natl Assn of Counties, 1986-; Home Economics Advisory Bd, Broward School Board, 1987-89; committee mem, Mt Hermon AME Church Credit Union 1988-; bd mem, Code Enforcement City of Lauderdale Lakes, 1988-; mem, Minority Recruitment Broward County School Board, 1989. **BUSINESS ADDRESS:** Director, Broward County Government, 115 South Andrews Ave, Rm 336U, Fort Lauderdale, FL 33301.

GILLIS, WILLIAM FREEMAN
Business administration. **PERSONAL:** Born Jul 09, 1948, Henderson, KY; divorced; children: Jeffrey, Janeen, Kevin. **EDUCATION:** Purdue Univ, BS Elec Engrg 1970. **CAREER:** RCA Consumer Electronics, r&d engr 1970-73, spec mkt rep 1973-75, adv prod plnng mgr 1975-76, mkt dev mgr 1976-77, mkt mgr 1977-78; Bell System, mkt mgr 1978-81; Mattel Electronics, vp, gen mgr 1981-83; Charles Schwab & Co Inc, exec vice pres 1983-85; Medlink Inc, pres 1985-. **ORGANIZATIONS:** Mem Kappa Alpha Psi 1967-; vstg prof Urban League Black Exec Exchange Prog 1979-80. **HONORS/ACHIEVEMENTS:** Articles on Engrg, Electronics, Marketing and the Home of the Future in various publ 1971-. **MILITARY SERVICE:** USAF 2nd lt 1 yr.

GILLISPIE, WILLIAM HENRY
Aerospace engineering. **PERSONAL:** Born Jan 08, 1927, Hanna, WY; son of Nathan Gillispie and Susie Anderson Gillispie; married Laura, Dec 21, 1977; children: Vincent, Shiela, Richard. **EDUCATION:** Lincoln Univ, BSME 1950; Washington Univ, Univ of Missouri Rolla & St Louis, grad study. **CAREER:** USA Aviation Syst Comm, mgr aircraft div 1973-, special asst to commanding gen for pro mgmt USA .1970-73, dep chief it observation helicopter field office USA 1963-70, special asst for R&D USA 1962-63, oper rsch analyst USA 1961-62; A/C Proj Office USA, ch test 1953-61; part in mgt, devel, prod & support of all curr Army fixed & rotary winged aircraft 1953-88; aerospace and management consultant 1989-. **ORGANIZATIONS:** Chmn St Louis Sec AIAA 1977; chmn CFC camp USA Aviation Syst Comm 1974; lectr aerospace St Louis Public Schools; pres Lincoln Univ Missouri State chap 1975-76; mgmt of trans of Aviation Rsch & Devel resp 1960; command work in the act of the AUS Mobility Comm 1963; pres Lincoln Univ Alumni Assn 1979-85. **HONORS/ACHIEVEMENTS:** Army Civilian Merit Award 1971; Award AIAA Sect Leadership Award 1977; Distinguished Alumni Award Lincoln Univ of Missouri 1977; Army Commanders Award for Civil Serv 1980; AIAA Serv Award 1980; President's Award Natl Assn for Equal Opportunity in Higher 1985; Outstanding Serv Award Lincoln Univ 1985; Commanders Award for Meritorious Achievment 1988. **MILITARY SERVICE:** AUS air corps 1945. **BUSINESS ADDRESS:** President, WHG Engineering and Management Counsultants, 1915 Claymills Dr, Chesterfield, MO 63017.

GILLUM, RONALD M.
State educational administrator. **PERSONAL:** Born May 21, 1939, Gates, PA; son of Roger O Gillum and Edna R Gillum; married Harriette A Coleman, Dec 21, 1963; children: Ronald Jr, Rhonda, Robin. **EDUCATION:** Western MI Univ BS 1963; Wayne St Univ, MEd 1972, EdD 1975. **CAREER:** MI Dept of State, dir prog devel 1978-80; Detroit Pub Sch, teacher, 1963-70 admin 1969-71; Wayne Co Comm Coll, inst 1969-71; MI O Reg Lab Detroit, demon inst 1967; Detroit Pub Sch, inst 1963-69; Boy's Club of Amer, recreation dir; MI Dept of Educ, Lansing, MI, Adult Educ, deputy dir 1980-83, state dir 1983-. **ORGANIZATIONS:** Mem MI Alliance of Black Sch Educators; mem MI Assn of Pub Adult Comm Edn; mem Nat All Black Sch Educators; co-founder Black Tchr Workshops Detroit; mem Urban League Lansing; mem NAACP; mem PTA Lansing; bd of directors, Amer Assn for Adult & Continuing Educ 1987-; policy fellow, Educ Policy Fellowship Program, Natl Inst for Educ Leadership. **HONORS/ACHIEVEMENTS:** Hon mem Sheet Metal Workers Intl Asso; recip Focus & Impact Awd Cotillion Club Inc Detroit; MI State Bd of Educ Distinguished Service Award, 1987; Pres Award, MI Assn of Adult & Continuing Educ 1989; Outstanding Leadership Award in Literacy, US Dept of Educ 1985; "MI Is Learning How to Close Its Literacy Gap" Detroit Free Press, 1987; "Adult Literacy-Can We Handle the Problem" OPTIONS 1987. **HOME ADDRESS:** 1817 Kingwood Drive, Lansing, MI 48912. **BUSINESS ADDRESS:** State Director, Adult Extended Learning Services, Michigan Dept of Education, PO Box 30008, Lansing, MI 48909.

GILMORE, AL TONY
Educator. **PERSONAL:** Born Jun 29, 1946, Spartanburg, SC; married Beryl Sansom; children: Jack S, Genevieve M. **EDUCATION:** NC Central Univ, BA 1968, MA 1969; Univ of Toledo, PhD 1972. **CAREER:** Howard Univ, prof of history; Univ of MD, prof of history; Natl Afro-Amer Museum Project, consultant director; ASALH, researcher; Natl Educ Assoc, program develop specialist. **ORGANIZATIONS:** Bd dirs Assoc for the Study of Afro Amer Life & History 1977-88; consultant dir Natl Afro-American Museum Project Columbus OH 1979-82; mem Organization of Amer Historians, Amer Historical Assoc, Natl Conference of Black Political Scientists, pres, The Forum for the Study of Educ Excellence. **HONORS/ACHIEVEMENTS:** Author of several books "The Natl Impact of Jack Johnson" 1975, "Revisiting the Slave Community" 1979; book reviews have appeared in Washington Post, New York Times, New Republic, American Scholar and others; lectured at over 40 colleges and univs including Harvard, Brown, UCLA, Morehouse and others. **HOME ADDRESS:** 9707 Hill St, Kensington, MD 20895. **BUSINESS ADDRESS:** Program Develop Specialist, Natl Education Association, 1201 16th St NW, Washington, DC 20036.

GILMORE, ARTIS
Professional athlete. **PERSONAL:** Born Aug 21, 1948, Chipley, FL; married Enola Gay; children: Shawna, Priya, Tiffany, Otis, James. **EDUCATION:** Jacksonville Coll, BS 1971. **CAREER:** Chicago Bulls, player 1978-82; San Antonio Spurs 1982-. **ORGANIZATIONS:** Mem Amer Basketball Assn. **HONORS/ACHIEVEMENTS:** All Star Team 1972; Named Rookie of the Yr Amer Basketball Assn 1972; Player of the Yr 1972; All Amer 1971. **BUSINESS ADDRESS:** San Antonio Spurs, Hemis Fair Arena, San Antonio, TX 78292.

GILMORE, CARTER C.
Elected official, business executive. **PERSONAL:** Born May 30, 1926, Grapeland, TX; married Elizabeth Mae Hampton; children: Carl E, Clifford E, Donald A, Carol E, Rodney C, Janet E. **EDUCATION:** Merritt Coll, attended. **CAREER:** Granny Goose Foods, bus mgr; City of Oakland, councilman. **ORGANIZATIONS:** Mem Oakland City Council 1977-; vice mayor 1979-81; chairperson Rules & Procedures Comm of the Council, Community Action Bd, Personnel & Finance Comm; mem Public Safety Comm of the City Council, Exec Comm & Coord Comm, East Oakland Youth Ctr Bd of Dir, Alameda Cty Fair Bd of Dir, League of CA Cities, League of CA Cities Adv Bd; former chmn Civic Action Comm of the City Council; former mem Legislative Comm of the City Council; mem NAACP, Bethel Baptist Church, Boy Scouts Jr Achievment. **HONORS/ACHIEVEMENTS:** Outstanding Comm Leadership Oakland Comm Org; Civil Rights Leadership Awd NAACP; Outstanding Comm Leadership Awd Granny Goose Foods, Five Year Participant Awd Bay Area Black Cowboys; Outstanding Serv to Youth Awd I Oakland Youth Devel; Delegate to China representing City of Oakland; Delegate to Natl Council of Mayors; Delegate to Japan representing City of Oakland. **MILITARY SERVICE:** USN. **BUSINESS ADDRESS:** Councilmember, City of Oakland, 1 City Hall Plaza, Oakland, CA 94612.

GILMORE, CHARLES ARTHUR
Retired educational administrator. **PERSONAL:** Born Sep 23, 1919, Columbia, SC; son of Arthur William Gilmore (deceased) and Rosa Amelia Scott Gilmore (deceased); married Josephine Specter; children: Charles A Jr, Michael, Martha, J Andrew. **EDUCATION:** Temple Univ, BS 1949; Univ of PA Philadelphia, MGA 1960. **CAREER:** City of Phila, admin asst 1957-58, training ofcr 1958-62; NY State Dept Labor, manpower training spec 1963, asst dir 1963-64; US Dept Labor Wash, DC, manpower dev spec 1964, chf div of prgm demonstration 1965-67; Comm Coll of Phila, asst to pres 1967-69, dir div of comm serv 1967-72, dir div ofsoc and behav scis 1969-72; PA Dept Comm Affairs Harrisburg, chf div of municip emp training 1972-74; PA Dept Educ Harrisburg, high educ assoc 1974-79,coord for state-related universities 1979-82, educ and govt administ consultant 1982; retired. **ORGANIZATIONS:** Amer Soc for Training and Dev; Amer Acad of Political and Soc Sci; Amer Soc for Publ Administration; The Academy of Polit Sci; Natl Cncl on CommServ for Comm and Jr Colleges; Natl Exec Bd Wharton Grad Sch Alumni; bd dir PA Inst for Law and Justice; mem Center for Study of the Presidency; mem Natl Center for Public Serv Internship Programs; bd dir Wharton Graduate - Philadelphia Chptr; trustee, Harrisburg Area Community Coll, 1988-. **MILITARY SERVICE:** AUS Lt Col served 9 years. **HOME ADDRESS:** 2715 N 4th St, Harrisburg, PA 17110.

GILMORE, EDWIN
Physician. **PERSONAL:** Born Mar 27, 1931, New York, NY; married Dorothy; children:

Pamela, Jonathan, Gregory. **EDUCATION:** CCNY, BS 1952; SUNY, MD 1956; Upstate Med Ctr. **CAREER:** Coll of Med & Dent of NJ, chf serv dept radiology; Montefiore-Morrijania Affliation, asso dir 1964-75; Grasslands Hosp, asst dir 1960-64; Am Bd Radiology, diplomate. **ORGANIZATIONS:** Mem Am Coll of Radiology; Am Trauma Soc; NY Roentgen Soc; Radiol Soc N Am Mem Harlem Lions. **BUSINESS ADDRESS:** 65 Bergen St, Newark, NJ 07107.

GILMORE, JOHN T.
Educator. **PERSONAL:** Born Aug 01, 1935, Prescott, AR; married Curley Usher. **EDUCATION:** BS 1957; MSIE 1970; PhD 1971. **CAREER:** Univ of AR, prof; Boeing Air Co, assoc engineer 1958-60, statistical cons, computer prog cons; Real Estate Broker; Trinity Church, admin asst; Univ of AR Pine Bluff, dir of engineering; Diversified Unlimited Corp Inc, sec bd of trustees. **ORGANIZATIONS:** Mem Am Inst of Indsl Engr Inc; mem Pine Bluff Planning Commn; bd chmn Trinity Ch God Christ. **HONORS/ACHIEVEMENTS:** Beta Kappa Chi Scientific Hon Soc; Alpha Pi Mu Indsl Eng Hon Soc; mem Alpha Kappa MUniv Nat Honor Soc; Who's Who Am Coll & U; Outstndg Math Student. **MILITARY SERVICE:** AUS e3 1962. **BUSINESS ADDRESS:** 1116 State St, Pine Bluff, AR.

GILMORE, MARSHALL
Clergyman. **PERSONAL:** Born Jan 04, 1931, Hoffman, NC; married Yvonne Dukes; children: John M, Joan M. **EDUCATION:** Paine Coll Augusta, GA, BA 1957; Drew Theol Sem Madison, NJ, MDiv 1960; United Theol Sem Dayton, OH, DMin 1974. **CAREER:** Bray Temple CME Chicago, IL, pastor 1960-62; W Mitchell St CME Ch Atlanta, 1962; Allen Temple CME Ch Detroit, 1962-64; Phillips Temple CME Ch Dayton, 1964-; Payne Theol Sem Wilberforce, OH, instr 1972-73. **ORGANIZATIONS:** Pres Dayton NAACP 1971-72; mem bd Phillips Sch of Theol 1966-; Paine Coll 1969-; Gen Conn Bd CME Ch 1966-. **MILITARY SERVICE:** USAF airman 1-C 1950-54. **BUSINESS ADDRESS:** 2050 Germantown St, Dayton, OH 45408.

GILMORE, RICHARD G.
Business executive. **PERSONAL:** Born Jun 09, 1927, Waterbury, CT; married Elizabeth Redd; children: Richard Jr, Bruce S, Carol Gilmore Wright;s. **EDUCATION:** VA State Coll, BS Business Admin 1951; Wharton Sch Univ of PA, MBA 1982; Additional study Temple Univ Grad Sch of Business; Professional Seminars at Columbia and Harvard. **CAREER:** Penn Fruit Co Phila, PA, finan analyst/budget dir/asst to vptreas 1954-66; Sch Dist of Phila, budget dir 1967-69, exec dir of finance 1969-70, dep supt for administration 1970-71; Girard Bank, vice pres of holding co/vp 1972-73, vice pres of holding co/sr vice pres 1973-76, exec vice pres 1976-81, exec vp/treas 1981-83; City of Philadelphia, dir of finance 1984-86; Philadephia Electric Co, Sr Vice Pres of finance/chief financial officer 1986-. **ORGANIZATIONS:** Dir Philadelphia Elec Co; former dir Comcast Cablevision of Phila; former dir Comcast Corp; former dir Carver Loan and Invest; former dir Philadelphia Tribune Co; trustee Albert Einstein Med Cntr Phila; trustee The Philadelphia Award (former chmn); vice pres Philadelphia Fellowship Comm; mem bd mgrs Franklin Inst; mem GreaterPhiladelphia Partnership; dir Hero Scholarship Fund of Phila; mem Urban Bankers Coalition of Denver Valley; mem Finan Executives Inst (former dir); Alpha Phi Alpa Frat; Frontiers Intl Philadelphia Club; Sigma Pi Phi Frat; Sunday Breakfast Club Phila; The Philadelphia Club; Southeastern PA Chptr American Red Cross, director; Franklin Institute, trustee; director, William Penn Foundation, CSS Inc, Data Access Systems Inc, Meritor Saving Banks. **MILITARY SERVICE:** AUS Corpl 1945-46; Inactive Reserve 2nd Lt 1951-53. **BUSINESS ADDRESS:** Sr VP/Financial Officer/Dir, Philadelphia Electric Co, Philadelphia, PA 19101.

GILMORE, ROBERT MCKINLEY, SR.
Educator. **PERSONAL:** Born May 14, 1952, Houston, TX; son of Marvin Gilmore and Olan Gilmore; married Letha LaVerne Stubbs; children: Robert Jr, Reshun. **EDUCATION:** TX Southern Univ, BA 1980, MA 1981, MA 1984; Univ of Houston, EdD 1985; Mount Hope Bible Coll, BTh; Houston Graduate School of Theology M.D.v. l987-89. **CAREER:** City of Houston, asst dir 1982-84; Texas Southern Univ, instructor 1981-83; Univ of Houston, grad asst 1982-85; Prairie View A&M Univ, asst prof 1985-; Houston Graduate School of Theology urban ministry program director. **ORGANIZATIONS:** Asst to pastor Barbers Memorial Bapt Church 1979-; radio producer and host KTSU and KPVU 1980-; pres Real Productions 1980-; consultant Baptist Ministers Assoc 1985-; mem Phi Delta Kappa Univ of Houston 1985-, Prairie View A&M Univ 1986-; dir of Drug Training Programs Independent Missionary Baptist Assn; pres Real Educ Alternatives for Leadership & Learning l989; pres One Church/One Child l988-; drug educ consultant City of Houston. **HONORS/ACHIEVEMENTS:** Who's Who in South & Southwest Houston 1985; Outstanding Young Men of Amer 1986; publication "Effective Communication a Drug Education Solution," 1986; PV Choice Award Prairie View A&M Univ l989. **MILITARY SERVICE:** USAF sgt 1971-75; Natl Security Awd 1971. **BUSINESS ADDRESS:** Program Director Urban Ministry, Houston Graduate School of Theology, 6910 Fannin, Ste 207, Houston, TX 77030.

GILOTH, RICHARD PETER (KING R. GILOTH-DAVID)
Clergyman, editor. **PERSONAL:** Born Dec 23, 1940, White Plains, NY; son of Henry and Frances Giloth Cook Koch; married Mary Lou; children: Laura Lee, Daniel Peter, Matthew David, Jonathan Henry, King David. **EDUCATION:** Univ of Notre Dame, BA Political Science 1963, MA Teaching 1965. **CAREER:** The Reformer Newspaper Inc, S Bend IN, editor, publisher 1967-; The Drummer,publisher 1989. **ORGANIZATIONS:** Dir Christian Democratic Center, S Bend IN 1964-87; chmn Christian Democratic Movement 1968-; sec bd of dir St Joseph Co Comm Federal Credit Union 1980-82; dir Reg Fed Anti-Poverty Agency 1980-82; dir Center for Christian Democratis Socialism 1987-; coordinator Christian Democratic Socialist Party 1987-; manager Volkswagen Remanufacturing Cooperative 1988. **BUSINESS ADDRESS:** Editor, The Reformer Newspaper Inc, 1040 W Jefferson Blvd, South Bend, IN 46625.

GILOTH-DAVID, KING R. See GILOTH, RICHARD PETER

GILPIN, CLEMMIE EDWARD
Educator. **PERSONAL:** Born Aug 12, 1942, Beaverdam, VA; children: 5 Children. **EDUCATION:** VA State Coll, AB 1966; OH U, MA 1970. **CAREER:** Nigeria, peace corps volunteer 1966-68; Vista, recruit 1969-71; PA State Univ Capital Campus, instructor 1971-. **ORGANIZATIONS:** Assn ofr Study Afro-Am Life & History; United Nations Assn Harrisburg; African Liberation Support Com Founder Capitol Campus & Model United Nations. **BUSINESS ADDRESS:** PA StateUniv, Capitol Campus, Middletown, PA 17057.

GILREATH, COOT, JR.
Educator. **PERSONAL:** Born Jun 03, 1937, Wilkesboro, NC; married Rosalind Delores Petty; children: Greg, Amy. **EDUCATION:** Appalachian St Univ, BT 1978, MA 1981. **CAREER:** Chatham Mfg, industrial engr 1963-73; Wilkes Comm Coll, dir affirmative action 1973-. **ORGANIZATIONS:** Mem NC Assoc Coordinators of Vet Affairs 1979-, Amer Assoc of Affirmative Action 1984-. **MILITARY SERVICE:** USAF A/3C 1 yr. **HOME ADDRESS:** Rt 1 Box 99, Roaring River, NC 28669. **BUSINESS ADDRESS:** Dir of Affirmative Action, Wilkes Community College, PO Box 120, Wilkesboro, NC 28697.

GILVEN, HEZEKIAH
Deputy executive director. **PERSONAL:** Born Jul 01, 1927, Birmingham, AL; married Juanita Gilven; children: Ronald, Edwin, Curtis, Phyllis. **EDUCATION:** Evergreen State Coll, BA sociology 1975. **CAREER:** Tacoma Housing Auth, dep exec dir 1979-; Tacoma-Pierce County Drug Prog, dir drug treat prog 1973-79; Comprehensive Mental Hlth Cntr, mental hlth worker 1972-73; Met Devel Council, mental hlth worker 1971-72; Met Devel Council, bd of dir 1972-73; Health Clinic, bd of dir 1973-74; Citizen Affirmative Action Council, bd of dir 1974-76; Pacific Matrix Soc, bd of dir 1975-76; Tacoma Urban League, bd of dir 1974-79; Oppor Industr Cntr, bd of dir 1976-78. **ORGANIZATIONS:** Mem Gov Adv Council on Drug Abuse 1973-79; commr City of Tacoma Human Relation Comm 1975-78; mem Private Industry Council City of Tacoma 1979-; Tacoma Ministerial Credit Union; CETA Adv Counc; Dept Social & Hlth Serv Adv Counc; Tacoma Sch Dist Affirm Action & Adv Com; Precinet Com person; Black Forum. **HONORS/ACHIEVEMENTS:** Recip Combat Arms; Oak Leaf Cluster; Purple Heart. **MILITARY SERVICE:** AUS staff sgt 1945-69. **BUSINESS ADDRESS:** Tacoma Housing Authority, 1728 E 44th St, Tacoma, WA 98404.

GIOVANNI, NIKKI
Poet. **PERSONAL:** Born Jun 07, 1943, Knoxville, TN; children: Thomas Watson. **EDUCATION:** Fisk Univ, BA (with honors) 1967; Univ PA Sch Soc Work, postgrad 1967; Wilberforce Univ, LHD (hon) 1972; Worcester Univ, LHD 1972; Ripon Univ,DLitt 1974; Smith Coll, D Litt 1975. **CAREER:** Publishing firm TomNik Ltd, founder 1970; poet; writer; lecturer; author of, "Black Feeling, Black Talk" 1968; "Black Judgement" 1969; "Re-Creation" 1970; "Broadside Poem of Angela Yvonne Davis" 1970; "Night Comes Softly" 1970; "Spin a Soft Black Song" 1971; "Gemini" 1971; "My House" 1972; "A Dialog, James Baldwin and Nikki Giovanni" 1973; "Ego Tripping and Other Poems for Young Readers" 1973; "A poetic Equation, Conversations Between Nikki Giovanni and Margaret Walker" 1974; "The Women and the Men" 1975. **ORGANIZATIONS:** Vol worker/life mem Natl Cncl Negro Women. **HONORS/ACHIEVEMENTS:** Recorded album "Truth Is On Its Way" 1972; TV appearances, "Soul!" Natl Educ TV network; numerous talk shows incl the Tonight Show; particip "Soul at the Center" Lincoln Center Performing Arts New York City 1972; Recip Mademoiselle Mag Award Outstanding Achievement 1971; Omega Psi Phi Award; Ford Found Grantee 1967. **BUSINESS ADDRESS:** 303 Hampton Ct, Rolastsburg, VA 24066.

GIPSON, ARTHUR A.
Dentist. **PERSONAL:** Born Aug 24, 1935, Clarksdale, MS; divorced; children: Arthur III, Vickie. **EDUCATION:** TN State U; HowardUniv Sch Dentristry; Holy Rosary Inst Sch Lafayette Parish; MS Indsl Coll; AUS Med Field Serv Sch; Armed Forces Inst Pathology; Symposium Fear & Pain Control Am Analgesic Soc; Am Inst Hypnosis. **CAREER:** Dental Group Inc Memphis, pres chmn; Nat Spectographic Lab Cleveland, jr spectographer 1958; Chf Dental Serv Rochfort, France, command ofc 1961-63; Paris, chf operative dentistry 1961-63; Dewitt Army Hosp Ft Belvoir, VA, rotation assign;Univ TN Coll Dentistry, instr, 1st black to teach at; M T Mfg Co, dir vp; Vic-Art Optics Inc Memphis, pres; Memphis Health Center, bd dir dental dir; W TN Dem Club, chmn; Beale St Blue Light Corp Memphis. **ORGANIZATIONS:** Mem Royal Soc Hlth London; Shelby Co Dental Soc; Am Analgesic So; Aca Gen Dentistry; Am Acad Forensic Odontology; Am Dental Soc; Nat Dental Assn; Am Acad Dental Med; Assn Mil & Surgeons US; Pan-TN Dental Soc; Am Endodontic Soc; Am Inst Hypnosis; Shelby Co Dental Soc; Faculty ClubUniv TN mem Royal Soc Hlth London; mem Collegium Inter Oris Implantatorum; Fellow Royal Soc Hlth London; Am Acad Dental Med. **HONORS/ACHIEVEMENTS:** Clinican Awd Oral Med; Green Awd PUSH; Mosby Scholar Book Awd Scholastic)?"Ellence Howard U; citation Memphis Dairy Council; Founders Club; Goodwill Boys Club; Who's Who S & SW. **BUSINESS ADDRESS:** 2344 Park Ave, Memphis, TN 38114.

GIPSON, BERNARD FRANKLIN, SR.
Surgeon. **PERSONAL:** Born Sep 28, 1921, Bivins, TX; married Ernestine Wallace; children: Bernard F Jr, Bruce Edward. **EDUCATION:** Morehouse Clge, BS 1944; Howard Univ Clge of Med, MD 1947; Diplomat of the Amer Bd of Surgery, 1956. **CAREER:** Private Prac Surgery 1956-. **ORGANIZATIONS:** Clin assc prof of surgery Univ of CO Schl of Medicine 1985; chrmn Dept of Surgery Mercy Med Ctr 1968; life mem NAACP 1980; chrmn Emancipation Proclamation Schlrshp Fund of Newhope Baptist Church 1974. **HONORS/ACHIEVEMENTS:** Comm srv award Methodist Conf of Western States 1984; article Denver Post 1984; Story of my Life Denver Post Newspaper 1984. **MILITARY SERVICE:** USAF capt. **HOME ADDRESS:** 2375 Monaco Pkwy, Denver, CO 80207. **BUSINESS ADDRESS:** Surgeon, Private Practice, 1633 Fillmore St Ste 104, Denver, CO 80206.

GIPSON, FRANCIS E.
City official. **PERSONAL:** Born Apr 25, 1923, Huntington, WV; married Clara; children: Francis, Jr, Linda, Pamela, Teresa, Constance. **EDUCATION:** KY State Coll, BS bus admin 1950; (At Rec & Parks Assn, atnd forums & workshops sponsored by. **CAREER:** Conservation Corps Dept of the interior, br chf of young adults 1974-; City of E Cleveland, former city ofcl dir parks & rec, vice city mgr 1973. **ORGANIZATIONS:** Former mem E Cleveland bd of edn; mem Lake Erie Assn; Amateur Athletic Union; num other professional orgns; former asst dist mgr Equitable Life Assurance Soc of US. **BUSINESS ADDRESS:** Dept of the Interior, 18th & C St NW, Washington, DC 20240.

GIPSON, LOVELACE PRESTON, II
Dentist. **PERSONAL:** Born Jan 09, 1942, Clarksdale, MS; married Amanda; children: Lovelace III, Tamitha, Teresa, Tinile. **EDUCATION:** Am&N CollDd BS 1963; St Louis U, 1965;Univ MO, 1966; A&L U, 1967;Univ TN Sch Dentistry, DDS 1970-73. **CAREER:** Pvt Pract, dentist; Hamilton Co Chattanooga Hlth Dept, staff dentist 1974; St Louis & E St Louis Bd Edn, tchr 1965-70; Nashville, AR, bd of Educ 1963-64. **ORGANIZATIONS:** Mem Nat Bus League; pres Professional Corp 1977; mem PK Miller Youth Orgn 1955; Nat Dental Assn; Am Den Assn; Memphis Shelby Co Dental Soc; NAACP; UAPB Alumni Assn; Elks Lodge; Chickasaw Cncl BSA; Urban League; hon del TN Constl Conv; mem Am Endodontic Soc; Fndrs Club The Memphis Goodwill Boy's Club. **HONORS/ACHIEVEMENTS:** Recip Ford Found Flwsp St LouisUniv 1965; NSF GrantUniv MO & AtlantaUniv 1966-67. **BUSINESS ADDRESS:** 1216 Thomas, Memphis, TN 38107.

GIPSON, MACK, JR.
Educator, geologist. **PERSONAL:** Born Sep 15, 1931, Trenton, SC; son of Mack Gipson, Sr (deceased) and Artie Mathis Watson; married Alma Gadison, Jul 22, 1956; children: Jacquelyn, Deborah, Mack, Byron. **EDUCATION:** Paine Coll, BA 1953; Univ of Chicago, MS 1961; Univ of Chicago, PhD 1963. **CAREER:** Augusta GA, teacher 1953-54, 1956-57; VA State Coll, prof dept chmn 1964-75; Exxon Co, exploration geologist 1973-74; Exxon Prod Rsch Co, 1975-82; NLERCO, mgr Plastic Geology 1982-84; Aminoil Inc/Phillips Petroleum Co, explorationist II 1984-86; Univ of SC, prof of Geology 1986-. **ORGANIZATIONS:** Mem Amer Geological Inst Educ Com 1968-71; dir Natl Science Found Earth Science Inst 1964-74; mem Grad Records Exam Com 1971-76; mem Amer Assn of Petroleum Geology; fellow Geological Soc of Amer; mem Amer Geological Inst Minority Advisory Com; mem US Dept of Interior Minority Advisory Com 1972-74; mem Kappa Alpha Psi Fraternity; mem Natl Consortium for Black Prof Devel; mem bd of trustees Paine Coll 1979-; mem NAACP; mem Soc of Sigma Xi, Beta Kappa Chi; numerous professional articles. **HONORS/ACHIEVEMENTS:** J Elmer Thomas Fellowship in Geology 1961-63; Distinguished Science Award Natl Consortium for Black Professional Devel 1976; numerous plaques and certificates. **MILITARY SERVICE:** AUS sp-3 1954-56. **HOME ADDRESS:** 7424 Coachmaker Rd, Columbia, SC 29209.

GIST, JESSIE M. GILBERT
Director. **PERSONAL:** Born Mar 07, 1925, Passaic, NJ; daughter of David Julian Gilbert and Annie Iora Nelson Gilbert; married James Fredrick Jr (deceased); children: David Allan, Sandra Thorpe, James Fredrick III, Stephanie DuBois. **EDUCATION:** Tombrock Coll, AA 1972; Montclair State Coll, MA 1976. **CAREER:** Passaic Co Comm Coll, dir of spl prog; Paterson Task Force for Comm Action Paterson NJ, center dir 1965-69; Tombrock Coll W Paterson, NJ, asst to pres for comm affairs 1969-73; Passaic County Comm Coll Paterson NJ, dean of students 1978-80; County Coll of Morris Randolph NJ, dir, educ oppty fund prog. **ORGANIZATIONS:** Life mem NC Negro Women 1977; bd mem & life mem NAACP 1978-80; treas trustee Paterson Regional Devel; chmn Council on Social Serv City of Paterson 1983,84; pres, bd of dir Paterson Task Force for Comm Action Inc 1986-87; treas Natl Council on Black Amer Affairs A Council of the Amer Assoc of Comm &Jr Colls; Council on Comm Serv Am Assn of Jr Comm Coll, pres l975; Commn on Legis, mem; Am Assn of Comm Jr Coll, bd of dir; NJ Educ Oppor Fund Dir Assn, pres l978-80; bd mem, Citizen's Alliance for the Prevention of Drug Abuse l988-; vice pres Coalition of l00 Black Women; bd mem/treasurer Natl Assn of Negro Business & Prof Women's Clubs l980-86. **HONORS/ACHIEVEMENTS:** Corp Woman of Yr Nat Council on Comm Serv & Continuing Educ Midlantic Region 1976; Community Serv Awd EFA Fitness Center Paterson NJ 1986; Outstanding Serv Awd NJ Educ Oppty Fund Professional Assoc 1986; 20 Year Service Award N.J. Dept of Higher Educ l989; 20 Year Oustanding Service N.J. Educ Opportunity Fund Prof Assn l989. **HOME ADDRESS:** 86-88 17th Ave, Paterson, NJ 07513.

GIST, KAREN WINGFIELD
Educator. **PERSONAL:** Born May 14, 1950, Harrisburg, PA; daughter of Raleigh Wingfield and Mary Gooden Wingfield; divorced; children: Maya Jemelle. **EDUCATION:** Clarion State Univ, BS 1972; Univ of Pittsburgh, MEd 1974; California State Univ, attended 1983. **CAREER:** Pittsburgh Board of Education, secondary teacher. **ORGANIZATIONS:** Instructor Community Coll of Allegheny County 1974-84; fellow Western Pennsylvania Writing Project 1983-; mem Lambda Kappa Mu Sor Inc Zeta Chapter; mem Pittsburgh Federation of Teachers; mem Natl Council of Teachers of English; mem Urban League. **BUSINESS ADDRESS:** Secondary Teacher, Pittsburgh Board of Education, 341 So Bellefield, Pittsburgh, PA 15213.

GIST, LEWIS ALEXANDER, JR.
Retired government official. **PERSONAL:** Born Nov 17, 1921, Richmond, VA; son of Lewis Gist Sr and Leonia Hill Gist; married Grace Naomi Perry, Dec 25, 1948; children: Marilyn, Lewis III. **EDUCATION:** VA Union U, BS 1947; Howard U, MS 1949; IA State U, PhD 1956. **CAREER:** SPI SE Nat Sci Found, div dir 1976-82; OEEO NSF, dir 1974-76, asso prgm dir 1964-74; Norfolk St Coll, prof dept chmn 1958-64; VA Union U, asso prof head chemistry dept 1956-58; GW Carver Found Tuskegee Inst, rsrch asst, asst prof 1949-52, 56; Howard U, instr 1949, tchng asstshp 1947-49. **ORGANIZATIONS:** Consult Govt of India 1967,69, Rep of S Africa 1972; fellow WA Acad of Sci, Amer Inst of Chemists; exec sec Beta Kappa Chi 1962-64; mem Amer Chem Soc; pres Natl Inst of Sci 1963-64,71-72; mem Amer Assn for Advancement of Sci, Sigma Xi. **HONORS/ACHIEVEMENTS:** Merit Serv Awd NSF 1976; publ Jour of Am Chem Soc; Jour of Organic Chem; Beta Kappa Chi Bulletin; Transactions of Nat Inst of Sci. **MILITARY SERVICE:** AUS staff sgt 1942-46. **HOME ADDRESS:** 1336 Locust Rd NW, Washington, DC 20012.

GITE, LLOYD ANTHONY
Journalist. **PERSONAL:** Born Oct 16, 1951, Houston, TX. **EDUCATION:** North TX State Univ Denton, bachelor's degree 1971-74; Southern Methodist Univ Dallas, master's program 1976-77; Univ of MI Ann Arbor, master's/radio-TV-film 1979-80. **CAREER:** KNOK AM/FM Dallas, news dir 1977-78; Black Forum Dallas, host/producer ABC program 1977-78; Sheridan Broadcasting Network, corres 1980-83; Natl Black Network, corres 1975-83; WTVS TV Detroit, reporter/producer 1981-83; writer for several natl magazines incl Essence, Black Enterprise, USA Today, Gentlemen's Quarterly, Working Woman, Monthly Detroit, 1981-; KRIV TV, reporter/producer 1983-. **HONORS/ACHIEVEMENTS:** Chosen by Essence Mag as an Essence Man 1976; recipient of Press Club of Dallas Media Awd 1977; chosen by US Jaycees as one of the Most Outstanding Young Menin America 1978; selected by Ebony Mag as one of the Fifty Leaders of the Future 1978; recipient Natl Assoc Black Women Entrepeneurs Mentor of Year Awd 1982; recipient of Lincoln Univ UNITY Awd in Media 1982, 1983; Houston Press Club Awd for Media 1984. **BUSINESS ADDRESS:** Reporter/Producer, KRIV-TV, 3935 Westheimer, Houston, TX 77027.

GITHII, ETHEL WADDELL
Educator. **PERSONAL:** Born Jul 23, Atlanta, GA. **EDUCATION:** Spelman Coll Atlanta, AB 1957; Columbia Univ NY, MA 1965; Tufts Univ Medford, MA, PhD 1980; Harvard Univ Cambridge, MA; Oxford Univ Oxford England. **CAREER:** GA Inst of Tech, Atlanta, asst prof 1977-; Morehouse Coll English Dept, asst prof 1976-77; Harvard Univ Cambridge, tutor in English & African & literature 1975-76; Boston State Coll Boston, MA, lecturer, English 1974-75; Harvard & Radcliffe Univ Cambridge, undergraduate admissions recruitment offcr 1973-75; Tufts Univ, Medford, MA graduate teaching asst 1973-75; Harvard Univ Cambridge, consult Afro-Amer studies dept 1970-71; Westminster Coll of Educ Oxford, England, lectr in English 1968-70; Oxford Univ Oxford, England, lecturer in English 1968-70; Univ of East Africa Nairobi Kenya E Africa, lecturer. **ORGANIZATIONS:** Mem, Modern Lang Assn; mem African Studies Assn; mem So Center for Intl Studies; mem Natl Urban League; mem Amer Cancer Soc; mem African Wildlife Assn; mem Met Opera Guild. **HONORS/ACHIEVEMENTS:** Danforth Found Award Danforth Found, 1961; Boy Scouts of Amer Award for Serv in interpreting to deaf, 1971; Travelled througout the world. **BUSINESS ADDRESS:** 225 N Ave, Atlanta, GA 30317.

GITTENS, JAMES PHILIP
Attorney. **PERSONAL:** Born Jul 18, 1952, Somerville, NJ. **EDUCATION:** Rutgers Coll, BA 1974; Rutgers Law Sch, JD 1977; Georgetown Law Sch Wash, LlM (pending) 1981. **CAREER:** US Dept of Hous & Urban Devel, atty 1979-, congress Liason 1978-79; NJ Dept of Correct, asst to comm of correct 1977-78; Gov Brendan Byrne's Campaign, minority camp coord 1977; Newark Munic Cts, law clerk 1975-77; Rutgers U, adm ofcr 1974. **ORGANIZATIONS:** Mem Asso of Black Law Stud 1974-77; mem PA Bar Assn; mem Nat Conf of Black Lawyers; pres Challenge (Civic Orgn in Neward); sec appt as Congress Liason 1978-79. **BUSINESS ADDRESS:** 451 Seventh St SW, Washington, DC 20410.

GIVENS, DONOVAHN HESTON
Physician, educator. **PERSONAL:** Born Dec 31, 1930, Chicago, IL; married Shirley; children: Linda, Rachel, Donna, Elizabeth. **EDUCATION:** Univ PA; Wayne State U;Univ MI Med Sch, MD 1961. **CAREER:** Oakland Internist Asso, owner; Wayne State U, clinical asst prof 1965-; St Joseph's, resd 1962-65; St Joseph Mercy Hosp, intern 1961-62. **ORGANIZATIONS:** Mem Nat Med Assn; Detroit Med Soc; Wayne Co Med Soc; MI Med Soc; AMA; Am Soc of Internal Med; Am Coll of Phys; mem Vis Com to Med Ctr for AlumniaeUniv of MI; Adv Plann Com forUniv Outpaitent Clinic 1971-72; publ "Urinary Salt Wasting in Chronic Renpl Failure" Grace Hosp Billiton 1970. **MILITARY SERVICE:** USAF 1951-55. **BUSINESS ADDRESS:** 23077 Greenfield, Southfield, MI 48075.

GIVENS, E. TERRIAN
Retired business executive. **PERSONAL:** Born Mar 08, 1930, Spartenburg, SC; daughter of Josephine Porter Smith (deceased); married Howard; children: Darrick H, Dermot D. **EDUCATION:** Univ of Detroit, BS 1970, MS 1972. **CAREER:** Mayor's Comm for Human Resources Devel, staff coord 1965-71; Detroit Youth Bd, coord summer activ 1971-73; Detroit Mayor Roman S Gribbs, exec asst (1st female exec asst to any mayor in hist of Detroit) 1973-74, admin asst (Grade III) assigned to Detroit Bicent 1974; City of Detroit, principal soc planning & devel asst; City of Detroit, admin asst (Grade IV) in Detroit Planning Dept, retired after 38 years of service. **ORGANIZATIONS:** Established 1st Sub-Center in US under Poverty Prog, Natl Assn Comm Developers; Soc Workers of Metro Detroit, pres 1973-75, 1st vice pres 1972; Detroit Black Coalition; 2nd vice pres Tri-City Business & Professional Women's Club; Citizens Adv Council, Southeastern Michigan Transit Authority; Metro Summer Comm Detroit UCS, 1972-73; mem Women's Econ Club; chairperson Assn of Municipal Professional Women; sec, treas, bd dir Hancock Residential Care Center 1975-; bd dir St Peter's Home for Boys 1973-; Natl Round Table of Christians & Jews; NAACP; Natl Drifters Inc; Intl Afro-Amer Museum; Marion Park Civic Club; YMCA; mem, bd dir Detroit Assn for Retarded Children; pres Detroit Jet Setters. **HONORS/ACHIEVEMENTS:** WJLB Radio's Citizen of Day 1967; Boy Scouts of Amer, Toppers Club Citation 1970; Optimist Club 1971; Now Black Woman of the Yr, Natl Drifters Inc 1974-75; Woman of the Year, Amer Business Women's Assn 1976-77; Certificate of Appreciation, Detroit Assn of Retarded Citizens 1976; Appreciation Award, Conastoga Coll Kitchner, Ontario, Canada 1979; Notary Public 1972-; Detroit Public Schools Serv Award 1981; Detroit Black United Fund, Certificate of Appreciation 1984-87; Booster Club, United Negro Coll Fund l987-88.

GIVENS, HENRY, JR.
College president. **CAREER:** Harris-Stowe State College, St Louis MO, president. **BUSINESS ADDRESS:** Harris-Stowe State College, St Louis, MO 63103. *

GIVENS, JOSHUA EDMOND
Marketing executive. **PERSONAL:** Born Jun 12, 1953, Norfolk, VA. **EDUCATION:** Northwestern Univ, BS Speech 1975, MS Journalism 1977. **CAREER:** WGN-TV, promotional writer 1974, news writer 1974-75; Benton & Bowles, acct exec 1977-79; Natl Black Network Radio, acct exec 1979-80; Ebony Magazine, acct exec 1980-81; Caldwell Reingold Adv, acct super 1981; Revlon, Inc, dir of marketing 1981-86, vp, dir of mktg ethnic retail markets 1987-. **ORGANIZATIONS:** Mem, Natl Black MBA Assn NY Chapter, Natl Assn Market Devel; NAACP. **HONORS/ACHIEVEMENTS:** Editor-in-chief high school newspaper 1970-71; Acad Scholarship Northwestern Univ, 1971-75, 1976-77. **BUSINESS ADDRESS:** Vice President of Marketing, Revlon, Inc, 767 Fifth Ave, New York, NY 10153.

GIVENS, LEONARD DAVID
Attorney. **PERSONAL:** Born Sep 10, 1943, Elmira, NY; married Patricia. **EDUCATION:** Mansfield State Coll, BS 1965; Howard Law Sch, JD 1971. **CAREER:** Miller, Canfield, Paddock & Slone, atty 1971-; NLRB Wash, law clerk 1970-71; AFSCME Wash, law clerk 1968-69; IBM Owego, NY, admin asst 1965-68. **ORGANIZATIONS:** Mem ABA; NBA; Detroit Bar Assn; Oakland Co Bar Assn; MI State Bar Assn; Am Judicature Soc bd dir Homes for black children; Gr Detroit Soc for Blindsec; Law Journal invitee Moot Ct Team. **BUSINESS ADDRESS:** 2500 Detroit Bank & Trust Bldg, Detroit, MI 48226.

GIVHAN, MERCER A., JR.
Business executive. **PERSONAL:** Born Dec 28, 1943, Birmingham, AL; married Annetta Foster; children: Mercer III, Carrie. **EDUCATION:** Morehouse Coll, BA econ 1965. **CAREER:** Shearson Loeb Rhoades, sr vice pres investments; Shearson Loeb Rhoades, investm broker 1969-. **ORGANIZATIONS:** Pres council Shearson Loeb Rhoades 1975-80. **MILITARY SERVICE:** A1c a/c 1965-68. **BUSINESS ADDRESS:** Shearson Loeb Rhoades, 30 S 17th St, Philadelphia, PA 19103.

GIVINS, ABE, JR.
Goverment official, insurance consultant. **PERSONAL:** Born Apr 22, 1951, Columbus, MS; married Linda Sue Robinson; children: Abe III, Ryan Eugene. **EDUCATION:** Central State Univ, BS Ed 1974-77. **CAREER:** Normandy School Dist, teacher 1980-82; City of Pine Lawn MO, alderman 1982-; Insurance Agency, insurance broker 1982-; City of Pine Lawn, alderman. **ORGANIZATIONS:** Mem Normandy Municpal League 1982-, MS Municipal League 1982-, Normandy Democratic Club 1982-. **HOME ADDRESS:** 3712 Manola, Pine Lawn, MO 63121.

GLADDEN, BRENDA WINCKLER
Attorney. **PERSONAL:** Born May 29, 1943, Baltimore, MD; married Major Paul Gladden MD; children: Miriam P, Paul B. **EDUCATION:** Cedar Crest Coll Allentown PA, BA 1965; Howard Univ School of Law WA DC, JD 1973. **CAREER:** NY HOsp NY, chemist 1965-67; US Dept op HUD WA DC, attny 1974-. **ORGANIZATIONS:** Mem Phi Alpha Delta Law Frat 1971-, DC Bar Assoc, PA Bar Assoc, Amer Bar Assoc, 1974-, Delta Sigma Theta, Jack & Jill of Amer Inc, Aux to Medico-Chirurgical Soc DC, Aux to Natl Med Assoc, The Nat'l Bar Assoc, Links Inc, Law Review Invitee Howard 1972. **HONORS/ACHIEVEMENTS:** Outstanding Young Women of 1976; DC Ct of Appeals 1974; Supreme Ct of PA 1974; US Dist Ct DC 1974; US Ct of Appeals DC Circuit 1980; US Supreme Ct 1980. **BUSINESS ADDRESS:** Attorney, US Dept of HUD, 451 7th St SW, Washington, DC 20410.

GLADDEN, MAJOR P.
Orthopedic surgeon. **PERSONAL:** Born Dec 08, 1935, Chester, SC; son of Joseph Gladden and Isabelle Gladden; married Brenda Winckler; children: Miriam P, Paul B. **EDUCATION:** Morgan State Coll, BS 1957; Howard Univ, MD 1961; Amer Bd of Orthopaedic Surgery, cert 1969, recertified 1983. **CAREER:** DC Gen Hosp, internship 1961-62; Mt Alto VA Hosp, res training (gen surg) 1962-63; DC Gen Hosp, res ortho 1963-64; Bronx Municipal Hosp, residency ortho 1964-66; Albert Einstein Coll of Med Bronx, instr 1966-68; Howard Univ Coll of Med, asst prof 1969-80; DC Genl Hosp, chief orthopaedic surg1968-80; Howard Univ Coll of Med, assoc prof ortho surg 1980-. **ORGANIZATIONS:** Mem Alpha Phi Alpha Frat 1954-; team physician & ortho consul Howard Univ 1969-; volunteer in Orthopaedics Medico Prog (CARE) Dominican Rep 1978; examiner Amer Bd of Ortho Surg Chicago 1979; vol ortho surg Olympic Training Ctr Colorado Springs 1984; mem bd of dirs Morgan State Univ Found 1984; chief physician DC Boxing & Wrestling Comm 1984. **MILITARY SERVICE:** AUS maj 1957-71. **BUSINESS ADDRESS:** Assoc Prof Ortho Surgery, HowardUniv Coll of Med, 1140 Varnum St NE, Suite l08, Washington, DC 20017.

GLADNEY, MARCELLIOUS
Public health chief. **PERSONAL:** Born May 14, 1949, West Point, MS; married Elizabeth F Jones; children: Scott, Tarik M, Tonia M. **EDUCATION:** St Johns Univ, BS Pharmacy 1972; Univ of Med & Dent of NJ, DMD 1977. **CAREER:** Eli Lilly and Co, pharm sales rep 1972-74; US Public Health Svcs, asst dental surgeon 1977-80; Mercer McDowel Dental Group, pres/founder 1980-; US PublicHealth Svcs, chief dental officer 1986-. **ORGANIZATIONS:** Mem Amer Dental Assoc 1979-87; mem Princeton WV Civitans 1982-85; pres Southern WV Roadrunners Club 1983-86; bd mem Princeton Comm Hosp 1984-86; sire archon Alpha Upsilon Boule Sigma Pi Phi 1985; consultant Blue Cross/Blue Shield 1985-86. **HONORS/ACHIEVEMENTS:** Public Health Serv Scholarship 1975; Natl Health Service Grant 1980; PHS Citation Awd. **HOME ADDRESS:** New PHS Housing #2026-1, PO Box 177, Crown Point, NM 87313. **BUSINESS ADDRESS:** Dept Chief Dental Services, US Public Health Service, Rte 7 Box R50, Philadelphia, MS 39350.

GLANTON, LUTHER T., JR.
Judge. **PERSONAL:** Born Jan 01, 1916, Murfreesboro, TN; married Willie S. **EDUCATION:** TN St U, BS; Drake U, LLB; SorbonneUniv Paris, adv stud; Northwestern U;Univ of VA. **CAREER:** Dist ct judge 1976-; asso judge 1973-76; mun ct judge 1958-73; general law pract; Polk Co, asst co attny. **ORGANIZATIONS:** Past co-chrm Gov UN Com; past corr sec AAUN; past mem exec bd Gov Commn on Human Rts; past mem Des Moines Commn on Human Rts; past mem Family Serv Bd; good will amb to Africa Cypress & SE Asia US State Dept 1962; past mem pres exec comm Bd of Intl Edn; mem Am Bar Assn; Nat Bar Assn; IA Bar Assn; Polk Co Bar Assn; past pres IA Conf of Mun Ct Judges; past chrm trustee bd Corinthian Bapt Ch; mem exec bd IA br BSA; past memexec bd Nat Conf of Christ & Jews; past pres Des Moines Area Cncl of Chs; mem Shrine & Prince Hall Masonic Order; mem Omicron Delta Kappa Frat DrakeUniv Chapt; mem Order of Elks; fdr chrm of bd United Blk Fed; past mem exec bd Des Moines Chap of Big Bros of Am; past pres exec bd Goodwill Inds of Am; mem exec bd Goodwill Inds of Am Inc; mem exec bd Nat Goodwill Inds of Am Inc; mem exec bd Am Red Cross; mem exec bd Arthritis Found; state dir Omega Psi Phi Frat; candidate 33 degree Mason. **HONORS/ACHIEVEMENTS:** Man of the yr Omega Pso Phi 1963. **MILITARY SERVICE:** AUS lt c. **BUSINESS ADDRESS:** Polk Co Ct House, 5th & Mulberry, Des Moines, IA 50309.

GLANTON, LYDIA JACKSON
Educator. **PERSONAL:** Born Jul 11, 1909, Rockvale, TN; married Simon Henry Glanton; children: Thelma Louise Rogers Lawson. **EDUCATION:** TN State Univ, BS (w/honors), 1948; Fisk Univ, Postgraduate 1950; George Peabody Coll, 45 hrs towards Masters degree, 1968. **CAREER:** Rutherford County Schools, teacher, 1931-38; Rutherford County Schools, Little Hope School, principal, 1938-45; Rutherford County Schools, teacher 1965-74; Rutherford County Bd of Educ, bd mem 1975-84; Rutherford Cty Schools, special educ task force 1986. **ORGANIZATIONS:** life mem, Natl Educ Assn, 1945; pres, Rutheford County Teachers Assn, 1966-67; pres Murfreesboro County Fed, 1970-78, TN Fed Colored Women's Club 1973-77; life mem Natl Assoc CWC 1976-; adv bd Patterson Comm Ctr 1977-; cancer bd 1980; pres Rutherford Cty Retired Teachers 1982-83; bd Local Heart Assoc 1982-84; pres Heart of TN Amer BWS Women Assn 1983-84; judging comm Murfreesboro Chamber of Comm Christmas Parade 1983; vice pres Mid Cumberland Agency Co 1984-85; pres, treas, committees, Criterian Literary & Art Club; mem Dynamic Club; life mem Natl Assoc of Colored Womens Clubs Washington DC; mem League of Women Voters Murfreesboro Chapt, Southeastern Assoc of Colored Womens Clubs; Murfreesboro City Sign Commission 1985; Murfreesboro City Planning Comm 1986-89. **HONORS/ACHIEVEMENTS:** Helped write curriculum guide for Rutherford Cty Schools 1965; Head Start Vol Serv head Start Dept of Mid Cumb 1973-78; Outstanding Serv Rutherford County School Bd 1975-84; Hon Staff Mem of TN House of Rep Certificate of Merit 1976; Murfreesboro Masonic Lodge Citizen of the Year Awd 1977; Certificate of Appreciation Mid Cumb Comm Action Agency 1978; Hon Sgt at Arms of TN House of Rep James R McKinney Speaker of House of Rep; Certificate of Award, Kappa Alpha Psi 1978; Outstanding Serv TN School Bd Awd 1982-83. **HOME ADDRESS:** 615 East Castle St, Murfreesboro, TN 37130. **BUSINESS ADDRESS:** Special Education Task Force, Ruth Co Schools, 467 South Hancock, Murfreesboro, TN 37130.

GLANTON, SADYE LYERSON
Executive secretary. **PERSONAL:** Born Jul 05, 1900, Nashville; widowed. **EDUCATION:** A&IUniv Nashville TN, BS 1918;Univ of Cincinnati, BS 1930;Univ of Cincinnati, grad work. **CAREER:** Organized Nat Coun of Negro Women, pres 1955-58, 70-74; Zeta Phi Beta Sorority, organizer dir job corps for girls training 1964-68; Springfield NAACP, exec sec; Dramatics Cincinnati Recruiter, dir 1940-48. **ORGANIZATIONS:** Organizer mem Bapt Ch; mem of choir 20 yrs; pres Zeto Phi Beta Sorority 1922-24; pres Nat Coun of Negro Women 1930 & 1954; participent conv Dayton OH. **HONORS/ACHIEVEMENTS:** Citation for comm work Trenton Meth Ch; award of merit for outstanding contribution by Affiliate Contractors of Am Inc 1972; award from YMCA.

GLANVILLE, CECIL E.
Psychiatrist. **PERSONAL:** Born Jan 15, 1925; married Mattie E Lynch; children: Kenneth, Douglas. **EDUCATION:** Teachers Coll Port of Spain Trinidad West Indies, Teachers Diploma 1946; Howard Univ Coll of Liberal Arts, BS (cum laude) 1959; Howard Univ Coll of Medicine, MD 1963. **CAREER:** Manhattan Psychiatric Center, NY City, unit chief; Harlem Hospital, Manhattan Psychiatric Center, affiliate unit 1967-69; Speedwell Servs for Children, NY City, clinical dir 1969-72; W Harlem Mental Health Council, NY City, medical dir Washington Heights 1973-80; Private Practice; Bergen Pines County Hospital, Paramus NJ, staff psychiatrist. **ORGANIZATIONS:** Gen mem Amer Psychiatric Assn 1967-, Amer Medical Assn 1967-, Natl Medical Assn 1969-; chrmn Youth Guidance Council Teaneck NJ 1974-86; mem Amer Heart Assn 1983-85. **BUSINESS ADDRESS:** 185 Cedar Lane, Teaneck, NJ 07666.

GLASCO, ANITA L.
Educator. **PERSONAL:** Born Oct 24, 1942, Kansas City, KS. **EDUCATION:** UUniv So CA, AB 1964; Harvard Univ Law Sch, JD 1967. **CAREER:** Univ of Chicago Law Sch, master of comparative law 1970; Southwestern Univ Sch of Law, prof of law 1975-; SW, Asso prof of law 1972-75; Smith & Glascod partner 1971-72; Lewis & Clark Coll, visting prof of law 1975; Univ of Wash, visting prof of law 1974; Univ of TN knoxville, vis prof of law 1980. **ORGANIZATIONS:** Mem CA State Bar Assn 1968-; mem Black Women Lawyers Assn; mem CA Assn of Black Lawyers; chpn Elect of Minority Groups Sect of Assn of Am Law Schs1977; chmn Minority Groups Sect of Assn of Law Schs 1978; fellow Inst French Lang & CivilUniv of Geneva 1968; fellow Inst of French Lang & CivilUniv ofPau 1969; fellow Inst French Lang & CivilUniv of Paris 1969; comparative law fellowUniv of Aix-Marseilles 1969-74. **HONORS/ACHIEVEMENTS:** Outst Young Woman of Am honoree 1971. **BUSINESS ADDRESS:** SWUniv School of Law, 675 S Westmoreland, Los Angeles, CA 90005.

GLASGOW, DOUGLAS G.
Educator. **EDUCATION:** Brklyn Coll, BA 1959; Clmb U, MSW 1961;Univ of So CA, DSW 1968. **CAREER:** Natl Urban League Inc, wash oper; Howard Univ School of Social Work, prof, dean 1971-74; Univ of CA Los Angeles, assoc prof, School of Social Welfare 1970-71; Council on Social Work Educ LA, juvenile delinquency comm 1969-70; The Center for the Stdy of Afro-Amer Historical Culture UCLA, interim dir 1969-70; HEW Office of Juvenile Delinquency Youth Devel LA, prin invest 1968-69. **ORGANIZATIONS:** Mem Nat Assn of Soc Wrks; Intl Coun on Soc Wlfr Inc; The Acad of Cert Soc Wrkrs; Am Acad of Pol & Soc Sci; Nat Assn of Blck Soc Wrkrs; Nat Assn of Soc Wrkrs; bd mem Coun on Soc Wrk Ed; co-chmn Blck Fclty Staff UCLA 1969; CSWE Struc Rvw Com 1971-72, bd dir 1972-74, adv com on Comm Coll Gdlns 1969, Rvw Dsgn Com 1972; v chmn Div Prog NCSW Cntnl Conf 1973; edtrl bd NASW Jrnl of Soc Wrk 1970-73, Gls Comm Jvnl Dlnqncy Adlt Crm 1969-70; US Prog Com ICSW 1973; bd dir Untd Blck Fund Inc Wash; mem adv com HwrdUniv Inst on Drug Abs & Adctn 1973. **HONORS/ACHIEVEMENTS:** Recip M J Palevsky Fnd Awd 1970; Flwshp Awd Dnfrth Fnd 1971; NIMH Sr Stpnd Awd 1975. **BUSINESS ADDRESS:** HowardUniv Sch of Social Work, Washington, DC 20059.

GLASS, JAMES
Labor administrator. **PERSONAL:** Born Jan 27, 1928, Birmingham, AL. **EDUCATION:** Miles Coll, Birmingham AL, 1951; Detroit Inst of Technology, Detroit MI, BA Sociology, 1976; Wayne State Univ, Labor School, Detroit MI. **CAREER:** Chrysler Assembly Plant, 1952-54; Detroit General Hospital, 1952-55; Wayne County Juvenile Court, 1955-81; Todd Phillips Children's Home, 1965-78; AFSCME Council 25, exec vice pres, elected 1981, pres, 1982-. **ORGANIZATIONS:** Mem 1982-, advisory bd mem 1982-, United Foundation, 1982-; chmn, Council 25 Exec Bd, 1982-; exec bd mem, Michigan AFL-CIO, 1982-; vice pres, intl exec bd, AFSCME, 1983-; mem, Coalition of Black Trade Unionists, 1983-; governor's appointee, Michigan Job Training Coord Council, 1983-; bd dir, NAACP, 1983-; exec bd mem, Michigan Trade Union Council for Histadrut. **HONORS/ACHIEVEMENTS:** Dedicated Committeeman, AFSCME Local 409, 1981; Distinguished Service, Coalition of Black Trade Unionists, 1981; testimonial dinner honoree, AFSCME, 1985; Outstanding Leadership, AFSCME Local 1985. **MILITARY SERVICE:** US Navy, honorable discharge, 1947. **BUSINESS ADDRESS:** President, Michigan AFSCME Council #25, 1034 N Washington, Lansing, MI 48906.

GLASS, MICHELE ROLES
Communications account executive. **PERSONAL:** Born Jul 10, 1945, Berkeley, CA; married Joseph Harris. **EDUCATION:** Univ of San Francisco, BS 1978. **CAREER:** Johnson Publishing Co (Ebony Magazine), account exec 1983-84; American Heritage Publishing, eastern regional sales mgr 1984-86; The Gannett Co, account exec 1986-. **ORGANIZATIONS:** Asst account exec Ted Bates Adv 1977-82; account exec Essence 1982-83; co-chair communi-

cations comm The EDGES Group Inc 1986-. **HOME ADDRESS:** 457 West 153rd St, New York, NY 10031.

GLASS, ROBERT DAVIS
Judge. **PERSONAL:** Born Nov 28, 1922, Wetumpka, AL; married Doris Powell; children: Robert Jr, Roberta Diane, Rosalyn Doris. **EDUCATION:** NC Coll Durham NC, AB 1949, LLB 1951, JD 1971. **CAREER:** Private pratice, attny 1951-53; Private practice, New Bern NC, attny 1953-60; CT Labor Dept, claims examiner 1961-62; Private practice Waterbury CT, attny 1962-66; US Attny Office Dist of CT, 1st black asst attny 1966-67; CT Juvenile Ct, 1st black judge 1967-78; CT Superior Court, judge 1978-. **ORGANIZATIONS:** Mem Eastern NC Counsel NC Conf of NAACP 1953-60, Waterbury Comm on Human Rights 1964; reg vchmn CT Council on Human Rights 1964; mem bd of dir Pearl St Neighborhood House Waterbury 1965-66; pres CT State Fed of Negro Dem Clubs 1965-67; former bd mem of corps Waterbury Savings Bank 1973-84; mem CT Bar,NC Bar, Amer Bar Assoc; life mem Natl Bar Assoc, Amer Judicature Soc, Jucicial Council of Natl Bar Assoc, CT Bar Assoc, Waterbury Bar Assoc, Assoc for Study of Afro-Amer Life & History, NAACP. **HONORS/ACHIEVEMENTS:** Amer Campaign Medal Asiatic Pacific Campaign Medal; Cert 3 Wks Training Prog Natl Council of Juvenile Ct Judges; Cert 2 Wks Grad Training Natl Coll of Juvenile Justice 1974. **MILITARY SERVICE:** AUS 1943-46. **BUSINESS ADDRESS:** Judge, Connecticut Superior Court, 300 Grand St, Waterbury, CT 06720.

GLASS, RONALD
Performer. **PERSONAL:** Born Jul 19, 1945, Evansville, IN. **EDUCATION:** Univ of Evansville, BA 1968. **CAREER:** Actor Detective Harris Barney Miller series 1974-82; TV guest appearances Hawaii Five-O, Maude, Bob Newhart Show, Streets of San Francisco, Sanford & Son, GoodTimes, All in the Family, num others; theater actor num shows Tyrone Guthrie Theater 1968-72; Slow Dance on the Killing Ground 1972; Day of Absence Seattle Rep Co, Happy Ending Theater W 1970; TV movie Shirts & Skins 1973; TV show The New Odd Couple 1982-83. **ORGANIZATIONS:** Mem Screen Actors Guild, Hollywood Acad of TV Arts & Scis, AFTRA, AEA, Alpha Psi Omega. **HONORS/ACHIEVEMENTS:** Blue Key Scholastic Hon Soc; Alumni Cert of Excellence Univ of Evansville 1975; Dionysus Awd Hollywood Club Forum Intl 1977; Comm Awd LA Sentinel Entertainment Writer Gertrude Gibson 1975; Comm Awd Phil Wilkes Freddie Jett 1976; Who's Who in Amer Colls 1967-68; only student in Univ of Evansville to win 3 SAMMY's; Pearl Le Compte Awd; Wm A Gumbertz Awd 1968; Medal of Honor Univ of Evansville. **BUSINESS ADDRESS:** c/o Lawrence Kubik, PO Box 4669, Los Angeles, CA 90046.

GLASS, VIRGINIA M.
Tennis consultant. **PERSONAL:** Born Dec 14, 1927, Manila, Philippines;daughter of Tomas N. McKinney and Maria Noreto; divorced; children: Sidney Glass, Luis Glass. **EDUCATION:** Fordham Univ, undergrad work; Columbia Univ, BA; Columbia Univ School of Library Science, graduate work; Hunter Coll; Queens Coll School, graduate work, Educ, 1977. **CAREER:** Self-employed, Consultant in Promotions, Publicity, Community Devel and Educ; Pres, Community Tennis Serv, presently; Head Librarian, LaJolla Country Day School, 1980-81; Dir, Community Serv, City Coll, 1978-80; Educ Coordinator, San Diego Human Relations Commn, 1974-78; Dir, Public Relations, San Diego Urban League, Consultant, Univ of CA, San Diego, 1972-74; Consultant, San Diego City Schools, 1970-72; High School Admin, NY City School Dist, 1952-70; Librarian, Brooklyn Public Library, 1949-52. **ORGANIZATIONS:** Founder/past pres, Mt. View Tennis Club; Pres, San Diego Dist Tennis Assn; Contemporary Black Arts, UCSD; Commr, Chrysler LeBaron Series; Coordinator, USTA Volvo League; USTA Stadium Umpire and Referee; Editor, Black Tennis Magazine; Coordinator, Jr Olympic Tennis; Natl Jr Tennis League, Coordinator for San Diego; Pres, Amer Tennis Assn; Advisory Staff for Matchmate and Yonex; Bd Mem, Black Tennis and Sports Found; Exec Bd Mem, Southern California Tennis Assn; Natl Conf of Christians & Jews. **HONORS/ACHIEVEMENTS:** Southeast Community Theatre Award; USTA Community Serv Award, 1977; Mildred Pierce Award for Contribution to Tennis in San Diego; San Diego City Coll Citizens Council Award; Honor Roll, NCCJ; San Diego Dist Tennis Award for Outstanding Serv; California Federation of Black Leadership Serv Award; Ranked #4 in the US Sr Women's Tennis & #2 in Southern California, 1989; Ranked #1 in the World, 1989; Leadership Award for Community Serv, 1985; Elected to Tennis Hall of Fame.

GLAUDE, STEPHEN A.
Business executive. **PERSONAL:** Born Jul 25, 1954, Washington, DC; son of William Criss Glaude and Phyllis Taylor Glaude; married Rhonda Roland; children: Koya, Shani, Khary. **EDUCATION:** Morgan State Univ, BS 1977. **CAREER:** Capitol East Children's Ctr, asst dir 1977-79; DC Assoc for Retarded Citizens, vocational evaluator 1979-80. **ORGANIZATIONS:** Founder/pres Institute for Life Studies 1970-; chairperson/bd of directors Capitol East Children's Ctr 1979; bd member Montgomery Mental Health Assn 1980;mem President's Task Force on Private Sector Initiatives 1981; chairperson/fundraising membership devel cmte Black Child Development Inst 1984; mem Council for Blk Economic Agenda 1985. **HONORS/ACHIEVEMENTS:** President's Second Mild Awd 1977; Mental Health Community Service Awd 1977. **BUSINESS ADDRESS:** Executive Dir, Natl Assn of Neighborhoods, 1651 Fuller NW, Washington, DC 20009.

GLEASON, ELIZA
Librarian. **PERSONAL:** Born Dec 15, 1909, Winston-Salem, NC; married Maurice F Gleason; children: Joy Carew. **EDUCATION:** Fisk Univ, AB 1926-30; Univ IL, BS 1930-31; Univ CA, MA 1935-36; Univ Chicago, PhD 1937-40. **CAREER:** Louisville Mun Coll, asst librarian 1931-32, librarian 1932-36; Fisk Univ, asst prof 1936-37; Talladega Coll, dir libraries 1940-41; Atlanta Univ, prof 1941-46; Univ Chicago, guest lecturer 1953; Chicago Tchrs Coll, asso prof 1954-65; IL Tchrs Coll, assoc prof 1965-67; IL Inst of Tech, prof 1967-70; John Crerar Lib, asst librarian 1967-70; Chicago Public Library, asst chief librarian 1970-73; No IL Univ, prof 1974-75; Self Employed, library cons. **ORGANIZATIONS:** Women's Aux of Cook Co Physicians Assn 1940-; Women's Aux of Meharry Med Coll Alumni Assn 1940-; Hyde Park-Kenwood Comm Conf 1950-; SE Chicago Commn 1952-; Ind Voters of IL 1952-; Women's Aux of Intl Coll of Surgeons 1961-; co-chmn Fisk Univ Centennial Campaign 1963-65; exec comm Fisk Univ Alumni Assn 1964-; mem Phi Beta Kappa, Beta Phi Mu Natl Hon Soc in Lib Sci, Amer Library Assn. **HONORS/ACHIEVEMENTS:** Fellow 1938-40; Fisk Univ Alumni Award 1964; former ALA Counselor; numerous publs.

GLEASON, MAURICE FRANCIS
Physician. **PERSONAL:** Born Mar 07, 1909, Mobile, AL; married Eliza; children: Joy, Carew. **EDUCATION:** John Carroll Univ, BS 1931; Meharry Med Coll, MD 1940; Cleveland City Hosp, intern 1940-41; Provident Hosp, resident 1941-43. **CAREER:** State & 51st St Shopping Ctr, partner; Hyde Park Fed Savings & Loan Assn, former dir; private practice, physician. **ORGANIZATIONS:** Mem AMA, IL State Med Soc, Chicago Med Soc, Natl Med Assn, Prairie State Med Assn, Cook County Physicians Assn; fellow Amer Coll, Amer Soc Abdominal Surgeons, Intl Coll Surgeons, IL Soc Med Rsch; mem Amer Assn Maternal & Infant Health, Pan Amer Cytologican Soc, Intl Fertility Assn, Amer Soc Study Sterility, Amer Heart Assn, Hyde Park-Kenwood Neighborhood Redevel Corp, Hyde Park-Kenwood Comm Conservation Council, SE Chicago Comm Hyde Park-Kenwood Community Conf, Hyde Park Neighborhood Club, Hyde Park & WA Park YMCA, Urban League; life mem NAACP, Chicago Art Inst, Museum of Natural Hist, Planetarium soc, Cosmopolitan C of C, Ind Voters IL, League Women Voters, S Christ Leadership Conf PUSH, Amer Democratic Action, The Chicagoans, Royal Coterie Snakes, Original 40 Club Chgo; mem Alpha Phi Alpha, Kappa Pi Hon Med School Soc 1939. **MILITARY SERVICE:** AUS maj 1943-46.

GLEE, GEORGE, JR.
Business executive. **PERSONAL:** Born May 03, 1938, Madison, FL; son of George Glee Sr and Zera Glee; children: Knigi S. Glee. **EDUCATION:** VA Union Univ, BS 1963. **CAREER:** Mobile Oil Corp, financial analyst 1967-69; Bedford Stuyvesant Restoration Corp, consultant, vice pres dir, mgr mgr of housing, sr analyst 1969-78; John Whitney Foundation, consultant 1978-79; Vannguard Urban Improvement Assoc Inc, exec dir 1979-. **ORGANIZATIONS:** Mem coord comm Brooklyn Chamber of Commerce; mem Bedford Stuyvesant Businessmen's Assoc, Brownstoners of Bedford Stuyvesant, Natl Business League Washington DC, Volunteers of Minisink New York City Mission Soc, Kappa Alpha Psi; bd mem Soc for the Preservation of Weeksville & Bedford-Stuyvesant History; bd mem Educ Actional Develop Ctr, NY City Housing Develop Corp. **HONORS/ACHIEVEMENTS:** New York Recorder Special Citizen Awd 1982; 79th Precinct Comm Cncl Operation Gratitude Awd 1983; Mt Pisgah Christian Acad Comm Serv Awd 1984; NYS Black & Puerto Rican Legislative Caucus Serv Awd 1985; Brooklyn Alumnae Chap Delta Sigma Theta Sor Inc Comm Serv at Home & Abroad Awd 1985; VIDA Outstanding Comm Serv Awd 1985. **BUSINESS ADDRESS:** Executive Dir, Vannguard Urban Improv Assoc, 613-619 Throop Ave, Stuyvesant Height Office Complex, Brooklyn, NY 11216.

GLENN, CECIL E.
Educator. **PERSONAL:** Born Dec 18, 1938, Nashville; children: Cecil LaVel, Gerald Glenn. **EDUCATION:** BA; MA; PhD 1975. **CAREER:** Univ of CO, prof Social Science, head Ethnic Studies; Chicago Dept of Educ, Public Health Serv Civil Rights Envolvement, 10 yrs; teahcer 15 yrs; Higher Educ, area urban sociologist 5 yrs; Mental Health Inc, serv in mental health field chmn 5 yrs. **ORGANIZATIONS:** Chmn Malcolm X Mental Inc; mem NAACP. **HONORS/ACHIEVEMENTS:** Recip awds Nat Alliance of Business 1975; Mt Plains Comm Coll Ldshp 1974; Partners corrective progs 1974. **BUSINESS ADDRESS:** 1100 14 St, Denver, CO 80202.

GLENN, EDWARD C., JR.
Senior sales representative. **PERSONAL:** Born Jan 08, 1922, Akron, OH; married Sitella Rodriguez. **EDUCATION:** Wayne State U, attended; MI U, student. **CAREER:** Superior Life Ins Soc, asst Mgr 1953-57; Mammoth Life Ins Co Detroit, dir training field supr 1957-60; Metropolitan Life Ins Co, sr sales rep. **ORGANIZATIONS:** Bd mem Detroit Asso Life Underwriters; ch educ comm 1972-74; former ch Metropolitan Life's Pres Conf 1972-73; past pres Cotillion Club inc 1970-72, bd ch 1973; pes Bagley Pub Sch PTA 1969; life mem NAACP 1971-. **HONORS/ACHIEVEMENTS:** Cited for prof Ebony & Life Mag 1966, 1972; Nat Quality Awd 1965-73, Detroit News 1970-73; man of yr Metropolitan Life Ins Co 1968, 1969, 1970, 1971, 1972, 1973. **BUSINESS ADDRESS:** 28225 Hoover Rd, Warren, MI 48093.

GLENN, PATRICIA CAMPBELL
Mediator. **PERSONAL:** Born Dec 15, 1942, Brandon, MS; daughter of James Alvin Campbell and Ewnice Agnes Finch; divorced; children: Allison, Jennifer, Lee. **EDUCATION:** Ohio State Univ, Columbus OH, BS Educ, 1970; Univ of Illinois, Chicago IL, MS Educ Admin, 1985. **CAREER:** Gast High School, Columbus OH, teacher, 1971-74; Ohio Civil Rights Comm, Columbus OH, supvr, investigator, 1974-78; US Dept of Justice Community Relations Serv, Chicago IL, sr conciliation specialist, 1978-. **ORGANIZATIONS:** Natl Council Negro Women, 1980-; pres, Major Charles L Hunt VFW Post, 1984-85; dist commr, Boy Scouts, 1987-89. **HONORS/ACHIEVEMENTS:** Humanitarian Award, Columbus Metropolitan Community Action Org, 1980; Outstanding Performance Award, Attorney General, 1984; Human Relations Service Award, 1985; Certificate of Appreciation, Kiwanis Award, 1987; Silver Beaver, Chicago Area Council, 1989.

GLENN, WYNOLA
Elected official. **PERSONAL:** Born Jan 27, 1932, Farmville, VA; married James L Glenn; children: Denise Mercado, Cheryl Mitchell, Anita Bonet, Delana, Tanya, James L Jr. **EDUCATION:** Baruch Coll CUNY, attended; Coll of New Rochelle, attended. **CAREER:** Harlem Primary Care Governing Bd, pres 1983-; Zeta Amicac Sor, pres 1984-; Community School Bd #5, pres 1983-. **BUSINESS ADDRESS:** School Board President, Board of Education, 433 W 123rd St, New York, NY 10027.

GLOSTER, HUGH MORRIS
Educator. **PERSONAL:** Born May 11, 1911, Brownsville, TN; married Beulah V Harold; children: Alice, Evelyn, Hugh Morris. **EDUCATION:** Morehouse Coll, BA 1931 Atlanta U, MA 1933 NY U, PhD 1943. **CAREER:** Morehouse Coll, pres 1967-87; dean fac 1963-67; Hampton Inst, prof 1946-67; assoc regional exec 1944-46; USO, program dir 1943-46; Morehouse Coll, prof 1941-43; LeMoyne Coll, instructor, assoc prof 1933-41; Hiroshima Univ, fulbright prof 1953-55; Amer Lit Univ Warsaw Poland, visiting prof 1961-72; lecturerr tours 1933-55, 56, 59. **ORGANIZATIONS:** Mem commn on ldrshp devel in higher educ Am Cncl on Edn; commn on coll adminstrn Assn Am Coll; v chmn GA postsec Educ Commn; mem Pres's Councl Am Forum for Intl Studies; Inst European Studie; mem bd nom Am Inst for Pub Svc; mem exec com Coll Entrance Exam Bd 1967-71; bd dir United Bd for Coll Devel; com on Econ Devel; So Christian Ldrshp Conf; bd dir trustee United Negro Coll Fund; trustee AtlantaUniv Morehouse Coll Interdenominational Theol Ctr Educ Testing Svc; Phi Beta Kappa; Sigma Pi Phi Boule; Alpha Phi Alpha. **HONORS/ACHIEVEMENTS:** Rschr grant Carnegie Found 1950-51; Disting Contbns Awd Coll Lang Assn 1958; Centennial Med Hampton Inst 1968; Alumnus of Yr Awd LeMoyne Coll 1967; author "Negro Voices in Am"

1948; co-ed "The Brown Thrush an Anthology of Verse by Negro Coll Students" 1935; "My Life-My Country-My World Coll Readings for Modern Living" 1952; contrib ed "Phylon the AtlantaUniv Review of Race and Culture" 1948-53; Adv Ed Coll Lang Assn Jour 1957; cited among the nations 100 Most Effective College Leaders Jet Dec 15, 1986; Hon Doctor of Humane Letters Morehouse Coll. **BUSINESS ADDRESS:** President, Morehouse Coll, 830 Westview Dr SW, Atlanta, GA 30314.

GLOSTER, JESSE E.
Educator. **PERSONAL:** Born Apr 15, 1915, Ocala, FL; married Norma Robinson. **EDUCATION:** Lincoln U, AB 1941;Univ of Pittsburgh, MA 1947;Univ of Pittsburgh, PhD 1955. **CAREER:** TX Southern Univ, prof of economics 1948-; NC Mutual Life Insurance Co, Afro-Amer Life Insurance Co, insurance representative. **ORGANIZATIONS:** Organizer TX SoUniv Fed Credit Unoin; organizer chrmn bd TX So Financer Corp; co-organizer Riverside Nat Bank. **HONORS/ACHIEVEMENTS:** Author book "Econ of Minority Groups"; publ NC Mutual Life Ins Co Arno Press NY Times subs 1976; authored "Minority Econ Pol & Soc Devel"Univ Press of Am 1978; also numerous publs for professional jour; recip ins research grant 1951f grant TX SoUniv 1957; case inst fellow Econ-in-Action 1960; fac research grants TX SoUniv 1964, 67; Ford Found Grant 1968-69. **MILITARY SERVICE:** AUS 1st lt 1942-46. **BUSINESS ADDRESS:** Chairman, Texas Southern Investment Corp, 3003 Holman St, Houston, TX 77004.

GLOSTER, JOHN GAINES
Executive. **PERSONAL:** Born Jan 01, 1928, Baltimore, MD; married Augustine Brown; children: John G. **EDUCATION:** Amherst Coll, AB cum laude 1948; Columbia U, MA Pol Sci 1951; Harvard Grad Sch of Bus, MBA 1955. **CAREER:** Opp Funding Corp, pres 1970-; Nat Urban Coalition, dir for econ dev 1969-70; HUD, dep dir for optns model cities prog 1968-69; US St Dept, for serv off 1962-68; Morgan St Coll, bus mgr asst to pres 1958-62; Cit Tr Bk, 1953-58; Coppin St Coll, instr 1950-51; Brooklyn Coll, instr 1949-50. **ORGANIZATIONS:** Chrm bd of dir Syn Comm Inc; mem Min Contractors Asst Proj Loan Adv Com; adv com Min Bus Res Cntr Dept of Transp; Am Bankers Assn Urban Task Force Adv Com; mem bd of dir Robert P Morton Mem Inst; bd of dir Provident Hosp of Balt; mem comm Health Cncl of MD; mem Nat Urban Coalition Steering Com. **HONORS/ACHIEVEMENTS:** Auth "Min Entry to Mainstream Mkts" NY Times 1975; "Flex Guaranties" Bkrs Mag 1973; awd Exemplary Support & encouragement of Com & Econ Devel Goals Nat Cong for Comm Econ Devel Citation 1975. **MILITARY SERVICE:** AUS corpl 1951-53f. **BUSINESS ADDRESS:** 2021 K St NW, Washington, DC 20006.

GLOVER, AGNES W.
Educational administrator. **PERSONAL:** Born Mar 06, 1925, Orangeburg, SC; daughter of Ben I Williams and Victoria Glover Williams; married Freddie V. **EDUCATION:** SC State Clge, BS Ed 1956; Hunter Clge, MS Ed E Chhd Ed 1973; Queens Clge, MA Supr and Admin 1983. **CAREER:** Natl Sor of Phi Delta Kappa Inc Beta Omicron Chapter, 3rd Anti Basileus 1965-67, tamias 1967-69, basileus 1969-71, chrmn of bd of dir Big Sister Educ Action and Srv Ctr 1972-; Hallet Cove Child Dev Ctr, dir. **ORGANIZATIONS:** Dir Grosnenor DC 1968-72; 1st vice pres Flushing Branch NAACP 1982, pres 1974-78; Basileus Natl Sor Phi Delta Kappa Div Beta Omicron Chap 1969-71, chrmn bd dir Big Sister 1972-; life mem, NAACP 1987; mem, South Carolina State College Chapter Phi Delta Kappa 1988. **HONORS/ACHIEVEMENTS:** Srv and dedication Big Sister Educ Aciton and Srv Ctr 1978; Cert of Appreciation La Guardia Comm Clge 1981, Flushing Branch NAACP 1984; Outstanding Service, Flushing Branch NAACP 1984; for Outstanding Service, The Council of Supervisors and Admin of New York City 1987; Dedicated Service, The National Sorority of Phi Delta Kappa Inc, Beta Omicrom Chapter Big Sister Educational Action and Service Center 1987.

GLOVER, ARCHIBALD F.
Civil engineer. **PERSONAL:** Born Oct 16, 1902, Brooklyn, NY; widowed. **EDUCATION:** Cooper Unoin, BS 1930;Univ of State of NY, teaching cer 1935; St John's U, LLD 1954. **CAREER:** Mason & Hanger Silas Mason Co Inc, proj engr 1972-; WPA NYC, asst civil engr 1932-36; NYC, civil engr various dept 1928-32, 1936-70; State of NY, licensed professional engr. **ORGANIZATIONS:** Life mem Nat Soc of Professional Engr; mem Nat Tech Asn; mem Bd of Higher Educ New York City 1952-57; commnr New York City Commn on Human Rights 1968-72; trustee St FrancisColl Brooklyn 1969-73; trustee Cath Med Center Diocese of Brooklyn 1969-72; life mem NAACP; mem AAS. **HONORS/ACHIEVEMENTS:** Cert Fallout Shelter Analyst #1TT 341-63 Ofc of Civil Def; recop Archbishop Thomas E Molloy Awd for Interracial Justice 1967; Brooklyn Alumni Sodality Med 1969. **MILITARY SERVICE:** NY State Guard cpt corps of engr 1941-44. **BUSINESS ADDRESS:** 347 Madison Ave, New York, NY 10022.

GLOVER, ARTHUR LEWIS, JR.
Retired counselor. **PERSONAL:** Born Sep 29, 1912, Los Angeles, CA; son of Arthur Glover (deceased) and Lucille Lewis Glover (deceased); married Beatrice Louise Jones Glover, Sep 10, 1944; children: Beatrice Louise Schine. **EDUCATION:** Univ of CA Santa Barbara, AB 1937; Freedmens Hospital, Certificate of Nutrition 1939; Univ of Southern CA, MA 1952, ME 1956; Nova Cluster Univ, doctoral studies. **CAREER:** Tuskegee Inst AL, chief dietitian 1939-42; Andersen's Frozen Foods Buellton, product mgr 1946-50; Thomas Jefferson High School, instructor & counselor 1950-69; West LA Community Coll, prof of English & counselor emeritus 1969-84. **ORGANIZATIONS:** Bd dir Culver City Mental Health Clinic; Di Di Hirsch Guidance Clinic; Culver City Police Dept; mem Phi Delta Kappa; past moderator Culver City Educ Comm; mem Mariners Nautilus Ship LA; exec sec DiDi Hirsch Mental Health Clinic; sec Kayumanggi Lions Club; district chmn Lions World Serv Day; social action chmn Omega Psi Phi Frat; chmn Lords of Inglewood; dist chmn Lions Fundraiser for The City of Hope; vice pres, Di Di Hirsch Community Mental Health Center. **HONORS/ACHIEVEMENTS:** First Black man admitted to Amer Dietitic Assoc 1939; Man of Yr Lambda Omicron 1970; Lion of Yr Culver City Lions Club 1973, Beverly Hills 1980; Counselor of the Year 1982-83 Los Angeles Community Coll Dist (7 colleges). **MILITARY SERVICE:** AUS med corp sgt 1942-46.

GLOVER, BERNARD E.
Dentist. **PERSONAL:** Born Apr 09, 1933, Suffolk, VA; married Juanita Cross; children: Cheryl, Kevin. **EDUCATION:** Morgan State Coll, BS 1959; Meharry Med Coll, DDS 1963; St Elizabeth Hosp, inter 1964. **CAREER:** Pvt Prac 1964-. **ORGANIZATIONS:** Mem bd, dir Obici Hosp; mem bd dir Nansemon Credit Unoin; mem Suffolk City Forum; mem John L McGriff Dental Soc; Am Nat & Old Dominoin Dental Assn;Am Endodontic Soc; mem Suffolk City Sch Bd; Tidewater Regional Health Council; C of C; Bi-racial Council; Obia Hosp Staff. **HONORS/ACHIEVEMENTS:** E end bapt ch schlshp awd Morgan State Coll 1955-59; Mosby Schshp Awd 1962; man yr Kappa Alpha Si 1974; Elks awd en 1975. **MILITARY SERVICE:** AUS pfc 1963-65. **BUSINESS ADDRESS:** 384 E Washington St, Suffolk, VA 23434.

GLOVER, CLARENCE ERNEST, JR.
Educator, educational administrator. **PERSONAL:** Born Apr 19, 1956, Shreveport, LA; son of Clarence E Glover, Sr (deceased) and Elizabeth Bradford Glover. **EDUCATION:** Grambling State Univ, BA 1978; Southern Methodist Univ, Master Theology 1982; Harvard Univ, post grad 1985. **CAREER:** St Duty CME Church, pastor 1974-75; Washington Temple CME Church, pastor 1978-80; Caddo Bossier Assoc for Retarded Citizens, instructor/supervisor 1978-79; El Centro College, campus minister 1979-80; Clarence Glover Ministries, Inc, pres 1981-; Southern Methodist Univ, asst to the chaplain 1980-81, coordinator intercultural education African-American student serv 1980-89; adjunct prof of African-Amer Studies, 1987; Clarence Glover & Assoc, professional lecturing & consulting agency, 1987; dir, Intercultural Educ, 1989;. **ORGANIZATIONS:** African- american cultural consultant Dallas Independent Sch Dist 1980-; mem TX Assoc of Coll and Univ Student Personnel Administrators 1980-; natl coord Natl Black Christian Student Leadership Consultation 1985-; third vice pres TX Assoc of Black Personnel in Higher Educ 1985-; mem NAACP; mem Christian Leadership Conf; mem Natl Assoc of Student Personell Admin; mem American Cancer African-American Task Force; co-host Cable TV Show Religion in Foucus; lecturer & consultant on African-American Religion and Culture; mem Black Male-Female Relations; mem The Life and Time of Dr King the Civil Rights movement andInter-Cultral Relations and Racism. **HONORS/ACHIEVEMENTS:** Outstanding Young Men of Amer US Jaycees 1982-83, 1986; WE DuBois Awd 1980; Advisor of the Year Awd Natl Christian Student Leadership Consultation 1983; consultant/interviewer "In Remembrance of Martin" the First Natl Martin Luther King Jr PBS Natl Documentary 1986; Humanitarian Serv Awd El Centro Coll/Street Acad 1986; Spirituality: An African View, Interview in Essence Magazine, 1987; On Being African-American: The Challenge of a New Generation, Natl Society of Black Engineers Journal, 1988; Honorary Mayor of San Antonio, TX, 1988. **BUSINESS ADDRESS:** Director, Southern Methodist University, Intercultural Education, Box 355 SMU Station, Dallas, TX 75275.

GLOVER, DANNY
Actor. **PERSONAL:** Children: Mandisa. **EDUCATION:** Attended, San Francisco State Univ. **CAREER:** Movies, Mad Max, Places in the Heart, Silverado, Witness, Mister in "The Color Purple", Lethal Weapon; Plays, Athol Fugard's "The Blood Knot", "The Island", "Sizwe Banzi is Dead" South Africa; HBO TV film "Mandela", played part of Nelson Mandela.

GLOVER, DIANA M.
Personnel executive. **PERSONAL:** Born Apr 19, 1948, Buffalo, NY. **EDUCATION:** Cornell U, BA Sociology 1971; Gen Motors Inst, liberal arts cer 1973. **CAREER:** GNC Chev Div Tonawanda Motor, supr labor rel 1978-; GMC Che Div Tonawanda Motor, supr salaried pers adm 1976-78; GMC Chev Div Tonawanda Motor, supremployee benefits 1976; GMC Chev Div Tonawanda Motor, EEO rep 1975-76; GMC Chev Div Tonawanda Motor, asst supv employment 1974-75; GMC Chev Div Tonawanda Motor, employment interviewer 1973-74. **ORGANIZATIONS:** Mem Indsl Rela Assn of Western NY 1976-80; dir Center for Women in Mgmt 1978-80; adv coord Jr Achievement 1975-78; mem Buffalo Urban League 1976-; mem NAACP 1978-. **HONORS/ACHIEVEMENTS:** Black achvmt awd 1490 Jefferson Enterpises Inc 1976. **BUSINESS ADDRESS:** Assistant Personnel Dir, General Motors, CPC Tonawanda Engineering Plt, PO Box 21, Buffalo, NY 14240.

GLOVER, EULA E.
Educator. **PERSONAL:** Born Dec 27, 1907, Norfolk; married Julius E; children: Julius E, Jr, Jeanette M, Monroe T. **EDUCATION:** VA Unoin U, BS 1950. **CAREER:** S Hill VA, teacher 1929-34; Norfolk Public Schools, 1950-72. **ORGANIZATIONS:** Mem NEA; VA Educ Assn; Nat Assn Classroom Tchrs; past anti-basileus Alpha Kappa Alpha; area chmn Nat Cancer Soc; bd dirs TWCA; United & Comm Fund; Women Pol Action; Women Comm Serv.

GLOVER, GLEASON
Association executive. **PERSONAL:** Born Jun 14, 1934, Newport News, VA; son of Josesh Glover and Rachel Glover; married Dr Sharon Tolbert; children: Gleason Edward, Maury Todd, Stephanie Marie. **EDUCATION:** Norfolk State Coll, BA Sociology 1961; Case Western Reserve Univ, MSSA Social Serv Admin 1963. **CAREER:** Cleveland Neighborhood Youth Corp, project dir 1961; Golden Age Center of Cleveland, project dir 1963-65; Cleveland Urban League O J T Program, project dir 1965-66; Minneapolis Urban League, exec dir, pres/CEO, 1967-. **ORGANIZATIONS:** Instr Univ of MN 1968-73; comm Minneapolis Civil Serv Comm 1968-71; pres Council of Exec Dir Natl Urban League, 1974-77; mem Governor's Appointment Commission, 1977-78; mem Governor's Commn on Technology and Job Creation, 1981-; exec comm MN Wellspring 1981-; vice pres Citizens League 1983-; mem Social Work Licensing Board, 1988-91; mem Academy of Certified Social Work. **HONORS/ACHIEVEMENTS:** Outstanding Admin, Minneapolis Urban League Staff 1980; Citation of Honor, State of Minnesota 1978; Serv Award, City of Minneapolis 1972; Achievement Award, Natl Alliance of Busisness 1968. **MILITARY SERVICE:** USAF airman first class 1955-59. **BUSINESS ADDRESS:** Executive Dir, Minneapolis Urban League, 2000 Plymouth Ave N, Minneapolis, MN 55411.

GLOVER, KENNETH ELIJAH
Investment banker. **PERSONAL:** Born Feb 24, 1952, Washington, DC; son of Elijah B Glover (deceased) and Eunice Washington Glover (deceased); married Lauren Dugas, Apr 23, 1988. **EDUCATION:** Amherst Coll, Amherst MA, BA, 1974; Univ of Maryland, College Park MD, MA, 1976. **CAREER:** Maryland Gen Assembly, Annapolis MD, staff dir, 1975-76; Prince George's County MD, Upper Marlboro MD, admin asst, 1976-78; Natl League of Cities, Washington DC, project dir, 1978-79; South Shore Bank, Chicago IL, vice pres, 1979-83; Mayor Washington Transit Team, Chicago IL, dir, 1983; Drexel Burnham Lambert, New York NY, managing dir, 1983-. **ORGANIZATIONS:** Dir, Natl Assn of Securities Professionals, 1985-88, Natl Black Child Devel Inst, 1987-, Harold Washington Found, 1987-; dir, chmn, Corporate Advisory Council/Natl Forum, 1989. **HONORS/ACHIEVEMENTS:** America's Best & Brightest, Dollars & Sense Magazine, 1989. **BUSI-**

NESS ADDRESS: Managing Director, Drexel Burnham Lambert, 60 Broad Street, 7th Floor, New York, NY 10004.

GLOVER, ROBERT G.
Chemist. **PERSONAL:** Born Jul 04, 1931, Bradley, AR; married Mary; children: Mary, Andrew, Alvin, Shirley, Dedra, Robert. **EDUCATION:** Printing Ink Inst of LeHighUniv Phila, attended. **CAREER:** St Clair & Valentine Co; Printing Ink Inst of LeHigh Univ, lab 8 yrs; Quality Printing Ink Co Houston, president. **ORGANIZATIONS:** Mem Litho Club, Craftsman Club, PTA of Houston. **HONORS/ACHIEVEMENTS:** Only black owner of form which mfg printing inks of all types for distrb throughout world. **BUSINESS ADDRESS:** President, Quality Color Printing Ink, 1803 Cleburne, Houston, TX 77004.

GLOVER, SARAH LOUISE
Public relations director. **PERSONAL:** Born Apr 27, 1954, Detroit, MI. **EDUCATION:** Shaw Univ, Raleigh NC, BS in Behavioral Science, 1976; Univ of Chapel Hill, Chapel Hill NC, attended, School of Journalism Writing for Publication, 1984; North Carolina Central Univ, Durham NC, Graduate School, Media Educ, 1985-. **CAREER:** Southland Corp, Raleigh & Durham NC, store clerk, asst mgr, mgr, 1977-79; Bloodworth St YMCA, Raleigh NC, activity asst public relations dir, 1981; Garner Rd Family YMCA, Raleigh NC, public relations dir, 1981-. **ORGANIZATIONS:** Order of Eastern Stars, Detroit, MI, 1974; mem, Public Relations Soc of Amer, 1983-, Natl Professional YMCA Directors, 1985-. **HONORS/ACHIEVEMENTS:** Citizen of the Week Award, WLLE-AM 57, 1982; Chairman's Award, Garner Road Family YMCA, 1984; Citizen of the Week Award, WAUG-AM 750, 1988. **BUSINESS ADDRESS:** Public Relations Director, Garner Road Family YMCA, 2235 Garner Rd, Raleigh, NC 27610.

GLOVER, VICTOR NORMAN
Educator. **PERSONAL:** Born Jul 25, 1948, Chicago, IL; married Kathlyn Jane Harris; children: Alexis, Mia, David. **EDUCATION:** St Francis College, BS 1979, MS 1981. **CAREER:** Marion Chronicle Tribune, reporter 1971-76; WKJG-TV, newsman 1976-81; Manchester Coll, dir minority affairs 1981-85, counselor foreign student adv instr in psy. **ORGANIZATIONS:** Dir Manchester Baseball Assn 1983-84; Wabash Co IN Mental Health Assn 1983-85. **HONORS/ACHIEVEMENTS:** First Place (Feature) Hoosier St Press Assn 1972; TV PSA Merit Natl Assn Businessmen 1980; TV PSA Merit Natl Red Cross 1981. **MILITARY SERVICE:** Army Medical Corps Spec 5 1968-71; Purple Heart, Distinguished Flying Cross, Vietnamese Cross of Gallantry, Air Medal, Combat Medic Badge. **BUSINESS ADDRESS:** Director, Minority Programs, ValparaisoUniv, 606 Freeman St, Valparaiso, IN 46383.

GODBEE, THOMASINA D.
Research associate. **PERSONAL:** Born Apr 10, 1946, Waynesboro, GA; married Cornelius; children: William Jr, Cornelius Tremayne II. **EDUCATION:** Paine Coll, BS 1966. **CAREER:** Butts Co Bd Educ Jackson GA, chem instr 1966-67; EI du Pont de Nemours & Co, lab tech 1967-69; Grady Meml Hosp, lab tech 1970-71; Univ CA Irvine,staff rsch assoc nuclear physics 1971-. **ORGANIZATIONS:** Mem NAACP; Paine Coll Alumni Club; United Presb Women; Natl Assn of Univ Women; Westminster United Presb Ch Soloist Paine Coll Concert Choir 1966;second vice pres, scrapbook co-chmn, first vice pres, membership com chmn NAUW. **HONORS/ACHIEVEMENTS:** English & Soc Sci Awds 1960 1962; Natural Sci Awd 1961; Outstanding Serv to the Comm Awd NAUW 1977; Special Performance Awd Univ of CA 1984.

GODBOLD, DONALD HORACE
Community college administrator. **PERSONAL:** Born Oct 03, 1928, Detroit, MI; married Delores; children: Donald Terrance, Michelle, Monique Toi, Darwyn. **EDUCATION:** Wayne State Univ, BS 1950, MEd 1956; Univ of MI Ann Arbor, PhD 1967. **CAREER:** Wayne State Univ, supervising teacher 1953-67; Oakland Comm Coll Orchard Ridge Campus, dean of student serv 1967-68, provost & chief exec 1968-70; Univ of No CO, guest prof sociology black history & culture, counselor 1971-74; Community Coll of Denver Auraria Campus, dean of campus & founding chief exec 1970-71, campus dir & chief exec 1971-72, vice pres & chief exec 1972-73; Merritt Coll, pres 1973-77; Peralta Comm Coll Dist, vice chancellor educ serv 1977-80, chancellor 1980-. **ORGANIZATIONS:** Natl chmn/bd mem Council on Black Amer Affairs Council of the Amer Assoc of Comm & Jr Colls 1972-87; commn mem Amer Concil on Educ Commn on Collegiate Athletics 1977-80; mem City of Oakland Private Industry Cncl 1978-; chmn accreditation team Western Assoc of Schools & Colls 1979; mem bd of dirsChildren's Hospital Medical Ctr 1980-; mem Convention Adv Comm CA Assoc of Comm Colls 1983; mem Commn on Urban Comm Colls Amer Assoc of Comm & Jr Colls 1983-87; mem adv comm Amer Cncl on Educ 1984-87; mem Amer Coll Personnel Assoc, Amer Personnel & Guidance Assoc, CO Assoc of Comm Jr Colls, Cncl for Exceptional Children, Natl Assoc of Student Personnel Administrators, MI Acad of Scis Arts and Letters, Natl Vocational Guidance Assoc; dir Univ of MI Chap Phi Delta Kappa; mem Wayne State Univ Coll of Educ Alumni Assoc, Wayne State Univ Alumni Assoc, Univ of MI Alumni Assoc, Assoc ofCA Comm Coll Administrators; bd mem Urban League of CO Inc. **HONORS/ACHIEVEMENTS:** Clifford Woody Memorial Scholar Awd for Outstanding Promise in Professional Educ Univ of MI 1966; Comm Coll of Denver Faculty Awd for Outstanding Leadership in the Establishment of the Comm Coll of Denver Auraria Campus 1971; Disting Serv Awd Western Region Cncl on Black Amer Affairs 1976; Meritorious and Unselfish Leadership and Serv Awd as Natl Chairperson (1974-79) in the Founding of the Org Cncl on Black Amer Affairs Natl Chairperson 1980; Leonard F Saine Awd Esteemed Black Alumni Awd Univ of MI 1982; Leadership and Supportive Serv Awd North Central Region Cncl on Black Amer Affairs 1986; recognition The Effective President a natl survey funded by the Exxon Educ Foundation 1986; 13 pulications. **MILITARY SERVICE:** AUS pfc 3 yrs. **HOME ADDRESS:** 6201 Clive Ave, Oakland, CA 94611.

GODFREY, EMILE SYLVESTER, JR.
Executive. **PERSONAL:** Born Jul 19, 1950, New Orleans, LA; married Pamela O'Leary; children: Jennifer. **EDUCATION:** Harvard Coll, AB 1972. **CAREER:** Mayor's Office of Public Serv Boston, admin asst 1972-73; Federated Dept Stores, vice pres govt affairs 1978-83; Democratic Natl Comm, exec dir business council 1983-84; Highland Corp, chairman/ceo 1984-86; First Chicago Corp, sr vice pres corporate affairs. **HONORS/ACHIEVEMENTS:** YMCA Black Achiever; White House Fellowship finalist; Rhodes Scholar finalist. **BUSINESS ADDRESS:** Sr Vice Pres Corporate Affairs, First Chicago Corp, One First Natl Plaza, Chicago, IL 60670.

GODFREY, WESLEY
Chief executive. **CAREER:** Security National Bank, Shreveport LA, chief executive. **BUSINESS ADDRESS:** Security National Bank, 2800 N Hearne Ave, Shreveport, LA 71107. *

GODFREY, WILLIAM R.
Financial administrator. **PERSONAL:** Born May 18, 1948, Gay, GA; son of John Godfrey and Iula Godfrey; married Joyce Lincoln; children: Runako, Kenan, Nyasha. **EDUCATION:** Clark College, BBA 1970; State Univ of New York, MBA 1973. **CAREER:** US General Accounting Office, senior auditor 1973-80; US General Serv Adm Office of the Inspector General, senior auditor 1980; Fulton County, assistant dir of finance. **ORGANIZATIONS:** Treasurer, Mental Health Assoc of Metro Atlanta, 1984-. **HOME ADDRESS:** 2917 Dodson Dr, East Point, GA 30344.

GODWIN, I. LAMOND
Busines executive. **PERSONAL:** Born Jun 30, 1942, Mobile, AL; married Thelma Quillings; children: Agnes Marie, Lamond Charles. **EDUCATION:** Harvard U, Summer Sch 1964; Clark Clg, BA 1964;Univ of IL, MA 1967. **CAREER:** Ford Foundation, prog consultant 1967-71; Metropolitan Applied Rsrch Ctr, sr fellow 1970-71; Rutgers U, prof Labor Studies Dept 1971-74; Lamond Godwin Ltd;; pres 1971-; Southern Regional Council, asso dir 1974-76; Natl Rural Ctr, asso dir 1976-77; US Dept of Labor, adm Natl Prog 1977-81; US Dept of Labor, spec asst to US Sec of Labor 1977-81. **ORGANIZATIONS:** Pol strategy adv to Rev Jesse L Jackson 1981-; prog consultant Ford Foundation 1967-72; sr consultant Rockefeller Foundation 1981-84; bd of dir Rexon Gas & Oil Co Inc 1984-; consultant 1st Bank Natl Asso 1983-; bd of dir Operation Push Inc 1981-; founding trustee Natl Rainbow Coalition Inc 1984-; mem Omega Psi Phi Frat 1961-. **HONORS/ACHIEVEMENTS:** Rsrch flwshpUniv of IL 1964-67; Author (With Ray Marshall) "Cooperatives & Rural Poverty" Baltimore, Jophns HopkinsUniv Press 1971. **BUSINESS ADDRESS:** HarvardUniv Grad Sch Govt, 79 John F Kennedy St, Room 6402, Washington, DC 20213.

GOFF, REGINA MARY
Retired professor of education. **PERSONAL:** Born Aug 06, 1917, St Louis, MO. **EDUCATION:** Northwestern U, BS 1935; Columbia U, MA 1940, PhD 1948; Natl Clg of Educ Washington Sch of Psychiatry, 1954. **CAREER:** Morlgan State Coll, chair Dept of Educ & chair Div of Social Sciences 1950-65; Intercultural Coop Agency, Dept of State, consultant, ministry of educ of Iran 1955-57; Univ of MD, prof of educ 1971-77. **ORGANIZATIONS:** Psychometrist Catholic Charities of MD 1951-55; therapist Harriet Lane Clinic Johns Hopkins Sch of Med 1952-55; bd of dirs United Nations of MD 1956-63; pres bd of dir Baltimore Urban League 1961-64; core prof Union Grad Sch 1977-80; bd UNICEF of MD 1981-84. **HONORS/ACHIEVEMENTS:** Rockefeller Foundation Genl Educ Awd (Fellowship) 1946-47; Leadership in Educ Alpha Kappa Alpha Sor New York 1966; Educ & Community Serv NJ Federation ofWomens Clubs 1967; Appreciation of Ldrshp HEW US Dept of Educ 1971; authored several books; contributor to professional journals; listed in Who's Who in Amer; Who's Who in Of Amer Women; Who's Who in the World; Pi Lambda Theta; Kappa Delta Pi; Psi Chi.

GOFF, WILHELMINA DELORES
Educational administrator. **PERSONAL:** Born Jun 18, 1940, Columbia, SC. **EDUCATION:** Morgan State Coll, BS 1962; John Carroll Univ, MA 1971; New York Univ, attended; Cleveland State Univ, EdSD. **CAREER:** Hillcrest Center for Children Bedford Hills, counselor 1962-64; Cleveland Public Schools, music teacher 1964-78, guidance counselor 1971-78; Cuyahoga Community Coll, coord/counselor job corps 1978-, assoc dir access/job corps act 1979-80; Cleveland, asst dean student personnel servs; Natl Council Negro Women, dir prog & devel. **ORGANIZATIONS:** Newsletter ed Phi Delta Kappa Reg dir Delta Sigma Theta Sor 1976-; pres OH Assn Non-White Concerns in Personnel & Guidance 1978-80; corres sec/mem at large NE OH Personnel & Guidance 1978-80; bd mem/chmn ed com Cleveland NAACP 1979-80; coord speakers bureau Gr Cleveland Com of IYC 1979; pres Delta Sigma Theta Tutoring & Nutrition Inc. **HONORS/ACHIEVEMENTS:** Awd for Congressman Stokes Cleve 1974; Pan-Hellenic Awd Cleveland 1976; Outstanding Serv to Delta New Orleans LA convention 1979; Key to the City Indianapolis IN 1980; Higher Educ Counselor of Yr NEOPGA 1980; Outstanding Serv to Teen Father Prog 1984; Proclamation City of Cincinnati 1982; Outstanding Serv OH Personnel & Guidance Assn; Outstanding Serv to Dyke Coll Student Body 1986; Outstanding Serv to Youth & Educ Cleveland Chap Negro Bus & Profession Women'sClub 1986. **BUSINESS ADDRESS:** Dir Program and Develop, Natl Council Negro Women, 701 N Fairfax St, Alexandria, VA 22314.

GOGGINS, HORACE
Dental surgeon. **PERSONAL:** Born May 14, 1929, Hodges, SC; divorced; children: Horace W. **EDUCATION:** SC State Coll, BS 1950; Howard Univ DDS 1954. **CAREER:** Self-Employed, dental surgeon Rock Hill SC. **ORGANIZATIONS:** Mem Natl Dental Assn; past pres Palmetto Med & Dental Assn 1973; mem SE Analgesia Soc; mem tri county Dental Soc; mem Piedmont Dental Soc; Beta Kappa Chi Sci Soc; mem Rock Hill Planning Commn; NAACP; Council Human Relations; Mt Prospect Bapt Ch deacon; Alpha Phi Alpha Frat; mem Sigma Pi Phi Frat (Boule); SC Dem Party; American Legion Elks. **HONORS/ACHIEVEMENTS:** Personalites in the S 1973-74; Who's Who in S & SW 1973-74. **MILITARY SERVICE:** AUS capt dental corps 1954-56; USAR maj. **BUSINESS ADDRESS:** 425 S Dave Lyle Blvd, Rock Hill, SC 29730.

GOINES, LEONARD
Educator. **PERSONAL:** Born Apr 22, 1934, Jacksonville, FL; son of Buford Goines and Willie Mae LaMar Goines; married Margaretta Bobo (divorced); children: Lisan Lynette. **EDUCATION:** Manhattan School of Music, BMus 1955, MMus 1956; Fontainbleu School of Music France, Certificate 1959; Columbus Univ, MA 1960, Professional Diploma 1961, EdD 1963; New School for Soc Rsch, BA 1980; New York Univ, MA 1980; Harvard Univ, CAS 1984. **CAREER:** Leonard Goines Quintet, trumpeter-leader 1960-; Symphony of the New World, trumpeter 1965-76; New York City Bd of Educ, teacher music 1959-65; Bedford Stuyvesant Youth in Action, dir of music 1965-66; Morgan State Coll, assoc prof of music 1966-68; York Coll CUNY, lecturer 1969; Queens Coll CUNY, lecturer; Howard Univ, assoc prof of music 1970-72; NY Univ, lecturer 1970-; DuBois Inst Howard Univ, postdoctoral fellow 1982-85; Shepard & Goines, partner org & educ arts consultants 1984-; Williams Coll, visiting prof music 1984; Vassar Coll, visiting prof music 1985; Lafayette Coll Easton PA, distinguished visiting prof of music 1986; Manhattan Commun Coll CUNY, prof music. **OR-**

GANIZATIONS: Folklore consultant Smithsonian Inst 1974-76; jazz consultant Creative Artists Public Serv Program 1980; jazz rsch consultant Natl Endowment for the Arts 1983; music consultant US Info Agency 1984; bd of trustees Natl Assn of Comm School & The Arts 1982-85; chmn special arts sect panel New York State Council on the Arts 1982-85; lecturer NYU 1970-, Manhattanville Coll 1976-; adv bd mem Universal Jazz Coalition Inc; adv bd mem Afro-Amer Music Bicentennial Hall of Fame & Museum Inc. **HONORS/ACHIEVEMENTS:** Public Serv Award US Dept of Labor 1980; Coll Teachers Fellowship Natl Endowment for the Humanities 1982-83; Faculty Rsch Grants Howard Univ State Univ of NY, CUNY 1971-73; Scholar Incentive Award CUNY 1983-84; Hon Citizenship Winnipeg Canada 1958; writer/contrib articles to Groves Dictionary of Music & Musicians, Black Books Bulletin, 1st World, The Black Perspective in Music, Jrnl of African & Asian Studies, Black World, Downbeat, Music Educ Journal, Allegro; devel series of music filmstrips for Educ Audio Visuals Inc 1975; 1st Annual New York Brass Conf for Scholarships Award 1973. **MILITARY SERVICE:** AUS Honorable Discharge 1958. **BUSINESS ADDRESS:** Professor of Music, Manhattan Community College, 199 Chambers St, New York, NY 10007.

GOINS, MARY G.
Educator. **PERSONAL:** Born Sep 08, 1929, Orange, TX; married Lee A Randle. **EDUCATION:** BA, MA. **CAREER:** Enterprise Jr High School, Compton CA, prin 1974-; various schools, instructor, prin since 1961. **ORGANIZATIONS:** 2nd vice pres Compton Educ Assn 1969-70; pres Assn of Compton Sch Counselors 1970-71; sec Assn of Compton Unified Sch Adminstrs 1971-72; mem Assn of CA Sch Adminstrs; CA Pers & Guid Assn; mem PTA; officer Exec PTA. **HONORS/ACHIEVEMENTS:** Recip finer womanhood awd XavierUniv 1948; life hon awd PTA 1972. **BUSINESS ADDRESS:** 2600 W Compton Blvd, Compton, CA 90220.

GOINS, N. WALTER
President/general manager. **CAREER:** KSTP, newsroom; KXLI-TV, president/general manager.

GOLDBERG, WHOOPI (CARYN E. JOHNSON)
Comedienne, actress. **PERSONAL:** Married David Edward Claessen. **CAREER:** Movie, "The Color Purple"; Comic Relief; movie "Fatal Beauty.". **BUSINESS ADDRESS:** Gallin/Morey Associates, 8730 Sunset Blvd, Penthouse West, Los Angeles, CA 90069. *

GOLDEN, ARTHUR IVANHOE
Attorney, insurance executive. **PERSONAL:** Born Jan 14, 1926, New York, NY; married Thelma O Eastmond; children: Thelma Ann, Arthur E. **EDUCATION:** NYU, BS 1959; Brooklyn Law School, JD 1973. **CAREER:** Golden & Golden Insurance, pres, 1957-; Harlem Branch New York County District Attorney's Office, mem of legal staff 1973-; Mayor's Office of Devel, project dir 1969-70; A Jackson High School, instructor 1966-69; Dept of Licensing NY, 1963-66; Dept Social Services Harlem 1960-63. **ORGANIZATIONS:** Past pres United Insurance Brokers Assn Inc; neighborhood sponser Queens DA Comm Crime Prevention Bureau; mem Black Amer Law Students Assn; mem Mayor's High School Career Guidance Conf 1966-72; mem advisory council SBA; mem One Hundred Black Men Inc; vice pres, bd of dir, Professional Insurance Agents of NY State; vice pres, bd of dir, Council of Insurance Brokers of Greater NY; state appointed public mem, governing committee, Automobile Underwriting Assn, chairman, Anti-Arson Committee; chairman, Property Management Division, Presbyterian of NY; ruling elder, First Presbyterian Church of Jamaica, treasurer of the session; mem Producer Liaison Committee, Insurance Services Office. **HONORS/ACHIEVEMENTS:** Moot court honor soc Brooklyn Law School 1971-73; Iota Nu Sigma ins hon soc NYU 1959. **MILITARY SERVICE:** AUS major 1950-54.

GOLDEN, DONALD LEON
Professor, attorney. **PERSONAL:** Born Jan 03, 1940, Walnut Cove, NC; children: Donna, Amber. **EDUCATION:** Howard Univ, BA 1972; Howard Univ Law School, JD 1972. **CAREER:** US Attorney's Office, law clerk 1971; Judicial Panel on Multi-Dist Litigation, temp rsrch asst 1971; Howard Law School Library, 1971-72; US Dist Court, law clerk 1972-73; Covington & Burling, assoc 1973-77; Howard Univ Law School, adjunct prof 1974-81; Asst US Attorney's Office, atty 1977-81; Howard Univ Law School, prof 1981-. **BUSINESS ADDRESS:** Professor, Howard Univ Law School, 2900 Van Ness St N W, Washington, DC 20001.

GOLDEN, EVELYN DAVIS
Attorney. **PERSONAL:** Born Jun 01, 1951, Moultrie, GA; married James T; children: Vivian Louise, Faye Jessica Maurine. **EDUCATION:** York Coll of the CityUniv of NY, BA1972;Univ of FL, JD 1976. **CAREER:** Dept of Legal Affairs, asst atty gen 1980-; Valencia Community Coll Orlando FL, instr prog dir 1977-79; Central FL Legal Serv, legal intern 1976-77; Pub Defender's Office Gainesville FL, legal intern 1974-75; Legal Aid Soc Brooklyn NY, legal asst 1973. **ORGANIZATIONS:** Mem FL Bar 1978-; mem FL Chap of the Nat Bar Assn 1978-; mem FL Assn of Women Lawyers 1979-; v chmn Ch 24 Seminole Co Prog Adv Com 1976-79; parli Delta Sigma Theta Sorority Inc 1979-80; bd of dir Citrus Council of Girl Scouts 1979-. **HONORS/ACHIEVEMENTS:** Outstd young women of Am Bd of Dir for Outstd Young Woman of Am 1977. **BUSINESS ADDRESS:** Dept of Legal Affairs, 125 N Ridgewood Ave, Daytona Beach, FL 32014.

GOLDEN, LOUIE
Educator. **PERSONAL:** Born May 02, 1940, Matthews, SC; married Batty Washington. **EDUCATION:** Claflin Coll, BS 1963; So IL U, MS 1971. **CAREER:** Sterling High School Greenville, coach, teacher 1963-65; Beck High School, coach, teacher 1965-70; Carolina High School, coach, teacher 1970-72; Riverside High School Greer, athletic dir 1973; Greenville County School Dist, athletic dir. **ORGANIZATIONS:** Coack clinic SC Basketball; SC Educ Assn; Greenville Co Educ Assn; NEA Council Math; SC HS League; master Mason; polemarch Kappa Alpha Psi Frat; Commn on Citizen of week for Co Council; Park & Tourist Commn for Appalachian Council Govt Park & recreation Commn Greenville C of C; mem v chmn trustee bd v chmn fin com chr treas St Matthew United Meth Ch. **HONORS/ACHIEVEMENTS:** First black head coach prodominent white sch; first black athletic dir Greenville Co Sch Dist; 750 winning percent basketball for ten yrs; one season 23 wins & no losses. **BUSINESS ADDRESS:** Riverside HS, Greer, SC 29651.

GOLDEN, MARITA
Novelist, college professor. **PERSONAL:** Born Apr 28, 1950, Washington, DC; daughter of Fancis Sherman Golden and Beatrice Reid Golden; children: Michael Kayode. **EDUCATION:** Amer Univ, Washington DC, BA, 1972; Columbia Univ, New York NY, MS, 1973. **CAREER:** WNET Channel 13, New York NY, assoc producer, 1974-75; Univ of Lagos, Lagos, Nigeria, asst prof, 1975-79; Roxbury Community Coll, Boston MA, asst prof, 1979-81; Emerson Coll, Boston MA, asst prof, 1981-83. **ORGANIZATIONS:** Exec dir, Inst for the Preservation and Study of African-Amer Writing, 186-87; consultant, Washington DC Commn on the Arts and Humanities, 1986-89, Washington DC Community Humanities Council, 1986-89; pres, African-Amer Writers Guild, 1986-. **HONORS/ACHIEVEMENTS:** Novels: Migrations of the Heart, 1983; A Woman's Place, 1986; Long Distance Life, 1989.

GOLDEN, RONALD ALLEN
Insurance supervisor. **PERSONAL:** Born Feb 06, 1944, St Louis, MO; married Clementina Joyce Thompson; children: Stephanie, Lisa, Ronald. **EDUCATION:** Southwest MO State, BS 1970; Am Educ Inst Inc, casualty claim law asso 1979. **CAREER:** The Travelers Ins Co, supr casualty prop claims 1968-; St Louis Bd of Edn, pe tchr 1968; McDonnell & Douglas Corp, tool & parts control spec 1966-68. **ORGANIZATIONS:** Mem Am Fed of Musicians Local 2-197 1973-; bus mgr Third World Band 1973-; bus mgr Simply Us Bank 1977-. **HONORS/ACHIEVEMENTS:** First black athlete to win track & field schlshp SMSU 1962-66; outstd freshman awd SMSU Track Team 1962; capt track team SMSU 1966; first black in CP Claim St Louis Office Trav Ins Co. **BUSINESS ADDRESS:** Sr Claim Law Associate, The Travelers Companies, 701 Market St, St Louis, MO 63101.

GOLDEN, SAMUEL LEWIS
Fire chief. **PERSONAL:** Born Dec 14, 1921, Althiemer, AR; married Bette R Hall; children: Leslie Freeman, Sammetra L Bircher. **EDUCATION:** St Mary's Coll, BA 1976. **CAREER:** Oakland Fire Dept, firefighter 1949-58, engr 1958-62, lt of fire 1962-66, capt of fire 1966-73, battalion chief 1973-81, fire chief 1981-. **ORGANIZATIONS:** Mem CA State Bd of Fire Svcs, NAACP, CA Fire Chiefs Assoc, Alameda Co Fire Chiefs Assoc, Intl Assoc of Fire Chiefs, Intl Metro Chiefs Assoc, CA MetroChiefs Assoc, Oakland Black Firefighters Assoc; chairman CA Metro Chiefs Assoc 1984-85; exec vice pres IABPFF. **HONORS/ACHIEVEMENTS:** 1st black pres of a firefighter union; 1st black fire chief; life mem in firefighters union; Outstanding Leadership Awd OBFFA; Affirmative Action Awd WomenFF; Outstanding Leadership Awd Black Amer Women's Movement; Leadership Awd Brothers United San Diego; Appreciation of Serv Oakland Assoc Ins Agents; Certificate of Appreciation CA State Bd of Fire Svcs; Commendation CA State Fire Marshal 1987; Certificate of Special Congressional Recog US Congress 1987. **MILITARY SERVICE:** AUS tech 5 1943-45. **BUSINESS ADDRESS:** Chief, Oakland Fire Department, 2808 Frye St, Oakland, CA 94602.

GOLDEN, WILLIE L.
Law enforcement officer. **PERSONAL:** Born Aug 16, 1952, Miami, FL; son of Willie S Golden and Louise Smith; married Myra E Jones Golden, Dec 19, 1979; children: Bryan, Kyle, Christopher, William Justin. **EDUCATION:** Southeast Florida Inst of Criminal Justice, Miami FL, Certificate of Completion, 1974; Miami-Dade Community Coll, Miami FL, AA, 1978; Biscayne Coll, Miami FL, BA, 1980; St Thomas Univ, Miami FL, MS, 1981. **CAREER:** Metro-Dade Police Dept, Miami FL, police officer, 1974-; Dade County School System, Miami FL, teacher, 1977-84; Dade County Citizen Safety Council, Miami FL, instructor, consultant, 1984-; Florida Memorial Coll, Miami FL, assoc prof, 1986-; Alexander & Alexander, Miami FL, public relations consultant, 1986-88; Metropolitan Police Inst, Miami FL, instructor, 1987. **ORGANIZATIONS:** Jr warden, Prince Hall Masons, 1974-; pres, Progressive Officers, 1975-; mem, Dade County Police Ben Assn, 1975-; parliamentarian, Natl Black Police Assn, 1977-; chaplin, Phi Beta Sigma Frat, 1984-; mem, NAACP, 1984-; mem, bd of dir, South Florida Inst of Traffic Safety Unlimited, 1985-. **HONORS/ACHIEVEMENTS:** Planned, Organized and Developed, The Community Oriented Police Unit for the Metro-Dade Police Dept, 1982; Outstanding POC Mem, Progressive Officers Club, 1985; Outstanding Young Man of Amer, Young Americans, 1986; Distinguished Serv Commendation, Metro-Dade Police, 1988.

GOLDSBERRY, RONALD EUGENE
Business executive. **PERSONAL:** Born Sep 12, 1942, Wilmington, DE; married Betty May Sanders; children: Ryan, Renee. **EDUCATION:** Central State Univ, BS Chem 1964; MI State Univ, PhD Inorganic Chem 1969; Stanford Univ, MBA Finance/Marketing 1973. **CAREER:** Univ of CA San Jose, asst prof of chem 1969-71; NASA Ames Rsch Ctr, rsch chemist 1969-72; Hewlett Packard Co, prod mgr 1972-73; Boston Consulting Group, mgmt consultant 1973-75; Gulf Oil Corp, dir corp planning 1975-78; Occidental Chem Corp, vice pres bus develop 1978-81, vice pres gen mgr surface treatment prods 1981-83; Parker Chem Co, pres 1983-. **ORGANIZATIONS:** Bd mem Cranbrook Educ Inst; bd mem MI State Univ Alumni Assn; bd mem Black Exec Exchange Prog; mem Amer Chem Soc; mem Natl Black MBA Assn; mem Natl Org Black Chemists & Chem Engrs; mem Assn of Consumer Growth; mem Comm Develop Assn; mem Amer Mgmt Assn; mem Economic Club; mem GreaterDetroit Chamber of Commerce; mem Omega Psi Phi Frat; bd of trustees WTVS Channel 56 Detroit; bd mem Amer Can Co. **HONORS/ACHIEVEMENTS:** Beta Kappa Chi Hon Soc 1962; Alpha Kappa Mu Hon Soc 1963; Omega Psu Phi Man of the Year 1971; Outstanding Alumnus of MI State Univ 1983; Outstanding Alumnus of NAFEO 1983; patent "Ultraviolet & Thermally Stable Polymer Compositions" 1974. **MILITARY SERVICE:** AUS capt 1971. **BUSINESS ADDRESS:** President, Parker Chemical Company, 32100 Stephenson Hwy, Madison Heights, MI 48071.

GOLDSBY, W. DEAN, SR.
Educational administrator. **PERSONAL:** Son of Louis Goldsby and Ola Lee Ellison Goldsby Lankford; married Laverne Gibson Goldsby, Dec 22, 1980; children: Cathy, Anthony, Ricky, W. Dean Jr., Sandy, Keith Gibson, Kenya, Khaaym, Kelly Eddings. **EDUCATION:** Campbell Jr College, Jackson, MS, AA, 1957; Allen Univ, Columbia, SC, BA, 1959; Univ of Arkansas, Fayetteville, MEd, 1966; Shorter College, Little Rock, AR, DHL, 1977. **CAREER:** Shorter College, North Little Rock, AR, dean of men, 1960-64, instructor, 1960-67, dean of students, 1964-67, director of fed work-study program, 1966-67, dean of weekend college, 1969, director of student services, vice pres, 1987-88, pres, 1988-. **ORGANIZATIONS:** Sec/treas, Natl Assn for Community Devel, 1973; trustee, Shorter Coll, Natl Community Action Trust Fund, and Bethel AME Church; pre, N Little Rock Coun on Human Rels; pres, AFSCME Local #1934; member, exec bd, AFSCME Coun 38 of AR; member,

bd of direcs, Greater Little Rock Chamber of Commerce. **HONORS/ACHIEVEMENTS:** Regional Omega Man of the Year, 1967. **BUSINESS ADDRESS:** W Dean Goldsby, President, Shorter College, 604 Locust Street, Suite 106, North Little Rock, AR 72114.

GOLDSON, ALFRED LLOYD
Hospital chairman. **PERSONAL:** Born Apr 09, 1946, New York; married Amy Goldson. **EDUCATION:** New York U, 1966; Hampton Inst, BS 1968; Coll of Med Howard U, MD 1972. **CAREER:** Dept of Radiotherapy Howard Univ Hosp, res 1973-75, asst radiotherapist 1976-79, chmn 1979-, prof of radiotherapy. **ORGANIZATIONS:** Consult Cancer Info Serv Cancer Communication for Met DC 1977; vol lecr smoking rel to teenagers Am Cancer Soc 1977-78; chmn adv com Coll of Allied Health Radiation Therapy HowardUniv 1977-78; mem Nat Med & Am Med Assn 1978-; mem of numerous other civil orgns; bd of trustees DC Div Amer Cancer Soc1979. **HONORS/ACHIEVEMENTS:** Cert of Merit Radiological Soc of N Am 1978; Serv Cit Explorers of Am 1978; Five Yr Serv Cit HowardUniv Hosp 1978; among top 50 sci & res in cancerfor 1978 Am Cancer Soc 21st Annual Seminar for Sci Writers 1979; Alpha Omega Alpha Natl Medical Honor Soc 1987-. **BUSINESS ADDRESS:** Professor, HowardUniv Hospital, Radiotherapy Dept, 2041 Georgia Ave NW, Washington, DC 20060.

GOLDSTON, NATHANIEL R., III
Food service executive. **PERSONAL:** Born Oct 20, 1938, Omaha, NE; married A Darleen; children: Nathaniel IV, Steven, Kimberly. **EDUCATION:** Univ of Denver, BA 1962. **CAREER:** Catering Mgmt Inc, food serv dir, dist mgr/regional vice pres 1963-74; Gourmet Serv Inc, pres & chmn of the bd 1975-. **ORGANIZATIONS:** Chmn of the bd Tuskegee Inst Food Service Task Force; bd of dirs Atlanta Regional Commn; natl bd of dirs Amer Business Council; mem Atlanta Chamber of Commerce, Amer Mgmt Assn, Private Industry Council, Natl Restaurant Assn, GA Hospitality and Travel Assn; bd mem School of Hospitality and Mgmt Wiley Coll; mem Univ of Denver Alumni Assn. **HONORS/ACHIEVEMENTS:** Minority Business Person of the Year, Urban Business Devel Center; Catalyst Award Most Outstanding New Business by Interracial Council of Business Opportunity 1976; Black Enterprise Magazine's Annual Achievement Award in the Area of Serv 1977; Columbia MO Restauranteur of the Year 1978; Leadership Atlanta 1980; Minority Business of the Year, Interracial Council for Business Opportunity 1981; Natl Urban League Certificate of Appreciation 1981. **BUSINESS ADDRESS:** President, Gourmet Services, Inc, 1100 Spring St Ste 450, Atlanta, GA 30367.

GOLDSTON, RALPH PETER
Assistant football coach. **PERSONAL:** Born Feb 25, 1929, Campbell, OH; son of Richard Goldston and Alice Goldston; married Sarah Sloan; children: Ralph, Jr, Ursula, Beverley, Monica. **EDUCATION:** Youngstown Univ, BS Educ 1952. **CAREER:** Seattle Seahawks, scout; Chicago Bears Club, asst football coach 1974-75; Univ of Colorado, coach 1973; Harvard Univ, 1971-72; Burlington Central High School, Burlington Ontario; Montreal Alouettes, 1966-69; NY Giants, scout 1970; Philadelphia Eagles, played 1952-55; Hamilton Tiger-Cats, 1956-64; Montreal Alouettes, 1965; City of Youngstown & Mahoning Co, surveyor during off-season; City of Philadelphia, rec dir 1952; Burlington Ontario, teacher 1962-67. **ORGANIZATIONS:** First black at Youngstown Univ 1950-51, Philadelphia Eagles 1952-55; pro coach Canadian Football League 1966; coach at Harvard Univ 1971-72; All-Pro def back CFL 1956-63; All-Co HS Mahoning Co Ohio 1945-46. **HONORS/ACHIEVEMENTS:** Letterman & capt, Youngstown Univ 1950-51; athletic scholarship Ind Univ. **BUSINESS ADDRESS:** Staff Scout, Seattle Seahawks, 11220 NE 53rd St, Kirkland, WA 98033.

GOLIDAY, WILLIE V.
Business executive. **PERSONAL:** Born Feb 22, 1956, Oxford, MS; married Mary Ann Cration. **EDUCATION:** Jackson State Univ, BS 1978, MBA 1980. **CAREER:** Delta Capital Corp, investment analyst 1980-82; Action Commun Co Inc, pres. **ORGANIZATIONS:** Advisor Jr Achievement 1981; mem JSU Alumni Assoc; dir Interchange Comm; vice pres Fayette Cable TV; State College Economic Development advisor. **HONORS/ACHIEVEMENTS:** Outstanding Young Man of Amer 1985. **HOME ADDRESS:** 233 Oktibbeha, Greenville, MS 38701. **BUSINESS ADDRESS:** President, Action Communications Co Inc, PO Box 588, Greenville, MS 38701.

GOLIGHTLY, LENA MILLS
Composer, radio producer. **PERSONAL:** Born in Horse Cave, KY. **CAREER:** Author, "Premonition of Last Christmas" 1947, "Top of the Mountain" 1967, "The Seventh Child" 1967; Composer, I Don't Worry 1955, Sugarpie Tears Easy Now 1955,Jack is Back 1957, Mis Bronzeville 1961, Eternal Flame 1964, Resurrection City USA 1968, Do Your Thing & I'll Do Mine 1969, King Drive 1969, I Had Too Much To Dream Last Night 1970; Poems, include Golden Chain of Friendship 1967, Amer You're Dying 1969; WBEE-Radio, Chicago 1967; Ada S McKinley Comm Svcs, activepub relations 1967; WXFM-Radio, Chicago 1966-. **ORGANIZATIONS:** Mem Natl Assn Media Women, Chicago Museum Assn; dir Civic Liberty League of IL; mem NAACP, Urban League, AME Church; dir Amer Friendship Club. **HONORS/ACHIEVEMENTS:** Amer Friendship Club Awd 1962-65; Awd of Merit WVON 1965, 1969; Chicago Mus Assn 1965; Awds Chicago No Dist Assn Federated Clubs 1966, WXFM 1966, Carey Temple 1966, WGRT Chicago 1970, Natl Acad Best Dressed Churchwomen 1972, 1973; Humanitarian Awd Baptist Fgn Mission Bur 1973; Dr Martin Luther King Jr Humanitarian Awd Love Meml Missionary Baptist Church 1974.

GOMES, PETER JOHN
Clergyman. **PERSONAL:** Born May 22, 1942, Boston, MA. **EDUCATION:** Bates Coll Lewiston ME, BA 1965; Harvard Univ, STB 1967-68; New England Coll, DD (hon) 1974; Waynesburg Coll, LHD (hon) 1978; Gordon Coll, Hum D (hon) 1985. **CAREER:** Amer Baptist Church, ordained to ministry 1968; Tuskegee Inst AL, instr history, dir fresmen exptl prog 1968-70; Meml Church Harvard Univ, asst minister, acting minister 1970-74, minister 1974-. **ORGANIZATIONS:** Fellow Royal Soc ARts; mem Royal Soc Ch Music, Colonial Soc MA, MA Hist Soc, Farmington Inst Christian Studies, Amer Bapt Hist Soc, Unitarian HistSoc; pres Signet Soc, Harvard Musical Assn; dir English-Speaking Union; mem Phi Beta Kappa; trustee Pilgrim Soc, Donation to Liberia 1973-, Bates Coll 1973-78,80-, Charity of Edward Hopkins 1974-, Boston Freedom Trail 1976-, Plimoth Plantation 1977-, Rosbury Latin School 1982-, Wellesley Coll 1985-, Boston Found 1985, Jordon Hosp, Plymouth Pub Library 1985-; pres, trustee Intl Fund Def & Aid in S Africa 1977-; natl chaplain Amer Guild Organists 1978-82. **HONORS/ACHIEVEMENTS:** Co-author Books of the Pilgrims; editor Parnassus 1970, History of the Pilgrim Soc 1970. **BUSINESS ADDRESS:** Minister, Memorial Church, Harvard University, Cambridge, MA 02138.

GOMEZ, DANIEL J.
Missionary. **PERSONAL:** Born Nov 26, 1926, Orange, NJ. **EDUCATION:** Seton Hall Univ, BS 1956. **CAREER:** Capuchin Missionary Zambia C Africa, 1967-; Hse of Novitiate Wilmington DE, confssr 3 yrs; St Ann's Parish Hoboken, asst pastor 2 yrs; Hse of Theology, tchr. **ORGANIZATIONS:** Mem NAACP; mem Order of Cross & Crescent Seton Hall U. **MILITARY SERVICE:** AUS 6 months; USAF corpl 3 yrs. **BUSINESS ADDRESS:** Capuchin-Franciscan Order, PO Box 6279, Hoboken, NJ 07030.

GOMEZ, DENNIS CRAIG
Personnel administrator. **PERSONAL:** Born May 14, 1948, Suffern, NY; son of Carlos and Elizabeth; married Henrietta McAlister; children: Camille, Mark, Brian. **EDUCATION:** S IL Univ, BA 1971. **CAREER:** Chase Manhattan Bank, credit corres 1971-72; Allstate Ins Co, office oper super 1972-73, claim super 1973, div super 1973-74, personnel assist 1974-76, personnel div mgr 1976-79, human resources mgr 1979-80, personnel serv mgr 1980-82, regional personnel mgr 1982-86, human resource director, customer relations dir 1987-88, field human resources director 1989-. **ORGANIZATIONS:** Mem ASPA; mem Urban League Phila; mem NAACP North Philadelphia Branch; OIC Fund Raising chmn Montgomery Co, PA 1985. **BUSINESS ADDRESS:** Field Human Resource Dir, Allstate Insurance Company, Allstate Plaza North, Northbrook, IL 60062.

GOMEZ, KEVIN LAWRENCE JOHNSON
Business executive. **PERSONAL:** Born Nov 27, 1950, Erie, PA; married Yvonne Ruth Stepp; children: McKenzie. **EDUCATION:** Univ of CO at Denver, BA 1972;Univ of MI at Ann Arbor, 1973;Univ of CO aT Denver, 1975-. **CAREER:** US Dept of Interior, envirnmntl protectn spec; Gary W Hart, asst US senator 1978-80; Floyd K Haskell, asst US senator 1975-78; Sam Brown, campaign mgr 1974;Univ of MI, stud advocate 1973; Student Health Conf of SW, Sam Brown for Dir 1975; Denver Affirmtv Action Commn, chmn 1975-77; Denver Dem CntrlCom, asst sec 1975-79, sec 1979-81; US Dept of Air Force, dir of fam support ctr 1982-. **ORGANIZATIONS:** Bd mem Am Friends Serv Com 1972-; vice pres CO Young Dem 1974-77; adv bd mem Sickle Cell Anemia gubernatorial appt 1976-81; vice pres Denver-Park Hill NAACP 1977-80. **HONORS/ACHIEVEMENTS:** Horace H Rackham Grad AwardUniv of MI 1973; Denver Regnl Cncl of Govts Grad Award in Pub AdminstrnUniv of CO 1975; del Nat Dem Midterm Conv 1978; Leadrshp Denver '80 Award Denver C of C 1979-80; Who's Who in Am Politics 1980. **BUSINESS ADDRESS:** Dir, USAF Family Support Ctr, 3415 ABG/FS Lowry AFB, Denver, CO 80230.

GOMILLION, CHARLES GOODE
Retired educator. **PERSONAL:** Born Apr 01, 1900, Johnston, SC; married Blondelia Elizabeth Graves; children: Mary Gwendolyn Gomillion Chaires. **EDUCATION:** Paine Clge Augusta GA, AB 1928; OH State Univ Columbus OH, PhD 1959; Howard Univ Wash DC, LL D 1965; OH State Univ Columbus OH, LL D 1967; Tuskegee Inst Tusk AL, LL D 1971. **CAREER:** Tuskegee Inst, instructor, high school and coll 1928-44, dean School of Educ 1944-49, dean of students 1949-58, prof of soc 1959-71. **ORGANIZATIONS:** Life mem Paine Clge Natl Alumni Assc, Natl Educ Assc; mem emeritus Southern Sociological Soc; life fellow Southern Regional Council; mem Omega Psi Phi Frat 1937-; life mem NAACP, Tuskegee Civic Assc AL; mem Christian Methodist Church 1914-. **HONORS/ACHIEVEMENTS:** Alumnus of Decade Paine Clge Augusta GA 1982; C S Johnson Awd FiskUniv Nashvl TN 1965; Natl Omega Man of Yr Omega Psi Phi Frat 1958; L B Johnson Freed Award AL Dem Conf 1975; Citation for Achievement OH State Univ 1976. **HOME ADDRESS:** 5601 13th St NW 306, Washington, DC 20011.

GONA, OPHELIA DELAINE
Research scientist, educator. **PERSONAL:** Born Jul 04, 1936, South Carolina; daughter of Joseph A DeLaine and Mattie DeLaine; married Amos; children: Shantha, Raj. **EDUCATION:** Johnson C Smith Univ, BS 1957; Yeshiva Univ, MS 1965; City Coll NY, MA 1967; City Univ NY, PhD 1971. **CAREER:** CCNY, resrch asst, teacher asst 1966-70; Peace Corps Volunteer Ghana, 1961-63; Eastern Dist High School Brooklyn, Biology teacher 1958-61; Cornell Univ Medical School, lab tech 1957-58; Montclair State Coll, asst prof Biology 1970-77; NJ Coll of Medicine & Dentistry, asst prof Anatomy; UMD-New Jersey Medical School, assoc prof of Anatomy 1986-. **ORGANIZATIONS:** Educ consult Hoffman LaRoche Pharms 1972-73; author science publications concrng 1972-77; mem AIBS, AAAS, Am Assn of Anatomists, ARVO, NY Acad of Sci. **HONORS/ACHIEVEMENTS:** Recipient of NIH grants for lens (eye) rsch Golden Apple Award for Excellence in Teaching of Medical Gross Anatomy; author of scientific publications concerning comparative endocrinology of prolactin cataracts of the lens of the eye. **BUSINESS ADDRESS:** Associate Professor, UMDNJ New Jersey Med School, Dept Anatomy, Newark, NJ 07103.

GONSALVES, JUNE MILES
Attorney. **PERSONAL:** Born Jun 24, 1939, Boston, MA; daughter of William D Miles and Gladyce Satterwhite Miles; married Manuel (divorced); children: Monique, Manuel. **EDUCATION:** Northeastern Univ (cum laude), BA 1962; Northeastern Univ Martin Luther King Jr Fellowship, JD 1973. **CAREER:** Gonsalves, pvt prac 1979-; Univ Lowell, assoc prof dept of criminal justice 1979-; affirmtv action offcr 1973-78. **ORGANIZATIONS:** Distngshd mem Affirmtv Action Offcrs in MA Pub & Pvt Edn; mem Lowell Bar Assn/MA Bar Assn; mem MA Black Lawyers Assn; mem Black Genesis Found 1974-; bd of dirs Urban League of Eastern MA 1978-82; pres Greater Lowell YWCA 1980; pres Merrimack Valley NAACP 1985-; mem Mass Black Women Attorneys; mem Mass women Lawyers; Invited Guest Speaker on many Occasions; bd of tustees, MA School of Law at Andover 1988-; bd dirs, First Foundation 1986-; chairperson, Lowell Human Rights Planning Committee 1987-. **HONORS/ACHIEVEMENTS:** Woman of the Yr Northeastern Univ 1962; Black Achievers Boston YMCA 1978; outstndg serv AAOMPHE 1979; Beulah Pierce Mem Award Greater Lowell Black Heritage Com 1980; Community Serv Awd YMCA 1985; Martin Luther King Jr Awd Univ of Lowell 1985; Certificate of Achievement, Tribute to Women in Industry, Lawrence YWCA 1988. **BUSINESS ADDRESS:** Law Office, 134 Middle St, Lowell, MA 01815.

GONZALEZ, CAMBELL
Project engineer. **PERSONAL:** Born Aug 26, 1918, Tampa, FL; married Juanita Nash; children: Amelia, Anita, John. **EDUCATION:** Howard Univ, BSEE, 1949; Stevens Inst,

graduate courses; Brooklyn Polytechnic Newark Coll of Engineering. **CAREER:** RCA, retired proj engr, 1970-82; design devel engr, 1955-70; applied engr, 1950-55; engr training, 1949. **ORGANIZATIONS:** Mem, IEEE; bd dir, YMCA Orange NJ; Alpha Phi Alpha Fraternity; planning bd, adv gr Reading Township; Sewer Adv Commn; teacher elder Flemington Pres Church; pres Inv Club Alumni. **HONORS/ACHIEVEMENTS:** Achievement award, Howard Univ, 1957; tech art pub in RCA Engr IRE Trans Electronics; Pat disclosure RCA. **MILITARY SERVICE:** AUS commanding officer, 1942-52.

GOOD, TRACY BATTEAST
Psychotherapist. **PERSONAL:** Born Dec 12, 1938, Chicago, IL; married Stuart W Good. **EDUCATION:** Univ of Dubuque, BS Pre-Med 1960; Columbia Pacific Univ, Mill Valley CA, MS Holistic Psychotherapy, MA 1979, PhD Holistic Psychotherapy & Analytical Psychology 1980. **CAREER:** Yeshiva Univ Grad School of Educ, New York, asst dir of rsch 1966-69; Apostolic Studios, New York, asst producer 1968-69; Queens Coll, New York, rsch devel 1970-71; The Woodstock Times, New York, poetry editor 1971-72; Berkshire Community Coll, Massachusetts, prog dir, counselor 1976-80; New Hampshire Coll, Connecticut, instructor 1980-81; Meridian House Found, psychotherapist 1980-82; Anuk Inc, psychotherapist 1980-83; Connecticut Psychotherapy Ctr, psychotherapist 1980-84; Ctr for Human Serv, dir/clinical supr 1982-84; Calgary Bd of Educ, employee assistance prog, 1985-87; private practice, Calgary, AB, Canada, psychologist 1985-. **ORGANIZATIONS:** Mem, ASCAP, 1963-65; prog dir, Berkshire Community Coll, 1976-80; mem, Bd of Regents, Columbia Pacific Univ, 1982-; mem, bd dir, 1979-80, co-chairperson, bd dir 1980-81, Anuk Inc; mem, bd dir, Berkshire Mental Health Assn 1977-79; bus admin, Ask Your Father Ltd Toy Store, 1973-75; mem, Canadian Assn for Transactional Analysis, 1985-.

GOOD, WILLA W.
Registered nurse. **PERSONAL:** Born Feb 05, 1915, Pittsburgh, PA; married Dr Edmund E; children: Willa, Phyllis, Sylvia. **EDUCATION:** Harlem Hosp Cntr Sch Nursing, RN; NY U, BS. **CAREER:** Harlem Hosp Cntr Harlem Hosp Svc, various nursg positions; Bellvue Hosp; Dr's Office; presntly retird. **ORGANIZATIONS:** Consult Fed Hosp Cncl; Health Care Faclts Svc; Health Serv & Mental Hlth Adminstrn; Nat Center for Hlth Serv Resrch & Devel; Dept Health Educ & Welfare; commr Mt Vernon Plnng Bd; chr Westchester Rent Guidlns; bd mem numerous offcs; coms Am Nurses Assn; NY State Nurses Assn; Nat League Nursing; Harlem Hosp Center Sch Nursng Alumni Assn; Chi Eta Phi Sor Omicron Chpt; Zeta Phi Beta Sor Gamma Xi Zeta Chpt; Women's Aux Loma LindaUniv Med Sch; Nat Cncl Women of US; Leag Women Voters; Philharmonic Symphony of Westchester Women's Com; Mt Vernon Women's Serv Leag; Intl Inst Women's Studies; Nat Women's Rep Club; sect chmn Mt Vernon Hosp Expansn Pgm Campaign; Hosp Admissns Com Mt Vernon-Eastchester Mental Hlth Cncl; numerous past appntmnts, community activities, pub speakng engagements. **HONORS/ACHIEVEMENTS:** Recip Mt Vernon Housng Authority Distngshd Serv Citation 1965; Mt Vernon United Community Fund Citation 1965; spl award Westchester Lighthse for the Blind 1968; placque Mt Vernon Women's Serv League 1969; Honoree Soror of Yr Chi Eta Phi Sor Omicron Chap 1971.

GOODALL, HURLEY C.
Administrator. **PERSONAL:** Born May 23, 1927, Muncie, IN; married Fredine Wynn. **EDUCATION:** IN Bus Coll, 1950; Purdue U, time & motion courses 1952. **CAREER:** DE Co IN, asst co engr 1978-80; Muncie Fire Dept, fire fighter 1958-78; Muncie Malleagle Co, time & motion steward 1950-58, factory wrkr 1944-50; Hur Co Inc, owner electrical supplies equipment & devices industrial & commercial; IN House of Reps, state rep 1978-. **ORGANIZATIONS:** Mem Muncie Human Rights Com 1964-70; mem Muncie Bd of Educ 1970-78; bd mem WIPB-TV Chan 49 Muncie PBS Sta 1974-80; chmn IN Black Leg Caucus; bd memIN Jobs Training Coord Council; mem govs commiss on Minority Bus Devel. **HONORS/ACHIEVEMENTS:** Co-author "History of Negroes in Muncie" Ball State Press 1974; Muncie Black Hall of Fame Multi-Serv Cntr of Muncie 1979; Govt Serv Award OIC of DE Co1980. **MILITARY SERVICE:** AUS pfc 1945-47. **BUSINESS ADDRESS:** State Representative, IN House of Reps, Indianapolis, IN 46204.

GOODE, CALVIN C.
City official. **PERSONAL:** Born Jan 27, 1927, Depew, OK; married Georgie M; children: Vernon, Jerald, Randolph. **EDUCATION:** Phoenix Coll, AA 1947; AZ State Coll, BS 1949; AZ State U, MA 1972. **CAREER:** Phoenix Union HS Dist, sch comm wrkr 1969-, sch bus mgr, asst proprty contrl dir, asst budget dir 1949-69; Goode & Asso Tax & Accntg Svc, owner & oper 1950-; Phoenix City Cnclmn, 1972-; Phoenix City V Mayor, 1974. **ORGANIZATIONS:** Bd mem Comm Council; dir Investmnt Opportnts Inc; mem CTA, AEA, NEA; mem United Fund Budget Com; mem Phoenix Urban Leag; mem NAACP; past bd chmn BT Washington Child Devel Cntr Inc; past co-chmn Child Care Project Comm Cncl; mem Omega Psi Phi Frat; mem Downtown Bkfst Optimist Club.

GOODE, GEORGE RAY
Elected official. **PERSONAL:** Born Feb 08, 1930, Clifton Forge, VA; married Doris Hatcher (deceased); children: Cassandra White, George Jr, Ava, Stanley, Kim Rickten, Carren, Stacey, Dana. **EDUCATION:** VA Seminary Ext, Assoc in Religious Educ 1976. **CAREER:** City of Clifton Forge, city councilman 1974, Mayor. **ORGANIZATIONS:** Chmn Greater Allegheny United Fund 1984. **HOME ADDRESS:** 700 Pine St, Clifton Forge, VA 24422.

GOODE, JAMES EDWARD
Clergyman. **PERSONAL:** Born Nov 18, 1943, Roanoke, VA. **EDUCATION:** Immaculate Conceptn Coll, BA 1969; Coll of St Rose, MA 1971; St Anthony Theol Sem, MDiv 1972, MTh 1974; PhD;Univ of Louvain Belgium, post-doctoral studies 1980. **CAREER:** Our Lady of Charity, pastor 1974-; CityUniv NY, adj prof 1975-, chaplain 1975-; Center for Positive Directn, dir 1976-; Black Religious Expernc Inst, co-dir; Directions A Jour of Black Ch/Comm Studies, editor; Black Cath Day, founder; Survival & Faith Inst of NY, cons; Juvenile Justice Task Force of Cntrl Brooklyn, cons; Offc for Black Ministry Diocese of Brooklyn, bd dirs; Bldg a Better Brooklyn, bd dirs; lectr, psychlgy & theology. **ORGANIZATIONS:** Mem New York City Comm Sch Bd; mem Central Brooklyn Yth & Fmly Svcs; mem Juvenile Prevntv Pgms Brooklyn; mem New York City Comm Plnng Bd; mem Culture & Worship Adv Bd Nat Offc for Black Cath; mem Coalition of Concerned Black Eductrs of NY; mem Black Ministers Cncl; mem Nat Black Cath Clergy; Nat Assn of Black Social Wrkrs; Educ Task Force for Positive Direction of NY Urban Commn; "Catholicsm & Slavery in US" Labor Press 1975; pub "Ministry in the 80's in the Black Comm" Liberation Press 1980; numerous publs. **HONORS/ACHIEVEMENTS:** Dr of Humane Letters VA Theol Sem; Preacher of First Black Cath Revival in US Chicago 1974; Martin Luther King Schlrshp NYUniv 1975-76; Black Cath Leadrshp Awrd; proclmtn declaring Nov 18 1978 Father James E Goode Day New York City 1978; proclmtn declaring Nov 16 1979 Father James E Goode Day Mayor of Brooklyn 1979; Nat Black Cath Clergy Tribute Award 1979; proclmtn NY State Assembly; lead Nat Protest Prayer Serv Against Budget Cuts in Human Servs. **BUSINESS ADDRESS:** 1669 Dean St, Brooklyn, NY 11213.

GOODE, MALVIN R.
Consultant. **PERSONAL:** Born Feb 13, 1908, White Plains, VA; married Mary Lavelle; children: Mal, Jr, Robert, Richard, Roberta, Ronald, Rosalia. **EDUCATION:** Univ of Pittsburgh, 1931. **CAREER:** Juvenile Ct, 2 yrs; Boys Work Pittsburgh YMCA, dir 6 yrs; Pittsburgh Courier, 14 yrs; Station WHOD Pittsburgh, 6 yrs; Station WMCK McKeesport, 1 yr; ABCNetwork, 11 yrs; Nat Black Network, retired cons. **ORGANIZATIONS:** Mem Assn of Radio & TV News Analysts 1967; Assn of Radio & TV News Dir 1952; NY 100 Black Mens' Club 1969; adv Ramapo Coll; NJ adv Norfolk State Coll; trustee First Bapt Ch Teaneck NJ; bd mem NAACP; bd mem Amistad Awards New Orleans; mem Teaneck Together. **HONORS/ACHIEVEMENTS:** Recip honorary Dr of Humanities Shaw U; Mary McLeod Bethune Award Bethune-Cookman Coll; keys to 35 Am cities; honorary cit Austin Tx 1971; Michelle ClarkAward Columbia Sch of Journalism 1974; Alpha Phi Alpha Man of Yr Award 1964; Alpha Phi Alpha Award Conv Milwaukee 1971; Polish Govt Award United Nations 1972. **BUSINESS ADDRESS:** Rm C-321, United Nations, New York, NY 10017.

GOODE, VICTOR M.
Director. **PERSONAL:** Born Nov 07, 1947, Monroe, LA. **EDUCATION:** Northwestern U, BA 1970; Rutgers Sch of Law, JD 1973. **CAREER:** Nat Conf of Black Lawyers, natl dir 1978-, asso dir 1975-78; Gen Counsel, vindicate soc asso dir 1974-75; City of Newark Ofc of Newark Studies, sr research asso. **ORGANIZATIONS:** Mem Assn of Bar Com on Courts 1980; mem of bar NJ/NY Pro hac vici; chmn of bd E Harlem Coll & Career Guidance Prog 1978-80; exec bd mem Nat Black United Fund 1978-80; bd Mem Nat Emergency Civil Liberties Com 1979-80. **HONORS/ACHIEVEMENTS:** Jr & Sr Mens Hon Soc NorthwesternUniv 1969-70; Comm Serv Award Black Am Law Students Assn 1979; Comm Serv Award City Coll SEEK Prog 1979; serv award Nat Conf of Black Lawyers 1980. **BUSINESS ADDRESS:** Nat Conf of Black Lawyers, 126 W 119th St, New York, NY 10026.

GOODE, W. WILSON
Mayor. **PERSONAL:** Born Aug 19, 1938, North Carolina; married Velma Williams; children: Muriel, Wilson Jr, Natasha. **EDUCATION:** Morgan State Univ, Undergrad Degree 1961; Univ of PA Wharton School, Master Govtl Admin 1968. **CAREER:** Philadelphia Council for Comm Advancement, pres ceo 1966-78; PA PUC, chmn 1978; City of Philadelphia, managing dir 1980-82; City of Philadelphia, Mayor 1984-. **MILITARY SERVICE:** AUS military police lt. **BUSINESS ADDRESS:** Mayor, City of Philadelphia, Office of the Mayor, City Hall, Philadelphia, PA 19102.

GOODEN, CHERRY ROSS
Educator. **PERSONAL:** Born Nov 07, 1942, Calvert, TX; married Lonnie J Gooden, Jr; children: Deron LeJohn, DeShaunda Lorraine. **EDUCATION:** Texas Southern Univ, BS 1960-64, MEd 1969-72; Univ of Houston, EdD 1987. **CAREER:** Houston Independent School District, teacher 1964-76; Texas Southern Univ, assistant professor 1976-. **ORGANIZATIONS:** Various School Districts in State, consultant 1981-; Natl Home & Health Care, board member 1984-; Lockhart Tech Acad, board member 1984-; Texas Southern Chapter of Phi Delta Kappa, president; Houston Chapter Jack & Jill of Amer, former treasurer & currently chaplain; Humble-Intercontinental Chapter Top Ladies of Distinction, top teen advisor; Houston Chapter Natl Women of Achievement, financial secretary; mem Ladies Aux Knights of Peter Claver Ct 151; mem Alpha Kappa Alpha Sor. **HONORS/ACHIEVEMENTS:** Outstanding Young Women of Amer 1979; Publication in Texas Tech Journal of Educ 1984; Publication in Journal of Educational Equity 1985; Appeared in Black Histor in the Making, Vol 1 Published by Riverside Hospital Houston, TX. **BUSINESS ADDRESS:** Assistant Prof of Education, Texas SouthernUniv, 3100 Cleburne EB 219, Houston, TX 77004.

GOODEN, DWIGHT EUGENE
Professional athlete. **PERSONAL:** Born Nov 16, 1964, Tampa, FL. **CAREER:** New York Mets, pitcher 1984-. **HONORS/ACHIEVEMENTS:** Named Natl League Rookie of Yr by Baseball Writers Assoc of Amer 1984; Led major leagues with 276 strikeouts becoming 1st teen-aged rookie ever to lead either AL or NL in strikeouts; ML record with avg 1139 strikeouts per nine innings; set Mets rookie record with 16 strikeouts in game; broke Natl League record for strikeouts in 2 consult games (32); set major league record with 43 strikeouts in 3 consult nine inning games; establ Mets record with 15, 10-plus strikeout games; established Mets Club mark for victories in season by a rookie righthander with 17-9 mark; youngest player selected to All Star Game; twice named NL Player of the Week; Topps Major League Rookie All Star Team; 1st Met pitcher to throw back to back shutouts; led Majors by permitting an average of 975 runners per 9 innings; Honoree Jackie Robinson Award for Athletics; 1985 Cy Young Awd winner (youngest pitcher ever to receive awd); Sporting News NL Pitcher of the Year; named Male Athlete of the Year by Associated Press 1985; named New York Athlete of the Year SportsChannel 1985; mem All Star Team 1984,86. **BUSINESS ADDRESS:** New York Mets, Shea Stadium, Flushing, NY 11368.

GOODEN, SAMUEL ELLSWORTH
Clergyman, educator. **PERSONAL:** Born Aug 25, 1916; married Elita Powell; children: Sharon, Rose. **EDUCATION:** Union Coll, BA 1949; Columbia U, MA 1958. **CAREER:** S Atlantic Conf of Seventh Day Adventists, dir of youth activts, supt of school, dir Office of Public Affairs & Religious Liberty, dir public relations; GA Council on Moral & Civic Concerns, vice pres; Africa, coll prin; W Africa, missionary; vice prin, high school; NYC, prin elementary school. **ORGANIZATIONS:** Mem Phi Delta Kappa; Alpha Phi Alpha; AASA chmn W Manor Comm Action Group 1975. **BUSINESS ADDRESS:** 235 Chicamauga Ave SW, Atlanta, GA 30314.

GOODEN, WINSTON EARL
Educator. **EDUCATION:** Muskingum College, BA; Yale Univ, MDiv, MS, PhD. **CAREER:** Two Churches in CT, pastored; Unoja Juvenile Program, co-founder & director; Univ

of IL at Chicago, asst prof; Fuller Theological Seminary, asst prof. **HONORS/ACHIEVEMENTS:** Published many articles; presented papers across the nation. **BUSINESS ADDRESS:** Asst Prof of Psychology, Fuller Theological Seminary, 135 N Oakland, Pasadena, CA 91101.

GOODLETT, CARLTON B.
Editor, publisher, retired physician. **PERSONAL:** Born Jul 23, 1914, Chipley, FL; son of Arthur Goodlett and Fannie Goodlett; divorced; children: Garry Marvin. **EDUCATION:** Howard Univ, BS 1935; Univ of CA, PhD 1938; Meharry Med Coll, MD 1944. **CAREER:** Private Practice, physician San Francisco 1945-83 (retired); San Francisco Sun Reporter, editor/publisher 1948-. **ORGANIZATIONS:** Former Pres Natl Black United Fund; former pres Natl Newspaper Publishers Assn; consult civil rights & role of minority newspapers in Amer Life; Del Intl Conf;mem Presidium; World Council of Peace; chmn bd Beneficial Devel Group; former tchr course entitled Group Conflict in Urban Amer San Francisco State Coll 1967-68; past pres San Francisco NAACP; pres San Francisco Found to Study our Schs; dir San Francisco Council BSA; mem Sigma Xi; Natl Com on Africa; chmn CA Black Leadership Conf; trustee 3rd Bapt Ch; chmn bd tst William L Patterson Found 1977; former vice pres San Francisco Council of Chs; mem, bd of overseers, Morehouse Med College. **HONORS/ACHIEVEMENTS:** Cited for Disting Serv by local groups. **BUSINESS ADDRESS:** Editor &Publisher, San Francisco Sun Reporter, 1366 Turk St, San Francisco, CA 94115.

GOODLOE, CELESTINE WILSON
Educational administrator. **PERSONAL:** Born May 07, 1954, Brooklyn, NY; married John W Goodloe, Jr; children: Jasmine R. **EDUCATION:** Bennett Coll, BS 1976; Miami Univ, MS 1982. **CAREER:** Bennett Coll, admin counselor 1979-81; Coll of Wooster, asst dir, coordinator of minority 1982-84; Xavier Univ, assoc dir of admin, dir of minority 1984-. **ORGANIZATIONS:** OH Assn of Coll admin Counselors, mem 1980-; NACAC, mem 1982, panel participant 1985; Amer Personnel & Guidance Assn, mem 1981-82. **HONORS/ACHIEVEMENTS:** Miami Univ, graduate assistantship 1981-82; Bennett Coll, marie clapp moffitt scholarship 1975; Xavier Univ, honored at the black student assn banquet for increasing the number of black students 1986. **BUSINESS ADDRESS:** Assoc Dir of Admissions, Xavier University, 3800 Victory Pkwy, Cincinnati, OH 45207.

GOODMAN, GEORGE D.
Association executive. **PERSONAL:** Born Sep 13, 1940, Saginaw, MI; son of George V Goodman and Thelma Kaigler Goodman; married Judith A Mansfield; children: George, Mark. **EDUCATION:** BA 1963; MA 1970. **CAREER:** Eastern Michigan Univ, instr 1967-68; Univ Michigan, asst dir admissions 1968-73; Opportunity Program, dir 1973-82; City Ypsilanti, mayor 1972-82; exec dir Michigan Muncipal League. **ORGANIZATIONS:** Mem Michigan Municipal League; chmn Michigan Conf of Mayors 1976-77; chmn Urban Affairs Comm 1974-75; mem Emanon Club 1967-; life mem Alpha Phi Alpha Frat; mem NAACP; bd mem Huron Valley Girl Scout Council; mem Michigan Municipal Bond Authority; mem Washtenaw Community Coll Found Exec Bd 1983-; mem United Way of Michigan Bd of Dir 1987-; mem Coll of Wooster, Ohio Bd of Trustees 1987-; pres Ann Arbor Summer Festival Comm 1988-. **HONORS/ACHIEVEMENTS:** Distinguished Serv Award Ypsilanti Area Jaycees 1973; 1 of 5 Outstanding Young Men of Michigan 1974; Public Serv Achievement Award Common Cause 1987. **MILITARY SERVICE:** AUS capt 1963-67. **BUSINESS ADDRESS:** Executive Dir, Michigan Municipal League, 1675 Green Rd, Ann Arbor, MI 48105.

GOODMAN, JAMES ARTHUR, SR.
Medical school executive. **PERSONAL:** Born Apr 22, 1933, Portsmouth, VA; son of Accie Goodman and Viola James Goodman; married Gwendolyn Jones, Apr 12, 1956; children: James A Jr, Rhonda. **EDUCATION:** Morehouse Coll, Atlanta GA, AB, 1956; Atlanta Univ, Atlanta GA, MSW, 1958; Univ of Minnesota, Minneapolis MN, PhD, 1967. **CAREER:** Natl Acad of Sciences, Inst of Medicine, Washington DC, sr professional assoc, 1973-75; Univ of Minnesota, School of Social Work, Minneapolis MN, prof, dir, 1975-77; State Dept, Office of Intl Training, Washington DC, dir, 1977-79; Inst of Public Mgmt, Washington DC, exec vice pres, 1979-83; Morehouse School of Medicine, Atlanta GA, exec vice pres, 1980-89, pres, 1989-. **ORGANIZATIONS:** Natl Accreditation Comm, Council on Social Work Educ; Natl Assn of Social Workers; Acad of Certified Social Workers; Council on Social Work Educ; Amer Sociological Assn; mem, bd of dir, Atlanta Urban League, 1981-88, HealthSouth Inc, 1982-88; mem, DeKalb County Hospital Authority, 1984-88, Natl Advisory Council on Educ for Health Professionals, 1985-89, Rotary Intl. **HONORS/ACHIEVEMENTS:** Editorial Advisory Bd Mem, Mental Health Digest, 1971-73; author of "The Health Community: Perspective for the Future," 1973; author of The Dynamics of Racism in Social Work Practice, 1973; author of "The Social Health of Disadvantaged Black Coll Students," Amer Journal of Coll Health, 1974; author of "Race and Reason in the 1980's," Social Work, 1975; Oustanding Achievement, Atlanta Medical Assn, 1985; delivered the Dean Brailsford Brazeal Lecture, Morehouse Coll, 1986; Outstanding Contribution to Medical Educ, Natl Assn of Medical Minority Educ, 1988; Frankie V Adams Award for Excellence, Atlanta Univ, 1988; Fanon Scholar, Charles Drew Postgraduate Medical School. **BUSINESS ADDRESS:** President, Morehouse School of Medicine, 720 Westview Dr SW, Atlanta, GA 30310-1495.

GOODMAN, ROBERT O., JR.
Military officer. **PERSONAL:** Born Nov 30, 1956, San Juan, Puerto Rico;son of Robert Oliver Goodman Sr and Marylyn Joan (Dykers) Goodman; married Terry L Bryant, Jun 02, 1979; children: Tina, Morgan. **EDUCATION:** US Naval Academy, Monterey CA, Annapolis MD, Bachelors Operations Analysis 1978; US Naval Post Graduate School, Masters Systems Technology (Space) 1987. **CAREER:** US Navy, navigator and bombardier. **MILITARY SERVICE:** USN, lt commander 1978-.

GOODRICH, HAROLD THOMAS
Educator. **PERSONAL:** Born Aug 01, 1931, Memphis; married Verastine Goodrich; children: Ivan DeWayne, Michael Rene. **EDUCATION:** LeMoyne-Owen Coll, BS 1956; Memphis State Univ, MA 1969; additional studies, 1974. **CAREER:** Capleville Elementary School, Memphis, English teacher, 1956-65; coord 1965-67; Adult Basic Ed, teacher 1966; supvr of instructors, 1967-74; Title I Consult & Bolivar City, 1967-70; Adult Basic Educ, supvr 1967-69; Consult AV 1971; Natl Technical Corps, team leader, 1972-74. **ORGANIZATIONS:** Chmn mem Vis Com of Southern Assn of Coll & Schls 1974-76; delegate to NEA 1971, 74; mem NEA, TEA, WTEA, SCEA, TASCD, AECT, ASCD, Dem, Omega Psi Phi; vice pres GAIA Investment Club; deacon, mem finance com, mem housing com Mt Vernon Bapt Ch. **HONORS/ACHIEVEMENTS:** Recipient, Phi Delta Kappa Award 1969; Outstanding Educator in Amer for 70's. **MILITARY SERVICE:** AUS pfc hon gd 1953-55. **BUSINESS ADDRESS:** Capleville Elem Sch, 4326 Shelby Dr, Memphis, TN 38118.

GOODRICH, THELMA E.
Insurance broker. **PERSONAL:** Born Apr 19, 1933, New York, NY; daughter of James Goodrich and Evelyn Goodrich; married Lawrence Hill, Jan 24, 1960. **EDUCATION:** Baruch City Coll, New York NY, Assoc Degree, 1952; Coll of Insurance, New York NY, Certificate, 1960; Coll of New Rochelle, New York NY, attended, 1985; Empire State Coll, New York NY, attending. **CAREER:** Fay Weintraub-Sterenbuck, New York NY, sec, 1953; Thelma E Goodrich, New York NY, owner/mgr, 1959; Goodrich/Johnson Brokerage, New York NY, pres, CEO, 1980-. **ORGANIZATIONS:** Dir, United Mutual Life Insurance Co, 1983-86, New York Porperty Fire Insurance Org, 1983-; treasurer, East Harlem Reinvestment Group, 1985-; dir, Aaron Davis Hall, 1987-, 100 Black Women, 1987-; pres, Harlem Business Alliance, 1989; dir, Professional Insurance Agents, 1989, Council of Insurance Brokers, 1989, Greater Harlem Real Estate Bd, 1989; 1st vp, New York Club, Natl Assn of Negro Business & Professional Women Club Inc, 1989. **HONORS/ACHIEVEMENTS:** Business, Iota Phi Lambda Sorority, 1975; Business, New York City Negro Business & Professional Women, 1978; Insurance Broker, Council of Insurance Brokers, 1980; Community Serv, Insurance Women of New York State; Community Serv, New York City Business & Professional Women, 1988; Community Serv, New York State Black & Public Relations Caucus, 1989.

GOODSON, ANNIE JEAN
Government official. **PERSONAL:** Born in Camp Hill, AL; married Adolph. **EDUCATION:** AL State U, BS (cum laude) 1954; Fisk U, grad study 1956; Howard Univ Sch of Soc Work, MSW 1962. **CAREER:** Family Serv Adminstrn, acting adminstr 1980-; DC Dept of Human Resrcs, dep bur chief 1976-80; DC Dept of Human Svcs, chief spl serv div 1971-76; Med Eval & Rehab Svcs, chief 1967-71; St Elizabeths Hosp, psychiatric soc wrkr 1962-67; DC Dept of Pub Welfare, caseworker 1958-60; DC Children's Ctr, tchr 1957-58; E Highland HS Sylocauga AL, pub sch tchr 1954-56. **ORGANIZATIONS:** Adv bd Washington DC UpJohn Homemaker Servs; mem Nat Assn of Soc Workers; Acad of Certfd Soc Wrkrs; mem John Wesley AME Zion Ch; Delta Sigma Theta Inc Sor; pres Montgomery Co Alumnae Chap Delta Sigma Theta Inc 1975-77. **HONORS/ACHIEVEMENTS:** Nom Fed Woman's Award 1975; Soror of Yr Award Delta Sigma Theta Sor 1975; Phelps-Stokes Flwshp Cert Grp Therapy St Elizabeths Hosp. **BUSINESS ADDRESS:** 122 C St NW, Washington, DC 20001.

GOODSON, ERNEST JEROME
Orthodontist. **PERSONAL:** Born Dec 16, 1953, Concord, NC; married Patricia Timmons, Nov 17, 1984; children: Ernest Jerome Jr (Sonny), Aaron Timmons. **EDUCATION:** Univ of NC Chapel Hill, BSD 1976, Sch of Dentistry DDS 1979; Univ of London Royal Dental Hosp, Fellowship of Dental Surgery 1980; Univ of CA-San Francisco, MS 1984. **CAREER:** Central Piedmont Comm Coll, faculty 1980; MA General Hosp Boston, general practice residency 1981; Pasquotank-Perquimans- Cander- Chowan Dist Health Dept, dir of dental servs; Univ North Carolina School of Dentistry, adjunct faculty 1981-82; Elizabeth City State Univ, lecturer math 1981-82; Nash-Edgecombe-Halifak Counties, dir of dental serv, 1984-85; Fayetteville State Univ, lecturer math 1985-86; private practice, orthodontist. **ORGANIZATIONS:** Tutor First Baptist Math-Science Tutorial Prog 1986-. **HONORS/ACHIEVEMENTS:** Most Outstanding Young Men of Amer 1979; Acad of General Dentistry Scholarship 1985; rsch and publications "Detection and Measurement of Sensory Illusions" with Dr Barry Whitsell and Dr Duane Dryer, Dept of Physiology, Univ of NC, School of Medicine and School of Dentistry; "The London Experience" Dental Student 1981; "Dental Education in England" The Dental Asst 1981; "Orthodontics for the Public Health Dentist" NC Dental Public Health 1986. **BUSINESS ADDRESS:** 907 Hay St Ste 100, Fayetteville, NC 28305.

GOODSON, FRANCES ELIZABETH
Educational administrator, author, poet. **PERSONAL:** Born in Nashville, TN; married David Goodson; children: Shereen, David Hughes. **EDUCATION:** Hofstra Univ, Admin Eval Seminar 1978, Negotiations Seminar 1979; Natl Assn of Educ Negotiators, Negotiations Seminar 1980; Computer Educ, Management Seminar 1980; Natl Sch Bd Journal, Public Relations Seminar 1982-83, Admin Eval Workshops 1983-84. **CAREER:** Roosevelt Council of PTA's, pres 1973-74; Legislative Liaison for Bd of Educ, NYS 1981-; Adv Council to Gov NYS, state human rights 1984-; Roosevelt Public Schools, bd of educ pres. **ORGANIZATIONS:** Mem Adult Basic Educ Bd 1975; pres Bd of Educ 1977-; mem Natl Caucus Black Sch Bd 1978-; mem bd of dirs NCBSBM 1978-80, chairperson election comm1982; mem Elem Educ Accrediation Comm 1983; regional pres Natl Caucus of Black Sch Bd Members 1983, 1984; Gov's appointment on Comm on Child Care 1984-; mem bd of dirs Natl Caucus Blk Bd members; NY State Liaison representing Roosevelt Bd of Educ 1982-; mem State Human Rights Adv Council 1983-84; vice pres Northeast Region Natl Caucus Black Sch Bd members 1983-84; pres Roosevelt Bd of Educ 1981-82; vice pres Roosevelt Bd of Educ 1983-84; pres Roosevelt Bd of Educ 1984-85; Gov's apptmt NYS Comm on Child Care 1985; mem of Natl Political Congress of Black Women; exec vice pres Natl Caucus of Black School Bd Members 1986-87, 1987-88. **HONORS/ACHIEVEMENTS:** Black Faces in High Places 1979; Outstanding Member Awd NCBSBM 1982, President's Awd of Appreciation 1983; Natl Pres Awd Natl Black Caucus 1983, 1984, 1985; Student Awd Frances E Goodson Awd Est 1980; Democratic Club of Roosevelt Awd 1984; Northeast Region Vice President's Awd NCBSBM 1984; poetry (anthology) Our World's Most Beloved Poems 1985; Natl Woman of the Year Awd 100 Black Men Inc 1985; New York State Senate Commendation Resolution 1985. **HOME ADDRESS:** 236 Beechwood Ave, Roosevelt, NY 11575.

GOODSON, JAMES ABNER, JR.
Advertising manager. **PERSONAL:** Born Jul 11, 1921, Cuero, TX; married Emma E; children: James III, Theresa Jasper, Johnny L, Jerome K. **EDUCATION:** Metropolitan Coll Los Angeles, 1943; Harold Styles Sch of Radio Announcers, 1952. **CAREER:** Tire salesman 1940; BF Goodrich, 1944; JAGME Found, pres; Natl Record Newspaper, publisher, pres. **ORGANIZATIONS:** Pres Cosmopolitan Rep Voters Club Inc; mem NAACP 20 yrs, Urban League 25 yrs; mem Hollywood Community Police Council 1977,81, Southside C of C of Los Angeles, Happiness Project, Masonic Lodge, New Hope Baptist Church. **HONORS/ACHIEVEMENTS:** Recipient Exceptional Achievement Awd NAACP 1971; recipient Personal & Professional Achievement Awd Hon Mike Roos 46th Assembly Dist, Hon Maxine Waters 48th Assembly Dist, Hon David Roberts 23rd Senatorial Dist 1980; recipient Cert of

Apprec County of Los Angeles 1980; recipient Cert of Commendation Republican Central Comm Los Angeles County 1985; recipient Plaque of Appreciation Young Men's Christian Assoc 1986. **MILITARY SERVICE:** AUS engr 1945. **BUSINESS ADDRESS:** President, Publisher, The Record Publishing Co, 6404 Hollywood Blvd, Hollywood, CA 90028.

GOODSON, LEROY BEVERLY
Physician. **PERSONAL:** Born Feb 11, 1933, Elyria, OH; married Evelyn Wimmer; children: Earl, Kenneth, Parker. **EDUCATION:** Univ MI, BS 1953-55; Univ MI Med Sch, MD 1955-59; Kenyon Coll, 1951-53. **CAREER:** St Rita's Hosp, intern 1959-60; Carl S Jenkins, partner 1960-61; Wilberforce Univ, med dir 1960-62; Private Practice, physician 1963-72; Wright PattersonAF Base, 1966-68; Clark Co Drug Control Cnsl, med dir 1971-; Private Practice, physician 1972-; Wright State Univ, consult 1973-75; HK Simpson Ctr Maternal Hlth, instr physical diag & anemia 1973-; Wright State Univ, assoc clinical prof family practice 1975-; Alcohol Chem Detox Unit, med dir 1975-83. **ORGANIZATIONS:** Mem Clark Co Med Soc 1960-, sec 1968-70, pres 1971; Comm Hosp Med Staff 1960-, vice pres 1973; OH Acad of Family Physicians 1960-; Hosp Com 1971-;diplomate Amer Bd Family Practice 1973-; mem Operation Big Sister 1968-70, pres bd 1970; Amer Red Cross 1968-71, exec com mem 1969-71; Comm Hosp BdMem 1968-71, exec com mem 1969-71; chmn bd Ronez Apt Inc 1972-74. **HONORS/ACHIEVEMENTS:** Outstanding Serv to Comm Frontiers Intl Inc 1973; Amer Red Cross Serv Awd 1971; Comm Hosp Serv Awd 1971; listed Who's Who in the Midwest 1973; Who'sWho in the US 1975; Men of Achvmt 1973; Men of Achvmt in the US 1975; Amer Biog Inst 1977. **MILITARY SERVICE:** AUSMC capt 1961-63. **BUSINESS ADDRESS:** Medical Dir, Alcohol Chem Detox Unit, PO Box 1223, Springfield, OH 45501.

GOODSON, MARTIN L., JR.
Educator. **PERSONAL:** Born Feb 14, 1943, Boligee, AL; children: Monique. **EDUCATION:** Stillman Coll, BS 1964; IN State Univ, MS 1970; IN Univ, EdD 1975. **CAREER:** Rochelle High School, Lakeland FL, biology teacher 1964-65; Druid High School Tuscaloosa, physics teacher 1965-66; Seagrams Distilling Inc, lab technician 1967; IN State Univ, instructor 1970-72; AL A&M Univ Huntsville, assoc prof 1975-77; Delta Coll MI, assoc prof. **ORGANIZATIONS:** Consult Amer Inst Physics 1973-75; outside CollUniv Ctr MI 1977-; Outside evaluator Proj Impact throughout state of IN 1973-75; consult & evaluator POT Modules 1973-75; keeper of records & seals Omega Psi Phi Frat 1963-64; pres NAACP Terre Haute 1970-72; adv IN State Univ 1968-75; sec Omega Psi Phi Frat 1963-; bd mem Amer Baptist Theol Sem 1978-; mem Phi Delta Kappa 1974-; mem Natl Assn of Rsch in Sci Teaching; Phi Delta Kappa; AL State pres Natl Pres New Farmers Assn 1959-60. **HONORS/ACHIEVEMENTS:** Woodrow Wilson Flwshp 1964; "The Effect of Objective-Based Diagnostic Test on Physical Science Students" Journal of Coll Science Tchng 1978. **MILITARY SERVICE:** ROTC Tuskegee Inst 1959-62. **BUSINESS ADDRESS:** Associate Professor, Delta Coll, University Center, MI 48710.

GOODWIN, DENNIS MICHAEL
Pharmacist. **PERSONAL:** Born Jan 09, 1950, Ozan, AR; married Gloria Jean Winston; children: Natasha, Natesha. **EDUCATION:** TX Southern Univ Sch of Pharmacy, BS 1975; TN State Univ, PharmD 1981. **CAREER:** Skillerns Drugs, pharmacist & store mgr 1978; Target Stores, pharmacist & asst dept 1980; Super-X Drugs, pharmacist & asst mgr 1981; Meharry Medical Coll, asst rschr & lecturer 1981-82; Riverside Adventist Hosp, chief & dir of pharmacy 1982-84; Dennis Goodwin Enterprises, pharmacy consultant 1984-87; Jack Eckerd Corp, pharmacist & mgr 1987. **ORGANIZATIONS:** Mem NAACP 1968-84; mem Omega Psi Phi Frat. **HONORS/ACHIEVEMENTS:** Billion Dollar Club Target Store 1980; Management Awd Target Store.

GOODWIN, E. MARVIN
Educator. **PERSONAL:** Born Sep 05, 1936, Chicago, IL; married Ann M Hudson; children: Pamela Denise, Eric Winston, Marvin E II. **EDUCATION:** Chicago State Univ, BA History 1970, MA History, Pol Sci 1972; Fulbright Scholar, 1983. **CAREER:** AB Dick Co, chief admin clerk 1968-72; Kennedy-King Coll, asst prof of history 1972-83, title III coord 1978-81, coll registrar 1985-, history prof, social sci 1984-. **ORGANIZATIONS:** History consult Chicago Metro-History Fair 1976-83; sr consult Ed Mgmt Assoc 1981-85; pres Assoc for the Study of Afro-Amer Life & History 1982-; mem IntlHistory Honor Sco Phi Alpha Theta, Amer Assoc for Higher Ed, Phi Theta Kappa. **HONORS/ACHIEVEMENTS:** Fulbright Scholarship US Dept of Ed 1983; "Black Migration An Uneasy Exodus" publ by ERIC 1984. **MILITARY SERVICE:** USAF airman 2nd class 1955-58. **BUSINESS ADDRESS:** Prof of History, Social Sci, Kennedy-King College, 6800 South Wentowrth, Chicago, IL 60621.

GOODWIN, EVELYN LOUISE
Personnel administrator. **PERSONAL:** Born May 20, 1949, Columbus, GA; daughter of Alfred Goodwin Jr and Annie Hinton Goodwin. **EDUCATION:** Tuskegee Univ, BS 1971; USAF Air Command and Staff Coll, graduate 1982; Webster Univ, MA 1985. **CAREER:** Military Airlift Command USAF, labor relations officer 1982-84; Air Force Office of Personnel, personnel administrator 1984-85; Secretariate of the Air Force, personnel administrator; USAF Appellate Review Agency, hearings examiner/complaints analyst. **ORGANIZATIONS:** Vice pres Federal Mgrs Assoc Norton AFB Chap 1983-84; public relations officer Tuskegee Airmen Inc San Antonio Chap 1984-85; mem Blacks in Govt; Order of Eastern Star-PHA; Theta Chap Lambda Kappa Mu Sor Inc; pres, Kittyhawk Chapter, Intl Training in Communication, 1989-; mem, Dayton, OH Intergovt Equal Employment Opportunity Council, 1989-. **HONORS/ACHIEVEMENTS:** Martin Luther King Jr Humanitarian Awd; Afro-Culture Workshop Clark AB Philippines 1982. **HOME ADDRESS:** 2417 Marcia Dr, Bellbrook, OH 45305. **BUSINESS ADDRESS:** Hearings Examiner/Comp Analyst, USAF Appellate Review Agency, Wright Patterson AFB, OH 45433.

GOODWIN, FELIX L.
Retired educator. **PERSONAL:** Born Nov 24, 1919, Lawrence, KS; married Esther Brown (deceased) (deceased); children: Cheryl G Washington, Sylvia E, Judith G Barnes. **EDUCATION:** Univ of MD, BS 1958; Univ of AZ, MPA 1965; Univ of AZ, Educ Specialist 1974; Univ of AZ, EdD 1979; School of Journalism, Univ of Wisconsin, Madison. **CAREER:** Army 1939-1945; Army Officer 2nd Lt to Lt Col 1945-1969; Univ of AZ, asst prof 1968-69; Univ of AZ, asst to pres 1969-83. **ORGANIZATIONS:** Alpha Phi Alpha; Beta Gamma Sigma business hon; Alpha Delta Delta; Phi Delta Kappa; Kiwanis Intl; NAACP Life Mem; Chmn AZ Bicentennial Comm; Chrmn Pima Cnty Personnel Merit Syst Comm; Pima County Law Enforcement Comm; Natl Urban League; Knights of Comm Disabled Amer Veterans; Amer Legion; Natl Orig Legal Problem in Educ; Natl Assn Black Schl Educators; Assn of US Army; Chmn Natl Consultant for Black Professional Devel. **HONORS/ACHIEVEMENTS:** 2 Bronze Letters of Appreciation by Mayor/City Council, Tucson; Certificate of Appreciation/plaque Pima Cnty Bd of Supvrs; Honorary Citizen of Sierra Vista, AZ, 1st Sr Distinguished Serv Award in Affairs, Univ of AZ, Distinguished Serv Awards for Serv in the Western Region. **MILITARY SERVICE:** AUS lt col; Legion Merit, Meritorious Serv Medal, Army Commendation Medal, Oak Leaf Cluster. **HOME ADDRESS:** 7065 N Stardust Cir, Tucson, AZ 85718.

GOODWIN, HUGH WESLEY
Minister. **PERSONAL:** Born May 06, 1921, Steelton, PA; married Frances Jones; children: Hugh Jr, Paul Kelley, Anna Euphemie, Tom. **EDUCATION:** Howard Univ Wash DC, BA 1939-43; Harvard Law Schl Cambridge MA, LLB 1945-48. **CAREER:** Private Prac 1949-67; Fresno Cty CA, asst pub def 1967-76; Fresno CA, judge of municipal ct 1976-79; Follow Up Ministries, prison ministries 1979-. **MILITARY SERVICE:** Infantry Quartermaster 2nd lt 1943-45. **BUSINESS ADDRESS:** 3160 W Kearney Blvd, Fresno, CA 93706.

GOODWIN, JAMES OSBY
Attorney. **PERSONAL:** Born Nov 04, 1939, Tulsa, OK; married Vivian Palm; children: Jerry, Davey, Anna, Jeanne, Joey. **EDUCATION:** Univ of Notre Dame, BA 1961;Univ of Tulsa, JD 1965. **CAREER:** Atty; OK Eagle Newsppr, publisher. **ORGANIZATIONS:** Chmn Tulsa Human Srvc Agncy 1978-80; bd chmn Tulsa Comprhnsv Hlth Ctr 1973; mem Tulsa City Co Bd of Hlth; mem OK Bar Assn; Am Trial Lawyers; sec, vice pres OK Trial Lawyers; mem Tulsa Co Bar Assn; Tulsa Co Legal Aid; ACLU Award for Serv as Chmn Tulsa City Co Bd of Hlth 1975. **HONORS/ACHIEVEMENTS:** Award for Serv as mem bd chmn Tulsa Comprehensive Hlth Ctr 1973. **BUSINESS ADDRESS:** 122 N Greenwood, Tulsa, OK 74120.

GOODWIN, JESSE FRANCIS
City labs. director. **PERSONAL:** Born Feb 07, 1929, Greenville, SC; son of Jesse Goodwin (deceased) and Frances Byrd Goodwin; married Della M Mcgraw; children: Gordon Francis, Paula Therese, Jesse Stephen. **EDUCATION:** Xavier Univ, BS Pharm 1951; Wayne Univ, MS 1953, PhD 1957. **CAREER:** Wayne State Univ Clge Med, res assc 1958-59; Wayne Cty Gen Hosp; clin biochem 1959-63; Gen Clin Res Ctr Chidlrens Hosp Wayne StateUniv Sch Med, lab dir 1963-73; Detroit Health Dept, dir labs 1973-. **ORGANIZATIONS:** Pres Gamma Lambda Chap Alpha Phi Alpha Frat 1972-76; bd trustees Horizon Health Systems 1982-, Detroit Osteopatric Hosp Corp 1980-, Marygrove Clge 1977-; 1st vice pres Det Branch NAACP 1982-84, 2nd vice pres 1978-82; commissioner MI Toxic Substance Control Commn 1986-; bd dirs MI Catholic Conf 1986-; bd dirs Amer Assoc for Clinical Chemistry 1987-90; bd dir Natl Acad Clinical Biochemistry 1987. **HONORS/ACHIEVEMENTS:** Chrmn MI Section AACC 1964; author 36 Sci Publ 1958-; listings Who's Who Midwest Amer Men Sci 1964-; Distg Serv Award Detroit Branch NAACP 1983. **BUSINESS ADDRESS:** Dir of Laboratories, Detroit Health Dept, 1151 Taylor, Detroit, MI 48202.

GOODWIN, KELLY OLIVER PERRY
Pastor-emeritus. **PERSONAL:** Born Dec 24, 1911, Washington, DC; daughter of Oliver Perry Goodwin and Martha Gertrude Duncan Goodwin; married Emmalene E Hart Goodwin, Dec 24, 1940. **EDUCATION:** Howard Univ DC, AB 1935; United Theol Sem, MDiv 1943; Shaw U, DD 1960; NC Bapt Hosp & Bowman Gray, Med Cert 1948. **CAREER:** Zion Bapt Ch Reading PA, pastor 1936-47; Mt Zion Bapt WS NC, pastor 1946-77; WS StUniv NC, chaplain 1958; WS NC, commissioner of Public Housing 1958-77; WS Human Relations Commission, 1st Chmn 1978-80; Housing Task Force, chm 1984-85; Cedar Grove Bapt Ch, pastor 1970-. **ORGANIZATIONS:** Past pres WS Bapt Min Conf & Asso; past pres Forsyth Ministers Flwshp; A Fdr WS Day Care Asso & Past Pres; adv cncl WS Chronical (Wkly Paper); bd Mem WS Patterson Ave YMCA; bdmem Old Hickory Cncl BSA; A Mem Natl Asso Housing & Redev Officals; A Bd/Mem NAACP Local & St; bd mem Crisis Control Ministry W-S, W-S Industries for the Blind. **HONORS/ACHIEVEMENTS:** Silver Beaver BSA Old Hickory Cncl NC; Ford Fndtn Grant Urban Training Ctr Chicago IL; Lily Fndtn Grant VA UnionUniv Richmond PA; WS Dstgshd Citizen Awd Sophisticated Gents 1985; Charles McLean Community Service Award, Sara Lee Corp, 1989. **HOME ADDRESS:** 501 W 26th St, Winston-Salem, NC 27105.

GOODWIN, MERCEDIER CASSANDRA DE FREITA
Govt. official. **PERSONAL:** Born in Chicago, IL; married Quentin Goodwin; children: Horace Milano Mellon. **EDUCATION:** LincolnUniv Jefferson MO, BHE 1944; Chicago Tchrs Clg Chicago IL MEd 1957; De PaulUniv Chicago IL, MA 1961; Northern Il Univ De Kalb, Il, EdD 1974; HowardUniv Summer Sch J F Kennedy Sch of Govt 1976. **CAREER:** Central YMCA Comm Clg Chgo, inst in ed 1961-64; Argo, Summit, Bedford Park Summit IL dir of spec ed 1964-68; IL Tchrs Clg Chicago IL instr 61965-66; Garfield Sch Blue Island IL, prin 1968-69; Graves Sch Bedford Pk IL, prin 1969-71, dir of spec ed 1970-73; Walker Sch Bedford Pk IL, prin 1971-75; IL St Bd of Ed Springfield & Chgo, mem 1974-79; Malyors Office of Employment & Trianing Chgo, dep dir 1975-81; Chicago Dept of Health/Bd of Health, spec asst to commr 1981-, EEO officer. **ORGANIZATIONS:** Mem Exec Women 1981-; chp Early Outreach, Comm Urban Hlth Prog,Univ of IL Med Ctr Chicago 1978-; mem Comm of Visitors Northern ILUniv 1978-; mem Commof Visitors Northern ILUniv 1978-; career education coord & mem Chicago United Task Force 1978-80; mem Pres Carters Youth Motivation Task Force on "Bridging the Gap between Education and Labor" (conduct seminars at major universities); mem bd of dir Midwest Asso for Sickle Cell Anemia Inc 1974-79; position papers in Spec Ed & Early Childhood Ed; "A Comparative Study of Progressive & Traditional Attitudes of Elem Sch Tchrs & Principals in Cook Co IL" March 1974; "St Bd of Education Goals Statement" Jan 1976; "Future Plans of the St Bd of Ed Affecting the Principalship" IL Principals Journal Vol 8 No 3 Mar 1977; "Identifying Pressures on Children" Dec 1969; "Women in Todays Labor Force" Ivy Leaf Vol 54 Fall 1977 pp 10-11; "Learning in America (By Dr Ralph W Tyler) The Center Mag Vol 10 Nov/Dec 1977 pp 50-62 (panel presentation). **HONORS/ACHIEVEMENTS:** Recipient of & listed in Alive Black Women publ tribute from members of Western Region Iota Phi Lambda Sor Inc Feb 1980; biography in "Whos Who Among BlackAmericans" 1977-78; mem Chicago Comm on Animal Care & Control (appointed by Mayor Byrne 1978-); recipient of Dist Alum Awd DePaulUniv 1976; selected 2nd woman mem of Spring Conf 1976; selected to serve on Dept of Labor Comm for selecltion Of CETA Woman of Yr 1975; recd Intl Woman of Yr Awd in Govt 1975; selected 3 Listed by Ebony & Black Enterprise Magavines among top black females who have achieved in Govt & Ed in US 1975. **HOME ADDRESS:** 601 E 32nd St,

Chicago, IL 60616. **BUSINESS ADDRESS:** Spec Assistant to Commissioner, Chicago Dept of Health, Daley Center, 55 W Washington Rm 255, Chicago, IL 60601.

GOODWIN, NORMA J.
Physician, health care administrator. **PERSONAL:** Born May 14, 1937, Norfolk, VA; daughter of Stephen Goodwin and Helen Goodwin. **EDUCATION:** Virginia State Coll, BS 1956; Medical Coll of Virginia, MD 1961. **CAREER:** Kings County Hospital Center Brooklyn, internship residency 1961-65; Downstate Medical Center, dir clinical asst, asst prof clinical, asst prof medicine 1964-72; Natl Inst of Health, postdoctoral & fellow nephrology 1965-67; Kings County Hospital, Den & State Univ NY, Downstate Medical Center Brooklyn, served; Kings County Hospital, clinical dir hemodialysis unit 1967-69 1969-71; Univ Hospital Downstate Center, attending physician 1968-75; Health & Hospitals Corp, vice pres, sr vice pres 1971-75; Dept Family Practice, clinical asst prof 1972-; Howard Univ School of Business & Public Admin, adjunct prof 1977-; AMRON Mgmt Consult Inc, pres 1976-; Columbia Univ Teachers Coll, adjunct professor. **ORGANIZATIONS:** Mem staff Kings County Hospital Center 1965-; charter mem bd dir NY City Comp Health Planning Agency 1970-72; 2nd vice pres Natl Medical Assn; 1st vice pres Empire State Med Soc State Chapter Natl Medical Assn, sec v speaker & house del 1972-74 exec comm 1974; regional advisory group NY Metro Regional Medical Program; past pres Provident Clinical Soc Brooklyn Inc 1969-72; consultant Dept Health Educ & Welfare; mem Health Serv Research Study Section Dept HEW; chmn com comm med Kings Co Med Soc; 1st vice chmn Bedford Stuyvesant Comp Health Plan Council; mem NY Amer & Intl Soc of Nephrology Amer Public Health Assn; bd trust Atlanta Univ Center; NY Coll of Podiatric Med; bd dir NY Assn Ambulatory Care; NY Heart Assn; Public Health Assn NYC; bd dir mem Amer Red Cross of Greater NY; past mem Health Sci Careers Advisory Comm; LaGuardia Comm Coll City Univ of NY; mem Natl Assn C omm Health Centers Inc; mem Med Adv Bd on Hypertension New York City Health Dept; mem Leg Comm Med Soc Co of Kings; subcom Hospital Emer Servs Med Soc Co of Kings; mem Task Force Emer Med Care NY St Health Plan Comm; founder & pres, Health Watch Information and Promotion Service Inc, 1987-. **HONORS/ACHIEVEMENTS:** Natl Found Fellow 1958; Jesse Smith Noyes & Smith Douglas Scholarships; mem Alpha Kappa Mu Natl Honor Soc; Beta Kappa Chi Natl Science Honor Soc; Soc Sigma Xi; author or co-author of more than 30 publications; Health Watch News, brochures on cancer and AIDS; Videos on AIDS. **BUSINESS ADDRESS:** President, AMRON Mgmt Consult Inc, 3020 Glenwood Road, Brooklyn, NY 11210.

GOODWIN, ROBERT T., SR.
Business executive. **PERSONAL:** Born Nov 25, 1915, Camden, SC; married Neal McFadden; children: Robert, Jr, Myrna. **EDUCATION:** Tuskegee Inst, MEd 1962; SC State Coll, 1938; PA State U. **CAREER:** GG&F Devel Co Tuskegee Inst, pres 1973-; Consolidated Constrn Co, owned operated 1957-73; Tuskegee Inst, master instr Building Sci 1968-53; BuildingTrades Pub Schs Lancaster, instr 1945-52; Building Trds Pub Schs Moultrie GA, instr 1938-41. **ORGANIZATIONS:** Pres Tuskegee Area Hm Bldrs Assn; mem SE Alabama Self Help Assn; pres Greenwood Cemetery Inc Tusxkegee Inst Ruling elder Westminster Presb Ch Tuskegee; supt Westminister Presb Ch Sch 1960-65; Polemarch Tuskegee Alumni Chap Kappa Alpha Psi 1967-68. **HONORS/ACHIEVEMENTS:** Hon mention Builder of Hse of Yr 1967 sponsrd by AIA & Better Hms & Grdns; submitted in Nat Competition Wade & Hight Architects; co-designed with son Robert T Jr Goodwin Model SEASHA Home model low cost Housing Brochure. **MILITARY SERVICE:** AUS t/5 1941-45. **BUSINESS ADDRESS:** PO Box 1264, Tuskegee Institute, AL 36088.

GOODWIN, WILLIAM PIERCE, JR.
Physician. **PERSONAL:** Born Sep 18, 1949, Harrisburg, PA; son of William P Goodwin Sr MD and Joan L Robinson-Goodwin; married Gloria Baker, Sep 27, 1980. **EDUCATION:** Dillard Univ New Orleans, BA (Magna Cum Laude) 1972; Meharry Medical Coll, MD 1976. **CAREER:** Univ of OK, assoc prof 1981-85; Martin Army Community Hospital, resident family practice program 1985-88; Reynolds Army Hospital, Ft Sill OK, family practice. **ORGANIZATIONS:** Mem National, American Medical Assocs; mem Amer Assoc of Family Practice 1985, Amer Geriatrics Soc 1986; mem, American Academy of Family Physicians. **HONORS/ACHIEVEMENTS:** Alpha Chi 1971; Beta Kappa Chi Natl Honor Soc 1971. **MILITARY SERVICE:** AUS Lt Col 12 years; Overseas Ribbon, Service Awd, Army Commendation Medal. **HOME ADDRESS:** 2804 NE Heritage Lane, Lawton, OK 73507-3307.

GOODWIN-FULGHAM, ROIETTA
Educator. **PERSONAL:** Born Jan 28, 1948, Oakland, CA; daughter of Roy Goodwin and Dovie Goodwin; children: Keia Syreeta. **EDUCATION:** Utah State Univ Logan UT, BS 1971, MS 1977. **CAREER:** Area Voc Ctr Ogden UT, off occupations supv 1971-75; Yosemite Jr Coll Dist Modesto, instructor 1975-76; Los Rios Comm Coll Dist ARC, instructor 1976-. **ORGANIZATIONS:** Mem Natl Western CA Business Educ Assoc 1976-; mem Natl Educ Assn/CA Teachers Assn 1976-; sec NAACP Central Area Conf 1976-87; vice pres NAACP California State Conf 1988-89; state council rep CA Teachers Assn 1979-85; natl teller NAACP 1980-81; sec Utah State Univ Black Alumni Assn 1980-; chairperson NAACP West Coast Region 1982-83, NAACP ACT-SO Prog Sacramento Branch 1982-85; chairperson Outstanding Business Student Program California Business Educ Assn 1983; office mgr IDS Financial Serv 1985-86; support analyst Wang Labs Inc 1986; consultant Westroots Business Writing Systems 1986-. **HONORS/ACHIEVEMENTS:** Outstanding Program Utah State Univ Alumni Assn 1980; Certified Business Educator Business Educ Certification Council 1976; Certified Professional Sec Professional Sec Intl 1982; Outstanding Young Woman of Amer 1982; NAACP Golden Gavel Award NAACP Northern Area Conf 1984; Outstanding Instructor of the Year Amer River Coll 1986. **HOME ADDRESS:** 6600 Branchwater Way, Citrus Heights, CA 95621. **BUSINESS ADDRESS:** Instructor, Los Rios Comm Coll Dist, American River College, 4700 College Oak Dr, Sacramento, CA 95841.

GOOSBY, ZURETTI L.
Dentist. **PERSONAL:** Born Oct 19, 1922, Oakland, CA; married Jackieline. **EDUCATION:** Univ Ca; BA 1946, DDS. **CAREER:** Priv practice 30 yrs. **ORGANIZATIONS:** Mem SF Human Rights Commn 1968-70; mem past pres San Francisco Bd Educ 5 yrs; mem Nat, Am, CA, San Francisco Dental Assns; chmn Prgm Com BlackLdrshp Forum; bd dirs TV & Sta KQED 1973, 74; Exploratorium Museum 1970-75; mem State Commn Educ Mgmt Evaluatn 1973, 74. **HONORS/ACHIEVEMENTS:** Man of Yr San Francisco Sun-Reporter 1970. **MILITARY SERVICE:** AUS capt 1943-45. **BUSINESS ADDRESS:** 2409 Sacramento St, San Francisco, CA.

GORDEN, FRED A.
Brigadier general. **PERSONAL:** Born Feb 22, 1940, Anniston, AL; son of P J Gordon and Mary Ethel Johnson Harper; married Marcia Ann Stewart; children: Shawn Nicole, Michelle Elizabeth. **EDUCATION:** US Military Academy (West Point), graduate; Middlebury Coll, M Spanish Language & Literature; Attended, Armed Forces Staff Coll, Natl War Coll. **CAREER:** 7th Infantry Div, asst div commander; Office of the Assistant Sec of Defense for Intl Security Affairs Washington DC, dir; Army Office of the Chief of Legislative Liaison, exec officer; Division Artillery 7th Infantry Div, commander; Eighth US Army in Korea, artillery battalion exec officer; field artillery battalion commander,25th infantry div; 25th Infantry, div inspector general; US Military Academy, commandant of cadets. **HONORS/ACHIEVEMENTS:** Defense Disting Serv Medal; Legion of Merit; Bronze Star Medal with V Device; Meritorious Serv Medal; Air Medal; Army Commendation Medal w/one Oak Leaf Cluster; Honorary Dr of Human Letters, St Augustine Coll, 1988; Candle in the Dark, Morehouse Coll, 1989; Alumnus of the Year, Amer Assn of Community & Junior Coll, Middlebury Coll, 1988. **MILITARY SERVICE:** AUS brigadier general. **BUSINESS ADDRESS:** Commandant of Cadets, United States Military Acad, West Point, NY 10996.

GORDON, AARON Z.
Educator. **PERSONAL:** Born Oct 11, 1929, Port Gibson, MS; divorced; children: Aaron, Jr, Aaryce, Alyta. **EDUCATION:** Univ Mi, BS 1952; Wayne State U, MA 1956;Univ Mi, PhD 1974. **CAREER:** Ft Monmouth, Assoc Officers Signal Course 1952; Communications Center Qualification Course, 1952; Teletype Operators School, asst officer in charge; Message Center Clk School, officer in charge; SW Signal School Training Center, Camp San Luis Obispo CA; 3rd Infantry Div AFFE Korea, communication center officer, asst cryptographic officer 1953-54; Br Officers Advance Signal Officers Course, 1963; Command & Gen Staff Coll Ft Levenworth; ICAF, 1974; Air War Coll Maxwell Air Force Base; personnel Officer 1965; S1 5064 USAR Garr, 1967-69; 5032 USAR School, branch officer advanced course instructor 1969-71, dir 1971-73. **ORGANIZATIONS:** Mem Hlth & Curriculum Wrkshp Detroit Pub Schs 1963; co-author Guide to Implementation of Unit of Smiking & Hlth 1963; asst dist ldr E Dist & Dist Ldr 1961-63; com chmn Hlth & Phys Ed Tchrs Inst Day E Dist 1964; sch dist rep Last Two Millage Campaigns Educ TV Tchr Channel 56 Detroit Pub Schs 1964; mem Detroit Orgn Sch Admnstrs & Suprs; Phi Delta Kappa; pgm chmn Detroit Sch Mem's Clu Metro; Detroit Sco Black Educ Admn; Natl All Black Ed; MI Assc Elem Sch Admn Region 1; com mem Midwest Dist AAHPR Conv Detroit 1964; mem Pgmd Educ Soc Detroit 1965; speaker Blue Star Mothers Detroit1963; Carter CME Ch Detroit; bd dir mem Troop 775 BSA 1964; participating guest Focus Negro Life & History Six Wk Work Shop 1967; coordntr Annual Spelling Bee 1967; participant Maximizing Benefits from Testing Workshop Test Admn 1968; participant Ed Admn Workshop 1970-73; dir Professional Skills Dev Workshop Metro Detroit Soc Black Ed Admn Ann Arbor 1973; spkr Hampton Sch Detroit 1973; spkr Joyce Sch Grad 1973. **HONORS/ACHIEVEMENTS:** Bronze Star Decoration; do-holder worlds record Outdoor Distance Medley Relay; co-holder world's record Indoor Distance Medley Relay; co-holder am record Indoor Two Mile & Relay 1951. **MILITARY SERVICE:** USAR col. **BUSINESS ADDRESS:** 15000 Trojan, Detroit, MI 48235.

GORDON, ALEXANDER H., II
Director. **PERSONAL:** Born Jun 13, 1944, Phoenix, AZ; son of Alexander Houston Gordon and Elizabeth DeLouis Davis Gordon; married Loretta Perry, Jan 28, 1967; children: David Anthony, Ellen Alicia. **EDUCATION:** Marquette Univ, BA Speech/Radio TV, 1962-67; LaSalle Correspondence School, Diploma, Business Admin 1965-67. **CAREER:** WTMJ-TV, sales promotion & merchandising dir 1968-69; AVCO Broadcasting Corp, corporate adv/promotion writer 1969-70; WLWI-TV, dir promo publicity 1970-71; WPVI-TV, dir audience promotion, 1971-72, mgr advertising & promotion, 1972-74; WPXI-TV, dir advertising & promotion 1974-77, dir community rel 1977-80; Church of God of Prophecy Donora, PA, pastor 1979-83; WPXI-TV, account exec 1980-87; Church of God of Prophecy Wilkinsburg, PA, pastor 1983-; Dir of Community Serv & Sales, Pittsburgh Pirates, 1988-present. **ORGANIZATIONS:** promotion intern, WTMJ AM-FM TV 1965, promotion asst 1965-67, audience promotion dir 1967-68; chmn Day Camp Com Allegheny Trails Council Boy Scouts Amer, 1978-; pres Neighborhood Centers Assn 1978-83; bd mem Greater Pittsburgh Guild for the Blind 1980-83; vice pres com activities Pittsburgh Ad Club 1975-77; bd mem Hand in Hand Inc 1974-81; mem George Washington Carver Day Com 1977-; mem United Way Review Com II 1977-82; bd mem Urban Youth Action 1981-83; advisory bd mem Booth Mem Home Salvation Army 1977-81; treasurer Broadcasters Promotion Assn 1976-77, bd mem, 1974-77; mem, Marquette Univ Alumni Assn 1980-; pres The Mews of Towne North Owners Assn 1977-79 & 1982-83, 1984-85; bd mem Wilkinsburg Community Ministries 1984-85; Three Rivers Youth Inc, bd mem, 1988-present. **HONORS/ACHIEVEMENTS:** Honorable Pastor Church of God of Prophecy PA 1980-81, 1983-84, 1987; Appreciation Award Allegheny Trails Council Boy Scouts of Am 1985; Clio Awards Comm for Advertising 1975; Golden Reel Award Pittsburgh Radio TV Club 1976; Whitney Young Award for work with minority scouts 1986; Silver Beaver Award, Boy Scouts of America, 1988; Salute to Negro League Baseball, The Homestead Grays and the Pittsburgh Crawfords, 1988. **MILITARY SERVICE:** AUS specialist 5th class 1966-72; Sharpshotter. **BUSINESS ADDRESS:** Dir, Community Serv & Sales, The Pittsburgh Pirates, 600 Stadium Circle, Pittsburgh, PA 15212.

GORDON, ALLAN M.
Educator. **PERSONAL:** Born Aug 31, 1933, Seminole, OK; son of Allan M Gordon and Edith Bruner Gordon; married Delores Aldridge; children: Mark Edward, Angela Catherine. **EDUCATION:** BA 1955; MA 1962; PhD 1969. **CAREER:** CSUS CA, prof art 1969-; OH U, tchg flw 1966-69; Prairie View Clg, asst prof 1964-66. **ORGANIZATIONS:** Mem Natl Conf of Artists; Clg Art Assc of Am Inc; mem Alpha Phi Alpha Frat; mem NAACP; bd dirs Crocker Art Gallery Assc Sacramento 1970-74; bd dirs Amistad II Exhib Recip; Awards Comm Chair, Sacramento Metropolitan Arts Commn. **HONORS/ACHIEVEMENTS:** Awrd for distinguished publications in Art Criticism Fisk Univ 1974-75; fellow Natl Endowment for the Humanities 1979; Echoes of Our Past: The Narrative Artistry of Palmer C Hayden 1988; distinguished alumni Natl Conf of Blacks in Higher Educ 1989. **MILITARY SERVICE:** USAF 1955-59. **HOME ADDRESS:** 5940 Annrud Way, Sacramento, CA 95822.

GORDON, BERTHA COMER
Educator. **PERSONAL:** Born Feb 27, 1916, Louisville, GA; married Carlton. **EDUCATION:** NY U, BS 1945; Hunter Coll, MA 1955. **CAREER:** Bronx NY, asst supt 1972-74, supt 1974-78; Eli Whitney Vocational High School, dept head 1962-69, counselor 1952-62; Manhattan School, teacher 1950-52; NY City Dept Hospital, registered nurse 1937-50. **ORGANIZATIONS:** Mem NY City Admin Women in Educ 1970; past pres & life mem NAACP

Nat Assn Scdry Assn; Scdrry Sch Prin; NY City Supts Assn; Am Assn Sch Admin; Am Vocat Educ Assn; Am NY State NY City Dist 14 Nurses Assn; Doctorate Assn NY City Edn; exec bd Assn Study African Am Life & Hist Hunter Coll NYUniv Alumni Assn. **HONORS/ACHIEVEMENTS:** Hall of Fame Kappa Delta Pi; pres Gr NY Alumni bd; Club Women's City of NY.

GORDON, BRUCE S.
Marketing executive. **PERSONAL:** Born Feb 15, 1946, Camden, NJ; son of Walter Gordon and Violet Gordon; married Genie Alston, Feb 20, 1970; children: Taurin S. **EDUCATION:** Gettysburg Coll, Gettysburg, PA, BA, 1968; Univ of Illinois, Bell Advance Mgmt, 1981; University of PA, Wharton Exec Mgmt; M.I.T. Sloan School of Mgmt, Boston, MS, 1988. **CAREER:** Bell Atlantic Corp, Arlington, VA, init mgmt devel, 1968-70, business officemgr, 1970-72, sales mgr, mktg, 1972-74, personnel supvr, 1974-76, market mgmt supvr, 1976-78, mktg mgr, 1978-80, div staff mgr, 1980-81, div operations mgr, 1981, div mgr, phone center, 1981-83, mktg mgr II, 1983-84, gen mgr, mktg/sales, 1985, vice pres mktg, 1988-. **ORGANIZATIONS:** Founder and past vice-pres, Alliance of Black Mgrs; member, Toastmasters Intl; member, bd of trustees, Gettysburg Coll; direc, Urban League, 1984-86; member, bd of direcs, Inroads of Philadelphia, 1985-88; chair, United Negro Coll Fund Telethon, 1985-86; volunteer, United Way, 1986-88. **HONORS/ACHIEVEMENTS:** Mass Inst of Tech, Alfred P Sloan fellow, 1987.

GORDON, CHARLES D.
Housing official. **PERSONAL:** Born Aug 10, 1934, Memphis, TN; married Hazel D Mannings; children: Debra, Charles, Jr, Marshall, Kenneth, Derrick, Carlton. **EDUCATION:** Univ WY; TN State; Hampton Inst; Roosevelt U. **CAREER:** Chicago Hous Auth, clk, mgmt training prog, asst mgr, hous mgr I, hous mgr II 1961-. **ORGANIZATIONS:** Mem NAHRO; mem Cntrl Southside Comm Workers; bd dir Horizon House; lectr various schs; mem Dist Ii Educ Counc; mem Area A Besea Coun Dep commr hit basketball league, hous invitational tour; bd dir Afro-Am touch football league; bd dir housing bowling leadue. **HONORS/ACHIEVEMENTS:** Won commnr flag beautification grounds within CIIA 1971-74; placed 3rd City Chicago beautif grounds mgr Wentworth Gardens 1974; achvmnt plaque for outstndg achvmnt as hous mgr Comm Wentworth. **MILITARY SERVICE:** USAF s/sgt 1955-61. **BUSINESS ADDRESS:** 3640 S State St, Chicago, IL 60609.

GORDON, CHARLES EUGENE
Educator. **PERSONAL:** Born May 31, 1938, Gallatin, TN; married Barbara Gibbs. **EDUCATION:** History Western MI U, BS 1962; Wayne State U, MEd spl educ for emotion disturbed 1970;Univ of MI, PhD higher educ admin 1976. **CAREER:** Wayne State Univ, dir Office of Special Student Serv Programs 1970-; Project Upward Bound, dir 1968-70; Detroit Youth Home, boys counselor, supvr 1965-67; Detroit Public Schools, secondary teacher Social Studies, Special Educ 1962-65. **ORGANIZATIONS:** Mem ANWC bd dirs; past pres Region V Trio Adv Coun; past pres MI Coun of Educ opp progs; past exec bd mem Nat Alliance ofr grad & professional Edn;exec bd mem Nat Assn of Minority Financial Aid Admin; numerous professional & bus orgns; mem Am Assn of Higher Edn; Am Pers & Guid Assn; Nat Coord Coun of Educ Opp Progs; Nat Vocat Guid Assn; Mid-West Assn of Educ Opp Prog Personnel; MI Coun of Educ Opp Progs; Nat Alliance for Grad & Professional Edn; Am Educ Res Assn. **HONORS/ACHIEVEMENTS:** Recip Region V citation of merit US Ofc of Edn; Distingd Serv Awd MI Coun of Educ Opp Progs; Outstndg Serv Awd The MI Inter-Assn of Black Bus & Engineering Students; Three-yr Appntmt to Nat Adv Coun on Finan Aid to Sutdents, Hon Casper W Weinberger; pres exec dir Cybernetic Res Systems Inc; author Employer Attitudes in Hiring Culturally Different Youth, Careeer Educ Implications for Counseling Minority Students Career Edn; Short Steps on a Long Journey & The Devel Sys Model as a Tool of Prog Adminst & Eval, several art in professional jour. **MILITARY SERVICE:** AUS radio operator.

GORDON, CHARLES FRANKLIN
Physician. **PERSONAL:** Born Oct 31, 1921, Ward, AL; married Marion; children: Charles Jr, Jacquelyn, Jan. **EDUCATION:** Fisk U, BA 1943; Meharry Med Coll, MD 1947. **CAREER:** Self, physician; Golden State Med Assn, bd dir 1972-77; Perris Valley Comm Hosp, 1972-77; Riverside Comm Hosp, 1970-73; LA Co Hlth Dept & LA City Hlth Dept, radiology & pulmonary resd; LA City Hlth Dept; Polemarch Riv Alumni Chap KAY Frat; fndr. **ORGANIZATIONS:** Life mem KAY Frat; pres Perris Rotary Club 1971-72. **HONORS/ACHIEVEMENTS:** 25 yr serv awd Meharry 1972; Perris Comm Serv Awd 1975; 30 yr serv awd KAY Frat 1977. **MILITARY SERVICE:** AUS MC capt 1954. **BUSINESS ADDRESS:** 2226 Ruby Dr, Ste 5, Perris, CA 92370.

GORDON, CLIFFORD WESLEY
Clergyman. **PERSONAL:** Born Jul 14, Youngstown, OH; married Janet E Jones; children: Carole, Brenda, Brian, Constance, Marie. **EDUCATION:** Nat Coll of Massage & Phys Therapy; Mckinley Roosevelt U; Wilberforce U; Payne Theol Sem; Chicago Theol Sem; Antioch Coll; OH U; Monrovia Coll;Univ Chgo. **CAREER:** Gospel Bethel AME Ch, pastor ministe; OH, KY, PA, MI, pastored in; Jr Coll in OH, tch; Periodicals, writer; OH Ann Conf, sec; 5th Dist Ct Berrien Co, MI, magistrate. **ORGANIZATIONS:** MI civil rights worker. **HONORS/ACHIEVEMENTS:** Cited by Am Legion, Omegas, city of Benton Harbor, Monrovia Coll of Liberia, W Africa; Sickle Cell Anemia Worker Berrier Co. **BUSINESS ADDRESS:** 414 W Vermont St, Indianapolis, IN 46202.

GORDON, DARRELL R.
Business executive. **PERSONAL:** Born May 18, 1926, Philadelphia, PA; married Joan. **EDUCATION:** Univ of Pennsylvania, BS. **CAREER:** Gordon Buick Inc, pres bd chmn 1972-; Gordon Buick Cadillac Oldsmobile Inc, Pres & Bd Chmn, 1988-. **ORGANIZATIONS:** Dir, Philadelphia Industrial Development Corp, 1988-; Dir, Pennsylvania Automobile Assn, 1987-. **BUSINESS ADDRESS:** President/Board Chairman, Gordon Buick, Inc, Broad St & Roosevelt Blvd, Philadelphia, PA 19140.

GORDON, EDMUND W.
Educator. **PERSONAL:** Born Jun 13, 1921, Goldsboro, NC; married Susan Gitt; children: Edmond T, Christopher W, Jessica G, Johanna S. **EDUCATION:** Howard Univ, BS 1942, BD 1945; Amer Univ, MA 1950; Columbia Univ Tchrs Coll, EdD 1957. **CAREER:** Ferkauf Graduate School Yeshiva Univ, chmn dept of special educ 1959-60; Albert Einstein Coll of Medicine Yeshiva Univ, resident, asst prof of pediatrics 1961-; Project Head Start, dir div of rsch & evaluation 1965-67; Ferkauf Univ, chmn dept of educ, psychology & guidance 1965-68; Columbia Univ, chmn dept of guidance 1968-73; Teachers Coll, dir div of health serv science & educ 1970-73; Amer Journal of Orthopsychiatry, editor 1978-83; Columbia Univ, prof dept of applied human devel & guidance 1979; "Review of Research in Education", editor 1981-84; Yale Univ Graduate School & Coll of Medicine, prof Psychology 1979-. **ORGANIZATIONS:** Consult Rand Corp 1972-; NIE 1970-; Educ Testing Svc; fellow Amer Assn for Advancement of Sci; Amer Psychol Assn; mem Educ Com Amer Educ Rsch Journal; NY Statewide Com on Educ Oppor; com on tests Amer Psychol Assn; trustee Pub Educ Assn; assoc trustee Svgs Bank of Rockland Co Monsey; fellow &mem Educ Bd Amer Orthopsychiatric Assn; mem Assn of Black Psychologists; APGA; AAUP; AERA; Child & Family Develop Res Review Com Office of Child Develop 1974-77; bd dir Natl Health Inst. **HONORS/ACHIEVEMENTS:** Awd for Outstanding Achievements in Educ Howard Alumni 1973; elected Natl Acad of Educ 1978. **BUSINESS ADDRESS:** Professor of Psychology, YaleUniv Coll of Med, Box 11a Yale Station, New Haven, CT 06520.

GORDON, ETHEL M.
Educator. **PERSONAL:** Born Nov 16, 1911, Antreville; married Maxie S Gordon; children: Maxie S, Thomas A. **EDUCATION:** Benedict Coll, BA 1939; Temple Univ, MEd 1955; MI State Univ, further study 1966; Harvard Univ, further study 1969. **CAREER:** Starr SC, public school teacher 1934-38; Pendelton SC, 1938-42, asst librarian, 1944-45, bookstore mgr, 1945-54; Dept of Elementary Educ, chmn 1955-69; Benedict Coll, elementary teacher trainer 1970-. **ORGANIZATIONS:** Mem World Traveler; NEA; SC Reading Assn; Intl Reading Assn; Assn Tchr Educs; SC Educ Assn; Natl Assn Univ Women; SC Coun of Human Relat; League of Women Voters; mem Queen Esther Chap Eastern Star; mem Sigma Gamma Rho Sor; mem Jack & Jills of Amer Inc; historian Woman's Conv Aux; Natl BaptConv USA Inc; fdr SC Assn Ministers Wives pres 2 yrs; statistician SC Women's Missionary & Educ Conv; asst sec Gethsemane Assn; instr Natl Sunday Sch & BTU Cong; mem Phi Delta Kappa Univ SC Chap 1977. **HONORS/ACHIEVEMENTS:** Publ book "Unfinished Business" 1976; Appreciation Plaque Sr Class Benedict Coll 1966, 1975; Women's Conv Aux to Natl Baptist Conv USA Inc 1971; Hon LLD Morris Coll Sumter SC 1975. **BUSINESS ADDRESS:** Elem Teacher Trainer, Benedict College, Columbia, SC 29204.

GORDON, FANNETTA NELSON
Educator. **PERSONAL:** Born Nov 29, 1919, Hayneville, AL; divorced. **EDUCATION:** Univ of Pittsburgh, BA 1941, MEd 1960;Univ of WA, MA 1967; Franklin & Marshall Coll, 1970. **CAREER:** PA Dept of Secondary Language Educ, sr adv st coord 1973-; PA Dept of Educ, german educ adv 1969-73; Fillion Music Studios, teacher Piano, French & German 1964-69; Pittsburgh Bd of Educ, teacher German, Engligh Language background english for foreigners 1955-69; State Dept of Welfare Allegheny County Bd of Asst, social worker 1944-45, 1947-50; Dept of Commerce, weather man plttng supvr 1943; City of Pittsburgh YMCA, youth advisor 1941-43; Fanneta Nelson Gordon Music & Dance Studio, owner & operator 1941-69; Cole Tutoring Serv, tutor French, German, English 1960-65; Penn Hall Acad Private School, teacher summer school. **ORGANIZATIONS:** Alpha Kappa Alpha Kappa Alpha 1938-; st yth adv in PA NAACP 1942-44; mem NAACP 1936-; fdr mem PA Blk Conf on Higher Educ 1971-; liaison with PA Dept of Educ PA Blk Conf on Higher Edn; fdr finan sec mem govrning counc liaison with PA Dept of Educ PA Conf on Blk Basic Edn; mem steering com Natl Blk Alliance on Grad Level Edn; Natl Assn for Blk Child Devel 1976-; Am Counc on the Tchng of Frgn Lang 1969-; Nat Counc of St Supr of Frgn Lang 1969-; PA St Modrn Lang Assn 1960-; Nat Assn on Bilingual Educ 1973-; Tchrs of Eng to Spkrs of Other Lang 1972-; Nat Counc of Negro Wmn;Univ of Pittsburgh Alumna Assn;Univ of WA Alumna Assn; YMCA; Ch of the Holy Cross (Episcpl); st coord Indochinese Refugee Asst Edn. **HONORS/ACHIEVEMENTS:** 1 of 22 German tchrs from the cntry named as Fellows in the Exprncd Tchr Fllwshp PrgmUniv of WA 1966-67; Nat Def Educ Act FlwshpUniv of WA German; Nat Def Educ Act Flwshp StanfordUniv Bad Boll Germany; articles " Articulation in the Tchng of German" 1969; "The Soc Purpose of Lang Lrng" 1974; "The Status of Frgn Lang Educ & What Tchrs Can Do to Improve It" 1973; "Strategies for Improving the Status of Lang Tchng Lrng" 1976; "Is Frgn Lang Educ Necessary" 1977; "Frgn Lang Lrngng an open door to the world" 1976; "frgn lang for the gifted & talented"; citat serv to the cmmnwlth Gov Milton J Shapp PA; schlrshp Dawson Studios; schlrshp Fillion Mus Studios. **BUSINESS ADDRESS:** Bur of Curriculum Services PA, Box 911, Harrisburg, PA 17126.

GORDON, HELEN A.
Attorney. **PERSONAL:** Born Jul 20, 1923, New York; married Joseph A Bailey; children: Josette, Jonathan, Gordon. **EDUCATION:** Brooklyn Law Sch, LlB, JD 1950; Hunter Coll of City of NY, AB 1947. **CAREER:** Priv Prac Gordon & Wilkins, atty; AAA, arbitrator. **ORGANIZATIONS:** Mem bd trustees Grahan Sch for Child Hastings on Hudson, NY; mem bd of dir E Tremone Child Care Cntr; mem Bronx & Women's Bar Assn; Gothamettes Inc of NY; lecturer in continuing educ City Coll NY. **BUSINESS ADDRESS:** Attorney at Law, Gordon & Wilkins, 304 W 138th St, New York, NY 10030.

GORDON, JOSEPH G., II
Scientist. **PERSONAL:** Born Dec 25, 1945, Nashville, TN; son of Joseph Gordon and Juanita Gordon; married Ruth Maye Gordon. **EDUCATION:** Harvard Coll, AB 1966; MIT, PhD 1970. **CAREER:** CA Inst of Tech, asst prof chem 1970-75; IBM San Jose Rsch Lab, rsch staff mem 1975-, interfacial electrochem mgr 1978-84, interfacial science mgr 1984-86, technical asst to dir of research 1986-88; interfacial chemistry & structure mgr 1988-. **ORGANIZATIONS:** Mem Amer Chem Soc, Royal Soc of Chemistry, Electrochemical Soc, Sigma Xi, Amer Assoc Advanc Science; Caltech Y, bd of dir 1973-75, chmn 1975; treas San Francisco Sect of Electrochem Soc 1982-84, pres 1984-85; sec San Francisco Bay Area Chap of the Natl Orgn for Prof Advancement of Black Chemists & Chem Engrs 1983-86; Gordon Research Conference on Electrochemistry, chmn 1987; mem American Physical Society; mem of exec bd, National Organization for the Professional Advancement of Black Chemists & Chem Engineers 1986-92. **HONORS/ACHIEVEMENTS:** NSF Predoctoral Fellow MIT 1967-70; 3 patents; 50 articles in professional journals. **BUSINESS ADDRESS:** IBM Research Division, Almaden Research Center, K33/801, 650 Harry Rd, San Jose, CA 95120-6099.

GORDON, LANCASTER ANTHONY
Professional athlete. **PERSONAL:** Born Jun 24, 1960, Jackson, MS. **EDUCATION:** Louisville, Recreation 1984. **CAREER:** Los Angeles Clippers, guard 1984-. **HONORS/ACHIEVEMENTS:** Named 2nd Team All-Am by The Sporting News & 3rd Team All-Am by Bsktbl Weekly; voted to the 2nd Team All-Metro Conf for the 2nd consecutive season; was oneof final cuts on Bobby Knight's USA Olympic Bsktbl team that competed in 1984 Olym-

pics in Los Angeles; named to 1984 Mideast Region All-Tournmnt team after scoring 25 pts agnst KY. **BUSINESS ADDRESS:** Los Angeles Clippers, 3939 S Figueroa St, 777 Sports St, Los Angeles, CA 90037.

GORDON, LEVAN
Judge. **PERSONAL:** Born Apr 10, 1933, Philadelphia, PA; married Vivian J Goode; children: Shari-Lyn L Pinkett. **EDUCATION:** Lincoln Univ Pennsylvania, AB; Howard Univ Law Sch, LLB; Pennsylvania State Univ. **CAREER:** Gov Commn Chester, PA, assoc counsel 1964; Philadelphia Housing Info Serv, exec dir 1966-68; Pennsylvania Labor Rel Bd, hearing examiner 1971-74; Municipal Court of Philadelphia, judge, appointed 1974, elected 1975 Court of Common Please of Philadelphia, elected judge 1979; Temple Univ School of Criminal Justice, instructor 1980-; Georgetown Univ Intensive Session in Trial Advocacy Skills, instructor 1984-; Court of Common Pleas, judge. **ORGANIZATIONS:** Mem Alpha Phi Alpha, Zeta Omicron Lambda, Lincoln Univ Alumni Assn, W Philadelphia HS Alumni Assn, Philadelphia & PA Bar Assn, Lawyers Club of Phila, Amer Judicature Soc, Amer Bar Assn, Natl Bar Assn, Pennsylvania Conf of Trial Judges; bd of dir Columbia N Branch YMCA; mem Philadelphia Tribune Charities, Philadelphia Tribune Bowling League, Chris J Perry Lodge Elks IBPOE of W, Natl Bowling Assn, Amer Bowling Congress, AFNA Preceptor Program, Natl Assn of Blacks in Criminal Justice, World Assn of Judges, Governors Advisory Comm on Probation; bd of dir Natl Kidney Found S PA, Wharton Centre, Men of Malvern, Supportive Child/Adult Network (SCAN); chmn bd of trustees/s upr of jr ushers Tindley Temple United Methodist Church; Black Methodist for Church Renewal; bd of trustees Lincoln Univ; bd dir Natl Assn of Black in Criminal Justice. **HONORS/ACHIEVEMENTS:** Distinguished Serv Award Liberty Bell Dist Philadelphia Council Boy Scouts of Amer; Community Serv Award Strawberry Mansion Civic Assn Puerto Rican Comm Serv Award; Lincoln Univ Alumni Achievement Award; Man of the Yr Zeta Omicron Lambda Chap Alpha Phi Alpha 1975; The Assn of Business & Professional Women of Philadelphia & vicinity Man of the Year Award 1984; McMichael Home & School Assn Distinguished Serv Award; The Methodist Men Tindley Temple United Methodist Church 1986 Award of Excellence; member, West Philadelphia High School Hall of Fame. **MILITARY SERVICE:** AUS 1953-55; USNR Reserve 1958-61. **BUSINESS ADDRESS:** Judge, Court of Common Pleas, 1004 One E Penn Sq, Philadelphia, PA 19107.

GORDON, LOIS JACKSON
Music educator. **PERSONAL:** Born Feb 03, 1932, Springfield, OH; children: Joan, Catherine. **EDUCATION:** Fisk U, AB 1953;Univ Cincinnati, MusM 1971. **CAREER:** Voorhees Jr Coll, tchr 1953-54; Cincinnati Pub Sch, 1961-66;Univ Cincinnati, pvt instr 1969-; Kenner Gen Mills Found Talent prog, dir. **ORGANIZATIONS:** Mem Wmn's Com Cincinnati Symphony; Am Schlshp Assn; Music Ed Nat Conf Alpha Kappa Alpha Sor. **BUSINESS ADDRESS:** U Cincinnati Colls Conservator, Cincinnati, OH.

GORDON, MAXIE S., SR.
Educator, clergyman, world traveler, town leader. **PERSONAL:** Born Dec 10, 1910, Greenville, SC; married Ethel Mae McAdams; children: Maxie Jr, Dr Thomas A Gordon. **EDUCATION:** Benedict Coll, BA, BD; Oberlin Coll, MA, STM; Vanderbilt-Oberlin, MDiv; Univ Chicago, grad study; Attended, Sorbonne via Temple, Harvard Univ; Benedict Coll, DD Hon. **CAREER:** Friendship Jr Coll, Rock Hill SC, teacher 1939-42; Benedict Coll, teacher 1942-; Royal Baptist Church, Anderson SC, pastor 1939-45; New First Calvary, Columbia SC, pastor/builder 1945-. **ORGANIZATIONS:** SC rep Foreign Mission Bd Natl Bapt Conv 1962-; author-ed Vestpocket Commentary (Flashlights); offcl rep Natl Bapt Conv Ghana's Independence 1957;mem Mayor's Youth Comm & Comm Human Relations Council 1955-72; SC Commn on Aging 1967-73; Gr Carolina Human Rights Commn 1970-; Urban League; life mem NAACP; mem Amer Acad of Religion; mem Phi Delta Kappa Professional Frat; mem SCLC; mem various civic & professional organizations; official delegete to World Council of Churches 1954; Omega Psi Phi; 32 Degree Mason Prince Hall Affiliate. **HONORS/ACHIEVEMENTS:** Special Awd for 30 yrs of Teaching at Benedict Coll; listed in many biographical volumes.

GORDON, MILTON A.
Educator. **PERSONAL:** Born May 25, 1935, Chicago, IL; married Louise J Townsend; children: Patrick Francis, Vincent Michael. **EDUCATION:** Xavier Univ New Orleans, BS 1957; Univ of Detroit, AM 1960; IL Inst of Tech, PhD 1968. **CAREER:** Univ of Chicago Math Lab Applied Science, educator; Chicago Public School System, educator; Loyola Univ of Chicago, educator; IL Inst of Tech, educator; Univ of Detroit, educator; Chicago State Univ, prof of math 1978-; Coll of Arts & Science, dean 1978-. **ORGANIZATIONS:** Dir Afro-Amer Studies Prog Loyola Math Assoc of Amer, Chicago Math Club, African Assoc of Black Studies, Sigma Xi, Assoc of Social & Behavioral Sci; mem City of Evanston Youth Commiss; chmn Archdiocese of Chicago School Bd 1977-79; bd dir Dem Party of Evanston; mem State of IL Data Comm, Phi Delta Kappa, Amer Conf of Acad Deans, Counc of Coll & Arts & Sci NSF 1964, IL Inst of Tech, Afro-Amer Studies KY State Coll 1971; Rice Univ 1972, Univ of WI 1972, Amer Men & Women of Sci 1972. **HONORS/ACHIEVEMENTS:** Outstanding Educators of Amer 1973; listed in Who's Who in Midwest; honorary registrar of West Point Mil Acad 1973; author "Enrollment Analysis of Black Students in Inst of Higher Ed from 1940-72", "Correlation Between HS Performance & ACT & SAT Test Scores by Race & Sex". **BUSINESS ADDRESS:** Dean, College of Arts & Science, 6525 N Sheridan Rd, Chicago, IL 60626.

GORDON, ROBERT FITZGERALD
Dentist. **PERSONAL:** Born Nov 07, 1928; married Mabel Enid Welds; children: Wayne, Gregory. **EDUCATION:** Howard U, BSc 1958, DDS 1964. **CAREER:** Jersey City Med Cntr, dental intern 1964-66; Somerset, NJ, pvt prac 1966-; Somerset Co Rural Sch Dental Hlth Svc, trustee. **ORGANIZATIONS:** Mem Am Dental Assn; NJ Middlesex Co Commonwealth Dental Soc; mem Alpha Phi Alpha. **BUSINESS ADDRESS:** 812 Hamilton St, Somerset, NJ 08873.

GORDON, ROBERT L.
Assoc. consultant & psychologist. **PERSONAL:** Born Jun 23, 1941, Lexington, KY; married Mamie R Baker; children: Kimberly; Cedric. **EDUCATION:** Edwards Waters College, BS 1964; Florida A&M Univ, 1965; College of Finger Lakes, MA Psychology 1967. **CAREER:** Waycross, GA, psychology teacher & baseball coach 1964-65; New York Harlem Astronauts, pro basketball player 1965-67; Ford Motor Co, labor relations 1969-84;Premier Personnel Placement Consultant, Inc, president 1984-85; Kappa Alpha Psi Fraternity, Inc, grand polemarch. **ORGANIZATIONS:** Chairman War Chest Com Nat Assault on Illiteracy 1984-85; member President Reagan's Task Force on Priv Sec 1984-85; board member Kappa Alpha Psi Foundation, 1984-85; co-chairman Labor & Industry Committee NAACP, Ann Arbor Branch 1984-85. **HONORS/ACHIEVEMENTS:** 100 Most Influential Blacks (Ebony) 1982-85; received more than 40 awards throughout the US 1982-85; Honorary Citizen's Award State of Kentucky 1983; Kentucky Colonel State of Kentucky 1983; received more than 200 plaques and awards. **BUSINESS ADDRESS:** Grand Polemarch, Kappa Alpha Psi Fraternity Inc, Natl Headquarters, 2320 N Broad St, Philadelphia, PA 19132.

GORDON, RONALD EUGENE
Production supervisor. **PERSONAL:** Born Feb 22, 1946, Springfield, OH; married Felicity Ralph; children: Mark, Rebecca, Ryan. **EDUCATION:** Central State Univ, BS 1973; Xavier Univ, MBA 1976. **CAREER:** Continental Can Co, production supervisor 1971-77; Formica Corp, production supervisor 1977-79; Miller Brewing Co, production supervisor 1979-. **HONORS/ACHIEVEMENTS:** The Olubandek Dada Awd Dept of Business Admin Central State Univ 1973. **MILITARY SERVICE:** USAF sgt 4 yrs. **BUSINESS ADDRESS:** Production Supervisor, Miller Brewing Co, PO Box 1170, Reidsville, NC 27320.

GORDON, VIVIAN V.
Educator. **PERSONAL:** Born Apr 15, 1934, Washington, DC; daughter of Thomas Verdell and Susie Verdell; married Thomas & Susie Verdell; Ronald Clayton Gordon (divorced); children: Ronald Clayton Jr, Susan Gordon Akkad. **EDUCATION:** VA State Univ, BS 1955; Univ of PA, MA Sociology 1957; Univ of VA Charlottesville, PhD Sociology 1974. **CAREER:** Women's Christian Alliance Child Welfare Agency, social work child welfare 1956-57; Library of Congress, resch asst 1957; House Comm on Educ & Labor, coord of rsch 1963; Legislative Reference Serv Library of Congress, educ & social sci analyst 1957-63; Upward Bound Project Univ of CA, asst dir 1966-67; CA State Coll Educ Participation in Comm Prog, dir 1967-69; Univ of VA Dept of Sociology, teaching asst 1971-73; Univ of VA Dept of Sociology, asst prof & chrprsn 1974-79, assoc prof Dept of Soc 1979-84; State Univ of NY, chairperson & assoc prof dept of African & African-Amer Studies 1984-85. Assoc Prof, 1985. **ORGANIZATIONS:** mem Amer Sociology Assn 1969-71, 1973-75, 1978-80; mem So Sociological Soc 1971-; chmn MACAA; mem Natl Council for Black Studies; mem edit bd The Negro Educ Review; author of The Self-Concept of Black Am Univ of Amer 1977; numerous publications & lectures including "Black Women/Feminism/Women's Studies" The Caucus of Black Women Conf on Black Women Chicago 1983; "African American Woman, Feminism & Black Liberation" Third World Press Chicago 1984; "A Focus Upon Afrocentricity and the Curriculum Perspective in Higher Education" presented in a series of lectures to faculty & students, Savannah State College 1984; "Afrocentricity, The Scholarly Tradition and Implications for Law Education" Natl Bar Assn/Amer Bar Assn Legal Educ Conf Washington DC, 1984; Other papers, 1985-89; Consultant, Albany Annual Critical Black Issues Conf; Coordinator, NCBS Student Contest, 1984-89; Coordinator, SUNY, Albany African American Family Symposium, 1989. **HONORS/ACHIEVEMENTS:** Outstanding Serv Award, Parents Assn of Jordan HS 1968; Bethune-Roosevelt Awd for Outstanding Contributions to Race Relations at the Univ The Soc of Artemas Univ of VA 1974; Black Scholar in Residence, Gettysburg Coll 1978; rep VA Comm Serv Progs White House Meeting on Comm Action 1980; Visiting Black Scholar Ball State Univ 1981; Martin Luther King Awd for Serv to Students, Alpha Phi Alpha 1982; course selected for Directory of Model Courses Inst of the Black World Atlanta GA "African Amer Women" Contemporary Issues" 1983; Awd for Distinguished Serv to Students & Comm NAACP UVA Branch 1983; Visiting Mentor in Residence Savannah State Coll 1984; Distinguished Serv to Students Awd Council of Black Student Org, Univ of VA, 1984; Outstanding Serv to African Students, SUNY, African Students Assn, 1985; The Albany Black Arts & Culture Award, 1985; SUNY, Outstanding Black Woman, 1989; SUNY, Outstanding Serv to Black Students, 1989. **BUSINESS ADDRESS:** Assoc Prof, State Univ of NY, Dept of African-Amer Studies, Albany, NY 12222.

GORDON, WALTER CARL, JR.
Surgeon. **PERSONAL:** Born Oct 25, 1927, Albany, GA; married Suzanne Patterson; children: Walter III, Tia. **EDUCATION:** Hampton Inst, BS 1947; Tuskegee Inst, MS 1948; Meharry Med Coll, MD 1955; Letterman Army Hosp, intern 1956; Walter Reed Army Hosp, resd 1961. **CAREER:** Phoebe Putney Meml Palmyra Pk Hosp, surgeon; Fitzsimmons Gen Hosp, chf gen sur 1966-68; Am Coll of Surgeons, flw. **ORGANIZATIONS:** Mem AMA; Dougherty Co Med Assn; GA State Med Assn; Pan-Am Med Assn; field fac Meharry Med Coll; dipl Am Coll of Surgeons; bd dir Albany ChptAm Cancer Soc; guest lctr Emergency Med Tech; chf emer room com Phoebe Putney Meml Hosp; mem Alpha Phi Alpha Frat; bd dir FL A&M; Albany State Coll; mem Criterion Club; Albany C of C. **HONORS/ACHIEVEMENTS:** Recip 3 Commendation Med AUS; Legion of Merit. **MILITARY SERVICE:** AUS lt col 12 1/2 yrs. **BUSINESS ADDRESS:** 401-A S Madison St, Albany, GA 31701.

GORDON, WALTER LEAR, III
Attorney at Law. **PERSONAL:** Born Mar 06, 1942, Los Angeles, CA; married Teresa Sanchez; children: Maya Luz. **EDUCATION:** Ohio State Univ, BA 1963; UCLA, MPA 1965, JD 1973, PhD 1981. **CAREER:** UCLA Law School, lecturer 1978-82; private practice, attorney. **ORGANIZATIONS:** Bd mem SCLC-West 1980-85; mem Langston Bar Assoc 1986. **HONORS/ACHIEVEMENTS:** Published "The Law and Private Police," Rand 1971, "Crime and Criminal Law," Associated Faculty Press 1981; has also published several articles. **BUSINESS ADDRESS:** Attorney at Law, 2822 S Western Ave, Los Angeles, CA 90018.

GORDON, WINFIELD JAMES
Retired broadcast journalist/anchorman, political staffer. **PERSONAL:** Born Oct 18, 1926, Camden, NJ; son of Rev Winfiled Arandas (deceased) and Tabitha (Payton) Gordon; married Genevieve Emily Owens, Jun 01, 1946; children: Brenda Seri Law, Winfield James Jr, James Noble. **EDUCATION:** Graduate of various military schools to qualify as a broadcast journalist, public speaker, reporter/researcher. **CAREER:** KFMB-TV,TV news report; US Navy, sr chf journ 1965; WHIM, disc jcky 1955-56; WPFM, disc jcky 1955-56, news reader 1953-55; WRIB, disc jcky 1967-68; AFRTS-LA, news annc 1964-66; Ethnic Faces, host prod 1972-75; Interntl Hour, host 1970-72; weekend anchor 1976-81; council and mayoral staff positions 1983-86. **ORGANIZATIONS:** Mem Sigma Delta Chi; mem SD Prof Chptr 1973-; mem SD Cntry Boy Scout Cncl 1974-; mem dir bd Encanto Boys Club 1974-; mem AFTRA & Fra Br 9 1972. **HONORS/ACHIEVEMENTS:** Honor Golden Hill United Pres Chrc 1976; Comm Serv Awd Omega Psi Phi Frat 1978; Comm Serv Awd Pub Comm; nominated for a Bronze Star for service in Vietnam as the NCOIC of the Amer Forces Vietnam Network

key station: Saigon. **MILITARY SERVICE:** USN 1943-69; AF/USMA Vietnam war; nominated for Bronze Star.

GORDONE, CHARLES
Playwright, actor, director. **PERSONAL:** Born Oct 12, 1925, Cleveland, OH; son of William Gordone and Camille Morgan Gordon; married Jeanne Warner, 1959; children: Stephen, Judy, Leah Carla, David. **EDUCATION:** CA State Univ, Los Angeles, BA, 1952; also attended NY Univ, Univ of CA, Los Angeles, and Columbia Univ. **CAREER:** Actor in plays, including "Of Mice & Men", 1953, "The Blacks," 1961-65, and "The Trials of Brother Jero", 1967; director of plays, including "Rebels and Bugs," 1958, "Peer Gynt," 1959, "Tobaco Road," 1960, "Detective Story," 1960, "No Place to Be Somebody," 1967; "Cures," 1978, and "Under the Boardwalk," 1979. Co-founder of Comm for the Employment of Negro Performers, 1962; mem, Commn on Civil Disorders, 1967; instructor, Cell Block heatre, Yardville and Bordontown Detention Ctrs, NJ, 1977-78; judge, MO Arts Coun Playwriting Competition, 1978; instructor, New School for Social Research, 1978-79; mem, Ensemble Studio Theatre and Actors Studio. **HONORS/ACHIEVEMENTS:** Author of play, No Place To Be Somebody, prod in NYC at Sheridan Sq Playhouse, Nov, 1967, Bobbs-Merrill, 1969; Obie Award for best actor, 1953, for perf in "Of Mice and Men"; Pulitzer Prize for drama, LA Critics Circle Award, and Drama Desk Award, all 1970, all for No Place to Be Somebody; Vernon Rice Award, 1970; grant from Natl Inst of Arts & Letters, 1971. **BUSINESS ADDRESS:** Charles Gordone, Springer-Warner Productions, 365 West End Ave, New York, NY 10017.
*

GORDY, BERRY, JR.
Business executive, producer, composer,. **PERSONAL:** Born in Detroit, MI; divorced; children: Berry IV, Terry James, Hazel Joy, Kerry A, Kennedy W Stefan K. **CAREER:** Opened record store; worked in auto factory; wrote song "Reet Petite" for Jackie Wilson which became 1st Gordy hit; wrote "You Made Me So Very Happy"; then promoted & dist records himself; started Tamla record label w/Smokey Robinson & the Mircales as first group record "Way Over There" sold 60,000 copies, "Shop Around" sold over a million copies; formed Motown Record Corp signed stable of little known singers who later became famous, Temptations, Four Tops, Supremes, Martha Reeves & the Vandellas; co moved hdqrs to Hollywood 1970; controls 8 subsidiaries formed to produce movies "Lady Sings the Blues"; "Mahagony"; Motown Records among top 3 rcrd co; Motown Picts,exec prod; Motown Ind, bd chmn, pres. **ORGANIZATIONS:** Mem Dirs Guild Amer; chmn Motown Ind entertainment complex. **HONORS/ACHIEVEMENTS:** Bus Achievement Awd Interracial Cncl for Bu Oppt 1967; 2nd Ann Amer Music Awd for Outstanding Contrib to Indus 1975; One of Five Leading Entrepreneurs of Nation Babson Coll 1978; Whitney M Young Jr Awd Los Angeles Urban League 1980; exec producer film "Berry Gordy's The Last Dragon" 1984; elected a Gordon Grand Fellow at Yale Univ 1985. **BUSINESS ADDRESS:** Chairman, Motown Records, 6255 W Sunset, 18th Floor, Los Angeles, CA 90028.

GORDY, DESIREE D'LAURA
Attorney. **PERSONAL:** Born Jul 14, 1956, Long Beach, CA; married Terry J Gordy Sr; children: Terry James Jr, Whitney Jade. **EDUCATION:** San Diego State Univ, BA 1978; Southwestern Univ Sch of Law, JD 1982. **CAREER:** Work Records a div of MCA Records, outside counsel and business affairs 1987-; Jobete Music Co Inc, Motown Productions Inc, Motown Record Corp, in-house counsel to all three corporations 1983-. **ORGANIZATIONS:** Mem Black Women Lawyers Assoc, John Langston Bar Assoc, CA Women's Lawyers Assoc, Women Lawyers Assoc of Los Angeles; volunteer Bradley for Governor Campaign 1986; volunteer All Africa Games in Kenya 1987; sponsor of children in underdeveloped nations; concert promoter, artist management, songwriter. **HONORS/ACHIEVEMENTS:** Top 100 Black Business and Professional Women 1986. **BUSINESS ADDRESS:** In-house Corporate Counsel, Motown Record Corp, 6255 Sunset Blvd, Los Angeles, CA 90028.

GORE, BLINZY L.
Educator, attorney. **PERSONAL:** Born Jun 13, 1921, Hinton, WV; son of Isaiah E Gore and Cora Pack Gore; married Gloria A Bultman; children: Brian, William. **EDUCATION:** IA Univ, JD 1950; NY Univ, MA 1958, PhD 1967; WV State, BS 1966. **CAREER:** SC State Coll, prof of law, assoc prof soc sci 1966-67; Claflin Coll, Orangeburg, SC, vice pres for academic affairs; private practice, attorney 1950-; South Carolina Coll, Orangeburg SC prof law 1950-66. **ORGANIZATIONS:** Mem IA Bar & SC Bar; Pi Gamma Mu 1974; life mem NAACP; exec comm Edisto Fed Credit Union; past pres Assn of Coll Deans, Registrars and Admissions Officers mem trustee bd Orangeburg Regional Hosp; bd dir Wesley Found; United Methodist Church. **HONORS/ACHIEVEMENTS:** Founders Day Award NY Univ 1967; Kappa Man of 1975 Orangeburg Alumni Chap Kappa Alpha Psi 1975. **MILITARY SERVICE:** AUS 1942-46. **BUSINESS ADDRESS:** Attorney, 1700 Belleville Rd, Orangeburg, SC 29115.

GORE, DAVID L.
Attorney. **PERSONAL:** Born Dec 17, 1937, Horry County, SC; son of Samuel B Gore and Sadie Anderson Gore; married Mary L Andrews; children: David Jr, Sheila. **EDUCATION:** Allen Univ, BA 1959; SC State Coll, MEd 1966; Howard Univ Sch of Law, JD 1969. **CAREER:** Natl Labor Relations Bd, legal asst to chmn 1969-70; Kleiman, Whitney, Wolfe & Gore, partner 1982-; United Steelworkers of Amer, asst genl counsel 1970-81, dist counsel 1982-. **ORGANIZATIONS:** Mem IL & PA Bar Assocs, 3rd 6th 7th and DC Court of Appeals, Phi Alpha Delta Legal Frat. **MILITARY SERVICE:** AUS sgt 1960-63. **BUSINESS ADDRESS:** District Counsel Dist 31, United Steelworkers of Amer, One E Wacker Dr, Chicago, IL 60601.

GORE, JOSEPH A.
Educational administrator. **PERSONAL:** Born in Sypply, NC; married Gloria Gardner; children: Duane K. **EDUCATION:** Livingstone Clge, BS 1952; Univ of MI, MS 1960; Yale Univ, MPH 1970; Univ of MA, EdD 1977. **CAREER:** Mary Holmes Coll, dean of men and science instructor 1956-58; Mary Holmes High School, prin 1958-59; Mary Holmes Coll, dean of students 1959-62, acad dean 1962-68, dir health servs 1968-70; Tougaloo Coll, acad dean 1970-72; Mary Holmes Coll, pres 1972-. **ORGANIZATIONS:** Mem FAFEO, Amer Pub Assc, Natl Educ Assc, Clay Cty Chamber of Comm, Bd of Dir I M Hosp. **HONORS/ACHIEVEMENTS:** Ped D degree Mary Holmes Clge 1972; LL D degree Lake Forest Clge 1984; Kellogg Fellow St Louis Univ 1964; Natl Sci Fellow Univ NC 1965. **MILITARY SERVICE:** AUS medic 82nd airborne div 1953-55. **BUSINESS ADDRESS:** President, Mary Holmes Coll, PO Drawer 1257, West Point, MS 39773.

GOREE, JANIE GLYMPH
Elected official. **PERSONAL:** Born Jan 24, 1921, Newberry, SC; married Charlie A Goree; children: Henry L Suber, Denice, Michael, Charles, Winifred Drumwright, Juanita, Darryl. **EDUCATION:** Benedict Coll, BS 1948; Univ of CO, MBS 1958; Univ of SC, attended; Univ of WY, attended; Univ of Notre Dame, attended, SC State Coll, attended. **CAREER:** Union Cty School, teacher 1948-81; Town of Carlisle, mayor/judge 1978-. **ORGANIZATIONS:** Exec person Democratic Party 1976-82; vice chairperson SC Conf of Black Mayors 1980-; treas World Conf of Mayors 1984-; mem Delta Sigma Theta Sor, Alpha Kappa Mu Natl Hon Soc; sec Grassroot Rural Devel Advisory Bd; rep & del Natl Conf of Black mayors to Interamer Travel AGents Soc Inc; del Natl Conf of Black Mayors to Japan, China, US, People Republic of China; del World Conf of Mayor in Africa. **HONORS/ACHIEVEMENTS:** Valedictorian Benedict Coll 1948; Star Teacher Sims High School 1968; Outstanding Awd Serv to Comm State & Nation Personality of the South Amer Biographical Inst 1978-79; First elected Black Woman Mayor of SC-SC Conf of Black Mayors 1980; Spec Tribute to Black Women Mayors Natl Conf of Black Mayors 1983; Natl salutes to 31 Black Female Mayors for Outstanding Political Achievement Metropolitan Women Democratic Club of Washington DC; Drum Major for Justice Southern Christian Leadership Con 1984; Hon Citizen Liberia, West Africa 1984. **BUSINESS ADDRESS:** Mayor, Town of Carlisle, PO Box 305, Carlisle, SC 29031.

GORHAM, SANDRA W. See WILLIAMS, SANDRA K.

GORHAM, THELMA THURSTON
Educator. **PERSONAL:** Born Feb 21, 1913, Kansas City, MO; married Richard Redwine Gorham Jr; children: Darryl Theodore. **EDUCATION:** Univ of MN, BA 1935; Univ of MN, MA 1951; Univ of MN/FL State Univ, ABD 1968-70, 1971-74. **CAREER:** The Kansas City Call, editor feature writer 1935-41; Hampton Univ, asst pr dir/teacher 1941-42; US Army Ft Huachuca AZ, editor/teacher/pr 1942-44; Lincoln Univ, journalism prof 1947-51; Central Sr High School Kansas City, teacher/publs advisor 1962-63; FL A&M Univ, assoc prof journalism 1963-68; Univ of MN, communications instructor 1968-71; FL A&M Univ, assoc prof journalism 1971-88. **ORGANIZATIONS:** Writing awd judge Stringer Jet and Ebony NNPA 1954-84; public school volunteer/advisor; comm & mass media collective bargaining team mem United Faculties ofFL Natl Educ Assoc; civilian/non-military Serv Command Unit 1922 Editor of Post Newspaper. **HONORS/ACHIEVEMENTS:** Kellog Fellow in Mass Comm 1977-78; Dr Martin Luther King Freedom Awd Natl Educ Assoc FAMU Student Govt 1985; First Black Communicator Hall of Fame Awdby Tallahassee Chap Natl Assoc of Black Journalists 1986; cited in Who's Who and Why of Successful Florida Women. **BUSINESS ADDRESS:** Prof of Journalism & Mass Comm, Florida A&M University, FAMU School of Journalism, Tallahassee, FL 32307.

GORING, WILLIAM S.
Educator. **PERSONAL:** Born Feb 01, 1943, New York; married Eloise Langston; children: Quijuan, Zurvohn, Kwixuan. **EDUCATION:** Univ Columbia, BA 1959;Univ San Francisco, JD 1963. **CAREER:** Mutual of NY Secur; Minority Educ Devel Univ of San Francisco, dir; Special Opportunity Scholarship Programs Univ of CA Berkeley, exec dir; E Bay Home Care Serv Inc, part owner 1975; Trio Educ Disadvantage Health Educ & Welfare, task force chmn. **MILITARY SERVICE:** AUS sgt. **BUSINESS ADDRESS:** 10 Eastmont Mall, SUITE 303, Oakland, CA 94605.

GORMAN, GERTRUDE ALBERTA
Executive officer. **EDUCATION:** Case Sch of Applied Sci, cert elec engr 1943; CWRU Cleveland Coll, BA polit phil 1949; ColumbiaUniv NYC, MA polit sci 1950. **CAREER:** NAACP, field dir 1949-79; Signal Corps USA War Dept, design & devel ofcr elec engr 1943-45; NAACP Cleveland, sec exec com 1941-43; NPORC NYC, natl pub opinion pollster 1949-51. **ORGANIZATIONS:** Golden heritage life mem NAACP (CONS) 1979-; mem Am Engineering Soc 1943-51; mem Am Sociol Soc Nat Counc on Fam Relations 1949-62; life mem Alpha Omega Chap Alpha Kappa Alpha Sorority Inc 1979. **HONORS/ACHIEVEMENTS:** Nat Distgshed Serv Awd Nat NAACP 1973; NDSA Outstndg Contrib NAACP Convention 1974; hon citizen cert Indianapolis 1975; Cert of Apprec Inter City Sertoma Club 1976. **BUSINESS ADDRESS:** 1790 Broadway, New York, NY 10019.

GOSLEE, LEONARD THOMAS
Physician. **PERSONAL:** Born Aug 05, 1932, Salisbury, MD. **EDUCATION:** Howard Univ, BS; Boston Univ, MS; Meharry Med Coll, MD. **CAREER:** Detroit Genl Hosp, internship 1958-59; Children's Hosp of MI, residency 1959-62, chief residency 1962-63; Laguardia Med Group Inc, physician 1964-. **ORGANIZATIONS:** Mem Natl Med Assn, Amer Acad of Pediatrics, NY State Med Assn, Queens Co Med Assn, Amer Assn of Pediatrics, Sch Health Planning Program. **BUSINESS ADDRESS:** Laguardia Med Group Inc, 11218 Springfield Blvd, Queens Village, NY 11429.

GOSS, CLAYTON
Playwright. **PERSONAL:** Born 1946, Philadelphia, PA. **CAREER:** Author "Children"; author num plays includ "Homecookin", "Of Being Hit", "Space in Time", "Bird of Paradise", "Ornette", "Oursides", "Mars", "Andrew"; Howard U Wash, DC, playwright-in-residence.

GOSS, FRANK, JR.
Business executive. **PERSONAL:** Born Jun 14, 1952, Chicago, IL. **EDUCATION:** Kendall Coll, AA 1972; Roosevelt, BS, BA 1975; Gov State U, MAB. **CAREER:** Continental IL Nat Bank, fed funds trdr cash pos mgr 1975-; IL Bell Tel, 1974; Spec in Monetary Policy, mgmt cons, student senator 1973; Black Bus Adv Grp Soc for Advcmt of Mgmt. **ORGANIZATIONS:** Mem Phi Theta Kappa 1972. **HONORS/ACHIEVEMENTS:** Ford Found schlrsp awd 1972. **BUSINESS ADDRESS:** 231 S La Salle, Chicago, IL 60693.

GOSS, THERESA CARTER
Educator, librarian. **PERSONAL:** Born Aug 22, 1932, Latham, AL; daughter of Columbus Carter and Willie D Carter; married James Calvin. **EDUCATION:** AL State Univ Montg,

BS; NC Central Univ Durham, MLS; Nova Univ Ft Lauderdale, EdD. **CAREER:** Jackson State Univ, librarian 1954-55; FL A&M Univ, librarian 1956; Pinellas HS, librarian 1956-66; St Petersburg Jr Coll, librarian 1966-81; MM Bennett Library SPSC, dir 1981-. **ORGANIZATIONS:** Mem League of Women Voters 1957-; mem Amer Assn of Univ Women 1958-; mem NAACP 1964-; mem Amer Assn of Univ Prof 1979-; mem Women's Adv Com Eckerd Coll 1979-; mem FL Library Assn, Amer Library Assn, Southeast Library Assn, FL Assn of Comm Coll, Phi Delta Kappa, Amer Assn of Univ Women; mem Alpha Kappa Alpha Sor, Links Inc, Silhouettes of Kappa Alpha Psi. **HONORS/ACHIEVEMENTS:** Girl Scout Leadership Awd 1959; PCPTa Awd for Outstanding Serv 1960; Religious Comm Serv Awd 1961; SOUL Awd for Outstanding Serv 1971; Library Bd Mem Awd City of Clearwater 1976; Alpha Kappa Alpha Awd Outstanding Accomplishments 1979; "Model Library Serv for the Hearing Handicapped" Major Applied Rsch Project Ft Lauderdale Nova Univ 1978, various other publications; Kappa Alpha Psi Awd; Links Awd for Outstanding Serv in Library Science; pres Clearwater Adult Adv Comm. **BUSINESS ADDRESS:** Dir, MM Bennett Library, 6605 5th Ave N, St Petersburg, FL 33710.

GOSS, WILLIAM EPP
Business executive. **PERSONAL:** Born Feb 03, 1941, Baltimore, MD; married Charlotte; children: Maisha, Zuri, Malaika. **EDUCATION:** Univ Chicago Grad Sch Bus, MBA 1975, MA soc serv admin 1970; Morgan State U, BA 1968. **CAREER:** Talent Asst Prgm Inc, exec dir 1976-; Minority Bus, mgmt cons; Talent Asst Prgm, asso dir 1975-76; Henry Booth House Settlement-Hull Hse Assn, ctr dir;Univ IL, Jan) Addams Sch Sch Work, field instr; Hull House Assn, bd dir. **ORGANIZATIONS:** Mem Nat Assn Soc Workers; Assn Black MBA'S; Assn Black Soc Wrkrs. **HONORS/ACHIEVEMENTS:** Chicago Assn Commerce & Ind Bicentennial Awd Grt Am Excell in Econ 1976; Outsdng Comm Serv Chicago Police Dept 173; FlwspUniv Chicago Grad Sch Soc Serv Admin 1969-70. **BUSINESS ADDRESS:** 19 S La Salle, Chicago, IL 60603.

GOSSETT, LOUIS, JR.
Actor. **PERSONAL:** Born May 27, 1936, Brooklyn, NY; divorced; children: Sate. **EDUCATION:** NYU, BA Drama. **CAREER:** Actor, made Broadway debut in "Take A Giant Step";"The Desk Set" Broadway; "Lost in the Stars" Broadway; "Raisin in the Sun" Broadway; "The Blacks"; "My Sweet Charlie"; "Carry Me Back to Morningside Heights"; "The Charlatan"; "Tell Pharoah"; "Roots"; "The Choirboys" feature film; "The Landlord"; "The Deep"; "River Niger"; "The Laughing Policeman"; "An Officer and a Gentleman"; "Enemy Mine". **ORGANIZATIONS:** Mem Motion Picture Arts & Sciences Acad; mem SAG/NAG/AEA/AFM/Alpha Phi Alpha/AGVA; Legal Def Fund NAACP. **HONORS/ACHIEVEMENTS:** Starred in TV movie "Sadat" 1983; Emmy Award for role of Fiddler in "Roots"; Oscar Best Supp Actor for role in "An Officer and a Gentleman" (3rd Black to win an acting Oscar). **BUSINESS ADDRESS:** c/o Tri-Star Pictures, 1875 Century Park East, Los Angeles, CA 90067.

GOTHARD, BARBARA WHEATLEY
Educator. **PERSONAL:** Born Nov 23, 1937, Springfield, IL; married Donald L; children: Donald Jr, Ann Marie. **EDUCATION:** Mt Mary Coll Milwaukee, WI, BA 1959; Long IslandUniv Greenvale, NY, MS 1972; MI StateUniv E Lansing, MI, PhD stud 1977. **CAREER:** Utica High School MI, assoc prin 1977-; MI State Univ, instructor 1980; Utica Comm School, art teacher 1973-77; Crimel Oakland Univ, Rochester MI, free lance graphic artist 1972-73; Union Free School Dist #4, Northport NY, art teacher 1966-71; Milwaukee Public Schools, art teacher 1959-64. **ORGANIZATIONS:** Mem Chairprsn publ com MI Assn of Secondary Sch, prin 1977-; mem Nat Assn of Secondary Sch Prin 1977-; mem MI Counc for Women in Sch Admin 1978-; bd of dir Meadowbrook Art Gallery OaklandUniv 1973-76; bd of dir Xochipilli Gallery 1974-76; mem Utica Cultural Arts Counc Exhibits of Paintings include Main Streams "74" Marietta Coll OH, Detroit Artists Market "Woman Works"Univ of MI, Midwest Artists Milwaukee Performing Arts Cntr, Macomb Co Bi-Centennial Exchange Prog Coventry England; solo shows at Delta Coll,Univ City MI, Art Gallery Central MI U, Mt Mary Coll Milwaukee, WI, Xochipilli Gallery MI; newspr reviews prv collections 1972-80. **HONORS/ACHIEVEMENTS:** Outstdng Young Women of Am 1973; edited weekly col "Cultural Arts Events" The Advisor Newspr Utica, MI 1973-75; publ "Art Tchr, Admin" Secondary Educ Today Jour of the MI Assn of Second Sch Prin 1978. **BUSINESS ADDRESS:** Utica High School, Utica Community Schools, 47255 Shelby Rd, Utica, MI 48087.

GOTHARD, DONALD L.
Executive engineer. **PERSONAL:** Born Dec 02, 1934, Madison, WI; son of William H. Gothard and Lorraine Williams Gothard; divorced; children: Donald Jr, Ann Marie. **EDUCATION:** Univ Notre Dame, BSEE 1956; Graduate ROTC 1956; GMI Tech Staff Management Program, Cert 1974. **CAREER:** GM AC Sparkplug Div, jr engineer production engineering 1956; GM AC Electron Div, design sys engineer Mace Missile Guidance & Navig Equip 1958-62; GM AC Electron Div Milwaukee & Wakefield, MA, engineer Apollo Ground Support Syst 1962-66; GM Delco Electron Div, lab supr Apollo Guidance Sys Lab 1966-71; GM Auto Electron Contrl Syst Devel 1971; GM Instrumentation Sect Test Dept, supr engineering staff 1972; GM Engineering Staff, asst manager 1973-76; GM Chevrolet Motor Div, sr design engineer 1976-77, asst staff engineer 1977-79, staff engineer 1979-82; GM Truck & Bus Engineering Operations, chief engineer electrical components 1982-85, exec engineer adv vehicle engineering 1985-. **ORGANIZATIONS:** Sec Shelby Township Cable TV Reg Comm 1980-84; Soc of Auto Engineers 1976-; Shelby Utica Athletic Fedn 1975-81; Macomb Co Comm Coll Citizens Com on Ednl & Finan Needs & Resources 1976; sec steering com Finance Com; chmn 500 mem Citizens Adv Com Utica Comm Schools 1974-75; past pres vice pres PTA 1972-74; vol YMCA Youth Basketball Program 1971-87; Meadow Brook Art Gallery Assn 1972-80; vol Little League Baseball Program 1969-70; GM Co Athl program 1958-81; Photography 1956-; Local Human Relations Org 1967-70; asst coach Utica Eisenhower High School Girls Basketball 1985-87. **HONORS/ACHIEVEMENTS:** Certificate of Appreciation Macomb County Comm Coll 1976; Disting Serv Award Utica Educ Assn 1975-76; Certificate of Appreciation Utica Comm Schools 1972-74; NASA Apollo Achievement Award 1969; MIT Cert Commend Apollo Program 1969; name carried to moon on first two lunar landings 1969; Society of Automotive Engineers (SAE) Excellence in Oral Presentation 1987. **MILITARY SERVICE:** US Army Ordnance, 1st lt 1956-58; Distinguished Military Graduate Award from Notre Dame 1956. **BUSINESS ADDRESS:** Exec Engr Adv Vehicle Engrg, GM Truck & Bus Engr Operations, 1996 Technology Drive, MC 1902-11, Troy, MI 48007-7057.

GOUDY, ANDREW JAMES
Educator. **PERSONAL:** Born Apr 15, 1943, Martins Ferry, OH; son of Sidney Goudy and Bertha Goudy. **EDUCATION:** IN Univ of PA, BS 1967, MS 1971; Univ of Pittsburgh, PhD 1976. **CAREER:** Cameron Cty HS, tchr 1968; Bald Eagle Nittany HS, tchr 1969; Canon Mcmillan HS, tchr 1971; West Chester Univ, prof 1977, chrmn dept chem, 1983-87. **ORGANIZATIONS:** Mem Amer Chem Soc 1976-, Intl Assc Hydrogen Energy 1982, NAACP; Natl Org for the Prof Advancement of Black Chemists & Chem Eng. **HONORS/ACHIEVEMENTS:** Article publ J Less Common Metals 99 1984, J Less Common Metals 91 1983; Research Grants: Petroleum Research Fund, 1982; NSF, 1986. **BUSINESS ADDRESS:** West Chester Univ, West Chester, PA 19383.

GOUGH, WALTER C.
Physician. **PERSONAL:** Born Apr 24, 1943, Pittsburgh, PA; son of Walter C Gough Sr and Kathryn Scott Grinage Gough; married May Ella Bailey, Sep 24, 1974; children: Wanda, Marcus, Henry, Lynette, Kathryn, Nora. **EDUCATION:** Tarkio Coll, AB 1965; Meharry Medical Coll, MD 1970; Mercy Hospital Pittsburgh, intern resident 1970-72; Mehary Medical Coll, resident (pediatrics) 1973. **CAREER:** Mound Bayou, MS, medical dir 1974-; Black Belt Family Health Center, medical dir 1973; Delta Comm Hospital & Health Center, physician 1974-; Choctaw Indian Hospital, medical dir 1976-78; Natl Health Serv, medical dir 1978-81; Spectrum ER Care, dir 1981-84; Gough's Family & Ped Clinic, owner 1984-. **ORGANIZATIONS:** Mem Allegheny Co Medical Co 1971-72; AMA, NMA 1973-74; Omega Psi Phi 1967-; mem MS Heart Assn 1974; surgery intern Mercy Hospital 1970-71; resident anesthes Mercy Hospital 1971-72; resident pediatrician Hubbard Hospital 1972-76; medical dir Taboman Hospital 1972-75; bd of trustees Delta Health Center 1986-89, WQSZ 1989-. **HONORS/ACHIEVEMENTS:** First black graduate at Tarkio Coll; Man of the Year Award, Pittsburgh Jaycees 1972; Outstanding Alumnus 15 yrs, Tarkio Coll 1974; Distinguished Alumni, Tarkio Cool 1974; Bronze Medal Tarkio Coll 1965; Best Scientific Article, Meharry Coll 1966; Student Christian Med Soc 1967; Jaycee's Man of the Year 1970; Board Certified, American Bd of Physicians, 1977, 1983, 1989; Board Certified, American Bd of Emergency Medicine, 1983, 1989; Man of the Year, Omega Psi Phi 1986; #1 Award Iota Omicron Charter 1986. **BUSINESS ADDRESS:** Physician, Gough's Family & Peds Clinic, 189 N Main St, Drew, MS 38737.

GOUGIS, LORNA GAIL
Marketing manager. **PERSONAL:** Born Aug 19, 1948, New Orleans, LA. **EDUCATION:** Newcomb Coll, BA Psych 1969. **CAREER:** Ginn & Co, test editor 1972-74; Wallace & Assoc, rsch dir 1975-79; Mgmt Intern Progr, intern coord 1980; Omega Group Inc, dir rsch 1981-83; Polytech Inc, reg sales dir 1983-86; field supervisor Arbitron Ratings, current. **ORGANIZATIONS:** Vp, bd mem Treadwell & Wallace 1984-; Conf of Minority Transp Official sec, Minority Affairs Comm, Amer Public Transit Assoc 1984-. **HONORS/ACHIEVEMENTS:** Outstanding Young Woman of Amer 1979. **HOME ADDRESS:** 1836 Metzerott Rd, #1623, Adelphi, MD 20783. **BUSINESS ADDRESS:** Field Supervisor, Arbitron Ratings, 312 Marshall Ave, Laurel, MD 20707.

GOULBOURNE, DONALD SAMUEL, JR.
Social worker, health care administrator. **PERSONAL:** Born May 05, 1950, New Rochelle, NY; son of Donald Samuel Goulbourne Sr and Girthel Grayson Goulbourne; children: Antoine Donald. **EDUCATION:** Columbia Union Coll, Takoma Park MD, BA, 1973; Columbia Univ School of Social Work, New York NY, MS, 1977; Albert Einstein Coll of Medicine/Yeshiva Univ, Post-Graduate Certificate, 1984. **CAREER:** New Rochelle Bd of Educ, New Rochelle NY, teachers asst, 1974-75; Washington Heights Community Center, New York NY, social work trainee, 1975-76; Family & Children Serv, Stamford CT, clinical social worker, 1977-79; Natl Health Serv Corps, Einstein Medical Coll, New York NY, social work coord, 1979-84; Dept of Social Serv, Albert Einstein Coll of Medicine, New York NY, 1984-89; Lincoln Ave Clinic, The Guidance Center, New Rochelle NY, dir, 1989-. **ORGANIZATIONS:** US Reserve Officers Assn, 1989; US Commissioned Officers Assn, 1989; Natl Assn of Social Workers, 1989; Soc of Clinical Work Psychotherapists Inc, 1989; volunteer group leader, Minority Task Force on AIDS, 1989; vice pres, Westchester Townhouse Condominium Assn, 1989; professional counselor, Community Adult Patients, 1989. **HONORS/ACHIEVEMENTS:** Letter of Commendation, New York State Dept of Health, 1981; Clinical Assoc Nomination, Dept of Sociology, Herbert H Lehman Coll of the City Univ of New York, 1982; Serv Citation, New York City Dept of Public Health, 1983; Certificate of Appreciation, Yeshiva Univ, 1986, 1987. **BUSINESS ADDRESS:** Director, Lincoln Ave Clinic, The Guidance Center, 95 Lincoln Ave, New Rochelle, NY 10801.

GOULD, WILLIAM B.
Attorney. **PERSONAL:** Born Jul 16, 1936, Boston; married Hilda; children: William, V, Timothy, Bartholomew. **EDUCATION:** Univ RI, AB 1958; Cornell Law Sch, LIB 1961; London Sch Econ, grad study 1963;Univ Cambridge, MA 1975. **CAREER:** United Auto Wkrs, asst gen counsel 1961-62; Nat Lab Relat Bd Washg, atty 1963-65; Battle Fowler & Stokes, Kheel, NY, asso 1965-68; Wayne State Law Sch, prof law 1968-71; Harvard Law Sch, vis prof law 1971-72; Stanford Law Sch Overseas Fellow Churchill Coll Cambridge, prof law 1975; Univ Tokyo Law Faculty, vis scholar 1975. **ORGANIZATIONS:** Mem Nat Acad Arbitrat; Labor Law Sect; Am Bar Assn atty; racial discrim class act involving Detroit Edison Co Intl Bro Teamsters; Am Fed Mus; del Dem Party mid-term conv 1974. **HONORS/ACHIEVEMENTS:** Author articles lab law & unions Stanford, Yale, Duke, Cornell, Penn & other law jour; contrib NY Times, Manchester Guard London Econ, Nation, New Rep Commonwealth, New Leader. **BUSINESS ADDRESS:** Stanford Law Sch, Stanford, CA 94305.

GOURDINE, SIMON PETER
Government official. **PERSONAL:** Born Jul 30, 1940, Jersey City, NJ; son of Simon and Laura; married Patricia Campbell; children: David Laurence, Peter Christopher, Laura Allison. **EDUCATION:** The City Clge of NY, BA 1962; Fordham Univ Law Schl, JD 1965; Harvard Univ Grad School of Business Cert Prog for Mgmt Develop 1979. **CAREER:** US Atty Southern Dist of NY, asst US atty 1967-69; Celanese Corp, atty 1969-70; Natl Basktbl Assc, deputy comm 1970-81; NY City Dept Consumer Affairs, commissioner 1982-84; The Rockefeller Fnd, sec 1984-86; Metropolitan Transportation Authority, dir of labor relations 1986-. **ORGANIZATIONS:** Dir Police Athletics League 1974-, 100 Black Men Inc 1974-; commissioner NY City Commn on Human Rights 1978-81; mem NY State Banking Bd 1979-; comm NY City Civil Srv Comm 1981-82; mem Mayors Comm Taxi Reg Issues 1981-82, Exec Adv Comm on the Admin of Justice in NY State 1981-83; mem Mayor's Adv Comm on Police Mgmt and Personnel Policy 1985-87; dir Fresh Air Fund 1985-; commr, New York City Charter Revision Commn 1988-. **MILITARY SERVICE:** AUS capt 1965-67; Army Comm

Medal Meritorious Srv Vietnam. **BUSINESS ADDRESS:** Dir of Labor Relations, Metropolitan Trans Authority, 347 Madison Ave, New York, NY 10017.

GOVAN, RONALD M.
Research physicist, staff associate. **PERSONAL:** Born Jan 20, 1931, Los Angeles, CA. **EDUCATION:** Pacific StateUniv Coll of Elec Engr, BSEE 1962. **CAREER:** USC, physics dept resrch asso; Ryan Aircraft, elec main & calibration tech a; Hughes Aircraft, elec fabric tech a elec main tech a; USN ET2, main of radar, sonar & commun equip;Univ of So CA LA, physics dept asst in resrch 1962-64, chem dept instrument design 1964-66; Rockwell Intl Sci Cntr, staff asso physics 1966-;Univ of CA Santa Barbara Dept of Urban Affairs, conf coord 1969. **ORGANIZATIONS:** Mem Educ Counc of Coll &Univ Ventura Co; chmn local bd 81 selec serv Ventura Co; mem bd dir So CA Comprehen Hlth Plann Bd; vice pres So Area ConfNAACP; vice pres Ventura Co NAACP; lab chmn Educ Chmn; mem Camarillo Jaycees; chmn John C Montgomery Forum on Welfare; mem Camarillo Boys Club bd dir; mem United Fund Ventura Co Budget & Com Task Force chmn; chmn Ventura Co Comm Action Commn; mem Ventura Co Criminal Justice Planning Delegate Conf on Crim Just Sci & Tech Wash, DC 1972; found past pres Camarillo Dem Club; mem Task Force On Excellence in Educ Pomona 1972; CA State Dept of Edn; lectr paid consult Ventura Co Human Relat Comm; Task Force on Housing Ventura Co Plann Dept; Equal Oppor Com; CA State Personnel bd adv com on Career Oppor Devel; mem Gov's Conf on Law Enforcement Standards Crime Control Com; Publs Spectroscopy Grp; Atmospheric Sci Grp. **HONORS/ACHIEVEMENTS:** Recip outstdg Contrib Awd NAACP So Area Conf; recip Comm Serv Awd & 1967 outstdg Comm Interest Awd; Jaycee of Month awd; Distgshd Serv Awd; Commen for High Svc. **MILITARY SERVICE:** USN electronics tech 2nd class 1949-54. **BUSINESS ADDRESS:** 1049 Camino Dos Rios, Thousand Oaks, CA.

GOWARD, RUSSELL A.
Government official. **PERSONAL:** Born Aug 25, 1935, St Louis, MO; married Dolores Thorton; children: Russell II, Monika. **EDUCATION:** Hubbards Bus Coll; Harris Tchrs Coll;Univ MO, 1969. **CAREER:** State rep 1966-; House Com on Soc Serv & Medicade Ins, asst majority floor ldr chmn; broker, real estate broker; R G Lynch & Asso Inc, pres; Freedom Residents, bd dir; Yeatman Corp; Soc Serv Inc. **HONORS/ACHIEVEMENTS:** Legislator of Yr MO Beauticians Assn 1967; merit serv MO Nursing Home Assn 1968, 69, 77; 1 of top 10 legis St Louis Mag; MO Assn of Pub Employ; Outst Legislator 1977. **MILITARY SERVICE:** USN quarter master 3rd class 1952-56. **BUSINESS ADDRESS:** Capitol Bldg, St Louis, MO 65101.

GRACE, MARCELLUS
Educator, pharmacist. **PERSONAL:** Born Oct 17, 1947, Selma, AL; married Laura Dunn; children: Syreeta Lynn, Marcellus Jr;K'Chebe M. **EDUCATION:** Xavier Univ of LA; BS Pharm 1971; Univ of MN, MS Hosp Pharm 1975, PhD Pharm Admin 1976. **CAREER:** Tulane Med Ctr Hosp & Clinic, dir of pharm serv 1976-77; Xavier Univ of LA Coll of Pharm, asst prof & dir of prof exp pro 1976-78; Howard Univ Coll of Pharm & Pharmacal Sci, asst dean for serv ed 1979-82, chmn dept pharm admin 1982; Xavier Univ of LA, dean coll of pharm 1983-. **ORGANIZATIONS:** Vp New Orleans Parish Coord Council for High Blood Pressure Control 1978; pres Washington DC Soc of Hosp Pharm 1982-83; mem New Orleans Historical Pharm Commiss 1983-; pres Assoc of Minority Health Professions Schools. **HONORS/ACHIEVEMENTS:** Eli Lilly Achievement Awd Eli Lilly Co Indianpolis In 1971; Recipient of Fellowship Natl Fellowship Fund Grad Fellowship for Black Amer 1975-76; mem Rho Chi Natl Pharm Honor Soc 1977; Outstanding Young Men of Amer US Jaycees Montgomery AL 1979-80. **MILITARY SERVICE:** USN Reserve lt comm 1976-. **BUSINESS ADDRESS:** Dean, College of Pharmacy, Xavier University of LA, 7325 Palmetto St, New Orleans, LA 70125.

GRADY, MARY FORTE
Regional coordinator, government official. **PERSONAL:** Born Nov 19, 1921, Chicago, IL; daughter of Cyril Forte and George Forte; married Leonard Grady Jr, Jul 26, 1947; children: Leonard Grady III, Graham C Grady. **EDUCATION:** Wilson Jr Coll; Chicago Conservatory. **CAREER:** US Dept of Commerce, coord comm serv; US Census Bureau, Chicago, IL, regional coord 1969-. **ORGANIZATIONS:** Mem United Way; prog audit comm Chicago Urban Affairs Council; mem United Negro Coll Fund; League of Black Women Unit Char; assoc bd dir Cosmopolitan C of C; mem Chicago Urban League; Coalition against Crime; Chatham Lions Club Women's Auxiliary. **HONORS/ACHIEVEMENTS:** Bronze Medal, US Dept of Commerce 1974. **BUSINESS ADDRESS:** Regional Coordinator, US Census Bureau, 175 W Jackson, Suite 557, Chicago, IL 60604.

GRADY, WALTER E.
Chief executive. **CAREER:** Seaway National Bank of Chicago, Chicago IL, chief executive. **BUSINESS ADDRESS:** Seaway National Bank of Chicago, 645 E 87th St, Chicago, IL 60619. *

GRADY, ZEDEKIAH L.
Clergyman. **PERSONAL:** Born Mar 28, 1931, Laughman, FL; married Carrie; children: Zedekiah II, J. **EDUCATION:** Edward Waters Coll, BTh 1954; AllenUniv & Dickerson Theol Sem, BS BD 1957; Union Theol Sem, 1969; Urban Tgrng for Missions, 1970; Allen U, hon DD 1964; Ritrell Coll 1962. **CAREER:** Morris Brown AME Ch, minister 1962-; Grtr St Stephen AME Ch, minister 1959-62; Bethel AME Ch Anderson, SC, minister 1958-59; Bethel AME Ch Lauren, SC, minister 1954-58; Cedar AME Ch, minister 1953; Shady Oak AME Ch, minister 1951-52. **ORGANIZATIONS:** Past pres Interdenom Ministerial Alliance; past mem Strateby Com Charleston Area for Civil Rights 1963; co-chmn Voter Registration Dr 1965-66; co-chmn Concerned Clergy Com 1969; prs Comm Relat Com; mem bd of trsts Allen U; bd of dir Citizens & So Housing Corp; bd of dir Citzns Com; bd of dir Charleston Charter Commin Mason; mem Phi Beta Sigma Frat.

GRAHAM, ALBERTHA L.
Educator. **PERSONAL:** Born in Georgetown, SC; married Sam Ellison; children: Kezia Ellison. **EDUCATION:** Morris Coll, 1965; NY Univ, Cert Ldrshp Devel Training 1968; Erikson Inst, MEd 1971;Univ of Pittsburgh, grad stud. **CAREER:** Chopee High School, teacher 1965-67, summer librarian 1966; Brookhaven HS, head start teacher 1967-68; Cent Brookhaven Head Start Program, dir 1968-70; Suffolk Co Summer Head Start Patchoque NY, dir 1970; Kezia Enterprises, counselor; CA Univ of PA, state training officer, assoc prof, dir of affirmative action/human relations, counselor. **ORGANIZATIONS:** Mem Nat Assn Educ Young Child; Nat Council Black Child Devel; PA Reg Adv Com Day Care Person Proj conduc EPI 1973; mem Educ Com Pgh Chap NAACP;nat pres Black Women Assn Inc; init & spon "You The Black Woman" in a series of seminars for the Black Wom Assn Inc 1975-; prov training & tech asst toreg Iii agency for Child You & Fam; vol & adv bd mem Nat Cncl of Jewish Women Pgh Sec Friends Indeed Proj 1975-; mem Afric Am Inst; bd mem Inst for Women Ent NAWBO; mem Greater Pgh Commn for Women. **HONORS/ACHIEVEMENTS:** Business Woman of the Year Awd Alleghenians LTD Inc. **BUSINESS ADDRESS:** Box 13 LRC, California, PA 15419.

GRAHAM, CATHERINE S.
Director of health & human services. **PERSONAL:** Born Apr 08, 1920, Norfolk, VA; daughter of Sye Stoney and Irene Stoney; married Robert (deceased); children: Antoine. **EDUCATION:** Trenton State Coll, BA 1973, MA 1977; Rider Coll, cert in ins 1968. **CAREER:** Trenton Ed Devel Corp; Educ Advo Prog City of Trent, form dir; Mercer Co Ct, prin docket clk; St Hm for Girls, supv; City Hall Trenton NJ, health & human serv dir. **ORGANIZATIONS:** Mem Will H Dinkins Real Est; bd dir Unit Prog Inc; mem Foll Through Prog; Hd Start Pol Counc; Spl Educ Adv Counc; Hd Start; Educ Supp Tm;former pres Urb League Met Trenton; past pres NAACP; mem Jack & Jill; bd dirs Nat Counc for Black Child Devel Inc; adv comm Mercer County Human Svcs; mem Mercer County Dem Black Caucus. **HONORS/ACHIEVEMENTS:** Recpt comm spons testim dinner; awds From Omega Phi Psi 1968; frontiersman 1968; Fai Ho Cho Club 1967; City of Trent 1972; Bronzettes 1967; Usher Counc of NJ 1964; Head St Par Action Counc 1974; Carver Cntr YMCA 1972;AKA Recog Achieve 1972; NJ Conf of Christ & Jews Achieve & Awd 1979. **BUSINESS ADDRESS:** Dir Health & Human Serv, City Hall, 319 East State St, Trenton, NJ 08608.

GRAHAM, CHESTIE MARIE
Educator. **PERSONAL:** Born Nov 07, 1917, Louisburg, NC; married Samuel; children: Samuel Jr, Barbara, Karen. **EDUCATION:** Fayetteville State U, BS 1944; PA State U, MEd 1952. **CAREER:** Dist of Columbia Bd of Educ, elementary school counselor; teacher 1944-64. **ORGANIZATIONS:** Am Sch Couns; Elem Sch Couns Assn; DC Sch Couns Assn; The Am Personn & Guid Assn; Delta Sigma Theta; YWCA; Nat Counc of Negro Wom; Bus & Prof Wom; Nat Cap Person & Guid Assn; mem NAACP; pres Elem Sch Couns Assn 1974-75; Adv Nghbrhd Commn Wd 6 1976-80; sec DC Sch Couns Assn1974-75. **HONORS/ACHIEVEMENTS:** Chpn Human Res & Ag Com in ANC 6b; induct into Pi Lambda Theta Hon Sor; served 5 yrs on Chap Com St Monica's Epis Ch; vol 25 yrs plus With Am Red Cross; served 7 yrs with Girl Scouts; test at hearing on State Plan for DC 1975; part in pres "Mirror Mirror Mirror On The Wall" 1975; outst couns DC Rsrch Club 1975-76; outst achvmt in Advance of Comm & Sch Act James E Coates 1976; outst achvmts Jerry A Moore 1976; reg of atten at Apga Wkshp Am Pers & Guid Assn 1976; cert of apprec serv render Superior Ct 1977; cert of apprec outst serv in DC Empl One Fund Dr; rec cert Assn for one-whhite conc in person & guid for exemp serv to the assn & the conc of minor in the field of couns & guid 1978; 1st pres DC assn for non-white conc inperson & guid; publ sev art.

GRAHAM, DELORES METCALF
Educator. **PERSONAL:** Born Aug 04, 1929, Frankfort, KY; divorced; children: Tanya, Gregory, Derrick. **EDUCATION:** KY State Coll, BS 1952; Georgetown Coll, MA 1982. **CAREER:** State Of KY, child welfare social work 1957-58; Franklin County Bd of Educ, special reading teacher, classroom teacher. **ORGANIZATIONS:** Mem Franklin Cnty Centr KY KY Nat Educ Assn; mem Delta Sigma Theta Sor; Nat Counc Negro Wom; mem Alpha Delta Kappa, Foster Care Review Bd; trustSt John AME Church. **HONORS/ACHIEVEMENTS:** Out Elem Tchrs in Am 1973. **BUSINESS ADDRESS:** Teacher, Franklin Co Bd of Education, 916 E Main St, Frankfort, KY 40601.

GRAHAM, FREDERICK MITCHELL
Educator. **PERSONAL:** Born Feb 07, 1921, Des Moines, IA; son of Fred Graham and Anna Mae Graham; married Lillian Louise Miller; children: Frederick, Stephen, Anita Wardlaw. **EDUCATION:** Drake U, 1943; IA State U, BS 1948, MS 1950, PhD 1966. **CAREER:** Prairie View A&M TX, dept civil eng head 1950-59; IA State U, prof of eng sci & mechanics 1961-87. **ORGANIZATIONS:** Consulting engr McDonnell-Douglas & Meredith Publishing Co Etc 1965-; mem ASEE; mem ASCE; former lay reader St John's Episcopal Ch. **HONORS/ACHIEVEMENTS:** Elected Tau Beta Pi IA State U; elected by stdnts Knights of St Patrick; awarded 2 Nat Sci Found Fac Fellowships; chosen Outstand Prof 1978, 1984; pres of local NSPE 1984; elected to Nat GRE Com of Engineering Examiners 1982-86; chosen outstanding prof 1984, 1988; SIRE ARCHON, Gamma Eta Boule. **MILITARY SERVICE:** USAF m sgt 1943-46. **HOME ADDRESS:** 134 S Franklin, Ames, IA 50010. **BUSINESS ADDRESS:** Prof of Engineering Sciences, IA StateUniv, 209 Lab of Mechanics, Ames, IA 50011.

GRAHAM, GEORGE WASHINGTON, JR.
Government official. **PERSONAL:** Born Feb 16, 1949, Kinston, NC; son of George W Graham Sr (deceased) and Mattie L Graham; married Marilyn, Jun 18, 1988; children: Marilyn, George III, Alicia, Brandi. **EDUCATION:** Fayetteville State Univ, BS, 1971; North Carolina State Univ, MS, 1975, doctoral program, currently. **CAREER:** US Post Office, Fayetteville, NC, mail handler, 1967-71; Simone Jr High School, instructor & athletic coach, 1971-72; Lenoir Community Coll, Kinston, NC, adult basic educ dir, 1972-76, admin asst to the pres & resource devel officer, 1977-79; Dobbs School, Kinston, NC, dir, 1979-. **ORGANIZATIONS:** Mem: Omega Psi Phi, NAACP, St Augustus AME Zion Church, Jaycees, Masons, Kinston Rotary Club, N Carolina Assn of Black Elected Officials, Lenoir County Black Artist Guild; Lenoir County Bd of Commissioners; bd of dirs, Lenoir County Chamber of Commerce; bd of dirs, Lenoir Memorial Hospital; bd of dirs, Untied Way; Lenoir County Commn of 100; Lenoir County Health Bd of Dirs; N Carolina General Assembly Special Legislative Commn on Fairness in Taxation; N Carolina Assn of County Commrs Taxation & Finance Steering Comm; chmn, bldg commn, St Augustus AME Zion Church; bd of dirs, N Carolina Assn of County Commrs. **HONORS/ACHIEVEMENTS:** Teacher of the Year, 1971; Jaycee of the Month, 1973; Outstanding Educ of the Year, 1974; Outstanding Educ of Amer, 1974-75; Outstanding Black Educ, 1976; Jaycee Boss of the Year, 1979; Man of the Year, Omega Psi Phi, 1979; Distinguished Service Award Nominee, Kinston, Lenoir County Chamber of Commerce, 1980; Governor's Award for Excellence Nominee, 1987. **BUSINESS ADDRESS:** Dir, Dobbs School, Route 7, Box 180, Kinston, NC 28501.

GRAHAM, HELEN W.
Educator (retired). **PERSONAL:** Born Dec 24, 1924, New York, NY; daughter of Ray-

mond Wilson and Pauline W Crayton; married Fitzroy, Jun 26, 1949; children: Rosalyn, Shelle. **EDUCATION:** Howard Univ, Washington DC, BA, 1950; Hunter Coll, New York NY, MS, 1974. **CAREER:** S Siegel Inc, New York NY, bookkeeper, office, payroll, typist, 1950-55; Brooklyn Bd of Educ, Brooklyn NY, teacher, 1962-89. **ORGANIZATIONS:** Treasurer, Natl Sorority of Phi Delta Kappa Inc, Beta Omicron Chapter, 1987-; vice pres, Key Women of Amer Inc, 1989-. **HONORS/ACHIEVEMENTS:** Teacher of the Year, PTA, PS 37Q, 1975. **HOME ADDRESS:** 134-19 166th Place #10A, Jamaica, NY 11434.

GRAHAM, JO-ANN CLARA
Educational administrator. **PERSONAL:** Daughter of James Harold Graham and Clara Polhemus Graham. **EDUCATION:** New York Univ, BS 1962, MA 1968, PhD 1982. **CAREER:** Bronx Comm Coll, prof 1970-, chairperson of communications, division coordinator of humanities. **ORGANIZATIONS:** Exec bd New York State TESOL 1970-73; mem commercial panel Amer Arbitration Assn 1976-; bd of dir Assoc Black Charities 1982-; consultant Mayor's Voluntary Action Center, New York City Bd of Educ, Major New York City Law Firm, McGraw-Hill, Addison Wesley, Macmillan, North Hudson Language Devel Ctr, Haryou-Act; vice pres G/S Associates-Human Communication. **HONORS/ACHIEVEMENTS:** Fellowship Univ of Puerto Rico, New York Univ 1966; co-author The Public Forum, A Transactional Approach to Public Communication, Alfred 1979; chosen 1 of 100 top women in mgmt nationwide to participate in Leaders for the '80's, 1983. **BUSINESS ADDRESS:** Div Coordinator of Humanities, Bronx Community College, 181 St &Univ Ave, New York, NY 10453.

GRAHAM, JOHN H.
Clergyman, educator. **PERSONAL:** Born Apr 06, 1915, Corinth, MS; children: James Arthur, Patricia V. **EDUCATION:** Clark Coll, AB 1939; Gammon Theol Sem, BD 1940; Drew U, MA 1941; Boston U, grad stud; Rust Coll, DD 1950. **CAREER:** Univ & Young Adult Min Ofc Bd of Global Min The Un Meth Ch, staff mem 1960-; Gammon Sem, prof 1953-60; Holly Springs MS, pastor 1951-53; Amory MS, pastor 1951; Upper MS Conf, dist supt 1944-50; Holly Springs, pastor 1941-44. **ORGANIZATIONS:** Mem Phi Beta Sigma. **BUSINESS ADDRESS:** 475 Riverside Dr, New York, NY 10027.

GRAHAM, LARRY, JR.
Musician. **PERSONAL:** Born Aug 14, 1946; married Tina. **CAREER:** Graham Cent Sta Mavimus Prodns, pres 1973-77; Sly & The Family Stone, bass play 1967-73; Dell Graham Jazz Trio, 1951-67. **ORGANIZATIONS:** Mem Jehovah's Witness. **HONORS/ACHIEVEMENTS:** Top star awd; best dress male art 1973; best dress art 1973-74; top big band 1975; ent of yr 1975; #1 black contemp & sing rec all trades cashbox billbd rec wor black rad exclus gavin report jet "One in a Million You".

GRAHAM, LEROY MAXWELL, JR.
Pediatrician. **PERSONAL:** Born Feb 14, 1954, Chicago, IL; married Patrice T Gaspard MD; children: Arianne Marie, LeRoy Maxwell III. **EDUCATION:** St Joseph Coll, BS (cum laude); Georgetown Univ, MD 1979. **CAREER:** Fitzsimmons Army Medical Ctr, pediatric resd 1979-82; US Army Community Hosp Seoul Korea, asst chief ped svcs, chief newborn nursery 1983-84; Fort Knox KY, chief of ped serv 1984-86; Fitzsimons Army Med Ctr Auora Co, clinical priviledges 1986-; Univ of CO Health Scis Ctr, fellow ped pulmonary med 1986-, clinical instr in ped 1987-, fellow cardiovascular pulmonary rsch lab 1987-; The Childrens Hospital, emergency room attending 1988-; chief, pediatric Pulmonary Serv, dir, pediatric intensive care unit, Fitzsimons Army Medical Ctr 1989-. **ORGANIZATIONS:** Cert Amer Bd of Peds 1983; mem Alpha Phi Alpha; dir of educ Delta Psi Lambda; mem Alpha Omega Alpha Hon Med Soc; mem bd of dirs, Black American West Museum. **HONORS/ACHIEVEMENTS:** First black student to be elected to Alpha Omega Alpha Honor Medical Soc at Georgetown Univ School of Med 1979. **MILITARY SERVICE:** AUS 1979-; Meritorious Serv Medal; Army Commendation Medal, Army Achievement Medal, Foreign Serv Medal. **HOME ADDRESS:** 4130 So Roslyn St, Denver, CO 80237.

GRAHAM, LOUISE MCCLARY
Business executive. **PERSONAL:** Born Sep 27, 1903, Ethel, GA. **EDUCATION:** St Petersburg Jr Coll, AA. **CAREER:** Florence Nightingale Center for Retarded, foun pres 30 yrs; City of St Petersburg, supr arts & crafts 26 yrs; Amer Legion Hospital, head train For retarded 1949-60; Sid & Saunders-sheriff, private nurse 1925-50; Florence Nightengale Cntr for Retarded, dir 1949. **ORGANIZATIONS:** Founder Spl Olympics for Handicapped 1968; deaconess Bethel Commn Bapt Ch 1959; mem chmn Daught Elks 1940-50. **HONORS/ACHIEVEMENTS:** Outst serv Dept of Hlth & Rehab Serv 1978; spl serv City of St Petersburg 1956, 1968-77; woman of the yr awd Zeta Phi Beta Sor 1965; mer Awd Pinellas Co Govt 1959. **BUSINESS ADDRESS:** Florence Nightengale Center, 1885 12th St S, St Petersburg, FL 33705.

GRAHAM, MARIAH
Artist, business executive. **PERSONAL:** Born Nov 03, 1946, South Carolina. **EDUCATION:** The Sch of Visual Arts, cert of grad 1968. **CAREER:** Mariah Graham Studios, pres owner 1969-; NY Times, freelance art 1968-80; Marymount Coll, instr 1977-; Fashion Inst of Tech, instr 1978-. **ORGANIZATIONS:** Mem Soc of Illust; mem Graphic Art Guild; mem Drama & Guild Broadway. **HONORS/ACHIEVEMENTS:** Cert of apprec Baruch Coll 1976; the One Show Merit awd The Art Direct Club 1976; cert of merit The Soc of Illust 1978; cert of merit New York City Coll 1979. **BUSINESS ADDRESS:** 670 W End Ave, New York, NY 10025.

GRAHAM, MICHAEL ANGELO
Editor, producer. **PERSONAL:** Born Dec 15, 1921, Savannah, GA. **EDUCATION:** Savannah State Coll, attended. **CAREER:** New Observer DC, editor 1973-; Capitol Times DC, 1954-55; Metro-HERALD Beltsville MD, 1972; Afro-Amer Newspaper Natl, theatre writer 1960-; Pittsburgh Courier Natl, 1939-58; AK Spotlight Anchorage, feature writer 1952-54; Savannah Herald, orig staff mem; WA Informer DC, 1969; Black Voice Landover MD, 1973; Vista Raceway MD, pub dir 1970-72; Black & White Scotch DC, 1964-65; Town of Glenarden MD, 1971-72; Theatre Producer Promoter & Publ Lucky Mill Orchest NYC; Howard Theater DC, resident producer & emcee 1956-75; Fun For Fighters Camp Shows DC, dir production 1945-50; Harold Jackson Rad Show. **ORGANIZATIONS:** Mem NAACP; Columbia Lodge of Elks; Prince Hall Mason; Amer Cancer Soc & Pub Comm; Amer Guild of Variety Acts; US Pres Inaugural Entertainment Comm. **HONORS/ACHIEVEMENTS:** Young mem New Orleans Mus Stock Co 1942; recip Red Cross Donors Awd 1962; Q'Pettes Club apprec awd 1969; Bakers Assn honor cit 1974; Nat Negro OperaAwd 1953; ed of the yr awd 1975; VFW Ladies Aux Comm Awd; am Canc Soc Awd; Shriners Awd; Petey Green Theat Awd; Orig Entert of Yr awd 1954. **MILITARY SERVICE:** US Merchant Marine 1941-42. **BUSINESS ADDRESS:** 811 Florida Ave NW, Washington, DC 20001.

GRAHAM, ODELL
Chief scientist. **PERSONAL:** Born Mar 31, 1931, Chicago, IL; married Loretta Harriet Lewis; children: Karyn, Cynthia, Jessica. **EDUCATION:** Univ of CA Los Angeles, BS Physics 1961, MS Engineering 1966, PhD Engineering 1976. **CAREER:** Microwave Dept Hughes Aircraft Co, asst mgr 1961-; Hycon Mfg Co, elec engr 1960-61; Hughes Aircraft Co, resrch & asst 1954-60. **ORGANIZATIONS:** Sr mem Inst of Elec & Elect Engr 1972-; chmn Los Angeles Chap Anten & Prop Soc Inst of Elec & Electron Engr; mem NAACP. **HONORS/ACHIEVEMENTS:** Howard Hughes Doct fellow; Hughes Aircraft Co Miss Syst 1967-76. **MILITARY SERVICE:** USMC corpl 1952-54. **BUSINESS ADDRESS:** Hughes Aircraft Co, 8433 Fallbrook Ave, Canoga Park, CA 91304.

GRAHAM, PATRICIA
Educator. **PERSONAL:** Born Mar 09, 1949, Saluda, SC; daughter of Eddie R Graham and Lillian Graham; divorced. **EDUCATION:** Rutgers Univ, BA 1972; Antioch Coll, MEd 1974. **CAREER:** Morrell School for Girls, group leader 1972-74; Widener Univ, counselor 1974-77; East Stroudsburg Univ, assoc prof/counselor 1977-. **ORGANIZATIONS:** Chair Interprofessional Relations PA Counseling Assoc 1984-; bd dirs Women's Resource's Monroe County 1986-; vice pres Pocono Chap Phi Delta Kappa 1986-87; mem NAACP, Amer Assoc Counseling & Develop, Amer Assoc Univ Professors. **HONORS/ACHIEVEMENTS:** Who's Who in the East 1979; Outstanding Young Women in Amer 1980; Appreciation Awd Black Student Assoc E Stroudsburg Univ 1981.

GRAHAM, PETER EDGAR
Physician. **PERSONAL:** Born Jan 17, 1948; married Jennifer; children: Gordon, Peter Anthony, Tiffanie. **EDUCATION:** Brooklyn Coll, 1969; Downstate Med Sch, MD 1973. **CAREER:** Dept Med Downstate Med Sch, asst instr 1977-; Intern Med Comm Med Mt Sinai Hosp;; resd 1974-77; Intern Med Kings Co Hosp, intern 1973-74. **ORGANIZATIONS:** Mem Student Nat Med Assn; Am Pub Hlth Assn; resrch fellow Dept of Neoplast Dis Mt Sinai Sch of Med 1979; fellow Am Cancer Soc 1980; mem NY Acad of Scis 1980; mem Am Coll of Physic 1980; chmn Union Carribbean Stud 1967; mem Jamaica Prog League 1969.

GRAHAM, PRECIOUS JEWEL
Educational director. **PERSONAL:** Born May 03, 1925, Springfield, OH; daughter of Robert Lee Freeman (deceased) and Lulabelle Malone Freeman (deseased); married Paul Nathaniel Graham; children: Robert; Nathan. **EDUCATION:** Fisk Univ, BA 1946; Case Western Reserve Univ, MSSA 1953; Univ of Dayton, JD 1979. **CAREER:** YWCA, prog dir 1946-53; Antioch, other positions 1964-69; Antioch College, prof soc welfare 1969-89; Antioch College, director of institute of human development 1984-89. **ORGANIZATIONS:** Mem OH Bar 1979-; dir Yellow Springs Instrument Co 1981-; pres Yellow Springs Comm Fnd 1980, Pres, YWCA of USA 1979-85; bd dir, Meadville Lombard Theological Seminary 1983-87; president, World YWCA 1987-91. **HONORS/ACHIEVEMENTS:** Faculty lecturer Antioch College 1979-80; Soc Wrkr of Year Miami Valley NASW 1975; Danforth Assc Danforth Fnd 1971-; Greene County Women's Hall of Fame Greene Cty OH 1982; Ten Top Women of Miami Valley, Dayton Daily News 1987; Ohio Women's Hall of Fame 1988. **BUSINESS ADDRESS:** Dir Human Development Inst, Antioch College, Yellow Springs, OH 45387.

GRAHAM, RICHARD A.
Dentist. **PERSONAL:** Born Feb 13, 1936, Boston. **EDUCATION:** Norwich U, BS 1956; HowardUniv Dental Sch, DDS 1966. **CAREER:** Crownsville State Hosp, staff dent 1969-70; Western Hlth Dent Clin Balti, clin dir 1970-. **ORGANIZATIONS:** Md Dental Soc; Am Dental Soc pvt ofce; W Balti Fedn; NAACP. **MILITARY SERVICE:** AUS lt 1956-60, capt 1966-70. **BUSINESS ADDRESS:** 3502 N Rogers Ave, Baltimore, MD.

GRAHAM, SAUNDRA M.
Government official. **PERSONAL:** Born Sep 05, 1941, Cambridge, MA; children: Carl Jr, Rhonda, Tina, Darryl, David. **EDUCATION:** Univ of MA. **CAREER:** MA State Legis, state rep; Cambridge City Counc, 1971-; Cambridge, v mayor 1975-. **ORGANIZATIONS:** Mem Wom Cau MA State Leg; MA Black Cau; Cambridge Black Concl; chmn Housing & Land Use Com; bd of dir Riverside Cambridgeport Comm Corp 1971-76. **HONORS/ACHIEVEMENTS:** Sojourner Truth awd; Nat Assn of Negro Bus & Professional Wom Clubs 1976 dist Citz Awd; MA Assn of Afro-AM Pol 1974. **BUSINESS ADDRESS:** State Rep, Rm 156 State House, Boston, MA 02133.

GRAHAM, TECUMSEH XAVIER
Clergyman. **PERSONAL:** Born Mar 14, 1925, Washington, DC; married Loreda Branch; children: Tecumseh X, Jr, Marjorie Ella. **EDUCATION:** Livingstone Coll, BA 1955; Hood Theol Sem, BD, MDiv 1958, 1974; Xavier U, LlD 1971; Cincinnati Tech Coll, DTL 1973; Cincinnati Bible Coll Seminary, DD 1980; Livingstone Coll, DD 1983. **CAREER:** Cleveland Co, Shelby NC Pub Schs, Portland OR State Even Coll, Xavier Univ Univ of CT, tchr & lecturer; Sag Horbor Long Island, pastor 1950-53; BelmontNC, pastor 1953-56; Shelby NC, pastor 1956-60; Portland OR, pastor 1960-64; St Mark AME Zion Ch, clergyman 1964-79; Coun of Christ Comm, exec dir 1972-;Broadway Temple AME Zion Church, pastor 1979-. **ORGANIZATIONS:** Vp Local NAACP 1965-66; pres Interdenom Minist Alli 1966-68; Am Assn ofUniv Profs 1968-72; pres Bd of Educ 1972; chmn Bd of Trust Cinc Tech Coll 1973; Mem Citizens Com on Yth; mem YKRC-TV Dial Pan 1967-; city councilman Cincinnati OH 1978-79; pres KY Council of Churches 1985-; mem many other civic org. **HONORS/ACHIEVEMENTS:** Outstanding Serv Awd NAACP 1959; Civic Leadership Cit 1959; many other leadership awds and citations. **BUSINESS ADDRESS:** Pastor, Broadway Temple AME Zion Ch, 662 South 13th St, Louisville, KY 40203.

GRAHAM, THEODORE N.
Physician. **PERSONAL:** Born Feb 05, 1930, Detroit; married Celestine Stanton; children: Theodore Kevin, Douglas Hiram, Gregory Stanton. **EDUCATION:** Wayne U, BS 1952; Meharry Med Coll, MD 1960. **CAREER:** Biochem Lab Harper Hosp, chief med tech 1954-56; St Jos Mercy Hosp, int med res 1961-64;Univ MI Hosp, 1962-63; St Jos Mercy Hosp, chief

res 1963-64; priv pract. **ORGANIZATIONS:** *Mem Speak Bur MI Heart Assn; Wayne Co Med Soc; MI Med Soc; Am Med Assn; MI Diab Assn; Det Canc Club; Det med dir Martin Luther King's Poor Peop Mar 1968; exec bd St Jos Mer Hosp 1969; mem Omega Psi Phi Frat; Jack & Jill Am Inc; Founders Soc Det Inst Arts; John Jay Asso Colum U;Meharry Alumni Assn; NAACP; co-found Quest Cult Club chmn 1965-68. **HONORS/ACHIEVEMENTS:** Publs in field. **MILITARY SERVICE:** AUS 1952-54.

GRANBERRY, JAMES MADISON, JR.
Clergyman. **PERSONAL:** Born Apr 29, 1914, Coweta, OK; married Ethel Lee Hymes. **EDUCATION:** Western U, AA 1934; Lane Coll, AB 1936; OK Sch of Rel, 1941-42; Fisk U, grad wk 1954-55; Minist Inst TN State U, 1960-61; Campbell Coll, hon DD 1954; Monrovia Coll, hon LlD 1955; Bethel Ch, ordained Deacon 1940; Ward Chapel AME Ch, ordained Elder 1944. **CAREER:** Camps Chap AME Ch, pastor; Handy Chapel & AME Ch; Cooper Chapel AME Ch; Bethel AME Ch; Metro AME Ch; St Peters AME Ch; St John AME Ch; St Paul AME Ch. **ORGANIZATIONS:** Sec treas pension dept AME Ch 1964; admitted to ann conf 1939; mem NAACP; mem Comm on struct for Mission 1972; mem Gen Assemb of Nat Counc of Chs 1966; mem IBPOE Pride of TN; Masonic Lodge; Mt Hope 96. **HONORS/ACHIEVEMENTS:** Outst cit of Nash 1960; chart mem Beta Pi Chap of Alpha Phi Alpha 1936; outst minis awd; Payne Sem 1964; cit OK State House of Reps 1970; Chaplainof day Mar 12 1973; gen assemb TN ldrs of Black Am; Who's Who in Rel; Pers of the S; Who's Who in TN 1973.

GRANDISON, EARL MICHAEL
Singer, actor. **PERSONAL:** Born Mar 24, 1950, Baltimore. **EDUCATION:** Peabody Conservatory Mus, BMus 1972; Operatic Performance Curtis Inst, cert 1974. **CAREER:** Lake George Opera Co NY, professional operatic debut 1970; Scott Joplin's Opera Treemonisha Wolf Trap Park Wash, prin role; Resident Co Wolf Trap , mem 2 seasons; concert & recital appearances frequently in MD, PA, NY, NJ, VA, Wash DC; Philadelphia Orchestra, 1975; Opera, Concert, Mus Comedy Tv, singer actor; Settlement Mus Sch Phila, faculty. **ORGANIZATIONS:** Baltimore Urban Mus Theater 1971; Playward Bus Theater Co 1975; Wilmington Opera Soc 1974; Young Audiences Inc of Philadelphia since 1972; summer concerts Goldman Band NY 1972-73; PBS TV Network 1975; heard overseas via Voice Am 1973. **HONORS/ACHIEVEMENTS:** Marian Anderson prize 1st place 1972; flwshps Wolf Trap Found 1972, 73; Omega Psi Phi Talent Hunt 1968; 1st prize dist 3rd regnl Myra Grand Chap Eastern Star talent contest 1st Place 1968; first place talent Intl Platform Assn 1974.

GRANGER, CARL VICTOR
Physician. **PERSONAL:** Born Nov 26, 1928, Brooklyn, NY; son of Carl Granger and Marie Granger; married Joanne Ghee; children: Glenn, Marilyn. **EDUCATION:** Dartmouth Coll, AB 1948; New York Univ, MD 1952. **CAREER:** Yale New Haven Hosp, faculty 1961-67; Tufts New England Medical Ctr, faculty 1967-77; Brown Univ, faculty 1977-83; SUNY at Buffalo, prof 1983-. **MILITARY SERVICE:** AUS 1st lt to major 1954-61. **BUSINESS ADDRESS:** Prof Rehabilitative Medicine, SUNY at Buffalo, 100 High St, Buffalo, NY 14203.

GRANGER, EDWINA C.
Artist. **PERSONAL:** Born Oct 15, Yonkers, NY; daughter of Paul Weldon and Christina White Weldon Small; widowed. **EDUCATION:** New York Univ, Courses & Cert Sculp Ceramic 1952; Caton Rose Inst of Fine Arts, Landscape Anatomy 1958; Art Student League New York, Portrait Fig 1962; Rutgers Univ, Certificate in Real Estate 1978; New Mexico Univ, Composition Abstract 1965. **CAREER:** Creative Arts McGuire AFB, tchr 1963-64; exhibiting artist throughout USA and Azores 1964-84; African & Afro-Amer People Exhibits, original pen & ink prints 1973-84; Doll Shows Applehead Ceramic, dollmaker 1976-80. **ORGANIZATIONS:** Festival art consultant 1980, art judge 1984, Garden State Art Center 1980; Meadow Lands Race Track 3 Shows 1979-84; mem, NAACP, 1985; mem, Natl Conf of Artists; mem, Natl League of Amer Pen Women, 1965-81; mem Southern Christian Leadership Conf Women 1988-89. **HONORS/ACHIEVEMENTS:** Alexander Medal of Honor, Walton High School; Outstanding Achievement Art Award, NBPW, Willingboro, NJ; first prize in many art shows, Illinois, New Mexico, New York, New Jersey, Azores; currently working on Martin Luther King Show/Prints/Oil/Pen/Ink; completed fine art print, "The Spectators," Color Print Limited Edition 500, 1988. **HOME ADDRESS:** 7145 Chestnut Lane, Riverdale, GA 30274.

GRANGER, SHELTON B.
Planning consultant, executive director. **PERSONAL:** Born Feb 21, 1921, Harrisburg, PA; son of Dr. Augustus T Granger and Katherine H Granger; married Dorothy Steele (deceased); children: Carol Nesmith, Katherine, Diane Bowman, Shelton H, Richelle Shelton. **EDUCATION:** Howard U, AB 1942; Columbia U, MS 1947. **CAREER:** Cleveland Urban League OH, dir of industrl rel 1947-51; MN Urban League MN, exec dir 1951-58; Cleveland Urban League OH, exec dir 1958-62; Pres Com on Juvenile Delinquency Dept of Justice, consult 1962; Youth Develmntl Div Childrens Bureau Dept of Hlth/Educ & Welfare, dir 1962-63; Human Resources Devel Div Latin Am Bureau Agency for Intl Devel, dir 1963-65; Dept of Hlth/Educ & Welfare, deputy asst sec 1965-66; Intl Affairs Dept of Hlth/Educ & Welfare, deputy asst sec 1966-69; Macalester Coll St Paul, MN, asso prof/cons on urban affairs. **ORGANIZATIONS:** Field worker Urban League of Greater NY; recruitment specialist Peace Corps Cleveland, OH; consult Ford Found Social & Govt Agencies; guest lecturer Univ of MN & Univ MD Sch of Soc Work; field instructor Sch of Applied Soc Sci at Case-Western Reserve U; field instructor Atlanta Univ Sch of Soc Work; field instructor Univ of MN Sch of Social Work; founder/owner of Private Consltng Firms; asso prof Lincoln Univ PA. **HONORS/ACHIEVEMENTS:** Publications, "The Urban Crisis-Challenge for the Century" Paul S Amidon & Asso Inc Minneapolis, MN 1970; The Ebony Success Library; Community Leaders & Noteworthy Am. **MILITARY SERVICE:** AUS 1st lt 1942-46. **HOME ADDRESS:** 5307 Woodbine Ave, Philadelphia, PA 19131.

GRANT, ANNA AUGUSTA FREDRINA
Educator. **PERSONAL:** Born in Jacksonville, FL; married Thomas Ray Grant; children: Kimberly Anne-Renee, Donna Dianna-Raye. **EDUCATION:** FL A&M Univ, BA; Fisk Univ, MA; WA State Univ, PhD; OD Assn, Cert Orgnl Devel Change Agent. **CAREER:** WA State Univ, teacher & resch asst 1951-55, counselor 1954-55; Dillard Univ, asst prof & freshman counselor 1956; Grambling Coll, assoc prof sociology 1956-57; Fisk Univ, dean of students & assoc prof 1957-59; LA State Special Educ Team, prof soc & coord of comm studies & psychiatric soc work 1959-63; Morehouse Coll, prof of sociology & dept head. **ORGANIZATIONS:** Visiting prof & lecturer to numerous sch, coll, univ in Amer & abroad; Amer Personnel & Guidance Assn; GA Psychological Assn; Amer Assn of Univ Prof; So Sociological Soc; mem League of Women Voters; NAACP; Natl Counc of Negro Women; YWCA; YMCA; Delta Sigma Theta; Phi Beta Kappa. **HONORS/ACHIEVEMENTS:** Who's Who of Amer Women; Who's Who in Edn; Who's Who in S & SE; Intl Dictionary of Biography; Pers of the So; Amer Men & Women of Sci; FL Meml CollAchiev Award 1976; FAMU Alumni Achiev Award 1984; Wash State Univ Alumni Award 1982; Eminent Scholar Norfolk State Univ 1972; NAACP Natl Urban League Black Family Summit 1984; Frederick Douglass Inst Disting Prof Serv Award 1972; Bronze Woman of the Year in Educ Iota Phi Lambda 1972; Dogwood Festival Award 1974. **BUSINESS ADDRESS:** Prof of Sociology, Morehouse College, Box 733, Atlanta, GA 30314.

GRANT, ARTHUR H.
Attorney. **PERSONAL:** Born Oct 23, 1930, Louisiana; married Bonnie Connors; children: Arthur H, Jr, Charlotte, Norman. **EDUCATION:** Wilson Jr Coll, 1951; John Marshall Law Sch, JD 1954. **CAREER:** Arthur H Grant Ltd, attny; Major Lance noted enter, past mgr; Barbara Atklin; Johnny Williams; Profit Publ Co Lucky Labels Inc, pres; Jabita & Co Imprtrs, v p. **ORGANIZATIONS:** Mem NBA; Cook Co Bar Assn; IL Bar Assn. **MILITARY SERVICE:** AUS spec 4/C 1955-56. **BUSINESS ADDRESS:** 30 W Washington, Chicago, IL 60602.

GRANT, CEDRIC STEVEN
Government administrator. **PERSONAL:** Born Aug 10, 1952, New Orleans, LA. **EDUCATION:** Xavier Univ of Louisiana, BA Political Science 1970-74; University of New Orleans, HUD Fellow, MPA 1978-81. **CAREER:** US Army, army officer 1974-77; City of New Orleans, economic development planner 1980-81, housing administrator 1981-82; Downtown Development District, dir of capital projects 1982-. **ORGANIZATIONS:** Member Intl City Management Assoc 1979-84; member American Society for Public Administrators 1979-84; board member Community Food Distribution Center 1983-84; member Natl Forum of Black Public Administrators 1984; member Metropolitan Area Committee Forum 1984; bd mem Natl Forum For Black Public Admins 1986-88. **HONORS/ACHIEVEMENTS:** Graduate Fellowship Department of Housing & Urban Development 1979-81. **MILITARY SERVICE:** AUS Captain 10; Natl Defense Medal-1974 Army Reserve Achievement Medal 1984. **HOME ADDRESS:** 3523 Piedmont Dr, New Orleans, LA 70122. **BUSINESS ADDRESS:** Dir of Capital Projects, Downtown Development Dist, 301 Camp St, New Orleans, LA 70130.

GRANT, CHARLES TRUMAN
Business executive. **PERSONAL:** Born Oct 10, 1946, Chicago, IL; son of Charles Grant and Mildred Grant; divorced; children: Jordanna Lynn. **EDUCATION:** DePaul Univ, BA 1969, MBA 1975; Licensed Real Estate Broker 1986; Licensed Mortgage Broker 1987. **CAREER:** V Mueller Div Amer Hosp Supply Corp, staff accountant, chief accountant, gen acctg mgr, cost acctg mgr 1970-73; Rand McNally & Co, gen credit mgr, dir internal audit 1973-75; Amer Hosp Supply Corp, corp dir, acctg & reporting, div controller officer, 1975-78; Mead Corp, oper admin, vice pres 1978-80; Ft Dearborn Paper Co, ceo, pres 1980-82; Acquisition Mgmt, evp 1982-84; Mid Amer Inc, pres, ceo 1985-; Mergers & Acquisitions, vp; Baird & Warner Inc, 1986-87; Grant-Eaton Ventures, Inc, pres 1985-. **ORGANIZATIONS:** Pres Natl Black MBA Assoc; bd of dir CEDCO Capital Inc, MESBIC Venture Capital; mem NY Credit & Fin Mgmt Assoc; fin adv Jr Achievement. **HONORS/ACHIEVEMENTS:** Article in Ebony Mag 1977, Black Enterprise 1978, Chicago Trib, Crain's Chicago Bus, Chicago Defender, Ebony Mag, Black Enterprise; Ten Outstanding Prof of the Year Blackbook Dollars & Sense Mag 1982; Outstanding Young Man in Amer Jaycees 1982; Outstanding MBA of the Year Natl Black MBA Assoc 1982; DePaul Univ Disting Alumni Awd; publ in Bus & Soc Review Mag 1984-85; Listed in DuSable Museum Chgo. **MILITARY SERVICE:** AUSR 1968-74. **HOME ADDRESS:** 1240 N Lake Shore Dr, Apt 6B, Chicago, IL 60610.

GRANT, CHERYL DAYNE
Attorney. **PERSONAL:** Born Jan 03, 1944, Cincinnati, OH; married Daniel R. **EDUCATION:** Univ of Cin, BA 1966;Univ of Cincinnati Law Sch. **CAREER:** CD Grant & Asso Co LPA, asst OH atty gen 1979-80; Univ of Cincin, asst prof 1976-78; City of Lin Hgts OH, dir legal svcs; Cong Thomas A Luken House of Rep, admin aide of 1974-; Legal Aid Soc, atty 1973-74; Cincinnati Lawyers for Hsing (ABA Proj) 1972; Cin, police Offcr 1968-70; Mem Comm Ctr, soc wrkr 1966-68; ABC'S of Law WCIN-RADIO, co-mod. **ORGANIZATIONS:** Mem bd dir Wom Cty Club; mem bd NAACP; mem bd of Cit Com on Just & Corr; mem pres bd Mem Comm Ctr; mem Alpha Kappa Alpha; mem Cincinnati Bar Assn; OH Bar Assn; ABA; cin Lawyers Club; Black Lawyers Assn of Cin. **HONORS/ACHIEVEMENTS:** Listed in outst yng wom in amer; appoint OH Yth Adv Bd 1974-77; appoint OH Juv Just Adv Comm OH 1976-; NAACP scholar 1970-73; Regin Heber Smith fellow Howard U. **BUSINESS ADDRESS:** Ste 2125 Krover Bldg, Cincinnati, OH 45202.

GRANT, CLAUDE DEWITT
Educational administrator. **PERSONAL:** Born Dec 20, 1944, New York, NY; son of Claude Allen Grant and Rose Levonia Nelson Chenault; married Gloriana B Waters; children: Damian A;Tahra L. **EDUCATION:** US Armed Forces Inst Germany, 1 yr coll equiv; Bronx Comm Coll, (with Honors) 1970-72; Hunter Coll, BA Social Sci 1972-74; Mercy Coll Long Island, Masters Program Psychology not completed. **CAREER:** NY Psychiatric Inst, psych intern 1973-74; Yonkers Youth Svcs, adolescent counselor 1974-76; Jamaica Comm Adol Progassoc psych, sr soc wkr 1976-79; Bronx Comm Coll, coord prog & cultural affairs 1979-1986;Dir, BUsiness & Professional Development Inst. **ORGANIZATIONS:** Admin ed/fiscal officer Blind Beggar Press 1977-; spec proj dir Unity & Strength of BCC 1981-; mem Coll Media Advisers 1982-, Assoc for Ed in Journalism 1983-; consult Bronx Council on the Arts 1983-;Community College Journalism Assoc; 1984; Free Lance Contributor to;Essence Magazine, Amsterdam News, etc;"Jazz, Lost Legacy of A People"? (Univ of Ca at Berkeley), " Creativity, Imagination Help Preserve Quality Programs on a Limited Budget" (Bulletin of Assoc of College Unions International) Papers presented at BCC 1986, Pace University 1985, Howard University 1987; Books Published, " Keeping Time" 1981, " Images in a Shaded Light" 1986. **HONORS/ACHIEVEMENTS:** Deans List/BCC Bronx CC 1970,71,72; Serv Awds Bronx CC 1972,80,81,83,84; Listed in Directory of Disting Amers 3rd ed, Intl Who's Who in Poetry (Great Britain), Biographical/Bibliog Dir of Black Amer Writers (Univ of WI), Dir of Amer Poets & Fiction Writers (Poets & Writers Inc) 1985-86;Int'l Author's and writers Who's Who, Who's Who in US Writers, Editors & Poets, BCC Meritorious Service Awards 1972-1986. **MILITARY SERVICE:** AUS corpl 3 yrs;medical technician/medical records clerk Texas, Germany. **HOME ADDRESS:** 1783 Bussing Avenue, Bronx,

NY 10466. **BUSINESS ADDRESS:** Dir Business & Professional Development Inst, Bronx Community College, West 181 St &Univ Ave, Bronx, NY 10453.

GRANT, DEBORA FELITA
Minister. **PERSONAL:** Born Jul 28, 1956, Georgetown, SC; daughter of Rev Joseph J Grant and Lillie M Ward Grant. **EDUCATION:** Clark Coll, Atlanta GA, BA Mass Communications, 1981; Interdenominational Theological Center, Atlanta GA, Master of Divinity Pastoral Care and Counseling, 1987. **CAREER:** DHR/Div of Youth Serv, Atlanta GA, court serv worker, 1977-85; Flipper Temple AME Church, Atlanta GA, asst minister, 1985-; Morris Brown Coll, Atlanta GA, chaplain, 1987-. **ORGANIZATIONS:** Mem, Black Women In Church and Soc, 1986-89; exec sec, Concerned Black Clergy of Metro Atlanta, 1987-89; mem, NAACP, 1987-89, AME Ministers Union, 1988-89, Natl Assn of College & Univ Chaplains, 1989, Natl Black Campus Ministers Assn, 1989, SCLC Women, 1989. **HOME ADDRESS:** 249 Fielding Ln SW, Atlanta, GA 30311. **BUSINESS ADDRESS:** Chaplain, Morris Brown College, 643 Martin Luther King Jr Dr, Atlanta, GA 30311.

GRANT, DELL OMEGA
Journalist. **PERSONAL:** Born Nov 23, 1951, Georgetown, SC; daughter of Rev Joseph James Grant and Lillie Mae Ward Grant. **EDUCATION:** Columbia Coll, Columbia SC, Natl Science Found Certificate, 1968; St Olaf Coll, Northfield MN, BA, 1973; Parsons School of Design, attended, 1977; Columbia Univ, Graduate School of Journalism, MS, 1984. **CAREER:** Georgetown County Schools, Georgetown SC, teacher, 1973-74; New York City Bd of Educ, New York NY, staff analyst, 1975-79; AME Z Overseas Missions, New York NY, admin, assoc editor, 1980-83; The New York Times, New York NY, editor, 1984-85; New York City Dept of Corrections, New York NY, public affairs editor, 1988-. **ORGANIZATIONS:** Pres, Georgetown United Tutorial Serv (vista), 1967; founder, exec dir, Georgetown Dance Theatre Inc, 1974-75; exec sec, New York Assn of Black Journalists, 1988-89; mem, Nat Assn of Black Journalists, 1989; life mem, Kitani Found (defunct), Columbia SC. **HONORS/ACHIEVEMENTS:** General Excellence, St Cyprian, 1965; Mother Butlor's Acad Scholarship, Bronx NY, 1965; Natl Science Found Scholarship, Columbia Coll SC, 1968; Valedictorian, and various academic, club & citizenship awards, Howard High School, 1969; St Olaf Scholarship, St Olaf Coll, 1969-73; "De Profundis," a 3-movement dance, choreographer, performed with band, choir and dancers at "Young Choreographer's Night," Walker Arts Center in Minneapolis MN; performed on tour throughout midwest and in Washington DC; later "Precious Memories," performed at young choreographer's night at the Walker Center, 1969-73; recruitment brochure, First for St Olaf Chicago Urban Studies South Side, Associated Colleges of the Midwest, 1972; Dance Theatre of Harlem Scholarships, Dance Theatre of Harlem, 1972, 1974-75; Interdisciplinary Honors, St Olaf, 1973; Outstanding Young Woman of Amer, 1977; Scholarships in the Arts for New York City High School Students (booklet), 1979-80; The Missionary Seer Magazine, 1980-83; New York Times Scholarship, The New York Times, 1983-84; Correction News, Newsletter, 1988-.

GRANT, GARY RUDOLPH
Business executive. **PERSONAL:** Born Aug 19, 1943, Newport News, VA; divorced. **EDUCATION:** NC Central Univ, BA 1965; Shaw Univ, post grad studies attended; NC Wesleyan Coll, post grad studies attended; East Carolina Univ, post grad studies attended. **CAREER:** Halifax Cty Schools, teacher 1965-79; Tillery Casket Mfg Inc, gen mgr 1979-. **ORGANIZATIONS:** Bd mem Concerned Citizens of Tillery 1979-, NC Hunger Coalition 1982-, Halifax Cty Bd of Ed 1982-86; chairperson Committee to Save Black Owned Land 1983-. **HONORS/ACHIEVEMENTS:** Gary Grant Day Tillery Comm 1978; 4-H Club Halifax Cty; Gov Volunteer Awd Gov James B Hunt 1982. **BUSINESS ADDRESS:** General Manager, Tillery Casket Mfg Inc, PO Box 68, Tillery, NC 27887.

GRANT, GEORGE C.
Library administrator. **PERSONAL:** Born Oct 22, 1939, Memphis, TN; son of Willie L Grant Sr and Clara Lawson Grant; married Alice Morgan Grant, Mar 16, 1963; children: Genine M, Melanie C. **EDUCATION:** Owen Jr Coll, Memphis TN, AA, 1959; Morehouse Coll, Atlanta GA, BS, 1961; Atlanta Univ, Atlanta GA, MSLS, 1962; Univ of Pittsburgh, SLIS, Pittsburgh PA, PhD, 1981. **CAREER:** Owen Jr Coll, Memphis TN, head librarian, 1962-65; Southern Illinois Univ, Edwardsville IL, E St Louis Campus, chief librarian, 1965-67, assoc dir of library, 1967-76; Morgan State Univ, Baltimore MD, library dir, 1976-81; Stockton State Coll, Pomona NJ, library dir, 1981-86; Rollins Coll, Winter Park FL, dir of libraries, 1986-. **ORGANIZATIONS:** Mem, Amer Library Assn, 1967-, Black Caucus of ALA, 1971-; exec bd mem, Black Caucus of ALA, 1980-; editor, newsletter, Black Caucus of ALA, 1980-; chair, 1982-86, advisory comm, 1982-88, ALA Office of Library Outreach Serv; editor, membership directory, Black Caucus of ALA, 1984-; mem, Florida Library Assn, 1986-; mem, bd of dir, Central Florida Soc of Afro-Amer Heritage, 1987-; mem, steering comm, Preserve the Eatonville FL Community, 1988-; steering comm, Central Florida Library Network, 1988-; advisory comm, Florida State Library, LSCA, 1988-. **HONORS/ACHIEVEMENTS:** Fellowship for PhD Studies, Univ of Pittsburgh, 1974-75; Council on Library resources Acad, Library Internship Yale Univ, 1975-76; Newsletter of the Black Caucus of ALA, 1980-88; Membership Directory, Black Caucus of ALA, 4th edition, 1984, 5th edition, 1986, 6th edition, 1988; Preserve the Etonville Community Inc Serv Award, 1989. **BUSINESS ADDRESS:** Director of Libraries, Rollins College, Olin Library, Winter Park, FL 32789.

GRANT, HOWARD P.
Civil engineer. **PERSONAL:** Born Jul 28, 1925, Houston, TX; married Julia. **EDUCATION:** Univ Of CA, BS. **CAREER:** City & Cnty of San Franc, civil Eng 1948-. **ORGANIZATIONS:** Mem Natl Soc of Prof Eng; mem North CA Counc of Black Prof Eng; mem Eng Manpower Train Comm; mem Alpha Phi Alpha; mem Commonwealth Club Of CA; bd of dir Bethany Sr CitHm; mem Boy Scout Comm 1970; Mem Big Bros 1965. **MILITARY SERVICE:** USAF 1944-45.

GRANT, JACQUELYN
Educator. **PERSONAL:** Born Dec 19, 1948, Georgetown, SC. **EDUCATION:** Bennett Coll, BA 1970; Interdenominational Theol Ctr, MDiv 1973; Union Theol Seminary, MPhil 1980, PhD 1985. **CAREER:** Union Theol Seminary, tutor & relief teacher 1975-77; Harvard Divinity School, assoc in rsch 1977-79; Candler School of Emory/Theol Univ, visiting lecturer 1981; Princeton Theol Seminary, visit lectr 1985; Interdenominational Theol Center, asst prof 1980-. **ORGANIZATIONS:** Assoc minister Allen AME Church 1973-80; itinerant elder African Methodist Episcopal Church 1976; assoc minister Flipper Temple AME Church 1980; founder/dir Black Women in Church & Soc 1981; bd of dirs Black Theology Project in the Americas. **HONORS/ACHIEVEMENTS:** DuBois Fellowship Harvard Univ 1979-80; Dissertation Fellowship Fund for Theological Educ 1979-80; Amer Black Achievement Awd nominee Johnson Publishing Co 1982; Woman of the Year in Religion nominee Iota Phi Lambda Sorority 1984. **BUSINESS ADDRESS:** Asst Prof of Systematic Theol, Interdenominational Theological Ctr, 671 Beckwith St SW, Atlanta, GA 30314.

GRANT, JAMES
Educational administrator. **PERSONAL:** Born Dec 28, 1932, Ruffin, SC; married Maggie Ruth Harrison; children: Christopher, Kevin, Karen. **EDUCATION:** Adelphi Univ, BBA 1959, MBA 1973. **CAREER:** Adelphi Univ, asst controller 1970-73, controller 1973; CUNY-Medgar Evers Coll, assoc dean of admin 1973-78, dean of admin 1978-79; SUNY-College at New Paltz, vice pres for admin. **ORGANIZATIONS:** Consultant MD State Higher Educl 1984 & 1985; consultant Middle States Assn 1985; pres Auxillary Compus Enterprises Inc 1979-; mem Eastern Assn of Univ & Coll Business Officers 1970-; pres State Univ of NY Business Officers Assn 1983-85. **MILITARY SERVICE:** AUS sp4 2 yrs. **BUSINESS ADDRESS:** Vice President Administration, SUNY/The College at New Paltz, Hab 905, New Paltz, NY 12561.

GRANT, JOHN H., SR.
Manager. **PERSONAL:** Born May 11, 1927, Philadelphia, PA; married Carolyn Sawyer; children: John Jr, Marsha L. **EDUCATION:** Tuskegee Inst, graduated 1949. **CAREER:** Boeing Vertol, inspector, supervisor, genl supervisor, asst mgr contract maintenance mgr, quality assurance corrective action unit, quality assurance rep, quality control final assembly supervisor, sr product assurance analyst, coord of quality control functions, supervisor dynamic components 1961-. **ORGANIZATIONS:** Mem and past pres Boeing Mgmt Assoc; dir emeritus Northeastern Regional, Tuskegee Inst Alumni Assoc Inc; mem Amer Helicopter Soc Inc; past vice chmn exec bd Natl Tuskegee Alumni Inc; chmn trustee bd New Bethlehem Bapt Church 1975-85. **HONORS/ACHIEVEMENTS:** Deputy/Lecture Awd Outstanding Worshipful Master 1st Dist Prince Hall Masons; 33 Degree Mason, United Supreme Council, Northern Jurisdiction 1988. **MILITARY SERVICE:** AUS motor sgt 1946-50. **HOME ADDRESS:** 267 East Meehan Ave, Philadelphia, PA 19119.

GRANT, JOSEPH N.
Educator. **PERSONAL:** Born Apr 04, 1925, Tarboro, NC; married Maye Holden. **EDUCATION:** NC Coll, BS 1948, MS 1949; Tchrs Coll Clmb U, MEd;Univ CT, PhD. **CAREER:** Wash High School, Rdsvl NC, teacher coach 1949-51; DE State Coll, chmn bio dept 1953-61; Mnstry Educ Nigeria, sci educ adv fed 1961-63; New Brtn Office Economic Opportunity, exec dir 1965-68; Univ of CT Storrs, assoc prof 1968-. **ORGANIZATIONS:** Mem Sch Sci Consult Team; wrkshp ldr Svrl Colls & U; mem Am Assn Advncmnt Sci; AIBT; AAPSS; invtn to mem NC Acad Sci; mem AAUP; Phi Delta Kappa; Beta Kappa Chi; NEA; CSTA; corp N Brtn Gen Hosp 1967; Rtry Intl 1967; bd tst CT Jnt Cncl Econ Educ 1971-; Cncl Hum Rghts OppUniv CT 1974-; bd dir St Mchl's Cntr Hrtfrd 1973-. **HONORS/ACHIEVEMENTS:** 3 Nat Sci Fnd Schlr; Who's Who Am Edn; Who's Who Am Sci; Who's Who CT 1974; Beta Kappa Chi; Phi Delta Kappa; Omega Psi Phi. **MILITARY SERVICE:** AUS 1945-47. **BUSINESS ADDRESS:** University of Connecticut, Storrs, CT 06268.

GRANT, KINGSLEY B.
Physician. **PERSONAL:** Born Feb 13, 1931, Central Amer; married Margaret; children: Ward, Conrad Maxwell. **EDUCATION:** Univ London, BA 1948; Howard Univ, BS 1955, MD 1959; Amer Bd of Pathology, cert 1964; Amer Bd of Pathology & Dermatopathology, cert 1980. **CAREER:** LA Co Harbor General Hosp, resident anatomic & clinical pathologist, 1962-64, chief resident, 1963-64; St Lukes Hospital, resident anatomic & clinical path 1960-62, assoc pathco-dir path 1970; dir dept pathology & lab serv 1975-88. **ORGANIZATIONS:** Staff St Lukes Hosp 1964-; bd dir United Way 1966-71; Hawkeye Area Comm Action Prog 1968-69; CR chap Natl Conf Christians & Jews 1969; Am Soc Clin Path Chmn Cedar Rapids Commn Human Rights 1969; pres PTA 1969; clin asst prof Coll Med Univ IA 1973-; exec comm mem IA Assn Pathologists 1974-; pres St Lukes methodist Hosp Med/Dental Staff 1981; fellow Amer Coll Pathologists; mem Commn Race & Religion IA United Meth Ch, Rotary Club, Educ Oppor Prog Comm Coll Med Univ IA; mem AMA, NMA, Intl Acad Pathologists; delegate Coll of Amer Pathologists; secty-treasurer/pres, Iowa Assn of Pathologists, 1986-present. **HONORS/ACHIEVEMENTS:** Phi Beta Kappa 1955; Comm Bldr Awd B'nai B'rith 1970; Certificate of Appreciation City of Cedar Rapids 1974. **BUSINESS ADDRESS:** 9 Cottage Grove Woods, SE, Cedar Rapids, IA 52403.

GRANT, MCNAIR
Educator. **PERSONAL:** Born Aug 09, 1925, Fort Smith, AR; married Angela I; children: Mc Nair, Jr, Reme, Donna. **EDUCATION:** George Williams Coll, BA 1950; NWU, MA 1955. **CAREER:** Chicago Bd of Educ, assoc supt 1975-; area assoc supt 1972-75; dist supt 1965-72; prin, teacher 1950-65. **ORGANIZATIONS:** Mem Stratton Educ Assn; Nat Assn of Black Sch Edctrs; Am Assn of Admin; mem NAACP; Urban League. **HONORS/ACHIEVEMENTS:** Class pres George Wms Coll 1950; hon soc Kappa Delta Phi 1950; 1st vice pres Kappa Delta Phi 1970. **MILITARY SERVICE:** AUS sgt 1943-46. **BUSINESS ADDRESS:** 228 N La Salle, Chicago, IL.

GRANT, NATHANIEL
Corporate officer. **PERSONAL:** Born Sep 08, 1943, Washington, DC; married Patricia A; children: Monica D, Nathaniel D. **EDUCATION:** Norfolk State Coll, business admin courses 1964-66. **CAREER:** Communications Satellite, admin super 1966-69; Amer Assoc of Univ Women, production mgr 1969-73; Natl Public Radio, admin mgr 1973-77. **ORGANIZATIONS:** Mem Natl Forum for Black Public Administrators 1984-87. **HONORS/ACHIEVEMENTS:** Bd Resolution for Outstanding Serv Neighborhood Housing Serv of Amer 1982; Bd Resolution and Monetary Awd Neighborhood Reinvestment Corp 1986,1988. **MILITARY SERVICE:** USN yeoman 2nd class 4 yrs. **HOME ADDRESS:** 13713 Town Line Rd, Silver Spring, MD 20906. **BUSINESS ADDRESS:** Dir Personnel & Administration, Neighborhood Reinvestment, 1325 G St NW Ste 800, Washington, DC 20005.

GRANT, ROBERT C.
Educator. **PERSONAL:** Born Mar 14, 1943, Montgomery, AL; married Sandra Bates; children: Robert Jr, Angela Aileen. **EDUCATION:** AL State Univ, BA 1965. **CAREER:** Grambling Univ, instructor 1965; Urban League, vet affairs coordinator employment counsel-

or 1969-70; Meharry Medical Coll, assoc dir devel & dir alumni affairs 1970-83; Grant Enterprises Inc, owner/president. **ORGANIZATIONS:** Past exec sec Meharry Med Coll; mem Amer Alumni Council; TN Alumni Relations Council; Black Coll Fund; mem Civitan Intl; mem NAACP, YMCA; adv Kappa Chap Kappa Alpha Psi Frat; part owner/mem bd dirs WVOL Radio Station in Nashville; mem bd dir WMAK Radio Station in Nashville; apptd bd MTRMPC. **HONORS/ACHIEVEMENTS:** Who's Who Among Small Colls & Univs; Cert Plaques Alumni Meharry Med Coll Outstanding Svcs; Awded Cert for Outstanding Contrib to White House Conf onSmall Business by Pres Jimmy Carter 1980. **MILITARY SERVICE:** USAF s/sgt 1965-69. **BUSINESS ADDRESS:** President, Grant Enterprises Inc, 1005 18 Ave N, Nashville, TN 37208.

GRANT, TIMOTHY JEROME
Social worker. **PERSONAL:** Born Aug 06, 1965, Greenville, SC; son of John M Grant Sr and Mamie J Rosemond Grant. **EDUCATION:** Univ of South Carolina, Columbia SC, BS, 1987. **CAREER:** South Carolina House of Representatives, Cola SC, legislative aide, 1987-89; Richland County Dept of Social Serv, Cola SC, social serv specialist I, 1987-89, social serv specialist II, 1989-. **ORGANIZATIONS:** Phi Beta Sigma Frat, 1984-; Notary Public, South Carolina Notary Public, 1987-. **HONORS/ACHIEVEMENTS:** Undergraduate Brother of the Year, Phi Beta Sigma, 1986; Order of Omega Honor Soc, USC Greeks, 1987; Outstanding Young Men of Amer, OYM, 1987; Outstanding Coll Students of Amer, 1987; Serv Award, South Carolina House of Representatives, 1987. **HOME ADDRESS:** 1035 Comanchee Trail, Apt 0-2, West Columbia, SC 29169.

GRANT, WILLIAM W.
County official. **PERSONAL:** Born Oct 06, 1934, Guyton, GA; divorced; children: 1. **EDUCATION:** Mt Unoin Coll, 1960; Lee Inst, 1963; Ford Fellow, 1974-75; Shaw U, BA. **CAREER:** Ins Co, 1961-64; NC Mutual Life Ins Co, undrwrtr inves 1965-71; comm organizer & devel 1971-; Beaufort Co, co councilman 1972-; Grant Grant & Asso, owner. **ORGANIZATIONS:** Legislative com Hunger Malnutrition 1969-72; chmn bd dir Beaufort Jasper Comprehensive Health Serv 1971-73; chmn bd dir Beaufort Council for Handicapped1971-; Nat Consumer Conf 1973; SC Assn Councils 1974. **HONORS/ACHIEVEMENTS:** Cert merit Am Hosp Assn 1973; cert of awd & apprecn Beaufort-Jasper Mental Retardation 1977; cert of awd & apprecn Sons & Daughters Veterans & ReliefCorps; cert of awd Beaufort Co SC Bicentennial Commn; bldg named in honor W W Grant Jr Adult Devel Cntr. **MILITARY SERVICE:** AUS 1952-55. **BUSINESS ADDRESS:** Grant, Grant & Associates, PO Box 6093, Hilton Head Island, SC.

GRANT, WILMER, JR.
Educator. **PERSONAL:** Born Jul 29, 1940, Ahoskie, NC; married Ruth Dale Ford. **EDUCATION:** Hampton Inst, BA 1962; IN U, MS 1967; IN U, PhD 1974. **CAREER:** Univ of Toledo, asst prof 1973-; Univ of MO, asst dean 1972-73; IN Mil Acad, instructor 1966. **ORGANIZATIONS:** Mem Am Physical Soc; Am Inst of Physics; ctrl OH Black Studies Consortium; Nat Concl of Black Studies; consult DHEW 1976f Assn for the Study of Afro-Am Life & Hist 1976-; mem Alpha Phi Alpha 1961-; Sigma Pi Phi 1977-; Comm Chest Budget Com 1975; bd of tsts Cordelia Martin Ngbrhd Hlth Ctr 1974-76; Toledo Cncl for Bus 1975-77. **HONORS/ACHIEVEMENTS:** Omega Psi Phi talent contest State of VA 1958; comndtn AUS 1961; cert of merit Kappa League 1977f develpr "Famous Black Symphomic Composers' & Their Works"1976. **MILITARY SERVICE:** AUS 1st lt capt 1962-64. **HOME ADDRESS:** 4323 Terrace View N, Toledo, OH 43607.

GRANTLEY, ROBERT CLARK
Electric utility company executive. **PERSONAL:** Born Aug 30, 1948, Atlanta, GA; son of Robert Charles Grantley and Edith Clark Grantley; married Sandra Prophet Grantley, Nov 22, 1979; children: Michael, Robyn. **EDUCATION:** Howard Univ, Washington DC, BSEE, 1971; Catholic Univ, Washington DC, JD, 1983. **CAREER:** Challenger Research Inc, Rockville MD, electronics engineer, 1971-73; Potomac Electric Power Company, Washington DC, start-up engineer, 1973-75, site mgr, 1975-78, construction coord, 1978-84, mgr, Energy Use Mgmt, 1974-87, mgr, Customer Serv, 1987-. **ORGANIZATIONS:** Mem, Washington DC Bar Assn, 1983-, Maryland Bar Assn, 1983-; bd of dir, Metropolitan Police Boys & Girls Club, 1984-; mem, Edison Electric Inst Customer Serv Comm, 1987-; bd of dir, Washington DC Assn for Retarded Citizens, 1987-; vice chmn, United Way Campaign Program for Potomac Electric Power Company, 1989. **BUSINESS ADDRESS:** Manager, Customer Service, Potomac Electric Power Company, 1900 Pennsylvania Ave NW, Room 204, Washington, DC 20068.

GRANVILLE, WILLIAM, JR.
Petroleum business executive. **PERSONAL:** Born Dec 06, 1940, Warner Robbins, GA; son of William Granville Sr and Marian Hicks; married Jessica Katherine Hilton; children: Cheryl Lynn, Michelle Marie, William Lamont. **EDUCATION:** Delaware St Coll, BS Math (cum laude) 1962, Doctor of Humane Letters, Honoris Causa 1987. **CAREER:** Dept of Army, mathematician 1962-65; Mobil Rsch & Develop Corp, res math 1965-69; Mobil Intl Div, intl planning analyst 1969-70, intl rel exec 1970-76; Mobil Oil Corp, mgr Middle East training oper 1976-81, mgr tech transfer Middle East 1981-; Mobil Intl Consulting Serv Inc, exec vice pres 1983-. **ORGANIZATIONS:** Woodrow Wilson Fellow; bd of trustees Rider Coll; bd of dir US Black Engineer and US Hispanic Engineer magazines. **HONORS/ACHIEVEMENTS:** Community Serv Award NAACP 1984; Distinguished Alumnus Award, DE State Coll 1984; Award Natl Assn for Equal Opportunity in Higher Educ Washington; Hon DHL Delaware State Coll; mem Omicron Delta Kappa Honorary Society. **BUSINESS ADDRESS:** Executive Vice President, Mobil Intl Consult Serv Inc, 150 E 42nd St, New York, NY 10017.

GRATE, ISAAC, JR.
Emergency physician. **PERSONAL:** Born Dec 20, 1952, Georgetown, SC; married Frankie Lee Young; children: Chelsea. **EDUCATION:** Howard Univ, attended 1971-74; Meharry Medical Coll, MD 1978; UCLA School of Public Health, Graduate School 1979-80. **CAREER:** Martin Luther King Jr General Hosp, intern 1978-79; Johns Hopkins Hosp, resident 1980-82; Texas Tech Univ, instructor surgery/em 1982-84; St Lukes Episcopal Hospital, dir of emergency svcs. **ORGANIZATIONS:** Mem Univ Assoc of Emergency Physicians 1982-85, Soc of Teachers Emergency Med 1982-85, Amer Coll of Emergency Physicians 1982-87; instructor ACLS Amer Heart Assoc 1984-87; mem Houston Medical Forum 1987-, Southwest Texas Emergency physicians 1987-, Natl Medical Assoc 1987-, NAACP 1987; flight surgeon USAF Reserves 1987. **HONORS/ACHIEVEMENTS:** Dir Medical Educ Texas Tech Univ Sch of Medicine Div Emergency Medicine 1981-82; Fellow Amer College Emergency Physicians 1986-. **MILITARY SERVICE:** USAF Reserves major 1 yr. **HOME ADDRESS:** 11811 Pepperdine Ln, Houston, TX 77071.

GRAVELY, MELVIN J.
Councilman. **PERSONAL:** Born Jul 29, 1940, Canton, OH; married Sarah; children: Jewel, Melvin II. **EDUCATION:** Kent State Univ, BBA; Akron Univ, working on MA. **CAREER:** Diebold Inc, supvr 1960-73; IBM, sales rep 1973-76; Canton City Council, councilman 1976-, majority leader 1984-85 (first black to ever hold position); Roach Reid Lanier, sales rep 1977-; MJ Consultant, dir 1977-. **ORGANIZATIONS:** Hiram Abiff Lodge #72 Masonic Masonry 1968-; coach Mdgt Ftbl League 1965-; Vol Prob Officer 1974-; Can Urban League; NAACP; Youth Bd Dntn YMCA 1975-; Can Negro Old Timers Ath Club 1976-; Elks #287 1976-; Natl Blk Conf Local Elected Ofcls 1976-; Peoples Bapt Ch. **HONORS/ACHIEVEMENTS:** Outstanding Contrib to Can Human Res Corp & Pov Residents 1976; Green Co Social Club Comm Awd 1978. **MILITARY SERVICE:** USAF A/2c 1959-65. **BUSINESS ADDRESS:** Dir, MJ Consultant, 218 Cleveland Ave SW, Canton, OH 44702.

GRAVELY, SAMUEL L., JR.
Vice admiral. **PERSONAL:** Born Jun 04, 1922, Richmond, VA; son of Samuel L Gravely and Mary George Gravely; married Alma Bernice Clark; children: Robert (dec), David, Tracey. **EDUCATION:** Virgina Univ, BA History 1948, LLD (hon) 1979; Dr Social Science (hon) 1988. **CAREER:** US Navy, vice adm (0-9) 1942-80; Third Fleet, commander 1976-78; Defense Communications Agency, dir 1978-80; AFCEA, exec dir educ & training; PSE senior corp adv. **ORGANIZATIONS:** Vice pres ABSS 1983; vice pres CTEC 1981-82; mem Ruritan Intl 1981-; mem Navy League 1982-; PWC community serv bd 1984-. **HONORS/ACHIEVEMENTS:** Scottish Rite Prince Hall Masonic Bodies of MD Prince Hall Founding Fathers Military Commanders Award 1975; Savannah State Coll Major Richard R Wright Award of Excellence 1974; Alpha Phi Alpha Frat Alpha Award of Merit 1971; Los Angeles Chap Natl Assn of Media Women Inc Communications Award 1972; San Diego Press Club Military Headliner of the Year 1975; Golden Hills United Presb Church Military Service Award 1967; San Diego Optimists Club Good Guy Award; Distinguished Virginian by Governor Holton 1972; WW II Victory Medal; Naval Reserve Medal (for 10 years serv in USN Naval Reserve; Amer Campaign Medal; Korean Pres Unit Citation; Natl Defense Medal with one bronze star; China Serv Medal; Korean Serv Medal with two bronze stars; United Nations Serv Medal; Armed Forces Expeditionary Medal; Antarctic Se rv Medal; Venezuelan Order of Merit Second Class. **MILITARY SERVICE:** USN Vice Admiral 34 years; Legion of Merit with gold star; Bronze Star Medal; Meritorious Serv Medal; Joint Serv Commendation Medal; Navy Commendation Medal. **HOME ADDRESS:** 15956 Waterfall Rd, Haymarket, VA 22069.

GRAVENBERG, ERIC VON
Educator. **PERSONAL:** Born May 18, 1950, Oakland, CA; son of Allen Gravenberg and Myrtle LeBlanc-Gravenberg; married Deborah Elaine; children: Roshan, Ashande. **EDUCATION:** California State Univ, BA Black Studies 1972, MPA Public Admin 1974. **CAREER:** California State Univ Chico, dir educ opportunity personnel 1979-80; California State Univ Hayward, dir educ resource ctr 1980-81; Office of the Chancellor California State Univ, assn dean educ programs 1981-86; Univ of California Riverside, dir undergrad admissions 1986-; Renaissance Enterprises Private Consulting Company, pres 1989-; Institute for Contemporary Leadership, dean of faculty 1989-. **ORGANIZATIONS:** Mem Affirmative Action Comm Adv Bd Univ of California Irvine 1985-86; bd mem Western Assn of Educ Opportunity Personnel 1985-86; mem Natl Council on Access Services College Bd 1985-; organizational development consultant California State Univ-Chico 1986; chmn minority affairs, Western Assn of Coll Admission Counselors 1988-. **HONORS/ACHIEVEMENTS:** Achievers Awd WESTOP Long Beach 1983; Outstanding Young Men of Amer 1983; President's Award Natl Council of Educ Opportunity Assoc Washington DC 1984; published "Learning Assistance Programs," 1986; exec producer, writer, director of theatrical production On the Edge of a Dream, 1988; writer, producer, host of over 25 multicultural television productions, 1976-78. **BUSINESS ADDRESS:** Dir Undergrad Admissions, Univ of CA-Riverside, 1101 Administration, Riverside, CA 92521.

GRAVES, CAROLE A.
Labor union administrator. **PERSONAL:** Born Apr 13, 1938, Newark, NJ; daughter of Philip Burnett Anderson and Jennie Valeria Stafford Anderson; married David Leon Graves, Nov 04, 1962. **EDUCATION:** Kean College, Newark, BA, 1960; Rutger Inst of Labor and Mgmt Rels, labor rels specialist certificate, 1976. **CAREER:** Newark School System, Newark, NJ, special education teacher, 1960-69; Newark Teachers Union, Local 481, Amer Fedn of Teachers, Newark, NJ, president, 1968-. **ORGANIZATIONS:** Vice-pres, NJ State AFL-CIO; vice-pres, NJ State Indus Union Coun; vice-pres, Essex West/Hudson Central Labor Coun; vice-pres, NJ State Fedn of Teachers; member, Rutgers Lacor Alumni Exec Bd; member, A Philip Randolph Inst; member, Coalition of Labor Union Women. **HONORS/ACHIEVEMENTS:** Named one of Labor's Outstanding Black Women, Natl Org of Black Leaders, 1973; Martin Luther King Award, NJ Labor Press Council, 1973; inducted into NJ Labor Hall of Fame, Newark Community Action Team, 1977; Labor Achievement Award, Women's Affirmative Action Comm, IUC/AFL-CIO, 1983. **BUSINESS ADDRESS:** Mrs Carole A Graves, President, Newark Teachers Union, Local 481, 30 Clinton St, Newark, NJ 07112.

GRAVES, CLIFFORD W.
Government official. **PERSONAL:** Born Mar 30, 1939, San Francisco, CA. **EDUCATION:** Univ of CA Berkeley, BA 1961, M City Planning 1964. **CAREER:** City of Santa Rosa, asst city planner 1961-62; E Sussex Co, town planner & civic designer 1964-66; San Francisco Bay Consult & Dev Commn, assoc planner 1966-69; special projects officer, 1969-70; Comprehensive Planning Asst Div, dir 1970-71; Office of Planning & Mgmt Asst, dir/asst dir 1971-72; Sec for Comm Planning & Mgmt, dep asst 1972-74; Office of Mgmt & Budget, dep assoc dir eval & prog implem; County of San Diego, chief admin officer. **ORGANIZATIONS:** Lectr Howard Univ 1970-73; lectr Univ of CA Berkeley 1968-69; mem Amer Inst of Planners; Amer Soc of Planning Ofcl; Amer Soc of Pub Adminstrn; Natl Assn of Planners. **HONORS/ACHIEVEMENTS:** HUD Disting Serv Award 1972; Wm A Jump Found Award 1972; Student Award Amer Inst of Planners 1972. **BUSINESS ADDRESS:** Chief Administrative Officer, County of San Diego, 1600 Pacific Highway, Room 209, San Diego, CA 92101.

GRAVES, CURTIS M.
Agency official. **PERSONAL:** Born Aug 26, 1938, New Orleans; son of Joseph F Graves and Mable Haybel Graves; married Joanne Gordan; children: Gretchen, Christopher, Gizelle. **EDUCATION:** Xavier U, atnd; TX So U, BBA 1962; Union Bapt Bible Sem, awd hon doc; Princeton Univ, Woodrow Wilson Fellow 1984-85. **CAREER:** Educ & Comm Affairs Br of NASA, chief 1977-, dep dir civil affairs; Ldrship Inst for Comm Devel in Wash DC, training ofcr tchng state & local govt procedures; Standard Savs Assn of Houston, mgr 1962-66; TX House of Reps, elected 1966-72. **ORGANIZATIONS:** Mem steering com Nat Congress of Aerospace Edn; pres, World AerospaceEduc Org; mem Wash Alumni Chap Kappa Alpha Psi Frat; pres, World Aerospace Education Organization 1983-. **HONORS/ACHIEVEMENTS:** Publ book "Famous Black Amers". **BUSINESS ADDRESS:** Deputy Dir Civil Affairs, NASA, Code XD, Washington, DC 20546.

GRAVES, EARL G.
Editor, publisher. **PERSONAL:** Born Jan 09, 1935, Brooklyn, NY; son of Earl G Graves (deceased) and Winifred; married Barbara Kydd; children: Earl Jr, John Clifford, Michael Alan. **EDUCATION:** Morgan State Coll, BA 1958. **CAREER:** Senator Robt F Kennedy, admin asst 1965-68; Earl G Graves Ltd, Earl G Graves Pub Co Inc, Earl G Graves Assoc, Earl G Graves Mktg & Rsch Co, Earl G Graves Develop Co; Black Enterprise Magazine, publisher. **ORGANIZATIONS:** Bd dirs Rohn & Haas Corp; Mag Pubs Assn; Natl Minority Purchasing Council Inc; mem Natl Bd Exec Comm Interracial Council for Bus Oppor; mem Natl Bus League; mem NY State Econ Devel Bd; mem exec comm Grtr NY Council BSA; bd selector Amer Inst Pub Svc; trustee Amer Mus Natural History; mem NAACP; SCLC Mag Pub'rs Assn; Interracial Council; Sigma Pi Phi; Statue of Liberty Ellis Island Centennial Comm; visiting comm Harvard Univ's John F Kennedy Sch of Govt; Pres's Council for Business Admin Univ of Vermont; bd mem New York City Partnership; trustee New York Economic Club; bd dirs, New York Urban Development Corp; chmn, Black Business Council; exec comm, Coun of Competitiveness; Stroh's Advisory Coun; natl commissioner and mem exec bd, Natl Boy Scouts of Amer; Natl Minority Business Coun; trustee coun, Business Economic Development; bd mem, NY City Partnership. **HONORS/ACHIEVEMENTS:** LLD, Morgan St Univ, 1973, VA Union Univ, 1976, FL Memorial Coll, 1978, J C Smith Univ, 1979, Wesleyan Univ, 1982, Talladega Coll, 1983, Baruch Coll, 1984, AL St Univ, 1985, Mercy Coll, 1986, Iona Coll, 1987, Elizabeth City St Univ, 1987, Brown Univ, 1987, Lincoln Univ, 1988, Central St Univ, 1988, Howard Univ, 1989, Livingstone Coll, 1989; honorary doctorates, Rust Coll, 1974, Hampton Inst, 1979, Dowling Coll, 1980, Bryant Coll, 1983, St Josephs, NY, 1985, Morehouse Coll, 1986, Suffolk Univ, 1987, Meharry Medical Coll, 1989; Scroll of Honor Natl Med Assn; 1 of 100 Influential Blacks, Ebony Mag; Black Achiever, Talk Mag; 1 of 10 Most Outstanding Minority Businessmen in US, ex-Pres Nixon; 1 of 200 Future Leaders in US, Time Magazine; Broadcaster of the Yr, Natl Assn of Black Owned Broadcasters; Poynter Fellow, Yale Univ; Recipient of the Boy Scouts Natl Awards, Silver Buffalo 1988, Silver Antelope 1986 and Silver Beaver 1969. **MILITARY SERVICE:** AUS Capt. **BUSINESS ADDRESS:** Publisher, Earl G Graves Pub Co, Inc, 130 Fifth Ave, New York, NY 10011.

GRAVES, IRENE AMELIA
Educational administration. **PERSONAL:** Born Feb 22, 1906, St Louis, MO; married Willis M Graves Esq (deceased). **EDUCATION:** Wayne State Univ, AB 1932; McGill Univ, MA 1934; attended Univ of Chicago, CO State Coll, Middlebury Coll, Univ of MN, Univ of MI, Univ of Paris (La Sorbonne); 67 hours beyond MA. **CAREER:** Detroit Public Schools, teacher 1924-66; Stay-at-Home Camp YWCA, dir 1938; Coll of Ed, dir tchr 1941-47, recruiter 1932-53; Fuller Prod Co Jam Handy Audio Visual Writer, writer in sch serv dept, French translations of English masterpieces 1966-71. **ORGANIZATIONS:** Mem Alpha Kappa Alpha Great Lakes Reg Dir 1938, 1940; chmn social studies teacher Detroit Bd of Ed 1948-60; chmn NAACP 1952; vice chair Cherboneau Condo 1960-62; chair women's comm UNCF 1960; history chair Detroit Branch NAACP 1970-83; 1st black female chair Detroit Windsor Intl Fest Luncheon 1975; chair woman's comm NAACP Life Mem Comm 1976; mem comm Women's Econ Club 1977-85; founder Detroit Chap Barristers Wives, Silhouette Chap Kappa Wives; organizer Largest Group of Inductees Top Ladies of Distinction Inc. **HONORS/ACHIEVEMENTS:** 5 State Awds Governor-Senator 1966-84; 10 City Awds Mayor-Detroit Common Council 1966-84; Carter G Woodson Awd of Distinction Natl Assoc for the Study of Negro Life 1967; Teacher of the Year MI 1975; NAACP Highest Female Seller Life Mem Awd 1978-84; Volunteer of the Week Detroit Free press 1982; Activist on Home Front (one of 3 chosen) 1984; Black Episcopalian Awd Church Comm Activities 1984; Alpha Kappa Alpha Sor of the Year Urban League; 2 Medallions; Highest Award from NAACP for being highest woman salesperson of life membership June 1985; Jefferson Awd Community Serv Nal Organ Medallion 1986; Heart of Gold, United Foundation 1989; Highest Woman Salesperson of Life Memberships in the USA, NAACP 1987-89. **HOME ADDRESS:** 1585 Cherboneau Condo, Detroit, MI 48207.

GRAVES, JACKIE
Personnel administrator. **PERSONAL:** Born Mar 10, 1926, Santa Anna, TX; married Willie G Clay; children: Roderick L, Sheila R, Jackie A. **EDUCATION:** TX Coll, BA 1948. **CAREER:** Philadelphi Eagles Football Club, asst dir of player person 1975-; Phil Eagles Football Club, player person scout 1972-75; CEPO, player person scout 1970-72; Boston Patriots Football Club, player person scout 1965-70; AG Spalding Bros, natl sales rep 1965-70; TX So U, asst football coach head golf coach 1950-58; TX Coll, asst head football coach 1958-61; Continental Bowling Lanes Inc, vice pres gen mgr 1961-65. **ORGANIZATIONS:** Mem Almeda Rotary Club; mem Pop Warner Football; mem Almeda Little League Baseball. **HONORS/ACHIEVEMENTS:** Football super scout awd Black Sprots Mag 1972; gentleman of the year Phil Eagles Football Club 1978. **BUSINESS ADDRESS:** Veterans Stadium, Broad St & Pattison Ave, Philadelphia, PA 19148.

GRAVES, JERROD FRANKLIN
Dentist. **PERSONAL:** Born Sep 25, 1930, Greensboro, NC; son of Everett Graves and Lola Graves; married Earnestine Ross; children: Jerrod M, Gwendolyn Graves Irowa. **EDUCATION:** Johnson C Smith Univ, BS 1951; A&T Univ, MS 1955; Meharry Medical Coll, DDS 1959. **CAREER:** Harlem Hosp, intern/resident oral surgery 1959-61; Private Practice, dentist. **ORGANIZATIONS:** Mem Omega Psi Phi Frat 1949-, NAACP; 32 Degree Mason; mem 369th Veterans Assn; mem Natl Dental Assn, Acad General Dentistry, Amer Soc Anestheologist, Amer Endodontic Soc; Amer Soc of Military Surgeons. **HONORS/ACHIEVEMENTS:** Mizzy Award Best in Oral Surgery. **MILITARY SERVICE:** Dental Corp col 15 years; Bronze Star, Army Achievement, Overseas Medal, Army Commendation Medal, Good Conduct Medal 1952-; United Nations Ribbon; Amy Reserve, 1951-present; 1 Oak Leaf Cluster. **BUSINESS ADDRESS:** 327 Victory Blvd, Staten Island, NY 10301.

GRAVES, RAY REYNOLDS
Judge. **PERSONAL:** Born Jan 10, 1946, Tuscumbia, AL; married Lola Larice Glass; children: Claire Elise Glass Graves. **EDUCATION:** Trinity Clge CT, BA 1967; Wayne State Univ, JD 1970. **CAREER:** Private Law Practice, atty 1971-81; US Bankruptcy Court, US bankruptcy judge. **ORGANIZATIONS:** Trustee MI Cancer Fnd 1979-; bd dir Natl Conf of Bankruptcy Judges 1984-. **HONORS/ACHIEVEMENTS:** Esquire Magazine;s Registrrer; America's Under 40 Leadership, 1985. **BUSINESS ADDRESS:** US Bankruptcy Judge, US Bankruptcy Court, 1063 Univ S Courthouse, 231 West Lafayette, Detroit, MI 48226.

GRAVES, RAYMOND LEE
Clergyman. **PERSONAL:** Born Jan 03, 1928, Yanceyville, NC; married Pauline H. **EDUCATION:** Winston-Salem State U, BS 1951; NC Central U, MA 1954; Colgate Rochester-Crozier-Bexley Hall Div Sch, MDiv 1968. **CAREER:** New Bethal CME Ch Rochester NY, rev 1973-; Rochester Econ Oppor Cntr, instr 1969-73; States of VA & GA NY SC, min 1959-80; Sch Bd Danville VA, tchr 1954-62. **ORGANIZATIONS:** Founder Rochester Affiliate of OIC 1978; exec dir Rochester OIC; pres United Ch Ministry; orgn bd mem Action for a Better Comm 1963-65; co-founder FightOrgn 1964; bd mem Push-Excel Rochester Chap 1979-80. **HONORS/ACHIEVEMENTS:** Recip Martin Luther King Prof Chair Awd Colgate Rochester Div Sch 1968; serv awd Urban League of Rochester 1978; Colgate Rochester-Crozier-Bexley Hall achmnt awd Colgate Rochester Div Sch 1980. **MILITARY SERVICE:** USAF 1951-53. **BUSINESS ADDRESS:** New Bethel CME Church, 270 Scio St, Rochester, NY 14606.

GRAVES, RODERICK LAWRENCE
NFL scout. **PERSONAL:** Married Alesia. **EDUCATION:** Texas Tech, BS Economics; Attended, Strake Jesuit Coll Pre Houston. **CAREER:** Philadelphia Stars USFL, personnel scout, asst dir of player personnel 1983; Chicago Bears, regional scout. **BUSINESS ADDRESS:** Scout, Chicago Bears, Halas Hall, 250 North Washington, Lake Forest, IL 60045.

GRAVES, SHERMAN TEEN
Miner. **PERSONAL:** Born Sep 11, 1905, Freeman, WV; married Estella Mae Ward; children: JoAnn, Sherman, Dwight, Debbie, Wanda. **CAREER:** Miner retired; notary pub 27 yrs; Comm Action, orgnr 1945-46; City of Bramwell, v mayor cnclmn; 1st black mayor; former city judge; Mercer Co, bd of dir. **ORGANIZATIONS:** Indsl Park Devel Assn; chmn Personal Com Rock Dist Clinic Assn; vice pres WV Br NAACP; vice pres Mercer Co OEO; grand rcdr Royal Craft Grand Lodge; F & AAY Masons; pres BHS PTA; treas Mercer Co PTA Cncl; bd of dir Miners Black Lung Hlth Assn; deacon yth adv Bluestone Bapt Ch; rep Black Lung Compensation; Miners Pensions; Unepmt Compensation. **HONORS/ACHIEVEMENTS:** Congressman Nick J Rahall's Adv Com.

GRAVES, VALERIE JO
Business executive. **PERSONAL:** Born Feb 27, 1950, Pontiac, MI; daughter of Spurgeon Graves and Deloris Graves; married Alvin E Bessent; children: Brian. **EDUCATION:** Wayne State Univ, attended 1969-73; NY Univ, Filmmaking Program, 1985-. **CAREER:** D'Arcy MacManus & Masius Ad Agency, copywriter 1974-75; BBDO Inc Ad Agency, copywriter 1975-76; Kenyon & Eckhardt Boston Ad Agency, copywriter 1977-80; J Walter Thompson USA Ad Agency, sr copywriter 1981-82; Ross Roy Inc, vice pres assoc creative dir; Uniworld Group, vp/assoc creative dir. **ORGANIZATIONS:** Former mem Harvard Univ Black Comm & Student Theater 1979-80; mem Adcraft Club of Detroit 1982-; consultant 1984-, dir 1984- The Creative Network Inc; mem Natl Assoc Black Women Entrepreneurs 1985; mem, Advertising Club of New York. **HONORS/ACHIEVEMENTS:** Corporate Ad Award Boston Ad Club Francis Hatch Award 1981; Merit Award Art Dirs Club of NY 1982; CEBA Award of Excellence Black Owned Comm Assoc NY 1983; Graphic Excellence Merchandising Graphics Award Competition 1984; Notable Midwest Adwoman Adweek Magazine Chicago 1984; Profile Ebony Magazine Nov 1984; CEBA Award of Excellence, 1987, 1988. **BUSINESS ADDRESS:** Vice Pres Creative Group Head, Uniworld Group Inc, 1250 Broadway, New York, NY 10001.

GRAY, ANDREW JACKSON
Business executive. **PERSONAL:** Born Jun 20, 1924, Charlotte, NC; married Lucille Jackson; children: Andrew, Jr, Amizie. **EDUCATION:** Morehouse Coll, BA 1946; NC State U, addl studies. **CAREER:** Andrew J Gray Accounting Firm, acct 1962-; NC Con NAACP Br, auditor. **ORGANIZATIONS:** Mem Nat Soc of Pub Accnt; NC Sor of Accnt; Nat Assn of Enrolled Agents; Nat Assn of Black Accnt; mem Kappa Alpha Psi; NAACP; St Paul Bapt Chl; YMCA. **BUSINESS ADDRESS:** 2202 Beatties Ford Rd, Charlotte, NC 28216.

GRAY, ARTHUR D.
Clergyman. **PERSONAL:** Born Jan 17, 1907, Sheffield, AL; married Edna. **EDUCATION:** Talladega Theol Sem, AB 1929; Chicago Theol Sem, MVD 1934, hon DD 1948. **CAREER:** Congregational Ch of Park Manor Chgo, minister; ch at Talladega Coll, minister 1944-52; Talladega Coll, pres 1952-62; Plymouth Congregational Ch Wash DC, minister 1934-44; Talladega, asst to pres 1930-32. **ORGANIZATIONS:** Trst Talladega; vice pres mem bd Dirs Comm Renewal Soc; mem United Ch of Christ Minister for Racial & Social Justice; mem United Black Chruchmen of United Ch of Christ; former pres Wash Bdc Br NAACP; former asst natl moderator fomer chmn exec com Gen Council of Congregational Chris Ch; former mem bd dirs United Negro Coll Fund. **BUSINESS ADDRESS:** 7000 S King Dr, Chicago, IL 60637.

GRAY, ARTHUR L.
Retired police chief. **PERSONAL:** Born Dec 25, 1918, Plymouth, MA; married Eunice N Fisher; children: Arthur Griffin, Christopher Wells. **CAREER:** Town of Plymouth Police Dept, patrolman 1946-58, sgt shift commander & court prosecutor 1958-76, cpt administ asst 1976-77, chief of police 1977-78, retired police chief after 32 years of service 1978. **ORGANIZATIONS:** Town meeting mem Town of Plymouth 1958; corporator Plymouth Sav Bk 1976; mem Plymouth co Prosecutors Assn 1976. **MILITARY SERVICE:** USAF Tech Sgt 1941-45; Bronze Star & N Africa Campaign Citation 1943. **HOME ADDRESS:** 16 Oak St, Plymouth, MA 02360.

GRAY, C. VERNON
Educational administrator, professor, county councilman. **PERSONAL:** Born Jul 30, 1939, Sunderland, MD; son of Major Gray and Virgina Gray; married Sandra Lea Trice; children: Michael, Angela. **EDUCATION:** Morgan State Univ, BA 1961; Atlanta Univ, MA 1962; Univ of MA, PhD 1971. **CAREER:** Philander Smith Coll, instr 1961-66; Oakland Univ, instr 1970-71; Joint Ctr for Political Studies, Washington DC, 1971-72; Morgan State Univ, assoc dean for soc sci 1974-75; Goucher Coll, visiting prof 1974; Univ of MD, visiting prof 1978-79; Univ of MD College Park, visiting prof 1980-81; Morgan State Univ, chmn political sci 1972-87; Morgan State Univ, dir public serv internship program 1972-87; Morgan State Univ, prof political sci 1972-; Morgan State Univ, chmn political sci & intl studies 1984-87. **ORGANIZATIONS:** Exec council Natl Capitol Area Political Sci Assoc 1976-; pres elect Natl Conf of Black Political Sci 1976-77; chmn Political Action Comm MD State Conf of NAACP 1976-77; bd of dir Meals on Wheels of Central MD 1976; chmn Ad Hoc Contribs Comm Meals on Wheels 1976-77; pres Natl Conf of Black Political Sci 1977-78; nominating comm Southern Political Sci Assoc 1977-78; chmn Ethnic & Cultural Pluralism Award Comm Amer Political Sci Assoc 1977-78; political analyst WJZ, WBAL 1977-; host, producer Politics Power & People 1977-80; speakers bureau United Way of Central MD 1977-78; allocations panel United Way of Central MD 1977-78; adv comm Ctr for Urban Environmental Studies 1977-80; resources bd Minority Energy Tech Asst Program Ctr for Urban Environ Studies 1978; bd of dir Natl Policy Studies Inst Goucher Coll 1978; chmn program comm Alpha Phi Alpha 1979-80; dir Educ Activities Alpha Phi Alpha 1979; Election Laws Revision Comm MD 1979-80; chmn county council Howard County MD 1985-87; bd dir MD Assn of Counties, Natl Assn of Counties; bd of dir MD Museum of African Art; bd of dir Howard County Red Cross; chmn United Negro Coll Fund Howard County Campaign. **HONORS/ACHIEVEMENTS:** WEAA-FM Awd for Serv 1978; Community Serv Awd United Way of Central MD, 1978; Appreciation Awd Calvert Cty NAACP 1978; Community Serv Admin Certificate of Training 1979; Certificate of Merit Black Women's Consciousness Raising Assoc 1979; Community Serv Awd Howard Community Action 1980, Natl Conf of Black Political Sci 1980; Awd for Distinguished Serv Natl Conf of Black Political Sci 1980; Outstanding Faculty Awd for Community Serv Morgan State Univ 1980; Alpha Man of the Year 1982; mem Pi Sigma Alpha, Ford Found Fellowship, Crusade Scholar, Southern Found Scholar; chmn Educ Comm MD Assn of Counties 1983-84; mem Educ Subcomm/Health and Educ Steering Comm of Natl Assn of Counties; mem bd trustees Howard County Gen Hosp Capital Fund Inc; chmn Howard County Council 1985; first black elected to Howard County Council 1982; Citizen of the Year, Omega Psi Phi Fraternity 1987; Outstanding Service Award, Alpha Kappa Alpha Sorority 1989; Honorary 4-H member; Outstanding Achievement Award, Maryland State Teachers Assn. **BUSINESS ADDRESS:** Chairman, Political Science, Morgan StateUniv, Hillen Rd & Coldspring Ln, Baltimore, MD 21239.

GRAY, CAROL COLEMAN
Pediatrician. **PERSONAL:** Born Jun 22, 1946, Wharton, TX; married James Howard Gray MD; children: Nakia, James. **EDUCATION:** Univ of Texas, BS 1967, Medical School MD 1972. **CAREER:** Walter Reed Army Medical Center, pediatric internship 1972; Univ of MD Hospital, pediatric residency 1977; Dallas Independent School Dist Project Find, medical coord 1979-83; Southwestern Medical School, clinical facility 1981-; Baylor Univ Medical Center, assoc attending 1981-; Private Practice, pediatrician 1981-. **ORGANIZATIONS:** Bd mem Child Care Dallas; mem Amer Medical Assoc, Natl Medical Assoc, CV Roman Medical Soc, NAACP, Amer Heart Assoc Preschool Comm. **HONORS/ACHIEVEMENTS:** Civilian Achievement Award, Walter Reed Army Medical Center 1978; Dallas Independent School Dist Black Women Against the Odds Award; 2nd Annual Salute to America's Top 100 Black Business & Professional Women, Dollars & Sense Magazine 1986; Dream Maker's Award, Southeast Dallas Business and Professional Women; publication "Wednesday's & Thursday's Children, Medical Assessment of the Child with a Handicap" Early Periodic Diagnosis & Treatment Progs. **MILITARY SERVICE:** AUS capt 1972-73; Internship Certificate 1973. **BUSINESS ADDRESS:** Pediatrician, 3600 Gaston Ave #760, Dallas, TX 75246.

GRAY, CHARLES HENRY
Business executive. **PERSONAL:** Born Feb 24, 1919, Smithfield, VA; married Mary Phillips; children: Loris J Jones, Charles Henry Jr, LaVerne Smith, Tammy Riddick, Evelyn Anderson. **EDUCATION:** Isle of Wight Co Training Schl, 1934-38; Norfolk State Univ, Pub Rel 1954-55; Hampton Inst, Human Rel Brick Masonry 1956-57. **CAREER:** Smithfield Packing Co Inc, laborer 1939-53; Employee Benefit Assc Labor Union, organizor 1953; Smithfield Packing Co Inc, supr 1953-55, employment mgr 1955-75, asst to chrmn of bd 1975-. **ORGANIZATIONS:** Chrmn trustee bd Smithfield Elk's Lodge 1940-80; mem Main St Baptist Church 1925-; exec com VA Pork Comm of Smithfield VA 1975-79. **HONORS/ACHIEVEMENTS:** Humanitarian Award Smithfield HS 1973-80; Outstanding Booster Norfolk State Univ 1979-. **HOME ADDRESS:** PO Box 71e St, Smithfield, VA 23430-9998. **BUSINESS ADDRESS:** Asst to Chairman of Board, The Smithfield Packing Co Inc, Hwy 10, PO Box 447, Smithfield, VA 23430.

GRAY, CHRISTINE
Manager specialist. **PERSONAL:** Born Nov 27, 1922, Cuthbert, GA; married Herman C; children: Dianne, Donna. **EDUCATION:** Adminstrv Sch WAAC, 1943; Sch Comptometer, 1944; Exxon, math keypunch 1971. **CAREER:** Kolodney & Meyers Hartford, payroll clk 1940-46; Hop Equip, customer serv rep 1970-71; Credit Unoin, sec 1965-67; Thompson & Weinman Co, asst office mgr 1967-70; Unoin Co OIC, keypunch instr 1971-73; 1975; Unoin Co Dept Youth Svcs, sec; Unoin Co OIC, mgr spec. **ORGANIZATIONS:** Charter mem NCNW Vauzhall Sect; pres Burnet Jr High PTA; inter club pres YWCA 1942-45; Jr Dgt Ruler Emma V Kelly Elks 1940-42; jr ckl Hopewell Bapt Ch 1941-46; sec Concerned Citizens Vauxhall; sec Citizens Council Vauxhall; pres Jefferson Sch PTA; pres Nat Council Negro Women Vauxhall Sect; chairlady Consumer Educ NCNW; dist ldr Dist 8 Unoin Co Girl Scout Ldr; bd mem Unoin Co Anti-proverty bd; sec Calvary Bapt Ch 1959-67, 1970-77; chrtr mem Gary Family Assn; Cancer Soc; Comm Vacation Bible Sch; Calvary Bapt Sunday Sch; Census Bur 1960-70; Calvary Bapt Ch 1973. **HONORS/ACHIEVEMENTS:** Gold pin Girl Scouts; plaque Nat Council Negro Women Vauxhall Sect 1972 & 1973; cert NCNW; guest part Esther Roll Thresa Merritt; Maude Johnson Cultural Awd 1976. **MILITARY SERVICE:** WAAC 1943. **BUSINESS ADDRESS:** Coordinator, Union Twp Comm Action Org Inc, 2410 Springfield Ave, Vauxhall, NJ 07088.

GRAY, CLARENCE CORNELIUS, III
Agricultural research science administrator. **PERSONAL:** Born Jul 23, 1917, Ridge Springs, SC; son of Clarence Gray and Maude Gray; married Shirley Brown; children: Michele, Clarence, Jennifer. **EDUCATION:** VA State Coll, BS 1943; MI State Coll, MS 1942, PhD 1947; School Adv Intl Studies Johns Hopkins Univ, Certificate 1963; Foreign Serv Inst US Dept of State, Certificate 1967. **CAREER:** VA State Coll, asst/assoc/and prof 1948-58; Agency for Intl Dev/US Dept of State, foreign serv officer 1958-70; Rockefeller Foundation, prog off/principal off 1970-83 (retired); Virginia Polytechnic Inst & State Univ, prof 1983-89; prof emeritus 1989. **ORGANIZATIONS:** Trustee/chmn of bd Intl Rice Rsch Inst Philippines 1971-83; consultant United Nations Develop Prog 1973-74; trustee/chmn of bd General Educ Bd 1973-84; mem adv cncl NY Coll of Agr Cornell Univ 1976-82; mem Agr Projects Review Govt of Nepal 1979; mem Governor of Virginia's Intl Trade Adv Cncl 1987-; mem Alpha Phi Alpha, Sigma Pi Phi, National Guardsmen. **HONORS/ACHIEVEMENTS:** Certificate of Merit VA State Coll 1978; Doctor of Laws Morehouse Coll 1979, Virginia State Univ 1982; The W Averell Harriman Intl Serv Awd Intl Ctr Albany 1981. **MILITARY SERVICE:** AUS major 25 yrs; Army Commendation Medal 1946, and various serv medals 1943-56. **BUSINESS ADDRESS:** CCG Associates, 9934 Great Oaks Way, Fairfax, VA 22030.

GRAY, EARNEST
Professional athlete. **PERSONAL:** Born Mar 02, 1957, Greenwood, MS. **EDUCATION:** Memphis State, attended. **CAREER:** NY Giants, professional football player wide receiver 1979-. **HONORS/ACHIEVEMENTS:** All NFL Rookie Honors UPI & Pro Football Weekly & Professional Football Writers Assn & Football Digest; All-American; played in Sr Bowl & E-w Shrine Games. **BUSINESS ADDRESS:** New York Giants, Giants Stadium, East Rutherford, NJ 07073.

GRAY, EDWARD WESLEY, JR.
Government official. **PERSONAL:** Born Mar 15, 1946, Gary, IN; married Cheryl Bernadette Leggon; children: Robert RL. **EDUCATION:** Univ of Chicago, BA Soc 1967; Columbia Univ Law Schl, Juris Doctor 1970; Parker Schl of Foreign and Corporate Law, Cert 1980. **CAREER:** Kirkland and Ellis, assc atty 1970-73; RR Donnelley and Sons Co, atty 1973, sr atty, gen atty, Pres Comm on Exec Exch, participant exchange XV 1984-; US Gen Acct Office, spec asst dir gen govt div US gen acct office. **ORGANIZATIONS:** Numrans Bar Assc Amer Arbitration Assc. **HONORS/ACHIEVEMENTS:** Who's Who in the Land; Who's Who in Real Estate; Who's Who in the World. **BUSINESS ADDRESS:** Special Assistant to Dir, US Gen Acct Office, 441 G St NW, Washington, DC 20548.

GRAY, FRED DAVID
Attorney evangelist. **PERSONAL:** Born in Montgomery, AL; married Bernice Hill; children: Deborah, Vanessa, Fred David Jr, Stanley. **EDUCATION:** Nashville Christian Inst, Diploma; AL State Univ, BS 1951; Case Western Reserve Univ, JD 1954. **CAREER:** Sr mem of law firm of Gray, Langford, Sapp, Davis & McGowan, with offices in Montgomery & Tuskegee, AL; cooperating attorney with NAACP Legal Defense Fund, Inc; city attorney for city of Tuskegee; AL Education Assoc, general counsel; Tuskegee Univ, local general counsel; Erlanger Health Services, Inc, John A Andrew Hospital, local general counsel; first civil rights attorney for Dr Martin Luther King, Jr and attorney for Rosa Parks in the Montgomery Bus Boycott. **ORGANIZATIONS:** Bar comm 5th Judicial Circuit of AL 1983-86; pres elect Natl Bar Assc 1984-85; pres Natl Assc Cty Civil Attys 1982-83; rep AL State Leg 1970-74; bdmem SW Christian Clge; mem Amer Bar Assc, Omega Psi Phi Frat Inc; elder Tuskegee Church of Christ; Natl Bar Assoc, president 1985-86; Southwestern Christian Coll, chairman, bd of trustees. **HONORS/ACHIEVEMENTS:** The Man in the News NY Times 1966; First Annual Equal Justice Award Natl Bar Assc 1977; Drum Major's Award MLK Jr Mem Southern Christian Ldrshp Conf 1980; Pres Award Natl Bar Assc 1982; World Conference of Mayors, the legal awd 1985; Case Western Reserve Univ, law alumni assoc - graduate of the yr 1985, school of law - Society of Benchers 1986; Women at Work of Los Angeles CA & Southwestern Christian Coll, man of the yr awd 1986; WA Bar Assoc, Charles Hamilton Houston Medallion of Merit 1986. **BUSINESS ADDRESS:** Senior Partner, Gray, Langford, Sapp, Davis, PO Box 239, Tuskegee, AL 36083.

GRAY, GEORGE W., III (SKIP)
Attorney. **PERSONAL:** Born Sep 28, 1945, Denver, CO; married Janice Gross; children: Sean Michael, Aaron Christopher. **EDUCATION:** Mesa Coll, AA, Freshman Scholarship for Music, 1965; Univ of Denver, BA, Joint Honor Scholarship, USOE, 1968, Fellowship School of Educ, 1971, JD, Sam Carey Bar Assn Scholarship, 1985; Univ of Northern Colorado, attended 1969. **CAREER:** Job Corps, youth worker 1965-67; Bureau of Reclamation, pres; Denver Public School, jr high soc studies teacher 197-73; Met State Coll Denver, assoc dir financial aid 1973-78; Coloradoans to Re-Elect Richard Lamm Gov, staff aid-constituent groups 1978; Colorado Office of Energy & Conservation of the Gov, mgr IBGP 1978-82; Governor's Office, sr staff aide 1981; Yellow Cab Co, driver 1982-84; Manville Corp, law clerk 1984; Holland & Hart, assoc 1985-. **ORGANIZATIONS:** Mem Phi Delta Kappa 1970-80; mem Black Educ Adv Comm Denver Pub School 1972-78; chmn sub comm on budgets, Black Educ Adv Comm, Denver Public School 1974-75; co-chair, Greater Park Hill Comm Inc 1974-75; sec, Colorado Assn of Financial Aid Admin 1975-76; dir, Park Hill Chap Bd, NAACP 1977; mem, Amer Assn of Blacks in Energy 1977-82; mem, Denver Entry to Engrg Educ Adv Bd to Denver Public School 1979-82; incorporator, Natl Assn of Inst Bldgs Grants Prog Admin mem 1980-82; precinct committeeman 1980-84; capt-at-large, Denver Democratic Party 1982-83; senator, Student Bar Assn, Univ of Denver Coll of Law 1982-83; mem hon bd, Univ of Denver Coll of Law 1984-85; mayor's appointee mem of bd, Denver Opportunity Inc 1985; mem Colorado Office of Energy Conservation Adv Comm 1985-; dir, chmn nominating comm ACLU of Colorado 1987-; mem, Denver Bar Assn 1986-; mem Colorado Bar Assn 1986, Amer Bar Assn 1986, Natl Bar Assn 1986, Sam Carey Bar Assn 1986-.

GRAY, JAMES AUSTIN, II
Attorney. **PERSONAL:** Born Aug 06, 1946, Scotlandville, LA; married Ernestine Steward; children: Cheryl Artise, James Austin III. **EDUCATION:** Morehouse Coll, BS 1967; Harvard Law Sch, JD 1973. **CAREER:** Jefferson Bryan & Grayd partner; gary & taylor, partner 1975-77; LA state u, law prof 1973-77; headquarters u SMC, 1970; USMC, 1967-68. **ORGANIZATIONS:** Chmn Lewis & Sewell Boy Scout Dist; dir Big Bros New Orleans; mem New Orlaens C of C; mem Lous A Mertinet Legal Soc; Original IL Club; pres HeritageSquare Devel Corp; mem New Orleans Revenue Revision Task Force; mem Kappa Alpha Psi; mem Educators to Africa 1973-75. **MILITARY SERVICE:** USMC capt 1967-70. **BUSINESS ADDRESS:** 3828 1 Shell Sq, New Orleans, LA 70139.

GRAY, JAMES E.
College president. **CAREER:** Natchez Junior College, Natchez MS, president. **BUSINESS ADDRESS:** Natchez Junior College, Natchez, MS 39120. *

GRAY, JAMES HOWARD
Physician. **PERSONAL:** Born May 20, 1943, Kaufman, TX; married Carol Coleman; children: Nakia, James. **EDUCATION:** North Texas State Univ, B 1966, M 1967; Univ of Texas Medical School, MD 1971; Johns Hopkins Hospital, Wilmer Ophthalmology Inst, attended 1975-78. **CAREER:** Bexar Co Hospital, internal medicine intern 1971-72; Wilmer Ophthalmology Inst Johns Hopkins Hospital, resident 1975-78; Khalili Hospital Ophthalmology Dept Shiraz Iran, visiting instructor 1978; Baylor Univ Med Ctr, assoc/attending 1978-; Southwestern Medical School, clinical faculty 1979-; TX Instrument & Terrell State Hospital, eye consultant 1979-81; Private Practice, ophthalmologist 1978-. **ORGANIZATIONS:** Fee review comm Dallas County Medical Soc 1985-; bd mem Good St Baptist Church; mem NAACP, YMCA, Amer Heart Assoc, Soc to Prevent Blindness, Dallas Black Chamber of Commerce; Amer Medical Assoc, Johns Hopkins Hospital Resident's Assoc, Wilmer Resident's Assoc. **HONORS/ACHIEVEMENTS:** Legislative Merit Scholarship; Galaxy of Starts Award, Dallas Independent School District; Social Service Award XZ; First place and best of show awards TX Med Assoc; First place awards Medical Illustration SNMA Wyeth Natl Contest. **MILITARY SERVICE:** AUS MC major 1972-75. **BUSINESS ADDRESS:** Ophthalmologist, 3600 Gaston Ave #760, Dallas, TX 75246.

GRAY, JERRY
Professional athlete. **PERSONAL:** Born Dec 02, 1961, Lubbock, TX. **EDUCATION:** Attended, Texas State. **CAREER:** Los Angeles Rams, cornerback 1985-. **HONORS/ACHIEVEMENTS:** Mem Pro Bowl team 1987. **BUSINESS ADDRESS:** Los Angeles Rams, 2327 Lincoln Ave, Anaheim, CA 92801.

GRAY, JOANNE S.
Educator. **PERSONAL:** Born Dec 19, 1943, Headland, AL; daughter of Charlie Stoval and Gussie Jones Stovall; married Kenneth Byron Gray; children: Kina Carisse. **EDUCATION:** Chicago City Coll, AA 1965; Chicago State Coll, BS 1970; Governor State Univ, MS 1979; Univ of Chicago, attended 1975-86. **CAREER:** Chicago Bd of Educ, dist chairperson science fair 1983-, chairperson citywide academic Olympics 1985-86, science dept chairperson 1984-, ECIA coord 1986, teacher 1970-87. **ORGANIZATIONS:** Papers-Science Fair Success and Encouraging Females in Science related Activites 1978-; bd of dir Pre-medical and Allied Health Prog Chicago St Univ 1978-81; sec, vice pres Rebecca Circle United Methodist Women 1980-86; Phi Delta Kappa 1984-86; prog chmn Natl Assn of Biology Teachers 1984; coord/facilitator Natl Sci Educ Comm 1984; science curriculum bd of governors St Univ 1986; bd mem Women's Div of Global Ministries 1987; area teen advisor Top Ladies of Distinction Inc 1987-89. **HONORS/ACHIEVEMENTS:** Celebrated Teacher by Beta Boule' Sigma Pi Phi 1981; Ora Higgins Youth Foundation Award 1981; Exceptional Serv to Students Blum-Kovler Foundation 1981; Principal Scholars Prog Serv Award 1982; Master Teacher Award Governor of IL 1984; Textbook Revision Team Biological Science Curriculum Study 1985; Science Curriculum Writer Chicago Bd of Educ 1985-87; Fellowship Fry Foundation Univ of Chicago 1986; Outstanding Biology Teacher Natl Assn of Biology Teachers 1986.

GRAY, JOHNNIE
Professional athlete. **PERSONAL:** Born Dec 18, 1953, Lake Charles, LA; married Barbara. **EDUCATION:** CA Fullerton, attended. **CAREER:** Greenbay Packers, professional football player defensive back 1975-. **HONORS/ACHIEVEMENTS:** Has amassed more than 100 solo tackles in each of last three seasons 1977-79; selected All-Conf All Four Years in Coll; All-Conf PCAA Honors. **BUSINESS ADDRESS:** Green Bay Packers, 1265 Lombardi Ave, Green Bay, WI 54303.

GRAY, JOSEPH WILLIAM
Physician. **PERSONAL:** Born May 31, 1938, Memphis, TN; married Jacquelyn Cooper; children: Joseph IV, Jaylynn, Jeffrey, Jerron, Jerome. **EDUCATION:** St Augustine's Coll, BA; Meharry Med Coll, MD 1963; Santa Monica Hosp, Intern 1963-64; GW Hubbard Hosp, Res 1966-69. **CAREER:** Physician 1985. **ORGANIZATIONS:** Natl Med Assn; AMA; Toledo & Lucas Ped Soc; OH Chap of Amer Acad of Ped; fellow Amer Acad of Pediatrics; certified Amer Bd of Pediatrics; life mem NAACP; Sigma Pi Phi; Alpha Phi Alpha; Alpha Kappa Mu. **MILITARY SERVICE:** USN 1964-66. **BUSINESS ADDRESS:** Physician, 2700 Monroe St, Ste E, Toledo, OH 43606.

GRAY, KEITH A., JR.
Elected government official. **PERSONAL:** Born Nov 03, 1947, Camden, NJ. **EDUCATION:** Career Ed Inst, Cert 1975; Pierce Jr Coll, Associate 1977; Rutgers Univ, Cert 1983. **CAREER:** Conrail, customer rep 1982; Juveniles In Need of Suprv, counselor 1984; Cumberland Cty Welfare, intake maintenance 1985. **ORGANIZATIONS:** Adb bd Fairfield Twp Schools, 1983; leg comm Adv Comm on Women 1984; bd of dir NJ Citizen Action 1985; mem Natl Conf of Black Mayors 1985, NJ Assoc of Mayors 1985, NJ Conf on Mayors 1985. **HONORS/ACHIEVEMENTS:** Cert NJ State Assembly 1984; Cert SCOPE 1984; Placque Concerned Citizens of Fairfield 1984; Cert Concerned Citizens of Fairfield 1984. **MILITARY SERVICE:** USAF E-4 4 yrs. **BUSINESS ADDRESS:** Mayor, Fairfield Twp Comm, P O Box 125, Fairton, NJ 08320.

GRAY, LARUTH H.
Retired educational administrator. **PERSONAL:** Born in Texarkana, TX; daughter of Curtis Hackney and Hazel Johnson; married Joseph Morgan; children: Phillip Anthony, Dierdra Alyce. **EDUCATION:** Howard Univ, BA 1954; Columbia Univ, MA 1957; Nova Univ, EdD 1975. **CAREER:** New Rochelle NY Public Sch, chmn English Dept, principal/ed support center, dir of instructional serv, asst supt 1980-83; Abbott Univ Free School District, Supt of Schools 1983-89. **ORGANIZATIONS:** Mem bd comm White Plains YWCA; mem Comm on Aging City of New Rochelle; past chair Urban Affairs Comm NYS Assoc Super & Curr Develop; past vice pres NY State English Council; chair standing comm on minorities Amer Educ Rsch Assoc 1983-85; pres bd of dirs Martin Luther King Child Care Ctr 1980-; mem Council for the Arts 1986-; vice pres bd of trustees New Rochelle Public Library 1986-90; mem of bd of dir NY State Alliance of Art 1989-91; Westchester (Children's) Assn 1989-91. **HONORS/ACHIEVEMENTS:** Outstanding Educator New Rochelle Branch NAACP 1973; Outstanding Educator Natl Council of Negro Women 1975; Outstanding Educator Natl Assoc of Minority Bankers 1976; Community Serv Awd West Salute Comm 1984; Cert Recognizing Unique Contribution to Educ US Congressional Black Caucus 1984; 100 Top Educators US and North Amer 1986; Outstanding Supt in the Arts, Kennedy Center DC Arts Alliance 1988. **BUSINESS ADDRESS:** Executive Asst, Metro/New York Univ, School of Educ, Press Bldg, Suite 72, 32 Washington Pl, New York, NY 10003.

GRAY, LEO MILTON, JR.
Executive director. **PERSONAL:** Born Jun 25, 1946, Hornlake, MS; married Allie Macklin; children: Angelique, Leah. **EDUCATION:** Lane Coll, BS 1968; Memphis State Univ, MEd 1976; Memphis Theological Seminary, MDiv 1986. **CAREER:** St Louis Public Sch System, coach and instructor 1968-69; Lane College Jackson TN, dir alumni affairs and public relations 1969-73; St Mark Missionary Baptist Church, pastor & ceo 1976-; Memphis Comprehensive Program for Sickle Cell Disease, coord of comm serv 1973-. **ORGANIZATIONS:** Mem Omega Psi Phi Frat Inc, NAACP Memphis Branch, Operation PUSH Inc; bd dirs Memphis Urban League; 2nd vice pres Natl Assoc for Sickle Cell Disease Inc; chmn TN Human Rights Commn; vice pres Memphis Satellite of Oper PUSH; Royal Arch Mason/Shriner. **HONORS/ACHIEVEMENTS:** Dr Martin Luther King Jr Awd Memphis Army Defense Depot 1980; Memphis Spiritual Support Awd Afro-Amer Police Assoc 1980.

GRAY, LEON
Professional athlete. **PERSONAL:** Born Nov 15, 1951, Olive Branch, MS. **EDUCATION:** Jackson StateUniv Jackson MS, BS 1972; 16 hrs grad study 1973-74. **CAREER:** Houston Oilers, player 1979-; New Engl Patriots, offensive tackle 1973-79. **ORGANIZATIONS:** Nat Football League Player Kappa Alpha Psi Frat; Jackson StateUniv Alumni Assn MS; Assn Health Physical & Educ & Rec. **HONORS/ACHIEVEMENTS:** Who's Who Among AmUniv & Coll Students; Who's Who Among AmUniv & Coll Athletes; Am All Acad Team; MS Nat Football Hall of Fame Honor Student; valed Health Physical Educ & Rec Class 1972; magna cum laude grad; professional sprots All Am; Pittsburgh Courier All Am; Mutual Black Sports All Am; named All NFL AP/NEW/PFWA; winner Seagram Seven Crowns Awd Top Off Line Man NFL Pro Bowl 1976, 78, 79; All Star Squads Playboy, Ebony. **BUSINESS ADDRESS:** c/o Houston Oilers, POB 1516, Houston, TX 77001.

GRAY, MACEO
Engineering supervisor. **PERSONAL:** Born Dec 22, 1940, Dallas; married Annie P Hatcher; children: Karen, Kathleen. **EDUCATION:** Prairie View A&M U, BS EE 1963;Univ MO, grad engineering work. **CAREER:** Bendix Corp, jr engr 1963; Test Equip Design Dept, engineering supr 1969; Electrical Products, engineering supr. **ORGANIZATIONS:** Dir comm proj by Bendix Mgmt Club 1973-74; vice pres spl events Bendix Mgmt Club 1975-76; term vice pres Camp Fire Bowling League; adv Jr Achvmnt Co 1970. **HONORS/ACHIEVEMENTS:** Received numerous outstndg serv awrds Bendix Mgmt Club Work.

GRAY, MARCUS J.
County clerk. **PERSONAL:** Born Sep 22, 1936, Kansas City, MO; married Abbey Dowdy; children: Marcus, III, Sean, Yolanda. **EDUCATION:** BBA. **CAREER:** Cahoun Co, co clk register 1972-; co clk 1964-72; Eaton Mfg, prod insp chief clk quality con commercial trans clk; Kellogg Co, machine operator. **ORGANIZATIONS:** Mem exec com Calhoun Co Dem Party; Haber & Commn on Polit Reform in Elections; sub-com chmn MI Non-Partisan Election Commn; imm past pres MI Assn of Co Clks; pres Nat Assn of Co Recorders & Clks 1979; mem United Co Officer's Assn; pres Battle Creek Area Urban League; pres Battle Creek Area Council of Ch. **HONORS/ACHIEVEMENTS:** Les Bon Amie Club awd outstd sev; cert of merit Dem Party of MI & Calhoun Co Dem Women's Club; recog Comm Ldrs of Am; Who' Who in Am Pol; clerk of the yr MI Assn of Co Clks. **MILITARY SERVICE:** USAF a/2c. **BUSINESS ADDRESS:** County Clerk's Office, Calhoun County, Marshall, MI.

GRAY, MARVIN W.
Attorney. **PERSONAL:** Born Aug 12, 1944, Chicago; married Taffy; children: Derek, Jason, Meagan. **EDUCATION:** So IL U, 1966; IL Inst Tech, 1972. **CAREER:** Chicago Pub Sch, tchr 1966, 1970-72; Aetna Life & Casualty Ins, claims rep 1967-70; Cook Co, asst pub defndr 1972-74; Harth Vital Stroger Boarman & Williams, atty; Braud Warner & Neppl, atty; Firm of Ward & Gray, prtnr; Montgomery & Holland, asso & self-employed 1967-79; Pvt Prac Chgo, atty. **ORGANIZATIONS:** Consult Opera PUSH 1973-74; couns 10 Dist Omega Psi Phi Frat; mem IL Trial Lawyers Assn; mem Phi Delta Phi Intl Legal Frat; mem Nat Cook Co IL & Am Bar Assns. **HONORS/ACHIEVEMENTS:** Moran fund scholarship 1968; IL Inst Tech scholarship 1970. **BUSINESS ADDRESS:** Marvin W Gray Ltd, 31st Natl Plaza, Ste 1400, Chicago, IL 60602.

GRAY, MATTIE EVANS
Educator. **PERSONAL:** Born Nov 22, 1935, Pascagoula, MS; married James C Gray, Jr; children: Robert, Kenneth, Michael. **EDUCATION:** Fisk Univ, BA (Magna Cum Laude) 1959; TX Southern Univ, MA 1963. **CAREER:** Univ of CA-Davis, learning skills counselor 1975-79; Sacramento & San Joaquin County Schools, prog consult standard english 1980-84; CA State Univ Sacramento, instructor 1983-86, curriculum consultant 1986-; consultant "Building Self-esteem to Promote Academic Achievement," CA, PA, LA educators inservice trng 1988-89. **ORGANIZATIONS:** Developed & narrated "Issues In Education" KXTV Sacramento 1978; presenter Language Symposium CA State Dept of Educ 1983, 1985, 1989; Far West Region Co-chair, Alumni Assn, Fisk Univ 1987-; mem Sacramento valley Chap Natl Council of Negro Women; mem Natl Coalition for Sex Equity in Educ 1988-. **HONORS/ACHIEVEMENTS:** Column "Issues in Education," Sacramento Observer 1982-83; "The Untold History of the Black Man in America," 1971,72,73; "Images" CA State Dept of Ed 1988; "Sketches" 1974; Mary McLeod Bethune Award, Natl Council of Negro Women 1988; presenter, Natl Coalition for Sex Equity in Ed Annual Conf 1988; "Booker T Washington Revisited" Circle Project, CSU Sacramento 1989. **MILITARY SERVICE:** WAC splst 3rd class 1954-56. **HOME ADDRESS:** 300 Yampa Circle, Sacramento, CA 95838. **BUSINESS ADDRESS:** Curriculum Consultant, CIRCLE Project CA StateUniv, 655 University Ave Ste 109, Sacramento, CA 95825.

GRAY, MELVIN DEAN
Professional athlete. **PERSONAL:** Born Sep 28, 1948, Fresno, CA; married Ginger. **EDUCATION:** Ft Scott Comm Coll, attended;Univ MO, attended. **CAREER:** St Louis Cardinals, wide rec, drafted in 6th round 1971; Pro Bowl 1974,75,76,77. **HONORS/ACHIEVEMENTS:** Led NFL in passes caught for TD's 1975; "Sporting News" NFC All Star Team 1975-76. **BUSINESS ADDRESS:** Wide Receiver, St Louis Cardinals, 200 Stadium Plaza, St Louis, MO 63102.

GRAY, MOSES W.
Automotive company executive. **PERSONAL:** Born Apr 12, 1937, Rock Castle, VA; son of Moses Young and Ida B Young; married Ann Marie Powell, Nov 22, 1962; children: Tamara Ann, William Bernard. **EDUCATION:** IN Univ, BS Phys Educ 1961; Detroit Diesel Allison Apprentice Training Program, journeyman tool & die maker 1967. **CAREER:** Indianapolis Warriors, professional football player; DDAD Indianapolis, inspector 1962-63, apprentice tool & die maker 1963-67, journeyman tool & die maker 1967-68, production supervisor 1968-69, supervisor-tool room 1969-73, genl supv tool room 1973-76, asst supt master mechanic 1976-79, dir comm relations 1979-83, mgr mfg serv 1983-88, general supt mfg engineering 1989-. **ORGANIZATIONS:** Bds, Indianapolis Business Develop Found, Black Adoption Comm, Children's Bureau of Indianapolis, Child Welfare League of America, Indianapolis Urban League, Comm Serv Council, IN Vocational Tech Coll, United Way of Greater Indianapolis, NAACP, The Volunteer Bureau, The Office of Equal Oppor-City of Indianapolis, Channel #20 Public Service TV, Black Expo, Indianapolis C of C Corporate Comm Affairs Discussion, Black Child Develop Institute, United Way Agency Relations Adv Comm, Oppor Indus Ctr, Madame Walker Urban Life Ctr, The Wilma Rudolph Foundation; pres, Indianapolis Chapter Sigma Pi Phi Fraternity. **HONORS/ACHIEVEMENTS:** B'nai B'rith Man of the Yr 1974; Gold Medal Winner Genl Motors Awd for Excellence in Comm Serv 1978; Outstanding Achievement in Pub & Comm Serv 1982 Bus & Profls of Indianapolis; Who's Who in the Mid-West 1978-84; Public Citizen of the Year Natl Assoc of Social Workers 1986; Citizen of the Year Omega Psi Phi frat 1986; Moses Gray Awd (first recipient) for Outstanding Service of Special Adoptions 1986. **BUSINESS ADDRESS:** General Supt, Mfg Engineering, Detroit Diesel Allison Div, P O Box 894, 4700 West 10th St, Indianapolis, IN 46206.

GRAY, MYRTLE EDWARDS
Educational administrator. **PERSONAL:** Born Nov 20, 1914, Tuscaloosa, AL; married Samuel Alfred Gray; children: Myrtle Imogene, Samuel A. **EDUCATION:** Alabama State Univ, BS, MEd 1950; Univ of Alabama, EdS 1971; Wayne State, Marquette Univ, Auburn Univ, Univ of So Alabama, further study. **CAREER:** Tuscaloosa Cty School Dist, elem teacher 1935-36, 1936-54, principal elem schools 1954-63, suprv principal 1963-80. **ORGANIZATIONS:** Bd dir YMCA 1975-80, Salvation Army 1975-80; chmn Westside Cancer Dr 1979; vice pres Alabama Baptist State Women's Conv; 2nd vice pres Natl Assn Colored Women's Clubs Inc 1980-; pres NW Dist 1981-; mem Alabama Educ Assn, Elem Principals Assn; mem Univ of Alabama Alumni Assn; mem Natl Baptist USA Womens Auxiliary, Nightingale, Cosmos Study; past pres Tuscaloosa City Fed; mem Tuscaloosa C of C; pres Alabama Baptist State Northwest Dist Women's Convention 1981, Natl Assn Colored Women's Clubs Inc 1984-88. **HONORS/ACHIEVEMENTS:** Hon Doct Selma Univ 1986.

GRAY, NAOMI T.
Business executive. **PERSONAL:** Born May 18, 1924, Hattiesburg, MS. **EDUCATION:** Hampton Inst, BS 1945; IN Univ Sch of Soc Svc, MA 1948. **CAREER:** Sheltering Arms Children's Serv NY, caseworker 1948-50; Planned Parenthood Fed of Amer NY, director, field consult 1952-61, dir of field serv 1961-68, vice pres field serv 1968-70; Naomi Gray Assoc, president. **ORGANIZATIONS:** Comm Serv Soc 1948-50; bd mem Natl Assn of Soc Workers NY Chap 1969-71; Natl Conf on Soc Welfare 1967-68; Pvt Sch Placement Prog for Disadvantaged Students 1969-71 NY; past pres Educ Access Cable TV Corp of San Francisco 1974-76; mem Commn on Accreditation Council on Soc Work Educ 1968-71; Soc Welfare & Health Commn Natl Urban League 1965-69; Black Agenda Council San Francisco; vice chmn bd dirs Pyramid Savs & Loan Assn San Francisco; mem vice pres public affairs Fort Mason Ctr Golden Gate natl Recreation Area San Francisco; Amer Pub Health Assn; Amer Pub Welfare Assn; Natl Conf of Social Welfare; Natl Assn of Soc Workers; NAACP; Black Leadership Forum of San Francisco. **HONORS/ACHIEVEMENTS:** Who's Who Amer Women 1966-67; Citation IN Disting Cit 1976; Indianapolis Black Bicentennial Comm; Citation bd dir Natl Assn for Sickle Cell Disease 1973; Citation for Outstanding Achievements in field of bus; Omega Psi Phi SF May 1974. **BUSINESS ADDRESS:** President, Naomi Gray Assoc, 1726 Fillmore St, San Francisco, CA 94115.

GRAY, PEARL SPEARS
Educational administrator. **EDUCATION:** Wilberforce Univ, BA Soc 1968; Antioch-putney Grad Schl of Educ, MAT Sec Educ 1970; OR State Univ, PhD Educ Admin in progress. **CAREER:** Teachers Corp Project, Providence RI, exec LEA asst coor 1971-73; OR State Univ School of Educ, Portland OR, assc dir 1973-76; OR State Univ, dir 1976-. **ORGANIZATIONS:** Bd of dir Natl Human Rel Task Force 1981-; chrprsn bd mem Black Clges Comm Inc 1980-; bd mem Public Health Adv Bd 1985; mem Zonta Intl 1984, Amer Mgmt Assc 1984, Amer Assc of Univ Women, Delta Sigma Theta Inc 1967-. **HONORS/ACHIEVEMENTS:** Outstanding Srv Award Council of Natl Alumni Assc 1983; Women of Excel Award in Educ Delta Sigma Theta Portland Alumnae 1983; One of 100 Most Influential Persons Black Journal 1976; Boss of Year Natl Assc Educ Secr 1976-77. **BUSINESS ADDRESS:** Director, Affirmative Action, OR StateUniv, Ads A 600, Corvallis, OR 97331.

GRAY, RAYMOND LEROY, SR.
Retired association executive. **PERSONAL:** Born Mar 26, 1915, Washington, DC; married Henry Etta Davenport; children: Raymond L Jr. **EDUCATION:** HowardUniv Econs, 1940-41; Rutgers Univ Amer Univ Fed City Clge, Spec Courses Soc Prob Clge Barg Prob Race and Labor 1967-69. **CAREER:** AFGE Wash DC AFL CIO, dir fair dept 1969-83; AFL CIO Wash DC, mem civil rights comm prac 1970-72; Amer Inst of Parlimntrns Natl, mem AIP 1972-; Univ of DC, adjunct prof 1980- (retired). **ORGANIZATIONS:** Asst dir Educ Dept ELFGE Natl Office 1968-69; chmn Pastor Parish Rd Ebenezer United Meth Church 1969-74; chrmn bd trustee Most Worshipful Grd Lodge 1971-73; pres Interdenominational Church Ushers Assoc DC 1973-83; pres Chap #2881 Capitol Hill AARP 1984-; parliamentarian Capitol Cab Cooperative Assoc Inc1984-; pres Junior Investors Club 1984-. **HONORS/ACHIEVEMENTS:** Pres Emeritus Sr Usher Bd EbenezerUniv M Church 1979-; trustee Emeritus MWPHGLF and PHA 1974-; hon pres ICUA of DC Inc 1984-. **HOME ADDRESS:** 303 Dias Dr, Fort Washington, MD 20744.

GRAY, ROBERT DEAN
Mayor. **PERSONAL:** Born Jun 30, 1941, Clarksville, TN; married Gloria F Enochs. **EDUCATION:** MS Vlly State U, BS 1964; TX Southern U, Further Stud 1968. **CAREER:** Bolivar Co Sch Dist #3, tchr/coach 1964-67; TX Southern U, asst coach 1967-68; Bolivar Co Headstart Pgm, headstart dir 1968-71; Shelby, MS, city cncl 1968-76. **ORGANIZATIONS:** Owner/operator Gray's Trucking & Serv Station 1969-77; mayor City of Shelby 1976-; mgr/treas Shelby Fed Credit Union 1970-; mem WAJ Morgan Lodge #20 (Mason) 1967-; mem/trustee IT Montgomery Lodge #664 (ELKS) 1967-; chmn bd of trustees Zion Grove Ch (Baptist) 1967-. **HONORS/ACHIEVEMENTS:** Hall of Fame MS Vlly StateUniv Iha Bena 1981; Outstand Young Men of Am 1975; Govt Serv Award by Jackson Advocate Newspaper 1983; chmn MS Conf of Black Mayors 1978-; 1st vice pres Nat Conf of Black Mayors 1982-84. **BUSINESS ADDRESS:** Mayor, City of Shelby, MS, PO Box 43, Shelby, MS 38774.

GRAY, ROBERT R.
Government official. **PERSONAL:** Born Jun 13, 1910, Lakeland, MD; married Mildred W. **EDUCATION:** Bowie Normal, 1928-30; Morgan State, BS 1949; NY Univ, MA 1951. **CAREER:** Talbot Cty, elem schl prin 1930-34; Fairmount Hghts, elem schl prin 1934-70; PGCo Tchrs Assc Fed Credit Union, educ and info offr 1970-76; Town of Fairmount Hghts, mayor 1977-. **ORGANIZATIONS:** Mem County and State Retired Tchrs Assc, NEA, NAACP. **HONORS/ACHIEVEMENTS:** President MD Chap Natl Conf of Black Mayors. **MILITARY SERVICE:** AUS battalion supply sgt 1942-45. **HOME ADDRESS:** 5502 Addison Rd, Fairmount Heights, MD 20743.

GRAY, RUBEN L.
Attorney. **PERSONAL:** Born Nov 06, 1938, Georgetown, SC; married Jean Dozier; children: Ruben, Jr, Valencia, Valerie. **EDUCATION:** SC Stae Coll, BS 1961; SC State Coll, LLB 1963; Nat Moot Ct Competitor, grad 1st in class. **CAREER:** Finney & Gray, atty 1973-; Morris Coll, vice pres for devel 1970-73; SC Econ Opp Bd Inc, exec dir 1968-70. **ORGANIZATIONS:** Mem SC State Elections Commn; mem bd trst Sumter Sch Dist 17; mem ABA, NBA; SC Bar Assn; chmn Sumter Co Child Uplift Bd Inc; pres Sumter Br NAACP; mem UMCA; Goodfellows; Sumter Co Black Polit Caucus; Sumter Co Dem Exec Com. **HONORS/ACHIEVEMENTS:** Recip Comm Leader of Am Awd 1968. **MILITARY SERVICE:** AUS 1963-65f. **BUSINESS ADDRESS:** 110 S Sumter St, Sumter, SC.

GRAY, STERLING PERKINS, JR.
Criminal court judge. **PERSONAL:** Born Dec 24, 1943, Nashville, TN; married Kristin Byard; children: Cezanne, Sterling P III. **EDUCATION:** FL A&M Univ, BS 1963; Nashville Law School, JD 1973; Certificate of Completion, Natl Judicial Coll 1984, Harvard Univ 1983. **CAREER:** Division I Circuit Court, criminal court judge. **ORGANIZATIONS:** Bd of dirs Nashville Symphony Assoc 1978-81, Leadership Nashville 1985-87, Napier Looby Bar Assoc; mem criminal justice comm Nashville Bar Assoc. **HONORS/ACHIEVEMENTS:** Most Disting Grad of the Nashville Law School 1986; commencement speaker Nashville Law Sch 1986. **BUSINESS ADDRESS:** Judge of Division I, Circuit Court, 601 Metro Courthouse, Nashville, TN 37201.

GRAY, WILFRED DOUGLAS
Paper company executive. **PERSONAL:** Born Oct 01, 1937, Richmond, VA; son of Richard L Gray and Lula B Duvall Gray; married Shirley M Durant, Nov 23, 1957; children: Alden D, Kathleen Y. **EDUCATION:** Dale Carnegie, Buffalo NY, attended, 1971; State Univ of New York at Buffalo, Buffalo NY, BA, 1974; Printing Industry of Metropolitan Washington, Washington DC, attended, 1981. **CAREER:** Republic Steel, Buffalo NY, scarfer, inspector, 1962-76; Buffalo Envelope, Buffalo NY, sales representative, 1976-80; Envelopes Unlimited, Rockville MD, sales representative, 1980-81; Gray Paper Products Inc, Washington DC, pres, 1981-. **ORGANIZATIONS:** Mem, District of Columbia Chamber of Commerce, 1984-, NAACP, 1987-; bd of dir, Boys and Girls Clubs of Greater Washington, 1987-; mem, Amer Assn of Retired Persons, 1987-, Natl Assn of Black Public Officials, 1988-, Upper Georgia Ave Business & Professional Assn 1988-, Natl Business Forms Assn, 1988-, Rotary Club of Washington DC, 1988-. **HONORS/ACHIEVEMENTS:** President's Award, Federal Envelope, 1979; Score, Certificate of Training, 1987; Certificate of Appreciation, Browne Jr High School, 1987. **MILITARY SERVICE:** US Navy, Airman, 1956-60; Honorable Discharge, 1960. **BUSINESS ADDRESS:** President, Gray Paper Products Inc, 7600 Georgia Ave NW, Suite 205, Washington, DC 20012.

GRAY, WILLIAM H., III
Government official. **PERSONAL:** Born Aug 20, 1941, Baton Rouge, LA; married Andrea Dash; children: William H IV, Justin Yates, Andrew Dash. **EDUCATION:** Franklin & Marshall Coll, attended 1963; Drew Seminary, grad deg 1966; Princeton Theol Sem, grad deg 1970; Univ of PA, Temple Univ, Mansfield Coll ofExford Univ England, grad work. **CAREER:** Union Baptist Church Montclair NJ, pastor 1964-72; Bright Hope Baptist Church Philadelphia, sr pastor 1972-; Philadelphia Mortgage Plan, helped design; Philadelphia, US Congressman 1978- (5th term). **ORGANIZATIONS:** Mem Dem Steering Com 96th US Congress; sec Cong Black Caucus; mem House Com on Foreign Affairs; mem Com on the Budget; mem Com on the Dist of Columbia; appointed by Pres Carter to US Liberia Presl Commn; vice chmn Congressional Black Caucus; sponsored the emergency food aid bill for Ethiopia 1984; authored the House version of the Anti-Apartheid Acts of 1985,86. **HONORS/ACHIEVEMENTS:** Man of the Yr Natl Federation of Housing Counselors 1980; Recip 1985 The Martin Luther King Jr Award for Public Serv for leadership as chairman of the Budget Committee of the US House of Reps, for contrib as mem of the Congressional Black Caucus, and for political achievements as Dem mem of the House from Philadelphia. **BUSINESS ADDRESS:** US Congressman, 204 Cannon House Office Bldg, Washington, DC 20515.

GRAY-LITTLE, BERNADETTE
Psychologist, educator. **PERSONAL:** Born Oct 21, 1944, Washington, NC; daughter of James Gray and Rosalie Lanier Gray; married Shade Keys; children: Maura M, Mark G. **EDUCATION:** Marywood Coll, BA 1966; St Louis Univ, MS 1968, PhD 1970. **CAREER:** Univ of NC, asst prof 1971-76, assoc prof 1976-82, prof 1982-. **ORGANIZATIONS:** Mem Amer Psychol Assn, Sigma Xi; dir Clinical Psychology Program Psychology Dept; school consultant Assoc of IRSS. **HONORS/ACHIEVEMENTS:** Phi Beta Kappa Fulbright Fellow; recipient of grants Social Science Research Council, Carolina Population Center, Spencer Found, Natl Research Council. **BUSINESS ADDRESS:** Professor, Univ of NC, Psychology Dept Davie Hall, Chapel Hill, NC 27514.

GRAYDON, WASDON, JR.
Educational administrator. **PERSONAL:** Born Sep 22, 1950, Fort Mammoth, NJ; son of Wasdon Graydon and Lenora Graydon; married Veronica Brooks; children: Tremayne, Jasmaine. **EDUCATION:** Abraham Baldwin Agr Coll, AS Sec Educ 1970; GA Southern Coll,

BS Soc Sci 1972; Valdosta State Coll, Med History 1974. **CAREER:** Special Serv Prog, dir 1973-76; Upward Bound Special Serv Prog, dir 1973-76, special serv/min adv prog 1983-87; Tift County, commissioner dist 2 1984-88; G&M Enterprises, partner 1985-87; Abraham Baldwin Agr Coll, dir of special serv. **ORGANIZATIONS:** Treasurer Georgia Assn of Special Prog Inc 1980-84; consultant mem Georgia Statewide Health Coor Council 1980-83; mem Phi Delta Kappa 1975-83; bd mem SW Georgia Health System Agency Inc 1976-81; mem Tift Co NAACP 1980-87; trustee Everette Temple CME Church 1980-87; mem The PROMISE Club 1983-84; trustee Tifton Tift Co Public Library 1984-88; mem Tift Co Arts Councils 1984-87; bd mem Tifton-Tift Co United Way 1986-88; mem Tifton-Tift Co C of C 1986-87; bd of dir Tifton-Tift Co Main St Prog 1986-87. **HONORS/ACHIEVEMENTS:** Outstanding Young Men of Amer 1976; GASPP Outstanding Serv Awd 1983; SAEOPP Certificate of Recognition 1984. **HOME ADDRESS:** 4030 Martin Ave, Tifton, GA 31794. **BUSINESS ADDRESS:** Dir of Special Services, Abraham Baldwin Agr Coll, PO Box 21 ABAC Station, Tifton, GA 31793.

GRAYS, MATTELIA BENNETT
Educational administrator. **PERSONAL:** Born Jul 26, 1931, Houston; married Horace. **EDUCATION:** Dilliard U, BA cum laude;Univ of MI, MA spl edn. **CAREER:** Will Rogers Research & Devel Center for Houston Independent School Dist, educator admin operator, duties corr to those of school prin, has total resp for acad & curr of enrollees staff devel & mgmt function. **ORGANIZATIONS:** Mem Intl Assn of Childhood Edn; exec bd mem Nat Pan Hellenic Council Inc; natl pres Alpha Kappa Alpha Sor Inc. **BUSINESS ADDRESS:** 3101 Weslayan, Houston, TX 77027.

GRAYSON, BARBARA ANN
Educational administrator. **PERSONAL:** Born Oct 10, 1954, Van Buren, AR; daughter of Vallard Campbell, Sr and Beatrice Schoate Campbell; married Norman J Grayson; children: Lamar. **EDUCATION:** Northeastern State Univ, BA 1976, MEd 1980. **CAREER:** Alluwe Public Schools, special ed inst 1977; East Central Univ, counselor 1977-80; Connors State College, counselor 1980-. **ORGANIZATIONS:** Member past sec & bd of directors OK Division of Student Assistance 1977-; member/past board Southwest Region Student Assistance 1977-; member-public relations Phi Delta Kappa 1983-; member NAACP. **HONORS/ACHIEVEMENTS:** Outstanding Woman Outstanding Young Women of America 1982, 1983. **BUSINESS ADDRESS:** Counselor, Connors State College, Box 711 CSC, Warner, OK 74469.

GRAYSON, ELSIE MICHELLE
Counselor. **PERSONAL:** Born May 05, 1962, Fairfield, AL. **EDUCATION:** The Univ of AL-Tuscaloosa, BS; Univ of AL at Birmingham, MA Educ. **CAREER:** Child Mental Health Svcs, teaching parent 1983-84; AL Dept of Human Resources, social worker 1984-. **ORGANIZATIONS:** Mem Alpha Kappa Alpha Sor Inc Omicron Omega Chapt; mem Eastern Star Corine Chap 257; choir dir/pres/asst teacher New Mount Moriah Bapt Church. **HOME ADDRESS:** 322 Knight Ave, Hueytown, AL 35023.

GRAYSON, HARRY L.
Educator. **PERSONAL:** Born Jul 07, 1929, Corinth, MS; married Valeris Maxine Porter; children: 7. **EDUCATION:** Rust Coll, BA 1956; Jackson State Coll, MA 1966. **CAREER:** Lowe's High School Guntown, teacher, coach 1952-53; Poplar High School Saltillo, prin 1953-60; Green St Elementary School Tupelo, first prin 1960-62; George Washington Carver High School Tupelo, prin 1962-. **ORGANIZATIONS:** Mem Spring Hill Bapt Ch Tupelo; YMCA; United Supreme Council 33rd Mason; First Dist Tchrs Assn MAT Nat; Educ Asnn US; Nat Assn Secondary Schs Prin; Young Dem Club MS; Tupelo Civic Improv Club; Phi Beta Sigma Frat Inc; state off State & Nat Funeral Dirs & Mort Assn; bd mem Comm devel Found; pub rel man Kirksey & Grayson-Porterhs Mortuary; pres Ebony Saving Club; treas Astronaut Saving Club; adv bd BSA; exec sec 1st Dist MTA; chosen as del rep MTA to Nat Educ Assn Atlantic City; past pres 1st Dist Tchrs Assn MTA; past sunday sch supt Spring Hill Ch; past chmn McIntoch Dist BSA; past exalt ruler trst Henry Hampton Lodge 782. **HONORS/ACHIEVEMENTS:** NJ awd outstd ldrshp 1st Dist MTA. **BUSINESS ADDRESS:** George Washington Carver HS, Tupelo, MS 38801.

GRAYSON, JOHN N.
Business executive. **PERSONAL:** Born Sep 04, 1932, Brooklyn, NY; married Dorothy Lane; children: Lois, Theresa (Wallace), Susan, April. **EDUCATION:** BSEE 1959f. **CAREER:** UNIVOX CA Co, pres; Unified Ind Alexandria VA, dir energy problems proj on minority bus enter 1973; prod line mgr mgr-manu engr test sec; Electronics Harward Operations, sub-proj mgr; Guidance & Nav Lab TWR Sys Redondo Beach CA, bus mgr 1962-71; Hughes Aircraft Co El Segundo CA, proj engr 1955-62. **ORGANIZATIONS:** Mem Nat Assn of Black Manu; Inst of Elec & Electronics Engr Inc; chrtr pres Consolidate Comm Action Assn; mem pres Youth Motivation Task Force; Urban League; NAACP; assisted in organization & devel of comm sel-help group in Mexican Am Comm in E LA; assisted & adv in forming of Oriental-Am Caucus; ruling elder Westminster Presb Ch LA; commr 181st Gen Assembly United Presb Ch 1969; past moderator Synod of So Bca UPCUSA; past chmn com which restructured the Synod of So CA; mem The Gen Assembly Mission Council UPCUSA; cmn The Section on Eval UPCUSA. **HONORS/ACHIEVEMENTS:** Man of yr awd Westminister Presb Ch 1972; outsnd serv awd Nat Assn of Black Manuf 1974f. **MILITARY SERVICE:** AUS sgt 1st class 1950-55. **BUSINESS ADDRESS:** UNIVOX CA Co, 4505 W Jefferson Blvd, Los Angeles, CA 90016.

GRAYSON, ROBERT
Chief executive. **CAREER:** Metro Lincoln-Mercury Inc, Charlotte NC, chief executive. **BUSINESS ADDRESS:** Metro Lincoln-Mercury Inc, 7301 South Blvd, Charlotte, NC 28209. *

GREAR, EFFIE C.
Educational administrator. **PERSONAL:** Born Aug 15, 1927, Huntington, WV; daughter of Rev Harold J Carter and Margaret Tinsley Carter; married William A Grear; children: Rhonda Kaye, William A Jr. **EDUCATION:** WV State Clge, BMus 1948; OH State Univ, MA 1955; Nova Univ, Doctor of Educ 1976. **CAREER:** Excelsior High WV, music and band tchr 1948-49; FAMU HS Tallahassee FL, band and chorus tchr 1949-51; Smith-brown HS Arcadia FL, band and chorus tchr 1952-56; Lake Shore HS Belle Glade FL, band and chorus tchr 1956-63, dean 1963-66, asst prin 1966-70; Glades Cnt HS Belle Glade FL, asst prin 1970-75, prin 1975-. **ORGANIZATIONS:** Pres Elite Comm Club Inc Belle Glade 1971-82; pres Belle Glade Chamber of Comm Beautification 1974-80; bd of dirs Mental Health Assc Palm Beach Cty 1984-; pres City Assc of Belle Glade 1984-, mem bd of dirs Palm Beach County Mental Health Agency 1984-; pres Belle Glade City Assoc of Women's Clubs 1985-; bd of governors Everglades Area Health Educ Ctr 1986-; sec, Florida Assn of Women's Clubs 1988-90; bd of dir, Florida High Sch Activities Assn, 1987-88; bd of dir, Glades ACTS, 1987-. **HONORS/ACHIEVEMENTS:** Outstanding Comm Ach by FL Atlantic Univ 1977; Woman of Year Elite Comm Club 1979 1982; Outstndng Achmt Hnry Mem Glades Correctional Jaycees Unit 1979; Special Recognition FL Sugar Cane League for Lobbying for Sugar Industry Washington DC 1985; Srv Awd United Negro College Fund Telethon 1985; Zeta Phi Beta Educator of the Yr 1984; Educator of the Yr Phi Delta Kappa Palm Beach Co FL 1986; Hon Chap Farmer of the Future Farmers of Amer local chap 1986; Honored by Gov Bob Graham of FL during first celebration of Martin Luther King Jr Natl observance 1986; Woman of the Yr FL Assoc of Women's Clubs 1986; Citizen of the Yr Belle Glade Chamber of Commerce 1986; Community Service Award, El Dorado Civic Club, 1987; Martin L. King, Jr. Humanitarian Award West Palm Beach Urban League 1988; Community Service Award Palm Beach County NAACP Branch 198 9. **HOME ADDRESS:** 661 SW 4th St, PO Box 262, Belle Glade, FL 33430. **BUSINESS ADDRESS:** Principal, Glades Central HS, 425 W Canal St, Belle Glade, FL 33430.

GREAR, WILLIAM A.
Business owner. **PERSONAL:** Born Sep 16, 1923, Russelville, KY; son of Charles C Grear and Oretha Williams Grear; married Effie Carter; children: Rhonda, William Jr. **EDUCATION:** Palm Beach Jr Clge. **CAREER:** City of Belle Glade FL, city comm 1968-83; Wee Care Child Dev Ctr, dir 1973-79; City of Belle Glade FL, vice mayor 1974; City of Belle Glade FL, mayor 1975; B and E Rubber Stamps and Trophies, owner mgr 1976-. **ORGANIZATIONS:** Bd of dir Solid Waste Authority Palm Bch Co, Katherine Price Fnd Belle Glade 1985, Habilitation Ctr of Belle Glade. **HONORS/ACHIEVEMENTS:** Man of Year Omega Psi Phi Frat 1969; Citizen of Year Elite Comm Club Inc 1975; Comm Srv Award Eldorado Civic Clb 1980; Community Service Award by Governor Graham during 1st Martin Luther King Jr birthday observance 1986. **BUSINESS ADDRESS:** Manager, B & E Rubber Stamps-Trophies, 661 SW 4th St, PO Box 262, Belle Glade, FL 33430.

GREAVES, WILLIAM
Film producer, director, writer. **PERSONAL:** Born Oct 08, 1926, New York, NY; married Louise; children: David, Taiyim Maiya. **EDUCATION:** City College of New York, attended 1944-45; Film Institute City College, attended 1950-52. **CAREER:** Natl Film Bd of Canada, filmmaker 1952-60; United Nations Television, filmmaker 1963-64; Canadian Drama Studio, artistic dir 1952-63; Lee Strassberg Theatre Inst in NYC, taught acting for film & tv; Univ Pictures' Bustin Loose, exec producer; produced written & directed, The Marijuana Affair, Symbiopsychotaxiplasm, TAke One, Ali the Fighter; directed dramaticTV in both the US and Canada; produced & directed multi-media production "Tribute to Paul Robeson" at Carnegie Hall for the Paul Robeson Archives; exec producer & co-host for Black Journal; William Greaves Productions, pres/filmmaker 1964-85. **ORGANIZATIONS:** Mem NY Actors Studio. **HONORS/ACHIEVEMENTS:** Black Filmmakers Hall of Fame 1980; special hommage in Paris at First Black Amer Independent Film Festival; honored at Joseph Papp's Public Theatre; Emmy Awd1970 for Black Journal; NY Actors Studio Dusa Awd; Dr of Humane Letters King Mem Coll; listed in Who's Who in Amer, Who's Who in the World; winner of over60 film festival awards. **BUSINESS ADDRESS:** President, William Greaves Productions, 80 Eighth Ave Ste 1703, New York, NY 10011.

GREEN, A. C.
Professional basketball player. **EDUCATION:** Attended Oregon State Univ. **CAREER:** Los Angeles Lakers, Inglewood CA, professional basketball player. **BUSINESS ADDRESS:** c/o Los Angeles Lakers, P O Box 10, Inglewood, CA 90306. *

GREEN, AARON ALPHONSO
Attorney. **PERSONAL:** Born Jul 22, 1946, Gainesville, FL; married Carolyn Speed; children: Ava, Adrienne, April. **EDUCATION:** FL A&M Univ, BS Political Science 1966; Univ of FL, JD 1972. **CAREER:** Self-employed Aaron A Green Law Office, atty 1973-; Gainsville City Commn, youngest person elect 1975; Gainesville FL, mayor commr 1977-78. **ORGANIZATIONS:** Mem FL Bar Assn; FL Acad Trial Lawyers; Natl Bar Assn 8th Judiciary & Cir Nom Commn; mem chrt class Natl Coll Criminal Defense Lawyers & Public Defenders. **HONORS/ACHIEVEMENTS:** Youngest mayor elected; re-elected for second term of city comm 1978. **BUSINESS ADDRESS:** 410 S E 4th Ave, Gainesville, FL 32602.

GREEN, AL
Clergyman, recording artist, business executive. **PERSONAL:** Born Apr 13, 1946, Forrest City, AR. **EDUCATION:** Lane Coll, Hon BA Music 1976; Lemoyne Owen, Hon BA Music 1977. **CAREER:** Green Enterprises Inc, owner/pres 1970; Al Green Music Inc, owner/pres/recording artist 1970-; Full Gospel Tabernacle Church, pastor 1976-; formerly recording artist w/Bell then Hi-Records; songs include Rhymes, Lets Stay Together, Tired of Being Alone, How do You Mend a Broken Heart, Back up train, Love and Happiness; appeared in Broadway production "Your ARms Too Short to Box with God" 1982; album He is the Light 1986. **ORGANIZATIONS:** Mem NARAS 1970-, AGVA 1970-; spec deputy Memphis Sheriffs Dept 1976-; hon capt Bolling AFB Washington DC 1976-; pres Lee County Publ Co 1983-; mem Econ & Devel City Hall 1984-. **HONORS/ACHIEVEMENTS:** Tribute in the Music Ind Sullivan Awd 1982; Grammy Precious Lord NARAS 1983; Grammy I'll Rise Again NARAS 1984; Dove Awd Gospel Music Assoc 1984. **HOME ADDRESS:** 3208 Winchester, Memphis, TN 38118.

GREEN, ANGELO GRAY
Financial administrator. **PERSONAL:** Born Sep 20, 1950, Mobile, AL; married Joyce Wright; children: Angela Latifa, Jasmine Niya. **EDUCATION:** Clark Coll, BA Econ 1968-72; Univ of MI, MPP Public Finance 1972-74. **CAREER:** Cunningham Art Products, cost accountant 1974; City of Atlanta Employment & Training Office, financial analyst II 1974-78; City of Atlanta Fin Dept, financial analyst III 1978-83, fin chief analyst. **ORGANIZATIONS:** Consult United Negro Coll Fund 1979, Southern Ctr for Public Policies Studies 1980,82; mem NAACP 1981-85, Atlanta Urban League 1982-84, Natl Forum for Black Public Admin 1984-85. **HONORS/ACHIEVEMENTS:** Publ "Manpower Devel & Training, An Evaluation" Southern Ctr for Public Policy Studies Clark Coll 1971; Employee of the Year City of Atlanta Employment & Training Office 1977; Manager of the Year City of Atlanta

Employment & Training Office 1978. **BUSINESS ADDRESS:** Financial Chief Analyst, City of Atlanta, 902 City Hall, Atlanta, GA 30335.

GREEN, ARTHUR L.
Executive director. **PERSONAL:** Born Oct 21, 1928, New London, CT; married Betty L Mokowski; children: Judith, Adam, Susan. **EDUCATION:** Univ of MA, MEd 1974;Univ of MA, EdD 1976. **CAREER:** CT Commn on Human Rights & Opport, exec dir 1966-; Commn on Opport Rights & State, field rep 1960-66; CT Dept of Labor, clms exam 1959-60. **ORGANIZATIONS:** Past chmn CT Civil Liberties Union; Intl Assn of Officl Human Rights Agy; mem of Gov Coun on Opport for Spanish-Speaking; Gov Plann Com on Crimnl Adminstrn; Gov Exec Com on Human Rights & Opport; mem Adv Coun for State Dept of Comm Affrs; mem bd dir Intl Assn of Offcl Human Rights Agy; convn chmn CT State Conf of NAACP Br; mem bd dir CT State NAACP Conf of Br St. **HONORS/ACHIEVEMENTS:** Benedict awd Greater Hartford Cath Inter-racial Coun 1969; oustndg young man of am US Jr C of C 1965; man of yr CT Conf of NAACP 1972. **MILITARY SERVICE:** USAF s/sgt 1949-52. **BUSINESS ADDRESS:** CT Common on Human Rights & Op, 90 Washington St, Hartford, CT 06115.

GREEN, BRENDA KAY
Educator. **PERSONAL:** Born Dec 07, 1947, Baton Rouge, LA; daughter of Jackson Willis Green and Lillian White Green George. **EDUCATION:** Southern Univ, Baton Rouge LA, BS, 1969; Northwestern Univ, Evanston IL, MA, 1973; Louisiana State Univ, Baton Rouge LA, post graduate studies, 1980-82. **CAREER:** East Baton Rouge Parish Schools, Baton Rouge LA, teacher, 1969-89. **ORGANIZATIONS:** Pres, Beta Alpha Chapter, Zeta Phi Beta, 1968; mem, Natl Educ Assn, 1969-, Louisiana Educ Assn, 1969-72, Louisiana Assn of Educ, 1972-, Phi Delta Kappa, 1974-89; 3rd vice pres, Mu Zeta Chapter, Zeta Phi Beta, 1976-80; mem, Natl Council of Negro Women, 1980-; Louisiana State dir, Zeta Phi Beta Sorority Inc, 1980-88; 1st vice pres, Mu Zeta Chapter, Zeta Phi Beta, 1984-88; Natl 2nd vice pres, Zeta Phi Beta Sorority Inc, 1988-; chmn of scholarship, Natl Educ Found, ZOB, 1988-. **HONORS/ACHIEVEMENTS:** Teacher of the Year, Louisiana Educ Assn (local school), 1973, 1974; Outstanding Young Educ, Scotlandville LA Jaycees, 1974; Honorary Dist Atty, East Baton Rough Parish Dist Attorney's Office, 1983. **HOME ADDRESS:** 1514 N 25th St, Baton Rouge, LA 70802.

GREEN, CALVIN COOLIDGE
Educator, clergyman. **PERSONAL:** Born Jul 19, 1931, Laneview, VA; son of Rev James Herman Green (deceased) and Consula Levallia Deleaver Green (deceased); married Ella Mary Osbourne; children: Robert Caesar, Carroll Anthony, Charles Conrad. **EDUCATION:** VA State Coll Petersburg, BS Biology 1956; A&T Coll of NC Greensboro, MSEd Chem 1965; Grad Sch Med Coll of VA,Physiology 1968-71;Sch of Theology VA Union U, MDiv Theology 1982; Intl Bible Inst & Seminary Orlando, ThD Cnslng 1983; Nova Univ, Ft Lauderdale FLA Ed D Program 1987. **CAREER:** Downingtown Industrial Sch PA, sci tchr 1956-57; Med Coll of VA Heart Lung Project, surgical Lab Tech 1957-59; Armstrong HS Richmond, tchr of sci1959-62; Armstrong HS Richmond, prof of military sci/commandant of cadets 1963-69; pastor Lebanon Bapt Church New Kent, VA 1977-82; pastor Calvary Bapt Ch Saluda, VA 1979-; Thomas Jefferson High School, dept head science 1969-78; Jefferson-Hugeunot-Wythe HS, Dept sci head 1978-, Chmn Sci Dept 1980-85; Sci Dept Chmn, Thomas Jefferson High School 1985-. **ORGANIZATIONS:** Mem VA Acad of Sci Com 1981-85; General Board of Baptist General Convention of VA; mem, gen bd of Baptist Gen Convention of VA 1985-89; Chaplain, dept of VA ROA 1983-88; mem Phi Delta Kappa 1988-89; mem National Society for the study of education 1986-89. **HONORS/ACHIEVEMENTS:** ROTC Hall of Fame VA State Coll 1969-; chief plaintiff US Supreme Court Decision, "Green v New Kent" 1968; author, "Counseling, With the Pastor and CPE Stdnt in Mind" Vantage 1984; chaplain VA Dept of Reserve Offcrs Assn (ROA) 1984-; honorarium & banquet by New Kent NAACP 1989; plaque from Professional Business Women's Orgn, Middlesix & Vic 1989. **MILITARY SERVICE:** AUS Med Serv col 23 yrs; Chaplain Corps col 2 yrs; Occupation Medal (Japan); Korean Svc; Armed Svcs; Armed Forces Reserve 1951-Adjanct Faculty, Command and General Staff College, 1986; continuous military (USAR) since 1951; officer 1956-; Korean War; enlisted service 1951-53. **HOME ADDRESS:** Rt 2 Box 820, Quinton, VA 23141.

GREEN, CHARLES A.
Educator, psychologist. **PERSONAL:** Born Oct 17, 1927, Detroit, MI; divorced; children: Iris, Robin Charles. **EDUCATION:** BA 1952; MEd 1957; PhD 1974. **CAREER:** Detroit Bd of Educ, teacher Special Educ 1953-52; Northville State Hospital, 1958-62; Detroit Bd of Educ, psychology clinic 1962-68; Rsch & Evaluation Dept Detroit Bd of Educ, rsch assoc 1968-. **ORGANIZATIONS:** Fellow-Am Assn on Mental Defieciency; Am Assn Advncmt of Sci; Am Acad of Polit & Social Sci; Phi Delta Kappa; co-fndr & 1st pres MI Assn Tchrs of Emtnlly Dstrbd Children 1960; Alpha Phi Alpha; Bro-Big Sister Orgn 1968-72; Evltn Com New Detroit Inc 1970-; chrmn Thunderbird Dist; chmn Boy Scoutsof Am 1974; chmn MI Assn of Black Psychol, MI Acad of Polit & Social Sci 1978-79; Am Educ Rsrch Assn. **HONORS/ACHIEVEMENTS:** Lstd in ldrs in am sci 1960; comm ldrs of am 1970; men of achvmnt 1974. **BUSINESS ADDRESS:** 10100 Grand River, Detroit, MI 48204.

GREEN, CICERO M., JR.
Business executive. **PERSONAL:** Born Oct 08, 1930, Durham, NC; married Dora Jenkins; children: Andrea, Michael. **EDUCATION:** NC Central U, BS 1957; NC Central U, MS 1966;Univ NC, Cert 1974. **CAREER:** NC Mutual Life Ins Co spl home off rep 1957; asst mgr 1959; contrlrs staff asst 1962; adminstrv asst 1966; admin staff 1968; asst treas 1969; treas 1972; vice pres 1974; sr vice pres finance. **ORGANIZATIONS:** NC CentralUniv Endwmnt Fund 1975-; adv bd DukeUniv Med Cntr 1979-; bd of dirs Northwestern Nat Bank 1979-; bd dirs Mgmt Devel Inc; bd dirs-NC Mutual Life Ins Co; Pres and mem of Bd Dir of NCM Life Comm, Inc; bd dirs, executive comm and treas of Amer Citizens Life Ins Co, Chrmn, bd dirs and pres of American Capital Life Ins Co; Chrmn, bd dirs Opportunity Funding Corp; Advisory Bd to Duke Univ Hospital; Bd dirs of Mngmnt Devlpmnt, Inc; local bd dirs First-Union Natl Bk; bd dirs Durham Bd of Realtors; Mortgage Banker's Assoc; Financial Analyst Fed; NC Society of Financial Analysts. **HONORS/ACHIEVEMENTS:** Who's Who in Finance & Industry; Who's Who in the Southwest. **MILITARY SERVICE:** USAF 1950-54. **HOME ADDRESS:** 902 Jerome Rd, Durham, NC 27713.

GREEN, CLIFFORD SCOTT
Judge. **PERSONAL:** Born Apr 02, 1923, Philadelphia, PA; married Mabel Wood; children: Terri Alice, David Scott. **EDUCATION:** Temple Univ Sch of Business, BS 1948; Temple Univ Sch of Law, JD 1951. **CAREER:** Co Ct of Phila, judge 1964; US Dist Ct Eastern Dist of PA, judge 1971-. **ORGANIZATIONS:** Bd trustees Temple Univ; lectr Law Temple Univ Sch of Law; bd dir Crime Prevention Assn of Phila; White House Fellows Philadelphia Regional Panel; emeritus mgr Children's Hosp. **HONORS/ACHIEVEMENTS:** Hon LLD Temple Univ. **MILITARY SERVICE:** USAF 1943-46. **BUSINESS ADDRESS:** Judge US District Court, US Dist Court Eastern Dist PA, 15613-601 Market St, Philadelphia, PA 19106.

GREEN, CLYDE OCTAVIOUS
Medical doctor. **PERSONAL:** Born Oct 06, 1960, St Elizabeth, Jamaica;married Cheryl E Wilson; children: Juliet, Elise. **EDUCATION:** Univ of South Carolina, BS 1982; Howard Univ, MD 1986. **CAREER:** Student Christian Fellowship, minister 1979-82; Student Natl Medical Assoc, parlimentarian 1982-86; Triumph The Church of New Age, asst pastor 1979-. **ORGANIZATIONS:** Mem Medical Assoc of GA; rsch asst Howard Univ 1984-86; consultant Natl Council on Aging 1985-86; mem Amer Medical Assoc 1986-. **HONORS/ACHIEVEMENTS:** Dean's List 1981,82; President's List 1982; founder/pres Intl Student Professional Assoc 1983-86. **HOME ADDRESS:** 3729 Tinley Dr, Macon, GA 31204. **BUSINESS ADDRESS:** Physician, Medical Ctr of Central GA, 777 Hemlock St, Macon, GA 31201.

GREEN, CONSUELLA
US Navy officer. **PERSONAL:** Born Mar 14, 1946, New Orleans, LA; daughter of Nancy Mae Green Anderson. **EDUCATION:** Southern Univ, Baton Rouge LA, BS, 1971; InterAmerican Univ, Puerto Rico, MA, 1976. **CAREER:** US Navy, Great Lakes IL, dir, Race Relations Center, 1973-75, Roosevelt Roads PR, port serv, Base Educ Serv, 1975-77, Navy Reserve Officer Training Corps, asst prof, Naval Science, 1977-80, Washington DC, Devel & Implementation of Navy Training Plans, 1980-83, Little Rock AR, Military Entrance Processing Station, commanding officer, 1984-86, San Diego CA, dir of training & exec officer, Fleet Training Center, 1986-90. **HONORS/ACHIEVEMENTS:** Certificate of Community Serv for the Neighborhood House Assn Head Start Child Devel Program; Community Serv & Professional Achievement Award, Lambda Kappa Mu; Leadership Award, YWCA Tribute to Women In Industry; Young Outstanding Woman of America Award, 1978. **MILITARY SERVICE:** US Navy, Commander (0-5), 1972-.

GREEN, CURTIS E.
Business executive. **PERSONAL:** Born Dec 20, 1923, Franklin, LA; married Juanita; children: Curtis Jr, Sandy, Ricky. **EDUCATION:** SF State Coll, BS. **CAREER:** SF Muncpl Rlwy, gen mgr present; bus opertr; serv insp; chief of insps; Bur of Persnnl & Safty, dir; Operations & Adminstrns SF Muncpl Rlwy,dep gen mgr. **ORGANIZATIONS:** NAACP; Black Leadership Forum. **MILITARY SERVICE:** USMC platoon sgt 1942-45.

GREEN, DARRELL
Professional athlete. **PERSONAL:** Born Feb 15, 1960; married Jewell Fenner. **EDUCATION:** Attended, Texas A&I Univ. **CAREER:** Washington Redskins, cornerback 1983-. **ORGANIZATIONS:** Spokesperson Big Brothers of Amer DC Chapt; hon chmn Red Cross Northern VA Chapt. **HONORS/ACHIEVEMENTS:** Name to Football Coaches all-American Division II team in coll; Lone Star Conference Defensive Player of the Yr; selected to AP first team Little all-Amer; won title of NFL's Fastest Man; named to Football Digest and AP all-rookie first teams; Super Bowl Punt Return record 1983; Pro Bowl Starter 1984; mem 1987 ProBowl team. **BUSINESS ADDRESS:** Washington Redskins, PO Box 17247, Dulles Intl Airport, Washington, DC 20041.

GREEN, DEBORAH KENNON
Attorney. **PERSONAL:** Born Aug 14, 1951, Knoxville, TN. **EDUCATION:** Knoxville Coll, BA (Hon Grad) 1973; Georgetown Law Ctr, JD 1976. **CAREER:** David N Niblack Wash DC, legal intern, law clerk, attny 1976-77; DC Govt Rental Accommodations Office, hearing examiner 1977-78; Govt Oper Arrington Dixon, comm clerk 1978-79; Council of DC Office Arrington Dixon, leg asst to chmn 1979-80; US Dept of Labor, attny. **ORGANIZATIONS:** Co-chmn 7th Annual Conv Natl Assoc of Black Women Attny 1978-; mem WV Bar Assoc 1979, WA Bar Assoc 1980, God's Universal Kingdom 1984. **HONORS/ACHIEVEMENTS:** Listed in Who's Who Among Amer Coll & Univ Knoxville Coll 1972-73; Tuition Scholarship Georgetown Law Ctr Wash DC 1973-76; Earl Warren Legal Training Scholarship 1973-74; Special Awd of Merit DC Bar 1979; Outstading Young Women in Amer 1983. **BUSINESS ADDRESS:** Attorney, US Dept of Labor, 4015 Wilson Blvd, Arlington, VA 22203.

GREEN, DENNIS
Coach. **PERSONAL:** Born Feb 17, 1949, Harrisburg, PA; married Margie; children: Patty, Jeremy. **EDUCATION:** Iowa State Univ, BS in Educ 1971. **CAREER:** British Columbia Lions Canadian Football League, starting tailback; Iowa State, grad asst 1972, quarterbacks/receivers coach 1974-76; Dayton, offensive backs/receivers coach 1973; Stanford, offensive coord 1980; Northwestern, head coach (5 seasons); San Francisco 49ers', running back coach 1979, receivers coach. **HONORS/ACHIEVEMENTS:** Big 10 Coach of the Year 1982. **BUSINESS ADDRESS:** Assistant Coach, San Francisco 49'ers, 711 Nevada St, Redwood City, CA 94061.

GREEN, DENNIS O.
Government official. **PERSONAL:** Born Nov 14, 1940, Detroit, MI; son of Arthur S Green and Olive M Dean McCaughan; married Katherine F, Aug 12, 1961; children: Damon, Leslie. **EDUCATION:** Wayne State Univ, BS 1967; State MI, CPA. **CAREER:** Arthur Andersen & Co, staff sr 1967-69; Wells & Green Prof Corp, pres 1969-71; Arthur Andersen & Co, audit mgr 1971-73; Sec City of Detroit Bldg Auth, former fin dir; Office of Mgmt & Budget Wash DC, assoc dir exec of the Pres 1977-78; Ford Motor Co, gen auditor, 1978-. **ORGANIZATIONS:** Mem, Amer Inst of CPA's, MI Assn of CPA's, Natl Assn of Black Accountants; mem, 1984-, Intl Treasurer, 1989-, Inst of Internal Auditors. **BUSINESS ADDRESS:** General Auditor, Finance Staff, Ford Motor Co World Headquarters, American Rd, Room 145, Dearborn, MI 48121-1899.

GREEN, EDWARD L.
Business executive. **CAREER:** USMC, lt col 1960-81; Eastern Airlines, spec in mktg svcs, mgr ground support svcs, vice pres sales & svc. **HONORS/ACHIEVEMENTS:** Highest-ranking black xec working for a major carrier in the airline industry. **MILITARY SERVICE:** USMC lt col 1960-81. **BUSINESS ADDRESS:** Vice President Sales & Service, Eastern Airlines NE Div, 10 Rockefeller Plaza, Room 901, New York, NY 10020.

GREEN, ELIZABETH LEE (NEE DOLES)
Clergyman. **PERSONAL:** Born Feb 09, 1911, Montgomery. **EDUCATION:** Weslyan Smith Coll. **CAREER:** Betty Lee Modiste Shop, owned & opertd 14 yrs; Thompson Mem Ch, pstr; Mem AME Zion Ch, asso pstr; Lomax Templ, asso pstr; Martin Chpl, pstr; Vista Trvl Serv, owner & Oprtr. **ORGANIZATIONS:** Mem Booker T Washington Businessmens Assn; Meth Detroit Minstrl Allnc; Wmn Home & Foreign Missnry Soc; vice pres Inter Am Travl Agent Soc Am; mem MAACP; Community Serv Com; Order Eastern Stars; Study Negro Life & Histry Organiz; Benevolent Daughter Elks; Salvation Army. **HONORS/ACHIEVEMENTS:** Mothers club awd HowardUniv 1958; mother yr MI Chronicle 1968; hon mem Wayne StateUniv African Student Assn 1963. **BUSINESS ADDRESS:** Pastor, Vista Travel Services, Inc, 8401 Woodward Ave, Detroit, MI 48202.

GREEN, ERNEST G.
Investment banker. **PERSONAL:** Born Sep 22, 1941, Little Rock, AR; son of Ernest G Green, Sr and Lothaire S Green; married Phyllis; children: Adam, Jessica, McKenzie. **EDUCATION:** MI State Univ, BA 1962, MA 1964. **CAREER:** A Philip RAndolph Educ Fund, dir, 1968-76; US Labor Dept, asst sec of labor 1977-81; Green & Herman, partner 1981-85; E Green & Associates, owner 1985-86. **ORGANIZATIONS:** Mem natl bd NAACP; bd mem Winthrop Rockefeller Foundation; natl bd March of Dimes; mem Omega Psi Phi. **HONORS/ACHIEVEMENTS:** Rockefeller Public Service Princeton Univ 1976; NAACP Spingarn Awd. **BUSINESS ADDRESS:** Investment Banker, Shearson Lehman Hutton Inc, 1627 I St NW, Suite 1100, Washington, DC 20006.

GREEN, FORREST F.
City official, business executive. **PERSONAL:** Born Feb 02, 1915, E Point, GA; married Mamie E Logan; children: Forrest, Jr, Saul A, Darryl L. **EDUCATION:** Morehouse Coll, BA 1937; Wayne State U, MA 1967. **CAREER:** City of Detroit, city ombudsman present; bus exec 1947-74; social workr 1938-46; Vocational Sch, pres owner. **ORGANIZATIONS:** Mem Intl Bar Assn Ombudsman & Adv Com; Am Arbitrtn Assn; Intl Persnnl Mgmt Assn; Greater C of C; Detroit Rotary Club; first black mem MI Civil Serv Commn 1961-68; first black mem Detroit Parks & Recreation Commn 1962-69; mem Detroit's Charter Revisn Comm 1970-73. **HONORS/ACHIEVEMENTS:** State cert of hon MI Acad of Voltr Ldrshp 1964; outstndg cit awd Detroit Urban League 1965; cert for serv to youth WayneUniv 1968; liberty bell awd Detroit Bar Assn 1969. **BUSINESS ADDRESS:** 114 City Co Bldg, Detroit, MI 48226.

GREEN, FRANKLIN D.
Attorney. **PERSONAL:** Born May 19, 1933, Staunton, VA; married Shirley Lomax. **EDUCATION:** Coll Liberal Arts; Howard Univ, BA 1959; Howard Univ Sch Law, JD 1963. **CAREER:** US Dept Labor, 1964-72; Moore & Green Law Firm, pvt prac law 1972-. **ORGANIZATIONS:** Nat Bar Assn; Am Bar Assn; PA Bar Assn; Philadelphia Bar Assn; Barrister's Club Phila; NW Br Philadelphia NAACP; Howard Univ Alumni Club Phila; Am Civil Lbrts Union Philadelphia Chpt; Omega Psi Phi Frat Mu Omega Chpt. **MILITARY SERVICE:** AUS sgt first class 1950-53. **BUSINESS ADDRESS:** 1 N 13 St, Ste 708, Philadelphia, PA 19107.

GREEN, FREDERICK CHAPMAN
Physician, educator. **PERSONAL:** Born Oct 07, 1920, Fort Wayne, IN; son of Oliver Green and Loretta M Green; married Lucille; children: Frederick C MD, Sharman L. **EDUCATION:** IN Univ, BS 1942; IN Univ School of Medicine, MD 1944; Harlem Hospital New York City, internship & residency 1947. **CAREER:** New York City, private practice pediatrician 1947-67; AUS Hospital, chief pediatrician 1951-53; Sydenham Hospital NY, dir of pediatrics 1961-71; Pediatric Ambulatory Care Roosevelt Hospital NY, dir 1967-71; US Children's Bureau DHEW, assoc chief 1971-73; Children's Hospital Natl Medical Center, assoc dir 1973-; Child Health Advcy Children's Hospital Natl Medical Center, dir ofc 1973-; Child Health & Devel George Washington Univ School of Medicine & Health Science, prof 1973-; US Nat Commn on the Intl Year of the Child, commr 1979; George Washington Univ School of Medicine, asst dean for prog planning, prof emeritus child health devel. **ORGANIZATIONS:** Chmn Mayor Marion Barry's Interagncy/Interdprtmntl Com on Child Abuse & Neglect 1975-; chmn Mayor Marion Barry's Blue Ribbon Com on Infant Mortality Washington DC 1979-; bd or dirs UNICEF Amer Humane Assn Nat Com for Citizens in Educ 1979-; pres Natl Comm for Prevention of Child Abuse 1986-. **HONORS/ACHIEVEMENTS:** Citation & outstanding serv rendered as mam of com on Community healh servs Am Acad of Ped 1975; distinguished black am fellow Phelps-Stokes Fund 1975-76; guest editor Ped Annuals 1979; pres medal for distinguished comm serv The Catholic Univ of Am & Madison Nat Bank 1979; Hildrus Poindexter Awardee Amer Public Health Assn Black Caucus 1983; Washingtonian of the Year Washingtonian Magazine 1984. **MILITARY SERVICE:** AUS cpt 13 yrs. **BUSINESS ADDRESS:** Prof Emeritus-Child Health Dev, George Washington University, 2300 Eye St NW, Washington, DC 20037.

GREEN, GEORGIA MAE
Attorney. **PERSONAL:** Born Apr 15, 1950, Knoxville, TN. **EDUCATION:** Knoxville Coll, BA (cum Laude) 1972; Howard Univ Sch of Law Washington, DC, JD 1976. **CAREER:** Dept of Corrections, attorney. **ORGANIZATIONS:** Mem WV Bar Assn 1979-; conv co-chmn Natl Assn of Black Women Atty 1980-; 1st vice pres Amer Fed of Govt Employees Local 1550 DC Dept of Corrections Union1984; mem District of Columbia Bar Assoc 1985-. **HONORS/ACHIEVEMENTS:** WV Ambassador of Good Will Among All People, WV Sec of State 1979; Who's Who Among Outstanding Young Women in America 1983; Who's Who Among Young American Women 1984. **BUSINESS ADDRESS:** Attorney, District of Columbia, Central Facility, PO Box 25, Lorton, VA 22079.

GREEN, GERALDINE D.
Attorney. **PERSONAL:** Born Jul 14, 1938, New York, NY; daughter of Edward Chisholm and Lula Chisholm. **EDUCATION:** City Coll of NY Baruch Sch of Bus, BBA 1964; St John'sUniv Law Sch, JD 1968. **CAREER:** Law Offices of Geraldine D Green 1987-; pres Geraldine's Restaurant-Cocktail Lounge 1987-; Burke, Robinson & Pearman, attorney of counsel 1985-86; Rosenfeld Meyer & Susman, partner 1983-85; CA Corp Comnr 1980-83; Atlantic Richfield Co, sr atty asst corp sec 1972-80; IBM Corp, staff atty 1968-72; Coopers & Lybrand CPA's, tax accountant 1966-68; LA Traffic Commn, commr; Business Law & Finance, Dillard Univ, FL Mem Coll, visiting prof; CA State Bar Comm on Corp 1974-76. **ORGANIZATIONS:** Pres Beverly Hills/Hollywood Br NAACP 1979-82; spec coun LA Urban League; Black Women Lawyers of CA; Women Lawyers of LA; CA Women Lawyers; Langston Bar Assn; Natl Bar Assn; Southern Poverty Law Ctr; Natl Legal Aid & Defender Assn; Youth Motivation Task Force; Finance Lawyers Conf. **HONORS/ACHIEVEMENTS:** LA Urban League Comm Serv Awd 1973 ; NAACP Freedom Awd Cit 1973; YWCA Cert of Achievement 1976; Geraldine D Green Day in City of Los Angeles 1984; Certificate of Achievement California State Legislature 1986; Certificate of Appreciation California State Senate 1984; Certificate of Appreciation City of Los Angeles 1981. **BUSINESS ADDRESS:** Attorney at Law, Law Offices of Geraldine Green, 3325 Wilshire Blvd, Suite 1250, Los Angeles, CA 90010.

GREEN, HUGH
Professional football player. **PERSONAL:** Born Jul 27, 1959, Natchez, MS. **EDUCATION:** Univ of Pittsburgh. **CAREER:** Tampa Bay Buccaneers, player 1981-. **HONORS/ACHIEVEMENTS:** Coll, selected to The Sporting News all-time All-America team; winner of 1980 Lombardi Trophy; runner up in 1980 Heisman Trophy voting; won four Natl Player of the Year Awards in 1980; selected Player of the Year by touchdown clubs in Cleveland, Columbus and Washington; first team All-America in 1978 by UPI and Walter Camp and second team NEA All-America; as a junior named best defensive player in the country by New York Times; played in Hula Bowl and Japan Bowl; profl, two consec Pro Bowls; first team All-Pro from The Sporting News, Sports Illustrated and Football Digest; All-NFC from UPI and Pro Football Weekly; finished 1983with 138 tackles to lead the team for second straight season; selected All-Pro and St Petersburg Times Buc MVP by media vote; 1982 first team All-Pro from ProFootball Writers, Football Digest, Sports Illustrated and College & Pro Football Newsweekly. **BUSINESS ADDRESS:** Tampa Bay Buccaneers, One Buccaneer Place, Tampa, FL 33607.

GREEN, JAMES L.
Physician. **PERSONAL:** Born Feb 02, 1945, Hampton, VA; son of Dr and Mrs J L Green; married Cheryl A Lewis; children: Timothy B, Jenifer L. **EDUCATION:** Hampton Inst, BA 1967; Meharry Med Coll, MD 1973. **CAREER:** Hubbard Hosp, intern 1973-74, resident 1975-77; VA Hosp Tuskegee AL, chief retina sect 1978-79; Univ of IL, asst prof of clinical opthol 1980-; Univ ofIL, fellow vitreous surgery 1979-81, asst prof of opth 1980-; Michael Reese Hospital & Medical Ctr, attending surgeon 1981-; Retinal Vitreal Consultants; Mercy Hospital & Medical Center, chief of retina service, 1986-. **ORGANIZATIONS:** Fellow American Acad of Opthalmology 1979-; certified Amer Bd of Opthalmology 1979-; mem NMA, Chicago Opthalmological Society. **HONORS/ACHIEVEMENTS:** Rowe Awd in Ophthalmology 1973; Merk Awd 1973; 7 publications. **BUSINESS ADDRESS:** Retinal Vitreal Consultants, 8th Floor Eye Center, Mercy Hospital & Medical Center, Stevenson Expressway & King Dr, Chicago, IL 60616.

GREEN, JOSEPH, JR.
Electrical/logistics engineer. **PERSONAL:** Born Jun 14, 1950, Oakley, SC; married Betty A; children: Quentin E. **EDUCATION:** South Carolina State Coll, BSEE 1973. **CAREER:** GE/RCA Corp, logistics engr and management coordinator and Logistics Program Plannning for the AEGIS ORDALT Program. **ORGANIZATIONS:** Affiliations w/ Philadelphia Regional Introd of Minorities to Engrg 1986-87, Black Exec Exchange Prog 1986-87; mem Soc of Logistics Engrs; mem The Soc of Black and Hispanic Engrs. **HONORS/ACHIEVEMENTS:** Letter of Achievement Recogniton from RAdm Wayne Myers for Successful DDG-51 Logistics Audit 1982; Dale Carnegie Honors 1985; AEGIS Tech Awd for producing several logistics support analysis plans as a mgmt tool for the surface Navy & other representative utilization; development of an intergrated logistics ORDALT Plan for AEGIS ILS Disciplines. **BUSINESS ADDRESS:** Logistics Engineer, GE/RCA Corp, Marne Hwy, Moorestown, NJ 08057.

GREEN, LARRY W.
Councilman/businessman. **PERSONAL:** Born Nov 07, 1946, Louisville, KY; married Delmira M Hinestroza Labalsa; children: Larry Jr, Carmen, Diana. **EDUCATION:** Chicago Acad of Fine Art, 1964-66;Univ of KY E'Town Comm, 1971-72. **CAREER:** Metropolitan Life, rep 1973-82; City of Elizabeth KY, city cnclmn 1974-82; L&D Home Prod Dstrbtrs, pres 1974-84; Rize Unlimited Inc, regional coord; NewHorizons Fin Svc, anlyst ownr. **ORGANIZATIONS:** Legal chrmn Cntrl KY Life Underwriters 1975-80; liason KY Cmrc Cabinet 1972-; oprtng bd Wesley Hilltop Comm Cnt 1972-75; mem Intrntl Platform Assc 1983-; KY State Manpower Comm Reg Crime Comm 1974-78; pres Hardin Cnty Youth Athletic Assc 1974-; regional comm on economic development 1985-. **HONORS/ACHIEVEMENTS:** Serv Above Self Rotary Clb of Elizabethtown 1981; "Leadership Elizabethtown" Chmbr Of Cmrc City 1985. **MILITARY SERVICE:** USAF stf sgt; Viet Nam Era Overseas. **HOME ADDRESS:** Rt 6 119 Pear Orchard Rd, Elizabethtown, KY 42701.

GREEN, LESTER L.
Electrical engineer, business executive. **PERSONAL:** Born Jun 27, 1941, Lynchburg, VA; married Lucille Withers. **EDUCATION:** HowardUniv Sch Archit & Engr Wash DC 1966; BSEE 1966. **CAREER:** Elect Switching System Western Elect Co, proj engr 1966-; Comm Commun Res Inc, pres 1973-; Am Tel & Tel Co Silver Spring MD, transmsn man 1964-65. **ORGANIZATIONS:** Chmn Cablecommunication Task Force for Develop Reg Learning Cntr Morgan State Coll Baltimore 1973-74; chmn bd dir Comm Commun Sys Inc Baltimore 1970-; indstl mem rep for WE Co HowardUniv Cluster; mem Soc Cable TV Engr; Inst Electrcl & Electrnc Engrs; Alpha Phi Alpha Frat; mem Urban Reg Learning Cntr Policy Bd; exec bd NW Baltimore Corp; charter mem Pk Heights Comm Corp Inc Baltimore; charter mem & vice pres Beacon Hill Tenants Assn Baltimore; charter mem Oxford Manor Tenants Assn Wash DC. **HONORS/ACHIEVEMENTS:** Cost reductn awd WE Co 1974; citznshp & ldrshp awd HowardUniv 1961; author "The Design and Economics of an Urban Cable & Distrbtn Sys" 1973. **HOME ADDRESS:** 737 Stoney Spring Dr, Baltimore, MD 21210.

GREEN, LILLER BERNICE
Educator. **PERSONAL:** Born Dec 01, 1928, Atlanta, GA; daughter of Walter Parrott and Henrietta Johnson Parrott; married William Clarence Green; children: Pamela A, Jan A.

EDUCATION: Morgan State Univ, BA (Magna Cum Laude) 1951; Bryn Mawr Coll, MSW 1953. **CAREER:** Children's Adolescents, Psychiatric Clinic, dir of social work 1957-59; Child Study Center, dir of social work 1959-60; Bryn Mawr Coll, field instr consultant 1963-65; Ivy Leaf School, dir 1965-. **ORGANIZATIONS:** Mem Grace Baptist Church 1952-; golden life mem Delta Sigma Theta 1949-; life mem NAACP 1960-; mem bd dir YWCA 1983-85; mem Elementary Educ Study Group 1985-86. **HONORS/ACHIEVEMENTS:** Eliza Jane Cummings Awd Morgan State Univ 1951; Richard Allen Awd Community Serv Mother Bethel AME 1982; Zeta Outstanding Woman of the Year Beta Delta Zeta 1983; Citizen of the Year Omega Psi Phi 1985. **BUSINESS ADDRESS:** Dir, Ivy Leaf School, 1196 E Washington Ln, Philadelphia, PA 19138.

GREEN, OLIVER WINSLOW
Labor union officer. **PERSONAL:** Born Aug 18, 1930, Baltimore, MD; son of William S Green and Ethel I Gray Green; married Loraine E Johnson, Sep 07, 1951; children: Oliver W Jr, Michael G. **EDUCATION:** Attended Morgan State Univ, Baltimore MD. **CAREER:** Baltimore Tansit Co, Baltimore MD, operator, 1953-69; Mass Transit Admin, Baltimore MD, operator, 1969-70; Amalgamated Transit Union, Baltimore MD, financial sec, 1970-75, Washington DC, vice pres, 1975-. **ORGANIZATIONS:** Bd mem, United Way of Central Maryland, 1972-75, President's Comm on Employment, 1985-; mem operating comm, A Philip Randolph Inst, 1985-; pres, 43/44 Democratic Club, 1986-. **MILITARY SERVICE:** US Army, staff sergeant, 1951-53.

GREEN, RAYMOND A.
Government official. **PERSONAL:** Born Aug 18, 1944, Gary, IN; married Lucille McConnell; children: Caleb, Adam. **EDUCATION:** BA, Indus Engineering. **CAREER:** State of IN, asst state senator 1972-76; Lake Cty Council, asst councilman 1978-85; Lake County Commn, Commn Engr, 1980-85; Govt Center, chief deputy, Lake County recorder 1985-. **BUSINESS ADDRESS:** Chief Deputy Lake County Recorder, Govt Center, 2293 N Main St, Crown Point, IN 46307.

GREEN, REUBEN H.
Clergyman, educator. **PERSONAL:** Born Jun 14, 1934, Wright City, OK; married Mildred Denby; children: Reuben H, Howard D. **EDUCATION:** Bishop Coll, BA 1955; Oberlin Grad Sch of Theo, BD 1959; Iliff Sch of Theo, STM 1969; VanderbiltUniv Div Sch, DMin 1973. **CAREER:** Cntrl Bapt Ch Inc, minstr 1968-; Philosy Lemoyne-Owen Coll, asso prof 1968-; Lemoyne-Owen Coll, chapln 1974-; Bells Chapl Bapt Ch, pstr 1964-68;OT OK Sch of Relgn, dean of students instr. **ORGANIZATIONS:** Mem Omega Psi Frat; Knights of Pythians; Prince Hall A F&M; past vice pres Memphis Br NAACP; dean Memphis SS & BTU Congress; mem TN Ldrshp Educ Cong; dean TN Bapt Sch of Rel. **BUSINESS ADDRESS:** 320 W Joubert Ave, Memphis, TN.

GREEN, RICHARD
Educator. **PERSONAL:** Born Mar 03, 1940, Louisville, KY; married Dorothy Reed; children: Kim, R. **EDUCATION:** Concordia Coll, BA 1961; North Dakota State Univ, MS 1963; Univ Louisville, PhD 1969. **CAREER:** Girdler Catalysts Louisville, research chemist 1965-66; Kentucky State Univ Frankfort, instr chemistry 1966-68; Concordia Coll, prof chemistry, asst dean students 1969-72; State Univ Coll Buffalo, asst to pres 1972-74; SW Residential Coll, Univ of Massachusetts at Amherst, prof chemistry master dir 1974-. **ORGANIZATIONS:** Amer Chem Soc; Amer Assn Higher Educ; Amer Assn School Admin; NAACP; Urban League; bd regents Concordia Coll 1972-75; bd dir Research & Planning Coun Comm Services Erie Co NY 1972-74; Western NY Adv Comm on the Role of Campus Ministry in Higher Educ 1973-74; Phi Lambda Upsilon Hon Chem Soc; Phi Delta Kappa; Phi Kappa Phi. **HONORS/ACHIEVEMENTS:** Young Educator of Yr Nominee 1972; John Binford Award Grad School Honors Univ Louisville 1970; NASA Sci Research Fellow 1968-69.

GREEN, RICHARD CARTER
Family therapist. **PERSONAL:** Born Oct 28, 1947, Brooklyn, NY; married Florence Elayne Parson; children: Damani Saeed Tale, Taiesha Tene Tale, Khalid Abdu Tale. **EDUCATION:** Central State Univ, BA 1969; Wright State Univ, MS 1983. **CAREER:** Montgomery County Juvenile Court, probation officer 1969-70; US Army 1st Lt Infantry, instructor of offensive tactics 1970-72; Montgomery Co Juvenile Court, probation counselor 1972-73; Tale Retail and Wholesale Co, owner 1985-; Nicholas Residential Treatment Ctr, family resource counselor 1973-. **ORGANIZATIONS:** Mem Omega Psi Phi Frat Inc 1966-; mem Greater Dayton Jaycees 1972; mem Nguzo Saba Family Educ and Unity Club 1980-; master mason Prince Hall Free MasonryAncient Square Lodge #40 1982-; lecturer Child Discipline and Residential Treatment 1984-; fellow Menninger Foundation 1985. **HONORS/ACHIEVEMENTS:** Certificate of Participation in Seminary on Adolescence Menninger Foundatin 1978; Outstanding Young Men of Amer US Jaycees 1980; Computers Today/Computer Literacy Sinclair Comm Coll/Computer Tech 1983; Gerontological Counseling Wright State Univ 1985; Licensed Professional Counselor OH Counselor and Social Worker Bd 1985. **MILITARY SERVICE:** AUS Infantry 1st lt 1970-71; Natl Defense Serv Medal 1970, Master Tactician US Army Infantry School 1971. **HOME ADDRESS:** 811 Neal Ave, Dayton, OH 45406.

GREEN, ROBERT L.
Educator. **PERSONAL:** Born Nov 23, 1933, Detroit, MI. **EDUCATION:** San Francisco State Coll, BA 1958; San Francisco State Coll, MA 1960; MI State U, PhD 1963. **CAREER:** USOE Grant Chicago Adult Educ Project, Southern Christian Leadership Conf, dir 1967; Southern Christian Leadership Conf, educ dir 1965-66; Cen for Urban Affairs, dir; MI State Univ, prof 1968-73; Coll Urban Devel, dean; MI State Univ, prof 1973-; Univ of Dist of Columbia; NCJW Center for Research in Educ Disadvantages Hebrew Univ Jerusalem, visiting lecturerr 1971;Univ Nairobi Kenya, 1971. **ORGANIZATIONS:** Mem Am Psychology Assn; Am Assn Black Psychologists; Am Research Assn; bd dirs Martin Luther King Jr Center for Social Change. **MILITARY SERVICE:** AUS 1954-56. **BUSINESS ADDRESS:** President, University of DC, 4200 Connecticut Ave NW, Washington, DC 20008.

GREEN, ROLAND, SR.
Transportation executive. **PERSONAL:** Born Aug 26, 1940, Washington, DC; son of Robert Green Sr and Mary Sophie Welch; married Elverna Coleman, Dec 31, 1966; children: Rolanda Michelle, Robin Yvette, Roland Green Jr. **EDUCATION:** Univ of Maryland, College Park MD, 1963-64; Bowie State Univ, Bowie Maryland; Univ of Dist of Columbia, Washington DC. **CAREER:** Washington DC Gen Hospital, Washington DC, physical therapy asst, 1960-66; Washington DC Transit Inc, Washington DC, bus operator, 1966-71; United Planning Org, Washington DC, transportation coord, 1971-77, branch chief, 1977-81; Washington Elderly Handicapped Transportation Serv, United Planning Org, Washington DC, gen mgr, 1982-. **ORGANIZATIONS:** Mem, Washington DC Devel Disabilities Council, 1979-81; pres, Owens Rd Elementary School PTA, 1984-86; mem, Conf Minority Transportation Officials, 1984-89; vice pres, Capital Area Community Food Bank, 1985-87; mem, Natl Forum Black Public Admin, 1987-89; mem, Natl Council on Aging, 1989-, Amer Public Transit Assn, 1989-. **HONORS/ACHIEVEMENTS:** Meritorious Serv, Kiwanis Club, Eastern Branch, 1977; Vietnam Vets Award, Natl Black Veterans, 1978; Master Mason of the Year, Prince Hall of Masons, Washington DC, 1979; Appreciation, Washingtron DC Urban League, 1986. **MILITARY SERVICE:** US Army Medical Corp, specialist 4, 1958-64, Good Conduct Medals, Overseas Serv. **HOME ADDRESS:** 4923 Mavry Pl, Oxon Hill, MD 20745.

GREEN, ROY
Professional football player. **PERSONAL:** Born Jun 30, 1957, Magnolia, AR. **EDUCATION:** Attended Henderson State Univ. **CAREER:** St Louis Cardinals, wide receiver 1979-. **HONORS/ACHIEVEMENTS:** Tied NFL record for longest kickoff return game (106 yards) against Dallas Cowboys 1979; Named as kick returner to The Sporting News NFC All-Star Team 1979; Named to The Sporting News NFL All-Star Team 1983,84; Played in Pro Bowl NFL All-Star Game following 1983,84 seasons. **BUSINESS ADDRESS:** Wide Receiver, Phoenix Cardinals, PO Box 888, Phoenix, AZ 85001.

GREEN, RUTH A.
Clinic administrator. **PERSONAL:** Born Feb 02, 1917, Oklahoma; widowed. **EDUCATION:** BS 1936. **CAREER:** Social wrkr; probtn offcr; Step Parent Adoptn; Social Svc, dir; Sr Citzns Prevntv Hlth Care Serv for Elderly Minrty, clinic adminstr. **ORGANIZATIONS:** All professional jobs San Diego Pres Comm Hosp of San Diego Aux 1973-74; past reg pres of CA Probtn & Parole Assn; past couns to Youth in Free Clinics as Vol; apptd bd dir by Pres Nixon to Small Bus Bur San Diego; apptd by Bd of Supvs to Charter Review Com; past pres NAACP; 2nd vice pres Urban League; past grand sec of Charity; Order of Eastern Star; orgn San Diego Chap The Links Inc; found Civic Orgn Women Inc; apptd by Mayor of San Diego to Housing AdvBd; The Gvrn of CA To intergvrnmntl Relations Counc & to the CA State Commn On Aging 1974-75. **HONORS/ACHIEVEMENTS:** Serv awds YMCA, NAACP, Bus & Professional Womens Clubs; Probation Offcr of Yr Awd 1971. **BUSINESS ADDRESS:** 446 26 St, San Diego, CA 92102.

GREEN, SHIRLEY
Government official. **PERSONAL:** Born Jun 01, 1935, Newark, NJ; children: Aaron, Jason, Allen. **EDUCATION:** Caldwell Coll, BA 1972; RutgersUniv Grad Sch of Social Work, MSW 1973; Wharton Sch of Bus, attended 1974. **CAREER:** City of Newark, dir div of pub welfare 1978-; Newark Rent Contrl Bd City of Newark, adminstr 1974-78; Office of Bus & Admin City of Newark, admin asst 1972-74; Rutgers Proj On Aging RutgersUniv Newark, rsrch analyst 1971-72; Essex Co Coll Dept of Behavioral Sci Newark NJ , adj prof 1979-80. **ORGANIZATIONS:** Bd mem Essex Co Mental Hlth Assn 1978-; bd of dir Nat Leased Housing Assn; mem Am Pub Welfare Assn/Municipal Welfare Assn; mem Kenneth A GibsonAssn. **HONORS/ACHIEVEMENTS:** Newark Outstndg Woman of Am Awd 1971; frontiers achvmnt awd Intl Frontiersman 1979; best del awd Women and Pop Commn Intl Affairs Assn Univ of PA; Pres Counc on Youth Opport. **BUSINESS ADDRESS:** 2 Cedar St, Newark, NJ 07102.

GREEN, SIDNEY ANTHONY
Professional athlete. **PERSONAL:** Born Jan 04, 1961, New York, NY; married Dee Dee; children: LaShawn. **EDUCATION:** Univ of NV Las Vegas, 1979-83. **CAREER:** Chicago Bulls, forward 1983-. **HONORS/ACHIEVEMENTS:** Ended coll career as most honored plyr ever to wear UNLV uniform; was selected first team All-Am by US Basketball Writers Assn; was A 2nd team selection bythe Sporting News Bsktbl Times after leading team to 28-3 season. **BUSINESS ADDRESS:** Chicago Bulls, 333 N Michigan Ave, 777 Sports St, Chicago, IL 60601.

GREEN, STERLING
Associate executive, clergyman. **PERSONAL:** Born Oct 08, 1946, Washington, DC; married Sophie Ann Pinkney; children: Sterlicia Sophia, Tamika Tamara. **EDUCATION:** Williams Coll MA, 1964-67; USASATC&S Ft Devens MA, 1967. **CAREER:** United House of Prayer, ordained as elder 1967, asst minister 1971; DC Govt Adv Neighborhood Comm, vice chmn, commr, 1978-85; United House of Prayer, ordained as apostle 1984, dir of special proj for Bishop W McCollough. **ORGANIZATIONS:** Elected adv neighborhood Commiss 1978; bd mem SHAW Proj Area Comm 1979; delegate DC Fed of Civic Assn 1979; mem Mayors Commiss on Coop Econ Devel 1980; natl comm mem McCollough Property Invest Comm 1980; asst to ex dir McCollough Scholarship Coll Fund 1984. **HONORS/ACHIEVEMENTS:** Harvard Book Awd Washington DC 1964; Participant White House Briefing on the Cities 1980; Washington Post Article "Remap or Outmap" Census Mapping 1981. **MILITARY SERVICE:** AUS 1967-69; Vietnam Campaign, Outstanding Trainee. **HOME ADDRESS:** 602 Emmanuel Court NW #104, Washington, DC 20001. **BUSINESS ADDRESS:** Dir Special Projects, United House of Prayer, 616 Emmanuel Court NW #102, Washington, DC 20001.

GREEN, THEODIS GUY
Mayor, educator, poet, novelist. **PERSONAL:** Born Nov 06, 1930, Wright City, OK; son of Mack Green and Della Green; married Mary Lois Burris; children: Theodis Jr. **EDUCATION:** Langston Univ, BS; OK State Univ, MS. **CAREER:** City of Langston, mayor; Langston Univ, prof & asst chmn 1977-87. **ORGANIZATIONS:** Life mem Alpha Phi Alpha Frat; mem Prince Hall Masons; pres NAACP; mem OEA, LEDC, NEA; past mem OK Tech Soc; mem bd of trustees Mt Bethel Bapt. **HONORS/ACHIEVEMENTS:** Teacher of the Week, Langston Univ, 1980; Mayor of the Year, OK Conf of Black Mayors; Awarded plaque as a Bronze Ambassador at OSU; Honorary Dr Degree, TN Univ School of Religion; Published poems/novel. **BUSINESS ADDRESS:** Professor-Asst Chairman, LangstonUniv, Langston, OK 73050.

GREEN, THOMAS L.
Assoc. administrator. **PERSONAL:** Born Sep 09, 1940, Bronxville, NY; married Patricia S; children: Thomas II, Jennifer. **EDUCATION:** State Univ of NC, BS 1959-63; AFL-CIO Labor Studies Ctr, Post Grad Work 1971-72; Univ of UT, Post Grad Work 1975-76. **CAREER:** Manufacturer Traders Trust Co, asst mgr 1966-69; Recruitment Training Program, field rep 1969-71; Westchester Affirmative Action Agency, exec dir 1971-73; NYS Dept Labor, job training spec 1973-83, assoc employment cons. **ORGANIZATIONS:** Relocation dir Urban Renewal Agency 1962-64; resource consult US Dept of HEW 1964-69; proj dir Pres Comm Juvenile Delinquent & Youth Devel 1964-70; prog dir Urban Ed Ctr 1965-68; consult Southern IL Univ 1966-67; cons/proj dir Central State Univ 1967-68; prog dir Urban League of Westchester 1969-70. **HONORS/ACHIEVEMENTS:** Author 2 years study Juvenile Delinquent & Youth Devel 1965-66; 32 degree United Supreme Council 33 AASR of Free Masonry USA; Community Serv Awd Westchester/Rockland Boy Scouts of Amer. **BUSINESS ADDRESS:** Assoc Employment Consultant, New York City Dept of Labor, Two World Trade Center, New York, NY 10047.

GREEN, VERNA S.
Broadcast executive. **PERSONAL:** Born Oct 09, 1947, Columbus, GA; daughter of Oscar L Crouch and Evelyn Robinson Crouch. **EDUCATION:** Wayne State Univ, Detroit MI, BS Business Admin, 1973; Michigan State Univ, E Lansing MI, MBA, 1976. **CAREER:** General Motors Corp, Detroit MI, org devel specialist, 1970-76; Visiting Nurse Assn, Detroit, MI, personnel dir, 1977-78; Detroit Medical Center, Detroit MI, assoc dir public affairs, dir support serv, mgr training & devel, 1979-81; Booth American Co, WJLB-FM, Detroit MI, vice pres, gen mgr, 1982-. **ORGANIZATIONS:** Mem, NAACP, 1982-, Urban League, 1982-; alumni bd, Wayne State Univ Business School; research comm, Natl Assn of Broadcasters; Leadership Detroit, Graduate of Class #7, 1986; bd mem, YWCA of Metro Detroit, 1986-87, Women's Advertising Club, 1986-87, Michigan Assn of Broadcasters, 1987-; advisory bd, Wayne State Univ Journalism Institute for Minorities, 1987-; bd mem, Detroit United Fund, 1987; mem, Michigan Women's Forum, 1987-; bd mem, Children's Aid Soc, 1989. **HONORS/ACHIEVEMENTS:** General Manager of the Year, Black Radio Exclusive, 1986; Most Outstanding Woman in Radio Management, Detroit Chapter of Amer Women in Radio & Television, 1986; Woman of the 80's Award, J C Penney Co, 1987; Distinguished Alumnus Award, Wayne State Univ Business School, 1988; General Manager of the Year, Young Black Programmer's Coalition, 1988; Corporate Leadership Award, Wayne State Univ, 1989. **BUSINESS ADDRESS:** Vice President/General Manager WJLB-FM, Booth American Company, 645 Griswold, 2050 Penobscot Building, Detroit, MI 48226.

GREEN, WALLACE ORPHESUS
Government official. **PERSONAL:** Born Mar 26, 1948, Washington, DC; married Mary Lassiter; children: Jewell Elizabeth. **EDUCATION:** Morgan State Univ, AB Polit Sci 1970; Boston Univ, MS Comm/Pub Relations 1971. **CAREER:** Abramson Himelfarb Inc, advertising acct exec 1972-74; US House of Reps, staff dir DC subcomm 1974-75; Jt Comm on Bicentennial US Congress, staff dir 1975-76; Interior Dept Washington, exec asst to under sec 1977-78, dep under sec 1978-80; Terr & Intl Affairs US Dept Interior, asst sec 1980-81;Council on Foundations, vice pres 1981-82; Able Machining & Electronics, ceo 1984-; Able Supply Co, Able Machining & Electronics, ceo 1981-. **ORGANIZATIONS:** Consul AL Nellum Assoc; consul Mark Battle Assoc; consul Roy Littlejohn Assoc; consul Ofield Duke Assoc; mem Amer Fed of State Co & Municipal Employees; bd mdm Minority Legislative Educ Prog Washington; bd mem Landmark Serv (Tourmobile) Washington DC; bd mem Durham Bus & Professional Exchange; mem Gov Small Bus Council. **HONORS/ACHIEVEMENTS:** Scholarship Boston Univ Sch of Pub Comm 1970; Directed Compilation First Complete Collection of Photographs of Black Mem of Congress & Developed Rsch Project on 45 Black Amer Congressmen who served or who are now serving in US Congress; directed Biog & Photographic Rsch Project on US Congresswomen. **BUSINESS ADDRESS:** Chief Executive Officer, Able Supply Co, Able Machining & Electronics, 7826 Eastern Ave NW, Washington, DC 20012.

GREEN, WALTER
Business executive. **PERSONAL:** Born Sep 05, 1924, Coconut Grove, FL. **EDUCATION:** Miami-Dade Coll Sch of Continuing Educ 1971-72. **CAREER:** Walt's Laundromat, owner 1972-80; real estate investr 1947-80. **ORGANIZATIONS:** Pres fdr Black Grove Inc; New Frontiers in Envirnmtl Understndg; Human Comm & Social Justice 1970-80; co-author Black Grove a plng model for am Miami Interactn 1973; pres Grove Golfers Assn 1960-70; mem Proj Area Com HUD 1967-70; dir Black Grove Com Design Ctr 1970-76; exec com Intl Optimist Club of Coconut Grove 1972-76; mem Coconut Grove Plng Task Force 1974-76; mem Comm of Man Proj Com 1976. **HONORS/ACHIEVEMENTS:** Conf partic in 1st Nat Seminar on Environmtl Quality & Social Justice in Urban Am The Consrvtn Found 1972; Who's Who in FL 1973-74; Voice of Am Intervw for W African Nats 1976. **MILITARY SERVICE:** Pfc WW II 1943-46. **BUSINESS ADDRESS:** 3565 Grand Ave, Miami, FL 33133.

GREEN, WILLIAM EDWARD
Educator. **PERSONAL:** Born May 17, 1930, Pittsburgh, PA; married Betty Jayne Garrison; children: William Jr, Bobbi Brookins, Nancy Hill, Kenneth. **EDUCATION:** Univ of Pgh, BS 1953, MEd 1958, EdD 1969. **CAREER:** Herron Hill Jr HS, teacher 1955-60; Westinghouse HS, couns 1960-65, vice prin 1965-68, exec asst to supt 1968-69, asst supt 1969-75; Pittsburgh Public Sch, asst supt middle schs 1976-81, asst supt pupil serv 1981-85 retired; W PA Conf United Methodist Church, dir of ethnic minority concerns 1985-. **ORGANIZATIONS:** Prince Hall Mason (Boaz 65) 1959-; Phi Eta Sigma 1949-53; dissertation Sch Coll Orientation Prog 1969; bd dir Need 1969-87; Univ of Pgh Alumni Council 1974-77 1979-; chmn PACE 1974-80; PA State Adv Council on Voc Educ 1974-78; State ESEA Title IV Adv Council 1975-78; mem Alpha Phi Alpha; exec dir Pgh Upward Bound Prog; Omicron Delta Kappa; Phi Delta Kappa; lecturer Carnegie Mellon Univ; treas Warren United Methodist Church 1980; chmn Ethnic Minority LocalChurch Coord Comm Western PA Conf United Methodist Church 1980-84; delegate 1984 United Methodist General Jurisdictional Conf; Pace Board 1984-. **HONORS/ACHIEVEMENTS:** Who's Who in Religion 1976-79. **MILITARY SERVICE:** USAF capt 1953-55. **BUSINESS ADDRESS:** Dir Ethnic Minority Concerns, W PA Conf United Meth Ch, 1204 Freedom Rd, Mars, PA 16046.

GREEN, WILLIAM ERNEST
Attorney. **PERSONAL:** Born Nov 19, 1936, Philadelphia; married Loretta Martin; children: Billy, Roderic, Nicole. **EDUCATION:** Univ of Pittsburgh, BS 1957; DuquesneUniv Sch of Law, LlB 1963. **CAREER:** Palo Alto CA, atty pvt prac; CA, NY & US Patent Off, admtd; Palo Alto Area Chptr Am Red Cross, dir. **ORGANIZATIONS:** Mem Palo Alto City Plann Commn; mem Charles Houston Bar Assn; Palo Alto Area Bar Assn; San Mateo Co Bar Assn; Bar Peninsula Patent Law Assn; SF Patent Law Assn; Am Bar Assn; asst gen couns Boise Cascade Corp 1971-73; atty Sybron Corp 1963-71; chemist US Steel Corp; Applied Rsrch Lab PA 1957; past chmn Rochester City Plann Commn five yrs; chmn bd trustees World of Inquiry Sch; rep Co & Regnl Plann Councls; bd dir Rochester Savngs Bank;Comm Chest; Rochester Urban League; Rochester Hlth Serv Corp; Ind Training Sch; Rochester Monroe Co Chap Am Red Cross; Planned Parenthood League of Rochester & Monroe Co; PTA Bd of Sch #1; mng edt Law Review DuquesneUniv Sch of Law. **HONORS/ACHIEVEMENTS:** Rec Folette Greeno Pub Awd 1966; NY State Jaycees Distngshd Serv Awd 1967; cand for NY State Assm 1968. **BUSINESS ADDRESS:** William Green & Associates, 550 Hamilton Ave, Palo Alto, CA 94301.

GREENBERG, REUBEN M.
Educator. **PERSONAL:** Born Jun 24, 1944, Houston. **EDUCATION:** San Francisco State U, BA 1967;Univ CA, MPA 1969;Univ CA, MCP 1973; PhD expected 1975. **CAREER:** City & Co San Francisco, undersheriff 1971-73; first black undersheriff CA hist; CA StateUniv Hayward, asst prof sociology 1969-73; City Berkeley, human rel offr 1967-69; Univ NC Chapel Hill, presently asst prof polit sci. **ORGANIZATIONS:** Enfrcmnt consult numerous Sheriff's & Police Dept; sec No CA Police Comm Rel Assn 1971-74; instr San Mateo Basic Police Acad 1972-73; mem Chapel memChapel Hill Flying Club; mem Sausalito Yacht Club; San Francisco Sheriff's Mounted Posse; Fac ClubUniv NC; Life mem NAACP. **HONORS/ACHIEVEMENTS:** NIMH fellow 1969-71; elected memUniv NC Fac Counc. **BUSINESS ADDRESS:** Dept Polit Sci, U NC, Chapel Hill, NC 27514.

GREENE, AURELIA
Legislator. **PERSONAL:** Born Oct 26, 1934, New York, NY; daughter of Edward Henry and Sybil Russell Holley; married Jerome Alexander Greene; children: Rhonda, Russell. **EDUCATION:** Livingston at Rutgers, BA 1975. **CAREER:** Bronx Area Policy Bd #6, exec dir 1980-82; New York State, assemblywoman. **ORGANIZATIONS:** District leader 76th Assembly District Bronx 1979-82; mem Comm Sch Bd #9 1985; exec officer Bronx Unity Democratic Club 1986; education advisor MorrisaniaEduc Cncl 1986; mem NAACP, Urban League. **HONORS/ACHIEVEMENTS:** Woman of the Year NAACP; Brotherhood Awd NY State Employees; Organizational Impact Awd Alpha Kappa Alpha. **BUSINESS ADDRESS:** Assemblywoman, New York State, 1188 Grand Concourse #D, Bronx, NY 10456.

GREENE, CAROLYN JETTER
Educator. **PERSONAL:** Born Jun 28, 1942, Paulsboro, NJ; divorced. **EDUCATION:** Douglass Coll, attended 1959-61; Newark State Coll, BA 1963; Wayne State U, MA 1967. **CAREER:** Chabot Coll, presently counselor. **ORGANIZATIONS:** Mem Nat Assn Black Psychol 1970-80; educ com Bay Area Assn Black Psychol 1970-80; CA Persnnl & Guid Assn 1968-80; Western Reg counc on Black Am Affairs 1975-80. **HONORS/ACHIEVEMENTS:** Author "Seventy Soul Secrets of Sapphire" 1973; "Sapphires Second Set of Soul Secrets" 1977; publs artcl in field. **BUSINESS ADDRESS:** 25555 Hesperian Blvd, Hayward, CA 94545.

GREENE, CECIL M., JR.
Employment executive. **PERSONAL:** Born Oct 10, 1932, Pass Christian, MS; married Joaquina Lizama; children: Joaquina Deborah, Cecil Gregory. **EDUCATION:** Central State U, BS 1952;Univ Chicago, grad work. **CAREER:** Argonne Nat Lab, 1956-66; Univ Chicago, 1966-71; Enroci Fermi Inst, adminstrv asst 1966-71; Montgomery Ward & Co, regional personnel employment mgr 1971-; Adminstrative Services, dir. **ORGANIZATIONS:** Mem Chicago & Nat Urban Affairs Council 1971-; Nat Alliance Businessmen; Coll Placement Assn; bd dir Chicago Mental Health Assn; Wabash YMCA; NAACP; Kappa Alpha Psi Frat; personnel com S Shore Commn. **MILITARY SERVICE:** 1st lt 1952-54. **BUSINESS ADDRESS:** Dir of Admin Services, Knoxville College, 901 College St NW, Knoxville, TN 37921.

GREENE, CHARLES ANDRE
Business executive. **PERSONAL:** Born May 17, 1939, Blocton, AL; divorced. **EDUCATION:** TX So Univ Sch Bus; Wayne State Univ Sch Mortuary Sci. **CAREER:** Greene Home for Funerals, v pres. **ORGANIZATIONS:** Mem Nat Funeral Dir & Mortcns Assn; bd dir Greater Flint Oppor Industrl Cntrs Inc; Vehicle City Lodge No 1036 IBPOE of W; bd mem Tall Pine Counc BSA; Epsilon Nu Delta Mortuary Frat; elected fin chmn 5th Ward Charter Revision Commn 1974; appntd asst exec sec Nat Funeral Dir & Mortcns Assn Inc 1974; mem Foss Ave Bapt Ch; found dir Foss Ave Fed Credit Union; mem Wayne StateUniv Alumni Assn; TX SoUniv Alumni Assn; Urban League Urban Coalition; Centl Optimist Club. **HONORS/ACHIEVEMENTS:** Rec NAACP Achvmnt Awd 1913; v pres Genesee Co Funeral Dir Assn; chmn Educ Com Nat Funeral Dir & Mortcns Assn 1972-73; Youth Splst Nat Funeral Dir & Embalmer Mag; dist gov Dist 4 Nat Funeral Dirs & Mortcns Assn 1973-74; Foss Ave Ldrshp Awd as pres of Credit Union 1973-74; Big Bro & Distngshed Serv Awd 1973; awd mer Flint Fire Dept for saving life of citz 1974.

GREENE, CHARLES EDWARD (MEAN JOE GREENE)
Professional athlete. **PERSONAL:** Born Sep 24, 1946, Temple, TX. **EDUCATION:** N TX State U. **CAREER:** Pittsburgh Steelers, def tackle present; AFC Champ Game 1972/74/76/78/79; Pro Bowl 1975/76/78/79; NFL Champ Game 1974/75/78/79; drafted by Pitts 1st round 1969. **ORGANIZATIONS:** Sporting News Coll All Start 1968; Sporting News NFL Eastern Conf All Stars 1969; Sporting News AFC All Stars 1970-74/79. **BUSINESS ADDRESS:** Pittsburgh Steelers, 3 Rivers Stadium, Pittsburgh, PA 15212.

GREENE, CHARLES EDWARD CLARENCE
Government official. **PERSONAL:** Born Apr 01, 1921, Philadelphia, PA; son of Raymond Greene and Christine Greene; married Julia Castenedes; children: Ruth Gumbs, Martin, Rene, Vincent Cocom, Gamel Bowen. **EDUCATION:** LaSalle Ext, LLB 1940; Univ Church of Brotherhood, DD 1955; TV Southwest Coll, Ref Courses. **CAREER:** actor, producer, writer, director, 1937; Negro Cowboys Assn; Rodeo Champ, Natl Pres, 1945-49; Step Inc, Chmn of Bd, 1970-71; Black Political Assn, pres; Independent Prod Assoc, Pres, 1971-72; Casey Coll exec vp; Universal Brotherhood Churches, serge archbishop; Lbr & Indus Comm, NAACP, chmn; Trans-Oceanic Indus Inc, pres; Adelphi Business Coll, public relations con-

sultant; Most Worshipful Prince Hall Grand Lodge F&AM CA & HI Inc, Public Relations Consultant; CA Sr Legislative Sr Senator. **ORGANIZATIONS:** Sr Senator CA, Sr Legislator, 1983-; commr, Los Angeles County Obsenity & Porngraphy Comm 1980-; pres Sr Coalition Political Action Com 1983-; sr deacon James H Wilson Lodge 68 Pha 1985; very rev asst gr chaplin MW Prince Hall Grand Lodge of CA Inc 1984-; pres Inglewood Southbay Br NAACP 1979-, Independent Producer & Assc. **HONORS/ACHIEVEMENTS:** Graduate inspector general 33rd Degree Supreme Council PHA 1985. **MILITARY SERVICE:** AUS sgt. **HOME ADDRESS:** 2328 West 30th St, Los Angeles, CA 90018.

GREENE, CHARLES LAVANT
Educator. **PERSONAL:** Born Feb 22, 1938, Headland, AL; married Delores Johnson; children: Charles L. **EDUCATION:** Univ of Akron OH, BS Biology 1962; Univ of Pittsburgh PA, MSW 1967; Akron Law Sch OH, JD 1977. **CAREER:** Kent State Univ, asst prof & asst dean for stud life 1972-, asst prof soc & anthr 1970-, asst prof & coord vol & comm serv 1971-72; CAC Program, Syracuse NY, dep dir for admin 1968-70; E Akron Comm House, coord of comm devel 1967-68. **ORGANIZATIONS:** Vp urban affair Tomorrow's People Inc Consult Firm 1972-; bd mem Alpha Homes Inc Akron OH 1979-; bd sec Ebony Blackstar Broadcast Corp 1980; bd mem Urban League Akron OH 1977-; bd mem Fair Housing Contact Serv Akron OH 1977-; bd mem Mental Hlth Assn of Summit Co Akron OH 1977-80. **HONORS/ACHIEVEMENTS:** Commend medal AUS; US Pub Hlth Scs ScholrshpUniv of Pittsburgh 1965-67; found Law Firm Davison Greene Holloway & Walker 1977; frat awd Kent State 1979. **MILITARY SERVICE:** AUS capt 1962-65. **BUSINESS ADDRESS:** Davidsn Greene Hollowy & Walke, Akron, OH 44308.

GREENE, CHARLES RODGERS
Physician, educator. **PERSONAL:** Born Jul 08, 1926, Lawrence, NY; married Arlene D Hopkins; children: Allyson Gail, Carca Gay, Wendy Leigh. **EDUCATION:** HowardUniv Coll of Liberal Arts, 1926; HowardUniv Coll of Med. **CAREER:** Dept of Family Practice State Univ of NY Downstate Medical Center, assoc prof; Dept of Family Practice, assoc chmn; Coll of Medicine Downstate Medical Center, assoc dean . **ORGANIZATIONS:** Mem Comm Adv Bd Kings Co Hosp Ctr; Am Coll of Physicians; Metro Com for Minrty Grps in Med; Hlth Rsrch Counc of City of NY; Downstate Med Ctr Prgm Com. **HONORS/ACHIEVEMENTS:** Diplmt Am Bd of Internal Med NY Acad of Med Allergic Reactns to Dipasis Disease of Chest 1957; Electrocardiogram of Hlthy Adult Negro 1959. **MILITARY SERVICE:** AUS 1944-46. **BUSINESS ADDRESS:** 450 Clarkson, Brooklyn, NY 11225.

GREENE, CLIFTON M.
Cosmetic distributor. **PERSONAL:** Born Apr 05, 1916, Thomasville, GA; married Cleo Collins; children: Princetta Berry, Clifton, Jr. **EDUCATION:** Tuskegee Inst, BS 1938. **CAREER:** Veeder-Root Corp, chief chef 1943; Self-Employed, restaurant owner 1946-51; Allen Mfg Co & Putnam-Phalanx Hartford, food concessions 1946-51; Ethnic Cosmetics, distribr 1951-. **ORGANIZATIONS:** Charter mem Tuscan Lodge #17 F&AM Masons PHA Affiliations, treas 3 yrs, past master; charter mem The Adah Chap #22 OES, PHA; grand treas Most WorshipfulPrince Hall Grand Lodge of CT PHA Affil; adv bd mem Prince Hall Acres Lebanon CT & co-founder; mem Alpha Chi Psi Omega Frat of beauticians & barbers; treas & trustee Ind Social Ctr 1943-46; institutional rep Pack & Boy Scout Troop #205; mem NAACP Hartford; mem Urban League of Gr Hartford; mem Hartford C of C;bd mem Inner City Exchange of Hartford CT; area bd Soc for Svgs Hartford; mem Hartford Devel Commn; co-founder bd mem Pioneer Budget Corp; apptd toCT Emergency Resources Corp as adv on State Prince Control Bd 1970. **HONORS/ACHIEVEMENTS:** Prince Hall Mason of Yr 1966; Citation from Natl Council of Negro Women 1972.

GREENE, CLIFTON S.
Business executive. **PERSONAL:** Born Oct 21, 1920, Georgetown, SC; son of Walley Greene and Janie Greene; married Irene. **EDUCATION:** SC State Coll, 1940. **CAREER:** Cliff Greene's Wines & Liquors Brooklyn, owner 1948-74; Wally-Thel Inc, pres 1959-69; Greenoung Enterprises, pres 1966; Green-Harris Enterprises, Inc, chmn chief exec ofcr 1966; Ebony Enterprises, Inc, pres 1972. **ORGANIZATIONS:** Pres sole stockholder Nu-way Investors Corp; mem NAACP; Urban League; Prince Hall Mason 32nd Degree; Shriner; Widow's Son Lodge #11; Long Island Consistory #61; Imperial Council; AEAONMS, Inc (Inactive); Amer Legion (Inactive); mem 100 Black Men Inc; Retired Army Officer's Assn; Ft Hamilton Officer'sClub. **HONORS/ACHIEVEMENTS:** 1st Black in US to file with FCC for UHF TV station; 1st Black or white to build multi-million dollar housing for elderly in Bedford Stuyvesant, Brooklyn; published "Unique & Mae" magazine; various articles, Stock Market Fundamentals 1966. **MILITARY SERVICE:** AUS Staff Sgt to Captain in 29 mo 1943-45; honorable discharge Nov 1946. **HOME ADDRESS:** 1333 President St, Brooklyn, NY 11213.

GREENE, DE REEF ANTHONY
Business executive. **PERSONAL:** Born Jul 02, 1929, Washington, DC; married Yvonne Cruz; children: Diana, Richard, Rebecca. **EDUCATION:** Univ of NE, BE 1965. **CAREER:** Sun Apparel Inc, dir of adminstrn 1977. **ORGANIZATIONS:** Bd of dir El Paso Dept of Human Devel; YMCA-USO; State Ctr for Human Devel; St Margarets Ctr for Emotnly Distrbd Children; El Paso Concl for Intl Visitors; Hlth Serv Com TX Counc of Govts; Urban League; NAACP; Omega Psi Phi Frat. **HONORS/ACHIEVEMENTS:** Sec of army awd for best Army-wide EEO Prgm 1975; Excellnc In Oratory AwdUniv of NE; Freedoms Found Essay Awd 1967; Dept on Human Devel Awd 1976; City of El Paso Awd 1976; NAGE 1975; outstng mil comdr 1973. **MILITARY SERVICE:** AUS col 1951-77. **BUSINESS ADDRESS:** 2430 Texas Ave, El Paso, TX 79901.

GREENE, DWIGHT L.
Attorney. **EDUCATION:** Wesleyan Univ Middletown CT, BA 1970; Harvard Law Sch, JD 1974. **CAREER:** SDNY, asst US atty; Davis Polk & Wardwell, assoc 1974-75 & 1976-78; NY City Ct of Appeals, law asst to chf jdg 1975-76; Wesleyan U, sch com 1974; Pace Univ Sch of Law, adv bd 1979. **BUSINESS ADDRESS:** US Dept of Justice, One Saint Andrew's Plaza, New York, NY 10007.

GREENE, F. DENNIS
Performer. **PERSONAL:** Born Jan 11, 1949, New York, NY. **EDUCATION:** Columbia U, BA 1968-72. **CAREER:** Sha Na Na TV Concert Rock Group, prtnr & fndng mem 1969-80; Gonzaga Entrprs Pub & Prdn Co, pres & fndr 1974-80. **ORGANIZATIONS:** Mem bd of Gov NY Chap Nat Acad of Rec Arts & Sco 1980. **HONORS/ACHIEVEMENTS:** Mem Alpha Phi Alpha Frat 1969-80; mem Friars Club 1975-80.

GREENE, FRANK S., JR.
Business executive. **PERSONAL:** Born Oct 19, 1938, Washington, DC; son of Frank S Greene Sr and Irma O Swygert Greene; married Nilene D, Sep 1985; children: Angela, Frank, III, David, Christopher. **EDUCATION:** Washington Univ, BS 1961; Purdue Univ, MS 1962; Univ of Santa Clara, PhD 1970. **CAREER:** Technology Develop Corp, chmn bd 1985-; ZeroOne Systems Inc, pres chmn bd 1971-87; Sterling Software Inc (subsidary of ZeroOne Systems Group), 1987-. **ORGANIZATIONS:** Mem Inst of Elec & Electronic Engrs 1960-; asst chmn lecturer Stanford Univ 1972-74; mem IEEE Computer Soc Gov Bd 1973-75; bd dir Natl Conf of Christians & Jews 1978-; bd of dir Security Affairs Support Assn 1980-83; bd of regents Univ of Santa Clara 1983-; mem Amer Electronics Assoc; mem Bay Area Purchasing Council; dir Comsis Corp 1984; mem Natl Cont Mgmt Assn; mem Eta Kappa Nu, Sigma Xi; mem NAACP. **HONORS/ACHIEVEMENTS:** Author of 10 tech articles 2 indl textbooks; 1 patent received. **MILITARY SERVICE:** USAF cpat 1961-65. **BUSINESS ADDRESS:** President/Chairman of Board, ZeroOne Systems Inc, Sterling Software Inc, 4401 Great Amer Bldg, Santa Clara, CA 95054.

GREENE, FRANKLIN D.
Business executive. **PERSONAL:** Born Jan 23, 1950, Hot Springs, AR; son of John Greene and Jessie Green; divorced. **EDUCATION:** The School of the Ozarks Point Lookout, MO, BS 1972. **CAREER:** Cit Financial Serv, customer serv rep 1972-73; Ford Motor Co, Kansas City, MO, zone mgr 1973-81; Indian Springs Ford Kansas City, MO, pres 1981-83; Republic Ford Inc, pres 1983-; Columbus Ford, Mercury, Columbus, KS, president 1987-; Zodiac Lounge, Springfield, MO, president 1988-. **ORGANIZATIONS:** Bd dir Big Brothers and Sisters of Springfield, MO 1985-; pres of bd 1986, volunteer Big Brothers and Sisters of Springfield, MO 1984-; pres School of the Ozarks Springfield Alumni Assn 1986-87; bd mem Metro Credit Union 1987-; bd mem American Red Cross 1987-. **HONORS/ACHIEVEMENTS:** Republic Ford listed as one of Black Enterprise's Top 100 Auto Dealers, 1984-88; Meritorious Achievement Award, School of the Ozarks, 1989. **BUSINESS ADDRESS:** President, Republic Ford Inc, PO Box S, Republic, MO 65738.

GREENE, GRACE RANDOLPH
Elected official. **PERSONAL:** Born Oct 05, 1937, Washington, DC; divorced; children: Denise, Samuel, Michael, Annette, Wayne, Katerina, Grace E, Deloris. **EDUCATION:** Spingarn Sr HS, 1954. **CAREER:** Dept of Housing & Comm Devel, retired 1982; Advisory Neighborhood Commiss, commiss 1982-84; Friends & Anacostia Library, mem 1984; Central Baptist Church Library, co-chairperson; Central Baptist Church Women's Dept, mem. **ORGANIZATIONS:** Acting mgr-mgmt aide Dept of Housing & Comm Devel 1969-82; volunteer for community; mem Library of Central Baptist Church, Women's Dept of Central Baptist; volunteer Friends of Anacostia Library. **HONORS/ACHIEVEMENTS:** Cert OES Chap #5 Prince Hall 1972; Cert Women's Dept of Central Baptist Church 1984. **HOME ADDRESS:** 1924 Naylor Rd SE, Washington, DC 20020.

GREENE, HORACE F.
Physician, administrator. **PERSONAL:** Born May 05, 1939, Tuscaloosa, AL; married Stephanie Rodgers; children: Amanda, David, Jason. **EDUCATION:** Fisk U, BA 1960; Meharry Med Sch, MD 1964. **CAREER:** Area C Comm Mental Hlth Cntr, dir adlscnt svc, dir Yth svc, clncl dir, part time stf Psychiatrist, supr Evng Clinic 1970-74; GeorgetownUniv Sch Med, asst prof clncl & Psychiatry 1970; VA Hosp Washington, consult Drug Trtmnt & Rsch Prgm 1971; HowardUniv Sch Med, consult Residency Training Prgm 1973; Alexandria Comm Mntl Hlth Cntr, dir 1971-74; Pvt Practice; Bur Mntl Hlth Serv NHA , DC, dep admin chf 1974; VA Hosp, consult dept psychiatry 1974; N VA Prison Aftercare Prgrm, consult 1974-75. **ORGANIZATIONS:** 1975 N ASMHPD Task Force Nat Hlth Ins Adv Cncl; Adv Councl Estrn Area Alcohol Educ & Training Prgrm Inc Beta Kappa Chi Hon Sci; Kappa Alpha Psi Frat Inc; pres ALL Progress Psychiatry; Washington Psychiat Soc; Am Psychiat Assn; Washington Soc & Adlscnt Psychiatry; Psychiat Adv Cncl Mntl Hlth Admin Washington; chmn Professional Adv Com Mntl Hlth Assn Inc; Washington Cncl Child Psychiatry; APA Task Force Psychosurgery; nominating Com Wash Psychiatry Soc 1974; Peer Rvw Comm Wshngtn Psychiatry Soc Nat Med Fnd; WA Hosp Ctr, vchmn of clinical affairs dept of psychiatry 1987-. **HONORS/ACHIEVEMENTS:** Who's Who Am Coll & U's 1960. **MILITARY SERVICE:** USNL med offcr 1965-67. **BUSINESS ADDRESS:** Vice Chairman Clinical Affairs, Washington Hospital Center, 4600 Comm Ave, NW #224, Washington, DC 20008.

GREENE, JEROME A.
Educator, public administrator, clergyman. **PERSONAL:** Born Mar 12, 1941, Welch, WV; married Aurelia; children: Rhonda, Russell. **EDUCATION:** City Coll of NY, BA 1964; Brooklyn Coll, grad studies; Attended, Columbia Univ, Univ of Detroit, CCNY; Special Studies, Turtle Bay Sch of Music, Henry St Settlement Sch of Music, MA Bowie State Coll 1983. **CAREER:** Morrisania Comm Corp, dir prog eval educ & training 1967-70; Afro-Amer Ethnic Orientation Soc, exec dir 1970-71; New York City Bd of Educ Dist #9, dir auxiliary personnel & special programs 1971-73; Lehman Coll, instructor & coordinator teacher training 1972-74; Dist #9 Comm School Bd, 10 yrs pres 1975-; New York City Bd of Educ Dist 5, pres dir of funded prog 1975-78; Touro Coll, prof; Peoples Devel Corp, exec dir 1979-. **ORGANIZATIONS:** Treas Comm Planning Bd #4; pres Morrisania Educ Counc Inc 1970-; co-pres Bronx Educ Alliance; former Bronx chmn NY Assn of Black Educators 1972-74; mem Amer Assn of Sch Admin; pastor & founder Bronx Christian Charismatic Prayer Fellowship Inc; mem Natl Alliance Black Sch Educators; assoc min Morrisania Comm Ch; mem Natl Caucus Black Sch Bd; chmn Area Policy Bd #4; NY State Cert as Sch Admin & Sch Dist Admin; adv bd LaGuardia Comm Coll;former wekly educ columnist Big Red Newspaper; vice chmn Local Draft Bd #133; former Bronx rep NY Assn of Comm Sch Bds. **HONORS/ACHIEVEMENTS:** Humanitarian Awd Bronx Counc Bapt Ministers 1972; Man of Yr Bronx NAACP 1973; Outstanding Comm Ldr Awd Morrisania Educ Council 1975; Outst Fed Prog Admin Awd 1977; Outstanding Educator Awd City Tabernacle 1978; Man of Yr E Bronx NAACP 1979; Cited in Resolution NY State Assembly for estab Morrisania Educ Counc; Outstanding Educator Awd 1984. **BUSINESS ADDRESS:** Executive Dir, Peoples Develop Corp, 1162 Washington Ave, Bronx, NY 10456.

GREENE, JEROYD X. **See EL-AMIN, SA'AD**

GREENE, JOANN LAVINA
Educator. **PERSONAL:** Born in Columbus, OH; divorced; children: David. **EDUCATION:** San Jose State Univ, BS 1969; Univ of California San Francisco, MS 1970; Univ Southern California, PhD. **CAREER:** VA Hospital Mental Hygiene Clinic, head nurse 1970-72; San Jose State Univ, instr psych nursing 1972-74; West Valley Coll, instr psych tech program 1974-76; West Valley Mission Coll, dir psych tech program 1976-. **ORGANIZATIONS:** Mem CNA 1972-, ANA 1972-, FACCC, Phi Kappa Phi, Sigma Theta Tau, Alpha Kappa Alpha Sor 1960-62; pres California Assn of Psychiatric Tech Educators 1980-83. **HONORS/ACHIEVEMENTS:** Delta Sigma Theta Scholarship; NIMH Fellowship; Dean's List, President Scholar Phi Kappa Phi; Florence Nightingale Award 2 years; Sigma Theta Tau Natl Nursing Hon. **BUSINESS ADDRESS:** Dir Psychiatric Tech Program, Mission College, 3000 Mission College Blvd, Santa Clara, CA 95051.

GREENE, JOE
Assistant coach. **PERSONAL:** Born Sep 24, 1946, Temple, TX. **EDUCATION:** Attended, No Texas State Univ. **CAREER:** Pittsburgh Steelers, defensive tackle 1969-81; CBS-NFL Today, color commentator 1983; Private Business, 1983-. **HONORS/ACHIEVEMENTS:** Named to Sporting News NFL Eastern Conf All-Star team 1969; named to Sporting News AFC All-Star team 1970-74, 1979; played in Pro Bowl 1970-76, 1978,79,82; named to Natl Football Hall of Fame 1987. **BUSINESS ADDRESS:** Assist Coach, Pittsburgh Steelers, Three Rivers Stadium, 300 Stadium Circle, Pittsburgh, PA 15212.

GREENE, JOHN SULLIVAN
Educator, consultant. **PERSONAL:** Born Oct 27, 1921, Long Branch, NJ; son of John and Dortia; married Linda Ray Lichtenstein; children: Lynda Greene Bookhard, Joshua, Benjamin. **EDUCATION:** Boston U, BS 1948; Boston U, MEd 1951. **CAREER:** Dist supt 1973-77; Chasrles Drew Jr HS, prin 1968-73; asst prin 1962-67; tchr of history 1948-62; Brooklyn Jewish Hosp Sch of Nrsng, Sociology Instr. **ORGANIZATIONS:** Nat Assn of sch adminstrs; Assn of asst Comm supts; Morrisania Educ Cncl; chmn bd dirs Jefferson Twrs Inc. **HONORS/ACHIEVEMENTS:** NAACP Edctr of Yr 1975; Hispanic Ldrshp Conf; Outst Commtmnt & Educ Ldrshp 1975; Morrisania Educ Cncl; Outst Serv in Bronx Comm State Senate 1976; Awd Excptnl Achvmnt JHS Mayor of NY 1969. **MILITARY SERVICE:** USN 1943-46.

GREENE, JOSEPH DAVID
Business executive. **PERSONAL:** Born Oct 18, 1940, Emanuel Co, GA; married Barney L Robinson; children: Cathy, J David. **EDUCATION:** Augusta Clg, BBA 1972;Univ GA, MA 1973; Am Clg, CLU 1982. **CAREER:** Pilgrim Life Insurance Co, salesman 1959-66; Augusta Coll, instructor 1973-84; Pilgrim Life Insurance Co, vice pres 1973-85. **ORGANIZATIONS:** Bd mem McDuffie Cnty Brd of Ed 1972-84; Thomson-mcDuffie Chmbr of Comm 1978-81; regent GA Bd of Regents 1984-. **HONORS/ACHIEVEMENTS:** Outstndng Yng Man Thomas Jaycees 1973; man of the yr Thomson Prgrsvc Civic Clb 1974; thesis publdUniv of GA 1973; agcy ofcr of yr Natl Ins Assc 1982. **MILITARY SERVICE:** AUS e-5. **HOME ADDRESS:** P O Box 657, Thomson, GA 30824.

GREENE, JOSEPH P.
Author, composer. **PERSONAL:** Born Apr 19, Spokane, WA; married Marthella Wilson; children: Lee Anthony, Larue, Jonathan. **CAREER:** RCA Victor, artist & repertoire dir 1954-55; A & R Vee Rcds, 1956-58; Liberty Recds, 1957-59; Carson-paramount Prdctns. **ORGANIZATIONS:** Mem ASCAP Westrn Regnl Com 1974-75. **HONORS/ACHIEVEMENTS:** Recip Urbanleg Awd 1947; over 100 published & rcded songs; author of numerous novels, New Am Library, Warner Paper Back Libr; Screen Play, 1973, 20th Century Fox "Together & Bros" in collaboration; scored six pictures, United Commonwealth Corp 1963-66. **BUSINESS ADDRESS:** Paramount Studios, Hollywood, CA.

GREENE, LIONEL OLIVER, JR.
Research scientist. **PERSONAL:** Born Apr 28, 1948, Brooklyn, NY; children: Tera Ann. **EDUCATION:** CA StateUniv Los Angeles, BA 1970; Stanford U, PhD 1978. **CAREER:** Natl Aeronautics & Space Admn, rsrch scntst 1973-77,79-81; MA Inst of Tech, rsrch assc 1977-79; Lockheed Missiles & Space Co, rsrch scntst 1981-84;MacDonnel Douglas Astronautics, sr eng/scntst 1984-85; AT&T Bell Laboratories, sr engr sci human fctrs 1985-. **ORGANIZATIONS:** FAA Pilots License 1972; US Navy High Altitude Test Certification 1975; mem Soc for Neuroscience 1978-; Mission Spec Astronaut candidate 1978; Aerospace Med Assc 1979-; Assc of Black Psychologists; mem Amer Defense Preparedness Assoc 1986-; FCC Radiotlphn License DJ 6 Yrs. **HONORS/ACHIEVEMENTS:** Ford Found fellow Washingon DC; NASA Predoctoral Fellow Washington DC; NIH Postdoctral Fellow Natl Inst of Hlth Washington DC NRC/NAS Postdoctral Fellow; Natl Rsrch Fellow/Natl Acad of Sci Bethesda MD; 12 research publications 1975-. **MILITARY SERVICE:** AUS capt; Air Defense Artillery Co (Hawk Missiles) 1970-82. **BUSINESS ADDRESS:** Sr Engineer Sci Human Fctrs, A&T Bell Laboratories, #1 Whippany Road, Whippany, NJ 07981.

GREENE, MAMIE LOUISE
Government administrator. **PERSONAL:** Born Jun 11, 1939, Midland, TX; divorced; children: Roy A, Lucille J, Laurie A, Alice R, Ruth E Simmons. **EDUCATION:** San Diego HS, 1958. **CAREER:** 300 Club of San Diego, sec 1983-; Employment Development Dept, program specialist. **ORGANIZATIONS:** Mem, sec NAACP; sec Natl Council Negro Women 1979; vice pres Black Advocates in State Serv 1980 & 1981; bd mem Black Federation 1980-82; bd mem San Diego Co Bd of Health 1981-82; comm mem Welfare Human Care 1985; mem Black Advocates in State Serv 1979-; bd mem Educ Cultural Complex 1981-; mem Mt Zion Missionary Baptist 1983-. **HONORS/ACHIEVEMENTS:** Citizen of the Yr Omega Psi Phi 1980; Citizen of the Year Omega Psi Phi 1982; Citizen of the Month Co Supervisor Jim Bates 1982; Community Awareness Action Enterprises 1982. **BUSINESS ADDRESS:** Employment Program Specialist, Employment Development Dept, 5328 Caminito Mindy, San Diego, CA 92105.

GREENE, MARION O., JR.
Business executive. **PERSONAL:** Born in Athens, GA; children: Stephany, Brett. **EDUCATION:** Morehouse Coll, BS 1961; Atlanta Univ, 1962; Howard Univ 1964. **CAREER:** Mktg Data Prep Wash DC, dir 1967-68; Intl Bus Serv Inc Wash DC, pres 1969-. **ORGANIZATIONS:** Mem Assn Computer Machinery, Amer Mgmt Assn, Natl Assn Minority Consultants & Urbanologists, Natl Assn of Black Mfgrs, NAACP, Urban League, Natl Bus League, DC C of C, Met Wash Bd of Trade. **HONORS/ACHIEVEMENTS:** Natl Awd of Excellence US Dept of Commerce 1972; featured in a film US C of C 1973; Natl Outstanding Serv Awd Natl Assn Black Manufacturers 1974; featured in Nation's Business Magazine Feb 1983; featured in Forbes Magazine July 1983.

GREENE, MARVIN L.
Retired educator, consultant. **PERSONAL:** Born Nov 17, 1915, Greenville, AL; children: David, Marcia, Glenn. **EDUCATION:** Wayne State Univ, BA 1942, MA 1948, EdD 1968. **CAREER:** Detroit Public Schools, tchr 1948, dept head 1960, asst prin 1963, supr 1965, asst reg supt 1968, region supt 1970-. **ORGANIZATIONS:** Mem MCTE, NCTE, IRA, MRA, Detroit English Club; Met Linguistics Club pres 1963-69, ASCD, MASCD, AASA, MASA; mem Natl Alliance Black Sch Educators, MetroDetroit Black Educ Admins; Metro Alliance of Black Sch Educators; mem Reserve Officers Assn; Phi Delta Kappa; com mem Boy Scouts Amer; chmn bd dirsBooth Meml Hosp 1975-78; pres Natl Alliance Blk Sch Ed 1981-83; asst supt Curriculum & Staff Dev 1979-83. **HONORS/ACHIEVEMENTS:** Martin Luther king Awd 1972; Nu Omega Man of Yr 1953. **MILITARY SERVICE:** Lt col 1942-46, 1950-52.

GREENE, MITCHELL AMOS
Educator. **PERSONAL:** Born Nov 02, 1927, Georgetown, SC; children: Charles Myers, Mitchell III, Ann Eileen, Hilliard Dwane, Lois Elizabeth. **EDUCATION:** Dillard Univ, BA 1952; Case Western Reserve Univ, MS 1956; Univ of IA, PhD 1972. **CAREER:** Orleans Parish Dept of Social Servs, social caseworker 1953-54; Logansport State Hospital, psychiatric social worker 1956-59; Univ of IA, instructor dept of pediatrics 1959-65; IA Office of Economic Opportunity, tech asst 1965-66; IA Wesleyan Coll, asst prof sociology 1966-70; Black Hawk-Grundy Mental Health Center, consultant 1977-; Univ of No IA, assoc prof educator/clinician 1970-. **ORGANIZATIONS:** Mem Baptist Church, Democratic Party, Omega Psi Phi Frat; articles published in professional journals. **MILITARY SERVICE:** AAF pfc 1946-48. **BUSINESS ADDRESS:** Associate Professor, Univ of Northern Iowa, Cedar Falls, IA 50613.

GREENE, NATHANIEL D.
Chief executive. **CAREER:** Empire Ford, Inc, Spokane, WA, chief executive, 1986-. **BUSINESS ADDRESS:** Empire Ford, Inc, West 423 Third Ave, Spokane, WA 99204. *

GREENE, NELSON E., SR.
Business executive. **PERSONAL:** Born May 20, 1914, Danville, VA; married Gloria Kay; children: Nelson, Jr, Terry F. **EDUCATION:** Shaw Univ, AB 1941; Renourd School of Embalming NY, 1948. **CAREER:** Greene Funeral Home Alexandria, funeral dir owner; Langston HS Danville, tchr 1941-42. **ORGANIZATIONS:** Mem bd dir, Alexandria Bd of Trade; commr, Alexandria Redevel & Housing & Authority 1966-69; VA bd of Funeral Dir & Embalmers 1972; Natl Funeral Dir Assn; bd dir, VA Mortician Assn; mem NAACP; Urban League, Masons, Elks, Shrine; bd dir Alexandria Hospital 1970; sr warden, Meade Episcopal Church 1969-72, vestry 1974. **MILITARY SERVICE:** Military serv major 1942-46, 1951-53.

GREENE, PERCY
Editor, publisher. **PERSONAL:** Born Sep 07, 1900, Jackson, MS; married Francis Reed; children: Frances, Gwendolyn. **EDUCATION:** Jackson Coll, 1915-16, 1921-22; AUS Sch, cert Law, Bookkeeping Acct. **CAREER:** Jackson Advocate, fndr, edtr 1939-77; Tuskee Inst, apprntcd 1939. **ORGANIZATIONS:** Mem Nat Nwspr Pub Assn; fndr Nat Assn Negro War Vet 1927; mem Mason & 33rd Degree Shriner; KP; Elks; Rosicrucian; MW King Hiram Grand Lodge. **HONORS/ACHIEVEMENTS:** Inducted Jackson St Coll Hall Fame Sports 1974; Spkr Stevenson & Sparkman Campaign 1952; Spl recog Black Jour in MS by St 1975; LLD Outst Pub Svc,Chicago Defndr 1946-48; guest Dem Nat Conv 1952, 48; 1st black cast ballot dem primary MS hist. **MILITARY SERVICE:** AUS pfc. **BUSINESS ADDRESS:** 115 E Hamilton St, Jackson, MS 39202.

GREENE, R. W.
Minister. **EDUCATION:** Simmons U; Simmons Theol Sem;Univ So CA;Univ Divine Sci, BD, AB 1936, MTh 1937, MA 1938, ThD 1939, PhD 1940; Numerous Grad Wrk. **CAREER:** Tchr, pastor, lectr; Empire Journal AME Ch St of GA, dir of pub rel, 6th episcopal Dist & Edtr. **ORGANIZATIONS:** USS Const Mus Fnd; Natl Trust for Historic Prsrvtn; The Smithsonian Inst; The Early Am Soc; The Natl Histroical Soc; The Academy of Polit Sci; United Cnc of Ch of Am; mem Untd Cncl Chs Am; Librarian Soc; Vancover Folk Festival Soc; GA Press; pres Pub Rltns Cncl; Quad State Athletic Assn FL; mem GA Cncl on Human Reltns; Columbus Urban League Inc; Shriner 32 Deg Mason; S GA Annual Conf AME Ch; Phi Beta Kappa. **HONORS/ACHIEVEMENTS:** Who's Who Among Black Americans; Scholarship Club, Wash DC Publ "A Letter to Am of Segregation" 1959; "Who Wants What?" 1963; "Crime Stoppers Voice" 1966; "Philosophical Food for Am" 1967; "Southland USA Dimple of the World" 1968; "The New Dimension & In (Am) Hell" 1970; "Shoplifting Is A Crime" 1972; "Peace, Joy, Love" 1973; "Human Touch" 1974; "The Osculation of Humankind" 1974; "Law & Order" 1976; "Faith, Justice, Hope" 1977; A Big Brother To Mankind Numerous Publs on race & crime prevention. **BUSINESS ADDRESS:** 19 Mathew Dr, Columbus, GA 31903.

GREENE, RICHARD T.
Bank president. **PERSONAL:** Married Virginia Lea; children: Cheryll Greene, Richard T Greene, Jr. **EDUCATION:** Hampton Univ, Hampton, VA, BS, 1938; attended NY Univ, 1955-64. **CAREER:** Citizens and Southern Bank and Trust, Philadelphia, PA, former asst treasurer; Associated Pubrs Inc, New York, business mgr, 1945-58; Interstate United Newspapers, sec and business mgr, 1958-60; Carver Federal Savings Bank, New York, exec asst, 1960, mgr of Brooklyn branch office, 1961, asst vice pres, 1963-66, vice pres, 1966-68, exec vice pres, 1968-69, pres and dir, 1969-. **ORGANIZATIONS:** Elder, Westminster Presbyterian Church; member, Hampton Alumni Club; member, Omega Psi Phi; member, Pres Coun of Museum of City of NY; former trustee, Citizens Budget Comm; direc, Amer League of Financial Instns; member, One Hundred Black Men Inc; direc, Financial Services Corp, Thrift Assns Service Corp, Harlem Urban Devel Corp, and Fed Home Loan Bank. **MILITARY SERVICE:** US Army, captain, 1941-45; Army commendation medal; Army Res, major. **BUSINESS ADDRESS:** Mr Richard T Greene, Carver Federal Savings Bank, 75 W 125th Street, New York, NY 10027.

GREENE, RONALD ALEXANDER
Business executive. **PERSONAL:** Born Nov 01, 1945, Greenwood, SC; married Margaret St Mark; children: Ronald Jr, Jennifer. **EDUCATION:** SC St Coll, BS 1965-68. **CAREER:** Blue Cross Blue Shield, mgr telecommunications 1979; Blue Cross Blue Shield, telecomm Coordntr 1978-79; Blue Cross Blue Shield, mgr data entry 1976-78; Blue Cross Blue Shield, prgrmr analyst 1975-76; prgmr analyst. **MILITARY SERVICE:** AUS 1974-75; oak leaf cluster; AUS capt 7 yrs. **BUSINESS ADDRESS:** I 20 and Alpine Rd, Columbia, SC.

GREENE, SARAH MOORE
Educator, political leader. **PERSONAL:** Born Feb 22, 0917, Madisonville, TN; daughter of Isaac Moore and Mary Toomey Moore; married William J Green (deceased), Oct 03, 1939 (deceased). **EDUCATION:** A & I State Coll, Nashville TN, 1932-34. **CAREER:** Monroe County School Bd, Sweetwater TN, teacher, 1934-36; North Carolina Mutual Insurance Co, Knoxville TN, special agent, 1936-46; Knoxville TN, private kindergarten proprietor, 1946-66; State of Tennessee, Nashville TN, pardon/parole bd mem, 1967-69; Knox County, Knoxville TN, sec of finance comm, 1971-80; US Government, Knoxville TN, staff aide, 1980-85. **ORGANIZATIONS:** Chairperson, bd of dir, YWCA, 1956-62, KOIC, 1964-88; bd mem, Community Action Comm, 1965-71; mem, Knoxville Bd of Educ, 1969-85; sec, NAACP. **HONORS/ACHIEVEMENTS:** Certificate of Appointment to NCEDC, President Gerald Ford, 1975; Torch Bearer Award, Opportunity Industrial Corp, 1976; Honorary Mem, Alpha Kappa Alpha Sorority Inc, 1976; Civic Serv Award, Greater Knoxville Minority Business Bureau, 1978; Honor Serv Award, Knoxville Opportunity Industrial Corp, 1988. **HOME ADDRESS:** 2453 Linden Ave, Knoxville, TN 37917.

GREENE, WILLIAM
Minister. **PERSONAL:** Born Sep 13, 1933, Rowland, NC; son of Joe Greene and Margaret Brunson Greene; married Wilhelmenia O. Greene, Dec 28, 1953; children: Wanda Greene. **EDUCATION:** Anchorage Community College, Anchorage, AK, AA, 1982; Alaska Pacific Univ, Anchorage, AK, BA, 1983. **CAREER:** US Air Force, fuel supt, 1953-80; Shiloh Missionary Baptist Church, Anchorage, AK, chairman, 1974-79, admin, 1979-85; chaplain with state of Alaska, 1980-; Eagle River Baptist Church, Eagle River, AK, pastor, 1985-. **ORGANIZATIONS:** Pres, Interdenominational Ministerial Alliance, 1987-; pres, Chugiak Food Pantry, 1988-; chair, Black Edn Task Force, 1988-; chair, Minority Community Rels Police Task Force, 1988-. **HONORS/ACHIEVEMENTS:** Man of the Year Award, Alaska State Assn of Colored Women, 1987; Outstanding Leadership Award, Alaska Black Caucus, 1988; military awards inc Korean Service Medal, Korean Pres Unit Citation, UN Service Medal. **HOME ADDRESS:** Rev William Greene, 7310 East 17th Ave, Anchorage, AK 99504. **BUSINESS ADDRESS:** Rev William Greene, Eagle River Missionary Baptist Church, 16331 Business Park Blvd, P O Box 775188, Eagle River, AK 99577-5188.

GREENE, WILLIAM HENRY L'VEL
University president. **PERSONAL:** Born Jul 28, 1943, Richburg, SC; married Ruth Lipscomb Greene; children: Omari; Jamila. **EDUCATION:** Johnson C Smith Univ, BA 1966; Michigan State Univ, MA 1970; PhD 1972. **CAREER:** Univ of Massachusetts, asst prof 1972-76; Univ of Massachusetts, Center for Urban Educ, dir in-service teacher educ 1974-76; Fayetteville State Univ, asst to chancellor, dir of devel relations 1976-79; Johnson C Smith Univ, dir career counseling 1979-83; Livingstone Coll, pres 1983-. **ORGANIZATIONS:** NC Internship Council, member 1986; (Phi Delta Kappa), Outstanding Yount Men of America, Fayetteville Business League, Exec Brd 1986;Board of Directors, 1986 Salisbury Chamber of Comm;First Union Nat'l Bank; Salisbury Rowan Symphony Society; Salisbury YMCA. **HONORS/ACHIEVEMENTS:** Black Caucus, Outstanding Black Educator 1976; Fayetteville State, Advisor of the year 1978-79; American Heart Assoc, Achievement Recognition Awd 1984; Charlotte NC (Delta Zeta Chapter) Comm Serv Awd 1984. **BUSINESS ADDRESS:** President, Livingstone College, 701 W Monroe St, Salisbury, NC 28144.

GREENE, WILLIAM J.
Analyst. **PERSONAL:** Born Aug 02, 1912, New York, NY; married Gertrude A; children: Vida, Janice. **CAREER:** NYS Leg, analyst 1977; NY Cnty Fam Crt, clerk 1972-77; NYS Sup Crt, clerk 1962-72. **ORGANIZATIONS:** Mem NYS Crt Clerks Assoc; pres NAACP 1968; chmn bd of dir NAACP Pro Rebound; mem adv bd Borough Manhattan Comm Coll; mem Interracial Colloquy; mem 100 Blackmen, Inc. **HONORS/ACHIEVEMENTS:** Mem Dist IV Mort Pool; life mem NAACP Golden Her; dist serv Proj Rebound.

GREENE-THAPEDI, LLEWELLYN L.
Attorney. **PERSONAL:** Born in Guthrie, OK; daughter of Latimer Hamilton Greene and Fannye M Gaines; married Dr Isaac Thapedi, Aug 11, 1966 (divorced); children: Severn Latimer Deck, Letha Llewellyn Deck, Sheryl Renee Deck, Andre Martin Thapedi, Anthony Isaac Thapedi. **EDUCATION:** Langston University, OK, BA; University of Saskatchewan, MA; Loyola University, Chicago, IL, JD. **CAREER:** University of Saskatchewan, Canada, instructor, 1971-72; Amoco Oil Company, Chicago, IL, attorney, 1976-81; Chicago State University, Chicago, IL, instructor in business law, 1977-78. **ORGANIZATIONS:** Delivery of Legal Services Standing Committee, Illinois State Bar Association, 1976-85; member, officer, Cook County Bar Association, 1978-88; member of board of directors, Public Interest Law Internship, 1982-83; member of board of directors, Chicago Bar Association, 1983-85; member of board of directors, Illinois Institute for Continuing Legal Education, 1985-87; member, Citizen's Advisory Committee of the Circuit Court, 1987; member, Illinois Trial Lawyers Association, 1978-88; member of board of directors, National Bar Association, 1987-88; president, Cook County Bar Association, 1987-88; member of hearings committee, Attorney Registration and Disciplinary Committee, 1989-90; member, Urban League; member, NAACP; member, Delta Sigma Theta. **HONORS/ACHIEVEMENTS:** Meritorious Service Award, 1983; National Association for Equal Opportunity in Education Award, 1984; Legal Assistance Foundation Award, 1984; Richard E Westbrook Award for legal excellence, 1986; Kizzie Award for community service, 1987; Martin Luther King Teen Leadership Award, 1988. **BUSINESS ADDRESS:** Bell Federal Savings Building, 205 West Randolph, Suite 1250, Chicago, IL 60603.

GREENFIELD, ELOISE
Freelance writer. **PERSONAL:** Born May 17, 1929, Parmele, NC; married Robert J; children: Steven, Monica. **EDUCATION:** Miner Tchrs Coll, 1946-49. **CAREER:** US Patent Office, clerk typist 1949-56, supv 1956-60; DC Unemploy Compensation Bd, sec 1963-64; Case Cntrl Tch Wrk & Training Oppty & Ctr, 1967-68; DC Dept of Occptn & Profns, admin 1968; DC Writers Workshop, staff mem 1971-74; DC Commn of the Arts, writer in residence 1973; freelance writer. **ORGANIZATIONS:** Mem African Amer Writer's Guild, Authors Guild, Black Literary Umbrella. **HONORS/ACHIEVEMENTS:** Cit Council on Interracial Books for Children; Cit DC Assn of School Librarians; Cit Clbrtns in Lrnng; short stories & articles, for Negro Digest, Black World, Scholastic Scope, Ebony Jr, Negro Hist Bull, num chldrn's Books; Carter G Woodson Book Awd 1974; NY Times Outst Book; Irma Simonton Black Book Awd 1974; Jane Addams Chldrn's Book Awd 1976; Coretta Scott King Awd 1978; Am Library Assn Notable Book; Awd from Natl Black Child Development Inst 1981; producer of childrens recordings 1982; works reviewed & dramatized on publicTV (Reading Rainbow); Awd Black Women in Sisterhood for Action 1983; Wash DC Mayor's Art Awd for Lit 1983; Inst for the Preservation & Study of African Amer Writing 1984; grants DC Comms on the Arts & Humanities. **BUSINESS ADDRESS:** Author, PO Box 29077, Washington, DC 20017.

GREENFIELD, ROBERT THOMAS, JR.
Physician. **PERSONAL:** Born Jul 08, 1933, Washington, DC; son of Robert T Greenfield and Avis Greenfield; married Wilma Sue Robertson; children: Kimberly, Karyn, Robert III, Richard. **EDUCATION:** Howard Univ, BS 1954; Howard Univ Coll of Med, MD 1958. **CAREER:** US Army, capt med corps 1958-63; Madigan General Hosp, internship 1958-59; Freedmen's Hosp, res phys ob/gyn 1963-67; Howard Univ Coll Med, clinical instr 1976-; Georgetown Univ, instructor clinical 1978-; Drs Clark, Greenfield Chartered, physician, pres 1969-; Chartered Health Plan medical dir. **ORGANIZATIONS:** Bd dir Columbia Hospital for Women 1981-85; mem Joint Perinatal Site Visit Task Force for Washington DC 1982-85; chief of staff Columbia Hosp for Women 1983-85; chmn, bd dir Colmesh Inc 1985-86; mem adv bd DC Maternal & Infant Health; mem Joint Venture Medical Staff & Columbia Hospital; vice chmn Washington DC Sect Dist IV Amer Coll of Ob/Gyn; chmn Washington DC Section Dist IV Amer Coll of Obs/Gyn; chmn Perinatal Mortality Comm Dist IV Amer Coll of Ob/Gyn. **HONORS/ACHIEVEMENTS:** Mem Alpha Omega Alpha Med Scholastic Frat. **MILITARY SERVICE:** AUS capt 5 yrs. **HOME ADDRESS:** 2010 Spruce Dr NW, Washington, DC 20012. **BUSINESS ADDRESS:** President, Drs Clark, Greenfield Charter, 665 E St SW, Washington, DC 20024.

GREENFIELD, ROY ALONZO
Retired chairman/director, consumer education. **PERSONAL:** Born May 07, 1915, Washington, DC; son of Eugene Greenfield and Roy Marie Greenfield; married Mathilde Camille DePoidras. **EDUCATION:** Howard Univ, BS Liberal Arts, MA, PhD Higher Educ Admin; New York Univ, PhD Psychology; New York Univ, postdoctorate courses, Psychology. **CAREER:** US Federal Govt, first black hospital administrator under Genl Omar Bradley, Veterans Administrator, Washington DC, first black interpreter of French and Spanish WW II under Genl Eisenhower; State College for Colored Students Dover State Delaware, prof of foreign languages; Vet Adm NYRO, psychologist/psychometrist; US Federal Trade Commn, first black chmn dir consumer educ NY regional office. **ORGANIZATIONS:** Mem, Federation National Des Anciens Combattants, NAACP, Urban League, Alliance Francaise, NY Acad of Science, Natl Soc for the Advancement of Ethical Culture; lecturer to staff members at Blair House on how to improve their educ helping them in their educ programs; consultant to mem of Diplomatic Corps connected with foreign embassies Washington DC; French and Spanish interpreter at Washington Natl Airport for Delta, Eastern, Piedmont, Pan Am Airlines; USO volunteer 5 yrs Washington DC; mem, Natl Assoc of Federal Investigators 1958-. **HONORS/ACHIEVEMENTS:** First Black member admitted NY Acad of Science 1939; Only bona fide US Federal Black fur expert, textile expert and wool expert in USA trained by United States Federal Government; Outstanding Guest Speaker for the Natl Urban League; publication "Speak 5 Languages Instantly for Travellers," 1987. **MILITARY SERVICE:** Graduated from Camp Ritchie MD Sch of Military Intelligence as an interpreter of French.

GREENFIELD, WILBERT
College president. **CAREER:** Virginia State University, Petersburg, VA, president. **BUSINESS ADDRESS:** Virginia State University, Petersburg, VA 23803. *

GREENFIELD, WILLIAM RUSSELL, JR.
Physician. **PERSONAL:** Born Sep 15, 1915, Williamsport, TN; married Mae Rivers Ward; children: William R, Albert, Mae Helaine, Mary Jewel Howard, Theolya Louise, William Ward. **EDUCATION:** TN St U, BS 1938; Meharry Med Coll, MD 1949. **CAREER:** Physician Prvt Prac Dothan AL 1951; TN St 1937-45. **BUSINESS ADDRESS:** 904 DuBoise St, Dothan, AL 36302.

GREENIDGE, JAMES ERNEST
Publicity director. **PERSONAL:** Born Feb 25, 1949, Cambridge, MA; son of Beresford and M Norma. **EDUCATION:** Northeastern Univ, BA 1971. **CAREER:** Boston Record Amer, news reporter 1971-72; Albany NY Knickerbocker News, sportswriter 1972-73; Rensselaer Polytech, sports info dir 1973-82; Harvard Univ, sports info dir 1982-84; New England Patriots, publicity dir 1984-. **HOME ADDRESS:** 17-3 Old Colony Lane, Arlington, MA 02174. **BUSINESS ADDRESS:** Publicity Dir, New England Patriots, Sullivan Stadium, Rt 1, Foxboro, MA 02035.

GREENLEAF, LOUIS E.
Chief of investigators. **PERSONAL:** Born Apr 09, 1941, Newark, NJ; married Cynthia Robinson Conover; children: Bridget, Michael, Brectt, Towanna. **EDUCATION:** Essex Co Coll, AS 1973; John Jay Coll of Criminal Justice, BS 1975; Rutgers School of Law, JD 1978. **CAREER:** Private Law Practice, attorney 1983-86; City of Newark, police dept 1968-87. **ORGANIZATIONS:** Mem NJ Bar Assoc 1985-; mem Natl Org of Black Law Enforcement Execs; bd of trustees Garden State Bar Assoc; vice chmn bd of trustees NJ Juvenile Insts; Bd of Dir Newark Emr Services for Families. **MILITARY SERVICE:** AUS E-4 2 yrs; Vietnam Service, Good Conduct 1964-66. **BUSINESS ADDRESS:** Chief of Investigators, Essex County Prosecutors Office, New Courts Bldg, Newark, NJ 07102.

GREENLEE, PETER ANTHONY
Attorney. **PERSONAL:** Born Feb 18, 1941, Des Moines; married Marcia McAdoo. **EDUCATION:** Univ Wash, BA 1965; Howard Univ Law Sch, JD 1971. **CAREER:** Univ of OR, instr; Job Corps, 1965-66; US Peace Corps Euthiopia, 1966-68; Reginald Heber Smith Fllw Nghbrhd Lgl Srvcs, Atty 1970-72; Redvlpmnt Lnd Agncy, 1972-74; Dept Energy. **ORGANIZATIONS:** Mem Am Bar Assn; Nat Bar Assn; Delta Theta Phi; mem Intl Trade

& Finance Div; DC Bar. **HONORS/ACHIEVEMENTS:** Conferee World Peace Through Law Conf 1973. **BUSINESS ADDRESS:** Dept of Energy Office Gen Coun, Washington, DC.

GREENLEE, ROBERT DOUGLASS
Journalist. **PERSONAL:** Born Sep 12, 1940, Washington, DC; married Julia Ann Colbert; children: Chris (deceased), Ronald, Raymond (deceased), Richard. **EDUCATION:** South Central Community Coll, AS 1969-71; Univ of Chicago, Urban Journalism Fellow 1972; Univ of MA, BA 1973-75. **CAREER:** The Crow Newspaper, assoc editor/publisher 1967-70; The New Haven Register, reporter/columnist 1971-82; Chicago Daily Defender, staff writer 1972; Prince George's Journal Daily Paper, staff writer 1982; Planned Parenthood of CT Inc, public relations coordinator; author, playwright. **ORGANIZATIONS:** Charter mem Natl Assn Black Journalists 1975-77; mem Omega Psi Phi Fraternity/Chi Omicron Chapter 1976-; founder, past pres Knights of Ebony Inc 1967-73. **HONORS/ACHIEVEMENTS:** Urban Journalism Fellowship, Univ of Chicago 1972; Danforth Award for Leadership HS 1956; numerous journalism awards from community and civic groups 1971-82; published books, articles and essays 1973-83. **MILITARY SERVICE:** USAF airman 1st cls e-4. **BUSINESS ADDRESS:** Public Relations Coordinator, Planned Parenthood CT Inc, 129 Whitney Ave, New Haven, CT 06517.

GREENLEE, SAM
Author. **PERSONAL:** Born Jul 13, 1930, Chicago, IL; married Nienke. **EDUCATION:** Univ of WI, BS, 1952; Univ of Chicago, grad study, 1954-57; Univ of Thessaloniki, Greece, grad study, 1963-64. **CAREER:** Author; US Info Agency, foreign serv officer in Iraq, Pakistan, Indonesia, and Greece, 1957-65; LMOC, deputy dir, 1965-69. **HONORS/ACHIEVEMENTS:** Author of The Spook Who Sat by the Door, Baron, 1969, Blues for an African Princess, Third World Press, 1971, Baghdad Blues, Bantam, 1976; contributor of articles & short stories to magazines and journals. **MILITARY SERVICE:** US Army, first lieutenant, 1952-54. **HOME ADDRESS:** 6240 S Champlain Ave, Chicago, IL 60637. *

GREENWOOD, CHARLES H.
Educational administrator. **PERSONAL:** Born Jul 30, 1933, Anderson, IN; married Theresa M Winfrey; children: Lisa Renee, Marc Charles. **EDUCATION:** Ball State Tchrs Coll, BS 1956; CO Coll, 1956-58; Ball State U, MA 1961; IN U, EdD 1972. **CAREER:** Ball State Univ, graduate asst 1958-59; E Chicago Public Schools, teacher 1959-61; Ball State Univ, instructor 1961-63, assoc prof 1973-; N IL Univ, visiting prof 1973-74; Undergraduate Program Ball State Univ, asst dean 1974-84; School of Continuing Educ, asst dean 1984. **ORGANIZATIONS:** Mem Am Assn of Higher Educ 1974-; mem Assn for Supervision & Curriculum Devel 1974-78; mem Assn of Acad Affairs Admin 1974-78; mem Adult Educ Assn of IN 1978; mem Phi Delta Kappa 1976-; evaluator Am Cncl of Educ 1984; vp/pres Kiwanis Club of Muncie IN 1980-81; lt gov Wapahanl Div IN Dist Kiwanis Intl 1982-83; vice pres Jr Achievement 1979-81; sec YMCA Bd 1978; mem Sigma Iota Epsilon 1986; educational coord Acad Comm Leadership; liaison officer Washington Center (DC). **HONORS/ACHIEVEMENTS:** Who's Who in IN 1967; Nat Bronze Award Jr Achievement 1980; Dictionary Intl Biography 1967-68; Community Leaders Noteworthy Am 1975-76; Disting Lt GovKiwanis Intl 1983. **MILITARY SERVICE:** AUS sp 4 1956-58; Civil Air Patrol USAF Aux CAP major 1976-; Good Conduct; Aerospace Educ Mem 1956-83. **BUSINESS ADDRESS:** Assistant Dean, Ball State Univ, 2000 University Ave, Muncie, IN 47306.

GREENWOOD, DAVID
Professional athlete. **PERSONAL:** Born May 27, 1957, Lynwood, CA; married Joyce; children: Tiffany Crystal Marie. **EDUCATION:** UCLA, BA History 1979. **CAREER:** Chicago Bullets, basketball player-forward. **ORGANIZATIONS:** Taught basketball clinics Western US 1980. **HONORS/ACHIEVEMENTS:** NBA First Team All Rookie Team 1978-79.

GREENWOOD, JOHN T.
Educator. **PERSONAL:** Born Feb 02, 1949, Winston-salem, NC; son of Joseph Jackson Greenwood and Elizabeth Millner Greenwood. **EDUCATION:** Cornell, AB 1971; Harvard, JD 1974; Business Admin, Business Law, Criminal Law, Health Law, Civil Rights, Legal Studies. **CAREER:** Mudge Rose Guthrie & Alexander, atty 1972; Inst of Gov Univ of North Carolina at Chapel Hill, asst prof, asst dir 1974; NC A&T State Univ, asst prof business admin 1975; WS State Univ, asst prof business admin 1976; Barber Scotia Coll, asst prof & dir test-taking & learning skills 1977; Gulton Femco, asst mgr of personnel 1978; WS Urban League, dir of prog 1978; Div of Business Shaw Univ, assoc prof chmn 1979; Mgmt Educ & Real Estate, consulant; JTG Assoc, pres. **HONORS/ACHIEVEMENTS:** Phi Beta Kappa; Alpha Kappa Mu.

GREENWOOD, L. C.
Professional athlete. **PERSONAL:** Born Sep 08, 1946, Canton, MS. **EDUCATION:** AR A&M Coll, BA 1969. **CAREER:** Pitts Steelers, defensive end. **HONORS/ACHIEVEMENTS:** AFC Champ Game 1976; NFL Champ Game 1974, 75; Pro Bowl, 1973-79; drafted Pitts, 10th round 1969; Played In Four Superbowls With Pitts Steelers 1974-75, 78-79. **BUSINESS ADDRESS:** President, Greenwood Enterprise, Inc, 745 Washington Ave, Bridgeville, PA 15017.

GREENWOOD, THERESA M. WINFREY
Writer, musician, educator. **PERSONAL:** Born Dec 28, 1936, Cairo, IL; daughter of Hubert Winfrey and Lillian T Williams Winfrey; married Dr Charles H Greenwood; children: Lisa Renee, Marc Charles. **EDUCATION:** Millikin Univ, MusD 1959; Ball State Univ, EdM 1963, EdD 1976. **CAREER:** E Chicago Pub Schools, music teacher 1959-61; Muncie Pub Schools, teacher 1962-68; Ball State Univ, acad counselor 1971-72; Ball State Univ Burris Lab School, asst prof educ 1979-, teacher of gifted/talented program 1986-. **ORGANIZATIONS:** Past pres Sigma Alpha Iota 1958; music adjudicator NISBOVA 1961-; bd of dir United Way, ARC, Huffer Day Care, WIPB-TV 1969-75; mem Kappa Delta Pi 1972-73; mem & state sec Natl League Amer Pen Women 1973-78; testified White House Conf on Families 1980; mem Eastern IN Community Choir; ed bd White River State Park 1983; judge Social Study History Days; adv bd Social Studies Council Natl Publ 1982; recipient Ind & MI Electric Co Mini-Grant 1987; Kodak (Newsletter Pub 1985 & Prie Time Newsletter Pub) 1986; editorial bd Natl Soc Studies Journal; speaker HS Young Writers Conf 1986; media volunteer Pan-American Games 1987. **HONORS/ACHIEVEMENTS:** Scholarship Tri Delta Millikin Univ 1958; IN Soc Studies Grant 1982; Commendation IN Gov Orr 1982; published, Psalms of a Black Mother Warner Press 1970, Gospel Graffiti M Evans NY 1978, weekly newspaper column, Muncie Eve Press Poems, "Black Like It Is/Was" 1974, "Break Thru (Upper Room Anthology)" 1972, "Crazy to be Alive in Such A Strange World" 1977; bibliographic, Ladies Home Journal 1976, Essence Mag 1975, Church Herald 1972; article "Cross-Cultural Educ for Elementary School" The Social Studies Teacher 1983; IN All-Amer Family Awd Family Weekly Mag, Eastern Airlines 197; fellowship Natl Fellowship Funds Emory Univ l973-76; NAACP Award l980; published poems in the Saturday Evening Post, l974; students gained extensive publicity for "Dear World" letters to Pres Reagan and Gen Sec Mikhail Gorbachev during Washington Summit (exhibited l0 months at World's Largest Children Museum), l988; BSU Minority Achievement Award, Minority Student Development, l989, currently developing "Tap the Gap," a program for at-risk students. **BUSINESS ADDRESS:** Assistant Professor Education, Ball StateUniv, Burris Lab School, 2000Univ, Muncie, IN 47304.

GREER, CURTIS WILLIAM
Professional football player. **PERSONAL:** Born Nov 10, 1957, Detroit, MI. **EDUCATION:** Univ of MI, BS Speech Communication 1979. **CAREER:** St Louis Cardinals, defensive end 1980-. **BUSINESS ADDRESS:** Defensive End, Phoenix Cardinals, PO Box 888, Phoenix, AZ 85001.

GREER, EDWARD
Realtor. **PERSONAL:** Born Mar 08, 1924, Gary, WV; married Jewell Means; children: Gail Lyle, Michael, Kenneth. **EDUCATION:** WV State Coll, BS 1948; George Washington U, MS 1967. **CAREER:** Gunaca & Asso Realtors, vp. **HONORS/ACHIEVEMENTS:** Awarded, Distgshd Serv Medal; Silver Star; Legion of Merit; Oak Leaf Cluster; Bronze Star & Medal, Oak Leaf Cluster; Air Medal; Joint Srvc Cmmndtn Medal; Army Cmmndtn Medl; Alumnus of Yr WV St Coll 1963. **MILITARY SERVICE:** 2d lt to mjr Genrl AUS; brigadier genrl; AUS 1944. **BUSINESS ADDRESS:** Gunaca & Asso Realtors, 8815 Dyer, Ste 101, El Paso, TX 79904.

GREER, MICHAEL
Real estate executive. **PERSONAL:** Born May 23, 1956, Shreveport, LA; married Pandora Roberson; children: Jonathon Michael. **EDUCATION:** Louisiana Tech Univ, attended 1977. **CAREER:** JS Clark Jr High, instructor 1977-78; LA Campbell & Assoc, district mgr 1977-79; Financial Concepts, pres 1979-84; Pro Star Mgmt, pres 1985; Texas Realty Financial Group, chmn of the bd 1986; Texas Realty Ventures Inc, president/ceo 1984-. **ORGANIZATIONS:** Mem RESSI, Houston Chamber of Commerce, NAACP, Austin Chamber of Commerce, Intl Assoc of Financial Planners, Grand Club YMCA, Omega Psi Phi Frat; contributor Sickle Cell Foundation, UNCF; speaker Natl Assoc of Black Accountants. **HONORS/ACHIEVEMENTS:** Listing Outstanding Young Man of Amer 1982-86; feature story Black Enterprise Magazine 1986, Houston Post 1985, 86, Austin American Statesman 1984; local newsstory Channels 2,8,11,26,39; radio show KLBJ Longhorn RadioUniv of T.

GREER, ROBERT O.
Assistant superintendent. **PERSONAL:** Born Mar 16, 1915, Coalwood, WV; married Mary Gentry; children: Robert, Darryl, Dwight. **EDUCATION:** Bluefield St Coll, BS 1938; OH St U, MA 1948; Temple U, PhD Cand; Spl Studies, Intl Rltns, Cite Universitaire Paris France. **CAREER:** OH Dept Pub Instr, asst supt 1968; Sch Systm of Gary IN, princ 1949-68; OH St U, grad asst 1949-68; McDowell Co Bd Edn, instr 1942-49; Bluefield St Coll, librarian 1938-39. **ORGANIZATIONS:** Mem Phi Delta Kappa, NASSP; AASA Nat Acad for Sch Execs 1973; chmn N Cntrl Assn Pacfc Evl Team, DOD Schs 1973; pres Gary & Lake Co IN Prin, Pres Commn on Nat Goals 1961; chf St Sch Ofcr's Staff Dvl Task Frc 1975-76; OH Crmnl Justice Adv Comm 1976-77; mem OH Crmnl Jstc Supv Com 1971-74; coord Ann Evls N Cntrl Assn of Coll's & Scndry Schls 1977; mem various other prfnl orgns; mem bd dir United Fund 1954-64; YMCA Bd; pres Comm Wlfr Cncl 1955-57; Urban Redvl Commn; Mayor's Adv Com on Human Rghts; mem bd dir OH Cncl of chrchs, OH Mntl Hlth Assn; other civic orgns. **HONORS/ACHIEVEMENTS:** John Hay Fellow CO Coll 1964; Dist Alumni Cntnl Awd OH StUniv 1970; Gov's Awd for exclnc in Educ 1972; NASE, AASA Professional Dvl Awd 1974; citation for excellence in Educ 110th Gen Asmbly OH Senate 1973; Listed in IN Lives; Who's Who in Midwest; Comm Ldrs of Am. **MILITARY SERVICE:** AUS 1st lt 1942-46. **BUSINESS ADDRESS:** OH Dept of Educ, 65 S Front St, Columbus, OH 43215.

GREER, ROBERT O., JR.
Educator. **PERSONAL:** Born Mar 09, 1944, Columbus, OH; son of Robert O Greer Sr and Mary A Greer; married Phyllis Ann Harwell. **EDUCATION:** Miami Univ Oxford OH, AB 1961-65; Howard U, DDS 1965-69; Boston U, ScD MD 1971-74. **CAREER:** Dept of Pathology Univ of CO Hlth Sci Cntr, asst prof 1974-77; Dept of Pathology UCHSC, assc prof 1977-80; Div of Oral Pathology & Oncology Univ of CO Sch of Dentistry, prof & chrmn 1980-; Dept of Pathology UCHSC, prof 1984-. **ORGANIZATIONS:** Pres & chief pathologist Western States Regnl Pthlgy Lab; sec Mile High Med Soc 1978-79, pres 1983-85; mem Alumni Bd of Dir Miami Univ 1984-;Editor, High Plains Library Review. **HONORS/ACHIEVEMENTS:** David Swing Acad Schlrshp Miami Univ 1961-63; tuition schlrshp Howard Univ 1965-69; NIH postdoctoral rsrch flwhsp Boston Univ 1970-74; investigative rsch grants Am Cancer Soc Natl Cancer Inst Smokless Tobacco Cncl 1980-; three texbooks Tumors of the Head & Neck. **MILITARY SERVICE:** USCG lt cmdr. **BUSINESS ADDRESS:** Professor & Chairman, Div Oral Pathlgy & Oncology, Univ of CO Hlth Sci Cntr, Box C285 4200 E 9th St, Denver, CO 80262.

GREGG, HARRISON M., JR.
Attorney. **PERSONAL:** Born Sep 24, 1942, Longview, TX; son of Harrison Gregg and Ola Timberlake Gregg; married Arizona Johnson Gregg, Jun 18, 1963; children: Sherri Kimberly. **EDUCATION:** Texas Southern Univ, BA, 1968, JD, 1971; Master Barber 1958. **CAREER:** State of Texas, 2nd Admin Region, 4D Master (judge), 1987-; Instructor, Texas Paralegal Sch, 1976-; Gregg Okehie & Cashin, atty, 1972-; barber 14 yrs. **ORGANIZATIONS:** Mem Houston Bar Assn; TX State Bar; Houston Lawyer Assn; TX Crimnal Defense Lawyers; Harris Co Criminal Defense Lawyers; Nat Bar Assn; Am Bar Assn. **HONORS/ACHIEVEMENTS:** Phi Alpha Delta; mem Free & Accepted Prince Hall Mason; volntr UNCF. **MILITARY SERVICE:** AUS. **BUSINESS ADDRESS:** Gregg Okehie & Cashin Law Offices, 608 Fannin #440, Houston, TX 77002.

GREGG, LUCIUS PERRY
Business executive. **PERSONAL:** Born Jan 16, 1933, Henderson, NC; married Doris Marie Jefferson. **EDUCATION:** US Naval Acad, BS 1955; MA Inst Tech, MS 1961; Cath U, doctoral candidate 1961-63; Grinnell Coll, hon DSc 1973; Aspen Inst Exec Prog, 1974; Adv Mgmt Prog Harvard Bus Sch, 1975. **CAREER:** USAF Office Scientific Rsrch, proj dir in space tech 1961-65; Northwestern U, asso dean of Scis & dir rsrch coord 1965-69; Alfred P Sloan Found, prgm ofcr 1969-71; 1st ChicagoUniv Finance Corp, pres 1972-74; 1st Nat Bank Chgo, vice pres 1972-. **ORGANIZATIONS:** Bd dirs Corp for Pub Brdcstng 1975-; acad bd US Naval Acad 1971-; mem HarvardUniv Trsts Visiting Comm in physics 1973-; Pres's Com on White HouseFellows Midwest Reg Selec Com 1974-; mem Nat Acad of Sci Found Com on Human Rsrcs (chmn Com on Minorities in Sci) 1973-; bd mem Fermi (AEC) NatAccel Lab 1967-77f RooseveltUniv 1976-; Garrett Theol Sem 1974-; TulaneUniv Bd of Visitors 1972-; Chicago Coun on Foreign Rel 1975-; Harvard Bus Sch of Chicago 1977f mem MIT Trsts Visiting Con in Aero & Astronautics; Harvard Club of Chicago 1975-; memUniv Club Chicago 1972-; Econ Club Chicago 1967-. **HONORS/ACHIEVEMENTS:** Hon mem Sigma Gamma Tau 1969; 1 of 10 outstndg young men of 1966 Chicago Assn Commerce & Indus; outstndg young engr of 1964 Wash Acad Sci; Who's Who inAm 1968; Am Men of Sci 1970. **MILITARY SERVICE:** USMC pfc 1950-51; USAF 1955-62.

GREGORY, BERNARD VINCENT
Business executive. **PERSONAL:** Born Nov 05, 1926, New York, NY; son of Horace Gregory and Winnifred Gregory; married Marion Arnetha Buck; children: Bernard II, Michele Verne, Rodney Glenn. **EDUCATION:** Wilberforce Univ, attended 1943-45; Central State Univ, BS 1948. **CAREER:** Beneficial Life, general mgr 1954-60; Supreme Life, assoc brokerage supvr/asst agency dir/dir educ & training 1960-72; Chicago Metro Mutual, ordinance agency mgr 1972-75; Afro-Amer Life, vp/agency dir 1975-77; Prudential Insurance, assoc mgr advertising & sales promotion, 1977-79; Winston Mutual Life Ins Co, agency dir 1979-81; Jacksonville Chamber of Commerce, minority youth empl dir 1984; Southern Bell, acct exec asst mgr, telemarketing mgr. **ORGANIZATIONS:** Chmn, Jacksonville Equal Opportunity Commission, 1987-91; 3rd vice pres, Jacksonville Branch, NAACP, 1987-89; bd mem, First Coast, Black Business Investment Corp, 1987-89, Private Indus Council, Jacksonville Chamber of Commerce, 1989, United Way of Northeast Florida, Amer Lung Assn of FL, northeast branch, Jacksonville Community Council Inc, Clara White Mission Inc; Mem, Mayor's Comm on Blodget Homes; Jacksonville Commn on Crime, Strikeforce, Duval Assn of Retarded Citizens, Tots 'N' Teens, Jacksonville, YMCA, Southern Bell Florida Inc; Life Mem, Kappa Alpha Psi Fraternity, NAACP, Central State Univ General Alumni Assn; Jacksonville Blood Bank. **HONORS/ACHIEVEMENTS:** Outstanding Alumnus of the Year, Central State Univ, 1970; Rutledge H Pearson Memorial Award, Jacksonville Branch, NAACP, 1987; Outstanding Leadeship and Dedicated Serv, 1987, Jacksonville Urban League, bd of dirs, 1988; Outstanding Community Serv, Tots 'N' Teens Theatre Inc, 1989; Honorary Citizen, City of Houston, TX, 1975; Minority Youth Employment Program, Jacksonville Chamber of Commerce, 1981; Contribution to the Devel of Jacksonville, Bd of Govs, Jacksonville Chamber of Commerce, 1988; Volunteer of the Month, Jacksonville Chamber of Commerce, 1989. Exemplary Leadership, Northwest Council, 1988; Achievers' Club, Southern Bell, 1988-89; Outstanding Leadership, A. Philip Randolph Northside Skills Center, 1989; Certificate of Appreciation, Edward Waters Coll, 1987; Hornsby Trophy, Soc for the Advancement of Mgmt, Central State Univ, 1965; 1st black agent with a black insurance company to sell a $500,000 policy, Black Enterprise Magazine, 1969; For Dedicated Serv, Community Economic Devel Council, 1987. **MILITARY SERVICE:** USNR 1945-46. **HOME ADDRESS:** 8430 Sophist Cir E, Jacksonville, FL 32219.

GREGORY, DICK **See GREGORY, RICHARD CLAXTON**

GREGORY, FREDERICK DREW
Astronaut. **PERSONAL:** Born Jan 07, 1941, Washington, DC; married Barbara Ann Archer; children: Frederick Jr, Heather. **EDUCATION:** USAF Acad, BS 1964; George Washington Univ, MSA 1977. **CAREER:** USAF, helicopter & fighter pilot 1965-70; USAF/NASA, research test pilot 1971-78; NASA/USAF, astronaut 1978-. **ORGANIZATIONS:** Mem Soc of Experimental Test Pilots; mem Tuskegee Airmen Inc; mem Am Helicopter Soc; mem Nat Tech Assn; mem USAF Acad Assn of Grads; mem Omega Psi Phi; mem Sigma Pi Phi. **HONORS/ACHIEVEMENTS:** Distinguished Nat Scientist Nat Soc of Black Engineers 1979. **MILITARY SERVICE:** DFC/MSM/SAMS/AFCM USAF Colonel served 20 years. **BUSINESS ADDRESS:** Astronaut, USAF/NASA, Johnson Space Center, Houston, TX 77058.

GREGORY, HENRY C., III
Minister. **PERSONAL:** Born Jul 31, 1935, New York, NY; married Muriel Edwards; children: Lisa, Henry IV. **EDUCATION:** Howard U, BA 1956; Drew U, MDI 1959f Harvard U, THM 1968; Oxford U, cert 1970. **CAREER:** Shiloh Bapt Chr, sr minister 1977; The Shiloh Hour WYCB 1340 AM, radio broadcaster; Shiloh Chr, pastor 1964-67; 5th St Bapt Chr, pstr 1967-72; VA Unoin U, tchr 1970-72; Howard U, asst to dean 1957; VA Unoin U, u pastor 1970-72; Richmond Theo Ctr, lect 1970-72; McCormick Theo Sem, prof 1976; WRUA,radio commtr 1971. **ORGANIZATIONS:** Chrm Theo Comm Ntl Bapt Conv; chrm Human Rel Comm Bapt Comm; chrm bd of dir WA Metro PUSH; bd of dir Legal Aid Soc; adv bd DrewUniv Sch ofTheo; mem Harvard Club of WA; mem Harvard Div Shc Alumni/Ae Counc; mem Alpha Phi Alpha Frat; mem Ionic Ldg; mem Ets Sigma Phi; mem Bapt in the AM Experience 1976. **HONORS/ACHIEVEMENTS:** PHP Schlsp Harvard U; cit Outstdn Serv to City; distg rel achv Bus & Prof Women's Club. **BUSINESS ADDRESS:** 1500 9th St NW, Washington, DC 20011.

GREGORY, KARL DWIGHT
Educator, business executive. **PERSONAL:** Born Mar 26, 1931, Detroit, MI; married Tenicia Ann Banks; children: Kurt David, Sheila Therese, Karin Diane. **EDUCATION:** Wayne State Univ, BA Econ 1951, MA Fin 1957; Univ of MI, PhD Econ 1962; Brown Univ, Postdoctoral Micro Econ. **CAREER:** Detroit Housing Commiss, tech aid-acct 1951-53; Federal Reserve Bank St Louis, economist 1959; Office of Mgmt & Budget, Washington DC, economist 1961-64; Wayne State Univ, prof 1960-61, 1964-67; Fed for Self-Determination, exec dir 1968-69; Accord Inc Housing Rehabilitation Detroit, pres, CEO, bd chmn 1970-71; SUNY Buffalo, visiting prof 1974; Congressional Budget Office, exec staff, sr economist 1974-75; 1st Independence Natl Bank, interim pres 1980-81; Karl D Gregory & Assoc, managing dir; Oakland Univ, prof finance & strategic planning. **ORGANIZATIONS:** Dir Natl Econ Assoc, Black Econ Rsch Ctr 1968-75, Inner City Bus Improvement Forum 1968-; dir, chief org, chmn of the bd 1st Independence natl Bank 1970-81; bd of trustees Protestant Episcopal Diocese of MI 1972-74,84-86; dir Inner City Capital Access Ctr 1973-, Detroit Capital Access Ctr 1973-; adv comm US Census of the Black Populations 1976-79, US Trade Negotiations tokyo Round 1978-81; dir Detroit Br Fed Reserve Bank of Chicago 1981-86, Barden CableVision of Detroit 1982-, Detroit Metro Small Bus Investment Corp 1982-, Detroit Econ Growth Corp 1982-; bd of trustees Oakland Cty Bus Attraction & Expansion Comm 1983-84; mem Gov Blanchards Entrepreneurs & Small Bus Corp 1984-; vice pres Econ Club of Detroit 1984-. **HONORS/ACHIEVEMENTS:** Num comm serv & acad awds; num publs in acad jrnls; expert witness on econ matters; consult to natl office of the NAACP & other civil rights orgs. **MILITARY SERVICE:** AUS artillery 1st lt 1953-56. **BUSINESS ADDRESS:** Professor of Finance & Strategic Planning, Oakland University, School of Business Administration, Rochester, MI 48063.

GREGORY, O. GRADY
Business executive. **PERSONAL:** Born Nov 04, 1895, Meridian, MS; married Lillian; children: Ronald, Katherine, Phyllis. **EDUCATION:** Ralladega Coll, BA;Univ Chicago. **CAREER:** Maner Realty Col, real estate salesman; Chicago Inter-Alumni Cncl, pres emeritus; United Negro Coll Fund, tst; Ch of the Good Shepherd, emeritus; United Ch Christ. **ORGANIZATIONS:** Mem Nat Alliance Postal & Fed Empl 1928-78; natl sec Welfari Com Coinv Nat Alliance Postal & Fed Emply 1934; vice pres Mens Club; deacon bd Ch of Good Shepherd United Ch of Christ; mem Umpires Assn. **HONORS/ACHIEVEMENTS:** First black gen foreman Chicago PO; author "From the Botton of the Barrell" 1977. **MILITARY SERVICE:** AUS pvt 1918. **BUSINESS ADDRESS:** 8055 Cottage Grove, Chicago, IL 60619.

GREGORY, RICHARD CLAXTON (DICK GREGORY)
Civil rights activist, comedian, author. **PERSONAL:** Born Oct 12, 1932, St Louis, MO; married Lillian Smith; children: Michele, Lynne, Paula, Pamela, Stephanie, Gregory, Christian, Ayanna, Miss, Yohance. **EDUCATION:** Southern Illinois Univ at Carbondale, attended 1951-53 1955-56. **CAREER:** Entertained at Esquire Club Chicago; opened nightclub Apex Robbins IL; MC Roberts Show Club Chicago 1959-60; appeared in night clubs in Milwaukee Akron San Francisco Hollywood numerous other cities 1960-;TV guest appearances Jack Parr Show others; rec include "Dick Gregory in Living Black & White", "Dick Gregory, The Light Side-Dark Side" others; lecturer univs throughout US; American Prog Bureau, lecturer 1967-; Peace & Freedom Party Candidate 1968; Dick Gregory Health Enterprises Chicago, chmn 1984-. **HONORS/ACHIEVEMENTS:** Author "From the Back of the Bus", "Niggar" 1964, "What's Happening" 1965, "The Shadow That Scares Me", "Write Me In", "No More Lies" 1971, "Dick Gregory's Polit Primer" 1971, "Dick Gregory's Natural Diet for Folks Who Eat Cookin' With Mother Nature" 1973, "Dick Gregory's Bible & Tales with Commentary" 1974, "Up FromNigger" (with Mark Lane) 1976; "The Murder of Martin Luther King Jr" 1977; Winner No Mile Championship 1951 1952; Outstanding Athlete So IL Univ 1953; Ebony-Topaz Heritage & Freedom Awd 1978; Doctor of Humane Letters, Southern Illinois Univ at Carbondale, 1989. **MILITARY SERVICE:** AUS 1953-55. **BUSINESS ADDRESS:** Chairman, Dick Gregory Health Enterprises, 39 South LaSalle, Chicago, IL 60603. *

GREGORY, ROBERT ALPHONSO
Business executive. **PERSONAL:** Born Jun 21, 1935, Hertford, NC; married Barbara Ann White; children: Alan, Christopher. **EDUCATION:** Elizabeth City State Univ NC, BS 1956. **CAREER:** Rheingold Breweries Inc, acct sales rep 1963-68; Faberge Inc, acct exec 1968-72; 3M Duplicating Prod Div, area sales rep 1972-74, natl market coord 1974-75; 3M Copying Prod Div, natl sales devel coord 1975-; Office Systems Div 3M, competitive analysis supr 1980-82; System Business Dev Unit OSD/3M, market development supr 1982-83; LES/Ed Markets OSD/3M, natl public sector marketing coord 1983-. **ORGANIZATIONS:** Chap organizer Alpha Phi Alpha Frat Inc 1955-56; presenter St Paul C of C 1974; family mem St Paul Urban League 1975-76; natl coord Copying Prod Div3M 1975-80; finance com spokesman Guardian Angels Parish Counc 1977-80. **HONORS/ACHIEVEMENTS:** Author market resource books 3M Copying Prod Div 1974-75; author awareness bulletins 3M Copying Prod Div 1975-80; author competitive awareness books 3M Copying Prod Div 1977-80; prod VTR Series on Competition 3M Copying Prod Div 1979-80. **MILITARY SERVICE:** AUS Corpl 1957-60. **BUSINESS ADDRESS:** Natl Pub Sect Market Coord, LES/Ed Markets OSD/3M, 3M Center-220-10E, St Paul, MN 55144.

GREGORY, TENICIA ANN
Corporate officer. **PERSONAL:** Born Sep 28, 1933, Detroit, MI; married Karl Dwight Gregory; children: Karin Diane, Sheila Therese, Kurt David. **EDUCATION:** Wayne State U, BS 1955, MA 1961. **CAREER:** Detroit Pblc Sch, tchr 1957-63, 64-69; MDTA Washington DC, tchr 1963; Oakland Comm Clg, assc prof english 1969-75; Feminist Fed Credit Union, bd of dir/credit com mem 1971-75; WGPR Inc, vp/sta mgr. **ORGANIZATIONS:** Mem bd dir WGPR Inc 1975-; pub mem Greater Detroit Area Hlth Cncl; mem Zonta Intl Women's Orgnztn; mem bd dir Intl Masons Inc 1975-; mem Eastern Star of Int Masons Chptr; Delta Sigma Theta Sorority Inc Det Alumnae Chptr. **HONORS/ACHIEVEMENTS:** Spirit of detroit Detroit City Cncl 1977; Natl Black Women's Pol Ldrshp Causus Awrd 1980; 1983 Superstar Awrd Women In Cmnctn Inc 1983. **BUSINESS ADDRESS:** Vice President/Station Manager, WGPR Inc, 3140-6 E Jefferson, Detroit, MI 48207.

GREGORY, THEODORE MORRIS
Business executive. **PERSONAL:** Born May 21, 1952, Middletown, OH. **EDUCATION:** ColumbiaUniv NYC, BA 1970-74. **CAREER:** Salomon Brothers, vice pres 1975-, generalist sales 1974-75. **ORGANIZATIONS:** Mem Prince Hall Masons Boyer Lodge # 1 New York City 1975-; mem Alpha Phi Alpha Frat 1971-; mem football adv com ColumbiaUniv 1976-; mem bd of dir of alumni & assn ColumbiaUniv 1978-; Co-capt/All Ivy League/All East ColumbiaUniv Varsity Football Team 1971-73. **HONORS/ACHIEVEMENTS:** Merit award for participation in youth Motivation Task Force Central StateUniv Nat Alliance Of Businessmen 1975. **BUSINESS ADDRESS:** Salomon Brothers, 1 New York Plaza, 41st Floor, New York, NY 10004.

GREGORY, WILTON D.
Clergyman. **PERSONAL:** Born Dec 07, 1947, Chicago, IL; son of Wilton D Gregory and Ethel D DuncanGregory. **EDUCATION:** Niles College of Loyola Univ, BA 1969; St Mary of the Lake Seminary, STB 1971, MDiv 1973, STL 1974; Pontifical Liturgical Inst Sant'Anselmo Rome Italy, DSL 1980. **CAREER:** St Mary of the Lake Seminary, teacher;

Titular Bishop of Oliva; Archdiocese of Chicago, auxiliary bishop 1983-. **ORGANIZATIONS:** Mem Catholic Theol Soc of Amer, North Amer Acad of Liturgy, Midwestern Assoc of Spiritual Dirs; mem of NCCB/USCC comms as follows Bishops Comm on the Liturgy, Black Liturgy Subcomm of the Bishops' Comm on the Liturgy, Bishops' Comm on the Permanent Diaconate; bd of trustees Natl Shrine of the Immaculate Conception, US Catholic Bishops Adv Comm. **HONORS/ACHIEVEMENTS:** Chicago's First Black Bishop. **BUSINESS ADDRESS:** Auxiliary Bishop, Archdiocese of Chicago, PO Box 733, South Holland, IL 60473.

GRIER, ARTHUR E., JR.
Business executive. **PERSONAL:** Born Mar 21, 1943, Charlotte, NC; married Linda Clay; children: Anthony, Eugene Grier, III. **EDUCATION:** FL A&M U; Central Piedmont Comm Coll; Cincinnati Coll of Mortuary Sci, grad 1969. **CAREER:** Grier Funeral Svc, pres gen mgr. **ORGANIZATIONS:** Mem Funeral Dirs & Mort Assn of NC; Western Dist Funeral Dirs & Mort Assn of NC Inc; Nat Funeral Dir p Mort Assn of NC Inc; bd mem Nat FD; mem chmn Funeral Dirs & Mort Assn of NC Inc; mem Black Caucus; Big Bros Assn; Epsilon Nu Delta Mortuary Frat; Grier Heights Masonic Lodge #752; Ambassadors Social Club; bd dir Big Bros Assn; vice pres Western Dist Funeral Dirs; Eastside Cncl. **HONORS/ACHIEVEMENTS:** Ousts serv by funeral dirs & mort Assn of NC 1972; professional of yr Western Dist Funeral Dirs & Mort Assn of NC Inc 1974. **MILITARY SERVICE:** AUS sp/5-e5 1963-66. **BUSINESS ADDRESS:** 2310 Statesville Ave, Charlotte, NC 28206.

GRIER, BOBBY
Offensive backfield football coach. **PERSONAL:** Born Nov 10, 1942, Detroit, MI; married Wendy; children: Chris, Michael. **EDUCATION:** Univ of Iowa, Grad 1964. **CAREER:** Eastern MI, coaching staff; Boston Coll, offensive backfield coach; Northwestrn Univ, offensive coord; New England Patriots, college scout, offensive backfield coach. **HONORS/ACHIEVEMENTS:** In coll named honorable mention All-Big Ten as a junior & senior; led the team in rushing as a senior with 406 yds in 98 carries. **BUSINESS ADDRESS:** Offensive Backfield Coach, New England Patriots, Schaefer Stadium Route 1, Foxboro, MA 02035.

GRIER, DAVID ALAN
Actor. **PERSONAL:** Born Jun 30, 1956, Detroit, MI. **EDUCATION:** Univ of MI, BA 1978; Yale Univ Sch of Drama, MFA 1981. **CAREER:** Films, A Soldiers Story, Corpl Cobb 1982; Streamers Roger 1982; Beer Elliot 1984; From the Hip Steve 1986, Saigon, Rogers 1987; Theatre, (Broadway) Jackie Robinson, A Soldier's Play CJ Memphis Negro Ensemble Company, (Broadway) Dream Girls James "Thunder" Early; TV, All My Children. **HONORS/ACHIEVEMENTS:** Theatre World Awd for the musical "The First" 1981; The Golden Lion for best actor in a film Venice Film Festival for "Streamers" 1983. **BUSINESS ADDRESS:** Cherokee Stat PO Box 20075, New York, NY 10028.

GRIER, JENNIFER ANN
Educational administrator. **PERSONAL:** Born Apr 29, 1953, Gastonia, NC; daughter of Robert E Grier and Susie Kithcart Grier. **EDUCATION:** Univ of Rhode Island, BA 1975; Rhode Island Coll, MA 1983. **CAREER:** Atlanta Bd of Educ, comm organizer 1977-78; Rhode Island Educ Oppt Center, follow-up counselor 1980; Comm Coll of Rhode Island, counselor access prog 1981-83; Rhode Island Coll, coord minority prog 1983-86, asst dir of student life/minority affairs 1986-. **ORGANIZATIONS:** Mem NAACP, CPARI; Providence Christian Outreach Ministries, 1988-; vice president, URI Minority Alumni Council, 1987-. **HONORS/ACHIEVEMENTS:** Wrote and directed gospel play, "Thy Will Be Done", 1985; co-wrote and directed gospel play, "Tis The Season", 1987. **HOME ADDRESS:** 160 Calla St, Providence, RI 02905. **BUSINESS ADDRESS:** Assistant Director of Student Life for Minority Affairs, Rhode Island Coll, 600 Mt Pleasant Ave, Providence, RI 02908.

GRIER, ROOSEVELT (ROSEY GRIER)
Football player, actor, community activist. **PERSONAL:** Born Jul 14, 1932, Cuthbert, GA; son of Joseph Grier and Ruth Grier; married Margie Hanson; children: Roosevelt Kennedy, Cheryl Tubbs. **EDUCATION:** Pennsylvania State Univ, University Park PA, BS, 1955. **CAREER:** New York Giants, New York NY, professional football player, 1955-62; Los Angeles Rams, Los Angeles CA, professional football player, 1963-68; National General Corp, public relations director; television and film actor, 1968-77. **ORGANIZATIONS:** Mem, board of dir, Americans for Children Relief, Anti-Self-Destruction Program, Soulville Foundation, Direction Sports, Teammates, and Giant Step; affiliated with Kennedy Foundation for the Mentally Retarded. **HONORS/ACHIEVEMENTS:** Member of Los Angeles Rams' Fearsome Foursome, 1963-67; actor in films, including In Cold Blood, 1968, Skyjacked, 1972, and Evil in the Deep, 1977; actor on television shows, including The Danny Thomas Show, Kojak, Daniel Boone; host of The Rosey Grier Show and On Campus With Rosey; consultant to numerous committees on youth and senior citizens' affairs; author of The Rosey Grier Needlepoint Book for Men, Walker, 1973; author of autobiography The Gentle Giant, 1986; interviewed in And Still We Rise: Interviews With 50 Black Role Models, Gannett New Media Services, Inc, 1988. **MILITARY SERVICE:** US Army, 1957-59. **BUSINESS ADDRESS:** 11656 Montana, #301, Los Angeles, CA 90049. *

GRIER, ROSEY See GRIER, ROOSEVELT

GRIFFEY, DICK
Company executive. **PERSONAL:** Born Nov 16, 1943, Nashville, TN; children: 3 children. **EDUCATION:** Attended, TN State Univ. **CAREER:** Guys & Dolls Night Club, co-owner; Soul Train Records, partner; SOLAR Records, ceo/president. **ORGANIZATIONS:** Founding mem Black Concert Promoters Assn. **HONORS/ACHIEVEMENTS:** Solar listed 11th in 1986 Black Enterprise List of the Top 100 Black Owned Businesses. **BUSINESS ADDRESS:** Chief Executive Officer, Solar, 1635 N Cahuenga Blvd, 6th Floor, Los Angeles, CA 90028.

GRIFFEY, GEORGE KENNETH
Professional athlete. **PERSONAL:** Born Apr 10, 1950, Donora, PA; married Alberta Littleton; children: George Jr, Craig. **CAREER:** Cincinnati Reds, 1973-81; NY Yankees, outfielder/1st Base 1982-84. **HONORS/ACHIEVEMENTS:** 1980 Reds MVP & MVP of All-Star game; 1972 named to Eastern League All-Star team and in 1973 to Amer Assc All-Star team; tied Major League rec ord for most at-bats, game, since 1900, 7, June 13, 1975; tied Eastern League lead in double plays by outfielders with 6 and tied lead in err ors by outfielders with 15 in 1972; led Gulf Coast League outfielders in errors with 10 in 1969. **BUSINESS ADDRESS:** New York Yankees, Yankee Stadium, Bronx, NY 10451.

GRIFFIN, ARCHIE
Professional athlete. **PERSONAL:** Born Aug 24, 1954, Columbus, OH; married Loretta; children: Anthony, Andr. **EDUCATION:** Columbus OH State, BS 1976. **CAREER:** Cincinnati Bengals, running back, drafted in 1st round. **HONORS/ACHIEVEMENTS:** 1st coll player in hist win Heisman Trophy twice 1974, 75; gained 625 yrs rushing in 138 carriers for 3 TDs 45 yrds per carry adv; caught 6 passes for 138yds 86 yds per cath avg; All-Am 3 times; inducted into Football Hall of Fame.

GRIFFIN, BERTHA L.
Business owner. **PERSONAL:** Born Feb 08, 1930, Blythewood, SC; daughter of Dock Cunningham and Lula Cunningham; married James Griffin, Feb 01, 1947; children: Wayne Griffin, Denise E. Bryant, Geoffrey L. Griffin. **EDUCATION:** Greystone State Hospital, NJ state psychiatric technician training course, 1956; attended Riverton Bio-Analytical Laboratory School, Newark, NJ, 1959. **CAREER:** Greystone State Hospital, Newark, NJ, psychiatric technician, 1953-56; Drs. Burch and Williams, Newark, office mgr, 1957-63; Girl Friday Secretarial School, Newark, director, 1963-71; Newark Manpower Training, Newark, director, 1971-73; Porterhouse Cleaning, Edison, NJ, president, 1973-. **ORGANIZATIONS:** Sec, Natl Assn of Negro Business and Profl Women, 1961-63; member, Natl Key Women of Amer, 1978-83; sec, Edison, NJ Bd of Edn, 1978-84; delegate, White House Conf on Small Businesses, 1980; member, Small Business Unity Coun and NJ Braint Trust Comm on Small Business. **HONORS/ACHIEVEMENTS:** Minority Business Woman of the Year, Newark Minority Business Dev Ctr, 1984; Entrepreneur of the Year, YMCA of NJ, 1987, NJ Black Achievers, 1987, and Venture Magazine, 1988; recognition award, Natl Council of Negro Women, 1987. **BUSINESS ADDRESS:** Mrs Bertha L Griffin, Porterhouse Cleaning, 6 Moyse Pl, Edison, NJ 08820.

GRIFFIN, BETTY SUE
Educator. **PERSONAL:** Born Mar 05, 1943, Danville, KY. **EDUCATION:** Fisk Univ, BS 1965; OR State Univ, MEd 1976, EdD 1985. **CAREER:** Overbrook HS Philadelphia, teacher 1968-70; Model Cities Portland OR, placement dir 1970-72; OR State Univ, dir, field prog 1972-, prof educ psych, dir tchr training prog; KY Dept of Education, dir beginning teacher internship prog 1986-. **ORGANIZATIONS:** Mem Outstanding Young Women of Ame 1977; ed consult Portland Public Schools 1978-; mem KY Col Assoc 1979, Delta Sigma Theta, Soroptomist; ed consult Portland Comm Coll 1984-; keynote speker Black Achievers Scholarship Prog; mem KY Natl Honor Soc, Morehead State Univ. **HONORS/ACHIEVEMENTS:** Bd mem OR Governors Commiss 1978; Danford Fellow OR State Univ; mem Faculty Networking Stanford Univ 1980; OR Governors Commn on Black Affairs 1985; Governors Scholars Selection Committee 1986. **HOME ADDRESS:** 509 Russell St, Danville, KY 40422. **BUSINESS ADDRESS:** Dir Internship, Kentucky Dept of Education, Frankfort, KY 40602.

GRIFFIN, BOOKER
Broadcast journalist. **PERSONAL:** Born Oct 01, 1938, Gary, IN; married Lynette. **EDUCATION:** Bladwin-Wallace Coll, BA psychology. **CAREER:** Radio Sta KGFJ in LA, brdcst journ news dir comm rel dir; reviews news to be broadcast designs executes various comm relations progs coord pub serv announcements & sta serv to listeners. **HONORS/ACHIEVEMENTS:** Extraordinarily popular & news commentator; pub speaker in LA area; feature columist for LA Sentinel Newspaper.

GRIFFIN, EDNA WESTBERRY
Retired educator. **PERSONAL:** Born Nov 25, 1907, Philadelphia, PA; married William E Griffin (deceased). **EDUCATION:** Univ PA, BS 1931; Columbia Univ, MA 1942; additional study. **CAREER:** Temple Univ Philadelphia Public Schs, teacher, supr cons; Civic Ctr Museum Univ Akron, presently retired. **ORGANIZATIONS:** Mem Philadelphia Teachers Assn pres 1957-60; chmn 1st of Race; (1st of Race) Classroom Tchrs SE PA; ethics comm PA State Educ Assn; 1st of Race delegate State Natl Convens; numerous coms; Natl Educ Assn; Amer Tchrs Assn; bd dirs CARE; mem Student Welfare Council; 1 of founders of Haesler Fund; mem Alpha Kappa Alpha, AAUW, NAACP; bd Natl Council for Accreditation of Tchr Educ Coll. **HONORS/ACHIEVEMENTS:** Afro-Amer Newspaper Awd; Awd Radio Station WDAS; Awd Natl Sor Phi Delta Kappa, Alpha Kappa Alpha, Natl Council Negro Women, Bus & Professional Women, AME Church, Monumental Baptist Church.

GRIFFIN, ERVIN VEROME
Educator. **PERSONAL:** Born May 15, 1949, Welch, WV; son of Roy Griffin and Martha Griffin; children: Ervin Jr. **EDUCATION:** Bluefield State Coll, BS 1971; Western IL Univ, MS 1974; VA Polytechnic Inst & State Univ, Cert of Advanced Grad Study in Higher Educ 1979, Doctorate of Education 1980. **CAREER:** McDowell Co Bd of Educ, spec educ teacher 1971-72; Western IL Univ, asst head resident advisor 1972-74; Southwest VA Comm Coll, dir of student financial aid 1974-78 (first Black admin); VA Polytechnic Inst & State Univ, counselor 1978-79; Southwest VA Comm Coll, coord of cocurricular activities 1979-84; Patrick Henry Comm Coll, (first Black admin) dir of student develop 1984-89; West VA State Coll, vice pres of student affairs, 1989-. **ORGANIZATIONS:** Mem Amer College Personnel Assoc; mem Amer Assoc of Non-White Concerns; mem Amer Personnel & Guidance Assoc; elected to Comm XI Directorate Body Amer College Personnel Assn 1984-87; bd of dirs Tazewell Co Helpline 1984-86; Martinsville-Henry Co NAACP 1985-86; Martinsville-Henry Co Men's Roundtable 1985-86. **HONORS/ACHIEVEMENTS:** Who's Who Among College Students Bluefield State Coll 1971; Outstanding Young men of America Jaycees SVCC 1978; multiple publications and presentations including "Educational Opportunity Programs—Educative or Not?" 1980; "The Pareto Optimality Problem" Minority Educ 1981; "Adults Making the Commitment to Return to School" 1985; "Cocurricular Activities Programming, A Tool for Retention and Collaboration" 1985; Graduate Fellowship Western IL Univ 1972-74; Innovative Practices and Devel in Vocational Sex Equality, a monograph 1988; The Alliance for Excellence: A Model for Articulation Between the Community Coll and the Black Church 1988. **HOME ADDRESS:** Box 330, Institute, WV 25112. **BUSINESS ADDRESS:** Vice Pres for Student Affairs, West Virginia State Coll, Box 188, Institute, WV 25112.

GRIFFIN, EURICH Z.
Attorney. **PERSONAL:** Born Nov 21, 1938, Washington; son of Eurich and Lucille; divorced; children: Jennifer, Eurich III. **EDUCATION:** Howard U, BA cum laude high honors in economics 1967; Harvard Law School, JD 1970. **CAREER:** Carlton Fields Ward Emmanueal Smith & Cutler PA, atty; US Fifth Cir Court of Appeals Judge Paul H Roneyd law clk 1971. **ORGANIZATIONS:** Mem ABA; Natl Bar Assn; Hillsborough Co FL Bar Assn; pres Harvard Club of the West Coast FL 1974-; mem St Petersburgh Kiwanis Club 1971-74. **MILITARY SERVICE:** USAF airman 2nd class 1959-63. **BUSINESS ADDRESS:** Carlton, Fields, Ward, PO Box 3239, Tampa, FL 33601.

GRIFFIN, GERALD
Business associate. **PERSONAL:** Born Oct 01, 1944, Chicago, IL; married Laura Dominic Ingersol. **EDUCATION:** DeLaSalle Inst, diploma 1962; IL State Univ, BA 1966, MS 1970, ABD 1974-82. **CAREER:** Joliet IL Public Schools, instructor 1966-69, title III coord 1969-70, principal 1970-73; IL State Univ Teacher Training Ctr, dir instructor 1973-74; Univ of New Mexico-Washington, sen mgmt dir 1977-79; Miranda Associates, sr assoc 1979-. **ORGANIZATIONS:** Mem IL Accreditation Assn Team 1970, 1971; mem Mid-West IL Office of Ed Advis Council 1971-74; pres Will Co Big Brothers Bd of Dirs 1972-75; rsch consultant Univ of MD Competency Study 1979; grant review panelist Office of Education/HEW 1979; consultant Washington Youth Problems Comm 1980-81; vice pres Southwest Comm Hse Bd of Dirs 1980-83; sec/treas Bd of Dirs MUSCLE Inc 1980-; mem WA Adv Neighborhood Comm 2d 1980-; elected to WA DC Adv Neighborhood Commiss Dist 1980-82. **HONORS/ACHIEVEMENTS:** Nomination to Phi Delta Kappa 1969; nomination for Outstanding Young Educator 1970; awd Outstanding Young Men in America 1973; nomination to Kappi Delta Pi 1974; fellowship Amer Assn of School Admin 1974; Natl Fellowship Univ Council of Educ Admin 1975-76; Outstanding Prog Develop Miranda Assoc 1983. **BUSINESS ADDRESS:** Senior Associate, Miranda Associates, Inc, 401 M St SW, East Tower, Washington, DC 20024.

GRIFFIN, JAMES STAFFORD
Retired law enforcement. **PERSONAL:** Born Jul 06, 1917, St Paul, MN; son of William Griffin and Lorena Waters Griffin; married Edna S; children: Linda Garrett, Helen Anderson, Vianne (dec). **EDUCATION:** Attended St Thomas College, St Paul, MN, WV State College, and MI State Univ, East Lansing, MI; Northwestern Univ, Evanston, IL, 1973; Metro State Univ, St Paul, MN, BA, 1974. **CAREER:** St Paul Police Dept, patrolman, 1941-54, police sergeant, 1955-68, spec, 1968-70, captain, 1970, station commander, dep chief, 1972-84; retired. **ORGANIZATIONS:** Bd of trustees St Paul Police Benevolent Assoc presently; bd of dir St Paul Municipal Basketball Assoc, mem Amer Legion Post 449, Hallie Q Brown Comm Ctr, NAACP, St Paul Police Fed, Big Brothers Inc, HIRE, St Paul Bd of Ed; life mem Kappa Alpha Psi; mem Intl Assoc of Chiefs of Police, NOBLE; treas St Paul Bd of Educ; mem vestry St Philips Epis Church. **HONORS/ACHIEVEMENTS:** Author "Blacks in the St Paul Police & Fire Dept 1885-1976"; article about St Paul Police Dept 1975 Fall ed MN History; Outstanding Police Work Natl Urban League 1949; Vol Work with Youths HQ Brown Ctr 1952; WCCO Good Neighbor Awd 1974; Kappa Man of the Year 1974; 1st black sgt, capt & dep chief of police State of MN; Highest Ranking Black Police Officer selected by competitive written civil serv examination in metro police dept in US 1972; article on minority recruitment in the Police Chief 1977; received St Paul Urban League SE Hall Award for outstanding community service; received NOBLE (Natl Association of Black Law Enforcement Executives) Natl Walter E Lawson Award for outstanding community service; Significant Contribution to the Social History of St Paul citation, St Phillips Episcopal Church and Kappa Alpha Psi St Paul/Minneapolis chapter; outstanding school board member from Ramsey County citation, MN State Fair, 1978; cited as outstanding school bd mem, Mn Association of School Bds, 1986; Distinguished Alumni Award, North Central Province of Kappa Alpha Psi, 1986-87; Central High School Stadium in St Paul renamed the Jim Griffin Stadium, 1987; honorary Doctor of Letters, Concordia College, St Paul, MN, 1988; Spurgeon Award for outstanding community service and career achievement, 1989; elected to MN High School Football Coaches Hall of Fame, 1989. **BUSINESS ADDRESS:** Board of Education, Saint Paul Public Schools, 360 Colborne St, Saint Paul, MN 55102.

GRIFFIN, JEAN THOMAS
Educator. **PERSONAL:** Born Dec 26, 1937, Atlantic City, NJ; married James A Griffin; children: Lillian Hasan, Tallie Thomas, Karen Brondidge, James A IV, Wayne. **EDUCATION:** Temple Univ, BA Psychol 1969, MEd Psychol 1971, EdD Ed Psychol 1973; Natl Training Lab, training internship 1973; Yale Univ, clinical internship 1974-75; Univ of PA, physicians Alcohol Educ Training Prog 1976. **CAREER:** Yale Univ, asst prof dir 1972-76; Solomon Canter Fuller MHC, clinical dir 1976-77; Union Grad School, core prof 1976-; Univ MA Boston, assoc prof 1979-. **ORGANIZATIONS:** Comm on racism & sexism Natl Educ Assn 1975; women's career development Polaroid Corp 1977; trainer Natl Training Lab 1977-83; pres of bd Women Inc 1977-84; consultant/ed Univ OK College of Nursing 1978-81; fellow Amer Orthopsychiatric Assn 1978-85; assoc of blk psych Eastern Representative 1979; consultant/training Bank of Boston 1980-84; racism workshop Boston State Coll 1981; adv to dir Roxbury Comm Sch 1981-82. **HONORS/ACHIEVEMENTS:** Grant Prof Growth & Develop 1974; Fellow Mellon Faculty Develop Awd 1982; article West African & Blk Amer Working Women published Journal Black Psychol 1982; chapter in Contemporary Blk Marriage 1984; numerous publications including Exploding the Popular Myths Review of Black Women in the Labor Force Equal Times 1982. **HOME ADDRESS:** Univ MA Boston, Boston, MA 02125. **BUSINESS ADDRESS:** Associate Professor, Univ of MA-Boston, 77 Tampa St, Mattapan, MA 02126.

GRIFFIN, JOHNNY
Professional jazz musician. **PERSONAL:** Born Apr 24, 1928, Chicago, IL. **EDUCATION:** Du Sable High School Chicago. **CAREER:** Lionel Hampton Band, musician 1945-47; Joe Morris Band, musician 1947-57; Monk's Band, musician 1958; Johnny Griffin, jazz musician 1959-.

GRIFFIN, LOUIS G., III
Curator. **PERSONAL:** Born Sep 14, 1943, Bremerton, WA; divorced. **EDUCATION:** TX Tech U, BA 1965;Univ MO Columbia, MA 1969; TX Tech U, MA 1970. **CAREER:** Univ KS, bibliographer 1969-72; KS CollectionUniv KS, curator 1972. **ORGANIZATIONS:** Am AssnUniv Profs; Soc Am Archivist; Western Hist Assn; Orgn Am Hists; KS Libr Assn Field Humanist KS Com for Humanities 1973-; adv com DouglasCo Bicentennial Com; presUniv KS Chap Am AssnUniv Profs 1975-76. **HONORS/ACHIEVEMENTS:** Phi Alpha Theta History Hon 1967.

GRIFFIN, LULA BERNICE
Educator. **PERSONAL:** Born Oct 16, 1949, Saginaw, MI. **EDUCATION:** Tuskegee Inst, BSN 1967-71;Univ MI, Addtl Grad Study 1973-74; Med Clg of GA, MS Nrsng 1976-77. **CAREER:** Univ AL Hosp B'Ham AL, stf rn psychiatry 1971-73; Comm Hosp Birmingham AL, stf rn; Cooper Green Hosp Birmingham AL, stf rn high risk Nrsng 1982-83; Lawson State Comm Clg Birmingham AL, nrsng instr Level II coord 1974-85. **ORGANIZATIONS:** Mem Chi Eta Phi Sorority Inc 1969; Am Nurses Assc; AL State Nurse Assc; Sixth Ave Bapt Ch; Help One Another Clb Inc 1981; fin sec Tuskegee Inst Nurses Alumni 1982; vol diaster serv Am Red Cross 1984-85. **HONORS/ACHIEVEMENTS:** Biographee Who's Who Among Blck Am, Outstndng Young Women of Am 1984; certified psychiatric & mental hlth nurse Am Nurses Assc Cert Bd for Psychiatric& Mental Hlth Practice 1985-89. **BUSINESS ADDRESS:** Nurse Instructor, Lawson State Comm Clg, 526 Beacon Crest Cir, Birmingham, AL 35209.

GRIFFIN, PERCY LEE
District supervisor. **PERSONAL:** Born Dec 10, 1945, Jackson, MS; divorced; children: Gregory T. **EDUCATION:** Jackson St Univ, BS; IN Univ, MS Recreation Admin. **CAREER:** Jackson State & Univ Alumni Assn of Indianapolis, vp; Detroit Lions, 1969; Indianapolis Capitols, football player 1969-74; Indianapolis Caps Pro-Football Team, owner, pres 1976-; City of Indpls, distr supv, admin sewer maint div. **ORGANIZATIONS:** Mem Small Bus Assn. **HONORS/ACHIEVEMENTS:** Small College All-Amer Pitts Courier. **BUSINESS ADDRESS:** Administrator, Department of Public Works, 3915 E 21st St, Indianapolis, IN 46218.

GRIFFIN, PLES ANDREW
Educator. **PERSONAL:** Born Apr 05, 1929, Pasadena, CA; married Lora Lee Jones. **EDUCATION:** Univ CA, BA 1956; USC, MS 1964. **CAREER:** CA Dept of Educ, chief office intergroup relations; US Office of Educ, consultant 1969-; Pasadena City Coll, counselor 1964-66; Pasadena School Dist, educator, counselor 1960-66; Pasandena Settlement Assn, exec dir 1953-59. **ORGANIZATIONS:** Mem Nat All Balck Sch Educators; Assn CA Sch Adminstr; AssnCA Intergroup Rel Educators; mem NAACP Sacramento Urban League; Alpha Phi Alpha; Episc Ch. **HONORS/ACHIEVEMENTS:** Listed in Who's Who in the W 1967-68, 1972-73. **MILITARY SERVICE:** UAS military intell 1953-55. **BUSINESS ADDRESS:** 721 Capitol Mal, Sacramento, CA 95814.

GRIFFIN, RAY EUGENE
Professional athlete. **PERSONAL:** Born Jun 29, 1956, Columbus, OH; married Lynn; children: Raymond Jr, Rashad. **EDUCATION:** OH St Univ. **CAREER:** Cincinnati Bengels, cornerback 1978-85. **HONORS/ACHIEVEMENTS:** Mem of Cinc Super Bowl club in 1982; four letters as def back at OH St Univ; All-Amer as a sr; played AL in the Sugar Bowl; played in two Rose Bowls and one Orange Bowl.

GRIFFIN, RICHARD GEORGE
Librarian. **PERSONAL:** Born Jun 24, 1927, Tampa, FL; married Dolores; children: Felicia Rene, Eric Hubert. **EDUCATION:** Morehouse Coll, AB 1949; Atlanta U, MLS 1951; Sch of LawUniv of TN, postgrad 1958. **CAREER:** TX So U, circulation libr 1950-54, univ libr 1954-57, instr govt 1953-57; Knoxville Coll, asst libr 1957-58; NY Inst Tech Old Westbury, dir libr 1959-79; Wilmington Coll New Castle DE, libr consult 1968-71; US Merchan Marine Acad Kings Pt NY, chief libr 1979-. **ORGANIZATIONS:** Mem NY Libr Assn; Am Assn Univ Prof; ALA; Assn for Higher Edn. **MILITARY SERVICE:** AUS 1946-47. **BUSINESS ADDRESS:** US Merchant Marine Academy, Kings Point, NY 11024.

GRIFFIN, RONALD C.
Attorney, educator. **PERSONAL:** Born Aug 17, 1943, Washington; married Vicky Lynn Tredway; children: David R, Jason R. **EDUCATION:** Hampton Inst, BS 1965; Harvard Univ, attended 1965; Howard Univ, JD 1968; Univ VA, LLM 1974. **CAREER:** Office Corp Counsel Dist of Columbia Govt, legal intern 1968-69, legal clerk 1969-70, asst corp counsel 1970; the JAG School AUS, instructor 1970-74; Univ of OR, asst prof; Notre Dame Univ, visiting prof 1981-82; Washburn Univ, prof of law. **ORGANIZATIONS:** Mem Legal Educ Com Young Lawyers Sect Amer Bar Assn; Young Lawyers Liaison Legal Educ & Admission to Bar Sect Amer Bar Assn; mem Bankruptcy Com Fed Bar Assn; mem OR Consumer League 1974-75; grievance examiner Mid-West Region EEOfC 1984-85; mediator N E Kansas Region Consumer Protection Complaints Better Business Bureau 1984-87, pres 1987-88. **HONORS/ACHIEVEMENTS:** Rockefeller Found Grant; Outstanding Young Men of Amer Awd 1971; Outstanding Educators of Amer Awd 1973; Intl Men of Achievement 1976; Outstanding Young Man of Amer Awd 1979; William O Douglas Awd Outstanding Prof 1985-86. **MILITARY SERVICE:** AUS capt 1970-74. **BUSINESS ADDRESS:** Associate Professor, WashburnUniv, School of Law, Topeka, KS 66621.

GRIFFIN, THOMAS J.
Clergyman. **PERSONAL:** Born Jul 04, 1917, Coila, MS; married Geneva Estella Brown; children: Robert Eugene, Thomas J. **EDUCATION:** Jarvis Christ Coll Hawkins TX, BA cum laude 1947; Garrett Theol SemEvanston IL, MDiv 1950; Jarvis Christ Coll Hawkins TX, DD 1978. **CAREER:** Jarvis Christ Coll Hawkins TX, pastor instr 1979-; Christ Ch Disciples of Chirst Indpls, dir of reconcil 1969-78;Univ Christ Ch Houston, pastor 1961-69; United Christ Missionary Soc Indlps, dir ch comm 1957-61; E 6th St Christ Ch Oklahoma City, pastor 1951-56. **ORGANIZATIONS:** Mayor's commn on civil rights City Govt Oklahoma City 1953-56; consult Ofc of Educ Opportunity Houston 1965-69; consult 6th Pan African Congress Tanzania E Africa 1974; bd mem NAACP 1951-56; vice pres TX Assn of Christ Ch 1962-63; dir Change Though Invilvement 1965. **HONORS/ACHIEVEMENTS:** Shepherd of dist awd Nat Christ Missionary Conv 1960; What It Means to be A Negro in TX Today Inter-Faith Movement on Civil Rights 1964; alumni serv awd Jarvis Coll Nat Alumni Assn 1974; cit for serv rendered Nat Reconcil 1976. **BUSINESS ADDRESS:** Jarvis Christian College, Hawkins, TX 75765.

GRIFFIN-JOHNSON, LORRAINE ANTIONETTE
City official. **PERSONAL:** Born Apr 15, 1951, Tyler, TX; married Willie Johnson. **EDUCATION:** Tyler Jr Coll, AA 1971; Stephen F Austin State Univ, BSE 1973; Univ of TX, MA 1977. **CAREER:** TX Comm for the Blind, orientation & mobility specialist 1973-75; Region VII Education Service Ctr, educ consultant 1975-79; City of Tyler, planner 1979-80,comm development dir 1980-83; City of Wichita, dir human resources dept 1983-. **ORGANIZATIONS:** Basileus anti basileus parliamentarian Alpha Kappa Alpha 1972-; Top Ladies of Dis-

tinction 1976-; member SRS Advisory Council 1983-; member Chamber of Commerce employ and training task force 1983-; member Community Task force 1983; Black Women's Conference 1983-. **HONORS/ACHIEVEMENTS:** Who's Who Among Students in Colleges & Univs Stephen F Austin Univ 1972-73; Outstanding Young Women in America 1977; Outstanding Alumni Tyler Jr College Alumni 1982; loaned exec United Way 1982; KS Leadership/Class 1985. **BUSINESS ADDRESS:** Dir Human Resources, City of Wichita, 455 N Main St, Wichita, KS 67202.

GRIFFITH, BARBARA J.
Educator. **PERSONAL:** Born Sep 09, 1935, Cincinnati; married Maurice; children: Marcus, Sean, Keir. **EDUCATION:** Univ Cincinnati, EdD 1974, M 1969. **CAREER:** Science Resource Inc, curr dir 1969; Univ of Cincinnati, instructor educ consultant to vice pres co-dir 1970-74; Xavier Univ, asst prof 1974; Univ of AZ Tucson, special events coordinator 1979-. **ORGANIZATIONS:** Mem Intl Reading Assn; Montessori Soc; Nat Counc Tchrs Engl; Phi Delta Kappa; Coll Tchrs Reading Urban League Guild; trust Comm Chest progs & allocations Planning bd com; Alpha Kappa Alpha Sor; Jack & Jill Inc Am; St Mark's Cath Ch speaker Intl Reading Assn NY 1978.

GRIFFITH, ELWIN JABEZ
Educator. **PERSONAL:** Born Mar 02, 1938; married Norma Joyce Rollins; children: Traci. **EDUCATION:** Long Island Univ, BA 1960; Brooklyn Law Sch, JD 1963; NYU, LLM 1964. **CAREER:** Modern HS, teacher 1955-56; Chase Manhattan Bank, asst couns 1964-71; Cleveland Marshall Law Sch, asst prof 1968; Tchrs Ins & Annuity Assn, asst consl 1971-72; Drake Univ, asst dean & asst prof 1972-73; Univ of Cincinnati Coll of Law, assoc dean & prof 1973-78; DePaul Law School, dean & prof 1978-85; FLorida State Univ Coll of Law, prof 1986-. **ORGANIZATIONS:** Barbados Indp Com 1966; Bedford-Stuyvesant Jr C of C 1970-72; mem Black Exec Exchg Prof 1971; mem NY State Bar Assn; Amer Bar Assn. **HONORS/ACHIEVEMENTS:** Outstanding Young Men of Amer 1972; publ "Final Payment & Warranties Under the Uniform Commercial Code" 1973; "Truth-in-Lending & Real Estate Transactions" 1974; "Some Rights & Disabilities of Aliens" 1975; "Deportation of Aliens - Some Aspects" 1975; Who's Who in Amer Law 1977; "The Creditor, Debtor & the Fourteenth Amendment Some Aspects" 1977. **BUSINESS ADDRESS:** Law Professor, Florida StateUniv, College of Law, Tallahassee, FL 33306.

GRIFFITH, EZRA EDWARD
Physician. **PERSONAL:** Born Feb 18, 1942; married Brigitte Jung. **EDUCATION:** Harvard Univ BA 1963; Univ of Strasbourg, MD 1973. **CAREER:** French Polyclinic Hlth Ctr, intern 1973-74; Albert Einstein Coll, chief res psych 1974-77; Yale Univ Schl of Med, asst prof 1977, assoc prof of Psychiatry & Afro-American Studies 1982-; CT Mental Health Center, assoc dir 1986-. **ORGANIZATIONS:** Mem Black Psychs of Am; Am Psych Assn; Am Med Assn FALK Flwshp Am Psych Assn 1975-77; traveling fellow Solomon Fuller Inst 1976; fellow WK Kellogg Found 1980. **HONORS/ACHIEVEMENTS:** Fellow American Psychiatric Assoc; mem & editorial bd "Hospital and Community Psychiatry"; editor-in-chief "Yale Psychiatric Quarterly". **BUSINESS ADDRESS:** Assoc Professor of Psychiatry, and Afro-American Studies, Yale University, School of Medicine-34 Park St, New Haven, CT 06519.

GRIFFITH, JOHN A.
Utilities manager. **PERSONAL:** Born Dec 14, 1936, Greensburg, PA; married Patricia Cuff; children: Pamela, Gail, Jennifer. **EDUCATION:** INUniv of PA, BS Educ 1960; Fairleigh Dickinson U, MBA Mgmt 1985. **CAREER:** Dept of Pblc Asst Beaver Co PA, soc worker 1960-1962; Allencrest Juvenile Detention Cntr Beaver PA, cnslr 1963-64; Nutley Pub Sch NJ, tchr coach 1964-68; Montclair Pub Sch NJ, gdnc cnslr 1968-1969; PSE&G, mgr prsnl dev. **ORGANIZATIONS:** Mem Bd Natl Bnk Advsry Bd 1979-; Intercl Cncl Bus Oprtnts 1985-; Edges Inc 1970-; Am Soc Training & Dev 1980-; mem pres Bd Ed Montclair NJ 1979-85; trustee Urban League of Essex Co NJ 1970-. **HONORS/ACHIEVEMENTS:** 75 achvrs awrd Black Media Inc Corporate Comm Serv. **MILITARY SERVICE:** AUS sp 4th cls. **HOME ADDRESS:** 23 Stephen St, Montclair, NJ 07042.

GRIFFITH, JOHN H.
Educator. **PERSONAL:** Born Aug 28, 1931, Pittsburgh; married Euzelia Cooper; children: Nell, Ronald (dec). **EDUCATION:** LincolnUniv PA, BA 1954f AtlantaUniv Atlanta, Ma 1964; US InstnlUniv San Diego, PhD 1979. **CAREER:** Coahoma Jr Coll, Clarksdale MS, instructor, basketball coach 1955-63; Atlanta Univ, instructor summer school 1964; City School Dist of Rochester NY, counselor manpower devel & training program 1964-66; head counselor 1966-67; dir of testing 1967-68; planning & research dir 1968-71; San Diego City Schools, asst dir planning & research dept 1971-76, dir planning & research 1976-84, dir of research 1984-. **ORGANIZATIONS:** Phi Delta Kappa Educ Frat 1966-; CA Tchr Assn San Diego Sch Admin Assn; Amer Assoc of School Administrators; Amer Educ Research Assoc. **HONORS/ACHIEVEMENTS:** Rockefeller Found Suprt Training Internship 1970-71. **BUSINESS ADDRESS:** 4100 Normal St, San Diego, CA 92103.

GRIFFITH, REGINALD WILBERT
Architect. **PERSONAL:** Born Aug 10, 1930, New York, NY; married Linden James; children: Courtney, Crystal, Cyrice. **EDUCATION:** MCP MIT, 1969; MIT, BA 1960; Inst of Intl Edn, traveling flw in W Africa 1961-62. **CAREER:** Reg Griffith Asso, owner city planner architech; Am Inst of Planners, 1st vice pres 1977-; Nat Capitol Planning Commn, commr v chmn 1974-; Howard Ud profl1970-; howard u, chmn dept of city reg plng 1971-74; MICCO, dep exec dir 1967-70; boston redevel auth, archt 1962-67. **ORGANIZATIONS:** Bd of dir Am Soc of Planning Ofcls 1974-76; bd od dir AIP Found 1971-; bd dir mem Am Inst of Archt; Georgetown Day Sch 1972; chmn Urban Trans Com of Consortium ofUniv 1972-73; mem MIT Educ Cncl 1971-F AIP Bd of Examiners 1972-. **MILITARY SERVICE:** AUS 1st lt 1956-58. **BUSINESS ADDRESS:** 1200 15th St NW, Washington, DC 20005.

GRIFFITH, THOMAS LEE, JR.
Superior court judge. **PERSONAL:** Born Mar 05, 1902, Albia, IA; married Portia Louise Broyles; children: Thomas Lee III, Greta Louise, Liza Jane. **EDUCATION:** Univ So CA, 1922-26; Law Sch, 1925-26; Southwestern U, LLB 1928. **CAREER:** Admitteed to CA Bar 1931; Pvt prac Los Angeles; Los Angeles, mun ct judge 1953-69; Los Angeles, supr ct judge 1969-. **ORGANIZATIONS:** Mem Am Judicatur Soc; Los Angeles Co Muncpl Ct Presideng Judge 1962; chmn Mun Judge Assn 1968-; Am Bar Assn; Los Agneles Bar Assn; mem Omega Psi Phi; Rep; Bapt. **BUSINESS ADDRESS:** 111 N Hill St, Los Angeles, CA 90012.

GRIFFITH, VERA VICTORIA
Educator, city official. **PERSONAL:** Born May 30, 1920, Pittsburgh, PA. **EDUCATION:** Univ of Pittsburgh, BS 1942; Wayne State, MI teaching cert 1943;Univ of MI, MA 1954;Univ of MI, addl stud. **CAREER:** City of Detroit, deputy dir consumer affairs; Detroit Bd of Educ, elementary school admin 1956-74, elementary school teacher 1943-56. **ORGANIZATIONS:** Dir local sch Headstart Prof Detroit 1967-68; taugh & admin summer sch prog Detroit; thcr Evening Sch for Adults Detroit; asst dir Comm Arts Prog at MI State Fair; Alpha Kappa Alpha; Urban Alliance; Am Civic Liberties Assn; vchmn 13th Dist Dem Orgn; past pres bd trst Detroit Optometric Inst &Clinic. **BUSINESS ADDRESS:** Consumer Affairs Dept 312 City, Detroit, MI 48226.

GRIFFITHS, BERTIE BERNARD
Educator. **PERSONAL:** Born Jul 14, 1930, Darliston, Jamaica;married Barbara Jane Heslop; children: Bradley B, Bonnie J. **EDUCATION:** Univ of WI, BS 1958, MS 1960; Univ of West Indies, PhD 1972. **CAREER:** Univ of West Indies 1961-74; Univ of So AL, assoc prof 1974-75; Univ of West Indies, lecturer 1976-77; Oral Roberts Univ, assoc prof 1978-. **ORGANIZATIONS:** Adv Caribbean Students to US Univs 1962-77; adv Scientific Consultants 1968-77; adv Jamaica Bureau of Standards 1976-78; mem Amer Soc for Microbiology1958-; mem The Amer Soc of Tropical Medicine & Hygiene 1979-; mem Bixby Optomist Club 1983-; mem Amer Assoc of Dental Schs 1982-. **HONORS/ACHIEVEMENTS:** Fellowship Natl Inst of Health 1960-61; Fellowship Rockefeller USA 1963; Indefinite tenure Univ of WG 1977; Fellowship (offered but not accepted) Pan Am Health Organ 1977. **HOME ADDRESS:** 11405 So 98th E Ave, Bixby, OK 74008. **BUSINESS ADDRESS:** Associate Professor, ORU School of Medicine, 8181 S Lewis Ave, Tulsa, OK 74137.

GRIFFITHS, PEGGY S.
Attorney. **PERSONAL:** Born Apr 23, 1925, Roanoke, VA; married Norman; children: Stephanie, Michael, Manel, Dwight, Arthur, Deneen. **EDUCATION:** Howard U, 1946; Howard U, JD 1949; Cath U, MA 1958. **CAREER:** Sen Adlai Stevenson of IL, atty leg asst; Appeals Review Bd US Civil Serv Commn, former chmn 1968-77; US Dept of Labor, atty adv 1960-68; VA, spl asst to dir person 1968; Howard U, instr 1947-51, 55-58; Am Univ Cairo Egypt, vis lect 1955-58. **ORGANIZATIONS:** Mem Nat Bar Assn; Am Bar Assn; chmn Parish Sch Bd of St Francis DeSales Sch for 2 yrs; chrmn Commn on Christian Educ for the DC Archdiocese. **HONORS/ACHIEVEMENTS:** Recip Fellowship in Congress Rel; mem Ph Gamma Mu Nat Honor Soc in Soc Sci.

GRIGGS, ANTHONY
Journalist. **PERSONAL:** Born Aug 13, 1946, Chicago, IL. **EDUCATION:** Eastern IL U, BS 1968. **CAREER:** Bell Tel Lab, pub rel 1975-; Ebony Mag, jrnlst 1974-75; Nashville TN, rptr 1974-75; Chicago Dailey Defender, 1970-74; Sir George WmsUniv Libr, 1968-70. **HONORS/ACHIEVEMENTS:** Musical achvmt Waukegan-Lake Co Philharmic Soc 1964; 1st place LincolnUniv 1974; Outstng Yng Man of Am 1977.

GRIGGS, ANTHONY
Professional football player. **PERSONAL:** Born Feb 12, 1960, Lawton, OK. **EDUCATION:** OH State Univ, attended; Villanova Univ, degree in communications. **CAREER:** Philadelphia Eagles, 1982-86; Cleveland Browns, linebacker 1986-. **BUSINESS ADDRESS:** Linebacker, Cleveland Browns, Cleveland Stadium, Cleveland, OH 44114.

GRIGGS, BERTRAM S.
Association executive. **PERSONAL:** Born Feb 12, 1921, Birmingham; married Evelyn; children: Stephen III, Diane. **EDUCATION:** Morehouse Coll Atlanta, BA 1942;Univ So CA Ch Social Work, grad cert 1951;Univ So CA Sch Publ Admin, grad work 1951-52; HarvardUniv Law Sch Cntr Crim Justice, 1970-71. **CAREER:** CA Inst for Men, super 1971-; Parole & Comm Serv Div, parole admin 1967-71; Sacramento Bca, dir serv Cntr prog 1966-67; Dept Corrections LA, regnl adminstr 1961-63; Narcotic Treatment Control Unit LA, asst dist supr 1956-61; Dept Corrections LA, parole agt 1952-56; Commercial Firms, pub relunit mgr; Office Price Adminstr, invest; LA Co, social worker. **ORGANIZATIONS:** Consult Dept Housing & Urban Devel Washington DC 1967; consult Dept Corrections DC 1969-70; consult Dept Corrections MA 1973; consult Comm on Accreditation forCorrectiosn Rockville MD 1979-; reg soc worker; mem CA Probation Parol & Correctional Assn; mem Chino Rotary Club; mem bd dir Volutneers of Am; membd dir W End United Fund; mem Prog Alcoholics & Drug Addicts; Criminal Justice Council LA Co 1969-70; Inst of Gov Studies Case Studies in Intergov Rel The CA Serv Cntr Prog. **HONORS/ACHIEVEMENTS:** Publ "Community-Based Correctional Prog a survey & analysis". **MILITARY SERVICE:** AUS. **BUSINESS ADDRESS:** 14901 S Central Ave, Chino, CA 91710.

GRIGGS, HARRY KINDELL, SR.
Educational administrator. **PERSONAL:** Born Mar 26, 1910, Reidsville, NC; married Mary S; children: Harry K Jr, Gary M. **EDUCATION:** Shaw Univ, BS 1934; Univ of MI, MA 1948, 1952. **CAREER:** Roanoke Inst, teacher 1934-36; Yanceville School, teacher 1936-40; Riedsville City Elementary & High Schools, teacher 1940-48, high school principal 1948-59, retired sr high school principal 1959-74. **ORGANIZATIONS:** Mem bd dir United Fund 1960-70; mem Reidsville C of C 1968-87; mem Natl Lib Trustee Assoc 1968-87; mem NC Public Lib Trustee 1968-87; trust County Publ Lib Prin Section 1987. **HONORS/ACHIEVEMENTS:** "The Education of Blacks From Slavery to Covert Enforced Integration" 1987. **HOME ADDRESS:** 1713 Courtland Ave, Reidsville, NC 27320.

GRIGGS, JAMES C.
City councilman. **PERSONAL:** Born Aug 24, 1907, Milledgeville, GA; married Azelma Mobley. **EDUCATION:** Paine Coll, AB 1934; Columbia Univ, AM 1951; Atlanta Univ, 1936,49. **CAREER:** Boggs Acad, teacher 1934-42; Cousins Jr High School, Sardis GA, principal 1948-58; Blakeney Elementary School Waynesboro, principal 1958-75; City of Waynesboro, city councilman. **ORGANIZATIONS:** Notary public-at-large GA 1973-83; pres Burke Cty Retired Teachers Assoc 1978-81; mem, master mason Aurora Lodge 54 Waynesboro 1937-85; mem, organist New Springfield Bapt Church, Smith Chapel AME Zion Church Girard GA, Neely Grove CME Church Waynesboro GA; mem Burke Cty & Natl NAACP, Retired Teachers Unit of GA Assoc of Ed; mem Burke Cty Improvement Assoc,

Burke Cty Citizens for Better Gov. **HONORS/ACHIEVEMENTS:** Awd for 27 Yrs Outstanding Serv as School Principal Burke Cty Bd of Ed 1948-75; Awd for Serv to Youth of Burke Cty Girard Elem School 1977; Presidential Alumni Achievement Awd Paine Coll Augusta GA 1978; Cert of Appreciation for an invaluable contrib of time & interest to the membership devel of Burke Cty NAACP 1980; Disting Serv Awd for outstanding & sustaining interest in & contribs to public ed in Burke Cty GA; Paine Coll recognizes & commends James C Griggs for notable contribs to civic & comm affairs & for exemplary embodiment of the Paine Coll Ideal 1981. **MILITARY SERVICE:** AUS sgt 1942-45; Good Conduct Medal 1942-45. **BUSINESS ADDRESS:** City Councilman, City of Waynesboro, 1628 Myrick St, Waynesboro, GA 30830.

GRIGGS, JAMES CLIFTON, JR.
Educational administrator. **PERSONAL:** Born Oct 24, 1930, Chicago, IL; married Alice Rebecca Cox; children: Eric James. **EDUCATION:** Roosevelt Univ, BA 1954; IL State Teachers Coll, Master of Educ 1964; DePaul Univ, Doctor of Laws 1977. **CAREER:** Comm on Youth Welfare City of Chicago, asst dir 1960-65; Chicago Comm on Urban Oppor City of Chicago, dir div of training 1965-68; Univ of IL, dir educ assist pro 1968-77; Malcolm X College, pres. **ORGANIZATIONS:** Mem exec comm Metro Chicago Chapter March of Dimes 1981-83; mem bd of dir Goodwill Industries 1985; mem bd of dir Midwest Comm Council 1985. **HONORS/ACHIEVEMENTS:** Outstanding Leadership and Citizenship Dept of Human Services City of Chicago 1978; Human Relations Comm on Human Relations City of Chicago 1979. **MILITARY SERVICE:** AUS specialist 3rd class 1954-57. **BUSINESS ADDRESS:** President, Malcolm X College, 1900 W Van Buren St, Chicago, IL 60612.

GRIGGS, JOHN W.
Business executive. **PERSONAL:** Born Dec 20, 1924, Birmingham; married Leola Griggs; children: Sylvia, Linda. **CAREER:** E Linwood Lawnview Dev Corp, pres. **ORGANIZATIONS:** Mem bd trst Cleveland Model Cities 1967-73; chmn Model Cities Housing Com 1967-73; unoin comman Local #188 United Steel Workers Am Jone Laughlin Steel Corp 1970-72; mem past jr sr warden Upper Lawnveiw St Club 19712. **HONORS/ACHIEVEMENTS:** Bd Fundamental Educ Awd 1969; United Steel Workers Educ Awd 1971; Parents of Yr Awd 1971; housing and urban dev cert Cuyahoga Comm Coll 1969; housingspec awd Coyahoga Comm Coll 1970.

GRIGGS, JUDITH RALPH
Educator. **PERSONAL:** Born May 02, 1946, Pittsburgh; married Phillip L. **EDUCATION:** Cheyney State Coll, BS 1968; Carnegie-Mellon U, MA 1969;Univ of Pgh, doc studies. **CAREER:** Westinghouse HS St & Kieran Elementary School Pittsburgh, teacher 1968; Pittsburgh St Acad Program, teacher 1969-70, head teacher acting dir 1971-72; Counseling & Learning Dept Duquesne Univ, asst dir 1972-75; Learning skills Program Duquesne Univ, assoc dir. **ORGANIZATIONS:** Mem An Psychol Guidance Assn; educ consult Pittsburgh Model Cities; adv bd mem sec adv bd WDUQ Radio Sta & TV Sta Duquesne U; adv bd mem Action Prgm Point Park Coll; fac adv Blck Student Unoin DuquesneUniv Gospel Choir; mem Alpha Kappa Alpha Sor; mem bd dir Harambee Bookstore 1969-71; a founder Together Inc 1967-71. **HONORS/ACHIEVEMENTS:** Richard Humphrey Schlshp Cheyney State Coll; cert schol achvmt Cheyney State Coll; prospective tchr fellwship english Carnegie-MellonUniv 1968; cert Pub Sch in PA area comp English; & pvt acad schs in PA area english reading educ Dir of pvt acad schs. **BUSINESS ADDRESS:** Duquesne Univ Counseling & Learni, Pittsburgh, PA.

GRIGGS, MILDRED BARNES
Educator. **PERSONAL:** Born Mar 11, 1942, Marianna, AR; married Alvin Scott; children: Scott, Paul. **EDUCATION:** AR A M & N Coll, BS 1963;Univ of IL, MEd 1966;Univ of IL, EdD 1971. **CAREER:** Univ of IL Coll of Educ, assoc prof 1976-; Univ of IL, asst prof 1971-76; Champaign School Dist, teacher 1966-68. **ORGANIZATIONS:** Mem Phi Delta Kappa 1976-; consult Nat Inst of Educ 1979-80; vice pres Am Home Econs Assn 1979-81; mem Delta Sigma Theta Sorority 1960-; mem Urban League; mem NAACP. **HONORS/ACHIEVEMENTS:** Recip outstd undergrad teaching awdUniv of IL 1975. **BUSINESS ADDRESS:** U of IL Coll of Educ, Urbana, IL 61801.

GRIGSBY, CALVIN BURCHARD
Investment banker. **PERSONAL:** Born Dec 24, 1946, Uscola, AR; son of Uzziah P. Grigsby and Janever Burch Grigsby; married Cheryl, Feb 24, 1968; children: James, Janene, Calvin, Jr.. **EDUCATION:** Univ of AZ, BA, 1968; Univ of CA, JD, 1972. **CAREER:** Pillsburg, Madison & Sutro, San Francisco, CA, corporate lawyer, 1972-75; Univ of San Francisco, San Francisco, CA, securities law prof, 1975-76; Itel Corp, San Francisco, CA, natl mktg mgr, municipal finance, 1975-79; Fiscal Funding, San Francisco, CA, chief exec officer and gen counsel, 1979-; Grigsby, Brandford Powell Inc, San Francisco, CA, chief exec officer and chmn of bd, 1981-. **ORGANIZATIONS:** Member, CA Bar Assn, 1972-; member, Charles Houstion Bar Assn, 1973-; vice chair, Natl Assn of Securities Profls, 1985-; member, Natl Bar Assn, 1987-; member, bd of trustees, San Francisco Symphony, 1987-; member, bd of direcs, Boalt Hall Alumni Assn, 1987-. **HONORS/ACHIEVEMENTS:** Author of "Financing Duties of Bank Trustees," Calif Law Rev, 1972; speaker at Public Admin Conf, New Orleans, 1988; author of "Buy, Borrow or Lease?, 1988. **MILITARY SERVICE:** US Navy Reserve, 1968-71. **BUSINESS ADDRESS:** Calvin Burchard Grigsby, Grigsby Brandford Powell Inc, 230 California, 6th Floor, San Francisco CA 94111.

GRIGSBY, CHARLES T.
Chief executive. **CAREER:** Scott and Duncan Co Inc, Boston, MA, chief executive, 1988-. **BUSINESS ADDRESS:** Scott and Duncan, 504 Dudley St, Boston, MA 02119. *

GRIGSBY, DAVID P.
Business executive. **PERSONAL:** Born Mar 06, 1949, Greenville, MS; divorced; children: Reginald, Kayla Ann, Jasohn. **EDUCATION:** MS Valley State Univ, BS 1970; AMA Mgmt Acad Saranac Lake NY, Mgmt 1970-71; St Johns Univ Jamaica NY, MBA 1973; Donald T Regan School of Advanced Fin Mgmt, 1984. **CAREER:** NBC TV NY City, coord, sales devel & promo 1971-73; Metromedia TV Sales NY City, dir, rsch & sales promo 1973-75; Arbitron TV NY City, acct exec, easterntv sales 1975-78; WENZ-AM Drum Commun Inc, pres 1978-81; Merrill Lynch Pierce Fenner & Smith, investment broker, asst vice pres sr finl consultant. **ORGANIZATIONS:** 2nd vp, bd of dir Natl Assoc of Black Owned Broadcasters 1979-81; adv bd mem US Small Bus Admin Reg III 1979-81, TV for All Children/Viewer PromoCtr 1979-80; chmn media comm Fed Arts Council 1979-80; publ speaker, broadcasting Temple Univ, Hunter Univ, Union Univ, Howard Univ; mem Manhattan Stockbrokers Club 1984-; adv bd mem US Small Bus Admin Reg II 1984-87; selection comm Small Bus Person of the Year Reg II 1985-87; issues specialist White House Conference on Small Business 1986. **HONORS/ACHIEVEMENTS:** Outstanding Sales US Arbitron TV Sales 1977; Outstanding Serv to Youth Salvation Army Boys Club 1979; March of Dimes Serv Awd Natl Found March of Dimes 1979; Awd of Appreciation "To Be Ambitious Gifted & Black" Hunter Coll 1979; Cert of Appt Small Bus Admin 1979,81; Outstanding Officer Cand, Gov Awd NY Militia Awd; Awd of Appreciation Assoc of Black Accountants 1984; President's Club Merrill Lynch. **MILITARY SERVICE:** NYARNG 1st lt Gov Awd; NY Militia Awd. **HOME ADDRESS:** 360 West 22nd St, New York, NY 10011. **BUSINESS ADDRESS:** Asst VP, Sr Finl Consultant, Merrill Lynch, 1185 Avenue of the Americas, 19th Floor, New York, NY 10036.

GRIGSBY, JEFFERSON EUGENE, JR.
Artist, retired educator, author. **PERSONAL:** Born Oct 17, 1918, Greensboro, NC; son of Jefferson E and Purry; married Rosalyn Thomasena M; children: J Eugene III, Marshall C. **EDUCATION:** Johnson C Smith Univ, 1934-35; Morehouse Coll, BA 1938; OH State Univ, MA 1940; NY Univ, PhD 1963; The Amer Artists School, 1938-39. **CAREER:** Johnson C Smith Univ, artist-in-residence 1940-41; Bethune Cookman Coll, art instr, dept head 1941-42; US Army, m/sgt 1942-45; Phoenix Union HS, art teacher, head dept 1946-66; AZ State Univ, prof art 1966-. **ORGANIZATIONS:** Vice pres Pacific Region Natl Art Educ 1972-74; chmn Minority Concerns Comm NAEA 1978-82; consulting editor African Arts mag 1968-80; contrib ed School Arts Mag 1978-83; bd mem Phoenix Oppty Ind Ctr 1968-; bd mem Phoenix Arts Coming Together, BTW Child Devel Ctr; bd dir Phoenix Urban League, AZ Job Colleges, OIC; bd chair COBA Consortium of Black Orgs for the Arts AZ; contrib editor Arts & Activities Mag 1983-. **HONORS/ACHIEVEMENTS:** Booker T Washington Child Devel Ctr, SW Ensemble Theatre; DFA Philadelphia School of Art 1965; Medallion of Merit Natl Gallery of Art 1966; 75th Anniversay Medallion of Merit Univ of Arizona; Distinguished Rsch Fellow Arizona State Univ 1982-83; elected Danforth Assoc Fellow 1974; elected pres, Arizona Art Educ Assn 1988-90; Art Educ of the Year Natl Art Educ Assn 1988; Received the 8th annual Govt Award in the Arts for a living individual who has made a signficant contribution to the arts in Arizona 1989. **MILITARY SERVICE:** AUS m/sgt 1942-45. **HOME ADDRESS:** 117 N 9th St, Phoenix, AZ 85006.

GRIGSBY, LUCY CLEMMONS
Educator. **PERSONAL:** Born Dec 27, 1916, Louisville, KY; daughter of Clarence Clemmons and Ophelia Bryant Clemmons; married J Howard Grigsby, Aug 14, 1946; children: Richard Howard Grigsby. **EDUCATION:** Louisville Municipal College, Louisville, KY, BA, 1939; Atlanta Univ, Atlanta, GA, MA, 1941; attended Univ of WI, Madison, WI, 1944-45, 1949-50. **CAREER:** Atlanta Univ, Atlanta, GA, research fellow, 1941-42, instructor to prof, 1942-87, prof emerita, 1988-, chairperson of English dept, 1969-87. **ORGANIZATIONS:** Consultant, Lang Arts, Phelps-Stokes Fund Project for Improv of Secondary School Instruction, 1956-58; sec, Coll Assn, 1969-; direc, curriculum programs at Memphis State Univ, Fisk Univ, and Atlanta Univ, 1970-75; consultant, Inst for Serv to Edn, 1971-75; comm member, Evaluation of Teaching of Writing, Conf on Coll Composition and Communication, 1980-87; member, Coll English Assn; member, Langston Hughes Soc; member, Zora Neal Hurston Soc. **HONORS/ACHIEVEMENTS:** Assoc Editor, Phylon magazine, 1954-; Excellence in Teaching Award, Atlanta Univ, 1963; Award for Disting Serv, Coll Language Assn, 1974; Prof of the Yr Award, Toastmasters Intl; DLit, Atlanta Univ, 1988. **BUSINESS ADDRESS:** Mrs Lucy Clemmons Grigsby, English Dept, Atlanta University, Atlanta, GA 30314.

GRIGSBY, MARGARET ELIZABETH
Educator, physician. **PERSONAL:** Born Jan 16, 1923, Prairie View, TX. **EDUCATION:** Prairie Veiw Coll, BS 1943;Univ of MI Med Sch, MD 1948; Homer G Phillips Hosp, intern 1948-49; Homer G Phillips, asst resd med 1949-50; Freedmen'sHosp, 1950-51. **CAREER:** HowardUniv Coll Med, prof med 1966-; HowardUniv Coll Med, adminsitrv asst asso prof med lctr chf infectious deseases sect asst prof med instr med 1952-62; Peace Corps, expert adv 1964-; DC Asian Influenza Adv Com, adv com 1957-58; DC Gen Hosp, atdg phys 1958-; Mt Alto VA Hosp, 1958-64;cons 1964-66; Freedmen's Hosp, phys 1952-63;Univ Ibadan Nigeria, hon vis prof 1967-68; Harvard Med Sch, tchr rsrch flw 1951-52. **ORGANIZATIONS:** Asso mem Am Coll Phys 1957-62; mem AMA; Nat Med Assn; Med Soc DC; Medico-Chirugical Soc DC; Sigma Xi Sci Soc Howard U; Assn Former Interns & Resd Freedmen's Hosp; Pasteur Med Reading Club; Alpha Epsilon Iota Med Sor; Royal Soc Tropical Med & Hygiene; flw Am Coll Phys 1962; Am Soc Tropical Med & Hygiene; Nigerian Soc Hlth; Royal Soc Hlth; Royal Soc Med; Nat Geog Soc; Soc Med Assn; bd gov Medico-Chirugical Soc 1960-62; sec HowardUniv Sigma Xi 1960-62; mem DC Citz for Better Pub Edn9; St Luke's Episc Ch; Centruy Club-Bus & Professional Women's Club; NAACP; Urban League; All-Saints Anglican Ch 1967-68; Ibadan Rec Club 1967-68; Ibadan Motor Club 1968; Alpha Kappa Alpha. **HONORS/ACHIEVEMENTS:** Flwsp Rockefeller Found 1951-52; flw Chinca Med Bd 1956; dip Nat Bd Med Exmrs 1949; am Bd Internal Med 1956; dipUniv Loncon 1963; NIH flwsp 1962-6 USPHS 1966; num honors & publ. **BUSINESS ADDRESS:** Professor Dept of Medicine, Howard University, 520 W Street, NW, Washington, DC 20059.

GRIGSBY, MARSHALL C.
Educational administrator, clergyman. **PERSONAL:** Born Aug 18, 1946, Charlotte, NC; married Germaine A Palmer; children: Rosalyn Kimberly, Michelle Alexandria. **EDUCATION:** Morehouse Coll, BA 1968; Univ of Chicago Div Sch, MTh 1970, DMn 1972. **CAREER:** Black Legislative Clearing House, exec dir 1970-72; First Unitarian Church of Chicago, assoc minister 1970-75; S Shore Comm Planning Assn, project dir 1972; Assn of Theology Schools, assoc dir 1973-75; Howard Univ School of Religion, asst dean 1975-. **ORGANIZATIONS:** Ordained minister Unitarian Universalist Ch 1970-; mem Soc for the Study of Black Religion 1973-; consult Assn of Theol Schs 1975-; natl selection panel Fund for Theol Educ Inc 1976; consult Religion Div of the Lilly Endowment 1977-; mem Natl Counc of Negro Women 1979-. **HONORS/ACHIEVEMENTS:** Fellowship recipient So Fellowships Fund Inc 1968-71; Fellowship recipient Fund for Theol Educ Inc 1969-71; Outstanding Young Men in Amer 1972, 1979; Regional Finalist White House Fellows Program 1978. **BUSINESS ADDRESS:** Assistant Dean, HowardUniv School of Religion, 1240 Randolph St NE, Washington, DC 20017.

GRIGSBY, TROY L.
Urban planner. **PERSONAL:** Born Oct 25, 1934, Holly Grove, AR; son of Roy Vell and Velma Vell; children: Shari, Gloria, Alexis, Troy, Jr. **EDUCATION:** Wayne State Univ, BA 1958, MUP 1964. **CAREER:** State of MI Dept Pub Welfare, soc worker 1959-62; Ypsilanti MI Dept Urban Renewal, asst dir 1962-64; Inkster MI Dept Planning & Urban Renewal, 1964-66; Greater Cleveland Growth Assn, mgr community dev 1968-71; State of OH Dept Urban Affairs, deputy dir 1971-72; State of OH Dept Econ & Community Devel, dep dir 1971-75; Dept of Community Devel Highland Park, MI, admin 1976-79; US Dept of HUD Omaha, NE, deputy area mgr 1979-82; US Dept of HUD Milwaukee, WI, mgr 1982-86; US Dept of HUD Oklahoma City OK, dept mgr 1986-. **ORGANIZATIONS:** Mem Amer Soc Planning Officials; mem Cleveland City Club 1969-71; Cleveland Citizens League 1969-71; Mayor's Commn Crisis in Welfare 1968; Mayor's Commn Urban Transportation 1968; bd dirs Plan Action for Tomorrow Housing 1970-71; Cleveland Contractor's Asst Corp 1970-71; mem Mayor's Commn on Trans & Redevelopment 1970-71; sec OH State Bd Housing 1971-75; dir Dayton State Farm Devel Bd 1973-75; Gov Housing & Community Devel Adv Commn 1971-74; OH Water & Sewer Rotary Commn 1971-75; state rep Appalachian Reg Commn 1971-75; Council Appalachian Govs 1971-75; Council State Housing Finance Agencies Task Force on Natl Housing Policy 1973-74; Council State Dept Comm Affairs Agencies 1974; Natl Govs Conf Task Force on Natl Regional Devel Policy 1973; OH Dept Transportation Adv Comm for Highways, Terminals & Parking 1971-72; OH Comprehensive Health Planning Adv Council 1972-74; Fed Reg Council Task Force Intergovernmental Relations 1974. **BUSINESS ADDRESS:** Department Manager, US Dept of HUD, 200 NW 5th St, Oklahoma City, OK 73102.

GRILLO, ANIVAL J.
Attorney. **PERSONAL:** Born Dec 24, 1913, Tampa; married Dorothy Roseberry. **EDUCATION:** JD 1956. **CAREER:** Private Practice. **ORGANIZATIONS:** Past chmn DC Cit Traffic Bd; past dir Assn Plaintiffs Trial Atty; mem Am, Nat, Wash & DC Bar Assn; Nat Assn Immigration & Naturalizaion Lawyers. **HONORS/ACHIEVEMENTS:** Otstndng Cit Assn, Plaintiffs Trial Atty 1973.

GRIMES, CALVIN M., JR.
Chief executive. **CAREER:** Grimes Oil Company, Inc, Boston, MA, chief executive, 1940-. **BUSINESS ADDRESS:** Grimes Oil Company Inc, 165 Norfolk St, Boston, MA 02124. *

GRIMES, DOUGLAS M.
Attorney. **PERSONAL:** Born Aug 11, 1942, Marshall, TX; married Bernadette. **EDUCATION:** CA St Coll BA 1965; Howard Univ Sch of Law, JD 1968. **CAREER:** Pvt Practice, Grimes, Barnes & Gill, atty 1971-; Univ of IL Coll of Law, asst prof of Law & dir Comm Involvement 1970-71; Cont IL Nat Bank & Co Chicago, adm asst 1968-70. **ORGANIZATIONS:** Has taught real estate IN U; asst city atty City of Gary; Police Civil Serv Commn; Gary Fire Commn; pres Legal Aid Soc of Gary; pres Thurgood MarshallLaw Assn; legal adv Minority Businessmens Steering Com; legal adv Lake Co Corner; mem Gary Jaycees; Urban League of NW IN Inc adv bd NW IN UrbanLeagbue; mem Gary Frontiers Serv Club; sec treas bd mem Gary Leased Housing Corp; mem IN St Black Assembly; mem Gary chap IN St Black Assembly; del Nat Black Assembly Conv 1972-74; bd dir Gary Gus Resource Ctr; past mem Chicago Jaycees, Southend Jaycees; former public dfndr, Gary City Ct; former legal & counsel IN Jaycees. **BUSINESS ADDRESS:** 562 Washington St, Gary, IN.

GRIMES, JOHN J.
Attorney. **PERSONAL:** Born Dec 10, 1939, New York, NY; son of John Thomas Grimes and Rhoda A Gordon. **EDUCATION:** John Jay Coll of Crim Justice, BS 1967, MPA 1970; NY Univ, PhD Publ Admin 1970; Harvard Law School, JD 1973. **CAREER:** Fish & Neave, summer assoc 1971; Fried Frank Harris Shriver & Jacobson, summer assoc 1972; Shea & Gould, assoc 1973-77; Trans World Airlins Inc, gen attny litigation 1977-84, staff vice pres sec 1984-1986; New York City Police Dept, Asst Commr Civil Matters 1986-88, General Counsel Civilian Complaint Review Board 1988-89; Grimes & Zimet, partner 1989. **ORGANIZATIONS:** Mem NY State Bar Assoc, NY Cty Lawyers Assoc, The Assoc of the Bar of NYC; fin sec Harlem Lawyers Assoc; mem Fed Bar Council, Queens Cty Bar Assoc; Natl Org of Black Law Enforcement Executives. **BUSINESS ADDRESS:** Grimes & Zimet, 95 Deerfield Lane N, Pleasantville, NY 10570.

GRIMES, JOHN T.
Attorney. **PERSONAL:** Born Nov 15, 1919, Cedar Hill, TN; married Dorothy M Ellison; children: Willa, Jennifer, Joyce. **EDUCATION:** IN U, AB 1949; IN Univ Sch of Law, JD 1952. **CAREER:** City Ct, Kokomo IN, municipal judge 1971-79, chief dep pros atty 1953-58; Gen Prac of Law, 1952-. **ORGANIZATIONS:** Past pres Howard Bar Assn; mem C of C; Rotary Club; IN St Youth & Council; IN St Bar Assn; Nat Bar Assn. **MILITARY SERVICE:** AUS; s/sgt. **BUSINESS ADDRESS:** 123 N Buckeye St, Kokomo, IN 46901.

GRIMES, VONI B.
Retired educational administrator. **PERSONAL:** Born Dec 23, 1922, Bamberg, SC; son of McKinley Grimes and Mittie Grimes; married Lorrayne; children: Johnsie Silas, Edgar Gibson, Naomi Davis, Beverly Devan, Toni McKinney. **EDUCATION:** Penn State Univ, attended 1948-51, certificate 1971-73; Univ of KY, certificate 1982, 1983, 1985. **CAREER:** Philadelphia Ship Yard, sheet metal mechanic 1942-44; York Hoover Corp, sheet metal worker/oper 1947-49; Cole Steel Equip/Litton Ind, supervisor 1949-70; Penn State Univ/York Campus, dir business serv 1970-88. **ORGANIZATIONS:** Past master Soc Friendship #42 PHA 1950-; mem Nimrod Consistory #9, PHA 1950-; mem Himyar Temple #9 PHA 1951-; bd dirs Indus Mgmt Club 1965-; trustee Small Memorial AME Zion Church School 1970-; advisory bd pres York Co Vocational-Tech School 1974-; budget chmn York County Red Cross 1978-; bd dir 70001 (for drop-out students); mgr City of York Business Entrepreneur Resource Center 1983-; pres, East York Lions Club 1988-89; 33 degree inspector general The United Supreme Council 1986-. **HONORS/ACHIEVEMENTS:** Honored by Smalls Memorial AME Zion Church School for service as superintendent 1970; honored by York Recreation Commission 1976; honored by Deborah #26 OES, PHA 1980; October 31, 1984 designated "Voni B Grimes Day" by the Mayor of the City of York, PA; renamed gymnasium to "Voni B Grimes Gym" by resolution (passed by mayor & council) October 31, 1984; received 33rd Degree inspector general the United Supreme Council PHA 1986; York Yacht Club Honoree. **MILITARY SERVICE:** Corpl 2 yrs; Good Conduct Medal, served in Guam. **HOME ADDRESS:** 112 Lynbrook Dr So, York, PA 17402.

GRIMES, WILLIAM THOMAS, SR.
Clergyman, business executive. **PERSONAL:** Born Jul 14, 1909, Martin Co; married Tedia M Galloway. **CAREER:** W T Grimes Barber Shop & Sales Agcy, operator 1944-74; Missionary Bapt Ch, pastor 1966-74. **ORGANIZATIONS:** Tchr cnslr & prchr CA Prison 1966-74; past vice pres treas NAACP; ministger & Music 1945-; pres Hampton Choir Dir & Organist Guild 1946-50; mem Voters League; Ministers Conf 1964-74. **HONORS/ACHIEVEMENTS:** Recognition, Biographical Dir Negro Ministers; Cert & Pin 25 yrs mbrshp & ldrshp, Choir Dir & Organist Guild.

GRIMES, WILLIAM WINSTON
Business executive. **PERSONAL:** Born Feb 07, 1927, Gorgas, AL; married Bettie Jane Howell; children: Clinton Alan, Kevin Eugene. **EDUCATION:** OH State Univ, BChE 1950; Case Western Reserve, grad work 1952-53. **CAREER:** Standard Oil Co Engr Dept, sr engrg supvr 1969-73; Standard Oil Co Refining Dept, proj coord mgr 1973-74; BP Oil Co(a wholly-owned subsidiary of Standard Oil Co) Marcus Hook Refinery, operations mgr 1974-78, refinery mgr 1978-81; The Standard Oil Co, refinery mgr. **ORGANIZATIONS:** Chmn of bd Lima Area C of C 1985; vice pres United Way of Greater Lima 1983-85; dir Amer Inst of Chem Engrs 1984-. **HONORS/ACHIEVEMENTS:** Disting Alumnus The OH State Univ Engrg Dept 1975. **MILITARY SERVICE:** AUS PFC 1946-47.

GRIMMETT, SADIE A.
Psychologist. **PERSONAL:** Born Jan 31, 1932, Talladega, AL. **EDUCATION:** Univ of OR, BA 1952, MA 1962; George Peabody Coll for tchr, PhD 1969. **CAREER:** Elemtary Portland OR Pub Sch, tchr 1952-66; Early Childhood Educ CtrUniv Of AZ, research Asso 1969-70; Syracuse U, asst prof 1970-73; IN U, asso prof 1973-; Standard & Rsrch Inst, consult 1969-70; Nat Follow Through, consult 1971-73; Guamanian Project, NW Regional Lab, 1970, Dir Facilitative Environmental Devel, BEH Proj 1974-75. **ORGANIZATIONS:** Mem Educ Adv Bd; Training of Tchr Trainers 1972-73; Am Psych Assn 1971-; Am Educ Rsrch Assn 1965-; Soc for Rsrch in Child Devel 1966; mem Delta Sigma Theta Sor 1950-; Portland OR Urban League Bd 1958-66; Portland OR League Of Women Voters Bd 1963-64; mem Pi Lambda Theta 1952; Pi Delta Phi 1952; DeltaTau Kappa 1975; Delta Kappa Gamma 1966. **HONORS/ACHIEVEMENTS:** Recipient St of OR Schlrshp 1948-50; NDEA Foreign Lang Flwshp 1960; ESEA Grad Training Flwshp 1966-69. **BUSINESS ADDRESS:** Inst for Child Study, Bloomington, IN 47401.

GRIMMOND, ARLENE PATRICIA
Physician. **PERSONAL:** Born Jul 03, 1944, Georgetown, Guyana. **EDUCATION:** Coll of Liberal Arts Howard Univ, BS 1970; Coll of Medicine Howard Univ, MD 1980. **CAREER:** DC General Hosp, surgical intern 1980-81; Dept of Radiology Howard Univ Hosp, radiology resident 1981-84; Univ of CT Affil Hosp, resident nuclear medicine 1985-. **ORGANIZATIONS:** Mem Amer and Natl Medical Assocs 1978-; mem Soc of Nuclear Medicine 1985-, Amer Assoc Women Radiologists 1986-. **HONORS/ACHIEVEMENTS:** 6 articles published including "Hepatic Mass Functioning Metastatic Thymona 22 Years After Radiation Therapy," w/RP Spencer Clin Nucl Med 11 1986.

GRIMSLEY, ETHELYNE
Consultant. **PERSONAL:** Born Jun 13, 1941, Clayton, AL; married Calvin H Grimsley; children: Kelvin, Karen. **EDUCATION:** NY Comm Coll, AS 1975. **CAREER:** Staten Island Devel Cntr, social work 1962-80; NJ School Assoc 1980-; Roselle School Board, mem 1980-; Lankmark Travel, travel consultant. **ORGANIZATIONS:** Pres Union Cty School Board Assoc 1983-85; mem NAACP; Union Cty Negro Business & Professional Women's Club. **HONORS/ACHIEVEMENTS:** Women of Achievement Awd Leadership & Community Serv Phileman Baptist Church 1983. **BUSINESS ADDRESS:** Travel Consultant, Lankmark Travel, 207 Morris Ave, Springfield, NJ 07081.

GRINSTEAD, AMELIA ANN
Business executive. **PERSONAL:** Born Jul 24, 1945, Hopkinsville, KY. **EDUCATION:** Fisk U, BA biology 1967. **CAREER:** J Walter Thompson Co, print media buyer 1967-68, media planner 1968-71, media supr 1972-74, vice pres assoc media dir 1974-; Test Mkt Media Planning Advertising AgeMedia Workshop, faculty 1973-75; The Pillsbury Co, mgr of media serv 1981-85; Miller Meester Adv Inc, vice pres media 1985-86, sr vice pres media dir 1986-. **ORGANIZATIONS:** Mem Our Chalet Com World Assn of Girl Guides Girl Scouts 1972-; dir asst sec Girl Scouts 1972-78, 3rd vice pres 1978-; US Delegate UNESCO/WAGGGS East-West Cul Conf New Delhi, India 1964; staff mem pub relations GSUSA East-West Cultural Conf Hawaii 1966. **HONORS/ACHIEVEMENTS:** Black Achvrs Awd YMCA Harlem Branch; film subject United Negro Coll Fund 1979. **BUSINESS ADDRESS:** Sr Vice Pres Media Dir, Miller Meester Adv Inc, 2001 Killebrew Dr, Minneapolis, MN 55420.

GRISSETT, WILLIE JAMES
Educator/educational administrator. **PERSONAL:** Born Aug 19, 1931, Atmore, AL; married Glender Wilson; children: Frasquita G McCray, Johannice W, Zina E Myers, Tchetha J, Weida S, Deri K. **EDUCATION:** Knoxville Coll, AB 1953; Univ of South AL, MA 1975. **CAREER:** Clark Co Training School, music inst & choral dir 1953-55; Escambia Co Training School, music inst & choral dir 1955-68; Escambia Co Middle School, administrator 1968-. **ORGANIZATIONS:** Dir Atmore Comm Male Chorus 1971-; mem AL Assoc of School Administrators 1980, AL Middle Level School Administrators 1981, Natl Assoc of School Administrators 1985. **HONORS/ACHIEVEMENTS:** Education and Humaniterian Awd United Civic Clubs 1981; Special Service Awd Gamma Theta Chap Phi Delta Kappa Inc 1981; Special Service Awd Kappa Alpha Psi Frat 1981. **HOME ADDRESS:** 171 N 8th Ave, Atmore, AL 36502. **BUSINESS ADDRESS:** School Administrator, Escambia County Middle School, P O Box 486, Atmore, AL 36504.

GRIST, ARTHUR L.
Educator. **PERSONAL:** Born Apr 29, 1930, Tampa, FL; son of Edwin Grist and Eleanor Grist; married Nancy Jackson; children: Michelle, Arthur, Michael. **EDUCATION:** Univ of Michigan, MPH; Ohio State Univ, BS. **CAREER:** Cleveland Div Health, public health sanitarian 1955-61; So Illinois Univ, 1961-; Health Zoning & Housing, comm consult 1961-65; Sol IL Univ, asst to vice pres 1965-70, asst to pres 1970-76, sp asst to vice pres bus affairs 1976-79, asst prof 1968-82, assoc prof 1982-. **ORGANIZATIONS:** Mem APHA, NEHA, Madison City Mental Health Bd, Edwardsville City Planning Comm, Zoning Bd Appeals 1975-, YMCA, United Fund, United Way; treasure Metro E Labor Council; vice pres Alliance Reg Comm Health MO & IL, Reg Adv Group IL, Reg Med Program; vice pres, St Clair City

Health & Welfare Council 1974-; mem Black Caucus of Health Workers APHA 1969-; treasure St Louis Health Systems Agency 1970-78; pres Metro East Health Serv Council Inc 1978-80; Alderman City of Edwardsville 1986-89; Ward 4 Park & Recreation Bd 1985-86; Alderman Ward 4 Edwardsville, IL 1989-93. **HONORS/ACHIEVEMENTS:** Serv Award Tri-City Health & Welfare Council 1972; Hildrus A Poindexter Disting Serv Award 1975. **MILITARY SERVICE:** US Army, 1953-55; OARNG 1955-61; US Army Reserve Medical Serv Corps, rank O-6 col, 1961-88, retired; Meritorious Serv, 1983, 1988. **HOME ADDRESS:** 1912 McKendree Dr, Edwardsville, IL 62025.

GRIST, RAYMOND
Artist. **PERSONAL:** Born Jan 31, 1939, New York, NY; son of Arthur Grist and Ena Francis Grist; married Adrienne Daniel, Apr 04, 1986; children: Lisa Grist. **EDUCATION:** School of Visual Arts, New York, certificate of fine arts; attended Baruch School of Business, New York, Poliakoff School of Stage Design, New York, MOK Studio, New York, Printmakers Workshop, New York, New School for Social Research, New York, and Art Students League, New York. **CAREER:** East River Houses Research Project, New York, NY, pres and project dir; former co-chair, dept of the arts, Malcolm/King: Harlem Coll Extension, NY; former teacher at UN Intl School, E Harlem Protestant Parish, Thompsons Rehabilitation Ctr, Grant Day Care Ctr, New Mews, BOCES of S Westchester, NY, and with "Artists in the Schools" program, New York City. **HONORS/ACHIEVEMENTS:** One man exhibitions at Cinque Gallery, New York, 1970, Shooting Star Gallery, New York, 1971, Metro Applied Research Ctr, New York, 1974, Alaska State Museum, Juneau, AK, 1974, Cellar Gallery, New York, 1984, Studio Museum in Harlem, New York, 1984. **MILITARY SERVICE:** US Army, 1962-64. **HOME ADDRESS:** Raymond Grist, 595 Main St, Apt 602, Roosevelt Island, NY 10044.

GRIST, RERI
Coloratura soprano, professor of voice. **PERSONAL:** Born in New York, NY; married Dr Ulf Thomson; children: Mareka. **EDUCATION:** Queens Coll, BA, Music, 1954. **CAREER:** Various performances on Broadway, plays and musicals; original cast, West Side Story, 1957; opera debut, Santa Fe Opera Co, 1959; New York City Opera, 1959; queen of the night in Magic Flute, starring role in The Nightingale, Cologne, Germany Opera; leading performer, San Francisco Opera, 1963-77, 1981, 1990, Vienna State Opera, 1963-88, Salzburg Festival, 1964-77, Metropolitan Opera, 1966-77, Munich State Opera, 1967-84; appearances with other major houses including Chicago Lyric, Covent Garden, La Scala; specialized in lyric-coloratura roles in operas by Mozart, R Strauss, Verdi, Rossini, Donizetti; concert and opera performances with conductors Leonard Bernstein, Karl Boehm, Herbert V. Karajan, James Levine, Zubin Mehta, Seiji Osawa, and with the major orchestras including New York Philharmonic, Vienna Philharmonic; solo recitals throughout Europe, US; numerous operatic productions for German and Austrian television including two biographical portraits; 15 recordings, DGG, RCA Victor, EMI, CBS; prof of voice, Indiana Univ, Bloomington, 1981-83, 1989, Hochschule f. Musik, Munich, Germany, 1984-. **HONORS/ACHIEVEMENTS:** Blanche Thebom Award for Voice, 1958; Bayerische Kammersaengerin, Munich State Opera (first and only black to be given award); Alumni Assn Award, Queens Coll; Marian Anderson Award; Whitney Award; Rockefeller Grant. **BUSINESS ADDRESS:** c/o Ronald Wilford, Mgr, Columbia Artists, 165 W 57 St, New York, NY 10019.

GRIST, RONALD
Corporate finance officer. **PERSONAL:** Born in New York, NY; married Joyce. **EDUCATION:** City Coll of NY, New York, BBA. **CAREER:** Aetna Business Credit, New York, NY, former vice pres; Fidelity Bank, Philadelphia, PA, former sr vice pres; Fidelcorp Business Credit Corp, New York, NY, exec vice pres. **HOME ADDRESS:** Ronald Grist, 1921 Lark Ln, Cherry Hill, NY 08003.

GRISWOLD, A. J.
Organization member. **PERSONAL:** Born May 01, 1905, Starkville, MS; widowed. **EDUCATION:** Cleve Miller Public School, Detroit, 1923. **CAREER:** Peoples Bapt Church, sec, teacher, Sunday school asst supt; Sr Citizens MEDCCE, instr; Peoples Baptist Church, gen chmn 1982-84, pres dept of missions. **ORGANIZATIONS:** Missionary Metro Dist Assoc 1984-85; leader Christian Soc Rel Wolverine State Baptist Conv 1984-85; co-chmn Natl Bapt Conv on Aging & Volunterrism; mem Church Women United; leader Sunday School Natl Bapt Convention, Missionary Met Dist Assoc; mem Field of Chris Soc Relations, Womens Aux, NAACP, Keep Detroit Beautiful, E Side Concerned Citizens, Mayors Prayer Breakfast, Church Women Concerned, Church Women United, Metro Dist Ministers Wives; volunteer driver Amer Red Cross; chmn of bd Election Dist 3; co-chmn CWU, Ecumenical Action for Volunteer Serv Oper Layette, Ecumenical Action Citizens, Task Force on Battered Women; mem Wolverine State Ministers Wives; mem 13th Congressional Dist. **HONORS/ACHIEVEMENTS:** Heart of Gold Metro Detroit 1969; Comm Serv Pin Metro Detroit 1972; Missionary Year Eastern Star Detroit 1983; Life Membership, Natl Bapt Conv 1980; State Resolution; Cty & City Resolutions; Certs & Honors. **HOME ADDRESS:** 2508 Holcomb St, Detroit, MI 48214.

GROCE, HERBERT MONROE, JR.
Priest. **PERSONAL:** Born Apr 17, 1929, Philadelphia, PA; son of Herbert M Groce Sr and Gertrude Elaine McMullin; married Linda Jane Rosenbaum; children: Eric H, Cheryl M, Karen D, Herbert M III, Lauren S. **EDUCATION:** La Salle Coll Phila, PA, 1955-60; Gen Theol Sem New York, 1972-74; Inst of Theol Cathedral of St John the Divine, New York City 1975-78. **CAREER:** Lincoln Center for Performing Arts Inc, dir of operations 1978-; Coll of Medicine & Dentistry of Newark, NJ, vice pres for human resources 1971-78; Delta Found Greenville, MS, exec dir 1970-71; The Singer Co (Link Div) Binghamton, NY, admin 1964-69; Fairchild-Hiller Inc Hagerston, MD, engineering planner 1963-64; Mutual Benefit Fund Newark, dir 1977-; St Stephen's Pearl River, NY, episcopal priest asst 1978-; Trinity Cathedral, Trenton, asst 1980-84; Rector, St Andrews Church, New York City 1984-. **ORGANIZATIONS:** Vice pres/unit Serv Boy Scouts of Amer, NE Region 1978-; mason 32 degree Ancient Accepted Scottish Rite, NY 1979; shriner Mecca Temple, AAONMS NY 1980; MBF-MBL Growth Fund Inc, dir 1982-; MBF-MAP-Government Fund Inc, dir 1982-; Grand Chaplain, Grand Lodge of New York 1984-; Grand Chaplain, Grand Chapter of Royal AR-Masons 1986-. **HONORS/ACHIEVEMENTS:** Good Conduct Medal, Korean War USAF 1951-55; Law Day Award, Broome/Tioga Bar Assn 1968; Silver Beaver & Silver Antelope Awards, BSA 1975; Whitney M Young Jr/Serv Award, BSA, 1979; Supreme Council 33 degree Ancient Accepted Scottish Rite of Freemasonry, Northern Masonic Jurisdiction, US of Amer 1989; Honorary Alumnus, Gen Theol Seminary 1983. **MILITARY SERVICE:** USAF s/sgt 1951-55. **HOME ADDRESS:** 875 Berkshire Valley Road, Wharton, NJ 07885.

GROFF, REGIS F.
Legislator, educator. **PERSONAL:** Born Apr 08, 1935; son of Eddie Groff (deceased) and Fenimore Groff (deceased); married Ada; children: Peter, Traci. **EDUCATION:** Urban Affairs Inst, 1972; Univ of Denver, 1972; Western Illinois Univ, 1962; JFK School Harvard Univ, Program for Sr Execs in State & Local Govt Grad 1980. **CAREER:** Cook Co Dept of Public Aid, case worker 1962-63; Denver Public Schools, teacher 1963-66; Rockford Public Schools, teacher 1966-67; Univ of Denver, instr black history 1972-73; Metro State Coll, instr black politics 1972-73; CO State Univ, instr black history 1972-73; Univ of CO, instr black history 1974-75; elected Democratic senate minority leader 1978,1980; Natl Democratic Leader Caucus, vice pres 1980-82; CO State Senate, state senator 1974-. **ORGANIZATIONS:** Vice pres Denver Fed of Tchrs 1968-70; staff participant History of Minorities Univ of Denver 1969; pres Black Educators United 1970-72; bd mem Denver of Tchrs 1967-71; bd mem CO Dept of Educ Steering Comm 1970-72; instr Natl Comm of Christians & Jews Annual Summer Youth Conf 1971-73; bd mem Black Educ Adv Com 1971; del Nat Black Conv 1972; bd Mem Black Educators United 1972; cert Urban Studies 1972; staff person Natl Council of Social Sci 1972; chmn Rachel Noeb Scholarship Fund; participant Black Studies Seminar 1973; visiting instr Santa Clara Univ Ext 1973; mem Natl Black Caucus of State Legislature Exec Comm 1977-87; co-founder Natl Black Caucus of State Legislature 1977; lecturer in Nigeria 1980, Vienna Austria 1981; mem Natl Conf of State Legislature Exec Bd 1981-84; mem Democratic Planning Bd Gov Commission of Children & Their Families; housing study throughout West Germany 1983; economic development trade missions Kingston Jamaica 1984; chamn Natl Conf of State Legislature Energy Comm 1986-; chmn Natl Conf of State Legislature Educ Comm 1988-; bd mem Amer/Israel Friendship League 1988-. **HONORS/ACHIEVEMENTS:** Legislator of the Year Awd Assoc Press 1981; lecture on democracy, Nigeria 1980; Presentation of paper on South African Apartheid Intl Center Vienna, 1981; Co-op Educ Workshop, St Johns, Newfoundland 1988; housing study, West Germany 1983; Anti-Defamation League Mission, Israel 1985. **MILITARY SERVICE:** USAF 1953-57; highest rank attained Adm 1C. **BUSINESS ADDRESS:** State Senator, Colorado Senate, 2841 Colorado Blvd, Denver, CO 80207.

GROFFREY, FRANK EDEN
Educational administrator. **PERSONAL:** Born Dec 23, 1944, Charleston, SC; married Andrea Ollivierra; children: Frank Jr, Marlin, Shannon. **EDUCATION:** St Augustines, BS Bus 1967; TX Southern, MBA 1971; Harvard Univ, MPA 1979, EdD 1983. **CAREER:** Hampton Inst, instructor 1971-75; NASA, contracting officer 1974-80; St Augustines Coll, dir alumni affairs 1984, chmn div of bus. **ORGANIZATIONS:** Assoc dir Ctr for Minority Bus Devel 1972; adj faculty St Leo Coll 1975-78; rsch asst Harvard Univ 1980-82; bd of advisors Martin Luther King Open School 1982-83; tutor Elliott Congregational Church 1983. **HONORS/ACHIEVEMENTS:** Natl scholar Alpha Kappa Mu 1966; Ford Fellow TX Southern Univ 1969-71; EPM Fellowship NASA/Harvard Univ 1978-79; Whitney Young Fellow 1983. **MILITARY SERVICE:** AUS Spec 5th Class 2 years; Army Commendation Oak Leaf Cluster 1968. **BUSINESS ADDRESS:** Chairman, Div of Business, St Augustines College, Raleigh, NC 27610.

GROOMES, EMRETT W.
Business executive. **PERSONAL:** Born Mar 22, 1930, Madison, FL. **EDUCATION:** Tuskegee Inst, BS; NY U, MA, PT; Cornell U, MBA. **CAREER:** Tchr 7 asst princ 1951-57; Roosevelt Hosp, consult phys therapist 1958-64, admin residency 1965; Rochester Regnl Hlth & Hosp Council, assoc dir 1966-68; Michael Reese Hosp & Med Cntr, asst dir 1968-71, assoc 1968-75; Midsouthside Hlth Planning Orgn, exec dir; New City Hlth Center, exec dir. **ORGANIZATIONS:** Past chmn Assembly of Outpatient & Home Care Inst, Am Hosp Assn; assn of Adminstr of Ambulatory Svc, Chicago Hosp Council; past first vice pres Nat Assn of Health Serv Exec Inc; past pres Midwest Chap Nat Assn of Health Serv Inc; past mem Ambulatory Care Com, Am Hosp Council; Am Coll of Hosp administr; Am Pub Health Assn; mem Voc Adv Com, Dunbar HS;past mem Professional Adv Com VNA; treas KOMED Bd, KOMED Health Cntr Chicago Orgn. **MILITARY SERVICE:** USAFR Med Serv Corp Lt Col, ret. **BUSINESS ADDRESS:** Executive Dir, New City Health Center, 5500 South Damen Ave, Chicago, IL 60636.

GROOMES, FREDDIE LANG
Educator. **PERSONAL:** Born Sep 02, 1934, Jacksonville, FL; married Dr Benjamin H Groomes; children: Linda, Derek. **EDUCATION:** FL A&M Univ, BS 1962, MEd 1963; FL State Univ, PhD 1972. **CAREER:** Project Upward Bound, coordinator, counselor 1965-68, assoc dir 1968-70; FL A&M Univ, dir inst rsch 1970-72; FL State Univ, asst pres & dir human affairs 1972-. **ORGANIZATIONS:** Consult HEW,Univ & Coll Inst for Serv to Educ, State Govt, priv bus & indus, Amer Council on Educ, Coll & Univ Pers Assn; chpsn FL Gov Comm on the Status of Women; mem FL Human Relat Commn; FL Cncl on Indian Afrs; exec bd Amer Assn for Affirm Action. **HONORS/ACHIEVEMENTS:** Rockefeller Fellow 1976; Outstanding Educators of Amer; Kappa Delta Pi Natl Hon Soc; Who's Who in Amer Colls & Univs; Outstanding Young Women of Amer. **BUSINESS ADDRESS:** Asst Pres & Dir Human Affrs, FL StateUniv, 201 Westcott, FL State Univ, Tallahassee, FL 32306.

GROOMS, HENRY RANDALL
Engineer. **PERSONAL:** Born Feb 10, 1944, Cleveland, OH; son of Leonard A Grooms and Lois Pickell Grooms; married Tonie Marie Joseph; children: Catherine, Zayne, Nina, Ivan, Ian, Athesis, Shaneya, Yaphet, Rahsan, Dax, Jevay. **EDUCATION:** Howard U, BCE 1965; Carnegie-Mellon U, MS Civil Eng 1967, PhD Civil Eng 1969. **CAREER:** DC Highway Dept Wash, DC, hwy engr 1962; Peter F Loftus Corp Pittsgh, PA, structural Engr 1966; Blaw-Knox Co Pittsgh, PA, structural engr 1967-68; Rockwell Intl Downey, CA, structural engr 1969-, engineering mgr. **ORGANIZATIONS:** Mem Tau Beta Pi 1964-; mem Sigma Xi 1967-; mem Kappa Alpha Psi 1963-; mem Am Soc of Civil Engrs 1965-; scoutmaster Boy Scouts of Am 1982-; coach, Youth Basketball 1984-; coach, Youth Soccer 1985-. **HONORS/ACHIEVEMENTS:** Engineer of the Yr Rockwell Intl Space Div 1980, Coll Recruiter of the Yr 1979-80; Alumni Merit Award Carnegie-Mellon Univ 1985; Honoree, Western Reserve Historical Society, Cleveland OH, Black History Achives Project 1989; author or co-author of 12 technical papers. **BUSINESS ADDRESS:** Engineering Manager, Rockwell International, 12214 Lakewood Blvd, Downey, CA 90241.

GROSS, MELVIN A.
Business executive. **PERSONAL:** Born Dec 26, 1941, Marshall, TX; married Jessie Laverne Allen. **EDUCATION:** Bishop Coll Dallas, BS Chemistry 1959-63; BaylorUniv Waco, TX, MS Chemistry 1967-68. **CAREER:** Sherwin-Williams Co, vice pres & dir mfg 1979-, mgr distrib ctrs 1977-79, plant mgr Newark, NJ 1975-77, prodn Mgr Detroit 1974-75, prodn mgr Newark 1972-74, quality control dir 1971-72. **ORGANIZATIONS:** Mem Am Chem Soc/Fedn of Soc for Paint Technology/Nat Paint & Coating Assn. **HONORS/ACHIEVEMENTS:** Fellowship, NSF 1967-68; publ "Hepatic Lipidasis Asso With L-Asparaginase Treatment" 1969; Plant Mgr of the Year, Sherin-Williams 1976.

GROSVENOR, VERTA MAE
Writer. **PERSONAL:** Born Apr 04, 1938, Fairfax, SC; children: Kali, Chandra. **ORGANIZATIONS:** People United to Save Humanity (PUSH). **HONORS/ACHIEVEMENTS:** Author of Vibration Cooking, Doubleday, 1970; Thursday and Every Other Sunday Off, Doubleday, 1970; and Plain Brown Rapper, Doubleday, 1975; author of food column in Amsterdam News and Chicago Courier. **BUSINESS ADDRESS:** Penn Center, PO Box 126, Frogmore, SC 29920. *

GROVE, DANIEL
Government official. **PERSONAL:** Born Dec 14, 1923, Milport, AL; married Mary E; children: Elbert, Donnie, Robert, Maxie. **EDUCATION:** Stillman Coll, BA; Brook Army Med Ctr, M. **CAREER:** CO State Bd of Parole, v chmn 1974-; Motor Veh Div, dir 1971-74; Loretto Hts Coll, instr 1971-72; Juvenile Hall, supt 1970-71, asst supt 1966-70; Juvenile Ct, probtn couns 1960-66; Juvenile Hall Boys, 1959-60, supt 1958-59, admns clerk 1958; CO Mil Dist, adminstrv asst 1955-58; Fitzsommons Army Hosp, 1951-55. **ORGANIZATIONS:** Mem CO House of Reps 1965-69; CO Work-Release Prgm; CO Prison Ind Law; CO Chidlren's Code; White House Conf 1966; mem Zion Bapt Ch; bd dirs Curtis Park Comm Ctr 1966-68; Red Shield Comm Ctr 1964-67; Mayor's Commn on Human Rel 1965-68; spl com, Gov 1967; bd dirs Boys Club of Denver 1969-73; Mile High Chap Am Red Cross 1969-74; commr Denver Housing Authority 1969-; bd of tsts Multiple Sclerosis Soc of CO 1971-; liaison rep United Fund City & Co of Denver 1971-72; bd dirs CO Prison Assn 1964-. **BUSINESS ADDRESS:** 888 E Iliff, Denver, CO 80210.

GROVES, DELORES ELLIS
Educational administrator. **PERSONAL:** Born Jan 29, 1940, Shelby Co, KY; daughter of David I Ellis and Mary Powell Ellis; married Clyde Groves, Dec 20, 1969; children: Angela D Payden, Robin L. **EDUCATION:** Spalding Coll, BS Ed 1966; John Carroll Univ, MA Ed 1972; Clevelalnd State Univ, admin certificate, 1976-79; Univ of Akron, EdE candidate 1981-. **CAREER:** Shaker Heights City School District, elementary principal. **ORGANIZATIONS:** Pres & organizer VIP's Social & Civic Club 1973-75; dean of pledges Phi Delta Kappa 1979-80; mem Phi Delta Kappa 1981-; consultant & workshop leader NAESP Conferences 1982-83; presenter AASA Summer Conf 1983; treas LSAC 1983-85; consultant Cuy Sp Educ Serv Ctr 1983-85; delegate & county rep OAESA 1984-87; health fair coord Shaker Hts Int Group 1985; fund raiser co-chair Delta Sigma Theta 1985-87; delegate to rep assembly NAESP 1985-87; natl nominating chairperson 1986 convention NABSE. **HONORS/ACHIEVEMENTS:** OAESA, lead school to 1st "Hall of Fame" Award 1984-85; Natl Assn of Negro Business & Professional Women Inc, Professional of the Year, 1985; "Salute to Black Women Recognition, Call & Post newspaper, 1989; Intervention Assistance Team Trainer, OAESA & State of OH, 1988-89; workshop planner & leader, Natl Sor PDK, Pre-Conf, 1989. **BUSINESS ADDRESS:** Elementary Principal, Mooreland School, 16500 Van Aken, Shaker Heights, OH 44120.

GROVES, HARRY EDWARD
Educational administrator. **PERSONAL:** Born Sep 04, 1921, Manitou Springs, CO; son of Harry Groves (deceased) and Dorothy Cave Groves; married Evelyn Frances Apperson; children: Sheridan Hale. **EDUCATION:** Univ of CO, BA 1943; Univ of Chicago, JD 1949; Harvard Univ, LLM 1959. **CAREER:** TX So Univ, dean/sch of law 1956-60; Univ of Singapore, dean/faculty of law 1960-64; Central State Univ, pres 1965-68; Sch of Law of Cincinnati, prof 1968-70; NC Central Univ Durham, dean/sch of law 1976-81; Univ of NC, prof sch of law 1981-86; Memphis State Univ, Herbert Heff visiting prof of law, 1989-90. **ORGANIZATIONS:** Elected mem City Council Fayetteville NC 1951-52; chmn Gov's Task Force on Sec & Privacy 1979-; bd of dir Mutual Svgs & Loan Assn 1979-80; pres NC Prisoner Legal Serv Inc 1979-81; pres Legal Serv of NC 1983-85; mem Sigma Pi Phi, Alpha Phi Alpha Frat; mem NC, TX, OH Bar Assns; vice pres bd of gov NC Bar Assn 1986-87; mem bd of dir Amer Bar Found 1986-88, NC Museum of Art 1989-. **HONORS/ACHIEVEMENTS:** "Comparative Constitutional Law Cases & Materials" Oceana Publs Inc 1963; "The Constitution of Malaysia" Malaysia Publs Ltd 1964; pub more than 30 other books & articles; Phi Beta Kappa; Phi Delta Kappa; Kappa Delta Pi; president, Wake County North Carolina Phi Beta Kappa 1989-; sire archon, Alpha Tau Chapter of Sigma Pi Phi 1986-88; The Constitution of Malaysia, 4th ed. (with Sheridan) 1979; Malayan Law Journal (PTE.) LTD; Tun Abdul Razak Memorial Lecturer, Kuala Lumpur Malaysia 1983. **MILITARY SERVICE:** AUS capt 1943-46 1951-52. **BUSINESS ADDRESS:** Professor Emeritus, Univ of North Carolina, School of Law, Chapel Hill, NC 27514.

GUDGER, ROBERT HARVEY
Business executive, attorney. **PERSONAL:** Born Nov 17, 1927, Mamaroneck, NY; married Priscilla Kirby; children: Margo T, Gail T, Robin. **EDUCATION:** Univ of Redlands CA, BA Polit Sci 1953; ColumbiaUniv NYC, MA Psychol 1958; NY Law Sch NYC, JD 1961. **CAREER:** Xerox Corp, mgr higher educ prgms 1971-; Am Airlines Inc, mgr labor relations 1962-65, 1967-71; Rochester Urban League, exec dir 1965-67; Urban League Westchester, asso dir 1959-62; NY State Dept of Edn, rehab couns 1957-59; NY State Dept of Labor, employment couns 1955-57. **ORGANIZATIONS:** Bd mem Comm Savings Bank, Rochester 1974-76; bd mem Girl Scouts of Am, Rochester 1974-76; bd mdm Meml Art Gallery Rochester 1975-76; bd mem Jr Achvmnt of Stamford 1979-; bd mem Drug Liberation Inc, Stamford 1979-; bd mem United Way of Stamford 1980; Intl Legal Frat, Phi Delta Phi 1961. **HONORS/ACHIEVEMENTS:** Frederick Douglas Award, Comm Serv Rochester 1966; Black Achievers Award, YMCA New York City 1971; Who's Who East Am 1975-76. **BUSINESS ADDRESS:** 800 Long Ridge Rd, Stamford, CT 06904.

GUESS, FRANCIS S.
Appointed government official. **PERSONAL:** Born Jun 14, 1946, Nashville, TN. **EDUCATION:** TN State Univ, BS 1972; Vanderbilt Univ Owen Sch of Mgmt, MBA 1976. **CAREER:** TN State Prison, classification counsl 1971-72; TN Housing Devel Agy, financial mgmt spec 1974-78; Meharry Med Coll, instructor 1978; TN Dept of Personnel, asst commr 1979-80; TN Dept of Gen Serv, commr 1980-83; US Comm on Civil Rights, commr serving 6-yr term 1984-; TN Dept of Labor, commr 1983-. **ORGANIZATIONS:** Vp Nashville-Middle TN Muscular Dystrophy 1984; mem Nashville Urban League; bd mem TN Human Rights Comm 1977-84; bd mem Govt Monitoring Com on Juvenile Corrections 1978-80; v chrmn TN Vietnam Vet Leadership Program 1983-84. **HONORS/ACHIEVEMENTS:** Delegate Amer Council of Young Political Leaders - Africa Study Tour 1981. **MILITARY SERVICE:** AUS Spec 5/E-5 1968-70. **BUSINESS ADDRESS:** Commissioner, State of TN, Dept of Labor, 501 Union Bldg, 2nd Floor, Nashville, TN 37219.

GUICE, GERALD
Chief executive. **CAREER:** Sentinel Computer Services, Oak Brook, IL, chief executive, 1982-. **HOME ADDRESS:** 400 Plaza Dr, Westmont, IL 60559. **BUSINESS ADDRESS:** Sentinel Computer Service Inc, 1010 Jorie Blvd, Oak Brook, IL 60521. *

GUICE, LEROY
Judge. **PERSONAL:** Born Dec 12, 1944, Fayette, MS; married Rosemary Thompson; children: Leroy, Cedric. **EDUCATION:** Co-Lin Jr Coll, continuing ed 1974-76; MS Coll, continuing ed 1983-84; Univ of MS, continuing ed 1984-. **CAREER:** USAF, aircraft frame tech 1964-68; Thomasville Furniture Co, plant production suprv 1972-85; Jefferson Cty, justice court judge 1984-. **ORGANIZATIONS:** Brother mem United Methodist Church 1972-; mason brother Jefferson Lodge 1984; judge Justice Court Judges Assoc 1984-. **MILITARY SERVICE:** USAF airman 1st class 4 yrs; Vietnam Veteran. **HOME ADDRESS:** Rt 2 Box 35, Fayette, MS 39069. **BUSINESS ADDRESS:** Judge Justice Court, Jefferson Co Dist 1, PO Box 1047, Fayette, MS 39069.

GUICE, RALEIGH TERRY
Business executive. **PERSONAL:** Born Jun 11, 1940, Chicago, IL; married Norma W; children: Raleigh Jr, Tracey, Gregory. **EDUCATION:** Univ of IL, BS Acct 1963;Univ of Chicago Grad Bus Sch, MBA 1972. **CAREER:** Raleigh Guice Oldsmobile-Cadillac, pres/owner 1975-; IL Bell Telephone Co, mgr 1967-72; US Treas Dept IRS, treas agt 1963-67; Guice & Sons Driftwood Creation, mgr & salesman 1951-64. **ORGANIZATIONS:** Bd of dir Innercity Foods Inc 1971-75; bd of dir Hamilton Assn of Trade & Industry 1977-; mem Nat Assn of Auto Dealer 1976-; bd or dir Fairfield C of C 1977-; bd of dir United Way of Butler Co OH 1977-; bd of dir Am Bus Council 1978-. **MILITARY SERVICE:** AUS 1st lt 1964-72. **BUSINESS ADDRESS:** 5251 Dixie Hwy, Fairfield, OH 45014.

GUIDRY, ARREADER PLEANNA
Counselor. **PERSONAL:** Born Jan 27, Sour Lake, TX. **EDUCATION:** XavierUniv New Orleans, 1938; OH StateUniv Columbus, 1940-42; Prairie View A&MUniv TX, MS 1958. **CAREER:** Port Arthur Ind School Dist, counselor 1962; Prairie View A&M Univ, assoc prof 1968, instructor 1959; Port Arthur Ind School Dist, teacher, coach1949; Xavier Univ, Lake Charles LA, instructor 1939. **ORGANIZATIONS:** Com person Nat Merit Scholarship Corp 1980; dir Prairie View Off-Campus Ctr 1976; consult Texas A&M Vocational Doctoral Prgm 1972; mem Delta Sigma Theta Sor Inc/Nat Educ Assn/Am Personnel & Guidance Assn/TX Classroom Tchrs Assn/TX State Tchrs Assn; sec-treas Assn of Coll Educ & Suprs; pres Delta Sigma Theta Sor 1975; coord guidance & serv Lincoln HS 1962. **HONORS/ACHIEVEMENTS:** Phi Delta Kappa Award; Outstanding Edn, Prairie View A&MUniv 1977. **BUSINESS ADDRESS:** Port Arthur Ind Sch Dist, PO Box 1388, Port Arthur, TX 77640.

GUILLAUME, ALFRED JOSEPH, JR.
Educator. **PERSONAL:** Born Apr 10, 1947, New Orleans, LA; married Bernice Forrest; children: Alfred III. **EDUCATION:** Xavier Univ of LA, BA 1968; Brown Univ, AM 1972, PhD 1976. **CAREER:** Xavier Univ, coord of admissions 1977-78, dean of freshman studies 1978-80, dean of arts & sci 1980-. **ORGANIZATIONS:** Bd codofil Council of Devel of French in LA 1976-; asst treas Coll Lang Assoc 1978-81;section chmn South Central Modern Lang Assoc 1978-79; pres LA Collegiate Honors Council 1980-81; mem Amer Conf of Acad Deans, Natl Assoc of Coll Deans Registrars & Admissions Officers, LA Council of Deans of Arts & Sci, Assoc of Amer Coll, Amer Assoc of Teachers of French, Coll Lang Assoc; gov appointee & mem acad advisory council Devel of French in LA; pres LA Collegiate Honors Council 1980-81; Louisianais Athenee; assoc mem Sociedad Nacional Hispanica; reader title III proposals Dept of Ed; presentor & discussion leader Competency Assessment in Teacher Ed; panelist Ed Testing Serv Workshop on Testing Dallas TX; consult Methods of Improving Oral Communication in the Target Language. **HONORS/ACHIEVEMENTS:** Fulbright-Hays Teaching Assistantship Intl Inst of Ed 1974-75; Baudelaire & Nature" South Central Modern Lang Assoc Convention 1977; "Conversation with Leopold Sedar Senghor on His Poetry & Baudelaire's" French Review 1978; "The Baudelairian Imagination, Positive Approaches to Nature" Coll Lang Assoc Jrnl 1979; "To Spring" (Au Printemps) New Laurel Review 1980; "Women and Love in the Poetry of the Free People of Color" South Central Modern Lang Assoc Conv 1980; "The Emotive Impulse & the Senghorian Response to Nature" Coll Lang Assoc Conv 1980; "Literature in Nineteenth Century LA, Poetry & the Free People of Color"Jambalaya Public Library Lecture Series 1980; "Jeanne Duval as the Cornerstone of the Baudelairian Imagination" South Central Modern Lang Assoc Convention 1982; "Love Death & Faith in the New Orleans Poets or Color" Southern Quarterly 1982; "Joanni Questi, Monsieur Paul" LA Literature 1984; "Le Divin Mystere, Religious Fervor in the Literature of the Free People of Color" Southern Conf on Christianity in Literature 1984. **MILITARY SERVICE:** AUS sp4 2 yrs; Commendation Medal, Bronze Star 1970. **BUSINESS ADDRESS:** Dean of Arts & Sciences, Xavier University of LA, 7325 Palmetto St, New Orleans, LA 70125.

GUILLAUME, ROBERT
Actor/director/producer. **PERSONAL:** Born in St Louis, MO; married Donna; children: 4 children. **EDUCATION:** Attended, St Louis Univ, Washington Univ. **CAREER:** Theater credits include, Golden Boy, Tambourines to Glory, Othello, Porgy & Bess, Purlie, Jacques Brel; bit parts on, All in the Family, Sanford & Son, The Jeffersons, Marcus Welby MD; starred in, Soap, Benson. **HONORS/ACHIEVEMENTS:** 2 Emmy Awards; 4 NAACP Image Awards. **BUSINESS ADDRESS:** Peters Entertainment Prod Inc, 1438 No Gower, Los Angeles, CA 90028.

GUILLEBEAUX, TAMARA ELISE
Educator, choreographer, administrator/development. **PERSONAL:** Born Mar 29, Philadelphia, PA. **EDUCATION:** Robt Joffrey Sch of Ballet, scholarship 1971; Butler Univ IN, BA 1972; NY Univ, MA 1974; PA Ballet Co Sch of Dance; Judimar Sch of Dance; Marion Cuyjet; Essie Marie Dorsey Sch of Dance. **CAREER:** "Open Space Program" NY Univ, instructor 1973-74; Citidance Dance Co, founder co-dir choreographer 1976; Coll of New Rochelle, asst prof dance/history/movement 1976-77; Bronx Arts Project, asst instructor dance 1978; Fund for Higher Educ, admin asst rsch/fundraising & records 1981-83; Rod Rodgers Dance Co Inc, asst artistic dir 1974-86; Metropolitan Opera Lincoln Center, admin devel dept 1986-. **ORGANIZATIONS:** Asst choreographer off broadway "The Prodigal Sister" 1977; cultural emissary intl tour to Africa, Syria, Portugal US Intl Communic Agency 1978; model Danskin Inc 1979; asst choreographer/commercials Japan Suntory Whiskey Corp 1983; benefit comm member UNICEF "For Our Children's Sake" 1984; mem Alpha Kappa Alpha Sor Inc 1970-; bd of dirs Saraband Ltd 1976-; dir Scholarship Devel Saraband Ltd 1985-. **HONORS/ACHIEVEMENTS:** Rosenblith Scholarship Awd 1970-71; soloist 51st Boule AKA Sor 1984; participant Intl Olympics Black Dance Art Festival 1984; co-producer "Spring Flowering of Arts" Saraband Ltd Scholarship Prog 1983-; consultant Career Counseling in Dance & Dance Educ; choreographerTV commercials. **BUSINESS ADDRESS:** Admin Development Dept, Metropolitan Opera, Lincoln Center, New York, NY 10023.

GUILLORY, JOHN L.
Real estate broker. **PERSONAL:** Born Jul 28, 1945, Oakland; divorced; children: John, Leann. **EDUCATION:** Standord U, BA 1967; Pepperdine U, MBA 1977. **CAREER:** Grubb & Ellis Co, commercial leasing splst 1970-; Cincinnati Bengals, professional football 1969-70; CT Gen Life Ins Co, est, bus & pension planning dept 1968; Lockheed Electronics, Downey, prod control coordntr 1967-68; Oakland Raiders, professional football 1967-68; grieff & Ellis Commrcl Brok Co, asst dist mgr, sales mgr. **ORGANIZATIONS:** Dir Alameda Cnty Taxpayers Assn; mem Intl Cncl of Shopping Ctrs; mem Oakland Airport Ctr; Phi Kappa Sigma Frat; mem Block "S" Letter Soc; presBay Area Black Caucus; sec bd dir Charilla Found; adv com Cath Charities; former mem bd regents John F Kennedy Coll; former dir Cath Socl Svc; former dir Comm Devel Corp; past pres Lay Black Cath Caucus Oakland; mem Philip A Buchanan Lodge 63; Prince Hall Masons CA Inc; former mem Intl 20-30 Club; mem Nat Assn Security Dealers; dir Nat Office Black Cath; pres Nat Lay Black Cath Caucus; bd dir Real Estate Bd; chmn bd tsts Oakland Met Enterprises. **HONORS/ACHIEVEMENTS:** All Coast Honors 3 yrs football, Stanford U; Salesperson of Yr, Grubb & Ellis Co 1974-75. **BUSINESS ADDRESS:** 1333 Broadway, Oakland, CA 94612.

GUILLORY, JULIUS JAMES
Law officer. **PERSONAL:** Born Feb 04, 1927, Opelousas, LA; married Charity Belle Morris. **EDUCATION:** LA State U; So U. **CAREER:** Opelousas, LA, asst police chief 1970-; police capt 1965-70; police lt 1960-65; patrolman 1954-60. **ORGANIZATIONS:** Mem LA Chief Assn; LA Preace Officers Assn; Magnolia State Peace Officers Assn; Municipal Police Officers Assn of LA; Nat Black Police Assn; Nat Org of Black Police Exec; Am Legion; BSA; Foxes Social Club; Frontiers Internat; Holy Ghost Ch Ushers Club; Knights of Peter Claver; NAACP. **HONORS/ACHIEVEMENTS:** KPC Silver Medal Nat Counc, Knights of Peter Claver 1973; KPC Knight of the Year, Knights of Peter Claver 1972; VFW Officer of the Yr 1972; Officer of the Yr, Magnolia State Peace Officers Assn 1970; Nat Black Police Assn Workship 1975-76. **MILITARY SERVICE:** AUS 1945-46. **BUSINESS ADDRESS:** PO Box 669, Opelousas, LA 70570.

GUILLORY, WILLIAM A.
Educator. **PERSONAL:** Born Dec 04, 1938, New Orleans, LA; children: William Jr, Daniel S. **EDUCATION:** Dillard Univ, BA 1960; Univ CA, PhD 1964. **CAREER:** Howard Univ, asst prof 1965-69; Drexel Univ, assoc prof 1969-74; Univ of UT, assoc prof Chemistry 1974-76, prof & chmn Chemistry 1976-. **ORGANIZATIONS:** Consult Naval Ordnance Station 1967-76; adv com EPA 1972-75; adv panel NSF 1974-77; natl chmn Professional Black Chemists & Chemical Engrs 1972-; consult Natl Acad Scis 1973-74; author num publs; mem Amer Chem Soc; mem Beta Kappa Chi; mem Sigma Xi, Alpha Chi Sigma, Amer Physical Soc, AAAS, NY Acad Sci, Phi Kappa Phi. **HONORS/ACHIEVEMENTS:** NSF Postdoctoral Fellow Univ Paris 1964-65; Alfred P Sloan Found Fellow 1971-73; Outstanding Educators Amer 1972; Merit Awd City New Orleans 1974; DanfortFound Assn 1975. **BUSINESS ADDRESS:** Chairman of Chemistry, Univ Utah, Dept of Chemistry, Salt Lake City, UT 84112.

GUILMENOT, RICHARD ARTHUR, III
Business executive. **PERSONAL:** Born Mar 15, 1948, Detroit, MI; married Melanie Williams. **EDUCATION:** Fisk U, BA 1970; Northwestern U, M BA 1972. **CAREER:** Ted Bater Adv, acct exec 1972-74; BBDO Adv, acct supr vice pres 1974-77; Mingo Jones Guilmendt, vice pres dir client serv 1977-79; Warner Am Satellite Ent Co, vice pres mktg 1980-82; GCI, pres. **ORGANIZATIONS:** Dir Natl Urban League 1978-81; advsr Amsterdam News 1977-82; barileur Omega Psi Phy 1970-. **BUSINESS ADDRESS:** President, GCI, 90 Grandview Ave, Great Neck, NY 11020.

GUILTON, HENRIETTA FAYE BRAZELTON
Business executive. **PERSONAL:** Born Oct 30, 1941, Springfield, IL; married Harvie Guiton Jr; children: Nichele Monique. **EDUCATION:** Mills Coll, BA 1974; CA State Univ, MS 1975; Univ of CA , Berkeley, EdD candidate. **CAREER:** Mills Coll, asst dean of students/int head of ethic studies 1975-76; Marcus Foster Educational Inst, exec dir 1976-79; Kaiser Aluminum & Chem Corp, admin mgr planning & control 1979, vice pres, general mgr. **ORGANIZATIONS:** Mem Phi Lambda Theta 1975-; mem, Amer Mgmt Assn 1977-; advisory bd World Coll West 1979-80; bd dirs No CA NAACP Legal Defense Fund 1979-80; bd dirs Oakland Visitors & Convention Bureau 1980-81; Bd dirs KQED, Channel 9, 1980-81; bd dirs Univ YWCA Berkeley 1976-77; mem, Natl Soc of Fund Raising Execs; mem, Pacific Child & Family Counseling Center 1977-; mem Develop Execs Roundtable; mem LWV. **HONORS/ACHIEVEMENTS:** Citizen of the Day KABL 1976; Distinguished Public Award, CA BSU Convention 1979; Distinguished Alumni Oakland Public School 1979.

GUINIER, EWART
Educator. **PERSONAL:** Born May 17, 1910, Ancon, CZ; married Eugenia Paprin; children: Clotilde, Lani, Sary, Marie. **EDUCATION:** Harvard Univ, 1929-31; CCNY, BS 1935; Columbia, MA 1939; NYU, JD 1959; Harvard Univ, hon MA 1969. **CAREER:** Harlem Rsch Labs Inc, supvr 1933-35; YWCA Harlem Trade School, teacher 1935-37; NY City, personnel examiner 1935-39; Serv Rating Bureau, dir 1940-42; Army Univ Pacific, teacher 1945; CIO Public Workers, intl sec-treasurer 1946-53, consult 1953-; UN, research 1961-62; Brownsville Comm Council, exec dir 1965; Intra-Am Life Insurance Co, assoc dir agency 1966; Urban Center Columbia Univ, assoc dir 1968; Harvard Afro-Amer Studies Dept, prof, chmn 1969. **ORGANIZATIONS:** Exec asst Harlem Affairs Com 1953-55; Jamaica Coor Council on Urban Renew & Neighborhood Consult 1961-; chmn Queens Urban League 1961-67; mem Acad Political Sci; NY Urban League; Pub Educ Assn; Douglass Urban Corp; mem Alpha Phi Alpha Organ of Am Historians; mem Natl Exec Counc Assn; mem Study Afro-Am Life & Hist; mem Natl Counc for Black Studies; NAACP; adv bd Black Heritage; trustee Ctr for Urban Edn; Queens Coll Speech and Hearing Serv Ctr. **HONORS/ACHIEVEMENTS:** Recipient of Carter G Woodson Award for Promotion of Black History NY Br Assn for the Study of Afro Am Life & Hist; Official Citation MA State Senate; author monographs and articles in professional journals. **MILITARY SERVICE:** AUS 1942-46. **BUSINESS ADDRESS:** Chmn Afro-American Studies, Harvard University, 77 Dunster St, Cambridge, MA 02138.

GUITANO, ANTON W.
Broadcast company financial executive, corporate officer. **PERSONAL:** Born Jul 05, 1950, Brooklyn, NY; son of Whitney J Guitano and Blanche Epps Guitano; married Leslie Marie Ferguson, Jun 15, 1975; children: Jessica Lynn, Jennifer Whitney, Jason Antonn. **EDUCATION:** St Peters Coll, Jersey City NJ, BS, 1971. **CAREER:** Price Waterhouse, New York NY, sr auditor, 1971-78; CBS Inc, New York NY, sr dir auditing, 1978-83; CBS Television Stations, New York NY, controller, 1983-86; CBS Television Network, New York NY, controller, 1986-88; CBS Inc, New York NY, vice pres, gen auditor, 1988-. **ORGANIZATIONS:** Mem, Amer Inst of Certified Public Accountants, 1979-, NYSSCPA, 1979-; pres, Walden & Country Woods Homeowners Assn, 1980-84; mem, Broadcast Financial Mgmt Assn, 1983-, Natl Assn of Broadcasters, 1983-. **HONORS/ACHIEVEMENTS:** Certified Public Accountant, New York State Dept of Educ, 1979. **BUSINESS ADDRESS:** Vice President & General Auditor, CBS Inc, 51 W 52nd St, Room 2164, New York, NY 10019.

GUITON, BONNIE
Government official. **PERSONAL:** Born Oct 30, 1941, Springfield, IL; daughter of Henry Frank Brazelton and Zola Elizabeth Newman Brazelton; divorced; children: Nichele M. **EDUCATION:** Mills Coll, Oakland CA, BA, 1974; California State Univ, Hayward CA, MS, 1975; Univ of California, Berkeley CA, EdD, 1985. **CAREER:** Mills Coll, asst dean of students 1974-76; Marcus Foster Educ Inst, exec dir 1976-79; Kaiser Ctr Inc, vice pres & genl mgr 1979-84; US Postal Rate Commn, commissioner 1984-87; US Dept of Educ Washington, DC asst sec 1987-89; US Office of Consumer Affairs, Washington DC, special adviser to the pres & director 1989-; US Dept of Education, Office Vocational & Adult Education, Washington DC, asst secretary, 1989-. **ORGANIZATIONS:** Mem Northern CA NAACP Legal Defense Fund 1979-84, bd of directors Northern CA Conf of Christians & Jews Assoc 1983-86, Natl Urban Coalition 1984-85; mem Urban Land Inst 1982-84, Natl Assoc of Regulatory Utility Comrs 1984-87, Exec Women in Govt 1985-; bd of directors, Natl Museum for Women in the Arts 1988-89; mem Independent Agency. **HONORS/ACHIEVEMENTS:** Tribute to Women in Intl Industry YWCA 1981; Outstanding Comm Leader & Humanitarian Awd NAACP Legal Defense Fund 1981; CANDACE Awd Natl Coalition of 100 Black Women 1982; Equal Rights Advocate Awd 1984; Distinguished Meritorious Award DC Human Services 1987; Honorary Doctorate Tougaloo Univ 1988. **BUSINESS ADDRESS:** US Dept of Education, Asst Secretary, Office of Vocational & Adult Education, 400 Maryland Ave, Washington, DC 20202. *

GULLATTEE, ALYCE C.
Physician, educator. **PERSONAL:** Born Jun 28, 1928, Detroit; married Latinee G; children: Jeanne, Audrey, Nat. **EDUCATION:** Univ CA, BA 1956; HowardUniv Coll Med, MD 1964. **CAREER:** St Elizabeth's Hosp & DC Gen Hosp, rotating intshp 1964-65; St Elizabeth's Hosp, med officer, gen prac 1965-66, Med Officer in Psychiatry 1968-71; St Elizabeth's Hosp & George WashingtonUniv Hosp, residency psychiatry 1965-68; HowardUniv Coll Med, asst prof psychiatry 1970-, clinical asst prof FamilyPractice 1970-; Nat Inst Mental Health, career tchr Addictive Substances Abuse 1974-77. **ORGANIZATIONS:** Mem ed bd Jour Nat Med Assn 1967-; consult Juvenile & Domestic Relations Ct, Arlington Co 1968-; recording sec All Psychiat Progress 1967-70; chiefcons Drug Educ Prgm Juvenile Ct, Arlington 1969; v chmn 1969-70, chmn elect 1970-71, chmn 1971-72 Psychiatry-Neurology Sect, Nat Med Assn; mem Ho of Dels, Nat Med Assn 1968-75; obsvr consult Council Intl Ogrgn, Am Psychiat Assn 1969-73; consult EEO 1969-70; co-coordntr Drug Abuse Seminar, Nat Council Juvenile Ct Judges 1970; chmn ad hoc com HEW, Poor Children & Youth 1969-; rep Am Psychiat Assn Chicago 1970; mem Com Psychiat & Law, Am Psychiat Assn 1973-; chmn Prgm Com, Am Psychiat Assn 1974-75; chmn Grad Com Intl Prgms, HowardUniv 1974-; chief consult Arlington Co Drug Abust Treatment Prgm, Prelude 1969-; Nat Psychiat Consult & Prgm Developer Nat Council Negro Women 1972-; chmn Com Intl Med, Nat Med Assn, Med-surgical Soc 1974-78; sr adv, co-founder Student Nat Med Assn, Washington; mem Nat Inst Drug Abuse Task Force 1975-. **HONORS/ACHIEVEMENTS:** Outstanding Tchr Award, HowardUniv Coll Medicine 1973; Career Tchr Award, Nat Inst Mental Health 1974-; Academic Honors Zoology,Univ CA 1956; first award Clinical Acumen, HowardUniv Coll Medicine 1964; Magna Cum Laude Internship Award, St Elizabeth Hosp 1965; Citizens Award - Outstanding Contbns to Comm, Santa Monica NAACP 1960; Outstanding Black Woman of 1970, Nat Med Assn; nominee TV Emmy award by Washington Chap Nat Acad TV Arts & Scis, NBC Spl The Disabled Mind; mem by apptmt of Pres of US to Nat Adv Com Juvenile Justice & Delinquency Prevention, US Dept Justice 1975-76; fellow Inst Soc, Ethics & Life Scis Hastings-on-Hudson 1975-77.

GULLEY, WILSON
Business executive. **PERSONAL:** Born Oct 06, 1937, Buckner, AR; married Katherine Richardson; children: Debbie Renee Collins, Wilson Jr, Bruce Edward, Keith Ramon. **EDUCATION:** Univ of Wash, AA, BA 1966-68; NY U, post grad 1968-69. **CAREER:** F & G Constrn Inc, pres 1977-; Omni Homes Inc, pres 1979-; United Inner City Devel Found, pres 1971-75; Nat Bus League Seattle Chpt, pres 1970-79. **ORGANIZATIONS:** Exec dir Rotary Boys Club, Seattle 1968-70; institutional rep Boy Scouts of Am 1968-70; credit com chmn Central Area Fed Credit Union 1968-73; couns/fdr Youth in Bus Orgn 1971-72; Boys Club (Pres Nixon), Boys Club of Am 1969; comm devel Seattle Police & Fire Depts 1969. **HONORS/ACHIEVEMENTS:** Outstndg bus proposal Roxbury Bus Inst 1972; spl recognition Seattle Kiwanis Club 1971; scholarshipUniv CA Berkeley, Nat Council for Equal Bus Opportunies 1972; scholarship toUniv of Chicago, United Mortgage Bankers of Am 1973f

community Devel Award, SER Seattle Chap 1973. **MILITARY SERVICE:** USAF a/2c 1956-60. **BUSINESS ADDRESS:** 1924 Franklin Ave E, Seattle, WA 98102.

GULLIVER, ADELAIDE CROMWELL
Educator. **PERSONAL:** Born Nov 27, 1919, Washington, DC; divorced; children: Anthony C Hill. **EDUCATION:** Smith Coll, BA 1940; Univ of PA, MA 1941; Bryn Mawr, Cert in Soc Work 1952; Radcliffe Coll, PhD 1952. **CAREER:** Hunter Coll, mem faculty 1942-44; Smith Coll, mem faculty 1945-46; Boston Univ, mem faculty 1951-, dir Afro-Amer studies, prof emerita sociology. **ORGANIZATIONS:** Adv comm Corrections Commonwealth MA 1955-68; adv comm Voluntary AID 1964-80; mem Natl Endowment for the Humanities 1968-70; dir African Studies Assoc 1966-68; adv comm, to dir census 1972-75 IRS; mem Natl Ctr of Afro-Amer Artists 1970-80, African Scholars Council 1971-80; bd mem Wheelock Coll 1971-72; mem Commonwealth Inst of Higher Ed 1973-74; mem Natl Fellowship Fund 1974-75, Bd Foreign Scholarships 1980-84; mem Bd on Sci & Tech for Intl Devel 1984-86; mem African Studies Assoc, Amer Soc Soc, Acad of Arts & Sci, Council on Foreign Relations. **HONORS/ACHIEVEMENTS:** Mem Phi Beta Kappa; Grand Master of Ivory Coast 1967; Univ of Southwestern MA LHD 1971; Alumnae Medal Smith Coll 1971; TransAfrica Africa Freedom Awd 1983. **BUSINESS ADDRESS:** Prof Emerita Sociology, Boston University, 138 Mountfort St, Brookline, MA 02146.

GUMBEL, BRYANT CHARLES
TV host. **PERSONAL:** Born Sep 29, 1948, New Orleans, LA; married June Baranco; children: Bradley. **EDUCATION:** Bates Coll, BA 1970. **CAREER:** Black Sports Magazine, editor-in-chief 1972; KNBC-TV, weekend sportscaster 1972-73, sportscaster 1973-76; NBC's Rose Bowl Parade & coverage, co-host 1975-; NBC's Grandstand Show, co-host 1976-; Super Bowl XI, co-host 1977; 19 Inch Variety Show, 1977; performer co-host KNBC Shows What's Going On, News Conference, Prep Sports World, Brainworks 1977; KNBC-TV, sports director; NBC-TV, sportscaster; NBC Today Show, co-host 1983-. **ORGANIZATIONS:** Mem AFTRA, SCSBA, NATAS. **HONORS/ACHIEVEMENTS:** 9 Emmy Awds Sportscasting 1973-; prod wrote & hosted Olympic Reflections A Handful of Dreams; Golden Mike Awd Los Angeles Press Club 1978,79. **BUSINESS ADDRESS:** NBC Today Show, 30 Rockefeller Plaza, Ste 1508, New York, NY 10020.

GUMBS, OLIVER SINCLAIR
Retired physician. **PERSONAL:** Born Oct 31, 1913, Aetna, NY; married Muriel Francene Burruss; children: Mignon, BJ, Carol, John, Oliver, Antoinette. **EDUCATION:** Attended, Cornell Univ, Virginia Union Univ; Meharry Medical School, MD 1941. **CAREER:** St Martin De Pours Hosp, chief of staff of surgery; Twin Oaks Nursing Home, director/physician; Gateway Drug Prog, director; Private Practice, physician/surgeon 1941-83; Mobile Mental Health Clinic, physician; Searcy Mental Hospital, 1983-86 (retired). **ORGANIZATIONS:** Mem The Utopian Social Club, Florida Guardsmen; mem 32 degree Masons 1946-; mem Mobile Bay Medical Assoc; one of founders Gulf Coast Medical Assoc; one ofincorporators State Medical Assoc for Blacks. **HONORS/ACHIEVEMENTS:** State Resolution for Accomplishment AL State Legislature 1980; Ebony's 100 Most Influential Ebony Magazine 1981; Grand Polemarch Kappa Alpha Psi Frat 1981; rec'd Keys to the Cities of Chicago, Indianapolis, Mobile and New Orleans.

GUMBS, PHILIP N.
Attorney. **PERSONAL:** Born Apr 29, 1923, Perth Amboy, NJ; married Rachel Valentine; children: Robina, Philip Kelvin. **EDUCATION:** Seton Hall U, AA 1948; Lincoln U, JD 1952. **CAREER:** Township Matawan, councilman 1971-73, mayor 1974; Worker's Compensation Ct NJ Bd Edn, judge 1955-58; Matawan Twp Zoning Bd Admustment, 1964-71. **ORGANIZATIONS:** Bd dirs Monmouth Co United Fund; mem Monmouth Co NJ Bd of Chosen Freeholdes 1974, dir 1975; chmn bd tsts, supt Sunday Sch St Marks AME Ch 1953- ;mem Monmouth Co Am, NJ State, Nat Bar Assns chmn Amaricanization & Citizenship Com. **HONORS/ACHIEVEMENTS:** Brotherhood Award, Nat Conf Christians & Jews 1975; Life Fellow, Am Co Govt 1976; Comm Serv Award, The Nat Caucus of the Black Aged Inc 1979. **MILITARY SERVICE:** AUS sgt 1942-45. **BUSINESS ADDRESS:** 1 Ct House Sq, Freehold, NJ 07728.

GUMMS, EMMANUEL GEORGE, SR.
Clergyman & educational administrator. **PERSONAL:** Born Jan 16, 1928, Opelusas, LA; married Shirley Mae Griffen (dec) (deceased); children: Emanuel Jr; Salyria, Valenti. **EDUCATION:** Leland College, AB cum laude 1954; Union Seminary, BD 1955; Inter Baptist Theological, ThD 1974, LLD 1976; Universal Bible Institute, PhD 1978; Straigth Business Coll, exec sec 1960. **CAREER:** West NO Baptist Assn, president 1972-76; LA Cristian Training Institute, president 1973-75; Christian Bible College of LA, academic dean 1976-; First New Testament B C, pastor 1958-. **ORGANIZATIONS:** Supervisor LSU Dental School 1971-77; secretary Jefferson Parish Ministers Union 1973-81; bd chairman Jefferson Parish Voters League 1975-84; general secretary LA Progressive Baptist Assn 1978-; chaplain Veterans of Foreign Wars #2403 1981-. **HONORS/ACHIEVEMENTS:** Outstanding leadership 2nd Congress LBA 1978; communicator West Bank American Muslem 1980; dedicated service ML King Community Center 1981. **MILITARY SERVICE:** AUS sfc5 6 yrs; OCC MED(J); OCC MED(K); KSM 2 BSS UNSM 1950-56. **BUSINESS ADDRESS:** Pastor, First New Testament BC, 6112 W Bank Expressway, Marrero, LA 70072.

GUNN, ALEX M., JR.
Educator. **PERSONAL:** Born May 09, 1928, Newkirk, OK; divorced; children: Alexis Lamb, Michael Clay. **EDUCATION:** LangstonUniv & Friends U, BA 1953; CA Polytechnic, MA 1962. **CAREER:** Bureau of Intergroup Relations CA State Dept of Educ, cons; CRA Youth Auth Whittier, dir 1970-71; supvr of acad instruction 1970; Parole & Serv Sacramento, supvr of acad instruction 1969-70; Paso Robles, supvr of acad instr 1965-69, teacher 1965-70, youth auth & teacher 1958-65; boys group supvr 1956-58. **ORGANIZATIONS:** Mem ACIRE; Black Sch Bd mem & Adminstrs; Council of Excptnl Chldrn; chrtr mem ASCA Black Edctrs Assn; past pres CEC Chap 39; NAACP; Assn of CA Sch Adminstr; past pres & vice pres So Co Chap Dist #12 Toastmaster & Intl Gov; pblcty chmn OEO No Co Area Grtr Whittier Fair Hsng Com & Human Rels Com; pres 3 times PRSB Tchr Assn; adv BSA; past membrshp chmn CPPCA; mem Assn of CA Intrgrp Rels Edctrs; CA Council for Intergrated Edn. **MILITARY SERVICE:** AUS 1950-51. **BUSINESS ADDRESS:** CA State Dept of Educ, 721 Capitol Mall, Sacramento, CA 95814.

GUNN, ARTHUR CLINTON
Educator. **PERSONAL:** Born Apr 29, 1942, New Castle, PA; son of John O Gunn Sr and Magnolia Hill Murray. **EDUCATION:** Wilberforce Univ, Wilberforce OH, BS Educ, 1964; Atlanta Univ, Atlanta GA, MS Library Science, 1969; Univ of Pittsburgh, Pittsburgh PA, PhD, 1986. **CAREER:** Delaware State Coll, Dover DE, librarian, 1969-71; Howard Univ, Washington DC, librarian, 1971-76; Univ of Maryland, College Park MD, adjunct prof, 1972-76; Univ of Pittsburgh, Pittsburgh PA, librarian, 1983-86; Wayne State Univ, Detroit MI, prof, 1986-. **ORGANIZATIONS:** Mem, Amer Library Assn, 1969-, Amer Library and Information Science Educ, 1986-; consultant, General Motors Corp, 1988-; pres, Assn of African-Amer Librarian, 1988-. **HONORS/ACHIEVEMENTS:** Chair, Govt Relations Comm of the Assn for Library and Information Science Educ. **BUSINESS ADDRESS:** Wayne State University, Library Science Program, 106 Kresge Library, Detroit, MI 48202.

GUNN, BILL See GUNN, WILLIAM HARRISON

GUNN, GLADYS
Educational administrator. **PERSONAL:** Born Apr 28, 1937, Columbus, GA; daughter of John Gunn and Jessie Gunn. **EDUCATION:** Cntrl State U, BS Elem Ed 1959; Miami U, MEd 1964; OH State U, 1971-72. **CAREER:** Dayton Publ Schls, teacher 1959-66, interviewer for federally funded prgm 1966-69, assoc in personnel 1969-71; OH Youth Cmsn, asst supt 1972-73; CSU W & CSU Training Ins, dir 1973-77; Cntrl Stae U, training & emplymnt pgm 1977-78, crdntr SDIP 1978-80; Dept Hlth & Human Serv, spec asst 1980-81; Dayton Pblc Sch, crdntr evltn 1982-86; Dayton Publ Schls, spec asst for administration & ident of grants 1986-. **ORGANIZATIONS:** Mem of, Alpha Kappa Alpha Sorority, Soroptimist Intl, Assc Suprvsn & Crclm Dev, Phi Delta Kappa, Subcommittee on Ed of the Ad Hoc Committee on Civil Rights, City of Dayton Comm on Ed; bd mem Daymont Mental Health Prgm; elected mem Inner West Priority Bd; bd mem Comprehensive Manpower Training Cntr; mem, Amer Assn of School Admin, 1989-. **HONORS/ACHIEVEMENTS:** Prsdtl apptment Natl Advsry Cncl on Women's Edctnl Pgm 1978-80; presappt Spec Asst for Spec Grps 1980-81. **HOME ADDRESS:** 1541 Earlham Dr, Dayton, OH 45406. **BUSINESS ADDRESS:** Special Asst for Admin, Dayton Pblc Sch, 348 W First St, Dayton, OH 45402.

GUNN, VERA
Business executive. **PERSONAL:** Born Dec 25, 1925, Philadelphia, PA; married Mitchell E Harden. **EDUCATION:** West Chester State Coll, BA 1953; PA School of Social Work, 1966; Rutgers Univ, Cert Professional Counseling 1970; Temple Univ, Cert Public Relations 1973. **CAREER:** Woman's Christian Alliance, social worker interviewer 1954; Fellowship Commiss, intergroup relations rep 1964; Heritage Honor Ed Cultural Ctr, exec dir 1969; WDAS Sunday Breakfast Show, public relations dir 1973; Vera Gunn Assoc Inc, pres 1980. **ORGANIZATIONS:** Pres Natl Assoc Media Women 1969; 1st female pres Natl Assoc Market Devel 1972; 1st female pres, 1st female bd chairperson Natl Assoc of Mkt Developers 1974-85; bd mem Temple Univ Recreation Council 1976-85; founder, bd mem Afro-Amer Historical & Cultural Museum 1976-85; bd mem Boys & Girls Club Metro 1980; bd mem Natl Coalition of 100 Black Women 1982-85; consult DE Valley Pepsi Cola Bottling Co; founder Afro-Amer Cultural Museum; trustee PhiladelphiaChap United Way. **HONORS/ACHIEVEMENTS:** Serv Awd NAACP Disting Serv Awd 1962; Mktg Awd Natl Assoc Mkt Devel Awd 1970; Woman of the Year Natl Council of Negro Women 1971; Comm Serv Awd OIC Bicentennial Awd 1976. **HOME ADDRESS:** 6466 Ross St, Philadelphia, PA 19119.

GUNN, WILLIAM HARRISON (BILL GUNN)
Writer/director. **PERSONAL:** Born Jul 15, 1934, Philadelphia, PA; son of William Harrison Gunn and Louise Alexander Gunn. **CAREER:** Writer/director; author of plays: "Marcus in the High Grass," 1958, "Black Picture Show," 1975; novelist: All the Rest Have Died, Delacorte, 1963, Rhinestone Sharecropping, Reed, Cannon, 1981; screenplays: "The Landlord" 1970, "Angel Levine" 1970, "Don't the Moon Look Lonesome," 1970, "Ganja and Hess," 1973, and "The Greatest: The Muhammed Ali Story," 1976; films directed "Ganja & Hess" 1973. **HONORS/ACHIEVEMENTS:** Emmy Award, Natl Acad of Television Arts and Sciences, for TV screenplay "Johnnas," 1972; "Ganja and Hess" chosen one of ten Best Amer Films of the Decade, Cannes Film Festival, 1973; Audelco Award for Best Play of the Year, for "Black Picture Show," 1975; John Simon Guggenheim Mem Found Fellowship Award in filmmaking, 1980. **MILITARY SERVICE:** US Navy. *

GUNN, WILLIE COSDENA THOMAS
Educator, school academic counselor. **PERSONAL:** Born Dec 24, 1926, Seneca, SC; daughter of Fletcher Gideon and Mattie Riley Gideon; married Willie James Gunn, Dec 24, 1975; children: Dr John Henderson Thomas III. **EDUCATION:** Benedict Coll, BS 1946; Univ of MI, MA Educ 1967, MA Guidance 1970; Urban Bible Coll, Detroit, MI, doctorate, 1987. **CAREER:** Emerson Jr HS, tchr common learnings & scis 1956-64; Headstart Prog, super 1965; Title I Operation Summer Prog, super 1967-73; MI State Univ, tchr supervisor 1962-64; Emerson Jr HS, guidance counselor 1964-76; Mott Coll, instr social sci 1969-78; Flint Open Sch, guidance counselor 1976-82; Jordan Coll, instr social sci dept 1981; Southwestern HS, guidance counselor 1982-88; Southwestern Acad, guidance counselor, 1988-. **ORGANIZATIONS:** Flint City Adv Comm League of Women Voters; Voter Educ Coalition Drug Abuse Task Force; bd dirs WFBE Pub Radio Station; bd dirs Natl Assn of Media Women; life mem & past pres Zeta Phi Beta Sor; life mem & past pres Natl Sor of Phi Delta Kappa; mem Amer Assn of Univ Women; life mem Natl Assn of Negro Business & Professional Women; mem NAACP, Urban League, Africa Care, Natl Council of Negro Women; Genesee Area Assn of Counseling Devel; United Teachers of Flint; Natl Educ Assn; Michigan Educ Assn; mem, Metropolitan Chamber of Commerce, 1984-; 2nd vice pres, Top Ladies of Distinction, 1985-; public relations dir, Black Panhellenic Council, 1987-. **HONORS/ACHIEVEMENTS:** Woman of the Yr Natl Assn of Media Women 1976; Sepia Awd Natl Assn of Media Women 1978; Zeta Phi Beta Sor Woman of the Yr 1982; Zeta Phi Beta Sor Zeta of the Yr 1969; Panhellenic Woman of the Yr 1972; Educational Awd Natl Sor of Phi Delta Kappa 1974; Achievement Award Rsch Alcoholism Univ WI 1967; March of Dimes Comm Serv Awd 1971; author & counselor consultant Comm Educ Network Proj 1983; Woman of the Year, Natl Assn of Media Women, 1988; Bigger & Better Business Award, Phi Beta Sigma Fraternity, 1989; Hall of Fame, Zeta Phi Beta Sorority, 1989; Counselor of the Year, Genesee Area Assn of Counseling Devel, 1989; author, Black Achievement Register; co-author, Feelings (poems), 1971; author, Countdown to College, 1984; co-author, Career Planning, 1988. **HOME ADDRESS:** 1511 Church St, Flint, MI 48503.

GUNNEL, JOSEPH C., SR.
Government official. **PERSONAL:** Born May 02, 1918, St Louis, MO; married Annie P

Fields; children: Kathleen, Joseph, Jr, Charles, Ronald. **EDUCATION:** Lincoln U, 1936-39; TN A&I State, AB 1947-49; Washington U, MSW 1966-68. **CAREER:** State of MO, admin ofcr/EEO spclst 1958-; Lackland AF Base Scott AF Base, training instr 1955-58. **ORGANIZATIONS:** Bd of dir USO; past & mem Model City Bd of DirF MOUniv Extension Ctr; past consult Juvenile Deliquency Sub-com Mayor's Commn on Crime & Law Enfrcmnt; past commr BSA; past bd of dir Page-Park YMCA; past pres Epsilon Lambda; past vice pres Alpha Phi Alpha Bldg Fdn; host Accent on Youth 1963-74; clmnst St LouisAm 1951-60; St Louis Argus 1973-. **HONORS/ACHIEVEMENTS:** Man of Year Alpha Phi Alpha 1963; Alpha Phi Alpha Midwest Hall of Fame 1965; Citz of Wk Comm Serv Awrd KATZ 1965; Mayor's Civic Awrd 1970; Outstdng & meritorious serv Comm Devel & Pub Civic Activity Awrd Iota Phi Lambda 1970; hon St Louis Cardinal 1970; cert Am Correction Assn 1970; St Louis Ambassadors1969-71; cert Am Mgmt & Assn 1971; Meritorious Serv to Alpha House of St Louis 1973; Prsnl Mgmt for EEO Spclst 1975; Basic Consult Skills Lab 1975;Univ of MO 1975. **MILITARY SERVICE:** USN yeoman 1944-46.

GUNNELL, JAMES B.
Educator. **PERSONAL:** Born Oct 27, 1929, Palmyra, VA; married Virginia Mabrey; children: Soraya. **EDUCATION:** VA State Coll, BS 1956;Univ Notre Dame, MS 1962; NM State U, EdD 1969. **CAREER:** OH State Univ Columbus, assoc prof 1969-74; VA State Coll Petersburg, instructor math 1962-66; various high schools, instructor math 1956-62; VA Union Univ Richmond, dir institutional rsch & planning; James B Gunnell & Assoc Inc Richmond, pres. **ORGANIZATIONS:** Nat Educ Assn; Am Educ Rsrch Assn; Assn Institutional Rsrchrs. **HONORS/ACHIEVEMENTS:** Mu Epsilon Math Honor Soc; Phi Delta Kappa Educ Honor Soc; Nat Sci Found Fellow; Educ Rsrch Training Pgrm Fellow. **MILITARY SERVICE:** AUS ofcr 1952-54. **BUSINESS ADDRESS:** 2924 Chamberlayne Ave, Richmond, VA 23220.

GUNNINGS, THOMAS S.
Educator. **PERSONAL:** Born Feb 08, 1935, Gastonia, NC; married Barbara. **EDUCATION:** Univ of OR, PhD 1969; OR State Univ, DMA 1967; Winston-Salem Teachers Coll, BS 1958. **CAREER:** MI State Univ Coll of Human Med, adjunct prof psych, prof of psych; G & P Properties, vice pres; Meridian Professional Psych Consult Inc, pres. **ORGANIZATIONS:** Natl consult to many fed state & local agencies; mem Kappa Delta Phi Hon Soc, Natl Inst of Mental Health Training Grants; vstg scientists, vstg psych Amer Psych Assn 1969-72; mem Amer Psych Assn; bd dir Assn of Black Psych mem Natl Assoc of Counseling & Development. **HONORS/ACHIEVEMENTS:** Fellow of APA and many other honors. **BUSINESS ADDRESS:** President, Meridian Professional Psychol Consul, 5031 Park Lake Rd, East Lansing, MI 48823.

GUNTER, LAURIE
Educator. **PERSONAL:** Born Mar 05, 1922, Navarrow Cty, TX; children: Margo Alyce Gunter Toner, Lara Elaine Bonow. **EDUCATION:** TN A&I State Univ, BS 1948; Univ of Toronto, Cert Nursing Ed 1948-49; Fisk Univ, MA 1952; Cath Univ of Amer, 1956; Univ of CA Berkeley, 1959; Univ of Chicago, PhD 1959. **CAREER:** George W Hubbard Hosp, staff nurse 1943-44, head nurse 1945-46, suprv 1947-48; Meharry Med Coll School of Nursing, asst instr 1948-50, instr 1950-55, asst prof 1955-57, acting dean 1957-58, dean 1958-61; UCLA, asst prof nursing 1961-63, assoc prof 1963-65; IN Univ Med Ctr, prof nursing 1965-66; Univ of WA, prof 1969-71; PA State Univ, prof of nursing human devel 1971-87. **ORGANIZATIONS:** Mem Amer Nurses Assoc 1948-, Natl League for Nursing 1948-87, Amer Assoc of Univ Prof, 1949-87, Gerontological Soc 1959-; rsch proj grants 1965-; mem Amer Assoc of Coll of Nursing 1971, Amer Publ Health Assoc 1974-87; consult HRA/Natl Ctr for Health Serv Rsch 1976-; reviewer HEW 1976-; mem steeringcomm PA Nurses Assoc, Council of Nurse Rsch, Amer Nurses Assoc; ad hoc ed, adv comm Div of Geriatric Nursing Pract, Amer Nurses Assoc; proj dir Composite Ed Prog for Geriatric Nursing 1976-77; mem Amer Acad of Nursing 1979-, Inst of Medicine of the Natl Acad of Sci 1980-. **HONORS/ACHIEVEMENTS:** Charles Nelson Gold Medal Meharry Med Coll School of Nursing 1943; Foster Mem Prize Meharry Med Coll School of Nursing 1943; Alpha Kappa Mu Hon Soc TN A&I State Univ 1948; Fellowship Rockefeller Found 1948-49; Rockefeller Found 1953-55; 1nd Training Inst in Soc Gerontology Univ of CA 1959; Golden Anniv Citation Spec Competence in Nursing TN Agr & Indust Univ 1963; invitee White House Conf on Food Nutrition & Health 1969; guest lecturer Japanese Nurses First Rsch Conf 1971; author, co-autor num articles & audiovisual prod 1949-. **BUSINESS ADDRESS:** Professor of Nursing, PA StateUniv, 309BHenderson, Human Devel Bldg, University Park, PA 16802.

GUNTHORPE, URIEL DERRICK
Educator, dentist. **PERSONAL:** Born Jun 25, 1924, Asheville, NC; married Elaine. **EDUCATION:** Howard U, BS 1952, DDS 1956; Columbia U, MPH 1969. **CAREER:** CMDNJ NJ Dental School, assoc prof; private practice, dentist 1958-74; Provident Clinical Soc, dental dir 1969-70; med rev dentist City NY, clinician 1959-68; Dental Consult & Headstart Program Region II PHS of HEW; DAU Program NJ Dental School, dir; Coll of Medicine & Denistry NJ, apptd 1976. **ORGANIZATIONS:** Mem Bergen Co Mental Hlth Bd first black male past sec 1976. **HONORS/ACHIEVEMENTS:** 3 Campaigne Battle Stars. **MILITARY SERVICE:** WW II AUS. **BUSINESS ADDRESS:** 100 Bergen St, Newark, NJ.

GURLEY, DOROTHY J.
Educational administrator. **PERSONAL:** Born Dec 13, 1931, Livingston, AL; daughter of Edward Johnson and Ethel Conley Johnson; married James E Gurley, Jan 02, 1952; children: Dr Marilyn G. Foreman, Beverly G. Lampley, Darryl E, Kenneth A. **EDUCATION:** AL A&M Univ, BS 1951; Tuskegee Univ, MEd 1961; AL A&M Univ, "AA" Certificate 1974; Univ of Alabama, EdD 1988. **CAREER:** Education Improvement Prog Huntsville City Schs, childhood educ 1966-71; Comprehensive Child Care Prog, program coord 1971-73; Educ Improvement Prog, curriculum specialist 1974-79; Rolling Hills Elem Sch Huntsville, asst principal 1979-88; Alabama A&M Univ, assoc prof 1988-. **ORGANIZATIONS:** Grand dist deputy IBPO of Elks of the World; mem Natl Educ Assoc, Assoc for Supervision and Curriculum Develop, AL Educ Assoc, Huntsville Educ Assoc; vice pres, Alabama Assn for the Educ of Young Children 1983-85; mem, Alabama State Advisory Committee for Early Childhood Educ 1974-; mem, Alabama Public TV Citizen Advisory Bd 1983-85; basileus, Epsilon Gamma Omega Chapter Alpha Kappa Alpha Sorority Inc 1975-77; Phi Delta Kappa. **HONORS/ACHIEVEMENTS:** Inducted in to Alpha Kappa Alpha Hall of Fame Epsilon Gamma Omega 1980; Disting Alumni Awd NAEFO 1984; Distinguished Alumni Awd, Natl Assn for Equal Opportunity for Higher Education 1984; Class Achievement Awd, Alabama A&M Natl Alumni Normalite Assn 1986; Effective Schools Program, Rolling Hills Elementary 1986-88; Teachers' Perceptions Toward Causes of Discipline Problems in the Elementary Grades of Huntsville City Schools 1988; Resolution of Recognition, Huntsville City School Board; Basileus of the Year Award, Southeastern Region, Alpha Kappa Alpha Sorority Inc; Cum Laude Graduate from Alabama A&M Univ; Southern Education Foundation Fellow; Panelist, Tri-State Early Childhood Education Project. **BUSINESS ADDRESS:** Associate Professor, Department of Secondary Education, Alabama A&M University, P O Box 357, Normal, AL 35762.

GURLEY, HELEN RUTH
Administrator. **PERSONAL:** Born Dec 05, 1939, Ogemaw, AR; daughter of Rev & Mrs Curtis Hildreth (deceased); married Archie Gurley, Sr; children: Archie Jr, Thomas Jeffrey, Vallissia Lynn. **EDUCATION:** Natl Univ San Diego, MBA 1975. **CAREER:** Univ of CA, counselor 1971-77; Nueces County MHMR Comm Ctr, service dir 1977-79; City of Corpus Christi, admin human relations 1979-83; Del Mar Coll, EEO/affirmative action officer 1985-. **ORGANIZATIONS:** Consultant Mary McLeod Bethune Day Nursery Inc 1983-85; pres Littles-Martin House Fund Inc 1984-89; pres Corpus Christi Branch NAACP 1984-89; chairperson United Way of the Coastal Bend Agency Council 1984-86; chairperson Coastal Bend Council of Govt Health Adv Comm 1985-; bd mem Natl Conf of Christians and Jews; treasurer, Amer Assn for Affirmative Action, 1988-. **HONORS/ACHIEVEMENTS:** Woman of the Year Corpus Christi Alumnae Chap Delta Sigma Theta Sorority 1983-84; Unsung Heroine Natl NAACP 1985. **MILITARY SERVICE:** USN E-3 seaman 3 yrs; USAR E-8 MSG 13 yrs; Army Commendation; Army Achievement; Humanitarian Service Medal. **HOME ADDRESS:** 1322 Southbay Dr, Corpus Christi, TX 78412. **BUSINESS ADDRESS:** EO/AA Officer, Del Mar College, 101 Baldwin Blvd, Corpus Christi, TX 78404-3897.

GUSTUS, RUDOLPH C.
Business executive. **PERSONAL:** Born Feb 04, 1933, Philadelphia, PA; married Harvadene M; children: Camille, Angela. **CAREER:** General Motors Assembly Division, assembly-line worker 1956-59; June Oil Co, driver 1959-63; G&M Fuel Oil Company, partner 1963-76, executive president 1976-82, president 1982-. **ORGANIZATIONS:** Member President's Round Table 1982-; member Greater Baltimore Committee 1982-. **BUSINESS ADDRESS:** President, G & M Oil Co Inc, 1549 N Warwick, Baltimore, MD 21216.

GUTHRIE, CARLTON LYONS
Automotive supplier/president/ceo. **PERSONAL:** Born Sep 15, 1952, Atlanta, GA; married Dr Danielle K Taylor; children: Carille, Adam. **EDUCATION:** Harvard Coll, AB (Cum Laude) 1974; Harvard Business School, MBA 1978. **CAREER:** Jewel Companies Chicago, internal consultant 1978-80; McKinsey & Co Chicago, sr assoc 1980-82; James H Lowry & Assoc Chicago, exec vice pres 1982-85; Trumark Inc, pres 1985-. **ORGANIZATIONS:** Consultant United Christian Churches Cooperative Soc Chicago 1980-; dir Ctrs for New Horizons Chicago 1980-, Urban League Lansing MI 1986-, Boys & Girls Club Lansing MI 1986-. **HOME ADDRESS:** 1230 E 46th St, Chicago, IL 60653. **BUSINESS ADDRESS:** President & CEO, Trumark, Inc, 1820 Sunset, Lansing, MI 48917.

GUTHRIE, MICHAEL J.
Executive. **PERSONAL:** Born Sep 19, 1950, Lithonia, GA; married Valorie C Walker; children: Lauren. **EDUCATION:** Harvard Coll, AB 1972; Harvard Law School, JD 1975. **CAREER:** Sonnenschein, Carlin, Nath & Rosenthal, atty 1975-79; Johnson Products Co Inc, serv atty 1979-83, vice pres corp planning 1979-85; Trumark Inc, co-owner, exec vice pres 1985-. **ORGANIZATIONS:** Bus adv bd Lansing Comm Coll. **BUSINESS ADDRESS:** Executive Vice President, Trumark, Inc, 1820 Sunset Ave, Lansing, MI 48917.

GUY, ADDELIAR DELL, III
District court judge. **PERSONAL:** Born Nov 01, 1923, Chicago, IL; son of Addeliar D Guy II and Hattie P Brown Guy; married Alice Rosalyn Banks Guy; children: Addeliar D IV, Pamela D Guy Anderson, Michael Lawrence. **EDUCATION:** St Norbert Coll, 1941-42; Wilson Jr Coll, 1948; Loyola Univ School of Law, LLB 1957. **CAREER:** Peterson Johnson & Guy, attorney, 1958-64; City of Chicago asst corp counsel 1960-64, admin asst district atty office 1964-66, dep district attorney 1966-70, chief deputy district attorney 1970-75; State of NV Clark Cty 8th Judicial Dist Court, chief judge, 1985, judge, 1975-. **ORGANIZATIONS:** Mem IL Bar, NV Bar, US Dist Court, IL Dist Court, US Court of Appeals, US Supreme Court, US Military Court of Appeals, US Court of Appeals, Jr C of C, Cosmo C of C, S Side Comm, 3rd Ward Young Dem, 3rd Ward Regular Dem, Comm So NV Human Relat, Comm Housing Auth of Las Vegas, NAACP, Fitzsimmons House,N Las Vegas Rotary; adv bd AD Guy Boys Club; mem Clark Cty Dem Cntrl Com; exec bd March of Dimes, VFW, Saints & Sinners, Help Them Walk Again, Civilian Mil Counc USCG 1942-46; mem, exec bd, Boulder Dam Area Council, Boy Scouts of Amer, 1979-; mem, exec bd, Judicial Council of the Natl Bar Assn. **HONORS/ACHIEVEMENTS:** Outstanding Achievement as Judge, NAACP; Silver Lily Award, Easter Seal Soc of Nevada, 1979; Distinguished Achievement Award, Judicial Council of the Natl Bar Assn, 1980; Certificate of Appreciation, Freedom Fund NAACP, 1984; Addeliar D Guy III Law School Scholarship Fund, established 1987; Silver Beaver Award, Boulder Dam Area Boy Scouts of Amer, 1989. **MILITARY SERVICE:** AUS 1949-54; IL Natl Guard 1955-65; NV Natl Guard 1965-76; Purple Heart AUS 1950; Korean Campaign Battle Stars AUS 1950-51; Airborne 1949; Rangers 1952; RetLt Col 1976. **BUSINESS ADDRESS:** District Court Judge, State of Nevada County of Clark, 200 S Third St, Dept XI, Las Vegas, NV 89155.

GUY, GEORGE V.
Educator. **PERSONAL:** Born Mar 20, 1921, Windsor, Ontario, Canada;son of Dr William Elihu Guy and Della Edythe Vance; married Clementyne M Turner, Jan 23, 1946; children: Karen M, G Kenneth, Kathleen M. **EDUCATION:** Univ of Illionis, BA 1948, MA 1949, PhD 1957. **CAREER:** UUniv Illionis Urbana, grad asst 1948-50, instr 1950-51, visiting lecturer summer 1960; A&T Coll NC, Greensboro, prof educ 1951-55; Portland Extension Center & Portland State Coll, asst prof educ 1955-59; Portland State Coll, assoc prof educ 1959-63, head dept educ 1961-65, school of educ asst dean & grad coord 1965-68; Portland State Univ, prof educ 1963; NCATE Portland State Univ, dir 1971-73; School of Educ Portland State Univ, asst dean 1979-86, prof emeritus. **ORGANIZATIONS:** Fellow Philosophy of Educ Soc 1976-; mem The Society of Professors of Educ; mem The John Dewey Soc; editorial bd The Journal of Educ Theory 1975-76, 1977-78, 1979-80, 1981-82, 1983-84; mem Northwest Philosophy of Educ Soc, Phi Delta Kappa, Kappa Delta Pi, Amer Educ Studies Assoc. **HONORS/ACHIEVEMENTS:** Frederick Douglass Scholar Award Pacific Northwest Re-

gion Natl Council for Black Studies; numerous publications; Ralph Metcalfe Chair, Marquette Univ, Milwaukee, WI 1988-89. **MILITARY SERVICE:** AUS, 1942-46. **BUSINESS ADDRESS:** Professor Emeritus, Portland StateUniv, School of Education, PO Box 751, Portland, OR 97207.

GUY, JASMINE
Actress and dancer. **PERSONAL:** Born in Boston, MA; daughter of Dr. William Guy and Jaye Rudolph. **CAREER:** Alvin Ailey American Dance Theater, New York, NY, dancer; appeared in television series Fame, The Equalizer, Loving, Ryan's Hope, and A Different World; appeared in stage shows The Wiz, Bubbling Brown Sugar, and Beehive; appeared in motion picture School Daze. **BUSINESS ADDRESS:** NBC Inc, 30 rockefeller Plaza, New York, NY 10020. *

GUY, LYGIA BROWN
Business executive. **PERSONAL:** Born Apr 23, 1952, Charleston, SC; married Peter Steele; children: Aja Steele. **EDUCATION:** Spelman Coll, 1969-72; Fashion Inst of Amer, AA Merchandising/Design 1973; Pepperdine Univ, BA Sociology 1974. **CAREER:** Chelsa Records, promo coord 1975; Greedy Records, promo coord 1976; ABC Records, promo coord 1977; Connections, dir & owner of co, personnel agent 1984; RCA Records, merchandising mgr, West Coast regional promo. **ORGANIZATIONS:** Mem, NAACP, 1969; mem Acad of Country Music, 1980; mem, AFTRA, 1980; mem, NARAS, 1982; mem, Black Music Assn. **HONORS/ACHIEVEMENTS:** Promo Mgr of the Yr BRE Mag 1984. **BUSINESS ADDRESS:** Promotion Manager, RCA Records, 6363 Sunset Blvd, Hollywood, CA 90028.

GUY, MILDRED DOROTHY
Educator. **PERSONAL:** Born Apr 16, 1929, Brunswick, GA; daughter of John Floyd (deceased) and Mamie Smith Floyd (deceased); divorced; children: Rhonda Lynn. **EDUCATION:** Savannah State Coll, BS 1949; Atlanta Univ, MA 1952; Univ of Southern California, Post Grad Studies 1953-81; Univ of N Colorado, Colorado Univ Foreign Study League-Europe, Post Grad Studies 1953-81. **CAREER:** LS Ingraham High School, Sparta GA, chmn soc studies dept 1950-56; N Jr High School Colorado Springs Sch Dist #11, tchr soc studies & English 1958-84, retired teacher. **ORGANIZATIONS:** Originator Annual Minority Student Recognition Prog 1973; trustee Pikes Peak Comm Coll 1976-83; CSTA delegate to Delegate Assembly Colorado Springs Tchrs Assn 1978; life mem NEA, Colorado Council for Soc Studies, ASALH, Friends of Pioneers Museum 1974-; basileus pres Iota Beta Omega Chap of AKA 1984-86; local bd mem & life mem NAACP 1979-83; UL 1972-75; NHACS Bd 1984-89; delegate to Dem Pty Assemblys & Conv 1974-84; AAUW; ADK; LWV; Pikes Peak Ctr Fundraiser; CS Fine Arts Ctr; nominating comm Wagon Wheel Council Colorado Springs CO, 1985-86. **HONORS/ACHIEVEMENTS:** Outstanding Soror Award of Mid-Western Region (AKA) 1980; Outstanding Black Educator of Sch Dist #11 1980; Honorable Mention, Colo Tchr of Yr St Bd of Educ 1983; Outstanding Achievemnt in Ed Award; NHACS Award 1984; Iota Omicron Lambda Chap Alpha Phi Alpha Awd 1985; CBWPA Sphinx Awd 1986; Outstanding Grad Chap President Awd Mid-Western Region of Alpha Kappa Alpha 1986; Salute to Women 1986; Recognition Gazette Telegraph Colorado Springs CO 1986; Distinguished Educator of the Year, Black Educators of District Eleven, 1984. **HOME ADDRESS:** 3132 Constitution Ave, Colorado Springs, CO 80909.

GUY, ROSA CUTHBERT
Author. **PERSONAL:** Born Sep 01, 1925; married Warner Guy; children: Warner Jr. **EDUCATION:** New York Univ, attended. **CAREER:** Bird at My Window 1966, The Friends 1973, Ruby 1981, Edith Jackson 1979, The Disappearance 1980, Mother Crocodile 1981, Mirror of Her Own 1981, New Guys Aroundthe Block 1983, A Measure of Time 1983, author. **ORGANIZATIONS:** Comm mem Negro in the Arts; org Harlem Writers Guild. **BUSINESS ADDRESS:** c/o Holt, Rinehart & Winston, Attn: Linda Pennel, 385 Madison Ave 8th Floor, New York, NY 10017.

GUY, TALMADGE CARTER
Educational administrator. **PERSONAL:** Born Sep 15, 1948, Cleveland, OH; married Jaqueline Thomas. **EDUCATION:** Fisk Univ, BA 1971; Univ of Abidjan Ivory Coast, 1971; Northwestern Univ, MA 1973. **CAREER:** Gary Oppor Indus Center, deputy dir 1973-78; Chicago Urban Skills Institute, dir of personnel 1979, vice pres for admin services 1979-84, exec dir 1984-. **ORGANIZATIONS:** Mem Targeted Assistance Grant Adv Com Jewish Fed 1983-85; mem 23rd Dist World's Fair Task Force 1984-85; mem First Congressional Dist Sub-Committee on Educ 1984-85; chmn Adult Educ Area Planning Council 1985; adv mem Chicago Youth Centers Adv Com 1985. **HONORS/ACHIEVEMENTS:** Service Awd Gary OIC 1975; Service Awd Lake County CETA Adv Council 1977; Outstanding Young Men of America New York NY 1984; Phi Beta Kappa Fisk Univ 1971. **BUSINESS ADDRESS:** Executive Dir, Chicago Urban Skills Institute, 3901 S State St, Chicago, IL 60609.

GUY, WILLIAM I.
Educator. **PERSONAL:** Born Jan 04, 1939, Philadelphia, PA; married Karen Woodley; children: Leslie, Lisa, Lauren. **EDUCATION:** TempleUniv Philadelphia, BA 1963; TempleUniv Philadelphia, MA 1980. **CAREER:** W Chester State Coll, dir acad devel progs & instructor of sociology 1974-; Opportunities Industrialization Center, research mgr 1968-74; Prudential Insurance Co, exec sales 1965-68; First PA Co Banking & Trust, jr mgmt 1957-65; Consultant Youthwork Inc, Washington DC, vice pres; Alpha Phi Alpha Frat Inc Rho Chapter 1970-75. **ORGANIZATIONS:** Dir United Cerebral Palsy Assn of Philadelphia 1972-80; dir Fellowship House of Philadelphia 1976-80. **HONORS/ACHIEVEMENTS:** Recipient Writing Across the Curriculum Award Nat Endowment for the Humanities 1978. **BUSINESS ADDRESS:** W Chester State Coll, 131 New Library, West Chester, PA 19380.

GUYTON, ALICIA V.
Pharmacist, government official. **PERSONAL:** Born Nov 12, 1951, Wolfe, WV; daughter of Dr M B Guyton and Susie Hayes Guyton; children: Mychal B, Erik W, Guyton Boyd (twins). **EDUCATION:** New York City Comm Coll, AS 1974; Brooklyn Coll of Pharmacy of Long Island Univ, BS 1977; Columbia Pacific Univ, MS 1986. **CAREER:** MCEOC, alcohol counselor 1980-81; Children's Home Soc of WV, asst dir counselor 1981-82; WV Job Service, interviewer 1982-83; Veterans Admin Medical Ctr, pharmacist 1983. Veterans Admin Medical Center, Iowa City, IA, asst chief BMS 1989-. **ORGANIZATIONS:** Mem Delta Sigma Theta Sor, Bluefield Alumnae Chap; chairperson Comm on Youth Serv, Links Inc, So WV Chap; mem Educ Commn, Berkeley Chap, NAACP; mem Register official WV Secondary Schools Athletic Commn; mem Links Inc So WV Chapt, Natl Council of Negro Women; sanctioned ASA softball umpire; mem Eastern Panhandle Officials Assoc, Berkeley County Umpires Assoc. **HONORS/ACHIEVEMENTS:** First black female USSSA-ASA sanctioned umpire in the State of WV 1978; Outstanding Delta, Bluefield Alumnae Chap, Delta Sigma Theta Sor 1982; first black female umpire to work the State Class C Men's slow-pitch softball championships 1982; first black woman to officiate a boys' varsity basketball game in the State of WV 1985. **BUSINESS ADDRESS:** Assistant Chief Building Management Service, Veterans Affairs Medical Center, Highway 6, Iowa City, IA 52246.

GUYTON, BOOKER T.
Business executive, educational administrator. **PERSONAL:** Born Dec 27, 1944, Clarksville, TX; married Mary Allen Guyton; children: Booker Jr, Roxann, Keisha, Katrina. **EDUCATION:** Univ of the Pacific, BSEd 1971, MA Religion 1972. **CAREER:** Facilities Mgmt & Inst for Personnel Devel, dir; Humanities & Intercultural Ed Div, chmn; Mgmt Svcs, admin asst to vp; affirm action officer; Johnson & Johnson, suprv mfg; John F Kennedy Ctr, exec dir; Fed Teacher Corps prog, teacher intern; Parks Chapel AME Church, pastor; San Joaquin Delta Comm Coll, instr. **ORGANIZATIONS:** Mem North Stockton Rotary, Assoc of CA Comm Coll Admin, CA Comm Serv Assoc, Natl Ed Assoc, CA School Bd Assoc, Official Black Caucus of Natl Ed Assoc, Kappa Alpha Psi; bd of dir Dameron Hosp Found; pres McKinley Improvement Assoc, State Council Oppty Indust Ctr State of CA. **HONORS/ACHIEVEMENTS:** Numerous awds incl New Educators Awd CA Assoc, Man of the Year Kappa Alpha Psi 1979, Community Serv Awd City of Stockton, Comm Serv Awd Black Teachers Alliance Stockton CA, Cert of Appreciation of Serv CA Black Student Union Assoc, Community Serv Awd League of Black Voters Stockton CA. **MILITARY SERVICE:** USMC staff sgt 6 yrs. **HOME ADDRESS:** 148 W 8th St, Stockton, CA 95207.

GUYTON, PATSY
Educator. **PERSONAL:** Born Jun 16, 1949, Mobile, AL; daughter of Wes Guyton and Marie Johnson Guyton. **EDUCATION:** Bishop State Jr Coll, Mobile AL, Associates in Psychology, 1969; Alabama State Univ, Montgomery AL, BA Sociology, 1971; Springhill Coll, Mobile AL, attended, 1979-83; Xavier Univ, New Orleans LA, Masters in Theology, 1989. **CAREER:** Boca Raton Middle School, Boca Raton FL, teacher, 1971-75; Christian Benevolent Insurance Co, Mobile AL, debit mgr, 1975-76; St Mary's Children Home, Mobile AL, child care worker, 1976-79; Marion Corp, Theodore AL, personnel specialist, 1979-82; Parish Social Ministry, Mobile AL, coord, 1982-88, dir of religious educ, coord of ministries, 1988-. **ORGANIZATIONS:** Alpha Kappa Alpha Sorority, 1970-; bd mem, Valentine Award, Catholic Social Services, 1982-; religious educ consultant, Archdiocese of Mobile AL, 1985-; bd mem, Natl Assn of Lay Ministry, 1985-. **HONORS/ACHIEVEMENTS:** Debit Mgr. Present Presidents' Club, Christian Benevolent Insurance Co, 1975; Outstanding Debit Mgr, Christian Benevolent Insurance Co, 1975. **HOME ADDRESS:** 915 Luther Ave, Prichard, AL 36610.

GUYTON, TYREE
Artist. **PERSONAL:** Born Aug 24, 1955, Detroit, MI; son of George Guyton (deceased) and Betty Solomon Guyton; married Karen Smith Guyton, Jul 19, 1987; children: Carmen, Darren, Sean, Tyree, Jr, Towan, Omar. **EDUCATION:** Northern High School Adult Training; Franklin Adult Educ; Center for Creative Studies, Detroit, MI. **CAREER:** Ford Motor Co, Dearborn, MI, inspector; Northern High School, Master Residence Art Program, Detroit, MI, teacher; Heidelberg Community Street Art Inc, Detroit, MI, pres, 1987-; painter, sculptor. **HONORS/ACHIEVEMENTS:** David A Harmon Memorial Scholarship, 1989; nominated for Spirit of Detroit Award, 1989; work shown at Detroit Artists Market, Michigan Gallery, Le Minotaure, Ann Arbor MI, Cade Gallery, Royal Oak MI, Trobar Gallery; featured in People, Aug 15, 1988, Detroit News, Detroit Free Press Magazine, April 2, 1989, City Arts Quarterly, Winter 1988/89, Detroit Monthly, Detroit City Guide, Connoisseur Magazine, local television commentaries. **MILITARY SERVICE:** AUS, E-2, 1972; honorable discharge. **HOME ADDRESS:** 11151 Findlay, Detroit, MI 48205.

GWALTNEY, JOHN L.
Anthropologist. **PERSONAL:** Born Sep 25, 1928, Orange, NJ; son of Stanley Gwaltney and Mabel Harper. **EDUCATION:** Upsala Coll, BA 1952; New Sch Soc Rsrch, MA 1957; Columbia U, PhD 1967. **CAREER:** Syracuse U, prof anthropology; NE US Urban Afro-Ams, ethnographer 1973-74; Allopsychic Res Proj NY, ethnographer 1961; LI NY, ethnographer among Shinnecock & Poospatuck Indians 1969; Oaxaca Mexico, ethnographer among Highland Chiantec 1963-64; StateUniv of NY, assoc prof 1967-71; Ctr Intl Coop Ottawa,sem 1969. **ORGANIZATIONS:** Mem Com on Oppty in Sci & Resource Group; proj on the handicapped in sci AAAS; mem Amer Found for the Blind Sem on Visual Impairment & Ethnicity NY 1977; guest lecturer Smithsonian Inst, Onondaga Public Library, Wellfleet Public Library, 1st Parish Brewster, Amer Found for the Blind, Navser Reg HS, Robt F Kennedy Meml Inst, Amer Red Cross, Boy Scouts of Amer, AAAS, Applied Anthropology Soc, Amer Anthropological Assoc, Amer Folklore Soc, Amer Assoc of Oral History, Brown Columbia Northwestern Univ of MI Jackson State Univ, Univ of Scranton; grant-in-aid, Syracuse Univ 1979,81; fellow Prog in Black Amer Culture Smithsonian Inst 1982; fellow Natl Endowment for the Humanities 1983-84; bd dir NY Council for the Humanities, Smithsonian Inst Folk Life Council. **HONORS/ACHIEVEMENTS:** Hon DSc Bucknell Univ 1979; Hon Litt D Upsala Coll 1980; Assoc of Black Anthropologists Publ Awd 1980; Robt F Kennedy Book Awd Hon Mention 1981; semi-finalist, 1986 Chancellor's Citation for Exceptional Acad Achievement Syracuse Univ 1983; 13th Annual Unity Awd in Media Educ Reporting, Natl Print Div Lincoln Univ 1983; Best of Show Awd Cultural Resources Council Syracuse NY 1983,86; selected publs, Miss Mabel's Legacy Readers Digest 1982, A Native Replies Natural History 1976, Drylongso, A Self-Portrait of Black Amer NY Random House 1980, 81; The Dissenters, Voices from Contemporary Amer NY Random House 1986. **BUSINESS ADDRESS:** Professor, Syracuse University, 500 University Pl, Syracuse, NY 13244.

GWIN, WILIVIGINIA FASZHIANATO (CORA)
Educator, administrator. **PERSONAL:** Born Feb 02, 1954, Mobile, AL; daughter of Ernest L Gwin (deceased) and Willie V Gwin. **EDUCATION:** Bishop State Jr Coll, AS 1974; AL State Univ, BA 1975, MS 1978. **CAREER:** Amer Cancer Soc, program dir 1975-79; Upjohn Healthcare Servcs, Service Dir 1979-80; Univ of Southern AL, admissions counselor 1980-85, dir of minority affairs 1983-85, dir of affirmative action & academic counseling 1985-; Department of Developmental Studies, academic adviser, 1987-89. **ORGANIZATIONS:** Mem Business & Professional Women's Club 1977; mem Alpha Kappa Alpha Sor Inc 1980; mem Assoc of Admissions Counselors 1980-; bd mem AL Assoc for Counseling &Develop 1985-87;

bd mem Univ of So AL Affirmative Action Monitoring Comm 1985-; mem AL New South Coalition 1986-; bd dirs AL Assoc of Counseling & Develop; mem Mobile County Urban League, Mobile Comm Concerts Assoc. **HONORS/ACHIEVEMENTS:** AL Literary Soc Award 1st place 1973; Alumni Leadership Scholarship AL State Univ 1974; Kappa Delta Pi Natl Honor Soc 1977; Omicron Delta Kappa Natl Honor Soc USA 1984; Univ of So AL Affirmative Action Develop Scholarship 1986; Abeneefoo Kuo Honor Soc; Pi Sigma Pi Natl Honor Soc. **HOME ADDRESS:** P O Box 5026, Mobile, AL 36605. **BUSINESS ADDRESS:** Academic Adviser, Dept of Developmental Studies, University of South Alabama, Alpha Complex East Hall, Rm 232, Mobile, AL 36688.

GWYNN, FLORINE EVAYONNE
Educator, counselor, administrator. **PERSONAL:** Born Jan 16, 1944, Beckley, WV; daughter of Flauzell Calhoun and Jean Daisy Wright Calhoun; married Herman L Gwynn, Aug 05, 1979; children: Towanna M, Catherine S, Alvin, Calvin, Robert. **EDUCATION:** Beckley Coll, AS 1970; Bluefield State Coll, BS 1977; WV Coll Graduate Studies, MS 1982; WV Union Coll of Law, Morgantown WV, attended 1986-88. **CAREER:** Raleigh County, youth/sr citizens dir 1969-72; Fed Prison for Women, fed correctional officer 1972-75; Nutrition for the Elderly, project dir 1979-80; Raleigh County Comm on Aging, exec dir 1980-81; Social Security Admin, hearing asst 1982-; Bluefield State Coll, asst prof Criminal Justice program 1982-; NCWVCAA, Kingwood WV, counselor/coordinator 1988-. **ORGANIZATIONS:** Mem Bluefield State Coll Alumni 1977-, WV Coll of Graduate Studies 1979-; bd of dir Domestic Violence Center 1984-; treasurer Raleigh Co Rainbow Coalition 1984-; mem Phi Alpha Delta Law Fraternity 1986-; coordinator Tygart Valley Baptist Assn Sunday School Congress 1988-, Youth Action Inc 1989-; bd mem Sex Equity-Teen Pregnacy Project 1989-. **HONORS/ACHIEVEMENTS:** Appreciation for Serv Amer Legion Aux #70 1969; Community Serv Bluefield State Coll Beckly Chapter Alumni 1984; Bluefield State Coll Teacher of the Year 1985; Service Award, Bluefield State Coll Alumni 1986. **HOME ADDRESS:** 1401 Anderson Ave, Morgantown, WV 26505.

GWYNN, TONY
Professional athlete. **PERSONAL:** Born May 09, 1960, Los Angeles, CA; married Alicia; children: Anthony II, Anisha Nicole. **CAREER:** San Diego Padres, player 1981-. **HONORS/ACHIEVEMENTS:** Win Clark Award Top Southern CA Baseball Player Los Angeles Anaheim Baseball Writers; Career best in 33 stolen bases; voted to start in All-Star Game in Candlestick Park; selected outfielder The Sporting News Nat League All-Star Team; Finished 3rd in balloting for league MVP Award; Northwest Leagues Most Valuable Player Award; Golden Glove winner for Defensive Excellence; mem 1985 and 1986 All Star Team; 3 time winner Padres/Broadway Player of the Month Awd 1986; honored by Hall of Champions as San Diego's Professional Athlete of the Year. **BUSINESS ADDRESS:** San Diego Padres, PO Box 2000, San Diego, CA 92120.

H

HABERSHAM, ROBERT
Clergyman. **PERSONAL:** Born Feb 16, 1929, Savannah; married Olga Hyatt; children: Robert, Mabel Estelle. **EDUCATION:** Bethune Cookman Coll, AB 1956; Boston U, STB 1958; MDiv; Brantridge Forest, PhD 1970. **CAREER:** St Peters Comm Meth Ch CA, minister 1959-66; Calvary Meth Ch CA, 1966-67; Hamilton United Meth Ch CA, 1967-; Franklin Life Ins Co, life & disability agt 1971-; variable annuity agt 1973-. **ORGANIZATIONS:** Mem LA Co Dist Atty Adv Council 1967-; Wilshire Div Police Council 1973-; SW Clergy Police Council 1974-; mem NAACP; Shriner; Mason 33; founder& organizer Willard W Allen Lodge #102; Prince Hall; LA Consistory #26; Assembly CA Legislature 1965; co bd supr LA Co 1974. **HONORS/ACHIEVEMENTS:** Merit award NAACP; LHD Balcombe Sussex 1966; spl award BSA; resolution City Compton CA 1965; resolutcion City LA CA 1965. **MILITARY SERVICE:** USAF 1952. **BUSINESS ADDRESS:** 6330 S Figueroa St, Los Angeles, CA 90003.

HACKER, BENJAMIN THURMAN
Naval officer. **PERSONAL:** Born Sep 19, 1935, Washington, DC; married Jeanne Marie House; children: Benjamin, Bruce, Anne. **EDUCATION:** Wittenberg Univ, BA 1957; US Naval Postgrad School, Engrg Sci 1963; George Washington Univ, MSA 1978. **CAREER:** US Navy, commd ensign 1958 advanced through grades to rear adm 1980; Naval Facility Barbados WI, commanding officer 1967-69; FL A&M Univ, comdg officer, prof naval sci 1972-73; Patrol Squadron 24 Jacksonville FL, comdg officer 1974-75; US Naval Air Sta Brunswick, comdg officer; US Mil Enlistment ProcessingCommand Ft Sheridan IL, comdr 1980-82; Fleet Air Mediterranean Naples Italy, comdr 1982-84; Navy Dept Washington DC, dir total force training 1984-86; Naval Training Ctr San Diego, commander 1986-. **ORGANIZATIONS:** Mem US Naval Inst, Natl Naval Officers Assoc, Alpha Phi Alpha, F&AM, PHA. **HONORS/ACHIEVEMENTS:** EdD (HS) George Washington Univ 1986. **MILITARY SERVICE:** USN, rear admiral; Legion of Merit; Defense Superior Service Medal. **BUSINESS ADDRESS:** Commander, Naval Training Center, 937 North Harbor, San Diego, CA 92132.

HACKETT, OBRA V.
Administrator. **PERSONAL:** Born Sep 09, 1937, Osyka, MS; son of James Hackett and Letha T Williams; married A Carolyn Evans; children: Obra V Jr. **EDUCATION:** Jackson State Univ, BS 1960; Atlanta Univ, MA 1967; attended Mississippi State Univ 1967-68. **CAREER:** Henry Weathers HS, math teacher 1960-62, asst principal 1962-64; Carver HS, counselor 1965-66; Utica Jr Coll, vocational counselor 1966-69, dean of students1969-73; Jackson State Univ, dir pub inform 1973-77, dir develop 1977-84; JSU Dev Found, exec sec 1984-87; Jackson State Univ, asst to the Dean for Career Counseling & Placement 1987-. **ORGANIZATIONS:** Charter mem Coll Pub Relations Assn MS 1970; bd of dir Hinds Co Heart Assn 1974-79; sec bd of dir Goodwill Indus MS 1979-; commr of scouting Seminole Dist Andrew Jackson Council BSA 1979-83; pres Callaway HS PTA 1986-87; 3rd vice pres Jackson Cncl PTA 1986-88; key communicator JPS 1986-; 1st vice pres Jackson Council PTA 1988-90; treasurer Jackson State Univ Natl Alumni Assn 1988-. **HONORS/ACHIEVEMENTS:** Outstanding Educators of Amer 1971; Personalities of the South 1973; nominee Intl Biographies 1976. **BUSINESS ADDRESS:** Assistant to the Dean, Career Counseling & Placement, Jackson State University, 1400 1600 John R Lynch Street, Jackson, MS 39217.

HACKETT, RUFUS E.
Retired business executive. **PERSONAL:** Born Feb 04, 1910, Baltimore, MD; son of Edward and Charlotte; married Charlotte E Parrott; children: Veronica L Fullwood, Rufus E, Jr. **EDUCATION:** Morgan State Coll, BS 1934; Life Ins Agency Mgt Assn Inst, 1962. **CAREER:** NC Mutual Life Ins Co, comb agt 1934-35, spec ordinary agt 1935-41, asst mgr 1941-61, dist mgr Baltimore 1961-67, asst agency dir 1967-73, reg agency dir 1973-76, retired. **ORGANIZATIONS:** V chmn Meth Bd of Publn Inc NC Christian Advocate Offic Newsp of the United Meth Ch 1980; past pres MD Underwriters Assn; bd mem Atlantic Alumni Assn; past bd mem Provident Hosp; dist chmn BSA; Econ Dev Commn; co-chmn Emp Subcom Mayor's Task Force on Equal Rights; bd mem Vol Council on Equal Oppor; bd of mgrs YMCA; life mem NAACP; Morgan State Coll Alumni Assn; Alpha Phi Alpha; bd dir Ret Sr Volun Prgm; coord coun Sr Citizen's; past bd mem Div of Laf Life & Work Durham Dist United Meth Ch. **HONORS/ACHIEVEMENTS:** Life Underwriters Hon Soc Alumnus of Yr Morgan State Coll 1958; Morgan State Coll Athletic Hall of Fame 1972; numerous awards from NC Mutual Life Ins Co. **BUSINESS ADDRESS:** Regional Agency Dir, NC Mutual Life Ins Co, 411 W Chapel Hill St, Durham, NC 27701.

HACKETT, WILBUR L., JR.
Coordinator. **PERSONAL:** Born Oct 21, 1949, Winchester, KY; married Brenda. **EDUCATION:** Univ of KY, BA 1973. **CAREER:** Louisville Reg Criminal Justice Commn, comm coord; Gen Elec Louisville, supr 1973; Erwin House, bd dir. **ORGANIZATIONS:** Russel Area Youth Adv Com; adv Urban League Youth Program; vice pres Concerned Young Men of Louisville; adv Project Way-Out; mem Sickle Cell Anemia Found of KY,; Com for Restoration of Black Hist. **HONORS/ACHIEVEMENTS:** First black capt in SF-CUniv of KY; hon mention All-SEC Linebacker. **BUSINESS ADDRESS:** 400 S 6th St, MSD Bldg, Louisville, KY 40203.

HACKLEY, LLOYD VINCENT
Educational administrator. **PERSONAL:** Born Jun 14, 1940, Roanoke, VA; son of David W Hackley Sr (deceased) and Ernestine Parker Hackley (deceased); married Brenda L Stewart, Jun 12, 1960; children: Dianna Hackley-Applin, Michael R. **EDUCATION:** MI State Univ of Political Science, BA (Magna Cum Laude) 1965; Univ of CO Dept of Psychology, grad studies in psychology 1966-67; Univ of NC at Chapel Hill Dept of Polit Science, PhD (Honors) 1976; Government Exec Inst, School of Business Admin, Univ of NC Chapel Hill 1980. **CAREER:** USAF, retired as major 1958-78; Univ of NC General Admin, assoc vice pres for academic affairs 1979-81; Univ of NC at Chapel Hill, faculty govt execs inst sch of business admin 1980-81; Univ of AR at Pine Bluff, chancellor chief exec officer 1981-85; Univ of NC General Admin, vice pres for student serv and special programs 1985-88; USAF Acad, coach track & cross country, 1974-78; USAF Acad, assoc prof, course dir political science, 1974-78; Fayetteville State Univ, Fayetteville NC, chancellor 1988-. **ORGANIZATIONS:** Mem exec comm Triangle World Affairs Center 1978-79; mem bd dirs United Fund Carrboro-Chapel Hill 1978-80; mem bd trustees The Village Company Foundation 1980-81; mem exec comm NC Comm on Intl Educ 1980-81; mem adv bd Natl Ctr for Toxicological Rsch 1983; mem adv comm Univ of AR Grad Inst of Tech 1983; chmn subcomm on curriculum and student matters AR Quality Higher Educ Study Comm 1984; chmn subcomm on middle and jr high schools AR Educ Standards Comm for Elementary and Secondary Schools 1983-84; third vice pres United Way of Jefferson Co 1985; vice pres bd dirs AR Endowment for the Humanities 1985-86, 1984-85; chmn AR Adv Comm to the United States Commn on Civil Rights 1985; mem Strategic Planning Team, Cumberland County Board of Educ 1989; mem, Fayetteville Area Economic Devel Corp. **HONORS/ACHIEVEMENTS:** Scholastic Achievement Award, Dean's List Award, Univ of MD European Div 1961; Outstanding Young Man in Amer, United States Jaycees 1977; Governor of AR Traveler Award 1982; AR Certificate of Merit 1983; Key to City Flint MI 1984; Resolution of Tribute by MI Legislature 1984; Community Serv Award in Educ, Pine Bluff/Jefferson County AR 1984; also numerous papers and publications; Hackley, Lloyd V, "Disadvantaged Students": Testing Education Not Cultural Deprivation, American Middle School Education, 1983; Hackley, Lloyd V, "The Agony of Orthodoxy in Education," Congressional Record, Vol 129, Number 161, Part III, 1983; Resolution of Commendation, Arkansas Legislature, 1985. **MILITARY SERVICE:** US Air Force major (retired) 20 yrs, 1958-78; Outstanding Airman Rosas Air Station Spain 1961; Distinguished Military Grad Officer Training Sch 1965; Vietnam Cross of Gallantry 1968; Bronze Star for Meritorious Serv in Combat with Valor Vietman 1968; Man of the Hour Headquarters Europe 1970; Bronze Star & Meritorious Serv Medal, Europe, 1971; Aircraft Control & Warning School, Honor Grad 1958. **BUSINESS ADDRESS:** Fayetteville State Univ, 1200 Murchison Rd, Fayetteville, NC 28301.

HADDEN, EDDIE RAYNORD
Attorney, pilot. **PERSONAL:** Born May 25, 1943, Many, LA; son of Eddie and Emma; married Kay Dupree; children: Eugene. **EDUCATION:** Univ of TX El Paso, BA Journalism 1965; Geo Washington Univ, incomplete MBA 1971; Hofstra Univ Sch of Law, JD 1979. **CAREER:** JF Small Adv, vice pres 1973-74; Eastern Airlines, pilot 1972-; US Navy, officer/aviator 1965-72; Private Practice, lawyer 1980-. **ORGANIZATIONS:** Vice pres Bergen Co NJ NAACP 1980-83; pres Bergen Co NJ Urban League Housing Auth 1981-85; bd of dir Org of Black Airline Pilots Inc 1981-85; city councilman at large City of Englewood NJ 1983-86. **HONORS/ACHIEVEMENTS:** Elected official Englewood NJ City Council 1983; Youth Serv Awd Tuskegee Airm Inc Natl Conv 1984. **MILITARY SERVICE:** USN commander 21 yrs. **BUSINESS ADDRESS:** Attorney/Aviator, Priv Pract/Eastern Air Lines, 20 N Van Brunt St Ste 200, Englewood, NJ 07631.

HADDOCK, MABLE J.
Executive director. **PERSONAL:** Born Jun 20, 1948, Clover, VA; children: Kevin. **EDUCATION:** Mercy Coll, BA 1974; NBC Fellow Kent State Univ, MA 1976; Wharton Bus School, Cert 1982. **CAREER:** HEOP Mercy Coll, asst dir 1974-76; NBC, writer/rschr 1977-78; Canton Cultural Ctr, urgan arts dir 1978-80; Natl Black Programming Consortium, exec dir1980-. **ORGANIZATIONS:** Mem women in Commun, OH Arts Council Minority Arts Task Force 1980-82; consult OH Arts Council 1980-82; bd of dir YWCA 1982; bd mem Columbus Cable Commiss1982-83; mem Columbus Comm Calbe Access 1983-. **HONORS/ACHIEVEMENTS:** Participated conf on Media in Africa held in Senegal 1981; Co-Produce "Fannie Lou Hamer Story" 1983; Proj Dir "State of Black Amer" 1984, "Forum of Black Amer" 1985, "Mandela" currently in production; selected by the UN as rep on "Seminar on the Intensification of Intl Media Action for the Immediate Independence of Namibia" held in Brazzaville, Congo March 25-29 1985.

HADEN, MABEL D.
Attorney. **PERSONAL:** Born Feb 17, Virginia; married Russell George Smith. **EDUCA-**

TION: Howard U, LLB 1948; Georgetown U, LLM 1956. **CAREER:** Self-employed atty 1948-; DC, real estate broker 1959-; DC Pub Schs, tchr 1941-50. **ORGANIZATIONS:** Mem ABA; NBA; Washingtion Bar Assn; Nat Assn of Black Women Attorneys; mem Am Civil Liberties Union; Women's Equity Action League. **HONORS/ACHIEVEMENTS:** Honoree Iota Phi Lambda Sor Gamma Chap 1977; Marquis Who's Who in Am Law 1977; articles Case & Comment Lawyers' Co-operative Pub Co 1975. **BUSINESS ADDRESS:** 506 5 St NW, Washington, DC 20001.

HADLEY, HOWARD ALVA, JR.
Physician. **PERSONAL:** Born Jul 14, 1941, Miami, FL; married Cynthia Barnes. **EDUCATION:** FL A&M U, BS 1963; Howard U, MD 1967. **CAREER:** S Dade Commn Hlth Ctr, emergency rm phys; Mt Sinai Hosp, intern 1967-68; Dade Co Hlth Dept, gen med clinic 1970; Dept of Family MedUniv Miami, clinical asst prof 1976. **MILITARY SERVICE:** AUS med corps, capt 1968-70. **BUSINESS ADDRESS:** 11277 SW 152nd St, Miami, FL 33157.

HADLEY, ROBERT EARL
Assoc. executive. **PERSONAL:** Born Mar 11, 1937, New York, NY; married Sharon; children: Earl Nkrumah. **CAREER:** Frederick Douglas Book Center, assistant 1963-68; Afro-American Book Center, owner/operator 1973-. **MILITARY SERVICE:** USMC PFC. **BUSINESS ADDRESS:** President, Institute Operatnal Afro-Amer, PO Box 608, New York, NY 10035.

HADNOT, THOMAS EDWARD
Engineer. **PERSONAL:** Born Jul 23, 1944, Jasper, TX; married Gay Nell Singleton; children: Wanda Rideau Carrier, Sonja Armstrong, James E Rideau III, Clint D Rideau, Tomi L. **EDUCATION:** Univ of MD, 1967; Prairie View A&M Univ, BS Civil Engrg 1972. **CAREER:** Exxon Chem Amer, proj engr 1972-73, 1975-76, design engr, 1973-75, start-up engr 1976-77, scheduling engr 1977-79, coord sec supv 1979-81, prod coord/bus planner 1981-83, mfg supr 1983-86, dept mgr 1986-. **ORGANIZATIONS:** Tau Beta Pi. **HONORS/ACHIEVEMENTS:** Phi Beta Sigma Alpha Beta Sigma Chapt; Alpha Kappa Mu Hon Soc. **MILITARY SERVICE:** USAF e-4 sgt 3 1/2 yrs. **HOME ADDRESS:** PO Box 3664, Baytown, TX 77520. **BUSINESS ADDRESS:** Manager, Exxon Chemical Company, PO Box 4004, Baytown, TX 77522.

HADNOTT, BENNIE L.
Business executive. **PERSONAL:** Born Nov 23, 1944, Prattville, AL; son of Jame and Flura; children: Danielle, Johnathan. **EDUCATION:** Bernard M Baruch, BBA 1971; Iona Coll, MBA 1976. **CAREER:** Watson Rice & Co, partner 1981. **ORGANIZATIONS:** Am Inst of CPA'S; Assn of Govt Acctnts; NY/NJ Intergovt Audit Forum; Municipal Finance Offcr Assn of the US & Canada; NY State Soc of CPA'S, State & Local Govt & Health Care Comm; AICPA'S Govt Acctng & Auditing Educ Subcommittee; AICPA Fed Acquistion Committee Wash, DC; treas Berger County Br NAACP; treas PIC Council Bergen County; AICPA Future Issues Committee. **MILITARY SERVICE:** USAF Airman 1st Class 1962-67. **BUSINESS ADDRESS:** Managing Partner, Watson Rice & Co, 928 Broadway, New York, NY 10010.

HADNOTT, GRAYLING
Community investment funds officer. **PERSONAL:** Born Apr 07, 1950, New Iberia, LA; divorced; children: Roxanne. **EDUCATION:** Univ of Southwestern LA, BA 1973, MBA 1980; Attended, Univ of OK, Natl Consumer Credit School. **CAREER:** St Martin Parish Schools, english teacher 1972-79; Univ of Southwestern LA, english teacher 1973-75; Community Investment Funds, officer/supervisor; Iberia Svgs & Loan Assoc, comm investment funds officer 1980-87. **ORGANIZATIONS:** Mem Assoc of MBA Execs 1981-87, NBMBA Detroit Chap 1983-87; bd of dirs Sugarland Optimists' Club 1984-85, Friends of the Library 1985-87; mem LA Assocof Student Aid Administrators 1986-87. **HOME ADDRESS:** 1105 Field, New Iberia, LA 70560. **BUSINESS ADDRESS:** Community Invest Funds Ofcr, Iberia Svgs & Loan Assoc, PO Box 1000, New Iberia, LA 70561.

HAGER, JOSEPH C.
Educator. **PERSONAL:** Born Jun 11, 1944, Washington, DC. **EDUCATION:** Marist Coll Poughkeepsie NY, BA 1967; Sherwood Sch of Music Chicago, certificate of music 1960; candidate MA. **CAREER:** American Univ, camp counselor 1960-61; Family & Child Services; Marist House Formation St Joseph Novitiate, asst dir music; Marist Coll, asst dir music 1965-66; Marist Coll, dir music 1966-67; St Mary Parish Poughkeepsie, CCD instructor 1964-65; Mt St Michael Acad Bronx, secondary educ teacher 1967-70; Emmaculate Concoption Bronx teacher adult educ 1968; Our Lady Perpetual Help Pelham NY, CCD tchr 1968; New Rochelle HS religion, CCD secondary teacher 1968-70; New Rochelle HS religion, CCD training instructor 1968-69; New Rochelle HS religion, CCD curriculum developer 1969-70. **ORGANIZATIONS:** Staff consult Nat Office Black Caths 1970-73; exec dir Nat Black Cath Clergy Caucus 1970-73; dir religious educ St Benedict the Moor Wash DC; 1973-74; Alpha Kappa Psi Frat; DC bicentennial com; Nat Educ Assn; Nat Cath Educ Assn; Nat Black Cath Clergy Causus; bd mem camping programs Family & Child Services; Delta Psi Omega; Nat Office Black Caths; consult DESIGN; Carter G Woodson Com; Nat Black Churchmen Com. **HONORS/ACHIEVEMENTS:** Black Cath Secretariat Who's Who in Am Univs & Colls. **BUSINESS ADDRESS:** Woodward Bldg Archdiocese of W, 733 15 St NW #725, Washington, DC 20005.

HAGER, ROSCOE FRANKLIN
Consultant. **PERSONAL:** Born Jul 13, 1941, Gaston Cty, NC; married Anna Evans; children: Roscoe F Jr, Angela, Dorothy R. **EDUCATION:** Elizabeth City State Univ, BS 1963; WI State Univ Eau Claire, MS 1969; Appalachian State Univ Boone NC, MA 1980. **CAREER:** Anson Cty Bd of Educ, teacher, athletic dir, asst principal 1965; WI State Univ, instructor, counselor 1972; Conner Homes, sales mgr 1973-75; Anson Tech Coll, asst to pres & dir of inst rsch 1976-79; Govt Exec Inst UNC Chapel Hill, 1981; NC Dept of Public Educ Affirmative Action, 1979-. **ORGANIZATIONS:** Manpower chmn Anson Cty Boy Scouts 1976-79; vchmn Anson Cty Grass Roots Art Council 1977-79; chmn Anson Cty Scout Show 1978-79; mem NAACP, Alpha Phi Alpha, NC State Employees Assoc, NC Chap of the Intl Personnel Mgmt Assoc; chmn Wake Forest Comm School Adv Council. **HONORS/ACHIEVEMENTS:** Corpl Elizabeth City State Football Team 1962; listed in Who's Who in Coll & Univ Elizabeth City State 1962; NSF Fellowship WI State Univ 1967-69; Outstanding Young Man Awd Jaycees 1978. **BUSINESS ADDRESS:** Federal Compliance Consultant, NC Dept of Community Colleges, 114 W Edenton St, Raleigh, NC 27611.

HAGGINS, JON
Fashion designer. **PERSONAL:** Born Sep 05, 1943, Tampa, FL; son of John Haggins and Willie Mae Haggins; divorced. **EDUCATION:** Fashion Inst of Tech, AAS, 1964. **CAREER:** "Off the Avenue" (first studio), designer 1966; Reno Sweeney in Greenwich Village, Copa, Once Upon a Stove, Dangerfield's" singer; Jon Haggins Inc, pres/fashion designer, 1980-. **HONORS/ACHIEVEMENTS:** First recognized black designer and one of the youngest designers nominated for The Coty American Fashion Critics Awd; one of designs named "The Dress of the Year" by Bill Cunningham; honored for achievements with 9 other black designers by Harvey's Bristol Cream 1980, 1981, 1983; Black Designer of the Year 1981; Key to the City, Baltimore, MD, 1982; honored by Cornell Univ with an exhibition of his work, 1988; Artist-in-Residence, Cornell Univ, 1988; made numerous TV appearances; clothes featured in magazines & newspapers including Cosmopolitan, Harper's Bazaar, Vogue, Town & Country, New York Times, Essence, Ebony, and many more. **BUSINESS ADDRESS:** Pres, Jon Haggins Inc, 250 W 35th St, New York, NY 10001.

HAGINS, JEAN ARTHUR
Attorney. **PERSONAL:** Born Jun 25, 1947, Goldsboro, NC. **EDUCATION:** Fisk Univ Nashville, BA (His) 1969; Notre Dame Univ Sch of Law London Eng, 1971; Valparaiso Univ Sch of Law Valparaiso IN, JD 1972. **CAREER:** Alameda Co Pub Defender, atty; US Equal Employment Opportunity Commn, trial atty 1974-75; San Francisco Neighborhood Legal Asst, staff atty 1973; Shropshire Hatcher & Allen Gary IN, law clk 1970. **ORGANIZATIONS:** Mem Pub Defenders Assn 1975-; treas Black Women Lawyers Assn 1976-; mem Charles Houston Bar Assn; Nat Endowment for Humanities FellowshipUniv CA Berkeley 1972-73. **HONORS/ACHIEVEMENTS:** Listed Outstanding Women in Am 1979. **BUSINESS ADDRESS:** Alameda Co Pub Defender, 1225 Fallon St, Oakland, CA 94612.

HAGLER, MARVELOUS MARVIN
Professional boxer. **PERSONAL:** Born May 23, 1954, Newark, NJ; married Bertha Joann Dixon; children: Gentry, James, Celeste, Marvin Jr, Charelle. **CAREER:** World Boxing Assoc Professional Middleweight Boxer, World Boxing Champion 1980-; professional record 57 wins, 2 losses, 2 draws. **ORGANIZATIONS:** Mem World Boxing Assoc, US Boxing Assoc, World Boxing Council. **HONORS/ACHIEVEMENTS:** Won the Natl Am Middleweight Championship 1973; Outstanding Fighter Awd; Won AAU Championship 1973; Became Middleweight Champion 1980; Successfully defendedhis championship 8 times; Honored as Boxer of the Year World Boxing Council 1984; 1st in middleweight div to earn a $1 million purse; 1985 Honoree The Jackie Robinson Award for Athletics for accomplishments as simultaneous holder of the World Boxing Assn, World Boxing Council and Intl Boxing Federation middleweightdiv titles and for successful defense of his titles. **BUSINESS ADDRESS:** Marvelous Enterprises Inc, 28 Ward St, Brockton, MA 02401.

HAILE, RICHARD H.
Business executive. **PERSONAL:** Born Aug 02, 1910, Camden, SC; married Bessie E Pickett; children: Sylvia Nelson, Ralph H. **EDUCATION:** Claflin Coll, BS 1932; Orangeburc SC; Gupton-Jones Coll of Mortuary Sct Nashville TN, 1933. **CAREER:** Hickman Elem Sch, prin 1934-43; Haile's Funeral Home, owner 1944-. **ORGANIZATIONS:** Pres SC Morticians Assn Inc 1945-52; pres Nat Funeral Dir & Morticians Assn Inc 1959-61; mem Exec Com Nat Funeral Dir & Morticians Assn Inc 1961-; past basalus Omicron Phi Chpt; Omega Psi Phi Frat Columbia SC; basalus Chi Chi Chap Omega Psi Phi Frat Camden SC; past chmn Voter Educ Project Fifth Dist SC; past chmn Camden-Kershaw Co Br NAACP; mem, bd dir Office of Econ Opportunity Kershaw Co SC; past orshipful master Compostie Lodge #372 Masonic Order; past illustrous potentate AL Bar Temple Shriners; officer Trinity Unied Meth Ch. **BUSINESS ADDRESS:** Rutledge at Ch St, Camden, SC.

HAILES, EDWARD A.
Clergyman, association executive. **PERSONAL:** Married Nettie Drayton; children: Edward, Jr, Gregory, Patricia. **EDUCATION:** VA Union Univ, 1950; VA State Coll, Certificate; Harvard & Boston Univs, advanced studies; Howard Univ, Certificate. **CAREER:** Union Baptist Church New Bedford, pastor 1951-63; Inter-Church Council of Greater New Bedford, supr religious educ 1954-61, exec sec 1963-66; MA Public Sch Syst, substitute teacher 1962-63; DC Branch NAACP, exec sec 1963-66; Opportunity Industrialization Ctr, exec dir; 19th St Baptist Church Washington, DC, assoc pastor 1978-; pastor Mount Moriah Baptist Church. **ORGANIZATIONS:** Comm Adv on Equal Employment 1967-71; natl bd dir NAACP, pres DC Branch 1968-72; bd dir Housing Dev Corp 1969-74; Health & Welfare Council 1969-; mem Commn on Criminal Justice Stand & Goals 1970-71; v chmn Project Build Inc 1972; mem Mayor's Com Project HOME Washington 1973-; adv panel Adult Educ Demonstration Proj 1974-; pres DC Branch NAACP 1978-; natl vice pres NAACP 1980-; mem bd dir DC Chamber of Commerce 1983-; pres Charitable Found, United Supreme Council Ancient and Accepted Scottish Rite of Freemasonry Prince Hall Affil 1984-; bd dir United Givers Fund; DC chap US Civil Rights Commn. **HONORS/ACHIEVEMENTS:** Chamber of Commerce Award for role in march on Washington 1963; Created Grand Insp Gen of 33rd Degree The United Supreme Council of the Sovereign Grand Inspector General of the 33rd & Last Degree of the Ancient & Accept Scottish Rite of Freemasonry Prince Hall Affil 1974; Man of the Year Award Shiloh Men's Club Shiloh Baptist Ch 1980; Citizen of the Year Omega Psi Phi Chapters of Washington, DC 1981; Distinguished Serv Award United Supr Coun Ancient & Accept Scottish Rite of Freemasonry Prince Hall Affiliate; Outstand Young Citizen of Yr Jr Chamber of Commerce New Bedford. **BUSINESS ADDRESS:** Clergyman, 19th St Baptist Church, 3224 16 St NW, Washington, DC 20010.

HAILEY, PRISCILLA W.
Associate publisher. **PERSONAL:** Born Oct 22, 1947, Georgia; married Howard L. **EDUCATION:** Savannah State Coll, BS 1969. **CAREER:** The Medium Newspaper Seattle, assoc publisher 1970-; Dublin GA Bd of Educ, tchr 1969-70; Kaiser Gypsum Co, credit sec 1969; Head Start, tchr 1967-68. **ORGANIZATIONS:** Mem bd dir, treas Tilober Publ Co Inc; NAACP; Black Educ & Economics Conf; trainer-supr SeattleUniv Minority Stud Newspaper 1971-73; team capt Neighborhood Cancer Soc; Nat Educ Assn 1969-70; GA Educ Assn 1969-70; vol accountant to inner city residents vol trainer-typesetter Garfield HS Messenger 1970-71. **HONORS/ACHIEVEMENTS:** Recipient Model Cities Citizen Participation Award; Black Comm Unsung Hero Award. **BUSINESS ADDRESS:** 2600 S Jackson, Seattle, WA 98144.

HAINES, CHARLES EDWARD
Art director. **PERSONAL:** Born Apr 20, 1925, Louisville, KY; married Junetta; children: Charles Jr. **EDUCATION:** IN Univ, AB 1950, MFA 1953, MA 1959. **CAREER:** Free lance adv art; IN Univ, graduate asst; Sarkes Tarzian Inc, art dir; Avco Broad, art dir; Crosley Broad, art dir; Marian Coll, lecturer; Purdue Univ, lecturer; IN Univ, lecturer; WTHR TV, art dir. **ORGANIZATIONS:** Mem Coll Art Assoc Amer; mem Dean's Select Comm Search & Screen to appt new dean, Herron Sch of Art Indianapolis. **HONORS/ACHIEVEMENTS:** Black Expo Feat in "Ebony Mag" 1957; Exhibitions & Awds various state fairs; art work IN Basketball Hall of Fame; painting Atlanta Univ Collection. **MILITARY SERVICE:** AUS Corp of Engrg pfc 1944-46. **BUSINESS ADDRESS:** Art Dir, WTHR TV, 1000 N Meridian St, Indianapolis, IN 46204.

HAIR, JOHN
Educator. **PERSONAL:** Born Oct 08, 1941, Gulf Port, MS; son of John Hair and Julia Hair; married Beverly Ann Coffman; children: John Saverson, Melissa Dion. **EDUCATION:** Wayne State Univ, BS Ed 1969, MS Ed 1971; GA State Univ, EdS 1978; Western MI Univ, EdD 1986. **CAREER:** Detroit Public Schools, band dir 1969-71; Grand Rapids OIC, exec dir 1973-77; Grand Rapids Job Corps, mgr of educ 1981-82; Davenport Coll, faculty 1982-, dir of minority affairs 1983-88; dean of minority affairs, Michigan Council for the Arts Music Proposal Consultant 1988-. **ORGANIZATIONS:** Mem Phi Delta Kappa 1980-, MI Academy of Sci Arts & Letters 1983-; higher educ comm mem NABSE 1984-; mem IL Comm Black Concern in Higher Educ 1985-; secondary/higher educ comm AAHE 1986-; adv bd mem Grand Rapids Cable TV 1986-; mem industrial adv council Grand Rapids OIC; mem Grand Rapids Urban League; mem exec adv comm Sara Allen Family Neighborhood Ctr; bd mem, Grand Rapids Public School 1987-. **HONORS/ACHIEVEMENTS:** Grad Rsch Asst GA State Univ 1976-77; Band Leader 13 piece band Amway Grand Hotel 1982-85; "GIANTS" Phyllis Scott Activist Award 1988; "HEROES" Hispanic Community Service (non-Hispanic) Award of Merit 1988; chair personnel and Junior College Conn Grand Rapids Public School Board 1988-. **MILITARY SERVICE:** AUS pfc 3 yrs. **BUSINESS ADDRESS:** Dean of Minority Affairs, Davenport College, 415 E Fulton, Grand Rapids, MI 49503.

HAIRSTON, EDDISON R., JR.
Dentist. **PERSONAL:** Born Apr 04, 1933, York Run, PA; married Audrey Barnes; children: Eddison, Jr, Robert Eugene. **EDUCATION:** Lincoln U, AB 1954; HowardUniv Dental Sch, DDS 1962. **CAREER:** Self-employeed dentist 1963-; HowardUniv Comm Dentistry Chronically Ill & Aged Prog, clin asst prof 1967-. **ORGANIZATIONS:** Consult Armstrong Dental Asst Prog 1973-74; mem Robt T Freeman Dental Soc; Am & Nat Dental Assns; DC Dental Soc; Am Soc of Dentistry for Children; Omega Psi Phi; Wash Urban League; NAACP; many other ch, civc & professional orgns. **MILITARY SERVICE:** AUS dental tech 1954-57. **BUSINESS ADDRESS:** 3417 Minnesota Ave, SE, Washington, DC 20019.

HAIRSTON, JERRY WAYNE
Professional athlete. **PERSONAL:** Born Feb 16, 1952, Birmingham, AL; married Esperanza Anellano; children: Jerry Jr, Justin, Scott, Stacey Lynn. **CAREER:** Chicago White Sox, 1973-76; Chicago White Sox & Pittsburgh, 1977; Chicago White Sox, outfielder 1981-84. **BUSINESS ADDRESS:** Chicago White Sox, Dan Ryan & 35th St, Chicago, IL 60616.

HAIRSTON, JESTER
Actor, singer, composer. **PERSONAL:** Born in North Carolina; married Margaret Lancaster, 1938 (deceased). **EDUCATION:** Attended Univ of Massachusetts; received music degree from Tufts Univ, Boston MA, 1930; attended Juilliard School of Music, New York NY. **CAREER:** Broadway singer, music instructor, composer, conductor, and actor. **HONORS/ACHIEVEMENTS:** Actor for twenty years on Amos 'n' Andy; composer of Broadway musical Green Pastures; composer of film scores with Dmitri Tiomkin; actor in films including The Alamo, In the Heat of the Night, Lady Sings the Blues, and The Last Tycoon; plays part of Rolly Forbes on television series Amen. **BUSINESS ADDRESS:** 5047 Valley Ridge Ave, Los Angeles, CA 90043. *

HAIRSTON, JOSEPH HENRY
Attorney. **PERSONAL:** Born May 08, 1922, Axton, VA; married Anna L Allen; children: Nancy R, Naomi, JoAnn, Victoria M. **EDUCATION:** Univ Maryland, BS 1957; Am U, JD 1960; Georgetown U, LLM 1961. **CAREER:** Office of Solicitor Dept Labor Wash, atty 1960-61; Admin Serv Div IRS, retired dir 1976-85. **ORGANIZATIONS:** Mem Wash DC Am Nat Bar Assns; founding mem Nat Laywers Club; mem Am Inst Parliamentarians; past pres, vp, bd dirs Neighbors Inc; past v chmn, d trustees Takoma Park Bapt Ch; moderator Takoma Park Bapt Ch; founder, pres Nat Neighbors 1969, 1975; del Shepherd Park Citizens Assn; exec com DC Federation Citizens Assns 1970-73; Shepherd PTA; Takoma PTA; Officers Club Walter Reed Army Med Ctr; Nat Assn Uniformed Serv. **HONORS/ACHIEVEMENTS:** First black atty apptd sr exec IRS. **MILITARY SERVICE:** AUS 1940-60.

HAIRSTON, OSCAR GROGAN
Physician. **PERSONAL:** Born Jun 08, 1921, Winston-Salem, NC; married Lillian F. **EDUCATION:** Hampton Ins, 1949; Meharry Med Coll, 1958; Harvard Univ, PG 1953; Reynold Hosp, PG surgical residency. **CAREER:** Geo Washington Carver HS, sci & math teacher 1952-54; physician . **ORGANIZATIONS:** Twin City Med Soc; Oln N St Med Soc; Forsythe Co Med Soc; Amer Academy of Family Practitioners AOA; life mem NAACP. **HONORS/ACHIEVEMENTS:** Fellow Amer Academy of Family Practice. **MILITARY SERVICE:** USAAC 1942-46. **BUSINESS ADDRESS:** 2206 No Patterson Ave, Winston-Salem, NC 27105.

HAIRSTON, OTIS L.
Clergyman. **PERSONAL:** Born Apr 28, 1918, Greensboro, NC; son of John Wright and Nancy Wright; married Anna Cheek; children: Mrs Emma Lois Belle, Otis Jr. **EDUCATION:** Shaw Univ, 1940. **CAREER:** Bapt Informer, ed 1941-56; Shaw Univ, dir publ 1950-51; Brookston Bapt Church, pastor 1952-60; Bapt Supply Store, mgr 1956-58; Shiloh Bapt Church. **ORGANIZATIONS:** Mem PTA, Wake Cty Credit Union, Natl Shaw Univ Alumni Assoc, Shaw Univ Theol Alumni, Raleigh Citizens Assoc, Gen Bapt State Conv, Rowan Bapt Assoc, Org Greensboro Human Rel Comm, Greensboro Ministers Fellowship, Pulpit Forum, Citizens Assoc, Citizens Emergency Comm, NAACP, Hayes-Taylor YMCA; bd memIndust for the Blind; exec comm Gen Bapt St Convention of NC, Greensboro C of C, United Comm Svc, Comm Plnng Council, United Day Care Svc, Comm Christian Soc Ministeries of NC Council Chs, Bd of Ed, Dem Party, Phi Beta Sigma; bd of trustees L Richardson Mem Hosp; adv comm Friends Home; chaplain on call Wesley Long Hosp; bd of trustees Bennett Coll. **HONORS/ACHIEVEMENTS:** Ford Fellow 1966; Peacemaker Awd 1974; Cert Distinction Lott Carey Bapt Foreign Mission 1973,74; Hon DDiv Shaw Univ 1974; Zeta Phi Beta Sor Awd 1968; YMCA Awd 1971; NAACP Man of the Year Awd 1978; Hayes Taylor YMCA Awd for Leadership to Youth 1971; Citizen of the Year Awd for Meritorius Serv to Greensboro & The Ed Syst Tau Omega Chap of Omega Psi Phi Frat Inc; Brotherhood Citation Awd Natl Conf of Christian & Jews 1983. **BUSINESS ADDRESS:** Minister, Shiloh Baptist Church, 1210 S Eugene St, Greensboro, NC 27406.

HAIRSTON, ROWENA L.
Examiner. **PERSONAL:** Born Mar 17, 1928, Mohawk, WV; married Charles B; children: Anthony William. **EDUCATION:** Central Night Sch Columbus OH, 1956-58. **CAREER:** Bur of Employment Servs , examiner data control 1970-; Bur of Employment Servs Columbus, typist & clk 1961-70. **ORGANIZATIONS:** Nat aux pres Nat Alliance of Postal Fed Employees 1975-; life mem NAACP; natl rep Leadership Conf on Civil Rights 1972-. **HONORS/ACHIEVEMENTS:** Recognition plaque Local #605 Aux NAPFE Columbus 1975; key to city Mayor of Kansas City MO 1977; gold medallion Mayor of Atlantic City NJ 1978.

HAIRSTON, WILLIAM
Playwright, author, business administrator. **PERSONAL:** Born Apr 01, 1928, Goldsboro, NC; son of William Russell Hairston and Malissa Carter; married Enid Carey; children: Ann Marie. **EDUCATION:** Univ No CO, BA; NY Univ and Columbia, writing studies. **CAREER:** Play author-Walk in Darkness, Curtain Call Mr Aldridge, Black Antigone, and Swan Song of the 11th Dawn; The World of Carols, bk author; DC Pipeline, editor; Democratic Natl Committe, radio news editor & correspondent; 1968 Presidential Campaign, radio news editor; USIA, writer for films and TV prog; NY Shakespeare Fest, theatre manager; Greenwich News Theatre, prod coord; Arena Stage, admin intern; Washington City Government, public admin 1970-. **ORGANIZATIONS:** Chmn DC Police & Firefighters Retirement & Relief Bd; mem Boy Scouts of Amer, Authors League of America, Dramatists Guild. **HONORS/ACHIEVEMENTS:** Ford Found grantee 1965; Natl Endowment for the Arts grantee 1967; Playwrights Festival Award, The Group Theatre, Seattle, WA 1988; The Silver Beaver Award, The Boy Scouts of America, National Capital Area 1988; "IRA Aldridge (The London Conflict)" The Group Theatres Multi Cultural Playwrights Festival Winner 1988. **HOME ADDRESS:** 5501 Seminary Road, Falls Church, VA 22041.

HAIRSTONE, MARCUS A.
Dean arts and sciences. **PERSONAL:** Born Oct 16, 1926, Reidsville, NC. **EDUCATION:** Livingstone Coll, BS 1949; Duquesne Univ, MS 1950; Univ of Pittsburgh, PhD 1956. **CAREER:** Univ of NE, dir dental res labs 1957-59; Rockefeller Univ, rsch assoc 1962-64; Columbia Univ, rsch assoc 1964-66; Amer Univ Cairo, prof 1972-74; Natl Institutes of Health, health sci admin 1977-86; Cheyney Univ, dean 1986-. **ORGANIZATIONS:** Mem Amer Assoc Adv Sci 1950-, NY Acad of Sci 1969-; consultant/prof Tabriz Univ Iran 1971-72; consultant/prof USAID Addis Ababa Univ Ethiopia 1974-75; chair Africa Comm Amer Soc Publ Admin 1978-79; mem Mayor's (DC) Intl Adv Comm 1983-86. **HONORS/ACHIEVEMENTS:** Fulbright Fellowship Egypt 1966-67, Iran 1969-71; Mayor's Adv Comm International Washington DC 1984-86. **MILITARY SERVICE:** AUS non-comm officer 2 yrs. **BUSINESS ADDRESS:** Dean Arts and Sciences, Cheyney University, Cheyney, PA 19319.

HAIZLIP, ELLIS BENJAMIN
Producer. **PERSONAL:** Born Sep 21, 1929, Washington, DC; divorced. **EDUCATION:** Howard U; Malcolm X Coll, Dr Humanities. **CAREER:** Educ Broadcasting Corp, exec producer 1965-82; Lincoln Center, producer 1975-79; WOR-TV, developer & producer 1972; Victoria Intl Co, developer & producer 1971; Schomburg Center NY Public Library 1985-; The Ellis B Haizlip Co, pres. **ORGANIZATIONS:** Bd of dir Alvin Ailey City Ctr & Dance Thtr; Symph of New World; Gospel Workshop of Amer; The Jrnl of NATAS; Brewery Puppet Troup; NY State Task Force for the Arts; NY State Council on the Arts; Natl Council of Negro Women; Martin Luther King Players of NY; mem Manhattan Community Bd 5; mem First Mondays Literary Soc. **HONORS/ACHIEVEMENTS:** NATAS Emmy Award 1968, 1970; Black Rose Encore Mag 1972; excellence NATRA; excellence NY City Diamond Jub; human award Morrisania Comm Serv Ctr; publ "Sing Sing Sounds" 1976. **BUSINESS ADDRESS:** President, The Ellis B Haizlip Co, 275 Fifth Ave, Ste 3A, New York, NY 10016.

HAKIMA, MALA'IKA
Physician. **PERSONAL:** Born Aug 25, 1950, Kansas City, KS; married Larry Linstrome Hodge Hakima; children: Habiibah Nuurah-Salaam, Rabi'a Mala'ika, Mahmoud Abdul, Ihsan-Karim, Yasmin Rahimah, Isa Najm Sulayman. **EDUCATION:** Grinnell Coll, BA 1972; Meharry Medical Coll, MD 1984. **CAREER:** King/Drew Medical Ctr Los Angeles, intern 1984-85; Self-employed, physician 1985-. **ORGANIZATIONS:** Physician Comm Health Ctr of West Wilcox Co 1986-. **HONORS/ACHIEVEMENTS:** Southern Medical Assoc Scholarship 1980; Alpha Phi Alpha Awd 1981. **BUSINESS ADDRESS:** PO Box 101, Orrville, AL 36767.

HALE, CECIL I., II
Business executive. **PERSONAL:** Born Aug 03, 1945, St Louis, MO; married Patricia Jean Thomas; children: Juanita Patrice, Tasha Arnice. **EDUCATION:** So IL U, 1963-66; IntlUniv of Communications, MA 1973-75; Union Grad Sch, PhD 1975-78. **CAREER:** Capitol Records Inc, vp; Phonogram Inc, natl dir 1977-78; WVON Radio Chicago, asst prog dir announcer 1970-77; Soul Communications Inc, vice pres 1972-75; WNOV Radio Milwaukee, operations mgr announcer 1968-70; WMPP Radio Chicago, asst mgr announcer 1966; consult frelance announcer lctr TV. **ORGANIZATIONS:** Nat pres Nat Assn of Radio/TV Artists 1973-75; natl div chmn Black Music Assn 1978-; mem Nat Acad of Rec Arts & Scis; Alpha Phi Alpha; Sigma Beta Gamma; NAACP; Urban League. **HONORS/ACHIEVEMENTS:** Excellence in communications keynote spkr NY; key to city LA-New Orleans-Nashville; Fred Hampton Image Award; Operation PUSH Nat Award; city resolution LA. **BUSINESS ADDRESS:** Capitol Records Inc, 1750 N Vine St, Hollywood, CA 90028.

HALE, CLARA MCBRIDE
Humanitarian. **CAREER:** Hale House (home for children born addicted to drugs), founder 1970-. **HONORS/ACHIEVEMENTS:** During 1985 State of the Union Address Pres Reagan honored Clara Hale as an American Hero one of two individuals selected out of 200 million people; Leonard H Carter Humanitarian Awd 1987. *

HALE, CYNTHIA LYNNETTE
Minister, pastor. **PERSONAL:** Born Oct 27, 1952, Roanoke, VA; daughter of B Harrison Hale and Janice Hylton Hale. **EDUCATION:** Hollins Coll, Hollins VA, BA Music, 1975; Duke Divinity School, Durham NC, Master of Divinity, 1979; United Theological Seminary, Dayton OH, Doctorate of Ministry, 1989. **CAREER:** Fed Correctional Institution, Butner NC, Chaplain, 1979-85; Ray of Hope Christian Church, Decatur GA, pastor, 1986-. **ORGANIZATIONS:** Mem, Natl Council of Churches New York, 1978-83; vice pres, bd of dir, Greenwood Cemetery Co, 1979-80; pres, Natl Convocation Christian Church (DOC), 1982-88; mem, General Bd of Christian Church (DOC), 1982-88; vice pres, Concerned Black Clergy Inc, 1987-. **HONORS/ACHIEVEMENTS:** Outstanding Young Woman of Amer, 1982, 1986-88; "My Story, My Witness," Program for Compelled by Faith, 1983-84; Liberation Award, Natl Convocation CCDC, 1984. **BUSINESS ADDRESS:** Pastor, Ray of Hope Christian Church, 3936 Rainbow Dr, Decatur, GA 30034.

HALE, EDWARD HARNED
Physician. **PERSONAL:** Born Sep 15, 1923, Nashville, TN; son of William J. Hale (deceased) and Harriett Hodgkins Hale (deceased); married Della Ellis Miller; children: Pamela, Deborah, Nancy, Barbara, Rudolph Miller, Maria Miller. **EDUCATION:** TN State Coll, BS 1941; Meharry Med Coll, MD 1945; Univ of IL, MS 1947. **CAREER:** Harlem Hosp NYC, intern 1945-46; Univ of IL, fellow med 1947-48; Freedman's Hosp, resident 1948-50; West Penn Hosp, staff mem; Howard Univ, instr med 1950-53; VA Hosp Pgh, chief med serv 1955-58; Private Practice, specializing in internal med and pulmonary disease 1958-. **ORGANIZATIONS:** Mem Amer Bd Intl Med 1952, 1979-; fellow Fed Clin Rsch; contrib articles to professional jours; treas PA Soc of Intl Med 1976-77; fellow Amer Coll of Physicians 1979. **MILITARY SERVICE:** AUS MC 1953-55. **BUSINESS ADDRESS:** Physician, 211 N Whitfield St, Pittsburgh, PA 15206.

HALE, FRANK W., JR.
Educator. **PERSONAL:** Born Mar 24, 1927, Kansas City, MO; married Ruth Saddler; children: Ruth, Frank III, Sherilyn. **EDUCATION:** Univ NE, AB 1950; MA 1951; OH State U, PhD 1955; London, postgrad study 1960. **CAREER:** OH State Univ, provost for minority affairs, prof of law, vice provost 1978-, dean graduate school 1971-78; Oakwood Coll, pres 1966-71; Central State Univ, prof, dept chmn 1959-66; Andrews Univ, visiting prof 1957; OH State Univ, asst instructor 1954-55, assoc prof 1955-59, asst to pres 1957-59, dept head 1955-59; Oakwood Coll, instructor, dir public relations 1952-53. **ORGANIZATIONS:** Mem Am Assn Coll & U; Am Assn Sch Adminstr; Assn Study Afro-Am Life & Hist; Nat Coun Tchrs Eng; OH Eng Assn; OH Speech Assn; Speech Assn Am; Mod Lang Assn; Assn Grad Schs; bd dirs Black Campus Ministry 1972-; Buckeye Boys Ranch 1975-; United Christian Ctr 1975-; United Negro Coll Fund 1965-71; bd dirs AL Ctr Higher Educ 1967-71; Coop Coll Libr Ctr 1969-71; Comm Welf Coun 1967-71; Harding Hosp 1971-; Huntsville C of C 1967-71; Huntsville Lit Assn 1970-71; Laymen's Ldrshp Conf 1959-65; Loma LindaUniv 1968-71; Mayor's Bicent Commn 1974-; Mental Hlth Assn 1968-71; Operation PUSH 1974-; Riverside Hosp 1966-71; So Missionary Coll 1966-71; Top AL Reg Coun Govt 1969-71; 7th Day Adventist Commn Higher Edn1968-71; Minority Affairs in the OH StateUniv Grad Sch; Com on Instnl Coop; Conf on Equal Oppor in Higher Edn, ofc of Women's Affairs INUniv 1976; 5 Yr Experiment in Affirm Action Jour of Proceedings 1976; The Blacks (Blacks in OH) The Ohioana Lib Yrbk Ethnic Groups 1977. **HONORS/ACHIEVEMENTS:** Cons, lectr, publ nem art most recent are, A Sprinkle of Pepper the ste of black influence in white coll & u journal of non-White concerns 1975; Black Protest past & present 200 yrs of black r*esistance to oppression negro educ review 1976; %cert merit central state u 1965; coop libr Ldrshp Award 1969; alumni awd Oakwood Alumni Assn 1970; Black Heritage Awd AL A&MUniv 1970; achvmt awards Oakwood Coll Faculty 1971; Disting Alumnus of Yr OH StateUniv 1970; Adminstr of Yr OH StateUniv 1971-73. **BUSINESS ADDRESS:** Vice Provost & Prof of Law, Ohio State University, 190 N Oval Mall, Columbus, OH 43210.

HALE, GENE
Association executive. **PERSONAL:** Born in Birmingham, AL. **EDUCATION:** California State Univ Dominquez Hills, BS 1980. **CAREER:** G&C Equipment Corp, pres; Gence Corporation, pres. **ORGANIZATIONS:** Mem NAACP; chmn advisory bd CA State Dept of Transportation; chmn Black Business Assn of Los Angeles, Congressional Task Force on Minority Business Set Aside (private sector). **HONORS/ACHIEVEMENTS:** Black Business of the Year Black Business Assoc of Los Angeles 1984; Outstanding Minority Business State of CA 1985. **MILITARY SERVICE:** AUS sgt 2 yrs. **BUSINESS ADDRESS:** Chairman, Black Business Association, 1875 W Redondo Beach Blvd, Ste 102, Gardena, CA 90247.

HALE, PHALE D.
Legislator, clergyman. **PERSONAL:** Born Jul 16, 1915, Starksville, MS; married Cleo; children: Phale, Jr, Janice Ellen, Marna A, Hilton Ingram. **EDUCATION:** Morehouse Coll, AB; Gammon Theol Sem, MDiv; Cincinnati Bapt Theol Sem, DD. **CAREER:** OH, Hilton Ingram mem; OH Dist 31, state rep 1966-80; Union Grove Bapt Church Columbus, pastor 37 yrs; OH Civil Rights Commission, chmn. **ORGANIZATIONS:** Chmn, past chmn Health & Welfare Com.

HALE-BENSON, JANICE ELLEN
Educator, researcher. **PERSONAL:** Born Apr 30, 1948, Ft Wayne, IN; daughter of Rev Phale D Hale Sr and Cleo Ingram Hale; married Keith Benson, May 19, 1984; children: Keith A Benson Jr. **EDUCATION:** Spelman Coll, BA 1970; Interdenominational Theol Center, MRE 1972; GA State Univ, PhD 1974. **CAREER:** Early Childhood Educ Clark Coll, asso prof; Dept of Psychol Yale Univ, rsrch asso; Afro-Am Studies Prog, lecturer 1980-81; Cleveland State Univ, assoc prof. **ORGANIZATIONS:** Exec dir Visions for Children, Afro-Amer Early Childhood Educ Rsch Demonstration Prog; governing bd mem, Natl Assn for the Educ of Young Children; consulting editor, Young Children, Journal of NAEYC. **HONORS/ACHIEVEMENTS:** Publications "Christian Educ for Black Liberation" in For You Who Teach in th Black Church 1973; "The Woman's Role The Strength of Blk Families" in 1st World, An Intl Jrnl of Black Thought 1977; "De-Mythicizing the Educ of Black Children" 1st World, An Intl Journal of Black Thought 1977; numerous other publications; recipient of grant Spencer Found; numerous presentations on Research for the following institutions and assns, Black Child Devel Inst, Natl Council for Black Child Devel, Natl Assn for the Educ of Young Children, NC Assn for the Educ of Young Children, Univ of SC, SC State Coll, Spelman Coll, Morehouse Coll, GA State Univ, Univ of the West Indies, NY Univ, Head Start Prog of Omaha NE, CO Springs, CO Public School; one of ten outstanding young people of Atlanta 1978; author of "Black Children, Th eir Roots Culture and Learning Styles," John Hopkins Univ Press revised edition 1986; 50 Future Leaders, Ebony Magazine, 1978; Distinguished Alumna, College of Educ, Georgia State Univ 1982. **BUSINESS ADDRESS:** Assoc Prof, Cleveland State University, Early Childhood Education, 24th at Euclid Aves, Cleveland, OH 44115.

HALES, EDWARD EVERETTE
Attorney. **PERSONAL:** Born Feb 13, 1932, Leechburg, PA. **EDUCATION:** Baldwin-Wallace Coll, 1955;Univ of WI Madison Law Coll, 1962. **CAREER:** Hales Hartig, atty 1979-; Hales Harvey & Neu, atty 1973-79; Goodman Hales & Costello, atty 1965-73; City of Racine, asst city atty 1965-67; State of MN, legal asst, atty general 1962-63; Intl Fellowship, consultant; VISTA, consultant; State of MI OEO, consultant; IA Urban Rsch Center, consultant; AIM Jobs, board. **ORGANIZATIONS:** Spec arbitrator Bd of Arbitration US Steel Corp Unite Steel Workers of Am; spec arbitrator Fed Mediation Serv; spec arbitrator WI Employment Rel Commn; spec arbitrator Bd of Arbitration State of MN NAACP; Urban League; Nat Bar Assn; Am Bar Assn; WI State Bar Assn; WI Council Criminal Justice; WI Higher Educ Aids Bd; WIUniv Merger Implementation Com; Alpha Ph Alpha; chmn Finance Com Bd of RegnestsUniv of WI System 1975-77; pres Bd of RegentsUniv of WI System 1977-79; bd of trustees Assn of Gov Bds ofUniv & Coll 1977-; selection com US 7th Circuit & Judicial Court 1978-79; bd of dirs Pub Broadcasting Service 1979-80; bd of trustees Assn for Pub Broadcasting 1979-; arbitrator Am Arbitration Assn 1980-; bd of trustees Ripon Coll Ripon WI1980-; Offiec of Econ Oppty 1967. **HONORS/ACHIEVEMENTS:** Urban Serv Award 1967; effort award Kings Daughter Club 1974. **MILITARY SERVICE:** AUS 1956-58. **BUSINESS ADDRESS:** 524 Main St, Racine, WI 53403.

HALES, MARY ANN
Educator, bail bond agent. **PERSONAL:** Born Jul 27, 1953, Fayetteville, NC; daughter of Dorothy M Allen Melvin; divorced; children: Michelle, Mario, Dominique. **EDUCATION:** Fayetteville State Univ, BS Psych (magna cum laude) 1981; Masters in Educ; Fayetteville Tech Inst, Certificate Industrial Supervision 1984; Fayetteville Real Estate Acad, Certified Real Estate Salesperson 1987; Fayetteville Tech Inst, Certificate Enhancing Educ Opportunity with Quality Indus. **CAREER:** Foxe's Surety Bail Bonding Co, admin chief 1978-81; Fayetteville Tech Inst, adult basic educ instructor 1981-88; WFBS Radio, radio communications operator 1982-83; HSA Cumberland Psychiatric Hospital, mental health counselor 1985-87; Century 21 Odyssey Real Estate, salesperson 1987-; All American Bail Bonding Company, owner/agent 1987-; Long Hill Elementary School, teacher 1989-. **ORGANIZATIONS:** Vice pres Cumberland Co Chapter of Bail Bondsmen 1978-81; notary public State of NC 1980-; mem NC Assoc of Adult Educators 1981-; sr friend Fayetteville Urban Ministries Find-A-Friend Program 1986-; mem NC Bail Bondsmen Assn 1987, Nor Carolina Assn of Educators 1989-, Natl Education Assn 1989-, Assn of Teacher Educators 1989-. **HONORS/ACHIEVEMENTS:** Permanent mem Natl Dean's List 1978-; Alpha Kappa Mu Natl Honor Society 1979. **HOME ADDRESS:** 1834 Cascade St, Fayetteville, NC 28301. **BUSINESS ADDRESS:** Long Hill Elementary School, 6546 Ramsey St, Fayetteville, NC 28301.

HALES, WILLIAM ROY
Editor, publisher. **PERSONAL:** Born Aug 18, 1934, Girard, GA; married Inez Hales; children: Wilbert R. **EDUCATION:** Univ of Hartford, 1954. **CAREER:** NAACP, bd mem 1956; Ebony Businessmens League, past pres 1968-71; CT House of Reps, cand ct ho 1968-72; State of CT Justice of Peace, justice of peace 1968-74; Hartford Devel Commiss, commissioner 1984-86; Focus Magazine, editor/publisher; The Inquirer Newspaper Group, editor publisher. **HONORS/ACHIEVEMENTS:** Cert of Appreciation Greater Hartford Jaycees 1971. **BUSINESS ADDRESS:** Editor & Publisher, The Inquirer Newspaper Group, 3281 Main St, Hartford, CT 06120.

HALEY, ALEXANDER PALMER
Author, lecturer. **PERSONAL:** Born Aug 11, 1921, Ithaca, NY; children: William, Lydia, Cynthia. **EDUCATION:** Elizabeth City Tchrs Coll, attended 1937-39; Simpson Coll, LittD 1970; AL A&M Univ, attended 1937-39; Hon Doctorates, Seaton Hill Univ 1974, Williams Coll 1975, Howard Univ 1974, Simpson Coll 1971, Capitol Univ 1975. **CAREER:** USCG, chief journalist 1949 retired 1959; self employed author/lecturer. **ORGANIZATIONS:** Bd mem New Coll of CA 1974; presidential appointee Amer Revolutionary Bicentennial Comm 1975; pres The Kinte Found, The Kinte Corp; mem Authors Guild,Soc Mag Writers; mem King Hassan's Royal Acad; commissioned by Gov of TN to write Tennessee's Official History to be completed in 1996 the state's bicentennial. **HONORS/ACHIEVEMENTS:** Author "The Autobiography of Malcolm X", "Roots"; Springarn Medal NAACP 1977; Spl Pulitzer Prize 1977; "Roots, The Saga of an American Family" 1979; nom Black Filmmakers Hall of Fame for Producing "Palmerstown USA" 1981; book "Roots" had largest printing for a hard cover book in US publishing history. **BUSINESS ADDRESS:** Kinte Corporation, PO Box 3338, Beverly Hills, CA 90212.

HALEY, DONALD C.
Business executive. **PERSONAL:** Born Mar 15, 1928, Peoria, IL; married Janice C Wilson; children: Randle, Gordon, Steven. **EDUCATION:** Univ IL, BS 1950; Western Reserve U, MBA 1958; Cleveland StateUniv Coll of Law, JD cum laude 1963. **CAREER:** IRS Cincinnati, ast dist dir 1967-68; IRS Cleveland, various mgmt supr positions 1954-67; Allied Drug Co Cleveland, acct 1953-54; Standard Oil CoOH, vice pres accounting. **ORGANIZATIONS:** Mem bd trustees Financial Execs Inst NE OH 1980; Cleveland Scholarships Inc 1980; Bar Assn Gr Cleveland 1973-; Urban League of Cleveland 1972-; Karamu House 1974-; Harvard Comm Serv Cntr 1970-; present & past memberships various civic bds & commisions. **MILITARY SERVICE:** AUS sgt 1950-52. **BUSINESS ADDRESS:** 255 Midland Bldg, Cleveland, OH 44115.

HALEY, EARL ALBERT
Business executive. **PERSONAL:** Born May 18, 1933, Newark, NJ; son of Earl Haley and Ada Haley; married Pearl L Hall; children: Earl Jr, Derek. **EDUCATION:** Fairleigh Dick-

inson Univ, BS Industrial Engineering 1967. **CAREER:** Machintronic & Engrg Co, machinist inspector 1951-55; Western Electric Co, detail maker 1955-66, numerous positions 1957-66; Becton Dickinson, mgr special recruiting 1969-71, coord 1973-74, dir EEO, corp staffing & compliance 1985-. **ORGANIZATIONS:** Past chmn Bergen Co Advisory Com; bd of dir, Urban League, NAACP, United Way, Consortium Black Professional Devel; chmn Bergen Co JSIP; bd of dir, Amer Cancer Society, Boy Scouts of Amer, Industry Labor Council, Natl Assoc of Manufacturers, NJ Liaison Group, TWIN, Washington Study Group. **MILITARY SERVICE:** AUS corpl 1953-55. **BUSINESS ADDRESS:** Dir Staffing/Compliance, Becton Dickinson & Co, Paramus, NJ 07652.

HALEY, GEORGE WILLIFORD BOYCE
Attorney. **PERSONAL:** Born Aug 28, 1925, Henning, TN; married Doris Elaine Moxley; children: David Barton, Anne Palmer. **EDUCATION:** Morehouse Coll, BA with high honors 1949; Univ of AK, LLB 1952. **CAREER:** Kansas City KS, deputy city attorney 1954-64; State of KS, KS state senate 1964-68; US Urban Mass Trans Admin, chief counsel 1969-73; US Information Agency, gen'l counsel & congressional liasion 1975-76; George W Haley Prof Corp, president. **ORGANIZATIONS:** Lay-leader Methodist-KS-MO-CO Conference 1956-68; pres, Wyandotte Cty Kansas Young Republicans 1959-60; UNESCO monitoring panel US State Dept 1984; bd ofdirectors Universal Bank 1985; bd of directors Antioch Sch of Law 1985. **HONORS/ACHIEVEMENTS:** Comments editor AR Law Review 1951-52. **MILITARY SERVICE:** USAF sgt 3 yrs. **HOME ADDRESS:** ate Dr, Silver Spring, MD 20906. **BUSINESS ADDRESS:** President, Geo W Haley Prof Corp, 1511 K St NW, Ste 940, Washington, DC 20005.

HALEY, JOHNETTA RANDOLPH
Educator. **PERSONAL:** Born Mar 19, 1923, Alton, IL; daughter of Rev John Randolph and Willye Smith Randolph; divorced; children: Karen Douglas, Michael. **EDUCATION:** Lincoln Sr HS, Diploma 1941; LincolnUniv Jeff City, MO, BS 1945; Southern ILUniv at Edws, MM 1972. **CAREER:** Lincoln HS E St Louis, IL, vocal/genl music teacher 1945-48; Turner Jr HS Kirkwood, MO, vocal music teacher/choral dir 1950-55; Nipher Jr HS Kirkwood, MO, vocal/gen music teacher/choral dir 1955-71; Title I Program for Culturally Disadvantaged Childrn Kirkwood, MO, teacher of black history/music 1966; Human Devel Corp St Louis, MO, program specialist 1968; St Louis Cncl of Black People St Louis, MO, interim exec dir 1970; School of Fine Arts S IL Univ at Edwardsville, IL, grad res asst 1971-72, asst prof of music 1972-77; TX S U, visiting prof 1977; So IL Univ, prof of music 1982-, dir E St Louis Br 1982-. **ORGANIZATIONS:** Amer Assn of Univ Prof; The Coll Music Soc; Music Educators Natl Conf; IL Music Educators Assn; Natl Choral Dir Assn; Mu Phi Epsilon; Intl Prof Music Frat; Assn of Teachers Educators; Mid-West Kodaly Music Educators; Organ of Am Kodaly Educators; Artist Presentations Soc; Pi Kappa Lambda; Music Hon Soc; Alpha Kappa Alpha Sor Inc; Jack & Jill Inc; Las Amigas Social Club; Friends of the St Louis Art Museum; Top Ladies of Distinction Inc; United Negro College Fund Inc; Urban League; past pres Las Amigas Club; past sec St Louis Co Elem Music Teachers Assn past pres St Louis Chap; past pres Jack & Jill Inc; past pres St Louis Alumni Chap; co-founder St Louis Cncl of Black People; Metro Youth Commn 1966-69; St Louis Mayor's Committee for Protection of the Innocent; initiated Worlds Largest Garage Sale 1977; initiated Pilot Cnslr Aide Program in St Louis Public School for Delinquent Students; initiated 1st Exhibit of Black-Artist at St Louis Art Museum; advisory bd Help Inc; chairperson, Illinois Comm on Black Concerns in Higher Educ; bd of Trustees, Lincoln Univ 1974-83; bd of Trustees, Stillman Coll 1984-; bd of Dir, Assn of Governing bds of Univs and Colls; Links Inc. **HONORS/ACHIEVEMENTS:** Woman of the Yr Greyhound Bus Corp 1969; Disting Citizen Award St Louis Argus Newspaper 1970; Comm Serv Award Las Amigas Club 1970; Key to the City Mayor R Hatcher 1972; Serv to Music Award MO Music Educators 1972; Serv to Educ Award Kirkwood Sch Dist 1972; Duchess of Paducah Award Paducah, KY 1974; Signel Hon Award for Outstand Comm Serv St Louis Sentinel Newspaper 1974; Pi Kappa Lambda Intl Music Hon Soc 1977; Disting Alumni Award LincolnUniv 1977; 1988 Woman of Achievement/Education KMOX radio & surburban newspaper. **HOME ADDRESS:** 30 Plaza Sq, St Louis, MO 63103.

HALFACRE, FRANK EDWARD
Association executive. **PERSONAL:** Born Jun 21, 1936, Youngstown, OH; son of Walter Melvin Halfacre and Consuelo Stewart; married Mary Tyson; children: Lyle, Laura, Keith, Frank, Mary, Madelyn, Walter. **EDUCATION:** Youngstown State Univ, BA Telecommunications/Speech 1980. **CAREER:** Youngstown Park & Rec Commn, caretaker 1955-65; WWOW-WFIZ, newsman/announcer; WFAR, disc jockey, music & program dir, 1966; WNIO & WJMO Radio, disc jockey 1968; James Brown Prod,1969; Starday King Records, promotions; pub affairs & research positions, 1970-72; Afro-Amer Mus Hall of Fame & Mus Inc Rsch Center, exec dir 1973-. **ORGANIZATIONS:** Mem Natl Assn TV & Radio Announcers; FORE; Black Indsl & Econ Union; mem DAV; mem PTA; Lexington Players; co-founder 7-11 Club; founder Kleen Teens; vice pres Youngstown Sickle Cell Found; Emanon Jaguars Track Club; co-chmn/coach Youngstown Rayen Girls Track; track coach Rayen Boys Freshman State Edward Jr HS; Youngstown State Univ Track Club. **HONORS/ACHIEVEMENTS:** Man of the Year OH Assn of Beauticians 1968; Disting Serv Award NATRA 1969; Free Lance Writing including, Buckeye Review (Jazz & Sports); Call and Post (Jazz & Sports); The Voice (Jazz & Sports); Hit Kit (Jazz, Rhythm & Blues); Stringer reporter for Jet & Ebony; voted into Youngstown Area Curb Stone Coaches Hall of Fame for Track Field 1987. **MILITARY SERVICE:** AUS 1951-53. **BUSINESS ADDRESS:** Executive Dir, Afro-American Hall of Fame, PO Box 2120, Youngstown, OH 44504.

HALIBURTON, LAWRENCE E.
Attorney. **PERSONAL:** Born Oct 29, 1917, Great Bend, KS; married Reba J; children: Lawrence E, Jr. **EDUCATION:** Howard U; Temple U; John Marshall Law Sch; Northwestern Law Sch; IL Kent Coll of Law. **CAREER:** Gen Practice, jr atty. **ORGANIZATIONS:** Mem Am Bar Assn; mem IL State Bar Assn; mem Cook Co Bar Assn.

HALL, ADDIE JUNE
Educational administration. **PERSONAL:** Born Apr 11, 1930, Houston, TX; children: Sharmane C, Dr LeRoy B Jr DVM PhD. **EDUCATION:** Washington Jr Coll, AA 1953; Bethune-Cookman, BS 1955; Columbia Univ, MA 1962; FL State Univ, PhD 1975; Emory Univ, Certificate, Theol 1981. **CAREER:** Agat Guam, instr 1955-58; Escambia Cty School Bd, instr 1959-69, curriculum coord 1969-71, instr coord 1971-73; FL State Univ, grad instr 1973-74, instr 1974-75; Pensacola Jr Coll, asst prof 1975-78, dir of adult ed & prof 1978-. **ORGANIZATIONS:** Minister United Methodist 1971-, mem Kappa Delta Pi 1972-, Phi Delta Kappa 1974-; parliamentarian FL State Adv Council 1983-; mem adb bd Dept of Corrections Reg 1983-; mem NAACP, Links, Tiger Bay Club, FL Admin 1983; TV appearances Adult Educ, Black History 1983, 1984; radio WBOP 1983, 1984; journalist Delta Sigma Theta 1985-; marcher March of Dimes, Arthritis, Leukema Soc; lecturer, counselor Churches Schools Inst; mem Natl Pol Congress of Blackwomen, AAACE, US Senate Educ Adv Council; president, Pensacola Chapter Links, Inc 1988-90. **HONORS/ACHIEVEMENTS:** Pensacola Women 1978; Outstanding Ed Delta Sigma Theta 1982, 1986; Articles publ "The New Amer" 1983, "The Self-Concepts & Occupational Aspiration Level of ABE Students" 1983; Pensacola Leadership Chamber of Commerce 1984-85; Nominee of BIP Prog Chamber of Commerce 1984-85; many certificates of appreciation; certificate from Gov Graham 1986; cert from Senator Hawkins for serving on the US Senate Educ Adv Council 1986; Supervisor of the Year, College Assn of Educ Office Personnel, Pensacola Junior College, 1986; Lady of Distinction, Pensacola Chapter Top Ladies of Distinction, 1987; Community Service Award, and A Believer in the Under Achiever Award, Jordan Street SDA Church, 1987 & 1988. **BUSINESS ADDRESS:** Dir Adult Basic Educ, Pensacola Junior College, 1000 College Blvd, Pensacola, FL 32504.

HALL, ALBERT
Professional athlete. **PERSONAL:** Born Mar 07, 1959, Birmingham, AL. **CAREER:** Atlanta Braves, left fielder 1984. **ORGANIZATIONS:** 120 runs scored that season is still a Richmond Braves record; Carolina League All-Star 1980. **BUSINESS ADDRESS:** Atlanta Braves, PO Box 4064, Atlanta, GA 30302.

HALL, ANTHONY W., JR.
Elected government official. **PERSONAL:** Born Sep 16, 1944, Houston, TX; married Carolyn Joyce Middleton; children: Anthony William, Ursula Antoinette. **EDUCATION:** Howard Univ, BA 1967; Turgood Marshall School of law, JD 1982. **CAREER:** Harris Cty Commiss Bray Houston, asst 1971-72; Williamson Gardner Hall & Wiensenthal, partner; State of TX, state rep; City of Houston, city councilmember. **ORGANIZATIONS:** Mem Rules Budget & Fin Coms, TX Dem Party; state dem exec committeeman Sentatorial Dist 13; delegate 1972,74,76,80 Dem Natl Conv; mem Kappa Alpha Psi, Sigma Pi Phi; Natl Municipal League; mem bd mgrs YMCA Houston; mem Masons, Shriner, OES, Houston Bus & Professional Mens Club; bd dir, past vp, immed past pres Riverside Lions Club; exec bd mem United Negro Coll Fund, Gr Zion Bapt Church; mem Natl Bar Assoc, TX Bar, Amer Bar, Houston Bar Assoc, Houston Lawyers Assoc. **HONORS/ACHIEVEMENTS:** Black Achiever Awd YMCA 1972; Cotton Hook of the Year Awd ILA Local 872 1973; Citation for Outstanding Comm Serv NAACP 1972. **MILITARY SERVICE:** AUS capt 1967-71. **BUSINESS ADDRESS:** City Councilmember, City of Houston, P O Box 1562, Houston, TX 77251.

HALL, BRIAN EDWARD
Transportation company executive. **PERSONAL:** Born May 05, 1958, Cleveland, OH; son of William D Hall; married Susan Reed, Mar 14, 1987. **EDUCATION:** University of Cincinnati, Cincinnati OH, BBA, 1980; Baldwin-Wallace College, Berea OH, MBA, 1987. **CAREER:** Industrial Transport, Cleveland OH, dispatch administrator, 1980-81, operations manager, 1981-83, general manager, 1983-85, president, 1985—. **ORGANIZATIONS:** Ohio Trucking Assn; Michigan Trucking Assn; Council of Small Enterprise and Contractors Assn; Big Brothers of America; Leadership Cleveland; board member, Excel Corp; trustee and treasurer, Cleveland Business League, 1989-90; Kappa Alpha Psi. **HONORS/ACHIEVEMENTS:** Outstanding Men of America, 1982, 1983; Kappa Alpha Psi Award for Entrepreneurship, 1987, Outstanding Achievement Award, 1989; Minority Business Executive Program scholarship, 1988; nominee for business excellence, Crain's Cleveland Business, 1989. **BUSINESS ADDRESS:** President, Intrans Inc/Industrial Transport, 2330 East 79th St, Cleveland, OH 44104.

HALL, CHARLES HAROLD
Business executive. **PERSONAL:** Born Mar 10, 1934, Sapelo Island, GA; son of Charles Hall and Beulah Hall; divorced; children: Ronald Charles, Reginald Harold. **EDUCATION:** Morehouse Clge, BS 1955; DT Watson Schl of Physiat, phys therapy dip 1956; Air Univ USAF, Cert 1957. **CAREER:** Therapeutic Serv Inc, pres chf exec ofcr prof 1970-; VA Hosp, supv phys therap 1961-69; Total Living Care Inc, admin 1976-; Jefferson Twshp OH Dev Corp, treas 1970-. **ORGANIZATIONS:** 1st Black chmn OH Chptr Amer Phys Therap Assc 1967-69; 1st black chf deleg OH Chap Amer Phys Therap Assc 1969-71; 1st black treas pvt pract sect APTA 1975-76; 1st Black pres pvt prac sect APTA 1976-; bd dir BS of Amer 1972-; mem NAACP 1960-. **HONORS/ACHIEVEMENTS:** Sup Perf Award VA Hosp; Outst Srv Award APTA; guest spkr APTA. **MILITARY SERVICE:** USAF 1st lt 1957-61; USAFR lt col 1977-. **BUSINESS ADDRESS:** President, Prof Therapeutic Services Inc, 45 Riverside Drive, Dayton, OH 45405.

HALL, DANIEL A.
Physician/administrator. **PERSONAL:** Born Nov 16, 1933, Philadelphia, PA; married Shirley Louise Conway; children: Joy, Patricia. **EDUCATION:** Howard Univ, BS 1955; Temple Univ, MD 1959; Columbia Sch of Public Health, MPH 1968. **CAREER:** Gen med Philadelphia 1962-66; Philadelphia Health Dept, resident 1966-69; Health Dist 5, dept dir 1969-72; Temple Univ, assoc prof 1973-78; Prudential Ins Co, dir med serv 1978-. **ORGANIZATIONS:** Finance comm Zion Baptist Church 1967-; mem Philadelphia Boy Scouts Exec Council 1968-72; bd of dirs W Nicetown Neighborhood Health Ctr 1969-71; bd of dirs Temple Univ Med Alumni Assn 1971-73; bd of mgrs N Br YMCA 1972-76; mem Amer Pub Health Assn Awds Comm 1974-77; Med Soc of Eastern PA 1974-; PA Medical Care Found 1984-86. **HONORS/ACHIEVEMENTS:** Scholarship Howard Univ 1951-55, Phi Beta Kappa 1954; Natl Med 1956-59; Outstanding Young Man of the Yr 1968; Charles Drew Awd 1978. **MILITARY SERVICE:** USN capt 1960-62. **BUSINESS ADDRESS:** Dir Medical Services, Prudential Ins Co, 7700 Stenton Ave, Philadelphia, PA 19118.

HALL, DAVID
Ecucator. **PERSONAL:** Born May 26, 1950, Savannah, GA; son of Levi Hall and Ethel Glover Hall. **EDUCATION:** Kansas State Univ, BA (political sci) 1972; Univ of Oklahoma, MA (human relations) 1975, JD 1978; Harvard Law School, LLM, 1985, SJD, 1988. **CAREER:** Federal Trade Commission, staff attorney 1978-80; Univ of Mississippi Law School, asst prof of law 1980-83; Univ of Oklahoma Law School, assoc prof of law 1983-85; Northeastern Univ School of Law, assoc professor of law, 1985-88, assoc dean & professor, 1988-. **ORGANIZATIONS:** Member, Natl Conference of Black Lawyers 1978-80; member, Oklahoma Bar Assn 1978-; attorney, Fed Trade Commn, Chicago, IL, 1978-80; Amer Bar

Assn. **HONORS/ACHIEVEMENTS:** Outstanding Senior Award Oklahoma Bar Assn 1978; Professor of the Year Oxford Miss Branch of NAACP; Floyd Calvert Law Faculty Award Univ of Oklahoma Law School 1984; Order of the Coif Univ of Oklahoma Law School Chapter 1984; Robert D Klein, Northeastern Univ; Floyd Calvert Law Faculty, Univ of OK; professor of the year, NAACP, Oxford, MS; Outstanding KS State Student. **BUSINESS ADDRESS:** Assoc Dean of Academic & Student Affairs, NortheasternUniv Sch of Law, 400 Huntington Ave, Boston, MA 02115.

HALL, DAVID ANTHONY, JR.
Dentist. **PERSONAL:** Born Sep 19, 1945, San Francisco, CA; married Pamela. **EDUCATION:** So U, BS 1967; Meharry Med Sch, DDS 1972. **CAREER:** Dentist 1973-; Health Power Asso, dentist 1972-73. **ORGANIZATIONS:** Rhodes United Fidelity Funeral Home, dir tchr. **HONORS/ACHIEVEMENTS:** ADA, NDA pres Pelican State Dental Assn 1980; LDA 6th Dist Dental Assn; Capital & City Dental Assn Scottlandville Jaycees; Baton Rouge Alumni, Kappa Alpha Psi; Mt Zion 1st Bapt Ch; SoUniv Alumni Assn; life mem Meharry Med Coll Alumni Assn. **MILITARY SERVICE:** Whos Who in LA 1976; Outst Young Men of Am 1977. **BUSINESS ADDRESS:** 1704 Convention St, Baton Rouge, LA 70802.

HALL, DAVID MCKENZIE
Executive. **PERSONAL:** Born Jun 21, 1928, Gary, IN; son of Alfred M Hall and Grace E Hall; married Jacqueline V Branch, Apr 30, 1960; children: Glen D, Gary D. **EDUCATION:** Howard Univ, BA Business 1946-51; Univ North Carolina, MS Ed Soc 1962-66; North Carolina Agricultural and State Univ, Greensboro, NC, MS, 1962-66; MIT, Cambridge MA, Certificate, 1976. **CAREER:** Scott AFB IL USAF, deputy base cmndr 1974-75, base cmndr 1975-76; Air Force Logistics Cmd USAF, deputy cmptrlr 1976-77, cmptrlr 1977-83; Delco-Remy Div of Gen Motors, dir data prcsg 1983-84; Electr Data Systems Corp, acct manager 1985-88; Electronic Data Systems, Saginaw,MI, regional manager. **ORGANIZATIONS:** Pres Am Soc of Miltry Cmptrlrs 1981-83; vice pres Am Defense Preparedness Assc 1980-83; mem Air Force Assc 1960-; natl bd mem Boy Scouts Am 1983-; bd mem Anderson Boys Clb 1984-, Madison Cty NAACP 1984-; cmsnr Anderson Housing Authority 1984-; mem Steward Allen Chapel AME Church 1985-; life mem NAACP, Kappa Alpha Psi. **HONORS/ACHIEVEMENTS:** Key to city Gary, IN 1981; hon citizen of City Of E St Louis 1976; crtfd systms eng Assc for Systms Management 1984; crtfd cost anlyst Assc of Anlyst 1983; Computers in Combat, AF Comptroller Magazine 1967. **MILITARY SERVICE:** USAF brigadier gen; Dstngshd Serv Medal 1983; Legion of Merit 1974; Meritorious Serv Medal 1976, 71. **HOME ADDRESS:** 49 West Hannum Blvd, Saginaw, MI 48602-1938. **BUSINESS ADDRESS:** Regional Manager, Electronic Data Systems, 3900 Holland Road, Saginaw, MI 48605.

HALL, DELILAH RIDLEY
Educational administrator. **PERSONAL:** Born Aug 23, 1953, Baton Rouge, LA; married Holmes G Hall, Sr; children: Holmes, Byron, Marsha, Michael, Monica. **EDUCATION:** Jarvis Christian Coll, BS 1975; East Texas State Univ, MS 1977. **CAREER:** East Texas State Univ, coord 1975-77; Longview Independent School Dist, ind instructor 1978; Jarvis Christian Coll, upward bound prog counselor 1978, asst to the dean of academic affairs 1980, asst to the president 1981-. **ORGANIZATIONS:** Mem JCC/SCI Natl Alumni & Ex-Student Assoc 1975; sec Hawkins Elementary PTA 1985-87; mem Zeta Phi Beta Sorority, Inc. **HONORS/ACHIEVEMENTS:** Who's Who in Amer Colls & Univs 1974; Outstanding Young Women of Amer 1980; mem Alpha Kappa Mu. **HOME ADDRESS:** P O Box 37, Hawkins, TX 75765. **BUSINESS ADDRESS:** Educational Administrator, Jarvis Christian Coll, P O Drawer G, Hawkins, TX 75765.

HALL, DELORES
Actress. **PERSONAL:** Born Feb 26, Kansas City, KS; married Michael Goodstone. **EDUCATION:** Harbor Jr Coll, LACC. **CAREER:** Broadway Show, "Your Arm's Too Short To Box With God"; "Godspell", "Hair", major roles & night club performer; toured with Harry Belafonte, Tommy Smothers. **HONORS/ACHIEVEMENTS:** Recorded album RCA 1973-74; Antoinette Perry Awd, Best Supporting Actress in a Musical 1977; Toro Awd Young Woman of Am nominee Chs of NJ; music awds; White House performance 1977.

HALL, DOLORES BROWN
Educational administrator. **PERSONAL:** Born in Brooklyn, NY; married Rev Kirkwood M Hall; children: Alexander Chapman. **EDUCATION:** Brooklyn Hosp School of Nursing, RN Diploma 1962; Long Island Univ, BS 1966; Adelphi Univ, MS 1969; NY Univ, PhD 1977. **CAREER:** Medgar Evers Coll NIMH Rsch Proj, project dir 1975-77; Delaware State Coll, assoc prof 1977-79; Health & Human Serv NIMH St Elizabeth Hosp, dir nursing ed 1979-84; Edison State Coll, dir BSN Prog 1984-. **ORGANIZATIONS:** Workshop leader Delaware Home for the Aged 1976; bd of dir Good Shepard Home Health Aide Prog 1977-79; mem Mental Health Plan Task Force 1978-79; book reviewer Nursing Outlook Addison & Wesley 1980,82; mem USPHS Cont Ed Review Comm 1980-83; consult Charles Drew Neighborhood Health Ctr. **HONORS/ACHIEVEMENTS:** Traineeship Grant Natl Inst of Mental Health 1964-65; EPDA/Southern Fellowship NY Univ 1971-75; Sr Level Rating 14 Fed Govt 1979-84; Postdoctoral Fellowship Gerontological Soc of Amer 1985. **BUSINESS ADDRESS:** Dir of BSN Program, Thomas A Edison State College, 101 W State St CN 545, Trenton, NJ 08625.

HALL, EDWARD CLARENCE
Performer. **PERSONAL:** Born Jan 11, 1931, Roxbury, MA. **EDUCATION:** Howard U, BA 1949-53. **CAREER:** Philip Morris Playhouse on Bdwy Radio, actor 1951; Arena Stage Wash DC, actor 1952; "The Climate of Eden" Bdwy, actor 1952; "No Time for Sgts" Bdwy, actor 1957-58; actor "Joe Turner's Come and Gone" Bdwy 1988; actor "Driving Miss Daisy" Old Globe 1989. **ORGANIZATIONS:** Actor "A Raisin in the Sun" 1958-60, "Blues for Mr Charlie", Trinity Sq Rep Co 1965-, "Baby I'M Back" TV 1971-78; mem RI Black Heritage Soc 1984-85. **HONORS/ACHIEVEMENTS:** RI Comm Serv Awrd Found for Rep Theatre 1983; nominee New York Drama Desk Award 1988; nominee Helen Hayes Award 1988. **MILITARY SERVICE:** AUS sp-3. **BUSINESS ADDRESS:** Trinity Rep Co, 201 Washington St, Providence, RI 02903.

HALL, ELLIOTT S.
Executive, lawyer, lobbyist. **PERSONAL:** Married Shirley Ann Robinson Hall; children: Fred, Lannis, Tiffany. **EDUCATION:** Wayne State Univ, Detroit MI, BA, law degrees. **CAREER:** Govt of Wayne County MI, Detroit, MI, chief asst prosecutor; Dykema Gossett Spencer Goodnow & Trigg, Detroit MI, law partner; Ford Motor Company, Dearborn MI, lawyer, lobbyist, vice pres of govt affairs, 1987-. **HONORS/ACHIEVEMENTS:** Distinguished alumnus award, Wayne State Univ. **BUSINESS ADDRESS:** Ford Motor Company, American Rd, Dearborn, MI 48126. *

HALL, ETHEL HARRIS
Educator. **PERSONAL:** Born Feb 23, 1928, Decatur, AL; daughter of Mr and Mrs Harry Harris; married Alfred James Hall, Sr; children: Alfred Jr, Donna Hall Mitchell. **EDUCATION:** AL A&M Univ, BS 1948; Univ of Chicago, MA 1953; Univ AL, DSW 1979. **CAREER:** Jefferson City Bd of Ed, teacher 1955-66; Neighborhood Youth Corps, dir 1966-71; Univ Montevallo, assoc prof 1971-78; Univ AL, assc prof 1978-. **ORGANIZATIONS:** Pres AL Personnel & Guidance Assn 1972-73, AL Conf of Child Care 1977; AL Conf of Soc Work 1981-82; AL Assc Womens's Clubs 1984-88; mem Social Work Bd of Examiners; mem AL State Board of Educ 1987-91. **HONORS/ACHIEVEMENTS:** Leadership award AL Personnel & Guidance Assn 1974, 1976 , 1977; Alumus of the Yr AL A&M Univ 1975; Serv Award AL Conf of Social Work 1982; fellowship Intrntl Study Dept of State Jamaica, West Indies 1975. **BUSINESS ADDRESS:** Associate Professor, Univ of AL, PO Box 1935, PO Box 1935, University, AL 35486.

HALL, EVELYN ALICE (EVELYN MANNING)
Physician. **PERSONAL:** Born Oct 31, 1945, Paterson, NJ; married Dr Macy G Hall Jr. **EDUCATION:** Howard Univ, BS 1967; Howard Univ Clge of Med, MD 1973; Columbia Univ, MPH 1977. **CAREER:** Rockville Centre Group Hlth Assc, physician if chief 1977-; Columbia Univ, fellow pediatric ambulatory care 1975-77; Roosevelt Hosp, resd 1974-75. **ORGANIZATIONS:** Cand Amer Acad of Pediatrics; bd Elgible Amer Pediatric Bds; DC Med Soc 1977; Howard Univ Med Alumni; Alpha Omega Alpha Med 1973. **BUSINESS ADDRESS:** 6111 Executive Blvd, Rockville, MD.

HALL, FRED, III
Accountant, elected official. **PERSONAL:** Born Feb 09, 1945, St Louis, MO; married Pattie M Burdett; children: Fred IV, Rose M. **EDUCATION:** Sinclair Coll, AS Engrg Tech 1968; Univ of Dayton, BS Engrg Tech 1976. **CAREER:** Delco Pod Div GMC, lab tech 1968-73, sales coord 1973-78, sales engrg 1978-85, acct mgr 1985-. **ORGANIZATIONS:** Bd mem Camp Fire Girls 1975-77; city commiss City of Xenia 1977,81-; sec Xenia-Wilberforce Dem Club 1979-82; pres Wilberforce-Xenia Optimist Club 1981-82; chmn bd of zoning appeals City of Xenia 1982,83,85; vice pres Chi Lambda Chap Alpha Phi Alpha 1984-85; deputy mayor City of Xenia 1984-; plnng commiss, chmnCity of Xenia 1984. **HONORS/ACHIEVEMENTS:** Awd for Excellence in Community Activities General Motors Corp 1979. **HOME ADDRESS:** 3272 Wyoming Drive, Xenia, OH 45385. **BUSINESS ADDRESS:** Account Manager, Delco Products, 2000 Forrer Blvd, Dayton, OH 45424.

HALL, FREDERICK THEODORE
Dentist. **PERSONAL:** Born Sep 23, 1951, New York City, NY; married Gwendolyn Grace Smith; children: Carole G. **EDUCATION:** Lincoln Univ Chester Co PA 1946; Meharry Med Clge Nashville, DDS 1948; Univ of WI. **CAREER:** Carter Comm Health Ctr; So Ozone Park Med Bldg Jamaica NY, owner 1960-. **ORGANIZATIONS:** Treas Queens Clinical Soc LI 1977-; mem Lutheran Ch of Resurrection St Albans NY 1954; treas Scene Realty Co St Albans NY 1978; exec bd mem Jamaica Mental Health Clinic Jamaica NY 1979; mem Phi Beta Sigma Frat Inc Gamma Rho Sigma Chap Long Island NY; one of Fndrs Carter Comm Health Ctr Jamaica NY 1970-. **MILITARY SERVICE:** AUS capt 1954-56. **BUSINESS ADDRESS:** Sutphin Blvd, Jamaica, NY 11432.

HALL, HANSEL CRIMIEL
Company executive. **PERSONAL:** Born Mar 12, 1929, Gary, IN; son of Alfred M Hall (deceased) and Grace Eliz Crimiel Hall; divorced; children: Grace Jean. **EDUCATION:** IN Univ, BS 1953; Industrial Coll of the Armed Forces, Certificate Natl Security Mgmt 1971; Blackstone School of Law, BLaws 1982. **CAREER:** US Dept of Housing & Urban Devel, program specialist 1969-73, dir FH&EO div MN 1973-75, dir FH&EO div IN 1975-79; US Dept of Interior, dir office of human resources 1979-88. **ORGANIZATIONS:** Pres Crimiel Ltd (consulting) 1979-; pres MN-Dakota Conf NAACP 1981-86; pres bd of dirs Riverview Towers Homeowners Assoc 1985-87; life mem Indiana Univ Alumni Assoc, Omega Psi Phi Fraternity Inc; golden heritage mem NAACP; life mem VFW; bd of dirs Cedar Riverside Project Area Committee 1989-. **HONORS/ACHIEVEMENTS:** Area Governor Toastmasters Intl 1982-83; Distinguished Toastmaster Award Toastmasters Intl 1986; Outstanding Leadership Award NAACP Region IV 1986. **MILITARY SERVICE:** USAF Reserve lt col 25 yrs; United Nations Serv Medal, Korean Serv, Reserve Officers Assn, Air Force Overseas. **BUSINESS ADDRESS:** President, Crimiel Communications Inc, PO Box 65650, St Paul, MN 55165.

HALL, HAROLD EUGENE
Physician. **PERSONAL:** Born Dec 05, 1922, Pittsburgh, PA; children: Harold II, Lynn. **EDUCATION:** Prairie View AM, BS 1947; Howard Univ, MS 1950, MD 1959; Univ WA, rsrch flw 1963-65. **CAREER:** USPHS Hosp, chf dept pathology 1968-77; Sch Med Howard Univ, instr res chem 1951-55; NIH, res chem 1950-51; Chester TX HS, instr 1947-48; Kirkland Land Assc Inc, general partner 1971-; Educ Commn States, consult 1977; Clge Amer Pathologist, flw 1969. **ORGANIZATIONS:** Mem AMA Bd Gov Evergreen State Clge Fnd 1977-; WA State Bd Educ 1982; bd dir Nueva Learning Ctr 1977-; mem Rotary Intl 1964-; NAACP Rsrch flwNatl Polio Fnd 1956; Citz Day Award 1968; flw Clge Amer Pathologists 1970; mem Natl Task Force Alcohol Abuse 1973-77. **HONORS/ACHIEVEMENTS:** Distg Srv Award Educ Commn States 1977; num publ USPHS Med Dir. **BUSINESS ADDRESS:** 6505 108th NE, Kirkland, WA 98033.

HALL, HAROLD L.
Chief executive. **CAREER:** Delta Enterprises, Inc, Greenville MS, chief executive. **BUSINESS ADDRESS:** Delta Enterprises Inc, 819 Main St, Greenville, MS 38701. *

HALL, HORATHEL
Educator/artist. **PERSONAL:** Born Dec 03, 1926, Houston, TX; married Howard D; chil-

dren: Kenneth A, Admerle J, Horace D. **EDUCATION:** Prairie View A&M U, BA 1948; NM Highlands Las Vegas, MFA 1962; W African States Art Research, fellowship HISD 1975. **CAREER:** Houston Independent Sch Dist, art tchr/Artist 1980-; Worthing High Sch, art tchr & dept chmn 1951-80; TX So U, art prof 1964-79; Adept New Am Folk Gallery, crafts consult 1977-79; Eliza Johnson Home for the Elderly, crafts consult 1977-79; Houston Comm Coll, art prof 1975-77. **ORGANIZATIONS:** Affiliated mem Nat Art Educators Assn 1951-80; treas Houston Art Educators Assn 1976-80; affiliated mem Nat Conf of Artists 1976-80; vP Contemporary Handweavers of Houston 1968-69; sec E Sunny Side Civic Club of Houston 1970-80; sec Orgn of Black Artist 1975-80; spl publ Black Artist of the New Generation 1977; The Arts & the Rural & Isolated ElderlyUniv of KY 1980. **HONORS/ACHIEVEMENTS:** Pub "Contemporary Concepts of the Liberian Rice Bag Weave" vol 27 no 2 Contemporary Handweavers of TX Inc 1975; Arrowmont Scholarship Pi Beta Alumnae ClubGatlingburg TN 1980. **BUSINESS ADDRESS:** Houston Independent Sch Dist W, 9215 Scott St, Houston, TX 77051.

HALL, HOWARD RALPH
Dentist. **PERSONAL:** Born May 01, 1919, Cincinnati; married Dorothy; children: Lillian, Howard, VIII, Juanita. **EDUCATION:** Wilberforce U, BS 1943; Meharry Med Coll, DDS 1947. **CAREER:** Dover DE, intern 1948-49; Cincinnati Bd Health, 1953-63; pvt practic 1953-; Model Cities Dental Prog KY, proj dir 1970-74. **ORGANIZATIONS:** Mem Nat Am & KY Denatl Assns; bd mem Cincinnati ARC 1973-; mem Kappa Alpha Psi Frat; asst dir pub Nat Dental Assn 1970-. **HONORS/ACHIEVEMENTS:** Outstanding Grad Meharry Coll 1972; Bronze Star Medal 1952. **MILITARY SERVICE:** AUS capt 1949-53. **BUSINESS ADDRESS:** 502 Copplin Bldg, Covington, KY 41011.

HALL, IRA DEVOYD
Business executive. **PERSONAL:** Born Aug 25, 1905, Colbert, OK; married Rubye Maie Hibler; children: Iris Marie Bruce, Carole Anitrice Hardeman, Janice LaMarne, Ira DeVoyd Jr, John Anthony, Jessilyn Anne White. **EDUCATION:** Langston U, BBA 1932;Univ of OK, MS in Sch Admin 1951. **CAREER:** Shoemake Consolidated Schools, Colbert OK, principal 1933-37; Clearview Public Schools, supt 1937-39; Kingfisher's Douglas School, principal 1939-41; Hall Fidelity, real estate/insurance broker 1946-71; OK State Dept Educ, asst dir secondary educ 1947-56; OK City 1st Integrated Schools Creston Hills, principal 1956-60; Inman Page School, principal 1960-71; Pre-Marital & Family Life Agencies, owner. **ORGANIZATIONS:** Pres Nat LangstonUniv Alumni 1980-82; pres Southern OK Tchrs Assn; pres LangstonUniv Coalition 1979-; pres OKC Boys Club of Am; pres OKC Alpha Phi Alpha; 50 yr honoree/charter mem LU Campus Chap; OK PTA of Colored Parents 1938-42; chmn NAREB; Nat Project Pride; dir Tabernacle Ch Educ Activities;former dir OK TX Area United Negro Coll Fund Drive; mem YMCA; mem NAACP; founder Local Urban League. **HONORS/ACHIEVEMENTS:** Disting Alumni Langston U; Alpha Man of the Yr; named Gov Hon Col; Hon OKC Mayor; articles, "How & Why Children Learn", "The Upper Third Teacher" ; established LangstonUniv Alumni Hall of Fame. **HOME ADDRESS:** 733 NE 20th St, Oklahoma City, OK 73105. **BUSINESS ADDRESS:** Owner Consulting Agencies, Pre-Marital & Family Life, 1523 N Lottie St, Oklahoma City, OK 73117.

HALL, JESSE J.
Educator. **PERSONAL:** Born Dec 16, 1938, Clover, SC; married Nancy Thorne; children: Nathaniel Craig, Yoland Yevette. **EDUCATION:** State Tchrs Clg Fayetteville NC, BS 1962;Univ of NV, MEd Sc Admn 1970;Univ of San Francisco, Doctoral 1984. **CAREER:** Washoe Co School Dist, Orvis Ring and Sierra Vista Schools, prin 1971-72, Glen Duncan School, prin 1972-80, Lloyd Diedrichsen School, prin 1981-84. **ORGANIZATIONS:** Mem Intrntl Reading Assc 1962; Natl Assc of Elem Sc Prins 1971; NV Assc of Sc Admn 1972; Phi Delta Kappa 1968; Eql Opprtnty Bd UNR 1980; NV StateTextbk Cmsn 1969-79; bd of dir panel chrmn United Way NV 1972-78. **HONORS/ACHIEVEMENTS:** Dist serv awrd Negro Bus & Profsnl Women's Assc 1980; man of the yr Second Bapt Ch Reno 1978; distgshd serv awrd NAACP 1978. **BUSINESS ADDRESS:** Principal, Lloyd Diedrichsen Sch, 1735 Del Rosa Way, Sparks, NV 89431.

HALL, JOHN ROBERT
House painter, community activist. **PERSONAL:** Born Jun 29, 1920, Mitford, SC; married Ruth. **CAREER:** House Painter self-employed. **ORGANIZATIONS:** Mem Deacon Bd, church treas, Sunday school supt Pine Grove Bapt Church; co-organizer Great Falls Br NAACP; organizer Young Men's Council for Political Action; pres Home & Comm Improvement Club; pres Great Falls Br NAACP; organizer Chester Co Voters Assn; pres 1st Vice Pres Chester Co Dem Party; past pres Fairfield Bapt Sunday School Conv of Fairfield Co 1958-62; former mem Chester Co Adv Council on Adult Educ; former mem Carolina Comm Action Bd 1968-70; Gov West's Adv Commn on Human Relations in SC 1970-72; Great Fall Inc Commn; mem Voters Educ Project of SC 5th Congressional Dist; instrumental in getting relief for black citizens treated unjustly in retirement system procedures, helped get black deputy sheriff's policeman jobs for both black & white.

HALL, JOSEPH A.
Consultant & educator. **PERSONAL:** Born May 30, 1908, Chester, WV; son of Isaac Hall and Lottie Hall; married Marguerite L Clemmons; children: JoAnn, Joseph Andrew. **EDUCATION:** Wilberforce Univ, BS, 1931; Western Reserve, MSW, 1944. **CAREER:** Family Serv Bureau, caseworker, 1933-35; Dept of Public Welfare, caseworker 1935-1940; Juvenile Court Cleveland, OH, probation officer, 1942-45; Cleveland Urban League, industrial rel dir, 1945-46; Urban League of Greater Cincinnati, exec dir, 1946-73; School of Soc Work Univ of Cincinnati, assoc prof, 1979-. **ORGANIZATIONS:** Natl Conf of Soc Welfare, 1935-73; pres, Ohio Welfare Conf, 1956; mem Natl Assn of Soc Workers 1949-; pres, Ohio Advisory Council for Voc Educ, 1972; mem Ohio Housing Bd, 1961-72; chmn, Models City, 1973-74, Ohio State Advisory Comm, 1964-70; vice chmn, Childrens Home 1975- . **HONORS/ACHIEVEMENTS:** Man of the Year Cinncinnati Prsnl Assc, Cincinnati, OH, 1965; distinguished serv, United Black Comm Orgs, 1969; Man of the Year, Ohio Voc Assn, 1973; Honorary Degree, FFA Ohio Chapter, 1971. **HOME ADDRESS:** 3543 Amberacres Dr 409 W, 2101 Grandin #404 -, Cincinnati, OH 45237.

HALL, KATIE
Educator, city government official. **PERSONAL:** Born Apr 03, 1938, Mount Bayou, MS; daughter of Jeff L Green and Bessie Mae Hooper Green; married John H Hall, Aug 15, 1957; children: Jacqueline, Junifer, Michelle. **EDUCATION:** MS Valley State Univ, BS, 1960; IN Univ, MS, 1967. **CAREER:** City of Gary Schs, tchr 1960-; IN 5th Dist, state rep 1974-76; IN 3rd Dist, state senator, 1976-82; US Congress, Congresswoman, IN 1st Dist, 1982-84; City of Gary, IN, city clerk, 1985—. **ORGANIZATIONS:** Pres Gary Cncl for Soc Studs 1972-74; vice chpsn Gary Housing Bd of Commr 1975; House Comm on Afrs of Lake & Marion Cos 1975-76; chpsn Senate Educ Comm 1977; life mem NAACP; Amer Assn of Univ Women; pres, Gary IN branch, Natl Council of Negro Women; Natl Black Political Caucus; Natl Organization for Women; IN State Tchrs Assn; NEA; Amer Fed of Tchrs; US Congressional Black Caucus; US Congressional Caucus on Women's Issues; Alpha Kappa Alpha Natl Sor; exec bd and secretary-treas, Congressional Steel Caucus; chair House sub-comm on census and the US population. **HONORS/ACHIEVEMENTS:** Outstanding Lgsltr Awd NAACP 1975; Outstanding Woman in Politics City of Gary 1975; Outstanding Serv to Comm Gary Com on Status of Women 1976; OutstandingWomen in Politics IN Blk Polit Assn 1975; only Black from IN to serve in US Congress; wrote and served as chief sponsor of the Martin Luther King Jr Natl Holiday Law in 1983; wrote and served as chief sponsor of King Holiday Comm Law in 1984; rec more than 200 awds for serv to religion, educ, politics, civic & comm groups; Gary Branch NAACP's Mary White Irvington Awd 1984. **BUSINESS ADDRESS:** Gary City Clerk, 401 Broadway, Gary, IN 46407.

HALL, KENNETH
Legislator. **PERSONAL:** Born May 20, 1915, E St Louis; married Anne; children: Kenneth, Jr, Maurice, Mark, Thomas. **EDUCATION:** Park Coll. **CAREER:** IL State, senator asst major ldr 57th Dist; aptd to State Rent Cntrl Bd Gov Adlai Stevenson 1949; St Clair Co Housing Auth E St Louis Park Dist, commnr 1959; St Clair Co Sheriffs & Dept, former investigator; Licensed ins broker; state House of Rep 2 terms, election to Senate 1970. **ORGANIZATIONS:** Mem St Clair Co Welfare Serv Com; chmn E St Louis City Dem Cntrl Com; mem NAACP; Knights of Columbus. **BUSINESS ADDRESS:** Illinois General Assembly, 121 A State House, Springfield, IL 62706.

HALL, KIM FELICIA
Educator. **PERSONAL:** Born Dec 25, 1961, Baltimore, MD. **EDUCATION:** Hood Coll, BA (Magna Cum Laude) 1983. **CAREER:** Democratic Natl Convention, communications coord 1984; Univ of PA, graduate fellow 1985-86; Committee to re-elect Clarence Blount, campaign coord 1986; Swarthmore Coll, visiting instructor; Friends of Vera P Hall, public relations dir 1986-87. **ORGANIZATIONS:** Vice pres Grad English Assoc Univ of PA 1985-86; mem Renaissance Soc of Amer; sec Grad English Assoc 1984-85. **HONORS/ACHIEVEMENTS:** Mem Phi Kappa Phi 1983; Hood Scholar 1983; Mellon Fellowship in the Humanities Woodrow Wilson Natl Fellowship Foundation; Outstanding Young Woman of Amer 1986; Folger Inst Fellowship Washington DC 1986; Governor's Citation Gov Harry Hughes MD 1986. **BUSINESS ADDRESS:** Visiting Instructor-English, University of Pennsylvania, English Dept, Philadelphia, PA 19104.

HALL, KIRKWOOD MARSHAL
Health official. **PERSONAL:** Born May 13, 1944, Montclair, NJ; son of Marshal Eugene Hall and Alice Chapman Hall; married Dolores Brown; children: Malaika Estelle, Dalili Talika, Alexander Chapman. **EDUCATION:** VA Union Univ, BA Sociology 1967; Pittsburgh Theological Sem, MDiv 1974; Univ of Pittsburgh School of Public Health, MPH 1978. **CAREER:** Hill Mental Health Team, mental health clinician 1970-74; Western Psych Inst & Clinic, dir 1974-75; NJ Dept of Public Advocate Div of Mental Health, suprv field rep 1975-77; Project SAIL, dir 1977-79; Henry J Austin Health Ctr, clinic suprv mental health. **ORGANIZATIONS:** Asst dir Black Campus Ministries Inc 1971-; chmn Nieghborhood Comm on Health Care 1974; elder Unification Assoc of Christian Sabbath 1976-80; mental health clinician Univ of Med & Dentistry Newark, NJ 1980-82; assoc pastor Union Bapt Church Trenton, NJ 1981-; vice pres Samuel DeWitt Proctor Greater NJ Alumni Chap VA Union Univ 1983-84; assoc pastor, St Paul AME Zion, Trenton NJ 1987-. **HONORS/ACHIEVEMENTS:** Service Awd Neighborhood Adv Bd Mercy Hosp Pittsburgh 1971-75; Cited in Black Amer Writers Past & Present Ed Rush 1975; Publ "Chapman New Black Voices" Davis Spectrum in Black, "Haynes Voices of the Revolution" Jones & Neal Black Fire, "Porter Connections" Univ of Pittsburgh Jrnl of Black Poetry Periodical; Presenter 62nd Annual Meeting Amer Orthopsychiatric Assn "Suggestions for the Utilization of the Job Training Partnership Act" NY City April 22, 1985. **BUSINESS ADDRESS:** Clinic Supervisor Mental Hlth, Henry J Austin Health Center, 321 N Warren St, Trenton, NJ 08618.

HALL, LAWRENCE H.
Journalist. **PERSONAL:** Born Jan 28, 1944, Elizabeth, NJ; married Linda. **EDUCATION:** Rutgers U, 1966. **CAREER:** Star-Ledger Newspaper, journalist 1969-; Irving L Straus Assoc NY, financial public relations 1968-69; WOR Radio NY, public relations dir 1967-68; NY Daily News, reporter 1965-67; WJRZ Radio Newark NJ, commentator 1962-65; WNJR Radio Newark, 1972-73. **BUSINESS ADDRESS:** Star Ledger Plaza, Newark, NJ.

HALL, LLOYD DALTON, JR.
Clergyman. **PERSONAL:** Born Sep 11, 1935, Dallas; married Virginia A; children: Clyde, Lloyd, Keith, Kammille. **EDUCATION:** Bishop Coll, BA 1959; Howard U, MDiv 1962; TX Christian U, PhD 1968; CA Grade Sch of Theol. **CAREER:** Mt Calvary Bapt Ch Tuscon, minister 1969-77; Tabernacle Bapt Ch Wichita KS, minister 1977; Beth-eden Bapt Ch Dallas, founder 1965-69; Bishop Coll, asst dean of men, dir student work, asst prof of religion & christian educ 1962-68. **ORGANIZATIONS:** Mem Assn ofUniv Prof; Bapt Ministers Alliance; Interdenom Ministers Alliance; Interdemon Ministers Alliance of Wichita; Interseminary Movement; Alpha Phi Alpha; Am Academy of Religion; vP Bapt Fellwoship of Wichita; Inter-city Parish; Clergymens Cancer Conf; past pres Tucson Assn Child Care 1973-74; first v chmn Day Care Task Force appt by Mayor Co Commr & Counc; treas Tucson Urban League; mem Tucson Ecumenical Council; United Way; Commr Civil Rights & Equal Employment Oppor Commn; dir Christian Educ for State of KS; instr Christian Educ Nat Bapt Conv USA; treas Paradise Bapt State Conv. **HONORS/ACHIEVEMENTS:** Rockefeller Theol Award 1962; Pastoral Award HowardUniv 1962; Whos Who Among Negro Clergymen in Am 1965; Greater Educators of TX 1967. **BUSINESS ADDRESS:** Wichita, KS.

HALL, LLOYD EUGENE
College administrator. **PERSONAL:** Born Jul 22, 1953, Indianapolis, IN; married Susan D Dale; children: Nathan Tucker. **EDUCATION:** Indiana Univ, BA 1975. **CAREER:** Clairon State Univ, asst to dean of students 1977-81; Colby Coll, asst dean of admissions 1981-84; Lawrence Univ, assoc dir of admissions 1984-. **ORGANIZATIONS:** Mem Natl Assoc of Coll Admissions Counselors 1981-; mem IL Assoc of Coll Admissions Coun 1984-; bd dir

A Better Chance 1984-; bd dir Fox Valley Fair Housing Council 1986-; planning task force for recruitment Relations of Black Minority Students Profls Assoc Colls of the Midwest 1986-. **BUSINESS ADDRESS:** Assoc Dir of Admissions, Lawrence University, Admissions Office, Appleton, WI 54912.

HALL, MILDRED MARTHA
Physician. **PERSONAL:** Born Jan 24, 1949, Nassau, Bahamas;children: Nikechia. **EDUCATION:** Howard Univ, BS 1973, Coll of Medicine MD 1977. **CAREER:** Howard Univ Hosp, intern 1977-78, resident 1978-82; Cheverly Drug Treatment Ctr, med dir 1982-; Progressive Health Assoc, team coord 1983-; DC General Hosp, clinical instructor 1984; Private Medical Practice, physician/owner 1982-. **ORGANIZATIONS:** Mem Medical Soc of Dist of Columbia 1982; physician mem Prince Georges Volunteer Health Clinic 1982-; mem Prince George's Assoc of Health Profls 1984; diplomate Amer Bd of Ob/Gyn 1984; fellow Amer Coll of Ob/Gyn 1986. **HONORS/ACHIEVEMENTS:** Mem Alpha Omega Alpha Medical Honor Soc 1977; Citizen Awd Dist of Columbia Boxing Commn 1983. **HOME ADDRESS:** 9348 Cherry Hill Rd, Apt 222, College Park, MD 20740. **BUSINESS ADDRESS:** 601 60th Place, Fairmount Heights, MD 20743.

HALL, PERRY ALONZO
Educational administrator. **PERSONAL:** Born Sep 15, 1947, Detroit, MI. **EDUCATION:** Univ of MI, BA Psychology 1969; Harvard Univ, EdD Educ & Soc Policy 1977. **CAREER:** Northeastern Univ, inst 1974; Wayne State Univ, ext prog coord 1974-76, asst prof 1977-80, dir 1980-. **ORGANIZATIONS:** Exec bd mem Natl Council for Black Studies 1978; consultant Chicago Ctr for Afro-Amer Stud & Rsch 1982; consultant State of MI Office of Substance Abuse Serv 1982; Substance Abuse Comm New Detroit Inc 1974-; adv bd mem Equal Oppor Center 1983-. **HONORS/ACHIEVEMENTS:** Doctoral Fellowship Ford Found 1971; listing Outstanding Young Men of America 1980. **BUSINESS ADDRESS:** Dir Center for Black Studies, Wayne State University, Center for Black Studies, 5980 Cass Ave, Detroit, MI 48202.

HALL, RAYMOND A.
Administrator. **PERSONAL:** Born Apr 17, 1914, Washington, DC; married Correne A McDonald; children: Jean M Freeman, Kendall L. **EDUCATION:** Natl Radio Inst Washington DC, grad 1952. **CAREER:** Dept of Army Bd of Engrs for Rivers & Harbors, retired clk 1940-72; AAF Sch Pueblo CO, airplane mechanic; Rivers & Harbors Dept of Defense, vice pres empls assn bd of engrs for rivers & harbors 1971; City of N Brentwood MD, mayor. **ORGANIZATIONS:** Trustee St Paul CC Ch 1945-; exec bd NCBM vice pres MD Chap 1977-80; pres N Brentwood Citizens Assn 1968; chmn human relations commn exec bd Northwestern HS PG Co 1972; com mem Transp Study PG Co. **HONORS/ACHIEVEMENTS:** Meritorious Serv Awd Recreat Dept Prince George Co; Outstanding Pub Ofcl MD Intl Rotary Club; cited for 32 yrs serv bd of engrs for rivers & harbors Dept of Def; Golden Anniv Cert of Appreciation MD Natl Park & Planning Commn 1978. **MILITARY SERVICE:** AAF pfc 1944-46; Good Conduct Medal; Amer Theater Ribbon; Victory Ribbon. **BUSINESS ADDRESS:** Mayor, N Brentwood MD, 4507 & Church St N, Brentwood, MD 20722.

HALL, REGINALD LAWRENCE
Physician. **PERSONAL:** Born Jun 19, 1957, Whiteville, NC. **EDUCATION:** Baltimore Polytech Inst, 1975; St Vincent Coll, summa cum laude BS chem 1979; Duke Univ School of Med, 1983; Duke Univ Med Ctr, 1st yr resd 1983-84, jr asst resd 1984-85, resd orthopedic surg 1985-87. **CAREER:** St Vincent Coll, chem lab asst; Mayor's Coord Council on Criminal Justice Baltimore, work/study alumni devel office intern; Rsch & Plng Dept of Mass Transit Admin Baltimore, intern; Rsch & Plng Dept of Mass Transit Admin, mayor's coord council on criminal justice; St Vincent Coll, chem lab asst, work/study alumni devel office; Duke Med Ctr, phlebotomist, rsch fellow div of ped cardiology, orthopedic surg resd; Cornell Med Coll, summer fellowship; Duke Med Ctr Clinical Chem Lab, orthopedic surg resd. **ORGANIZATIONS:** Mem Black Student Union, Freshman Orientation Comm, Dean's Coll Subcomm, Resd Adv Council, Alumni Telethon, Duke Univ Med School Admiss Comm, DavisonCouncil Student Govt, Student Natl Med Assoc, Amer Med Student Assoc, Dean's Minority Affairs Subcomm; adv Duke Univ Undergrad Premed Soc. **HONORS/ACHIEVEMENTS:** Listed in Who's Who in Amer Coll & Univ; CV Mosby Book Awd; Dean's List. **HOME ADDRESS:** 4129 Forest Park Ave, Baltimore, MD 21207.

HALL, ROBERT JOHNSON
Educational administrator. **PERSONAL:** Born Jun 05, 1937, Crumrod, AR; married Jerlean. **EDUCATION:** N Coll Pine Bluff AR, BS & AM 1963; UCA Conway AR, MA 1972; UA Fayetteville AR, adminstrv spec 1977. **CAREER:** Wabbaseka School Dist, supt 1975-; UAPB, assoc dean students 1972-75; AM & N Coll, asst dean of men 1967-72; JS Walker High School, teacher 1967-68; Tucker Rosenwald High School, prin 1966-67, teacher 1963-66. **ORGANIZATIONS:** Phi Delta Kappa Educ Frat; NEA AR Adminstr Assn; Phi Beta Sigma Frat; Royal Knight Soc Deacon Pine Hill Bapt Ch 1969; pres Gamma Psi Sigma Chap Phi Beta Sigma Frat 1974; bd mem OIC 1976. **HONORS/ACHIEVEMENTS:** Outstndg Young Man of Am 1976. **BUSINESS ADDRESS:** PO #210, Wabbaseka, AR 72175.

HALL, ROBERT JOSEPH
Physician. **PERSONAL:** Born Dec 21, 1929, Natchitoches, LA; married Ida; children: Wayne, Robi, Krystal. **EDUCATION:** So Univ A&M, BS 1950; Howard Univ Sch of Med, MD 1960. **CAREER:** Freemans Hosp, intern 1960-61; Freedmans & DC Gen Hosp, resd internal medicine 1961-64; Physician self. **ORGANIZATIONS:** Mem Baton Rouge Alcohol & Drug Abuse Ctr; staff mem Margaret Dumas Mental Health Clinic; mem Phi Beta Sigma Frat, Amer Legion, Mason, Mt Zion First Baptist Church. **MILITARY SERVICE:** AUS commun sgt 1951-53. **BUSINESS ADDRESS:** 8818 Scotland Ave, Ste B, Baton Rouge, LA 70807.

HALL, ROBERT L.
City administrator. **PERSONAL:** Born Apr 01, 1937, Stuart, FL; married Rose Ann. **CAREER:** City of Stuart, supt of parks & cemetery; City of Stuart, mayor. **ORGANIZATIONS:** Past pres Martin Co Dem Mens Club; past potentate FL St Nursing Home Investigator; chmn Ombudsment Com for nursing home; mem Stuart Volunteer Fire Dept; 32 degree Mason; Shriner; So Assn of Cemeteries; Park Personnel Assn; Mason. **HONORS/ACHIEVEMENTS:** Many awards from Civic & Church Organizations; award for Serving as Commnr & Mayor City of Stuart; award for Voters Registration Participation Supr of Election. **BUSINESS ADDRESS:** Supt of Streets Department, City of Stuart, 121 SW Frazer Ave, Stuart, FL 33494.

HALL, RUBYE MAIE
Educator. **PERSONAL:** Born Feb 27, 1912, Eufaula, OK; married Ira DeVoyd; children: Iris Marie Bruce, Carole Anitrice Hardeman, Janice LaMarne, Ira DeVoyd Jr, John Anthony, Jassilyn Anne White. **EDUCATION:** Langston U, BA in Engl 1932;Univ of S CA, Spcl Stud Drama 1943;Univ of OK, MA in Engl/Speech 1959; OU Hlth Sci Ctr, Sp Pathology/Neurology Spec St. **CAREER:** OK Pubic Schools, teacher, English, Math, Music 1932-41, speech pathologist 1949-64, psychometrist, diagnostician 1964-70, consultant 1970-75; Developmental Communication Assoc, owner. **ORGANIZATIONS:** Consult Speech Pathology VariousUniv By Inovation; founder bd of dir Central OK Learning Disabil; founder bd of dir OK Speech/Hearing Assn; mem OK Regents for Higher Educ 1974-80, chmn 1978-79; pres OK Fed of Colored Womens Clubs 1978-83; chmn exec cncl Nat Assn Colored Womens Clubs 1982-; natl pr chmn LangstonUniv Alumni Assn 1980-; founder/coord NEOSA Com OK Symphony Orchestra 1982-. **HONORS/ACHIEVEMENTS:** Regent of the Yr Award OK Higher Educ Alum Organ 1980; 1st Annual Pub Serv Award OK Affirmative Action Assn 1980; Equal Oppor Award OKC Urban League1982; OK Afro-Am Hall of Fame NTU Art Assn 1983; Alumni Hall of Fame LangstonUniv 1983; Bd of Dir Award OK Symphony Orchestra 1984. **HOME ADDRESS:** 733 NE 20th, Oklahoma City, OK 73105. **BUSINESS ADDRESS:** Develpmntl Communctn Assoc, 1523 N Lottie, Oklahoma City, OK 73117.

HALL, SHIRLEY ROBINSON
Administrator. **PERSONAL:** Born Jun 11, 1942, Detroit, MI; married Elliott Sawyer Hall; children: Tiffany. **EDUCATION:** Wayne State Univ, BA 1974. **CAREER:** Vice Pres Hubert H Humphrey, exec sec 1967-69; US Rep James H Scheuer, cong aide 1969-70; MI Democratic State Central Comm, field rep 1970-72; Model Neighborhood Devel Corp, program spec 1972-73; MI Consult Gas Co, mgr 1975-79; US Bureau of the Census, dep dir 1979-80; Detroit Symphony Orchestra; dir spec grants 1983-; public relations consult 1986-. **ORGANIZATIONS:** Mem exec bd Detroit NAACP 1972-86; mem Democratic natl Comm 1972; mem Jack & Jil of Amer 1982-, Exec bd Metro Detroit YWCA 1983-84; commiss MI Sesquicentennial Commiss 1985-; mem Links Inc Detroit Chap 1986-, Convention Site Comm 1986-87, Dem Natl Comm 1988.

HALL, WILLIE GREEN, JR.
Dentist. **PERSONAL:** Born May 23, 1947, Prattville, AL; son of Rev. Willie G. Hall, Sr. and Kattie R. Hall; married Cheryl F Wesley, Jan 30, 1971; children: Darius, Dashia. **EDUCATION:** Howard Univ, BS 1971, DDS 1978. **CAREER:** People's Drug Store, pharmacist/asst mgr 1969-72; Standard Drugs, pharmacist 1972-74; Syracuse Comm Hlth Ctr, dentist 1979-80; Southeast Dental Assoc, partner/pres 1984-; East of the River Health Assoc, dental dir 1980-1988. **ORGANIZATIONS:** Mem Natl & Amer Dental Assocs 1986-87, Natl Pharm Assoc 1986-87, Omega Psi Phi Frat 1986-87, Robert T Freeman Dental Soc 1986-87; Howard Univ Pharmacy & Dental Alumni Assocs; D.C. Dental Society 1988-1989; Intl Assn for Orthodontics 1988-1989. **HONORS/ACHIEVEMENTS:** Outstanding Young Men of Amer 1982; DC Dept Recreation Special Act Volunteer Awd 1984; Capital Head Start Comm Awd 1984; Washington Seniors Wellness Ctr Awd for Volunteer Serv 5/86 and 9/86. **HOME ADDRESS:** 4905 LaSalle Rd, Hyattsville, MD 20782.

HALL, YVONNE BONNIE
Director. **PERSONAL:** Born in New York, NY; children: Gilda, Glenn. **EDUCATION:** Adelphi U, BS 1974; Hunter Sch of Soc Work, MSW 1982. **CAREER:** Coll for Human Svcs, actg reg 1967-73, asst dir 1974-77, dir of agency devel 1977-83; Sadie Amer Lyfe Center, social work coord 1985-. **ORGANIZATIONS:** Asst publicity dir Bedford Stuyvesant Youth in Action 1965-67; vlntr Adoption Worker Assn of Black Social Workers 1979-; adoption spec Lutheran Comm Svcs. **HONORS/ACHIEVEMENTS:** Alvin I Brown Fellowship Aspen Inst 1975; Woman in Hist S I Boro Pres 1982. **HOME ADDRESS:** 9 Davis Ct, Staten Island, NY 10310.

HALL-KEITH, JAQUELINE YVONNE
Judge. **PERSONAL:** Born Jan 08, 1953, Detroit, MI; daughter of William H Hall and Evelyn V Callaway Hall; married Luther A Keith, Sep 17, 1988. **EDUCATION:** General Motors Inst, B Indus Admin 1971-76; Detroit Coll of Law, JSD 1976-80. **CAREER:** Gen Motors Corp, coll co-op 1971-76; Ford Motor Co, mgmt trainee 1976-78, personnel analyst 1978-80, staff atty 1980-84; State of MI Dept of Labor, Admin Law Judge. **ORGANIZATIONS:** Mem Amer, MI, Wolverine Bar Assoc; mem GMI & DCL Alumni Assoc, Assoc of Black Judges of MI, MI Assoc of Admin Law Judges, NAACP, Museum of African Amer Hist, Founders Soc; advisor UOD Natl Black Alumni Assoc; Delsprites, sponsor Delta Sigma Theta Sorority Inc 1984-. **HONORS/ACHIEVEMENTS:** Speaking of People Ebony Mag 1984. **BUSINESS ADDRESS:** Administration Law Judge, State of MI, Dept of Labor, Bureau of Workers' Dis Comp, 1200 Sixth St, Detroit, MI 48226.

HALLIBURTON, WARREN J.
Professor, writer, editor. **PERSONAL:** Born Aug 02, 1924, New York, NY; son of Richard H Halliburton and Blanche Watson Halliburton; married Marion Jones, Dec 20, 1947; children: Cheryl, Stephanie, Warren, Jr, Jena; married Francis Fletcher, Feb 11, 1971. **EDUCATION:** New York Univ, BS, 1949; Columbia Univ, MEd, 1975, DEd, 1977. **CAREER:** Prairie View Agricultural and Mechanical College (now Univ), Prairie View TX, English instructor, 1949; Bishop College, Dallas TX, English instructor, 1951, assoc, Inst of Intl Education, 1952; Recorder, New York NY, reporter and columnist, 1953; Brooklyn NY, teacher and dean at high school, 1959-60; coordinator for New York City Board of Education and assoc of New York State Dept of Education, 1960-65; McGraw Hill, Inc., New York NY, editor, 1967; Hamilton-Kirkland Colleges, Clinton NY, visiting prof of English, 1971-72; Columbia Univ, Teachers College, New York NY, editor, research assoc and dir of scholarly journal, govt program, and Ethnic Studies Center, 1972-77; Reader's Digest, New York NY, editor and writer; free-lance edi tor and writer. **HONORS/ACHIEVEMENTS:** Author of Some Things That Glitter (novel), McGraw, 1969; author of The Picture Life of Jesse Jackson, F. Watts, 1972, 2nd edition, 1984; author of Harlem: A History of Broken Dreams, Doubleday, 1974; editor of Short Story Scene, Globe, 1973; contributor of about one hundred short stories, adaptations, and articles to periodicals; writer of fifteen filmstrips and a motion picture titled "Dig.". **MILITARY SERVICE:** US Army Air Forces, 1943-46. **HOME ADDRESS:** 22 Scribner Hill Rd, Wilton, CT 06897. *

HALLUMS, BENJAMIN F.
Educator. **PERSONAL:** Born Mar 06, 1940, Easley, SC; married Phyllis; children: Jacqueline, Bernard, Maisha. **EDUCATION:** BA 1970; MEd 1972; 6 Yr Cert 1973. **CAREER:** Quinnipiac Coll, counselor 1971-75; Allied Health Prgram, counselor 1974; School for the Mentally Retarded, counselor 1972-73; Quinnipiac Coll, asst prof Blk Studies 1973-75, asst prof Fine Arts 1972-75. **ORGANIZATIONS:** Mem Assn Blk People Hghr Educ 1970-75; Estrn Allnc Blk Couns 1974-75; Nat Blk Coll Choir Annl Fest; CT Liason Prgm 1973; Mnrty Coll Couns 1973; rep United Mnstry Hghr Edn; Nat Coll Choirs; sec Coaltn Blk Prnts 1975; vice pres Couples Inc. **HONORS/ACHIEVEMENTS:** Dist Inst Mnrty Coll Couns 1973; citat Mnrty Stdnts 1974; Testmnl 1974; citat Orgn Stdnt Sngng Grp 1974; citat Adv Orgn 1974. **MILITARY SERVICE:** AUS e5 1961-64. **BUSINESS ADDRESS:** College Counselor, Quinniiac College, Mt Carmel Ave, Hamden, CT 06518.

HALPERT, LEONARD
Business executive. **PERSONAL:** Born 1922, Boston, MA. **EDUCATION:** Wesleyan Univ, 1944; Columbia Univ, 1948. **CAREER:** Cocoline Chocolate Co, vchmn, dir. **ORGANIZATIONS:** Dir Halrin Slcaks Inc; chmn Chocolate Mfgs Assoc of the US, Assoc of Mfgrs of Confectionery Chocolate Inc; vchmn, dir Amer Best Chocolate Inc; dir Freedom Natl Bank NY. **BUSINESS ADDRESS:** Vice Chairman, Cocoline Chocolate Co Inc, 689 Myrtle Ave, Brooklyn, NY 11205.

HALSEY, GEORGE
Business executive. **PERSONAL:** Married Ruth; children: Karen H Smith, John B Hampton. **CAREER:** Amway, distributor; Halsey & Assoc Inc, chmn of bd. **HONORS/ACHIEVEMENTS:** Amway's only black Triple Diamond Direct Disbributors. **BUSINESS ADDRESS:** Chairman of the Board, Halsey & Associates, Inc, 515 College Road, Ste 11, Greensboro, NC 27410.

HALYARD, ARDIE ADLENA
Business executive. **PERSONAL:** Born in Covington, GA; married Wilbur. **EDUCATION:** Atlanta Univ Normal Preparatory, 1917; Atlanta Univ Normal School, 1919; Univ of Wisconsin Extnsn, 1924; Wisconsin savings & Loan Inst, 1945. **CAREER:** Milwaukee Goodwill Inds, prsnl dir 1923-43; Columbia Svg & Loan Assc, sec treas 1925-69. **ORGANIZATIONS:** Organizer & pres Various NAACP Units 1923-85; trustee Calvary Baptist Churc; vice pres Wisconsin Voc Tech & Adult School 1971-79. **HONORS/ACHIEVEMENTS:** Distgshd Serv Award Milwaukee Metropolitan Civic Alliance 1980; Mt Mary Coll Pro Urbe Metal 1981; Radcliffe Coll Women of Courage 1983. **HOME ADDRESS:** 7407 W Glendale Ave, Milwaukee, WI 53218..

HALYARD, MICHELE YVETTE
Physician. **PERSONAL:** Born Apr 13, 1961, Buffalo, NY; married Paul Edward Leroy Richardson; children: Hamilton. **EDUCATION:** Howard Univ, BS (Summa Cum Laude) 1982; Howard Univ Coll of Medicine, MD 1984. **CAREER:** Mayo Clinic, fellow radiation oncology 1987-89; Howard Univ Hosp, resident radiation oncology 1984-87. **ORGANIZATIONS:** Mem Natl & Amer Medical Assocs, Phi Beta Kappa Honor Soc, Alpha Omega Alpha Medical Honor Soc, Alpha Kappa Alpha Sor Inc. **HONORS/ACHIEVEMENTS:** Amer Medical Women's Assoc Awd for Scholarship Achievement; Grandy Awd for Internal Medicine; Awd for Clinical Excellence in Psychiatry; Frederick M DRewAwd for Outstanding Performance in Radiation Therapy; article "The Use of Intraoperative Radiotherapy and External Beam Therapy in the Management of Desmoid Tumors," w/JoAnn Collier-Manning MD, Ebrahim Ashayeri MD, Alfred Goldson MD, Frank Watkins MD, Ernest Myers MD in Journal Natl Medical Assoc 1986. **BUSINESS ADDRESS:** Third Year Resident, Howard University Hospital, 2041 Georgia Ave NW, Washington, DC 20060.

HAM-YING, J. MICHAEL
Physician. **PERSONAL:** Born Mar 16, 1956, Gainesville, FL; son of John Russeel Ham-Ying DO and Dorothy McClellan Ham-Ying; married Franeco Cheeks, Jun 24, 1989. **EDUCATION:** Oakwood Coll, BA Biology 1977; Meharry Medical Coll, MD 1981. **CAREER:** King Drew Medical Ctr, residency 1981-84, asst medical dir 1984-85; Los Angeles Doctors Hosp, exec staff sec 1984-85; South Eastern Coll of Osteopathic Med, asst clinical prof 1985-; Clewiston Comm Health Ctr, asst medical dir 1985-; executive medical director, Florida Community Health Centers, Inc 1987-. **ORGANIZATIONS:** Mem Amer Medical Assn, Amer Acad of Family Physicians FL Chap 1983; bd certified Amer Bd of Family Practice 1984; attending physician Hendry General Hosp 1985-. **HONORS/ACHIEVEMENTS:** Geriatric Fellow Dept of Family Medicine King-Drew Medical Ctr 1985. **BUSINESS ADDRESS:** Medical Director, Florida Community Health Centers, Inc, 3500 Forty-fifth Street, Suite 12, West Palm Beach, FL 33407.

HAMBERG, MARCELLE R.
Physician. **PERSONAL:** Born Jul 04, 1931, Anderson, SC; son of Robert Clark Hamberg and Pauline Hamlin Hamberg; married Cheryl Jones; children: Marcelle Jr, Gabrielle. **EDUCATION:** Hampton Inst, BS 1953; Meharry Med College, MD 1957. **CAREER:** Univ of Louisville, instr in urology 1967; Meharry Med Coll, chief div of urology 1976; physician Nashville, TN. **ORGANIZATIONS:** Newman Van Hugh spl fellow in cancer urology Meml Hosp for Cancer & Allied Diseases New York 1962-63; Amer Bd of Urology 1968; mem Amer Urological Assn1969. **BUSINESS ADDRESS:** 1916 Patterson St, Ste 603, Nashville, TN 37203.

HAMBERLIN, EMIEL
Educator. **PERSONAL:** Born Nov 08, 1939, Fayette, MS; married Minnie; children: Emiel III, Mark. **EDUCATION:** Alcorn State Univ, BS 1964; Univ of IL, MEd 1978, PhD 1982. **CAREER:** Chicago Bd of Educ DuSable HS, professor. **ORGANIZATIONS:** Mem Omega Psi Phi Frat 1964-; mem Natl Geographic Soc 1970-; mem Operation PUSH 1972; mem Natl Biology Assoc 1974-; mem Intl Wildlife Federation 1974-; mem IL Teachers Assoc 1975-; mem Phi Delta Kappa 1976-; mem IL Science Teachers Assoc 1978-; hon mem Kappa Delta Pi 1979-; bd mem Ada McKinley Highland for Special Children 1980. **HONORS/ACHIEVEMENTS:** The Governors Awd World Flower Show 1972; Professional Personnel in Environmental Educ IL Environ Educ Assoc 1975; Omega Man of the Year 1977; Those Who Excell Awd State of IL 1977; Illinois Teacher of the Year 1977; Outstanding Educator Awd Lewis Univ 1980; Phi Delta Kappa Educator 1981; IL Master Teacher Governor of IL 1981; Ora Higgins Leadership Awd 1985; Distinguished Alumni of Black Univs Natl Assoc for Equal Oppor in Higher Educ 1986; Outstanding Achievements as an Educ in Horticulture Mayor H Washington 1986; One of the Heroes of Our Time Newsweek 1986. **HOME ADDRESS:** 8500 S Winchester, Chicago, IL 60620. **BUSINESS ADDRESS:** Professor, DuSable High School, 4934 S Wabash, Chicago, IL 60615.

HAMBRICK, HAROLD E., JR.
Association director. **PERSONAL:** Born Feb 17, 1943, New Orleans, LA; married Margaret; children: Tyra, Jeffery, Sharon. **EDUCATION:** Pepperdine U, BS 1976. **CAREER:** Western Assn of Comm Hlth Ctrs Inc, exec dir 1974-; Watts Hlth Fdn Inc, sr Acct 1969-75; New Communicators Inc, bus mgr 1967-69; IBM Corp, ofcmgr, Trn 1966-67. **ORGANIZATIONS:** Treas Nat Assn of Comm Hlth Ctrs Inc 1974-76; fndng pres Western Assn of Comm Hlth Ctr Inc 1973-75; v pres Hambricks Mort Inc 1975-; pres Employees Serv Assn 1972-74; bd mem Watts United Credit Union Inc 1974-75; mem Am Soc of Assn Exec 1976-; State of CA Dept of Hlth Advsry Cncl; AmPubl Hlth Assn 1973-; Nat Notary Assn 1972-; Nat Assn of Tax Consult 1972-; CA Assn of Tax Consult 1972-. **HONORS/ACHIEVEMENTS:** Whos Who Am Assn Exec 1976; Outstanding Yng Men of A 1978. **BUSINESS ADDRESS:** 320 E 111th St, Los Angeles, CA 90061.

HAMBY, ROSCOE JEROME
Attorney. **PERSONAL:** Born Jun 08, 1919, Tupelo, MS; married Mary Lean Farr; children: Roscoe Jr, William. **EDUCATION:** TN A&I State Univ, AB 1944; Kent Coll, LLB 1948. **CAREER:** Private practice, attny. **ORGANIZATIONS:** Mem TN Bar, Amer Bar, Natl Bar, Fed Bar, Amer Trial Lawyers Assoc; deacon Pleasant Greek Bapt Church; mem IBPOE, Elks, Amer Legion Post #6; past exalted Rulers Council; mem Black Masons Intl Union of Amer 35 yrs; bd of trustees MS Minestineal Inst & Coll. **HONORS/ACHIEVEMENTS:** Listed in Who's Who Among Amer Construction Craftman 1955; Dick Slater Awd Cook Cty Trowel Trades Assoc. **BUSINESS ADDRESS:** Attorney, 2702 Jefferson St, Nashville, TN 37208.

HAMER, JUDITH ANN
Training specialist. **PERSONAL:** Born Jan 03, 1939, Brooklyn, NY; daughter of Frank Leslie Thompson and Martha Louise Taylor Thompson; married Martin J Hamer; children: Kim T, Fern S, Jill T. **EDUCATION:** Cornell Univ, BA 1960; Smith Coll, MAT 1961; Columbia Univ, PhD 1984. **CAREER:** CCNY, instructor 1971-76; Columbia Univ, adjunct instructor 1977-83; Learning Intl, consultant writer 1984-86; PaineWebber Inc, dp trainer 1986-. **ORGANIZATIONS:** Mem Coalition of 100 Black Women Stamford CT. **HONORS/ACHIEVEMENTS:** Ford Foundation Fellowship for Black Americans 1976-81. **BUSINESS ADDRESS:** AVP, Paine Webber Inc., 1200 Harbor Boulevard, 2nd Floor, Weehawken, NJ 07087.

HAMILL, MARGARET HUDGENS
Educator. **PERSONAL:** Born Mar 09, 1937, Laurens, SC; children: Beatrice Chauntea. **EDUCATION:** Benedict Coll, BA 1958; St Peter's Coll, Ed diploma 1962. **CAREER:** No 5 Public School, educator 1966-68; Frank R Conwell, educator 1968-74; Joseph H Brensinger, educator 1974-. **ORGANIZATIONS:** School rep NJEA 1985-; advisor Tauette Club 1985-; bd of dirs Bayonne Chap Natl Conf of Christians and Jews 1985-; pres Young Women's League FriendshipBapt Ch 1986-; 1st vice pres Bayonne Youth Ctr Inc 1986-; sgt-of-arms Tau Gamma Delta Sor Psi Chapt. **HONORS/ACHIEVEMENTS:** Comm Serv Awd Bayonne NAACP 1979; Who's Who Amer Women Marquis publ 1981-84; Brotherhood Awd Natl Conf of Christians & Jews 1985; Mary McLeod Bethune Awd 1985. **HOME ADDRESS:** 42 W 18th St, Bayonne, NJ 07002.

HAMILTON, ART
State legislator. **PERSONAL:** Born in Phoenix, AZ. **CAREER:** Began as public affairs representative; Arizona State Legislature, Phoenix AZ, state representative, District 22, House Minority Leader. **BUSINESS ADDRESS:** House of Representatives, State House, Phoenix, AZ 85007. *

HAMILTON, ARTHUR N.
Judge. **PERSONAL:** Born Jan 21, 1917, New Orleans; married Mary; children: Lisa. **EDUCATION:** Kent Coll Law, JD 1950; Nat Coll Juvenile Ct Judges Univ NV, grad 1973. **CAREER:** Cook County Circuit Ct, assoc judge 1971-; Chicago Park Dist, 1st asst gen atty; Illinois, special asst atty gen; Cook County, asst states atty; City of Chicago, asst corp counsel. **ORGANIZATIONS:** Mem bd, Augustana Hosp; bd mem, Inter-Relig Conf Urban Affairs; bd mem, Ch Fedn Greater Chicago; bd mem, Pkwy Comm House; delegate, Natl Conv Lutheran Church of Amer 1970. **HONORS/ACHIEVEMENTS:** Advocacy for Children Award Lake Bluff Chicago Homes Children 1974. **BUSINESS ADDRESS:** Circuit Court of Cook Co Daley, Chicago, IL 60602.

HAMILTON, AUBREY J.
CEO, janitorial/food services. **CAREER:** Southeastern Enterprises, Inc, Groton, CT, chief executive officer, 1973—. **BUSINESS ADDRESS:** Southeastern Enterprises, Inc, 643 North Rd, PO Box 1146, Groton, CT 06340. *

HAMILTON, CHARLES S.
Clergyman. **PERSONAL:** Born May 12, 1927, Cedartown, GA; married Lillie Mitchell; children: Ronald, Charletta, Rachael. **EDUCATION:** Morehouse Coll, AB 1950; Morehouse Sch Rel, BD 1953, ITC STM 1964; Colgate Rochester Div Sch, DMin 1975. **CAREER:** Tabernacle Baptist Church, minister. **ORGANIZATIONS:** Past pres Augusta Baptist Ministers Conf; GA Humane Relations Council; v moderator Walker Baptist Assn; mem City Council Augusta 1966-71; bd dir Morehouse Sch Rel 1969-75; Human Relations Comm 1971-74; mem Progressive Natl Baptist Conv; pres Comm Civil Rights; mem NAACP; Civil Serv Comm Augusta GA 1974-78; pres New Era Missionary Baptist Conv of GA; Augusta-Richmond Planning & Zoning Comm. **HONORS/ACHIEVEMENTS:** Martin Luther King Jr Fellow 1972. **MILITARY SERVICE:** AUS 1946-47. **BUSINESS ADDRESS:** Minister, Tabernacle Baptist Church, 1223 Laney Walker Blvd, Augusta, GA 30901.

HAMILTON, EDWARD N., JR.
Sculptor. **PERSONAL:** Born Feb 14, 1947, Cincinnati; married Bernadette S Chapman. **EDUCATION:** Louisville Sch Art, 1965-69;Univ Louisville, 1970-71; Spalding Coll, 1971-73. **CAREER:** Iroquois HS, tchr 1969-72; Louisville Art Workshop, 1972; Louisville Speed Mu-

seum, lectr 1974; self-employed sculptor. **ORGANIZATIONS:** Mem Alpha Phi Alpha Frat; mem Nat Conf of Artists 1980; bd mem Renaissance Devel Corp; mem Art Circle Assn; bd mem St Frances HS Louisville; bd mem KY Minority Businessmen. **HONORS/ACHIEVEMENTS:** Award KY Black Achievers 1980; Bronze St Frances of Row St Frances of Row Ch Louisville; numerous exhibitions group shows pub commns works in private collections.

HAMILTON, EDWIN
Educator. **PERSONAL:** Born Jul 24, 1936, Tuskegee, AL; son of Everette Hamilton and Julia Sullins Hamilton; married Alberta Daniels, Aug 03, 1960; children: Michelle, Stanley, Gina, Carl. **EDUCATION:** Tuskegee Univ, BS 1960, MEd 1963; The Ohio State Univ, PhD 1973. **CAREER:** Macon County Schools, dir 1965-70; Ohio State Univ, rsch asst 1971-73; FL International Univ, prof 1973-74; Howard Univ, prof 1974-. **ORGANIZATIONS:** Mem AAACE/ASTD 1975-87; presidential assoc Tuskegee Univ 1980-87; mem Intl Assoc CAEO/ICA 1984-87; rsch rep Phi Delta Kappa Howard Univ 1986-87; adjunct prof Univ of DC 1986; educ leader Professional Seminar Consultants's (Russia) 1986; adjunct prof OH State Univ 1987; pres, Howard Univ PDK, 1989-89; elections judge, P G Bd of Elections, Uppermarlboro, MD, 1986-87; chief elections judge, 1988. **HONORS/ACHIEVEMENTS:** Fulbright Scholar (Nigeria) CIES/USIA 1982-83; Writer's Recognition Univ of DC 1984; Certificate of Appreciation Phi Delta Gamma Johns Hopkins Univ 1986; Certificate of Awd Phi Delta Kappa Howard Univ 1987-89; Distinguished Alumni Citation NAFEO/Tuskegee Univ, 1988; President's Award Howard Univ, PDK, 1989; designed study-travel to China Tour, 1989. **MILITARY SERVICE:** AUS sp E-4 1954-56; Good Conduct Medal, Honorable Discharge 1956; Active Army Reserve, 1956-63. **BUSINESS ADDRESS:** Professor of Education, Howard University, School of Education, Washington, DC 20059.

HAMILTON, FRANKLIN D.
Educator. **PERSONAL:** Born Oct 30, 1942, Aucilla, FL; children: Kayla, Ebony, Nikki. **EDUCATION:** FL A&M Univ, BS 1964; Univ of Pittsburgh, PhD 1969. **CAREER:** Univ of Pittsburgh, USPHS pre-doctoral fellow 1964-69; SUNY, USPHS postdoctoral fellow 1969-71; Univ of TN, asst prof 1971-74, assoc prof 1974-79; Univ CA Berkeley, visiting prof 1986-87; Atlanta Univ, assoc prof 1979-. **ORGANIZATIONS:** Vice-chair Sci Adv Comm to the Natl Assoc for Equal Opportunity in Higher Edn; consult Natl Inst of Hlth; consult Robert Wood Johnson Found; consult premed rev com United Negro Coll Fund; AAAS; Amer Soc for Cell Biol; Amer Soc of Biol Chem; comm mem MARC Review Comm, NIGMS, NIH; comm mem NSF Pre-doctoral Fellowship Review Comm. **HONORS/ACHIEVEMENTS:** Published, "Minorities in Sci, A Challenge for Change in Biomedicine" 1977; "Proceeding of the Conference on Health Professional Educational Programs" 1980; "Participation of Blacks in the Basic Sciences, An Assessment in Black Students in Higher Education in the 70's, Conditions and Experiences" edited by Gail Thomas, Greenwood Press 1981. **BUSINESS ADDRESS:** Associate Professor, Atlanta University, Chemistry Dept, Atlanta, GA 30314.

HAMILTON, GRACE TOWNS
Government official. **PERSONAL:** Born Feb 10, 1907, Atlanta, GA; married Henry. **EDUCATION:** Atlanta U, AB 1927; OH St U, MA 1929. **CAREER:** GA House of Representatives, general assembly 1965-; Atlanta Charter Comn, vice chmn 1971-73, comm relations conselor 1961-67; Atlanta Youth Council, dir 1966; YWCA, natl bd 1960-61; Atlanta Urban League 1943-61; So Reg Council Inc, 1954-55; YWCA, natl bd 1936-43; Durvey of White Collar & Skilled Negro Workers, dir 1935-36; Lemoyne Coll, instructor 1930-34; Clark Coll, instructor 1928-30; Atlanta School of Social Work, instructor 1928-29; YMCA, sec 1927-28. **ORGANIZATIONS:** Bd trustee Meharry Med Coll Atlanta U; mem GA Register Review Bd; exec bd Atlanta Landmarks Inc; mem Nat Order of Women Legislators; Gate City Day Nursery Assn; mem Govs Spec Council on Family Planning; bd dir Atlanta Arts Festival; Citizens Adv Com for Urban Renewal; Nat Citizens Adv Com on Environmental Quality 1966-71. **HONORS/ACHIEVEMENTS:** Liberty Bell Award Atlanta Bar Assn 1974; Good Neighborhood Award Nat Conf of Christians & Jews 1973; Non Partisan Comm Serv Award Fulton Co Rep Women 1971; Achievement Award NJ Chap Links Inc 1966; numerous other honors.

HAMILTON, H. J. BELTON
Judge. **PERSONAL:** Born Jun 01, 1924, Columbus, MS; married Midori Minamoto; children: Konrad, Camille. **EDUCATION:** Stanford Univ, AB Pol Sci 1949; Northwestern Sch of Law Lewis & Clark Coll, JD 1953; Univ of OR, postgrad studies in pub affairs 1960-61. **CAREER:** Genl Practice of Law, attorney 1953-54; State Bureau of Labor, asst atty genl state of OR & staff atty 1955-58; US, admin law judge; Social Security Dept, admin law judge. **ORGANIZATIONS:** Sec treas Freedom Family Ltd; pres Alpha Develop Invest Corp; mem OR State, Amer Bar Assns; mem Amer Trial Lawyers Assn; World Assn of Judges; chmn Admin Law Sec of Natl Bar Assn; mem Natl Urban League Quarter Century Club; mem OR State Adv Com to US Commn on Civ Rights; OR State Adv Council; co-founder former chmn legal counsel & Parliamentarian of Intl Assn of Official Hum Rights Agencies; former mem Natl Urban League New Thrust Task Force for institutional reorientation; former pres Urban League of Portland; Boltol-Cedar Oak PTA; Portland chap of Alpha Phi Alpha; TV host of PBL-Spin off; former moderator of radio "Great Decisions" prog. **HONORS/ACHIEVEMENTS:** Outstanding Civic Contributions to Comm Alpha Phi Alpha; Who's Who in Govt; named in Martindale & Hubbell as atty with high legal skill & ability & highest recommendation; Ford Found Fellow 1960-61; author of legislation atty gen opinion & scholarly articles on wide range of subjects; guest lecturer at most OR colls & univs. **MILITARY SERVICE:** AUS s/sgt 1943-46.

HAMILTON, JAMES G.
Genealogical researcher, ethnic relations consultant, educator. **PERSONAL:** Born Jun 22, 1939, Washington, DC; son of John Henry Hamilton Jr and Ruth Aura Hamilton Proctor. **EDUCATION:** Rochester Inst Tech, AAS with Hons 1970; RIT, BS with high Hons 1972; Univ Rochester, MA 1974; Univ Orthodox Coll Nigeria, Hon Doctorate African Hist 1981. **CAREER:** Rochester, New York Museum & Science Center, comm consultant 1972-74; Eastman Kodak Co, tech sales rep in graphic arts 1975; Aetna Life & Casualty, sr graphic arts consultant 1976-83; SBC Management Corp, pr consultant 1983-85; Freelance Consultant and Lecturer, black history, ethnic relations and genealogy; The Melting Pot A Genealogical Publ, ethnic rel consult & assoc ed; genealogical researcher and ethnic relations consultant and coll instructor, Manchester, CT Comm Coll. **ORGANIZATIONS:** Founder/exec dir Ankh-Mobile Proj Inc 1977-81; founder/pres Rochester, NY Branch of the Assn for the Study of Afro-Amer Life & Hist; former mem Amer Film Inst; former mem Connecticut Hist Soc Hartford, CT; life mem Disabled Amer Veterans; life mem NAACP; former mem Natl Geographic Soc Wash, DC; former mem Natl Historical Soc Gettysburg, PA; former mem Natl Trust for Historic Preserv Wash, DC; former mem Smithsonian Inst; former mem Photographic Soc of Amer; former mem Connecticut Computer Soc 1985; mem Natl Huguenot Soc 1984; mem Connecticut Huguenot Soc 1984; former mem Amer Vets Boston MA; former mem Natl Pres Photographers Assoc Wash DC; mem Connecticut Soc of Genealogist; mem Maryland Genealogical Soc; former mem Intl Platform Assoc, Cleveland Heights, OH; former Natl Archives Trust Fund Assoc, Washington DC; former mem Camera Club of Fitchburg, MA; former county Committeeman, Monroe County Democratic Committee, Rochester, NY. **HONORS/ACHIEVEMENTS:** Fellowship Social Work Educ NY State Council on the Arts 1972. **MILITARY SERVICE:** AUS Staff Sgt E-6 1957-67; 3 Good Conduct Medals. **HOME ADDRESS:** 134 B2 Central Ave, East Hartford, CT 06108.

HAMILTON, JOHN JOSLYN, JR.
Government official. **PERSONAL:** Born Dec 16, 1949, New York, NY; children: Issoufou K. **EDUCATION:** Basic Elec & Electronic School, certificate 1969; Sonar Tech School, certificate 1970; Natl Assn of Underwater Instructors, certified scuba diver certificate 1971; College Level Exam Program; Keane Coll, 1972-75; Vol Probation Counselor Training Program, certificate; Dept of Corrections Behavious Modification, staff training certificate; Grantsmanship & Proposal Writing, State of NJ Dept of Health certificate 1980; State of NJ, comm skills/counseling tech certificate; Amer Legion Leadership Coll, basic & advanced certs 1982; Amer Legion Serv Officers School, certificate 1985. **CAREER:** First Class Auto Body, payroll & office mgr 1972-74; Musician, performer 1972-80; Kean Coll, audio visual tech 1973-74; Essex County Highway Dept, traffic signal electrician 1975; Private Limousine Serv, mgr chauffeur 1978-80; Beitler Public Relations, acct exec/artist 1978-80; Employment Dynamics, consultant, public relations counselor 1980-81; House of Hope, dir, counselor 1981-84; Veterans Admin Med Center, program specialist, public relations 1984-87; Essex-Newark Legal Services, community legal educ coordinator 1987-, dir Homeless Prevention Program 1987-. **ORGANIZATIONS:** Performed Carnegie Hall, New York All City Chorus 1964; performed world's fair with Bronx Boro Chorus 1964; public relations chmn Third World Organ Kean Coll 1973-75; bd mem co-curricular program bd Kean Coll 1973, 1974; co-founder, public relations chmn, counselor RAPIN 1972-75; vol probation counselor Union Co Probation Dept 1973-82; vol assisting handicapped individual Hand in Hand Inc 1978-79, 1981-82; voluntary serv volunteer Veterans Admin 1983-84; commander Amer Legion Post #251 Montclair 1983-; consultant State Program Coordinator N Amer Wheelchair Athletic Assn 1985-; Public speaker, Civic Activist North-East Regional Conference; youngest County Vice Commander Amer Legion 1986-; county chmn NJ POW/MIA Committee 1987-; site coordinator Newark Literacy Campaign 1987-; bd mem Newark Transitional Supervised Living Program 1988, Essex County CEAS Committee 1988. **HONORS/ACHIEVEMENTS:** Hall of Fame Award, St Vincent De Paul New York 1959; Natl Defense Service Medal 1968; Keane Coll Award of Merit 1973-74; Special Commendation for participation in the Intl Conf on Morality & Intl Violence 1974; #1 Artist musician, performer 1978 & 1979; Union Co Volunteer of the Year 1980; ranked #3 in the Nation by the Natl Assn of Volunteers in Criminal Justice 1981; twice recognized and presented resolutions passed by the Essex County Bd of Chosen Freeholders 1984; Jerseyan of the Week, The Star Ledger 1984; 1984 Pride in Heritage Award, Male Volunteer of the Year; 1984 Natl Good Neighbor Award recipient presented by Natl Comm of the Amer Legion Natl Vol of the Year 1984; Federal Distinguished Public Serv Award 1985; IBPOE of W Cmmunity Serv Award 1986; Citizens' Service Award, Cult-Art Associates 1987; Elected Essex County Commander, The American Legion 1989; Producer, Host of Community Crisis (Cable TV Show) 1988-. **MILITARY SERVICE:** US Nave petty officer 3rd class 1968-74; served in Amphibious Forces and regular Navy. **HOME ADDRESS:** 38 Lexington Ave, Montclair, NJ 07042. **BUSINESS ADDRESS:** Community Legal Education Coordinator, Essex-Neward Legal Services, 8-10 Park Place, 4th, Newark, NJ 07102.

HAMILTON, JOHN M.
Savings and loan chief executive. **CAREER:** Washington Shores Savings Bank, FSB, Orlando, FL, chief exec. **BUSINESS ADDRESS:** Washington Shores Savings Bank, FSB, 715 South Goldwyn Ave., Orlando, FL 32805. *

HAMILTON, JOHN MARK, JR.
Dentist. **PERSONAL:** Born Oct 02, 1931, Washington, DC; son of Mr and Mrs John M Hamilton; married Dorothy Wilson; children: John M III, Sheree R. **EDUCATION:** US Military Academy at West Point NY, BS, 1955; US Army Command and General Staff College, 1964; US Army War College, 1977; Univ of Medicine & Dentistry of New Jersey, DMD, 1982. **CAREER:** 101st Airborne Division, Vietnam, brigade deputy commander, infantry battalion commander, 1970-71; US Army Command and General Staff College, Fort Leavenworth KS, faculty member, 1971-74; US Military District of Washington DC, chief of human resources division, 1974-75; Office of US Secretary of Defense, military advisor, 1975-78; private practice, dentist, 1982-; JB Johnson Nursing Center, consulting dentist, 1985-; East of the River Health Center, consulting dentist, 1984-; John M Hamilton Jr, DMD, PC, director 1988-; Hamilton Professional Enterprises Inc, president, 1988-. **ORGANIZATIONS:** Mem Kappa Alpha Psi Fraternity 1951-; vice pres Wee Care Youth Academy 1974-; consultant Lawrence Johnson & Assoc 1983; mem Robert T Freeman Dental Soc 1984-; vice pres Investors Consolidated Assoc Inc 1985-87; mem bd of dir Ethel James Williams Scholarship Foundation 1986-; mem bd of dir La Mirage Beauty Enterprises 1986-87. **HONORS/ACHIEVEMENTS:** Harvard Prize Book Award, Harvard Club of Washington DC; Recruiting Award, US Air Force Recruiting Service, 1982. **MILITARY SERVICE:** AUS Infantry col 23 yrs; Ranger Tab, Parachute Badge, Army Commendation Medal with Oak Leaf Cluster, Vietnam Gallantry Cross with Palm, Legion of Merit, Air Medal with 13th Oak Leaf Cluster, Bronze Star with 1st Oak Leaf Cluster, Vietnam Gallantry Cross with Silver Star, Combat Infantryman Badge. **HOME ADDRESS:** 10806 Braeburn Rd, Columbia, MD 21044. **BUSINESS ADDRESS:** President, Hamilton Professional Enterprises Inc, 10806 Braeburn Rd, Columbia, MD 21044.

HAMILTON, JOSEPH WILLARD
Manager, educator. **PERSONAL:** Born Mar 12, 1922, Lake Charles, LA; married Lou Wilda Bertrand; children: Joseph W. **EDUCATION:** Leland Coll, BS 1948; Bishop Coll, MEd 1955. **CAREER:** Hamilton's Enterprise, mgr; Science Dept Plaisance High School, head 1953-76; Plaisance High Sch, head coach 1950-73; St Landry Parish Classroom Teachers, pres 1960-65; Plaisance High School, counselor 1950-60; Elba Elmentary School, prin 1948-50. **ORGANIZATIONS:** Fdr pres St Joseph Cath Ch Counc 1967-77; vice pres Frontiers Internatl Opelousas Club 1976-77; commn BS of Amer 1972-75; dir confirm classes St

Joseph Par Cath Ch 1970-77; JW Hamilton Annual Relays Plaisance High Sch 1977; particip Citiz Fgn Pol Forum US Sec of State 1960; Fo. **HONORS/ACHIEVEMENTS:** Coach of Yr CCOA 1959; Expt Rifleman 1943; Good Cond Med 1945; ribbon Pacif Theater of War 1945. **MILITARY SERVICE:** Sgt mjr 1943-45. **BUSINESS ADDRESS:** 948 E Laurent St, Opelousas, LA 70570.

HAMILTON, LA VERNE M.
Editor. **PERSONAL:** Born Jan 31, 1940, Springfield, MO; married Harry L Hamilton Jr; children: David Mc Daniel, Lisa La Verne. **EDUCATION:** Beloit Coll, BA 1961. **CAREER:** Scott Foresman & Co, editorial consult 1975, 1967-72;Univ of NY Albany, publ splst 1966-67; Scott Foresman & Co, editorial asst 1964-65; Cleveland Pub Sch, tchr 1961-63. **ORGANIZATIONS:** Corr sec Albany NAACP 1968-; bd dir NE NY Speech Cntr 1971-72; delegate Dem Nat Conv 1972; chmn Canvass Com of NAACP Voter Registration Dr 1972; bd dir Blue Cross of NE NY 1973-; mem Exec com; mem League of Women Voters 1973-74; mem Albany Co Blue Corss Advis Commit 1976-; Nat Women's Political Caucus 1973-76; Women's Press Club 1973-; Dem Com Woman 1974-; Bethlehem Dem Action Group 1973-75; nominating com Urban League 1970-; editor Albany NAACP newsletter 1967-76. **HONORS/ACHIEVEMENTS:** Comm serv award Federated Clubs of Albany 1973; Who's Who in Am Politics 1973; Intl Who's Who in Comm Serv 1975; five natl awards for NAACP Newsletter since 1967; NAACP Outstanding Serv Award 1975.

HAMILTON, LYNN (LYNN JENKINS)
Actress. **PERSONAL:** Born Apr 25, 1930, Yazoo City, MS; daughter of Louis Hamilton and Naney Hamilton; married Frank S Writer. **EDUCATION:** Goodman Theatre, BA 1954. **CAREER:** Writer; Sanford & Son; The Waltons; Gunsmoke; Ironside; The Rockford Files; Good Times; Starsky & Hutch; Lady Sings the Blues; Buck & the Preacher; Bro John; Leadbelly. **BUSINESS ADDRESS:** PO Box 3612, Los Angeles, CA 90036.

HAMILTON, MCKINLEY JOHN
Clergyman. **PERSONAL:** Born Nov 24, 1921, Lake Charles, LA; married Mary Stone. **EDUCATION:** Butler Coll, AA 1943; Bishop Coll, BA1945; Crozer Theol Sem, 1945-46; Howard U, MD 1958. **CAREER:** First Bapt Ch Rocky Mt VA, pastor 1958-; Shiloh Bapt Ch Washington DC, asst pastor 1947-58; Good Samaritan Bapt Ch, pastor 1955-57; St James Bapt Ch & New Hope Bapt Ch Alto TX, pastor 1942-43. **ORGANIZATIONS:** Bd mem T & C Ministers; vice pres Dist SS Conf 1962-; past pres Fr Cty Ministerial Assn; Am Cancer Soc; moderator Bapt Pigg River Assn; bd mem Sheltered Workshop Comm Action of Fr Co; mem Fr Co Hist Soc; Mental Health; NAACP; United Fund; Cancer Soc; vol Sr Nutrition Program for Sr Citizens. **HONORS/ACHIEVEMENTS:** Plaque for outstanding contribution to Comm of Franklin Co; plaque for being mem of Cneturion Club Ferrum Coll 1975. **BUSINESS ADDRESS:** 117 Patterson Ave SE, Rocky Mount, VA 24151.

HAMILTON, PAMELA MARIE
Marketing manager. **PERSONAL:** Born Oct 30, 1962, Rantoul, IL; daughter of Earl P Hamilton and Lula F Hamilton (deceased). **EDUCATION:** Old Dominion Univ, BSBA 1984; Syracuse Univ, MBA 1986. **CAREER:** Bristol Labs Bristol Myers Co, marketing asst 1985; IBM Corp, marketing support asst 1985-86; Bristol Myers Co The Drackett Co, asst product mgr 1986-88, product manager 1989-. **ORGANIZATIONS:** Mem Delta Sigma Theta Sor 1981-; mem Amer Mktg Assoc 1982-88; vice pres for admin 1987, mem Natl Black MBA Assoc 1985-. **HONORS/ACHIEVEMENTS:** Grad and Professional Oppor Prog Fellowship Syracuse Univ 1984-86; Beta Gamma Sigma Business Honor Soc Syracuse Univ 1986. **BUSINESS ADDRESS:** Product Manager, Bristol-Myers The Drackett Co, 201 E 4th St Ste 1800, Cincinnati, OH 45202.

HAMILTON, PAUL L.
Educator. **PERSONAL:** Born Apr 01, 1941, Pueblo, CO; divorced; children: John. **EDUCATION:** Univ of Denver, BA 1964, MA 1972; Univ of N CO, EdD 1975. **CAREER:** Denver Public Schools, teacher 1964-; Denver Head Start Family Camps, asst dir 1967; Denver Area Consortium for Improvement of Teacher of Histories of Minorities, assoc dir 1969; State of CO, representative 1969-73; Univ of Denver, instructor weekend & evening coll soc problems 1971, lecturer & rsch asst 1971-72; Gen Asst Center Greeley, consultant 1974-; Denver Push-Excell (on loan from Denver Public Schools) dir. **ORGANIZATIONS:** Mem Denver Fed of Teacher 1965-, AFT Natl Comm for Effective School 1968-71; org, chmn Ed vs Racism Conf 1968; org Colelctive Bargaining Election 1967; exec comm Denver Fed of Teacher 1966-68; sec Denver Fed of Techer 1966-68; mem Kappa Delta Pi, Phi Kappa Delta, Omicron Delta Kappa, Alpha Kappa Delta. **HONORS/ACHIEVEMENTS:** Co-author "Effective School Progs in Denver" 1966; listed in Who's Who in Amer 1975-87. **BUSINESS ADDRESS:** Teacher, Denver Public Schools, 451 CLermont, Denver, CO 80206.

HAMILTON, PHANUEL J.
Government official. **PERSONAL:** Born Aug 03, 1929, Detroit; children: Thieda, Deborah, Gregory. **EDUCATION:** Eastern MI U, BA 1951; Northwester U, grad sch speech; DePaul U; Chicago State U; KY Christian U, MA 1973. **CAREER:** Mayor's Ofc Sr Citizens Chicago, dir field servs 1970-; Human Motivation Inst, consult 1969; OEO, manpower 1966-69; Cook Co OEO, dir 1965-66; Comm Youth Welfare, dir 1964-66; tchr 1956-64. **ORGANIZATIONS:** Mem Am Assn Retarded Persons 1973-75; Cerontological Soc 1975; Nat Coun Aging 1974-75; Nat Assn Soc Wrkrs; Nat Assn Comm Devel; Kappa Alpha Psi; Sigma Phi; Pi Kappa Delta; Urban League; NAACP; Shiloh Bapt Ch Mgmt Devel. **HONORS/ACHIEVEMENTS:** Award 1971; Comm Efford Orgn Cert Merit; achievement award Kappa Alpha Psi. **MILITARY SERVICE:** USAF 1st lt 1951-56. **BUSINESS ADDRESS:** 330 S Wells, Chicago, IL.

HAMILTON, RAYMOND
Attorney. **PERSONAL:** Born Dec 14, 1950, Hobbs, NM; married Helen Ann; children: Richard, Steven. **EDUCATION:** Univ of NM, BA 1972; Harvard Law School, JD 1975. **CAREER:** NM Attny Gen, asst 1976; NM Public Defender, asst 1977-78; private law practice, 1978-79; US Attny Office NM, asst attny 1980-. **ORGANIZATIONS:** Bd of dir Legal Aid Soc of Albuquerque 1978-; adj prof of law Univ of NM School of Law 1981-84; legal redress chmn NAACP 1986-; gen counsel, past presNM Black Lawyers Assoc. **HONORS/ACHIEVEMENTS:** Attny General's Cert of Award 1981; Outstanding Young Albuquerquean 1987. **HOME ADDRESS:** 4819 Royene NE, Albuquerque, NM 87110.

HAMILTON, RAYMOND L.
Professional athlete. **PERSONAL:** Born Jan 20, 1951, Omaha, NE; married Paula Kay; children: Kadar, Damon. **EDUCATION:** Univ of OK, BBA 1973; SuffolkUniv Boston, MPA 1977. **CAREER:** New England Patriots, defensive tackle, assistant defensive line coach. **ORGANIZATIONS:** Mem Charlestown Sav Bank; USTA Tennis Umpire; mem Alpha Phi Alpha. **HONORS/ACHIEVEMENTS:** Two time All Big 8 selection at Oklahoma; All-Big Eight player 1971, 1972; set team record for quarterback sacks 1973; Johnny Unitas winner 1977. **BUSINESS ADDRESS:** Asst Defensive Line Coach, New England Patriots, Schaefer Stadium, Rt 1, Foxboro, MA.

HAMILTON, RICHARD NATHANIEL
Business executive. **PERSONAL:** Born Dec 18, 1941, Dayton, OH; married Blanche Gurganus; children: Richard Andrea, Tarae Sonya, Shanna Elizabeth. **EDUCATION:** Howard U, 1977; Empire State Coll, 1979. **CAREER:** ECO Systems Industries Inc, pres 1977-; Nat Black Vet Orgn, exec dir 1976-77; Nat Center on Black Aged, exec dir 1975-76; Wash Tech Inst, dir of marketing & distrib 1973-75. **ORGANIZATIONS:** Mem DC C of C 1978; mem DC Bd of Trade 1979; bd pres Nat Black Vet Orgn 1978-; mem NAACP; planning com mem Manpowe Serv Planning Adv Council 1979-81. **MILITARY SERVICE:** AUS sgt 1960-65. **BUSINESS ADDRESS:** 2115 Bryant St NE, Washington, DC 20018.

HAMILTON, ROSS T.
Physician. **PERSONAL:** Born Jun 05, 1946, Yonkers, NY; married Toni Plaskett; children: Neil, Ross T, Tonisha. **EDUCATION:** Syracuse U, BA1968; Columbia U, MD 1972; ColumbiaUniv Internal Med, 1975; ColumbiaUniv Gastroenterology, 1977. **CAREER:** Pvt practice internal med gastroenterology; Columbia U, instr, asst clinical prof of medicine; disease control NYC, dir of professional rel; United Harlem Drug Fighters Inc, asst med dir; St Lukes Hosp attending physician; Harlem Hosp attending physician; Hosp for Joint Diseases; sponsor and medical dir Genesis. **ORGANIZATIONS:** Mem Nat Med Assn; mem Nat Assn of Postgrad Physicians; mem Med Soc of State of NY; mem Am Coll of Physicians; mem Manhattan Cental Med Soc; mem American Society for Gastrointestinal Endoscopy; mem American Gastroenterology Assoc; Deacon Abyssinian Baptist Church; mem NYS Bd of Regents; mem Bdof Managers Harlem YMCA. **HONORS/ACHIEVEMENTS:** Publ Esophageal TB a Case Report 1977. **BUSINESS ADDRESS:** 630 Lenox Ave, New York, NY 10037.

HAMILTON, SAMUEL CARTENIUS
Attorney. **PERSONAL:** Born Mar 29, 1936, Hope, AR; married Flora Elizabeth; children: Leslie Terrell, Sydne Carrigan; Patrice Alexan. **EDUCATION:** Philander Smith Coll, BS 1958; Howard U, JD 1970. **CAREER:** Roy M Ellis & Louise Eighnie Turner Gen Prac of Law Silver Spring MD, asso; Montgomery Co MD, asst states pros atty; Lilver Spring MD, pvt pract of law; Legal Aid Clinic US Dist Attys Off DC; Off of Chief Counsel Fed Highway Adminstrn Litigation Div, legal intern; Ft Detrick MD, res asst. **ORGANIZATIONS:** Mem MD State Bar Assn; Am Bar Assn; Nat Bar Assn; past pres Frederick Co Branch NAACP; vice pres MD State Conference Of NAACP Branches; co-chmn; Comm to Uphold State Pub Accomodationlaw; mem Prince Hall Masons; Kappa Alpha Psi Soc Frat; Phi Alpha Delta Legal Frat; mem bd of dir Comm Action Agency. **HONORS/ACHIEVEMENTS:** Frederick Co Award for Service & Leadership Student Bar Assn HowardUniv Sch of Law; Am Legion Outs Citizen Award; NAACP Outs Ser Award; Prince HallMasons Ser Award. **BUSINESS ADDRESS:** 8605 Cameron St, Silver Spring, MD 20910.

HAMILTON, THEOPHILUS ELLIOTT
Educational administrator. **PERSONAL:** Born Feb 06, 1923, Detroit, MI; married Fannie L; children: Millicent. **EDUCATION:** Eastern MI Coll, MusB 1955, MA 1962; Eastern MI Univ, Spec of Arts Degree in Leadership & School Admin 1967. **CAREER:** Pickford Public Schools, teacher, dir vocal & instumental music 1955-62; Highland Park Public Schools, vocal music teacher 1962-64, asst principal 1964-67; Eastern Michigan Univ, asst dir of personnel 1967-69, asst dir of career planning & placement center 1969-. **ORGANIZATIONS:** Past sec, treas, mem MI Coll & Univ Placement Assoc; admin appt, mem Eastern MI Univ Judicial Bd 1977-78; apptd mem Soc Ministry Comm MI Synod of the Luth Church of Amer 1977-78; assoc mem MI Assoc for School Admin; mem Great Lakes Assoc for Coll & Univ Placement, Coll & Univ Personnel Assoc, School Admin & Prin Assoc, Kappa Alpha Psi, Black Faculty & Staff Assoc at EMU; faculty adv Delta Nu Chap EMU; mem Ypsilanti Twp Plnng Comm; membd of dir Washtenaw Cty Black Caucus Comm, Washtenaw Cty Citizens Comm for Econ Oppty; chmn Ypsilanti Citizens Advising Comm for OEO; affirm action comm Ypsilanti Publ Schools. **HONORS/ACHIEVEMENTS:** Alumni Achievement Awd Kappa Alpha Psi 1974; Dedication & Serv to Comm Awd Kappa Alpha Phi; Best Teacher Awd EMU Personel. **MILITARY SERVICE:** AUS 1943-46. **BUSINESS ADDRESS:** Asst Dir Career Planning, Eastern MichiganUniv, Career Planning & Placement Cn, Ypsilanti, MI 48197.

HAMILTON, VIRGINIA
Author. **PERSONAL:** Born Mar 12, 1936, Yellow Springs, OH; daughter of Kenneth James Hamilton and Etta Belle Perry Hamilton; married Arnold Adoff, Mar 19, 1960; children: Leigh Hamilton, Jaime Levi. **EDUCATION:** Attended Antioch Coll, 1952-55, OH State Univ, 1957-58, and New School for Social Research. **CAREER:** Author of children's books: Zeely, Macmillan, 1967, The House of Dies Drear, Macmillan, 1968, The Planet of Junior Brown, Macmillan, 1971, M C Higgins, the Great, Macmillan, 1974, Paul Robeson, The Life & Times of a Free Black Man, Harper, 1974, Arilla Sun Down, Greenwillow, 1975, Justice & Her Brothers, Greenwillow, 1978, Dustland, Greenwillow, 1980, The Gathering, Greenwillow, 1980, Jahdu, Greenwillow, 1980, Sweet Whispers, Brother Rush, Philomet, 1982, The Magical Adventures of Pretty Pearl, Harper, 1983; A Little Love, Philomel, 1984, Junius Over Far, Harper, 1985, The People Could Fly: American Black Folktales, Knopf, 1985, The Mystery of Drear House, Greenwillow, 1987, A White Romance, Philomel, 1987. **HONORS/ACHIEVEMENTS:** Nancy Block Meml Award, Downtown Community School Awards Comm; The House of Dies Drear won the 1969 Edgar Allan Poe Award for Best Juvenile Mystery; Ohioana Literary Award, 1969; John Newbery Honor Book Award, 1971, for The Planet of Junior Brown; Lewis Carroll Shelf Award, Boston Globe-Horn Book Award, 1974, John Newbery Medal and Natl Book Award, both 1975, all for M C Higgins, the Great; John Newbery Honor Book Award, Coretta Scott King Award, Boston Globe-Horn Book Award, and Amer Book Award nomination, all 1983, all for Sweet Whispers, Brother Rush; Horn Book Fanfare Award in fiction, 1985, for A Little Love; Coretta Scott King Award, NY Times Best Illus Children's Book Award, and Horn Book Honor List selection, all 1986, all for The People Could Fly. **BUSINESS ADDRESS:** Virginia Hamilton, c/o Dorothy Markinko, McIntosh & Otis Inc, 475 Fifth Ave, New York, NY 10017. *

HAMILTON, WILBUR WYATT
Business executive. **PERSONAL:** Born Jan 28, 1931, San Antonio, TX; married Joy Coleman. **EDUCATION:** Trinity Jall Sem, DD; Simpson Bible Coll, BTh; San Francisco City Coll, AA; Golden Gate U. **CAREER:** San Fran Hous Auth, acting exec dir; San Fran Redevel Agy, exec dir 1977-, dep exec dir 1974-77, asst exec dir for adm 1971-74, area dir 1969-71; Am Pres Line, trmnl chf 1965-69. **ORGANIZATIONS:** Sec San Fran Intrdenom Minstrl Allnc; judge field fclty CORO Found; pres No CA Regn NAHRO; pres Pacific SW Regn NAHRO; dir yth serv No CA Ch of God in Christ; past agency commr San Fran Redevel Agy; NAACP; exec counc Am Arbtrn Assn; Intl Lngshrmn/Wrhsmn Union; pastor Hamilton Meml COGIC San Fran; mem St Mary's Hosp Comm Bd; bd trstUniv HS. **HONORS/ACHIEVEMENTS:** Cert of dist Bd of Supvr City & Co of San Fran; chrchmn of yr Nat Conf of Ch of God in Christ; outst grad acad achvmnt Ch of God in Christ Internat. **BUSINESS ADDRESS:** San Francisco Housing Authorit, 440 Turk, San Francisco, CA 94103.

HAMILTON, WILLIAM NATHAN
Attorney. **PERSONAL:** Born Dec 09, 1926, New Haven, CT; married Maelorie Delores; children: Mark, Lori. **EDUCATION:** h. **CAREER:** Self-employed atty 1955-. **ORGANIZATIONS:** Mem CT Bar Assn; Bd of GovUniv of New Haven; bd mem Dixwell Plaza Brnch New Haven Nat Bank; past vice pres CT Credit Union Leag; pres CT Credit Union Leag 1969-71. **MILITARY SERVICE:** AUS 1945-46. **BUSINESS ADDRESS:** 152 Temple St, New Haven, CT 06510.

HAMILTON-RAHI, LYNDA DARLENE
Public administrator. **PERSONAL:** Born Oct 22, 1950, Chicago, IL; daughter of Leonard O Hamilton and Mabel C Clenna' Hamilton; divorced; children: Mumtaza, Toshmika, Courtney Lyons. **EDUCATION:** Univ of Hawaii, Honolulu HI, 1968-71; Univ of Cincinnati, Cincinnati OH, BS, MPA, 1976; Woodrow Wilson Coll of Law, Atlanta GA, 1979-81. **CAREER:** City of Cincinnati, Cincinnati OH, program mgr, 1976; Riviera Beach Hsq Authority, Riviera Beach FL, exec dir, 1976-77; City of Marietta, Marietta GA, planner, 1977; Butler Co CAC, Hamilton OH, exec dir, 1977-78; City of Marietta, Marietta GA, planning admin, 1979-83; City of Phoenix, Phoenix AZ, mgmt asst, 1983-, program mgr, 1988-. **ORGANIZATIONS:** Bd mem, Community Serv Bd, 1978; regional coord, Women's Division, Amer Planning Assn, 1981-83; pres, founder, Conf of Minority Public Admin, Arizona Chapter; comm mem, Intl City Mgmt Assn; bd mem, Arizona Governor's 20th Year Civil Rights, 1984; chair, Phoenix Child Care Task Force, 1984, Phoenix Minority Devel Working Comm, 1985; mem, Phoenix Women's Issue Comm, 1985-87; pres, Amer Soc for Public Admin, Arizona Chapter, 1988-89, bd mem, 1989-90. **HONORS/ACHIEVEMENTS:** Talent Show Judge, Marietta Parks Dept, 1980; Outstanding Young Woman of Amer, 1986; Rideshare Coord of the Year, Rapid Public Transit Authority, 1988; Leaderhsip, Amer Soc for Public Admin, 1988. **BUSINESS ADDRESS:** Program Manager, City of Phoenix, Community & Economic Development, One N 1st St, 7th Floor, Phoenix, AZ 85004.

HAMLAR, PORTIA Y. T.
Attorney. **PERSONAL:** Born Apr 30, 1932, Montgomery, AL; children: 1 child. **EDUCATION:** AL State Univ, BA 1951; MI State Univ, MA 1953; Univ of Detroit School of Law, JD 1972; Univ of MI, Wayne State Univ, Post Grad Studies. **CAREER:** Univ of MI; acad counselor 1957-58; Pontiac HS, vocal music instr 1963-65; Hyman Gurwin Nachman & Friedman, legal sec 1966-68; MI Appellate Defender Detroit, legal rschr 1971-73; Amer Bar Assoc Lawyers for Housing Prog LA, admin asst 1973; Gr Watts Model Cities Housing Corp LA, legal counsel 1973; Chrysler Corp, atty; DE Law School of Widener Univ, asst prof of law 1980-82; MI State Bar Atty Grievence Commiss, assoc counsel 1982-. **ORGANIZATIONS:** Organist, choir dir St Andrews Presby Church 1955-72; vocal music instr Detroit Pub Schools 1953-71; adj prof law Univ of Detroit School of Law; org Resources Counselors Occupational Safety & Health Lawyers Group bd of ed Hazardous Matls Mgmt Jrnl; mem MI State Bar, Detroit Bar Assoc, Delta Sigma Theta, Kappa Beta Pi, Alpha Kappa Mu, Mu Phi Epsilon; law review staff Univ of Detroit 1970-72; mem literature & rsch Amer Bar Assoc Com on Real Prop Law 1971-72; mem ABA Com on OSHA Law 1978-. **HONORS/ACHIEVEMENTS:** Publs "Landlord & Tenant" 1971, "HUD's Authority to Mandate Effective Mgmt of Pub Housing" 1972; "Defending the Employer in OSHA Contests" 1977, "Minority Tokanism in Amer Law Schools" 1983.

HAMLET, JAMES FRANK
Retired army major general. **PERSONAL:** Born Dec 13, 1921, Alliance, OH; son of Frank Hamlet and Rhoda Hamlet. **EDUCATION:** Tuskegee Univ; St Benedict's Coll; US Army Command & General Staff Coll; US Army War Coll. **CAREER:** Joint Spl Operations & Spl Weapons Div Ft Leavenworth, project officer later doctrinal devel officer 1963-66; 11th Aviation Group 1st Cavalry Div Vietnam, operations officer 1966; 227th Aviation Battalion, commanding officer later exec officer 1966-67; Doctrine & Systems Div Ft Leavenworth, chief airmobility br 1968-69; 11th Aviation Group 1st Cavalry Div Vietnam, commanding officer 1970-71; 101st Airborn Div Vietnam, asst div comdr 1971; 3rd Brigade, 1st Cavalry Div, Vietnam, commanding genl 1971-72; 4th Infantry Div Ft Carson, commanding genl 1972-74; US Army Headquarters, Washington DC, deputy the inspector general, 1974-81; retired, 1981. **ORGANIZATIONS:** Bd dirs Wall St Petroleum Co; bd trustees Rider Coll; bd commnrs Trenton City Museum; pres Officers & Non-Comm Officers Retiree Counsel at Ft Dix NJ; commissioner, Trenton City Museum; bd of dirs, Mercer Medical Center; commissioner, Mercer County Community Coll; mem, Governor's Aviation Educ Advisory Council; trustee, AUSA; chmn, steering comm, Trenton YMCA; mem, First Cavalry Div Assn, Fourth Infantry Div Assn, 366th Infantry Veterans Assn. **HONORS/ACHIEVEMENTS:** Distinguished Serv Medal (w/ Oak Leaf Cluster); Legion of Merit (w/2 Oak Leaf Clusters); Distinguished Flying Cross; Soldier's Medal; Bronze Star (w/Oak Leaf Cluster); Air Medal (49 awards); Army Commendation Medal (w/3 Oak Leaf Clusters); Combat Infantryman Badge; Parachutist Badge; Master Army Aviator Badge; Army Aviation Hall of Fame; US Army Infantry Hall of Fame; Toastmaster's Intl. **MILITARY SERVICE:** US Army, major general, 1942-81.

HAMLIN, ALBERT T.
Attorney. **PERSONAL:** Born Jun 06, 1926, Raleigh, NC; married Jacqueline Peoples; children: Alan C. **EDUCATION:** Shaw U, BS 1944; Howard U, JD with honors 1956. **CAREER:** Office for Civil Rights Chief Counsel, dir 1977-80; hew Civil Rights Div; Gen Coun for Litigation, dep asst 1966-72; US Dept of Just, exec gbr & leg liaison 1965-66; Off of Alien Prop, chief of litigation 1963-65; Settlement of Societe Internationale Pour Participations Industrielles et Commerciales SA (Interhande IG Chemit vs Kennedy), gov coun; Gen Aniline & Film Corp, sale of Gov's 11,166,438 shares of stock 1963-65; Reeves Robinson Rosenberg Duncan & Hamlin, Ptnr 1960-63; US Dept of Just, tri atty 1956-60. **ORGANIZATIONS:** Mem NAACP Legal Redress Com 1960-63; co-fndr Asst Ed HowardUniv Law Journal; mem Urban Problems Com; Fed Bar Assn. **HONORS/ACHIEVEMENTS:** Outstndg Stud Award Howard Law Sch 1953; Outstndg Atty Award US Dept of Just 1965. **MILITARY SERVICE:** USN 1944-46.

HAMLIN, ARTHUR HENRY
Educator. **PERSONAL:** Born Jan 04, 1942, Bastrop, LA; son of Elmore Hamlin and Augustine Hamlin; married Deloris E; children: Eric, Erica. **EDUCATION:** Grambling State Univ, BS 1965; Northeast LA Univ, Master 1970, 30 Plus 1975. **CAREER:** CTA, business oper 1966-67; City of Bastrop, gym super 1973-76; City of Bastrop, councilman 1977-; Morehouse Parish Sch Bd, teacher-coach 1966-; Morehouse Parish Drug Free Schools and Communities, coordinator. **ORGANIZATIONS:** Oper Greenview Club 1971-72; past pres Morehouse Comm Improv Org 1973; past pres Morehouse Concerned Citizens 1979; past secretary Club 21 1981; mem Gents Civic & Social Club. **HOME ADDRESS:** 2302 Bonnie Ave, Bastrop, LA 71220.

HAMMETT, WILLIE ANDERSON
Educator. **PERSONAL:** Born Apr 19, 1945, Sumerton, SC; children: Jamal. **EDUCATION:** Hudson Valley Comm Coll, AAS 1966; WV State Coll, BS 1968; SUNY Albany, MS 1971, EdS 1977. **CAREER:** Troy School System, guidance counselor 1969-71, basketball coach 1969-71; Hudson Valley Comm Coll, counselor 1971-72, asst basketball coach 1971-72, dir educ opportunity program 1972, vice pres student serv 1972-. **ORGANIZATIONS:** Bd of dir Camp Fire Girls 1969-72; vice pres Troy Jaycees 1969-72; pres NA-MAL Enterprises Inc 1977-79; mem Council on Black Amer Affairs 1977-; bd of trustees Troy YWCA Troy NY 1972-; bd of dir Samaritan Hosp Troy NY 1978-; vchairperson, exec bd NY State Spec Prog Personnel Assoc 1979-. **HONORS/ACHIEVEMENTS:** Listed in Outstanding Young Men of Amer 1972. **BUSINESS ADDRESS:** Vice President Student Serv, Hudson Valley Comm College, 80 & Vandenburgh Ave, Troy, NY 12180.

HAMMOCK, EDWARD R.
Government official. **PERSONAL:** Born Apr 20, 1938, Bronx, NY; married Jeanne Marshall; children: Erica, Rochelle, Regina. **EDUCATION:** Brooklyn Coll, BA 1959; St John'sUniv Law Sch, LLB 1966. **CAREER:** NY State Parole Bd, chief exec ofcr/chmn for the div of parole 1976-; NY City Dept of Investigation, dep commr 1973-76; Dept of Law NY State Criminal Investigation Attica Prison Riot, spec asst atty gen 1971-73; Daytop Village Inc, exec dir 1969-72; NY Co Homicide Bur, asst dist atty 1966-69; Supreme Ct Kings Co, probation officer 1963-66; Youth Council Bur, caseworker 1960-63; St John's Univ Sch of Law, adj prof; Nat Inst on Drug Abuse, spec cons; Proj Return Inc, bd dir. **ORGANIZATIONS:** 100 Black Men; NY Co Lawyers Assn; NY State Bar Assn; pres Student Bar Assn St John'sUniv Sch of Law. **BUSINESS ADDRESS:** 1450 Western Ave, Albany, NY 12203.

HAMMOND, BENJAMIN F.
Educational scientist. **PERSONAL:** Born Feb 28, 1934, Austin, TX; son of Dr. Virgil T Hammond. **EDUCATION:** Univ of KS, BA 1950-54; Meharry Med Coll, DDS 1954-58; Univ of PA, PhD 1958-62. **CAREER:** Univ of PA School Dental Med, inst micro 1958, asst prof micro 1962-65, assoc prof micro 1965-70, prof micro 1970-, chmn of dept 1972-, assoc dean for acad affairs 1984-. **ORGANIZATIONS:** Com mem Philadelphia Clg of Art, Museum of Art of Philadelphia; invited stockholder Athenaeum of Philadelphia; American Assoc for Dental Research vice pres 1977, pres 1978-79. **HONORS/ACHIEVEMENTS:** EH Hatton Intrntl Assc for Dental Rsrch 1959; Lindback Awrd Distngshd Tchng at theUniv of PA 1969; Medaille D'Argent City of Paris France 1976; Pres LectureUniv of PA 1981; R Metcalf Chair-Distinguished Visiting Prof Marquette Univ 1986; Dean's Lecture Northwestern Univ Med Ctr 1987. **BUSINESS ADDRESS:** Professor of Microbiology, Univ of Pennsylvania, School Dental Medicine, 4001 Spruce St, Philadelphia, PA 19174.

HAMMOND, DEBRA LAUREN
Educator. **PERSONAL:** Born Jan 15, 1957, Plainfield, NJ. **EDUCATION:** Rutgers Univ, BA 1979. **CAREER:** Cook College-Rutgers Univ, asst to the dean minority affairs 1980, instructor educational opportunity fund 1980-84, asst dir Cook Campus Ctr 1980-82, asst dean of students, dir Cook Campus Ctr 1982-. **ORGANIZATIONS:** Co-founder public relations officer 1975 Scholarship Committee 1976-82; mem Natl Assn for Campus Activities 1981-; chairperson mem Educ Oppor Fund Comm Adv Bd Cook College 1981-; mem Young Women's Christian Assn 1981-; sec bd of dirs Ensemble Theatre Co 1982-84; mem Natl Assn for Executive Females 1982-; educ comm conference comm 1985, 86; committee on minority programs coord Assoc of Coll Unions Intl 1986. **HONORS/ACHIEVEMENTS:** Paul Robeson Outstanding Faculty/Staff Awd Students Afro-Amer Soc Rutgers Univ 1982; Outstanding Young Women of Amer Outstanding Americans 1982, 83; Outstanding Faculty/Administrator Awd Natl Assocs of Negro Business & Professional Women's Club Beta Psi Chap 1983. **HOME ADDRESS:** CPO 82, Cook College, New Brunswick, NJ 08903. **BUSINESS ADDRESS:** Asst Dean of Students, Cook College-RutgersUniv, Cook Campus Ctr, Biel Road, New Brunswick, NJ 08903.

HAMMOND, JAMES A.
Executive. **PERSONAL:** Born Nov 11, 1929, Tampa, FL; son of William and Lucile; married Evelyne L Murrell; children: Kevin, Gary, Lisa. **EDUCATION:** Hampton University BS Inds Voc Ed 1951; US Command & General Staff Coll, 1971; Inds Clgof the Armed Forces, 1974. **CAREER:** Hammond Elect Contracting Inc, pres 1951-65; Comm of Comm Rltns City of Tampa, admn dept head 1965-70; AL Nellum & Assc Inc, vice pres 1969-73; Impact Assc Inc, pres 1972-74; Walter Industries, Inc. dir eo progs 1974-; Impac Communications Inc, pres & ceo 1983-. **ORGANIZATIONS:** Dir Comm Fed Savings & Loan Assn 1967-; Tampa Urban League 1967; Am Assc for Affirmative Action 1977-81; mem Kappa Alpha Psi Fraternity; chmn City Civil Serv Bd 1980-87; mem NAACP; Commsn on Access to Legal Syst 1984; Commissioner, Unemployment Appeals Commission-State of Florida. **HONORS/ACHIEVEMENTS:** The Governor Award State of FL 1967; Outstanding Alumnus Hampton Inst 1971; Whitney Young Awrd Tampa Urban League 1978. **MILITARY SERVICE:** AUS lt col; Distinguished Serv 1951-79. **BUSINESS ADDRESS:** Dir of Equal Opportunity Programs, Walter Industries Inc., P.O. Box 31601, Tampa, FL 33631.

HAMMOND, JAMES MATTHEW
Educator. **PERSONAL:** Born Jul 10, 1930, Keanansville, NC; married Carol Howard;

children: Endea Renee, Renata Melleri, Rona Meiata, James Matthew Jr. **EDUCATION:** Oakwood Coll, BA 1953; SC State Coll, MSc 1960; Catholic Univ of Amer, MA 1975; Friendship Coll, DDiv 1963; S IL Univ, PhD 1973. **CAREER:** Atkins HS, guidance counselor 1960-61; Sci Dept Bekwai Teachers Coll, chair 1961-68; Seventh Day Adventist Church of Sierra Leone, pres 1968-70; SDA Church of North Ghana, exec dir 1972-74; Metro Family Life Council, mem 1979; Pan African Develop Coop, bd mem 1981; MD Psychological Assoc, mem 1982-; Columbia Union Coll, chair/prof of psychology. **ORGANIZATIONS:** Mem Metro Family Life Council 1979; bd mem Pan African Develop Coop 1981; mem MD Psychological Assoc 1982; chaplain (maj) Civil Air Patrol 1983. **HONORS/ACHIEVEMENTS:** UNESCO Fellow United Nations Organs 1972; Phi Delta Kappa mem SIU Chap 1972. **HOME ADDRESS:** 3200 Fullerton St, Beltsville, MD 20705. **BUSINESS ADDRESS:** Chair/Prof of Psychology, Columbia Union College, 7600 Flower Ave, Takoma Park, MD 20912.

HAMMOND, KENNETH RAY
Educational administrator, clergy. **PERSONAL:** Born Jul 28, 1951, Winterville, NC; son of Rev. and Mrs. Hoyt Hammond; married Evelyn Patrick; children: Kennetta, Brandon. **EDUCATION:** East Carolina Univ, BA History 1973, MAEd Counselor Ed 1983, CAS Counselor Ed 1985; Shaw Univ, M Divinity 1978; NC State Univ, ABD 1986-. **CAREER:** Mendenhall Student Ctr ECU, asst prog dir 1973-74; Cedar Grove Baptist Church, pastor 1974-79; Mt Shiloh Baptist Church, pastor 1980-; East Carolina Univ Mendenhall Student Ctr, prog dir 1974-85; East Carolina Univ, asst dir university unions 1985-; East Carolina Univ, assoc dir of Univ Unions and Student Activities. **ORGANIZATIONS:** Chmn Pitt Co Adolescent Sexuality Task Force 1979-81; mem Alpha Phi Theta Honor Hist Soc 1972-; mem Assn of College Unions Intl 1973-; mem Natl Assn for Campus Activities 1973-; mem Natl Baptist Convention 1975-; mem bd of dirs Pitt Co Arts Council 1984-; mem NC Assoc for Counseling & Development 1985-; mem Alpha Phi Alpha Fraternity 1971-; NC Coll Personnel Assn 1986; Amer Assoc for Counseling and Development 1987; Amer Coll Personnel Assn 1987. **HONORS/ACHIEVEMENTS:** Coach of the Year Eastern Carolina Conf 1973; Joint Council on Health & Citizenship DSA 1979; mem Phi Alpha Theta Honor History Soc 1972-; Alpha Phi Alpha ML King Jr Community Service Award 1986; The Honor Society of Phi Kappa Phi 1988. **HOME ADDRESS:** 111 Ravenwood Dr, Greenville, NC 27834. **BUSINESS ADDRESS:** Assoc Dir University Unions, East CarolinaUniv, Mendenhall Student Center, Greenville, NC 27858-4353.

HAMMOND, KENNETH T.
Architect. **PERSONAL:** Born Mar 25, 1926, Providence; children: 2 Children. **EDUCATION:** Howard U, BA 1955. **CAREER:** Pvt draftsman 1955-63; Redevelopment Land Agency DC, sr rehabilitation architect 1963-69; pvt practice 1960-; DC Zoning Commn Office, deputy dir 1969-. **ORGANIZATIONS:** Mem Am Inst Architects; Nat Assn Housing Devel; Nat Tech Assn; mem HowardUniv Archit Alumni Assn; Wash Bldg Congress; DC Bd Appeals & Review. **HONORS/ACHIEVEMENTS:** Outstanding performance rating DC Govt 1973; licensed archt DC, MD, MA. **MILITARY SERVICE:** AUS 1944-46; USAF capt 1950-53. **BUSINESS ADDRESS:** 1329 E St, Rm 600 NW, Washington, DC 20004.

HAMMOND, MELVIN ALAN RAY, JR.
Dentist. **PERSONAL:** Born Feb 06, 1949, Austin, TX; children: Melvin AR III. **EDUCATION:** Huston-Tillotson Coll, BS 1971; Howard Univ Coll of Dentistry, DDS (w/Honors) 1981. **CAREER:** Harris Co Hosp Dist, staff dentist 1981-83; Private Practice, dentist 1981-. **ORGANIZATIONS:** Vice pres Charles A George Dental Soc 1984 & 85; pres elect Gulf States Dental Assoc 1986-; mem Amer, TX and Natl Dental Assocs, Houston Dist Dental Soc, Gulf States Dental Assoc, Charles A George Dental Soc. **HONORS/ACHIEVEMENTS:** Mem Omega Psi Phi Frat Rho Beta Beta 1976-; Outstanding Young Men of Amer 1982; Estelle Coffey Young Memorial Awd; Robert Hardy Jr Memorial Awd. **BUSINESS ADDRESS:** Dentist, 1213 Herman Dr, Ste 840, Houston, TX 77004.

HAMMOND, ULYSSES S., JR.
Manager/treasurer. **PERSONAL:** Born Jun 16, 1919, Calvert, TX; married Florida M. **EDUCATION:** Huston-Tillofson Coll, BA 1941; Schiff Sch for Scout Execs, grad 1946. **CAREER:** Tyler, dist scout exec 1946-58; Tyler, field dir 1958-71; Dallas, 1971-; St John Fed Credit Union, manager/treasurer. **ORGANIZATIONS:** Faculty mem Butler Coll 1948-68; pres St John Fed Credit Union 1972-74; bd dirs Downtown Kiwanis Club 1973-74; mem Dallas County Selective Serv Bd 1972-74; basileus Theta Alpha Cpht Omega Psi Phi 1972-74; Theta Alpha Chap 1974. **HONORS/ACHIEVEMENTS:** Omega Man of Yr SW Region 1964. **MILITARY SERVICE:** AUS sgt 1941-46. **BUSINESS ADDRESS:** Manager/Treasurer, St John Fed Credit Union, 2600 S Marsalis, Dallas, TX 75216.

HAMMOND, W. RODNEY
Psychologist educator. **PERSONAL:** Born Jan 12, 1946, Hampton, VA; son of William R Hammond, Sr and Mildred R Looper Hammond; married Andrita J Topps; children: William Rodney III. **EDUCATION:** Univ of IL Champaign/Urbana, BS 1968; FL State U, MS 1970, PhD 1974. **CAREER:** FL State U, instr 1973; Univ of TN, asst prof Psychology 1974-76; Meharry Med Clg CMHC, asst prof Psychiatry 1976-83, dir chldrns serv 1976-83; Wright State Univ, assoc prof and asst Dean School of Professional Psychology. **ORGANIZATIONS:** Mem Amer Psyclgl Assoc 1975-; pres TN Behavior Therapy Assoc 1980-81; cnlsltn Natl Center on Child Abuse 1980; full partner Univ Psycholoical Serv Assoc Inc 1984-; bd chmn Cnty Bd of Mental Retardation 1988; mem Ohio Developmental Disabilities Planning Council 1986-; bd of dirs Amer Assoc of Gifted Children 1986; bd of professional affairs Amer Psychological Assoc 1988-90; chmn Montgomery County Bd of Mental Retardation, 1989-. **HONORS/ACHIEVEMENTS:** "100 Outstanding Seniors", Univ of IL at Champaign/Urbana, 1968; Pub Health Sr. Fellow, Natl Inst of Mental Health, 1968-70; Grant Child Youth & Family Serv, NIMH, 1976-82; Grant Matl Center on Child Abuse & Neglect, 1981-83; President's Awd for Outstanding Contribution in Teaching Research and Serv, Wright State Univ, 1986. **HOME ADDRESS:** 2046 Harvard Blvd, Dayton, OH 45406. **BUSINESS ADDRESS:** Assoc Prof of Psychology, Sch of Psychology, Wright StateUniv, Dayton, OH 45435.

HAMMONDS, ALFRED
Business executive. **PERSONAL:** Born Feb 06, 1937, Gary, IN; married Pearlena J Donaldson; children: Alfred, Jr, Danelle J. **EDUCATION:** Bus Coll Hammond IN, cert accounting 1963; Am Inst Banking, 1968. **CAREER:** Gary Nat Bank, baker asst vice pres & branch mgr 1963-. **ORGANIZATIONS:** Mem Am Inst Banking; pres Gary Frontiers Serv Club; vice pres Urban League; bd US Selective Serv Bd #44. **HONORS/ACHIEVEMENTS:** 1st Black salesman HC Lyttons & Co Gary 1961-63. **MILITARY SERVICE:** USAF 1955-59. **BUSINESS ADDRESS:** Gary Natl Bank, 1710 Broadway, Gary, IN 46407.

HAMPTON, DELON
Engineering, architectural, planning & design company executive. **PERSONAL:** Born Aug 23, 1933, Jefferson, TX; son of Uless Hampton and Elizabeth Lewis Hampton; divorced. **EDUCATION:** Univ of Illinois, Urbana IL, BSCE, 1954; Purdue Univ, West Lafayette IN, MSCE, 1958, PhD, 1961. **CAREER:** Consulting activities, 1961-; Kansas State Univ, asst prof, 1961-64; Eric H Wang Civil Engineering Research Facility, assoc research engineer, 1962-63; IIT Research Inst, sr research engineer, 1964-68; Howard Univ, Washington DC, prof of civil engineering, 1968-85; Gnaedinger, Banker, Hampton & Assoc, pres, 1972-74. **ORGANIZATIONS:** Vice pres, Housing and Public Facilities, Montgomery County Chamber of Commerce, 1983-85; pres, Amer Soc of Civil Engineers, Natl Capital Section, 1984-85; bd of dir, Amer Public Transit Assn, 1985-86, 1987-89; chmn, exec comm, Amer Soc of Civil Engineers, Engineering Mgmt Div, 1985-89; mem, Transportation Coordinating Comm, Greater Washington Bd of Trade; mem, bd of dir, Washington DC Chamber of Commerce, 1985-86; vice pres, Amer Consulting Engineers Council, 1987-89; mem, President's Forum, Montgomery Coll Found, 1987-. **HONORS/ACHIEVEMENTS:** Featured in Philadelphia Electric Co's permanent exhibit of 24 outstanding black engineers from 1862-; Edmund Friedman Professional Recognition Award, Amer Soc of Civil Engineers, 1988; Theodore R Hagans Jr Memorial Achievement Award, Outstanding Business Man of the Year, Govt of the Dist of Columbia, Office of Human Rights, 1988; Award for Outstanding Contributions in the Field of Engineering, Los Angles Council of Black Consulting Engineers; author, co-author of over 40 publications. **MILITARY SERVICE:** US Army, sp2, 1955-57; US Naval Reserve, lieutenant, 1967-72. **BUSINESS ADDRESS:** President, Delon Hampton & Associates, Chartered, 111 Massachusetts Ave NW, Suite 400, Washington, DC 20001.

HAMPTON, EDWIN HARRELL
Musician, educator. **PERSONAL:** Born Feb 05, 1928, Jacksonville, TX; son of Joe Hampton and Lela Barnett; married Rosaline, Jun 01, 1951. **EDUCATION:** Xavier Univ, Grad 1952; Northwestern Univ, Vandercook Coll, further study. **CAREER:** St Augustine HS, band dir 1952-. **ORGANIZATIONS:** Mem LMEA, NCBA, NBA, Musicians Union Local, Alpha Phi Omega, Phi Beta Mu; leader Royal Dukes of Rhythm Band; mem 33rd Army Band 1940; Lay Advisory Board, Josephite Fathers, 1987-; Mayors Advisory Board Mardi Gras, 1986-. **HONORS/ACHIEVEMENTS:** Dand Director of the Year, Louisiana, 1967; Key to City, New Orleans, 1969; Doctor of Humane Letters, Baptist Christian College 1988. **MILITARY SERVICE:** Med Corps sgt 1946-49. **BUSINESS ADDRESS:** Band Dir, St Augustine HS, 2600 A.P. Tureaud Avenue, New Orleans, LA 70119.

HAMPTON, ELWOOD
Association executive, city official. **PERSONAL:** Born Nov 07, 1924, Philadelphia. **EDUCATION:** Cloucester Co Comm Coll; Baltimore Comm Coll; Cornell U. **CAREER:** Nat Maritime Union Am AFL-CIO, union ofcl region rep 1966-; Paulsboro NY, mayor 1974-. **ORGANIZATIONS:** DeHugo Consistory #2; 32 Degree; Greater Paulsboro Dodge #575; Tuscan Lodge #49; Paulsboro Lions Club; Gloucester Co Devel Council; Gloucester Co Animal Shelter; George Patton Jr VFW Post #678 Paulsboro; trustee 2nd Bapt Ch; NAACP. **HONORS/ACHIEVEMENTS:** Man of Yr Award Gloucester 1974; hon citizenship award VFW Post #678; 1974. **MILITARY SERVICE:** USCG 1942-46; US merchantmarine 1946-66. **BUSINESS ADDRESS:** 346 W 17 St, New York, NY 10011.

HAMPTON, FRANK, SR.
Business executive, city official. **PERSONAL:** Born Jan 02, 1923, Jacksonville; married Willa D Wells; children: Frank, Jr. **EDUCATION:** Edward Waters Coll, 3 1/2 yrs. **CAREER:** Hampton's Gulf Serv Stn, owner, oper; Hampton's Fuel Oil; Hampton Villa Apts; H & L Adv & Pub Rel; councilman 8th Dist. **ORGANIZATIONS:** Chmn, trust bd Mt Ararat Bapt Ch; pres Duval Co Citizens Bene Corp Char Org; 1st vice pres Donkey Club of Jacksonville; chmn Youth Adv Com ARC; Gov Coun on Crim Just; mem Gator Bowl Assn; NAACP; YMCA; Jacksonville C of C; Boy Scouts of Am; commnr Civil Liberites Elks Lodge IBPOE of W. **HONORS/ACHIEVEMENTS:** Lead the fight for 1st black pol officers 1950; FL's 1st black beverage supr 1953; desegregated Jacksonville's golf courses 1958; filed Omnibus Suit in Fed Ct which desegregated all mun rec facil 1960; placed blacks in city & state offices 1961; apptd by Gulf Oil to vis Africa Angola to invest discrim pract in jobs salary & liv conds; spon Open Golf Tournament annu allproceeds going to indigent familes; Who's Who in FL 1973-74; num awards for outstndg serv to comm. **MILITARY SERVICE:** AUS WWII 1943-45. **BUSINESS ADDRESS:** 3190 W Edgewood Ave, Jacksonville, FL.

HAMPTON, GRACE
Educator. **PERSONAL:** Born Oct 23, 1937, Courtland, AL. **EDUCATION:** Art Inst Chicago, BAE 1961; IL State U, MS 1968; AZ State U, PhD Dec 1976. **CAREER:** IL State Univ, prof Art Educ; Northern IL Univ; School Art Inst Chicago; CA State Univ Sacramento; Univ of OR. **ORGANIZATIONS:** Mem Nat Art Educ Assn; Nat Conf of Black Artist; Artist-in-residence Hayden House Phoenix; presented papes local & natl conferences; del Festac 1977. **BUSINESS ADDRESS:** Art Dept CA State Univ, Sacramento, CA.

HAMPTON, LEROY
Business executive. **PERSONAL:** Born Apr 20, 1927, Ingalls, AR; married Anne; children: Cedric, Candice. **EDUCATION:** Univ of CO, BS pharmacy 1950; Denver U, MS chem 1960. **CAREER:** Dow Chem Co Midland MI, mgr issue analysis; analyzes fed & state legis regulatory & other issues as related to health & environment; held positions of devel chemist, devl leader, recruiting mrg, mgr, EEO; Dow Chm Co, 24 yrs promoted to present position 1975. **ORGANIZATIONS:** Mem Am Chem Soc Midland Kiwanis Club; mem Presb Ch.

HAMPTON, LIONEL LEO
Musician. **PERSONAL:** Born Apr 12, Louisville, KY. **EDUCATION:** Univ So CA, studied 1934; Allen Univ, Mus D (hon) 1975; Pepperdine Coll, Mus D (hon); Xavier Univ, PhD Mus (hon) 1975; Howard Univ, PhD Mus (hon) 1979; USC, PhD Music 1982; State Univ of NY, PhD (hon) 1981; Glassboro State Coll, PhD Music 1981; Daniel Hale Williams

Univ, Univ of Liege Belgium, PhD. **CAREER:** Benny Goodman Quartet, mem 1936-40; Lionel Hampton Orch, organ/dir 1970-; composer conductor entertainer; broke segregation barrier when joined Goodman quartet; recorded with Dizzy Gillespie, Ben Webster, Coleman Hawkins and others; Hampbon Band grads include Quincy Jones, Dexter Gordon, Cat Anderson, Ernie Royal, Joe Newman, Charles Mingus, Wes Montgomery, Fats Naverro, Art Farmer, Joe Williams, Dinah Washington. **ORGANIZATIONS:** Chmn bd Glad Hamp Records Glad Hamp Music Pub Co; Swing & Tempo Music Pub Co Lionel Hampton Development Group; Lionel & Gladys Hampton Found; Lionel Hampton Eng; 33rd Degree Mason Imperial Dir of Band; goodwill ambassador for Imperial Shriners; Friars Club; mem Alpha Phi Alpha; grand band master Elks; New York City Culture Com; Lionel Hampton Jazz Endowment Fund; Human Rights Commnr City of New York; chmn New York Republicans for Reagan/Bush; mem Eagles; launches "Who's Who in Jazz" series with artists like Woody Herman, Earl Hines, Dexter Gordon, etc 1982. **HONORS/ACHIEVEMENTS:** Papel Medal from Pope Paul VI; Key to City of New York/LA/Chicago/Detroit; New York City Highest Culture Award Geo Frederick Handel 1966; Appeared London Jazz Expo/Newport Jazz Festival/Carnegie Hall/Town Hall/Avery Fischer Hall; toured Europe/Japan/Africa/Australia/Middle East; compositions, "Hamp's Boogie Woogie", "Airmail Special", "Flyin Home"; films, "Pennies From Heaven", "A Song is Born", "The Benny Goodman Story"; saluted at White House by Pres & Mrs R Reagan 1982; Best Rock Instrumental Performance for Vibramatic 1984; Performance by a Big Band for Ambassador at Large 1985; Performance by a Big Band for Sentimental Journey Atlantic 1986; Lionel Hampton Sch of Music established at Univ of ID 1987.

HAMPTON, MICHAEL EUGENE
Manager. **PERSONAL:** Born Feb 17, 1955, Nashville, TN. **EDUCATION:** Fisk U, BS 1976; Rutgers U, MBA 1979. **CAREER:** Meharry Med Coll, bus mgr 1980-; Fisk U, instr 1979-80; Polytech Inc, economist 1979-80; Hampton Supply Co, pres; consult to various business ventures; Rutgers Bus Devel Cntr, intrnat trade analysist 1977-79. **ORGANIZATIONS:** Mem Nashville Area C of C; mem Big Bros of Am; mem Assn of Am Med Colls; mem Assn of MBA Execs; mem Am Mgmt Assn; mem Nat Assn of Financial Planners; bd of adv N Nas Community Counc 1980; Kappa Alpha Psi Franternity 1974. **HONORS/ACHIEVEMENTS:** 4 yr football scholarship FiskUniv 1972-76; Outst MBA Cand Black Enterprise 1979; Outstanding Man of Yr Nat Jaycees 1980. **BUSINESS ADDRESS:** Sch of Med, Meharry Medical Coll, Nashville, TN.

HAMPTON, OPAL JEWELL
Educator. **PERSONAL:** Born Jul 04, 1942, Kansas City, KS; daughter of W A Blair and Mary Overton Blair; divorced; children: Kenton B Hampton. **EDUCATION:** Emporia State Univ, Emporia KS, BSE, 1966; Asuza Pacific Univ, Azusa CA, MA, 1974. **CAREER:** Kansas City United School Dist, Kansas City KS, teacher, 1964-66; Pasadena United School Dist, Pasadena CA, teacher, 1966-. **ORGANIZATIONS:** Usher, First AME Church, 1966-; mem, Natl Sorority PDK Inc, 1985-87; regional dir, Natl Sorority Phi Delta Kappa Inc, 1987-91; mem, Richard Allen Theater Guild, First AME Church, 1987-.

HAMPTON, PHILLIP JEWEL
Educator. **PERSONAL:** Born Apr 23, 1922, Kansas City, MO; married Dorothy Smith (deceased); children: Harry J, Robert Keith. **EDUCATION:** KS St Clg, 1947-48; Drake U, 1948-49; KS City Art Inst, BFA-MFA 1949-52; KS City U, 1950-52. **CAREER:** Savannah State Coll, dir art, assoc prof 1952-69; Southern IL Univ Edwardsville, prof of painting 1969-. **ORGANIZATIONS:** Instr painting Jewish Ed Alliance Savannah 1967-68; bd mem Savannah Art Assc Savannah GA 1968-69; Citizens Advsry Cncl Edwardsville IL 1973-74. **HONORS/ACHIEVEMENTS:** Who's Who in Am Art RR Bowker Co 1954; cert of excellence Savannah Chptr Links 1960; "Schemata of Ethnic & Spec Stds" 1980; Danforth Assc Danforth Found 1980-86. **MILITARY SERVICE:** AUS s/sgt 3 yrs; ETO 5 Campaign Stars 1945. **BUSINESS ADDRESS:** Professor of Painting, Southern IL Univ at Edwardsvl, PO Box 1774, Edwardsville, IL 62026.

HAMPTON, ROBERT L.
Educator. **PERSONAL:** Born Nov 18, 1947, Michigan City, IN; son of Rev T L Hampton and Anne A Williams; married Cathy M Melson; children: Robyn, Conrad. **EDUCATION:** Princeton Univ, AB 1970; Univ of Michigan, MA 1971, PhD 1977. **CAREER:** Connecticut Coll, asst prof 1974-83; Harvard Med School, lectr of ped 1981-89; Connecticut Coll, assc prof 1983-89, prof 1989-. **ORGANIZATIONS:** Consultant Urban Inst 1975; consultant Women in Crisis 1979-82; consultants Childrens Hospital Boston 1982; mem exec com Peguot Comm Found 1983-86; chr Oprtns Dev Corp 1977-78; pres of bd Child & Family Agency 1987-90; New London County Child Sexual Abuse Task Force. **HONORS/ACHIEVEMENTS:** Danfurth Assc Danfurth Found 1979; NIMH Post Doc Flwshp 1980; NRC Flwshp Natl Rsrch Cncl 1981; Rockfeller Flwshp Rockefeller Found 1983. **MILITARY SERVICE:** AUSR cpt; Army Cmltn Medal. **BUSINESS ADDRESS:** Dean of the College, Connecticut College, New London, CT 06320.

HAMPTON, RONALD EVERETT
Police officer. **PERSONAL:** Born Jan 05, 1945, Washington, DC; son of Memory J Hampton and Annie L Hunt-Hampton; married Quintina M Hoban, Aug 27, 1982; children: Candace, Ronald Quinten. **EDUCATION:** American Univ, Washington DC, BS, 1978. **CAREER:** US Air Force, Dover Air Force Base, staff seargent, 1968-72; Washington DC Metropolitan Police Dept, Washington DC, police officer, 1972-; Natl Black Police Assn, Washington DC, exec dir, 1987-. **ORGANIZATIONS:** Regional chmn, Eastern Region, Natl Black Police Assn, 1982-84, natl chmn, 1984-86, exec dir, 1987-. **HONORS/ACHIEVEMENTS:** Police Officer of the Year, Eastern Region, Natl Black Police Assn, 1983; writings on Community/Police Relations, 1988; Extended Community Policing, 1989; Outstanding Community Relations Officer, Washington DC Police Dept, 1989. **MILITARY SERVICE:** USAF, staff seargent, 1968-72, US Air Force Good Conduct Medal, 1970, Vietnam Valot, 1969. **HOME ADDRESS:** 303 Allison St NW, Washington, DC 20011. **BUSINESS ADDRESS:** Executive Director, National Black Police Association, 1919 Pennsylvania Ave NW, Suite 300, Washington, DC 20006.

HAMPTON, THOMAS EARLE
Transportation service executive. **PERSONAL:** Born Sep 28, 1950, Greenville, SC. **EDUCATION:** Morgan State Univ, BA Pol Sci & Govt 1973; Univ of Baltimore MPA 1984. **CAREER:** Baltimore Mayor's Office, admin aide 1974-83; Mass Transit Admin Office of Public Affairs, comm relations officer 1983-. **ORGANIZATIONS:** Mem Kappa Alpha Psi Frat 1971-; bd mem Northwest Baltimore Comm Corp 1978-82; sales consul MD Real Estate Comm 1981-; host/coord "Inside the Criminal Justice System" public affairs radio show 1979-83; coord logistical arrangements for intl visitors touring the Baltimore metro; coord logistical arrangements for two regional Mass Transportation confs; mem Kappa Alpha Psi Frat; provided techn asst to fed grant recipients regarding Fed guidelines & regulations; guest speaker before various comm & business groups. **HONORS/ACHIEVEMENTS:** Recipient of the Outstanding Young Man of the Yr Awd 1978; United Way Comm Serv Awd 1978-79-80-81; two Mayoral Citations issued by Wm Donald Schaefer Mayor Baltimore City Council resolution recognizing 9 yrs of svcs. **BUSINESS ADDRESS:** Community Relations Offcr, Baltimore Mass Transit Admin, 300 W Lexington St, 6th Floor, Baltimore, MD 212013415.

HAMPTON, THURMAN B.
District attorney. **PERSONAL:** Born Feb 05, 1949, Chatham Co, NC; son of Joseph Hampton, Jr and Ernestine Rogers Hampton; married Maria Hopp, Oct 17, 1978; children: Kathryn Adair. **EDUCATION:** NC A&T Univ, BS 1970; State Univ of IA, JD 1973; Judge Advocate General's Officers Basic Course 1973, Military Judge's Course 1983; Officer Advanced Course 1984. **CAREER:** NC Central Univ, asst prof of law 1976-79; Thurman B Hampton Atty at Law 1979-82; 17-A Judicial Dist, asst district atty, district atty in general 1986; State of NC, Rockingham Co NC, asst district atty 1982-85. **ORGANIZATIONS:** Mem IA Bar Assn, NC Bar Assn, Omega Psi Phi Frat; dir Eden Branch Wachovia Bank & Trust Co 1980-; mem NC Conf of District Attys; mem NC District Atty's Assn; dir Rockingham Co Youth Involvement Program; trustee, Morning Star Baptist Church; dir Tri-City Rescue Squad; dir Hospice of Rockingham Co. **HONORS/ACHIEVEMENTS:** Appointed Military Judge US Army Reserves; first Black DA in State of NC; one of 3 elected black DA's in the state of NC; Outstanding Young Democrat (NC) 1984; Eden NAACEP Meritorious Community Service 1983. **MILITARY SERVICE:** AUS capt 1973-76; AUS Commendation Medal; AUS Reserves major. **BUSINESS ADDRESS:** District Attorney, 17-A Judicial Dist, PO Box 35, Wentworth, NC 27375.

HAMPTON, WILLIE L.
Mortician. **PERSONAL:** Born May 09, 1933, Montgomery Co, TN. **EDUCATION:** Mortuary Sch, MS 1970. **CAREER:** Winston Fun Home, licensed fun dir & embalmer, owner & oper 1971-. **ORGANIZATIONS:** Mem So KY Econ Opp Council; Russellville City Council; Cemetary Commr; Asst Police Commr 1971-; mem Men's Welfare League; 32 Deg Mason; mem Am Legion; mem Ra Council Exec Bd; mem, bd dir The Electric Plant Bd. **HONORS/ACHIEVEMENTS:** 1st Black apptd bd dir The Electric Plant Bd. **MILITARY SERVICE:** AUS corpl 1953-55. **BUSINESS ADDRESS:** 162 S Morgan St, Russellville, KY.

HANBERRY, ANNIE E.
Retired educator. **PERSONAL:** Born Mar 15, 1903, Columbia, SC; married TJ Hanberry. **EDUCATION:** Benedict Coll, AB 1940; Columbia Univ, MA 1954; Benedict Coll, LittD (Hon) 1972. **CAREER:** Finley High Shcool, Chester SC, Bethel High School Blythwood, teacher 1935-70; Richland School Dist #2, gen suprv 1970-71; Annie E Hanberry High Shcool, principal 1958-70 retired. **ORGANIZATIONS:** Mem SC Ed Assoc, NEA; vice pres Columbia Br Natl Assoc Univ Women 1970-75; bd mem GSA 1952-67, 1969-75; mem Richland Cty Teacher Fed Credit Union 1965-;vp Richland Cty Chap Natl Found March of Dimes 1974-; vice pres Columbia YWCA 19790-74; se reg dir Zeta Phi Beta 1965-70. **HONORS/ACHIEVEMENTS:** Elected to Pi Lambda Theta Natl Hon & Professional Assoc in Ed 1954; listed in Who's Who Among Amer Women 1966-67, Personalities of the South 1970; Zeta Woman of the Year 1971.

HANCOCK, ALLEN C.
Educator. **PERSONAL:** Born Feb 27, 1908, Cherokee Co, TX; married Jewell. **EDUCATION:** TX Coll, BA 1932;Univ of CO, MEd 1947;Univ of CO, DEd 1951. **CAREER:** TX Coll, Tyler TX, pres; Jarvis Christian Coll, formerly dean; Hampton Inst, dir graduate studies; Christ Methodist Episcopal Church, ordained minister. **ORGANIZATIONS:** Mem Phi Delta Kappa Idn Hon Soc; Alpha Kappa Mu; Nat Educ Assn; Nat Vocational Guid Assn. **BUSINESS ADDRESS:** 2404 N Grand Ave, Tyler, TX 75701.

HANCOCK, EUGENE WILSON WHITE
Educator. **PERSONAL:** Born Feb 17, 1929, St Louis, MO. **EDUCATION:** Univ of Detroit, BM 1951; Univ of Michigan, MM 1956; Union Theological Seminary School of Sac Music, SMD 1967. **CAREER:** Catholic Church of St John the Divine, asst org and choirmaster 1963-66; New Calvary Baptist Church, dir of music 1967-70; St Philip Episcopal Church, org and choirmaster 1974-82; West End Presbyterian Church, organist and choirmaster 1982-; Manhattan Community College, prof of music. **ORGANIZATIONS:** Natl counsellor Amer Guild of Organists 1977-82; chmn Prof Concerns New York City Chap AGO 1984; St Wilfrid Club, Natl Assn of Negro Musicians, Amer Soc of Un Composers. **MILITARY SERVICE:** AUS corpl 1951-53. **HOME ADDRESS:** 257 Central Park West 10C, New York, NY 10024. **BUSINESS ADDRESS:** Professor of Music, Borough of Manhattan Comm Coll, 190 Chambers St, New York, NY 10017.

HANCOCK, GWENDOLYN CARTER
Business executive. **PERSONAL:** Born Feb 23, 1933, Philadelphia, PA. **EDUCATION:** West Philadelphia High School, comm diplo 1952. **CAREER:** Southeastern Pennsylvania Transportation Authority, superintendent 1959. **HONORS/ACHIEVEMENTS:** SEPTA, first female to become a district superintendent. **BUSINESS ADDRESS:** Superintendent, SE Pennsylvania Trans Auth, 11th & Grange, Philadelphia, PA 19141.

HANCOCK, HERBERT JEFFREY
Composer, pianist, publisher. **PERSONAL:** Born Apr 12, 1940, Chgo, IL; married Gudrun Meixner. **EDUCATION:** Grinnel Coll, 1956-60; Roosevelt U, 1960; Manhattan Sch Music, 1962; New Sch Social Research, 1967. **CAREER:** Hancock Music Co, owner-pub; scored film "Blow Up"; "Death Wish" 1974; composer "Watermelon Man" 1962; "Chameleon" 1973; "Maiden Voyage" 1973; perfomed with Miles Davis Quintet 1963-68; Donald Byrd 1960-63; Coleman Hawkins 1960; Chicago Symphony Orch 1952. **ORGANIZATIONS:** Mem Jazz Musicians Assn; Nat Acd TV Arts & Scis; Nat Cad Rec Arts & Scis; Boradcast Music; pres Harlem Jazz Music Cntr; mem Grinnel Coll Pioneer Club. **HONORS/ACHIEVEMENTS:** Recipient citiation of achievement Broadcast Music Inc 1963; Jay Award Jazz Mag 1964; critics poll for talent deserving wider recognition Down Beat Mag

1967; 1st place piano category 1968-70; composer award 1971; All-Star Brand New Artist Award Record World 1968; named top jazz artist Black Music Mag 1974; appeared Carnegie Hall "An Evening With Herbie Hancock" 1974-75; appeared Newport Jazz Festival 1976; appeared City Center 1976; Radio City Music Hall 1976; records "Crossings"; "Fat Albert Rotunda"; "Mwandishi"; "Secrets"; "Head Hunters"; "VSOP"; Academy Awd for Best Original Score in the film Round Midnight. **BUSINESS ADDRESS:** c/o Adams Dad Mgmt, 827 Folsom St, San Francisco, CA 94107.

HANDON, MARSHALL R., JR.
Clinical pastoral psychologist. **PERSONAL:** Born Jul 03, 1937, Philadelphia, PA; son of Marshall R Handon; divorced; children: Marcia, Marvette, Mavis, Traci, Maia. **EDUCATION:** Rider Coll, Trenton NJ, BA; New School for Social Research, New York NY, MA; Temple Univ, Philadelphia PA, PhD; Amer Theological Seminary, Milledgeville GA, PhD. **CAREER:** Ben Hill United Methodist Church, Atlanta GA, minister, 1963-; Arthur Brisbane Child Treatment Center, Farmingdale NJ, dir QA, 1978-79; Ancora Psychiatric Hospital, Hammonton NJ, clinical dir, 1980-82; Physical Mental Health Clinical Ass, College Park GA, clinical psychotherapist, 1982-89; Asbury Park Drug Treatment Center, Asbury Park NJ, psychologist; private practice, Asbury Park NJ, psychologist. **ORGANIZATIONS:** Mem, NAACP, 1960-, Amer Assn of Clinical Pastoral Educ Inc, 1985-; dist dir,Young Adult Ministries, College Park Dist, United Methodist Church, 1985-; mem, Natl Assn of Black Psychologists, 1989-. **HONORS/ACHIEVEMENTS:** Community Leader of Amer, Urban Amer Inc, 1959; Man of the Year, Jaycees, 1960; Gang Members, The Police & Delinquency, 1969; The Microcosm, 1973; Case Work/Case Management, 1979; The Joy of Sharing, 1980; The Real Jesus Christ, 1986; The Ben Hill Phenomena, 1989. **MILITARY SERVICE:** US Navy, Fleet Marine Force/USMC, lieutenant, 1954-59, 1965-67, Purple Heart.

HANDY, DELORES
Anchor/reporter. **PERSONAL:** Born Apr 07, 1947, Little Rock, AR; daughter of Rev George G Handy and Myrtle Carr Handy; married James Lawrence Brown, Jun 24, 1989. **EDUCATION:** Univ of Arkansas, graduate 1970. **CAREER:** WTTG-TV Channel 5 Washington DC Ten O'clock News & Black Reflections, anchorperson & host 1978-; Six O'clock News WJLA-TV Channel 7 Wash DC, co-anchor 1976-78; CBS-KNXT-TV, reporter, anchorperson 1974-76; KABC-TV LA, reporter June 1973, April 1974; WHBQ-TV Memphis, reporter, anchorperson 1972-73; FKAAY Radio Little Rock, reporter, announcer 1970-72. **ORGANIZATIONS:** Hollywood-Beverly Hills Chapter Nat Assn of Media Women; Am Women in Radio & TV; Radio & TV News Assn of So CA; charter mem Sigma Delta Chi AR Chapter; bd of dirs Jr Citizens Corps Washington DC; exec comm Natl Capital Area March of Dimes; volunteer Big Sisters of Amer Washington DC Chapter; mem Washington Chapter Amer Women in Radio & TV. **HONORS/ACHIEVEMENTS:** Outstanding Young Woman in Am 1973-; Journalist of the Year Award Capitol Rpess Club 1977; awards Natl Council of Negro Women/United Black Fund for Excellence in Community Serv; awards Journalistic Achievement Univ of DC; Emmy Award for America's Black Forum Special on Jesse Jackson 1985; Emmy Award for Testing the Class of '87 (Channel 7-Boston) 1987; Honored on 350th anniversary of Black Presence in Boston as one of 350 people who represented Black Presence in Boston 1988. **BUSINESS ADDRESS:** WNEV-TV Channel 7, 7 Bulfinch Place, Boston, MA 02114.

HANDY, JOHN RICHARD, III
Saxophonist, composer. **PERSONAL:** Born Feb 03, 1933, Dallas; divorced. **EDUCATION:** City Coll NY, 1960; San Francisco State Coll, BA 1963. **CAREER:** Modern jazz groups, rhythm & blues bands San Francisco-oakland CA area 1948-58, Charleie Mingus, Randy Westen, Kenny Dorham 1959-62; toured Europe 1961; concerts own band Carnegie Recital Hall 1962, 67 Santa Clara CA Symphony 1967; Newport Jazz Festival 1967; Hollywood Bowl CA 1966; Monterey Jazz Festival 1964-66; Antibes Jazz Festival 1967; head jazz band San Francisco prodn opera "The Visitation" 1967; collaborated with Ali Akbar Khan 1970-71; duets tabla players Shandar Ghosh & Zakir Hussein; quest soloist major symphonies coll & univ symphony orchs, concert bands, stage bands, natl. **ORGANIZATIONS:** Mem Jazz Arts Soc mus dir 1960-61; San Francisco Interim Arts Adv Com 1966-67. **HONORS/ACHIEVEMENTS:** Recipient Downbeat Poll Award; 1st Place Award Record World All-star Band 1968. **BUSINESS ADDRESS:** 618 Baker St, San Francisco, CA 94117.

HANDY, JOHN WILLIAM, JR.
Retired educational administrator. **PERSONAL:** Born Jan 10, 1918, Harrisburg, PA; married Lois E. **EDUCATION:** Shaw U, BS; Drew U, 1942;Univ CO, MEd 1959; NY U, MA 1961;Univ CO, EdD 1971. **CAREER:** St James Methodist Church MD, pastor 1942-43; St Lude United Meth NY, 1959-61; Hampton Inst, asst prof 1969-70, assoc prof 1970-71, dept chmn 1971-73, prof 1973-; Div Graduate Studies Hampton Inst, dir 1973-76; Hampton Inst, acad dean 1976-80; Hampton Inst, retired dir School of Business 1980-. **ORGANIZATIONS:** Mem City Mgmt Study Com 1971-72; va Minority Affairs; delegate Rep Nat Conv 1972; VA Commn Educ Tv; C of C; Girl Scout Council; Nat Aeromautics & Space Adminstrn 1973-74; mem Am Personnel & Guidance Assn; VA Personnel & Guidance Assn; Am Psychological Assn; va Psychol Assn; AssnUniv Prof; ResOfficers Assn US; Military Chaplains Assn; Nat Vocational Guidance Assn. **HONORS/ACHIEVEMENTS:** Urban League Fellowship Jones & Laughlin Steel Corp 1972-73; Outstanding Educ Am 1971; Man Yr Alpha Phi Alpha 1972; Hon Citation Mayor Hampton 1973; C of C Citation 1973; Peyton Randolph Lectureship Award 1974; Whos Who Meth Ch 1963; Personalities of the S 1975-76; Whos Who in S & SW 1975-76; Legion Merit Award w/Oak leaf cluster 1967-68 & 68-69; Bronze Star Commendation Medal w/3 oak leaf clusters; many other Serv medals & awards 1943-69. **MILITARY SERVICE:** AUS col 1943-69.

HANDY, WENDELL TAYLOR
Business executive. **PERSONAL:** Born Jan 28, 1928, Tyler, TX; married Adelaide; children: Wendell, Anthony, Darryl. **EDUCATION:** Univ of So CA, 1947; Met Bus Coll, 1947; Santa Ana City Coll, 1974-. **CAREER:** UT Handy & Sons Whse Co Gov Reagans Adv Com for Children & Youth, owner. **ORGANIZATIONS:** Mem Credentials & Reules Com CA Speakers Bur 1966-76; mem CA State Ctrl Com; CA Campaign Dir Nixon-agnew; rep del Nat Conv 1976; rep del Nat Conv 1978, 76; chmn 55th Assembly Dist Rep; mem Legislative Steering Com; mem Bus & Professional Mens Assn; rep cand State Assembly 1966; CA rep cand Secof State 1970-74; clk, sec, pres Compton Sch Bd of Trustees 1966-75; CA Sch Bd Assn 1966-75; del assembly mem CA Legis Rep or Sch Bd mem NatSch Bds Assn; chmn Mid-cities Sch Trustees Assn. **HONORS/ACHIEVEMENTS:** Comm Serv Award for Outst Merits; Compton Jr Coll Award; Merit Award Outst Civic Achvmts CA Senate Rules Com; Merit Award Bd of Educ City of Compton; num other awards.

HANDY, WILLIAM T., JR.
Clergyman, association executive. **PERSONAL:** Born Mar 26, 1924, New Orleans; married Ruth. **EDUCATION:** Dillard U, AB 1948; Gammon Theol Seminary, MDiv 1951; Boston U, STM 1952; Tillotson Coll, DD; Wiley Coll, DD 1973. **CAREER:** United Meth Pub House, vP & pub rep 1968-70; St Mark Meth Ch, pastor 1959-68; Newman Ch, 1952-59; LA Conf Bd Ministry, chmn 1958; ATL Region Consultation Task Force Theol Edn; bd trustees Interdenom Theol Cntr; Gammon Theol Sem; Juris Confs, del gen 1964, 66, 68, 70, 72, 76; World Meth Conf del 1966, 71, 76. **ORGANIZATIONS:** Mem bd dir United Meth Neighborhood Cntr; bd dir Nashville Area United Way; Frontiers; LA State Adv Com Civil Rights 1959-68; Mayors Bi-racial Adv Com 1965-66; life mem NAACP. **HONORS/ACHIEVEMENTS:** Man Yr Frontiers 1963; 33 degree Mason. **MILITARY SERVICE:** AUS s/Sgt 1943-46. **BUSINESS ADDRESS:** 201 8 Ave S, Nashville, TN 37202.

HANDY-MILLER, D. ANTOINETTE
Flutist. **PERSONAL:** Born Oct 29, 1930, New Orleans; married Calvin M Miller. **EDUCATION:** New Eng Conservatory Music, BMus; Northwestern U, MMus; Paris Nat Conservatory, dip. **CAREER:** Natl Endowment for the Arts, asst dir of music pgrm; VA State Coll, asst prof music 1975-; soloist; symphony orch mem; recording artist; recitalist; lectr. **ORGANIZATIONS:** Mem Pi Kappa Lambda; music consult Head Start Trainee Prgm; clinician, Dept Music Richmond Pub Schs; humanities coord Upward Bound, VA State Coll; mem ASALH; NAACP; VA Alliance Arts Edn. **HONORS/ACHIEVEMENTS:** Writer; World Who's Who Musicians 1975; Personalities of S 1974.

HANEY, DARNEL L.
Director, student life. **PERSONAL:** Born Feb 06, 1937, Phoenix, AZ; son of Walker Lee Haney and Pearlie Marie Johnson Haney; married Marie Packer Haney, Nov 24, 1962; children: Norman Darnel Haney, Keith Lyman Walker Haney, Raven Rebecca Haney. **EDUCATION:** Phoenix Jr Coll, 1959; UT State U, 1960-65; UT State Univ Grad Sch, 1970. **CAREER:** Weber State Coll Ogden UT, asso dean of students; Inst of Ethnic Studies Weber State Coll, minority vocational counselor; Thiokol Clearfield Job Corps, supvr of counseling 1966-71; Parks & Job Corps Cntr Pleasanton CA counselor 1965-66; Oakland Unified Sch Dist, sub tchr 1962-65; Oakland Rec Dept Oakland, part-time rec dir 1962-65; Oakland Raiders Defensive End, professional football player 1961-62; Black Cultural Arts Group of UT, organizer dir. **ORGANIZATIONS:** Bd dirs Childrens Aid Soc of UT; Black Adv Council to the Gov of the State of UT Coll Com; Affirmative Action; Athletic Com; spl chmnshp City Govt Cultural Washington Terrace; Oddessey Hse Drug Prospective Preventive Progs for Addicts; Human Potential Instr for Positive Behavior; Nat consulting with Trinity Univ on Cultural Awareness; bd mem UT Endowment for Humanities; worked with drug & training prog in Identifying who are minorities & what they are in the Black experience; Title IV Prog in WY & CO; counseling advising AR Art Cntr in Little Rock Black Cultural Awareness and Drug training; consult to state of UT Hwy Patrol Title IV Progs Ogden City Sch. **HONORS/ACHIEVEMENTS:** Crystal Crest-William P Miller Friend of Students Award, Associated Students WSC 1982; Whitney M Young Jr. Service Award, Boy Scouts of America. **MILITARY SERVICE:** USCG 1957-59. **HOME ADDRESS:** 131 E 4900 S, Ogden, UT 84405.

HANEY, DON LEE
Newsman. **PERSONAL:** Born Sep 30, 1934, Detroit, MI; married Shirley; children: Karen Lynn, Kimberly Joy. **EDUCATION:** Wayne State U, Radio-TV Arts Maj 1959; Wayne State U, Polit Sci & Law 1974. **CAREER:** WXYZ-TV TV Talk Show, host-anchr nwsmn 1968-; WJR, staff announc 1963-68; CFPL-TV, host, wkly pub affairs prog 1967-68; WCHD-FM 1960-63; WQRS-FM & WLIN-FM; WGPR-FM, prog dir 1959-60; CKCR, staff announc 1957-59; WSJM, staff announc 1956-57; free lance exp/motion pict slide films, TV, radio. **ORGANIZATIONS:** Mem New Detr Inc Commun Com; mem bd dir Am Fed of TV & Radio Arts Union; mem bd dir Suddne Infant Death; mem bd Eq Just Counc; chmn Mus Dyst Assn of Am; mem Detr City Airpt Commin. **BUSINESS ADDRESS:** 2405 W Mc Nichols Rd, Detroit, MI 48221.

HANEY, NAPOLEON
Elected official. **PERSONAL:** Born Oct 01, 1926, Texas City, TX; married Sylvia C; children: Lorraine, Katherine, Angela, Lynette, Napoleon. **EDUCATION:** Central High School 1944. **HONORS/ACHIEVEMENTS:** Awd Men of Progress Kankakee 1983; Awd $3,500,000 Sewer Grant for Village, State, IL 1984. **HOME ADDRESS:** Rt 4 Box 47Y, St Anne, IL 60964.

HANFORD, CRAIG BRADLEY
Commissioned officer/aviator. **PERSONAL:** Born Sep 04, 1953, Washington, DC; son of Lexie B Hanford and Boris A Davis Hanford; married Cassandra G Hurse Hanford, Jan 30, 1988; children: Craig J Dumas, Ashley F. **EDUCATION:** US Military Acad West Point, BS 1975; Univ of So CA, MSSM 1982; Georgia Tech, MS 1985; Flight School, Army Aviator 1978; Defense System Mgmt Coll, Program Mgr Quality 1987. **CAREER:** US Army, special asst aviation center 1979-81, flight operations officer korea 1981-82, ch tech transfer office info system eng command 1985-87, PEO Stamis, Ft Belvoir, VA, exec officer, 1987-88; A CO, 4-58 AVN, APO, SF, co commander, 1988-89. **ORGANIZATIONS:** Comm chmn Kappa Alpha Psi Inc 1976, 1980, 1985-87; mem Tuskegee Airman Inc 1979,80; mem Army Aviation Assoc of Amer 1983-89, Assoc of Computing Mach 1986-89, IEEE 1986-89; comm chmn Rocks Inc 1986, 1987. **MILITARY SERVICE:** US Army mayor 14 yrs Army Aviator 12 yrs; Computer/Software Engr 4 yrs; Meritorious Serv Medal 1979, 1988-89; Army Astronaut Nominee 1985-87, 1989; Army Commendation Medal 1986; Army Achievement Medal 1986, 1988. **BUSINESS ADDRESS:** Student, US Army, Class 86, Armed Forces Staff Coll,, 7800 Hampton Blvd, Norfolk, VA 23511.

HANKERSON, ELIJAH H.
Educator, pastor. **PERSONAL:** Born May 15, 1912, Stark, FL; children: Tom, Eunice, Esther. **EDUCATION:** FL Meml Coll, BTh 1939; Pacific Lutheran U, AB 1968. **CAREER:** Tacoma Comm Coll, prof History; St Paul Baptist Church, pastor; organized Shiloh-Tacoma Church 1952; St Paul 1964; Ministers Alliance, pres 1969-71; N Pac Baptist Convention, pres 1971-; state vice pres NBC, USA; Minority Affairs, co-chmn 1970. **ORGANIZATIONS:** Mem NAACP. **HONORS/ACHIEVEMENTS:** Valuable Service Award Urban League; plaque State of AK & Anchorage bringing N Pac Bapt Conv. **MILITARY SERVICE:** USAF chaplain 1944-64; ret lt col. **BUSINESS ADDRESS:** Tacoma Comm Coll, 1200 S 12 St, Tacoma, WA 98465.

HANKINS, ANDREW JAY, JR.
Radiology department chairman. **PERSONAL:** Born Jul 15, 1942, Waukegan, IL; son of Andrew J Hankins Sr and Julia Lampkins Hankins; married Margaret Roberts; children: Corbin, Trent, Andrea. **EDUCATION:** Univ IA, BA 1960-64; Univ MI Med Sch, MD 1964-68. **CAREER:** Michael Reese Hosp & Med Cntr, intern 1968-69; Univ of Chicago, resdnt 1971-74; Dept of Radiology Univ Chicago, instr 1974-75; Milton Communit Hosp, stf rdlgst 1975; Wayne State Univ, clinical asst prof 1977-; SW Detroit Hosp, radiologist 1975-80, vice chmn dept radiology 1980-83, chrmn radiology 1984-. **ORGANIZATIONS:** Cnsltnt radio pharmaceutical drug advsry com FDA 1982-84; pres Equip Lsng Firm Hankins Ervin Goodwin & Assc 1984-; vice pres Goodwin Ervin & Assc PC 1980-; mem Hartford Memrl Bapt Ch 1984-; mem NAACP; mem Detroit Med Society, Natl Med Assn, & Wayne County Med Society; mem RSNA, SNM, & AIUM; mem Iowa Black Alumni Assn; mem YMCA. **HONORS/ACHIEVEMENTS:** Distinguished Young Alumni, Univ IA Alumni Assn 1977; Phi Beta Kappa Alpha Chptr IA 1964; Omicron Delta Kappa Univ IA Cir 1963. **MILITARY SERVICE:** USAF capt 1969-71. **BUSINESS ADDRESS:** ChairmanDepartment of Radiology, Southwest Detroit Hospital, 2401 20th Street, Detroit, MI 48207.

HANKINS, FREEMAN
Business executive. **PERSONAL:** Born Sep 30, 1918, Brunswick, GA; married Dorothy; children: Bernadette. **EDUCATION:** Friendship Sch Pittsburgh; Selden Inst Brunswick Temple U, Dolans Coll of Embalming 1943. **CAREER:** Freeman Hankins Funeral Home, funeral dir; State of PA, senator. **ORGANIZATIONS:** Mem PA State Senate 1967-; PA House of Rep 1960-67; mem Nat Funeral Assn; PA Funeral Dir Assn; Quaker City Funeral Dir Assn; Am Legion; NAACPlife mem; Masonic Bodies; George W Gaines Lodge; leader Philadelphia Sixth Ward Dem Com; third v-chmn Philadelphia Dem City Com; treas Met Bapt Ch; me Humanitarian Asso; AMVETS; Am Woodmen; Philadelphia Elks Lodge. **HONORS/ACHIEVEMENTS:** YWCA Man of Yr 1961; Man of Yr Boy Scouts 1970; Humanitarian Award Sickle Cell Anemia Assn & Tribune Charites Assn. **MILITARY SERVICE:** AUS med corps 1944-47. **BUSINESS ADDRESS:** State Senator, Senate of Pennsylvania, 458 Main Capitol Bldg, Harrisburg, PA 17120.

HANKINS, GERARD S.
Bank chief executive. **CAREER:** Gateway Natl Bank of St Louis, St Louis, MO, chief exec. **BUSINESS ADDRESS:** Gateway Natl Bank of St Louis, 3412 Union Blvd, St Louis, MO 63115. *

HANLEY, J. FRANK, II
Attorney. **PERSONAL:** Born Mar 11, 1943, Charlotte, NC; son of Frank and Robert D; married Elizabeth Booth; children: Laura Elizabeth, Melinda Lee. **EDUCATION:** Attended Hampton Inst; NC Central Univ School Law, LLB 1968. **CAREER:** State of IN, deputy atty general 1969-71; Standard Oil Div Amer Oil Co, real estate atty 1971-72; Marion County, deputy prosecutor 1972-73; IN Employment Security Div, mem review bd 1974; private practice, attorney 1974-; public defender 1985-88. **ORGANIZATIONS:** Mem, Marion Co Bar Assn; mem, Indianapolis Bar Assn. **HONORS/ACHIEVEMENTS:** Tennis Doubles Champion, Central Inter-Atlantic Assn, 1965; Tennis Doubles Champion, NCAA Atlantic Coast, 1965. **BUSINESS ADDRESS:** Attorney, 302 N East St, Indianapolis, IN 46202.

HANNA, CASSANDRIA H.
Educator, musician. **PERSONAL:** Born Jan 01, 1940, Miami, FL. **EDUCATION:** St Augustines Coll, BA 1961;Univ of Miami, MusM 1971;Univ of Miami, attended; IN U, attended. **CAREER:** Episcopal Church St Agnes, organist, choir dir; Miami Dade Comm Choir; concerts on radio & TV co-dir; Comm Coll in FL, presented various lecture-recitals; performed with Greater Miami Symphony Soc Orchestra Grieg Piano & Concerto & Beethoven 3rd Piano Concerto; pianist-lecturer recitalist; Miami Dade Comm Coll, assoc prof of music, sr prof of music. **ORGANIZATIONS:** Mem MENC, NEA, FEA, FCME, Natl Human Fac, FHEA, Alpha Kappa Alpha, Phi Kappa Alpha, AABWE, Natl Guild of Organists; pres of Cardiney Corp/Diversified Investments; pres of Cassie's Cookies. **HONORS/ACHIEVEMENTS:** Who's Who of Women 1977; Who's Who in FL; featured performer Nat Black Music Colloqim & Competition at the Kennedy Cntr 1980. **BUSINESS ADDRESS:** Senior Professor of Music, Miami Dade Comm College, 11380 NW 27 Ave, Opa-Locka, FL 33167.

HANNA, HARLINGTON LEROY, JR.
Optometric physician. **PERSONAL:** Born Sep 24, 1951; married Helen; children: Lauren, Kristen. **EDUCATION:** Univ of Houston, BS, MEd 1977, OD 1977; Memphis State Univ, JD 1985. **CAREER:** Optometric Physician, private practice Memphis; H & H Productions USA, pres (record production); Perkins Hanna & Assocs, attorney; Southern Coll of Optometry, assoc prof 1977-. **ORGANIZATIONS:** Mem Amer Optometric Assn, Natl Optometric Assn, Natl Eye Rsch Found, Amer Pub Health Assn; bd of trustees & fellow Amer Coll of Optometric Physicians; bd of govs Memphis health Ctr 1979-; pres Mid S Health Prof Assn 1980-81; mem Amer, Natl & TN Bar Assocs; mem Assoc of Trial Lawyers of Amer. **HONORS/ACHIEVEMENTS:** Bausch & Lomb Rsch Awd Bausch & Lomb Softlens Div 1976-77; publ "Cytological Contraindications in Contact Lens Wear" Contacto 1979; Outstanding Young Men of Amer US Jaycees 1979. **BUSINESS ADDRESS:** Associate Professor, S Coll of Optometry, 1245 Madison Ave, Memphis, TN 38114.

HANNA, ROLAND
Musician. **EDUCATION:** Eastman School of Music; The Julliard School. **CAREER:** Benny Goodman Orchestra, pianist; Charles Mingus, pianist; Thad Jones-Mel Lewis Band, 1970's. **BUSINESS ADDRESS:** Abby Hoffer Enterprises, 223 1/2 E 48th St, New York, NY 10017.

HANNAH, HUBERT H., SR.
Association executive. **PERSONAL:** Born Jul 06, 1920, Hill Top, WV; married Edith C; children: Hubert, Jr, Dwayne, Judith, Marc, Don. **EDUCATION:** Depaul U, EDP computer uses in accounting 1968; OH State U, MBA 1952; Bluefield State Coll, BS 1942; OH State U, BS 1949. **CAREER:** J Cameron Wade & Asso Chicago , mgmt consult accountant 1969-72; Statistical Sect Gen Office Intl Harvester Co Chicago, supr & Accounting 1963-69; Steel Div Intl Harvester Co, divisional accountant 1952-63; Antioch Bookplate Co Yellow Springs, chief accounting officer 1949-51; Dept Budget & FinanceHealth & Hosps Governing Commn Cook Co Hosp Financial Mgmt Assn, bus mgr 1975. **ORGANIZATIONS:** Omega Psi Phi Frat; Trinity United Ch chmn bd trustees 1973-75; Urban League; Beta Alpha Psi Hon Accounting Frat 1951. **MILITARY SERVICE:** AUS s/Sgt 1942-45. **BUSINESS ADDRESS:** 1900 W Polk St, Chicago, IL 60612.

HANNAH, MACK H., JR.
Savings and loan chief executive. **CAREER:** Standard Savings Assoc, Houston, TX, chief exec. **BUSINESS ADDRESS:** Standard Savings Assoc, 4702 Old Spanish Tr., Houston, TX 77021. *

HANNAH, MARC REGIS
Electrical engineer. **PERSONAL:** Born Oct 13, 1956, Chicago, IL. **EDUCATION:** IL Inst of Tech, BSEE 1977; Stanford Univ, MSEE 1978, PhD EE 1985. **CAREER:** Silicon Graphics, co-founder & mem of the tech staff 1982-85, principal scientist 1986-. **ORGANIZATIONS:** Mem IEEE; ACM, NCCBPE, NTA. **HONORS/ACHIEVEMENTS:** ITT Alumni Assoc Professional Achievement Awd 1987; NTA Professional Achievement Awd 1987. **BUSINESS ADDRESS:** Principal Scientist, Silicon Graphics, 2011 Stierlin Rd, Mountain View, CA 94043.

HANNAH, MELVIN JAMES
Elected goverment official. **PERSONAL:** Born Apr 19, 1938, Winslow, AZ; married Shirley Rae Stingley; children: Melvin Jr, Marcellus, Michelle, Reginald, Derek, Ashley. **EDUCATION:** East AZ Jr Coll Thotchen AZ, AA 1959; North AZ Univ Flagstaff AZ, BA 1961. **CAREER:** City of Flagstaff, city councilman. **ORGANIZATIONS:** Pres NAACP Flagstaff; mem Residential Utility Consumer Officer. **HOME ADDRESS:** 3060 Hemberg Dr, Flagstaff, AZ 86001. **BUSINESS ADDRESS:** City Councilman, City of Flagstaff, 211 West Aspen Ave, Flagstaff, AZ 86001.

HANNAH, MOSIE R.
Banking executive. **PERSONAL:** Born Jul 11, 1949, Lake City, SC; married Doris Horry; children: Michelle, Brandon. **EDUCATION:** Voorhees Clg, BS 1967-70;Univ MI, Grad Sch & Bkng 1980-81;Univ OK, Retail Bnkg Sch 1983. **CAREER:** Security Norstar Bk, brnch mgr 1973-75, avp 1975-79, vice pres 1979-84, sr vice pres 1984-. **ORGANIZATIONS:** Dir United Nghbrhd Cntrs of Am 1984-; Vstg Nurses Serv Monroe Cnty 1984-; Rochester Bus Oprtnts Corp 1982-; mem allocaties Com United Way of Greater Rochester. **HOME ADDRESS:** 31 Crystal Spring Ln, Fairport, NY 14450. **BUSINESS ADDRESS:** Senior Vice President, Norstar Bank, 1 East Ave, 1 E Ave, Rochester, NY 14638.

HANNIBAL, ALICE PRISCILLA
Statesman, journalist, educator. **PERSONAL:** Born Dec 06, 1916, Metuchen, NJ; daughter of Charles J Stateman (deceased) and Hester Robinson Stateman (deceased); married Dr John Jacob Hannibal Jr; children: Alice L, John J III, Marcia E McCall; Myriam A, Gregor J, Charles J, Rhonda A. **EDUCATION:** Middlesex Jr Clge Perth Amboy NJ, Diploma 1939; LaSalle Extension Univ, lifetime charter membership 1968; East Carolina Univ Greenville NC, BA English/Journalism 1975, MA Educ 1978. **CAREER:** Amer Red Cross, home nursing civil defense instr 1950-70; Volunteer Adult Educ Instr 1950-; City of Kinston NC, councilwoman 1959-61; Caswell Ctr NC, staff dev spec 1979-83; Folk Heritage Presentations, consultant/exhibitor 1983-; Notary Public 1986-; public speaker. **ORGANIZATIONS:** Kappa Delta Pi 1978-; Council of Negro Women 1960; exec council Assc Negro Life & History 1959; alternate delegate Natl Democratic Convention 1972; nominated distg Woman of NC Status of Women Council 1985; NAACP life mem; Zeta Phi Beta (Delta Rho Zeta Chapter) AARP. **HONORS/ACHIEVEMENTS:** Natl Clubwomen Award Woman's Home Companion 1954-55; First Afro-Amer Woman Alderman in History of South 1959-61; Emma V Kelly Civic Awd 1960; listed among women eligible for Appointment by Pres Kennedy 1961-63; Civil Rights Awd United Eastern Bapt Convention 1962; finer womanhood Delta Rho Zeta Chptr Zeta Phi Beta 1966; poetry publ World Poetry Press 1983-84; Silver Poet Awd 1985, Golden Poet Awd 1986 World of Poetry Press; life mem NAACP 1986; Delta Rho Zeta Woman of the Yr Awd 1987; Disting Women of North Carolina Awd 1987. **BUSINESS ADDRESS:** PO Box 924, Kinston, NC 28501.

HANSEN, JOYCE VIOLA
Teacher, writer. **PERSONAL:** Born Oct 18, 1942, Bronx, NY; daughter of Austin Hansen and Lillian Dancy Hansen; married Matthew Nelson, Dec 18, 1982. **EDUCATION:** Pace Univ, New York NY, BA English, 1972; New York Univ, New York NY, MA English Educ, 1978. **CAREER:** New York City Bd of Educ, teacher 1973-. **ORGANIZATIONS:** Soc of Children's Book Writers, 1980-; Harlem Writer's Guild, 1982-. **HONORS/ACHIEVEMENTS:** Author of: The Gift-Giver, 1980, Home Boy, 1982, Yellow Bird and Me, 1986, Which Way Freedom?, 1986, Out From This Place, 1988; Parent's Choice Award, 1986; Coretta Scott King Honor Book Award, 1987.

HANSEN, WENDELL JAY
Radio & TV executive. **PERSONAL:** Born May 28, 1910, Waukegan, IL; married Eunice Ervine; children: Sylvia Larson, Dean C. **EDUCATION:** Cleveland Bible Inst, grad 1932; Wm Penn Coll, AB 1938; Univ of IA, MA 1940, PhD 1947. **CAREER:** Menomonie Broadcasting Co, pres 1952-72; Mid-IN Broadcasting, pres & chmn of bd 1969-; White River Broadcasting Co, pres & chmn of bd 1970-; WESL Inc, pres & chmn of bd 1971-. **ORGANIZATIONS:** Dir St Paul Inter-racial Work Comp 1939; chmn MN Joint Refugee Comm 1940-41; pres dir Great Comm Schools 1956-60; mem East St Louis Kiwanis Club 1981-; dir East St Louis Chamber of Commerce 1982-; advisor Indianapolis Prosecutor 1985 shared platform w/Rev Jesse Jackson. **HONORS/ACHIEVEMENTS:** Awd Natl Religious Broadcasters 1970; Boss of the Year Hamilton Co Broadcasters 1979; awd Women of Faith, Inc 1984. **BUSINESS ADDRESS:** President, WESL, Inc, 149 S 8th St, East St Louis, IL 62201.

HANSON, CHARLES M., JR.
Consul general. **PERSONAL:** Born Jun 18, 1917, NYC; married Muriel A; children: Ann Marie, Margaret, Mary Ann. **EDUCATION:** AB 1937; MS 1941; Coll of City of NY;Univ of Havana; Nat AutonomousUniv of Mexico. **CAREER:** Attached US Del 32nd session UN Gen Assembly NYC; New York City Govt 1938-42; US Foreign Serv Liberia 1948-50; Switzerland 1950-55; India 1956-58; Wash DC 1958-60; Trinidad 1961-64; Wash DC 1964-66; Nigeria 1966-70; Liberia 1970-72; Ghana 1972-75; Netherlands Antilles 1975-77; Washington DC-NYC 1970. **ORGANIZATIONS:** Mem Omega Psi Phi; Sigma Delta Pi Spanish Hon; ABA Foreign Serv Assn. **MILITARY SERVICE:** AUS 1st lt 1942-46. **BUSINESS ADDRESS:** Dept State, Washington, DC 20520.

HANSON, JOHN L.
Journalist, producer. **PERSONAL:** Born Aug 05, 1950, Detroit, MI; son of Cavirin Colline; children: Kacey. **EDUCATION:** Huston-Tillotson Coll, 1968-72. **CAREER:** KHRB-AM Lockhart, disc jockey 1970-71; KUT radio Austin, disc jockey 1974-80, producer In Black America radio series 1980-, executive producer 1984-. **ORGANIZATIONS:** Pres John Hanson & Assoc 1970-; bd of directors Black Arts Alliance 1985; bd of directors Camp Fire 1985; pres Austin Assn of Black Communicators 1986-87; bd of directors, Natl Assn of Black Journalists 1987-89. **HONORS/ACHIEVEMENTS:** Community Service Awards, Greater Austin Council on Alcoholism, Cystic Fibrosis Foundation, Federal Correctional System/TX, Univ of TX; Over the Hill, Inc, Comm Serv Award; Austin Black Art Alliance/ The Friends of Phoenix; Phoenix Award. **BUSINESS ADDRESS:** Executive Producer, Longhorn Radio Network, Comm Bldg B/UT Austin, Austin, TX 78712.

HAQQ, KHALIDA ISMAIL
Educational administrator. **PERSONAL:** Born Jul 11, 1946, Cape Charles, VA; children: Hassana, Majeeda, Thaky, Hussain, Jaleel, Jameel. **EDUCATION:** Rutgers NCAS, BA Psych, Black Studies (with honors) 1980; Rutgers GSE, MEd Counseling Psych 1983. **CAREER:** Rutgers Univ, counselor 1976-80; Plainfield Bd of Ed, sub teacher 1980-81; Rutgers Univ, rsch asst 1981-82; New Brunswick HS, career ed intern 1982;Caldwell Coll, counselor 1982-84, coord-eof counseling/tutor 1984-; Rider Coll, eop asst dir, counselor 1985-. **ORGANIZATIONS:** Mem Irvington Parent Teachers Assoc, NJ Assoc of Black Ed 1980-, Assoc of Black Psychologists 1982-, NJ Ed Opportunity Fund Professional Assoc 1982-, Amer Assoc for counseling & Devel 1982-; mem NAACP 1985, Community Awareness Now 1986-, Mercer County Black Dem Caucus 1986; leadership adv bd Rutgers Minority Community. **HONORS/ACHIEVEMENTS:** Martin Luther King Jr Fellowship Recipient 1982; Soroptimist Scholarship Recipient 1978. **BUSINESS ADDRESS:** E O P Asst Dir, Counselor, Rider College, 2083 Lawrenceville Rd, Lawrenceville, NJ 08648.

HARDAWAY, ERNEST, II
Oral and maxillofacial surgeon. **PERSONAL:** Born Mar 03, 1938, Col, GA; son of Ernest and Virginia L. **EDUCATION:** Howard Univ, BS 1957, DDS 1966, OSurg 1972; John Hopkins Univ, MPH 1973. **CAREER:** Bureau of Med Svcs, dep dir 1980; Public Health Washington DC, dep commiss 1982; Public Health Wash DC, commiss 1983-84; Federal Employee Occupational Health Prog HHS Region V, dir 1985; Howard Univ, asst prof of oral & maxillofacial surgery 1970-. **ORGANIZATIONS:** Chief policy coord Bur of Med Serv 1978. **HONORS/ACHIEVEMENTS:** PHS Plaque 1980; Commendation Medal USPHS 1973; Meritorious Serv Medal; Outstanding Unit Citation Commendation Medal Unit Commendation Medal, USPHS; Dentist of the Year 1983; Distinguished Dentist of the Year Natl Dental Assoc 1984; Fellow Amer Coll of Dentists Natl Dental Assoc Found; Fellow Intl Coll of Dentists; Fellow Amer Assoc of Oral & Maxillofacial Surgeons; Fellow Acad of Dentistry Intl; Disting Serv Awds. **MILITARY SERVICE:** USPHS, col 16 yrs.

HARDAWAY, YVONNE VERONICA
Psychologist. **PERSONAL:** Born Oct 14, 1950, Meridian, MS. **EDUCATION:** Memphis State U, BS 1970; So ILUniv at Carbondale, MA 1972;Univ of Louisville, PhD 1978. **CAREER:** LA State Univ, asst prof of psychology 1980-; Baylor Univ, asst prof of psychology 1978-80; Vanderbuilt-Peabody Internship Program, clinical psychology intern 1977-78; Jefferson Comm Coll Louisville, instructor of psychology 1975-77; SIU-CARBONDALE Couns Center, counselor 1972-74; Jeff Co Mental Health Center IL, counselor intern 1972. **ORGANIZATIONS:** Mem League of Women Voters 1978-; mem Delta Sigma Theta Sor 1979-; bd of Dir Freeman House Halfway House; Nat Achievement Scholar Nat Scholarship Serv & Fund New York City 1976-70. **HONORS/ACHIEVEMENTS:** Co-author "Facilitating Assertive Training Groups" 1975; participant "The Nature of Morality & Moral Devel" cntr for Advanced Study in the Behavioral Sciences Stanford CA 1979; various publs. **HOME ADDRESS:** 6700 Old Briarstown Dr, Waco, TX 76710.

HARDCASTLE, JAMES C.
Educational administrator. **PERSONAL:** Born Aug 20, 1914, Dover, DE; married Edith E; children: Frank J, Carmen E. **EDUCATION:** DE State Coll, BS 1935; NY U, MA 1951; Temple U, U, U;Univ of DE; DE State Coll, LlD 1979. **CAREER:** Capital School Dist, Dover DE, dir of personnel 1966-; William W M Henry Jr Sr High School, Dover DE, supt of schools 1954-66; BTW Jr High School, Dover DE School System, teacher, coach 1935-54. **ORGANIZATIONS:** Life mem NEA 1942-; mem DE Assn Sch Adminstrs 1954-; mem Am Assn of Sch Adminstrs 1955-; sec bd of Trustees DE State Coll 1962-; varoius others 1968-; various positions with YMCA 1946-; mem NAACP 1943; mem various frat 1946-; mem barious alumni assns 1954-; various postions United Meth Ch1972-. **HONORS/ACHIEVEMENTS:** Omega Man of the Year Award Psi Iota Chap Omega Psi Phi Frat Inc 1962 & 1975; Merit Ward Frontierman of Am DE Chap 1694; Outstanding Alumni Award DE Coll 1970; YMCA Outstanding Citizens Award Dover YMCA 1974; barious other & awards educators & frats 1978-79; EW Buchanan Distinguished Serv Award C of C 1980. **BUSINESS ADDRESS:** 945 Forest St, Dover, DE 19901.

HARDEMAN, CAROLE HALL
Publishing executive. **PERSONAL:** Born in Muskogee, OK; divorced; children: Paula Suzette. **EDUCATION:** Fisk Univ, BA Music; Univ of OK, MA Human Relations 1975, PhD Ed Admin 1979. **CAREER:** Univ of OK, program devel spec 1975-82; Coll of Educ & Human Relations OU, adj prof 1980-85; Center for Human Relations Studies, dir 1982-85; Univ of OK, admin officer 1982-85; Adroit Publ Inc, pres. **ORGANIZATIONS:** Founder/ natl review bd CENTERBOARD Jrnl of OU Ctr 1982; bd of dir United Cerebral Palsy of OK 1983-; exec bd Natl Alliance/Black School Ed 1983-; founder OK Alliance for Black School Educators 1984; cons/speaker NABSE, NAFEO, US Dept of Ed, Natl Conf of Christians & Jews, NSTA; pres & co-founder TwelveInc; mem Links Inc, Jack & Jill Inc, NABSE, Urban League, NAACP, NAMPW, AASA, ASCD, AERA, Alpha Kappa Alpha, YWCA, Assoc of Women in Math; kyenote speaker, Univ of DE, Univ of Pittsburgh, Univ of OK, State Dept of Ed-PA, DC Public Schoosl, Chicago IL, New Orleans Chap One, Las Vegas; num workshops on study skills for sorors & school dists; mm Natl Task Force on Multicultural Ed. **HONORS/ACHIEVEMENTS:** Regents Doct Fellow OK State Regents for Higher Ed 1975-79; The Black Student on the White Coll Campus Univ Press 1983; Outstanding Faculty/Staff Univ of OK 1984; Sounds of Sci Sci Curriculum Publ 1984; The Math Connection Math Curriculum Publ 1985; Commiss by Natl Ctr for Ed Stat US Dept of Ed Rsch &Stat Div to write paper addressing policy issues & admin needs of Amer ed syst through the year 2001; Spec Consult for Sci Projects Harvard Univ; publ "Profile of the Black Coll Student" Urban League's The State of Black OK; Roscoe Dungee Awd for Excellence in Print Journalism OK Black Media Assoc 1984; num papers, articles publ by US Dept of Ed & Natl Sci Found. **HOME ADDRESS:** 7201 German Creek Park, Memphis, TN 38125. **BUSINESS ADDRESS:** Assoc Dean for Lifelong Learning, LeMoyne-Owen College, 807 Walker Ave, Memphis, TN 38126.

HARDEMAN, JAMES ANTHONY
Social worker. **PERSONAL:** Born Feb 02, 1943, Athens, GA; divorced; children: Maria, Brian. **EDUCATION:** Howard Univ, BA 1967; Boston Coll, MSW 1973; Harvard Univ, MPA 1974. **CAREER:** Dept of Corrections, prison warden 1975-78; Dept of Mentah Health, sr social worker 1978-79; Ex-Office of Human Serv State House Boston, deputy dir of planning 1979-83; Polaroid Corp, dir of counseling 1983-. **ORGANIZATIONS:** Bd mem Boston Coll Bd of Directors 1981-83; pres Boston Coll Grad Sch of Social Work Alumni Assoc 1981-83; vice pres Natl Assoc of Social Work MA 1982; bd mem Mayflower Mental Health Assoc 1983-, Catholic Charities 1983-, Crime and Justice Foundation Boston 1985-. **HONORS/ACHIEVEMENTS:** Natl Delegate Rep Natl Assoc of Social Workers MA Chap 1981. **MILITARY SERVICE:** USAF capt 1967-71. **HOME ADDRESS:** 55 Main St, Kingston, MA 02364. **BUSINESS ADDRESS:** Dir of Counseling, Polaroid Corp, One Upland Rd, Norwood, MA 02062.

HARDEMAN, STROTHA E., JR.
Dentist. **PERSONAL:** Born Oct 26, 1929, Ft Worth; married Wllie Mae; children: Sharon Kaye, Keith Dion. **EDUCATION:** VA Union U, BS 1950; Meharry Med Coll, DT 1956; Meharry Med Sch, DDS 1963. **CAREER:** Gulf State Denatl Assn, dentist pres. **ORGANIZATIONS:** Mem NT Wallis Dental Soc; Ft Worth Dental Soc; TX Denatl Assn; Am Dental Assn; mem Ambassadore Club; Jack & Jill Am Inc. **MILITARY SERVICE:** AUS med corp 1950. **BUSINESS ADDRESS:** 612 NW 25 St, Fort Worth, TX 76106.

HARDEN, MARVIN
Artist educator. **PERSONAL:** Born in Austin, TX; son of Theodore Roosevelt Harden and Ethel Sneed Harden. **EDUCATION:** Univ of CA Los Angeles, BA Fine Arts 1959, MA Creative Painting 1963. **CAREER:** Univ CA Los Angeles, extension instr art 1964-68; Los Angeles Harbor Clge, eve div instr art 1965-68; Univ High Adult Schl, instr art 1965-68; Santa Monica City Clge, eve div instr art 1968; CA State Univ Northridge, prof art 1968-. **ORGANIZATIONS:** MemNatl Endowment for Arts Visual Arts Flwshp Painting Panel 1985; mem Los Angeles Municipal Art Gallery Assc Artist's Adv Bd 1983-; mem bd dir "Images & Issues" 1980-84; co-fndr Los Angeles Inst of Contemporary Art 1973. **HONORS/ACHIEVEMENTS:** Distg Prof Award & Excep Merit Srv Award CA State Univ Northridge 1984; Flw John Simon Guggenheim Mem Fnd 1983; Flw Awards in Visual Arts 1983; Flw-Natl Endowment for Arts 1972; One Man Shows, Whitney Museum of Amer Art, Irving Blum Gallery, Los Angeles Municipal Art Gallery, Newport Harbor Art Museum; Eugenia Butler Galleries, James Corcoran Gallery, David Stuart Galleries, Ceeje Galleries, Brand Library Art Ctr, Group Shows, L A Cty Museum Of Art, BrooklynMuseum, Chicago Museum of Contemporary Art, Equitable Gallery, NYC, Nagoya City Museum Japan, Contemporary Art Assc Houston, Philadelphia Civic Ctr Museum, San Francisco Museum of Art, High Museum of Art, Minneapolis Inst of Arts, Univ of CA Los Angeles, US State Dept tour of USSR, Franklin Furnace NYC, San Diego Fine Art Gallery. **BUSINESS ADDRESS:** Professor of Art, CA StateUniv Northridge, 18111 Nordhoff St - ART2, Northridge, CA 91330.

HARDEN, ROBERT JAMES
Physician. **PERSONAL:** Born Jul 16, 1952, Washington, GA; married Margaret Ellanor Hemp; children: Robert Jr, John Phillip. **EDUCATION:** Univ of IL Chicago, BS 1975; Meharry Medical Coll, MD 1979. **CAREER:** Weiss Memorial Hosp, medical intern 1980-81; US Public Health Svcs, asst surgeon general 1981-83; Timberlawn Psychiatric Hosp, psychiatry resident 1984-87,child & adolescent fellow 1987-89. **ORGANIZATIONS:** Resident mem of exec council TX Soc of Psychiatric Physicians 1986-87. **HONORS/ACHIEVEMENTS:** S01 W Ginsburg Fellowship Group for the Advancement of Psychiatry 1987-89. **BUSINESS ADDRESS:** Resident Staff Psychiatrist, Timberlawn Psychiatric Hosp, 4600 Samuell Blvd, Box 11288, Dallas, TX 75223.

HARDIE, ROBERT L., JR.
Business executive. **PERSONAL:** Born Oct 22, 1941, Portsmouth, VA; son of Robert L Hardie, Sr and Janie Norman Hardie; married Marianne Lowry; children: Levon, Robin, F Gary Lee (stepson). **EDUCATION:** Hampton Inst, BS 1963; Univ of MD, Southern IL Univ, Grad Studies for MBA. **CAREER:** US Army Security Agency Warrenton, chief elect engrg 1964-66; Bunker-Ramo Corp Silver Spring, system integration engr 1966-69; Vitro Lab Automation Ind Inc Silver Spring, proj leader 1969-72; Raytheon Serv Co Hyattsville, sr systems engr 1972-73; Systems Consultants Inc Washington, sr systems engr 1973-75; Scientific Mgmt Assoc Inc, prog mgr 1975-85; sr systems engr Evaluation Research Corp Interntl 1985-86; pres Sentel Corp, Maryland 1986-. **ORGANIZATIONS:** Mem Amer Soc Naval Engrs 1974-, Navy League 1974-87, Naval Inst, Inst Elec Electronic Engrs 1965-70, 1975-; pres Greenbelt Jaycees 1973-74; deacon, asst to pastor at church, chaplain, church choir; chmn Greenbelt Comm Relations Adv Comm 1974-76; vice pres Mutual Hum Concerns Inc 1974-77; vice pres Greenbelt Labor Day Festival Comm; bd of dirs Camp Springs Boys & Girls Club 1979-; mem Greenbelt Rep Transp Citizen Adv Comm Met Washington Council Govts; mem Natl Assn of Minority Business 1984-. **HONORS/ACHIEVEMENTS:** Greenbelt Jaycees Keyman Awd 1973, 1975; Jaycee of the Month 1971, 1972; Graduated with dept honors, grad with honors; Distinguished Military Grad; co-authored & publ "Let's Design Out EMI" 1981; Gold Plaque Award, letter of appreciation Naval Sea Systems CMD 1985. **MILITARY SERVICE:** AUS 1st lt 1964-66. **BUSINESS ADDRESS:** President, Chief Executive Officer, Sentel Corporation, 1735 Jefferson Davis Highway, Suite 407, Arlington, VA 22202.

HARDIMAN, PHILLIP THOMAS
Governmental official. **PERSONAL:** Born Nov 07, 1935, Chicago, IL; married Loretta; children: Phillip Jr, Christopher. **EDUCATION:** Lewis U, BA 1974; Roosevelt U, MPA 1976; Chicago State U, MS 1977. **CAREER:** Cook Co Dept of Corrections, exec dir 1977-; Cook Co Sheriffs Police, capt 1974-77; Cook Co Sheriffs Police, lt 1969-74; Cook Co Shefeffs Police, sgt1967-69; Cook Co Sheriffs Police, patrolman 1964-67. **ORGANIZATIONS:** Bd mem Nat Blacks in Criminal Justice 1979-; bd mem SCLC Chicago Chap 1979-; bd mem IL Correctional Assn 1979-. **HONORS/ACHIEVEMENTS:** Twelve commendations Cook Co Sheriffs Police 1964-77; Law Award Phi Alpha Delta Law Frat 1975; Dr Martin Luther

King Award SCLC Chicago Metro Chap 1980. **BUSINESS ADDRESS:** 2700 S California, Chicago, IL 60608.

HARDIN, BONIFACE
Clergyman. **PERSONAL:** Born Nov 18, 1933, Louisville. **EDUCATION:** St Meinrad Sem, 1947-59;Univ Of Note Dame, addl studies 1962-63. **CAREER:** Martin Center Inc, exec dir 1969-; St Meinrad Archabbey, monk; Holy Angels Ch Indianapolis, assoc pastor 1965-69; St Meinrad, asst treas 1959-65;Afro-am Studies, fdr & dir of inst 1970; Afro-am Journal, fdr & ed 1973; Afro-am Indianapolis WIAN FM & WFYI-TV, producer & host; Indianapolis Sickle CellAnemia Found, co-fdr; IN Sickle Cell Cntr, dir of com serv; Nego-jewish Dialogue, co-fdr; Hum Relations Consortium; NW Action Council, dir & frd; Action Project Commitment; Indianapolis Black Coalition, co-chmn. **ORGANIZATIONS:** Mem State Penal Reform Com; Vol Adv Corps Citizens for Progress Com Comm Service 1971; Comm Ser in Sickle Cell Guys & Dolls 1971. **HONORS/ACHIEVEMENTS:** Citizen of Year Award Zeta Epsilon; Citizens of Yr Award Zeta Phi; Hum Rights Award in Comm ldrshp Indianapolis Educ Assn 1974; founder & pres Martin Center Coll 1977. **BUSINESS ADDRESS:** 3561 N Coll Ave, Indianapolis, IN 46205.

HARDIN, EUGENE
Educator/physicians. **PERSONAL:** Born Dec 06, 1941, Jacksonville, FL; widowed; children: Jeffrey, Gregory. **EDUCATION:** FL A&M Univ, BS Pharm 1964; Univ So FL, MD 1977. **CAREER:** Walgreens, asst mgr pharmacist 1964-66; VA Hosp, staff pharmacist 1966-74; King-Drew Med Ctr, physician specialist 1980-, asst prof internal medicine 1980-. **ORGANIZATIONS:** Med dir Carson Medical Group 1981-; mem Natl Medical Assoc 1984-87, Drew Med Soc 1985-87, Carson Chamber of Commerce 1985, SCLC 1986-; chmn Joint Practices Comm Martin Luther King Hosp 1987; med dir Physician Asst Prog King Drew Med Ctr. **HONORS/ACHIEVEMENTS:** Most Outstanding Residence Internal Medicine Martin Luther King Hosp 1980; published paper "The Dynamics of Parental Abuse," 1987. **MILITARY SERVICE:** AUS sp-5 2 yrs; Foreign Serv Medal 1969. **HOME ADDRESS:** PO Box 901, Harbor City, CA 90710.

HARDIN, HENRY E.
Educator, businessman, clergyman. **PERSONAL:** Born 1912, Ft Motte, SC; married Carrie; children: Isadora Wallace, Henrietta Butler. **EDUCATION:** Benedict Coll, BA 1944; Benedict Coll, BD 1945; NY U, MA 1947; NYUniv Union Theol Sem City Coll of NY, pursued addl grad studies. **CAREER:** St Paul Bapt Ch, pastor; Morris Coll Sumter SC, pres; prof dean of Instr elected by trustees to head Coll 1970; dean dir coll financial aid prog recruited students in large numbers expanded on campus & ext progs; Centennial Celebration of SC Bapt Conv, inst. **ORGANIZATIONS:** Mem numerous professional orgns spl honors include Nat Humanities Flw DukeUniv 1971; mem on Staff of Colgate-rochester Seminar on Black Ch Curr 1969; pres Commn on Equal Opp. **BUSINESS ADDRESS:** Morris Coll, Sumter, SC 29150.

HARDIN, HERBERT G.
Attorney. **PERSONAL:** Born Sep 02, 1915, Knoxville, Tunisia;married Thelma; children: Marilyn, Herbert, Jr. **EDUCATION:** Morgan State Coll, AB 1937; Howard Sch of Law, LlD 1940. **CAREER:** Commonwealth of PA, asst atty gen 1946-49. **ORGANIZATIONS:** Mem NBA; Philadelphia Bar Assn; Alpha Phi Alpha. **MILITARY SERVICE:** Nat guardsmen capt Ordnance Dept 1941-45. **HOME ADDRESS:** 6492 Anderson St, Philadelphia, PA 19119.

HARDIN, JOHN ARTHUR
Educator. **PERSONAL:** Born Sep 18, 1948, Louisville, KY; son of Albert A and Elizabeth; married Maxine Randle; children: Jonathan. **EDUCATION:** Bellarmine Coll, BA 1970; Fisk Univ, MA 1972; Univ of MI, PhD Candidate 1978-. **CAREER:** Univ of Louisville, lecturer 1972-84; KY State Univ, asst prof 1976-84, area coord 1978-80; Univ of KY, visiting asst prof 1980-81; Eastern WA Univ, asst prof 1984-. **ORGANIZATIONS:** Mem exec comm KY Assoc of Teachers of History 1976-80; state dir Phi Beta Sigma Frat Inc 1981-83; club pres Frankfort Kiwanis Club 1983-84; mem KY History Preservation Review Bd 1983-84, Publ Advisory Comm Historical Soc 1983-84, Natl Council on Black Studies Region X 1984-87, KY Historical Soc 1984-; NAACP, 1984-. **HONORS/ACHIEVEMENTS:** Lenihan Awd for Comm Serv Bellarmine Coll 1969; Three Univ Fellowship Fisk Univ 1970-72; J Pierce Scholarshp Univ of MI Dept of History 1976; Distinguished Alumni Gallery Bellarmine Coll 1979-80; Pres Awd, Natl Council For Black Studies-Region X (1987); author, Onward and Upward: A Centennial History of Kentucky State University 1886-1986. **HOME ADDRESS:** PO Box 149, Cheney, WA 99004. **BUSINESS ADDRESS:** Assistant Professor, Eastern Washington University, Black Education Program, Monroe Hall 104 Mail Stop 164, Cheney, WA 99004.

HARDING, ED
Retired government offical. **PERSONAL:** Born Oct 23, 1924, Portsmouth, VA; son of Cammie Kadosa Harding and Bernice Cook Harding; married Edna Moore; children: Robin. **EDUCATION:** Howard Univ, 1950-52; CCNY, 1959; Amer Theatre Wing, Drama Cert 1950. **CAREER:** Theatre/Films/TV/Radio, actor 1946-64; Africa Pavillion/NY Worlds Fare, dir 1964; Ed Hardings Freeport NY, restaurateur 1965-69; Nassau Cty Govt Svcs, dir1971-; Glen Cove Coop Ctr, dir. **ORGANIZATIONS:** Past dir Freeport Chamber of Commerce 1972, Nassau Cty Sickle Cell Anemia 1978; mem The Edges Group Inc 1979-85; past dir Nassau Cty Hispanic Coalition 1982; Nassau Co Republican Comm Republican committeeman Freeport, NY for 16 yrs; vice pres Freeport Home Rule Pary 1986. **HONORS/ACHIEVEMENTS:** Mem Amer Legion 1970, Natl Urban League 1979; Certificate of Recognition Nassau Cty Youth Bd 1980; life mem Disabled Amer Vets 1982. **MILITARY SERVICE:** AUS 2 years; Bronze Star, Victory Medal, Asiatic Pacific Campaign Medal 1943-44; USN Hon Discharge 1941.

HARDING, JOHN EDWARD
Port authority director. **PERSONAL:** Born May 28, 1938, Nashville, TN; son of James A Harding and Helen E Harding; married Delores Evon Kelly Harding, Dec 18, 1960; children: Sheri Harding Daley. **EDUCATION:** Tennessee A&I State Univ, Nashville TN, BS Civil Engineering, 1960. **CAREER:** US Army, Directorate of Civil Engineering, Ohio, civil engineer, 1960-67; Air Force Logistics Command, Ohio, civil engineer, 1967-71; Virgin Islands Dept of Public Works, St Thomas VI, commr, 1971-75; Virgin Islands Port Authority, St. Thomas VI, dir of engineering, 1975-77, exec dir, 1977-. **ORGANIZATIONS:** Mem, Amer Soc Civil Engineers, Airport Operators Council Intl, Amer Assn of Port Authorities, Southeastern Airport Managers Assn, Southeastern and Caribbean Port Authorities, Amer Assn of Airport Executives. **MILITARY SERVICE:** USAF, 1963-64. **BUSINESS ADDRESS:** Executive Director, Virgin Islands Port Authority, PO Box 1707, St Thomas, Virgin Islands of the United States 00801.

HARDING, ROBERT E.
Attorney, educator, labor arbitrator. **PERSONAL:** Born May 31, 1930, Danville, KY; son of Robert Sr (deceased) and Olivia(deceased); married Iola Willhite; children: Roberta, Olivia. **EDUCATION:** KY State Univ, BA 1954; Univ KY, JD 1957. **CAREER:** USPHS, corr officer 1952-58; Natl Labor Relations Bd, atty 1958-74; EEO consultant 1980-86; labor arbitrator 1981-; Univ New Mexico, tchr Afro-Amer studies 1974-. **ORGANIZATIONS:** Mem KY, NM, Natl, Fed, Inter-Am, Albuquerque Bar Assns; mem US Dist Ct NM; mem US Court of Appeals 10th Circuit; US Ct Appeals DC & Supreme Ct; mem Natl Conf Black Lawyers; Amer Arbitration Assn, Soc of Profls in Dispute Resolution, Soc of Fed Labor Relations Profls, Amer Assn of Univ Prof; mem Phi Alpha Delta Legal Frat; pres, bd dir Albuquerque Child Care Centers 1980-81; mem NM Adv Comm to the US Commiss on Civil Rights 1981-. **MILITARY SERVICE:** AUS 1946-47. **BUSINESS ADDRESS:** Teacher Afro-Amer Studies, Univ New Mexico, P O Box 14277, Albuquerque, NM 87191.

HARDING, VINCENT
Historian, educator. **PERSONAL:** Born Jul 25, 1931, New York City; married Rosemarie Freeney; children: Rachel, Jonathan. **EDUCATION:** City Coll NY, BA 1952; Columbia, MS 1953;Univ of Chgo, MA 1956; PhD 1965. **CAREER:** Seventh Day Adventist Church Chicago, sply pastor 1955-57; Woodlawn Mennoite Church Chicago, lay assoc pastor 1957-61; Mennonite Central Com Atlanta, so rep serv com 1961-64; Spelman Coll Atlanta, asst prof History, dept chmn History Social Sciences 1965-69; Martin Luther King Jr Library Project, dir 1968-70; Inst of Baclk World, dir 1969-. **HONORS/ACHIEVEMENTS:** Author "must walls divide" 1965; cntbg ed, mem, ed bd concern chrstnty & crisis chrstn cntry; others, also poems, short stories, articles, sermons to professional publs; Kent fellow Soc Rel in Hghr Edn. **BUSINESS ADDRESS:** % Harcourt, Brace & Jovanovich, Trade Publicity Department, 111 Fifth Ave, New York, NY 10003.

HARDISON, RUTH INGE
Sculptor. **PERSONAL:** Born Feb 03, 1914, Portsmouth, VA; daughter of William Hardison and Evelyn Jordan Hardison; children: Yolande. **EDUCATION:** TN State A&I, 1934-35; Art Stdnts League, 1935; Vassar Coll, 1942-44. **CAREER:** Cmmsnd Sclptrs By Old Taylor Whiskies, "Ingenious Amers" 1966; New York City Bd of Educ, "New Genration" 1975; New York City Dept Cultural Affairs, Jackie Robinson Portrait 1980; Black Alumni of Princeton Univ, Frederick Douglas Portrait 1982; creator of on-going series "Negro Giants in History" begun in 1963 includes, Harriet Tubman, "The Slave Woman," Frederick Douglass, Dr WEB DuBoise, Dr Mary McLeod Bethune, Dr Geo Washington Carver, Sojourner Truth 1968, Dr ML King Jr 1968,1975,Paul Robeson Sojourner Truth Pin; new series "Our Folks" begun in 1984 one of a kind collectibles sculptures of ordinary people in everyday scenes. **ORGANIZATIONS:** Prsntn WISH Assc Margaret McCaden on Sculpture and The Spoken Word; founding mem Harlem Cultural Council 1964, Black Acad of Arts and Letters 1969. **HONORS/ACHIEVEMENTS:** Anna Arnold Hedgeman Awrd 1957-59; self discovery workshops granted by Harlem Cultural Council 1975; school children studio visits Cottonwood Found 1980; Cultural Achievement Award, Riverside Club of the Natl Business and Professional Women's Clubs, 1987; exhibition of 26 photographs, Portsmouth Museum 1988; latest edition to series "Views from Harlem," Phillis Wheatley, poet 1989. **HOME ADDRESS:** 444 Central Park W 4b, New York, NY 10025.

HARDISON, WALTER L., JR.
Business executive. **PERSONAL:** Born Mar 20, 1921, Chicago, IL; married Helen Youngblood. **EDUCATION:** Attended, Herzel Jr Coll, Temple Univ; Mutual of Omaha Natl Sales Training Acad, grad. **CAREER:** Golden State Mutual Life Chicago, dist mgr 1948, agency mgr 1955; Rolling Green Memorial Park Wilmington DE, branch mgr 1952; Dept of Revenue City of Chicago, dist supr 1962-; W L Hardison Jr & Assocs Genl Ins Agency, pres 1958-. **ORGANIZATIONS:** Triangle Club YMCA; Tee Birds Gold Club; Hyde Park-Kenwood Comm Conf; Operation PUSH; Urban Gateways; Comm coord for 5 Ward Regular Dem Orgn & Urban League; solicited over 100 cash memberships for Operation PUSH 1973; coord 100 youths attending Urban League's Football Classic 1973; originator & editor of comm newsletter 1973; coord 100 percent membership of Unity Mutual Life's Staff & Field w/Chicago Urban League 1958; baptized mem St John Church Baptist 1984.

HARDMAN-CROMWELL, YOUTHA CORDELLA
Educator. **PERSONAL:** Born Jan 10, 1941, Washington, DC; daughter of Esther Willis Jubilee; married Oliver W Cromwell, May 28, 1988; children: Darnell Whitten, Wayne Whitten, Debra Whitten. **EDUCATION:** George Washington Univ, AA, 1960, BS Math 1963; Troy State Univ AL, MS Ed 1971; Univ of VA, EdS Math, Ed 1984; Howard Univ, MDiv 1986. **CAREER:** Mountain Home Primary School ID, 2nd grade teacher 1964-67; Garrison Elementary School DC, 2nd grade teacher 1967-68; Fledgling School AL, 1st grade teacher 1968-70; Misawe Dependents School Japan, chmn Math dept & teacher 1972-75; Elmore County HS AL; Math teacher 1975; Stafford Sr HS VA, Math teacher 1976-79; Germanna Comm Coll, assoc prof Math 1979-86; Woodlawn United Methodist Church VA Conf, pastor, 1986-89; Howard Univ School of Divinity, coordinator of Field-Based Fellowship Program, 1987-; lecturer, Practical Theology, 1989. **ORGANIZATIONS:** Mem Rappahanock-Rapidan Teachers of Math, VA Council of Teachers of Math, Math Assoc of Amer; political action chmn Orange County NAACP 1978-86; commission Planning Dist Nine VA 1979-84; bd mem Orange County Recreation Assoc 1979-80; bd mem Orange County Library Bd 1982-84; pres Black Caucus VA Conf UMC 1986-88; Consultant, Secretary, Churches in Transitional Communities, 1987-; Mem, VA Conf Commission on Religion and Race, 1987-. **HONORS/ACHIEVEMENTS:** Outstanding Teacher Dept of Defense Dependent Schools Japan 1974; Serv Awd NAACP Orange County 1982, 1983; Dir 7th Annual Devel Studies Conf VA Community Coll 1983; Benjamin Mays Fellow Howard Univ Divinity School 1984-86; Published Poem "The Sound of Your Laughter" Journal of Religious Thought Fall-Winter 1984-85; Anderson Fellow 1985-86; Deans Award 40 Ave, Henry C Maynard Award for Excellence in Preaching & Ministry, Staff Award for Exceptional Performance, gave welcome address at Howard Univ graduation as rep of all graduates Howard Univ Divinity School 1986; Assistantship American Univ, 1989-90; Women of Color Doctoral Fellowship, 1989-90. **HOME ADDRESS:** 2015 13th St, NW, Washington, DC 20009.

HARDNETT, CAROLYN JUDY
Librarian. **PERSONAL:** Born Aug 12, 1947, Washington, DC; daughter of Freddie P Hardnett and Ada West Hardnett. **EDUCATION:** Hampton Inst, Hampton VA, 1965-68. **CAREER:** First & Merchants Natl Bank, Pentagon & Arlington VA, 1968-70; Chicago Tribune, Washington DC, librarian, 1970-85; The Baltimore Sun, Baltimore MD, chief librarian, 1985-. **ORGANIZATIONS:** Sec/treasurer, Special Libraries Assn, News Division, 1982-83, conference planner, 1983-84, chair, 1984-85, dir, Baltimore Chapter, 1986-88, bd of dirs, 1987-89; mem, Natl Assn of Black Journalists, 1985-. **HONORS/ACHIEVEMENTS:** Award of Merit, Special Libraries Assn, News Division, 1985; Certificate of Recognition, Black Enterprise Professional Exchange & Networking Forum, 1989. **BUSINESS ADDRESS:** Director of Library Services, The Baltimore Sun, 501 N Calvert St, Baltimore, MD 21278.

HARDWICK, CLIFFORD E., III
Educator. **PERSONAL:** Born Sep 04, 1927, Savannah, GA; children: 2 children. **EDUCATION:** Savannah State Coll, BS 1950; Univ of Pittsburgh, LittM 1959; Howard Univ, NC Coll, Atlanta Univ, Univ of GA, Mott Leadership Inst, attended; Morris Brown Coll, LLD 1975. **CAREER:** Effingham Cty Training School, teacher; instructor, physical science lecturer, gen inorganic chem 1951-52; Springfield Terrace Elementary School, teacher 1952-53; Alfred E Beach High School, chmn biology dept 1953-61; Secondary Educ, supvr 1961-68; Comm Educ Savannah, dir 1968-70; Continuing Educ Program Univ of GA, asst prof, dir 1970-; Coastal Georgia Center for Continuing Ed ASC/SSC, asst to the dean. **ORGANIZATIONS:** 1st black elected to serve as foreman on grand jury 1974; ordained as itinerate elder AME Church 1980; mem Natl Univ Ext Assoc, Natl Comm School Ed Assoc, GA Adult Ed Council; adv comm Adult Basic Ed, Alpha Phi Alpha; pres Greenbriar Children Ctr, Savannah Tribune; dir Carver State Bank; exec bd Savannah Chap NAACP; mem Comm of Christian Ed St Philip AME Church, Savannah State Coll Alumni Assoc; mem Cardiovascular Nutrition Comm; vchmn, bd of dir Amer Red Cross Savannah Chapt; mem Hospice Savannah Bd; mem Amer Heart Assoc; exec comm Coastal Area Council Boy Scouts of Amer, United Way Allocations Panel. **HONORS/ACHIEVEMENTS:** Man of the Year Alpha Phi Alpha 1962; listed in Who's Who in Amer Ed 1965-66; Outstanding Personalities of the South 1968; Comm Leaders of Amer 1969-70; Creative & Successful Personalities of the World 1970; Model Cities Recognition Awd for Leadership 1971; Citizen of Day WTOC 1974; Cirus G Wiley Disting Alumnus Awd Savannah State Coll 1974; Community Serv Awd Savannah Bus League 1976. **BUSINESS ADDRESS:** Assistant to the Dean, Coastal Georgia Center for Continuing Education, University of Georgia, Athens, GA 30602.

HARDY, CHARLIE EDWARD
Business executive. **PERSONAL:** Born Jan 19, 1941, Montgomery, AL; son of William H Hardy and Sarah W Hardy; married Lillie Pearl Curry; children: Randall Charles, Christa Valencia. **EDUCATION:** AL State Univ, BS Secondary Ed 1962; IN State Univ, attended 1967; Life Underwriters Training, Council Grad 1972. **CAREER:** Brewton City School System, dir of bands 1962-66; Macon Cty Public School, dir of bands 1966-69; Metropolitan Life, sr sales rep 1969-, assoc branch mgr 1988, sr acct exec 1969. **ORGANIZATIONS:** Mem Natl Assoc of Life Underwriters 1969, NAACP, Tuskegee Civic Assoc, 33 Degree Mason Shriner; life mem Alpha Phi Alpha Frat Inc; deacon Greenwood Missionary Baptist Church; legislative liason Tuskegee Civic Assn 1989. **HONORS/ACHIEVEMENTS:** Outstanding Alumnus AL State Univ 1972; Alpha Man of the Year Alpha Phi Alpha Frat Inc 1975; Salesman of the Year Metropolitan Life Montgomery Dist 1979; Alpha Man of the Year Alpha Phi Alpha Frat Tuskegee 1984; Distinguished Alumnus AL State Univ 1985; Inducted as Veteran for 20 Years of Service, Metropolitan Life & Affiliated Companies 1989. **BUSINESS ADDRESS:** Associate Branch Manager, Metropolitan Life & Affil Comp, 1102 W Old Montgomery Rd, Tuskegee Institute, AL 36088.

HARDY, DOROTHY C.
Professional administrator. **PERSONAL:** Born in Town Creek, AL; children: Althea J Mootry. **EDUCATION:** AL St U, BS; Xavier U, MEd;Univ of Cincinnati, EdD. **CAREER:** Univ of Cincinnati, Grps & Univ Progms, asst dean stdnts 1973-77; KS St U, asst prof & emp/rcrtmnt Spec;Univ of Cincinnati, instr; Cincinnati LifeAdj Inst, pres 1980-83; OH Dept Mental Hlth, comm div bus adm 1983-84; Southeast Missouri State Univ,. **ORGANIZATIONS:** Human Invlvmnt Prog 1979; bus act Madisonville Jabos Training 1982; consult Archdiocese of Grtr Cincinnati 1983; Prog Assoc for Economic Dev; mnrty coord Issues 2 & 3 Ctzns for Gov Richard F Celeste 1983-84; training dir Mondale/Ferraro Camp 1984. **HONORS/ACHIEVEMENTS:** Brodie Rsrch Awd #1000 Plus 1975; Otstndg Comm Serv 1976; Otstndng Women NAACP 1981; Background Player "The Jesse Owens Story" Paramount Studio for ABC TV 1984; Cert of Mert for the Fiction (Writer's Diegest) Poetry (Creative Enterprise, World of Poetry) Pebble in the Pond 1985; Golden Poet Awd 1986. **BUSINESS ADDRESS:** Southeast Missouri StateUniv, Rockwood & Henderson, Cape Girardeau, MO 63701.

HARDY, FREEMAN
Educator. **PERSONAL:** Born May 22, 1942, Winona, MS; married Cozetta Hubbard; children: Tonya, Tasha. **EDUCATION:** AR AM&N Coll, BS 1964; Howard Univ, DDS 1970; Georgetown Univ, MSc 1974. **CAREER:** AR AM&U Coll, lab instructor 1964; Howard Univ, instructor 1970-72; Georgetown, post-grad training 1972-74; HUCD, asst prof 1974-77, assoc prof 1977-83, prof 1983-; Howard Univ Coll of Dentistry, prof. **ORGANIZATIONS:** Consult Howard Univ Hosp; Oral Cancer Soc Chi Delta Mu; Omicron Kappa Upsilon; ADA; Robert T Freeman Dental Soc; NDA; Amer Coll of Prosthodontics; AADR; IADR; Sigma Xi; DC Dental Soc; Alpha Phi Alpha; Diagnosis & Treatment Planning for Rem Partial Dentures 1976; Comparison of Fluid Resin & Compression Molding Methods in Processing Dimensional Changes 1977.

HARDY, JAMES
Professional athlete. **PERSONAL:** Born Dec 01, 1956, Knoxville, AL. **EDUCATION:** San Francisco 1978. **CAREER:** UT Jazz, professional basketball player forward. **HONORS/ACHIEVEMENTS:** NBA All-rookie Team Basketball Digest Mag.

HARDY, JOHN LOUIS
Educational administrator. **PERSONAL:** Born Feb 22, 1937, Rayville, LA; married Bernetta; children: Mike, David, John. **EDUCATION:** Pasadena City Coll, AA 1958; CA State Poly Univ Pomona, BS 1961; Azusa Pacific, MA 1970. **CAREER:** Azusa School Dist, teacher 1963; Pasadena City Coll, counselor 1970; Pasadena City Coll Extended Opportunity Program, dir. **ORGANIZATIONS:** Pres Sugar Ray Youth Found 1975; chmn Pasadena Comm Serv Comm 1976; pres, bd of ed Pasadena School Dist 1978-79. **BUSINESS ADDRESS:** Dir, Pasadena City Coll, Extended Oppty Prog, 1570 E Colorado Blvd, Pasadena, CA 91106.

HARDY, LARRY
Professional athlete. **PERSONAL:** Born Jul 09, 1956, Mendenhall, MS. **EDUCATION:** Jackson State Univ, Phys Ed. **CAREER:** New Orleans Saints, tight end 1978-. **HONORS/ACHIEVEMENTS:** All-Southwest Athletic Conf; caught only TD scored at Chicago in Saints win 1982; 71 yard TD catch vs Atlanta was team's longest pass play 1978.

HARDY, MICHAEL LEANDER
Marketing manager. **PERSONAL:** Born Feb 21, 1945, Petersburg, VA; married Jacqueline; children: Sheila Jacqueline, Michelle Lorraine. **EDUCATION:** ColumbiaUniv New York City NY, BS 1966; Rollins Coll Winter Park FL, MCS 1973. **CAREER:** The Carborundum Co, mge maint servs & repairs pangborn 1979-; The Carburundum Co Pangborn Div, mgr market planning & control 1973-79; Martin-marietta Corp Orlando Div, prog planning analyst 1967-71; Martin-marietta Corp Orlando Div, asso engr 1966-67. **ORGANIZATIONS:** Bd mem Bethel Corp 1979-; mem Citizens Adv Com Wash Co Bd of Edn; bd mem Big Bros of Wash Co; past pres Orange Co FL Br NAACP 1971-73. **BUSINESS ADDRESS:** Pangborn Blvd, Hagerstown, MD 21740.

HARDY, WALTER S. E.
Physician. **PERSONAL:** Born Oct 09, 1920, Alcoa, TN; married Edna D; children: Cheryl. **EDUCATION:** Johnson C Smith Univ, BS 1938; Meharry Univ, MD 1950. **CAREER:** Private practice, physician. **ORGANIZATIONS:** Mem NMA, AMA, AAFP; bd chmn Hillcrest Med & Nursing Inst; past pres Volunteer State Med Assoc; bd mem Home Vstg Nursing Assoc; vice pres Knoxville Ambulance Auth; bd chmn Knoxville Area Urban League; Squire Knoxville Cty Court; past pres Volunteer Bowling League; mem Better Bus Bureau Knoxville, C of C; mem Selective Svc, TN State Voters Council; bd mem Girls Club of Amer; comm man-at-large Knoxville United Way; dir Health Serv Knoxville Coll. **HONORS/ACHIEVEMENTS:** Omega Man of the Year 1970. **MILITARY SERVICE:** AUS warrant officer 1942-45. **BUSINESS ADDRESS:** 2210 Vine Ave, Knoxville, TN 37915.

HARDY, WILLIE J.
Legislator. **PERSONAL:** Born Jul 18, 1922, St Louis, MO; daughter of James White and Willie White; widowed; children: Charles, DeSales, Joan, Linda, Marinne, Diana, Lloyd. **EDUCATION:** Atlantic Business School; George Washington Univ. **CAREER:** Council of DC, chwmn councilwoman; Dept of Environ Svcs, dep dir; Ofc of Mayor, dep dir; Sen Phillip Hart Toastmistress Intl Toastmistress Club, staff asst; Com on Housing & Econ Devel, chwmn. **ORGANIZATIONS:** Life mem Nat Council of Negro Women; mem PA Ave Devel Corp; adjunct prof Antioch Sch of Law; mem Com on the Judiciary; mem Comm on Finance & Revenue; mem Com on Finance & Revenue; chwman Comm Task Force for Safety of Children & Youth 1973; exec dir Metro Comm Aid Council 1967-71; exec dir HowardUniv Nghbrhd Council; instr Fed City Coll; partic CORE effort to deseg food establ; partic SCLC voters regis drive; coord DC residents attng Selma-to-montgomery March. **HONORS/ACHIEVEMENTS:** Outst Woman of WA Phi Lambda Theta Sor 1967; Woman of Yr Afro-am Newspapers & Greyhound & Corp 1972; Comm Serv Award Metro Police Dept 1974; Kiwanis Award Kiwanis Intl 1976; Antioch Sch of Law Fdrs Award 1976. **BUSINESS ADDRESS:** Dist Bldg, Washington, DC 20004.

HARDY-HILL, EDNA MAE
Psychologist. **PERSONAL:** Born Feb 14, 1943, Thomasville, GA; daughter of Leroy and Hagar; married Davis Vincent, Jun 22, 1974; children: Davis Vincent Jr, Michael A. **EDUCATION:** Bennett Coll, AB 1965; Howard Univ, MS 1968. **CAREER:** Natl Inst of Mental Health, health scientist admnstr 1974, resch psycgst 1968-74. **ORGANIZATIONS:** Treas Assoc of Black Psychologist 1983 Natl Conv; mem Peoples Congregational Church, Assoc of Black Psychologists, Amer Psychological Assoc, Bennett Coll Alumnea Assoc. **HONORS/ACHIEVEMENTS:** Hnr soc Chi Beta Kappa Chi; Pi Gamma Mu; Psi Chi; Howard Univ Flwshp 1966-67; Bennett Coll Flwshp 1961-65; Outstanding Work Performance NIMH 1982, 85, 87; NIMH Dir Award for Significant Achievement 1989. **BUSINESS ADDRESS:** Chief Research Development, Natl Inst of Mental Health, 5600 Fishers Lane 9C15, Rockville, MD 20857.

HARE, JULIA REED
Journalist. **PERSONAL:** Born Nov 07, 1942, Tulsa, OK; married Dr Nathan Hare. **EDUCATION:** Langston Univ, BA 1964; Roosevelt Univ Chicago, MMEd 1966; DC Teachers Coll, certified elem educ 1967. **CAREER:** Chicago Public Schs, teacher 1966; DC Teachers Coll, supr student teachers 1967-68; Natl Comm Against Discrimination in Housing, pub relations dir 1969-72; Univ of San Francisco, instructor 1969-70; Golden W Broadcasters KSFO radio, dir comm affairs 1973-. **ORGANIZATIONS:** Mem No CA Broadcasters Assn 1973-; hon bd Sickle Cell Anemia Devel Rsch Found 1976-; bd Afro-Amer Cultural & Hist Soc 1978-; bd of dirs Bay Area Black United Fund 1979-; publ "Black Male/Female Relationships" 1979-. **HONORS/ACHIEVEMENTS:** Outstanding Educator of the Yr World Book Ency & AmUniv 1967; Abe Lincoln Awd for Outstanding Broadcaster of the Yr 1975; Cert of Appreciation Sickle CellAnemia Rsch & Educ 1976; Meritorious Comm Serv Awd CA NG 1979; Special Serv Awd CA Soc of CPA 1980. **BUSINESS ADDRESS:** Dir Community Affairs, Golden W Broadcasters, 1801 Bush St #127, San Francisco, CA 94109.

HARE, LINDA PASKETT
Educational administrator. **PERSONAL:** Born Jun 10, 1948, Nashville, TN; daughter of Hulit Paskett (deceased) and Juanita Hicks Paskett; married divorced (divorced); children: Nicole, Brian. **EDUCATION:** Tennessee State Univ, BA (w/Distinction) 1969; Indiana Univ, MS 1974; Tennessee State Univ, EdD 1984. **CAREER:** Gary IN Schools, english teacher 1969-80; Tennessee State Univ, adjunct english instructor 1980-; Meharry Medical Coll, asst dir/corp & fdn relations 1983-84, special asst & deputy to the vice pres 1983-87, asst vice pres for institutional advancement. **ORGANIZATIONS:** Consultant Natl Baptist Publishing Bd 1983-84; mem Phi Delta Kappa 1984-; mem Tennessee Planning Comm of Amer Council on Educ (ACE), Natl Identification Program (ACE/NIP) 1986-. **HONORS/ACHIEVEMENTS:** Graduate Fellowship TN State Univ 1980-81. **BUSINESS AD-**

DRESS: Asst Vice Pres for Inst Advancement, Meharry Medical College, 1005 DB Todd Blvd, Nashville, TN 37208.

HARE, NATHAN
Publisher. **PERSONAL:** Born Apr 09, 1933, Slick, OK; son of Seddie Hare and Tishia Hare Farmer; married Julia Reed, Dec 27, 1956. **EDUCATION:** Langston U, AB 1954;Univ of Chicago, MA 1957;Univ of Chicago, PhD Sociology 1962; CA Sch of Professional Psychology, PhD Clinical Psychology 1975. **CAREER:** The Black Scholar The Black World Found, founding pub; Howard U, asst prof sociology 1964-67; Black Male-female Relationships, editor 1979-82; priv practice & clinical psychology 1977-; San Francisco State Coll Dept of Black Studies, chmn 1968-69; Instr 1961-63 & 1957-58; San Francisco Stat, lecturer part-time; private practice, psychology; The Black Think Tank, chairman of the board 1979-82. **ORGANIZATIONS:** Mem bd dir Univ of Chicago Bay Area Club; bd Dir No Am Zone Second World Black & African Festival of Arts & Culture; mem Black Speakers Club. **HONORS/ACHIEVEMENTS:** co-editor Contemporary Black Thought 1973; co-editor Pan-Africanism 1974; Author of The Black Anglo Saxons, The Endangered Black Family 1984, Bringing the Black Boy to Manhood 1985 & various articles in mag & journals; Distinguished Alumni Award Langston Univ 1975; presidential citation Natl Assn of Blacks in Higher Education 1981; Natl Awd Natl Council for Black Studies 1983; Crisis in Black Sexual Politics 1989. **MILITARY SERVICE:** AUS reserve 1958-64. **BUSINESS ADDRESS:** Chairman of the Board, The Black Think Tank, 1801 Bush St, Ste 127, San Francisco, CA 94109.

HARELD, GAIL B.
Regional human resource manager. **PERSONAL:** Born Apr 20, 1954, Providence, RI. **EDUCATION:** College of Our Lady of the Elms, BA 1976; Springfield Coll, MA 1979. **CAREER:** Digital Equipt Corp, production skills instructor 1976-80; WMAS radio, news anchor; Burroughs Corp, manufacturing production skills instructor 1980-83, corp opers quality standards coord 1983; Burroughs World Headquarters, mgr after hours prog 1983-84, project mgr human resources 1984-85; Burroughs Corp, reg area human resource mgr; Unisys Corp, regional human resource mgr/organizational devel specialist 1985-87. **ORGANIZATIONS:** Mem Providence Urban League 1976-87; mem Impact Assocs of Philadelphia 1981-82, Natl Black MBA Assoc Detroit Chap 1984-87, ASPA Amer Soc for Personnel Admin 1987; personnel comm Morris County C of C 1985-87. **HONORS/ACHIEVEMENTS:** Comm Serv Awd Impact Assocs of Philadelphia 1982; Certificate/Plaque Most Outstanding Young Women of Amer 1983; Burroughs Exemplary Action Awd 1986. **BUSINESS ADDRESS:** Regional Human Resource Mgr, Unisys Corp, 3 Becker Farm Rd, Roseland, NJ 07068.

HAREWOOD, DORIAN
Actor. **PERSONAL:** Married Ann. **EDUCATION:** Univ of Cincinnati Conserv of Music, attended. **CAREER:** Roots, The Next Generations, Tank, Against All Aodds, The Jesse Owens Story, Jesus Christ Superstar, Two Gentlemen of Verona, Miss Moffat, Streamers, The Mighty Gents, Sparkle, High Ice, Looker, Grey Lady Down, Beula Land, Strike Force, Trauma Ctr, actor.

HARGRAVE, BENJAMIN
Educational administrator. **PERSONAL:** Born Dec 18, 1917, Wakefield, VA; son of Bennie Hargrave and Laura Blow Hargrave; married Carolease Faulkner, Aug 31, 1943 (deceased). **EDUCATION:** Springfield Coll, Springfield, MA, BS 1941; San Francisco State Univ, San Francisco, CA, MA 1951. **CAREER:** Livingstone Coll, athletic dir 1941-42; Oakland Public Schools, teacher, principal 1941-68; California State Employment Serv, deputy dir 1969-74; Self-employed, educ consultant 1974-. **ORGANIZATIONS:** Pres California Assn Secondary School Admin 1966-68; mem bd of dir Ind Educ Council of California 1963-76; mem Natl Council Upward Bound 1964-66; mem Natl Advisory Council Nrs Training 1965-67; mem bd of dir NAACP, Oakland Branch; mem bd of dir Alameda Co Mental Health Assn 1951-56; pres Men of Tomorrow 1966. **HONORS/ACHIEVEMENTS:** Distinguished Alum Award, Springfield Coll 1971; Governors Award Vocational Educ California 1974; NAACP Freedom Fund Award 1988. **MILITARY SERVICE:** AUS staff sgt 1942-46. **HOME ADDRESS:** 3468 Calandria Ave, Oakland, CA 94605.

HARGRAVE, CHARLES WILLIAM
Scientist. **PERSONAL:** Born May 12, 1929, Dandridge, TN; son of Walter Clarence and Electa Snapp Hargrave; married Iona Lear Taylor. **EDUCATION:** Johnson C Smith Univ, BS 1949; Washington Univ St Louis, AM 1952. **CAREER:** Dept of the Navy, physicist 1954-55; US Atomic Energy Commission, scientific analyst 1955-62; Natl Aeronautics and Space Admin, technical information 1962-. **ORGANIZATIONS:** Advisory neighborhood commissioner DC Government 1979-84; pres District Police Adv Cncl 1985-88; mem Mayor's Adv Comm on Budget and Resources; SW Neighborhood Assembly; Omega Psi Phi. **HONORS/ACHIEVEMENTS:** Award of Merit JCSU Alumni Association 1979; Spaceship Earth NASA 1982, 1988; Alumni Award UNCF, Washington 1983. **MILITARY SERVICE:** AUS 1952-54; USNR Capt retired; reserve unit co 1984-86. **HOME ADDRESS:** 600 Third St SW, Washington, DC 20024. **BUSINESS ADDRESS:** Technical Information Manager, Natl Aero Space Admin, NASA Headquarters (NTT-4), Washington, DC 20546.

HARGRAVE, THOMAS BURKHARDT, JR.
Association executive. **PERSONAL:** Born Oct 05, 1926, Washington, GA; married Meredith Higgins; children: Kenneth, Anna. **EDUCATION:** Knoxville Coll, AB 1951; Springfield Coll, grad study. **CAREER:** James Welden Johnson Br YMCA FL, exec dir 1960-64; Pasadena YMCA, asst gen exec 1964-68; YMCA of LA, assoc gen exec 1968-71; YMCA of Metro Washington, pres 1973-. **ORGANIZATIONS:** Mem Rotary Club Intl; adv bd Studio Theatre; adv comm Tom Sawyer Training School; mem YMCA African Crisis Comm. **HONORS/ACHIEVEMENTS:** Good Conduct USAF 1947; Cert of Civ Rights, FL NAACP 1964; author "Private Differences-General Good, A History of the YMCA of Metropolitan Washington," 1985. **MILITARY SERVICE:** USAF sgt 1945-47. **BUSINESS ADDRESS:** President, YMCA Metropolitan Washington, 1625 Massachusetts Ave, NW, Ste 700, Washington, DC 20036.

HARGRAVES, WILLIAM FREDERICK, II
USAF command pilot. **PERSONAL:** Born Aug 18, 1932, Cincinnati, OH; married Maurine Collins; children: William III, Jock, Charles. **EDUCATION:** Miami Univ, BS (Cum Laude) 1954, MA 1961. **CAREER:** USAF, rsch physicist 1961-65, aircraft commander 1965-70, air liaison ofcr 1970-71; Miami Univ, asst prof air sci 1971-74; Wright Patterson AFB, chief flight deck develop 1974-78; Pentagon Washington DC, deputy div chief 1978-82; Central State Univ, asst prof. **ORGANIZATIONS:** Founder Alpha Phi Alpha Miami Univ Chapt; leader/founder Pilgrim Baptist Men's Chorus; vice commander Veteran of Foreign Wars 1986; mem Phi Beta Kappa (first black in Miami chapt), Omicron Delta Kappa, Kappa Delta Pi, Pi Mu Epsilon; mem Sigma Pi Sigma, Phi Mu Alpha; charter mem Phi Kappa Phi. **HONORS/ACHIEVEMENTS:** Rhodes Scholar candidate 1950; computer science advisor on North Central Evaluation Team and US Dept of Educ Washington DC; 6 publications "Magnetic Susceptability of Manganese Compounds," "The Effect of Shock Waves on various Plastic Nose Cone Materials"; Length, Mass, Time, & Motion in One Dimension (software program) 1986. **MILITARY SERVICE:** USAF col 28 yrs; Air Force Commendation Medal w/two Oak Leaf Clusters, Flying Cross and Air Medal for Meritorious Achievement, Vietnam Serv Medal w/five Bronze Stars, Republic of Vietnam Commendation Medal, Natl Defense Service Medal. **HOME ADDRESS:** 123 W Walnut St, Oxford, OH 45056. **BUSINESS ADDRESS:** Assistant Professor, Central State University, 210 Banneker Hall, Wilberforce, OH 45384.

HARGRETT, JAMES T., JR.
Business executive. **PERSONAL:** Born Jul 31, 1942, Tampa; married Berlyn; children: Crystal Marie, James T, III. **EDUCATION:** Morehouse Coll, AB 1964; Atlanta U, MBA 1965. **CAREER:** US Comptroller Currency, natl bank examiner 1965-67; Life & Casualty Co, commercial property under writer aetna 1967-68; Leadership Devel Prog Tampa Urban& League, dir 1968-69; Fed Sav & Loan Assn Tampa, exec Vice Pres mgr 1969-;Univ So FL Commr Tampa Housing Authority, tchr 1968-71. **ORGANIZATIONS:** Treas Urban League 1971-75; cit adv com Hillsborough Co Sch Bd 1974-; Dem Exec Com 1974; past chmn St Peter Claver Day Care Center; Tampa United Way. **HONORS/ACHIEVEMENTS:** Omega Man Yr Omega Psi Phi Frat 1971; Meritorious Comm Serv Housing Urban League 1971. **BUSINESS ADDRESS:** Representative District 63, State of Florida, PO Box 11986, Tampa, FL 33680.

HARGROVE, ANDREW
Engineer, educator. **PERSONAL:** Born Apr 01, 1922, Richmond, VA; children: Andrea Marie, Larry. **EDUCATION:** City Coll of NY, BEE 1966; NYU, MS 1968; PA State Univ, PhD 1975. **CAREER:** New York City Bd of Educ, teacher 1960-62; New York City Transit Auth, elec engr 1962-68; PA State Univ, instructor 1972-74; Tuskegee Inst, prof 1979-83; Andrew Hargrove Consulting Engineer, proprietor 1986-; Hampton Univ, prof. **ORGANIZATIONS:** Committeeman NY Co 1966-70; registered prof engr NY, VA; mem Power Engrg Soc, Control Systems Soc, Inst of Elec & Electronic Engrs, Natl Soc of Prof Engrs, Amer Soc for Engrg Educ, Natl Tech Assn, Alpha Kappa Mu, Omega Psi Phi; mem Virginia Waste Mgmt Bd 1986-88. **HONORS/ACHIEVEMENTS:** Mem Alpha Kappa Mu Honor Soc, Eta Kappa Nu Electrical Engineering Honor Soc; numerous books published. **BUSINESS ADDRESS:** Professor, HamptonUniv, P O Box 6592, Hampton, VA 23668.

HARGROVE, JOHN E.
Labor relations consultant. **PERSONAL:** Born Dec 28, 1903, Texas. **EDUCATION:** Wilberforce U, BS; WesternUniv bus law & commerce 1922; KS state coll, grad work; u of CA, special work in labor. **CAREER:** Wells Fargon, labor rel consultant; tchr 5yrs; Fed Govt, labor rel advisor 1943u of CA, special work in labor; 47; LA Co Grand Jury 1944 & 1971. **ORGANIZATIONS:** Pres SE Symp Assn; Our Authors Study Club; chmn bd dir Urban League; mem NAACP; Panhellenic; Comm Chest-united Way Campaign. **HONORS/ACHIEVEMENTS:** Plaque Kappa Alpha Psi 1970; CA State Senate 1973; 34yr diamond feather United Way; Award of life membership for organizing Dining Car Employees on a majorA-1 railroad Local Union No 465 AF of L-cIO served as dist dir 12 yrs Pacific Coast Regional chmn of Joint Council 6 yrs; Whos Who in Labor & Ind Rel; elec mem adv com LA City Unified Sch Dist Vol & Tutorial Prgms; mem Adv Com LA City Recreation Parks Dept Festival in Black; CA St Dir ofBr Assn for the Study of Afro-am Life & History; Cleveland OH Wilber ForceUniv Natl Alumni Assn awarded 50 yr Gold Cert & Gold Green Pin Hon & given Cert for Meritorious Community Serv by LA Human Rel Commn 1977. **BUSINESS ADDRESS:** 1200 Commonweatlh Ave, Fullerton, CA.

HARGROVE, JOHN R.
Judge. **PERSONAL:** Born Oct 25, 1923, Atlantic City, NJ; married Shirley Ann Hayes; children: John R, Jr, Steven L, Janet Ruth, Lora Frances. **EDUCATION:** Morgan State Coll, 1941-43; Army Spec Training Prog Engring, 1943-44; Howard U, BA 1946-47;Univ of MD Law Sch, LLB 1947-50. **CAREER:** Supreme Bench of Baltimore City, judge; Dist Ct of MD # 1 Baltimore City, judge 1971-74; Munic Ct of Baltimore City, asso judge 1968-71; Howard & Hargrove, asso with law firm 1963-68; Peoples Ct Baltimore City, asso judge 1962-63; desig deputy US atty 1957-62; MD Dist, asst US atty 1955; gen prac 1950-55; MD Ct of Appeals, admitted to prac 1950. **ORGANIZATIONS:** Mem Baltimore City Bar Assn; Monumental City Bar Assn; MD State Bar Assn; Character Comm Ct of Appeals of MD; Nat Bar Assn; mem Adv Bd of Trustees Sheppard Pratt Hosp; bd of trusteesUniv of MD Alumni Assn Internatl; Exec Com MD Judic Council; former chmn Character Comm Eighth Cir Ct of App; Adv Bd of Correc State of MD; Good Samaritan Hosp; Commis on Revision Crim Law & Proc; dele MD Const Conv; mem Comm on Judic; State ConstConv Commn; mem Comm on the Judic. **MILITARY SERVICE:** AUS sgt 1943-46. **HOME ADDRESS:** 3524 Ellamont Rd, Baltimore, MD 21215.

HARGROVE, MILTON BEVERLY
District superintendent, clergyman. **PERSONAL:** Born Oct 25, 1920, Birmingham, AL; married Blanche; children: Beverly III, Gayle, Ruth, William, John. **EDUCATION:** Miles Coll, AB; Birmnghm AL; Gammon Theol Sem. **CAREER:** Trinity Untd Meth Ch, pastor; United Meth Ch, dist supt; E Meth Balta MD, pastor; Asbury Meth Hagerstwn MD; Buena Vista Pitts PA; Simpson Meth Charlestn WV; St Marks United Meth Montclair NJ. **ORGANIZATIONS:** Mem Xi Alpha Chap of Omega Psi Phi Frat. **HONORS/ACHIEVEMENTS:** John A Holmes Lodge # 89 Free & Accep Masons Hon Cit Town of Montclair 1968; sub of not Vol II, Dict of Intl Biogrphy. **BUSINESS ADDRESS:** Trinity United Methodist, 581 Clinton Ave, Newark, NJ 07108.

HARGROVE, TRENT
Attorney. **PERSONAL:** Born Aug 25, 1955, Harrisburg, PA; son of Willie Clarence Hargrove Sr and Odessa Daniels Hargrove; married Eugenia Russell Hargrove, Sep 08, 1984; children: Channing Leah, Tyler Trent. **EDUCATION:** Buchnell Univ, Lewisburg PA, BA,

1977; Dickinson Law School, Carlisle PA, JD, 1980. **CAREER:** Office of Attorney General, Harrisburg PA, deputy atty, 1979-81; Pennsylvania Housing & Finance Agency, Harrisburg PA, asst counsel, 1981-86; McNees Wallace & Nurick, assoc, 1987-. **ORGANIZATIONS:** Mem, Harrisburg Jaycees, 1984-, Dauphin County Bar Assn, 1986-; pres, Harrisburg Black Attorneys, 1986-87; bd mem, Volunteer Center, 1986-; external vice pres, Harrisburg Jaycees, 1986-87; mem exec comm, NAACP, 1987-; chmn mgmt comm, Volunteer Center, 1988-; bd mem, Harrisburg Sewer & Water Authority, 1988-. **HOME ADDRESS:** 3212 N Fifth St, Harrisburg, PA 17110.

HARKINS, ROSEMARY KNIGHTON
Director. **PERSONAL:** Born Aug 05, 1938, Amarillo, TX; daughter of Herbert Knighton and Cloteal Knighton; divorced. **EDUCATION:** Amarillo Jr Coll, AA 1957; West TX State Univ, BS 1964; Univ of OK, MS 1971; Univ of OK Health Scis Ctr, PhD 1972; Central State Univ, BS 1976. **CAREER:** Veterans Admin Medical Center, hematology supvr 1968-70; Univ of OK Coll of Allied Health, asst prof 1972-77; Schoo of Allied Health Professions Univ of OK, dir & assoc prof 1977-81; Univ of OK Coll of Allied Health, assoc dean & prof 1981-88; Howard Univ, Dean, College of Allied Health Sciences 1988-. **ORGANIZATIONS:** Consul Petroleum Training & Tech Serv Workman Inc 1978; consul Bd of Regents FL State Univ System 1983; consul Amer Physical Therapy Assn 1983; chmnbd dirs OK Minority Business Develop Center US Dept of Commerce 1982-88; vice chair bd of trustees OK Inst for Child Advocacy 1983-87; natl sec bd dirs Amer Soc of Allied Health Professions 1982-84; bd dirs mem Natl Adv Comm on Accreditation & Inst Eligibility 1981-83. **HONORS/ACHIEVEMENTS:** Fellow Amer Soc of Allied Health Professions Washington DC 1984; Fellowship for Advanced Studies Ford Found 1971-72. **MILITARY SERVICE:** USAR lt col 5 yrs. **BUSINESS ADDRESS:** Dean, College of Allied Health Sciences, Howard University, Washington, DC 20059.

HARKLESS-WEBB, MILDRED
Educator. **PERSONAL:** Born Aug 17, 1935, Cedar Lane, TX; daughter of Mayfield Harkless and Cody Powell Harkless; married James E Webb, Jun 27, 1981. **EDUCATION:** Prairie View A&M, BS 1957; San Francisco State Univ, MA 1976. **CAREER:** Webb's Pest Control, vice pres 1979-; Everett Middle School, teacher. **ORGANIZATIONS:** Sponsor Scholarship Soc 1968-; mem NEA, CTA, ISBE, WBEA, CBEA, ABE 1970-; mem NAACP 1974-; staff rep ALC SFCTA 1976-; presenter NBEA 1976-; sponsor Black Student Club 1983-; mem, Commonwealth Club of California, 1988-. **HOME ADDRESS:** 35 Camellia Pl, Oakland, CA 94602. **BUSINESS ADDRESS:** Teacher, Everett Middle School, 450 Church St, San Francisco, CA 94114.

HARKNESS, JERRY LAVELLE
Professional athlete. **PERSONAL:** Married Judy; children: Gerald; Julie. **EDUCATION:** Indiana Pacers, prof athlete,TV analyst 1983-. **CAREER:** Morning sports anchor for WTLC Radio; dir of New Horizon for the United Way; coached CYO basketball for 10 yrs. **ORGANIZATIONS:** 1963 NCAA Champs Loyola of Chgo. **BUSINESS ADDRESS:** Indiana Pacers, 300 E Market St Market Sq Arena, Indianapolis, IN 46204.

HARLESTON, BERNARD WARREN
Educational administrator. **PERSONAL:** Born Jan 22, 1930, New York, NY; son of Henry Mitchell Harleston and Anna Tobin H; married Marie Ann Lombard; children: David Warren, Jeffrey Stuart. **EDUCATION:** Howard Univ, BS 1951; Univ of Rochester, PhD 1955. **CAREER:** Univ of Rochester, instructor 1954-55, asst prof 1955-56, rsch assoc 1956; Lincoln Univ, provost & prof of psychology 1968-70, acting provost 1970; Tufts Univ, asst prof & prof of psychology 1956-68, 1970-80, prof psychology dean faculty arts & scis 1970-80, Moses Hunt prof psychology 1980-81; city coll of the City Univ, pres of the city coll 1981-. **ORGANIZATIONS:** Mem Corp of MA Inst of Tech 1982-87; mem Visiting Comm to the Dept of Psychology & Social Rela at Harvard Univ 1982-; mem Bd of the Josiah Macy Jr Found 1984-; mem Mayor's Commn on Black New Yorkers of the City of New York 1986-, Mayor's Task Force Commn on the Homeless of the City of NY 1986-, Bd of the African Amer Inst 1986-; mem adv cncl presidents to the Assoc of Governing Bds of Univs and Colls 1986-; Assn of Amer Coll Bd Member, 1982-86, chmn 1985-86; chmn, Mayor's Commn for Science and Technology of New York City 1984-87, bd mem, 1987-; mem and co-chmn of the New York State Educ Department's Task Force on Ch ildren and Youth at Risk; mem, Bd of the New York Hall of Science, 1988-; mem, Advisory Comm to the New York Historical Society, 1988-; mem, Bd for the Fund for New York City Public Educ, 1988-; mem, the Council on Foreign Relations, 1989-. **HONORS/ACHIEVEMENTS:** John H Franklin Awd from Tufts Univ African-Amer Cultural Ctr 1980; Psychologist of the Yr Awd from NY Soc of Clin Psychol 1983; Honorary Degrees Dr of Sci Univ of Rochester 1972, Dr of Laws Temple Univ 1982; New York Urban League's Frederick Douglass Awd 1986; Dr of Laws Hon Doctorate Lincoln Univ 1986; Distinguished Educator Award from the New York City Assn for Supervision and Curriculum Devel, 1988; recipient of invitation to participate in the Japan Foundation's Short-Term Visitors Program, 1988; Howard Univ Alumni Award for Distinguished Postgraduate Achievement in the Fields of Educ and Admin, 1989. **BUSINESS ADDRESS:** President, CityUniv of New York, Convent Ave at 138th St, New York, NY 10031.

HARLEY, DANIEL P., JR.
Government employee. **PERSONAL:** Born Feb 16, 1929, Shelby, NC; married Lillian L Dent; children: Daniel, III. **EDUCATION:** SC State Coll, BS 1954; Atlanta U, MSW 1956;Univ IL, 1957-58. **CAREER:** House, comm 1954-57; Kenwood Ellis Comm Center, 1957-60; Parkway Comm House, exec dir 1960-65; Neighborhood Youth Corps US Dept Labor Wash 1965-66; New York City BWTP, dep regional dir 1966-68; Bur Work Training Programs, regional dir 1968-70; Chicago, asso regional manpower adminstr 1970-72; Equal Employment Opportunity US Dept Labor, dir 1972-; Harrisburg PA, on loan to commonwealth of PA to head office of affirmative action 1976-78. **ORGANIZATIONS:** Mem Nat Assn Social Workers; Acad Certified Social Workers; NAACP; Chicago Urban League; Chicago Hearing Soc; Alpha Phi Alpha Frat; mem bd dir Chicago Hearing Soc Cosmopolitan C of C. **HONORS/ACHIEVEMENTS:** Outstanding Citizen Award 1971; Certificate Performance Award US Dept Labor Manpower Adminstrn 1974. **MILITARY SERVICE:** 1st lt 1946-51. **BUSINESS ADDRESS:** Chicago, IL 60604.

HARLEY, PHILIP A.
Educator. **PERSONAL:** Born in Philadelphia; married Ireleen I; children: Anthony, Antoinette, Richard, Michael, Bruce, Annette, Terri. **EDUCATION:** Morgan State Coll, BA 1945; Temple U;Univ Cincinnati; CapitalUniv Sch Theol; Garrett Theol Sem, MDiv 1956. **CAREER:** IL, IN, OH, SD, WI, pastor; Garrett Theol Seminary, assoc prof. **ORGANIZATIONS:** Chmn Regional Consultative Com Race; Mayors Com Human Relations; dist dir Research & Devel; ministries educ IN, SD; prog leadership devel Prog Council Northern IL Conf; v chmn Leadership Devel Com N Central Jurisdictron; regional vice pres Nat Com Black Churchmen; chmn Chicago Coordinating Com Black Churchmen; v chmn Serv Review Panel Comm Fund; Ch Federation Met Chicago; Chicago Conf Religion & Race; mem bd dir Welfare Council Met Chicago. **MILITARY SERVICE:** USNR sp/x 1944-46. **BUSINESS ADDRESS:** Garrett-Evangelical Seminary, Field Education Office, 2121 Sheridan Road, Evanston, IL 60201.

HARMON, JAMES F., SR.
Business executive. **PERSONAL:** Born Apr 18, 1932, Savannah, GA; married Clarissa V Poindexter; children: James F Jr, Valerie H Seay, Laurence E, Wendell E. **EDUCATION:** NC A&T Coll, BS 1954; Troy State Univ, MS 1974; Air Univ, Sqd Officer School 1960-61. **CAREER:** Atlanta Marriott Hotels, personnel dir 1975-80; Marriott Hotels, reg dir of training 1980-82; Courtyard by Marriott Hotels, prop mgr 1983; Atlanta Perimeter Ctr Marriott, res mgr 1982-. **ORGANIZATIONS:** Mem Alpha Phi Alpha 1952-; pres Atlanta Falcon Club Inc 1983-; chmn Ed Comm of Natl Hosp Ed Mgr Assoc 1983. **MILITARY SERVICE:** USAF lt col 1954-74; Command Pilot DFC, Air Medal, DSM, Vietnam Serv Medal. **HOME ADDRESS:** 3945 Somerled Trail, College Park, GA 30349. **BUSINESS ADDRESS:** Manager, Marriott Hotel, 246 Perimeter Center Pkwy, Atlanta, GA 30346.

HARMON, JESSIE KATE See PORTIS, KATTIE HARMON

HARMON, JOHN H.
Attorney. **PERSONAL:** Born Feb 10, 1942, Windsor, NC. **EDUCATION:** BA 1963; Bach of Law 1965. **CAREER:** US Dept of Labor, solictor's off 1965-66; US House of Rep Com on Educ & Labor, asst coun 1966-67; Harmon & Raynor, owner 1967-. **ORGANIZATIONS:** Mem Fed Bar Assn, Craven Co Bar Assn, Nat Conf of Blacklawyers NC Academy of Trial Lawyers, Omega Psi Phi Frat; pres NC Assn of Black Lawyers; mem NAACP, SCLC, Black Prog Businessmen Inc; pres New Bern Chap NC Central Univ Alumni Assoc; pres Craven County Bar Assoc 1985-86. **HONORS/ACHIEVEMENTS:** Merit Awd NC CentUniv Sch of Law 1974. **MILITARY SERVICE:** USAR e-5 1966-72. **BUSINESS ADDRESS:** Owner, Harmon & Raynor, 1017 C Broad St, New Bern, NC 28560.

HARMON, M. LARRY
Industrial relations executive. **PERSONAL:** Born Nov 15, 1944, Kansas City, MO; son of E Morris Harmon and Vivian N Harmon; married Myrna L (Hestle); children: Robert T , M Nathan, Dana E. **EDUCATION:** Rockhurst Coll, Kansas City MO, BA Industrial Relations, 1971; Univ of Massachusetts, Amherst MA, MBA, 1972. **CAREER:** Joseph Schlitz Brewing Co, Milwaukee WI, corporate employee mgr, 1978, Syracuse NY, industrial relations mgr, 1978-80; Anheuser-Bush Inc, Syracuse NY, industrial relations mgr, 1980-85, St Louis MO, sr exec asst, 1985-87, Baldwinsville NY, employee relations mgr, 1987-. **ORGANIZATIONS:** Mem, Amer Soc Personnel Admin, 1976-; Kappa Alpha Phi, 1982-; exec bd mem, Personnel Mgmt Council, 1987-; bd of dir, Onondaga County Uran League, 1987-. **HONORS/ACHIEVEMENTS:** Black Achievers in Indus, YMCA of Greater New York, 1979; NAACP Image Award, Outstanding Men Achievers, 1989. **MILITARY SERVICE:** US Navy, petty officer, 1962-66, Vietnam Serv Medal. **BUSINESS ADDRESS:** Employee Relations Manager, Anheuser-Bush Inc, PO Box 200, Baldwinsville, NY 13027.

HARMON, SHERMAN ALLEN
Retired community relations representative. **PERSONAL:** Born Aug 06, 1916, Washington, IN; son of Sherman Harmon and Rosa Lawhorn Harmon; children (previous marriage): John Charles, Josephine Harmon Williams, Allen Sherman; married Lena Hinson Epperson, Oct 01, 1966; children: Epperson Bolling. **EDUCATION:** Hampton Institute, BS, 1939. **CAREER:** Centre Ave YMCA Pgh, prog exec, 1941-47; Moreland YMCA, Dallas TX, exec dir, 1947-49; Christian St YMCA, Philadelphia PA, prog dir, 1949-52; NC Mutual Life Co, Philadelphia PA, insurance counselor, 1952-54; Philadelphia United Way FUnd, peer counselor, 1954-57; Redevelopment Auth of Phila, dir com rels, 1957-80. **ORGANIZATIONS:** Mem Metro Bd, mem Intl Comm of Natl Council, chair exec comm of Natl Youth Workers, YMCA; intl pres, Y's Men Intl, 1973-74; bd of Natl Council of YMCAs; NAACP; Urban League; mem Philadelphia Presbytery; chmn joint comm on merger of Faith & Second Presbyterian Churches into Germantown Comm Presbyterian Church. **HONORS/ACHIEVEMENTS:** Man of the Year Y's Men of Philadelphia 1971; Family Man of the Year Natl Conf of Black Families 1980; 1st black intl dir for PA, 1st black intl serv coord, 1st black elected to Intl Exec Comm, 1st black vp; 1st black pres YMCA Men's Intl. **HOME ADDRESS:** 134 W Upsal St, Philadelphia, PA 19119.

HARMON, WILLIAM WESLEY
Educator. **PERSONAL:** Born May 26, 1941, Charlotte, NC; son of Evelyn M Norman; married Beverly J Pines; children: Hilary. **EDUCATION:** Johnson C Smith Univ, BS 1968; Seton Hall Univ, MA 1978; Kansas State Univ, PhD 1984. **CAREER:** University Rsch Corp, consultant 1969-70; Univ of Medicine & Dentistry of NJ, dir student affairs 1970-80; The Wichita State Univ, asst dean 1980-85, dean 1985-. **ORGANIZATIONS:** Consultant NC Public Health Adv Council 1968; pres Boys Club of Newark, NJ 1974; chairperson Council for Higher Educ Newark, NJ 1974-75; mem Health Professions Educ Adv Council NJ 1976-79; chairman Community Adv Bd Kean College NJ 1978-80; mem United States Jaycees 1980; mem Accreditation Team Amer Medical Assoc 1982-; pres Youth Development Service 1984. **HONORS/ACHIEVEMENTS:** Mem Phi Delta Kappa 1981; mem Phi Kappa Phi 1982; Leadership Kansas KS Chamber of Commerce 1986; 20 articles in professional journals; 25 presentations at natl meetings. **MILITARY SERVICE:** AUS E-4 3 yrs; Honorable Discharge 1962. **HOME ADDRESS:** 2021 Siefkin, Wichita, KS 67208. **BUSINESS ADDRESS:** Assoc Vice Pres & Dean of Univ Coll, Wichita StateUniv, 1745 Fairmount Ave, Box #6, Wichita, KS 67208.

HARPER, ALPHONSA VEALVERT, III
Dentist. **PERSONAL:** Born Feb 05, 1948, Alexander City, AL; son of Alphonza V Harper and Barbara B Harper; married Debra Sanders; children: Niaya A Harper. **EDUCATION:** TN State Univ, BS 1969; Meharry Med Coll, DDS 1975. **CAREER:** Alphonza Vealvert Harper III, dentist. **ORGANIZATIONS:** Mem Amer Dental Assoc, Natl Dental Assoc, Greater St Louis Dental Soc, Mound City Dental Soc 1975-, NAACP 1980-; vice pres Nor-

mandy Kiwanis Club 1979-. **BUSINESS ADDRESS:** Dentist, 4503A Page Blvd, St Louis, MO 63113.

HARPER, BERNICE CATHERINE
Government official. **PERSONAL:** Born Feb 24, Covington, VA; widowed; children: Reginald. **EDUCATION:** VA State Coll, BS 1945; Univ of So CA, MSW 1948; Harvard Univ, MSC 1959. **CAREER:** Childrens Hospital, social worker 1947-57; City of Hope Medical Ctr, dir social work 1960-74; Dept of HEW, chief nh branch 1970-72, dir div of ltc 1973-77, spec asst to the dir hsqb 1977-79, medical care advisor. **ORGANIZATIONS:** Mem Bd Intl Hospice Inst, Bd Intl Council of SW US Comm; mem steering comm NASW. **HONORS/ACHIEVEMENTS:** Ida M Cannon Awd AHA 1972; PHS Superior Serv Awd 1977; Better Life Awd AHCA 1978; HCFA Admin Awd 1982. **BUSINESS ADDRESS:** Medical Care Advisor, Dept of Health & Human Serv, 330 Independence Ave SW, Washington, DC 20201.

HARPER, BEVERLY A.
Business executive. **PERSONAL:** Born Apr 29, 1942, Philadelphia, PA. **EDUCATION:** Temple Univ, BS Educ 1964. **CAREER:** Temple Univ, asst tchr math workshop for experienced tchrs; Montgomery County OIC, dir of training; Portfolio Associates Inc, founder/pres. **ORGANIZATIONS:** Pres The Brain Trust 1981-; vice pres Edwards & Harper Inc 1985-; bd & exec comm mem Urban Affairs Partnership; exec dir The Arts Mgmt Corp; bd mem COMCAST Cablevision of Phila; adjunct faculty Antioch Univ; bd mem PA Coalition of 100 Black Women; mem Natl Assnof Media Women; mem Mayor's Econ Round Table; adv bd Philadelphia Dance Co; panelist 2nd Minority Bus Dev Workshop by Philadelphia Urban Coalition; panelist "A Media Workshop for Women - Spreading the Word"; speaker/panelist Ann Meeting of Intl Assn of Official Human Rights Agencies; workshop leader "How to Use the Media" Women Today Forum YWCA of Phila; guest lecturer "Starting Your Own Business" Temple Univ; speaker/panelist Ann Meeting Natl Assn of Chain Drug Stores; formal testimony pres at White House Conf onSmall Business Washington, DC; formal testimony hearings on overall sm business issues by US House of Representatives Comm on Sm Business Phila, PA; guest speaker Wilmington Women in Business Organization Wilmington, DE; keynote speaker at seminar spons by Central PA Sect Amer Soc Civil Engrs. **HONORS/ACHIEVEMENTS:** One of five Outstanding Young Leaders of the Yr Philadelphia Jaycees 1975; Outstand Achiev Award for Emerging Female Communicator Intl Women's Yr Natl Assn ofMedia Women; author of sect of econ dev publn "The State of Black Philadelphia" award from Urban League of Phila; Award for Serv on Citizen's Adv Comm on Transp Quality from US Dept of Trans; Award from Eboni Women for Leadership in the Business Community; Ms Magazine Award for Achievements and as Friend of Equality; Award for Serv as a Commissioner from PA Comm for Women; Haven House - Martin Lugher King Freedom Meml Disting Serv Award for Outstanding Contrib to the Advancement of Econ, Political and Educ Progress in Philadelphia Black Community; Award for Comm Serv from Bd of Dirs of Philadelphia Tribune Charities; Award for Comm Serv from Natl Black MBA Assn; Award for Achiev in Founding and Dev of a Minority Business into the Mainstream from Natl Freedom Day Assn; featured in natl magazines "Ms", "Black Enterprise", "Redbook" and "Working Woman"; numerous appearances on TV and radio in Delaware Valley; subject of an in-depth profile publ in Sunday Mag of Philadelphia Inquirer Aug 19, 1984. **BUSINESS ADDRESS:** President, Portfolio Assoc, Inc, 325 Chestnut St #815, Philadelphia, PA 19106.

HARPER, BRUCE
Professional athlete. **PERSONAL:** Born Jun 20, 1955, Englewood, NJ. **EDUCATION:** Kutztown State PA, attended. **CAREER:** New York Jets, football player runningback 1977-. **HONORS/ACHIEVEMENTS:** Pro Rookie of the Year NJ Sportswriters Assoc 1977; Led AFC in All-Purpose Yardage; Tied NFL Record with 55 Kickoff Returns 1978; Holds 9 Jets Records Punt & Kickoff Return. **BUSINESS ADDRESS:** New York Jets, 1000 Fulton Ave, Hempstead, NY 11550.

HARPER, CONRAD KENNETH
Law partner. **PERSONAL:** Born Dec 02, 1940, Detroit, MI; son of Archibald L Harper and Georgia F Hall Harper; married Marsha L Wilson; children: Warren, Adam. **EDUCATION:** Howard U, BA 1962; Harvard Law Sch LLB 1965. **CAREER:** NAACP Legal Defense Fund, law clk 1965-66, stf lwyr 1966-70; Simpson Thacher & Bartlett, assoc 1971-74, partner 1974-. **ORGANIZATIONS:** Rutgers Law Schl lctr 1969-70; Yale Law Schl Lctr 1977-81; US Dept HEW consltnt 1977; NY Pub Lib Trustee 1978—; Museum of the City of NY trustee 1983—; Chrmn Exec Comm NY City Bar 1979-80; mem brd of editors AM Bar Assoc Jrnl 1980-86; Comm on Admissions and Grievances US Crt of Appeals (2nd Cir) 1983, Chrmn 1987; Brd of Dir, co-chair, Lawyers Comm for Civil Rights under Law, 1987-89; Vestryman St Barnabus Epis Chrch, Irvington NY 1982-85;Fellow Am Bar Fndtn; Fellow Am Coll of Trial Lawyers; mem Cncl on Foreign Rltns; chancellor, Epis Diocese of NY, 1987—; Council of Amer Law Inst, 1985—; Bd of managers, Lewis Walpole Library. **BUSINESS ADDRESS:** Attorney, Simpson Thacher & Bartlett, 425 Lexington Ave, New York, NY 10017.

HARPER, CURTIS
Educator, research scientist. **PERSONAL:** Born May 13, 1937, Auburn, AL. **EDUCATION:** Tuskegee Inst, BS 1959; Tuskegee Instit, MS 1961; IA State U, MS 1965;Univ of MO, PhD 1969. **CAREER:** Univ of NC Sch of Med, assoc prof 1976-; Nat Inst of Envrnmtl Hlth Scs, sr staff flw 1972-76; Ept of PharmclgyUniv of NC, instr 1971-72; Dept of BiochemUniv of NC, resrch assoc 1970-71; Dept of Biochem & Moleculr Biophysics Yale U, resch assoc 1969-70. **ORGANIZATIONS:** Mem Am Chem Soc; Am Asn for Advmnt of Sci; Soc of Sigma Xi; Soc of Toxicology; Am Soc for Pharyclgy & Expmtl Thrptics Human Relat Commin 1970-74; Drug Act Com 1971-73; Interch Counc Soc Act Com 1971-74; bd mem NC Civ Lib Union 1976-; bd mem Interch Counc Housing Author 1977-. **MILITARY SERVICE:** USAR capt 1963-65. **BUSINESS ADDRESS:** Dept of Pharmacology, Sch of Med Univ of NC, Chapel Hill, NC 27514.

HARPER, DAVID B.
President. **PERSONAL:** Born Dec 03, 1933, Indianapolis, IN; married Mae McGee; children: Vicki Clines, Sharon Chaney, Wanda Mosley, Lydia Restivo, Kathleen Bass, Carol, Kyra, David, Daniel, Ralph. **EDUCATION:** Arizona State Univ, BS 1963; Golden Gate Univ, MBA 1968. **CAREER:** First Independence Natl Bank Detroit, pres 1969-76; Gateway Natl Bank St Louis, pres 1976-83; County Ford Inc, president 1983-. **ORGANIZATIONS:** Dir Student Loan Mkt Assoc 1972-; K-Mart Corporation 1975-; vice chmn St Louis Chap Amer Red Cross 1981-. **HONORS/ACHIEVEMENTS:** Hon Doctor of Laws degree Eastern MI Univ 1970. **MILITARY SERVICE:** USAF staff sgt 4 yrs. **BUSINESS ADDRESS:** President, County Ford, Inc, 9000 West Florissant, St Louis, MO 63136.

HARPER, DEREK ANTHONY
Professional athlete. **PERSONAL:** Born Oct 13, 1961, New York City, NY; married Sheila. **EDUCATION:** Illinois, 1984. **CAREER:** Dallas Mavericks, guard 1983. **ORGANIZATIONS:** Played in NBA exhibition against the 1984 Olympians at Iowa City last summer. **HONORS/ACHIEVEMENTS:** One of six NBA rookies to play in every game; second-team all-Am by AP as a jr; led the Big Ten in steals and assists as a soph & in steals as a jr. **BUSINESS ADDRESS:** Dallas Mavericks, Reunion Arena, 777 Sports St, Dallas, TX 75207.

HARPER, EARL
Educator. **PERSONAL:** Born Jul 07, 1929, Jackson, MS; married Clara Louise; children: Felicia, Denise, Julie, Earl, Andre Robinson. **EDUCATION:** Grand Rapids Jr Coll, Associate Voc Studies 1964; Western MI Univ, BS Ind Suprvsn 1968, MS Tech 1970, MBA Mgmt 1973, SpA Mgmt 1974; TX Tech Univ, DBA Mgmt 1974. **CAREER:** F E Seidman School of Business, chmn dept mgmt; Grand Valley State Coll, prof of mgmt 1971-; Doehler-Jarvis, training dir, asst to plant mgr; Harper & Assoc Mgmt Consulting & Training, pres. **ORGANIZATIONS:** Developed Grand Rapids MI Model Cities Career & Acad Counseling Ctr 1971; devel Gen Acad Prog Grand Rapids & Muskegon Inner-City Coll Ed Prog for Grand Valley State Coll 1971; worked with comm to devel Higher Ed Prog Grand Rapids Model Cities 1972-73. **MILITARY SERVICE:** AUS corpl 1951-53. **BUSINESS ADDRESS:** President, Harper & Assoc Mgmt Consult, 2029 Wolfboro Drive, Kentwood, MI 49508.

HARPER, ELIZABETH
Management consultant health services. **PERSONAL:** Born Jul 10, 1922, Cleveland, OH; married Kendrick Harper. **EDUCATION:** Homer G Phillips School of Nursing, RN 1945; St John's Univ, BSN 1963; C W Post Coll, MPS 1975. **CAREER:** Homer G Phillips Hospital, staff nurse 1945-50; New York City Dept of Hospitals, staff nurse 1950-54, head nurse 1954-60, supervisor of nurses 1960-63; New York City Health & Hospital Corp, asst dir of nursing 1963-70, assoc dir of nursing 1970-72, dir of nursing 1972-81, nurse management consultant 1981-. **ORGANIZATIONS:** Mem Amer Nurses Assn 1968-; Licensed Nursing Home Adminis 1978-; mem Natl League for Nurses 1979-; state committeewoman 27th AD Queens Co 1982-; mem NY State Federation of Republican Women 1982-; mem Republican Senatorial Inner Circle 1984-; mem Flushing Suburban Civic Assn; Flushing Council of Women's Organs Inc; Long Island Fed of Women's Clubs; Nassau County Fed of Republic Women; Nat'l Republican Congressional Comm; Judicial Dist Dir-11th Judical Dist NY ST Fed of Republican Women; Queens County Exec Comm 1982-; State Committeewoman 1982-; Republican Senatorial Inner Circle 1984-. **HONORS/ACHIEVEMENTS:** Numerous awards including Distinguished Serv Award 1972, Certificate of Serv 30 yrs 1980, Nurses Recognition Day Award 1981 New York City HHC Bird S Coler Hospital; City Council Citation City of New York 1981; Legislative Resolution Senate #1083 State of New York 1981; New York City HHC Bird S Coler Hospital Recognition Award 1981; Certificate of Recognition Natl Republican Congressional Comm 1984; Humanitarian Serv Award Queens Co Pract Nurses Assn 1981; Apprec and Dedication Award New York City HHC Assn of Nursing Dir 1981; Comm Adv Bd Recognition Award New York City HHC Bird S Coler Hospital 1981; Del Rep Pres Conv 1984; Certificate in Health Care Employee and Labor Rel from The Center to Promote Health Care Studies in cooperation with The Health Care Management Group 1985; New York ST Fed of Republican Women-President's Award, Honored 1986; Natl Republican Congressional Comm Certificate of Recognition 1985; Republican Party Presidential Achievement Award 1987; Delegate Republican Presidential Convention 1984 and 1988; guest of Vice Pres and Mrs. Dan Quayle at their Home 1989. **BUSINESS ADDRESS:** Nurse Managment Consultant, Ctr to Promo Hlth Care Studies, 14 Colvin Rd, Scarsdale, NY 10583.

HARPER, GERALDINE
Educator. **PERSONAL:** Born Jan 27, 1933, Memphis, TN; daughter of James Edward Seay and Janie Lee Bolden Seay; married Charles N Harper, Mar 04, 1954; children: Dr Deborah Harper Brown, Elaine Harper Bell, Charles Terrence Harper. **EDUCATION:** LeMoyne-Owen, Memphis TN, BS Education, 1955; Chicago State Univ, Chicago IL, MS Education, 1977. **CAREER:** Chicago Bd of Educ, Chicago IL, teacher, 1958-76, teacher-librarian, 1976-. **ORGANIZATIONS:** Chicago Teacher Librarians Assn, mem, 1980-, rooms comm chair, 1986-87, reservations sec, 1987-88, correspondence sec, 1988-; mem, Delta Sigma Theta Sorority; dir, Vacation Bible School, Lilydale First Baptist Church Chicago, 1983-; chair, Senior Citizens Comm, Top Ladies of Distinction Inc, Chicago Chapter, 1987-89. **HONORS/ACHIEVEMENTS:** Laday of the Year, Top Ladies of Distinction Inc, Chicago Chapter, 1989.

HARPER, HARRY DANDRIDGE
Physician. **PERSONAL:** Born Jul 15, 1934, Ft Madison, IA. **EDUCATION:** Lincoln U; IA Wesleyan Coll; Grinnell Coll, BS; Howard Med Sch, MD 1963; Drake U;Univ of IA. **CAREER:** E%Xcalibur 9tl W Inc, pres; Sacred Heart Hosp Med Staff, pres 1971; Lee Co Med Soc vice pres 1971; Co Mental Hlth Ctr, dir 1971; IA State Penitentiary, sr cons; Mt Pleasant Mental Hlth Inst, cons; Lee Co Welfare Dept, inst; Planned Parenthood of SE IA; Headstary Mothers, recp; pvt prac psychiatry. **ORGANIZATIONS:** Mem Nat & Am Med Assns; Am & IA Psych Assn; Lee Co & IA Med Assn; Nat Assn of Interns & Resd IA Nat Guard; NAACP; Kappa Alpha Psi; Kiwanis Internat; YMCA; IA Commn for Blind; Keokuk Country Club; FM Country Club; C of C; Lee Co Crime Commn; IA Bd of Family Planning; past dir Boy Scouts of SE IA. **HONORS/ACHIEVEMENTS:** "Who's Who Personalities in the W; presented paper to Nat Med Assn Atlanta GA 1970; "Comm Psychiatry" paper presented to Assn of Med Suprs of Mental Hosp Houston TX; prestented paper to World Fedn of Mental Hlth "Family Planning in Mental Hosp" 1970. **MILITARY SERVICE:** Military serv IA NG comdr. **BUSINESS ADDRESS:** 3766 Mill St, Reno, NV 89502.

HARPER, JOSEPH W., III
Educator. **PERSONAL:** Born Jan 10, 1931, Charlotte, NC; married Mary A Turner; children: Delcia Marie, Lisa Yvette, Jonette Michelle. **EDUCATION:** Johnson C Smith U, BS1955; A&T State U, MS 1963; A&T State U, NSF grants; Unive CA at Berkeley, cert molecular biol 1968; Western MI U; Univ NC at Charlotte. **CAREER:** E Mecklenburg Sr High School, asst prin 1974-; E Mecklenburg Adult Educ Center of Central Piedmont Comm Coll, dir, biology teacher 1969-73, teacher, coach 1955-74. **ORGANIZATIONS:** Mem NEA;

NCEA; NC Prins Assn; adv bd Upward Bound Program Johnson C Smith U; past pres NC Southwestern Dist Ath Assn 1960-62, 1964-65; pastdir NC State Basketball Tourn Western Div AA Confs 1966-68; mem Model Cities Task Force; YMCA; Helping Hand Scholarship Adv Bd; Charlotte-MecklenburgRec Commn; Pan-Hellenic Coun; Omega Psi Phi. **HONORS/ACHIEVEMENTS:** Dem Omega Man of Yr Award Pi Phi Chap 1974; sixth dist 1975; Bell & Howwel Schs Fellowship Award 1973; Most Understanding Tchr 2d Ward HS 1969; Outstanding Ldrshp Award Lincoln Co PTA 1967; outstandin serv plaque 1966; cert merit NC Sci Tchrs Symposium 1965; Coach of Yr NCHSAA Western Div football 1966; basketball 1967. **MILITARY SERVICE:** AUS pfc 1952-54. **BUSINESS ADDRESS:** Assistant Principal, East Mecklenburg High School, 6800 Monroe Rd, Charlotte, NC 28212.

HARPER, KENDRICK
Administrator. **PERSONAL:** Born Sep 14, 1919, New York, NY; married Elizabeth Maxwell. **CAREER:** New York City Parks Recreation & Cultural Afrs, admin. **ORGANIZATIONS:** Bd mem Selective Serv Syst 1968-76; pres Robt A Taft Repub Club Queens 1973-75; bd chmn Gov Taft Club 1972-76; life mem 369th Vet Assn; life memVFW Proct Hobson Post 1896; mem Blk Reps NY State; exec mem Queens Cty Rep Com Honoree Awds in Black 1973; alternate delegate Rep Pres Conv 1980; alternate delegate Rep Pres Conv 1984; mem US Senatorial Club 1985, Rep Senatorial Inner Circle 1985, Capitol Hill Club 1985; 27th AD Queens County, county comm chairman 1987; Flushing Suburban Civic Assoc New York City 1987; Empire Club 1987. **HONORS/ACHIEVEMENTS:** John S Snyder Meml Award Robt A Taft Rep Club 1983; Disting Serv Award Queens Rep Co Comm 1983; Rep Natl Comm Campaign Victory Certificate 1983; Robt A Taft Awd 1976; Selec Serv Syst Merit Serv Award & Med 1976; del Rep Pres Conv 1976; guest of Pres & Mrs Ford 1976; City of New York Parks & Recreation, certificate of appreciation of 24 yrs of faithful service 1985; State of New York Legislative Resolution Senate No 940 by Senator Knorr 1986; alternate delegate Presidential Convention New Orleans, LA 1988; guest of Vice President and Mrs. Dan Quayle at their Home 1989. **MILITARY SERVICE:** AUS 1939-45.

HARPER, LEONARD ALFRED
Educational administrator. **PERSONAL:** Born Nov 10, 1920, New York, NY; married Lovette Washington; children: Peter Alan, Radiah Sumler. **EDUCATION:** Tuskegee Inst, BS 1943; NY U, MA 1952; NY U, pre-doctoral studies 1960-64; Hofstra U, grad studies 1968-69. **CAREER:** Educ Opportunity Center Westchester Community Coll, dir 1971-; Ossinging High School, asst prin 1969-71; Plainedge Public Schools, dept head Math & Inds Arts 1958-59; Tuskegee Indonesia Tech Educ Project, admin asst 1955-57; Elizabeth Irwin High School, teacher 1950-58; Training Thru-Sight Assn, writer 1946-50. **ORGANIZATIONS:** Pres bd of dir Yonkers Community Action Prog 1975-76; chmn personnel Westbury Community Action Prog 1965-68; mem Assn for Supervision & Curriculum Devel; NAACP. **HONORS/ACHIEVEMENTS:** Award for leadership Yonkers Community Action Prog 1976; for leadership Westbury Community Action Prog 1967; collaborated on five books bupl Doubleday/Prentice-Hall/Duel Sloan & Pearce 1947-49. **MILITARY SERVICE:** AUS corpl 1943-45. **BUSINESS ADDRESS:** Educational Opportunity Ctr, Westchester Community Coll, 41 Main St, Yonkers, NY 10701.

HARPER, MARY L.
Accountant. **PERSONAL:** Born Feb 24, 1925, Emporia, KS; married Edward J. **EDUCATION:** LincolnUniv Jeff City MO; Emporia State Tchrs Coll Emporia KS; State Coll LA, LA. **CAREER:** Self Employ, accountant tax couns 1965-; LA Co Prob Dept Juvenile Reim Sect, invest 1960-63, girls coun; Cong Dist Dem Union, special asst. **ORGANIZATIONS:** Treas Dem Coal of Pomona Valley; Pol Action Chmn Pomona Valley NAACP bd pres NAACP So CA Area Conf 1971-73; treas NAACP So CA Area Conf 1966-71; commissioner City of Pomona; vice chmn Parks & Rec Commn; Pol Act Chmn NAACP So CA Area Conf 19 73-; bd dirs YMCA Outreach. **HONORS/ACHIEVEMENTS:** Recip serv awd So Area Conf NAACP 1969, 71; elec Delegate Dem Chrtr Conf KC, MO 35th Cong Dist 1974 only blk cand in field of 12, one of two females.

HARPER, MARY STARKE
Association executive. **PERSONAL:** Born Sep 06, 1919, Ft Mitchell, AL; widowed. **EDUCATION:** PhD 1963; MS 1952; BS 1950; diploma RN 1941; credential competent in four professions, clinical pscychology, nursing, sociology, secondary edn. **CAREER:** Cntr for Minority Group Mental Health Progs, asst chief; Dept of HEW Nat Inst of Mental Health DHEW; positions in nursing, staff head nurse, supervisory, adminstrv, mgmt, cons, nurse edn, nurse adminstrs in Vets Adminstrn u of mN, instr; ULCA st mary's coll; dir nursing edn; Interdisciplinary Clinical Research, cons, research chief 1964-68; St Mary's Coll, instr sociology. **ORGANIZATIONS:** Mem, bd dirs Nat League for Nursing; bd dirs Westchester Mental Health Assn; pres Mental Health Assn Peekskill Br Commnr Nursing Res 1969-74; chmn Adv Com to DC Mental Health Adminstrn 1972-; bd dirs DC Mental Health Assn. **HONORS/ACHIEVEMENTS:** Listed in Who's Who Among Am Women; Who's Who in Am Edn; Intl Dir of Scholars 1973.

HARPER, MICHAEL STEVEN
Educator. **PERSONAL:** Born Mar 18, 1938, Brooklyn, NY; son of Walter Harper and Katherine Harper; married Shirley Ann; children: Roland Warren, Patrice Cuchulain, Rachel Maria. **EDUCATION:** CA State Univ, BA, MA 1961-63; Univ of IA, MA 1963; Brown Univ, ad eundem 1972. **CAREER:** Harvard Univ, visiting prof 1974-77; Yale Univ, visiting prof 1976; Carleton Coll Northfield MN, benedict prof 1979; Univ of Cincinnati, Elliston poet 1979; Brown Univ, prof of English 1970-; Distinguished Minority Professor, Univ of DE 1988; Distinguished Visiting Professor, Creative Writing, Macalester Coll, MN 1989. **ORGANIZATIONS:** Council mem MA Council Arts & Humanities 1977-80; judge Natl Book Awd Poetry 1978; Bicentennial poet Bicentennary Exchange, Britain/USA 1976; Amer spec ICA State Dept tour of Africa 1977; lecturer German Univ ICA tour of nine univ 1978; appt IJ Kapstein Prof of English 1983; ed special issue of Carleton Miscellany 1980 on Ralph Ellison; bd mem Yaddo Artists Colony Saratoga Springs NY; ed bd TriQuarterly, the Georgia Review, Obsidian; ed Collected Poems of Sterling A Brown; publ Amer Journal by Robert Hayden 1978. **HONORS/ACHIEVEMENTS:** Guggenheim Fellowship Poetry John Simon Guggenheim Found 1976; NEA Creative Writing Awd 1977; Melville-Cane Awd for Images of Kin New & Selected Poems Univof IL Press 1978; Natl Humanities Distinguished Prof Colgate Univ 1985; books of poems, "Dear John, Dear Coltrane" 1970, "History Is Your Own Heartbeat" 1971, "Song, I Want A Witness" 1972, "History As Apple Tree" 1972, "Debridement" 1973, "Nightmare Begins Responsibility" 1975, "Images of Kin" 1977, "Healing Song For The Inner Ear" 1985, "Chant of Saints" 1979; Honorary Doctorate of Letters, Trinity College, CT 1987. **BUSINESS ADDRESS:** Professor of English, BrownUniv, English Dept, Providence, RI 02912.

HARPER, NEVILLE W.
Physician. **PERSONAL:** Born in New York, NY; married Gladyce; children: 1 daughter. **EDUCATION:** Coll City NY, BS 1947; Coll Med Howard Univ, MD 1954. **CAREER:** Nassau Med Ctr, asst path 1963-66; Suffolk Co, dep med examiner 1966-68; dir lab Rose Hosp, Rome Hosp & Murphy Mem Hosp 1968-; Mohawk Valley Clinical & Path Asso, pres. **ORGANIZATIONS:** Mem bd dir Oneida Co Health Dept 1974-; past pres bd trustees Jervis Libr Assn; past pres Rome Acad Med; past pres med staff Rome Hosp; past pres Oneida Co Med Soc; pres Lorkim Clinical & Diagnostic Lab Inc; consult pathologist AF Hosp GAFB Rome NY; mem NY State Bd for Medicine 1982-. **MILITARY SERVICE:** AUSR col. **BUSINESS ADDRESS:** Dir of Laboratories, Rome/Murphy Memorial Hospital, Dept of Pathology, 1500 No James St, Rome, NY 13440.

HARPER, ROBERT LEE
PERSONAL: Born Oct 03, 1920, Longview, TX; married Eldora; children: Robert Jr, Beverly. **EDUCATION:** Jarvis Christian Coll, 1939-42; Wiley Coll, BA 1945-48; Meharry Med Coll, DDS 1948-52. **CAREER:** Dentist pvt prac 1952-77; Jarvis Christian Coll, 1960-77. **ORGANIZATIONS:** Mem sec E TX Med Dental & Pharm Assn 24 yrs; pres Gulf State Dental Assn 1962; mem E TX Dist Dental Soc; TX Dental Assn; Am Dental Assn; Nat Dental Assn; Gulf State Dental Assn; Am Soc Dentistry Children; Am Acad Gen Dentistry; mem bd dir Logview C of C 1977; bd Parks & Rec Prgm 1969-75; Piney Woods Am Red Cross; chmn, adv bd Good Samaritan Nursing Home; bd mem Mental Hlth Assn Gregg Co; E TX Area Cncl BSA; past mem, bd Vocational Tech Training Longview Ind Sch Dist Hon; kkper of In mem Omega Psi Phi Frat; mem Kappa Sigma Pi Hon Dental Frat. **HONORS/ACHIEVEMENTS:** Recpt Clinical of Dentistry 1952; Omega Man Yr 1967; candidate City Commr Longview 1967; recpt Silver Beaver Award BSA 1966. **MILITARY SERVICE:** USN yeoman 1st class 1942-45. **BUSINESS ADDRESS:** 1002 S Martin Luther King Blvd, Longview, TX 75602.

HARPER, ROLAND
Professional athlete. **PERSONAL:** Born Feb 28, 1953, Seguin, TX. **EDUCATION:** LA Tech, BA. **CAREER:** Chicago Bears, professional football player (runningback) 1975-. **HONORS/ACHIEVEMENTS:** NCAA Coll Div Champs 1974; Brian Piccolo Award 1975; Bear MVP NEA 1978. **BUSINESS ADDRESS:** Chicago Bears, PO Box 204, Lake Forest, IL 60045.

HARPER, RONALD J.
Attorney. **PERSONAL:** Born Dec 20, 1945, W Palm Beach; married Betty Vance; children: Ronald, Jr, Jennifer. **EDUCATION:** Temple U, BA economics 1968; Temple Law Sch, JD 1971. **CAREER:** Haper & Paul, atty; OIC of Am Inc, atty; Comm Legal Serv Phila, atty 1971; NY Life Ins Co, salesman 1970; Metro Life Ins Co, salesman 1968. **ORGANIZATIONS:** Mem Nat Bar Assn; Philadelphia Bar Assn; Philadelphia Barristers Assn; Am Bar Assn; mem Bd of Mgrs TempleUniv 1974; Zion Bapt Ch; bd Community Legal Svcs. **BUSINESS ADDRESS:** Attorney, 140 W Maplewood Ave, Philadelphia, PA 19144.

HARPER, RUTH B.
Business executive. **PERSONAL:** Born Dec 24, 1927, Savannah; married James; children: Catherine, Deloris (deceased). **EDUCATION:** Beregan Bus Sch Philadelphia, grad; Flamingo Modeling Sch, grad; LaSalle Coll. **CAREER:** 196th Legislative Dist, state legislator 1979-; Ruth Harper's Modeling & Charm Sch, owner/dir; Gimbel's Dept Store, sales; Gratz HS, instr; Strawberry Mansion Jr HS, instr; Miss Ebony PA Schlrsp Pageant, producer. **ORGANIZATIONS:** Mem Nat Dem Com Women; mem PA Council on the Arts; fdr pres N Cent Philadelphia Women's Pol Caucus; bd mem YMCA Columbia Br; bd mem ARC SE Chpt; vice pres Zion BC Ch Womens Serv Guild; mem NAACP; Urban League; Itaga Civic League; Philadelphia Variety Club 1964; bd mem Piladelphia Univ. **HONORS/ACHIEVEMENTS:** Recip citation of honor Philadelphia Tribune Newspaper 1963; NAACP Serv Award 1964; Bright Hope BC Ch Award 1965; Black Expo Award 1972; Cosmopolitan Club Award 1969; LaMode Mannequins Inc Achvmt Award 1969; Freedom Award NAACP 1978; Women in Politics Cheynew State Coll 1978; service award YMCA 1979.

HARPER, SARA J.
Judge. **PERSONAL:** Born Aug 10, 1926, Cleveland. **EDUCATION:** Western Reserve U, BS; Franklin Thomas Backus Sch of Law Western Reserve U, LLB; Nat Coll of State JudiciaryUniv of NH Naval Justice Sch. **CAREER:** Cleveland Municipal Ct, military law elected judge 1971-, 6 yr term; apptd by Gov James A Rhodes Cleveland Muni Ct, judge 1970; Air Pollution Control Dept, atty in charge; Dept of Human Resources & Econ Dev, atty in charge; Law Dept City of Cleveland, asst dir of law 1969-70; Legal Aid Soc, atty in charge 1966-68; pvt prac law 1952-66; William Saxbe, special asst OH atty gen. **ORGANIZATIONS:** Mem Women Lawyers Assn of Cleveland; mem John M Harlan Law Club; Nat Abar Assn; Cleveland Bar Assn; past sec, treas Greater Cleveland Muni Judges Assn; chmn elect Jud Council of Nat Bar Assn; mem, bd of trustees Hope House; Comm Adv Com; Jr League Of Cleveland Inc; bd of trustees Metro Job Council; mem NAACP; Urban League Forest City Hosp Aux; (At Assn of Fashion & Accessories Designers Cleveland Chpt. **HONORS/ACHIEVEMENTS:** Recip Tribute to Greatness Award Nat Council of Negro Women 1971; appreciation award Cleveland Br NAACP 1971; hon mem Cts of Calanthe 1971; Woman ofYr Award 1972. **MILITARY SERVICE:** USMC reserve military judge maj. **BUSINESS ADDRESS:** Judge, Cleveland Municipal Court, Justice Center #14A, 1200 Ontario St, Cleveland, OH 44113.

HARPER, SARAH ELIZABETH
Engineer. **PERSONAL:** Born in Detroit, MI; married Arnell Harper. **EDUCATION:** Lawrence Inst of Tech, mech engrg; LA Harbor Coll, cert E/M engrg; Livingstone Coll. **CAREER:** Hughes Aircraft Co, sr assoc engr 1953-61, 1977-82; TRW Syst Grp, design engr 1967-69; Teledyne Sys Co, project design engr 1969-70; Rockwell Intl, mem tech staff 1970-77; Presently, consultant. **ORGANIZATIONS:** Mem Soc of Women Eng; mem Coll of Fellows; mem Alpha Kappa Alpha Sor; NAACP; Crenshaw Neigh Comm Housing & Beautif; mem Inst for the Advancement ofEngrg; mem Engrg Adv Comm E LA Coll; mem Urban League; mem Town Hall of CA; mem LA Counc of Engrs & Scientists; rep Hughes Aircraft Co ActiveCitizenship; speaker at high schools and colls on careers in engrg. **HONORS/**

ACHIEVEMENTS: Selected for biog & pict inclusion of 2nd ed 1974 The World Who's Who of Women; selected for inclusion in the Alpha Kappa Alpha Sor Heritage Series on "Women in Sci & Engrg" 1979; elected to grade of Fellow by Inst for the Advancement of Engrg 1977.

HARPER, T. ERROL
Automobile dealership executive. **PERSONAL:** Born Feb 12, 1947, Birmingham, AL; son of Rev Theophilus E Harper and Callie O'Bryant Harper; married Elaine Betz, Mar 26, 1975; children: Rena Nicole, Zachary Jordan. **EDUCATION:** Morris Brown Coll, Atlanta GA, BA, 1970. **CAREER:** Ernst & Ernst, Philadelphia PA, auditor, 1970-73; Philadelphia '76 Inc, Philadelphia PA, controller, 1973-74; Dupont Co, Wilmington DE, staff accountant, 1974-76; Ford Motor Co, Dearborn MI, dealer trainee, 1977-78; Phillips Ford Inc, Conshohocken PA, business mgr, 1978-79; Harper Pontiac Inc, Upper Darby PA, pres, 1979-82; Heritage Lincoln-Mercury, Hackensack NJ, pres, 1983-. **ORGANIZATIONS:** Dir, Commerce & Indus Assn of New Jersey, 1985-, United Way of Bergen County, 1985-; mem, Hackensack Lions Club, 1987-; dir, Black Ford & Lincoln-Mercury Dealer Assn, 1989-91. **MILITARY SERVICE:** USMCR, Corporal, 1970-74. **BUSINESS ADDRESS:** President, Heritage Lincoln-Mercury Sales Inc, 55 Hackensack Ave, Hackensack, NJ 07601.

HARPER, TERRY
Professional athlete. **PERSONAL:** Born Aug 19, 1955, Douglasville, GA. **CAREER:** Atlanta Braves, left fielder 1982. **HONORS/ACHIEVEMENTS:** Braves Minor League Player of the Month for April & May 1982. **BUSINESS ADDRESS:** Atlanta Braves, PO Box 4064, Atlanta, GA 30302.

HARPER, TOMMY
Professional athlete. **PERSONAL:** Born Oct 14, 1940, Oak Grove, LA; married Bonnie Jean Williams. **CAREER:** Cincinnati Reds, baseball player 1963-67; Cleveland Indians, baseball player 1968; Seattle Pilots, baseball player 1969; Milwaukee Brewers, basebal player 1970-71; Boston Red Sox, 1972-74, first base coach; CA Angels, 1975-76; Baltimore Orioles, 1976; Boston Red Sox, special asst to genl mgr. **BUSINESS ADDRESS:** Special Assistant to Gen Mgr, Boston Red Sox, Fenway Park, 24 Jersey St, Boston, MA 02215.

HARPER, WALTER EDWARD, JR.
Educator. **PERSONAL:** Born Jul 10, 1950, Chicago, IL; son of Walter Edward Harper Sr and Elizabeth Mercer Harper. **EDUCATION:** Loyola Univ, Chicago IL, AB History, 1972, MA Counseling Psychology, 1978; Inst for Psychoanalysis, Chicago IL, Certificate, Teacher Educ Program, 1979; Loyola Univ, Chicago IL, post-graduate studies, 1982-86. **CAREER:** Precious Brood Grammer School, Chicago IL, teacher, 1972-74; Loyola Univ, Chicago IL, admin, 1974-79; North Park Coll, Chicago IL, teacher, counselor, 1979-86; Brown Univ, Providence RI, asst dir financial aid, 1986-. **ORGANIZATIONS:** Bd mem, Eisenberg Chicago Boy & Girls Club, 1978, Loyola Univ Upward Bound Program, 1978; mem, C G Jung Center, 1980; bd mem, Friendship House/Chicago, 1981; mem, Illinois Psychological Assn, 1982, Phi Delta Kappa, Loyola Univ Chapter, 1982, Assn of Black Admission and Financial Aid Admin in the Ivy League & Sister Schools, 1986, Eastern Assn of Financial Aid Admin. **HONORS/ACHIEVEMENTS:** Certificate of Merit, Chicago Youth Center, 1975; Most Eligible Bachelor/Promising Minority Professional, Ebony Magazine, 1976; Fellow, Soc for Values in Higher Educ, 1982; Workshop Leader, High School Summer Intern Program, Philadelphia Daily News, 1987; Workshop Leader, Atlanta Dream Jamboree, three day program for high school youth in Atlanta, 1988, 1989. **BUSINESS ADDRESS:** Financial Aid Officer, Brown University, 8 Fonce Alley, Financial Aid Office, Providence, RI 02912.

HARPS, WILLIAM S.
Corporation executive. **PERSONAL:** Born Jul 03, 1916, Philadelphia, PA; married Justine; children: Richard, Eunice. **EDUCATION:** Howard U, BS 1943. **CAREER:** John R Pinkett Inc, first vice pres 1939-; WA Bd of Realtors, chmn; Harps & Harps Inc Real Estate Appraisers & Counselors, pres 1984-. **ORGANIZATIONS:** Mem, intl pres Am Inst Real Estate Appraisers 1968-81; Soc Real Estate Appraisers; natl past pres Nat Soc Real Estate Appraisers; mem NY Real Estate Bd, WA Real Estate Brokers Assn, Lambda Alpha On Land Economics; bd dir Met Police Boys Club 1963- mem, bd trustees Fed City Council 1969-; vp, bd trustees Childrens Hosp 1969-; bd mem Tax Equalization & Review 1970-74; Mayors Economic Dev Comm 1970-74; DC Commn Judicial Disabilities & Tenure 1971-75; bd dirs Columbia Title Ins Co; Nat Bank WA 1971-86; Pepertual Fed Sav & Loan Assn 1971-87; pres WA Chapter #18 Amer Inst Real Estate Appraisers 1976; pres WA Bd of Realtors 1977; Investors 15 Inc; consult District Title Ins 1984-; mem Soc of Real Estate Counselors. **HONORS/ACHIEVEMENTS:** Metro Womens Dem Club Awd 1971; Alumni Awd Howard Univ 1972; Jos Allard Awd Amer Inst Real Estate Appraisers 1974; Realtor of the Year 1980. **BUSINESS ADDRESS:** President, Harps & Harps Inc, 1522 K Street, NW, Ste 430, Washington, DC 20005.

HARRELL, ANTHONY JAMES
Physician. **PERSONAL:** Born May 19, 1954, Richmond, VA. **EDUCATION:** Morgan State Univ, BS 1976; Univ of MD, MS 1980; Meharry Medical Coll, MD 1984. **CAREER:** Baptist Hosp, internal medicine resident 1984-87; MD Health physicians Assoc, internist 1987-. **ORGANIZATIONS:** Mem Amer Medical Assoc; assoc Amer Coll of Physicians. **HONORS/ACHIEVEMENTS:** Publication The Journal of the Baltimore Coll of Dental Surgery "The Effect of Dexamethasone on the Replication of Herpes Simplex Virus in Human Giugiual Fibroblest Cultures," 1982.

HARRELL, CHARLES H.
Automobile dealership chief executive. **CAREER:** Harrell Chevrolet-Oldsmobile Inc, Flat Rock, MI, chief exec. **BUSINESS ADDRESS:** Harrell Chevrolet-Oldsmobile Inc, 26900 Telegraph, Flat Rock, MI 48134. *

HARRELL, H. STEVE
Chief executive. **CAREER:** Shelby Dodge, Memphis TN, chief executive. **BUSINESS ADDRESS:** Shelby Dodge Inc, 2691 Mt Moriah Rd, Memphis, TN 38115. *

HARRELL, OSCAR W., JR.
State gpvernment official. **PERSONAL:** Born in Bristol, VA; married Sophia M Bailey; children: Oscar W III, Stafford B. **EDUCATION:** Virginia Union Univ, BA 1957-60; Assumption Coll, Massachusetts, CAGS 1972-74; Brandeis Univ, PhD candidate 1982-; research fellow Northeastern Univ, 1987-. **CAREER:** Leonard Training School NC Bd of Corr, head counselor 1963-64; Gardner State Hospital, psych Soc Worker 1964-67; Rutland Heights Hosp, coord of rehab 1967-72; Mt Wachusett Comm Coll, faculty 1968; Fitchburg State Coll, asst dir of admiss, dir of minority affairs/AID 1974-81; Fitchburg State Coll, faculty 1976-77; Tufts Univ, dir of african amer center 1981-87; deputy asst comm, Massachusetts Department of Mental Retardation, 1987-. **ORGANIZATIONS:** Mem Alpha Phi Alpha Frat, Amer Psych Assoc 1976-78, Amer Personnel Guidance Assoc 1976-78, Amer Rehab Counseling Assoc 1976-78; mem & bd of dir MA Mental Health Assoc 1969-, MA Halfway House Assoc; former pres MA Branch NAACP; sec & pres Soc Organized Against Racism 1982-; treas Greater Boston Interuniversity Cncl; vice pres MA Assoc for Mental Health; comm mem, Racial Justice Comm, Natl YWCA, currently; bd of dirs, Community Change Inc, Boston MA, currently. **HONORS/ACHIEVEMENTS:** City rep Gardner Massachusetts Opportunity Council 1970-72; comm & chmn Sudbury Park & Recreation 1978-81; mem Governor's Advisory Comm to Correction 1980-82; Citation, Governor of Massachusetts, 1981; Citation, Massachusetts Senate 1987; Citation, Massachusetts House of Representatives 1987; performer (non-professional) in the play "The Man Nobody Saw". **MILITARY SERVICE:** AUS E-5 1960-62. **HOME ADDRESS:** 15 Bent Brook Road, Sudbury, MA 01776.

HARRELL, ROBERT L.
Attorney. **PERSONAL:** Born Aug 16, 1930, Ahoskie, NC; married Alice Fay Jamison; children: Anthony, Robert, Jr, Kyle, Kevin. **EDUCATION:** NCCU, AB 1955; NCCU Law Sch, LLB 1958; NCCU Law Sch, JD 1970. **CAREER:** NY Co Bunlombe, asst pub defender 1973-; pvt prac 1965-73; Dailey & Harrell, partnership 1963-65; pvt prac 1960-63; Asso Coun & Legal Defense Fund Reorganized Hartford Co Cits Organ, atty 1961. **ORGANIZATIONS:** Chmn Assheville-Buncombe Co Cit Orgn 1965-70; mem Better Schs Com Buncombe 1965-69; delegate Nat Dem Conv 1972. **MILITARY SERVICE:** AUS pfc 1951-53. **BUSINESS ADDRESS:** PO Box 7154, Asheville, NC.

HARRELL, RUTH J.
Staff developer, executive director. **PERSONAL:** Born Apr 16, 1927, Elkhart, IN; daughter of Lexie Brown and Cora Green Brown; married Dr Thomas H Kiah Jr, Sep 18, 1980; children: Richelle Renee Dade. **EDUCATION:** Wayne State Univ, BS 1948; Wayne State Univ, MEd 1954, EdD 1975; Marygrove Coll, grad work; Oakland Univ; Wayne State Univ, doctoral candidate. **CAREER:** Mercy Coll Reading Methods Course, instr 1966-67; Mercy Coll, consultant 1962-74; facilitator of change needs assessment problem & analysis for school staff 1972-74; Office of Adult Cont Educ Detroit Public School coordinator 1967-72; dept of staff devel & tchr training detroit public sch, tchr corps coordinator, prof growth cntr 1972-; Detroit Pub Sch, tchr; Detroit Public Schools Management Academy, on camera teacher reading 1962-67; WTVS 50, administrative asst 1984; Detroit Public Schools College of Eduation, Wayne State Univ, exec dir 1984-. **ORGANIZATIONS:** Mem Delta Kappa Gama 1966-74; Met Det Soc of Black Adminstr 1970-74; Women Admin 1974; Org of Admin & Supr 1970-74; MI Reading Assn 1962-74; Am Women in Radio & TV 1965-70; Met Detroit Reading Assn 1958-74; Beta Sigma Phi Fellowship 1966; Detroit Urban League Guild 1966; Detroit Urban League Educ Component 1974; Delta Sigma Theta Sorority 1948; St John Christian Meth Ch On Camera TV; mem Women's Economic Club Assoc Prof 1985-; bd of dirs Friends of International Institute 1978-; sec bd of dirs Michigan Coalition of Staff Development and School Improvement 1987-; bd of dirs Effective Instruction Consortium 1987; mem Assn of Supervisors and Curriculum 1980; mem Phi Delta Kappa, Wayne State University Chapter 1985. **HONORS/ACHIEVEMENTS:** Author of several books; award in recognition & of creativity pioneering spirit & serv to youth Womens Fellowship & Youth Ministry Plymouth United Ch of Christ Detroit 1971; Quarterly Publications Professional Development Programs with Thematic Inservice Modules 1984-; A Multi Faceted Approach to Staff Development and Its Relationship to Student Achievement 1975. **HOME ADDRESS:** 2360 Oakman Blvd, Detroit, MI 48238. **BUSINESS ADDRESS:** Executive Dir, Detroit Center for Professional Growth & Devel, Wayne State Univ, 155 College of Education, Detroit, MI 48202.

HARRIGAN, RODNEY EMILE
Consultant. **PERSONAL:** Born Jul 23, 1945, New York City, NY; married Elaine Mims; children: Pamela, Sherrice. **EDUCATION:** Paine Coll, BS Math 1967; IBM System Rsch Inst, 1969; Howard Univ, MS Computer Sci 1975. **CAREER:** Royal Globe Ins Co, programmer 1968; Fed City Coll, assoc prof 1977; Howard Univ, assoc prof 1977; IBM, systems engr 1968-72, staff programmer 1972-75, proj mgr 1975-76, adv proj mgr 1976-77, systems engrg mgr 1977-79; Post Coll, instructor 1980-81; IBM, employee relations mgr 1979-81, spec proj mgr 1981-82, faculty loan prof 1982-. **ORGANIZATIONS:** Mem Assn for Computing Machinery; mem Data Processing Mgmt Assn; mem IEEE Computer Soc; mem Alpha Kappa Mu Honor Soc; mem Omega Psi Phi Frat. **HONORS/ACHIEVEMENTS:** Alpha Kappa Mu Scholar of the Yr 1966; Honor Grad Awd 1967; Paine Coll Pres Awd 1967; IBM Golden Circle Awd 1975; IBM Symposium Awd 1972-74-75-76; IBM 100% Club Awd 1977-78 1981; Young Exec of Hartford Leadership Awd 1982; Operation Push Hartford Chap Awd 1981-82; NCA&J State Univ ACM Awd 1984. **BUSINESS ADDRESS:** System Engr/Adjunct Prof, IBM, 1100 W Market St, Greensboro, NC 27411.

HARRINGTON, CHARLES E.
Educator. **PERSONAL:** Born Jul 10, 1923, Raeford, NC; divorced; children: Karen, Charles, Jr, Lois, Candice, Kimberly. **EDUCATION:** Howard U, BS physics 1950; MA physics 1959; George Wash U, grad study systems engrng. **CAREER:** Office of Educ HEW, educ specialist, admin officer 1970-72; Naval Ordance Stata of MD, physicist 1960-70; Natl Bureau of Standards, research physicist 1950-60; School of Public Finance Atlanta Univ, consultant. **ORGANIZATIONS:** Chmn Greater Wash Area Black Unitarian Universalist Caucus; mem Banneker City Club; chief rep Local 2607 Ofc fo Educ HEW. **HONORS/ACHIEVEMENTS:** Recip fellow HowardUniv Physics 1958. **MILITARY SERVICE:** AUS 1943-45. **BUSINESS ADDRESS:** Ofc of Educ 7 & D Sts SW, Washington, DC 20202.

HARRINGTON, ELAINE CAROLYN
Educator. **PERSONAL:** Born Aug 31, 1938, Philadelphia, PA. **EDUCATION:** Tuskegee Inst, BS Elem Educ 1961; A&T State Univ, grad study 1962-64; Univ of CT Storrs, MA Supr Adm 1972. **CAREER:** JC Price School, teacher 1961-71; A&T State Univ, demonstration teacher 1965; Shiloh Baptist Church, dir cultural prog 1967; A&T State Univ, matls coord mus inst for jr high students 1968; Passaic Comm Coll, prof & acting dean of students 1972-80, prof acad founds 1980-. **ORGANIZATIONS:** Soloist Radio City Music Hall New

York City 1958; mem/pres/secty NCEA & NJEA Educ Organs 1961-80; mem NEA 1961-80; mem/secty Zeta Phi Beta Sor Inc 1963-; mem Natl Alliance of Black Sch Educators 1973-; mem Amer Personnel & Guidance Assoc 1976-; commn mem NAACP; mem YWCA; mem Christ Ch United Meth. **HONORS/ACHIEVEMENTS:** Outstanding Young Educator Awd Greensboro Public Schs NC 1968; Participant Leadership Seminar Guilford Co Schs NC 1969; Grad Scholarship Zeta Phi Beta Sor Inc 1971; 15 month Grad Fellowship EPDa Univ of CT 1971-72; NEH 1980 Seminar Fellowship Univ of Pgh 1980. **BUSINESS ADDRESS:** Prof Acad Founds, Passaic Co Comm Coll, Coll Blvd, Paterson, NJ 07509.

HARRINGTON, PHILIP LEROY
Educator. **PERSONAL:** Born Apr 27, 1946, Southern Pines, NC; son of Neville W Harrington and Blanche McNeil Harrington; married Chandra Salvi, Sep 15, 1968; children: Kafi Nakpangi, Kamala Nwena. **EDUCATION:** North Carolina Central Univ, Durham NC, BS, 1968. **CAREER:** Roxbury Multi-Serv Center, Boston MA, educ program dir, 1972-74; Lena Park Community Devel Corp, Boston MA, program dir, 1974-76; Action for Boston Community Devel, Boston MA, admin, 1976-81; Dover-Sherborn Regional Schools, Dover MA, 1981-; Indeprep School, Boston MA, founder, dir, 1985-88; Freedom House, Boston MA, consultant, 1988-. **ORGANIZATIONS:** Educator, Massachusetts Dept of Educ, 1974-77; mem, Youth Motivation Task Force for Natl Alliance of Business, 1975-78; bd mem, Inner City Council for Children, 1976-80; dir, Boston Youth Devel Program, 1978-80; mem, Omega Psi Phi Frat, Iota Chi Chapter, 1982-; pres, founder, Parents of Black Students of Buckingham, Browne & Nichols, 1984-88; review comm, Massachusetts Arts Council, 1984-87; bd mem, Natl Alliance of Black School Educators, 1987-; vice pres, Black Educators Alliance of Massachusetts, 1988-. **HONORS/ACHIEVEMENTS:** Performed in Black Nativity, produced by Natl Center of Afro-American Artists, Boston MA, 1984-89; Honoree, Museum of Afro-American History, Boston MA, 1988; Certificate of Recognition, Mayor of Boston, 1988. **HOME ADDRESS:** 27 Walden St, Cambridge, MA 02140.

HARRINGTON, ZELLA MASON
Director, nurse. **PERSONAL:** Born Jan 29, 1940, St Louis, MO; married Melvyn A; children: Melvyn A, Jr, Kevin Mason. **EDUCATION:** Jewish Hosp Sch of Nursing, diploma 1957-60; Webster Coll, BA1976; Webster Coll, MA 1977. **CAREER:** Nursing & Health Servs ARC, dir 1969-; Urban League of St Louis, health specialist 1968-69; Cardinal Ritter Inst, chief nurse trainer 1966-68; St LouisBd of Edn, practical nursing instr 1966; Vis Nurses Assn, sr staff nurse 1960-65; Nursery Found of St Louis, nurse consult 1963-65. **ORGANIZATIONS:** Mem, past pres, sec, treas, MO State Bd of Nursing 1974-; pres, vice pres Family Planning Council Inc Bd of Dirs 1976-77; faculty panel mem St LouisUniv Sch of Comm Med 1976-79; mem Health Adv Com Human Devel Corp 1977-; bd of dirs Maternal & Child Health Council Inc 1978-; comm consult Maternal & ChildHealth Council Inc 1979-; mem ANA 1961-80; mem Jack & Jill of Am Inc 1970-; mem Nat League for Nursing 1977-80. **HONORS/ACHIEVEMENTS:** Assisted with pub "Handbook for Home Health Aides" Cardinal & Ritter Inst 1968; listed Outstanding Young Women of Am 1972; listed Outstanding Contributions of Blacks in Health Care Delta Sigma Theta Sorority 1977; recipient George Washington Carver Award Sigma Gamma Rho Sororty 1978. **BUSINESS ADDRESS:** American Red Cross, 4050 Lindell Blvd, St Louis, MO 63108.

HARRIS, AL CALVIN
Professional athlete. **PERSONAL:** Born Dec 31, 1956, Bangor, ME. **EDUCATION:** Arizona State, BS 1979. **CAREER:** Chicago Bears, linebacker 1979-. **HONORS/ACHIEVEMENTS:** Has overcome injury problems and changing positions to become solid performer; started 8 games at DRE, 3 at LB in 1983; finished 8th on club in tackles (57) despite missing three games with turf toe; started 7 games at DRE in 1982 & last 11 games there in 1981. **BUSINESS ADDRESS:** Chicago Bears, Halas Hall, P O Box 500 Sta M Montreal, Lake Forest, IL 60045.

HARRIS, ARCHIE JEROME
Rehabilitation company executive. **PERSONAL:** Born Dec 02, 1950, Atlanta, GA; son of Richard E Harris Sr and Essie Lee Brown Harris; children: Ajeenah K Harris. **EDUCATION:** Morehouse Coll, BA 1972; Univ of GA, MEduc 1978. **CAREER:** Atlanta Public Sch System, sub teacher 1972-74; AP Jarrell Pre-Vocational Ctr, work adjustment inst 1974-75; Bobby Dodd Rehab & Industry Ctr, vocational eval 1975-77; Rehabilitation-Exposure Inc, pres 1983-; GA Dept of Human Resources Div of Rehab Serv, sr rehab counselor 1977-88; Rehabilitation-Exposure Inc, Atlanta, GA, pres, 1988-. **ORGANIZATIONS:** Chairperson JF Kennedy Ctr Adv Bd 1983-; co-chmn comm programming subcomm Mental Health Assoc of Metro Atlanta Inc 1983-; exec bd mem Statewide Minority Advocacy Group against Alcohol & Drug Abuse 1984-86; pres Atlanta Chap of the Assoc of Black Psychologists 1984-86; vice chmn The Atlanta Exchange Inc 1987-; pres, Atlanta Chapter of the Statewide Minority Advocacy Group for Alcohol & Drug Prevention, 1987-; bd mem, Mental Health Assn of Metropolitan Atlanta, 1989-. **HONORS/ACHIEVEMENTS:** Awards for Outstanding Serv & Dedication SMAGADAP 1983-86; Outstanding Young Men of Amer 1984-85; Outstanding Serv Awd Nigerian Student Council 1985; Bobby E Wright Community Serv Award, Assn of Black Psychologists, 1987; Mentor of the Year Award, Big Brothers/Big Sisters of Metropolitan Atlanta, 1988. **HOME ADDRESS:** 1948 Creekside Ct, Decatur, GA 30032. **BUSINESS ADDRESS:** Pres & Project Dir, Rehabilitation-Exposure Inc, 756 W Peachtree St, Atlanta, GA 30309.

HARRIS, ARTHUR LEONARD, III
Educator. **PERSONAL:** Born Jul 12, 1949, Pittsburgh, PA; divorced; children: Arthur L IV, Wesley P. **EDUCATION:** Comm Coll of Allegheny Co, AS 1971; Temple Univ, BA 1973; Univ of MA, MEd 1976, EdD 1986. **CAREER:** Univ of MA, grad asst 1973-74; Bd of Educ Springfield MA, classroom instructor 1974-82; Penn State Schuylkill Campus, program asst 1982-84; Penn State Hazleton Campus, dir continuing educ 1984-. **ORGANIZATIONS:** Bd mem Hazleton Leadership; past master Mt Nebo 118 Prince Hall Affiliated; mem Natl Univ Continuing Educ Assoc; mem Hazleton Area Chamber of Commerce. **HOME ADDRESS:** 319 N Third St, Pottsville, PA 17901. **BUSINESS ADDRESS:** Dir Continuing Education, Penn State Hazleton, Highacres-Acres, Div of Continuing Educ, Hazelton, PA 18201.

HARRIS, BARBARA ANN
Associate judge. **PERSONAL:** Born Jul 18, 1951, Atlanta, GA; daughter of Rev & Mrs Thomas Harris Sr. **EDUCATION:** Harvard Univ, AB (cum laude) 1973; Univ of MI Law Sch, attended 1976. **CAREER:** Justice Charles L Weltner, law clerk 1976-77; Northern Dist of GA, asst US atty 1977-82; Atlanta Municipal Court, assoc judge 1982-. **ORGANIZATIONS:** Mem Eta Phi Beta 1980-; exec comm Leadership Atlanta 1987-88; mem State Bar of GA; bd mem Determine Fitness of Bar Applicants Supreme Court of GA; exec comm Gate City Bar Assoc 1985; founder GA Assoc of Black Women Attys; bd mem United Servicemen's Organization, Amer Bar Assn, Natl Conf of Special Court Judges; judicial council Natl Bar Assn. **HONORS/ACHIEVEMENTS:** HO Smith Awd 1969; Jane L Mixer Awd Univ of MI 1976; Awd for Outstanding Public Serv One of GA's 50 Most Influential Black Women GA Coaltion of Black Women 1984; NAACP Awd 1985. **BUSINESS ADDRESS:** Associate Judge, Atlanta Municipal Court, 165 Decatur St SE, Atlanta, GA 30335.

HARRIS, BARBARA CLEMENTE
Episcopal bishop. **EDUCATION:** Attended Urban Theology Unit, Sheffield England, 1979. **CAREER:** Sun Oil Co, public relations manager; ordained Episcopal priest, 1979; St Augustine of Hippo Episcopal Church, Norristown PA, priest-in-charge, 1980-84; Episcopal Church Publishing Co, exec dir, 1984-89; Massachusetts Diocese of the Episcopal Church, Boston MA, bishop, 1989-. **HONORS/ACHIEVEMENTS:** Consecrated first female Episcopal Bishop, 1989. **BUSINESS ADDRESS:** Episcopal Diocese of Massachusetts, 138 Tremont, Boston, MA 02111. *

HARRIS, BETTY WRIGHT
Scientist. **PERSONAL:** Born Jul 29, 1940, Monroe, LA; daughter of Henry Jake Wright and Legertha Wright; married Alloyd Harris Sr (divorced); children: Selita, Jeffrey, Alloyd. **EDUCATION:** Southern Univ Baton Rouge, BS 1961; Atlanta Univ Atlanta, GA 1963; Univ of NM, PhD 1975. **CAREER:** Los Alamos Natl Lab, research chemist 1972-; Solar Turbines Inc, chief of chemical technology, 1982-84 (on leave from Los Alamos); CO Coll, chemistry teacher, 1974-75; MS Valley State Univ, math, physical science & chemistry teacher 1963; Southern Univ New Orleans, chemistry teacher 1964-72; Los Alamos Sci Lab, vis staff mem summers 1970-72; Intl Business Machines, vis staff mem summer 1969; Univ of OK, research asst summer 1966. **ORGANIZATIONS:** Mem Delta Sigma Theta Sororitiy 1959-; sec Central NM Section Am Chem Soc 1964-; mem Nat Consortium for Black Professional Devel 1975-; mem US Dept of Labor Women in Comm Serv 1978-; Sunday school, catechism teacher, Lutheran Ch Council; chmn, bd of dirs, Self-Help Inc; chmn, Mission Outreach Bd, sec, Multicultural Commn, Rocky Mountain Synod of the Evangelical Lutheran Church of Amer; mem, Women United for Youth, Albuquerque Public Schools; mem, outreach program, Los Alamos Natl Laboratory; mem, Planning Conf on the Status of Women in Sci, Washington DC (AAAS & NSF), 1977; natl mem NAACP 1975; mem Sigma Xi 1980-; mem Nat Tech Assn 1979-; Natl Assn of Parlimentarians, 1989-; legislative chmn & parlimentarian, Business & Professional Women, Los Alamos, 1987-. **HONORS/ACHIEVEMENTS:** Area Gov of Yr Award, 1978, Able Toastmaster Award, 1979, Distinguished Toastmaster Award, 1980, Distinguished District, 1981, Toastmasters Hall of Fame; author of 6 articles published in professional journals & 8 internal reports for Los Alamos & Solar Turbines Inc; awarded patent in 1986. **BUSINESS ADDRESS:** Research Chemist, Los Alamos Natl Laboratory, PO Box 1663, Mail Stop C920, Los Alamos, NM 87544.

HARRIS, BILL
Musician. **PERSONAL:** Born Apr 14, 1925, Nashville, NC; married Fannie Huthinson; children: Joseph, Clovia, Charles. **EDUCATION:** Washington Jr Coll of Music, diploma 1948. **CAREER:** Wash Jr Coll of Music, tchr 1949050; Mr Papps Sch, tchr 1957, 1958, 1959; Clovers Quartet, arranger & conductor guitarist 1950-57; performing & tchng 1957-; lectures Howard U, Fed City Coll; tchng pvt students; home studio; Pigfoot Restaurant Washington DC, owner operator & performer 1975-; completed musical score for movie Sincerely The Blues MORBEC 1974. **ORGANIZATIONS:** Participated D'Jango Reinhardt; mem Fest Paris 1974. **HONORS/ACHIEVEMENTS:** Recip Nat Endowment of Arts Fellow for Jazz Composers 1972; Cash Box Gold Record 1954; appeared on natl TV many times; recip Silver Star. **MILITARY SERVICE:** AUS pvt.

HARRIS, BRYANT G.
Consulting engineer. **PERSONAL:** Born Nov 05, 1916, Topeka, KS; son of Carl Harris and Georgia Harris; married Eugenia; children: Bryant II, Michael B. **EDUCATION:** KS State Univ, BS 1939; IL Inst Tech, further studies course advanced testing methods; Small Bus Admin, courses business mgmt; Howard U, seminars intergroup relations; Cornell U, Wilhelm Weinberg seminars labor mgmt public interest; Amer Univ, course facilities mgmt; Control Data Corp, advanced tech course. **CAREER:** Natl Youth Admin, journeyman electrician 1939-42; Reliable Electric Co Local 134 AFL Chicago, 1939-40; Howard Univ, instr engrg defense training courses 1942-44; War Dept Field Inspections Office, elect engr 1943-45; KDI Corp, consult 1968-69; Howard Univ, asst to vice pres for admin 1969-84, retired asst to vice pres for business & fiscal affairs 1986; private practice, cons; JAM Corp, part owner; Harris Elect Co Inc, founder, pres 1946-69, stand-by operations 1969-; Washington DC, professional engineering board 1987-. **ORGANIZATIONS:** Am Inst Elec Electronic Engrs; Illuminating Engineering Soc; mem Nat Tech Assn DC Chpt; Assn DC Univ Phys Plant Mgrs; vice chmn Greater WA Business Cntr; bd advs Nat Alliance of Businessmen; Score; bd dir Better Business Bureau; pres, treas Bureau Rehabilitation; bd mem, pres DC Chamber of Commerce; bd dir Natl Business League; mem SE Neighbors; mem Public Interest Civic Assn; chmn DC Electrical Bd; bd mem Bureau of Rehabilitation; mem Natl Council of Engineering Examiners 1988-; mem Natl Society of Professional Engineers 1988-. **HONORS/ACHIEVEMENTS:** Outstanding Contribution to Civic Betterment of Washington Comm; Outstanding Serv to District of Columbia Chamber of Commmerce; Business Perpetuation Awd Washington Area Contractors Assoc; Outstanding Service on Behalf of the Engineering Profession, NHL Society of Professional Engineers 1988; Outstanding Service as Commissioner from MBOC, The Business Exchange Networks 1986. **HOME ADDRESS:** 3135 Westover Dr SE, Washington, DC 20020.

HARRIS, BURNELL
Educator. **PERSONAL:** Born Oct 19, 1954, Fayette, MS; married Dyann Bell; children: Tomika Tantrice, Tineciaa, Tiaura Tichelle. **EDUCATION:** Alcorn State Univ, BA 1975, MS 1976. **CAREER:** West District Jr High School, instructor of history 1976-77; AJFC Comm Action Agency, instructor of adult ed 1977-78; Alcorn State Univ, instructor of history 1978-81; Grand Gulf Nuclear Station, bechtel security 1981-83; Jefferson County, circuit clerk 1984-. **ORGANIZATIONS:** Member Jefferson Co NAACP 1970-; member Phi Beta Sigma Fraternity 1976-; secretary Mountain Valley Lodge #6 1978-; member MS Circuit Clerks Assn 1983-; potentate Arabia Shrine Temple #29. **HONORS/ACHIEVEMENTS:** Outstanding Leadership Award Governors Office of Job Development and Training 1978.

BUSINESS ADDRESS: Clerk Circuit Court, Jefferson County Circuit Court, PO Box 305, Fayette, MS 39069.

HARRIS, CALVIN D.
Educator. **PERSONAL:** Born Aug 27, 1941, Clearwater, FL; married Ruth H Owens; children: Randall, Cassandra, Eric. **EDUCATION:** Univ of So FL, BA 1966; Northeast MO State Univ Kirksville, MA 1970; Nova Univ Ft Lauderdale, EdD 1975. **CAREER:** St Petersburg Jr Coll, provost open campus 1979-, dir spl prgm 1975-79, dir student comm & Serv 1970-75; Pinellas Co School System, instructor, history 1966-70. **ORGANIZATIONS:** Mem State Employment & Training Council/ Pinellas Co Coord Council/Pinellas Manpower Planning Consortium; mem State Of FL Standing Com for Continuing Edn; chmn Pinellas Co Arts Council 1980; chmn Ponce de Leon Elementary Sch Adv Com; dep commr Clearwater Babe Ruth Baseball; del White House Conf on Families; guest columnist Evening Indep Newspaper; chmn Juvenile Welfare Bd; mem bd of dir Amer Red Cross, YMCA; mem adv bd 1st Union Bank; mem bd of dir Upper Pinellas Assoc for Retarded Children, Employment & Devel Council. **HONORS/ACHIEVEMENTS:** Past-Pres Award, Clearwater Am Little League 1978; Certificate of Appreciation, Pinellas Co Sch Bd 1978; David Bilgore Memorial Award, Clearwater Kiwanis Club 1989. **MILITARY SERVICE:** AUS sp/4th class 1960-63. **BUSINESS ADDRESS:** Provost, St Petersburg Jr College, P O Box 13489, St Petersburg, FL 33733.

HARRIS, CARL GORDON
Educator. **PERSONAL:** Born Jan 14, 1936, Fayette, MO; son of Carl Harris, Sr. **EDUCATION:** Philander Smith Coll, AB (Cum Laude) 1956; Univ of MO at Columbia, AM 1964; Vienna State Acad of Music, attended 1969; Univ of MO at Kansas City Conservatory of Music, DMusA 1972; Westminster Choir Coll, attended 1979. **CAREER:** Philander Smith Coll, choral dir asst prof of music 1959-68; VA State Univ, choral dir professor/chmn 1971-84; Norfolk State Univ, choral dir prof/head 1984-. **ORGANIZATIONS:** Organist Centennial United Methodist Church 1968-71; organist/dir Gillfield Baptist Ch 1974-84; organist/dir Bank St Memorial Bapt Ch 1984-; bd dirs Choristers Guild Dallas TX 1981-87; dean Southside VA Chap Amer Guild of Organists 1984-85; adv panel VA Commn of the Arts 1980-84; mem exec bd Tidewater Chap American Guild of Organists 1987-; VA State chmn Jazz and Show Choirs; mem Amer Choral Directors Assoc 1987-. **HONORS/ACHIEVEMENTS:** Disting Alumnus Awd Philander Smith Coll, 1975; Outstanding Alumnus Achievement Awd Conservatory of Music Univ of MO Kansas City 1982; AR Traveler Awd Gov Frank White State of AR 1982; published article on "Negro Spiritual" Choristers Guild Letters 1985; published article "Conversation with Undine Smith Moore, "Black Perspective in Music 1985; Outstanding Teaching Award Norfolk State Univ, 1987. **HOME ADDRESS:** 1515 Versailles Ave, Norfolk, VA 23509. **BUSINESS ADDRESS:** Professor/Head, Norfolk State University, Box 2479 NSU, Dept of Music, Norfolk, VA 23504.

HARRIS, CAROLYN ANN
Systems analyst. **PERSONAL:** Born Jun 01, 1953, Lynchburg, VA. **EDUCATION:** Brown Univ, BA 1975; Rutgers Univ Graduate School of Mgmt, MBA 1984. **CAREER:** New Jersey Bell, computer programmer 1976-82; AT&T, mem programming staff 1982-. **ORGANIZATIONS:** Mem, Delta Sigma Theta Sorority Inc, 1976-; membership chair 1980-82, 1986-, recording sec, 1980-82 New Jersey Chap Black Data Processing Assoc; mem, AT&T Alliance of Black Employees, Crossroads Theater Guild & Benefit Commn; financial sec, Central Jersey Alumnae, Delta Sigma Theta Sorority, Inc, 1989-. **BUSINESS ADDRESS:** Programming Staff, AT&T, 100 Atrium Dr, Rm 2C63, Somerset, NJ 08873.

HARRIS, CASPA L., JR.
Association executive. **PERSONAL:** Born May 20, 1928, Washington, DC. **EDUCATION:** Amer Univ, BS 1958; Amer Univ Wash Coll of Law, JD 1967. **CAREER:** Peat Marwick Mitchell & Co, sr auditor 1958-62; Howard Univ, vice pres for bus & fiscal affairs, treas, comptroller 1965-71, chief internal auditor 1962-65, professor law sch 1967-. **ORGANIZATIONS:** Mem bd dir United Natl Bank; Columbian Harmony Soc; Natl Harmony Memorial Park; mem State of VA Treasury Bd; mem Supreme Court Bar; Amer, DC, VA Bar Assns; Amer Inst of CPA's; VA Soc of CPA's; The Academy of Mgmt; Financial Executives Inst; Natl Assn of Coll & Univ Bus Officers; mem of various other orgs; commr Fairfax Co Redevel & Housing Auth 1970-73; consult Natl Inst of Health.

HARRIS, CHARLES ALBERT
Physician. **PERSONAL:** Born Sep 07, 1952, Cleveland, OH; married Karen Marcia Brown; children: Gabriel M, Joy M, Joel T. **EDUCATION:** Macalester Coll, BA 1975; Howard Univ Coll of Medicine, MD 1979. **CAREER:** Womack Army Hospital, intern family practice 1979-80; 731st General Dispensary West Germany, commander & chief physician 1980-83; Tripler Army Medical Ctr, resident general surgery 1983-85; USAHC Pentagon Washington, officer-in-charge surgery section 1985-. **ORGANIZATIONS:** Mem candidate group of Amer Coll of Surgeons 1983-85, ministerial intern Alexandria Church of God 1986-; missionary to Haiti Nov 1986; radio bible teacher w/Mother B Harris on WFAX VA and WPJL NC "Solid Rock" program. **HONORS/ACHIEVEMENTS:** OT Kathryn Walter Awd Macalester Coll 1974; publication "Potentiation of d-TC Neuromuscular Blockade in CATS by Lithium Chloride," w/BN Basuray 1977; publication "Cassette Album w/Mother Barbara Harris "The Incomparable Teachings of Jesus Christ," 1986; physician assigned to Pres & Vice-Pres on Pres Reagan's visit to Pentagon April 8, 1987. **MILITARY SERVICE:** AUS major medical corps 9 yrs; Army Medal of Commendation; USMC plc prog 1972-74.

HARRIS, CHARLES CORNELIUS
Project manager. **PERSONAL:** Born Mar 02, 1951, Arkadelphia, AR; married Marva Lee Bradley; children: Charla Nicole. **EDUCATION:** Stanford U, MCE 1974, BCE 1973. **CAREER:** Procter & Gamble Cincinnati, OH, Affrmtv Action spclst 1975-76, cost engr 1974-75, bldg design engr 1976-81, proj engr 1981-84, proj mgr 1984-. **ORGANIZATIONS:** Adv Jr Achvmnt 1978-81; cnsltnt Cincinnati Mnrty Cntrctrs Asst Corp 1981; chm deacon bd Mt Zion Bapt Ch Woodlawn, OH 1983-; mem Kappa Alpha Frat 1969-; Sun Sch tchr Mt Zion Bapt Ch Woodlawn, OH 1979-. **HONORS/ACHIEVEMENTS:** EIT St of OH 1976; Schlrshp StanfordUniv 1968-73. **HOME ADDRESS:** 7337 Quail Run, West Chester, OH 45069. **BUSINESS ADDRESS:** Project Manager, Procter & Gamble, 6105 Center Hill Rd (Peawii), 6100 Center Hill Rd, Cincinnati, OH 45224.

HARRIS, CHARLES F.
Journalist director. **PERSONAL:** Born Jan 03, 1934, Portsmouth, VA; married Sammie Jackson; children: Francis, Charles. **EDUCATION:** VA State Coll, BA 1955; NY Univ Grad Sch, attended 1957-63. **CAREER:** Doubleday & Co Inc, rsch analyst to editor 1956-65; John Wiley & Sons Inc, vice pres gen mgr Portal Press 1965-67; Random House Inc, managing editor & sr editor 1967-71; Howard Univ Press, exec dir 1971-. **ORGANIZATIONS:** Mem Natl Press Club; mem bd dirs Reading is Fundamental; mem Assn of Amer Publishers; mem Assn of Intl Scholarly Publishers; mem Washington Area Book Pusblishers; adjunct prof of journalism Howard Univ; mem bd dirs Assn of Amer Univ Presses 1984; dir Laymen's Natl Bible Comm 1985. **MILITARY SERVICE:** AUS 2nd lt 1956; Honorable Discharge. **BUSINESS ADDRESS:** Executive Dir, HowardUniv Press, 2900 Van Ness St NW, Washington, DC 20008.

HARRIS, CHARLES SOMERVILLE
Educator/athletics. **PERSONAL:** Born Aug 22, 1950, Richmond, VA; married Lenora Billings. **EDUCATION:** Hampton Inst, BA/BS 1972; Univ of Michigan, MS 1973. **CAREER:** Hampton Inst, aduio-vis specialist 1972-73; Newsweek, staff writer 1973; Univ of Michigan, asst athletic dir 1973-79; Univ of Pennsylvania, dir of athletics 1979-85; Arizona State Univ, dir of athletics. **ORGANIZATIONS:** Mem Kappa Alpha Psi 1971-; mem Valley Big Brother 1985-; mem Valley of the Sun YMCA 1986-; mem Sigma Pi Phi 1987-; mem numerous natl collegiate athletic assoc comms. **BUSINESS ADDRESS:** Dir of Athletics, AZ StateUniv, University Activity Center, Tempe, AZ 85287.

HARRIS, CHARLES WESLEY
Educator. **PERSONAL:** Born Sep 12, 1929, Auburn, AL; children: Neeka, Angela. **EDUCATION:** Morehouse Clg, BA 1949;Univ of PA, MA 1950;Univ of WI, PhD 1959; Harvard U, 1964;Univ of MI, 1966. **CAREER:** TX Coll, asst prof of political science 1950-53; Tuskegee Inst, asst prof political science 1954-56; Grambling State Univ, assoc prof of political science 1959-61; Coppin State Coll, assoc prof political science 1961-70; Howard Univ, prof of political science. **ORGANIZATIONS:** Rsrch assoc Xerox Corp 1968; div chf & sr spec Govt Div Cong Res Serv 1974-74; Indep Res Ford Grant Ford Fndtn 1969; mem Alpha Phi Alpha Frat. **HONORS/ACHIEVEMENTS:** James Fund FellowshipUniv of WI 1956-58; Ford Res Grant Ford Fndtn 1969; Pi Gamma Mu Hon SocUniv of PA Chap 1951; Alpha Kappa Mu Hon Soc. **MILITARY SERVICE:** AUS t-4 1947-48. **BUSINESS ADDRESS:** Professor of Political Science, Howard University, 2400 6th St NW, Howard Univ, Washington, DC 20059.

HARRIS, CLIFTON L.
Construction & real estate contractor, mayor. **PERSONAL:** Born Feb 03, 1938, Leland, MS; son of Willie Harris and Gertrude Harris; married Maxine Robinson; children: La'Clitterfer Charisse Harris. **CAREER:** Harris Construction Co, Arcola MS, owner, 29 years; C & M Realty Co, Arcola MS, owner, 9 years; Town of Arcola, Arcola MS, mayor, 1986-. **ORGANIZATIONS:** Mem, NAACP, 1969; Elk Lodge, 1984, Deercreek Natl Gas Dist, 1986-, Salvation Army, 1986. **HONORS/ACHIEVEMENTS:** Certificate of Achievement, Delta Jr Coll, 1983-84; Certificate of Achievement, Howard Univ, 1988.

HARRIS, CURTIS ALEXANDER
Investment banking. **PERSONAL:** Born Jul 23, 1956, San Diego, CA. **EDUCATION:** US Military Acad West Point, BS 1978; Wharton School at Univ of PA, MBA 1985. **CAREER:** Smith, Barney, Harris, Upham & Co, assoc public finance 1985-87; W R Lazard & Co, 1987-89; Kidder, Peabody & Co, asst vice pres 1989-. **ORGANIZATIONS:** Mem Alpha Phi Alpha 1980-, Black MBA Assoc 1985-, West Point Soc of NY 1985-, Natl Assoc of Securities Prof 1986-. **MILITARY SERVICE:** USA capt 5 yrs; US Paratroopers Badge, Sr Instructor & Ordnance Corp 1978-83. **BUSINESS ADDRESS:** Kidder, Peabody & Co, 10 Hanover Square, New York, NY 10005.

HARRIS, DAISY
Disc jockey. **PERSONAL:** Born Apr 22, 1931, Hattiesburg, MS; divorced; children: James, Jr, Anthony, Harold. **EDUCATION:** Pearl River Jr Coll, Sec Cluster Course. **CAREER:** WDAM-TV, sec, receptionist 2 yrs; WORV Radio, dj, sec; CORE, sncc, complete ofc work. **ORGANIZATIONS:** NAACP; MFDP; civil rights work 1963-68; sec 5th dist Loyalist Dem Party; third class FCC Radio Lic; vol worker SCLC; chmn Voter Registrn. **HONORS/ACHIEVEMENTS:** Most Popular Disc Jockey; award for work in Civil Rights; honored for work in comm serv 1973-74.

HARRIS, DAVID, JR.
Clergyman. **PERSONAL:** Born Apr 12, 1931, Dallas, TX. **EDUCATION:** Wiley Coll, BS 1957; Southwestern Seminary, BD 1967, MRE 1969; Teomer Sch of Religion, LLD 1981; Southwestern Seminary, MA 1983. **CAREER:** NAACP, advisor 1970-80; Suburban Tribune, publisher 1983-85; Second Corinthian Church, pastor 1970-. **ORGANIZATIONS:** Advisor Urban League 1980-85; pres Wiley Coll Alumni 1981-83; advisor Black Coll Alumni Assn 1984-85; mem Master Masons AF & AM. **HONORS/ACHIEVEMENTS:** "Jesse Jackson, Is He a Phony?" the Suburban Tribune; "The Jubilee Year" Dallas Post Tribune 1984; "The Story of Pacific Ave School in Dallas TX" the Post Tribune 1983; "What Happened to Booker T Washington Trophies?"; Who's Who in Amer; Who's Who in the South & Southwest; Intl Congress of Who's Who; Personalitiesof the South; KY Col Honors; Hons from the City of Atlanta GA; Honors from the City of Detroit MI. **HOME ADDRESS:** 4220 E Grand, Dallas, TX 75223. **BUSINESS ADDRESS:** Pastor, Second Corinthian Church, 1803 Browder St, Dallas, TX 75215.

HARRIS, DAVID ELLSWORTH
Pilot. **PERSONAL:** Born Dec 22, 1934, Columbus, OH; children: Camian, Leslie. **EDUCATION:** Ohio State Univ, BS 1957. **CAREER:** Amer Airlines, capt 1964-. **ORGANIZATIONS:** Mem, pres Organization of Black Airline Pilots; former mem NAI. **HONORS/ACHIEVEMENTS:** Black Achievement in Indus Award, YMCA 1971. **MILITARY SERVICE:** USAF cpt 1958-64. **BUSINESS ADDRESS:** Captain, American Airlines, Logan Intl Airport East, Boston, MA.

HARRIS, DELONG
Attorney. **PERSONAL:** Born in New Orleans, LA; married Dr Laline O; children: De Long Jr. **EDUCATION:** VC Jones Teachers Coll, attended; Dillard Univ, attended; Howard Univ, attended; Robert H Terrell Law School in Dist, valedictorian of class 1944. **CA-**

REER: Private practice, lawyer 1944-. **ORGANIZATIONS:** Mem Bar of Supreme Ct of US, US Ct of Appeals for DC Circuit; past pres Wash Bar Assoc 1958-60; past mem bd dirs Wash Bar Assoc 15 yrs; mem Natl Assoc of Trial Attnys; mem Law Enforcement Council of DC 1958-; chmn bd trustees Asbury United Meth Church 1979-81; past pres Mott School PTA; mem Health & Welfare Council DC Br; mem YMCA, Eureka Lodge, Mason; legal counsel Mecca Temple; past gen counsel Most Worshipful Prince Hall Grand Lodge; past exec vice pres Acacia Masonic Hall Assoc past pres Commanders of the Rite 33 Degree Masons. **HONORS/ACHIEVEMENTS:** Cert Recog of Coop & Serv Urban Leag 1959; Lawyer of the Year Awd WA Bar Assoc 1965; Counsel for petitioner & argued the cause in Man's House is His Castle ruling of US Supreme Ct Miller v US 357, US 301, 2L Ed 2d-1332, 78 S Ct 1190. **BUSINESS ADDRESS:** Attorney, 1816 Eleventh St NW, Washington, DC 20001.

HARRIS, DOLORES M.
Educational administrator. **PERSONAL:** Born Aug 05, 1930, Camden, NJ; daughter of Roland H. Ellis (deceased) and Frances Gatewood Ellis; children: Morris E Jr, Sheila D Rodman, Gregory M. **EDUCATION:** Glassboro State Coll, BS 1959, MA 1966; Rutgers Univ, EdD 1983. **CAREER:** Glassboro Bd of Educ, tchr adminstr 1959-70; Camden Welfare Bd, supvr adult ed ctr 1968; SCOPE Glassboro Ctr, dir Headstart 1969-70; Natl ESL Training Inst Jersey City State Coll, assoc dir 1971; Glassboro State Coll, dir cont educ 1970-; Glassboro State Coll Glassboro, N.J. Acting vice pres for Academic Affairs 1989. **ORGANIZATIONS:** Bd dirs Adult Educ Assn of USA 1973-79; consul NJ Gov's Conf on Libraries & Info Serv 1979; examiner NY Civil Serv 1976-; chair of adv bd Women's Educ Equity Comm Network Project 1977-78 1980; bd dirs Glassboro State Coll Mgmt Inst 1975-; consul Temple Univ 1978-79; consul NY Model Cities Right toRead Natl Training Conf 1973-81; comm NJ Task Force on Thorough & Efficient Educ 1976-78; legislative comm Amer Assn for Adult & Continuing Educ 1982-; mem Gloucester Co Private Industry Cncl 1984-; 1st vice pres Natl Assn of Colored Women's Clubs Inc 1984-; vice pres at large Northeastern Fedn of Colored Women's Clubs Inc 1983-; pres vice pres other offices NJ State Fedn of Colored Women's Clubs Inc 1972-80; pres South Jersey Chap of Links Inc 1984-; pres vice pres other offices Gloucester Co United Way 1968-; fndr chair of bd Glassboro Child Develop Ctr 1974-82; pres Glassboro State Coll Alumni Assn 1975-77; delegate Intl Women's Yr Natl Conf 1978; vice chair Commn on Status of Women Gloucester Co NJ 1983-; Commission on Women of Gloucester Cnty NJ, chair 1986-; Nat'l Council of Women, exec comm & education chair; pres Natl Assn of Colored Women's Clubs, Inc. 1988-. **HONORS/ACHIEVEMENTS:** Disting Serv to Adult Educ OIC Inc Camden 1974; Clubwomen of the Yr Outstanding Serv Awd NJ State Fedn of Colored Women's Clubs Inc 1972 1973; Disting Serv Awd Assn for Adult Educ of NJ 1974; Disting Alumna Awd Glassboro State Coll NJ 1971; fndr editor of Newsletter "For Adults Only" Glassboro State Coll NJ 1970-74; editor of Newsletter AEA/USA Commn on Status of Women Washington DC 1973-75; Comm Serv Awd Holly Shores Girl Scouts NJ 1981; President's Awd United Way of Gloucester Co Woodbury NJ 1985; co-author "Black Studies Curriculumfor Corrections" Garden State Sch Dist Trenton NJ 1975; Gloucester Cnty Business & Professional Women's Club, woman of the year awd 1985; Holly Shores GirlScouts, citizen of the year awd 1987; Ebony 100 Most Influential Black Americans May, 1989; Rose Award Delta Kappa Gamma, Alpha Zeta State 1989; Woman of the year Zeta Phi Beta, Gamma Nu Zeta 1989.

HARRIS, DON NAVARRO
Biochemical pharmacologist. **PERSONAL:** Born Jun 17, 1929, New York, NY; son of John Harris and Margaret Vivian Berkeley-Harris; married Regina B; children: Donna Harris-Wolfe, John Craig, Scott Anthony. **EDUCATION:** Lincoln Univ PA, AB 1951; Rutgers Univ, MS 1959, PhD 1963. **CAREER:** Colgate Palmolive Research Ctr, sr res 1963-64; Rutgers Univ, asst research specialist 1964-65, assoc prof 1975-77; Squibb Inst for Med Rsch, rsch fellow 1965-. **ORGANIZATIONS:** Mem Amer Assoc Adv of Sci 1966-; mem, treas, bd dir Frederick Douglass Liberation Library 1970-82; steering comm 1975-, sec 1986- Biochem Pharmacology Discussion Group of the NY Acad of Sci; mem Philadelphia Physiological Soc 1978-, Amer Soc for Pharmacology and Exp Ther 1980-; consultant US Army Sci Bd 1981-85; reviewer Natl Science Foundation 1981-; advisory comm Biochem Section of NY Acad of Sci 1983-; vstg lecturer Lincoln Univ PA 1983-; participant Natl Urban League Black Exec Prog; lecturer TX Southern Univ 1984; editorial bd mem Journal of Enzyme Inhibition 1985-; mem Sigma Xi, NY Acad of Sci, Amer Heart Assoc, Amer Chem Soc, Theta Psi Lambda Chapter of Alpha Phi Alpha, Mu Boule, Sigma Pi Phi; lecturer So Univ Baton Rouge LA 1987. **HONORS/ACHIEVEMENTS:** Author or co-author of 40 scientific papers, 40 scientific abstracts and 4 patents; Recipient of Harlem YMCA Black Achievers Award 1984. **MILITARY SERVICE:** AUS Medical Corp speclst 2 yrs. **BUSINESS ADDRESS:** Research Fellow, Squibb Inst for Medical Rsch, Dept of Pharmacology, PO Box 4000, Princeton, NJ 085434000.

HARRIS, DONALD J.
Economist. **EDUCATION:** UCWI-LONDON U, BA 1961;Univ CA Berkeley, PhD 1966. **CAREER:** Univ IL Champaign, asst prof 1965-67;Univ WI Madison, assc prof 1968-71; Stanford U, prof 1972-. **ORGANIZATIONS:** Consultant United Nations Conf Trade & Devel 1966-67; researcher & lecturer Univ & Inst Mexico Holland England Brazil Italy India Africa Caribbean; mem bd editor Journal of Economic Lit 1979-84. **HONORS/ACHIEVEMENTS:** Natl Rsch Council Ford Found Fellowship 1984-85; numerous publications Professional Journals & Books. **BUSINESS ADDRESS:** Dept of Economics, Stanford Univ, Stanford, CA 94305.

HARRIS, DOUGLAS ALLEN
Entrepreneur. **PERSONAL:** Born Feb 07, 1942, Burlington, NJ; son of Milton Harris and Marvel Clark Harris; married Myrna L Hendricks. **EDUCATION:** Trenton State Coll, BA Educ 1964; Rutgers Univ Graduate School of Educ, MEd 1973; Fordham Univ Graduate School of Bus, MBA Mgmt & Mktg 1980. **CAREER:** NJ Bd of Educ, teacher 1964-69; Webster Div McGraw-Hill Book Co, dir of mktg serv 1969-76; RR Bowker, mgr Educ Admin book div 1976-79. **ORGANIZATIONS:** Mem Council of Concerned Black Exec 1975-78, Amer Assn for Adult Continuing Ed 1980-; founding bd mem Literacy Volunteers of Chicago 1982-; vice pres bd Simek Mem Counseling Ctr 1983-; vice pres Sanctuary Choir Second Bapt Church of Evanston 1984-; dir of marketing, American Dental Assn 1986-88; dir, Middle Atlantic Assn of Temporary Services 1989. **HONORS/ACHIEVEMENTS:** Volunteer of the Year, North Shore Magazine 1985; Gold Award/Marketing Training, American Marketing Assn 1987; Ordained Baptist Deacon 1985. **BUSINESS ADDRESS:** Owner, Todays Temporary of Greater Philadelphia, 500 N Gulph Rd, Suite 320, King of Prussia, PA 19406.

HARRIS, EARL
City official. **PERSONAL:** Born Jan 01, 1922, Dawson, GA. **EDUCATION:** Newark Jr Coll. **CAREER:** Newark City Council, pres, first black to hold this position. **ORGANIZATIONS:** Over 20 yrs active partic in political field; active Dr Martin Luther King's voter regis drives in S; enlisted support of 10 black Elected ofcls from NY& NJ to help Dr King initiate voter regis drive; Essex Co Bd of Freeholders 1962. **BUSINESS ADDRESS:** 920 Broad St, Newark, NJ.

HARRIS, EARL L.
State representative. **PERSONAL:** Born Nov 05, 1941, Kerrville, TN; son of Collins Harris and Magnolia Hall Harris; married Donna Jean Lara, 1969. **EDUCATION:** Indiana University-Northwest, 1961-62; Purdue University, Calumet IN, 1966-67. **CAREER:** Inland Steel Company; Amer Maize Products Co, laboratory tester; Kentucky Liquors and Kentucky Snack Shop, owner/operator; General Assembly, state representative, 1983-86. **ORGANIZATIONS:** Mem, NAACP; mem, East Chicago Black Coalition. **BUSINESS ADDRESS:** 4114 Butternut St, East Chicago, IL 48312. *

HARRIS, EDWARD E.
Educator. **PERSONAL:** Born Feb 27, 1933, Topeka, KS. **EDUCATION:** Lincoln U, AB 1954;Univ IA, AM 1958, PhD 1963; WI U, post grad 1972. **CAREER:** IN Univ, Perdue Univ Indianapolis, assoc prof sociology 1968-; CA State Coll, asst prof 1965-68; Prairie View A&M Coll, TX, assoc prof 1963-64. **ORGANIZATIONS:** Mem Am & No Central Sociological Assns ed bd Coll Student Journal 1971-; contrib articles to professional jrnls. **HONORS/ACHIEVEMENTS:** Who's Who Midwest, 15th ed. **MILITARY SERVICE:** AUS 1965-56. **BUSINESS ADDRESS:** Sociology Dept, IN Univ PurdueUniv, Indianapolis, IN 46208.

HARRIS, ELBERT L.
Educator. **PERSONAL:** Born Feb 16, 1913, Baltimore, MD; married Claudette Archer; children: Susan, Elbert Jr. **EDUCATION:** West Chester State Coll, BS 1937; Howard Univ, MA 1939; Univ of MI, 1940; Oxford Univ, 1945; Univ of PA, PhD 1959. **CAREER:** St Paul Ind School, instructor 1940, acting dean 1941-42; Livingstone Coll, instructor 1946-59; DE State Coll, dept head language & literature 1959-60, dept head social science 1962-65; Cheyney State Coll, prof 1965-69; Swarthmore Coll, visiting lecturer 1968; Rutgers Univ, dir black studies and prof of history 1969-82, prof emeritus 1982. **ORGANIZATIONS:** Mem Assoc for Study of Negro Life & History. **HONORS/ACHIEVEMENTS:** Author, Killers of the City, The Athenian, Sojourn in Persepolis, Private Undre Luneville of Harlem; listed in Who's Who in the East; Plaque Livingstone Coll;Awd for Serv to Black Students Rutgers 1972; Acad of Human Serv 1974; 2 Gen Ed Bd Grants; Danforth Fellow. **MILITARY SERVICE:** AUS 1942-45. **BUSINESS ADDRESS:** Professor Emeritus, RutgersUniv, 5 & Penn Sts, Camden, NJ 08102.

HARRIS, ELIHU MASON
Legislator/attorney. **PERSONAL:** Born Aug 15, 1947, Los Angeles, CA; son of Elihu Harris, Sr. and Frances Harris; married Kathy Neal. **EDUCATION:** CA State at Hayward, BA 1968; Univ CA Berkeley, MA 1969; Univ CA Davis,JD 1972. **CAREER:** Congresswoman Yvonne Burke, legislative asst 1974-75; Natl Bar Assn, exec dir 1975-77; Alexander Millner & McGee, partner 1979; State of CA, assemblyman. **BUSINESS ADDRESS:** Assemblyman, State of CA, State Capitol, Sacramento, CA 95814.

HARRIS, EUGENE EDWARD
Personnel administrator. **PERSONAL:** Born Feb 10, 1940, Pittsburgh, PA; married Marva Jo. **EDUCATION:** PA State U, BA Labor Econ;Univ of Pittsburgh, MPA Public Admin 1969; DuquesneUniv Law Sch, JD 1980. **CAREER:** US Steel, mgr employment 1978-; asst mgr/mgr labor relations 1973-78, prog coord Gary Proj 1969, labor contract adminstr 1968, labor contract admnstr Clairton Works 1965, pers serv analyst 1964. **ORGANIZATIONS:** Chmn Gary Concentrated Employ Prgm 1969-73; chmn Gary Econ Devel Corp 1970-73; dir Gary Urban League 1970-72; treas Comm Partners Corp 1975-. **HONORS/ACHIEVEMENTS:** Capt PA StateUniv Basketball team 1962; hon mention, All-Am 1962. **MILITARY SERVICE:** AUS sp4 1963-68. **BUSINESS ADDRESS:** 600 Grant St, Pittsburgh, PA 15230.

HARRIS, FRANCO
Retired professional athlete. **PERSONAL:** Born Mar 07, 1950, Ft Dix, NJ; son of Cad Harris and Gina Parenti; married Dana Dokmanovich; children: Franco Dokmanovich Harris. **EDUCATION:** Pennsylvania State Univ, University Park, PA, BS 1972. **CAREER:** Pittsburgh Steelers, running back 1972-84. **HONORS/ACHIEVEMENTS:** AFC Champ Game 1972/74/75/78/79; Pro Bowl 1972-78; tied NFL record for most consecutive games of 100 yards or more rushing in a season, with 6 straight games1972; Rookie of Yr, rushed for more than 1,000 yds 1972; gained over 1,000 yds in 4 out of 5 yrs in NFL; led NFL in TD's with 14 in 1976; Sporting News AFCAll-Star Team 1972/75/77; Distinguished Alumnus of Pennsylvania State Univ 1982. **BUSINESS ADDRESS:** PresVinial Street, Franco's All Naturel, 800 Vinial St, Suite D, Pittsburgh, PA 15212.

HARRIS, FRANK
Military officer. **PERSONAL:** Born in Arcadia, LA; children: Wilma A, Rosalind L, Ronald R. **EDUCATION:** United Coll of San Antonio, BA; Our Lady of the Lake Univ San Antonio TX 1975. **CAREER:** Natl Bank of Commerce San Antonio, bank clerk 1967-68; HEB Food Stores San Antonio, groc store mgr 1968-69; USAF Logistic Command, suprv, supply clerk 1970-80. **ORGANIZATIONS:** Mem OLL Univ Alumni Assoc 1975-80, Kelly AFB Mgmt Club 1978-80, Black Employees Org for Progress 1978-80. **HONORS/ACHIEVEMENTS:** Asiatic Pacific Campaign Medal; Natl Defense Medal; Korean Serv Medal w/2 BB Stars; Vietnam Serv Medal w/1 BB Star; Army Good Conduct Medal/AF Longevity Serv Medal; Korean Pres Unit Citation; Vietnam Pres Unit Citation; United Nation Serv Medal; United Nation Republic of Vietnam Medal. **MILITARY SERVICE:** USAF s/sgt 1946-67; Disting Flying Cross Awd; Air Medal w/16 OLC; Pres Unit Citation w/1 Clasp; Outstanding Unit Awd w/2 clasps; Victory WW II Medal. **BUSINESS ADDRESS:** Supervisor, Supply Clerk, USAF Logistic Command, Directorate of Distrib SAALC, Kelly AFB, TX 78241.

HARRIS, FRED
Editor, publisher. **PERSONAL:** Born Sep 27, Gary, IN. **EDUCATION:** Indiana Univ;

Columbia Univ. **CAREER:** Gary American Newspaper, editor, publisher; Vet in Politics, PR man; Amer Legion Post 498, comdr. **ORGANIZATIONS:** Mem NAACP. **HONORS/ACHIEVEMENTS:** Vet in Politics Award 1973; Am Legion Award 1972-75. **MILITARY SERVICE:** AUS pfc. **BUSINESS ADDRESS:** 2768 Broadway, Gary, IN.

HARRIS, FREEMAN COSMO
Publisher. **PERSONAL:** Born Jul 14, 1935, Andrews, SC; married W Mae Harris; children: Audrey, Angela, Bontrice, Carla, Dane, Ronnie, Edwana. **EDUCATION:** Adjutant Gen Sch, Ft Ben Harrison, IN; RCA, NY; ATS, NY. **CAREER:** Denver Weekly News, publ; KBPI, sta mgr, commercial mgr, prgm dir, air personality; KFML Radio, air personality; KFSC Radio AE & AP; KDKO AM; WVOERadio AE & AP; WYNN Radio AE & AP; WATP Radio AE & AP; Channel 4 Gospel Experience, host; Signal Sch of Broadcasting, instr; Denver Chronicle Newspapers, columnist, acct exec. **ORGANIZATIONS:** Mem Nat Newspaper Pub Assn; CO Press Assn; Advtsng Club of Denver; chmn bd & pres Dark Fire Publ House Inc; owner Tasta Printing Co; bd of dirs US Black C of C; pres emeritus Denver Black C of C; mem Black Media Inc; chmn E Neighborhood Anti-Crime Adv Counc. **HONORS/ACHIEVEMENTS:** Refused to accept awards or honors from anyone or Orgn. **MILITARY SERVICE:** USAF a2c. **BUSINESS ADDRESS:** Denver Weekly News, 8720 E Colfax Ave, Denver, CO 80220.

HARRIS, GARY LYNN
Educator. **PERSONAL:** Born Jun 24, 1953, Denver, CO; son of Norman Harris and Gladys Weeams; married Jennifer Dean, May 19, 1984; children: Jamie Harris. **EDUCATION:** Cornell Univ, Ithaca, NY, BSEE, 1975, MSEE, 1976, PhD in EE, 1980. **CAREER:** Natl Research & Resource Facility for Sumicron Structures, Ithaca, NY, asst, 1977-80; Naval Research Laboratory, Washington, DC, visiting scientist, 1981-82; Howard Univ, Washington, DC, assoc prof, 1980-; Lawrence Livermore Natl Laboratory, consultant 1984-. **ORGANIZATIONS:** mem, Sigma Xi, Inst of Electrical & Electronic Engineers; chmn, IEEE Electron Devices, Washington Section, 1984-86; mem of selection comm, Black Engineer ofthe year, 1989. **HONORS/ACHIEVEMENTS:** IBM Graduate Fellow, 1978-80; author of on the Origin of Periodic Surface Structure of Laser Annealed Semiconduct, 1978; Robert Earle Fellowship; 1980; author of SIMS Determinations on Ion Implanted Depth Distributions, 1980; author ofAn Experimental Study of Capless Annealing on Ion Implanted GaAs, 1983; author ofElectronic States of Polycrystalline GaAs & Their Effects on Phtovoltaic Cells, 1983; author of Geltering of Semi-Insulation Liquid Incapsulated GaAs for Direc t Ion Implanation, 1984. **BUSINESS ADDRESS:** Dr. Gary L Harris, Materials Science Research Center (MSRCE), Howard Univ/Eng, 2300 6th St, NW, L K Downing Hall, Washington, DC 20059.

HARRIS, GEORGE DEA
Educator. **PERSONAL:** Born Mar 26, 1945, Pittsburgh, PA; married Judith Anne Flurry; children: Ebon Lee. **EDUCATION:** Scottsbluff Jr Coll, working towards BS 1965; Univ of Eastern NM, BS 1967; Univ of Pittsburgh, MEd 1973, PhD 1981. **CAREER:** Pittsburgh Board of Education, community agent 1968-69; Duquesne Univ, dir of Counseling & Learning Dept for Black Students 1969-76, dir Learning Skills/Act 101. **ORGANIZATIONS:** Bd of directors Pittsburgh Coll YMCA, Pittsburgh Council on Pub Educ, Information & Vol Serv of Allegheny Cty; chrmn NAACP Educ Committee; mem Omega Psi Phi Black Arts Fest comm; consult C-Map Office-Carnegie-Mellon Univ 1973-78, Urban Yth Action 1975-78; advisory brd Duquesne Univ grad dept ofCounselor Educ 1979-80; consultant Office of Cmty Affairs - Univ of Pgh 1980-82. **HONORS/ACHIEVEMENTS:** Gold Medallion Black Catholic Ministry; Citizen of the Year Awd, Distinquished Educ Awd- Talk Magazine; All Amer Hon Ment Scottsbluff Jr Col; All ConfFirst String Awd - Univ of Eastern NM. **BUSINESS ADDRESS:** Dir, Dusquesne University, Room 314 Administration Bldg, Pittsburgh, PA 15282.

HARRIS, GERALDINE E.
Scientist, microbiologist. **PERSONAL:** Born in Detroit, MI; divorced; children: Reginald, Karen. **EDUCATION:** Wayne State Univ Med Tech, BS 1956; Wayne State Univ, MS Microbiology 1969, PhD Microbiology 1974. **CAREER:** Detroit General Hosp, med tech 1956-60; Parke Davis & Co, asst res microbiol 1961-66; Wayne St Univ Dept of Biol, rsch asst 1967-68; Wayne State Univ Coll of Med, tutor/advisor post baccal prog 1971-73; Drake Inst of Sci, consult 1971-73; Met Hosp Dt, microbiol 1975; Winston-Salem State Univ, asst prof microbiol 1975-77; Clinical Microbiology Group Health Assn Inc, chief; Allied Health Prog Devel Amer Assn State Colls & Univs Washington, assoc coord; Food & Drug Admin Center for Food Safety & Applied Nutrition, consumer safety officer 1980-. **ORGANIZATIONS:** Reg Amer Soc Clinical Pathology MT #28926 1956-; Amer Soc for Microbiol 1967-; Assn Univ Prof 1968-; Sigma Xi; Assn for Advance of Sci 1975-; consult Natl Caucus on Black Aged 1976; partic Educ Computers in Minority Inst 1977; mem Alpha Kappa Alpha Sor, Urban League, Orphan Found. **HONORS/ACHIEVEMENTS:** NIH Pre-Doctoral Fellow 1968-71. **BUSINESS ADDRESS:** Consumer Safety Officer, Food & Drug Admin, 200 C St SW, Washington, DC 20204.

HARRIS, GIL W.
Educator. **PERSONAL:** Born Dec 09, 1946, Lynchburg, VA; married Paula Bonita Gillespie; children: Deborah Nicole Gillespie-Harris. **EDUCATION:** Natl Acad of Broadcasting, dipl radio &TV 1964-65; Winston-Salem Coll, AS 1969-71; Shaw Univ, BA 1977-80; NC A&T St Univ, MS 1981-82; Pacific Western Univ, PhD 1986. **CAREER:** WEAL/WQMG Radio Stations, oper dir 1972-79; Shaw Univ, dir of radio broadcasting 1979-81; Collegiate Telecommunications, system producer, sport dir 1981-84; SC St Coll, asst prof of broadcasting 1984-. **ORGANIZATIONS:** Mem Omega Psi Phi, Prince Hall Mason, NAACP. **HONORS/ACHIEVEMENTS:** Citizen of the Week WGHP TV High Point NC 1977; Radio Announcer of the Year Dudley HS 1979; Outstanding Media Serv Triad Sickle Cell 1979; Outstanding Media Serv Mid-Eastern Athletic Conf 1983; Outstanding Media Serv Central Intercoll Athletic Assoc. **MILITARY SERVICE:** USA sp5-e5 3 yrs; Army Commendation with "V" Device 1965-68. **HOME ADDRESS:** 416 Robinson St NE, Orangeburg, SC 29115.

HARRIS, GLEASON RAY
Chief estimator. **PERSONAL:** Born Jun 19, 1952, Norfolk, VA; married Jacqueline Theresa; children: Devanae Nicole, Deondra Laneese. **EDUCATION:** Attended, Univ of Louisville 1983; Louisville Voc/Tech Inst, A 1978. **CAREER:** Anderson & Assoc Architects, sr designer 1978-80; Kamex Construction, estimator/designer 1980-83; Tidewater Design Assocs, pres/designer 1984-86; Public Storage Inc, chief estimator 1986-. **ORGANIZATIONS:** Mem Amer Inst for Design & Drafting 1983, Louisville Minority Contractors Assoc 1984, KY State Highway Minority Contractors Assoc 1984; mem Louisville Urban League 1985. **BUSINESS ADDRESS:** Chief Estimator, Public Storage Inc, 4707 Eisenhower Ave, Alexandria, VA 22304.

HARRIS, HARCOURT GLENTIES
Physician. **PERSONAL:** Born Apr 16, 1928, New York, NY; married Charlotte L Hill; children: Harcourt Jr, Michael, Brian, Andrea. **EDUCATION:** Fordham U, BS 1948; Howard U, MD 1952. **CAREER:** Physician, pvt pract 1960-; UAH, staff pos 2 yrs; Dearborn UAH, resdnt 3 yrs; Harlem Hosp, internship 2 yrs; Bd Certified Internist 1962; Highland Park Gen Hosp, chf of med, dir med educ 1973-76; Wayne State U, clin asst prof 1975-. **ORGANIZATIONS:** Life mem NAACP. **MILITARY SERVICE:** AUS 1953-55. **BUSINESS ADDRESS:** 15521 W Seven Mile Rd, Detroit, MI 48235-2927.

HARRIS, HASSEL B.
Clergyman, administrator. **PERSONAL:** Born Jul 10, 1931, Garrard Cty, KY; married Elizabeth Ann Green; children: Dominico, Eric. **EDUCATION:** Morehouse Coll, AB 1955; Simmons Bible Coll, DD 1972; Univ of MO, Grad Study 1966; Union Coll, attended. **CAREER:** Benedict Coll Columbia SC, dir mens personnel & publ rel 1955-58; Summer Work Camp Simsubry CT, dir 1955-58; St Paul Bapt Church, pastor 1960-70; Knox Cty OEO & Cumberland Valley OEO, personnel dir, acting dir 1965-70; Union Coll, 1st black staff mem dir fin aid 1969-73; Mt Moriah Ch, pastor 1970-; Cumberland River Comp Care Ctr (8 counties), occupational prog consult 1973-74, admin catchment b 1975-77; State Mental Health, mgr oper 1977-; Gen Assoc of KY Baptists, moderator 1984-. **ORGANIZATIONS:** Moderator London Dist Assoc 1962-; chmn Cumberland River Mental Health-Mental Retardation Bd 1970-73; bd dir Knox Gen Hosp 1975-77; exec bd Gen Assoc 1962-; mem Human Relations Comm 1972. **HONORS/ACHIEVEMENTS:** JJ Starks Awd Best Man of Affairs 1955; Commissioned KY Col 1968.

HARRIS, HELEN B.
Educator. **PERSONAL:** Born Mar 06, 1925, High Point, NC; daughter of Willie Boulware and Hattie Whitaker Boulware; married Dr Wendell B Harris, Sep 04, 1951; children: Wendell B Jr, Charles B, Dr Hobart W. **EDUCATION:** Bennett Coll, BA 1945; Univ of IA, MA 1952. **CAREER:** Prismatic Images Inc, exec producer. **ORGANIZATIONS:** Appointed by gov of state, mem St Neighborhood Educ Auth; bd mem Flint Public Schools; exec dir YWCA High Point NC 1945-48; program dir YWCA Des Moines 1948-51; sec Mayors Adv Comm; charter mem Flint Chap Delta Sigma Theta; mem Jack & Jill; pres League of Women Voters 1965; pres, bd of ed Flint 1973-74,75-76; life mem NAACP, Delta Sigma Theta, Urban League, ACLU; bd mem, NBD Genesee Bank 1980-89; trustee, Comm Found of Greater Flint 1986-89; pres, Flint Area Educ Found 1988-89; bd mem emeritus Questar School for Gifted 1987-89. **HONORS/ACHIEVEMENTS:** 1st female black mem & 1st woman pres elected to Flint Bd of Ed; produced movie "Chameleon Street", that is selected for entry in 1989 Venice Festival. **BUSINESS ADDRESS:** Executive Producer, Prismatic Images Inc, 124 W Kearsley St, Flint, MI 48502.

HARRIS, HORATIO PRESTON
Dentist. **PERSONAL:** Born Sep 25, 1925, Savannah, GA; married Barbara E Monroe; children: Gary P, Patricia L, Michael M, Dr Conrad W, Nancy E, Dr David M, Cathy C, Roxanne D, Robert H. **EDUCATION:** Howard U, BS 1951, DDS 1956. **CAREER:** VA, Wash, IBM splst 1949; St Elizabeth Hosp, intern, oral surgery 1956-57; priv prac dentistry, Wash 1957-; Bur Dental Health, dental ofcr 1960-65; Howard U, instr 1966-67, asst prof 1967-71; minister 1973-82. **ORGANIZATIONS:** Mem courtesy staff oral surgery, Freedman's Hosp; mem Am/Nat/DC Dental Assns; RT Freeman Soc; mem Omega Psi Phi. **HONORS/ACHIEVEMENTS:** Honored UAU. **MILITARY SERVICE:** USNR 1943-46.

HARRIS, HOWARD F.
Association executive. **PERSONAL:** Born Apr 19, 1909, Monticello, AR; married Ozepher; children: Howard, Helen, Ozepher. **EDUCATION:** Atlanta U, BA 1929. **CAREER:** Independent consult on pub housing; Housing Authority, City of Tampa, FL, exec dir ret 1977; field of pub housing 26 yrs; Monsanto Chem Co, nitric acid prod 6 yrs; Lincoln HS Bradenton, FL, science tchr 5 yrs; Booker Washington HS Tampa, tchr 4 yrs; Lee Co Training Sch Sanford, NC, science tchr 1 yr. **ORGANIZATIONS:** Past pres FL Housing & Redevel Ofcls; past mem Exec Council Southeastern Regional Council of Housing & Redevel Ofcls; mem White House Council on Aging1971; mem Omego Psi Phi 1926-; NAACP; bd dirs Big Bros; Tampa Chap Frontiers of Am Inc; N Tampa Optomist Club. **HONORS/ACHIEVEMENTS:** Omega Cit of Yr 1969; award for excellence in adminstrn, Frontiers of Am 1968. **BUSINESS ADDRESS:** 1514 Union St, Tampa, FL 33607.

HARRIS, J. ROBERT, II
Marketing analyst. **PERSONAL:** Born Apr 01, 1944, Lake Charles, LA; son of James Robert Harris and Ruth E Boutte Harris; widowed; children: Evan, April. **EDUCATION:** Queens Coll, BA psychol 1966; City Univ of NY, MA soc 1969; Berlitz School Langs, postgrad 1974. **CAREER:** Equitable Life Ins Co, rsch analyst 1965-66; NBC, mktg rsch supvr 1966-69; Gen Foods Corp, grp mktg rsch mgr 1969-72; Pepsi Co Intl, assoc dir rsch 1972-74; Intern Mktg Res Pepsico Inc, plans, sup sur polls stud 130 count to provide info necessary for mktg co food & beverage products around world, assoc dir; JRH Markting Servs Inc, pres. **ORGANIZATIONS:** Mem Amer Mktg Assn (one of org of groups Min Employee Prog which was inst in hir many blacks & other min mem into mktg res field); pres JRH Mktg Serv 1975-; dir rec lectr math & french proj Upward Bound 1966-67; mem European Soc for Opinion & Mkt Rsch; pres, bd dir Qualitative Rsch Consult Assn 1987-89; consult Volunteer Urban Consulting Group Inc. **HONORS/ACHIEVEMENTS:** Recipient, Key of Success Mex City 1973; NY State Reg School 1961-65; David Sarnoff Fellow 1967; grant HowardUniv 1961-65; Franklin & Marsh Coll 1961-65; NAACP; Omega Psi Phi; Roman Catholic. **BUSINESS ADDRESS:** President, JRH Marketing Serv Inc, 29-27 41st Ave, Long Island City, NY 11101.

HARRIS, JACK
Radio owner. **PERSONAL:** Born Jul 08, Chicago, IL; married Janis A; children: Cindie M, Linda S, Jackie R, Esther, Charlene A, Trisha J, Jack II. **EDUCATION:** Lincoln Univ, Govt 1959; Roosevelt Univ, 1964; Brown Inst of Broadcasting Engrs; 1970; Marquette Univ 1972. **CAREER:** Former Chess recording artist; record producer and writer; Harris Family

Publishing, pres; WCKX Radio Columbus/KBWH Radio Omaha, pres/gen mgr. **ORGANIZATIONS:** Mem NAACP; AQA FAT. **HONORS/ACHIEVEMENTS:** Billboard Prog Dir & Announcer of Yr 1969; Who's Who Among Black Amers 1975-76; Citizen Awd for Outstanding Leadership 1983. **MILITARY SERVICE:** USAF a2c 4 yrs. **BUSINESS ADDRESS:** President/General Manager, WCKX/KBWH, 696 E Broad St, Columbus, OH 43215.

HARRIS, JAMES A.
Association executive. **PERSONAL:** Born Aug 25, 1926, Des Moines; married Jacquelyn; children: James, Jr, Jerald. **EDUCATION:** Drake U, BA 1948, MFA 1955; Drake Div Coll, post grad work; OK A&M. **CAREER:** Nat Educ Assn, pres 1974-, vice pres 1973; Des Moines, art, human rel tchr 1954; Kansas City, elem tchr 1948; Langston U, tchr 1953-54. **ORGANIZATIONS:** Dir NEA; mem NEA Budget Com; mem Steering Com NEA Consti Conv; mem first ofcl delegation of Am Educators to Peoples Rep of China; spkr Nat Assem for Educ Research, Yamagata, Japan 1974; co-chmn with Dr Wise NEA Com on Am Revol - Bicen; served on many com of IA State Educ Assn, Des Moines Educ Assn; past dir Red Cross refugee shelter during Kansas City flood; bd mem Am Friends Serv Com; adminstr comm relations Forest Ave Baptist Ch; served on Mayor's task forces on educ & police-comm relations; NAEA Bd of Dirs liaison with Nat Assn of Art Edn; mem IA Assn of Art Educators; mem NAACP; Kappa Alpha Psi; dir Des Moines Chap Boys Clubs of Am. **MILITARY SERVICE:** USAF pilot WwII. **BUSINESS ADDRESS:** 1201 16 St NW, Washington, DC 20036.

HARRIS, JAMES ANDREW
Scientist, business executive. **PERSONAL:** Born Mar 26, 1932, Waco, TX; married Helen L; children: Cedric, Keith, Hilda, Kimberly, James. **EDUCATION:** Huston-Tillotson Coll Austin, TX, BS 1953; CA StateUniv Hayward, CA, MPA (pending thesis) 1975. **CAREER:** Tracer Lab Inc Richmond CA, radiochemist 1955-60; Lawrence Berkeley Lab, nuclear chemist Beta Spectroscopy Group 1960-66, nuclear chemist 1966-69, group leader/rsch chemist Heavy Isotope Prodn Group 1969-74, post doctoral recruiter Chem & Physics Div 1974-77, asst to div head, staff scientist Engrg & Tech Serv Div 1977-. **ORGANIZATIONS:** Mem Nat Soc of Black Chemists & Chem Engrs; bd mem Far WHS; mem PTA Pinole CA. **HONORS/ACHIEVEMENTS:** Most Outstanding Youn Man Awd; listed in Who's Who in Amer Soc, Who's Who in Sci; lectr at num univs & colls; Rsch Display at Oakland Museum & City Hall of Providence RI; DSc Degree Houston Tillotson Coll 1973; Cert of Merit Natl Urban League; Scientific Merit Awd City of Richmond; Outstanding Achievement Awd Marcus Foster Inst. **BUSINESS ADDRESS:** Staff Scientist, Lawrence Berkeley Lab, Univ of CA, 1 Cyclotron Rd, Berkeley, CA 94720.

HARRIS, JAMES E.
Educational administrator. **PERSONAL:** Born Sep 24, 1946, Castalia, NC; married Justine Perry; children: Kasheena, Jamillah. **EDUCATION:** Montclair State Coll, BA 1968, MA 1970; Pub Serv Inst of NJ, 1974; Harvard U, summer 1974; NY U, 1973-. **CAREER:** Montclair State Coll, assoc dean 1986-, cross country coach 1975-, asst dean of students 1970-, counselor 1969-70; Bamberger's, Newark, asst to dir comm relations 1968; Montclair State Coll, res counselor Upward Bound Project summer 1966-67; Elko Lake Camp, NY, counselor 1965; Montclair State Coll, asst librarian 1964-67; Camp Weequahic, Lake Como, PA, porter 1964. **ORGANIZATIONS:** Consult Educ Testing Svc, Am Coll Testing Inc; Ctr for Opportunity & Personnel Efficiency, NJ; Nat Orientation Director's Assn; pres, Montclair State Coll Assn of Black Faculty & Adminstrv Staff; pres Educ Oportunity Fund Comm Adv Bd of Montclair State Coll; pres NJ Assn of Black Educators 1973-; mem No NJ Counselors Assn; Nat Assn of Personnel Adminstr; Am Personnel & Guidance Assn; Am Coll Personnel Assn; v-chmn NJ Amateur Athletic Union Women Track & Field Com; bd mgr NJ Assn of Amateur Athletic Union of Am; bd tsts Leaguers Inc; dir, coach, fdr Essex Co Athletic Club of Newark; Cross Country Coach at Montclair State Coll; mem Legislative Aide Com to Assemblyman Hawkins; N Ward Block Assn; cert mem NJ Track & Field Officials Assn;Amateur Athletic Union Officials; chmn NJ Black Issues Convention Educ Task Force 1986-; pres NAACP Montclair Br 1983; mem Montclair Civil Rights Commiss1979-; chmn Presidents Council on Affirmative Action Univ of Med & Dentistry of NJ; mem Urban League of Essex County. **HONORS/ACHIEVEMENTS:** Outstanding Black Educator Awd; Montclair State Coll Student Leadership Awd; Essex Co Volunteer Awd; Athlete of the Year Awd for Montclair St Coll. **MILITARY SERVICE:** NJ NatlGuard cpt. **BUSINESS ADDRESS:** Assoc Dean of Students, Montclair State College, Upper Montclair, NJ 07043.

HARRIS, JAMES G., JR.
Executive director. **PERSONAL:** Born Oct 27, 1931, Cuthbert, GA; son of James Harris Sr and Eunice Mitchner Harris; married Roxie Lena Riggs; children: Peter C, Robin M. **EDUCATION:** Hillyer Coll, Assoc Bus Admin 1956; Univ of Hartford, BS Bus Admin 1958; New Hampshire Coll, Hon DL 1984. **CAREER:** State of CT, social worker 1958-59; EJ Korvette, acct payable supvr 1959-60; State of CT, social worker 1060-65; State Office of Economic Oppor, asst dir 1965-66; Gov John Dempsey, spec asst to gov 1966-70; Greater Hartford Comm Renewal Team, exec dir state civil rights coord 1970-82; CT Dept of Human Resources, commnr 1983-87; Data Institute Inc, consultant 1987-89; Bethol Center for Humane Services, consultant 1987-89. **ORGANIZATIONS:** Pres legislative chmn CT Assoc for Comm Action 1975-83; vice pres & panelist New England Comm Action Assoc 1977-80; mem Gov's Task Force on the Homeless 1983-; mem Adult Educ Study Commn 1984-; pres life mem Greater Hartford Branch NAACP 1962-64; chmn State Conf of NAACP chmn emeritus 1967-70; sec Alpha Phi Alpha 1964-66; mem Priorities Comm United Way 1984-; Gov's Designee Femia Distrib Comm 1984. **HONORS/ACHIEVEMENTS:** Who's Who Among Students in Amer Colls & Univs, Univ of Hartford 1958; Comm Leaders of Amer 1972-81; Who's Who in the East 1982-85; Who's Who in Amer 1984-85; Outstanding Serv Awd New England Chap of NAACP 1962; Charter Oak Leadership Awd Chamber of Commerce of Hartford 1964; Disting Serv Awd Phoenix Soc of Hartford 1979; Outstanding Serv New England CAP Dirs Assn 1981-83. **MILITARY SERVICE:** USAF sgt 4 yrs. **HOME ADDRESS:** 42 Tower Ave, Hartford, CT 06120.

HARRIS, JASPER WILLIAM
Educator/psychologist. **PERSONAL:** Born Dec 10, 1935, Kansas City, MO; son of Jasper Harris and Mary P Harris; married Joann S Harper; children: Jasper Jr. **EDUCATION:** Rockhurst Coll, BS Biology 1958; Univ of Missouri, MA 1961; Univ of Kansas, EdD 1971, PhD 1981. **CAREER:** Univ of Kansas research assoc 1969-77; Kansas City School Dist, teacher 1963-69, assoc supt 1977-86, superintendent 1986-. **ORGANIZATIONS:** Mem Phi Delta Kappa Frat, Alpha Phi Alpha Frat, Jr Chamber of Commerce, Rockhurst Coll Alumni Assoc, Univ of MO Alumni Assoc; vice chmn United Negro Coll Fund; mem adv bd & chmn educ and youth incentives comm Urban League; mem Science Teachers Assoc, Amer Educ Rsch Assoc, Amer Psychological Assoc, Univ of KS Alumni Assoc; life mem NAACP; mem Assoc for Supervision and Curriculum Develop, Personnel Rsch Forum; theta boule Sigma Pi Phi Frat; consultant Kaw Valley Medical Soc Health Careers Prog 1971-; participant in the Pres of the US Comm on Employment of the Handicapped White House Washington DC1980; selected reviewer for manuscripts submitted for publication in Exceptional Children 1984-85; apptd to MO State Dept Funding Comm Study Group by Commnr of Educ 1985; apptd assoc editor Exceptional Children Journal 1985. **HONORS/ACHIEVEMENTS:** SPOKE Awd US Jaycees for Comm Svcs; Outstanding Young Man of Amer 1970; Outstanding Young Educator of Greater Kansas City Jr Chamber of Commerce; Life-time Teaching Certificate in Science for the State of MO; Life-time Administrative Secondary Certificate for the State of MO; Life-time Superintendent's Certificate; Special Educ Certification; apptd by the Office of the Sec of Educ Dept of Educ Washington DC to a review panel for identifying exemplary secondaryschools Washington DC 1985; numerous publications. **BUSINESS ADDRESS:** Superintendent, Kansas City MO School Dist, 1211 McGee St, Kansas City, MO 64106.

HARRIS, JAY TERRENCE
Executive editor. **PERSONAL:** Born Dec 03, 1948, Washington, DC; married Anna Christine; children: Taifa Akida, Jamarah Kai, Shala Marie. **EDUCATION:** Lincoln Univ, BA 1970. **CAREER:** Wilmington News-Journal, gen assignment reporter 1970, urban affairs reporter 1970-71, investigative reporter 1971-73; Wilmington News-Journal Papers, special projects editor 1974-75; Northwestern Univ, instructor of journalism/urban affairs 1973-75, asst prof of journalism/urban affairs 1975-82; Frank E Gannett Urban Journalism Ctr, asst dir 1975-76, assoc dir 1976-82; Northwestern Univ Medill Sch of Journalism, asst dean 1977-82; Gannett News Svc, natl correspondent 1982-84; Gannett Newspapers and USA Today, columnist 1984-85; Philadelphia Daily News, exec editor 1985-. **ORGANIZATIONS:** Mem John S Knight Fellowship Prog Bd of Visitors; bd of dirs Dow-Jones Newspaper Fund; mem accrediting comm Accrediting Cncl on Educ in Journalism and Mass Communication; author Minority Employment in Daily Newspapers 1978-82; founder/former dir The Consortium for the Advancement of Minorities in JournalismEduc; head Minorities and Communication Div Assoc for Educ in Journalism and Mass Communication. **HONORS/ACHIEVEMENTS:** Co-authored series of articles on heroin trafficking in Wilmington DE that won Public Serv Awds of the Assoc Press Managing Editors Assoc and Greater PhilaChap Sigma Delta Chi; Special Citation for Investigation of Minority Employment in Daily Newspapers Natl Urban Coalition 1979; Par Excellence Awd for Disting Serv in Journalism Operation PUSH 1984; Drum Major for Justice Awd Southern Christian Leadership Conf 1985. **BUSINESS ADDRESS:** Executive Editor, Philadelphia Daily News, 400 N Broad St, Philadelphia, PA 19101.

HARRIS, JEAN LOUISE
President & CEO. **PERSONAL:** Born Nov 24, 1931, Richmond, VA; daughter of Vernon J Harris and Jean Pace Harris; married Leslie J Ellis; children: Karin Denise, Cynthia Suzanne Ellis. **EDUCATION:** VA Union U, BS 1951; Med Clg VA, MD 1955;Univ Richmond, DSC Hon 1981. **CAREER:** DC Dept Hlth, dir bur rsrcs dev 1967-69; Natl Med Assc Found, exec dir 1969-73; Med Clg VA, prof fam prac 1973-78; VA Cabinet Post, sec of human rsrcs 1978-82; Control Data Corp, vice pres 1982-88; Ramsey Foundation St Paul MN, pres & CE0 1988-. **ORGANIZATIONS:** Mem Natl Acad Sci Inst of Med, Recominant DNA Cmn NIH, Pres Tsk Force Pvt Sec Initiatives 1981-82; bd trustees Univ Richmond 1982-; Links Inc 1973-, VA State Bd Hlth 1982-84; v chn Pres Tsk Force Alcholism & Abuse; council mem, Eden Prarie City Council, Rotary International 1987-91. **HONORS/ACHIEVEMENTS:** Magnificent Seven VA Women's Pol Action Grp 1983; distngshd serv Natl Govr Assc 1981; nwsmkr of yr VA Press Women 1979; otstndg woman govt YWCA 1980; Top 100 Black Business & Prof Women, Dollars & Sense Magazine 1986; Recipient, First Annual SERWA Award Comm of 100 Black Women, Virginia Chapter, 1989. **HOME ADDRESS:** 10860 Forestview Cir, Eden Prairie, MN 55344. **BUSINESS ADDRESS:** President, Ramsey Foundation, Jackson St University Ave, St Paul, MN 55101.

HARRIS, JEANETTE G.
Business executive. **PERSONAL:** Born Jul 18, 1934, Philadelphia, PA; divorced. **EDUCATION:** Inst of Banking, 1959-70. **CAREER:** First PA Bank NA, banking ofcr, bank mgr; dept store bookkeeper, sales clerk. **ORGANIZATIONS:** Mem Urban League; bd dir YMCA; bd mem Philadelphia Parent Child Care Ctnr; mem & vis prof BEEP; mem Nat Assn of Black Women Inc; Philadelphia Black Bankers Assn; mem community orgn dealing with sr cit; past treas Ch Federal Credit Union; treas Merchants Assn Progress Plaza Shopping Ctnr. **HONORS/ACHIEVEMENTS:** First black female bank mgr in Phila. **HOME ADDRESS:** 4548 N Gratz St, Philadelphia, PA 19140.

HARRIS, JEROME C., JR.
City administrator. **PERSONAL:** Born Dec 15, 1947, New York, NY; married Rosemarie Mcqueen; children: Rahsaan, Jamal. **EDUCATION:** Rutgers Univ, BA Soc 1969, MS Urban Planning 1971. **CAREER:** Livingston Coll Rutgers, instr dept of community devel, asst to dean acad affairs 1969-73; Mayor's Policy & Devel Office Newark, dir urban inst 1973-74, urban devel coord 1974-75; Middlesex County Econ Opport Corp, dep exec dir mgmt & admin 1975-77; NJ Educ Opport Fund Dept of Higher Ed, asst dir, fiscal affairs 1977-78; Dept of Higher Ed, assoc dir budget & fiscal planning 1978-82; City of Plainfield, dir public works & urban devel 1982, dep city admin 1983, city admin 1983-. **ORGANIZATIONS:** Mem bd of dir Plainfield Econ Devel Corp; pres NJ Jaycees 1977; vice pres New Brunswick NAACP 1978-79; pres NJ Public Policy Rsch Inst 1979-84; chmn Middlesex Cty CETA Advisory 1979-83; 1st vice chmn NJ Black Issues Convention 1983-; mem Intl City Mgrs Assoc, Amer Soc of Public Admin, Conf of Minority Public Admin, Forum of Black Public Admin, NJ Municpal Mgrs Assoc. **HONORS/ACHIEVEMENTS:** Serv Awd NJ Black United Fund 1984; Outstanding Black Ed NJ Assoc of Black Ed 1983. **BUSINESS ADDRESS:** City Administrator, City of Plainfield, 515 Watchung Ave, Plainfield, NJ 07061.

HARRIS, JIMMIE
Attorney. **PERSONAL:** Born Jul 27, 1945, Winona, MS. **EDUCATION:** Univ of CA Berkeley, JD 1972;Univ of IL Champaign-Urbana, IL, BS Elec Engrng 1967. **CAREER:** Vidal Sassoon Inc, counsel; Daylin Inc Asso Irell & Manella, gen counsel. **ORGANIZATIONS:** Mem Beverly Hills Bar Assn; LA Co Bar Assn; Langston Law Club. **HONORS/ACHIEVEMENTS:** Pub articles, ed CA Law Review 1971-72. **BUSINESS ADDRESS:** 2049 Century Park East, Ste 3900, Los Angeles, CA 90067.

HARRIS, JOHN CLIFTON
Physician. **PERSONAL:** Born Jan 15, 1935, Greensboro, NC. **EDUCATION:** NY Coll of Podiatric Med, Dr of Podiatric Med; Howard U, grad courses 1964-65; NC A&T, BS 1962. **CAREER:** Dr of Podiatric Med, self-empl; Addiction Rsrch & Treatment Corp, 1972-; Lyndon B Johnson Comm Health Cntr, staff podiatrist 1974-77; Towers Nursing Home, staff podiatrist 1970-71; 125th St Comm Med Grp, 1970-74. **ORGANIZATIONS:** Podiatry So of State of NY; Am Podiatry Assn; Acad of Podiatry; NY Co Podiatry Soc; bd dir Harlem Philharmonic Soc Inc; diplomate Nat Bd of Podiatry; NAACP; YMCA. **MILITARY SERVICE:** USAF med serv spl, a/1c 1954-58. **BUSINESS ADDRESS:** 50 West 97th St, New York, NY 10025.

HARRIS, JOHN EVERETT
Educator. **PERSONAL:** Born May 31, 1930, New Haven, CT; married Emily Louise Brown; children: John E. **EDUCATION:** Yale U, BS 1953; Brown U, PhD 1958. **CAREER:** Boston Univ, assoc prof of science 1970-; MA Inst Tech, asst prof food toxicology 1965-70; Monsanto Rsch Corp, sr rsch chemist 1959-65; Yale Univ Medical School, rsch fellow 1957-59. **ORGANIZATIONS:** Mem Sigma Si; Am Chem Soc; Chem Soc, London; Am Assn for Advncmt of Sci; Am Acad of Sci; bd trustee SW Boston Comm Svcs; sci adv Cynthia Sickle Cell Anemia Fund Inc; past pres Stonybrook Civic Assn; mem Alpha Phi Alpha; NAACP; Urban League. **HONORS/ACHIEVEMENTS:** Listed in Am Men of Sci & Ldrs of Am Sci; articles publ in Jour of Am Chem Soc Jour of Organic Chem Analytical Biochem & Biochem Abstracts publ in Meetings of Am Chem Soc. **BUSINESS ADDRESS:** 871 Commonwealth Ave, Boston, MA 02215.

HARRIS, JOHN H.
Financial administrator. **PERSONAL:** Born Jul 07, 1940, Wynne, AR; married Adele E Lee; children: Cheryl E, Angela M. **EDUCATION:** So IL Univ, BS 1967; Southwestern Grad Sch of Banking 1973-74. **CAREER:** Gateway Natl Bank, vice pres, cashier 1967-74, exec vice pres 1975; Boatmens Natl Bank, operations officer 1976-77; School Dist of Univ City, dir of finance. **ORGANIZATIONS:** Mem Natl Bankers Assn 1967-, Amer Inst of Banking 1967-77, Bank Admin Inst 1968-73; adv Jr Achievement of MS Valley Inc 1967-77; dir treas St Louis Council Campfire Girls Inc 1972-73; former mem Phi Beta Lambda; mem Natl Assn of Black Accountants 1974-75; treas fund drive United Negro Coll Fund 1975; bd dir Inst of Black Studies 1977; mem NAACP, US Selective Serv Comm; dir treas Greely Comm Ctr Waring Sch PTA; dir King-Fanon Mental Health Ctr, Child Day Care Assoc; supervisory comm Educational Employees Credit Union; treas Block Unit #1144; dir Amer Cancer Soc. **BUSINESS ADDRESS:** Assistant Superintendent, Sch Dist of University City, 8346 Delcrest, St Louis, MO 63124.

HARRIS, JOHN H.
Educator. **PERSONAL:** Born Aug 12, 1940, Memphis, TN; married Dorothy Payne; children: Sean Kofi, Steven Kwesi. **EDUCATION:** LeMoyne Coll, BS 1962; Atlanta Univ, MS 1966. **CAREER:** US Peace Corps, pc volunteer Accra Ghana 1962-64; LeMoyne-Owen Coll, instructor 1967-. **ORGANIZATIONS:** Mem Natl Assoc of Mathematicians 1986-87, Black Data Processing Assocs 1986-87, Amer Mathematical Soc 1987. **HONORS/ACHIEVEMENTS:** UNCF Faculty Fellow 1978. **BUSINESS ADDRESS:** Assoc Prof of Math/Comp Sci, LeMoyne-Owen College, 807 Walker Ave, Memphis, TN 38126.

HARRIS, JOHN J.
Company executive. **PERSONAL:** Born Sep 18, 1951, Plymouth, NC; son of Jerome Harris. **EDUCATION:** California State Univ, Northridge CA, BA, 1972; Univ of California Los Angeles, MBA, 1974.

HARRIS, JOSEPH BENJAMIN
Director & chairman of board. **PERSONAL:** Born Jun 08, 1920, Richmond, VA; married Pauline Elizabeth McKinney; children: Paula Jo, Joseph C, Joya R. **EDUCATION:** VA Union U, BS 1949; Howard U, dds 1953. **CAREER:** CA Howell & Co, pres 1967-72, chmn bd 1972-. **ORGANIZATIONS:** Am Dental Soc 1953-; MI Dntl Soc 1953-; Det Dntl Soc 1953-; Nat Dntl Soc 1955-; Am Dntl Fund 1980; Sigma Pi Phi 1970; Omega Psi Phi 1947-. **HONORS/ACHIEVEMENTS:** Am Soc Dentistry for Children 1953. **MILITARY SERVICE:** AUS stf sgt 1943-46; Battle of Normandy; Good Conduct Medal; Vctry Medal World War II; Asiatic Pacific Theater with 1 Bronze Star 1944. **HOME ADDRESS:** 1190 W Boston Blvd, Detroit, MI 48202. **BUSINESS ADDRESS:** Dir & Chmn of Board, CA Howell & Co, 2431 W Grand Blvd, Detroit, MI 48208.

HARRIS, JOSEPH PRESTON
Business executive. **PERSONAL:** Born Apr 11, 1935, Rome, MS; married Otha L; children: Jacqui, Joe Jr. **EDUCATION:** Chicago Tchrs Coll, BE 1956; John Marshall Law Sch, JD 1964. **CAREER:** Allstate Ins, reg vp; Allstate Ins, mgmt dev rotational 5 yrs; Allstate Ins, atty law div yrs; Allstate Ins, adjuster 2 yrs; Chicago Bd of Edn,tchr 1956-64. **ORGANIZATIONS:** Bd of dir Maywood Proviso State Bank 1973-76; mem IL & Chicago Bar Asnn 16 yrs; mem NAACP. **BUSINESS ADDRESS:** 2431 W Grand Ave, Detroit, MI 48208.

HARRIS, JOSEPH R.
City official. **PERSONAL:** Born Jan 29, 1937, Philadelphia, PA; married Jean A Williams; children: Joseph R Jr, Keith A, Allison M. **EDUCATION:** La Salle Clg U, BA Govt 1954-58; Fordham U, MA Pol 1958-71; Hunter Clg CUNY, Urban Plng Course 1971; Fordham U, PhD Candidate 1975-. **CAREER:** US Peace Corps Cameroun W Africa, assoc dir 1964-66; NCCJ Natl Police Comm Relations, dir 1966-67; Manpower & Career Devel Agency NYC, spec asst cmsnr 1967-68; City Univ NY, dean, dir 1969-84. **ORGANIZATIONS:** Cnsltnt/evaluator Bureau of Equal Ed State of PA 1980-; Mdl States Cmsn on Hghr Ed 1973-82; cnslnt USAID Ed Msn to Africa 1974; bd dir Natl CoaltnAdult Ed Orgn 1970; bd dir pres Friends Plainfield Lbry 1980-83; v chm bd dir NJ Edctnl Oprtnry Fund 1981-; bd dir NY Univ School of Continuing Educ. **HONORS/ACHIEVEMENTS:** Vatterott Schor Vatterott Fdt St Louis MO Grad S 1958-60; otstndg yng man awrd Otstndg Am Fdt 1976; Ford Found Grant Ford Found 1981; Matsushita Found Grant 1987. **MILITARY SERVICE:** AUSR spec ii 1962-68. **BUSINESS ADDRESS:** Director, CDDP/Urban Project, City Univ of NY, 555 W 57th St Ste 1512, Ste 1512, New York, NY 10019.

HARRIS, JULIUS
Counselor. **PERSONAL:** Born Nov 13, 1940, Arcadia, FL; married Ernestine; children: Trina Dris, Shannon. **EDUCATION:** BS 1968; FL A&M U, MEd 1969. **CAREER:** Grand Rapids Public Schools, counselor; Calvin Coll, academic coordinator Upward Bound Program. **ORGANIZATIONS:** Bd dir YMCA 1972-75; exec bd Grand Rapids Educ Assn 1974-76; Nat Tchrs Assn 1969; MI Educ Assn; APGA; mem Masons; Elks; NAACP; Am Legion 59; educ com Urban League; chmn Minority Task Force; Human Relation Com. **HONORS/ACHIEVEMENTS:** Hon admission counselor USN Acad 1974. **MILITARY SERVICE:** AUS sp/4 1962-65. **BUSINESS ADDRESS:** 431 Fountain St NE, Grand Rapids, MI 49503.

HARRIS, LARRY VORDELL, JR.
Sales executive. **PERSONAL:** Born Jun 24, 1954, New York, NY; son of Larry Harris, Sr (deceased) and Marian Harris; children: Karena, Dell. **EDUCATION:** Drexel Univ, BS 1979, attended 1984-86; candidate for MBA, Finance. **CAREER:** Proctor & Schwartz, product specialist 1980-82; Exide Electronics, export sales mgr 1982-84; AMP Inc, sales engr 1984-1988; Senior Sales Engineering 1989-; 1988 District Performance Award Sales Performance, Industrial Division. **ORGANIZATIONS:** Mem Natl Black MBA Assoc, Prince Hall Masons of PA; co-founder Drexel Univ Black Alumni Assoc 1984; presiding partner Professional Investment Club of Philadelphia 1987-1989. **HONORS/ACHIEVEMENTS:** 1988 District Performance Award AMP Inc.1988. **BUSINESS ADDRESS:** Senior Sales Engineer, P.O. Box 2216, Willingboro, NJ 08046.

HARRIS, LEE
Reporter. **PERSONAL:** Born Dec 30, 1941, Bryan, TX; married Lois. **EDUCATION:** CA State U, 1968. **CAREER:** Los Angeles Times, reporter; San Bernardino Sun Telegra, 1972-73; Riverside Press, 1968-72. **MILITARY SERVICE:** AUS sp 4 1964-67. **BUSINESS ADDRESS:** Times Mirror Sq, Los Angeles, CA 90053.

HARRIS, LEE ANDREW, II
Marketing manager. **PERSONAL:** Born Mar 25, 1958, Akron, OH; married Karen D Swartz; children: Jason D. **EDUCATION:** Heidelberg Coll, BS 1985. **CAREER:** Summit Co Sheriff's Dept, deputy sheriff 1981-83; Copy Data Systems Inc, opers mgr 1985-86, mktg rep 1986-87, mktg mgr 1987-. **ORGANIZATIONS:** Bd of dirs, Copy Data Systs Inc, 1987-; admin bd, Lincolnia United Methodist Church, 1987. **HONORS/ACHIEVEMENTS:** Vice pres Black Student Union/Heidelberg 1984-85. **HOME ADDRESS:** 5701 121 Harwich Ct, Alexandria, VA 22311. **BUSINESS ADDRESS:** Marketing Manager, Copy Data Systems Inc, 8474C Tyco Rd, Tysons Corner, VA 22180.

HARRIS, LEODIS
Judge. **PERSONAL:** Born Aug 11, 1934, Pensacola, FL; married Patsy Auzenne; children: Courtney, Monique, Darwin. **EDUCATION:** Cleveland Coll Western Reserve U, 1952-57; Cleveland Marshall Law Sch, JD 1959-63. **CAREER:** Common Pleas Ct Juvenile Div, juvenile ct judge; pvt prac of law 1963-77. **ORGANIZATIONS:** Mem The Greater Cleveland Citizens League 1961-; mem Urban Affairs Com Cleveland Bar Assn 1975-77. **HONORS/ACHIEVEMENTS:** Service award Cleveland Jr Women's Civic League 1978; Freedom Award Cleveland NAACP 1979; Man of the Yr Cleveland Negro Bos & Prof Women 1979; Silver Award OH Prince Hall Knights of Templar 1980; publ features Ebony, Nat Star, Nat Enquirer, Cleveland Plain Dealer Sun Mag; media appearances Today Show, Good Morning Am Show, British Broadcasting, Canadian Broadcasting Corp, numerous local TV & radio shows; speaks German & Russian. **MILITARY SERVICE:** AUS spec 4th cl 1957-59. **BUSINESS ADDRESS:** Common Pleas Court, 2163 East 22nd St, Cleveland, OH 44115.

HARRIS, LEON L.
Union official. **PERSONAL:** Born in Nyack, NY; married Evelyn. **EDUCATION:** Hampton Inst, 1948-50; RI Coll Edn, AA 1953-56; Harvard U, 1963. **CAREER:** ASFCME AFL-CIO, intl rep 1960-64; Providence, New England phys educ instr 1954-60; John Hope Settlement Providence, athletic instr 1950-53. **ORGANIZATIONS:** Dir Civil Rights Research Educ Retail Wholesale Dept Store Union & AFL-CIO CLC 1964-; natl life mem Com NAACP; v chmn Manhood Found Inc; adv bd recruitment training program NY Black Trade Union Leadership Com; pres Greenwich Village NAACP 8 other chpts; former pres New Eng Golf Assn; natl vice pres United Golf Assn; Am Social Club; former chmn CORE Rochester; lectured several univ; mem A Philip Randolph Inst; Friends Nat Black Theater. **HONORS/ACHIEVEMENTS:** Am Legion Honor Award Outstanding Athlete 1947; 16 Letterman; first black New Eng to sign with St Louis Cardinals 1952; Kansas City Monarchs; negotiated 1stunion contract o include Dr Martin Luther King Jr as Nat Holida 1968. **BUSINESS ADDRESS:** Retail Whlsle & Dept Str Union, 30 E 29th St, New York, NY 10016.

HARRIS, LEONARD CALVIN
Professional athlete. **PERSONAL:** Born Nov 17, 1960, McKinney, TX. **EDUCATION:** Texas Tech. **CAREER:** Denver Gold, slot back, 1984-. **HONORS/ACHIEVEMENTS:** Gold single season reception yardage leader with 657 yds; team single season leader in kickoff returns; voted 2nd team All-SWC Sports Illustrated Offensive Player of Week; AP SWC Palyer of Week.

HARRIS, LEOTIS
Professional athlete. **PERSONAL:** Born Jun 28, 1955, Little Rock, AR; married Gloria; children: Leotis Jr, Derrick, Michael, Tony. **EDUCATION:** AR Univ, attended. **CAREER:** Ford Dealer, parts & serv rep off seasons; Green Bay Packers, offensive guard. **HONORS/ACHIEVEMENTS:** All Amer selection AR; Voted top offensive lineman in Southwest conf in 1977; 2 time All-Amer in football at Little Rock AR HS. **BUSINESS ADDRESS:** Green Bay Packers, 1265 Lombardi Ave, Green Bay, WI 54307.

HARRIS, LESTER L.
Administration. **PERSONAL:** Children: Michelle, Ernie, Leon, Lester. **CAREER:** Econ Oppty Cncl of Suffolk Inc, chmn. **ORGANIZATIONS:** Pres Deer Park NAACP 1973-74; vice pres Deer Park NAACP 1964-70; elected committeeman Babylon Dem Party; mem Suffolk Co Migrant Bd; mem Suffolk CoHansel & Gretal Inc; Deer Park Civic Assn; Negro Airman Intl Inc. **HONORS/ACHIEVEMENTS:** Suffolk Co Humanitarian Award Suffolk Co

Locality Mayor JF Goode & Ossie Davis 1973. **BUSINESS ADDRESS:** 244 E Main St, Patchogue, NY 11772.

HARRIS, LINDA MARIE
Performer, producer. **PERSONAL:** Born Aug 17, 1940, Canton, OH; married David; children: Camian, Leslie. **EDUCATION:** Goddard Coll Plainfield VT, BA 1975. **CAREER:** WBZ-TV, TV talent producer 1980-; WBZ-TV, consumer reporter 1979-80; "Linda's Great Escapes" PM/EVENING Magazine, host, producer 1978; WBZ-TV Boston, staff announcer 1975-77. **ORGANIZATIONS:** Mem, past bd mem League of Women Voters; mem Zonta Internat; corporator Veverly Savs Bank; corporator Beverly Hosp; bd mem Freedom House Roxbury MA; bd mem Operation Genesis. **HONORS/ACHIEVEMENTS:** Recipient Individual Achievement Award New Engl Emmy Nominee 1978; Women in Communications Award Kappa Lambda Mu 1979; Black Acieever Award Greater Boston YMCA 1979; Individual Achievement Award New Engl Emmy Nominee 1979. **BUSINESS ADDRESS:** WBZ-TV 1170 Soldiers Field Rd, Boston, MA 01915.

HARRIS, LORENZO W.
Physician. **PERSONAL:** Born Jun 11, 1921, Spring Lake, NJ; married Gertrude; children: Sharon Gail, Deborah Kay, Lorenzo, III, Nancy Ren?. **EDUCATION:** Howard U, BS 1943; HowardUniv Med Sch, MD 1947; Homer G Phillips Hosp St Louis, internship & residency. **CAREER:** Asbury Park NJ, pvt prac of medicine; Jersey Shore Med Cntr, staff affiliation. **ORGANIZATIONS:** Mem Joint Com of Interprofl Rel of Monmouth Co Med Soc; Am Heart Assn; NJ Pub Health Assn; med dir NJ State Assn; IEPOE of W; past pres Alpha Phi Alpha; vice pres Monmouth Co Men's Club; vchmn Asbury Park Council on Hum Rel; exec com Shore Area Br NAACP; lay reader & vestryman St Augustine's Episcopal Ch; chmn Black Am of Monmouth Co; vice pres of bd dir Monmouth Boys Club; bd dir Westside Comm Coalition. **HONORS/ACHIEVEMENTS:** Who's Who Among Students in Am Coll &Univ 1942-43; pptd by Gov Richard Hughes to NJ Migrant Labor Bd 1962; elected delegate Dem Nat Conventions 1964, 1968; elected to city council Asbury Park 1973; Nat Conf of Christians & Jews Brotherhood Award 1974; five awards from comm organizations. **MILITARY SERVICE:** USAF capt 1952-54.

HARRIS, LORETTA K.
Librarian. **PERSONAL:** Born Nov 20, 1935, Bryant, MS; daughter of Estella Kelley Parker; married James Joe Harris; children: Sheila Lynne Harris Ragin. **EDUCATION:** S Illinois Univ, 1952-54; Kennedy-King Coll, certificate, 1970-71; City Coll of Chicago-Loop, diploma, 1973-74; Chicago State Univ, BA, 1983. **CAREER:** Univ of Illinois Library, photographic tech 1957-59; S Illinois Univ Library, library clerk, 1959-63; John Crerar Library, order librarian, 1968-70; Univ of Illinois at Chicago, Library of Health Scis, library tech asst III, 1970-. **ORGANIZATIONS:** Council on Library/Media Tech Assts, mem chairperson, 1977-80, constitution chairperson, 1980-84, mem 1970-; mem Med Library Assn Midwest Chapter, 1976-; mem Health Science Librarians of Illinois, 1976-; mem Ontario Assn of Library Techs, 1977-; listed in Natl Deans List, 1982-83; mem Black women in the Middle West Project, 1984-, Amer Library Assoc, Standing Comm on Library Ed; mem Training of Library Supportive Staff Subcomm, 1979-81; mem Intl Federation of Library and Assn and Institutions Printing and Reproduction Committee IFLA annual meeting, 1985; mem Natl Council of Negro Women, 1986; Council on Library/Media Technical Assistants, Constitution chairperson, 1986-, chairperson nominating committee, 1988. **HOME ADDRESS:** 8335 S Colfax Ave, Chicago, IL 60617. **BUSINESS ADDRESS:** Library Technical Assistant, Univ of IL at Chicago, 1750 W Polk St, Chicago, IL 60612.

HARRIS, M. L.
Professional athlete. **PERSONAL:** Born Jan 16, 1954, Columbus, OH; married Linda; children: Michael Lee II, Joshua. **EDUCATION:** Kansas State; Tampa. **CAREER:** Canadian Football League, 1976-80; Cincinnati Bengals, tight end 1980-. **ORGANIZATIONS:** Founded ML Harris Outreach; Sports World Ministries. **BUSINESS ADDRESS:** Cincinnati Bengals, 200 Riverfront Stadium, Cincinnati, OH 45202.

HARRIS, MARGARET R.
Pianist, conductor, composer, arranger. **PERSONAL:** Born Sep 15, 1943, Chicago, IL; daughter of William Harris and Clara Harris. **EDUCATION:** Juilliard Sch of Music, BS 1960-64, MS 1964-65. **CAREER:** Natl Endowment for Arts, cnsltnt 1971-74; Natl Opera Inst, cnsltnt 1971-76; Afilliate Artists Inc, panelist 1972-82; Hillsborough Comm Clg, artist-in-residence; Bd of Educ NY, consultant; conductor, Chicago, St Louis, Grant Park, San Diego, Detroit, Winston-Salem, Minneapolis, American Symphonies; conductor, Los Angeles Philharmonic; guest soloist, Los Angeles Philharmonic, Zubin Mehta Conducting-M Harris Second Piano Concerto. **ORGANIZATIONS:** Judge Natl Assc of Negro Musicians 1980-; mem Mu Phi Epsilon Prof Music Sorority 1961-; Natl Assc Negro Muscisians 1978-. **HONORS/ACHIEVEMENTS:** Distnguished alumni Prof Children's Sch 1971; distinguished musician Natl Assc Negro Musicians 1972; ooutstanding mem Mu Phi Epsilon Music Sorority 1964; dame honour & merit Knights of Malta Order of St John 1986. **HOME ADDRESS:** 165 W End Ave, New York, NY 10023.

HARRIS, MARION HOPKINS
Government official. **PERSONAL:** Born Jul 27, 1938, Washington, DC; daughter of Dennis Hopkins and Georgia Hopkins; children: Alan Edward MD. **EDUCATION:** Univ of Pittsburgh, MPA 1981; USC, MPA 1985; Univ of Southern California, DPA 1985. **CAREER:** Westinghouse Corp Pittsburgh, housing consult 1970-71; Dept of Urban Renewal & Econ Devel Rochester NY, dir program planning; Fairfax Cty Redevel & HousingAuth, exec dir 1971-72; HUD Detroit Area Office, dep dir of housing 1973-75; US Gen Acct Office Wash DC, managing auditor 1975-79; Dept of Housing & Urban Devel Office of the Asst Sec, sr field officer for housing 1979-. **ORGANIZATIONS:** Pres USC-WPAC Doctoral Assoc Wash DC 1979; exec bd mem SW Neighborhood Assembly Wash DC 1979; mem Black Women's Agenda 1980; chmn Housing Comm DC League of Women Voters 1980-82; Advisory Neighborhood Commissioner 1986; mem Amer Acad of Social and Political Science, Amer Evaluation Assoc; chmn Educ Comm Caribbean Amer Intercultural Org. **HONORS/ACHIEVEMENTS:** Carnegie-Mellon Fellow Univ of Pittsburgh 1970-71; Fellow Ford Found 1970-71; Outstanding Performance Award HUD 1984; Certificate of Achievement HUD 1988. **BUSINESS ADDRESS:** Senior Field Officer, Dept Housing & Urban Devel, Office of Asst Sec, 451 Seventh St SW, Washington, DC 20410.

HARRIS, MARION REX
Business executive. **PERSONAL:** Born Jun 30, 1934, Wayne County, NC; married Aronul Beauford Edwards; children: Amy, Angelique, Anjanette. **EDUCATION:** LaSalle Ext Corres Law Sch, 1970; A&T State Univ, Hon Doc of Humanities 1983. **CAREER:** NC Dept of Trans, bd mem 1972-76; Off of Min Bus Enterprise Adv Bd, bd mem 1970-; Custom Molders Inc, bd of dirs 1976-83; Vanguard Investment Co, chief exec officer 1982-84; Rexon Coal Co, chmn of the bd 1981-; Intl & Domestic Develop Corp, chmn of the bd. **ORGANIZATIONS:** Mem Fayetteville Area Chamber of Commerce 1965-; chmn/proprietor A&H Cleaners, Inc 1965-; chmn/proprietor A&H Coin Operated Laundromat Inc 1970-; mem NC Coal Institute 1976-; dir Natl Business League 1980-; chmn Rexon Coal Co 1982-; dir Middle Atlantic Tech Ctr 1983-; bd of trustees St Augustine's Coll1983-, A&T State Univ 1985-. **HONORS/ACHIEVEMENTS:** Recognition in Black History Sears Roebuck Co 1969; Letter of Recognition/Excellence in Business US Dept of Commerce Off of Minority Business Enterprise 1972; Businessman of the Yr Natl Assn of Minority Certified Public Accountants 1982; "Driven" Business NC Magazine 1983; Horatio Alger Awd St Augustine's Coll 1983; Par Excellence Operation PUSH 1983. **MILITARY SERVICE:** 82nd airborne E7 12 yrs; Silver Star; Good Conduct Medal; Army Accom. **BUSINESS ADDRESS:** Chmn of the Board, Intl & Domestic Dev Corp, 4511 Bragg Blvd, Fayetteville, NC 28303.

HARRIS, MARJORIE ELIZABETH
Educator, educational administrator. **PERSONAL:** Born Dec 08, 1924, Indianapolis, IN; daughter of T Garfield Lewis and Violet T Harrison-Lewis; married Atty Richard Ray Harris, Nov 20, 1965; children: Frank L Gillespie, Grant G Gillespie, Gordon L Gillespie, Jason Ray Harris. **EDUCATION:** West Virginia State Coll, Institute WV, BS, 1946; Univ of Michigan, Ann Arbor MI, MA, 1975, PhD, 1981. **CAREER:** Lewis Coll of Business, Detroit MI, faculty, 1946-60, admin asst, 1960-65, pres 1965-. **ORGANIZATIONS:** Bd of trustees, Lewis Coll of Business, 1950-; bd of commissioners, Detroit Public Library, 1970-86; regional dir, Gamma Phi Delta Sorority, 1989. **HONORS/ACHIEVEMENTS:** Mayor's Award of Merit, Mayor City of Detroit, 1979; Spirit of Detroit, City of Detroit, 1979; 50 Most Influential Women in Detroit, Detroit Monthly Magazine, 1985; Excellence in Educ, Assn of Black Women in Higher Educ, 1986; Community Service, Detroit Urban League, 1988. **BUSINESS ADDRESS:** President, Lewis College of Business, 17370 Meyers Rd, Detroit, MI 48221.

HARRIS, MARY LORRAINE
Business executive. **PERSONAL:** Born Jan 18, 1954, Durham, NC; daughter of Greenville E Harris (deceased) and Mable Freeland Harris; married Raynard K Williams, Oct 11, 1987. **EDUCATION:** NC Central Univ, BA 1975; Univ of Miami, MS 1980. **CAREER:** Metro-Dade Transportation Admin, program analyst 2 1978-80, program analyst 3 1980-81, principal planner 1981-83, chief urban init unit 1983-84, asst to the exec dir 1984-88. **ORGANIZATIONS:** Mem Natl Forum for Black Public Admins, Women's Transportation Seminar, Natl Assn for Female Executives, Amer Heart Assn of Greater Miami, NAACP; mem Conference of Minority Transit Officials and chair 1988-; mem bd of dirs COMTO Mid-Year Conf League of Women Voters of Dade County; mem task force Inner City "Say No To Drugs"; mem Metro Dade County United Way Cabinet; Metro-Dade Office of Rehabilitative Services, Miami, FL, asst to dir, 1989; mem, Metro-Dade, Women's Assn. **HONORS/ACHIEVEMENTS:** Gold Awd United Way; Honored by Gov Bob Graham as Outstanding Black American in the State of Florida 1986,. **BUSINESS ADDRESS:** Assistant to Dir, Metro-Dade County Office of Rehabilitative Services, 111 NW 1st St, Suite 2150, Miami, FL 33056.

HARRIS, MARY STYLES
Scientist. **PERSONAL:** Born Jun 26, 1949, Nashville, TN; married Sidney E Harris. **EDUCATION:** Lincoln Univ, BA Biology 1971; Cornell Univ, PhD Genetics 1975; Rutgers Med Sch, Post-Doctoral Study 1977. **CAREER:** Sickle Cell Found of GA, exec dir 1977-79; Morehouse Coll Sch of Med, asst prof 1978-; WGTV Channel 8 Univ of GA, scientist in residence 1979-80; Atlanta Univ, asst prof of biology 1980-81; GA Dept of Human Resources, dir genetic svcs. **ORGANIZATIONS:** Mem Public Health Assn 1977-; mem Amer Soc of Human Genetics 1977-; adj pub serv asst GA Bd of Regents Univ of GA 1979-80; comm adv bd Univ GA Pub TV Station WGTV 1980-83; mem Cong Black Caucus Health Brain Trust; mem Gov's Adv Council on Alcohol & Drug Abuse; mem GA Human Genetics Task Force. **HONORS/ACHIEVEMENTS:** Gen Rsch Support Grant, Rutgers Med Sch 1975-77; Outstanding Young women of Amer 1977-78; Outstanding Working Woman of 1980 Glamour Mag 1979-80. **BUSINESS ADDRESS:** Dir, GA Dept of Human Resources, Genetic Serv, 878 Peachtree St, 1st Floor, Atlanta, GA 30309.

HARRIS, MARYANN
Educational administrator. **PERSONAL:** Born Jun 10, 1946, Moultrie, GA; married John W Harris; children: Paul, Justin. **EDUCATION:** Knoxville Coll, BS 1969; Wayne State Univ, MA 1971; Nova Univ, EdD 1986. **CAREER:** Case Western Reserve Univ, gerontology suprv 1972-74; Cuyahoga Comm Coll, gerontology consult 1975-80; City of Cleveland, gerontology consult 1980-81; Project Rainbow Assoc Inc, exec dir & founder 1980-; East Cleveland City Schools, bd mem; UAW- Ford Devel and Trainging Prog, reg coord. **ORGANIZATIONS:** Mem school bd East Cleveland City School Dist 1979-; gerontology consult Council of Econ Oppty of Greater Cleveland 1980-84; grants devel Cleveland Adult Training 1980-; pres & sr assoc Grantsmanship Rsch Council 1980-; exec comm mem Cuyahoga Cty Demo Party 1984; chmn youth comm NAACP 1985; 2nd vice pres Alpha Kappa Alpha 1985. **HONORS/ACHIEVEMENTS:** Gerontology Study Grant USA Admin on Aging 1969-71; Career Mother of the Year Cleveland Call & Post Newspaper 1984; Developing Intergenerational Comm Serv Prog Natl Alliance of Black School Ed 1984; Grandparents Riddles Proj Rainbow Assoc 1984; Women's Rights, Practices Policies Comm Serv Awd 1984. **HOME ADDRESS:** 1326 E 143 St, East Cleveland, OH 44112.

HARRIS, MAURICE A.
Military. **PERSONAL:** Born Oct 17, 1942, Baltimore, MD; son of Herbert L Harris (deceased) and Elsie L Harris (deceased); married Marcelite; children: Steven Eric, Tenecia Marcelite. **EDUCATION:** NC A&T Coll, BS 1960-64; LA Tech Univ, MA 1972-73; Dept of Defense Race Relations Inst, graduate 1973; Air Command and Staff Coll, graduate 1975; Air War Coll, grad 1983. **CAREER:** USAF, B-52 pilot 2d Bomb Wing 1966-70, chief/mission support operations 1970-71, chief/wing social actions 1971-73, chief/wing social actions 51st air base wing 1973-74, KC-135 flight commander & instructor pilot 97th air refueling squadron 1974-77, commander cadet sqaudron 5 USAF Acad CO 1977-79, instructor pilot/exec officer 1979-80, lt col chief command control div 384th air refueling wing 1980-83, dir of in-

spection 313th air div 1983-86, chief of safety 1986-. **ORGANIZATIONS:** Mem Air Force Assn 1964-; mem US Coast Guard Aux 1986 (Flotilla 37); mem Mt Lebanon Lodge #20; mem JO Banfield Consistory 1972-. **HONORS/ACHIEVEMENTS:** Natl Defense Medal 1964; All Star Award as Best Individual Crew Mem 2nd Bomb Wing USAF 1969; Air Medal w/2 Oak Leaf Clusters 1969; Outstanding Unit Award with "V" Device for Valor 1969; Vietnam Cross of Gallantry with Palm 1969; Vietnam Campaign Medal w/3 Campaign Stars 1969; Vietnam Serv Medal 1969; Combat Readiness Medal 1970; Armed Forces Expeditionary Medal 1972; Air Force Commendation Medal w/Two Oak Leaf Cluster 1973-74; Meritorious Serv Medal w/One Oak Leaf Cluster 1980. **MILITARY SERVICE:** USAF lt col 22 yrs served. **HOME ADDRESS:** 14020 Puerto Dr, Ocean Springs, MS 39564.

HARRIS, MELVIN
Government official. **PERSONAL:** Born Feb 09, 1953, Oxford, NC. **EDUCATION:** NC Central Univ, BA 1975; The Amer Univ, MPA 1977; Natl Assn of Schools of Public Affairs and Public Admin, fellowship. **CAREER:** US Office of Personnel Mgmt, personnel mgmt specialist 1977; Amer Fed of State Co & Municipal Auth, rsch analyst 1977-78; Prince Georges Co MD, personnel/labor relations analyst 1978-79; Dist of Columbia Government, labor relations officer 1979-. **ORGANIZATIONS:** Pres Alpha Phi Omega NC CntrlUniv 1973-75; Conf of Minority Pub Adm Amer Soc for Pub Adm 1978-; rndtbl coord Natl Capitol Area Chap Amer Soc for Pub Adm 1980-83; chmn VA Voter Regis Educ Task Force 1984; co-fndr/treas Natl Young Prof Forum Amer Soc for Pub Adm 1981-83; bd of dir Natl Cncl of Assns for Policy Sci 1984-85; bd of dir Natl Capitol Area Chap Amer Soc for Pub Adm 1980-82 & 1984-85; AmerUniv Title IX Adv Comm 1984-; Alexandria Forum 1983-; co-chmn Young Prof Forum Natl Capitol Area Chap ASPA; publications "New Directions In Personnel" 1975-76, co-auth "The Supreme Ct & Pub Employment" 1975-76; author Starting a County Prog for Alcoholic Employees" 1977; co-auth Labor-Management Relations 1977; camp dir Alex Young Dem 1982;Spnsr N VA Voter Reg Coalition 1983; Alex Dem Exec Comm 1983-84; pres Alex Young Dem 1983-84; exec vice pres Va Young Dem 1984-; chrmn Va Young Dem NVA Fundraiser 1985. **HONORS/ACHIEVEMENTS:** Who's Who in Amer Colleges & Univs 1975; fellowship Natl Assn of Schools of Public Affairs and Public Admin Amer Univ 1975; Outstanding Young Man of America 1979-80-83; Chap Service Awd Natl Capitol Area Chap Amer Soc for Public Admin 1983. **BUSINESS ADDRESS:** Labor Relations Officer, District of Columbia, 415 12th St NW, Washington, DC 20004.

HARRIS, NARVIE J.
Retired educator. **PERSONAL:** Born Dec 19, Wrightsville, GA; married Joseph L Harris; children: Daryl H Griffin. **EDUCATION:** Clark Clg, AB 1939; Atlanta U, MED 1944; Tuskegee Inst;Univ GA ; GA State U; TN State U; Wayne State Univ, Detroit Mich. **CAREER:** Decatur County GA, home economics & elementary teacher 1939-41; Henry County GA, home economics & elementary teacher 1941-42; Calhoun County GA, home economics teacher 1942-43; Albany State GA State Univ, teacher; Dekalb School System, instructor coord 1944-83. **ORGANIZATIONS:** Cnsltnt Morris Brown Clg & Atlanta U; supr GA Assc Instctnl; sec-tres ASCD GA; ch sch bells awrd pgm GA Assc Edctrs; vice pres Borders Courtesy Guild 1982-87; pres GA Congress Clg PTA 1967-71, Royal Oaks Manor Clb 1961-87;Brd of Dir De Kalb Historical Soc;Joseph B Whitehead Boys Club. **HONORS/ACHIEVEMENTS:** Bronze woman of yr Iota Pi Lambda Sorty 1965; Dynamic Delta Delta Sigma Theta Sorority Inc; Clark Clg Alumni Dynamic Edctr 1982; co authored History GA Congress Col PTA History 1970; co authored History Royal Oaks Manor Comm Clb 1979;Honary Assoc Superintendent Dekalb Schls 1985;Clark Coll Dist Alumni Achievement Awd 1986; Ambassador from Georgia to Brazil 1974,England 1977,Africa 1972;Korea 1980;Cali Colombia 1981; Also to Kyoto & Tokyo Japan. **BUSINESS ADDRESS:** DeKalb Sch Systm, 3775 N Dekalb Rd, Decatur, GA 30032.

HARRIS, NATE CALVIN
Professional athlete. **PERSONAL:** Born Sep 28, 1962, Longview, TX. **EDUCATION:** Univ of Tulsa, Acctng Major. **CAREER:** Denver Gold, strong safety 1985-. **HONORS/ACHIEVEMENTS:** All-Missouri Valley Conf pick this season; voted honorable mention All-Am.

HARRIS, NATHANIEL C., JR.
Business executive. **PERSONAL:** Born Jan 01, 1941, Hackensack, NJ; son of Nathaniel C Harris Sr and Susan Satterwhite Harris; married Frazeal Larrymore, Feb 01, 1969; children: Courtney. **EDUCATION:** Hampton Inst Hampton, BS 1964; Pace Univ NY, MBA 1979. **CAREER:** Aetna Life & Casualty, engrg account mgr 1966-68; Real Estate & Constr Div, dept head foreign collection/data processing 1968-71, acct officer 1971-73; Urban Affairs, staff officer 1973-75; RE Comm Devel, sr acct officer 1975-78; Citibank NA, asst vp, real estate-mktg/plnng 1979-80; Chase Manhattan Bank, vice pres real estate 1980-. **ORGANIZATIONS:** Chmn fin comm, bd of dir Energy Task Force 1979-81; mem Omega Psi Phi, NAACP; bd of dir 1980-87, vice pres 1987- Neighborhood Housing Serv of NY City Inc pres bd of directors 1988-; pres, Urban Bankers Coalition Inc New York City 1985-87; vice pres Natl Assoc of Urban Bankers 1986-87; pres, National Assoc of Urban Bankers 1987-88; pres, Neighborhood Housing Services of New York City Inc 1988-. **HONORS/ACHIEVEMENTS:** Banker of the Year, Urban Bankers Coilition Inc, New York New York Inc 1989. **MILITARY SERVICE:** AUS capt 1964-70; Vietnam Serv Medal; Vietnam Campaign Medal; Natl Defense Serv Medal. **BUSINESS ADDRESS:** Vice President Real Estate, Chase Manhattan Bank NA, 80 Pine St, New York, NY 10081.

HARRIS, NELSON A.
Architect. **PERSONAL:** Born Jan 11, 1922, Youngstown; married Dorothy; children: Gayle Elizabeth, Nelson Jr. **EDUCATION:** Univ IL, BA 1961. **CAREER:** 5th AUS Hdq, asst post eng 1956-60; Harris & Isensee, partner 1960-63; Nelson A Harris & Asso, principal 1963-; IL reg arch; IN; WI; MI; OH; PA. **ORGANIZATIONS:** Mem Am Inst Architects; Nat Org Minority & Architects; Guild Rel Archit;Consult City Chgo; mem NAACP; Urban League; Masons. **HONORS/ACHIEVEMENTS:** Design award Guild Rel Architecture. **MILITARY SERVICE:** AUS 1st sgt 1943-46. **BUSINESS ADDRESS:** 9110 S Ashland Ave, Chicago, IL 60620.

HARRIS, NOAH ALAN, SR.
Physician. **PERSONAL:** Born Apr 02, 1920, Baltimore, MD; married Dorothy W; children: Noah Jr, Merle. **EDUCATION:** Howard U, BS 1942, MD 1945. **CAREER:** Physician. **ORGANIZATIONS:** Mem Monu Med Soc; Observ & Gyn Soc of MD; Chi Delta Mu Frat; mem Alpha Phi Alpha Frat. **MILITARY SERVICE:** AUS capt 1953-55. **BUSINESS ADDRESS:** 4200 Edmondson Ave, Baltimore, MD 21229.

HARRIS, NORMAN W., JR.
Physician. **PERSONAL:** Born Sep 30, 1924, Washington, DC; married Helen; children: Karen, Patricia, Norman III, Charyl, Kathleen. **EDUCATION:** Howard U, BS 1945, MD 1947; Harlem Hosp, intern; Provident Hosp, resd 1951; Freedmen's Hosp 1956. **CAREER:** HowardUniv Coll Med, urol 1956-; anat 1957-61; path 1947-48; HowardUniv Hosp, chf urol clin 1971-; exec com 1975-; PSRO, physic adv 1975-; amb care1975-. **ORGANIZATIONS:** Chm MCE Com 1975-78; chmn util rev Com 1977-; vd com 1976; mem Nat Cap Med Found 1975-; chmn Peer Review Commn NCMF 1978-80; staff mem Freedmen's Hosp 1956-75; Hadley Meml 1961-75; Cafritz Meml 1966-68; VA Hosp 1964-71; HowardUniv Hosp 1975-; mem WA Urol Soc; Med Soc DC; Medico-chir Soc; NMA; AMA; Dan Hale Will Med Club; HowardUniv Med Alumni; St Lukes PE Ch; mem Asso Photo Intern; What Good Are We Club; crucifer St Lukes Ch 1940-43; mem Alpha Phi Alpha Frat. **HONORS/ACHIEVEMENTS:** Publ "Hematuria" "Comm Genito Urin Prob" "Genito-urin Compl of Sickle Cell Hemo" "Treat of Sickle Cell Dis Compl" "Prost & Thrombo-embol". **MILITARY SERVICE:** AUS pfc 1943-46; USAF MC capt 1951-53. **BUSINESS ADDRESS:** 1628 S St NW, Washington, DC 20009.

HARRIS, OSCAR L., JR.
Elected official. **PERSONAL:** Born Jun 27, 1945, Chiefland, FL; married Alice Mae Wilson; children: Aurthur, Melissa, Lori, Corey. **EDUCATION:** Univ of MA, MRP 1982. **CAREER:** Santa Fe Comm Coll, teacher 1975; Alchua Cty Schools, coach 1972-76; Archer Comm Progressive Org Inc, dir 1978-81; Archer Daycare Center, pres 1980-81; FL Assoc for Comm Action Inc, pres; Central FL Comm Action Agency Inc, exec dir. **ORGANIZATIONS:** Fellow Southeastern Leadership Devel Program Ford Found 1976-77; councilman City of Archer 1980; gubernatorial appointee North Central Regional Planning Council 1980-82; fellow Natl Rural/Urban Fellows Program 1981-82; mem Gainesville Chamber Leadership 1984, Natl Assoc of Black Public Admin 1984; mem Private Industry Council; mem state bd Coord Council on Transportation Disadvantaged; mem Vision 2000, Affordable Housing Coalition, Hunger Coalition; bd mem United Way. **HONORS/ACHIEVEMENTS:** Grant Ford Found 1976, Natl Urban Fellows 1981; Housing Affordability Book Dept of Comm Affairs 1982; Ebony Award Gainesville Police Dept 1985; Alpha Phi Alpha Leadership and Achievement Award 1986; Oscar Harris Day in City of Gainesville Feb 4, 1986. **HOME ADDRESS:** PO Box 125, Archer, FL 32681. **BUSINESS ADDRESS:** Executive Dir, Central Florida Community, Action Agency, 1204 NW 8th Ave, Gainesville, FL 32601.

HARRIS, OSCAR LEWIS
Business executive. **PERSONAL:** Born Oct 06, 1943, Pittsburgh, PA; married Sylvia; children: Myka Jene, Todd Oscar, Tarik Lewis. **EDUCATION:** Lincoln Univ, BA Math 1965; Carnegie Mellon Univ, MA 1971; Howard Univ, Post Graduate 1972. **CAREER:** Parsons Brickerhoff-Tudor Consulting Firm, design mgr 1974-77; Turner Assoc/Architects & Planners Inc, pres 1977-. **ORGANIZATIONS:** Pres GA State Bd of Examination Qualification/Registration of Arch 1984-86; sec Intl Business Fellows 1985-86; mem and past pres State Bd of Examination Qualification & Registration of Architects GA; mem Soc of Intl Business Fellows; bd mem Natl Cncl of the Boy Scouts of Amer; mem adv bd Atlanta Business Chronicle; bd of dirs Atlanta Chamber of Commerce; mem Atlanta Business League and Central Atlanta Progress. **HONORS/ACHIEVEMENTS:** Crescent Awd Atlanta Regional Minority Purchasing Cncl 1982; Pres State Bd of Architects GA 1984-86; Comm Leadership Awd INROADS/Atlanta 1985; Minority Entrepreneur for 1985 by the US Dept of Commerce. **BUSINESS ADDRESS:** President, Turner Associates, 55 Park Place 6th Fl, Atlanta, GA 30303.

HARRIS, PAUL E.
Chief executive. **CAREER:** Protective Industrial Insurance Co of Alabama Inc, Birmingham AL, chief executive. **BUSINESS ADDRESS:** Protective Industrial Insurance Co, 237 Graymont Ave, Birmingham, AL 35204. *

HARRIS, PERCY G.
Physician. **PERSONAL:** Born Sep 04, 1927, Durant, MS; married Evelyn Lileah Furgerson; children: 12 children. **EDUCATION:** IA State Teachers Coll, 1947-49; Howard Univ, BS 1953, MD 1957. **CAREER:** St Lukes, asst med dir 1958-59; Linn Cty , dep coroner 1958-61, med examiner 1961-; Out Patient Clinic, dir 1959-61, comm chmn med records, utilization audit 1962-75, vice pres med staff 1973-76; Linn Cty Med Soc, physician 1970-77; Private practice, physician. **ORGANIZATIONS:** Mem IA Found for Med Care 1977; mem 1960-69, pres 1967-69 Jane Boyd Comm House Bd; pres Cedar Rapids Chap NAACP 1964-66, Cedar Rapids, Marion Rels Cncl 1961-67; mem Mayors Comm Low Cost Housing IA 1967; mem 1969, vice pres 1973- Non-Profit Housing Corp 1969; mem Black Culture Adv Bd 1968-78, United Way 1969-72, Ad Hoc Comm 1975-76 founder, pres Cedar Rapids Negro Civic Org 1961-67, Linn Cty Psych Bd 1974-82, Comm Cable Corp; apptd 6 yr term IA Bd of Regents 1977; mem, med adv comm Kirkwood Comm Coll 1976-. **HONORS/ACHIEVEMENTS:** Listed in Who's Who in the Midwest; 8 articles publ in Cedar Rapids Gazette & 1 article in Med Economics. **BUSINESS ADDRESS:** MD, 119 & 3rd St NE, Cedar Rapids, IA 52401.

HARRIS, PETER J.
Editor/publisher. **PERSONAL:** Born Apr 26, 1955, Washington, DC. **EDUCATION:** Howard Univ, BA 1977. **CAREER:** Baltimore Afro-Amer, staff reporter/editor 1977-78, sports & culture columnist 1979-84; Genetic Dancers Magazine, editor/publisher. **ORGANIZATIONS:** Public relations consultant Council Independent Black Inst 1983-. **BUSINESS ADDRESS:** 7102 Lockraven Rd, Temple Hills, MD 20748-5308.

HARRIS, RAMON STANTON
Physician. **PERSONAL:** Born Oct 02, 1926, Nashville, TN; married Ruthie Lois Chatman; children: Richard S, Sandra Corrado, Frances Lynn. **EDUCATION:** Fisk U, student 1945; John Carroll U; Case Western Reserve U; Meharry Med Coll, MD 1963. **CAREER:** Hubbard Hosp Nashville, intern 1963-64; Kings Co Hosp Bklyn, resident 1964-67; staff & anesthesiologist 1967-68; Meharry Med Coll, chief of anesthesiology 1968-73; Nashville, prac med spec in anesthesiology. **ORGANIZATIONS:** Mem TN Soc Anesthesiologists; Soc Acad

Anesthesia; chmn Am Soc Anesthesiologists. **MILITARY SERVICE:** AUS 1945-46. **BUSINESS ADDRESS:** 1005 18 Ave N, Nashville, TN 27308.

HARRIS, RAY, SR.
Business executive. **PERSONAL:** Born Jun 30, 1947, New York, NY; married Gina Carol Carpenter; children: Stacey Lynn, Ray Kwesi Jr. **EDUCATION:** Bernard Beruch Clg, MBA 1967-70. **CAREER:** RCA Records Inc, dir r&b promotion 1974-76, dir r&r promtn & mrchds 1976-78, div vice pres blck msc mktg 1978-80, div vice pres blck msc 1980- 82; Solar Rcrds Inc, pres. **ORGANIZATIONS:** Acct exec Atwood Richards Advertising Inc 1971-74; media buyer Ted Bates Advertising Agency 1970-71; bd dir Black Music Assc 1979-84, Black United Fund 1980-82. **HONORS/ACHIEVEMENTS:** Ray Harris Hall of Fame Delaware Valley Jobs Corp 1980; young black achvr awrd YMCA 1978; spec rcntn awrd Black Entrmnt Law Assc 1983. **BUSINESS ADDRESS:** President, Solar Records Inc, 1635 N Cahuenga Blvd, Hollywood, CA 90028.

HARRIS, RICHARD, JR.
Appraiser. **PERSONAL:** Born Feb 26, 1923, Lima, OK; married Clarice V; children: Teresa K Hollid, Jay R, Marcia H, Rocklyn E. **EDUCATION:** Milwaukee Sch of Engrg, electronic tech 1947-49. **CAREER:** US Post Office, letter carrier 1950-72; Homefinders Realty, real estate broker 1973-, appraiser 1975-. **ORGANIZATIONS:** Mem Natl Assn of Realtors 1973-; state chmn Equal Oppor KS Assn of Realtors 1978; sec vice pres pres Wichita Met Area Bd of Realtors 1978-80; mem S Central Economic Devel Bd 1973-74; mem KS Office of Minority Bus Enterprise 1975-77; mem Wichita Real Estate Adv Bd 1977-80; commr KS Real Estate Commn 1977-. **HONORS/ACHIEVEMENTS:** Walter Morris Realtor of the Yr Awd 1982. **MILITARY SERVICE:** AUS sgt 1943-45; Good Conduct Medal; Sharp Shooter Medal. **BUSINESS ADDRESS:** Appraiser, Homefinders Realty, 1521 N Hillside, Wichita, KS 67214.

HARRIS, ROBERT ALLEN
Professor, conductor, composer. **PERSONAL:** Born Jan 09, 1938, Detroit, MI; son of Major L Harris and Ruina Marshall Harris; married Mary L Pickens, Jun 08, 1963; children: Shari Michelle. **EDUCATION:** Wayne State Univ, BS 1960, MA 1962; Michigan State Univ, PhD 1971. **CAREER:** Detroit Public Schools, teacher 1960-64; Wayne State Univ, asst prof 1964-70; MI State Univ, assoc prof, prof 1970-77; Northwestern Univ, prof 1977. **ORGANIZATIONS:** Dir of music Trinity Church of the North Shore 1978-. **HONORS/ACHIEVEMENTS:** Disting Alumni Awd Wayne State Univ 1983; Publ, Composer Boosey & Hawkes, Carl Fisher Inc, Mark Foster Publ, Heritage Music Press, Oxford Univ Press. **BUSINESS ADDRESS:** Professor of Conducting, NorthwesternUniv, School of Music, 711 Elgin Rd, Evanston, IL 60201.

HARRIS, ROBERT D.
Manager. **PERSONAL:** Born Aug 31, 1941, Burnwell, WV; married Barbara. **EDUCATION:** WV State Coll, BA 1966;Univ Akron Sch of Law, JD. **CAREER:** Firestone Tire & Rubber Co, indsl rel trainee 1966-67; Akron, indsl rel rep plant 1967-69; Fall River MA, mgr indsl rel 1969-71; Akron, mgr labor rel 1971-73; Akron, mgr indsl rel 1973-. **ORGANIZATIONS:** Mem Employers & Assn; exec com Summit Co; commr Civil Serv Comm Akron 1977; mem Am OH & Akron Bar Assns; adv bd YMCA; Nat Alliance of Businessmen's Youth Motivation Task Force; W Side Nghbrs; Alpha Phi Alpha frat; Akron Barristers Club; admitted to OH Bar 1976. **HONORS/ACHIEVEMENTS:** Who's Who Am Coll &Univ 1966; Black Exec Exch Prog Nat Urban League; Ebony Success Story. **MILITARY SERVICE:** AUS sgt E-5 1959-62. **BUSINESS ADDRESS:** 1200 Firestone Pkwy, Akron, OH 44317.

HARRIS, ROBERT EUGENE PEYTON
Financial analyst. **PERSONAL:** Born Sep 05, 1940, Washington, DC; son of Dr & Mrs John F Harris; married Yvonne Ramey; children: Lisa, Johanna. **EDUCATION:** Morehouse Coll, BA 1963; Long Island Univ, MBA 1981. **CAREER:** Equitable Life Assur Soc, exp exam; Bronx Community Coll Assn Inc, operations manager. **ORGANIZATIONS:** Mem 100 Black Men 1976; vice pres Battle Hill Civic Assn 1977; Illustrious Potential Elejamal Temple Shrine 1987; worshipful master Bright Hope Masonic Lodge 1981; mem Council of Concerned Black Exec New York City 1980. **MILITARY SERVICE:** USAR ltc 1964-89. **HOME ADDRESS:** 20 Jefferson Ave, White Plains, NY 10606. **BUSINESS ADDRESS:** BCC Assoc Inc, W 181st & University Ave, Bronx, NY 10453.

HARRIS, ROBERT F.
Government employee. **PERSONAL:** Born May 15, 1941, Knights, FL; married Lydia Patricia Dunn; children: Roger, Lisa. **EDUCATION:** FL A&M U, BS 1964. **CAREER:** Subcommittee on Govt Oper US Sen, chief clk dep staff dir; Bd Pub Instr of Polk Co, tchr & coach 1966-72. **ORGANIZATIONS:** Chmn bd dir Neighborhood Serv Cntr Inc of Lakeland; bd Cath Soc Serv of Central FL; mem Council of Concerned Citizens of Lakeland; Pi Gamma Mu. **HONORS/ACHIEVEMENTS:** All Conf Track & Field; Cleve Abott Award for Track 1963; various track record awards. **MILITARY SERVICE:** Airborne 1st lt 1964-66. **BUSINESS ADDRESS:** 119 D St NE, Senate Annex II, Washington, DC.

HARRIS, ROBERT L.
Attorney. **PERSONAL:** Born Mar 04, 1944, Arkadelphia, AR; children: Anthony, Regina. **EDUCATION:** Merritt Coll, AA 1963; San Francisco State Univ, BA 1965; Univ of CA School of Law Berkeley, JD 1972. **CAREER:** Alameda Cty Probation Office, dep probation officer 1965-69; Pacific Gas & Electric Co, attny 1972-. **ORGANIZATIONS:** Pres Natl Bar Assoc 1979-80; admin mem Blue Shield of CA 1979-; chmn Publ Law Sect CA State Bar 1980-81; pres Western Reg Kappa Alpha Psi 1975-79; bd mem San Francisco Lawyers Comm 1978-; mem grand bd of dir Kappa Alpha Psi 1980-; pres Wiley Manuel Law Found 1982-; sec Natl Bar Inst 1982-; lawyer fellowship adv comm RH Smith Comm Howard Univ School of Law 1981-; chmn Legal Comm of Oakland Br NAACP 1983-. **HONORS/ACHIEVEMENTS:** Listed in Who's Who in Amer Law, Who's Who in the West 1979-80, Personalities of Amer 1979, Intl Who's Who in Comm Svc. **BUSINESS ADDRESS:** Central Division Manager, Pacific Gas & Eleectric Co, 1919 Webster St, Oakland, CA 94612.

HARRIS, RUBIE J.
Director field personnel. **PERSONAL:** Born Feb 16, 1943, Hearne, TX. **EDUCATION:** Texas Southern Univ, BA 1966; The Johns Hopkins Univ, MEd 1973, Certificate for Advanced Study 1974; Univ of WI-Madison, PhD 1980. **CAREER:** Johns Hopkins Univ, asst dir of adms academic counselor/res staff asst 1969-74; Coppin State Coll, sr counselor 1974-78; Internal Revenue Svcs, educ specialist 1981-85; Motorola Computer Systems, dir field personnel 1985-. **ORGANIZATIONS:** Bd of dirs Cupertino C of C 1985-87, Comm Sch of Music and Arts 1985-; vice pres Quota Club of Cupertino 1986; career counselor Resource Ctr for Women 1986-. **HONORS/ACHIEVEMENTS:** Top 100 Black Business and Professional Women Dollars and Sense Magazine 1986; Tribute to Women and Industry YWCA 1986. **HOME ADDRESS:** 49 Showers Dr Apt X158, Mountain View, CA 94040. **BUSINESS ADDRESS:** Dir Field Personnel Serv, Motorola Computer Systems, Inc, 10700 N De-Anza Blvd, Cupertino, CA 95014.

HARRIS, RUTH COLES
Educational administrator. **PERSONAL:** Born Sep 26, 1928, Charlottesville, VA; married John Benjamin; children: John Benjamin Jr, Vita Michelle. **EDUCATION:** VA State Univ, BS 1948; NY Univ Grad School of Bus Admin, MBA 1949; The Coll of William & Mary, EdD 1977. **CAREER:** VA Union Univ, instructor 1949-64, head of commerce dept 1956-59, assoc prof commerce dept 1964-69, prof, dir div of commerce 1969-73, dir Sydney Lewis School of Business Admin 1973-81; Sidney Lewis School of Bus Admin, mem mgmt team 1985-. **ORGANIZATIONS:** Mem State Adv Council Community Serv Continuing Ed Prog 1977-80; bd of dir Amer Assembly of Collegiate Schools of bus 1976-79; mem adv bd Intercollegiate Case Clearing House 1976-79; mem Equal Oppty Comm AACSB 1975-76; bd of dirs Richmond Urban League 1979-; agency eval comm United Way of Greater Richmond 1980-85; appointed chmn 1983-85 by gov Tobb to Interdepartmental Comm on Rate Setting for Children's Facilities; bd mem Richmond VA Chap Natl Coaltion of 100 Black Women. **HONORS/ACHIEVEMENTS:** Co-author Principles of Accounting Pitman Publ Co 1959; 1st black woman to pass exam for CPA in VA 1962; Outstanding Achievement in Bus Delver Womans Club 1963; Faculty Fellowship Awd United Negro Coll Fund 1976-77. **BUSINESS ADDRESS:** Management Team, VA UnionUniv, Sydney Lewis School of Bus, 500 N Lombardy St, Richmond, VA 23220.

HARRIS, SARAH ELIZABETH
Administrator. **PERSONAL:** Born Dec 31, 1937, Newnan, GA; daughter of Dan W Gates and Sarah L Gates; married Kenneth Eugene; children: Kim Y Harris. **EDUCATION:** Miami Univ, BS 1959, MEd 1967, PhD 1973. **CAREER:** Career Oppty Prog, univ coord 1970-73; FL School Desegregation Expert, consult 1971-77; General Electric Co, mgr supp serv 1973-75; Urban Rural Joint Task Force ESAA Proj, proj dir 1975-76; Sinclair Coll, consult 1976; Inst for Educ Leadership George Washington Univ, educ policy fellow 1977-78; Cleveland School Desegregation Exp, consult 1977; Citizens Council for OH Schools, staff assoc 1978-79; Dayton Urban League Inc, exec dir 1979-; Dayton Power & Light Co, dir community relations 1985; Dayton/Montgomery County Public Educ Fund, sr consult 1986; Montgomery County, treasurer 1987-. **ORGANIZATIONS:** Community affairs council Dayton Women's Network; mem bd of trustees Univ of Dayton, Wright State Univ, Miami Univ Found; mem Amer Assn of Blacks in Energy, Twentig Inc, Corinthian Baptist Church. **HONORS/ACHIEVEMENTS:** Children's Serv Awd; Jack & Jill of Am Dayton 1975; Outstanding Woman of the Year Iota Phi Lamba Dayton 1978; Salute to Career Women YWCA 1982; Outstanding Grad Awd Dayton Public Schools 1983; Top Ten Women 1983; Induction into the OH Women's Hall of Fame 1984; Martin Luther King Natl Holiday Celebration Meritorious Awd for Community Social Svcs; Miami Univ Bishop Alumni Medal, Outstanding Community Leader Awd Great Lakes Midwest Region of Blacks in Govt 1986; Dayton Champion Awd Natl Multiple Sclerosis Soc. **BUSINESS ADDRESS:** Treasurer, Montgomery County, Dayton, OH 45422.

HARRIS, TEREA DONNELLE
Physician/internist. **PERSONAL:** Born Aug 05, 1956, St Louis, MO; daughter of Dr Samuel E Harris and Mrs Dixie Gardner Harris. **EDUCATION:** Fisk Univ, BA 1978; Meharry Medical Coll, MD 1982. **CAREER:** Henry Ford Hosp, resident 1983-86; Health Alliance Plan, staff physician 1986-88; Outer Drive Hospital, Lincoln Park MI, internist, 1988-. **ORGANIZATIONS:** Mem Natl Medical Assn, The Links Inc, Alpha Kappa Alpha Sor Inc, Detroit Fisk Club. **BUSINESS ADDRESS:** Internist/House Physician, Outer Drive Hospital, 26400 Outer Drive, Lincoln Park, MI 48146.

HARRIS, THOMAS C.
Business executive. **PERSONAL:** Born Mar 23, 1933, Paterson, NJ; married Betty M Kennedy; children: Thomas Jr, Michael, Elaine Jefferson, Brenda. **EDUCATION:** Fairleigh Dickinson Univ, Teaneck NJ, BS Chemistry 1970; Columbia Univ NY, Cosmetic Science 1972; Fairleigh Dickinson Univ, Teaneck NJ, Surface Active Chemistry 1973. **CAREER:** Shulton Inc, chemist 1968; Revlon Inc, sr chemist 1974; American Cyanand Co, group leader research & devel 1977; Harris Chemical Co Inc, pres 1977-. **ORGANIZATIONS:** Bd dir Chamber of Commerce; Rotary Club Intl; bd trustee St Joseph's Medical Center; assoc minister Mission Church of God; natl correspondence secy Natl Mens Org; mem Cosmetic Chemistry Soc; Sales & Allied Chemistry Indus; advisor Youth for Christ. **HONORS/ACHIEVEMENTS:** Gold Medal Atlantic Richfield Co Prime Sponsor of Olympic 1984; Excellence in Business US Olympics in LA. **MILITARY SERVICE:** AUS Signal Corp sp 3/c 3 yrs; Natl Defense Serv Medal 1953-56. **HOME ADDRESS:** 602 14th Ave, Paterson, NJ 07504. **BUSINESS ADDRESS:** President, Harris Chem Co Inc, 546 E 30th St, Paterson, NJ 07504.

HARRIS, THOMAS WATERS, JR.
Physician. **PERSONAL:** Born Mar 12, 1915, Annapolis, MD; married Elsie. **EDUCATION:** Morgan Coll, BS 1937; HowardUniv Med Sch, 1941. **CAREER:** Physician pvt prac; VA, med ofcr; Prov Hosp, chf dept radiol 1960-70; Nat Cancer Inst, flw radiol 1949-51. **ORGANIZATIONS:** Bd dir Dukeland Conval & Nurs Hm 1967—; med asso Vilge Med Cntr; Mediso Inc; mem Monu Med Soc; MD State Med Soc; Nat Med Soc; Balti City Med Soc; AMA; ACR; Kappa Alpha Psi; Chi Delta Mu Frat; YMCA; NAACP; Mediso Club; Liberterian Inc. **HONORS/ACHIEVEMENTS:** Flwsp Nat Canc Inst 1949-51; achvmt awd VA 1974, 1977. **MILITARY SERVICE:** AUS MC capt 1941-46. **BUSINESS ADDRESS:** 4200 Edmondson Ave, Baltimore, MD 21229.

HARRIS, TOM W.
Playwright, librarian. **PERSONAL:** Born Apr 30, 1930, New York, NY. **EDUCATION:** Howard Univ, BA 1957; UCLA, MA 1959; USC, MLS 1962. **CAREER:** LA Publ Library, librarian; Voice of Amer, writer 1953-55; Studio West Channel 22 LA, writer, dir; Inner City

Cult Ctr LA, teacher 1968; Actors Studio, writer 1967-74; Pasadena Playhouse, playwright; LA Citizens Co, producer/dir. **ORGANIZATIONS:** Mem NAACP, Librarians Black Caucus; LA Black Playwrites; Dramatists Guild; Playwrites Co. **HONORS/ ACHIEVEMENTS:** Writer 25 plays & short stories, 2 books of fiction; publ New Amer Plays Vol III; listed in several bibliographies & Antho; Outstanding Contrib to Theatre in LA Citation LA City Council 1967; All CIAA, All Tournament Howard Univ 1956. **MILITARY SERVICE:** AUS Ord Korea 1951-53.

HARRIS, TRUDIER
Educator, scholar. **PERSONAL:** Born Feb 27, 1948, Mantua, AL; daughter of Terrell Harris (deceased) and Unareed Burton Moore Harris. **EDUCATION:** Stillman Coll, Tuscaloosa AL, BA, 1969; Ohio State Univ, Columbus OH, MA, 1972, PhD, 1973. **CAREER:** The Coll of William and Mary, Williamsburg VA, asst prof, 1973-79; Univ of North Carolina, Chapel Hill NC, assoc prof, 1979-85, prof, 1985-88, J Carlyle Sitterson prof, 1988-; Univ of Arkansas, Little Rock AR, William Grant Cooper Visiting Distinguished, prof, 1987; Ohio State Univ, Columbus OH, visiting distinguished prof, 1988. **ORGANIZATIONS:** Mem, The Modern Language Assn of Amer, 1973-, Amer Folklore Soc, 1973-, Coll Language Assn, 1974- South Atlantic Modern Language Assn, 1980-, The Langston Hughes Soc, 1982-, Zeta Phi Beta Sorority Inc. **HONORS/ACHIEVEMENTS:** NEH Fellowship for Coll Teachers, 1977-78; Carnegie Faculty Fellow, The Bunting Inst, 1981-83; Fellow, Natl Research Council/Ford Found, 1982-83; Creative Scholarship Award, Coll Language Assn, 1987; Teaching Award, South Atlantic Modern Language Assn, 1987; Natl Endowment for the Humanities Fellowship, 1988-89; author of: From Mammie To Militants: Domestics In Black American Literature, 1982; Exorcising Blackness: Historical and Literary Lynching And Burning Rituals, 1984; Black Women In The Fiction Of James Baldwin, 1985; editor of: Afro-American Writers Before The Harlem Renaissance, 1986; Afro-American Writers From The Harlem Renaissance To 1940, 1987; Afro-American Writers From 1940 To 1955, 1988. **BUSINESS ADDRESS:** J Carlyle Sitterson, Professor of English, University of North Carolina at Chapel Hill, CB# 3520 Greenlaw, Chapel Hill, NC 27599-3520.

HARRIS, VANDER E.
Educational administrator. **PERSONAL:** Born Dec 27, 1932, Nashville, TN; married Janie Greenwood; children: Vander E Jr, Jason G. **EDUCATION:** Fisk Univ, BS Math 1957; TN State Univ, Engineering Specialist, 1957-58; MIT, Facilities Mgmt 1973; Century Univ, MS Engineering 1979. **CAREER:** Ft Valley State Coll, supt of bldgs & grounds 1960-67; AL A&M Univ, coord of phy fac 1967-79; Fisk Univ, dir of phy plant 1969-76; Univ of TN Nashville, asst dir of phy plant 1976; Benedict Coll, dir of ply plant 1976-84; Fisk Univ, dir of phy plant 1984-. **ORGANIZATIONS:** Mem AME Meth Church 1936, APPA 1960, NSPE 1969-, SC Soc of Engrs 1979-, Amer Inst Plant Engrs 1980-; adv bd, Who's Who 1983; bd of dir Crittenton Serv 1984. **HONORS/ACHIEVEMENTS:** Publ Utilities Systems NACUBO 1972; Received Acad of Educ & Devel $10,000 Energy Awd 1980; Appointed Tech Asst ISATIM UNCF Schools 1982; Cert Plant Engrs Designation 1983. **MILITARY SERVICE:** Army Med Serv corpl 1953-55. **BUSINESS ADDRESS:** Dir Physical Plant Oper, Fisk University, 17th & Meharry, Nashville, TN 37203.

HARRIS, VERA D.
Retired county extension agent. **PERSONAL:** Born Nov 10, 1912, Palestine, TX; daughter of Caesar A Dial and Estella M Dial; married James A Harris, Sep 25, 1963 (deceased). **EDUCATION:** Prairie View Coll, BS 1935; TX Co So U, MS 1950. **CAREER:** So Newsp Feat Dallas, home econ lectr 1935-37; TX Agr Extens, co extens agent 1937-73 (retired). **ORGANIZATIONS:** Mem sec Order East Stars 1945-46; mem Prairie View Alumni Assoc 1945-47; sec 1968-72, chmn const & bylaws 1969-70, chmn budget comm Gamma Sigma Chapt; pres 1945-47, sec 1972-77 Cambridge Village Civic Club; NRTA & AARP; pres Gardenia Garden Club; reprtr Optim 13 Soc Club 1970-72; life mem YMCA 1973; chmn Hlth Comm Houston Harris Co Ret Tchrs Assoc 1974; hist Home Econ in Homemaking 1980; Am Home Econ Assn; Prairie View Alumni Club; Sigma Gamma Rho Sor; Epsilon Sigma Phi Frat; TX Home Econ Assn; Home Econ in Homemaking; Am Home Econ Assn; Houston Harris Co Ret Tchrs Assn; Clint Pk Unit Meth Ch; Nat Assn Exten Home Econs & Nat Assn Ret Fed Employ Sec; Houston Negro C of C; pres TX Negro Home Dem Agts Assn; mem Pine Crest Home Demo Club; pres Houston Harris Co Ret Tchrs; mem NARFE (Nat Assn of Fed Employ) Assn; Greater Houston Golden Kiwanis Club. **HONORS/ACHIEVEMENTS:** Certificate of Recognition TX Negro Home Demo Agts Assoc 1947; Prairie View & TX So Woman of the Week The Informer 1954; Cert of Awd Natl Assoc Fash & Access Design 1957; Distinguished Serv Awd TX Negro Home Demo Agts Assn 1962; Sigma of Yr Merit Awd 1973; "Palm Branch & Laurel Wreaths" Pal Negro Bus & Professional Wom Club 1976; 100 Plus Club The Prairie View Devel Fund 1976-78; Cooperative Extension Program, Prairie Vew A&M Univ 1986; Houston Harris County Retired Teachers Assn 1988. **HOME ADDRESS:** 5110 Trail Lake, Houston, TX 77045.

HARRIS, VERNON JOSEPH
Retired manager. **PERSONAL:** Born May 18, 1926, Washington, DC; son of Dr Vernon J Harris Sr and Beatrice V Robinson; married Georgetta Mae Ross; children: Elliott F, Cassandra Harris Lockwood, Georgette E, Wayne J,Verna J H Agen, Dolores A (deceased). **EDUCATION:** Catholic Univ of Amer, BEE 1952. **CAREER:** General Elec AESD, mgr, sr engr, cons, project engr, design engr, jr engr 1952-87. **ORGANIZATIONS:** Past pres, past lt governor of the NY District of Kiwanis & mem Kiwanis Club of N Utica 1962-; mem Coll Council SUNY Coll of Technology Utica 1968-84; mem Provost Post Amer Legion 1970-; past comdr Provost Post Amer Legion 1974-76; treas Central NY Chap Amer Heart assn 1975-80; treas NY State Affiliate Amer Heart Assn 1978-80. **HONORS/ ACHIEVEMENTS:** Elfun Territorial Awd for Pub Serv Utica Elfun Soc Gen Elec AESD 1974-75; Elfun Man of Year Utica Chap Utica Elfun Soc Gen Elec AESD 1975; nominee Phillippe Awd for Pub Serv Gen Elec Co Fairfield CT 1977; Phillippe Awd winner for Pub Serv Gen Elec Co Fairfield CT 1978. **MILITARY SERVICE:** Hon discharge 1946 from US Army Air Corp with rank of Sgt, was NCO in charge of base signal office with 387th ASG, Godman Fld KY, Freeman Fld IN, and Lockbourn Fld OH.

HARRIS, WESLEY YOUNG, JR.
Clergyman. **PERSONAL:** Born Jan 14, 1925, Medford, MA; children: Wesley Y III, Wayne Preston. **EDUCATION:** Wilberforce Univ OH, BS 1951; School of Social Work Boston Univ, 1961; SUNY Buffalo, MS 1964. **CAREER:** West Medford Comm Center MA, exec dir 1959-61; Comm Action for Youth Clevland OH, supvr couns serv 1964-66; Psy Dept Wilberforce Univ, dir counc & test, chmn 1965-66; OH Bureau of Vocational Rehabilitation, Columbus OH, supvr spec serv 1966-69; Montgomery Cty Opportunity Ind Center Dayton, exec dir, consultant 1969-70; Syracuse Univ, lecturer, supvr 1969-71; State Univ Coll Potsdam NY, dir office of special programs 1971-75; State Univ Coll Brockport, dir ed opportunity center 1975-79; 1st Genesis Baptist Church, asst minister, min of christian educ 1980; Mon Co Dept of Social Servs, examiner 1981-. **ORGANIZATIONS:** Comm mem Natl Alliance of Bus Dayton 1969-70; mem Human Relations Council Dayton 1969-70; mem Alpha Phi Alpha 1948-, Amer Personnel & Guidance Assoc 1962-, Natl Rehab Assoc 1962-; chmn Natl Comm on Racism, Amer Rehab Couns Assoc 1972; mem Rotary Intl 1973-, Phi Delta Kappa 1974-; ed comm mem NAACP 1969-71, Madison HS Redesign Comm Rochester NY 1973-75; exec comm Greater Boston Settlement House Assoc 1959-71. **HONORS/ACHIEVEMENTS:** Cert VRA Mgmt Trgn Manpower Devel Univ of OK 1967; Cert Workshop on Rehab of the Publ Offender Univ of Cinn 1968; Cert Human Relations Dept of State Personnel OH 1968; Cert Intergroup Relations Dept of State Personnel OH 1968. **MILITARY SERVICE:** AUS capt 17 yrs; Good Conduct; Sharp Shooter; CBI Theater; Infantry Man's Badge; Asiatic Pacific; Korea Medals.

HARRIS, WILLA BING
Educator. **PERSONAL:** Born Mar 12, 1945, Allendale, SC; daughter of Van Bing (deceased) and Willa M L Bing; married Dr Jake J Harris; children: KeVan Bing. **EDUCATION:** Bennett Coll, BA 1966; Bloomsburg State Coll, MEd 1968; Univ of IL, EdD 1975. **CAREER:** White Haven State School & Hospital, classroom teacher, 1967-69; Albany State Coll, instructor, 1969; SC State Coll Orangeburg, asst prof & suprv of graduate practicum students, 1969-70; Univ of Illinois at Urbana-Champaign, head counselor, 1971, asst to major advisor, 1971-73; Barber-Scotia Coll, asst prof of educ & psychology 1975-76; Alabama State Univ, Montgomery, coord, Central AL Regional Educ In-Serv Center, coord 1985-88, dir, Rural & Minority Special Educ Personnel Preparation, 1988, assoc prof & coord for special educ, 1976-. **ORGANIZATIONS:** Consult Head Start 1977-80, 1984-85; lay delegate annual conf AL-West FL Conf United Meth Church 1980-; bd of dir United Meth Children's Home Selma AL 1984-87, ASU Credit Union 1984-87, Nellie Burge Comm Ctr 1985-; mem Amer Assoc on Mental Deficiency-Mental Retardation, AAUP, AL Consortium of Univ Dirs Spec Ed, Black Child Devel Inst, Council for Excep Children, Council for Children with Behavior Disorders, Div for Children with Commun Disorders, Div for Mental Retardation, Teacher Ed Div, IL Admin of Spec Ed, Kappa Delta Pi, Natl Assoc for Ed of Young Children, Natl Assoc for Retarded Citizens, Montgomery Cty Assoc for Retarded Citizens, Phi Delta Kappa, ASU Grad Faculty, AL State Univ Woman's Club, Montgomery Newcomers Club, Tot'n'Teens, Peter Crump Elem School PTA State & Natl Chapt, Metropolitan United Methodist Church, Adult II Sunday School Class, Committee Chmn Fund Raising Choir Robes, Organizer of United Meth Youth Fellow, Admin Bd. **HONORS/ACHIEVEMENTS:** USOE Fellow Univ of IL 1970-73; Ford Found Fellow Univ of IL 1972-73; Ed of Year AL Assoc Retarded Citizens 1982; Outstanding Educ, Montgomery County Assn for Retarded Citizens, 1982; Volunteer Services Award, Montgomery County Assn for Retarded Citizens, 1985; Distinguished Alumni Award, C V Bing High School, Allendale, SC, 1988. **HOME ADDRESS:** 2613 Whispering Pines Drive, Montgomery, AL 36116. **BUSINESS ADDRESS:** Assoc Prof of Spec Educ, Alabama State Universiy, Box 288, Montgomery, AL 36101-0271.

HARRIS, WILLIAM H.
Educational administrator. **PERSONAL:** Born Jul 22, 1944, Fitzgerald, GA; married Wanda F Harris; children: Cynthia Maria, William James. **EDUCATION:** Paine Coll, AB 1966; IN Univ, MA 1967, PhD 1973. **CAREER:** Paine Coll, instr of history 1967-69; IN Univ, assoc instr, lecturer of history 1972-77, dir cic minorities fellowships prog 1977-82; Paine Coll, pres 1982-. **ORGANIZATIONS:** Mem Augusta Chamber of Commerce/ Augusta Rotary 1982-, Leadership Augusta/Leadership GA 1982-, Augusta Jr Achievement Bd of Dir 1984-, ETS Bd of Trustees 1984-, UNCF Bd of Dir 1984-, NAFEO Comm on Intercoll Athletics 1984-, Lilly Endowment Inc Commiss on Lilly Open Fellowship 1984-87, Boy Scouts of Amer; bd dir NAFEO 1985-; GA Commission on the BiCentennial of the USConstitution 1986-88. **HONORS/ACHIEVEMENTS:** Susan O'Kell Memorial Awd IN Univ Bloomington 1971; Keeping the Faith Univ of IL Press 1977; Fulbright Fellow Univ of Hamburg 1978-79; The Harder We Run Oxford Univ Press 1982. **BUSINESS ADDRESS:** President, Paine College, 1235 Fifteenth St, Augusta, GA 30910.

HARRIS, WILLIAM H., JR.
Attorney. **PERSONAL:** Born Sep 08, 1942, New Orleans, LA; son of William and Victoria; married Cynthia; children: Alisa Carol, William H, III. **EDUCATION:** Xavier Univ, BA 1965; Howard Univ, JD 1968. **CAREER:** Pohoryles Goldberg Station & Harris PC, atty 1969-88; Office of Ice, atty; Greenstein Delorme & Luchs, PC, partner, 1989-. **ORGANIZATIONS:** Mem US Court of Appeals Wash DC; mem US Dist Ct; mem US Ct of Claims; mem NAACP; mem Am Dist of Colum & Nat Bar Assns; DC mayor's commiss on Rental Housing Production; mem Natl Assoc of Security Profls; Alpha Phi Alpha Fraternity. **BUSINESS ADDRESS:** Partner, Greenstein Delorme & Luchs, PC, 1220 19th Street NW, Suite 300, Washington, DC 20036-2400.

HARRIS, WILLIAM HENRY
Business executive. **PERSONAL:** Born Mar 06, 1948, New Orleans, LA. **EDUCATION:** Univ of California, BS 1972; Univ of California, MS 1977. **CAREER:** Fairchild Cam & Instru, 1973-; Afric Sci Inst, ofcr 1977. **ORGANIZATIONS:** Mem Tau Beta Pi; Eta Kappa Nu; No CA Assn of Black Professional Engrs Edison Found Flwshp 1966; Kaiser Found Flwshp 1972. **BUSINESS ADDRESS:** 646 Ellis, Mountain View, CA 94040.

HARRIS, WILLIAM J.
Government employee. **PERSONAL:** Born Aug 26, 1924, Birmingham; married Josephine Brown; children: William, Jr, Sheila, Carol, Michael, Mark. **EDUCATION:** BS 1949. **CAREER:** Ofc Investig Compli US Dept Labor, dir 1974-; Ofc Comm Manpower Progs, dep dir 1973-74; Ofc Train Prog Admin, dir 1971-73; Operat Plan & Res & Alloc Staff, dir 1970-71. **ORGANIZATIONS:** Mem Intern Assn Person Employ Sec; Tam Tri Civ Assn. **HONORS/ACHIEVEMENTS:** Dist ach awd 1971; apprec awd Span Herit Day Com 1973. **MILITARY SERVICE:** AUS 1942-45. **BUSINESS ADDRESS:** Dir, Office of Civil Rights, US Dept of Labor, 200 Constitution Ave NW, Washington, DC 20210.

HARRIS, WILLIAM J.
Educator, author. **PERSONAL:** Born Mar 12, 1942, Fairborn, OH; son of William Lee Harris and Camilla Hunter Harris; married Susan Kumin, Aug 25, 1968; children: Kate Elizabeth Harris. **EDUCATION:** Central State Univ, Wilberforce OH, BA, 1968; Stanford Univ,

Stanford, CA, MA, 1971, PhD, 1974. **CAREER:** Cornell Univ, Ithaca NY, asst prof, 1972-77; Epoch Magazine, poetry editor, 1972-77; Univ of California, Riverside CA, asst prof, 1977-78; State Univ of New york, Stony Brook NY, asst prof, 1978-85; Harvard Univ, Cambridge MA, mellon faculty fellow, 1982-83; State Univ of New York, Stony Brook NY, assoc prof, 1985-; The Minnesota Review, poetry editor, 1988-; The Norton Anthology of Afro-Amer Literature, advisory editor, 1988-. **ORGANIZATIONS:** Mem, Modern Language Assn of Amer, 1971-. **HONORS/ACHIEVEMENTS:** Cornell Univ Faculty Grant, Cornell Univ, 1974; SUNY Faculty Fellowships, 1980, 1982; Andrew W Mellon Fellowship in the Humanities, Harvard Univ, 1982, 1983; W E B Dubois Fellow, Harvard Univ, 1985; Outstanding Academic Book for The Poetry and Poetics of Amiri Baraka, Choice Magazine, 1986; author of: Hey Fella Would You Mind Holding This Piano a Momement, 1974; In My Own Dark Way, 1977; The Poetry and Poetics of Amiri Baraka: The Jazz Aesthetic, 1985. **HOME ADDRESS:** 152 Baltic St, Brooklyn, NY 11201.

HARRIS, WILLIAM M.
Educational administrator. **PERSONAL:** Born Jan 19, 1932, Middletown, OH; married Mary Buchanan; children: William, Walter, Adrienne. **EDUCATION:** OH State, BS 1954;Univ ND, MS 1968. **CAREER:** Univ of MS Amherst, dir camp center 1977-; Rutgers Univ, dir camp center & stud act 1971-77; Rutgers Univ, asst dean of students 1969-71; Essex Co Coll, counselor 1968-69. **ORGANIZATIONS:** Mem Com on Minor Prog; Asso Coll Union Intern 1971-; help alien yo Uth E Orange Bd Educ 1970-74; Vind Soc 1971-. **MILITARY SERVICE:** USAF Reserves lt col. **BUSINESS ADDRESS:** Campus Center, U of MA, Amherst, MA 01002.

HARRIS, WILLIAM MCKINLEY, SR.
Professor of city planning. **PERSONAL:** Born Oct 29, 1941, Richmond, VA; children: Rolisa. **EDUCATION:** Howard U, BS Physics 1964;Univ Washington, MUP Urban Plng 1972, PhD Urban Plng 1974. **CAREER:** Cntr for Urban Studies Western Washington State Clg, dir 1973-74; Black Studies Dept Portland St U, chrmn 1974-76; Off Afro Am Afrs, dean 1976-81; Univ of Virginia, prof of city planning, 1987-; planning consultant, 1987-. **ORGANIZATIONS:** NAACP Charlottesville Branch 1980-87; chmn bd Charlottsville Planning Commn, 1981-87; PH F&M Masons (Prince Hall) 32nd degree 1983-85; mem bd Rural VA 1984-87; Charlottesville Anglrs Club 1983-87; mem Comm Dev Soc 1987; bd mem, Devel Training Inst. **HONORS/ACHIEVEMENTS:** Danforth Assc Danforth Found VA 1980; otstndg serv Comm Dev Soc VA 1984. **MILITARY SERVICE:** USAF rotc cadet. **BUSINESS ADDRESS:** Prof of City Planning, Univ of Virginia, School of Architecture, Charlottesville, VA 22903.

HARRIS, WILLIAM R.
Clergyman. **PERSONAL:** Born Jan 03, 1915, Concord, NC; married Doris Elaine Davis; children: Elaine Jeanne, Pauline, Marie. **EDUCATION:** BS MDiv 1945. **CAREER:** Siloam Bapt Ch, minister. **ORGANIZATIONS:** 5 evang teams Africa 1969, 72, 77; dir audio vis educ & spl asst Sec For Miss Bd Nat Bapt Conv USA 1963-; sec Bapt Min & Conf Pittsburgh 1952-56; v moderator Allegheny Union Bapt Assn 1952-56; dean Rel W Theol Sem 1947-51; mem sec Mont Co Ment Hlth Cntr; bd Cent Mont Co Tech Sch;Allan Wood Steel Schol Com; dir Norris Area Sch Dist 11 yrs nonconsec term 11-77; United Fund. **HONORS/ACHIEVEMENTS:** Gr Philad Fund; mem 1st black preach team S Africa Nat Bapt Conv USA 1975.

HARRIS, WINIFRED CLARKE
Educator. **PERSONAL:** Born Sep 13, 1924, Norfolk, VA. **EDUCATION:** Delaware State Coll, BS 1943; New York Univ, MA 1953; Univ of Delaware, graduate. **CAREER:** Booker T Washington Jr High School, chair english dept 1947-53; William Henry High School, chair english dept 1953-66; Delaware State Coll, chair dept ofenglish 1966-72; Delaware State Coll, dir federal relations and affirmative action, exec asst to president. **ORGANIZATIONS:** Exec comm Natl Consortium of Arts and Letters for Historically Black Colls & Univs 1974-; corporate rep Delaware State Coll Amer Assoc of Univ Women 1975-; mem Tri-State Commn on Educ 1984-; pres Dover Chap of The Links Inc 1986-; vice chair Delaware Humanities Forum; former chair Natl Sor of Phi Delta Kappa Inc; Phi Delta Kappa. **HONORS/ACHIEVEMENTS:** Distinguished Comm Serv Awd Natl Sor of Phi Delta Kappa Eastern Region 1978; Woman of the Year in Educ Wilmington Chap of Natl Assoc of Univ Women 1983; publ "Dialogue with a Teacher of Listeners, Readers, and Writers," DE State Dept of Public Instruction 1967. **BUSINESS ADDRESS:** Exec Asst to the President, Delaware State College, 1200 North Dupont Hwy, Dover, DE 19901.

HARRIS, ZELEMA M.
Education administrator. **PERSONAL:** Born Jan 12, 1940, Newton Cty, TX; married J Oliver (divorced); children: Narissa Bond, Cynthia Bond, James Jay. **EDUCATION:** Prairie View A&M Coll, BS 1961; Univ of KS, MS 1972; Univ of KS, EdD 1976. **CAREER:** Metro Comm Coll, coord of eval 1976-78, dir of eval 1978-80, dir of dist serv 1980; Pioneer Comm Coll, pres 1980-87; pres Penn Valley Comm Coll and Pioneer Campus 1987-. **ORGANIZATIONS:** Eval spec Office of Ed 1976; consult McMannis Assoc 1978-80; consult Natl Ctr for voc ed 1979; bd mem Black Econ Union 1981-85, Urban League of Gr KS City 1981-85; pres NAACP 1982-86; mem steering comm Mayor's Prayer Breakfast; mem Full Employment Council, Natl Conf of Christians & Jews, Downtown MinorityDevel Corp, Public Bldg Auth, Quality Ed Coalition; former co-chair KS City's Jazz Commiss. **HONORS/ACHIEVEMENTS:** 60 Women of Achievement Mid Continent Council of Girl Scouts 1983; Mary McLeod-Bethune Alpha Phi Alpha 1983; Jefferson Awd Channel 4 TV NBC 1984; 100 Most Influential Women Globe Newspaper 1983-; Ed Awd Oper PUSH 1981; Ed Awd KS City Metro Reg Commiss on Status of Women 1982; Recognition for Serv Adv Comm onthe House Select Comm on Children Youth & Females 1984; Recognition for Outstanding Participation the UNCF Lou Rawls Parade of Stars Fund-Raising TV spec 1983; One of the Most Powerfull Women in KS City KS Citian publ by C of C 1984; named gen chmn, Greater Kansas City, Missouri, United Negro Coll Fund Campaign, 1988; published as part of selected papers from the 1988 North Central Assn of Coll and Schools Annual Meeting, "Institutional Commitment to Cultural Diversity," 1988; name d "One of 30 Women of Conscience" by the Panel of American Women, 1987; Kansas City Spirit Award sponsored by the Gillis Center of Kansas City, Missouri, and the Kansas City Star Company, 1987; received "Citation Award" as "Protestant of the Year" sponsored by the Natl Conf of Christians & Jews, 1986; Named "One of Nations Most Influential Black Women" by Dollars & Sense Magazine, 1986. **BUSINESS ADDRESS:** President, Penn Valley Community College, 3201 Southwest Trafficway, Kansas City, MO 64111.

HARRIS-EBOHON, ALTHERIA THYRA
Educator, business executive. **PERSONAL:** Born Jun 26, 1948, Miami, FL; daughter of Andrew Harris and Mary White-Harris; married John Ikpomwenosa Ebohon, Dec 25, 1987. **EDUCATION:** Miami-Dade Community Coll, AA 1968; FL Atlantic Univ, BA 1970; Morgan State Univ, MS 1972; FL Atlantic Univ, EdS 1976; Nova Univ, EdD 1981; Post Doctoral Studies Barry Univ, Florida Intl Univ; Univ of Miami. **CAREER:** Dade County Public Schools, 20 years, educator; businesswoman 1988-. **ORGANIZATIONS:** 33 year mem New Mt Zion Missionary Baptist Church of Hialeah; mem Natl Educ Assoc 1970-; baptist training union directress New Mt Zion Missionary Baptist Church of Hialeah 1980-; bd mem Florida Baptist Conv, Inc 1986; life fellow Intl Biographical Assn, Cambridge, England, 1988-, Amer Biographical Inst 1988-. **HONORS/ACHIEVEMENTS:** 1st place art display Miami-Dade Comm Coll Library Exhibit 1968; Awds Banquet Honoree by Senator Bob Graham, St Augustine, FL 1986. **HOME ADDRESS:** 475 NW 90th St, El Portal, FL 33150. **BUSINESS ADDRESS:** NIAM Inc of Florida, USA, 10150 NW 7th Ave, Miami, FL 33150.

HARRIS-MCKENZIE, RUTH BATES
Retired human relations consultant, author, lecturer. **PERSONAL:** Daughter of Harry B Delaney and Florence Phillips; married Alfred U Mckenzie, Aug 25, 1987; children: Bernard, Charles. **EDUCATION:** FL A&M Univ, BS; New York Univ, MBA 1957. **CAREER:** District of Columbia Human Relations Commn, exec dir and equal employment opportunity officer DC 1960-69; Montgomery County MD Public Schools, dir human relations dept 1969-71; NASA, dept asst admin 1971-76; Dept of Interior Washington DC, human relations officer 1978-87. **ORGANIZATIONS:** Lecturer; pres Cosmopolitan Business and Professional Women's Club; mem natl pr comm, bd mem Tuskegee Airmen Inc, East Coast Chapter; mem natl adv comm Federally Employed Women; mem natl adv comm Amer Univ Women's Inst; Golden life mem Delta Sigma Theta Sor; life mem, Natl Council of Negro Women; mem, bd of dir, East Coast Chapter Tudkegee Airmen Inc; Federally Employed Women; Natl Advisory Committee; Amer Univ Womens Institute Advisory Commission. **HONORS/ACHIEVEMENTS:** Keys to Cities of Cocoa Beach and Jacksonville FL 1980; Omega Psi Phi Chapter Award; Sigma Gamma Rho Awd; Alpha Phi Alpha Chapter Award; Delta Sigma Theta Award; Hon Iota Phi Lambda; honored at annual luncheon Blacks in Sisterhood for Action as one of 12 Disting Black Women in the Nation 1986; One of Outstanding Women in Washington Area Washington Women Magazine; one of top 100 Black Business and Professional Women in Amer Dollars and Cents Magazine Editorial Bd; author "Trigger Words,"; recipient of over 100 awards; author "Handbook for Careerists" and "Personal Power Words"; featured in The Real Story of integration of astronauts corps in NASA with foreword by Astronauts Alan Shepard and Guion Bluford; two poems in her honor, one by Lt Uhuru, Star Trek Actress; Women of Distinction Award; Andrews Air Force Base Chapter, Air Force Assn; Meritorious Service Award, Dept of the Interior, 1987.

HARRISON, A. B.
Physician. **PERSONAL:** Born 1909, Portsmouth, VA. **EDUCATION:** VA State Coll, BS; Meharry Med Coll, MD 1930. **CAREER:** South Hampton Meml Hosp, staff mem1945; Franklin VA, pvt pract 1936-; Provident Hosp, intern. **ORGANIZATIONS:** Mem Franklin VA City Cncl 1968-74; v mayor 1974-76; mayor 1976-. **BUSINESS ADDRESS:** City Hall, Franklin, VA.

HARRISON, ALGEA OTHELLA
Educator. **PERSONAL:** Born Feb 14, 1936, Winona, WV; children: Denise, Don Jr. **EDUCATION:** Bluefield State Coll, BS (Magna Cum Laude) Ed 1956; Univ of MI, MA Ed 1959, PhD Psych, Ed 1970. **CAREER:** Detroit Public School System, teacher; Inkster School System, Rsch Design, Urban Action Needs Analysis, Wayne County Headstart Program, MI Dept of Educ, consultant 1962-66; Highland Park School System, school diagnostician 1968-69. **ORGANIZATIONS:** Mem Amer Psych Assoc, MI Psych Assoc, Assoc of Black Psych, Soc for Rsch in Child Devel, Assoc of Soc & Behavioral Sci; bd trustees New Detroit Inc, Roeper City & Cty Schools; mem Founders Soc, Your Heritage House A Black Museum, Natl Org for Women, Child Care Coord Council. **HONORS/ACHIEVEMENTS:** Horace Rackham Predoctoral Fellow 1969-70; US Publ Health Grant 1965-66,67-68; grad second highest mem of class; listed in Comm Leaders & Noteworthy Amers1973-74. **BUSINESS ADDRESS:** Associate Professor Psychology, OaklandUniv, Psychology Dept, Rochester, MI 48063.

HARRISON, BEVERLY E.
Attorney. **PERSONAL:** Born Jun 17, 1948, Port Chester, NY. **EDUCATION:** SUNY Oneonta, BA 1966-70; Univ of IL Coll of Law, JD 1970-73. **CAREER:** Counselor for Housing & Spec Equal Oppty Prog, grad asst 1970-73; SUNY Oneonta Legal & Affirm Action Affairs, asst to pres for employment 1974-81; SUNYStony Brook, spec asst to pres affirm action & equal employment 1981-83; Nassau Comm Coll, assoc vice pres personnel & labor relations 1983-. **ORGANIZATIONS:** Faculty adv Varsity Cheerleaders SUNY 1974-81; bd mem Amer Assoc of Univ Women 1978-79, bd mem Planned Parenthood of Otsego & Delaware Cty 1978-80; mem Amer Assoc for Affirm Action Nominating Comm 1979-80, Univ Faculty Senate Fair Employment Practices Comm 1979-81, State Univ Affirmative Action Council 1981-83; bd mem Amer Red Cross of Suffolk Cty 1981-83, Suffold Comm Devel Corp 1981-83; mem NY State Public Employer Labor Relations Assoc, Indust Relations Rsch Assoc, Metropolitan Black Bar Assoc, Committee of Minority Labor Lawyers, Natl Conf of Black Lawyers, Natl Assoc of Black Women Attny; bdmem Suffolk Cty Girl Scout Council; founder Assoc of Black Women in Higher Ed. **HONORS/ACHIEVEMENTS:** Bell & Dragon Honor Soc; Leadership Soc; SUNY Oneonta; Public Serv Awd The 100 Black Men of Nassau/Suffolk Inc 1985. **BUSINESS ADDRESS:** Assoc Vice Pres Persnl & Labor Rel, Nassau Community College, Stewart Ave, Garden City, NY 11530.

HARRISON, BOB
Football coach. **PERSONAL:** Born Sep 09, 1941, Cleveland, OH; married Anna Marie Bradley; children: Lorraine Ellen, Barbara Annette. **EDUCATION:** Kent State Univ, BS 1964, MEd 1969. **CAREER:** John Adams HS Cleveland, OH, asst head football coach 1964-66, head football coach 1967-68; Kent State Univ, assoc admission dir/asst football coach 1969-70; Univ of IA Iowa City, asst football coach 1971-73; Atlanta Falcons, asst coach. **ORGANIZATIONS:** Offensive coord Cornell Univ Ithaca, NY 1974; asst football coach NC State Raleigh 1975-76; asst football coach Univ TN Knoxville 1977-82; mem NAACP1982-.

HARRISON, BOOKER DAVID (MULE BROTHER)
Mechanical engineer. **PERSONAL:** Born Apr 23, 1908, Grant Par-colfax, LA; married

Ernestine Carroll. **EDUCATION:** So U, BS 1933; MI State ms 1947; tuskegee inst IN state u pra. **CAREER:** Carver Branch YMCA Fed Cred Un, treas mgr 1968-; Agr Exten Svc, aso co agt 1950-68, asso co agt 1933-50. **ORGANIZATIONS:** Pres Nat Negro Co Agts Assn 1957-58; pres SoUniv Nat Alumni Fedn 1960-64; chmn fin com SoUniv Bd of Suprs 1976-80; fin sec Evergreen Bapt Ch 1948-; basileus Omega Phi Psi Frat 1954-59; sec Shreveport Metro Plan Com 1978-. **HONORS/ACHIEVEMENTS:** Agt of the yr Co Agt Assn 1955; plaque Compl of 30 yr serv US Dept of Agr 1966; cert of apprec of serv LA StateUniv 1969; cert dist out servComm Lead of Am 1971; plaque out serv SoUniv Alumni Fedn 1971-75; achieve awd Negro C of C 1976; various other awds YMCA & frat 1977-79. **BUSINESS ADDRESS:** 405 Hearne Ave, Shreveport, LA 71103.

HARRISON, BOYD G., JR.
Automobile dealership executive. **PERSONAL:** Born Feb 23, 1949, Detroit, MI; son of Boyd G Harrison Sr and Jessie Mae Trussel Harrison; married Alfreda Rowell, Jul 19, 1969; children: Deonne, Devon. **EDUCATION:** Detroit Coll of Business, Computer Science, 1972. **CAREER:** Ford Motor Co, Dearborn MI, inspector, 1968-72; Chevrolet Central Office, Warren MI, computer operations, 1972-85; Ford Motor Co Minority Dealer Training Program, Detroit MI, dealer candidate, 1985-86; West Covina Lincoln Mercury, W Covina CA, dealer, 1986-. **ORGANIZATIONS:** Dir, West Covina Chamber of Commerce, 1988-. **BUSINESS ADDRESS:** Dealer Principal, West Covina Lincoln Mercury Merkur, 2539 E Garvey, West Covina, CA 91791.

HARRISON, CAROL L.
Educator. **PERSONAL:** Born Nov 15, 1946, Buffalo. **EDUCATION:** English Psychology, BA 1968; PhD 1970. **CAREER:** Medailla Coll English Dept, instructor, asst prof, chmn 1970-73; Media-Communications Medaille Coll, acting dir, assoc prof 1974-; SUNY AB english educ colloquim 1972-; Am Assn Univ Prof 1968-; Modern Language Assn 1969-; Intl Plaform Assn 1972-74; Univ Buffalo Alumni Assn 1968-; Academic Com Buffalo Philharmonic 1971-73. **ORGANIZATIONS:** Vol work Buffalo Childrens Hosp 1972; Western NY Consortium English & Am Lit Prof 1974; Nomination Am AssnUniv Womens Educ Found. **HONORS/ACHIEVEMENTS:** Award 1974; Outstanding Educators Am Award 1974; Comm Leaders Am Biog Inst 1973; Modern Language Assn Directory Women Scholars 1973; Outstanding Young Women Am Award 1975; Worlds Whos Who of Women Intl 1977; World Whos Who of Women in Educ 1977; Comm Leaders & Noteworthy Am 1977. **BUSINESS ADDRESS:** 18 Agassiz Circle, Buffalo, NY 14214.

HARRISON, CHARLIE J., JR.
State representative. **PERSONAL:** Born May 16, 1932, W Palm Beach, FL; married Marquita Jones; children: Cheryl, Charlie III, Marcella, Mark, Cynthia. **EDUCATION:** Attended, Detroit Inst of Dry Cleaning, Wayne State Univ. **CAREER:** State of MI, state rep 62nd dist 1973-, Appropriations Subcommittee on Natural Resources & Environment, chmn 1989-90; Appropriations Subcommittee on Agriculture, chmn 1989-90. **ORGANIZATIONS:** Dem Precinct Delegate; del Natl Dem Conv 1972, 76; pres St John United Meth Ch; Gibralter Lodge No 19; Oakland County NAACP; mem Urban League; mem Appropriations Committee; mem Pontiac Dem Club; 100 Club Oakland Co Dem Com; bd of dir Pontiac Opp Indus Ctr; Maracci Temple #2; Sylvan Lake Lodge #723; Carr St Block Club; Wolverine Consistory #6; Pontiac Neighborhood Serv Ctr; mem natl Black Caucus of State Leg; Reg 9 chmn NBCSL; adv council mem Boy Scouts of Amer Oakland Chapt; mem, Michigan Housing Coalition 1988-89; mem, Executive Committee of the Oakland County Democratic Party; honorary mem, Society of African American Police. **HONORS/ACHIEVEMENTS:** Doctor of Humanism Degree, Highland Park Community College 1988; Distinguished Community Service Award, Omega Psi Phi Fraternity 1988. **BUSINESS ADDRESS:** State Representative 62nd Dist, State of MI, State Capitol, Lansing, MI 48913.

HARRISON, DAPHNE DUVAL (DAPHNE D. COMEGYS)
Educator. **PERSONAL:** Born Mar 14, 1932, Orlando, FL; daughter of Alexander Chisholm Duval and Daphne Alexander Duval Williams; married Daniel L Comegys Jr; children: Michael A, Stephanie D. **EDUCATION:** Talladega Coll, BMus 1953; Northwestern Univ, MMus 1961; Univ of Miami FL, EdD 1971. **CAREER:** Marion & Broward Co FL, music tchr 1953-66; Broward Co FL,TV instr 1966-68; FL Atlantic Univ, asst prof educ 1969-70; Hallandale Middle Sch FL, dean of girls 1970-71; Benedict Coll, asso prof fine arts 1971-72; Univ of MD Balitmore, proj dir summer inst African & African-Amer History culture & literature 1984-85; assoc prof and chairperson African Amer studies dept 1981-. **ORGANIZATIONS:** Proj dir Racism Intervention Develop Proj UMBC 1975-77; social planner New Town Harbison SC 1971-72; consult FL Sch Desegregation Consult Ctr 1965-70; ch music dir St Andrews Ch Hollywood FL 1960-70; bd mem CTD FL Educators Assn 1965-67; bd mem FL State Tchrs Assn 1963-65; mem Natl Assn of Negro Business & Professional Women, Alpha Kappa Alpha, Assn for the Study of Afro-Amer Life & Hist; Co-chair Black Family Committee of African American Empowerment Project; Commissioner of the Maryland Commission on Afro-American History & Culture; Sonneck Society; Intl Assn for Study of Popular Music. **HONORS/ACHIEVEMENTS:** NEH African Humanities Fellow UCLA 1979; Moton Ctr for Independent Studies Fellow Philadelphia 1976-77; So Fellowships Univ of Miami 1969-70; Theodore Presser Awd Talladega Coll 1951; Fulbright Fellow 1986; Outstanding Faculty of the Year, Black Student Union, UMBC 1988-89; Black Pearls: Blues Queens of the 1920's, Rutgers Univ Press 1988; Most Favorite Faculty Student Government Assn, UMBC 1989; The Classic Blues and Women Singers, Blackwell Press Guide to the Blues 1989. **BUSINESS ADDRESS:** Assoc Prof, Chairperson, Univ MD Baltimore, African-Amer Studies Dept, 5401 Wilkens Ave, Baltimore, MD 21228.

HARRISON, DIAN JOHNSON
Social service. **PERSONAL:** Born Jun 02, 1948, Los Angeles, CA; married Dr Darryll R Harrison; children: Darryll Jr. **EDUCATION:** CA State Univ, Bachelors 1971; Western MI Univ, Masters 1973. **CAREER:** Planned Parenthood, dir of comm affairs and teen clinics 1976-81; Meharry Medical Coll, program admin 1981-83; United Way, campaign dir 1982-83; Fisk Univ, vice pres 1983-84; Austin Area Urban League, pres 1984-. **ORGANIZATIONS:** Mem Women in Management; bd Lone Star Girl Scout Council; bd Black Arts Alliance; participant Leadership TX; mem Delta Sigma Theta; mem Assoc of Black Social Workers; mem Natl Conf Christians/Jews; bd mem Laguna Gloria Art Museum; bd mem Heart Assn of TX Metro Austin. **HONORS/ACHIEVEMENTS:** Comm Serv Natl Assoc Social Workers 1973; Woman on the Move Awd Womens political Caucus 1982; Leadership Awd Womens Political Caucus 1983. **BUSINESS ADDRESS:** 3109 N Hwy IH, Austin, TX 78722-2202.

HARRISON, DON K., SR.
Educator. **PERSONAL:** Born Apr 12, 1933, Nashville, NC; married Algeo O Hale; children: Denise, Don K. **EDUCATION:** North Carolina Central Univ, BA 1953; Wayne State Univ, MA 1958; Univ of Michigan, PhD 1972; Licensed Psychologist. **CAREER:** Univ of Michigan Rehabilitation Rsch Inst, assoc prof and dir 1976; Univ of Michigan Rehabilitation Counseling Educ, assoc prof and dir 1975; Guidance and Counseling Program, Univ of Michigan, chmn 1974-77; Guidance and Counseling Program, Univ of Michigan, asst prof 1972-76; Vocational Rehabilitation, Wayne State Univ, adjunct asst prof 1972. **ORGANIZATIONS:** Dir PRIME Inc Detroi MI 1970-80; mem Am Psychol Assn; mem Personnel & Guidance Assn Rehab Couns Traineeship Rehab Srv Admin 1975. **HONORS/ACHIEVEMENTS:** Outstanding Srv Awd MI Prsnl & Guid Assn 1976. **MILITARY SERVICE:** AUS sgt 1953-55. **BUSINESS ADDRESS:** Univ of Michigan Rehabilitation Research, 1360 School of Educ, Ann Arbor, MI.

HARRISON, EMMA LOUISE
Educational administrator, author. **PERSONAL:** Born Apr 13, 1918, Mexia, TX; daughter of Ulysess C McDonald and Lula Bell Glasco McDonald; married Jesse Harrison, Mar 24, 1939. **EDUCATION:** Houston-Tillotson, BA 1939; Univ of So CA, MS 1942, Doctorate 1944; Grad Study Tour, Scandinavian countries. **CAREER:** City Schs of Waco, teacher/supervisor 1932-57; Summer School Los Angeles City Schs, teacher 1939-41; Paul Quinn Coll, prof/dean 1957-60; Huston-Tillotson, coll prof 1952-54, 1954-69; Baylor Univ, prof 1969-71; Waco Indep Sch Dist, trustee, 1976-. **ORGANIZATIONS:** Trustee & church hostess St Luke AME Church Waco 1935; Alpha Kappa Alpha Sor former natl officer Chicago 1945; charter mem/org Doris Miller YWCA Waco 1947; charter mem/org Blue Triangle YWCA Waco 1950; bd mem Eco Opp Adv Corp 1965-83; bd of advisors KXXV 25 1980-; bd of adv mem Central TX Economic Devel District 1981-; bd of advisors Eco Opp Adv Corp 1984-; bd Legal Aid 1966-70; bd sec Centennial 1985-; mem/voter, League of Women Voters, 1975-; mem, Amer Cancer Soc, 1976-; Bell Ringer, Salvation Army Christman Cheer, yearly; charter org mem, NAACP, 1969-. **HONORS/ACHIEVEMENTS:** Liberty Bell Awd Young Lawyers of Waco 1976; Liberty Bell Awd Young Lawyers of TX 1977; Yellow Rose of TX gov of TX 1978; pres Thos Jefferson KCEN-TV Corp Waco 1981; Disting Serv Award Alpha Kappa Alpha Sorority, Inc Chicago; honored in publication by Essai Seay; Black Women Role Models, 1986; Outstanding Woman of the Year, Delta Sigma Theta, 1986-87; Baylor Univ Founders Club as a Baylor Family Mem, Baylor Univ, 1989; Certificate of Appreciation, Amer Kidney Assn, 1989; author of 10 books. **BUSINESS ADDRESS:** Trustee, Waco Indep Sch Dist, 1018 Taylor Ave, Waco, TX 76704.

HARRISON, ERNEST ALEXANDER
Association executive. **PERSONAL:** Born Apr 10, 1937, Morganton, NC; son of Mid Milton Harrison and Laura Mae Happoldt; married Karen Yvonne Perkins; children: Darius, Desiree'. **EDUCATION:** NC Centrl U, BA; NC Cntrl U, MA 1961;Univ of MI, PhD 1977. **CAREER:** Highland Park Comm Coll, exec asst to the pres & vice pres 1979; Highland Park Comm Coll, dir of personnel 1977-79; Highland Park Comm Coll, dir of evnng sch 1975-77; Highland Park Comm Coll, dir Black Studies 1972-75; Albany State Coll, prf History 1961-64; Univ of Rochester, consult Black History 1972; Detroit Pub Sch Systm, consult Black Hist 1974-76; Highland Park Comm Coll, chief lbr Negotiator 1976. **ORGANIZATIONS:** Mem Kappa Alpha Psi Frat; mem NAACP; mem MI Comm Coll Personnel Admin Assn; mem Natl Alliance of Black Sch Edctrs; mem N Central Assn of Jr Coll; mem Phi Delta Kappa; advisory bd, Grosse Pointe Academy. **HONORS/ACHIEVEMENTS:** Merit Award United Negro Coll Fund. **HOME ADDRESS:** 19023 Muirland, Detroit, MI 48221. **BUSINESS ADDRESS:** Assistant Superintendent, School District of the City of Highland Park, 20 Bartlett, Highland Park, MI 48203.

HARRISON, GREGORY W.
Life underwriter. **PERSONAL:** Born Mar 01, 1928, Wash, DC; married Lillie Moss; children: Michael, Mark, Jeffrey, Kent. **EDUCATION:** Howard U, BS Engrng. **CAREER:** Mutual of NY, life underwriter. **ORGANIZATIONS:** Regnl ofcr estrn regn MONY Hnr Clb 1976; mem Million Dollar Rnd Table; mem MONY'S Hall of Fame; mem Natl Assn of Life Underwriters; mem DC & Life Undrwrtrs Assn Regnl Vice Pres Nat Bus League; past pres on bd of dirs DC C of C; bd dirs Interracial Council for Bus Opp; United Givers Fnd; Wash Tech Inst; bd of cncllrs Fed City Coll; mem Mayor's Econ Dev Com; Mayor's Com for Drug Addiction Prevntn & Rehab; mem Brandywine Dem Club; bd dirs Better Bus Bureau of Wash; Metro Wash Urban Coalition. **HONORS/ACHIEVEMENTS:** Recip Nat Quality Award Winner; consistant qualifier MONY'S Pres Council; MONY'S Top 50 1976. **MILITARY SERVICE:** AUS first lt Korean War; maj AUSR.

HARRISON, HARRY PAUL
Elected official. **PERSONAL:** Born Jan 10, 1923, Lawrenceville, VA; married Teressa H; children: Vera, Zelma, Agatha. **EDUCATION:** St Pauls Coll, BS 1952. **CAREER:** Greenville Co School System, teacher 1952-55; Bruns Co School System, teacher (retired) 1955-85; Bd of Supervisors, chmn. **ORGANIZATIONS:** Supt of Sunday School 1957-83; pres Brunswick Teachers Assoc 1968-69; pres Brunswick Ed Assoc 1970-71; chmn Poplar Mt Church's Bldg Comm 1977; chmn Brunswick Co Dem Comm 1978-; treas Brunswick Co NAACP 1978-; dir Emergency Services Brunswick Co 1980-. **HONORS/ACHIEVEMENTS:** Back Bone NAACP 1976, 1980; Citizen of the Year Omega 1981. **MILITARY SERVICE:** AUS corpl 1946-47; Army Occupation Medal; WWII Victory Medal. **BUSINESS ADDRESS:** Chairman, Bd of Supervisors, Rt 2 Box 48, Lawrenceville, VA 23868.

HARRISON, HATTIE N.
Delegate. **PERSONAL:** Born Feb 11, 1928, Lancaster, SC; married Robert; children: Robert, Philip. **EDUCATION:** J C Smith; Community Educ Devel; Antioch Coll. **CAREER:** Dist 45, delegate; sr commn aide 1968-73; del sub-tchr 1962-73; mayors rep 1974; NH Sch Pub Reltns Assn, consult 1970; NH Aerospace Conv; Comm Sensitivity Training Comm Sch Div . **ORGANIZATIONS:** Fndr chmn Dunbar Comm & Cncl; mem Steering ComUniv MD; NAACP Comm Sch Wrkshp; fndr & spnsr Douglass Teen Club; ward ldr Mothers March 1950-60. **HONORS/ACHIEVEMENTS:** Outstndng Ldrshp Awrd 1974; Wmn Yr Alpha Zeta 1974. **BUSINESS ADDRESS:** MD State Delegate, MD General Assembly, 2503 E Preston St, Baltimore, MD 21213.

HARRISON, JAMES, JR.
Phamacist. **PERSONAL:** Born Oct 14, 1930, Pittsburg, PA; married Eunice Kea; children: Wanda, James III, Donna. **EDUCATION:** BS 1954; Registered Pharmacist NJ 1956;Univ Freeman's Hosp, Intern 1 Yr. **CAREER:** Harrison Pharmacy Inc, pres; Berg Pharmacy, purchased 1971. **ORGANIZATIONS:** Sunday Schl Tchr; Boy Scout Ldr; mem adv bd Bloomfield HS; past pres & treas N Jersey Pharm; mem bd of dir Essex Co Pharm Soc. **BUSINESS ADDRESS:** Harrison Pharmacy, 641 High St, Newark, NJ 07102.

HARRISON, JEANETTE LAVERNE
TV news reporter. **PERSONAL:** Born Dec 04, 1948, Kyoto, Japan;married James Michael Sullivan; children: Katherine, James Brady. **EDUCATION:** CO State Univ, BA (French) 1968; Univ of CA Berkeley, MJ 1973. **CAREER:** KPIX-TV San Francisco CA, TV news agent 1973-74; KTVU-TV Oakland CA, editor & apprentice 1973-74; KQED-TV San Francisco CA, reporter 1974-75; KGW-TV Portland OR, TV news reporter 1975-78; WTCN-TV Minneapolis MN, TV news reporter 1978-; KARE-TV, TV news reporter. **ORGANIZATIONS:** Mem Limited Thirty Black Prof Womens Orgn; Natl Hon Phi Sigma Iota 1970-; freelance jrnlst & wrtr. **HONORS/ACHIEVEMENTS:** Comm serv Vet Frgn Wars Waite Park 1984; comm serv Gannet Corp MN 1984; missing chldrn Wrote & Prod 5 TV Series. **BUSINESS ADDRESS:** TV News Reporter, KARE-TV, 441 Boone Ave, Minneapolis, MN 55427.

HARRISON, LINCOLN J.
Accountant. **PERSONAL:** Born Jul 07, 1919, Tylertown, MS; married Joyce; children: Lincoln J, Jr, Huelon A. **EDUCATION:** Southern U, BS 1938; Atlanta U, MA 1944; Univ IL, MS 1946; OH State U, PhD 1953; CPA Cert LA 1946. **CAREER:** SthrnUniv Baton Rouge, prof Acctg 1974; LA State Dept Rev, dep Cllctr Admnstv Servs 1973-74; Sthrn U, dean coll bus 1958-73; So U, instr 1942-47. **ORGANIZATIONS:** Chmn Commerce Dept Cntrl StateUniv 1947-52; mem Com Mnrty Recxruit Am Inst CPA'S; Am Acctg Assn; adv bd Gov's Coun Consumer Prot; AAA AICPA ComDoct Fellows & Vstng Schlrs; bd dirs Oprtn Upgrade; C of C Ford Found. **HONORS/ACHIEVEMENTS:** Post doct fellowship 1962; dist serv awd OH StateUniv 1970. **BUSINESS ADDRESS:** Coll Bus Southern Univ, Baton Rouge, LA 70813.

HARRISON, PAUL CARTER
Producer, director, writer, professor. **PERSONAL:** Born Mar 01, 1936, New York, NY; son of Paul Harrison (deceased) and Thelma Carter Harrison; married Wanda Malone, Aug 06, 1988; children: Fonteyn. **EDUCATION:** New York Univ, New York City, 1952-55; Indiana Univ, Bloomington IN, BA, 1957; New School for Social Research, New York City, MA, 1962. **CAREER:** Howard Univ, Washington DC, asst prof of theatre arts, 1968-70; Kent State Univ, Kent OH, assoc prof of Afro-American literature, 1969; California State Univ, Sacramento CA, prof of theatre arts, 1970-72; Univ of Massachusetts at Amherst, prof of theatre arts and Afro-American studies, 1972-76; Columbia College, Chicago IL, artistic producer and chairman of theatre/music dept, 1976-80, writer-in-residence, 1980-. **ORGANIZATIONS:** Mem of theatre panel, Illinois Arts Council, Chicago IL, 1976-79; cultural consultant, Choice Magazine, 1973-83; contributing editor/theatre, Elan Magazine, 1981-83; contributing/advisory editor, Callaloo Magazine, 1985-88; curriculum consultant/cultural diversity, The Evergreen College, Olympia WA, 1986. **HONORS/ACHIEVEMENTS:** Director of plays Junebug Graduates Tonight, 1967, Ain't Supposed to Die a Natural Death, 1970, My Sister, My Sister, 1981, The River Niger, 1987, and Anchorman, 1988; producer of play Black Recollections, 1972; developer and producer of television film Leave 'Em Laughin', CBS-TV, 1981; author of plays The Experimental Leader, 1965, Tabernacle, 1970, and The Great MacDaddy, 1974; author of The Drama of Nommo (essays), Grove Press, NY, 1973; editor of Kuntu Drama (anthology), Grove Press, NY, 1974; author of screenplays Lord Shango, 1974, Youngblood, 1978, and Gettin' to Know Me, 1980; Obie award for best play, 1974, for The Great MacDaddy; Audelco Development Committee Recognition Award, 1981, for Tabernacle; Humanitas Prize, 1981, for Leave 'Em Laughin'; Illinois Art Council grant, 1984; fellowships from National Science Foundation, 1984, and Rockefeller Foundation, 1985; author of Totem Voices, Grove Press, NY, 1989, and In the Shadow of the Great White Way, Thunder Mouth Press, 1989. **HOME ADDRESS:** P O Box 143, Leeds, MA 01053. **BUSINESS ADDRESS:** Department of Theater/Music, Columbia College, 600 South Michigan Ave, Chicago, IL 60605.

HARRISON, PEARL LEWIS
Arts & culture executive director. **PERSONAL:** Born Jun 08, 1932, East Orange, NJ; married John Arnold Harrison; children: Lauren Deborah, Adrianne Carol. **EDUCATION:** Julliard School of Music NY, Certificate 1952. **CAREER:** Pearl Lewis Harrison Piano Studio, dir 1953-83; Governor's Task Force to est the Suburban Essex Arts Cncl, mem 1978; City of East Orange, coord arts/culture 1979-80; City of East Orange, acting dir public relations 1986; East Orange Arts & Culture Inc, exec dir 1987-. **ORGANIZATIONS:** Mem New Jersey Music Educ Cncl 1960-77, Suburban Essex Arts Cncl 1978-82, Friends of NJ Opera 1982-, Essex Co Arts & Culture Planning Bd 1983-86; bd of trustees United Way of Essex & Hudson Co 1985-86; mem Black Composers Inc 1985-; mem NJ Motion Picture Commission 1986-. **HONORS/ACHIEVEMENTS:** White House Citation from Mrs Nancy Reagan for music/comm spirit 1983; Pride & Heritage Women of the Year Awd Int Year of Environ Concerns 1983; Resolution for Cultural Expertise Essex Co Bd 1983; State of New Jersey for Excellence Awd NJ State Senate 1983; Certificate of Appreciation for Comm Serv City of East Orange 1983. **BUSINESS ADDRESS:** Executive Dir, East Orange Arts & Culture Inc, City Hall Plaza, East Orange, NJ 07019.

HARRISON, ROBERT WALKER, III
Educator. **PERSONAL:** Born Oct 13, 1941, Natchez, MS; son of Robert Harrison and Charlotte Harrison; married Gayle Johnson; children: Robert, Seth. **EDUCATION:** Tougaloo SC Coll, BS 1961; Northwestern Univ, MD 1966. **CAREER:** Vanderbilt Univ Sch of medicine, instructor 1972-74, asst prof 1974-81, assoc prof 1981-85; Univ of AR for Medical Sci, prof 1985-. **MILITARY SERVICE:** USN lt comm 1968-70. **BUSINESS ADDRESS:** Professor of Medicine, Univ of Arkansas for Med Sci, 4301 W Markham Slot 587, Little Rock, AR 72205.

HARRISON, RONALD E.
Corporation executive. **PERSONAL:** Born Jan 11, 1936, New York, NY; married Pauline; children: Richard, David, Katherine. **EDUCATION:** City Coll NY, BBA 1958; Boston Coll, Corp Comm Relations Prog 1986-87. **CAREER:** Pepsi Cola Metro Bottling Co NY, vp, area mgr; Pepsi-Cola Inc, Cincinnati dir special mkts 1966, control div Chicago dir training 1969, mgmt inst Phoenix dir training 1970, franchise devel NY dir 1972; area vice pres Pepsi Bottling Co 1975-79; no div vice pres Pepsi-Cola Co owned plants New England, Pgh, Milwaukee, vice pres 1979-81; Pepsi-Cola Inc, natl sales dir 1981-86; PepsiCo, dir comm relations. **ORGANIZATIONS:** Nat Assn Mktng Devel; Sales Exec Club NY; bd trst NY Orphan Asylum Soc; bd Educ Spl Sch Dist Greenburgh. **BUSINESS ADDRESS:** Dir Community Relations, PepsiCo, Anderson Hill Rd, Purchase, NY 10607.

HARRISON, ROSCOE CONKLIN, JR.
Public affairs director. **PERSONAL:** Born Sep 20, 1944, Belton, TX; married Sandra K Smitha; children: Corinne. **EDUCATION:** Temple Jr Clg, AA 1963-65; Prairie View A&M U, 1965-66;Univ Mary Hardin Baylon Belton TX, BA Jrnslm 1966-67. **CAREER:** San Antonio Exprs News, rprtr 1967-68; Jet Mag, assc edtr 1968-69; TX Atty Gen, deputy press sec 1976-79; Dallas Times Hearld, rprtr 1969; KCEN-TV, pblc afrs dir. **ORGANIZATIONS:** Mem Sigma Delta Chi/Soc Profsnl Jrnls; Omega Psi Phi Frat; Natl Assc Black Jrnlst; Temple NAACP; bd memUniv Mary Hardin Baylor Ed Found; Cntrl TX Goodwill Inds. **HONORS/ACHIEVEMENTS:** Ostdng young men of am US Jaycees 1972-79; pblc afrs awrd TX State Tchr Assc 1982; pblc afrs awrd TX Assc Brdcstrs 1976. **HOME ADDRESS:** 3806 Wendy Oaks, Temple, TX 76502. **BUSINESS ADDRESS:** Public Affairs Dir, KCEN-TV, P O Box 188, Temple, TX 76503.

HARRISON, WILLIAM EDGAR
Educator. **PERSONAL:** Born Jan 16, 1912, Asheville, NC; married Catherine; children: Linda, William E III. **EDUCATION:** Morehouse Coll, BA; OH St U, MA; OH St U, MBA; Miami U. **CAREER:** Dayton Bd of Edn, asst supt 1973; Carlson Elem Sch, prin 1970-73; Westwd Elem Sch, prin 1969-70; Wright StU, inst 1966-70; Dunbar HS, asst prin 1950-68; Dunbar HS, tchr 1941-50; FLA A & M, tchr 1939 -41; Whitmore Arms, devel 1965; GHR Empl Fed Cr Union, treas 1963; Fleetline Cab Co, stockh & opr 1948-58; J B Blayton & Co Acct, prtnr 1944-60; Wright-patterson AFB, stat 1941-44; NC Mutual Life Ins Co, asst mgr & aud 1932-37. **ORGANIZATIONS:** Alpha Phi Alpha Frat; past pres Dayton Trav Aid; past-pres Dayton Urban Leg; mem US Comm on Civil Rights; mem Dayton YMCA Friend Trvlrs. **BUSINESS ADDRESS:** 348 W 1st St, Dayton, OH 45402.

HARROLD, AUSTIN LEROY
Clergyman, counselor. **PERSONAL:** Born Jan 28, 1942, Omaha; married Gussie; children: Sabrina Butler, Austin Harrold, Jr, Sophia Harrold. **EDUCATION:** Lane Coll TN, BA Sociology 1964; Interden Theological Ctr & Phillips School of Theological Atlanta, MDiv 1968. **CAREER:** Barr's Chapel CME Church Paris TN, first appointment; St Mary CME Church, prev pastor; W Mitchell CME Church Atlanta, prev asst pastor; Lane Chapel CME Church, prev pastor; Turner Chapel CME Church Mt Clemens, formerly pastor; Calvary CME Church Jersey City, pastor; Phillips Mem CME Church, pastor; Russell CME Church, pastor; Mayor of Jersey City, exec sec 1981-85; US Dept of Commerce Bureau of the Census, community awareness specialist 1986-; Interdenominational Christian Comm Church, pastor and founder 1985-. **ORGANIZATIONS:** Prev Can for Dem Nomination to the KS House of Reps from 45th Dist; 1st vice pres Jersey City Branch NAACP; sec Interdenom Ministerial All of Jersey City BrNAACP; sec Interdenom Ministerial All of Jersey City & Vicinity; chpln Topeka Jaycees; co-chmn Employment Task Force coord com of Black comm; sec Interdenominational Ministerial Alliance of Topeka Vic; substitute teacher Mt Clemens HS; active in the nations War on Poverty; central manger NE Macomb Act Center; mem Bd Dirs Macomb Co Child Guidance Clinic; mem Mt Clemens Minis Assn; pres Macomb Co Chapter NAACP; pres Christ Clemens Elem School PTA; WM Excelsior Lodge; past first vice pres Macomb Co Comm Human Relations Assn; dean Detroit Dist CME Church Leadership Training School; mem bd of pension MI-IN Annual Conf Third Episcopal Dist of CME Church; sec MI dele to Natl Black Conv 1972; mem MI Dept Educ Vocational Rehabilitation Serv Vocational Rehabilitation; coun Mt Clemens Dist Office; chmn Mt Clemens Chapter Youth for Understanding; cand Mt Clemens City Comm; appointed to Macomb Co Office of Substance Abuse Advisory Council; bd mem Operation PUSH. **HONORS/ACHIEVEMENTS:** Certificate of Merit Third Episcopals Dist of Christ Methodist Episcopal Church for work in Civil Rights movement 1960-62; selected to spend summer 1963 in Sierra Leone W Africa in Operation Crossroads Africa Project 1963; Dept of Sociology Award Dept of Religion & Philosophy Award; Effective Christ Leadership 1960-64; Outstanding Young Men of Amer Bd of Edns 1970, 1976. **BUSINESS ADDRESS:** Minister, Founder -Interdenominational Christian Community Church, 2 Oxford Ave, Jersey City, NJ 02304.

HARROLD, JEFFERY DELAND
Clergy. **PERSONAL:** Born Oct 16, 1956, Detroit, MI; married Monica Jackson; children: Jeffrey Deland II, Jennifer Dianne, Jason Darnell. **EDUCATION:** University of MI, BA Economics 1978; Trinity Evangelical Divinity School, MDiv. **CAREER:** ADP Network Services Inc, tech analyst 1983-84; Bethel AME Church, asst pastor 1984-; Trinity AME Church, assoc pastor 1984-; Trinity Coll, dir of minority student develop 1985-. **ORGANIZATIONS:** Mem Assoc of Christians in Student Develop 1986-87; student council pres Trinity Evangelical Div Sch 1986-87; mem Omega Psi Phi Frat. **HONORS/ACHIEVEMENTS:** Outstanding Young Men of Amer 1983; Kearney Black Achievement Awd Trinity Evangelical Divinity School 1985; Who's Who in Amer Colls and Univs 1987. **BUSINESS ADDRESS:** Dir, Minority Student Dev, Trinity College, 2077 Half Day Rd, Deerfield, IL 60015.

HARROLD, LAWRENCE A.
Production management. **PERSONAL:** Born Apr 04, 1952, Belle Glade, FL; married Phyllis Lea; children: Lawrence Jr, Lamont, James. **EDUCATION:** Hillsborough Comm Coll, AA 1975; San Francisco State Univ, BA 1977, MBA 1979. **CAREER:** Pacific Telephone, mktg office supervisor 1980-81; Westvaco Corp, production supervisor. **ORGANIZATIONS:** Mem Black MBA. **MILITARY SERVICE:** USAF sgt 4 yrs. **HOME ADDRESS:** 2079 Brighton Dr, Pittsburg, CA 94565. **BUSINESS ADDRESS:** Production Supervisor, Westvaco Corporation, 5650 Hollis, Emeryville, CA 94608.

HARRY, JACKEE (JACKEE)
Actress. **PERSONAL:** Born in Winston-Salem, NC. **EDUCATION:** Attended Music & Art High School, New York City; Long Island Univ, Brooklyn Ctr, BA. **CAREER:** Television actress, playing "Sandra" on "227" series, NBC, 1985-. Former actress on "Another World" soap opera, and in Broadway prodns of "Eubie!," "The Wiz," and "One More Time." Former teacher at Brooklyn Tech High School. **HONORS/ACHIEVEMENTS:** Emmy

Award, Natl Acad of Television Arts and Sciences, 1987, for outstanding performance by a supporting actress. *

HART, BARBARA MCCOLLUM
Educator. **PERSONAL:** Born Oct 14, 1937, Pittsburgh, PA; married Charles E; children: Brian Charles. **EDUCATION:** Cheyney St Coll, BA 1966;Univ of Pittsburgh, MPA 1969; Univ of Pittsburgh, PhD 1986. **CAREER:** PA State Univ, asst prof 1970; PA House of Representatives, admin asst 1975-76; Model Cities, wlfr planner 1970; Hill House Assn, neighborhood devel specialist 1968-70; Urban League of Pittsburgh, dir rsch & planning 1966-68; Allegheny Co OEO, planning consultant 1970-74; Penn State-McKeesport, dir learning center. **ORGANIZATIONS:** Bd mem PARC 1970; bd mem PACE 1973; mem Pres Adv Com on Black Student Life PA St 1975; pres Pgh Alumnae 1978-80; Delta Sigma Theta Inc. **HONORS/ACHIEVEMENTS:** Jessie Smith Noyes Flwshp 1967; Who's Who Among Students in AmUniv & Coll 1965;Dean's List 1964-66; pres Honor Soc 1965; 1st Scholar of Yr 1964-65; OutstSrv Awd; Alpha Phi Sigma 1966; Master's Thesis Relocation implications for families in Carnegie, PA 1969; Doctoral Dissertation, A Description & Analysis ofPA's Efforts to Equalize Educational Oppty 1986. **BUSINESS ADDRESS:** Dir, Penn State University, University Dr, McKeesport, PA 15132.

HART, CHRISTOPHER ALVIN
Attorney. **PERSONAL:** Born Jun 18, 1947, Denver, CO; son of Judson D Hart and M Murlee Hart; married Celeste Eileen. **EDUCATION:** Princeton Univ, BSE 1969, MSE 1971; Harvard Law Sch, JD 1973. **CAREER:** Peabody Rivlin & Lambert, assoc 1973-76; Air Transport Assoc, attorney 1976-77; US Dept of Transportation, deputy asst genl counsel 1977-79; Hart & Chavers, managing partner 1979-. **ORGANIZATIONS:** Mem Natl, Amer, Washington Bar Assocs 1973-; mem Princeton Engrg Adv & Resource Cncl 1975-; dir/pres Beckman Place Condo Assoc 1979-83; mem FederalCommunications Bar Assoc 1981-; dir WPFW FM 1983-. **HONORS/ACHIEVEMENTS:** "Antitrust Aspects of Deepwater Ports," Transportation Law Journal 1979; "State Action Antitrust Immunity for Airport Operators," Transportation Law Journal 1981. **HOME ADDRESS:** 1612 Crittanden St NW, Washington, DC 20011. **BUSINESS ADDRESS:** Managing Partner, Hart & Chavers, 1120 20th St NW, Ste 610, Washington, DC 20036.

HART, DARYL CALVIN
Professional athlete. **PERSONAL:** Born Jan 10, 1961, Memphis, TN. **EDUCATION:** Lane Coll. **CAREER:** Oakland Invaders, cornerback 1984-. **HONORS/ACHIEVEMENTS:** Named All-Southern Intercoll Athletic Assn as a jr & sr.

HART, EDWARD E.
Physician. **PERSONAL:** Born May 08, 1927; married Joycelyn Reed; children: Edward, Janet, Reed, Cynthia, Jonathan. **EDUCATION:** Univ Toledo, BS 1946; Meharry Med Sch, MD 1949; Am Coll of Surgeons, FACS Fellow 1960. **CAREER:** Pvt Practice. **MILITARY SERVICE:** USAF 1954-56. **BUSINESS ADDRESS:** 1301 Tremonsburg, Ithaca, NY 14850.

HART, EMILY
Educator. **PERSONAL:** Born Oct 29, 1940, St Joseph, LA; divorced; children: Tammylynn, Lynnella. **EDUCATION:** SoUniv Baton Rouge LA, BS Spch & Hrng 1966;Univ CA Los Angeles, Post Grad Wrk; PepperdineUniv LA CA, MS Sch Mgmt & Admin 1974. **CAREER:** Compton Unified School Dist, teacher 1978-80, consultant 1975-78, teacher & speech therapist 1969-75; NV Countys, speech therapist 1968-69; Orleans Parish New Orleans, teacher 1978. **ORGANIZATIONS:** Vp Compton Comm Coll 1978; Los Angeles Co Trustee Assn 1977; pres Compton Comm Coll bd of trustees 1980; adv dirUniv of So CA Acad for Educ Mgmt 1978-79; mem CA Dem Prty Affrmtv Actn 1979-80; dir CA St Long Bch Math Engrng & Sci Achvmnt Bd; Accrdtatn Tm mem W Hills Coll. **HONORS/ACHIEVEMENTS:** 1st black woman elected tro trustee compton Comm Coll 1975; 1st black woman elected Los Angeles Co Trustee Assn 1977; Love & Dvtn For Chldrn Awd, ParentAdv Cncl Compton 1972; Woman of Year Awd, Nat Cncl of Negro Women 1973; Outstndng Comm Serv Awd NAACP 1975. **BUSINESS ADDRESS:** Compton Comm Coll Bd of Truste, 1111 E Artesia St, Compton, CA 90221.

HART, HAROLD RUDOFF
Business executive. **PERSONAL:** Born May 06, 1926, Washington, DC. **EDUCATION:** CathUniv Washington DC;Univ Madrid Spain. **CAREER:** Martha Jackson W Gallery NY, vice pres dir. **BUSINESS ADDRESS:** 156 W 86th St, New York, NY 10024.

HART, JACQUELINE D.
Educator/adminstrtor. **PERSONAL:** Born in Gainesville, FL; daughter of Mrs Edna M Hart. **EDUCATION:** Lane College, Jackson, TN, BS 1959; IN Univ, Bloomington, IN, 1965; Univ of FL Gainesville, FL, MEd 1970, EdS 1972, PhD 1985. **CAREER:** Alachua Public Schools, instructor 1967-70; Santa Fe Coll, instructor 1972-74; Univ of FL, dir/equal opp prog 1974-88; University of Florida, Gainesville, Florida, assistant vice president, 1988-. **ORGANIZATIONS:** Amer Assn of Affirmative Action, nominating committee; Delta Pi Epsilon; Kappa Delta Pi; League of Women Voters, former bd secty; City Commission on the Status of Women, legislative committee 1983-83; Delta Sigma Theta, Inc, former pres/life mem; Amer Cancer Soc Bd, 1984-; United Way of Alachua Cty, 1985-; Allocation Reviewer Committee; Institute of Black Culture Advisory Board, 1988; bd mem, United Nations Assn, Florida Division,1989. **HONORS/ACHIEVEMENTS:** Leadership Gainesville VIII-City of Gainesville 1983; Leadership Achievement Awd Alpha Phi Alpha 1981; Administrative Leadership Awd City of Gainesville 1986; Distinguished Alumni Award, Natl Assn for Equal Opportunity in Higher Educ, 1989; Societas Docta, Inc 1988. **HOME ADDRESS:** 1236 SE 13th St, Gainesville, FL 32601. **BUSINESS ADDRESS:** Assistant Vice President, University of Florida, Affirmative Action Office, 352 Tigert Hall, Gainesville, FL 32611.

HART, NOEL A.
Fire marshal. **PERSONAL:** Born Dec 14, 1927, Jamaica, NY; married Patricia Spence Cuffee; children: Noel Jr, Alison, Ira, Jonathan. **EDUCATION:** NY U, BA 1954. **CAREER:** Exec Devel Program Natl Fire Acad, Emmitsburg MD, training instructor; Peoria Fire Dept, fire marshal 1977; NY City Fire Dept 1954-77; John Jay Coll, team leader, lecturer; Promotional & Career Training Program, prof; FEMA US Fire Admin, fire prevention specialist. **ORGANIZATIONS:** Past pres Comus Scl Clb; mem trustee Port Chester Pub Library; bd dir Port Chester Carver Ctr; warden vestryman St Peters Episcopal Ch, Prince of Peace Episcopal Church; Diocese Cncl Episcopal Diocese Central PA. **MILITARY SERVICE:** AUS pfc 1945-47. **BUSINESS ADDRESS:** Fire Prevention Specialist, FEMA US Fire Administration, 16825 S Seton Ave, PO Box 147, Emmitsburg, MD 21727.

HART, RONALD O.
Elected official & educational administrator. **PERSONAL:** Born Jul 09, 1942, Suffolk, VA; married Ethel D; children: Aprill Jenelle, Ryan O. **EDUCATION:** NCA&T State Univ, BS Biol 1964; Hampton Inst, MS Biol 1968; Old Dominion Univ, Certification in Admin 1976. **CAREER:** John F Kennedy HS, 1964-76; Metropolitan Church Fed C Union, 1966-; Ruffner Jr HS, 1976-; Suffolk City Council, vice-mayor Cypress rep. **ORGANIZATIONS:** Mem Omega Psi Phi Frat 1962-; mem & adv Stratford Terrace Civic League 1975-; mem Norfolk, VA, Natl Educ Assns 1976-; mem Tidewater Regional Trans Comm 1978-; mem Odd Fellows Lodge 1978-; adv Cypress Comm League 1978-. **HONORS/ACHIEVEMENTS:** Outstanding Educator Elks Lodge Suffolk VA 1975; Man of the Year Omega Psi Phi Frat Suffolk 1979. **BUSINESS ADDRESS:** Vice Mayor Cypress Rep, Suffolk City Council, 129 County St, Suffolk, VA 23434.

HART, TOMMY
Assistant defensive line coach. **PERSONAL:** Born Nov 11, 1944; married Cherrie Ann; children: Sebrina, Ywakita, Tanya, Crystal. **CAREER:** Chicago Bears, 1978,79; New Orleans Saints, 1980; Tommy Hart's Sport Store, owner/operator; San Francisco 49ers', asst defensive line coach.

HART, TONY
Corrections counselor, college instructor. **PERSONAL:** Born Jul 27, 1954, Harlem, NY; married Judy Murphy; children: Tonya. **EDUCATION:** SUNY, graduated (Cum Laude) 1978; SUNY New Paltz, M Humanistic Educ 1987. **CAREER:** Highland Educational Occupational Ctr for Juvenile Offenders, Orange County Jail, Marist Coll HEOP Program, counselor; Green Haven Correctional Facility, correction counselor; Marist Coll Humanities Dept, part-time coll instructor. **ORGANIZATIONS:** Mem New York State Coalition for Criminal Justice; bd mem Coalition for Peoples Rights; mem Natl Rainbow Coalition, Newburgh Black History Comm, Redeeming Love Christian Center; staff advisor Black Solidarity Comm at Green Haven Correctional Facility. **HONORS/ACHIEVEMENTS:** Special Academic Awd SUNY 1977; Outstanding Service Awd PreRelease Ctr Green Haven Correctional Facility 1986; Martin Luther King Jr Awd Newburgh Memorial Comm 1987; Black Humanitarian Awd Newburgh Free Academy 1987; Most Deserving Black Award, Newburgh Black History Comm, 1989. **HOME ADDRESS:** PO Box 1007, Newburgh, NY 12550.

HART, WILLIAM L.
Police chief. **CAREER:** Detroit Police Dept, Detroit MI, chief of police. **BUSINESS ADDRESS:** Chief of Police, City of Detroit Police Department, 1300 Beaubien, Detroit, MI 48226. *

HART-NIBBRIG, HAROLD C.
Attorney. **PERSONAL:** Born Aug 16, 1938, Los Angeles, CA; married Deanna T McKenzie; children: Nand, Jaunice, Lauren. **EDUCATION:** Political Sci, BA 1961, JD Law 1971. **CAREER:** Manning & Hart-Nibbrig, atty. **ORGANIZATIONS:** Vice pres LA Black Congress 1968; Western Ctr on Law & Pov 1968-71; Com Educ Devel & Referral Serv 1969-; Black Law Ctr Inc 1971-73; bd of dirs Amer Civil Liberties Union 1973-79; chmn bd Viewer Spon TV Found KVST-TV 1973-74; mem LA Co Bar Assn, LA Co Bar Assn Judiciary Comm; mem John M Langston Law Club. **HONORS/ACHIEVEMENTS:** Order of Golden Bruin UCLA 1960; Martin Luther King Fellow Woodrow Wilson Fellow Found 1968; Serv Awd CA Jobs Agents Assn 1974; SCLC West Law & Justice Awd 1979; Image Awd NAACP 1980. **MILITARY SERVICE:** AUS pfc 1961-64. **BUSINESS ADDRESS:** Attorney, Manning & Hart Nibbrig, 4929 Wilshire Blvd, Ste 1020, Los Angeles, CA 90010.

HARTAWAY, THOMAS N., JR.
Director. **PERSONAL:** Born Mar 28, 1943, Lonoke County; married Arnice Slocum; children: Katina, Carla, Keith, Thomas III, Britt. **EDUCATION:** Henderson St Tchrs Coll AR; Harding Coll, 1972-73; Inst of Pol Gov Batesville Coll, 1971-72. **CAREER:** Dixie Ch of Christ, pastor; Ch of Christ, st dir of chrstn edn; Carter Mondale Camp, st dep cam coord 1976; Hartaway Assoc Adv & Pub Rel, pres 1974-76; OKY Radio, gen sales mgr 1972-74; Ch of Christ, minister 1968-71; The AR Carrier Nwspr, publ 1975-76; The Black Cnsmr Dir, publ 1976-77. **ORGANIZATIONS:** Bd mem No Little Rock Dwntwn Dev Com; adv bd mem NLR Comm Dev Agy; bd mem Cntrl AR Chrstn Coll; bd mem consult HOPE Inc No Little Rock AR. **HONORS/ACHIEVEMENTS:** Outst Yng Men of Am Awd 1976; best serv awd Pulaski Co Shrf Dept; outst ldrshp awd Conf of CME Chs. **BUSINESS ADDRESS:** Dixie Church of Christ, 916 "H" St, North Little Rock, AR 72114.

HARTH, RAYMOND EARL
Attorney. **PERSONAL:** Born Feb 04, 1929, Chicago, IL; married Fran Byrd; children: Cheryl, Raymond Jr, Douglass. **EDUCATION:** Univ of Chicago Law Sch, JD 1952. **CAREER:** Attorney, self-employed. **ORGANIZATIONS:** Pres IL Conf of Brs NAACP 1962-65; chmn 1960-62, 66-69, hndled Num Civil Rghts Cases in State & Fed Cts 1960-72. **MILITARY SERVICE:** ANG 1st lt 1948-64. **BUSINESS ADDRESS:** One N La Salle St, Chicago, IL 60602.

HARTMAN, HERMENE DEMARIS
Educator. **PERSONAL:** Born Sep 24, 1948, Chicago, IL; daughter of Herman D Hartman and Mildred F Bowden; married David M Wallace (divorced). **EDUCATION:** Roosevelt Univ, BA 1970, MPh 1974, MA 1974. **CAREER:** WBBM-TV-CBS, prof & asst mgr comm affairs 1974-75; Soul publ, columnist 1978-79; The Hartman Group, pres 1978-80; City Coll of Chicago, prof 1980-83, dir of develop & comm 1983-88; vice chancellor of External Affairs 1988-. **ORGANIZATIONS:** Mem Amer Acad of Poets 1979; adv comm on the Arts John F Kennedy Ctr 1979; adv bd Univ of IL Sch of Art & Design 1979; exhibit com Chicago Public Library Cultural Ctr 1979; exec com natl adv coun the John F Kennedy Ctr Wash DC 1980; producer of "Conversations with the Chancellor" Channel 20 Chicago; edited and compiled "A Lasting Impression, A Collection of Photographs of Dr Martin Luther King Jr". **HONORS/ACHIEVEMENTS:** Chicago Emmy nomination for "Conversations with the Chancellor" TV show; Pioneer's Awd Natl Assn of Media Women Chicago Chap 1975; article pub

"TV in Amer Culture" Crisis Mag 1978; "Great Beautiful Black Women" Johnson Products Co 1978; CEBA Awd PR Communications to Black Audiences 1979; "The Quest of the Black Woman in the 80's US Black & The News 1980; Media Awds, Chicago Emmy Awd 1984-86; "Up and Coming Black Business & Professional Women" 1985; Silver Quill Awd 1985; Communicator of the Year 1986; Gold Quill Awd 1986; Paragon Awds 1986; Merit Awd 1986; Grand Gold Medals 1986; Communications Excellence to Black Audiences 1986; 2 Silver Awds 1985 & 1987; Gold Awd 1987. **HOME ADDRESS:** 5555 S Everett, Chicago, IL 60637. **BUSINESS ADDRESS:** Vice Chancellor of External Affairs, City Colleges of Chicago, 226 W Jackson #1422, Chicago, IL 60606.

HARTSFIELD, ARNETT L., JR.
Educator, attorney. **PERSONAL:** Born Jun 14, 1918, Bellingham, WA; married Kathleen Bush; children: Maria Riddle, Paula Ellis, Charlean, Arnett, Barbara. **EDUCATION:** Univ of So CA, BA Econ 1951; USC, LLB 1955. **CAREER:** CA State Univ Long Beach, assoc prof 1974, asst prof 1972-74; United Way, asst dir 1970-71; Comm Mediation Center, chief mediator 1967-69; Los Angeles Neighbrhood Legal Servs, exec dir 1965-67; CA Fair Employment, assoc counselor 1964-65; Private Practice, 1955-64; City of Los Angeles, fireman 1940-61. **ORGANIZATIONS:** Bd trustees S BayUniv Coll of Law; pres Los Angeles City Cvl Serv Commn 1973-76; vice pres 1974-75. **HONORS/ACHIEVEMENTS:** Man of Yr Comm Rltns Conf of So CA 1962; mem Cvl Serv Commn 1973, pres 1973-74, 75-76, vice pres 1974-75. **MILITARY SERVICE:** 1st lt 369th infantry 1943-46. **BUSINESS ADDRESS:** 7 & Bellflower, Long Beach, CA 90815.

HARTSFIELD, HOWARD C.
Assistant superintendent. **PERSONAL:** Born Jul 30, 1926, Chicago, IL; children: Eric, Mark. **EDUCATION:** Morgan State Univ, BS 1954; HI & IL Univs, advance study. **CAREER:** AUS, platoon leader, operations officer, battalion comdr, instr infantry & armor tactics; Baltimore City Pub Sch, asst supr & bus mgmt. **ORGANIZATIONS:** Mem BSA, USO, NAACP, Morgan State Univ Alumnae Assn; Purple Heart Assn AUS; Natl Alliance Black Sch Educators; Amer Assn Sch Admins; mem Res Officers Assn US; Assn Sch Bus Ofcls; Supts Assn MD; Pub Sch Transp Liaison Com. **HONORS/ACHIEVEMENTS:** Distinguished Citizenship Awd State of MD 1979; Bus Admins Awd Registered Sch 1980; Purple Heart; Meritorious Serv Medal. **MILITARY SERVICE:** AUS retired lt col 1954-72; Soldier's Medal Heroism; Bronze Star 1 & 2 Oak Leaf Clusters; Air Medal 1 & 2 Oak Leaf Clusters; Army Commendation Medal. **BUSINESS ADDRESS:** Asst Supr & Bus Mgmt, Baltimore City Public Sch, 3 E 25th St, Baltimore, MD 21218.

HARTSHORN, HERBERT HADLEY
Retired educational administrator. **PERSONAL:** Born Apr 25, 1909, St Joseph, MO; married Goldie Reid; children: Gail Patricia, Hadley Reid. **EDUCATION:** Lincoln U, BS 1930; AMUniv MN, 1940;Univ MN, PhD 1948. **CAREER:** TX Southern Univ Coll of Arts & Science Houston, dean, vice pres 1968-70, vice pres 1970; Lincoln Univ, asst prof educ 1940-48, prof educ 1948, dean of students 1948-50; Lab High School, teacher 1936-40, prin 1940-48; St Louis, social worker 1935-36; Samuel Houston Coll, Austin TX, dir extension schools 1932-33; St Philip's Jr Coll San Antonio, dean 1931-32. **ORGANIZATIONS:** Sec YMCA 1930-31; mem TX Tchrs Assn; Coll Prsnnl Assn; mem Phi Delta Kappa; Psi Chi.

HARTY, BELFORD DONALD, JR.
Restaurant franchisee. **PERSONAL:** Born Nov 03, 1928, New York, NY; married Nell. **EDUCATION:** Lincoln U, BA; Real Estate Inst; Post Coll. **CAREER:** Real Estate, sales, purch, syndication; Burger King Franchisee; Hotel Owner. **ORGANIZATIONS:** Gtr Harlem Real Estate Bd; mem 100 Black Men; Nat Assn of Real Estate Brkrs; PAC Com; state coord Realtists in NY. **HONORS/ACHIEVEMENTS:** Several plaques Assn of RE Brkrs. **MILITARY SERVICE:** AUS corpl 1952-54. **BUSINESS ADDRESS:** 2289 5th Ave, New York, NY 10037.

HARTY, DONALD K.
Fast-food executive. **CAREER:** The Charisma Group Inc, New York, NY, chief exec. **BUSINESS ADDRESS:** Chief Executive, The Charisma Group Inc, 2370 Adam Clayton Powell Jr Blvd, New York, NY 10027. *

HARTZOG, ERNEST E.
Educational administrator. **PERSONAL:** Born Jan 08, 1928, York, PA; married Jeanne Leatrice Shorty; children: Daniel, Sharon. **EDUCATION:** San Diego St U, BA 1955; San Diego St U, MA 1962; NY U, MA 1964; US Intl U, PhD 1969. **CAREER:** Portland Public Schools, asst supt comm relations staff devel 1972; Govt Studies System Philadelphia, program mgr 1970-72; Philadelphia Public Schools, rockefeller intern; Detroit Public Schools, 1969-70; Lincoln High School San Diego, prin 1967-69; San Diego High School, vice prin 1966-67; San Diego Public Schools, dir Neighborhood Youth Corps; San Diego Urban League, 1964-66; San Diego Public Schools, counselor 1961-63, teacher 1956-61. **ORGANIZATIONS:** Pres Nat Alliance of Black Sch Edctrs; mem Am Assn of Sch Admnstrs; mem Cnfdn of OR Sch Admnstrs; Alliance of Black Sch Edctr; OR Sch Actvts Assn; OR St Chmn; United Negro Coll Fund; screening com Martin Luther King Schlrshp Fund; mem NAACP; mem African Meth Epis Ch. **HONORS/ACHIEVEMENTS:** Blue Key Nat Honor Soc. **MILITARY SERVICE:** AUYS sgt 1946-49 1950-51. **BUSINESS ADDRESS:** 501 N Dixon St, Portland, OR 97227.

HARVARD, BEVERLY BAILEY
Police chief. **PERSONAL:** Born Dec 22, 1950, Macon, GA; married Jimmy Harvard. **EDUCATION:** Morris Brown Coll, BA 1972; GA State Univ, MS 1980. **CAREER:** Atlanta Police Dept, police officer 1972-79; Atlanta Dept of Public Safety, affirmative action spec, 1979-80, dir of public info 1980-82; Atlanta Police Dept, dep chief of police 1982-. **ORGANIZATIONS:** Mem Leadership Altanta, Atlanta Univ Criminal Justice Inst Advisory Bd, Governor's Task Force on Police Stress, Natl Org of Black Law Enforcement Exec; mem of police training committee Intl Assoc of Chiefs of Police; parliamentarian Delta Sigma Theta Sor Inc 1979-; adv bd Atlanta Victim-Witness Asst; bd of dirs Georgia State Univ Alumni Assoc. **HONORS/ACHIEVEMENTS:** Outstanding Atlantan 1983; Personalities of the South; Graduate Fed Bureau of Investigations Natl Acad 1983; Listed in World's Who's Who of Women; Alumni ofthe Year Morris Brown Coll 1985. **HOME ADDRESS:** 3541 Cumberland Rd, East Point, GA 30344. **BUSINESS ADDRESS:** Deputy Chief of Police, Atlanta Police Bureau, 175 Decatur St SE, Atlanta, GA 30335.

HARVELL, VALERIA GOMEZ
Librarian. **PERSONAL:** Born Jun 27, 1958, Richmond, VA. **EDUCATION:** VA State Coll, BS 1978; Pittsburgh Theol Seminary, MDiv 1983; Univ of Pittsburgh, MLS 1983. **CAREER:** Burr Oaks Regional Library System, chief librarian 1984-85; Newark Public Library, branch mgr 1985-86; Penn State Univ, head librarian 1986-. **ORGANIZATIONS:** Mem Amer Library Assoc, Amer Theol Library Assoc, PA Library Assoc, Black Librarian Caucus, Black Librarians Caucus. **HOME ADDRESS:** 900 E Pittsburgh St, Greensburg, PA 15601. **BUSINESS ADDRESS:** Head Librarian, Penn State Univ/Fayette Campus, PO Box 519, Uniontown, PA 15401.

HARVEY, BEVERLY ANN
Assistant manager/finance. **PERSONAL:** Born Mar 25, 1957, Sorrento, FL. **EDUCATION:** Oral Roberts Univ, BA 1979; Amer Inst of Banking, Certificate 1980; Rochester Inst of Tech, accounting. **CAREER:** First Natl Bank of Rochester, acctg clerk/note teller 1979-81; Citibank NYS, acctg clerk 1981, opers supervisor 1981-83, mis specialist 1983-85, financial analyst 1985-. **ORGANIZATIONS:** Assoc dir newsletter Natl Assoc of Accountants 1985-86; mentor Citicorp Fellows Program 1987; treas NBMBA Western NY 1987. **HONORS/ACHIEVEMENTS:** Outstanding Volunteer Serv Awd Baden St Settlement Inc 1985; Certificate of Disting Serv Urban League of Rochester 1986; Disting Achievement Comm SvcsJolyettes of Rochester 1986. **BUSINESS ADDRESS:** Assistant Manager, Citibank/Citicorp, 99 Garnsey Rd, Pittsford, NY 14534.

HARVEY, CLARIE COLLINS
President of funeral home and insurance company. **PERSONAL:** Born Nov 27, 1916, Meridian, MS; daughter of Malachi C Collins and Mary Rayford Collins; married Martin L Harvey, Aug 01, 1943 (deceased). **EDUCATION:** Spelman College, Atlanta GA, BA, 1937; Indiana College of Mortuary Science, Indianapolis IN, 1942; Columbia University, New York NY, MA, 1951; School of Metaphysics, Jackson MS, 1983-84. **CAREER:** Freelance bookkeeper, Jackson MS, 1937-39; Collins Funeral Home and Insurance Companies, Jackson MS, general mgr, 1940-70, president, 1970-; Unity Life Ins Co, chairman of board and chief executive officer, 1980-. **ORGANIZATIONS:** National Council of Negro Women; NAACP; Links Inc. **HONORS/ACHIEVEMENTS:** First Woman of the Year, National Funeral Directors Association, 1955; outstanding alumni award, Spelman College, 1966; named outstanding citizen of City of Jackson MS, 1971; Top Hat Award, New Pittsburgh Courier, 1974; Clarie Collins Harvey Day in Mississippi declared by Governor William Waller, December 30, 1974; Churchwoman of the Year Award, Religious Heritage of America, Inc, 1974; International Upper Room Citation, 1976; named outstanding small business woman, central region, National Council of Small Business Management Development, 1976. **BUSINESS ADDRESS:** Collins Funeral Home, Inc, 415 North Farish St, Jackson, MS 39202.

HARVEY, DENISE M.
Educational administrator. **PERSONAL:** Born Jul 22, 1954, Knoxville, TN. **EDUCATION:** Oxford Coll of Emory Univ, AA 1974; George Peabody Coll for Teachers, BA 1976; Univ of TN, MSSW 1978. **CAREER:** Natl Inst of Publ Mgmt, rsch assoc 1978; Natl Inst for Adv Studies, rsch analyst 1978-80; Howard Univ, info spec 1980-81; Univ of TN, dir affirmative action 1982-. **ORGANIZATIONS:** Mem Amer Field Serv 1971-; adv UTK Black Cultural Programming Comm 1982-; mem Natl Assn for Equal Opportunity 1983-; advisory bd Knoxville Women's Ctr1983-; mem Amer Assn for Affirm Action 1984-; speakers bureau Knoxville Coll 1984-. **HONORS/ACHIEVEMENTS:** Exchange Student Peabody in Denmark, Univ of Denmark, Copenhagen 1975; Rsch Fellow Natl Inst of Public Mgmt WA DC 1978; Outstanding Young Women of Amer; Outstanding Young Amers AL 1981,82. **HOME ADDRESS:** 4000 McDonald Rd, Knoxville, TN 37914. **BUSINESS ADDRESS:** Dir of Affirmative Action, Univ of TN, 405E Andy Holt Tower, Knoxville, TN 379960144.

HARVEY, GERALD
Elected official. **PERSONAL:** Born Feb 21, 1950, Macon, GA; married Cotilda Qanterman; children: Marcia, Gerald. **EDUCATION:** Tuskegee Inst, BS Pol Sci 1972; GA Coll, MEd Behavior Disorder 1977. **CAREER:** GA Psycho-Educ Center, therapist 1973-85; City of Macon, councilman 1979-85. **HOME ADDRESS:** 1572 Canterbury Rd, Macon, GA 31206. **BUSINESS ADDRESS:** Councilmember, City of Macon, PO Box 247, Macon, GA 31298.

HARVEY, HAROLD A.
Physician, educator. **PERSONAL:** Born Oct 24, 1944; married Mary; children: 3 children. **EDUCATION:** Univ W Indies, MB, BS 1969; Tufts Med New Eng Med Ctr Hosp, med Resd Flw 1970-74. **CAREER:** PA St U, asso prf Med; PA SUniv Milton S Hershey Med Ctr, asso prof med, med oncologist, cancer rsrch 1974. **ORGANIZATIONS:** Mem Am Fedn Clncl Rsrch, Am Soc & Clncl Oncology, Amer Assoc for Cancer Rsch. **BUSINESS ADDRESS:** Physician, MS Hershey Med Ctr, Hershey, PA 17033.

HARVEY, JACQUELINE U.
Health educator. **PERSONAL:** Born Jan 21, 1933, Louisiana; married Herbert J Harvey; children: Cassondra Dominique, Gretchen Young, Herbert, Yolonda. **EDUCATION:** Natl Voc Coll, Vocational Counseling 1951-53; So Univ New Orleans, Soc Mktg Cert 1968-69; Xavier Univ, Spec Training 1969-70; Loyola Univ, Adv Studies 1978; Univ of New Orleans, presently. **CAREER:** LA Family Planning Prog New Orleans, family health counselor supr comm activity workers 1974-, sect supr family hlth cnslr 1970-74; Family Health Inc,team supr aux hlth wrkr 1968-69; LA Family Planning Prog New Orleans, aux hlth wrkr I 1967-68; Ctr for Health Trng, training mgr; Family Plng, dir of community svc. **ORGANIZATIONS:** Training mgr The Ctr for Health Training 1982-; consult Volunteer Mgmt 1967-; consult Outreach in Family Plng 1967-; pres Easton Community Schools Adv Council; mem Amer Publich Health Assoc, NAACP; pres Minority Women for Progress. **HONORS/ACHIEVEMENTS:** Recip Merit Award Family Health Found 1971; Comm Involvement Plaque Proj Enable 1967; Community Serv LA Black Women for Progress 1976; Outstanding Achievement Women in History NO LA 1976; Serv Awd Noteworthy Commun Leaders LA 1981; Merit Awd NO Human Relation 1982. **HOME ADDRESS:** 2669 Gladiolus St, New Orleans, LA 70122. **BUSINESS ADDRESS:** Dir of Community Services, Family Planning, 325 Loyola Ave, New Orleans, LA 70112.

HARVEY, LOUIS-CHARLES
Educator, theologian. **PERSONAL:** Born May 05, 1945, Memphis, TN; married Sharon Elaine Jefferson; children: Marcus Louis, Melanee Charles. **EDUCATION:** LeMoyne-

Owen Coll, BS 1967; Colgate Rochester Divinity School, MDiv 1971; Union Theological Seminary, MPhil 1977, PhD 1978. **CAREER:** SColgate Rochester-Divinity School, prof 1974-78; Payne Theological Seminary, dean 1978-79; United Theological Seminary, prof 1979-; Payne Theological Seminary, pres 1989-. **ORGANIZATIONS:** Speaker, preacher, writer, workshop leader African Methodist Episcopal Church 1979-. **HONORS/ACHIEVEMENTS:** Articles published Journal of Religious Thought 1983, 1987; Rsch grant Assn of Theological Schools 1984-85; pioneered study of Black Religion in Great Britain, 1985-86; biographer of William Crogman in Something More Than Human Cole, 1987. **BUSINESS ADDRESS:** President, Payne Theological Seminary, Box 384, Wilberforce, OH 45384.

HARVEY, NORMA BAKER
Educator, business counselor. **PERSONAL:** Born Nov 23, 1943, Martinsville, VA; daughter of Mrs N H Baker; married Dr William R Harvey; children: Kelly R, Christopher, Leslie D. **EDUCATION:** VA State Univ, BS Elem Educ 1961-65; Fisk Univ, MA Educ Media 1976. **CAREER:** VA and AL, elem sch teacher 1965-68; State of MA Planning Office, admin asst 1968-70; Tuskegee Inst, rsch asst 1974-78; Hampton Univ, business counselor 1982-; Kelech Real Estate Corp, pres 1981-; Pepsi Bottling Company of Houghton Inc, secretary/treasurer 1985-. **ORGANIZATIONS:** Bd of dirs Amer Heart Assn 1981-83; panelist VA Comm for the Arts 1983-84; bd of dirs VA Symphony 1983-; bd dirs United Way 1978-80; bd mem, Peninsula Council for the Arts 1978-80; mem, Planning & Research Committee for the United Way 1978-82; trustee, United Way 1985-. **HONORS/ACHIEVEMENTS:** Intl Progs at Tuskegee Behavioral Sci Rsch Tuskegee Inst 1976. **BUSINESS ADDRESS:** Business Counselor, HamptonUniversity, 55 E Tyler St, Hampton, VA 23668.

HARVEY, RAYMOND
Music director. **PERSONAL:** Born Dec 09, 1950, New York, NY; son of Lee Harvey and Doris Walwin Harvey. **EDUCATION:** Oberlin Coll, Oberlin, OH B Mus 1973, M Mus 1973; Yale Univ, New Haven CT, MMA 1978, DMA 1984. **CAREER:** Indianapolis Symphony, exxon/arts endowment conductor 1980-83; Buffalo Philharmonic, assoc conductor 1983-86; Springfield Symphony Orchestra, music dir 1986-. **HONORS/ACHIEVEMENTS:** Recent engagements have incl, Detroit Symphony, New York Philharmonic, Buffalo Philharmonic, Indianapolis Symphony, Houston Symphony, Louisville Orchestra; has conducted opera in US Canada and Italy. **BUSINESS ADDRESS:** Conductor, Springfield Symphony Orchestra, 1391 Main St, Suite 1006, Springfield, MA 01103.

HARVEY, RICHARD R.
Savings and loans executive. **CAREER:** Tuskegee Federal Savings & Loan Assn, Tuskegee, AL, managing officer. **BUSINESS ADDRESS:** Tuskegee Federal Savings and Loan Association, 301 North Elm St, Tuskegee, AL 36083. *

HARVEY, WARDELLE G.
Clergyman. **PERSONAL:** Born Jun 12, 1926, Booneville, IN; married Marsha G; children: Marian Jeanette, Wardell, Monica Perirr. **EDUCATION:** Tri-State Bapt Coll, 1957; Evansville Coll, 1958; Inter-Bapt Theol Sem, 1962, BTh, DD 1963, DCL 1970. **CAREER:** Paducah Public Housing, commiss 1966-67; City of Paducah, city commiss 1968-75, mayor protem 1970-72; Greater Harrison St Bapt Church Paducah, pastor; Cosmopolitan Mortuary, founder, owner; WGHarvey manor, owner. **ORGANIZATIONS:** Mem Mayors Adv Bd 1964-66; vice pres KY Bapts Assoc 1964-66; past pres Bapt Ministers Alliance of Paducah Area 1965-67; auditor 1st Dist Assoc 1965; mem State Voca Ed Bd Chmn Comm Chest 1965; pres founder Non-Partisan League; mem Inter-Denominational Ministers Alliance, NAACP, Christ Ldrshp Conf KY Col, Duke of Paducah. **HONORS/ACHIEVEMENTS:** Civic Beautification Awd; Optimist Club Blue Ribbon Awd; Voca Indust Ed Awd; Beta Omega Omega Chap of Alpha Kappa Alpha Pol Know-How. **BUSINESS ADDRESS:** WG Harvey Manor, 1429 Reed Ave, Paducah, KY 42001.

HARVEY, WILLIAM JAMES, III
Clergyman. **PERSONAL:** Born Jun 18, 1912, Oklahoma City, OK; son of Dr William J Harvey, Jr and L Mae Johnston Harvey; married Betty JenkinsJean Nelson, Dec 25, 1983; children: William J, IV, Janice Faith, Edward, Jr. **EDUCATION:** Fisk Univ, Nashville, TN, BA, 1935; Chicago Theological Seminary, M.Div, 1938. **CAREER:** Phila, pastor 1939-50; Okla City, pastor 1950-53; Pitts, pastor 1954-66; VA Union Univ, guest preacher 1946-48; Fisk Univ, guest preacher 1949; Cheyney State Teachers Coll, guest preacher 1949; Hampton Univ, guest preacher 1950; Prairie View State Coll, guest preacher 1951-52; OK State Univ, guest preacher 1953; Church History School Langston OK, prof of homiletics religion 1951-53; Pinn Memorial Baptist Church, Philadelphia, PA, pastor, 1939-50; Calvary Baptist Church, Oklahoma City, OK, pastor, 1950-54; Macedonia Baptist Church, Pittsburgh, PA, pastor, 1954-66. **ORGANIZATIONS:** Mem exec bd foreign mission bd Natl Baptist Convention 1949-50, exec sec 1961-; auditor PA Baptist Convention 1945-50; vice pres Philadelphia Baptist Ministers Conf 1950; pres Oklahoma City Ministers Alliance 1953; del const Convening Convention Natl Council Churches 1951; Natl Baptist Conv to World Baptist Allaiance London England 1955; vice pres Pitts Baptist Ministers Conf 1961; treasurer Allegheny Union Baptist Assn 1961-62; Ministers Conf 1961; preinvest editor World Bapt Alliance Rio de Janeiro Brazil 1959; mem Alpha Phi Alpha; Sigma Pi Phi; assoc editor Mission Herald 1950-54; bd of dir, Natl Baptist Convention USA, INC, 1961-; bd of dir, Bread for World, 1986-; bd of dir, Africa News, 1987-; bd of dir, Philadelphia Urban League, life mem, NAACP. **HONORS/ACHIEVEMENTS:** Mason author of Baptist Fundamentals in an Emerging Age of Freedom 1958; various articles; Missionary Worker's Manual, 1963; Mission Educ for Tomorrow's Leaders, 1965; Sacrifice and Dedication, 1980. **BUSINESS ADDRESS:** Exec Sec St, Foreign Mission Bd,, Natl Baptist Convention USA, Inc, Philadelphia, PA 19146.

HARVEY, WILLIAM M.
Psychologist. **PERSONAL:** Born Jan 25, 1933, Jackson, MS; son of William Harvey and Sarah McNeamer. **EDUCATION:** Tougaloo Coll, BA 1954; Washington Univ, PhD 1966. **CAREER:** St Louis State Hosp, chief psychologist 1967-69; Washington Univ, lecturer in psychology 1966-72, adjunct prof; MS Enterprise Newspaper, editor; Narcotics Serv Council Inc, exec dir. **ORGANIZATIONS:** Mem Natl Adv Council Natl Inst on Drug Abuse 1977-83; vice pres Natl Mental Health Assoc 1978-85. **HONORS/ACHIEVEMENTS:** Fellow Menniger Foundation; US Public Health Rsch Fellow Washington Univ. **BUSINESS ADDRESS:** Executive Dir, Narcotics Service Council Inc, 2305 St Louis Ave, St Louis, MO 63106.

HARVEY, WILLIAM R.
Educational administrator. **PERSONAL:** Born Jan 29, 1941, Brewton, AL; married Norma Baker Harvey; children: Kelly Renee, William Christopher, Leslie Denise. **EDUCATION:** Talladega Coll, AB 1961; Harvard Univ, EdD 1971; Salisbury State Coll, Honorary LHD 1983. **CAREER:** Secondary school teacher 1965-66; Harvard Univ, admin coord Harvard Intensive Summer Studies Prog 1969, asst to dean for govt affairs 1969-70; Fisk Univ, admin asst to pres 1970-72; Pepsi Cola Bottling Co of Houghton MI, owner; Tuskegee Inst, vice pres student affairs 1972-74, vice pres admin services 1974-78; Hampton Univ, pres. **ORGANIZATIONS:** Bd of dirs Newport News S&L 1980; bd of visitors Univ of VA 1981; bd of dirs Natl Merit Scholarship Corp 1981. **HONORS/ACHIEVEMENTS:** Admin Fellow Harvard Univ 1969; Martin L King Fellow Woodrow Wilson Found 1968-70; Woodrow Wilson Intern Fellowship Woodrow Wilson Found 1970-72; Who's Who in Amer 1982. **MILITARY SERVICE:** AUS Natl Guard Reserve lt col 1981-. **HOME ADDRESS:** 612 Shore Rd, Hampton, VA 23669. **BUSINESS ADDRESS:** President, HamptonUniv, Pres Office HamptonUniv, Hampton, VA 23668.

HARVEY-BYRD, PATRICIA LYNN
Journalist. **PERSONAL:** Born Nov 13, 1954, Detroit, MI; married Prentiss Lewis Byrd; children: Michelle Renee. **EDUCATION:** Attended, Mercy Coll of Detroit 1972-73, Univ of Detroit 1976-79, Saginaw Valley State Coll 1979-81. **CAREER:** WGPR TV & Radio Detroit, radio host 1976-77; WJBK TV Detroit, staff announcer 1977-79; WNEM TV Saginaw, anchor/reporter 1979-81; Cable News Network, anchor/corres 1981-85; WGN TV News Chicago, anchor/reporter 1985-. **ORGANIZATIONS:** Bd of governors Natl Acad of TV Arts & Scis 1986-; mem Chicago Assoc of Black Journalists 1986-; public serv work Girl Scouts of Amer 1987; board member, Governor's Task Force on Public-Private Child Care 1989; board member, Academic Development Institute 1988; Muscular Dystrophy Association 1988. **HONORS/ACHIEVEMENTS:** Comm Serv Awd Buena Vista Township 1980; Chicago's Up & Coming Business & Professional Women 1986; IL Coalition Against Domestic Violence 1986; Emmy Award for AIDS Reporting National Academy of TV Arts & Sciences 1988; Peter Lisagore Award for Investigative Journalism into Pap Industry 1988; Journalist of the Year , National Association of Black Journalists 1988; Associated Press Award for Investigative Journalism Re: Pap Industry 1989; Illinois Broadcasters Association Award for Aids Reporting 1989; Blackbook's Business & Professional Award 1989. **BUSINESS ADDRESS:** Anchorwoman, WGN News, 2501 W Bradley Place, Chicago, IL 60618.

HARVIN, ALVIN
Reporter. **PERSONAL:** Born Feb 20, 1937, NYC; married Norma Ellis; children: A Jamieson, Khary, Demetria. **EDUCATION:** CCNY, BA 1967. **CAREER:** NY Post, sports reporter; NY Times, sports reporter. **ORGANIZATIONS:** Mem Baseball Writers Assn Am. **BUSINESS ADDRESS:** Reporter, New York Times, 229 W 43 St, New York, NY 10036.

HASAN, AQEEL KHATIB
Personnel administrator. **PERSONAL:** Born Sep 10, 1955, Augusta, GA; married Venita Lejuene Merriweather; children: Aqeel. **EDUCATION:** Augusta Area Tech Sch, diploma 1976-78. **CAREER:** Augusta News Review, columnist 1978-79; WRDW Radio, broadcaster 1978-80; Black Focus Magazine, columnist 1982; Richmond Co Bd of Educ, mem 1982-, pres 1983-84; Richmond Co Bd of Health, mem 1983-84; Employment Planning Consultants Inc, pres 1985. **ORGANIZATIONS:** Counselor Richmond Co Correction Inst 1876-80; minister American Muslim Mission 1977-80. **HONORS/ACHIEVEMENTS:** Best athlete Augusta Area Tech School 1978; Citizen of the Year Omega Psi Phi Frat 1983; Citizen of the Year Augusta News Review 1983; Outstanding Young Man of America Jaycees Natl 1984. **MILITARY SERVICE:** USMC lance corpl 2 yrs. **HOME ADDRESS:** 1015 Carrie St, Augusta, GA 30901.

HASAN, RASHAD
Television producer. **PERSONAL:** Born Dec 10, 1954, Asheville, NC; son of Roland R and Anna Edgarton; married Shirley M Robertson; children: Shah D. **EDUCATION:** Univ of MN-Minneapolis, BA 1975. **CAREER:** Insight Communications, sales mgr 1977-79; Equitable Life Assurance Soc, sales rep 1979-81; TV Forum Magazine, publisher 1981-; Satban Music Television, executive producer 1984-. **ORGANIZATIONS:** Chmn educ comm Prince Hall Masons Palestine Lodge #7 1980-83. **HONORS/ACHIEVEMENTS:** Producer documentary Law Enforcement in the Black Community WCCO-TV 1983, dailyTV show Satban Music TV KXLI-TV 1984-, documentary Queen Mother Audrey Moore 1986; produced documentary on "Reparations" (40 Acres & a Mule) Satban 1986. **MILITARY SERVICE:** AUS sgt e-5 3 yrs; Good Conduct Medal, NDSL. **HOME ADDRESS:** 1515 Washburn Ave No, Minneapolis, MN 55411.

HASBROUCK, ELLSWORTH EUGENE
Physician. **PERSONAL:** Born Oct 27, 1913, Syracuse, NY; married June Seay; children: Ellsworth Jr. **EDUCATION:** SyracuseUniv Coll of Liberal Arts, AB 1934; HowardUniv Sch of Med, MD 1937; NovaUniv Grad Prgm, DPA Candidate 1977. **CAREER:** Prvdnt Hosp , consult srgn asso atndng srgn 1946-48, jr atndng srgn 1943-46, inst 1937-49; Jcksn Pk Hosp, consult srgn; Cook Co Hosp, consult srgn, instr 1942; Chicago Med Csh, asso in srgry 1955-, lectr 1953-63, instr 1951-55. **ORGANIZATIONS:** Chmn div of gen srgry Prvdnt Hosp 1948-55, v chmn 1948-50; exmng bd Cnddts of Intl Coll of Srgns 1966-; plng com Am Coll of Srgns 1961; press rel com Am Coll of Srgns 1961; Nat Conv 1967; spl adv com Member Com Chicago Srgcl Soc 1965; mem Adj Com IL Blue Shld 1966-76; v regent Intl Coll of Srgns 1970-; great exmr Am Bd of Srgry 1971; mdwt regl itrvwr HowardUniv Med Sch 1950-70; mem Hlth & Hosp Govng Commn Cook Co 1972-; chmn Prgn Com HHGC 1975-; chmn Ethcl Rel Com US Sect Intl Coll of Srgns 1976-; Am Med Wrtrs Assn; Nat Med Assn; AMA; il State Med Soc; Chicago Med Soc; Prairie St Med Soc; Cook Co Phscns Assn; mem bd trst Hektn Inst for Med Rsrch 1975-; DuSable Mus of Afro-Am His 1975-; IL Srgcl Soc 1976-81. **HONORS/ACHIEVEMENTS:** Fellow Am Coll of Srgns 1950; fellow Intl Coll of Srgns 1951; publ The Behavior of a Trnsplntd Hrt 1954, Trauma to the Abdomen 1956, Pr 1957, Effof Ascites form on Rspns to Rapid Water Sdm & Dxtrn Loads in Intct & Dbts 1958. **BUSINESS ADDRESS:** 200 E 75th St, Chicago, IL 60619.

HASHIM, MUSTAFA
Political activist. **PERSONAL:** Born Mar 18, 1935; married Hamida; children: Ishmail, Munira, Rasheeda. **EDUCATION:** Islamic & African Inst of PA, 1962. **CAREER:** African-Amer Repatriation Assn Philadelphia, political activist, pres. **ORGANIZATIONS:** Goal of assn is to obtain land in Africa for the voluntary repatriation of African Americans

who are the descendants of slaves, and to petition the US govt to cooperate with willing African states in programs to achieve this goal. **BUSINESS ADDRESS:** 5119 Chestnut St, Philadelphia, PA 19139.

HASKINS, JAMES S.
Author, English professor. **PERSONAL:** Born Sep 19, 1941, Demopolis, AL; son of Henry Haskins and Julia Brown Haskins. **EDUCATION:** Georgetown University, BA, 1960; Alabama State University, BS, 1962; University of New Mexico, MA, 1963; New York Institute of Finance, certificate of Work of the Stock Exchange, 1965; attended New School for Social Research and City University of New York. **CAREER:** New York City Public Schools, Brooklyn NY, teacher, 1966-68; New School for Social Research, New York NY, part-time teacher, 1970-72; State University College, New Paltz NY, part-time teacher, 1970-72; Staten Island Community College, Staten Island NY, associate professor, 1970-76; Elisabeth Irwin High School, New York NY, teacher, 1971-73; Weekend College, Indiana University/Purdue University, Indianapolis IN, visiting lecturer, 1973-74; Manhattanville College, Purchase NY, visiting lecturer, 1972-76; College of New Rochelle NY, visiting professor, 1977—; University of Florida, Gainesville FL, professor of English, 1977—; consultant to numerous educational and governmental groups, and to publishers. **ORGANIZATIONS:** Authors Guild; National Book Critics Circle; member, Africa Roundtable, Phelps-Stokes Fund, 1987—; National Education Advisory Committee of the Commission on the Bicentennial of the Constitution, 1987—; New York Urban League; Phi Beta Kappa, Kappa Alpha Psi. **HONORS/ACHIEVEMENTS:** Best Western Juvenile nonfiction book finalist, Western Writers of America, 1975; Coretta Scott King Award, 1977; Children's Book of the Year award, Child Study Association, 1979; Deems Taylor Award for writing in the field of music, ASCAP, 1979; fourteen books selected as Notable Children's Books in the field of social science, Social Studies magazine; author of The Cotton Club, Random House, 1977; author of over twenty-five biographies for children; author of numerous nonfiction books on social issues. **HOME ADDRESS:** 325 West End Ave, 7D, New York, NY 10023. **BUSINESS ADDRESS:** Department of English, University of Florida, 4326 Turlington, Gainesville, FL 32611.

HASKINS, JAMES W., JR.
Public relations representative. **PERSONAL:** Born Dec 01, 1932, Sandusky, OH; married Janie L Moore; children: Lisa, Scott, Karen, Laura, Ronald, Sondra, Iona. **EDUCATION:** Bowling Grn St U, BA 1959;Univ of PA, MSEd 1975, Doct Cand Educ Adm. **CAREER:** DuPont Invtn, editor 1971-, rsrch sci wrtr 1969-71; Chem & Engr & News, asst ed bur head 1966-69; US Atmc Enrgy Com, chem 1963-66; Cntrls RdtnInc, tech 1961-63; Prvdnc Hosp Sch Nrsng, sci instr 1962, bctrlgst-tech 1960-63; IUPAC Bk on Org Chem, editor; US Acad of Sci Host, mcrmlclr chem 1971. **ORGANIZATIONS:** Mem Am Chem Soc; AAAS; Nat Assn Sci Wrtrs Inc; Soc Tech Commnctn; Sigma Delta Chi; Intl Assn Bus Commnctrs; mem Blck Educ Forum; Urban League; NAACP; Alpha Phi Alpha; Wynfld Rsdnts Assn. **HONORS/ACHIEVEMENTS:** Sci Wrtr Yr NY Voice 1972; Legion Hon; member Chpl 4 Chplns 1973; Phi Delta Kappa 1975. **MILITARY SERVICE:** USMC sgt 1954-57. **BUSINESS ADDRESS:** Pub Affairs Dept EI, Du Pont de Nemours & Co Inc, Wilmington, DE 19898.

HASKINS, JOSEPH, JR.
Bank chief executive. **CAREER:** Harbor Bank of Maryland, Baltimore, MD, chief exec. **BUSINESS ADDRESS:** Harbor Bank of Maryland, 21 W Fayette St, Maryland, MD 21201. *

HASKINS, MICHAEL KEVIN
Public relations consultant. **PERSONAL:** Born Mar 30, 1950, Washington, DC; son of Thomas Haskins and Frances (Datcher) Haskins; divorced. **EDUCATION:** Lincoln Univ, Oxford PA, BA Economics, 1972; LaSalle Univ, Philadelphia PA, MBA Finance, 1980. **CAREER:** Fidelity Bank, Philadelphia PA, asst mgr, 1972-76; First Pennsylvania Bank, Philadelphia PA, mktg specialist, 1976-77; Greater Philadelphia CDC, Philadelphia PA, sr project mgr, 1977-80; Emerson Electric, Hatfield PA, mktg analyst, 1980-82; Cooper Labs, Lang Horn PA, product mgr, 1982-83; First Pennsylvania Bank, Philadelphia PA, asst vice pres, 1983-89; Crawley Haskins & Rodgers Public Relations, Philadelphia PA, exec vice pres, 1989-. **ORGANIZATIONS:** Vice pres, Greater Philadelphia Venture Capital, 1983-; dir, Pennsylvania Minority Business Devel Authority, 1988-; pres, Richard Allen Museum Bd, 1989-. **HONORS/ACHIEVEMENTS:** Mother Bethel AME Bicentennial Award, 1987; Group Leader, Urban League of Philadelphia, 1988. **BUSINESS ADDRESS:** Executive Vice President, Crawley, Haskins & Rodgers Public Relations, The Bourse, Suite 900 Independence Mall, Philadelphia, PA 19106.

HASKINS, MORICE LEE, JR.
Financial administrator. **PERSONAL:** Born Jun 09, 1947, New Brunswick, NJ; son of Morice L. Haskins, Sr. and Mary Toombs Haskins; divorced. **EDUCATION:** Colgate U, BA 1969; HofstraUniv Sch of Law, JDL 1978. **CAREER:** First TN Bank Corp, vice pres & trust officer l979-; NY State Educ Dept Albany, exec sec commn on educ oppor 1974-75; NY State Educ Dept, asso in higher educ 1971-75; StateUniv of NY at Oswego, asso dean dir full oppor prog 1969-71; Colony S Settlement House Brooklyn, coor soc studies curric 1969. **ORGANIZATIONS:** Mem Assn for Equality & Excellence in Educ 1978-; mem Nat Bar Assn Memphis 1979-; mem Am Inst of Banking Memphis 1979-; mem Nat Conf of Black PolitScis 1970-; mem Tau Kappa Epsilon Mediator Memphis City Ct Dispute Prog 1979-l98l; vchmn LaRose Sch Title I Comm Adv Com 1979-l98l; Chicasaw Counc Boy Scouts of Am 1981-84; mem bd dir Memphis Black Arts Alliance 1982-; loan comm mem TN Valley Center for Minority Econ Dev 1984-; chmn, bd of dir Dixie Homes Boys Club 1988-l990. **BUSINESS ADDRESS:** Trust Administrator/Officer, First Tennessee Bank Natl Assn, P O Box 84, Memphis, TN 38107.

HASKINS, WILLIAM J.
Executive director. **PERSONAL:** Born Oct 16, 1930, Binghamton, NY; married Bessie White; children: Billy, Terri, Wendell. **EDUCATION:** Syracuse Univ, BA 1952; Columbia Univ, MA 1953; NY Univ, cert adm 1954. **CAREER:** Boys Club of Amer, Milwaukee 1957-60, Richmond 1960-62; Natl Urban League, exec dir Eliz NJ 1962-64, mideastern reg 1964-66, deputy dir 1966-69; Natl Alliance of Businessmen, natl dir comm rel 1969-72; Arthur D Little, sr staff consult 1972; Eastern Reg Natl Urban League, dir; Human Resources Social Serv Natl Urban League, natl dir; Urban League Whitney M Young Jr Training Exec Develop and Continuing Educ Ctr, dir 1986. **ORGANIZATIONS:** Mem Natl Counc Urban League; exec mem NAACP; mem Pres Commn on Mental Health; pub mem Pres's Strategy Council on Drug Abuse; bd mem Natl Cncl onBlack Alcoholism; Alpha Phi Alpha Frat; chmn Human Environ Ctr Washington DC. **HONORS/ACHIEVEMENTS:** Many athletic awds 1948-53; Athlete Yr 1951; Man of Yr 1970; Letterman of Distinction Syracuse Univ 1978; Pacesetters Awd Syracuse Univ Black Alumni 1979; 1982 inducted into NY State Athletic Hall of Fame. **BUSINESS ADDRESS:** Natl Dir, Human Res Soc Serv Urban Leag, 500 E 62nd St, New York, NY 10021.

HASSELL, FRANCES M.
Business executive. **PERSONAL:** Born Mar 26, 1925, Woodstock, TN; divorced; children: Marian Hassell Whitson. **EDUCATION:** Shelby Co Training Sch, Vldctrn 1943; Lane Coll, 1947; TN State U; Memphis State U. **CAREER:** Adv Life Ins Unvrsl Life Ins Co, vice pres asst sec pub rltns 1980-, asst vice pres pub rltns 1971-80, admin asst 1958-71, sec to vice pres 1950-58, br ofc clerk 1947. **ORGANIZATIONS:** Mem Life Advtrs Assn; past mem LOMA Educ Com; life mem YWCA; vice pres NIA HO Sect 1978-80; bd of dirs NIA; NAACP; Memphis Vol Plcmnt Com; instr secLOMA Staff Unvrsl Life Ins Co; chmn HO Pub Rltns Com; mem Memphis Panel of Am Wmn; mem Memphis Chap PRSA Loma Curric Com 1976-77; mem Mt Olive CME Ch; chmn PR Com; pub spkr NIA, Nat Inst Asso, Orgn of Blck Ins Co. **HONORS/ACHIEVEMENTS:** Recip LAA; Award of Exclnc 1973, 1974; An Otstndng Woman Who Work Memphis 1973; Hon by DillardUniv New Orlns as Prin Spkr During Woman Wk 1964; ed & rsrchr Black His; compiled Blck His Clndrs; ed Blck His Bklt. **BUSINESS ADDRESS:** Universal Life Insurance Co, 480 Linden Ave, Box 241, Memphis, TN 38101.

HASTINGS, ALCEE LAMAR
Judge. **PERSONAL:** Born Sep 05, 1936, Altamonte Springs, FL; divorced; children: Alcee II. **EDUCATION:** Fisk U, BA 1958; Howard U; FL A&M Univ, JD 1963. **CAREER:** 17th Crct St of FL, frmr crct ct jdg; Tri-City News, part owner oprtr; W Side Gazette, col wrtr; Southern District of FL, district judge. **ORGANIZATIONS:** Mem Brwrd Co Bar Assn; FL Bar Assn; Am Bar Assn; Nat Bar Assn; Am Trial Lwyrs Assn; Brwrd Co Trial Lwyrs Assn; Brwrd Co Crmnl Def Atty Assn; World Peace Thrgh Law Ctr; Am Arbtrtn Assn; Gov Conf on Crmnl Jstc; frmr lgl counsel NAACP; Brwrd Co Clsrm Tchrs Assn; mem Gov Jdcl Cncl; Brwrd Co Cncl on Human Rels; FL Grdsmn; frmr mem Am Civil Lbrts Union; Comm Serv Cncl of Brwrd Co; num other afltns; host WPLG Pride. **HONORS/ACHIEVEMENTS:** FL Who's Who 1966; Freedom Award NAACP; Man of Yr Kappa Alpha Psi Orlando Chpt; NAACP Co Award 1976; Humanitarian Awd Broward County Young Democrats 1978;Citizen of the Year Awd Zeta Phi Beta 1978; Sam Delevoe Human Rights Awd Comm Relations Bd of Broward County 1978; named Man of Year Com Italian Amer Affairs 1979-80; Judge Alcee Hastings Day proclaimed for City of Daytona Beach in his honor Dec 14, 1980; Glades Festival of Afro Arts Awd Zeta Phi Beta 1981. **BUSINESS ADDRESS:** US District Judge, Southern District of Florida, Federal Courthouse Square, 301 N Miami Ave Ste 517, Miami, FL 33128.

HASTON, RAYMOND CURTISS, JR.
Dentist. **PERSONAL:** Born Jul 24, 1945, Lexington, VA; married Diane Rawls; children: Lisa, Crystal, April, Tasha. **EDUCATION:** Bluefield State, BS 1967; Howard Univ, DDS 1977. **CAREER:** Appomattox Public School Systems, teacher 1967-68; Milton Sumners HS, teacher 1969; DC Public School System, teacher 1969-73; Private Practice, dentist. **ORGANIZATIONS:** Mem Natl Dental Assoc 1987, Amer Dental Assoc 1987, General Acad of Dentistry 1987; mem Alpha Phi Alpha Frat, NAACP. **HONORS/ACHIEVEMENTS:** Natl Science Foundation Scholarships 1971-72. **HOME ADDRESS:** 6425 Battle Rock Dr, Clifton, VA 22024.

HASTY, KEITH A.
Chief executive of packaging materials firm. **CAREER:** Best Foam Fabricators Inc, Chicago, IL, chief exec. **BUSINESS ADDRESS:** Best Foam Fabricators Inc., 9633 S Cottage Grove Ave, Chicago, IL 60628. *

HATCHER, ESTER L.
Educator. **PERSONAL:** Born Jan 02, 1933, College Grove, TN. **EDUCATION:** TN State Univ, BS 1954; Univ of TN, MS 1970. **CAREER:** Univ of TN Knox Blount Anderson, extension agent 1954-65; Univ of TN Madison Cty, extension agent 1965-69; Univ of TN, asst prof, 1970-77, assoc prof 1977-84, prof 1984-. **ORGANIZATIONS:** Mem Amer Home Econ Assoc 1965-87; counselor Equal Employment Oppty Univ of TN 1973-87; mem Century Club Univ of TN 1975-87; chmn nom comm TN Home Econ Assoc 1977; treas Home Demo Agents of TN 1978-80; mem Soc of Nutrition Ed 1978-87. **HONORS/ACHIEVEMENTS:** Publ"Teaching Nutrition to Youth", "SPIFFY Food Science", "Food & Nutrition Grades K-3", "Ideas for Visuals". **BUSINESS ADDRESS:** Professor, Univ of Tennessee, PO Box 1071, Knoxville, TN 37901.

HATCHER, JEFFREY F.
Manager. **PERSONAL:** Born in East Orange, NJ; son of John Cornelius Hatcher and Cordella Garnes; divorced; children: Troy. **EDUCATION:** TN State Univ, attended 1965-69; The New School of Social Rsch, attended 1977-78. **CAREER:** Spot Time Ltd Natl TV Station Representatives, sales mgr 1979-82; MCA Television, account exec 1982-84; Channel Syndication Corp, marketing dir 1984-85; USA Network, regional mgr affiliate relations 1985-. **ORGANIZATIONS:** Mem Natl Acad of TV Arts & Scis, Intl Radio & TV Soc Inc, Natl Assoc of Minorities in Cable NY Chapter. **BUSINESS ADDRESS:** Regional Mgr Affiliate Relations, USA Network, Eastern Region, 1230 Avenue of the Americas, New York, NY 10020.

HATCHER, LILLIAN
Representative. **PERSONAL:** Born May 30, 1915, Greenville, AL; widowed; children: Carlene, John, Gloria. **CAREER:** UAW Intl Union, intl rep (1st Black woman appointed). **ORGANIZATIONS:** Commr vice chairperson Human Rights Comm; delegate MI Constl Conv 1961-62; vice chpsn 13th Congr Dist Chpsn Women's Com of the Bicent Commn 1976; Women's Comm bd mem NAACP Flight for Freedom Dinner 1977; precinct delegate 1948-; coalition Black Trade Unionists; Women's Economic Club of Detroit. **HONORS/ACHIEVEMENTS:** Awd Intl Order of the Elks. **BUSINESS ADDRESS:** International Representative, UAW Intl Union, 8000 E Jefferson Ave, Detroit, MI 48214.

HATCHER, RICHARD GORDON
Consultant, lawyer. **PERSONAL:** Born Jul 10, 1933, Michigan City, IN; son of Carlton Hatcher and Catherine Hatcher; married Ruthellyn; children: Ragan, Rachelle, Renee. **EDUCATION:** IN Univ, BS 1956; Valparaiso Univ, JD 1959. **CAREER:** Lake Co IN, deputy prosecuting atty 1961-63; City of Gary, city councilman 1963-67, mayor 1967-88; Hatcher and Associates, pres, 1988—. **ORGANIZATIONS:** Dem Conf of Mayors 1977; instr IN Univ NW; many publs; chmn Human & Resources Devel 1974; mem Natl League of Cities; past pres, US Conf of Mayors; Natl Conf of Black Mayors; Natl Black Polit Conv; former vice chair, Natl Dem Comm; Mikulski Commn report dem party policy; Natl Urban Coalition; natl chmn bd dir Operation PUSH; mem IN Exec Bd NAACP; mem Natl Dem Comm on Delegate Selection (co-author Com Report); founder Natl Black Caucus of Locally Elected Officials; Natl Black Caucus; IN State Dem Central Com; Assn Councils Arts; chair TransAfrica Inc; Jesse Jackson for Pres Campaign; pres Natl Civil Rights Museum and Hall of Fame; mem bd of dirs Marshall Univ Socof Yeager Scholars; fellow, Kennedy School of Govt, Harvard U; chair, African American Summit, 1989. **HONORS/ACHIEVEMENTS:** Outstanding Achievement Civil Rights 10 Annual Ovington Awd; life mem & Leadership Awd NAACP; Man of Yr Harlem Lawyers Assn; Disting Serv Awd Capital Press Club; Disting Serv Awd Jaycees; Employment Benefactors Awd Intl Assn Personnel Employment Security; Serv Loyalty & Dedication Awd Black Students Union Prairie State Coll; Outstanding Cit Yr Awd United Viscounts IN; Inspired Leadership IN State Black Caucus; among 100 Most Influential Black Americans Ebony Magazine 1971; among 200 most outstanding young leaders of US, Time Magazine, 1974; Urban Leadership award, IN Assn of Cities and Towns, 1986; Natl League of Cities President's Award, 1987; Natl Black Caucus of Local Elected Officials Liberty Award, 1987; honorary doctorates, Coppin St College, Duquesne U, Fisk U, Valparaiso U, Clevland St U. **BUSINESS ADDRESS:** Hatcher and Associates Inc, 2210 Hayes St, Gary, IN 46404.

HATCHETT, ELBERT
Attorney. **PERSONAL:** Born Jan 24, 1936, Pontiac, MI; married Laurestine; children: 4 children. **EDUCATION:** Central State Coll of OH, attended; Univ of MI, attended; FL A&M Univ, LLD. **CAREER:** Hatchett Brown Watermont & Campbell, attny 1969; Circle H Ranch Otter Lake MI, owner; Hatcett Dewalt Hatchel & Hall, sr parnter, attny. **HONORS/ACHIEVEMENTS:** Num awds from local & state orgs for serv to community & outstanding contribs to the pursuit of human rights; Disting Alumni Awd FL A&M Univ. **BUSINESS ADDRESS:** Trial Attorney, Sr Parnter, Hatchett,DeWalt,Hatchett,Hall, 485 Orchard Lake Ave, Pontiac, MI 48053.

HATCHETT, JOSEPH WOODROW
Judge. **PERSONAL:** Born Sep 17, 1932, Clearwater, FL; married Betty Lue Davis; children: Cheryl Nadine Green, Brenda Audrey. **EDUCATION:** FL A&M Univ, AB 1954; Howard Univ, JD 1959; Naval Justice Sch, Certificate 1973; NY Univ, Appellate Judge Course 1977; Amer Acad of Jud Educ, Appellate Judge Course 1978; Harvard Law Sch, Prog Instruction for Lawyers 1980. **CAREER:** Private Law Practice, Daytona Beach FL 1959-66; City of Daytona Beach, contract consul 1963-66; US Attorney, asst Jacksonville FL 1966; US Atty for the Middle Dist of FL, first asst 1967-71; Middle Dist of FL, US magistrate 1971-75; Supreme Court of FL, justice 1975-79; US Court of Appeals for the 5th Circuit, US circuit judge 1979-81; US Court of Appeals for the 11th Circuit, US circuit judge 1981-. **ORGANIZATIONS:** Mem FL Bar, Amer Bar Assn, Natl Bar Assn; bd dir Amer Judicature Soc; mem Jacksonville Bar Assn; mem DW Perkins Bar Assn; mem FL Chap of Natl Bar Assn; mem Phi Delta Phi Legal Frat, Phi Alpha Delta Legal Frat, Omega Psi Phi Frat. **HONORS/ACHIEVEMENTS:** Stetson Law Sch Dr Laws 1980; FL Memorial Coll Honoris Causa Dr Laws 1976; Howard Univ Post Grad Achievement Awd 1977; High Risk Awd State Action Cncl1977; President's Citation Cook Co Bar Assn 1977; Most Outstanding Citizen Broward Co Natl Bar Assn 1976; Bicentennial Awd FL A&M Univ 1976; Comm SvcsAwd Edward Waters Coll 1976; An Accolate for Juristic Distinction Tampa Urban League 1975; Medallion for Human Relations Bethune Cookman 1975; Man of the YrAwd FL Jax Club 1974; Who's Who in the S & SW; Who's Who in American Law; the American Bench; Who's Who in Amer; Notable Amers; Notable Black Amers; firstblack person apptd to the highest court of a state since reconstruction; first black person elected to the highest court of a state; first black person elected to public office in a statewide election in the south; first black person to serve on a federal appellate court in the south; several publs including "Criminal Law Survey-1978" Univ of Miami Law Review; "1978 Developments in FL Law" 1979; "Pre-Trial Discovery in Criminal Cases" Fedl Judicial Ctr Library 1974. **MILITARY SERVICE:** AUS 1st lt 1954-56; USMCR lt col 1977-. **BUSINESS ADDRESS:** Judge, 11th Circuit Ct of Appeals, PO Box 10429, Tallahassee, FL 32302.

HATCHETT, PAUL ANDREW
Bank executive. **PERSONAL:** Born May 27, 1925, Clearwater, FL; married Pearlie Young; children: Mrs Paulette Simms, Mrs Pamela Hunnicutt, Paul A II. **EDUCATION:** Hampton Inst Hhmptn VA, BS 1951; FL A&MUniv Tlhs, MEd. **CAREER:** Clearwater Federal Savings & Loan, asst vice pres 1978-, personnel dir mktg 1972-78; Pinellas Co School System FL, teachar admin 1951-71. **ORGANIZATIONS:** Pres Clrwtr Kwns Club E 1974-; dir Clrwtr Slvtn Army 1973-76; chmn Pinellas Co Hsng Athrty 1974-; bd of trsts St Ptrsbrg Jr Coll 1978-; bd of trsts Med Cntr Hosp 1978-. **HONORS/ACHIEVEMENTS:** Serv award St Ptrsbrg Jr Coll; serv award Pinellas Co Hsng Auth 1979. **MILITARY SERVICE:** AUS 1st lt korean cnflct. **BUSINESS ADDRESS:** PO Box 4608, Clearwater, FL 34618.

HATCHETT, WILLIAM F. (BUCKY)
Personnel/training executive. **PERSONAL:** Son of William F. Hatchett; married Ora; children: Craig, Kimberley, Karen. **EDUCATION:** Rutgers Univ, BS 1950. **CAREER:** Verona Publ Schools, staff; Eastern PA League, pro basketball; McCoy Job Corps Ctr Sparta WI, set up & oper recreation & phys ed prog; RCA Corp, mgr 1966-68, employment admin & resources 1966-; Performance Training Inc, vice pres 1987-. **ORGANIZATIONS:** Consult & presentations Moods & Attitudes Black Man; past mem Lions Club; past dir Little League Prog; past bd of dir ARC; former commiss State NJ Publ Broadcasting Auth; adv council Econ Career Ed, State Bds Ed, Higher Ed; mem EDGES Group Inc; past mem Student Council, Crown & Scroll, Cap & Skull; chmn Natl Urban League, Whitney M Young Jr Training Center. **HONORS/ACHIEVEMENTS:** 1st black elected pres Sr Class; former record holder 120 yrd high hurdle; Natl Recogn Football, Basketball; 10 Varsity Letters. **MILITARY SERVICE:** AUS 1st lt 1951-53. **BUSINESS ADDRESS:** Vice President, Performance Training, Inc, 118 Federal City Road, Lawrenceville, NJ 08648.

HATHAWAY, ANTHONY, JR.
Staff manager. **PERSONAL:** Born Apr 19, 1921, Edenton, NC; married Etta Hankins; children: Elizabeth, Teresa, Anthony, Roger, Edna, Gary. **CAREER:** NC Mtl Life Ins Co, staff mgr; AME Zion Ch, pastor; Mach Hlpr;R. **ORGANIZATIONS:** Fireman; mem NAACP; Good Nghbrhd Cncl; PTA Nat Ins Assn. **HONORS/ACHIEVEMENTS:** Cldbrst Cert. **MILITARY SERVICE:** AUS staff sgt. **BUSINESS ADDRESS:** PO Box 91, Edenton, NC.

HATHAWAY, MAGGIE MAE
County commissioner. **PERSONAL:** Born Jul 01, 1925, Louisiana; divorced; children: Ondra Lewis. **EDUCATION:** UCLA. **CAREER:** Studied golf under 4 prfls; LA Co, comm on alcoholism; Frederick Douglas Child Devel Cntr, soc wrkr 1967-. **ORGANIZATIONS:** Golf ed LA Sentinel News, 1st blck female golf ed; 1st blck female golfer to become mem Women's Pub Links; 1st blck female to become found of Bev Hills Hollywood NAACP; 1st blck female Commr on Alcoholism, 1st blck female golfer to organize a LA Co Youth Golf Found, donalted $30,000 by LA Co to train minority youth, Minority Asso Golfers, founded the "Image Awds" of Bev Hills NAACP, Image Awds raised $200,000 in past 5 yrs, placed by Comm on Alchlsm in Crts Div 80 to help place Minority Alcoholics in Clinics. **BUSINESS ADDRESS:** Commission on Alcoholism, Los Angeles County, 313 N Figueroa, Los Angeles, CA 90012.

HATTER, HENRY
Engineer. **PERSONAL:** Born May 21, 1935, Livingston, AL; married Barbara King; children: Marcus, Kelly, Henry II. **EDUCATION:** Sgnw Valley Coll, BS 1966; E U, MS Physics 1972. **CAREER:** Buick Mtr Div GMC, sr engr 1973-, chem engr 1965-69; GM, prod supv 1970-73, tech 1971. **ORGANIZATIONS:** Sec Gns Co Rep Pty 1972-76; alt del Nat Conv GOP 1976; Elctrl Coll 1976; 7th dist chmn GOP 1977, 1978; chmn Old Nwsbys Bck Mtr Div 1976; bdof dir Old Nwsbys; Gns Co Bcntnl Comm; Flint Riv Beautif Wrkshp; Clio Bcntnl Comm 1975; mem MI Trvl Commn 1979; vice pres Old Nwsbys of Gns Co 1979;rep GM Area Wide C of C. **HONORS/ACHIEVEMENTS:** MI Snt Cit G Rckwl 1974; nom Awrd of Exclnc GM 1977, 1979; Dstngshd Almns Awrd Sgnw Vly Coll 1978. **BUSINESS ADDRESS:** Sen Eng Buick Motor Div GMC, 902 E Hamilton St, Flint, MI 48550.

HATTON, BARBARA R.
Educator. **PERSONAL:** Born Jun 04, 1941, LaGrange, GA; divorced; children: Kera. **EDUCATION:** BS 1962; MA 1966; MEA 1970; PhD 1976. **CAREER:** Tuskegee Inst, dean school of educ; Atlanta Public School System, teacher; Howard Univ, counselor; Federal City Coll Washington, asst dir, admin asst, dean student servs; Stanford Urban Rural Inst; assoc dir; Stanford Univ School of Educ, acting asst prof educ; Stanford Urban Coalition Task Force on Educ, 1974. **ORGANIZATIONS:** Com Yearbook 1974-75; chprsn Ravenswood City Sch Dist bd trust; co-directed Iniative Imprvmnt Educ Governance 1973; East Palo Alto; vol comm activities. **HONORS/ACHIEVEMENTS:** EPDA flw 1969-71; NDEA Flw 1965-66. **BUSINESS ADDRESS:** Dean, Tuskegee University, School of Education, Tuskegee, AL 36088.

HAUGABROOK, JOHN R.
Business executive. **PERSONAL:** Born Nov 03, 1931, Montezuma, GA; son of Robert Haugabrook and Elnora Harris Haugabrook; married Ivradell W; children: Kathy Elaine, Karen Renee. **EDUCATION:** FL A&M Univ, BS 1958; IN Univ, MBA 1965. **CAREER:** FL A&M Univ Hosp Tallahassee, sr accnt 1958-59, bus mgr 1959-64; Jewel Food Stores, trainee 1965-66, personnel mgr 1966-67, resident suprv 1967-68, asst div sales mgr 1968-69, dist mgr 1969-75, grocery oper mgr 1975, vice pres area oper 1975-80; vice pres personnel oper 1980-82; vice pres training & commun, 1982-84. **ORGANIZATIONS:** Exec comm Jackson Park Hosp Bd of Dir; mem Policy Bd Inroads Chgo, mem, treas FL A&M Univ Alumni Chicago Chapt; bus adv council Chicago Urban League; mem Natl Urban Affairs Council, Chicago Chap Urban Affairs Council; vice pres Community Affairs Jewel Food Stores 1984-1985; exec vice pres Jackson Park Hospital & M.C. 1985-; Black MBA Assoc Natl Assoc of Health Services Executives, Ill Hospital Assn; Metro Chicago Health Council Life member NAACP, Indiana Univ Alumni Assn. **HONORS/ACHIEVEMENTS:** Commendation Natl Alliance of Businessmen 1972; Spec Recog Awd Malcolm X Coll 1972; Wol Workers Awd Cosmopolitan C of C 1972; WJPC Great Guy Awd 1974; Metro YMCA Black Achievers Awd 1974; Wildwood/JRE Lee High School Hall of Fame. **MILITARY SERVICE:** AUS pfc 1952-54. **HOME ADDRESS:** 9137 Dr Korczak Terrace, Skokie, IL 60076.

HAUGHTON, JAMES G.
Physician, director. **PERSONAL:** Born Mar 30, 1925, Panama City; married Vivian; children: James Jr, Paula. **EDUCATION:** Pacific Union Coll, BA 1947; Loma Linda Univ, MD 1950; Unity Hosp, Intern 1949-50, Fellowship 1951-55; NYU Med Sch, postgrad 1959-60; NY City Health Dept, Resident 1960-62; Columbia Univ, MPH 1962. **CAREER:** Private Pract, physician 1952-66; New York City Health Dept, child health clinician 1958-60; Demonstration Proj, asst dir 1962; New York City Health Dept, asst exec dir 1962-63, dir med care serv indigent & med indigent aged 1963-65, exec dir med care serv 1965-66; New York City Dept Hosp & Med Welfare, first dep commr 1966; New York City Health Serv Adminstrn, first dep admin 1966-70; Cook Co Hosp, dir 1970-71; Cook Co Health & Hosp Gov Commn, exec dir 1970-79; Charles R Drew Postgrad Med Schl, vice pres finance and admin 1980-83; City of Houston, dir public health 1983-85; City of Houston, dir Health & Human Services 1985-. **ORGANIZATIONS:** Mem Amer & IL Hosp Assn; Amer Pub Health Assn; Cncl Urban Health Providers; mem Chicago Hosp Cncl; Com Natl Health Ins; DHEW; Emerg Med Serv Commn; Harvard Univ Adv Com Inst Med Chicago; Natl Urban League; Adv Cncl on Aging; Amer Hosp Assn; AMA; Hospice Inc; Human Serv Inst; IL Hosp Assn; Inst Med & Natl Acad Scis; Natl Urban Coalition; Econ Club Chicago; US Conf of Local Health Officers; TX Med Assn; Harris County Med Assoc. **HONORS/ACHIEVEMENTS:** Merit Award NY City Pub Health Assn 1964; Achvmnt Award Immigrants Serv League 1971; Award Merit Richard T Crane Evening Sch 1971; Hon D Sc Chicago Med Sch 1971; Outstanding Devotion & Contbns Pub Health 1971; IL Assn Clinical Lab 1971; Health Award Woodlawn Orgn 1971; James B Anderson Jr Award Montford Point Marine Assn 1971; Black Man Month Holy Angels Ch 1971; Humanitarian Award Natl Assn Health Serv Exec 1972; Natl Register Prom Amer & Intl Notables 1973; Image Award League Black Women 1974; Dr Mary McLeod Bethune Award natl Cncl Negro Women 1972; matthew B Rosenhaus Lecture Amer Pub Hlth Assn 1974; Award in Apprec of Devoted & Inval Serv Rendered to Res of Chicago & Cook Co Health Awareness Cncl Chicago 1979; Merit Award for Long & courageous Serv to Chicago & Cook Co Lu Palmer Found 1979; Award for Except Perf as Exec Dir of Health & Hosps Governing Comm of Cook Co 1970-79; Recogn of Disting Efforts on Behalf of People of Coo Co & Outstanding Achievements in Pub Health Admin Health & Hosps Govern Commn of Cook Co 1979. **MILITARY SERVICE:**

USNR med corps 1956-58. **BUSINESS ADDRESS:** Dir Publ Hlth & Humn Serv, City of Houston, 1115 N MacGregor Dr, Ste 178, Houston, TX 77030.

HAUGSTAD, MAY KATHERYN (NEE HILL)
Plant physiologist. **PERSONAL:** Born Oct 18, 1937, Dallas, TX; married Paul Haugstad; children: Monika Moss, Veronica Moss, Karsten. **EDUCATION:** So Univ, BS 1959; Yale Univ, MS 1960; Cath Univ, PhD 1971. **CAREER:** Howard Univ, rsch asst 1961-63, instructor 1963-66; Fed City Coll, asst prof 1968-69; Univ of NH, asst prof 1969-75, dept chmn 1972-73; Univ of Oslo, researcher 1977-. **ORGANIZATIONS:** Mem Delta Sigma Theta Sor, Sigma Xi. **HONORS/ACHIEVEMENTS:** Publ The Effect of Photosynthetic Enhancement on Photorespiration in Sinapis Alba, Physiologia Plantarum 47, 19-24 1979; Determination of Spectral Responses of Photorespiration in Sinapis Alba by CO2 Burst Effect of O2 & CO2 Compensation Conectrations, Photosynthetica 1980; several publ incl, Effect of Abscisic Acid on CO2 Exchange in Lemna Gibba, Yield of Tomato & Maize in Response to Filiar & Root Appl of Triacontanol, Photoinhibition of Photosynthesis, Effect of Light& the Selective Excitation of the Photosystems on Recovery. **BUSINESS ADDRESS:** 8108 Elkhorn Mountain, Austin, TX 78729.

HAUSER, CHARLIE BRADY
Educational administration, legislator. **PERSONAL:** Born Oct 13, 1917, Yadkinville, NC; son of Rev and Mrs DM Hauser; married Lois Elizabeth Brown; children: Lois H Golding, Fay E Hauser. **EDUCATION:** Winston-Salem State Univ, BS 1936-40; Catholic Univ of Amer, 1941; Univ of PA, MS EdD 1946-47, 1956; TX Southern Univ, 1968. **CAREER:** 14th St Elementary School Winston Salem NC, teacher 1940-42; WV State Coll, instr 1947-50; Mary H Wright Elem School, principal 1951-55; Allen Univ, prof 1955-56; Winston-Salem State Univ, prof 1956-77, director of Teacher Educ 1968-76. **ORGANIZATIONS:** Bd mem Inter Municipal Coop Comm 1958-60; bd mem Dixie Classic Fair 1978-82; trustee Forsyth Tech Coll 1977-; chmn bd Northwestern Reg ALANC; life mem/life mem chmn NAACP; chmn bd Patterson Ave Branch YMCA, bd Mental Health Assn Forsyth Cty; rep NC Gen Assembly 39th Dist 1983-84, 67th Dist 1985-86; life mem, NEA and Omega Psi Phi Fraternity; Forsyth Nursing Home Community Advisory Comm, Community Corrections Resources, Inc; Urban Arts Advisory Committee. **HONORS/ACHIEVEMENTS:** Cited by Bd of Governors of Univ NC 1977; Inducted Winston-Salem State Univ & CIAA/Sports Hall of Fame; Omega Man of the Year 1966 & 1984; plaques from various charitable, civic, educ and religious assns. **MILITARY SERVICE:** AUS staff sgt; ETO Ribbon with 5 Battle Stars, Good Conduct Medal; 1942-45. **HOME ADDRESS:** 2072 K Court Ave, Winston-Salem, NC 27105.

HAWK, CHARLES N., JR.
Educator. **PERSONAL:** Born Aug 10, 1931, Madison Hts, VA; married Amarylyiss Murphy; children: Charles Nathaniel III, Lloyd Spurgeon, Natalyn Nicole. **EDUCATION:** Northwestern Univ School of Ed, BS 1953; Loyola Univ, MA 1966. **CAREER:** Chicago Public Schools, teacher 1953-56; Hoke Smith High Scool Atlanta, principal 1957-. **ORGANIZATIONS:** Mem Natl, Atlanta & GA Elem Prins Assoc, Natl Assoc Sec School Prins, NEA, Atlanta & GA Assoc Ed, Alpha Phi Alpha, Phi Delta Kappa, Mason,; bd mgrs YMCA; bd dirs Ralph C Robinson Boys Club, BSA. **HONORS/ACHIEVEMENTS:** Outstanding Leadership Awd Boy Scouts Atlanta Reg 1969; Outstanding Leadership Awd YMCA 1974; Outstanding Leadership Awd Alpha Phi Alpha 1975. **BUSINESS ADDRESS:** Principal, Hoke Smith High School, 535 Hill St SE, Atlanta, GA 30312.

HAWK, CHARLES NATHANIEL, III
Attorney & educational administrator. **PERSONAL:** Born Oct 25, 1957, Atlanta, GA. **EDUCATION:** Morehouse Coll, BA cum laude 1979; Georgetown Univ Law Center JD 1982. **CAREER:** Cooper & Weintraub PC, assoc 1982-83; Morehouse Coll, dir office of alumni affairs. **ORGANIZATIONS:** Sec Deacon Bd Friendship Baptist Church 1978-; mem Council for Advancement and Support of Educ 1983-; chmn United Way Campaign Morehouse Coll 1983-; mem GA Bar Assn 1983-; of counsel Law Firm Cooper & Assoc 1983-; legal counsel Natl Black Alumni Hall of Fame 1983-; legal counsel Hank Aaron Found Inc 1984-; legal counsel Council of Natl Alumni Assoc Inc 1984-. **HONORS/ACHIEVEMENTS:** Who's Who in Amer Colleges & Univs 1978 & 1979; writer and dir of "Balls, Balloons, and Butterflies" presented 1981 Washington DC; artistic achievement Georgetown Univ Church Ensemble 1982; writer & dir "Black Gold" 1982 Washington DC; Serv Awd United Negro Coll Fund 1985. **BUSINESS ADDRESS:** Dir of Alumni Affairs, Morehouse College, 830 Westview Dr SW, Atlanta, GA 30314.

HAWKES, DIANA R.
Administrator. **PERSONAL:** Born Sep 11, 1947, Brooklyn, NY; married Alden; children: Kimberly, Tracey. **EDUCATION:** NY Enst of Tech, BFA 1978. **CAREER:** Nassau Co Blck His Mus, mus supr; Frlnc, cmptr grphcs Oprtr 1978-; WLIW/TV Plnvw NY, cmr prsn nws shw 1978-79; NYIT Video Cntr Old Wstbry NY, flm tech 1977-78; WLIW/TV 21 Grdn Cty NY, prod asst 1975; Nassau Co Yth Bd Mnl NY, dnc spl 1968-72; Rsvlt Mtl Hlth Cntr, afrcn am his lectr 1976-77; Jazz Hrtg Assn, afrcn am his consult 1977-79. **ORGANIZATIONS:** Mem Oystr Bay Arts Cncl 1977-79; mem consult Afrcn Am Hrtg Assn of Lng Islnd 1978-; vice pres bd of dir Enly Lowe Glry 1980. **HONORS/ACHIEVEMENTS:** Aprctn for Dstnctv Contrib Smthsn Inst 1974-75; Aprctn for Serv Art Wrkshp Glry Mus Rsvlt 1975; Otstndng Twn of Hmpstd Bcntnl Commn 1976; Aprctnfor Serv Jazz Hrtg Soc NY 1977. **BUSINESS ADDRESS:** Nassau Co Black History Museum, 106 A Main St, Hempstead, NY 11550.

HAWKINS, ALEXANDER A.
Educator. **PERSONAL:** Born Sep 03, 1923, Gainesville, FL; married Mable Emanuel; children: Alexander Jr, Clinton M. **EDUCATION:** Bethune-Cookman Coll, AA 1944; Morehouse Coll, AB 1946; Univ of Pittsburgh School of Social Work, MSW 1949; Univ of Pittsburgh School of Educ, PhD 1970; Mnrv Coll Mnrv Liberia, DD 1967. **CAREER:** Dept of Public Asst Pittsburgh, sr vis 1949-50; Amer Red Cross, caseworker 1951-54; VA Hosp Pittsburgh, counselor social worker 1954-60; African Methodist Episcopal Church, ordained elder 1955-; Salvation Army Pittsburgh, supr of crctnl serv 1960-62; PA Bureau of Correction, dir social serv 1962-64; St Petersburgh, dir of comm relations 1967-68; CMHR Center Inst, soc caseworker of med dept of psy 1964-67; Univ of Pittsburgh School of Social Work, asst prof chief of social svc, assoc prof chmn juvenile & adult criminal justice specialization 1972-; Univ of Pittsburgh, chairperson. **ORGANIZATIONS:** Mem Amer Ortho Assn, Council on Social Work, Urban League; consult PA Bur of Correction Central Office, Inst of Pittsburgh Pstrl Inst 1971-75; co-plannerof conf Univ of Pittsburgh 1977; mem Public Safety Comm 1978; mem Bd of Commiss 1978-. **HONORS/ACHIEVEMENTS:** Key To The City Of St Ptrsbrg FL; lstd Comm Ldrs in Am/Dict of Blck Am Biog/Dict of Intl Biog/Who's Who Amng Blk Am/Who's Who in the E; various publs. **MILITARY SERVICE:** AUS pvt 1942-43. **BUSINESS ADDRESS:** Chairperson, University of Pittsburgh, Justice Social Problem Area, Pittsburgh, PA 15260.

HAWKINS, ANDRE
Educational administrator. **PERSONAL:** Born Aug 01, 1953, Jacksonville, FL; son of Sylvester Hawkins and Emma J Hawkins; married Annette Campbell; children: Anika, Alicia, Antoinette. **EDUCATION:** Univ of So CA, BA History 1971-75; FL Atlantic Univ, MEd Admin & Super, EdS Admin & Super 1976-85. **CAREER:** FL School for Boys, occupational counselor 1975-76, classroom teacher 1976-79; Indian River Comm Coll, academic counselor 1979, dir of educ 1979-82, dir of instructional serv 1982-86, asst dean of instruction 1986-. **ORGANIZATIONS:** Mem Univ of S CA Fla Atlantic Univ Alumni Assn 1976-; mem New Hope Lodge #450 1981-; mem Southern Regional Council on Black Amer Affairs 1981-; mem FL Adult Educ Assn 1981-; mem FL Adult & Comm Educ Assn 1982-; mem Amer Assn of Adult & Continuing Educ FACC 1982-; mem Ft Pierce Chamber of Comm St Luce Leadership I 1983-; pres 1986, chmn 1987 FL Assn of Comm Colls Indian River CC Chapt; bd of dirs St Lucie Co Learn to Read Literary Prog 1985-87; bd dirs FL Assn of Comm Colls 1987, St Lucie Co YMCA 1987; bd of dir, NY Mets Booster Club, 1987-; second vice pres, Florida Assn of Conn Colleges 1988, vice pres, 1989; bd of dir, Indian River Comm Mental Health Assn Inc 1989-; treasurer, Martin Luther King Jr Commemorative Comm,1989-. **BUSINESS ADDRESS:** Asst Dean of Instruction, Indian River Community College, 3209 Virginia Ave, Fort Pierce, FL 34981.

HAWKINS, AUGUSTUS F.
Congressman. **PERSONAL:** Born Aug 31, 1907, Shreveport, LA; married Elsie. **EDUCATION:** Univ of CA, AB Economics 1931; attended grad classed Univ So CA Inst of Govt. **CAREER:** Elected to CA State Assembly 1934; US House of Reps 29th Dist of CA, congressman 1962-. **ORGANIZATIONS:** In Congress, chmn House Educ & Labor Comm, chmn House Sub-comm Elementary, Secondary, and Vocational Ed, sponsored Economic Oppor Act, Vocational Educ Act, Equal Employment Oppor Sect of 1963 Civil Rights Act, sponsored the Humphrey-Hawkins Full Employment & Balanced Growth Act, Pregnancy Disability Act, JobTraining Partnership Act, Youth Incentive Employment Act, Effective Schs Development in Educ Act; involved in many comm action progs including SE LA Improvement Action Council founder; Methodist; Mason. **HONORS/ACHIEVEMENTS:** Authored or co-authored more than 300 laws including one establishing CA low-cost housing prog one which removed racial designations from all state documents. **BUSINESS ADDRESS:** Congressman, US House of Rep 29th Dist CA, 2371 House Office Bldg, Washington, DC 20515.

HAWKINS, BENNY F., SR.
Dentist, periodontist. **PERSONAL:** Born Feb 27, 1931, Chattanooga, TN; son of Bennie Hawkins and Corinne Hawkins; married E Marie Harvey; children: Benny F Jr, Christopher Thomas. **EDUCATION:** Morehouse Coll, BS 1952; Meharry Med Coll, DDS 1958; Univ of IA, MS 1972, Certificate in Periodontics 1972. **CAREER:** USAF Dental Corps, lt col (retired) 1958-78; Univ of IA Coll of Dentistry, assoc prof periodontics 1978-. **ORGANIZATIONS:** Vestry Trinity Episcopal Church Iowa City 1980-83; bd dirs Iowa City Rotary Club 1982-84; Human Rights Commission Iowa City 1983-86; vice pres Univ Dist Dental Soc 1984-85; pres Iowa Soc of Periodontology 1985-86; mem Amer Dental Assn, Amer Acad of Periodontology, Amer Assn of Dental Schools, Intl Assn for Dental Rsch; Omicron Kappa Upsilon Honorary Dental Fraternity, Iowa, president 1988-89. **HONORS/ACHIEVEMENTS:** Omicron Kappa Upsilon Hon Dental Frat Iowa 1980; Fellow Intl College of Dentists 1984; Distinguished Alumni of the Yr Awd (Meharry) Natl Assn for Equal Opportunity in Higher Educ 1986. **MILITARY SERVICE:** USAF Dental Corps lt col 1958-78; Air Force Commendation Medal 1976. **BUSINESS ADDRESS:** Peridontics Graduate Dir, Univ of IA, Coll of Dentistry Periodontics Dept, Iowa City, IA 52242.

HAWKINS, CALVIN D.
Attorney, clergyman. **PERSONAL:** Born Jun 14, 1945, Brooklyn; married Lennie E James; children: Alia, Alex, Jason. **EDUCATION:** Huntington Coll, AB 1967; Howard U, JD 1970; Wesley Theol Sem, MDiv 1974. **CAREER:** US Dept Just, atty 1971-74; Am U, asso chapl 1971-72; US Dept Just, comm rel splst 1971; Supreme Ct IN, admitted 1971; So Dist Ct IN, 1971; DC Ct Appeals, 1973; Dist Ct DC, 1973; Untd Ct Appeals DC, 1973; Supreme Ct USA 1974; Shropshire & Allen, Gary, IN, atty 1974-. **ORGANIZATIONS:** Mem Am IN & Gary Bar Assns; DC Bar Unified; Thurgood Marshall Law Assn; ABA, Council on Urban State Local Govt Law Section; Huntington Coll, bd of trustees; Indiana Republican Platform Comm. **HONORS/ACHIEVEMENTS:** Nom Gov's Awd outstndg black coll student IN Civil Rights Comm 1965; social theol awd Martin Luther King Jr Hood Theol Sem 1971; Jonathan M Daniels Fellow Awd 1974; alumnus of yr awd Huntington Coll 1975; fellow awd Chicago Theol Sem 1976. **BUSINESS ADDRESS:** Reverend, Shropshire & Hawkins, 2009 Broadway, Gary, IN 46407.

HAWKINS, CONNIE
Retired professional basketball player. **PERSONAL:** Born Jul 17, 1942. **EDUCATION:** Univ of IA. **CAREER:** Pitts, bsktbl plyr; MN, bsktbl plyr; Phnx Suns, bsktbl plyr 1969-73; LA Lakers, bsktbl plyr 1973-74. **ORGANIZATIONS:** Am Bsktbl Assn 1967-69.

HAWKINS, DORISULA WOOTEN
Educational administrator. **PERSONAL:** Born Nov 15, 1941, Mt Pleasant, TX; married Howard Hawkins; children: Darrell, Derek. **EDUCATION:** Jarvis Christian Coll, BS 1962; East TX State Univ, attended 1965; Prairie View A&M Univ, MS 1967; TX A&M Univ, attended 1970; Univ of Houston, EdD 1975. **CAREER:** Jarvis Coll, sec & asst public relations dir 1962-63; Roxton School Dist, instructor business 1963-66; Prairie View A&M Univ, assoc prof head general business dept 1966-. **ORGANIZATIONS:** Adv bd Milady Publishing Co; exec bd mem TX Assn of Black Personnel in Higher Educ 1978-83; bd mem TX Bus Educ (TBEA) Assn 1978-83; pres Alpha Kappa Alpha 1982-85; chmn TX Business Thcr Educ Cncl 1985-; mem Natl Bus Educ Assoc; mem Jarvis Christian Coll Bd of Trustees, pres Natl Alumni Assoc 1986. **HONORS/ACHIEVEMENTS:** Dist Business Tchr of the Yr TBEA 1981; Disting Alumnus Jarvis Coll 1982; nominee State Tchr of Yr TBEA 1982; "Can Your Office Administration be Justified" TX Business Educator 1979; Disting Alumni Citation (NAFEO)

1986; listed in Who's Who in the South & Southwest 1986, Who's Who in America 1986, Personalities of America 1987. **BUSINESS ADDRESS:** Head, General Business Dept, Prairie View A&MUniv, Hobart Taylor Hall Rm 222, Prairie View, TX 77446.

HAWKINS, ELDRIDGE
Assemblyman, attorney. **PERSONAL:** Born Sep 04, 1940, Orange, NJ. **EDUCATION:** Rutgers U, BS Polit Sci 1962; Seton Hall Law Sch, JD 1966. **CAREER:** St of NJ, st asmblymn; Hwkns & Rossi Esqs, atty; City of E Orng, frmr pros; US Eql Emplymnt Opp Comm, spl lgl cnslr; Nwrk Lgl Svcs, staff atty; E Orng Dem Co Com, lgl cnsl. **ORGANIZATIONS:** Dir Monmth Co Lgl Serv Proj; admtd to prac bfr NJ & US Sprm Cts; mem 3rd Ward Dem Club; E Orng Dem Club; Essx Co Wlfr Bd Cswrkr; dir E Orng Jycs; Nat Conf of Chrst & Jews; trst Day Care Comm Cntr; trst Vctry Hs Comm Actn Prog Com; mem Cncrnd Lgl Asso; mem Nat Assn for Comm Dev; mem NJ St Dem Plcy Cncl; chmn E Orng Hrt Fund Camp. **HONORS/ACHIEVEMENTS:** Won Jr Nat AAU Brd & Trip Jmp Chmpnshps NJ St AAU Chmpn in Brd & Trpl Jmps; Recip 1972 E Orng Jyc Man of Yr; All Am Ftbl Hon; set sch rcrds in trck. **BUSINESS ADDRESS:** 110 S Munn Ave, East Orange, NJ 07018.

HAWKINS, ERSKINE RAMSAY
Retired musician. **PERSONAL:** Born Jul 26, 1914, Birmingham, AL; married Gloria Dumas. **EDUCATION:** AL State Teachers Coll, 1931. **CAREER:** Concord Hotel, Kiamesha Lake, NY, musical bandleader composer trumpeter 1967-89; RCA, recording artst; Svry Ballroom music; Uproar Hs, music; Ubng Club, music 1934-55; Alabama St & Collgns, bandleader Ella Fitzgerald, accompanist; Nat King Cole, accompanist; Jane Morgan accompanist; Della Reese, accompanist; Billy Daniel, accompanist; Txd Jc, composer 1939. **ORGANIZATIONS:** Inducted as mem Arts Hall of Fame Birmingham; inducted as mem Jazz Hall of Fame Birmingham; mem ASCAP.

HAWKINS, GENE
Educator. **PERSONAL:** Born in Henderson, NC; son of Argenia Hawkins and Roxie Hawkins; divorced. **EDUCATION:** Glassboro State, BS 1955; Temple Univ, MA 1969; Nova Univ, DEd 1976. **CAREER:** Dept Ford Twp Public Schools, math tchr 1955-64, chmn math dept/counselor 1957-67; Gloucester County Coll, dir financial aid 1968-74; The College Board, dir finan aid svcs. **ORGANIZATIONS:** Consultant ETS Upward Bound College Bd 1970-74; consultant Financial Aid Inst 1968-78; consultant HEW 1970-76; staff NJ Assn Coll & Univ Presidents 1982; treasurer Eastern Assn Financial Aid Adm 1973-75; mem Natl Councl Natl Assn Financial Aid Admin 1973-75; exec dir Glou County Economic Devel 1970-72; publicity dir NAACP 1963-66. **HONORS/ACHIEVEMENTS:** Distinguished Alumni Award Glassboro State 1971; Black Student Unity Movement Award Glou County Coll 1970-71; Ten Yr Serv Award College Bd 1985; Distinguished Educator NJFOF Dir Assn 1979; Special Recognition NY Bd Educ 1982; Distinguished Service Award, New Jersey Student Financial Aid Administrators, 1989. **MILITARY SERVICE:** USMC Corpl 1951-53. **HOME ADDRESS:** 3440 Market St, Ste 410, Philadelphia, PA 19104.

HAWKINS, HOWARD P.
Clergyman. **PERSONAL:** Born Oct 19, 1900, Princeton, LA. **EDUCATION:** Wshbrn Coll, BA 1931; Gmmn Theol Sem, BD 1934. **CAREER:** Christ Meth Epis Ch, ret mnstr; Ordnd Elder, 1931; Clrgymn, 45yrs itnrnt svc. **ORGANIZATIONS:** Pres Pasco WA Br NAACP 1962-66; mem Pasco Mnstrl Alli; Tri-Cities Mnstrl Alli; affil with Comm Actn & Com; Bntn-Frnkln Mtl Hlth Assn; Human Rights Com Srved on Ctzns AdvCom of Pasco Sch Dist No 1 1966-69; mem St Jms Chrstn Meth Epis Ch; mem AK-PCFC Conf of CME Ch; VFW. **HONORS/ACHIEVEMENTS:** Mason Recip Am Thtr Mdl; 2 Brnz Bttl Strs; Vctry Mdl; Nat Def Mdl; Krn Serv Mdl; UN Serv Mdl; Armd Frcs Rsrv Mdl; helped to build 2 new chrs. **MILITARY SERVICE:** AUS capt ret 1943-56; chpln.

HAWKINS, JAMES
Educational administrator. **PERSONAL:** Born Jul 02, 1939, Sunflower, MS; married Vivian D; children: Lisa, Linda. **EDUCATION:** Western Michigan Univ, BS 1963; Wayne State Univ, MA 1967; Michigan State Univ, PhD 1972. **CAREER:** Pontiac Public School, teacher 1963-67, project dir 1967-68, principal 1968-72; Jackson MI Public School, asst supt 1973-75, deputy supt 1975-78; Benton Harbor Area School, supt 1978-84; Ypsilanti Public Schools, supt 1984-. **ORGANIZATIONS:** Mem Mayors Urban Entrp Com 1983-84, N Cntrl Regnl Lab 1984-85; State Prntshp Sch Rlthnshp Task Force 1984-85; Kappa Alpha Psi; Rotary Intl; NAACP; pres Mdl Cities Ed Assc 1984-85; mem Gamma Rho Boule 1986; bd of dirs United Way. **HONORS/ACHIEVEMENTS:** Otsdg com serv Benton Harbor Citizens Awrd 1983; man of yr Negro Bus & Prof Womens Clb 1977; guest aprnc Phil Donahue Show 1982; featured Articles People Mag Minimal Skills No Nonsence Ed 1982. **BUSINESS ADDRESS:** Superintendent of Schools, Ypsilanti Pblc Sch, 1885 Packard Rd, Ypsilanti, MI 48197.

HAWKINS, JAMES C.
Director of technical services. **PERSONAL:** Born Mar 26, 1932, Apalachicola, FL; son of Harold Hawkins and Prudence Hawkins; married Gloria M Edmonds; children: Brian, Cynthia. **EDUCATION:** Univ of RI, BSME 1959; Northeastern Univ, MSEM 1971; MIT Sloane Sch 1977. **CAREER:** Rayethon Co & MIT Labs, sr engr 1966-68; Natl Radio Co, mgr of engrg 1968-70; Consult 1971-77; Polaroid Corp, mgr 1973-77, sr mgr 1978-; division mgr 1984; director 1989. **ORGANIZATIONS:** Int & ext consult various organs; past grand knight K of C; mem Actors Guild, ASME; CCD instructor; org & coach basketball team, tennis player, tutor, inst Karate; Vice President, Board of Directors-Chamber of Commerce, Cambridge MA, Corporator-East Cambridge Savings Bank. **HONORS/ACHIEVEMENTS:** Scholarship LaSalle Acad; Cambridge Chamber of Commerce, pres 1989. **MILITARY SERVICE:** USAF 1951-55. **BUSINESS ADDRESS:** Director of Technical Services, Polaroid Corp, 750 Main St-1C, Cambridge, MA 02139.

HAWKINS, JOHN RUSSELL, III
Public affairs officer (AUS). **PERSONAL:** Born Sep 07, 1949, Washington, DC; married Michelle Mary Rector; children: John R IV, Mercedes Nicole. **EDUCATION:** Howard Univ, BA 1971; Amer Univ, MPA 1976; Amer Univ Law Sch, JD 1979; Univ of London Law Faculty England, independent study. **CAREER:** Federal Trade Commn and US EEOC, personnel mgmt spec 1972-75; Pentagon Counterintelligence Forces US Army, admin ofcr 1975-77; Theoseus T Clayton Law Firm, law clerk 1979-80; US EEOC Public Affairs, asst dir for Public Affairs 1981-85; AUS Public Affairs, major 1986-. **ORGANIZATIONS:** Mem Phi Delta Phi Intl Law Frat 1978-; pres and chief counsel HRH Commercial Farms Inc of NC 1979-; cub scout leader Pack 442 1985-; treas St John the Baptist Home School Assoc 1986-; mem Kappa Alpha Psi. **HONORS/ACHIEVEMENTS:** Sustained Superior Performance Federal Govt 1979-85; editorial writer for Washington Informer & Washington Afro 1985-86; Outstanding Young Men of Amer 1986. **MILITARY SERVICE:** AUS major 10 yrs; Army Commendation Medal, Army Achievement Medal. **HOME ADDRESS:** 2123 Apple Tree Lane, Silver Spring, MD 20904. **BUSINESS ADDRESS:** Public Affairs Officer, Dept of the Army, Pentagon, Washington, DC 20310.

HAWKINS, LAWRENCE C.
Educator, management consultant. **PERSONAL:** Born Mar 20, 1919, Greenville, SC; son of Waymor Hawkins and Etta Hawkins; married Earline Thompson; children: Lawrence Charles Jr, Wendel Earl. **EDUCATION:** Univ of Cincinnati, BA History 1941, BEd 1942, MEd 1951, EdD 1970; Univ of Cincinnati, AA (Hon) 1970, Wilmington College. **CAREER:** Cincinnati Public School, cert school supt, secondary teacher 1945-52, school principal, dir 1952-67; Eastern MI Univ Ypsilanti, visiting asst prof 1955-60; Cincinnati Public Schools, asst supt 1967-69; Univ of Cincinnati, dean 1969-75, vice pres 1975-77, sr vice pres 1977-84; Omni-Man Inc, president, CEO 1981-. **ORGANIZATIONS:** Bd of dir Wilimgton OH Coll 1980, Inroads/Cincinnati 1981; bd of dir Bethesda Hosp Deaconess Assn Cincinnati 1980; vice chmn Greater Cincinnati TV Ed Found WECT-TV 1983; co-chmn Cincinnati Area Natl Conf of Christians & Jews 1980;mem, Kappa Alpha Psi; bd of trustees Childrens Home 1978; adv bd on policy Cincinnati Council on World Affairs; mem, bd of directors, Mount St Joseph College 1989-. **HONORS/ACHIEVEMENTS:** Awd of Merit Cincinnati Area United Appeal 1955, 1973; Certificate Presidents Council of Youth Opportunity 1968; City Cincinnati 1968; Charles P Taft Gumption Awd 1984; mem, Sigma Pi Phi, Kappa Delta Pi, Phi Delta Kappa; Cincinnati Area Natl Conference of Christians and Jews, Distinguished Service Award, 1988; Great Living Cincinnatian Award, Greater Cincinnati Chamber of Commerce 1989. **MILITARY SERVICE:** USAAF, lietenant, 1942-45. **BUSINESS ADDRESS:** President, Omni-Man Inc, 3909 Reading Rd, Cincinnati, OH 45229.

HAWKINS, MARY L.
Vocational counselor. **PERSONAL:** Born in Columbus, GA; daughter of Bruno Hawkins and Eva P Hawkins-Robinson. **EDUCATION:** Meharry Med Coll, Cert Dntl Hygn 1961; MI St U; Western MI U, BS 1976, MA 1979, SPADA, 1985; MI St Univ, rehabilitation cert candidate. **CAREER:** MI Rehabiliation, Kalamazoo MI, substance abuse and vocational rehabilitation counselor, 1988—; Brrn Co Hlth Dept, sr dntl hygnst beg 1967; Priv Prac, dntl hygnst 1961-67. **ORGANIZATIONS:** Pres Nat Dntl Hygnst Assn 1973-75, pres elct 1971-73, vice pres 1970-71; mem Am Dntl Hygnst Assn 1961-; Business and Professional Women; Amer Assn of Univ Women; Natl Counselors Assn; Meharry Alumni Assn; spl consult Mnrty Affrs Com 1973-75; Tri-Co Hlth Plnrs Com 1970-75; mem NAACP 1963-; YWCA 1965-; Blossomland United Way, 1983-89; Operation PUSH, 1980—; Mrch of Dms 1970. **HONORS/ACHIEVEMENTS:** Outstanding Dental Hygienist, Meharry's Alumni 1974; President's Award, Natl Dental Hygienists Assn, 1975; won 1st EEOC-Detroit Dist Office job discrimination suit, 1988. **BUSINESS ADDRESS:** Vocational Counselor, Michigan Rehabilitation, 4210 South Westnedge Ave, Kalamazoo, MI 49008.

HAWKINS, MORRIS M.
Executive committeeman. **PERSONAL:** Born Sep 12, 1920, Lake Vlg, AR; divorced; children: Rese, Carolyn, Warren, Madelyn, Mauricia. **EDUCATION:** US Army Clerical School; Tucker Business Coll. **CAREER:** Rcrd Cntr, 1946-48; VA Ins Div, 1948-49; US Pstl Serv, 1949-; Velda Village Hills, alderman 1981-85, mayor 1983-84; Amvet Post 67 St Louis, MO, from ways and means chmn to post commander, represented MO Amvets to Washington, DC 1974-78, presently trustee and pres of the building housing for post 67. **ORGANIZATIONS:** Mbr Prince of Hall Mason; Lodge Frank J Brown 80; Shriners Medinah Temple 39; 9th Dist Commander Amvets (3 terms). **HONORS/ACHIEVEMENTS:** Honorary Attorney General State of LA 1970-74; Distinguished Citizens Awd St Louis Argus Newspaper 1978; The White Clover Awd; The Distinguished Service Awd; listed Honorable Americans from SC, Biography Book of Outstanding Amers. **MILITARY SERVICE:** AUS 1944-46; 2 Bronze Stars; Unit Citation. **BUSINESS ADDRESS:** Amvet Post 67, 5022 San Francisco, St Louis, MO 63115.

HAWKINS, MURIEL A.
Educational admin. & educator. **PERSONAL:** Born Apr 22, 1946, Norfolk, VA; daughter of George Hawkins and Frieda Robinson-Hawkins; children: Jamal Scott. **EDUCATION:** Univ of Health Scis Chicago Med Sch, BS 1974; The Citadel, MEd 1979; Loyola Univ of Chicago, PhD 1988. **CAREER:** Meharry Med Coll, radiographer/instructor 1967-70; Cook Co Hosp, clinical instructor 1970-76; Med Univ of SC/VA Med Ctr, instructor allied health 1976-79; Chicago State Univ, admin & asst prof 1980-. **ORGANIZATIONS:** Mem Phi Delta Kappa; mem Amer Soc Allied Health Prof; mem IL Soc Allied Health Prof; mem Amer Educ Rsch Assn; mem Midwest Rsch Assn; mem Assn of Supv & Curric Developers; mem Natl Soc of Allied Health; mem IL Comm on Black Concerns in Higher Educ; site visitor Joint Review Comm on Accreditation Radiography 1977-; recruitment specialist Clark Coll 1983; student affairs consultant/counseling Natl Coll of Educ 1984-88; enrollment mgt consult West Chester Univ 1985. **HONORS/ACHIEVEMENTS:** Kellogg Fellow Amer Soc of Allied Health Professions 1983-84; "Role Modeling as a Strategy for the Retention of Minorities in Health Professions" presentation at annual ICBC meeting 1983 & Midwest Allied Health Symposium 1984 subsequently published in Journal of Ethnic Concerns; "Deaning in the Allied Health Professions," presentation at the ASAHP Annual Meeting Pittsburgh, PA 1986; ICEOP Fellow 1986-87; "Successful Coping Strategies for Black Graduate Students" Natl Conf of the AAHE Chicago, IL 1987. **HOME ADDRESS:** 810 S Austin, Oak Park, IL 60304. **BUSINESS ADDRESS:** Admin & Asst Prof, Chicago State University, 9501 S King Dr, Chicago, IL 60628.

HAWKINS, REGINALD A.
Dentist, minister. **PERSONAL:** Born Nov 11, 1923, Beaufort, NC; married Catherine Elizabeth Richardson; children: Pauletta, Reginald Jr, Wayne, Lorena. **EDUCATION:** Johnson C Smith Univ, BS 1948, BD 1956, MDiv 1973; Howard Univ, DDS 1948. **CAREER:** Private Practice Charlotte NC, dentist 1948-; United Presbyterian Church, minister 1956-. **ORGANIZATIONS:** Chmn bd SE Reg Investment Corp; past pres Old N State Dental Soc, Charlotte Dental Soc; chmn Voter Reg Dr Mecklenburg Cty, Mecklenburg Org on Pol Affairs; guest lectr Princeton Univ 1966; fellow Royal Soc of Health 1973; mem Cncl on Admin Serv for United Presybterian Church USA; moderator/interim pastor of several churches in

Catawba Presbytery; one of founders/mem Commn on Religion and Race of the United Presbyterian Church USA. **HONORS/ACHIEVEMENTS:** Kappa Alpha Psi Awd 1960; Middle East Prov Outstanding Achievement Awd; Dentist of the Year 1962; Omega Citizen of the Year Alpha Kappa Alpha 1962; Hon Drof Laws 1962; Scroll of Honor 1964; testified before US Sen Sub-Com on poverty 1965; Bruce W Klunder Meml Awd 1966; Alumni Awd Outstanding Achievement 1967; gubernat cand NC Dem pri 1968; Black Econ Devel Counc SBA 1968; Citation of Merit Old North St Dental Soc 1968; Awd Outstanding Civic Cont 1968; Dist Serv Awd Alpha Kappa Alpha Sor 1969; sued NC Dental Soc resulting in desegregation; sued NC Dept of Human Resources for reinstatement of medicaid benef its to adult dental patients & correction of other iniquities 1978; filed 1st civil rights suit against a YMCA which resulted in the admission of Negroes to all facilites; litigant in the case challenging NC Pearsall Plan allowing state grants for students to private segregated schools; litigant against City of Charlotte challenging zoning laws, public discrimination & jobs; litigant against Charlotte-Mecklenburg School Bd for discrim. **BUSINESS ADDRESS:** Minister, United Presbyterian Church, 951 S Independence Blvd, Charlotte, NC 28208.

HAWKINS, THEODORE F.
Obstetrician, gynecologist. **PERSONAL:** Born Apr 06, 1908, E Orange, NJ; married Shirley R; children: Shirley C, Karen, Theodore Jr. **EDUCATION:** Lincoln U, AB 1931; Meharry Med Coll, MD 1937; Grad Sch Med Univ PA, 1950. **CAREER:** Ob/Gyn, pvt pract present. **ORGANIZATIONS:** Hosp affil Med Coll of PA & Hosp Miser Hosp; dip Am Bd Obs/Gyn; fellow Am Coll Obs/Gyn; fellow Am Coll Surg; mem Philadelphia Co Med Soc; Nat Med Soc; East PA Med Soc; bd YMCA; Wissahickon Boy's Club; Youth Serv; Plann Parenthood; Christian St Y'S Men's Club; NAACP; Med Com Civil Rights. **HONORS/ACHIEVEMENTS:** Dist alumnus Lincoln U; man of yr Chi Delta Mu; dist serv awd St Paul's Bapt Ch.

HAWKINS, WALTER LINCOLN
Engineering consultant. **PERSONAL:** Born Mar 21, 1911, Washington, DC; married Lilyan B Bobo; children: W Gordon, Philip L. **EDUCATION:** Rensselaer Polytechnic Ins, ChE 1932; Howard U, MS 1934; McGill U, PhD 1938; Monclair State Clg & Kean Clg, LLD Hon 1975, 81; Stevens Inst of Tech, DEng Hon 1979; Howard U, DSci 1984. **CAREER:** McGill U, sessnl lctr 1938-41; Bell Lab, mem tech stf 1942-63, supr apld rsrch 1963-72, dept head apld rsrch 1972-74, asst dir chem rsrch lab1974-76; Plastics Inst of Am, rsrch dir 1976-84; cnlsnt in matrl eng. **ORGANIZATIONS:** Frmr mem Bd of Trustees Montclair State 1963-74; mem Bd of Dir NACME 1980-. **HONORS/ACHIEVEMENTS:** Sigma Xi; hon scroll Am Inst of Chem 1970; Percy L Julian Awrd 1977; Intl Awrd Soc of Plastic Eng Inc 1984. **BUSINESS ADDRESS:** Consultant in Materials Eng, Self Employed, 26 High St, Montclair, NJ 07042.

HAWKINS, WILLIAM DOUGLAS
Business executive. **PERSONAL:** Born May 14, 1946, Los Angeles, CA; son of William D. Hawkins and Marian Parrish Hawkins; married Floy Marie Barabino; children: William D, Yonnine, Kellie, Todd. **EDUCATION:** Howard University, BA 1968. **CAREER:** US Congressman Samuel S Stratton, administrative assistant 1968-70; Security Pacific Natl Bank, commercial loan officer 1970-73; Natl Economic Management Association, sr vice president 1973-76; Korn Ferry Intl, managing associate 1976-84; The Hawkins Company, president 1984-. **ORGANIZATIONS:** Ed chair Black Businessmen's Assn of LA 1975; board of directors Boy Scouts of America, LA Council 1979-82; fundraiser LA Chapter United Negro College Fund 1984; member California Executive Recruiters Assn 1985; member NAACP; chairman Josephite Lay Advisory Bd 1988-1992. **HONORS/ACHIEVEMENTS:** Award of Merit Boy Scouts of America 1977; Silver Beaver Boy Scouts of America 1989. **BUSINESS ADDRESS:** President, The Hawkins Company, 5120 Brynhurst Ave, Los Angeles, CA 90043.

HAWTHORNE, ANGEL L.
TV producer. **PERSONAL:** Born May 31, 1959, Chicago, IL. **EDUCATION:** Columbia Coll, BA 1981. **CAREER:** WLS-TV, desk asst 1980; ABC News, desk asst 1980-81, assignment editor 1981-85, field producer 1985-. **BUSINESS ADDRESS:** Field Producer, ABC News, 190 N State St, Chicago, IL 60601.

HAWTHORNE, KENNETH L.
Business executive. **PERSONAL:** Born in Mobile, AL; married Eugenia; children: Cecilia Hawthorne Patterson, Bruce, Bart. **EDUCATION:** Pacific Western U, BBA;Univ of Pittsburgh, Tchng Cert. **CAREER:** New York City Dist Gulf Oil Corp, sales mgr 1971-73, mrktng mgr 1973-76; Gulf Trading & Transp Co (Gulf Oil Sub), vice pres 1976-81; Gulf Tire & Supply Co (Gulf Oil Sub), pres 1981-83; Gulf Oil Corp, mgr mgnt training dev. **ORGANIZATIONS:** Mem Assoc Pet Inst 1978-84; mem Am Mgmt Asso 1978-; mem Am Soc for Training & Dev 1983-; bd mem Harlem YMCA Bd Mgr 1972-84; bd mem Houston Bnaacp Dinner Comm 1984; chm pub Houston UNCF Campaign 1984. **HOME ADDRESS:** 342 Tynebridge Ln, Houston, TX 77024. **BUSINESS ADDRESS:** Manager of Mgmt Devel & Training, Gulf Oil Corp, 1301 McKinney, Houston, TX 77010.

HAWTHORNE, LUCIA SHELIA
Educator. **PERSONAL:** Born May 06, Baltimore, MD; married Rev Ward S Parham. **EDUCATION:** Morgan State Univ, BS Lang Arts 1964; Washington State Univ, MAT Speech 1965; PA State Univ, PhD Speech Comm 1971. **CAREER:** Washington State Univ, teaching asst 1964-65; Morgan State Univ, instructor 1965-67; PA State Univ, teaching asst 1967-69; Morgan State, asst prof 1969-72, assoc prof 1969-72, assoc dean of humanities 1974-75, prof 1975-, chmn dept of speech comm & theatre 1972-75, 1984-. **ORGANIZATIONS:** Chmn Commn on the Profession & Social Problems Speech Comm Assn 1972-75; mem Commn on Freedom of Speech Speech Comm Assn 1973-75; mem Bi-Lingual and Bi-Cultural Educ rep to TESOL for Speech Comm Assoc 1975-77; mem Speech Comm Assn, Eastern Comm Assn, MD Comm Assn, Assn of Comm Administrators; bdtrustees Morgan Christian Ctr; life mem NAACP; Golden Heritage mem NAACP; Golden Life mem Delta Sigma Theta Sor Inc. **HONORS/ACHIEVEMENTS:** Alpha Kappa Mu; Kappa Delta Pi; Lambda Iota Tau; Phi Alpha Theta; Promethean Kappa Tau; Alpha Psi Omega; Alpha Lambda Delta; Phi Eta Sigma; Danforth Assoc Danforth Found 1978-85; Academic Adminstrn Intern Amer Cncl on Educ 1974-75. **BUSINESS ADDRESS:** Professor/Chairman, Morgan State University, Dept Speech Comm & Theatre, Baltimore, MD 21239.

HAWTHORNE, NATHANIEL
Attorney. **PERSONAL:** Born Nov 21, 1943, Alliance, OH; married Sylvia Bush; children: Natalie, Austin K. **EDUCATION:** Mount Union Coll, BA 1966; OH No Univ, JD 1969. **CAREER:** Youngstown Legal Serv, staff atty 1969; City of Youngstown, asst law dir 1970-71; OH Atty Gen Office, asst atty gen 1971-74; Amer Tele & Teleg Co,atty 1976-79; Ohio Bell, atty. **ORGANIZATIONS:** Mem Amer, OH State, Dist of Columbia Bar Assns; former mem Franklin Co Juvenile Probation Council; former mem Mt Union Coll Annual Fund Comm, Mt Union Coll Alumni Council; bar admissions OH Supreme Ct, US Dist Court Northern OH, US Dist Court Southern OH, US Supreme Ct, Dist of Columbia Court of Appeals, US Court of Appeals DC Circuit, US Dist Court Dist of Columbia. **HONORS/ACHIEVEMENTS:** Outstanding Young Men of Amer 1971. **BUSINESS ADDRESS:** Attorney, Ohio Bell, 45 Erieview Plaza, Cleveland, OH 44114.

HAYATT, LESTER
Designer. **PERSONAL:** Born Apr 21, 1948, Panama; children: Tiffany. **EDUCATION:** Parsons Sch of Desing, BFA 1973. **CAREER:** Sportstreet, designer; Lady Madonna Maternity Boutiques, design 1974-; Giorgio St Angelo, asst design 1 yr. **HONORS/ACHIEVEMENTS:** Lady Madonna designs in such pub as Mademoiselle, Glamour, Essence, Ebony, Vogue, Harpers Bazaar; NY Times & LA Times, Chicago Tribune, NY Post, NY Daily newspapers; Young Designer of Am Awd 1972; did Inaugural wardrobe for Caron Carter 1977; designed costumes for Image Awards Show 1977.

HAYDEL, JAMES V., SR.
Life insurance chief executive. **CAREER:** Majestic Life Insurance Co Inc., New Orleans, LA, chief exec. **BUSINESS ADDRESS:** Majestic Life Insurance Company Inc., 1833 Dryades St., New Orleans, LA 70113. *

HAYDEN, JOHN CARLETON
Clergyman, educator. **PERSONAL:** Born Dec 30, 1933, Bowling Green, KY; married Jacqueline Green. **EDUCATION:** Wayne State, BA 1955;Univ of Detroit, MA 1962; Coll of Emmanual & St Cha, LTh honors 1963; Howard U, PhD 1972. **CAREER:** St Mary's School for Indian Girls, Springfield SD, teacher; Detroit Public School, teacher 1956-59; St Chad's Secondary School, instructor 1962-64; Univ of Saskatchewan, anglican chaplain 1963-67; Univ of Saskatchewan, instructor in history 1965-68; Howard Univ, asst prof of history 1972-78, scholar in ch history 1978-79; Dept of History Morgan State Univ, chmn 1979-; Frostburg State Coll, prof of history 1986-. **ORGANIZATIONS:** Mem Ch Historical Soc; asso editor " Historical Mag of the Protestant Episcopal Ch"; bd dir Assn for Study of Afro-Am Life & History; Am Historical Assn; Southern Historical Assn; Unoin of Black Episcopalians; mem pres Saskatchewan Assn for Retarded Children 1966-68; chmn youth conf Saskatchewan Centennial Corp 1964-67; Com for com Improvement; pres Black Episopal Clergy 1974-75; bd of dirs Washington Urban League 1980-; bd of dirs St Patrick's Episcopal Day School 1981-. **HONORS/ACHIEVEMENTS:** Recipient Angus Dun Fellow 1973, 74, 78; Facutly Research Prog in the Social Sciences Award 1973 & 1974; Spencer Found Award 1975; Am Philosophical Soc Award 1976; grant Commn for Black Mins 1976-78; fellowship Bd For Theol Educ 1978-79; fellowship Robert R Moton 1978-79; Abscam Jones Awd 1987. **BUSINESS ADDRESS:** Professor of History, Frostburg State College, Frostburg, MD 21532.

HAYDEN, ROBERT C., JR.
Educator, historian, author. **PERSONAL:** Born Aug 21, 1937, New Bedford, MA; son of Robert C Hayden Sr and Josephine Hughes Hayden; divorced; children: Dr Deborah M Hayden, Kevin R, Karen E. **EDUCATION:** Boston Univ, Boston MA, BA, 1959, EdM, 1961; Harvard Univ, Cambridge MA, Certificate, 1966; Massachusetts Institute of Technology, Cambridge MA, Certificate, 1977. **CAREER:** Xerox Educ Division, editor, 1966-69; Metropolitan Council for Educ Opportunity, Boston MA, exec dir, 1970-73; Educ Devel Center, Newton MA, project dir, 1973-80; Northeastern Univ, Boston MA, adjunct faculty, 1978-; Massachusetts Inst of Technology, Cambridge MA, dir, 1980-82; Boston Public Schools, Boston MA, exec asst to supt, dir project devel, 1982-86; Massachusetts Pre-Engineering Program, Boston MA, exec dir, 1987-; Boston Coll, Newton MA, adjunct faculty, 1987-; Bentley Coll, Waltham MA, adjunct faculty, 1989-. **ORGANIZATIONS:** Kappa Alpha Psi Frat, 1957; Natl Assn of Black School Educators, 1976-; Black Educators Alliance of Massachusetts, 1980-; mem, Natl Exec Comm, Washington DC Assn for Study of Afro-Amer Life and History, 1986-; Massachusetts Advocacy Center, 1988-. **HONORS/ACHIEVEMENTS:** Educ Press All-Amer Award, Educ Press Assoc of Amer, 1968; NAACP Serv Award, NAACP, 1973; Human Relations Award, Massachusetts Teachers Assn, 1979; Carter G Woodson Humanitarian Award, Omega Psi Phi, 1985; Martin Luther King Jr Award, Boston Public Schools, 1986; Humanitarian Serv Award, The Spiritual Assembly of the Baha'is of Boston, 1987; author of Seven Black American Scientists (1970), Eight Black American Inventors (1972, 1989), Nine Black American Doctors (1976), Boston's NAACP History 1910-1982 (1982), Faith, Culture and Leadership: A History ofthe Black Church in Boston (1985); Singing For All People: Roland Hayes—A Biography (1989). **BUSINESS ADDRESS:** President, RCH Associates, PO Box 5453, Boston, MA 02102.

HAYDEN, WILLIAM HUGHES
Investment banker. **PERSONAL:** Born Apr 26, 1940, New Bedford, MA. **EDUCATION:** Southeastern MA Univ, BS, BA 1962; New Eng Sch of Law, JSD 1967; New Sch for Social Rsch, cert 1968. **CAREER:** Atty Generals Office MA, 1963-67; US Dept of Treasury, 1966-67; Pres Comm on Civil Disorders, asst dir cong relations 1967-; NY State Urban Devel Corp, reg dir 1968-73; Grapetree Bay Hotels Co, gen partner 1973-75; E End Resources Corp, pres 1973-75; Metro Applied Rsch Ctr, sr fellow 1974-75; First Boston Corp, managing dir 1975-84; Bear Stearns & Co, managing dir, partner 1984-. **ORGANIZATIONS:** Former dir Wiltwyck Sch for Boys 1976-78; bd of dirs Urban Home Ownership Corp 1977; bd of dirs United Neighborhood Houses New York City 1977-; former dir First Women's Bank of NY 1979; trustee Citizen's Budget Comm City of NY 1981-; dir natl Assoc of Securities Profls. **BUSINESS ADDRESS:** Managing Director, Partner, Bear Stearns & Co, 55 Water St, New York, NY 10041.

HAYE, CLIFFORD S.
Attorney. **PERSONAL:** Born Dec 20, 1942, New York; married Jenelyn; children: Angela, Christopher. **EDUCATION:** MI State Univ, NC Coll, BA 1966; Columbia Law Sch, JD 1972. **CAREER:** US Dept of Justice, trial attorney 1972-73; NY Stock Exchange, enforcement atty 1973-74; Teachers Ins Ann Assn, asst gen counsel 1974-. **ORGANIZATIONS:**

Comm to elect Charles Evers Gov 1971; vol atty Comm Law Offices 1974-78; atty Indigent Panel Kings Co 1975-79; exec comm The Edges Group 1982-; bd mem Citizens Advocates for Justice 1983-. **HONORS/ACHIEVEMENTS:** Outstanding Young Man of Amer 1977. **MILITARY SERVICE:** AUS 1st lt 1966-1969. **BUSINESS ADDRESS:** Assistant General Counsel, Teachers Insur & Annuity Assoc, 730 3rd Ave, New York, NY 10017.

HAYES, ALBERTINE BRANNUM
Educator. **PERSONAL:** Born Apr 03, Lake Providence, LA; married James T. **EDUCATION:** So U, BS 1940;Univ of MI, MA 1952; George Peabody Coll for Tchr, specialist in edn;Univ of OK, EdD. **CAREER:** Caddo Parish Sch Bd, asst supt for comm affairs; Natchitoches Paris Sch LA, thcr; Lake Charles City Sch LA, tchr; Caddo Parish Sch LA, tchr; Booker T Washing HS Caddo Parish Sch, asst prin in charge of instr; Caddo Parish Sch, supr math sci edn; Centenary Coll LA, lecturer in edn; SoUniv LA, prof of edn; NE StateUniv LA, guest prof. **ORGANIZATIONS:** Vp Pride of Carroll Burial Ins Co Inc Lake Providence LA; vice pres Hayes Flower Shop Inc Shreveport LA; vice chmn United Way 1974; bd dir Intergrated Youth Svc; bd Dir United Way 1975; bd dir Shreveport Chap Am Red Cross. **HONORS/ACHIEVEMENTS:** Zeta Woman of Yr 1965; Eucator of Yr. **BUSINESS ADDRESS:** 1961 Midway, PO Box 37000, Shreveport, LA.

HAYES, ALVIN, JR.
Attorney. **PERSONAL:** Born Apr 11, 1932, Cedar Rapids, IA; married Julia Wilburn; children: Alvin Douglas III, Robert Ellis. **EDUCATION:** BA 1958;Univ of Bsd Law Sch, BLegal Languages 1961. **CAREER:** Agrico Chem Co, labor and EEO cnsl; WA State Hum Rights Commn, dir 1973-74; Priv Prac, law 1961-69; Woodbury Co, asst atty 1964-69. **ORGANIZATIONS:** Mem William Frank & Powell Consistory; Decatur Lodge #14; NAACP; Urban League; Share through Adoption; bd dir Alvin Douglas Hayes III Corp; mem Citizens Task Force; IA Bar Assn9; Sioux City Bar Assn; LS Dist Ct for No Dist fo IA; OK Bar Assn; Fed Dist Ct for the N Dist of OK. **HONORS/ACHIEVEMENTS:** Award for outstanding performance in field of civil rights from Gov Robert D Ray 1973; award Outstanding Exec Dir of the IA Civil Rts Commin 1977. **MILITARY SERVICE:** AUS sp3 1953-55. **BUSINESS ADDRESS:** PO Box 3166, Tulsa, OK 74101.

HAYES, ANNAMARIE GILLESPIE
Educator. **PERSONAL:** Born Sep 06, 1931, Flint; married Emery M; children: Colon, Marcus. **EDUCATION:** MI St, BA, MA, MS, PhD. **CAREER:** Pontiac Public Schools, Inkster Public Schools, public school teacher; MI-OH Regional Lab, teacher trainer; MI State Univ, educ specialist; Univ WI Madison, rsch assoc; Coll of Educ Wayne State Univ, presently assoc prof. **ORGANIZATIONS:** Nat Assn Negro Bus & Professional Women; Nat Assn Black Fin Aid Adminstr; Nat All Black Educ; Am Educ Resrch Assn; Assn Study Negro Life & Hist; bd dir Intl Afro-Am Museum; Shrine Black Madonna Detroit; Councilwoman Erma Henderson Women's Concerns Conf. **HONORS/ACHIEVEMENTS:** Woman of yr awd MI StateUniv 1971; USAF Europe awd 1972; fellow resrch Williams Coll.

HAYES, CHARLES
Elected official. **PERSONAL:** Born Oct 14, 1943, Catherine, AL; married Muriel. **EDUCATION:** Selma Univ, Assoc 1971; Wallace Comm Coll, diploma 1973; Mobile Bus Coll, diploma 1970; Univ of S Alabama, further study 1983; Dale Carnegie, 1984. **CAREER:** 4th Judicial Circuit, spec investigator dist atty, indigent def comm; Wilcox Co, commissioner. **ORGANIZATIONS:** Mem Alberta Comm Health Clinic 1981-84; dir Alberta Comm Club 1983-85; mem Assn of Co Commissioners 1982-; deacon Salem Baptist Church 1982-; dir Alberta Comm Fire Dept 1984-; mem Wilcox Co Democratic Conf; mem AL Democratic Conf Black Caucus. **HONORS/ACHIEVEMENTS:** Outstanding Leadership Awd Alberta Comm Club-Alberta AL 1984. **MILITARY SERVICE:** AUS sgt E-5 1964-69; Code of Conduct Awd. **HOME ADDRESS:** Gen Post Del Hwy 28, Prairie, AL 36736.

HAYES, CHARLES A.
Business executive. **PERSONAL:** Born Feb 17, 1918, Cairo, IL; married Edna J; children: Barbara Delaney, Charlene Smith. **EDUCATION:** Attended, Sumner HS Cairo IL. **CAREER:** Carpenters Local 1424, pres 1940-42; UPWA Grievance Comm, chmn 1943-49; UPWA, field rep 1949-54; Dist #1 UPWA, dist dir 1954-68; Amalgamated Meatcutters-Union, dist dir and intl vice pres 1968-79; United Food & Commercial Workers Intl Union AFL-CIO & CLC, intl vice pres & dist dir region 12 1979-83; 1st Congressional Dist Chicago, congressman 1983-. **ORGANIZATIONS:** Serves on Educ & Labor Commns, Small Business Commns; exec vice pres Coalition of Black Trade Unionists; vice pres Operation PUSH; exec bd mem ChicagoUrban League; IL St Commn on Labor Laws. **BUSINESS ADDRESS:** Congressman, Chicago's 1st Dist, House of Representatives, Washington, DC 20515.

HAYES, CHARLES LEONARD
Educator. **PERSONAL:** Born Dec 16, 1921, Baton Rouge, LA; married Bette Harris; children: Charles Jerome, Jaime. **EDUCATION:** Leland Coll, AB 1947; Loyola U, EdM 1949;Univ No CO, EdD 1958. **CAREER:** Chicago, teacher 1948-49; NC A&T State Univ, instr 1949-52, asst prof 1952-56, prof 1958-61, chmn 1961-66; George Washington Univ, ace fellow 1966-67; US Office of Educ HEW, chief 1967-69; Albany State Coll, pres 1969-80; NC A&T State Univ, chmn 1980-. **ORGANIZATIONS:** Am Assn ofUniv Profs; Assn of Higher Edn; NEA; Phi Delta Kappa; Am Personnel & Guidance Assn; Am Coll Personnel Assn; Assn of Counselor Educators & Suprs; NC Psychol Assn; Kappa Delta Pi; bd dir Albany Urban League; Albany USO Council; exec bd Chehaw Council Boy Scouts of Am; Nat Conf of Christian& Jews; YMCA; Citizens Adb Com; mem Drug Action Council, Volunteers to the Courts. **HONORS/ACHIEVEMENTS:** Personalities of the S; Who's Who in N Am 1976-77. **MILITARY SERVICE:** USN skd1c 1942-46. **BUSINESS ADDRESS:** Chairperson, NC A&T State University, 1601 E Market St, Greensboro, NC 27411.

HAYES, CURTISS LEO
Educator/substitute teacher. **PERSONAL:** Born Jan 10, 1931, Glasgow; married Opal Juanita Owens; children: Janice R Almond, Curtiss L Jr, Collin L. **EDUCATION:** Morningside College, BA 1956; AZ State Univ, MA 1974; Dallas Theological Seminary, ThM 1980. **CAREER:** Secondary Public Schools, teacher 1956-75; Sudan Interior Mission, Christian educ coord 1980-84; Liberian Baptist Theol Seminary, theology instructor 1982-83; Dallas Bible College, missionary in residence 1984-85; Dallas Independent School Dist, substitute teacher. **ORGANIZATIONS:** Mem NAACP 1956; pres Desert Sands Teachers Assoc 1972; mem Stull Bill Steering Comm 1973; mem Natl Educ Assoc 1973; licensed minister Mt Zion Baptist Church 1980; instructor Monrovia Bible Inst 1982. **HONORS/ACHIEVEMENTS:** College Orator Morningside College 1954; Diamond Key Awd Natl Forensic League 1972; Masters Rsch Project AZ State Univ 1974; Masters Thesis Dallas Theol Seminary 1980. **MILITARY SERVICE:** AUS corpl 2 yrs; Honorable Discharge. **BUSINESS ADDRESS:** Dallas Independent Sch Dist, 3807 Ross St, Dallas, TX 75204.

HAYES, EDWARD, JR.
Attorney. **PERSONAL:** Born Jun 19, 1947, Long Branch, NJ; son of Edward Hayes and Bessie Hayes; married Alice Hall; children: Blair Hall, Kia Hall. **EDUCATION:** Wesleyan Univ, BA 1969; Stanford Law Sch, JD 1972. **CAREER:** Commr Mary Gardner Jones FTC, clerk 1971; Citizens Communications Center, atty 1972-74; Hayes & White, partner atty 1974-84; Baker & Hostetler, partner atty 1984-. **ORGANIZATIONS:** Mem Congressional Black Caucus Communications Task Force, WA Bar Assn; adv comm African Development Fund; mem budget comm DC; bd mem Inst of Intl Trade & Devel; bd mem, So Others Might Eat, 1979; vice chmn, DC Chamber Intl Trade Comm 1988; bd mem, Stop the Madness, 1989-. **HONORS/ACHIEVEMENTS:** Articles publ Natl Bar Assn; Natl Assn of Broadcasters; Natl Assn of Black Owned Broadcasters; Cablelines Magazine. **BUSINESS ADDRESS:** Partner, Baker & Hostetler, 3206 Morrison St NW, Washington, DC 20036.

HAYES, ELVIN
Professional athlete. **PERSONAL:** Born Nov 17, 1945, Rayville, LA; married Erna; children: Elvin Jr, Erna Jr, Erica, Ethan. **CAREER:** San Diego Professional Basketball Team, played 1968-71; Houston Rockets, player 1971-72; Baltimore Bullets, player 1972-73; Capital Bullets, player 1973-74; Washington Bullets, player 1974-81; Houston Rockets, player 1981-. **HONORS/ACHIEVEMENTS:** All Star every year in the NBA; All Amer every year at Houston; Coll Player of the Yr 1968; only player in NBA history to have more than 1,000 rebounds every year; missed only six of 984 games in pro career; 4th all time minutes played (highest of active players); top active player in rebounds (5th all time);7th all time scorer (one of 6 NBA players to score 20,000 pts & pull down 10,000 rebounds; 8th in NBA scoring 1979; 5th in rebounding; 5th in blocked shots. **BUSINESS ADDRESS:** Houston Rockets, The Summit, Ten Greenway Plazar, Houston, TX 77046.

HAYES, FLOYD WINDOM, III
Educator. **PERSONAL:** Born Nov 03, 1942, Gary, IN; son of Charles Henry Hayes and Thelma Ruth Person Hayes; married Charlene Moore; children: Tracy, Keisha, Ndidi, Kia-Lillian. **EDUCATION:** Univ of Paris, Cert d'Etudes 1964; NC Central Univ, BA (Cum Laude) 1967; Univ of CA Los Angeles, MA (w/Distinction) 1969; Univ of MD, PhD 1985. **CAREER:** Univ of CA Los Angeles, instruction specialist 1969-70; Princeton Univ, lecturer dept of pol exec sec Afro-Amer studies 1970-71; Swarthmore Coll, vstg lecturer dept of history 1971; Univ of MD, asst coord Afro-Amer studies 1971-73, instructor 1971-77; Cornell Univ, instructor Africana studies 1977-78; Close Up Found, prog instructor 1979-80; Howard Univ, res asst, res fellow inst for the study of ed policy 1980-81, 1981-85; US Equal Employment Oppor Com, special asst to chmn 1985-86; San Diego State Univ, asst prof Afro-Amer studies 1986-. **ORGANIZATIONS:** Consultant Union Township Sch System 1971, Comm Educ Exchange Prog Columbia Univ 1972, MD State Dept of Educ 1973-75; mem Early Childhood Educ Subcomm FICE US Dept of Educ 1986. **HONORS/ACHIEVEMENTS:** Outstanding Young Men of Amer 1977; Phi Delta Kappa Professional Educ Frat Howard Univ Chap 1982; "The Future, A Guide to Information Sources," World Future Soc 1977; "The African Presence in America Before Columbus," Black World July 1973; "Structures of Dominance and the Political Economy of Black Higher Education," Institute for the Study of Educational Policy Howard Univ 1981; "The Political Economy, Reaganomics, and Blacks," The Western Journal of Black Studies 1982; "Politics and Education in America's Multicultural Society," Journal of Ethnic Studies 1989; "Governmental Retreat and the Politics of African American Self-Reliant Development," Journal of Black Studies 1990. **BUSINESS ADDRESS:** Asst Prof, Afro-American Studies, San Diego State University, Dept of Afro-American Studies, San Diego, CA 92182.

HAYES, GRAHAM EDMONDSON
Attorney. **PERSONAL:** Born Nov 02, 1929, Horton, KS; children: Sondra, Karen, Graham II, Alisa. **EDUCATION:** Washburn U, AB 1956; Washburn U, JD 1957. **CAREER:** Sedgwick Co, dep dist atty 1958-62; KS Commn on Civil Rights, atty 1970-74; Wichita Commn on Civil Rights, examiner 1974; Wichita Commn on Civil Rights, atty 1975-; Private Practice, attorney at law. **ORGANIZATIONS:** Mem Supreme Ct of US; US Ct of Claimes; Tax Ct of US; US Dist Ct; Circuit Ct of US; Supreme Ct of KS; USAF Bd for Correction of Mil Records; St Bd of Law Examiners of KS; bd of dirs KS Trial Lawyers Assn; Am Trial Lawyers Assn; Nat Assn of Criminal Def Lawyers; past pres Urban League of Wichita; mem VFW Post 6888; Kappa Alpha Psi. **HONORS/ACHIEVEMENTS:** Appt ExmnR 1976; KS State Bd for Admission of Attorneys 1979. **MILITARY SERVICE:** USAF 1948-52. **BUSINESS ADDRESS:** Attorney at Law, 2225 E 21st, Ste #4, Wichita, KS 67214.

HAYES, ISAAC
Entertainer, business executive. **PERSONAL:** Born Aug 20, 1942, Covington, TN; children: 4 Children. **CAREER:** As youth sang with various gospel & rythm & blues groups; played piano and saxophone in nightclubs; began writing songs with David Porter for Stax Records 1962; composer musical score film Shaft; appeared on Rockford Files. **HONORS/ACHIEVEMENTS:** Albums recorded incl, Black Moses, Hot Buttered Soul, Enterprise, His Greatest Hits, Hotbed, Isaac Hayes Movement, To Be Continued, Greatest Hit Singles(with Dionne Warwick), A Man and A Woman; winner of numerous awards incl Oscar, Grammy, Acad of Motion Picture Arts & Sci 1972. **BUSINESS ADDRESS:** c/o Poly Gram Records Inc, 810 7th Ave, New York, NY 10019.

HAYES, LEOLA G.
Educator. **PERSONAL:** Born in Rocky Mount; married Spurgeon S. **EDUCATION:** BS; MA; MS Prof Diploma; PhD 1973. **CAREER:** William Paterson Coll of NJ, chmn spl educ dept; Fair Lawn NJ, supvr spl educ 1957-64; Fair Lawn NJ, tchr handicapped children; Blind Chgo, consult 1954-57; Blind NY Inst for Blind, tchr 1953-54. **ORGANIZATIONS:** Mem CEC; Voc Rehab Soc; AAMD; NJEA; mem Drug Abus Prog 1973-; Young Peopl Econseling Session. **HONORS/ACHIEVEMENTS:** Recip Human Relations Award; Nat Bus & Professional Women; Nat Comm Ldrs Award; Hannah G Solomon Award; Who's Who in Edn; Who's Who Internatl. **BUSINESS ADDRESS:** Professor of Special Education, William Paterson College, 300 Pompton Rd, Wayne, NJ 07470.

HAYES, LESTER
Professional football player. **PERSONAL:** Born Jan 22, 1955, Houston, TX. **CAREER:** Oakland Raiders, football player 1977-81; Los Angeles Raiders, football player 1982-. **HONORS/ACHIEVEMENTS:** Played in Pro Bowl NFL All-Star Game following 1980-84 seasons. **BUSINESS ADDRESS:** Professional Football Player, Los Angeles Raiders, 332 Center St, El Segundo, CA 90245.

HAYES, MARION LEROY
Educator. **PERSONAL:** Born Dec 23, 1931, Jefferson Co, MS; son of Lindsey J Hayes and Irene Rollins Hayes; married Louise. **EDUCATION:** Alcorn St Univ, BS 1961; South Univ, MEd 1971. **CAREER:** Hazelhurst Pub Sch, teacher 1961-66; Jefferson Co Sch, asst prin tchr 1966-75. **ORGANIZATIONS:** Mem Amer Assn of Sch Admin, Natl Educ Assn, MS Assn of Sch Supts, MS Assn of Educ, Jefferson Co Tchrs Assn; bd mem Copiah-Lincoln Jr Coll; planning bd chmn town of Fayette; bd of gov Educ Secur. **HONORS/ACHIEVEMENTS:** Star Teacher MS Econ Coun 1970-72. **MILITARY SERVICE:** USAF E-5 1950-54; AUS E-5 1956-60. **BUSINESS ADDRESS:** Supt of Educ, Jefferson Co, PO Box 157, Fayette, MS 39069.

HAYES, RICHARD C.
Association executive. **PERSONAL:** Born Dec 13, 1938, Carbondale, IL; married Joyce L; children: Clinette, Rachaelle, Richard. **EDUCATION:** BA 1967; MA 1975. **CAREER:** So IL U, asso u affirm action ofcr; internal compliance ofcr; Gov's Ofc Human Resources, dir; IL State Employment Svc, employemetn coord; SIU, acad adv gen studies; Carbondale, planning operator 1963-66. **ORGANIZATIONS:** Mem chmn Affirmative Action Officers Assn 1972-; consult AA/EEO; exec com Nat AAAO; NAACP; Bethel AME Ch. **MILITARY SERVICE:** USN 1956-58. **BUSINESS ADDRESS:** AA Ofc Personnel Servs SIU-C, Carbondale, IL.

HAYES, ROLAND HARRIS
Attorney. **PERSONAL:** Born Feb 04, 1931, Winston-Salem, NC; son of John Hayes and Juanita Hayes; married Barbara Spaulding; children: Roland Jr, John F, Reba J. **EDUCATION:** Winston-Salem State Univ, BS 1952; NC Central Univ School of Law, JD 1971. **CAREER:** Wachovia Bank & Trust Co, asst cashier 1952-68; Legal Aid Soc of Forsyth Cty, staff atty 1971-72; Richard C Erwin Atty at Law, assoc atty 1972-74; General Practice, atty 1974-84; State of NC, Dist Court Judge, 1984-present. **ORGANIZATIONS:** Mem Forsyth Cty Bar Assn 1971-, NC Bar Assn 1971-, Amer Bar Assn 1971-; mem NC Assn of Black Lawyers 1974-; mem Winston-Salem Bar Assn 1974-; Elder Cleveland Ave Christian Church; life mem NAACP; mem Omega Psi Phi Frat; mem Phi Alpha Delta Law Frat, mem Bachelor Benedict Club; mem, Family Violence Advisory Comm; mem, Exchange/SCAN Board; mem, Youth Opportunity Honor Board. **BUSINESS ADDRESS:** District Court Judge, State of NC, PO Box 1411, Winston-Salem, NC 27102.

HAYES, VERTIS
Painter, sculptor, educator, lecturer. **PERSONAL:** Born May 20, 1911, Atlanta, GA; married Florence Alexander; children: Vertis Jr, Gregory. **EDUCATION:** Attended Natl Acad of Design, Florence Kane Sch of Art, Art Students League NY. **CAREER:** Fed Art Proj NYC, mural painter 1934-38; LeMoyne Coll TN, tchr chmn dept fine art 1938-49; Hayes Acad of Art, founder dir 1947-52; CA State Coll Immaculate Heart Coll, painter sculptor lecturer 1971-74. **ORGANIZATIONS:** Mem Painting & Sculpture Commn; mem Family Savs & Loan Assn, Home Savs & Loan Assn, Harrison-Ross ortuaries; 32 Degree Mason; past mem Harlem Artists Guild 1936-38; artists union. **HONORS/ACHIEVEMENTS:** Carter Found Grant 1965; Founding Fellow Black Acad of Arts & Letters Inc 1969; Creative Comm Awd Art Inst of Boston 1971; Hon Degree Art Inst of Boston 1971.

HAYES, WALLACE S.
Retired pharmacist. **PERSONAL:** Born May 11, 1889, Atlanta, GA; married Esther F Fields. **EDUCATION:** Acad of Howard Univ, 1920; Columbia Univ Coll of Pharmaceutical Sci, PhG 1923. **CAREER:** Railway, postal clerk 1908-09; Jacksonville FL, letter carrier 1910-17; Washington DC, forestry serv 1917-20; New York City Post Office, clerk 1921-50; retired as supr;pharmacist 1950-68. **ORGANIZATIONS:** Mem NY State Pharmaceutical Soc, NJ State Pharm Assoc, Natl Pharm Assoc; past mem Elks Lodge Jacksonville & Washington. **HONORS/ACHIEVEMENTS:** NAACP Golden Life Time Mem Cert Natl Alliance of Postal & Fed Employees; Gold Card mem NALC; Awarded Jewel Studded Lapel Pin 60 yrs NALC; Awd Half-Century Cert & Hon Life Mem Alumni Assoc Univ of Columbia Coll of Pharmaceutical 1974; Saluted as an Outstanding Citizen grad class of Stanton HS; Plaque for 70 Yrs continued membership Natl Assoc Letter Carriers Wash DC.

HAYES-GILES, JOYCE V.
Gas company executive. **PERSONAL:** Born Dec 08, 1948, Jackson, MS; daughter of Isaac Hayes and Myrtle Stigger Hayes; married Ronald Giles; children: Kristen, Erica. **EDUCATION:** Knoxville Coll, BA 1970; Univ of Detroit, MBA 1978; Wayne State Law Sch, JD 1985. **CAREER:** Chrysler Corp, salary admin analyst/supv 1971-76; Auto Club of MI, compensation adminr 1976-78; MichCon Gas Co, dir matl mgmt & other managerial positions 1978-. **ORGANIZATIONS:** Mem Natl Black MBA Assoc 1978-; exec comm & bd mem Amer Red Cross 1984; mem Detroit Bar Assoc 1985-, MI Bar Assoc 1986-; mem Natl Purchasing Assoc 1986-; chairperson personnel com vice pres of bd YWCA 1986-; life mem NAACP; mem Links Inc, Delta Sigma Theta Sor Inc; pres, Metropolitan YWCA 1988-89. **HONORS/ACHIEVEMENTS:** Outstanding Young Women of Amer 1981; Leadership Detroit Grad Chamber of Commerce 1982; Minority Achiever in Industry YWCA 1984; NAACP 100 Club Awd. **BUSINESS ADDRESS:** Dir, Administrative Services, MichCon Gas Co, 500 Griswold, Detroit, MI 48226.

HAYGOOD, WIL
Journalist. **PERSONAL:** Born Sep 19, 1954, Columbus, OH. **EDUCATION:** Miami Univ, BA 1976. **CAREER:** The Columbus OH Call & Post, reporter 1977-78; Community Info & Referal, hotline operator 1978-79; Macy's Dept Store NYC, exec 1980-81; The Charleston Gazette, copy editor 1981-83; The Boston Globe, feature reporter. **ORGANIZATIONS:** Reporter The Pittsburgh Post Gazette 1984-85. **HONORS/ACHIEVEMENTS:** Natl Headliner Awd Outstanding Feature Writing 1986; author of "Two on the River" Atlantic Monthly Press 1987. **BUSINESS ADDRESS:** Feature Reporter, The Boston Globe, 135 Morrissey Blvd, Boston, MA 02107.

HAYLING, WILLIAM H.
Gynecologist/obstetrician. **PERSONAL:** Born Dec 07, 1925, Trenton, NJ; married Carolyn Anne Mitchem; children: Pamela Hoffman, Patricia Price. **EDUCATION:** Boston Univ, Pre-med 1943-45; Howard Univ, MD 1949. **CAREER:** NJ Coll of Medicine/Dentistry, assoc prof ob/gyn 1960-80; King/Drew Medical Ctr, asst prof ob/gyn 1981-87, chief ambulatory ob/gyn 1981-87. **ORGANIZATIONS:** Pres 100 Black Men of NJ 1975-78; bd Jersey City State Coll NJ 1975-80; pres Natl 100 Black Men of Amer Inc 1987; founder/pres 100 Black Men of LA Inc. **HONORS/ACHIEVEMENTS:** Image Awd 100 Black Men of LA 1982; LA Sentinel Awd LA Sentinel Newspaper 1983; Presidential Awd Alpha Phi Alpha Frat 1984. **MILITARY SERVICE:** AUS Medical Corps capt 1951-53; Bronze Star, Combat Medical Badge. **BUSINESS ADDRESS:** Chief Ambulatory Ob/Gyn, King/Drew Medical Center, 3660 Imperial Hwy, Lynwood, CA 90262.

HAYMAN, WARREN C.
Educator. **PERSONAL:** Born Oct 01, 1932, Baltimore, MD; married Jacqueline; children: Warren Jr, Guy, Julia. **EDUCATION:** Coppin State Coll, BS 1961; Stanford U, MA 1967; Harvard U, EdD 1978. **CAREER:** Coppin State Coll, dean of edn; Ravenswood City Sch Dist, supt 1973-77; Ravenswood, asst supt 1971-73; Belle Haven, elem prin 1968-71; Baltimore City Schs, elem tchr 1961-66; Stanford Univ, faculty resident 1970-73; San Francisco State Univ, instr 1971-74; US Office of Educ, consult 1968-76. **ORGANIZATIONS:** Chmn bd dir Nairobi Coll 1970-76; chmn bd of dir Mid-Peninsula Urban Coalition 1973-75; reg dir of educ Phi Beta Sigma Frat Inc 1980. **HONORS/ACHIEVEMENTS:** Circuluc schol honor soc Coppin State Coll 1961; elem math tchr fellow Nat Sci Found 1966; exper tchr flwshp US Ofc of Educ 1966; higher educ flwshp Rockfeller Found 1976-78; good conduct ribbon AUS 1955-57. **MILITARY SERVICE:** AUS sp/2nd class 1955-57. **BUSINESS ADDRESS:** Coppin State Coll, 2500 W North Ave, Baltimore, MD 21216.

HAYMORE, TYRONE
Elected government official. **PERSONAL:** Born Mar 12, 1947, Chicago, IL. **EDUCATION:** Thornton Jr Coll, AA 1969; Northeastern IL Univ, BA Ed 1983. **CAREER:** Village of Robbins, trustee. **ORGANIZATIONS:** Minister of music Christ Crusaders Ch, Bethesda GT, St John Comm 1962-85; rapid transit clerk Chicago Transit Auth 1968-; treas Robbins Historical Soc 1981; trustee Village of Robbins 1983; dir Commiss on Youth Bremen Twp 1983; treas Black Elected Officials of IL 1984; mem IL Civil Air Patrole. **HONORS/ACHIEVEMENTS:** Christian Leadership Christ Crusader Church Robbins 1965; Music Scholarship to Summer Music Camp Eastern IL Univ 1965; Achievement Awd Mayor of Robbins for Ambulance Fund Drive 1984. **BUSINESS ADDRESS:** Trustee, Village of Robbins, 3327 W 137th St, Robbins, IL 60472.

HAYNES, ALPHONSO WORDEN
Educational administrator. **PERSONAL:** Born in Brooklyn, NY; married Margaret S Alvarez; children: Thomas, Pia, Mia, Pilar, Alphonso III, Alejandro. **EDUCATION:** Long Island U, BA 1965; Columbia U, MS 1967, MA 1974, EdD 1978. **CAREER:** New York City Dept of Welfare, admin & recreation 1953-67; Harlem Hospital Center, ped social worker 1967-69; Long Island Univ, dean of students 1969-79; Norfolk State Univ School of Social Work, assoc prof & program dir 1979-81; Old Dominion Univ, asst dean of student affairs. **ORGANIZATIONS:** Mem Natl Asso of Soc Wrkrs 1967-; mem Acdmy of Cert Soc Wrkrs 1969-; staff training consult Chesapeake Soc Serv 1979-80; bd mem Yng Adult & Campus Ministry 1983-; mem VA Asso of Stdnt Personnel Adm 1981-; mem Rsrch Focus in Black Ed 1980-; bd mem Columbia Univ Schl of Social Work Alumni Assoc. **HONORS/ACHIEVEMENTS:** Pi Gamma Mu Soc Sci Hnr Soc 1962; Karagheusian Mem Flwshp ColumbiaUniv 1965-67; outstndng edctr in Am. **BUSINESS ADDRESS:** Asst Dean of Student Affairs, Old DominionUniv, 1401 W 49 St, Multicultural Center, Norfolk, VA 23508.

HAYNES, BARBARA ASCHE
Educator, nurse. **PERSONAL:** Born Jun 26, 1935, Rochester, PA; married Donald F Haynes. **EDUCATION:** Chatham Coll, BSNE 1958; Univ of Pgh, MNE 1967, PhD 1984. **CAREER:** Allegheny Gen Hosp Sch of Nursing Pittsburgh, instr nursing 1959-67; Allegheny Comm Coll, asst prof nursing 1967-70, assoc prof/dept head 1970-74, dean of life sci/dir nursing prog 1974-79; Coll of DuPage, instr nursing 1979-80; Univ of IL Chicago Coll of Nursing, asst prof gen nursing/dir student serv 1981-. **ORGANIZATIONS:** Sec Univ of Pgh Sch of Nursing Alumnae Assn 1967-69; bd of dirs PA Nurses Assn 1973-77; chmn nominating comm Univ Pgh Sch of Nursing Alumnae Assn1974; bd of dirs United Mental Health of Allegheny Co1975-79; professional adv com NW Allegheny Home Care Prog 1976-79; v chmn conf grp on teaching PA Nurse's Assn 1977-79; comm on nursing educ PA Nurses Assn 1977-79; adv comm BSN Prog LaRoche Coll 1978-79; reg continuing educ adv comm Duquesne Univ Group 1978-79; pub "The Practical Nurse" & "Auto-Education" PA Nurse 1972; speaker "Multi-Media in Nursing Educ" Tchrs Coll Columbia Univ 1972; speaker "Coping with Change through Assessment & Evaluation" Natl League for Nursing-Council of Asso Degree Progs NY 1974; mem Sigma Theta Tau Alpha Lambda Chapt. **BUSINESS ADDRESS:** Asst Prof of Gen Nursing, Univ of IL Coll of Nursing, 845 S Damen Ave, Chicago, IL 60680.

HAYNES, ELEANOR LOUISE
Business executive. **PERSONAL:** Born in Warrenton, GA; widowed; children: SFC Jeffrey M Thomas. **EDUCATION:** Fashion Inst, 1953; Sobleshon Inst 1972; Queensboro Comm Coll, Small Bus Mgmt 1978; Queens Coll, 1983-. **CAREER:** Garment Industry, fashion designer 1951-74; NY Voice, columnist 1968-; Good Serv & Group Travel, travel agency 1976-78; Coler Mem Hosp, dir public relations1978-, appointed liaison, adv bd 1987-. **ORGANIZATIONS:** Mem ViVants Soc & Civic Org 1969-; mem & officer Natl Assoc Negro Bus & Prof Women 1972-80; sec, treas Allied Fed Savings & Loan Assoc 1980-83; publ relations dir SE Queens Reg Dem Club 1980-; mem Natl Assoc Female Execs 1980-; mem Edges Group Inc 1980-; vice pres Council of PR Dir Health & Hosp Corp 1981-; 1st natl vice pres Natl Assoc Media Women 1981-; elected delegate Judicial Convention State of NY 1982-; mem Manhattan Chamber of Commerce 1983-, Jamaica Branch NAACP; elect pres Cncl PR Directors Health & Hospitals Corp City of NY 1985; judge Easter Boardwalk Parade Atlantic City NJ 1987. **HONORS/ACHIEVEMENTS:** 30 awds & certs incl Excellence in-Serv Awd Natl Assoc Media Women 1983; Media Woman of the Year Long Island Chap Media Women 1983; Excellence in Journalism Awd SE Queens Dem Club 1982; Best Perf Awd Dunton Presbyterian Church 1981; Mother of the Year Awd from Assemblyman Guy R Brewer Queens Cty 1976. **HOME ADDRESS:** 231-16-126 Ave, Laurelton, NY 11413.

HAYNES, EUGENE, JR.
Educator, composer. **EDUCATION:** Juillard Sch of Music in NY, earned undergrad grad degrees in comp piano. **CAREER:** Lincoln U, prof; intl known as concert pianist; So IL Univ East St Louis Campus, prof of music & artist in residence 1979-; artist in residence at univ 1960-79; tchs advanced courses in piano improvisation music history; "The Wonderful World of Music" radio sta KSD St Louis, host classical music prog. **HONORS/ACHIEVEMENTS:** Made New York City debut at Carnegie Hall 1958; since appeared there; appeared in every major city of Europe & Latin Am; featured on severalTV spls; orginal comps include String Quartet, Song Cycle, Symphony, Fantasy for Piano & Orchestra; awarded Maurice Loeb Prize for excellence in grad studies Julliard Schl of Music in NY. **BUSINESS ADDRESS:** So IL Univ, East St Louis Campus, East St Louis, IL 60201.

HAYNES, FRANK L., JR.
Attorney, executive. **PERSONAL:** Born Aug 26, 1944, New York. **EDUCATION:** Horace Mann Sch New York, 1962; Yale Coll, BA 1966; Yale Law Sch, LlB 1969. **CAREER:** Prudential Ins Co of Am; asst gen cns vice pres of law dept; Milbank, Tweed, Hadley & Mccloy, asso 1970-76; Western Cntr on Law & ProvertyUniv of S CA Law Cntr LA, asso 1969-70; NAACP Legal Def & Educ Fund NY, legal intern summer 1968. **ORGANIZATIONS:** Admitted to bar 1971. **HONORS/ACHIEVEMENTS:** Recip Fiske Stone Moot Ct Awd Yale Law Sch 1967. **BUSINESS ADDRESS:** Vice President of Law Dept, Prudential Insurance Co of Am, Prudential Plaza, Newark, NJ 07101.

HAYNES, GEORGE E., JR.
Educator. **PERSONAL:** Born Oct 23, 1920, Victoria, TX; children: George E III, Elizabeth (jemison). **EDUCATION:** Tuskegee Inst, BS 1942; NY ll, MA 1947. **CAREER:** Human Relations Dept Houston Ind Sch Dist, asst supt; TX So U, vis prof; Kashmere Sr HS, prin 2 yrs; I M Terrell Jr High, prin 2 yrs; Kashmere Gardens Jr/Sr HS, asst prin; FL A&M Coll, summer vis prof 1955 & 1957; Tuskegee Inst AL, dept head 3 yrs; NY U, tchr. **ORGANIZATIONS:** Mem NEA Workshop "Deveoloping an Instructional Prog to Implement Cultural Pluralism"; mem Houston Council of Edn; TX Assn of Secondary Sch Prin; Houston Prin Assn; Nat Assn of Secondary Prins; pres Tuskegee Nat Alumni Assn; mem Phi Delta Kappa; Smithsonian Asso; mem Epsilon Pi Tau Honorary Industrial Frat; Alpha Phi Alpha Frat; Assn for Study of Afro-Am Life & History; Asso musicians of NY Local #802; mem NAACP; YMCA Century Club; Com of Religion &Race Unitedmeth Ch. **MILITARY SERVICE:** Sgt 1943-46.

HAYNES, GEORGE EDMUND, JR.
Unit supervisor. **PERSONAL:** Born Jul 17, 1912, New York, NY; married Daisy A; children: George Edmund III, Alan Ross (dec), Bruce Daniel. **EDUCATION:** WilberforceUniv Wilberforce OH, BS 1938; AtlantaUniv Schl of Social Work Atlanta GA, MSW 1947; ColumbiaUniv Sch of Social Work; Temple U. **CAREER:** State of NY Exec Dept Parole Div, unit supr; Neighborhood House Morristown NJ, dir 1948-49; Forrest House Bronx NY, program dir 1947-48; Colonial Park Day Nursery Inc, treas 1957-59. **ORGANIZATIONS:** Mem 100 Black Men Inc; mem Councilliers Inc; affiliate AMAS Repertory Theatre Inc. **MILITARY SERVICE:** AUS 1943-46. **BUSINESS ADDRESS:** State of New York, 260 East 161st, Bronx, NY 10451.

HAYNES, JAMES H.
Educational administrator. **PERSONAL:** Born Nov 27, 1953, Pensacola, FL. **EDUCATION:** Pensacola Jr Coll, AA 1973; Morebouse Coll, BA 1975; Georgia State Univ, MEd 1977; Univ of IA, PhD 1979. **CAREER:** Atlanta Public Sch System, teacher 1975-77; Philadelphia Training Center, asst dir 1979-80; FL A&M Univ, dir of planning 1980-83; Morgan State Univ, dir of inst research 1983-84, vice pres of planning 1984. **ORGANIZATIONS:** Woodrow Wilson Nat'l Fellowship Foundation, 1980; Title III Prog Bowie State Coll, counsultant 1984-; Assoliation of Minority Hlth Profession Sch, consultant 1982; supervisor of admin for NTE, GMAT 1984-; Alpha Phi Alpha, Baltimore Morehouse Alummi Club, sec; NAACP; Morehouse Coll Nat'l Alumni Assoc. **HONORS/ACHIEVEMENTS:** Honorary membership in Promethean Kappa Tau, Phi Delta Kappa, Phi Alpha Theta. **HOME ADDRESS:** 1655 Kingsway Ct, Baltimore, MD 21218. **BUSINESS ADDRESS:** Vice President for Planning, Morgan State University, Cold Spring Ln & Hillen Rd, Baltimore, MD 21239.

HAYNES, JOHN K.
Life insurance chief executive. **CAREER:** Superior Life Insurance Co, Baton Rouge, LA, chief exec. **BUSINESS ADDRESS:** Superior Life Insurance Co., 7980 Scenic Hwy, Baton Rouge, LA 70807. *

HAYNES, JOHN KERMIT
Educator. **PERSONAL:** Born Oct 30, 1943, Monroe, LA; son of John K Haynes Sr and Grace Ross Haynes; married Carolyn Ann Price. **EDUCATION:** Morehouse Coll, BS 1964; Brown Univ, PhD 1970, Post Doctoral 1971; MA Inst of Tech, Post Doctoral 1973. **CAREER:** Brown Univ, teaching asst 1964-70; MIT, post doctoral & teaching asst 1971-73; Meharry Medical Coll, asst prof 1973-78; Morehouse Coll, prof & dir of health professions 1979-, chmn dept biology 1985-. **ORGANIZATIONS:** Mem Amer Assn for the Adv of Science; mem Natl Assn of Advisors for the Health Professions; peer reviewer Natl Sci Found; chmn bd dir Afro Arts Ctr 1970-72; mem bd dir Sickle Cell Found GA 1980-; mem bd trustees Morehouse Coll 1984-. **HONORS/ACHIEVEMENTS:** Predoctoral Fellow Brown Univ 1964-70, 1970-71; Postdoctoral Fellow MIT Cambridge 1971-73; David Packard Chair Morehouse Coll 1985-. **BUSINESS ADDRESS:** Chairman Biology/Dir Health Profs, Morehouse College, 830 Westview Dr SW, Atlanta, GA 30310.

HAYNES, LEONARD L., JR.
Clergyman, educator. **PERSONAL:** Born Mar 16, 1923, Austin, TX; son of Leonard L Haynes Sr and Thelma Haynes; married Leila Louise; children: Leonard III, Walter, Angeline, Leila. **EDUCATION:** Huston Tilloston Meth Gammon Theol Sem, AB 1945; Boston Univ, ThD 1948. **CAREER:** Philander Smith Coll, dean 1948; Morristown Jr Coll, pres 1958; So Univ, prof 1960-; Wesley United Meth Church, minister 1960-. **ORGANIZATIONS:** Prchr Eng 1948, Orient 1972; chmn Human Relations Council 1967; lecturer Atlanta 1972; black task force LA Assn of Business & Indus; mem, exec comm LA Assoc of Business & Ind; ed The Black Comm within the United Methodist Church; dir OIC Baton Rouge LA; mem 33 Degree Mason; chairperson, Christians for Good Government 1989-90; mem, President George Bush Republican Task Force, 1989-. **HONORS/ACHIEVEMENTS:** Meth Crusade Scholar 1947; Distinguished Alumnus Awd Boston Univ 1972; Outstanding Coll Teacher 1973; chmn bd Professional Psychotherapy 1977; JK Haynes Foundation Awd 1981; Natl Assn for Equal Oppor in Higher Educ Black Church Awd 1985; State of LA recognized 2/15/87 as LL Haynes Jr Day. **BUSINESS ADDRESS:** Minister, Wesley United Methodist Church, 605 France, Baton Rouge, LA 70821.

HAYNES, MICHAEL E.
Government official, clergyman. **PERSONAL:** Born May 09, 1927, Boston, MA. **EDUCATION:** Berkshire Christian Coll; New Eng Shch Theo, ABM 1949; Shelton Coll. **CAREER:** Commonwealth MA State Parole Bd, mem; 12th Bapt Ch, sr minister 1965-; House Reps 7th Suffolk Dist, mem 1965-69; Norfolk House Crt, soc work staff 1957-64; Commonwealth MA Yth Serv Div, 1955-57; Robert Gould Shaw House, asst boys wrkr 1953-58; Breezy Meadows Camp, prgm dir 1951-62. **ORGANIZATIONS:** Chmn Metro Boston Settlement Assn 1965-67; bd dir New Eng Bapt Hosp; mem Citz Training Grp Boston Juv Ct; Cushing Acad; Gordon-Conwell Theo Sem ; Malone Coll; Boys' Club Boston; Roxbury Clubhouse; Mayor's Com Violence 1976; New Boston Com; City Boston Charitable Fund; chmn gov adv com State Chaplains; Ministerail Alliance Grtr Boston. **HONORS/ACHIEVEMENTS:** Recpt LLD Gordon Coll 1969; Dr Pub Serv Barington Coll 1971; DD NortheasternUniv 1978; publ "Christian-Secular Coop" Urban Mission 1974; "Five Minutes Before Midnight" Evang Missions 1968; Intervarsity Press Champion Urban Challenge 1979. **BUSINESS ADDRESS:** 100 Cambridge St, Boston, MA 02202.

HAYNES, MICHAEL JAMES
Professional athlete. **PERSONAL:** Born Jul 01, 1953, Dennison, TX; married Julie Anne Imdieke; children: 3 children. **EDUCATION:** Attended, AZ State U. **CAREER:** New Eng Patriots, defensive back. **HONORS/ACHIEVEMENTS:** MVP 1973 Fiesta Bowl; Most Valuable Defensive Player 1976 Japan Bowl; 3 yr all WAC; Kodac All-Amer; Sports Writers All-Amer 1975; led natl in interceptions 1974; led team in interceptions 1976-78; Defensive Rookie of Yr Amer Football Conf 1976; All Conf 1976; New England's all time punt return leader; unanimous pick by The Associated Press, Newspaper Enterprise Assoc and Pro Football Writers Assoc as All-Pro; mem NFL Pro Bowl teams 1986, 1987. **BUSINESS ADDRESS:** Los Angeles Raiders, 332 Center St, El Segundo, CA 90245.

HAYNES, NEAL J.
Clergyman, educator. **PERSONAL:** Born Aug 16, 1912, Eddyville, KY; married Ollie Hart; children: Marian. **EDUCATION:** AB BTh MRE DD 1950. **CAREER:** St Louis & St Louis Co, elem tchr pub schs; Theology Wetern Bapt Bible Coll, instr; Western Bapt Bible Coll dean instrn; western bapt Bible CollSt Louis Center, dir; Antioch Dist Assn, mod; Missionary Bapt State Conv MO, exec sec; First Bapt Ch, pastor; Webster Groves Ministerial Alliance, pres 1960-61 & 1973. **ORGANIZATIONS:** Pres Gamma Tau Frat; mem Alpha Theta Zata Frat; mem In-Ter Faith Clergy 1970-74; chmn Audio-Visual Aid Dept Nat Bapt Conv USA Inc 1973-74; Mem Bapt Training Unoin Bd Nat Bapt Conv USA Inc; mem Preaching Team IV S Afrca 1975; chmn Ethics Com Bapt Pastor's Conf St Louis. **HONORS/ACHIEVEMENTS:** Plaque Youth Dept Antioch Dist Assn 1972; outstanding membership award Antioch Dist Assn 1973. **MILITARY SERVICE:** USAF first sgt 1943-46. **BUSINESS ADDRESS:** 159 E Kirkham Ave, Webster Groves, MO 63119.

HAYNES, ORA LEE
Executive director. **PERSONAL:** Born Sep 13, 1925, Cooter, MO; married Joseph; children: Claudia, Joseph. **EDUCATION:** Lane Coll Jackson Tenn, BA 1949f Howard Univ Grad Sch Social Work, 1949-50; Univ Kansas Sch Social Work, MSW 1955. **CAREER:** Baltimore City Schs, social worker 1958-62; Washington DC, clin social worker 1962-63; Long Beach Cal, 1963-65; Los Angeles City Schs, 1965-66; Gillis Home KC MO, case worker supr 1967-69; KCMC Day Care Corp, exec dir 1970-77; Family Servive Assn of Rio Hondo Area Santa Fe Springs CA, exec dir. **ORGANIZATIONS:** Mem Soroptomist Intl Whitter CA; mem SCAEYC; mem NASW; mem NAACP; mem Alpha Kappa Alpha. **HONORS/ACHIEVEMENTS:** Outstanding Serv Award Community 1974; Outstanding Serv as Exec Dir 1974. **BUSINESS ADDRESS:** 7702 Washington Ave, Ste C, Whittier, CA 90602.

HAYNES, SAMUEL LLOYD
Actor. **PERSONAL:** Born Oct 19, 1934, So Bend, IN; divorced. **EDUCATION:** Oceanside Carlsbad Coll, attended;Univ of IN Extension; Los Angeles City Coll; San Jose State Coll. **CAREER:** Modomac Indus, dir of mktg; Room 222, 79 Park Ave, Rosemary's Baby #2, Marcus Welby, Emergency, Julia, Felony Sqd, The FBI, Star Trek, Batman, various other TV Shows, TV actor; Ice Station Zebra, Madigan, The Mad Room, Assault on the Wayne, The Greatest, Good Guys Wear Black, movie actor; Hollywood Shakespeare Fest, stage actor; Night Club Circuit, folksinger; Film Indus Workshop Inc, instr phys educ lab; Quigley Prodns, prodn asst; Los Angeles, tech illustrator. **MILITARY SERVICE:** USNR lt comdr.

HAYNES, SUE BLOOD
Educational administrator. **PERSONAL:** Born Mar 21, 1939, Pine Bluff, AR; married Joe Willis; children: Rodney, Joe B. **EDUCATION:** Seattle U, BA MA 1974; Unoin Grad Sch, PhD 1979; Bryn Mawr Coll, mgmt cert 1979. **CAREER:** S Seattle Comm Coll, dir spl prog 1974-; Seattle U, head couns 1972-74; IBO Data Processing Co Inc, exec officer owner 1969-76; The Boeing Co, systems analysts 1960-69. **ORGANIZATIONS:** Bd of dirs Educ Talent Search 1977-; bd of dir New Careers Found 1978-; editorial bd The Western Jour of Black Studies 1978-; mem Alpha Kappa Alpha Elta Epsilon Omega 1977-; vice pres bd of dir Counc on Black Am Affairs Western Region 1978-79; chairperson founder The Inner-City Health Careers Proj-jack & Jill of Am 1978-79. **HONORS/ACHIEVEMENTS:** Community serv awardUniv of Chicago 1974; pub sch vol award Seattle Pub Sch 1978; Martin Luther King Jr Meml Award Blanks Wooten Prodn 1980; dedicationto black educ award Western Regional Counc on Black Am Affairs 1980; Fellowship Grant-Bryn Mawr Coll Puget Sound Minority Consortium 1980. **BUSINESS ADDRESS:** 6000 16th Ave SW, Seattle, WA 98106.

HAYNES, ULRIC ST. CLAIR, JR.
Diplomat. **PERSONAL:** Born Jun 08, 1931, Brooklyn, NY; son of Ulric S Haynes and Ellaline (Gay) Haynes; married Yolande Toussaint; children: Alexandra, Gregory. **EDUCATION:** Amherst Coll, BA 1952; Yale Law Sch, LL B 1956; Harvard Business School Advanced Mgmt Prgm 1966; Fisk Univ, IN Univ, AL State Coll, John Jay Coll, honorary doctorates. **CAREER:** US Dept of State, foreign serv officer 1963-64; Natl Security Council, stf 1964-1966; Mgmt Formation Inc, pres 1966-70; Spencer Stuart & Assn, sr vice pres 1970-

72; Cummins Engine Co, vice pres mgmt devel 1972-75, vice pres Mid-East & Africa 1975-77; Am Embsy-Algeria, amb 1977-81; Cummins Engine Co, vice pres intl business planning 1981-83; Self-Employed, consultant 1984-85; SUNY Coll at Old Westbury, acting pres 1985-86; AFS Intl/Intercultural Programs, pres 1986-87, consultant 1987-. **ORGANIZATIONS:** Mem bd dir Amer Broadcasting Co 1981-84, Rohm & Haas Co 1981-84, Marine Midland Bank 1981-; mem sel comm Henry Luce Federation Scholars 1975-; mem Council on Foreign Rel 1968-; vice chrmn Assn of Black Amer Ambassadors 1984-; trustee Pratt Univ; dir Inst for Study of Diplomacy; mem US-S African Leader Exchange Program; Intl Sponsor's Council, Howard U, Cncl of Amer Ambassadors, The Yale Club of NYC; honorary chrmn Indiana United Negro Coll Fund Drive; mem Intl Exec Bd Sister Cities Internatl; mem bd of dirs Salzbur-Seminar; mem bd of dirs Smithsonian Associates; mem bd of dirs Technoserve. **HONORS/ACHIEVEMENTS:** Martin Luther King Humanitarian Awd; Black Chrstn Caucus Riverside Church, New York City Martin Luther King Award; student bar assn; Howard Univ Law Schl; resolutions of commendation from IN State Senate & Assbly, CA State Senate, City of Detroit & LA; Alumni Award, Class of 1952; Amherst Coll, Afro-Amer Student Assn, Harvard Busn Schl; Liberty Bell Award IN Young Lawyers Assn; Freedom Award; IN Black Expo 1981; certified, US Dept of State; hon LLDs IN Univ AL State Univ, Fisk Univ, John Jay Coll. **HOME ADDRESS:** 8 Brookwood Ln, Weston, CT 06883. **BUSINESS ADDRESS:** DBM, 100 Park Ave, New York, NY 10017.

HAYNES, WALTER WESLEY
Dentist. **PERSONAL:** Born Nov 16, 1919, St Matthews, SC; children: Saundra, Donald. **EDUCATION:** Lincoln U, AB 1943; Howard Univ Coll Dentistry, DDS 1946. **CAREER:** 1st Presbyterian Ch of Hampstead, deacon 1962-67; Queens Gen Tribro Hosp, 1960-65; Hampstead School, dentist 1962-. **ORGANIZATIONS:** Pres Queens Clinical Soc 1961-62; Ethical Dent Soc 1975-77; mem ADA; NDA; 10th Dist Dental Soc; Beta Kappa Chi; Omega Psi Phi. **HONORS/ACHIEVEMENTS:** Man of the Year Lincoln Univ 1967; Fellow of the Acad of Gen Dentistry 1984. **MILITARY SERVICE:** AUS capt 1946-48. **BUSINESS ADDRESS:** Dentist, 151 Bennett Ave, Hempstead, NY 11550.

HAYNES, WILLIAM J., JR.
Judge. **PERSONAL:** Born Sep 05, 1949, Memphis, TN; son of William J Haynes Sr and Martyna Q McCullough; married Carol Donaldson; children: Paz, Anthony, Maya. **EDUCATION:** Coll of St Thomas, BA 1970; Vanderbilt School of Law, JD 1973. **CAREER:** TN State Atty Gen Office, asst atty general 1973-77; TN State Antitrust & Consumer Protection, dep atty general 1978-84, spec dep atty general for special litigation 1984; US District Court Middle District of TN, magistrate 1984-. **ORGANIZATIONS:** Mem Amer Bar Assn 1978, 1985, 1988; mem 1st vice pres Nashville Bar Assn 1980-84; dist atty gen pro tem Shelby Cty Criminal Court 1980; mem Rotary Intl 1980-; mem bd of dir Cumberland Museum & Sci Ctr 1981-87; mem bd of professional responsibility TN Supreme Court 1982-84; mem bd of dir Napier Lobby Bar Assn 1983-84; chmn antitrust planning comm Natl Assn of Atty General 1984; mem, bd of advisors, Corporate Practice Series, Bureau of Natl Affairs; Lecturer-in-law Vanderbilt School of Law. **HONORS/ACHIEVEMENTS:** Bennet Douglas Bell Awd Vandervilt School of Law 1973; author, "State Antitrust Laws" published by the Bureau of National Affairs, 1988. **HOME ADDRESS:** 6576 Sunnyside Court, Brentwood, TN 37027. **BUSINESS ADDRESS:** US Magistrate, US District Court, 649 US Courthouse, Nashville, TN 37203.

HAYNES, WILLIE C., III (BUTCH)
Educational administrator, elected official. **PERSONAL:** Born Nov 23, 1951, Opelousas, LA; married Rebecca M Smith; children: Markisha A, Willie C IV. **EDUCATION:** Southern Univ Baton Rouge, BS 1973, MAEduc 1976. **CAREER:** Clark Lodge #186, jr deacon 1975-88; Melville HS, asst principal 1982-88; St Landry Parish Police Jury, District 5 Juror, 1988-91. **ORGANIZATIONS:** Mem NAACP 1981-88; mem Governor's Council on Physical Fitness & Sports 1984-87; mem Acidiana Principal's Assn 1984-88; mem bd of dirs St Landry Parish Council on Aging 1985-88. **BUSINESS ADDRESS:** Asst Principal & Sci Teacher, Melville High School, PO Box 466, Melville, LA 71353.

HAYNES, WORTH EDWARD
Educational administrator. **PERSONAL:** Born Apr 20, 1942, Webb, MS; married Linden C Smith; children: Natasha C, Worth Edward. **EDUCATION:** Alcorn StateUniv Lorman MS, BS 1965; WI StateUniv River Falls, MST 1971; IA StateUniv Ames, PhD 1977. **CAREER:** Alcorn State Univ, youth camp dir 1964; Eva H Harris HS Brookhaven MS, tchr vocational agr 1964-69; Hinds Co AHS Utica, tchr vocational agr 1969-72; Utica Jr Coll, dir vocational tech educ 1972-74; IA State Univ Ames, instr agr educ dept 1974-76, grad student adv 1976-77; Utica Jr Coll, dir vocational-tech educ 1977-; Governors Office of Job Develop & Trng, exec dir 1985-86; Div of Industrial Serv & Fed Prog, asst state dir 1987-. **ORGANIZATIONS:** Pres Utica Comm Devel Assoc 1978-80; pres Post Secondary Voc Dirs Assoc MS 1979; chmn Post Secondary State Evaluation Comm Voc Educ MS 1980; vice pres laymen assoc, mem New Hope Bapt Church Jackson MS 1981-; sunday school teacher New Hope Church 1982-. **HONORS/ACHIEVEMENTS:** Outstanding Tchr Awd MS Econ Devel Council Eva Harris High Sch Brookhaven MS 1967-69; Outstanding Young Men of Am 1972; Man of the Year Awd Alpha Phi Alpha Frat Natchez MS 1972; Achievement Awd Gamma Sigma Delta Honor Soc of Agr Ames IA 1976; Outstanding Contributions to Agr Educ IA Vocational Educ Assn Ames 1976; Outstanding Serv to Utica Jr Coll 1984. **BUSINESS ADDRESS:** Assistant Dir, Div of Industrial Svc/Fed Prog, 301 Pearl St, Jackson, MS 39206.

HAYRE, RUTH WRIGHT
Educator. **PERSONAL:** Born in Atlanta, GA; daughter of Richard R Wright, Jr and Charlotte Crogman Wright; married Talmadge B Hayre (deceased); children: Sylvia E Hayre Harrison. **EDUCATION:** Univ of PA, BS, MA, PhD 1948. **CAREER:** Wash DC/Phila, tchr 1942-52; Wm Penn HS Phila, PA, vice principal 1952-56, principal 1956-63; Philadelphia Sch Dist, dist supt 1963-75; Univ of PA Phila, adj prof 1976-79; Philadelphia Sch Dist, school bd mem. **ORGANIZATIONS:** Mem Am Assn of Sch Admin, bd of trustees Citizens Commn on Public Educ Temple Univ Phila, PA 1968-80; bd of trustees Blue Cross of Greater Philadelphia 1978-; mem Philadelphia Bd of Educ 1985-. **HONORS/ACHIEVEMENTS:** Afro-Am Mus Distinguished Daughter of PA, 1960; Philadelphia (BOK) Award, 1976; Award of Distinction, Grad School of Educ Univ of PA 1977; Alumnae Award, Univ of PA; honorary degree L.H.D. Temple Univ 1989; honorary degree L.L.D. Univ of Pennsylvania 1989; Natl PUSH Award Operation PUSH 1989; Philanthropist established fund to pay coll educ for 119 students 1988. **HOME ADDRESS:** 1420 Locust St, 13C, Philadelphia, PA 19102.

HAYS, BUTCH ANTHONY
Professional athlete. **PERSONAL:** Born Sep 16, 1962, Omaha, NE. **EDUCATION:** Univ of CA, BA 1984. **CAREER:** Chicago Bulls, guard 1985-. **HONORS/ACHIEVEMENTS:** Finished Cal career with 1,145 career points good for 10th place in Cal history. **BUSINESS ADDRESS:** Chicago Bulls, 333 N Michigan Ave, Ste 510, Chicago, IL 60601.

HAYSBERT, RAYMOND VICTOR, SR.
Business executive. **PERSONAL:** Born Jan 19, 1920, Cincinnati, OH; son of William Haysbert and Emma Haysbert; married Carol Evelyn Roberts; children: Raymond V Jr, Reginald, Nikita M, Brian R. **EDUCATION:** Wilberforce Univ, BS Math CL 1948; Central State Univ OH, BS Bus Admin CL 1949; Univ of MD, Dr Pub Serv 1984. **CAREER:** City of Cincinnati, boiler oper 1941-42; Central State Univ, instr 1947-52; Parks Sausage Co, genl mgr exec vice pres 1952-74, pres 1974-. **ORGANIZATIONS:** Dir Equitable Bancorp 1971-; dir South Baltimore General Hosp 1973-84; dir C&P Telephone Co 1975-85; pres The Hub Orgn 1979-84; dir Richmond Dist Fed Reserve Bank 1984-; trustee Univ of MO Med System 1984-; dir Bell Atlantic Corp 1985-; mem, The President's Roundtable 1983-. **HONORS/ACHIEVEMENTS:** Man of Yr Baltimore Marketing Assn 1971; Man of Yr Baltimore Business League 1968; Disting Citizens Square/Compass Club 1973; Irving Blum Awd United Way Central MO; Honorary Doctor Public Serv Univ of MD; Baltimore Business Hall of Fame, Junior Achievement Metropolitan Baltimore 1986. **MILITARY SERVICE:** USAF; Civilian Aide to Sec of Army 4 yrs; various awds 1981-. **BUSINESS ADDRESS:** President & CEO, Parks Sausage Co, 501 W Hamburg St, Baltimore, MD 21230.

HAYWARD, ANN STEWART
Producer/director/writer. **PERSONAL:** Born Aug 23, 1944, Philadelphia, PA. **EDUCATION:** Simmons Coll, AB 1966; NY U, grad 1967-70; Am Film Inst Directing Workshop for Women 1977-78; Stanford U, professional jour fellow 1978-79. **CAREER:** Group Visionary Prodns Inc, writer reprtr prdcr 1980; KPIX TV Westinghouse Brdcstng Co, video prod 1979-80; ABC TV Network News Docum Div "Ams & All", prod dir writer 1976-78; ABC TV Network News Docum Div "Closeup", assoc prod 1973-77; ABC TV Network News, dir of research 1972-73. **ORGANIZATIONS:** Mem Dirs Guild of Am; mem Guild of Am.

HAYWARD, JACQUELINE C.
Journalist. **PERSONAL:** Born Oct 23, 1944, East Orange, NJ; married Sidney G. **EDUCATION:** Howard U, BA 1966. **CAREER:** WTOP TV 9, anchorwoman; WAGA TV 5, 1970-72; V Mayor's Ofc, asst to v mayor 1970; City of Miami, dir of Training 1969-70. **ORGANIZATIONS:** Delta Sigma Theta Sor; Nat Counc of Negro Women; Nat Bus & Professional Women; NAACP; Nat Assn of Social Workers. **HONORS/ACHIEVEMENTS:** Women of the 70's Capitol Press Club; Outst Woman, Am Assn ofUniv Women; woman of Achvmt, Nat Multiple Sclerosis Soc; publ Citizen of Yr Kiwanis Club, Toastmasters Club; Delta Sigma Theta. **BUSINESS ADDRESS:** W-USA, 4001 Brandywine St NW, Washington, DC 20016.

HAYWOOD, BERTRON DON
Physician. **PERSONAL:** Born Apr 13, 1934, Garner, NC; married Myrtle Marie Owens; children: Carla, Donna. **EDUCATION:** Shaw U, BS 1957; Meharry Med Coll, MD 1970; NC Cen U, MS 1963; Hubbard Hosp, 1974. **CAREER:** Private Practice Raleigh, 1975; Meharry Medical Coll, instructor 1974; Winston-Salem State Univ, instructor 1963-66; NC Public Schools, teacher 1957-62; S&D Leasing Co, vice pres. **ORGANIZATIONS:** Trustee Bd of Triangel Health Svcs; mem Wake Co Unit of Am Cancer Soc; pres LA Scruggs Med Soc; Am Coll of Ob-gyn; Nat Med Assn; Old N St Med Soc; mem Kappa Slpha Psi; Widow Son Lodge; Sunnybrook Med Ctr. **HONORS/ACHIEVEMENTS:** Academic Scholarship ShawUniv 1953; grantUniv MI Nat Sci Found 1959-60; Upjohn Achievement Award 1970. **BUSINESS ADDRESS:** 100 Sunnybrook Rd, Raleigh, NC 27610.

HAYWOOD, EMMETT L.
Business executive. **PERSONAL:** Born May 28, 1937, Cuero, TX; married J Frances Marie; children: Eric William, Kirsten Lee. **EDUCATION:** KS StateUniv Manhattan KS, BA 1960; Univ of OK, Master of Reg & City Planning 1966; OK Cntr for Urban & Reg Studies Norman OK, research asst 1964-66; Boulder CO, asst planning dir 1966-68; Model Cities & Agency Kansas City MO, chief planning 1968-69; ResrDevel Corp Denver, chief planner 1969-70; US Dept Housing & Urban Devel Denver, urban planner 1970-72; Comprehensive Planning Div US Dept HUD Denver 1972; Grad Dept of City Reg PlanningUniv of CO, lectr 1973-75. **ORGANIZATIONS:** Treas CO Chapter Am Inst of Planners 1968; pres CO Chapter Am Inst of Planners 1973-75; life mem Alpha Phi Alpha Frat; mem Nat Nominating Com Am Inst of Planners 1973-74; chmn Nat Nominating Com Am Inst of Planners 1974-75; mem Am Inst of Planners; mem bd of dir Am Soc of Planning Ofcl 1975-78. **HONORS/ACHIEVEMENTS:** Recip Lew Wentz SchlrshpUniv of OK 1965-66; dept of Reg & City Planning Book AwardUniv of OK 1966; dean's listUniv Of OK 1964-66. **MILITARY SERVICE:** AUS 1961-64. **BUSINESS ADDRESS:** Office of CPD US Dept HUD 19, Stout Fed Bldg, Denver, CO 80202.

HAYWOOD, HIRAM H., JR.
Deacon. **PERSONAL:** Born Jan 08, 1921, Key West, FL; married Charlean Peters; children: Hiram III, Yolanda, Yvonne. **EDUCATION:** 2 yrs college. **CAREER:** US Naval Gun Factory Washington & Naval Ordnance Sta Indian Head MD, 32 yrs; Catholic Archdiocese Washington, permanent deacon. **ORGANIZATIONS:** Knights of Columbus 4th deg. **HONORS/ACHIEVEMENTS:** Fed Superior Accomplishment Awds 1960 1972. **MILITARY SERVICE:** USAAF cadet & sgt 1943-46. **BUSINESS ADDRESS:** Deacon, Catholic Archdiocese Wash, St Joseph's Seminary, 1200 Varnum St NE, Washington, DC 20017.

HAYWOOD, L. JULIAN
Physician, educator. **PERSONAL:** Born in Reidsville, NC; son of Thomas W Sr and Louise V; married Virginia; children: Julian, Anthony. **EDUCATION:** Hampton Inst, BS 1948; Howard U, MD 1952, (Dist Alummi Award) 1982. **CAREER:** Univ of So CA, asst prof 1963-67; LAC/USC Med Ctr, dir, CCU 1966-; Univ of So CA, assoc prof 1967-76; Cmprhnsv Sickle Cell Ctr LAC/USC, dir 1972; Loma Linda U, clncl prof of med 1973-78;Univ of So CA, prof of med 1976-; LAC/USC Med Ctr, sr physician. **ORGANIZATIONS:** Pres Sickle Cell Disease Res Found 1978-89; past pres AHA/Greater Los Angeles Aff 1983; gvnrs comm Amer Coll of Phys 1981-; consltnt Martin Luther King Jr Hosp 1970-; flw Amer Coll of Car-

diology 1968-, Amer Coll of Physcns 1964-, Amer Heart Assoc 1983-; cnsltnt CA State Dept of Health Hypertnsn Cntrl Prog, consultant, NHLBI; various committees, HCT Div PHS. **HONORS/ACHIEVEMENTS:** Certf of Merit City of Los Angeles 1982; Certf of recogntn Natl Med Assoc 1982; Newsmaker of the Year Nat Assoc of Medica Women 1982; dist Service Award AHA/GLAA 1984; Louis Russell Award, AHA 1988; Heart of Gold Award, AHA 1989; over 400 scientific papers and abstracts. **MILITARY SERVICE:** USN lt 1954-56. **BUSINESS ADDRESS:** Professor of Medicine, LAC/USC Medical Center, 1200 N State St Box 305, Los Angeles, CA 90033.

HAYWOOD, MARGARET A.
Senior judge. **PERSONAL:** Born Oct 08, 1912, Knoxville, TN; daughter of Jonathan Austin and Mayme Austin; divorced; children: Geraldine H Hoffman. **EDUCATION:** Robert H Terrell Law Sch, LLB 1940. **CAREER:** General Practice, attorney 1940-72; DC Coun, mem 1967-72; Superior Court Dist of Columbia, assoc judge 1972-82. **ORGANIZATIONS:** Natl grand basileus Lambda Kappa Mu Sor Inc 1948-52; moderator United Church of Christ 1973-75; mem DC, Wash, Amer Bar Assns; mem Women's Bar Assn; Bar Assn of the DC; Natl Bar Assn; mem Cosmopolitan Bus & Prof Women's Club; mem People's Congregational United Ch of Christ; mem Zonta Intl. **HONORS/ACHIEVEMENTS:** Cited Lambda Kappa Mu Sor Outstanding Sor of Yr 1947; NAACP Trophy 1950; one of Am Outstanding Women Natl Coun of Negro Women 1951; elected to Afro-AmerNewspaper Honor Roll 1951; Women of Yr Barrister's Wives Inc 1954; cited by Sigma Delta Tau Legal frat for Outstanding Prof Serv 1957; cited People's Congregational Church Meritorious Serv 1961; cited Lambda Kappa Mu Sor elected to Disting Serv Key Chap 1967; cited Lambda Kappa Mu Sor Outstanding Sor of Yr 1968; Natl Bar Assn Awd 1968; Woman of Yr by Oldest Inhabitants 1969; cited Lambda Kappa M Sorority, Outstanding Soror of year 1972; Woman Lawyer of Yr Women's Bar Assn 1972; Awarded Hon Degree Dr of Humanics Elmhurst Coll 1974; Hon Doctor Humane Letters Carleton Coll Northfield MN 1975; Hon DL Catawba Coll Salisbury NC 1976; honorary doctor of laws degree, Doane Coll, Crete, Nebraska, 1979; awarded Charles Hamilton Houston Medallion of Merit, by the Washington Bar Assn for contribution to jurisprudence, 1980. **BUSINESS ADDRESS:** Senior Judge, Superior Court DC, 500 Indiana Ave NW, Washington, DC 20001.

HAYWOOD, NORCELL D.
Business executive, architect. **PERSONAL:** Born Jan 23, 1935, Bastrop, TX; children: Natalie Dawn, Nan Deliah, David Norcell. **EDUCATION:** Prairie View A&M Coll, 1954-55;Univ of TX, BA 1955-60. **CAREER:** Prarie View A&M Coll, instr schl of engineering 1960-61; planning dept 1961; Eugene Wukasch, architect eng TX 1961-63; O'Neil Ford & Assoc San Antonio, 1963-68; Norcell D Haywood & Asoc San Antonio, 1968-72; Haywood Jordan Mc Cowan Inc, pres 1972. **ORGANIZATIONS:** Mem Am Inst of Architects; TX Soc of Architects; San Antonio Chap Am Inst of Architects; Construction Specifications Inst; past pres 1971-73 Minority Architects Inc of TX & LA M Arch; Greater San Antonio C Of C; bd dir San Antonio BRC; life mem Alpha Phi Alpha; BBB of San Antonio Inc; bd of Prof FREE; bd dir Met YMCA; bd dir Mid Am Region YMCA; sec Nat Org of Min Architects; bd dir Healy Murphy Learning Cntr; Alamo Area Coun of Govt Regional Devel & Review Com; bd dir Nat Coun of YMCA;Univ of TX Schl of Architecture Dean's Coun; bd dir San Antonio Bus Resource Cntr; coach bd of dir San Antonio Symphony Soc; chmn Alamo City C of C. **HONORS/ACHIEVEMENTS:** Recip Merit Award 2nd Bapt Ch San Antonio Am Inst of Architects Design Award Prog San Antonio Chap 1968; certificate of commendation Houston Municipal Art Commn 1973-74. **BUSINESS ADDRESS:** 1802 S WW White Rd, PO Box 20378, San Antonio, TX 78220.

HAYWOOD, ROOSEVELT V., JR.
Business executive. **PERSONAL:** Born Feb 06, 1929, Mount Bayou, MS; married Adel; children: 6 Children. **EDUCATION:** IN U. **CAREER:** Haywood Ins Agy, owner. **ORGANIZATIONS:** City Councilman at Large Gary; state chmn Fair Share Orgn; fndr pres United Cncl Midtown Bsnsmen; fndr pres Gary's Midtown Voters League; mem adv bdGary Urban League; vice pres Gary NAACP; co-foundr pres Gary Toastmasters; natl mem trustee Pilgrim Bapt Ch. **BUSINESS ADDRESS:** 1983 Broadway, Gary, IN.

HAYWOOD, SPENCER
Professional basketball player. **PERSONAL:** Born Apr 22, 1949, Silver City, MS. **CAREER:** European League Italy, basketball player; NY Knicks, basketball player; LA Lakers, basketball player. **HONORS/ACHIEVEMENTS:** NBA A-All Star Team 1972, 73, 74, 75. **BUSINESS ADDRESS:** NY Knicks Madison SQ Garden, Four Pennsylvania Plz, New York, NY 10001.

HAYWOOD, WARDELL
Association executive. **PERSONAL:** Born Feb 21, 1928, Chicago, IL; married Pearline Pope; children: Wardell Jr, Doris Akasania, Lorraine Johnson, Sharon Johnson, Stephanie Johnson. **EDUCATION:** Harvard Bus Sch, AMP 1975; Chicago St U, Soc 1978. **CAREER:** South Shore YMCA, exec dir; YMCA of Met Chgo, vice pres 1964-;Univ of Chgo, inhltn thrpst 1964; United Pcknghs Wkrs Union, trade union orgnzr 1950-57; IL Bell Tel Co, consult 1966-68; KUUMBA Wrkshp, consult 1978-80. **ORGANIZATIONS:** Mem Harvard Club of Chicago 1975-80; mem Chicago Urban Leag 1977-80. **HONORS/ACHIEVEMENTS:** Recip outst prsn awd Ebony Mag Chicago 1967; WGRT grt guy awd WGRT Radio Chicago 1970; outst ldrshp awd Leag of Blk Wmn Chicago 1977. **BUSINESS ADDRESS:** Executive Dir, South Shore YMCA, 1833 E 71st St, Chicago, IL 60649.

HAYWOOD, WILLIAM H.
Company executive. **PERSONAL:** Born Nov 04, 1942, Raleigh, NC. **EDUCATION:** St Augustines Coll, 1960; NC State at Raleigh, 1961; Univ of NC at Chapel Hill, 1964. **CAREER:** R & B Prod Phonogram Inc, vice pres 1977; Phonogram Inc, natl program mgr 1975-77; Bill Haywood Inc, pres 1973-75; DJ Prod, pres 1972-73; WOL Radio, DJ program dir 1967-72; WOOK Radio, program dir 1965-67; WLLE Inc, program dir 1962-65; Kirby Co, sales mgr 1960-62. **ORGANIZATIONS:** Dir, Washington Baltimore Chapter NATRA 1971; head Broadcast Commn BMA 1979. **BUSINESS ADDRESS:** Phonogram Mercury Inc, 810 7th Ave, New York, NY 10019.

HAYWOODE, M. DOUGLAS
Attorney, educator. **PERSONAL:** Born Feb 24, 1938, Brooklyn; divorced; children: Alyssa, Arthur. **EDUCATION:** Brooklyn Coll, BA 1959; Brooklyn Law Schl, JD 1962; LLM 1967; New Sch Social Resrch, MA 1970; PhD Cand. **CAREER:** Private Practice Law, 1962; City of NY, prof Political Science 1969; New York City Branch NAACP, counsel 1962-64; Human Resources Admin NYC, assoc gen counsel 1972-74. **ORGANIZATIONS:** Mem New York City Bar Assn; Nat Conf Black Lawyers; Am Soc Intl Law; Intl African Centre. **HONORS/ACHIEVEMENTS:** Governor personal Appointee, New York Housing Corp. **BUSINESS ADDRESS:** 60 East 86th St, New York, NY 10028.

HAZARD, BENJAMIN W.
Curator. **PERSONAL:** Born May 30, 1940, Newport, RI; children: Mark. **EDUCATION:** Solano Community Coll Fairfield CA, 1963-65; CA Coll of Arts & Crafts, BA 1965-68;Univ of CA, MA 1968-69. **CAREER:** Oakland Mus, curator 1970; Stanford U, instr 1971-72; Merritt Coll, 1970;Univ of NV, 1969-70; Berkeley Unified Sch Dist 1968-69. **ORGANIZATIONS:** V chmn AAM Educ Com; BART Art Cncl; bd of dir Far West Schl; Alliance of CA Arts Cncls; mem CA Alliance for Art Edn; CA Coll of Arts & Crafts; mem Nat Endowment for Humanities; appointee Nat Mus Serv Bd by Pres Carter 1978-80. **HONORS/ACHIEVEMENTS:** 1st Awrd Vallejo Art Exhibit 1964-65; Joseph P Herger Award 1965; CA Coll of Arts & Crafts Schrsp 1967-68; Ford Award 1969; listed Personalities of West &Midwest. **BUSINESS ADDRESS:** 1000 Oak St, Oakland, CA 94607.

HAZELWOOD, HARRY, JR.
Judge. **PERSONAL:** Born Oct 08, 1921, Newark; married Ruth Gainous; children: Harry, Stephen. **EDUCATION:** Rutgers Univ, BA 1943; Cornell Law School, LLB 1945. **CAREER:** Atty, 1948; Co Prosecutor, asst 1956-58; City of Newark, municipal judge 1958-74; City Newark, chief judge 1970-74; Essex Co Ct, judge 1974-79; Essex Co, superior Ct judge 1978. **ORGANIZATIONS:** Mem Am Essex Co NJ; Natl Bar Assn. **BUSINESS ADDRESS:** Judge, State of New Jersey, Essex County Cts Bldg, Room 706, Newark, NJ 07102.

HAZZARD, TERRY LOUIS
Educational administrator. **PERSONAL:** Born Jul 08, 1957, Mobile, AL; son of Milton Hazzard and Ora D Sheffield Hazzard; married Tanya Finkley Hazzard, Jun 27, 1981. **EDUCATION:** AL A&M Univ, BS 1979; Univ of AL, MA 1980; The Florida State University, Tallahassee, Florida, Doctoral Student. **CAREER:** Univ of AL, financial aid peer counselor 1979-80, residence hall asst dir 1980, coord/coop educ 1980-81; Spring Hill College, counselor/upward bound 1981-85; Bishop State Community Coll, asst dean of students. **ORGANIZATIONS:** Alpha Phi Alpha Frat; actor Whole Backstage Performer 1979-80; choir Greater Mt Olive # 2 Baptist Church; actor/entertainer Mobile Theatre Guild; vocalist Mobile Opera; SAEOPP; AAEOPP; AL Assoc for Guidance/Counseling; AL Assoc of Deans of Students; mem bd of dir Mobile (AL) Opera; mem, 3rd vice pres, Alabama A&M Alumni Assn. **HONORS/ACHIEVEMENTS:** Cum Laude AL A&M Univ 1979; broadway audition Detroit Music Hall 1979; Kappa Delta Pi Honor Soc Sch of Educ 1979-81; Honor Roll & Dean's List student 1978-79; vocalist, Miss USA Pagent, 1989; publications in the Eric System, "Attitudes of White Students Attending Black Colleges and Universities," 1989, "Affirmative Action and Women in Higher Education," 1989. **HOME ADDRESS:** 1700 W Princeton Woods Dr, Mobile, AL 36608.

HAZZARD, WALT (MAHDI ABDUL RAHMAN)
Basketball coach. **PERSONAL:** Born Apr 15, 1942, Wilmington, DE; son of Dr Walter R Hazzard Sr and Alexina Ayers Hazzard; married Jaleesa Patricia Shull Shephard; children: Yakub, Jalal, Khalil, Rasheed. **EDUCATION:** Univ CA at LA, BS Kiniesiology 1964. **CAREER:** Pro basketball player, Los Angeles Lakers 1964-67; Seattle Supersonics 1967-68; Buffalo Braves 1971-73; Golden State Warriors 1972-73; UCLA, college basketball coach; Compton Community College; Chapman College; UCLA, asst vice-chancellor. **ORGANIZATIONS:** Mem Olympic Team 1964; dir Comm Relations Fulton Mills; Kappa Alpha Psi Frat; 100 Black Men. **HONORS/ACHIEVEMENTS:** Selected charter mem of UCLA Athletic Hall of Fame; Coach of 1985 Natl Invitation Tournament championship team; 1964 NCAA Player of the Year; 1964 NCAA Tournament Most Outstanding Player; Eighth-leading career scorer in UCLA history; Pacific Ten Conference Coach of the Year 1987; Father of the Year; Athletes and Entertainers for Kids.

HEACOCK, DON ROLAND
Psychiatist. **PERSONAL:** Born Jun 02, 1928, Springfield, MA; married Melba Fiorentino; children: Stephan, Roland, Maria. **EDUCATION:** Colby Coll, BA 1949; HowardUniv Coll of Med, MD 1954. **CAREER:** Bronx Psychiat Ctr, dir adolescent Serv 1975-79; Mt Sinai Coll of Med, clinical asst prof in psychiatry; Knickerbocker Hosp, dept of psychiatry 1970-72. **ORGANIZATIONS:** Mem Am Psychiat Assn; NY Dist Br of APA; NY State Med Assn; Am Ortho Psychiat Assn; NY Cncl on Child Psychiatry; fellow Am Acad of Child Psychiatry. **HONORS/ACHIEVEMENTS:** Diplomate Am Bd Psychiatry & Neurology 1962; diplomate Am Bd Child Psychiatry 1965; editor "A Psycodynamic Approach to Adolescent Psychiatry" 1980; author Black Slum Child Problem of Aggression 1977; num other papers. **MILITARY SERVICE:** AUS capt 1956-58. **BUSINESS ADDRESS:** 5 Kingswood Way, South Salem, NY 10590.

HEAD, EDITH
Elected official. **PERSONAL:** Born Nov 16, 1927, Autaugaville, AL; married Toysie Lee Head; children: Alberta, Patricia A, Timothy L, Robert W. **EDUCATION:** Wilkins Cosmetology Sch, graduated 1955; Market Training Inst, graduated 1968; Cuyahoga Comm Coll. **CAREER:** Clinic Inn Motel, desk clerk 1969-72; East Cleveland Public Library, front office aide 1972-74; Villa Angela School, media aide 1974-75; City of East Cleveland, commissioner 1978-. **ORGANIZATIONS:** Pres Orinoco St Club 1968-82; pres Comm Action Team 1975; mem Cuyahoga Democratic Party 1975-; mem Natl League of Cities 1978-; mem OH Municipal League 1978-; pres The Comm for East Cleveland Black Women 1983-. **HONORS/ACHIEVEMENTS:** Honorary Citizen City of Atlanta GA 1979; Special Recognition ECCJC E Cleveland 1980; Certificate of Appreciation City of E Cleveland 1984; Outstanding Work Citizens of E Cleveland 1982. **HOME ADDRESS:** 1816 Taylor Rd, Cleveland, OH 44112. **BUSINESS ADDRESS:** Commissioner, City of East Cleveland, 14340 Euclid Ave, East Cleveland, OH 44112.

HEAD, HELAINE
Artist. **PERSONAL:** Born Jan 17, Los Angeles. **EDUCATION:** Univ San Francisco, BA 1968. **CAREER:** Am Conservatory Theatre, stage mgr 3 yrs; NY Shakespeare Festival; Spoleto Festival Italy, prod stage mgr "Your Arm's Too Short To Box With God" 1975;

broadway prods, "Ain't Suppose To Die a Natural Death", "Raisin", "The Royal Family"; "Porgy & Bess"; Lincoln Center-mitzi Newhouse Theatre, dir; Afro-am Total Theatre; "Porgy & Bess" 2nd European Tour; Am Conservatory Theatre; Negro Ensemble Co; Urban Arts Corp; Marin Shakespeare Festival; Brooklyn Acad Music; Henry St Settlement; Frank Silvera Writer's Workshop; Harlem Cultural Ctr; Vest Pociket Thr; Richard Allen Center for Culture & Art. **HONORS/ACHIEVEMENTS:** 2nd Annual Audelco Recob Award 1974.

HEAD, LAURA DEAN
Educator. **PERSONAL:** Born Nov 03, 1948, Los Angeles, CA; daughter of Marvin Head and Helaine Head. **EDUCATION:** San Francisco State Coll, BA 1971; Univ of MI, MA 1974, PhD 1978. **CAREER:** Univ of CA Riverside, 1973-76; Urban Inst for Human Develop, project dir 1978-80; Far West Lab for Educ Rsch & Develop, project dir 1980-81; San Francisco State Univ, prof black studies 1978-. **ORGANIZATIONS:** Chmn of bd Marin City Multi Serv Inst 1978-; chair Black Child Develop Inst 1978-81; mem Comm on Sch Crime CA State Dept of Educ 1981; mem bd of dir Oakland Men's Project 1988-; mem Committee to organize the 20th anniversary commemoration of the 1968 San Francisco State University student strike 1988. **HONORS/ACHIEVEMENTS:** Fellowship Minority Fellowship Prog Amer Psych Assoc 1976-77; Meritorious Promise Awd San Francisco State Univ 1984. **HOME ADDRESS:** 3614 Randolph Ave, Oakland, CA 94602. **BUSINESS ADDRESS:** Professor of Black Studies, San Francisco StateUniv, 1600 Holloway Ave, San Francisco, CA 94132.

HEAD, RAYMOND, JR.
City official, business executive. **PERSONAL:** Born Feb 23, 1921, Griffin, GA; son of Raymond Head Sr and Pauline Head; married Ceola Johnson; children: Cheryl Johnson, Raylanda Anderson, Raymond III. **EDUCATION:** Tuskegee Inst, BS 1943. **CAREER:** Griffin Co, city commnr, 1971, mayor 1977, 1985, mayor pro tem, 1975, 1986, 1989; Cleanwell Cleaners, partnerand tailor, 1956—. **ORGANIZATIONS:** Mem treas steward Heck Chapel United Meth Ch 1948; comdr 1946-51 quartermaster 1951—, Vaughn-Blake VFW Post 8480; chrtr mem Morgan-Brown Am Legion Post 546; mem Spalding Improv League; Spalding Jr Achvmt; C of C GA Assoc of Retarded Children; Spalding Pike Upson Co Dept of Labor 1972; bd of Family & Children Serv 1970; del to Natl Dem Conv 1976; vol worker for Am Cancer Soc Inc Spalding Co Unit; Cert Lay Sprk United Meth Ch; chrmn Pastor Parish Rel Heck Chapel Red Oak Charge; mem Griffin Dist Commn on Bldg & Loc; United Meth N GA Conf Com on Ethnic Minority Local Ch; convener Griffin Spalding Co Commn Human Reltns; pres NAACP; bd dir Spalding & Convalescent Cntr; mem trustee bd N GA Meth Conf; mem Griffin Spalding Hosp Authority 1971; v chmn bd dir State McIntosh Trail Area Planning & Dev l Commn 1975; appointed by GA Gov Carter to State Hosp Advisory Cncl 1972; GA Municipal Assn 6th Dist Dir 1974-75; Dem Natl Convention delegate; GMA Municipal Commission; Spalding Co Health Bd. **HONORS/ACHIEVEMENTS:** Outstdng Community Serv Citizens of Spalding Co 1969; Dedicated Serv Laciso Club 1971; Outstdng Serv Awds 1st Black Elected Offical Caballeros Dlub 1972; Civic Improv League 1976; Heck Chapel United Meth Ch 1977; 8 St Bapt Ch 1977; Bicentennial Awd Griffin Spalding Bicentennial Comm 1976 Awd for 30 yrs of dedicated Svc; Vaughn-blake VFW Post 8480 1977; Disting Serv Awd Mayor, Businessman, Religious Ldr, & Civic Ldr 1977; Ft Vlly St Coll 38th Ann Awd; Man of yr Awd; Griffin Spalding NNBPW Club 1977; proclamation by City of Griffin; Mayor Raymond Head Jr, lifetime mem Vauhn-blake VFW Post 8480; citation, Locust Grove Masonic Lodge 543; Griffin Branch NAACP citation, 1977, Roy Wilkins Freedom Awd, 1985; Tuskegee U and Spalding County Athletic Halls of Fame, 1985; certificates of appreciation, American Heart Assn; Amer Legion Post 546; General Griffin Chamber of Commerce award, 1989. **MILITARY SERVICE:** AUS s sgt 1943-46. **BUSINESS ADDRESS:** 118 N 8 St, Griffin, GA 30223.

HEAD, SAMUEL
County government official. **PERSONAL:** Born Nov 20, 1948, Tampa, FL; divorced; children: Samuel S, Jr, Shauna D. **EDUCATION:** Florida A & M University, Tallahassee FL, BS, 1970; Valdosta State College, Valdosta GA, certificate in govt management, 1980; National University, MS, 1989; Golden Gate University, Las Vegas NV, MPA candidate, 1986—. **CAREER:** Atlanta Board of Education, Atlanta GA, educator, 1970-73; Harold A Dawson Real Estate Brokers, Atlanta GA, real estate executive, 1973-81; Federal Emergency Management Agency, Atlanta GA, management specialist, 1976-82; Cuban Refuge Operation, Key West FL, deputy federal coordinating officer, 1980; EG & G Inc, Las Vegas NV, assistant personnel security administrator, 1982-84; NV Economic Development Co, Las Vegas NV, director of commercial revitalization, 1984-85; Clark County Manager's Office, Las Vegas NV, economic development specialist, 1985—. **ORGANIZATIONS:** American Society of Public Administrators; Conference of Minority Public Administrators; National Forum for Black Public Administrators; National Association of Human Rights Workers; Florida A & M National Alumni Association; chairman, Governor's Advisory Council on Black Economic Development, 1988—; member, NV State Job Training Coordinating Council, 1988—; chairman, Clark County Minority/Women Business Council, 1987—; Toastmasters International; president, Uptown Kiwanis International Club, 1987—; president, Las Vegas chapter, Alpha Phi Alpha Fraternity, 1983—; Prince Hall Free and Accepted Masons. **HONORS/ACHIEVEMENTS:** Meritorious Award, Uptown Kiwanis Club, 1988. **BUSINESS ADDRESS:** Economic Development Specialist, Clark County Manager's Office, 225 Bridger Ave, Las Vegas, NV 89155.

HEADLEY, DE COSTA ONEAL
Government official. **PERSONAL:** Born Mar 03, 1946, New York, NY; married Geraldine Gibson; children: DeCosta Jr, Kimberly, Natasha. **EDUCATION:** Shaw Univ, BA 1977. **CAREER:** Fed of Addiction Svcs, exec admin 1968-70; Ashford Group Home, dir 1970-77; Comm Alliance for Youth Action, exec dir 1977-83; College for Human Svcs, consultant 1982-83; US Congress, special asst 1983-. **ORGANIZATIONS:** Mem Comm Sch Bd Dist 19 1980-; mem Interfaith Hosp Comm Adv Bd 1980-; mem Comm Bd #5 1980-. **HONORS/ACHIEVEMENTS:** Comm Serv Awd NY Jaycees 1980; Comm Serv Awd St John's Hosp 1980; US Flag US Congress 1980; Comm Serv Awd Delta Sigma Theta 1980. **BUSINESS ADDRESS:** Special Assistant, US Congress, 276 Stuyvesant Ave, Brooklyn, NY 11221.

HEARD, GARFIELD
Professional athlete. **PERSONAL:** Born May 03, 1948, Hogansville, GA; children: Yaasmeen, Gyasi. **EDUCATION:** Univ of OK, grad 1970. **CAREER:** Professional basketball player, Seattle, 1970-72, Chicago Bulls 1972-73, Buffalo Braves 1973-76, Phoenix Suns 1976. **HONORS/ACHIEVEMENTS:** All Big Eight Conf; MVP in the Big Eight 1970; MVP in Marshall Univ Tournament 1970.

HEARD, LONEAR WINDHAM
Corporate executive. **PERSONAL:** Married James T. Heard, 1864 (died 1981); children: four daughters. **EDUCATION:** Rust Coll, BA, 1964; Atlanta Univ, GA, MBA. **CAREER:** Rust Coll, sec to dir of public relations, sec to pres; Amer Natl Bank and Trust, statistical sec; James T. Heard Mgmt Corp, Cerritos, CA, co-mgr, became owner and pres; Rust Coll, vice pres of bd of trustees; Vermont Slauson, mem bd of dir. **HONORS/ACHIEVEMENTS:** McDonald's Golden Arch Award, 1986. **BUSINESS ADDRESS:** James T. Heard Management Corp., 16627 S. Valley View Ave., Cerritos, CA 90701. *

HEARD, NATHAN CLIFF
Author. **PERSONAL:** Born Nov 07, 1936, Newark, NJ; son of Nathan E. Heard and Gladys Pruitt Heard; children: Melvin, Cliff, Natalie. **CAREER:** CA State Univ, Fresno, guest lecturer in creative writing, 1969-70; Rutgers Univ, New Brunswick, NJ, asst prof of English, 1970-72. **ORGANIZATIONS:** Mem, Natl Soc of Literature and the Arts. **HONORS/ACHIEVEMENTS:** Author of Howard Street, Dial, 1968, To Reach a Dream, Dial, 1972, A Cold Fire Burning, Simon & Schuster, 1974, When Shadows Fall, Playboy Paperbacks, 1977, The House of Slammers, Macmillan, 1983. Author's awards from NJ Assn of Teachers of English, 1969, and Newark Coll of Engineering, 1973. **BUSINESS ADDRESS:** Nathan Cliff Heard, c/o Macmillan Publishers, Publicity Dept, 866 Third Ave, New York, NY 10022. *

HEARN, ROSEMARY
Educational administrator. **PERSONAL:** Born May 01, 1929, Indianapolis, IN; daughter of Oscar Thomas Hearn and Mabel Lee Ward Hearn. **EDUCATION:** Howard University, BA 1951; Indiana University, MA 1958, PhD 1973. **CAREER:** Lincoln University, Jefferson City MO, english prof 1958—, dir of honors program 1968-72, executive dean/acad affairs 1983-85, spec asst to pres for acad affairs 1985-87; dean, College of Arts and Sciences 1989—. **ORGANIZATIONS:** Natl Assn of Teachers of English; College Language Assn; Delta Sigma Theta; Jefferson City United Way, secretary, board of directors 1983-; Missouri Community Betterment Awards Competition, judge 1983; Mo State Planning Committee, American Council on Education, Natl Identification Program, member 1983-; Planning Committee, Natl Association of State Land Grant Colleges and Universities, member 1985-; Mid-Missouri Associated Colleges & Universities, vice-chairperson executive committee mid-Missouri; mem Missouri Assn for Social Welfare; reviewer/consultant, Amer Assn of Univ Women; advisory panel, MO Council on Arts, 1987—; reviewer, Amer Library Assn; reviewer/consultant, US Dept of HEW, 1977-79. **HONORS/ACHIEVEMENTS:** Outstanding teacher, Lincoln U, 1971; Development Proposals, Dept of HEW, district reader 1977-79; Phelps-Stokes (West Africa, 1975) NEH, grants received 1977-80; NEH, Division of Research Programs, proposal reviewer 1980-81; American Library Association, CHOICE, consultant-reviewer 1985-; Comm Serv Award, Jefferson City United Way, 1987. **BUSINESS ADDRESS:** Dean of College of Arts and Sciences, Lincoln University, 820 Chestnut St, Jefferson City, MO 65101.

HEARNS, THOMAS
Professional boxer. **PERSONAL:** Born Oct 18, 1958, Memphis, TX; children: Natasha. **CAREER:** Professional boxer; World Boxing Assoc Super-Welterweight Champion 1982-. **ORGANIZATIONS:** Volunteer policeman Detroit Police Dept. **HONORS/ACHIEVEMENTS:** Super Welterweight Champion; Amateur Boxer of the Yr Award 1977; Natl Golden Gloves 139 lb Champ 1977; Natl AAU 139 lb Champ 1977; Won WBA (World Boxing Assn) World Welterweight Championship 1980; Fighter of the Yr "Ring Magazine" 1980; Fighter of the Yr Boxing Writers Assn 1980; Won World Boxing Council Super Welterweight Championship 1982; Fighter of the Yr "Ring Magazine" 1985; Won WBC Middleweight Championship. 1987. **BUSINESS ADDRESS:** c/o Emanuel Steward, 19600 W McNichol St, Detroit, MI 48219. *

HEATH, BERTHA CLARA
Humanitarian/historian. **PERSONAL:** Born Jul 22, 1909, Middletown Township, NJ. **EDUCATION:** Harlem Hosp Sch of Nursing, Diploma 1930; New York Univ, BS 1948; Columbia Univ, MA 1958. **CAREER:** New York Dept of Hospitals, clinician 1931-74; Clinton P and Mary E Heath Ctr, co-founder with Mon Co Park System NJ 1974-80. **ORGANIZATIONS:** Mem Harlem Hosp Alumni Assoc 1930-, NAACP 1930-, Natl Assoc of Grad Negro Nurses 1937-, Amer Red Cross 1940-, New York Public Library Assoc 1944-; lecturer Focus on Black History The Heath Family 1944-; mem Amer Assoc of Retired Persons 1974-, Monmouth Co Historical Soc 1975-, Middletown Township Historical Soc 1975-; charter mem Belford NJ Prayer Group 1979-; commissioner Middletown Human Rights Commn 1983-; mem Amer Assoc of Univ Women 1984-; mem Amer Library Assoc NIAB Club NJ 1987-; pres, trustee bd Clinton Chapel AME. **HONORS/ACHIEVEMENTS:** Proclamation Human Rights Middletown Twp NJ 1986; Proclamation Afro Amer/Black History (Mayoral) Middletown Township NJ 1986; honorary mem Natl Police Officers Assoc of Amer NJ State Chap 1987-; saluted as a Black Historian and Humanitarian by The Asbury Park Press, Red Bank Register, Newark Star Ledger, Middletown Township Courier; Humanitarian Awd East Central Dist of the NJ State Fed of Colored Women's Clubs Inc 1987. **HOME ADDRESS:** 179 Harmony Rd, Middletown, NJ 07748. **BUSINESS ADDRESS:** Founder, Clinton P & Mary E Heath Ctr, Tatum Park - Red Hill Rd, Middletown, NJ 07748.

HEATH, COMER, III
Educational administrator. **PERSONAL:** Born Feb 22, 1935, Eastman, GA; married Lois J Burke. **EDUCATION:** Wayne State Univ, BS 1962; Univ of MI, MA Couns & Guidance 1965; Wayne State Univ, EdD Educ 1961. **CAREER:** Wayne State Univ, guidance counselor 1968-75; City of Highland Park, sch comm coord 1975; Highland Park Comm Coll, dir admin/records 1976, vice pres for coll serv 1977, dean liberal arts & scis 1981; pres 1978-. **ORGANIZATIONS:** Mem Kappa Alpha Psi Frat 1960-; mem Phi Delta Kappa 1962-; consult Interdisciplinary Approach to Counseling Wayne State Univ 1969; asst prof guidance/psychol St Clair Coll Windsor Canada 1971; consult Sch Liaison for Boy Scouts of Amer 1972; prof guidance couns Wayne State Univ European Prog Turkey/Germany 1972; mem Highland Park City Council 1984. **HONORS/ACHIEVEMENTS:** Humanitarian Awd Radio Station WJLB-Detroit 1968; "Where Do We Go From Here?" MI Chronicle 1975; Outstanding Achievement Awd Alumni Chapt/Highland Park Comm Coll 1978; African Puppets in Global Context El Instituto Mexicana Del Seguro El Departmento Del Distrito Fed 1979.

MILITARY SERVICE: AUS spec/4 1958-60. BUSINESS ADDRESS: President, Highland Park Comm Coll, Glendale at Third Ave, Highland Park, MI 48203.

HEATH, JAMES E.
Musician, educator. **PERSONAL:** Born Oct 25, 1926, Philadelphia; married Mona Brown; children: Mtume, Roslyn, Jeffrey. **EDUCATION:** Theodore Presser School of Music, Studied Saxophone; Prof Rudolph Schramm, studied Orchestration. **CAREER:** Composer, over 80 compositions; played saxophone with Howard McGhee, Miles Davis, Dizzy Gillespie, Art Farmer, Clark & Terry & Own Bands; recorded 8 Albums; performed on 75 albums with other jazz greats; Aaron Copland School of Music, Queens Coll, New York City, prof 1987-. **ORGANIZATIONS:** Mem Jazz Repetory Co; mem Heath Bros Quartet, Jimmy Heath Quartet; advisor, Thelonious Monk Inst, 1090-; advisor, Louis Armstrong House, 1987-. **HONORS/ACHIEVEMENTS:** Jazzmobile performed "The Afro-Amer Ste of Evolution" 1976; currently Teacher for Jazzmobile of New York City; instructor for Woodwinds, Housatonic Comm Coll Bridgeport; Jazz Pioneer Award BMI City Coll of New York 1985; Jimmy Heath Day in Wilmington NC 1985; Hon Doctor of Humane Letters Sojourner-Douglass Coll Baltimore MD 1986; Jazz Masters Award Afro-Amer Museum Philadelphia, PA; composed first symphonic work "Three Ears", 1988.

HEBERT, STANLEY PAUL
Attorney, business executive. **PERSONAL:** Born Jun 18, 1922, Baton Rouge, LA; married Mary Lou Usher; children: 13. **EDUCATION:** Univ of WI, PhB 1947; Marquette Univ Law School, JD 1950. **CAREER:** Bank of Amer, vice pres asst sec 1971; US EEOC, gen counsel 1969-71; US Govt Dept of Navy Office of Gen Counsel Washington DC, dep gen counsel 1963-69; State of WI & Pub Serv Commn of WI, commnr 1961-63; City of Milwaukee, City Atty's Offc, asst city atty 1958-61; atty private practice Milwaukee, 1956-58; atty private practice, Columbus GA, 1955-56; NC Coll Law School, assoc prof of law 1952-55; So Univ Law School, asst prof 1951-52; US Govt Office of Price Stabilization Milwaukee, investigator atty 1951. **ORGANIZATIONS:** Mem Amer Bar Assn; Fed Bar Assn; WI Bar Assn; WI Acad of Sci Arts & Letters; chmn Exec Comm Natl Catholic Comm Serv; vice pres mem Exec Comm & Bd Dir United Serv Orgns Inc; chmn Pastoral Commn's Comm on Role of Church in Changing Metro, Diocese of Washington DC; mem Bd Gov John Carroll Soc & Pastoral Commn, Archdiocese of Washington; mem Exec Comm WI Welfare Council; Exec Comm Intl Inst of Milwaukee; Exec Comm Madison Commn on Human Relations; exec comm Milwaukee & Madison Chapters of NAACP; mem bd trustees Voorhees Coll; adv bd CA State Univ Hayward; pres Natl Catholic Conf for Interracial Justice; Bay Area Urban League; chmn CA Atty Gen's Adv Commn on Comm Police Relation. **HONORS/ACHIEVEMENTS:** Recip Pub Serv Award Delta Chi Lambda Chap Alpha Phi Alpha Frat Inc 1962. **MILITARY SERVICE:** Served USAF WW II a/c; CDR USNR law Co 12-4. **BUSINESS ADDRESS:** General Counsel, Port of Oakland, 66 Jack London Square, Oakland, CA 94607.

HEBERT, ZENEBEWORK TESHOME
President, CEO. **PERSONAL:** Born Apr 01, 1942, Addis Ababa, Ethiopia;married Maurice Robert Hebert; children: Teshome, Rachel. **EDUCATION:** Univ of IL Coll of Pharmacy, BS 1967. **CAREER:** Michael Reese Hosp, pharmacist 1967-70; South Chicago Comm Hosp, pharmacist 1971-74; The Life Store, owner/mgr 1974-; Arthur Treacher Fish & Chips, owner/mgr 1978; Hebert & Moore Store for Men, owner/mgr; Hebert Montissore School, owner; Hebert Enterprises, president/ceo. **ORGANIZATIONS:** Mem Jack & Jill of Amer Inc, SNOB Inc; vice pres & mem 87th St & Stony Island Business Assoc. **HONORS/ACHIEVEMENTS:** One of the Top 10 Black Business Women in Chicago; One of the Top 10 Best Dressed Women in Chicago. **BUSINESS ADDRESS:** Chief Executive Officer, Hebert Enterprises, 1651 E 87th St, Chicago, IL 60617.

HEDGEPATH, LESLIE EUGENE
Physician. **PERSONAL:** Born Dec 16, 1922, Chilliothe, OH; married Ruth Harris; children: Leslie Eugene, Gregory. **EDUCATION:** Howard U, MD 1947. **CAREER:** Harlem Hosp NYC, intern 1947-48; admit phys 1948-49; Freedmen's Hosp Wash, asst res in med 1953-54; chief res in med 1954-55; Wash, priv prac med spec in internal med 1959-; Howard U, instr med 1955-56; instr phys 1959-64; VA Hosp Pitts, asst chief med serv 1956-58; VA Hosp Pittsburgh, chief med serv 1958-59; Freedmen's Hosp HowardUniv Med Serv DC Gen Hosp, attndg phys 1959-; Wash Hosp Cntr, sr attndg phys 1961-; trustee 1974-. **ORGANIZATIONS:** Mem AMA Nat Med Assns; Med Soc DC (bd credentials 1962-64 exec bd 1971-73); Am Soc Internal Med; resrch in hemodynamic & angiocardiographic observ in adult with persistent left super Vena Cava draining into the coronary sinus; cong cardio-vascular anomalies in adults; incidence & sign of bacter in female diab. **HONORS/ACHIEVEMENTS:** Dec silver star bronze star with oak leaf cluster AUS; rec serv awrd HowardUniv 1968; fellow ACP. **MILITARY SERVICE:** AUS WWII 1949-52. **BUSINESS ADDRESS:** 106 Irving Street, NW, Washington, DC 20010.

HEDGEPETH, CHESTER MELVIN, JR.
Educator. **PERSONAL:** Born Oct 29, 1937, Richmond, VA; married Thelma Washington; children: Chester III. **EDUCATION:** Blackburn Coll, BA 1960; Wesleyan Univ, MA 1966; Harvard Univ, EdD 1977. **CAREER:** Maggie Walker HS, teacher 1960-65; Macalester Coll, instr in english 1968-71; VA Union Univ, instr english 1966-68, 1971-75; VA Commonwealth Univ, coord of Afro-Amer studies 1978-; Univ of MD, dean arts & scis chmn english & languages. **ORGANIZATIONS:** Mem Phi Delta Kappa Harvard Chap 1976-; mem Eastern VA Intl Consortium 1978-; mem S Atlantic Modern Lang Assn 1978-; usher & Christian Educ Comm Brandermill Ch 1979-; secty/treas VA Humanities Conf 1980-; Black philos writingUniv Press of Am 1980; pres VA Humanities Conf 1983; "Afro-Amer Perspectives in the Humanities" Collegiate Pub Co 1980. **HONORS/ACHIEVEMENTS:** Danforth Assoc Danforth Found 1980-86. **BUSINESS ADDRESS:** Dean/Chmn Arts & Scis, Univ of Maryland, Eastern Shore, Princess Anne, MD 21853.

HEDGEPETH, LEONARD
Bank chief executive. **CAREER:** United National Bank, Fayetteville, NC, chief exec. **BUSINESS ADDRESS:** United National Bank, P. O. Box 1450, Fayetteville, NC 28302. *

HEDGESPETH, GEORGE T., JR.
Financial administrator. **PERSONAL:** Born Aug 09, 1949, Richmond, VA; married Portia Meade; children: George III, Sheldon. **EDUCATION:** LincolnUniv PA, BA 1971; Central MI, MA 1978. **CAREER:** Miami Dade Community Coll FL, dir of financial aid & vet affrs 1978; Moton Consortium Washington DC, asst dir 1977-78; Lincoln Univ PA, dir of financial aid 1974-77; Univ of Rochester NY, asst dir student activities 1972-74; Lincoln Univ PA, accountant 1971-72. **ORGANIZATIONS:** Comm mem on Need Analysis The Coll Bd; institutional rep Nat Assn of Student Financial Aid Administr; mem So Assn of Student Fin Aid Adminstrs; mem FL Assn of Student Financl Aid Adminstrs; mem Omega Psi Phi Frat. **HONORS/ACHIEVEMENTS:** Outst young men in am Jaycees of Am 1978; scroll of hon for serv to stdnt Omega Psi Phi Frat Beta Chap 1977. **BUSINESS ADDRESS:** VP for Business & Finance, Johnson C Smith University, 100 Beatties Ford Rd, Charlotte, NC 28216.

HEDGLEY, DAVID R.
Retired clergyman. **PERSONAL:** Born Apr 22, 1907, Mobile, AL; son of Noah Hedgley and Pauline Hedgley; married Maybelle; children: David Jr, Christine. **EDUCATION:** VA Union Univ, AB 1931; Univ Chicago, AM 1935; N Baptist Theological Sem, BD 1945; Shaw Univ, DD 1955; VA Union Univ, DD 1957. **CAREER:** FL A&M Univ, chaplain 1936-44; Evergreen Church, pastor 1940-44; 1st Baptist Church, pastor 1944-74; Pastor Emeritus, 1974; Rising Star Baptist Church, pastor 1953-74; retired 1975. **ORGANIZATIONS:** Ministers Conf Rowan Bapt Assn; State Baptist Convention; ordained to ministry Baptist Church; asst pastor Olivet Baptist Church 1931-36; mem Mayor's Goodwill Com 1962-65; Phi Beta Sigma; Mason; Lott Cary Foriegn Missions Convention; Natl Baptist Convention; NAACP; 32 Degree Mason has held many exec postions. **HONORS/ACHIEVEMENTS:** Hon certificate Mayor 1972; hon Plaque Ministers 1969; plaque YMCA; hon pin Urban League 1965; minister yr NAACP 1972. **BUSINESS ADDRESS:** 700 N Highland Ave, Winston-Salem, NC 27101.

HEDGLEY, DAVID RICE, JR.
Mathematician. **PERSONAL:** Born Jan 21, 1937, Chicago, IL; son of Dr David R Hedgley, Sr; children: Angela Kay Garber, Andrea Kim. **EDUCATION:** VA Union Univ, BS Biology 1958; MI State Univ, BS Math 1964; CA State Univ, MS Math 1970; Somerset Univ PH.D (computer science) Ilminister, England 1986-1988. **CAREER:** So Adhesive Corp, chemist 1958-59; Ashland Sch System, teacher 1961-65; Richmond Sch System, teacher 1965-66; NASA Dryden Flight Rsch Facility, mathematician 1966-. **ORGANIZATIONS:** Asst prof AU Coll 1975-78; consultant Manufacturing Tools Inc 1982-86; bd mem Local Black Adv Group 1984-87; consultant Univ of Washington 1984-. **HONORS/ACHIEVEMENTS:** Superior Sustained Awd Recognition Awd, etc 1966-87; numerous scientific publications 1974-87; Best Paper of Year (Scientific) 1976; Natl Exceptional Engr Awd NASA 1983; Natl Julian Allen Awd NASA 1984; Natl Space Act Awd NASA 1984; Special Achievement NASA 1988. **MILITARY SERVICE:** AUS E-4 2 yrs. **HOME ADDRESS:** PO Box 1674, Lancaster, CA 93537.

HEFLIN, JOHN F.
Educator. **PERSONAL:** Born Apr 07, 1941, Sweetwater, TX; married Anita Blaz; children: Kyle, Jonathan. **EDUCATION:** NM Highlands U, BA 1963; Stanford U, MA 1972, PhD 1977. **CAREER:** Portland St U, asst prof ed admn 1976-; OR Dept D, eeo pgm coord 1974-76; Stanford U, asst to dean 1971-74; Merced Union High Sch Merced, CA, tchr coach 1965-70; US Dept Interior Denver, CO, Cartographer 1964-65. **ORGANIZATIONS:** Mem Portland Urban League; OR Assembly for Black Afrs; OR Alliance of Black Sch Educators; mem CA Tchrs Assc; OR Educators Assc; NEA; Natl Cncl Soc Stds; Policy Stdnt Orgn; Phi Delta Kapp; bd dir Mid-Peninsula Task Force Integrated Ed; Am Ed Rsrch Assc; ed dir NAACP; Natl Alliance of Black Sch Educators; natl chmn Rsrch Focus on Black Ed (Am Ed Rsrch Assc); commnr Protland Met Human Realtions Comm; Assc for Supervision & Curriculm Dev. **HONORS/ACHIEVEMENTS:** NW Assc of Black Elected & Officials; found ldrshp Dev Pgm Fellow 1970-71. **BUSINESS ADDRESS:** Portland StUniv, P O Box 751, Portland, OR 97207.

HEFNER, JAMES A.
Educator. **PERSONAL:** Born Jun 20, 1941, Brevard, NC; married Edwina Long; children: Christopher, Jonathan, David. **EDUCATION:** North Carolina A&T State Univ, BS 1961; Atlanta Univ, MA 1962; Univ of CO, PhD 1971. **CAREER:** Prairie View A&M College, teacher 1962-63; Benedict College, teacher 1963-64; FL A&M Univ, teacher 1964-65; Univ of CO, teacher 1965-67; Clark College, teacher 1967-71; Atlanta Univ, teacher 1973-74; Morehouse College, teacher 1974-82; Tuskegee Institute, provost 1982-84; Jackson State Univ, president 1984-. **ORGANIZATIONS:** Consult Congrsmn Hawkins & Mitchell; United Negro Coll Fund; mem NAACP; Labor & Indstry Com; I-20 Coaltn; AtlantaUniv Ctr Fclty Forum; economic and business consultant to many organizations in the public and private sectors; consultant Congressional Black Caucus, Natl Institute of Public Management, the Dept ofTransportation; mem Amer Economic Assn, Industrial Relations Rsch Assn, Natl Institute of Public Management. **HONORS/ACHIEVEMENTS:** Hghst endwd chair AtlantaUniv Ctr; 1 grant train HS Grads & Drpts; author of more than 50 articles on economic research; authored or co-edited two books "Black Employment in Atlanta", "Public Policy for the Black Community, Strategies and Perspectives"; apptd by Gov Bill Allain as Mississippi's rep on the Southern Regional Educational Bd; Phi Beta Kappa; mbrshp MENSA; NAFEO Achievement Awd in Research; listed in Who's Who in America. **BUSINESS ADDRESS:** President, Jackson State University, 1400 J R Lynch St, Jackson, MS 39217.

HEGEMAN, CHARLES OXFORD
Surgeon. **PERSONAL:** Born Jun 15, 1940, Detroit, MI; married Jessye Davis; children: Elisabeth, Veronica, Charles Jr. **EDUCATION:** Dartmouth Clg, AB 1962; Howard U, MD 1966. **CAREER:** Pvt Prac; West Adams Comm Hosp, attending surgeon 1973; Cedars of Lebanon Hosp, 1974; Queen of Angels Hosp, 1973; Kaiser Found Hosp, 1971; Charles R Drew & Postgrad Sch of Med, asst prof surg; Residency in Intergrated Surgical ResidenciesUniv of CA Irvine, surgical residencies 1971; LA Co Gen Hosp, intern 1967; Am Clg of Surgeons, fellow 1976. **MILITARY SERVICE:** AUS mjr 1971-73. **BUSINESS ADDRESS:** 1818 S Western Ave, Los Angeles, CA 90006.

HEGMON, OLIVER LOUIS
Clergyman. **PERSONAL:** Born Feb 28, 1907, Boling, TX; son of J.C. Hegmon and Martha Robin Hegmon; married Emma Louise Jones; children: Paul E, Beverly Ann. **EDUCATION:** Conroe Normal & Indus Coll, BTh 1937; Union Bapt Theol Sem, Hon DD 1950; Union Bapt Sem Inc, Hon LLD 1953; Bishop Coll, BA 1970. **CAREER:** Antioch Missionary Bapt Ch, pastor; Truth Seekers Bible Sch (broadcast over sevrl radio & TV stations since 1936), pres; Var Pastorates, 1933-. **ORGANIZATIONS:** Vp Prgm Voters League of TX

1947-49; Mayor's Com on Human Relat 1949-51; pres Bapt Min Union 1951-56; pres McLennan Co Br NAACP 1955-59; vice pres bd dir Ft Worth Area Counc of Chs; life mem NAACP; bd mem United Fund 1970-71; Mayor's Com on Human Resources 1973-74; mem Nat Ch Pub Rel Com Bishop Coll 1973-74; vice pres Ft Worth Area Counc of Chs 1974-75. **HONORS/ACHIEVEMENTS:** Recip ldr of yr award Doris Miller Br YWCA 1950; dist serv award TX State Conf of Br NAACP 1974; KNOK Radio Sta Award 1974. **BUSINESS ADDRESS:** 1063 E Rosedale St, Fort Worth, TX 76104.

HEGWOOD, GORDON F.
Vice president, finance. **PERSONAL:** Born Dec 08, 1935, Guthrie, OK; married Muriel; children: 1 Daughter. **EDUCATION:** NW U, BA 1964; DePaul, NW, Roosevelt U, Grad Work. **CAREER:** Borg-Warner, staff acctnt sr staff acctnt asst controller & mgr 1964-. **ORGANIZATIONS:** Dir CEDCO; MESBIC; Chicago Econ Club; Am Inst Certified Pub Acctnts; MI Inst of CPA's; IL Soc Pub Acctnts; bd mem Counc Comm Svc; lctr Urban League Black Exec Exchange Prgm; CPA. **BUSINESS ADDRESS:** Trans Eq Grp Borg Warner Corp, 3001 W Big Beaver Rd, Troy, MI 48084.

HEGWOOD, WILLIAM LEWIS
Retired biochemist. **PERSONAL:** Born Oct 05, 1918, San Antonio, TX; son of William L Hegwood and Mary B Hegwood. **EDUCATION:** Tuskegee Univ, BS 1939; New York Univ, MS 1947. **CAREER:** Biochemist; Artist. **ORGANIZATIONS:** Reserve Officer Assoc, mem; Retired Officers Assoc, mem; Kappa Alpha Psi 1942. **HONORS/ACHIEVEMENTS:** Exhibited Metropolitan Museum, artist 1976. **MILITARY SERVICE:** Army Chemical Corps, retired Lt Colonel Aus. **HOME ADDRESS:** PO Box 254, New York, NY 10035.

HEIDT, ELLEN VIRGINIA
Educator. **PERSONAL:** Born Aug 27, Brunswick, GA; daughter of Benjamin Sullivan and Lucille Baker Sullivan; widowed; children: Arnold Joseph Heidt Jr, Benjamin Darwin Heidt. **EDUCATION:** Savannah State Coll, Savannah GA, BS, 1946; Columbia Univ, New York NY, MA, 1950; Univ of Miami, Miami FL, IA, 1971; Florida Intl, Miami FL, 1986-88. **CAREER:** Dade County School Bd, Miami FL, teacher, 1956-; Miami Northwestern Sr High, dept chmn of English, 1967-70; Norland Sr High, dept chmn of English, 1970-74; Dade County School Bd, Miami FL, program coord, 1974-88. **HONORS/ACHIEVEMENTS:** Outstanding Serv in Educ, Alpha Phi Alpha Frat, 1978; Scroll of Friendship, City of Miami FL, 1980; Certificate of Appreciation, City of Miami FL, 1984; Natl Council of Negro Women, 1988; Plaques, Certificates for Years of Dedication, Miami Northwestern Sr High School; auhor of a proposal and initiator of successful program to improve students' SAT scores at Miami Northwestern Sr High School. **HOME ADDRESS:** 5621 NW 19th Ave, Miami, FL 33142.

HEIGHT, DOROTHY I.
Civil rights activist. **PERSONAL:** Born Mar 24, 1912, Richmond, VA. **EDUCATION:** NY Univ, MA; Attended, NY Sch of Social Work. **CAREER:** New York City Welfare Dept, caseworker 1934; Young Women's Christian Assn, dir Ctr for Racial Justice; Natl Council of Negro Women Inc, natl pres 1957-. **ORGANIZATIONS:** Served on numerous commns bds including NY State Social Welfare Bd 1958-68; US Dept of Def Adv Com on Women 1952-55; ARC bd govs 1964-70; past pres Delta Sigma Theta Sor 1947-58; pres's comm for Employment of the Handicapped; mem ad hoc comm Public Welfare Dept Hlth Educ & Welfare; consult African Affairs to Sec State; mem women's comm Office Emergency Planning Pres's Comm on Status of Women; pres's comm for Equal Employment Oppor; bd dir CARE; Comm Rel Serv; bd govs ARC; natl bd YWCA; dir YMCA Ctr for Racial Justice; currently holds bd mem with 15 orgns. **HONORS/ACHIEVEMENTS:** Written numerous articles; rec'd 14 awds including Disting Service Awd Natl Conf on Social Welfare 1971. **BUSINESS ADDRESS:** President, Natl Council of Negro Women, 1211 Connecticut Ave, Washington, DC 20036-2701.

HEINEBACK, BARBARA (NEE TAYLOR)
Director. **PERSONAL:** Born Dec 29, 1951, New York, NY; daughter of John Taylor and Robella Taylor; children: 1 Son. **EDUCATION:** Howard Univ, BA TV Comm 1971; Univ of Stockholm, Lang Arts 1975. **CAREER:** CBS TV, asst to prod "Face the Nation" 1969-71; Swedish Natl Radio Stockholm, free-lance journalist 1972-75; the White House, press asst to the first lady; Communications Satellite Corp (COMSAT), mgr pub relations 1976-87; Scripps Memorial Hospital, San Diego CA 1988-. **ORGANIZATIONS:** Special consultant public relations firms & Univ producer radio prog Sweden; dir Washington Urban League; dir Chamber of Commerce, Chula Vista CA; mem PRSA; Natl Assoc Health Developers, Natl Society Fund Raising Executives; Sunrise Bonita Rotary. **HONORS/ACHIEVEMENTS:** Articles in Stockholm's major morning daily "Dagens Nyheter"; Plaques of Appreciation, President Carter, Pres Tolbert (Liberia); San Diego Arts Board; United Negro College Fund Steering Committee of San Diego. **HOME ADDRESS:** PO Box 214, La Jolla, CA 92037.

HEINS, HENRY L., JR.
Physican/educator. **PERSONAL:** Born Feb 09, 1931, New Orleans, LA; children: Karen, Henry L III. **EDUCATION:** Univ of Pittsburg, BS 1951;Univ of Pittsburgh, MD 1955. **CAREER:** UCLA Med Cntr, asso clin prof in ped present; Cardiol Div Childrens Hosp, asst attndg phys 1961-; Cedars-Sinai Med Cntr, clin staff in ped 1961-. **ORGANIZATIONS:** Mem of cardiac team UCLA Med Cntr 1961-; mem LA Heart Assn; mem Charles Drew Med Soc; mem CA Med Assn; mem Nat Med Assn; mem Am Med Assn; mem Kappa Kappa Psi; mem Physic Handicapped Children's Bd Crippled Children Servs of CA; mem CA Soc for Ped Cardiol; fellow Am Acad of Ped; fellow Am Coll of Cardiol; fellow Am Coll of Chest Phys. **HONORS/ACHIEVEMENTS:** Sci achiev awd Am CA Soc of Cardiol 1976; many publs & lectr. **MILITARY SERVICE:** USN inactive res 1951-56; USN active duty 1956-58. **BUSINESS ADDRESS:** 101 N LaBrea, Ste 401, Inglewood, CA 90301.

HEISKELL, MICHAEL PORTER
Attorney. **PERSONAL:** Born Sep 11, 1951, Ft Worth, TX; married Gayle Regina Beverly; children: Marian Phenice, James Dewitt II. **EDUCATION:** Baylor U, BA 1972; Baylor Law Sch, JD 1974. **CAREER:** Dawson Dawson Smith & Snodd, law clerk 1974-75; Galveston Co, asst dist atty 1975-80; Johnson Vaughn & Heiskell, atty; United States Atty, asst atty 1980-84; Johnson Vaughn & Heiskell, partner 1984-. **ORGANIZATIONS:** Del Phi Alpha Delta Law Frat Conv 1974; mem Galveston Co Bar Assn; vice pres sec Galveston Co Young Lawyers Assn 1977-78; Am Bar Assn 1976-77; TX St Bar Assn; TX Dist & Co Attys Assn; bd dir mem Gulf Coast Legal Found; Disaster Relief Com; TX Yng Lyrs Assn; Min Recruit Com Baylor Law Sch; pres Pi Sigma Alpha Baylor U; pres Agiza Funika Soc Serv Club Baylor U; pres elect Fort Worth Black Bar Assoc; vice pres Tarrant County Criminal Defense Lawyers Assoc; assoc dir TX Criminal Defense Lawyers Assoc. **HONORS/ACHIEVEMENTS:** Mr Navarro Jr Coll Corsicana TX 1971; 1st black to grad from Baylor Law Sch; 1st black asst DA Galveston Co. **BUSINESS ADDRESS:** Partner, Johnson, Vaughn & Heiskell, 815 Throckmorton, Ste 609, Fort Worth, TX 76102.

HELM, WILLIAM C.
Retired police captain. **PERSONAL:** Born Feb 14, 1925, Roachport, MO; married Dolores Jean Sanders; children: Carolyn Williams, William Jr, Craig. **EDUCATION:** Dickinson Bus Coll, attended 1946-48; Bradley Univ, attended 1948-50. **CAREER:** Phoenix Products Inc, former vice pres; City of Peoria, patrolman, detective, sgt, lt, capt retired 1983. **HONORS/ACHIEVEMENTS:** Policeman of the Yr Awd 1962. **MILITARY SERVICE:** USN 3/C 1943-46.

HELMS, DAVID ALONZO
Attorney. **PERSONAL:** Born Jul 05, 1934, Evanston, IL; son of Hugh Judson Helms Sr and Edna J Peterson-(Helms) Holmes; divorced; children: Donald Anthony, Cybil Estelle. **EDUCATION:** Northwestern Univ Evanston, BS Bus Admin 1957; Boalt Hall Sch of Law, JD 1969; Attended, John F Kennedy Sch of Govt; Harvard Univ Cambridge; 1985 Teaching Fellow. **CAREER:** Matson Navigation Co, mgr marketing rsch 1959-66; Paul Weiss Rifkind Wharton & Garrison, assoc atty 1969-73; State of CA, special asst to gov 1973-75; NAACP Natl Office & Western Regional Office, consul 1974-78; Bar Assn, exec sec civil rights 1974-79; IL Inst of Tech Chicago Kent Coll of Law, asst dean & faculty 1979-81; Cases of Air Traffic Controller Terminations, 1981; Office of Regional Cnsl Fed Aviation Adminstrn, genl aviations attorney, 1982-84;Dr Hycel B Taylor Natl Pres Operation PUSH, legal counsel 1986; David A Helms & Assocs, atty/consultant 1974-. **ORGANIZATIONS:** Bd mem Public Advocates San Francisco 1973-76; bd mem KQED Channel 9 PBS San Francisco 1974-78; mem Natl Bar Assn 1973-; bd mem Family Focus Evanston 1983-; proj dir Chicago Volunteer Legal Serv Fndtn Chicago 1983-; consul NAACP Natl Ofc & Western Regional Ofc San Francisco New York City 1974-78; mem CA Assn of Black Lawyers 1975-79; mem Cook Co Bar Assn Chicago 1980-; mem Amer Bar Assn 1979-; mem Chicago Bar Assn 1979-; mem Urban League Chicago 1982-. **HONORS/ACHIEVEMENTS:** One of Ten Outstanding Young Men Jr Chamber of Commerce San Francisco 1965-66, New York City 1970; Dean's Awd Boalt Hall Sch of Law Univ of CA Berkeley 1969; Image Awd NAACP Beverly Hills/Hollywood Branch 1974. **MILITARY SERVICE:** USN aerographer's mate first class 1956-60; Disting Serv Medal Joint Task Force 7 Operation Redwing 1956. **HOME ADDRESS:** 1802 Hovland Ct, Evanston, IL 60201. **BUSINESS ADDRESS:** Attorney/Real Estate Broker, David A Helms & Associates, 53 W Jackson Blvd, Suite 1040, Chicago, IL 60605.

HEMBY, DOROTHY JEAN
Educational administrator. **PERSONAL:** Born Aug 21, Greenville, NC. **EDUCATION:** Essex Co Coll, AS Liberal Arts (Cum Laude) 1975; Montclair State Coll, Sociology & Social Studies (honor soc) 1975; Kean Coll of NJ, Student Personnel Serv (Summa Cum Laude) 1977. **CAREER:** Newark Bd of Educ, tchr 1974-76; Kean Coll of NJ, coll counselor 1976-77; Passaic Co Coll, coll counselor/admin 1978-. **ORGANIZATIONS:** Chairperson Passaic Co Coll Student Life 1983-84; mem NJ Black Issues Assoc 1984; comm mem NJ Assoc of Black Educators 1979-; chairperson HOPE Orgn 1978-82; mem NJ EOF Professional Assoc Inc 1978-; exec bd/secty Passaic Co Admin Assoc 1984-; counselor The Love of Jesus Ministry 1983-; advisor/consul Passaic Co Newman Christian Club 1983-; exec bd/treas Passaic County Coll Admin Assoc 1985-88; mem Amer Assoc for Counseling and Develop. **HONORS/ACHIEVEMENTS:** Who's Who Among Women Cambridge England Biographical 1979-80-81-83; Who's Who in the East Marquis 1980-86; Who's Who in the World Marquis 1984-85; Comm Leaders & Noteworthy Amers Biographical Inst of Amer 1979-80-81-83-84-85; Graduate Scholarship NJ Personnal Guidance Assoc 1976-77; Who's Who of Amer Women Marquis 1987-88. **BUSINESS ADDRESS:** College Counselor/Admin, Passaic County College, College Blvd, Paterson, NJ 07509.

HEMMINGWAY, BEULAH S.
Educator. **PERSONAL:** Born Mar 11, 1943, Clarksdale, MS; married Theodore Hemmingway; children: Kofi Patrice, Julius Chaka. **EDUCATION:** Coahoma Jr Coll, 1962; Alcorn State Univ, BS 1964; NC Central Univ, MA 1965; FL State Univ, PhD 1981. **CAREER:** Southern Univ, teacher 1965-66; Voorhees Coll, teacher 1966-67; Benedict Coll, teacher 1967-72; FL A&M Univ, assoc prof lang & lit 1972-. **ORGANIZATIONS:** Mem Natl Council of Teachers of English, Coll Lang Assoc, FL Coll, English Teachers, Undergrad Council for the Coll of Arts & Sci 1982-, Role & Scope Comm 1976, Library Resource Comm 1977, Curriculum Comm for Lang & Lit, Southern Assoc of Coll & Schools Editing Comm, Homecoming Comm 1983; chairperson Poetry Festival 1975-82; advisor Lambda Iota Tau 1975-82; search comm for vice pres acad affairs FL A&M Univ 1982; mem task force Coll Level Acad Skills Test; reader for scoring state-wide essays holistically; bd of dir LeMoyne Art Found 1980-82, Mothers March of Dimes 1982-; vice pres Natl Council of Negro Women 1982-, Jack & Jill of Amer 1979-81; prog chairperson 112 anniv Bethel Baptist Church; mem Tallahassee Urban League, NAACP; panelist FL Division of Cultural Affairs 1986; mem American Popular Culture Assn 1988; mem Drifters Inc 1989. **HONORS/ACHIEVEMENTS:** Various publ incl, "Critics Assessment of Faulkners Black Characters FL A&M Univ" 1978; "A Comparative Pilot Study by Sex & Race of the Use of Slang" Soc for Gen Syst Rsch 1978; conducted a seminar on "Black Women Writers" 1983; workshop for Bay Cty English Teachers in Panama City FL "Teaching English Composition"; "Abyss-Gwendolyn Brooks Women" FL A&M Univ Bulletin; read paper 45th Annual Convention of Coll Lang Assoc 1985 "Can Computer Managed Grammar Make a Difference That Makes a Difference?"; Teacher of the Year FL A&M Univ 1987-88; Meritorious Service Award FL A&M Univ 1988; "Through the Prism of Africanity: A Preliminary Investigation of Zora Neale Hurston's Mules and Men," presented paper at American Popular Culture Assn 1989. **HOME ADDRESS:** 545 Victory Garden Dr, Tallahassee, FL 32301. **BUSINESS ADDRESS:** Assoc Prof Lang & Lit, Florida A&M University, Tallahassee, FL 32307.

HEMPHILL, DARRYL CALVIN
Professional athlete. **PERSONAL:** Born Mar 29, 1960, San Antonio, TX. **EDUCATION:** West TX State. **CAREER:** Baltimore Colts, strong safety 1982-; New York Jets,

strong safety 1982-; Denver Gold, strong safety 1984-. **HONORS/ACHIEVEMENTS:** AP honorable mention All-Missouri Valley Conf honors as a sr; earned second team All-Conf honors.

HEMPHILL, FRANK
Educator. **PERSONAL:** Born Nov 16, 1943, Cleveland; married Brenda; children: Tracie, Dawn, Frank John Parker, Jr. **EDUCATION:** W KY U, BS 1968; Kent State U, MEd 1975. **CAREER:** Assoc Dean Students, Dir Acad Assts, 1975-; Tching Asst Biology, 1971-73; Shaw HS E Cleveland, biology teacher 1968-71. **ORGANIZATIONS:** Mem Minority Educ Serv Assn; vice pres Black Studie Consortium NE OH. **HONORS/ACHIEVEMENTS:** Martha Jennings Fellowshp 1971; outst contrib award Alliance Black Consciousness Assn Hiram OH. **BUSINESS ADDRESS:** Dean Students Ofc, Hiram Coll, Hiram, OH 44234.

HEMPHILL, GWENDOLYN
Government administrative assistant. **PERSONAL:** Born Apr 04, 1941, Johnstown, PA; married Lawrence; children: Cheryl, Karen, Larry. **EDUCATION:** Trinity Coll, 1977. **CAREER:** The White House, exec asst 1977-; Am Fed of State Co & Municpal Employees, adminstrv asst 1968-76; Dept of Transp, adminstrv asst 1965-68; US Office of Edn, asst 1963-65. **ORGANIZATIONS:** 2nd vice pres Ward 4 Dem Club 1974-76; exec com mem DC People United to Help Club 1974-76; mem DC Dem Womens Club; mem NAACP; mem PUSH. **BUSINESS ADDRESS:** 1600 Pennsylvania Ave NW, Washington, DC 20050.

HEMPHILL, MILEY MAE
Educator. **PERSONAL:** Born Jan 08, 1914, Gwinnett Co; married John R. **EDUCATION:** Morris Brown Coll, AB 1950; Atlanta U, MA 1957. **CAREER:** Tchr Prin 23 Yrs; Gwinnett-Jackson Co & Winder City Sch, curriculum dir 9 Yrs; GA Dept of Edn, reading-english splst 8 yrs. **ORGANIZATIONS:** Mem Nat Assn NEA; GEA; GTEA; ACS; pres Atlanta GA Jeanes Cirriculum Dirs; dir Region IV Fine Arts; pres Royal Oaks Manor Comm Club; mem YMCA. **HONORS/ACHIEVEMENTS:** Recip hon LLD Union Bapt Sem 1974; Outst Personalities of The S 1970; Bronze Woman of Yr in Educ 1966; listed Who's Who Outst Women of the World 1973; biographical sketches London England; listed Who's Who Among Prin & Supv in GA 1965. **BUSINESS ADDRESS:** 896 Woodmere Dr NW, Atlanta, GA.

HEMPHILL, PAUL W.
Director. **PERSONAL:** Married Vernal. **EDUCATION:** Wayne U, BA 1947. **CAREER:** Mayor's Ofc for Sr Citizens & Handicapped, dir field serv 1973-; Corrections & Yth Svc, dep dir 1970-73; Chicago Com on Urban Oppor, asst dir personnel 1968-70. **ORGANIZATIONS:** Mem Nat Counc of Soc Workers; mem Nat Assn for Comm Devel; Am Gerontological Soc; Am Soc for Pub Adm; Kappa Alpha Psi Frat. **HONORS/ACHIEVEMENTS:** VIP award outst comm serv State of IL Lt Gov Ofc; award for outst serv to human family Chicago's "We Do Care" Com; award for outst training in comm resources HEW Region. **MILITARY SERVICE:** USN. **BUSINESS ADDRESS:** 330 S Wells, Chicago, IL 60606.

HEMSLEY, SHERMAN
Actor, comedian. **PERSONAL:** Born Feb 01, 1938, Philadelphia, PA. **EDUCATION:** Attended, Philadelphia Acad Dramatic Arts; studied with Negro Ensemble Co NY, Lloyd Richards. **CAREER:** Actor "All in the Family", "The Jeffersons", new series "Amen"; Gitlow Broadway's Purlie; appearances "Don't Bother Me I Can't Cope", "The Odd Couple" in regional theaters, "Norman, Is That You?" in Las Vegas; owner production co Love Is Inc. **ORGANIZATIONS:** Mem AFTRA; mem Vinnette Carroll's Urban Arts Corps. **HONORS/ACHIEVEMENTS:** NAACP Image Awd 1976. **BUSINESS ADDRESS:** Herb Tobias & Assocs Inc, 1901 Ave of the Stars, Ste 840, Los Angeles, CA 90067.

HENCE, MARIE J.
Violinist. **PERSONAL:** Born Jul 02, 1936, Trenton, NJ. **EDUCATION:** New Eng Conservatory Music, BM, MM 1958-60; Tanglewood, 1956-58; Yale Summer Sch Music & Art, 1960. **CAREER:** Musicians on Broadway, 1st female music contractor; Shubert Theatres, 1961-74.

HENDERSON, AUSTRALIA TARVER
Educator. **PERSONAL:** Born Feb 08, 1942, Ft Worth; married William. **EDUCATION:** Univ IA, ABD 1975; OH U, MA 1965; Fisk U, BA 1964. **CAREER:** Univ IA, tchng resrch fellow 1971-74; FL A & M, instr 1968-71; Pontiac N HS, tchr 1966-69; MI Valley St Coll, instr 1965-66; AWAKE, tchr dir 1969; Prog Plan Proj Upward Bound, instr 1968, 1971-72; FL A&MUniv Midwest Modern Lang Assn, present asst prof 1973-74; S Atlantic Mod Lang Assn, present; Coll Lang Assn present. **ORGANIZATIONS:** Organ staff Camp COCO Tallahassee 1970-71; retreat consult Race Rel FL Coll Campuses 1970. **HONORS/ACHIEVEMENTS:** Four yr coll scholar Mary Gibbs Jones-Jesse H Jones Scholar 1960-64; fellow Nat Fellow Fund 1973-74.

HENDERSON, BUTLER THOMAS
Educator. **PERSONAL:** Born Jun 20, 1919, Knoxville, TN; son of John H Henderson and Rainey Henderson; married Charlie Lee Scott. **EDUCATION:** Morehouse Coll, AB 1944; NY Univ, AM 1947; Univ of AR at Pine Bluff, LLD (honors) 1972; Morehouse Coll, LLD (honors) 1985. **CAREER:** Univ of AR, Pine Bluff, asst prof chm eco & bus 1944-60; Morehouse Coll, asst to the pres 1960-68; United Bd for Coll Devel, dir 1968-70; United Negro Coll Fund, asst dir 1971-72; Earl Warren Legal Training Prog of NAACP Legal Defense & Educ Fund, exec dir 1972-. **ORGANIZATIONS:** Exec sec/grand grammateus Sigma Pi Phi Frat The Boule 1979-; life mem NAACP; mem Omega Psi Phi Frat; mem Prince Hall Masons Southern 33 Deg; mem shriners. **HOME ADDRESS:** 69 Fifth Ave 9g, New York, NY 10003. **BUSINESS ADDRESS:** Executive Dir, Earl Warren Legal Training Pgm, 99 Hudson St, Ste 1600, New York, NY 10003.

HENDERSON, CHARLES
Engineer. **PERSONAL:** Born Jul 30, 1937, Okolona, MS; married Janice Roberts; children: Eric, Marc. **EDUCATION:** Northeastern U, BS 1960; UCLA, MS 1969, PhD 1973. **CAREER:** Aerospace Corp, dir data sys 1977-, sect mgr 1975-77, mem tech staff 1973-75; Aerojet Gen CA, engr spl 1970-73; N Am Rockwell CA, sr rsrch engr 1968-70; Autonetics CA, rsrch

engr 1960-68; DHE W, dev an automated human serv info sys; pub of sev tech papers on computer-aided med idagnosis; copenhagen Denmark, presented phD dissert at conf 1974. **ORGANIZATIONS:** Mem IEEE Biomed Engrng Soc; Eta Kappa Nu; mem PTA. **MILITARY SERVICE:** AUS Signal Corps 2nd lt 1961-63. **BUSINESS ADDRESS:** 2350 E El Segundo Blvd, El Segundo, CA.

HENDERSON, CRAWFORD, SR.
Mechanical engineer. **PERSONAL:** Born Apr 08, 1931, Granville Co, NC; married Doris L; children: Susan L, Crawford Jr, Raymond G, Benjamin D. **EDUCATION:** A&T Coll, insl arts study 1950-53; NC A&T U, BS in Engineering 1959; Geo WashUniv Wash DC; OH State U. **CAREER:** US Postal Serv Wash DC, retired prog mgr 1971-86; Naval Ship Engrg Ctr, proj engr 1966-71; Ft Belvoir VA, proj engr res & dev lab 1959-66; Visiting Scientist & Engrs, student tchr radio fund A&T Sci Fair Judge mem 1959-67. **ORGANIZATIONS:** Past v pres Cen Arlington Civic Assn; past mem YMCA Com; past Inst Rep Cub Scouts Arlington Delegate Co Fed. **HONORS/ACHIEVEMENTS:** Merit badge couns BSA Comm Leaders & Noteworthy Ams 1977; recipient Nat Capitol Award for Engrg Achievement 1963; author articles on snow tunnel maint in "Military Engr" & Popular Science 1963. **MILITARY SERVICE:** USMC sgt 1953-56.

HENDERSON, D. RUDOLPH
Attorney. **PERSONAL:** Born Jan 09, 1921, Cleveland, OH; married Irene Price. **EDUCATION:** Case Western Reserve U, BA 1943; Case Western Reserve U, LLB 1954. **CAREER:** US Dept of State, dep asst legal adviser for consular affairs; Dept of State, staff asst to legal adviser 1977-; Office of the Legal Adviser US Dept ofState, 1966-76; Pvt Practice Cleveland OH, atty 1954-66. **ORGANIZATIONS:** Mem Greater Cleveland & Cuyahoga Co & OH State Bar Assn 1954-. **BUSINESS ADDRESS:** Deputy Asst Legal Adviser, Department of State, Consular Affairs, 2201 C St NW, Washington, DC 20520.

HENDERSON, DAVE LEE
Professional athlete. **PERSONAL:** Born Jul 21, 1958, Dos Palos, CA; married Loni. **CAREER:** Seattle Mariners, outfielder 1981-. **HONORS/ACHIEVEMENTS:** Centerfielder on CA League Champion San Jose Missions 1979; named to All-Star team; selected by coaches as the circuit's Best Defensive Outfielder & Outfielderwith the Best Arm. **BUSINESS ADDRESS:** Seattle Mariners, PO Box 4100, Seattle, WA 98104.

HENDERSON, DAVID
Author/poet. **PERSONAL:** Born in New York, NY. **EDUCATION:** Bronx Comm Coll, 1960; Hunter Coll NY, 1961; New School for Social Rsch, 1962; East West Inst, 1964; Univ Without Walls Berkeley 1972. **CAREER:** SEEK prog City Coll of NY, lecturer 1967-69; CCNY, poet-in-resd 1969-70; Univ of CA Bekreley, lecturer 1970-72; full time author 1973-79; Umbra Publ, editor 1962-. **ORGANIZATIONS:** Vstg prof Univ of CA San Diego 1979-80, Manopa Inst CO 1981; consult Natl Endowment for the Arts 1967-68,80, Arts Commiss City of Berkeley 1975-77, Ed Dept City of Berkeley 1969; consult Berkeley Public School System 1968, NY Publ School Systems; mem Intl PEN 1972-, Afro-Amer Triad World Writers Union 1980-. **HONORS/ACHIEVEMENTS:** Great Lakes New Writers Awd 1971; Felix of the Silent Forest poetry NY 1967; The Mayor of Harlem poetry NY 1970; The Low East poetry CA 1980; Voodoo Child biography NY 1979; Poetry in Permanent Archives Libr of Congress 1978.

HENDERSON, EDDIE L.
Engineer. **PERSONAL:** Born Feb 25, 1932, Quincy, FL; married Velma Dean Hall; children: Tracy, Dionne. **CAREER:** Professional Fighter 1955-64; Freedmen's Hosp, 1961-67; Amer Broadcasting Co News Washington DC, NABET engr. **ORGANIZATIONS:** Mem Local 644 Intl Alliance Theatrical Stage Employees; Hillcrest Hts Bapt Ch; mem White House News Photographers Assn. **HONORS/ACHIEVEMENTS:** Amateur fighter Golden Gloves NY 1949-50; So Conf Air Force Japan 1953. **MILITARY SERVICE:** USAF 1951-55. **BUSINESS ADDRESS:** Engineer, ABC, 1717 DeSales St, Washington, DC 20036.

HENDERSON, ELMER W.
Government attorney. **PERSONAL:** Born Jun 18, 1913, Baltimore; married Ethel; children: Lee, Stephanie, Jocelyn. **EDUCATION:** Morgan State Coll, AB 1937;Univ of Chgo, AM 1939; GeorgetownUniv Law Sch, JD 1952. **CAREER:** US Ho of Reps, sr couns of com on govt ops. **ORGANIZATIONS:** Mem bd dirs Supreme Life Ins Co of Am; former exec dir IL Commn on Condition of the Urban Colored Population; served as Chicago regional dir Pres Roosevelt's Fair Employment Prac Com 5 yrs; exec dir Am Counc on Human Rights 7 yrs. **BUSINESS ADDRESS:** 1640 Upshur St NW, Washington, DC 20011.

HENDERSON, ERMA L.
City official. **PERSONAL:** Born Aug 20, 1917, Pensacola, FL; divorced; children: 2 Children. **EDUCATION:** Wayne Co Comm Coll Spl Course in Crim; Univ of MI; Master's Sch of Soc Work Wayne State U; Shaw Coll, Hon Dr of Humane Letters. **CAREER:** Detroit City Counc, elected 1972-; Equal Justice Coun Inc, exec dir; Nat Maritime Un port sec; lb arwin co, priv sec; arden ent inc, exec sec; Fuller Prod Co, recruiter; Personal Sec Svc, owned oper; Interfaith Act Counc, staff counc. **ORGANIZATIONS:** Bd mem Nat Counc on Crime & Delin; Leag of Women Voters; Nat Assn Soc Work Inc; MI Acad of Sci Arts & Letters; Assn of Black Soc Work WS U; mem Am for Dem Act Bd; mem Interfaith Act Coun; life mem NAACP; Nat Coun Negro Women; hon mem Uni Sisterhd Wolverine St Bapt Conv; bd mem Black-Polish Conf; orgnzr Women's Conf of Concerns; bd chwm MI Coalition against Redlining; co-fdr Black Rsrch Found; Delta Sigma Theta Inc; Alpha ChptGamma Phi Delta Sor; past chwm Women in Municipal Govt; Nat Leag of Cities; mem other pol & rel orgns. **HONORS/ACHIEVEMENTS:** Hon mem Eta Phi Beta Sor Alpha Chpt; Past Grand Daugh Rul Elks; Grand Nat Pub Rel; num awards for outst serv to Comm; 1st black to win against white in head-up city-wide non-partisan election in polit hist of Detroit MI. **BUSINESS ADDRESS:** President, Detroit City Council, 1340 City County Bldg, Detroit, MI 48226.

HENDERSON, FREDDYE SCARBOROUGH
Travel company executive. **PERSONAL:** Born Feb 18, 1917, Franklinton, LA; married Jacob R Henderson; children: Carol Tyson, Jacob, Jr, Gaynelle Long, Shirley. **EDUCA-

TION: So Univ, BS 1937; NY Univ, MS 1950; attended Traphagen Sch Fashion Design 1949, McDowell Sch of Costume Design 1944. **CAREER:** Spelman Coll, asst prof applied art 1950-61; Asso Negro Press Chicago, fashion editor 1951-56; WERD Radio, commentator 1953-56; Pittsburgh Courier, columnist 1961-63; Henderson Travel Serv Atlanta, vice pres 1961-. **ORGANIZATIONS:** Mem pres Natl Assn Fashion & Accessory Designers 1950-54; pres Inter-Amer Travel Agts Soc 1966-68; bd of YWCA 1966-72; bd of Atlanta Council of Intl Vis 1967-; bd Gate City Day Nursery Assn 1970-75; bd Martin Luther King Jr Ctr for Social Change 1972-; mem Natl Bus & Professional Women's Clubs, League of Women Voters; mem adv bd Small Bus Devel Ctr; gov's appointee to White House Conf on Balanced Economic Growth; mem Women's C of C, Amer Soc of Travel Agents, Amer Assn of Univ Women. **HONORS/ACHIEVEMENTS:** World Mother of 1951 Atlanta Daily World; Specl Achiev Awd Black Enterprise Mag 1975; Catalyst Awd Interracial Council Bus Oppor; listed in Who's Who ofAmer Women, Who's Who in Amer; designated Certified Travel Counselor; African Trophy Awd; Martin Luther King Jr Center for NVSC; Rosenbluth Awd from AmerSoc of Travel Agents; YWCA's Acad of Women Achievers; Candace Awd in Bus from Coalition of 100 Black Women; Togo Govts Highest Civilian Awd the Order of the Mono. **BUSINESS ADDRESS:** Vice President, Henderson Travel Service, 931 Martin Luther King Jr Dr, Atlanta, GA 30314.

HENDERSON, GEORGE
Educator. **PERSONAL:** Born Jun 18, 1932, Hurtsboro, AL; son of Kidd L Henderson and Lula Mae Crawford Fisher; married Barbara Beard; children: George Jr, Michele, Lea, Joy, Lisa, Dawn, Faith Mosley. **EDUCATION:** Wayne State U, BA 1957, MA 1959, PhD 1965. **CAREER:** Church Youth Svc, soc caseworker 1957-59; Detroit Housing Commn, soc economist 1960-61; Detroit Urban League, com serv dir 1961-63; Detroit Mayors YouthCommn, pgm dir 1963-64; Detroit Pub Sch, asst supt 1965-67; Univ of OK, prof of human relations. **ORGANIZATIONS:** Disting visiting prof USAF Acad 1980-81; consult US Dept of Def, US Dept of Justice, US Commn on Civil Rights, Social Sec Admin, Am Red Cross; mem Kappa Alpha Psi Frat; mem Am Sociological Assn; mem Assn of Black Sociologist; mem Assn for Supr & Curriculum Devel. **HONORS/ACHIEVEMENTS:** S N Goldman Distinguished Prof, Univ of Oklahoma, 1969; Citation for Achievements in Human Relations, Oklahoma State Senate, 1978; Distinguished Community Serv Award, Urban League of Oklahoma City, 1981; Citation for Affirmative Action Activities in Higher Educ, Oklahoma House of Representatives, 1984; David Ross Boyd Distinguished Prof, Univ of Oklahoma, 1985; Civilian Commendation, Tinker AFB, Oklahoma, 1986; Outstanding Faculty Award, Univ of Oklahoma Black People's Union, 1987; Outstanding Contributions, Osan Air Base, Korea, 1987; Trail Blazer Award, Oklahoma Alliance for Affirmative Action, 1988; Outstanding Teacher, Univ of Oklahoma Black Alumni Assn, 1988; Books: "Foundations of Am Edn" 1970; "Tchrs Should Care" 1970; "Am Other Children" 1971; "To Live in Freedom" 1972; "Educ for Peace" 1973; "Human Rel" 1974; "Human Rel in the Military" 1975; "A Religious Found of Human Rel" 1977; "Intro t o Am Edn" 1978; "Understanding & Counseling Ethnic Minorities" 1979;"Police Human Rel" 1981; "Transcultural Hlth Care" 1981; "Physician-Patient Communication" 1981; "The State of Black OK" 1983; "The Human Rights of ProfsnlHelpers" 1983; "Psychosocial Aspects of Disability" 1984; "Mending Broken Children" 1984; "College Survival for Student Athletes," 1985; "Intl Business & Cultures" 1987. **MILITARY SERVICE:** USAF a 2c 1953-55. **HOME ADDRESS:** 2616 Osborne Dr, Norman, OK 73069. **BUSINESS ADDRESS:** Professor, University of OK, 601 Elm Room 730, Norman, OK 73019.

HENDERSON, GERALD EUGENE
Chief executive officer. **PERSONAL:** Born Oct 06, 1928, Strongburg, NE; married Josephine W; children: Gerald M, Kaul B. **EDUCATION:** NE Wesleyan U, BA 1957. **CAREER:** City of Lincoln Commn on Human Rights, exec dir 1968-; Lincoln Action Prgm, prgm dir 1967-68; Malone Comm Ctr, dep dir 1964-67; Fairmont Foods Co, salesman 1961-64. **ORGANIZATIONS:** Treas NE Chap Human Right Worker 1978; pres Family Serv Assn 1978; 1st vice pres Malone Comm Ctr 1980; pres Comm Action Lincoln Action Prgm 1969-80; bd mem Lincoln Salvation Army 1978-80. **HONORS/ACHIEVEMENTS:** Recip NAACP Serv Award Lincoln Br 1964; JC Good Govt Award Lincoln JC's 1969; distngshd serv award United Nation Day 1976. **BUSINESS ADDRESS:** Comm on Human Rights, 129 N 10th St, Lincoln, NE 68521.

HENDERSON, HENRY FAIRFAX, JR.
Electronics company executive. **PERSONAL:** Born Mar 10, 1928, Paterson, NJ; married Ethel Miller; children: Kathleen Carter, Kenneth, David, Elizabeth. **EDUCATION:** State Univ of NY Alfred, Cert, 1950; William Paterson Coll, Seton Hall Univ; New York Univ. **CAREER:** Howe Richardson Scale Co, engr 1950-67; HF Henderson Industries, founder (on part-time basis), 1954-67, pres/CEO (full-time), 1967-. **ORGANIZATIONS:** Commr Port Auth of NY & NJ; chmn Governor's Commission on Intnl Trade; dir NJ State Chamber of Commerce; mem World Trade Inst of the Port Authority of NY & NJ Advisory Board; advisory bd mem Curriculum at State Univ of NY Agricultural & Tech Inst of Alfred, St Vincents's Schl, Newark; mem Coalition of Northeast Governors, Port Authority of NY & NJ trade missions; bd mem, the Partnership for NJ; bd of trustees, Stevens Inst of Tech; advisory council mem Rutgers Graduate Schl of Management; bd of dirs, General Public Utilities Corp; bd of dirs, Natl Urban League; bd of trustees, Community Found of New Jersey. **HONORS/ACHIEVEMENTS:** Outstand Bus Achievement Award; NJ Black Chamber of Commerce; Edmond L Houston Foundation 1979; Most Outstand Minority Bus Award; Recog of Bus Achievement 1982 & Black Achievers Entrepreneur of the Yr 1982 Awards from Leaguers Inc; US Small Bus Admin Contractor of the Yr 1983; Outstand Achievement in Bus & Pub Serv Award; Urban League of Essex Co Award; The Nat Assn of Negro Bus & Profesnl Womens Clubs Inc Award; Man of the Yr Award; Nat Conf of Christians & Jews Inc Brotherhood Award 1984; Man of the Yr 100 Black Men of NJ Inc; Company of the Yr Black Enterprise 1984; Distinguished Business Citizenof the Year from the NJ Business & Ind Assoc; received 28th annual Essex Awd for Outstanding Serv to Business, Industry & Humanity 1986; Natl Black MBA Assoc awd for outstanding contributions to the busniness community & the Passaic Valley HS Distinguished Alumni Awd 1986; Berean Award, United Minority Business Brain Trust Inc, 1988. **HOME ADDRESS:** 315 Rifle Camp Rd, West Paterson, NJ 07424. **BUSINESS ADDRESS:** President/Chief Executive Officer, HF Henderson Industries, 45 Fairfield Pl, West Caldwell, NJ 07006.

HENDERSON, HERBERT H.
Attorney. **PERSONAL:** Married Maxine D McKissick; children: Cherly Lynne, Sherri Avis Willoughby, Gail Henderson-Staples, Leslie Jeanine, Michael Renaldo. **EDUCATION:** WV State Coll, BS 1953; George Wash Univ Coll of Law, JD 1958. **CAREER:** Attorney, civil rights & general practice; Marshall Univ, part-time instructor in black history, 1967-80; Henderson & Henderson General Practice, Huntington, WV, sr partner, currently. **ORGANIZATIONS:** Mem Cabell Co Bar Assn; bd dir WV Trial Lawyers Assn; WV State Bar; Nat Bar Assn; Am Trial Lawyers Assn; Mountaineer Bar Assn; mem bd dir Region III Assn of Mental Hlth; chmn bd trustees Huntington Dist united Methodist Ch; state United Meth Ch Conf; pres Meth Men's Club; Ebenezer Meth Ch; mem Kappa Alpha Psi Frat; mem, bd of trustees, Morristown Coll; mgr & supvr, WV NAACP Jobs Program, 1978-; state pres WV NAACP, 1966-; mem, natl bd of dirs, NAACP, 1980-. **HONORS/ACHIEVEMENTS:** W Robert Ming Award, NAACP Bd of Dirs; Justitia Officium Award, West Virginia Univ Coll of Law, 1989. **MILITARY SERVICE:** US Army, 1946-49; US Army, Korean Conflict, artillery officer, 1953-55. **BUSINESS ADDRESS:** 317 Ninth St, Huntington, WV 25711.

HENDERSON, HUGH C.
Government official. **PERSONAL:** Born Dec 03, 1930, Poughkeepsie, NY; married Sandra V Bell; children: Hugh III, Denise. **EDUCATION:** Kent Univ; Univ of Indiana; Univ of Illinois; Univ of Wisconsin. **CAREER:** State Dept of Employment Relat, sec 1979-; State of Wisconsin, indsl commr 1978-79; United Steel Workers of Amer, staff rep 1968-78; Valley Mould And Iron Co, maintenance electrician 1949-68. **ORGANIZATIONS:** Mem Intl Personnel Management Assn 1979-; mem bd of dir Milwaukee Urban Leage 1974-79; pres Milwaukee Frontier Club 1977-79; mem natl bd natl OIC 1978-; chmn of the bd Milwaukee Opport Industrialization Center 1971-. **HONORS/ACHIEVEMENTS:** Certificate of appreciation OIC Bd of Dir 1978; outstanding commun effort award Dane Cty State Employees Combined Campaign 1979; enlightened ldrshp dedicated Commun Svc Award Milwaukee Frontiers Club 1980; serv Awards; Combat Infantry Medal. **MILITARY SERVICE:** AUS 1950-53. **BUSINESS ADDRESS:** Commissioner, State of Wisconsin, Labor & Ind Review Commission, PO Box 8126, Madison, WI 53708.

HENDERSON, I. D., JR.
Government official. **PERSONAL:** Born Jul 23, 1929, Lufkin, TX; married Jerlean Eastland; children: Brenda Kay Heads, Lara Wayne Parker, Gwendolyn Joyce McKinley, Bruce Anthony. **CAREER:** Recinct #2 Angelina Co TX, county commr 1979-F Home Savings & Loans Assn, building supr 1972-79; Lufkin Foundry Inc, material control 1971-72. **ORGANIZATIONS:** Master mason Franfurt Germany 1962-65; master mason Mistletoe Lodge #31 Lawton OK 1966-77; master mason Southgate Lodge #42 Lufkin TX 1978-; deacon Mt Calvary Bapt Ch Lufkin TX; pres Angelina Co C of C 1979-. **HONORS/ACHIEVEMENTS:** Recipient KSM w/1 Bronze SV Stara; NDSM; GMC w/5 Loops; Purple Heart AUS. **MILITARY SERVICE:** AUS sfc-e-7 1951-70. **BUSINESS ADDRESS:** Commissioner, Angelina County, PO Box 908, Lufkin, TX 75901.

HENDERSON, ISAIAH HILKIAH, JR.
Clergyman. **PERSONAL:** Born Aug 16, Lexington, MS; married Ophelia; children: Georgia, Ruth. **EDUCATION:** Am Bapt Theo Sem, BA MT DD HHD. **CAREER:** Friendship Bapt Ch, pastor minister; Pleasant Green Bapt Ch, minister pastor 1944. **ORGANIZATIONS:** Past moderator New Era Dist Assn; past pres Inter-denominational Ministers Alliance 1961; pres Missionary Bapt State Conv MO; pres Friendship Village; mem Human Rela Commn KS City; denom rep Metro Inter-Ch Agy; asst sec Nat Bapt Conv USA Inc; dir gen Nat Bapt Congress Christian Edn; partcpBapt World Alliance 1955, 70; mem Evang Crusade to Austrilia 1964; Bahama Isl 1965. **HONORS/ACHIEVEMENTS:** Recpt Urban Design Award Munc Arts Commn KC 1972; award bd dir K C Bapt Comm Hosp 1972; outsdng achvmt award SN Vass 1975; spl citation Mayor KC Charles Wheeler & Jackson Co Legislators 1974. **BUSINESS ADDRESS:** 2701 E 43, Kansas City, MO 64130.

HENDERSON, JACOB R.
Business executive. **PERSONAL:** Born Jun 27, 1911, Abbeville, SC; married Freddye Scarborough; children: Carole, Jacob Jr, Gaynelle, Shirley. **EDUCATION:** SC State Coll, BS 1932; Atlanta Univ, MA 1934. **CAREER:** US Housing Auth, fiscal acctg clerk 1934-37, housing mgr 1941-63; W/EDA, economic devel rep; Henderson Travel Serv Inc, pres 1955-75, bd chmn 1976-. **ORGANIZATIONS:** Pres emeritus Atlanta Urban League Bd Dir; bd mem Butler St YMCA; trustee 1st Congregational Ch; former regional vice pres Alpha Phi Alpha Frat for So Region; Thirty-third Degree Mason & Shriner; mem Sigma Pi Phi Frat; mem NAACP; radio moderator Butler State YMCA; Hungary Club Forum & one of its founders;mem Alpha Phi Alpha Frat; former Boy Scout Leader; mem exec comm Atlanta Univ Alumni Assn; mem City of Atlanta Charter Comm 1971-72. **HONORS/ACHIEVEMENTS:** Atlanta's 200 "City Shapers"; 25 Yr Serv Pin Bd Dir Urban League YMCA; Membership Campaign Awd; Urban League Equal Oppor Day Awd. **BUSINESS ADDRESS:** President, Henderson Travel Serv Inc, 931 ML King Dr NW, Atlanta, GA 30314.

HENDERSON, JAMES H.
Educator/government official. **PERSONAL:** Born Apr 20, 1937, Lexington, NC; son of Haney Henderson and Callie Spindell Henderson; married Joan E Woods; children: Tonya L, James H Jr, James, Jennifer, Janet, Jacqueline. **EDUCATION:** Community Coll of the Air Force, AAS Mgmt, AAS, Ed Methology 1978-81; Pikes Peak Comm College, AA General Studies 1978; Univ of Southern CO, BS 1979; Webster Univ, MA Mgmt 1982; Univ of Northern CO, MA Counseling 1983; Harvard Univ, Graduate School of Educ, Institute for the Management of Lifelong Education. **CAREER:** Univ S Air Force, educ supt 1955-81; Ed Ctr Hurlburt Fld FL, educ counselor 1982-84; HQ Strategic Air Command, command educ counselor 1984-; USAF Civil Serv, HQ SAC/OPAE, assistant dir education services 1989. **ORGANIZATIONS:** Mem Recorder Kadesia Temple #135 1975-; mem Amer Assn for Adult Continuing Educ 1978-; mem Amer Numismatic Assn 1982-; mem Amer Assn for Counseling Development 1982-; midwest coord Military Educators/Counselors Assn 1983-; natl certified counselor Natl Bd of Certified Counselors 1984-. **HONORS/ACHIEVEMENTS:** Counselor Guide (Military) 1984; Education Services Officer's Guide 1989. **MILITARY SERVICE:** USAF smsgt (E-8) 26 years; Good Conduct Medal; Commendation Medal; Meritorous Service Medal. **HOME ADDRESS:** 2320 Georgetown Pl, Omaha, NE 68123. **BUSINESS ADDRESS:** Command Education Counselor, Strategic Air Command Hdqtrs, HQ SAC/DPAE, Offutt AFB, NE 68113.

HENDERSON, JAMES H. M.
Educator. **PERSONAL:** Born Aug 10, 1917, Falls Church, VA; married Betty Francis; children: Ellen Wimbish, Dena Sewell, James F, Edwin B II. **EDUCATION:** Howard Univ,

Wash DC, BS 1939; Univ of WI Madison, MPh 1940, PhD 1943. **CAREER:** Univ of Chicago Toxicity Lab, rsrch asst 1943-45; Carver Research Fnd Tuskegee Inst, rsrch asso 1945-48/1950-68; CA Inst of Tech, resrch fellow 1948-50; Biology Dept Tuskegee Inst, prof & head 1957-68; Carver Resrch Fndtn Tuskegee Inst, dir 1968-75; MBRS Program Tuskegee Inst, prog dir 1973-87; Div of Natural Sci Tuskegee Inst, chm 1975-. **ORGANIZATIONS:** Nom comm Am Asso Adv of Sci Fellow; mem Am Soc of Plant Physgsts; mem Tissue Culture Asso; mem bd trustees Montreat-Anderson Coll 1973-78; bd mem Soc of the Sigma Xi 1982-85; mem bd of trustees Stillman Clg Tuscaloosa AL 1981-. **HONORS/ACHIEVEMENTS:** Alum Awd HowardUniv 1964 & 1975; eminent faculty awd Tuskegee Inst 1965, faculty Awd 1976 & 1980; UNCF Awd for Dist Schlrs 1982; Distinguished Serv Awd SS-ASPP 1984; Lamplighters Awd Beta Kappa Chi 1984. **BUSINESS ADDRESS:** Chairman, Div of Natural Sci, Tuskegee University, Carver Research Laboratories, Tuskegee Institute, AL 36088.

HENDERSON, JAMES HENRY, SR.
Dentist. **PERSONAL:** Born Jan 29, 1925, Henderson, NC; son of James Henderson and Sarah Evans Henderson; married Mabel J White; children: Eryn Janyce, Edith Janelle, James Henry Jr. **EDUCATION:** Hampton Univ, BS 1948; Meharry Med Coll, DDS 1953; FRSH 1972; FAGD 1979; FADI 1986. **CAREER:** VA Hospital, intern 1955-56; LA State Dept Hospital, 1956-59; Private Practice, 1957-; Iberia Parish Hospital, Dauterive Hospital, Found Hospital, mem staff; NO Charity Hospital, visiting staff. **ORGANIZATIONS:** Mem Pelican Dental Assn; Chicago Dental Soc; Acad Gen Dentistry; Am Endodontic Soc; fellow of Royal Soc Health England; mem LA Com Human Relations 1965-75; mem LA Dental Assn; mem Am Dental Assn; life mem NAACP; fellow Acad of Gen Dentistry; chmn Counc on Dental Health & Planning of LDA; consult HEW; House of Delegates LDA; founder pres Community Progress League 1960-63; mem House of Delegates NDA CH of Credentia; state bd 1962-72, treas NAACP 1969-70,; dir Bacmonila Ltd 1969-; bd LA Sugar Cane Festival; mem Beta Kappa Chi Sci Soc; life mem Alpha Phi Alpha; Shriner; Royal Vanders Social Club; trustee Mt Cal Bapt Ch; PTA; HS Booster Club; ESSA Com New Iberia Bicentenial Com 1974-; pres Pelican State Dental Assn 1974-75; reference com NatL Dental Assn 19 73-; dir Natl Dental Assn Foundation; mem Acadiana Dental Soc; trustee Natl Dental Assn; delegate Amer Dental Assn 1986-88; pres Natl Dental Assn 1989-; Iberia Parish Recreation & Playground Bd 1975-; consultant, Health and Human Serv 1989-; 33 degree Prince Hall Mason 1978-. **HONORS/ACHIEVEMENTS:** Civic Achievement Awd Omega Psi Phi 1962; Awd of Merit LA Beauticians 1968; NAACP Talheimer Awd 1969, 70, 72; 5 NAACP Certificates of Merit; Alpha Phi Alpha Man of the Year Awd 1975-76; R B Jones Consistory #298 Outstanding Community Serv Awd; Notable Amer of Bicentennial Era; Merit Awd for Dedicated Service to Dentistry in LA Acadiana Dist Dental Soc; New Iberia Freshman High School Service Awd (10 years); Distinguished Service Award, Louisiana Recreation and Park Assn 1988. **MILITARY SERVICE:** AUS sgt 1943-46; AUS Dental Corp 1952-55; US Army Reserve 1st lt 1955-59. **HOME ADDRESS:** 400 Curtis Drive, New Iberia, LA 70560. **BUSINESS ADDRESS:** PO Box 9580, New Iberia, LA 70562.

HENDERSON, JAMES J., SR.
Retired business executive. **PERSONAL:** Born Jan 22, 1908, Bristol, TN; son of William T and Sallie Ann; married Julia Mildred Hicks; children: C Ann, James Jackson, Jr. **EDUCATION:** Hampton Inst, BS 1932. **CAREER:** Bankers Fire Insurance Co Durham, NC, 1932, asst sec 1937, dir 1937; NC Mutual Life Inc Co, asst treasurer 1953-62, asst vice pres 1962-64, treasurer 1964, vice pres 1970-72, financial vice pres 1972-, consultant 1974-; retired. **ORGANIZATIONS:** Trustee Mechanics & Farmers Bank Durham; dir chmn & mem exec com Mutual Savings & Loan Assn 1979; Durham Homes Inc 1976-; mem bd Harrison Construction Co; mem exec com Durham Com Negro Affairs 1940-; chm Durham Civic Co 1950-58; vice chm Durham Housing Authority 1958-71, chm 1971-78; mem Citizen Adv Com Durham 1961-; bd of dirs Durham Chamber of Commerce 1979-80; former mem Gov Adv Com on Low Income Housing; trustee vice chm mem exec com Hampton Inst 1964-71, chm 1971-; co-organizer Durham Business School 1949, pres 1949-52, bd dir 1949-57; bd dir John Avery Boys Club; pres chmn bd dir Daisy E Scarborough Nursery School; former vice pres dir exec com Durham Mem Nat Bus League; finci sec Natl Hampton Alumni Assn 1945-48; past pres Durham Chapter NC Conf; mem St Joseph's AME Church vice chmn sr bd trustees. **HONORS/ACHIEVEMENTS:** Hamptonian of Year Award 1954; past grandkeeper records exchequer past mem bd dirs exec com Kappa Alpha Psi Fraternity; mem Durham Alumni Chapter Keeper of Records 1933-58, Polemarch 1958-75; recipient Alumni award Hampton Inst 1967; Centennial Medallion 1968; first annual award City of Durham Human Relations Comm 1969; Outstanding Alumni Award Middle Eastern Province Kappa Alpha Psi 1971; civic award Durham Com on Negro Affairs 1972; Laurel Wreath Award highest award of Kappa Alpha Psi Fraternity 1974; New 5 million dollar 9 story high physical devel named "J J Henderson Housing Center" Housing Authority City of Durham 1979.

HENDERSON, JAMES R.
Dentist. **PERSONAL:** Born Nov 15, 1919, Jacksonville; married Geneva Coleman; children: Stephanie Denise. **EDUCATION:** FAMU, BS 1938; Howard U, DDS 1953. **CAREER:** Brideport Brass Co, caster 1942-43; US Postal Serv NY, postal clk 1946-48; FL A&M U, maintenance 1948; Dental Surgery FL, dentist 1953-. **ORGANIZATIONS:** Mem NAACP; Nat Urban League 1955-56; Acad Gen Dentistry; Health Adv Bd 1973; FAMU Found 1974; C of C 1973-74; mem FL Med Dental & Pharm Assn 1953-; Am Dental Assn 1949-53; FL Jak Club 1955; NE FL Dental Assn 1965-; bd mem Gateway Girl Scout Day Care Serv. **HONORS/ACHIEVEMENTS:** Combat Infantry Badge; Good Conduct Medal. **MILITARY SERVICE:** AUS sgt 1943-45. **BUSINESS ADDRESS:** 1366 Kings Rd, Jacksonville, FL.

HENDERSON, JAMES ROBERT
Business executive. **PERSONAL:** Born in Abbeville, LA; children: David Matthias, James Martin, Monique Marie. **EDUCATION:** Grambling Univ, BS Pol Sci (cum laude) 1958; Univ of Oregon, MEd 1964; Univ of Washington, Doctoral studies 1972-76. **CAREER:** Our Lady of Lourdes, teacher 1960-65; Tongue Point Job Ctr, super 1965-67; Advanced Corpsman Inst, instructor/act mgr 1967-68; Seattle-King Co New Careers Project, exec dir 1968-72; Public Employ Prog King-Snohomish Manpower Consortium, dir 1975-79; Natl Office for Black Catholics, exec dir. **ORGANIZATIONS:** Consul Mind Inc 1969; consul Natl Black Lay Catholic Caucus Washington DC 1978-80; consul Church Council of Gr Seattle Regional Office 1979-81; consul Archdiocese of Seattle 1979-81; bd mem Natl Catholic Conf for Interracial Justice 1982-85; mem Natl Assn Black Pol Scientists 1984-85; mem NAACP 1955-. **HONORS/ACHIEVEMENTS:** Serv Awd United Inner City Devel Found Seattle 1976; Serv Awd Seattle Blk Lay Catholic Caucus 1981; Achievement Awd Archdiocese of Seattle Catholic Charities 1981; Honorary Citizen Mayor City of New Orleans 1984; Leadership Awds Housing Advocacy WA DC 1985. **MILITARY SERVICE:** USAR e-5 specialist 6 yrs; Adjutant General Sch among top three of 50 1967. **BUSINESS ADDRESS:** Executive Dir, Natl Office of Black Catholics, 3025 Fourth St, NE, Washington, DC 20017.

HENDERSON, JOHN L.
Educator. **PERSONAL:** Born Apr 10, 1932, Evergreen, AL; married Theresa Crittenden; children: Dana, Nina, John. **EDUCATION:** Hampton Inst, BS 1955;Univ Cincinnati, M Ed 1967, Ed D 1976; Inst Afro-Am Studies Earlham Coll, 1971. **CAREER:** Univ of Cincinnati, dean student devel 1972-76; Univ Urban Affairs, dir; Xavier Univ Cincinnati, lecturer Psych Ed 1970-72; Raymond Walters Coll, instr Psychology Ed 1969-70; Univ Cincinnat, asst dean students 1968-69; Xavier Univ, research asst 1967-68; Univ Cincinnati, 1957-67; US Public Health Serv Cincinnati, research asst; Sinclair Comm Coll, Dayton OH, Amer Assn Higher Educ, vice pres for student services; Amer Coll Personnel Assn. **ORGANIZATIONS:** Mem Council on Black Am Affairs; bd of dirs Dayton Urban League 1977-; bd of Dirs Miami Valley Lung Assn 1978; bd of dirs Miami Valley Counc on Aging 1979; bd of dirs Miami Vlley Educ Oppor Ctr 1978; editorial bd Journal of Developmental and Remedial Educ 1980; Assn Non-White Concerns; Nat Assn Student Personnel Adminstrs; Phi Delta Kappa 1971; commr Cincinnati Human Relations Comm; Cincinnati Branch NAACP 1969; chmn Educ Com; Special Task Forceto Study Racial Isolation Cincinnati Pub Schs 1972-73; Cincinnati Manpower Planning Council 1971-72; bd trustees Cincinnati Sch Found 1973-75; appointed Chmn bd commrs Cincinnati Human Relations Comm; Developemental Educ Adv Com OH Bd Regents 3 yr term 1974; editorial bd NASPA Jour 1974. **HONORS/ACHIEVEMENTS:** Hon chmn Cincinnati Black Expo 1971. **MILITARY SERVICE:** AUS 1st lt 1955-57. **BUSINESS ADDRESS:** Sr Asst to President, Cincinnati Technical College, 3520 Central Parkway, Cincinnati, OH 45223.

HENDERSON, JOYCE ANN
Educational administrator. **PERSONAL:** Born Jan 12, 1947, Oklahoma City, OK; married William Gerald; children: Kevin G, Wm Kelly. **EDUCATION:** LangstonUniv Ok, BS 1969; Central StateUniv Edmond OK MS 1973. **CAREER:** OK City School System Adult Educ, prin 1980-; Harvard Middle School OK City School System, asst prin 1978-80; Life Guthrie Job Corps Center, supvr basic educ & dept head of center 1976-78; Orchard Park Girls School Ok City School System, counselor 1974-76; Teacher Corps Univ of OK & OK City School System, teacher corps supvr 1972-74. **ORGANIZATIONS:** Bd mem Central StateUniv Alumni Assn 1977-; sec & bd mem United Nations Assn OK City Chap 1977-; mem OK Educ Assn Prins Assn; 1978- sec OKC ChptAlpha Kappa Alpha Sor 1973-77; mem OKC Chap Jack & Jill of Am Inc 1975-; bd mem & v chairwoman OK Crime Comn 1978-; co-authored Tchr's Guide Black History OK OKC Sch Sys 1970. **HONORS/ACHIEVEMENTS:** Who's Who among Leaders of Secondary Educ 1971; Who's Who among Women in Am 1977; second pl Midwestern Region Outstanding Soror Alpha Kappa Alpha Sor 1977. **BUSINESS ADDRESS:** 715 N Walker, Oklahoma City, OK 73102.

HENDERSON, LEMON
Auto dealership chief executive. **CAREER:** Broadway Ford Inc, Edmond, OK, chief exec; Quality Ford S ales Inc, Little Rock, AR, chief exec. **BUSINESS ADDRESS:** Quality Ford Sales, Inc., 11200 W. Markham St., Little Rock, AR 72211. *

HENDERSON, LENNEAL JOSEPH, JR.
Educator, consultant. **PERSONAL:** Born Oct 27, 1946, New Orleans; son of Lenneal Henderson and Marcell Henderson; married Joyce E Colon, May 07, 1989; children: Lenneal C, Lenneal Jr III. **EDUCATION:** Univ of CA Berkeley, AB (cum laude) 1968; Univ of CA, MA Political Science, Public Admin 1969; Univ of CA, PhD Political Science 1977. **CAREER:** San Jose State Univ Afro-Amer Studies, lecturer 1973-75; Shepard & Assoc, 1973-74; Morrison & Rowe, sr analyst 1974; Dukes Dukes & Assocs San Francisco, assoc consultant 1974-75; Howard Univ Washington, visiting prof Political Science 1975, prof school of business and public admin; Howard Univ 1979-87; Univ of TN Knoxville, head, prof of political science 1988-89; Federal Exec Inst, Charlottesville VA, prof 1989; Schaefer Center for Public Policy, Univ of Baltimore, sr fellow 1989-. **ORGANIZATIONS:** Mem, bd of dirs, acting pres Children & Youth Serv Agency; pres San Francisco African Amer History & Cult Soc; Campaign Human Devel; co-ed "Journal on Political Repression"; affiliate Joint Center for Political Studies Washington 1971-; Conf of Minority Public Administrators 1972-; Amer Assn Univ Prof 1972-; educ bd The Black Scholar Mag; chmn Citizens Energy Advisory Comm Washington 1981-; Natl Rsch Council 1983-84; Ford Foundation Postdoctoral Fellow; Johns Hopkins School of Advanced Intl Studies Washington; visiting black scholar Fairfield Univ; bd of trustees Population Reference Bureau; bd of dirs Decision Demographics, Natl Civic League. **HONORS/ACHIEVEMENTS:** Outstanding Serv Award, San Francisco Afro-Amer History Soc 1975; Outstanding Educator Amer 1975; Distinguished Faculty Award, Howard Univ; Kellogg Natl Fellow 1984-87; author "Black Political Life in the US" 1972. **HOME ADDRESS:** 4530 Mustering Drum Way, Ellicott City, MD 21043.

HENDERSON, LEROY W., JR.
Visual artist. **PERSONAL:** Born May 27, 1936, Richmond, VA; married Helen Foy; children: Kerby, Keith. **EDUCATION:** VA State Coll, BS 1959f Pratt, MS 1965f certificate educ broadcasting corp TV training sch 1971; Nat Acad TV Arts & Sci Film & TV Workshop, certificate 1973. **CAREER:** Free-lance photographer 1967-; Bedford-Lincoln Neighborhood Mus Brooklyn, art tchr 1968-70; Brooklyn Mus Educ Dept, art tchr 1968; New York City Sch System, art tchr 1962-66; Richmond Pub Sch System, art tchr 1959. **ORGANIZATIONS:** Bd mem Aunt Len's Doll & Toy Mus NY; mem Kappa Alpha Psi Frat Full Opportunities Com Acad of TV Arts & Sci 1970-73; Emergency Cultural Coalition 1968. **HONORS/ACHIEVEMENTS:** Recipient certificate of excellence in design photography Mead Library of Ideas Mead Paper Co 1972; one show merit award photography Art Dir Club Inc & Copy Club of NY, 1974f Photo-Graphis Intl Annual Award of Outstanding Art & Photography; commendation for Heroic Performance from concerned parents & students of HS of Mus & Art New York City 1968. **MILITARY SERVICE:** AUS sp/4 1959-61.

HENDERSON, LLOYD D.
Educational administrator. **PERSONAL:** Born Jan 28, 1945, Monroe Co, AL; married Sarah A; children: Cheryl. **EDUCATION:** AL State Univ, BS 1964; Univ of WY, MS 1971; Auburn Univ, grad study 1972. **CAREER:** Monroe Co Training Sch, coach head of math dept 1964-70; Monroe Co Monroeville AL, instr adult educ 1965; Univ of WY, instr physics 1971; Lurleen B Wallace State Jr Coll, instr math & physics 1971-74, dir div of student sup-

port & spec prog 1974-. **ORGANIZATIONS:** Mem AEA, NEA, SAEOPP; chmn trustee bd First Bethlehem Baptist Ch; mem Covington Co Civic Organ; mem Free & Accepted Masons of AL. **HONORS/ACHIEVEMENTS:** Cert of Achievement FL A&M Univ 1970; Outstanding Young Men of Amer 1977; Personalities of the So 1977-78. **BUSINESS ADDRESS:** Dir Div of Student Support, Lurleen B Wallace St Jr Coll, PO Box 1418, Andalusia, AL 36420.

HENDERSON, NANNETTE S.
Educator. **PERSONAL:** Born Jun 09, 1946, Washington, DC; daughter of Percival Carlton Smith and Edith Richardson Smith; married Lyman Beecher Henderson, Nov 29, 1969; children: Kara Michelle, Kristi Bynn. **EDUCATION:** Howard U, BS 1967, MS 1969; NC State U, PhD 1973. **CAREER:** Vance Granville Comm Coll, dir coll transfer prgm; NC State Univ Raleigh, asst prof plant pathology. **ORGANIZATIONS:** North Carolina Assn of Educators Amer Assn of Junior & Community Colleges; North Carolina Assn of Two-Year and Community College Biologists. **HONORS/ACHIEVEMENTS:** Phi Kappa Phi Hon Soc; mem Beta Kappa Chi Hon Soc; creator of Live Animal Substitute, Ribbit 1980; Excellence in Teaching NC Dept of Community Colleges 1987; C.A.S.E. Teaching Award 1988; Tar Heel of the Week, News & Observer Newspaper 1988. **HOME ADDRESS:** 516 W Ridgeway St, Warrenton, NC 27589. **BUSINESS ADDRESS:** Chair, Science Dept, Vance Granville Community College, PO Box 917, Henderson, NC 27536.

HENDERSON, RAMONA ESTELLE
Government appointee. **PERSONAL:** Born Oct 03, 1952, Baltimore, MD; daughter of Robert Henderson and Doris Green Henderson. **EDUCATION:** Morgan State U, BS 1975; Morgan State U, candidate MBA 1982. **CAREER:** Arthur Young & Co, sr auditor; Linwood Jennings PA CPA's, asso 1977-79; Constant Care Comm Health Center Inc, controller 1976-77; Ernst & Ernst, auditor 1975-76; Wayne State Univ, director internal audit, 1985-87; Wayne County Govt, auditor general, 1987-. **ORGANIZATIONS:** Mem Am Inst of CPA's 1976-; mem MD Asso of CPA's 1977-; president Nat Assn of Black Accountants; mem NAACP; mem Big Brothers & Sisters of Am. **HONORS/ACHIEVEMENTS:** "How to Start a Small Business" Afro-Am Newspaper 1977; Outstanding mem, Natl Assn Black Accountants 1983. **HOME ADDRESS:** 8200 E Jefferson #1203, Detroit, MI 48214.

HENDERSON, RICKEY
Professional athlete. **PERSONAL:** Born Dec 25, 1958, Chicago, IL. **CAREER:** Oakland A's, left fielder baseball player; New York Yankees, player 1985-. **HONORS/ACHIEVEMENTS:** All-Amer honors as a running back in hs; dozen football scholarship offers from coll incl UCLA, Univ of So CA; Stole 130 bases in 1982 to shatter the single-season record of 118; Brock, Maury Wills & Henderson are the only three major leaguers to have stolen more than 100 bases in a single season; Gold Glove Awd for his outstanding defensive play in the outfield; named outfielder on The Sporting News Amer League Silver Slugger team 1981,85; Sporting News Silver ShoeAwd 1982; Sporting News Golden Shoe Awd 1983; mem All Star Team 1980,82,83,84,85,86. **BUSINESS ADDRESS:** New York Yankees, Yankee Stadium, New York, NY 10451.

HENDERSON, ROBBYE R.
Librarian. **PERSONAL:** Born Nov 10, 1937, Morton, MS; son of Robert Allen Robinson (deceased) and Aljuria Myers Robinson (deceased); children: Robreka Aljuria. **EDUCATION:** Tougaloo So Christian Coll, BA 1960; Atlanta Univ, MSLS 1968; So IL Univ, PhD 1976. **CAREER:** Patton Lane HS, head librarian 1960-66; Utica Jr Coll, head librarian 1966-67; MS Valley State Univ, acquisitions librarian 1968-69; MS Valley State Univ, dir of tech serv 1969-72, univ librarian 1972-. **ORGANIZATIONS:** Consult Office of Health Resources Oppor 1976-78; instr So IL Univ Carbondale 1976; consult MS Assn of Coll Council on Study Accreditation 1970; pres Progressive Faculty & Staff Women's Club 1978-; owner/partner Itta Bena Nursey 1978; financial sec Alpha Kappa Omega 1979. **HONORS/ACHIEVEMENTS:** Fellowship Library Admin Dev Prog 1973; Internship Mellon ACRL Prog 1974; Fellowship Developing Leaders in Developing Instns 1974-76; Fellowship cum laude1976. **BUSINESS ADDRESS:** Univ Librarian, MS Valley StateUniv, J H White Library, Itta Bena, MS 38941.

HENDERSON, ROMEO CLANTON
Educator. **PERSONAL:** Born Apr 23, 1915, Salisbury, NC; married Jestina Tutt; children: Gwynette, Patricia. **EDUCATION:** Livingstone Coll AB 1936; Cornell Univ, MA 1938; PA State Univ, EdD 1950. **CAREER:** Swift Memorial Jr Coll Rogersville TN, instr dean 1939-43; SC State Coll Orangeburg, prof, chmn social sci, dean school of grad studies 1952-60; DE State Coll, prof educ, dean instrn. **BUSINESS ADDRESS:** Professor Emeritus, Delaware State College, Dupont Highway, Dover, DE 19901.

HENDERSON, STANLEY L.
Educator, musician. **PERSONAL:** Born Oct 08, 1909, Albia, IA; widowed. **EDUCATION:** Milwaukee State Tchrs Coll, BEd 1953;Univ of MI, MMus 1949;Univ of IA, PhD 1959. **CAREER:** Harris Tchrs Coll St Louis, prof of music chmn music dept 15 yrs; St Louis Pub Schls, educator 25 yrs; prof act incl num piano & organ reci radio & TV appear with vocal art & chorus. **ORGANIZATIONS:** Pres Negro MO Mus Educ Assn 1940-44; chmn Music Coun St L Pub HS; vice pres St L Mus Educ Assn 1965-67f vice pres MO Music Educ Assn Coll Dept 1974; org choir dir St James Ch 1935-37; Berean 7th Day Adv Ch 1936-40, 1951-54; Centenial Chris Ch 1951-53; 1st Bapt Ch 1958-66; Nat Assn Negro Mus; chmnSchol Memship St L Music Educ Assn ofUniv Prof; Music Educ Nat Assn; NAACP; YMCA; Edl Berean 7th Day Adv Ch St L 1953; chmn Schol Com St L Br Nat Assn of Missourians 1969. **HONORS/ACHIEVEMENTS:** Writ book "Resources in Afr-Am Music" now being pub by MO St Dept of Educ for use in schl & coll in MO; award Mo St Dept of Educ 25 yrs; Merit Serv 1965; Kappa Delta Pi Hon Soc; oustndg citi award Mayor Cervantes St Louis 1965; muesher medal Musice Dept St Loui Pub Schls outstng work in instrumMusic 1940. **MILITARY SERVICE:** WW II bandsman medic ts-4 1944-46.

HENDERSON, STEPHEN E.
Educator. **PERSONAL:** Born Oct 13, 1925, Key West, FL; son of James Henderson and Leonora (Sands) Henderson; married Jeanne Holman, Jun 14, 1958; children: Stephen E., Jr., Timothy A., Philip L., Alvin Malcolm. **EDUCATION:** Morehouse Coll, A.B., 1949; Univ of Wisconsin, M.A., 1950, Ph.D., 1959. **CAREER:** Virginia Union Univ, Richmond, VA, teacher, 1950-62; Morehouse Coll, Atlanta, GA, prof of English and chmn of dept, 1962-71; Howard Univ, Washington, D.C., prof of Afro-Amer studies, 1971—, dir of Inst for the Arts and the Humanities, 1973—. **ORGANIZATIONS:** Natl Council of Teachers of English, Amer Assoc of Univ Profs, Coll Languag e Assoc, S Atlantic Modern Language Assoc, Phi Beta Kappa. **HONORS/ACHIEVEMENTS:** Danforth research grant; Southern Fellowships Fund grant; Amer Council of Learned Societies, General Educ Board grant; co-author of The Militant Black Writer in Africa and the United States, 1969; author of Understanding the New Black Poetry: Black Speech and Black Music as Poetic References, 1973. **MILITARY SERVICE:** U.S. Army, 1944-45. **HOME ADDRESS:** 1703 Lebanon St., Langley Park, MD 20783. **BUSINESS ADDRESS:** Institute for the Arts and the Humanities, 2400 Sixth St., Howard University, Washington, DC 20059. *

HENDERSON, THELTON EUGENE
Federal judge. **PERSONAL:** Born Nov 28, 1933, Shreveport, LA; children: Geoffrey A. **EDUCATION:** Univ of CA Berkeley, BA 1956, JD 1962. **CAREER:** US Dept Justice, atty 1962-63; FitzSimmons & Petris, assoc 1964-64; San Mateo County Legal Aid Soc CA, directing atty 1966-69; Stanford CA Univ Law School, asst dean 1968-76; Rosen, Remcho & Henderson San Francisco, partner 1977-80; US Dist Court No Dist CA San Francisco, judge 1980-. **ORGANIZATIONS:** Assoc prof School Law Golden Gate Univ San Francisco 1978-80; mem Natl Bar Assn, Charles Houston Law Assn. **MILITARY SERVICE:** AUS 1956-58. **BUSINESS ADDRESS:** Federal Judge, U S District Court, 450 Golden Gate Ave, San Francisco, CA 94102.

HENDERSON, VIRGINIA RUTH MCKINNEY
Psychologist. **PERSONAL:** Born Feb 19, 1932, Cleveland, OH; daughter of Dr Wade Hampton McKinney and Ruth Berry McKinney; married Perry A; children: Sheryl, Virginia, Perry Jr. **EDUCATION:** Spelman Coll, AB Psych Bio 1953; Boston U, MA Psych 1955 Univ of NM, PhD 1974. **CAREER:** Mad Metro School Dist, school psychology 1976-;Univ of NM, psychology asst prof ped psychology 1968-76; Seattle, school psychology 1967-68; Cleveland Metro General Hosp, psychology 1963-65; Cleveland Guidance Center, psychology 1957-59; Muscatatuck St School, dir nurse educ psychology 1955-57. **ORGANIZATIONS:** Am Psychol Assn 1965-; Am Assn on Mental Def 1964-; consultant Model Cities Day Care Center 1972-74; certified admin Brazelton Neonatal Behavior Assessment Scale; bd of dir All Faiths Receiving Home 1973-76; bd of trustees Mazano Day School 1974-76; bd dir TWCA 1977; First Baptist Church of Mad WI 1976-; bd of dirs Visiting Nurses Assn 1978-; bd of dirs Madison Urban League 1979-F mem Natl Assn of School Psychologist 1979-; pres, Women in Focus, 1987-; General Board, Amer Baptist Churches USA, 1983-; bd of dir, Green Lake Conference Center, 1982-; Wayland Board, Univ Wisconsin, 1987-; chair, Minority Student Achievement Committee, Madison School District, 1988-; United Way Allocation Comm, 1987-. **HONORS/ACHIEVEMENTS:** Grand Magna Cum Laude Spelman Coll 1953. **BUSINESS ADDRESS:** Madison Metropolitan Sch Dist, 545 W Dayton St, Madison, WI 53703.

HENDERSON, WILLIAM C., II
Artist, designer. **PERSONAL:** Born Nov 03, 1941, Birmingham, AL; married Australia Tarver. **EDUCATION:** AL State Coll Montgomery, BS 1964; Cranbrook Acad of Art, MFA 1969. **CAREER:** Henderson Osborne & Khan Manu Ent Port-Au-Prince, Haiti, West Indies, Sr Ptr;Univ level tchr; Erzulie Proj Inc apparl des. **ORGANIZATIONS:** 12 natl & Intl gr exh; 7 One-man exh. **HONORS/ACHIEVEMENTS:** Pres hon cit scholar AL St Coll; Commn Container Corp of Am Great Ideas of West Man; Consing Cont Ringling Museum Sarasota. **MILITARY SERVICE:** USMCR.

HENDON, LEA ALPHA
Human resources administrator. **PERSONAL:** Born Mar 27, 1953, Hartford, CT; daughter of Charles Martin and Willie Mae Wilcox Martin. **EDUCATION:** Boston Coll, Chesnut Hill MA, BA Education, 1975; Eastern New Mexico Univ, Portales NM, MA Psychology, 1979. **CAREER:** Boston Public Schools, Boston MA, teacher, 1975-77; Allstate Insurance Co, Farmington CT, office operations supvr, 1979-80; Aetna Insurance Co, Hartford CT, business systems analyst, 1980-83; Hartford Insurance Group, Hartford CT, office automation consultant, 1983-85; Aetna Life & Casualty, Hartford CT, recruiter, consultant, 1986-. **ORGANIZATIONS:** Advisory Bd, DP, Post Coll, 1987-88; mem, Amer Soc for Personnel Admin, 1988-; pres, Black Data Processing Assoc, Hartford Chapter, 1989-90; sec, ITC-Gavel, 1990-91; mem, Delta Sigma Theta Sorority.

HENDRICKS, BARBARA
Opera singer. **PERSONAL:** Born Nov 20, 1948, Stephens, AR; children: 2 children. **EDUCATION:** Univ of NE, BS; Julliard School of Music NY, BMusic; Studied with Jennie Tourel. **CAREER:** Debut with San Francisco Spring Opera in Ormindo 1974; performed with maj opera co's in US, Europe incl Boston Opera, St Paul Opera, Santa Fe Opera, Deutsche Opera, Berlin, Aix-en-Provence Festival, Houston Opera, De Nederlandse Operastichting, Glyndebourne Festival Opera; recitial & appearances with symphony orchs incl Boston Symphony Orch, NY Philharm, Los Angeles Philharm, Cleveland Symphony Orch, Philadelphia Orch, Chicago Symphony, Berlin Philharm, Vienna Philharm,London Symphony Orch, Orchestre de Paris, Orchestre Nationale de France. **HONORS/ACHIEVEMENTS:** Grand Prix due Disque 1976; Commandeur des Arts et des Lettres given by French Govt 1986; has made over 30 recordings.

HENDRICKS, BARKLEY L.
Artist, educator. **PERSONAL:** Born Apr 16, 1945, Philadelphia. **EDUCATION:** YaleUniv Sch Art, BFA; MFA 1972; Bpa Acad Fine Arts, cert 1967. **CAREER:** CT Coll, artist, asst prof art 1972-; Un Saskachewan, vis artist 1974; Glassboro State Coll, 1974; PA Acad Fine Arts, instr 1971, 72. **HONORS/ACHIEVEMENTS:** Num group & one man exhibns; pvt colls 1st prize NE Photography Exhbn Mt Holyoke Coll Art Mus 1973; 2nd prize Cheltenham Art Cntr Exhbn PA 1974; 1st prize CT Artist Annual 1974; num other prizes. **BUSINESS ADDRESS:** Asst Professor of Fine Arts, Connecticut College, New London, CT 06320.

HENDRICKS, BEATRICE E.
Attorney. **PERSONAL:** Born Sep 19, St Thomas, Virgin Islands of the United States. **EDUCATION:** Morgan State Coll, BS 1962; Howard Univ Law School, JD (Cum Laude) 1972. **CAREER:** William Morris Agency NY, jr acctn 1962-64; IRS, field agent 1964-69; Ford Motor Co, staff attny 1972-74; Acacia Mutual Life Ins, attny 1974-76; Acacia Mutual,

asst counsel 1976-79; Dept of Housing & Comm Devel, asst corp counsel 1980-; A&B Household Serv Inc, president, half-owner 1979-. **ORGANIZATIONS:** Mem Natl Bar Assoc, Amer Bar Assoc, DC Bar Assoc, Detroit Bar Assoc, Alpha Kappa Alpha Sor Inc, Inez W Tinsley Cultural Soc, Natl Assoc of ColoredWomen Clubs Inc. **BUSINESS ADDRESS:** President, A & B Household Services Inc, 1133 N Capital St NE, Washington, DC 20002.

HENDRICKS, ELROD JEROME
Professional athlete. **PERSONAL:** Born Dec 22, 1940, St Thomas, Virgin Islands of the United States;married Merle; children: Ryan, Ian. **CAREER:** Baltimore Orioles, 1968-72; Chicago Cubs, 1972; Baltimore Orioles, 1972-76; New York Yankees, 1976-77; Baltimore Orioles, coach 1977-. **ORGANIZATIONS:** Operated a two-week baseball camp for youngsters the past 3 summers. **HONORS/ACHIEVEMENTS:** Selected first "Man of the Year" by the Baltimore cphtr Natl Conf of Christians & Jews. **BUSINESS ADDRESS:** Catcher, Baltimore Orioles, Memorial Stadium, Baltimore, MD 21218.

HENDRICKS, JON
Professional musician. **PERSONAL:** Born Sep 16, 1921, Newark, OH; son of Rev Alexander Brooks Hendricks and Willie Carrington Hendricks; married Judith, Mar 26, 1959; children: Jon Jr, Michele, Eric, Colleen, Aria. **EDUCATION:** Univ of Toledo, pre-law 1948-51. **CAREER:** Lambert, Hendricks & Ross, singer & songwriter 1960's; taught jazz at, Cal St, Sonoma, UC Berkeley, UCLA, Stanford; sang with and wrote for King Pleasure, Count Basie, Duke Ellington, Louis Armstrong, Dave Brubeck, Carmen McRae; Jon Hendricks & Co, singer & songwriter. **ORGANIZATIONS:** Appointed to bd of the Kennedy Center Honors Committee Washington, DC; Artistic Dir and Host of the Annual San Francisco Jazz Festival. **HONORS/ACHIEVEMENTS:** Peabody Award and Emmy Award for Best Documentary of the Year for "Somewhere to Lay My Weary Head, The Story of the Dunbar Hotel" for KNXT; Voted Number One Jazz Singer in the World by London's Melody Maker 1968-69; 1981 Intl Critics Poll of Down Beat Magazine as the vocal group most deserving of wider recognition; Awarded Grammy for lyrics to the Manhattan Transfer's hit verstion of "Birdland"; created and performed on current Manhattan Transfer album "Vocalese" Playwrite,won 5 Grammy's; wrote produced directed & starred in hit show "Evolution of the Blues" which ran five years on broadway 1974-78; ran one year in Westwood Playhouse Los Angeles where nothing had ever run over six weeks; group Lambert Hendricks & Ross won 1st Grammy for Jazz Vocals. **MILITARY SERVICE:** USA 1942-46 Cpl. **HOME ADDRESS:** Gateway Plaza 400, 375 Southend Ave, New York, NY 10280-1025.

HENDRICKS, JUANITA
Housing developer. **PERSONAL:** Born Jun 11, 1935, St Louis; widowed. **EDUCATION:** Vashon, courses accounting & bookkeeping 1965; St Louis Iniv, majoring Psychology 1953; Wash Univ, certificate Bus Adminstrn 1970; Wash Univ, certificate Community Devel 1967. **CAREER:** St Louis Head Start Aide, human devel corp 1966; housing specialist 1969; housing developer 1972-; Internal Revenue, tax counselor 1965; Gerriatric Center LA, supr 1962-64; St Louis City Hosp Mental Health Div, 1955. **ORGANIZATIONS:** Nat Assn Housing & Redevelopment Officials through Human Devel Corp; Nat Assn Community Devel Police Community Relations; dir Summer youth program Grace & N Min Presb Chs; United Block Inc; mem volunteer sec Volunteered assisting League Women Voters in Voting Educ Workshops; volunteered with Aunts & Uncles Shoe Distribn Workshop; volunteered 22rd Ward Dem Orgn. **HONORS/ACHIEVEMENTS:** Merit achievement awrd Police Community Relations. **BUSINESS ADDRESS:** 1321 Clark Ave, St Louis, MO 63103.

HENDRICKS, LETA
Librarian. **PERSONAL:** Born May 22, 1954, Galesburg, IL. **EDUCATION:** Western IL Univ, BA (w/Honors) 1977; Atlanta Univ, MA 1979; Univ of Illinois, MS 1989. **CAREER:** Carl Sandburg Coll, instructor 1983; Knox Coll, reader services librarian 1986-; Galesburg Public Library, specl col lib 1980-; Knox College, reference assistant 1986-, instructor winter 1989. **ORGANIZATIONS:** Mem NAACP 1967-, NSWA 1982-, Feminist Writers Union 1982-. **HONORS/ACHIEVEMENTS:** Foundation Scholar Western Il Univ 1976. **HOME ADDRESS:** PO Box 775, Galesburg, IL 61402.

HENDRICKS, MARVIN B.
Scientist. **PERSONAL:** Born Dec 04, 1951, Newnan, GA; son of Jimmie L Hendricks and Margaret Petty Hendricks; married Helen Talley, Dec 26, 1971; children: Bridget. **EDUCATION:** Massachusetts Inst of Technology, Cambridge MA, BS, 1973; Johns Hopkins Univ, Baltimore MD, PhD, 1980. **CAREER:** Fred Hutchinson Cancer Research Center, Seattle WA, post-doctoral fellow, 1980-84; Integrated Genetics, Framingham MA, staff scientist, 1984-87, sr scientist, 1987-. **ORGANIZATIONS:** Mem, Amer Assn for Advancement of Science, 1976-, New York Academy of Science, 1984-86. **HONORS/ACHIEVEMENTS:** MIT Scholarship, Massachusetts Inst of Technology, 1969; Valedictorian, Central High School, Newnan GA, 1969; 16 articles in intl research journals, 1976-; co-author of articles in two books, 1980-; Post-doctoral Fellowship Awards, Amer Cancer Soc, 1980, Ann Fuller Fund (Yale Univ), 1980, Natl Inst of Health, 1980; featured in Ebony Magazine, 1988. **HOME ADDRESS:** 21 Perry H Henderson Dr, Framingham, MA 01701.

HENDRICKS, RICHARD D.
Business executive. **PERSONAL:** Born May 26, 1937, Glen Cove, NY; married Madelyn Williams; children: Pamela, Jeannette, Natalie. **EDUCATION:** Hofstra Univ, BBA 1960. **CAREER:** Abraham & Straus Dept Stores NY, dept mgr 1960-65; Johnson Pub Co, adv sales rep 1965-66; JC Penney Co, buyer 1966-. **ORGANIZATIONS:** Founder bd mem QNS Assoc Inc; founder pres LISA Prodns; spl lectr Black Exec Exchange Prog; lectr State Univ of NY; mem Urban League; AME Zion Ch; trustee treas 1963-64; Mason Doric Lodge; Black Artist Assn; NAACP. **HONORS/ACHIEVEMENTS:** Outstanding Achievement Awd Intl Key Women of Amer 1974; Comm Serv Awd Black Media Inc 1975. **BUSINESS ADDRESS:** Buyer, JC Penney Co, 1301 Ave of the Americas, New York, NY 10019.

HENDRICKS, STEVEN AARON
Public relations mgr. **PERSONAL:** Born Feb 05, 1960, Kansas City, KS. **EDUCATION:** Wichita State Univ, BA Journalism 1982. **CAREER:** Wichita Eagle-Beacon Newspaper, adv rep 1981; Pizza Hut Inc, comm asst 1982, operations mgr 1982-83; State of KS, aide to the governor. **ORGANIZATIONS:** Mem Withita State Univ Football Team 1978-82; mem WSU Advertising & PR Club 1980-82; mem Fellowship of Christian Athletes 1981-82; mem Adv & PR Club of Whichita 1981-82; mem Kappa Alpha Psi Frat 1982-; mem Black Democratic Caucus 1984-. **HONORS/ACHIEVEMENTS:** Top Ad/PR Student WSU Adv & Public Relations Club 1980; Outstanding Student Stephan Adv Agency 1981; Student of the Year Adv & PR Club of Wichita 1981; Outstanding Young Man of America 1984. **BUSINESS ADDRESS:** Aide to the Governor, State of KS, State Capitol-Gov's Office, Topeka, KS 66612.

HENDRIETH, BRENDA LUCILLE
Purchasing planning analyst. **PERSONAL:** Born Oct 28, 1955, Detroit, MI. **EDUCATION:** MI State Univ, BA 1977; Wayne State Univ, MBA 1984. **CAREER:** Hudsons Dept Store, asst mgr 1977-78; Detroit Bd of Educ, purchasing agent 1978-86; Chrysler Motors, forward model timing analyst 1986-. **ORGANIZATIONS:** Mem Purchasing Mgmt Assoc 1982-84; human resources co-chmn Natl Black MBA Assoc 1985; mem NAACP, Alpha Kappa Alpha. **HONORS/ACHIEVEMENTS:** Golden State Minority Awd WSU 1983. **HOME ADDRESS:** 19511 Greenfield, Detroit, MI 48235.

HENDRIX, DANIEL W.
Educator. **PERSONAL:** Born Oct 16, 1922, Sylvania, GA; children: Gia Michelle, Piaget Descartes, 3 grown Children. **EDUCATION:** FL Atlantic U; Auburn U;Univ OK; OH State U; Atlanta U, MS; Savannah State Coll, BS. **CAREER:** Palm Beach Jr Coll, Roosevelt Jr Coll, Carver HS, Washington HS, teacher; Washington HS, asst prin. **ORGANIZATIONS:** 1st black elected mem Palm Bch Sch Bd; Christian Bus Yng Mens Com; bd trustees Sci Planaterium of Palm Bch Co; bd dir United Way; facutly sponsor Phi Theta Kappa Palm Bch Jr Coll; life mem Phi Beta Sigma; natl dir Bigger & Better Bus Phi Beta Sigma; exec bd Gulf Stream Council BSA; FL State Action Council; FL State Voters League; Gold Coast Voters League; Urban League; Nat Business League; Wmn's Political Caucus. **HONORS/ACHIEVEMENTS:** Who's Who FL; Outstanding Educators America 1972.

HENDRIX, MARTHA RAYE
Educator, mayor. **PERSONAL:** Born Aug 17, 1939, Mineral Springs, AR; daughter of Lewis Turner and Flossie Johnson Turner; married Clarence Henderix Jr, Aug 05, 1963 (divorced); children: Marcia, Clarisse Renee', Christal Lynn. **EDUCATION:** Shorter Coll, N Little Rock AR, AA, 1959; Philander Smith, Little Rock AR, BA, 1961; Henderson State Univ, Arkadelphia AR, post graduate studies. **CAREER:** Howard County High School, Mineral Springs AR, teacher, 1961-70; Saratoga School, Saratoga AR, teacher, 1970-89; Town of Tollette, Tollette AR, mayor, 1989. **ORGANIZATIONS:** Mem, Amer Educ Assn, 1961-89, Natl Educ Assn, 1961-89, Day Card Bd of Dir, 1975-80, EHC, 1985-89, Literacy Council, 1987-89; mem, advisory bd, Municipal League, 1988-89. **HOME ADDRESS:** Route 1 Box 325-C, Mineral Springs, AR 71851.

HENDRY, GLORIA
Actress, producer, singer, director, entrepreneur. **PERSONAL:** Born Mar 03, 1943, Winterhaven, FL; daughter of George Hendry and Lottie Hendry. **EDUCATION:** Essex Coll of Bus; 1963; LA City Coll 1979. **CAREER:** Actress/films in many plays including Bare Knuckles, Savage Sisters, Hell Up In Harlem, Black Belt Jones, Live & Let Die, Slaughter's Big Rip-Off, Black Caesar, Appleman, For Love of Ivy, TV Blue Knight, CBS Flip Wilson Special, Love Amer Style, As the World Turns, producer Live Every Moment, W Indies Fest, Doin It variety show; Plays including Owl & the Pussycat, Raisin in The Sun, Medea, Stage Door, The Fantasticks, Who's Afraid of Virginia Woolf, as well as several TV and Radio shows such as Morning Show with Julie Shaw, Hostess Radio NYC, completed over 200 commercials; Singing shows/revues/clubs Light House, LaCafe, Mission Inn, Gardenia Cafe, New York Bell-Faces of This Land, Travellers Club, benefit OOP's, 69 Playboy Club; and a few records. **ORGANIZATIONS:** Kwanza Foundation exec dir Women in the Performing Arts Los Angeles; mem AEA/AFTRA, SAG; mem Greenwich CT NAACP. **HONORS/ACHIEVEMENTS:** Hon Phi Beta Omega Frat Inc Rho Iota Chapt; Black Achiever in US Awd; Natl Assn of Tennis Awd; After Hours News Awd Newark; I Am Somebody Awd; Outstanding Celebrity Awd; Key to City Birmingham AL Mayor George G Seibels; Key to City Mayor Kenneth Gibson Newark NJ; Kathleen Brown Rice Tennis Awd; Buffalo Soldiers Awd 10th Calvary. **BUSINESS ADDRESS:** c/o Cunningham Escot & Dipine, 261 S Robertson Blvd, Beverly Hills, CA 90211.

HENINGBURG, GUSTAV
Business executive. **PERSONAL:** Born May 18, 1930, Tuskegee, AL; children: Anne Renee', Gustav Jr. **EDUCATION:** Hampton Inst, BS 1950. **CAREER:** United Negro Coll Fund, alumni dir 1957-63; NAACP Legal Defense & Educ Fund, asst to pres 1963-68; Grtr Newark Urban Coalition Inc, pres 1968-80; New Jersey Nightly News, chief corres 1980-82; Gustav Heningburg Asso Inc, pres and chief exec officer 1980-. **ORGANIZATIONS:** Host Positively Black WNBC-TV 1973-; chmn NJ Educ Oppty Fund; past chmn of bd Archt's Comm Design Ctr; Newark Constrn Trades Training Corp; trustee Fundfor NJ; fdr Nat Assn of Urban Coalition Dir; past bd dir Regnl Plan Assn Disting. **HONORS/ACHIEVEMENTS:** Grad Awd Hampton Inst 1970; Trustees Disting Serv Awd Fairleigh DickinsonUniv 1976; State of NJ Governor's Awd; Alice Paul Humanitarian Awd (highest awd the gov of the state can present to a civilian) 1987; num awds for civil rights, educ & comm serv, civic & comm assns. **MILITARY SERVICE:** AUS Counter Intelligence Corp 1950-57. **BUSINESS ADDRESS:** President, Gustav Heningburg Associates, 40 Clinton St, Ste 200, Newark, NJ 07102.

HENLEY, CARL R.
Business administrator. **PERSONAL:** Born Jul 04, 1955, Los Angeles, CA. **EDUCATION:** CA State Univ LA, BA Psychology 1977, MS Public Adminstr 1980. **CAREER:** Universal Artists, asst to spl projects 1977-; Black Leadership Conf CSULA, adv 1977-; Backyard Prods, vice pres bd of dirs 1978-; LA United Sch Dist, couns asst 1979; Los Angeles Co, comm devel analyst asst 1979-; Universal Artists, assoc producer; NAACP Youth & Coll Div, reg dir 1980-82; HME Subsidiaries, vice pres 1982-. **ORGANIZATIONS:** Pres & cofounder LA NAACP Youth & Coll Div 1977-80; mem LA Cnty Dem Central Comm 1978-; exec bd mem S Central Planning Council of United Way of Amer 1979-80; del CA Dem State Party 1982-84. **HONORS/ACHIEVEMENTS:** Hon Life Mem Award CSULA 1977; Hon Pres Emeritus LA NAACP Youth & Coll Div 1980; Comm Serv Resolution LA City Council 1980. **BUSINESS ADDRESS:** Vice President, HME Subsidiaries, 2040 Ave of the Stars, Ste 400, Los Angeles, CA 90067.

HENLEY, VERNARD W.
Business executive. **PERSONAL:** Born Aug 11, 1929, Richmond, VA; son of Walter A

Henley and Mary Crump Henley; married Pheriby Christine Gibson; children: Vernard W Jr, Wade G, Adrienne C. **EDUCATION:** Virginia State Univ, BS 1951. **CAREER:** Mechanics & Farmers Bank Durham, NC, asst note teller 1951-52, cashier/head of personal loan dept 1954-58; Consolidated Bank & Trust Co, sec & cashier 1958-69, bd of dir 1961, vp/sec 1961; Unity State Bank Dayton, OH, chief exec ofcr 1969; Consolidated Bank & Trust Co, exec vice pres 1969-71, chmn of bd, pres and trust officer 1983-84, chmn of bd, chief exec officer and trust officer 1984-. **ORGANIZATIONS:** Bd of dir Maymont Found 1973, pres 1983-84, bd mem of exec & finance committees; mem Downtown Devel Commission 1974-85; mem exec committee DowntownDevel Unlimited 1975-85; bd of dir Children's Hosp 1975-85; bd of trustees St Paul's Coll 1976-84, bd of assoc 1984; bd of dir The Federated Arts Council of Richmond, Inc 1979-85; Citizens Legislative Comm 1981-85; mem Governor's Economic Adv Council 1982-84; bd of trustees VA Museum of Fine Arts 1983,mem of exec exhibition and finance comm; bd of dir Richmond Renaissance, Inc, mem of exec and finance comm; vice chmn Audit Comm City of Richmond 1983-88, chmn 1986-88; bd of trustees J Sargeant Reynolds Coll Found 1984; bd of trustees VA Union Univ 1984, mem, exec and finance committees; lay mem, bd of dir Old Dominion Bar Assoc 1985; bd of trs VA Council on Economic Ed 1985; bd of dir VA Bankers Assoc 1986-; bd of Trustees Univ Fund VA Commonwealth Univ 1986; mem, adv bd Black Museum 1986; bd of trustees, Historic Richmond Found 1986-; bd of dirs, Retail Merchants Assn of Greater Richmond 1986-; mem Kiwanis Club of Richmond, 1978-, mem Natl Corp Comm of the United Negro Coll Fund, 1975-; bd of dirs, Atlantic Rural Exposition, 1976-; mem advisory bd, The Arts Councy of Richmond, Inc. 1986-; mem advisory council, bd of trustees Salvation Army Boys Club 1970-. **HONORS/ACHIEVEMENTS:** Order of Merit Boy Scouts of Am 1967; Man & Boy Awd Salvation Army Boys Club 1969; Citizenship Awd Astoria Beneficial Club 1976; Brotherhood Awd Richmond Chap Natl Conf of Christians & Jews 1979; Order & Citizenship Awd Indep Order of St Luke 1981; recipient of "The Quest for Success Award" for Black Entrepreneurs in America, sponsored by Miller Brewing Company and Philip Morris USA. **MILITARY SERVICE:** AUS 1st lt 2 yrs; Bronze Star 1954. **HOME ADDRESS:** 1728 Hungary Rd, Richmond, VA 23228. **BUSINESS ADDRESS:** Chief Executive Officer, Consolidated Bank & Trust Co, 320 N 1st St, PO Box 10046 23240, Richmond, VA 23219.

HENNINGS, KENNETH MILTON
Mangement consultant. **PERSONAL:** Born Aug 03, 1943, Chicago, IL; married Bonnie; children: Alison, Kenneth. **EDUCATION:** Univ IL, BA 1967; Univ Chicago, MBA 1970. **CAREER:** Amrour Dial's Pharm, controller budget dir 1968-70; Sivart Mortgage, vice pres 1970-72; Chicago State Univ, asst prof 1972-; Deluxol Labs, controller 1973-76; Hennings Mgmt Group Inc, pres 1976-78; Soul-Chef Inc, pres 1978; DSM Inc, pres 1980-. **ORGANIZATIONS:** Chprsn Assn for Systems Mgmt 1975; treas Chicago C of C & Ind 1976; acting treas 1975; Chicago Midwest Serv Corp; Natl Asn of Credit Mgmt; mem Natl Assn of Accountants; Natl Black MBA Assn; SAM; Chicago Cosmopolitan C of C. **BUSINESS ADDRESS:** President, DSM Inc, 9220 S Cottage, Chicago, IL 60619.

HENRY, AARON E.
Association executive. **PERSONAL:** Born Jul 02, 1922, Coahoma Co, MS; married Noelle Michael; children: Rebecca E. **EDUCATION:** Xavier U, 1950. **CAREER:** NAACPT MS State, pres 1953-; NAACP, mem natl bd dir 1965-. **ORGANIZATIONS:** Mem of following MS Pharm Soc 1955-; Dem Nat Com 1972-; chmn MS Dem Exec Com; campaign mgr Residential Campaign 1972; mem Medgar Evers Meml Fun Soc; pres Nat Pharm Assn 1963; natl dir pres MS Con NAACP; mem Coahoma Co C of C; Am Legion; VFW; Omega Ssi Phi; natl bd dir Southern Christian Leadership Conference; Southern Regional Council; ms Council Human Relations; chmn COFO Movement; Freedom Dem Party; MS Action Progress; mem Nat Council on Aging; vice pres chmn Nat Black Caucas on Aging; vchmn Nat Rural Am Inc; chmn Nat Rural Housing Colition; adv con Retires Sr Citizens Vol Program of Coahoma Co MS; Coahoma Opportunities Inc; office Economic Opportunity; Registered Lobbyist; owner operator 4th St Drug Store. **HONORS/ACHIEVEMENTS:** Listed in Who's Who Am Southeast Am; Politics Am; Outstanding Southerners Am; recpt Rosa Parks award S Christian Ldrshp Conf; Outsdng Ciz award Office Econ Opportunity. **MILITARY SERVICE:** AUS 1943-46. **BUSINESS ADDRESS:** 213 4 St, Clarksdale, MS 38614.

HENRY, ALBERTA (NEE HILL)
Educator. **PERSONAL:** Born Oct 14, 1920, Hosston, LA; married Harold Lloyd; children: Wendell Lloyd, Julia Armenta Cosby. **EDUCATION:** Univ of UT, BS (cum laude) 1980. **CAREER:** Ritz Theater Topeka, projectionist & cashier 1940-45; Jenkins Cafe Topeka, comgr 1947-49; Head Start Day Care Ctr, comm relations spec 1967-72; Salt Lake City Sch Dist, cntrl office minority 1972-86 retired. **ORGANIZATIONS:** Founder & chmn Alberta Henry Educ Found 1967; founder Rainbow Honor Soc of Salt Lake City Sch Dist 1972; instituted & set up Utah Oppors Indus Ctr Inc 1974; fdr chmn UT Adv Comm to US Comm on Civil Rts 1975-79; chmn Gov Black Policy Adv Counc 1975-77; vice pres 1973-79, pres 1981-, NAACP; fdr chmn Blacks Unlimited 1974-; mem & officer Altrusa 1973-85, pres 1979-80; pres Travelers Aid Soc 1977-79; consultant & moderator TV show "Blacks in UT" 1974-79; UT Endowment for the Humanities 1974-78; Comm on State House Fellows 1973-79. **HONORS/ACHIEVEMENTS:** Hon Doctor of Humane Letters Univ of UT 1971; commendation from former Pres Richard Nixon 1970; Outstanding Citizens Awd Beehive Lodge of Elks 1970; GoldenDeeds Awd Exchange Club of Salt Lake City 1975; Disting Woman of the Yr Awd 1976 Women's Resource Ctr Univ of Utah; Comm Serv Awd Westminster Coll 1977; Who's Who in Politics 1977-78; Personalities of the West & Midwest 1977-78; inducted into Salt Lake Council of Women's Hall of Fame 1983.

HENRY, BRENT LEE
Attorney. **PERSONAL:** Born Oct 09, 1947, Philadelphia, PA; son of Wilbur Henry and Minnie Adams; married Sarita Wardlaw; children: Adam, A'isha. **EDUCATION:** Princeton Univ, BA 1969; Yale Law Sch, JD 1973; Yale Univ, Master of Urban Studies 1973. **CAREER:** New Haven Housing Information Ctr, counsel 1973-74; Yale Univ, lecturer in Afro-Amer studies 1973-74; Jones Day Reavis & Pogue Cleveland, atty 1974-78; NYCHuman Resources Adminstrn, dept adminstr 1978-79; Jones Day Reavis & Pogue, atty 1979-82; Howard Univ School of Business Admin, adjunct prof; Greater Southeast Comm Hospital Found, dir of business and govt affairs 1982-84; Medatlantic Healthcare Group, vice pres/gen counsel 1985-. **ORGANIZATIONS:** Bd of trustees Princeton Univ 1969-72; mem adv council Woodrow Wilson School of Pub & Intl Affairs Princeton Univ 1969-72; author "The Provision of Indigent Defense Services in Greater Cleveland" Cleveland Found authored as staff mem of Concerned Citizens Commn on Criminal Justice 1975; mem Amer, Natl, OhioBar Assocs, Dist of Columbia Bar Assoc, Natl Health Lawyers Assoc; bd of dirs, Mental Health Law Project 1987-; bd of dirs, Combined Health Appeal of the National Capital Area 1989-. **BUSINESS ADDRESS:** Vice Pres/General Counsel, Medlantic Hlth Care Grp, 100 Irving St NW, Washington, DC 20010.

HENRY, CALVIN O. L.
Business executive, educator, author. **PERSONAL:** Born May 10, 1940, Texarkana, TX; married Muriel M Wilkerson. **EDUCATION:** Wiley Coll Marshall, TX, BS w Hon Math 1962; OR StateUniv Corvallis, MS Math & Chem 1975. **CAREER:** Calmax Corp Corvallis, pres; Equal Opportunity Human & Race Relations, consultant 1970-; Salem's Oregon Statesman & Capitol Journal Newspapers, weekly columnist 1976; Univ of OR, grad asst; ERIC, legal educ res; OR State Univ, grad asst in Math 1971, teaching asst in Chem 1970; UAF & OR Air Nat Guard, held many pos of leadership; State of OR, sec of state. **ORGANIZATIONS:** Bd mem Corvallis Indsl Eco Coun; chmn Benton-Linn Co Eco Opport Coun 1972-73; pres Corvallis Br NAACP 1971-74; pres Wiley Coll Stu Body 1961-62; pres Beta Chap Phi Beta Sigma Frat Wiley Coll 1961-62; pres TX North Dist 4-H Coun 1968; mem Corvallis Human Resource Center Adv Com 1972-; bd mem Corvallis Indsl Econ Coun 1972-74; mem Benton Co Mental Hlth Adv Com 1973-76; mem Corvallis Area C of C Toastmasters. **HONORS/ACHIEVEMENTS:** Authored Sev Pub Sel as one of Personalities of West & MW 1972; Am Biog Inst 1972-73; Who's Who in Am Coll & U's. **MILITARY SERVICE:** USAFR capt. **BUSINESS ADDRESS:** Room 122 Secretary of State, State Capitol, Salem, OR 97310.

HENRY, CHARLES D., II
Athletic commissioner. **PERSONAL:** Born Sep 25, 1923, Conway, AR; married Jeanette Mouton; children: Charles, III, Nannette. **EDUCATION:** PhiLander Smith Coll, BA (cum laude) 1946; Univ IA, MA 1948, PhD 1954. **CAREER:** Intercollegiate (big ten) Athletic Conf, asst athletic commr 1985; Grambling Coll, prof & head dept HPER 1955-74; PhiLander Smith Coll, head dept HPER 1949-55. **ORGANIZATIONS:** Mem AAHPER; IAHPER; Am Coll Sports Med; Phi Epsilon Kappa; Sigma Delta Psi; CCA; Omega Psi Phi. **HONORS/ACHIEVEMENTS:** 9th Dist Man of Yr Omega 1963, 1969; Phys Educator of Yr 1967; So Ist AHPER Hon Award 1974; Who's Who Am Educ 1962; Outstanding Educators Am 1971; Ethnics Serv Com Hon Award AHPER 1975. **MILITARY SERVICE:** AUS 1942-45. **BUSINESS ADDRESS:** Big Ten Conference, 1111 Plaza Drive, Schaumburg, IL 60172.

HENRY, CHARLES E.
Educator. **PERSONAL:** Born Apr 14, 1935, Palestine, TX; son of Rev E W Henry Sr and Mrs Ophelia Spencer Henry; married Janice Normandyne OBrien; children: Melvin Wayne, Carolyn Janiece Henry Ross. **EDUCATION:** Texas Coll Tyler, TX, BS 1956; Texas Tech Univ, MEd 1971, EdD 1974. **CAREER:** Lubbock Indp School Dist, sci inst 1956-72; Texas Tech Univ Project Upward Bound, cons/inst 1968-72; Texas Tech Univ HSC School of Med, coord/inst 1972-76; Henry Enterprises, educ cons/owner/manager. **ORGANIZATIONS:** Mem Intl Platform Assn 1984-85; mem Amer Soc of Professional Cons; exec dir Mntl Health Assn Lubbock 1976-80, pres bd of dir 1972-76; vice pres Phi Delta Kappa Educ Fraternity 1975-76; life mem Alpha Phi Alpha Frat Inc 1980; mem NAACP; mem Texas Mental Health Counlrs Assn; Phi Delta Kappa, life mem 1986; Amer Assoc of Professional Hypnotherapists, mem. **HONORS/ACHIEVEMENTS:** Citation of Excell Texas Coll Tyler 1980; Community Serv Award Alpha Kappa Alpha Sor 1978; area 3-G coord Phi Delta Kappa Educ Fraternity 1977-78; Presidents Award Estacado HS PTA 1975-76. **BUSINESS ADDRESS:** Educator Consultant, Henry Enterprises, 2345 - 50th, Lubbock, TX 79412.

HENRY, DANIEL JOSEPH
Attorney. **PERSONAL:** Born Jan 03, 1945, New York, NY; married Leona A Macon; children: April V. **EDUCATION:** Columbia Univ School of Law, JD 1967-70. **CAREER:** Rubin Wachtel Baum & Levin, assoc 1969-71; Bernard M Baruch Coll, adj lecturer 1971-72; NY State Spec Comm on Attica, asst counsel 1971; NY State Supreme Ct, law sec 1971-73; Carver Dem Club, counsel 1972-76; Montgomery Ward & Co, sr attny 1973-74; Caterpillar Tractor Co, attny 1976-84; Univ of MN, assoc attny. **ORGANIZATIONS:** Mem Amer Bar Assoc, Natl Bar Assoc, Intl Law Sec Council, IL State Bar Assoc 1979-80; vchmn Natl Urban Coaltion Salute to Cities Dinner 1980. **BUSINESS ADDRESS:** Associate Attorney, University of Minnesota, 333 Morrill Hall, 100 Church St SE, Minneapolis, MN 55455.

HENRY, EGBERT WINSTON
Educator. **PERSONAL:** Born Apr 28, 1931, New York, NY; married Barbara Jean. **EDUCATION:** Queens Coll, BS 1953; Brooklyn Coll, MA 1959; CityUniv of NY, PhD 1972. **CAREER:** Oakland Univ, prof 1974-; Herbert H Lehman Coll, prof 1969-74; Wayne State Univ, prof 1966-69; Marygrove Coll, prof 1973; NY State Maritime Coll prof 1973-74; Bronx Comm Coll, prof 1970-72. **ORGANIZATIONS:** Mem Soc of the Sigma Xi; Am Soc of Plant Physiolgst; Smithsonian Soc; Plant Growth Reg Wrkng Grp; MI Electron Microscopy Forum. **HONORS/ACHIEVEMENTS:** Rsch Award Soc of the Sigma Xi 1971, 1974; Grant Herbert H Lehman Coll 1973; OaklandUniv Biomed Sci 1976; OaklandUniv Rsch Grant 1976. **MILITARY SERVICE:** AUS 1953-56. **BUSINESS ADDRESS:** Oakland Univ, Rochester, MI 48063.

HENRY, FOREST T., JR.
Educator. **PERSONAL:** Born Jan 02, 1937, Houston; married Melba J Jennings; children: Felicia Denise, Forest III. **EDUCATION:** Howard U, BS 1958; TX So U, M Ed 1971, adminstrv cert 1972. **CAREER:** Evan E Worthing Sr High Sch Houston, prin 1978-; Carter G Woodson Jr HS Houston, prin 1974-, asst prin 1971-74, teacher physical educ, head football coach & athletic dir 1968-70, golf coach 1960-70, asst football coach 1959-68, teacher 1959-68; F T Henry Income Tax & Real Estate Serv, 1958-. **ORGANIZATIONS:** Pres Greater Fifth Ward Citizens League 1972-; exec bd Bhouston Prin Assn 1972-; mem BSA; YMCA; TX Assn of Econdary Sch Prin; Nat Assn of Secondary Sch Prin; bd of dir N Side Sr Citizens Assn; Houston Assn of Supervison & Curriculum Develop; TX State Tchrs Assn; Alpha Phi Alpha. **HONORS/ACHIEVEMENTS:** Worthing Scholarship; Nat Sci Summer Fellowship in Biology; Comm Serv Award Religious Heritage of Am. **BUSINESS ADDRESS:** Carter G Woodson Jr HS, 10720 Southview St, Houston, TX 77047.

HENRY, FRANK HAYWOOD
Composer, musician. **PERSONAL:** Born Jan 10, 1913, Birmingham, AL; son of James Madison and Sara; married Arvenell, Jun 03, 1973; children: Fabian, Dianne. **EDUCA-**

TION: Attended, AL State Univ. **CAREER:** Bama State Collegions, musician; Erskine Hawkins Orch; Earl Hine; Sy Oliver; Duke Ellington Orch's; NY Jazz Repretore Co, musician; Intl Arts of Jazz Europe Soviet Union British Islands 1975 1984; Broadway Shows, Hair, Cindy, Dr Jazz, Ain't Misbehavin; Sophisticated Ladies; Album, "Haywood Henry-The Gentle Monster"; Haywood Henry Quartette; Black & Blue Paris, France 1986. **HONORS/ACHIEVEMENTS:** Cert for Outstanding Achievements in Athletics; World Class Sprinter 1933 100 yrds-95 AL State; Key to City Birmingham AL; Awd in Black NY City; Jazz Hall of Fame Birmingham AL.

HENRY, JAMES T., SR.
Retired educator. **PERSONAL:** Born Sep 20, 1910, St Louis, MO; married Vivian Snell; children: 11 Children. **EDUCATION:** Univ of IL, BS 1933; IBIDMA, 1938; Ford Found Fellowship Univ of MI, 1966. **CAREER:** Central State Univ, retired prof of geography 1977; FL A&M, visiting prof of Geography 1950, 1952, 1955; Morgan State, visiting prof, Geography 1940; AL State, visiting prof, Geography, 1937, 1939; Danforth Fellowship Consortium Univ, 1960-70; Small Coll Consortiom ClarkUniv Worcester, 1960; Univ WI Milwaukee, consultant 1968; Xenia United Nations Comm, gov chmn, 1968; Serv Acad Review Bd Airforce, 1968-69; City of Xenia, mayor 1969-72. **ORGANIZATIONS:** Life mem, Alpha Phi Alpha; 25 year certificate. **HONORS/ACHIEVEMENTS:** Civic awards Alpha Phi Alpha; Omega Psi Phi; Phi Beta Sigma; Amer Legion; 2nd 51 Force Comm Aging; Third Degree KOFC; Alpha Phi Gamma Journalism; Phi Alpha Theta history; Pershing Rifles; Coauthor numerous articles 1971-74; Prof Emeritus Earth Science CSU 1977; Affirmative Action Rev Spec Inertial Guidance Center Newark, 1st black elect to Xenia OH Cty Comm 1953, 1st ever to be re-elected to 6 consecutive 4 yr terms.

HENRY, JOHN W., JR.
Educator. **PERSONAL:** Born Jun 03, 1929, Greensboro, NC; children: Dawn Yolanda, John W III. **EDUCATION:** NC A&T State Univ, BS 1955; Chicago State Univ, MEd 1965. **CAREER:** Malcolm X Coll, City Coll of Chicago, vice pres acad affairs 1971-73; Denmark Tech Educ Center, assoc dir 1973-77, interim dir 1977, dir 1977-80, pres 1980-. **ORGANIZATIONS:** Bd mem Chicago Westside Plnng Comm; mem O'Keefee PTA Chgo; bd mem So Reg Council on Black Amer Affairs 1979-, Bamberg Cty Indust Devel Comm, SC Tech Ed Assoc, SC State Employees Assoc. **HONORS/ACHIEVEMENTS:** Superior Performance Awd VA Rsch Hosp 1967; Outstanding Educator of the SE 1973; Outstanding Ed of Amer 1973; Dictionary of Intl Biography Cambridge England 1974,75; Personality of the South 1973,75; Men of Achievement 1975,79; listed in Who's Who in the South & SW 1976,79, Notable Amer of 1976-77. **MILITARY SERVICE:** AUS 1947-51. **BUSINESS ADDRESS:** President, Denmark Tech College, P O Box 327, Denmark, SC 29042.

HENRY, JOSEPH A.
Retired insurance executive. **PERSONAL:** Born Jul 17, 1917, Cranford, NJ; married W Regania; children: 1 daughter. **EDUCATION:** Tuskegee Inst, BS 1941; Univ MI, MBA 1952; Life Ofc Mgmt Inst, FLMI 1959. **CAREER:** Central Life Ins Co FL, pres 1978-83; pres 1985-. **ORGANIZATIONS:** Mem Beta Alpha Psi, Amer Legion, Urban League. **MILITARY SERVICE:** AUS warrant officer JG 1942-44. **BUSINESS ADDRESS:** President, PO Box 3286, Tampa, FL 33601.

HENRY, JOSEPH KING
Educator, recruiter. **PERSONAL:** Born Aug 02, 1948, St Louis, MO; son of King Henry and Geraldine Henry; married Diana Edwards. **EDUCATION:** Lincoln Univ, BS Educ 1973; Boston Univ, MA 1974. **CAREER:** Humboldt Elem Sch St Louis, teacher 1972-73; Metro Council for Educational Oppor Inc, coord 1974-77; Univ of IA Special Svcs, academic counselor 1985-86, grad outreach counselor 1986-; Univ of IA, graduate outreach counselor 1986-87; Univ of IA, graduate outreach coordinator 1987-; mem Natl Council of Black Studies 1988; mem The Society for the Study of Multi-Ethnic Literature in the US 1988; mem Organization of American Historians 1988. **ORGANIZATIONS:** Counselor Univ of Iowa Upward Bound Program 1980; pres Afro-Amer Studies Grad Student Assoc 1982-83; instructor, grad teaching asst American Lives 1982; presented papers at the Midwest Modern Language Assoc Conf 1982, 11th Annual Conference on South Asia 1982, Tenth Annual Conference on the Black Family 1983; instructor, grad teaching asst Introduction to Afro-Amer Society; grad rsch asst The Univ of IA Office of Affirmative Action 1983-85; lecturer in history Cornell Coll Mt Vernon, IA 1985; presented a paper on the Rev Dr Martin Luther King at the Annual Special Support Serv Honors Recognition Day Prog 1986. **HONORS/ACHIEVEMENTS:** Martin Luther King Fellowship to Boston Univ 1973; Phi Alpha Theta Intl Honor Soc in History 1974; "A Melus Interview, Ishmael Reed," The Journal of the Soc for the Study of the Multi-Ethnic Literature of the United States Vol II No 1 1984; Black Awds Honor Certificate of Recognition Univ of IA 1984; "Preliminary Afro-Amer Observations on Goan Literature," The Journal of Indian Writing in English V13 No 1 1985; "Public spiritual Humanistic Odyssey of Malcolm X," The Western Journal of Black Studies V 9, No 2 1985; "High-Tech, Higher Education, and Cultural Pluralism, A Systems Approach to New Prospects," The Journal of the Assoc for General and Liberal Studies V 15, No 3 1985; published articles in The Challenger and The Daily Iowa newspapers. **BUSINESS ADDRESS:** Graduate Outreach Coordinator, TheUniv of Iowa, Special Support Serv, 310 Calvin Hall, Room 310, Iowa City, IA 52244.

HENRY, JOSEPH LOUIS
Educator. **PERSONAL:** Born May 02, 1924, New Orleans, LA; son of Varice S Henry, Jr and Mabel Mansion Henry; married Dorothy Lilian Whittle; children: Leilani Smith, Joseph L Jr, Ronald, Joan Alison, Peter D. **EDUCATION:** Howard Univ, DDS 1946; Xavier Univ, BS 1948, ScD 1975; Univ of IL, MS 1949, PhD 1951; IL Coll of Optometry, DHL 1973; Harvard Univ, MA 1975. **CAREER:** Howard Univ, instructor to prof 1946-51, dir of clinics 1951-65, dean 1965-75, Harvard School of Dental Medicine, assoc dean/prof and chmn, oral diagnois and oral radiology. **ORGANIZATIONS:** Vp/fellow Amer Assoc for Advancement of Sci 1952 & 1972; pres Intl Assoc for Dental Res DC Section 1968; mem NIH Natl Adv Cncl on Hlth Professions 1968-72; pres Greater Washington Periodontal Soc 1970; commr US Commn on Educ Credit 1973-74; chmn Assoc of Black Fac & Admin Harvard Univ 1981-83; mem Inst of Medicine of the Natl Acad of Sciences 1981-; chmn bd of trustees IL Coll of Optometry 1982-86; Natl Res Cncl/Inst of Medicine Comm on an AgingSoc 1984-; mem Amer Optometric Assoc Cncl on Clinical Optometric Care 1984-; chmn Amer Assoc of Dental Schools Sect on Oral Diagnosis and Oral Medicine 1984-85; Academy of Oral Diagnosis, radiology and medicine, founding mem, chmn, Admin Bd-Council of Sections, Amer Assoc of Dental Schools, 1988. **HONORS/ACHIEVEMENTS:** Awards from Urban League, NAACP, UNCF 1970; Distinguished Faculty Award Harvard Univ 1971; Dentist of the Yr Natl Dental Assn 1972; Dentist of the Year in DC 1973; DC Mayors Award for Serv to the City 1975; Natl Dental Assoc Presidential Awd 1976, 1978; Dean Emeritus Howard Univ Coll of Dentistry 1981; Distinguished Faculty Award Harvard School of Dental Medicine 1981; Natl Optometric Assoc Founder's Award 1985; Howard Univ Alumni Achievement Award 1986; Citation from Maryland Legislative House of Delegates for "Outstanding Contribution to Dentistry and Commitment to Excellence in Higher Education" 1986; over 100 articles published in journals in Dentistry, Dental Educ, Optometry & Health Sci 1948-. **MILITARY SERVICE:** USAR 2nd St; 2515 Serv Unit pfc 1942-45; Good Conduct Medal 1944. **BUSINESS ADDRESS:** Associate Dean, Prof & Chmn, Harvard School of Dental Med, 188 Longwood Ave, Boston, MA 02115.

HENRY, KARL H.
Attorney. **PERSONAL:** Born Jan 21, 1936, Chgo; married Dolores Davis; children: Marc, Paula. **EDUCATION:** Fisk U, Atnd; LA City Coll; Northwestern U; SouthwesternUniv of Law LA, JD 1969; USC Law Shc Prac Aspects of Recording Indus, Post Grad. **CAREER:** Pvt Prac, atty 1970-; Juv Ct, referee 1975-76; Spartan Missile Proj McDonnel Douglas Corp, sr contracts negotiator 1969-70, sr Employee relations rep 1968-69; Green Power Found, mktng sales mgr 1968; Pabst Brewing Co, mchdsng salesman 1964-68; Sys Outlet Shoes, asst mgr 1962-63. **ORGANIZATIONS:** Mem LA Co Bar Assn; Am Bar Assn; Juvenile Cts Bar; Langston Law Club; LA Trial Lawyers Assn; past pres Englewood Youth Assn; mem Nat Police Assn; mem John F Kennedy Club; bd dirs Green Power Found; adv bd STEP Inc; bd dirs NAACP; pres Hollypark Homeowner Assn; dir Spec Prog PUSH. **BUSINESS ADDRESS:** Attorney, 4050 Buckingham Rd, Los Angeles, CA 90008.

HENRY, MARCELETT CAMPBELL
Educator. **PERSONAL:** Born Apr 16, 1928, Langston, OK; married Delbert V Jr; children: Jacqueline M, Sharon R, Delbert V III, Andrea D. **EDUCATION:** Langston Univ, BS 1949; Univ of OK Norman, ME 1963; San Fran State Univ, ME Admin 1969; Walden Univ, PhD Admin 1973. **CAREER:** Anchorage Comm Coll AK Voc Homemaking Courses, tchr 1954-55; Anchorage Indep Sch Dist AK Lang Arts/Soc Stud, tchr 1956-59; Anchorage Comm Coll AK Adult Edn/Curriculum Devel, tchr/coord for summer tchrs wrkshps 1958-59; Anchorage Indep Sch Dist AK, tchr/homemaking 1960-65; Tamalpais Union HS Dist Mill Valley, CA, dept chmrn/tchr/dir of occupatnl training pgm 1966-74; CA State Dept of Edn, mgr summer sch/cons planning & devel/coord alternative edn/project mgr/cons secondary edn/state staff/liaison to co supts/dir 1974-. **ORGANIZATIONS:** Real Estate Training 1959; curr spclst AK Dept of Educ 1964; mem Marin Co Home Ec 1966-68; Poject FEAST City Coll San Fran 1968; consult Pace Ctr Sys Analysis Wrkshp Tamalpais HS Dist 1969; adv com/edn JC Penny Bay Area 1969-74; consult CA State Dept Voc Educ 1970; consult Marin Co Supt Offc Corte Madera, CA 1970; devel model curr "System Analysis" Tamalpais Union HS Dist 1970; state exec bd Delta Kappa Gamma Chi 1971; consult "Project Breakthrough" Tamalpais HS Dist 1972; CA State Dept 1973; review/eval panelist Right to Read Pgm HEW 1973; participant US Senate Select Com on Nutrition & Human Needs Wash, DC 1973; sub-com CA Attys Genl Consumer Educ 1975; rep State Supt of Pub Instr in Select of State Century III Leaders 1976-78; chmn/conf "Reform Thru Research" Phi Delta Kappa 1976; chmn Phi Delta Kappa Dist II 1977, mem PDK Adv Bd; pres Sacramento Phi Delta Kappa 1977-78; cand Supt Co Off of Educ 1978; mem US Presidential Task Force 1981. **HONORS/ACHIEVEMENTS:** Mother's Day Recog Awd for Outstand Contrib in Educ 1959; KBYR Radio Station Bouquet of the Day 1964; Delta Kappa Gamma Schlrshp 1966; Delta Kappa Gamma Chi State Mini Grant 1972; CA State Dept of Educ Research Grant 1972; Award of Merit CA Dept of Justice/Educ 1975; Award for Leadership in State BicentennialActiv State Dept of Educ ARBC of CA 1976; Women of the Yr Delta Delta Zeta Cha Zeta Phi Beta San Fran 1976; Nat Sch Journlsm Award for Sch Publ Bicentennial Film Brochure 1977. **BUSINESS ADDRESS:** Dir of Special Programs, CA Dept of Educ, 721 Capitol Mall, Sacramento, CA 95814.

HENRY, MILDRED M. DALTON
Educator. **PERSONAL:** Born in Tamo, AR; children: Delano Hampton, Alvia Hampton Turner, Lawrence Hampton, Pamela Hampton Ross. **EDUCATION:** AM&N College Pine Bluff, BS Music Ed 1971; S IL Univ Edwardsville, MSED Counselor Ed 1976; S IL Univ Carbondale, PhD Counselor Ed 1983. **CAREER:** AM&N Coll, sec bus office 1949-51; St Paul Public Library, library asst 1956-58; AM&N Coll, lib asst/secty 1968-71; Pine Bluff School Dist, music teacher 1971-75; S IL Univ Edwardsville, library asst 1975; Watson Chapel Sch Dist, counselor 1976-77; Univ of AR at Pine Bluff, counselor 1978-80; S IL Univ at Carbondale, grad asst 1981; Carbondale Elem Sch Dist, teacher 1981-83; CA State Univ San Bernardino, asst prof 1983-. **ORGANIZATIONS:** Adv bd Creative Educators Inc Riverside 1983-; city com Fontanta CA 1984-; exec bd Rialto/Fontana NAACP 1984-; pres Provisional Educ Services Inc 1984-; Amer Assn of Univ Profs; Natl Educ Assn CA Faculty Assn; CA Teachers Assn; CA Assn of Counseling Develop; Assn of Teacher Educators; CA Black Faculty and Staff Assn; CA State Employees Assn, Inland Empire Peace Officer Assn, NAACP; Natl Council of Negro Women; steering comm San Bernardino Area Black C of C; mem San Bernardino Private Industry Council. **HONORS/ACHIEVEMENTS:** Leadership Awds Atlanta Univ & UCLA 1978 & 1979; Citizen of Day Radio Station KOTN Pine bluff 1980; Dean's Fellowship S IL Univ Carbondale 1980-81; Outstanding Scholastic Achievement Black Affairs Council SIUC 1981; publication "Setting Up a Responsive Guidance Program in a Middle School" The Guidance Clinic 1979. **BUSINESS ADDRESS:** Assistant Professor Education, California StateUniv, 5500 University Pkwy, San Bernardino, CA 92407.

HENRY, NANCY L.
Business executive. **PERSONAL:** Born Jul 18, 1940, Somerville, NJ; divorced; children: Lionel Jr, Robert. **EDUCATION:** Rutgers Univ, 1973-75; Trenton State Coll, 1976-77. **CAREER:** Johnson & Johnson, exec asst 1959-77; Natl Conf Ctr, coord 1977-78; State of NJ Office of the Gov, spec asst to the gov 1978-79; State of NJ, dir resources and comm participation 1979-81, sales coord 1981-82; Scanticon-Princeton, admin asst purchasing mgr 1982-; Mayor of Franklin Twp; Henry's DomesticsInc, pres. **ORGANIZATIONS:** vice chairperson Franklin Twp Democratic Mun Comm 1979, 1980; vice pres NJ Fed of Democratic Women 1982; vice pres Somerset Co Fed of Democratic Women1982; councilwoman Franklin Twp 1977, 1981; Natl Council of Negro Women. **HONORS/ACHIEVEMENTS:** Nominated Third Annual Women in Business & Indus Luncheon Raritan Valley Chamber of Commerce 1981. **BUSINESS ADDRESS:** President, Henry's Construction, Inc, 15 Dewald Ave #1, Somerset, NJ 08873.

HENRY, RAGAN A.
President, attorney. **PERSONAL:** Born Feb 02, 1934, Sadiesville, KY; married Regina A Goodwin; children: Vincent A, Joseph A, Richard A, Leah A, Ralph Brower III. **EDUCATION:** Harvard Coll, AB 1952-56; Harvard Law Sch, LLB 1959-61; TempleUniv Grad Sch, Attended 1963. **CAREER:** Broadcast Enterprises Nat Inc, pres 1973-; Wolf Block Schorr & Solis-Cohen Law Firm, partner 1977-; SyracuseUniv SI Newhouse Sch of Comm, vis prof 1979-; LaSalle Coll, lectr 1971-73; Goodis Greenfield Henry & Edelstein Law Firm, partner 1964-77. **ORGANIZATIONS:** Bd of dirs Continental Bank; bd of dirs Abt Asso Inc; pres Nat Assn of Black Owned Broadcasters; bd of dirs LaSalle Coll; bd of dirs Hops of theU of PA; chmn John McKee Scholarship Com; fellowships Noyes & Whitney Founds 1956-57, 1959-61. **HONORS/ACHIEVEMENTS:** Scholarship Harvard Law Sch 1957-61. **MILITARY SERVICE:** AUS 1957-59. **BUSINESS ADDRESS:** Broadcast Enterprises Nat Inc, 1422 Chestnut St, Philadelphia, PA 19107.

HENRY, ROBERT CLAYTON
Funeral director. **PERSONAL:** Born Jul 16, 1923, Springfield, OH; married Betty Jean Scott; children: Robert C II, Alan Stefon, Lisa Jennifer. **EDUCATION:** Cleveland Coll of Mortuary Sci, attended 1948-49; Wittenburg Univ, attended 1950-51. **CAREER:** City of Springfield, commr 1963-66, mayor 1966-68; Robert C Henry & Son Funeral Home, funeral director. **HONORS/ACHIEVEMENTS:** LLD Central State Univ 1968. **MILITARY SERVICE:** USAF t/sgt 1943-45; Pacific Theatre Bronze Star; Amer Theatre 1943-45. **BUSINESS ADDRESS:** Funeral Dir, Robt C Henry & Son Funeral Hom, 527 S Center St, Springfield, OH 45506.

HENRY, SAMUEL DUDLEY
Educator. **PERSONAL:** Born Oct 09, 1947, Washington, DC; son of Rev Dudley Henry and Shendrine Boyce Henry; married Ana Maria Meneses Henry, Dec 23, 1988. **EDUCATION:** DC Teachers Coll, BS 1969; Columbia Univ, MA 1974, EdD 1978. **CAREER:** Binghamton, eng/soc studies teacher 1971-73; HMLI Columbia Univ Teachers Coll, rsch assoc 1975-77; Sch of Ed Univ MA Amherst, asst prof 1977-78; Race Desegregation Ctr for NY, NJ, VI & PR, dir 1978-81; San Jose State Univ, dir of Equal Opportunity & Affirmative Action; CSU Northridge, Northridge CA, School of Education, assoc dean (acting) 1988-; San Jose State Univ, San Jose CA, School of Social Sciences, assoc dean 1987-88. **ORGANIZATIONS:** Exec bd Greenfield Secondary Sch Comm 1977-79; sponsor Harlem Ebonetts Girls Track Team 1980-81; exec bd Santa Clara Valley Urban League 1982-83; exec bd CAAAO,CA Assoc of Affirmative Action Off 1983-84; mem Prog Comm No CA Fair Employ Roundtable 1983-85; mem ASCD Assoc of Supr of Curr Ser 1984-85; mem bd of dirs Campus Christian Ministry 1984-85; San Jose Roundtable, chair-drug prevention task force. **HONORS/ACHIEVEMENTS:** Outstanding Serv Awd Disabled Students SJSU 1982-83; Commendation Curr Study Comm East Side Union HS Dist 1984; AA in Higher Educ/2nd Annual Conf on Desegregation in Postsecondary 1984. **MILITARY SERVICE:** ANG 1967-; AUSR 1972-. **HOME ADDRESS:** 21450 Burbank # 108, Woodland Hills, CA 91367. **BUSINESS ADDRESS:** Assoc Dean, School of Education, California State University Northridge, 18111 Nardhoff St Montercy Hall, Northridge, CA 91330.

HENRY, THOMAS
Educator. **PERSONAL:** Born Nov 27, 1934, St Louis; married Gemalia Blockton. **EDUCATION:** LincolnUniv bs 1957; harris tchrs coll, atnd. **CAREER:** Turner Middle School St Louis, head art dept 1985; St Louis Co Transportation Commn by Co Supr Gene McNary, appointed; St Louis System, teacher 14 yrs; Free Lance 1 Yr, commercial artist 1962. **ORGANIZATIONS:** Bd dirs St Louis Co Grand Jury First Black Man to Head 1974-77; bd dirs Bicentennial for St Louis St Louis Co; chmn Distri Aunts & Uncles Give NeedyKids Shoes; resource dir Inner City YMCA; painted Portraits of Many Movie Stars & Celebs. **HONORS/ACHIEVEMENTS:** Recip Cit of Week KATZ Radio; Honor Rehab Educ at Leavenworth KS; Honor Sigma Gamma Rho for Outstanding Artist in MO; Commissioned to Paint Portraits BillTriplett & Bill Contrell of Detroit Lions, Elston Howard of NY Yankees, Redd Fox, TV Star, Painting of Sammy Davis Jr Elvis Presley James Brown Ron Townsend of 5th Dimension. **MILITARY SERVICE:** AUS pfc 1958-60. **BUSINESS ADDRESS:** 2815 Pendleton Ave, St Louis, MO.

HENRY, WALTER LESTER, JR.
Physician, educator. **PERSONAL:** Born Nov 19, 1915, Philadelphia, PA; son of Walter Lester Henry and Vera Robinson Henry; married Ada Palmer. **EDUCATION:** Temple Univ, AB 1936; Howard Univ Med Sch, MD 1941 (1st in class). **CAREER:** Howard Univ, asst & assoc prof 1953-63, chmn dept med 1962-73, prof med 1963-. **ORGANIZATIONS:** Mem AMA, Natl Med Assn, Endocrine Soc, Assn Amer Physicians; certified in Endocrinology & Metabolism Amer Bd of Int Med; NAACP; Urban League; Sixth Presbyterian Church; Amer Bd Internal Med; regent Amer Coll Physicians (1st & only Black regent) 1974-; faculty trustee Howard Univ 1971-75. **HONORS/ACHIEVEMENTS:** American College of Physicians, Master, 1987. **MILITARY SERVICE:** USMC maj WW II; US Army Bronze Star, cluster to Bronze Star 1942-44. **BUSINESS ADDRESS:** Professor Medicine, HowardUniv, Dept of Medicine, Washington, DC 20060.

HENRY, WARREN ELLIOTT
Educator. **PERSONAL:** Born Feb 18, 1909, Evergreen, AL; married Jeanne Sally Pearlson; children: Eva Ruth. **EDUCATION:** Tuskegee Inst, BS 1931; Atlanta Univ, MS 1937; Univ Chicago, PhD 1941; Lehigh Univ, Hon ScD 1983. **CAREER:** Spelman & Morehouse Colls, instr 1934-36; Tuakegee Inst, instr 1936-38, 1941-43; MA Inst Tech, staff mem radiation lab 1943-46; Univ Chicago, instr 1946-47; Morehouse Coll, acting head dept physics 1947-48; Naval Rsch Lab Wash, super physicist 1948-60; Lockheed Missiles & Space Co, staff scientist srstaff engr 1960-69; Minority Participation in Physics, consult chmn com 1970-; Howard Univ, prof physics 1969-. **ORGANIZATIONS:** Fellow Amer Phys Soc; mem Amer Assn Physics Tchrs; Fedn Amer Scientists (chmn chap 1957-59); mem Inst Intl du Froid; Sci Rsch Soc Am (pres Naval Rsch Lab Br 1955); fellow AAAS; vice pres Palo Alto Fair Play Council 1968-69; presidential assoc Tuskegee Inst; grantee So Educ Found 1970-; mem Sigma Xi; author of articles & chapts in books.

HENRY, WILLIAM ARTHUR, II
Attorney. **PERSONAL:** Born Feb 11, 1939, Canalou, MO; married Alice Faye Pierce; children: William III, Shawn. **EDUCATION:** Lincoln U, BS 1962; GeorgetownUniv Law Ctr, JD 1972. **CAREER:** Xerox Corp, patent atty; US Patent Ofc, patent exam 1966-72; IBM, rep 1964-66. **ORGANIZATIONS:** Mem DC Bar; DC Bar Assn; PA Bar; Am Bar Assn; Urban League; Nat Patent Law Assn; Rochester Patent Law Assn; Alpha Phi Alpha Frat. **MILITARY SERVICE:** AUS 1/lt 1962-64. **BUSINESS ADDRESS:** Counsel, Rochester Patent Opns, Xerox Corporation, Xerox Square, 20A, Rochester, NY 14644.

HENSON, CHARLES A.
Clergyman. **PERSONAL:** Born Jan 05, 1915, Dallas, TX; married Helen M Hoxey; children: Helen Marie. **EDUCATION:** Friends U, AB 1951; Union Bapt Sem, LlD; Prov Bapt Theol Sem, DD. **CAREER:** Zion Bapt Ch, pastor; CA State Congress of Christ End, pres; Martin Luther King Hosp, chpln. **ORGANIZATIONS:** Mem bd dirs LA Coun of Chs; past group leader World Bapt Youth Congress Beirut, Lebanon; chmn Adv Bd LA Sickle Cell Cntr; traveled extensively Europe, Asia, Africa, Holy Land 1955, 63, 68; mem CA Gen Adv Coun; served Preaching Mission Japan 1972. **HONORS/ACHIEVEMENTS:** Commended outstanding serv to state of CA CA State Assembly 1967. **BUSINESS ADDRESS:** 600 W Rosecrans Ave, Compton, CA 90220.

HENSON, DANIEL PHILLIP, III
Business executive. **PERSONAL:** Born Apr 04, 1943, Baltimore, MD; son of Daniel P Henson, Jr and Florence Newton; married Delaphine S; children: Darren P, Dana S. **EDUCATION:** Morgan St Univ, BA 1966; Johns Hopkins Univ, 1968-70. **CAREER:** Baltimore City Pub Sch, tchr 1966-67; Metropolitan Life Ins Co, assoc mgr 1967-74; Guardian Life Ins Co Am, gen agent 1974-77; US Small Bus Adm, reg adm 1977-79; Mnrty Bus Dev Agcy, dir 1979-81; Greater Baltimore Comm, dir 1981-82; G & M Oil Co Inc, vice pres 1982-84; Struever Bros Eccles & Rouse Inc, vice pres 1984-. **ORGANIZATIONS:** Pres Dan Henson & Asso Inc 1966-67; chmn bd Devel Credit Fund, Inc 1982-; mem Grtr Baltimore Comm 1982-; mem Maryland Chamber of Commerce 1983-; bd mem Baltimore Urban League 1982-88; bd mem Baltimore Sch for the Arts 1982-; 1981-; chmn of bd Investigators Baltimore, Inc; bd mem Johns Hopkins Univ Inst of Policy Studies; mem Home Builders Assn of of MD. **BUSINESS ADDRESS:** Vice President, Struever Brs Eccles/Rouse Inc, 519 N Charles St, Baltimore, MD 21201.

HENSON, WILLIAM FRANCIS
Physician. **PERSONAL:** Born May 21, 1933, Washington, DC; married Lucile Thornton; children: Rhonda Elaine Poole, David T, Russell Francis, Alan Everett. **EDUCATION:** Lincoln Univ, AB 1955; Howard Univ Sch of Medicine, MD 1959. **CAREER:** VA Medical Ctr, staff physician 1963-64, section chief 1964-77, acting chief med 1977-78, chief medicine 1978-. **ORGANIZATIONS:** Mem Natl Medical Assoc 1964-, Medical Assoc of State of AL 1980-, Macon Co Medical Soc 1980-, AL State Medical Assoc 1982-; 33rd degree masonry, 1st lt commander, 2nd Lt commander Booker T Washington Consistory 1983-87, commander-in-chief 1987-89; high priest and prophet Mizraim Temple # 119 1986-88. **MILITARY SERVICE:** AUS Army Reserve Medical Corps major 15 yrs; Outstanding Officer 1207th US Hospital. **BUSINESS ADDRESS:** Chief, Medical Services, VA Medical Ctr, Tuskegee, AL 36083.

HENTREL, BOBBIE KUYKENDALL
Educator. **PERSONAL:** Born Sep 09, 1938, Batesville, MS; married Percy; children: Michael Louell. **EDUCATION:** BS MEd 1964; PhD 1975. **CAREER:** Brace-Lederle Elementary School, prin; Southfield, MI Public School System, first & only black school administrator; elementary sec & jr coll teacher; Univ of MI, lecturer; Upward Bound; Community School; Adult Educ, teacher; Highland Pk Bd of Educ, accountant. **ORGANIZATIONS:** Mem Nat Educ Assn 1960-76; MI Educ Assn 1960-76; Ofc Educ Assn 1969-74; MI Assn of Scndry Sch Prins; Nat Assn of Scndry Sch Prins Pres, Justice, Unity, Generosity & Svc; Delta Sigma Theta Inc, vp; Pi Omega Pi Hon Soc. **HONORS/ACHIEVEMENTS:** Listed in Who's Who Among Students in Am Coll & Univ, Who's Who in Amer; Phi Delta Kappa; Pi Lambda Theta; Fulbright-Hays Awd 1975-76; Most Outstdg Student 1974-75Univ of MI. **BUSINESS ADDRESS:** President, Kuykendall Enterprises, 18575 W 9 Mile Rd, Southfield, MI 48075.

HERBERT, BENNE S.
Mediator. **PERSONAL:** Born Sep 06, 1946, Bronx, NY; divorced; children: Ainah Reid. **EDUCATION:** Ithaca Clg, BA 1969; Cornell U, Cert 1968-70; Hampton Inst, Cert 1970; Cleveland St, Cert 1984-85. **CAREER:** Ithaca Clg, asst dean of stdnts 1969-70; Am Arbitration Asso, dir 10-75; Arbitration & Mediation Serv, Inc, pres 1975-78; Home Owners Warranty Corp,dir of cncltn 1978-80; Natl Acad Cncltrs, vice pr 1980-82; Travis & Staughn Cnsltnts Labor Rltns, vice pres 1982-84; Vstng Nurse Asso, vice pres 1984-87. **ORGANIZATIONS:** Sr consult D A Browne Asso 1978-87; sr consult Herbert Grp Mgrs 1984-; mem Am Arbtrtn Asso 1985; pres Negotation Spclts Corp 1982-85; mem Black Prof Asso of Cleveland 1984-85. **HONORS/ACHIEVEMENTS:** Deans list Ithaca Clg 1968-69; Outstanding Sr Awd; author "How" Settles Consumer Complaints" 1979, "Preparing for Negotiation" 1984, "Disputes Settlement inChicago Housing" 1979, "Arbitration of Minor Criminal Complaints" 1974. **HOME ADDRESS:** 2045 Revere, Cleveland Heights, OH 44118. **BUSINESS ADDRESS:** Vice-President Resource Mgmt, Visiting Nurse Asso, 3300 Chester Ave, Cleveland, OH 44114.

HERBERT, JOHN TRAVIS, JR.
Attorney. **PERSONAL:** Born Feb 17, 1943, Montclair, NJ; divorced; children: Stephanie, Travis, Suzanne. **EDUCATION:** Seton Hall Law School, JD 1974. **CAREER:** Johnson & Johnson, atty, corp dir 1974-76, manager 1972-74; Allied Chem, corp staff 1969-72; Rugers Univ, adjunct prof 1973-; Central Jersey OIC, bd atty; Pitney Bowes, Stamford, CT, vice pres Corp Facilities & Admin 1983-. **ORGANIZATIONS:** Vol in Parole 1974-; chmn BALSA Seton Hall Law School 1973-74; coach Pop Warner Football 1975-77; organized Franklin Township Youth Athletic Assn 1976-77; mem Franklin Township Bd of Educ; Amer Bar Assn; Natl Bar Assn; New Jersey Bar Assn; Middlesex Co Bar Assn 1979-80; bd sec, gen counsel Rutgers Min Bus Co 1980; bd of Westchester Fairfield City Corp Councils Assoc 1985-; bd of mayors Transportation Management Round Table 1985-; corp liason, Natl Urban League of Stamford 1986-. **HONORS/ACHIEVEMENTS:** Outstndg Young Men of Am 1980. **BUSINESS ADDRESS:** 501 George St, New Brunswick, NJ 08903.

HERCULES, FRANK E. M.
Educator, author. **PERSONAL:** Born Feb 12, 1917, Port of Spain, Trinidad and Tobago;son of Felix Eugene Michael Hercules and Millicent Dottin Hercules; married Dellora C. Howard, 1946; children: John, Eric. **EDUCATION:** Attended Univ Tutorial Coll, 1934-35,

and Hon Soc of the Middle Temple of Inns of Court, 1935-39, 1950-51. **CAREER:** Loyola Univ, New Orleans, LA, visiting scholar; Xavier Univ, New Orleans, writer-in-residence. **ORGANIZATIONS:** Mem, final review panel, Natl Endowment for the Humanities. **HONORS/ACHIEVEMENTS:** Author of novels: Where the Hummingbird Flies, Harcourt, 1961, I Want a Black Doll, Simon & Schuster, 1967, On Leaving Paradise, Harcourt, 1980; contributor to periodicals; Fletcher Pratt Memorial fellowship, Bread Loaf Writers Conf, 1961; Rockefeller fellowship for distinguished scholarship in the humanities, 1977. **BUSINESS ADDRESS:** c/o Trade Publications, Harcourt, Brace & Jovanovich, 111 5th Ave, New York, NY 10003. *

HERD, JOHN E.
Educator. **PERSONAL:** Born May 29, 1932, Colbert Co, AL; married Eleanor; children: Arnold, Garland. **EDUCATION:** BS MS 1966, AA Cert 1976. **CAREER:** Russa Moton HS Tallassee, AL; instr; Cobb HS Anniston, AL, instr; Brutonville Jr HS AL, prin; Alexandria HS AL, prin; Calhoun Co Educ Assn, vice pres 1971, pres 1972, past pres 1973, second vice pres 1974. **ORGANIZATIONS:** Mem Alpha Phi Alpha; 1st Black pres of Calhoun Co Educ Assn 1972. **MILITARY SERVICE:** USAF sgt 1/c 1951-55. **BUSINESS ADDRESS:** PO Box 38, Alexandria, AL 36250.

HEREFORD, SONNIE WELLINGTON, III
Physician. **PERSONAL:** Born Jan 07, 1931, Huntsville, AL; married Martha Ann Adams; children: Sonnie IV, Kimela, Lee, Linda, Brenda, Martha. **EDUCATION:** AL A&M U, BS 1955; Meharry Med Coll, MD 1955. **CAREER:** Oakwood Coll, campus phys 1957-73; AL A&M Univ, team physician 1962-, campus physician 1962-73, prof of histology 1960-68, prof of psychology 1960-68. **ORGANIZATIONS:** Chmn com for Desegragation of Huntsville, AL 1962-63; consult sickle cell anemia Delta Sigma Theta 1971-75. **HONORS/ACHIEVEMENTS:** Distinguished Serv Award Voter Coord Com Huntsville, AL 1962; Distinguished Serv Award Oakwood Coll Huntsville, AL 1973. **BUSINESS ADDRESS:** 930 Franklin, Huntsville, AL 35801.

HERENTON, WILLIE W.
Educator. **PERSONAL:** Born Apr 23, 1940, Memphis, TN; married Ida Jones; children: Errol, Rodney, Andrea. **EDUCATION:** LeMoyne-Owen Coll, BS 1963; Memphis State Univ, MA 1966; So IL Univ, PhD 1971. **CAREER:** Memphis City Sch System, elementary sch tchr 1963-67, elementary sch prin 1967-73; Rockefeller Found, fellow 1973-74; Memphis City Schs, dept supt 1974-78, supt of schs 1979-. **ORGANIZATIONS:** Bd dir Natl Urban League; bd dir Natl Jr Achievement; mem Amer Assn of Sch Adminstr 1969-80; mem Natl Alliance of Black Educators 1974-; bd dirJr Achievement of Memphis 1979-; mem Natl Urban League Educ Adv Council 1978; bd dir United Way of Greatr Memphis 1979-. **HONORS/ACHIEVEMENTS:** Raymond Foster Scholarship Awd So IL Univ 1970; Rockefeller Found Fellowship Rockefeller Found 1973; Alumnus of the Yr LeMoyne Owen Coll 1976; Named oneof Top 100 Sch Adminstrs in US & Can Exec Educator Journal 1980, 1984. **BUSINESS ADDRESS:** Supt of Schools, Memphis City School System, 2597 Avery, Memphis, TN 38112.

HERMAN, ALEXIS M.
Government official. **PERSONAL:** Born Jul 16, 1947, Mobile, AL. **EDUCATION:** Savier Univ, BA 1969. **CAREER:** Cath Soc Serv Mobile, AL, soc worker 1969-72; Recruitment Training Prog Pascagoula, MS, outreach worker 1971-72; Black Women Empl Prog So Regional Cncl, dir 1972-74; Dept Labor Recruitment Training Prog, consult supr 1973-74; Women's Prog for Minority Women Empl Atlanta, natl dir 1974-77; Women's Bur Washington, dir 1977-.

HERMAN, KATHLEEN VIRGIL
Communications administration. **PERSONAL:** Born May 17, 1942, Buffalo, NY; children: Jonathan Mark. **EDUCATION:** Goddard Coll, BA 1976; Boston Univ, MS Commun 1980. **CAREER:** Public Info Boston Edison, consult 1979; Minority Recruitment Big Sister Assoc, coord 1980; Council on Battered Women, comm educ dir 1980; Access Atlanta Inc, dir 1981; City of Atlanta, coord cable commun. **ORGANIZATIONS:** Mem Minorities in Cable, Natl Assoc of Telecom, Natl Fed of Local Programmers, Women in Cable; NAACP Media Comm, co-chair; American Women in Radio & TV. **HONORS/ACHIEVEMENTS:** Publication, "Minority Participation in the Media", sub-committe on Telecom Consumer Protection & Finance of the Committee on Energy & Commerce, US House ofRepresentatives, 98th Congress. **BUSINESS ADDRESS:** Coord Cable Communications, City of Atlanta, 68 Mitchell St SW, Atlanta, GA 30335.

HERMANUZ, GHISLAINE
Educator. **PERSONAL:** Born in Lausanne, Switzerland;daughter of Max Hermanuz and Manotte Tavernier Hermanuz; children: Dahoud Walker. **EDUCATION:** ETH/Lausanne Switzerland, Arch Diploma 1967; Harvard Grad School of Design, 1968-69; Columbia Univ, MS Urban Planning 1971. **CAREER:** Candilis, Josic & Woods, architect 1964-65; Llewelyn-Davies & Weeks, architect 1967-68; Architects' Renewal Comm in Harlem, architect 1969-71; Urban Design Group City Planning Dept, urban designer 1972-73; Columbia Univ Grad Sch Architecture, prof of architecture; City Coll of New York, dir, City College Architectural Center. **ORGANIZATIONS:** Principal PHD Assoc 1983-87; principal Hermanuz Ltd 1988-. **HONORS/ACHIEVEMENTS:** Fellowship Fulbright 1968, German Marshall Fund of the US 1979, Natl Endowment for the Arts 1982; Grant NY State Council on the Arts 1984, 1986, 1988. **BUSINESS ADDRESS:** Director City College Architectural Center, City Coll of New York, Convent Ave at 138th St, New York, NY 10031.

HERNANDEZ, AILEEN CLARKE
Business executive, urban consultant. **PERSONAL:** Born May 23, 1926, Brooklyn, NY; daughter of Charles Henry Clarke Sr and Ethel Louise Hall Clarke; divorced. **EDUCATION:** Howard U, BA (cum laude) 1947;Univ Oslo, postgrad (internat student exchange prog) 1947; NY U, 1950; Univ CA at LA; Univ of So CA; Intern Ladies Garment Workers Union, grad labor coll 1951; LA State Coll, MA 1961. **CAREER:** Intl Ladies Garment Workers Union LA, org asst educ dir 1951-59, dir pub relat & educ 1959-61; State Dept So Amer Countries, specialist in labor educ toured 1960; CA Fair Employ Prac Commn, asst chief 1962-65; San Francisco State Univ, lecturer/instructor in political sci 1968-69; Univ of CA Berkeley, instructor urban planning 1978,79; Hernandez & Assoc San Francisco, owner/pres 1966—; commissioner, US Equal Employment Opportunity Prog, 1965-66. **ORGANIZATIONS:** Western vice pres Nat Orgn Women 1967-70, pres 1970-71; co-found mem Black Women Organized for Act San Fran & Nat Hookup of Black Women chair, Sec Adv Com on Rights & Responsibilities of Women HEW, mem Task Force Employ of Women of Twentieth Century Fund; trust Urban Inst Wash; DC bd mem MS Found for Women; bd dirs Nat Com Against Discrim in Housing 1969; Am Acad Politic & Soc Scis; Indus Relat Rsch Assn; mem Am Civil Liberties Union; bd mem Foreign Policy Study Found Commn to Study US Policy towards S Africa; exec com Common Cause; mem steering exec com Nat Urban Coalition; bd of trustees Working Assets Money Fund; bd of overseers Inst for Civil Justice Rand Corp; advisor Natl Inst for Women of Color; treas Eleanor R Spikes Memorial Fund; advisory comm, prog for Rsch on immigration policy, Rand and Urban Inst; ed comm chair, Death Penalty Focus; bd mem, Meiklejohn Civil Liberties Union; CA Comm on Campaign Financing; NAACP; Alpha Kappa Alpha; Bay Area Urban League; Natl Comm against Discrimination in Housing; co-founder, Coalition for Economic Equity. **HONORS/ACHIEVEMENTS:** Named Woman of Yr Comm Relations Conf So CA 1961; recip Bay Area Alumni Club Disting Postgrad Achvmt Awd Howard Univ 1967; Charter Day Alumni Postgrad Achvmnt in Labor & Pub Serv Awd 1968; named one of 10 Most Distin Women Bay Area San Fran Examin 1968; Southern Vermont Coll Hon DHL 1979; Awd from Equal Rights Advocates 1981; Friends of the Commn on the Status of Women Awd 1984; SF League of Women Voters Awd "Ten Women Who Make a Difference" 1985; Parren J Mitchell Award, SF Black Chamber of Commerce, 1985; distinguished service award, Natl Urban Coalition, 1987. **BUSINESS ADDRESS:** President/Owner, Hernandez & Associates, 818 47th Ave, San Francisco, CA 94121.

HERNDON, CRAIG GARRIS
Photographer. **PERSONAL:** Born Jan 23, 1947, Washington, DC; son of Garris Harndon and Lucy Mills Herndon; married Valerie Ingrid Naylor, Aug 01, 1988; children: Stacey Arlene, Robert Eric. **EDUCATION:** Howard U, BA 1970. **CAREER:** WA Post, photographer 1972-; Potomac Magazine, news aide 1968-72; White House News Photographers Assn. **BUSINESS ADDRESS:** 1150 15th St NW, Washington, DC 20071.

HERNDON, GLORIA E.
Business executive. **PERSONAL:** Born Aug 09, 1950, St Louis; married Brent Astaire. **EDUCATION:** Johns Hopkins U, MA 1972; So IL U, BA 1970; Ahmadu Bello Univ, PhD 1978. **CAREER:** Amer Embassy London, financial economist; Ahmadu Bello Univ Nigeria, research 1978-79; Brooking Insat, research asst; Johns Hopkins, research asst; African-Amer Inst, prog asst; Dept State, escort interpreter; Carnegie Endowment Intl Peace Council Foreign Relations, research asst; Equitable Financial Services, insurance company executive 1984-. **ORGANIZATIONS:** Mem Accomplished Musician; Mu Phi Epsilon; Nat Economic Assn; Am Soc Intl Law; Nat Conf Black Political Scientist; Nat Council Negro Women; Nigerian-Am C of C; US Youth Council Research initial Black Caucus 1970- 71; planner United Minority Arts Council. **HONORS/ACHIEVEMENTS:** Distinguished Serv Award So ILUniv 1970; Nat Assn of Honor Students; Nat Negro Merit Semifinalist 1967; Magna Cum Laude Woodrow Wilson Fellow Finalist 1970; recip Rockefeller Found Fellow. **BUSINESS ADDRESS:** Insurance Executive, Equitable Financial Services, 1803 Research Blvd, Rockville, MD 20850.

HERNDON, JAMES
Attorney. **PERSONAL:** Born May 14, 1925, Troy, AL; children: 2 Children. **EDUCATION:** Morehouse Coll, AB 1948; Howard U, LlB 1951. **CAREER:** Garry, Dreyfus, McTernan, Brotsky, Herndon & Pesonen; atty. **ORGANIZATIONS:** Pres San Francisco African Am Historical & Cultural Soc. **BUSINESS ADDRESS:** 1256 Market, San Francisco, CA 19402.

HERNDON, LANCE H.
Information systems consultant executive. **PERSONAL:** Born Apr 04, 1955, New York, NY; son of Russell Herndon and Jackie Herndon; married Jeannine Price Herndon, May 27, 1989. **EDUCATION:** LaGuardia Community Coll, New York NY, BS Computer Science; City Univ, New York NY, BS Computer Science, 1978. **CAREER:** Generation Science, New York NY, consultant, 1973-78; Insurance Systems of Amer, New York NY, product consultant, 1978-80; ACCESS Inc, Atlanta GA, pres, 1980-. **ORGANIZATIONS:** Mem, Atlanta Business League, Atlanta Chamber of Commerce, Black Data Processing Assn, Information Systems Consultant Assn, Natl Assn of 8 (a) Contractors; founding mem, Inc Council of Growing Companies; charter mem, Natl Civil Rights Museum and Hall of Fame; mem, Butler Street YMCA Century Club, Mothers Against Drunk Driving, NAACP, Operation PUSH, United Negro Coll Fund. **HONORS/ACHIEVEMENTS:** Outstanding Business Achievements, Atlanta Minority Business Devel Center; Certificate of Appreciation, Amer Red Cross; Supplier of the Year, Atlanta Business League, 1987, 1988; 500 Fastest Growing Companies, INC magazine, 1988; articles: "Young Tycoons," Ebony Magazine, 1988, "Still Making It," Black Enterprise Magazine, 1988; Georgia Trend Magazine, 1988; Atlanta Tribune, 1988. **BUSINESS ADDRESS:** President, ACCESS Inc, 4882 Old Mountain Park Rd, Roswell, GA 30080.

HERNDON, LARRY LEE
Professional athlete. **PERSONAL:** Born Nov 03, 1953, Sunflower, MS; married Faye Hill; children: Latasha, Kamilah, Maya, Larry Darnell. **EDUCATION:** TN State Univ, attended. **CAREER:** San Francisco Giants, 1976-81; Detroit Tigers, outfielder 1982-84. **HONORS/ACHIEVEMENTS:** July 26-Aug 10 AL Player of Week 1982; voted "Willie Mac Award" (MVP) by Giant teammates 1981; Sporting News' NL Rookie of Year 1976. **BUSINESS ADDRESS:** Detroit Tigers, 2121 Trumbull Ave, Detroit, MI 48216.

HERNDON, PHILLIP GEORGE
Investment banker - import/exports. **PERSONAL:** Born Jul 03, 1951, Little Rock, AR; son of James Franklyn Herndon and Georgia Mae Byrd Herndon. **EDUCATION:** Villanova Univ, PA, 2 years; Amer Legion Boy's State, 1968. **CAREER:** Pulaski Co, AR, surveyor; Just for Kicks Inc retail shoe store, owner 1973-74; KATV Little Rock, news reporter 1972; Black Rel Dir Youth Div Gov Winthrop Rockefeller's Re-Election Campaign, 1970; Pulaski Co, elected co-surveyor & 1st black elected official, 1972; Lt Governor Amer Legions Boys State, 1st Black elected 1968; Kip Walton Productions (TV/Motion Pictures), Hollywood, CA, production asst 1974-78; US Assoc Investment Bankers, Little Rock, AR, investment banker, 1985-87; Blinder, Robinson & Co, Denver, CO, asst manager Bond Department 1987-88; consultant, Colorado African/Carribbean Trade Office 1988-; consultant, Anisco Enterprises (import/export) 1988-. **ORGANIZATIONS:** Dir of Community Relations

GYST House, (fund raiser drug rehabilitation program). **HONORS/ACHIEVEMENTS:** Natl HS Track Champ Natl & state record holder high hurdles 1968; 1st Black inducted into Little Rock Central HS Hall of Fame 1969; recip over 200 full scholarship offers from coll & Univ nationwide 1969; Million Dollar Club, Blinder, Robinson & Company 1988.

HERNTON, CALVIN COOLIDGE
Educator. **PERSONAL:** Born in Chatanooga, TN; children: Antone. **EDUCATION:** Talladega Coll, BA Sociology 1954; Fisk Univ, MA Sociology 1956; Columbia Univ, Sociology 1961. **CAREER:** Central State Univ, poet in residence 1970; Oberlin Coll, black writer in residence 1970-72, prof black studies/creative 1973-; ABC Warner Bros TV, Burbank CA, technical consultant for A Man Called Hawk 1988-. **ORGANIZATIONS:** AL A&M Coll, instr sociol 1958-59; Edward Waters Coll, instr social sci 1959-60; instr sociol Southern Univ 1960-61. **HONORS/ACHIEVEMENTS:** "The Coming of Chronos to the House of Nightsong" poetry Interim Books 1963; "Sex and Racism in Amer" Doubleday 1964; "White Papers for White Amer" Doubleday1966; "Coming Together" Random House 1971; "The Cannabis Experience" Peter Owen 1974; "Scarecrow" novel Doubleday 1974; "Medicine Man" Reed Cannon & Johnson 1977; "The Sexual Mountain & Black Women Writers, Adventures in Sex, Literature & Real Life" Doubleday 1987. **BUSINESS ADDRESS:** Professor of Black Studies, Oberlin College, Rice Hall, Oberlin, OH 44074.

HERRELL, ASTOR YEARY
Administrator. **PERSONAL:** Born Feb 13, 1935, Fork Ridge, TN; son of Clarence Herrell and Charity Herrell; married Doris Vivian Smith; children: Patricia Faye. **EDUCATION:** Berea Coll KY, BA 1957; Tuskegee Inst AL, MS Ed 1961; Wayne State Univ MI, PhD (inorg chem) 1973; Wayne State Univ, Science Faculty Fellow 1970-72. **CAREER:** St Augustine's Coll, instr 1961-63; Knoxville Coll, prof & chmn 1963-79; Winston-Salem State Univ, chmn physical sciences dept 1979-. **ORGANIZATIONS:** Chemist New Brunswick Lab NJ summers 1964-65; rsch chemist Sandia Lab NM summer 1975; consult Fisk UNCF Summer Inst summers 1977-83; mem Amer Chemical Soc 1969-; consult Winston-Salem/Forsyth County Schools 1983-85; bd of dir Forsyth County Environmental Affairs Board; Sigma Xi 1985-. **HONORS/ACHIEVEMENTS:** Biography display Martin Luther King Libr DC 1984; several publns in natl and international science journals - last article publ in 1984. **MILITARY SERVICE:** AUS Reserves Pfc served 6 yrs. **BUSINESS ADDRESS:** Chairman, Physical Sci Dept, Winston-Salem State University, PO Box 13236, Winston-Salem, NC 27110.

HERRIFORD, MERLE BAIRD
Physician. **PERSONAL:** Born Jun 10, 1919, Kansas City, MO; married Barbara; children: Wayne, Carla, David. **EDUCATION:** Univ NE, AB 1939; Howard U, MD 1942. **CAREER:** Homer G Phillips Hosp, dir urology; St LouisUniv Sch Med, sr instr urol 1949-77; Homer G Phillips, resd urol 1947-48; Howard U, instr urol 1946-47, resd urol 1945-46, asst resd & surgery 1943-46. **ORGANIZATIONS:** Mem Am Urol Assn; Nat Med Assn; St Louis Urol Assn; past chmn Sect Urol Nat Med Assn bd dir St LouisUniv HS; vice pres Parochial Bd Educ St Louis; bd medm MO Assn Non-pub Sch. **HONORS/ACHIEVEMENTS:** 25 yr serv recg Homer Phillips Hosp; 25 yr serv vol faculty St LouisUniv Sch Med. **BUSINESS ADDRESS:** 2715 N Union Blvd, St Louis, MO 63113.

HERRING, BERNARD DUANE
Educator. **PERSONAL:** Born in Massillon, OH; son of James and Eva; married Odessa Appling; children: Kevin, Duane, Terez, Sean. **EDUCATION:** Kent State U, BS (magna cum laude) 1952; Univ of Cinci Med Sch, MD 1956; LaSalle U, LLB 1963. **CAREER:** San Fran Gen Hosp, intern 1956-57; Brooklyn Vet Hosp, resident 1957-58; Crile Vet Hosp, resident 1958-59; Merritt Hosp, teaching 1966-84; Univ of CA Med Sch SF, asst clin prof of med. **ORGANIZATIONS:** Candidate CA Bar; bd cert Am Bd of Family Med; candidate Am Bd of Internal Med; Sabteca Music Co; Real Estate License CA; Am Soc of Internal Med; fellow Am Coll of Legal Med; Am Med Writers Assn; Am Diabetes Assn; mem Am Coll of Physician; Am Soc of Composers & Authors; Am Med Assn; Am Heart Assn; Pres Sunshine Vitamin Co; fellow Am Academy of Family Physicians 1983; mem Am Geriatric Society 1989; presiding overseer Watchtower Bible and Tract Society 1980-89. **HONORS/ACHIEVEMENTS:** Cited by Phi Beta Kappa, staff Kent State Univ 1952; article "Kaposi Sarcoma in The Negro" 1963 Jama; Article "Hospital Priviledges" 1965 Cleveland Marshall Law Review; article "Pernicious Anemia and The American Negro" American Practitioner 1962; article "Hepatoma with Unusual Associations" J. National Medical Assn 1973; article "Cancer of Prostate in Blacks" J. Natl Medical Assn 1977; Listed Best Doctor in Am 1979; article, "Unravelling Pathophysiology of Male Pattern Baldness" 1985. **BUSINESS ADDRESS:** Assistant Clinical Professor, U of CA Med Sch SF, 400 29th St, Oakland, CA 94609.

HERRING, LARRY WINDELL
Dentist. **PERSONAL:** Born Jul 08, 1946, Batesville, MS; married Phyllis D; children: Cedric, La Canas Nicole, Yolanda. **EDUCATION:** TN St U, BA 1967; Meharry Med Coll, DDS 1971. **CAREER:** Dentist, pvt prac. **ORGANIZATIONS:** Mem Nat Den Assn; Am Den Assn; Pan-TN Den Assn; Tri-Lakes Study Club; Shelby Co Den Soc; mem NAACP; Omega Psi Phi; Masonic Lodge; W Camp MB Ch. **MILITARY SERVICE:** USAF capt 1971-73. **BUSINESS ADDRESS:** 114 Wood St, Batesville, MS 38606.

HERRING, LEONARD, JR.
Business executive. **PERSONAL:** Born Oct 01, 1934, Valdosta, GA; children: Leonard III, Lynne Rene. **EDUCATION:** Univ of Cincinnati, BA 1960, BS 1964. **CAREER:** Colgate-Palmolive Co NYC/San Fran, mrktng staff asst 1963-64; Market-Cincinnati Bell Tele OH, accnts mgr staff asst 1964-66; Armco Steel Corp Middletown, OH, asst personnel 1966-67; Leonard Herring, Jr Pub Rel Ltd & Mgmnt, dir/pres ceo 1967-. **ORGANIZATIONS:** Life mem Kappa Alpha Psi 1960-; mem Univ of Cinci Aumni Assn 1964-; mem Am Tennis Professnl 1970-; mem Univ of Cinci 100 Disting Alumni 1970; mem US Tennis Writers Assn 1970-; mem Advertising Assn of Am 1972-; vice pres Pub Rel Soc of Amer 1972-76; vice pres US Lawn Tennis Assn 1975-76; mem Men of Achievement in the World 1976; bd mem United Way Los Angeles 1984-. **HONORS/ACHIEVEMENTS:** Pub rel consult Movies, "The Amityville Horror", "A Piece of the Action", "Part II Sounder", "Cross Creek"; donfidante of Arthur Ashe; coached Cinci Chap of the Nat Jr Tennis Leagues Boys & Girls to 3 consecutive championships at US Tennis Open Forest Hills, NY 1972-74; pres/producer Celebrity Tennis Tournaments Ltd. **MILITARY SERVICE:** AUS lt; news coorespondent for the Stars & Stripes in Europe 1954-56. **BUSINESS ADDRESS:** President/Chief Executive Ofcr, Leonard Herring, Jr Pub Rel, 900 Hammond Towers, Ste 434, Beverly Hills, CA 90069.

HERRING, WILLIAM F.
Manager. **PERSONAL:** Born Jul 28, 1932, Valdosta, GA; married Janet L; children: William Jr, Paul, Kristi. **EDUCATION:** Wayne State U, BA 1961. **CAREER:** Buick Motor Div GM Corp, mgr dealer development 1979-, asst zone mgr 1977-79; Detroit Coca-Cola Bottling Co, dir of indsl relations 1973-75; Houdaille Industries, mgr indsl relations 1970-73. **ORGANIZATIONS:** Mem Detroit Police Comm Relations 1972; life mem NAACP 1976; mem Car & Truck Renting & Leasing Assn (CATRALA) 1977. **HONORS/ACHIEVEMENTS:** Achievement Award United Found 1972. **MILITARY SERVICE:** AUS cpt 1952-54. **BUSINESS ADDRESS:** Buick Motor Div GM Corp, 902 E Hamilton Ave, Flint, MI 48550.

HERRON, BRUCE WAYNE
Educational administrator. **PERSONAL:** Born Apr 14, 1954, Victoria, TX; married Joyce LaDell Freeman; children: Monica Yvonne, Bruce Wayne Jr. **EDUCATION:** Univ of New Mexico, Bachelors 1977. **CAREER:** Miami Dolphina, player 1977-78; Chicago Bears, player 1978-83; Accurate Air Express, owner 1982-83; Metro Media TV Channel 32, acct exec 1984; Chicago State Univ, dir of athletics 1984-. **ORGANIZATIONS:** Dir Big Brothers/Big Sisters; volunteer Better Boys Found; hon chmn Sicle Cell Anemia 1982. **HONORS/ACHIEVEMENTS:** Man of the Yr Big Brothers/Big Sisters; Byron Wizzard White Natl Football League Players Assn. **HOME ADDRESS:** 8504 S Calumet, Chicago, IL 60619. **BUSINESS ADDRESS:** Dir of Athletics, Chicago State University, 95th St at King Dr, Chicago, IL 60628.

HERRON, VERNON M.
Consultant. **PERSONAL:** Born Oct 07, 1928, Charlotte; children: 3 Children. **EDUCATION:** Shaw U, AB 1951; Johnson C Smith U, mdiv 1958; penn state u, MPA 1978; pittsburgh theol sem, dmin 1978. **CAREER:** Pub Prgms, consult adminstr mgmt 1975-; Am Bapt Ch Hdqrs, asst sec div soc ministries 1968-75; 2nd Bapt Ch Joliet, pastor 1962-68; Friendship BaptCh Pittsburgh, pastor 1955-62; 1st Bapt Dallas, pastor 1952-55; Valley Forge, plng budget obj 1974, plng prgm obj 1973; Urban Training Ctr Chicago 1970; Valley Forge, strategic plng 1969-74; MI State U, conf plng 1968; Allentown State Hosp, clin psych 1959; Harrisburgh State Hosp, clin psych 1958. **ORGANIZATIONS:** Mem Alpha Phi Alpha Frat; Prince Hall Mason. **HONORS/ACHIEVEMENTS:** Who's Who AmgUniv & Coll 1950-51.

HERVEY, BILLY T.
Aero space technologist. **PERSONAL:** Born Apr 02, 1937, Naples, TX; married Olivia M Gray; children: Jewel, Marcus, Patrick. **EDUCATION:** BS 1960. **CAREER:** Space Shuttle Pgm Ofc, currently assigned; Phys Schi Tech Mgr, served; Mission Control Ctr Houston on Greini & Apollo Flghts, nasa flight controller 1966-71; NASA/JOHNSON Space Center Houston; Kennedy Space Ctr Cape Kennedy, nasa & mehanical engr 1964-65; Gen Dynamics Corp Atlas F Missile Pgm Altus, OK,mech design engr test conductor; AUS Corps Engrs Ballistic Missle Ofc Atlus, mech Engr 1960-62. **ORGANIZATIONS:** Mem Gulf Coast Soc; mem Trinity United Meth Ch; Prince Hall Free & Accepted Masonry; Douglas Burrell Consistory No 56; Ancient Accepted Scottist Rite; Ancient Egyptian Arabic Order Noble of Mystic Shrine N & S Am. **HONORS/ACHIEVEMENTS:** Received group achvmnt awrd for support Gemini Missions; grp achvmnt flight operation awrd; Prsidential Medal of Freedom Awrd; participation on Apollo XiiiMission Operations Team; Johnson Spacecraft Ctr EEO Awrd. **MILITARY SERVICE:** AUS 1962-64. **BUSINESS ADDRESS:** Johnson Spacecraft Center, Houston, TX 77058.

HERVEY, RAMON TRICHE, II
Public relations consultant. **PERSONAL:** Born Oct 18, 1950, Chicago, IL; married Vanessa Lynne Williams. **EDUCATION:** Whittier Coll, BA 1972. **CAREER:** Pan Am Airlines, in-flight attendant 1972-74; Hamlett/Marsh Publishers, editor-in-chief 1975-76; Motown Records, writer/publicist 1976-77; Rogers & Cowan Inc,vice pres talent 1977-80; The Group, pres/partner 1980-86; Hervey & Company, pres 1986-. **ORGANIZATIONS:** Have represented and/or consulted entertainment clients including Richard Pryor, Bette Midler, Natalie Cole, George Benson, Bee Gees, Herb Alpert, Little Richard, Vanessa Williams, Chaka Khan, "The Wiz" Motion Picture Soundtrack; mem NAACP, Publicists Guild 1978-; mem Black Music Assoc, Black Public Relations Soc,Natl Acad Recording Arts & Scis. **BUSINESS ADDRESS:** President, Hervey & Company, 8271 Melrose Ave, Los Angeles, CA 90046.

HERZFELD, WILL LAWRENCE
Clergyman. **PERSONAL:** Born Jun 09, 1937, Mobile, AL; married Thressa Mildred Alston; children: Martin, Katherine, Stephen. **EDUCATION:** Attended, AL Lutheran Acad; Immanuel Luth Coll, AA 1957; Immanuel Luth Sem, MDiv 1961. **CAREER:** Christ Lutheran Church, pastor 1961; CA & NV Dist, urban minister 1966; Lutheran Council USA, regional mission exec 1968; Bethlehem Lutheran Church, pastor 1973-; Assn of Evangel Lutheran Church, vice pres 1976-, presiding bishop 1984. **ORGANIZATIONS:** Pres Tuscaloosa Chap SCLC 1963; vice pres Luth Human Relations Assn 1973-74; commr Alameda Cty Human Relations Commn 1977-78; vice pres Alamo Black Clergy 1973-; dir Natl Conf of Black Churchmen 1974-76; dir Black Theology Project. **HONORS/ACHIEVEMENTS:** Outstanding Citizen Tuscaloosa Businessmen's League 1961-66; 3 Service to Youth Awds Barnes YMCA Tuscaloosa AL 1961-66; DD Ctr for Urban Black Studies 1975; Man of the Yr Mother's for Equal Educ 1976. **BUSINESS ADDRESS:** Assn of Evangel Luth Chs, 959 12th St, Oakland, CA 94607.

HESTER, ARTHUR C.
Army officer. **PERSONAL:** Born Mar 05, 1942, Columbus, MS; married Mae J Howard; children: Zina, Karen, Lisa, Arthur III. **EDUCATION:** US Military Acad, BS 1965; Stanford U, MS 1970. **CAREER:** AUS, mjr; 11th Armored Cavalry Regiment Fulda West Germany, intelligence Ofcr; Admissions & Equal Admsn Oppr , asst dir; USMA & West Point, ofcr 1970-73; US Vietnam Germany, various command stf postions. **ORGANIZATIONS:** Mem Naacp; Assc of US Army; Armor Assc; Blackhorse Assc; Master Mason; past mem Assc of Black Bus Stdnt NYU; trustee Assc of Graduates USMA 1970-73; mem German-am Cncl Fulda, W Germany 1973-; mem bd Dir Am Youth Activities Fulda W Germany 1974-. **HONORS/ACHIEVEMENTS:** Recipient Silver Star, Bronze Star, Purple Heart; meritorous serv medal; Vietnamese Cross of Gallantry with Silver Star; nominee outst jr ofcr of yr 1st Army 1971. **MILITARY SERVICE:** AUS 1965-. **BUSINESS ADDRESS:** Hqs 11 Armored Cavalry, Reg APO, New York, NY 09146.

HEWING, PERNELL HAYES
Educator. **PERSONAL:** Born May 13, 1933, St Matthews, SC; married Joe B; children: Rita, Johnny. **EDUCATION:** Allen Univ, BS 1961; Temple Univ, MEd 1963; Univ WI, PhD 1974. **CAREER:** Palmetto Leader Newspaper, linotypist genl printer 1952-57; Allen Univ, supr dept printing 1958-61, instr 1961-62; Philadelphia Tribune, linotypist 1962-63; Allen Univ Columbia, asst prof business educ 1963-71; Palmetto Times Newspaper, woman's editor 1963-64; Palmetto Post Columbia SC, mgr editor 1970-71; Univ of WI Whitewater, prof business communications 1971-. **ORGANIZATIONS:** Delta Pi Epsilon Hon Bus Orgn; Pi Lambda Theta Natl Honor & Professional Assn Women Educ 1972; mem Natl Bus Educ 1950; Amer Bus Communications Assn; founder/dir Avant-Garde Cultural & Devel Orgn; Sigma Gamma Rho Sor Inc 1962; dev chptsUniv WI Madison 1973;Univ WI Whitewater 1974; mem WI Coord Council Women Higher Educ. **HONORS/ACHIEVEMENTS:** Who's Who Am Coll & Univ 1961; Outstanding Educators Amer 1971; co-founder Palmetto Post weekly newspaper 1970. **BUSINESS ADDRESS:** Professor Bus Comm, Univ of Wisconsin, 4010 Carlson Bldg, Whitewater, WI 53190.

HEWITT, BASIL
Clergyman. **PERSONAL:** Born Jan 31, 1926, Colon, Panama;married May Shirley; children: Nidia, Gloria, Chris. **EDUCATION:** KY So Coll, BA 1969; So Baptist Theol Sem, MDiv 1973. **CAREER:** Fifth St Baptist Church, asst pastor 1967-73; Emmanuel Baptist Church, pastor 1973-. **ORGANIZATIONS:** Mem C of C; decty Laurel Clergy Assn 1974-75; exec comm Citizen's Adv Coun Pkwy. **BUSINESS ADDRESS:** Pastor, Emmanuel Baptist Church, 11443 Laurel-Bowie Road, RR 2, Laurel, MD 20707.

HEWITT, JOHN H., JR.
Retired editor. **PERSONAL:** Born Aug 20, 1924, New York, NY; son of John H Hewitt and Agatha B Hewitt; married Vivian Davideson; children: John H III. **EDUCATION:** Harvard Coll, 1941-43; NY Univ, BS 1948; NY Univ, MA 1949. **CAREER:** Medical Tribune, med writer 1961-72; Hosp Practice, sr edtr, mgng edtr 1972-75; Med Tribune, asso edtr 1975-80; Emerg Med, sr edtr 1980-82; Self-Employed 1982-86; retired 1986. **ORGANIZATIONS:** Mem Am Med Writer Assn 1965-; mem Natl Assn of Sci Writers 1976-80; Trustee Manhattan Cntry Sch 1971-; trustee, treas Schomburg Corp 1980-; vestryman St Philip's Ch 1982-. **HONORS/ACHIEVEMENTS:** J H Hewitt, "The Sacking of St Philip's Church, NY" Hstrcl Mag of the Protestant Epscpl Ch, Vol XLVIV, No 1, 03/80; J H Hewitt, "New York's Black Episcopalians, In the Beginning, 1704-1722"; Afro-Americans in NY Life & History, Vol 3, No 1, Jan 1979.

HEWITT, RONALD JEROME
Business executive. **PERSONAL:** Born Oct 31, 1932, Welch, WV; married Deanna Cowan; children: Ronald Jr, Kevin, Robert, Jonathan, Mkonto. **EDUCATION:** Fisk U, BA 1955. **CAREER:** Detroit Housing Comm, supt of operations 1969, asst dir 1971, dir 1973; Comm & Econ Dev Detroit, exec dep dir 1974, dir 1974-79; Mayor Coleman A Young, exec asst 1979-; Detroit Planning Dept, dir. **ORGANIZATIONS:** Downtown Dev Authority; Detroit Econ Dev Corp; Ford Hosp/VA Joint Ventura Corp; Cncl for Urban Econ Dev;; CORD; SE MI Cncl of Govt; Detroit FinancialCenter Task Force; Afro-American Museum bd of dir; Detroit Foreign Trade Zone; Detroit Economic Growth Corp; Strategic Plan Bd; Detroit-Wayne Port Authority liaison. **MILITARY SERVICE:** AUS 1956-58. **BUSINESS ADDRESS:** Dir, Detroit Planning Dept, 2300 Cadillac Tower, Detroit, MI 48226.

HEWITT, VIVIAN DAVIDSON
Librarian. **PERSONAL:** Born in New Castle, PA; daughter of Arthur Robert Davidson and Lela Mauney Davidson; married John H; children: John H III. **EDUCATION:** Geneva Coll, BA 1943; Carnegie-Mellon, BS in LS 1944; Univ of Pittsburgh, Grad Stud 1947-48; Geneva Coll, LHD 1978. **CAREER:** Carnegie Lib of Pittsbgh, sr asst lib 1944-49; Atlanta Univ Sch Lib Sci, instructor/librarian 1949-52; Crowell-Collier Publishing Co, researcher asst to dir 1954-56; Rockefeller Found, librarian 1956-63; Katharine Gibbs Sch, dir lib info svcs 1984-86; Carnegie Endowment for International Peace NY 1963-83 (retired); Council on Foreign Relations 1987-88; Univ of Texas, Austin, faculty, Graduate School of Library & Informaiton. **ORGANIZATIONS:** Librarian Carnegie Endowment for Intl Peace 1963-83; contributor to Professnl Journals; lecturer Library Schools; mem US, Canada IFLA; pres Spcl Libraries Assn 1978-79; exec com/sec of bd Graham-Windham Child Care & Adoption Agency 1969-87; exec com/sec Laymens Club The Cathedral of St John the Divine NY. **HONORS/ACHIEVEMENTS:** Distinguished Alumni Award Carnegie-Mellon Univ 1978; Distinguished Alumni Award Univ of Pittsburgh 1978; Distinguished Serv Black Caucus Amer Lib Assn 1979; Hall of Fame Special Lib Assn 1984.

HEWLETT, ANTOINETTE PAYNE
Government official. **PERSONAL:** Born in Martinsburg, WV; children: Adora. **EDUCATION:** WV State Coll, BA; Columbia Univ, MA 1961. **CAREER:** Jefferson Co, teacher 1960; San Francisco Redevelop, relocation asst 1962-66; Oakland Redevelop, planner/reloc super 1967-76; City of Oakland, dir commdevelop 1976-. **ORGANIZATIONS:** Mem Oakland Museum Assoc; mem Friends of Ethnic Art; mem Natl Forum for Black Public Admin; mem Amer Soc Public Admin; mem Natl Assoc Housing & Redevelopment Officials; mem Comm Club of CA; mem bd of directors Natl Comm Develop Assoc 1984-. **BUSINESS ADDRESS:** Dir, Community Development, City of Oakland, 1417 Clay St, Oakland, CA 94612.

HEWLETT, DIAL, JR.
Physician. **PERSONAL:** Born Jul 26, 1948, Cleveland, OH; son of Dial Hewlett and Lydia Hewlett; married Janice M Chance; children: Kwasi, Tiffany, Whitney Joy, Brandon. **EDUCATION:** Attended Univ of WI Madison; Univ of WI School of Med, MD 1976. **CAREER:** Harlem Hosp Center, internship & residency 1976-79; Harlem Hospital Center, chief med residency 1979-80; Montefiore Hospital & Albert Einstein Coll of Med, fellowship infectious diseases 1980-82; NY Med Coll, asst prof of med 1982-; Our Lady of Mercy Hospital, chief of infectious diseases. **ORGANIZATIONS:** Attending physician internal med, chief of infectious diseases Lincoln Med & Mental Health Center 1982-84; mem Amer Soc for Microbiology 1983-; ed bd Hospital Physicians Joyrnal 1984-; consult infectious diseases Our Lady of Mercy Hospital 1984-, Bronx Lebanon Hospital 1984-, Mt Vernon Hospital 1984-, Calvary Hospital for Terminally Ill 1985-; mem Infectious Diseases Soc of Amer 1986-; consult infectious diseases Lawrence Hospital 1987-; mem Manhattan Central Medical Society INMA. **HONORS/ACHIEVEMENTS:** Co-captain Track Teach Univ of WI Big Ten Champions 1969-70; Diplomate Specialty Internal med Amer Bd of Internal Med 1980; Publs on, Tuberculosis & AIDS, Tropical Splenomegaly Syndrome, AIDS in Socially Disadvantages Groups, Chagas Disease in Diabetic Animals 1980-; Diplomate Subspecialty Infectious Diseases Amer Bd of Internal Med 1984. **BUSINESS ADDRESS:** Chief of Infectious Diseases, Our Lady of Mercy Hospital, 600 East 233rd St, Bronx, NY 10466.

HEWLETT, EVERETT AUGUSTUS, JR.
Attorney. **PERSONAL:** Born Mar 27, 1943, Richmond, VA; married Clothilde. **EDUCATION:** Dickinson Coll Carlisle PA, BA 1965; Golden Gate Univ Law Sch, JD 1975. **CAREER:** USAF, information spec 1965-69; Univ of CA Berkeley, writer-editor 1970-75; Bayview-Hunters Point Comm Defender San Francisco, staff atty 1976-80; Private Law Practice, attorney 1980-86; San Francisco Superior Court, court commissioner 1986-. **ORGANIZATIONS:** Bd dirs SF Neighborhood Legal Asst Found 1979-; bd dir SF Neighborhood Legal Asst Found 1979-; hearing officer SF Residl Rent Stabilization & Arbitration Bd 1980-82; bd dir CA Assn of Black Lawyers 1980-; vice pres Counseliers West 1980; pres William Hastie Bar Assn 1984; vice chmn SF Neighborhood Legal Asst Found 1984; parliamentarian Wm Hastie Bar Assn 1980-86; mem State Bar Comm on Legal Specialization 1982; mem CA State Bar Legal Serv Trust Fund Comm 1984-85. **HONORS/ACHIEVEMENTS:** Editor of Best Newspaper in its class USAF Hamilton CA & Nakhon Phanom 1967 & 1968. **MILITARY SERVICE:** USAF sgt 1965-69. **BUSINESS ADDRESS:** Superior Court Judge, San Francisco Superior Court, 375 Woodside Dr, Youth Guidance Center, San Francisco, CA 94117.

HEYWARD, DON H.
Association executive. **PERSONAL:** Born Oct 19, 1931, South Carolina; married Hilda. **EDUCATION:** SC State Coll, BS 1952; SC State & NY Univs, Columbia Sch of Social Work, post-grad studies. **CAREER:** CT Family Health Plan, vice pres; Bridgeport MOdel Cities Agency, dir; CT Mental Health Ctr New Haven, dir; Career Devel Ctr Gen Learning Corp CT, dir; Bridgeport Housing Auth, exec dir; Metropolitan Business Assoc, exec dir. **ORGANIZATIONS:** Mem bd Bridgeport Area Mental Health Council; adv bd Mental Retardation; CT Mental Health Assn; NAACP; United Way of Eastern Fairfield; Bridgeport Economic Devel Corp. **MILITARY SERVICE:** AUS maj 1952. **BUSINESS ADDRESS:** Executive Dir, Metropolitan Business Assoc, 1302 Stratford Ave, Bridgeport, CT 06607.

HEYWARD, ILENE PATRICIA
Systems engineer manager. **PERSONAL:** Born Apr 09, 1948, Plainfield, NJ; daughter of William Nesbitt Jr and Bonlyn Pitts Nesbitt; children: Eric Eugene. **EDUCATION:** Farleigh Dickinson Univ, BS Chem/Math 1976; New York Univ, 1982-88 MS Chem. **CAREER:** AT&T Bell Labs, tech assoc 1976-77, sr tech assoc 1977-79, assoc mem of tech staff 1979-81, mem of tech staff 1981-. **ORGANIZATIONS:** Lecturer Women and Mathematics 1979-; mem Natl Organ for the Advancement of Black Chemists & Chem Engrs 1980-; mem Amer Chem Soc 1980-; mem Amer Assoc for the Advancement of Science 1982-; bd mem Plainfield Science Center 1983-; conducts workshops pertaining to Black Women in the Corp Environment 1985-. **HONORS/ACHIEVEMENTS:** Authored and co-authored many articles in technical journals such as ACS and Journal of the Society of Plastic Engrs 1976-; authored chap in ACS Symposium Monograph Series 1985; featured in cover story of Black Enterprise 1985; Honored during Womens History Month by Bell Communications Rsch 1985. **BUSINESS ADDRESS:** AT & T Bell Labs, Crawfords Cornor Road, Holmdel, NJ 07733.

HEYWARD, ISAAC
Radio announcer, sales manager. **PERSONAL:** Born Apr 30, 1935, Charleston, SC; son of Rev St Julian Heyward (deceased) and Chrestina Capers Heyward; children: Regina Vermel Heyward, Bryant Isaac Heyward. **EDUCATION:** Radio Broadcast Inst, New York NY, Certificate, 1967; Morris Coll, School of Religion, Orangeburg Extension, Certificate, 1975. **CAREER:** WHBI Radio, Newark NJ, program announcer, sales mgr, 1965-67; WRNW Radio, Mt Kisco NY, am announcer, dir, 1967-71; WQIZ Radio, St George SC, am announcer, sales mgr, 1971-85; WTGH Radio, Cayce SC, am announcer, sales mgr, 1985-. **ORGANIZATIONS:** Assoc ordained minister, St Paul Baptist Church, Orangeburg SC, 1971; Gospel Music Workshop of Amer (Announcers Guild), 1974; NAACP, South Carolina Brancy, 1974; Baptist Assn, Orangeburg SC, 1985; mem, Boy Scouts of Amer Council, 1986; pres, Go Gospel Radio Consultant, 1987. **HONORS/ACHIEVEMENTS:** Second Runner-up DJ, Gospel of the Year, Lamb Records, 1978; Best Radio Gospel Program, Lee's Publication, 1979; Gospel Promotion, Gospel Workshop of Amer, 1982; Community Service, Amer Cancer Soc, 1982, 1983; Living Legacy, Natl Council of Negro Women, 1984; Boy Scouts of Amer Service, Boy Scouts of Amer, 1986. **HOME ADDRESS:** Colonial Villa, 7645 Garnes Ferry Rd, Columbia, SC 29209.

HEYWARD, JAMES OLIVER
Educator. **PERSONAL:** Born Jul 17, 1930, Sumter, SC; son of Julian H Heyward Sr (deceased) and Lue Heyward; married Willie Mae Thompson; children: Julian. **EDUCATION:** South Carolina State Coll, BS 1953; Armed Forces Staff Coll, 1969; Shippensburg State University, MA 1972. **CAREER:** US Army, Deputy Cmdr Military Comm 1974-75; Cmdr TRADOC Field Element 1976-79 Alabama A&M Univ, prof of military science 1979-83, dir of admissions 1984-. **ORGANIZATIONS:** Amer Assn Collegiate Registrars & Adm Ofcrs, Equal Oppor Committee 1986-87; Phi Delta Kappa; chmn, Membership Comm, NAACP, 1983-84; Alpha Phi Alpha, Chapter Vice Pres 1984-87, pres, 1987-; mem Human Relations Council Huntsville AL; mem, Steward Bd, St John AME Church, 1985-. **HONORS/ACHIEVEMENTS:** Mt Pisgah AME Church, Outstanding Son 1973; SC State College, ROTC Hall of Fame 1979. **MILITARY SERVICE:** US Army, Colonel 1953-83; Legion of Merit, Bronze Star, Joint Services Commendation, US Army Commendation Medal, Senior Parachutist Badge; Meritorious Serv Medal. **HOME ADDRESS:** 747 Bluewood Drive SE, Huntsville, AL 35802. **BUSINESS ADDRESS:** Dir of Admissions, Alabama A&M University, P O BOX 284, Normal, AL 35762.

HIATT, DANA SIMS
Educational administration. **PERSONAL:** Born in Chickasha, OK; married James H Hiatt. **EDUCATION:** Langston U, BA History (summa cum laude) 1968;Univ of KS Sch of Law, JD 1971. **CAREER:** Chicago IL, Oklahoma City OK, RH Smith Comm, law fellow 1971-73; City of Oklahoma, asst municipal atty 1974; Darrell, Bruce, Johnson & Sims Assoc, private practice law 1975-77; CO State Univ, title IX coord cncltn officer 1979-82, dir office of equal opportunity. **ORGANIZATIONS:** The Denver Chapter of Links Inc, Am Asso of Univ Women, Amer Assoc for Affrim Action, Higher Educ Affirm Action Dirs. **HONORS/ACHIEVEMENTS:** Whos Who Amg Stnts in Am Clgs Univs 1968; Otstndng Yng

Woman Zeta Phi Beta Sor Okla City, OK 1975; R H Smith Law Fellowship. **BUSINESS ADDRESS:** Dir Ofc of Eq Opptnty, Colorado State University, 314 Student Services Bldg, Fort Collins, CO 80523.

HIATT, DIETRAH (NEE CHAPMAN)
Journalist, school counselor. **PERSONAL:** Born Sep 23, 1944, Washington, DC; married Robert Terry; children: Stephanie Gail, Benjamin Jesse. **EDUCATION:** Howard U, BA 1965. **CAREER:** The Pierre Times, editorial columnist present; Sen George Mcgovern, comm rep; Nyoda Girl Scout Council, brownie ldr resource person 1976-77; Pierre Indian Learning Cntr, sch counselor; Pierre-Ft Pierre Head Start Prgm, vol tchrs asst 1973-74; Huron SD Daily Plainsman, reporter 1973-74; DC Dept of Pub Assistance, social serv rep caseworker 1968-70; US Peace Corps Vol Rep of Panama 1965-67. **ORGANIZATIONS:** Alpha Kappa Alpha; Am Assn ofUniv Women 1972-74; treas Short Grass Arts Council 1974-75; membership chpn 1976; publicity chpn present; vice pres Nat Orgn for Women Central SD Chap 1975-; Dem Party precinct woman 1976-; chpn Hughes Co Dem Com; co-chpn Candidate Task Force SD Womens Caucus; mem Nat Abortion Rights Action League; mem State Professional Practices & Standards Commn of Dept of Educ & Cultural Affairs present. **HONORS/ACHIEVEMENTS:** Choreographed & performed rev of dance & history for AAUW Cultural Study Group 1973; performed in modern & native Am dance recital for Arts Festival arts wrkshp 1973; nominated for Outstdng Young Woman of Am 1973, 77; candidate for Pierre Sch Bd 1976; candidate for SD State Senate 1978. **BUSINESS ADDRESS:** 404 E Sioux Ave, Pierre, SD 57501.

HIBBERT, DOROTHY LASALLE
Educator. **PERSONAL:** Born Sep 17, 1923, New York, NY; daughter of Arthur Hilbert, Sr and Lily Roper Hilbert. **EDUCATION:** Hunter Coll, BA 1945; Teachers Coll Columbia Univ, MA 1949; City Coll Graduate Div, PD 1983. **CAREER:** Bd of Educ New York City, PS 186 teacher 1947-59, HS 136 math teacher 1959-68, PS 146 & 36 asst principal 1969-79, PS 138 acting interim principal 1979-81, PS 93 asst principal 1981-85, PS 146 principal 1985-. **ORGANIZATIONS:** Vice pres 1976-86, sec 1987 Intl League of Human Rights; planning participant New York State Conf on Status of Women; sec Amer Commn on Africa 1979-; asst examiner Bd of Examiners 1982; chairperson for conf New York City Bronx Reading Council 1985; mem NAACP; mem Assoc of Black Educators of NY 1986. **HONORS/ACHIEVEMENTS:** Outstanding Educator City Tabernacle Church 1980; Outstanding Principal of the Year Morrisana Educ Council 1980; publications "The Role of the Nefers in Egyptian History," 1979, "Nubian Egypt and Egyptian Nubia," 1979, "Big Red Newspaper," Brooklyn NY; PHD candidate Walden Univ, 1989. **HOME ADDRESS:** 90 Meucci Ave, Copiague, NY 11726. **BUSINESS ADDRESS:** Admin, Bd of Education, City of New York, Bronx, NY 10455.

HICKERSON, O. B. See SMITH, OTRIE

HICKLIN, FANNIE
Educator. **PERSONAL:** Born in Talladega, AL; divorced; children: Ariel Yvonne Ford. **EDUCATION:** Talladega Coll, BA; Univ Michigan, MA; Univ of Wisconsin at Madison, PhD. **CAREER:** Magnolia Ave HS, Avery Inst, Burke HS, Tuskegee Inst, AL A&M Coll, Univ of Wisconsin at Madison, previous teaching experience; Univ of Wisconsin at Whitewater, assoc dean faculties 1974-88. **ORGANIZATIONS:** Bd of curators State Hist Soc of Wisconsin; Cen States Communication Assn; speech comm assn; Theta Alpha Phi; Alpha Kappa Alpha; bd, Wisconsin Alliance for Art Educ.

HICKMAN, GARRISON M.
Educator. **PERSONAL:** Born Jan 14, 1945, Washington, DC; married Cynthia Burrowes; children: Michael Barrington. **EDUCATION:** VA Union U, BA 1967; Howard U, MDiv 1971. **CAREER:** Student Affairs & Affirmative Action Capital Univ & Abiding Saviour Lutheran Church, assoc dean present; Neighborhood Youth Corps Dept of Defense, teacher counselor 1967-68; Washington Concentrated Employment Program, 1968-70; DC City Govt, counselor 1971. **ORGANIZATIONS:** Mem Am Assn of Higher Edn; Nat pres Am Assn for Affirmative Action 1976-77; Nat chmn Conf on Inner City Ministries 1975-76; Nat Collegiate Honor Soc; coord com on Nat Crises Conf on Inner City Ministries; Coalition of Minority Profls in Am Lutheran Ch Collegs &Univ 1974-75; natl sec Conf on InnerCity Ministries 1973-74; OH reg chmn Coord Com on Nat Crisis 1973-75. **HONORS/ACHIEVEMENTS:** Who's Who in Religion 1975-76. **BUSINESS ADDRESS:** 2199 E Main St, Columbus, OH 43209.

HICKMAN, JERRY A.
Administrator. **PERSONAL:** Born Oct 03, 1946, Philadelphia, PA. **EDUCATION:** Philadelphia Com Coll, AA 1971. **CAREER:** Parkview Hosp Phila, instr of inserv educ, asst supr of nursing 1973-76; nursing 1973-76; Philadelphia Coll of Osteo Medicine, operating room supr 1971-73, admin of primary health care ctr 1976-82. **ORGANIZATIONS:** Mem TREA Peoples Health Serv of W Philadelphia 1976-78; bd of dir W Philadelphia Com Mental Health Consortium 1976-82; bd dir Philadelphia C of C 1976-82; lay reader St Andrew St Monica Episcopal Ch 1976-; council mem Philadelphia Council Boy Scouts of Amer 1978-; bd mem, chair Consortium CA #4 Inc Comm Mental Health & Mental Retardation Progs 1979-82. **MILITARY SERVICE:** USN 2/c petty officer (e-4) 1964-67. **BUSINESS ADDRESS:** Dir of Nursing Services, Greenwich Home for Children, 2601 South 9th St, Philadelphia, PA 19148.

HICKMAN, THOMAS CARLYLE
Physician. **PERSONAL:** Born Dec 25, 1932, St Paul, MN; married Norma; children: Thomas Jr, Staci, Michael, Eric. **EDUCATION:** Univ Denver, BA 1953;Univ CO Med Sch, 1953-57;Univ MI Wayne Co Gen Hosp, resd 1957-62. **CAREER:** Univ CO Med Sch, surg self asst clin prof; Denver Gen Hosp, clin instr. **ORGANIZATIONS:** Annual lectr Alpha Epsilon Delta; past med dir Malcom X Drug Abuse Prgm dir counc for pubTV denver channel 6 PBS; city park manor; past chf med dir Air Force Attng & Fin Ctr; consult Gen Surg Lowry AF Clinic; mem State Bd Soc Serv; mem Mile High Med Soc; mem phys adv bd Blue Shield Blue Cross of CO; flw Am Coll Surg; dir Am Cancer Soc; mem CO Heart Assn; past pres Denver Chap NAACP; reg v chmn NAACP ; dir Alumni ComUniv of CO MedSch; mem Kappa Alphs Psi Frat; Southwestern Surg Cong; Owls Club Denver. **HONORS/ACHIEVEMENTS:** Publ "Abdominal Paracenteses" Surg Clinics N Am 1969; "Duodenal Obstruction & Second to Aortic Ansurrysm". **BUSINESS ADDRESS:** Medical Dir, East Denver Health Care Center, MD FACS, 2800 Race St, Denver, CO 80205.

HICKMON, NED
Physician. **PERSONAL:** Born Dec 05, 1934, Bishopville, SC; married Consuella Anderson; children: Ned Norman, David Wesley, Chery A. **EDUCATION:** SC St Clg, BS 1955; Meharry Med Clg Nashville, TN, MD 1959. **CAREER:** Huron Rd Hosp Cleveland OH, intrn 1959-60; HG Phillips Hosp St Louis, MO, res ob/gyn 1960-62; G W Hubbard Hosp Meharry Med Clg Nashvl, chf resob/gyn 1962-63 us army hosp bremerhaven, germany, chief ob/gyn 1963-66; patterson army hosp ft monmouth, nJ, asst chf ob/gyn 1966-67; Private Prctc Hartford, CT, obstetrics & gyn 1968-. **ORGANIZATIONS:** Dir, pres Comm Hlth Serv Hartford, CT 1972-; mem Alpha Phi Alpha Frat Inc Sigma Pi Phi Frat Inc; dir CT Unit of Am Cancer Soc. **MILITARY SERVICE:** 'US Med Corps capt 4 yrs. **BUSINESS ADDRESS:** President, Ned Hickmon, M D P C, 140 Woodland St, Hartford, CT 06105.

HICKS, ARTHUR JAMES
Educator. **PERSONAL:** Born Feb 26, 1938, Jackson, MS; married Pearlie Mae Little; children: Arnetta Renee, Roselyn Marie. **EDUCATION:** Tougaloo Coll, BS 1960; Univ Illinois, PhD 1971; Missouri Botanical Gdns, NEA Postdoctoral Fellowship 1975-76; Natl Inst Health Extramural Assoc 1982; Inst of Educ Management, Harvard Univ 1989. **CAREER:** Grenada City School, biology & gen sci teacher chmn sci div 1960-64; Botany Dept Univ Illinois, grad stud 1965-71; Botany Dept Univ of Georgia, asst prof 1971-77; Natl Sci Foundation, vstg grants officer 1987; Biology Dept NC A&T, prof & chmn 1977-88; dean, Coll of Arts and Sciences 1988-. **ORGANIZATIONS:** Amer Inst of Biological Sci; Amer Soc of Plant Taxonomists; Assn of SE Biologists; Botanical Soc of Amer; Georgia Acad of Sci; Intern Assn of Plant Taxonomists; Mississippi Academy of Sci; Sigma Xi; Torrey Botanical Club; past co-pres Gaines School PTA Athens 1973-74; bd of dir NE Girl Scouts of Amer 1977; bd of trustees Hill First Bapt Church Athens 1977; mem Swim Bd of Gov Athens Park & Rec Dist Athens 1977; mem Natural Areas Adv Com to North Carolina Dept of Natural Resources & Comm Devel 1978; adv bd Guilford Co NC Environmental Quality 1979-; mem Alpha Phi Alpha. **HONORS/ACHIEVEMENTS:** Hon mem Beta Kappa Chi Sci Honor Soc 1960; sr bio award Tougaloo Coll 1960; NSF Summer Fellowship SIU Carbondale 1961; Univ Illinois Botany Fellowship Urbana 1968-69; So Fellowship Found Fund Fellow Univ Illinois Urbana 1969-71; NEA Fellowship Missouri Bot Gdn St Louis 1975-76; auth "Apomixis in Xanthium?" Watsonia 1975 "Plant mounting problem overcome with the use of self-adhesive plastic covering" Torreya 1976; co-auth "A Bibliography of Plant Collection & HerbariumCuration" Taxon 27(1) 63-99 "botany lab manual" u GA bookstore 1974 "botany lab manual" paje pub co atlanta 1976. **BUSINESS ADDRESS:** Dean, NC A&T StateUniv, College of Arts and Sciences, 312 N Dudley St Crosby Hall, Greensboro, NC 27411.

HICKS, CLAYTON NATHANIEL
Educational administrator, association executive, optometrist. **PERSONAL:** Born May 02, 1943, Columbus, OH; son of Amos Nathaniel Hicks and Augusta Louvenia Hicks. **EDUCATION:** OH State Univ, BS 1964, OD 1970. **CAREER:** OH Dept of Health, microbiologist 1965-70; OSU Coll of Optomertry, clinical instr 1970-; Driving Park Vision Ctr, optometrist 1970-; OH Dept of Human Svcs, optometric consult 1977-; Natl Optometric Assn, pres, meeting/conference planner 1984-; Annette 2 Cosmetiques, consultant, 1989-. **ORGANIZATIONS:** Pres Columbus Panhellenic Council 1975-80, Columbus Inner City Lions Club 1977-80, Neighborhood House Inc, Bd of Dir 1979-81, Martin Luther King Holiday Observance Comm 1981-83, Alpha Phi Alpha Frat 1981-83, Natl Optometric Assn 1983-85; Driving Park Mental Health Comm 1984; Nat'l Coalition of Black Meeting Planners 1984; consultant, Annette Cosmetiques, 1989-; president, Alpha Rho Lambda Educ Foundation 1989-. **HONORS/ACHIEVEMENTS:** Outstanding Serv Awd Alpha Phi Alpha Frat 1981; Optometrist of the Year Natl Optometric Assn 1983; Citizen of the Week WCKX Radio 1986; Political Leadership Awd 29th Dist Citizens Caucus. **BUSINESS ADDRESS:** President, Natl Optometric Assn, 1489 Livingston Ave, Columbus, OH 43205.

HICKS, DAISY C.
Educational administrator. **PERSONAL:** Born Feb 13, 1919, Conyers, GA; married James Hicks; children: Norma Robinson, Schoni Skrug. **EDUCATION:** Miner Teachers Coll Wash, DC, BS elem educ 1941; Queens Coll Flushing, NY, Professional Cert Guidance 1962; NY Univ, MA early childhood educ 1952; NYU/Queesns Coll/City Coll, NY State Cert Dist Admin/School Admin 1982; NY Univ NY, candidate for doctoral degree 1979-85. **CAREER:** US Treasury, Washington DC, sales US Treasury Bonds 1941-45; Afro-Amer Newspaper, fashion editor 1945-49; Div Personnel Bureau of Educ Staffing, asst to the dir 1972-76; New York City Bd of Educ Div of Personnel, head Bureau of Special Recruitment 1976-81, administrator, dir 1979-. **ORGANIZATIONS:** Pres NY Assn of Black Educators 1975-79; pres 402 W 153rd St Coop New York City 1983-85; exec dir Skills Review for Black Youth Seeking Scholarships for Higher Educ 1978-85. **HONORS/ACHIEVEMENTS:** Woman of the Yr Zeta Phi Beta Sorority 1975; listed Who's Who Among Black Americans 1981; Comm Leader Award AKA Sorority (Bronx Chpt) 1985; Natl Educational Leadership Award NAACP 1981. **HOME ADDRESS:** 402 West 153rd St, New York, NY 11301. **BUSINESS ADDRESS:** Dir Bureau of Spec Recruitmn, NY City Bd of Educ Div Personne, 65 Court St, Brooklyn, NY 11201.

HICKS, DELPHUS VAN, JR.
Sheriff. **PERSONAL:** Born Feb 06, 1939, Ashland, MS; married Frankie Marie Hamer; children: Early Hue, James Earl, Diane Lanell. **EDUCATION:** TN Law Enforcement Acad, attended 1974. **CAREER:** Hardeman Co Sheriff Dept, sheriff 1978-; chief dep sheriff 1974, 78; Hardemann Co, dep sheriff 1969-74; Leadman Reichhold Chem Inc, mixer/ insp 1967-69; Williams Candy Co, stockman 1960-62. **ORGANIZATIONS:** Mem Hardeman & Fayette Law Assn 1974-80; mem Mason Goodwill Lodge #253 1977-80. **HONORS/ACHIEVEMENTS:** Recipient Soldier of the Year Award AUS 1964; Good Conduct Medal AUS 1964; First Black Chief Dep Sheriff Hardeman Co 1974; First Black Sheriff State of TN 1978. **MILITARY SERVICE:** AUS sgt e-5 1962-67. **BUSINESS ADDRESS:** Hardeman Co Sheriff Dept, 315 E Market St, Bolivar, TN 38008.

HICKS, DORIS ASKEW
Retired educational administrator. **PERSONAL:** Born May 24, 1926, Sulphur Springs, TX; married George P; children: Sherra Daunn. **EDUCATION:** Butler Coll, AA 1946; Bishop Coll, BA 1948;Univ of TX, MLS 1959. **CAREER:** Rochester City Sch Dist Rochester NY, dir learning resources 1973-; Rochester City Sch Dist Rochester, sch librarian 1969-

73; Macedonia Sch Dist Texarkana, sch librarian 1962-69; Bowie Co Common & Independent Sch, multi sch librarian 1654-62; Naples Independent Sch Dist, tchr librarian 1952-54; Quintman Independent Sch Dist, tchr 1950-52. **ORGANIZATIONS:** Vp Sch Library Media Section/NY Library Assn; vice pres elect Sc H Library Media Section/NY Library Assn; pres/unit V chmn Am Assn of Sch Librarian/ALA 1979-80; mem Mt Olivet Bapt Ch Scholarship Com 1976-; bd mem Hillside Children's Center 1977-; chair felloship com Rochester Chap of Zonata 1979-80. **HONORS/ACHIEVEMENTS:** NDEA grant Fed Govt Coe Coll IA 1964; NDEA grant Govt SyracuseUniv NY 1973; sch library & media program of year Am Assn of Sch Librarians 1975.

HICKS, E. B.
Clergyman. **PERSONAL:** Born Jul 11, 1907, Wichita, KS; married Roena S Sayers; children: 6 children. **EDUCATION:** Central Bapt Sem, BTh 1934; Washburn Univ, BA 1951;Central Bapt Sem M Div 1986; Monrovia Coll & Industrial Inst DD 1961. **CAREER:** 1st Bapt Church Paxico KS, pastor 1934-37; 2ncd Bapt Church Holton KS, pastor 1936-38; Calvary Bapt Church Duluth MN, pastor 1938-42; Missionary of the Missionary Bapt State Conv of KS, exec sec 1945-56; Amer Bapt Home Mission Soc, field rep 1956-61; Comm Witness Prog, assoc dir 1961-66; Inner City WorkAmer Bapt Home Mission Soc, prog asst 1966-67; Div of Parish Devel Amer Bapt Home Mission Soc, asst sec 1969-71; Amer Bapt Church of the South, reg exec min 1971-76; OH Bapt Conv ABC, minister of coop relationships (retired 1984),. **ORGANIZATIONS:** Mem bd of dir Chicago Bapt Inst Chicago 1957-72; bd dir Brooklyn Bapt Ed Ctr Brooklyn NY 1957-72; bd dir Bapt Ed Ctr New York City 1962-72; bd of dir TopekaBoys Club Topeka KS 1966-69; mem Amer Bapt Ministers Council 1971-76, Atlanta Bapt Ministers Union 1971, Natl Staff Council of Amer Bapt Church 1972-76;Butler St YMCA 1972-76; bd trustees Morehouse School of Religion 1973-77. **HONORS/ACHIEVEMENTS:** Churchmanship Citation Central Bapt Sem Kansas City 1971; 25 yrs Serv Awd Amer Bapt Home Mission Soc; 1st Black Exec Minister of Region/State/City in Amer Bapt Church of USA;Major Contributor to ABC-PNC Fund of Renewal; Service Awd from Foreign Mission Brd, Nat'l Bapt Conv USA, Inc; Service Awd Amer Bapt Black Caucus; PIoneer Awd for service 1937-1984 to Black Amer Bapt Churches; Service to Columbus Ohio Churches, Baptist Pastor's Conference; Distinguished Bridge-Builder Award for 52 continues years Ohio Baptist Convention, affiliated with Amer Bapt CHurches; Awd from Exec Ministers of Amer Bapt Regions, States and Citiesfor the Interracial Ministry throughout the United States. **MILITARY SERVICE:** AUS chaplain 1942-54.

HICKS, EDITH A.
Elected government official, educational administrator. **PERSONAL:** Born Sep 06, 1939, Barnwell, SC; married James Adams; children: Ronald, Curtis, Craig, Paul, Paula, Kevin. **EDUCATION:** Antioch Coll, BA 1974, MA 1976. **CAREER:** Bd of Educ NYC, paraprof 1967-69; Morrisania Comm Corp, training sp 1969-70; Children Circle Day Care, day care dir 1970-75; Comm Sch Bd NYC, exec asst 1975-77; Bd of Educ NYC, asst principal. **ORGANIZATIONS:** Vice pres Comm Sch Bd of NYC; adjunct prof Touro Coll; instructor College of New Rochelle; female dist leader 78th Assembly Dist NYC; chairperson People's Development Corp, mem Comm Planning Bd #3. **HONORS/ACHIEVEMENTS:** Sojourner Truth Black Women Business & Prof Group New York City Chapt; Woman of the Yr Morrisania Comm Council; Outstanding Comm Serv Bronx Unity Democratic Club. **HOME ADDRESS:** 575 E 168th St, Bronx, NY 10456.

HICKS, ELEANOR
Government official, educator. **PERSONAL:** Born Feb 21, 1943, Columbus, GA. **EDUCATION:** Univ of Cincinnati, BA (fgn affairs cum laude) 1965; John Hopkins Sch of Advanced Intl Studies (SAIS), MA Intl Relations 1967. **CAREER:** Dept of State US Embassy Cairo, deputy polit sect present; Dept of State Central Am Affairs, deputy 1976-78; Dept of State, policy analyst 1975-76; US consul to Monaco & in Nice Dept of State, 1972-75; Thailand Dept of State, desk officer 1970-72. **ORGANIZATIONS:** Bd mem Women's Action Orgn Dept of State 1978; mem Middle East Inst; mem Alpha Kappa Alpha; mem Phi Beta KappaUniv of Cincinnati (UC) 1964-. **HONORS/ACHIEVEMENTS:** Honorific award Chevalier De Tastevin 1973; civic award in Intl Realm Cavalieri Del Nouvo Europe (Italy) 1974; scholarship award named after her for outstanding arts & sci student (UC) Annual Eleanor Hicks Award 1974; legendary woman award St Vincent's Birmingham AL 1975. **BUSINESS ADDRESS:** Professor of Political Science, Univ of Cincinnati, Clifton Ave (ML627), Cincinnati, OH 45221.

HICKS, H. BEECHER, JR.
Clergyman. **PERSONAL:** Born Jun 17, 1944, Baton Rouge, LA; son of H. Beecher Hicks and Eleanor Frazier Hicks; married Elizabeth Harrison; children: H Beecher III, Ivan Douglas, Kristin Elizabeth. **EDUCATION:** Univ of AR Pine Bluff, BA 1964; Colgate Rochester, MDiv 1967, Dr of Ministry 1975; Richmond Virginia Seminary LLD honorary. **CAREER:** Second Baptist Church, intern pastorate 1965-68; Irondequoit United Church of Christ, minister to youth 1967-68; Mt Ararat Baptist Church, sr minister 1968-73; Antioch Baptist Church, minister 1973-77; Metro Baptist Church, senior minister 1977-. **ORGANIZATIONS:** Chmn Bd of Funeral Dirs 1985; vp, Eastern Reg Natl Black Pastors Conf; admin Natl Black Pastors Conf; bd Council for Court Excellence; asst sec Progressive Natl Baptist Convention, Co-chair American Baptist Ministers Council of D.C., pres Kerygma Assoc, A Religious Consulting Service; pres Martin Luther King Fellows, Inc; co-chair Ministers in Partnership (Pregnancy Prevention). **HONORS/ACHIEVEMENTS:** "Give Me This Mountain" Houston TX 1976; "Images of the Black Preacher, The Man Nobody Knows" Valley Forge PA 1977; "The Black Church as a Support System for Black Men on the Simon Syndrome" Howard Univ; Comm Leaders & Noteworthy Amers 1977; Gubernatorial Citation for Serv 1977; Outstanding Personalities of the South 1977; Martin Luther King Fellowship in Black Church Studies 1972-75; Preaching Through A Storm Zondervan Press 1987. **BUSINESS ADDRESS:** Senior Minister, Metropolitan Baptist Church, 1225 R St NW, Washington, DC 20009.

HICKS, HENDERSON
Business executive. **PERSONAL:** Born Jul 11, 1930, Fairmont, WV; married Barbara; children: Alan H, Eric A. **EDUCATION:** City Coll NY, BBA 1958. **CAREER:** Mark IV Travel Serv NYC, officer owner 1968-75; NY Met Trans Auth, dep asst contrlr 1968-; Neighbrhd Bds HARYOU-ACT, coord contrlr 1965-68; NY State Atty Gen Office & NYS Housing & Fin Agy, auditor investigator 1962-65; NYC, catering mgr 1958-62; Gr NY Ballroom Assn, rep 1960-62. **ORGANIZATIONS:** City Coll Alum Assn; Nat Assn Black Accnt 1971-72; NAACP; NY Urban League; dir 100 Black Men Inc; bd of gov Pathways for Youth (Boys Athletic League)New York City 1985-; trustee Metro Suburban Bus Authority/TWU Pension & Welfare Fund 1985-. **MILITARY SERVICE:** AUS adj gen corp 1951-53. **BUSINESS ADDRESS:** Deputy Comptroller, Metropolitan Trans Authority, 347 Madison Ave, New York, NY 10017.

HICKS, HENRY BEECHER, SR.
Clergyman. **PERSONAL:** Born Sep 21, 1912, Uniontown, AL; married Eleanor Frazier; children: Sandra H Beecher, Jr, William J. **EDUCATION:** Leland Clg, BA; Oberlin Grad Sch of Theol, MDiv, 1944; Leland Clg, DD 1947; Central State U, DD 1963. **CAREER:** Mt Olivet Bapt Ch Columbus, sr Minister 1946-; Hicks Travel Serv Inc, fdr 1966; Mt Olivet Credit Union, fdr 1960; Mt Olivet Bapt Ch, designer & construction supr; Bapt World Alliance, exec comm. **ORGANIZATIONS:** Past pres La HS Principals Assc; chptr mem Omega Psi Phi; mem Natl Cncl Chs; pgm chmn Progressive Natl Bapt Con. **HONORS/ACHIEVEMENTS:** Churchmanship awrd OH Bapt Gen Assc Inc; awrd in theology & soc welfare Omega Psi Phi; frontiers intrntl pres's citiation Columbus Chpt; man of yr Prince Halle Masons; awrd for distngshd ldrshp in ed Columbus Bd Ed.

HICKS, HILLY GENE
Actor. **PERSONAL:** Born May 04, 1950, Los Angeles, CA; children: Hilly Jr. **EDUCATION:** Occidental Coll, AB 1973; Am Bapt Sem. **CAREER:** ActorTV & motion pictures; filmes include, "They Call Me Mr Tibbs"; "Halls of Anger" 1970; "The New Centurions" 1972; TV includes, "Bill Cosby Show", "Mod Squad", "Night Gallery", "Adam-12", "Mash", "Cannon", "Barnaby Jones", "Roots". **ORGANIZATIONS:** Co-pastor New Shiloh Bapt Ch. **HONORS/ACHIEVEMENTS:** Spl citation People's Choice 1977; protestant ministers flwsp 1972.

HICKS, JOHN J.
Clergyman. **PERSONAL:** Born Feb 13, 1916, Bronwood, GA; married Pollie Bledsoe; children: John Jr, Eldon, Paula, Raiford, Emma. **EDUCATION:** Paine Coll, AB 1938; Gammon Sem, BD 1941; USC, MTh 1944; Reid Sch of Religion, DD 1954; Gammon Sem, DD 1957. **CAREER:** St Mark's United Meth Ch, pastor present; Meth Ch Barnesville, pastor; St John's Meth Ch LA; Union Mem Ch St Louis. **ORGANIZATIONS:** Pres bd of Educ St Louis 1959-64; pres Comm Sch Bd #5 NY 1974-; mem bd of Educ Dist #6 New York City 1965-69; mem NAACP Urban League; bd of mgrs Harlem YMCA 1972-; bd dir Harlem Counselling Ser; pres Manhattan Council of Ch1973-; Omega Psi Phi. **BUSINESS ADDRESS:** 49 Edgecombe Ave, New York, NY 10030.

HICKS, LEON NATHANIEL
Educator. **PERSONAL:** Born Dec 25, 1933, Deerfield, FL. **EDUCATION:** Univ KS State, BS;Univ IA Stanford, MA post grad. **CAREER:** FL A&M Univ Concord, Lincoln Univ, Lehigh Univ, Webster Coll, teaching present. **ORGANIZATIONS:** Coll Art Assn; Nat Conf Artists; Intl Platform Assn; Brandywine Graphic Workshop; Creatadrama Soc; Kappa Alpha Psi; chmn bd exec & vice pres Hicks Etchprint Inc Philadelphia 1974. **HONORS/ACHIEVEMENTS:** State rep Nat Conf Artists MO first prizes prints art work; Dictionary Intl Biography 1974; Black Artists Art publs 1969; Am Negro Printmakers 1966;Directions Afro Am Art 1974; Engraving Am 1974; Albrecht Art Mus St Joseph. **MILITARY SERVICE:** AUS 1953-56. **BUSINESS ADDRESS:** Webeter Coll Art Dept, 470 E Lockwood, St Louis, MO 63119.

HICKS, LOUIS CHARLES, JR.
Curator. **PERSONAL:** Born Aug 31, 1951, Austin, TX. **EDUCATION:** Univ of TX-Austin, BA 1974, BFA 1978. **CAREER:** Austin Public Library, librarian Carver Museum 1980-83; Austin Parks & Rec Dept, curator Carver Museum 1983-. **ORGANIZATIONS:** Ex officio mem Black Arts Alliance 1984-86; mem Austin Comm for UNICEF 1984-86; advisor Austin Children's Museum 1986-87; mem Amer Assoc of Museums, TX Assoc of Museums, African Amer Museums Assoc, Amer Assoc State & Local History. **HONORS/ACHIEVEMENTS:** Field Reviewer Inst of Museum Serv 1985; 1985 Councilor at Large African Amer Museums Assoc 1985; Adv Comm mem Fine Arts Continuing Educ Comm 1985-86;Project Dir of Prod Exhibit Street, The Image of the Black Enterpreneur 1986-87. **BUSINESS ADDRESS:** Curator, Carver Museum, 1165 Angelina St, Austin, TX 78702.

HICKS, MARYELLEN
Judge. **PERSONAL:** Born Mar 10, 1949, Odessa, TX; daughter of Albert G. Whitlock and Kathleen Durham; divorced; children: Erin Kathleen. **EDUCATION:** TX Womans Univ, BA, Grad Work 1971; TX Tech Sch of Law, DJ 1974. **CAREER:** Bonner & Hicks, atty at law 1975-77; City of Ft Worth, mncpl ct jdg 1977-82; 231st Judicial Dist Ct, dist jdg 1983-85. **ORGANIZATIONS:** Fellow Natl Endwmnt for the Humanities 1980; con sec Natl Women Achvmnt 1985; State Bang TX; Natl Bar Assn; vice pres Natl Cncl of Negro Women; D Elta Sigma Theta Sor Jack & Jill Inc; pres Font Work Black Bar Assoc; vice pres Sojourner Truth Cmty Theatre. **HONORS/ACHIEVEMENTS:** Outstndng Black Wmn 1982; Outstndng Black Lawyer 1982; Female Newsmaker 1 Yr Press Club 1982; Citizen Awd Black Pilots of Amer 1986; Citizen of the Year SS Dillow Elem Schl 1987; Alumna Award Texas Woman's Univ 1989. **BUSINESS ADDRESS:** District Judge, Tarrant County, 100 N Houston, Fort Worth, TX 76102.

HICKS, RICHARD LOUIS, JR.
Clergyman. **PERSONAL:** Born Nov 17, 1921, Alexandria, LA; married Pearl; children: Cynthia Delores, Patricia Agnes, William Joseph, Richard Lami. **EDUCATION:** FL A&M U, BA 1949; Case Western Reserve U, MA 1952; Baxley Hall, MDiv 1956. **CAREER:** FL A&M, instructor 1949-52; St Andrews, curate 1956-57; Cuttington Clg Divinity Sch, chaplain 1957-60; Trinity Pro Cathedral, rector 1957-60; Ch Redeemer,vicar 1960-64; A&T U, Campus Minister 1960-64; St Andrews Ch, rector 1964-67; St Philips Ch, rector 1967-69; Diocese PA, campus minister 1969-. **ORGANIZATIONS:** Mem Natl Campus Ministries Assc; Episcopal Soc Mnstry Higher Ed; Ch Society Clg Work; PA Campus Ministers Assc; Pride Inc; Natl Com Black Churchmen; Ministries Blacks Higher Ed; Union Black Episcopalians; NAACP; PA Transactional Analysis Seminar; E Inst Transactional Analysis & Gestalt; Intrntl Analysis Assc; mem Mayor's Com Race Relations 1962-64; pres Black Ministers Forum 1962-64; vice pres Integrated Ministers Assc 1962-64; chmn Ctzns & Coordinating Com 1963; founder Cincinnati OIC 1965; exec minister Chester Co Campus & Brandywine Deanery. **HONORS/ACHIEVEMENTS:** Canon watson awrd Ecellency Reading 1955; canon watson flwshp 1964; order afrcn redemption Liberia 1959; plaque Cincinnati OIC 1967.

HICKS, RICHARD R.
Clergyman. **PERSONAL:** Born Oct 20, 1931, Milford, DE; married Thelma Miller; children: Terri Lynn, Stephanie, Georgie Sue, Marjorie Louise. **EDUCATION:** Hampton Inst, BS 1958; Crozer Theol Sem, MDiv 1964; VA Theol Sem;Univ MD; Howard U. **CAREER:** Williams VA, tchr 1958-59; Charlotte NC 1959-60; ferris Sch ofr Boys, counselor 1961-62; United Meth Chs, Townsend, DE, pastor 1961-63; Chestertown, MD1963-67; Princess Anne, MD 1967-70; Wesley FoundUniv of MD Eastern Shore, dir 1967-70; Mt Joy United Meth Ch Wilm DE, pastor 1970-71; SE Reg Sec United Ministries in Higher Ed, 1971-74; Ministries to Blacks in Higher Edn, exec dir 1975-79; Howard Univ Wash DC, United Methodist chaplain 1977-80; Huntingtown Chg United meth Church, pastor 1980-85; Morgan State Univ Baltimore, instr religious studies 1985-; Morgan Christian Center, dir 1985-. **ORGANIZATIONS:** Bd dir Black Meth for Ch Renewal 1972-75; SE coord Nat Campus Min Assn; Minority-in-Serv Training & Scholarship Com 1976-76; Nat Conf Black Churchmen; past chmn Chestertown MD NAACP exec com; mem ACLU Cons, numerous papers & publs in field. **MILITARY SERVICE:** AUS first lt 1952-55.

HICKS, VERONICA ABENA
Laboratory manager. **PERSONAL:** Born Feb 22, 1949, Awate, Ghana;daughter of Stephen Kwani Kokroko and Salone Atawa Dzeble, Kokroko; married Anthony M Hicks, Jun 06, 1980; children: Esi, Gloria, Tania. **EDUCATION:** Univ of Ghana, Legon, BSc 1971, graduate diploma, 1972; Iowa State Univ, Ames, IA, MSc, 1976, PhD, 1980. **CAREER:** Ministry of Agriculture, Accra Ghana, nutrition consultant, 1976-77; ISU Dept Biochemistry & Biophys, Ames, IA, postdoctoral research fellow, 1980-81; Kellogg Company, Battle Creek, MI, nutritionist 1981-82, mgr nutrition research, 1982-84, dir nutrition, 1984-86, dir chemistry & physiology, 1986-. **ORGANIZATIONS:** Mem, Advisory Bd, Iowa State Coll of Consumer & Family Sciences, 1985-88; mem, Infant Health Advisory Bd, Calhoun County Dept of Health, 1983-. **BUSINESS ADDRESS:** Dir, Chemisty & Physiology, Kellogg Co, Science & Technical Center, 235 Porter St, Battle Creek, MI 49017.

HICKS, WILLIAM H.
State official. **PERSONAL:** Born Aug 27, 1925, Littleton, NC; married Margaret; children: Chiquita, Patricia, William, Linda. **EDUCATION:** William Patterson Coll, BA. **CAREER:** State Co Housing, dir present; NJ State, assemblyman 1971-75. **ORGANIZATIONS:** Bd dir Paterson Boys Club; Damon House adv om equal opportunities ramapo coll; alderman patersons 4th ard 1966-71; mem am legion post 268. **MILITARY SERVICE:** USN air corps 1943-46. **BUSINESS ADDRESS:** State County, 317 Pennsylvania, Paterson, NJ 07503.

HICKS, WILLIAM J.
Physician. **PERSONAL:** Born 1948. **EDUCATION:** Morehouse College, BS, 1970; University of Pittsburgh, School of Medicine, Pittsburgh, Pa, MD, 1974. **CAREER:** University Hospital of Pittsburgh, Pittsburgh, PA, intern and resident, 1974-79; Grant Medical Center and Saint Anthony's Hospital, Columbus, OH, staff member. **ORGANIZATIONS:** President, National Black Health Planners Association, Washington, DC. **BUSINESS ADDRESS:** St Anthony's Hospital, 1450 Hawthorne Avenue, Columbus, OH 43203. *

HICKS, WILLIAM L.
Professional engineer, general contractor. **PERSONAL:** Born Jan 19, 1928, Yoakum, TX. **EDUCATION:** Coll of Engr UC Berkeley, BS 1954. **CAREER:** Corps of Engrs LA, engr trainee; Daniel Mann Johnson & Mendenhall LA, design engr; Ralph M Parsons Co LA, design engr; Mackintosh & Mackintosh LA, civil engr; Hick Constrn Co, owner. **ORGANIZATIONS:** Mem Am Soc & Civil Engrs.

HICKS, WILLIE LEE
Business executive. **PERSONAL:** Born Jan 31, 1931, Bartow, GA; married Doris B Culley. **EDUCATION:** Baruch Sch of Bus & Pub Admin, BBA 1960; Heffley & Brown Sec Sch, attended 1955-56. **CAREER:** Durojaye Assn, retailer distributor mfg 1968-73; African Investment Partnership Ltd, 1974; Durojaye Trading & Commodity Corp, 1976-; United Mutual Life, 1975-. **ORGANIZATIONS:** Sec Nile-Niger Corp 1957; pres Durojaye Trading & Commodity Corp 1959-62; HKM Intl 1967; sec Natl Postal Alliance 1956; NAACP 1956; sec Angola Refugee Rescue Com; vice pres Soc of African Descendents; African-Amer Tchrs Assn; numerous other affiliations. **MILITARY SERVICE:** USAF A/1C 1951-55. **BUSINESS ADDRESS:** Agent, United Mutual Life, 310 Lenox Ave, New York, NY 10027.

HICKS-BARTLETT, SHARON THERESA
Social scientist. **PERSONAL:** Born Nov 22, 1951, Chicago, IL; married David Charles Bartlett; children: Alani Rosa Hicks. **EDUCATION:** Roosevelt Univ, BA 1976, MA 1981; Univ of Chicago, MA 1985. **CAREER:** IL Council on Cont Medical Educ, prog & activities sec 1975-78; Amherst Assocs, office mgr 1978-80; Univ of Chicago, convocation coord 1980-81; Univof Chicago Urban Family Life Project, rsch asst 1985-. **ORGANIZATIONS:** Instructor Thornton Comm Coll 1982 & 1987; rsch asst Univ of Chicago 1983; freelance researcher Better Boys Foundation 1985; volunteer East Chicago Heights Comm Serv Ctr 1986-; literacy tutor (adults) Literacy Volunteers of Amer 1987-. **HONORS/ACHIEVEMENTS:** Art & Science Scholar Awd Roosevelt Univ 1980-81; Title IX Fellowship for Grad Study Univ of Chicago 1981-85; Danforth-Compton Dissertation Awd Univ of Chicago 1986-87; Amer Sociological Soc Dissertation Awd Univ of Chicago 1986-87. **HOME ADDRESS:** 66 Water St, Park Forest, IL 60466. **BUSINESS ADDRESS:** Research Asst/Doctoral Student, Univ of Chicago, Urban Family Life Project, 5811 So Kenwood Ave, Chicago, IL 60637.

HICKSON, EUGENE, SR.
Business executive. **PERSONAL:** Born Jun 10, 1930, Arcadia, FL; married Verlene Deloris Stebbins; children: Eugene Jr, Vergena, Edward. **EDUCATION:** Gubton-jones Clg of Mortuary Sci, 1952. **CAREER:** Hickson Funeral Home;; owner; Arcadia FL, mayor. **ORGANIZATIONS:** 32 Degree Mason; Shriner; deacon Elizabeth Bapt Ch; chmn C of C; 2nd vice pres FA Martician Assc. **HONORS/ACHIEVEMENTS:** FL Mortician Assoc Awd Sarasota Womens Clb 1971; FL Mortician Assoc 1972; FL Mortician Assoc1975.

HICKSON, SHERMAN RUBEN
Dentist. **PERSONAL:** Born Apr 03, 1950, Ridgeland, SC; son of Glover Hickson and Justine Hickson; married Eavon Holloway; children: Sherman Jr (dec), LaTonya, Thurston, Adrienne. **EDUCATION:** SC State Coll, BS 1971; Meharry Medical Coll Sch of Dentistry, DDS 1975. **CAREER:** Southside YMCA Augusta GA, Korean karate instructor 1986-87; Private Practice, general dentistry 1977-87. **ORGANIZATIONS:** Mem SC Dental Assoc 1975-, Palmetto Medical Dental & Pharm Assoc 1976-87, Natl Dental Assoc 1976-87, Acad of General Dentistry 1978-87; mem Dickerson Lodge #314 Mason Prince Hall 1981-87, CC Johnson Consistory #136 1982-87, Cairo Temple #125 Shriners 1982-87, Orion Chap #135 Eastern Star 1986-87; 2nd degree black belt World Tae Kwon Do Assoc mem 1982-87; trustee, Friendship Baptist Church; life mem, NAACP; life mem, Omega Psi Phi Fraternity Inc. **MILITARY SERVICE:** AUS capt 2 yrs; Letter of Commendation 1975-77. **BUSINESS ADDRESS:** Dentist, 500 Richland Ave E, Aiken, SC 29801.

HICKSON, WILLIAM F., JR.
Dentist. **PERSONAL:** Born Aug 27, 1936, Aiken, SC; married Charlestine Dawson; children: Nina R, William F, III, G G Oneal. **EDUCATION:** SC State Clg, BS 1956; Meharry, DDS 1962. **CAREER:** GG Oneal Dentist, pvt prac. **ORGANIZATIONS:** Am Natl SC Palmetto Dental Assc; Cty dental dir OEO State; pres Palmetto Dental Assc; reg consult HEW Dist IV; mem Beta & Kappa Chi; Omega Psi Phi; past basileus Alpha Iota Boule; past sire Archon; Natl Bd Missions United Presbyterian Ch; mem NAACP; Fed Dental Cons. **MILITARY SERVICE:** AUS capt 1963-65. **BUSINESS ADDRESS:** Dentist, 109 Treadwell St, Orangeburg, SC 29115.

HIGGINBOTHAM, A. LEON, JR.
Judge. **PERSONAL:** Born Feb 25, 1928, Trenton, NJ; children (previous marriage): Stephen, Karen, Kenneth; married Evelyn Brooks. **EDUCATION:** Antioch Coll, BA 1949; Yale Law Schl, LLB 1952. **CAREER:** US Dist Ct of PA, US dist judge 1964-77; Fed Trade Comm, commissioner 1962-64; Norris, Green Harris & Higginbotham, partner 1954-62. **ORGANIZATIONS:** Lecturer Harvard Law School; adjunct prof Univ of PA. **HONORS/ACHIEVEMENTS:** Author, more than 100 published articles; author "In the Matter of Color; Race and the American Legal Prcess," Oxford Univ Press 1978; over 40 honorary degrees. **BUSINESS ADDRESS:** Circuit Judge, US Court of Appeals, 22613 United States Courthouse, Philadelphia, PA 19106.

HIGGINBOTHAM, KENNETH DAY, SR.
Clergyman. **PERSONAL:** Born May 01, 1928, Worcester, MA; married Ruth Kidd; children: Kenneth Jr, Maretta, Michael, Paul, Stephen, Keith, Andrea, Christopher. **EDUCATION:** Trinity Coll, BA 1950; Berkeley Div Sch, MDiv 1954; Yale-Berkeley Div Sch, STD 1983. **CAREER:** St Philips Ch, rector 1957-68; Fisk Univ, Meharry Med Coll, TN State Univ, chaplain 1968-70; Fed City Coll, chaplain 1970-72; Episcopal Diocese of WA, asst to bishop 1971-79; Christ the Good Shepherd Ch LA, rector 1979-. **ORGANIZATIONS:** Mem Franklin Co Welfare Bd 1965-68; chaplain Crenshaw Ctr Hosp; pres of bd Good Shepherd Ctr for Independent Living; chmn Diocese An Urban Caucus; mem Program Group on Christian Educ & Leadership Training for Diocese of LA; Union of Black Episcopalians; bd mem Encl of Chs Columbus OH; Green door; standingcom Diocese of So OH; chmn Commn on Black Ministries; mem Commn on Ministry; GOE reader; deputy General Convention 1985; public advisory dir Blue Cross of California 5/1989-5/1990. **HONORS/ACHIEVEMENTS:** Pres MED USA Coll Sr Hon Soc; Fellow Bexley Hall Div Sch. **BUSINESS ADDRESS:** Rector, Christ the Good Shepherd Chrch, 3303 W Vernon Ave, Los Angeles, CA 90008.

HIGGINBOTHAM, PEYTON RANDOLPH
Physician. **PERSONAL:** Born Aug 21, 1902, Lynchburg, VA; married Miriam; children: Lynn. **EDUCATION:** Howard Univ Coll, BS Liberal Arts 1923; Howard Univ Sch Med, MD 1926; Freedman's Hosp, intern 1926-27. **CAREER:** WV State Bd Hlth, 1948-; Bluefield State Coll, 1932-; Private Practice, physician. **ORGANIZATIONS:** Mem exec com So WV VA Reg Hlth Cncl; mem WV State Med Assn; AMA; WV Med Soc; NMA; staff mem St Luke's Hosp; assoc mem Beckley Appalachian Reg Appalachian Regional Hosp; mem Princeton Meml Comm Hosp; Mercer Co Planning Commn; bd dir Bluefield Comm Hosp; mem Alpha Phi Alpha Frat; Sigma Pi Phi; HM Club Am; Physician for Welfare Rev Bd Mercer Monroe & Summers Co; mem Scott St Bapt Ch; NAACP. **HONORS/ACHIEVEMENTS:** Plaque Appalachian OH-9 Hlth Cncl; WV Med Soc; League for Serv; Freedman's Hosp; past pres plaque 50 yrs Continuous Serv; plaque Howard Univ Med Alumni Assn; plaque former interns & resd Freedmen's Hosp Med Res Capt. **BUSINESS ADDRESS:** 725 1/2 Bland St, Bluefield, WV 24701.

HIGGINBOTHAN, MAURICE JAMES
Clergyman. **PERSONAL:** Born Jun 14, 1914, Chgo; married Marian; children: Gloria Heddy, Thomas. **EDUCATION:** Lewis Inst of Chgo, BA; Garrett Theol Sem, BD; Chicago Theol Sem Roosevelt U, Grad Courses; Wilberforce U, Hon DD; Edward Waters Clg, Hon LHD. **CAREER:** Bethel AME Ch Detroit, pastor; Chicago , Evanston, pastored chs. **ORGANIZATIONS:** Chmn Finance of MI Annual AME Ch Conf; chmn Fourth Episc Dist Dels to Gen Conf of 1972; trustee Hutzell Hosp; chmn Med Dist Cncl.

HIGGINS, BENNETT EDWARD
Educator, mortician. **PERSONAL:** Born May 05, 1931, Athens, AL; married Shirley Webb; children: Bennett Dion, Melessa Shawn. **EDUCATION:** AL A&M U, BS 1953; Temple U;; Attended; Athens Clg, adv study. **CAREER:** Clements HS, Limestone Co Bd of Educ, teacher science 1957-; Peoples Funeral Home, mortician & funeral dir 1968-, owner founder 1965-; Atlanta Life Insurance Co, salesman 1953; Forniss Printing Co Birmingham, linotype operator 1953. **ORGANIZATIONS:** Pres Limestone Co NAACP 1978-; sec Limestone Dem Conf; chmn Boy Scout Troup No 154; mem Kappa Alpha Psi Frat. **HONORS/ACHIEVEMENTS:** Recipient good conduct & rifle medals AUS 1954; orgnzr Local NAACP 1968; Keep Am Beautiful City of Athens 1977; achvmnt awrd Kappa Alpha Psi Frat 1978; outst serv awrd NAACP 1980. **MILITARY SERVICE:** AUS corpl 1953-55. **BUSINESS ADDRESS:** Clements High Sch, Athens, AL 35611.

HIGGINS, CHESTER A., SR.
Journalist. **PERSONAL:** Born May 10, 1917, Chicago, IL. **EDUCATION:** KY State Coll, Frankfurt KY, 1 year; Louisville Municipal Coll, Univ of Louisville, 2 years. **CAREER:** Commr of Fed Communications Hon Benj L Hooks, special asst; Howard Univ, part-time lectr 1972-; Louisville Defender Weekly Newspaper, reporter, feature writer; Ford Motor Co & Chrysler Motor Co, industrial & ordinary ins salesman, hourly worker; Detroit Courier,

editor; Jet magazine, assoc editor, sr editor; Ebony & Tan magazines, contrib editor; Malcolm X Coll, teacher of Pioneering Black Journalism Course 1971-72; MI State Univ Ctr for Urban Affairs, lectr 1972-73; Michigan State Univ's Radio-TV Sr Class, MSU Sch of Communications, lectr 1973. **ORGANIZATIONS:** Participant Soul Mus Preservation Conf Virgin Islands 1969; intrntl orgnzr United Elec Radio & Machine Workers of Am 1951-52; exec sec Natl Negro Labor Cncl Louisville Chap 1952; mem Capital Press Clb, Natl Press Clb; WA Press Clb; Natl & Broadcasting Clb; Washington, DC Chpt; Natl Acad of TV Arts & Sci; Natl Com of Black Lawyers; vice chmn Communications Com; Com for Commeration of Birthday of Dr Martin Luther King, Jr; Search for Dean of Sch of Communications HowardUniv 1974; mem Metropolitan (DC) YMCA; bd mem Project Build VOICE; mem NAACP. **HONORS/ACHIEVEMENTS:** Recipient First Annual Black Heritage Series' Natl Black Excellance Awrd for Contrib to Black Experience Through the art of Communications Omaha, NE 1974; author "Committee for KY" Prize Winning Essay Over All Clg Stdnts in KY 1946; Exemplary Serv Awrd Detroit; pres awrd for outst & significant serv DetroitAlumni Chap WilberforceUniv 1964; first & congressional dist awrd Detroit 1963; freedom citation for outst serv in Behalf of the Emancipation Centianial YrCommermoration Detroit 1963; Detroit Courier Nwspr Stf Appreciation Awrd 1964; NNPA Second Place News Feature Awrd 1966; NPA First Place News Feature Awrd1967. **MILITARY SERVICE:** AUS sgt WWII.

HIGGINS, CHESTER ARCHER, JR.
Journalist. **PERSONAL:** Born Nov 06, 1946, Lexington, KY; children: Nataki, Chester III. **EDUCATION:** Tuskegee Inst, BS 1970. **CAREER:** Exhibits NY & World-Wide Retrospective; USIA, sent to 65 countries 1975-76; NY Univ, instr 1975-78; NY Times, staff photographer 1975-. **ORGANIZATIONS:** Mem Natl Congress of Men, Intl Center of Photography, Pan Asian Repertory; represented by Photo Researchers. **HONORS/ACHIEVEMENTS:** Works in Mus of Modern Art; Intrnat Ctr of Photography; Library of Congress; Vassar Coll; Tuskegee Inst Archive Ford Found Fellow 1972-74; Rockefeller Grant 1973; Nat Endowment on the Arts Grant 1973; author Black Woman McCalls 1970; Drums of Life Doubleday 1974; Sometime Ago Doubleday 1978; African Disting Lectr 1975; United Nations Award; Am Graphic Design Award; Graphics Mag Award; Intl Ctr of Photog Grant; Art Dir Club of NY Award.

HIGGINS, CLARENCE R., JR.
Pediatrician. **PERSONAL:** Born Sep 13, 1927, E St Louis, IL; son of Clarence Higgins and Louise Higgins; married Edwina Gray; children: Rhonda, Adrienne, Stephen. **EDUCATION:** Fisk Univ, 1948; Meharry Med Coll, 1953. **CAREER:** Homer Phillips Hospital St Louis, internship 1953-54, ped res 1954-56; Baylor Coll Med, res flwshp 1956-57, asst clinical prof peds; Peds Sec NMA, self-employed Ped, chmn 1973-; St Joseph Hospital, dir. **ORGANIZATIONS:** Alpha Phi Alpha Fraternity; Diplomat Amer Bd Peds; Fellow Amer Acad Peds. **MILITARY SERVICE:** USAF 1957-59. **BUSINESS ADDRESS:** 4315 Lockwood, Houston, TX 77026.

HIGGINS, CLEO SURRY
Educator. **PERSONAL:** Born Aug 25, 1923, Memphis, TN; widowed; children: Kyle Everett, Sean Craig. **EDUCATION:** LeMoyne Clg, BA 1944;Univ WI, MPh 1945, PhD 1973. **CAREER:** Bethune-Cookman Coll, acting acad dean 1976-; Div of Humanities Bethune-cookman Coll, chmn 1973-76; Div of Humanities, acting chmn 1970-73; Humanities St Johns & River Jr Coll, instructor 1964-70; Collier Blocker Jr Coll, dean students prsnl registrat instructor 1960-63; Central Acad HS, instructor reading 1958-60. **ORGANIZATIONS:** Chmn Div of Humanities Bethune-Cookman Clg 1948-56; vis prof WV State Clg 1948; chmn Bethune-cookman Clg 1946-48; instr Bethune-cookman Clg 1945-46;Fessenden Acad, instr 1943-44; mem Am Dialect Soc; mem Natl Cncl of Tchrs of Engl; mem Natl Cncl of Clg Pub Advsrs; mem Am Assc ofUniv Women;mem Putnam Co Hist Soc; mem Emanuel United Meth Ch; chptr mem Daytona Br Chap of Links Inc 1956; fdr mem Beta Iota Sigma Sigma Gamma Rho Sor 1948; standing mem Vis Com of S Assc of Secondary Schs & Clgs 1948-56; organizer The Woemsn Serv league; spkr St Louis George Washington Day Observance 1959; natl pres Sigma Gamma Rho Sor 1962-63; asst chmn coordn team SACS Vis Team 1962; chmn planing grp Bilingualism in W Indies 1963; mem exec bd Putnam Co Chap Natl Found March of Dimes 1964; mem Bi-Racial Com Putnam Co 1964-70; vol sec Putnam City Comm Action Pgm 1966; consult In-Serv Ed Meeting Putnam Co Sec Schs 1966; mem FL Citizens Com for Humanities 1972-73. **HONORS/ACHIEVEMENTS:** Outst Educators in Am 1970; schlr in dept of englUniv WI 1971; rec Charles Dana Faculty SchlrshpUniv NCF 1972-73; oratorical contest judge VFW Voice of Democracy Natl Pgm 1975; woman of yr Bethune-Cookman Clg 1975; panelist a Humanities Pgm for Disadvantaged 1976. **BUSINESS ADDRESS:** Bethune Cookman Coll, 640 2nd Ave, Daytona Beach, FL 32017.

HIGGINS, ORA A.
Assistant personnel manager. **PERSONAL:** Born Sep 24, 1919, Birmingham, AL; married William Higgins, Sr; children: Murrell Duster, William, Jr. **EDUCATION:** Northwestern Univ, BS 1946, MA 1955; Northwestern Univ Bus Law, grad work. **CAREER:** Spiegel Inc, asst personnel mgr 1946-. **ORGANIZATIONS:** Mem Chicago Comm on Human Relations Employment Com, State of IL Dept of Personnel Grievance Com; mem Natl Bus League, Chicago Guid & Personnel Assn Inc, Manpower Commn State of IL, Civil Serv Commn Oral Panel; adv bd Midwest Day Care Ctr; bd dir Rehab Workshop Assn; chmn DuSable HS Exemplary Project; sec bd dir Joint Negro Appeal; treas Jones Comm HS adv coun; Cosmopolitan C of C; chmn Youth Motivation Prog Chicago Assn of Commerce & Indus; gov bd, pres women's auxiliary, mem Tabernacle Comm Hosp & Health Ctr; mem Women's Div Natl Conf of Christians & Jews; natl chmn Women in Industry Federated Women's Clubs; faculty mem Dunbar Voc Evening Sch; chmn Awd Com Dunbar Voc HS adv council; Provident Hosp Women's Aux; personnel chmn Met YWCA; Corp Com Fund of Chicago; Personnel Mgmt Com Comm Fund; tech adv com Dawson Skill Ctr City Coll of Chicago; personnel mgmt com Comm Fund; engineered Integration Prog for Loop dept stores 1950; Alpha Gamma Phi Sor; mem Greenview Comm Council. **HONORS/ACHIEVEMENTS:** Awd from Chicago Assn of Commerce & Indus 1975; Awd Add Info Contrib to Bus World Cosmo Sec NCNW 1978; Merit Employ Awd Chic Assnof Commerce & Ind 1978; Woman of the Week WBEE Radio 1973; Assoc Orgn for Vocational Achievement 100th Yr Anniversary Emancipation Proclamation Merit Awd 1963; Chicago Daily Defender Round Table of Commerce 1961; Rosa Gregg Awd Bus & Indus of Natl Assn of Colored Women's Clubs Inc 1964; Alpha Gamma Phi Sor Outstanding Progressive Woman 1967; Disting Serv Awd Tuskegee Inst 1967. **BUSINESS ADDRESS:** Asst Personnel Mgr, Spiegel Inc, 1040 W 35 St, Chicago, IL 60609.

HIGGINS, ROD ANTHONY
Professional athlete. **PERSONAL:** Born Jan 31, 1960, Harvey, IL; children: Fresno State Univ: 1982. **EDUCATION:** Fresno State Univ, 1982. **CAREER:** Forward 1982-. **HONORS/ACHIEVEMENTS:** Played in final 42 games including 6 starts near the end of season; scored in double figures 20 games including a season high 18 points twice. **BUSINESS ADDRESS:** Chicago Bulls, 333 N Michigan Ave, Ste 510, Chicago, IL 60601.

HIGGINS, SAMMIE L.
Clergyman, educator. **PERSONAL:** Born May 11, 1923, Ft Worth; married Elizabeth; children: Pam, Don, Benita, Kim, Garry. **EDUCATION:** Univ Denver, BS 1954; Western Theol Sem, BTh 1963; Merritt Clg, AA 1969;Univ UT San Fran State Clg. **CAREER:** Rev Higgins Has Been Very Active Politically in Various Rel Appts & in Tchg, meth clrgymn edctr. **ORGANIZATIONS:** Mem Variety of Assc & Coms; mem NAACP; Omega Psi Phi. **HONORS/ACHIEVEMENTS:** Who's Who In Am Politics 1973; outst cit of Ogden 1964; outst Fin Ed Ofcr Poletechnic HS 1970; outst Faculty Mem & Tchr 1972.

HIGGINS, STANN
Art director. **PERSONAL:** Born May 16, 1952, Pittsburgh, PA. **EDUCATION:** Columbia Coll of Communication Arts, BS, graphics/advt 1979; Art Inst of Chicago Jr Sch. **CAREER:** Jordan Tamraz Caruso Advt, art dir 1985, prod mgr 1979; Bentley Barnes & Lynn Advt, asst prod mgr 1978; Starstruk Prods, creative dir 1985; Raddim Intl Musicpaper, art dir, production mgr 1986. **ORGANIZATIONS:** Bd of dirs, chmn of graphics Yth Communications 1985. **HONORS/ACHIEVEMENTS:** Work selected for, recip 2 hon mentions Art Inst of Chicago 1965; Dist Art Award Maywood Bd of Ed 1966; Cert of Apprec as Guest Speaker in Advertising Triton Coll 1981.

HIGGS, FREDERICK C.
Business executive. **PERSONAL:** Born Jul 03, 1935, Nassau, Bahamas;married Beryl Vanderpool; children: Rory, Linda, Saundra. **EDUCATION:** St John's Coll, 1947-51. **CAREER:** Lisaro Ent Ltd, pres 1973-; Charlotte St Prop, properties mgr 1971-73; Bahamas Airways, sta mgr 1965-70; New Providence Div of BGA. **ORGANIZATIONS:** Vice chmn, trnmnt dir, New Providence Div of BGA; first vice pres, Bahamas Confed of Amateur Sports; mem, Mental Health Assn Exec; mem, Scout Assn of Bahamas; sec, Amateur Boxing Assn of Bahamas. **HONORS/ACHIEVEMENTS:** Intl Golf Tour Champion, Nairobi 1973. **BUSINESS ADDRESS:** Bahamas Golf Assn, PO Box 4568, Nassau, Bahamas.

HIGGS, MARY ANN SPICER
Veteran affairs executive. **PERSONAL:** Born May 10, 1951, South Bend, IN; daughter of Bobby Higgs Jr and Willa B Thornton; married Jack Spicer IV, Dec 25, 1977; children: Jack V. **EDUCATION:** North Texas State Univ, Denton TX, BA Psychology, 1973; Abilene Christian Univ, Abilene TX, MPA, 1975. **CAREER:** Veterans Affairs Recruitment Office, Waco TX, Dallas TX, Lincoln NE, Knoxville IA, 1973-. **ORGANIZATIONS:** Veteran's Administration, Natl Civil Rights Advisory Council, 1986-, EEO Counselor trainer (Dist), Natl Trainer for Supervisor's EEO; natl parliamentarian; Zeta Phi Beta Sorority, 1982-86, natl vice pres, 1986-.

HIGH, FREIDA
Artist, educator. **PERSONAL:** Born Oct 21, 1946, Starkville, MS. **EDUCATION:** Graceland Coll, AA 1966; No IL U, BS 1968;Univ WI, MA 1970, MFA 1971. **CAREER:** Univ WI, asst prof of art dept of Afro-Amer studies; artist-in-residence 1971; Contemporary African & Afro-Amer Art, rsch; Univ WI, dept studies various exhibitions 1970-; Trad African Art, major shows curator 1971, 72; Prints & Paintings Afro-Amer Art, curator 1972; WI Acad of Arts Letter Sci, one woman show latest reflections 1974; Studio Museum NY, 1976; KY State Univ, 1974. **ORGANIZATIONS:** Mem Nat Conf of Artists. **HONORS/ACHIEVEMENTS:** Outs Young Women in Am 1972; WI Arts Bd Visual Arts Grant 1977; City Arts Grant Cultural Com Ofc of Mayor 1977; Who's Who Among Women 1976-77. **BUSINESS ADDRESS:** Univ of Wisconsin-Madison, Room 4223-Humanities, 455 N Park St, Madison, WI 53706.

HIGHSMITH, CARLTON L.
Packaging company chief executive. **CAREER:** Specialized Packaging International Inc, New Haven, CT, chief exec. **BUSINESS ADDRESS:** Specialized Packaging International Inc., 100 Crown, New Haven, CT 06510. *

HIGHSMITH, CHARLES ALBERT
Retired education administrator. **PERSONAL:** Born Jan 08, 1921, Wilkes-Barre, PA; married Magnolia White; children: Charles Jr, Karen Lynn, Pamela Fern Highsmith Johnson. **EDUCATION:** Cheyne Univ, BS 1943; Univ of PA, MS 1947; Univ of PA-Temple Univ, grad work; Shaw Coll at Detroit, MI, Hon Dr 1981. **CAREER:** Philadelphia Bd of Ed, prin 1959-67, dist supt 1967-72, assoc supt 1972-78, dpty supt of schls 1978-83, acting supt of schl 1982-83 (retired). **ORGANIZATIONS:** Schoolmens Club; Phi-beta Sigma Frat; ACSA & Cheyney Alumni Assn; Epsil on Pi Tau Frat; past pres Dr Virginia M Alexander Schlrshp Fnd; instr Nicetown-Boys Club; bd dir Downingtown Ind Schl; ARC; past commtman BSA Troop; bd dir, Germantown Settlement Hse; chmn Educ Schlrshp Co M Zion Bapt Ch; pres Cheyney Alumni Assoc; mem Germantown Comm Cncl, Sch Comm Cncl; Educ Equality League; E Mt Airy Neighborhood Assn; Men Clivden NW br Cancer Soc. **HONORS/ACHIEVEMENTS:** Richard Humphreys Schlrshp Cheyney, 1939-41; Vaux Schlrshp 1941-43; Stdnt Tchr Award 1943; ldrshp awd Reynolds Sch, 1963; honoree Dr V M Alexander Schlrshp Foun 1965; Educ Achvmnt award Opportunities-Ind Ctr 1966; awrd Educ Achvmnt Salem Bapt ch, 1966; achvmnt award Philos Annl 1966; cit award Germantown HS 1968; educ achvmnt award Adelphi Club 20 1968; educ award NuSigma Chap Phi Beta Sigma Frat, 1969; citation Men Clivededn 1969; ldrshp award Russell Tabernacle 1969; cert achvmnt NASE 1970; achvmnt award Phi Beta Sigma Frat, 1971; educ award Kiwanis Club 1973, Elks Inc, 1973. **MILITARY SERVICE:** AUS 1st lt 4 yrs; Commendation Ribbon 1946.

HIGHTOWER, ANTHONY
Attorney, city councilman. **PERSONAL:** Born in Atlanta, GA; son of John Vincent Hightower (deceased) and Erie Beavers Hightower. **EDUCATION:** Clark Coll, Atlanta GA, BA, 1983; Univ of Iowa, Iowa City IA, JD, 1986. **CAREER:** City of College Park, College Park GA, councilman, 1986-; Self-employed, College Park GA, attorney, 1986-; Clark Coll, Atlanta GA, teacher, 1988-. **ORGANIZATIONS:** Mem, NAACP, 1979-, Alpha Phi Alpha

Frat, 1980-; bd mem, Clark Coll, 1982-83; natl bd mem, Alpha Phi Alpha Frat Inc, 1982-83; mem, State Bar of Georgia, 1986-, Natl Bar Assn, 1986-, Amer Bar Assn, 1986-, Natl League of Cities, 1986-, Natl Black Caucus of Local Elected Officials, 1986-, Georgia Municipal Assn, 1986-; bd mem, Fulton County Public Safety Training Center, 1989-. **HONORS/ACHIEVEMENTS:** Selected for Membership, Alpha Kappa Mu Honor Soc, 1981, Pi Gamma Mu Intl Honor Soc, 1981; Oustanding Young Men of Amer, 1987; Participated and Completed Inaugural Class of South Fulton Leadership, 1987; Golden Rule Awards Panel, United Way/J C Penny, 1988; Appreciation Award, Metro Atlanta Private Indus Council, 1988; Political Service Award, Delta Sigma Theta Sorority Inc, 1988. **HOME ADDRESS:** 2210 Ross Ave, College Park, GA 30337.

HIGHTOWER, CHARLES H., III
Journalist, editor. **PERSONAL:** Born Jul 24, 1934, Chgo; divorced. **EDUCATION:** Univ of IL, 1952-54; Roosevelt U, 1956. **CAREER:** United Meth Pub Hse, jrnlst, asso ed 1985; DuSable Museum of African Am Hist, dev dir 1973-74; Am Com on Africa, washington dir 1970-73; Guardian Newsweekly NY, staff corr 1968-70; Toronto Star Canada, paris corr 1966-68; Pan Am World Airways Chgo, passenger sales agent 1964-66. **ORGANIZATIONS:** Mem St Mar United Meth Ch Chgo. **MILITARY SERVICE:** AUS pfc 1956-58. **BUSINESS ADDRESS:** 1661 N Northwest Hwy, Park Ridge, IL 60068.

HIGHTOWER, DENNIS FOWLER
Business executive. **PERSONAL:** Born Oct 28, 1941, Washington, DC; married Denia Stukes; children: Dennis F Jr, Dawn D. **EDUCATION:** Howard Univ, BS 1962; Harvard Business School, MBA 1974. **CAREER:** Xerox Corp Rsch & Engrg Group, mgr org plnng 1970-72; McKinsey & Co Inc, sr assoc& engagement mgr 1974-78; Gen Electric Lighting Bus Group, mgr oper plnng 1978-79; Gen Electric Mexico Lighting Affiliate, vice pres & gen mgr 1979-81; Mattel Inc, vice pres corp plnng 1981-84; Russell Reynolds Assoc Inc, exec dir 1984-86; managing dir and manager Los Angeles office 1986-. **ORGANIZATIONS:** Mem Kappa Alpha Psi 1960-, Harvard Club of NY City 1977-, Howard Univ Alumni Assoc 1978-, Bus Roundtable US Consulate Monterrey Mexico 1979-81; bd mem Monterrey Mexico Amer School Found 1979-81, Monterrey Mexico Chamber of Commerce 1980-81, Harvard Bus School Assoc of So CA 1983-; bd mem So CA Ctr for Nonprofit Mgmt 1984-; mem steering comm Public/Private Partnership Prog DC Publ Sch System 1985-; mem Jonathan Club 1987-. **HONORS/ACHIEVEMENTS:** COGME Fellow Harvard Business School 1972-74; Outstanding Young Men of Amer 1976; Listed in Who's Who in Black Corp Amer 1982; Alumni Achievement Awd Howard Univ Alumni Assn So CA 1984; Disting Alumni Citation Natl Assn for Equal Opport in Higher Ed 1985; Howard Univ distinguished postgraduate achievementawd-business & admin service 1986. **MILITARY SERVICE:** AUS maj 8 yrs; 2 Bronze Stars, 3 Air Medals, Joint Serv Commend Medal; 5 Army Commend Medals with "V", Purple Heart, Vietnam Honor Medal 1st Class; Ranger;senior parachutist. **BUSINESS ADDRESS:** Managing Dir, Russell Reynolds Assoc Inc, 333 S Grand Ave, 42nd Floor, Los Angeles, CA 90071.

HIGHTOWER, EDWARD STEWART
Salesman. **PERSONAL:** Born Feb 07, 1940, New York, NY; married Ola Cherry; children: Meredith, Allyson. **EDUCATION:** Bloomfield Coll, BA 1964; Yeshiva U, MS 1971. **CAREER:** Kronish Agy, asso 1979-; Kings Co Hosp Ctr, exec asst, comm bd 1970-72, asso dir 1972-79; Gen Lrng Corp, reg mrkt dir 1969-70; Manpower Dev Training Prog, cnslng supr 1969; Williamsburg Adult Training Ctr, asst tchr in charge 1967-69. **ORGANIZATIONS:** Bd of dir Commerce Labor Ind Corp of Kings 1973-80; mem Nat Assn of Life Underwriters 1980; pres Concerned Citizens for Ed of Gifted & Talented Children 1978-79; chmn City of NY Community Planning Bd #9 1979; pres Prospect Lefferts Gardens Neighborhd Assn 1979-80. **HONORS/ACHIEVEMENTS:** Outstndng Young Men of Am 1970; Community Ldrs of Am 1972; Community Activist Award Nat Concl of Negro Women Flatbush Sec 1979; Outstndng Community Ldr Bedford Stuyvesant Jaycees 1980. **BUSINESS ADDRESS:** Mony Financial Services, 475 Park Ave, South, New York, NY 10016.

HIGHTOWER, HERMA J.
Government executive. **PERSONAL:** Born Jul 03, Mesa, AZ; son of Oliver Harris and Mae Kemp Harris; married Dr Claude George, Aug 03, 1984; children: Valerie, Kimberly. **EDUCATION:** AZ State Univ, BA 1963, MA 1966, PhD 1977. **CAREER:** Roosevelt School Dist, classroom teacher 1963-70; AZ State Personnel Comm, training officer 1970-71; AZ Dept of Educ, educ program consultant 1971-74, dir ESEA Title I 1974-76, deputy assoc supt of schools 1976-78; Internal Revenue Servs, asst to dir 1978-79, asst dir 1980-81, asst district dir 1985-, district dir 1988-. **ORGANIZATIONS:** Adv bd AZ State Univ Model for Mobility of Women 1976; adhoc consultant Natl Inst of Educ, Natl Coaltion of Title I Parents, Lawyers Comm for Civil Rights Under Law 1976; mem Seattle Oppor Indus Ctr 1980-81; bd of dirs Seattle Urban League 1980-81; mem Bus Adm Tech Comm Seattle Jr Coll 1980-81; mem City of Phoenix Human Relations Comm 1977; bd of dirs Phoenix Urban League 1977-79; adhoc consultant Amer Educ Rsch Assn 1977; bd of dirs Phoenix Oppor Indus Ctr 1978-79; visited People's Republic of China before formalization of relations 1978; mem Senior Executive Assn 1980-; mem exec comm Resurgens Atlanta 1983-; bd of dirs YWCA 1985-; natl speaker on motivation/goalsetting; bd of dir United Way of Greater Des Moines 1988-; mem Rotary Club of Greater Des Moines 1988-. **HONORS/ACHIEVEMENTS:** 10 Top Sr Women AZ State Univ 1963; Community Serv Awd Delta Sigma Theta Sor 1976; Special Friend Award YWCA 1977; First Black female in the history of IRS to be selected for its Executive Prog 1978; First Black to be selected to Exec position in the IRS 1979; Distinguished Serv Awd Natl Assoc of Black Accountants 1982; Contributor to Equal Employ Opportunity 1984; "Parental Involvement-A Happening Author and Prod Consultant in Educ" 12 min videotape presentation for natl state & local dissemination 1976; "Zero-Base Planning & Budgeting, A Tool for Systematic Evaluation of Programs in the AZ Dept of Educ" AZ Dept of Educ 1977; Keynote speaker Governor's Salute to Black Women AZ 1986; Certificate of Merit, City of Atlanta 1988; First Black Female Director in History of IRS 1988; First Femal Executi ve in nine-state region 1988; Proclamation: Dr Herma Hightower Day, City of Atlanta 1988; Partnership in Administration Award, General Serv Admin 1989; various EEO related awards, honors. **HOME ADDRESS:** 535 Valley West Court, West Des Moines, IA 50265.

HIGHTOWER, JAMES HOWARD
Psychologist. **PERSONAL:** Born Feb 21; married Marie Oliver; children: James Howard II, Tiffany Iwanonski, Terrance Remon, Mira Alyssa. **EDUCATION:** Edward Waters Coll, BS 1969, LLD 1979; Michigan State Univ, MA 1971, PhD 1973; Nova Univ, Post-Doctoral Program in Clinical Psychoanalysis 1983-84; category I CME, American Psychiatric Assn, 1986-89. **CAREER:** FL Div of Vocational Rehabilition, counselor 1970-71; MI State Univ Oseteopathic Medicine, clinical instructor in comm medicine 1972-73; FL A&M Univ, grad psychology instructor 1975-76; Tri-County Comm Health Bd Drug Abuse Treatment Program, chief psychologist asst program dir 1971-74; Edward Waters Coll, dept chairman of psychology; FL Community College at Jacksonville, prof of psychology; private practice, consulting psychologist; PPPAA, president #F00701. **ORGANIZATIONS:** Consulting clinical psychologist, Head Start Programs; chief clinical psychologist, dir of psychology, Youth Study Unit, Hope Haven Children's Hospital; psychology mentor, FL Comm Coll at Jacksonville, 1985-; life mem, NAACP; dactylologist; "The Psychology Corner" series, The Jacksonville Advocate, and The Truth in Politics. **HONORS/ACHIEVEMENTS:** Published book, Conflict Resolution, PPPAA, 1980; Copley Publishing Group-MA, 1985; author of numerous other articles and books; received Special Award, The Natl Assn of Negro Women; Distinguished Alumni Citation of the Year, Natl Assn for Equal Opportunity in Higher Educ, 1986; published "Famanotophobia," in which a new type of phobia is isolated, NY Vintage Press, Inc, 1987. **MILITARY SERVICE:** USMC. **BUSINESS ADDRESS:** President, PPPAA, 1881 Powell Place, Jacksonville, FL 32205.

HIGHTOWER, MICHAEL
Elected official, personnel administrator. **PERSONAL:** Born in College Park, GA. **EDUCATION:** Clark Coll Atlanta, BA Music 1979. **CAREER:** GA State Univ Atlanta, admin coord, asst to dir of physical plant oper 1979-; City Hall College Park, councilman, mayor pro-tem. **ORGANIZATIONS:** Mem Clark Coll Bd of Trustees; pres, vice pres Alpha Phi Chap of Alpha Phi Alpha; mem Friendship Baptist Church 1965-, Eta Lambda Chap Alpha Phi Alpha 1979-, GA Municipal Assoc 1980-, Natl League of Cities 1980-; vice chmn Fulton Cty CETA Youth & Adv Council 1980-82;; mem South Fulton Chamber of Commerce 1980-, Airport Intl Jaycees 1982-, Fulton Cty Private Ind Council 1982-83; mem bd of dir Jesse Draper Boy's Club 1983-. **HONORS/ACHIEVEMENTS:** Outstanding Serv to HS & Comm Atlanta Airport Rotary Club 1975; Man of the Year Awd Alpha Phi Alpha 1979; Outstanding Young Men of Amer Awd Amer Jaycees1980,83; Disting Alumni Awd from Men of Clark Coll 1980; Outstanding Young People of Atlanta Awd 1980; Disting Comm Serv Awd Woodward Acad 1981; Disting Comm Serv Awd Friendship Baptist Church 1983; Awd of Appreciation Flipper Temple AME Church 1984. **BUSINESS ADDRESS:** Councilman, Mayor Pro-Tem, City Hall College Park, 3667 Main St, College Park, GA 30337.

HIGHTOWER, MONTERIA
Librarian. **PERSONAL:** Born Nov 20, 1929, Texas. **EDUCATION:** Butler Coll, BS 1951;Univ Maryland, MA 1968. **CAREER:** Butler Coll, div tchr sec to pres 1951-53; LA Pub Library, libr asst 1953-67; Prince George's County Libr, children's libr 1967-68; New Haven Free Pub Libr, bd dir 1968-71; Maryland State Dept Educ Div Libr Dev & Serv, spls 1972-73; DC Pub Libr, head pub serv dept 1973-; Seattle Pub Library,central libr serv dir. **ORGANIZATIONS:** Mem Am Conn New England DC Libr Assns; Nat Book Com; New Haven Sch Bd Lectr surv consult in field. **HONORS/ACHIEVEMENTS:** Num grad credits cert; pub "Ommanilities & Diversities in Pub Lib Prgmng in a Pluralistic Soc Serving our Ethnic Pub" PLA Am Lib Assn 1976; "Prgm Plng & Evaluation" Designing Lib Educ Prgms Progress in Urban LibrarianshipUniv of WI Milwaukee 1974; "The Personnel Manual an Outline for Libraries" Am Lib Assn Chicago 1977 Ad Hoc Com to Revise the ALA Personnel Organ & Procedure Manual. **BUSINESS ADDRESS:** Central Library Services Dir, Seattle Public Library, 1000 Fourth Ave, Seattle, WA 98104.

HIGHTOWER, WILLAR H., JR.
Purchasing manager. **PERSONAL:** Born Aug 08, 1943, Greenville, SC; married Josephine Holman; children: Willia J, Terri T. **EDUCATION:** NC Coll at Durham, 1964-65; SC State Coll, BS Math 1964. **CAREER:** US Army, battery commander 1965-67; USAR Defense Personnel Support Ctr, logistician 1981-; E I DuPont, computer pgrmr 1967-79, buyer 1979-80, asst purchasing agent 1980-. **ORGANIZATIONS:** Mem Augusta Area Purchasing Manag Assoc 80-, Amer Mgmnt Assoc 1980-, Reserve Officers Assoc 1968-; NAACP 1967-; brd of dir Aiken Chapter Am Red Cross1984-; city cnclmn City of Aiken, SC 1981-86; Aiken County Councilman 1986-. **HONORS/ACHIEVEMENTS:** Presented Key to the City of Aiken 1986. **MILITARY SERVICE:** AUS lt col 20 yrs; USAR 15 yr medal 1980; 81st ARCOM Cert of Achvmnt 1979. **HOME ADDRESS:** 682 Edrie St, Aiken, SC 29801. **BUSINESS ADDRESS:** Assistant Purchasing Agent, E I DuPont, Savannah River Plant, Aiken, SC 29808.

HIGHTS, WILLIAM E.
Clergyman. **PERSONAL:** Born in Cape Girardeau, MO; children: Dana Marie, Phyllis Ann. **EDUCATION:** St Louis U; Wstrn Bapt Sem. **CAREER:** John Missionary Bapt Ch Sacramento, pastor 1962-; Third Bapt Ch San Francisco, asst to Dr FD Haynes 1959-62. **ORGANIZATIONS:** Moderator N Dist Bapt Assn; chmn Civic Com Sacramento Bapt Minister Conf; pres CA St Bapt Congress of Christian Ed; mem adv bd to supt of Sacramento Unified Sch Sys; pres Ch Srv Bureau of Sacramento; bd dirs Nat Bapt Conv USA Inc Off. **BUSINESS ADDRESS:** 2130 4 St, Sacramento, CA 95818.

HILDEBRAND, RICHARD ALLEN
Clergyman. **PERSONAL:** Born Feb 01, 1916, Winnsboro, SC; married Anna Beatrix Lewis; children: Camille Ylonne. **EDUCATION:** Allen Univ, BA 1938; Payne Theol School, BD 1941; Boston Univ, STM 1948; Wilberforce Univ, DD 1953; Morris Brown Coll, LLD (hon) 1975. **CAREER:** African Meth Episcopal Church, ordained to ministry 1936, elected bishop 1972; Columbia & Sumter SC, pastor 1936-38; Jamestown & Akron OH, pastor 1938-45; Providence, pastor 1945-48; Bayshore NY, pastor 1948-49; Wilmington DE, pastor 1949-50; Bethel AME Church NYC, pastor 1950-65; Bridge St AME Church Brooklyn, pastor 1965-72; AME Church GA 6th Dist, presiding bishop 1972-76, 1st Dist Philadelphia 1976-. **ORGANIZATIONS:** Pres Manhattan Dirs Protestant Council 1956-60; chmn Chs for New Harlem Hosp New York City 1957-65; mem, pres New York City br 1962-64 NAACP; mem Alpha Phi Alpha, Masons;pres Atlanta N GA Conf AME Fed Credit Union 1972-76; chmn, bd dirs Morris Brown Coll, Turner Sem Interdenominational Theol Ctr 1972-76, Payne TheolSem 1976-; pres Council of Bishops AME Church 1977-.

HILDRETH, GLADYS JOHNSON
Educator. **PERSONAL:** Born Oct 15, 1933, Columbia, MS; married Dr Eddie Hildreth Jr; children: Bertina, Dwayne, Kathleen, Karen. **EDUCATION:** So Univ Baton Rouge LA, BS 1953; Univ of WI Madison, MS 1955; MI State Univ East Lansing, PhD 1973. **CAREER:** So Univ, assoc prof 1960-68; LA State Univ School of Home Econ, prof family studies

1974-. **ORGANIZATIONS:** Chmn jr div adv council LA State Univ 1979-80; state chmn aging serv LA Home Econ Assoc 1978-; consult Natl Assoc for Ed of Young Children 1974-; task force on aging Natl Council on Family Relations 1976-; ctr for the family Amer Home Econ Assoc 1977-79; sec Delta Sigma Theta 1970-73; mem Phi Upsilon Omicron So Univ Home Econ 1974, Omicron Nu MI State Univ Human Ecology 1971. **HONORS/ACHIEVEMENTS:** Grad School Fellowship MI State Univ Human Ecology 1970; Thelma Porter Fellowship MI State Univ Human Ecology 1970; Recipient of the LA Home Econ Assoc Disting District & State Serv Awd 1986; Nominated for Amer Council on Educ Fellow 1979. **BUSINESS ADDRESS:** Professor, Louisiana StateUniv, Sch of Home Economics, Baton Rouge, LA 70803.

HILL, AL CALVIN
Professional athlete. **PERSONAL:** Born Jul 17, 1959, Kansas City, MO. **EDUCATION:** Arizona, BS Business. **CAREER:** Oakland Invaders, wide receiver 1984-.

HILL, ALFRED
Business executive. **PERSONAL:** Born Dec 25, 1925, Atlanta; divorced; children: Alfred II, Gordon, Stanford. **EDUCATION:** Howard U, BA 1952. **CAREER:** Newark Lamp Plant, empl specl; Equal Oppty & Urban Affairs & Hourly Skill Tng, Lighting Bus Grp, mgr; Euclid Lamp Plant Gen El Co, mgr empl & unionrel 1985. **ORGANIZATIONS:** Mem Nat Urban Affairs Cncl 1972-; Corp Minority Panel; adv Lamp Bus Div Minority Panel; mem Hum Rels Cncl Cleveland; chmn United Torch-Affirm ActCom; Community Ldrshp Com; pres, bd mem Collinwood Community Srv Ctr; bd mem Karamu House Cleveland Area Cncl Hum Rels; mem Resrch & Dev Com Cleveland Urban Leag; mem Empl Com Who's Who in The E 1959-. **HONORS/ACHIEVEMENTS:** Frontiersman Community Srv Award 1960. **MILITARY SERVICE:** USAF capt. **BUSINESS ADDRESS:** General Electric Co, 1814 E 45 St, Cleveland, OH 44103.

HILL, ANDREW WILLIAM
Pianist, composer. **PERSONAL:** Born Jun 30, 1937, Chicago, IL; married Laverne Miller. **CAREER:** Organist, composer 1940-; recorded series of 10 released record LPS 1963-; records, "Point of Departure" 1964, "Judgement" 1964, "Black Fire" 1963; Roland Kirk Quartet, 1962; Lighthouse Grp, pianist 1962; Dianh Washington, accompanist 1954; compositions include, Symetry, Black Monday, Le Groits, Duplicity, Alfred, Reconciliation, Legacy, Premonition, Moon Child, Ghetto Lights, Violence, Hope, Illusion, Golden Spook 1970. **ORGANIZATIONS:** Bd dir, Fdr, Andrew Hill & Asso Inc 1966-. **HONORS/ACHIEVEMENTS:** Nat Endowment Art Grantee 1971, 1974, 1976, 1979; Smithsonian Inst Prfmng Artist's Fellow 1972-76; NY St Cncl of the Arts Grantee 1974-75; Schlrshp New Coll of CA San Francisco 1979-80.

HILL, ANNETTE TILLMAN
Educator. **PERSONAL:** Born Nov 09, 1937, Copiah County, MS; daughter of Fayette Tillman and Martha Coleman Tillman; divorced; children: Gerri Lavonne Hill Chance. **EDUCATION:** Tougaloo Coll, BS 1956; Chicago State Univ, MS Educ 1971; Attended, Jackson State Univ, Univ of MS. **CAREER:** Parrish High School, science/math teacher 1956-60; Chicago Public Schools, science teacher 1960-69; Wendell Phillips High School Chicago, counselor 1969-71; Jackson State Univ, counselor 1971-81; Hazlehurst High School, counselor 1981-. **ORGANIZATIONS:** Mem MS Counselors Assn, Amer Assn of Counseling & Devel, Multicultural Assn Counseling & Devel, Hazlehurst Public Schools PTA; bd of dirs Central MS Chap Amer Red Cross 1978-81, 1985-; adv commn mem Juvenile Justice State of MS 1981-; chairperson Emergency Food & Shelter Adv Comm Copiah Co 1985-; sec Hazlehurst Branch NAACP. **HONORS/ACHIEVEMENTS:** Certificate of Achievement Life Career Develop System 1976; Certificate of Appreciation Natl Foundation for Cancer Rsch 1982; Certificates of Appreciation for Healthfest Central MS Chap Amer Red Cross 1982, 1983; Natl Appreciation Awd Soc of Distinguished HS Students 1983. **HOME ADDRESS:** 321 N Massengill St, Hazlehurst, MS 39083. **BUSINESS ADDRESS:** Counselor, Hazlehurst High School, 431 Monticello St, Hazlehurst, MS 39083.

HILL, ARTHUR BURIT
Transportation company executive. **PERSONAL:** Born Apr 02, 1922, New York, NY; son of Alton Hill and Victoria Ellis; married Patricia Ruth Smith, Aug 05, 1956; children: Arthur Jr, Ernest, Victoria, Joanne. **EDUCATION:** City Univ, NY, MPA 1973, BS 1966; City Univ NY MPA 1973. **CAREER:** NYPD, patrolman 1946, sgt 1956, lt 1960, capt 1964, deputy insp 1967, inspector 1969 asst chief 1971-73; United Parcel Serv, mgmt trainee 1973, vice pres public affairs 1975; vice pres United Parcel Service 1973-. **ORGANIZATIONS:** Dir Harlem Commonwealth Cncl 1966-; life mem NAACP; dir Guy R Brewer Dem Club 1981-; Alternate delegate to Democratic Natl Conv 1980 & 1984; Kappa Alpha Psi; Sigma Pi Phi-Alpha Sigma Boule; Guardsman; 32 degree Mason. **HONORS/ACHIEVEMENTS:** Comdtn Honor Legion NY PD 1950; lay reader NY Diosese Epsicopal Church 1960-; William A. Dawson Award Congressional Black Caucus 1988. **MILITARY SERVICE:** AUS corpl 1942-46. **HOME ADDRESS:** 187-10 Ilion Ave, Hollis, NY 11412. **BUSINESS ADDRESS:** Vice President, United Parcel Service, GOP 5, Greenwich, CT 06836.

HILL, ARTHUR JAMES
Business executive. **PERSONAL:** Born Jul 04, 1948. **EDUCATION:** FL Memorial Coll, BS 1971; Univ of FL, MA 1973. **CAREER:** Southeast Bank NA, asst vice-pres 1975, head money market dept 1979, vice-pres corporate lending 1979-83; Amerifirst Federal S&L, vice-pres regional mgr 1984; Peoples Natl Bank of Commerce, pres and chief exec officer 1984-. **ORGANIZATIONS:** Mem Economic Society of S FL; mem Miami Bond Club; mem Miami Herald Bd of Economists; pres & chief exec officer Peoples Natl Bank of Commerce 1984-. **HONORS/ACHIEVEMENTS:** Disting Alumni of the Year Citation Natl Assn for Equal Oppor in Higher Educ 1983; Outstanding Young Man of America US Jaycees 1983. **HOME ADDRESS:** 10294 NW 9th St Circle, Miami, FL 33172. **BUSINESS ADDRESS:** President, Peoples Natl Bank of Comm, 3275 NW 79th St, Miami, FL 33147.

HILL, AVERY
Optometrist. **PERSONAL:** Born May 24, 1924, Evanston, IL; son of William Hill, Sr. and Julia Wesley Avery Hill; married Eleanor; children: Colette. **EDUCATION:** IL Coll of Optometry, D Optometry 1948. **CAREER:** IL Visions Serv Inc Chicago, dir; staff mem Daniel Hule Williams Neighborhood Health Ctr 1972, Near N Childrens Ctr of Childrens Mem Hosp; Optometrist-consultant St. Mary of Nazareth Hosp Chicago. **ORGANIZATIONS:** Mem Optometric Assn, IL Optometric Assn, Central City Optometric Assn; mem Evanston Twp HS lay adv comm 1964-67, bd educ 1969-78, pres pro-temp 1972; Evanston Human Relations Commr 1968; steering comm Evanston N Suburban Urban League; bd of trustees Ebenezer Primm Towers; mem NAACP, Norshore Twelve Inc; trustee Garrett Theo Sem; family counseling serv of Evanston; bd of trustees Abbeville Assn of Evanston. **HONORS/ACHIEVEMENTS:** NAACP Service to the Community Awd. **MILITARY SERVICE:** USAF 1943-45; ETO Decoration Bronze Star with Oak Leaf Cluster. **BUSINESS ADDRESS:** Optometrist, 5650 W Madison, Chicago, IL 60644.

HILL, BARBARA ANN
Educator. **PERSONAL:** Born Mar 31, 1950, Brooklyn, NY; married Larry Hill; children: Vaughn, Kinshasa. **EDUCATION:** Long Island Univ CW Post Ctr, BS 1974, MS 1984. **CAREER:** Howard T Herber Middle School, educator. **ORGANIZATIONS:** Mem NY State Public High Sch Athletic Assoc 1976-; founder/advisor Malverne Girls Varsity Club 1976-; track chairperson Nassau Co HS Girls Track 1978-84;Nassau Girls Athletic Rep 1979-; mem Black Educator Coalition of Malverne HS 1984-; founder/advisor Carter G Woodson Black Studies Club 1984-; sec Nassau Co Volleyball Coaches Assoc 1985-; workshop coord Hempstead Pre-K Reading Workshop 1984-; pres Ludlum PTA 1985-. **HONORS/ACHIEVEMENTS:** Coach of the Year 1984, 5 time coach County Championship Track & Field Girls 1976,77,78,79,84; eight times Girls Track & Field Divisional & Conference Champions. **BUSINESS ADDRESS:** Teacher, Howard T Herber Middle School, Ocean Ave, Malverne, NY 11565.

HILL, BENNETT DAVID
Educator. **PERSONAL:** Born Sep 27, 1934, Baltimore, MD; son of David B Hill and Muriel Clarke Hill. **EDUCATION:** Princeton Univ, AB 1956; Harvard Univ, AM 1958; Princeton Univ, Ph D 1963. **CAREER:** Univ IL, chmn dept of History 1978-81, prof Dept of History 1975-81; Univ of Western Ontario, London CN, asst prof 1962-64; Univ of MD, visiting prof 1984-87; Georgetown Univ Visiting Professor 1987-; Roman Catholic Priest, ordained 1985. **ORGANIZATIONS:** Consltnt Natl Endowmnt for the Humanities 1978, Woodrow Wilson Natl Fdtn 1982; bd of dir American Benedictine Review. **HONORS/ACHIEVEMENTS:** Flw Amer Cncl of Learned Soc 1970-71; author of "English Cistercian Monasteries and Their Patrons in the Twelfth Century" 1970, "Church and State in the Middle Ages" 1970; co author A History of Western Society, 1979 3rd edition, 1986, "A History of World Societies" 1983 2nd edition.

HILL, BETTY J.
Manpower programs director. **PERSONAL:** Born Aug 11, 1948. **EDUCATION:** Los Angeles Harbor Jr Coll, AA 1970; California State Univ, BA 1973. **CAREER:** Compton Urban Corps, counselor 1973-74, chief counselor 1974-75; City of Compton Urban Corps, asst dir 1975-76, urban corps dir 1976-78; City of Compton, manpower program chief 1978-80, manpower programs dir 1980-. **ORGANIZATIONS:** Mem Employment Training Adv Comm, Natl Assoc for Female Execs, Veterans Comm, Compton NAACP, Prime Agent Council, Los Angeles Regional Coalition of Serv Providers, Human Resources Develop Comm, United Way Southeast Agenxcy Exec Comm, Natl Forum for Black Public Administrators, Young Men's Christian Assoc. **BUSINESS ADDRESS:** Manpower Program Dir, City of Compton, 205 So Willowbrook Ave, Compton, CA 90220.

HILL, BOBBY L.
Attorney. **PERSONAL:** Born Jul 24, 1941, Athen, GA; divorced; children: Ashley Conrad. **EDUCATION:** Savannah State Coll, BS (cum laude); Howard Univ Sch of Law, JD 1966. **CAREER:** Hill Jones & Assoc, sr pres law firm. **ORGANIZATIONS:** Former chmn GA Legislature Black Caucus; coop counsel NAACP Legal Defense Fund Inc NYC; bd dirs Natl Assembly for Social Policy & Develop; Chatham Co Cits Adv Com on comm improvement & urban renewal; Young Lawyers & Criminal Law Sections of GA; Am, Savannah Bar Assns; Savannah Area C of C; State Adv Bd; Amer Civil Libs Union; Adv Bd GA Serv Cntr for Elected Officials div of Clark Coll Pub Ctr; bd chmn IDEA Inc; adv bd Exec Inns of Amer; GA State Rep House Dist 127 serves on the educ judiciary and welfare comms of the GA Gen Assembly; serves on the Fiscal Affairs sub-comm of the GA General Assembly; pres GA Assn of Black Elected Officials (4 yrs); chmn and sr ranking mem Chatham Legislative delegation; former Youth Field Dir Region V NAACP; part-time asst law firm Van Arkle & Kaiser Washington DC; mem Natl Steering Comm Frontlash 1968; Nat Voter Educ Proj USYS; bd of dirs UN Assn of USA; chmn Youth Work Comm Savannah Br NAACP; delegate at large US Youth Council; editorial editor Unity News Savannah GA. **HONORS/ACHIEVEMENTS:** Listed Personalities in the South 1968, Outstanding Young Men in Amer 1968, Who's Who in Amer Politics 1969-70; Disting Alumnus Awd Student Bar Assn HowardUniv Sch of Law 1969; Man of the Yr Beta Phi Lamba Alpha Phi Alpha Frat 1969-70; Awd for Outstanding Achievement in Politics Savannah State Coll Natl Alumni Assn 1969; attended three day conference in Rome sponsored by European & North Amer Comm EURANAC 1970; Mayor Richard Wright Awd continuous sponsorship oflegislation to relieve human suffering & deprivation 1972; elected as a delegate to the Democratic Natl Convention in 1976 and 1980 NY; elected to the "Hallof Wisdom" 1980; Special Counsel to Pres Carter during his term of office; was counsel in Furman v Georgia which struck the death penalty in the US in 1971; was counsel in the Thikol explosion with winning claims of $770,000,000.

HILL, BRANDON T.
Security services chief executive. **CAREER:** Hill's Capitol Security Inc, Silver Spring, MD, chief exec. **BUSINESS ADDRESS:** Hill's Capitol Security Inc., 816 Thayer Ave., Silver Spring, MD 20910. *

HILL, CALVIN
Businessman/consultant. **PERSONAL:** Born Jan 02, 1947, Baltimore; married Janet McDonald; children: Grant. **EDUCATION:** Yale U, BA 1969. **CAREER:** Dallas Cowboys, running back 1969-74; Hawaiians WFL, running back 1975; Washington Redskins, 1976-78; Cleveland Browns, 1978-81; Baltimore Orioles, bd of dirs. **ORGANIZATIONS:** Consultant NFL Cleveland Browns. **HONORS/ACHIEVEMENTS:** NFL Champ Games 1970-71; Pro Bowl NFL All-Star Game 1969, 1972, 1973-74; named NFL Rookie of Yr 1969; Sporting News NFL Estrn Conf All-Star Team 1969; All NFL (Pro Football Writers Am) 1969, 1973; 1000 Yd Club 1972; Sporting News NFC All-Star 1973; mem Maryland Hall of Fame. **BUSINESS ADDRESS:** Baltimore Orioles, Memorial Stadium, Baltimore, MD 21218.

HILL, CARL M.
Educator. **PERSONAL:** Born in Norfolk; married Helen Collins Rose. **EDUCATION:** Hampton Inst, BS 1931; Cornell U, MS 1935;Univ PA, Grad Studies 1938-40, PhD 1941;Univ KY, LLD 1966;Univ of Louisville, DSc; Estrn KYUniv DSc. **CAREER:** Hampton Inst Hampton VA, asst prof, hs sci tchr 1931-41; NC A&T StUniv Greensboro NC, assoc prof chem 1941-44; TN StUniv Nashville, prof, headdept chem 1944-51; TN St U, chmn ch arts & sci, prof chem 1951-58, dean faculty, dean sch arts & sci, prof chem 1958-62; KY StUniv Frnakfort, pres 1962-75; Hampton, emeritus 1976-; Inst Higher Ed Opptny KY C of C, instr policy com, bd dir. **ORGANIZATIONS:** Bd of dir United VA Bk Citizen Marine; fellow, past ed Journal 1955-63; TN Acad Sci; mem, ed Bulletin 1949-62; pres Beta Kappa Chi Sci Soc 1962-63; mem, past pres Nat Inst Sci 1948; mem, past pres Soc Sigma Xi 1953-54; mem Nat Adv Com Tchr Exams NJ; mem KY Acad Sci; mem Nat Ed Assn;mem KY Ed Assn; mem Am Assn Sch Admin; mem NY Acad Sci; Optimist & Internatl, Frankfort Club; Omega Psi Phi Frat Inc; Sigma Pi Phi Frat; Mason 33 deg; mem,elder S Frankfort Presb Ch; bd trustees Stillman Coll; bd World Mission Presb Ch; KY Cncl Publ Higher Ed; KY Com Higher Ed; bddir KY Heart Assn; adv com KY Authority Ed TV; exec com Nat Com Accrediting; adv cncl KY Sci & Tech; bd dir, publ com Am Heart Assn; bd, exec com S Regional Ed; adv com Accreditation & Institutional Eligibility, US Off Ed; bd dir, exec com KY Blue Cross Hosp Plan; gen exec bd, exec com Gen Assembly Presb Ch; bd Am Red Cross; bd dir, chmn United. **HONORS/ACHIEVEMENTS:** Citizen Yr Award, Omega Psi Phi Frat Inc Psi Tau Chap 1974; Outstndng Alumnus at Large Award Hampton Inst 1969; commissioned KY Col; author & co-author Textbooks; numerous resrch papers pub. **BUSINESS ADDRESS:** KY State Univ, Frankfort, KY.

HILL, CHARLIE H.
Business executive. **PERSONAL:** Born Dec 05, 1926, Lakewood, FL; married Alberta; children: Charlie Jr, Wanda J, Warren A. **EDUCATION:** FL A&M Univ, BS 1949, MS 1956. **CAREER:** Brooks Elem School, prin 13 yrs; WE Combs HS, prin 5 yrs; Eglin AFB, asst equal employmnt oppty officer. **ORGANIZATIONS:** Mem Bi-Racial Comm, Citizens Adv Comm, Spec Comm on Minority Housing, Comm Action Program, C of C Military Affairs Comm, Reg I Human Rights Adv Comm; mem trustee bd & steward bd Meth Church Mem Bd, Red Cross; appt by Hon Bob Graham to bd of trustees OWJC 1983. **HONORS/ACHIEVEMENTS:** Cert of Apprec for Outstanding Contrib to Air Force EEO Prog 1971; Nominated for Personalities of S 1974; 1st black to serve on City Council in Ft WaltonBeach FL for 8 yrs. **BUSINESS ADDRESS:** Asst EEO Officer, Eglin Airforce Base, 3201 ABGP/DPCM, Eglin AFB, FL 32542.

HILL, CLARA GRANT
Educator. **PERSONAL:** Born Oct 05, 1928, Hugo, OK. **EDUCATION:** Philander Smith Coll, BA 1952; Memphis St U, MA. **CAREER:** Longview Elementary School, teacher 1985, chairperson, sixth grade teachers 1963-77; Memphis Educ Assn, faculty rep 1963-; Professional Growth Com, chairperson 1973-; acting prin 1972-77. **ORGANIZATIONS:** Com mem Curriculum Dev Elem Ed, apptd by St Commr of Ed 1977; mem Memphis Ed Assn; W TN Ed Assn; TN Ed Assn; mem Nat Ed Assn; mem, exec bd MEA 1973-76; chpsn, mbshp com MEA 1974-76; chpsn Status of Women in Ed MEA 1977; chpsn Screening Com Hiring Staff MEA 1977-78; chpsn Black Caucus MEA 1977; mem Credntls Com TEA 1976; mem Resltns Com TEA 1977; pres Dept of Clsrm Tchrs TEA 1976-78; NAACP; exec bd mem, chpsn Xmas Seals 1975-76; basileus Sigma Gamma Rho Sor 1973-75; chpsn Outstnd Sigma Woman of Yr 1973-74; mem Mbrshp Com Reg & Nat Chpts of Sor; mem YWCA; pres Optimistic Chrtbl Soc Club 1969; mem Philander Smith Alum Assn; chpsn Constitution Com 1976; mem, pres Les Demonselles Brdg Club 1972; comm wkr Heart Fund; Cancer Fund; Birth Defects; tchr Sun Sch 1964-; pres Usher Bd 1972; dir Christian Ed 1966-67; adv Jr Usher Bd 1970-; chpsn Birthmonth Flwshp 1973; mem Ada Cir of Missionary Soc; pres Dept of Clsrm Tchr TEA 1977. **HONORS/ACHIEVEMENTS:** Five Outstndng Srv Awards MEA 1974-77; Ldrshp Training Award NEA 1976; 2 Comm Srv Awards, US Congressman Harold Ford TN 1976-77. **BUSINESS ADDRESS:** 1085 Stafford Ave, Memphis, TN 38106.

HILL, CURTIS T., SR.
Business executive. **PERSONAL:** Born Jun 30, 1929, Vernon, OK; children: Sonya L, Curtis. **EDUCATION:** BS 1950; Dental Tech 1953; Adviced Life Ins 1971. **CAREER:** State Farm Ins Co, agent; Jr HS, tchr. **ORGANIZATIONS:** Mem Natl Assc of Life Underwriters; vice pres Elkhart Co Life Underwriters; pres NAACP Chpt; pres Elkhart Urban League; bd dir Amer Cancer Soc; mem Natl Black Caucus of Sch Bd Mem; former life mem Chr of Elkhart NAACP; former bd mem Jaycees; former mem Elkhart Sch Bd. **HONORS/ACHIEVEMENTS:** Rec Outst Historian Award IN Jaycees 1960; Award for Outst Contrib to Educ IN Sch Bd Assc 1974; mem Life Ins Millionaires Club 1972; first black candidate for Mayor of Elkhart. **MILITARY SERVICE:** AUSR lt col. **BUSINESS ADDRESS:** State Farm Insurance Co, 2408 S Nappanee St, Elkhart, IN 46514.

HILL, CYNTHIA D.
Attorney. **PERSONAL:** Born Feb 05, 1952, Bethesda, MD; daughter of Melvin L Hill and Mamie Landrun Hill (deceased). **EDUCATION:** Wellesley Coll, BA 1974; Georgetown Univ Law Ctr, JD 1977. **CAREER:** DC Office of Consumer Protection, law clerk to admin law judge 1977-78; League of Women Voters Educ Fund, staff atty litigation dept 1978-84, acting dir litigation dept 1984-85, dir of election serv and litigation 1985-. **ORGANIZATIONS:** Mem Women's Div Natl Bar Assoc 1977-, Washington Bar Assoc 1978-, Women's Bar Assoc of the District of Columbia 1979-, Washington Council of Lawyers 1986-; bd of dirs, Metro Washington Planning and Housing Assn, 1980-89. **HONORS/ACHIEVEMENTS:** Outstanding Young Women of Amer 1980; Phi Beta Kappa. **BUSINESS ADDRESS:** Dir Elect Serv & Litigation, League of Women Voters, Education Fund, 1730 M St NW 10th Fl, Washington, DC 20036.

HILL, DAVID
Professional athlete. **PERSONAL:** Born Jan 01, 1954, San Antonio, TX. **EDUCATION:** TX A&I, Maj Journ. **CAREER:** Detroit Lions, pro ftbl tight end 1976-. **HONORS/ACHIEVEMENTS:** All Am; Japan Bowl; EW Shrine; All Am Bowl; All-Rookie Team 1976. **BUSINESS ADDRESS:** L A Rams, 2327 W Lincoln, Anaheim, CA 92801.

HILL, DEBORAH
Personnel administrator. **PERSONAL:** Born Oct 15, 1944, Long Beach, CA. **EDUCATION:** CA State Coll Long Beach, BA 1967; Western State Univ Coll of Law, JD 1975. **CAREER:** Shell Oil Co, analyst 1968-76, sr emp rel analyst 1976-78, employee rel rep 1978-82, employee rel assoc 1982-85; service manager 1985-86; empl rel asso 1986-. **ORGANIZATIONS:** Chmn personnel comm Alpha Kappa Alpha Sor Inc 1982-86; historian Intl Assn for Personnel Women 1983; Top Ladies of Distinction 1980-; trustee bd Wesley Chapel AME Church 1983-; Links, Inc 1986-. **HONORS/ACHIEVEMENTS:** Outstanding Young Woman of Amer 1978. **HOME ADDRESS:** PO Box 90354, Long Beach, CA 90809.

HILL, DIANNE
Educator. **PERSONAL:** Born Mar 06, 1955, Newark, NJ; children: Tania Regina, Gary Robert. **EDUCATION:** Caldwell Coll, BA Elem Educ 1977; Rutgers Univ, Certificate Early Childhood 1982; Jersey City State Coll, MA Spec Educ 1985. **CAREER:** Newark Bd of Educ, teacher 1976-77; Friendly Fuld Headstart Prog, teacher/policy comm mem 1977-80; Caldwell Coll, dir educ oppor fund prog 1980-. **ORGANIZATIONS:** Public relations officer NJ Educ Oppor Fund Professional Assoc 1982-86; mem policy council Friendly Fuld Headstart 1983-85; bd mem Irvington Comm Develop 1985-86, Women's Employment network; private sector rep Assoc of Independent Colls & Univs in NJ. **HONORS/ACHIEVEMENTS:** Outstanding Black Women of the Year 1985; Outstanding Alumnae Awd Caldwell Coll BSCU & Faculty 1985. **BUSINESS ADDRESS:** Dir, Educational Oppor Fund Prog, Ryerson Ave, Caldwell, NJ 07006.

HILL, E. SHELTON
Retired association executive. **PERSONAL:** Born Mar 13, 1903, Caddo, OK; son of Lewis and Alice; married Helloise Conley; children: Edwina. **EDUCATION:** Western Univ, BS 1925; OH State Univ, Grad Work 1937; Univ of OR, 1950-51. **CAREER:** Base comdr Portland Army Air Base, race relations adv 1943-45; Vancouver Housing Auth, tenant rel adv 1945-47; Portland Urban League, dir indus relations 1947, exec dir 1959-74; NS Docum Film Co, exec dir. **ORGANIZATIONS:** Mem Natl Assn Soc Workers, Acad of Cert Social Workers, NAACP, Govt Task Force Jobs Vets, City Club, Mayors Cit Adv Com, United Way; City-Cty Comm Aging; Civil Serv Custodial Comm Title VII Adv Comm; exec bd Railroad Sr Cit Assn, NNE Mental Health Council, Scholarship Assn Concordia Coll. **HONORS/ACHIEVEMENTS:** Achievement Awd USAF; Natl Serv Awd Alpha Chi Pi Omega Sor; Leadership Awd Mina Temple 68; Civil Rights Awd Billy Webb Lodge 1050; Cert Disting Achievement Anti-Defamation League; Certificate of Hon, Portland Public School; Dedication Awd League Albina Woman; Hadassah Awd Civil Rights; Aubry S Wutsek Awd NW Pioneers 1978; Soc Work of the Year NASW 1978; Outstanding Contrib Awd Portland Public School 1979.

HILL, ELLYN ASKINS
Librarian. **PERSONAL:** Born Mar 13, 1907, Chicago; married Roosevelt T. **EDUCATION:** Nrthwstrn U, 1925-26;Univ Chicago, 1927-28, 1936, 1940, 1955-56. **CAREER:** UFBL Bookstore, mgr 1975-80; Chicago Pub Lib, libn (ret) 1924-70 Johnson Pub Co, asst libn 1972. **ORGANIZATIONS:** Mem Local 1215 AFL-CIO; NAACP; Assn Study Afro-Am & Hist; Art Inst; ALA; Coretta Scott King Awards Com; Urban Leag exec bd YWCA; Friends of Chicago Pub Lib; life mem Universal Found for Better Living Inc; Christ Universal Temple; staff assn Chicago Pub Lib. **HONORS/ACHIEVEMENTS:** Srv Award YWCA 1957-58; ofcl del ALA 1945, 1953, 1969; ofcl delUniv WI Lib Conf 1967.

HILL, ERROL GASTON
Educator. **PERSONAL:** Born Aug 05, 1921; son of Thomas David and Lydia Caroline Gibson Hill; married Grace Hope; children: Da'aga, Claudia, Melina, Aaron. **EDUCATION:** Yale Coll, BA (Summa Cum Laude) 1962; Yale School of Drama, MFA 1962, DFA 1966; Royal Acad Drmatic Art, London Univ Diploma in Drama 1951. **CAREER:** Author, director, playwright; US Engineers Trinidad, 1941-43; BBC London, announcer & actor 1951-52; Creative Arts Univ WI, tutor 1953-58; Univ Ibadan Nigeria, tch fellow 1965-67; Richmond Coll, CUNY, assoc prof drama 1967-68; Dartmouth Coll, prof of drama and play director 1968-89. **ORGANIZATIONS:** Consult Natl Humanities Faculty 1971-80; Natl Assn Schools of Theatre; Amer Society for Theatre Research; Assn for Theatre in Higher Educ; Amer Drama Society; Intl Federation for Theatre Research. **HONORS/ACHIEVEMENTS:** Brit Coun Scholarship 1949-51; Rockefeller Found Fellow 1958-60; Theatre Guild Amer Fellow 1961-62; Gold Med Govt Trinidad & Tobago 1973; publs, "Collections of Caribbean Plays" 1958-79, "The Trinidad Carnival" 1972, "The Theatre of Black Amers" 1980, 1987, "Shakespeare in Sable, A History of Black Shakespearean Actors" 1984; Plays on Black Heroes 1989; Bertram Joseph Award for Shakespeare Studies 1985; Bernard Hewitt Award for Outstanding Research in Theatre History 1985; Guggenheim Fellowship 1985-86; Fulbright Fellowship 1988.

HILL, ESTHER P.
Art educator. **PERSONAL:** Born Jun 07, 1922, Rocky Mount, NC; married Samuel W; children: Samesta Elaine. **EDUCATION:** Columbia U, BS 1943, MA 1954; NY U, Matriculated in PhD 1962. **CAREER:** Univ NC Charlotte, asso prof art 1972-; Charlotte-Mecklenburg Schs, art tchr, asst supr, cons, prog asst 1951-72; professional exhibitor of prints, jewelry, paintings; S Ed Fund, text & earth paintings in Invitatinl Black Artists Exhibition 1985. **ORGANIZATIONS:** Chmn div higher ed, mem NC Art Ed Assn 1979-81; reg rep NAEA Com Minority Concerns 1978-81; life mem NEA; Am AssnUniv Women; Phi Delta Kappa; Alpha Kappa Alpha Sor; The Moles; 1st Bapt Ch; black adv bd WBT; natl pres Guys & Dolls Inc; bd trustees Mint Museum of Art Personalities of S 1974. **HONORS/ACHIEVEMENTS:** Srv Award Plaque Guys & Dolls 19698 1975; nominee Salute to Women Who Work 1969; Nc del S Arts Fed Conf Atlanta 1979; recip Doctoral Award NC Bd of Govs 1979-80; Afro-Am Cultural Ctr, Spirit Sq Honore for Contributions in Arts in the Comm, Gala Celebration 1981. **BUSINESS ADDRESS:** Crestive Arts Dept, UNCC Sta, Charlotte, NC 28223.

HILL, FANNIE E.
Associate executive. **PERSONAL:** Born in Americus, GA; widowed; children: Lt Col George F. **EDUCATION:** BA 1927. **CAREER:** MS, GA, OK, educator 1927-37; YPD 12th Episcopal Dist AME Ch, AR, OK, dir 1947-67; RSVP Tulsa Metro Ministry, assoc dir 1985; OCOMS Bd ofRegents, vice chmn. **ORGANIZATIONS:** Dir Youth Cncl; mem TMM City of Tulsa 1971-75; Ch Women United City of Tulsa 1950-80; St of OK; mem YWCA; life mem Woman's Missionary Soc AME Ch; mem Urban Leag; mem NAACP; Mayor's Cncl on Aging; Govs Status of Women; Zeta Phi Beta; Vernon AME Ch; pres Hands of Frndshp; pres Pastor's Wives Cncl Intrdnmntl; mem Govs Commn on Status of Women; Nat Cncl of Negro Women; assoc dir Retired Senior Volunteer Program in Tulsa; mem

UMCA; bd MortonHealth Ctr. **HONORS/ACHIEVEMENTS:** Thw Wife of the Yr 1971; 100% Attend Award, Connectnl Young Peoples Dept 1964; Mem of Yr, Vernon AME 1969; Humanitarian Award, Tulsa Yth 1973; Liberty Bell Award, Bar Assn 1974; Newsmaker Award, Women in Communicatns; Perfect Attendance Award, SS Tchr 1965; Violet Anderson Award for Finer Womanhood, Zeta Phi Beta 1975; Woman of Yr, NCCJ 1975; del Nat Dem Conv, Carter Div 1976; hostess at the Inaugural in Washington DC; apptd by Gov of State of OK as Ambassador of Goodwill. **BUSINESS ADDRESS:** Chairman, Board of Regents, Osteopathic College, 1111 West 17th St, Tulsa, OK 74107.

HILL, GEORGE C.
Educator. **PERSONAL:** Born Feb 19, 1939, Moorestown, NJ. **EDUCATION:** Rutgers U, BA 1961; Howard U, MS 1963; NY U, PhD 1967. **CAREER:** Univ Cambridge, England, NIH spl resrch fellow 1971-72; Squibb Inst Med Resrch, resrch invstgtr 1969-71; Univ KY Med Ctr, NIH post-doctoral fellow 1967-69; CO State Univ, assoc 1972-85; Meharry Medical College, dir Div of Biomedical Sci. **ORGANIZATIONS:** Mem AAAS; AIBS; Am Soc Protozoologists; Am Soc Parasitologists; Soc Biological Chem; Sigma Xi. **HONORS/ACHIEVEMENTS:** NIH Res Career Dev Award 1974-79. **BUSINESS ADDRESS:** Dir Div of Biomedical Sci, Meharry Medical College, Div of Biomedical Sciences, 1005 D B Todd Blvd, Nashville, TN 37208.

HILL, GEORGE CALVIN
Surgeon/occupational physician. **PERSONAL:** Born Aug 29, 1925, Johnstown, PA; son of George C Hill and Mosetta Pollard; married Valentine Kay Johnson, Jun 12, 1959; children: Georgia Anne, Janet Marietta, Ellen Valentine. **EDUCATION:** Univ Pittsburgh, PA, BS 1948; MS 1954; Meharry Medical Coll, Nashville, TN, MD 1954-58. **CAREER:** Harper Grace Staff, jr attend 1976; Hutzel Hospital, jr attend 1974; Brent Gen Hospital, sr attend 1972; Harper Hospital, 1971; Detroit Gen Hospital, 1971; Wayne St & Med School, asst lectr 1971; Private Practice, 1966-69; VA Hospital, staff surg 1966; Dearborn 1965-66; Saginaw Mi 1964-65; Am Bd Surg, diplo 1964; Dearborn VA Hospital, instr 1963-64; gen surg res 1959-63; Mercy Hospital, intrnshp 1958-59; self employed Detroit, Michigan, surgeon, 1966-87; Chrysler Corp, Detroit, Michigan, plant physician 1983-. **ORGANIZATIONS:** Am Coll of Surgeons Am Trauma Soc; Intl Coll of Surgeons; Detroit Surg Assn; Detroit Surg Soc; diplomate Am Bd of Surg; Am Med Writers Assn;AMA; Wayne Co Med Soc; Natl Med Assn; Detroit Med Soc; Wolverine Med Soc Spkrs Bur; Am Cancer Soc; bd dirs United Health Org 1985-; chmn, Comm Occupational Health Safety, Wayne County Medical Society 1989-. **HONORS/ACHIEVEMENTS:** Dr. Clarke McDermont Award 1962, 1963, Chi Delta Mu 1957. **MILITARY SERVICE:** USN 1944-46; US Army Medical Corp, Active Reserve, col 1983-. **BUSINESS ADDRESS:** Plant Physician, Outer Drive Manufacturing Technical Center, Chrysler Corp, 3675 E. Outer Drive, Detroit, MI 48234.

HILL, GEORGE HIRAM
Business executive. **PERSONAL:** Born Apr 13, 1940, Detroit, MI; married Alma Matney; children: Dylan Foster. **EDUCATION:** Wayne State Univ, BA 1963, graduate work. **CAREER:** MI Bell Telephone Co, comm consultant employment supr/comm supvr 1963-68; Assist Negro Youth Campaign, exec dir 1967; Job Oppty Line WJBK-TV, host 1968-73; Chrysler Corp, labor rel supr/corp personnel staff 1968-71; Foster Chemicals Inc, pres 1971-. **ORGANIZATIONS:** Asst treasurer, Greater Detroit Chamber of Commerce; bd of advisors, Univ of Detroit Business School. **HONORS/ACHIEVEMENTS:** Honored by Boy Scouts of Amer MI Dist 1973; Jr Achievement Award 1973; Citation Distinguished & Significant Contributions Wayne Co Comm Coll; Minority Businessman of the Year State of MI 1978; Outstanding Small Businessman of the Year State of MI 1979. **BUSINESS ADDRESS:** President, Foster Chemicals Inc, 15477 Woodrow Wilson, Detroit, MI 48238.

HILL, GERTRUDE BEATRICE
Psychologist. **PERSONAL:** Born Apr 27, 1943, Birmingham, AL. **EDUCATION:** Howard Univ, BA 1971; Univ of DC, MA 1979. **CAREER:** Federal City Coll, intl stud counselor 1972-74; Operations Crossroads Africa, DC coord africa leadership prog 1975; For Love of Children, family work coord 1980-83; FL Memorial Coll, adjunct prof of psych 1984-85; Nova Univ Clinic, staff psychologist 1983-84; Early Childhood Develop, family therapist 1985-. **ORGANIZATIONS:** Volunteer feeder at DC Village for Aged and Handicapped 1975-83; consultant US Dept of Educ 1979-80; mem Congress Black Scholars Urban League FL 1983-85; mem Natl Forum Black Public Adminis 1983-; co-chair Cmte for Non-White Concerns Comm Serv Council 1983-84; 1st black counseling psychologist hired by NovaUniv 1983-84; consultant La Fierta Child Devel Ctr Mgmt 1986-. **HONORS/ACHIEVEMENTS:** Awarded Family Systems Therapy Training Grant by Uniformed Serv Univ MD 1981; Workshop Presenter at FL Child Care Conf 1986.

HILL, HENRY
Automobile dealership chief executive. **CAREER:** East Tulsa Dodge Inc, Tulsa, OK, chief exec. **BUSINESS ADDRESS:** East Tulsa Dodge Inc., 4627 South Memorial Dr., Tulsa, OK 74145. *

HILL, HENRY, JR.
Banking executive. **PERSONAL:** Born Mar 19, 1935, Nashville, TN; married Mary E Hill; children: Michael E, Terrill E, Veronica E. **EDUCATION:** Weaver Sch of Real Est, cert; Amer Inst of Banking, diploma 1981. **CAREER:** Citizens Svngs Bank & Trust Co, branch mgr/loan ofcr 1963-76, executive vice pres 1976-84, interim pres/CEO 1984, pres/CEO 1984-. **ORGANIZATIONS:** Bd dir Better Busn Bureau; bd dir Amer Inst Banking; bd dir Citizens Savings Bank & Trust Co; bd dir March of Dimes Birth Defectd Fd; chmn bd dir South St Comm Cntr; chmn trustees bd Progressive Bapt Ch; Man of the Year 1986; Natl Assoc of Negro Bus and Prof Women's Club, Inc 1986 Graduate of Leadership Nashville. **HONORS/ACHIEVEMENTS:** Profiled Nashville Banner (newspaper) 1984; Profiled Nashville Tennessean (newspaper) 1984; Cert of Apprec South St Comm Center 1980. **BUSINESS ADDRESS:** President & CEO, Citizens Savings Bank & Trust, Fourth & Charlotte Aves, Nashville, TN 37219.

HILL, HOWARD HAMPTON
Attorney. **PERSONAL:** Born Mar 29, 1915, Aiken, SC; son of Adam P. Hill, Sr. and Savannah Dunbar Hill; married Jane Washington Graves, Jul 22, 1975; children: Sylvia Maria, Howard Maurice, Charles III. **EDUCATION:** DePaul U, 1949; VA Union U, JD 1939. **CAREER:** Raymond C Sufana, Lk Co IN, pros atty 1985; LC Bar Assn, pres; IN St, parole ofcr; dep pros atty; Dept Redev, cnsl, legal Adv. **ORGANIZATIONS:** Mem St Juvenile Justice Div; mem, trustee Bd 1st Bapt Ch; NAACP; Boy Scouts of Am; Frontiers of Am; Roosevelt Alumni Assn; bd dir Gary Urban Leag; CIO Union; fdr Gary Alumni Chpt, Kappa Alpha Psi 1935. **HONORS/ACHIEVEMENTS:** 1st Black Asst Corp Cnsl, Gary IN 1952; All Am, All CIAA 1939. **HOME ADDRESS:** 3354 W 21st Ave, Gary, IN 46404.

HILL, JACQUELINE R.
Attorney. **PERSONAL:** Born May 23, 1940, Topeka, KS; daughter of Boyd Alexander Hill (deceased) and Noblesse Demoss Lansdowne; children: Dana Alesse Jamison, MD. **EDUCATION:** Univ of CA Berkeley, BA 1957-62; Univ of Southern CA, Teachers Credential 1965-66; Southwestern Univ School of Law, JD (cum laude) 1968-72; California State Univ, Long Beach, Certitificate in Calligraphy 1987-89. **CAREER:** Univ of CA Lawrence Radiation Lab, admin exec 1963-66; L A Unified School Dist, math teacher 1966-1973; LA Comm Coll Dist, evening instr 1972-75; Los Angeles City, deputy dist atty. **ORGANIZATIONS:** Mem NCTM CMC CACTMA NEA CTA UTLA AFT 1966-1972; Langston Law Clb; CA State Bar; Amer Bar Assc; CA Dist Attys Assc; Assc of Dpty Dist Attys 1972-; CA State Adv Grp Juvenile Justice and Delinquency Prevention 1983-; bd dir Didi Hirsch Comm Mental Health Ctr 1979-;Society of Calligraphy; mem Societas Docta, Inc 1987-89. **HONORS/ACHIEVEMENTS:** Legal Book Awards Southwestern Univ School of Law 1969-72; Outstanding Women of Amer 1973-74. **BUSINESS ADDRESS:** Deputy District Attorney, Los Angeles County, 210 W Temple St, Los Angeles, CA 90012.

HILL, JAMES, JR.
Certified public accountant. **PERSONAL:** Born Aug 20, 1941, Baltimore, MD; married Carole; children: James III, Brian. **EDUCATION:** Central State Coll, BS 1964; Univ of Chicago, MBA 1967. **CAREER:** Union Carbon, cost accountant 1964-65; Alexander Grant & Co, auditor 1967-69; Chicago Economic Devel Corp, deputy dir 1969-71; Hill Taylor & Co, managing partner. **ORGANIZATIONS:** Bd of dirs Chicago Commons Assoc 1970-; various comms Amer Inst of CPA's 1977-; state bd of accountancy State of IL 1980-; bd of dirs IL CPA Soc 1983-86, Provident Hosp 1983-86, Better Government Assoc 1987-. **HONORS/ACHIEVEMENTS:** Certificate of Appreciation Central State Univ 1981-82; Citation of Achievement Inst of Internal Auditors 1981. **BUSINESS ADDRESS:** Managing Partner, Hill Taylor & Co, 116 South Michigan 11th Floor, Ste 705, Chicago, IL 60603.

HILL, JAMES A., JR.
Attorney general. **PERSONAL:** Born Apr 23, 1947, Atlanta, GA; married CJ Van Pelt; children: Jennifer Joy. **EDUCATION:** MI State Univ, BA 1969; IN Univ, MBA 1971, JD 1974. **CAREER:** OR Dept of Revenue, hearing ofcr; OR Dept Justice, asst atty gen, law clk; Judge Adv Gen Corp 1972; Bankers Trust Co 1970. **ORGANIZATIONS:** Mem OR State Bar Assc 1975-; mem Salem OR Chpt; NAACP; chrt mem OR Assembly for Black Affairs. **HONORS/ACHIEVEMENTS:** Flwshp The Consortium Grad Study in Bus for Blacks IN Univ.

HILL, JAMES A., SR.
Minister, educator. **PERSONAL:** Born Jun 10, 1934, Chicago, IL; son of Mr Robert E Hill Sr and Mrs Fannie M Whitney Hill; divorced; children: Carl J, Jewell Davis, Fannie M, James A Jr, Robert E. **EDUCATION:** Chicago Baptist Coll, Sem Dept 1959; Blackstone School of Law, LLB 1962; Clarksville School of Theology, BD 1966, THD 1979; Amer Bible & Divinity Coll, ThM 1966; St John's Univ, BA 1974; Trinity Coll, MSSc 1976; Faith Evangelical Luthern Seminary, Tacoma WA, Doctor of Ministry 1989; Gradelupa College & Seminary, San Antonio TX, Doctor of Humanities 1988. **CAREER:** Wayne County EOE, dep dir 1967-69; Wayne County Probation Dept, probation officer 1969-72; Memphis Urban League, dep dir 1975-80; Methodist CME Church, minister 1950-. **ORGANIZATIONS:** Mem Gov's Comm on Human Rights, Fairbanks Human Relations Council; exec bd Fairbanks USO, United Fund Comm; chmn Boy Scouts of Amer; mem Fairbanks Ministerial Assoc, Anchorage Ministerial Assoc, The Amer Acad of Political & Soc Sci; asst state chaplain Elks State of MI Assoc; asst grand chaplain Elks Natl Assoc of the IBPOE of W; professional mem Adult Educ Assoc of USA; life mem AMVETS; mem The Amer Counselors Soc, Amer Ministerial Assoc, Natl Assoc of Social Workers Inc. **HONORS/ACHIEVEMENTS:** Letters of Appreciation Govs Comm on Human Rights State of AK; Letters of Appreciation Fairbanks Human Relations Council; The NAACP State Level Svcs; Letters of Appreciation Univ of AK; Letters of Appreciation Mayor of the City of Fairbanks AK; First and only black mem of the clergy listed in the AK Literary Dir for the State of AK 1964; Plaques from the Eastern Star & Masonic Order; meritorious Serv Cert Masonic Order; Meritorious Serv Plaques Inkster Br of the US Jaycees 1967-68; Meritorious Serv Plaques Golden Gate Lodge, Sunset Temple, IBPOE of W; Certificate of Appreciation South Bend Urban league for Oustanding Community Leadership; Plaque Laymen Chapel CME Church for serv beyond the call of duty; Community Serv Awd The Hon Harold E Ford US Congressman 1977; Man of the Year, Christian Information & Service Center 1988, Outstanding Big Brother Award, Angelina County Juvenile Probation Serv 1988; Outstanding Family & Community Serv, The Hon Charles Wilson US Congressman 1988; Let's Study the Bible 1987; Evangelism for Today 1985. **HOME ADDRESS:** 3733 Juneau Street, P O Box 18616, Seattle, WA 98118. **BUSINESS ADDRESS:** Minister, Curry Temple CME Church, 172 23rd Ave, Seattle, WA 98122.

HILL, JAMES H.
Public relations executive. **PERSONAL:** Born Aug 11, 1947, Cleveland, OH; son of Cassie Hill; married Cynthia Carter, Mar 05, 1988. **EDUCATION:** Ohio Univ, Athens OH, BS Journalism, 1969; Ohio Univ Graduate School, Athens OH, attended. **CAREER:** Owens-Corning Fiberglas, Toledo OH, merchandise supvr, 1970-75; WGTE-TV FM (PBS), Toledo OH, dir public information, 1975-77, producer/writer, 1977-80; S C Johnson, Racine WI, mgr operations, public relations, 1980-82; Sara Lee Corp, Chicago IL, dir of public relations, 1982-86; Burrell Public Relations Inc, Chicago IL, pres/CEO, 1986-. **ORGANIZATIONS:** Bd mem, NAACP/Toledo, 1973-75; mem, PCC, 1983-, PRSA, 1983-; co-chairman/fundraising, UNCF/Chicago, 1983; bd mem, Children and Adolescent Forum, 1984-86; mem, BPRSA, 1985-; membership comm, UNCF, 1985-; bd mem, Travelers & Immigrant Aid, 1989-; public relations advisory comm, Chicago Urban League, 1989-. **HONORS/ACHIEVEMENTS:** Gold Trumpet, PCC, 1981; Silver Trumpet, PCC, 1981, 1986, 1989; CINE Golden Eagle, 1981; Gold Quil IABC, 1984; Silver Anvil (2), 1986. **BUSINESS ADDRESS:** President/CEO, Burrell Public Relations Inc, 20 North Michigan Ave, Chicago, IL 60602.

HILL, JAMES L.
Association executive. **PERSONAL:** Born Aug 21, 1928, Austin, TX; married Geraldine

Holmes; children: Jacqueline (Howard). **EDUCATION:** Huston-Tillotson Coll, BA Ed 1953;Univ of TX, MEd 1962. **CAREER:** TX St Bd of Ed, dir, Off of Urban Ed 1985; CTB/MCGRAW Hill, Manchester MO, eval splst 1973-74; Pt Arthur, dir, pupil prsnl 1968-73, dir testing 1964-68; Abilene, guidance cnslr 1959-64. **ORGANIZATIONS:** Mem NEA; TX St Tchr Assn; TX Prsnl & Guidance Assn; Am Prsnl & Guidance Assn; Phi Delta Kappa; past mem, bd dir Jefferson Co Ec Oppor Commn; mem TX Urban Adv Cncl; TX Urban Curriculum & Evaluation Cncls, Huston-Tillotson Coll. **HONORS/ACHIEVEMENTS:** Spl Alumni Award 1972; chosen as one of 30 educators to tour Viet Nam with Bob Hope Troupe to present MEMO. **MILITARY SERVICE:** USN 1948-53. **BUSINESS ADDRESS:** TX Educ Agency, 201 E 11 St, Austin, TX 78701.

HILL, JAMES LEE
Educational administrator. **PERSONAL:** Born Dec 10, 1941, Meigs, GA; son of Mr & Mrs Willie L Hill (deceased); married Flo J; children: Deron James, Toussaint LeMarc. **EDUCATION:** Fort Valley St Coll, BS English 1959-63; Atlanta Univ, MA English 1963-68; Univ of IA, PhD American CIV 1971-76; Purdue Univ, post doctoral study 1981; John Carroll Univ, post doctoral study 1984; Univ of Texas, post doctoral study, 1989. **CAREER:** Winder City Schs, instructor English 1964-65; Hancock Central High, chmn Eng dept 1965-68; Paine Coll, instructor English 1968-71; Benedict Coll, chmn Eng dept 1974-77; Albany State Coll, chmn Eng dept 1977-, dean arts & sciences 1981-. **ORGANIZATIONS:** Consultant natl Rsch Project on Black Women 1979-81; sec Albany Urban League Bd 1979-81; chair Assoc Assit Conf on Coll Comp & Comm 1980-83; chairvice chair GA Endowment for Humanities 1981-83; mem Exec Comm NCTE 1982-83; pres Beta Nu Sigma Phi Beta Sigma Frat 1983-85; chair Academic Comm on English-GA 1983-84; vice pres S Atlantic Assn of Dept of English 1984-85; bd dir Natl Fed State Humanities Councils 1984-87; mem Coll Section Comm Natl Council of Teachers of English 1985-89; dir NEA Writer-in-Resd Prog ASC 1982-85; dir NEH Summer Humanities Inst ASC 1983-85; regional dir Southern RegionPhi Beta Sigma; visiting scholar Nat'l Humanities Faculty. **HONORS/ACHIEVEMENTS:** NEH Fellow Atlanta Univ 1969; NEH Fellow Univ of IA 1971-74; Governor's Award in the Humanities, State of Georgia, 1987. **HOME ADDRESS:** 2408 Greenmount Dr, Albany, GA 31705. **BUSINESS ADDRESS:** Dean of Arts & Sciences, Albany State College, 504 College Dr, Albany, GA 31705.

HILL, JAMES O.
City employee. **PERSONAL:** Born Sep 05, 1937, Austin; married Eva Marie Mosby; children: Eva Marie, James O II, Dudley Joseph. **EDUCATION:** Howard Univ, BA 1964; Nova Univ, MPA 1975. **CAREER:** City of Ft Lauderdale, asst city mgr, manpower analyst, admin asst 1971-; Boys Clubs of Broward Co FL, dir 1968-71; Boys Clubs of Newark, asst dir 1964-68. **ORGANIZATIONS:** Mem Intl City Mgrs Assc 1972-; Amer Soc of Pub Admin 1973-; ARC 1971-; Govs Crime Prevention Task Force 1971-; Elks 1970-; KC 1968; Seminole Hist Soc 1975; Ft Lauderdale Chamber of Comm 1971-. **HONORS/ACHIEVEMENTS:** Educ achievement award USAF 1961; Youth Srv Award 1970; 3 Boys Club Srv Awards 1964-70. **MILITARY SERVICE:** USAF a/1c 1958-62. **BUSINESS ADDRESS:** PO Box 14250, Fort Lauderdale, FL 33301.

HILL, JEFFREY RONALD
Marketing manager. **PERSONAL:** Born Nov 14, 1948, Philadelphia, PA. **EDUCATION:** Cheyney State Clge, bS Sci 1972; Penn State Univ PA, mrkt cert 1974. **CAREER:** Nabisco Inc, mrkt sales mgr; Hilltop Promotions Philadelphia, dir 1979-; Second Story/Catacombs Disco Complex Phila, mgr 1978-79; 3rd Jazz Record Co & Retail Phila, mgr 1975-76; Philip Morris Tobacco Co NY, sales mgr 1972-75. **ORGANIZATIONS:** Mem Natl Hist Soc 1968-77; mem Black Music Assc; mem Amer Film Inst. **HONORS/ACHIEVEMENTS:** Merit Achievement Award Amer Legion Philadelphia Post 1963. **BUSINESS ADDRESS:** Navisco Inc, 201 Precision Dr, Horsham, PA 19044.

HILL, JESSE, JR.
Business executive. **PERSONAL:** Married Azira Gonzalez; children: Nancy, Azira. **EDUCATION:** Univ MD, BS 1947; Lincoln Univ, BA; Univ of MI, M Bus Admin. **CAREER:** Atlanta Life Ins Co, pres ceo. **ORGANIZATIONS:** Chmn campaign of Andrew Young 1972; campaign of Maynard Jackson; past chmn Natl Alliance of Businessmen; dir Marta; mem bd dir Delta Airlines; past chmn Atlanta Crime Commn; pres Enterprise Investments Inc; mem Amer Acad of Actuaries, Atlanta Actuarial Club, SE Actuarial Club; mem bd dir chmn Bldg Com of Martin Luther King Ctr for Social Change; mem bd dir Natl Urban Coalition Oppor Funding Inc; Natl Urban League; Voter Educ proj; bd Boy Scoutsof Amer, Bethune Cookman Coll, Provident Hospital; bd dirs Sperry Hutchinson Co, Communications Satellite Corp, Morse Shoe Co, Trust Co of GA, Knight Ridder Newspapers Inc, Natl Serv Industries Inc. **HONORS/ACHIEVEMENTS:** Received numerous honors & awds from civic & civil rights orgns; Annual Natl Urban League EOE Awd 1965; Most Disting Alumni Awd MO Lincoln Univ 1970; Abe Goldstein Awd Anti-Defamation League of B'nai B'rith 1973; Hon LLD Morris Brown Coll, Clark Coll 1972 1974; Chung-Ang Univ 1976. **MILITARY SERVICE:** Veteran Korean war. **BUSINESS ADDRESS:** President/CEO, Atlanta Life Ins Co, PO Box 897, Atlanta, GA 30301.

HILL, JOHN C.
Education administrator. **PERSONAL:** Born Jan 30, 1926, Terre Haute, IN; married Alyce Adams. **EDUCATION:** IN State Teachers Coll, BS 1947, MS 1950; IN Univ, EdD 1965. **CAREER:** IN Schols, sci & math teacher 1947-50, hs principal 1950-56, supt of schools 1956-63; IN State Univ, prof ed admin 1965-, asst interim dean 1967-. **ORGANIZATIONS:** Exec dir IN Leg Study Comm 1963-65; consult Facility Plng to Architects/Schools 1965-; chmn CEFP I Great Lakes Reg 1969-72; ed bd Contemporary Ed 1972-, Black Amer Lit Forum 1969-, CEFP I Jrnl 1978-; mem Phi Delta Kappa 1954-, Phi Kappa Phi 1982-, IN Assoc of Public School Supts 1963-. **HONORS/ACHIEVEMENTS:** Cert of Recognition Phi Delta Kappa 1979; Serv Citation Awd CEFP I 1972; Outstanding Educators of Amer OEA 1972,73,74,75,76; 1st Design Awd Progressive Architecture 1972. **MILITARY SERVICE:** AAF sgt 1944-46; Air Medal, DFC, Good Conduct, Unit Service Citation 1945. **BUSINESS ADDRESS:** Asst Dean Admin & Inst Serv, Indiana StateUniv, School of Education, 1117 ISU, Terre Haute, IN 47809.

HILL, JOHNNY R.
University administrator. **PERSONAL:** Born Apr 27, 1944, Hot Springs, AR; son of Simmie Hill and Lusbirda Hill; married Etta Jo; children: Kenyetta, Johnny Ray Jr. **EDUCATION:** KY State Univ, BA 1967; Western KY State Univ, MA 1969; Miami Univ OH, PhD 1972; Univ of WI, 1973; Harvard Univ, Post Doctoral 1980. **CAREER:** KY State Univ, prof, ed psych, dean of students 1972-74; Univ of Louisville, asst to pres 1974-75; Natl Assoc of State Univ & Land Grant Coll, execdir Off for Advancement of Pub Negro Colls 1975-78; Bowie State Coll, vice pres acad affairs, dean 1978-81; Prairie View A&M Univ, vice pres for devel & univ rel 1981-85; State Comm Coll, pres 1985-86; Chicago State Univ, vice pres for student affairs 1986. **ORGANIZATIONS:** Vp West Louisville Med Group 1974-75; public mem Foreign Serv US State Dept 1976-; adv comm mem US Dept Agriculture 1978; mem Alpha Phi Alpha 1964, Phi Delta Kappa 1982, Alpha Kappa Mu 1966, APGA, River Reg Mental Health Bd 1973-75, Louisville & Atlanta Urban League, Amer Assoc of Higher Ed, Council forAdvancement Ed; bd of dir St Louis Urban League, Chicago Urban League. **HONORS/ACHIEVEMENTS:** Mayor Flynn Citizenship Awd Frankfort KY 1966; author "A Study of the Public Assisted Black Coll Presidency" 1972; authored a variety of articles in jrnls 1972-78; Urban League Awd 1973; Outstanding Young Man in Amer 1972; Outstanding Educator Citation; Star of David Award 1986. **BUSINESS ADDRESS:** Vice President, Chicago State Univ, 95 at King Dr, Chicago, IL 60628.

HILL, JOSEPH HAVORD
Attorney, director of labor relations. **PERSONAL:** Born Aug 19, 1940, Luverne, AL; son of Huey Hill and Arneta Williams Hill; married Jacqueline Bryant, Jun 30, 1963; children: Jason Joseph Kent Hill. **EDUCATION:** Central State Univ, Wilberforce OH, BS, 1962; Akron Univ, Akron OH, JD, 1972. **CAREER:** Goodyear Tire and Rubber Co, Akron OH, chemist, 1965-69; Natl Labor Relations Bd, Cleveland OH, attorney, 1972-76; Montgomery Ward, Chicago IL, sr labor relations attorney, 1976-78; McDonald's Corp, Oakbrook IL, sr labor relations attorney, 1978-81, staff dir labor relations, 1981-83, dir of labor relations, 1983-. **ORGANIZATIONS:** Life mem, Alpha Phi Alpha Frat, 1959-; bd of dir, Alpha Phi Alpha Homes Inc, Akron OH, 1972-76; pres, Alpha Phi Alpha Frat, Eta Tau Lambda, Akron OH, 1974-76; mem, NAACP, 1981, Uran League of Chicago, Amer Bar Assn, 1981-, Natl Bar Assn, 984-. **HONORS/ACHIEVEMENTS:** Akron Univ Law Review, 1980; President's Award, McDonald's Corp, 1981. **MILITARY SERVICE:** US Army, Artillery (Field), captain, 1963-65. **BUSINESS ADDRESS:** Director of Labor Relations, McDonald's Corporation, Office Campus Building, Jorie Blvd, Oak Brook, IL 60521.

HILL, JULIA H.
Educator. **PERSONAL:** Born Sep 28, Kansas City, MO; married Quincy T (deceased). **EDUCATION:** Lincoln Univ, Jefferson City MO, BS (cum laude) 1943; Univ of Southern CA, LA, CA, Master's degree 1954; Nova Univ, Ft Lauderdale, FL, Doctorte of Educ 1982. **CAREER:** Kansas City, MO School Dist, elementary school teacher 1943-66, consultant/urban affairs 1966-67, coord Title I paraprofessional 1968-75, elementary school prin 1975-76; Pioneer Comm Coll, comm serv coord 1976-79, coord Northland Work and Training Unit 1980-81, evening coord Kansas City Skill Center 1982-85; Pioneer Comm Coll, coord of coll relations 1985-. **ORGANIZATIONS:** Mem Kansas City, MO School Bd 1984-; mem Kansas City Campus Ministers 1984-; mem SW Bell Tele Adv Comm 1981-; former pres Kansas City, MO NAACP Branch 1971-80; life mem chairperson Kansas City, MO NAACP Branch 1984-; mem Alpha Kappa Alpha Sorority Beta Omega Chapter; life mem/golden heritage life mem NAACP. **HONORS/ACHIEVEMENTS:** Dist Servs, Kansas City, MO Leon M Jordan Mem Award 1971; Citizen of the Year Omega Phi Psi Fraternity Kansas City, MO 1973; Ldrshp & Civil Rights, KS City, MO Baptist Ministers Union 1974; SCLC Black Woman on the Move in Civil Rights 1975; Othell G Whitlock Meml Award Comm Involvement 1976; Outstanding Serv Natl NAACP Civil Rights Award 1976; Afro-Amer Student Union Disting Comm Leadership 1977; Zeta Phi Beta Sor Outstanding Leadership; Greater Kansas City Business and Prof Women Sojourner Truth Award; Outstanding Civil Rights 1978; Outstanding Women of the Year Award; Beacon Light Seventh Day Adventist Church Outstanding Comm Serv 1979; Operation PUSH, Dr Martin Luther King Jr Awards; Girl Scouts of Amer Awd; Civil Rights Black Archives Award 1980-81; selected for list of 100 Most Influential Blacks of Kansas City 1986-88. **HOME ADDRESS:** 5100 Lawn Ave, Kansas City, MO 64130.

HILL, JULIUS W.
Physician. **PERSONAL:** Born Jun 12, 1917, Atlanta, GA; married Luella Blaine; children: Sheila Lorraine. **EDUCATION:** Johnson C Smith Univ, BA 1933; Univ of IL, BS, MS 1973; Meharry Med Coll, MD 1951; USC, Orthopedic Surgery 1956. **CAREER:** MD Orthopedic Surgery self-employed. **ORGANIZATIONS:** Past pres Natl Med Assn 1969-70; mem bd dir LA Co Hosp Comm 1963-; Natl Med Fellowships Inc 1970-; Charles R Drew Postgrad Med Sch 1971-; Riverside Natl Bk Houston; pres Emeritus Golden State Med Assn 1960-72; pres Natl Med Assn Fnd 1974-; bd dir Martin Luther King Hosp LA; mem Amer Med Assn; CA State Med Assn; various assn clubs & comm; mem Phi Beta Kappa; Sigma Xi; Kappa Alpha Psi; Masons. **HONORS/ACHIEVEMENTS:** Distinguished Serv Award Natl Med Assn 1970-71; outstanding serv award Charles R Drew Med Soc LA. **MILITARY SERVICE:** AUS maj 1941-46.

HILL, KENNETH D.
Business executive. **PERSONAL:** Born Jan 22, 1938, Bryn Mawr, PA; married C Irene Wigington; children: Kimberly Diane. **EDUCATION:** Temple Univ, Assoc Arch Tech 1958; Univ of PA, Indust Mgmt 1972; Harvard Business School, PMD 1980. **CAREER:** Sun Co Inc, central sales training mgr 1969-71; Alliance Enterprise, pres 1971-73; Sun Co Inc, dist mgr 1973-75, proj mgr corp human resources 1975-76, div mgr mktg 1976-79, mgr corp citizenship 1979-84, vice pres publ affairs 1984-. **ORGANIZATIONS:** Chmn council of trustees Cheyney State Univ 1981; bd of trustees Comm Leadership Seminar 1983; pres Amer Assn of Blacks in Energy 1984-86; bd dir Private Industry Cncl 1984. **HONORS/ACHIEVEMENTS:** Ebony Women's Awd for Comm Serv Womens Resource Network 1982; James McCoy Founder's Awd NAACP 1982; Centennial Awd for Advancement & Image Bldg Cheyney Univ 1983; Comm Serv Awd Urban League of Philadelphia 1983. **MILITARY SERVICE:** AUS spec 4 1960-62; Good Conduct Medal, Soldier of the Month 1960-62. **BUSINESS ADDRESS:** Vice Pres Public Affairs, Sun Refining & Marketing Co, 1801 Market St, Philadelphia, PA 19103.

HILL, KENNETH RANDAL
Mechanical designer. **PERSONAL:** Born Aug 01, 1952, Detroit, MI; married Sherin Gauff; children: Kenneth Anthony; Kalonn Christopher. **EDUCATION:** Wayne State Univ, attended 1970-72; Art Ctr Coll of Design, BS (honors) 1975. **CAREER:** WTVS Channel 56, graphic/artist 1975-76; freelance/self-employed consultant 1976-85; General Motors Corp, creative designer 1976-82, sr designer 1982-. **ORGANIZATIONS:** Mem NAACP/

Detroit Chap 1972; mem Industrial Designers Soc 1973-75; mem Art Center Alumni Assn 1985; mem Detroit Inst of Arts Founders Soc 1985-86; treas Intl Designers Assoc. **HONORS/ACHIEVEMENTS:** Scholarship Ford Motor Co 1972; Honors/Degree Art Center Coll of Design 1975. **BUSINESS ADDRESS:** Senior Designer, General Motors Corp, G M Tech Center, Warren, MI 48090.

HILL, KENT
Professional athlete. **PERSONAL:** Born Mar 07, 1957, Americus, GA; married Suzette Irving. **EDUCATION:** Georgia Tech, Industrial Mgmt degree. **CAREER:** Los Angeles Rams, guard 1979-. **HONORS/ACHIEVEMENTS:** Played in Senior Bowl; All-NFC UPI and Pro Football Weekly 1980; All-NFL by Pro Football Weekly 1980; first Carroll Rosenbloom Awd winner honoring the club's Rookie of the Yr 1983; All-Rookie honors from Football Digest 1983; first team All-NFL by Sporting News; first team All-NFC by UPI 1983; second team All-NFL byAssoc Press 1985; second team All-NFC by UPI 1985; mem 1986 Pro Bowl team.

HILL, LAWRENCE THORNE
Physician. **PERSONAL:** Born Jan 15, 1947, Washington, DC; married Greta Dixon. **EDUCATION:** Muhlenberg Coll, BS 1968; Howard Univ Coll of Medicine, MD 1972. **CAREER:** Georgetown Univ Rad Med, assoc dir 1976-84; Howard Univ, assoc prof radiation oncology 1976-; Washington County Hosp Rad Oncol, dir 1984-. **ORGANIZATIONS:** Bd dirs Amer Cancer Soc Washington County 1984-; chmn cancer comm and tumor bd, mem hospice comm, mem radiation safety comm Washington County Hosp;chmn Intl Cancer League; mem tumor bd Frederick Memorial Hosp; dir US Virgin Island Cancer Project; mem Intl Hospice Comm, Radiation Therapy Tech Howard Univ Coll of Allied Health; consultant Pan Amer Health Org. **HONORS/ACHIEVEMENTS:** Junior Clinical Fellowship in Radiation Oncology Amer Cancer Soc 1977-80; AMA Physician Recognition Awd 1977,82,86; 11 publications including "Radiation Risks in Pregnancy," w/KL Mossman Obste and Gynecol 1982. **BUSINESS ADDRESS:** Dir Radiation Oncology, Washington County Hospital, 251 East Antietam St, Hagerstown, MD 21740.

HILL, LEO
Business administrator. **PERSONAL:** Born Mar 27, 1937, Columbus, TX; married Jacquelyne; children: Leo, Stacy. **EDUCATION:** LA City Coll, 1955-58; LA State Coll, BA 1958-61; LA State Coll, Grad Work 1961-62; CA Tech, 1969; Pepperdine, 1970; Univ of CA, 1973; Univ of CA LA, Cert Ind Rel 1979, Cert Personnel Mgmt 1979; Inst of Cert Professional Mgrs, Cert Certified Mgr 1984. **CAREER:** RCA Serv Co, sr job devel admin; Hughes Aircraft Co, head eeo/affirm action prog 1977-81; Lockheed-CA Co, mgr equal oppor programs 1981-. **ORGANIZATIONS:** Dir comm prog Greater LA Community Action Agency; dir Program Monitoring, Neighborhood Youth Corps, Narcotics 1973; asst eeo 1972, dir personnel 1972 Economic & Youth Oppty Agency Gr LA; personell dir 1966-71, acting admin officer 1968-69 Neighborhood Adult Participation Proj Inc; rec dir Bethune Co Park; mem comm Florence-Firestone Coord Council & Case Conf; mem LA Area C of C Ed Comm, Men of Tomorrow, Hunters Elite Gun Club, Narcotics Task Force, Amer Soc Training & Devel; vice pres 1961, treas 1960 LA State Coll Inter-Frat Council; pres Kappa Psi Frat. **HONORS/ACHIEVEMENTS:** All W State Conf 2 yrs; All S CA 2 yrs; Sam Berry Tournament Most Valuable Player; Broke-Tied 11 Records Jr Coll Career; CCAA 1st team 3 yrs; Leading Scorer NCAA Most Valuable; All Amer 2 yrs; CA State Univ Los Angeles Hall of Fame (Basketball) 1985. **BUSINESS ADDRESS:** Manager Equal Oppor Programs, Lockheed-Calfornia Co, PO Box 551, Burbank, CA 91520.

HILL, MARNESBA D.
Librarian, educator. **PERSONAL:** Born Mar 30, 1913, La Crosse, WI; married Irving C Northover; children: Suzanne, Marnesba, Patricia, Stephanie. **EDUCATION:** Langston Univ, BS 1940; Atlanta Univ, BLS 1947; Columbia Univ, MA 1963; Univ London, postgrad 1953. **CAREER:** Atlanta Univ, libr 1947-58; Herbert H Lehman Clge City Univ NY, chief libr, prof, asst libr 1958-. **ORGANIZATIONS:** Mem Natl Libr Week Comm Amer Libr Assc 1967-70; vice pres Libr Assc City Univ NY 1967-69; mem Delta Kappa Gamma; Kappa Delta Pi vice pres 1972-73; consult NY State Dept Health Educ Materials Ctr 1970-71; Univ Nigeria Libr 1960-62; mem Libr Com Riverside Ch 1970—78. **BUSINESS ADDRESS:** Herbert H Lehman Coll, Bedford Park Blvd W, Bronx, NY 10468.

HILL, MARY ALICE
Assoc. executive. **PERSONAL:** Born Sep 15, 1938, Marlow, GA; married Elton E Hill. **EDUCATION:** NJ Coll of Commerce, Public Admin 1956; Univ Coll, Urban Studies 1972; Rutgers Univ, Certified Public Manager 1986; Natl Council of Negro Women, pres. **CAREER:** City of Newark, sr budget analyst 1972-83, mgmt info spec 1985, pres natl council of negro women. **ORGANIZATIONS:** Mem Amer Mgmt Assoc; mem Natl Assoc of Black Public Admin; pres Newark Sect Natl Council of Negro Women Inc; chmn US Selective Service Bd #33; mem NJ State Univ of Med & Dentistry; bd pres Council on Affirm Action; chair Metropolitan BC Women's Day 1983; mem NJ Bethune Recognition Team Steering Comm 1985; officer Bethany 43, OES PHA Newark NJ; chair NJ Rainbow Coalition. **HONORS/ACHIEVEMENTS:** Nomination Mayor's Comm Service Awd 1980; Rainbow Coalition Serv Awd 1984; chmn UMDNJ-PCAA 1987. **HOME ADDRESS:** 351 Seymour Ave, Newark, NJ 07112. **BUSINESS ADDRESS:** President, Natl Council of Negro Women, PO Box 295, Newark, NJ 07102.

HILL, MERVYN E., JR.
Producer. **PERSONAL:** Born Jul 12, 1947, St Louis. **EDUCATION:** Grand Valley State Clge, BA; Wm James Clge; Allendale MI 1974. **CAREER:** WGVC-TV Allendale MI, asst to prod 1975-; Black Free Form Theatre Co Grand Rapids, actor, asst dir 1971-72; Living Arts Proj Grand Rapids Bd Educ, drama dir 1971-72; WOTV Grand Rapids, mgr 1973. **HONORS/ACHIEVEMENTS:** Prod consult "Arbitration Mr Businessman"; assc prod ed "Portrait of African Journey"; author screenplay "The Neighborhood". **BUSINESS ADDRESS:** WGVC TV 35, Allendale, MI 49401.

HILL, MICHAEL EDWARD
Editor. **PERSONAL:** Born Nov 28, 1943, St Paul, MN. **EDUCATION:** Coll St Thomas, BA 1965; Univ of Minnesota, M 1978. **CAREER:** Minneapolis Trib, reporter, asst city ed 1965-70; WA Post, copy ed, asst city ed, day sports ed, asst style ed, TV ed 1970-. **ORGANIZATIONS:** Mem Kappa Tau Alpha Univ Minnesota 1967. **HONORS/ACHIEVEMENTS:** Recip coll scholarship Minneapolis-St Paul Baseball Writers Assn Amer 1965; Nieman flwshp Harvard Univ 1980-81.

HILL, NORMAN CALVIN
Professional athlete. **PERSONAL:** Born Jan 05, 1961, Nashville, TN. **EDUCATION:** TX Tech, Recreation Major. **CAREER:** Denver Gold, running back 1984-. **HONORS/ACHIEVEMENTS:** All-State linebacker; Adidas All-Am team; Top 100 Players in Am as sr; school's Trackman of the Year.

HILL, NORMAN S.
Association executive. **PERSONAL:** Born Apr 22, 1933, Summit, NJ; married Velma Murphy. **EDUCATION:** Haverford Clge, BA 1955. **CAREER:** A Philip Randolph Inst, pres, exec dir 1975-79, assc dir 1967-74; AFL/CIO, legislative rep & civil rights liason indsl union dept 1964-67; CORE, staff 1961-64. **ORGANIZATIONS:** Mem bd trustees Freedom House; bd dir League Industrial Democracy; Wrkrs Def League; World Withouth War Coun; Frontlash; exec com Coalition for Dem Majority; acctblty comm NY Bd Educ Arts. **HONORS/ACHIEVEMENTS:** Pub AFL/CIO journals, Federationist. **MILITARY SERVICE:** AUS 1956-58. **BUSINESS ADDRESS:** A Philip Randolph Inst, 260 Park Ave S, New York, NY 10010.

HILL, OLIVER W.
Attorney. **PERSONAL:** Born May 01, 1907, Richmond, VA; son of William Henry White Jr and Olivia Lewis White Hill; married Beresenia Walker, Sep 05, 1934; children: Oliver W Jr. **EDUCATION:** Howard Univ, AB 1931; Howard Univ Sch of Law, JD 1933. **CAREER:** Roanoke VA, lawyer 1934-36; Law Practice, 1939-61; FHA, asst to commr 1961-66; Hill Tucker & Marsh, attorney 1966-. **ORGANIZATIONS:** Mem City Council Richmond 1948-50; mem Pres Com on Gov Contracts 1951-54; founder Old Dominion Bar Assn 1942; chmn Legal Com VA State Conf NAACP 1940-61; mem Richmond Dem Com 1955-61, 1966-74; founder Global Assn for the Liberation & Advncmt of Civilized Human Earthlings & the Devel of Universalists 1974; bd mem mem leg com NAACP; mem Urban League; mem bd VA Reg Med Prog; mem NBA Richmond Bar Assn & Old Dominion Bar Assn; mem Omega Psi Phi, Sigma Pi Phi; numerous other civic orgs; mem VA State Bar Discipl Bd 1977-82; mem VA State Bar Judicisary Comm 1977-; former mem bd trustees St Paul's Coll; mem VA Bar Foundation 1985; pres Old Dominion Bar Assoc Foundation 1985; fellow, American College of Trial Lawyers 1987-; mem, Omicrom Delta Kappa Honor Society 1989; mem, Commission on Constitution Revision for Commonwealth of VA 1968-69; trustee, George C Marshall Foundation 1989-. **HONORS/ACHIEVEMENTS:** Chicago Defender Merit Awd 1948; Howard Univ Alumni Awd 1950; co-recipient Russwurm Awd natl Publ Assn 1952; Omega Man of the Yr Omega Psi Phi 1957; VA State Conf Awd NAACP 1957; Lawyer of Yr NBA 1959; Hon LLD St Paul's Coll 1979; William Robert Ming Adv Awd NAACP 1980; Democratic Party of Virginia Wm P Robinson Memorial Awd 1981; Hon LLD VA State Univ 1982; Brotherhood Citation Natl Conf of Christians & Jews 1982; Oliver W Hill Black Pre-Law Assoc Univ of VA 1983; Richmond Amer Muslims Mission Ctr Pioneer Awd 1984; NAACP Legal Defense and Educational Fund, Inc The Simple Justice Awd 1986; Honorary Doctor of Laws, Virginia Union Univ 1988; The Judicial Council of National Bar Assn Awad 1979; The Charles H Houston Medallion of Merit, Washington Bar Assn 1976; Francis Ellis Rivers Award,NAACP Legal Defense and Educational Fund 1976; The Hill-Tucker Public Service Award, The Bar Assn of the City of Richmond VA 1989; Outstanding Contribution to the Legal System Award, The Virginia Commission on Women and Minorities in the Legal System 1987. **MILITARY SERVICE:** AUS s/sgt 1943-45. **HOME ADDRESS:** 3108 Noble Ave, Richmond, VA 23222.

HILL, PATRICIA LIGGINS
Educator. **PERSONAL:** Born Sep 18, 1942, Washington, DC; divorced; children: Sanya Patrice, Solomon Philip. **EDUCATION:** Howard Univ Wash DC, BA cum laude 1965; Univ of San Francisco, mA Eng 1970; Stanford Univ CA, PhD Eng/Am Lit 1977. **CAREER:** Univ of San Francisco, assoc prof English 1979-, dir ethnic studies 1977-, asst prof English 1977-79; Stanford Univ, teaching asst English 1974-77; Univ of San Francisco, instructor English 1971-77; Urban Inst for Human Serv Inc, research consultant 1976-80; Upper Midwest Tri-Racial Center Univ of MN, resource consultant 1977-78. **ORGANIZATIONS:** Bd dir Westside Mental Health Ctr 1971-78; mem SF Comm Clge Bd 1972-78; mem CA Council of Black Educ 1973-. **HONORS/ACHIEVEMENTS:** Recpt of Flwshp Natl Endowment for Humanities 1978; pub "The Dark/Black-Bad Light/White-Good Illusion in Joseph Conrad's 'heart of Darkness' & 'Nigger of the Narcissus'" Western Jour of Black Studies 1979; pub "Roots for a Third World Aesthetic Found in Black & Chicano Poetry" De Colores 1980; pub "The Violent Space, An Interpretation of the Function of the New Black Aesthetic in Etheridge Knight's Poetry" Black Amer Lit Forum 1980. **BUSINESS ADDRESS:** U of San Francisco, 2130 Fulton St, San Francisco, CA 94117.

HILL, PAUL G.
Educator. **PERSONAL:** Born Mar 15, 1933, Gary, IN; son of Daniel Hill and Naomi Hill; divorced; children: Kenneth de Rouen-Hill. **EDUCATION:** IN State Univ, PhD 1973; Kent State Univ, Adv cert 1965; TN A&I State Univ, MA 1965; IN State Univ, BA 1955. **CAREER:** Chicago Publ School, instr 1955-61, couns 1961-67, coord of guid in career devel prog 1967-68; IN State Univ, doctoral fellow 1968-70; Govs State Univ,dir stud serv & prof of human learning & devel 1970-73, disting univ prof of human learning & devel 1973-1989. **ORGANIZATIONS:** Workshop IL Coll Personnel Assoc 1972; conflict resolution team Rich Twp Schl dist 1972-73; co-dir Non-Whites in NASPA 1975-76; mem Natl Assoc of St Personnel Admin 1974-77, Amer Personnel & Guid Assoc 1973-77, World Future Soc 1975, IL Assoc for Non-White Concern 1974-75, Amer Assoc for Higher Ed 1974-75; rsch task force handicapped Bur for Ed of Handicapped & Ed Testing Serv 1975; bd of dir Gavin Meml Found 1974-76; dir Proj Aquarius 1977; career devel workshop Amer Personnel & Guid Assoc Conf 1975; mem Amer Asson for Counseling and Devel. **HONORS/ACHIEVEMENTS:** Blue Key Natl Scholastic Hon Soc; Pi Gamma Mu Hon Soc; Hulman 40 Ave Scholarship Cert IN Univ; Kappa Delta Pi Hon Soc. **MILITARY SERVICE:** USN petty officer 1955-56. **BUSINESS ADDRESS:** Prof Human Learning & Devel, Governors StateUniv, University Park, IL 60466.

HILL, PEARL M.
Educational administrator. **PERSONAL:** Born Apr 07, 1949, Portland, OR; children: Marla Dene. **EDUCATION:** Univ of OR, BS Sociology 1971, MS Counseling/Psych 1973. **CAREER:** Univ of OR, academic coord 1970, counseling coord 1971, asst dir upward bound

1971, dir upward bound 1972-. **ORGANIZATIONS:** Sec Natl Council of Educ Oppor Assoc; mem Amer Personnel & Guidance Assn 1973-75; adv bd mem Univ of OR Financial Aid 1976-77; mem Northwest Assn of Special Progs 1977-80; mem Northwest Assn of Special Progs 1977-; founder Northwest Assn of Special Progs 1977; coord of First Annual Conf at PortLudlow 1977; mem Natl Coord Cncl of Educ Oppor Assns 1977-81; mem OR Alliance of Black Sch Educators 1978; mem Natl Alliance of Black Sch Educators1978; mem Urban League of Portland 1979; mem Natl Cncl of Educ Oppor Assns 1980-82; sec 1981; chair of adv bd Howard Univ Leadership Training 1981-82; founding mem Natl Cncl of Educ Oppor Assns Inc 1981; mem bd of trustees St mark's CME Church 1981; adv mem BOOST Educ Talent Srch Prog 1975-; mem NAACP 1978-; mem Delta Sigma Theta Sor 1982-. **HOME ADDRESS:** 2380 Riverview St, Eugene, OR 97403. **BUSINESS ADDRESS:** Director-Upward Bound, Univ of Oregon, 1859 E 15th, Eugene, OR 97403.

HILL, RAY ALLEN
Educator. **PERSONAL:** Born Sep 16, 1942, Houston, TX; son of Cal Hill Jr (deceased) and Ann Stewart Hill. **EDUCATION:** Howard Univ, Washington DC, BS 1964, MS 1965; Univ of California Berkley, PhD 1977. **CAREER:** Southern Univ, Baton Rouge LA, instructor 1965-66; Howard Univ, Washington DC, instructor botany 1966-75; Fisk Univ, Nashville TN, asst prof 1977-80; EPA, Washington DC, staff scientist 1978; NASA, Washington DC, staff scientist 1979; Univ of CA, San Francisco CA, visiting research assoc prof 1985; Lowell Coll Preparatory School, San Francisco CA, instructor 1986-; Purdue Univ, W Lafayette IN, visiting prof botany & plant pathology 1989; Alpha Distributors, owner, 1989-. **ORGANIZATIONS:** Mem Natl Inst of Science 1968-85, Amer Assn of Advanced Science 1972-85, Amer Soc Cell Biology 1972-85, Botanical Society of Amer 1972-85, Information Visitors Center 1975-, Alpha Phi Alpha Fraternity 1980-; bd mem Big Brothers of East Bay 1986. **HONORS/ACHIEVEMENTS:** F E Worthing Fellow, F E Worthing Trust 1960-64; Faculty Fellow, Howard Univ 1972; Fellow, Ford Found 1975-77; Faculty Fellow, Natl Science Found 1975; NASA/ASEE Fellow, Stanford Univ 1983-84; published "Ultrastructure of Synergids of Gossypium Hirsutum," 1977, and "Polarity Studies in Roots of Ipomea Balatas In Vitro," 1965.

HILL, RAYMOND A.
Engineer. **PERSONAL:** Born Jul 11, 1922, Savannah, GA; son of Raymond Hill and Mary Hill; married Lois Holmes; children: Lopez, Keith. **EDUCATION:** A&T State Univ, BS 1950; George Washington Univ, advance study numerous certificates 1954-58. **CAREER:** Dept Agric Washington DC, cartographic aide 1951; BuShips DC, electronic engr 1951-58, sr engr 1958-59, supr electronic engr 1959-66; Naval Electronics System Command DC, 1966-70, electrons solid state devices unit head 1970-74; SEM Microelectronics & Mfg Tech, sect head, consult 1974-retired. **HONORS/ACHIEVEMENTS:** Publs "Transistors Are They Reliable?" Military Electronics 1957; Military Transistor Specifications Bur Ships Journal 1957; "Radioactive Tubes" BuShips Journal 1957; "Radioactive Tubes Philco Tch" Rep Bulletin 1958; "Radioactive Tubes Danger" Military Electronics 1959; Spl Achievement Awd Tech Asst Electron Tubes by Def Supply Agency 1967; Spl Achievement Awd Tech Assistance DOD on Electron Tube Solid State Devices; DOD-AGED Awd 16 yrs professional svc. **MILITARY SERVICE:** AUS 1943-46.

HILL, REUBEN BENJAMIN
Attorney. **PERSONAL:** Born Aug 01, 1938, Indianapolis, IN; son of Joe Hill and Flossie Hill; married Sheila; children: Philip, Martin, Nicholas. **EDUCATION:** IN Univ, 1969; IN Univ Law Sch (cum laude) 1969-73. **CAREER:** IN State Police/Trooper, legal adv; Bingham Summers Welch & Spilman, assoc 1974-75; Marion Co, pros dep 1975-; Flanner House of Indianapolis, exec dir 1975-; Social Serv Agency, atty/exec dir; Butler Brown & Blythe, attorney. **ORGANIZATIONS:** Mem Indianapolis Lawyers Commn; bd dir IN Lawyers Commn; bd mem WYFI-20 Pub Broadcasting Svc; Childrens Museum; bd dir Metro Arts Council; Amer Bar Assn; Indianapolis Bar Assn; IN Bar Assn; Natl Bar Assn Adv Bd; Indianapolis Repertory Theatre; Kiwanis Club; Indianapolis Balpt Soc Adv Com; Indianapolis Museum of Art Adv com; adv bd Indianapolis Urban League; Inner-City Y's Men Club; Indianapolis 500 Festival Bd Dir IN IU Law Sch Min Enrollment Adv Com; Greater IN Progress Com; IN State Dept of Mental Health Bd Dir; Golden Glove Offcial IN; bd mem, Selective Service System. **HONORS/ACHIEVEMENTS:** Outstanding IN Citizen IN Black Bi-Centenial; WTLC Indianapolis Citizen of the Day; WTLC Man of the Year 1978. **MILITARY SERVICE:** USAF 1957-61.

HILL, RICHARD NATHANIEL
Educational administrator. **PERSONAL:** Born Nov 20, 1930, Port Chester, NY; married Mayme Kathryn Hegwood; children: Richard H Jr, Lori S, Mark E. **EDUCATION:** Chaminade Univ of Honolulu, MBA 1984; Univ of So CA, Ed D 1977; Chapman Coll, MA 1969; Univ of the Philippines, BA 1959. **CAREER:** Chaminade Univ of Honolulu, acting asst dean 1984-, dir 1972-84; Pacific Air Forces, educ admn 1970-72; Allan Hancock Coll, dir 1969-70. **ORGANIZATIONS:** Consultant Federally Emplyd Women 1983, Amer Assn for Adult & Cont Ed 1982, Waikiki Comm Cntr 1978; dir Univ of S CA-HI Alumni 1979-; mem Wrld Affrs Forum of HI 1977-; pres Kiwanis Intrl Waikiki 1978-79. **HONORS/ACHIEVEMENTS:** Outstanding Serv Awd Phi Delta Kappa,Univ of HA 1984; Certfct of Apprectn Federally Emplyd Women, Wash, DC 1983, Am Assn for Adult & Cont Ed, San Antonio, TX 1982; Dist Press Award Kiwanis Interntl—cA, NV, HI Dist 1980. **MILITARY SERVICE:** USAF ret ofcr, commendation medal 1969. **BUSINESS ADDRESS:** Acting Assistant Dean, ChaminadoUniv of Honolulu, 3140 Waialae Ave, Honolulu, HI 96816.

HILL, ROBERT BERNARD
Director. **PERSONAL:** Born Sep 07, 1938, Brooklyn, NY; divorced; children: Bernard, Renee. **EDUCATION:** City Coll of NY, BA 1961; ColumbiaUniv NYC, PhD 1969. **CAREER:** Bureau of Soc Sci Rsrch, vice pres sr rsrch assoc; Nat Urban League, dir of rsrch; Nat Urban League Rsrch Dept, dep dir of rsrch 1969-72; Bureau of Applied Soc Rsrch ColumbiaUniv NY, rsrch asso 1964-69; PrincetonUniv Fordham U, adj faculty 1969-73; HowardUniv Wash, DC, vis scholar soc dept sch of Human ecology 1975-77; Bur of the Census, chmn mem adv com on blck population 1974-. **ORGANIZATIONS:** Pres Wash, DC Sociological Soc 1975. **HONORS/ACHIEVEMENTS:** "The Strengths of Black Families" Nat Urban League New York City 1971; "Informal Adoption Among Black Familie" NUL Rsrch Dept Wash, DC 1977; "The Illusion of Black Progress" NUL Rsrch Dept Wash, DC 1978.

HILL, ROBERT J., JR.
Architectural engineer. **PERSONAL:** Born Feb 23, 1943, Wilmington, NC; married Sheila G. **EDUCATION:** A&T State Univ, BS 1971. **CAREER:** Norfolk Naval Shipyard, archit engr pub works. **ORGANIZATIONS:** Mem Soc Prof Naval Engr; Kappa Alpha Psi; YMCA; 35th St Karate Club; A&T Alumni Club. **HONORS/ACHIEVEMENTS:** Letter Commendation Shipyard Comdr 1974. **MILITARY SERVICE:** AUS 1962-65. **BUSINESS ADDRESS:** NNSY Public Works, Bldg 65, Portsmouth, VA 23509.

HILL, ROBERT K.
Business executive. **PERSONAL:** Born May 12, 1917, San Antonio, TX; married Mildred. **EDUCATION:** Univ of NE; Inst of Banking 1951-54. **CAREER:** Union Pacific RR, 1937-42; Epply Hotel Co, maitre d' 1942-46; self-employed 1946-50; Federal Reserve Bank 1950-54; Hill Enterprises, founder/mgr 1954-. **ORGANIZATIONS:** Score couns Small Business Admin; sec/treas NE Placement Assn; Ins Underwriter; Notary Public; mem Omaha Real Estate Assn; bd dir Omaha C of C; Business Devel Corp; United Comm Svc; Natl Conf Christians & Jews; Gene Epply Boys Club; Omaha Safety Coun; Legal Aid Soc; founder & dir Comm Bank of NE; Intl past pres Frontiers Intl; Natl Federation of Independent Business; Central State Golf Assn (pres 5 yrs); past master Excelsior Lodge 2 Masonic Order; dir Natl Bus League. **BUSINESS ADDRESS:** Founder/Manager, Hill Enterprises, 1023 N 105, Omaha, NE 68114.

HILL, ROSALIE A.
Educator. **PERSONAL:** Born Dec 30, 1933, Philadelphia, PA; daughter of Joseph Behlin (deceased) and Anna Mae Elliott; divorced; children: Bernadette Hill Amos. **EDUCATION:** FL A&M Univ, Tallahassee, FL, BS MEd, l96l; FL State Univ, Tallahassee, FL, Ph.D, l985. **CAREER:** RA Hill & Assoc, educ consultant, Univ of S FL, dir, Equal Opportunity Affairs, FL State Univ, rsch assc; Leon Interfaith Child Care Inc, dir; Univ of FL, cnslr; Best Day of Week Program, staff dir; Taylor Co Adult Inst, basic educ teacher; FL A&M, counselor; Taylor Co Head Start Program, dir; Jerkins HS, music teacher. **ORGANIZATIONS:** Secr/vp/pres Taylor Co Educ Assc 1966-69; Taylor City Teachers Assn 1961; pres 1963-65; vice pres FL State Teachers Assc 1965; chairperson Dist III 1960-66; chairperson FL State Teachers Assn 1965-66; exec bd mem Dist Iii 1963-65; FL Educ Assn Small Co Prob Com 1967-69; chairperson Jerkins HS 1964-79; bd mem Taylor Co Sch Bd; PK Yonge Lab Sch; Leon City School Bd 1974-75; secr FL A&M Univ Alumni Assn 1974-76; Natl Assn 1974-; mem Amer Higher Educ Assn; Amer Assn of Affirmative Action Officers; Zeta Phi Beta Sor; Taylor Co Improvement Club Inc; Tri-Co Econ Cncl; FL Forest Festival; Miss Woodland Pageant; Taylor Co Bi-racial Com; Region III Drug Abuse Com; Miss Black Amer Pageant; Amer Cancer Soc; Hillsborough Co Commn on Status of Women; special projects dir, United Negro Coll Fund-Tampa Exec Comm, l985-; sec, Friends of Coll Hill Library, l986-; special projects coord, FL A&M Univ Natl Alumni Assn, l985-; dist music dir, Tampa Conf AME Churches, l985-; dir, St Luke AME Church, Tampa Chapter of the NAACP and Greater Tampa urban League. **HONORS/ACHIEVEMENTS:** Recp Lewis State Scholarship 1952-56; Teacher of Year Jerkins HS 1960; Yearbook Dedication Jerkins HS 1960; Tampa Bay Most Influential Blacks, l983; FL A&M Univ, Outstanding Alumni Hall of Fame, l987; Martin Luther King Educ Award, Start Together on Progress, Inc, l988; co-founder, FL Statewide Alumni Consortium of Historically Black Insts, l985; founder, Conf on the Educ of Blacks, Tampa, l982; served as role model for state, gave impetus to establishment of state activity. **BUSINESS ADDRESS:** Pres, Ra Hill & Assoc, PO Box 75543, Tampa, FL 33675-0543.

HILL, RUFUS S.
Clergyman. **PERSONAL:** Born Apr 08, 1923, Raymond, MS; son of Rev O A Hill and Mary Dixon Hill; married Ruth (divorced); children: Rufus, Thomasine, Beverly, Daphane. **EDUCATION:** MS Indust Coll, AB 1951; MS State Univ, MA 1971. **CAREER:** Shannon MS, teacher 1951-55; Houston MS, teacher 1955-61; New Albany MS, teacher 1961-66; Clay Cty MS, teacher 1966-72; Christian Meth Episcopal Church, clergyman; Universal Life Ins, 1963-65; Union Fed Life Ins, 1965-66; Dixie Car Craft Cen, owner; 4-Way Pest Control Co, owner. **ORGANIZATIONS:** Past chmn Union Co Comm Devel Council 1963-66; vice pres Clay Cty Comm Fed Credit Union 1971-74; mem MS Loyal Dem Party, Amer Legion Post #252 New Albany, FA Mason Lodge #171; founder of chap NAACP New Albany Devel Club, Union Co Life mem of Amvet. **MILITARY SERVICE:** AUS corporal 1943-46; Campaign Medal, Good Conduct Medal; Bronze Star.

HILL, SAM
Building & construction contractor. **PERSONAL:** Born Feb 22, 1918, Starkville, MS; married Martha Lue; children: Sammie Louis Moore, Julia McCarter, Butten, Hattie, Laura, Marilyn. **EDUCATION:** US Army Inst of Educ, HS diploma 1947. **CAREER:** FHA Organization, contractor 1976-81; Loundes Co, carpenter 1954-88; Brown Ridge MB Church, asst minister 1978-; Lowndes Co, constable 1972-86. **ORGANIZATIONS:** Contractor for Future Home Admin 1976; minister Southern Baptist 1979; fireman Crawford MS 1978-82. **HONORS/ACHIEVEMENTS:** Fireman's Awd Lowndes-Crawford 1978; Constable Awd Columbus MS. **MILITARY SERVICE:** AUS sgt 10 yrs. **BUSINESS ADDRESS:** NAACP, PO Box 91, Crawford, MS 39743.

HILL, SANDRA PATRICIA
Social worker. **PERSONAL:** Born Nov 01, 1943, Peidmont, AL; daughter of Theotis Hill and Edith Palmore Hill. **EDUCATION:** Berea Coll Berea, KY, BS (Home Ec) 1966; Southern Baptist Theo Smnry, MRE (Social Work) 1968; Univ of Michigan, MSW 1977; Cornell Univ, attending 1982-. **CAREER:** Harvard St Baptist Center, Alexandria, Virginia, assoc dir 1968-73; Harvard St Baptist Center, dir 1974-75; Home Mission Bd, S Baptist Convention, consultant 1977-1986; Southern Baptist Theological Seminary, Louisville, KY, Visiting Prof, Social Work 1987-88; Home Mission Bd/SBC, Atlanta, GA, Careers Fatus Reserve 1987-. **ORGANIZATIONS:** Various Assn of Black Social Workers 1974-; various Fold, Inc, Alexandria, VA 1970-75 sec/treasurer Social Serv Assn, 1977-; bd of dir, Reach Out Inc Atlanta, 1980; mem NAACP. **HOME ADDRESS:** 122 N Sunset Dr, Ithaca, NY 14850.

HILL, SONNY See HILL, WILLIAM RANDOLPH, JR.

HILL, SYLVIA IONE-BENNETT
Educator. **PERSONAL:** Born Aug 15, 1940, Jacksonville, FL; daughter of Paul T. Bennett, Sr. and Evelyn Harker Bennett; children: Gloria Angela Davis. **EDUCATION:** Howard U, BS 1963;Univ of OR, MS 1967, Ph D 1971. **CAREER:** UDC/Dept of Crimnl Justice,

prof 1974-; Union for Exprmntng Coll & Univs, part-time core prof 1976-; Macalester Coll, asst prof 1972-74. **ORGANIZATIONS:** Sec gen Sixth Pan African Congress 1974; fndr and co-chrpsn Southern Africa Support Proj 1978-; founder/mem Strng Comm Free S Africa Movement 1984-; treasurer/bd TransAfrica Forum 1984-; bd mem TransAfrica 1984-1990; bd mem New World Foundation 1988-. **HONORS/ACHIEVEMENTS:** Nat'l Certfd Cnslr/Natl Brd for Certified cnslrs 1984-89. **BUSINESS ADDRESS:** Professor of Criminal Justice, University District Of CO, 4200 Connecticut Ave NW, Washington, DC 20008.

HILL, THADDEUS EARL
Manager. **PERSONAL:** Born Oct 16, 1938, Raleigh, NC; married Cornelia Gregg; children: Thaddeus Jr, Diane, Geraldine, Michael, Michelle. **EDUCATION:** VA State U, BS 1957. **CAREER:** Sanders Broadcasting, vice pres natl sales mgr Sheridan Broad Network, midwest sales mgr; Sinclair Broad WANT Radio Sta, gen mgr 1975-76; Atlas Comm WJPC Radio, eastern sales mgr 1974-75; New Broadcasting WLIB/WBLS Radio, regional sales mgr 1968-74; Doubleday Co, account exec mgr 1962-68. **ORGANIZATIONS:** Mem NY Sales Mgmt Assn CAC 1975-80; mem Urban League 1976-80; mem NAACP 1977-80. **HONORS/ACHIEVEMENTS:** Recip Peabody AwdUniv of GA 1970. **MILITARY SERVICE:** USAF a/1st class 1958-61.

HILL, THELMA W.
Instructor. **PERSONAL:** Born Dec 22, 1933, Baltimore; divorced; children: Linda Joan. **EDUCATION:** Coppin State Clge, BS Ed 1956; Morgan State Clge, BS Art Ed 1965; Howard Univ 1963; Johns Hopkins Univ, 1958; Towson State 1968. **CAREER:** Baltimore City Public Schools, teacher 1956-63; Coppin State Coll, demonstr teacher; Baltimore City Public Schools, art resource teacher instructor art 1965; Supr Student Teachers Art1972; Afro-Arts Center, art consultant 1970; Artist-in-Residence 1971-72; Morgan State Coll, dir Childrens Art Class 1965-. **ORGANIZATIONS:** Commentator fashion show; poetess; watercolorist; piano & organ concerts; N & N Soc; Natl Conf Artists; visiting staff Provident Hosp; adv & consult Christ Ch Balto Comm Afro-Arts Ctr. **HONORS/ACHIEVEMENTS:** Humanitarian Award Christ Church; Outst Christian Woman Maryland Ch God 1965. **BUSINESS ADDRESS:** Morgan St Coll Murphy Fine Art, 5 Cold Spring Ln at Hillen Rd, Baltimore, MD 21239.

HILL, TONY
Professional athlete. **PERSONAL:** Born Jun 23, 1956; married Mildred; children: Cassidy, Kelli. **EDUCATION:** Stanford Univ, Political Science degree. **CAREER:** Tony Hill's Cowboy Catfish Restaurant Garland TX, owner; Dallas Cowboys, wide rec 1977-. **ORGANIZATIONS:** Chrmn Dallas Juvenile Diabetes Fund 1980; org Tony Hill Sports Camp. **HONORS/ACHIEVEMENTS:** Athlete of Year Long Beach CA 1978; led Cowboys in rec & touchdowns scored; NFL 7th leading rec in total yards; had NFC Top Yardage Game; 2 time Pro Bowl selection 1978-79; set club playoff record with 9 receptions; broke all of former 49ers All-Pro Gene Washington's receiving records at Stanford; mem 1986 NFL Pro Bowl team.

HILL, VELMA MURPHY
Association executive. **PERSONAL:** Born Oct 17, 1938, Chicago; married Norman Hill. **EDUCATION:** No IL Univ Dekalb IL; Roosevelt Univ Chicago 1960; Harvard Univ, MEd 1969. **CAREER:** United Fedn Tchrs, asst to pres; New York City Training Inst, consult 1967-68; Amer Dem Action Washington, exec dir 1965-66; OEO summer recruit dir 1964-65; CORE, 1960-64. **ORGANIZATIONS:** Mem Labor Adv Com OEO 1970-71; Trade Union Com Histadrut Labor Seminar Israel 1969; Commn Status Women 1975. **BUSINESS ADDRESS:** 260 Park Ave S, New York, NY 10010.

HILL, VONCIEL JONES
Municipal judge. **PERSONAL:** Born Sep 23, 1948, Hattiesburg, MS; married Charles Edward Hill. **EDUCATION:** Univ TX at Austin, BA 1969; Atlanta Univ, M Lib Sci 1971; Rice Univ, M Hist 1976; Univ TX at Austin, JD 1979. **CAREER:** Atlanta, GA Publ Schools, tchr 1969-70; Prairie View A&M Univ, asst circulations librarian 1971-72; TX Southern Univ, asst law librarian 1972-76; Public Utility Comm of TX, staff atty 1979-80; Dallas/Ft Worth Airport, asst city atty; City of Dallas Municipal Court Judiciary, municipal court judge 1987-. **ORGANIZATIONS:** Chair/bd dir Methodism's Breadbasket 1983-85; committee chair Dallas Bar Assn 1985; sec JL Turner Legal Assn 1985; treas State Bar of TX Women & the Law Section. **HONORS/ACHIEVEMENTS:** Univ Fellow Rice Univ 1974-76; Ford Found Fellow Atlanta Univ 1970-71. **BUSINESS ADDRESS:** Municipal Court Judge, City of Dallas, 2014 Main St, Dallas, TX 75201.

HILL, WENDELL T., JR.
Educator. **PERSONAL:** Born Dec 17, 1924, Philadelphia, PA; son of Wendell T Hill, Sr and Mildred Bailey Hill; married Marcella Washington, Aug 25, 1951; children: Dr Wendell T Hill, III, Philip Hill. **EDUCATION:** Drake Univ, Des Moines, IA, BS Pharmacy, 1950; VA Center Residency, Los Angeles, CA, Residency Hospital Pharmacy, 1952-54; Univ Southern CA, Los Angeles, CA, MS Pharmacy, 1954, Pharmacy D. 1970. **CAREER:** Rhodes Medical Supply, St Louis, MO, pharmacist, 1950-52; VA Center Hospital, Los Angeles, CA, pharmacy resident, 1952-54; VA Center Hospital, Los Angeles, CA, chief pharmacy-teaching, 1954-56; Owl Drug Co, Los Angeles, CA, pharmacist, 1953-57; UCI Medical Center, Orange County, CA, chief pharmacist, 1957-70; Detroit Gen Hospital, Detroit, MI, dir, pharm. services 1970-77; Wayne State Univ, Detroit MI, assoc prof, 1970-77; Howard Univ, Washington, DC, dean, coll of pharmacy, 1977-. **ORGANIZATIONS:** Pres, bd mem, comm chmn, Amer Society of Hospital Pharmacists (ASHP), 1968-72; bd of dir/pres, Natl Council of Pharmacy Continuing Educ, 1974-76; mem, Mayor's Drug Abuse Advisory Comm, 1984-87; bd of trustees/task force, Drake Univ, 1989; chmn, Private Colls of pharmcy, Amer Assn of Colls of Pharmacy (AACP); pres-elect, Natl Pharmaceutical Assn (NPhA), mem, Amer Soc of Consultant Pharmacists (ASCP), bd of dir, Metropolitan Detroit Pharmaceutical Assn; Advisory Comm, GLAXO Pharmaceutical Inc; Accreditation Team Member: Middle States Assn of Colls & Schools Commn on Higher Educ; Phil Pharmacy Coll, Periodic Review Report Session. **HONORS/ACHIEVEMENTS:** Outstanding Alumnus of the Year, Univ of Southern CA, 1979; Pharmacist of the Year, DC Pharmaceutical Assn, 1982-83; Alumnus of the Year, Univ of Southern CA, 1983; Pharmacy Educ for the Inst Pharmacy Practioner, DC Soc of Hospital Pharmacists Annual Meeting, Ocean City, MO, 1985; contributing editor, Pharmacy Times Magazine, 1988-; author of A Profession in Transition: Then Changing Face of Pharmacy, Pharmacy Times, 1988; author of Prescription Drug Provisions, Medicare Catastrophic Coverage Act, Pharmacy Times, 1988; Harvey A K Whitney Lecture Award, Amer Soc Hospital Pharmacists, 1989; author of UNC Pharmacy Students Receive the First AIDS Awareness Award, Pharmacy Times, 1989; author of FDA Interim Rule for Expedited Devel and Approval of Drugs for Life Threatening Illness, Pharmacy Times, 1989; author of The Changing Healthcare System: The Patient at Home, NABP Annual Meeting, Char leston, SC, 1989. **MILITARY SERVICE:** US Army, T3, World War II; Honorable Discharge. **BUSINESS ADDRESS:** Dr Wendell T Hill, Jr, Howard Univ Coll of Pharmacy & Pharmacal Sciences, 2300 Fourth St, NW, Rm #107, Washington, DC 20059.

HILL, WILLIAM BRADLEY, JR.
Attorney. **PERSONAL:** Born Mar 03, 1952, Atlanta, GA; married Melba Gayle Wynn; children: Melba Kara. **EDUCATION:** Wash & Lee Univ Lexington VA, BA 1974; Wash & Lee Univ Schl of Law Lexington, JD 1977. **CAREER:** State Law Dept Atlanta GA, asst atty gen 1977. **ORGANIZATIONS:** Mem State Bar of GA 1977; exec chmn Wash & Lee Univ Black Alumni Fnd 1980-. **HONORS/ACHIEVEMENTS:** Listed Who's Who Among Amer High Schl Students 1970; Outst Young Men of Amer 1978. **BUSINESS ADDRESS:** State Law Dept, Atlanta, GA 30334.

HILL, WILLIAM RANDOLPH, JR. (SONNY HILL)
Sports editor. **PERSONAL:** Born Jul 22, 1936, Philadelphia, PA; married Edith Hughes; children: K Brent. **CAREER:** CBS TV, editor 1977; Teamsters Local 169, sec, treasurer, bus agt & trust, 1960-; Lancaster Red Roses Bsktbl Team, owner 1975; Eastern Basketball League, basketball player; WPEN Lct Sports & Humanitarian, analyst 1966-; Sonny Hill/John Chaney Basketball Camp, co-owner 1975-. **ORGANIZATIONS:** Pres Charles Baker Meml Summer League 1960-; adv bd MacDonald's HS All Amer Team 1978-80; bd dir Big Brothers Assc Natl Comm opr PUSH; mem NAACP;Big Brothers; PUSH; pres, founder Sonny Hill Community Involvement League Inc. **HONORS/ACHIEVEMENTS:** Outst Com Srv Award Sports Mag 1970; human rights award Commin on Human Rel 1972; good nghbr award WDAS Radio 1973; Oxford Circle JC Award 1973; Man of Year award Fishtown 1973; Man of Year Nite Owl 1972-73; Tribune Charities 1976; Bsktbl Wkly Plyr Dev Award Toyota Motors 1977; Mutual Radio Broadcaster of NBA Championship 1980; Mellon Bank Good neighbor Awd 1985; John B Kelley Awd 1986; City of Hope Spirit of Life Awd. **MILITARY SERVICE:** ANG 1959-65. **BUSINESS ADDRESS:** Secretary, Treasurer, Teamster Union Local 169, 1355 Cheltenham Ave, Philadelphia, PA 19126.

HILL, XACADENE AVERYLLIS
Physician. **PERSONAL:** Born Aug 12, 1909, Yazoo City, MS; widowed; children: Walter Fox Jr. **EDUCATION:** Univ of NE, AB 1933; Meharry Med Coll, MD 1937; Howard Univ, 1942. **CAREER:** St Louis Schools, school physician 1945-48; St Mary's Infirmary, instr venereal disease 1945-; St Marys Infirmary, instr 1946-52; Homer G Phillips Hosp,clinic physician, dir 1962-76; Private practice, semi-retired physician 1979-. **ORGANIZATIONS:** Mem St Louis Med Soc, MO State med Assoc, Mound City Med Forum, Natl Med Assoc, Amer Acad Family Physician, MO Acad Family Physician, Pan Med Assoc, Alpha Kappa Alpha 1929, NAACP; exec bd St Louis Acad Family Physician 1972-75; contribution memshp YWCA, Howard Univ 1942.

HILL-LUBIN, MILDRED ANDERSON
Educator. **PERSONAL:** Born Mar 23, 1933, Russell County, AL; daughter of Luther Anderson and Mary Anderson; married Dr Maurice A Lubin; children: Walter H Hill, Robert T Hill. **EDUCATION:** Paine Coll Augusta, GA, BA English Honors 1961; Western Reserve Cleveland, MA 1962; Indiana, 1964; Univ of Minnesota, 1965-66; Howard Univ & African-Amer Inst,1972; Univ of Illinois Urbana-Champaign, PhD English & African Studies 1974. **CAREER:** Paine Coll, instructor/asst prof 1962-65 & 1966-70; Hamline Univ, exchange prof 1965-66; Paine Coll, asst prof English/dir EPDA program 1970-72; Univ of IL, tchng asst/instructor 1972-74; Univ of Florida; assoc prof of English/dir English program for special admit students 1974-77; Univ of Florida, asst dean of graduate school 1977-80, assoc prof of English & African Studies 1982-. **ORGANIZATIONS:** Proj assoc Council of Chief State School Officers Washington, DC 1981-82; consultant Amer Council on Educ 1981-; panel mem Adv Cncl Mellon Humanities Grant UNCF College Fund 1980-; discipline comm in African Lit Fulbright Awards 1983-86; exec comm Coll Comp & Comm (CCCC) 1977-80; exec comm African Lit Assn 1983-86; pres Gainesville Chap of the Links 1985-87; pres FOCUS 1978-79; bd dir Gainesville/Alachua Co Center of Excell 1985-; Alpha Kappa Alpha Sor; vice pres & pres elect African Literature Assoc 1986-88; pres, African Literature Assn 1987-88; dir, Gainesville-Jacmel Haiti Sister Cities Program, 1987-90; pres, The Visionaires, 1988-90. **HONORS/ACHIEVEMENTS:** Alpha Kappa Mu Honor Soc Paine Coll 1960; Travel-Study Grant to W Africa African-Amer Intl 19; Trainer of Teachers Fellowship Univ of Illinois 1973-74; Outstanding Paine Coll Alumna DC Chap 1982; co-editor of "Towards Defining the African Aesthetic" and articles in, "Southern Folklore Quarterly," "Coll Lang Assn Journal"; "Presence Africaine"; "Okike"; Leadership and Achievement Award, Nu Eta Lambda Chapter Alpha Phi Alpha Fraternity 1988; article, "The Black Grandmother in Literature," in Ngambika 1986. **HOME ADDRESS:** 2119 NW 31st Ave, Gainesville, FL 32605. **BUSINESS ADDRESS:** Assoc Prof Engl & African Studies, University of Florida, Dept of English, 4008 GPA, Gainesville, FL 32611.

HILLIARD, ASA GRANT, III
Educator. **PERSONAL:** Born Aug 22, 1933, Galveston, TX; married Patsy Jo; children: Asa IV, Robi Nsenga Bailey, Patricia Nefertari, Hakim Sequenenre. **EDUCATION:** Univ of Denver, BA Psych 1955, MA Counseling 1961, EdD Ed Psych 1963. **CAREER:** Denver Public Schools, teacher 1955-60; Univ of Denver, teaching fellow 1960-63; San Francisco State Univ, prof, dean of educ 1963-83; GA State Univ, disting prof of educ 1980-. **ORGANIZATIONS:** Dir of rsch Automated Serv Inc 1970-72; consult testing African History Child Devel; bd of dir Natl Black Child Devel Inst 1973-75, Amer Assn of Coll for Teacher Educ 1974-76; mem Natl Assn for the Ed of Young Children 1974-; bd of ethnic & minority affairs Amer Psych Assn 1982-84. **HONORS/ACHIEVEMENTS:** Natl Defense Ed Act Fellow Univ of Denver 1960-63; Knight Commander of the Human Order of African Redemption 1972; Disting Leadership Awd Assn of TeacherEd 1983; Outstanding Scholarship Assoc of Black Psych 1984. **MILITARY SERVICE:** Armored Infantry 1st lt 2 yrs. **BUSINESS ADDRESS:** Professor of Education, Georgia StateUniv, PO Box 243, Atlanta, GA 30303.

HILLIARD, DELORIES
Public administrator, court executive. **PERSONAL:** Born in Texas; daughter of Rufus Wilson Sr and Ethel Wilson. **EDUCATION:** Texas Woman's Univ, Denton TX, BS, MS, Univ Texas, Arlington TX, PhD candidate. **CAREER:** Dallas County MHMR, Dallas TX, qual-

ity assurance coord, clinical psychology specialist; City of Dallas, asst to dir (housing), court admin. **BUSINESS ADDRESS:** Court Systems Administrator, City of Dallas, Dept of Court Services, 2014 Main St #100-B, Dallas, TX 75208.

HILLIARD, EARL FREDERICK
Government official & attorney. **PERSONAL:** Born Apr 09, 1942, Birmingham, AL; son of William Hilliard and Iola Frazier Hilliard; married Mary Franklin, Jun 09, 1966; children: Alesia, Earl Jr. **EDUCATION:** Morehouse Coll, BA 1964; AtlantaUniv Sch of Business, MBA 1970; HowardUniv Sch of Law, JD 1967. **CAREER:** AL State U, asst to pres 1968-70; Pearson & Hilliard (Law Firm), partners 1972-73; Bham Legal Aid Soc, rgnl heber fellow 1970-72; State of AL state rep1970-72, state senator 1980-. **ORGANIZATIONS:** Pres Amer Trust Life Ins Co 1977-; pres Amer Trust Land Co 1980-; chmn AL Black Legsltv Caucus; life mem NAACP 1984, Natl Bar Assoc 1979, Morehouse Coll Natl Alumni Assoc 1983, Alpha Phi Alpha Frat Inc 1980; mem bd of Trustees Miles Law School 1984-; mem bd of Trustees Tuskegee Univ 1986-. **HONORS/ACHIEVEMENTS:** Published The Legal Aspects of the Franchise Contract 1970; published How To Play Bid Whist 1984; father of the year Natl Orgnztn of Women 1981; outstanding ldrshp award Alpha Phi Alpha Frat, Inc 1980. **BUSINESS ADDRESS:** Attorney, 1614 3rd Avenue North, Birmingham, AL 35203.

HILLIARD, GENERAL K.
Cardiologist. **PERSONAL:** Born Dec 12, 1940, Hempstead, TX; married Ida R McCree; children: Denise, Renee, Brian. **EDUCATION:** Prairie View, BS 1960; Meharry Medical Coll, MD 1968. **CAREER:** Univ CA-Davis, int med 1972, cardiovas div 1974; AHA Alameda Cty Chapt, pres 1983-84; AHA Cal Affil, chmn elec prog comm; Peralta Hosp, dir cardiovas svcs. **ORGANIZATIONS:** Fellow Amer Coll of Cardiology 1976-87; bd of dir Assoc of Black Cardiol 1986. **HONORS/ACHIEVEMENTS:** Mem Alpha Omega Alpha Honor Med Soc. **MILITARY SERVICE:** AUS capt 1960-62. **HOME ADDRESS:** 46 E Albrinda Dr, Orinda, CA 94563. **BUSINESS ADDRESS:** Dir Cardiovascular Serv, Peralto Hospital, 3100 Telegraph Ave, Oakland, CA 94609.

HILLIARD, ROBERT LEE MOORE
Physician. **PERSONAL:** Born Jan 01, 1931, San Antonio, TX; son of Otho Hilliard and Robbie Moore Hilliard; married Mary Lou Moreno; children: Ronald, Bennie Karen Brown, Porfia Denise Byas, Robert Jr, Rudyard,Robbie Lesly, Ruby Lucinda. **EDUCATION:** Howard Univ, BS 1951; Univ of TX Medical Branch, MD 1956. **CAREER:** Natl Med Assn, trustee 1975-81, 1983-84; Natl Med Assn, pres 1982-83; TX Bank, dir 1975-; Natl Medical Fellowships, dir 1982-; St Mary's Univ, trustee advisory bd 1983-; TX State Bd of Med Examiners, mem 1984-; Women's Clinic of San Antonio, sr Ob/Gyn. **ORGANIZATIONS:** Chmn San Antonio Housing Authority 1969-71; councilman San Antonio City Council 1971-73; commissioned as Admiral TX Navy State of TX 1978; comm San Antonio Fire & Police Civil Serv Comm 1978-80; Hon Div Surgeon 1st Calvary Div US Army 1983; vice chmn United Negro Coll Fund 1971-; vice chmn City Water Bd San Antonio 1980-85; chmn City Water Bd 1986-. **HONORS/ACHIEVEMENTS:** Dedicated Serv 1973, Distinguished Leadership 1982 United Negro Coll Fund; Benefactor de la Communidad City of San Antonio 1981; Certificate of Appreciation State of TX House of Reps 1983; Achievement Award S Central Region AKA Sorority 1983. **MILITARY SERVICE:** USAF capt flight surgeon 1957-60. **BUSINESS ADDRESS:** Womens Clinic of San Antonio, 710 Augusta, San Antonio, TX 78215.

HILLIARD, WILLIAM ALEXANDER
Clergyman. **PERSONAL:** Born in Greenville, TX; married Edra Mae. **EDUCATION:** Western Univ, AB; Shaeffer Theol Sem Western Univ, BD; Hood Theol Sem, DD. **CAREER:** African Meth Episcopal Zion Ch, bishop; ministerial pastorates in KS MO SC NC; AME Zion Ch, elected to Episcopacy; overseas mission work Zion Ch Ghana,Nigeria, Liberia, West Africa 1960; Zion Conf in GA OK KS MO CA WA OR, supr. **ORGANIZATIONS:** Chmn Div of Overseas Minis Natl Cnsl of Ch of Christ; trustee Livingstone Clge; mem Nom Comm of Degrees; chmn Land Use Comm; mem World Cnsl of Ch; natl Cnsl of Churches; NAACP; Urban League; Christian Com Cnsl of Detroit; Knight Great Band Liberia West Africa 1975; selected srv ldr Amer Relig Del to visit Taiwan China to survey & observe tech, ind educ dev of China. **HONORS/ACHIEVEMENTS:** John Bryan Sm African Cen Mem Cit 12th Episcopal Dist AME Zion Ch; 1st AME Zion Rest Home Cit Laurinburg Dist Cen NC Conf; awards, Office of the Mayor, Mayor John H Reading; Office of Com Cnsl Mel Ravitz; 77th Legis of City of Detroit St of MI; OH House of Rep AL Concione; Father of Year MI Conf 1975; City of Los Angeles Thomas Ley Office. **BUSINESS ADDRESS:** 690 Chicago Blvd, Detroit, MI 48202.

HILLMAN, GRACIA
Business administrator. **PERSONAL:** Born Sep 12, 1949, New Bedford, MA; married Robert E Bates Jr; children: Hillman Martin. **EDUCATION:** Univ of MA Boston, Coll of Public & Comm Svc, attended 1978. **CAREER:** MA Legislative Black Caucus, admin 1975-77; MA Dept of Correction, exec asst to commissioner 1977-79; MA Port Authority, public & govt affairs spec 1979;Joint Center for Political Studies, project dir 1979-82; Natl Coal on Black Voter Partic, exec dir 1982-87. **ORGANIZATIONS:** Mem Natl Political Congress of Black Women; sec United Front Homes Devel Corp New Bedford MA 1972-76; pres United Front Homes Day Care Center New BedfordMA 1973-76; pres ONBOARD Community Action Prog New Bedford MA 1974-76; chairperson MA Govt Serv Career Prog 1977-78; v chairperson Center for Youth SvcsWashington DC 1985-; prog devel consult Congressional Black Caucus Found 1987. **HONORS/ACHIEVEMENTS:** Appointed to MA Post Secondary Education (1202) Commission 1975. **HOME ADDRESS:** 3524 Texas Ave SE, Washington, DC 20020. **BUSINESS ADDRESS:** Executive Dir, Natl Coalition on Black Voter, Participation, 1101 14th St, NW, Ste 925, Washington, DC 20020.

HILLS, JAMES BRICKY
Pharmacist. **PERSONAL:** Born Oct 01, 1944, Opelousas, LA; married Beatrice M Hubbard. **EDUCATION:** TX Southern Univ Coll of Pharmacy, BS 1971. **CAREER:** TSU School of Pharmacy Alumni, bd of dir 1978; Christian Coll of Amer, bd of dir 1985-86, vice chmn bd of regents 1985-86; La Porte Neighborhood Ctr, bd of dir 1986; La Porte Apothecary, owner. **ORGANIZATIONS:** Bd of dir Harris Co Pharm Assoc 1982; career consultant North Forest ISD Health Prof 1984; chmn USAC, COGIC 1985; instructor Greater Emmanuel Bible Inst 1985; consultant Eastwood Health Clinic 1985; mem by-law & constitution comm TX Pharm Assn 1986; mem TX Pharmaceutical Assoc, NAACP, LaPorte Chamber of Commerce, Law Memorial COGIC; fellow Amer Coll of Apothecaries 1987. **HONORS/ACHIEVEMENTS:** Outstanding Educator of SS TX SC COGIC 1982; Outstanding Board Mem HCPA 1984; Outstanding Board Mem CCA 1986. **MILITARY SERVICE:** AUS E-5 2 yrs. **BUSINESS ADDRESS:** Pharmacist, La Porte Apothecary, 410 E Fairmont Pkwy Ste B, La Porte, TX 77571.

HILLSMAN, GERALD C.
Association executive. **PERSONAL:** Born Jul 07, 1926, Dayton, OH; married Julia. **EDUCATION:** Marjorie Webster Jr Coll, AA 1975; Natl Inst Drug Progs, Cert 1975. **CAREER:** VA Hosp Brentwood CA, drug consult 1971-72; VA Hosp, drug consult 1972-73; USC Hosp, drug cons; Central City Bricks/Kick Proj, founder, prog dir 1970-. **ORGANIZATIONS:** Pres Partners for Progress; hon mem, bd dir W Coast Assoc of Puerto Rican Substance Abuse Workers Inc; adv bd mem Central City Substance Abuse TrngLA. **HONORS/ACHIEVEMENTS:** Outstanding Comm Serv Awd Alliance Drug Ed & Prevention Tehachapi 1974; Outstanding Serv Young People San Bernardino 1974; Dynamic Leadership Awd Friends of Bricks 1974; Resolution CA State Assembly 1974; Congressional Medal of Merit Congressman Augustus F Hawkins 1976; num plaques; listed in Who's Who in CA 1981-82, Intl Who's Who of Intellectuals 1981, The Dir of Disting Amer 1981, Who's Who of Intl Intellectuals Certs 1981. **BUSINESS ADDRESS:** Program Dir, Central City Bricks/Kick Proj, 1925 S Trinity St, Los Angeles, CA 90011.

HILTON, STANLEY WILLIAM, JR.
Business executive. **PERSONAL:** Born in Philadelphia, PA; son of Stanley W Hilton, Sr and Jennie Parsons Cooper; divorced; children: Richard H Hilton. **EDUCATION:** Fisk Univ, BA 1959; Temple Univ, Grad Study 1959. **CAREER:** Mill Run Playhouse Niles IL, treas 1969-70; Shubert Theatre, co mgr "Hair" 1969-70; Orpheum Theatre San Francisco, mgr 1970-74; "My Fair Lady", "Jesus Christ Superstar", "No Place to be Somebody" San Francisco, co mgr; Park & Theatre Opers Art Park Lewiston NY, dir 1974; Evanston Theatre Co IL, bus mgr; Blackstone Theatre Chgo, mgr 1974-86. **ORGANIZATIONS:** Coord ed & vocational couns Concentrated Employment Prog, Comm Coll Dist San Fran 1971-73; ofc mgr Cook Cty Dept of Publ Aid Chicago 1966-70; exec asst sec Bd of Pensions Meth Ch IL 1965-66; mem Assoc of Theatrical Press Agt & Mgr NY 1970-; reg soc worker IL 1966-; cert teacher & vocational couns CA 1971-. **MILITARY SERVICE:** NGR 1960.

HILYARD, TOMMY LEE
Manager. **PERSONAL:** Born Dec 02, 1948, Tacoma, WA; married Marti Virginia Joe Jones; children: Jahid, Uzuri Malaika Marcia Anne. **EDUCATION:** Western WA State Coll, BA 1967-71; State Univ of NY Albany, ABE Cert 1972; Univ of Puget Sound ICMA, Urban Plng Cert 1975. **CAREER:** Tacoma Comm Coll, asst for instr & devel 1971-72; Tacoma Urban League, comm devel 1972-74; Human Devel City of Tacoma, comm tech asst 1974-77, progdevel spec 1977-79, sr prog devel spec 1979-; Pierce Cty Comm Action Agency, mgr 1982-. **ORGANIZATIONS:** Pres Citizens Affirm Action Counc 1972-77; vice pres Afro-Amer Grant Fund Inc 1975; pres Tacoma Chap WA Conf on Black Ed & Econs; chmn Reg V Citizens Adv Counc WA State Dept Soc & Health Serv 1975-79; bd mem Tacoma Urban League 1975, Tacoma Pierce Cty OIC 1977-78.

HINCH, ANDREW LEWIS, SR.
Government official. **PERSONAL:** Born Sep 28, 1919, Mexico, MO; married Mary Ann; children: Andy Jr, Terry, Jaqueline, Henry, Shelia, Charles, Brenda, Lewis. **EDUCATION:** Lincoln Univ Jefferson City MO, attd; Hampton Inst VA, attd 1944; IN Sch of Educ Indianapolis, attd; Joliet Jr Clge IL, attd. **CAREER:** Dist 5 City of Joliet, councilman; V W Detective Agcy, capt over investigators 1976-78; US Post Office, mail carrier. **ORGANIZATIONS:** Pres Natl Assc of Retired Fed Employees Local 655; mem Natl Assc of Letter Carriers; mem Joliet Chamber of Comm; past mem Metro Bd of Joliet YMCA; mem Briggs St YMCA Bd; mem Sr Citizen Bd; mem Drug Coordination & Info Cnsl; mem Comm Action Bd; pres Brooklyn Home Owners Assc; former scoutmaster; Bethelehem Luth Ch & Buffalo Post Amer Legion Troops; mem Amer Legion Post 1284. **HONORS/ACHIEVEMENTS:** Beyond the Call of Duty Award US Post Office; 1st Black to hold Taxi-License Franchise City of Joliet; 1st Black to be elected to Joliet City Council 5th Dist. **MILITARY SERVICE:** USN cm2 1943-68. **BUSINESS ADDRESS:** City Of Joliet, 150 W Jefferson, Joliet, IL 60431.

HINDS, LENNOX S.
Attorney. **PERSONAL:** Born in Port of Spain, Trinidad and Tobago;son of Arthur Hinds and Dolly Stevens Hinds (deceased); married Bessie; children: Brent, Yvette, Renee. **EDUCATION:** City Coll, BS; Rutgers School of Law, JD 1972. **CAREER:** Natl Conf Of Black Lawyers, natl dir; Prisoner's Rights Org Def, dir 1971-72; Heritage Fnd, dir 1969-72; Citgo Corp, rsch sect chf 1964-69; Rutgers State Univ, prof of Criminal Law, chmn Administration of Justice Program. **ORGANIZATIONS:** Permanent del UN Non Govt Org; Intl Assc of Dem Lawyers; mem Intl Bd Org of Non-Govt Org; mem NJ Bar Assc; com on Cts & Criminal Procedure; Natl Minority Adv Commn for Criminal Justice; Natl Adv Council for Child Abuse; bd mem So Mobilization Legal Proj; past natl secretary Black Amer Law Students Assc; past bd mem Law Students Civil Rights Rsch Council; mem Task Force; mem State Bar of New York, New Jersey. **HONORS/ACHIEVEMENTS:** J Skelly Wright Civil Rights Award; Assn of Black Law Students Comm Serv Award 1973; Distguished Alumnus Award Black Amer Law Students 1974; numerous publichations. **HOME ADDRESS:** 42 Van Doren Ave, Somerset, NJ 08872. **BUSINESS ADDRESS:** Lennox S Hinds, Esq, Stevens, Hinds & White PC, 116 W 111th St, New York, NY 10026.

HINE, DARLENE CLARK
Educator. **PERSONAL:** Born Feb 07, 1947, Morley, MO; children: Robbie Davine. **EDUCATION:** Roosevelt Univ of Chicago, BA 1968; Kent State Univ Kent OH, MA 1970, PhD 1975. **CAREER:** Purdue Univ, assoc prof 1979-; Africana & Res Center Purdue Univ, interim dir 1978-79; Purdue Univ, asst prof 1974-79; SC State Coll, asst prof 1972-74. **ORGANIZATIONS:** Editorial Bd Jour of Negro History 1979-; exec counc mem Assc for Study of Afro-Amer Life History 1979-81; editor Truth, Newsletter of ABWH 1979-80; dir of publs Assc of Black Women Historians 1979. **HONORS/ACHIEVEMENTS:** Authored "Black Victory, The Rise and Fall of the White Primary in TX" 1979; Flwshp Rockefeller Fnd; Flwshp for Min Grp Schlrs 1980. **BUSINESS ADDRESS:** Purdue University, West Lafayette, IN 47907.

HINES, CARL R., SR.
State representative. **PERSONAL:** Born Mar 23, 1931, Louisville, KY; married Teresa Churchill; children: 4 Children. **EDUCATION:** Univ Louisville, BS; Louisville Sch Law. **CAREER:** Housing Opportunity Ctr, exec dir 1974; KY Gen Ass Louisville, state rep 1985; Housing Opportunity Centers Inc, city dir, exec dir. **ORGANIZATIONS:** Mem Housing Task Force Louisville C of C; mem Mayor's Housing Task Force under Mayor Frank Burke; mem Nat Assn Comm Devel; bd dir State KY Housing Corp; mem Housing Com Louisville C of C 1985; couns Nat Center Housing Mgmt Wash; adv com Non-Profit Housing Center; v chmn Jefferson Co Bd Edn;mem Dist Lines Subcom Charter Com for Merger Louisville & Jefferson Co Schs; former mem bd Louisville NAACP, W Louisville Optimist Club; past chmn Shawnee Dist Boy Scouts Am; cur pres Just Men's Civic & Social Club; exec sec mem Louisville & Jefferson Co Comm Action Commn; v Chmn bd mgrs YMCA; Louisville Bd Educ 1968; re-elected 1968 & 1972; chmn Fifth Region KY Sch Bds Assn; gov's adv Cncl Edn; mem Fed Relations Network Nat Sch Bd Assn; dir Nat Caucus Black Sch Bd Mems & Chmn State KY. **MILITARY SERVICE:** USAF 3 yrs.

HINES, GREGORY
Actor. **PERSONAL:** Born Feb 14, 1946, New York, NY; married Pamela Koslow; children: Daria, Jessica Koslow, Zachary Evan. **CAREER:** Appeared with Hines Kids 1949-55; Hines Brothers 1955-63; Hines & Dad 1963-73; Theater performances, appeared in "Severence," "Eubie," "Comin Uptown," "Sophisticated Ladies" 1981; Movies incl "Wolfen" 1981, "History of the World Part I" 1981, "The Deal of the Century," "The Cotton Club," "White Nights," "Running Scared.". **ORGANIZATIONS:** Mem Actors Equity, Screen Actors Guild, AFTRA. **HONORS/ACHIEVEMENTS:** 3 Tony Nominations 1979, 1980, 1981; Theater World Award; TOR Award; Dance Educators Am Award; Co-Host 1984 Oscars; Honoree 1985 Dramatic Arts Award for achievements as a stage and screen actor, and for contributions to the motion picture, "The Cotton Club". **BUSINESS ADDRESS:** Fran Saperstein, 919 Victoria Ave, Venice, CA 90291.

HINES, J. EDWARD, JR.
Attorney. **PERSONAL:** Born Feb 26, 1908, Alexandria, LA; married Willie B Smith; children: Ethel Hines Battle, J E III, Zelda Ruth Turner. **EDUCATION:** Parish of Rapiedes State of LA, asst dist atty 1972-; Alexandria, asst city atty 1971-72. **CAREER:** Mem LA State Bar; mem Alexandria Bar; pres Rapides Parish Voters League yrs; pres Alexandria Civ & Improvement Council 11 yrs; admin bd Newman United Meth Ch; mem Sch Bd Bi-Racial Com; appointed mem Bi-Racial Com of State of LA; alternate delegate To Dem Nat Conv 1968; mem Omega Psi Phi; 32 Deg Mason; Kisatchie-Delta Reg Planning & Dev Dist Inc; Cenla Health Planning Council. **ORGANIZATIONS:** Outstanding Citizen of the Comm 1965; Omega Man of the Yr Omega Psi Phi 1974. **BUSINESS ADDRESS:** 1330 8 St, Alexandria, LA 71301.

HINES, KINGSLEY B.
Attorney. **PERSONAL:** Born Mar 27, 1944, Pasadena; married Anne; children: Tiffany, Garrett. **EDUCATION:** USC, BA 1966; Loyola U, JD 1969. **CAREER:** So CA Edison Co, atty 1972-; Eng Sq Law Cntr LA 1970-71; Family Law Cntr, leg servs 1969-71. **ORGANIZATIONS:** Mem CA Bar Assn; LA Co Bar Assn; Langston Law Club. **BUSINESS ADDRESS:** 2244 Walnut Grove Ave, Ste 341, Rosemead, CA 91770.

HINES, LAURA M.
Psychologist. **PERSONAL:** Born Oct 29, 1922, Covington, VA; divorced. **EDUCATION:** VA St Univ, BA; NY Univ, MA; Fordham Univ, PhD. **CAREER:** Byrd S Coler Hosp Metro Hosp, psychologist 1960-65; Bd of Educ NYC,psychologist 1965-74, supr psychologists 1974-79; Columbia Univ, consult psychologist; Yheshiva Univ, asst prof. **ORGANIZATIONS:** Consult Greater Harlem Compr Gdnc Ctr 1979-; pres sch div NYS Psychological Asso 1983-84; bd of trustees Lexington Sch for the Deaf 1985; mem Am Psychological Asso; fellow Am Orthopsychiatric Asso; mem Natl Asso of Sch Psychologists. **HOME ADDRESS:** 156-20 Riverside Dr W, New York, NY 10032.

HINES, MORGAN B.
Dental surgeon. **PERSONAL:** Born Aug 11, 1946, New York, NY; son of Edgar D Hines and Emmie E Marshall; children: Morgan B Jr. **EDUCATION:** Toledo Univ, attended 1964-68; Meharry Medical Coll, DDS 1973. **CAREER:** Hubbard Hosp, intern 1973-74; Maury Co Health Dept, dentist 1974-75; Meharry Medical Coll Dept of Oral Pathology, assoc prof 1975-76; Columbia TN, professional hypnosis practice 1976-; Private Practice Columbia TN, dentist 1974-. **ORGANIZATIONS:** Professional artist pen and ink, sculpture, oils, pencil; art showing at TN Arts League, TN Performing Arts Ctr, Columbia State Comm Coll, TN State Univ; chmn Maury County Fine Arts Exhibit 1983; piece in collection of art Mid State TN Regional Library 1985; mem TN Art League, Columbia Creative Arts Guild, Columbia Cof C; hospital staff Maury County Hosp; mem Amer Dental Assoc, Omega Psi Phi Frat Inc, TN Sheriff Org, TN Black Artist Assoc; bd of dirs Nashville Amateur Boxing Assoc, Maury Co Creative Art Guild, TN/AL/GA Amateur Boxing Hall of Fame. **HONORS/ACHIEVEMENTS:** Coach of the Year Awd Spirit of Amer Tournament Decatur AL 1981; TN Special Deputy Sheriff; numerous art awds; numerous appreciation awds for dedication to youth and boxing; three articles Amateur Boxing Magazine 1980,81,82; poem published in "The World Book of Poetry" 1981. **BUSINESS ADDRESS:** 418 West 6th St, Columbia, TN 38402.

HINES, RALPH HOWARD
Business executive. **PERSONAL:** Born May 15, 1927, Chicago, IL. **EDUCATION:** Univ of IL, BS 1949; Univ of Copenhagen, MA 1951; Univ of IL, PhD 1955. **CAREER:** USIA-US State Dept, cultural affairs officer 1955-60; AL State Univ, prof sociology 1960-63; Howard Univ, prof assoc sociology 1963-65; Meharry Med Coll, exec vice pres 1966-82, prof soc psychiatry 1965-. **ORGANIZATIONS:** Editor Journal Social & Behavioral Sci 1968-75; consult HEW Washington DC 1970-75 chmn bd Metro Transit Authority 1971-81; vice chmn bd TN Housing Devel Agency 1973-75; mem bd Comm Fed Savings Assn 1975-; pres Assn Social & Behavorial Sci 1975; mem Nashville Gas Co 1978; mem bd Comm Fed Savings Assn 1975-. **HONORS/ACHIEVEMENTS:** Harold D West Awd Meharry Med Coll 1972; Fellow Amer Pub Health Assn Washington DC 1973; Doctor of Letters (LLD), Meharry Medical College 1976. **BUSINESS ADDRESS:** Prof Soc Psychiatry, Meharry Med Coll, 3808 John Merritt Blvd, Nashville, TN 37209.

HINES, WILEY EARL (CHIC)
Dentist. **PERSONAL:** Born Apr 29, 1942, Greenville, NC; married Gloria D Moore; children: Wandria, Wiley, Derrick. **EDUCATION:** Knoxville Coll, BS 1963; Meharry Med Coll, DDS 1971. **CAREER:** Oak Ridge Natl Labs, biologist 1963-65; Melpar, biologist 1965-67; St of NC, publ health dentist 1971-73; Howard Univ, asst clinical prof 1975; Private practice, dentist 1973-. **ORGANIZATIONS:** Mem Amer Dental Assoc, NC Dental Assoc, Old N St Dental Assoc, E Med, Dental Pharm Soc, Alpha Phi Alpha, IBPOE, Prince Hall Mason. **HONORS/ACHIEVEMENTS:** Listed in Who's Who in N Amer. **MILITARY SERVICE:** USNR 1971-73. **BUSINESS ADDRESS:** 608 E 10th St, Greenville, NC 27834.

HINES-HAYWARD, OLGA LORETTA
Librarian. **PERSONAL:** Born in Alexandria, LA; daughter of Samuel James and Lillie George Hines; married Samuel E Hayward Jr (deceased); children: Anne Elizabeth, Olga Patricia Hayward Ryer. **EDUCATION:** Dillard Univ, AB 1941; Atlanta Univ, BS in LS 1944; Univ of Michigan, MA in LS 1959; Louisiana State Univ, MA History 1977; Louisiana State Univ, further study. **CAREER:** Marksville, LA, HS teacher 1941-42; Grambling Coll, head librarian 1944-46; New Orleans Public Library, librarian 1947-48; Southern Univ Baton Rouge, head of reference dept 1948-74, dir collection develop librarian 1984-86, head of reference dept 1986-88; head of Social Sciences Collection 1974-84. **ORGANIZATIONS:** Sec treas, vice pres, pres LA Chap Special Libraries Assn; mem Baton Rouge Cncl on Human Relations 1981-; banquet comm mem Baton Rouge Conf for Christians & Jews 1982-; vice chair 1985-86, chair 1986-87 LA Library Assoc Subject Specialists Sect; mem steering comm LA Comm for Develop of Libraries 1987-. **HONORS/ACHIEVEMENTS:** "Annotated Bibliography of Works By and About Whitney M Young" Bulletin of Bibliography July/Aug 1974; "Spotlight on Special Libraries in LA" LA Library Assn Bulletin 41 Summer 1979. **HOME ADDRESS:** 1632 Harding Blvd, Baton Rouge, LA 70807. **BUSINESS ADDRESS:** Prof of Library Science, Southern University, Baton Rouge, LA 70813.

HINKLE, JACKSON HERBERT
Clergyman. **PERSONAL:** Born Dec 17, 1943, Arkansas; children: Herby, Jack. **EDUCATION:** Philander-Smith Coll, BA; Greenville Indus Coll, DD 1966; Northwestern U, grad sty. **CAREER:** Catherdral of Faith Inkster, MI, pastor cath hdqtrs 1975-; New Hebron Bapt Ch Little Rock, AR & St Bethel Bapt Ch Chgo, pastor; Stinson Cathedral Funeral Home, establ; Mobil Vido Tape Co, vp; Cath of Faith E Detroit, fdr pastor. **ORGANIZATIONS:** Fdr chmn Back to God Am Com; fdr pres Cathedral Christian Acad; fdr dir Nat Assn Black Soul Winning Chs 1974. **HONORS/ACHIEVEMENTS:** Apprec cert Gov; outstdg serv awd New Bethel Bapt Ch 1973; author lectr evangelist. **BUSINESS ADDRESS:** Founder, Pastor, Cathedral of Faith, PO Box 279, Inkster, MI 48141.

HINNANT, OLLEN B.
Attorney, business executive. **PERSONAL:** Born Jan 16, 1931, Lexington, KY; married Ella M Lilly; children: Denise, Gregory, Cheryl. **EDUCATION:** KY State U, BA 1952;Univ KY, JD 1955. **CAREER:** Prudential Ins Co Am, asst gen couns 1964-; Pvt Law Pract 1975-; KY Bar , adm 1955; NJ 1963; US Sup Ct 1963. **ORGANIZATIONS:** Nat bd mem Planned Parenthood Fed of Am; Nat Bar Assn; Broadcast Enterprises Network; YMWCA; NAACP; chmn Inst Lawyers' Sect NBA; chmn Am Assn of Inst Lawyers; Alpha Phi Alpha; Newark Fresh Air Fund; Union Bapt Ch; Phi Delta Phi Intl Legal Frat. **HONORS/ACHIEVEMENTS:** Num Civic Orgns; Hon Mention Charcoal Paint Geo W Carver Prudential Art Cont 1972; Outstanding Coll Student Leaders Am 1952; Who's Who in E; Men of Achiev of the World; Dict of Intl Biography; Pub in Am Bar Assn "FORUM" Mag 1975-76; Am Bar Assn Journal 1974; NJ Bar Assn Journal 1974; Who's Whoin Am Law. **MILITARY SERVICE:** AUS 1955-57.

HINTON, ALFRED FONTAINE
Artist, educator. **PERSONAL:** Born Nov 27, 1940, Columbus, GA; son of Eddie H Hinton and Johnnie Mae Sipp Hinton; married Ann Noel Pearlman, Aug 05, 1965; children: Adam, Melina, Elizabeth. **EDUCATION:** Univ of IA, BA 1967; Univ of Clincinnati with honors, MFA 1970. **CAREER:** Toronto Argonauts, professional football player, 1963-67; Khadejha Primitive Prints Toronto, design consultant, 1967-68; Dickinson Coll, Carlisle, PA, instructor, 1969; Western Michigan Univ, asst prof of painting & drawing, 1970-77; Univ of Michigan School of Art, assoc prof in painting, 1977-82, prof in painting, 1982-. **ORGANIZATIONS:** Mem Visual Arts Adv Panel MI Council for Arts 1973-; coord Visual Arts MI Academy of Sci Arts & Letters 1972-74; exhibiting artist Gallery 7 Detroit 1970-; bd mem, Michigan Council for the Arts, 1980-84; exec bd mem, Concerned Citizen's for the Arts Michigan, 1983-86; panelist, Ongoing Michigan Artist Program, Detroit Inst of Arts, 1986-88; mem, Master Panel Bd, Detroit Council for the Arts, 1987-. **HONORS/ACHIEVEMENTS:** Research Grant, Western Michigan Univ 1972-73; Flint Inst of Arts All MI Exhibition Purchase Award 1972; 16 one person shows; 40 invitational & group exhibitions; All-Amer, Co-captain, Most Valuable Player, Univ of IA Football Team 1961; Creative Artist Grant, Michigan Council for the Arts, 1985; State of Michigan Commission on Art in Public Places, 1986. **BUSINESS ADDRESS:** Prof, School of Art, Univ of Michigan, 2000 Bonisteel Blvd, Ann Arbor, MI 48109.

HINTON, CHRIS
Professional athlete. **PERSONAL:** Born Jul 31, 1961, Chicago, IL; married Carol. **EDUCATION:** Northwestern Univ, Sociology degree. **CAREER:** Indianapolis Colts, tackle 1983-. **ORGANIZATIONS:** Active in Adopt-A-Family, Special Olympics. **HONORS/ACHIEVEMENTS:** Selected first team All-America by Sporting News; second team All-America by UPI and NEA; chosen Northwestern Wildcat's MVP by teammates; named to the 1982 All-Amer Strength Team; played in 1983 Blue-Gray game, Senior Bowl; earned AP second-team All-Pro, UPI first-team All-AFC and NEA second team All-NFL honors; UPI NFL All-Rookie Team 1983; Football Digest NFL All-Rookie Team 1983; UPI AFC All-Star Second Team 1983; Pro Football Writers All-AFC 1983; PFWA All-Rookie Team 1983; AP All-Pro Second TEam 1985; UPI All-AFC First Team 1985; NEA All-NFL Second Team 1985; mem Pro Bowl teams 1986,87. **BUSINESS ADDRESS:** Indianapolis Colts, PO Box 24100, Indianapolis, IN 46224.

HINTON, CHRISTOPHER JEROME
Photographer, studio co-owner. **PERSONAL:** Born Sep 23, 1952, Raleigh, NC; son of J D Hinton and A M Hinton. **EDUCATION:** Winston-Salem State Univ, Winston-Salem NC, BA Music, 1975. **CAREER:** J D Hinton Studio, Raleigh NC, photographer, 1976-. **ORGANIZATIONS:** Phi Beta Sigma Frat, 1972-; Garner Road Family YMCA Back-A-Child Campaign; United Nero Coll Fund Campaign, 1989; NAACP Freedom Fund Banquet,

annual. **HONORS/ACHIEVEMENTS:** Phi Beta Sigma Frat Award; Business Award, Raleigh Alumnae Chapter Delta Sigma Theta; photography works featured in natl publications such as: Jet Publication, Black Radio Exclusive, Ohio Historical Soc. **BUSINESS ADDRESS:** Co-owner, J D Hinton Studio, 515 South Blount St, Raleigh, NC 27601.

HINTON, FLOYD
Association executive. **PERSONAL:** Born Jan 19, 1924, Richmond, VA; married Daisy C; children: Marguerite, Gary, Vanessa. **EDUCATION:** Essex Co Comm Coll. **CAREER:** Freedholders, assn exec 1985; Passaic Co Sheriff's Dept. **ORGANIZATIONS:** Mem, pres Paterson Br NAACP; 3rd vice pres NJ Conf NAACP Brs; Calvary Bapt Ch; Neg Com of PBA Local 197; Falls City Post Am Legion; mem Mayor's ManpowerCom; council of Agencies for Family Planning Serv Passar Co; Paterson Council Social Svcs. **HONORS/ACHIEVEMENTS:** Recip Membership Award NAACP 1973; Cert of Appreciation Calvary Bapt Ch 1970; Brotherhood Award for Meritorious Serv Action Now Ctr of Paterson 1971-72; Comm Award Unit #9 Beautician Assn 1974. **MILITARY SERVICE:** AUS. **BUSINESS ADDRESS:** Passaic Co Courthouse, Hamilton St, Paterson, NJ 07509.

HINTON, GREGORY TYRONE
Attorney. **PERSONAL:** Born Nov 22, 1949, Barrackville, WV; son of Nathan Hinton and Amelia Hinton; married Carol Jean Suggs; children: Gregory T II, Hamilton H, Carol Princess Jean. **EDUCATION:** Fairmont State Coll, AB 1978; WV Univ Coll of Law, JD 1981. **CAREER:** Thorofare Markets Inc, stock clerk/carry-out 1968-69; Hope Natl Gas Co, casual rouster 1970-71; Montana Power Co, elec clerk 1972-73; Gibbs & Hill, elec clerk 1973-75; N Central Opportunity Indus Ctr, exec dir 1975-78; Fairmont City Council, councilmember 1977-86, mayor 1983-85; WV Univ Coll of Law, consultant; attorney private practice. **ORGANIZATIONS:** Mem Montana Valley Assn of Health Ctrs Inc 1974-; deacon Good Hope Baptists Church 1974-; corp banking & business law & minority affairs comm WV State Bar 1984-86; vstg comm WV Univ Coll of Law 1984-87; adv bd WNPB-TV 1984-86; bd mem Fairmont Gen Hosp 1985-86; consul WV Univ Coll of Law 1985-; WV Adv Comm to US Commn on Civil Rights 1985-89; pres MT State Bar Assn 1986-88; ethics comm WV State Bar 1986-87; NAACP Legal Redress Comm. **HONORS/ACHIEVEMENTS:** 1st black elected Mayor to a major city in WV 1983; Hon Mem Magnificent Souls 1983; Outstanding Young Man of Amer Jaycees 1979, 1984; WV Outstanding Black Atty Black Amer Law Student Assn Morgantown WV 1984; WV Outstanding Black Atty; Spec Award as Mayor from WV State Assn and PER-PDR Tri-State Conf ofCouncils IBPOEW PA-OH-WV 1984; Spec Award as Mayor from Dunbar HS class of 1947 1984; Honorary Mem Amer Soc for Nondestructive Testing Fairmont State Coll Sect 1984; Black Amer Law Student Assn Morgantown WV 1985; Outstanding WV Black Attorney. **HOME ADDRESS:** 202 Maple Ave, Fairmont, WV 26554. **BUSINESS ADDRESS:** Attorney, 301 Security Bldg, Fairmont, WV 26554.

HINTON, HORTENSE BECK
College administrator. **PERSONAL:** Born Apr 27, 1950, Charlottesville, VA; married Walter M Hinton; children: Shani O, Adisa A, Ajamu A. **EDUCATION:** State Univ of NY, BA Psychology 1971; Univ of District of Columbia, MA Counseling 1977. **CAREER:** Univ of District of Columbia, sr counselor/asst dir special serv program 1971-78; Univ of VA, assoc dean/director summer preparatory program office of afro-amer affairs 1978-. **ORGANIZATIONS:** Mem Amer Assoc for Counseling & Develop, Natl Assoc Women's Deans & Counselors, Amer Assoc of Univ Women, Amer Assoc for Affirmative Action; memNatl & VA State Conf NAACP; clerk, choir mem, youth advisor Free Union Baptist Church. **HONORS/ACHIEVEMENTS:** Community Serv Awd Culpepper Branch NAACP 1983; Martin L King Jr Faculty Awd Alpha Phi Alpha Inc Univ of VA 1986-87; Gubernatorial apptmt VA State Equal Employment Oppor Council 1986-90. **HOME ADDRESS:** RT 4 Box 366B, Culpeper, VA 22701. **BUSINESS ADDRESS:** Assoc Dean Afro-Amer Affairs, University of Virginia, #4 Dawson's Row, Charlottesville, VA 22903.

HINTON, WARREN MILES
Chemist. **PERSONAL:** Born Feb 18, 1920, Corona, NY; married Sadie J; children: Warren G, Beverly Reynold, Roslyn Curseon. **EDUCATION:** Pratt Inst, BS Chemistry 1949. **CAREER:** Kollsman Instrument Corp, lab asst 1943-49; chemist 1949-68, mgr/eeo 1968-75; Dept of Labor-OSHA, industrial hygienist 1977-. **ORGANIZATIONS:** Mem Amer Chem Soc 1949-83; mem Omega Psi Phi Frat 1958; charter mem EDGES Group 1969; mem Amer Inst of Chemists 1970. **BUSINESS ADDRESS:** Industrial Hygienist, Dept of Labor/OSHA, 90 Church St, New York, NY 10007.

HISLE, LARRY EUGENE
Professional athlete. **PERSONAL:** Born May 05, 1947, Portsmouth, OH; married Sheila; children: Larry Jr. **EDUCATION:** OH State & OHUniv (Portsmouth). **CAREER:** Milwaukee Brewers, player 1978-; Minnesota Twins, player 1973-77; Philadelphia Phillies, player 1969-71; Baseball & BB, prep all Am 1965; All-State HS BB 1964-65. **ORGANIZATIONS:** All-Rookie Team 1969; set Twins record with 4 steals in one game 1976; Amer League All-Star Team 1977-78; topped League with 119 RBI 1977; Brewer MVP & 3rd in League MVP 1978; named to "Sporting News/AP/UPI & Baseball Bulletins" All-Star Teams 1978; 2nd in League in Homers (34) 1978; 3rd in League in RBI's (115) 1978. **BUSINESS ADDRESS:** Milwaukee Brewers, Milwaukee County Stadium, Milwaukee, WI 53214.

HITE, NANCY URSULA
Public relations. **PERSONAL:** Born Aug 01, 1956, White Plains, NY. **EDUCATION:** Spelman Coll, BA 1978; Iona Coll, MS 1985. **CAREER:** WOVX-Radio Station, reporter 1978-79; Potpourri WVOX Radio, producer 1982-; Freelance journalist newspapers and magazines throughout the US, 1982-; Natl PhotoNews Service, managing editor 1985-; Louis-Rowe Enterprises, public relations 1979-, exec sec to corp. **ORGANIZATIONS:** Assoc editor New Rochelle Branch NAACP Newsletter 1985-86; Black Women's Political Caucus Advisory New Rochelle NAACP Youth Council 1987; mem Alpha Kappa Alpha Sor. **HONORS/ACHIEVEMENTS:** Certificate The Publicity Club of New York 1981,82; Researcher "Break Dancing" pub by Shron Publication 1984; entertainment articles pub in "Right On" & "Class" Magazines Edri Communications; 1986 Outstanding Young Women of Amer. **BUSINESS ADDRESS:** Exec Sec to the Corporation, Louis-Rowe Enterprises, 455 Main St Ste 103-105, New Rochelle, NY 10801.

HIXSON, JUDSON LEMOINE
Administrator. **PERSONAL:** Born Jun 10, 1950, Chicago, IL. **EDUCATION:** Univ of Chicago, BA 1972, MA Ed 1973, PhD candidate. **CAREER:** IL Bell Telephone, installer, repairman 1968-70; Univ of Chicago, counselor, instr pre-freshman prog 1970-72, dir pre-freshman prog 1970-72, rsch, therapist dept of psych 1974-76; Loyola Univ School of Social Work, instr 1976-79; Chicago Urban League, ed dir 1976-80; City Comm Detroit MI, asst to pres 1981; Chicago Public Schools Equal Educ Opportunity, coord for admin 1981-. **ORGANIZATIONS:** Pres, treas Henry Booth House Bd of Trustees 1975-; bd of dir IL Assoc for the Advancement of Blacks in Voc Ed 1977-80; pres Natl Council of Urban League Ed Specialists 1978-80; founder, Spirit Records 1979-; pres City-Wide Adv Comm Chicago Bd of Ed 1979-80; mem WSSD Radio 1980; pres, founder Four "M" Co Multi-Media Prod & Mgmt; consult Valpariaso & Northeastern IL Univ; bd of dir Girl Scouts of Chgo, Chicago United Ed Task Force, Hull House Assoc, IL Consultation on Ethnicity in Ed; consult US Congressional Black Caucus, Natl Urban League, IL Office of Ed, Human Resource Devel Columbia Coll School Dist in Seattle, Pittsburgh, New Orleans, San Diego, Dallas, Blue Island IL; consult Catholic Charities of Chgo. **HONORS/ACHIEVEMENTS:** Howell Murray Alumni Awd for Achievement Univ of Chicago Alumni Assoc 1972; Comm Serv Awd Chicago Jr Assoc of Commerce & Ind 1978; Fifty Leaders of the Future Ebony Mag 1978; Ten Outstanding Young Citizens Chicago Jr Assoc of Commerce & Ind 1980; Outstanding Young Men of Amer 1980; Rsch Spec & Publ, testing,classroom mgmt, desegregation, student motivation, teacher/parent trng. **BUSINESS ADDRESS:** Coordinator for Administration, Chicago Public Schools, Equal Ed Oppty, 1819 W Persking Rd 6 East, Chicago, IL 60609.

HOAGLAND, EVERETT H., III
Educator. **PERSONAL:** Born Dec 18, 1942, Philadelphia, PA; divorced; children: Kamal, Nia, Ayan. **EDUCATION:** Lincoln Univ PA, BA 1964; Brown Univ, MA 1973. **CAREER:** Philadelphia School System, English teacher 1964-67; Lincoln Univ, asst dir admissions 1967-69; Claremont Coll Black Studies, instr Afro-Amer poetry 1969-71; Brown Univ, univ fellow 1971-73; Southeastern MA Univ, assoc prof of English. **ORGANIZATIONS:** Mem Bahia Faith 1973-; clerk of corp/bd mem New Bedford Foster Grandparents Prog 1976-82; weekly columnist New Bedford Standard-Times 1979-82; contrib editor Amer Poetry Review 1984-;Wm Carney Acad New Bedford 1985; mem NAACP 1985. **HONORS/ACHIEVEMENTS:** Univ Fellowship by Brown Univ 1971-73; Silvera Award for Creative Writing Lincoln Univ 1964; Gwendolyn Brooks Award for Fiction by Black World Mag 1974; Creative Artists Fellowship state-wide annual MA Arts & Humanities Competition 1975; NEH Fellowship 1984; Fellowship from Artists Foundation Annual State Wide Poetry Competition 1986. **BUSINESS ADDRESS:** Southeastern Massachusetts Univ, Group I Bldg, Room 323, Old Westport Rd, North Dartmouth, MA 02747.

HOARD, WALTER B.
Clergyman, educator. **PERSONAL:** Born Mar 10, 1925, Nicholasville, KY; married Georgia Jackson; children: David Walter. **EDUCATION:** OH Central State U, BS 1951; Oberlin Coll, BD 1957; Vanderbilt U, MDiv 1972; New Testament Studies Mansfield Coll of OxfordUniv England, cert in theology 1967; CA W U, PhD 1979. **CAREER:** Olney St Baptist Church RI, pastor 1958-60; St Paul Baptist Church NY 1960-65; Calvary Capt Church WI 1965-70; Amer Baptist Conv PA, assoc gen sec 1970-73; Chicago Baptist Inst, exec dean; Black Religious Educ Research Counselling Resource Center Ltd, exec dir 1985. **ORGANIZATIONS:** Past pres NAACP Utica NY 1963-65; pres NAACP Milwaukee 1965-68; pres State Conf of NAACP Br of WI 1965-68. **HONORS/ACHIEVEMENTS:** Chmn & Founder N Milwaukee State Bank First & Only Black Bank in Wi 1969-70; Co-founder of Milwaukee OIC; Author of Numerous Publs; Cited by NY & WI for Serv in Civil Rights 1964-68.

HOBBS, JOHN DANIEL
Educator, legislator. **PERSONAL:** Born Oct 13, 1931, Washington, DC; married Mary A Saxon; children: Danielle A, John D Jr, Harold Krause, Karen Krause. **EDUCATION:** Univ of Redlands CA, BA, MA 1962-69. **CAREER:** City of San Bernardino, councilman 1975-; Redlands Unified Sch Dist, tchr 1962-; Norton AFB CA, computer prog/syst analysis 1965-69; Past Polemarch San Bernardino Alumni Chap Southern CA Const Oppt Prog, educ consult & tutor 1968-75. **ORGANIZATIONS:** Kappa Alpha Psi 1967-69; mem Prince Hall Lodge #17 Masonic 1985; mem Govs Commn for Solar Energy 1985; mem Urban League NAACP NCMW 1985. **HONORS/ACHIEVEMENTS:** Airman of the Month USAF 1954; Outstanding Achievement & Dedication to Serv NCMW SB Chpt/Westside Community Development SB/Operation Second Chance/Kappa Alpha Psi SB Chptr 1976-79. **MILITARY SERVICE:** USAF s/sgt 1952-56. **BUSINESS ADDRESS:** 300 North D St, San Bernardino, CA 92408.

HOBBS, JOSEPH
Physician, educator. **PERSONAL:** Born Aug 05, 1948, Augusta, GA; married Janice Polk. **EDUCATION:** Mercer U, BS 1970; Med Coll of GA, MD 1974. **CAREER:** Med Coll of GA, asst prof family med 1979-, instr family med 1978, chief res 1977, family prac res 1976, med intern 1975. **ORGANIZATIONS:** Mem Richmond Co Med Soc 1978; vice pres Stoney Med Dental Pharm Soc 1979; team physician T W Josey High Sch. **HONORS/ACHIEVEMENTS:** Recipient Commendation Family Practice Resident Med Coll of GA 1978; Fellowship Am Acad of Fam Practice 1979. **BUSINESS ADDRESS:** Med Coll of GA, 15th St, Augusta, GA 30912.

HOBBS, THADEAUS H.
Educator. **PERSONAL:** Born Mar 26, 1924, Guthrie, OK; married Evelyn Fields. **EDUCATION:** LangstonUniv 1941-43; HowardUniv 1944;Univ Study Cntr Florence Italy 1945; UCLA, BA 1948; USC, MA 1961; USC, Addl Study PhD. **CAREER:** Locke High Sch LA, prin 1971-; Lafayette Jr High Sch, tchr 1953-55; Adams Jr HS 1955-67; Nightingale Jr HS, boys vice pres 1967-68; Locke HS 1968-71. **ORGANIZATIONS:** Mem Claremont Coll Bd Dirs 1971-74; WindsorUniv Adv Council 1973-; Town Hall CA 1974; Kedren Mental Health Cntr 1971-74; LA Assn Secondary Sch Adminstrs; LA Sr High Sch Prins Assn; mem Area Gifted Students Adv Bd Founder Promethian Eng Soc; various positions BSA; dir Big Brothers of Gr LA; council Black Adminstrs; pres Inter-Fraternal Basketball Council 1956-61; Org 1st NJROTC; LA Unified Sch Dist Locke HS (1st All-Black Unit W MS Rvr) 1971; western vice pres AOA 1970-75; ch & higher educ com mem UMC 1974-; dir So Central ARC; chrm com on Discipline & Greviances AOA 1976-; dir So Central LA Child Devel Ctr; mem 1st Work Team Germany UMC 1949. **HONORS/ACHIEVEMENTS:** Phi Delta Kappa Man of Yr 1967; Who's Who W Coast; YMCA 500 Club. **MILITARY SERVICE:** Serv 92d INF

DIV WW II; 90mM AAA Bn Korea. **BUSINESS ADDRESS:** 325 E 111 St, Los Angeles, CA.

HOBBS, WILBUR E.
Business executive. **PERSONAL:** Born Sep 17, 1921, Philadelphia, PA; married Imogene Denny; children: Wilbur E Jr. **EDUCATION:** PA State Univ, BS 1943; Univ of PA, MSW 1951. **CAREER:** Youth Devel Cntr PA, supt 1961-66; Greenleigh Assoc, sr mgmt consult 1966-70; Comm Scis Inc, founder & pres 1970-; Office Children & Youth Commonwealthof PA, commr 1975-79; PA Dept of Pub Welfare, dep sec 1975-79; Crime Prevent Assn Phila, PA, exec dir 1979-81; Dept of Human Serv City of Philadelphia, dep commissioner 1981-83; Hobbs and Assoc, pres 1983-. **ORGANIZATIONS:** Mem Acad Cert Soc Workers; Natl Assn Soc Workers; Natl Assn Urbanologist & Min Cons; Amer Pub Welf Assn; trustee Beaver Coll Glenside, PA; dirPhiladelphia Citizens for Children & Youth; dir/assoc trustee Univ of PA; dir Urban League of Phila; exec bd Philadelphia Council BSA 1978-; mem Frontiers Intl-Philadelphia Chapter; 1st vice pres & chmn Charitable Contributions; Smithsonian Assoc; Alpha Phi Alpha; dir Crime Prevention Assn; dir Comm Serv Planning Council. **HONORS/ACHIEVEMENTS:** 1st Black appointed Adj Gen Staff Commonwealth of PA; 1st Black appointed Supt State Inst for Juveniles; Recipient Humanitarian Gold Award Adult Trainees Found for Retarded Citizens 1976; Outstanding Gold Achievement in Human Serv Award OIC's of Amer 1978. **MILITARY SERVICE:** USAR 1942-62; Maj (ret). **BUSINESS ADDRESS:** President, Hobbs and Associates, 1617 J F Kennedy Blvd, Ste 1420, Philadelphia, PA 19103.

HOBSON, CAROL J. See SMITH, CAROL J.

HOBSON, CHARLES BLAGROVE
Television producer. **PERSONAL:** Born Jun 23, 1936, Brooklyn, NY; son of Charles Samuel Hobson and Cordelia Victoria Hobson; divorced; children: Hallie. **EDUCATION:** Attended, Brooklyn Coll, Emory Univ Grad Sch 1974-76. **CAREER:** WBAI-FM, production dir 1965-68; ABC-TV, producer 1966-71; Clark Coll, dir of communications 1971-76; WXIA, exec producer 1972-73; The Dance Exchange, trustee 1977-80; WETA-TV, sr vice president. **ORGANIZATIONS:** Consultant Natl Endowment for the Arts 1976-87, NEH; bd mem Amer the Beautiful Fund 1977-87; exec producer The Africans, From Jumpstreet, Global Links; mem Writer's Guild of Amer, African Studies Assn; consultant, Greycom International; consultant, National Black Arts Festival; bd mem, America The Beautiful Fund. **HONORS/ACHIEVEMENTS:** Capital Press Club Awd 1968; Emmy Awd NATAS 1968; Governor's Awd Natl Acad Arts & Scis 1976; WC Hardy Awd 1981; Natl Black Prog Consortium Awd 1985; Ohio State Award 1987; One of the Leading TV Producers, Millimeter Magazine. **MILITARY SERVICE:** AUS pfc 1962-63. **HOME ADDRESS:** 175 Warrren St, Brooklyn, NY 11201.

HOBSON, DONALD LEWIS
Judge. **PERSONAL:** Born Jan 11, 1935, Detroit, MI; son of Oscar Collins Hobson and Theresa Lewis Hobson; divorced; children: Donna Lynne. **EDUCATION:** Attended, OH State Univ; Eastern MI Univ, BSc History; MI State Univ, MA; Detroit Coll of Law, JD; Post Graduate Work, Univ of MI, Wayne State Univ Law School, Hampton Inst, US Naval Academy, US Naval Justice School, Natl Judicial College. **CAREER:** Detroit Public Sch System, social science teacher 1957-64; Detroit Bd of Educ Job Upgrading Prog, coord; US Dept of Justice Washington; Goodman Eden Millender Goodman & Bedrosian Detroit, assoc partner; Common Pleas Ct for the City of Detroit, judge; Recorders Ct of Detroit, judge. **ORGANIZATIONS:** Arbit panelist mem Detroit Regional Adv Cncl Amer Arbitration Assn; natl exec bd & adv bd Detroit Chap Natl Lawyers Guild; exec bd Amer Trial Lawyers Assn; Natl Bd Cncl on Legal Educ Oppors; hearing referee MI Civil Rights Comm; sec Income Tax Review Bd City of Detroit; MI Supreme Court's Spec Comm on Landlord-Tenant Problems; Natl Bd Natl Bar Assn; State Bar of MI Rep Assembly; counsel State Bar Grievance Bd; Wolverine Bar Assn treas vice pres pres & bd of dirs; Natl Assn for Equal Oppor in Higher Educ. **HONORS/ACHIEVEMENTS:** Eastern MI Univ Alumni Honors Awd 1974; Hon Doctor of Humane Letters by Shaw Coll Detroit 1977; Hon Doctor of Laws Degree & Hon Doctor of Divinity Degree; Black Lawyers, Law Practice and Bar Associations; 1844-1970: A Michigan History, 1987, The Wayne Law Review vol 33, No 5. **MILITARY SERVICE:** USNR commander. **HOME ADDRESS:** 2136 Bryanston Crescent, Detroit, MI 48207. **BUSINESS ADDRESS:** Judge, Recorders Court of Detroit, 1441 St Antoine St, # 802, Detroit, MI 48226.

HOBSON, PATRICIA PINNIX
Business executive. **PERSONAL:** Born Aug 20, 1947, Martinsville, VA; daughter of Mrs Ida W Pinnix; married Johannes Allasandro Chauncey; children: Hans, Tiffany. **EDUCATION:** Bennett College, BS 1969. **CAREER:** General Electric Co, Inc, systems analyst 1970; Norfolk & Western Railway, systems analyst 1971; Ethyl Corporation, systems analyst 1972; EI DuPont de Nemours, staff assist to area head 1973-77; Miller Brewing Co, production services manager 1977-. **ORGANIZATIONS:** Secretary Business and Professional Woman 1983; vice pres Toastmasters Master Brewers of America 1983; bd of directors Citizens Against Family Violence 1984-86; bd of trustees Carlisle School 1984-86. **HONORS/ACHIEVEMENTS:** Natl Merit Finalist 1965; Summa Cum Laude Bennett College 1969; Kizzie Award Black Women Hall of Fame 1984; Top Black Achiever New York YMCA 1984. **BUSINESS ADDRESS:** Production Services Manager, Miller Brewing Co, PO Box 3327, Eden, NC 27288.

HOBSON, ROBERT R.
Government official. **PERSONAL:** Born Oct 20, 1930, Memphis, TN; children: Mafara, Alicia. **EDUCATION:** Tennessee State Univ, BA Government 1952; Howard Univ, 1956-57; Johns Hopkins Univ, 1958-59. **CAREER:** President's Committee on Equal Employment/Office of Fed Contract Compliance, senior compliance advisor 1963-71; Natl Urban Coalition, asst to the President 1971-73; Office of Federal Contract Compliance, assoc dir 1973-82; White House, senior staff member. **HONORS/ACHIEVEMENTS:** OFCCP Labor Department awards, 2 Merit Awards 1967 & 1969, Distinguished Service Career 1974, Special Achievement 1975-79, Commendation Excellent Service 1976. **BUSINESS ADDRESS:** Senior Staff Member, The White House, Washington, DC 20500.

HOBSON, WILLIAM D.
Business executive. **PERSONAL:** Born Apr 02, 1908, Martinsville, VA; married Virgia B; children: William D Jr. **EDUCATION:** Piedmont Christian Inst, Attended; Knoxville Coll. **CAREER:** Hobson's Esso Station, previously owner; W End Laudromat; City of Martinsville, councilman 1968-72; vice mayor 1974-; Martinsville, mayor 1976. **ORGANIZATIONS:** Mem bd dirs sec Imperial Bldg & Loan Assn; mem Central Bus Dist Commn Martinsville VA; mem Trans & Safety Commn Martinsville VA; bd trustee Fayette St Christian Ch; bd dirs Martinsville-Henry County C of C; MARC Workshop; commn mem W Piedmont Planning Dist; chmn Enviroment Com; personnel com Virginia Municipal League; Martinsville-Henry County Voters Registration League; mem Martinsville Men's Round Table Club Office.

HOBSON-SIMMONS, JOYCE ANN See SIMMONS, JOYCE HOBSON

HODGE, ADELE P.
News coordinator. **PERSONAL:** Born Jun 05, 1942, Chicago; divorced; children: Michael, Sandra. **EDUCATION:** Wayne State U; Northwood Inst Adv Study Prog 1971; Electronics Inst Tech 1966; John Robert Powers Finshing Sch 1966-71. **CAREER:** WWJ-TV,TV sales asst 1970-72; ABC WXYZ-TV,TV traffic coordinator 1968-70; NBC WWJ-TV,TV news prodcuer-writer 1971-. **ORGANIZATIONS:** Mem Detroit Press Club; Wmn Adv Club Detroit; Founders Soc Detroit; lectr Schs & Youth Groups. **BUSINESS ADDRESS:** 622 W Lafayette, Detroit, MI 48231.

HODGE, CHARLES MASON
Educational administrator. **PERSONAL:** Born Jun 25, 1938, Seguin, TX; son of Clifford D Hodge and Goldie M Campbell; married Elizabeth Howze; children: Gwendolyn, Clinton. **EDUCATION:** Univ of AR at Pine Bluff, BA 1960; N TX State Univ, MEd 1969, EdD 1976. **CAREER:** Terrell HS Ft Worth, high sch teacher 1964-69; Jarvis Christian Coll, instr social studies educ 1969-73; AR Desegregation Ctr for Public Schs, assoc dir 1973-74; AR Dept of Higher Educ, coord for human resources 1974-76; Univ of Central AR, assoc prof teacher educ 1976-80; AR Dept of Higher Educ, asst dir rsch & planning 1980; Univ Central AR, asst vice pres acad affairs 1980-83, dean college of educ 1983-89; Lamar Univ, Beaumont TX, dean of college of education, 1989—. **ORGANIZATIONS:** State rep AR Omega Psi Phi Frat 1976-80; bd of dirs Aldersgate Inc 1976-85; bd of dirs Amer Assn for Affirmative Action 1978-80; dir Region VI Amer Assn for Affirmative Action 1978-80; natl treas Amer Assn for Affirmative Action 1980; mem Sch Deseg Monitoring Team US Dist Ct 1980; Unit Accreditation Bd of Nat'l Council for the Accred for Teacher Ed, mem 1986-; AR State Council for Econ Ed, mem 1987-; member of, NAACP, Phi Delta Kappa, PTA, Comm Arts, Editorial Review Bd- Am Middle School Ed Journal, Education & Youth Task Force - Urban League of AR. **HONORS/ACHIEVEMENTS:** Ford Fellow Ford Found 1971; Gubernatorial Appt AR Gov's Task Force on Mgmt 1979; AR Teacher Educ Certification Evaluation Comm 1984. **BUSINESS ADDRESS:** Dean, College of Education, Lamar University, Beaumont, TX 77710.

HODGE, CYNTHIA ELOIS
Educational administrator. **PERSONAL:** Born Feb 23, 1947, Troop, TX; daughter of Robert Spencer and Doris Lydia Spencer; divorced; children: Delwyn Ray Madkins. **EDUCATION:** Univ of Denver, Pre-dental 1973-75; Univ of OR Health Sciences Center School of Dentistry, DMD 1979; Univ of NC at Chapel Hill, Certificate 1985. **CAREER:** Dentistry for Children, assoc dentist 1979-82; Post Graduate Training Univ of NC, 1982-85; Meharry Medical Coll, chairperson dept of hospital dentistry 1985-; Meharry Medical Coll, School of Dentistry, Nashville, TN, dir, general practice residency program, 1985-. **ORGANIZATIONS:** Dental consultant Multnomah County Health Dept Portland OR 1979-81; dental consultant Health Advisory Bd, Albina Ministerial Alliance, Headstart Program 1980-82; dental coordinator regional Natl Dental Assn 1981-82; Headstart Program; Infections Disease Control Comm, TN Dental Assn, 1987. **HONORS/ACHIEVEMENTS:** Certificate of Recognition Washington Monroe High School; Awd for Participation in Dental Field Experiences Washington Monroe HS Portland OR 1981; valuable contribution to the "Scientific Session," Natl Dental Assn. 1988; publisher and pres of Nashville Pride, Inc (weekly newspaper,) 1988. **BUSINESS ADDRESS:** Dir Genl Practice Residency, Meharry Medical Coll, School of Dentistry, 1005 DB Todd Blvd, Nashville, TN 37208.

HODGE, DEREK M.
Government official. **PERSONAL:** Born Oct 05, 1941, Frederiksted, VI; son of Enid Hodge; divorced; children: Marisol, Jonathan. **EDUCATION:** Michigan State Univ, BA 1963; Georgetown Univ Law Center, JD 1971. **CAREER:** Law Firm of Hodge Sheen & Finch, partner 1972; Private Practice, attorney 1978-84; USVI Legislature, senator/pres 1984-86; Govt of the Virgin Islands, lt governor 1986-. **ORGANIZATIONS:** Pres VI Partners for Health 1980-81; chmn, bd of dirs St Dunstan's Episcopal School 1983-84; titular head Democratic Party of the VI 1983-86; pres VI Bar Assoc 1984-86; mem VI Govt Comms Rules, Trade Tourism & Economic Devel, Conservation Recreation & Cultural Affairs 1984-86. **HONORS/ACHIEVEMENTS:** Appreciation plaque 4-H Club of VI 1984; Certificate of Merit Small Business Devel Center 1986; Recognition plaque Lutheran Social Serv of VI 1986; Proclamation Fulton Co GA 1987; Certificate of Membership Joint Center for Political Studies Assoc Program 1987. **MILITARY SERVICE:** AUS 1967; Army Natl Guard captain, staff judge advocate 1979-83. **BUSINESS ADDRESS:** Lieutenant Governor, US Virgin Islands, 18 Kongens Gade, Charlotte Amalie, St Thomas, Virgin Islands of the United States 00802.

HODGE, ERNEST M.
Automobile dealership chief executive. **CAREER:** Colonial Cadillac Sterling, Virginia Beach, VA, chief exec. **BUSINESS ADDRESS:** Colonial Cadillac-Sterling, 5524 Virginia Beach Blvd., Norfolk, VA 23502. *

HODGE, JOHN EDWARD
Retired scientist, educator. **PERSONAL:** Born Oct 12, 1914, Kansas City, KS; son of John Alfred Hodge and Anna Belle Jackson Hodge; married Justine Mitchell; children: John Laurent, Jay Mitchell, Justina Louise, Judith Ann. **EDUCATION:** Univ of KS, (Cum Laude) AB 1936, MA 1940; Bradley Univ, post-grad studies 1946-60; KS Tchrs Certificate 1936; Fed Executives Inst, diploma 1971; Phi Beta Kappa (scholastic); Pi Mu Epsilon (honorary mathematics). **CAREER:** KS State Dept Inspections, chief oil chemist 1937-39; Western Univ, prof of chemistry 1939-41; USDA Northern Regional Rsch Ctr, rsch chemist 1941-61; USDA

NRRC, supervisory rsch chemist 1961-80; Grain Processing & Brewing Industries, consul 1981-84; Univ of Campinas SP Brazil, visiting prof of chemistry 1972; Bradley Univ, adjunct prof chemistry 1984-86. **ORGANIZATIONS:** Editorial adv bd "Carbohydrate Rsch" Intl Journal 1965-75; grant officer US Dept Agriculture US & Foreign 1962-75; chmn Div Carbohydrate Chem Amer Chem Soc 1964; consul Prog Review Natl Rsch Cncl 1964-80; chmn Carbohydrate Div Amer Assn Cereal Chemists 1971; consul Natl Acad of Scis US Army Natick Labs 1970-80; lecturer Amer & German Univs 1960-80; visiting prof of chem Organization of Amer States 1972; dir Carver Comm Ctr 1952-58; sec Citizens Comm for the Peoria Public Schs 1953; sec Mayor's Commn for Sr Citizens 1982-86; adv bd Central IL Agency for the Aging Peoria 1981-82. **HONORS/ACHIEVEMENTS:** Superior Serv Awd US Dept Agriculture Wash DC 1953; Rsch Team Awds (2) US Dept Agriculture Wash DC 1955 1960; Founding Honorary & Emeritus mem Phi TauSigma Soc;"Citation Classic" (most cited scientific journal article in food sci) "Current Contents" 1979; 65 articles in scientific journals; 9 book chapters; 9 US patents; editor book "Physiological Effects of Food Carbohydrates" 1975. **HOME ADDRESS:** 1107 W Groveland Ave, Peoria, IL 61604.

HODGE, LIONEL
Elected official. **PERSONAL:** Born Oct 29, 1943, Fairfield, CA; married Jacquelyn Clemons; children: Torrance, Keisha, Rahman. **EDUCATION:** UC Berkeley, BA Sci Econ 1970-73; Columbia Univ NY, Architect/Planning 1973; Stanford Univ, Civil Engrg 1973-74; Univ of Southern CA, MPl City Planning 1974-76. **CAREER:** United Technologies-Chem Syst Div, project planner 1976-78; Lockheed Missiles & Space Co, planner analyst 1978-81; Urban/Reg Subsystems, pres, owner, consult 1981-; City of Vallejo, councilman/vice mayor. **ORGANIZATIONS:** Chmn/mem Natl Planning Network 1975-; mem Natl Inst of Planners 1975-; mem NAACP 1975-; voting delegate Natl & CA League of Cities 1981-; mem Natl Black Caucus/LEO 1981-; chmn/mgr Lionel Hodge Campaign 1981-; bd of dir Bay Area Black United Fund 1982-. **HONORS/ACHIEVEMENTS:** Scholastic Achievement Merritt Coll Oakland CA 1968, 1969; Cum Laude UC Berkeley 1973; Publication Residential Environ Trade-Off Preferences USC 1976; Magna Cum Laude USC 1976; Vice Mayors City of Valleyjo 1984. **BUSINESS ADDRESS:** Councilman Vice Mayor, City of Vallejo, 1530 Solano Ave, Vallejo, CA 94590.

HODGE, MARGUERITE V.
Social worker. **PERSONAL:** Born May 21, 1920, Avondale, PA; married Dee; children: Dee. **EDUCATION:** Howard U, BA 1943;Univ of Chicago 1947. **CAREER:** Lung Assn, regional dir 1970-; Placement Student, field instr 1974; Information & Referral Serv, supr 1968-70; UCLA, field instr 1969-70; Prof & Vol Serv, supr 1965-68; UCLA, field instr 1966-67; Agency Co Ord 1960-64; Field Rep 1953-60; Municipal TB Santorium, med social worker 1949-51; Provident Hosp, med social worker 1947-48; Provident Hosp, psychiatric social worker 1948-49; Provident Hosp, med social worker 1944-46. **ORGANIZATIONS:** Mem Nat Conf of Social Welfare; Nat Assn of Social Workers; licentiate mem Royal Acad of Health; consult S Central Area Welfare Planning Coun; adv comLA Urban League Health & Welfare Com Headstart; SEARCH Bd USC Sch of Med; serv & rehab com Am Cancer Soc CA Div Cervical Cancer Screening Sub-com; Prog Planning Com So CA Pub Health Assn; LA Co Inter-agy Coun on Smoking & Health; Mayor's Adv Coun for Handicapped 1974; adv com Area IX Regional Med Prog; bd dir CA Assn for Mental Health 1973; discussion leader Alcholism Conf Welfare Plng Coun 1962; discussion leader Conf on Home Care Welfare Plng Coun & City of Hope 1962; registration chmn Pacific SW Regional Inst NASW 1966; panel participant for TB Assn; Numerous Other Com; mem Westminster Presb Ch; Alpha Kappa Alpha Sor. **HONORS/ACHIEVEMENTS:** Recipient Spl Recognition Award Bd Dir Lung Assn 20 yrs Serv 1974; Spl Award King-Drew Sickle Cell Cntr 1974; Spl Recognition Award S Central Area Plng Coun 1973; Spl Award Kedren Comm Mental Health Cntr; Comm Serv Award El Santo Nino Comm Devel Proj of Cath Welfare Bur 1972; Volunteer Serv AwardPatton State Hosp 1965-66. **BUSINESS ADDRESS:** 1670 Beverly Blvd, Los Angeles, CA 90026.

HODGE, NORRIS
Broker, appraiser. **PERSONAL:** Born Apr 03, 1927, Kingsville, TX; married Ruby Faye; children: Brenda, Theodora, Myrna. **EDUCATION:** BBA MS 1962-64. **CAREER:** TX Southern Univ, asst prof; Friends Univ Wichita KS, asst prof. **ORGANIZATIONS:** Mem Am Economic Assn. **HONORS/ACHIEVEMENTS:** So Economic Assn Recipient Ford Foundation Fellowship; Western Econ Assn; General Electric FellowshipUniv of Chicago. **BUSINESS ADDRESS:** Hodge & Co, Realtors, 13027 Hiram Clarke, Houston, TX 77045.

HODGE, PAGET T.
Meat products managing chief executive. **CAREER:** Atlantic Brands Inc, Boston, MA, chief exec. **BUSINESS ADDRESS:** Atlantic Brands Inc., 133 Newmarket Sq., Roxbury, MA 02118. *

HODGE, W. J.
Bible college president. **CAREER:** Simmons Univ Bible Coll, Louisville, KY, pres/chancellor. **BUSINESS ADDRESS:** Simmons University Bible College, Louisville, KY 40210. *

HODGES, CLARENCE EUGENE
Government official. **PERSONAL:** Born Oct 01, 1939, Princeton, NC; married Yvonne Mitchell; children: Clarence Jr, Courtney, Cassandra, Cathleen. **EDUCATION:** Hamilton Inst, adv certificate 1966; Yale Univ, Urban Studies fellow 1973; Univ of Iowa, BA 1975; Occidental Coll, MA 1976, PhD Political Sci, Public Admin 1987. **CAREER:** St Louis Concentrated Employment Program, exec dir 1969-73; Dept of Human Resources City of Indianapolis, dir 1974-76; US Senator Richard Lugar, sr staff asst 1977-81; US Dept HHS, comm 1981-83; US Dept of State, deputy asst sec. **ORGANIZATIONS:** Chmn St Louis CORE 1967-69; vice pres St Louis Co NAACP 1968-69; pres/chair Indianapolis CAAP 1980-81; pres Profs Diversified Inc 1980-85; mem bd of trustees Oakwood Coll 1982-85; bd trustees Washington Inst for Contemp Issues; bd of trustees, Jarvis Coll. **HONORS/ACHIEVEMENTS:** CE Hodges School named for by Chicago Soc for Children; Fellowship Natl Urban Fellows 1973-74; Man of Year Natl Assn of Business & Prof Women 1976; Intl Manof Achievement 1977; Brotherhood Award 100 Black Men 1984; Doctor of Laws 1986. **MILITARY SERVICE:** USAF 4 yrs. **HOME ADDRESS:** 4901 Dalton St, Temple Hills, MD 20748. **BUSINESS ADDRESS:** Deputy Assistant Secretary, US Dept of State, 2201 C St NW, Washington, DC 20520.

HODGES, COTHER L.
Owner, administrator. **PERSONAL:** Born Nov 10, 1920, Candler Co, GA; married Juanita Byrd; children: Percy London, Malinda Patrick White, Yvonne. **EDUCATION:** Swainsboro Sch of Tech Swainsboro GA, GED 1971; LaSalle U, Bus Mgmt 1972. **CAREER:** Pleasant View Health Care Facility, owner/operator 1975-; Pleasant View Nursing Home, owner/operator 1969-; CL Hodges & Son Inc, funeral home owner 1973-; Hodges Properties, real estate owner 1948-; Farm Owner/Operator 1946-. **ORGANIZATIONS:** Pres Candler Co Farm Bureau 1955-58; mem GA Health Care Assn/Am Health Care Assn 1970-; mem Nat Fedn of Ind Bus 1971; asst sec 1st Congr Dist SCLC 1965-68; mem NAACP 1965-; pres Candler Co Recreation Bd 1965-; organizer/pres Candler Co Voters League 1967-70; bd mem GA Altamaha Area Planning& Devel Commn 1970-73; mem Labor Relations Com GA Health Care Assn 1976-; mem Am Health Care Assn. **MILITARY SERVICE:** AUS t-5 1942-46. **BUSINESS ADDRESS:** 303 Anderson St, Metter, GA 30439.

HODGES, CRAIG ANTHONY
Professional athlete. **PERSONAL:** Born Jun 27, 1960, Park Forest, IL; married Carlita Hodges; children: Jibril. **EDUCATION:** Long Beach St Univ, 1978-82. **CAREER:** Guard. **HONORS/ACHIEVEMENTS:** Named to Basketball Digest's Second Team All-Rookie squad in 1982-83. **BUSINESS ADDRESS:** c/o The Chicago Bulls, 980 N Michigan Ave, Suite 1600, Chicago, IL 60611.

HODGES, DAVID JULIAN
Educator, anthropologist. **PERSONAL:** Born Jan 11, 1944, Atlanta, GA. **EDUCATION:** NY U, PhD 1971, MA 1969; Morris Brown Coll Magna Cum Laude, BA 1966; SophiaUniv Tokyo, Spl Grad Study 1967; ColumbiaUniv 1965-66; EmoryUniv GA 1965; Harvard U, Post Grad Study 1973. **CAREER:** Hunter Coll, prof Anthropology 1985; Heritage Musem NY, curator 1971-73; Cornerstone for Change Inc, pres founder 1974-; Amer Anthrop Assn; Amer Assn Advancement of Science; Soc Applied Anthropology; Natl Soc Study Educ; Amer Assn Univ Prof Educ Action Specialist NY Comm Devel Agency 1969-71; Nassau Comm Coll Garden City, instr 1970; Voorhees Tech Inst NY, part time instr 1969-70; New York City Youth Bd, sr st club worker 1965-69. **ORGANIZATIONS:** Mem adv bd YMCA 1970-; PGM Serv Com YMCA Greater NY. **HONORS/ACHIEVEMENTS:** NYUniv Founder's Day Award 1973; Outstanding Young Mem Am 1970; Who's Who Am Coll 1965; Phi Delta Kappa Hon Soc; Alpha Kappa Delta Hon Soc; Alpha Kappa Mu Hon Soc; Woodrow Wilson Fellowship 1965; So Educ Found Fellowship 1965; Doctoral Fellowship So Fellowships Fund 1969-71. **MILITARY SERVICE:** AUS 1966-68. **BUSINESS ADDRESS:** 695 Park Ave, New York, NY 10021.

HODGES, EDWARD N., III
Retired assistant vice president. **PERSONAL:** Born Jan 27, 1920, Springfield, IL; married Beatrice Officer; children: Pamela Hodges-Porter. **EDUCATION:** Wayne State Univ, JD 1951. **CAREER:** Natl Assn of Human Rights, vp; MI Employment Sec Comm, minority group consult 1946-48; MI Dept of Corrections, parole officer 1948-56; MI Fair Employment Prac Comm, dir of conciliation; MI Fair Employment Practices Comm, exec dir 1962-63; Personnel MI Bell Tele Co, retired asst vice pres 1985. **ORGANIZATIONS:** Mem Ind Rel Research Assn; metro dir Nat Alliance of Businessmen; mem NAACP; dir & exec Com Mem United Found; trustee Rehabilitation Inst; trusteeBotsford Gen & Zeiger Hosp; v chmn Osteopathic Hosp of Detroit Inc; vice pres dir & exec com mem United Found; former vice pres Nat Assn of Human Rights Workers; former metro dir Nat Alliance of Bus; trustee Intl Inst; chrmn Council on Governace-MI Hosp Assoc; chrmn Bd of Dir Botsford General Hosp; MI State Bar Assoc. **HONORS/ACHIEVEMENTS:** Distinguished Alumnus Award Saginaw Eastern HS 1964; Gold Key Award Greater Oppts Indsln Ctr Detroit. **MILITARY SERVICE:** USN Seabees machinist mate 1st class 1943-45.

HODGES, HAROLD EARL
Association executive. **PERSONAL:** Born Sep 15, 1934, Little Rock. **EDUCATION:** Central StateUniv Wilberforce OH, BS (cum laude) 1956; Mgmt Sci Lab Washington, DOD 1969; Harvard Grad Sch Bus, PMD 1971; Lctr Mgmt Orgns & Human Behaviro Detroit Inst Tech 1985. **CAREER:** Detroit Edison Co 1972; Personnel & Pay Servs Dept Def Saigon Vietnam, chief ofcr. **ORGANIZATIONS:** Mem Am Mgmt Assn Harvard Club E MI; Assn Master Bus Adminstrn Execs; Edison Luminaries of Businessmen; Small Bus Adminstrn; Citizens Crusade Against Crime Detroit. **HONORS/ACHIEVEMENTS:** Bronze Star Medal; Vietnam Campaign Medal; Meritorious Unit Citation; Army Commendation Medal; Oak Leaf Cluster. **MILITARY SERVICE:** Commissioned officer Overseas 2 1/2 yrs; AUS Vietnam Serv 1966-67.

HODGES, LILLIAN BERNICE
Owner. **PERSONAL:** Born Apr 02, 1939, Rosebud Island Mar, AR; married Alzetl Joe Nathan; children: Lillian L. **EDUCATION:** Shorter Jr Coll N Little Rock AR, Attended 1957-58; TX WomenUniv Denton TX, Attended 1965. **CAREER:** 19 Countried of NAACP, liaison officer 1985; Local 282 United Furniture Workers of Am, rep 1977-80; Mr Tax of Am, mgr 1968-74;Univ of AR, nutritionist 1967; E Central Economical Corp, outreach person 1965-66. **ORGANIZATIONS:** Dir L R Jackson Girls Club of Am; Beautiful Zion Bapt Ch, sunday sch tchr 1976-80; Demo Women of Critt Co, vp; Critt Co Improvement Assn, ex-sec; NAACP Critt Co, pres 1972-78; State NAACP, vice pres 1973-75; Bd of METOG for Youth Services, bd mem 1973-75; Coalition for Better Broadcast, vice chmn 1968-71. **HONORS/ACHIEVEMENTS:** Outstanding Religious Work Non-Denominational Council 1979; Outstanding Serv Award NAACP Local 1976; Outstanding Award for Minority Bus Minority Bus DeveOp 1975; Outstanding ParticipationUniv S Census Bus 1970. **BUSINESS ADDRESS:** President, Hodges & Sons, West Memphis, AR 72301.

HODGES, MELVIN SANCHO
Attorney. **PERSONAL:** Born Jan 01, 1940, Columbia, SC; son of Hilliard Hodges and Aubrey Hodges; married Ugertha Birdsong; children: Melvin II. **EDUCATION:** Morehouse Coll, 1957-60; UC Santa Barbara, BA 1964-65; UC Berkeley, JD 1965-69. **CAREER:** IBM Corp, atty 1969-72; Hastings Law Coll, prof 1972-73; St of CA, dpty atty gen 1976-78; Chevron USA Inc, atty 1978-. **ORGANIZATIONS:** Asst treasurer Amer Assn Blacks in Energy 1984-86; mem California Bar Assn 1974-;mem San Francisco Bar Assn 1980-; mem Charles Houston Bar Asso 1973-; fin com Bay Area Black United Fund 1982-. **HONORS/ACHIEVEMENTS:** Outstanding Legal Serv San Francisco Bar Asso 1983-84; outstanding Legal Serv California Bar Asso 1983-84. **HOME ADDRESS:** 705 Grizzly Peak Blvd,

Berkeley, CA 94708. **BUSINESS ADDRESS:** Attorney, Chevron USA Inc, 575 Market Street, Room 2756, San Francisco, CA 94105.

HODGES, VIRGIL HALL
Government executive. **PERSONAL:** Born Dec 06, 1936, Atlanta, GA; son of V W Hodges and Ruth Hall Hodges; married Verna McNeil; children: Virgil Arthur III, Ruth Ercile. **EDUCATION:** Morris Brown Coll, BA 1958; New York Univ, MA 1959, 6th Year Certificate 1961. **CAREER:** Coney Island Family Center, exec dir 1967-69; New York State Narcotic Control Comm,fctly Dir 1969-76; New York State Dept of Labor, Dir CETA Div 1977-81, Dpty Comm 1981-; area admin New York City Youth bd dir 1961-67; asst prof Philander Smith Coll 1959-61. **ORGANIZATIONS:** Bd of dir Labor Branch NAACP; bd of trustees MLK Jr Center for Nonviolent Soc Change; pres Minority Organizers for Voter Educ & Registration. **HONORS/ACHIEVEMENTS:** Man of the Year Award Coney Island Comm 1968; Alumni Award Morris Brown Coll 1978; Public Serv Award New York State NAACP 1982; Humanitarian Award New York Martin Luther King Jr Support Group 1983; New York Alumni Award Morris Brown Coll 1987; Disting Serv Award of New York State Black & Puerto Rican Caucus 1987; Disting Serv Labor Branch NAACP 1987; Potoker Award of The New York State Brotherhood Comm 1988. **HOME ADDRESS:** 9 Compass Ct, Albany, NY 12205. **BUSINESS ADDRESS:** Deputy Commissioner, NY St Dept of Labor, St Off Bldg 12Ste 564, 566 Washington Ave, Albany, NY 12240.

HODGSON, CARLTON ROY
Corporate director. **PERSONAL:** Born Nov 19, 1930, New York, NY; married Jocelyn Smith; children: Carla, Corey. **EDUCATION:** Fisk U, BA 1952; Basel U, MD 1965; Basel U, PhD 1967. **CAREER:** Delbuy Rsch, asst med dir 1970-; Bronx VA Hosp, res anest 1968-70; Albert Einstein Coll of Med, fellowship-Pathology 1966-68; Albert Einstein Coll of Med, internship 1965-66; Interfaith Hosp Nat Econ Growth Reconst Orgn, med dir 1970-71; NMA 1966-; Westchest Sickle Cell Orgn 1972-73; pres Fisk Club FiskUniv Alumni of NY 1977-79. **ORGANIZATIONS:** Mem ex com FiskUniv 1977-81; Am Leaders 1951; Who-Who in Am Colls 1952. **MILITARY SERVICE:** AUS scientist & prof 1956-58. **BUSINESS ADDRESS:** 25 Morgan Ln, West Haven, CT.

HODGSON-BROOKS, GLORIA J.
Psychotherapist, visual artist. **PERSONAL:** Born Nov 28, 1942, Hartford, CT; daughter of Charles O Gill and Marion S Jackson Gill; married Peter C Brooks. **EDUCATION:** Bennett Coll, BA 1965; Smith Coll Sch of Social Work, MSW 1979; Hartford Family Institute, Gestalt-Body Centered Psychotherapy 1976-83; Natl Assn of Social Workers certificates, 1982; state of CT cert in Social Work, 1987; Amer Bd of Examiners in Clinical Social Wrk certified dipl, 1988; studied visual arts at several colleges and seminars. **CAREER:** Child & Family Serv Inc, social worker 1974-77; Inter-Agency Svcs, social worker 1974-77; Hartford Family Inst, intern 1976-78; Private Practice, psychotherapist 1976-78; Child & Family Serv Inc, clinical social worker 1979-80; Dr Isaiah Clark Family & Youth Clinic, dir 1980-81; Hartford Family Inst, associate 1978-85; Private Practice, psychotherapist 1978-85; Psychotherapy & Counseling Assocs, psychotherapist/partner 1985—; Brooks & Brooks Ltd, Hartford CT, president, 1985—; Solitude Visual Arts Studio, Hartford CT, partner, 1989—. **ORGANIZATIONS:** Mem Natl Assoc of Black Social Workers 1972-, NAARPR 1977-85, Natl Assoc of Social Workers 1977-; counseling minority students Trinity Coll 1982-85; staff training Directions Unlimited 1984-85; mem CT Caucus of Black Women for Political Action 1984-86; assoc mem PRO Disabled Entrepreneur 1985-86; workshop leader on goal setting PRO Disabled Entrepreneur Goal Setting Workshops 1985-86; staff training communication Sandler Sales Inst 1986; administrative consultant CT Ctr for Human Growth & Develop 1986; mem Farmington Valley Arts Ctr 1986-; adv bd IAM Cares 1986-; Intl Sculpture Center; Amer Craft Council; Amer Craft Museum; charter mem, Natl Museum of Women in the Arts; Natl Trust for Historical Preservation. **HONORS/ACHIEVEMENTS:** Program & Function Mem Commn to Study the Consolidation of Children's Serv mandate of the 1974 Session of the CT General Assembly 1974; published "An Exploratory Study of the Diagnostic Process in Gestalt Therapy," Smith College Library 1975; Social Worker for Justice Awd Smith Coll Sch for Social Work 1979; award for starting Dr Issiah Clark Family & Youth Clinic, 1988; art exhibits: Intl Biographical Centre, 1989, ECKANKAR Creative ARt Festival, 1987, 1988, New England Hardweavers, 1987. **BUSINESS ADDRESS:** President, Brooks & Brooks Ltd, 17 Litchfield St, Hartford, CT 06112.

HOEHNE, FELICIA HARRIS See FELDER-HOEHNE, FELICIA HARRIS

HOFF, NATHANIEL HAWTHORNE
Educator. **PERSONAL:** Born Jan 10, 1929, Baltimore, MD; children: Victoria Forbes, Annette, Yvette Boschulte, Nathaniel Jr, Ronald, Yvonne Bell, Christopher, Kevin. **EDUCATION:** Morgan State Coll, BS (Magna Cum Laude) Biology/Sci Educ 1950; Johns Hopkins Univ, MEd Educ (Cum Laude) 1959; Post Grad Work, Morgan State Coll 1959, Cornell Univ 1962, Butler Univ 1964, Hampton Inst 1966, Western MD Coll 1973. **CAREER:** Anne Arundel Co Public Sch System, genl sci tchr 1952-54; Baltimore City Public Sch System, biology tchr 1954-67; MD State Tchrs Assn, field serv rep1967-68, assoc in field serv 1968-; Public Sch Tchrs Assn, dir of field serv 1962-73, exec uniserv dir 1973-79; Prince George's Co Education Assn, MSTA Uniserv dir 1979-84; Baltimore City Tchr Assn, MSTA uniserv dir 1984-; MD State Tchrs Assn, assoc in field svcs. **ORGANIZATIONS:** Founding mem Kappa Phi Lambda Chap Alpha Phi Alpha Frat 1975-; mem Natl Staff Orgn 1979-; MSU bd liaison Morgan State Univ Found 1977-79; sec bd of regents Morgan State Univ 1975-80; assn evaluator of Norfolk Educ Assn Natl Education Assn 1970 1972; pres Grace AME Keglers 1980-; life mem MD StateTchrs Assn 1983; mem Professional Staff Assn 1983; life mem Delta Lambda Chap Alpha Phi Alpha Frat 1986-; mem Mayor's Task Force on Educ 1968-70; bd dirs MD Congress of Parents & Tchrs Assn 1973-74; mem NAACP, Urban League 1986-89; life mem Natl Alpha Phi Alpha Frat 1986-. **HONORS/ACHIEVEMENTS:** Author of awd winning poems "War & Peace and the Negro" 1950; author of over 300 poems; Hon Scholarship Awd Morgan State Coll 1970-71; Resourcefulness Plaque Minority Affairs Comm Prince George's County Educ Assn 1982; plaque for Outstanding & Dedicated Serv to Minority Educators Black Caucus MD State Tchrs Assn 1982; Serv Awd Minority Affairs Comm Prince George's Co Educators Assn 1983; Certificate of Appreciation Prince George's Co Educators Assn 1983; inducted into Athletic Hall of Fame Morgan State Univ 1985. **MILITARY SERVICE:** Armored Infantry acting sgt s-3 operations 1951-53; Amer Spirit of Honor Medal 1951. **HOME ADDRESS:** 10529 Morning Wind Ln, Columbia, MD 21044. **BUSINESS ADDRESS:** Associate in Field Service, Maryland State Teachers Assoc, 344 N Charles St, Baltimore, MD 21201.

HOFFLER, RICHARD WINFRED, JR.
Physician. **PERSONAL:** Born Jun 22, 1944, Lynchburg, VA; married Sylvia C; children: Edward, Erika. **EDUCATION:** Hampton Inst, BA 1966; Meharry Med Coll, MD 1970. **CAREER:** Youngstown Hosp, intern 1970, resd 1971-74; Private practice, physician 1974-. **ORGANIZATIONS:** Mem AMA, Norfolk Acad of Med, Norfolk Med Soc, Nat'l Med Assoc, Colonial VA Found for Med Care, Norfolk Comm Hosp, Bayside Hosp, Chesapeake Gen Hosp; state agency med consultant 1974-; Tidewater Disability Determination Services, chief medical consultant 1980-. **HONORS/ACHIEVEMENTS:** Scholarship Student Hampton Inst 1963-64. **BUSINESS ADDRESS:** physician, R W Hoffler, Jr, MDPC, PO Box 898, Norfolk, VA 23501.

HOFFMAN, JOSEPH IRVINE, JR.
Physician. **PERSONAL:** Born Apr 14, 1939, Charleston, SC; married Pamela Louise Hayling; children: Katherine, Kristen, Kara. **EDUCATION:** Harvard Coll, AB 1960; Howard Univ, MD 1964. **CAREER:** Lenox Hill Hosp, internship 1964-66; Hosp for Special Surgery NY, orthopedic resd 1968-71; Joseph Hoffman MD, PC, pres. **ORGANIZATIONS:** Mem natl Med Assoc, AMA; pres Atlanta Med Assoc; mem NAACP, Urban League, Atlanta C of C, Omega Psi Phi; cert Amer Bd of Orthopedic Surgery 1973; fellow Amer Rheumatism Assoc 1972, Acad of Orthopedic Surgery 1977; pres, l00 Black Men of Atlanta. **MILITARY SERVICE:** USN 1966-68. **BUSINESS ADDRESS:** President, Joseph Hoffman MD, PC, 2945 Stone Hogan Rd, Atlanta, GA 30331.

HOGAN, CAROLYN ANN
Workers compensation representative. **PERSONAL:** Born Jul 13, 1944, New Orleans, LA; daughter of Elijah Hogan, Sr (deceased) and Yolanda Getridge Hogan Mosley. **EDUCATION:** Dillard Univ, BA 1966; Fisk Univ, MA 1969. **CAREER:** Dillard Univ, instructor 1969-73; Southern Univ New Orleans LA Instructor 1973-75; Orleans Parish Sch Bd, psychologist 1974-75; City of New Orleans, evaluation specialist 1976-79; Natl Opinion Rsch Ctr,opinion rscher 1980-82; Natl Testing Svcs, opinion rscher 1981; Transit Mgmt of Southeast LA, benefits specialist 1985-86, workers compensation rep 1986-. **ORGANIZATIONS:** Consultant Albert Wicker School's Special Educ Class Orleans Parish Sch Bd 1978; Gestalt Inst Psychodrama 1978-79; panelist on WDSU-TV Spectrum 50 entitled"A Salute to Women" 1979; Touro Infirmary and LSU Medical Ctr Psychiatry Seminar 1979; mem New Orleans Neighborhood Police Anti-Crime Council 1983-86; StressManagement Workshop Career Track Seminars 1985; scholarship comm Crescent City Chap of Conference of Minorities in Transportation 1986-87. **HONORS/ACHIEVEMENTS:** APA ABPSI Natl Sci Foundation Vstg Scientist in Psychology 1971; US Public Health Serv Traineeship in Psychology So IL Univ 1973-74; researcher for President's Civil Adv Commn; publication "A Black Woman's Struggles in Racial Integration," and "In Defense of Brown," in integrated education in 1980,84 Horace Mann Bond Ctr for Equal Educ. **HOME ADDRESS:** 1334 Pacific Ave, New Orleans, LA 70114. **BUSINESS ADDRESS:** Workers Compensation Rep, Transit Mgmt of Southeast LA, 101 Dauphine at Canal Street, Fourth Floor, New Orleans, LA 70112-3125.

HOGAN, FANNIE BURRELL
Head librarian. **PERSONAL:** Born Apr 06, New Orleans, LA; daughter of Alexander Burrell, Sr. and Lorenza Nicholas Burrell; children: Mrs Erica Whipple Jones, Ms Maria Monique Whipple. **EDUCATION:** Dillard Univ, BA 1945; Atlanta Univ, MSLS 1950; Atlanta Univ, MA Eng 78; Atlanta Univ, Natl Deans List 1982; Ed D 1985 (Educational Administration and Supervision). **CAREER:** Gilbert Acad New Orleans LA, Teacher 1942-45; Claflin Coll SC, head Librn 1950-54; Clark Coll Atlanta GA, head Librarian 1954-81; The Atlanta Univ Center Robert W Woodruff Library, head of Biographic Instructor 1981-; Asst in the Government Documents Dept, The Atlanta Univ Center Robert W Woodruff Library and Computer Literature Search Librarian for the Administration, Faculty, and Students of Atlanta Univ; Head of Curriculum Material and Editor of the Library's Official Newsletter "The Diversified Hexagon" 1987-. **ORGANIZATIONS:** Head librarian wrote Proposal for Library Orientation for Clark Coll Funded by NEH 1975-80; specially funded Program by the Lilly Endowment Inc for Clark Colltchr of Bibliographic instruction 1984-86; Amer Library Assoc mem; GA Library Assoc mem; Alpha Kappa Alpha Sorority mem; Bibliographic Instr Group Computer Programmer; Phi Delta Kappa Educational Fraternity mem of Research Comm and Newsletter Comm. **HONORS/ACHIEVEMENTS:** Study tour to Poland Clark Coll and the Untd Meth Bd of Ed 1973; schlrshp for doctoral study Untd Meth Bd of ed 1981; schlrshp Dept of Ed Atlanta Univ 1982; Poem "All Ages Can Learn" published in the 1989 Anthology of Southern Poetry. **HOME ADDRESS:** 1981 Valley Ridge Dr S W, Atlanta, GA 30331. **BUSINESS ADDRESS:** Head of Bibliographic Instr, AUC Robert W Woodruff Libr, 111 James P Brawley Dr S W, Atlanta, GA 30314.

HOGAN, JAMES CARROLL, JR.
Biologist. **PERSONAL:** Born Jan 03, 1939, Milledgeville, GA; son of James C Hogan, Sr and Leanna Johnson Hogan; married Izola Stinson, Nov 29, 1959; children: Pamela Hogan Robertson, Gregory Karl, Jeffrey Daneyl. **EDUCATION:** Albany State Coll, BS 1961; Atlanta Univ, MS 1968; Brown Univ, PhD 1972. **CAREER:** Hancock Co Bd of Educ, teacher/Science dept chmn 1961-66; Atlanta Public Schools, teacher Science 1967-68; Atlanta Univ, instructor 1967; Yale Univ, rsch assoc 1973-76; Howard Univ, asst prof dept of Anatomy 1976-78; Howard Univ, asst prof graduate school 1976-78; Univ of CT, assoc prof Health Science 1979-; UCONN Health Ctr, assoc prof & univ dir 1982-. **ORGANIZATIONS:** Founder and chmn Rhode Island Comm on Sickle Cell Disease 1970-72; founder UCONN Health Sci Cluster Program's Parents Auxilary 1979; vice pres CT's Black Health Professionals Network 1982-86; mem Omega Psi Phi Fraternity Inc; bd advisors The Sickle Cell Assoc of CT Inc; mem Urban League, Atlanta Univ Honor Soc, Sigma Xi; mem AAAS, Amer Inst of Biological Sci, Amer Soc for Cell Biology, Natl Assoc of Medical Minority Educators Inc; mem New York Academy of Sciences, Alpha Eta Soc; asst clinical prof, Univ of Hartford, W Hartford, CT, 1988-; founder & pres, N Haven (CT) Assn of Black Citizens, 1988-. **HONORS/ACHIEVEMENTS:** Post-doctoral Fellowship Yale Univ 1972-73; Macy Scholar Marine Biological Lab Woods Hole MA 1978-80; Rsch Foundation Grant Univ of CT 1979-80; Post-doctoral Fellow Ford Foundation 1980-81; Pres Natl Assoc Medical Minority Educators 1985-86; 13 publications including "An Ultrastructural Analysis of Cytoplasmic Makers in Germ Cells of Oryzias laptipes," J Ultrastruct Res 62,237-250; "Regeneration of the Caudal Fin in Killfishes (Oryzias laptipes and Fundulus heteroclitus" J Cell Biol 91(2), pt2,p 110a, also numerous presentations. **HOME ADDRESS:** 51 Pool Rd, PO Box 146, North Haven, CT 06473. **BUSINESS ADDRESS:** State of Connecticut, Dept of Health Serv, Bureau of Laboratories,, l0 Clinton St, Hartford, CT 06473.

HOGAN, JOHN A.
Bank chief executive. **CAREER:** Connecticut Savings and Loan Assoc, Hartford, CT, chief exec. **BUSINESS ADDRESS:** Connecticut Savings and Loan Association, 915 Main St., Hartford, CT 06103-1206. *

HOGAN, OGELIA M.
Retired. **PERSONAL:** Born Aug 13, 1904, Sulphur Springs, TX; married Wayman; children: Vandora Irving, Gwendolyn Hooks, Davetta Austin, Cecil Hooks, Joseph Hooks. **EDUCATION:** LangstonUniv 1919-23. **CAREER:** Tatums Comm Action Agy, cafeteria supr 1965-68; Hooks Gen Mdse 1933-38. **ORGANIZATIONS:** Pres Women Missionary Bethel Bapt Ch 1973; pres Tatks Gen Mdse 1933-38; Tatums Farm Womens Club 1933-39; pres Country Council 1946-48; pres PTA 1952-53; OES SEX 1957-; asst dir Carter Co Free Fair 1958-59; fin sec Bethel Bapt Ch 1960-65; Econ Oppor Gov's Council 1966-; Carter Co Comm Act Found Inc 1966-67; Organized Sr Cit Ctr; nyc vol supr Afternoon Study Prgm for Comm Youth. **HONORS/ACHIEVEMENTS:** Outstnd Cit of Am 1967; Outstnd Serv for the Comm Award 1971; Cert of Apprec for Outstnd; Serv in the Comm 1976.

HOGANS, WILLIAM ROBERTSON, III
Dentist/military. **PERSONAL:** Born May 18, 1945, Bristol, VA; son of William R Hogans, Jr. and Alma G McDowell Hogans; married Grace Valdine Blaylock; children: William IV, Adrienne, Elliott, Bryon, Michael. **EDUCATION:** Knoxville Coll, BS 1967; Meharry Medical Coll, DDS 1976; US Army Command and General Staff Coll Ft Leavenworth KS, Graduate 1986; resident post doctor training in fixed prosthodontics: Walter Reed Army Medical Center; Washington D.C. **CAREER:** US Army Dental Corps; sr. resident in fixed prosthodontics. **ORGANIZATIONS:** Mem Amer Dental Assoc 1976-; vice pres 1977-78, pres 1978-79 Phi Beta Sigma Frat Inc; vice pres Meadow Village Elem PTA 1977-78; vice pres San Antonio TX Region II PTA1978-79; mem Assoc of Military Surgeons 1982-, Rock's Military Social Club 1983-. **HONORS/ACHIEVEMENTS:** Acad of Dental Radiology Awd for Outstanding Achievement Meharry Medical Coll 1976; Outstanding Young Men of Amer US Jaycees 1979; selected as US Army Dental Corps Representative to the Postgraduate Course in Fixed Prosthodontic at Canadian Forces Dental Serv Sch in Borden Ontario, Canada 1987. **MILITARY SERVICE:** AUS lt col 13 yrs; Air Force Outstanding Unit Citation 1977; Air Force Commendation medal w/1 Oak Leaf Cluster 1979, Expert Field Medical Badge 1983, US Army Commendation Medal 1983, US Army Achievement Medal 1983, Overseas Serv Ribbon 1983; Meritorious Service Medal 1988. **BUSINESS ADDRESS:** US Army Dental Corps, USADENTAC W Reed Army Med Ctr, Washington, DC 20307.

HOGGES, RALPH
Educational administrator. **PERSONAL:** Born Aug 03, 1947, Allentown, GA; married Lilia N Pardo; children: Genithia L; Alicia I. **EDUCATION:** Tuskegee Isnt Tuskegee, AL, BS 1971; Tuskegee Inst Tuskegee, AL, MEd 1972; NovaUniv Ft Lauderdale, EdD 1977. **CAREER:** FL Intl Univ Miami, assoc dean of student affairs 1978-; The Center for Minority Rsch Inc Miami, exec dir 1979-; FL Intl Univ Miami, admin asst to the dean 1974-78, coordinator of coll work-study program 1973-74, prsnl tech 1972-73. **ORGANIZATIONS:** Bd trusee Am InterdenominationalUniv 1978-; bd dir The Ctr for Minority Rsrch Inc 1979-; mem Kappa Delta Pi 1971-; mem FL Clg Stdnt Afrs Assc 1978-; mem Phi Delta Kappa 1978-. **HONORS/ACHIEVEMENTS:** Outst serv in ed Phi Beta Sigma Frat Miami 1978. **BUSINESS ADDRESS:** Tamiami Trail Campus, Miami, FL 33199.

HOGU, BARBARA J. JONES
Artist, educator. **PERSONAL:** Born Apr 17, 1938, Chicago, IL; married Jean-Claude Hogu; children: Kuumba. **EDUCATION:** Howard Univ, BA 1959; Chicago Art Inst, BFA; Illinois Inst of Technology, MS. **CAREER:** Chicago Post Office, clerk 1961-64; Robt Paige Designs, designer 1968-69; lecturer 1968; Chicago Public High Schools, Art Inst high schs, 1964-70; Malcolm X Coll, asst prof. **ORGANIZATIONS:** Mem Bd Southside Comm Center 1971-; staff artist Third World Press 1973-; vice pres Natl Conf of Artists 1973-; lecturer Art History School of the Art Inst 1974-; mem Afri Cobra, African Commune of Black Relevant Artists; mem Union Black Artists; innumerable group shows, one woman shows & exhibitions. **HONORS/ACHIEVEMENTS:** Art History Honor Art Inst of Chicago 1962; Scholarship Art Inst of Chicago 1962-64; 1st Print Award Black Aesthetics "69" Serv Award; Natl Conf of Artist for 1972 & 1974; Malcolm X Umoja Award 1973. **BUSINESS ADDRESS:** Assistant Professor, Malcolm X College, Humanities Dept, 1900 W Van Buren, Chicago, IL 60612.

HOLBERT, RAYMOND RAY
Educator. **PERSONAL:** Born Feb 24, 1945, Berkeley, CA; son of James Albert Holberrt and Carolyn Bernice Gary; married Susan Demersseman, May 26, 1989; children: Onika Valentine, Lauren Dakota, Brian Jaymes. **EDUCATION:** Laney Coll, AA 1964; CA Coll of Arts & Crafts, BA 1966; Univ of CA, AB 1972, MA 1974, MFA 1975. **CAREER:** San Fran Comm Coll, prof art. **ORGANIZATIONS:** Mem Artists Books Advocate, Natl Conf of Artists. **HONORS/ACHIEVEMENTS:** Exhibits at, San Francisco Art Museum 1972, Oakland Art Museum 1973, Berkeley 1974, Baylor Univ Waco TX 1975, Studio Museum Harlem NY 1977, Studio Museum Harlem NY 1979, Howard Univ Washington DC 1980, Helen Euphrat Gallery CA 1982, Brockman Gallery LA 1982, Grand Oak Gallery 1983; LA Mus of African Amer Art Printmakers 1984, CA Museum of African Amer Art 1986, San Francisco Art Commiss Gallery 1987. **BUSINESS ADDRESS:** 3326 Adeline, Berkeley, CA 94703.

HOLDEN, DOROTHY M.
Educator. **PERSONAL:** Born Oct 11, 1928, Centralia, IL; married Hesper A Jackson. **EDUCATION:** Meharry Med Clg, MD 1952; Hurley Hosp, Intern 1952-53; Homer Phillips Hosp, Resident 1953-56. **CAREER:** Univ of MI Hospital, jr clinical instructor rsch 1955-56; State Univ of NY, instructor asst prof dept med 1967-. **ORGANIZATIONS:** Hosp apptmnt Research Flw 1956-58; Asst Visiting Phys 1958-67; assc Visiting Phys 1967-70; Visiting Phys 1968-; attending phys Brooklyn VA Hosp; dir Spec Hematology Lab; Kings Co Hosp; Adult Sickle Cell Anemia Clinic Kings Co Hosp; Comprehensive Care Sickle Cell Ctr; mem Med Adv Bd Sickle Cell Anemia; Scientific Adv Com Natl Assc Sickle Cell Disease Inc; chmn Sub-com Hematology; Kings Co Med Soc; mem AAAS; provident clncl Soc; natl med assc; NY Soc Med Jurisprudence; mem Soc of the Sigma Xi; Natl Cncl of Negro Women. **BUSINESS ADDRESS:** Downstate Med Center, 450 Clarskon Ave Box 20, Brooklyn, NY 11203.

HOLDER, GEOFFREY
Dancer, producer, director, choreographer. **PERSONAL:** Born Aug 01, 1930, Port-of-Spain, Trinidad and Tobago;married Carmen de Lavallade; children: Ed. **EDUCATION:** Queens Royal Coll Port-of-Spain, student native dances in W Indies. **CAREER:** Roscoe Holder's Dance O Trinidad, stage debut 1942; formed own dance co 1950; toured PR and the Caribbean 1953; US/Broadway debut, House of Flowers 1954;Met Opera, solo dancer 1956-57; dramatic debut Waiting for Godot 1975; Show Boat, solo dancer 1957; concerts with Geoffrey Holder Dance Co New York City 1956-60; appeared at Festival of Two worlds Spoleto, Italy 1958; Festividadi Ballet Hispanico NY 1979; Brouhaha, choreographer 1960; Actor's Studio prodn Mhil Daiim 1964, I Got a Song 1974; Josephine Baker's Review, dancer 1964; choreog/costume designer, Three Songs for One; costume des, The Twelve Gates 1964; dir/costume designer, The Wiz Broadway 1975; dir/costume des/choreog Timbuktu 1978. **ORGANIZATIONS:** Mem AFTRA, Screen Actors Guild, Actors Equity Assn, AGVA. **HONORS/ACHIEVEMENTS:** Movie appearances incl, All Night Long 1961; Everything You've Always Wanted to Know About Sex 1972; Live and Let Die 1973; Swashbuckler 1976; Annie 1982; appeared in night clubs; TV appearances incl, The Man Without a Country; paintings exhibited at Barbados Mus San Juan, PR; Barone Gallery NYC; Gallery of Brooks Atkinson Theatre NYC; Gropper Gallery Cambridge, MA; Griffin Gallery NYC; Grinnel Galleries Detroit; recorded albums of W Indian songs and album of song stories; author, Black Gods, Green Islands 1957; Geoffrey Holder's Caribbean Cookbook 1974; contrib articles to Playbill; Guggenheim fellow in painting 1957; DramaDesk Award for The Wiz 1975; Tony Award for Best Dir of a Musical The Wiz 1975 (also for costume design); recip United Caribbean Youth Award 1962; Monarch Award Natl Cncl Culture and Art 1982. **BUSINESS ADDRESS:** c/o Donald Buchwald Assoc, 10 E 44th St, New York, NY 10017.

HOLDER, IDALIA
Personnel administrator. **PERSONAL:** Born Mar 19, 1947; divorced; children: Aisha Margaret. **EDUCATION:** Northeastern Univ, BSc (Cum Laude) 1973. **CAREER:** Harvard Univ Sch of Business Admin, admin asst 1971-73; The Carnegie Foundation for the Advancement of Teaching, admin asst 1976-78; Carnegie Corp of New York, personnel asst 1974-76, personnel administrator 1976-78, personnel dir 1978-83, asst sec & dir of personnel 1983-86, dir of personnel. **ORGANIZATIONS:** Bd of dir Natl Black Child Develop Inst; mem NY Personnel Mgmt Assoc, Assoc of Black Foundation Execs, Amer Soc for Personnel Admin, Women in Human Resources Mgmt, Intl Assoc for Personnel Women; mem chairperson & treas NY Affiliate Natl Black Child Develop Inst; mem Administrative Mgmt Soc. **HONORS/ACHIEVEMENTS:** Mem Sigma Epsilon Rho Northeastern Univ Honor Soc 1973. **BUSINESS ADDRESS:** Dir of Personnel, Carnegie Corp of New York, 437 Madison Avenue, New York, NY 10022.

HOLDER, JULIUS H.
Association executive. **PERSONAL:** Born Jul 17, 1918. **EDUCATION:** Benedict Clg, BA 1955; Urban Planning NY U, M 1964;Univ of Manchester England & Harvard U, Grad Studies. **CAREER:** Environmental Design Collaborative (Resource Dev), urban plnr; Town Planning San Diego State U, lectr; LA Co, frmly stf plnr 1968-70; San Mateo Co, reg plnr 1966; NY Bureau of Urban Afrs, sr urban plnr 1963-65; Co of San Luis Obisop, asst plng dir 1961-62; Landscape Arch New York City Bd of Ed, asst 1955-59; Environ Design Collaborative, consult assc. **ORGANIZATIONS:** Mem Laucks Found 1974; living contrbtr mem Rotary Intrntl Rotary Found 1973-74; mem past comm rel chmn NAACP; frmr mem svd 5 yrs Santa Barbara Housing & Redevel Bds; past mem Sec of Peace League; inter-Am Friendship Centre; Am Inst of Certified Plnrs; Harvard Grad Sch of Design Assc; Town & Country Plng Assc. **HONORS/ACHIEVEMENTS:** Authored Proposal, Design for Coop ed. **BUSINESS ADDRESS:** EDC & Environmental Design Col, 320 W Cedar, San Diego, CA 92101.

HOLDER, REUBEN D.
Government official, management consultant. **PERSONAL:** Born Mar 21, 1923, New York, NY; son of Richard Holder and Orneata Holder; married Iris A Lumsby, Apr 03, 1948; children: Gregory Stewart Holder. **EDUCATION:** City Coll of New York; Queens Coll City Univ of New York Urban Affairs, BA; Exec Seminar Center Kings Point New York; Fed Exec Inst Charlottesville Virginia. **CAREER:** New York Post Office, asst employment officer 1968; New York Reg US Post Office, reg manpower dev specialist 1969; US Civil Serv & Commn, fed reg equal employment opportunity rep 1971; US Govt Office of Personnel Management, chief reg staffing div 1973-; self employed, cons, lecturer 1971-; Holder Management Systems Inc, management cons, lecturer; chmn of bd dirs, UHURV Joint Development Corp 1988-; area rep, New York City Planning Bd # 12, 1989-. **ORGANIZATIONS:** Mem 100 Black Men 1976-; life mem, 1st vice pres Queens Dist, natl bd of dir 369th Vet Assc 1978; pres Black Fed Exec 1980; bd of dir Queens Br NY Urban League 1986-87. **HONORS/ACHIEVEMENTS:** Alpha Sigma Lambda, Upsilon Chap NY; Deans List Queens College. **MILITARY SERVICE:** AUS sgt 1942-46; Bronze Star w/ 6 Battle Stars. **HOME ADDRESS:** 177-53 Leslie Rd, Springfield Garden, NY 11434.

HOLLAND, EDITH BRYANT
Retired. **PERSONAL:** Born Feb 01, 1912, Evansville, IN; married Bishop Harrison J Bryant; children: Cynthia Pitts, Hazel, Harrison Jr, John, Eleanor Graham. **EDUCATION:** Wilberforce U, BS 1934; OH State U, Grad Sch; Univ of MD Sch of Social Work 1960. **CAREER:** E HS, tchr; Baltimore Welfare Bd, social worker 1955-63; Spring Grove State Hosp, 1963-46; Field Enterprise Educ Inst, area supr 1963-65; World Fed Meth Women, official corrs 1976-81; Sunday Sch, tchr 1976; Bethel AME Ch. **ORGANIZATIONS:** Bd mem Nat Conf of Black churchmen; dir Promotion Missionary Educ of Women's Missionary Soc of African Meth Episcopal Ch; dir Christian Edn, Balt Conf, AME Ch 1956-64; supr of missions WMS of AME Ch 1964; author "Working Together With God" 1947; African Meth Epis ABC Book 1947; "Do You Want To Be A Christian" 1968.

HOLLAND, ETHEL M.
Nurse. **PERSONAL:** Born Oct 31, 1946, Washington, DC; married Donald R. **EDUCATION:** Immaculate Conception Acad, Washington, DC, HSD 1964; Mt Mrty Coll Ynktn SD, BS 1968; Nursing Catholic Univ of Amer Washington DC, MS 1974. **CAREER:** Childrens Hospital Natl Med Center Washington DC, unit coordinator, 1974-; DC General Hospital, clinical nurse, dept of pediatrics 1970-73; 91st E Vac Hospital Vietnam, asst head nurse, 1969-70; Walter Reed Army Hospital Washington DC, staff nurse, 1968-69. **ORGANIZATIONS:** Vice pres, Registered Nurse Examination Bd 1979-; mem Black Nurses Assn of Greater Metro Area 1978-; mem District of Columbia Nurses Assn 1968-; charter mem Ethnic Nurses for Adv of Health Care Among Minorities 1978-; vol Ancst Neighborhood Clinic, Washington, DC 1974; Sigma Theta Tau Kappa Chapter Washington DC 1974. **HON-**

ORS/ACHIEVEMENTS: Inducted into Natl Hon Soc for Nurses; Army Cmndtn Medal Mrtrs Serv Vietnam 1970; papers presented Nurse Care of Pts who Fail to Thrive 1979; Patterns of Elimination, 1976; Nursng Care of Patients with Sickle Cell Anemia, 1975. **MILITARY SERVICE:** AUS 1st lt. **BUSINESS ADDRESS:** Dir, Children's Hospital Natl Med Center, 3 Orange Nursing Service, 111 Michigan Ave NW, Washington, DC 20010.

HOLLAND, J. ARCHIBALD
Direct marketing consultant, author. **PERSONAL:** Born in Wilmington, DE; son of Archibald Holland Sr and Helen (Holland) Stanley. **EDUCATION:** Lincoln Univ, Lincoln Univ PA, AB; Columbia Univ, New York NY, 3 years' graduate school. **CAREER:** Amer Mgmt Assn, New York NY, advertising promotion writer, 1960-63; Holt, Rinehart & Winston, New York NY, sr copywriter, 1963-65; Grolier Educ Corp, New York NY, asst advertising dir, 1966-69; Grey Advertising Agency, New York NY, writer in residence, 1979-83; George G Garmus Assoc, New York NY, public relations assoc, 1983-85; Panamericana Co, New York NY, pres, 1985-. **ORGANIZATIONS:** Direct Mktg Assn, 1963-69; Natl Writers Union, 1988-. **HONORS/ACHIEVEMENTS:** New York Area Speech Champion, Intl Toastmasters, 1971; speech presentations: Eulogy for a Dying City, 1971, The Harlem Renaissance, 1988-89, The Legacy of Langston Hughes, 1988-89; author of "Freedom to Kill," magazine article read in Congress by Senator Edward Kennedy, 1974; author of "The Case for Calling Blacks Black," magazine article; author of novel, The Chinese Pagoda. **MILITARY SERVICE:** US Army Air Corps. **HOME ADDRESS:** 5008 Broadway #3B, New York, NY 10034.

HOLLAND, LAURENCE H.
Analytical chemist. **PERSONAL:** Born Nov 08, 1926, Tampa, FL; son of Albert Holland Jr and Hazel Symonette Holland; married Rose Withers, Sep 1982. **EDUCATION:** Central State Univ, BS; Studies NY Univ Rutgers Univ & City Univ of NY, Grad. **CAREER:** Lederle Lab Amer Chem Soc, analytical chem; Amer Soc Qulaity Control. **ORGANIZATIONS:** Mem Legisltaive Penal Com; mem bd dir ROCAC; past pres life mem NAACP; exec bd Lederle Fed Credit Union; trustee, St Charles AME Zion Church; Alpha Phi Alpha. **MILITARY SERVICE:** USN 1945. **HOME ADDRESS:** 63 Western Hwy, Orangeburg, NY 10962. **BUSINESS ADDRESS:** Mr. Laurence H Holland, Lederle Laboratories, Bld 130, Room 401 C, Pearl River, NY 10965.

HOLLAND, ROBIN W.
Educator. **PERSONAL:** Born May 23, 1953, Columbus, OH; daughter of Robert R Jackson and Elizabeth W Jackson. **EDUCATION:** Ohio State Univ, BS 1974, MA 1975. **CAREER:** Columbus Public Schools, reading teacher 1975-76, gifted/talented teacher 1977-80, classroom teacher 1976-86, consulting teacher 1986-89. **ORGANIZATIONS:** Mem Natl Educ Assoc 1975-, Assoc of Supervision and Curriculum Develop 1986-; chairperson-Educ Comm Central OH Club/Natl Assoc of Negro Business & Professional Women 1984-87; mem St Philips Episcopal Church. **BUSINESS ADDRESS:** Consulting Teacher, Columbus Public Schools, 52 Starling St, Columbus, OH 43215.

HOLLAND, SPENCER H.
Educator, psychologist. **PERSONAL:** Born Sep 11, 1939, Suffern, NY. **EDUCATION:** Glassboro State Clg, AB 1965; Columbia U, AM 1968; Columbia U, PhD 1976. **CAREER:** Burnet Jr HS, teacher 1965-67; Essex Co Coll, asst prof 1968-73, chmn psychology dept 1970-73; Harlem Interfaith Counseling Serv, prev mental health teacher 1974-75; Child Abuse & Neglect Proj Div of Pupil Personnel Serv Washington DC Public Schools, coord 1976-. **ORGANIZATIONS:** Mem Am Psycological Assc; mem Assc Black Psychologists 1972-. **HONORS/ACHIEVEMENTS:** Natl flwshp fund flw 1973-76; (cum laude) Glassboro State Clg 1965. **MILITARY SERVICE:** USAF 1957-60.

HOLLAND, VERNON E. (SUKI)
Professional athlete. **PERSONAL:** Born Jun 27, 1948, San Antonio. **EDUCATION:** Hlth & Physical Ed, BS 1971. **CAREER:** Cincinnati Bengals, professional ftbl plyr 1971-. **ORGANIZATIONS:** Buying & Selling Real Estate Personal Use; Trying to Start Summer Camp Black Kids of Low Income; Masons Lodge 33 Sherman, TX. **HONORS/ACHIEVEMENTS:** All am TN StateUniv Nashville; rookie of yr New Pitt Courage All Am 1971; all afc Benals; most improved plyr 2 Yrs Bengals.

HOLLAND, WILLIAM MEREDITH
Attorney, judge. **PERSONAL:** Born in Live Oak, FL; son of Isaac Holland and Annie Holland; children: William M, Jr, Maurice, Gian, Gaelim, Shakira. **EDUCATION:** FL A&M Univ, AB 1947; Boston Univ Law Sch, JD 1951. **CAREER:** Atty; civil rights advocate; pres with Law Firm of Holland & Smith; municipal judge 1973-1977. **ORGANIZATIONS:** Mem Legal Def NAACP; Amer Bar Assn Comm on Indiv Rights & Responsibilities; Amer Civil Liberties Union. **HONORS/ACHIEVEMENTS:** NAACP Achievement Award; Amer Bicentennial Resource Inst; Phi Beta Sigma Achiev Award; Omega Psi Phi Man of the Year; Optimist Achiev Award; Phi Delta Kappa Award; Zeta Phi Beta Award. **MILITARY SERVICE:** AUS Corpl 1943-46. **BUSINESS ADDRESS:** Attorney, Holland and Smith, PO Box 2648, 605 Clematis, West Palm Beach, FL 33402.

HOLLAND-CALBERT, MARY ANN
Registered nurse. **PERSONAL:** Born Jul 12, 1941, New York, NY; daughter of James Kirkland and Doris Wiles Vance; married Clarence E Calbert, May 23, 1987; children: Toussaint Michael Holland. **EDUCATION:** Washington Technical Inst, AAS, 1976; Univ of District of Columbia, BSN, 1987-. **CAREER:** St Elizabeth Hospital, Washington DC, psychiatric nurse coord, 1970-88; Greater Southeast Community Hospital, Washington DC, psychiatric nurse, 1988-. **ORGANIZATIONS:** Mem, Natl Council of Negro Women, 1976-; Chi Eta Phi Sorority Inc, mem 1976-, exec sec 1983-88; mem, Top Ladies of Distinction, 1986-; St Mark Presbyterian Church. **HOME ADDRESS:** 11963 Autumnwood Ln, Fort Washington, MA 20744.

HOLLAR, MILTON CONOVER
Physician. **PERSONAL:** Born May 06, 1930, Newark, NJ; son of Hector R and Ruth L; children: Michael C, Melia C, Marc C, Milton C. **EDUCATION:** New York Univ, BA 1955, MA 1957; Howard Univ Coll Medicine, MD 1962; New York Psychoanalytic Inst, Graduated 1975. **CAREER:** Yeshiva Univ Albert Einstein Coll of Medicine, asst clinical prof psy; Bronx Psy Center, faculty mem 1976-; New Rochelle Guidance Center Lincoln Ave Clinic, med dir 1966-88. **ORGANIZATIONS:** Half-Way House Ex-offenders; mem New Rochelle CAA; mem Natl Med Assc; Amer Psychiatric Assc; Amer Psychoanalytic Assc; New York Pscyhoanalytic Soc Diplomate; Amer Bd of Psychiatry & Neurology; pres New York Metro Black Psychiatrists of Amer; mem Comm Social Responsibility Amer Psy Assoc; mem New York County Med Soc public health Comm on Minorities; mem Physicians Adv Comm Visting Nurse Serv Westchester. **HONORS/ACHIEVEMENTS:** Published "Minority Students Psychological Notes for the 1980's" Journal Natl Assn of Student Pers Admin; co-chmn & coord, Apsychoanalya workshops "Impact of AIDS", 1988-;. **MILITARY SERVICE:** AUS maj 1951-53. **BUSINESS ADDRESS:** 838 Pelhamdale Ave, Suite Q, New Rochelle, NY 10801.

HOLLEY, CHARLES J.
Clergyman. **PERSONAL:** Born Dec 05, 1943, Phil, PA; married Phyllis Holley. **EDUCATION:** TN St U, BS;Univ Chic, BD, MS, MDiv. **CAREER:** Little Rock Bapt Ch, pastor; Stdnt Aff Shaw Clg Detroit, vp. **ORGANIZATIONS:** Pres Operation Push Detroit; intern chapln Elgin St Hosp 1967; comm Worker St Gangs Chic, 1966; asst chapln TN StUniv 1962-65; bus mgr Hamburger Fran 1961-62; mgr Super Mkt 1958-59; Alpha Phi Alpha; Assc Christian Ed Dirs; cncl Bapt Pstrs; Black Econ Cncl; SCLC Chpt; v chmn Hannibal Fund Inv Corp; Natl Bapt Conv; Am Bapt Conv; mem NAACP; CERV; bd of Payne-Pulliam Trade Sch. **MILITARY SERVICE:** USN 1944-46.

HOLLEY, JAMES W., III
Dental surgeon. **PERSONAL:** Born Nov 24, 1926, Portsmouth, VA; married Mary W; children: James IV, Robin. **EDUCATION:** West Virginia State Coll, BS 1949-; Howard Univ, DDS 1955. **CAREER:** Maryview Hospital/Portsmouth General Hospital, dental staff. **ORGANIZATIONS:** Norfolk Comm Virginia State Dental Assn; Virginia Tidewater Den Soc; Old Dominion Den Soc; Natl Dental Assn; Amer Den Assn; Pierre Fauchard Acad; Portsmouth Den Soc;Chicago Den Soc; Cen Civic Forum; United Civic League; Miller Day Nursery; Gosport Dist Boy Scouts of Amer; Tidewater Council Boy Scouts of Amer;YMCA; United Fund; Portsmouth C of C; Citizens Planning Assn. **HONORS/ACHIEVEMENTS:** Portsmouth Teachers, School Bell Award, 1960; Boy Scouts of Amer, Achievment Award,1962; Natl Den Assn, Pres Award, 1963; Omega, Man of Year, 1963; Boy Scouts of Amer, Silver Beaver Award, 1963; Old Dominion Den Soc, Dentist of Year 1968; Old Dominion Soc, Pres Award, 1969; numerous other honors & awards. **MILITARY SERVICE:** WW II. **BUSINESS ADDRESS:** 446 Effingham St, Portsmouth, VA 23704.

HOLLEY, SANDRA CAVANAUGH
Speech-language pathologist. **PERSONAL:** Born Mar 30, 1943, Washington, DC; daughter of Clyde Howard Cavanaugh and Rebecca Arthur Cavanaugh; children: David Marshall Holley. **EDUCATION:** George Wash U, AB 1965, AM 1966;Univ of CT, PhD 1979. **CAREER:** So CT State Univ, prof/spch-lang pathologist 1970-; Rehab Ctr of Eastern Fairfield Co, spch pathologist 1966-70; Am Speech-lang Hearing Assc, leg cnclr 1973-81. **ORGANIZATIONS:** Chmn humane commn City of New Haven 1977-86; bd of dir Am Natl Red Cross S Central Chap 1978-84; exec bd CT Speech & Hearing Assc 1971-83; bd dir New Haven Vis Nurse Assc 1977-79; vice pres for Adminstration, Amer Speech-Language-Hearing Assn 1983-85; mem bd of dir The Foote School Association 1985-89; pres American Speech-Language-Hearing Assn 1988. **HONORS/ACHIEVEMENTS:** Danforth flw So CT State Clg 1973-80; Leadership in Communications Award Howard Univ 1987; Honorary Doctor of Public Service Degree George Washington Univ 1989. **BUSINESS ADDRESS:** 501 Crescent St, New Haven, CT 06515.

HOLLIDAY, ALFONSO DAVID
Physician. **PERSONAL:** Born Jun 10, 1931, Gary, IN; married Iris; children: Kathy, Alfonso III, Tony, Leroy, Ronnie, Dawn. **EDUCATION:** IN Univ, BA 1952; IN Univ Sch Med, MD 1955; Univ of Chicago, MBA Health Adminstrn. **CAREER:** Self-employed, physician/surgeon 1960-75; Family Nurse Practitioner Program, co-dir 1975-; Med Ctr Gary, exec dir 1975-78; IN Univ NW, adj asst prof of nursing 1978; Group Health of NW IN Inc, pres 1979-; Holliday Health Cou PC, pres 1980-; Lake Co Jail Crown Point IN, med dir 1982-; Gary Police Dept Gary IN, police surgeon 1982-. **ORGANIZATIONS:** Diplomat Amer Bd Surgery 1964; flw Amer Coll Surgeons 1964; Amer Acad of Med Dir; Amer Med Assn; Hosp Fin Mgmt Assn; IN State Med Assn; nominee Amer Coll of Hosp Adminstr; Natl Med Assn; Hoosier State Med Assn; Lake Co Med Soc; mem certified physician executive Amer Coll of Physician Executives 1984; accreditation surveyor fot the Accreditation Assn for Ambulatory Health Care Inc 1979-; certified by the Amer Coll of Physician Executives 1984. **HONORS/ACHIEVEMENTS:** Awd for Activities in field Human Rights NAACP 1976; IN Univ Don's Awd 1976; Disting Serv Midwest Assn of Com Health Ctrs Inc 1979; Natl HMO Management Fellow Georgetown Univ Sch of Medicine 1980. **MILITARY SERVICE:** USAF capt 1960-62. **BUSINESS ADDRESS:** Police Surgeon, Gary Police Dept, 504 Broadway, Gary, IN 46402.

HOLLIDAY, BERTHA GARRETT
Psychologist. **PERSONAL:** Born Nov 15, 1947, Kansas City, MO. **EDUCATION:** Univ of Chgo, BA 1969; HarvardUniv Sch of Ed, EdM 1970;Univ Of TX at Austin, PhD 1978. **CAREER:** Peabody Coll of Vanderbilt Univ, asst prof 1978-; Austin State Hospital, psychology consultant 1975-76; Model Cities Program Urban Affairs Dept Kansas City, MO, specialist project mgmt specialist 1971 -74; Greater Kansas City Mental Health Found, counselor 1970-71; Univ of Chicago, student admin 1968-69. **ORGANIZATIONS:** Mem Assc of Black Psychologists 1978-; mem Am Psychol Assc Natl Blk Child Dev Inst 1978-; consult Westinghouse Hlth Syst 1979-; mem Delta Sigma Theta Sor Inc 1973-. **HONORS/ACHIEVEMENTS:** Schlrshp for Fgn Study Am Field Serv 1964-65; Nu Pi Sigma Hon Soc; Howell Murray AwrdUniv of Chicago 1969; 4 Yr Grad Flwshp Danforth Found 1974-78; apptd HEW Natl Adv Com on Blk Higher Educ 1977-. **BUSINESS ADDRESS:** Congressional Fellow, US Senate, Hart Bldg #619, Washington, DC 20510.

HOLLIDAY, BILLIE
Deputy commissioner. **PERSONAL:** Born in Florida; married Jackie Hayes; children: John W II. **EDUCATION:** NY Univ, Grad; New School for Social Rsch NYC, MHuman Resources. **CAREER:** New York City Office of Probation, court reporting officer, probation officer; NY Dept of Social Svcs, caseworker; Pre-Trial Serv Agency of Vera Inst of Justice NYC,exec dir 1974-76; NY State Parole Board, commissioner 1976-84; NY Police Dept, dep commiss for community affairs 1984-. **ORGANIZATIONS:** Mem Delta Sigma Theta; vice pres Black Resources & Issues Now; mem NY Chap Coaltion 100 Black Women; exec bd Natl

Org of Black Law Enforcement Execs; bd dir Manhattan Urban League, Manhattan NAACP. **HONORS/ACHIEVEMENTS:** Amer Top 100 Black Women 1985; Humanitarian Awd NY Chap of Continental Soc Inc 1985; Sojourner Truth Loyalty Awd Coalition of Black Trade Unionists 1986; Achievement Awd Fed of Negro Civil Assoc of NY 1986. **BUSINESS ADDRESS:** Deputy Commiss Commun Affairs, New York Police Dept, 1 Police Plaza, New York, NY 10038.

HOLLIDAY, FRANCES B.
Educator. **PERSONAL:** Born in Chicago, IL; married Oliver M Holliday; children: David E Brown. **EDUCATION:** DePaul Univ, BA 1949, MA 1962; Union Grad Sch, PhD 1977. **CAREER:** Chicago Public Schs, teacher 1950-68; Headstart Chicago, exec dir 1965-66; Loyola Univ, teacher 1969-70; Urban Teacher Educ Univ IL, instructor 1970-71; Title III Program in Early Childhood Dev Dist 65, dir 1971-74; NEU, instructor 1971-74; Title VII Emer Sch Aid Act Dist 65, director; Ctr for New Schools, pres & chmn of bd; Chicago Educ Corps, dir volunteer serv unit. **ORGANIZATIONS:** Mem Natl Alliance Black Sch Educators, Black Child Dev Inst; mem bd Assn Black Child Advocates; editorial adv bd mem Journal of Negro Educ; columnist author in field. **BUSINESS ADDRESS:** Dir, Chicago Education Corps, 1819 W Pershing Rd, Chicago, IL 60609.

HOLLIDAY, JENNIFER
Singer. **CAREER:** Broadway, "Dreamgirls", w/Grammy Awd winning song "And I'm Telling You I'm Not Going" 1981; Albums, Feel My Soul, Say you Love Me; Stage Work/Traveling Production of "Sing, Mahalia, Sing" a musical tribute to Mahalia Jackson. **HONORS/ACHIEVEMENTS:** Grammy Award, Tony Award for Dreamgirls 1981.

HOLLIDAY, PRINCE E.
Health insurance company executive. **PERSONAL:** Born Sep 29, 1935, Chambers County, AL; married Marcia E Cypress; children: Eric, Morgan. **EDUCATION:** Attended, Clark Coll Atlanta 1954-55; Univ of Detroit, AB 1975. **CAREER:** Blue Cross and Blue Shielf of MI, mgr phy & prov serv 1968-74, asst vice pres gov mktg 1974-75, assoc dir cust affairs 1975-78, exec asst ext affairs 1978-83, dir civic affairs 1983-85, vice pres comm affairs 1985-. **ORGANIZATIONS:** Pres Metro Detroit Youth Foundation; bd of dirs Police Athletic League; chmn bd of dirs Northside Family YMCA 1986-87; vice chmn Intl Freedom Festival 1986-87; mem Greater Detroit Chamber of Commerce; apptd by mayor Detroit Private Industry Cncl; pres Blue Cross and Blue Shield of MI Employee's Five Year Club 1986-87; sec Blue Cross and Blue Shield of MI HAP/PAC 1986-87; dist dir Public Relations MI District of Kiwanis 1986-87; exec comm Clark Coll C Eric Lincoln Lectureship; mem Detroit Kiwanis Club #1; golden heritage life mem NAACP; life mem Kappa Alpha Psi Frat; mem Booker T Washington Business Assoc; lt gov MI Dist of Kiwanis 1987-88; mem bd of dirs Junior Achievement Southeastern MI; mem bd of dirs Intl Inst of Detroit; mem bd of trustees Boys & Girls Clubs of Detroit. **HONORS/ACHIEVEMENTS:** Spirit of Detroit Awd Detroit City Cncl 1984; Testimonial Resolution Detroit City Council 1986; Metro Detroit YMCA Minority Achiever in Industry Awd YMCA Metro Detroit 1986; lay mem MI Assoc of Osteopathic Physicians and Surgeons. **MILITARY SERVICE:** USN usntn 1955-56; Honroable Discharge. **BUSINESS ADDRESS:** Vice Pres Community Affairs, Blue Cross/Blue Shield of MI, 600 Lafayette East #2003, Detroit, MI 48226.

HOLLIDAY-HAYES, WILHELMINA EVELYN (BILLIE)
Government official. **PERSONAL:** Born Sep 10, Jacksonville, FL; daughter of John Holliday and Leah Ervin Holliday; married John (Jackie) Hayes, Aug 25, 1970. **EDUCATION:** NY U, BS; Columbia Sch Social Work, Grad Stds; New Sch for Soc Rsrch, MA; Inst for Mediation & Conflict Resolution, Cert Mediator. **CAREER:** New York City Police Dept, dep commissioner for community affairs, 1984—; Bd of Parole NY State, commissioner, 1976-84; Vera Inst of Justice & Pretrial Serv Agy, borough dir 1974-76; New York City Police Dept, asst dir exec dir 1968-74; New York City Ofc of Probation, Ct reporting ofcr 1961-68; New York City Dept of Soc Svcs, Caseworker 1954-61. **ORGANIZATIONS:** Vp bd dir Wiltwyck Sch for Boys; chpn bd dir Wiltwyck Brooklyn Div; mem bd dir Exodus House; consult Equal Opp & Womans Career Mags; flw orgnzr Harlem Improvement Proj; mem Coalition of 100 Black Women NY State 1976-78; hon pres Friends of Northside Ctr for Child Dev 1974-; mem Delta Simga Theta; vice president, Black Resources and Issues Now (BRAIN); Mid Manhattan NAACP; advisor, Greater NY Councils of Boy Scouts of Amer and Law Enforcement Explorer Scouts; consultant, Key Women of America; Manhattan Urban League; Women in Criminal Justice. **HONORS/ACHIEVEMENTS:** Govt and community service award, Natl Council of Negro Women, 1989.

HOLLIE, DOUG CALVIN
Professional athlete. **PERSONAL:** Born Dec 15, 1960, Detroit, MI. **EDUCATION:** Southern Meth Univ. **CAREER:** Oakland Invaders, defensive end 1984-. **ORGANIZATIONS:** Working in degree in criminal justice at SMU during offseason.

HOLLINGSWORTH, ALFRED DELANO
Business executive. **PERSONAL:** Born Oct 26, 1942, Jackson, MS; married Hattie. **EDUCATION:** Univ of CO, BS; Univ of WA, MA. **CAREER:** Crown Zellarbach, jr exec sales dept 1965-67; Fiberboard Corp, sales mgr 1967-68; Sheet Plant Corp, pres 1968-; Squat Corp, pres, owner 1970-. **ORGANIZATIONS:** Bd of dir Black Bus Assn; LAC of C Chmn "Hot Seat" prog; Rotary Club; founder Christian Bus Ministries, Youth for Bus Prog. **HONORS/ACHIEVEMENTS:** Black Businessman of Month Nat Assn Mkt Devel; awds US Dept Commerce. **BUSINESS ADDRESS:** President, Sqwat Corporation, 23441 Goldensprings Dr, Diamond Bar, CA 91765.

HOLLINGSWORTH, JOHN ALEXANDER
Educator. **PERSONAL:** Born Sep 25, 1925, Owego, NY; son of John Alexander Hollingsworth Sr (deceased) and Florence Eve Haley Hollingsworth (deceased); married Dr Winifred Stoelting; children: 5. **EDUCATION:** NC A&T St Univ, BS Agriculture 1950; NC Central Univ, MS Biology 1960; Cornell Univ, Academic Yr 1962-63; NC A&T St Univ, MS Adult Educ 1985. **CAREER:** Fayetteville City Schools, science tchr 1959-68, science & math coordinator 1968-83; NC A&T St Univ, grad student 1983-85, staff develop intern; Consultant/Writer, 1985-. **ORGANIZATIONS:** Pres Fayetteville City Unit NCTA 1968-70; pres Fayetteville City Unit NCAE 1970-71; st Pres NC Sci Tchrs Asso 1971-73; mem Fayetteville Airport Com 1973-79; grad stdnt intern Major Int In Stress Mgmt & PrvnTV Hlth Care 1983-85; mem NEA, NCAE; life mem NEA-R; Arkansas Art Center, American Vision Foundation, Black World Foundation, Common Cause. **HONORS/ACHIEVEMENTS:** Writer/Dir ESAA Pilot Proj In Math 1974-80. **MILITARY SERVICE:** AUS captain 1943-46 1949-57; Served in Germany, Korea, and Hawaii. **HOME ADDRESS:** 61 Otalco Dr, Cherokee Village, AR 72542.

HOLLINGSWORTH, PERLESTA A.
Attorney. **PERSONAL:** Born Apr 12, 1936, Little Rock, AR; son of Perlesta G Hollingsworth and Eartha Mae Frampton Morris (deceased); married Ada Louise Shine; children: Terri, Tracy, Perlesta, Jr, Maxie. **EDUCATION:** Talladega Clg, AB 1958;Univ AR Law Sch, JD 1969. **CAREER:** Legal Extradition Ofcr of AR City Cncl, prosecuting atty 1971-; Little Rock City Bd, 1973-76, asst mayor 1975-76; Arkansas Supreme Court, assoc justice 1983-85; Hollingsworth Law Firm P A, attorney. **ORGANIZATIONS:** Mem Urban League, NAACP, Alpha Phi Alpha, Natl Bar Assc, Am Bar Assc, Sigma Pi Phi Frat. **HONORS/ACHIEVEMENTS:** Omega Citizen of the Year 1975. **MILITARY SERVICE:** AUS 1958-60. **BUSINESS ADDRESS:** Attorney, Hollingsworth Law Firm P A, 415 Main St, Main Place Bldg, Little Rock, AR 72201.

HOLLINGSWORTH, PIERRE
Commissioner. **PERSONAL:** Born Mar 30, 1931. **EDUCATION:** NY Inst of Tech, AS. **CAREER:** Atlantic City, city commr. **ORGANIZATIONS:** State bd of dir NAACP; pres Atlantic City NAACP; v chpsn Conv Com Bd of Trade; mem Frontiers Intl; Profnl Firefighters; Firemen's Mut Benevolent Assc; Interntl Assc of Arson Investrs; Natl Assc of Fire Sci & Admnstr; co dir Peoples Causes. **HONORS/ACHIEVEMENTS:** Black summit awrd 1968-69; achvmnt awrd Lighthouse Lodge 1975; mainland awrd NAACP 1975; humanitarian awrd Holy Temple Ch of God in Christ 1975. **BUSINESS ADDRESS:** City Hall, Rm 604, Tennessee Ave, Atlantic City, NJ 08401.

HOLLINS, JOSEPH EDWARD
Educational administrator. **PERSONAL:** Born Dec 14, 1927, Baton Rouge, LA; married Louise T; children: Reginald, Larry, Patrice, Stephanie. **EDUCATION:** Leland Coll, BS 1952; NM Styland Univ, 1957; Southern Univ, ME 1969. **CAREER:** Thomas A Levy, 1950-60; Upper Marengauin, principal 1960-. **ORGANIZATIONS:** Alderman Town Of Maringouin 1970-. **HOME ADDRESS:** P O Box 156, Maringouin, LA 70757.

HOLLINS, LIONEL
Professional athlete. **PERSONAL:** Born Oct 19, 1953, Arkansas City, KS; married Angela; children: Anthony. **EDUCATION:** Dixie Jr Coll, attended 1972-73; AZ State Univ, attended 1974-75. **CAREER:** Portland Trailblazers, guard 1975-79; Philadelphia '76ers, guard 1980-82; San Diego Clippers, guard 1982-84; Houston Rockets, guard 1984-. **HONORS/ACHIEVEMENTS:** All Rookie First Team Honors 1975; Sporting News 1st Team All-Amer 1975.

HOLLINS, ROBERT ALPHONSO
Retired busniess manager. **PERSONAL:** Born Apr 04, 1915, Jenkinsville, SC; married Elizabeth Brown; children: John, Robert, Hattye. **EDUCATION:** Allen U, BA 1939; Fisk U, MA 1963. **CAREER:** Co & State Govt Fairfield Co, tres; Allen U, bus mgr 1976; Supreme Ins Co of Am Akron, dist mgr 1962-67, auditor 1960-62, dist mgr 1956-60, asstmgr 1953; Reed St HS, tchr 1941-42; NC Mutual, inst agt 1939, co clerk 1939. **ORGANIZATIONS:** Mem Dept of Bus Ed; Washington; Phi Beta Sigma; Lay Delegate Gen Conf Dallas 1972. **HONORS/ACHIEVEMENTS:** Dist mgr awrd Natl Ins Assc 1964; cert of achvmnt Natl Inst 1963; cert of Merit 1958.

HOLLIS, CLARENCE O.
Business executive. **PERSONAL:** Born Oct 29, 1913, Dixie, GA; married Jane H Jason; children: Lena, Clarence, Jr. **EDUCATION:** Hampton Inst, BS 1939; Wharton SchUniv PA, MBA 1951; Am Clg Life Underwriters, CLU Designation 1951, Diploma Agcy Mgmt 1964. **CAREER:** Pilgrim Hlth & Life Ins Co Augusta 1935, spl rep 1939-40, dist mgr 1940-50, & ordinary mgr 1950-51, ordinary supr 1952, asst agency ofcr dir Training 1953-58; assc agency dir 1958-62, dir 1959-, v pres agency dir 1962-68, 1st v pres 1968-. **ORGANIZATIONS:** Chmn bd dir Pilgrim Life 1979-; vice pres Natl Ins Assc 1959-60; tres 1965-72; 1st vice pres 1972-73; pres 1973-74; bd chmn 1974-75; mem bd Ofcrs Corp; Episcopal Diocese GA 1969-76; dioceasan rep GA Cncl Chs; mem Diocesan Cncl, GA 1972-75; mem Layreader; past vestryman past ch sch supt St Mary's Episcopal Ch; mem Com Structure & Orgn; mem Boy Scouts Am 1957-60; mem bd YMCA 1960-62; mem Exec com Augusta-Richmond Co & Govt Study Com; mem Am Soc CLU Omega Psi Phi; mem Tax Equalization Bd Richmond Cnty 1973-74; dir Augusta Taxpayers Assc Augusta 1973-74. **HONORS/ACHIEVEMENTS:** Recipient alumni awrd merit Hampton Inst 1959; graduate LIAMA 47th Agency Ofcrs Sch 1968; recipient agency sect Spl Serv awrd NIA 1970; recipient Natl InsAssc Pres Awrd 1974. **BUSINESS ADDRESS:** 1143 Gwinnett St, PO Box 1897, Augusta, GA 30903.

HOLLIS, MARY LEE
Real estate broker. **PERSONAL:** Born May 15, 1942, Miller, GA; married Albert H Hollis; children: Naomi M, Pat Ann. **EDUCATION:** Attended, Sacramento City and State Coll; Real Estate School, broker. **ORGANIZATIONS:** Adv bd Sacramento Bd of Realtors, Sacramento Assoc for Artists, Sacramento Assoc for Children; mem Trinity Church Choir. **BUSINESS ADDRESS:** Owner/Dir, #10 Space Court, Sacramento, CA 95831.

HOLLIS, MELDON S., JR.
Attorney. **PERSONAL:** Born Apr 22, 1945, Charleston, SC; married Teresa K Harris; children: Meldon A. **EDUCATION:** Univ of MD, BA 1971, MA 1974; Harvard Univ, JD 1977, MPA 1986. **CAREER:** US Dept of HEW, special asst to assist sec for educ 1977-79; Univ S Dept of Ed, dir of white house initiative on black coll and univ 1979-80; TX Southern Univ, vice pres for univ devel 1980-82; Harvard Univ, admin asst office of pres 1982-85; Northeastern Univ African-American Studies, lecturer 1982-86. **ORGANIZATIONS:** Report on the President's Black College Initiative 1980; Dist of Columbia Veterans Assoc, exec dir 1970-74; MD Black Coalition for Higher Ed, vice chairman 1972-74; Friends of the Nat'l Zoo, bd of trustees 1979-80; exec comm Black Faculty and Admin Harvard Univ 1983-85; MA Bay Comm Coll, bd of trustees 1985-87; exec dir Harvard Law Sch Black Alumni Org 1985-; mem Washington DC and MA Bar Assocs. **MILITARY SERVICE:** AUS, 1964-70;

US Military Acad 1965-68. **BUSINESS ADDRESS:** Attorney, Semmes, Bowen & Semmes, 250 W Pratt St, Baltimore, MD 21201.

HOLLIS, MICHAEL R.
Business executive. **EDUCATION:** Dartmouth Coll, attended; Univ of VA, LLD. **CAREER:** Three Mile Island, assoc chief counsel to investigate the nuclear disaster; Oppenheimer & Co, vp; Urban Mass Transit Admin, counsel; Bay Area Rapid Transit San Francisco, counsel; Hansell & Post, counsel; Private practice, atty; Air Atlanta, founder, chmn 1983-. **ORGANIZATIONS:** 1st black pres Amer Bar Assoc. **HONORS/ACHIEVEMENTS:** One of the youngest vp's at 26 Oppenheimer & Co; 1985 recipient The Business and Professions Award for his accomplishments as founder and CEO of the nation's first major Black-owned airline, Air Atlanta, and for his commitment to excellence.

HOLLOMAN, JOHN L. S., JR.
Public health administrator. **PERSONAL:** Born Nov 22, 1919, Washington, DC; son of John L S Holloman and Rosa V Jones; married Patricia A Tatjie; children: Charlotte, Ellen, Laura, Karin, Paul. **EDUCATION:** Virginia Union Univ, BS (cum laude) 1940; Univ of Michigan Med, MD 1943; Virginia Union Univ, DSc 1983. **CAREER:** Private Practice New York City, 1947-87; Health Insurance Plan of New York, vice pres 1972-74; New York City Health Hospital Corp, pres 1974-77; Univ of North Carolina Public Health, Visting prof 1977-78; US Congress Ways & Means Comm, professional staff 1979-80; Medical Officer USFDA, regional 1980-85; W F Ryan Health Center, medical dir. **ORGANIZATIONS:** Pres bd of trustee Virginia Union Univ 1962-83; trustee St Univ of New York 1968-85; life mem NAACP, Sigma Pi, Natl Guardsmen, Alpha Phi Alpha; Amer Society of Internal Medicine; vice pres African Fund 1968-. **HONORS/ACHIEVEMENTS:** Hausen Emerson Award New York Public Health Assn 1970; mem Inst of Med Natl acad of Science 1972; Ernst P Boas Award Social Med 1975; Frederick Douglass Award New York Urban League 1976. **MILITARY SERVICE:** AUS med corp captain 1944-46. **HOME ADDRESS:** 27-40 Ericsson St, East Elmhurst, NY 11369. **BUSINESS ADDRESS:** Medical Dir, W F Ryan Hlth Ctr, 2160 Madison Ave, New York, NY 10037.

HOLLOMAN, THADDEUS BAILEY
Executive vice president. **PERSONAL:** Born Jun 30, 1955, Newport News, VA; married Renee D Brown; children: Thaddeus Jr. **EDUCATION:** Howard Univ, BBA 1977; Old Dominion Univ, Advanced Study-Public Administration 1982-83. **CAREER:** Peat Marwick Mitchell & Co, auditor 1977-79; Student Loan Marketing Assoc, accountant 1979; Hampton Univ, accountant 1979-81; City of Newport News VA, auditor 1981-85. **ORGANIZATIONS:** Mem NAACP Newport News VA 1983-; mem Newport News Political Action Comm 1984-; treasurer Peninsula Habitat for Humanity 1985-. **BUSINESS ADDRESS:** Executive Vice President, Community Federal Savings, & Loan Association, 1512 - 27th St, Newport News, VA 23607.

HOLLON, HERBERT HOLSTEIN
Personnel administrator. **PERSONAL:** Born Aug 17, 1936, New York City, NY; married Margaret Catherine Zeitz; children: Herbert Holstein II, Christopher James. **EDUCATION:** Morgan St Coll, BA Sociology 1955-59. **CAREER:** Los Angeles Cnty, dpty prbtn offcr 1961-66; Thomas J Lipton Inc, sls trrtry Rep 1967-69, manpwr devel asst 1969-71; E R Squibb & Sons Inc, affrmtv actn mgr 1971-73; Chesebrough-Pond's Inc, mgr rcrtmn & mgmt devel 1973-75, dir equal opprtnty affrs 1975-79, dir prsnl admin 1979-. **ORGANIZATIONS:** Chrtr mem The Edges Group Inc 1969-; mem Xavier Univ of LA Cluster 1971-; mem past bd of dir Emp Mgmt Assoc 1973-; coach Juvenile Ftbl, Bsbl & Bsktbl 1977-; chrtr mem Julius Thomas Scty NUL 1979-; chrmn of bd Waterbury OIC 1982-; chmn of the bd Grtr Waterbury Area Prvt Indus Council 1985-. **BUSINESS ADDRESS:** Dir Personnel Administ, Chesebrough-Pond's Inc, 33 Benedict Pl, Greenwich, CT 06830.

HOLLOWAY, ALBERT CURTIS
Educator. **PERSONAL:** Born Apr 22, 1931, Oxford, MS; married Mary D Laing; children: Christopher Bondy. **EDUCATION:** Oberlin Sch Commerce, asso deg 1957; Ashland Coll, BS 1961; OH State U, MS 1967. **CAREER:** Mohican Youth Camp OH, supt 1966-68, lectr & couns; Ashland Coll, asst vis prof 1968-69; Scioto Vill, OH,, dir clinical & chf soc wrkr 1968-70; MI State Univ, assoc prof 1970-; Lansing MI Comm Coll, assoc prof, visiting & part time. **ORGANIZATIONS:** Mem Nat Assn Soc Wrkrs; Acad Cert Soc Wrkers; Nat Coun Crime & Delinq; Am Pol & Soc Scientists; Coun Soc Wk Edn; Am Correctional Assn NASW; adv bd OH Correct Ct Servs; Community Services & Referral Center, Lansing, MI, mem of bd; Housing & Community Development Comm, City of East Lansing, MI. **MILITARY SERVICE:** USAF s/sgt 1950-54. **BUSINESS ADDRESS:** Associate Professor, School of Social Work, Michigan State University, 254 Baker Hall, East Lansing, MI 48824.

HOLLOWAY, ANNE FORRESTER
Ambassador. **PERSONAL:** Born Jun 02, 1941, Philadelphia, PA; married Marvin; children: 2. **EDUCATION:** Bennington Clg, BA 1963; Howard U, MA 1968; Antioch/Union Grad Sch, PhD 1975. **CAREER:** Repub of Mali, ambassador 1979-; Ofc of US Ambassador to United Nations, spl asst & dir; Congressman Andrew Young, foreign afrs leg asst 1975-77; Black Studnt Fund Wash DC, exec dir 1975-77; So Christian Ldrshp Conf Wash Bureau, assc dir for leg afrs; StateUniv of NY at Buffalo, vis asst prof 1971; Drum & Spear Press Pblshg House, dir 1969-70; Howard U, lectr 1968-69; Northfield Sch E Northfield, MA, tchr 1963-66. **ORGANIZATIONS:** Mem Transafrica; mem Cncl on Frgn rltns. **BUSINESS ADDRESS:** Dept of State USA, Room 4250, Washington, DC 20520.

HOLLOWAY, ARTHUR D.
Computer systems analyst. **PERSONAL:** Born Aug 20, 1931, Pleasant Grove, MS; married Juanita Yvonne; children: Arthur, Cheryl, James, Deborah. **EDUCATION:** Natl Security Agency Professional Sch;Univ Md; Armed Forced Inst. **CAREER:** Natl Security Agency Field Operations, mgr 1960-66; Natl Security Agency Operational Ctr, mgr 1966-71; Johns Hopkins Med & Inst, devel & mgr dept, cmptr systm analyst & pgmr. **ORGANIZATIONS:** Mem Data Processing Mgrs Assc; mem Frat order free Masons; Baltimore Comm Orgn Ed Adv Bd; dir Black Semi-pro Golf Assc. **HONORS/ACHIEVEMENTS:** Letter commondation NATO Joint Serv Commedndation Medal US Dept Defense. **MILITARY SERVICE:** USAF m/sgt 1949-71. **BUSINESS ADDRESS:** Johns Hopkins Computer Center, 720 Rutland Ave, Baltimore, MD 21205.

HOLLOWAY, BRIAN
Professional athlete. **PERSONAL:** Born Jul 25, 1959, Omaha, NE; married Bette; children: David. **EDUCATION:** Attended, Stanford. **CAREER:** New England Patriots, left tackle 1981-. **ORGANIZATIONS:** Speaker MADD, SADD; natl spokesman against heavy drinking for NFL and Distillers Assoc; New England team rep NFL Players Assoc; elected exec counsel NFL Players Assoc. **HONORS/ACHIEVEMENTS:** Selected All AFC by Football News; All-Pro 2nd Team by AP; All-AFC 2nd Team by UPI; NBC AFC Superteams Competition; mem 1986 NFL Pro Bowl Team. **BUSINESS ADDRESS:** New England Patriots, Schaefer Stadium, Rt 1, Foxboro, MA 02035.

HOLLOWAY, CALLON WESLEY, JR.
Pastor. **PERSONAL:** Born Jan 01, 1953, New York, NY; married Laverne; children: Callon III, Aaron. **EDUCATION:** Gettysburg Coll, BA 1976; Lutheran Sch of Theology at Chicago, MDiv 1980; Univ of Chicago, CPE 1978. **CAREER:** Bd of Publication Lutheran Church in Amer, bookkeeper/accountant 1978-80; Lutheran Sch of Theology at Chicago, asst to dean of faculty 1979-80; United Theol Seminary, adjunct faculty 1982-; Westwood Lutheran Church, pastor 1980-; Lutheran Church in Amer, pastor. **ORGANIZATIONS:** Pres Montgomery Co Hunger Coalition 1982-; vice pres Bd of Publs in Lutheran Church 1983-; mem Mayor's Strategic Task Force City of Dayton 1985-86; advisor/founder Dayton Assoc of Neighborhoods 1985-; bd of dirs Trinity Theol Seminary Columbus 1986-; bd mem Dayton Ministries in Higher Educ 1986-; bd of trustees Lutheran Social Serv Miami Valley 1987-. **HONORS/ACHIEVEMENTS:** Fellow Fund for Theol Educ Rockafeller Found 1977,79,80; Man of the Year Youth Services Commn MLU 1985, Dayton Assoc of Civic Orgs 1986. **BUSINESS ADDRESS:** Pastor, Lutheran Church in America, 3011 Oakridge Dr, Dayton, OH 45417.

HOLLOWAY, DEREK CALVIN
Professional athlete. **PERSONAL:** Born Jan 17, 1961, Riverside, NJ. **EDUCATION:** Arkansas. **CAREER:** Oakland Invaders, wide receiver 1984-. **HONORS/ACHIEVEMENTS:** Led USFL with 208 avg per catch; scored on touchdown passes of 12 and 14 yds in USFL Chmpnshp Game giving Panthers 17-3 lead over Phila; set career record for kickoff returns with 55 for 1,209 yds (220 avg); appeared in Sugar, Hall of Fame, Gator & Bluebonnet bowls.

HOLLOWAY, ERNEST LEON
Educational administrator. **PERSONAL:** Born Sep 12, 1930, Boley, OK; married Lula M Reed; children: Ernest L Jr, Reginald, Norman. **EDUCATION:** Langston Univ, BS 1952; OK State Univ, MS 1955; Univ of OK, EdD 1970. **CAREER:** Boley HS, sci teacher, principal 1955-62; Langston Univ, asst registrar, registrar, dean of student affairs, prof, vice pres for admin, acting pres, pres 1963-. **ORGANIZATIONS:** Nat Assn Sch Personnel Adminstrn, OK Coll Personnel Assn, pres 1975, OK Personnel Guidance Assn, Phi Delta Kappa, Imperial Council Shrines NW Consistory 33 Degree, educ found Alpha Phi Alpha Frat Inc. **HONORS/ACHIEVEMENTS:** "100 Most Influential Friends" Black Journ 1977. **BUSINESS ADDRESS:** President, Langston University, PO Box 907, Langston, OK 73050.

HOLLOWAY, ERNESTINE
Educator. **PERSONAL:** Born May 23, 1930, Clyde, MS. **EDUCATION:** Tougaloo Clg, BS; NY U, MA; MI State U, NDEA. **CAREER:** Tougaloo Clg, dean stdnts 1965-, asst dean 1963-65, sect pres 1953-63; Coleman HS, tchr 1952-53. **ORGANIZATIONS:** Mem Natl Assc Stdnt Prsnl Admn 1976-78; mem Edtrl bd NASPA Jour 1972-75; mem Reg III Adv & Bd 1978; corp del Am AsscUniv Women; mem Vis ComSoc Assc Clg & Sch; mem Yth Task Grp Hinds Co Assc Mental Hlth; undergrad pgm adv Alpha Kappa Alpha Sor 1974-78, southeastern reg dir 1970-74; bd dir Opera S 1975-76; chtr mem Opera S Guild 1976-; mem Resr Com Jackson Mun Separate Sch Dist; Clg Com Natl Assc Women Deans & Cnslrs; consult Workshops & Conf Stdnt Prsnl Serv; mem Phi Delta Kappa Frat; MS Persnl Guid Assc; so Clg Prsnl Assc; mem Am Miss Assc; United Ch Christ for Study NYUniv Natl Def Ed. **HONORS/ACHIEVEMENTS:** Awrd MI State U; alumnus yr Tougaloo Clg 1971; MS Black Women Natl Assc Colored Women's Clb 1976.

HOLLOWAY, HARRIS M.
Field representative, funeral director. **PERSONAL:** Born Jan 26, 1949, Aiken, SC. **EDUCATION:** Livingston Clg, BS 1966-71; Hood Theol Sem, 1970-71; Am Acad-McAllister Inst of Funeral Serv, PMS 1974. **CAREER:** Gen Motors Accept Corp, field rep; Perry Funeral Home, funeral dir; Carnie P Bragg Funeral Homes Inc, funeral dir 1972-78; NJ Dept of Labor Industry, emplymnt interviewer 1971-73. **ORGANIZATIONS:** Mem Garden State Funeral Dirs 1977; tres Tchr Corp Comm Cncl of Peterson 1979; mem Paterson Jaycees 1975-76; mem Rotary Clg of Paterson 1977-78; master mason Mt Zion Lodge No 50 (PHA). **HONORS/ACHIEVEMENTS:** Named best lighting technician/best stage mgr/best Set Designer/most coop thespian Livingston Clg 1966-71. **BUSINESS ADDRESS:** Perry Funeral Home, 34 Mercer St, Newark, NJ 07103.

HOLLOWAY, HERMAN M., SR.
Legislator. **PERSONAL:** Born Feb 04, 1922, Wilmington, DE; married Ethel. **EDUCATION:** Hampton Inst; DE State Coll, LLD 1969. **CAREER:** DE Gen Assembly Dem, state sen (1st blck to serve in senate) 1974; active in state politics at dist level 20 yrs; DE House of Reps, served 1963. **ORGANIZATIONS:** Became 1st black to serve on Joint Finance Comm in Gen Assembly; played active role in passage of DE Pub Accommodations Act; introduced legislation for correctional reforms training prgms for welfare recips in state; building inspector Wilmington Savs Fund Soc. **HONORS/ACHIEVEMENTS:** Recip Outstanding Cit Award Alpha Phi Alpha Frat 1972; Distingshd Serv Awrd Wilmington Br NAACP 1972. **BUSINESS ADDRESS:** 2008 Washington St, Wilmington, DE 19802.

HOLLOWAY, HILIARY H.
Business executive, attorney. **PERSONAL:** Born Mar 07, 1928, Durham, NC; married Beatrice Gwen Larkin; children: Hiliary Jr, Janis L. **EDUCATION:** NC Central Univ, BS Business Admin 1949; Temple Univ, EdM Business 1956; Temple Univ School of Law, JD Law 1964. **CAREER:** St Augustines Coll, business manager 1950-53; Kappa Alpha Psi Frat, exec dir 1953-65; Private Practice of Law, atty 1965-68; Fed Res Bank of Phila; asst counsel 1968-72, vice pres & gen counsel 1972-82, sr vice pres & gen counsel 1982-. **ORGANIZATIONS:** Grand Polemarch natl pres Kappa Alpha Psi Frat 1976-79; bd of trustees NC Cntrl Univ 1977-85; bd of dir Philadelphia Museum of Art 1978-; Urban Banker Bankers Assn; Amer Inst of Banking; Natl Bar Assn; Fed, Phila, Am, & PA Bar Assn. **HONORS/**

ACHIEVEMENTS: Comm Serv Awrd Chapel of the Four Chaplains 1977; Martin L King Award Educators Round Table 1977; Laurel Wreath Award Kappa Alpha Psi Frat 1983. **HOME ADDRESS:** 2293 Bryn Mawr Ave, Philadelphia, PA 19131. **BUSINESS ADDRESS:** Sr Vice Pres & Gen Counsel, Fed Reserve Bank of Philadelphia, Ten Independence Mall, Philadelphia, PA 19106.

HOLLOWAY, J. MILLS
University executive. **PERSONAL:** Born Nov 17, 1924, Durham Co, NC; married Doris Moore; children: Jay, Ivan. **EDUCATION:** NC Coll at Durham, BSC 1950. **CAREER:** St Augustine Coll, vice pres financial aff 1970-, business mgr 1957-70; J C Smith Univ, bus mgr 1952-57; Voorhees Coll, accountant 1951-52. **ORGANIZATIONS:** Mem Natl Assn Coll & Business Officers; Southern Assn Coll & Univ & Business Officers; Natl Assn Aux Enterprises; Kappa Alpha Psi; Coll & Univ Pers Assn; Natl Assc Financial Planners; Natl Assc Ed Buyers; mem NAACP; camp tres NC Sen Cand; tres St Augustine Coll Chpl; tres Wake Credit Union. **HONORS/ACHIEVEMENTS:** Man of yr Kappa Alpha Psi 1972; evaluation team Southern Assc Coll 1973-74; consultant Title IX Higher Ed Act 1973. **MILITARY SERVICE:** AUS sgt 1943-46. **BUSINESS ADDRESS:** Vice President for Finance, St Augustine's College, 1315 Oakwood Ave, Raleigh, NC 27611.

HOLLOWAY, JAMES L. (RED HOLLOWAY)
Jazz musician. **PERSONAL:** Born May 31, 1927, Helena, AR. **EDUCATION:** Conservatory Mus Chicago. **CAREER:** Musician, Worldwide Clubs & Concert Halls With Coltrane, Charlie Parker, Billie Holiday, Duke Ellington, Lester Young, Lionel Hampton, Kenny Burrell, Ella Fitzgerald, Muddy Waters, John Mayall; Bandleader Musician, 1943-67; Parisian Room LA, talent coord & ldr of house bnd; Toured US & Canada With Jimmy Dean Show; John Mayall Combo, Tours; Appeared in LA With Ray Brown & Sweets Edison. **HONORS/ACHIEVEMENTS:** Performed on soundtrack "Lady Sings the Blues" performed at Jazz Wk Comm Concert LA 1974; records on Prestige Label, "Sax", "Strings & Soul", "The Burner","Kriss Kross" (Own Composition) outst contributions City of LA 1974; Perth Jazz Soc. **MILITARY SERVICE:** AUS bandmaster 5 Army Band.

HOLLOWAY, JERRY
Educator. **PERSONAL:** Born May 14, 1941, Chicago, IL; married Mary Bowie. **EDUCATION:** Parson Coll, BA 1959-63;Univ NV, M 1968-71. **CAREER:** Matt Kelly Elem Sch Las Vegas, tchr 1963-66; Las Vegas, coord rec prog elem stdnts 1965-66; coord summer work exprnc prog 1966; Washoe Co Sch Dist Reno, asstd in plcng & sprvsng disadvntgd stdnts in work experience prog 1966; Traner Jr HS Reno, tchr 1966-67, tchr, admin asst to prin, v prin 1968-69, dean of stdnts 1969-71; Traner Rec Prog City Reno Rec Dept, asst dir 1970-71; Washoe Co Sch Dist Reno, intergroup splst 1971-72, sch admin, curriculum coord. **ORGANIZATIONS:** Mem Reno-Sparks Br NAACP; chrtr mem past chmn Black Coalition Fair Housing Law Com; past chmn Human Rels Com NV State Educ Assn; past chmn, past com mem Cub Scouts Div BSA Las Vegas; sec treas Econ Oppor Bd Washoe Co; vchmn CETA Manpower Adv Plng Cncl; mem bd dir YMCA; chr retired sr ctzns vol prgm; commn Equal Rights Citizens. **BUSINESS ADDRESS:** 425 E Ninth, Reno, NV 89502.

HOLLOWAY, JOAQUIN MILLER, JR.
Educational administrator. **PERSONAL:** Born Dec 28, 1937, Mobile, AL; son of Joaquin M Holloway Sr and Ariel Williams Holloway; married Malvina Murray; children: Monica, Joaquin III, Josef. **EDUCATION:** Talladega Coll, AB 1957; IN Univ, MS 1958, EdS 1960; Univ of AL, PhD 1976. **CAREER:** TX S Univ, instr 1958-61; Central HS, instr 1961-65; Mobile Co Pub Sch System, media splst 1965-69; Univ of S AL, prof of business 1969-, sr librarian & head of the instructional media ctr. **ORGANIZATIONS:** Consult Intl Paper Co 1977-80; consult Necott Devel Co 1978; consult Middle States Assn of Coll & Schs 1978; bd mem YMCA Dearborn Br 1975-86; bd mem Cine-Tel Commn 1976-; cncl mem AL State Cncl on the Arts 1979—; vice pres Culture in Black & White 1969-; host "Holloway House" progressive jazz program, WKRG AM-WKRG FM Radio 1969-79; mem Assn for Educ Comm & Tech, Minorities in Media, Omega Psi Phi Frat, Phi Delta Kappa, Omicron Delta Kappa; licensed lay reader in the Episcopal Ch; co-host of local UNCF Telethon 1983, 1984, 1988. **HONORS/ACHIEVEMENTS:** Fifth Place Awd (photography) Allied Arts Council Competition 1974; Second Place Awd (photography) First Annual Fort Conde Arts Festival 1979; 3 First Place Awds Photog Mobile Soc of Model Eng 20th SER Conv 1980; one-man photog shows, including: Percy Whiting Gall, 1985, Tel Fair Peet Gall, Auburn U, 1986, Tacon Station Gall, 1986; George Washington Carver Mus, Tuskegee U, 1987, Fine Arts Mus of the South, 1987, Hay Center Art Gall, Stillman Coll, 1988, Isabel Comer Mus of Art, 1989. **BUSINESS ADDRESS:** Professor/Senior Librarian and Head of Instructional Media Center, Univ of South Alabama, Library Bldg, Mobile, AL 36688.

HOLLOWAY, NATHANIEL OVERTON, JR.
Dentist. **PERSONAL:** Born Jan 30, 1926, HollyGrove, AR; married Dorothy Gladys; children: Jacqueline, Nathaniel III, Rhoda. **EDUCATION:** TN State Univ, BS 1949; Meharry Med Coll, DDS 1953. **CAREER:** Private Practice, dentist. **ORGANIZATIONS:** Past pres Ypsilanti Business & Professional League/Washtenaw Dist Dental Soc; mem, Wolverine Dental Soc, MI State Dental Soc, ADA Dental Soc Chmn, Deacon bd & Trust bd, Plymouth Congregational Ch; past gen chmn, NAACP Freedom Fund Dinner; past pres Detroit Duffers Golf Assn; mem Alpha Phi Alpha, Beta Kappa Chi. **MILITARY SERVICE:** USN 1944. **BUSINESS ADDRESS:** 401 S Hamilton St, Ypsilanti, MI 48197.

HOLLOWAY, RED See HOLLOWAY, JAMES L.

HOLLOWELL, DONALD L.
Regional attorney. **PERSONAL:** Born Dec 19, 1917, Wichita, KS; married Louise Thornton. **EDUCATION:** Lane Coll Jackson TN, AB; LoyolaUniv Law Sch, JD; Lane Coll, hon LLD 1966. **CAREER:** USEEOC, reg dir 1966-; Law, prvt pract 1952-. **ORGANIZATIONS:** Mem bd trustees Spelman Coll; trustee Phillips Sch Theol; trustee Interdenom Theol Cntr; trustee Collins & Chapel Hosp; exec com Nat Conf Christians & Jews; Am, Natl & Atlanta Bar Assns; Gate City Bar Assn; State Bar GA; Fed Bar Assn; NAACP; Kappa Alpha Psi; Phi Alpha Delta; Sigma Pi Phi; Nat Alumni Council United Negro Coll Fund. **HONORS/ACHIEVEMENTS:** Lawyer of Year NAACP 1965; civil rts awrd Council Human Rel 1966; Civil Liberties Award ACLU 1967; 750 Award WSB Radio 1967, 1970; Equal Opportunity DayAward Atlanta Urban League 1969; Unsung Hero Awrd SE Reg NAACP 1973; Charles Houston Alumni Award Harvard Law Sch 1974; num other awards & citations. **MILITARY SERVICE:** AUS capt 1935-46. **BUSINESS ADDRESS:** 75 Piedmont Ave NE, Ste 1150, Atlanta, GA 30303.

HOLLOWELL, JOHNNY LAVERAL
Asst. chief USCG. **PERSONAL:** Born Sep 13, 1951, New Orleans, LA; children: Ivory D. **EDUCATION:** Utica Jr Coll, AA 1971; Alcorn A&M Univ, attended 1971-72; Columbia Coll, BA 1980. **CAREER:** Marine Safety Office, asst chief port opers dept. **ORGANIZATIONS:** Mem Big Brothers of Amer 1982-84; mem vice pres Natl Naval Officers Assoc 1982-; mem Omega Psi Phi Frat 1982-. **HONORS/ACHIEVEMENTS:** Outstanding Young Man of Amer 1985. **MILITARY SERVICE:** USCG lt 1972-; 2 Coast Guard Achievement Medals, Commandants Letter of Commendation, Good Conduct Medal, Meritorious Unit Commendation Awd, Commandants Unit Commendation Awd. **HOME ADDRESS:** 8105 Catalpa, Texas City, TX 77591.

HOLLOWELL, KENNETH LAWRENCE
Labor representative. **PERSONAL:** Born Mar 05, 1945, Detroit, MI; married Patricia J; children: Terrance L, Rhonda L. **EDUCATION:** Wayne County Comm Coll, AA 1979. **CAREER:** Cook Paint & Varnish Co, rsch tech 1967-71; Teamsters Local Union No 247, business rep 1971-80, trustee and business rep 1980-82, recording sec and business rep 1982-85, vice pres and business rep 1985-87, pres and business rep 1987. **ORGANIZATIONS:** Deputy imperial potentate Intl Shriners 1975-83; commissioner Civic Ctr City of Detroit 1976-; first vice pres MI Assoc Masonic Grand Lodges 1979-; grand master Ralph Bunche Grand Lodge Intl Masons 1979-81; bd of dirs United Way of MI 1980-, Metro Agency for Retarded Citizens 1981-, Economic Alliance of MI 1982-; adv comm Ctr for Volunteerism UCS 1981-87; deputy supreme grand master Intl Masons 1983-86; grand master Intl F&AM Masons 1986-. **HONORS/ACHIEVEMENTS:** Goodwill Ambassador Awd 1987 Minority Womens Network. **MILITARY SERVICE:** USMC sgt e-5 1963-67; Good Conduct Medal, Natl Defense Medal, Vietnam Service Medal, Vietnam Campaign. **BUSINESS ADDRESS:** Pres/Business Representative, Teamsters Union Local #247, 2741 Trumbull Ave, Detroit, MI 48216.

HOLLOWELL, MELVIN L.
Urological surgeon. **PERSONAL:** Born Nov 24, 1930, Detroit, MI; married Sylvia Regina Ports; children: Regina, Dana, Melvin Jr, Danielle, Christopher, Courtney, Sylvia. **EDUCATION:** Wayne State Univ, BS 1953; Meharry Medical Coll, MD 1959. **CAREER:** MI Branch Amer Urological Assoc, pres 1976-77; Hutzel Hosp, vice chmn dept of urology 1980-87; Harper Grace Hosp Detroit, medical bd 1983-85, exec comm 1983-85; Southeast MI Surgical Soc, pres 1983-84; North Central Sect Amer Urological Assoc, exec comm 1984-86; Samaritan Health Ctr Sisters of Mercy, exec comm 1985-87, chmn dept of surgery 1985-. **ORGANIZATIONS:** Clinical asst prof, Dept of Urology Wayne State Univ Coll of Medicine; life mem NAACP; mem Kappa Alpha Psi Frat; mem GESU Catholic Church. **HONORS/ACHIEVEMENTS:** Fellow Amer Coll of Surgeons; Amer Coll of Medical Directors Physician Executives; Royal Coll of Medicine; Amer Bd of Urology. **MILITARY SERVICE:** AUS Medical Corp capt 1958-62; US Army Commendation Awd/Medal 1961. **BUSINESS ADDRESS:** Urological Surgeon/Pres, Adult Pediatric Urology Assocs, 20905 Greenfield Rd, Southfield, MI 48075.

HOLLY, ELLA LOUISE
Management consultant. **PERSONAL:** Born Aug 22, 1949, Philadelphia, PA. **EDUCATION:** Mills Coll of Educ, BS 1971; Teachers Coll Columbia Univ, MA 1973; Case Western Reserve Univ, PhD 1986. **CAREER:** New York City Bd of Educ, teacher 1972-76; Natl Educ Assoc, educ specialist 1976-79; Cuyahoga Co Welfare Dept, dir career advancement prog 1980; Yale School of Organization and Mgmt, prof of organizational behavior 1986-. **ORGANIZATIONS:** Natl fellow Inst of Educational Leadership 1979-80; external mgmt consultant in public and private sector 1981-86; mem Assoc of Black Sociologists, Academyof Mgmt, Gestalt Inst, Natl Assoc of Women Studies, Amer Sociological Assoc. **HONORS/ACHIEVEMENTS:** Innovating Programming Amer Public Welfare Assoc 1980; Outstanding Work in Educ and Social Services Cuyahoga Comm Coll 1980; Outstanding Young Women of the Year Greater Cleveland Urban League 1981; Amer Sociological Minority Fellowship 1983-86. **BUSINESS ADDRESS:** Prof Organizational Behavior, Yale School of Org/Mgmt, 135 Prospect St, New Haven, CT 06520.

HOLMAN, ALVIN T.
Planning administrative manager. **PERSONAL:** Born Jul 21, 1948, Wash, DC; married Karen. **EDUCATION:** L A Harbor Coll, AA 1969;Univ WA, AB 1970; MI St U, M Urb-Plng 1972. **CAREER:** S CA Rapid Trans Dist, plng proj mgr; UHURU Inc, proj dir; City of Seattle, comm plng cnslt; Office Econ & Oppor Seattle, reg res cnslt; St of MI, urban plnr/comm plng spclst; Cunningham/Short/Berryman & Assoc, sr plng cnslt. **ORGANIZATIONS:** Mem Am Inst of Plnrs; Am Soc Plng Officials; Am Soc Plng Conslts Natl Assn Hsng & Rehab Offcls; Natl Assn Plnrs; Natl Assn Min Cnslts Urbans. **BUSINESS ADDRESS:** Gardner & Holman Consulting, 3761 Stocker St, Ste 103, Los Angeles, CA 90008.

HOLMAN, BENJAMIN F.
Author, journalist, educator. **PERSONAL:** Born Dec 18, 1930, Columbia, SC. **EDUCATION:** Lincoln U, 1950;Univ KS, BS 1952;Univ Chgo, 1956. **CAREER:** Chicago Daily News, reporter 1952-62; WBBM-TV, commentator reprtr 1962-63; CBS News, edtr rprtr 1963-65; US Dept Justice, asst dir media rel div comm rel serv 1965-68; NBC News, prod rprtr 1968-69; Dept Justice, dir comm rel serv 1969-77; u of MD, prof of jour 1978-. **ORGANIZATIONS:** Adv com Uban Dev MI State U; IL Counc for Freedom of Rsdnce; bd mem Friendship Hse; mem Beatrice Caffrey Youth Serv & Ada S Mckinley House; Indepen Voters of IL; Jr Achvmnt Co mem Ralph Bunche Prog United Nations Assn US of Am; Wash Urban League; natl adv Counc Nat Ctr for Dispurte Settlement Am Arbitration Assn; Assn for Educ Journ; MD-DE-DC Press Assn. **HONORS/ACHIEVEMENTS:** Author "Sports & Mass Commun" 1979; "The Sports Commun Explosion" 1981; "The Symbiotic Adversaries" 1981. **MILITARY SERVICE:** AUS 1952-54; AUS reserve 1st lt 1955-65. **BUSINESS ADDRESS:** Professor Sch of Journalism, University of Maryland, Journalism Building, Room 4121, College Park, MD 20742.

HOLMAN, DORIS ANN
Retired educator. **PERSONAL:** Born Feb 14, 1924, Wetumpka, AL; daughter of Willie G Westbrooks and Mattie Banks Westbrooks; divorced; children: DeWayne, Douglas, De-

siree, Glenn. **EDUCATION:** AL State Univ, BS 1944; Univ San Francisco, MA 1979. **CAREER:** Detroit City Schools; Compton Unified School Dist, teacher. **ORGANIZATIONS:** Mem NEA; Phi Delta Kappa Beta Phi; Natl Assn Univ Women; rep CA Teachers Assn St Council 1960-62; bd dir ATEB Corp; chmn Neg Council Compton Unified School Dist 1971-73; pres Compton Educ Assn 1971-74; bd dir Compton YMCA 1970-; regional dir Natl Tots & Teens 1972-; Neighborhood chmn GS of A; bd dir BS of A; bd dir Christian Day School Comm Lutheran Church; mem Intl Toastmistress Club; pres Women of the Church Comm Lutheran Church 1977; treasurer So Bay Conf Amer Lutheran Church Women 1977; sec Compton Educ Assn 1976-77; mem Compton School Dist Compens Educ Adv Council School Advisory Council; bd of dir Mid Cities Schools Credit Union 1988-91; elect to bd for College and Univ Serv of the Amer Lutheran Church 1982-88. **HONORS/ACHIEVEMENTS:** Pro Achievement Award Enterprise Teachers Assn 1968; Who Award CA Teacher Assn 1970; Teacher in Political Award Theological Bass Mem 1972.

HOLMAN, FOREST H.
Executive assistant. **PERSONAL:** Born Apr 02, 1942, Birmingham; children: Karriem Malik. **EDUCATION:** Tuskegee Inst, BS 1965; MI State U, MA 1971, PhD 1974. **CAREER:** MI Consol Gas Co Detroit, mgr envrnmntl plng 1978-; Wayne St U, adj prof of Pol sci 1974-80; Shaw Coll of Detroit, adj prof of philos & soc inst 1974-78; City Chicago, tchr; Chicago Vice & Lords St Acad Inst, 1968; OIC, instr 1967-68; State Mi, senate rsrchr 1970-72; Tuskegee Inst , dir Frshmn studies & asst prof 1972-73; City Detroit, exec asst mayor; MI State U, asst prof Race & Urban Studies 1974-75. **ORGANIZATIONS:** Cvons Dept of Black Studies Eastern MI U; cons-cnslr Highland Park Dept of Human Resources Highland Park MI; couns MI Dept Human Resources 1974-45; mem Assn Study Negro Life & History; Assn Social & Bhvrl Sci; mem Alpha Phi Omega & Kappa Alpha Psi Frat; guest panelist Summer Bus Inst Wayne State U; panelist Neighborhood Legal Svc. **HONORS/ACHIEVEMENTS:** Certificate Recognition Jacob A Citrin Meml Seminar & Gov Conf Unemployment. **BUSINESS ADDRESS:** Mayors Office City Detroit, Detroit, MI.

HOLMES, BARBARA J.
Educator & communication specialist. **PERSONAL:** Born Jun 26, 1934, Chicago, IL; married Laurence H Holmes; children: Carole, Helyne, Sheryl, Laurence. **EDUCATION:** Talladega Coll, attended 1951-53; Univ CO, BA 1973, MA 1974, PhD 1978. **CAREER:** Natl Assessment of Educ Progress, writer 1977-83; State Educ Policy Seminary Prog co-sponsored by Educ Commn of the States & the Inst for Educ Leadership, natl coord; Intl Reading Assn, Speech Comm Assn of Amer & other educ prof organs, presentations. **ORGANIZATIONS:** Mem Delta Sigma Theta Public Serv Sor; mem bd of dirs Whitney M Young Jr Memorial Foundation 1974-84; fellow Educ Policy Fellowship Prog 1982-83. **HONORS/ACHIEVEMENTS:** Phi Beta Kappa Hon Soc 1974; Acad Fellowships Whitney M Young 1973-74; published over 20 articles and reports.

HOLMES, CARL
Attorney. **PERSONAL:** Born Dec 13, 1925, New York, NY; son of Thomas Holmes and Kathleen Holmes; married Dolores Fennell, Aug 05, 1957; children: Deborah, Beverly. **EDUCATION:** New York City Coll, BS 1950; Brooklyn Law Sch, 1953, JD 1967. **CAREER:** NYC, litigation atty 22 yrs; NY State Govt, 11 yrs; Rutledge Holmes & Willis, pvt pract; State of New York, assoc attorney, retired 1987. **ORGANIZATIONS:** Past vice pres Sch Bd Queens; rsrch Brown vs Bd Educ 1953; mem NAACP; ACLU; Macon B Allen Black Bar Assn. **MILITARY SERVICE:** USNR 1944-46; storekeeper 3/class. **HOME ADDRESS:** 116-47 167th St, Jamaica, NY 11434-1721. **BUSINESS ADDRESS:** Attorney at Law, 115-06 Merrick Blvd, Jamaica, NY 11434-1852.

HOLMES, CARL
Business executive. **PERSONAL:** Born Jan 06, 1929, Oklahoma City, OK; married Marvella; children: Carla D. **EDUCATION:** Drake Univ, MBA 1951; LA State Univ, Fire Dept attended; Southern Methodist Univ, Fire Dept Admin attended; Univ of MD Fire Dept Staff & Command School, attended; Motivational Mgmt Schools, attended; OK Univ Equal Oppty Seminars, attended. **CAREER:** OK City Fire Dept, fire chief (retired) 1951-81; Carl Holmes & Assoc, dir 1980-. **ORGANIZATIONS:** Consult City of Ft Worth 1979, City of Atlanta 1980, City of San Francisco 1982, natl Fire Acad, WA DC Fire Dept; mem 26 affiliations incl Natl Fire Protection Assoc, Intl Assoc Fire Instr; assoc mem Natl Assoc of Black Mfgrs; fire serv training instr OK State Univ; cty chmn OK Lung Assoc; tech adv Training Mag; guest lecturer at 8 univ's incl Univ of MD, AZ, MI, AR; instr motivational mgmt for Phycol Chem Corp, Amer Airlines, TX Light & Power Inc, OK Natural Gas Inc, Continental Oil Inc, TX Instrument Inc. **HONORS/ACHIEVEMENTS:** 7 publ incl Admin Problems of a Fire Dept, Auto Extrication for Rescue, Equal Employment Oppty Commiss Approach to Fire Dept Employment, The Fire Serv of the Future; Designed & implemented many progs incl a system which promoted 26 chief level positions in Atlanta GA, consult by Cty Admin for Tech Asst Orlando FL; implemented a Fire Station Location Prog & Eval System of the current status of its dept Minnetonka MN; rewrote entire entry level employment system Little Rock AR. **BUSINESS ADDRESS:** Chief Executive Officer, Carl Holmes & Assoc, 4040 N Lincoln Blvd, Oklahoma City, OK 73105.

HOLMES, CARLTON
Marketing executive. **PERSONAL:** Born Apr 01, 1951, New York, NY; married Dr Thelma Dye; children: Kyle, Arianna. **EDUCATION:** Cornell Univ, BA 1973; Columbia Univ Grad Sch of Business, MBA 1975. **CAREER:** Lever Bros NYC, asst prod mgr 1975-77; Johnson & Johnson, product director 1977-82; Drake Bakeries, product mgr 1982-83; Block Drug Co Jersey City, director, new business development, 1983-89. **ORGANIZATIONS:** Mem Cornell Black Alumni Assn, Natl Black MBA Assn. **HONORS/ACHIEVEMENTS:** NYS Regents Scholar 1968; Natl Achievement Scholar 1968; co-founder Cornell Black Alumni Assn 1976. **HOME ADDRESS:** 175 West 87th St #14H, New York, NY 10024.

HOLMES, CLOYD JAMES
Labor union official. **PERSONAL:** Born Nov 23, 1939, Houston, TX; son of Haywood Holmes and Charlene Cooper; married Madelyn Holmes Lopaz, Sep 20, 1986; children: Reginald B, Patrice, Cloyd J Jr, Anthony, E'vett, Chakka, Charlene, Cloyd J II, Conchita Nickles.. **CAREER:** Ramada Inn, Houston TX, fry cook, 1960-63; Howard Johnson, Bay Shore NY, fry cook, 1964-66; C W Post Coll, Automatique Food Serv, Brookville NY, chef, shop stewart, 1966-70; USEU Local 377, Long Island City NY, business representative, 1970-71, financial sec, tres, 1971-72, pres 1972-. **ORGANIZATIONS:** Mem, Intl Found of Employee Benefit Plan, 1970-; exec bd mem, vice pres, Retail Wholesale & Dept Store Union, 1978; former sec, treasurer, The Negro Labor Comm; exec vice pres, Huntington Boy's Club; former vice pres, NAACP, Greenwich Village Branch; mem, A Philip Randolph Inst, 1986, Coalition of Black Trade Unionists, NAACP, Huntington Branch, The Amer Cancer Soc, Queen's Branch. **HONORS/ACHIEVEMENTS:** Greenwich Village NAACP Branch, 1980; The Trade Union Women of African Heritage, 1981; NAACP Man of the Year, 1983; Negro Labor Comm Man of the Year, 1984; Amer Cancer Soc Greater Jamaica Unit for Notable Serv in the Crusade to Conquer Cancer Award, 1984. **BUSINESS ADDRESS:** Labor Union President & Intl Vice President, United Service Employee's Union Local 377 RWDSU, AFL-CIO, 29-27-41st Ave #1006, Long Island City, NY 11101.

HOLMES, DOROTHY E.
Psychologist, psychoanalyst. **PERSONAL:** Born Mar 09, 1943, Chicago, IL; daughter of Major Moten Evans and Queen McGee Evans Pryor; married Raymond L M Holmes, Jun 29, 1985. **EDUCATION:** Univ of IL, BS 1963; So IL U, MA Psych 1966, PhD Clinical Psych 1968. **CAREER:** Dept of Psych Howard Univ Hosp, associate prof; pvt prac; Dept of Psych Univ of MD, asst prof 1970-73; Univ of Rochester, instr & postdoctoral fellow 1968-70. **ORGANIZATIONS:** Nat Inst of Mntl Htlh; fellow Am Psych Assn; Sigma Xi; mem Amer Psychoanalytic Assn; District of Columbia Psychological Assn; Baltimore-Washington Institute and Society for Psychoanalysis; bd of dir Natl Register for Health Service Providers in Psychology, 1988-; bd of dir Professional Examination Service, 1987-. **HONORS/ACHIEVEMENTS:** Publ 1 book & 7 sci articles and 3 book reviews. **BUSINESS ADDRESS:** Dir, Clinical Psych Intrnshp, Howard University Hospital, Dept of Psychiatry, 2041 Georgia Ave NW, Washington, DC 20060.

HOLMES, EVERLENA M.
Educational administrator. **PERSONAL:** Born Feb 15, 1934, Eufaula, AL; daughter of Oscar McDonald and Carrie Howell McDonald; divorced; children: Rufus James Holmes, Parvin Warnell Holmes Porsche, Gregory Warren Holmes. **EDUCATION:** KY State Univ, BS 1957; US Public Health Serv Sch for Med Record Administrators, RRA 1960; Baylor Coll of Medicine Univ of Houston, MEd 1974; VA Polytechnic Inst & State Univ, EdD 1981; Harvard Univ, Institute of Educ Mgmt, Post Doctorate, 1987. **CAREER:** Central Oregon Comm Coll, dir med record tech prog 1971-73; Eastern KY Univ, chair dept of health record science 1975-79; TN State Univ, asst dean of allied health 1982-84; The George Washington Univ, dir med record admin 1984-85; Hunter Coll/Sch of Health Scis, dean. **ORGANIZATIONS:** Mem, NAACP 1949-; mem Congressional Black Caucus Health Brain & Educ Brain Trust 1978-; bd dirs, pres elect, Natl Soc of Allied Health 1982-; public commissioner Commn on Dental Accreditation Amer Dental Assn 1984-; consultant Project HOPE 1985-; mem Natl Urban League of New York 1986; mem, Natl Assn of Health Services Executives 1987-; Advisory Council, Teen Programs of St Mary's 1987-;Advisory Commission, Health Careers Educ Advisory Commission, NYC Board of Educ 1987-;mem, Assn of Black Women in Higher Educ, 1988-; mem, Natl Assn for Women Deans, Administrators, and Counselors 1988-. **HONORS/ACHIEVEMENTS:** Noyes Fellowship 1973-74; Duiguid Fellowship 1980-81; article "Two-Plus-Two Concept in the Preparation of Health Record Practitioners," Medical Record News; article, "Operating Ratios & Inst Characteristics Affecting the Responsiveness of Black Colls & Univs to Professional Allied Health Progs" Rsch in Post Secondary Educ; book "Allied Health Issues Related to Selected Minorities, A Bibliographic Refernce"; Outstanding Achievement Award 1987; Phi Delta Kappa, Phi Kappa Phi Natl Hon Soc; 39th Forum of ACE/NIP Office of Women in Higher Educ.. **BUSINESS ADDRESS:** Dean, Hunter Coll/Sch of Health Scis, 425 East 25th St, New York, NY 10010.

HOLMES, GARY MAYO
Business executive. **PERSONAL:** Born Feb 03, 1943, Atlanta, GA; married Margie Cannon; children: Candace Nicole. **EDUCATION:** Morris Brown Coll, BA 1969; Emory Univ Law Sch, 1970; GA State Univ, Atlanta Univ, further study. **CAREER:** Atlanta Legal Aid Soc, investigator 1968-69; Office of Economic Oppor, law intern 1970; General Learning Corp, VISTA trainer 1970-72, sr VISTA trainer 1972-73; Housing Auth of City of Atlanta, district mgr 1974-77, asst dir of housing mgmt 1977-78; State of GA Dept of Defense, training officer 1973-74; Cityof Atlanta, dir bureau of housing & physical develop 1978-85; Office of Econ Development, chief 1985-. **ORGANIZATIONS:** Designed & implemented first municipal tri-party participation prog in nation; reorganized Bureau of Housing & Physical Develop; developed innovative public/private partnership with sev lenders; negotiated largest single FNMA rehab loan in history of FNMA; spearheaded the implemen of a natl demonstration prog bythe Natl Assn of Real Estate Brokers Develop Co; chmn of bd Atlanta Jr Gold Adv Comm 1983-84; mem Natl Assoc of Housing & Redevelop Off 1978-; prog chmn Extra Point Club, Inc 1979-; mem Amer Soc for Public Admin 1982-; mem Conf of Minority Public Adminis 1982-; comm chmn Atlanta Alumni ChaptKappa Alpha Psi Frat Inc; mem Natl Housing Rehab Assn; mem US Comm on Civil Rights GA State Adv Comm; mem Amer Mgmt Assn; mem Natl Comm Develop Assn; mem US Conf of Mayors; mem Natl League of Cities; mem Natl Leased Housing Assn; mem McDaniel Glen Falcons Youth Football; mem NAACP; mem chmn Northside Atlanta Jaycees; vol coord United Way; mem comm Young Men's Christian Assn; mem Forum for Black Publ Administrators 1983. **HONORS/ACHIEVEMENTS:** Cited in Natl Assn of Housing & Redevelop Officials "Journal of Housing" 1981; cited in "Mortgage Banking" magazine 1982; cited in Bureau of Natl Affairs "Housing and Develop Reporter" 1983; recipient of three HUD Natl Merit Awds for Comm Develop Partnerships 1983; Outstanding Young Public Servant of the Yr Jaycees 1977-78; numerous civic and public serv awards. **MILITARY SERVICE:** USAF airman 3rd class 2 yrs. **HOME ADDRESS:** 3330 Cascade Rd, SW, Atlanta, GA 30311. **BUSINESS ADDRESS:** Office of Economic Development, 650 Omni Int South, Atlanta, GA 30335.

HOLMES, HAMILTON EARL
Orthopaedic surgeon. **PERSONAL:** Born Jul 08, 1941, Atlanta, GA; married Marilyn; children: Hamilton Jr, Alison. **EDUCATION:** Univ of GA, BS 1963; Emory Univ Sch of Medicine, MD 1967. **CAREER:** Emory Univ, asst clinical professor. **ORGANIZATIONS:** Bd of trustees Univ of GA. **HONORS/ACHIEVEMENTS:** Phi Beta Kappa 1963; Phi Kappa Phi 1963. **MILITARY SERVICE:** AUS major 3 1/2 yrs. **BUSINESS ADDRESS:** Asst Clinical Professor, Emory University, 730 Peachtree, Atlanta, GA 30308.

HOLMES, HENRY SIDNEY, III
Attorney. **PERSONAL:** Born Apr 10, 1944, New York, NY; married Albertha C Middleton; children: Monique Elizabeth. **EDUCATION:** Columbia Univ, BA 1976; Hofstra Univ Sch of Law, JD 1979. **CAREER:** Lever Bros Co, acct mgr 1969-72; Black Life Discount Stores, owner 1970-76; Mudge Rose Guthrie Alexander & Ferdon, assoc atty. **ORGANI-**

ZATIONS: Mem Amer Bar Assn 1979-; mem NY Bar Assn 1979-; mem 100 Black Men Inc 1983-; bd of dirs Natl Assn of Securities Professionals 1985-86. **MILITARY SERVICE:** AUS finance corps spec 5th class 1966-68. **BUSINESS ADDRESS:** Associate Attorney, Mudge Rose Guthrie Alexander, & Ferdon, 180 Maiden Lane, New York, NY 10038.

HOLMES, HERBERT
Physician. **PERSONAL:** Born Sep 17, 1932, New York, NY; married Carol (divorced); children: Gerald, Christope, Kathleen. **EDUCATION:** Royal Coll of Surgeons Dublin Ireland, MD 1958. **CAREER:** United Hospitals of Newark, attending surgeon; Beth Israel Hosp, assoc attending surgeon; Univ of Med & Dentristry of NJ, clinical assoc prof. **ORGANIZATIONS:** Mem NJ State Med Soc, NJ Acad of Med, NJ St Soc of NMA, Essex Co Med Soc, NJ Soc of Ob-Gyn, NJ St Med Soc; bd of trustees Univ of Med & Dentistry of NJ 1972-; 100 Black Men of NJ; Royal Soc of Health; Amer Coll of Ob-Gyn; UMDNJ. **BUSINESS ADDRESS:** 2130 Millburn Ave, Maplewood, NJ 07040.

HOLMES, LARRY
Professional boxer. **PERSONAL:** Born Nov 03, 1949, Cuthbert, GA; married Diane; children: Listy, Lisa. **CAREER:** Car wash, rock quarry, rug mill, foundry, worker; Muhammad Ali, sparring partner; constr co, janitorial svc, 400 room hotel, training ctr, "Round 1" bar & disco, sportswear store, owner; professional boxer retired. **HONORS/ACHIEVEMENTS:** Won World Boxing Council from Ken Norton 1978; Resigned his title to become champion of Intl Boxing Fed 1984; Undefeated record of 45 professional fights with 31 being won by knockouts; One of Ten Outstanding Men in Amer Jr C of C. **BUSINESS ADDRESS:** c/o Holmes Enterprises Inc, 704 Alpha Bldg, Easton, PA 18042.

HOLMES, LEO S.
City manager. **PERSONAL:** Born Aug 19, 1919, Philadelphia, PA; married Mildred Evans; children: Artelia H. **EDUCATION:** Cheyney State Coll, BA;Univ of PA & Temple U, addl study. **CAREER:** City of Chester, prsnl mgr, councilmn; Frederick Douglass Jr HS, math tchr & home sch vstr. **ORGANIZATIONS:** USPO Negro Rep Council of Delaware Co; Negro Rep State Council; DE Co Rep Exec Com; chmn DE Co Manpower Adv CounAm Leg Chester Br; bd dir YMCA; past pres Cheyney Alumni Assn; John A Watts Lodge #224 IBPOE; United Supreme Council AASR of FM PHA 33 deg. **MILITARY SERVICE:** USAC 1942-45. **BUSINESS ADDRESS:** City of Chester Municipal Bldg, 5 Welsh Sts, Chester, PA.

HOLMES, LORENE B.
Educator. **PERSONAL:** Born Jul 27, 1937, Mineola, TX; daughter of William H Barnes (deceased) and Jessie M Barnes (deceased); married Charles M Holmes Sr; children: Charles Jr, James Henry, Jessyca Yvette. **EDUCATION:** Jarvis Christian Coll, BS 1959; Univ North Texas, M Bus Ed 1966, EdD 1970. **CAREER:** Jarvis Christian Coll, chairperson soc & behav sc div of eight coll prog 1971-75, chairperson business admin dir int progs 1975-78, chairperson div of social sci & business 1978-81, chairperson div of bus admin 1981-. **ORGANIZATIONS:** Mem National Business Educ Assn 1964-; mem Texas Business Educ Assn 1972-; treasurer Hawkins Alumnae Chapter of Delta Sigma Theta Sorority 1983-; proposal reader United States Dept of Educ 1986, 1989; bd mem Hawkins Helping Hands 1987-; staff director Presidential Search Committee Jarvis Christian Coll 1987-88; mem bd of dir Greater Hawkins Chamber of Commerce 1987-; bd mem/sec Hawkins Public Library Board 1988-. **HONORS/ACHIEVEMENTS:** Top Lady of the Yr Top Ladies of Distinction Inc 1982, 1985; Woman of the Yr Hawkins C of C 1982; Certificates of Honor E TX Chap of Links Inc Longview & Tyler TX 1980 1984; publs (approx 15) Professional Journals 1969-84; Certificate of Appreciation Amer Business Women's Assn, Lake Country Charter Chapter 1984; T A Abbott Faculty Excellence in Teaching Award 1988; Texas Business Education Assn, Business Teacher of the Year 1988; Certificate of Appreciation, Shawnee State Univ 1988; Certificate of Appreciation The Univ of North Texas Fxecutive on Campus Program 1989; 6 chapters in yearbooks, 16 articles published, editorial reviewer for 2 textbooks. **HOME ADDRESS:** PO Drawer 858, Hawkins, TX 75765. **BUSINESS ADDRESS:** Chairperson Div of Bus Admin, Jarvis Christian Coll, PO Drawer G, Hwy 80, Hawkins, TX 75765.

HOLMES, LOUYCO W.
Educator. **PERSONAL:** Born Apr 24, 1924, Washington, DC; married Carleen Watts; children: Richard L. **EDUCATION:** Howard Univ, 1941-43; Rutgers Coll Pharmacy, BS 1946-50; NJ Coll of Med & Dentistry, DMD 1962-67. **CAREER:** Holmes Pharmacy, owner 1954-63; Gen Dental Practice, dentist 1967-; NJ Dental Sch, dental ed, Profof Clinical Operative Dentistry 1967-. **ORGANIZATIONS:** Mem 1956-63, pres 1958-59 NJ Pharm Assoc; vp/pres elect Commonwealth Dental Assn 1977-79, pres 1979-; chmn Budget Com 1977; Chi Delta Mu Frat; Nat Dental Assn; mem House of Dels 1974-77; chmn Credentials Com 1975; bd of trustees RL Garner Trust & Fund. **HONORS/ACHIEVEMENTS:** Fellow of the Acad of Gen Dentistry 1982-. **MILITARY SERVICE:** AUS sgt 1943-46. **BUSINESS ADDRESS:** Prof Clinical Oper Denistry, CNDNJ NJ Dental School, 100 Bergen St, Newark, NJ 07103.

HOLMES, MARION
Tax planning, research. **PERSONAL:** Born Dec 16, 1940, Dermott, AR; married Julia Ann A Skinner; children: Nicholas Matthew, Monica Skinner. **EDUCATION:** Univ of MO, BS 1962; St LouisUniv Grad Sch of Commerce & Finance; George WashUniv Nat Law Center. **CAREER:** Bausch & Lomb, corp dir of taxes; Cummins Eng Co Inc, dir tax plng & rsrch 1976-, dir taxes 1973-76; Ernst & Ernst CPA Firm, supr natl dept 1968-73;IRS, tax law splst 1965-68; IRS St Louis, inter rev agt 1962-65; MD & IN, CPA. **ORGANIZATIONS:** MD Assn of CPA'S; Tax Commn in Assn of CPA'S; Am Inst of CPAS Inc; Nat Assn of Blck Account Inc; natl pres & mem natl bd dir Tax Exec Inst natl bd dir pres vice pres treas chmn of Intl Taxation Com IN Chpt; Intl Tax Inst bd dir Five County Big Bros Big Sis Inc; bd dir treas Driftwood Valley Arts Counc; mem Project Review Com for Compreh Hlth Plng Counc Inc Region Xi; bd dir treas Found for Youth; Pres of OH Valley Com onSelf Devel of People; mem ruling elder 1st United Pres Ch; Kappa Alpha Psi Frat; life mem Bloomington Alumni. **HONORS/ACHIEVEMENTS:** Recip IRS Sup Performance Awd, Cert of Apprec; Men of Achvmt. **BUSINESS ADDRESS:** Corporate Dir of Taxes, Bausch & Lomb, 42 East Ave, PO Box 743, Rochester, NY 14603.

HOLMES, MARY BROWN
Labor, industrial relations manager. **PERSONAL:** Born Oct 20, 1950, Charleston, SC; daughter of Rufus Brown and Vernell P Brown; married William Holmes; children: Hosea L Banks, Joya N. **EDUCATION:** Johnson C Smith Univ, BA 1971; Webster Coll, MA 1976. **CAREER:** Sea Island Comp Health, med social worker 1974-79; Trident Tech Coll, instructor 1980-82; Telamon Corp, deputy dir; South Carolina Dept of Corrections, admin judge, 1987-. **ORGANIZATIONS:** Elder St Paul Presby Church; mem Sea Island Comp Health 1973-74; mem Ocean Queen OES 1975; treas Charleston EOC Comm 1980; chair Natl Black Social Worker Org 1974-; mem SC School Bd Assn 1975-; chairperson St Paul Sch Bd 1975-. **HONORS/ACHIEVEMENTS:** Notary of SC 1976-86; Outstanding Young Women of America 1978. **HOME ADDRESS:** PO Box 237, Hollywood, SC 29449. **BUSINESS ADDRESS:** Administrative Judge, South Carolina Dept of Corrections, Lieber Correctional Institution, P O Box 208, Ridgeville, SC 29472.

HOLMES, ROBERT A.
Educator, state representative, real estate broker. **PERSONAL:** Born Jul 13, 1943, Shepherdstown, WV; son of Clarence Holmes and Priscilla Holmes; divorced; children: Donna Lee Vaughn, Darlene Marie Boyce, Robert A Jr. **EDUCATION:** Shepherd Coll 1964; Columbia Univ, MA 1966, PhD 1969. **CAREER:** Columbia Univ, instructor 1968; Harvard-Yale-Columbia Summer Studies Program, dir 1968-69; Southern Univ, assoc prof 1969-70; City Univ of New York-Bernard Baruch Coll, dir of SEEK 1970-71; Atlanta Univ, prof; Georgia House of Representatives 1975-; chmn Governmental Affairs Comm; real estate broker, Unique Realty Co, 1987-. **ORGANIZATIONS:** Adj fellow Joint Center for Polit Studies 1982-; pres Natl Conf of Black Political Educators 1973-74; pres Assn of Soc and Behavioral Scientists 1976-77; chmn/bd dir YMCA Southwest Atlanta 1976-78; pres/bd dir Rsch Atlanta 1978-79; pres Adams Park Residents Assn 1972-73. **HONORS/ACHIEVEMENTS:** Outstanding Young Man of the Year Atlanta Jaycees 1975; Outstanding Legislator's Award Amer Assn of Adult Educators 1978; Alumnus of the Year Shepherd Coll 1978; author/co-author of 13 monographs and books and 30 articles; Georgia Municipal Assn Legislative Serv Award 1989; Metropolitian Atlanta YMCA Layperson of the Year Award 1989. **BUSINESS ADDRESS:** Professor of Political Science, Atlanta University, 223 James P Brawley Dr, Atlanta, GA 30314.

HOLMES, ROBERT C.
Commissioner, attorney. **PERSONAL:** Born Mar 20, 1945, Elizabeth, NJ; divorced; children: 1. **EDUCATION:** Cornell U, AB 1967; Harvard Law Sch, JD 1971. **CAREER:** Roxbury, cir asso 1969-71; St of NJ, atty 1971; Newark Housing Devel & Rehab Corp Newark, exec dir 1971-74; NJ St Dep Comm Affairs, asst commr atty present. **ORGANIZATIONS:** NJ Bar Assn; Nat Bar Assn; Am Soc for Pub Adm; Garden St Bar Assn; NAHRO. **HONORS/ACHIEVEMENTS:** Nat hon soc Cornell U; Deans List; 4 yr Teagle Found Scholar; Sr Men's Hon Soc MA NG.

HOLMES, ROBERT ERNEST
Attorney. **PERSONAL:** Born Jul 24, 1943, NYC. **EDUCATION:** NY U, BA 1966; NY Univ Sch of Law, JD 1969; Manhattan Sch Of Music & Univ of So CA, addl study. **CAREER:** Paul Weiss Rifkind Wharton & Garrison, summer assoc 1968, part time atty 1968-69, assoc atty 1969-71; WA Sq Coll of Arts & Sci, guest lectr 1969-70, adj instr Amer Lit 1970-71; NY School of Continuing Educ, adj instr Black Amer 1969-70; Motown Record Corp, sr counsel 1971, legal counsel 1971; Columbia Pictures Music Group, sr vp, gen mgr, pres Columbia Pictures Music Publ Div. **ORGANIZATIONS:** Bd dir Pacific Psychotherapy Asso CA; bd dir NAACP; bd dir Constl Rights Found CA; bd dir Black Music Assoc; past pres Black Entertainment & Sports Lawyers' Assoc. **HONORS/ACHIEVEMENTS:** Dean's List TempleUniv & NYUniv Sch of Law; Univ Schlrshp NY U, NY State Schlrshp NY U; Leopold Schepp Fnd Schlrshp NY U; various debate & pub spkng awrds; Am Jurisprudence Prize in Copyright; Military History Award TempleUniv 1963; recipient Fulbright-Dougherty Travel Grant 1967; Samuel Rubin SchlrshpCarnegie Fnd Schlrshp; author of numerous publs. **BUSINESS ADDRESS:** Sr VP, Gen Manager, Pres, Columbia Pictures Music Publ, Columbia Plaza East, Room 231, Burbank, CA 91505.

HOLMES, ROBERT L., JR.
Composer. **PERSONAL:** Born Mar 29, 1934, Greenville, MS; married Lois E Mason; children: Ronda Lang, Reba Lynn. **EDUCATION:** TN State U, BS 1956, MA 1970. **CAREER:** Pub mgr composer, arranger 1961; Moss Rose Pub, 1963; Tuneville Mus, 1964; Nashboro Record Co, artist repertoire dir 1967; Night Train, dir & arranger 1965; Multimedia DivUniv of CA, consult 1973; TV Peace Corps, composer producer radio 1971-73. **ORGANIZATIONS:** Many adv panels. **HONORS/ACHIEVEMENTS:** Who's Who Musicians & Personalties S 1974; many schlrshps & grants. **MILITARY SERVICE:** AUS 6th army band. **BUSINESS ADDRESS:** Thompson House, FiskUniv, Nashville, TN.

HOLMES, THEODORE NEAL
Chief exec. officer/retail. **PERSONAL:** Born Jan 16, 1939, York, PA; divorced; children: Crystal, Fern, Falica, Kim. **EDUCATION:** San Diego City College, 1958-59; York City College, 1960-62. **CAREER:** McCory Corp, inventory control mgr 1965-67; Chassis System, personnel officer 1967-69; Joioj Industries, president 1979-86; Chicken George Chicken, Inc, president; APS Inc, pres 1969-. **ORGANIZATIONS:** Natl Food Tech Assn 1969-; Natl Restaurant Assn 1974-; Black Businessmen's Assn 1975-. **HONORS/ACHIEVEMENTS:** Businessman of the Year HUB Organization (Baltimore) 1981. **BUSINESS ADDRESS:** President, APS Inc, 2 East Fayette St, Baltimore, MD 21202.

HOLMES, WENDELL P., JR.
Mortician. **PERSONAL:** Born Feb 10, 1922, Brunswick, GA; married Vivian Altamese Broome; children: Wendell P Holmes III, Carolyn Holmes Nesmith. **EDUCATION:** Hampton Inst, Pres of Class BS 1943; Eckels Coll of Mortuary Science, Pres of class Mortuary Science 1947. **CAREER:** Duval County Sch Bd, chmn 1980-84; Holmes & West Funrl Hm PA, pres 1956-. **ORGANIZATIONS:** Past chrmn Duval Cnty Schl Bd 1969-, Century Natl Bank 1976-85; pres Heritage of Jacksonville, Inc 1984-; 1st vice chrmn bd of trustees Bethune Cookman Coll; 2nd vice chrmn Hampton Bd of Trustees; mem Steering Comm Council of Urban Bds of Educ NSBA. **HONORS/ACHIEVEMENTS:** Honoray Dr of Laws Degree Bethune-Cookman 1982; Small Bsnsmn of the Yr Jacksonville Area-Chamber of Comm; Meritorious Srvc in Area of Human Rel Alpha PhiAlpha Frat; Silver Bell Awrd For Significant Contrib to Educ Duval Cnty Clsrm Tchrs Assn. **MILITARY SERVICE:** AUS 1st lt GMC 3 1/2 yrs. **HOME ADDRESS:** 4022 Gillislee Dr, Jacksonville, FL 32209. **BUSI-**

NESS ADDRESS: Funeral Dir, Holmes & West Funeral Home, 2719 W Edgewood Ave, Jacksonville, FL 32209.

HOLMES, WILLIAM
Systems programmer. **PERSONAL:** Born Aug 19, 1940, Allendale, SC; married Diane T; children: Renada Irene, Eva Regina. **EDUCATION:** VoorHees Coll, BS Math (summa cum laude) 1973. **CAREER:** USAF, legal specialist 1961-69; DuPont, sr engr. **ORGANIZATIONS:** Sec SC Conf of Black Mayors; mem NAACP; coach Little League Baseball; mayor (elected) City of Allendale 1976-88; mem Allendale County Industrial Development Bd. **HONORS/ACHIEVEMENTS:** Who's Who Among Students in Amer Univs VoorHees Coll 1972; Alpha Chi Hon Soc Beta Chap VoorHees Coll 1972; Outstanding Young Men of Amer 1974. **MILITARY SERVICE:** USAF staff sgt 1961-69; Commendation Medal. **BUSINESS ADDRESS:** Engineer, Dupont Savannah River Plant, Bldg 707-CRoom 355, Aiken, SC 29801.

HOLMES, WILLIAM B.
Probation officer. **PERSONAL:** Born Jan 31, 1937, Trenton, NJ; married Helen Vereen; children: Mark Wm, Allen C. **EDUCATION:** VA Union U, BA 1959; Rutgers U, Grad Study. **CAREER:** E Dist of PA, US prbtn ofcr 1975-; State of NJ, parole ofcr 1966-75; Fed Job Corp, grp ldr 1966; State of NJ Div of Mntl Retardation, soc wrkr 1963-66; Mercer Co Welfare Bd, soc case wrkr 1962-63; Dept of Pub Welfare, soc case worker 1961-62; Fed Probation Ofcrs Assn, tchr 1960-61. **ORGANIZATIONS:** Past pres, vice pres Bd of Educ Lawrence Twnshp 1969-; bd dir Lawrence YMCA 1968-; mem past chmn Mercer Co Comm Coll EOF 1972-; exec bd NAACP Trenton; life mem past polemarch Kappa Alpha Psi Frat 1970-71. **HONORS/ACHIEVEMENTS:** Pioneer Awrd for Achvmt, polemarch awrd Kappa Alpha Psi Frat; serv awrd BSA; cert of recog Lawrence Twnshp Recreation Commn; cert of recog Lawrence Twnshp Non-Profit Hsng; Achvmt Award for Disting Serv Kappa Alpha Frat; Achvmt Awrd NAACP; Recog Award for Outst serv Lawrence Twnshp. **MILITARY SERVICE:** AUSR e-5 1960-66. **BUSINESS ADDRESS:** 601 Market St, Philadelphia, PA 19106.

HOLMES, WILLIE A.
Sales manager. **PERSONAL:** Born Jul 25, 1928, Warwick, VA; married Addie Smith; children: Audrey, Yolanda, Wendell. **EDUCATION:** Quinn Coll, BS 1961. **CAREER:** Equit Life, dist sls mgr 1970-, asst dist mgr 1969, agent 1968-69; Litton Med Prod, slsmn 1955-68. **ORGANIZATIONS:** Mem Natl Assn Life Undrwrtrs 1968-; Career Sales Club 1974-; apptd mem CT Devel Auth 1976; Grtr N Haven Bus & Prof Assn; vice pres Bus Vent Inc; dir Urbn Leag NAACP; mem Alpha Phi Alpha 1957; Quinn Coll Alum Assn; Imm Bapt Ch. **HONORS/ACHIEVEMENTS:** Prof First & only black mem apptd to CT Devel Auth; Man of Yr Alph Phi Alpha 1965; Awards NCA. **MILITARY SERVICE:** AUS stf sgt 1952-54. **BUSINESS ADDRESS:** 55 Church St, New Haven, CT 06508.

HOLMES, ZAN W., JR.
Educator. **PERSONAL:** Born in San Angelo, TX; married Dorothy Burse. **EDUCATION:** Huston-Tillotson Coll, BA 1956; U, BD 1959; So Meth U, STM 1968. **CAREER:** Perkins School of Theology Southern Methodist Univ, assoc prof Pract Theol assoc dir Intrn Program; St Luke Comm United Methodist Church, pastor; Dist 33 TX, state rep 1968-72; Hamilton Park United Methodist Church, pastor 1958-68. **ORGANIZATIONS:** Asst dir Dallas War on Poverty; Goals for Dallas Conf; pres Dallas Pastors Assn; dist supr The United Meth Ch; mem bd trustees So Meth Ch; mem Gtr Dallas Comm Rel Commn; apptd mem TX Constl Revision Commn Gov of TX; chmn Council of Professional Ministries; mem Dallas Assembly; mem past chmn Tri-Ethnic Com; dir Urban Affairs Ctr; mem bd dir Dallas Alliance; Dallas Urban League; Dallas Black C of C; Dallas Day Care Assn; Dallas Pastoral Counseling & Educ Ctr; John F Kennedy Br NAACP; Pub Communication Fnd for N TX; N Part Nat Bank; life mem NAACP; mem Alpha Phi Alpha Frat. **HONORS/ACHIEVEMENTS:** Father John LaForge Awrd The Cath Interracial Council 1971; WFAA-TV Awrd; outstndng contrib in fld of Govt 1971; Man of Yr Awd Com of 100 Dallas BlackC of C 1975; num other awds & cit.

HOLSENDOLPH, ERNEST
Reporter. **PERSONAL:** Born Oct 31, 1935, Quitman, GA. **EDUCATION:** Columbia Coll, BA 1958. **CAREER:** Cleveland Press, reporter 1961-65; E Ohio Gas Co, editor 1965-67; Washington Star, reporter 1967-69; Fortune Magazine, assoc editor 1969-71; NY Times, reporter 1972-. **ORGANIZATIONS:** Mem bd dirs Alumni Assn Columbia Coll. **MILITARY SERVICE:** AUS. **BUSINESS ADDRESS:** NY Times Washington Bureau, 1000 Connecticut Ave NW, Washington, DC 20008.

HOLSEY, LILLA G.
Educator. **PERSONAL:** Born Aug 26, 1941, San Mateo, FL; children: Linita "Reesie". **EDUCATION:** Hampton Inst VA, BS 1963; FL State U, Ms 1971, PhD 1974. **CAREER:** E Carolina Univ, assoc prof Home Economics 1974-; FL State Univ, graduate rsch asst 1971, 1973; Gainesville High School, Home Economics teacher 1970-72; Lincoln High School, 1964-70. **ORGANIZATIONS:** Mem Natl & Am Home Ec Assns; Am & Vocational Assn; NC Consumer Assn; Bethel AME Ch; bd trustees Alpha Kappa Alpha; Kappa Delta Pi & Omicron Nu hon soc; mem Phi Kappa Delta. **HONORS/ACHIEVEMENTS:** Ford Fndtn Flwshp 1973-74; Outstndng Young Women Am 1974; Danforth asso 1977; charter mem Putnam Co Educ Hall of Fame Palatha FL. **BUSINESS ADDRESS:** Associate Professor, East Carolina University, School of Education, Greenville, NC 27834.

HOLSEY, WILLIAM FLEMING, JR.
Surgeon. **PERSONAL:** Born Apr 18, 1923, New York, NY; son of William F Holsey Sr and Lurine Holsey; married Joyce Chambers; children: Denise, Dorine, William III. **EDUCATION:** NY City Coll, BS 1943; Howard Univ, MD 1946. **CAREER:** Private Practice, surgeon. **ORGANIZATIONS:** Chief of surgery St Mary's Hosp Tucson 1976-77; mem Tucson Metropolitan Energy Commn 1983-86; bd of dir Pima County Medical Soc; vice pres St Mary's Hosp Tucson. **HONORS/ACHIEVEMENTS:** Fellow Amer College of Surgeons; Certified, American Board of Surgery. **MILITARY SERVICE:** USAF capt 1952-54. **BUSINESS ADDRESS:** Surgeon, 1601 N Tucson Blvd, Tucson, AZ 85716.

HOLT, ALINE G.
Administrative manager. **PERSONAL:** Born Apr 02, 1942, Dallas, TX; married Richard Holt (deceased). **EDUCATION:** LA City College, attended 1942. **CAREER:** City of LA, property mgmt dir 1962-72; Crenshaw Neighbors Inc LA, exec dir 1972-74; LA City Council Councilwoman Pat Russell's 6th Dist, comm serv aging specialist; LA City Comm Develop Dept, rent stabilization div 1979-84; retired. **ORGANIZATIONS:** Pres 1981-82, treas/secty 1978-81,past pres 1973-89, Los Angeles County Commission on Aging; mem PTA; pres Life Mem LA 1950-69; Girl Scouts of Amer & Boy Scouts of Amer leader & den mother 1958-60;1st vice pres & parlimentarian Crenshaw C of C Women's Div 1973-74; budget com spec United Way Western Region LA 1975; pres bd dir Crenshaw Consortium LA 1973-74; pres Les Bienfaisontes Charity & Social Club 1970-89; elected Women's Assn Rsch & Educ Assn mem 1974-75; mem Natl Caucus on the Black Aged Inc 1976-77; Natl Assn Bus & Professional Women of Amer 1975; Toastmasters of America, Los Angeles Chapter 1988-89. **HONORS/ACHIEVEMENTS:** CA Legislature Assembly Concurrent Resolution; Women's Recognition & Equality Day in CA to Aline Holt 1973; Woman of Yr for Outstanding Serv to Crenshaw Comm Crenshaw Chamber of Commerce 1974.

HOLT, DELORIS LENETTE
Educator, author. **PERSONAL:** Born in East Chicago, IN; daughter of Willis Adams and Pearl Adams; married Chester A Holt. **EDUCATION:** Ball State Univ, BS Educ 1956; UCLA Pepperdine Univ, CA Credential 1969; Univ of San Francisco, MD Educ 1978. **CAREER:** LA City Schs, parent involvement coordinator; Cleveland Public Schools, teacher; LA City Schs, advisor proj Follow Through; LA Unified Sch Dist, tchr/author. **ORGANIZATIONS:** Mem Alpha Kappa Alpha. **HONORS/ACHIEVEMENTS:** Author bks published by Ward Ritchie Press 1971, Childrens Press 1973, LA City Unified School Dist 1974; Merit Awd CA Assn Tchrs of Eng 1973; published Black Hist Playing Card Deck US Games Systems Inc 1978; Resolution of Commndtn LA City Cncl 1972. **BUSINESS ADDRESS:** Teacher/Author, Los Angeles Unified Sch Dist, 419 W 98th St, Los Angeles, CA 90003.

HOLT, DONALD H.
Business executive. **PERSONAL:** Born Jan 22, 1941, Cleveland, OH; married Dianne Williford. **EDUCATION:** J Carroll U, BS, BA 1964; Case Wstrn Res U, MBA 1971;Univ Akron, JD 1976. **CAREER:** Prmr Indus Corp, asst vice pres for corp prsnl admin; E OH Gas Co, asst to pres 1969-, spec asst to pres 1968-69, cst anlyst 1967-68. **ORGANIZATIONS:** Tst Urban Leag of Grtr Clvlnd; City Club of Clvlnd; Untd Way Serv; Rtry Club of Clvlnd; Blcks in Mgmt; NAACP; Alpha Phi Alpha; Nat Urban Afrs Cncl; OH St Bar Assn. **HONORS/ACHIEVEMENTS:** Ldrshp Clvlnd Class of 1979-80; Alpha Kappa Psi Men of Achie 1977; 10 Outst Yng Men Jcs 1973; Who's Who Amng Blck Ams; Who's Who Blck OH 1970; Outst Yng Men of Am 1974. **MILITARY SERVICE:** AUS 1st lt.

HOLT, DOROTHY L
Educator administrator. **PERSONAL:** Born Nov 11, 1930, Shreveport, LA; married James S Holt, III; children: James IV, Jonathan Lamar, Roderick Lenard. **EDUCATION:** Wiley Coll Marshall TX, BS 1962; LA Tech Univ Ruston MS, 1973; Nrthwstrn St Univ, 1973-75; E TX St Univ Commerce, TX, EdD 1978. **CAREER:** Caddo Parish Educ Sec Assoc, pres & fndr 1954-62; Caddo Teachers Assoc, sec 1973-74; League of Women Voters of Shreveport, treas 1979-82, 1st vice pres 1982-83; LA Distributive Educ Assoc, treas 1979-80, pres 1980-81; Central High Alumni Assoc, treas 1980-85; Natl Assoc Adv of Black Amer, sec & bd mem 1983-85; Caddo Assn Educators, 2nd vice pres 1984-85; LA Assoc of Dist Educ Teachers Awards Comm, chairperson 1984-85; Caddo Parish School System, coord. **ORGANIZATIONS:** Chrmn Alpha Kappa Alpha Sor Smnrs 1983-85; 2nd vice pres Caddo Assn of Eductrs 1984-85; mem Phi Delta Kappa, Kappa Delta Pi, Natl Assoc of DE Tchrs, Amer Voc Ed Assoc, LA Assoc of DE Tchrs NEA, YMCA, YWCA; brd of trustees MDEA/AV Dist Ed Professional Devel Awrd; chrmn Caddo Parish Textbook Comm for Dist Educ Teachers; planner & presenter CPSB Professional Improvement In-Service Pgm; pres Ave BC Jr Mission; mem Allendale Branch YWCA Bd of Mgnt, Caddo Parish Teachers Fed Union, Ed Comm Ave Bapt Church Fed Credit Union; pres, Allendale Branch YWCA 1988-90. **HONORS/ACHIEVEMENTS:** Outstanding Leadership Awards Natl DE 1983: Ave BC Educational Award, 1984; Booker T Washington High School Student Council Award; Appreciation Award, Muscular Dystrophy, HS chmn; Educator of the Year, Finalist; Outstanding coordinator & Fellowship Award, Leadership Devel, USOE; LA Vocational Assn, Teacher of the Year Award; published articles Journal of Bisiness Educ & Business Educ Forum Mags; DECA Award; Shreveport Times Educator of the Year Award 1986; Outstanding Leadership Award Huntington HS; Southern Assoc Accreditation Chrprsn 1987. **HOME ADDRESS:** 306 Holcomb Dr, Shreveport, LA 71103. **BUSINESS ADDRESS:** Coord, Caddo Parish Schl Systm, 6801 Rasberry Ln, Shreveport, LA 71129.

HOLT, EDWIN J.
Educator. **PERSONAL:** Born in Shreveport, LA; son of James S Holt and Sammie L Holt; married Dr Essie W; children: Lisa Michele, Rachelle Justine. **EDUCATION:** Central St Univ, BA 1958; IN Univ, MS 1962; Univ of AR, EdD 1971; Univ of TN, Postdoctoral Study 1977. **CAREER:** Caddo Parish Sch Bd, classroom tchr 1959-67, guidance cnslr 1967-68, sch asst prin 1968-71, sch prin 1971-74, instr dir 1974-80, asst Supt 1980-. **ORGANIZATIONS:** Univ adj prof LSU-br Univ 1972, LA Tech Univ 1973-75, Northeast LA Univ 1973-75, Northeast LA Univ 1973, So Univ 1976-79, Grambling St Univ 1980-84; founder and co-chmn "H" Enterprises 1980-81; bd of dir Rutherford House 1980-84; dir of summer youth work study pgm Trinity Baptist Church 1980-; co-dir of Afro Am Hist Actvts Trinity Baptist Church 1980-; pres LA Alpha Phi Alpha Frat 1981-83; Shreveport Clean Comm Cmmn 1981-; bd of mgmt Caddo Dist PTA; 1981-; bd of dir Norwela Council BSA 1981-; appeal bd mem Selective Serv System 1981-; bd of dir Council of Aging 1982-84; bd of mgmt Carver Br YMCA 1982-; Shreveport Proj Sel Sufficiency Task Force 1984-; prof mem NEA, LEA, CAE, Phi Delta Kappa, Caddo Jt Adm Org; bd dir Youth Involvement Prog 1986-. **HONORS/ACHIEVEMENTS:** Southern Fellowship Fund Univ of AR 1970-71; NDEA Fellow State Coll of AR 1968; John Hay Fellow Williams Coll 1964; Caddo Parish Educ of Year 1966; Alpha Phi Alpha Fraternity Man of Year 1972. **BUSINESS ADDRESS:** Asst Supt Comm Srv/Info and Business Services, Caddo Parish Sch Bd, PO Box 32000, Shreveport, LA 71130.

HOLT, ESSIE W.
Educator. **PERSONAL:** Born in Sicily Island, LA; married Dr Edwin J Holt; children: Lisa Michelle, Rachelle Justine. **EDUCATION:** Grambling St Univ, BS 1965;Univ of Ar, MEd 1970;Univ of AR, Ed Spclst 1972;Univ of TN, EdD 1978. **CAREER:** Caddo Parish School Bd, classroom teacher 1965-71, guidance counselor 1971-78, LSU-Shreveport guest

lecturer 1973-76 1980; Caddo Parish School Bd, psychologist 1978-79, elementary prin 1979-85; elementary instructional supvr 1985-. **ORGANIZATIONS:** Co-fndr & co-chm "H" Enterprises 1980-81; APGA Conv 1980; prog prsntr on "The Magnet School Approach" Natl Elem Sch Prins Conv 1984; pres Alpha Kappa Alpha Delta Lambda Omega Chapter 1984-85; adjunct prof 1985; State PTA Conv 1985; NEA; LEA; CAE; NAESP; PTA; bd of dir United Way, Rutherford House, Juvenile Justice Prog Caddo-Bossier Day Care Asso Volunteer Sicke Cell Anemia Dr, Arthritis & Heart Foundation Drives. **HONORS/ACHIEVEMENTS:** Who's Who in S and SW 1980-85; Zeta Phi Beta Educator Awd 1981; Leadership Shreveport Grad 1983; CAE Educator of Yr awd 1985; LA Gov Comm For Women 1984-85; life mbrshp PTA recipient 1985. **HOME ADDRESS:** 208 Plano St, Shreveport, LA 71103. **BUSINESS ADDRESS:** Principal, Caddo Parish School Board, 1961 Midway, Shreveport, LA 71130.

HOLT, FRED D
Business executive. **PERSONAL:** Born Feb 07, 1931, Macon, GA; married Nancy Smith; children: Larry, Kenny, Tim, Tony, Clevetta Rogers. **EDUCATION:** Hartnell Coll, AA Human Sv 1980; Chapaman Coll, BA Sociology 1982; Goldengate Univ, 1983. **CAREER:** Salinas City Council candidate 1979-83; Salinas City Affirm Active Action Bd chp 1980-82; Sal Rent Mediation Bd mem 1981-83; St James CME Church Steward Bd chm 1983; Salinas NAACP mbrshp chm 1983-85; Holts Record Co v pres. **ORGANIZATIONS:** Sr deacon Fremont Masonic Lodge No 13 1958-82; mem Sal Chamber of Commerce 1972-83; owner M & H Restaurant 1973-76; pres Salinas NAACP 1974-75; owner NadonEnterprize 1981-85; life member NAACP 1984; KRS Omega Psi Phi Omicron Nu 1984-85. **HONORS/ACHIEVEMENTS:** Thalheimer Awd Class I NAACP 1975-76; Man Of The Year Awd NAACP 1979; Achievement Awd NAACP 1984. **MILITARY SERVICE:** AUS E-7 1st Sgt 26 yrs; 1951 Good Conduct Army Commendation; 1972 Meritorious Awd; 1973 Bronze Star. **HOME ADDRESS:** 1433 Shawnee Wy, Salinas, CA 93706.

HOLT, GRACE S.
Educational administrator. **PERSONAL:** Born Jun 28, 1922, Union, SC; divorced; children: Colette. **EDUCATION:** Spelman Coll, BA (Summa Cum Laude) 1942; Univ of Chicago, Cert in Teaching 1952-53; Univ of Chicago, Reading & Language Arts 1955; Northeastern IL Univ,MA 1969. **CAREER:** Chicago Schools, teacher 1949-67; Chicago Bd of Educ Dept of Curriculum, lang devel corps consultant 1965-67; Woodlawn Exp Schools Proj Chicago, master teacher 1966-68; Univ of IL at Chicago NDEA Inst Adv Grammar, instr summer 1968; Center for Inner City Studies Chicago, instr 1968-69; Chicago Consortium of Coll & Univ Urban Teacher Corps, instr summer 1969; Univ of IL at Chicago, assoc prof speach com 1969; Ford Found, language research fellow 1970-72; Univ of IL at Chicago, Black Studies coordinator 1971, prof speech com 1973, prof Black Study 1974, dir Black Study 1974; New City Devel Corp, program developer 1981-82; Univ of IL at Chicago, acting dir Black Study 1983-. **ORGANIZATIONS:** Delegate White House Conf on Children 1970; ed bd The Jrnl of Afro-Amer Issues 1975-77; mem Constitutional Conf the Natl Cncl for Black Studies 1976-77; discussant Dialogue of Ctr for Study of Dem Inst Chicago 1976-78; ed adv First World 1976-81; chair Ed Task Force Ntl Cncl Negro Women 1977; mem PresAssemb on St Policy Rsch atUniv of IL 1978; consult Cmnwlth Ed Div of Ind Rel 1980-81; mem Reg I Adv Cncl for Frgn Lang & Intl Stds Il St Bd of Ed 1980-81; trustee Elam Manision 1980; scrng brd IL Humanities Cncl 1980-81; ethnic ldr panel Heritage News Serv 1981; Blk Wmns wrkshp Org of Amer Hist &Assoc of Blk Wmn Hist 1981-82; mem CCCC Com on advis of Lang Stmt for 1980's & 1990's NCTE 1982-83; mem Wmns Netwk for Wash-Chicago 1982-83; conv Coll Stdnt for Harold Washington 1983; fndg conv Cmty Liaison & Neg Comm, bd of dir, wmns comm, 1992 Chicago World Fair 1983-84; edit adv bd TESOL Qtrly1983-; bd of dir K Dunham Retrospective 1983-; mem exec com, chrprsn, educ & rsch comm, Blk Womens History PurdueUniv 1984; mem mil acad adv comm First Cong Dist Chicago 1984. **HONORS/ACHIEVEMENTS:** Fellowship in Linguistics Northeastern IL Univ 1966-68; Outstanding Ed of the Year 1972; Patron's Choice Awd IL Arts Week The Cultural Ctr Chicago Public Library 1980; Awd for Excellence Council for Coll Attendance Natl Scholarship Serv for Negro Students 1981; Outstanding Contribs to the Psychological Welfare of of Afro-Amer Awd Black Students Psych Assoc Chicago State Univ 1981; Summer Scholarship the Program in Black Amer Culture & Scholarship Smithsonian Inst 1983; Invited Scholar Conf in the Study & Teaching of Afro-Amer History Amer Assoc Purdue Univ 1983; Awd for Professional Contrib in Community Political Action Women's Task Force 1st Congressional Dist Chicago 1984. **HOME ADDRESS:** 1226 East Madison Park, Chicago, IL 60615. **BUSINESS ADDRESS:** Prof Communications/Blk Stds, Univ of Illinois at Chicago, Black Studies Program, Box 4348 (m/c 069), Chicago, IL 60680.

HOLT, JAMES STOKES, III
Educator. **PERSONAL:** Born Sep 23, 1927, Shreveport, LA; son of James Holt and Sammie Lee Holt; married Dr Dorothy L Thomas; children: James IV, Jonathan Lamar, Roderick Lenard. **EDUCATION:** Central State Univ, BS 1949; LA State Univ, MEd 1956; Univ of AR, EdD 1973; Lincoln Graduate Center, San Antoine Texas, MSA (Master Senior Appraiser) 1989. **CAREER:** Caddo Parish Sch Bd, math bio chem inst 1950-66; Teacher Organ, pres caddo educ assn 1960-62; LA Educ Assn, pres 4th dist 1963; State Dept of LA, council mem state drug abuse 1972-74; Graduate School S Univ, faculty mem & advisor 1972-79; Southern Univ, div chmn 1972-79; HHH Real Estate Investments Co Co, pres 1981-89; MRA Natl Assn of Master Appraisers 1982-87; SU CAI Rsch Program, selected participant 1984-85; Southern Univ, prof of biology; Holt Real Estate Appraisal Co, Shreveport, owner 1987-90; Ruben Real Estate Co, Shreveport, LA, salesman, 1989. **ORGANIZATIONS:** Alpha Phi Alpha Frat 1947-89; Beta Kappa Chi Hon Soc 1948-89; LEA life mem teacher organ 1955-89; NEA life mem teacher organ 1960-89; Supt Sunday School Ave Baptist Church 1969-89; 3rd Degree Mason AF & AM 1970-89; sec Shreveport Metro Bd of Appeals 1975-89; pres Lakeside Acres Civic Assn 1968-89; mem YMCA, NAACP, LA Council on Human Rights; co-chmn Biology Scholarship Awd Comm 1989; mem 20 yr Celebration Steering Comm for SU-Shreveport; mem, LA Home Managers Assn 1987-90; mem, Natl Organization of Black County Officials (NOBCO) 1988-89; Mem Shreveport Black Chamber of Commerce 1988-90. **HONORS/ACHIEVEMENTS:** Assn of Classroom Teachers Awd by the Caddo Educ Assn 1962; Educator of the Year chosen by Shreveport Times newspaper 1962; FL State Univ Radiation Biology Awd 1963; Southern Fellowship in Higher Educ Awd Univ of AR 1972-74; LEA Fourth Distinguished Achievement Awd by LEA 1974; Boy Scout Training Dir Pioneer Div of Norwela Honors Awards 1975; State Council mem LA Conf of Colleges & Univs 1975; recipient of Scout Leaders Regional Tr Cert & Scoutmasters key; Natl Science Fellowship Biology Student, TSU 1958, Dillard Univ 1962; Phi Delta Kappa, University of Arkansas, 1971; Academic Year Grant, National Science Foundation, 1960; graduate of Bakers Professional Real Estate College 1979; Licensed Real Estate Salesman, LA Real Estate Commissio n, 1980. **HOME ADDRESS:** 306 Holcomb Drive, Shreveport, LA 71103.

HOLT, JOHN J.
Government official. **PERSONAL:** Born May 07, 1931, Richmond, VA; married Andrea; children: Gwen, Greg, John, Keth, Derek, Brandon. **EDUCATION:** VA Union Univ, BS 1961. **CAREER:** USAF, communications specialist 1952-56; Univ of MD, lab scientist 1963-69, personnel mgr 1969-74; MD Port Admin, human resource mgr 1974-. **ORGANIZATIONS:** Pres IPMA 1980-81; vice pres MAAAO 1985-87; mem Johns Hopkins Univ Metro Planning & Rsch Comm 1982-; bd dir United Way of Central MD 1985-87; chmn alloc United Way Comm Serv 1985; mem Venture Grant Comm (UWCS) 1984-. **HONORS/ACHIEVEMENTS:** Governor's Citation for Outstanding Serv Balt, MD 1981; Furture Business Leaders of Amer Balt 1979; Dr Richard H Hunt Scholarship Award Comm Serv MD Assn Affirmative Action Ofcrs 1981. **MILITARY SERVICE:** USAF Sgt served 4 yrs; Natl Defense Serv Medal; Good Conduct Medal. **BUSINESS ADDRESS:** Manager of Human Resources, Maryland Port Administration, 401 E Pratt St, Baltimore, MD 21202.

HOLT, LEO E.
Judge. **PERSONAL:** Born Jul 02, 1927, Chicago; married Dorothy Considine; children: Pamela, Paula. **EDUCATION:** John Marshall Law Sch, LLB 1959; Pvt Pract, law 1959. **CAREER:** Mem Cook Co Bar Assn; mem Kappa Alpha Psi Frat; Circuit Court of Cook County, judge. **HONORS/ACHIEVEMENTS:** Kappa Alpha Psi Achievement Awd 1971; Richard Westbrook Awd Cook County Bar Assn 1975; Robert R Ming Awd Cook County Bar Assn 1981; Oper PUSH Community Serv Awd 1981; South Suburban Leadership Council Community Serv Awd 1985. **MILITARY SERVICE:** USAF corpl 1945-47.

HOLT, MICHAEL L.
Editor. **PERSONAL:** Born Mar 12, 1952, Milwaukee, WI. **EDUCATION:** Univ of WI Milwaukee. **CAREER:** Milwaukee Comm Journ, edit 1976-; Milwaukee Star Times, mng edtr 1975-76, sports edtr photo journ 1974-75; Milwaukee Sentinel, intern 1968-69; Seabreeze Mag, Milwaukee edtr; DJ WCLG, asst prgm dir; Naval AP & Group Vietnam, hist writer 1971-72; Comnine Great Lakes IL, media rel ofcr 1972-73; Stringer Jet Mag, 1971-72. **ORGANIZATIONS:** Past mem NAACP Youth Coun; past co-chmn Black Awareness Study Group; Milwaukee Black Photo-Journ; WI Black Press; TUJU; vice pres Assn for Stud of Afro-Am Life & Hist. **HONORS/ACHIEVEMENTS:** Holt Enter Bbraggs & Brooks Sports Serv Awrd 1974; Letter of apprc for brdcstng 1972; Black Achvmt Awd 1976; Commnty Serv Awd UWM 1977; Comm Serv Awrd Black Stud Union 1977. **MILITARY SERVICE:** USN e5 1969-73;. **BUSINESS ADDRESS:** 3764 N Port Washington, Milwaukee, WI.

HOLT, VEITYA EILEENE (VICKYE)
Portfolio analyst. **PERSONAL:** Born Jun 16, 1962, Indianapolis, IN; daughter of Mack Ross, Jr and Janice Mai Thomas Ross; married Charles Holt, Jr, Sep 17, 1988; children: Jescika Nekole Holt. **EDUCATION:** Univ of WI-Whitewater, BBA 1983, MBA 1985. **CAREER:** Univ WI-Whitewater Alumni Center, supervisor/telemarketing 1983, minority business program graduate asst 1983-85; Mazur-Zachow, interviewing telemarketer 1985; Cardinal Industries Inc, documents controller 1986-87. **ORGANIZATIONS:** Mem Alpha Kappa Alpha Service Sorority 1981-, Natl Assn of Black Accountants 1983-85; treas Univ WI Whitewater Choir 1983-85; mem St Mark AME Celestial Choir 1985, Natl Assn of Black MBA's 1986-. **HONORS/ACHIEVEMENTS:** Black History Month Achievement Award; Silver Scroll Honor Society; Graduate Assistantship Univ WI-Whitewater 1982-83. **HOME ADDRESS:** 3530 Pleasantbrook Village Lane, #A, Doraville, GA 30340.

HOLTON, MICHAEL LAVELLE
Professional athlete. **PERSONAL:** Born Aug 04, 1961, Seattle, WA. **EDUCATION:** UCLA, 1980-84. **CAREER:** Phoenix Suns, guard 1984-. **BUSINESS ADDRESS:** Phoenix Suns, P O Box 1369, Ste 510, Phoenix, AZ 85001.

HOLTON, PRISCILLA BROWNE
Educator. **PERSONAL:** Born Dec 31, 1921, Hartford, CT; married John Lyle Holton; children: Mary Frances Dickerson, John Kingsley, Leslie Lucille Miles. **EDUCATION:** St Joseph Coll for Women, BS 1946; Antioch Univ, MEd 1971. **CAREER:** Green Tree School, principal 1969-74; Antioch Univ, dir of special educ dept 1974-77, MEd prog administrator 1977-80; City of Philadelphia, coord of head start 1980-83; Self-employed, consultant. **ORGANIZATIONS:** mem, chairperson Foster Grandparents, 1980-85; pres, Children's Village Adv Bd, 1980-85; exec bd mem, Council for Labor & Indus 1983-87; mem Delta Sigma Theta Sor, Youth Svcs, PA Acad of Fine Arts, Afro-Amer Museum, Smithsonian Inst, League of Women Voters, Natl Assoc for the Educ of Young Children; consultant Temple Univ, Community Coll, Beaver Coll, Wharton Settlement, Delaware Valley Assoc for Nursery/ Kindergarden Teachers, Penn State, YWCA, Parent Child Ctr, Head Start, Mill Creek Day Care Ctr; TV appearances for toy manufacturer. **HONORS/ACHIEVEMENTS:** Award for work done w/Children with Learning Disabilities VIP Serv Club 1980; Recognition of Comm Serv Chapel of Four Chaplains 1980; Disting Alumni AwdSt Joseph Coll 1983; Certificate of Appreciation Better Boys Found, 1986; publications Tips to ,Parents (weekly) Hartford Chronicle CT; co-authored Teachers Manual for Green Tree School.

HOLZENDORF, BETTY S.
State representative. **PERSONAL:** Born Apr 05, 1939, Jacksonville, FL; daughter of Fanny Holmes; married King Holzendorf Jr; children: Kim Valette Lockley, King L III, Kevin Joseph, Kessler Lenard. **EDUCATION:** Edwards Water Coll, BS 1965; Atlanta Univ, MA 1971; Univ of N FL, MEd 1973; Univ of FL, further study; FL A&M Univ, further study. **CAREER:** Duval Cty Public School, teacher 1965-70; Edwards Waters Coll, asst prof 1971-75; Edward Waters Coll, dir inst rsch 1972-75; City of Jacksonville, equal oppty coord 1975-79; City of Jacksonville, admin aide to mayor; Dept of Transportation, Labor Employment & Training Field Representative; House of Representatives, State Representative/ Jacksonville. **ORGANIZATIONS:** Mem Alpha Kappa Alpha, African Methodist Episcopal Church, Planned Parenthood, Urban League, NAACP, Governors Commiss on Employment of the Handicapped, Chamber of Commerce, Political Action Coord Comm; Natl Council for Negro Women, Florida Black Legislative Caucus and Natl Black Legislative Caucus. **HONORS/ACHIEVEMENTS:** 1st Black Female Legislative Liaison Aide to Mayor in Jacksonville FL; Atlanta Univ Science Honor Society 1971; Paper presented to Research Consortium Summer Session 1973, Developing an Institutional Research Office; Institutional Research Grant 1973; Outstanding Educator Award; Appreciation Award, Florida A&M Univ, 1985-88. **HOME ADDRESS:** 3041 Woodlawn Rd, Jacksonville, FL 32209. **BUSINESS**

ADDRESS: State Representative, District 16, State of Florida, 4940 Soutel A Drive, Jacksonville, FL 32208.

HOMER, RONALD A.
Business executive. **PERSONAL:** Born Mar 01, 1947, Brooklyn, NY; married Cheryl E Bell; children: R Scott, Brian. **EDUCATION:** Univ of Notre Dame, BA 1968; Univ of Rochester, MBA 1971. **CAREER:** Action Inc, center dir 1968-69; Marine Midland Bank NY, asst vice pres 1970-79; Freedom Natl Bank of NY, exec vice pres & coo 1979-83; Boston Bank of Commerce, pres & ceo 1983-. **ORGANIZATIONS:** Bd of dirs Cambridge Coll, MA Indus Finance Agency, Roxbury Multi Service Ctr Inc, New England Student Loan Marketing Assoc; mem New England Telephone and Telegraph Co, Natl Bankers Assoc, Boston Symphony, Greater Boston YMCA, Greater Boston Chamber of Commerce; mem Greater Boston Convention & Visitors Bureau; mem Freedom House Inc, The Boston Housing Partnership, Roxbury Comm Coll Foundation; chmn The Partnership; mem Black Achievers Commn, Governor's Minority Business Commn. **HONORS/ACHIEVEMENTS:** Fellowship Consortium for Grad Study in BusUniv of Rochester 1969-71. **BUSINESS ADDRESS:** President and CEO, Boston Bank of Commerce, 110 Tremont St, Boston, MA 02109.

HONABLUE, RICHARD RIDDICK
Physician. **PERSONAL:** Born Apr 01, 1948, Staten Island, NY; married Valrie Mae Biggs; children: Richard III, Xavier, Michael. **EDUCATION:** Long Island Univ, AA 1968; Wagner Coll Grymes Hill, BS 1970; Meharry Med Coll, MD 1974. **CAREER:** Pildes Opticians NY, optical dispenser 1968-70; CBS Radio News, editors desk asst 1969; United Negro Coll Fund Pre-Med Prog Fisk Univ, tutor 1971; Dede Wallace Comm Mental Health Serv, consult 1976; Medical Exam Ctr, med dir 1977; Duke Univ Dept of Family Prac, asst clinical prof 1981-87; Family Practice of Williamsburg & Family Practice of Gloucester, owner, physician. **ORGANIZATIONS:** Pres Resident's Assn of Meharyy 1976; asst clinical prof George Wash Univ School of Allied Health Sci 1979; diplomate Amer Bd of Family Practice 1980;med examiner Comm of VA; Lord Chamberlain Soc; Tidewater TV Adv Comm; mem Tau Kappa Epsilon, AMA, AAFP, VAFP; chmn Reg II NMA 1984-85; pres Williamsburg Men's Club 1984; mem AMSUS, Natl naval Officers Assn, Frontiers Intl; fellow AAFP; life mem NAACP. **HONORS/ACHIEVEMENTS:** Eagle Scout Awd 1966; Order of the Arrow. **MILITARY SERVICE:** US Army Reserves capt med corps 1975-77; USNR commander. **BUSINESS ADDRESS:** Owner, Family Pract of Williamsburg, 110 Cary St, Williamsburg, VA 23185.

HONORE, STEPHAN LEROY
Educator. **PERSONAL:** Born May 14, 1938, Urbana, OH; married Flor; children: Francis, Andrew, Stephanie. **EDUCATION:** Capital Univ, BS 1960; Univ of Toledo, JD 1974. **CAREER:** Peace Corps Columbia Dominican Rep, 1961-66; US State Dept AID, 1966-68; Trans Century Corp, 1968-69; Model Cities Prog Toledo, 1970-71; Peace Corps Dominican Rep, 1978-81; Thurgood Marshall School of Law, law prof 1974-84 (leave of absence 1978-81); Self-Employed Houston TX, attorney at law. **ORGANIZATIONS:** Student body pres Capital Univ 1960-69; presiding justice, student honor ct Univ of Toledo Coll of Law 1973-74; law reveiw, casenote editor Univ of Toledo Law 1973-74; bd of dir Immigration Counselling Ctr 1976-78; mem State Bar of TX, Natl Bar Assoc, Houston Bar Assoc, Amer Immigration Lawyers Assoc; pres 1984-86, mem Parochial Sch Bd 1983-. **HONORS/ACHIEVEMENTS:** Articles on criminal & labor law publ in Univ of Toledo Law Review 1973-74. **HOME ADDRESS:** 4131 Levonshire, Houston, TX 77025.

HOOD, ELIZABETH
Educator. **PERSONAL:** Born Jun 17, 1930, Madison, GA; daughter of Henry Flemister and Mary Flemister; married Nicholas Hood; children: Nicholas III, Emory (dec.), Stephen, Sarah. **EDUCATION:** Wayne State Univ, MEd 1960; Dillard Univ, BA (magna cum laude) 1972; Wayne State Univ, PhD 1971. **CAREER:** LA State Dept, pub asst 1952-55; New Orleans Pub Schs, teacher 1955-58; Detroit Pub Schs, teacher 1958-71; Detroit, educ cons; Wayne State Univ, assoc prof, assoc prof coll of educ. **ORGANIZATIONS:** Delta Sigma Theta Sor 1951; Natl Bd of Homeland Ministries United Ch of Christ 1964-69; exec dir Detroit Educ Consult 1971-76; consult Highland Park Pub Schs 1972-75; bd trustees Roeper City & Co Sch 1975; E MI Univ Task Force on Women in Ch & Soc United Ch of Christ 1975-76; consult to feminist organs Wayne State Univ; Assn of Women's Studies Detroit; life mem NAACP; mem Assn for the Study of Afro-Amer Life & History. **HONORS/ACHIEVEMENTS:** Publ "Educating Black Students, Some Basic Issues" 1973; columnist MI Chronicle 1975; Feminist of the Yr Natl Organ for Women 1976; publ in the following,Amer Personnel & Guidance Assn, Crisis, Essence, ed journals, Detroit News, religious journals. **BUSINESS ADDRESS:** Associate Professor, Wayne State University, 325 Educ Bldg, Detroit, MI 48202.

HOOD, ESTUS
Professional athlete. **PERSONAL:** Born Nov 14, 1955, Hattiesburg, MS; married Diane; children: Estus IV, Elexsia Danielle. **EDUCATION:** IL State Univ, attended. **CAREER:** Green Bay Packer, defensive back 1978-. **ORGANIZATIONS:** Co-chmn Natl CP Telethon; works with Special Olympians. **HONORS/ACHIEVEMENTS:** Inducted into ISU Hall of Fame, Kankakee HS Hall of Fame; ISU third-ranking punt returner in nation as sophomore.

HOOD, HAROLD
Judge. **PERSONAL:** Born Jan 14, 1931, Hamtramck, MI; son of W Sylvester Hood Sr and Leonore Elizabeth Hand Hood; married Lottie Vivian Barnes Jones; children: Harold Keith, Kenneth Loren, Kevin Joseph, Karen Teresa. **EDUCATION:** Univ of MI, BA (Phi Eta Sigma Scholastic Hononary) 1952; Wayne State Univ, JD (Bronze Key and Gold Key for Legal Scholarship) 1959 (Dist Alumni Awd 1984). **CAREER:** Hood, Rice and Charity, atty 1959-61; City of Detroit, asst corp cnsl 1961-69; E Dist of Mi, chief asst US atty 1969-73; Common Plea Ct of Detroit, judge 1973-77; Recorders Court of Detroit, judge 1977-78; 3rd Judicial Circuit of MI, judge 1978-82; MI Court of Appeals, judge 1982-. **ORGANIZATIONS:** Member Amer Bar Assn, St of MI Bar Assn, Detroit Bar Assn, Amer Judicature Soc, Natl Bar Assn, Judicial Cncl of NBA, Assn of Black Judges Of MI Founder; trustee/vice chmn Kirwood General Hosp 1974-79; bd Mbr/vice pres Old Newsboys-Goodfellows 1974-; member Detroit Renaissance Lions 1975-; bd mem NCA/NARCO Greater Detroit Area 1976-; bd mem/vice pres Natl Council on Alcoholism 1979-; Natl Judicial Coll, faculty 1980-82; adj prof Central MI Univ 1982-; Michigan Judicial Institute, faculty 1983-; Michigan Judicial Tenure Comm, commissioner 1986-; Michigan Supreme Court Committee on Standard Civil Jury Instructions 1987-; Old Newsboys-Goodfellows, president 1987-88; chmn, Michigan Supreme Court Task Force on Race/Ethnic Issues in Courts, 1987-; chmn, Supreme Court Committee on Standard Civil Jury Instructions, 1987-; director, Thomas M Cooley Law School, 1988-; president, Old Newsboys Goodfellows, 1988-89; commissioner, Office of Substance Abuse Services, State of MI, 1987-. **HONORS/ACHIEVEMENTS:** Ted Owens Awd Detroit Alumni Kappa Alpha Psi 1971; Fed Exec Bd Serv Awd 1972; Northern Province Achvmnt Awd Kappa Alpha Psi 1972; City of Inkster Merit Awd City of Inkster, Mi 1976; distinguished alumni Wayne St Univ Law Sch 1984; Wayne State Univ, Distinguished alumni award 1985; "Executive Alcoholism- A Special Problem," Labor-Management Journal, 1988. **MILITARY SERVICE:** USASC 1st lt 1952-54; Army Commendation Medal, Korean Serv Medal, Far East Service Medal 1954. **BUSINESS ADDRESS:** Judge, MI Court of Appeals, 900 First Federal Bldg, Detroit, MI 48226.

HOOD, LEAMON
Union executive. **PERSONAL:** Born Apr 20, 1937, Jackson, GA; married Gloria P Gooden; children: Leamon, Jr, Mellonee, Brian. **CAREER:** Pittsburg Plate Glass Co, 1960-62; Antlanta Bd Educ 1962-63; Atlanta Water Pollution Control Operation, 1963-67; AFSCME AFL-CIO Staff Training Prgm, 1967; Union Organizer, apptd area dir 1970; Am Fedn State Co & Municipal Employees Union. **ORGANIZATIONS:** Mem NAACP exec com Memphis; mem ACLU exec bd; mem PUSH CBTU Memphis Chpts; Urban League; Alpha Kappa Alpha Sor. **HONORS/ACHIEVEMENTS:** Meritorious Serv Labor 1972 1973; Polit Educ Awrd NAACP 1972. **MILITARY SERVICE:** USN po 3rd cls 1955-60. **BUSINESS ADDRESS:** 280 Hernando St, Memphis, TN 38126.

HOOD, MORRIS, JR.
Legislator. **PERSONAL:** Born Jun 05, 1934, Detroit; married Beverly; children: Denise, Morris, III. **EDUCATION:** Wayne State U. **CAREER:** MI House of Reps Lansing, mem; precinct del, campaign mgr. **ORGANIZATIONS:** Mem MI Black Caucus; Trade Union Ldrshp Council. **HONORS/ACHIEVEMENTS:** One of twelve Blacks elected to MI Hse of Reps in 1973. **BUSINESS ADDRESS:** Dist 6 Representative, 8872 Cloverlawn, Detroit, MI 48901.

HOOD, NICHOLAS
Councilman, minister. **PERSONAL:** Born Jun 21, 1923, Terre Haute, IN; married Elizabeth Flemister; children: Nicholas III, Emory, Stephen, Sarah Cyprian. **EDUCATION:** Purdue U, BS 1945; N Central Coll, BA 1946; Yale U, MA 1949; Olivet Coll, hon DD 1966; Divinity SchUniv of Chgo, hon LittD, LLD 1966; N Central Coll, hon DD 1966. **CAREER:** City of Detroit, city councilman; Plymouth Ch, sr minister; Dixwell Cong Ch, asst mnstr; Central Cong Ch, mnstr; Cong'l Chs of the US, vice mod; Non-Profit Hsg Ctr, pres; Fed Natl Mortg Assn Fndr Cyprian Ctr, adv com. **ORGANIZATIONS:** Bd mem Ministers Life & Cas Ins Co; mem bd trustees Hutzel Hosp; mem Indsl Hsg Study Tour Europe 1971; US rep World Conf on Non-Profit Hsg 1972. **HONORS/ACHIEVEMENTS:** Outst mem 1949 class Yale Divinity Sch 1974; Amistad Award outstndng serv to Am 1977. **BUSINESS ADDRESS:** 1340 City Co Bldg, Detroit, MI 48226.

HOOD, RAYMOND W.
Legislator. **PERSONAL:** Born Jan 01, 1936, Detroit; married Helen; children: Raymond, Jr, Roger. **EDUCATION:** Fullerton Jr Coll. **CAREER:** MI House of Reps, asst floor ldr, rep 7th Dist, elected 1964. **ORGANIZATIONS:** Chmn Pub Hlth Com; mem Elections Com; Conservation & Recreation Com; Educ Com. **HONORS/ACHIEVEMENTS:** One of the youngest Black legislators elected in House; reelected 1966, 1968, 1970, 1972, 1974, 1976, 1978. **BUSINESS ADDRESS:** Dir, Dept Licensing & Regulations, PO Box 30018, Lansing, MI 48909.

HOOKER, DOUGLAS RANDOLF
Business manager. **PERSONAL:** Born Mar 31, 1954, Moultrie, GA; son of H Randolph Hooker and Odessa W Hooker; married Patrise M Perkins, Feb 17, 1979; children: Douglas Patrick Hooker, Randi Michelle Hooker. **EDUCATION:** Georgia Inst of Technology, Atlanta GA, BS Mechanical Engineering, 1978, MS, Technology & Science, 1985; Emory Univ, Atlanta GA, MBA, 1987. **CAREER:** Bio-Lab Inc, Decatur GA, exec dir of admin, 1989. **HOME ADDRESS:** 1121 Veltre Circle, Atlanta, GA 30311.

HOOKER, ERIC H.
Clergyman. **PERSONAL:** Born in Waco, TX; married Lois Nelson. **EDUCATION:** Houston-Tillotson Coll, AB 1951; VA Union Univ, BD MDiv 1953; Prairie View Univ, MA 1979. **CAREER:** New Mt Zion Baptist Church, pastor 1970-82; Bishop Coll, dean of men 1970-79; 11th Congressional Dist, congressional aide 1979-85; McLennan Comm Coll, trustee; Second Baptist Church, pastor 1982-. **ORGANIZATIONS:** Mem Amer Assn Higher Educ 1985; 2nd vice pres Kiwanis Club 1985; pres Conference of Christians and Jews 1985; trustee bd McLennan Co Comm Coll 1982-. **BUSINESS ADDRESS:** Pastor, Second Baptist Church, 1205 M L Cooper Dr, Waco, TX 76706.

HOOKER, JOHN LEE
Singer, guitarist, songwriter. **PERSONAL:** Born 1917, Clarkdale, MS; children: 6 children. **EDUCATION:** Studied under Will Moore. **CAREER:** Riverside, Vee-Jay, Modern, ABC Records, recording artist. **HONORS/ACHIEVEMENTS:** Over 50 albums on the mrkt; Sang with spiritual groups since age 14; Toured N Amer 1951-, Europe & UK 1961-; Partic Newport Folk Fest 1959,60,63; Partic Newport Jazz Festival 1964, Amer Folk Blues Festival 1964,65,68; Best Blues Album Awd Jazz & Pop Mag 1968-69; Carnegie Hall 1971,83; TV appearances incl Midnight spec 1971; Blues Hall of Fame Awd Ebony Mag 1974; Don Kirshner's Rock Concert 1978; Partic Montreaux Jazz Fest 1983, North Sea Jazz Fest 1983; Writer numerous blues songs. **BUSINESS ADDRESS:** c/o The Rosebud Agency, PO Box 21013, San Francisco, CA 94121.

HOOKER, ODESSA WALKER
Assistant principal. **PERSONAL:** Born Sep 21, 1930, Moultrie, GA; divorced; children: Douglas R, Melanie Ann, David A, Margaret P, Darrell W. **EDUCATION:** Paine Coll, BA 1951; Atlanta Univ, Certification 1951; Univ of Cincinnati, MEd 1967. **CAREER:** Barnesville HS, english teacher 1951-53; Whittemore HS, english teacher 1954-55; Cincinnati Public Schools, elem teacher 1961-83, elem asst principal 1983-. **ORGANIZATIONS:** Co-

choir dir and organist 1955-, bible class teacher 1977-, Peoples Tabernacle Bapt Church; volunteer organist Chapel Serv Bethesda Oak Hosp 1983-. **HONORS/ACHIEVEMENTS:** 1st Black Pres Delta Psi Delta Kappa Gamma Intl Cincinnati OH 1986-88. **HOME ADDRESS:** 3906 Wess Park Dr, Cincinnati, OH 45217.

HOOKS, BENJAMIN LAWSON
Attorney. **PERSONAL:** Born Jan 31, 1925, Memphis, TN; married Frances Dancy; children: Patricia Gray. **EDUCATION:** LeMoyne Coll Memphis, attended 1941-43; Howard Univ, attended 1943-44; DePaul Univ, JD, LLB 1948. **CAREER:** Indv practice law Memphis, 1949-65 1968-72; Mut Fed Savs & Loan Assn Memphis, co-fndr/vice pres/dir 1955-69; Middle Bapt Memphis, pastor 1956-72; New Mt Moriah Bapt Detroit, pastor 1964-72; Shelby Co Criminal Ct Memphis, judge 1965-68; NAACP, exec dir 1977-. **ORGANIZATIONS:** Mem Natl, Amer, TN Bar Assns; Judicial Coun Natl Bar Assn; bd trustee LeMoyne Owen Coll; bd dir So Christian Leadership Conf 1968-72; grand chancellor Knights Pythias; bd trustees Hampton Inst VA; NAACP; bd dir TN Coun Human Rel 1966-68; producer/host TV prog Conversations in Black & White; co-producer Forty Percent Speaks; panelist What is Your Faith. **HONORS/ACHIEVEMENTS:** Hon DHL Howard Univ 1975; Hon LLD Wilberforce Univ 1975; Gold Medal Achievement Awd Masons 1972; Man of Yr Awd Masons 1964; Optimist Club Am Awd 1966; Lincoln League Awd 1965; TN Reg Bapt Conv Awd; Hon DHL Central State Univ 1974. **MILITARY SERVICE:** AUS 1943-46. **BUSINESS ADDRESS:** Executive Dir, NAACP, 186 Remson St, Brooklyn, NY 11201.

HOOKS, FRANCES DANCY
Educator. **PERSONAL:** Born Feb 23, 1927, Memphis, TN; married Benjamin Lawson; children: Patricia Louise, Gray. **EDUCATION:** Fisk Univ, BS 1949; TN State Univ, MS 1968. **CAREER:** Shelby Co Schools of TN, teacher 1949-51; Memphis City Schools, teacher 1951-59, counselor-admin hs 1959-73; Memphis City Schools, counselor-pregnant girls 1976-77; NAACP; vol sect apptmt. **ORGANIZATIONS:** Dir Youth Activities Mt Monah Bapt Ch 1973-75; dir Youth Activities Middle Bapt Ch 1973-75; organizer People Power Project 1968; pres/co-founder Riverview KS Comm & Day Care Ctr 1969-73. **HONORS/ACHIEVEMENTS:** Outstanding Serv to Comm Memphia Vol Placement Prog TN 1973; Youth Chap Scholarship Fund Richmond VA NAACP 1979; Membership Awd Boston NAACP 1980; Hon Chairperson Awd KY State NAACP 1980. **BUSINESS ADDRESS:** Volunteer Sect, NAACP, 186 Remsen St, Brooklyn, NY 10019.

HOOKS, JAMES BYRON, JR.
Educator. **PERSONAL:** Born Sep 23, 1933, Birmingham, AL; son of James Byron Hooks Sr and Bessie Ardis Hooks; married Marcell Elizabeth; children: Angelique L, James Byron III, Kimberly M, Jamal B, Joffrey B, Keisha M. **EDUCATION:** IN Univ, BS 1955; Roosevelt Univ, MA 1969; Northwestern Univ, PhD 1975. **CAREER:** J M Harlan High, asst principal 1969-75; Skiles Middle Sch, principal 1975; Haver Middle Sch, principal 1976; Whitney Young, teacher/dean 1980-89; Square One Income Tax, owner 1988-89. **ORGANIZATIONS:** Exec dir Talent, Inc 1971-87; bd of dir Sullivan House Local Serv Syst 1984-89. **MILITARY SERVICE:** USN airman 1st 1955-57. **BUSINESS ADDRESS:** Research Instructor, Whitney Young High, 211 S LaFlin, Whitney Young Magnet, Chicago, IL 60636.

HOOKS, MICHAEL ANTHONY
Govt. official/real estate appraiser. **PERSONAL:** Born Oct 13, 1950, Memphis, TN; married Janet Dean Perry; children: Michael, Jr, Kristian Nichole. **EDUCATION:** Lane College, Jackson, TN, 1968-69; Memphis State Univ, 1969. **CAREER:** Shelby County Assessor's Office, deputy tax assessor 1972-77; Gilliam Communications, Inc, account exec; State Technical Institute, lecturer/instructor; Michael Hooks & Assoc, president; Memphis, Tenn, city councilman. **ORGANIZATIONS:** Delegate Tenn Constitutional Conv 1977; councilman Memphis, TN 1979-; member NAACP; member PUSH, Inc; member of Knights of Pythion, Commitment Memphis, Omega Psi Phi Fraternity, Prince Hall Masonic Lodge, Memphis Downtown Photographic Society, Inc. **HONORS/ACHIEVEMENTS:** Tenn Assn of Assessing Officers; Intl Assn of Assessing Officers; Society of Real Estate Appraisers; Natl Assoc of Real Estate Brokers; Memphis Board of Realtors. **HOME ADDRESS:** 2143 South Parkway East, Memphis, TN 38114. **BUSINESS ADDRESS:** City Councilman, Dist 4, 993 South Cooper, Memphis, TN 38104.

HOOKS, MOSE YVONNE BROOKS
Educator. **PERSONAL:** Born in Jackson, TN. **EDUCATION:** DiskUniv Nashville, BA 1960; ColumbiaUniv NY, MA 1963;Univ of TN Knoxville, EdD 1973. **CAREER:** Div Of Educ Tech Shelby St Comm Coll, div chmn 1979-; Nat Endowment of the Humanities Shelby Cty Govt, researcher 1978-79; Memphis City Sch System, instructional reseasrcher 1973-76, modern & fireign lang chtr 1960-70; Arts & Letters LeMoyne Owen Coll Memphis, part time prof; Arts & Letters Memphis St U, part time prof. **ORGANIZATIONS:** Bd mem Memphis TN Council of Govt 1976-80; natl educ bd US China Peoples Friendship Assn 1978-; pres Linke Inc Memphis Chap 1979-. **HONORS/ACHIEVEMENTS:** Whos Who Among Students in Am Coll & U, FiskUniv Nashville 1960; Am Council on Educ Fellow in Acad Adminstrn, Am Council on Educ Washington DC 1978-79;citizen diplomat US China Peoples Friendship Assn 1976-80. **BUSINESS ADDRESS:** 1588 Union, Memphis, TN 38104.

HOOKS, ROLAND
Professional athlete. **PERSONAL:** Born Jan 02, 1954, Brooklyn, NY; married Earlene A Carter. **EDUCATION:** NC State U, BA hist 1975. **CAREER:** Buffalo Bills, professional football player 1975-80. **ORGANIZATIONS:** Class Pres & Beta Club 1970. **BUSINESS ADDRESS:** c/o Dee Rauch, NFL Players Association, 1300 Connecticut NW Ste 407, Washington, DC 20036.

HOOPER, GARY RAYMOND
Business executive. **PERSONAL:** Born Aug 26, 1946, West Point, NY; married Valerie Jean Thompson; children: Ericka Lynn, Daren Cayton. **EDUCATION:** Sierra Coll, AA 1964-66; Ca St Univ at San Jose, BS Mktng 1966-68; Univ of S Ca, MBA Mgmt 1973-74. **CAREER:** Sky Climber Inc, mrkt rsrch anal 1974-76, prod mgr 1976-78; Hyland Diagnostics Inc, prod mgr 1978, asst to the pres 1978-80; Genentech Inc, assoc dir of bus development. **ORGANIZATIONS:** Commerce Assoc 1973; S Ca Black MBA Assoc 1974-; Am Mrktng Asso 1974-; Nat'l Mgmt Asso 1974-82. **HONORS/ACHIEVEMENTS:** Grad bus fellowship Univ of S CA 1973-74; consortium for grad study in bus fellowshipUniv of S CA 1973-74; Beta Gamma SigmaUniv of S CA 1974. **MILITARY SERVICE:** USN lt 3yrs; USN Leadership Awd 1970; First Black Regimental Commander In Naval History 1970; Commanding Officer Letter Of Commendation 1972. **HOME ADDRESS:** 709 Somerset Ln, Foster City, CA 94404. **BUSINESS ADDRESS:** Assoc Dir of Bus Development, GenenTech Inc, 460 Point San Bruno Blvd, San Francisco, CA 94080.

HOOPER, GERALD F.
Educator. **PERSONAL:** Born Nov 19, 1923, Chicago; married Ann Marie Cooper; children: Gerald, Jr, Theresa, Ernest, Gwendolyn Joyce. **EDUCATION:** PA St U, EdD 1953;Univ WI, MA 1953. **CAREER:** Chicago Post Office, clerk 1948; Xavier Univ, instructor 1948-50; Central CT State, asst prof 1966; FL A&M Univ, assoc prof 1953-. **ORGANIZATIONS:** Mem Nat Art Educ Assn; Lemoyne Art Found; Tallahassee Arts Council. **HONORS/ACHIEVEMENTS:** Tchr yr 1958; purchase prize & hon mention, water colour AtlantaUniv 1956-69. **MILITARY SERVICE:** S/sgt 1943-45; t/5 1950-51. **BUSINESS ADDRESS:** Art Dept Vsl Arts & Humnts FL, Box 132, Tallahassee, FL 32307.

HOOPER, MICHELE J.
Corporate executive. **PERSONAL:** Born Jul 16, 1951, Uniontown, PA; daughter of Percy Hooper and Beatrice Eley Hooper; married Lemuel Seabrook III, Sep 04, 1976. **EDUCATION:** Univ of Pennsylvania, Philadelphia, PA, BA, 1973; Univ of Chicago, Chicago, IL, MBA, 1973-75; State of Illinois, CPA, 1981. **CAREER:** Baxter Corp, Chicago, IL, parenterals div, 1976-83, various finance positions, dir, coverage & reimbursement, 1983-85, vice pres, corporate planning, 1985-88; Baxter Corp Canada, pres, 1988-. **ORGANIZATIONS:** Chmn bd of Baxter Credit Union Directors, 1981-88; mem, bd of dir, 1985-89, bd chmn, 1988, Joseph Holmes Dance Theatre; mem, The Economic Club of Chicago, 1986-; mem, bd of dir, Lake Forest Graduate School of Mgmt, 1987-88, mem, bd, Medical Devices Canada, 1988-; mem, Young President's Org, 1989-; mem, Comm of 200, 1989-;. **BUSINESS ADDRESS:** Pres, Baxter Corp, 6695 Airport Rd, Mississauga, Ontario, Canada L4V IT7.

HOOVER, JESSE
Supervisor. **PERSONAL:** Born Sep 06, 1918, Tamo, AR; married Dorothy Franks. **EDUCATION:** Wayne St U, 1952. **CAREER:** US Postal Serv, personnel action & records supr 1946-77; Detroit Postal Employees Cr Un, vP 1946-77, 1st black bd dir. **ORGANIZATIONS:** Mem NAACP; Freedom Fund; The Moors Inc; 1st Nighters; Sagicornians; bd deacons & trustees Plymouth Cong Ch. **HONORS/ACHIEVEMENTS:** Recd the US Postal Serv Bicentennial Awd 1976; Cert of Appreciation from MAACP 1976; co-chmn Annual Easter Teas; Mens Club; Pilot Club Cert Merit, Mens Club 1968; Cert Appreciation Easter Tea. **MILITARY SERVICE:** AUS staff sgt 1941-45. **BUSINESS ADDRESS:** Personnel Div US Postal Serv, 1401 W Fort St, Detroit, MI 48233.

HOOVER, ODIE MILLARD, JR.
Clergyman. **PERSONAL:** Born Sep 21, 1921, Nashville, TN; divorced; children: Carole, Patricia, Odie M, III. **EDUCATION:** TN St U, BS 1946; Am Bapt Theol Sem, BTh 1946; Union Bapt Theol Sem, MTh; Boston U;Univ of Chgo; VA Union U; Yale U; FiskUniv under dir John Work Jr studied music; wilberforce u, lhd 1969. **CAREER:** Olivet & Inst Bapt Ch Cleveland, pastor; one of nations leading evangelists & singers; accompanied Dr Martin Luther King Jr to Oslo Norway for 1964 Nobel Peace Prize; since coming to Olivet 1952 have built modern sanctuary, comm cntr, playground. **ORGANIZATIONS:** Mem Martin Luther King Jr Found; Op PUSH, SCLS; Am Bapt Theol Sem; Mason; founder OM Hoover Rescue Mission for Boys; asso natl grand chaplain; IBPO Elks of World. **BUSINESS ADDRESS:** 8714 Quincy Ave, Cleveland, OH 44106.

HOOVER, THERESSA
Church executive. **PERSONAL:** Born Sep 07, 1925, Fayetteville, AR; daughter of James (deceased) and Rissie (deceased). **EDUCATION:** Philander Smith Coll, BBA 1946; NY Univ, MA 1962. **CAREER:** Little Rock Meth Church, assoc dir 1946-48; Woman's Div of Christian Svc, field worker 1948-58; Dept of Christian Soc Relations, sec 1958-65; Sect of Prog & Educ for Christian Mission, asst gen sec 1965-68; Women's Div Bd of Global Ministries United Meth Ch, assoc gen sec 1968-. **ORGANIZATIONS:** Bd trustees Paine Coll 1963-76; del World Council of Ch Assemblies Sweden 1968, Nairobi 1975, Vancouver 1983; bd mem Ch Women United 1968; Bossey Ecumenical Inst 1969-75; mem Nat Council of Ch 1969-72; Comm on Ch Participation in Devel 1970; bd trustees United Theol Sem; mem Nat Bd YWCA; bd curators Stephens Coll; mem exec com Nat Council of Negro Women; mem Central Comm World Council of Churches 1983-90. **BUSINESS ADDRESS:** Deputy Gen Sec Women's Div, United Methodist Church, 475 Riverside Dr, Room 1504, New York, NY 10115.

HOPE, JULIUS CAESAR
Clergyman, political and civil rights activist. **PERSONAL:** Born Sep 06, 1932, Mobile, AL; son of Rev Robert Hope and Zeola King Hope; married Louise Portis, May 21, 1959; children: Rev Julius Escous, Tonya Louise. **EDUCATION:** Alabama State College, Montgomery AL, BS, 1958; Interdenominational Theology Center, MST, 1961. **CAREER:** Zion Baptist Church, Brunswick GA, pastor, 1961-70; First Baptist Church, Macon GA, pastor, 1970-78; New Grace Missionary Baptist Church, Highland Park MI, pastor, 1979—; Political Action Chair, Brunswick GA branch NAACP, 1961-78; GA State Conference of NAACP Branches, president, 1967-78; NAACP Natl Office, New York NY, natl director of religious affairs, 1978—; NAACP Midwest Region III, regional director, 1988—. **ORGANIZATIONS:** Life member, NAACP; member, President's Commission on Civil Rights, 1977-81; member of board of directors, Project Smile, 1974-76; president, GA State Church School and Baptist Training Union Congress, 1974-78; director, Neighborhod Youth Corps, Coastal Ara of GA, 1967-78; Alpha Phi Alpha. **HONORS/ACHIEVEMENTS:** Rev Julius C Hope Day, Brunswick GA, 1970, 1987; citation from city of Glen Cove, NY, 1978; special tribute for community service from State of MI, 1982; Outstanding Service Award, Council of Natl Alumni Assn, 1983; honorary degree, Birmingham Baptist Bible College, 1984; given key to Youngstown, OH, 1988; given proclamation from US Senator Howard Metzenbaum, 1988; Outstanding Service Award, Ohio Tri-County NAACP, 1989. **MILITARY SERVICE:** US Air Force, airman first class. **BUSINESS ADDRESS:** New Grace Missionary Baptist Church, 25 Ford Ave, Highland Park, MI 48203.

HOPE, NEIL CALVIN
Professional athlete. **PERSONAL:** Born Mar 22, 1963, Memphis, TN. **EDUCATION:** Univ of Southern CA, Pblc Admin Major. **CAREER:** Denver Gold, linebacker 1985-. **HONORS/ACHIEVEMENTS:** Voted All-Pac 10 honorable mention.

HOPE, RICHARD OLIVER
Educator/sociologist. **PERSONAL:** Born Apr 01, 1939, Atlanta, GA; married Alice Anderson; children: Leah, Richard Jr. **EDUCATION:** Morehouse Coll, BA 1961; Syracuse Univ, MA 1964, PhD 1969. **CAREER:** Metro Applied Rsch Center, rsch assoc 1960-72; Brooklyn Coll, asst prof of Sociology 1968-72; Dept of Defense, dir of rsch 1972-74; Morgan State Univ, chmn & prof 1974-82; Indiana Univ at Indianapolis, chmn and prof dept of Sociology; MA Inst of Technology, exec dir, 1988-. **ORGANIZATIONS:** Assoc editor Journal of Inter-cultural Relations 1976-; visiting lecturer Univ of West Indies Mona Jamaica 1977; mem bd dirs Moton Foundation 1978-; mem bd dir Urban League, Flanner House of Indianapolis 1982-; mem Corporation Visiting Committee MIT 1982-. **HONORS/ACHIEVEMENTS:** Rsch Fellow Goddard Space Flight Center 1976-78; publications "Racial Strife in the US Military," Praeger Publishing 1979; "Black Leadership," Black Organizations Univ Press 1980. **MILITARY SERVICE:** Civilian GS-15 1970-74. **BUSINESS ADDRESS:** Exex Dir, Quality Educ for Minority Project, MA Inst of Technology 26-161, Cambridge, MA 02139.

HOPKINS, ALBERT E., SR.
Pharmacist. **PERSONAL:** Born Apr 03, 1928, Houston; married Joetta Carothers; children: Albert E, Jr. **EDUCATION:** Xavier U, BS 1949. **CAREER:** Pres Nat Pharmaceutical Assn Inc, Prescription Pharmacy pres 1974-75; Lone Star St & Houston Pharmaceutical Assns, past pres 1958-59, 69-71; Harris Co Pharmaceutical Assn, past vP 1973-74. **ORGANIZATIONS:** Mem YMCA; XavierUniv Alumni; Court Volunteers; mem Acres Home Civic Club; bd dir Who Cares. **HONORS/ACHIEVEMENTS:** Malyor Houston proclaimed Albert Hopkins Day 1973; Civic Awd, Prog Missionary Bapt Ch 1974. **BUSINESS ADDRESS:** 7808 W Montgomery Rd, PO Box 38260, Houston, TX 77088.

HOPKINS, BARRY L.
Clergyman. **PERSONAL:** Born Feb 15, 1943, Stamford, CT; married Elberta Fennell; children: 1. **EDUCATION:** VA Union Univ, BA 1968, MDiv 1971; Lancaster Theol Sem, DMin; Pastoral Training Inst, grad. **CAREER:** 6th Mt Zion Bapt Church, pastor 1967-70; Urban League, consult 1968-69; Jackson Ward Proj So Bapt Conv, consult 1968-70; PA Found of Pastoral Counseling Inc, pastoral psychotherapist; Sts Mem Bapt Church, pastor; W Philadelphia Pastoral couns cntr, dir; Dimension Comm Affairs Prgm, host of On Target. **ORGANIZATIONS:** Africa comm Natl Comm Black Churchmen 1970-71; mem exec comm div Overseas Ministries Natl Council Churchs 1971-; vice pres Church World Serv Dept Comm 1971-; comm World Mission & Evangelism World Council Church 1971-; consult Prog to Combat Racism 1971; us rep Ecumenical Sharing of Personnel Comm 1971-; sec Africa & Spec Svc, bd Intl Ministries; mem Amer Baptist Churchs; mem gen bd Amer Bapt Church USA Valley Forge PA; mem bd Philadelphia Bept Assoc; mem bd Natl Ministries Amer Bapt Church USA; mem Amer Assoc of Pastoral Counselors, elected rep gen bd Amer Baptist Churches USA. **HONORS/ACHIEVEMENTS:** Community Awd Jaycees 1958; Outstanding Man of the Year US C of C 1972; Business & Professional Women's Club, Comm Serv Awd 1980; The Chapel of 4 Chaplains Awd 1983; dir, Building Better Famalies Inc, a family homeless shelter, 1989. **BUSINESS ADDRESS:** Pastor, Sts Memorial Baptist Church, 47 Warner Ave, Bryn Mawr, PA 19010.

HOPKINS, CHARMAINE L.
Insurance underwriter. **PERSONAL:** Born Mar 14, 1946, Danville, VA; children: Cecily Hopkins Gray. **EDUCATION:** Indiana Univ, BS Educ 1968. **CAREER:** Indiana Univ, day care specialist 1970-73; Prudential Insurance, various positions 1973-80; United Presidential Ins, chief underwriter 1980-87. **ORGANIZATIONS:** Supervisor Marion County Crisis/Suicide Intervention; business consultant, Project Business-Junior Achievement 1989; first vice pres, Council 6 International Training in Communication, 1989. **BUSINESS ADDRESS:** Chief Underwriter, United Presidential Insurance, 217 Southway Blvd, Kokomo, IN 46902.

HOPKINS, DONALD RAY
Attorney, government official. **PERSONAL:** Born Nov 14, 1936, Tulsa, OK; son of Stacey McGlory and Carolyn McGlory; divorced; children: Yvonne Ann-Marie. **EDUCATION:** Univ of Kansas, BA 1958; Yale Univ, MA 1959; Univ of California Berkeley, JD 1965; Harvard Law School, LLM 1969; honors cum laude Phi Beta Kappa Pi Sigma Alpha Woodrow Wilson Fellow. **CAREER:** Univ of California Berkeley, teaching asst 1960-63, asst dean of students 1965-67, asst exec v chancellor 1967-68; NAACP Legal Defense Fund Inc, staff attorney 1969-70; Pacific Cons, exec vice pres 1970-71; Eighth California Cong Dist, dist admins 1971-; attorney in Private Practice 1981-. **ORGANIZATIONS:** Estate tax examiner US Treasury Dept 1965; coll teacher Univ of California Laney Coll 1966-68; mem Acad of Polit Sci; mem Arbitration Assn Bd of Arbitrators; bd dir Amer Civil Liberties Union No California 1969-71; bd dir Univ of California Alumni Assn 1976-79; bd dir African Film Soc; bd dir Travelers Aid Soc; mem Kansas/Yale/Harvard/Univ of California Alumni Assn; mem California State Bar Assn, Natl, Amer Federal, Alameda Cty Bar Assns; bd dir Chas Houston Bar Assn; Amer Trial Lawyers Assn; Natl Conference of Black Lawyers; Natl Lawyers Guild; California Assn of Black Lawyers; bd dir Volunteer on Parole. **HONORS/ACHIEVEMENTS:** Various achievement awds; contrib auth "Politics & Change in Berkeley" Nathan & Scott 1979; contrib author to several periodicals. **BUSINESS ADDRESS:** District Administrator, 8th CA Cong Dist, 201-13th St Ste 105, Oakland, CA 94612.

HOPKINS, EDNA J.
Educator. **PERSONAL:** Born Sep 29, 1924, Weathrfrd, TX; married Fritizer; children: Jr, Stephen. **EDUCATION:** TX Coll, BA 1952; Columbia U, mA. **CAREER:** Compton Unified School Dist, Task Force PIRAMID, coord 1974; Enterprise School Dist, Task Force Early Chldhd Ed 1970, Task Force New Ling Program, supvr teacher Educ Workshops 1965-67, teacher 1958; LA County Schools, teacher 1955; Diboll TX Abilene TX. **ORGANIZATIONS:** Chrpsn PR&R Comm Ed Assn 1965-68; mem CA Tchr Assn; Nat Ed Assn; Compton Ed Assn; Int Assn Chldhd Ed; Delta Sigma Theta Nat vP for Nat Cncl Negro Wmn Inc 1970-; mem White Hse Conf onf Food, Hunger & Nutrtn 1969-; mem Bd Advs Am Yth Actn Org Inc 1974-; Nat Corp Bd, "Womn in CommServ Inc" 1968-; chrprsn Grtr LA WIGS Bd 1970-; Dir Chrstn Ed LA Dist Chrstn Meth Epis Ch; Dir Chrstn Ed Philllip Tem CME Ch 1970; sec/chmn Chld Care & Dev Ser Inc; mem Int Assn Vol Eds; bd dir Womn Coal Com Comm Actn 1970-73; bd dir Teen Age & Mthrs, Harriet Tubman Sch 1970-74; bd dir LA Cncl of Chs 1970-72; Educ Adv Comm PUSH. **HONORS/ACHIEVEMENTS:** Apple Grammy Tchr of Yr 1968; awd Womn in 1972; Woman of Yr Chrstn Meth Epis Ch/Wmns Miss Soc 1972.

HOPKINS, ERNEST LOYD
Physician, educator. **PERSONAL:** Born Aug 14, 1930, Birmingham, AL; son of Claibourne Hopkins and Ada Fields; married Lillie Blanks, Apr 24, 1959; children: William, Loyd, Ernest. **EDUCATION:** Morehouse Coll, BS 1952; Howard Univ, MD 1957; Monrovia College, Monrovia Liberia, LHD 1962. **CAREER:** Howard Univ Coll of Med, prof OB-GYN; Howard Univ, assoc prof 1967, asst prof 1964; Andre Public Health Sem, career development 1963-64; Howard Univ College of Medicine, prof, chmn of ethics bd and curriculum 1988-; Howard Univ College of Medicine, dir of maternal & fetal medicine 1976-; Metropolitan Ambulatory Care Center, partner. **ORGANIZATIONS:** Spl fellow OB & Anesthesia Resrch Asso OB-GYN Western Res U; spl fellow OBv Hospital de Clinicas, Universidad de Sp Republica, Montenideo, Uraguay 1963-64; consult vice pres Hlth Affairs HowardUniv 1968; knighted by pres, cabinet of Liberia, W Africa 1962; Med Chirugical Soc of DC; Dist Med Soc Am Coll of OB-GYN; Intl Coll of Surgeons; Pan Am Cytslgy Assn; patron, Metropolitan Police Boys Clubs 1965-; mem, District of Columbia Political Action Committee 1988-; Academy of Medicine of Washington DC. **HONORS/ACHIEVEMENTS:** Diplomate of American Board of Sexology 1989. **BUSINESS ADDRESS:** President, Ernest Loyd Hopkins MD PC, 5501 16th St NW, Washington, DC 20011.

HOPKINS, ESTHER ARVILLA
Attorney. **PERSONAL:** Born Sep 18, 1926, Stamford, CT; married T Ewell Hopkins; children: Susan, Thomas Jr. **EDUCATION:** Boston Univ, AB 1947; Howard Univ, MS 1949; Yale Univ, MS 1962, PhD 1967; Suffolk Univ, JD 1976. **CAREER:** VA State Coll, faculty 1949-52; New England Inst Med Rsch, biophysicist 1955-59; Amer Cyanamid Cor, rsch chem 1959-61; Polaroid Corp, scientist 1967-73, patent atty 1973-78, sr project admins 1979-. **ORGANIZATIONS:** Bd of govs Assn of Yale Alumni; chair Yale Medal Comm; natl bd YMCA of USA; pres-elect Genl Alumni Assn Boston Univ; finance comm Town of FraminghamMA; corp mem Cambridge Family YMCA; hon mem Boston Univ Women's Grad Club; bd of dir past pres Framingham Reg YMCA; chmn bd of assessors trustee 1st Parish; mem Alpha Kappa Alpha Sor; Soc for Promoting Theo Educ; past dean Stamfort Chap Amer Guild of Organists; natl scholar Natl Assn Coll Women 1963; disting alumni Boston Univ Coll of Liberal Arts 1975; Phi Beta Kappa; Sigma Xi; Sigma Pi Sigma; Beta Kappa Chi; Scientific Rsch Soc of Amer. **HONORS/ACHIEVEMENTS:** Woman of the Yr Regional Family YMCA Framingham 1984; Boston Univ carlet Key; First Parish Awd 1977; Women of Achievement MA Fedn of Bus or Professional Women'sClub 1979; Woman of the Yr Framingham Bus & Professional Women's Club 1979; training grant USPHS 1962-66. **BUSINESS ADDRESS:** Senior Project Adminis, Polaroid Corp, 38 Henry St, Cambridge, MA 02139.

HOPKINS, JOHN DAVID
Educator, radiologist. **PERSONAL:** Born Mar 06, 1933, Trenton, NJ; son of John P Hopkins Sr and Edith Harvey Hopkins; married Lillian L Henry; children: John III, Kay, Lisa. **EDUCATION:** Lincoln Univ, AB 1954; Meharry Med Coll, MD 1958; OH State Univ, residency 1963; Vanderbilt Univ, Fellowship 1970. **CAREER:** Meharry Medical Coll, assoc prof 1963-75, dir 1970-75; Tuskegee VA Hosp, consult 1965-68; Riverside Hosp, dir 1972-75; VA Hosp, chief radiology 1973-75; Norfolk Comm Hosp, radiologist 1975-, pres of staff 1983-85, chief radiologist; Lake Taylor Hospital, consultant radiologist 1985-. **ORGANIZATIONS:** Amer Coll of Radiology; fellow Amer Coll of Nuclear Physicians; Soc of Nuclear Med; mem adv bd Comm Mental Health Ctr; Aeolian Club; Clinical Serv Com, East VA School of Med; bd dir United Givers Fund; bd of trustees Eastern VA Medical School; Natl Medical Assn; Amer Medical Assn; commissioner, Norfolk Public Health Dept 1983-. **HONORS/ACHIEVEMENTS:** Guest lecture; 8 publications; mem Alpha Omega Hon Med Soc, Sigma Pi Phi; examiner for Amer Bd of Radiology 1983-; Case Report, Adrenal Tumors, Journal of Computed Tomography 1988. **MILITARY SERVICE:** AUS lt col 1968-70. **BUSINESS ADDRESS:** Norfolk Comm Hosp, Norfolk, VA 23504.

HOPKINS, JOHN ORVILLE
Educator. **PERSONAL:** Born Jan 27, 1930, Missoula, MT. **EDUCATION:** Gonzaga U, BA 1956, MA 1957; Columbia U, MPhil, PhD 1976; ColumbiaUniv Rsrch Prof, prep knder-grad educ 1977-78. **CAREER:** State Univ of NY, prof 1976-77; MARC Public Educ Assn, educ dir 1970-74; Bd of Educ Baltimore, asst supt 1968-69; Fed Civil Rights Officer for Educ 1965-67; Amer Philos Assn, parish priest, teacher 1962-64. **ORGANIZATIONS:** Am Assn of Sch Adminstrs; NAACP; Assn fcor Study of Black Religion; Minority Parents Assn; African Studies Assn; corporate bds MD Day Care Council; dir S African Rsrch Progm. **HONORS/ACHIEVEMENTS:** ColumbiaUniv Pub Speaking AwdsUniv MT, Seattle U, Gonzaga U, Elks, Rotary Club. **BUSINESS ADDRESS:** 420 W 118th St 1318, New York, NY 10027.

HOPKINS, LEROY TAFT, JR.
Educator. **PERSONAL:** Born Aug 19, 1942, Lancaster, PA. **EDUCATION:** Millersville St Coll, BA 1966; Harvard U, PhD 1974. **CAREER:** Millersville State Coll, asst prof of German 1979-; Urban League of Lancaster Co Inc, acting exec dir 1979, asso dir 1976-79; Hedwig-Heyle-Schule (W Germany), instr English 1974-76; NE Univ, instructor German 1971-72. **ORGANIZATIONS:** Adv Com on Black History PA Hist & Mus Commn 1979-; com person City of Lancasters Overall Econ Devel Prog; Bd Mem Lancastger Co Library/ Lancaster Neighborhood Hlth Ctr 1977-; chmn PA Delegation to White House Conf on Libraries 1978-79. **HONORS/ACHIEVEMENTS:** Received Travelling Fellowship HarvardUniv 1969-70. **BUSINESS ADDRESS:** Montgomery Ward Plaza, Millersville, IL 60671.

HOPKINS, PAULENE A.
Educator. **PERSONAL:** Born Dec 13, 1919, Chambers Co, TX. **EDUCATION:** Wiley Coll, BA 1941; Columbia Tchr Coll, MA 1943;Univ of CA at Los Angeles, postgrad 1950-53; Wiley Coll, HHD 1976. **CAREER:** Willowbrook School Dist, teacher elementary school 1951-56; Compton Union High, grade counselor 1956-58; Los Angeles Sec Schools, teacher psychometrist counselor 1958-65, rsch & devel specialist 1965-66; comm relations specialist 1966-67; Demonstration School for Adults, asst dir 1968-69, vice prin 1969-77, prin 1977-.

ORGANIZATIONS: Pres Los Angeles Sect Nat Counc Negro Women 1966-68; chmn Nat Conv 1968, reg treas 1967-69; mem Women's Coalition for Comm Action 1968-; mem CA Sch Admin Assn; mem Nat Assn of Pub & Cont Adult Edn; mem CA Counc for Adult Edn; mem Adult Educ Assn of LA; past pres Women Educ 1973-75; past pres Women in Ldrshp 1975-78; mem Delta Sigma Theta. **HONORS/ACHIEVEMENTS:** Named Ind Educ Councs Outstndg Tchr 1964; reg educ of yr awd Nat Counc Negro Women 1965; awd cit adv coms Los Angeles City Schs 1968; Outsndg Vol Serv Awd 1968; Protestant Comm Servs 1976; res for merit serv to teh comm City of LA 1979.

HOPKINS, PEREA M.
Accountant. **PERSONAL:** Born Apr 13, 1931, Marshall, TX; daughter of Charles A McCane and Margaret Perea McCane; married Milton M Hopkins Jr EdD; children: Christina Elizabeth. **EDUCATION:** Seton Hill Coll Greensburg PA, BA 1953. **CAREER:** Ballistic Rsch Lab Aberdeen Proving Ground MD, mathematician 1954-60; Spacetrack System Div LG Hanscom Field MA, mathematician 1960-68; Dynatrend Inc Woburn MA, staff accountant 1972-81; IOCS Inc, fin asst 1981-83; Heritage Meetings & Incentives Inc, acctg mgr 1983-; Krikorian Miller Associates, Bedford MA, operationa mgr 1987-. **ORGANIZATIONS:** Mem Amer Assoc of Univ Women 1953-, Amer Math Assoc 1953-68, League of Women Voters of Bedford 1969-; chmn of human resources League of Women Voters of Bedford 1970-76; bd of dir Boston Childrens Svc; pres of bd of dir Roxbury Childrens Serv 1973-79; charter mem Middlesex County Chapter of Links Inc 1976-; pres, Middlesex County Chapter of Links 1976-77; corr sec Middlesex County Chapter of Links 1978-80; membership chairperson, Middlesex County Chapter of Links 1986-88, recording sec 1988-; membership chmn, AAUW (Bedford-Lexington Branch) 1986-88. **HOME ADDRESS:** 8 Hilltop Dr, Bedford, MA 01730.

HOPKINS, STEPHANIE COLBERT
Business executive. **PERSONAL:** Born Feb 13, 1948, New York, NY; married Tyrone A Hopkins. **EDUCATION:** Lincoln Univ, attended 1966-68; Univ of MD, BA Communications 1971; Univ of Notre Dame, advanced comm certificate 1980. **CAREER:** Natl Broadcasting Co, dir of press, publicity, comm affairs 1971-76; Greater Washington Bus Ctr, consul 1976-79; DC Voting Rights, dir of comms 1980-81; Geor Mason Univ, dir of pub rel 1981-82; Star Step Inc, pres 1975-. **ORGANIZATIONS:** Consul East of the River Health Ctr 1978-85; mem Amer Fed of TV & Radio Artists; co-fndr/former vice pres Washington Area Media Orgn; bd mem MD DanceThreater 1984-85; mem Natl Assn for Prison & Welfare Reform; bd dirs Univ of MD Dance Theatre; mem Purity Bapt Church Washington. **HONORS/ACHIEVEMENTS:** Newsmaker of the Yr Washington Informer Newspaper 1984; Conference Coord Minority Enterprises Develop Week 1983 1984; Who's Who of Amer Women 1977-; DC Voting Rights Appreciation Plaque 1980; Washington Area Media Orgn Disting Serv 1980; Appreciation Awd Easter Seal Soc 1978; Recognition Awd Women's Inst for Limitless Living 1977; Natl Girl Scouts of Amer 1976; United Way of Amer Comm Serv Awd 1975. **HOME ADDRESS:** 304 Meadow Way, Landover, MD 20735.

HOPKINS, THOMAS FRANKLIN
Educational administrator, researcher, teacher. **PERSONAL:** Born in Culpepper, VA; son of Thomas Hopkins and Dorothy L Atkins (Hopkins); married Jacquelyn S Copeland, Jan 02, 1982; children: Winifred Louise, Thomas M, Charles M, Arthur G. **EDUCATION:** Calvin Coolidge Coll Boston MA, BS 1955; MI St U, MS 1961; Boston Univ, PhD 1970. **CAREER:** UUniv of MD Eastern Shore, Dept of Nat Sci chmn 1975-; Univ of CT, asso prof of biology 1970-75; Worcester Found for Experimental Biology scientist 1960-70, research asst 1949-60. **ORGANIZATIONS:** Mem Am Physiol Soc 1970-; pub many Journ Articles 1952-; mem, American Physiological Society 1970-. **MILITARY SERVICE:** USMC corpl 1943-46. **BUSINESS ADDRESS:** Univ of MD, Eastern Shore, Princess Anne, MD 21853.

HOPKINS, VASHTI EDYTHE JOHNSON
Educator. **PERSONAL:** Born Aug 22, 1924, Virginia; daughter of Rev Louis T Johnson and Matilda Ann Robinson Johnson; married Haywood Hopkins, Sr; children: Haywood Jr, Yvonne Andrews, Sharon. **EDUCATION:** Virginia Seminary & Coll, BS 1963; St Paul's Coll, BS Elem Educ 1967; Univ of Virginia, MEd 1969; Southwestern Univ, PhD Educ 1984. **CAREER:** Amherst City Public Schools, teacher 1963-67; Lynchburg Public Schools, teacher 1967-74; Sandusky Middle School, teacher 1974-82; Virginia Seminary & Coll, prof of english 1982-. **ORGANIZATIONS:** Dep organizer Order of Eastern Star PHA 1967-; life mem Virginia Seminary & Coll Natl Advisory Bd 1984; mem Zeta Chap Zeta Phi Beta Sor; life mem NEA, VEA,LEA, Univ of Virginia Alumni Assoc, Century Club St Paul's Coll; mem Daughter of Isis, Golden Circle Past LL Ruler; pres Episcopal Church Women, Amity Soc, Bridgette Soc; mem Natl Sor of Phi Delta Kappa Inc Alpha Tau Chapter Lynchburg Virginia Chapter; Phi Delta kappa Fraternity, vice pres of membership. **HONORS/ACHIEVEMENTS:** Poetry published in Century Magazine 1960; Achievement Award Order of Eastern Star Chapter 40 1984; Outstanding Achievement Grand Chapter of Virginia OESPHA 1984; Golden Poet Award, World of Poetry 1989; poems published in 1989 Golden Treasury of Great Poems. **BUSINESS ADDRESS:** Professor of English, Virginia Seminary & College, Garfield Avenue, Lynchburg, VA 24501.

HOPKINS, WES
Professional athlete. **PERSONAL:** Born Sep 26, 1961, Birmingham, AL. **EDUCATION:** Attended, Southern Methodist Univ. **CAREER:** Philadelphia Eagles, free safety 1983-. **HONORS/ACHIEVEMENTS:** Played in 1983 Hula Bowl; named Most Valuable Defensive Player Cotton Bowl; selected first team all-pro by Newspaper Enterprises Assoc; first team All-NFC by Pro Football Weekly; first alternate to the AFC-NFC Pro Bowl; named Defensive Player of the Week by Sports Illustrated; Conference Defensive Player of the Week by NFL; named NFC Defensive Player of the Month in October; first team all-pro by AP, Newspaper Enterprise Assoc, Pro Football Writers of Amer, The Sporting News, Sports Illustrated, NFL Films; second team by College and Pro Football Newsweekly; first team All-NFC by UPI and Football News; Eagles Defensive MVP by teammates. **BUSINESS ADDRESS:** Philadelphia Eagles, Philadelphia Veterans Stadium, Broad St & Pattison Ave, Philadelphia, PA 19148.

HOPKINS, WILLIAM A.
Appointed official. **PERSONAL:** Born May 27, 1943, Americus, GA; married Desi Page; children: Ellen, Ryan, Christopher, Leslee. **EDUCATION:** Albany State Coll, BA 1968; GA State Univ, MPA 1984. **CAREER:** St Regis Paper Co, asst indust relations 1967-69; Sentry Ins, dist mgr 1969-72; Insurance Multi Line, territory mgr 1972-77; Piedmont Ins Agency, pres 1977-82. **ORGANIZATIONS:** Vp Atlanta Alumni KAY 1976-78; pres Albany State Alumni 1980-82; bd mem Morris Brown Coll. **HONORS/ACHIEVEMENTS:** Outstanding Young Men of Amer Indust Relations St Regis 1969-72; Lt Col State of GA Governor Staff 1982. **MILITARY SERVICE:** AUS capt 1962-66. **BUSINESS ADDRESS:** SpclAsstto the Commrof DOAS, Stof GA DirSmall BusAffairs, 200 Piedmont Ave #1416, Atlanta, GA 30334.

HOPPER, CORNELIUS LENARD
Educational administrator. **PERSONAL:** Born Aug 30, 1934, Hartshorne, OK; son of Claude Hopper and Hazel Pugh; married Barbara M Johnson; children: Adriane, Brian, Michael. **EDUCATION:** OH Univ Athens, OH, AB 1956; Univ of Cincinnati Coll of Med, MD 1960. **CAREER:** Univ of WI Neurology, instructor 1967-68, asst prof 1968-71; Tuskegee Inst, med dir 1971-74; Univ of AL School of Med, asst clin prof 1971-79; Univ of CA, special asst for health affairs 1979-83; Univ of CA, vice pres for health affairs 1983-. **ORGANIZATIONS:** Consultant to Office of Special Programs Bureau of Health Manpower Educ NIH 1972-79; consult Amer Public Health Assn Div of Intl Health Program 1974-; pres AL State Med Assn 1974-79; assoc mem Amer Acad Neurology Natl Med Assn; mem Amer Assn for Advancement of Sci; mem Assn of Academic Health Centers; mem Golden State Med Assn; mem DHEW Natl Advisory Council on Professional Standards Review Org (PSRO) 1974-78; mem Natl Adv Comm to the Robert Wood Johnson Found Comm Hosp-Med Staff Sponsored Primary Care Group Practice Program 1974-82; mem VA Med Sch Asst Review Comm 1975-76; mem Natl Adv Comm to the Robert Wood Johnson Found Nurse Faculty Fellowships Program 1976-82; mem CA Health Manpower Policy Comm 1981-; mem Epilepsy Found of Amer, Natl Info and Resource Center Advisory Comm 1982-. **HONORS/ACHIEVEMENTS:** Special Research Fellow in Demyelinating Diseases Natl Inst of Neurological Disease and Blindness 1967-68; Alumnus of the Year OH Univ 1985; Medal of Merit OH Univ 1985; publications including, PSRO, A Current Status Report Proceedings of Sixth Annual Conf on the Southern Region Conf on the Humanities and Public Policy May, 1976; The Health Care Delivery System, A Rural Perspective Contact '72 - Proceedings of the Governor's Health manpower Conference 174, 1972; with CG Matthews and CS Cleeland, Symptom Instability and Thermoregulation in Multiple Sclerosis Neurology 22, 142, 1972; with CS Cleeland and CG Matthews, MMPI Profiles in Exacerbation and Remission of Multiple Sclerosis Psychological Reports 27, 343, 1970. **MILITARY SERVICE:** USN Battalion Surgeon 4th Marines served 2 yrs. **BUSINESS ADDRESS:** Vice President Health Affairs, University of CA System, Room 764 University Hall, Berkeley, CA 94720.

HOPPER, JOHN DOWL, JR.
Director & pilot. **PERSONAL:** Born Nov 16, 1946, Clarksville, TN; married Patricia M Rhodes; children: John Matthew, Jessica Marie. **EDUCATION:** USAF Acad, BS 1969; USAF Inst of Tech, MS (w/Distinction) 1977. **CAREER:** USAF Taiwan, pilot C-130E 1970-72; 374th Military Airlift Wing USAF, pilot 1971-72; Pilot Training Wing USAF, instr pilot/academic 1972-76; USAF Acad CO, asstto dir cdt lgstc 1977-78, aide to supt 1978-79, dep dir cdt lgstcs 1979-; 438th Military Air Life Wing, asst oeprs officer, chief command post, commander 1982-; USAF, commander 438th field maint squadron. **ORGANIZATIONS:** Mem AF Assn 1975-, USAF Acad Assn of Grads 1977-, Soc of Lgstcs Engrs 1980-, Air Lift Assoc, Alpha Iota Delta 1977-, Tuskegee Airmen Inc. **HONORS/ACHIEVEMENTS:** Listed in Outstanding Young Men of Amer 1979. **MILITARY SERVICE:** USAF lt col 16 yrs; Disting Flying Cross; Air Medal; Meritorious Serv Medal; Commodation Medal; Disting Grad Squadron Officers School 1974; Disting Grad Air Force Inst of Tech 1976-77; Disting Grad Air Command & Staff Coll 1981-82; Disting Grad C-141 Pilot Course 1982. **HOME ADDRESS:** 22 Bretton Way, Mount Laurel, NJ 08054. **BUSINESS ADDRESS:** Commander 438th Field Mntc Sq, US Air Force, 438 FMS/CC, McGuire AFB, Trenton, NJ 08641.

HOPPES, ALICE FAYE
Maintenance administrator. **PERSONAL:** Born May 20, 1939, Tucumcari, NM; daughter of Harold Kent and Bessie Mae Gamble Kent; married Willard Paul Hoppes, Aug 24, 1968 (deceased); children: LaDonna Hall Gamble, Toia Hall Hezekiah, Deidra Hall Faulkner, Linda Gail Hoppes. **EDUCATION:** Eastern New Mexico Univ, Portales NM, 1963-65. **CAREER:** Mountain Bell, Albuquerque NM, operator, 1970-74, accounts clerk, 1974-80, order writer, 1980-82; US West Communications, Albuquerque NM, maintenance admin, 1982-. **ORGANIZATIONS:** Treasurer, Amer Business Women, 1981-82; chairperson, Black Child Devel Inc, 1983-84; pres, NAACP, 1984-; nominee, State of New Mexico, State Representative Dist 24, 1985-86; ward chair, Ward 24B Democratic Party, 1985-87; vice pres, Natl Council of Negro Women, 1985-86; treasurer, Democratic Women of Bernalillo County, 1985-86; vice pres, Democratic Council, New Mexico, 1985-; mem, Albuquerque City Minority & Women's Task Force, 1985-. **HONORS/ACHIEVEMENTS:** Outstanding Community Serv, Mountain Bell Found, 1986; Unsung Heroine, NAACP, 1986; Certificate of Appreciation, Outstanding Volunteer, Governor Toney Anaya, State of New Mexico, 1986; Certificate of Nomination, State of New Mexico, State Representative Dist 13, 1986; Outstanding Community Srv, Winnie Mandella Award, 1987; Certificate of Appreciation, Secretary of State, Rebecca Vigil-Giron, 1987; Toastmaster Intl Award, Toastmaster Intl, 1987; Omega Citizen of the Year, Omega Psi Phi Frat, 1987. **HOME ADDRESS:** 9216 Hilton NE, Albuquerque, NM 87111.

HOPSON, HAROLD THEODORE, II (SONNY)
Business executive. **PERSONAL:** Born Jan 24, 1937, Abington, PA. **EDUCATION:** Philadelphia Wirless Sch, 3 post grad courses, 3rd class Radlio Telephone Operators License 1965. **CAREER:** Harold Randolph & Harvey Schmidt, div Ins Investigator 1958-65; Philadelphia Tribune, writer/reporter 1965-66; Scene Philadelphia & Tribune, entertainment critic & reviewer 1966-67. **ORGANIZATIONS:** Pepsi Generation Come Alive Radio Personality 1965-66; communicators & radio personality Radio Station WHAT-AM Philadelphia 1965-71; proprietor Sonny Hopsons Celebrity Lounge 1969-73; pres founder of Concerned Communicators 1971-; mem NAACP 1957-; mem SCLC 1965-; mem organizer of People United to Save Humanity 1971-; mem Jazz at Home Club 1968-; mem Nat Assn of Radio TV Announcers 1965-; mem Nat Black Media Coalition. **HONORS/ACHIEVEMENTS:** Recipient Spl Serv Awd YMCA 1968 BSA CIT AWD 1967; INTER URBAN LEAG AWD oF PHILA 1967; DISC JOCKEY oF YR AWD 1969; MAYOR oF PHILA YOUTH 1970; Sickle Cell Anemia Research Awd 1966; Jazz at Home Club of Am Achvmnt Awd 1971; mention in Books The Sound of Philadelphia & The Greatest Muhammad Alli. **MILITARY SERVICE:** USAF 1954-57. **BUSINESS ADDRESS:** 4936 Wynnefield Ave, Philadelphia, PA 19131.

HOPSON, MELVIN CLARENCE
Association executive. **PERSONAL:** Born Jun 29, 1937, Sawyersville, AL; married Beverly M Fraction; children: Steven, Wayne, Myra. **EDUCATION:** Roosevelt Univ, BA English 1966. **CAREER:** Montgomery Ward, store Mgr 1968, dir EEO 1969-80; McDonalds Corp, dir 1980-. **ORGANIZATIONS:** Bd mem Chicago Urban League 1971; pres Chicago Urban Affairs Council 1983; bd mem Chicago NAACP 1984; polemarch Kappa Alpha Psi. **HONORS/ACHIEVEMENTS:** Man of year Chicago Urban League 1980; view from the top EEO Today Article 1980; Urban League. **MILITARY SERVICE:** USAF sgt 1957-61. **BUSINESS ADDRESS:** Dir Affirmative Action, McDonalds Corp, McDonalds Plaza, Oak Brook, IL 60521.

HORAD, SEWELL D., SR.
Educator. **PERSONAL:** Born Jan 26, 1922, Washington, DC; married Ella Garnett; children: Sewell D, Jr, Denise H. **EDUCATION:** Howard U, BS 1942; George Washington U, MA 1973. **CAREER:** Washington DC Public Schools, admin officer Special Educ present, teacher Mathematics, sci physically handicapped children 1958-72. **ORGANIZATIONS:** Prtcptd in summer sch, night sch prog 13 Yrs; instrumental in developing new techniques for tchng handicapped chldrn, some have been copyrighted; real estate salesman family owned bus 1946-; mem Mason; vice pres "What Good Are We" Club, oldest Black Clubs in DC; "Pro-duffers" Golf Club of DC; author "Fraction Computer", math book designed to solve fractional problems without finding least common denominator; invented an inf retrieval system. **MILITARY SERVICE:** AUS capt 1942-46. **BUSINESS ADDRESS:** 5511 Illinois Ave NW, Washington, DC 20011.

HORD, FREDERICK LEE
Educator. **PERSONAL:** Born Nov 07, 1941, Kokomo, IN; divorced; children: Teresa D, F Mark, Laurel E. **EDUCATION:** IN State Univ, BS 1963, MS 1965; Union Grad Sch, PhD 1987. **CAREER:** Wabash Coll, prof of black studies 1972-76; IN Univ, guest lecturer black studies 1976; Comm Serv Admin, research dir 1977-80; Frostburg State Coll, asst dir minority affairs 1980-84; Howard Univ, prof of afro-amer studies 1984-. **ORGANIZATIONS:** Performer/lecturer PANFRE 1981-; consulting editor Nightsun; regional consultant NAMSE; consultant on black studies Aframeric Enterprises. **HONORS/ACHIEVEMENTS:** Governor's Awd for being the Outstanding Black Male Scholar in Indiana Colls & Univs 1963; poems and articles in major black journals such as Black Books Bulletin, The Western Journal of Black Studies, Black American Literature Forum, Obsidian II; featured poet in Fall 1982 issue of The Western Journal of Black Studies; book of essays "The Rhythm of Home," Third World Press 1987; book of poems "Into Africa, The Color Black," Third World Press 1987; completing comprehensive analysis of "Choice" 1987; book of poems "After(h)ours," Third World Press 1974. **BUSINESS ADDRESS:** Prof of Afro-Amer Studies, Howard University, PO Box 746, Washington, DC 20059.

HORN, EVELYN B.
Administrator. **PERSONAL:** Born Jan 08, 1953, Danbury, CT; children: Maghan Kadijah. **EDUCATION:** Univ of CT Storrs, BA 1975. **CAREER:** CT State Dept of Correction, affirmative action officer 1976-77, personnel officer 1977-79, deputy warden 1979-84, warden 1984-. **ORGANIZATIONS:** Bd mem House of Bread 1982-83; vice pres bd Families in Crisis 1982-; volunteer counselor YWCA Sexual Assault Crisis 1982-; commnr City of Hartford Drug/Alcohol 1986-; mem CT Criminal Justice Assoc, Amer Correctional Assoc, North Amer Assoc Wardens/Supts, Middle Atlantic States Correctional Assoc. **HONORS/ACHIEVEMENTS:** CT Zeta of the Year Zeta Phi Beta Sor 1978; Comm Serv Awd Phoenix Soc Firefighters 1985; Comm Serv Awd Hope SDA Church & Metro AME 1985; Govt Service Recognition YWCA 1985; Outstanding Working Women Glamour Magazine 1985. **BUSINESS ADDRESS:** Warden, CT Dept of Corrections, 177 Weston St, Hartford, CT 06120.

HORN, LAWRENCE CHARLES
Educator. **PERSONAL:** Born Jul 07, 1938, Abilene, TX; son of Alonzo Horn and Isabella W Rhodes; married Lee Ester Cross; children: Kenya La Dawn. **EDUCATION:** TN St A&I Univ, 1956-57; Langston Univ, BMusEd 1957-61; Abilene Christian Univ, 1962; Univ of OK, MMED 1971. **CAREER:** AUS, infantry & bandman 1962-64; Woodson H S Abilene Pub Sch, Teacher 1964-65; Ms Valley St Univ, teacher 1965-. **ORGANIZATIONS:** Life mem Kappa Kappa Psi Hnry Band Frat 1959-; stdnt advsr Music Educators Natl Conf 1965-; mem AAUP 1965-; past pres coll div Ms Music Educ Assn 1982-83; sec Phi Delta Kappa 1982-; bd of dir Sch Of Religious Studies 1982-; basileus Omega Psi Phi Frat Inc 1983-; MVSU Mid-Delta summer band camp 1986; MVSU Honor Band 1987; adv Alpha Kappa Mu Hon Soc 1985-; pres LS Rogers Elem School PTA 1988-89; Collegiate Division Sponsor, Mississippi Music Educators Assn 1988-. **HONORS/ACHIEVEMENTS:** Service Lyceum Com MVSU Lyceum Com 1980; Omega man of yr Beta Rho Chap Omega Psi Phi Frat 1982; soloist Messiah MVSU Concert Choir 1983 & 84; Service Award Phi Delta Kappa Utica Chapter 1988; MVSU Teacher of Year Miss Legislature 1989. **MILITARY SERVICE:** AUS pfc 2 yrs; sharp shooter 1962-64. **HOME ADDRESS:** 216 Leflore Ave, Itta Bena, MS 38941.

HORNE, EDWIN CLAY
Dentist. **PERSONAL:** Born Feb 16, 1924, Greensboro, NC; son of Ellis Clay Horne and Annie Slade Horne; married Gene Ann Polk-Horne MD, Aug 23, 1982; children: Carol Anne Horne-Penn, Edwin Christian Horne. **EDUCATION:** NC A&T State Univ, BS 1947; School of Dentistry Univ of PA, DDS 1952. **CAREER:** Harlem Hospital, assoc attending dentist 1954—; Upper Harlem Comprehensive Care Ctr, attending dentist, dental supervisor 1985—; Private Practice, dentist; North Central Bronx-Montefiore Hosp Affiliation, clinical assoc supervisor 1973—, adj prof of clinical dentistry for Columbia Univ Sch of Dental and Oral Surgery. **ORGANIZATIONS:** Fellow, Am Coll of Dentists, 1988; Mem First District Dental Soc of New York 1952-; mem Omega Psi Phi Frat 1945-, Sigma Pi Phi Frat 1967-; mem Revielle Club of New York 1971-; mem Lions Intl Englewood NJ 1978-; corp mem, 1980—, brd 3rd vice pres, 1988-89, Schomburg Corp, Schomburg Ctr for Rsch in Black Culture; sire archon North East Region Sigma Pi Phi Frat 1987; mem North Carolina A&T State Univ Alumni; mem bd of dirs Univ of PA-Metro New Jersey Alumni Assoc 1987; exec bd, U of PA Dental School Alumni Soc, 1989-90; comm mem visual aids Annual November Dental Convention New York City past 10 yrs. **HONORS/ACHIEVEMENTS:** Man of the Year Awd Kappa Omicron Chap Omega Psi Phi Frat 1970; honored for 40 yrs Meritorious Membership Omega Psi Phi Frat August 1986 Washington DC. **MILITARY SERVICE:** AUS. **HOME ADDRESS:** 374 Miller Ave, Englewood, NJ 07631.

HORNE, GENE-ANN P. See POLK, GENE-ANN

HORNE, GERALD C.
Attorney. **PERSONAL:** Born Jan 03, 1949, St Louis, MO. **EDUCATION:** Princeton U, BA 1970; Univ C-Berkeley, JD 1973; Columbia U, M Phil & PhD 1979-82; Revson Fellowship City Coll of New York, 1980-81. **CAREER:** Affirmative Action Coord Center, dir counsel 1979-81; CCNY Revson Fellow, 1980-81; Natl Lawyers Cnilo, staff atty 1982; Sarah Lawrence Coll, prof of History and law 1982-; Natl Conf of Black Lawyers, exec dir; District 1199 - Health & Hospital Workers Union, counsel. **ORGANIZATIONS:** Vice chair equality comm Am Civil Liberties Union 1981-; editorial bd Nat'l Lawyers 1982-; bd of dir Nat'l Conf of Black Lawyers Wrence Coll 1982-; steering Comm Free So Africa Movement 1984-; mem of bar NJ and PA. **HONORS/ACHIEVEMENTS:** McConnell Fellowship Princeton Univ 1969; Nellon Fellowship Sarah Lawrence Coll 1983; Hope Stevens Awd Nat'l Conf of Black Lawyers 1983; Author Black & Rep WEB DuBois and the Am Response to the Cold War Suny Press 1985; Communist Front? The Civil Rights Congress (Fairleigh Dickinson Univ Press) 1987. **BUSINESS ADDRESS:** Counsel, Dist 1199-Hlth & Hosp Wkrs Un, 310 W 43rd St, New York, NY.

HORNE, JUNE C.
Business executive. **PERSONAL:** Born Sep 06, 1952, New York City, NY; daughter of Samuel Smith and Celiel Sledge Smith; married Frank Horne, Mar 30, 1972. **EDUCATION:** Lab Inst of Merchandising, AA 1971. **CAREER:** Saks Fifth Ave, exec trainee 1971-72, asst buyer swimwear/sportswear 1976-78, buyer swimwear 1977-79, buyer designer sportswear 1978-82; Saks Garden City Branch, 1st black female store gen mgr 1982-84; Saks Fifth Ave, assoc div merch mgr designer sportswear 1985-; Saks Fifth Ave, dir of Designer Sportswear 1986-. **ORGANIZATIONS:** Mem YMCA of Greater NY Black Achievers, Black Retail Action Group. **HONORS/ACHIEVEMENTS:** Black Achievers in Industry Awd YMCA of Greater NY 1979; Interviewed for NY Times Article "A Buyers View of the Busy World of Fashion" 1980; Buyer Achievement Awd Black Retail Action Group 1982. **BUSINESS ADDRESS:** Assoc Div Merch Mgr Dsgnr, Saks Fifth Avenue, 611 5th Ave, New York, NY 10022.

HORNE, JUNE MERIDETH
Psychiatric technician. **PERSONAL:** Born Feb 23, 1936, Chicago, IL; daughter of William Browder and Elizabeth Neal-Browder; married Brazell Horne, Oct 06, 1954 (deceased); children: Brazell Rodney. **EDUCATION:** Kennedy King Jr Coll, attended 1974-75. **CAREER:** Veterans Administration, psychiatric tech 1964-. **ORGANIZATIONS:** Pres Browder and Watts Inc 1985. **HONORS/ACHIEVEMENTS:** Emergency Escape Apparatus (invention) US Patent 4-498-557 1985. **HOME ADDRESS:** 1713 W 90th St, Chicago, IL 60620.

HORNE, LENA
Singer, dancer. **PERSONAL:** Born Jun 30, 1917, Brooklyn, NY. **CAREER:** Dancer Cotton Club 1934; toured recorded with Noble Sissle Orch 1935-36, w/Chas Barnet's Band 1940-41; cafe society singer; roles in motion pictures include "Panama Hattie", "Cabin in the Sky", "Stormy Weather", "As Thousands Cheer", "Two Girls & A Sailor", "Ziegfeld Follies", "Till The Clouds Roll By", "Words & Music", "The Wiz", "That's Entertainment"; numerousTV appearances including specials Harry & Lena 1970, Tony & Lena 1972, Jubilee 1976, The Sound of His Music (salute to Richard Rogers) 1976; recording artist; appeared Carnegie Hall, London Palladium, On Broadway in "Jamaica". **HONORS/ACHIEVEMENTS:** Author "In Person-Lena Horne" 1950; co-author "Lena" 1965; Page One Awd NY Newspaper Guild; Black Filmmakers Hall of Fame; "Special Tony" Disting Achievementin Theater; NY Drama Critics Circle Awd; Handel Medallion Highest Cultural Awd; Drama Desk Awd for Best Actress in a Musical; Third Annual Young Audiences Arts Awd; Ebony's Lifetime Achievement Awd.

HORNE, MARVIN L. R., JR.
Project manager. **PERSONAL:** Born Mar 05, 1936, Richmond, VA; married Vernell Bell; children: Marvin III, Tracy R, Carl E, Kelly M. **EDUCATION:** VA State Coll, BS Physics 1957; Howard Univ graduate school Physics, 1959-60; Univ of Rochester, MBA 1975. **CAREER:** US Naval Weapons Lab, math/physicist 1960-61; Gen Elec Co, physicist 1961-63; US Naval Weapons Lab, math/physicist 1963-65; Eastman Kodak Co, engrg mgr 1965-. **ORGANIZATIONS:** Mem Amer Inst of Aero & Astronautics 1963-67; mem Tech Marketing Soc of Amer 1978-; mem Sigma Pi Sigma 1954-57; mem Kappa Mu Episilon 1954-57; mem Alpha Phi Alpha Frat 1954-; mem Beta Gamma Sigma 1975-; chmn Rochester City Planning commn 1977-82. **MILITARY SERVICE:** AUS 1st lt 1957-59; Letter of Commendation. **BUSINESS ADDRESS:** Engineering Manager, Eastman Kodak Co, 901 Elmgrove Rd, Rochester, NY 14650.

HORNE, SEMMION N.
Business executive. **PERSONAL:** Children: Raymond N. **EDUCATION:** Dorchester Academy; Spring Garden Inst. **CAREER:** Horne & Howard Const Co, line mechanic 23 yrs; Somerset Hls & Co Natl Bank, Pres Adv Bd. **ORGANIZATIONS:** NAACP pres; mem Rent Leveling Bd; Community Church of God. **HONORS/ACHIEVEMENTS:** Awarded Life Mem Wise Owl Club.

HORNE, WESTRY GROVER
Administrator/educator. **PERSONAL:** Born Feb 20, 1913, Rocky Mount, NC; son of Westry Horne and Florida Horne; married Dorothy Bailey; children: DeLois Jacqueline Brown, Dorothy Judith Hamblin. **EDUCATION:** Clark Coll Atlanta, BS 1938; NY Univ, MA 1948; Univ of PA Phila, MS 1956. **CAREER:** Jasper Co Training Sch Monticello GA, prin 1938-39; Warren Co Training Sch Wise NC, asst prin & librarian 1939-40; Natl Youth Admin Prog A&T Coll Greensboro NC, prof & dir 1940-41; Natl Youth Admin for NC, dir 1941-43; USO Camp Edwards Hyannis MA, dir 1943-44; USO Prog Camp Kilmer, dir 1944-50; Harlem YMCA NY, gen prog sec 1950-58; Woodbridge Township Schs NJ, supv elem ed 1958-63; NJ State Dept of Ed, dir elem educ & coord of migrant educ 1963-67; Ofc for Civil Rights US Dept of HEW, dir ed div 1967-77; Fair Housing & Equal Oppor US Dept of Housing & Urban Devel, dir contract compliance 1977-78; Ofc Fed Contract Compliance Progs US Dept of Labor Newark, area dir 1978-. **ORGANIZATIONS:** Mem Edges Group Inc; mem Amer Library Assn; charter mem Natl Assn of Social Workers; mem Amer Educ Assn; mem NEA; state pres Frontiers Intl Serv Clubs; chmn NC Council on Employment Oppors; pres USO Staff Conf Camp Kilmer NJ; chmn Natl Youth Admin Adv Council for

NC; organizer vol groups from So NJ & New York City for couns & Hostesses for servicemen stationed & passing through Camp Kilmer NJ; mem Assn of Sec Intl YMCA; mem Masonic Order F & AM; mem Frontiers Intl Serv Clubs; mem NJ Duplicate Bridge Club; mem Amer Tennis Assn; mem Natl Rec Assn; mem Alpha Phi Alpha Frat; pres Coll Student Cncl;pres Coll Chap YMCA; pres Coll Dramatic Club; pres Alpha Phi Alpha Frat; vice chmn Watchung Area Council BSA; mem United Comm Fund Plainfield Area; bd dirs Plainfield Area YMCA; chmn adult prog & membership com Plainfield Area YMCA; supr Little Theatre Group Harlem; dir City & Statewide Tennis Activities. **HONORS/ACHIEVEMENTS:** Outstanding Educator of Amer Awd NEA 1967; Outstanding Comm Serv Awd Frontiers Intl Serv Clubs 1975; named Westry G Horne Day City of Plainfield NJ 1980; Feb 28 1980 Westry G Horne Day Gen Assembly of NJ 1980.

HORNE-MCGEE, PATRICIA J.
Educational administrator. **PERSONAL:** Born Dec 23, 1946, Ypsilanti, MI; daughter of Lacy Horne Sr and Louise Hardwick Horne; married Columbus McGee, Aug 04, 1979. **EDUCATION:** MI State Univ, BA 1968; Univ of MI, MSW 1971; Eastern MI Univ, MA 1973. **CAREER:** MI State Dept of Social Svcs, caseworker 1968-69; Ann Arbor Model Cities, social coord 1970-72; Washtenaw Co Comm Coordinated Child Care, exec dir 1971-74; Ferris State Coll, asst prof 1974-79; Mercy Coll of Detroit, assoc prof/program dir social work dept 1979-88; Wayne County Intermediate School District, assoc dir, 1987-; Wayne State Univ, adjunct prof, 1988-; Washtenaw Community Coll, Ann Arbor, MI, adjunct prof, 1989-. **ORGANIZATIONS:** Sec Huron Valley Assoc of Black Social Workers 1971-; consultant Head Start Wayne Co, Washtenaw 1980; planning commissioner City of Ypsilanti 1982-; bd mem, 1983-, 2nd Vice Pres, 1988-, Huron Valley Girl Scouts; pres Ann Arbor Delta Sigma Theta 1985-87; mem Natl Assoc of Social Workers; mem Zoning Bd of Appeals City of Ypsilanti; vice pres, Michigan Council, Delta Sigma Theta Sorority. **HOME ADDRESS:** 925 Frederick St, Ypsilanti, MI 48197.

HORNSBY, ALTON, JR.
Editor, educator. **PERSONAL:** Born Sep 03, 1940, Atlanta; married Anne R; children: Alton, III, Angela. **EDUCATION:** Morehouse Coll, BA 1961;Univ of TX, MA 1962, PhD 1969. **CAREER:** Tuskegee Inst, instr 1962-65; Dept of History Morehouse Coll, presently prof of History. **ORGANIZATIONS:** Mem Assn for Study of Afro-am Life & History, exec counc of Atlanta Br; Assn of Soc & Behvrl Scientists, mem budget Com; So Historical Assn Mem prog com; Phi Alpha Theta; NAACP; Alpha Phi Omega. **HONORS/ACHIEVEMENTS:** Recipient Woodrow Wilson Fellow 1961-62; So Educ Found Fellow 1966-68; Tchr of Yr Morehouse Coll 1971; editor "Journal of Negro History"; editor "The Cage; Eyewitness Accounts of the Freed Negro in So Soc 1877-1929"; author "The Black Almanac". **BUSINESS ADDRESS:** Morehouse College, The Journal of Negro Histroy, Box 721, Atlanta, GA 30314.

HORNSBY, B. KAY
Mortician. **PERSONAL:** Born Dec 09, 1906, Wolf City, TX; widowed. **EDUCATION:** Bishop Coll Marshall TX, NA 1928; Hampton sch of Embalming Dallas, cert of proficiency 1930; Worsham Coll of Mortuary Sci Chicago, BS 1935. **CAREER:** Fleming Fraternal Beaumont TX, mortician 1930-35; Thomas Funeral Home Hearn TX, mortician 1935-39; Thomas & Brooks Funeral Home Temple TX, mortician 1939-46; Hornsby Funeral Home Temple TX, mortician/owner/mgr 1946-79; Hornsby & Murcherson Funeral Home, mortician/owner/mgr 1979-. **ORGANIZATIONS:** Pres Natl Council of Negro Women 1949-53; mem comm relations com NAACP Temple Br 1939-; sec Epsilon Nu Delta Mortuary Chap Zeta 1945-; mem Ch Women of Temple 1950-. **HONORS/ACHIEVEMENTS:** Woman of the Yr Awd Independent Funeral Dir Assn of TX 1962; Dr T E Dixon Humanitarian Awd Temple NAACP 1977; David Henderson Jr Awd Temple Youth Council of NAACP 1977; 50 yrs Dedicated Serv Awd TX Funeral Dir Assn 1980. **BUSINESS ADDRESS:** Manager, Hornsby & Murcherson Funeral H, 201 S 8th St, Temple, TX 76501.

HORNSBY, WALTER SPURGEON, III
Business executive. **PERSONAL:** Born Sep 06, 1941, Augusta, GA; married Clara J; children: Walter IV, Wendell. **EDUCATION:** Morehouse Coll, BA 1957-61;Univ MI, grad sch 1963. **CAREER:** The Pilgrim Health & Life Ins Co, exec vice pres 1976-; Pilgrim Hlth & Life Ins Co, exec vice pres actuary 1975-76; Nat Ins Assn, actuary dir 1971-; St Josephs Hosp, dir 1977-. **ORGANIZATIONS:** Mem Augusta Port Authority 1975-; 1st Vp United Way of Richmond & Columbia Co & N Alugusta 1978, pres 1979; vice pres prog GA Carolina Council BSA 1979; sec The Sportsmans Boat Club Inc; 2nd vice pres treas chmn United Way 1974-; chmn trustee bd Antioch Bapt Ch 1975-; vchmn Augusta/Richmond Co Data Processing Com 1976-. **HONORS/ACHIEVEMENTS:** Whos Who in S & SW 1976-77; Whos Who in Ins 1972-; Outst Young Men of Am 1977. **MILITARY SERVICE:** AUS sp-5 1966-68. **BUSINESS ADDRESS:** 1143 Laney Walker Blvd, Augusta, GA 30901.

HORSFORD, ANNA MARIA
Actress, producer. **PERSONAL:** Born in New York, NY; daughter of Victor A Horsford and Lillian Agatha Richardson Horsford. **EDUCATION:** Attended Inter-American Univ of Puerto Rico, Puerto Rico, 1966-67. **CAREER:** Stage debut at New York Shakespearean Theater, New York NY, 1965; WNET-13 National Educational Television, New York NY, producer, 1970-81; film debut, 1978. **ORGANIZATIONS:** Mem, Variety Club of America; pres, Black Women in Theatre, 1983-84. **HONORS/ACHIEVEMENTS:** Outstanding leadership award, NAACP, Gary IN chapter, 1973; actress in films, including An Almost Perfect Affair, 1978, Times Square, 1979, The Fan, 1980, Love Child, 1981, Class, 1982, Crackers, 1982; actress on television shows, including The Doctors, Murder, Inc, Star Struck, Bill; played Clara Jones on The Guiding Light. **BUSINESS ADDRESS:** c/o Monty Silver, 200 West 57th St, New York, NY 10019. *

HORTON, CARRELL PETERSON
Educator. **PERSONAL:** Born Nov 28, 1928, Daytona Beach, FL; daughter of Preston S. Peterson and Mildred Adams Peterson; divorced; children: Richard. **EDUCATION:** Fisk Univ, BA 1949; Cornell Univ, MA 1950; Univ of Chgo, PhD 1972. **CAREER:** Fisk Univ, instr/res asso 1950-55; Meharry Med Coll, stat anal 1955-66; Fisk Univ, prof & adm 1966-, dir div of soc sci. **ORGANIZATIONS:** Bd of dir Rochelle Training Ctr 1968-84; consult Health Services Research 1977-1 980; bd of dir Wesley Foundation 1977; consult Nat'l Science Fndtn 1979; cons Nat'l Research Council 1979; bd of dir Samaritan Pastoral Counseling Ctr 1983; mem, Bd of Higher Educ & Campus Ministry, UM Church, 1983-. **HONORS/ACHIEVEMENTS:** Urban league awd Jacksonville, FL 1949; grad Assistantship Cornell Univ 1949-50; faculty fellowships Ford Found IBM 1969-70, Sum 1971; Article in Prof Journals; mem bd of Higher Educ & Campus Ministry, U.M. Church 1983-. **BUSINESS ADDRESS:** Dir Div of Soc Science, FiskUniv, FiskUniv, Nashville, TN 372034501.

HORTON, CLARENCE PENNINGTON
Physician. **PERSONAL:** Born Aug 29, 1910, Rome, GA; married Helen Annis Phillips; children: Clarence Jr, Chandler, Gregory, Lisa. **EDUCATION:** Bluefield St Tchrs Coll, BS; Meharry Med Sch, MD 1937. **CAREER:** Alton Meml Hosp, surg med staff; St Josephs Hosp, St Anthonys Hosp, St Josephs Hosp, head emgcy staff 1974-77. **ORGANIZATIONS:** Mem Gtr Alton C of C, Madison Co 708 Bd; Alpha Phi Alpha; 33 Degree Mason; fellow Asso Intl Coll of Surgeons. **HONORS/ACHIEVEMENTS:** Daniel Bowles Awd, Alpha Phi Alpha 1975. **BUSINESS ADDRESS:** 206 Market St, Alton, IL 62002.

HORTON, EARLE C.
Attorney. **PERSONAL:** Born Mar 09, 1943, Tampa, FL; married Mabel; children: Brett, Earle III. **EDUCATION:** Fisk U, BA 1964; Cleveland St U, JD 1968. **CAREER:** Thunder Bay Communications, pres; Graves Haley Horton, atty. **ORGANIZATIONS:** Mem 1st Black Law Firm in OH; spl counsel to Atty Gen OH; mem Am Bar Assn; oH St Bar Assn; Cleveland Bar Assn; John Harlan Law Club; Cleveland FiskUniv Club; mem NAACP, Urban League, Norman Minor Bar Assoc. **HONORS/ACHIEVEMENTS:** Recipient Meritorious Serv Awd, Cleveland Bar Asson 1971; Dist Serv Awd, John Harlan Law Club 1973. **BUSINESS ADDRESS:** Attorney, Graves, Haley, Horton, 100 Erieview Plaza, Cleveland, OH 44114.

HORTON, JAMES T.
Attorney. **PERSONAL:** Born Dec 06, 1918, E St Louis, IL; married Helen B; children: 4 children. **EDUCATION:** Loyola Univ, LLB, JD 1948. **CAREER:** Chicago Resident Training Ctr, football coach & athletic dir 1939-41; Prescott Burroughs Taylor & Carey Chgo, attny 1949-66; Cook Cty Chgo, asst state attny; Reciprocal Non-Support Div, chief 1959-61; Solicitor of Labor US Sec of Labor Ofc, gen counsel 1964-68; Publ Welfare Admin DC, hearing officer 1968-71; Fair Hearings & Reg Div, chief, admin judge 1974-. **ORGANIZATIONS:** Admitted to practice IL Bar, Fed Bar & Supreme Court of US; pres Cook Cty Bar Assoc 1954-56; mem bd dir Cook Cty Bar Assoc 1956-64; mem Natl Bar Assoc, Amer Bar Assoc, IL State Bar Assoc; pres Upsilon Sigma Chap Phi Beta Sigma Frat 1956-58; dir of soc action 1958-63; mem Natl Legal Counsel Phi Beta Sigma Frat 1960-; mem bd dir Chicago Com of 100; past asst Gen Counsel Cosmopolitan C of C Chgo; past mem Natl Coun of Christians & Jews; past mem Cath Interracial Soc; mem NAACP. **HONORS/ACHIEVEMENTS:** Phi Beta Sigma Man of the Year Awd 1962; Disting Serv Chap Phi Beta Sigma Frat 1968; Key to City Lovejoy IL 1973. **MILITARY SERVICE:** AUS 1943-45. **BUSINESS ADDRESS:** Chief, Admin Judge, Fair Hearings & Reg Div, 500 First St NW, Washington, DC 20001.

HORTON, LARKIN, JR.
Business executive. **PERSONAL:** Born Feb 18, 1939, Lenoir, NC; married Patricia Richardson; children: Larkin III, Gregory Derwin. **EDUCATION:** Catawba Valley Tech Inst, Assoc Elect 1960; General Electric Control School, Master Controls 1961; Clever-Brooks Pressure Vessels, Cert Pressure Vessels 1961; Caldwell Comm Coll, Cert Powder Activated Tools 1972. **CAREER:** World Police Congress, vice pres 1971; Intl Police Hall of Fame, bd of dir 1973-75, lifetime membership 1976; Intl Assoc of Elect Inspectors, inspector 1980-;profl photographer; City of Lenoir, councilman-at-large, Horton's Electric Co, electrical contractor. **ORGANIZATIONS:** Owner East Finley Auto Laundry 1972-; councilman at large, police committee 1983-, City of Lenoir; Trustee St Paul AME Church 1978-; bd of dir Natl Cancer Soc 1983-; mem Caldwell Friends Inc 1984-85; mem Gov Crime Prevention Comm. **HONORS/ACHIEVEMENTS:** Value Analysis Awd Burlington Ind 1980, 1981, 1982; Man of the Year The American Legion 1984. **HOME ADDRESS:** 445 Arlington Circle NW, PO Box 242, Lenoir, NC 28645. **BUSINESS ADDRESS:** Electrical Contractor, Horton's Electric Co, 445 Arlington Circle NW, PO Box 242, Lenoir, NC 28645.

HORTON, LARNIE G.
State employee. **PERSONAL:** Married Katrena B; children: Larnie Glenn, Jr, Langston Garvey. **EDUCATION:** Morris Brown Coll, AB;Univ NC-chapel Hill, completed degree & lang reqluirements for Masters Prog; Duke U, MDiv (Hon Dr); Nat Theo Sem & Coll. **CAREER:** Saxapaw, NC, pastor of ch 1960-64; Emanuel AME Ch, Durham, pastor 1964-66; Kittrell Coll NC, academic dean 1961-62, pres 1966-73; Gov for Minority Affairs, spl asst 1973-. **ORGANIZATIONS:** Mem bd trustees Vance Co Tech Inst 1968; mem bd dir Nat Lab for Higher Educ 1970; mem bd dir Soul City Found 1968; consult Am Assn of Jr Coll 1970-72; mem NAACP; Merchants Assn of Chapel Hill; Alpha Phi Alpha Frat; C of C of Henderson NC. **HONORS/ACHIEVEMENTS:** Grad Cum Laude, Morris Brown Coll; Whos Who in Am Coll & Univ; Woodrow Wilson & Rockefeller Fellow; Whos Who in S & Sw; voted 1970 Civic Achievement Awd, Morris Brown Coll Nat Alumni Assn; voted ond of Am Otstndng Young Men of 1970; presented Nat Alumni Assn Awd Stillman Coll 1970. **BUSINESS ADDRESS:** Gov Ofc Admin Bldg, 116 W Jones St, Raleigh, NC 27611.

HORTON, LEMUEL LEONARD
Agri-business manager. **PERSONAL:** Born Jun 29, 1936, Fort Valley, GA; married Yvonne Felton; children: Lorna Y Hill. **EDUCATION:** Fort Valley State Coll, BS 1963. **CAREER:** Civil Service Robins AFB GA, warehouseman 1958-65; State of GA, comm serv consultant 1965-68; Ft Valley State Coll, dir student union 1968-71; The Research GP, assoc 1971-73; New York Life, field underwriter 1973; Gold Kist Inc, mgr employee relations 1973-. **ORGANIZATIONS:** Pres 1980-81, mem Resurgens; mem Intl Assoc of Quality Circles, IRRA, US Army Reserves; bd mem GA Chap Epilepsy Foundation; pres TAPS Epilepsy Foundation. **HONORS/ACHIEVEMENTS:** Presidential Citation Natl Assoc for Equal Oppor in Higher Educ 1983. **MILITARY SERVICE:** AUS sp2 3 yrs; AUS Reserve command sgt major 30 yrs; Army Achievement Medal 1982, Army Commendation Medal 1983, Meritorious Serv Medal 1986. **BUSINESS ADDRESS:** Manager Employee Relations, Gold Kist, Inc, P O Box 2210, Atlanta, GA 30301.

HORTON, ODELL
Judge. **PERSONAL:** Born May 13, 1929, Whiteville, TN; married Evie; children: Odell Jr, Christopher. **EDUCATION:** Morehouse Coll, AB 1951; Howard Univ Law Sch, JD 1956; MS Indsl Coll, Hon LHD; Morehouse College, Hon LLD. **CAREER:** Western Dist

of TN, apptd asst US atty 1962; LeMoyne-Owen Coll, pres; Criminal Court Shelby Co, judge 1969-70; US Bankruptcy Court, judge. **ORGANIZATIONS:** Mem Amer Council on Educ; US Dist Court Judge Western Dist of TN 1980; Assn of Amer Coll & Univ Council on Higher Educ; Amer Bar Assn; credited with creating progressive pre-trial release prog for indigent persons charged with violations of criminal law. **HONORS/ACHIEVEMENTS:** Disting Alumni Awd Howard Univ; 1970 Bill of Rights Awd; LM Graves Meml Health Awd 1969; numerous other awds. **BUSINESS ADDRESS:** Judge, Tennessee Western District, Federal Bldg, Memphis, TN 38103.

HORTON, STELLA JEAN
Educator, educational administrator, business executive. **PERSONAL:** Born Aug 16, 1944, Durham, NC; children: Braheim Knight. **EDUCATION:** St Augustine's Coll, attended 1962-64; A&T State Univ, BS (magna cum laude) 1966; Rutgers The State Univ, MEd 1972, EdD 1986. **CAREER:** Orange Co Bd of Educ, teacher 1966-69; Rutgers The State Univ, assoc prof 1970-76; Alternative Sch Camden Bd of Educ, teacher/principal 1976-80; Juvenile Resource Ctr Inc, adm/exec dir 1980-. **ORGANIZATIONS:** Consul NJ Dept of Educ 1980-84; mem Urban League Camden Co 1981-83; Camden City Bd of Educ vice pres 1983-84, mem 1980-; mem 5th Legilsative Dist NJSch Bds 1983-. **HONORS/ACHIEVEMENTS:** Who's Who in Amer Colls & Univs 1966; Serv to Young People Juvenile Resource Ctr Inc 1979; Comm Serv NJ Assoc of Black Soc Workers 1982. **HOME ADDRESS:** 1412 Van Hook St, Camden, NJ 08104. **BUSINESS ADDRESS:** Executive Dir, Juvenile Resource Ctr Inc, 315 Cooper St, Camden, NJ 08102.

HORTON, WILLIE WATTISON
Professional baseball player. **PERSONAL:** Born Oct 18, 1942, Arno, VA; married Gloria; children: Darryl I, Al, Darryl II, Gil, Terri Lyn, April, Pam. **CAREER:** Seattle Mariners, pro baseball player 1979-; Oakland Athletics, pro baseball player 1978; Cleveland Indians, pro baseball player 1978; Detroit Tigers, outfielder 1964-77; Minor Leagues, baseball player 1962-64. **HONORS/ACHIEVEMENTS:** Led North Lg in total bases (203) 1962; played World Series 1968; named Outfielder Sporting News All Stars 1968; played in All Star Game 1965, 1968, 1970, 1973; tied major league record most put-outs & most chances accepted by left-fielder (11) 1 game 1969; hit 3 home runs 1 game 1970, 1977; played in AL Championship Series 1972; named designated hitter Sporting News AL All Stars 1975, 1979; led AL designated hitters in strikeouts (114) 1977; named AL Comeback Player of Yr Sporting News 1979; Mariners's MVP 1979; 1st Mariner to drive in 100 runs in season & set club record with 106 1979; 9th in AL game winning RBI's 1979; Club record for home runs 1 season (29) 1979; tied for 7th in AL home runs 1979; one of 6 League players to play all games 1 season 1979; had club record at bats (646)1979; ranked 3rd in league for at bats (646) 1979; Club record for total bases (209) & total hits (180) ranking 9th in League for both; "Willie Horton" Night at Seattle 1979.

HOSKINS CLARK, TEMPY M.
Educator. **PERSONAL:** Born Oct 25, 1938, Hazen, AK; married Wilber L Hoskins; children: Jamele, Monroe, Brian McKissic. **EDUCATION:** Philander Smith Clge, BA 1963; Western MI Univ, MA 1971. **CAREER:** Grand Rapids Bd of Educ, elementary prin; McKinley Upper Grade Center Chicago IL, vocal music teacher; S Middle School Grand Rapids MI, vocal music teacher, chmn. **ORGANIZATIONS:** Minister of mus True Light Bapt Ch Grand Rapids; bd dir Blue Lake Fine Arts Camp; pres Negro Bus & Prof Club Inc; mem Delta Sigma Theta Sor; pres of local chap Delta Sigma Theta; travel abroad summer 1972 with hs students to Belgium Holland England & France. **BUSINESS ADDRESS:** 50 Antoine SW, Grand Rapids, MI.

HOSTEN, ADRIAN
Physician, educator. **PERSONAL:** Born in Grenada, WI; married Claire C; children: Karen, Lester. **EDUCATION:** Atlantic Union Coll, BA 1958; Howard Univ, MD 1962. **CAREER:** Howard Univ, chief nephrology div 1967-; Med Intensive Care Unit Howard Univ Hospital, dir 1968-75; Bates Memorial HS, principal 1954-55, instructor 1966-68, asst prof 1968-72; Howard Univ, assoc prof 1972-82, prof 1982-. **ORGANIZATIONS:** Mem Natl Med Assoc 1968-, Amer Soc of Nephrology 1971-, Intl Soc of Nephrology 1973-. **BUSINESS ADDRESS:** Professor, HowardUniv, 2041 Georgia Ave NW, Washington, DC 20060.

HOTCHKISS, WESLEY AKIN
Retired educator, clergyman. **PERSONAL:** Born Jan 26, 1919, Spooner, WI; married Mary Ellen Fink; children: Tannia. **EDUCATION:** Northland Coll, BA 1944, ThD 1958; Univ Chicago, MS 1948, PhD 1950; Yankton Coll, DD 1956; Pacific Univ, LLD 1965; IL Coll, LitD 1979; Talladega Coll, LHD 1982; Ripon Coll, LHD 1982; HI Loa Coll, LitD 1983; Tougaloo Coll, LLD 1984. **CAREER:** Chicago Theol Sem, rsch assoc 1947-49; Greater Cinn Council Chs, rsch dir 1949-50; City Coll NY, lectr in geography 1960-; United Ch Bd, rsch dir 1950-55, sec 1955-58, gen sec for higher educ 1958-82 (retired). **ORGANIZATIONS:** Mem spl seminar higher educ Columbia 1962-; AAAS; Amer Sociol Assn; Religious Rsch Assn; former trustee Ripon Coll; Fisk Univ; Dillard Univ; Talladega Coll; Tougaloo Coll; Northland Coll; Huston-Tillotson Coll; Le Moyne-Owen Coll; Ripon Coll; Prescott Coll; Hawaii LOA Coll; trustee Affiliate Artists Inc; fellow Assn Amer Geographers. **MILITARY SERVICE:** AUS chaplain 1945-47.

HOUSE, CAROLYN JOYCE
Attorney. **PERSONAL:** Born Nov 11, 1952, Columbia, SC. **EDUCATION:** Univ of S FL, BA 1974;Univ of SC Law Center, JD 1977. **CAREER:** State Attys Ofc Hillsborough Co, asst state atty present; Jim Walter Corp, asso litigation couns 1977-80; Univ of SC Law Cntr, 1st black legal writing inst 1976-77; Law Inc Legal Serv to the Poor, legal intern 1976; Law Students Civil Rights Resrch Counc, legal intern 1975-76. **ORGANIZATIONS:** Spl consult to pres Nat Bar Assn; asst to pres FL Chap Nat Bar Assn 1979; CLE-CHRPSN & loan ofcr FL Chap Nat Bar Assn 1980; vice pres Alpha Kappa Alpha Sorority 1972-74; bd of dirs Tampa Orgn of Black Affairs 1980; bd of dirs Hillsborough Co Mental Hlth Assn 1980; bd of dirs Tampa Philharmonic Soc 1980. **HONORS/ACHIEVEMENTS:** Who's Who in Am Law Marquis Publisher's Co 1979-80; lectr FL Chap Nat Bar Assn 1979.

HOUSE, JAMES E.
Consultant. **PERSONAL:** Born Oct 06, Goldsboro, NC; son of Edward A House and Cleo Peoples House. **EDUCATION:** Howard Univ, BS Mech Engrg 1963. **CAREER:** McDonnell Douglas Corp St Louis, test & structural engr 1963-67; Fairchild Hiller Corp, stress analyst 1967-68; The Boeing Co Seattle, rsch engr 1968-72; WIPCO Inc St Croix, vice pres treas 1972-77; Progress Inc of Wash DC, Natl Assoc of Minority CPA Firms, Govt of DC, Jones & Artis Co Wash DC, consult 1981-86; JBH Associates, consultant 1986-87; The Eckenberge Group, Washington, DC, pres, 1987-. **ORGANIZATIONS:** Pres Student Govt School of Engrg & Arch Howard Univ 1962; chmn MD Frederick Douglas Scholarship Fund 1984-; mem VA Black Republican Council 1984-; mem VI C of C Econ Devel Comm, VI Businessmens Assoc, Minority Bus Devel Org, St Croix Howard Univ Alumni Assoc, Alpha Phi Omega; sec Republican Central Comm Prince Georges Cty MD 1982-; chmn Black Republican Council Prince Georges Cty MD 1984-; co-chmn Reagan-Bush 1984 Comm Prince Georges Cty MD 1984; chmn Maryland Black Republican Council 1985-87; 2nd vice chmn Maryland State Republican Party 1986-. **HONORS/ACHIEVEMENTS:** Civil Rights Student Leader 1959-62; Touring Debater Intl AFSC Peace Caravan 1960; Serv Awd Alpha Phi Omega 1961; Disting Military Student Awd 1962; listedin Who's Who in Amer Univ & Coll 1962; The News Amer Baltimore 1974; Mem of the Year Awd Natl Assoc of Black Mfgrs Inc 1975; Achievement Awd Estate Profit Civic Assoc of VI 1978; Achievement Awd Natl Assoc of Minority CPA Firms Wash DC 1978; Achievement Awd MD Minority Contractors Assoc 1986,87; Republican of the Year 1987; elected delegate, White House Conference on Small Business, 1986; Bush delegate, Maryland Republican National Convention 1988. **BUSINESS ADDRESS:** Pres, The Eckenberge Group, Washington, DC.

HOUSE, JESSE O.
Business executive. **PERSONAL:** Born Apr 13, 1935, Hennessey, OK; married Mildred; children: Loren, Fera, Mark. **EDUCATION:** NM State Univ, BS, MA 1964. **CAREER:** Crescent Engr Co, pres; White Sands Missle Range; Hollman Air Force Dev Ctr; McDonnell Douglas Corp NM State Univ, rsrch staff. **ORGANIZATIONS:** Mem bd dir Natl Assc Black Mfr; LA Sheltered Workshop for Handicapped; indsl coord United Way; natl vice pres Langston Univ Alumni Assc; mem LA Chamber of Comm; Carson Kiwanis Intl; mem Alpha Phi Alpha Frat; So CA Prof Eng Assc; Soc of Aero Mass Properties Engr; chmn Fedn of Black Ldrshp. **HONORS/ACHIEVEMENTS:** Outst achvmt award Natl Assc of Black Mfrs 1976; publ "Estimate Costs During Advance Design of Space Craft", "Justification of Measurement System Costs". **BUSINESS ADDRESS:** 12820 S Western Ave, Gardena, CA 90249.

HOUSE, KEVIN N.
Professional athlete. **PERSONAL:** Born Dec 20, 1957, St Louis, MO. **EDUCATION:** So IL, attnd. **CAREER:** Tampa Bay Buccaneers, professional football player present. **BUSINESS ADDRESS:** Tampa Bay Buccaneers, 1 Buccaneer Place, Tampa, FL 33607.

HOUSE, MILLARD L.
Educator. **PERSONAL:** Born Jan 28, 1944, Langston, OK; married Anna Shumate; children: Milton, Signee, Millard, II. **EDUCATION:** Langston Univ, BA 1966; Northeastern State Clge, MA 1971. **CAREER:** Dept Human Rel Tulsa Pub Sch, dir 1970-; Gilcrease Jr HS, soc sci instr 1966-70. **ORGANIZATIONS:** Mem NEA OK Educ Assc; Tulsa Assc Curriculum Supvrs & Dir; Tulsa Pub Sch Affirmative Action Com; Urban League; NAACP; Langston Univ Alumni Assc; YMCA; Kappa Alpha Psi; Phi Delta Kappa; Royal Housa Club; St John's Bapt Ch; Mayor's Commn Comm Relations. **HONORS/ACHIEVEMENTS:** Outst Young Men Amer Award US Jaycees 1973; Kappa of Yr Award Kappa Alpha Psi 1974-75; publ. **BUSINESS ADDRESS:** 3027 S New Haven, Tulsa, OK 74145.

HOUSTON, AGNES WOOD
Government executive. **PERSONAL:** Born in Westville, IL; divorced. **EDUCATION:** YMCA Bus Sch, 1940; Inst Bus Technique, 1960; courses sponsored by Civil Srv Commn 1967; courses at Univ IL & So IL Univ 1969; Lincoln Land Comm Clge; Sangamon State Univ. **CAREER:** State IL Dept Rev 1943-. **ORGANIZATIONS:** Pres NAACP; mem Govt Tech Staff on Youth; PTA; Sch Survey Com; Springfield & Sangamon Comm Action Prog; Springfield Fluoridation Com; pres Women's Intl League for Peace & Freedom 1978-80; mem IL Commn on Children 1980; YWCA; League of Women Voters; Assc Media Women. **HONORS/ACHIEVEMENTS:** Gold Cert NAACP; Frontiers Intl Comm Srv Award; PTA Cert Excel Prog Planning 1958; Comm Srv Award Urban League 1977; Webster Plaque NAACP 1978; First Woman of Springfield IL Award Springfield Women's Political Caucus 1979; cert NAACP Natl Conv; chrmn Springfield Fair Housing Bd.

HOUSTON, ALICE V.
Educator. **PERSONAL:** Born Dec 06, Baton Rouge, LA. **EDUCATION:** So Univ, BA 1953; LA State Univ, MEd 1956; Univ TX, PhD 1974; Additional Study, Atlanta Univ, Kent State Univ, Western Reserve Univ; Univ of WA, attended; Univ of VA, attended; OK City Univ, attended. **CAREER:** Various teaching positions 1953-68; S Greenville Elem Sch Baton Rouge, prin 1968-69; Beechwood Elem Sch E Baton Rouge Parish Sch Bd, prin 1969-75; EBaton Rouge Parish Sch, supr of rsch & prog evaluation 1976-77, supr of evaluation of state & fed progs 1976; OK City Pub Schs, dir of curriculum serv dept 1977-82; Seattle Public Schools, asst supt 1982-. **ORGANIZATIONS:** Mem Assn Supvrn & Curric Dev; exec council ASCD 1979-81; mem of exec bd Natl Alliance Black Sch Educators 1975-79; mem Phi Delta Kappa, Kappa DeltaPi, NAACP, Urban League, Zeta Phi Beta, Council for Basic Educ, Black Child Development Inst, Professional Black School Educ of Greater Puget Sound, Intl Assoc for Intercultural Educ, Assoc for the Study of Classical African Civilizations. **HONORS/ACHIEVEMENTS:** Awd plaque Girl Scouts 1964; serv United Meth Mission 1969; NDEA Grant 1965; Awd plaque Zeta Phi Zeta 1970; Awd Doctoral Fellowship to the Univ TX 1972-73; reception Hon Relig & Civic Act Hughes UMC, Zeta Phi Beta & Beechwood Elem Sch 1974; elected to Southern Univ Chap of Phi Delta Kappa 1975; Natl Alliance of Black School Educators Recognition for Outstanding Serv 1974-77,77-79; Outstanding Princ of Yr 1975; Outstanding Contributions in the Area ofEduc 1977; Omega Psi Phi Recognition as Citizen of the Year 1981; listed in Who's Who Among Amer Women 1981-82,83,84; Phi Beta Sigma, Alpha Phi Alpha, Benefit Guild; Awd for Knowledge & Understanding of the Art of Black Amers & Commitment to the Educ of All Students OK City OK Black Liberated Arts Center Inc 1982; nom President-Elect of Assoc for Supv & Curriculum Development 1984; present with the Benefit Guild Assoc Martin Luther King Jr Awd for providing Excellence in Educ 1985; received Awd of Merit for Community Serv Alpha Phi Alpha 1986. **BUSINESS ADDRESS:** Assistant Superintendent, Seattle Public Schools, 815 4th Ave N, Ste 1, Seattle, WA 98109.

HOUSTON, CORINNE P.
Business executive. **PERSONAL:** Born Mar 24, 1922, Birmingham; married Olin Houston;

children: Avis, David. **EDUCATION:** 2 Year coll; 3 years business coll. **CAREER:** Head cashier 15 yrs; first black female asst mgr; first black store mgr; first female for large supermarket chain in country; Personnel & Public Relations Specialist Allied Supermarkets Inc Sec Gotham Hotel. **ORGANIZATIONS:** Mem NAACP; chmn Drug Educ Comm; mem All Saints Episcopal Ch; former mem St Cyprians Episcopal Ch; first female Sr Warden; mem Urban League Guild; Sister Hood. **HONORS/ACHIEVEMENTS:** Certf Merit Natl Black White Consumer Club 1974; Cited MI Chronicle; Top 10 Black Women City Detroit; Testimonial Resolution City Detroit Hnrng Corinne Houston Day W Grand Blvd named Corinne Houston Blvd one week; Resolution State MI. **BUSINESS ADDRESS:** 13901 Joy Rd, Detroit, MI 48228.

HOUSTON, DAVID R.
Educational administration. **PERSONAL:** Born Sep 01, 1936, Tyler, TX; son of Rev W B Houston; married Lillian Scott. **EDUCATION:** TX Coll Tyler, BA 1957; North TX State Univ Denton, MA Music Ed 1964, EdD 1969; Univ of Houston TX, Post Doctorate 1972. **CAREER:** San Angelo TX Public Schools, teacher/band dir 1957-64; TX Coll Tyler, instructor of music/band dir 1964-67, prof of educ and chmn div of educ, dir ofteacher educ 1969-73; Ft Worth TX Public Schools, elem teacher 1968-69; Prairie View A&M Univ, adjunct prof of ed 1974-; Wiley Coll, vice pres acad affairs, admin asst to the pres 1973-88, exec vice pres 1988-. **ORGANIZATIONS:** Mem Natl Educ Assoc, Phi Delta Kappa, TX State Teachers Assoc, Assoc of Higher Educ, Amer Assoc of Colls for Teacher Educ, Southern Conf of Deans of Faculties and Academic Vice Presidents; life mem NAACP; mem YMCA, Boy Scouts of Amer; consultant Jamaica Hotel School Univ of the West Indies Kingston Jamaica 1979; pastor Smith Temple Church of God in Christ Jones Valley Comm Church of God in Christ Tyler TX; officer Mineola Dist Church of God in Christ; mem East TX Ministerial Alliance Church of God in Christ, Interdenominational Ministerial Alliance; state sunday sch superintendent TX Northeast Church of God in Christ. **HONORS/ACHIEVEMENTS:** Ford Grant Found Ford Found 1964; Outstanding Achievement Awd Alpha Phi Alpha Frat 1978; 3 publications. **BUSINESS ADDRESS:** Exec Vice President, Wiley College, Marshall, TX 75670.

HOUSTON, IVAN J.
Business executive. **PERSONAL:** Born Jun 15, 1925, Los Angeles, CA; son of Norman O Houston and Dons Talbot Young; married Philippa Jones; children: Pamela, Kathi, Ivan A. **EDUCATION:** Univ of CA Berkeley, BS 1948; Univ of Manitoba, actuarial science; Life Office Mgmt Inst, fellow; Amer Coll of Life Underwriters, charter life underwriter. **CAREER:** Accountant, 1948; Actuarial & Policyowners Serv Div, supr 1950, admin asst in charge 1952, asst sec actuarial 1954, actuary 1956, bd dir exec com mem 1959, vice pres actuary 1966; Golden State Mutual Life Ins Co, pres/ceo 1970, chmn of bd/ceo 1980-. **ORGANIZATIONS:** Assoc mem Conf of Actuaries in Pub Practice; mem Amer Acad of Actuaries; Amer Soc of Pension Actuaries; Intl Actuarial Assn; past pres Los Angeles Actuarial Club; mem Kappa Alpha Psi Frat; past mem bd of Regents Loyola Marymount Univ; corporate bd mem United Way of Los Angeles Inc; past mem bd dir CA C of C; past chmn of bd dir Los Angeles Urban League; past mem bd dir Pacific Indemnity Co; former chmn of bd dir M&M Assn; former mem bd dir Los Angeles C of C; former chmn of bd Life Ofc Mgmt Assn 1979-80; bd dir First Interstate Bank of CA, Pacific Thesis Group; former mem of bd, Kaiser Alum & Chem Corp, Family Savings and Loan. **HONORS/ACHIEVEMENTS:** First Black elected to bd dir Amer Life Ins Assn. **MILITARY SERVICE:** AUS sgt maj 1943-45; Purple Heart, Bronze Star, Combat Infantryman's Badge. **BUSINESS ADDRESS:** Chairman and Chief Executive, Golden State Mutual Life Ins, 1999 W Adams Blvd, Los Angeles, CA 90018.

HOUSTON, JOHNNY L.
Educator, administrator, mathematician, computer specialist. **PERSONAL:** Born Nov 19, 1941, Sandersville, GA; son of Bobby Lee Houston and Catherine Houston Vinson; married Virginia Lawrence; children: Mave Lawrence, Kaiulani Michelle. **EDUCATION:** Morehouse Coll, BA 1964; Atlanta Univ, MS 1966; Universite de Strasbourg, France, 1966-67; Univ of Georgia, 1969; Purdue Univ, PhD 1974. **CAREER:** Atlanta Univ, chmn math & comp sci 1975-81; Fort Valley State Coll, coord of comp sci 1981-83, Callaway prof of comp sci 1983-84; Elizabeth City State Univ, vice chancellor for acad affairs 1984-88, senior research professor of mathematics/computer science, 1988—. **ORGANIZATIONS:** Amer Math Society; Assn of Computing Machinery; Math Assn of Amer; Natl Assn of Mathematicians; Dir Black Cultural Ctr Purdue Univ 1972-73; exec sec Natl Assoc of Mathematicians 1975-89; vstg sci Natl Ctr for Atom Res 1976; co-dir Natl Conf Math & Physical Sci Boulder CO 1979; pres & chmn bd Intl Trade and Dev Corp 1979-86; vstg scientist Lawrence Livermore Natl Lab 1979, 83; consultant Math/Comp Sci Spec NIH-MARC Review Comm 1982-86; visiting sci, NASA Langley Res Center, 1989. **HONORS/ACHIEVEMENTS:** Merril Scholar Univ de Strasbourg France 1966-67; Disting Service Awd Invited Speaker Purdue Univ 1980; Invited Spkr XI Intl Symp on Math Programming Bonn Germany 1982; selected for Statewide Comp Sci Review Team Bd of Regents Commonwealth of MA 1986; invited Keynote Spkr 43rd Annual Mtg NIS/Betta Kappa Chi 1986. **HOME ADDRESS:** 602 West Main St, Elizabeth City, NC 27909. **BUSINESS ADDRESS:** Dept of Math and Computer Science, Elizabeth City StateUniv, 1704 Weeksville Rd, Elizabeth City, NC 27909.

HOUSTON, KENNETH RAY
Professional athlete. **PERSONAL:** Born Nov 12, 1944, Lufkin, TX; married Gustie Marie Rice. **EDUCATION:** Prairie View A&M, BSM in Guid Couns 1967. **CAREER:** Houston Oilers, draft pick 9th round 1967; Washington Redskins, def back 1973-. **HONORS/ACHIEVEMENTS:** AFL Champ Game 1967; Holds NFL record for most touchdowns on intercep lifetime with 9 in Houston from 1967-71; AFL All-Star Games 1968, 69; Pro Bowl 1970-76;tied NFL records for most touchdowns on intercep for a season 1971; TD's on intercep in a game 1971; named to all-AFC team 1971; named all-Pro or all-NFC 7 straight yrs 1973-79; Byron Whizzer White Awd for Humanitarian Serv NFL Players Assn 1980; inducted into Pro Football Hall of Fame 1986. **BUSINESS ADDRESS:** c/o Pro Football Hall of Fame, 2121 Harrison Ave NW, Canton, OH 44708.

HOUSTON, LILLIAN S.
Educator. **PERSONAL:** Born Oct 24, 1946, Tyler, TX; married David Houston. **EDUCATION:** TX Clge, BA 1966; E TX State Univ, studies; Stephen F Austin State Univ, studies; Prairie View A&M, studies; N TX State Univ, studies in Aging; E TX State Univ, MS Sociology 1975. **CAREER:** Nursing Home Admin Wiley Coll, instructor, program dir. **ORGANIZATIONS:** Sec Tyler ISD; Library & NTSU Denton; Library TX Clge Tyler; Library Tyler ISD Soloist, Original Gospel Templetts Recording Grp Concert Artist; implemented& directing vol training prog Wiley Clge Campus Marshall TX; TX Nrsg Home Assc; mem Natl Caucus on the Black Aged; mem Amer Assc of Retired Persons; mem Cole Hill CME Ch Tyler TX mem Local CYF Christian Youth Flwshp; dir Cole Hill CME Ch; mem bd of dir Tyler City Library Tyler TX mem AmerClge of Nrsg. **HONORS/ACHIEVEMENTS:** Home Admin in Outst Young Women of Amer 1976; Personalities of the S 1976. **BUSINESS ADDRESS:** Wiley Coll, Marshall, TX.

HOUSTON, MARSH S.
Consultant, coordinator. **PERSONAL:** Born Mar 04, 1918, Cornersville, TN. **EDUCATION:** TN State Univ, attd; Drake Univ, grad wk. **CAREER:** Des Moines Public Schools, consultant; New Horizons Project, asst coord; Model Cities, coord; Des Moines Public School, educ progs, teacher, math. **ORGANIZATIONS:** Vp Des Moines Educ Assc 1972-73; chmn 1973-74; Human Rel Com Aptd Des Moines Civil Serv Commn 1974 first black aptd to position; mem Omega Psi Phi Frat; Fndr Mu Omicron Chap in Des Moines. **MILITARY SERVICE:** AUS e-7. **BUSINESS ADDRESS:** 1214 E 15 St, Amos Hiatt Jr HS, Des Moines, IA.

HOUSTON, NORMAN OLIVER
Business executive. **PERSONAL:** Born Oct 16, 1893, San Jose, CA; married Edythe A Pryce. **EDUCATION:** Univ of So CA, BA; Univ of CA Berkeley. **CAREER:** Golden State Mutual Life Ins Co, chmn bd 1969-, chmn & chief exec ofcr 1967-69, pres 1949-67, pres & controller 1945-49, secr/treas 1925-45, co-founder 1925; Field Sec Liberty Savings & Loan Assc of LA, co-organizer 1924; Natl Life Ins Co of USA, salesman 192-24; Bd of Fire Underwriters of Pacific, clk 1917. **ORGANIZATIONS:** Mem Municipal Auditorium Commn; mem Bd dir Intl Exec Srv Corps; chmn S LA Comm Health Plan; CA State Chamber of Comm; Natl Rec & Parks Assc;mem bd dir Watts Manufacturing Co; past mem of, Inst of Life Ins; LA 1976 Olympic Com; CA State Athletic Commn; OEO; US Dept of Comm; LA Zoo Assc; Rec & Youth Council; CA Gov's Bus Adv Com; Housing, Home & Finance US Govt; Natl Conf of Christians & Jews; Intl Student Ctr Inc; treas bd trustees Crippled Children's Soc of LA Co; Children's Home Soc; YMCA; Amer Legion; life mem NAACP; First African Meth Episcopal Ch Hon LLD Bethune-Cookman Clge 1951; Wilberforce Univ 1951. **HONORS/ACHIEVEMENTS:** Wisdom Award; Fellow of Round Table of Commerce; Golden Book of Distg Srv YMCA 1963; Comm Serv Award United Way 1970; Benefactor Award; George Wash CarverMeml Award; Kappa Alpha Psi Frat; Sigma Pi Phi Frat; Men of Tomorrow bd dir. **MILITARY SERVICE:** AUS 2nd lt 1917. **BUSINESS ADDRESS:** 1999 W Adams Blvd, Los Angeles, CA 90018.

HOUSTON, SEAWADON LEE
Banking administrator. **PERSONAL:** Born Aug 29, 1942, Liberty, MO; son of Samuel Houston and Thelma Merical; married Carole L Floyd, Jun 1976; children: Brenda, Toni, George, Michael. **EDUCATION:** Golden Gate Univ, BA Business; Univ of WA, Banking School; Stanford Sloan Program, Graduate. **CAREER:** US Air Force, sgt 1960-65; Wells Fargo Bank, trainee 1965-66, several mgmt positions 1966-84, senior vice president 1984-. **ORGANIZATIONS:** Commiss Bayview Hunters Point Model Cities 1972-74; bd of dir San Mateo Devel Assn 1980-; bd mem San Mateo Boy Scout Council 1981-; bd of dir Mills Hospital Found 1982-; chmn of adv bd Bay Area Urban Bankers Assn 1984-; bd mem Public Relations Comm United Way Agency 1984-. **MILITARY SERVICE:** USAF sgt 5 yrs; Far East Airman of the Year 1963. **BUSINESS ADDRESS:** Senior Vice President, Wells Fargo Bank, 201 Third Street, San Francisco, CA 94463.

HOUSTON, W. EUGENE
Clergyman. **PERSONAL:** Born Jul 01, 1920, Hot Springs, AR; married Doris A Cobbs; children: Bjorn, Cheryl Hunter. **EDUCATION:** Johnson C Smith Univ, AB summa cum laude 1941, MDiv magna cum laude 1944, DD 1961; Columbia, phD 1952; Chicago, STD 1959; Mansfield Clge Oxford Univ, Cert 1971. **CAREER:** Eastern Area Rep Bd Pensions United Presby Ch USA, asst sec; St James Presby Ch NYC, interim pastor 1977; Westminster Presb Ch Cedar Manor Jamaica NY, pastor 198-75; Stated Clerk-Synod NE United Presb Ch, 1974-75; Rendall Mem Presb Ch Manhattan, pastor 1944-68; Dept Sanitation NY, chpln 1960-; NY Hosp Welfare Island & Elmhurst Queens, chpln 1950-60. **ORGANIZATIONS:** Exec dir Commn Religion & Race Presbytery of New York City 1963-65; dir Athletic Publ JC Smith 1942-44; Moderator-Synod NY 1962-63; v moderator Presbytery NY 1960-62; chmn Div Pastoral Care Queens Fed Chs 1969-74; pres Interdemoninational Ministers Meetings Greater NY 1970-74; pres Presb Council & W 1656-58; Polemarch NY Alumni Chap Kappa Alpha Psi 1958-60; pres General Alumni Assc Johnson C Smith Univ 1954-58; Kappa Alpha Psi; Alpha Kappa Mu; Delta Phi Delta; Chi Alpha; Assc Amer Protestant Hosp Chplns; Natl Presb Health & Welfare Assc; Insts Religion & Mental Health. **HONORS/ACHIEVEMENTS:** Publ poet composer & arranger music; bass-baritone recitalist; contrb many articles varied publ Who's Who Harlem 1950; Amer & Amer Clge & Univ Students 1940; Who's Who in Colored Amer 1948; Who's Who in the East 1964; Intl Dictionary famous Persons 1969; Comm Leaders Amer 1971; recieved Kappa Alpha Psi Grand Chap Individual Meritorious Achievement Award; Charter Trustee Eisenhower Clge. **BUSINESS ADDRESS:** 475 Riverside Dr, New York, NY 10027.

HOUSTON, WHITNEY
Singer. **PERSONAL:** Born in New Jersey. **CAREER:** Debut album Whitney Houston sold more than seven million copies, No 1 singles from that album include Saving All My Love for You, How Will I Know, The Greatest Love of All; sellout concert at Carnegie Hall. **HONORS/ACHIEVEMENTS:** Key to the City of Newark by Mayor Gibson; 2 American Music Awds; Grammy Awd Top Female Pop Vocalist; Multi-platinum debut album "Whitney Houston" No 1 on Billboard's chart for eight weeks.

HOUSTON, WILLIAM DEBOISE
Educational administration. **PERSONAL:** Born Mar 10, 1940, Quincy, FL; son of Albert Houston and Ada Houston; married Elizabeth Shorter; children: William Carril, Kendra, Karli, Kylean. **EDUCATION:** SC State Coll, BSEd 1963; NC A&T Univ, MEd 1972; Lehigh Univ, Admin Cert 1975. **CAREER:** Easton Area School dist, teacher 1964-74; Shawnee Intermediate School, asst principal 1975-. **ORGANIZATIONS:** Vp Easton City Council; chairperson Easton Econ Devel, Police Fire & Health Bd City of Easton; co-host Channel 39 Black Exposure TV Show; mem PA State Ed Assoc, Amer Assoc for Health Phys Ed & Recreation, Women's League of Voters, NAACP Exec Bd; bd mem Easton Boys Club, Private Indust Council; pres Pride & Joy Ed Nursery Inc, South Side Civic Assoc; bd of trustees Union AME Church; pres Easton City Council. **HONORS/ACHIEVEMENTS:** Certifi-

cate of Appreciation NAACP 1967, 1982; Rainbow Festival Awd Bahai 1981; First Black Councilman City of Easton PA Certificate NAACP; First Black City Council Pres City of Easton; pres Easton City Council 1985-87, 1988-90. **HOME ADDRESS:** 201 Reese St, Easton, PA 18042.

HOUZE, JENEICE CARMEL
Educator. **PERSONAL:** Born Mar 26, 1938, New Orelans, LA; married Harold Emmanuel Houze; children: Harold Emanuel Jr, Miles Peter. **EDUCATION:** Xavier Univ of LA, BA 1959; Univ of San Francisco, MA 1980, Admin Credential 1980. **CAREER:** Chicago Sch Dist, teacher 1959-65; Torrance Unified Sch Dist, teacher 1965-87. **ORGANIZATIONS:** Mem, sec 1983-87 Xavier Univ of LA Alumni 1965-87, CA Teachers Assoc 1966-87, Natl Educ Assoc 1966-87, Torrance Teachers Assoc 1966-87, Parent Teachers Assoc 1966-87; attended Dist Sci Workshop on Science Framework 1982-83; coord Career Awareness Prog Lincoln School 1982-84; staff develop clinical teaching Rowland Heights CA 1983-84; project writing team mem Lincoln Elem Sch 1983-84; Olympic Field Day chairperson, budgeting asst, coord ECT Musical Holiday Presentation 1983-84; facilitator Workshops Lincoln Elem Sch 1983-87; curriculum writer Gifted and Talented Prog Lincoln Elem Sch 1983-86; mem Univ ofSt Francis Alumni 1986-87; mem CA Assoc Gifted 1987. **HONORS/ACHIEVEMENTS:** Honorary Service Chairperson PTA Assoc 1983-84; Honorary Serv Awd Torrance PTA 1986-87. **BUSINESS ADDRESS:** Elementary Teacher, Torrance Unified Sch Dist, 2335 Plaza del Amo, Torrance, CA 90504.

HOWARD, AUBREY J.
Business executive. **PERSONAL:** Born Mar 23, 1945, Memphis, TN; married Patricia Claxton; children: Adrian K. **EDUCATION:** Southwestern at Memphis, BA 1972. **CAREER:** Belz Enterprises, proj dir new hotels & commercial devel 1986-; Belz/Curits Outdoor Oper, mgr of real estate oper 1985-; TESCO Devel, dir of devel 1983-85; Doyen Assn Inc, pres 1977-83; Beale St Nat Historic Found, exec dir 1975; Intergovernmental Coord Dept Shelby Cty Govt, assoc dir for resrch 1974; Project on the Aging, asst asst dir 1973; Preventive Med Cntr, acting dir 1972. **ORGANIZATIONS:** Fellow Natl Endowment for the Humanities 1977; chmn Midtown Memphis Mental Health Ctr 1980-82; pres Ballet S Inc 1980-82; mem Mason, NAACP; bd mem Memphis Oral School for the Death 1985, Memphis Crisis Stabilization Center 1985, State of TN Dept of Mental Health & Mental Retardation 1986-94. **BUSINESS ADDRESS:** Project Manager, Belz Enterprises, 5118 Park Ave, Memphis, TN 38117.

HOWARD, BILLIE JEAN
Educator, nurse. **PERSONAL:** Born Jul 31, 1950, Chicago, IL. **EDUCATION:** Univ of IL Chicago, BSN 1973; Loyola Univ, MSN 1976. **CAREER:** Univ of IL Hosp, staff nurse 1973-76; Univ of IL Coll of Nursing, instr 1976-77; Michael Reese Hosp, clinical spec 1977-78; Univ of IL Coll of Nursing, asst prof 1978-81; Chicago State Univ, asst prof nursing. **ORGANIZATIONS:** Suprv Univ of Chicago Hosp 1981-83; assoc dir of nursing Provident Med Ctr 1983-84; asst prof nursing Chicago State Univ 1984-; mem Sigma Theta Tau,March of Dimes Perinatal Nursing Adv Council. **HOME ADDRESS:** 5925 S Throop, Chicago, IL 60636. **BUSINESS ADDRESS:** Assistant Professor Nursing, Chicago StateUniv, 95th and King Dr, Chicago, IL 60619.

HOWARD, CALVIN JOHNSON
Police officer. **PERSONAL:** Born Oct 17, 1947, Miami, FL; son of Norman Howard and Mary Magalene Johnson Ferguson; married Laverne Maryland Hatchett, Jun 04, 1977; children: Tara Evette, Calvin Deon, Arlethia Michelle, LaTonya Linnell, Cortenay DeMaon, LaToya Linnett, Troy Everett, Jabari Deon. **EDUCATION:** Tarrant County Jr Coll, Hurst TX, AA Law Enforcement; Univ of Texas, Arlington TX; Abilene Christian Univ, Garland TX, BS Criminal Justice. **CAREER:** Dade County Seriff's Office, Miami FL, deputy Sheriff, 1969-70; Tarrant County Sheriff's Office, Ft Worth TX, deputy Sheriff, 1970-72; Dallas Police Dept, Dallas TX, police officer, 1972-. **ORGANIZATIONS:** Pres, Texas Peace Officers Assn, Dallas Chapter, 1975-77, 1st state vice pres, 1977-82; vice chmn, Southern Region, Natl Black Police Assn, 1980-84, chmn, 1984-, natl chmn, 1987-; NAACP, Congressional Task Force, Dallas Chapter, 1987; Thompson Chapel United Methodist Church, 1989; Dallas & Grand Prairie Texas NAACP, 1989. **HONORS/ACHIEVEMENTS:** Appreciation Award, Texas Peace Officers Assn, Dallas Chapter, 1986; Leadership Award, Southern Region NBPA, 1987; Community Relations Comm, 1988; Outstanding Law Enforcement Officer Award, Greater Dallas; Renault Robinson Natl Award, NBPA, 1988. **MILITARY SERVICE:** AUS, SFC, SA US Army Intelligence, USAF, SSG, Airborne, 1965-. **HOME ADDRESS:** 721 Pinoak Dr, Grand Prairie, TX 75051.

HOWARD, CHARLES PRESTON, JR.
Attorney. **PERSONAL:** Born Mar 09, 1921, Hampton, VA; married Audrey J Lattimore; children: Chas III, Catherine Marie, Chas L. **EDUCATION:** Howard U, BA, JD 1951-54; New York U, LLM 1955. **CAREER:** AOA vice pres 1971-75; NBA Foundation, pres 1974; NBA pres 1975; Bay College pres 1978. **ORGANIZATIONS:** Gen counsel and member Arena Players 1960-83; pres Monumental Bar Asso 1965-70; vice pres Boy Scouts Bd Central Md 1968; mem B of D Md Public Broadcasting 1969-75. **MILITARY SERVICE:** AUS staff sgt 1941-45.

HOWARD, CORLISS MAYS
Retired educational administrator. **PERSONAL:** Born Jan 19, 1927, St Louis, MO; daughter of Duffie L Mays and Celeste Ragan Mays. **EDUCATION:** AM&N Coll, BA (Magna Cum Laude) 1948; Syracuse Univ, MA (w/Honors) 1953. **CAREER:** Arkansas Public Schools, teacher counselor librarian asst principal 1947-65; Arkansas Employment Security Div, master counselor/mgr 1965-74; Arkansas Dept of Educ, coordinator supervisor 1974-87. **ORGANIZATIONS:** Mem Peace Links, Wilowe Inst, AR Arts Center; life mem AM&N Coll, Univ of AR at Pine Bluff Alumni Assoc; comm chair Delta Sigma Theta Inc; mem Links Inc, Urban League, NAACP, Alpha Kappa Mu Honor Soc, Heritage Club, UAPB Develop Cncl; mem Amer Assoc of Univ Women; charter mem Bd of AR Council on Human Relations; mem bd of dirs Goodwill Industries of AR, Assoc of Governing Bds of Colls and Univs, NEA, AEA, AR Literacy Council Bd; Natl Assoc of State Educ Media Professionals, Alpha Kappa Mu Natl Honor Soc; official delegate Pre-White House Conference on Library and Information Serv 1978; delegate to White House Conf on Library and Information serv Washington DC 1979; vice chairperson Arkansas State Bd of Higher Educ, 1989; elected natl pres of 15,000 mem graduates UAPB/AM&N Alumni Assn, 1988; mem, AR Literacy Council Bd, 1986-; mem, Task Force for Recruitment & Retention of Minority Teachers, 1985-. **HONORS/ACHIEVEMENTS:** AR Award of Merit Intl Assn of Personnel in Employment Security; cited in several books and articles; first woman to serve on state bd of higher educ; first black women to serve as pres of AR Branch AAUW; mem Pi Lambda Theta Natl Scholastic Honor Soc; Presidential Citation from Natl Assn for Equal Opportunity in Higher Educ; Doctor of Humane Letters, Univ of AR at Pine Bluff; Certificates of Recognition and Certificate of Merit, State of AR, 1987. **HOME ADDRESS:** 1209 East Twin Lakes Dr, Little Rock, AR 72205-6758.

HOWARD, DALTON J., JR.
Attorney. **PERSONAL:** Born in Vicksburg, MS; married Marian Hill. **EDUCATION:** Parsons Clge, BS 1964; Howard Univ Schl Law, JD 1974. **CAREER:** Nghbrhd Legal Serv Prog, managing atty 1975-; Wash Tech Inst, instr 1974-75; law student 1971-74; Mutual of NY, field underwriter 1968-69; Gary Schl Cty, tchr 1968-69. **ORGANIZATIONS:** Vp dir Movin' on Inc 1974-; Natl Bar Assc; Amer Bar Assc; Assc of Trial Lawyers of Amer; mem DC Bar Assc Sigma Delta Tau Legal Frat. **HONORS/ACHIEVEMENTS:** AUS Bandsman 1969-71. **BUSINESS ADDRESS:** Law Office of Howard Dalton, 1429 Good Hope Rd SE, Washington, DC 20002.

HOWARD, DARNLEY WILLIAM
Financial analyst. **PERSONAL:** Born Dec 24, 1957, Washington, DC. **EDUCATION:** Univ of PA Wharton Sch of Finance, BS Econ 1980; Univ of Chicago Grad Sch of Business, MBA 1984. **CAREER:** Xerox Corp, financial analyst. **ORGANIZATIONS:** Vice pres Western NY Chap Natl Black MBA Assoc; outside consultant to local small businesses.

HOWARD, DONALD R.
Engineer. **PERSONAL:** Born Oct 13, 1928, Wightman, VA; married Virdie M Hubbard; children: Jada Marni, Donald, Jr. **EDUCATION:** BS 1959. **CAREER:** IITRI 1956-64; Mobil Oil Corp 1964-68; Principal Chem Engr Commonwealth Edison Co 1968. **ORGANIZATIONS:** Mem AICHE; mem ACS; Prof Black Chemists & Chem Engrs; mem Carter Temple CME Ch. **MILITARY SERVICE:** USMC 1951-53. **BUSINESS ADDRESS:** 72 W Adams, Chicago, IL 60603.

HOWARD, ELIZABETH FITZGERALD
Educator, librarian. **PERSONAL:** Born Dec 28, 1927, Baltimore, MD; daughter of John M Fitzgerald and Bertha James Fitzgerald; married Lawrence C Howard; children: Jane Howard-Martin, Susan C, Laura L. **EDUCATION:** Radcliffe Coll Harvard Univ, AB 1948; Univ of Pittsburgh, MLS 1971, PhD 1977. **CAREER:** Boston Public Libr, childrens Librarian 1952-56; Episcopal Diocese of Pittsburgh, resource librn 1972-74; Pittsburgh Theol Sem, ref Librn 1974-77; Univ of Pittsburgh, visiting lecturer 1976-78; W VA Univ, asst prof 1978-85, on leave sr librarian Univ of Maiduguri Nigeria 1981-82, assoc prof 1985-. **ORGANIZATIONS:** Dir Radcliffe Alumnae Asso 1969-72; mem Brd of Trustees Ellis Sch Pittsburgh 1970-75; trustee Magee Womens Hosp 1980-; Episcopal Diocese of Pittsburgh Cathedral Chapter 1984-; Pittsburgh Chap of LINKS Inc; mem Amer Library Assoc, Children's Literature Assoc, Soc of Children's Book Writers; bd mem, QED Communications 1987-; bd mem, Beginning With Books 1987-. **HONORS/ACHIEVEMENTS:** Library science honor soc Beta Phi Mu; author Articles in Professional Journals; author children's books "Train to Lulu's House", "Chita's Christmas Tree" 1989, America As Story 1988; candidate for bd of dirs Harvard Alumni Assoc 1987. **HOME ADDRESS:** 919 College Ave, Pittsburgh, PA 15232. **BUSINESS ADDRESS:** Assoc Prof Library Science, WVUniv, Rm 101 Main Library, Morgantown, WV 26506.

HOWARD, ELLEN D.
Association executive. **PERSONAL:** Born Apr 08, 1929, Baltimore, MD; daughter of Lucious Norman Dolvey and Louise Tignor Dolvey; divorced; children: Harold H, Jr, Larry K. **EDUCATION:** Morgan State Coll, BS 1951; Johns Hopkins Univ, MA 1968. **CAREER:** Educ Talent Search US Office of Educ, exec dir; MD Educa Opportunity Center, exec dir. **ORGANIZATIONS:** Mem bd trustees Coll Entrance Exam Bd; DE DC MD Assc of Financial Aid Admin; 4th Dist Dem Org of Baltimore City; Natl Assc of Student Financial Aid Admin; Natl Council for Negro Women; MD Personnel & Guidance Assc; Natl Educ Assc; YWCA; NAACP; Baltimore Public School Teachers Assn; mem Delta Sigma Theta Inc; Baltimore Continental Soc for Underprivileged Children Inc; Town & Country Set; Baltimore Chap Moles Inc; Etc Ltd; Girl Scouts of Central MD Nominating Council; Natl volunteer planning progs in Mgmt & Audits for Girl Scouts of USA; mem Phi Delta Gamma, Gamma Chap Natl Hon Frat for Grad Women; Phi Lambda Theta Chi Chapter Natl Honor & Prof Assc of Women in Educ; Enon Baptist Church; mem Girl Scouts Central MD; mem MD Personnel and Guidance Association; mem Baltimore Urban League and League of Women Voters; mem Public S ool Administrators and Supervisors Association. **HONORS/ACHIEVEMENTS:** Author "Financial Aid for Higher Educ"; recip Certificate of Appreciation Amer Biog Inst 1975; Comm Serv Certificate 1974; Certificate of Achievement Morgan Coll ROTC 1974; Amer Legion Award; Intl Women's Yr Award; Outstanding Woman in Youth Devel Baltimore Alumni Chap of Delta Sigma Theta Inc; recip various awards & citations; Induction into the MECEO Hall of Fame as a founder; Mid-Eastern Association of Educational Opportunity Program Personel; MD State Award for Outstanding Services. **BUSINESS ADDRESS:** Executive Director, Maryland Educational Opportunity Center, 2700 Gwynns Falls Parkway, Baltimore, MD 21216.

HOWARD, GEORGE, JR.
Attorney. **PERSONAL:** Born May 13, 1924, Pine Bluff, AR; married Vivan Smith; children: Etoria, George III, Risie, Renee, Vivian Alycia. **EDUCATION:** Univ AR, BS, JD 1954; Morris-Booker Coll, LLD 1976. **CAREER:** Supreme Ct of AR, judge 1976-, apptd by Gov Pryor spc assoc justice; Eastern & Western Dists of AR, dist judge 1980-. **ORGANIZATIONS:** Comm on Professional Conduct; chmn AR State Claims Commn; pres Jeff Co Bar Assn; legal redress comm State Conf NAACP; past chmn AR Adv Com US Civil Rights Commn; mem Alpha Phi Alpha Frat; MW Prince Hall Grand Lodge; F & AM AR; past pres State Conf Branches NAACP Pine Bluff Br. **HONORS/ACHIEVEMENTS:** Honoree in AR Sesquicentennial Celebration. **MILITARY SERVICE:** USN seabees. **BUSINESS ADDRESS:** US Dist Judge, Eastern & Western Dists of AR, 329 1/2 Main St, Pine Bluff, AR 71601.

HOWARD, GLEN
Clergyman. **PERSONAL:** Born May 20, 1956, Oakland, CA; married Marian Byrd. **EDUCATION:** LA Tech Univ, BS Psychology 1980; Gammon Theological Seminary, MDiv 1984. **CAREER:** Marc Paul Inc, mgmt 1976-79; Xerox Corp, sales/marketing 1980-81; United Methodist Church Iowa Conf, pastor 1984-. **ORGANIZATIONS:** Sec Ankeny Ministerial Assn 1985. **BUSINESS ADDRESS:** Pastor, United Methodist Church, 206 SW Walnut, Ankeny, IA 50021.

HOWARD, GWENDOLYN JULIUS
Educator. **PERSONAL:** Born Nov 15, 1932, Brooklyn; divorced; children: Calvin, Lisa C. **EDUCATION:** Bethune Cookman Coll, BS 1956; Univ of No CO, MS 1974; Univ of No CO, EdD 1976. **CAREER:** Sunlight Beauty Acad-Kingston Jam Cri Deliq Task Force Mod Cities, assoc 1968-70; SE Reg NANB&PW Clubs, gov 1970-73; Gala Travel Inc Miami, co-owner; Dade Co Public Sch, school liaison juvenile justice support prog. **ORGANIZATIONS:** Mem Sigma Gamma Rho 1967-; pres Epsilon Chap Gamma Phi Delta 1978-81; pres Sigma Gamma Rho Gamma Delta Sigma Chap 1980-82; pres Miami Chap Top Ladiesof Distinction Inc 1983-87; YWCA NW exec bd 2 yrs; adv council Miami Dade Comm Coll 1984. **HONORS/ACHIEVEMENTS:** Appreciation Awd Equelloc Civic & Soc Club 1971; Personalities of the South 1971; Natl Assn of Bus & Professional Women's Club 1971; Achvmt Awds Sigma Gamma Rho 1976, MAB & P's Women Clubs 1976, Gamma Phi Delta Sor 1976; Who's Who Woman of the World 1976; nominee FL Women Hall of Fame 1984; Greater Miami Outstanding Influential Blacks 1984; Top Lady of the Year 1985-86. **BUSINESS ADDRESS:** School Liaison, Educ Spec, Dade Co Public Sch, Juvenile Justice Support Prog, 3300 NW 27th Ave, Miami, FL 33142.

HOWARD, HENRY L.
Business executive. **PERSONAL:** Born Jun 18, 1930, Augusta, GA; married Arnestine Chishom; children: Vincent, Karlton, Zachary, Henry DeWayne, Vertiz, Valerie, Jerrilynn. **CAREER:** Howard's Upholstery, owner; Supreme Fashion-Dot Inc, owner. **ORGANIZATIONS:** Pres CSRA Business League; mem BBB; D & B; Chamber of Comm; mem NFIB; chmn trustee bd Green Grove Bapt Ch; mem Optimist Club. **HONORS/ACHIEVEMENTS:** Businessman of the Year 1971, 1973; Citizen of the Year Award 1970. **BUSINESS ADDRESS:** 2047 Milledgeville Rd, Augusta, GA.

HOWARD, HOWELL J., JR.
Psychiatrist. **PERSONAL:** Born Mar 26, 1938, Washington, DC; son of Howell J Howard Sr and Consuelo Jones Howard; divorced. **EDUCATION:** Boston Univ Coll of Liberal Arts, AB 1959; Howard Univ Coll of Med, MD 1965. **CAREER:** Howard Univ, psychiatrist; Washington DC, private practice of psychiatrist 1970-73; Freedman's Hosp Howard Univ, res tng; Office of Forensic Psychiatry Dept Human & Resources Washington, staff psychiatrist. **ORGANIZATIONS:** Mem Med Soc of DC; Amer Med Assn; Natl Med Assn; Washington Psychiatric Soc; Amer Psychiatric Assn; Kappa Alpha Psi Frat. **MILITARY SERVICE:** AUS med corps 1966-69.

HOWARD, HUMBERT LINCOLN
Artist. **PERSONAL:** Born Jul 12, 1915, Phila, PA; married Beatrice Wood; children: David D, Humbert J. **EDUCATION:** Howard Univ, attended 1934; Univ PA, 1935; Barnes Found, 1961. **ORGANIZATIONS:** Artist exhibited one man shows at, Pyramid Club 1958, Philadelphia Art Alliance 56-58, Howard Univ 1959, Newman Gallery 1962, Grabar Gallery 1968; exhibited in group shows at, PA Acad Fine Arts 1951-54, 61, 69, PA Acad Living Philadelphia Mus Art Arts Festivals Green Hill 1969, McCleaf Gallery 1970; repres in permanent collections at PA Acad Fine Arts Philadelphia Civic Mus, Howard Univ, Sterne Sch, reproduced in, Amer Negro Art by Cedric Dover 1960, Ebony Mag 1963, The Barnes Found-Reality Vs Myth by Gilbert M Cantor 1963, 100 Yrs After the Emancipation by Jack Saunders 1965; instr Cheltenham Art Ctr 1962-66; Allens Lane Art Ctr 1967-71; mem Philadelphia Mus Art; Philadelphia Art Alliance; PA Acad Fine Arts; Artists Equity; mem Omega Psi Phi; Peale Club. **HONORS/ACHIEVEMENTS:** Recipient, Purchase Prize PA Acad Fine Arts 1951; Outstanding Achievement in Art Award; Amer Exhibiting Artists 1965; Woodmere Van Sciver Mem Prize 1968; writer of feature articles in Sunday Bull, 1969-70. **BUSINESS ADDRESS:** 1601 Walnut St, Philadelphia, PA 19102.

HOWARD, JAMES L.
Insurance company executive. **PERSONAL:** Born Sep 12, 1918, Lexington, MS; married Gloria King; children: Kyland, Dawn. **EDUCATION:** Tougaloo Coll, AB 1940; NYU, BS 1944; Brooklyn Univ, LLD 1954. **CAREER:** Carver Fed Savs & Loan Assn, vice pres & gen counsel 1961-64, vice pres mortg office 1964-69; Sol Masch & Co NYC, gen partner 1970-79; United Mutual Life Ins CoNYC, pres/CEO 1979-retirement. **ORGANIZATIONS:** Mem Amer Inst CPA's; mem NY State Soc CPA; mem Amer Soc Black CPA's; mem/past treas Harlem Lawyers Assn; banking com ABA; mem Alpha Phi Alpha; arbitrator Upper Manhattan Sm Claims Ct; guest lectr Columbia Univ; treas Harlem Busn Alliance; bd dir manhattan Comm Ctr; lectr Black Exec Exchange Prog Natl Urban League; mem 100 Black Man; Met Assn United Ch of Christ; Masons; mem NY Bar Assn 1956-. **HONORS/ACHIEVEMENTS:** Recipient Spl Inspiration Award Theater of Renewal Inc 1983. **BUSINESS ADDRESS:** President, retired, United Mutual Life Ins, 310 Lenox Ave, New York, NY 10027.

HOWARD, JOHN E.
Business executive. **PERSONAL:** Born Mar 12, 1938, Carrollton, AL. **EDUCATION:** Univ of So CA, attd. **CAREER:** Met Life Ins Co, sr sales rep. **ORGANIZATIONS:** Speaker to ins salesmen; bd dir Western Assc of Life Underwriters; mem Million Dollar Round Table; mem Pres Coun, only black sit on bd for Met Life. **HONORS/ACHIEVEMENTS:** Leading salesman for 1972-74. **MILITARY SERVICE:** USAF. **HOME ADDRESS:** 9623 Cresta Dr, Los Angeles, CA 90035.

HOWARD, JOHN ROBERT
Educator, attorney. **PERSONAL:** Born Jan 24, 1933, Boston, MA; married Mary Doris Adams; children: Leigh Humphrey. **EDUCATION:** Brandeix Univ, BA 1955; NY Univ, MA 1961; Stanford Univ, PhD 1965; J Du Pace Univ 1985. **CAREER:** Univ of OR, asst prof 1965-68; Rutgers Univ, assoc prof 1969-71; State Univ of NY, dean & prof 1971-80, State Univ of NY, prof of sociology 1971-; atty in private practice 1986-. **ORGANIZATIONS:** Bd mem UnitedWay of Westchester 1976-78; bd of advs Inst for Urban Design 1978-; vice pres Soc for the Study of Social Problems 1978-79; bd mem StreetTheater Inc 1978-80; bd Friends of the Nueberger Museum 1982-. **HONORS/ACHIEVEMENTS:** Publ Lifestyles in the Black, WW Norton 1969; The Cutting Edge, J B Lippincott Publ 1974; Urban Black Politics, Annals of the Am Acad 1978; various articles. **BUSINESS ADDRESS:** Professor of Sociology, StateUniv of NY, Lincoln Ave, Purchase, NY 10577.

HOWARD, JOSEPH CLEMENS
Judge. **PERSONAL:** Born Dec 09, 1922, Des Moines, IA; married Gwendolyn London; children: 1 son. **EDUCATION:** Univ of IA, BA 1950; Univ of Washington Law Sch, attd 1951; Drake Univ, LLB 1955, MA 1957, JD 1968; Morgan State Clge, hnry law degree 1972. **CAREER:** Howard & Hargrove Law Firm, atty 1960-64; City of Baltimore, asst states atty 1964-67, asst city solicitor; Supreme Bench of Baltimore, assoc judge 1968-79; US Dist Court, dist judge 1980-. **ORGANIZATIONS:** Mem bd of Counselors Drake Univ Law Sch 1970-73; chmn Judicial Council of Natl Bar Assc 1973-74; mem Bd of Gov Antioch Law Sch 1976-79; mem Task Force to Examine Criminal Justice System in China 1977; mem World Assc of Judges 1978-; mem All Natl & Local Bar Assc; mem Baltimore Urban Coalition; life mem NAACP; mem Mayor's Task Force on Community Relations; mem US Commn on Civil Rights. **HONORS/ACHIEVEMENTS:** Commendation From Brigadier Gen Trudo Philippine Command AUS 1945; first black admitted to Phi Alpha Delta Legal Frat 1952; first black elected to City-Wide Office Supreme Bench of Baltimore City 1968; Outst Srv in State's Attys Office Chief of Trial Section 1968; Bicentenial Judicial Award Black Amer Law Students Assc 1976; Man of Year Natl Assc of Bus & Prof Women's Clubs 1979; first black aptd to US Dist Ct for Dist of MD 1979; Spl Jud Serv Awd HerbertM Frisby Hist Soc 1980. **MILITARY SERVICE:** AUS 1st lt 1944-47. **BUSINESS ADDRESS:** U S District Court-Maryland, 101 W Lombard St, Ste 540, Baltimore, MD 21201.

HOWARD, JOSEPH H.
Retired dental director. **PERSONAL:** Born Jul 17, Chicago, IL; son of Dr. Joseph H. Howard, Sr.; married Tommye Berry (deceased); children: Brock, Viki. **EDUCATION:** Fisk Univ, AB 1935; Univ IL, DDS 1946; USC, MPH 1969. **CAREER:** Evanston Comm Hosp, dir dental serv 1948-50; City of Los Angeles, pub health dent 1966-70; LA Model City Dental Prog, coord 1969-70; Harbor Gen Hosp, dir comm dentistry 1970-73; UCLA, asst prof dentistry 1971-; Long Beach Genl Hosp, dental dir 1973-. **ORGANIZATIONS:** Inst chem Roosevelt HS; dental consult Suntown Palos Verdes Conv Hosp 1973; mem La Federation Dentaire Internationale; Amer Dental Assn; So CA Dental Soc; So CA Pub Health Assn; Amer Assn Pub Health Dentists; Western Soc of Periodontology; natl Dental Assn; Angel City Dental Assn; Amer Soc for Preventive Dentistry; Boys Work Sect YMCA 1936-37; mem LA Natl Library Week Com 1967; mem Dist Att Adv Council 1967; mem Mayor's Comm Adv Com 1967; Adv Bd Mahar House 1971; participant at lectures seminars & table clinics; author of numerous publications. **HONORS/ACHIEVEMENTS:** "Drums in the Americas" Oak pub l967; "Gifts From ILE IFE Black History Museum Phil PA l982; "Drums" l982. **MILITARY SERVICE:** USAF capt 1950-52. **HOME ADDRESS:** 1728 Victoria Ave, Los Angeles, CA 90019. **BUSINESS ADDRESS:** Dental Director-Retired, Long Beach General Hosp, 5220 W Washington Blvd, Los Angeles, CA 90016.

HOWARD, KEITH L.
Optometrist. **PERSONAL:** Born Feb 27, 1940, Buffalo, NY; son of Robert B Howard Sr and Annie C Howard; married Patricia; children: Jennifer, Kristopher. **EDUCATION:** AA, BS, OD 1966. **CAREER:** Optical Corp, partner 1968; pvt prac 1969; Melnick, Howard, Grzankowski Opt, prof corp formed 1974; Southern Tier Optometric Center, vice pres, partner 1979-. **ORGANIZATIONS:** Natl & Amer Optometric Assn; Natl Eye Research Fnd Optometric Extension Prog dir Olean YMCA; Olean Comm Chest; EGO Health Studios Inc; bd mem, State Board of Optometry, 1985-89, 1989-93; bd mem and Region I director, Natl Optometric Assn 1988-89. **HONORS/ACHIEVEMENTS:** Olean YMCA Man of Year 1970; one of two black optometrists in NY State. **BUSINESS ADDRESS:** 168 N Union St, Olean, NY 14760.

HOWARD, LAWRENCE CABOT
Educator. **PERSONAL:** Born Apr 16, 1925, Des Moines, IA; son of Charles P Howard and Maude Lewis Howard; married Elizabeth Fitzgerald; children: Jane, Susan, Laura. **EDUCATION:** Drake Univ, BA 1949; Wayne State Univ, MA 1950; Harvard Univ, PhD 1956. **CAREER:** Hofstra Univ, instr asst prof 1956-58; Brandeis Univ, asst prof 1958-63; Peace Corps, assoc dir 1961-63; Ctr on Inn NY St Dept of Educ, assoc dir 1964; Univ of WI, dir human rel inst 1964-67; Danforth Found, vice pres 1967-69; Univ of Pittsburgh, dean, Graduate School of Public and International Affairs, 1969-73, prof 1973-; Government of the Bahamas, management consultant 1986-. **ORGANIZATIONS:** Consult US Ofc Educ State Dept Bur Extnl Rsch; mem rsch & adv bd Com on Econ Devel; mem Natl Adv Comm Tchr Corps 1967-69; mem Pgh World Affrs Counc 1969-; Pgh Hist & Landmarks Found; mem exec council Natl Assn Sch Pub Affrs Adm 1971-73; Amer Soc Pub Admin 1972-; trustee Ch Soc for Coll Work, Drake Univ, St Augustine Coll, Seabury-Western Theol Sem, Epis Diocese of Pgh; Harvard Grad Soc for Advcmt of Study & Rsch; Deputy to Epis Diocesan Conv. **HONORS/ACHIEVEMENTS:** Man of the Yr Alpha Phi Alpha 1949; Disting Alumnus Awd Drake Univ 1971; contrib articles to professional jours; natl pres of COMPA 1979-80; co-author "Public Adminstrn, Balancing Power & Accountability"; Fullbright Professor Univ of Maiduguri Nigeria 1981-82; mem Phi Beta Kappa; author, US Involvement in Africa South of the Sahara before 1960 (1988). **MILITARY SERVICE:** AUS 1943-45. **BUSINESS ADDRESS:** Professor, University of Pgh, Grad Sch of Pub & Intl Aff, Pittsburgh, PA 15260.

HOWARD, LEON
Educator. **CAREER:** AL State Univ, pres 1984-. **BUSINESS ADDRESS:** President, Alabama State University, 915 S Jackson St, Montgomery, AL 36195.

HOWARD, LEON W., JR.
Business executive. **PERSONAL:** Born May 03, 1935, Pittsburgh, PA. **EDUCATION:** Univ of Pgh, attended 1974-; PA State Univ, attended 1968; licensed as broker 1971. **CAREER:** Robt C Golden, real estate 1956-57; Surety Underwriters Inc, vice pres 1970-73; Nationwide Ins Co, agency agreement 1972-. **ORGANIZATIONS:** Past chmn Labor & Indus Com Pgh NAACP 1974; past pres Pgh Branch NAACP 1975; past pres COPP; past vice pres PABU; past bd of dir Profit Making Prog for Black Catholic Ministries & Laymen's Council; exec bd mem Pgh Chap NAACP; exec bd mem Homewood-Brushton YMCA; commr City of Pgh Dept of City Planning; mem natl Assn of Sec Dealers; mem Pgh Life Underwriters Assn Inc; mem Natl Assn of Life Underwriters; mem Ins Club of Pgh Inc. **HONORS/**

ACHIEVEMENTS: Awd for Outstanding Contribution to the Struggle for Human Rights Western PA Black Polit Assembly. **MILITARY SERVICE:** AUS paratrooper. **BUSINESS ADDRESS:** Ins Broker/Agent, Nationwide Insurance Co, 564 Forbes Ave Ste 1006, Pittsburgh, PA 15219.

HOWARD, LESLIE KENYATTA
Public administrator. **PERSONAL:** Born Jun 18, 1950, Aberdeen, MD; son of Oliver Howard and Ethel Howard; married Corrine Felder; children: Kevin, Keith, Kenneth. **EDUCATION:** Howard Univ, BA 1980; Comm Coll of Balto, AA & Certificate Electronics 1971/1982; Baruch Coll CUNY, MPA 1984. **CAREER:** MD Dept of Human Resources, caseworker II 1975-77; Mayor of Baltimore, spec asst 1979-82; Neighborhood Housing Serv of Baltimore, prog dir 1982-83; Mayor of Detroit, spec asst 1983-84; Neighborhood Housing Serv of Baltimore, neighborhood coord asst dir, neighborhood dir 1985-87. **ORGANIZATIONS:** Mem Amer Muslim Mission 1977-82; founding mem Baltimore Chap Black Media coalition 1982-83; mem natl Forum of Black Public Admin 1984-85; producer/pres Be-More Productions Inc 1970-; mem Congressional Black Caucus Brain Trust Comm & Hous 1980-; mem Left Bank Jazz Soc; mem NAACP; adv bd mem Black United Fund of Gr Baltimore; pres MD Housing Coalition; mem MD State Rainbow Coalition; pres Alliance of Rosemont Cmmty Org, Inc; chmn Maryland Low Income Housing Information Serv; Westside Democratic Forum; executive bd mem, MD Assn Housing and Redevelopment Agencies (MAHRA); mem, Community Development Committee; Regional Planning Council. **HONORS/ACHIEVEMENTS:** Summer Scholarship Peabody Preparatory Sch 1967; Certificates Comm Serv RHATA Inc Calverton Jr High 1980, 1982; Natl Urban Fellowship Class of 1983-84; Concert Productions Hugh Masakela Leon Thomas et al 1970-; mem Phi Alpha Theta Intl Honor Soc in History; Governor's Certificate of Appreciation; Wilson Park Community Serv Awd; Mayor's Proclamation. **HOME ADDRESS:** 2322 Harlem Ave, Baltimore, MD 21216. **BUSINESS ADDRESS:** Housing Development Program Coordinator, Hartford County, 2205 Main Street, Office of Human Relations, Bel Air, MD 21014.

HOWARD, LYTIA RAMANI
Educator. **PERSONAL:** Born May 06, 1950, Atlanta, GA; daughter of G LaMarr and Gwendolyn Howard. **EDUCATION:** Spelman College, BA 1971; Univ of Tennessee, MACT 1973; Atlanta Univ, MA 1978, EdD 1979; Interdenominational Theological Ctr, MRE 1984. **CAREER:** Spelman Coll, instructor, asst prof 1973-83, asst dean academic 1983-85; GA Inst of Tech, dir of special programs 1985-. **ORGANIZATIONS:** Mem Alpha Kappa Delta Sociological Honor Soc, Mid-South Sociological Assn, Natl Assn for Women Deans Administrators and Counselors, Southern Christian Leadership Council, Phi Delta Kappa, Amer Soc for Engrg Educ; bd mem Natl Consortium for Grad Degrees for Minorities in Engrg Inc 1985-86; mem Natl Action Council for Minorities in Engrg, Natl Assn of Minority Engrg Program Administrators, United Assn of Christian Counselors; chairperson bd of dirs Hinsley Day Care Ctr 1986; bd of trustees New Hope Church of God in Christ 1986; intl pres, The Sunshine Band, Church of God in Christ, Inc 1986-. **HONORS/ACHIEVEMENTS:** Certificates Assoc of Colleges and Univs for International-Intercultural Affairs 1976; Alpha Kappa Delta Sociological Honor Soc; Central GA Scholarship Fund; Phi Delta Kappa; Proclamation City of Atlanta for Leadership in Community 1982; plaques Spelman Coll, New Hope Church, YWCA of Greater Atlanta, Central GA recognition; Proclamation, City of Detroit 1987; Plaque, Natl Assn of Business Women of America 1988. **HOME ADDRESS:** 371 Lynnhaven Dr SW, Atlanta, GA 30310. **BUSINESS ADDRESS:** Dir of Special Programs, Georgia Inst of Technology, Coll of Engineering-0360, Atlanta, GA 30332.

HOWARD, M. W., JR.
Clergyman. **PERSONAL:** Born Mar 03, 1946, Americus, GA; son of M William Howard, Sr and Laura Turner Howard; married Barbara Jean Wright; children: Matthew Weldon, Adam Turner, Maisha Wright. **EDUCATION:** Morehouse Coll, BA 1968; Princeton Theological Seminary, MDiv 1972. **CAREER:** Reformed Church in AM, exec dir of the Black Council, 1972-. **ORGANIZATIONS:** Ordained minister Amer Baptist Chs 1974; moderator Program to Combat Racism of the World Council of Churches 1976-78; pres Natl Council of Churches 1979-81; bd of trustees Natl Urban League 1981-88; bd of trustees Independent Sector 1981-86; trustee Childrens Defense Fund 1981-86; pres Amer Comm on Africa; provided X-mas services to US Hostages in Iran in 1979; Chaired Ecumenical delegation which accompanied Rev Jesse Jackson to obtain the release of Lt Robt Goodman in Demascus, Syria; Serves on Human Rights Advisory Group of the World Council of Churches. **HONORS/ACHIEVEMENTS:** Honorary Dr of Divinity Degree Miles Coll and Central Coll 1979-80; citations Mayors of Philadelphia, PA and Americus, GA 1981-84; distinguished alumnus award Princeton Sem 1982; Honorary Dr of Humane Letters Morehouse Coll 1984; Citations from the NJ ST Assembly; The City of Waterloo, Iowa; The Township of Lawrence, NJ; The Touissant Loverture Freedom Award by NY's Haitian Community; Chaired the Seminar against bank loans to South Africa in Zurich, Switzerland in 1982. **BUSINESS ADDRESS:** Exec Dir of Black Council, Reformed Church in Amer, 475 Riverside Dr, New York, NY 10115.

HOWARD, MAMIE
Educational administration. **PERSONAL:** Born Nov 24, 1946, Pascagoula, MS; daughter of Mr & Mrs E Howard. **EDUCATION:** Pensacola Jr Coll, AS 1971; USA, BS 1976; UAB, MS 1979; Univ of AL, PhD 1987. **CAREER:** DW McMillan Hosp, gen duty rn 1967-71, suprv 1971-76; Jefferson Davis Jr Coll, instr 1976-78; Pensacola Jr Coll, dept chair allied health ed. **ORGANIZATIONS:** Mem Amer Nurses Assoc 1971-, USA Alumni Assoc; consult Escambia Sickle Cell Disease Found 1979-82; mem UAB Alumni Assoc 1979-, Committee for Allied Health Ed 1981-, AAWCGC 1982-; bd of dir FL Lung Assoc 1983-; chief exec officer State Mgmt Ltd 1985-; dir at large Lung Assoc 1986; mem Alpha Kappa Alpha; chairman, PRIDE Committee of the Amer Lung Assn. **HONORS/ACHIEVEMENTS:** Honor Awd Kappa Delta Pi Grad Honor Soc 1981-; Selected as a Leader of the 80's FIPSE 1982; honored by the governor as an Outstanding Black American 1988. **BUSINESS ADDRESS:** Department Chairman Allied Health, Pensacola Junior College, 5555 Highway 98 West, Pensacola, FL 32507.

HOWARD, MILTON L.
Architect, associate executive. **PERSONAL:** Born Sep 03, 1927, Hurtsboro, AL; married Dolores Allen; children: Mark, James. **EDUCATION:** KY State Clge; Univ of IL. **CAREER:** Milton Lewis Howard Assc Architects, architect & owner. **ORGANIZATIONS:** Mem AIA; Natl Council Archit Registration Bds; Guild for Religious Arch Mem Arch Adv Panel GSA Region 1; Bldg Bd of Appeals City of Hartford; vice pres Hartford Comm Capital Corp. **MILITARY SERVICE:** AUS 1950-52. **BUSINESS ADDRESS:** 99 Pratt St, Hartford, CT 06103.

HOWARD, NORMAN
Industrial relations manager. **PERSONAL:** Born Jan 30, 1947, Johnson City, TN; married Nancy Goines; children: Erick, Nicole, Nichelle. **EDUCATION:** Georgetown Univ Inst on Comparative Political & Economic Systems, diploma 1972; Benedict Coll, BS 1974; Univ of Detroit, MBA 1979. **CAREER:** Ford Motor Co Casting Div and Transmission & Chassis Div, various positions in labor relations and salary admin 1974-81; Ford Motor Co Sales Opers Staff,affirmative action prog coord 1981-82; Ford Motor Co Livonia Trans Plant, supv sales pers & training 1982-83; Ford World Headquarters Pers & Org Staff, ind rels analyst 1983-85; Ford Motor Co Dearborn Glass Plant, mgr ind rels dept 1985-. **ORGANIZATIONS:** Pres Phi Bet Lambda 1973-74; mem Delta Mu Delta 1973-74; chairman Gesu Boy Scout Troop 191 Committee 1982-85; pres Detroit Chap Bendict Coll Alumni Club 1984-. **HONORS/ACHIEVEMENTS:** Outstanding Service Recognition Awds Gesu Boy Scout Troop 191 Detroit 1983, 84, 85; Distinguished Alumni Citation Natl Assoc for Equal Oppor in Higher Educ 1986. **MILITARY SERVICE:** USAF sgt E-4 4 yrs. **BUSINESS ADDRESS:** Mgr Industrial Relations Dept, Ford Motor Company, Dearborn Glass Plant, 3001 Miller Rd, Dearborn, MI 48121.

HOWARD, NORMAN LEROY
Administrator. **PERSONAL:** Born May 22, 1930, New York, NY; married Barbara; children: Karen, Dale, Steven. **CAREER:** Consolidated Edison Co of NY Inc, equal emplmt oppor coord; Inst Mediation & Conflict Resol, consult 1972-73; NYCPD, retired detective 1952-72; New York City Dept of Parks, playground dir 1948-51. **ORGANIZATIONS:** Mem 100 Black Men Inc; Boys of Yesteryear; 369th Vet Assc; K of C St Patricks Council; retired Guardians NYCPD; Intl Black Police Assc; Welterweight boxing champion amatuer New York City Dept of Parks 1943-44; Middleweight Champion Amatuer Met AAU 1945. **HONORS/ACHIEVEMENTS:** Combat Cross for Bravery NYCPD 1955; 15 awards for Bravery & Excellent Police Work NYCPD; 1st black detective assigned to 40th squad Bronx 1954. **MILITARY SERVICE:** AUS pvt e1 1950-52; Good Conduct Medal. **BUSINESS ADDRESS:** 4 Irving Pl, New York, NY 10003.

HOWARD, OSBIE L., JR.
Business executive. **PERSONAL:** Born Feb 09, 1943, Memphis, TN; married Rose O Ollie; children: John, Kendra, Nathan. **EDUCATION:** Memphis State Univ, BBA 1967; Washington Univ, MBA 1971. **CAREER:** TN Valley Center for Minority Economic Devel, exec vice pres 1979-; Shelby Cty Gvt, asst chief adminstn officer 1978-79; Banks's Findley White & Co CPA's, tax mgr 1974-78; Memphis Bus Resource Center, financial & specialist 1972-74; Exxon Co, financial analyst 1971-72; TN State Bd of Accountacy, CPA 1973. **ORGANIZATIONS:** Treasurer & co-founder Southern Memphis Development Corp, 1976; bd of dir JK Lewis Center for Senior Citizens 1978-; graduate Business School Fellowship Nconsortium for Graduate Study in Mgmt 1969. **BUSINESS ADDRESS:** Ste 1701, 8 N Third St, Memphis, TN 38103.

HOWARD, RAYMOND MONROE, SR.
Clergyman. **PERSONAL:** Born Sep 13, 1921, Many, LA; married Dorothy Mae Matthews; children: Raymond Jr, Sylvia Dean Norman, Sandra Laray Stuart, Shirley Ann Shields, Ralph Edgar, Sherry Marie Brown. **EDUCATION:** Skyline Coll San Bruno CA, AA 1972; San Francisco Theol Sem, M Div 1974. **CAREER:** Paradise Missionary Bapt Ch, pastor 1955-; Prog Educ & Dist Congress of Christian Edn, pres 1970; Prog Educ Dist Assn, sec of finance 1963. **ORGANIZATIONS:** Pres organizer Daly City Community for Childrens Serv 1976-77; bus mgr CA State Bapt Convention Inc 1980; candidate Daly City Councilman 1972; pres organizer Black Churchmens Assn 1972; pres organizer Ingleside Churches Assn 1973; Combat Eurpoe/Africa Campaign. **MILITARY SERVICE:** AUS mst sgt 1943-45. **BUSINESS ADDRESS:** 2595 San Jose Ave, San Francisco, CA 94112.

HOWARD, ROBERT BERRY, JR.
Retired city official. **PERSONAL:** Born Mar 29, 1916, Barnesville, GA; son of Robert B Howard and Annie C Collins; married Irene W Battle; children: Jean Margaret Holland. **EDUCATION:** Buffalo Collegiate Center. **CAREER:** Buffalo Artistic Upholstering Co, receiving clerk 1936-37; Semet Solvay Co, utility man 1937-43; Buffalo Fire Dept, lieutenant 1943-51, capt 1951-60, fire commissioner, retired fire commissioner. **ORGANIZATIONS:** Field rep Natl Fire Protection Assn 1973-76; bd dir many civic orgns 1968-73; Fire Adv Bd NY State 1972-73; sec Metro Comm Intl Fire Chiefs Assn 1970-73. **HONORS/ACHIEVEMENTS:** Man of the Yr Greater Niagara Frontier Adv Club 1970; Man of the Yr Jewish War Veterans Post 1969; chmn Brotherhood Week Natl Conf Christians and Jews 1968; chmn Cleanup Week Buffalo Chamber of Commerce 1969. **HOME ADDRESS:** 258 Sunrise Blvd, Amherst, NY 14221.

HOWARD, SAMUEL H.
Business executive. **PERSONAL:** Born May 08, 1939, Marietta, OK; son of Houston Howard and Nellie Howard; married Karan A; children: Anica, Samuel. **EDUCATION:** OK State Univ, BS 1961; Stanford Univ, MA 1963. **CAREER:** White House, spec asst fellow 1966-67; Howard Univ, dir 1967-68; HEW, consult to sec 1967-69; TAW Intl Leasing Corp, vice pres fin, sec, treas, 1968-72; Phoenix Comm Group Inc, founder, pres 1972-; Meharry Med Coll, vice pres fin 1973-77; Hosp Affiliates Intl Inc, vice pres 1977-81; Hospital Corp of Amer, vp, treas 1981-85; sr vice pres of public affairs Hospital Corp of America 1985-1988; Phoenix Holdings, chairman 1989-. **ORGANIZATIONS:** Mem Phi Kappa Phi, Blue Key, Beta Gamma Sigma, Delta Sigma Pi, Alpha Phi Alpha, Human Rels Council, Cordell Hall Council, Lariats, Sigma Epsilon Sigma, Fed of Amer Hosp, Fin Exec Inst, Nashville Br of Fed Reserve Bank of Atlanta, Nashville Urban League, United Way; chairman Nashville Convention Cntr Commission, Amer Hospital Assoc, dir of Scientific Leasing Inc, dir of Nashville Chamber of Commerce; dir Corporate Child Care; dir Genesis Health Ventures. **HONORS/ACHIEVEMENTS:** Outstanding Young Men of Amer 1969,71. **BUSINESS ADDRESS:** Chairman, Phoenix Holdings, Inc., Vanderbilt Plaza, 2100 West End Avenue, Suite 780, Nashville, TN 37203.

HOWARD, SHIRLEY M.
Educator. **PERSONAL:** Born Dec 15, 1935, Chicago; married Johnnie Howard; children: Patrice, Paula, Christopher. **EDUCATION:** Cook Co Sch Nursing, Diploma 1960; DePaul

Univ, BSN 1969, MS 1972. **CAREER:** Governors State Univ, prof Health Sci & Health Sci Instrctnl Prog Coord; Village Nursing Srv, co-owner; nursing admin, instr, publ health nurse. **ORGANIZATIONS:** Mem Natl League Nursing; Assc Rehab Nurses; Deans & Dirs Coun Baccalaureate & Higher Degree Progs; consult Robbins Human Resource Ctr; aux Independent Peoples Party; PTA; bd Family Health Ctr; adv Bd Kennedy-King Clge Nursing Alumni; bd Comprehensive Comm Health Planning & Dev Coun; Mini-grant ResearchProjs Gov's State Univ 1972-75. **HONORS/ACHIEVEMENTS:** Certf of Merit Youth Motivation Com & Chicago Merit Employment Com 1971-72; author & proj dir HEW proj nursing educ & research. **BUSINESS ADDRESS:** Governors State Univ, Park Forest South, IL 60466.

HOWARD, VERA GOUKE
Educator. **PERSONAL:** Born in Brooklyn. **EDUCATION:** Baruch Clge, BBA 1958; NY Univ, MA 1969. **CAREER:** NY Inst Technology, counselor 1971-; NY City Bd of Educ 1963-71; Brooklyn Coll, adjunct instructor; Manpower Devel Training, teacher; Brooklyn Coll, prog lecturer; Social Worker Investigator New York City Dept Welfare. **ORGANIZATIONS:** Mem New York City Personnel Guidance Assc; Black Alliance Educators; Long Island Assc Black Cnslrs; vol cnslr. **BUSINESS ADDRESS:** New York Tech, 268 Wheatley Rd, Old Westbury, NY 11568.

HOWARD, VIVIAN GORDON
Educator. **PERSONAL:** Born Apr 22, 1923, Warsaw, VA; married Dr Roscoe C Howard (deceased); children: Atty Linda G, Atty Roscoe C Jr, Roderick W. **EDUCATION:** VA State Univ, BS 1946, MS Elem Educ 1960, MS 1966, EdD Math Ed 1969; Hermenet of San Francisco, certified coach mgmt 1984; Action Technology, certified guide 1985. **CAREER:** Natl Institutes of Health, extramural assoc 1981; Longwood College, visiting prof of math 1983-84; VA Tech, visiting prof of math 1984-85; VA State Univ, prof of math 1969-; Howard Enterprises, founder w/daughter; VA State Univ & VA Tech Univ, exchange prof to promote integration in higher educ. **ORGANIZATIONS:** Consul Natl Inst of Educ 1974-76; dir Secondary Prog for Gifted in Math Sci & English for DC Schls Mediax Corp of CT 1976; math consul DC Schs putting math labs in Anacostia schs 1975-77; workshop leader on Natl Level-Metric System & Math Labs; VA coord & natl bd Natl Coalition of 100 Black Women establishing 6 chapts 1983-; VA coord Adolescent Pregnancy Child Watch of Children's Defense Fund 1984-. **HONORS/ACHIEVEMENTS:** Human Relations Awd in Educ Minority Caucus of the VA Educ Assn of NEA 1984; Outstanding Political Service Awd Womens Vote Project Atlanta 1984; Disting Teacher School of Natural Sciences VSU 1979; charter pres Kappa Delta Pi Honor Soc VSU; DuPont Fellow and 1st Black grad student assigned to teach in the classroom Univ VA; Metric Educ Plan for VA Richmond Dept of Educ Commonwealth of VA 1977; publ "Innovative Metric Educ Prog at VSU" presented in Miami & Denver and published in govt documents; Bronz Awd Intl Film Festival New York City and released in Washington DC "Roads to Mathematics through Physical Education Art Music and Educ" Industrial Arts VSU Prog comm by the US Office of Educ Dept of Health Educ & Welfare 1972. **BUSINESS ADDRESS:** Prof of Mathematics, VA StateUniv VA Tech Univ, 20413 Williams St, Ettrick, VA 23803.

HOWE, RUTH-ARLENE W.
Educator. **PERSONAL:** Born Nov 21, 1933, Scotch Plains, NJ; daughter of Curtis T Woods and Grace Louise R Wood (Randolph) (deceased); married Theodore Holmes Howe, Jun 29, 1957; children: Marian, Curtis, Helen, Edgar. **EDUCATION:** Wellesley Coll, BA 1955; Simmons Coll Sch of Social Work, SM 1957; Boston Coll Law School JD 1974. **CAREER:** Cleveland OH Catholic Youth Serv Bureau, casewkr 1957-61; Tufts Delta Health Ctr Mound Bayou MS, housing devel consultant 1969-70; Simmons Coll Sch of Social Work, instr soc pol 1970-78; Law & Child Dev Project DHEW/ACYF Funded B C Law Sch, asst dir 1977-79; Boston Coll Law Sch, asst prof of Law 1977-81; assoc prof of law. **ORGANIZATIONS:** Bd mem Boston League of Women Voters 1963-68; clerk Grimes-King Found for the Elderly Inc 1972-; guardian ad litem MA Family and Probate Court 1979-; ABA Tech to NCCUSL Uniform Adoption and Marital Property Acts 1980-83; reviewer CWLA Journal-Child Welfare 1984-93; mem MA Gov St Com on Child Support Enforcement 1985; mem MA Adv Comm on Child Support Guidelines 1986; mem MA Gov/MBA Commn on the Legal Needs of Children 1986-87; NCCUSL Uniform Putative and Unknown Fathers Act Reporter 1986-88. **HONORS/ACHIEVEMENTS:** Wellesley scholar Wellesley Coll 1955; Nat'l Inst of Mental Health Fellowship 1956-57; co-authored/Katz McGrath Child Neglect Laws in Am ABA Press 1976; cited for contribution to legal ed MA Black Lawyers Asso 1983; Honored by MA Black Legislative Caucus 1988. **BUSINESS ADDRESS:** Associate Professor of Law, Boston Coll Law Sch, 885 Centre St, Newton Centre, MA 02159.

HOWELL, AMAZIAH, III
Business executive. **PERSONAL:** Born Oct 12, 1948, Goldsboro, NC; son of Amaziah Howell Jr and Theresa Reid Howell; married Jessica McCoy, Jul 08, 1978; children: Joy Elizabeth, Aimee Denice. **EDUCATION:** Johnson C Smith Univ Charlotte NC, attended 1966-68; NY Inst of Credit, attended 1970; Amos Tuck Sch of Business, Dartmouth U, Minority Business Exec Program. **CAREER:** Howell Petroleum Products, Inc, Brooklyn NY, president, 1985—; Las Energy Corp, Roosevelt NY, vice pres, 1981-85; Assn of Minority Enterprises of NY Inc, exec dir 1976-77, 1979-81; Wallace & Wallace Fuel Oil Co, marketing mgr 1978-79; Ofc of US Senator James L Buckley, special assistant 1973-76; Manufacturers Hanover Trust Co, credit investigator 1968-72. **ORGANIZATIONS:** Mem NAACP 1960-; former pres & chairman, New York City Manhattan Jaycees 1970-71; co-chmn pub relations com Harlem YMCA Black Achievers Com 1975-; Future Promise Saturday Review World 1975; vice chair, Mayor's Black Business Advisory Bd; advisory bd, Long Island Univ Small Business Development Center; advisory bd, NY City Small Business Mentorship Prog; NY/NJ Minority Purchasing Council; bd mem, Westchester Minority Commerce Assn; Texaco Jobber Council; NJ Minority Business Braintrust; Brooklyn Chamber of Commerce; Greater Newark Chamber of Commerce; Natl Minority Business Council; NY State Business Council. **HONORS/ACHIEVEMENTS:** Outstanding Young Man of Am US Jaycees 1976; merit award St Albans Queens C of C 1977; achievement award Harlem YMCA 1978; outstanding minority business of the year, Natl Minority Business Council, 1987. **BUSINESS ADDRESS:** President, Howell Petroleum Products, Inc, Brooklyn Navy Yard, Building #292, Brooklyn, NY 11205.

HOWELL, GERALD T.
Business executive. **PERSONAL:** Born Sep 18, 1914, Columbia, TN; married Vera; children: Lynn Marie, Marian Rachelle. **EDUCATION:** TN State U, BS cum laude 1936. **CAREER:** Universal Life Ins Co Memphis, agt & other offices 1941-61, agency dir 1961-66, dir agys 1967, vice pres dir agys 1968-, 1st vp/secty/coo. **ORGANIZATIONS:** Mem Nat Ins Assn NAACP; Emmanuel Epis Ch Alpha Phi & Alpha; Mason; Shriner. **HONORS/ACHIEVEMENTS:** Sportsmen's club spl serv award Nat Ins Assn 1974; blount award exceptional performance Nat Ins Assn 1974. **MILITARY SERVICE:** AUS ETO 1st sgt 1942-45. **BUSINESS ADDRESS:** 1st VP/Secretary/COO, Universal Life Ins Co, 480 Linden St, Memphis, TN 38126.

HOWELL, JOSEPH L.
Educator, administrator. **PERSONAL:** Born Nov 25, 1930, So Bend, IN; married Joan C Alexander; children: Joseph Haywood, Eric Alexander. **EDUCATION:** Oberlin Coll, BA 1953; Wstrn Res U, MA 1963;Univ of MA, ABD. **CAREER:** Howell & Alexander Inc, pres; The Lilly Endowment Indianapolis, educ cons; African Region Peace Corps Washington DC, chief of operations 1972-73; OEO Washington DC, dir div of human resources 1970-72; Rsch Council of Greater Cities Washington, proj dir 1968-70; State of NJ, special asst to commr of educ 1967-68; Lincoln Job Corps Center Lincoln NE, program dir 1966-67; CAP US Office of Economic Opportunity Washington DC, program anlyst 1964-66; OH Civil Rghts Commn Cleveland, educ asst 1963-64; E Tech HS Cleveland, teacher coach 1954-63. **ORGANIZATIONS:** Mem Assn of Blck Fnd Ofcls; Am Assn of Sch Admin; Soc for Intrcltrl Educ Training & Rsrch. **HONORS/ACHIEVEMENTS:** Mst vlbl coach awd No OH Coaching Assn 1960; various awds as coach of bsktbl teams. **MILITARY SERVICE:** Usnr seaman 1950-54.

HOWELL, LAURENCE A.
Association executive. **PERSONAL:** Born Dec 13, 1943, Ft Wayne; married Mary E. **EDUCATION:** IN State U, BS 1973. **CAREER:** Upward Bound IN State U, dir; Rhoads Hall IN State U, dir 1973-74; Great Markwestern Pkg Co Detroit, asst dir personnel 1970-71, Vocational Industrial Therapy Ginsberg Rehab Cntr Ft Wayne State & Hosp, asst dir 1968-70. **ORGANIZATIONS:** Mem APGA; personnel Mid-Am Assn Educ Oppor Prog; IN Affiliate; Adv Black Student Union; adv bd Afro-Am Cultural Cntr & Afro-Am Studies Prog; Black Student's Psychol Assn; bd Charles T Hyte Comm Cntr; Vigo Co Lifetime; Vigo Co Economic Oppor Coun. **HONORS/ACHIEVEMENTS:** Certificates Appreciation & Trophies Black Student Union. **MILITARY SERVICE:** AUS sp/5 1965-68. **BUSINESS ADDRESS:** Upward Bound IN State Univ, Terre Haute, IN 47809.

HOWELL, MALQUEEN
Educator. **PERSONAL:** Born Apr 03, 1949, Calhoun Co, SC. **EDUCATION:** BA 1971, MA 1972. **CAREER:** Benedict Coll, English instructor. **ORGANIZATIONS:** Founding pres Calhoun Co Jr Improvement League 1966; mem NAACP; adv panel State Human Affairs Commn; Study & Preservation Black Hist; Art & Folklore Simons-Mann Coll 1973; voter educ proj & Heart Fund Campaign; United Way; Mt Carmel Bapt Ch Citation Conf Computing Minorit Instns. **HONORS/ACHIEVEMENTS:** Alpha Kappa Alpha; cert MI Sch Med Div Addiction Scis 1974; cert Proj Assist Action Prog 1968. **BUSINESS ADDRESS:** Benedict College, Harden & Blanding Streets, Columbia, SC.

HOWELL, ROBERT J., JR.
Business executive. **PERSONAL:** Born Feb 24, 1935, New York, NY; married Elestine. **EDUCATION:** New Sch, MA; NY U, PhD cand. **CAREER:** Human Resources Adminstrn, Personnel Adminstrn; Div of Emply dep dir 1972-74; Professional Recruitment & Replacement, chief 1968-72, spl asst dir personnel 1967-68; Cornell Grad Sch & Indsl Labor Rel, consult 1970-71; NY State Civil Serv Commn for Professional Cands Internal Pub Personnel Assn, oral examiner. **ORGANIZATIONS:** 100 Black Men. **MILITARY SERVICE:** Sp 4 1958-60. **BUSINESS ADDRESS:** 271 Church St, New York, NY.

HOWELL, ROSE COLE
Educational administrator. **PERSONAL:** Born Feb 14, 1949, Durham, NC; married SFC Calvin W Howell, Jr; children: Carli, Calvin, III, Cora Janiece. **EDUCATION:** Bennett College, BA Sociology 1971; United Christian Coll, BTh 1979; Eastern WA Univ, MS Counseling Psychology 1987. **CAREER:** Durham Co, NC Dept of Soc Serv, social worker 1978-80; Dept of Defense, site spvsr 1981-82; Eastern WA Univ, prog secretary Black Educ Prog 1984-85; Whitworth Coll, dir minority student affairs 1985-. **ORGANIZATIONS:** Mem Natl Council Black Studies; exec sec Natl Council Black Studies Pacific Northwest Region 1985-86; secretary Black Educators for Excellence 1985-86. **HONORS/ACHIEVEMENTS:** Ordained eldress Christ Holly Sanctified Church, Inc; mem NAACP-Spokane Chap; dir of Christian educ Solid Rock CHSC, Inc 1984-; mem Spokane Ministerial Alliance; Outstanding Young Women of Amer 1985. **HOME ADDRESS:** 9037 Carolina, Fairchild AFB, WA 99011.

HOWELL, VINCENT WYATT
Computer company executive. **PERSONAL:** Born Aug 21, 1953, Shelby, NC; married Carolyn Y Kelley; children: Naila S, Vincent Jr. **EDUCATION:** NC A&T State Univ, BSIT 1975; Salve Regina Coll, MA 1981; CA Coast Univ, PhD 1985; Colgate-Rochester Divinity Sch, Diploma 1986. **CAREER:** Ford Aerospace & Comm Corp, eng assoc qc 1975-77; Hughes Aircraft Co, quality assurance engr 1977-78; Raytheon Co, ind eng prod mgr ie supv 1978-82; Computer Consoles Inc, sr ie, prog mgr, ie mgr 1982-. **ORGANIZATIONS:** Mem Alpha Phi Alpha Frat 1973-; chap officer bd of dir Inst of Ind Engrg 1980-82, 1985-87; mem bd of dirs Child & Family Serv of Newport 1981, ML King Jr Ctr Newport 1981; mem Soc of Mfg Engrs 1982-; pastor St James AME Zion Church Ithaca NY 1985-; mem bd of dirs Roch Ind Eng Soc 1985-; editor/newsletter Roch Ind Eng Soc 1986-. **HONORS/ACHIEVEMENTS:** Certified Mfg Engr Soc of Mfg Engrs; Certified Systems Professional Assoc of System Mgmt; Author's Awd Raytheon Co 1981; Literary Awd Computer Consoles Inc 1985; Outstanding Young Mfg Eng Awd SME Natl 1985; Outstanding Young Eng of the Year Awd IIE Natl 1986; books "Quality Improvement Through Cont Educ," pub by ASQC 1986; "History of St James AME Zion Church"; author of 17 articles published; listed in Who's Who in Tech 1986. **HOME ADDRESS:** 4 Katsura Ct, Penfield, NY 14526. **BUSINESS ADDRESS:** Section Mgr, Mfg Quality, Computer Consoles Inc, 97 Humboldt St, Rochester, NY 14609.

HOWELL, WILLIAM B.
Clergyman. **PERSONAL:** Born Feb 19, 1932, High Point, NC. **EDUCATION:** Winston Salem State Coll, BS 1965; La SalleUniv Corr Sch Chicago, LLB; ITC Gammon Theol Sem M Div, 1970; Brantridge Forest Coll England, hon DD 1972; Daniel Payne Coll, DD 1975. **CAREER:** High Point NC, law enforcement officer 1953-62; So Pines Pub Sch NC tchr, 1965-

67; NC TN GA Conf, Pastorates; Turner Theol Sem Extension Prog, tchr of Theology 1973; ML Harris United Meth Ch, Minister. **ORGANIZATIONS:** Pres Columbus GA chap Operation PUSH; pres Columbus Phenix City Ministerial Alliance; mem NAACP; mem bd dir YMCA 1973-74; mem Gammon Sem Alumni Assn; ordained decon & elder United Meth Ch; past vice-chmnbd of missions S GA Conf 1972; vice chmn Ministry of S GA Conf 1972; mem commn on Religion & Race of S GA Conf Chpln of WK; GA State Senate 1972. **HONORS/ACHIEVEMENTS:** Humanitarian Award Am Red Cross 1974; scholarship award bd of United Meth Ch1967; Ada Stovall Award for Academic Achievement 1970; Dr Martin & Luther King Award for Distinguished Serv 1974. **BUSINESS ADDRESS:** 4309 Old Cusseta Rd, Columbus, GA 31903.

HOWELL, WILLIE R.
Chief of police. **PERSONAL:** Born May 27, 1926, Chicago, IL; married Evelyn; children: Barbara Ann Petty, William Roy, Gail Snoddy. **EDUCATION:** FBI Grand Valley Coll, basic police tng. **CAREER:** Muskegon Hts, chief of police 1976-, comdr of operations 1975, capt 1968, det Lt 1967, Det 1963; Nat Orgn Black Law Enforcement Execs, policeman 1954. **ORGANIZATIONS:** Internal Assn & Chiefs of Police; mem Frat Order of Police; mem Comm Orgn Black Businessmen; mem Urban League; mem NAACP; coord Boy Scout Troop 277 Explorer Post 17;mem Muskegon Hts Lions Club; United Appeal Bd of Finance 1968-71; mem Gtr Harvest Bapt H; Sunday Sch tchr 1969-73. **HONORS/ACHIEVEMENTS:** Police Officer of Year Muskegon Exchange Club 1966; Liberty Bell Award State Bar of MI 1967; Reverence for Law Award Mukegon Hts Eagles 1969; citation Blockade Com 1969; NWRO outstdng leadership award 1975. **MILITARY SERVICE:** USAF 1944-47. **BUSINESS ADDRESS:** 2715 Baker St, Muskegon Heights, MI 49444.

HOWZE, DOROTHY J.
Educator. **PERSONAL:** Born Nov 24, 1923, Detroit, MI; married Manuel; children: Karen, Gloria. **EDUCATION:** Wayne State U, BS;Univ MI, MS 1966. **CAREER:** Detroit Public Library, clerk 1947-49; Detroit Bd of Educ, teacher; Detroit Public Schools at Cerveny & Winship Middle School, specialist. **ORGANIZATIONS:** Memd Intl Reading Assn; Wayne Alumni Assn; Met Reading Assn; MI Reading Assn & Curricuium Devel task force NEC Proj; Human Relations Com; coordinator Summer Head Start Prog Black Catholics Action; sec bd dir Black Secretarial; sec Nat Black Lay Cath Caucus; MI Black Lay Cath Caucus; 1 salute Black Wmn; Black Secretariat 1972; Alpha Kappa Alpha Alpha Rho Omega Chap Detroit MI; mem Beta Sigma Phi Fellowship; mem MI Assn of Middle Sch Educators; coun pres religious educ coor Holy Ghost Cath Ch; bd of dir Inter-Parish Sharing; del Archdiocese Pastoral Assembly; bd of mgmt for vol & mem of memshp com Downtown Br YWCA. **BUSINESS ADDRESS:** 15055 Dexter, Detroit, MI 48238.

HOWZE, JOSEPH LAWSON
Clergyman. **PERSONAL:** Born Aug 30, 1923, Daphne, AL. **EDUCATION:** AL State Jr Coll, attended; AL State Univ, BS 1948; St Bonaventure Univ, grad 1959; Univ Portland, LLD 1974; Sacred Heart Coll Belmont NC, D of Humane Letters 1977; St Bonaventure Univ NY, LLD 1977; Manhattan Coll NY, LLD 1979; Phillips Coll Gulfport MS, Bus Mgmt degree 1980; Bible Crusade CollOcean Springs MS, DHL 1987. **CAREER:** Ordained priest Roman Catholic Ch 1959; pastor churches in, Charlotte, Southern Pines, Durham, Sanford, Asheville (all in NC) 1959-72; MS, aux bishop 1973-77; Biloxi, bishop 1977-. **ORGANIZATIONS:** Trustee Xavier Univ New Orleans; mem MS Health Care Commn; mem admistrv bd NCCB/USCC; mem educ comm USCC; mem Social Devel and World Peace Comm; liason com to natl Office of Black Catholics NCCB; bd dirs Biloxi Reg Med Cntr; Democrat; mem KC Knights of St Peter Claver; mem NCCB/USCC Vocation Comm. **HONORS/ACHIEVEMENTS:** Became one of few Black bishops in history of Catholic Church in US; 1st Bishop of the New Diocese of Biloxi MS 1977; 1st Black Catholic bishop to head a Cath-Diocese in the USA since 1900; second in contemporary history. **BUSINESS ADDRESS:** Bishop, Catholic Diocese Biloxi, PO Box 1189, Biloxi, MS 39533.

HOWZE, KAREN AILEEN
Corporate news executive. **PERSONAL:** Born Dec 08, 1950, Detroit, MI; daughter of Manuel Howze and Dorothy June Smith Howze; children: Charlene Howze, Karie Howze. **EDUCATION:** Univ of S California, BA 1972 (cum laude); Hasting Coll of Law, JD 1977. **CAREER:** Detroit Free Press, reporter 1971; San Francisco Chronicle, reporter 1972-78; Newsday, Long Island, asst editor 1978-79; Gannett Newspapers, Rochester NY, asst managing editor/Sunday features editor 1979-80; USA Today, founding editor 1981, managing editor/systems 1982-86, managing editor/International Edition 1986-88; Gannett Co Inc, Corporate News Systems, editor 1988-. **ORGANIZATIONS:** Mem Nat Assn of Black Journ; offcr SF Oakland Newspaper Guild; past mem Sigma Delta Chi; past mem Women in Commun; mem Alameda Co Comm Hlth Adv Bd; guest lectu local comm coll; mem, Amer Society of Newspaper Editors; vice-chair, Minority Opportunities Comm, Amer Newspaper Publisher's Assn. **HONORS/ACHIEVEMENTS:** Business Woman of the Year, Spellman Alumni, Washington DC 1986; Senior Editor, And Still We Rise, interviews with 50 Black Americans by Barbara Reynolds 1987. **BUSINESS ADDRESS:** Corporate News Systems Editor, Gannett Co Inc, PO Box 7858, 26th Floor, Washington, DC 20044.

HOYE, WALTER B.
College administrator. **PERSONAL:** Born May 19, 1930, Lena, MS; son of William H Hoye and Lou Bertha S Hoye; married Vida M Pickens; children: Walter B II, JoAnn M. **EDUCATION:** Wayne St Univ, BA 1954; UCSD Ext, Mngt Cert 1973. **CAREER:** MI Chronicle Nwspr, sprts ed/columnst 1964-68; San Diego Chargers Ftbl Clb, asst dir pblc rltns 1968-76; NFL media rltns/Super Bowl 1972-75; SD Urban League/Nghbrhd House Assn, pblc info off 1976; Educcultural Complex, dir support system. **ORGANIZATIONS:** 1st vice pres San Diego Urban League 1972-75; pgm review pnlst United Way/CHAD of San Diego Cnty 1972-74; brd of dirs Red Cross of San Diego Cnty 1975-77; nominator Outstndng Young Men/Women of Amer 1976-85; brd of dirs Pblc Access TV 1977-79; treas San Diego Career Guidance Assn 1981-82; Advisory Bd KPBS TV 15 1983-84. **HONORS/ACHIEVEMENTS:** Citizen of Month Cnty of San Diego 1979. **BUSINESS ADDRESS:** Dir Plcmnt/Pgm Support, Educational Cultural Complex, 4343 Ocean View Blvd, San Diego, CA 92113.

HOYE, WALTER B., II
Clergyman, educator. **PERSONAL:** Born Aug 20, 1956, Detroit, MI; married Carrie F Sims; children: Walter B III. **EDUCATION:** MI State Univ, BA Sociology 1979, MA Sociology 1980; US Int Univ, MBA 1985. **CAREER:** Allstate Ins Co, data processing super 1980-82; Calvary Baptist Church, assoc minister 1982-85; Pacific Bell, system analyst 1984-; St John Missionary Baptist Church, minister of educ 1985-. **ORGANIZATIONS:** Young Men of Amer Jaycees 1982-85; dir Pacific Coast Coll Extension 1983. **HONORS/ACHIEVEMENTS:** Outstanding Young Men of America Jaycees 1980-85. **BUSINESS ADDRESS:** Minister of Education, St John Mission Bapt Church, 1524 Lemon St, Oceanside, CA 92054.

HOYLE, CLASSIE
Educator. **PERSONAL:** Born Mar 26, 1926, Annapolis, MD; married Daniel C Hoyle; children: Dennis, Lynne. **EDUCATION:** Morgan State Univ, BS 1958, MS 1968; Univ IA, PhD 1977. **CAREER:** Lab scientist, 1958-59; sci tchr, 1960-68; Morgan State Univ, sci tchr 1968-73; grad tching asst, 1974-76; Cooperative Educ, coord 1976-77; Career Serv Placement Ctr, asst dir 1977-78; Univ of IA, dir affirmative action 1978-82; Clarke Coll, vice pres for academic affrs 1982-. **ORGANIZATIONS:** Admin asst Mt Lebanon Bapt Ch 1970-73; sec treas Fed Credit Union 1970-73; sec Morgan State Univ 1972-73; mem Natl Sci Tchrs Assn, Assn for theEduc of Tchrs of Sci, Natl Assn for Biology Tchrs; den mother Cub Scouts 1968, 1974; chairperson courtesy comm Morgan State Univ 1969-72; So Fellowship Fund 1975-76; Higher Educ Title III Grant 1973-75; Natl Sci Fellowships 1965-68; Senatorial Scholarship 1954-58; pres Phi Delta Kappa 1980; IA pres AmerCouncil on Educ Natl Identification Prog 1979-81; Kappa Delta Pi 1958; Beta Kappa Chi 1957; Alpha Kappa Mu 1957.

HOYT, THOMAS L., JR.
Educator. **PERSONAL:** Born Mar 14, 1941, Fayette, AL; married Ocie Harriet Oden; children: Doria, Thomas III. **EDUCATION:** Evansville Coll and Lane Coll, BA 1962; Interdenominational Theological Center, MDiv 1965; Union Theological Seminary, STM 1967; Duke Univ, PhD 1975. **CAREER:** Jefferson Park Methodist, assoc pastor 1965-67; St Joseph CME, pastor 1967-70; Fawcett Memorial, pastor 1970-72; Interdenominational Theological Center, professor 1972-78; Howard Univ, professor 1978-80; Hartford Seminary, professor 1980-. **ORGANIZATIONS:** Society of Biblical Literature, mem; American Academy of Religion, mem; Society for the study of Black Religion, mem; Theology Commission of Consultation onChurch Union, mem; CT Bible Society, board of directors; Christian Methodist Church, mem; Alpha Phi Alpha, mem; NAACP, mem; Faith and Order Commissionof Natl Council and World Council of Churches, mem; Institute for Ecumenical and Cultural Research, board of directors. **HONORS/ACHIEVEMENTS:** Rockefeller Doctoral Fellowship; Assoc of Theological Schools Fellowship; worked on Joint Committee which published an Inclusive Lectionary (year A,B,C,)1983-85; Natl Assoc for Equal Opportunity in Higher Education, award; Bilateral Dialogue between Methodist/Roman Catholic, participant; African Methodist Episcopal Zion/Christian Methodist Episcopal Unity Committee. **HOME ADDRESS:** 80 Girard Ave, Hartford, CT 06105. **BUSINESS ADDRESS:** Professor, Hartford Seminary, 77 Sherman St, Hartford, CT 06105.

HOYTE, ARTHUR HAMILTON
Educator. **PERSONAL:** Born Mar 22, 1938, Boston, MA; married Stephanie Hebron; children: Jacques. **EDUCATION:** Harvard Coll, BA 1960; Columbia Univ Coll of Phys & Surgs, MD 1964; SF Gen Hosp, intern 1965; Presb Hosp, resident 1968. **CAREER:** Georgetown Medical Center, asst prof 1971-; Office of Economic Opportunity, med officer 1970-71; East Palo Alto Neighborhood Health Center, 1969-70; Kaiser Found Hospital, 1968-70. **ORGANIZATIONS:** Consultant Health Care Serv 1971-; mem Presidential Task Force 1976; Med Cos of DC 1972-; Med Chrgcl Soc of DC 1974-; DC United Way; Coalition of Health Advs 1975-; Boys Club of WA 1975-; pres DC Sci Fair Assn 1976-77. **HONORS/ACHIEVEMENTS:** Civ Serv Awards WA Region Med Prog 1975; Mid Atlantic Regional Student Natl Med Assn 1975; US Senate Testimony on Ambulatory Health Serv in DC 1976. **MILITARY SERVICE:** AUSR 1969-74. **BUSINESS ADDRESS:** Georgetown University, Dept Community & Family Med, 3900 Reservoir Road, Washington, DC 20007.

HOYTE, JAMES STERLING
Lawyer. **PERSONAL:** Born Apr 21, 1944, Boston, MA; son of Oscar H Hoyte and Patti Ridley Hoyte; married Norma Dinnall, Dec 12, 1964; children: Keith Sterling, Kirsten Dinnall. **EDUCATION:** Harvard Coll, Cambridge MA, AB, 1965; Harvard Law School, Cambridge MA, JD, 1968; Harvard Graduate School of Business, Boston MA, MA, PMD Certificate, 1971; Kennedy School of Govt (Harvard), 1986. **CAREER:** Arthur D Little Inc, Cambridge MA, sr staff, 1969-74; Massachusetts Sec of State, Boston MA, deputy sec, 1975-76; Massachusetts Port Authority, Boston MA, sec/treasurer, dir of admin, 1976-79; Arthur D Little Inc, Cambridge MA, vice pres, 1979-82; Commonwealth of Massachusetts, Boston MA, cabinet sec, sec of Environmental Affairs, 1983-88; Coate, Hall & Stewart, Boston MA, Counsel, 1989-. **ORGANIZATIONS:** Mem, Amer Bar Assn, 1971-; sec, Massachusetts Black Lawyers Assn, 1976-78; mem, bd of dir, Opportunities Indusrialization Center of Greater Boston, 1976-83; mem, Natl Bar Assn, 1978-, Long Range Planning Comm, United Way of Massachusetts Bay, 1978; mem, bd of dir, Roxbury Multi Serv Center, 1979-87; chmn, bd of trustees, Environment Comm, Boston Harbor Assn, 1989-; exec comm, bd of dir, 1,000 Friends of Massachusetts, 1989-; bd of trustees, Univ Hospital, 1989. **HONORS/ACHIEVEMENTS:** Ten Outstanding Young Leaders, Greater Boston Jaycees, 1967; Black Achiever Award, Greater Boston YMCA, 1978; Alpha Man of the Year, Epsilon Gamma Lambda Chapter of Alpha Phi Alpha Frat, 1984; Governor Francis Sargent Award, Boston Harbor Assn, 1986; Frederick Douglass Award, Greater Boston YMCA, 1987. **BUSINESS ADDRESS:** Attorney, Choate, Hall & Stewart, 53 State St, Boston, MA 02109.

HOYTE, LENON HOLDER (AUNT LEN)
Curator, teacher. **PERSONAL:** Born Jul 04, 1905, New York, NY; daughter of Moses E Holder and Rose Best Holder; married Lewis P Hoyte, Sep 28, 1938 (deceased). **EDUCATION:** NY Teachers Training Schl, attended 1930; City Coll of NY, BS 1937; Columbia Univ, CRMD degree in education. **CAREER:** NY City Public Schs, art tchr 1930-70; Aunt Len's Doll & Toy Museum, New York NY, founder, dir and pres, 1966—. **ORGANIZATIONS:** Lay advisory bd Harlem Hosp; 1st Basileus Phi Delta Kappa Sor 1953; Beta Epsilon 1955; pres & sec Hamilton Terrace Block Assoc 1973; writes column "Our Museum" Doll News. **HONORS/ACHIEVEMENTS:** Name on Bronze plaque St Phillips Epis Ch; Harlem YWCA award, 1962; Awds in Black 1972; Notable Amer Awds The Bicentennial 1976-77; Who's Who Amer Women 1976; World's Who's Who of Women; Service Awd United Fedn of Doll Clubs Inc; Black History Before Your Eyes Westchester Urban League 1980; Brooklyn Tchr Humanitarian Awd 1983; Special Achievement Awd Harlem Week 1982; Building Brick Award, New York Urban League, 1985; Ethnic New Yorker Award, Mayor of City of New York, 1986; Educator of the Year award, City College of NY, 1988; Proclamation

award, office of the council president, 1988. **HOME ADDRESS:** 6 Hamilton Terr, New York, NY 10031.

HRABOWSKI, FREEMAN ALPHONSA, III
Educator. **PERSONAL:** Born Aug 13, 1950, Birmingham, AL; married Jacqueline Coleman; children: Eric. **EDUCATION:** Hampton Inst, BA 1970; Univ of IL, MA 1971, PhD 1975. **CAREER:** Univ of IL at Urbana-Champaign, math instr 1972-73, admin intern 1973-74, asst dean 1974-76; AL A&M Univ Normal, assoc dean 1976-77; Coppin State Coll Baltimore, dean arts & scis div 1977-81, vice pres academic affairs 1981-; vice provost, Univ of MD, Baltimore County. **ORGANIZATIONS:** Mem Alpha Phi Alpha Frat; sr class pres Hampton Inst 1969-70; brd of trustees, Baltimore City Life Musuems; Florence Crittenton Services, Inc, advisory council, Peabody Institute of the Johns Hopkins Univ; evaluator, Middle States Assn of Coll and Schls; consultant, MD ST Dept of Education; office of education; VA council of Education. **HONORS/ACHIEVEMENTS:** Scholarship for Study Abroad Amer Univ Cairo Egypt 1968-69; Who's Who Hampton Inst 1970; Phi Delta Kappa Univ of IL at Urbana-Champaign 1971; Outstanding Young Men of Amer 1977; Outstanding Alumni Awd, Hampton Univ (Baltimore Chapter); Outstanding Community Srv Awd, Tuskegee Univ. **BUSINESS ADDRESS:** Vice President Acad Affairs, Coppin State College, 2500 W North Ave, Baltimore, MD 21216.

HUBBARD, AMOS B.
Educator. **PERSONAL:** Born May 11, 1930, Dora, AL; son of Rev & Mrs A B Hubbard; married Irene Windham; children: Melicent Concetta. **EDUCATION:** AL State Univ, BS 1955; IN Univ, MS 1960; MI State Univ, Univ of Tulsa OK, additional study; Univ of TN, doctoral cond; Univ of AL Tuscaloosa, attended. **CAREER:** Carver HS Union Springs AL, teacher & coach 1955-58; Riverside HS Northport AL, teacher 1958-68; Coll Ed Ach Prog Stillman Coll, dir 1968-72, dir ed devel prog 1972-74, athl dir 1972-79, dir spec serv prog 1976-, coord instr, tch learning 1975-, dir spec progs 1977-87, Stillman Coll, dean of students 1988-. **ORGANIZATIONS:** Mem Tuscaloosa Alumni, Kappa Alpha Psi; mem Brown Mem Presbyterian Church, Kappa Delta Pi 1973, Phi Delta Kappa 1973; coord Stillman Coll Danforth Proj 1973-75; mem comm of mgmt Barnes Br YMCA 1965-68; mem Tuscaloosa Civic Ctr Commiss 1971, Family Counseling Serv 1974; Kiwanis of Tuscaloosa, Mental Health Board; Marashino City Sister City Commission; Tuscaloosa County Community Housing Resources Board Inc. **HONORS/ACHIEVEMENTS:** Cert of Achievement Awd Ed Improvement Proj of So Assoc of Coll & School 1973; Distinguished Serv Awd United Fund of Tuscaloosa Cty 1973. **MILITARY SERVICE:** AUS corpl 1951-53. **BUSINESS ADDRESS:** Dean of Students, Stillman College, PO Drawer 1430, Tuscaloosa, AL 35403.

HUBBARD, ARNETTE RHINEHART
Attorney. **PERSONAL:** Born Jan 11, Stephens, AR. **EDUCATION:** John Marshall Law Sch, JD 1969; So IL U, BS. **CAREER:** Pvt law practice 1972-; Lawyers Com for Civil Rights Under Law, Staff atty 1970-72, tchr 1961-66; Legal Def Com, pres elect chmn; Cook Co Bar Assn, judicial com; Cook Co Bar Found, vp; Judicial Com & Grants & Contracts, sec. **ORGANIZATIONS:** Mem Nat Bar Assn 1975-; mem IL State Bar Assn; mem past bd dir Wabash Ave YMCA; mem IL Family Plnng Counc Inc; IL Women's Bar Assn;; mem NAACP 1st female pres elect Cook Co Bar Assn. **BUSINESS ADDRESS:** Arnette R Hubbard & Assoc, 134 N LaSalle St, #908, Chicago, IL 60602.

HUBBARD, BRUCE ALAN
Attorney. **PERSONAL:** Born Feb 07, 1948, Chattanooga, TN; son of Robert McKinley Hubbard and Ruth Spratling Hubbard; married Constance Arrington, Jul 23, 1988; children: Read Spratling, Tate Hubbard. **EDUCATION:** Rutgers, AB 1969; Harvard Law, JD 1972. **CAREER:** Hale & Dorr, assoc 1972-73; US Dept HUD, atty/advisor 1973-75; The Continental Group, sr atty 1975-; Northville Ind Corp, gen counsel 1980-83; Davis Polk & Warpwell, assc 1985; private practice 1985-. **ORGANIZATIONS:** Trustee Rheedlen Found 1976-85; dir AIM 1978-87; House of Delegates NYS Bar Assoc 1978-81; Police Commissioner Stamford CT 1986-; trustee the King School Stamford CT 1985-; Nat'l Assn of Securities Professionals; Municipal Affairs Comm; Assn of the Bar of the City of NY 1979-; Rutgers Cares Program; Rutgers Fund; HBLSR; Harvard Fund; SCLA; chairman Police Comm, Stamford CT Police Dept 1985-; trustee King & Low-Heywood Thomas School 1985-. **HONORS/ACHIEVEMENTS:** Op-Ed NY Times 1978; Class of 1931 Award, Rutgers Alumni Assn 1979; Loyal Sons of Rutgers Coll, Cap & Skull 1986. **MILITARY SERVICE:** USAR 1st lt 1969-75; MA Military Academy 1971. **BUSINESS ADDRESS:** Pavelic & Levites, PC, Bruce A Hubbard, Esq, 645 Madison Ave, 6th Floor, New York, NY 10022.

HUBBARD, DONALD
Shoe designer. **PERSONAL:** Born Apr 26, 1943, Gary, IN. **EDUCATION:** Traphage School of Fashion, New York. **CAREER:** Shoe designer (designer of Projections line), Cantata Shoes Div of Latins, offices in Florence, Paris, and London, 1966; travels between Italy and Spain, supervising mfg aspects of shoes. **BUSINESS ADDRESS:** 43 Bramham Gardens, London SW6, England.

HUBBARD, HYLAN T., III
Insurance company executive. **PERSONAL:** Born Jan 26, 1947, Lynchburg, VA; son of Hylan Thomas Hubbard Jr and Florine Morris Hubbard; married Christine Richardson Hubbard, Feb 11, 1967; children: Hylan T Hubbard IV, Carmen D Hubbard. **EDUCATION:** Bowdoin Coll, Brunswick ME, AB, 1969. **CAREER:** Aetna Life & Casualty, Hartford CT, instructor/admin, 1974-75, Buffalo NY, mktg mgr, 1975-78, Hartford CT, regional dir, 1978-80, Harrisburg PA, gen mgr, 1980-82, Washington DC, gen agent, 1982, gen mgr, 1982-85, Hartford CT, vice pres S/C Region, 1985-. **ORGANIZATIONS:** Program chair, Buffalo Insurance Assn, 1976; mem, co-representative, Commissioner's Task Force on Take-Out, 1981-82; campaign co-chair, Amer Cancer Soc, 1981; mem, co-representative, Washington DC Assigned Claims Bd, 1982-83; bd chair, Univ of Washington DC, Bd of Counselors, 1985; bd of dir, Kappa Alpha Psi Frat, 1987-88; comm mem, IMPACT, 1988-; dir, Greater Hartford YMCA Bd, 1988-89. **HONORS/ACHIEVEMENTS:** America's Best & Brightest, Dollars & Sense Magazine, 1987; America's Best & Brightest Young Business & Professional Men, 1987. **BUSINESS ADDRESS:** Vice President, South/Central Region, PFSD, Aetna Life & Casualty, 151 Farmington Ave, RC3A, Hartford, CT 06156.

HUBBARD, JAMES MADISON, JR.
Dentist. **PERSONAL:** Born in Durham, NC; married Gloria Carter; children: Linda Rose, James III, Phillip. **EDUCATION:** NC Central U, BS 1945; Howard U, DDS 1949; UCLA; MPH 1974. **CAREER:** Jersey City Med Cntr, intern 1949-50; Durham, pvt prac 1950-62; Lincoln Hosp Durham, chief attending in oral surgery. **ORGANIZATIONS:** Pres of W Manchester Med Dental Cntr LA; staff mem Hollywood Presb Hosp Hollywood CA; bd dir & dental dir CompreCare Health Plan; bd mem, chmn 2nd Bapt Ch Credit Union; life mem NAACP; 32nd degree Mason & Shriner; Kappa Alpha Psi Frat. **HONORS/ACHIEVEMENTS:** Recipient of Alexander Hunter Dental Soc Award 1963; CA Dental Coll's Award for Achievement 1973. **MILITARY SERVICE:** AUS Dental Corps capt 1955-57. **BUSINESS ADDRESS:** 600 W Manchester Ave, Los Angeles, CA.

HUBBARD, JEAN P.
Educator. **PERSONAL:** Born Mar 05, 1917, Bedford, VA; married Portia. **EDUCATION:** Wilberforce U, BS 1941; OH State U, MA 1945; Dayton Art InstUniv of CA, further study; Tulane U. **CAREER:** TN State Univ, assoc prof 1947-50; Art Dept Central State Coll, chmn 1950-55; Southern Univ, instructor 1955-64; Dept of Fine Arts Southern Univ, chmn 1964-. **ORGANIZATIONS:** Mem Am Assn of Unive Prof; Coll Art Assn of Am Paintings in permanent collection at Carver Museum Tuskegee AL; commn Mural SoUniv New Orleans; Blacksof LA & their contribution to Culture of State of LA. **BUSINESS ADDRESS:** PO Box 10403, Southern Univ, Baton Rouge, LA 70813.

HUBBARD, JOSEPHINE BRODIE
Social service. **PERSONAL:** Born May 11, 1938, Tampa, FL; married Ronald C Hubbard; children: Ronald Charles, Valerie Alicia. **EDUCATION:** Fl A&M Univ, BS with honors 1958; Univ of South Fl, MA with honors 1968. **CAREER:** Howard W Blake H S, teacher 1958-63; Chicopee H S, teacher 1965-66; NB Young Jr H S, guid counselor 1968-69; Univ of South FL, proj upward bound counselor coord 1969-71, spec serv dir and acad adv; Wright State Univ, acad adv 1973; Edwards Air Force Base, sub teacher 1974-75, guidance counselor 1978-80; Dept of the Army West Germany, guidance counselor 1978-80, collateral duty assignment, ed services officer 1980-81; Nellis Air Force Base, guidance counselor 1981-83; Family Support Center, chief of programs 1983-87, asst educ serv officer 1987-. **ORGANIZATIONS:** Family Support Ctr, rep; Directors of Volunteers in Agencies Org, mem 1983-; Southern NV Chap Federally Employed Women Inc 1983-; mem Federal Women's Program Interagency Council 1983-; scholarship chairperson Nellis Noncommissioned Officers Wives' Club 1985. **HONORS/ACHIEVEMENTS:** Sustained Superior Performance Awd Family Support Ctr Chief of Programs 1985; Tactical Air Command Certificate of Recognition for Special Achievement 1985; Notable Achievement Awd Dept of the Air Force 1985; Sustained Superior Performance Awd Family Support Ctr Chief of Progs 1986. **BUSINESS ADDRESS:** Chief of Programs, Family Support Center, 554 CSG/FS, Nellis Air Force Base, Nellis Afb, NV 89191.

HUBBARD, MARILYN FRENCH
Entrepreneur, business executive. **PERSONAL:** Born Oct 19, 1946, Lansing, MI; daughter of Lester French (deceased) and Mabel Brown French; divorced; children: Paul Anthony Hubbard. **EDUCATION:** Ferris State Coll, Big Rapids, MI, Assoc of Arts, 1969; Univ of Detroit, Detroit, MI, Bachelor of Business Admin, 1974; Univ Assoc, LaJolla, CA, Certificate Human Resources Mgmt, 1978-79; Chrysler Corp, Troy, MI, Certificate Minority Dealer Devel Program, 1986-89. **CAREER:** Wayne County Comon Pleas Court, official ct reporter, 1969-76; Marilyn Hubbard Seminars, Detroit, MI, pres, 1976-; Natl Assn of Black Women Entrepreneur, Inc, founder & natl pres, 1978-; adjunct prof, several coll & univ, 1978-; Chrysler Corp, Troy, MI, dealer candidate, 1986-89. **ORGANIZATIONS:** Bd of dir, Detroit Economic Growth Corp, 1980-, Advisory bd, 1984-88; Minority & Women's Task Force, 1984-; bd of dir, Natl Coalition of Black Meeting Planners, 1985-87; chmn, Governor's Entrepreneurial & Small Business Commn; US Small Business Admin, Small Business Devel Center. **HONORS/ACHIEVEMENTS:** Natl 1980 Minority-Owned Business Advocate of the Year; Amer Top 100 Black Business & Prof Women, 1985; US Small Business Admin; Dollars & Sense Magazine; One of the first women to participate in Chrysler's Minority Dealer Devel Program; Success Story - Working Woman Magazine. **BUSINESS ADDRESS:** Founder & Natl Pres, Natl Assn of Black Women Entrepreneurs, Inc, PO Box 1375, Detroit, MI 48231.

HUBBARD, PAUL LEONARD
Foundation executive, consultant. **PERSONAL:** Born Oct 31, 1942, Cincinnati, OH; divorced; children: Paul Anthony. **EDUCATION:** Ohio U, BS Bus Ed 1961-65; Wayne State Univ-Detroit, MI, MSW 1969-71; IBM Exec Mgmt Training, Cert 1980; AMA Exec Training for Presidents, Cert 1982. **CAREER:** Stowe Adult Ed, instructor 1965; Detroit Public Sch, teacher 1965-71; Wayne County CC, consultant 1971-74; Downriver Family Neighborhood Service, associate dir 1971-74; New Detroit, Inc, sr vp, vice pres DHT transportation 1979-89, president, 1989—. **ORGANIZATIONS:** MI Bell Consumer Adv Group, mem (chmn 1984-89) 1980-; Metro Youth Prog, Inc, chmn 1983-87; Natl Assoc of Black Social Workers, natl vice pres 1982-86; US Selective Service Board, mem 1985-87; Internatl Exchange Bd of Directors, mem 1985-; MI Supreme Ct Subcommittee, chmn 1986-; pres Detroit Chap Natl Assoc Black Social Workers; Council of Political Education; bd of dir, Goodwill Industries of Greater Detroit. **HONORS/ACHIEVEMENTS:** Outstanding service award, Det chap, Natl Assn of Black Social Workers, 1975; Lafayette Allen Sr Distinguished Service Award, 1979; Detroit City Council Testimonial Resolution for Community Services 1980; Wayne St U chap NABSW alumni of the year award, 1981; Gentlemen of Wall St Service Award 1984; American Cancer Soc service award, 1985; Black Enterprise Magazine service award, 1987; Natl Welfare Rights service award, 1988. **HOME ADDRESS:** 18995 Birchcrest Ave, Detroit, MI 48221. **BUSINESS ADDRESS:** President, New Detroit, Inc, One Kennedy Square, Ste 1000, Detroit, MI 48226.

HUBBARD, PHIL LAVELLE
Professional athlete. **PERSONAL:** Born Dec 13, 1956, Canton, OH; married Dr Jackie Williams. **EDUCATION:** Michigan. **CAREER:** Detroit Pistons, forward 1979-82; Cleveland Cavaliers, forward 1982-. **ORGANIZATIONS:** Mem US teams that won Gold Medals at the 1976 Olympics in Montreal and The 1977 World Games; very active in num local charitable causes; svcd as Cavs' rep and as Honorary Coach for the OH Spcl Olympics the past 2 yrs & was torchbearer in the Games' opening ceremony; nom for 1984 Walter Kennedy Awrd, a citizenship awrd given annually to an NBA player for his charitable & civic conributions. **HONORS/ACHIEVEMENTS:** Emerged as a team leader & one of the best sixth men in the NBA last year; played in 80 games, but started only 6 times; was only Cavalier to play in all 82 regular season games 1982-83; & started 38 times; avgd 57 rebounds per game,

3rd best on team while his season total of 471 rebounds placed second on the Cavs behind Cliff Robinson. **BUSINESS ADDRESS:** Cleveland Cavaliers, The Colesium, Ste 510, Richfield, OH 44286.

HUBBARD, REGINALD T.
Automobile dealership chief executive. **CAREER:** Metrolina Dodge Inc, Charlotte, NC, chief exec. **BUSINESS ADDRESS:** Metrolina Dodge Inc, 8525 South Blvd., Charlotte, NC 28217. *

HUBBARD, WALTER T.
Consultant. **PERSONAL:** Born Oct 19, 1924, New Orleans, LA; married Frances Washington; children: Walter, Donna, Colette, Anthony. **EDUCATION:** Seattle U, bus course. **CAREER:** Local 17 AFL CIO Seattle, bus rep 1964-65; Project CARITAS, exec dir 1965-70; WA State Human Rights Com, contract compliance specialist 1970-; Am Arbitration Assn, Seattle center rep 1973-; Bangasser & Assoc, Business Planning, consultant; Washington State Board Prison Terms & Paroles, mem 1977-86. **ORGANIZATIONS:** Sec Model Capital Corp 1972-; bd mem Ecumenical Metro Ministry Seattle 1972-; bd mem Black Arts W Theatre Seattle 1975; pres Nat Office Black Cath 1972; Nat Cath Conf Interracial Justice 1968-73; chairperson Seattle Model Citizens Adv Council 1972-75; Civil Serv Commr King Co 1972-; pres Cntrl Area Civil Rights Com Seattle 1972; task force team mem No Ireland 1972; chairperson Black Higher Educ Seminar 1973; Wingspread; Johnson Found NCCIJ; mem Bd of-Prison Terms & Paroles WA 1977; mem bd of trustees Mattes Ricci Coll SeattleUniv & Seattle Preparatory Sch; mem Bd of Regents SeattleUniv 1974; mem Ecumenical group to White House Conf on Urban Policy 1978; Am del mem Elevation Archbishop Wash DC of Cardinal Wm Baum & 20 other cardinals around the world in Rome by Pope Paul VI; del to World Conf on Sov Jewry Brussel Belgium; participant in White House visit of Pope Paul II 1979; chair, Casey Family Program Foster Parents Services Seattle 1986-. **HONORS/ACHIEVEMENTS:** Dist serv award Nat Cath Conf Inbteracial Justice 1973; citizen participation Award Seattle Model City Program 1974; Nat Office Commendation Serv 1973; Nat Office Black Cath UJIMA Award Nat Black Conv Cath New Orleans 1973; awarded Man in the St annual recognition Baltimore Black Cath Lay Caucus Our Lady of Charity Ch Brooklyn NY. **MILITARY SERVICE:** AUS staff sgt 1943-45. **BUSINESS ADDRESS:** 1162 22nd Ave East, Seattle, WA 98112.

HUCKABY, HENRY LAFAYETTE
Physician. **PERSONAL:** Born Jul 26, 1934, Crockett, TX; married Audria Mae Rain; children: Seneca Kay, Arthur Craig, Sophia Katherine. **EDUCATION:** Prairie View A&M Univ, BS 1956; Meharry Med Coll, MD 1965. **CAREER:** Houston Indepen Sch, sch tchr 1959-61; Harlem Hosp NYC, internship-surg 1965-66, residency-gen surg 1966-70; Columbia-Presbyterian Hosp, residency plastic surgery 1970-72; Baylor Coll of Medicine, clinical instructor plastic surgery 1973-77; St Joseph Hosp, attending plastic surgeon 1974-87; Private Practice, plastic & reconstructive surgery 1974-87, hand surgery, cosmetic surgery, critical wound surgery, burn surgery 1974-87, micro-vascular surgery 1982-87. **ORGANIZATIONS:** Mem Houston Medical Forum, Natl Medical Assoc. **MILITARY SERVICE:** AUS 1st lt 1956-58. **BUSINESS ADDRESS:** Plastic Surgeon, PO Box 13687, 2619 Holman, Houston, TX 77219.

HUCKABY, HILRY, III
Attorney. **PERSONAL:** Born Jun 27, 1944, Shreveport, LA; married Pearl Aaron; children: Kimberly, Hilry IV, Kylaa G. **EDUCATION:** So U, BA 1966; So U, JD 1969. **CAREER:** Equal Employment Opportunity Commn, 1969-72; Huckaby & Piper, atty 1972-76; Huckaby & Asso, partner 1976-; Fifth Circuit Cort of Appeals US Dist Court EW & Middle Dist and all other LA Courts, licensed to practise; NAACP Legal Defense & Educ Fund of NYC, cooperating atty. **ORGANIZATIONS:** Mem Shreveport Bar Assn; Nat Bar Assn; Shreveport chap NAACP; Omega Psi Phi Frat; GW Carver Br YMCA; mem Cooper Rd Community Civic Club Inc; mem, bd dir CODAC Community Orgn for Drug Abuse & Control Shreveport; 32nd degree Mason; bd dir Am Civil Liberties Union; past pres BULL Blacks United for Lasting Leadership; mem St Mary Bapt Ch. **HONORS/ACHIEVEMENTS:** Listed in Who's Who Among Students in Am Coll & Univ; elected to Shreveport Council 1978; elected Chmn 1979. **BUSINESS ADDRESS:** Councilman, Shreveport City Council, 2600 Jewella Ave, Shreveport, LA 71109.

HUCKLEBY, HARLAN CHARLES (HUCK)
Professional athlete. **PERSONAL:** Born Dec 30, 1957, Detroit, MI; married Carol Ann. **EDUCATION:** Univ of MI, Ed Major. **CAREER:** New Orleans Saints, running back 1979; Green Bay Packers, running back 1980-. **HONORS/ACHIEVEMENTS:** Led team in KOR with 185 yard average for 41 returns 1983; Set 2 Packer records, most kickoff returns in a game (8) & most kickoff return yards in a game (208) both against Washington 1983 in the highest scoring Monday Night Football game in history; Packer's #2 rusher & was tied for runnerup scoring honors for season; 4th leading rusher in MI Univ history (2956 career yards) at time of grad; Played in Rose, Orange & Hula Bowls; Anchored MI Big Ten champion relay team in track. **BUSINESS ADDRESS:** Green Bay Packers, 1265 Lombardi Ave, Green Bay, WI 54307.

HUCLES, HENRY B., III
Rector. **PERSONAL:** Born Sep 21, 1923, NYC; married Mamie Adams; children: Henry, IV, Michael. **EDUCATION:** VA Union U, BS 1943; VA Theol Sem, BD 1946; MDiv 1970; DD 1976. **CAREER:** St George's Ch, rector; Brooklyn Epis Diocese of Long Island, archdeacon 1976-; Brooklyn House of Detention, protestant chpln 1957-74. **ORGANIZATIONS:** Sec bd mgrs St John's & Epis Hosps; bd Bedford/Stuyvesant Restoration; bd Bedford0Stuyvesant Design Works; bd Brklyn Interfaith; trustee Cathedral Incarnation NAACP; Protestant Coun Mayor's Com Aging; Alpha Phi Alpha. **HONORS/ACHIEVEMENTS:** Man of Yr Award Kings Co Med Soc 1965; serv cross Diocese Long Island Dist 1967; hon Canon Cath Incarnation Garden City Long Island. **BUSINESS ADDRESS:** 800 Marcy Ave, Brooklyn, NY 11216.

HUDGEONS, LOUISE TAYLOR
Educational administrator. **PERSONAL:** Born May 31, 1931, Canton, OH; married Denton Russell. **EDUCATION:** RsvltUniv Chgo, BS 1952;Univ of Chgo, AM 1958; INUniv Blmgtn, EdD 1974; Govs StUniv Pk Frst S IL, MBA 1977. **CAREER:** Central State Univ, dean School of Business Admin; Eastern NM Univ Coll of Business, dean 1978-; Chicago State Univ, asst prof, assoc prof, chmn, asst dean, acting dean 1969-78; State of IL, supvr Business Office Educ 1967-69; Chicago Public Schools, teacher 1955-67; MI Blvd Garden Apts, acct 1952-55. **ORGANIZATIONS:** Consult VA Plytchnc Inst 1966; consult IL StUniv 1971; consult Cntrl Sys Rsrch 1973; consult US Ofc of Educ 1975; consult Min Bus Opp Commn 1976-78; consJwl Osco Co 1977-78; consult Govs StUniv 1978; N Cntrl Assn Evltng Teams 1968-74; chmn Coll &Univ Div IL Bus Educ Assn 1970; chmn Evltn Supt Pub Schs IL 1972. **HONORS/ACHIEVEMENTS:** Co-author Your Career in Mrktng Mcgrw Hill 1976; Who's Who in Fin & Indus 1977; Ntbl Ams 1976; Who's Who in Wrld of Wmn 1977; flwshp Am & Asmbly of Clgt Schs of Bus 1978; Who's Who in Am 1980; num spkng engag; svrl artcls pub. **BUSINESS ADDRESS:** Central State University, Dean School of Business Admin, Wilberforce, OH 45384.

HUDLIN, WARRINGTON
Director. **EDUCATION:** Yale Univ, BA (cum Laude) Yale Scholar of the House 1974. **CAREER:** Black Filmmaker Found, co-founder/pres 1978—. **ORGANIZATIONS:** Bd of dirs Independent Feature Project 1979-; co-treas Independent Feature Project 1984-. **HONORS/ACHIEVEMENTS:** Prod/dir Black at Yale (documentary film) 1974; prod/dir St Corner Stories (feature film) 1977; prod/dir Capoeira of Brazil (documentary film) 1980; prod/dir Color (tv drama) 1983. **BUSINESS ADDRESS:** President, Black Filmmaker Foundation, 80 Eighth Ave Ste 1704, New York, NY 10011.

HUDSON, ANDREW HAROLD
Educator. **PERSONAL:** Born Jan 04, 1915, Lexington, MO; son of Andrew Hudson Sr and Edna Hudson; married Dorothy Taylor. **EDUCATION:** Langston Univ, BS 1935; State Univ of IA, MA 1952; addtnl grad study, Wayne Univ, Tulsa Univ, OK State Univ. **CAREER:** BT Washington HS Eufaula, OK, coach/sci tchr 1936-51; Carver HS Hominy, OK, principal 1951-55; Tulsa Elem Schls Tulsa, OK, instr 1955-59, principal 1959-79; retired educator 1979-. **ORGANIZATIONS:** Pres OK Elem Principals Assn 1976; pres Tulsa Elem Principals Assn 1975; mem Phi Delta Kappa 1968; pres Northeast Dist Teachers Assn 1949; bd mem Tulsa Assn for Retarded Children; pres Tulsa Retired Tchrs Assn 1983-84; pres North Tulsa Rotary Club 1974-75; treas NW Camp of Gideons Intl 1985. **HONORS/ACHIEVEMENTS:** Speaker Men's Day First Baptist Ch Tulsa, OK 1984; Man of the Year Kappa Alpha Psi Frat Tulsa Chap 1983; Distinguished Achiev Award in Tulsa Schools by Langston Univ Langston, OK 1982; Layman of the Year First Baptist Ch North Tulsa, OK 1982; Charter Mem Kappa Alpha Psi Alpha Pi Chapter 1933. **HOME ADDRESS:** 2247 N Rockford, Tulsa, OK 74106.

HUDSON, ANTHONY WEBSTER
Personnel administrator. **PERSONAL:** Born Mar 23, 1937, Durham, NC; son of Emanuel Hudson and Adele Nixon Hudson; married Glenda; children: April Lynn, Verna Lea. **EDUCATION:** Rutgers Univ, BA 1959; Columbia Univ, 1960-62. **CAREER:** Civil Service Comm, pers spec't 1962-70, dir prsnl 1970-74, dir eeo 1974-77; Defense Logistics Agcy, prsnl dir 1977-. **ORGANIZATIONS:** Chair Prsnl Admin Comm US Dept Agric Grad Schl 1969-; chair/mem Merit Brd MD/Nat'l Cap Park & Plng Comm 1974-; vice pres Brd of Dirs WAEPA 1982-. **HONORS/ACHIEVEMENTS:** William A Jump Award for Excellence in Public Admin 1969; Defense Logistics Agency, exceptional civilian service award 1986. **MILITARY SERVICE:** AUS 1st lt 8 Yrs with reserve. **HOME ADDRESS:** 7309 Pinehurst Pkwy, Chevy Chase, MD 20815. **BUSINESS ADDRESS:** Staff Dir Civilian Personnel, Defense Logistics Agency, DLA-K Cameron Station, Alexandria, VA 22314.

HUDSON, CHARLES
Professional athlete. **PERSONAL:** Born Mar 16, 1959, Ennis, TX; married Nikki. **EDUCATION:** Prairie View A&M Univ, BA. **CAREER:** Philadelphia Phillies, right hand pitcher 1983-. **HONORS/ACHIEVEMENTS:** Allowed 3 earned runs or less in 24 of 30 starts; Named Pitcher of the Year 1982; Named to Carolina League All-Star team 1982; Led league in ERA, wins & shutouts 1982; First rookie to hurl a complete game in NLCS history; named to Baseball Digest Rookie team 1983.

HUDSON, CLENORA FRANCES
Educational administrator. **PERSONAL:** Born Jul 23, 1945, Oxford, MS; divorced; children: Sharifa Zakiya. **EDUCATION:** LeMoyne-Owen Coll, BA 1967; L'Universite de Dijon, Cert French Studies 1969; Atlanta Univ, MA English 1971. **CAREER:** Southern Univ in New Orleans, asst prof of english 1976-77; DE State Coll, asst prof of english 1972-73, asst prof english, dir of Black studies 1982-. **ORGANIZATIONS:** Proj coord Council On Religion & Intl Affairs DE State Coll 1983; ed bd mem Western Jrnl for Black Studies WA State Univ; mem Natl Council for BlackStudies; bd mem Midwest Regional Representative African Heritage Studies Assoc; mem Coll Lang Assoc; mgr Rayfield Mooty Archival Collection on the Black Experience; from the Labor Union to the Civil Rights Movement; bd mem Midwest Regional Rep Natl Africana Womens Studies Assoc. **HONORS/ACHIEVEMENTS:** "1934-1968," poem Phylon 1970; "Prejudice," poem Phylon 1970; "Racial Themes in the Works of Gwendolyn Brooks," College Language Assoc 1973; recipient NEH Univ of PA 1981; CIC Internship OH State Univ 1983; author "Legitimacy of Violence in R Wright's Fiction, An Anthropological Perspective" 1983; co-author "Toni Morrison's World of Topsy-Turveydom, A Methodological Explication of New Black Literary Criticism," Western Journal for Black Studies 1986; Honorary OutstandingBlack Delawarean 1986; "The Triparthite Plight of the Black Woman in Their Eyes Were Watching God and The Color Purple," Journal of Black Studies 1987; Ford Fellowship 1986-87; Ford Doctoral Fellowship 1987-88. **HOME ADDRESS:** 913 N Gilbert St, Iowa City, IA 52240. **BUSINESS ADDRESS:** Dir of Black Studies, Delaware State College, DuPont Hwy, Dover, DE 19901.

HUDSON, ELBERT T.
Savings and loan chief executive. **CAREER:** Broadway Savings and Loan Assoc, Los Angeles, CA, chief exec. **BUSINESS ADDRESS:** Broadway Federal Savings and Loan Assn, 4501 South Broadway, Los Angeles, CA 90037. *

HUDSON, FREDERICK BERNARD
Business executive, television producer. **PERSONAL:** Born Oct 29, 1947, Chicago, IL; son of Joseph T Hudson and Nelle Parham Hudson. **EDUCATION:** Wayne State Univ, BA 1969; Yale Law Sch, attended 1970-71; New School for Social Rsch, MA 1975. **CAREER:** Elon Mickels & Assocs, planning dir 1978-79; Detroit City Council, staff analyst 1979-80;

Southern IL Univ, visiting asst prof and coord 1980-81; Frederick Douglass Creative Arts Ctr, dir of public relations 1981-82; Centaur Consultants, pres; faculty mem, City Univ of NY, 1975-76, Coll of New Rochelle, 1986-87, Amer Business Inst, 1986-89; producer of television movies, "Things We Take" and "The Undercover Man". **ORGANIZATIONS:** Mem Assn of Independent Video & Filmmakers; mem Amer Planning Assn; mem Amer Mgmt Assn; comm consultant AT&T 1974; comm consultant Coro Found 1980;comm consultant Reality House 1982. **HONORS/ACHIEVEMENTS:** Poems short stories published in Freedomways, NY Quarterly; Citation of Merit State of MO Annual Poetry Contest 1980; New Writers Citation PEN 1984. **HOME ADDRESS:** 312 Park Ave, Apt C5, East Orange, NJ 07017. **BUSINESS ADDRESS:** President, Centaur Consultants, 142 W 72nd St, Suite 2A, New York, NY 10023.

HUDSON, FREDERICK DOUGLASS
Business executive. **PERSONAL:** Born Mar 13, 1928, Miami, FL. **EDUCATION:** Univ of CA Berkeley, BA 1964;Univ of CA Berkeley Grad Sch. **CAREER:** Frederick Douglass Creative Art Center, pres/artistic dir 1971-; Paramount Pictures, screen writer 1973-74; World Edn, writer 1972-73; Physics L LibraryUniv of CA Berkeley, supr 1964-70; NY State Council on the Arts, film panel 1977-80; Kennedy Center for the Performing Arts, Black commr; TV & Radio Station WNYC, bd of advisors. **ORGANIZATIONS:** Mem Writer Guild of Am E; mem Dramatists Guild; mem adv bd Writers Guild of Am E Found. **HONORS/ACHIEVEMENTS:** Leadership award Exxon Comm 1974;the Educ of Sonny Carson produced by Paramount Pictures 1974; Andelco Award 1979. **MILITARY SERVICE:** USAF tech sgt 1950-54. **BUSINESS ADDRESS:** President/Artistic Dir, F Douglas Creative Art Ctr, 168 W 46th St, New York, NY 10036.

HUDSON, HERMAN C.
Educator. **PERSONAL:** Born Feb 16, 1923. **EDUCATION:** Univ MI, BA1945;Univ MI, MA 1946;Univ MI, PhD 1961. **CAREER:** IN U, prof 1978; Afro-Am Affairs, dean 1970-; Dept of AfroAm Studies IN U, chmn 1970-72; Dept of Applied Linguistics IN U, chmn 1969-70; IN U, asso prof 1968-69;Univ MI, ind reading 1967-68; TC ColumbiaUniv English Prgm in Afghanistan, asst prof, dir 1961-67; VA State Coll, consult 1960; NC Coll, asst prof 1959-60;Univ Puerto Rico, asst prof 1957-59;Univ MI, tchng fellow 1953-57; FL A&M U, instr 1946-51. **HONORS/ACHIEVEMENTS:** Publs; "The Black Studies Prgm Strategy & Structure" 1971; "From Paragraph to Theme" 1972; "From Paragraph to Essay" 1975; "How To Make It In Coll" 1977; "The Black Composer Speaks" 1978.

HUDSON, JAMES BLAINE
Educator. **PERSONAL:** Born Sep 08, 1949, Louisville, KY; married Bornwyn Carol Garrett; children: Maya F, Travis Ridley, Kenwyn Ridley. **EDUCATION:** Univ of Louisville, BS 1974, MEd 1975; Univ of Kentucky, EdD 1981. **CAREER:** School of Educ Univ of Louisville, admin coord 1974-75; West Louisville Educ Program Univ of Louisville, admin coord 1975-77, asst dir 1977-80, dir 1980-82;Univ of Louisville, assoc dir. **ORGANIZATIONS:** Mem APGA, KPGA, ACPA 1976-; MENSA 1984-. **HONORS/ACHIEVEMENTS:** Nat'l Merit Schlr 1967; Haggin FellowshpUniv of K 1977-78; Black Faculty/Staff Mem of the yrUniv of L 1982. **HOME ADDRESS:** 2418 W Madison, Louisville, KY 40211. **BUSINESS ADDRESS:** Associate Dir, Preparatory Division, University of Louisville, Louisville, KY 40208.

HUDSON, JEROME WILLIAM
Educator/executive. **PERSONAL:** Born May 09, 1953, Washington, DC. **EDUCATION:** Univ of MD, BA 1975; George Washington Univ, Grad Certificate 1980; Amer Inst of Hypnotherapy, PhD 1986. **CAREER:** YMCA, asst physical dir 1977-78; Wesley Early Childhood Ctr, dir 1978-79; Shore Up Inc, dir training & employment 1979-. **ORGANIZATIONS:** Adjunct faculty mem Salisbury State Coll 1978-80; governor's state adv cncl Office of Children & Youth 1978-; state adv comm mem Office Children & Youth1980-; selection comm mem Foster Care Review Bd 1980-; lecturer universities and colls 1980-; bd of dir Heart Assoc 1980-81; vice pres Wicomico Cnty Councilof Social Serv 1980-81; bd of dir Gemocratic Club Wicomico Cnty; Dance Instructor Salisbury City Hall Museum and Wicomico Cnty Recreation & Parks; Governors Task Force on Violence and Extremism; planning coord Lower Shore Career Day Prog; lec Afro-American History Week Phi Delta Kappa 1982; bd of dir MarylandPublic Braodcasting-Chemical People Adv Bd; bd of dirs March of Dimes 1983, YMCA 1984-; mem Salisbury Chap Jaycees 1986-. **HONORS/ACHIEVEMENTS:** Key to the City of Salisbury 1978; Outstanding Young Men of Amer US Jaycees 1981; Employee of the Year Shore Up Inc 1981; Producer Children & Youth Conf Governor of MD 1981; Enthusiastic Awd MD State Dept of Educ 1985-86. **BUSINESS ADDRESS:** Dir Employment/Training Div, Shore Up Inc, 520 Snow Hill Rd, Salisbury, MD 21801.

HUDSON, JOHN D.
Government administration. **PERSONAL:** Born May 16, 1927, Atlanta, GA; married Delores Harris; children: Renee, Tony. **EDUCATION:** Clark Coll, AB 1949; John Marshall Univ, JD 1968; Univ of LA, Police Admin 1969; Univ of GA, Cert Publ Admin 1972; GA State Univ, Publ Admin 1974. **CAREER:** Atlanta Police Dept, detective, vice squad, burglary squad, school detective, detective sgt 1967, internal security dist suprv detective lt 1968, commanding officer prostitution squad, internal security, commander of task force, crime prevention bureau, spec recruiting officer, training officer aide to police committee, police capt; Bureau Correctional Svcs, dir 1971-. **ORGANIZATIONS:** Bd mem Natl Assn Black in Criminal Justice, Amer Correctional Assn, Natl Org of Black Law Enforcement Exec; past pres Omega Chap Y's Mens Club, Douglas HS PTA; chmn bd of dir, YMCA Northwest Branch. **HONORS/ACHIEVEMENTS:** Outstanding Achievement in Law Enforcement Eta Sigma Chap 1973; Clark Coll Man of the Year 1974; Leadership Atlanta 1974-75; Frontiers Intl External Awd 1976. **HOME ADDRESS:** 1159 Mobile St NW, Atlanta, GA 30314. **BUSINESS ADDRESS:** Dir, Bureau of Corrections, 236 Peachtree St SW, Atlanta, GA 30335.

HUDSON, KEITH
Business executive. **PERSONAL:** Born Mar 04, 1954, St Louis, MO; married Janeice Fay Gipson. **EDUCATION:** O'Fallon Tech Sch Electronics, 1974. **CAREER:** Ted's One Stop Inc, vice pres Sales & mdse 1978-; Ted's One Stop, salesman 1975-78; Hudson Embassy, store mgr 1972-75; Metro Advt, acount exec 1977; Platinum Plus Records & Tapes, pres 1979. **ORGANIZATIONS:** Regular mem Dem Orgn 1973; mem Black Music Assn 1977. **HONORS/ACHIEVEMENTS:** Gold record sales over 500,000 on Evelyn "Champaign" King's single "Shame" RCA Records & Tapes 1977; platinum LP Michael Jackson's "Off the Wall" album 1980. **BUSINESS ADDRESS:** Ted's One Stop Inc, 3814 Page Blvd, St Louis, MO 63113.

HUDSON, LESTER DARNELL
Attorney. **PERSONAL:** Born Mar 04, 1949, Detroit, MI; married Vivian Ann Johnson. **EDUCATION:** Fisk U, BA 1971; Boston Coll, Law Degree; Law Sch Brighton MA, 1974. **CAREER:** Bell & Hudson, atty & sr partner; Boston Coll, legal internlegal asst 1973-74; City of Boston Law Dept, intern 1972-73; Boston Legal & Asst Proj, legal intern 1972. **ORGANIZATIONS:** Mem Detroit Bar Assn; mem NBA; mem ABA Young Lawyers sect; Urban Leag; PUSH Detroit; mem NAACP Crime Task Force com. **HONORS/ACHIEVEMENTS:** Recip Awd for Ldshp & Schlrshp Scott Paper Co Found 1971; listed "Who's Who Among Stu in Am Colls &Univ 1972; Martin Luther King Awd for Ldrshp & Comm Invlmnt 1974; listed "Outstndng Young Men of Am" 1978. **BUSINESS ADDRESS:** Bell & Hudson, 840 Buhl Bldg, Detroit, MI 48226.

HUDSON, LINCOLN THEODORE
Business executive. **PERSONAL:** Born Mar 12, 1916, Okmulgee, OK; married Chestine Macbeth; children: Lincoln Jr, Crystal, Chester. **EDUCATION:** Loyola Univ, BS 1951; Univ of Chicago Business Sch, attended. **CAREER:** Johnson Pub Co Inc, vice pres/midwest advertising sales dir/supvs staff of 9 salesmen & other personnel 1952-. **ORGANIZATIONS:** Mem Agate Club. **MILITARY SERVICE:** AUS WW II; parachuted from disabled aircraft over Czechoslovakia during escort duty captured & imprisoned at Nuremburg; Purple Heart. **BUSINESS ADDRESS:** Vice President, Johnson Publishing Co Inc, 820 S Michigan Ave, Chicago, IL 60605.

HUDSON, LOU
Retired professional athlete. **PERSONAL:** Born Jul 11, 1944, Greensboro, NC. **CAREER:** Atlanta Hawks 1967-77; NBA All-Star Team 1969-74.

HUDSON, MERRY C.
Government official. **PERSONAL:** Born Dec 25, 1943, Baltimore, MD; married Robert L Hudson; children: Alicia; Stephen. **EDUCATION:** Howard Univ, BA 1965, JD 1968; George Washington Univ, LLM 1972. **CAREER:** Equal Employment Opportunity Comm, supervisory attorney 1971-72; Univ of Maryland, affirmative action off 1975-76; Private Practice of Law, 1976-78; State of MD Comm on Human Relations, hearing examiner 1978-. **ORGANIZATIONS:** Univ of MD, eeo consultant 1976; Nat'l Assoc of Admin Law Judges, mem; Nat'l Bar Assoc, mem; DC Links, Inc, treasurer 1985-; Alpha Kappa Alpha, mem. **HONORS/ACHIEVEMENTS:** Howard Univ, academic scholarships 1961-68; State of MD Personnel Dept, cert of appreciation 1980; Nat'l Judicial Coll, citation for distinquished service, faculty advisor 1982, Nat'l Assoc for Equal Opp, distinguished Alumni awd 1986. **HOME ADDRESS:** 1216 Edgevale Rd, Silver Spring, MD 20910.

HUDSON, ROBERT L.
Educator, physician. **PERSONAL:** Born Oct 30, 1939, Mobile, AL; son of Robert L Hudson (deceased) and Claudia M Jackson Hudson Graham; married Merry Brock; children: Alicia, Stephen. **EDUCATION:** Lincoln Univ, BA 1962; Howard Univ, MD 1966. **CAREER:** Howard Univ Ctr for Sickle Cell Disease, physician coord 1971-72; Howard Univ, asst prof 1971-75; Howard Univ Ctr for Sickle Cell Disease, dep dir 1972-75; Private Practice, physician. **ORGANIZATIONS:** Attending staff Howard Univ Hosp; Children's Hosp; Natl Med Ctr; Columbia Hosp for Women; DC Genl Hosp; mem bd dir Capital Head Start 1971-75; medcons Capital Headstart 1971-76; Med Soc of DC; Amer Acad of Pediatrics; Medico Chirurgical Soc of DC; Amer Heart Assn. **BUSINESS ADDRESS:** Drs Crawford Hudson PC, 2600 Naylor Rd SE, Washington, DC 20020.

HUDSON, ROY DAVAGE
Pharmaceutical company executive, educator. **PERSONAL:** Born Jun 30, 1930, Chattanooga, TN; son of James Roy Hudson and Everence Wilkerson Hudson; married Constance Joan Taylor, Aug 31, 1956; children: Hollye Hudson Goler, David K Hudson. **EDUCATION:** Livingstone Coll, BS 1955; Univ of MI, MS 1957, PhD 1962; Lehigh Univ, LLD 1974; Princeton Univ, LLD 1975. **CAREER:** Univ of MI Med School, prof 1961-66; Brown Univ Med School, prof 1966-70; Brown Univ Graduate School, dean 1969; Hampton Univ, pres 1970-76; Parke-Davis, vice pres pharmaceutical research 1977-79; The Upjohn Co, dir pharmaceutical research, dir central nervous syst rsch, 1987-; vice pres, Pharmaceutical Research and Development Europe; Upjohn Co, Brussels, Belgium, vice pres pharmaceutical research and devel, 1987-. **ORGANIZATIONS:** Bd dir Parke-Davis Co 1974-76; bd dir Chesapeake and Potomac Telephone Co 1972-76; bd dir United Virginia Bankshares 1971-76; chmn VA State Comm for Selection Rhodes Scholars 1973; bd dir Peninsula Chamber of Commerce 1970-76; bd dir Amer Council on Educ 1973-76. **HONORS/ACHIEVEMENTS:** Danforth Fellow Danforth Foundation 1955-62; Outstanding Civilian Serv Award AUS 1972; Scholarship Award Omega Psi Phi Fraternity 1954-55; Distinguished Alumni Medallion Livingston Coll 1969; Award of Merit for Continuous Service to Humanity, Omega Psi Phi Fraternity, 1974; Award for Exemplary Leadership Omega Psi Phi Fraternity, 1978; M L King/C Chavez/R Parks visiting prof, Univ of MI, 1989. **MILITARY SERVICE:** USAF Staff Sgt 1948-52. **HOME ADDRESS:** Kastan Jedrief 14, B-1900 Overijse, Belgium. **BUSINESS ADDRESS:** The Upjohn Co, Pharmaceutical Research and Devel, Rue de Geneve 10, 1140 Brussels, Belgium.

HUDSON, SAMUEL WILLIAM, III
Attorney, government official. **PERSONAL:** Born Nov 06, 1940, Houston, TX; married Heney Suldon; children: Samuel IV, Cynric, Lelalois, Samzie, Stacie, Tracie, French Elle, William Henry. **EDUCATION:** TX Southern Univ, BS 1963; Thurgood Marshall School of Law, JD 1967. **CAREER:** Legal Found of Houston TX, staff attny 1967-68; Collin Radio Co, reg legal staff 1968-70; Daniel Investment, legal staff 1970-71; Fed Aviation Admin, legal staff 1972; TX Dist 100, state rep. **ORGANIZATIONS:** Appt chmn by gov Small Bus Interim Study Comm Mem JL Turner Legal Soc of Dallas 1974; mem NAACP, Natl Bar Assoc, TX Bar Assoc, Black C of C Dallas; elect sec So Reg of Natl Black Caucus of State Legisl. **HONORS/ACHIEVEMENTS:** Dallas Women's Club Trailblazer Awd 1969; Outstanding Leadership Awd Boy Scouts of Amer 1969; Legis Awd Dallas Cty Womens Pol Caucus 1976; A Phillip Randolph Legis Awd 1977. **BUSINESS ADDRESS:** State Representative, Dallas District 100, 2606 ML King Blvd #202, Dallas, TX 75215.

HUDSON, STERLING HENRY, III
Educator. **PERSONAL:** Born Jul 06, 1950, Hot Springs, VA; married Cheryl White; children: Tara L. **EDUCATION:** Hampton Univ, BA (w/Honors) 1973, MA 1979. **CAREER:** Hampton Univ, admissions counselor 1973-77, asst to dean of admissions 1977-78, asst dean of admissions 1978-82; Elizabeth City State Univ, dir of admissions/recruitment 1982-83; Morehouse Coll, dir of admissions 1983-. **ORGANIZATIONS:** Mem Natl Assoc of Coll Admissions Counselors 1973-, Amer Assoc of Coll Deans Registrars Adm Ofcrs 1973-, Kappa Delta Pi 1979-, Atlanta Urban League 1984-; rep Univ Ctr of GA 1984-86; council coll level serv Coll Bd 1985-. **HONORS/ACHIEVEMENTS:** Most Outstanding Grad Brother Iota Phi Theta 1980; writer Fin Aid for Minorities in Medicine, ed asst Fin Aid for Minorities in Medicine (series) Garrett Park Press 1980; Fleischman Foundation UNCF Study Grant 1986. **BUSINESS ADDRESS:** Dir of Admissions, Morehouse College, 830 Westview Dr SW, Atlanta, GA 30314.

HUDSON, THEODORE R.
Author, educator. **PERSONAL:** Born in Washington, DC; married Geneva Bess; children: Eric, Vicki. **EDUCATION:** Miner Teachers Coll, BS; NY Univ, MA; Howard Univ, MA, PhD. **CAREER:** Univ of DC, prof of English 1964-77; Amer Univ, adj prof of lit 1968-69; Howard Univ, grad prof English 1977-. **ORGANIZATIONS:** Mem Duke Ellington Soc; past pres Highland Beach Cit Assoc. **HONORS/ACHIEVEMENTS:** Most Disting Lit Scholarship Awd Coll Lang Assoc 1974; From LeRoi Jones to Amiri Baraka, The Literary Works Duke Univ Press 1973; num art in periodicals and books.

HUDSON, WILLIAM THOMAS
Government executive. **PERSONAL:** Born Dec 14, 1929, Chicago, IL; son of Cornelius and Mary Hudson. **EDUCATION:** Northwestern Univ, BS 1953; Univ of Chgo, MA 1954; Harvard Univ, 1982. **CAREER:** Bur Retirement & Survivors Ins Balt, claims authorizer 1963-64; Hders Retirement & Survivors Ins, employee devel ofcr; Comm on EEO WA, detailed to pres; Ret & Survivors Ins, spec asst for EEO to dir 1964-65; Ofc Sec Dept HEW WA, dep EEO Officer 1966-67; Ofc Sec Dept Transp WA, cons, prgm mgr internal EEO prog, Natl Urban league Conv, resource 1967-70; Office Civil Rights USCG WA, chief 1970-83; US Dept of Transportation, dept dir of civil rights 1983-. **ORGANIZATIONS:** Mem Natl Assoc Human Rights Workers, Phi Delta Kappa, Hon Soc for Men in Ed, Sec of Transportation. **HONORS/ACHIEVEMENTS:** Silver Medal for Meritorious Achievement 1974; Senior Executive Service Bonus 1984-88. **MILITARY SERVICE:** AUS 1954-56. **BUSINESS ADDRESS:** Dept Dir Civil Rights, US Dept of Transportation, 400 7th St SW, Washington, DC 20590.

HUDSON, WINSON
Educator. **PERSONAL:** Widowed. **EDUCATION:** Comm Educ Extension Mary Holmes Coll. **CAREER:** Leake Co Chapter NAACP, pres 1961-74; Leake Co Head Start, social serv specialist. **ORGANIZATIONS:** Mem MS Council on Human Relations; MS Assn for Health Care for the Poor; bd mem ACLU; chmn Dem Party Leake Co. **HONORS/ACHIEVEMENTS:** Recipient Many Awards for Outstanding Leadership in Civil Rights Movement.

HUESTON, OLIVER DAVID
Psychiatrist. **PERSONAL:** Born Oct 23, 1941, NYC; divorced; children: Michael, David. **EDUCATION:** Hunter Coll, BA 1963; Meharry Med Coll, MD 1968; Josiah Macy Fellow 1971-72; Columbia U, Attending Pediatrician 1971-72. **CAREER:** Harlem Hosp, chief Resident Pediatrics 1970-71; Harlem Hosp, gen psychiatric resident 1972-74, fellow child Psychiatry 1974-75; ColumbiaUniv Coll of Physicians & Surgeons, attending pediatrician 1971-72; Self Employed 1985. **ORGANIZATIONS:** Mem Pediatrician Flower 5 Ave Hosp Martin L King Evening Clinic 1971; clinical physician NY State Drug Abuse Control Com; dir Ambulatory Drug Unit #13 Harlem Hops; mem St Albans Martyr Episcopal Ch; Josiah Macy Fellow 1971-72. **HONORS/ACHIEVEMENTS:** USAFR 1968-71. **BUSINESS ADDRESS:** 100 Haven Ave, New York, NY 10032.

HUFF, EDGAR R.
Retired marine sergeant major. **PERSONAL:** Born Dec 02, 1919, Gadsden, AL; married Beulah M McCaskill; children: Dorothy Terrell, Barbara Jackson, Edgar R Jr. **EDUCATION:** MCI Washington DC, cert in introduction to personnel 1958; MCRD Parris Island SC, cert in personnel admin 1963. **CAREER:** USMC, guard chief French Morocco Africa Navy 214 1955-57, personal guard to Mohammed Ben Yusif 1955-57, 1st Black sgt major 1955-57; sgt maj MCB Camp Pendelton CA 1965-67, sgt maj 3rd Marine amphibious force Vietnam military police bn 1967, sgt maj 2nd air wing Cherry Point NC 1968-69, sgt maj USMC 3rd amphibious marine force Okinawa 1971 (retired). **ORGANIZATIONS:** Grand Inspector Genl of 33rd Degree & elevated to membership in the United Supreme Council of the Ancient & Accepted Scottish Rite of Freemasonry Prince Hall Affiliation for S Jurisdiction of the USA; bd dirs Staff NCO's Camp Lejeune NC 1957; chmn EEO Com Camp Lejeune NC 1963; bd dir CA Credit Union League 1965; mem Mt Hobert Lodge No 73; sr minister of state orator Lewis-Mingo Consistory No 316; mem Shriners Arabian Tample No 42 1968-80; judge advocate Amer Legion 1977-80; ceremonial chmn Natl Montford Point Marine Assn 1979-80. **HONORS/ACHIEVEMENTS:** Sec of Navy Commendation Medal USMC 1967; Pres Unit Citation Medal USMC 1968; Vietnamese Campaign Medal USMC 1968; received numerous other medals & citationsUSMC 1968-69; Purple Heart; 2 Bronze Stars 1968; Good Conduct Medal 1968; 4 Stars 1968; Combat Action Medal 1968; Hon Ambassador of Good Will State of LA 1978; inducted Hall of Fame Mason Strip New Orleans 1978; book "Roots of Two Black Marines Sgt Maj" 1978; Order of the Long Leaf Pine from Gov of the State of NC. **MILITARY SERVICE:** USMC sgt maj 30 yrs.

HUFF, LEON ALEXANDER
Producer, songwriter. **PERSONAL:** Born Apr 08, 1942, Camden, NJ; married Juanita Boone; children: Debbie, Detira. **EDUCATION:** Gamble-Huff Prodns & Philadelphia Intl Records Inc; Began Career as Studio Musician Playing Piano for Local Singing Groups; Now Composes & Produces Songs for Nation's Top Recording Artists; Recording Studios Are Among Fastest Growing Most Popular in Country. **CAREER:** Mem NATRA; Broadcast Music Inc; Nat Assn of Record Mfgs. **ORGANIZATIONS:** He & His Assoc were Named Best Rhythm & Blues Producers in Country Nat Assn of TV & Recording Artsits 1968-69; Awarded Five Gold Records Winthin 3 Months for Million-seller Records As , The Black Stabbers (The O'Jays), If You Don't Know Me By Now (Harold Melvin & The Blue Notes) Me & Mrs Jones (Billy Paul) Power of Love & Drowning in A Sea of Love (Joe Simon). **HONORS/ACHIEVEMENTS:** Recipient Key to City of Camden; Record World Producer-Writer of Decade Award. **BUSINESS ADDRESS:** 309 S Broad St, Philadelphia, PA 19107.

HUFF, LOUIS ANDREW
Educator & business consultant. **PERSONAL:** Born Jan 01, 1949, New Haven, CT; married Suzanne Elaine Cooke; children: Elaine Kai. **EDUCATION:** Howard Univ, BA Economics Bus Finance 1971, MA Economics 1974, PhD Economics 1981. **CAREER:** Fed Reserve Bd, economist 1971-74; Lincoln Univ, asst prof 1977-80; CBC Rsch Inst, pres 1980-82; Univ of New Haven, asst prof 1980-82; 1st Buffalo Corp, economist/stockbroker 1983-; PA State Univ, asst prof of economics. **ORGANIZATIONS:** Bd mem CBC Inc 1982-; mem Western Economic Soc 1983-; economic consultant RIE Ltd 1983-; host & producer Economist Corner 1984-; chairperson housing NAACP Reading Chap 1984-; mem Atlantic Economic Soc 1984-. **HONORS/ACHIEVEMENTS:** Rsch Study Awd Economics Natl Chap of Eastern States 1979; Outstanding Young Man in America Natl 1981; article published Atlantic Economic Journal 1985; Presented papers at num natl econ confs incl Montreal Canada 1983, Rome Italy 1985. **HOME ADDRESS:** 611 W 37th St, Wilmington, DE 19802. **BUSINESS ADDRESS:** Asst Prof Economics, PA StateUniv, RD #5 Box 2150, Reading, PA 19608.

HUFF, WILLIAM
Business executive. **PERSONAL:** Born Apr 10, 1920, Manchester, GA; married Beatrice; children: Ronald, Cherie Fae, Brian. **EDUCATION:** Youngstown U, AB 1951;Univ of Pittsburgh, MSW 1969; OH StateUniv Mgmt Devel Prog, Certificate 1968; Training Course Mattatuck Coll CT, Certificate of Housing Tech Training Course. **CAREER:** Plymouth Urban Cntr Louisville, exec dir 1973-; Pearl St Neighborhood House, exec dir 1970-73; Youngstown Area Comm Action Coun, asso dir 1965-70. **ORGANIZATIONS:** Fin chmn Commun Action Agency; mem CAC; Asso Neighborhood Cntr Hagstrom House US Military Reservation 1951-57; mem NAACP; Boys Wrk Com YMCA OH; Welf Rights Organz OH; past pres Prof Grp Wkrs OH; Stud Loan Com CT; Mod Cities Adv on Recreation; adv Teen Parent Club; co-chmn State Blk Polit Assemb KY; Black Social Workers of Louisville; Equal Justice Information Cntr Bd Louisville; LEAP Bd of Louisville Urban Leage; THETA Omega Chap of Omega PsiPhi; Russell Area Coun; adv com to WLKY TV of Louisville; Mayor's Human Relat Com OH. **HONORS/ACHIEVEMENTS:** Recipient Award by Freedom Inc as A Native Son Youngstown OH 1971f Certificate of Housing Technician Course 1969; Certificate from OH StateUniv Mgmt Devel Prog 1968; Hon KY Col. **MILITARY SERVICE:** USAF 1944-45. **BUSINESS ADDRESS:** 1626 W Chestnut, Louisville, KY 40203.

HUFFMAN, JASPER JEFFERSON, III
Chief executive officer. **PERSONAL:** Born Jan 07, 1944, Rochester, NY; divorced; children: Jasper J. **EDUCATION:** Univ of Buffalo, BA History 1971;Univ of Buffalo, BA Black Studies 1971. **CAREER:** Rochester Black United Fund Inc, chief exec officer 1985; FIGHT Inc, adminstr 1975-76; Urban League of Rochester, comm Planner/research spec 1974-75; StateUniv Coll Brockport NY, asst vice pres student affairs 1972-74. **ORGANIZATIONS:** Exec com bd mem Nat Black United Fund Inc 1977-; bd mem Comm Day Care Center Inc 1978-; pres chief exec officer JJH-KD Consult Inc 1979-; past pres& mem Rochester Black Polit Caucus 1974-; mem Rochester Black Bus Council 1979; bd mem Warzui Soc (Black Edn) 1980-. **HONORS/ACHIEVEMENTS:** Comm Recognition Award First Comm Interfaith Inst Inc 1980; Outstanding Black Achievement Fredrick Douglass Trans-Cultural Assn 1980. **BUSINESS ADDRESS:** Rochester Black United Fund In, 119 E Main St, Rochester, NY 14604.

HUFFMAN, RUFUS C.
Association executive. **PERSONAL:** Born Feb 05, 1927, Bullock Co, AL; married Callie Iola Harris; children: Rufus, Jr, Henry. **EDUCATION:** AL State U, BS 1952, MEd 1966; NY U, Further Study. **CAREER:** Tchr Prin Coach; Russell Co Bd Edn, prin 1947-49; Augusta Co Bd Educ Prattville AL 1951-53. **ORGANIZATIONS:** Bullock Co Bd Educ Union Springs AL 1953-56; Randolph Co Bd Educ Cuthbert GA 1956-63; coord treas mgr Seasha Fed Credit Union Tuskeegee Inst AL 1968-70; co-founder SE Self-Help Assn; organizer treas mgr SEASHA Fed Credit Union; consult OEO Comprehensive Health Program & Ford Found Leadership Devel Program; so educ field dir NAACP Spl Contrib Fund Inc 1985; pres Bullock Co Tchrs Assn; pres Bullock Co Athletic Assn; pres Union Springs NAACP 1966-70; chmn Bullock Co Coordntg Com 1966-70; chmn Bullock Co Recreational Bd 1973; life mem NAACP; v pres Bullock Co Improvement Orgn; mem bd dir So Poverty Law Center; Leadership Devel Program Selection Com; Union Springs Adv Com City Council; Great Books Western World Salesman; Distrib Success Motivation Inst. **HONORS/ACHIEVEMENTS:** Tchr of Yr Bullock Co 1963-64; Joshua A Smith Award Outstanding Leadership Educ Human Devel in S; Who's Who S & SE; Certificate Honor NAACP Club 100. **BUSINESS ADDRESS:** PO Drawer 190, Tuskegee Institute, AL 36088.

HUGER, JAMES E.
Business executive. **PERSONAL:** Born in Tampa, FL; married Phannye Brinson; children: James Ermine, Jr, Thomas Albert, II, John Leland. **EDUCATION:** Attended, Bethune Cookman Coll, West Virginia State Coll, Univ of MI. **CAREER:** Bethune-Cookman Coll, business mgr, admin asst to pres, assoc treasurer; Alpha Phi Alpha Frat Inc, genl secty; City of Daytona Beach FL, dir of community development. **ORGANIZATIONS:** Life mem Alpha Phi Alpha Frat, NAACP; mem Elks, Masons, American Legion, Assoc for the study of Negro Life and History, Sigma Pi Phi Frat, The Civic League, Civitan, Shrine; bd of dirs FL Health Care, FL League of Cities Intergovernmental Relations Comm, Stewart Treatment Ctr, SERC/NAHRO's Comm and Redevelop Comm, The United Methodist Church; bd of dirs Volusia Governmental Employees Credit Union; pres bd of dirs Rape Crisis Ctr of Volusia Co Inc; chmn United Nations Comm 1985, Dr Martin L King Birthday Commemoration Comm; pres Volusia County Assoc of Retarded Citizens; bd of dirs State Mental Health Assoc; The Review Panel, Developing Institutions HEW Washington DC; mem State Commn on Aging; mem FL Bar Grievance Comm, Southern Growth Policy Bd, Rotary Intl, Commn on the Future of the South; mem minority enterprises develop comm Dept of Commerce; mem urban admin comm FL League of Cities. **HONORS/ACHIEVEMENTS:** Charles W Green Award for Outstanding Serv to Humanity; Man of the Year Alpha Phi Alpha Frat; Bethune Cookman Coll Awd Administrator of the Year, Medallion for Outstanding Contribution to Local Govt; Awd of Achievement NAACP; Man of the Year 1975 Omega Psi Phi Frat; Humanitarian Awd NAACP; Equality Day Awd Natl Org for Women; named by City Commn July 1982 "James E Huger Park"; Awd of Thank You FL Assoc of Retarded Citizens and Volusia Assoc of Retarded Citizens; Disting Serv Awd United Nations 1985; Certificates

of Appreciation Halifax Hosp Med Ctr 1985, Links Inc 1985, Stewart Memorial United Methodist Ch 1986; Ray Sims Awd Outstanding Contribution in the Fight Against Heart Disease 1986; Disting Serv Awd Assoc of Retarded Citizens Volusia Co 1986; Dedicationof Jimmy Huger Circle Assoc of Retarded Citizens Volusia Co 1986; Plaque of Appreciation Mary McLeod Bethune Ctr 1986; Awd of Appreciation Rape Crisis Ctrof Volusia Co 1986; listed in Who's Who in the South and Southwest, Personalities of the South, Community Leaders and Noteworthy Amers, Amer Coll and UnivAdministrators, Men of Achievement. **MILITARY SERVICE:** USMC sgt major 4 yrs office.

HUGGINS, CLARENCE L
Physician. **PERSONAL:** Born Apr 25, 1926, Birmingham, AL; married Carolyn King; children: Patricia, Clarence III, Daphne. **EDUCATION:** Morgan St Coll, BS 1950; Meharry Med Coll, MD 1958; Huron Rd Hosp Cleveland, Intrn 1959, Srgcl Res 1959-63. **CAREER:** Cleveland Transit Sys, med dir 1969-72; Cleveland Acad of Med, bd of dir 1974-76; Medic-Screen Hlth Ctrs, pres 1974-84; Shaker Med Ctr Hosp, chf of surgery 1982-84; Private Practice, gen srgn. **ORGANIZATIONS:** Pres med stf Forest City Hosp Cleveland 1970-73; pres bd trustees Hough-Norwood Fam Hlth Ctr 1974-78; dir First Bank Natl Assn 1974-85; mem adv bd Robert Wood Johnson Found Natl Hlth Srvcs Prgm 1977-83; dir Ohio Motorist Assn AAA 1979-85. **HONORS/ACHIEVEMENTS:** Diplomate Am Bd of Surgery 1964; fellow Am Coll of Surgeons 1966; pres Cleveland Med Assn 1970-72; co-founder Buckeye Hlth Pln HMO 1974-78. **MILITARY SERVICE:** AUS 1st Lt Airborne Infntry 1944-46, 1951-52. **BUSINESS ADDRESS:** General Surgeon, Private Practice, 13944 Euclid Ave 102, Cleveland, OH 44112.

HUGGINS, HAZEL RENFROE
Business executive. **PERSONAL:** Born Jun 18, 1908, Chicago; divorced. **EDUCATION:** Chicago Normal Coll, Tchrs Cert;Univ Chicago, PhB 1933; Sorbonne-Paris Art History 1949-50; Painting Academie Julian Paris 1950; IL Inst Tech, MS Art Educ 1956; Northwestern U, Interior Design 1959-60. **CAREER:** Chicago Pub Schs, art instr 1927-70; YMCA Summer Camp Felsenthal Social Center, arts & crafts instr 1946-48; Moseley Sch Socially Maladjusted, headed art dept 1956-66; Initial Phase Nat Tchr Corps Program, selected by fed govt as master tchr 1966-67; Chicago Pub Schs, appointed supr art 1967; Emerita, art consult 1985; Renfroe Research, pres. **ORGANIZATIONS:** Mem Art Textbook Selection Com Chicago Bd Edn; mem City Wide Com Selected to Revamp Tchr Training Program DePaulUniv 1959; demonstrator teaching techniques Lectr on African & Afro-Am Art & Discussion Panelist for Spl Educ & Correctional Programs IL Art Educ Western ArtsUniv IL Natl Conf Artists; judge Model Cities Buckingham Fountain Art Competition 1974; judge Regl Div Nat Scholastic Arts Competition 1970-75; judge Intl Stock Show Art Contest 1975; mem N Central Assn 1975; founding mem S Side Comm Art Center Educ Chmn 1939; charter mem exec bd Metro Council Nat Council Negro Women; Served 3 Terms As presLambda Chap Delta Sigma Theta Sor 1938-41; Earnes Womens Defense Corps Army Uniform by Completing 100 Hrs Vol Serv WW II; Took Spl Training & Taught Gas Mask& Messenger Courses to Adults During WW II; Organized 250 mem Career Women for LBJ Directed Activities During 1964 Campaign; adv Com Contemporary African Art Exhibit Field Museum 1974; bd dir Creative Children's Arts Winnetka 1985; Bravo Chap Lyric Opera Guild. **HONORS/ACHIEVEMENTS:** Awarded HS Certificate Art Through Competitive Examination 1958; Selected to Organize Personnel & Direct Sales of Stamps Bonds During WW II Cited by TreasuryDept for Raising Unexpectedly Huge Amount Money; Awarded Delta Sigma Theta's Nat Scholarship 1949; Appointed by Gov Shapiro to IL Commn for Observance United Nations 25th Anniversary.

HUGGINS, HOSIAH, JR.
Management consultant. **PERSONAL:** Born Aug 17, 1950, Chicago, IL. **EDUCATION:** Univ of Akron, BA 1974; Newport Univ, MPA 1988. **CAREER:** Amalgamated Stationers, vice pres sales 1974-80; Xerox Corp, mktg exec 1980-83; Insight & Attitudes Inc, pres. **ORGANIZATIONS:** Bd of dirs Urban League of Cleveland 1978-80, YMCA 1979-85; natl pres Natl Assoc of Mgmt Consultants 1985-; assoc mem Institute of Mgmt Consult 1987. **HONORS/ACHIEVEMENTS:** Outstanding Scholastic Phi Beta Sigma 1974; Outstanding Young Man of Amer 1982; Man of the Year Bel-Aire Civic Club 1983; "1983 Most Interesting People" Cleveland Magazine. **BUSINESS ADDRESS:** President, Insight & Attitudes, Inc, 3101 Euclid Office Plaza, Ste 501, Cleveland, OH 44115.

HUGGINS, NATHAN IRVIN
Educator. **PERSONAL:** Born Jan 14, 1927, Chicago, IL; married Brenda Carlita Smith. **EDUCATION:** Univ of CA Berkeley, AB 1954, MA 1955; Harvard Univ, AM 1957, PhD 1962. **CAREER:** Long Beach State CA, asst prof 1962-64; Lake Forest Coll IL, asst prof 1964-66; Univ of MA Boston, asst prof 1966-69; Columbia Univ NY, prof 1970-80; Harvard Univ, prof 1980-. **ORGANIZATIONS:** Dir Libr of Amer 1978-; dir Amer Cncl of Learned Societies 1980-; editor Journal of Ethnic Studies 1979-; trustee Howard Thurman Trust 1966-; trustee Radcliff Coll 1985-. **HONORS/ACHIEVEMENTS:** Guggenheim Fellowship Guggenheim Found 1971-72; Fulbright Lecturer (France) 1974-75; Rockefeller Humanities Fellow Rockefeller Found 1984-85; Fellow Inst for Advanced Study Palo Alto, CA 1979-80. **MILITARY SERVICE:** AUS Corpl 1945-46. **BUSINESS ADDRESS:** WEB DuBois Prof of History, Harvard University, DuBois Institute, Cambridge, MA 02138.

HUGHES, ANITA LILLIAN
Educator. **PERSONAL:** Born Feb 16, 1938, French Lick, IN. **EDUCATION:** IN U, BS 1959; IN U, MS 1961; IN U, EdD 1967. **CAREER:** Lincoln HS IN, tchr 1959-60; IN Univ Counseling Dept, grad asst 1961-63; IN Univ NW Campus, asst dir of counseling 1963-67; IN Univ Counseling Center, counselor 1966-67; Howard Univ, sr counselor & asst prof 1967-68; Human Ecological Fed City Coll, prof & chmn 1968-; DHEW, consultant 1970-; EPDA Prog in USOE 1972; Natl Inst for Alcohol Drug Abuse & Mental Health 1972-; Natl Inst For Educ 1973-; Amer Coun on Educ 1973-; Assn of Amer Coll 1973-; Amer Personnel & Guidance Assn; Coun of Admin Women in Educ; Amer Coll Personnel Assn. **ORGANIZATIONS:** Chmn bd mem, State Membership HarvardUniv Inst for Educ Mgmt Prog; Am Physiol Assn Div of Comm Psychology; Groves Conf on Marriage & Family. **HONORS/ACHIEVEMENTS:** Recipient Honor Scholarship DrakeUniv 1955-56; Deans Honor List INUniv 1966-67; Outstanding Educator of Am Fed City Coll Student Govt Assn 1973. **BUSINESS ADDRESS:** 724 9 St NW, Washington, DC 20001.

HUGHES, CARL D.
Clergyman, educator. **PERSONAL:** Born in Indianapolis; married Louise. **EDUCATION:** WV State Coll Inst, BS 1942; Wharton Sch of FinanceUniv of PA, MA 1943; Christian Theol Sem, BD 1957; Christian Theol Sem, MA 1958; Centrl Bapt Theol Semin of IN, DD 1975; Christian Theol Sem, MDiv 1972; INUniv Sch of Law Wayne StateUniv &Univ of Detroit, Post Grad Studies. **CAREER:** Mt Zion Bapt Ch Indianapolis, ministers asst 1952; Second Bapt Ch Lafayette 1952-56; St John Missionary Bapt Ch 1956-60; Christian Educ Met Bapt ChDetroit, dir 1960-61; Bethel Bapt Ch East Detroit, pastor 1961; Hughes Enterprise Inc, vice pres treas; Detroit Christian Training Cntr, former dean; Bus Educ Detroit Pub Sch, former tchr; Ch Bldr & Bus Educ Detroit Pub Sch, dept hd; Calvary Dist Assn Detroit, former instr; Wolverine State Conv SS & BTU Cong MI, former instr; Nat Bapt SS & BTU Congress, former instr; Central Bible Sem, former instr. **ORGANIZATIONS:** Membership com YMCA; membership Com NAACP; former mem Grand Bd Dir Kappa Alpha Psi Nat Coll Frat; Mason; budget com Nat Negro Bus League; treas StEmma Military Acad Parent Assn of Detroit; chmn bd of trustees Todd-Phillips Children Home of the Wolverine State Missionary Bapt Conv Inc; chmn of Finance Pastors' Div of the Nat Bapt Congress of Christian Edn. **HONORS/ACHIEVEMENTS:** Listed in Who's Who in Am Coll & Univ 1943; Who's Who in Colored Am 1950; Received First John L Webb Award Nat Bapt Conv 1948; Author "The Ch Orgnzd For A Meaning Ministry" & "Financing the Local Ch Property". **BUSINESS ADDRESS:** Bethel Baptist Church East, 5715-33 Holcomb, Detroit, MI 48213.

HUGHES, CATHERINE LIGGINS
Radio station general manager. **PERSONAL:** Born Apr 22, 1947, Omaha, NE; daughter of William A Woods and Helen E Jones-Woods; children: Alfred Charles Liggins, III. **EDUCATION:** Creighton Univ, Omaha, NE, 1966-69; Univ of NE, Omaha, NE, 1969-71; Harvard Univ, Cambridge, MA, 1975. **CAREER:** Harvard Univ, Washington, DC, lecturer, 1971-73; WHUR-FM, Washington, DC, sales mgr, 1973-75, gen mgr, 1975-78; WYCB-AM, Washington, DC, gen mgr, 1978; WOL-AM, Washington, DC, gen mgr, 1980-89; WMMJ-FM, Washington, DC, gen mgr, 1986-89. **ORGANIZATIONS:** Bd mem, United Black Fund, 1978-88; bd mem, DC Boys/Girls Club, 1983-86; chmn, Community Comm Corp, 1985-87; Washington Post Recall Comm, 1987. **HONORS/ACHIEVEMENTS:** Woman of the Year, Washington Woman, 1987; 1988 People's Champion Award, Natl Black Media Coalition, 1988; 1988 Kool Achiever, Communications, 1988; Woman of the Year, Women at Work of the Natl Capital Area, 1989; The Cathy Hughes TV Show, 1989. **BUSINESS ADDRESS:** Owner/Gen Mgr, Almic Broadcasting T/A WOL-AM/WMMJ-FM, 400 H St, NE, Washington, DC 20002.

HUGHES, CHARLES W., JR.
Electronics engineer. **PERSONAL:** Born Jan 09, 1942, Hartsville, SC; married Alma Winborne; children: Alicia D, Dameron A, Cariel W. **EDUCATION:** So Univ Sch Engring, BElectronics 1965. **CAREER:** Norfolk Naval Shipyard Code 19122, electronics engr 1977; Naval Electronics Systems Engrg Ctr, communication systems analyst, project mgr, comsec project mgr 1977-. **ORGANIZATIONS:** Mem Omega Psi Phi; Zeta Iota. **HONORS/ACHIEVEMENTS:** Appreciation & Technical Assistance Awards Naval Activities. **BUSINESS ADDRESS:** Project Manager, Naval Electronics Sys Engrg, PO Box 55, Portsmouth, VA 23705.

HUGHES, DANIEL WEBSTER
Clergyman. **PERSONAL:** Born Nov 25, 1926, St Louis; married Ora Enochs; children: Hazel, Terease, Denise. **EDUCATION:** Harris Tchr Coll, BA; Am Bapt Sem, BD; Webster Coll, MA; St Louis U, Grad Work. **CAREER:** Mt Zion Bapt Ch MO, pastor 1958-61; Nat Alumni Assn Am Bapt Sem, pres 1967-70; E Star Bapt Ch MO, pastor 1961-; Missionary Bapt Educ Congress, pres 1973-. **ORGANIZATIONS:** Mem Nat Bapt Conv; bd mem St Louis Branch NAACP; vice moderator Berean Dist Assn; bd trustee Am Bapt Sem & Western Bapt Coll; mem Urban League;Ministers Union St Louis. **HONORS/ACHIEVEMENTS:** Minister Yr Berean Mem Nat Bapt Educ Congress; Pastors Div Nat Bapt Inc Educ Congress Dist Assn 1970; 100 Club St Louis NAACP. **MILITARY SERVICE:** USN 1943-46. **BUSINESS ADDRESS:** 3121 St Louis Ave, St Louis, MO 63106.

HUGHES, ERNELLE COMBS
Educator. **PERSONAL:** Born Jun 08, 1918, Martin, GA; daughter of Weyman Lee Combs and Bertha Johnson Combs; married Obieton (deceased). **EDUCATION:** Spelman Coll, AB 1947; Atlanta Univ, matriculated summers 1949,56,59; Univ of GA, MS 1975; Atlanta Univ, matriculated summers of 1949, 1956, 1959. **CAREER:** Bd of Educ Franklin Co GA, teacher 1945-46; Bd of Educ Hart Co GA, teacher 1947-80, mem 1982-87. **ORGANIZATIONS:** Sunday school teacher Maple Spring Baptist Church 1949-86; vice pres Savannah Missionary Bapt WMU 1962-84; program chmn Savannah River Bapt Cong of Christian Educ 1963-84; worthy matron Hart Co Chap Order of the Eastern Star 1980-86; mem Naomi Court #624 Heroines of Jericho; sec Community Action Committee 1982-86; volunteer work Crisis Pregnancy Counseling 1985-; mem NAACP; youth dir Smooth Ashlar Grand Lodge F&AAYM; worthy matron Order of the Eastern Star 1980-86; mem Heroines of Jericho; asst dean, Union Missionary Baptist Congress of Christian Education 1987-89; coordinator, Baptist Missionary Union District #3 1987-89. **HONORS/ACHIEVEMENTS:** Phelps-Stokes Scholarship Awd Atlanta Univ 1956; Regional Teacher of the Year GA State Chamber of Commerce 1967; Service Awd Smooth Ashlar Grand Lodge F&AAY Masons 1980; Portrait unveiled in the Masonic Hall of Fame in the Smooth Ashlar Masonic Temple in Atlanta GA 1981; Certificate awarded by GA Sch Bds Assoc and the Univ of GA Ctr for Continuing Educ for the GSBA Sch Bd Institute; Service Awd Hart Co Bdof Educ 1986. **HOME ADDRESS:** Route 1 Martin Dr, Martin, GA 30557.

HUGHES, ESSIE MEADE
Retired educator. **PERSONAL:** Born Dec 28, 1908, Baltimore, MD; daughter of Marshall Hughes and Mary Anderson Hughes. **EDUCATION:** Morgan State Univ, AB 1929; Univ of PA, MS 1942; NY Univ, Doctoral 1956-61; VA Seminary & Coll, Doctor of Humane Letters 1987. **CAREER:** Baltimore School System, teacher of latin 1929-34, sr high school latin teacher 1934-52, coord & supervisor 1952-59, special asst 1959-61, asst principal 1961-71; Western HS Baltimore MD, 1st appointed black admin; Baltimore MD Educ Syst, retired school admin; Baltimore School System, French teacher 1935-41, Spanish teacher 1942-52. **ORGANIZATIONS:** World traveler Canada, Africa, Europe, Middle East, Far East, South Amer, West Indies 1940-; adult educ teacher Baltimore School System 1945-52; mem NEA 1950-, Phi Delta Kappa Theta Lambda Pi 1960-; bd mem Baltimore Regional Red Cross 1969-79; mem MD Retired Teachers Assoc 1971-, AARP 1972-; educ consult for Consumer Product Safety Commission 1973-78. **HONORS/ACHIEVEMENTS:** Chester Katen

Kamp Brotherhood Natl Conf of Christians & Jews 1956; Planning & Executing City-Wide Educ Expo 1970; Awarded the Tannie Randall Humanitarian Honor 1973; Public Spirit Awd Heritage Church 1979; Outstanding Teacher Frederick Douglass High School 1981; Disting Awd Natl Assoc for Equal Oppor 1984; Educational Excellence Fund for Educ Excellence 1986; received Doctor of Humane Letters degree VA Sem & Coll 1987; selected as Maker of Negro History by the Iota Phi Lambda Sor. **HOME ADDRESS:** 1108 Harlem Ave, Baltimore, MD 21217.

HUGHES, GEORGE MELVIN
Educator. **PERSONAL:** Born Aug 26, 1938, Charlotte, TN; married Evelyn Benson; children: Vickie L, George M Jr. **EDUCATION:** TN State Univ, BS 1961, MEd 1963; Univ of WI-Milwaukee, Post Grad studies 1967-68; Cardinal Stritch Coll, Post Grad studies 1983; Indiana Univ, Post Grad studies 1986. **CAREER:** Lafollette Elem School, teacher 1963-68; Parkman Middle School, asst principal 1968-71; Garfield Elem School, asst principal 1971-74; Lee Elem School, principal 1974-. **ORGANIZATIONS:** Bd dir Carter Child Develop Ctr 1981, Girl Scouts of Amer 1987, Phi Delta Kappa Milwaukee Chap 1987; panelist US Dept of Educ Ctr for Systems & ProgDevelop Inc 1987; consultant Indianapolis Sch System 1987, Muscogee County Sch Dist Columbus GA 1987; life mem NAACP; consult Southwest Educ Devel Lab TX. **HONORS/ACHIEVEMENTS:** Special Recognition Lee School Parent-Teacher Org 1983; Special Visit US Educ Sec William J Bennett 1986; apptd to Property Tax Review Bd in Mequon 1986-; invited to the White House Rose Garden by the President to a reception for the release of a book entitled "What Works, Educating Disadvantaged Children"; received a Natl Recogniton by the US Dept of Education as part of the RISE (Rising to Individual Scholastic Excellence) effective school prog in Milwaukee Public Schools. **MILITARY SERVICE:** Air Force ROTC 2 yrs TN State Univ.

HUGHES, GEORGE VINCENT
Business executive. **PERSONAL:** Born Apr 08, 1930, New York, NY; children: Deirdre, Vincent. **EDUCATION:** Coll of City of NY, MBA 1954. **CAREER:** George Hughes Chevrolet, president. **HONORS/ACHIEVEMENTS:** Alpha Phi Alpha Frat 1950-present. **MILITARY SERVICE:** 82nd Airborne Inf captain 3 yrs. **BUSINESS ADDRESS:** President, George Hughes Chevrolet, U S Route 9, Freehold, NJ 07728.

HUGHES, HARVEY L.
Attorney. **PERSONAL:** Born May 07, 1909, Port DePosit, MD; married Ethel C. **EDUCATION:** Univ of Pittsburgh Terrell Law Sch, LLB 1944. **CAREER:** Harris & Hughes Law Firm, partner; N Capitol Corp, gen counsel; Accredited to Present Claims in Ofc of VA 1955. **ORGANIZATIONS:** Mem Wash Bar Assn 1946; DC Bar 1972; Nat Bar Assn 1954; mem Legal Frat Sigm Delta Tau 1946; mem Alpha Phi Alpha Frat Fairmount Heights Civic Club; counselor St Martin's Boys Club 1972. **BUSINESS ADDRESS:** 1840 North Capitol St, Washington, DC 20002.

HUGHES, HOLLIS EUGENE, JR.
Business executive. **PERSONAL:** Born Mar 14, 1943, Tulsa, OK; son of Hollis Eugene Hughes Sr and Suzan Marie Brummell Hughes; married Lavera Ruth Knight, Aug 26. **EDUCATION:** Ball State Univ, BS Soc Sci 1965, MA Sociology 1968. **CAREER:** S Bend Comm Sch Corp, tchr & coach 1965-69; Model Cities Prog/City of S Bend, exec dir 1969-74; Housing Allowance Office Inc, pres/dir 1974-. **ORGANIZATIONS:** Mem Amer Planning Assn 1975; mem, Natl Assn of Housing & Redevelopment Officials, 1978-; mem Amer Mgmt Assn 1979-; mem Alpha Phi Alpha Frat Inc 1966-; mem Alpha Phi Omega Serv Frat 1967-; mem pres elect Ball State Univ Alumni Council 1974-; former pres/bd mem Family & Children Ctr 1978-79; former trustee S Bend Comm Sch Corp/Pub Library; vice pres S Bend Com Sch Corp/Pub Library 1978-; vice pres S Bend Com Sch Corp 1980-81; life mem NAACP; pres S Bend Comm Sch Corp 1981-82; pres South Bend Public Library Bd of Trustees 1984-85; mem IN Adv Comm to the US Commn on Civil Rights; former mem bd trustees Art Ctr Inc S Bend; trustee for Memorial Hospital; bd of trustees for Memorial Hospital Found; bd mem Youth Services Bureau; bd mem Community Education Round Table; dir, S Bend-Mishawaka Chamber of Commerce, 1987-; dir, Project Future of St Joseph County, 1987-; trustee, Ball State Univ, 1989-. **HONORS/ACHIEVEMENTS:** Outstanding Citizen of IN Awd IN Civil Rights Commn 1976; George Awd for Outstanding Comm Serv Mishawaka Enterprise Record 1977. **HOME ADDRESS:** 6126 Miami Rd, South Bend, IN 46614.

HUGHES, ISAAC SUNNY
Mathematician, elected official. **PERSONAL:** Born Jun 29, 1944, Zachary, LA; married Anna Ceaser; children: Timothy, Troy, Jessica. **EDUCATION:** Grambling Univ, BA 1962-66; Univ of N CO, Public Admin 1971-74. **CAREER:** King George VA, co super 1984-; Naval Surface Weapons Ctr, mathematician 1967-. **ORGANIZATIONS:** Worshipful Master KG Masonic Lodge #314 1978; cub master Boy Scouts of Amer 1978-81; mem Bd of Zoning Appeals KG 1981; mem Wetland Bd KG 1982; tie breaker Bd of Supervisors KG 1983; bd of trustee-chair Antioch Baptist Church KG. **HONORS/ACHIEVEMENTS:** Dept of Navy, Outstanding Performance 1974, High Quality Performance 1978, Special Achievement 1983, Superior Performance 1984; Sec of the Yr Prince Hall Masons of VA 1984. **HOME ADDRESS:** Rt 1 Box 522, King George, VA 22485. **BUSINESS ADDRESS:** Supervisor Mathematician, Naval Surface Weapons Ctr, PO Box 666, Dahlgren, VA 22448.

HUGHES, JIMMY FRANKLIN, SR.
Police lieutenant. **PERSONAL:** Born Apr 10, 1952, Tuscaloosa, AL; son of Lee Marvin Hughes and Maryann Stanley Hughes; married Juanita Price, May 29; children: Trina Woodberry, Jimmy Jr, Jared. **EDUCATION:** Northwest Traffic Institute, Evanstan IL, SPSC, 1988; Ohio Peace Officers Training Academy Instructors, 1988; Youngstown State Univ, 1989-. **CAREER:** Youngstown Police Dept, Youngstown OH, patrolman, 1977; McGuffey Center Karate Club, instructor, 1980-; Youngstown Police Dept, Youngstown OH, detective, 1981; Harding Business Coll, instructor, 1987-; Youngstown Police Dept, Youngstown OH, lieutenant, 1988, juvenile div commander, 1988, self-defense instructor, 1989. **ORGANIZATIONS:** Mem, McGuffey Tae Kwon Do Club, 1980-, Natl Black Police Assn, 1981-; pres, Black Knight Police Assn, 1984-90; mem, Youngstown Urban League, 1989-. **HONORS/ACHIEVEMENTS:** Gold Medals, Ohio Police Olympics, 1980, 1983, 1985. **HOME ADDRESS:** 3239 Oak St, Youngstown, OH 44506.

HUGHES, JOHNNIE LEE
Mining engineer. **PERSONAL:** Born Nov 18, 1924, Coalwood, WV; son of George Hughes and Florine Westbrooke; married Sarah Etta Gibson; children: Leonard C Jones, Jacqueline Lee Jones, Moseley. **CAREER:** Osage West Virginia, mayor 1959-61, 1968-70; Ofc of Amer Asian Free Labor Inst Washington DC to Turkey, instr of mine safety 1979; Consolidated Coal Co, mine worker. **ORGANIZATIONS:** Pres UMVA 1978-80; mem Mine Com/Safety Com 15 yrs; mem Coal Miners Political Action Comm 4 yrs. **HONORS/ACHIEVEMENTS:** 1st Black chief of police Monongalia Co WV; 1st Black mayor State of WV; Miner to Mayor publ Ebony Edition 1972; consult to Turkey Publ Miner's Jour 1980. **MILITARY SERVICE:** USMC corpl 1942-46. **BUSINESS ADDRESS:** Consolidated Coal Co, Morgantown, WV 26505.

HUGHES, JOYCE A.
Educator, attorney. **PERSONAL:** Born Feb 07, 1940, Gadsden, AL; daughter of Solomon Hughes Sr and Bessie Cunningham Hughes. **EDUCATION:** Carleton Coll Northfield MN (magna cum laude), BA 1961; Univ Madrid Spaing 1961-62; Univ MN Law Sch (cum laude), JD 1965. **CAREER:** Northwestern Univ School of Law, prof, 1979-, assoc prof, 1975-79; Chicago Transit Authority, general counsel, 1984-88; Continental Illinois Bank, attorney, 1982-84; Univ MN Law Sch, assoc prof 1971-75; Peterson & Holtze Minneapolis, consult 1971-74; Auerbach Corp Philadelphia, consult 1970-71; LeFevere Lefler Hamilton & Peterson Minneapolis, atty 1967-71; Judge Earl R Larson Minneapolis, law clk 1965-67. **ORGANIZATIONS:** Mem, Amer Bar Assn, Natl Bar Assn, Illinois Bar Assn, Cook County Bar Assn; Chicago Bd of Educ, 1980-82; dir, Federal Home Loan Bank of Chicago, 1980-84; dir, First Plymouth Bank, 1971-82; trustee, Natl Urban League, 1972-78; trustee, Carleton Coll, 1969-. **HONORS/ACHIEVEMENTS:** Phi Beta Kappa, 1961; Fulbright Scholarship 1961-62; John Hay Whitney Fellowship 1962-63; Achievement Award Carleton College Alumni 1969; 100 Top Business & Professional Women, Dollars & Sense Magazine, 1986; Superior Public Service Award, Cook County Bar Assn, 1987. **BUSINESS ADDRESS:** Prof, Northwestern Univ School of Law, 357 E Chicago Ave, Chicago, IL 60611.

HUGHES, LEONARD S., JR.
Judge. **PERSONAL:** Born Jul 03, 1926, Kansas City, MO; married Mamie F Currie; children: Leonard, III, Kevin, Stefan, Shawn, Amy. **EDUCATION:** AB LLB 1952; Washburn U, MJ 1952. **CAREER:** State MO, magistrate judge. **MILITARY SERVICE:** USN WW II. **BUSINESS ADDRESS:** Municipal Court, 2519 Tracy St, Kansas City, MO 64108.

HUGHES, MAMIE F.
City official. **PERSONAL:** Born May 03, 1929, Jacksonville, FL; married Judge Leonard; children: Leonard, III, Kevin, Stefan, Patrick, Amy. **EDUCATION:** Fisk U, BA;Univ MO 1950-51. **CAREER:** Kansas City, tchr 1951-52, 1957-62; Greenville, tchr 1954-56; Fed Agency Reg Dir for Action 1985; Head Start, vol 1968-69; St Joseph Cath Sch, vol tchr 1962-63; Carver Neighborhood Center, mem adv commn 1985. **ORGANIZATIONS:** Cath Interracial Council 1959-63; former bd mem, HPEED 1965-66; foundling com Vol Serv Bur; bd mem United Campaign Vol 1964-68; vol Martin Luther King Jr HS; Greater KS Coordinating Com Intl Women's Yr; Jackson Co Child Welfare Adv Com; Panel Am Women; 1st v chmn Mid-Am Regional Council BdGovs; chmn Commn Aging; chairperson Fed Exec Bd; past chmn Health & Welfare Com; mem KC MO Fair Housing Commn; vol parent 1965-66; foster Parent 1966-67; St Joseph Sch PTA; pres Greater KC Minority Women's Coalition Human Rights; recording sec Greater KC Hearing & Speech Center; bd mem Truman Med-Center; Parker Sq Housing Corp; Lincoln Black Archives; KC Crime Commn; YMCA Urban Svcs; Manpower Adv Mem Nat Council Negro Women; NAACP; Jack & Jill Am Inc; Greater KC Links Inc Serv Urban Youth De LaSalle Educ Center; Beautiful Activists Vol Serv Woolf Bros & Germaine Monteil. **HONORS/ACHIEVEMENTS:** Comm Serv Award; Serv Award NAACP Freedom Fund Dinner Com. **BUSINESS ADDRESS:** Jackson Co Courthouse, 415 E 12 St, Kansas City, MO 64106.

HUGHES, ROBERTA V.
Attorney, educator. **PERSONAL:** Born in Detroit, MI; daughter of Dr & Mrs Robert Greenidge; married Wilbur B (deceased); children: Barbara, Wilbur B. **EDUCATION:** Univ of MI, PhD 1973; Wayne State Univ Law Sch, JD; Wayne State U, MEd. **CAREER:** Detroit Pub Sch, past sch social worker; Detroit Comm on Children & Youth, past dir; Shaw Coll, past vice pres for Academic Affairs; County Public Admin, practicing lawyer Michigan Courts & admitted to practice bar, District of Columbia and Supreme Court of USA; Lawrence, former prof; First Independence Nat Bank, inst organizer & dir. **ORGANIZATIONS:** Mem Am Bar Assn; mem MI Bar Assn; past mem Am & MI Trial Lawyers Assn; mem Oakland Co Bar Assn; mem Detroit Bar Assn; Wayne State Univ Law Alumni; Univ of MI Alumni Assn; AKA Sorority; life mem NAACP; mem Renaissance Club; million dollar mem Museum of African American History. **HONORS/ACHIEVEMENTS:** Recipient NAACP Freedom Award; MI Chronicle Newspaper Cit of Yr; Harriet Tubman Award; Alpha Kappa Alpha Sorority Recognition Award; Quality Quintet Award Detroit Skyliner Mag. **BUSINESS ADDRESS:** 29777 Telegraph Rd #2500, Southfield, MI 48034.

HUGHES, WILBUR B.
Business executive. **PERSONAL:** Born Mar 14, 1919, East Orange, NJ; married Roberta Greenidge; children: Barbara Allen, Wilbur. **EDUCATION:** Detroit Inst of Technology, BA. **CAREER:** Detroit Mem Pk, bd mem, general mgr 1985; Hughes Rlty & Reliable Brokers Inc, broker-owner; Community Assn Inc, pres; FHA Victory Loan Co, appraiser, vice pres, dir; Great Lakes Agency Co, pres. **ORGANIZATIONS:** Chmn State of MI Cemetery Commn; charter mem Fdr Det Cotillion Club; mem Grad Chap Alpha Frat; life mem NAACP; mem Det Chap Nat Guardsmen Inc. **HONORS/ACHIEVEMENTS:** Football Schlrshp BA Det Inst of Tech; Football & Track Letters Wayne State U. **MILITARY SERVICE:** AAF. **BUSINESS ADDRESS:** 4280 E 13 Mile, Warren, MI 48092.

HULETT, ROSEMARY D.
Educational administrator. **PERSONAL:** Born Sep 17, 1954, Chicago, IL; married Melvin D Hulett. **EDUCATION:** Chicago State Univ, BSEd 1975; MSEd 1980. **CAREER:** Archdiocese of Chicago Cath Sch Bd, head teacher 1975-77, headstart dir 1977-78; Chicago Bd of Educ, Special Educ teacher 1978-80; Chicago State Univ, dir of alumni affairs 1980-. **ORGANIZATIONS:** Mem River Oaks Coop Towne House Mem Comm; mem River Oaks Coop Towne House Finance Comm; mem Natl Assoc for the Educ of Young Children 1975-77; mem Council for Exceptional Educ 1978-79; exec secty/treas Chicago State Univ Alumni Assn 1980-; chmn CASE V Career Advancement for Women and Minorities Comm 1985-88;

bd mem Case V Bd of Dir 1987-89. **HONORS/ACHIEVEMENTS:** Teacher of the Year Award Natl Assoc for the Educ of Young Children 1976; Special Educ Teaching Certificate Chicago Bd of Educ 1979; Certificate of Recognition for Alumni Admin Council for the Advancement of Secondary Educ 1980; Outstanding Young Professional Award Chicago Coalition of Urban Professional 1986. **BUSINESS ADDRESS:** Dir of Alumni Affairs, Chicago State University, 95th St at King Dr, Chicago, IL 60628.

HULL, BERNARD S.
Research mechanical engineer. **PERSONAL:** Born Aug 01, 1929, Wetipquin, MD; married Marion Hayes; children: Karla L, Bernard S. **EDUCATION:** Howard U, BS 1951; Univ MD, grad credits mech engr. **CAREER:** Tamarach Triangle Civic Assoc, exec bd; White Oak Fed Credit Union, vice pres 1972-77; Naval Mat Command Wash DC, corp planning div hdqrs 1985; Naval SurfWeapons Ctr White Oaks MD, coll rela rep; Naval Suf Weapons Ctr Silver Spring MD, research mech engr adv planning staff. **ORGANIZATIONS:** Life mem NAACP. **HONORS/ACHIEVEMENTS:** Distinguished Able Toastmaster Award 1974. **MILITARY SERVICE:** AUS e-5. **BUSINESS ADDRESS:** Research Engineer, Naval Surface Weapon Center, White Oak, Silver Spring, MD 20904.

HULL, ELLIS L., SR.
Contractor. **PERSONAL:** Born Jun 04, 1928, Steele, MO; married Ollie Mae Hull; children: Ellis, Jr, Leroy, Carmella, Juan, Shango. **EDUCATION:** Andrews Univ Theology. **CAREER:** Anning & Johnson, 1952-64; H & H Constrn, 1964-; The Shoe Hull, owner; Williams & Hull Bonding Co, owner; Liberty Theatre, owner; Shango's Galley, owner; Pilgrim Rest Bapt Ch, asso minister. **ORGANIZATIONS:** Pres Benton Harbor-Benton Township Minority Contractors Assn; Urban Renewal Bd; Benton Harbor Schs Adv Bd; Deferred Prosecution Adv Bd; Berrien Co Rept Party Exec Bd; Bd to re-elect Gov Milliken; NAACP; co-chmn Benton Harbor-Benton Township Adv Bd. **HONORS/ACHIEVEMENTS:** Who's Who in MI 1974; Contractor of Yr 1973. **MILITARY SERVICE:** USN stm. **BUSINESS ADDRESS:** 172 E Main St, Benton Harbor, MI 49022.

HULL, EVERSON WARREN
Government official. **PERSONAL:** Born Oct 14, 1943, Nevis; married Melverlynn Surilina Spears; children: Randolph E, Cecilia A. **EDUCATION:** Howard Univ, BA 1970, PhD 1977; Univ of MD, MA 1974. **CAREER:** Federal Natl Mort Assoc, economist 1973-76; The Amer Petroleum Inst, sr economist 1976-78; TRW Inc, sr economist 1978-79; Congressional Rsch Svcs, head money/banking quantitative economics 1979-83; US Dept of Labor, deputy asst sec for policy 1983-. **BUSINESS ADDRESS:** Deputy Asst Sec for Policy, US Dept of Labor, 200 Constitution Ave NW, Washington, DC 20210.

HULL, GEORGE, JR.
Educator. **PERSONAL:** Born Sep 30, 1922, Indianola, MS; married Jewell; children: George Ronald, Sharon Elaine. **EDUCATION:** Alcorn A&M Coll, BS 1945; TN State Univ, MS 1949; OH State Univ, PhD 1957. **CAREER:** TN State Univ, chmn lower div of biology coord grad studies & rsch natl sci 1949-64; Grambling Coll, prof & head of dept of biological sci 1964-66; Fisk Univ, prof & chmn dept of biology/dir div natural sci & math 1966-. **ORGANIZATIONS:** Regional dir Natl Inst of Sci 1973-74; regional vice pres Beta Kappa Chi 1975; pres Fisk-Meharry-TN State Sigma Xi Club 1960-61; mem Sigma Xi; FrontiersIntl; Nashville Club pres 1973-75. **MILITARY SERVICE:** USN 1944-46. **BUSINESS ADDRESS:** Chmn Dept of Biology, Fisk University, Dept of Biology, Nashville, TN 37203.

HULL, GLORIA T.
Educator, writer. **PERSONAL:** Born in Shreveport, LA; children: Adrian. **EDUCATION:** So Univ, BA summa cum laude 1966; Purdue Univ, MA, PhD 1968, 1972. **CAREER:** Univ of Delaware, prof of English 1972-. **ORGANIZATIONS:** Co-project dir Black Women's Studies project 1982-84; Mellon Scholar Wellesley Ctr for Rsch on Women 1983; Fulbright Senior Lectureship Univ of the WestIndies-Jamaica 1984-86; mbr, commission co-chair Modern Language Assn; mem Natl Women's Studies Assn; advisor/consultant Black American Literature Forum, Feminist studies. **HONORS/ACHIEVEMENTS:** Fellowship Rockefeller Foundation 1979-80; Outstanding Woman of Color Natl Institute of Women of Color 1982; Books, "All the Women are White, All the Blacks are Men, but some of us are Brave," Black Women's Studies 1982; "Give Us Each Day, The Diary of Alice Dunbar," Nelson 1984. **BUSINESS ADDRESS:** Professor, Univ of Delaware, Dept of English, Newark, DE 19716.

HUMBER, TONI CHERYL
Educator. **PERSONAL:** Born Jan 06, 1946, Los Angeles, CA. **EDUCATION:** CA State Univ at Los Angeles, BA 1967; Loyola Marymount Univ, MEd 1975. **CAREER:** Los Angeles Unified Sch Dist, 2nd grade teacher 1968-72; LAUSD Non-Public Schools, math spec 1972-78, instruct advisor 1978-79; LAUSD English Prog for Black Learner, instruct advisor 1978-. **ORGANIZATIONS:** Consultant/lecturer Historical Contributions of Africans and African Amers to the World; mem Amenta and Southern Cradle Historical Organizations 1980-; founder Nubian Genius Historical Organization 1985-; co-chairperson Black History Month in Los Angeles 1987; mem Alpha Kappa Alpha Sor; extensive travel in Africa. **HONORS/ACHIEVEMENTS:** Outstanding Educator Community and Parents United for Children 1984; Outstanding Educator Images Unlimited 1985. **BUSINESS ADDRESS:** Instructional Advisor, LAUSD, 1320 W 3rd St, Los Angeles, CA 90017.

HUMES, EMANUEL I., SR.
Business executive. **PERSONAL:** Born Jan 12, 1928, Miami; married Lillie. **CAREER:** Menelek Construction Co Inc, chmn bd dir; Bethlehem Steel Corp, sub-foreman 1950-70; Niagra Frontier Housing Development, field supt; BAW Construction Co; supt & coordntr; Urban Systems Housing Co, mgr; Church of God of Prophecy, minister 1950-70; E I Humes Cleaning & Janitorial Serv 1971-; Manlil Mgmt Corp 1973-; Humall Enterprieses; E I Humes Construction 1971-; Ch of God of Prophecy, SS sput 1974. **ORGANIZATIONS:** Mem Greater Jefferson Businessmen's Assn; life mem NAACP. **HONORS/ACHIEVEMENTS:** Recipient achievement award Black Enterpise Mag; Top 100 1974; Natl Defense Service Medal. **MILITARY SERVICE:** AUS medical corp corpl 1953-55. **BUSINESS ADDRESS:** 302 Kensington Ave, Buffalo, NY.

HUMPHREY, ARTHUR
Bank executive. **CAREER:** First Bank National Assn, Cleveland, OH, chief exec. **BUSINESS ADDRESS:** First Bank National Assn, Terminal Tower, Cleveland, OH 44113. *

HUMPHREY, CLAUDE B.
Professional football player. **PERSONAL:** Born Jun 29, 1944, Memphis, TN; married Sandra K Harrell; children: Chandra Cheyenne, Claudia O'Lynn, Candice Cherokee. **EDUCATION:** TN State Univ, grad 1968. **CAREER:** Atlanta Falcons, player 1968-79; Philadelphia Eagles, player 1979-. **HONORS/ACHIEVEMENTS:** Played 1968 Sr Bowl Blue-Gray Game, Coaches All Amer Game, Coll All Star Game. **BUSINESS ADDRESS:** c/o Philadelphia Eagles, Pattison & Broad, Philadelphia, PA 19145.

HUMPHREY, HOWARD JOHN
Engineer. **PERSONAL:** Born Nov 05, 1940; son of Easton Humphrey; married Bernadette Barker; children: Hayden, Lynette. **EDUCATION:** NYU, BE 1969; Univ of MI, Am Elec Pwr Spons Mgmt Training Prgm 1976. **CAREER:** Am Elec Pwr Serv Corp, group mgr civil engineering div 1988-, mgr materials handling div 1983-88, section head in materials handling div, asst section head, sr engr, engr, assoc engr, engr tech 1967-; Cl Frd Power Plant Solid Waste Disposal, specialist. **ORGANIZATIONS:** Reg Professional Engr NJ, OH & WV; Am Soc of Civ Engr. **HONORS/ACHIEVEMENTS:** 1st Black Dept Head Amer Elec Power Serv Corp. **BUSINESS ADDRESS:** Group Mgr, Civil Engineering Div, American Electric Power Serv, One Riverside Plaza, Columbus, OH 43216.

HUMPHREY, HUBERT GRANT
Physician. **PERSONAL:** Born May 02, 1910, Westfield, NJ; married Juanita Thomas. **EDUCATION:** Howard Univ, BS 1931, MD 1935; Freedmens Hosp, Intrnshp 1935-36; Post Graduate Studies, Sefow Hall Univ, Harlem Hosp, Cornell Univ. **CAREER:** St Lukes Meth Church, chrmn of bd 1940-70; Bd of Hlth Scotch Plains, mem & vice pres 1951-72; Westfield Med Scty, pres 1958; Howard Univ Med Alumni Assn, pres 1966-68; NJ State Bd of Med Exmnrs, mem 1972-74; Westfield Comm Ctr, pres of bd. **ORGANIZATIONS:** Stf Muhlenberg Hosp Plainfield NJ 1941-85; past pres mem NJ Chap Natl Guardsman 1958-; mem Westfield Rotary Clb 1974-85; assco dir Franklin State Bank 1981-85; life mem NAACP, Omega Psi Phi Frat; mem Union Cnty Med Scty, Natl Med Scty, AMA, Westfield Med Scty, NJ Coll Observ & Gyn, PlainfieldMed Scty; mem HM Club of Amer 1985-. **HONORS/ACHIEVEMENTS:** The Gun African Safari Kenya, Uganda, Tanzania hunted "the big FIVE" Vide 1968; Ebony Mag 1969; MD Mag Coverage.

HUMPHREY, JAMES PHILIP
Elected official, public relations manager. **PERSONAL:** Born Jun 01, 1921, Sidney, OH; married Anna L Lloyd; children: Rebecca Breaston, Patricia Sheffield, Mary Weston, Janice Gaudy, James L, Helen Richard. **EDUCATION:** Morris Brown Coll, 1939-42; Cental States Coll of Physiatrics, DM. **CAREER:** Sidney Machine Tool Co, blueprint-dark room tech 1950-57, matl control mgr 1958-78, purchasing mgr 1979-84; Amos Press Inc, community relations dir 1984-. **ORGANIZATIONS:** Mayor-councilman City of Sidney 1975-; pres Lima Dist Church School & BTU Inst; adv bd Upper Valley Joint Vocational School of Practical Nursing; mem Sidney-Shelby Cty Chamber of Commerce, Kiwanis Club; chmn NAACP; mem Natl Conf of Black Mayors, Kappa Alpha Psi; mayor-councilman City of Signey 1975; deacon Mt Vernon Baptist Church; pres Ohio Tri-County NAACP. **HONORS/ACHIEVEMENTS:** Outstanding Serv NAACP OH Conf of Branches 1982; Cert of Apprec Southern Christian Leadership Conf 1984, Spec Olympics Prog 1984; Soft Cover for Booklet Martin Luther King Gallery Exhibits; Establishment of 6 Annual James P Humphrey Scholarships for Black Achievers. **MILITARY SERVICE:** AUS Med Corps sgt tech 3 1/2 yrs; Philappine Liberation Ribbon w/1 Bronze Star, Asiatic Pacific Theater Ribbon w/2 Bronze Serv Stars, Meritor Unit Awd. **HOME ADDRESS:** 1861 Fair Oaks Dr, Sidney, OH 45365. **BUSINESS ADDRESS:** Community Relations Dir, Amos Press, Inc, 911 Vandemark Road, Sidney, OH 45367.

HUMPHREY, KATHRYN BRITT
Educator. **PERSONAL:** Born Jan 24, 1923, Champaign, IL; widowed. **EDUCATION:** Parkland Jr Coll &Univ of IL, Attend. **CAREER:** Coll of Vet Medicine, Univ of IL, histologist, natural science lab asst 1985; Douglass Pk, jr youth dir 1941-46; Serv Men Center, Lawhead School, asst dir 1943-44. **ORGANIZATIONS:** Mem, bd ed Champaign Comm Sch Dist 1970-77; mem, bd dir Urban Leag & Opport Indstrlztn Ctr; mem Cntrl Reg Black Caucus of Sch Bd; mem Nat Black Caucuses of Sch bd mem Eyevett's Civic & Soc Sor Club, Chicago Hts IL; statistician Women's Conv of Bapt, Gen St Conv of IL; sec to bd trustees Mt Olive Bapt Ch; pres Gamma Upsilon Psi Soc; pres Women's Mission & Ed Conv of Cntrl Dist Assn; YWCA,Univ of IL; Affirm Act Equal Opport Comm,Univ of IL, Coll of Vet Med. **HONORS/ACHIEVEMENTS:** Recip Srv Award, Urban Leag, 5 Yr Pin; Srv Award, Young People's Dept of Cntrl Dist Assn; Srv Award, Bapt Gen St Conv of IL Young People's Dept 25 Yrs. **BUSINESS ADDRESS:** Coll of Vet Med Univ of IL, Urbana, IL 61801.

HUMPHREY, MARGO
Educator. **PERSONAL:** Born 1942, Oakland, CA. **EDUCATION:** CA St U, 1971; Stanford U, 1972-74. **CAREER:** Univ of CA, asst prof of art 1985; Stanford Univ, teaching asst 1972-74; Golden State Mutual Life Insurance Co, purchase 1968. **HONORS/ACHIEVEMENTS:** Num exhbns, colctns oakland mus, u art mus, golden st mut life ins co, lytton svngs & loan assn, san francisco art commn, mus of contmpry Art, Ctr of Visual Arts Gallery; Berkeley Post Nwspr Award 1966; Oakland Mus Purchase Award 1968; San Francisco Art Fest 1971; Bay Area Reg Graphics Exhbn 1972;City of San Francisco Spl Award Commn 1972-74; publ =Black Artists on Art" 1969; "CA Printmakers" 1973; full flw StanfordUniv 1971-74;Univ NM Whitney Mus of Am Art 1973; exhbtns The Black Artist/Recent Attitudes, CA StUniv Fresno 1974; exhbtn Black Graphics the Black Experience in Am Wstrn Assn of Art Mus1974-75; San Francisco Art Commn Prints, The Fine Arts Mus of SF Achenbach Found for Graphic Arts 1974; Mixed Media on Paper/Thirty E Bay Women Artists, Berkely Art Ctr CA 1978; impression/expressions; Black Am Graphics Studo & Mus Harlem NY HowardUniv Wash DC 1979; British Interntl Print Binealle, Cartwright Hall Lister Pk Bradford Eng 1979; "Eight" The Inst of Contmpry Art of the VA Mus Richmond 1980; The 1970's prints & drawings of afro-Ams, mus of the ctr of afro-Am artists inc boston 1980; recip post doctoral flwshp, ford found 1980-81.

HUMPHREY, MARIAN J.
Bank executive. **CAREER:** Medical Center State Bank, Oklahoma City, OK, chief exec. **BUSINESS ADDRESS:** Chief Executive, Medical Center State Bank, 1300 North Lottie, Oklahoma City, OK 73117. *

HUMPHREY, MELVIN
Public administrator, author. **PERSONAL:** Born Jan 02, 1921, St Louis; married Lois Bobbitt; children: Melvin Jr, Janice H. **EDUCATION:** Univ IL, BS 1948, MA 1950; PhD 1955. **CAREER:** US Dept of HUD, acting dir, dep dir; Hampton Inst, dir; STOP Norfolk, exec dir; CANDO Baltimore, exec dir Morgan St Coll, asso prof; Equal Empl Opport Commn US, dir resrch 1985. **HONORS/ACHIEVEMENTS:** Co-author Prin of Acting, Prin of Ec, Pub Fin, Pitman Book Co; author blk experience vs blk expectations EEOC 1977; case inst tech fellow 1958; Maury HS Outstndng Man of Yr 1966. **MILITARY SERVICE:** USAAF s/sgt 1942-45.

HUMPHREY, SONNIE
Executive assistant. **PERSONAL:** Born in Rocky Mount, NC; daughter of Frank Humphrey and Eva M McCullum Humphrey. **EDUCATION:** Hunter Coll, New York NY, BA, 1976. **CAREER:** Kaye Scholer, New York NY, 1967-. **ORGANIZATIONS:** Bd mem, YGB Leadership Training, 1971-; reporter, Hunter Coll News, 1974-76; coord, Luncheon/Fashion Event, 1980-89; award coord, Natl Coalition of 100 Black Women Candace Awards, 1982-89; talent coord, Motown Returns to Apollo; mem, UNCF Auxiliary Comm, 1984-; vice pres, New York Coalition of 100 Black Women, 1986-; pres, Zeta Delta Phi Sorority, 1987-; special events coord, UNCF Michael Jackson Benefit, 1988. **HONORS/ACHIEVEMENTS:** Outstanding Service, Zeta Delta Phi Sorority, 1974, 1977 1986; Service To Youth Award, Kennedy Community Center, 1975, 1978; poems, "Black Women," 1977, "Young, Gifted and Black," 1980; Arts Bulletin Editor, 1981; Outstanding Young Women, 1982; Achievement Award, New York Coalition of 100 Black Women, 1984; Community Service, Joseph P Kennedy Community Center, 1985; Souvenir Journal Editor. 1985-88; Sorority Manual, 1988; Editor-Newsletter, Zeta Delta Phi Sorority, current.

HUMPHRIES, CHARLES, JR.
Obstetrics/gynecology. **PERSONAL:** Born Apr 14, 1943, Dawson, GA; married Monica Tulio; children: Charlie Christopher. **EDUCATION:** Fisk Univ, BA 1966; Meharry Medical Coll, MD 1972. **CAREER:** Charlie Humphries Jr MD PC, president. **ORGANIZATIONS:** Mem Omega Psi Phi Frat, Dougherty Co Medical Soc, GA State Medical Assoc, Medical Assoc of GA; asst treas GA State Affiliate of Univ of IL 1972-73; alternate delegate to MAG Legislation Seesion; mem Southwest GA Black Hlth Care Providers. **MILITARY SERVICE:** USN lcdr 1976-78. **BUSINESS ADDRESS:** President, Charlie Humphries Jr MD PC, 907 N Jefferson St, Albany, GA 31701.

HUMPHRIES, FREDERICK S.
University president. **PERSONAL:** Born Dec 26, 1935, Apalachicola, FL; son of Thornton Humphries, Sr and Minnie Henry Humphries; married Antoinette McTurner, Aug 20, 1960; children: Frederick S, Jr, Robin Tanya, Laurence Anthony. **EDUCATION:** Florida A & M University, Tallahassee FL, BS (magna cum laude), 1957; University of Pittsburgh, Pittsburgh PA, PhD, 1964. **CAREER:** Private tutor of science and mathematics, 1959-64; Florida A & M University, Tallahassee FL, associate professor, 1964-66, University of Minnesota, assistant professor of chemistry, 1966-67; Florida A & M University, professor of chemistry, 1968-74, program director of thirteen-college curriculum program, 1967-68; Institute for Services to Education, Washington DC, program director of summer conference and thirteen-college curriculum program, 1968-74, three-universities graduate program in humanities, 1970-74, innovative institutional research consortium, 1972-73, study of science capability of black colleges, 1972-74, interdisciplinary program, 1973-74, and two-universities graduate program in science, 1973-74; Tennessee State University, Nashville TN, president, 1974-85; Florida A & M University, president, 1985—; consultant to numerous educational, social, and scientific organizations and commissions. **ORGANIZATIONS:** American Assn of Higher Education; American Assn for Advance of Science; American Assn of University Professors; American Chemical Society; American Assn of Minority Research Universities; NAACP; board of directors, American Cancer Society; board of directors, YMCA, 1987; MIT Visiting committee, 1982; Joint Committee on Agricultural Development, 1982; chairman, Advisory Committee of the Office of the Advancement of Public Negro College, 1982; secretary, American Council on Education, 1978; International Platform Association; National Merit Scholarship Corp. **HONORS/ACHIEVEMENTS:** Frederick S Humphries Day, City of Indianapolis, 1975; Outstanding Citizen of the Year Award, Nashville chapter Omega Psi Phi, 1976; certificate of appreciation, Governor of TN, 1982; certificate of appreciation, Dept of Health and Human Services, 1983; leadership grant, Prudential Life Insurance Co Foundation, 1988; Centennial Medallion, Florida A & M University; University Bicentennial Medal of Distinction and distinguished alumnus award, University of Pittsburgh; numerous service awards from civic and university groups. **MILITARY SERVICE:** US Army Security Agency, officer, 1957-59. **BUSINESS ADDRESS:** Office of the President, Florida A & M University, 302 Foote-Hilyer Administration Center, Tallahassee, FL 32307.

HUMPHRIES, JAY LAVELLE
Professional athlete. **PERSONAL:** Born Oct 17, 1962, Los Angeles, CA; married Carla Blair. **EDUCATION:** Colorado, 1980-84. **CAREER:** Phoenix Suns, guard 1984-. **HONORS/ACHIEVEMENTS:** Big Eight All-Conf Team; Honorable Mention All-Am & Big Eight All-Defensive Team; Big Eight's All-Freshman team. **BUSINESS ADDRESS:** Phoenix Suns, P O Box 1369, Ste 510, Phoenix, AZ 85001.

HUNIGAN, EARL
Personnel specialist. **PERSONAL:** Born Jul 29, 1929, Omaha; married Lazell Phillips; children: Kirk, Kris. **EDUCATION:** Univ MI, BBA 1952. **CAREER:** Civil Serv Comm, invstgtr 1956-60, prsnl splst 1962-63; USAF, mgmt analyst 1960-62; FAA, pers splst 1963-68; USCG, pers splst 1968-69; Dept Transp, spl asst, asst sec admin 1969-71; S Region FAA, exec ofcr 1971-73; Food & Nutrution Serv USDA, dept admin mgmt 1973-78; Smithsonian Inst, dir of prsnl training 1985; E&L Assoc, mgmt cons. **ORGANIZATIONS:** Alpha Phi Alpha; NAACP; Urban Leag Phalanx; Am Soc Pub Admin. **HONORS/ACHIEVEMENTS:** Sustained Superior Perf 1957-58, 1961, 1971; Quality Step Increase 1968; Spec Act 1963-73; Distngshd Military Instr Award 1969-71. **MILITARY SERVICE:** AUS Res col 1955-. **BUSINESS ADDRESS:** Management Consultant, E&L Associates, 409 Troon Circle, Fort Washington, MD 20744.

HUNN, DOROTHY FEGAN
Nursing administrator. **PERSONAL:** Born Sep 01, 1928, Chandler, OK; married Myron Vernon Hunn Sr DDS; children: Myron Vernon, Jonathan Scott, William Bruce. **EDUCATION:** Memorial Hosp School of Nursing, RN 1952; Compton Comm Coll, AA 1969; CSU Dominguez Hills, BA 1976; Pepperdine Univ, MPA 1977; CSU Long Beach, PhN 1984, postgrad 1982-84. **CAREER:** Kaiser Found Hosp, asst dir of nurses 1965-72; Martin Luther King Jr Hosp, asst dir of nurses 1973-77; Los Angeles Comm Coll Dist, nursing instr 1978-81; LAC/MC Sch of Nursing, nursing instr 1981-84; Watts Health Center, dir of nurses 1985-; Watts Health Found Inc Maxicare Medical Center, dir of nurses. **ORGANIZATIONS:** Mem Alpha Kappa Alpha Sor, Phi Delta Kappa Sor, Natl Assn of Univ Women; positions Auxillary to the Angel City Dental Soc, JUGS Civic/Community Club, Guidance Ch of Religious Science, The Links. **HOME ADDRESS:** 820 Clemmer Dr, Compton, CA 90221.

HUNN, MYRON VERNON
Dentist. **PERSONAL:** Born Aug 09, 1926, Sequndo, CO; married Dorothy Louise; children: Myron Jr, Jonathan, William. **EDUCATION:** LA State Coll, BA 1954; Howard Univ, DDS 1958. **CAREER:** Private Practice, dentist. **ORGANIZATIONS:** Mem Natl Dental Assn, Amer Dental Assn; bd dirs YMCA 1970-73; personnel bd City of Compton 1967-70; mem Comm Redev Agency; Compton Optimist Club 1967-; pres trustee bd United Meth Ch 1970-73; C of C 1964-71. **MILITARY SERVICE:** AUS 1951-54. **BUSINESS ADDRESS:** 1315 N Bullis Rd #4, Compton, CA 90221.

HUNT, BARBARA ANN
Educator. **PERSONAL:** Born Jul 26, 1931, Aberdeen, MS; divorced. **EDUCATION:** Bennett Coll Greensboro NC, BA 1948-52; Syracuse U, MSLS 1952-54; MSUniv for Women, MA 1969-73;Univ of IL, CAS 1971-73. **CAREER:** MS Univ for Women, dir curr lab 1977-; AL A&M Univ Huntsville, asst prof 1974-77; Bennett Coll Greensboro, head librn 1967-73; Dist 65 Evanston IL, librn cataloger 1961-66; Morgan State Coll, Baltimore MD, asst librn 1955-57; Rust Coll Holly Springs MS, head librn, assoc prof 1954-55; AL A&M Univ, acting dean 1975-76; S Assn of Coll & Schools, consult 1968. **ORGANIZATIONS:** Mem bd of dir Wesley Found MSUniv for Women 1979-; mem bd of trustees Millsaps Coll Jackson MS 1979-; coord Wesley Found St James Meth 1979-; cert lay asso United Meth Ch; co-chrprsn Local United Negro Coll Fund 1978. **HONORS/ACHIEVEMENTS:** Cerf Lib Admin Dev ProgUniv of MD Coll Pk; Janet Green Flwshp, NrthwstrnUniv 1980; Minority Flwshp St of MS 1979-; Ford Found & Flwshp 1970-73; Minority GrantUniv of IL 1972; cadetship SyracuseUniv NY 1952-54. **BUSINESS ADDRESS:** MSUniv for Women, Columbus, MS 39701.

HUNT, BETTY SYBLE
Elected official. **PERSONAL:** Born Mar 13, 1919, Forest, MS; married IP Hunt; children: Irvin D, Vera H Jennings, Garland H, Vernon. **EDUCATION:** Scott Co Training Sch, diploma 1935; Jackson State Univ, BS 1964; Univ of MS, Reading 1969; MS College, Communication 1979. **CAREER:** Jackson State Bookstore, asst Mgr 1950-65; Canton Public Schools, teacher 1968-73; Packard Elec, assembler 1973-85; Hinds Co MS, election commissioner. **ORGANIZATIONS:** Founder JSU Campus Ministry for Methodist Students 1957; chairperson United Givers Fund 1968-69; mem Election Comm Assoc of MS 1980; mem 100 Black Women Coalition 1982; delegate Co Democratic Convention 1984; re-elected Hinds Co Election Commissioner 1984; pres Women for Progress of MS Inc 1983-85; pres MS Chap Natl Coalition 100 Black Women. **HONORS/ACHIEVEMENTS:** Certificate March of Dimes 1968; community excellence General Motors 1974; awd pin United Methodist Women 1984; certificate Three Quarter Way House 1984. **HOME ADDRESS:** 1918 Dalton St, Jackson, MS 39204.

HUNT, EUGENE
Banker. **PERSONAL:** Born Jul 19, 1948, Augusta, GA; son of Alfred Hunt, Sr and Mabel Williams Hunt; divorced; children: Brian Eugene. **EDUCATION:** Augusta Coll, BBA 1971; Augusta Coll, post-baccalaureate study 1978-79. **CAREER:** Citizen & So Natl Bank, mgr 1975, dir 1976, asst banking officer 1977, banking officer & branch mgr 1980-; asst vice pres in charge of Govt Banking Div, 1984. **ORGANIZATIONS:** Treasurer, Good Shepherd Baptist Church Inc, 1971-; sec, Central Savannah River Area Business League, 1976; pres, Central Savannah River Area Business League, 1979; mem, tech advisory bd Opportunity Indus Center, 1977-80; bd of dirs, Augusta Sickle Cell Center, 1977; loan exec, Natl Alliance of Businessmen, 1979-80; mem, Governor's Educ Review Commn, 1983-84; present vice chmn, Georgia Dept of Technical & Adult Educ, 1985-. **HONORS/ACHIEVEMENTS:** Serv Award Natl Alliance of Businessmen 1977; Serv Award Good Shepherd Baptist Church Inc 1978; Appreciation Award Central Savannah River Area Youth Employment Opportunity Inc 1979; Businessman of the Year, Augusta Black Historical Soc, 1983; Businessman of the Year, Augusta Chapter Delta Sigma Theata, 1984. **BUSINESS ADDRESS:** Asst Vice Pres,, Citizen & Southern Natl Bank, PO Box 912, Augusta, GA 30903.

HUNT, ISAAC COSBY, JR.
Educational administrator, attorney. **PERSONAL:** Born Aug 01, 1937, Danville, VA; married Elizabeth Raucnell; children: Isaac III. **EDUCATION:** Fisk Univ, BA 1957; Univ of VA Law Schl, LLB 1962. **CAREER:** Securities & Exchange Comm, sttaf atty 1962-67; Natl Adv Comm on Civil Disordrs, fld team leader 1967-68; RAND Corp, rsch sttaf 1968-71; Catholic Univ of Amer, asst prof of Law 1971-77; Jones Day Renvis of Pogue, assoc 1977-79; Dept of Army, principal deputy general counsel 1979-81; Antioch School of Law, dean. **ORGANIZATIONS:** Visiting lectr Bryn Mawr Coll 1970-77; co-chair Dist of Columbia Consmr Goods Bd 1974-76; bd of Govnrs Scty of Am Law Tchrs 1976-79; troop comm mem Boy Scouts of Am Trp 52 1982-; bd of trust 1985-, chair 1987- Sasha Bruce Youthwork Inc. **HONORS/ACHIEVEMENTS:** Moderator Aspen Inst for Humanstc Stds 1973; Outstndng Civilian Serv Awrd Dept of the Army 1981. **BUSINESS ADDRESS:** Dean, Antioch Schl Of Law, 2633 16th St N W, Washington, DC 20009.

HUNT, JAMES, JR.
Business executive. **PERSONAL:** Born Oct 07, 1944, Hancock Co, GA. **EDUCATION:** BS 1968. **CAREER:** Baldwin Co Bd of Educ, teacher 1968-70; E Cntrl Com Opportunity, deputy dir, vice pres 1985. **ORGANIZATIONS:** Chmn Hancock Bd Ed; acting dir Ogeechees Lakeview Mgmt Co Inc; mem Hancock Co Chap Black Elected Officials; Dem Club. **HONORS/ACHIEVEMENTS:** Alumni Award, Kappa Alpha Psi 1971. **BUSINESS ADDRESS:** Central Adminstrn Bldg, Mayfield, GA.

HUNT, MAURICE
Educator. **PERSONAL:** Born Dec 16, 1943, Birmingham, AL; son of Percy Benjamin Hunt Sr and Ora Lee Lawson Hunt; married Mary Elizabeth Sain, Aug 06, 1966; children: Michael Phillip. **EDUCATION:** Washington H S East Chicago, IN, Diploma 1962; Kentucky State Coll, BS 1967; Iowa Univ, 1970-71; Drake Univ, MSE 1975. **CAREER:** Good Shepard H S, coach 1965-66; Glen Park Ambridge Elem Schools, instructor 1967-69, Tolleston H S, instructor/coach 1967-69; Grinnell Coll, instructor/coach 1969-77; Central State Univ, asst prof/coach 1977-79; Morehouse Coll, instructor/coach 1979-. **ORGANIZATIONS:** Mem Grinnell, IA Youth Comm 1969-71, Amer Football Coaches Assn 1970-; past mem Wrestling Fed 1970-73; mem Iowa Lions Club 1972-77; past mem Drake Relays Comm 1973-77; mem Iowa Human Rights Comm 1976-77; rater NAIA 1978; Sheridan Black Coll Pollster. **HONORS/ACHIEVEMENTS:** Coach of Year Atlanta Daily World Newspaper, Atlanta Constitution Journal, SIAC, 100 Per Cent Wrng Clb 1979, Atlanta Extra Point Clb 1980-83, 1987-88. **HOME ADDRESS:** 4463 John Wesley Dr, Decatur, GA 30035. **BUSINESS ADDRESS:** Head Football Coach, Morehouse Coll, B T Harvey Stadium, Atlanta, GA 30314.

HUNT, O'NEAL
Judge. **PERSONAL:** Born Jun 27, 1914, Palestine, TX; married Elnora Dorsey; children: Herbert, Jimmy, Norris, Amanda, Alice. **EDUCATION:** TX A&M Univ, Farm Welding 1964, Pasture 1966; Southwest TX State Univ, 1983-84;, Justice of Peace Training 1984-85. **CAREER:** Green Bay Comm Ctr, pres 1967-82; Anderson Cty Courthouse, justice of peace. **ORGANIZATIONS:** Pres Cty Bldg Prog Comm 1962-66. **HONORS/ACHIEVEMENTS:** Diamond Pin in Appreciation Awd Byrd-Frost Serv 1952; Statistician-Cert of Appt The Palestine Dist 1962; Cert of Recog East TX Leadership Forum 1975, And Cty Voters Comm 1975; Notary Public Comm 1982; Family of the Year Negro Bus & Professional Womens Club Inc 1982. **BUSINESS ADDRESS:** Justice Of The Peace, Anderson County Court House, Precinct 2 Place 1, Palestine, TX 75801.

HUNT, PORTIA L.
Counseling psychologist, educator, consultant. **PERSONAL:** Born Feb 12, 1947, East St Louis, IL; daughter of Luches Hunt and Ethel Hunt. **EDUCATION:** Southern IL Univ Edwardsville, BS 1971, MS 1972; Indiana State Univ Terre Haute IN, PhD 1975. **CAREER:** State Comm Coll, counselor 1971-73; Portia Hunt & Assocs, psychologist 1979-; Eclipse Mgmt Consultant Group, pres 1986-; Temple Univ, prof 1975-. **ORGANIZATIONS:** Natl program chair Assoc of Black Psychologists 1979; advisory bd pres Eastern Coll Cushing Counseling Act 101 1980-86; bd mem Church World Inst Temple Univ 1980-86; consultant Osage-Pine Comm Survivors W Philadelphia Consortium 1985-86, Philadelphia Desegration School Dist; Survivors of the "Move" Bombing in Philadelphia & W Philadelphia Consortium Mental Health Center; bd mem ABRAXAS Foundation 1985-; former pres Delaware Valley Assoc Black Psychologists 1976-. **HONORS/ACHIEVEMENTS:** Professional Affairs Serv Award Delaware Valley Assoc of Black Psych 1983; Psychology Award Serv to Black Comm Alliance of Black Social Worker 1985; Psychology Award Delaware Valley Assoc of Black Psychologists 1986; Kathryn Sisson Phillips Fellowship Scholar 1974.

HUNT, RICHARD HOWARD
Sculptor. **PERSONAL:** Born Sep 12, 1935, Chgo; divorced. **EDUCATION:** Art Inst of Chgo, bA 1957; Belli Bar, Studied Sculpture;Univ of Chgo, Undergrad Std 1953-55. **CAREER:** Advant-Grade Sculptures, sculptor, creator; Sch of the Art Inst of Chgo, tchr 1961;Univ of IL Chgo, dept arch & art 1962; vis prof, vis artist at 7 schs including Yale U, Purdueu 1965, NrthwstrnUniv 1968. **ORGANIZATIONS:** Perm coll of art, Mus in Chgo, Cleveland, Houston, NY, Buffalo, Milwaukee, Israel; work was exhibited in Artists of Chicago & Vicinity Exhbtn 1955-56; 62nd, 63rd, 64th Am Exhib of Art Inst of Chgo; Carnegie Intrnat Exhib in Pitts 1958; Mus of Mod New York City 1959; one-man Exhib in NYC, Chgo;participated in exhib Ten Negro Artists from US; First World Fest of Negro Arts, Dakar, Senegal 1966. **HONORS/ACHIEVEMENTS:** Recip 6 Major Awards & Flwshps. **BUSINESS ADDRESS:** 1017 W Lill St, Chicago, IL 60614.

HUNT, ROBERT S.
Executive director. **PERSONAL:** Born Sep 03, 1951, Toledo, OH; married Gay S Dolch; children: Jada, Lanell, Brande, Kaili. **EDUCATION:** Heidelberg Coll Tiffin OH, BS 1974. **CAREER:** NFL, prof football running back 1974-75; Aetna Life & Casualty, safety engr 1975-76; Tiffin YMCA, exec dir 1976-83; Hunt & Associates, marketing consultant. **ORGANIZATIONS:** Lectr on health & nutrition Comm & YMCA NW Dist 1977-; mem public relations com United Way of Tiffin & Seneca Co 1978-79; mem Rotary Intl 1979-. **HONORS/ACHIEVEMENTS:** Nominee Outstanding Young Men of Amer 1980. **BUSINESS ADDRESS:** Marketing Consultant, Hunt & Associates, 60 Autumn, Tiffin, OH 44883.

HUNT, RONALD JOSEPH
Educational administrator. **PERSONAL:** Born Dec 19, 1951, Uniontown, PA; married Karen Elaine Hill; children: Lynnette, Angela. **EDUCATION:** Slippery Rock St Coll, BS Health, Phys Ed 1973, MEd Admin & Curriculum 1975. **CAREER:** Slippery Rock St Coll, asst dir admsns 1979-, temp instr of phys ed 1979, acting coord spec srv 1974, grad asst 1973, asst ftbl coach 1973-77, asst bsktbl coach 1978-79. **ORGANIZATIONS:** Bd of dir Connie Hawkins Bsktbl Incorp 1978-80; bd of dir W Side Comm Act Ctr 1979-80; bd of dir Lawrence County Cncl of Comm Ctrs 1979-80. **HONORS/ACHIEVEMENTS:** Outstndng Athl in Am 1973; Outstndng Man in Comm, Jaycees 1979.

HUNT, SAMUEL D.
Senior relocation specialist. **PERSONAL:** Born May 21, 1933, Fresno, CA; married Ruby; children: Terry, Lanetta, Stanley, Steven, Brian. **EDUCATION:** 4 C's Coll, 1956; Fresno City Coll, Working Toward Degree in Public Admin. **CAREER:** Fresno Redevelopment Agency, senior relocation specialist, past west. **ORGANIZATIONS:** Reg dir Phi Beta Sigma Frat Inc; chrmn Fresno's Model Cities Ed Task Force; pres Epsilon Delta Sigma Chap, Phi Beta Sigma Frat Inc; pres 20th Cent Golf Club; pub rel chrmn Western St Golf Assn; mem King Soloman Lodge; Mt Sinai Consistory; prince hall aff spec rep Nat Urban Coal Conf 1973; paretn rep Fresno City Schs Atlanta. **HONORS/ACHIEVEMENTS:** Winner "Tray Award" Ach in Ed & Cit Part. **MILITARY SERVICE:** USAF 1951-55. **BUSINESS ADDRESS:** Ste 200, T W Patterson Bldg, Fresno, CA 93723.

HUNTER, ARCHIE LOUIS
Supervisor, educator retired. **PERSONAL:** Born May 07, 1925, Buffalo, NY; married Juanita; children: Jeffery, Wayne, Gail. **EDUCATION:** Univ of Buffalo, bA 1949; StUniv of NY, MSW 1965. **CAREER:** Dept of Social Serv, Erie County, unit supvr 1985; State Univ & Coll Buffalo, asst prof 1969-; Cent Police Acad of Eric County, lecturer 1971-. **ORGANIZATIONS:** Pres Fmly Life Consortium of Erie Co; chmn Allocations Com Untd Way of Buffalo & Erie Co; mem NAACP; Buffalo Negro Schlrp Found Inc; chmn FinCom, Soc, Wrkrs Club of Buffalo; mem StUniv at Buffalo Alumni Assn; trustee bd chmn, fin sec Trinity Bapt Ch; mem Manpower Adv Cncl of Erie Co; mem Omega Psi Phi Frat. **HONORS/ACHIEVEMENTS:** Srv Award United Way 1977; Buffalo Yth Bd Award; Grt Greeks on Am Campuses 1947. **MILITARY SERVICE:** AUS 1943-46. **BUSINESS ADDRESS:** 95 Franklin St, Buffalo, NY 14202.

HUNTER, CECIL THOMAS
Educator. **PERSONAL:** Born Feb 05, 1925, Greenup, KY; married Gloria James; children: Mildred C, Charlene James, Rosalind H Levy, Roderick, Gloria. **EDUCATION:** Washington Jr Coll; FL A&M Univ. **CAREER:** Brownsville Middle School, teacher of math. **ORGANIZATIONS:** Past chmn Catholic Soc Svcs; chmn Governmental Center Auth; chmn Escambia Co Health Facilities Auth; comm mem bd dir Sacred Heart Found; mem Saenger Mgmt bd dir; mem Finance Comm & Gen Govt Comm City Council; past mem Hospice - Northwest FL Area Agency on Aging; St Anthony's Catholic Ch; Knights of Columbus; Jack & Jill of Amer; Kappa Alpha Psi Frat; Prefect in Third Order of St Francis Secular Franciscans; mem NAACP. **HONORS/ACHIEVEMENTS:** Diocesan Medal of Honor; recip of Secular Franciscan Peace Award. **MILITARY SERVICE:** Veteran of WWII. **BUSINESS ADDRESS:** Teacher of Math, Brownsville Middle School, 3100 West Strong St, Pensacola, FL 32501.

HUNTER, CHARLES A.
Clergyman, educator. **PERSONAL:** Born May 07, 1926, Longview, TX; son of Wallace Alvin Hunter and Ivernia C Hunter; married Annie Alexander; children: Alpha A, Rhonda A, Rhasell D, Byron C, Rosalyn A. **EDUCATION:** Bishop Coll, BA 1947; Howard Univ, BD 1950; Philadelphia Divinity School, MTh, 1954, ThD 1958; North TX St Univ MS 71. **CAREER:** Bishop Coll, professor of sociology 1961-72; Hope Presbyterian Church, Dallas, pastor 1962-68; Dallas Independent Schl Dist, sociologicl rsrch 1969-72, 1974-75; St Luke Presbyterian Church, Dallas, assoc pastor 1969-80; Univ of TX at Arlington, assoc prof 1972-73; Bishop Coll, professor sociology 1975-88; Dallas County Community of Churches, dir church and community 1989-. **ORGANIZATIONS:** Dir United Cmps Christian Fllwshp 1959-61; coord Amigos 1968-; bd mem Greater Dallas Housing Opportunity Ctr 1969-, Dallas Theater Ctr 1974-83, Red Cross Dallas 1975-81; Grace Presbytery, moderator 1985. **HONORS/ACHIEVEMENTS:** Trail Blazer Award Business & Professional Women 1966; Outstanding Alumni Bishop Coll Alumni Assn 1966; Fair Housing Awrd Greater Dallas Housing Opportunity Ctr 1972; Vol Awrd First Lady's Volunteer TX 1980. **HOME ADDRESS:** Dr Charles A Hunter, Greater Dallas Community of Churches, Beilharz Block, 2800 Swiss Ave, Dallas, TX 75204.

HUNTER, CLARENCE HENRY
Public relations administrator. **PERSONAL:** Born Nov 01, 1925, Raleigh, NC; married Mary Ransom; children: Karen, Beverly, Katherine, Andrew. **EDUCATION:** NY Univ, BS 1950. **CAREER:** Jrnl & Guide Norfolk VA, reporter, bureau mgr 1950-53; Ebony Mag Chicago IL, assoc editor 1953-55; Post-Tribune Gary IN, reporter 1955-62; WA Evening Star WADC, reporter 1962-65; US Commiss on Civil Rights WA DC, dir info 1965-69; WA Journalism Ctr WA DC, assoc dir 1969-71; Howard Univ, dir univ rel& publ 1971-73; Rochester Products Div Gen Motors, dir commun & public rel. **ORGANIZATIONS:** Trustee WA Jrnlsm Ctr, Nat Cath Fnd of Wash DC; mem Public Rel Soc of Amer. **HONORS/ACHIEVEMENTS:** Howard Coles Assoc of Black Commun; Commun Awd Rochester Chap 1984. **MILITARY SERVICE:** USMC sgt 1944-46. **BUSINESS ADDRESS:** Dir of Commun & Public Rel, General Motors Rochester Prod, PO Box 1790, Rochester, NY 14692.

HUNTER, DAVID
Clergyman, educator. **PERSONAL:** Born Aug 03, 1941, Enterprise, MS; married Mary Williams; children: David Cornell, Christopher Dante. **EDUCATION:** Alcorn State Univ, BS 1964; Cleveland State Univ, MEd 1974; Central Bible Coll, BA 1976. **CAREER:** E Cleveland Schools, teacher 1969-82; Bright Star Bapt Church, pastor 1972-. **ORGANIZATIONS:** Life mem Alpha Phi Alpha 1965-; mem Oper PUSH, NAACP. **HONORS/ACHIEVEMENTS:** Acad Scholarship Alcorn State 1962. **BUSINESS ADDRESS:** School Board Member, E Cleveland City School Dist, 15305 Terrace Rd, East Cleveland, OH 44112.

HUNTER, DAVID LEE
Educational administrator. **PERSONAL:** Born Sep 10, 1933, Charlotte, NC; son of Mrs Annie L Boulware; married Margaret Plair; children: Karen Leslie, Jocelyn Jeanine. **EDUCATION:** Johnson C Smith Univ, BS 1951; Atlanta Univ, MS 1964; Nova Univ, EdD 1979. **CAREER:** Carver Coll & Mecklenburg Coll, instructor of math 1957-63; Central Piedmont Comm Coll, instructor of math 1963-71; Central Piedmont Comm Coll, coord coll trnsf prog 1971-73, dir of personnel 1973-75, vice pres (Dean), general studies 1975-. **ORGANIZATIONS:** Mem Amer Soc of Public Admins 1974-; mem North Carolina Assn of Comm Coll Instructional Admin 1975-; rep for CPCC League for Innovation in the Comm Coll 1979-; financial sec bd trustees Little Rock AME Zion Ch 1973; bd dir Charlotte Rehab Homes Inc 1978; bd dir ARC 1979; bd of dirs, Southern Regional Council on Black American Affairs; and North Carolina SRCBAA. **MILITARY SERVICE:** AUS corpl 1953-55. **BUSINESS ADDRESS:** Dean of General Studies, Central Piedmont Community College, PO Box 35009, Charlotte, NC 28235.

HUNTER, DEANNA LORRAINE
Educational administrator. **PERSONAL:** Born Dec 16, 1946, New York, NY; daughter of Harry Williams and Hazel Williams; divorced; children: Kimberly G. **EDUCATION:** Hofstra Univ, BA English 1971, MS Counseling 1977. **CAREER:** SUNY Farmingdale, career counselor 1979-80; Hofstra Univ, financial aid counselor 1980-82, asst dean of students 1982-85, school of law asst dean 1985-87, assistant dean University Advisement 1987-88, director CSTEp 1988-. **ORGANIZATIONS:** Lola T Martin Scholarship Assn, mem 1976-83; Dorothy K Robin Nursery School, mem/officer 1978-83; Hofstra Univ Alumni Senate, vice

pres 1979-, Counselor Education Alumni Assn, founding mem/past pres 1979-, Minority Women's Task Force, mem/officer; Human Connections Inst, human relations consultant 1984-. **HONORS/ACHIEVEMENTS:** Lola T Martin Scholarship Assn, community service award 1979; Hofstra Univ Alumni Senate, "Senator of the Year" 1985. **MILITARY SERVICE:** US Army Reserves, SSG 1975-83. **HOME ADDRESS:** 20 Wendell St Apt 9E, Hempstead, NY 11550. **BUSINESS ADDRESS:** Director, Collegiate Science & Technology Prog, 1000 Fulton Ave, Hempstead, NY 11550.

HUNTER, EDWINA EARLE
Music educator. **PERSONAL:** Born Dec 29, 1943, Caswell County, NC; daughter of Edgar Earl Palmer and Bessie Catherine Brown Palmer; married James Weldon Hunter, Sr, Jul 02, 1966; children: James W Jr, Anika Z, Isaac Earl. **EDUCATION:** Spelman Coll, BA 1964; Smith Coll, MAT 1966. **CAREER:** Vint Hill Farms Station, post chapel choir dir 1967-68; El Paso Comm Coll, instructor music 1975-76; Prince George's County Schools, music teacher 1969-72, 1979-. **ORGANIZATIONS:** Mem NAACP; sec Columbia Chap NAASC 1984-; MSTA Greater Laurel Music Teachers Assn NEA, MENC, MMENC; Suzuki Assn; pres Columbia Chapter Natl Alumnae Assn of Spelman College 1987-. **HONORS/ACHIEVEMENTS:** Recording "Children's Songs for Games from Africa," Folkways FCS 77855 1979; Outstanding Young Women of Amer 1979; distinguished Alumni Award NAFEO 1989. **HOME ADDRESS:** 10721 Graeloch Rd, Laurel, MD 20707. **BUSINESS ADDRESS:** Director of Vocal Music, Prince George's County Schs, 13710 Laurel-Bowie Rd, Laurel, MD 20708.

HUNTER, ELZA HARRIS
Educator. **PERSONAL:** Born Jul 14, 1908, Little Rock; married Melva W Pryor. **EDUCATION:** Langston U, BS;Univ of AR, MS; Atlanta U, NC St, Addl Study; Durham A&M Coll;Univ of OK; Shorter Coll, LLD 1957. **CAREER:** Shorter Coll Little Rock, acad dean 1973-77; Alumni Rel & Outreach, dir 1977-; N Little Rock Sch, dir instructnl srv & adult ed 1971-73; Jr HS, dir 1970-72; Jones HS, prin 1942-70, tchr 1935-42. **ORGANIZATIONS:** Mem N Little Rock Admin Assn; Nat Ed Assn; AR Ed Assn; Nat Assn of Secondary Sch Prin; Nat Assn for Pub Cont Adult Ed; bd trustees Shorter Coll; st mbrshp sec AR Sch Admin Assn; pres Urban Leag of Little Rock 1970-74; chmn N Little Rock Lib Commn; treas Urban Leag 1977-; bd of mgmt AW Young YMCA; met bd YMCA; pres Appollo Terr Housing Proj; Omega Psi Phi; sec Shorter Coll Grdns Housing Proj; IBP of Elks, Prince Hall Mason, 33 deg; Shriner Mohammed Temple #34; chmn, bd trustee Steward Bd, Miles Chapel CME. **HONORS/ACHIEVEMENTS:** Has received various awards including Man of Yr, Omega Psi Phi 9th Dist 1971; Family of Yr, Urban Leag Little Rock 1971. **BUSINESS ADDRESS:** Shorter Coll, 604 Locust St, North Little Rock, AR.

HUNTER, ERIC E.
Financial analyst. **PERSONAL:** Born May 03, 1960, Cleveland, OH; married Griselda E. **EDUCATION:** Swarthmore Coll, BA 1982; The Amos Tuck Sch of Business Admin Dartmouth Coll, MBA 1986. **CAREER:** Society Natl Bank, admin asst 1982-84; Norton Company, corp financial analyst 1986-87, sr corp financial analyst 1987-. **ORGANIZATIONS:** Mem Natl Black MBA Assoc 1986-; mem bd of dirs Worcester Comm Mental Health Ctr 1987-. **HONORS/ACHIEVEMENTS:** Council for Oppor in Grad Mgmt Educ Fellowship 1984; General Motors Fellowship 1985. **BUSINESS ADDRESS:** Corporate Financial Analyst, Norton Company, 120 Front St, Worcester, MA 01608.

HUNTER, FRANCES S. (NEE KRAFT)
Retired educator, scientist. **PERSONAL:** Born Apr 26, 1928, Washington, DC; daughter of Phillip M Simons and Effie Irine Simons; married Jehu; children: Benjamin, Leon. **EDUCATION:** Miner Tchrs Coll, BS 1946; Columbia Univ, MS 1951; So Univ Grad Sch, attended 1958; Columbia Univ, attended 1959; Montclair State Coll, attended 1962. **CAREER:** So Univ, instr 1946-59, asst prof 1959-61, adminstrv asst to chmn 1972-74; Washington DC Public Sch, tchr 1961-64; Howard Univ Sch of Medicine, instr acad reinforcement prog 1963-65, instr biometrist 1964-70, head sect on student achievement 1966-74, asst prof 1970-74, asst dean grad sch of arts & scis 1974-75, assoc prof 1974-. **ORGANIZATIONS:** Mem bd examiners So Univ Grad Sch 1961; consultant State Assn of Tchrs 1959; numerous other affiliations; mem Amer Physiol Soc; assoc mem Amer Physiol Soc 1971-73; Basic Sci Council; Amer Heart Assn; WA Heart Assn; Amer Assn of Univ Profs; Pi Mu Epsilon Natl Hon Math Frat; Natl Council of Tchrs of Math; DC Council of Tchrs of Math 1963-64; DC Educ Assn; numerous publications. **BUSINESS ADDRESS:** Associate Professor, HowardUniv Med Sch, Dept of Physiology, Washington, DC 20012.

HUNTER, FREDERICK DOUGLAS
Attorney. **PERSONAL:** Born Jan 30, 1940, Pittsburgh, PA; married Rosie M Kirkland; children: Frederick D, Deborah R. **EDUCATION:** Univ of Pittsburgh, BS 1961, PhD 1967; Univ of Maryland, JD 1974. **CAREER:** The Lubrizol Corp, Chief Patent Counsel; EI Dupont De Nemours & Co, corporate counsel 1972-89; W R Grace & Co, sr rsch chem 1967-72. **ORGANIZATIONS:** Amer Bar Assn; Delaware Bar Assn; District of Columbia Bar Assn; AOA Fraternity; AIPLA; mem Bethel AME Church. **HONORS/ACHIEVEMENTS:** Publ 5 papers various sci jour. **BUSINESS ADDRESS:** Chief Patent Counsel, The Lubrizol Corporation, 29400 Lakeland Blvd, Wickliffe, OH 44092-2298.

HUNTER, GERTRUDE T.
Physician, administrator. **PERSONAL:** Born Mar 23, 1926, Boston; married Charles. **EDUCATION:** Boston U, BA 1945; Howard U, MA 1946; HowardUniv Coll Med, MD 1950; HarvardUniv Grad Sch Bus Admin, PHMS 1972. **CAREER:** Pub Hlth Srv HEW, reg hlth adminstr 1973-; Boston, dep reg hlth dir 1971-72; Nat Ofc OEO & Head Start, sr ped 1965-71; Head Start, dir hlth srvs 1961-71. **ORGANIZATIONS:** Mem Am Acad Peds; HowardUniv Med Alumni Assn; Nat Med Assn; bd dirs Am Assn Sex Eductors & Cnslrs; Nat Family Guidance & Cnslng Srv; bd dirs Nat Cncl Black Child Dev; adv cncl Am Acad Med Dirs; Urban Leag; com to Improve Status of Women; Jack & Jill; NAACP; bd dirs People's Cong Ch; MA Heart Assn; bd dirs Boston Pub Housing Tenants Policy Cncl. **HONORS/ACHIEVEMENTS:** Num med publ; Who's Who Among Am Women; Beta Kappa Chi Hon Soc; Kappa Pi Hon Med Soc; Nat Contrbns Hlth Care NAACP 1973; Award Met Boston Consumer Hlth Cncl. **BUSINESS ADDRESS:** HowardUniv Coll of Medicine, Dept of Comm Hlth & Fmly Prac, Room 2400, Washington, DC 20059.

HUNTER, HARRIET LOUISE
Government official. **PERSONAL:** Born May 20, 1917, Orange, NJ. **EDUCATION:** Essex Co Vocational Sch, dental asst 1930. **CAREER:** MD Park & Planning Adv Comm, mem; Town of Eagle Harbor, commnr 1978-80; Branchwood Towers; pres of sr club. **ORGANIZATIONS:** Pres Sr Citizens Club 1984-85; precinct chmn Dem Party Prince George; mem dir MD Lung Assn; mem Dept Aging Adv Com. **HONORS/ACHIEVEMENTS:** Cert of Appreciation, Prince George Co Dept of Aging 1984, Prince George Med Serv 1980, MD Park & Planning 1980, MD Dept Human Resources 1984. **MILITARY SERVICE:** WAC sgt 1943-45; WAC Serv Ribbon; WW II Victory Medal.

HUNTER, HOWARD JACQUE, JR.
State official. **PERSONAL:** Born Dec 16, 1946, Washington, DC; son of Howard J Hunter, Sr and Madge Watford Hunter; married Vivian Flythe; children: Howard III, Chyla Toye. **EDUCATION:** NC Central Univ, BS 1971. **CAREER:** Hobson R Reynolds Elks Natl Shrine, mgr 1973-74; Hunter's Funeral Home Murfreesboro, owner 1974-; Hertford Co, commissioner, chmn of the bd, 1978-88; NC State Representative 5th District. **ORGANIZATIONS:** Trustee First Baptist Church Murfreesboro 1974-; scoutmaster Troup 123 BSA 1976-; past mem Gov Crime Commission 1980; life mem Kappa Alpha Psi. **HONORS/ACHIEVEMENTS:** Distinguished Serv Award Amer Jaycees 1980; Citizen of the Year NC Human Relations Comm 1981; Outstanding Young Men of Amer Jaycees 1974-75, 1977-79, 1981. **HOME ADDRESS:** 212 Third St, Murfreesboro, NC 27855. **BUSINESS ADDRESS:** State Representative, Northampton County, PO Box 418, Conway, NC 27820.

HUNTER, IRBY B.
Dentist. **PERSONAL:** Born Jul 12, 1940, Longview, TX; married Staphalene Johnson; children: Constance A, Irby B. **EDUCATION:** TX Coll Tyler, BS Chem 1961; Tuskegee Inst AL, MS Chem 1963;Univ TX Houston, DDS 1968. **CAREER:** Irby B Hunter DDS Inc Dallas, dentist gen 1971-; Dr WA Hembry Dallas, dentist gen 1968-70; Atlantic & Richfield Houston, chem (water) 1964-68; Houston ISD, tchr ad ed 1965-68. **ORGANIZATIONS:** Mem Am Dental Assn 1965-; pres MC Cooper Dental Soc Dallas 1974-78; pres Golf St Dental Assn of TX 1978-; mem of Steering Com, Small Sch Task Force Dallas ISD 1979-; mem of bd Comm Hlth Ctrs of Dallas Inc 1979-; Sir Orchun, Sigma Pi Phi Frat Dallas 1979. **HONORS/ACHIEVEMENTS:** Spec Alumni Award TX Coll Tyler TX 1980. **BUSINESS ADDRESS:** 2826 E Illinois, Dallas, TX 75216.

HUNTER, JERRY L.
Attorney. **PERSONAL:** Born Sep 01, 1942, Mt Holly, NC; son of Samuel Hunter and Annie B Hunter. **EDUCATION:** NC, BS; A&T State U, 1964; Howard Univ Schl of Law, JD 1967. **CAREER:** RoundTree Knox Hunter & Parker, Partner Law firm. **ORGANIZATIONS:** Mem US Supreme Court Bar; US Dist Court (MD & DC); US Court of Appeals & DC Court of Appeals; mem Natl Bar Assn; Am Bar Assn; DC Bar Assn; Assn of Plaintiffs Trail Atty; Sigma Delta Tau Legal Frat Alpha Kappa Mu Honor Soc; Kappa Pi Intl Honorary Art Soc. **HONORS/ACHIEVEMENTS:** Co-authored article "Current Racial Legal Developments" 12 How-L J 299, Spring 1966 No 2; received Am Jurisprudence Award for Academic Achievement in Legal Methods & History. **BUSINESS ADDRESS:** RoundTree, Knox, Hunter & Parker, 1822 11th Street, NW, Washington, DC 20019.

HUNTER, JOHN DAVIDSON
Insurance consultant. **PERSONAL:** Born in Alabama; married Lucile Chandler; children: Louise, John D Jr, Joshua, Phillip, Jackie Owens. **EDUCATION:** Graduate of Opelika HS, Selma Univ; extra corres courses in Business. **CAREER:** Protective Industrial Ins Co, rep 1962-81; Pilgrim Health Life Ins Co, rep 1981-. **ORGANIZATIONS:** Mem Tabernacle Baptist Church 1941-; mem NAACP 1950-; mem Dallas Cty Voters League 1975-; former mem The Selma City Council 1976-84; mem President's Democratic Club of AL 1977-85; mem Selma Black Leadership Council 1979-85; mem of exec comm Southwest AL Sickle Cell Anemia Assoc 1984-85; minister of the Rocky Branch Baptist Church 14 yrs. **HONORS/ACHIEVEMENTS:** Received twenty prof achiev awds and four comm service awds. **HOME ADDRESS:** 1818 Martin Luther King St, Selma, AL 36701.

HUNTER, JOHN W.
Elected official. **PERSONAL:** Born Apr 18, 1934, Union, MS; married RoseMary White, Jul 03, 1956; children: Eric, Shawn. **EDUCATION:** CS Mott Comm Jr Coll, Business Arts 1969. **CAREER:** 7th Dist Congressional Black Caucus Political Action Comm #659, chmn; Genesee County Bd of Health, bd of dir 1985-; Genesee County Bd of Commission, county commission 1974-86 retired. **ORGANIZATIONS:** Bd of dir Natl Assoc of Ctys Welfare & Soc Serv Comm, Genesee Mem Hospital 1975-84, Model Cities Econ Devel Corp; chairperson Genesee County Human Serv Comm; precinct delegate, former delegate State Democratic Convention; mem Urban League, NAACP, Elks Vehicle City Lodge 1036. **HONORS/ACHIEVEMENTS:** Leadership Award Black Business & Professional Womens Org 1978; Ambulatory Wing at Genesee mem Hospital in Flint MI was named The John W Hunter Wing 1984; The 1st black to be named to road commission, 5th black to serve in the State of MI as road commissioner; Fredrick Douglas Award Natl Assoc of Black Business & Professional Women Org 1987; A Phillip Randolph Civic Right Award, 1989. **BUSINESS ADDRESS:** Genesee County Rd Commn, 211 W Oakley St, Flint, MI 48532.

HUNTER, JOHNNIE L.
Educator. **PERSONAL:** Born Jul 12, Kansas City, MO; married Billy G Hunter; children: William, Jonathan. **EDUCATION:** Bnt Coll, BA 1951; Wayne St U, MSW 1968. **CAREER:** General Motors, dir of comm & civ affairs; State of MI, Brewster-Douglas Day Care Center 1965-67, supvr lic & fstr cr 1968-71; Pumpkin's Pal Pre- School. **ORGANIZATIONS:** Dir mem Natl Assn of Media Wmn; Natl Assn for Ed of Yng Chdrn; Nat Cncl for Blck Chld Devel; Am AssnUniv Wmn; mem NAACP; Urbn Leag; YWCA; fdng mem Your Hertg Hs Dtrt; com chmn Frnds of Schlr Contrm Dtrt; Dtrt Inst Arts Fndrs Soc. **HONORS/ACHIEVEMENTS:** Hon Untd Fndtn 1971-73. **BUSINESS ADDRESS:** Natl Assn of Media Women, 1185 Niskey Lake Rd, SW, Atlanta, GA 30331.

HUNTER, LLOYD THOMAS
Physician. **PERSONAL:** Born Feb 06, 1936, Des Moines, IA; married Janice; children: Cynthia, Laura, Elizabeth. **EDUCATION:** Univ NE, AB 1957, MD 1962. **CAREER:** Univ So CAUniv CA Los Angeles, Asso Prof. **ORGANIZATIONS:** Diplomate Am Bd of Pediatrics; fellos Am Acad of Pediatrics; past pres LA Pediatric Soc; mem Charles R Drew Med Soc; AMA; Nat Med & Assn; Golden State Med Assn; CA Med Assn; LA Pediatric Soc; Kappa Alpha Psi Frat; life mem NAACP; Los Angeles Urban League; Alpha Omega Alpha

Med Hon Soc. **HONORS/ACHIEVEMENTS:** Merit award Army commendation medal; 1962;Univ NE Regents Schlrshp 1961-62. **MILITARY SERVICE:** AUS med corps capt 1963-65. **BUSINESS ADDRESS:** 3719 S La Brea Ave, Los Angeles, CA 90016.

HUNTER, MACKIELL JAMES
Attorney, corporate officer. **PERSONAL:** Born Feb 07, 1946, Macon County, GA; son of Elton Hunter and Odessa Hunter; married Lorraine Dunlap; children: Adrienne, Michelle, Hillary. **EDUCATION:** Ft Valley State, BS 1968; Howard Univ, JD 1973. **CAREER:** US Equal Employment Oppty Comm, trial attny 1973-76, suprv trial atty 1976-78; M James Hunter & Assoc, principal partner 1978-81; M&M Products Co, Vice Pres and General Counsel (legal & human resources). **ORGANIZATIONS:** Bd mem Atlanta Judicial Commiss 1978-, Grady Hosp Bd of Visitors 1983-, Clayton Jr Coll 1984-;Atlanta Jr College Board 1986; Nexus Contemporary Arts Center Bd 1988, Bd of 100 Black Men of Atlanta, Inc 1989. **HONORS/ACHIEVEMENTS:** Knox Awd Ft Valley State 1968; Omega Psi Phi Award, 1968; Outstanding Young Men of America 1974; Outstanding Atlantans 1978; Outstanding Georgians 1984. **MILITARY SERVICE:** 1968, US Army Reserves, Airborne Division Honorable Discharge 1974. **BUSINESS ADDRESS:** VP & General Counsel, M & M Products, 4100 S. Central Avenue, #3, Atlanta, GA 30321.

HUNTER, NORMAN L.
Graphic artist. **PERSONAL:** Born Aug 28, 1932, Eutaw, AL; married Claudia M; children: Kim Derek, Marc Cedric. **EDUCATION:** Detroit Soc of Arts & Crafts; Art Inst of Chgo. **CAREER:** Jet & Black Stars mags, art dir; Supreme Beauty Products JPC Book Div; artist-designer; Ebony, designer of Books; Ebony Pictorial History of Black Am designed highly successful 3-vol set books 1972; Jet, Ebony, Black Stars, photographer; Johnson Library atUniv of Tex, photograph taken was accepted of Pres Lyndon B Johnson & Chicago Mayor Richard J Daley; Jet, page layouts & cover designs; Fashion Fair Cosmetics, artist, designer; Johnson Publ Co, art dir 1955-. **HONORS/ACHIEVEMENTS:** Merit Awd for Best Typography Nat Newspaper Pub Assn's 1972; book design CEBA Award "Dubois A Pictorial Biography"; Printers Industry Awd; book design BillCosby In Words & Pictures. **MILITARY SERVICE:** AUS. **BUSINESS ADDRESS:** Art Dir, Johnson Publishing Co, 820 S Michigan Ave, Chicago, IL 60605.

HUNTER, OLIVER CLIFFORD, JR.
Medical doctor. **PERSONAL:** Born Feb 20, 1935, Kilgore, TX; married Shirley; children: Oliver, III, Stephen, Stephanie, Sherri. **EDUCATION:** TX So U, BS 1956;Univ TX Med Sch, MD 1963. **CAREER:** Harris Co TX pvt practice 1967; Baylor Coll, instr 1967-73. **ORGANIZATIONS:** Mem Harris Co Med Soc; TX & Nat Med Assn; TX & Am Soc Intl Med; Houston Med Forum; life mem Kappa Alpha Psi;Univ of TX Med Br Alumni Assn 1974; TX SoUniv Alumni 1975; Trinity Meth Ch; mem MacGregory Pk Civic Club; Big Bro; Cal Farley's Boy's Ranch; Nat Jewish Hosp; diplomate Am Bd Intl Med1970; Nat Bd Med Examiners 1964. **HONORS/ACHIEVEMENTS:** Outstanding Alumnus TX Coll 1974. **MILITARY SERVICE:** AUS pfc 1963. **BUSINESS ADDRESS:** 2000 Crawford #830, Houston, TX 77002.

HUNTER, PATRICK J.
Educator. **PERSONAL:** Born Oct 29, 1929, Elberton, GA; married Mildred R Powell; children: Patrick J Jr, Kim M Brown, Michael A, Jeffrey M. **EDUCATION:** Univ of Bridgeport CT, BA 1958, MS 1959; NY Univ, PhD candidate. **CAREER:** CT Dept of Social Svcs, caseworker 1960-62; Birdgeport Inter-Group Council CT, exec dir 1963-66; Com on Training & Employment Stamford CT, exec dir 1966-68; Housatonic Comm Coll, dept chmn 1975-81, prof of psychology. **ORGANIZATIONS:** Mem Rotary Intl Bridgeport CT 1963-66; planning council United Way Greater Bridgeport; bd mem SW CT Mental Health; pres Southwest Regional Mental HealthBd 1986-87; mem CT State Mental Health Bd 1987; mem Greater Bridgeport Catchment ARea Cncl, Greater Bridgeport Regional Mental Health Adv Bd; vice presMental Health Social Club Greater Bridgeport Area. **HONORS/ACHIEVEMENTS:** Citizen of Yr Col Charles Young Post 1963; Achievement Awd Radio Station WICC 1963; Outstanding Educator 1972. **MILITARY SERVICE:** AUS corpl 1952-54; Korean Medal. **BUSINESS ADDRESS:** Prof of Psychology Dept Chmn, Housatonic Comm Coll, 510 Barnum Ave, Bridgeport, CT 06608.

HUNTER, RICHARD C.
Educator. **PERSONAL:** Born May 04, 1939, Omaha, NE. **EDUCATION:** Univ CA, DEd; San Francisco State Coll, M;Univ Omaha, BA. **CAREER:** Richmond Public Schools, supvr; Tokeyo, Japan, taught; Richmond CA, prin; Seattle, asst dep supvr; Richmond VA Bd, assoc supvr; Valentine Mus Dominion Natl Bank; Richmond Chamber of Commerce; St Paul Coll. **ORGANIZATIONS:** Kawanis; Kappa Alpha Psi; Phi Delta Kappa. **HONORS/ACHIEVEMENTS:** Selected for good govmnt awd Richmond 1st Club. **BUSINESS ADDRESS:** Richmond Pub Sch, Richmond, VA 23219.

HUNTER, ROBERT J.
Corporate administrator. **PERSONAL:** Born Aug 31, 1934, Clarksburg, WV; son of Robert Joseph Hunter, Sr and Marie Elizabeth Jackson; children: Robert Edward, Dawn Marie, Robin Denise, Michael Phillips. **EDUCATION:** Philadelphia Police Acad, 1963; Univ of PA, Philadelphia Bar Assoc Prog 1966-67; Philadelphia Govt Training Inst Mgmt, 1966-67, Master Barber 1970-72; Temple Univ Bus Admin, State Cert Bus Administrator 1976. **CAREER:** Hunters Employ Agency, owner-operator 1958-62; Philadelphia Police Officer, retired; McChatter Talk Mag, founder, editor-publisher 1976; Senate of PA, admin asst 1971-76; Found for Juvenile Decency, exec dir 1980-. **ORGANIZATIONS:** Mem promo & publ rel dir Shriners, Pyramid #1, Frat Order of Police Philadelphia #5; publ rel Amer Cancer Soc Com on Publ Info; founder, dir Committed & concerned Citizens Council Inc; life mem Volunteers in Aid to Sickle Cell Anemia; past chmn Troop 702 & past chaplain Troop 604 BSA; stewards bd, founder, past pres Mens Brotherhood of St John AME Church; past master Royal & Select Masters Council #3, Prince Hall Masonic Order, Star in the E Lodge #55; past grand lecturer PA Del Grand Council R&S of NY; past potentate Shriner, Pyramid Temple #1; exec dir Natl Grand Assembly of Squirrels & Found for Juvenile Decency Inc; Public Affairs Dir PA Shriners; Public Information Director United Supreme Council, 33 degree Masons 1989-. **HONORS/ACHIEVEMENTS:** 1 Bravery Awd, 8 Meritorious & Commendatory Citations Philadelphia Police Dept & FBI 1964-69; Disting Serv Awd Scottish Rite 32 & 33 Degree Mason; Meritorious Awd Star in the E Masonic Lodge; Comm Serv Awd PA Grand Lodge of Mason; Mason of the Year 1971; Matl Shriner Awd for Youth Concern & Involvement 1972; Masonic Publ Rel Awd State of PA 1973; PA Senate Candidate 1974; PA House of Rep Candidate 1980; Received Keys to Cities of Houston 1971, Detroit 1973, Newport 1974, Boston 1970; Chapel of Four Chaplains Legion of Honor Awd 1971; Natl Publ Rel & Publicity & Promo Dir Awd, The Imperial Council Shriners 1978-79; WPVI-TV Public Service Awd 1987; Liberty Bell, Mayor, City of Philadelphia PA 1989. **BUSINESS ADDRESS:** Executive Dir, Foundation for Juvenile Dcncy, 827 So 58th St, Philadelphia, PA 19143.

HUNTER, TONY WAYNE
Professional athlete. **PERSONAL:** Born May 22, 1960, Cincinnati, OH. **EDUCATION:** Notre Dame Coll, attended. **CAREER:** Buffalo Bills, professional tight end. **HONORS/ACHIEVEMENTS:** Named to num All-Rookie teams UPI & Pro Football Weekly; won 4 letters for the fighting Irsh; 2 time Playboy All-amer, NEA All-Amer as a sr; selected for the ABC/NCAA coll football tour in 1981; consensus All-Amer; OH Player of the Year as a sr.

HUNTER, WILLIAM ANDREW
Educator. **PERSONAL:** Born Sep 06, 1913, N Little Rock, AR; son of W J C Hunter and Jessie D Hunter; married Alma Rose Burgess. **EDUCATION:** Dunbar Jr Coll, Little Rock, AR, AA 1933; Wilberforce Univ Wilberforce, OH, BS 1936; Iowa St Univ, Ames, IA, MS 1948, PhD 1952. **CAREER:** Dunbar Hgh School, Little Rock, AR, instrctr Math & Science 1936-42; Tuskegee Inst AL, prof of Educ 1950-57, dean school of Educ 1957-73; AACTE, Washington, DC, dir of multicltrl rsch project 1973-74; Iowa St Univ, dir of rsrch inst for studies in educ 1974-79; Coll of Educ Iowa St Univ, prof of Educ 1979-83, prof emeritus of Educ, 1983-. **ORGANIZATIONS:** Mem Kappa Alpha Psi Frat 1936-; pres Amer Assn of Coll for Tchr Educ 1973-74; Natl Tchr Exam Adv Bd Educational Testing Service 1973-78; consultant IA Dept of Public Instruction on Human Relations 1975; life mem Tuskegee AL Civic Assn, Natl Educ Assn; mem Phi Delta Kappa, Kappa Delta Pi. **HONORS/ACHIEVEMENTS:** For Outstanding Service to the Teaching Profession Tuskegee 1972; Alumni Distinguishd Achievement Award Iowa State Univ 1973; Lagomarchino Lauerate Award Coll of Educ Iowa St; author-editor, Multicultural Education Through Competency-Based Teacher Educ, 1974; coauthor with Liem Nguyen: Educational Systems in Southeast Asia in Comparison with those in the United States, 1979. **MILITARY SERVICE:** AUS staff sgt 1942-46; good conduct Am, N African, European Theater. **HOME ADDRESS:** 2202 Country Club Ct, Augusta, GA 30904.

HUNTER, WILLIAM L.
Educator. **PERSONAL:** Born May 01, 1936, Spartenburg, SC; married Patricia Jenkins; children: Kerri. **EDUCATION:** Cardozo High School, Natl Honor Soc 1955; Central State Univ OH, BS cum laude 1959; Kent St Univ, MEd 1968. **CAREER:** Canton City School, principal 1969-73, exec principal 1973-76, dir of human relations 1976-78, dir of personnel 1978-. **ORGANIZATIONS:** Treasurer, Canton Classroom Teachers Assn, 1965-66; chrmn mem Canton Civil Srvc Comm 1969-83; trustee Faith United Christian Church 1970-; supreme council Omega Psi Phi Fraternity, Inc 1974-77; trustee Natl Urban League, Inc 1977-80; exec comm & vice pres United Way of Central Stark County 1980-; chmn guidance advisory bd Ohio Dept of Educ 1980-81; chmn Pro Football Hall of Fame Festival Security Comm 1986-. **HONORS/ACHIEVEMENTS:** Omega Citizen of Yr Omega Psi Phi 4th Dist 1973; Omega Man of Yr Omega Psi Phi 4th Dist 1974; Educ of Yr Canton Black, Hist Comm 1978; Business Assoc of Yr Am Business Wmns Assoc Canton Chptr 1980; United Way Volunteer of the Year "Gold Key" Award 1985. **BUSINESS ADDRESS:** Dir of Personnel, Canton City Schls, 617 Mc Kinley Ave S W, Canton, OH 44707.

HUNTER-GAULT, CHARLAYNE
Journalist. **PERSONAL:** Married Ronald Gault; children: 2 children. **EDUCATION:** Univ of Georgia, graduate. **CAREER:** The New Yorker, reporter; The New York Times, reporter; The MacNeil/Lehrer Report, reporter, natl affairs correspondent. **ORGANIZATIONS:** Series of reports Apartheid's People 1985. **HONORS/ACHIEVEMENTS:** Awds include Emmys, journalism awds; 1986 George Foster Peabody Awd for Excellence in Broadcast Journalism. **BUSINESS ADDRESS:** Correspondent, c/o MacNeil/Lehrer Report, WNET-TV, 356 W 58th St, New York, NY 10019.

HUNTER-LATTANY, KRISTIN EGGLESTON
Author, educator. **PERSONAL:** Born Sep 12, 1931, Philadelphia, PA; daughter of George L Eggleston and Mabel M Eggleston; married John I Lattany Sr; children: Leigh Lattany Norman, John I Jr, Ramona J, Andrew P. **EDUCATION:** Univ of PA, BS Ed 1951. **CAREER:** Pittsburgh Courier, columnist & feature writer 1946-52; Lavenson Bur of Advertising, copywriter 1952-59; Werner & Schorr Philadelphia, advertising copywriter 1961-62; Univ of PA Sch of Soc Work, research asst 1962; City of Philadelphia, info officer 1963-65; freelance writer, novels, journalism, fiction 1963-; Univ of PA, sr lecturer english 1972-. **ORGANIZATIONS:** Dir Walt Whitman Poetry Ctr 1977-79; mem Alpha Kappa Alpha, Modern Lang Assoc, PEN, Natl Council of Teachers of English, Authors Guild, NAACP; chair, fiction bd, Shooting Star Review, Pittsburgh PA 1989-. **HONORS/ACHIEVEMENTS:** Books, "God Bless the Child" 1964; "The Landlord" 1966; "The Soul Brothers and Sister Lou" 1968; "Boss Cat" 1971; "Guests in the Promised Land" 1973; "The Survivors" 1975; "The Lakestown Rebellion" 1978; "Lou in the Limelight" 1981; television, "Minority of One" CBS TV 1965; Fund for the Republic TV Documentqary prize1955; John Hay Whitney Oppty Fellowship 1959-60; Philadelphia Athenaeum Literary Awd 1964; Bread Loaf Writers Conf Fellowship 1965; Council on Interracial Books for Children Prize 1968; Sigma Delta Chi Best Mag Reporting Awd 1969; Univ of WI Childrens Book Conf Cheshire Cat Seal 1970; Silver Slate-Pencil & Dolle MinaAwds The Netherlands 1973; Chicago Tribune Book World Prize 1973; Christopher Awd 1974; Natl Book Awd Nom 1974; Drexel Univ Childrens Lit Awd 1981; NJ State Council on the Arts Prose Fellowship 1981-82, 1985-86. **BUSINESS ADDRESS:** Senior Lecturer, University of Pennsylvania, 119 Bennett Hall, English Department, Philadelphia, PA 19104-6273.

HUNTLEY, RICHARD FRANK
Educator. **PERSONAL:** Born Jan 25, 1926, Masury, OH; married Edith Marie Robinson; children: Dean, Lynn, Geoffrey, Steven, Donna Jean. **EDUCATION:** Youngtown State U, BA;Univ Akron, MA. **CAREER:** City Youngstown, chief draftsman 1964-65; Youngstown Planning Comm, research asst 1966-70, asso planner 1970-71; Youngstown Demonstration Agency, sr planner1971; Youngstown State U, instr 1971-72; Youngstown Vindicator, dir comm relations 1972-74; Youngstown State U, instr 1974-. **ORGANIZATIONS:** Chmn bd Buckeye Elks Youth Devel Ctr; bd mem Mental Health & Mental Retardation; Soc for Blind; Buckeye Review Publ Co; mem Mahoning County Selective Serv Bd; Vet Foreign Wars; Elks

Lodge #73; Masons F & Am; Am; Soc Planning Officials; Mayors Citizen Adv Com; dirs McGuffey Comm Ctr Bd; NAACP. **MILITARY SERVICE:** AUS 1944-45; USAF 1945-48. **BUSINESS ADDRESS:** 1098 Genessee Dr, Youngstown, OH 44511.

HURD, DAVID JAMES, JR.
Educator/musician. **PERSONAL:** Born Jan 27, 1950, Brooklyn, NY. **EDUCATION:** Julliard Sch NYC, attended 1959-67; Oberlin Coll, BMus 1967-71; Univ of NC Chapel Hill, attended 1972. **CAREER:** Trinity Parish, asst organist 1971-72; Duke Univ Durham NC, asst dir choral activities & asst chapel organist 1972-73; Ch of the Intercession NYC, organist & mus dir 1973-79; visiting lecturer Yale Inst of Sacred Music 1982-83; Commns from various insts orgns & persons, composer; Genl Theol Sem, prof of ch music & organist 1979-; organ faculty The Manhattan Schl of Music 1984-; music dr All Saints Church 1985-. **ORGANIZATIONS:** Mem v chmn The Standing Commn on Ch Music (Episcopal Ch) 1976-85; concert organist Phillip Trucken Brod Artist Rep 1977-; mem New York City Chap Amer Guild ofOrganists 1966-; mem Theta Chap Pi Kappa Lambda 1971-; aristic adv com mem Boys Choir of Harlem 1978-; mem Assn of Anglican Musicians 1979-; mem Liturgical Comm Diocese of NY 1982. **HONORS/ACHIEVEMENTS:** First Prize in Organ Playing Intl Congress of Organists 1977; First Prize in Organ Improvisation Intl Congress of Organists Philadelphia 1977; organ recitalist AGO Biennial Natl Conv Minneapolis 1980; diploma in improvision Stichting Int'l Orgelconcours Goud The Netherlands 1981; organ recitalist AGO Biennial Nat'l Conv 1986. **BUSINESS ADDRESS:** Professor of Church Music, Gen Theol Seminary, 175 9th Ave, New York, NY 10011.

HURD, JAMES L. P.
Musician, educator. **PERSONAL:** Born Aug 02, 1945, Bonham, TX. **EDUCATION:** Washburn U, Mus B(hon) 1967; Am Conservatory of Music, MusM 1968; Performance in OrganUniv of So CA, MusD 1973. **CAREER:** El Camino Clg, organ instr 1971- prof of music; First Presb Ch Inglewood , organist; Long Beach City Clg, organ instr 1973; Protestant Chapel KS BoysSch Topeka, organist choir dir 1964-67, 1968-69; Lawndale Presb Ch Chgo,choir dir 1967-68; Calvary Bapt Ch Topeka, KS, organist dir 1962-69; Ward AME Ch LA, CA, organist dir 1969-73; Blessed Sacremaent Cath Ch Chicago, IL, organist 1967-68; Cultural Arts Div Topeka Recreation Commn, head of music1965-67; CA State Univ-Dominguez Hills, CA State Univ Long Beach, organ prof. **ORGANIZATIONS:** Mem Am Guild of Organists; Kappa Alpha Psi; Phi Mu Alpha; Has Given Numerous Ogran Concerts Throuthouth KS, IL & CA; Adjuicator Music Tchrs Assc of CA;Orgn & Mgmt Analyst State Hwy Commn KS. **HONORS/ACHIEVEMENTS:** Listed in US Jaycees Outstanding Young Men of Amer 1980, Intl Who's Who in Music. **BUSINESS ADDRESS:** Professor of Music, El Camino College, 16007 Crenshaw Blvd, Torrance, CA 90506.

HURD, JOSEPH KINDALL, JR.
Chairman. **PERSONAL:** Born Feb 12, 1938, Hoisington, KS; son of Joseph K Hurd Sr and Mildred Ramsey Hurd; married Jean Challenger, Jun 20, 1964; children: Joseph III, Jason. **EDUCATION:** Harvard Coll, BA magna cum 1960; Harvard Med Schl, MD 1964. **CAREER:** Lahey Clinic Found, gynecologist 1972-. **ORGANIZATIONS:** Treas 1979-84, pres 1986-87 Obstetrical Soc of Boston 1979-84; pres New England Med Soc 1980; bd dir Freedom House Inc, Crispus Attucks Day Care Ctr, Roxbury Med Dntl Grp; adv comm, exec comm MA Section Amer Coll of Ob/Gyn; mem Amer Fertility Soc, Charles River Med Soc, AMA, NMA; councellor MA Med Soc; mem Am Uro-Gynecologic Soc, Amer Assoc Gynecologic Laporoscopy; mem bd of governors, bd of trustees, Lahey Clinic 1977-; mem, finance and executive committee, Lahey Clinic1987-; councillor, Harvard Medical Alumni Assn 1988-. **MILITARY SERVICE:** AUS major 2 yrs; Army commendation medal 1970-72. **BUSINESS ADDRESS:** Chairman, Dept of Gynecology, Lahey Clinic, 41 Mall Rd, Burlington, NJ 08105.

HURD, WILLIAM CHARLES
Physician/ophthalmologist. **PERSONAL:** Born May 17, 1947, Memphis, TN; son of Leon Hurd (deceased) and Doris Hurd; married Rhynette Northcross; children: Bill Jr, Ryan. **EDUCATION:** Univ of Notre Dame, BS 1969; MIT, MS 1972; Meharry Medical Coll, MD 1980. **CAREER:** General Electric Corp, systems engr 1969-70; TN State Univ, asst prof 1972-76; Univ of TN, intern 1980-81, resident physician 1982-85; Memphis Health Ctr, medical consultant 1981; Memphis Emergency Specialists, consulting physician 1982-84; Methodist Hospital, staff physician 1985-; Private Practice, physician. **ORGANIZATIONS:** Bd dirs Visiting Nurse Assoc 1985-. **HONORS/ACHIEVEMENTS:** Former All American Track Athlete at Nortre Dame 1697-69; Notre Dame Univ Athlete of the Year 1968; former World Record Holder at 300 yd Dash Indoors 1968-72; Rhodes Scholar Semi Finalist 1969; Prof Musician & Winner at serveral Natl Jazz Festival Competition; Hold US Patent on a Medical Instrument. **BUSINESS ADDRESS:** 1211 Union Avenue, Suite 495, Memphis, TN 38104.

HURDLE, EDMUND STEPHENSON
Business executive. **PERSONAL:** Born Feb 10, 1925, Brooklyn, NY; married Mary Mills; children: Edmund Jr, Kenneth, Celeste, David. **EDUCATION:** Howard U, BS 1953, MD 1958; Kings Co Hosp, Intern 1958-59; Kings Co Hosp, Resident 1959-62; Columbia U, MPH 1973; NY City Dept of Hlth, Resident 1971-74. **CAREER:** Bur of Med Serv, acting exec med dir 1977-; dep exec med dir 1976-77; dir 1974-76; dep dir 1974; cabinet mem 1973-74; reg hlth dir 1973-74; dep dir 1971-73; dir Kings Co Hosp 1969-71; asst to Chief 1966-69; coord 1965-66; clinician 1962-65; exec phys 1962-69. **ORGANIZATIONS:** Beta Kappa Chi; Natl Med Assc; Brooklyn Med Soc; Am Thoracic Soc; Am Soc Hlth Assc; Am Red Cross 1977-; tchg stf Downstate Med Clg 1967-72; assc attending Kings Co Hosp 1962-71; Unity Hosp 1962-; Downstate Hosp 1971-72; mem bd dir Am Red Cross 1977. **HONORS/ACHIEVEMENTS:** Num publs. **MILITARY SERVICE:** AUS t/4 1943-46; AUSR corpl 1946-49; lt 1953-55 . **BUSINESS ADDRESS:** 330 W & 34th St, New York, NY 10001.

HURDLE, HORTENSE O. MCNEIL
Educator. **PERSONAL:** Born May 20, 1925, Marlin, TX; married Clarence; children: Clarence, II, Gaile Evonne. **EDUCATION:** Prairie View U, BS 1947; Sacto State U, MA 1973; Sacramento State U, MS 1974. **CAREER:** Federal Govt, employee 1947-57; elementary teacher vice pres 1957-64; Compensatory Educ, dir 1964-68; elementary school prin 1968-; Del Paso & Heights School Dist, elementary school prin. **ORGANIZATIONS:** Mem Sacto Iota Phi Lambda Sor; Jack & Jill Am Inc; CA Adminstr Assc CTA; Ed Young Child; Natl Alliance Black Edctrs; Sacto Black Edctrs; Wmn Div Dem Wmn; NAACP; mem Phi Beta Delta Frat; XI Field Chpt; Negro Cncl Wmn; Camellia Federated Clb Sacto. **HONORS/ACHIEVEMENTS:** Woman of yr Parkside Congregational Ch 1966; distinguished comm serv awrd, C of C 1967; B'Nai B'Rith Outst Awrd Serv 1966; resolution 53 Assembly Dist & Progessive 12 1970; outst soror of the Far Western Reg of Iota Phi Lambda Sor 1980; Co-founder Concerned Citizens of Grt Sacto 1976. **BUSINESS ADDRESS:** 227 Fairbanks Ave, Sacramento, CA 95838.

HURDLE, VELMA B. BROOKS
Business executive. **PERSONAL:** Born Jan 07, 1931, Greenville, TX; married Finis Brooks; children: Sandra Renae Brewer, Terry Lamarr, Daryl Doen. **CAREER:** Beauty Acad, dir owner 1966-; CJ Walker Beauty Clge, instr 1959-66; cosm instr 1958, 1959. **ORGANIZATIONS:** Mem NAACP; mem YWCA; natl pres Alpha Chi Pi Omega Sor Inc; mem bd dir Sheer & Splen Prod Inc. **HONORS/ACHIEVEMENTS:** Bus Woman of Year Award Pylon Salesmanship Club Inc 1976; Trailblazers Award Bus & Prof Women's Club 1975; Dedicated Woman's Award Alpha Pi Chi Omegas 1973; 1st black mem OHFC; Hairstyling Champion of the World 1974. **BUSINESS ADDRESS:** #222 A Harris Oak Cliff Ctr, Dallas, TX 75224.

HURLEY, RUBY
Business executive. **EDUCATION:** Miner Tchr Clg & Robert H Terrell Law Sch, Attended. **CAREER:** NAACP, se reg dir. **ORGANIZATIONS:** Past mem St Paul Meth Ch; past pres Wesleyan Serv Guild; mem Warren Meml United Meth Ch; past pres United Meth Women; mem Pastor Parish Rel Com; sec Finance Com; mem Trust Bd Res & Plan Com N GA Conf of Unit & Meth Ch; Christ Soc Involve Mission Coord; N GA Conf of Unit Meth Women; bd life mem Atlanta License Rev; mem com Peace & World Order; bd on Ch & Soc. **HONORS/ACHIEVEMENTS:** Who's Who Among A Women; feature in "Look" & "Jet"; cit of yr awrd Birmingham Chap Omega Psi Phi; hon roll Democracy of Chicago Def; bronze woman of yr in Human Rel Delta Cpht Iota Phi Lambda Sor 1972; Spec Dist in Field of Civil & Human Rights; Natl Cncl of Negro Women; Outst Serv to Adv of World Understanding of Peace & Prosp Under Am Syst of Freedom Wilberforce U; Dynamic Christ Ldrshp in Flight for Freedom St Marks Meth Ch; 1st medgar evers awrd Cap Press Clb Wash DC; woman of yr awrd Utility Clb 1968; num awrds from NAACP.

HURSEY, JAMES SAMUEL
Educator. **PERSONAL:** Born May 09, 1931, Bridgeton, NJ; married Joyce Langston Washington; children: Joni Hursey-Young, Jennifer Elizabeth. **EDUCATION:** Glassboro State Coll, BS; VA State Coll, 1955. **CAREER:** Bridgeton Housing Authority, commiss 1958-84; Bridgeton City Council, councilman 1982-85; Bd of Dir Child Devel Ctr, mem 1984-; Bridgeton School System, teacher; Cumberland Co Utilities Auth, 1985-1990. **ORGANIZATIONS:** Mem NAACP, Natl Black Caucus, NJ Assoc Black Elected Officials; sec Hur-Ed Inc; chmn of bd Cedar Hill Mem Park 1980; past mem bd dir YMCA. **MILITARY SERVICE:** USN 1955-58. **HOME ADDRESS:** 31 Burt St, Bridgeton, NJ 08302.

HURST, BEVERLY J.
Association executive. **PERSONAL:** Born Jan 16, 1933, Oberlin, OH; married Dr Charles G Hurst Jr; children: Chaverly Kikanza. **EDUCATION:** Howard Univ, BA 1963, MA 1968. **CAREER:** Genl Acctg Office Washington, sec 1951-56; Crile VA Hosp, med sec 1956-61; Howard Univ, admin asst 1963-64, rsch asst 1964-67; DC Dept of Pub Health, rsch & training specialist 1967-68; New Careers Proj TRD, remedial educ supr 1968-69; Model Cities Tchr Aide Proj Kennedy-King Coll, coord 1969-70; IL Inst for Social Policy, eval analyst 1970-71; Chicago Urban League, rsch dir 1972-76; Comm Serv Admin, prog analyst 1980-82; US Railroad Retirement Bd,equal employment specialist 1982-84; US Corps of Engrs, equal employment oppor mgr 1984-. **ORGANIZATIONS:** Author of various articles papers & reports for professional journals; consult Youth Group Homes Proj DC Dept of Pub Welfare; comm splst Washington Concentrated Employment Proj United Planning Orgn; rsch consult Georgetown Univ Inst for Urban Serv Aides; AL Nellum & Assoc; consult to various other firms & assns; mem Amer Sociol Assn; Amer Acad of Polit & Social Sci. **BUSINESS ADDRESS:** EEO Manager, US Corps of Engineers, 4500 S Michigan Ave, Chicago, IL 60653.

HURST, CLEVELAND, JR.
Educator, counselor, educational consultant. **PERSONAL:** Born Sep 13, 1939, Montgomery, AL; divorced. **EDUCATION:** Wayne State Univ, BS 1961, MA 1971. **CAREER:** Educational Consultant 1972-; bowling instructor 1969-; Univ Admin Michigan 1962-64. **ORGANIZATIONS:** Reg basketball ofcl; mem Amer & Michigan Prsnl & Guid Assc; Univ Michigan Clb Gr Detroit; Natl Assc Vet Program & Admnstr; Detroit School Assc; Detroit Math Club; exec bd & rec sec Cntr Educ Returning Vets; pres bd of dirs, Virginia Park Comm Investment Assoc, Inc (2.1 mill assets); sec bd of dirs, Wayne State Univ Black Medical Assoc Schlarship Fund. **BUSINESS ADDRESS:** 11600 West 6 Mile Road, Detroit, MI 48240.

HURST, RODNEY LAWRENCE
City councilman. **PERSONAL:** Born Mar 02, 1944, Jacksonville, FL; married Ann; children: Rodney II, Todd. **EDUCATION:** FL Jr Clg; Edward Waters Clg. **CAREER:** Self Employed, ins slsm 1975-; City of Jacksonville, proj dir 1973-75; Greater Jacksonville Ec Opportunity, proj dir 1971-73. **ORGANIZATIONS:** Co-host "Feedback" WJCT-TV 1969-71; ins & underwriter Prudential 1965-69; mem Welfare & Soc Serv Plcy Steering Com; mem of the Natl Assc of Co; mem Jacksonville Cncl on Cit Invlm; mem City Cncl Fin & Rules Com; mem Cable TV Com; chmn Agr & Rec Com; mem NAACP; mem Urban Lea; bd mem Boy's Clb; advsr Ribault Sr HS; mem Consortium to Aid Neglected & Abused Children. **HONORS/ACHIEVEMENTS:** Man of yr Jacksonville Clb 1960; Flwshp grnt Corp for Pub Brdcstg 1969-70. **MILITARY SERVICE:** USAF a/2c 1961-65. **BUSINESS ADDRESS:** 220 East Bay St City Hall, Jacksonville, FL 32202.

HURT, JAMES E.
Business executive. **PERSONAL:** Born Sep 29, 1928, Chicago; married Suellen Gleason. **EDUCATION:** Am Inst Banking, Cert; Chicago State U, Presently Attending. **CAREER:** Drexel Natl Bank, vp, teller bkkpr field rep asst vice pres 1958-75; Inner-City Dev Corp, chmn bd. **ORGANIZATIONS:** Mem chmn adv bd Chicago Economic Devel Corp; bd Small & Bus Investment Corp; bd S End Jr C of C; Am Inst Banking; bd Untied Negro Clg Fund; Bus & Professional Men's Clb; adv bd Malcolm X Clg; adv bd Whitney Young Sch Bus; Urban Legue; YWCA. **HONORS/ACHIEVEMENTS:** One of 10 outst young men Chicago; awrd US Smal Bus Admn; cert Merit Chicago Pub Schs 1967; Color Inc; Century Clb

YMCA; outst serv awrd WBEE Radio; comm serv awrd 1971. **BUSINESS ADDRESS:** Drexel Nat Bank, 3401 S Dr ML King Jr Dr, Chicago, IL 60616.

HURT, LOUIS T., SR.
Association executive. **PERSONAL:** Born Jul 23, 1938, Kansas City, MO; married Ann Graham; children: Louis Jr, Jeffrey. **EDUCATION:** KS State Teachers, BS 1961; No Univ, Central MO State Univ, Grad Study. **CAREER:** Kansas City Teachers Union, 1st black pres 1967-71; Amer Fed Teachers Union, natl vice pres 1968-70,70-72, reg dir 17 state area 1971-74, natl dir Human Rights Comm Rel 1974-. **ORGANIZATIONS:** Vstg lecturer num colls & univs; life mem NAACP; former mem Freedom Inc; mem Alpha Phi Alpha, Sigma Theta Epsilon; ed commn former Gov Warren Hearnes 1969; consult Ford found Ed Task Force 1970-71, Ed Commn States Denver CO 1971, African Amer Labor Studies Ctr Ghana, Africa 1972, Leadership Conf Civil Rights WA 1974-. **BUSINESS ADDRESS:** Natl Dir, American Fed of Teachers, Human Rights Comm Relations, 1012 14 St NW, Washington, DC 20005.

HURTE, LEROY E.
Symphony conductor. **PERSONAL:** Born May 02, 1915, Muskogee, OK; son of Charles Hurte and Dora Grayson Hurte; married Hazel. **EDUCATION:** Los Angeles City Clg; Julliard Sch of Music; Tanglewood Music Workshop; Fresno State Clg. **CAREER:** Symphony Orch Inglewood Philharmonic Assc, condr; Angel City Symphony Orch, fdr-condr; Los Angeles Comm Symphony; guest condr; CA Jr Sympnony; Kings Co & Symphony; Fresno Philharmonic; Hanford Choral Soc, choral condr Tamarind Ave SDA Ch. **ORGANIZATIONS:** Mem bd dir Young Audiences; Assc of CA Symphony Orch; mem Natl Assc for Am Composers & Condrs; Am Symphony Orch League; Am Soc of Composers, Authors & Publshrs; mem bd Ladies of Song-Celeste Scott Meml Found; mem Rotary Clb; mem Natl Assn of Negro Musicians. **HONORS/ACHIEVEMENTS:** Achvmnt award Natl Assc of Media Women Inc 1973-74; commendation City of LA; commendation for Conducting Co of LA; edtr & pblshr Lyric Mag; author of 3 Books. **HOME ADDRESS:** 3500-279 W Manchester Blvd, Inglewood, CA 90305.

HUSSEIN, CARLESSIA AMANDA
Government administration. **PERSONAL:** Born Sep 01, 1936, Baltimore, MD; daughter of Nathan Minor and Amanda Minor; children: Monica. **EDUCATION:** Freedmen's Hosp School of Nursing, RN degree 1957; Univ of CA, San Francisco, BS Nursing 1966, MS Nursing 1967; Univ of CA, Berkeley, Dr of Public Health 1977. **CAREER:** Univ of CA-School of Public Health, associate dean 1971-73; Univ of CA-Epidemiology Dept, research dir 1974-77; Santa Clara County Health Planning Agency, executive dir 1977-80; LA County Health Planning Agency, executive dir 1980-83; LA County Fire Department, deputy health dir 1983-84; State Health Planning & Development Agency, dir 1984-. **ORGANIZATIONS:** Co-founder Bay Area Black Nurses Assn 1969; consultant Rural Health Project-Ecuador 1973; member CA Governor's Task Force on Cost Containment 1982; chair-planning committee Children's Home Society 1982-84; technical advisor LA Voluntary Health Planning Council 1983-83; founder LA County Black Female Manager's Assn 1984; mem Amer Health Planning Assn 1985; mem, John Hopkins Child Survival International Health Board of Directors. **HONORS/ACHIEVEMENTS:** Outstanding service Board of Supervisors-Santa Clara County 1980; recognition Board of Supervisors-Los Angeles 1984. **HOME ADDRESS:** 3001 Veazey Terr, #922 NW, Washington, DC 20008. **BUSINESS ADDRESS:** Public Health Advisor, Commission of Public Health, DC Government, 1660 L Street NW 12th floor, Washington, DC 20036.

HUTCHERSON, BERNICE B. R.
Educator. **PERSONAL:** Born Apr 14, 1925, Newton, KS; married Hubert W; children: Pamela Dineen, Karla Michelle. **EDUCATION:** Lanston Univ, BA 1950; Chicago Teachers Coll, 1952; Univ of KS, MSW 1969; Univ of Chicago, 1973. **CAREER:** Wichita State Univ, asst pross of soc work 1973; social worker 1954-72; Chicago, tchr 1950-54. **ORGANIZATIONS:** Pres KS co Social Workers Assn; Wichita Area Comm Action Program Inc; KS Conf on Social Welfare; mem Sedgwick Co; KS Mental Health Assn Boards; Sr Citizens Board; Nat Conf on Social Welfare; Am Pub Welfare Assn; Am Assn of Univ prof; charter mem Wichita OIC Board; mem Academy of Certified Social Workers; Suicide Prevention Service Counselor; past pres Youth Dept Calvary Baptist Church; Wichita Alumnea Delta Sigma Theta Inc; Matron KF Valley #97 OES; mem Nat Council of Negro Women; NAACP; professional adv com Family Planning Whichita Health Dept; KS Office of Minority Business Enterprises; bd educ #259 Professional Speakers Bureau. **HONORS/ACHIEVEMENTS:** Phi Kappa Phi; Honorary Citation & Wichita Comm Planning Council. **BUSINESS ADDRESS:** Box 25, Wichita, KS 67208.

HUTCHINS, BERTHA (NEE HUMPHREY)
Educator. **PERSONAL:** Born Jan 12, 1938, Waycross, GA; married Henry T. **EDUCATION:** Albany State Coll Albany GA, BA Eng 1956; AtlantaUniv Atlanta GA, MA Eng 1963; W CO U, PhD Eng 1979. **CAREER:** Monterey Peninsula Coll, ar prof English 1967-; AL State Univ, asst prof 1966; Monroe HS, instructor English 1960-65; Albany State Coll, instructor English 1959; Central HS, instructor English 1958. **ORGANIZATIONS:** Chnm ethnic st dept Monterey Peninsula Coll 1968-70; chmn eng dept Monroe HS 1963-65; mem Monterey Volunteers in Action 1978-; mem Am Assn ofUniv Women 1967-; mem Alpha Kappa Alpha Sorority 1954-. **HONORS/ACHIEVEMENTS:** Citation of Merit Am Assn of Bus Women 1980; Outstanding Tchr Award Monterey Asso Students 1976; Outstanding Citizen Award; Whos Who in the West 1968; Book "A Tree Has No Roots"; pageant pres 1968. **BUSINESS ADDRESS:** Monterey Peninsula Coll, 980 Fremont Blvd, Monterey, CA 93940.

HUTCHINS, FRANCIS L., JR.
Physician. **PERSONAL:** Born Jul 08, 1943, Ridley Park, PA; married Sandra; children: Keisha, Francis L. **EDUCATION:** Duquesne U, BS 1965; Howard U, MD 1969; Lankenau Hosp, intern 1969-70; OB-GYN, reds 1970-73. **CAREER:** OB-GYN Lankenau Hosp, dir of rsrch & out-patient educ dept 1977; Ob/Gyn Thomas Jefferson U, asst prof; TempleUniv Hosp, asst prof & dir family planning 1975-77; OB-GYN Lankenau Hosp, staff dept 1973; Navy Regional Ned Ctr, 1973-75. **ORGANIZATIONS:** Bd mem Family Planning Cncl Southerastern PA 1976-79; chmn Med Adv Bd FPCSP 1976-79; mem Nat Med Assn; sec Obstet Soc Phil 1976-79; sec Obstet Soc of Philadelphia 1980-; mem asv bd Concern for Hlth Options Info Care & Educ 1977-; phy adv bd Childbirth Educ Assn Grtr Philadelphia 1977-; Diplomat Nat Bd Med Exmnrs 1970; am bd OB-GYN 1975; flw Am Coll OB-GYN 1977; fellow Philadelphia Coll of Physicians 1979. **HONORS/ACHIEVEMENTS:** Many presentations & articles 1979-. **MILITARY SERVICE:** USN lt comdr 1973-75. **BUSINESS ADDRESS:** Ste 433 Lankenau Med Bldg, Philadelphia, PA 19151.

HUTCHINS, HENRY T.
Educator. **PERSONAL:** Born Oct 04, 1931, Albany, GA; widowed; children: Valoree A Renee. **EDUCATION:** Albany State Coll, BS 1956; NY Univ, MA 1957; OK Univ, EdD 1962. **CAREER:** Eureka HS, asst prin 1957-58; Albany State Coll, hazard lab sch 1958, dir of lab sch & asst prof of educ, assoc prof of educ & dir of student tchr, prof of educ & chmn div of educ 1958-67; AL State Univ, prof & grad dean 1967-68; Monterey Peninsula Unified Sch Dist, asst supt comm edn, asst supt elem educ 1970-73, asst supt instruction 1973-; Monterey Inst of Foreign Studies, adjunct prof of educ 1969-79; Mt Pleasant Sch Dist San Jose CA, supt of schs 1979-. **ORGANIZATIONS:** Mem CA Task Force for Integrated Educ 1969-; CA State Com Equal Educ Oppor 1972-; regional dir GA Tchr & Educ Assn; Natl Lab Sch Adminstr Assn; Natl Educ Assn; Amer Assn of CollTchr of Educ; CA Tchr Assn; Monterey Bay Tchr Assn; CA Black Educ Leadership Coun; Sch Sci & Math Assn Inc; organizer of Dougherty Co Resources & Devel Corp; regional dir GA Tchr & Educ Assn; exec sec ASC Alumni Assn; bd dir Lions Club; bd dir Reality House; bd dir Co Anti-Poverty Coun; past pres bd dir NAACP; bd dir Monterey Jazz Festival; bd dir Central Coast Devel; bd dir Children's Home Soc; bd dir Operation Shoe-String; bd dir Young Adults for Action; bd dir Boys Club; state EEOC-ACSA; mem Holy Name Soc; mem Knights of Columbus; mem supreme commander & chief 33 Degree Mason; mem Middle Atlantic State Philos Soc; Intl Platform Assn; Serra Intl. **HONORS/ACHIEVEMENTS:** Who's Who in Amer Educ; Outstanding Young Men of Amer; Outstanding Disting Personalities of the S 1967; Alpha Kappa Mu Natl Honor Soc; Sigma Rho Sigma natl Social Sci Honor Soc; Phelps-Stokes Fellowship 1958; So Educ Found Fellow 1961-63; Albany State Coll Academic Scholarship 1953-56; Miller-Unruh Mat 1970; Unified Sci & Math Elem Sch 1973; author of numerous publications; listed in Creative & Successful Personalities 1972; Two Thousand Men of Achievement1972; Presidential Awd Monterey Cotillion League; named Albany State Coll Outstanding Alumnus. **MILITARY SERVICE:** USAF 1948-52. **BUSINESS ADDRESS:** Supt of Schools, Mt Pleasant School Dist, 14265 Story Road, San Jose, CA 95127.

HUTCHINS, JAN DARWIN
Journalist. **PERSONAL:** Born Feb 11, 1949, Danville, IL; married Toni Lynn. **EDUCATION:** Yale Coll, BA 1971. **CAREER:** KRON-TV, sports dir; KPIX-TV Westinghouse, sports, anchor/reposter 1974-80; WIIC-TV Cox Broadcasting, sports reporter 1972-74; AT&T Long Lines, sales supr 1971-72. **ORGANIZATIONS:** Mem Health & Wisdom.

HUTCHINSON, CARELL, JR.
Physician, orthopaedic surgeon. **PERSONAL:** Born Sep 21, 1930, Chicago, IL; children: C. **EDUCATION:** Roosevelt U, BS 1958; HowardUniv Coll of Med, MD 1964. **CAREER:** Phys orthopaedic surg pvt prac 1969-; Howard U, orthopaedic surg res 1965-69; Freedmen's Hosp, intern 1965; various med staff appointmnts . **ORGANIZATIONS:** Chmn Polit Action Com Cook Co Phys Assn; Ins Mediation Com Chicago Med Soc; mem Peer Review Com Chicago Med Soc; IL St Adv Com on Pub Aid; 3yr appointmnt as alternate couns at large of Counc of Chicago Med Soc; chmn Med Com; mem Nat Bd of Dir John Howard Assn (Prison reform grp); orthopaedic consult Children's Hosp. **HONORS/ACHIEVEMENTS:** Outstndg Young Dem of Yr 1959; Intl Who's Who 1970; first prize winner Orthopaedic Res Resrch Paper Competition 1968.

HUTCHINSON, CHESTER R.
Business executive. **PERSONAL:** Born Mar 06, 1950, Birmingham, AL; married Lorraine Green; children: Treasure Genea, Reginald Chester. **EDUCATION:** Univ of Santa Clara, BS Bus 1972. **CAREER:** Univ of Santa Clara, asst dir housing 1971-72; Kelloggs Sales Co, territorial mgr 1972-74; Fairchild Camera & Instr, employee relations spec 1974-76; Crocker Natl Bank, employment mgr 1976-78; Paul Masson Vineyards, mgr labor relations recruitment & safety 1978-81, asst dir of human resources 1981-83; Joseph E Seagram & Sons Inc, dir human resources. **ORGANIZATIONS:** Pres Vintner Employers Assoc 1978-85; vice pres Winery Employers Assoc 1980-84; trustee CA Winery Workers Pension Plan Trust 1980-85; bd of trustees RFK Farm Workers Med Plan 1980-85, Juan De La Cruz Farm Workers Pension Plan 1980-85. **BUSINESS ADDRESS:** Dir of Human Resources, Joseph E Seagram & Sons Inc, PO Box 1852, Saratoga, CA 95070.

HUTCHINSON, GEORGE
Educational administrator. **PERSONAL:** Born Dec 19, 1938, Albuquerque, NM; son of John Hutchinson and Leona Hutchinson; married Gwen Pierce. **EDUCATION:** California State Univ Los Angeles, BS 1969, MS 1971; United States International Univ, PhD 1977; National University, San Diego, California, Post Doctoral Law 1988. **CAREER:** California State Univ, assoc dean educ support serv 1986-; San Diego State Univ, asst prof dept of recreation 1973-79, asst dean 1974-77 assoc dean 1978-81 college of professional studies and fine arts, assoc prof dept of recreation 1979-, dir student outreach serv dir 1981-,. **ORGANIZATIONS:** Mem Advisory Council for Minority Officer Recruiting US Navy 1977-; mem at large Industry Educ Council Greater San Diego 1980-; mem United Way Strategic Planning Program Comm 1980-; mem bd dirs and adv bd Higher Educ Access and Motivation 1982-; mem Phi Kappa Phi; mem bd dirs Educ Cultural Complex Foundations 1983-; mem bd dirs CA Advocates for Reentry Educ 1983-; mem bd dirs Amer Cancer Society 1984-; mem Athletic Adv Comm 1985-; mem United Way Management Assistance Program 1985-; mem Senate Comm Minority Underrepresentation 1985-; mem CA Academic Partnership Program 1985-; mem San Diego Comm Colleges Comm on Student Recruitment Retention and Transfer 1985-; mem Palomar Comm Coll Transfer Ctr Adv Comm 1986; mem Naval Reserve Officers Assn, Natl Naval Officers Assn, Navy League of the US; mem Urban League San Diego Chapt; mem Mexican American Political Assn; mem Third World Counselors Assn; bd mem, State Bar of California 1988-; pres, Boy Scouts of Amer Explorers Division, 1988-. **HONORS/ACHIEVEMENTS:** Letter of Commendation Coop Educ Program CA State Univ Los Angeles 1972; Prize Awd Amer Nursing Home Assn 1974; Golden Opportunity Awd San Diego County Vocational Guidance Assn 1976; Meritorious Awd for Serv City Council Los Angeles 1977; Letter of Commendation State of CA Developmental Disabilities Area Bd Thirteen 1977; Comm Serv Awd State of CA Governor Jerry Brown 1979; Honorary Mem US Navy ROTC Selection Bd Chief of Naval Opers Washington DC 1979-82; Distinguished Alumna San Diego Comm Leadership Develop 1980; Honorary Member Phi Kappa Phi San Diego State Univ 1980-86; 11 publications including "Trends Affecting Black Recreators in the Professional Society," California Parks and Recreation Society Magazine 1981; Role of Higher Educ in Educational Reform of Adolescents 1988; Meeting the Challenge of Technolo-

gy 1988. **MILITARY SERVICE:** USN captain 19 yrs; Letter of Commendation for Outstanding Serv to the Navy/Marine Selection Bd 1979; Meritorious Serv Medal 1980; Letter of Commendation1981; Gold Star for Excellence in Recruiting 1981; Gold Wreath Awd for Excellence in Recruiting 1982. **BUSINESS ADDRESS:** Director, San Diego StateUniv, Student Outreach Serv, San Diego, CA 92182.

HUTCHINSON, JAMES J., JR.
Business executive. **PERSONAL:** Born Sep 22, 1947, Chicago; divorced; children: Kelley, Jimmy. **EDUCATION:** Dartmouth Coll, AB 1969; Amos Tuck Sch of Bus Adminstrn, MBA 1971. **CAREER:** First Natl Bank of Chicago, copr loan officer 1971-74; South Side Bank, exec vice pres 1974-80; Inter-Urban Broadcasting Co, vice pres 1977-81; Inter-Urban Broadcasting of New Orleans Partnership, exec vp, gen partner 1980-86; Inter-Urban Broadcasting Co, pres 1984-; Inter-Urban Rental Systems, pres 1985-; Savannah Cardinals Baseball Club, sec 1986-; Inter-Urban Broadcasting Group, pres 1986-. **ORGANIZATIONS:** Adv bd mem New Orleans Reg Vo-Tech Inst 1982-; commiss New Orleans Exhibitions Hall Auth 1986-; chmn Urban League of Greater New Orleans 1986-; exec comm mem Chambers Small Bus Council 1984; radio vice pres Greater New Orleans Broadcasters Assoc 1984-85; mem YMCA of Greater New Orleans, United Way, Metropolitan Area Comm, LA Childrens Museum, Private Industry Council, Greater NO Tourist & Convention Commission, Mayor Morials Superbowl Task Force, AP Tureaud Comm, Mayor Morials Bus Devel Council, Bus Task Force on Educ. **HONORS/ACHIEVEMENTS:** Listed in Who's Who Among Black Amer, Who's Who in the Mid-West; Outstanding Achievement Awd Citizens Cultural Found 1978; recipient of one of the Ten Outstanding Black Businessmen in Chicago Awd 1979; Blackbook Urban League of Greater New Orleans Disting Serv Awd 1981; Metropolitan Area Comm Leadership Forum 1983; recipient of one of the Ten Best Dressed Men in New Orleans Men of Fashion. **BUSINESS ADDRESS:** President, Inter-Urban Broadcasting Group, PO Box 19066, New Orleans, LA 70179.

HUTCHINSON, JEROME
Association executive. **PERSONAL:** Born Jul 23, 1926, Louisville, KY; married Eleanor; children: Jerome, Jr, Seretha R. **EDUCATION:** Univ of Louisville, AB 1951; Sch of Bus Adminstrn & Seminars on Small Bus Adminstrn, grad. **CAREER:** Jerome Hutchinson & Asso Inc, pres 1971-; Jonah Enterprises Inc Louisville, vP 1970-71; Econ Devel & Now Inc Louisville , exec dir 1969-70; Small Bus Adminstrn, mgmt splst 1966-69; Falls City Brewing Co, sales & pub rel rep 1956-66; Admiral Finace Co, credit investigator 1954-55. **ORGANIZATIONS:** Bd mem Louisville OIC 1970-72; bd mem & chmn Finance Com River Reg Mental Health Corp 1974-75; chmn. bd dir Plymouth Urban Cntr 1974-; bd mem IMBE Washington 1969-70; chmn bd dir Continental Nat Bank of KY 1973-75. **HONORS/ACHIEVEMENTS:** Ambassador of Goodwill Citation City of Louisville 1974; Citizen of Day Award WLOU Radio 1973; SBA Regional Mgmt Award 1968. **MILITARY SERVICE:** USN 3rd class petty officer World War II. **BUSINESS ADDRESS:** 4307 Elliott Ave, Ste 5, Louisville, KY 40211.

HUTCHINSON, LOUISE DANIEL
Historian. **PERSONAL:** Born Jun 03, 1928, Ridge, MD; married Ellsworth W Hutchinson Jr; children: Ronald, David, Donna, Dana, Victoria. **EDUCATION:** Miner Teacher Coll, Prairie View A&M, Howard Univ, 1952; Amer History & Afro-Amer Studies, Grad Hrs in Sociol. **CAREER:** Natl Portrait Gall SI, rsch of harmon collection 1971, ed rsch spec 1972-73; Natl Capitol Parks E Washington, ed rsch spec 1973-74; Anacostia Museum Smithsonian Inst, historial, dir of rsch 1974-. **ORGANIZATIONS:** Bd mem SE Neighbor House 1968-70; bd of dir WA Urban League 1968-70; mem bd SE Unit Amer Cancer Soc 1969-; chmn supt Council on Arts in Ed DC Publ School 1972-74; mem Natl Assoc of Negro Bus & Professional Women's Club Inc 1973-; ex comm, bd DC Citizens for Better Publ Ed 1974-76; mem Frederick Douglass Mem & Hist Assoc 1974-, Douglass ad hoc comm Natl Capitol Parks E; plng comm for bicent Smithsonian Inst. **HONORS/ACHIEVEMENTS:** Author "The Anacostia Story, 1608-1930" 1977, "Out of Africa, From Kingdoms to Colonization", Smithsonian Press 1979, "Anna J Cooper, A Voice from the South" Smithsonian Press 1981; Exhibit Black Women, Achievements Against the Odds Smithsonian Traveling Exhib Svc. **BUSINESS ADDRESS:** Historian, Dir of Rsch, Smithsonian Inst, ANM Rsch Dept, 1901 Fort Pl SE, Washington, DC 20020.

HUTCHISON, PEYTON S.
Educational administrator. **PERSONAL:** Born Mar 24, 1925, Detroit, MI; son of Harry Greene Hutchison and Gladys Palace Smith; married Betty L Sweeney PhD; children: Peyton Jr, Allison Leigh, Jonathan Alan. **EDUCATION:** Wayne State Univ, BS Ed 1950, MEd 1955; Northern IL Univ 1969; MI State Univ, PhD 1975. **CAREER:** Detroit Public Schools, assistant principal 1964-65, admin asst 1966-73; City Coll of Chicago, suprv dir 1973-75; Chicago Urban Skills Inst, vice pres 1974-75; Chicago Urban Skills Inst,pres, 1975-84; Roosevelt Univ, part time faculty 1984-; City Coll of Chicago, exec dean; Hutchison Assoc (consulting business) currently. **ORGANIZATIONS:** Teacher Detroit Public Schools 1950-54; dir Green Pastures Camp Detroit Urban League 1959-65; asst principal Detroit Public School 1964-65; matl devel suprv Detroit Public Schools 1965-67; sr level rsch assoc MI State Univ 1968-69; chmn bd of dir Classic Chorales Inc 1983-; chmn Coll Univ Unit Amer Assoc of Adult Cont Ed 1983-; trustee Knoxville Coll 1984-; mem Alpha Phi Alpha; division director, Amer Association for Adult/Continuing Education. **HONORS/ACHIEVEMENTS:** Pres Phi Delta Kappa Wayne State Univ 1963; Mott Doctoral Fellowship Charles Stewart Mott Found 1968; Carl Sandburg Awd Friends of Chicago Public Libr 1984; Comm Serv Awd Univ of Chicago Intl Kiwanis 1985. **MILITARY SERVICE:** AUS sgt 1944-46. **HOME ADDRESS:** 688 Old Elm Rd, Lake Forest, IL 60045. **BUSINESS ADDRESS:** Executive Dean, City Colleges Of Chicago, Richard J Daley College, 7500 S Pulaski Rd, Chicago, IL 60652.

HUTSON, JEAN BLACKWELL
Retired librarian. **PERSONAL:** Born Sep 07, 1914, Summerfield, FL; daughter of Paul Blackwell and Sarah Myers Blackwell; married John Hutson, Jun 03, 1950 (deceased); children: Jean Frances. **EDUCATION:** Barnard Coll NY, BA 1935; Columbia Schl of Library Serv, BS 1936; King Mem Coll SC, LBD 1976. **CAREER:** Schomburg Ctr for Rsrch in Blck Culture, curator & chief 1948-80; City Coll of New York, adjunct prof 1960-72; Univ of Ghana West Africa, asst librarian 1964-65; Research Libraries NY Public Library, asst dir collection management and development 1980-84. **ORGANIZATIONS:** Pres Harlem Cultural Council 1965-70 1984-, 1st vice pres 1971-83; mem Arts & Lttrs Comm Delta Sigma Theta Sor 1972-; mem bd of Dirs Martin Luther King Ctr 1973-. **HONORS/ACHIEVEMENTS:** Publications, Harlem Cultural Hist Metropolitan Museum 1969; Schomburg Ctr Encyclopedia of Library & Info Sci 1978. **HOME ADDRESS:** 2255 5th Ave #8F, New York, NY 10037.

HUTT, MONROE L.
Business executive. **PERSONAL:** Born Mar 16, 1920, Evanston, IL; married LeJeune H; children: Monroe L Jr. **EDUCATION:** IL Inst of Tech, attended 1942; Chicago Sch of Real Estate, attended 1948; Roosevelt Univ Sch of Music & Tchr Training Prog, attended 1965. **CAREER:** US Vet Admin Chicago, adjudicator 1946-50; Gen Auto Prod Inc, plant supr 1950-63; AUS Army Corp (civ), maint supr 1963-65; Midway Tech Inst Chicago, 1965-68; Brunswick Corp Chicago, job dev 1968-69; Quinco Mfg Corp, pres chmn bd. **ORGANIZATIONS:** Pres's Coun Fellow Amer Inst of Mgmt; bd dir Chicago Minority Purchasing Council; mem IL Mfgrs Assn; mem Chicago S C of C; mem Amer Soc of Metals; mem VFW. **HONORS/ACHIEVEMENTS:** Nom "Small Bus Subcontractor of Yr" by SBA 1971; Supplier Performance Awd Chevrolet 1971-72; Top Rung Citation Chicago Oppor Indsl Ctr 1970; "Min Bus Achievement Awd" 1970; Top 100 Black Businesses 1973. **MILITARY SERVICE:** USN signalman 1942-46. **BUSINESS ADDRESS:** President/Board Chairman, Quinco Mgt Corp, 12010 S Paulina, Calumet Park, IL 60643.

HUTTON, DAVID LAVON
Educator. **PERSONAL:** Born in Kansas City, MO. **EDUCATION:** CMSU, BS 1963; Hall of Recognition, 1963; UMKC, MA 1974. **CAREER:** Paseo HS, teacher 1965-79; Lincoln Acad N, teacher 1981-. **ORGANIZATIONS:** Mem AFT 1965-; bd of dirs Ray Cnty Sesquicentennial Comm 1970-71; trustee Bethel AME Chrch 1979-; mem NAACP 1983-; mem Building and Expansion of Bethel AME Church 1983-, and choir. **HONORS/ACHIEVEMENTS:** Hall of Recognition CMSU 1963. **MILITARY SERVICE:** AUS sp/4 3 yr; medal of good conduct 1956-59. **BUSINESS ADDRESS:** Teacher Eng Department, Lincoln Coll Preparatory Acad, 2111 Woodland, Kansas City, MO 64108.

HUTTON, GERALD L.
Educator, consultant. **PERSONAL:** Born in Pittsburg, KS; married Marjorie. **CAREER:** Lincoln & HP Study Schs Springfield Mo, tchr; Springfield Pub Schls, pub infor rep; St Louis Northwest HS, athletic dir & bus educ instr; pub television-utilization consult St Louis Educ TV Comm Commr Zoning Park Bd; officer Ancient Egyptian Arabic Order Nobles Mystic Shrine of North & South Am. **ORGANIZATIONS:** Mem Am Guild of Variety Artists; mem Anerucah Fedn of TV & Radio Artists; mem Am Equity Assn; mem Royal Vagabonds St Louis Mens Civic Club; mem St Louis Area Bus Tchrs Assn; mem Kiwanis Club; mem NAACP St Louis Br; hon past potentate PHA Shriners; mem United Supreme Council PHA So Jurisdiction 33rd deg Soloist World Series Games St Louis 1967, 1968; life mem Kappa Alpha Psi. **HONORS/ACHIEVEMENTS:** Contrib Author "High Sch & Coll Typewriting" Textbooks; Festival Appreciation Award Sigma Gamma Rho Sorority Inc/Zeta Sigma chap Afro-am Arts.

HUTTON, MARILYN ADELE
Attorney. **PERSONAL:** Born Jul 21, 1950, Cincinnati, OH. **EDUCATION:** Fisk Univ, BA 1972; Harvard Law School, JD 1975; Hague Acad of Intl Law, Certificate 1983. **CAREER:** US Senator Lloyd M Bentsen, legislative aide 1975-76; The Procter & Gamble Co, corporate counsel 1976-81; Cincinnati Queen City Bowling Senate, corp sec 1980-82; NAACP, legislative cncl 1986-87; Natl Educ Assoc, atty human & civil rights spec. **ORGANIZATIONS:** Mem Metro Museum of Art 1983; legal adv comm Natl Bowling Assoc 1978-80; mem Intl Bar Assoc, Amer Soc of Intl Law, Amer & Federal Bar Assocs, District of Columbia Bar Assoc, Amer Assoc of Art Museums, Corcoran Gallery of Art; mem US Court of Military Appeals, US Court of Appeals for the Federal Circuit, US Court of Appeals for the District of Columbia Circuit, District of Columbia Courts of Appeals. **HONORS/ACHIEVEMENTS:** Author American Soc of Intl Law 1986 annual meeting report published 1987, 1987 annual meeting report to be published 1988. **HOME ADDRESS:** 1500 Massachusetts Ave NW, #660, Washington, DC 20005. **BUSINESS ADDRESS:** Attorney Human & Civil Rights, Natl Educ Assoc, 1201 16th St, Washington, DC 20036.

HUTTON, RONALD I.
Dentist. **PERSONAL:** Born Jul 23, 1949, High Point, NC. **EDUCATION:** Hampton Inst, BA 1971; HowardUniv Coll Dentistry, DDS 1975. **CAREER:** Winston-salem Dental Care Plan Inc, dentist; AUS Dental Corp, dentist 1976. **ORGANIZATIONS:** Mem bd trustees Promiseland Nurseries Inc; mem Assn of Mil Surgeons of US; Acad of Gen Dentistry; Old North State Dental & Soc; NC 2nd Dist DentalSoc; Am & Nat Dental Assns; Oral Cancer Soc; Robert Freeman Dental Soc. **HONORS/ACHIEVEMENTS:** Organized soc fellowship Campus of Hampton Inst 1969. **MILITARY SERVICE:** AUS capt 1976. **BUSINESS ADDRESS:** Winston-Salem Dental Care Plan, 201 Charlois Blvd, Winston-Salem, NC 27103.

HYATT, HERMAN WILBERT, SR.
Physician, minister. **PERSONAL:** Born Feb 19, 1926, S Pittsburgh, TN; son of Robert Hyatt and Wilma Hyatt; married Elizabeth; children: Monique, Monica, Hamilton, Richard, Robert, Herman Jr. **EDUCATION:** TN A&I State Univ, BS 1949; Meharry Med Coll, MD 1956; Lincoln Univ Law Sch, DJ 1972; Monrovia Coll, Honorary Doctor of Humanities 1987; San Jose City Coll, Honorary Assoc in Art 1988. **CAREER:** Kern Gen Hosp, res ped 1957-59, chf ped dept 1963; AME Church, dist dir youth cong 1964-75; St James African Meth, pastor 1967-77; No CA Conf AME Church, admin asst to presiding elder; Mt Herman African Methodist Episcopal Church, founder/pastor; Private Practice, pediatrician. **ORGANIZATIONS:** Chmn dept ped San Jose Hosp 1971-72, Alexian Brothers Hosp 1973-74; ordained itinerant elder Bishop H Thomas Primm 1966; life mem NAACP; mem Advisory; mem Parents Helping Parents; vice pres Interdenominational Ministers Alliance 1987-. **HONORS/ACHIEVEMENTS:** Alpha Kappa Mu Natl Honor Soc 1948; poems from a mountain 1980-81; special recognition Award Santa Clara Human Rights Commission 1988; Resolution from the CA Assembly 1989; Resolution from the House of Representative 1989; Commendation City of San Jose 1988; Special Award Urban League 1988. **MILITARY SERVICE:** AUS sgt 1946. **BUSINESS ADDRESS:** 12 S 15th St, San Jose, CA 95112.

HYDE, WILLIAM R.
Surgeon, educator. **PERSONAL:** Born Nov 09, 1923, StPaul, MN; married Opal Brown; children: William R Jr, David J, Drew S. **EDUCATION:** Howard Univ, BS (cum laude) 1944, MD 1947. **CAREER:** Harlem Hosp, internship; Freedmen's Hosp, residency; Colum-

bia Univ, 1949-50; Harlem Hosp, 1952-53; Howard Univ, asst prof of surgery; VA Hosp Washington, attending surgeon, Washington Hosp Ctr, DC Gen Hosp, Children's Hosp, Providence Hosp, sr attending surgeon; Howard Univ Coll of Med, surgeon; Washington Hospital Center, sr attending surgeon. **ORGANIZATIONS:** Mem DC Med Soc; NMA Fellow; Amer Coll of Surgeons 1958; diplomate Amer Bd of Surgery 1953; diplomate Natl Bd of Med Examiners; Washington Acad ofSurgery 1974; Alpha Phi Alpha Frat; Southeastern Surgical Assn. **HONORS/ACHIEVEMENTS:** Beta Kappa Chi, Kappa Pi Hon Soc. **MILITARY SERVICE:** AUS med corps capt 1953-55. **BUSINESS ADDRESS:** Senior Attending Surgeon, Washington Hospital Center, 3326 Georgia Ave NW, Washington, DC 20010.

HYDE-JACKSON, MAXINE DEBORAH
Physician, neurosurgeon. **PERSONAL:** Born Jan 18, 1949, Laurel, MS; daughter of Mr Sellus Hyde and Mrs Ann Huff McDonald; married James Jackson. **EDUCATION:** Tougaloo Coll, BS Biology (cum laude) 1966-70; Cleveland State Univ, MS Biology 1971-73; Case Western Reserve Univ, MD 1973-77; Univ Hosps, internship 1977-78, neurosurgery residency 1978-82. **CAREER:** Univ Hosps, internship general surgery 1977-78, residency neurosurgery 1978-82; Guthrie Clinic, neurosurgical staff 1982-; private practice neurosurgery. **ORGANIZATIONS:** The Bradford Co Med Soc; mem PA Med Soc; mem PA Neurosurgical Soc; mem Congress of Neurological Surgeons; mem Alpha Omega Alpha Med Hon Soc; publications "5-Hydroxytryptophan decarboxylase and monoamine oxidase in the maturing mouse eye" 1973; "The Maturation of 5-hydroxytryptophan decarboxylase in regions of the mouse brain" 1973; "The maturation of indoleamine metabolism in the lateral eye of the mouse" 1974; "The maturation of monoamine oxidase and 5-hydroxyindole acetic acid in regions of the mouse brain" 1974; "Re-expansion of previously collapsed ventricles" 1982. **HONORS/ACHIEVEMENTS:** Alpha Omega Alpha Honorary Med Soc 1977; featured story Ebony 1983; featured in first edition of Medica 1983; featured in First Register of Yearly Article on Young Professional Esquire 1984; featured story American Medical News 1984. **BUSINESS ADDRESS:** Neurosurgeon, 7230 Medical Center Drive #600, Canoga Park, CA 91307.

HYLTON, KENNETH N.
Attorney. **PERSONAL:** Born Jul 07, 1929, Roanoke, VA; married Ethel; children: Kenneth Jr, Keith, Kevin. **EDUCATION:** Talladega Coll, BA; Wayne State U, MA; BostonUniv Sch of Law, JD. **CAREER:** Dingell, Hylton & Ziemmol, atty 1956-; Wayne Co, pub admin 1976-. **ORGANIZATIONS:** Past pres Wayne Co Volters League; past pres Venice Spraggs Council Good Gov; past pres Noble PTA; past pres Talladega Alumni Assn; past Referee MI Civil Rights Comm; mem VA State Bar; MI State Bar; Detroit Bar Assn; Nat Lawyers Guild; Amer Judicature Soc; Workmens Comp Sec & Condemnation Com MI State Bar; Ch State Bar Grievance Bd; MI State Bar Trustee United Christian Ch Detroit; vice-ch State Dem Party MI; sec bd & legal counsel First Ind Nat Bank; life mem NAACP; ch bd dir Nat Housing Conf Inc. **MILITARY SERVICE:** US Army first lt 1953. **BUSINESS ADDRESS:** 2905 Cadillac Tower, Detroit, MI.

HYLTON, TAFT H.
Program analyst. **PERSONAL:** Born Jun 22, 1936, Washington, DC; divorced. **EDUCATION:** BS 1959; Washington Conservatory Music; Washington Inst Music. **CAREER:** Dept of Human Serv DC Govt, chief/Payments Br; Ofc Budget & Mgmt Sys DC Govt, budget & accounting analyst; choral conductor; tcht private piano; Voices of Expression Choral Ensemble, fndr dir. **ORGANIZATIONS:** Mem Am Choral Dir Assn; dir of sr choir New Bethel Bapt Ch; mem dir Anthem Choir Allen AME Ch; mem Cosmopolitan Choral Ensemble; Am Light OperaCo; Negro Oratorio Soc; 12th St Christian Ch; Univ Soc Piano Tchrs. **HONORS/ACHIEVEMENTS:** Work Performance Award; Pub Health Serv NIH 1963; Eligible Bachelor featured Ebony Mag 1974.

HYMAN, EARLE
Performer. **PERSONAL:** Born Oct 11, 1926, Rocky Mount, NC; son of Zachariah and Marie. **EDUCATION:** Studied with Eva Le Gallienne at the Amer Theatre Wing; studied with Robert Lewis at the Actors Studio. **CAREER:** NY State Amer Negro Theatre, performer 1943; TV, performer 1953; Films, performer 1954; The Bamboo Prison, The Possession of Joel Delaney, performed 1972; House Party Playhouse, various roles 1974; The Green Pastures, played Adam Hezdrel; Huckleberry Finn, played Jim; played title-role of Othello in Norwegian; US tour and Carnegie Recital Hall 1963; The Cosby Show, played Russell Huxtable. **ORGANIZATIONS:** Reader for Amer Found for the Blind; recorded Alex Haley's Roots 1977. **HONORS/ACHIEVEMENTS:** Show Bus Awd Othello 1953; Seagram Vanguard Awd 1955; Theatre World Awd 1956; GRY Awd for "Emporor Jones" Norwegian Oslo Norway 1965.

HYMAN, GEORGE E.
Business executive. **PERSONAL:** Born May 16, 1938, Newark, NJ. **EDUCATION:** Rtgrs U, BA 1964. **CAREER:** Urbana Inc, pres 1968-. **ORGANIZATIONS:** Mem Advertising Club of NJ; bd tst Boys' Club of Newark. **HONORS/ACHIEVEMENTS:** Good Conduct Medal AUS. **MILITARY SERVICE:** AUS sp-4-E-4 1961-63.

HYMES, JESSE
Business executive. **PERSONAL:** Born Feb 13, 1939, St Joseph, LA; married Addie B; children: Kenneth, Tracey, Trina. **EDUCATION:** Univ Chicago, MBA 1972; Purdue Univ, AAS 1970. **CAREER:** Joseph Schlitz Brewing Co, plant controller, asst controller 1975; control system adminstr 1975; plant accountant 1974; financial analyst 1972; Meade Elec Co, draftsman estimator 1969. **ORGANIZATIONS:** Bd dir Urban Arts 1976; pres PTA 1977; mem adv dom Boy Scouts of Am 1977; art council 1975-76; jr advisor Achievement 1975-76; NAACP. **HONORS/ACHIEVEMENTS:** Urban League Black Achiever Award NY YMCA 1977; cogme fellowship grant 1972. **MILITARY SERVICE:** AUS sp 4 1962-65. **BUSINESS ADDRESS:** 4791 Schlitz Ave, Winston-Salem, NC 27107.

HYNSON, CARROLL HENRY, JR.
Appointed official. **PERSONAL:** Born Dec 28, 1936, Washington, DC; son of Adel and Carroll; children: Michelle Hynson Green, Lejuene Tarra, Marcus Carroll, Brandee Carol. **EDUCATION:** Penn State Univ, 3 yrs Sociology & Political Science 1955-59; Amer Univ, summer course/Sociology; Morgan State Univ, BA 1960. **CAREER:** Sonderling Broadcasting Co, chief announcer/acting prog dir 1965-75; Hynson's Real Estate, office mgr 1975-76; Ceda Corp, public affairs specialist 1976-77; Provident Hosp Inc, asst vice pres for devel & pub relations 1978-80; Balt/Wash Intl Airport, dir office of trade dev 1980-84; MD State Lottery Agency, dep dir sales 1984-88; dep Director Public Affairs 1984-. **ORGANIZATIONS:** Vice pres Scholarship for Scholars Comm 1984; bd of dir Epilepsy Found of MD 1982-; adv bd Baltimore Convention Bureau 1982-; Kappa Alpha Psi Fraternity. **HONORS/ACHIEVEMENTS:** Life mem Phi Beta Pi Commerce Frat 1973; vice chmn Anne Arundel Co/Annap Bicentennial Comm; host/producer It Ain't Necessarily So-CBS 1976; host/producer The C Thing WRC-TV and Back to School Special Washington WHG-TV. **HOME ADDRESS:** 133 Clarence Ave, Severna Park, MD 21146. **BUSINESS ADDRESS:** Deputy Dir Public Affairs, Maryland State Lottery Agency, Plaza Office Center Ste 204, 6776 Reisterstown Rd, Baltimore, MD 21215.

HYTCHE, WILLIAM P.
Educator. **PERSONAL:** Born Nov 28, 1927, Porter, OK; married Deloris Juanita Cole; children: Pamelia, Jaqueta, William Jr. **EDUCATION:** Langston Univ, BS 1950; OK State Univ, MS 1958, EdD 1967. **CAREER:** Attucks Jr/Sr HS, tchr 1952-55; Ponca City Sr HS, tchr 1955-60; MD State Coll, asst prof 1960-66; Univ of MD, dept head assoc prof & dean of stud affairs 1968-73, acting chmn 1973-74, chmn of liberal studies 1974-75, acting chancellor 1975-76, chancellor 1976-. **ORGANIZATIONS:** Past pres Co-op Orgn Planning; mem bd dir Princess Anne Area C of C; mem Phi Sigma Soc; Alpha Phi Alpha; Holy Royal Arch Mason; Free & Accepted Mason; mem bd dir Natl Assoc for Equal Oppty in Higher Educ 1976-, Mid-Delmarva YMCA 1980-82; mem joint comm Agr R&D; mem bd dir InterFuture; mem Agribusiness Promotion Council 1985-; mem exec comm Natl Assoc of State Univs & Land-Grant Colls 1985-. **HONORS/ACHIEVEMENTS:** Acad of Arts & Sci Fellow OK State Univ 1978; Listed in NAFEO Disting Alumni of the Year Brochure 1980. **MILITARY SERVICE:** AUS 1950-52. **BUSINESS ADDRESS:** Chancellor, Univ of MD, E Shore, Princess Anne, MD 21853.

I

IBEKWE, LAWRENCE ANENE
Educator. **PERSONAL:** Born Apr 17, 1952, Onitsha, Nigeria;son of Eusebius Ibekwe and Marcelina Ibekwe Ozumba; married Theresa Ibekwe Nwabunie, Mar 23, 1989; children: Lynn Ibekwe. **EDUCATION:** Marshall Univ, Huntington, WV, 1979; Philander Smith Coll, Little Rock, AR, BA, Business Admin, 1980-81; Univ of AR, Fayetteville, AR, MS, Mgmt, 1982-83. **CAREER:** State School Board, Holy Rosary Teacher's Coll, Nigeria, library asst, 1975-78; AR Commemorative Comm (Old State House) Little Rock, AR, security officer, 1983-84; Philander Smith Coll, Little Rock, AR, instructor, 1984-; Shorter Coll, N Little Rock, AR, assoc prof, 1984-, academic dean, 1988-. **ORGANIZATIONS:** Advisor, Phi Beta Lambda, Philander Smith Coll, 1986-; advisor, Arkansas Assn of Nigerian Students, 1986-88; treasurer, Elite Social Club, 1987-; mem, Knight of Columbus (3rd degree) 1987-. **HONORS/ACHIEVEMENTS:** Dean's Lists, Philander Smith Coll, 1980-81; Outstanding Young Men of America Jaycees, 1981; Constitution Draft & Review, Intl Student Org, 1984-89; Award of Recognition (advisor) PBL, Philander Smith Coll, 1986-89; Award of Outstanding Leadership (chmn) Constitution Comm, 1986; Award of Outstanding Performance (chmn) Arkansas Assn of Nigerian Students, 1987; Award of Outstanding Contribution (advisor) Arkansas Assn of Nigerian Students, 1988; co-designer of Health Science Program, Shorter Coll, 1988. **HOME ADDRESS:** PO Box 164431, Little Rock, AR 72216.

IBRAHIM, ABDULLAH (DOLLAR BRAND)
Pianist, composer. **PERSONAL:** Born Oct 09, 1934, Cape Town; married Sathima; children: Tsakwe, Tsidi. **EDUCATION:** Univ of Cape Town, attended. **CAREER:** Marimba Mus Ctr & Ekapa Records, dir; AS-Shams Rec Co; Karate, instr Cape Town S Africa; Composer, Liberation Opera, Kalahari 1978; pianist, composer. **HONORS/ACHIEVEMENTS:** Rockefeller Grant 1968; Natl Endowment for the Arts; Talent Deserving Wider Recog Downbeat Mag 1975; Silver Awd 1973; Grand Prix Awd 1973. **BUSINESS ADDRESS:** 222 W 23rd St, Hotel Chelsea #314, New York, NY 10011.

ICE, ANNE-MARE
Pediatrician. **PERSONAL:** Born Mar 16, 1945, Detroit, MI; daughter of Lois Terry Ice and Garnet Tabor Ice. **EDUCATION:** Fisk Univ, BA Chem 1966; Howard Univ Coll of Med, MD 1970; Milwaukee Children's Hosp, Internship residency pediatrics 1970-73. **CAREER:** Private Practice, pediatrician 1973-. **ORGANIZATIONS:** Natl Med Assoc; Links, Inc; Delta Sigma Theta, Inc. **BUSINESS ADDRESS:** 15521 W Seven Mile Rd, Detroit, MI 48235.

IFORD, ROBERT (ROBERT FORD)
Business executive. **PERSONAL:** Born Dec 26, 1948, New Orleans, LA. **EDUCATION:** Grambling Coll. **CAREER:** Black Comm Devel & City Counc Untd Meth Ch; City of Charleston, SC, Mayor Pro Tem. **ORGANIZATIONS:** SCLC 9 yrs; SNCC 2 yrs; NAACP 16 yrs; CORE 2 yrs; work in over 200 comm in Country during Civil Rights Movement to vote reg drive; work in organ Labor Union; Direct Action Movement; Polit Educ drive in over 45 cities; mem NAACP; Nat Black Elec Official. **HONORS/ACHIEVEMENTS:** Youtstdng Young Men of Am; Citizen of Yr Awd; Soc Serv Awds.

IGHNER, BENARD T.
Musician. **PERSONAL:** Born Jan 18, 1945, Houston, TX. **CAREER:** Almo Publ Co, staff son writer; Dizzy Gillespie & Lalo Schifrin, worked with both; singer; musician; arranger. **MILITARY SERVICE:** AUS pfc 162-65. **BUSINESS ADDRESS:** c/o Alamo Music Corp, 1416 N La Brea, Los Angeles, CA.

IGLEHART, LLOYD D.
Attorney. **PERSONAL:** Born Apr 20, 1938, Dallas, TX; son of Lloyd Iglehart and Helen Waggoner Iglehart; married Vivian, Jun 20, 1964; children: Lloyd III, Stanley, Llauryn, Robyn. **EDUCATION:** Lincoln Univ of MO, BS 1961; Howard Univ, JD 1969; Columbia Univ, MPH 1976. **CAREER:** Met Life Ins Co, atty 1969-73; RCA Consumer Electronics, atty 1973-74; Private Practice, attorney 1983-. **ORGANIZATIONS:** Mem Natl Health Lawyers Assoc, Natl Conf Black Lawyers, ABA, Amer Civil Liberties Union, Natl Bar Assoc, Washington Bar Assoc, PA Supreme Court, Supreme Court of TX, DC Court of Appeals,

US Supreme Court, Phi Alpha Delta Law Frat, Alpha Phi Alpha Frat Inc. **MILITARY SERVICE:** AUS 1961-63. **BUSINESS ADDRESS:** Attorney, Law Offices L Iglehart & Assoc, 601 Indiana Ave NW, Washington, DC 20004.

IKE, REV. See EIKERENKOETTER, FREDERICK J., II

IMBRIANO, ROBERT J.
Managing editor. **PERSONAL:** Born Feb 10, 1944, Bronx, NY; married Clarice Cheatham; children: Robert II, Pierette. **EDUCATION:** Iona Coll, BA 1969; Michele Clark Fellowship Prog; ColumbiaUniv Grad Sch, journalism 1970. **CAREER:** Black Enterprise, managing ed; Earl G Graves Publ Co, vice pres 1975; Black Enterprise, asso editor; mng editor 1973; Newsday, reporter. **ORGANIZATIONS:** Mem Assoc Business Press Editors; mem bd adv Rainbow Print Art; Schlrsp Fund NY City; mem concerned council of Black executives. **BUSINESS ADDRESS:** 295 Madison Ave, New York, NY.

INCE, HAROLD S.
Dentist. **PERSONAL:** Born Jan 07, 1930, Bklyn; married Mary Ann Jackson; children: Nancy, Harold Jr. **EDUCATION:** BS 1951; DDS 1956. **CAREER:** Self-employed, dentist health dept new haven CT, dir. **ORGANIZATIONS:** Mem ADA; CT Dental Assn; New Haved Dental Assn; adv bd First New Haven Nat Bank; mem Urban League; trustee Bias Stanley Fund; Alpha Phi Alpha. **MILITARY SERVICE:** USAF capt 1956-58. **BUSINESS ADDRESS:** 1 Dixwell Ave, New Haven, CT 06511.

INGE, THEODORE R.
Physician. **PERSONAL:** Born Jul 25, 1901, Charlottesville, VA; married Virginia Robinson; children: Theodore R Jr, LaVerne Borden. **EDUCATION:** Univ of MN, AB 1924, BS 1925, BM 1927, MD 1928. **CAREER:** E Orange Gen Hosp, stf 1935-; Newark Beth Israel Hosp, stf 1940-60; Am Geriatric Scty, fellow 1960-; NJ Acad of Med, fellow 1960-; Es Cnty Geriatric Ctr, sr attend phys 1971-81; private practice. **ORGANIZATIONS:** Mem E Orange Chmbr of Comm 1950-; life mem NAACP 1963-; bd of dirs Westside Boys Clb 1965-; frmr pres Optimist Clb of E Orange 1965. **HONORS/ACHIEVEMENTS:** Tennis trophies 1929-; Man of Yr YMCA 1958; Citizenship Awrd YMCA 1966, 1975; Who's Who in NJ 1975. **MILITARY SERVICE:** AUSR 1st LT 1928-38. **BUSINESS ADDRESS:** 336 Halsted St, East Orange, NJ 07018.

INGRAM, ADELL, JR.
Social service administration. **PERSONAL:** Born Nov 25, 1948, Warren, OH; married Lori Ruth. **EDUCATION:** Ashland Coll, BS Ed 1970; Kent State Univ, MA Ed 1980. **CAREER:** Columbus Bd of Ed, teacher 1970-77; Vista Del Mar Jewish Fed, counselor 1978-79; Warren-Trumbull Urban League, employment dir 1981-84; Aurora Area Urban League, exec dir 1984-. **ORGANIZATIONS:** Mem Black Artists of Afro-Amer 1974-, Natl Urban League Council of Execs 1984-, Natl Urban League Religious Council 1984;, Private Indust Council 1984-, Minority Council of Aurora 1984-; vice chmn Big Brothers/Big Sisters Bd 1984-.

INGRAM, EARL GIRARDEAU
Educator. **PERSONAL:** Born Apr 18, 1936, Savannah, GA; married Carol L; children: Cheryl, Earl, Jr, Keith, Kevin. **EDUCATION:** IN U, MS; Savannah State Coll, BS. **CAREER:** US Dept of Edn, dir EEO 1971-; sr personnel staffing officer 1970-71; Youth Training Center, dir 1968-69; Svannah, tchr counselor. **ORGANIZATIONS:** NAACP. **HONORS/ACHIEVEMENTS:** 2 spec awards for EEO significant number of blacks recruited for Dept of Edn. **BUSINESS ADDRESS:** Director, EEO Staff, US Dept of Education, 400 Maryland Ave SW, Washington, DC 20202.

INGRAM, ELDRIDGE B.
Educator, director. **PERSONAL:** Born Feb 01, 1949, Pine Bluff, AR; married M Sandra Stephens. **EDUCATION:** AR State U, MS 1972;Univ AR, BA 1970. **CAREER:** Econ Devel & Employ Canton Urban League, dir 1974-; On-the-Job Training Prog, dir 1973-74; Forrest City Schs Forrect City, AR, tchr 1970-73. **ORGANIZATIONS:** Mem Omega Psi Phi Frat; OH Edn; Counc Execpt Children; Canton Urban League Inc; mem Mt Calvary 2nd Bapt Ch (sunday sch tchr); 32 deg Mason; alternate mem 1968 US Olympic Team; fellowship AR State Dept Higher Edn. **HONORS/ACHIEVEMENTS:** Track scholarship 1966-69. **BUSINESS ADDRESS:** 415 13 St SE, Canton, OH 44707.

INGRAM, JAMES WILLIAM
Deputy police chief. **PERSONAL:** Born Oct 17, 1937, Detroit, MI; married Gwendolyn Hunter; children: Abby, Chevon, Alandus, Rene, Crystal, Rahman, Ayana, James III, Gail. **EDUCATION:** Univ of MI, Journalism Fellowship 1973-74. **CAREER:** Mayor's Office City of Detroit, exec asst 1973-83; WJLB-FM Radio, commentator 1975-82; WGPR-TV Detroit, producer/host 1979-81; FBI Natl Acad, instructor devel sch 1985; Detroit Police Dept, dir of AV serv 1983-. **ORGANIZATIONS:** Columnist MI Chronicle newspaper 1970-; ring announcer State of MI Boxing 1971-; bd mem Concerned Citizens Council 1979-; master F&AM Abiff Lodge 21 Prince Hall 1981-. **HONORS/ACHIEVEMENTS:** Outstanding Citizen Awd Detroit City Council 1975; Disting Serv Awd New Detroit Inc 1975. **BUSINESS ADDRESS:** Deputy Chief of Police, Detroit Police Dept, 2310 Park Avenue, Detroit, MI 48201.

INGRAM, LAVERNE DOROTHY
Physician. **PERSONAL:** Born Mar 01, 1955, Lawrenceville, VA; daughter of James Artis Ingram (deceased) and Blanche Jones Ingram (deceased). **EDUCATION:** VA Union Univ, Richmond, VA, BS Biology, 1973-77; Harvard Univ, Cambridge, MA, 1975; Eastern VA Medical School, Norfolk, VA, MD, 1978-81; VA Commonwealth Univ, Richmond, VA, 1978. **CAREER:** Medical Coll of VA, Richmond, VA, lab asst, 1972-73, laboratory specialist, 1973-78; Howard Univ Hospital, Washington, DC, medicare intern, 1981-82, radiology resident, 1982-85; US Navy, Norfolk, VA, head, radiology dept, 1985-87; US Navy, Portsmouth, VA, staff radiologist 1987-. **ORGANIZATIONS:** Vice pres, Natl Naval Officers Assn, 1985-; mem, Soc Aid to Sickle Cell Anemia; Big Brother Big Sister, 1986-. **HONORS/ACHIEVEMENTS:** Outstanding Young Women of America, 1987; Mem of the Year, Natl Naval Officers Assn Tidewater Chapter, 1988; Distinguished Serv Award, Natl Naval Officers Assn, Natl Award, 1988. **MILITARY SERVICE:** US Navy, Lieutenant commander, 1985-, Navy Commendation ,1987, Certificate of Appreciation, 1988. **HOME ADDRESS:** 1529 Brendle Ct, Virginia Beach, VA 23464.

INGRAM, PHILLIP M.
Chief executive officer. **PERSONAL:** Born Nov 14, 1945, Detroit, MI; son of Henry Ingram and Marion Martin Lewis; divorced; children: Marc A Ingram. **EDUCATION:** Wayne State Univ, Detroit, MI, BFA, Industrial Design, 1971, MBA, 1978. **CAREER:** Gen Motors Engineering Staff, Warren, MI, project engr, 1964-78; Amer Motors Corp, Detroit, MI, principal engr, 1978-79; Systemation Corp, Detroit, MI, pres, 1979-80; Detroit Inst of Technology, Detroit, MI, assoc prof, 1980-81; Gen Automation, Detroit, MI, dist sales mgr, 1980-82; C G Enterprises, Inc, Southfield, MI, pres, 1982-. **ORGANIZATIONS:** Mem, Engineering Soc of Detroit, 1975. **HONORS/ACHIEVEMENTS:** Reviewer, Natl Science Found Cause Grant Programs, 1980. **BUSINESS ADDRESS:** Pres, C G Enterprises, Inc, 27704 Franklin Rd, Southfield, MI 48034.

INGRAM, WILLIAM B.
Consultant. **PERSONAL:** Born May 05, 1935, Lillesville, NC; married Dora Rebecca Plowden; children: Katrina, Eric, Elaine. **EDUCATION:** Lincoln Univ, BA 1961; Univ of Southern CA, M Public Admin, 1977. **CAREER:** Co-owner, D'Lora's Boys Home, 1968-73; LA Co Museum, chief museum opers 1970-73; Riverside City Coll, training consultant 1977-; B&D Financial Servs, owner, 1980-; Orange Co Probation, training consultant 1981-; Supervising Deputy Probations Officer, 1961-87 (retired); Teacher, Moreno Valley School, 1984-. **ORGANIZATIONS:** Pres CA Coalition Black Bd members 1982; vice pres CA School bd Assn 1979-; pres Natl Caucus Black Bd members 1982-84; dir Perris Valley Martin Luther King Found 1983-85; mem CA Correction, Probation & Parole Comm 1984-85; pres-elect Riverside Co School Bd Assn 1985-86; bd of dirs Coalition CA Black Bd members; commr Riverside County Juvenile Justice; Pres, California School Bd Assn, 1989. **HONORS/ACHIEVEMENTS:** Comm Serv Award Los Angeles Bd of Supvrs, 1980; Outstanding Bd Mem, Natl School Bd Assn, 1983; Proclamation Riverside Bd of Supvrs, Black supporter/Achievement 1984. **MILITARY SERVICE:** AUS corpl 1953-56. **HOME ADDRESS:** Box 1324, Perris, CA 92370.

INGRAM, WINIFRED
Retired educator. **PERSONAL:** Born Dec 15, 1913, Seattle, WA; daughter of LeRoy Robert Ingram and Ione Jeanette Clarke Williams. **EDUCATION:** Univ of WA, BA 1937, MA 1938; Northwestern Univ, PhD 1951. **CAREER:** Neuropsychiatric Inst Ann Arbor, MI, psychologist 1950-56; Univ of MI Summer Sch Educ, lecturer 1953-55; Univ of MI Sch of Med Dept Psychiatry, instr 1954-56; Hawthorn Center (for children), dir dept clinical psych 1956-72; The Evergreen State Coll, faculty mem 1972-81, faculty mem Emerita 1981-. **ORGANIZATIONS:** Cons, Delta Home for Girls Detroit 1963-66, Port Huron Area School Dist 1966-68, Ypsilanti Early Educ Proj 1968-70, Adv Comm on Training in Clinical Psych 1967-72; mem Amer Assn for Advancement of Sci; mem Amer Psychol Assn; Delta Sigma Theta Sor; bd dir Ann Arbor Family Serv 1964-70; bd dir Ann Arbor Black Theatre 1969-71; Comm Committee for Coord of Child Care & Devel 1968-69. **HONORS/ACHIEVEMENTS:** Community Scholarship 1933-34; US Public Health Serv Fellowship in Clin Psych Northwestern Univ 1948-50; Fellow of the Mary Ingraham Bunting Inst of Radcliffe Coll 1971; Alpha Kappa Delta Natl Soc Honor Soc 1936; Sigma Xi Natl Sci Honor Soc 1948; subject index to literature on Negro Art 1941 WPA editor; Marcus Garvey, a study of projected negro myths 1938; M.A. thesis Univ of Washington. **BUSINESS ADDRESS:** Mem of Faculty Emerita, Evergreen State College, Olympia, WA 98505.

INGRAM-GRANT, EDITH JACQUELINE
Judge. **PERSONAL:** Born Jan 16, 1942, Sparta, GA; married Roy L Grant. **EDUCATION:** Ft Valley State Coll, BS Elem Ed 1963. **CAREER:** Moore Elem Sch Griffin GA, tchr 1963-67; Hancock Central Elem Sparta GA, tchr 1967-68; Hancock Co, elected probate judge 1968-. **ORGANIZATIONS:** Mem State Natl & Intl Assoc of Probate Judges 1969; mem Voter Registration Assoc of GA 1972; comm chairwoman GA Coalition of Black Women 1980-, Hancock Co Womens Club 1964-, Macedonia Bapt Church Choir 1951-. **HONORS/ACHIEVEMENTS:** Cert of Merit Booker T Washington 1973; NAACP Achievement Awd 1969; Fulton County's Outstanding Citizen's 1978; Atlanta Br NAACP Outstanding Courage in Southern Polit Arena 1979. **BUSINESS ADDRESS:** Judge, Probate Court, PO Drawer G, Sparta, GA 31087.

INNIS, ROY EMILE ALFREDO
Racial equality director. **PERSONAL:** Born Jun 06, 1934, St Croix, VI; son of Alexander Innis and Georgianna Thomas Innis; married Doris Funnye; children: Cedric, Patricia, Corinne, Kwame, Niger, Kimathi. **EDUCATION:** City Coll of NY, 1952-56. **CAREER:** Harlem Commonwealth Council, dir 1967-68; Congress of Racial Equality, assoc dir 1968, natl dir 1968-81, natl chrmn 1981-. **ORGANIZATIONS:** Rsch chemist Vick Chemical Co 1958-63, Montefiore Hospital 1963-67; mem bd New York Urban Coalition, Haryou Act, Harlem Commonwealth Council. **HONORS/ACHIEVEMENTS:** Research Fellow Metropolitan Applied Rsch Center New York City 1967. **MILITARY SERVICE:** AUS sgt 2 Yrs. **BUSINESS ADDRESS:** Natl Chairman, Congress of Racial Equality, 1457-1463 Flatbush Ave, Brooklyn, NY 11210.

INYAMAH, NATHANIEL GINIKANWA N.
Educator. **PERSONAL:** Born Jan 21, 1934, Mbaise, Nigeria;married Catherine; children: Christian, Caroline, Grace, Deborah, Hope, Samuel. **EDUCATION:** Univ Nigeria, Diploma Tehol 1958; STM NW Seminary MN, BD MDiv 1969; Temple, MA 1973f Temple, PhD 1976;1971. **CAREER:** Nigeria, tchr 1951-53; Nigeria HS, 1954-55; Holy Trinity & Lutheran Nigeria, pastor 1959-66; LCA, asst & supply pastor; Camden NJ, teacher; positions in Nigeria Traditional Priest Earth Goddess; Trinity Lutheran Church, pastor & founder. **ORGANIZATIONS:** Bd dir & vice pres Lutheran Ch; pres Ezinihitte Cultural Union; vice pres Owerri Divisional Union; Owerri Provincial Union; WHO; exec mem Eastern Nigeria Soc Welfare Soc; youth prog dir; Utheran Commn Soc Equality Justice; Educ Com Minority Group; African Studies Assn. **HONORS/ACHIEVEMENTS:** Crowned chief Okonko Igbo Soc US Lutheran Missionary At Large 1967-71; Aid Assn Lutheran Ins Scholarship 1967; NW Students Assn Scholarship 1968; Lutheran Wmn Missionary & League Scholarship 1969; Elmer O & Ida Preston Educ Trust Award 1969-71; TempleUniv Gradh Sch Award 1972, 73. **BUSINESS ADDRESS:** PO Box 9786, Philadelphia, PA 19140.

IRBY, RAY
Business executive. **PERSONAL:** Born Jun 07, 1918, Meridian, MS; married Geraldine; children: 4. **EDUCATION:** DePaul U, Math 1969; Am Coll of Life Underwriters, CLU 1969. **CAREER:** Ouver 31 yr period held positions from Debit Builder to Pres in Supreme Life Ins Co. **ORGANIZATIONS:** Mem bd dir Pine Top Ins Co; Chicago Urban League Bus Adv Coun; fin com Operation PUSH; mem Chicago Crime Commin; mem Chicago United; mem Exec Club of Chicago; trustee Better Boys Found 1965; Park Manor Congreg Ch Cosmopolitan C of C Free Sch of Bus 1973. **HONORS/ACHIEVEMENTS:** Man of yr Southeast Community Organization 1973; mgr of yr Chicago Ins Assoc 1966. **MILITARY SERVICE:** AUS 1942-45. **BUSINESS ADDRESS:** 3501 S M L King Jr Dr, Chicago, IL 60653.

IRELAND, LYNDA
Entrepreneur/business leader. **PERSONAL:** Born Jan 02, 1950, Bronx, NY; daughter of Carwee Johnson and Margaret McNair Johnson; divorced; children: Francisco Marc & Maya Danielle Ireland. **CAREER:** African-Amer Inst, New York, NY, program dir, 1971-76; Hofstra Univ, Hempstead, NY, admin, 1979-84; Panache Professional Systems Inc, Hempstead, NY, CEO pres, 1979-84. **ORGANIZATIONS:** Bd mem, African Amer Hertiage Assn, 1981-85; bd mem, Minority Women's Task Force, NYS, N O W, 1985; delegate, White House Conf on Small Business, 1985-86; pres, Assn of Minority Enterprises of NYS, Inc, 1986-; bd mem, NYS Governor's Advisory Bd on Small Business, 1987-; Advisory Bd, Business Center, F.I.T., 1989. **HONORS/ACHIEVEMENTS:** Outstanding Achievement, AMENY, 1985; Leadership Citation, Nassau County, 1987; Citation, Mayor of NY, 1987; Leadership Award, Women on the Job, 1988; Leadership Citation, Town of Hempstead, 1988; Mothers at Work, Role Model of the Year Award (lst recipient), Morningside Community Day Care Centers; advisor to upcoming book by Prentice Hall on minority vendor programs of ethical corps (Fortune 500); Public speaker on Minority Business Devel. **BUSINESS ADDRESS:** Chief Exec Officer, Panache Professional Systems, Inc, 250 Fulton Ave, Suite 507, Hempstead, NY 11550.

IRELAND, RODERICK LOUIS
Judge. **PERSONAL:** Born Dec 03, 1944, Springfield, MA; divorced; children: Helen Elizabeth, Michael Alexander. **EDUCATION:** Lincoln U, BA 1966; Columiba Law Sch, JD 1969; Harvard Law, LLM 1975. **CAREER:** Boston Juvenile Ct, judge 1977-; Bd of Appeal on Motor Vehicle Policies & Bonds, chmn of bd 1977; Sec of Adminstrn & Finance MA, counsel 1975-77; Harvard Law Sch, teaching fellow 1975; Roxbury Defenders Com, dir 1971-74. **ORGANIZATIONS:** Bd of dirs Columbia Law Sch Alumni Assn; mem MA Bar Assn; mem Boston Bar Assn; mem ABA; mem MA Black Lawyers Assn; mem NY Bar Assn Bd Dirs Proj Aim; bd dirs First Inc; bd dirs Roxbury YMCA; bd dirs MA Minority Council on Alcoholism; mem Omega Psi Phi; mem Lincoln Alumni. **HONORS/ACHIEVEMENTS:** Recip 10 Outstndg yng ldrs of Boston award Boston Jaycees 1979; 10 outstndg men of Am award US Jaycees 1980. **BUSINESS ADDRESS:** Boston Juvenile Ct, 17 Somerset St, Boston, MA 02108.

IRMAGEAN
Artist. **PERSONAL:** Born Apr 09, 1947, Detroit, MI; daughter of Theodore Curry and Mamie Lee Sago Curry; divorced; children: Sundjata T Kone. **EDUCATION:** Wayne St Univ Monteith Coll, 1965-66; Grove Str Coll, AA 1974; CA Coll of Arts & Crfts, BFA 1976. **CAREER:** Isabelle Percy West Gallery CA Coll of Arts & Crafts Oakland, exhibit 1979; NY Carlsberg Glyptotek Museum Copenhagen Denmark, rep 1980; Los Medanos Coll Pittsburg, CA, exhibit artist 1980; Berkeley Art Center CA, exhibit 1981; Galerie Franz Mehring Berlin, Germany, exhibit 1981; SF Museum of Modern Art, exhibit 1981; Center for the Visual Arts Oakland CA, exhibit 1985; Spanish Speaking Citizens Found, Oakland, CA, guest art instructor, 1989; E Oakland Youth Devel Center, Oakland, CA, mural instructor, 1989; City Sites, CA Coll of Arts & Crafts, artist mentor, 1989; Berkeley Art Center, exhibitor, 1988; San Francisco State Univ, exhibitor, 1989. **ORGANIZATIONS:** Juror Vida Gallery SF, CA 1981; asst in orgn 11 Bienal del Grabado De Am Maracaibo, Venezuela 1982; juror, Festival at the lake, Craft/Art Market, Oakland, CA, 1989. **HONORS/ACHIEVEMENTS:** Amer Artist Today in Black & White Vol 11 1980 author Dr H L Williams; Directory of Distinguished Amers 1981; exhibit Dept De Bellas Artes Guadaljara, Mexico 1982; exhibit Brockman Gallery Prod LA, CA 1982; rep Hong Kong, China 1983-; Hon mem Sigma Gamma Rho Sor 1986; Daniel Mendelowitz "A Guide to Drawing" 3rd ed Holt Rinehart and Winston 1982, 4th ed revised by Duane Wakeham 1988; Sigma's Outstanding Women of the Twentieth Century, Sigma Gamma Rho Sorority, 1986; Certificiate of Appreciation, St Augustine's Church, 1988; feature, The Aurora, 1987, Sigma Gamma Rho Sorority, 1987; The CA Art Review, 2nd edition Amer Reference, Inc, 1988; Amer artist, 2nd edition, References, 1989. **BUSINESS ADDRESS:** Artist, P O Box 5602, Berkeley, CA 94705.

IRONS, GERALD DWAYNE
Athlete. **PERSONAL:** Born May 02, 1947, Gary, IN; married Myrna Joyce Wise; children: Gerald Jr, Jarrett. **EDUCATION:** MD Eastern Shore Coll, BS 1970;Univ of Chgo, MBA 1976. **CAREER:** The Woodlands Corp, dir of bus devel; Cleveland Browns, pro ftbl plyr 1977; Oakland Raiders, pro plyr 1970-75; Am Nat Bank & Trust Co, ofcr 1972-74;Cable TV Co, ofcr 1970-71;Univ of MD, admin aide 1967-69. **ORGANIZATIONS:** Vp Student Gov 1969; pres Men's Senate 1969-70; cpt ftbl team 1968-70; mem North Royalton OH Jaycees 1977; mem YMCA; Kappa Alpha Psi Frat; Atheletes in Action Rotary Internat; Flwshp of Christian Athl; Boys Club of Am; Physical Fitness Counc. **HONORS/ACHIEVEMENTS:** Hon mem Exchange Club of E Chicago; pro athlete of the yr Gary IN 1973-74; Assn Award for Achievement in Football Roosevelt High Alumni 1971; player of the Week NFL 1975; voted MVP Cleveland Browns 1977. **BUSINESS ADDRESS:** The Woodlands Corporation, PO Box 4000, OB-1, The Woodlands, TX 77380.

IRONS, SUE See FITTZ, SENGA NENGUDI

IRVIN, CHARLES LESLIE
Attorney. **PERSONAL:** Born Mar 02, 1935, Corpus Christi, TX; son of Joseph Irvin and Louise Irvin; married Shirley Jean Smith; children: Kimberley Antoinette, Jonathan Charles. **EDUCATION:** TX Southern Univ, BA 1964, LLB 1964; Cornell Univ, Exec Devel Course 1984; Wharton Sch of Business, Financial Course 1985. **CAREER:** US Dept of Labor Kansas City, MO, attorney 1964-67; US Dept of Labor Chicago, attorney 1967-73; Texaco Inc, senior attorney; division attorney Midland, Texas 1988-89; division attorney Denver, Colorado 1989-. **ORGANIZATIONS:** Mem TX Bar Assn 1964-; US Supreme Ct; 9th & 5th Cir Ct of Appeals; TX Bar Foundation; Director, Texaco Credit Union. **MILITARY SERVICE:** AUS Sgt E-5 1955-58. **HOME ADDRESS:** 16188 East Powers Place, Aurora, CO 80015. **BUSINESS ADDRESS:** Division Attorney, Texaco Inc, 4601 DTC Blvd, Denver, CO 80237.

IRVIN, LEROY
Professional athlete. **PERSONAL:** Born Sep 15, 1957, Fort Dix, NJ; married Roxanne; children: LeRoy III, Charles Julius, Sara Ashlee. **EDUCATION:** Attended, Kansas State, Cal State Fullerton. **CAREER:** Los Angeles Rams, cornerback 1980-. **HONORS/ACHIEVEMENTS:** Named Big-8 by AP and UPI after sr coll season; holds Ram records for punt returns, yards and touchdowns; Daniel F Reeves Memorial Trophy as teams MVP selected by Southern CA Sports Broadcasters Assoc; named AFC Defensive Player of the Week vs Tampa Bay 1985; UPI All NFC and AP All NFL (second teams); mem Pro Bowl teams 1986,87. **BUSINESS ADDRESS:** Los Angeles Rams, 2327 Lincoln Ave, Anaheim, CA 92801.

IRVIN, MONFORD MERRILL (MONTE)
Business executive. **PERSONAL:** Born Feb 25, 1919, Columbia, AL; married Dee; children: Mrs Pamela Irvin Fields, Mrs Patti Irvin Gordon. **EDUCATION:** Lincoln Univ Chester PA, attended 2 yrs. **CAREER:** Cuban Winter League, professional baseball player; NY Giants, professional baseball player 1949-55; Chicago Cubs, professional baseball player 1956; Office of the Baseball Commiss, spec asst to the commiss; Diversified Capital Corp, vp. **HONORS/ACHIEVEMENTS:** Elected to Baseball Hall of Fame 1973. **MILITARY SERVICE:** Buck sgt 1313 GS Engineers - ETO. **BUSINESS ADDRESS:** Senior Vice President, Office of the Baseball Commr, 350 Park Ave, New York, NY 10022.

IRVIN, TERRY CALVIN
Professional athlete. **PERSONAL:** Born Aug 14, 1962, Los Angeles, CA. **EDUCATION:** Colorado. **CAREER:** Denver Gold, linebacker 1984-. **HONORS/ACHIEVEMENTS:** 4-yr letterman for the Buffaloes.

IRVINE, FREEMAN RAYMOND, JR.
Educator. **PERSONAL:** Born Sep 12, 1931, Madison, FL; married Carolyn Lenett Green; children: Rodney, Charlton, Pamela, Fredreka, Freeman III. **EDUCATION:** FL A&M Univ, BS 1958; OK St Univ, Cert 1960; Oak Ridge Assocd Univs, Cert 1966; Univ of TN, MS 1968, EdD 1972. **CAREER:** SFL A&M Univ, electronics teacher 1958-61; Dillard Comp High School Ft Lauderdale, FL, electronics teacher 1961-63; FL A&M Univ, electronics & math teacher 1964-67; Univ of TN, rsch assoc 1967-69; FL A&M Univ, assoc prof of indus ed; chmn industrial arts and vocational educ dept. **ORGANIZATIONS:** Indus ed tchr FL A&M Univ 1969-74; pblctn comm mem FL Indus Arts Assn 1970-73; rsrch assoc FL St Univ 1974-75; head of indus ed dept FL A&M Univ 1976-82; fclty sen FL A&M Univ 1978-81; test coord NOCTI 1980-. **HONORS/ACHIEVEMENTS:** Comm Serv Awrd Sounds of Faith Radio Pgm 1979-80; A Smplication of Parallel Resistance Calcuation Schl Shop Mag 1982; Tchng Vctnl Ed to Hndicps 1985. **MILITARY SERVICE:** AUS stf sgt 3 yrs. **HOME ADDRESS:** 618 Brookridge Dr, Tallahassee, FL 32304. **BUSINESS ADDRESS:** Assoc Prof of Indstrl Ed, FL A&MUniv, Box 106 Famu P O, Tallahassee, FL 32307.

IRVING, CLARENCE LARRY, JR.
Attorney. **PERSONAL:** Born Jul 07, 1955, Brooklyn, NY. **EDUCATION:** Northwestern Univ, BA 1972-76; Stanford Univ Law School, JD 1976-79. **CAREER:** Kirkland E Ellis, summer assoc 1977; Breed Abbott & Morgan, summer assoc 1978; Hogan & Hartson, assoc 1979-83; US Rep Mickey Leland, legislative dir & counsel 1983-87; US House of Representatives Subcomm on Telecomm & Finance, sr counsel 1987-. **ORGANIZATIONS:** Precinct captain Washington DC Democratic Party 1983-84; mem Natl Bar Assn 1980-; mem Natl Conf of Black Lawyers Comm Task Force 1983-; mem Variety Club of Greater Washington 1985-; chair House of Representatives Fair Employment Practices Committee 1985-87; Board of Visitors, Stanford Law School. **HONORS/ACHIEVEMENTS:** Pres Stanford Law School Class of 1979; Outstanding Young Man of America Jaycees 1979. **BUSINESS ADDRESS:** Senior Counsel, US House of Representatives, Subcomm on Telecomm & Finance, Room 316 House Annex #2, Washington, DC 20515.

IRVING, HENRY E., II
Educational administrator. **PERSONAL:** Born Apr 21, 1937, Paterson, NJ; married Jocelyn Miller; children: Vian, Farrah, Herman III, Christopher. **EDUCATION:** Rutgers Univ, BA 1968; Seton Hall Univ, MA 1975; Princeton Univ, Prof Cert 1976. **CAREER:** Ayerst Labs, Inc, asst cr mgr 1968-71; Passonc County Community Coll, dean of students 1971-76; Catholic Diocese of Paterson, dir youth programs 1976-81. **ORGANIZATIONS:** Mem Mayors Council on Yth 1967-74, YMCA 1971-78; pres NJ Council Coll Deans & Stdnts 1974-75; mem Bd of Dirs Acts-Vim 1985; Efwc Diocese of Newark. **HONORS/ACHIEVEMENTS:** Citizenshp Awrd Lions Club Paterson 1971. **HOME ADDRESS:** 360 9th Ave, Paterson, NJ 07514.

IRVING, OPHELIA MCALPIN
Librarian. **PERSONAL:** Born Apr 04, 1929, Gadsden, AL; daughter of Jerry McAlpin and Lamae McAlpin; married Charles G, Jr; children: Cyretha C. **EDUCATION:** Clarks Coll, AB 1951; Atlanta Univ, 1952; Syracuse Univ, MLS 1958, 1973; Drexel Inst of Tech, 1966; NC Central Univ, 1982. **CAREER:** Center High School Waycross, GA, librarian 1951-54; Spencer Jr High School Columbus, GA, librarian 1954-55; St Augustine's Coll Raleigh, NC, librarian 1955-68; NC State Library Raleigh, NC, asst chief info series section 1968-. **ORGANIZATIONS:** Alpha Kappa Alpha Sor 1954-; NC Library Assn 1955-; Jack & Jill of Amer Inc 1961-73; Amer Library Assn 1963-; YWCA 1965-; NC On Line Users Group 1982-; Microcomputer Users Group NC 1983-; Top Ladies of Distinction. **HONORS/ACHIEVEMENTS:** Faculty Fellowship St Augustine Coll Raleigh, NC 1964. **BUSINESS ADDRESS:** Asst Chief Info Services, NC State Library, 109 E Jones St, Raleigh, NC 27611.

IRVING, REGGIE CALVIN
Professional athlete. **PERSONAL:** Born Dec 22, 1957, Baton Rouge, LA; married Florence; children: Tatum. **EDUCATION:** Grambling. **CAREER:** Oakland Invaders, guard 1984-. **HONORS/ACHIEVEMENTS:** Named All-Southwest Athletic Conf as sr.

IRVIS, K. LEROY
Speaker, Pennsylvania House of Representatives. **PERSONAL:** Born Dec 27, 1919, Saugerties, NY; married Cathyrn L Edwards; children: Reginald, Sherrie. **EDUCATION:** NY State Tchrs Coll, AB (summa cum laude); Univ of NY, MA; Univ of Pittsburgh Law Sch, LLB; Univ of Pittsburgh Law Sch, JD. **CAREER:** Pittsburgh Urban League Mag, ed; author; Baltimore school teacher; Pittsburgh Courier, newscaster; Asst DA 1957-63; elected to PA House of Representatives, 1958-; Minority Caucus, chmn 1963-64; Majority Caucus, chmn 1965-66; Minority Whip, 1967-68, 73-74; Majority Ldr, 1969-70, 71-72, 75-76, 77; Spkr 1977-78;elected mem Democratic Natl Comm 1982; Dem Natl Convention, del 1968,72,76,80,84; Minority Leader 1979, 1983-88. **ORGANIZATIONS:** Mem bd dirs Post-Gazette Dapper Dan Club; WQED-Pub TV; United Black Front; PA Council for Arts; Bidwell Cultural & Training Cntr; (TEAM) Training Employment & Manpower; Community Action of Pittsburgh; Urban League; Alumni Assn StateUniv of NY at Albany; mem bd trustees Univ Pittsburgh; mem Univ Pittsburgh Med Sch Adv Com; St Hwy & Bridge Auth; St Pub Sch Bldg Auth; PA Higher Educ Facilities Auth; Neighborhood Assistance Adv Bd; trustee PA Southwest Assn;treas Joint State Govt Commn; Phi Beta Kappa; Phi Delta Phi; Order of Coif; Practice law in Fed Dist & Commonwealth Cts; hon chmn Pub Defender Assn; sculpter, painter, writer. **HONORS/ACHIEVEMENTS:** Hon Dr of Laws Lincoln Univ 1979, Alma Mater St Univ of NY at Albany 1986; Man of the Year Awd B'Nai B'rith Anti Defamation League 1987. **BUSINESS ADDRESS:** 2170 Centre Ave, Pittsburgh, PA 15219.

ISAAC, BRIAN WAYNE
Employment administrator. **EDUCATION:** NY Univ, BA 1976, M Public Admin 1984. **CAREER:** Long Island Lighting Co, training & educ coord 1977-79, EEO admin 1979-84, employment serv admin 1984-. **ORGANIZATIONS:** Pres Manhattan Spokesman Club 1977-78; mem The Edges Group Inc 1982-. **HOME ADDRESS:** 326 E 92nd St, Brooklyn, NY 11212. **BUSINESS ADDRESS:** Employment Serv Admin, Long Island Lighting Co, 175 E Old Country Rd, Hicksville, NY 11801.

ISAAC, EPHRAIM
Educator, philologist, historian, scholar. **PERSONAL:** Born May 29, 1936, Nedjio, Ethiopia;son of Yishag and Ruth; married Dr Sherry Rosen; children: Devorah Esther, Raphael Samuel, Yael Ruth. **EDUCATION:** Concordia Coll, BA 1958; Harvard Univ Div School, BD 1963; Harvard Univ, PhD 1969. **CAREER:** Harvard Univ, instr 1968-69, lecturer 1969-71, assoc prof 1971-77; Hebrew Univ, visiting prof 1977-79; Inst for Advanced Study Princeton, fellow 1979-80; Princeton Theol Sem/Hunter Coll, visiting prof 1980-81; Bard Coll, visiting prof 1981-83; Lehigh Univ, visiting prof of religion Princeton Univ, visiting prof, 1983-85; Institute of Semitic Studies, dir 1985. **ORGANIZATIONS:** Dir general Natl Literacy Campaign of Ethiopia 1966-72; bd mem Amer Assn for Ethiopian Jews 1973-; pres Ethiopian Student Assn in North Amer 1959-62; vice chmn Ethiopian Famine Relief Comm 1984-; bd mem African Studies Heritage Assoc 1969-73; chmn Comm for Ethiopian Literacy 1963-68; treas Harvard Graduate Student Assoc 1962-65; chorale dir Harvard Graduate Chorale 1962-64. **HONORS/ACHIEVEMENTS:** Second Prize Ethiopian HS Matric Award 1954; Ethiopian Natl Prize for literacy (Humanity) 1967; Outstanding Educators of Amer 1972; Fellow Endowment for the Humanities 1979; NEH Rsch Grant 1976-77; Harvard Univ Faculty Fund Rsch Grants; Concordia Coll Scholarships 1956-58; Univ Coll of Addis Ababa Fellowship 1954-56; author of Ethiopic book of Enoch, Doubleday, 1983, a history of religions in Africa (Oxford, forthcoming.). **BUSINESS ADDRESS:** Dir, Inst of Semitic Studies, 195 Nassau St, Princeton, NJ 08540.

ISAAC, EUGENE LEONARD
Educator. **PERSONAL:** Born Aug 15, 1915, Natchez, MS; married Ardelma G Brown; children: Genette Leonardo, Doris Gene. **EDUCATION:** Alcorn A&M Coll, BS 1940; IA State Coll, MS 1950; Emporia State Univ, educ splst 1965. **CAREER:** Vocational Training Oak Park HS Laurel, teacher 1940-43, 1946-49; Utica Inst, counselor 1950-51; Savannah State Coll, head carpentry & woodworking dept 1951-58; MS Valley State Coll, chmn tech educ div 1958-75; Tech Edn, asso prof 1975-80, prof indust tech 1980-. **ORGANIZATIONS:** Chmn fin comm United Methodist Church 1968-; mem policy comm Tech Educ Dept Amer Vocational Assn 1977-79; chmn editorial & publ comm Amer Vocational Assn 1979-80; consult tech educ, mem Industrial Arts in Elem School; mem MS Teachers Assn, Amer Magnolia State Vocational Assn, Amer Council on Indus Arts Teacher Educ, Intl Platform Assn, Amer Legion, Phi Delta Kappa. **HONORS/ACHIEVEMENTS:** Meritorious serv Award Utica field chap Phi Delta Kappa 1965f recipient serv to Youth Award YMCA Savannah 1958; meritorious serv Award MS Valley State Coll YMCA 1967f man of the year award Utica Chap Phi Delta Kappa 1978. **MILITARY SERVICE:** AUS 1943-45.

ISAAC, JOSEPH WILLIAM ALEXANDER
Physician. **PERSONAL:** Born Dec 24, 1935; son of B Timothy Isacc and Agatha Henry Isaac; married Gertrude Harris; children: Charles, Zoe, Joseph A. **EDUCATION:** City Coll NYC, BS 1967; Howard U, MD 1971. **CAREER:** Freedmen's Hosp Wash DC, med & intern 1971-72; Howard Univ Wash DC, resident Ob/Gyn 1972-76; Norfolk Health Dept, family planning phys 1976-77; Portsmouth Gen Hosp, chmn dept of Ob/Gyn 1985-88; Norfolk & Portsmouth VA, private practice Ob/Gyn 1977-. **ORGANIZATIONS:** Mem AMA 1975-; mem Norfolk Med Soc 1976-; mem Norfolk Acad of Med 1977; mem Portsmouth Chamber of Commerce 1978-; mem Med Adv Com of Tidewater March of Dimes 1979-; diplomate Am Bd of Ob/Gyn 1978 fellow Am Coll of Ob/Gyn 1979; vice pres Old Dom Med Soc 1986-87; pres Norfolk Med Soc 1985-87. **MILITARY SERVICE:** AUS E-5 1959-62. **BUSINESS ADDRESS:** Physician, 549 E Brambleton Ave, Norfolk, VA 23510.

ISAAC, YVONNE RENEE
Business executive. **PERSONAL:** Born Apr 13, 1948, Cleveland, OH. **EDUCATION:** Sarah Lawrence Coll, BA 1970; Rensselear Polytechnic Inst, MS 1972; Ploytechnic Inst of NY, MS 1976. **CAREER:** Ehren Krantz Grp, architectural planner; Perkins & Will NYC, proj mgr 1978-; Mobil Oil Corp NYC, sr analyst 1976-78; Perkins & Will SPA/ REDCO Inc NYC& Chgo, sr asso 1972-76; Gen Elec Co Phila, rsrch analyst 1971-72; Pratt Inst Brooklyn, vis asso prof 1977; ColumbiaUniv NY, vis asso prof 1978-79. **ORGANIZATIONS:** Bd of dir Black Woman Collaborative 1975-; bd of dir Operation Open Cty 1977-; treas Sarah Lawrence Coll Black Alumni Assn 1979-. **HONORS/ACHIEVEMENTS:** Outstndg yng women of Am 1978-79; fellow to pursue doctoral studies Urban Mass Trans Adminstrn. **MILITARY SERVICE:** US DOT 1975-76.

ISAACS, DORIS C.
Computer company executive. **PERSONAL:** Born Jul 02, 1939, Columbus, OH; daughter of Dr. John D White, Jr and Lois Cox Boyce; married Thomas E Stallworth, Jr, Nov 03, 1987; children: Kelly Carroll Michaels, Thomas E Stallworth, III, Kaleb WinslowStallworth. **EDUCATION:** Kent State Univ, Kent, OH, BS Educ, 1956-59. **CAREER:** IBM Corp, Syst Engr-Dir, Educ Operations, 1966-. **ORGANIZATIONS:** Mem, Advisory Bd Cobb County YWCA, 1986-89. **HONORS/ACHIEVEMENTS:** Systems Eng Symposium, IBM, 1969, 1971-72; 100% Club, IBM, 1980-81; Systems Eng Mgr of the Year, IBM, 1975. **HOME ADDRESS:** 3685 Peachtree Rd, #8, Atlanta, GA 30319.

ISAACS, PATRICIA
Operations director. **PERSONAL:** Born May 06, 1949, Georgetown, Guyana;daughter of Violet Isaacs; children: Krystal Louise. **EDUCATION:** Dist of Columbia Teachers Coll; South Eastern Univ; Penn State. **CAREER:** McDonalds Corp, Michigan Region, dir of operations, 1975-. **ORGANIZATIONS:** Mem of Detroit Chamber of Commerce; bd mem, Homes for Black Children. **BUSINESS ADDRESS:** Dir of Operations, McDonalds Corp, 200 Town Center, Suite 700, Southfield, MI 48075.

ISAACS, STEPHEN D.
Administrative officer. **PERSONAL:** Born Feb 22, 1944, Boston, MA; children: Athelia, Stephanie. **EDUCATION:** Howard Univ, B Mech Eng 1969, MBA 1973. **CAREER:** Office of Mgmt & Budget, Operations Rsrch Analyst 1973-76; US Nuclear Reg Comm, program analyst 1976-77; US Nuclear Reg Commn, FOIA officer 1977-86; Federal Aviation Adminis, aviation safety inspector 1986-. **ORGANIZATIONS:** Am Soc of Mech Engs 1973-; Am Soc of Access Profls 1980-; acct exec Intrnl Monetary Founding Group, Inc 1984-86; bd of dirs Special Air Serv, Inc 1983-. **MILITARY SERVICE:** USCG E-4 intelligence specialist 1969-71. **HOME ADDRESS:** 1907 - 2nd St NW, Washington, DC 20001. **BUSINESS ADDRESS:** Aviation Safety Inspector, Federal Aviation Administration, Flight Standards District Office #27, P.O. Box 17325, Dulles International Airport, Washington, DC 20041.

ISADORE, HAROLD W.
Attorney, librarian. **PERSONAL:** Born in Alexandria, LA. **EDUCATION:** Southern Univ, BS 1967; Southern Univ Schl of Law, JD 1970; SUNY at Buffalo Law Schl, Cert 1978. **CAREER:** US Dept of Labor Office of the Solicitor, atty 1970-73; Baton Rouge Legal Aid Scty, atty 1973-74; Public Defender of Baton Rouge, atty 1974-75; Southern Univ School of Law, asst law libririan 1975-. **ORGANIZATIONS:** Mem Am Bar Assn, Natl Bar Assn, Delta Theta Phi Law Frat, Am Assn of Law Libraries, Kappa Alpha Psi Frat, Inc. **HONORS/ACHIEVEMENTS:** Serv awrd Stdnt Bar Assoc, SU Law Schl 1970; Hypotext on Security Devices Southern Univ Pblshr 1979; Hypotext on Civil Procedure Vols 1 and 11 SUniv Pblshr 1980-81. **BUSINESS ADDRESS:** Asst Law Librarian, SouthernUniv Law Schl, Baton Rouge Campus, Baton Rouge, LA 70813.

ISBELL, JAMES S.
Business executive. **PERSONAL:** Born Sep 13, 1918, Pittsburgh; married Ann B McLeary. **EDUCATION:** Northwester Sch Commerce; DePaul Sch Commerce. **CAREER:** Jackson Mut Life Ins Co, 1937; agency dir 1951-55; Chicago Met Mut Assur Co, sp rep 1956; asst agency dir 1957; adminstrv asst agency dir 1963; 2nd vice pres & adminstrv asst agency dir 1966f vice pres & adminstrv asst Agency dir 1967f vp-asso agency dir 1969; vp-agy dir 1970-. **ORGANIZATIONS:** Past chmn Agency Sect Nat Ins Assn; chmn Life Underwriters Hon Soc NIA; mem & past pres bd dir Chicago Ins Assn; chmn LUHS Nat Ins Assn;fndr Chicago chap Life Underwriters Hon Soc dist com; mem past chmn Oakland Dist Chicago Area Counc BSA; past bd mem RR Donnelly Boys Club; mem NAACP; Urban League. **HONORS/ACHIEVEMENTS:** The Olive H Crosthwait Award CIA 1970; Nat Ins Serv Award 1971. **MILITARY SERVICE:** AUS lt-col. **BUSINESS ADDRESS:** 4455 Dr Martin Luther King Jr, Chicago, IL 60653.

ISHMAN, SYBIL R.
Educator. **PERSONAL:** Born Jul 25, 1946, Durham, NC; married Reginald E Ishman. **EDUCATION:** Univ of NC (Greensboro), BA 1968; NC Central Univ, MA 1971; Univ of NC (Chapel Hill), PhD 1980. **CAREER:** NC Central Univ, grad asst 1969-71, instr 1970-72; NC State Univ, assist prof 1980-. **ORGANIZATIONS:** Mem Am Assn Univ Women; Modern Lang Assn; Natl Counc of Tchrs of English; mem TESOL; Natl Smart Set Durham Chpt. **BUSINESS ADDRESS:** Assistant Professor, NC StateUniv, 281 Tompkins Hall, Raleigh, NC 27695.

ISIBOR, EDWARD IROGUEHI
Engineer, educator. **PERSONAL:** Born Jun 09, 1940, Benin City, Nigeria;married Edwina Williams; children: Ekinadose, Emwanta. **EDUCATION:** Howard U, BSc 1965; MIT, MSc 1967; Purdue U, PhD 1970. **CAREER:** School of Engineering & Tech TN State Univ, dean 1975-; Civil Engineering FL Intl Univ, assoc prof & head urban systems prog 1973-75; NOACA Cleveland, transportation engr 1972; Afro-Am Cultural Center Cleveland State Univ, dir 1970-71; Purdue Univ, research asst 1967-69; MIT, research asst 1965-67. **ORGANIZATIONS:** Mem Am Soc Enrg Edn; Transportation Research Bd Washington, DC; OH Soc Professional Engrs; C of C Reg engr OH. **HONORS/ACHIEVEMENTS:** Who's Who Students Am Colls 1965; Sigma XI hon soc 1970; Tau Beta Pi hon Soc 1964. **BUSINESS ADDRESS:** Ofc of Dean Sch of Engineering & T, TN State Univ, Nashville, TN 37203.

ISLER, MARSHALL A., III
Company executive, businessman, real estate developer. **PERSONAL:** Born Jan 09, 1939, Kinston, NC; son of Marshall A Isler, Jr and Louise Douglas Isler (deceased0; married Ellen Sandra Jordan, Oct 20, 1963; children: Valerie L, Bryan C. **EDUCATION:** Howard Univ, BSEE 1962; George Washington Univ, MEA 1971; Harvard Univ, PMD 1977. **CAREER:** Johns Hopkins Univ Applied Physics Lab, space sys officer 1967; Naval Air Sys Command, satellite proj engr 1971; Natl Bureau of Standards Law Enforcement Standards, security syst prog mgr 1973; Sen John Tunney, sci adv 1974; Natl Bureau Standards Dept Commerce Center Consult Prod Tech, dep dir 1978; Parametric Inc, pres; Isler Assoc, pres. **ORGANIZATIONS:** Mem Howard Univ Alumni Assoc, Omega Psi Phi Frat, SBF Credit Union; assoc Urban Land Institute; vice pres Durham Business and Professional Chain; mem Durham Chamber of Commerce; mem Natl Home Builders Assoc; mem Mayor's Downtown Redevelopment Comm Durham; pres Abiding Savior Lutheran Church Durham, NC 1989-; vice pres Business & Prof Chain Duram, NC 1989-; Bd of Dir Dispute Settlement Center Durham, NC

1989-. **HONORS/ACHIEVEMENTS:** Congressional Fellowship 1973-74. **MILITARY SERVICE:** USN Lt 1962-67; USNR Comdr 1967-. **BUSINESS ADDRESS:** Isler & Associates Inc, PO Box 828, Durham, NC 27702.

ISMIAL, SALAAM IBN
Association president. **PERSONAL:** Born in Jersey City, NJ. **EDUCATION:** Robert Walsh School of Business, 1978-79; Kean Coll of NJ, 1980-82; Union Cty Coll, 1983. **CAREER:** Elizabeth Youth Council, pres 1982-84; Union Cty Coll, vice pres 1983; NAACP, youth pres 1984; EYC After School Prog Rec Dept, coord 1984-85; Elizabeth Youth Council, pres. **ORGANIZATIONS:** Youth leader Local Chap CORE 1973; chmn Kean Coll Black Student Union 1982; pres Elizabeth Youth Council 1982-85; mem Black Issue Convention, SouthernChristian Leadership 1984; Progressive Rainbow Alliance of NJ 1985. **HONORS/ACHIEVEMENTS:** Medal of Honor Elizabeth Boys Scouts 1972; Outstanding Serv Kean Black Student Union 1982; Community Serv Elizabeth Youth Council 1983; Life Time Membership NAACP 1984. **BUSINESS ADDRESS:** President, Elizabeth Youth Council, 455 Monroe Ave, Elizabeth, NJ 07201.

ITA, LAWRENCE EYO
Educator. **PERSONAL:** Born Dec 01, 1939, Calabar, Nigeria;married Autumn Dean; children: Eyo, Ekanem. **EDUCATION:** Univ of MI, PhD 1970; London U, BSC 1962. **CAREER:** Univ of NV, assoc prof 1978; Bureau of Asso Serv, dir 1974-77; Commonwealth Asso, engineering consultant 1970-72. **ORGANIZATIONS:** Mem Am Soc of Engineering Educ 1974-; mem Am Soc of Heat Refrig & Air-Cond Ewngrs 1976-; mem Intl Soc of Solar Energy 1975-. **HONORS/ACHIEVEMENTS:** Publs Jour of Chem & Engineering Data 1974-76. **BUSINESS ADDRESS:** 4505 Maryland, Las Vegas, NV 89154.

IVERY, EDDIE LEE
Professional athlete. **PERSONAL:** Born Jul 30, 1957; married Anna; children: Tauvia Edana, Eddie Lee Jr. **EDUCATION:** Georgia Tech, Indus Mgmt. **CAREER:** Green Bay Packers, prof football running back 1979-. **HONORS/ACHIEVEMENTS:** Career marks 609 carries & 3,517 rushing yds gained Georgia Tech; All-Time NCAA Single Game Rushing Record Sr Yr; Finished 8th in Balloting Heisman Trophy; Team capt & rep football squad Prestigious Tech Athletic Bd; teams leading rusher & reciever 1979 pre-season as rookie. **BUSINESS ADDRESS:** Green Bay Packers, 1265 Lombardi Ave, Green Bay, WI 54303.

IVERY, JAMES A.
Federal government official. **PERSONAL:** Born Jan 05, 1950, Zebulon, NC; son of Eugene Copeland and Dorothy Ivery; divorced; children: Jacinda D Ivery. **EDUCATION:** Fayetteville State Univ, Fayetteville, NC, BS, 1972; Bucknell Univ, Lewisburg, PA, MPA, 1982. **CAREER:** Wake County Public Schools, Raleigh, NC, instructor/coach, 1972-74; Internal Revenue Service, Raleigh, NC, revenue officer, 1974-76; US Dept of Health & Human Services, Washington, DC, policy analyst, 1976-. **ORGANIZATIONS:** Life mem, Alpha Phi Alpha Fraternity, 1977-; mem, Natl Forum for Black Public Administrators, 1986-; mem, Mt Olive Baptist Church, Arlington, VA, 1986-. **HONORS/ACHIEVEMENTS:** Outstanding Young Men of America, 1985; short story, Essense Magazine, "Say Brother Column," 1986; Distinguished Black College Graduate, Natl Assn for Equal Opportunity in Higher Education, 1988. **BUSINESS ADDRESS:** Special Asst to the Deputy Under Secretary, US Dept of Health & Human Services, 200 Independene Ave, SW, Rm 630F, Washington, DC 20201.

IVEY, HORACE SPENCER
Educator. **PERSONAL:** Born Nov 13, 1931, DeLand, FL; married Barbara Edwards; children: Lawrence, Derek, Chandra, Allegra, Elliot. **EDUCATION:** Smith Coll Sch for Soc Wrk; Syracuse U, 1962;Univ CT, MSW 1956fUniv Bridgeport, BA 1954. **CAREER:** SUNY Upstate Medical Center, assoc prof; State Univ Hospital, 1965, supvr 1961-62, social worker 1956-61, caseworker 1958-60. **ORGANIZATIONS:** Nat Assn of Social Workers; Acad of Certified Soc Workers; Med Social Work Sec; Unltd Prgm; Healther Serv Com Council on Aging; Am Hosp Assn Council on Volunteers; SyracuseUniv Rehab Council; num other affiliations. **HONORS/ACHIEVEMENTS:** Publs "Factors in Selection of Patients for Home Chemo-Therapy" 1956; "Hosp Abortion Prgm Implication for Social Work Planning & Serv Delivery 1971; numeralother publs. **BUSINESS ADDRESS:** Upstate Med Ctr, 750 E Adams St, Syracuse, NY 13210.

IVEY, MARK, III
Physician & pharmacist. **PERSONAL:** Born Apr 15, 1935, Ocala, FL; son of Mark Ivey and Mazie Ivey; married Evelyn Jacqueline Brown, Jun 05, 1958; children: Mark IV, Marlon, Michael. **EDUCATION:** FL A&M Univ, BS Pharmacy 1958; Meharry Med Coll, MD 1973; Akron Gen Med Ctr, Ob-Gyn residency 1978. **CAREER:** Summit Co Health Dept Akron, dep health officer 1973-78; Akron City Health Dept, dep health officer 1974-78; Delta Comm Hosp & Clinic Mound Bayou MS, Ob-Gyn dir 1975; Planned Parenthood of Summit Co, consultant 1976-78; Planned Parenthood of Central FL, med dir 1978-; Private Practice, physician & pharmacist. **ORGANIZATIONS:** Consult Intl Corr Soc of Ob-Gyn 197°-; bd dirs BSA Gulf Ridge Council FL 1978-80; co-dir United Negro Coll Fund Polk Co FL 1980. **HONORS/ACHIEVEMENTS:** Lehn & Fink Award Outstanding Sr Pharm of FL A&M Univ 1958; First Black Resident in Dept of Ob-Gyn Akron Gen Med Ctr 1973; First Black Chief Gynecological Serv of Lakeland Regional Medical Ctr Lakeland FL 1985; Margaret Sanges Award, Planned Parenthood of Central Fla, 1989. **BUSINESS ADDRESS:** Pharmacist-Physician, Lakeland Regional Med Center, 505 Martin Luther King Ave Suite #2, Lakeland, FL 33805.

IVORY, CAROLYN KAY
Physician. **PERSONAL:** Born Feb 21, 1944, Birmingham, AL. **EDUCATION:** Berea Coll, BA 1965f Meharry Med Coll, MD 1971. **CAREER:** Jefferson Co Hlth Dept, hlth med ofcr 1973-; Chidlren's Hosp, resd pediatrics 1972-73;Univ KS 1972-73;Univ KS, 1972-73; Meharry Med Coll, intern 1971-72. **ORGANIZATIONS:** Mem Nat Med Assn; Am Acad Pediatrics; Jefferson Co Pediatric Assn. **BUSINESS ADDRESS:** 1700 Ave E, Birmingham, AL 35218.

IVORY, HORACE ORLANDO
Professional athlete. **PERSONAL:** Born Aug 08, 1954, Ft Worth, TX. **EDUCATION:** Navario TX Jr Coll; OK U. **CAREER:** New England Patriots, professional football running back; CBS Star of Week 1978. **BUSINESS ADDRESS:** New England Patriots, Rt 1, Foxboro, MA 02035.

IVORY, LEE ALLEN
County commissioner. **PERSONAL:** Born Feb 10, 1910, Cottonton, AL; married Queen Ester; children: Robert, Eddie, Geraldine Hawkins, Fermer Wilson, Thurmond. **CAREER:** Medium Grocery Store, owner 1949-; Macon Co Dist 2, owner 1972-; Seaboard RR 30 yrs Deacon Pat Ch 1941-; Master Mason. **HONORS/ACHIEVEMENTS:** Award for outst job of operation Of gas station Bulf Gas & Oil Co.

J

JACK, STEPHANIE C.
Editor, actress, photographer. **PERSONAL:** Born Jan 09, 1950, San Francisco, CA. **EDUCATION:** BA 1972; MA 1975. **CAREER:** SFSU, dir of performing arts 1972-73; Grassroot Theatre Co, actress/pub relations dir; SFSU, asst vice pres 1973-74. **ORGANIZATIONS:** Adminstrv Dir Tutankhamun Communications; women's editor Sanfrancisco Sun Reporter; dir San Francisco Sisters Photo & Workshop; bd dir Fillmore/Fell Corp; bd dir Grassroots Theater Co Media Com BWOA; Communications Com Nat Coalition of Black Women in the Arts; mem & writer Nat Conf of Artists.

JACKEE See HARRY, JACKEE

JACKS, ULYSSES
Attorney. **PERSONAL:** Born Jan 15, 1937, Coatesville, PA; married Esterlene A Gibson; children: Marcus U, Eric D. **EDUCATION:** VA Union Univ, BS 1959; LaSalle Coll, accounting 1964-67; Howard Univ Law Sch, JD (Cum Laude) 1970. **CAREER:** Philadelphia Pub Schools, tchr 1964-67; Equal Empl Opp Commn, decision writer 1969-70; Howard Law Sch, admin asst univ counsel; Csaplar & Bok, assoc 1970-77; MA Dept of Public Works, deputy chief counsel 1977-. **ORGANIZATIONS:** Trustee Zion Bapt Church; bd dir Opportunities Indust Centers of Greater Boston; mem MA Black Lawyers; mem MA Bar Assn; mem Amer Bar Assn. **HONORS/ACHIEVEMENTS:** Development Editor Howard Univ Law Journal 1968-69; Tchng Fellow Howard Univ Law School 1969-70. **MILITARY SERVICE:** AUS Spec 5 1960-62. **BUSINESS ADDRESS:** Deputy Chief Counsel, MA Dept of Public Works, 10 Park Plaza, Boston, MA 02116.

JACKSON, ABBIE CLEMENT
Educator. **PERSONAL:** Born Mar 13, 1899, Salisbury, NC; married Clarence P. **EDUCATION:** Livingstone Coll Salisbury; KY State Coll; ColumbiaUniv NYC. **ORGANIZATIONS:** Past pres N Am World Fed Meth Women; vice pres Foreign Missions Nat Coun Chs; mem Nat Bd Dirs Nat Coun Negro Women; Woman's Com Japan Intl Christian U; Nat Adv Com Am Bible Soc; Nat Relig & Council Urban League; Louisville Women's Council Civil Rights; Mayor's Com Employment; del 1st Assembly WCC Amsterdam 1948; 2d assembly Evanston, IL 1953; pres N Am Area World Fedn Meth Women Oslo Norway 1961; pres's adv council Ursuline Coll Louisville; bd dirs Broadway Temple AME Zion Ch Only Black 1 of 10 Am Women Greatest Influence Relig Christian Century 1952; hon cit Indianapolis 1969f LittDLivingstone Coll 1961; hon mem Zeta Phi Beta 1952; del Nat Conf Relig & Race Chicago 1963f White House Conf Children. **HONORS/ACHIEVEMENTS:** Who's Who Am; Who's Who Am Women; Who's Who Methodism Extencsive Travel Incl Africa.

JACKSON, ACY LEE
Educational administrator. **PERSONAL:** Born Sep 14, 1937, W Bainbridge, GA; married Dawne Allette; children: Tsekani Allette. **EDUCATION:** Westminster Coll N Wilmington PA, BA 1958; Univ of Pittsburgh, MEd 1964; Columbia Univ NYC, MA 1970. **CAREER:** CTI HS Sialkot W Pakistan, English teacher, coach 1958-61; Armaghan English Lang Inst Teheran Iran, dir 1970-72; Coll of Wooster, instructor-at-large 1972-78, assoc dean of students, dir of career planning & placement 1972-78; Colgate Univ Hamilton NY, dir career planning center 1978-, asst dean for supportive servs. **ORGANIZATIONS:** Cons, guest lecturer Coll Placement Serv Bethlehem PA 1974-; consult US Office of Ed 1976-; cons, mem disting faculty Amer Mgmt Assoc 1978-; mem Coll Placement Council 1972-, Eastern Coll Pers Officers 1978-, Midwest Coll Placement Assoc 1972-78. **HONORS/ACHIEVEMENTS:** Listed in Who's Who in Amer Coll Y Univ 1958; author "The Conversation Class/Engl Teaching Forum Vol III" 1969; book reviewer Jrnl of Coll Placement 1972-78; author/poet "Black Forum", "The Poet", "Thistle" 1974-79. **BUSINESS ADDRESS:** Assistant Dean Supportive Serv, ColgateUniv, Hamilton, NY 13346.

JACKSON, ADA JEAN WORK
Educator. **PERSONAL:** Born Nov 16, 1935, Nashville, TN; daughter of Lucuis Work, Jr; divorced; children: Andrea Eva Fitzpatrick Collins. **EDUCATION:** TN State Univ, BS 1959, ME 1965; George Peabody Coll for Teachers, EdS guidance & counseling 1975; Vanderbilt Univ, PhD Educ Admin 1981. **CAREER:** Metro Public School, reading specialist 1964-76, careers spec 1976-77, guidance counselor 1977-79, asst principal 1979-83, coordinator of student referrals 1983-85, admin comprehensive hs 1985-. **ORGANIZATIONS:** Mem Alpha Delta Omega, Alpha Kappa Alpha 1957-, MNEA, TEA, NEA 1959-, Phi Delta Kappa 1972-, Natl Assoc of Secondary School Principal 1978-; natl pres Natl Pan-Hellenic Council Inc 1985-89. **HONORS/ACHIEVEMENTS:** Woman of the Year Gordon United Methodist Womens Honoree 1964; Natl Leader of Amer Awd Natl Assoc of Equal Oppty in Higher Ed 1980; Soror of the Year Alpha Kappa Alpha 1987; Woman of the Year Natl Business & Prof Womens Org 1987; Professional Woman of the Year Natl Assn of Negro Business and Professional Women 1987; Distinguished Service Award Tenn Black Caucus of State Legislators 1988. **BUSINESS ADDRESS:** Administrator, Metropolitan Nashville Schools, 3150 Mc Gavock Pike, Nashville, TN 37214.

JACKSON, ADELE MARTIN
Library administrator. **PERSONAL:** Born Oct 15, 1918, N Garden, VA; children: Reginal Jerome, Raymond Eugene, Ronald Keith. **EDUCATION:** VA State Coll Petersburg VA, AB 1938; Univ of MI Ann Arbor MI, ABLS 1946; LA State Univ Baton Rouge, attended; Univ of IL Urbanna, 1956-66. **CAREER:** Buckingham Cty Training School Dillwyn VA,

teacher 1938-43; Greenville Cty Training School Emporia VA, teacher 1941-42; Albemarle Cty Training School Charlottesville, teacher librarian 1943-45; Univ of MI Ann Arbor, library asst 1945; So Univ Libr Baton Rouge, cataloger & reference librn 1946-48; LA State Libr Baton Rouge, dir negro serv br 1948-51; Univ of MI Libr Lansing MI, library asst, acquisitions & map cataloguer 1951-52; So Univ Library, acting dir 1974-75;So Univ Library, assoc dir 1976-80 retired. **ORGANIZATIONS:** Mem NAWU; pres Baton Rouge Links Inc 1980-82; sec acad sect LA Library Assoc 1972-73; chmn documents com LA Libr Assoc 1972-74; admin internee Univ of CA San Diego 1975-76; exec bd mem ALA Black Caucus 1978-80; awds comm ALA 1978-80; bd of dirs YWCA 1973-75; sec Baton Rouge Links Inc 1974-76; vchmn exec bd Intl Hosp Found Baton Rouge 1978-80; mem Alpha Kappa Alpha. **HONORS/ACHIEVEMENTS:** Recipient Mellon ACRL Internship Assoc of Coll & Rsch Libraries ALA 1975-76.

JACKSON, AGNES MORELAND
Educator. **PERSONAL:** Born Dec 02, 1930, Pine Bluff, AR; married Harold A Jackson Jr; children: Barbara R Arnwine, Lucretia D Peebles. **EDUCATION:** Univ Redlands, BA (Cum Laude) 1952; Univ of WA, MA 1953; Columbia Univ, PhD 1960. **CAREER:** Spelman Coll Atlanta, instr 1953-55; Coll of Basic Studies Coll Lib Arts Boston Univ, instr, asst prof 1959-63; CA State Univ LA, asst & assoc prof 1963-69; Pitzer Coll & The Intercollegiate Dept of Black Studies The Claremont Coll, prof English 1969-. **ORGANIZATIONS:** Mem Soc for Values Higher Ed Central Comm 1971-74; bd of dirs 1985-88, mem Modern Lang Assoc, AAUP, Amer Assoc Univ Women, Danforth Assoc Prog 1971-; adv counc & panels/symposia at various english & other professional soc meetings; bd of trustees 1981-85 and 1985-89, pres 1983-84 Pomona Unified School Dist; mem nominating comm 1981-84, 1987-90 bd of dir 1984-86, 1988 Spanish Trails Girl Scout Council; mem Phi Beta Kappa Univ of Redlands 1982-. **HONORS/ACHIEVEMENTS:** United Church Christ Danforth Grad Fellowship 1952-59; So Fellowships Fund Awd 1955; Soc Values in Higher Ed Cross-Disciplinary Post-Doctoral Fellowship;Dist Serv Awd Univ Redland Alumni Assoc 1973. **BUSINESS ADDRESS:** Professor of English, Pitzer Coll/The Claremont Coll, 1050 N Mills Ave, Claremont, CA 91711.

JACKSON, ALEXIS CAMILLE
Investment banker. **PERSONAL:** Born in Los Angeles, CA; daughter of Alex and Roberta; children: Ebruh Fayeh Roberta Julia. **EDUCATION:** UCLA, BA 1966; Harvard Law School, JD 1970. **CAREER:** US Dept of the Interior, Assoc Solicitor 1978-81; Univ of CA, asst vice pres 1981-84; Bateman Eichler Hill Richards, vice pres 1984-87; Westpac Banking Corp, vp 1987-89; Clayton Brown & Associates, Inc 1989-. **ORGANIZATIONS:** Mem Admin Conf of US 1980; mem The Links Beverly Hills West Chap 1985-87; dir Natl Assn Securities Profls 1986-88. **HONORS/ACHIEVEMENTS:** Phi Beta Kappa UCLA 1966. **BUSINESS ADDRESS:** Clayton Brown & Assoc, 1801 Ave of the Stars, Los Angeles, CA 90067.

JACKSON, ALFRED THOMAS
Personnel administrator. **PERSONAL:** Born May 30, 1937, Issue, MD; married Clarice Cecelia Brooks; children: Michael, Karen, Damien. **EDUCATION:** Fisk U, BS 1964. **CAREER:** Employee Devel & Counseling 1980; dir of training NBC 1979-80; dir/orgn Devel NBC Bny 1978; mgr/orgn Devel NBC NY 1976; adminstr training & devel NBC NY 1976; Adminstr Training & devel 1975; Grand Union Co Elmwood Park NJ, mgr training & devel 1974-75f Grand Union Co Elmwood Park NJ Personnel Adminstr 1969-74; Grand Union Co 1965-69. **ORGANIZATIONS:** Pres Better Human Relations Council Bloomfield NJ 1973-78f chmn eof Com Adv Bd Bloomfield Coll 1973-77; bd of trustees Bloomfield Coll NJ, 1977-78. **HONORS/ACHIEVEMENTS:** Received Oustanding Trainee of the Cycle AUS 1960; Black Achievers Award Harlem Ymca NY 1971. **MILITARY SERVICE:** Aus E-2 1960. **BUSINESS ADDRESS:** NBC, 30 Rockefeller Plaza Rm 1616, New York, NY 10020.

JACKSON, ALPHONSE, JR.
State official. **PERSONAL:** Born Nov 27, 1927, Shreveport, LA; married Ruby McClure; children: Lydia, Angela. **EDUCATION:** So Univ, BA 1944; NY Univ, MA. **CAREER:** LEA, pres past vice pres; NEA, state dir; State of LA, state rep. **ORGANIZATIONS:** Mem Natl Dept Elem Prin; Shreveport Bicent Comm. **MILITARY SERVICE:** WW II. **BUSINESS ADDRESS:** State Representative, State of LA, Representative Dist 2, 3815 Lakeshore Dr, Shreveport, LA 71109.

JACKSON, ALTERMAN
Educator. **PERSONAL:** Born Feb 28, 1948, Bronx, NY. **EDUCATION:** Lincoln Univ, BA 1970; Millersville State Coll, ME 1973. **CAREER:** City of Lancaster, personnel asst 1970-71; School Dist of Lancaster, dir 1971-72; Millersville Univ, asst dir, counselor 1972-76; Lancaster Rec Commiss,; suprv 1974-76; Hahnemann Univ School of Med, dir, admissions 1976-. **ORGANIZATIONS:** Pres 307-Acad Fellowship 1968-69; mem Lancaster City Cty Human Rel Commiss 1971; comm mem King-Clemente Mem Scholarship Fund Trinity Luth Church 1972-77; reg rep PA State Ed Assoc 1972-77, PA Black Conf on Higher Ed 1973-76, NE Med Schools 1976-77; bd of dir Natl Assoc of Med Minority Ed 1976-87; reg rep Assoc Amer Med Coll 1977; past master Omega Psi Phi. **HONORS/ACHIEVEMENTS:** Dean's List Lincoln Univ 1968-69; Outstanding Young Men in Amer 1976. **BUSINESS ADDRESS:** Dir of Admissions, HahnemannUniv, School of Med, Univ Broad & Vine Sts, Philadelphia, PA 19102.

JACKSON, ALVIN B., JR.
Town administrator. **PERSONAL:** Born Mar 21, 1961, Miami, FL; son of Gussye M Bartley Jackson; married Debra Hinsey Jackson, Mar 12, 1983; children: Desarae, Tiffini. **EDUCATION:** Univ of MD, College Park MD, BS, 1982. **CAREER:** Urban Resources Consultant, Washington DC, admin aide, 1979-81; Birch & Davis Assn, Silver Spring MD, government conference coordinator, 1982-83; Ft Lauderdale Coll, Miami FL, dir of admin, 1984; Real Estate Data Inc, Miami FL, county coordinator, 1985-88; Opa-Locka Commercial Devel Corp, Opa-Locka FL, commercial revitalization specialist, 1988; Town of Eatonville FL, town administrator, 1988-. **ORGANIZATIONS:** Pastor, The Church of the Kingdom of God, 1984-88; mem, Amer Society for Public Administration, 1985; sec, The King of Clubs of Greater Miami, 1987-88; chairman, Day Care Committee, 1987-88, area pres, Dade County PTA/PTSA; mem, FL State Committee on Africa Amer History, 1988; mem, FL League of Cities Black Elected, 1988; mem, Preserve Eatonville Community Inc, 1988-; mem, Zora Neal Hurston Ad Hoc, 1988-90; state chairman, Progress Inc; council mem, FL State Historic Preservation Council, 1988-94; Bd of dir, The Center for Drug Free Living, 1989-.

JACKSON, ANDREW
Educator sociologist. **PERSONAL:** Born Feb 02, 1945, Montgomery, AL; married Dr Hazel Ogilvie; children: Yasmine Nefertiti. **EDUCATION:** Yale Univ, Study Prog 1966; Univ of Nairobi Kenya, Ed 1969-70; Univ of CA, MA Ed, Psych 1970, MA 1972, PhD Soc 1974. **CAREER:** Desegregation Inst Emergency School Aid Act, consult 1977; Fisk Univ, adj prof 1978-; US Dept of Labor, hbc faculty fellow 1980; Natl Assoc for Equal Oppty in Higher Ed, consult 1981; TN State Univ, prof of soc 1973-. **ORGANIZATIONS:** Pres Assoc of Social & Behavioral Scientists Inc 1983-84; mem Ed Bd Jrnl of Soc & Behavioral Sci 1984-; chairperson, bd of dir Sankofa Dance Theatre1984-; mem Amer Soc Assoc, Amer Acad of Political & Soc Sci, Southern Soc Assoc, Amer Assoc of Univ Prof, Kappa Alpha Psi, Islamic Ctr Inc; life mem Assn of Social and Behavioral Scientists Inc. **HONORS/ACHIEVEMENTS:** Delegate Crisis of Black Family Summit NAACP 1984; Article "Illuminating the Path to Community Self-Reliance" Journal of Soc & Behavioral Sci 1984; Textbook Sci of Soc, 1985; article "Apartheid, the Great Debate and Martin Luther King Jr" The AME Church Review Jan-March 1985. **BUSINESS ADDRESS:** Professor of Sociology, Tennessee StateUniv, 3500 John A Merritt Blvd, Nashville, TN 37203.

JACKSON, ANNA MAE
Educator. **PERSONAL:** Born Apr 10, 1934, Wetumpka, AL; daughter of Moses E Mitchell and Alice M Mitchell; children: Stevan, Sean. **EDUCATION:** Bowling Green State Univ, BA 1959; Univ of Denver, MA 1960; CO State Univ, PhD 1967. **CAREER:** State Home and Training Schl Lapeer MI, staff psych 1960-61; State Home and Training Schl Wheatridge CO, chief psych 1962-68; Univ CO Health Sciences Ctr, assc prof psych 1968-. **ORGANIZATIONS:** Consult US Homes Inc 1975-78; visiting lecturer Afro-Amer Studies Dept 1971-73; aqdv bd mem Schl of Comm and Human Srvs 1980-; pres Denver Rocky Mountain Chptr Assc of Black Psych; NAACP Park Hill Branch 1982-83; Denver Urban League. **HONORS/ACHIEVEMENTS:** Educ Ach CO Black Women for Political Action 1983; Woman of the Year Regina's Soc and Civic Club 1977; contrb to Minority Educ CO Schl of Medicine 1978; Woman of Ach Denver Alumnae Chptr Delta Sigma Theta Sor 1976; Founders Award Assn of Black Psychologists 1987; Distinguished Chapter Service Award Denver-Rocky Mountain Chapter Assn of Black Psychologists 1987. **BUSINESS ADDRESS:** Assc Prof of Psychiatry, Univ of CO Health Sciences, 4200 E 9th Ave C258, Denver, CO 80262.

JACKSON, ART EUGENE, SR.
Business executive. **PERSONAL:** Born Jan 14, 1941, St Louis, MO; married Nodie Elnora Scales; children: Andrea Annette, Art Eugene Jr. **EDUCATION:** Lincoln Univ, attended. **CAREER:** McDonnell Douglas, stock keeper 1966-69; Freeman Shoe Co, mgr, sales 1969-85; Mc Donnell Douglas-Tool & Parts Control Specialist. **ORGANIZATIONS:** Mem NAACP 1953; cub scout leader Boys Scout of Amer 1972; pres City of Northwoods 1974; treas/park bd City of Northwoods 1982; alderman City of Northwoods 1983-; treas Normandy Baseball League. **HONORS/ACHIEVEMENTS:** DECA Trainer St Louis Public School 1980-81. **MILITARY SERVICE:** USAF aic 4 yrs; Good Conduct, Sharp Shooting 1959-64. **HOME ADDRESS:** 4308 Oakridge, Northwoods, MO 63121.

JACKSON, ARTHUR D., JR.
Judge. **PERSONAL:** Born Oct 31, 1942; married Suellen Kay Shea; children: Christopher Daniel, Kyle Joseph, Courtney Kathleen. **EDUCATION:** OH No Univ, BS B Music Educ 1964, JD 1968. **CAREER:** City of Dayton Dept of Law, negotiator & asst city atty 1968-70; Jackson & Austin, atty at law 1969-71; City of Dayton, asst city prosecutor 1970-71; Dept of Justice So Dist of OH, asst US atty 1971-74; Dayton/Mont Co Crim Justice Ctr, legal spec/instr 1974-75; Skilken & Jackson, atty at law 1975-77; Dayton Municipal Ct, judge. **ORGANIZATIONS:** Deputy dir Pub Defender Assn 1975-76; instr Sinclair Comm Coll 1975-; adj prof of law Univ of Dayton Coll of Law 1977-; choir dir Epworth Meth Ch 1964-67; hearing officer OH Civil Rights Commn 1975-76; exec comm Mont Co Emergency Serv Cncl; Dayton Performing Arts Fund Bd; pres Dayton Ballet Co Bd. **HONORS/ACHIEVEMENTS:** Outstanding Actor-Musical Dayton Co 1980; State Certified EMT Paramedic 1981 & 1984. **BUSINESS ADDRESS:** Judge, 335 W 3rd St, Dayton, OH 45402.

JACKSON, ARTHUR HOWARD
Government official. **PERSONAL:** Born Mar 27, 1956, Bronx, NY. **EDUCATION:** Prince George CC, Assc Bus; South Eastern Univ, BA; Harvard Univ, Enrolled Masters Public Admin Prog 1985. **CAREER:** Bronx NY, mgr 1956; Stuart McGuire Fashions Inc, 1970; Gregory Apts, office aide 1971; United Comm Against Poverty Inc, maint engr 1972; Spencer for Senate campgn, polit consult 1974; NAACP, past regl v chrmn 1975; Fairmount Hghts MD, town Council 1975-. **ORGANIZATIONS:** Mem Amer Mgmt Assc 1982-, Amer Telemarketing Dir Assc 1984-, US Chamber of Commerce 1980-; pres Young Musical Mgrs Assc 1985; bd dir AIACA RecordCorp 1979-; bd governors Amer Civil Liberties Union State of MD 1974-82; senator adv consult Peoples Food Store Inc 1984-; elected 1975 youngest Cnclmn in US History; Councilman at Large City of Fairmount Hghts, MD 1975-86; Legislative Comm MD Municipal Assc 1977-84; PR Dir Help Families of Amer Inc 1980-. **HONORS/ACHIEVEMENTS:** Who's Who in Amer, Who's Who in Politics and Govt; Outstanding Young Man Leaders of Amer US Jaycees of Amer 1977; Black Comm Awd; Black Comm Council of MD 1972; Freedom Fund Award; NAACP MD Conf 1974; Robert F Kennedy Fnd Flwshp RFK Fnd Wash DC 1974. **BUSINESS ADDRESS:** City Councilman at Large, City of Fairmount Heights, 5943 Addison Rd, Seat Pleasant, MD 20743.

JACKSON, ARTHUR JAMES
Educator. **PERSONAL:** Born Jan 11, 0943, Union Springs, AL; married Beverly Fennoy; children: Monica D. **EDUCATION:** Wayne State Univ, BS 1972, Sch of medicine MS 1976, PhD 1979. **CAREER:** Wayne State Univ, grad asst 1 1974-76, grad asst 2 1976-79; Meharry Medical Coll, asst prof of anatomy 1979-. **HONORS/ACHIEVEMENTS:** Black Medical Assoc Awd for Excellence in Teaching WSU; Pre-Alumni Council Awd for Excellence in Teaching Meharry Med Coll 1980; Kaiser-Permanente Awd for Excellence in Teaching Meharry Medical Coll 1980. **BUSINESS ADDRESS:** Asst Prof of Anatomy, Meharry Medical College, 1005 DB Todd Blvd, Nashville, TN 37208.

JACKSON, ARTHUR MELLS, II
Surgeon. **PERSONAL:** Born Mar 29, 1915, Lynville, TN; married Florence Marie Edmonson; children: Gail Stephanie, Arthur Mells, III, Arnold Warren, Alan ?, Geoffrey. **EDUCATION:** Fisk U, Grad 1936; Meharry Med Sch, 1940. **CAREER:** Surgeon E St Louis, pvt prac 1944-; St Marys, mem hosp staff; Christian Welfare, hosp staff; Centreville Township,

hosp staff; Homer G Phillips hospstaff. **ORGANIZATIONS:** Num offices, coms & bds; St Clair Cnty Med Soc; IL State Med Soc; Am Med Assn; Mound City Forum; Nat Med Assn; Homer G Phillips Interns Alumni Assn; Boys Club E St Louis; United Fund of E St Louis; MS Valley Counc Boy Scouts Am; E St Louis C of C; Nurse Scholarship Com; St Louis Plng Counc & Commn; ARC; IL Children's Home & Aid Soc; St Clair Cnty Cancer Assn; Mental Hlth Soc; United Fund; Mayor Alvin G Fiels' Human Relations Com; num others. **HONORS/ACHIEVEMENTS:** Del Pres Dwight D Eisenhower's White House Conf on Youth 1960; man of yr Nu Chi Chap Omega Psi Phi Frat 1967. **BUSINESS ADDRESS:** 1324 Missouri Ave, East St Louis, IL 62201.

JACKSON, ARTHUR ROSZELL
Educator/college administrator. **PERSONAL:** Born Aug 16, 1949, Fort Dix, NJ; son of Arthur Jackson and Louise Fussell Jackson; married Celeste Budd, Jun 25, 1983; children: Kyle Arthur, Tamara Sheree. **EDUCATION:** State Univ of NY, BA 1971, MA 1977; Univ of MA, Amherst, MA, EdD, 1980-88. **CAREER:** Educ Opportunity Program, State Univ of NY, academic counselor 1971-72; State Univ of NY Binghamton, asst dir of student financial aide 1972-77; Financial Aid Serv Univ of MA, assoc dir 1977-82; Financial Aid Serv Univ of MA Amherst, dir 1982-. **ORGANIZATIONS:** Mem exec comm New England Coll Bd 1984-86; liaison/consultant Natl Consortium for Educ Access 1985-87; vice pres Eastern Assoc Student Financial Aid Administrators 1986; polemarch/pres Hartford Alumni Chap Kappa Alpha Psi 1986-87; bd of dir, MA Higher Educ Assistance Corp, 1988-. **HONORS/ACHIEVEMENTS:** Speaker Natl Assoc of Student Financial Aid Administrators 1986, Natl Conf on Black Retention 1986, College Bd Natl Forum 1986; pres, Eastern Assn of Student Financial Aid Admin, 1989. **BUSINESS ADDRESS:** Dir, Financial Aid Services, University of Massachusetts, 243 Whitmore Bldg, Amherst, MA 01118.

JACKSON, AUBREY N.
Dentist. **PERSONAL:** Born Feb 11, 1926, Lynchburg, VA; married Laura Thompson; children: Aubrey, Kelly, Carl. **EDUCATION:** Bluefield State Coll, BS 1949; Howard U, post-grad 1950; Meharry Med Coll, DDS 1954. **CAREER:** Dental Clinic Salem, pvt practice of dentistry & dir of dental clinic. **ORGANIZATIONS:** Mem NDA; Am Dental Assn; past pres WV Med Soc; WV State Dental Soc; pres Mercer-Mcdowell Dental Soc; Mcdowell Co Hlth Council; Chas Payne Dental Study Club; Bluefield Study Club; chmn Exec Comm NAACP; pol council Council of Southern Mountains; treas Alpha Zeta Lambda Chap Alpha Phi Alpha; treas Upsilon Boule Sigma Pi Phi. **MILITARY SERVICE:** USN PhM 3rd cl 1944-46. **BUSINESS ADDRESS:** Box 671, Keystone, WV 24852.

JACKSON, AUDREY NABORS
Retired librarian. **PERSONAL:** Born Jul 10, 1926, New Orleans, LA; daughter of Raymond Nabors and Beluah Carney Nabors; married Freddie Jackson Sr, Jul 26, 1946 (deceased); children: Claudia, Beverly, Freddie Jr (dec), Sharyll, Antria, Zefron. **EDUCATION:** Southern Univ Laboratory Sch Baton Rouge LA; Southern Univ & A&M College Baton Rouge LA, BA 1951, MEd 1966; Chicago Teachers College, 1959; Louisiana State Univ, 1954, 1956, 1960, 1968-73; Urban Geography Grantee, 1970; Audio-visual Grantee, 1968. **CAREER:** JS Dawson HS, librarian 1951-54; Southdown HS, librarian 1954-55; Chaneyville HS Zachary LA, librarian 1955-81, retired. **ORGANIZATIONS:** Greater Philadelphia Baptist Church usher; Delta Sigma Theta Sor Inc (Golden Life Mem) treas 1971-75, 1979—; YWCA Author Comm; Southern Univ Alumni Fed (Life Mem); Futura Social Club; Women of Elegance Civic & Social Club; Women in Mainstream (charter mem); LA Senate Docket leg sessions 1982-84; LA Womens Pol Caucus fin chair 1984-85, treas 1985—; Baton Rouge Womens Pol Caucus 1st vice chair 1984-85, treas 1985—; Friends Intl, treas 1982—; Audubon Girl Scout Council bd of dir 1983; LA Retired Tchrs Asso; LA Democratic Fin Cncl; Natl Retired Teachers Asso; Mayor Presidents Comm on Needs of Women 1982-85; Educators of Yesteryear Club; Head Start Bd sec 1983; Clerk of Courts Office abstractor 1982; Riverside Centroples Comm sec 1973-77; Comm Advancement Inc Bd sec 1971-77, 1974-77; LA Legislative Bureau sec 1979-80; Zachary Credit Union sec 1973—; exec bd of LLA sch librarian 1977-79; Human Resource & Dev Corp sec 1978-80; LA Asso of Educators pres Library Dept 1967-69, 1977-78; Rural Prog Adv Bd treas 1973, vice pres 1973-74; Natl Ed Asso; Chaneyville Comm Builders Inc pres 1971-81; LA Women in Politics treas 1986—; Baton Rouge Women's Politics treas 1986—; Southern Univ Alumni Federation (life mem); AARP; American Library Asso (life mem); American Asso of School Librarians. **HOME ADDRESS:** 23990 Reames Rd, Zachary, LA 70791.

JACKSON, BARBARA LOOMIS
Educator. **PERSONAL:** Born May 23, 1928, Detroit, MI; children: William E II, Caroline B. **EDUCATION:** Wellesley Coll MA, BA; Columbia Univ Teacher Coll, MA; Harvard Univ Grad School of Ed, EdD. **CAREER:** Great Neck Comm Nursery School, sec 1951-52; Elisabeth Morrow School NJ, music teacher 1958; Health & Welfare Council of Bergen Co Inc, exec dir 1959-64;Supplementary Ctr for Early Childhood Ed, acting coord 1966; Englewood School Devel Prog, rsch assoc 1964-67; Model City Admin, asst admin for ed & training 1969-72; Exper School St Acad Proj Natl Urban League, dir of eval 1972-73; Atlanta Univ, dir doctoral prog ed admin, assoc dean, assoc profed admin; Morgan State Univ, dean sch of educ 1979-81, prof of educ 1979-. **ORGANIZATIONS:** Bd of trustees Wellesley Coll MA; mem amer Ed Rsch Assoc; treas Natl Alliance of Black School Ed, Natl Soc for Study of Ed; mem Delta Sigma Theta, Wellesley Club of Baltimore, NAACP; bd of dirs Inst for Responsive Educ; mem ACE/NIP MD Planning Comm; mem AASA; mem Natl Commn on Excellence in Educational Administration. **HONORS/ACHIEVEMENTS:** Cert of Achievement in Soc Welfare Bergen Cty Chap Natl Council of Negro Women 1964; Awd for Outstanding Contrib in Field of Mental Health Soc of Clinical Psych of N NJ 1965; Woman of Achievement Citation Bus & Professional Womens Club of E Bergen NJ 1967; Disting Black Woman Awd Towson State Univ 1984; Public Service Awd Morgan State Univ 1984; auth of several publs. **BUSINESS ADDRESS:** Professor of Education, Morgan StateUniv, School of Education, Baltimore, MD 21239.

JACKSON, BENITA MARIE
Physician. **PERSONAL:** Born Aug 14, 1956, Englewood, NJ; daughter of Benjamin Jackson and Gloria Jackson. **EDUCATION:** Mount Holyoke Coll, AB, 1978; Howard Univ, Coll of Medicine, MD, 1982; Emory Univ, MPH, 1989. **CAREER:** resident, Public Health, Preventive Medicine, Morehouse School of Med, 1987-89; group health assoc, staff physician dept internal medicine. **ORGANIZATIONS:** mem, Natl Med Assn, Amer Coll of Physicians, Amer Soc of Microbiology; volunteer physician, Catholic Archdiocese of Greater Washington Area/Immaculate Conception Church; Amer Public Health Assn. **HONORS/ACHIEVEMENTS:** 1974 Natl Achievement Scholarship Finalist for Outstanding Negro Students. **BUSINESS ADDRESS:** Morehouse School of Medicine, Dept of Community Health & Preventive Medicine, 720 Westview Dr, SW, Atlanta, GA 30310.

JACKSON, BERNARD H.
Business executive. **EDUCATION:** CCNY, BA; Brooklyn Law Sch, JD; NY Law Sch, grad work. **CAREER:** Bronx Criminal Ct, judge; Police Dept, legal staff; US Atty, asst; Dyett Alexander Dinkins, atty; OEO NE Region, area co-ord; Civilian Complaint Rev Bd NY, exec dir; Pete Rozells Nat Ftbl Leag, asst to commr; Gov of NY, spl asst; Urban Crisis in Am WEVD Radio, host. **ORGANIZATIONS:** Mem bdi dir Settlement Hsng Fund; S Bronx Overall Econ Dev Corp; 100 Black Men; Police Athletic Leag NY; Nat Multiple Sclerosis Soc NY; Urban Leag; Mayor John Lindsay's Com Cty Marshals; Ctzns Union NYC; founding mem Nghbrhd Legal Serv Prgm; NAACP; Assn of Bronx Comm Orgns; Taft Yth & Adult Ctr; guest lectr John Jay Coll New Sch for Soc Rsrch Bernard M Baruch Coll; host The NY Urban Leag Presents WBLS-FM; mediator Cntr for Mediation & Conflict Resolution; arbitrator 1st Judicial Dept NY Bar; US Supreme Ct; US Customs Ct; Fed Circuit Dist Cts; Am Bar Assn; Fed Bar Counc; Bronx Co Bar Assn; Harlem Lawyers Assn. **BUSINESS ADDRESS:** Judge, Supreme Court, Bronx County, Bronx, NY 10451.

JACKSON, BEVERLY ANNE
Business executive. **PERSONAL:** Born Nov 29, 1947, Philadelphia, PA; children: Michelle Marie. **EDUCATION:** Penn St U, BA 1969; Chas Morris Price Sch of Advertising & Journalism, 1972. **CAREER:** KYW-TV, dir 1972-; KATZ-TV, sales rep, sales asst 1972-72; RCA Serv Co, instr; US Census Bur, adminstrv clk 1970-. **ORGANIZATIONS:** Dirs Guild of Am; Am Women in Radio & TV; Delta Sigma Theta; volunteer Big Sister; Big Sisters of Philadelphia 1980; mem Intl TV Assoc, Natl Acad of TV Arts and Sciences, Soc of Motion Picture and TV Engrs, Intl Brotherhood of Electrical Workers, Natl Black Media Coalition. **HONORS/ACHIEVEMENTS:** First and only black female dir ever hired at KYW-TV. **BUSINESS ADDRESS:** Producer/Dir, KYW-TV, Independence Mall East, Philadelphia, PA 19106.

JACKSON, BLYDEN
Educator. **PERSONAL:** Born Oct 12, 1910, Paducah, KY; son of George W Jackson and Julie Jackson; married Dr Roberta Hodges. **EDUCATION:** Wilberforce Univ, AB 1930; Univ MI, AM 1938, PhD (Rosenwald Fellow 1947-49) 1952. **CAREER:** Public Schs Louisville, tchr English 1934-45; Fisk Univ, asst then assoc prof 1945-54; Southern Univ, prof English head dept 1954-62, dean grad sch 1962-69; Univ NC, prof English 1969-81, assoc dean 1973-76, spl asst to dean 1976-81, prof English emeritus. **ORGANIZATIONS:** Mem Coll Lang Assn pres 1957-59; mem Natl Cncl Tchrs English, disting lectr 1970-71, chmn coll sect 1971-73, trustee rsch found 1975-; vice pres 1954-56, pres 1956-58 Coll Lang Assn; mem Speech Assn Amer; mem NC Tchrs English; mem Alpha Phi Alpha. **HONORS/ACHIEVEMENTS:** Author "The Waiting Years"; co-author "Black Poetry in America"; assoc editor CLA Bull; adv editor So Lit Journal; contrib articles to professional jours. **BUSINESS ADDRESS:** Prof of English Emeritus, University of NC Chapel Hill, Chapel Hill, NC 27514.

JACKSON, BOBBY L.
City official. **PERSONAL:** Born Feb 19, 1945, Fayetteville, NC; married Gwendolyn; children: Martin, Marquisha. **EDUCATION:** Essex Coll of Bus, sr accountant; St Peter College, acctg. **CAREER:** Hudson Co Operation PUSH, chmn bd 1978-81; Jersey City Certified Develop Corp, bd mem 1981-; Jersey City Democratic Organ, chmn; Commissioner Ins, comm; City of Jersey City, city council pres. **ORGANIZATIONS:** Campaign mgr for Jesse Jackson NJ; staff mem Ken Gibson for Governor. **HONORS/ACHIEVEMENTS:** Andrew Young Black Achievement Awd Lambda Omega Sor; Jesse Jackson Awd SC Chap Operation PUSH; Chap 1 Central Parent Council; Male of the Year CETA Inc Jersey City. **HOME ADDRESS:** 232 Wegman Parkway, Jersey City, NJ 07305. **BUSINESS ADDRESS:** President City Council, City of Jersey City, 280 Grove St, Jersey City, NJ 07302.

JACKSON, BURNETT LAMAR, JR.
Dentist. **PERSONAL:** Born Jan 31, 1928, Athens, GA; married Dorian Sara Gant; children: Burnett Lamar, Stephen Mouzon. **EDUCATION:** KY State Coll, BS 1950; Meharry Med Coll, DDS 1960. **CAREER:** Dentistry Tuskegee, AL, pvt prac 1961-68, Philadelphia 1969-; John A Andrew Hosp Tuskegee Inst, chief dental serv 1961-68; TempleUniv & Philadelphia, pub health dentist 1968-70; W Nice Town-Fioga Nghbrhd Hlth Ctr, chief dental serv 1970-. **ORGANIZATIONS:** Mem A&M & Philadelphia Co Dental Assn, Jackson sec 1969-70, New Era 1972; AL Dental Soc; John A Andrew Clinic Soc Sec1965-68; Acad Gen Dentistry; mem Com for a Greater Tuskegee, AL 1966-68; Macon Co Action Com 1965-68; contrib articles to professional jours. **MILITARY SERVICE:** AUS 1951-52. **BUSINESS ADDRESS:** 3450 N 17 St, Philadelphia, PA 19140.

JACKSON, C. BERNARD
Composer. **PERSONAL:** Born Nov 04, 1927, Brooklyn, NY. **EDUCATION:** Univ of CA Los Angeles, BA, MA; Attended, Brooklyn Coll. **CAREER:** Dept of Dance UCLA, staff mem 1957-61; Alvin Ailey Dance Co S Amer Tour, musical dir 1963; Graduate Concerts Dept of Dance UCLA, musical dir 1964; Neuropsychiatric Inst Mental Health Programs, musician/resource consultant 1965; Dept of Dance UCLA, lectr 1966-67; Inner City Cultural Ctr LA, exec dir 1966-; Dept of Ethnic Studies USC LA, sr lecture 1967-; Inner City Inst for Performing & Visual Arts LA, founding dir 1967; composer; CCNY Theatre Dept, chair 1981-; Inner City Cultural Ctr, artistic dir. **ORGANIZATIONS:** Bd mem CA Theatre Council; advisory bd Natl Arts Awards; arts advisory panel Univ of CA LA; arts advisory panel Amer Bicentennial Commn; arts advisory panel pres Commn on Mental Health; adv bd mem Radion Station KUSC; dance advisory panel Natl Endowment for the Arts; opera/musical theater panel Natl Endowment for the Arts, CA Arts Council Multi-Cultural Advisory Panel. **HONORS/ACHIEVEMENTS:** Musical compositions, Invisible Kingdom, Scudorama, Montage, Chameleon & the Lady, Two of Me, Arena, Blood of the Lamb; works for the theatre Fly Blackbird, Earthquake, The Second Earthquake, The Nutcracker Triology, Lemur, various others; Unity Award LA 1960; OBIE Award Best Musical (Fly Blackbird) 1961-62; Resolution of Special Commendation LA City Council 1969; Resolution of Special Commendation LA City Council 1978; 3rd Annual Theatre Awards Dramalogue writing & direction for "Iago" 1980; Award for Outstanding Achievement in the Area of Play Writing for play "Iago" LA Weekly Magazine; CITIES Comm Serv Awd for musical "What is to be Done?" 1986; NAACP-TrailBlazer Award, Frances E Williams Life time Achievement

Award. **BUSINESS ADDRESS:** Executive Dir, Inner City Cultural Center, 1308 So New Hampshire Ave, Los Angeles, CA 90006.

JACKSON, CAMERON W.
Clergyman. **PERSONAL:** Born Sep 08, 1939, Chattanooga, TN; married Margaret; children: Stephen, Michael, David, Charles. **EDUCATION:** Livingston Coll, BA; Hood Theol Sem, MDiv; Howard U, studied; Livingstone Coll, DD 1979; Temple U, cert in comm studies; ordained deacon 1959; ordained ch elder 1962. **CAREER:** First AME Zion Ch Columbus, pastorpresent; Shaw Temple AME Zion Ch Atlanta, pastor; Sandy Ridge AME Zion Ch Landis NC, pastor; John Wesley AME Zion Ch Wash DC, asst pastor; Hood Temple & Allen Chapel AME Zion Ch, pastor. **ORGANIZATIONS:** Pres Ministers & Laymen's Assn of AME Zion Ch; pres Bd of Black Campus Ministry OH St U; sec Budget & Fin Com OH AME Zion Annual Conf; chmn Black Clergy Council of Columbus; chmn bd ECCO Devel Corp; treas E Cntrl Cits Orgn; mem Bd of Chris Edn; adminstr Econ Opport Atlanta; mem Nat Bd of Oper PUSH; bd of dir Nat Black Theol Proj Nat Counc of Ch; mem Lions Club Internat; mem Alpha Phi Alpha. **HONORS/ACHIEVEMENTS:** Comm serv award Alpha Kappa Alpha Sor; listed Who's Who in Black Am/Ebony's 1000 & Outst Black Leaders.

JACKSON, CHARLES E.
Educator. **PERSONAL:** Born Nov 08, 1944, Charlotte, NC. **EDUCATION:** Lincoln Univ PA, AB 1967; Univ of NC Charlotte, MEd 1979; Univ of TX at Austin, PhD 1982. **CAREER:** DC Public Schools, teacher 1967-70; Peace Corps, 1971-72; Gethsemane Headstart, curriculum dir 1973-79; Eastern New Mexico Univ, 1982-84; Tarleton State Univ, asst prof/coord sec educ. **ORGANIZATIONS:** Pres Phi Delta Kappa of Stephenville; mem Assoc for Curriculum Devel, Amer Ed Rsch Assoc, Natl Council for the Soc Studies. **HONORS/ACHIEVEMENTS:** Kappa Delta Pi Univ of TX at Austin 1983-; Phi Delta Kappa Eastern NM Univ 1984-; Fulbright Scholar to Bangladesh 1985-88. **BUSINESS ADDRESS:** Asst Prof, Coord Sec Ed, Tarleton State University, Box T-399, Stephenville, TX 76401.

JACKSON, CHARLES E., SR.
Banking/financial officer. **PERSONAL:** Born Mar 18, 1938, Detroit, MI; married Maxine W; children: Melinda C, Charles E Jr, Summer M, David SW. **EDUCATION:** Attended, Highland Park Jr Coll. **CAREER:** MI Dept of Corrections, boys supervisor 1967-69; Security Insurance Group, inspector-safety engr 1969-70; Hartford Ins Group Detroit, underwriting coordinator 1970; MI Dept of Corrections, corrections specialist 1970-73; First Federal of Michigan, FSA, mortgage servicing officer-supervisor, asst vice pres. **ORGANIZATIONS:** Mem Natl Soc of Medical Rsch, Natl Assoc for Lab Animal Sci MI Chapt; mem Natl Assoc of Urban Bankers 1982, Urban Bankers Forum Inc 1982; pres Chap 19 MSEA Michigan State Employees. **HOME ADDRESS:** 15910 Greenlawn Ave, Detroit, MI 48238. **BUSINESS ADDRESS:** Assistant Vice President, First Federal of Michigan, 1001 Woodward Ave, Detroit, MI 48226.

JACKSON, CHARLES ELLIS
Educator. **PERSONAL:** Born Jan 30, 1930, Tampa, FL; married Nellie Grace Smith; children: Donovan Renee, Eric. **EDUCATION:** Clark Coll Atlanta, attended; Alaska Meth U, BS; AK Meth U, additional Studies. **CAREER:** AK Methodist Univ, assoc dean of students 1972-; Clinical Chem, chief 1955-70; AK Students Higher Educ Program, counselor 1970-72; Prov & Anchorage Comm Hospital, consultant 1955-70; Matunuska Maid Dairy, bacteriologist; AK Native Serv Hospital, med technologist; Valley Hospital; Elmendorf AFB AK Hospital, chief clinical chem. **ORGANIZATIONS:** Mem Nat Assn of Student Personnel Adminstr; Am Assn of Clinical Chemists; AK Soc of Med Technologists; Pacific Assn of Coll Deans & Admssns Officers; AK State Assn of Guidance Counselors; past pres Anchorage Rotary Club; past pres Anchorage Toastmasters Club; bd mem City of Anchorage Human Relations Commn; bd dir Lions Internat; mem Omega Psi Phi Frat; World Affairs Council; Am Cancer Soc; pres Elem & Secondary Sch PTA; bd dir Kings Lake Mus Camp; house chmn Anchorage Symphony; investigator Elmendorf AFB EED Commn; vestryman St Marys Episcopal Ch; chmn of Worship & Parish Life Com; scoutmaster; cub scouts & BSA. **HONORS/ACHIEVEMENTS:** Recipient Elks Oratorial Scholarship; Grand Union Pallsbearers Lodge Scholarship 1948; best dressed man 1974. **MILITARY SERVICE:** USAF aviation cadet 1952-55, lab officer 1953-55. **BUSINESS ADDRESS:** AK Meth Univ Univ Dr, Anchorage, AK 99504.

JACKSON, CHARLES N., II
Association executive. **PERSONAL:** Born Mar 16, 1931, Richmond, VA; married Marlene Mills; children: Renata, Andrea, Charles III. **EDUCATION:** VA Union U, BS 1958; Temple U, Post Grad 1976; MS Southeastern U, Post Grad 1976. **CAREER:** The Nat Urban Coalition, vice pres adminstrn & finan; Agcy Intl Devl, sr auditor chf accnt; IRS Intell Div, spec agt; Phila, auditor & trea vol tech. **ORGANIZATIONS:** Asst bd mem Wash Hosp Natl Assn Accts; natl Soc of Pub Accts Am Acctg Assn; Am Mgmt Assn Accredited; Accreditation Counc Acctg. **MILITARY SERVICE:** USAF 1951-55. **BUSINESS ADDRESS:** 1201 Connecticut Ave, Washington, DC 20036.

JACKSON, CHARLES RICHARD, JR.
Assistant director. **PERSONAL:** Born Jun 18, 1929, Yonkers, NY; married Mary Alice Crockett; children: Steven, Marc. **EDUCATION:** Lincoln Univ, attended 1948-50; Adelphi Univ, BA 1953; Baruch Sch, MPA 1959. **CAREER:** Yonkers Police Dept, det 1952-67; Westchester Co Sheriff Dept, chf criminal investigator 1968-72; 3 State Narcotic Strike Force, comdr 1970-72; Con Edison Urban Afrs, asst to vice pres 1973; City Mgr, asst 1974-75; Natl Football League, asst dir of sec 1975-. **ORGANIZATIONS:** Mem US Gov Presidential Task Force on Drug Abuse 1973; consult Polaroid Corp 1973-74; consult Boston PD 1973; Urban Afrs Task Force 1966; lectr Univ of OK 1973;Coll of Mainland 1973-75; mem Intl Narcotic Enformt Ofcrs Assn; Intl Assn of Chfs of Police; FBINA; NYPD Hon Legion; life mem Natl Sheriff Assn; NY State Assn of Chfs of Pol; Amer Soc for Indsl Security; pres Intl Narcotic Enforcement Ofcrs Assn 1977. **HONORS/ACHIEVEMENTS:** Dept Awds & Cit for Disting Police Serv 1952-73; New York City Det Educ Assn 1968; one of 10 Outstanding Police Officers in US W Grand Jurors Awd 1971; Humanitarian Awd Portchester Citizens Anti-Poverty Assn Inc 1975; publ "Coop With Police" 1968, "The Impact of Drugs on the Sport of Football" 1976. **MILITARY SERVICE:** AUS sp/4 1954-55. **BUSINESS ADDRESS:** Asst Dir of Sec, Natl Football League, 410 Park Ave, New York, NY 10022.

JACKSON, CLARENCE H.
Educator, attorney, business executive. **PERSONAL:** Born Aug 27, 1924, Pittsburg, TX; married Phyllis M Halliday; children: Anthony Lawrence, Phillip Michael. **EDUCATION:** Prairie View A&M Coll, BS 1948; TX SoUniv Sch Of Law, LLB. **CAREER:** Private Practice, attorney; tchr & instr 25 yrs; Oakland Small Bus Devel Cntr CA, proj dir; Pilgrim Life Ins Co, exec asst to pres; VA, asst toagy officer; Estate & Gift Tax U5 Treas Dept, examiner; San Joaquin Delta Community Coll Stockton CA, part-time instructor; Peral Peralta Coll Dist CA,presently Small Bus Mgmt Cons. **ORGANIZATIONS:** Mem CA Comm Coll; Am Mgmt Assn; former mem sch bd St Elizabeth Parish Oakland; editor & publisher of The Black Bus Newsletter; Black Bus Review; other black bus publs. **MILITARY SERVICE:** USNR 1943-46; AUSR 1948-54.

JACKSON, CLAUDE
Chief executive officer. **PERSONAL:** Born Sep 08, 1942, Aliceville, AL; married Drucilla Russ; children: Mikisha. **EDUCATION:** AL A&M Univ, BS 1972; Tuskegee Inst, attended; Los Angeles State, attended; Air Route Traffic Control Biloxi MS, attended. **CAREER:** Guy James Construction Co, civil engr 1972; Greene Cty Bd of Educ, chair math dept & teacher 1979; Sumter County Bd of Educ, attendance suprv 1983, public info officer 1984; Sumter County Bd of Commiss, chmn. **ORGANIZATIONS:** Trustee AL Assoc of Cty Commisss State Ins Bd 1983-; chmn Sumter Cty Bd of Commiss 1983-87; mem of the exec comm, bd of dir TN-Tombigbee WaterwayDevel Council; exec comm TN-Tombigbee Reg Commiss; ex-officio Cty Health Bd. **HONORS/ACHIEVEMENTS:** Designed 1st phase of Gainesville Lock to Corps Engrs Sepc; Program Participant Awd for the 56th Annual Convention of the Assoc of Cty Commiss of AL. **MILITARY SERVICE:** USAF E-4; Airman of the Month Awd. **BUSINESS ADDRESS:** Chairman, Sumter Co Bd of Commissioners, PO Box 70, Livingston, AL 35470.

JACKSON, CLINTON (THE EXECUTIONER)
Boxer. **PERSONAL:** Born May 20, 1954, Evergreen, AL; married Cindy Langford. **EDUCATION:** Univ of CO, 1973-75. **CAREER:** Sheriff's Youth Program, Davidson Co Sheriff's Dept, dir 1975-; Knoxville Utility Bd, electrician 1974; French & Hect Mfg Co, assembly line worker 1973; Briggs Mfg Co Knoxville, assembly line worker 1972. **ORGANIZATIONS:** Repr Athlete's Advisory Council 1977-; athlete's repr US Olympic Comm 1977-; mem & capt USA Boxing Team 1972-79; mem NAACP. **HONORS/ACHIEVEMENTS:** Numerous boxing awards & championships; Coll/Regional/Intl meets 1970-79; sportsman of the yr Olympian Mag 1976; official ambassador of good will City Of Nashville 1976; Clint Jackson Day NAACP of Evergreen AL 1977; Up Close & Personal NBC's Sports World 1979. **MILITARY SERVICE:** USAFR E-3 1973-76. **BUSINESS ADDRESS:** Davidson County Sheriff's Dept, 506 2nd Ave N, Nashville, TN 37201.

JACKSON, CORNELIA PINKNEY
Educator. **PERSONAL:** Born in Marietta, GA; married Ernest Jr; children: Andrea, Glenn. **EDUCATION:** Clark Coll, 1948; Wayne State U, MA; MI State U; CT State Coll. **CAREER:** Pontiac School Dist, resource teacher 1963-; elementary, 1955-63, 1948-50. **ORGANIZATIONS:** Pres Pontiac Educ Assn 1965-66; bd dir MI Educ Assn & NEA present; mem NEA Com & Prgm & Budget; fndr Theta Lambda Omega of AKA; dev NEA Conv 1967-; World Confedn Orgn Tchg Professions 1973, 1977. **HONORS/ACHIEVEMENTS:** Scholarship Clark College 1944; NDEA grant So CT State Coll 1966; Hilda Maehling Flwsp 1968; honoree Connie Jackson award 3rd World Ednr MI. **BUSINESS ADDRESS:** 131 Hillside, Pontiac, MI.

JACKSON, CURTIS M.
Education administrator. **PERSONAL:** Born Nov 15, 1938, Roselle, NJ; married Lillian Brenda; children: Stacey, Scott. **EDUCATION:** Newark State Coll, BA 1960; Seton Hall U, MA 1964; Fordham U, EdD 1976. **CAREER:** Elementary School, tchr 1960-64; Plainfield Jr High School, guidance counselor 1964-65; Upward Bound, counseling supvr 1964-66; Plainfield Sr High School, counselor 1967-68; Montclair State Coll, asst dir students 1968-69; Montclair State Coll, assoc dir 1969-. **ORGANIZATIONS:** Mem New Jersey PGA; APGA; mem Omega Phi Frat; Jr C of C; Black Coalition; consultant Exxon Research Corp 1968-72. **BUSINESS ADDRESS:** Montclair State College, Upper Montclair, NJ 07043.

JACKSON, DAVID M.
Business executive. **PERSONAL:** Born Aug 30, 1935, Vernon, TX; married Barbara. **CAREER:** Commercial Nat Bank, vice pres 6 years; fin collection exp 8 Yrs. **ORGANIZATIONS:** Asst scout master Troop #638; vice pres Pleasant Grove Kiwanis Club; chtr mem Circle K Intl Bethany Christian Ch. **HONORS/ACHIEVEMENTS:** AUS Sp-4. **MILITARY SERVICE:** AUS Sp-4. **BUSINESS ADDRESS:** 1551 So Buckner Blvd, Dallas, TX 75217.

JACKSON, DENNIS LEE
Educator. **PERSONAL:** Born Feb 18, 1937, Pachuta, MS; married Annie Earl Anderson; children: Donna, Danna, DeAnna, Dennis II. **EDUCATION:** Alcorn A&M Coll, BS 1959; Univ of Miami, MEd 1969, EdD 1977. **CAREER:** Oakley Training School, teacher 1959-64; Utica High School, teacher 1964-65, principal 1965-68; Orange County Public Schools, sr admin, 1971-. **ORGANIZATIONS:** Mem NAACP 1960-; mem AERA 1968-; mem FL Assoc Sch Admin 1971-; mem Leadership Orlando 1980-; supporter Urban League 1980-. **HONORS/ACHIEVEMENTS:** 4-H Club Scholarship 1955; NDEA Fellow Univ of Miami 1968. **MILITARY SERVICE:** AUS Spc-4 Army Reserve 10 yrs. **BUSINESS ADDRESS:** Senior Administrator, Orange County Public Schools, 434 N Tampa Ave, Orlando, FL 32805.

JACKSON, DONALD CLIFTON, JR.
Emergency room physician. **PERSONAL:** Born Sep 22, 1946, Chicago, IL; children: Donald III, Brion. **EDUCATION:** Fisk Univ, BA Biology 1968; Meharry Med Coll, MD 1972. **CAREER:** Charity Hosp of New Orleans, intern surgery 1972-73; Mt Carmel Hosp Detroit, resident surgery 1973-77; Kirwood Gen Hosp Detroit, clinical fellow 1978-79; Contractual Agreements Numerous Metro Detroit Area Hosp, ER Physician 1979-; DCJ Jr MD PC, pres. **ORGANIZATIONS:** Mem Amer Coll ER Physicians 1983-, Detroit Surgical Assn 1975, Wayne Cty Memorial Soc. **HONORS/ACHIEVEMENTS:** Biographee Who's Who Among Black Amer; Outstanding Young Mem of Amer 1983.

JACKSON, DONALD J.
Business executive. **PERSONAL:** Born Sep 18, 1945, Chicago, IL; married Rosemary; children: Rhonda, Dana. **EDUCATION:** Northwest U, BS Speech 1965. **CAREER:** Cent Cty Marktg Inc, pres; WVON-RADIO, sales mgr 1967-70; WBEE-RAD, acct exec 1966-67; RH Donnelly, salesman 1965-66; co-part Cent Cty Rack Serv1973. **ORGANIZATIONS:** Pres of Inner-Cty Merch Group 1976; mem bd of Merchg Exec Club 1975; mem Chic Forum 1974; bd Mem NWUniv "N" Men's Club 1974; mem Oper PUSH; mem Chic Urban Leag; mem AMA; mem Chic Symphony Soc; mem Art Inst of Chic. **HONORS/ACHIEVEMENTS:** Blackbook's Ten Outstand Black Bus People 1976; comm serv award IL Nurs Assn & Natl Med Assn 1975; Chic Jaycees award 1974; sickle cell anemia award1972. **MILITARY SERVICE:** USN lt jg 1972. **BUSINESS ADDRESS:** 1716 S Michigan, Chicago, IL 60616.

JACKSON, DOROTHEA E.
Educator. **PERSONAL:** Born Jul 18, Brooklyn; children: MI State Conv. **EDUCATION:** BS, MA 1958; cert spec educ 1957; Wayne State U, grad study in Team tchng & tchr trng; adv training in tchng reading. **CAREER:** Educable Mentally Impaired Detroit Bd of Educ, consultant presently; Detroit Bd of Educ; curriculum consultant; Para-Pro In-Serv, teacher trainer; Wayne State Univ, trainer 1970-71; reading coordinator, bd of educ 1967-69; Detroit Bd of Educ, special educ teacher 1957-67; YWCA Columbus, active dir 1943-47. **ORGANIZATIONS:** Mem NEA (ICEC) 12 years; Detroit Fed of Tchrs 18 years; Detroit Metro Rdng Coun; MI Reading Conf; ASAAH 20 years; pres Guild 1973-76; cntrl Regnl Coord Nat Counc of Urban League Guilds 1976; MI Assn for Emotionaally Disturbed Children; Detroit Friends of the Library; ACLD; NCNW; MI State Conv of StateOrganizers; pres Delta Sigma Theta; Kappa Frat; Silhouette Aux; Prov Coord 1970-76. **HONORS/ACHIEVEMENTS:** Winner Nat Adams Prize Debate Medal; IMRID award of merit Peabody Reading Proj; human rel schlrshp Nat Coun of Christians & Jews 1959; Outstanding vol serv award Delta Home for Girls; outstanding vol serv award Urban League; Detroit Pub Sch vol serv award; Kennedy camping Prog.

JACKSON, EARL, JR.
Microbiology specialist. **PERSONAL:** Born Sep 04, 1938, Paris, KY; son of Earl Jackson Sr. and Margaret Elizabeth Cummins Jackson. **EDUCATION:** KY State Univ, BS 1960; Attended, Univ of CT, Northeastern Univ, Univ of Paris; Northeastern Univ Boston MA, MS 1986. **CAREER:** Hydra Power Corp, chemical analyst 1964-68; Massachusetts General Hosp, sr rsch analyst dept of anesthesia 1968-81, microbiologist dept of medicine 1981-. **ORGANIZATIONS:** Mem Amer Soc for Microbiology, Amer Assoc for the Advancement of Science, KY State Univ Alumni Assoc. **HONORS/ACHIEVEMENTS:** Outstanding and Distinguished Community Leaders and Noteworthy Amers Citation 1977; NAFEO Disting Alumni of the Yr Citation 1986; special articles published "Hemoglobin-O2 Affinity Regulation, 43(4), 632-642" 1977 Journal of Applied Physiology, "Measurement of Levels of Aminoglycosides and Vancomycin in Serum" May 1984 pp 707-709 Journal of Clinical Microbiology. **HOME ADDRESS:** 89 Oxford St, Somerville, MA 02143.

JACKSON, EARL C.
Educator. **PERSONAL:** Born Aug 17, 1933, Alexandria, LA; son of Walter Jackson and Ethel Jackson; married Beverly A. **EDUCATION:** BS Mech Eng 1955; MS Math 1973; MS Educ Admin 1975; NY State, professional license; PhD Mathematical Physics. **CAREER:** Wyandanch Meml HS, zero-gravity test teacher; Cockpit Lunar Module, lead engr secondary structure; Grumman Aerospace Corp, design engr; Boeing & Co, design engr; Elastic Syst Design, owner; Telephonics Corp, asst to chief engr; Sedco Systems Inc, mgr of engrg analysis sect. **ORGANIZATIONS:** Chmn Math Dept Sgt. **MILITARY SERVICE:** 3 yrs military svc; 3rd Armored Div Germany sgt. **BUSINESS ADDRESS:** Manager Engrg Analysis Sect, Sedco Systems, Inc, 65 Marcus Dr, Melville, NY 11747.

JACKSON, EARL J.
Clergyman. **PERSONAL:** Born Mar 11, 1943, Chattanooga, TN; son of Mr James C Jackson and Mrs Kathryn C Jackson; married Ms Barbara Faye Anderson; children: Earl Darelwin, Roderick Lamar. **EDUCATION:** TN A&I State Univ, 1962-65; Am Baptist Theological Seminary, 1964-66; The Detroit Baptist Sem, ThG, BTh, DD 1969; The Emmanuel Bible Coll, BA, MDiv, MRE 1978. **CAREER:** KY Dept Human Resources, sr employment interviewer 1970-; New Bethel Baptist Ch, radio ministry 1969-. **ORGANIZATIONS:** Bowling Green Warren Co Chap NAACP; IAPES Employment Serv Organ; Bowling Green Alumni Kappa Alpha Psi Frat Bowling Green Noon Kiwanis Club; Bowling Green Warren Co Jaycees 1971-73; bd of dir Bowling Green War Memorial Boy's Club 1979-; asst chmn of bd Bowling Green Human Rights Commn 1976-79; bd of dirs, Bowling Green Noon Kiwanis Club; worshipful master, The House of Solomon #767 Ancient and Accepted Catfish Rife Masons of the World; past grand matron, The Flower's of Faith OFS #779, Bowling Green KY. **HOME ADDRESS:** 804 Gilbert St, Bowling Green, KY 42101. **BUSINESS ADDRESS:** Radio Minister & Pastor, New Bethel Baptist, 801 Church St, Bowling Green, KY 42101.

JACKSON, EARL K., SR.
Director (corporate). **PERSONAL:** Born Jan 17, 1938, Monroe, LA; married Emma M George; children: Felica C, Annoinette L, Jada E, Earl K. **EDUCATION:** Grambling State U, 1961; Robinson Bus Coll, Diploma Bus-Mgmt 1970; NLU & LSU-A, cert Var Courses in Construction 1961-78. **CAREER:** Programs & Urban Devel, prgms dir 1978-; Monroe Redevel, relocation rehab ofcr 1970-78; City of Monroe Dept, planner I 1969; Jackson Design & Construction Co, gen contractor 1961-; Jackson's Design & Assoc, designer (archtl) 1961-; Nat Assn of Housing Redevel Official Housing & Urban Devel, instr for section 312 loans 1970-. **ORGANIZATIONS:** Com mem Nat Conserv Bd for NAHRO Wash DC 1972-; consult various agys throughout cntry; supt mem Deuteronomy Bapt Ch Monroe LA; student in aviation (pvt pilot) McMahan Aviation Inc 1980; mem Nat Assn of Housing Redevel 1980. **HONORS/ACHIEVEMENTS:** Cert of merit Bldg Official Assn of LA 1973; hon state sen State of LA 1976; Staff Col Gov Edwards State of LA 1976; outst archit designer Nat Info Rsrch & Action Leag 1977. **BUSINESS ADDRESS:** 209 12th St, Monroe, LA 71201.

JACKSON, EARLINE
Education administrator. **PERSONAL:** Born Mar 26, 1943, Columbia, SC; children: Tanyl Lea, Tamara P Newsome. **EDUCATION:** Molloy Coll, BA Psych/Soc 1982; Adelphi Univ, MBA. **CAREER:** Cornell Univ FDC Pilot Prog, exec bd mem educ planning/assessment 1974-77; LI Minority Alliance Inc, educ/remedial serv prog coord 1978-82; ABWA Pandora Chapt, chairperson educ comm 1983; Molloy Coll, assoc dir HEOP. **ORGANIZATIONS:** Founder/exec dir FDC Assoc of Nassau Co Inc 1972-79; exec bd mem/Nassau Co Rep Licensed FDC Assoc of NYS Inc 1973-78; bd mem Daycare Council of Nassau Co Inc 1974-76-78; bd mem Comm Adv Bd Roosevelt NY 1976-78; Nassau Co Rep Connell Univ FDC Prog Planning Comm 1978; chairperson emerita FDC Assn of Nassau Co Inc 1979. **HONORS/ACHIEVEMENTS:** Meritorious Serv & Achievement FDC Assn of Nassau Co Inc 1978. **BUSINESS ADDRESS:** Assoc Dir, St Thomas Aquinas Program, Molloy Coll, 1000 Hempstead Ave, Rockville Centre, NY 11570.

JACKSON, EARNEST
Professional athlete. **PERSONAL:** Born Dec 18, 1959, Needville, TX. **EDUCATION:** TX A&M U. **CAREER:** San Diego Chargers, running back 1983-. **HONORS/ACHIEVEMENTS:** Selected in 8th round & was 22nd player in NFL Draft 1983; Blue-Gray Game.

JACKSON, EDGAR NEWTON, JR.
Educator. **PERSONAL:** Born Apr 20, 1959, Washington, DC; son of Edgar N. Jackson Sr. and Joan F. J. Clement. **EDUCATION:** Univ of the DC, Washington, DC, BS, 1987; Grambling State Univ, Grambling, LA, MS, 1989. **CAREER:** Warner Theatre, Washington, DC, box office mgr, 1979-81; Howard Univ, Washington, DC, aquatic mgr, 1981-, instructor, 1989-; Univ of the DC, Washington, DC, adjunct instructor, 1987-88; Grambling State Univ, Grambling, LA, instructor, 1988-89. **ORGANIZATIONS:** Member, Amer Alliance of Health, Physical Edn, Recreation and Dance, 1983-; member, Coun for Natl Cooperation in Aquatics, 1984-; chair, Aquatic Safety Comm, Amer Red Cross, 1985-; member, Natl Recreation and Park Assn, 1985-; member, Natl Org for Athletic Devel, 1987-; member, N Amer Soc for the Sociology of Sport, 1987-; member, Omega Psi Phi; life member, NAACP, Grambling State Univ Alumni Assn, and Univ of the DC Alumni Assn; member, Kappa Delta Pi. **HONORS/ACHIEVEMENTS:** Certif of apprec, Amer Red Cross, 1984; Outstanding Young Men of Amer Award, US Jaycees, 1985; Intl and Multicultural Award, Univ of the DC, 1987. **HOME ADDRESS:** Edgar Newton Jackson, Jr, 6635 Harlan Pl NW, Washington, DC 20012.

JACKSON, EDWARD W.
Attorney. **PERSONAL:** Born Aug 07, 1915, Baton Rouge, LA; married Gladys Childress; children: Christina L. **EDUCATION:** Howard Univ, AB (cum laude) 1937, LLB; USC, grad work psychology. **CAREER:** So Univ Law Sch Baton Rouge, prof law & visiting lectr 1950-55; Private Practice Baton Rouge, 1948-55; State of CA Dept Human Resources Dev, atty 1975-. **ORGANIZATIONS:** Pres Baton Rouge Chap NAACP 1951-53; mem Omega Psi Phi (Basileus 1953-55); Prince Hall Masons; Mt Zion First Bapt Ch. **BUSINESS ADDRESS:** Atty Dept Human Resources, State of CA, 1405 S Broadway, Los Angeles, CA 90015.

JACKSON, ELLEN SWEPSON
Administrator. **PERSONAL:** Born Oct 29, 1935, Boston, MA; married Hugh L; children: Ronica, Darryl, Sheryl, Troy, Stephanie. **EDUCATION:** State Tchrs Coll, BS 1954; Harvard Kennedy Sch of Gov't (Inst of Politics Research Fellow MIT) Dept of Urban Studies & Planng, teaching fellow 1970; HarvardUniv Grad Sch of Edn, EDM 1971. **CAREER:** Operation Exodus, founder/dir 1965-69; Black Women's Commnty Devel Found Inc, natl dir 1969-70; Title IV HEW, contract compliance/project dir 1964, 1971-74; Freedom Hse Inst on Schst Edn, dir 1974-78; Northeastern U, dean/dir affirmative action. **ORGANIZATIONS:** Dir Patriot Bancorp 1982-; trustee John F Kennedy Library Found 1983-; trustee Boston Children's Hosp 1982-; chmn Mass Governor's Commnty Devel Coord Cncl 1984; dir Lena Park Cmmnty Devel Cntr 1983-; mem New England Minority Women Admin 1982-; mem Am Assn for Affirmative Action 1978-. **HONORS/ACHIEVEMENTS:** Ellen S Jackson Children's Cntr Mission Hill Public Hsng 1983; Woman of Courage Black Women's Oral History Project Schesinger Lib Found 1984; hon degree dr of humanities NortheasternUniv 1976; hon degree dr of humane lettersUniv of MA 1984. **BUSINESS ADDRESS:** Dean/Dir Affirmative Act, NortheasternUniv, 360 Huntington Ave, Rm 175 RI, Boston, MA 02115.

JACKSON, ELMER CARTER, JR.
Attorney. **PERSONAL:** Born Oct 22, 1912, Kansas City, KS; married Lucile Victoria Wright. **EDUCATION:** Univ KS, BA 1933, BL 1935; Univ KS Sch of Law, Disting Alumnus Citation 1974. **CAREER:** Atty, pvt prac 1935-; State of KS, asst atty gen 1936-38; City Atty KS, asst 1939; Wyandotte Co Legal Aid Soc, gen counc 1963-68. **ORGANIZATIONS:** Exec dir Nat Bar Found 1968-72; pres Nat Bar Assn 1959-61; mem KS Bd of Regents 1970-; intl atty dir pub rel Frontiers Intl 1976-; chmn Legal Redress Com KS Br NAACP 1975-; commr Pub Housing Auth KS 1965-66; chmn KS Cty Zoning Appeal Bd 1953-65; trustee 1st AME Ch 1975-. **HONORS/ACHIEVEMENTS:** C Francis Stradford Award Nat Bar Assn 1965; 33rd Degree Mason US Supreme Counc No Jurisdiction; award Prince Hall Grand Lodge of KS outst & meritorious Serv 1970. **BUSINESS ADDRESS:** Jackson Law Office, 1314 N 5th St, Kansas City, KS 66101.

JACKSON, EMIL A.
Business executive. **PERSONAL:** Born Feb 02, 1911, Natchez, MS; married Mildred Mayo Mcgrew. **EDUCATION:** Univ Buffalo, 1948-50; Bryant & Stratton Bus Inst, 1952-54. **CAREER:** State Of NY Equal Employ Opp, retired field rep 1970; Majority Leader, gen clerk & aide 1968-70; engrossing clk 1967-68; New York Sen, sgt-at-arms 1966-67; Nelson & Rockefeller Minority Campaign, cmmttmn 1962; Nixon Minority Campaign, 1960; Emil Jackson Real Estate & Ins Agency Buffalo, ownr 1946-70; NY Central RR Dining Car Dept, waiter-in-charge 1929-43. **ORGANIZATIONS:** Past vice pres NAACP Buffalo; past exec bd mem Buffalo Urban League; past exec bd mem Buffalo Bd Realtors; past pres YMCA Bus & Prof Men Mens Club; vice pres Am Negro Labor Council; Civil Serv Empl Assn; Civil Serv Educ & Recreation Assn; Legis Counsel. **HONORS/ACHIEVEMENTS:** Received for meritorious service Presidential Citation; business award Phi Beta Sigma 1950; Iota Phi Lambda 1952; cert of merit NAACP 1958; polit sem cert Buffalo C of C 1960; serv award Buffalo Urban League 1962; merit & service Award YMCA Bus & Prof Mens Club 1964. **MILITARY SERVICE:** AUS s/sgt 1943-46.

JACKSON, EMORY NAPOLEON (SIPPY)
Association executive. **PERSONAL:** Born Oct 29, 1937, Magnolia, MS; son of Aaron Napoleon Jackson and Celia; married Adrea Perry; children: Lisa A, Charles L. **EDUCATION:** Newark State Coll, MA Counselling; Morehouse Coll, BA 1961; Adler Inst of Psychotherapy, 1974. **CAREER:** We Care About NY Inc pres 1986-; City of NY Dept Sanitation Deputy Commissioner 1983-86; DOE New York City Human Resources Admin, deputy commr 1980-; Urban League of Eastern MS, pres 1977-80; US Dept of Housing Urban Develop, spec & asst to sec 1976-77; Economic Devel Natl Urban League, deputy dir; Off Manpower Dev & Training Natl Urban Leag, natl dir; New York Urban League, comm org 1967; United Nations Intl Sch, tchr 1962; Natl Med Assn, cons; Intl Assn Official Human Rights Agencies, cons. **ORGANIZATIONS:** Vice pres US Team Handball Fed & Olypic Com Chmn Community Housing Resources Bd Boston; bd of dir Boston Private Ind; bd of dir Boston Metro Nab Natl Urban League Fellow; Natl Urban League 1969. **HONORS/ACHIEVEMENTS:** Highest scorer in team handball North Amer 1965-70; outstanding achievement Boston City Council Resolution 1980; Community Serv Boy Scouts-Brooklyn District 1987, 88 & 89; Community Serv Girl Scout Council of Greater NY 1988. **HOME ADDRESS:** 1333 President St, Brooklyn, NY 11213.

JACKSON, ESTHER COOPER
Editor. **PERSONAL:** Born Aug 21, 1917, Arlington, VA; daughter of George P Cooper and Esther Irving Cooper; married James E. **EDUCATION:** Oberlin Coll, AB 1938; Fisk Univ, MA 1940. **CAREER:** Soouthern Negro Youth Congress, exec sec 1940-50; Natl Urban League, educ dir 1952-54; Natl Bd Girls Scouts of Amer, social worker 1954-; Freedomways Magazine, editor. **ORGANIZATIONS:** Managing editor Freedomways Magazine 1961-; PTA. **HONORS/ACHIEVEMENTS:** Rosenwald Fellow 1940-41; Rabinowitz Fund Grant 1962-63; William L Patterson Foundation Award 1978; Natl Alliance of Third World Journalists 1981; Harlem School of the Arts Award 1987. **BUSINESS ADDRESS:** Editor, Freedomways Magazine, P O Box 1356, New York, NY 10276.

JACKSON, EUGENE D.
Business executive. **PERSONAL:** Born Sep 05, 1943, Waukomis, OK; married Brenda; children: Stephanie, Bradley, Kimberly. **EDUCATION:** Univ of MO Rolla, BS 1967; Columbia Univ, MS 1971. **CAREER:** Colgate Polmolive NYC, industrial engr 1967-68; Black Econ Union NYC, prod, proj engr 1968-69; Interracial Council for bus Oppty NYC, dir maj indust prog 1969-71; Unity Broadcasting Network, pres. **ORGANIZATIONS:** Bd of govs Intl Radio & TV Soc 1974-76; mem Natl Assoc of Black-Owned Broadcasters 1977-85; bd of dir Trans Africa 1977; mem Council on Foreign Relations 1978; bd of dirs Freedom Natl Bank 1978-85; mem World Admin Radio Conf 1979, Council of Concerned Black Exec, Howard Univ Intl Sponsors Council, Black Council on Africa, Alpha Phi Alpha. **BUSINESS ADDRESS:** President, Unity Broadcasting Network Inc, 10 Columbus Circle, New York, NY 10019.

JACKSON, EUGENE L.
Business executive. **PERSONAL:** Born Feb 14, 1939, Beckley, WV. **EDUCATION:** Amer Inst Banking San Francisco, attended 1969-70; San Francisco City Coll, attended 1976-77. **CAREER:** Chem AH Thomas Co Phila, expediter 1956-58; Wells Fargo Bank, 1/c negot 1968, asst operations ofcr, operations ofcr 1977, asst vice pres 1977-78, vice pres 1978-. **ORGANIZATIONS:** Planning bd mem Western Council Intl Banking 1978-70. **BUSINESS ADDRESS:** Vice President, Wells Fargo Bank NA, 475 Sansome St 18th Fl, San Francisco, CA 94144.

JACKSON, FELIX W.
Physician. **PERSONAL:** Born Sep 06, 1920, Woodville, MS. **EDUCATION:** IL Coll Optometry. **CAREER:** Am Sch, self instr optomoligist; Strip Founders Inc, purchasing agent; US Post Office, carrier; FW Jackson Enterprises, owner. **ORGANIZATIONS:** Pres NAACP 1965-67; bd exec vice pres Forsyth Century Art 1964-68; v Chmn Model Cities Bd 1968-70; co-chm Human Rel & Comm Forsyth Cent Art 1960-68; mem Winston Salem Redevel Commn 1974-. **HONORS/ACHIEVEMENTS:** Rep All Am City Event 1965; first black opth state NC; spl hon Orgn largest Pub Affairs Winston Salem; Lawrence Joel Day So Regional Concl for representing 5,000 in month. **MILITARY SERVICE:** AUS. **BUSINESS ADDRESS:** 533 N Liberty St, Winston-Salem, NC 27101.

JACKSON, FRANK DONALD
Business administrator. **PERSONAL:** Born Jul 25, 1951, Luling, TX; son of Robbie Jackson, Sr and Willie Louise Jackson; married Vanessa Williams; children: Tracy, Ayanna. **EDUCATION:** Prairie View A&M Univ, BA Geography 1973. **CAREER:** USS Long Beach CGN9, division off 1973-76; USS Coral Sea CU43, division off 1976-77; Naval Beach Group Det Mar 1-79, officer in charge 1979, 1st lt beachmaster unit II 1977-79; NROTC Prairie View, navigation/oper officer 1979-82; USN Reserves, lt comd; Mobile Mine Assembly Group Det 1310, comdg officer; The Prairie View Messenger, editor/pub; The Prairie View Vol Fire Fighter Assoc, pres; Prairie View A&M Univ, Memorial Student Center, dir 1982-87; dir of Auxiliary Services 1987-; Craft of Opportunity 2215 Galveston Texas, Commanding Officer, 1988-. **ORGANIZATIONS:** Mem Prince Hall Mason 1970; mem Alpha Phi Alpha Frat Inc 1971; mem Gamma Theta Upsilon 1972; mem Phi Alpha Theta 1983; mem Trail Blazer Sams 1984; mem NNOA Natl Naval Officers Assn 1985; city councilman City of Prairie View 1982-;chair City Planning & Zoning Commission; mem Chamber Commerce; mem Waller Cnty Juvenile Probation Bd; Waller Cnty Historical Commission and Society,1989-. **HONORS/ACHIEVEMENTS:** Outstanding Young Men-Outstanding Young Men of America 1983; Man of the Year Memorial Student Center Adv Bd 1985; publisher Prairie View Messenger 1984-; Staff Member of The Year, Prairie View A&M Univ 1988-89; honorary degree, Prairie View A&M Univ, 1988-89. **MILITARY SERVICE:** US Navy Reserves, commander, 1973-; 2 Navy Achievement Medal; Navy Commendation Medal 1989. **BUSINESS ADDRESS:** Director, Auxiliary Services, Memorial Student Center, Prairie View A&M Univ, PO Box 475, Prairie View, TX 77446.

JACKSON, FRANKLIN D.B.
Business executive/government official. **PERSONAL:** Born Mar 21, 1934, Cypress, AL; son of J Jackson and Mary Jackson; divorced; children: Franklin K, Debra R, Sabrina F, Delilah E, Jacquelyn R. **EDUCATION:** Univ of N CO Greeley, BS Bus Adminstrn 1976; Univ Of N CO, M Public Admin 1977; Webster Coll St Louis, M of Health and Hospital Admin 1979. **CAREER:** Jackson's & Enter Ltd, pres owner 1980; HUD, fair housing & ED spec 1978-; EEOC, employment opportunity specialist 1976-78; US Army Parotrooper. **ORGANIZATIONS:** Publicity chmn Univ of CO at Manuel 1972; bd of dir Occupational Industrialization Ctr 1977-; band leader Happy Jacks Combo And Dance Band; historian Kappa Alpha Psi Frat 1975-; mem Am Soc for Public Admin 1976-; research chmn Police Comm Denver 1977-78. **HONORS/ACHIEVEMENTS:** Award for academic achievement Fitzsimons Army Med Ctr 1976; certificate of appreciation Optimist Intl of NE Denver 1978; outstndng serv awd Denver Alumni Chap Kappa Alpha Psi 1978; Univ S leadership award Am Conf on leadership 1978; bronze stars meritorious svc; medal various other serv medals AUS; medal of Gallantry with palm. **MILITARY SERVICE:** AUS 1st sgt paratroopers. **BUSINESS ADDRESS:** PO Box 7096, Denver, CO 80207.

JACKSON, FRED H., JR.
Pilot. **PERSONAL:** Born Mar 12, 1933, Bridgeton, NJ; son of Fred H Jackson, Sr; children: Pamela, Lester Pierce, Antionette, Kerry Pierce, Cheri, Fred, II, Courtney Page. **CAREER:** Eastern Air Lines, pilot 1967-. **ORGANIZATIONS:** Mem Negro Airman Intl; asst scout master Troop 254 1969-74; mem Black Airline Pilot's Assn; mem NJ Bd Real Estate Slsmn. **MILITARY SERVICE:** USAF major 1953-67; Combat Crew Medal; NJ Air Natl Guard 1967-73.

JACKSON, FREDERICK
Business executive. **PERSONAL:** Born Dec 29, 1928, Washington, DC; married Emily E Smith; children: Noell, Hillary. **EDUCATION:** Howard U, BArch 1971. **CAREER:** Jackson & Tull Chartered Engr, pres 1974-; Ewell W Finley PC, vice pres 1970-74; Scrop S Nersesian Engr, chief eng 1965-70. **ORGANIZATIONS:** Mem Am Consulting Engrs Com 1974-; vice pres eastern region Nat Assn of Black Consulting Engrs 1976-77; pres Nat Assn of Black Consulting Engrs 1979-80;dist gov Intl 'y' Mens Clubs 1968-72; regional dir Intl 'y' Mens Clubs 1974-76. **HONORS/ACHIEVEMENTS:** Man of the year YMCA 12th St 'y' Men's Club 1970. **BUSINESS ADDRESS:** 2321 Wisconsin Ave NW, Washington, DC 20007.

JACKSON, FREDERICK LEON
Educator. **PERSONAL:** Born Aug 15, 1934, Albany, NY; married Mildred Helen Hagood; children: Leon K, Anthony W. **EDUCATION:** Oregon State Univ, BS 1976; Portland State Univ, MS 1977. **CAREER:** Portland Public Schools, handicapped teacher 1976-81, sixth grade teacher 1981-84, integration coord 1984-86, student transfer coord 1986-. **ORGANIZATIONS:** Dir Portland Assoc of Teachers 1978-86; KRS 1983-85, basileaus 1985-86 Omega Psi Phi; chair minority project Oregon Educ Assoc 1984-85; mem Oregon Alliance Black Sch Ed 1985-87. **HONORS/ACHIEVEMENTS:** Leadership Awd for Service Oregon Educ Assoc 1982; Leadership Awd Minority Oregon Educ Assoc 1984; Man of the Year Omega Psi Phi Zeta Nu 1986,87. **MILITARY SERVICE:** USAF E-6 tech sgt 1952-72; Outstanding Unit Awd. **HOME ADDRESS:** 2804 NE 25th, Portland, OR 97212.

JACKSON, GEORGE
Business executive. **PERSONAL:** Born Jul 03, 1942, Greenville, MS; married Leslie. **EDUCATION:** Wilson Jr Coll, AA; Roosevelt U;Univ Chicago. **CAREER:** Quaker Oats Co, mgr training & comm rels 1975-; empl rel supr 1973-75; empl supr 1972-73; EEO coord 1969-72; job analyst 1969. **ORGANIZATIONS:** Mem Rockford Personnel Assn; C Of Cmem bd tst St Anthony's Hosp; mem Rockford Rotary; v chmn City Co Plnng Comm; mem Winnebago Co Econ Devel Commn; v chmn United Cerebral Palsy; United Serv Bd; Winnebago Co Welfare Serv Com; Youth Planning Cncl; Ceta Adv Cncl. **HONORS/ACHIEVEMENTS:** Recpt Comm Limelight Award OIC 1976; named George Jackson Month Dec 1976; prod prgm "Minority Report" 1973-74.

JACKSON, GEORGE K.
Policeman. **PERSONAL:** Born Mar 08, 1919, Detroit, MI; married Dorothy W. **EDUCATION:** Morehouse Coll, BA 1941. **CAREER:** Detroit Police Dept, div commr 1973-; inspector 1971-73; lt 1970-71; sgt 1966-70; detective 1954-66; patrolman 1947-54. **ORGANIZATIONS:** Mem SE MI Chfs of Police Assn; mem Alpha Phi Alpha. **HONORS/ACHIEVEMENTS:** 27 meritorious citations Detroit Police Dept. **MILITARY SERVICE:** AUS capt 1941-46. **BUSINESS ADDRESS:** C/O Fred Murphy, Exec Secy, Pension Bureau, 510 City County Bldg, Detroit, MI 48226.

JACKSON, GERALD MILTON
Attorney. **PERSONAL:** Born Jan 08, 1943, Cleveland; married Patricia A Mullins; children: Alisa, Carmen. **EDUCATION:** Kent State U, BA 1967; Univ Of CO Sch of Law, post grad legal training 1968; Case Western Reserve Univ Sch of Law, JD 1971. **CAREER:** Alexander Jackson & Buchman, atty partner in law firm; Lawyers for Housing ABA & Cleveland Bar, asst dir 1972-75; Reginald Heber Smith Comm Lwyr Fellow, 1971-73; OH General Assembly, legislative advocate 1971-72; E Cleveland, asst to law dir 1971; EEO Commn US Govt, case analysis 1970; Cleveland Trust Co, accnt 1969; Minority Students Enrichment & Scholarship Prog Univ of CO, dir 1968; Cuyahoga Co Dept of Welfare, cswrkr 1967-68; Cuyahoga Co Juv Detention Home, supr 1965. **ORGANIZATIONS:** V chmn Cleveland Chap Nat Conf of Black Lawyers 1974-75; mem NBA; vice pres John M Harlan Law Club Inc 1975-76; dist rep OH Assn Of Blk Attys 1974-75; mem ABA; Bar Assn of Gr Cleveland; Cleveland Lawyers Assn; mem NAACP; Citizens Leag of Cleveland; Legal Aid Soc; City of Cleveland. **HONORS/ACHIEVEMENTS:** Recipient MLK & Award Baccus Law Sch 1970-71; organizer chm Black Am Law Students Assn Case WesternUniv Sch of Law 1970-71; co-designer BALSA Emblem 1971; cert of apprec Bar Assn of Gr Cleveland 1973-75. **BUSINESS ADDRESS:** 525 Terminal Tower, Cleveland, OH 44113.

JACKSON, GILES B.
Judge. **PERSONAL:** Born Mar 01, 1924, Richmond, VA; married Mary Cohn; children: Mignon, Yvette (Townsend), Yvonne (Watson). **EDUCATION:** VA State Coll Petersburg VA, AB 1948; SW Univ LA, JD 1953; Univ So CA LA, Grad Study Law 1971. **CAREER:** Private practice, 1954-68; Ct LA Cty Sup Ct, judge pro tem crim trial & dept se dist 1970-; LA Cty Sup Ct, referee juv ct 1970; LA Judicial Deist, judge 1977-. **ORGANIZATIONS:** Mem State Bar CA, LA Cty Bar Assoc, ABA, Omega Psi Phi, CA Sup Ct 1954, US Ct of Appeals 1955, US Dist Ct 1954, US Supreme Ct 1965. **MILITARY SERVICE:** USMC 1943-46. **BUSINESS ADDRESS:** Judge, Los Angeles Municipal Court, 110 N Grand Ave, Los Angeles, CA 90012.

JACKSON, GOVERNOR EUGENE, JR.
Financial administrator. **PERSONAL:** Born May 05, 1951, Linden, TX; married Linda

Kay Sueing; children: Governor Eugene III. **EDUCATION:** E TX State U, BS 1973; N TX State U, MEd 1978. **CAREER:** TX Woman's Univ, dir of financial aid 1976-; DeVry Inst of Tech, assoc dean of students 1973-76; E TX State Univ Sam Rayburn Memorial Student Center, bldg serv supr 1969-73. **ORGANIZATIONS:** Mem Nat Assn of Student Fin Aid Adminstr 1973-80; mem SW Assn of Student Fin Aid Admin 1973-80; mem nominating co TX Student Finan Aid Adminstrs 1979; mem adminstrv counc TX Woman'sUniv 1977-80; mem Voter Registration Com Dallas, 1978-80; mem Adminstrv bd St Luke Mehtodist Ch 1978-80. **HONORS/ACHIEVEMENTS:** Ldrshp award E TX State U, 1969-70, 1970-71; outst yng man of am Jaycees 1979. **BUSINESS ADDRESS:** Texas Woman's University, PO Box 22628 TWU Station, Denton, TX 76204.

JACKSON, GRANDVEL ANDREW
Retired educator. **PERSONAL:** Born Jul 17, 1910, Taylor, TX; married Cora Mary. **EDUCATION:** Huston-Tillotson Coll, AB 1936; San Francisco St Coll, MA 1955;Univ Of CA at Berkeley, postgrad 1951. **CAREER:** Human Rights Commn, coordinator 1964-; City & County of San Francisco, sr recreation dir 1946-64; Permanente Metals Corp, Richmond CA, pers cnsl 1943-44; Booker T Washington School Wichita Falls, teacher 1941-43; Wichita Falls, educ supr teacher public school 1937-44. **ORGANIZATIONS:** Commr Travelers Aid Soc 1968; bd mem BSA 1970; mem Arena Coun 1973; bd mem Allensworth Hist Adv Comm Proj 1969; commr Bay Area Soc Plan Coun1959-63; bd mem UN of San Francisco 1970-; org & consult OMI Comm Proj in San Francisco; consult Richmond dist comm proj; consult Haight Ashbury Comm Proj; bd dir treas Sickle Cell Anemia Dis Found 1973; bd pres 1959-60; pres No Area Conf of Brs 1973; exec Com NAACP San Fran Br 25 yrs; AlphaPhi Alpha. **HONORS/ACHIEVEMENTS:** Rec San Franciscan Foun Awd 1968. **MILITARY SERVICE:** USNR 1944-46.

JACKSON, GRANT DWIGHT
Professional athlete. **PERSONAL:** Born Sep 28, 1942, Fostoria, OH; married Millie; children: Debbie, Yolanda, Grant III. **CAREER:** Philadelphia Phillies, pitcher 1965-66; San Diego Padres, pitcher 1966; Philadelphia Phillies, pitcher 1967-70; Baltimore Orioles, pitcher 1971-76; NY Yankees, pitcher 1976; Pittsburgh Pirates, pitcher 1977-81; Montreal Expos pitcher 1981; kansas city royals, pitcher 1982; pittsburgh pirates, pitcher 1982; Pittsburgh Pirates, Qpitching coach 1983-. **HONORS/ACHIEVEMENTS:** Names to 1969 Natl League All-Star Team.

JACKSON, HAL
Broadcasting industry specialist. **PERSONAL:** Born Nov 03, 1922, Charleston; married Alice; children: Hal Jackson, Jewell McCabe, Jane Harley. **EDUCATION:** Troy Conf Acad VT; Howard Univ. **CAREER:** WBLS, grp chmn; Inner Cyt Brdcstng, vp; WLIB-AM, WBLS-FM Radio NYC, owners; Hal Jackson Prod, pres & exec; "Hal Jackson's Talented Teens Int" TalentPrgm, spon; Wash Afro-Am Newspapers, sports ed; ABC Radio Network, 1st black man on network radio reg sched prog; many other radio stations in MD, DC, NY, & NJ. **ORGANIZATIONS:** Leading pioneer in radio &TV inds estab many firsts as black man in this field; partic host natl telvsed cerebral Palsy Telethon; color comment for home games of NY Nets ABA Bsktbl Team; narra inter for natl synd radio spots for HEW to recruit yng peo for med & soc serv careers; NY Local & Nat Bd AFTRA; num other progs on radio & TV for various fund rais & civic causes. **HONORS/ACHIEVEMENTS:** Man of yr award Beverly Hills Chap NAACP; "Image Awards" recep of 1st pres award for brdcstng; award for work among youth Pres JF Kennedy; disc Jockey of yr Fair Play Com based on comm & charitable endeavors. **BUSINESS ADDRESS:** Group Chairman, Inner City Broadcasting Corp, WBLS, 801 Second Avenue, New York, NY 10017.

JACKSON, HAROLD
Professional athlete. **PERSONAL:** Born Jan 06, 1946, Hattiesburg, MS. **EDUCATION:** Jackson State, BS. **CAREER:** Philadelphia, player 1968-73; LA Rams, 1968, 1973-79; New England Patriots, wide receiver 1979, receivers coach. **ORGANIZATIONS:** Off season gives clinic for city's youth; mngs Little League Baseball Team. **HONORS/ACHIEVEMENTS:** Second Team ALL-NFC by UPL 1976; outst receiver 1973; leads NFL in receiving yards in 1969, 1972; played in Pro Bowl 1969, 1972, 1973, 1975, 197 7. **BUSINESS ADDRESS:** New England Patriots, Schaefer Stadium, Foxboro, MA 02035.

JACKSON, HAROLD BARON, JR.
Attorney. **PERSONAL:** Born Dec 28, 1939, Washington, DC; son of Harold and Julia; divorced; children: Julie, Tiffany. **EDUCATION:** Marquette U, BA 1964; MarquetteUniv Law Sch, Juris Doc 1967. **CAREER:** Milwaukee Cnty, 1st asst dist atty 1968; Milwaukee Bd of Sch Dir, pres 1970-72; Jackson & Clark Attys at Law, partner 1970-73; MarquetteUniv Law Sch, prof of law 1972-73; circuit court judge; Senior Counsel Milwaukee Metropolitan Sewerage District 1986. **ORGANIZATIONS:** Mem Exec Bd of Milwaukee Jr Bar Assn 1970; chmn Criminal Law Section Milwaukee Bar Assn 1972; pres bd of dir Sojourner Truth House; chmn bd of dir Benedict Cntr for Criminal Justice; mem bd of dir Athletes for Youth. **HONORS/ACHIEVEMENTS:** Outstand Jurist awarded by Friends in Law 1982; Man of the Yr Milwaukee Theological Inst 1978; winner of Am Jurisprudence Awards in Constitutional Law, Criminal Law & Jurisprudence. **HOME ADDRESS:** 1756 N Hi Mount Blvd, Milwaukee, WI 53208.

JACKSON, HENRY RALPH
Clergyman. **PERSONAL:** Born Aug 22, 1915, Birmingham, AL; married Cheri J Harrell; children: Zita J. **EDUCATION:** Daniel Payne Coll, BA; Jackson Theol Sem, BD; Wilberforce U, LlD; Monrovia Coll; Daniel Payne Coll; Campbell Coll, DD; Allen U, HHD. **CAREER:** N Memphis Dist AME Ch, presiding elder; Minimum Salary Dept AME Ch, fdr dir 16 yrs; AME Ch, pastor 25 yrs. **ORGANIZATIONS:** Fdr pres Brotherhood of AME Ch 8 yrs; mem gen bd AME Ch 8 yrs; del, gen conf AME Ch 1944-80; pres Christian Brotherhd Homes Inc 10 yrs, co-chmn Com on the Move for Equality; 32nd Degree Mason; mem State Dem Exec Com; hon mem State Co, Municipal Employees AFL-CIO; founding father Memphis Goodwill Boys Club. **HONORS/ACHIEVEMENTS:** Life mem NAACP Meritorious Serv Awards Brotherhd AME Ch; Goodwill Boys Club; Mallory Knights Charitable Orgn; Memphis Welfare Rights Orgn; JUGS Inc; Co-Ettes Inc Congressman Harold Ford; Man of Yr, IBPOE; Citizens Award, Local 1733, AFSCME; Outstdng TN Award Gov Ray Blanton. **BUSINESS ADDRESS:** 280 Hernando St, Memphis, TN 38126.

JACKSON, HERMOINE PRESTINE
Psychologist. **PERSONAL:** Born Mar 11, 1945, Wilmington, DE; daughter of Herman P Jackson, Jr and Ella Roane Jackson. **EDUCATION:** Elizabethtown Coll, BA 1967; OH State Univ, MA 1979, ABD 1984. **CAREER:** Wilmington Public Schools, teacher 1967-68; Philadelphia Public School System, teacher 1968-74; Central MI Univ, instr 1979-81; State of NY West Seneca Devel Ctr, psych 1981-. **ORGANIZATIONS:** Amer Psych Assoc; Amer Assoc on Mental Retardation; Coalition of 100 Black Women. **HONORS/ACHIEVEMENTS:** Outstanding Instr Centrl MI Univ 1981; Who's Who in the East Marguis Who's Who Inc 1984; Personalities of Amer Amer Biographical Inst 1983.

JACKSON, HORACE
Association executive. **PERSONAL:** Born Feb 19, 1935, Opelika, AL; son of Howard Taft Jackson and Emma L Lemnick; divorced; children: Michael, Karen M Stewart. **EDUCATION:** Tennessee A&I State Univ, BS, 1957; Washington Univ, MA Ed, 1969; Washington Univ, PhD, 1976. **CAREER:** Chattanooga Public Schools, cirriculum resource teacher, 1957-63; Rutgers Coll, lecturer, 1973-74; VA Polytechnic Institute, asst professor, 1974-75; East St Louis Center, coordinator of academic programs, 1976-77; St Louis Public Schools, divisional asst, 1978-83; Chattanooga Area Urban League, dir of programs, 1989-. **ORGANIZATIONS:** Mem, Kappa Alpha Psi, 1954-; mem, Kappa Delta Pi, 1970-. **HOME ADDRESS:** 5240 Polk St, Chattanooga, TN 37410.

JACKSON, IDA LOUISE
Retired educator. **PERSONAL:** Born in Vicksburg, MS. **EDUCATION:** Rust Coll, attended 1914; Dillard Univ, Normal Tchng Diploma 1917; Univ of CA Berkeley, BA 1922, MA 1923; Columbia Univ, further study. **CAREER:** Peck Sch of Domestic Science, asst sewing tchr; East Side HS Imperial Valley, CA, tchr; City of Oakland, tchr (1st Black person employed as tchr); Tuskegee Inst, dean of women 1937-38; City of Oakland, tchr until 1953; managed family's "Lookout Ranch" in Mendocina County, CA until 1970; retired educator. **ORGANIZATIONS:** Organizer/charter mem Rho Chapter Alpha Kappa Alpha Sor; head of newly defined Far Western Region 1926-32; organized, Alpha Gamma Chapter UCLA; Alpha OmicronChapter San Francisco State Coll; Alpha Sigma Chapter Phoenix, AZ; Alpha Nu Omega Chapter Berkeley; first Basileus of Rho Chapter; charter mem/first Basileusof Alpha Nu Omega Chapter; elected first Supreme Anti-Basileus 1932-35; elected Supreme Basileus 1934-37; organized sorority volunteers to launch Mississippi Health Project serving plantation workers in Holmes and Bolivar Counties, MS providing needed health care; served as dir of Family Serv Bureau; mem Mayor's Comm (Oakland) on Civic Unity; organizer of Women's Army for Natl Defense; estab 1st branch of Coll Women's Club west of the Rockies; co-organizer of Natl Council of Negro Women; served on local bd of NAACP 1921-24; pioneered orgn of Urban League in San Francisco; mem CA Farm Bureau Assn; mem Natl RetiredTeachers' Assn, Negro Hist and Cultural Soc of the Bay Area, CA Acad of Sci, Oakland Music Assn, AAUW, Intl Hospitality Center of the Bay Area. **HONORS/ACHIEVEMENTS:** Selected as member of the Berkeley Fellows; elected to Phi Beta Kappa membership; invitations to White House from Pres Franklin D Roosevelt and Eleanor Roosevelt; biography included in book "There Was Light" edited by Irving Stone - gives autobiographies of 39 of most disting alumni of Univ of CA; awarded BerkeleyCitation by Univ of CA; cited by East Bay Historical Soc for contributions to education and humanitarianism; Plaque from Personal Products Corp for Leadership in Womanhood; AAUW San Francisco Chapter has endowed a fellowship in her name.

JACKSON, IKE CALVIN
Professional athlete. **PERSONAL:** Born Jan 30, 1963, Ft Smith, AR. **EDUCATION:** Cameron, Marketing Major. **CAREER:** Denver Gold, quarterback 1984. **HONORS/ACHIEVEMENTS:** Honorable mention All-District 1984.

JACKSON, ISAIAH ALLEN
Symphony conductor. **PERSONAL:** Born Jan 22, 1945, Richmond, VA; son of Isaiah and Alma; married Helen Caroline Tuntland; children: Benjamin, Katharine, Caroline. **EDUCATION:** Harvard Univ, BA (Cum Laude) 1966; Stanford Univ, MA 1967; Juilliard School, MS 1969, DMA 1973. **CAREER:** Juilliard String Ensemble NYC, founder/conductor 1970-71; Amer Symphony Orch, asst conductor 1970-71; Baltimore Symphony Orch, asst conductor 1971-73; Rochester Philharmonic Orchestra, assoc conductor 1973-87; Flint Symphony Orchestra MI, music dir/conductor 1982-87; Dayton Philharmonic Orchestra, music dir 1987-; Royal Ballet London England, principal conductor 1986; music dir, 1987-. **ORGANIZATIONS:** Guest conductor San Francisco Symphony/Toronto Symphony 1984; guest conductor Boston Pops 1983; guest conductor NY Philharmonic 1978; mem bd dir Ralph Bunch Scholarship Fund 1974-; mem music panel NY State Council on the Arts 1978; guest conductor Berlin Symphony 1989; BBC Concert Orchestra, 1987; Orchestre de la Suisse Romande, 1985, 1988; Detroit Symphony Orchestra, 1983, 1985; Cleveland Orchestra, 1983-84, 1986-87, 1989. **HONORS/ACHIEVEMENTS:** First Governor's Awards for the Arts Commonwealth of VA Richmond 1979. **BUSINESS ADDRESS:** C/O United Arts, 3906 Sunbean Dr, Los Angeles, CA 90065.

JACKSON, JACQUELYNE JOHNSON
Educator. **PERSONAL:** Born Feb 24, 1932, Winston-Salem, NC; married Murphy Jackson; children: Viola Elizabeth. **EDUCATION:** Univ of WI, BS 1953, MS 1955; The OH State Univ, PhD 1960; Postdoctorals, Univ of CO Boulder 1961, Duke Univ 1966-68, Univ of NC Chapel Hill 1977-78. **CAREER:** Southern Univ Baton Rouge, asst/assoc prof 1959-62; Jackson State Coll, prof 1962-64; Howard Univ, asst prof 1964-66; St Augustine's Coll, visiting prof 1969-; Howard Univ, prof 1978-85; Duke Univ, instr-assoc prof of medical sociology 1966-. **ORGANIZATIONS:** Mem bd dir Carver Research Found of Tuskegee Univ 1970-87; life mem Tuskegee, AL Civic Assn 1959-; dir Natl Cncl on Black Aging 1975-; mem Amer Sociological Assn; mem Southern Sociological Soc; mem Gerontological Soc of Amer; Natl Cncl on Family Relations. **HONORS/ACHIEVEMENTS:** Author of, "These Rights They Seek" 1962; "Minorities & Aging" 1980; approximately 80 chapters in books and articles since 1962; John Hay Whitney Fellow 1957-59; NSF Fellow 1957-; NIH Fellow 1966-68 & 1977-78; former Pres of Assn of Social & Behavioral Scientists; former Chairman Caucus of Black Sociologists; recipof a number of awards from Amer Psychiatric Assn, ASBS, OSU, AAHA. **HOME ADDRESS:** PO Box 8522, Durham, NC 27707.

JACKSON, JAMES CONROY
Clergyman. **PERSONAL:** Born May 09, 1913, Scranton, PA; son of James and Ella Glascoe; married Daisy L Ledgister; children: Patricia Ann Cokley. **EDUCATION:** Cheyney State Coll, BS Educ 1938; Philadelphia Divinity Sch, MDiv 1949; Univ of South, MST 1973.

CAREER: St Philip's Epis Ch Dallas, vicar 1949-56; St Philip's Epis Ch Little Rock, AR, vicar 1956-62; Voorhees Coll, chaplain 1962-80; St Barnabus Epis Ch, priest-in-charge 1982-. **ORGANIZATIONS:** Asst prof Voorhees Coll 1980; dean of coll work Diocese of SC 1978-80; bd mem Tri-County Comm Alcohol & Drug Abuse 1973-80; officer/bd mem Bamberg County mental Health 1974-80; exec bd Mental Health Assoc in SC 1982-89; chmn bd Urban League 1960-62. **HONORS/ACHIEVEMENTS:** President Award Voorhees Coll 1979; NAACP Cited 1954; Big Brothers Dallas 1956; Parent Teachers Assn Little Rock, AR 1962; Rel Educ of Negro in SC prior to 1850 1965. **MILITARY SERVICE:** AUS Corpl 1942-45. **BUSINESS ADDRESS:** Priest-in-Charge, St Barnabus Episcopal Church, Rt 1 Box 162, Jenkinsville, SC 29065.

JACKSON, JAMES H.
Business executive. **PERSONAL:** Born Apr 24, 1939, Waterloo, IA; married Janet L Norman; children: Denise Rene, Jacqueline Lee, Stephanie Ann, Christine Lynn. **EDUCATION:** Univ of Northern IA, BA 1961; Univ of Detroit, 1968; NYU, 1974. **CAREER:** SIGNA Corp, sr vp; CT Gen Life Ins Co, second vice pres 1977-; Citibank NYC, vice pres 1973-77; ITT Corp NYC, exec 1971-73; Pepsi Cola Co, vice pres 1965-74; IAHo of Reps, former mem; N Milwaukee State Bank, bd of dir 1977-; Hartford Hosp CT, corporator 1978-; Children's Mus Hartford, bd of tsts 1979-;Computer Engineering Asso Avon MA, bd of dir 1980-. **ORGANIZATIONS:** Mem & former ofcr NAACP 1961-; mem Counc of Concerned Black Exec 1971-; sec Operation PUSH Hartford Chap 1979-; Black Achievers Harlem YMCA 1970; mem Zeta Boule Chap Sigma Pi Phi Frat 1977-.

JACKSON, JAMES HOLMEN
Construction management/owner/president. **PERSONAL:** Born Oct 05, 1949, Newark, NJ; married Lynda P Valrie; children: Lamarr. **EDUCATION:** Compu-Train, Computer Operator 1970; ICBO Rutgers Univ, Business Mgmt 1974; Bloomfield Coll, BA 1979. **CAREER:** Moldcast Lighting Div, asst mgr qc 1972-79; Condor Intl Corp, treas 1979-80; Internal Revenue Svcs, revenue officer 1980-83; Jacmin, Inc, pres 1982-. **ORGANIZATIONS:** Treas Citizens Improvement League 1979-82; pres Montgomery Ave Block Assoc Irv NJ 1979-83; chmn of the bd Sugar Bear Productions 1985-; bd of dirs People's Comm Corp 1986-, Budget Construction Co 1986-; consultant JS Minor Corp 1986-; chmn Tenant Assoc of 111 So Harrison East Orange NJ 1987-. **HONORS/ACHIEVEMENTS:** Editorials Irvington Herald Newspaper 1979-82. **MILITARY SERVICE:** AUS spec 4 military policeman 1 1/2; Honorable Discharge 1972. **BUSINESS ADDRESS:** Owner/President, Jacmin, Inc, 210 Pinehurst Ave, Scotch Plains, NJ 07076.

JACKSON, JAMES SIDNEY
Educator. **PERSONAL:** Born Jul 30, 1944, Detroit, MI; son of Pete J Jackson and Johnnie M Taylor; married Toni C Antonucci; children: Ariana Marie, Kendra Rose. **EDUCATION:** MI State U, BS Psychology 1966;Univ of Toledo, MA Psychology 1970; Wayne State U, PhD Social Psychology 1972. **CAREER:** Lucas Co Family Ct Toledo, OH, probation cnslr 1967-68; Univ of MI Ann Arbor, asst prof 1971-76, asso prof 1976-85, prof 1986-; Univ of MI Associate Dean of the Graduate School 1988-. **ORGANIZATIONS:** Faculty asso Inst for Social Research 1971-85; chair Social Psychology Training Prog Univ of MI 1980-86; faculty asso Ctr for Afro-Am & African Studies 1982-; chmn Nat Assn of Black Psych 1972-73; chmn Assn for the Adv of Psych 1978-80; mem bd of dir Public Comm on Mental Hlth 1978-83; mem comm on the status of black amers Natl Rsch Council 1985-; rsch scientist Inst for Social Rsch 1986-; mem bd of trustees Assoc for the Adv of Psychology 1986-;postdoctoral rsch fellow Groupe D'Etudes et Recher Caes Sur La Science Ecole Des Hautes En Science Sociaze Paris France. **HONORS/ACHIEVEMENTS:** Early Carrer Contrib to Psych in Pub Interest Am Psych Assn 1983; Dist Fac Ach Award Univ of MI 1975-76; Urban Studies Fellow Wayne St Univ 1969-70; Sr Postdoctoral Fellowship Ford Foundation 1986-87; The Black American Elderly: Research on Physical and Psychosocial Health 1988. **BUSINESS ADDRESS:** Prof of Psychology, The Univ of MI, 5118 Institute for Social Research, Ann Arbor, MI 48106.

JACKSON, JAMES TALMADGE
Dentist, educator. **PERSONAL:** Born Nov 23, 1921, Freeman, VA; married Louise; children: June, James Jr, Jane. **EDUCATION:** BS; DDS; FACP; FACD; FICD. **CAREER:** Howard U, asso dean clinical affairs; Georgetown U, prof; WA VA Hosp Central Dental Lab, chf. **ORGANIZATIONS:** Diplomate Am Bd Prosthodontists; flw Intl Coll & Prosthodontics; Intra-Theatre prosthodontic consult USAF bases. **MILITARY SERVICE:** AUS lt col 25 yrs. **BUSINESS ADDRESS:** 600 W St NW, Washington, DC 20001.

JACKSON, JANET
Entertainer. **PERSONAL:** Born 1967, Gary, IN; divorced. **CAREER:** First appeared with her 8 brothers and sisters on TV specials at age 9, 1975; Cast as Penny on CBS "Good Times"; appeared on TV's "Different Strokes"; joined cast of Fame 1984. **HONORS/ACHIEVEMENTS:** Top Female Singer/Dance Artist; 3rd album "Control" sold more than 5 million copies earned a Grammy and 2 American Music Awds 1986; Youngest artist to have No 1 pop album; Top 10 Artist. **BUSINESS ADDRESS:** 18321 Ventura Blvd, #580, Tarzana, CA 0475491.

JACKSON, JANICE TUDY
Agribusiness executive. **PERSONAL:** Born Sep 30, 1945, New York, NY; daughter of James Augustus Tudy, III and Mildred Reid Tudy-Johnston; children: Pamela E. **EDUCATION:** City Coll of New York, BA 1977; Univ of MI Labor/Industrial Relations, Certification 1983; Inst of Applied Mgmt & Law, Certification 1985; Cornell Univ/Baruch Coll NY, NY MS-ILR 1989. **CAREER:** St Luke's Hosp Sch of Nursing, asst registrar 1970-74; Continental Grain Co, research asst 1975-77, personnel admin 1977-79, EEO officer 1979-80, mgr coll relations 1980-82, regional personnel mgr 1982-84, corp labor relations mgr 1984-86, asst vice pres human resources 1986-88, vice pres labor relations 1988-. **ORGANIZATIONS:** Speaker/lecturer Cornell Univ, Purdue Univ, Atlanta Univ, Yale Univ, Howard Univ, Univ of IL 1979-; adv bd mem Atlanta Univ Grad Sch of Business 1979-82; panelist Women Business Owners of NY 1982,83; dir Tutorial Prog Manhattan Ctr for Science & Math 1985-; exec bd mem The EDGES Group Inc 1986-; life mem Delta Sigma Theta Inc 1986; aux mem NY City Commn on the Status of Women 1987-. **HONORS/ACHIEVEMENTS:** Natl Selection for Weinberg Natl Labor Mgmt Certificate; Graphic Art/Design Continental Grain Co Annual Employee Statement 1976-81; article "ET to Denny - Bossism or Crucifixion," The Esplanade News 1983; editorial "Miscarriage of Justice," NY Amsterdam News 1985. **BUSINESS ADDRESS:** Vice Pres, Labor Relations, Continental Grain Company, 277 Park Ave, New York, NY 10172.

JACKSON, JESSE L.
Business executive. **PERSONAL:** Born Feb 21, 1928, Groveton, TX; children: Jesse Jr, Nora. **EDUCATION:** Syracuse Univ. **CAREER:** Ascension Chem of Am Corp, pres, ETC Inc; H & Cream Cleaner; AEAONMS. **ORGANIZATIONS:** 100 Club of Buffalo; Buffalo C of C 1971; Urban League 1975.

JACKSON, JESSE LOUIS
Clergyman, civic leader. **PERSONAL:** Born Oct 08, 1941, Greenville, SC; married Jacqueline Lavinia Brown; children: Santita, Jesse Louis, Jonathan, Luther, Yusef DuBois, Jacqueline Lavinia. **EDUCATION:** Univ of IL, 1959-60; A&T Coll NC, BA Soc 1964; Chicago Theol Seminary, postgrad, DD (hon). **CAREER:** Greenville, SC Civil Rights Movement, leader 1960; directed a service of Statewide TV Prog 1962; Operation PUSH, natl pres 1963-64; Greensboro, NC Civil Rights Movement, mem 1963; NC Intercoll Councl on Human Rights, pres; Gov Stanford's Office, liaison officer; Congr of Racial Equality, field rep for so eastern region 1965; ordained to minister Bapt Church 1968; The Natl Rainbow Coalition, pres. **ORGANIZATIONS:** Assoc min Fellowship Missionary Bapt Ch; natl dir SCLC Operation Breadbasket by appointment of Dr Martin Luther King Jr 1967; natl dir Coordinating Council Comm Organizations 1966-71; Active Black Coalition for United Com Action; founder Operation PUSH Inc. **HONORS/ACHIEVEMENTS:** Listed in Who's Who in Amer Coll & Univ 1964; Greensboro Citizen of the Year 1964 Windsor Comm Rec Center; Chicago Club Frontier's Intl Man of the Year 1968; Natl Med Assn Presidential Award 1969; Humanitarian Father of the Year Natl Father's Day Comm 1971; Presidential Award Natl Med Assn; author "Straight From The Heart," Fortress Press Philadelphia PA 1987. **BUSINESS ADDRESS:** President, Natl Rainbow Coalition, 2100 "M" St NW, Washington, DC 20037.

JACKSON, JOHN
Mayor. **PERSONAL:** Born Jan 17, 1948, Hayneville, AL; married Katie Welch; children: Nina S, Kevin John. **EDUCATION:** Tuskegee Inst, Cert in Quality Control 1964-66; Univ of MI, Insurance Executive 1967-69. **CAREER:** Ford Motor Co, final inspector 1969-72; Life Ins of GA, ins exec 1973-79; City of White Hall, mayor 1980-. **ORGANIZATIONS:** Chmn of bd Sellers Memorial Christian Church; Student Non-violent Coord Comm. **BUSINESS ADDRESS:** Mayor, City of Whitehall, Rt 1 Box 191-B, Hayneville, AL 36040.

JACKSON, JOHN BERRYE
Surgeon. **PERSONAL:** Born Sep 23, 1919, Brainbridge, GA; married Eunice Mary Motte; children: Brenda Drake, Kenneth, Harold. **EDUCATION:** Morehouse Coll, BS 1942; Meharry Med Coll, MD 1946. **CAREER:** Herrick Hosp, chmn tissue comm; vstg surgeon training of resd; 10 local hosps, staff mem; gen surgery 1953-. **ORGANIZATIONS:** Bd mem W Oakland Cons; vice pres NAACP; exec vice pres Boy Scouts of Amer, Bay Area Urban League, Sinkler Miller Med Assoc; fellow Amer Coll of Surgeons, IntlColl of Surgeons, E Bay Surg Soc, Alameda Contra Costa Assoc Comm. **HONORS/ACHIEVEMENTS:** Diplomate of Amer Bd Surgery; Outstanding Teacher of the Year Attending Staff Surgery Highland Hosp 1975-76; Serv Awd NAACP 1977. **BUSINESS ADDRESS:** General Surgeon, 4346 San Pablo Ave, Emeryville, CA 94608.

JACKSON, JOHN H.
Civil engineer. **PERSONAL:** Born Jun 08, 1943, Boonville, MO. **EDUCATION:** Univ of MO, BS Civil Engrg 1968; Univ of Houston, MBA Finance 1975. **CAREER:** Dow Chemical, design engr 1968-72, project engr 1974-83; J F Pritchard & Co, design engr 1972-74; City of Miami, asst to dir public works. **ORGANIZATIONS:** Mem Amer Soc of Public Admin 1983-; mem Natl Forum for Black Public Admin 1984-. **BUSINESS ADDRESS:** Asst Dir Public Works, City of Miami, 275 NW 2nd St, Miami, FL 33128.

JACKSON, JOHNNY, JR.
Legislator. **PERSONAL:** Born Sep 19, 1943, New Orleans; married Ara Jean; children: Kenyatta Shabazz. **EDUCATION:** So U, BA 1965;Univ of New Orleans, 1965-66. **CAREER:** Dist 101, state rep 1973-77; Desire Comm Ctr, exec dir 1963-73; Social Welfare Plng Counc, comm orgn 1965-68; Sears Gentilly, porter 1961-65; Logan Cab Co, dispatcher 1958-61. **ORGANIZATIONS:** Mem LA Legislature elected Gov's Food Stamps Adv Com 1977; House Com on Ways & Means 1977; mem Joint Com on Legis Counc 1977; Municipal & Prochial Gov't Com 1972-77; Hlth & Welfare Com of the House 1972-77; Joint Com on Hlth & Welfare 1972-77; subcom Career & Secondary Educ 1972-77; House Com on Edn1972-77; subcom on Hlth & Mental Disorders 1972-77; joint com on Spec Educ 1972-76; specl com on Students Concerns 1974-76; Gov's Com of Ad Valorem Taxes 1975; Gov's Com St Revenue Sharing 1974; Gov's Blue Ribbon Com on SoUniv Crisis 1972; former bd mem NO Sickle Cell Anemia Found; bd mem Gtr NO Assn of Retarded Citizens; mem New Orleans Comm Sch 1973-77; Desire Credit Uniont 1975-77; pres OSEI Day Care 1975-77; New Orleans Jazz & Heritage Found; St Roch Comm Improvement Assn; Natl Black Sports Found; Desire Comm Housing Corp Affiliated; Desire Area Comm Counc Affiliated; Desire/FL Sr Citizens Prgm; Boy Scouts of Am; Urban League; NAACP; Free Southern Theatre; Desire Comm Ctr. **BUSINESS ADDRESS:** State Rep & Dist, 101 3413 Press St, New Orleans, LA.

JACKSON, JOSEPH H.
Clergyman. **PERSONAL:** Born in Rudyard, MS; married Maude; children: Kenny Jackson Williams. **EDUCATION:** Jackson Coll, BA; Creighton Univ, MA; Colgate-Rochester Div Sch, BD; Univ of Chicago, postgrad work theol; Jackson Coll Cntrl State Univ, Hon DD; Bishop Coll Coll of Monrovia Liberia, Hon LLD. **CAREER:** Olivet Baptist Church Chicago, pastor 1941-. **ORGANIZATIONS:** Mem Natl Baptist Conv USA 1953-; mem Phi Beta Sigma Frat; Alpha Sigma Nu; conducted preacing missions in more than 15 countries of Europe Africa S Amer. **HONORS/ACHIEVEMENTS:** Author "Stars in the Night", "The Eternal Flame", "Many But One", Unholy Shadows and Freedom's Holy Light", "Nairobi, A Joke, A Junket, or a Journey?", "A Story of Christian Activism, The History of the Natl Baptist Convention USA Inc". **BUSINESS ADDRESS:** Pastor, Olivet Baptist Church, 405 E 31 St, Chicago, IL 60616.

JACKSON, JOSEPH M.
Real estate broker. **PERSONAL:** Born Oct 21, 1912, Tulsa, OK; married Rhoda R; children: Sedrick E, Barbara Cole. **EDUCATION:** Met Jr Coll Los Angeles; Los Angeles Coll of Physiotherapy; Riverside City Coll;Univ of AK; Anchorage Comm Coll. **CAREER:** ABC Real Estate, owner 21 yrs. **ORGANIZATIONS:** Former mem Anchorage Real Estate Bd; Nat Assn of Real Estate Bd; Anchorage Co of C pres, Anchorage Cit Com; Highland Hts Lodge No 59; Prince Hall Grand Lodge; F & AM State of CA; md mem, treas United Churchmen Layman Conf; mem First Christian Meth Episcopal Ch; NAACP; invstgtr uncovering incidents of discrmntn in housing, the Armed Forces, employment, lending inst 5 yrs; legal redress chmn 10 yrs; mem adv com Anchorage City Council; mem 1970 AK Centennial Commn. **HONORS/ACHIEVEMENTS:** Dist Serv Award; Honorable Serv Award. **MILITARY SERVICE:** USN.

JACKSON, JOSEPH T.
Mechanical engineer. **PERSONAL:** Born Oct 30, 1916, Atlanta, GA; married Legretta. **EDUCATION:** Atlanta U. **CAREER:** Operating Engineers, master mechanic 1953-; Negro Am Labor Council (Westchester Chpt), chmn 1950-56; NY State NAACP Labor & Industry, chmn 1960-64; chmn of the bd Westchester/Putnam Affirmative Action Program 1972. **ORGANIZATIONS:** JF Kennedy Meml Award, Labor 1965; Civic Award New Rochelle Human Rights Commn 1978; Humanitarian Award Black Dem of Westchester 1978; Civic Westchester Affirmative Action Program 1978. **BUSINESS ADDRESS:** 61 Mitchell Pl, White Plains, NY 10601.

JACKSON, KARL DON
Publishing executive. **PERSONAL:** Born Apr 18, 1947, Baltimore, MD; son of Donald H Jackson and Jane Frances Jenkins; married Gloria Bagley, Nov 16, 1968; children: Karlyn Irene, Karl Daniel. **EDUCATION:** Baruch College, New York NY, 1968-74. **CAREER:** N W Ayer & Son, New York NY, account mgr, 1972-76; Black Enterprise Magazine, New York NY, advertising mgr, 1979-81; Amalgamated Publishers, Inc, New York NY, gen sales mgr, 1983-. **HONORS/ACHIEVEMENTS:** Silver Anvil, PRSA, 1970. **MILITARY SERVICE:** US Army, sergeant, 1966-68. **HOME ADDRESS:** 1771 Topping Ave, Bronx, NY 10457.

JACKSON, KEITH HUNTER
Educator. **PERSONAL:** Born Sep 24, 1953, Columbus, OH; married Violet Smallhorne; children: Kamilah, Akil. **EDUCATION:** Morehouse Coll, BS 1976; Georgia Tech, BSEE 1976; Stanford Univ, MS physics 1979, PhD 1982. **CAREER:** Hewlett Packard Labs, mem tech staff 1981-83; Howard Univ, asst prof 1983-. **ORGANIZATIONS:** Mem Amer Phys Soc, Optical Soc of Amer, Natl Soc of Black Physicists. **BUSINESS ADDRESS:** Asst Professor, Howard University, 2300 6th St NW, Washington, DC 20059.

JACKSON, KEITH M.
Executive. **PERSONAL:** Born Nov 22, 1948, Springfield, IL. **EDUCATION:** Dartmouth Coll, AB 1971; Columbia Univ, MS 1975. **CAREER:** Sahara Energy Corp, pres, Trans Urban East Orgn Inc NYC, consult econ dev & mkt analysis 1971-73; Rep Charles B Rangel US House Reps Wash, legis asst 1973-74; Congressional Black Caucus Inc, exec dir.

JACKSON, KENNELL A., JR.
Educator, historian. **PERSONAL:** Born Mar 19, 1942, Farmville, VA. **EDUCATION:** Hampton Inst VA, BA; King's Coll CambridgeUniv England, Historical Cert 1965; UCLA, PhD. **CAREER:** Stanford Univ Dept of History, asst prof 1969-. **HONORS/ACHIEVEMENTS:** Woodrow Wilson Scholar 1962; John Hay Whitney Scholar Univ Ghana 1963; Fulbright Scholar King's Coll Cambridge 1964-65; Foreign Fellows Scholar Kenya 1965-68; Lloyd W Dinkelspiel Award Serv Undergrad Educ StanfordUniv 1972; Mellon Faulty Rsrch Grant; Jr Fellow Soc for the Humanities CornellUniv 1977-78; NEH Summer Rsrch Grant. **BUSINESS ADDRESS:** Dept History, Stanford Univ, Palo Alto, CA 94305.

JACKSON, KENNETH WILLIAM
Physician. **PERSONAL:** Born Nov 12, 1924, Athens, PA; married Helen E Gormany; children: Janice Kaye Sherrill, Kenneth Michael. **EDUCATION:** Syracuse Univ, AB 1949; Meharry Med Coll, MD 1954. **CAREER:** Hubbard Hosp, resi instr 1955-58; Hubbard Hosp Meharry Med Coll, asst prof rad 1958-60; Vet Admin Hosp Brecksville, chief radiol serv 1961-. **ORGANIZATIONS:** Diplomate Amer Bd of Radiol; mem AOA Frat. **MILITARY SERVICE:** AUS sgt 1942-45. **BUSINESS ADDRESS:** Chief Radiol Serv, Vet Admin Hosp, 10000 Brecksville Rd, Brecksville, OH 44120.

JACKSON, LARRON DEONNE
Accountant, athlete. **PERSONAL:** Born Aug 26, 1949, St Louis, MO; divorced; children: Laresa, Temple, Larron Jr. **EDUCATION:** MO U, BS 1971. **CAREER:** Jackson & Asso Financial Svc, acctnt 1975-; Atlanta Falcons, football Player 1975-; Den Broncos, player 1971; Hous Oilers, player 1971; Jackson & Montgomery Tax & Acctg Serv, 1975; Touch-ross Co, jr & staff mem 1972-74, 76; Monsanto Chem, mgmnt intern trainee 1970; Soc of CPA's, assoc mem. **ORGANIZATIONS:** Mem Minority Recruit Comm; player rep NFL 1972-74; coord NFL strike 1974; mem Natl Mult Scler Soc; mem Kappa Alpha Psi Frat; exec mem Leg of Black Collegions 1969-71; stud sen MOUniv 1967; All Amer Schol Mag 1966; All Amer Coaches & Pepsi-Cola 1966; All-Amer NY News 1969; UPI & AP All-Am 1970. **HONORS/ACHIEVEMENTS:** Outstanding Coll Ath of Am 1971; NFL All-Pro Rookie team 1971; "Prof for a day" acctg dept MOUniv 1974; hon bd mem of Mathew-Dickey's Boy's Club 1971; "Who's Who Among Stud in Amer U'S & Coll's" 1971; vice pres Mystical Seven Hon Soc 1971. **HOME ADDRESS:** 3949 Veracruz Dr, Decatur, GA 30034.

JACKSON, LARRY EUGENE
Engineer. **PERSONAL:** Born Feb 18, 1943, Chicago, IL; married Roberta O Staples; children: Crystal, Robyn, Larry Jr. **EDUCATION:** Purdue U, BSME 1967. **CAREER:** Kaiser Eng Inc, proj eng 1977; Inland Stl Co, sr engr 1967-75. **ORGANIZATIONS:** Mem Amer Inst of Stl Engr Mem, Lake Area Untd Way Budgt Comm; Racing Chrmn, IN Ski Coun; pres bd of dir Gary & Bldg. **HONORS/ACHIEVEMENTS:** Auth; mem Alpha Phi Alpha; mem Front Intl Gary Chap Art Pub AISE 1970. **BUSINESS ADDRESS:** 35 E Wacker Dr, Chicago, IL 60601.

JACKSON, LENWOOD A.
Attorney. **PERSONAL:** Born Jan 11, 1944, Concord, GA; married Carolyn. **EDUCATION:** Morris Brown Coll, BA 1966; Emory Univ Sch of Law, JD 1969; Univ of MI; Harvard Univ Cambridge, MA. **CAREER:** Patterson, Parks & Franklin, atty; Latimer Haddon & Stanfield, asso atty 1971-72; Nat Labor Relations Bd LA, atty; GA Gen Assembly, intern 1969; City of Atlanta Planning Dept, intern 1967; OEO Reg Coun, law clerk 1968; Johnson & Jordan, law clerk 1968-69; Emory Neighborhood Law Ofc, legal asst 1969. **ORGANIZATIONS:** Mem Am Bar Assn Nat Bar Assn GA Bar Assn; Atlanta Bar Assn; Gate City Bar Asn; Nat Orgn on Legal Problems of Edn; Phi Delta Phi Legal Frat; Alpha Phi Alpha Frat; exec com NatCoun of Sch Attys; mem Butler St YMCA. **MILITARY SERVICE:** AUS res s/sgt 1969-. **BUSINESS ADDRESS:** 101 Marietta Tower Ste 2222, Atlanta, GA 30303.

JACKSON, LEO A.
Judge. **PERSONAL:** Born Mar 10, 1920, Lake City, FL; married Gilberta; children: Linda Sowell, Leonard Alan. **EDUCATION:** Morehouse Coll, AB 1943; Atlanta Univ, MA 1946; Cleveland-Marshall Law Sch, LLD 1950; Morehouse Coll, Honorary LLD 1977. **CAREER:** City of Cleveland, councilman ward 24 1957-70; 8th Ct of Appeals, chief justice 1976; 8th Dist Ct of Appeals, judge 1970-. **ORGANIZATIONS:** Mem Cuyahoga Co Dem Exec Comm 1963-70; Policy Com Cuyahoga Co Dem Orgn 1967-70; Elec Coll OH 1968; del Dem Natl Conv 1968; 21st Dist OH State Dem Exec Com 1970-; past mem bd trustee Forest City Hosp; AIM Job; Consumers League of OH; No OH Children's Perform Music Found & Lions Eye Clinic; published 150 opinions as of 1984; life trustee Cleveland Metro YMCA; sec mem bd trustees exec comm St Vincent Charity Hosp; mem plng com White House conf 1966; mem Amer Judicature Soc; Amer Bar Assn; OH Bar Assn; Natl Bar Assn; Cleveland Bar Assn; Cuyahoga Co Bar Assn; Press Bar Rel Com; NAACP; Citizens League; Glenville Area Comm Counc; Kappa Alpha Psi Frat; mem 1977-79, chmn 1979-80; Cleveland Works Selection Comm for Alcoa Found; Sons & Dau Schlrshp Com 1977-79 1979-80; apptd by Chief Justice Celebrezze to sit temporarily on OH Sup Ct 1979. **HONORS/ACHIEVEMENTS:** Testimonial dinner & plaque Citiz of Grtr Cleveland 1963; Outstanding Comm Serv Plaque Natl Coun Bus & Prof Women 1967; Outst Serv Plaque Glenville Youth Athletic Assn 1967; Comm Serv Awd Cleveland & Diocesan Union of Holy Name Soc 1968; Cleveland Bus Leag Awd of Honor; Bro Keeper Awd Cleveland Jewish Comm Fed 1969; hon life mem OH Congress of Parents & Tchrs 1961; Outst Ldrshp Plaque VFW 1961; KYW radio Docum 1963; Awd for Outst Judicial Serv OH Supreme Ct 1973; Outst Ldrshp Plaque NAACP Orange Co FL Br 1975. **MILITARY SERVICE:** AUS pvt 1942-43. **BUSINESS ADDRESS:** Judge, 8th Dist Ct of Appeals, 1 Lakeside Ave, Cleveland, OH 44113.

JACKSON, LEO EDWIN
Retired educator, elected government official. **PERSONAL:** Born Dec 30, 1925, Springfield, MA; son of Andrew J Jackson and Ethel Williams; married Barbara Lockwood; children: Reginald, Lionel T, Margo E. **EDUCATION:** Tuskegee Inst Tuskegee AL, 1944-45; Mitchell Coll New London, Bus Admin 1970-72. **CAREER:** Gen Dynamics Corp, engrg aid 1958-68, sugg analyst 1968-70, shipyard plcmt rep 1970-71, coord on job training 1971-76, sr instr 1976-80; Inst for Cert of Engrg Techs, sr engr tech 1968-; City of New London CT, mayor 1980-. **ORGANIZATIONS:** Bd of ed 1st Black Elected City of New London 1975-77; mem Electric Boat Mgmt Assoc, Biracial Comm of the Metal Trades Council; sec, treas Re-devel Agency; advsy capa Southeastern Reg Voctl Tech School; leading knight Victory Ldg of Elks IBPOE of W 1970-. **MILITARY SERVICE:** AAC avia cadet 1944-46. **BUSINESS ADDRESS:** Deputy Mayor, City of New London, City Hall, New London, CT 06320.

JACKSON, LEON
Business executive. **PERSONAL:** Born Mar 17, 1944, Helena, AK; married Ruby Evans; children: Eric, Jennifer. **EDUCATION:** Radio Logic Tech, BS 1971. **CAREER:** Urban Enterprises Corp, pres; Xerox Corp, sales rep 1972-74; Mt Sinai/Childrens Meml Hosp, radiologic tech 1961-74; Gen Foods Corp, chemist/food tech 1967-72. **ORGANIZATIONS:** Founding mem Am Bus Council 1977; mem Chicago Regional Purchasing Council; mem Neighborhood Inst Southtown Planning Assn chmn, Commn on Religion & Race of the UMC 1975-78; mem Council on Ministries No IL Conf United Meth Ch 1977; vchmn Marcy Newberry Assn 1979; mem Chicago Urban League; mem NAACP. **HONORS/ACHIEVEMENTS:** One of 10 Outstanding Young Citizens in Chicago Jaycees 1980. **BUSINESS ADDRESS:** 725 S Wells St, Chicago, IL 60607.

JACKSON, LEROY ANTHONY, JR.
Physician. **PERSONAL:** Born May 11, 1935, Shreveport, LA; married Ruth Ann. **EDUCATION:** Howard U, MD 1960. **CAREER:** Jackson Obstetrical PC, physician 1965-; Freedman's Hosp, intern 1960-61, resid training 1961-62; DC Gen Hosp, 1962-63; Freedmen's Hosp, 1963-65; Bur of Maternal & Child Hlth DC Hlth Serv Adminstrn, chief div of maternal hlth 1968-71; Maternity & Infant Child Proj, dir 1969-71; Shaw Comm Hlth Ctr NMA, dir 1971-73; Freedmen's Hosp, attending staff; Washington Hosp Ctr & Columbia Hosp for Women, courtest staff; Morris Cafritz Meml Hosp, active staff; HowardUniv Coll of Med Dept of Ob & Gyn, clinical instr part-time. **ORGANIZATIONS:** Certified by Am Bd of Ob & Gyn 1968; consNat Med Assn Found Inc 1970; Am Cancer Soc Uterine Site Com; DC Hlth & Welfare Counc Hlth Needs & Resources sub-com on Abortions; chmn Mayor's Task Force on Food Nutrition & Hlth; panel mem White House Conf on Food Nutrition & Hlth DC sub-panel & chmn; mem DC Med Soc; Medico-Chirurgical Soc; Washington Gyn Soc; Am Med Assn; Nat Med Assn; DC Pub Hlth Assn; mem Alpha Phi Alpha Frat; Alpha Kappa Mu Sci Frat; Chi Delta Mu Frat; charter mem Alpha Phi Omega Frat. **HONORS/ACHIEVEMENTS:** Fellow Am Coll of Ob & Gyn; fellow Am Fertility Soc; listed in Who's Who in Am Coll & Univ; author publs to professional jours. **MILITARY SERVICE:** AUS Reserve maj. **BUSINESS ADDRESS:** 4660 Martin L King Ave SW, Washington, DC.

JACKSON, LUKE
Dentist. **PERSONAL:** Born Sep 17, 1919, Recovery, GA; married Shirley Ann Lead; children: Charles L, Wayne D, Shirlee Barnetta, Shirlene Elizabeth, Luke Jr. **EDUCATION:** GA State Coll, BS 1942; Atlanta Univ, attended 1945-46; Meharry Med Coll, DDS 1951. **CAREER:** Meharry Med Coll, instr prosthetic dentistry 1951-53; Private Practice, dentist Chatanooga 1953-. **ORGANIZATIONS:** Bd orgnzr Peoples Bank of Chattanooga 1974-; diplomate Natl Bd Dental Examiners (pres 1957-59); Pan-TN Dental Assn; pres George W Hubbard Dental Soc 1953-; chmn Bus Div Chattanooga Council for Comm Action 1963-68; mem bi-racial Mayor's Comm 1963; Bapt (trustee 1955 coord bldg council 1970-71); mem bd mgmt Henry Br YMCA 1965-70. **MILITARY SERVICE:** USNR WW II. **BUSINESS ADDRESS:** 752 E 9 St, Chattanooga, TN 37403.

JACKSON, LUTHER PORTER, JR.
Educator. **PERSONAL:** Born Mar 07, 1925, Chicago, IL; married Nettie Lee; children: Luther P III, Lee Frazer. **EDUCATION:** VA State Univ, BA 1949; Columbia Univ Grad Sch of Journalism, MS 1951; Rutgers Univ Ford Found Fellow, 1962-63; Columbia Univ Russell Sage Fellow, 1967-68. **CAREER:** NJ Record, 1949; NJ Herald News, 1949-50; Balti Afro-Amer, 1950; Chicago City News Bureau, 1951; The Newark News, 1951-58; The Washington Post, reporter 1959-63; IBM News, Corp Headquarters Edition, editor 1963-65; Communicating Research on The Urban Poor, cross-tell dir 1965-67; NAACP, assoc dir public relations/assoc editor of Crisis 1968; Columbia Univ Grad Sch of Journalism, prof of journalism. **ORGANIZATIONS:** Exec bd Assn for Study of Afro-Am Life & Hist 1964-74; pres NY Branch ASAALH 1964-65; mem Omega Psi Phi Frat. **HONORS/ACHIEVEMENTS:** Research fellow Nat Endowment for The Humanities, subj "Black Towns in The US" 1974-75; visiting prof NC Agr & TechUniv 1981-82. **MILITARY SERVICE:** USMC sgt 1943-46. **HOME ADDRESS:** 6 S Poe St, Hartsdale, NY 10530. **BUSINESS ADDRESS:** Professor of Journalism, Columbia Univ Grad Sch Jour, Broadway at 116th St, New York, NY 10530.

JACKSON, MABEL I.
Business executive. **PERSONAL:** Born Oct 16, 1907, Leesville, LA; married Leonidas Jackson; children: Mary (coleman), Lucy (King), Leonidas Jr, William, Arnetta (Bartlow), Victor. **EDUCATION:** Univ Cal Ext Ctr Berkeley. **CAREER:** Lee's Auto Detail Ctr, sec-bookkeeper. **ORGANIZATIONS:** Mem East Bay Business & Pro Women's Club; Business & Pro Women's Town Council; Cal & Serv Alliance Bd; Dem Bd Berkeley; charter mem organizer Rainbow Sign Berkeley Nat com ch Nat Council Negro Women; mem Federated Women's Club; exec bd YWCA, Berkeley; mem Eastern Star; exec bd Berkeley PTA; mem Beth Eden Bapt Ch Woman of Yr, East Bay Area. **HONORS/ACHIEVEMENTS:** Outstanding community service awards Alpha Kappa Alpha Sor; YWCA; Nat Council Negro Women; Federated Women; Beth Eden Bapt Ch; Zeta Phi Beta Sor. **BUSINESS ADDRESS:** 3901 Telegraph Ave, Oakland, CA 94609.

JACKSON, MANNIE LEON
Business executive. **PERSONAL:** Born May 04, 1942, Illmo, MO; son of Emmett Leo. **EDUCATION:** Illinois Univ; Univ of Detroit Law Sch; Detroit Business Grad School. **CAREER:** Vice pres sales Marketing Comm Bldgs Group Honeywell Info Sys Newton, MA, dir employee & indus rel; vice pres gen mgr community serv; Harlem Globetrotters; Tech Tape Corp; Gen Motors Corp Cadillac Div, super labor rel; Honeywell Inc, dir per; Tampe Oper Univ So FL, instr. **ORGANIZATIONS:** Bd dir FL Am Soc Per Admin; ASPA; bd dir FL Sickle Cell Found; mem Urban Leag; NAACP; Minneapolis Children's Theater Bd, Bd of Honeywell Foundation, vice pres and bd of exec Leadership Council chairman, CEO of San Diego, NBA Franchise Inc. **HONORS/ACHIEVEMENTS:** Capt Univ IL Varsity Basketball Team; IL State Hall of Fame. **BUSINESS ADDRESS:** Commercial Buildings Group, Honeywell, Inc, MN 27-5177, Honeywell Plaza, Minneapolis, MN 55408.

JACKSON, MARVIN ALEXANDER
Educator, physician. **PERSONAL:** Born Oct 28, 1927, Dawson, GA; married Aeolian Loretta Mayo; children: Leigh, Brooke. **EDUCATION:** Morehouse Coll, BS 1947; Meharry Med Coll, MD 1951;Univ MI, MA 1956. **CAREER:** Univ of MI, instructor 1955-56, asst prof 1957-60, assoc prof 1960-68, prof 1968-; consult path NIH 1968-; Natl Naval Medical Center, toxicology unit 1964-71; Armed Forces Inst of Path 1971; VA Hospital 1960-71; NY, resident 1956-57; Univ of MI, resident 1953-56; US Naval Hospital, physician 1952-53; US Naval Hospital, intern 1951-52. **ORGANIZATIONS:** AAAS; Am Assn of Anatomists; Assn of Path Chmn; Am Assn of Path; Am Soc of Clinical Oncology; Am Assn ofUniv Profs; Coll of Am Path; Intl Acad of Path; NY Acad of Sci;Soc of Sigma Xi Sci publs 31; Am Bd Path 1957; Nat Sci Found Sr post doctoral fellowUniv Glasgow & Strangeways Research Lab Cambridge UK. **MILITARY SERVICE:** USNR lt 1951-56. **BUSINESS ADDRESS:** 423 13th St NW, Washington, DC 20004.

JACKSON, MARY
Purchasing manager. **PERSONAL:** Born Jan 07, 1932, Lumpkin, GA; daughter of Adie Beauford, Jr and Ida B Robinson Beauford; married Arthur L Jackson, Jul 02, 1965; children: Richard L George III, Cynthia A George. **EDUCATION:** Albany State Coll, Albany GA, B Educ, 1953; Anchorage AK Community Coll, Assoc Bus Admin, 1980. **CAREER:** Sheraton Hotel, Washington DC, payroll supervisor, 1963-68; Westover AFB MA, procurement clerk, 1966-68; Edwards AFB CA, procurement clerk, 1968-71; Elmendorf ABF AK, purchasing agent, 1971-78; Automotive Parts, Anchorage AK, purchasing agent, 1975-78; Alaska Village Electric, Anchorage AK, purchasing manager, 1978-. **ORGANIZATIONS:** Past state pres, Alaska State Federation BPW/USA, 1971-; past illustrious commandress, Daughter of Isis, 1977-; past dir, Intl Affairs Purchasing Management, 1977-; grand worthy matron, Prince Hall GC Order Eastern Star, 1977-; educational advisor, Anchorage Community Coll, 1977-79; committee mem, Kimo News Advisory Council on programming, 1978-80; state grand Loyal lady ruler, Order Golden Circle, 1982-; past sec, Soroptimist Intl, 1984-; past chairman, Job Service Executive Committee, 1985-; past chairman, Anchorage Community Block Grant Development (HUD), 1986-. **HONORS/ACHIEVEMENTS:** Delta Sigma Theta Sorority, 1952; Alpha Delta Zeta, Phi Theta Kappa Honor Society, 1978; Outstanding Service Award, purchasing management, 1983; Woman of the Year, Natl Business Women, 1984; Outstanding Achievement in Leadership, Prince Hall Masons F&AM, 1988; Community Service Award, Alaska Black Caucus, 1988; Community Service Award, Zeta Phi Beta Sorority, 1989. **HOME ADDRESS:** 4937 Tiffin Circle, Anchorage, AK 99508.

JACKSON, MATTIE J.
Labor official. **PERSONAL:** Born Oct 03, 1921, Livingston, TX; widowed; children: Gail Lavarra. **EDUCATION:** Attended, Johnson Business Coll, Healds Business Coll; San Francisco State Univ, Certificate of Completion Awd. **CAREER:** Koret of CA, garment worker/shop steward 1947-67; ILGWU, business agent 1967-70, intl vice pres. **ORGANIZATIONS:** Commnr SF Bd of Appeals 1967-; mem NAACP, Adv Bd SF Comm Coll, Social Concerns Commn Jones UM Church; exec bd SF Labor Council; exec bd Natl Negro Council of Women. **HONORS/ACHIEVEMENTS:** Salute to Women of Labor Awd Senate Indust 1983; Certificate of Appreciation USO 1984; Apri Salute to Labor A Philip Randolph Inst 1987. **BUSINESS ADDRESS:** Intl Vice President, ILGW Union, 660 Howard St, San Francisco, CA 94105.

JACKSON, MATTIE LEE
Director. **PERSONAL:** Born Jan 14, 1924, Miami, FL; married Thomas O; children: Thomas O, Richard K, Tammy Lynn. **EDUCATION:** Hampton Instr for Nurses, RN 1945; OK City U, BS 1974; OK City U, MA & Montessori Cert 1980. **CAREER:** NE Children's Montessori School N Eastern Ave Church of Christ Oklahoma City, dir 1979-; NE Child Develop Center, N Eastern Ave Church of Christ Oklahoma City, dir 1970-75; Job Corps Guthrie OK, dir of student nurses Health Occupation 1968-70; Kaiser Hospital, Portland OR, charge nurse 1960-66; Hoff Hospital & Clinic Victoria, TX, dir of surgery 1957-58; Univ Hospital Cleveland, staff nurse & private duty 1947-55; Jackson Memorial Hospital, Miami FL, charge nurse 1946-47. **HONORS/ACHIEVEMENTS:** World's Who' Who of Women 6th Edition 1981; Fellowship Grant (Montessari Intership) OK Community Found 1979; European Tour Early Childhood Educ OK CityUniv 1973; Woman of the Yr Christian Women Publ OK City 1972. **BUSINESS ADDRESS:** N Eastern Ave Ch of Christ, 4817 North Eastern Ave, Oklahoma City, OK 73121.

JACKSON, MAXIE C.
Administrator. **PERSONAL:** Born Mar 27, 1939, Gadsden, AL; married Carrie Baptiste; children: Maxie III, Lori, Dannielle. **EDUCATION:** BA 1966; MA 1969; PhD 1972. **CAREER:** Univ of the dis of Columbia, vice pres of acad affairs; Cntr for Urban Affairs Coll of Urban Devel, adminstr & faculty mem 1970-; MSU Vol Bur, dir 1969-70;MI Reformatory, prison couns 1967-68. **ORGANIZATIONS:** Vchprsn of adv com on Urban Devel Cntr for Urban Affairs Coll of Urban Devel 1974-75; coll rep Coun ofUniv Inst for Urban Affairs 1972-75; mem Phi Delta Kappa Educ Frat; Am Soc for Pub Admin & Comm Devel Soc; mem Gov's Commn on Vols in MI 1974-75; bd mem & com Chmn Grtr Lansing Urban Leag Voluntary Action Cntr of Grtr Lansing RSVP; consult NCVA Regional Network. **MILITARY SERVICE:** USAF weather observer 1962-65. **BUSINESS ADDRESS:** VP of Academic Affairs, University of DC, 4200 Connecticut Ave NW, Washington, DC 20008.

JACKSON, MAYNARD HOLBROOK
Government official. **PERSONAL:** Born Mar 23, 1938, Dallas, TX; married Valarie; children: Elizabeth, Brooke, Maynard III, Valerie Amanda, Alexandra. **EDUCATION:** Morehouse Coll, BA 1956; NC Central State Sch Law, JD 1959. **CAREER:** Atlanta, mayor, v mayor; Jackson Patterson Parks & Franklin, fndr & past ptnr; Nghbrhd Law Office Emory Comm Legal Serv Ctr, mgn atty; US NLRB, gen atty. **HONORS/ACHIEVEMENTS:** Youngest person to hold atlanta's highest office; youngest mayor of maj Am city; Greatest Pub Serv performed Am 35 yrs or under 1974; 200 Yng Ldrs Am Time Mag 1975; 100 Most Influencial Black Am Ebony Mag 1976. **BUSINESS ADDRESS:** Partner, Chapman & Cutler, 44 Broad St NW #500, Atlanta, GA 30303.

JACKSON, MICHAEL
Entertainer. **PERSONAL:** Born Aug 29, 1958, Gary, IN. **CAREER:** Lead singer Jacksons pop singing grp (Epic Label); introduced to Motown recording star Diana Ross with brothers Jackie Marlon Jermaine Tito; subsequently group went to Detroit to become biggest hit in Motown history; group soon recording both single records & albums "Got to be There", "Rocking Robin", "I Wanna Be Where You Are", "Ben", "With a Child's Heart", "We're Almost There"; appeared on Ed Sullivan Show, Hollywood Palace, The Andy Williams Show, Goin' Back to IN (their own special for ABC-TV); appeared in film "The Wiz" 1978; narrated ET, The Extra Terrestrial storybook 1982; leader of Jacksons US tour 1984. **HONORS/ACHIEVEMENTS:** Male Vocalist of the Yr 1971; Jacksons ranked top in single-record sales, in album sales for new artists 1970; group featured in animated cartoons onTV series 1971; Gold & Platinum record awds; performed Queen Elizabeth's Silver Jubilee 1977; Biggest selling solo album ever "Thriller" won 8 Grammy Awds, Album & Record of the Yr, won over 140 Gold & Platinum Awds in 28 countries & 6 continents; 1985 Recipient ABAA Music Award for efforts to aid African famine victims, and for conceiving and giving leadership to USA for Africa, producing the album and video, "We Are the World". **BUSINESS ADDRESS:** c/o Ziffren Brittenham Gullen, 2049 Century Park E, Ste 2350, Los Angeles, CA 90067.

JACKSON, MILES MERRILL
Educator, educational administrator. **PERSONAL:** Born Apr 28, 1929, Richmond, VA; son of Miles Merrill Jackson (deceased) and Thelma E Manning Jackson; married Bernice Olivia Roane, Jan 05, 1954; children: Miles, III, Marsha, Muriel, Melia. **EDUCATION:** VA Union U, BA 1955; Drexel U, MS 1956; Syracuse U, PhD 1974. **CAREER:** Free Library of Philadelphia, branch librarian 1956-58; Hampton Inst, head librarian 1958-62; Govt of American Samoa, territorial librarian 1962-64; Atlanta Univ, chief librarian 1964-69; State Univ of NY, assoc prof 1969-75; Univ of Hawaii at Manoa, dean and prof. **ORGANIZATIONS:** Bd of editors Intl Library Review 1984-; bd of editors Journal of Social Sci Information 1981-87; consultant Asia Found 1979-; consultant US Information Agency 1983-; consultant Natl Endowment for the Humanities 1979; chmn bd Hawaii Literacy 1985-86; bd of dir Central YMCA 1986-; pres Hawaii Literacy 1987. **HONORS/ACHIEVEMENTS:** Senior Lecturer fulbright US State Dept 1968-69; Bibliography of Negro History 1969; Ford Found Area Study grant for travel in Africa 1969; Sr Fulbright Lecturship, Univ of Tehran; Council on Library Resources Fellow 1970; Comparative and Intl Librarianship 1970; Intl Handbook of Intl Librarianship 1981; Pacific Islands Studies: A Review of The Literature 1986. **MILITARY SERVICE:** USN served 3 yrs. **BUSINESS ADDRESS:** Dean & Professor, Univ of Hawaii at Manoa, 2550 The Mall, Honolulu, HI 96822.

JACKSON, MILTON (BAGS)
Jazz musician. **PERSONAL:** Born Jan 01, 1923, Detroit, MI. **EDUCATION:** MI State Univ School of Jazz 1957. **CAREER:** Dizzie Gillespie NYC, musician 1945-; played piano & vibrahorn with Woody Herman Band 1949-50, Howard McGhee, Tadd Dameron, Thelonieus Monk 1950-52; Modern Jazz Quartet 1953-; School of Jazz Lenox, MA, faculty mem 1957; Town Hall Concert New York City 1958; European Tour 1957-58; appearances with Avery Fisher Hall/Newport Jazz Festival/Village Vanguard 1975. **HONORS/ACHIEVEMENTS:** Numerous recordings including, Jacksonville Opus de Jazz, Plenty Plenty, Soul Ballads in Blues, New Sounds in Modern Music, Modern Jazz Quartet, Bags & Flute, Bags & Trane, Jazz N'Samba, Milt Jackson Quintet Feelings, Live at the Museum of Modern Art; Numerous Downbeat Mag Awards 1955-59; Recip New Star Award Esquire Mag 1947; Encycl of Jazz Poll as "Greatest Ever" 1956; Metronome Poll Winner 1956-60; Playboy All-Stars Award 1959-60.

JACKSON, MONTE CARL
Professional athlete. **PERSONAL:** Born Jul 14, 1953, Sherman, TX. **EDUCATION:** San Diego Mesa Coll; San Diego State Coll; CA State Long Beach. **CAREER:** Oalkand Raiders, def back 1979-; Los Angeles Rams, cornerback 1975-79. **HONORS/ACHIEVEMENTS:** One of the premiere cornerbacks in teh league; AP, NEA Pro Football Writers Assn; Pro Football Weekly named All-NFL; All-NFC, UPI, AP, Pro Football Weekly Sporting News; Pro Bowl Nat Conf Coaches 1976; hon Ram's Outst Def Back; rookie of yr Rams All-Roockie UPI; NFC Champion Game 1975-76.

JACKSON, MURRAY EARL
Educator. **PERSONAL:** Born Dec 21, 1926, Philadelphia, PA; married Dauris Smart; children: Linda, David. **EDUCATION:** Wayne State U, MA 1954; Wayne State U, BA 1949. **CAREER:** Univ of MI, assoc prof Higher Edu, acting dir 1972-73; MI House of Representatives, comon colls & US, cons; N Cent Consult Examiner; Upward Bound Program Wayne State Univ, consultant adv; Detroit Council of Arts, 1975; Wayne County Community Coll, pres 1970-71, acting press 1969-70, exec dir 1969, exec sec 1968-69; Wayne State Univ, 1950-70; Urban Affairs, asst dean of students 1969-70, asst to vice pres; Coll Liberal Arts, exec asst 1955-64; Higher Educ Opportunity Com, coord dir 1963; Humanities, instructor 1958-60; Univ of MI, coord special projects 1965; Highland Park Jr Coll, instructor 1957-58. **ORGANIZATIONS:** Chmn Div 4 Sch of Educ 1972-74; mem Council ofUniv & Colls Mid-am Assn of Equal Oppty Prgm Pers; chmn Black Faculty Sch of Edn; mem TheUniv Evaluation Com; mem Career Planning & Placement Policy Com; mem Bd in Control of Intercoll Athl; mem Trio Prgm HEW Region 5; mem Cncl on Black Am Affr; mem Higher Educ Oppty Com Bd of dirs, 1st dist Dem Party MI 1965-69; Dem Party Educ Com; Citizens Adv Com to Det Pub Schs; Nat Bd for Theol Edn, Episcopal Ch 1971-73; pres Am Lung Assn of SE MI 1974-76; bd dir Nghbrhd Serv Orgn; bd dir Big Bro & Sister; The Detroit Council for Youth Serv Inc; Metro Detroit Citizens Devel Authority; Mayors Com for Rehab of Narcotic Addists; MI Episcopal Sch of Theology; mem NAACP; Polit Reform for Mayor, City of Detroit; Sr Citizen Commn City of Detroit; v chmn Urban Alliance; chmn Detroit Council of Arts; adv Proj 350 Wayne StateUniv Hon HHD ShawU;Mackenzie Honor Soc Wayne State U; commendation by House of Reps State of MI. **HONORS/ACHIEVEMENTS:** Awards in Learning; Elder W Diggs Award Kappa Alpha Psi; the Murray Jackson Serv Award Wayne Co Comm Coll; Citizen of Yr Award Unity Lodge 1975; Wayne CoComm Coll Founds Award Alumni Assn 1973; Disting Serv Award City of Detroit 1976. **BUSINESS ADDRESS:** Assoc Prof of Education, The University of Michigan, Ctr for Higher Education, 2007 School of Education Bldg, Ann Arbor, MI 48109.

JACKSON, NATHANIEL G.
Educator. **PERSONAL:** Born Sep 14, 1942, Elkins, WV; married Francis Lewis. **EDUCATION:** Purdue U, BA 1964;Univ of OK, MA 1966; Emory U, MEd 1970. **CAREER:** Elkins YMCA, dir; Job Corps, training staff, tchr, coach, secondary edn; Higher Ed, adminstr, professional cons; Alderson Broaddus Coll Real Estate broker, dir of financial aid. **ORGANIZATIONS:** Mem State Assn of Financial Aid Adm past pres, State Assn for Retarded Cit; trustee Shiloh Bapt Ch; mem Rotary; A & Fm; United Fund Bd; Sr Cit Bd;Master Mason Mt Zion Lodge #14. **HONORS/ACHIEVEMENTS:** Jaycee's Man of Yr 1969. **BUSINESS ADDRESS:** PO Box 437 Alderson Broaddus C, Philippi, WV 26416.

JACKSON, NOAH
Professional athlete. **PERSONAL:** Born Apr 14, 1951, Jack Bch, FL. **EDUCATION:** Univ of Tampa. **CAREER:** Chicago Bears, professional football guard 1975-. **HONORS/ACHIEVEMENTS:** Sm Coll All Am. **BUSINESS ADDRESS:** Chicago Bears, PO Box 204, Lake Forest, IL 60045.

JACKSON, NORLISHIA A.
Editor. **PERSONAL:** Born Oct 20, 1942, Washington, DC. **EDUCATION:** Howard Univ, BS 1964; Catholic Univ of Amer, MA 1966; Fed City Coll, advanced study. **CAREER:** Washington Urban League, dir information 1969-71; Natl Business League, dir information 1972-73; Natl Consumer Information Center, dir information & publications 1973-74; Delta Sigma Theta Publications, editor 1969-; YWCA Home for Girls, dir 1976. **ORGANIZATIONS:** Mem Am Personnel & Guidane Assn; Capitol Press Club; Assn ofUniv Women; mem YWCA, NCNW, Urban League. **HONORS/ACHIEVEMENTS:** Who's Who Among Students in AmerUniv & Coll 1964; Outstanding Young Women of Am 1970-71; Alumni Achievement Award 1971; Outstanding Serv Award HUU Ctr 1968; Women of the Yr Award Big Sisters of Am Inc 1980. **BUSINESS ADDRESS:** 636 E Capitol St NE, Washington, DC 20003.

JACKSON, NORMAN A.
Association director. **PERSONAL:** Born Nov 16, 1932, NYC, NY; married Nellie; children: Deborah, Norma, Leona. **EDUCATION:** BS, MA, PhD 1972. **CAREER:** FL Commn on Human Relations Commn, exec dir; Coll Entrance Examination Bd So Regional Office Atlanta, asst dir 1972-74; Minority Affairs FL State U, dir 1970-72; Student Comm Serv St Petersburg Jr Coll, dir 1965-70; St Petersburg, FL, chmn dept physical educ & athletic dir 1959-65;Univ AR, instr; Res Devel FL Jr Coll, asst dir. **ORGANIZATIONS:** Pres So Assn Black Adminstr 1973-74; cons, lecturer & writer FL Equal Access; mem Nat Council Measurement Edn; Phi Delta Kappa; Nat Assn Fin Asst Minority Students; Nat Alliance Black Sch Educator; AACJC; Am Pers & Guidance Assn; FL Assn Comm Coll; FL Assn Fin Aid Adminstrs; So Assn Financial Aid Adminstrs; FL Educ Research Assn; Nat Vocational Guidance Assn. **HONORS/ACHIEVEMENTS:** Basketball Coach Yr 1964; fellowships, Kellogg, NDEA, Seeing Eye Corp; grants, UOES, So Educ Found. **MILITARY SERVICE:** AUS 1 lt. **BUSINESS ADDRESS:** Florida Junior College, 21 W Church St, Jacksonville, FL 32202.

JACKSON, OCIE
Business executive. **PERSONAL:** Born 1904, Texas; widowed; children: Warren, Owen, Arthur Lee, Felix. **EDUCATION:** Hampton Inst, attended. **CAREER:** Jackson Brothers Ranch, Ocie Jackson & Properties, owner. **ORGANIZATIONS:** Regent Lamar Univ Beaumont TX; dir Golden State Mutual Life Ins Co CA. **HONORS/ACHIEVEMENTS:** One of the wealthiest black men in the US.

JACKSON, OSCAR JEROME
Physician. **PERSONAL:** Born Dec 17, 1929, Fairfield, AL; divorced. **EDUCATION:** Howard U, BS; Howard U, MD. **CAREER:** Gen Surgical, internship & residency; Private Practice, surgery 1963. **ORGANIZATIONS:** Mem Am Bd Surgery 1963; Fellow Am Coll Surgery 1967; clin instr surgeryUniv of CA; attending surgeon Mt Zion Hosp; dir John Hale Med Plan; chmn United Health Alliance; pres Business & Professional Assn; pres John Hale med soc; mem Omega Phi Psi Frat. **HONORS/ACHIEVEMENTS:** Professional Chemistry Prize Howard U; Comm Achievement Award MuhammedUniv of Islam. **MILITARY SERVICE:** Busaf capt 1956-59. **BUSINESS ADDRESS:** 1352 Haight St, San Francisco, CA.

JACKSON, PAUL L.
Educator, dentist. **PERSONAL:** Born Aug 01, 1907, Wilson, NC; married Catherine Mccain. **EDUCATION:** Livingstone Coll Salisbury, NC, BS 1930; Univ PA, MS 1933; TempleUniv Sch Dentistry, DDS 1943. **CAREER:** Temple Univ Comprehensive Health Servs Prog, chief, professional servs 1969-; Temple Univ School Dentisitry, instr 1966-69; Private Practice, dentistry 1947-69; Stephen Smith Home Aged, consult 1947-69; Mouth Hygiene Assn, clinical dentist 1947; Howard Univ, asst prof operative dentistry 1947. **ORGANIZATIONS:** Mem Am & PA (house del) Dental Assns; Acad Gen Dentristry; Am Assn Dental Anesthesiologists; Philadelphia Co Dental Soc; Am Assn Geriatric Dentists; chmn bd dir Stephen Smith Towers. **HONORS/ACHIEVEMENTS:** NAACP; Fellowship Commn; Franklin Inst; Smithsonian Inst; Nat Geographic So Who's Who in East 1966; British Dict 1967; Fellowship Acad Gen Dentistry Royal Soc Health; Fellow Royal Soc Health 1969; Fellow Acad Gen Dent 1969. **MILITARY SERVICE:** AUS dental corps maj 1943-46.

JACKSON, PAZEL
Business executive. **PERSONAL:** Born Feb 21, 1932, Brooklyn, NY; married Catherine M Faulkner; children: Karen, Pazel, Peter, Allyson. **EDUCATION:** City Coll of NY, BCE 1954, MCE 1959; Columbia Univ, MS Bus Admin 1972. **CAREER:** NYC, civil engr 1956-62; Worlds Fair Corp NYC, chief of design 1962-66; New York City Dept of Publ Works, dep gen mgr 1966-67; New York City Dept Bldgs, asst commiss 1967-69; Bowery Savings Bank NYC, sr vice pres 1969-86; Chemical Bank of NY, sr vice pres 1986-. **ORGANIZATIONS:** Chmn Mutual Real Estate Investment Trust 1975-; dir Natl Ho Partnership Corp NY State Urban Devel Corp, New York City Ho Devel Corp, Battery Park City Auth, Bedford Stuyvesant Restoration Corp; bd dir Com Serv Soc, Citizens Housing & Plnng Council; mem NY Professional Engrs Soc, ASCE, NY Bldg Congress, City Coll Alumni Assoc Lambda Alpha, Episcopalian Club. **HONORS/ACHIEVEMENTS:** Man of the Year Brooklyn Civic Assoc 1967; Spec Awd for Bldg Design Paragon Fed Credit Union 1968. **MILITARY SERVICE:** AUS lt 1954-56. **BUSINESS ADDRESS:** Senior Vice President, Chemical Bank of NY, 110 E 42nd St, New York, NY 10017.

JACKSON, PRINCE ALBERT, JR.
College professor. **PERSONAL:** Born Mar 17, 1925, Savannah, GA; married Marilyn Stuggles; children: Prince Albert, III, Rodney Mark, Julia Lucia, Anthony Brian, Philip Andrews. **EDUCATION:** Savannah State Coll, BS 1949; NY U, MS 1950;Univ KS, Post Grad 1961-62; Harvard, NSF Fellow 1962-63; Boston Coll, PhD 1966. **CAREER:** William James HS Statesboro, tchr sci math 1950-55; Savannah State Coll, faculty 1955-, asso prof, math physics 1966-71; Savannah State College, Savannah, GA pres 1971-78. **ORGANIZATIONS:** Chmn Natural Sci Div Dir Institutional Self Study 1967-71, pres 1971-78; prof Sch of Sci & Tech; athl dir St Pius X HS Savannah 1955-64; teaching fellowvis instr Boston Coll 1964-66; consult sci math vice pres Bd Pub Educ Savannah & Chatham Co 1971; mem Educ Com US Cath Conf 1971-; mem So Regl Educ Bd 1971; mem Chatham-Savannah Charter Study Com; United Way Bd of Dir; TACTICS Nat Policy Bd; St Jude Guild; adv bd March of Dimes; adv com Nat Assessment of Educ Progress; Am Assn of State Colls & U's; Nat Assn for Equal Educ Oppty; Nat Sci Found Panel; mem exec com So Regl Educ Bd 1973-74; Am AssnUniv Profs; NEA; GA Tchrs Educ Assn; Nat Sci Tchrs Assn; Nat Counc Tchrs Math; Am Educ Rsrch Assn; Nat Counc on Measurement in Edn; Nat Inst Sci Bd mgrs W Broad St YMCA Savannah 1962; v chmn St Pius X Educ Counc Savannah 1967-; mem NAACP Savannah 1968-; adv Comm Devel Corp1969; bd dirs GA Heart Assn; Goodwill Inds; ARC; BSA; trustee GA Econ Counc. **HONORS/ACHIEVEMENTS:** Recip outst ldrshp serv award Savannah State Coll Nat Alumni Assn 1967; liberty bell award Savannah Bar Assn 1973; Benedictine Medal of Excellence 1974; man of yr Alpha Phi Alpha 1960 & 67; outst educator award Nat Black Pub Assn 1975; S Region Man of Yr the Frogs Inc 1967. **MILITARY SERVICE:** USNR 1942-46.

JACKSON, RALPH LAVELLE
Professional athlete. **PERSONAL:** Born Oct 26, 1962, Los Angeles, CA. **EDUCATION:** UCLA, 1984. **CAREER:** Indiana Pacers, guard 1984-. **ORGANIZATIONS:** Natl Youth Sports Festival. **HONORS/ACHIEVEMENTS:** Co-winner of UCLA's Bruin Bench Awrd for most imprvmnt in all-around Play & Mental Attitude; All-Am acclaim. **BUSINESS ADDRESS:** Indiana Pacers, Two West Washington St, Ste 510, Indianapolis, IN 46204.

JACKSON, RANDOLPH
Justice. **PERSONAL:** Born Oct 10, 1943, Brooklyn, NY; son of James Titler and Rathenia McCollum Jackson; married Sarah McCall; children: two. **EDUCATION:** NY U, BA 1965; Brooklyn Law Sch, JD 1969. **CAREER:** Mudge Rose Guthrie & Alexander, asso atty 1969-70; Private Practice of Law, 1971-81; New York City Family Court, hearing examiner 1981; Civil Court, Housing Part, judge 1981-87; Civil Court, judge 1987-88; Supreme Court Brooklyn NY, justice 1988-. **ORGANIZATIONS:** Life mem Nat Bar Assn 1971-; mem Brooklyn Bar Assn 1971-; deacon Concord Baptist Ch 1982-; trustee Interfaith Med Cntr 1980-; dir Navy Yard Boys and Girls Club 1982-; mem Crown Hgts Lions Club 1980-; Sigma Pi Phi; mem Metropolitan Black Bar Assn of New York. **HONORS/ACHIEVEMENTS:** Book, "How to Get a Fair Trial By Jury" 1978. **BUSINESS ADDRESS:** Justice, Supreme Court, Kings County, Brooklyn, NY 11201.

JACKSON, RAYMOND T.
Educator. **PERSONAL:** Born Dec 11, 1933, Providence, RI; married Annette Barnhill; children: Andrea C. **EDUCATION:** New England Conservatory of Music, BMus (summa cum laude) 1955; Am Conservatory of Music Fontainebleau, France, Diploma 1960; Juilliard Sch of Music, DMA 1973, MS 1959, BS 1957. **CAREER:** Univ of RI, asst prof of music 1968-75; Mannes Coll of Music NY, instructor 1970-77; Concordia Coll Bronxville, NY, asst prof of music 1970-77; Howard U, prof of piano, chmn piano div and applied music studies. **ORGANIZATIONS:** Concert pianist US, Europe, S Am 1951; lecture/recitalist "The Piano Music of Black Composers" Adjudicator Coll &Univ Piano Master Classes 1963; organist/

choir dir Congdon St Baptist Ch Providence RI 1948-57; organist/choir dir Trinity Lutheran Ch Tenafly, NJ 1957-60; organist/choir dir Trinity Lutheran Ch Bogota, NJ 1961-72; organist 2nd Ch of Christ Scientist NY 1972-77; organist 1st Ch of Christ Scientist Chevy Chase, MD 1978; piano recording artist Performance Records Black Artist Series 1982; pres Raymond Jackson Music Forum; Baldwin Piano Roster of Disting Performing Artists. **HONORS/ACHIEVEMENTS:** Prizewinner Intl Piano Competition Rio De Janeiro 1965; prizewinner Marguerite Long Intl Piano Compet Paris 1965; prizewinner Jugg Inc NY Town Hall Debut Award 1959; prizewinner Nat Assn of Negro Musicians 1957; fellowship Ford Found 1971-73; fellowship Roothbert Fund 1971-73; fellowship John Hay Whitney Found 1965; fellowship Eliza & George Howard Found 1960, 1963; elected into RI Heritage Hall of Fame 1966; hon mem Chopin Club Providence, RI 1966; George W Chadwick Medal New Eng Conservatory of Music Boston 1955, grad 1st in class (summa cum laude) Black Am Music 2nd Ed (Roach); The Music of Black Am 2nd Ed (Southern); Blacks in Classical Music (Abdul); Black Americana by Richard Long (1986), p.129. **HOME ADDRESS:** 9205 Harvey Rd, Silver Spring, MD 20910. **BUSINESS ADDRESS:** Professor of Piano, HowardUniv, College of Fine Arts, Washington, DC 20059.

JACKSON, RAYNARD
Accountant. **PERSONAL:** Born Dec 23, 1960, St Louis, MO. **EDUCATION:** Oral Roberts Univ, BS Acctg 1983. **CAREER:** Fin consult to several bus in St Louis; MO Dept of Revenue, auditor. **ORGANIZATIONS:** Public speaker St Louis Bd of Educ 1979-; mem Oral Roberts Alumni Assoc 1983-; bd mem Metro Republican Forum 1984-; asst basketball coach Crusader's 1984-86; treas MO Chap Natl Black Republican Council 1984-; treas comm to elect Curtis Crawford Mayor 1985; treas Executive Elite 1985-; mem Full Gospel Businessmen Assoc 1986-; bd mem St Louis Squires 1986-; building fund comm Mt Zion Missionary Baptist Ch 1986-; bd mem Conf on Educ 1987-. **HONORS/ACHIEVEMENTS:** Outstanding Alumni Training Ctr for Service 1984; Citation from Mayor Role Model Experience Program 1986. **HOME ADDRESS:** 5830 Woodland Ave, St Louis, MO 63120.

JACKSON, REGINALD LEO
Educator, visual anthropologist, artist. **PERSONAL:** Born Jan 10, 1945, Springfield, MA. **EDUCATION:** Yale Univ School of Art & Architecture, BFA, MFA 1970; SUNY Stony Brook, MSW 1977; Union Grad School Cincinnati OH, PhD Commun, Visual Anthrop 1979. **CAREER:** Yale Univ School of Architecture, instr 1970; Quinnipiac Coll, asst prof, film making 1972; Biomedical Comm, asst media prod, dir 1972-74; Simmons College, tenured assoc prof photocommun, assoc prof commun 1974-. **ORGANIZATIONS:** Consult NY State HEOP Higher Ed Oppty Prog 1975; mem Poetry Lives Series McDougal Littel & Co 1976, African Herit Inst Simmons Review Photo/Essay-Ghana Simmons Coll 1976; co-chmn of legis Comm METCO—MA Council for Ed Oppty 1977-; consult English HS 1977-; consult Charles E Mackey Middle School Photo 1979-; mem Natl Conf of Artists. **HONORS/ACHIEVEMENTS:** Rsch Grants Simmons Coll 1975,77,80; Artist in Residence AAMARP Northeastern Univ Boston 1978-; MA Arts & Humanities Grant 1979; James D Parks Spec Awd Natl Conf of Artists 1979; Comm Fellowship MIT 1980; Fellowship Ford Found 1980-81; Ford Found Post Doctorate Fellowship MIT 1980; Smithsonian Rsch Fellowship Museum of Natural History 1981; John Anson Kitteridge Ed Fund Ella Lymon Cabot Trust 1982. **BUSINESS ADDRESS:** Associate Professor, Biomedical Communications, 300 The Fenway, Boston, MA 02115.

JACKSON, REGINALD MARTINEZ
Professional athlete. **PERSONAL:** Born May 18, 1946, Wyncote, PA. **EDUCATION:** Attended, AZ State Univ. **CAREER:** KS City, player 1967; Oakland A's, player 1968-75; Baltimore Orioles, player 1976; NY Yankees, player 1977-81; CA Angels, outfielder 1982-. **ORGANIZATIONS:** Former natl chmn Amyotrophic Lateral Sclerosis. **HONORS/ACHIEVEMENTS:** AL MVP 1973; led AL in RBI's & HR's in 1973 AL 1971-74; set major league World Series record for consecutive HR's in a game 1977; holds Amer League record for consecutive seasons of 100 or more strikeouts (12 seasons); hit a homer in each of 12 Amer League parks 1975; appeared in 10th All-Star Game 1980; 10 game World Series hitting streak; 9 Series home runs; 19th player ever to hit 20 or more homers 11 straight seasons; led Amer League in homers since 1974; Hon Big Brother of the Yr Big Brothers & Sisters Prog 1984. **BUSINESS ADDRESS:** CA Angels, Anaheim Stadium, 200 State College Blvd, Anaheim, CA 92806.

JACKSON, RENARD I.
Educational administration. **PERSONAL:** Born May 29, 1946, Chicago, IL; married Katherine Ann Fraizer. **EDUCATION:** Kennedy-King Coll, AA 1970; Northern IL Univ, BS Ed 1973, MS Ed 1977, EdD. **CAREER:** Abraham Lincoln Center, asst program dir 1968-70; Northern IL Univ, dir upward bound 1973-77; Elgin HS, asst principal 1977-80; IL Youth Center St Charles, dir of ed. **ORGANIZATIONS:** Pres Creative Cons; steering comm Council Mgr Govt; vice chmn Bd of Trustees Elgin Comm Coll; chmn Elgin Planning Commiss; mem Rotay Intl. **HONORS/ACHIEVEMENTS:** Past mem Elgin YMCA Coop Bd 1977-84; MWPM Marquette-Joliet Consistary #104; bd of dir Elgin United Way; active mem IL Assoc for Adv of Black Voc Ed. **BUSINESS ADDRESS:** Dir of Education, Illinois Youth Center, PO Box 122, St Charles, IL 60174.

JACKSON, RICHARD E., JR.
Mayor. **PERSONAL:** Born Jul 18, 1945, Peekskill, NY; married Ruth Sokolinsky; children: Tara, Alice, Abigail. **EDUCATION:** Univ of Bridgeport, BA Mathematics 1968. **CAREER:** Peekskill City Schools, math teacher 1968-; United Way of Westchester, board of directors 1969; Peekskill Field Library, board of directors 1974; Westchester County Republican Comm, county committeeman 1975; Peekskill City Republica; Comm, vice chairman 1976; Peekskill Housing Auth, board member 1982; City of Peekskill, councilman 1979-84; City of Peekskill, mayor. **ORGANIZATIONS:** Dir Neighborhood Youth Corps Comm Action Program 1968; education comm NAACP 1981-83; deputy mayor City of Peekskill 1982-84; Westchester County Board of Ethics 1984. **BUSINESS ADDRESS:** Mayor, City of Peekskill, Municipal Bldg Main St, Peekskill, NY 10566.

JACKSON, RICHARD H.
Engineering executive. **PERSONAL:** Born Oct 17, 1933, Detroit; married Arlena; children: Deirdre, Gordon, Rhonda. **EDUCATION:** Univ of MO;Univ of Wichita, Walton Sch of Commerce, postgrad 1971. **CAREER:** Nat Energy Corp IL, vice pres Ops 1975-; Gits Bros Mfg Co Chigo, vice pres engring; Boeing Corp, designed alternate landing gear sys & thrust reverser fail-safe sys for Boeing 747; disigned numerous components for various other air craft & space vehicles; Beech Aircraft, first black engr; Nat Aeronautics & Space Adminstrn Dept of Defense, cons, experiment team for Gemini space flights 5 through 12. **BUSINESS ADDRESS:** 1846 S Kilbourn Ave, Chicago, IL 60623.

JACKSON, RICKEY
Professional football player. **PERSONAL:** Born Mar 20, 1958, Pahokee, FL; married Norma; children: Rickeyah. **EDUCATION:** Attended, Univ of Pittsburgh. **CAREER:** New Orleans Saints, professional football player (linebacker) 1981-. **HONORS/ACHIEVEMENTS:** Played in Senior Bowl; was Defensive MVP in East-West Shrine Game; ABC Player of the Game vs Penn State 1980; selected to Pro Bowl second consec yr; was only Saint selected for 1984 Pro Bowl; led NFC linebackers in sacks (12) for second consec yr; fourth on team tackle chart with 199; led team in 1981 with eight sacks; mem NFL Pro Bowl teams 1986,87. **BUSINESS ADDRESS:** New Orleans Saints, 1500 Poydras St, New Orleans, LA 70112.

JACKSON, ROBERT, JR.
Associate executive/reporter. **PERSONAL:** Born Jan 15, 1936, Chicago; son of Robert and Lucille; divorced; children: Dawn, Robert, III, Randall. **EDUCATION:** CO State Coll, BA 1957; NorthwesternUniv Columbia Coll, Additional Study. **CAREER:** Intl News Svc, reporter 1958; Chicago Am Chicago Today, reporter 1958-69; WBEE Radio Chicago, reporter 1964; Chicago Bulletine, editor-writer 1965; Chicago Urban League, writer-producer 1966; CCUO, dir publ info 1969-70; Argonne Natl Lab, dir publ info 1970-73; Provident Hosp & Training School, dir publ rel; Reg Alcoholism Info Prog Natl Council on Alcoholism, field dir 1975-; Rocky Mountain News, reporter. **ORGANIZATIONS:** Chicago Newspaper Reporters Assn 1965; Sigam Delta Chi 1965; mem United Black Journalist 1968; Council for Advancement of Sci Writing 1971; Atomic IndustrialForm 1971; publ rel Soc of Amer 1971; bd dir S Shore YMCA 1972; Hosp Publ Rel Soc 1974. **HONORS/ACHIEVEMENTS:** Nom for Assn Press Award 1965; nom for Pulitzer Prize 1963, 1988. **BUSINESS ADDRESS:** Reporter, Rocky Mountain News, 400 W Colfax Ave, Denver, CO 80204.

JACKSON, ROBERT E.
Association executive. **PERSONAL:** Born Feb 10, 1937, Reading, PA; married Carol A Norman; children: Robert E, Jr, Jeannine, Monique, Gregory. **CAREER:** Food Serv Albright Coll, dir; Schuylkill Valley Restaurant Assn, pres 1974-76. **ORGANIZATIONS:** 2nd vice pres PA Assn Blind; pres Berks Co Assn Blind; bd dirs Camp Conrad Weiser; mem NACUFS. **MILITARY SERVICE:** AUSR E-5 1955-62. **BUSINESS ADDRESS:** Dir of Food Service, Albright College, 13th & Exeter Sts, Reading, PA 19604.

JACKSON, RONALD G.
Policy analyst/civil rights. **PERSONAL:** Born Sep 07, 1952, New Orleans, LA; married Brenda J Bellamy; children: Ronald Jr, Tiffany. **EDUCATION:** Jackson State Univ, BA 1974; Howard Univ, MSW 1975; Antioch School of Law, JD 1985. **CAREER:** Sen Thad Cochran, staff asst (1st Black on staff) 1974-77; So MS Legal Svcs, paralegal 1977; MS Gulf Coast Jr Coll, instructor 1978; Harrison Co HeadSTART Prog, project dir 1978-79; Univ of So MS, asst prof 1979-83; Natl Urban League, policy analyst. **ORGANIZATIONS:** Public relations officer Forrest Co NAACP 1979-84; mem Omega Psi Phi Inc 1981-; mem Midtown Montessouri School 1985-. **HONORS/ACHIEVEMENTS:** Outstanding Young Men in Amer 1978; Who's Who Among Amer Law Students 1985. **HOME ADDRESS:** 2217 Minnesota Ave SE #3, Washington, DC 20020. **BUSINESS ADDRESS:** Policy Analyst, Natl Urban League, 1111 14th St NW, Ste 600, Washington, DC 20005.

JACKSON, RONALD LEE
Educator. **PERSONAL:** Born Jul 13, 1943, Kansas City, MO; married Hattie Robinson; children: Taj, Yasmira. **EDUCATION:** Harris Jr Coll, AA 1963; Washington U, AB 1965; So ILU, addtl study 1974-76. **CAREER:** IL State Univ, admissions couns 1969-70; Washington U, asst dir of admissions 1970-73, asst dean 1973-; Higher Educ Coord Counc, adm Com 1970-73; StLouis Com on Africa, 1975-76; US Senator John Danforth, asst. **ORGANIZATIONS:** Contr to founding of Counc on Black Affairs IL StateUniv 1969-70; mem Leadership St Louis 1983; bd mem New City School 1984-86; mem Urban League Educ Comm 1984-; chmn United Way Comm Wide Youth Panel 1986-87; bd mem Cardinal Ritter Coll Prep HS 1987-; vice pres Westlake Scholarship Commn. **HONORS/ACHIEVEMENTS:** CORD Fellow 1973; Leadership St Louis 1982-83; Minority Business Advocate Eastern MO 1986. **MILITARY SERVICE:** AUS 1st lt 1966-69. **BUSINESS ADDRESS:** Assistant, US Senator John C Danforth, 815 Olive Room 228, St Louis, MO 63101.

JACKSON, ROSWELL F.
Educator, clergyman. **PERSONAL:** Born Jul 09, 1922, Madison, GA; son of William Jackson and Gertrude Jackson; married Frances L; children: Josephone Neal, Roswell F, Dwight. **EDUCATION:** Morehouse Coll, BS 1947; Morehouse School of Religion, BD 1950; Atlanta Univ, MA 1956; Interdenominational Theol, DMin 1974. **CAREER:** Mt Calvary Baptist Church, pastor 1950-; Morehouse Coll, instr, chmn dept of philos, religion 1950-. **MILITARY SERVICE:** AUS, 2nd lt 1942-45. **BUSINESS ADDRESS:** Chrmn Dept Philo/relgn, Morehouse College, 830 Westview Dr SW, Atlanta, GA 30314.

JACKSON, ROY J., JR.
Chemist. **PERSONAL:** Born Feb 08, 1944, Cottonport, LA. **EDUCATION:** So Univ, BS 1965, MS 1969; Univ of CA, PhD 1975. **CAREER:** Dow Chem Co, rsch chemist 1968; So Univ, instr 1969-70, grad asst 1967-69; Univ CA, teaching asst 1970-75; Shell Developing Co, rsch chemist, sr rsch chemist, exchange scientist at Koninklyke Shell Labs Amsterdam The Netherlands. **ORGANIZATIONS:** Mem Amer Chem Soc; Kappa Delta Pi; Alpha Phi Alpha Frat; Black Action Comm. **HONORS/ACHIEVEMENTS:** Numerous scholarships fellowships. **MILITARY SERVICE:** AUS capt 1965-67; Bronze Star Medal. **BUSINESS ADDRESS:** Senior Research Chemist, Shell Development Co, Westhollow Rsrch Cntr, Hwy 6 S, Houston, TX 77077.

JACKSON, ROY LEE
Professional athlete. **PERSONAL:** Born May 01, 1954, Opelika, AL; married Mary. **EDUCATION:** Tuskegee Inst. **CAREER:** NY Mets, 1977-79; Toronto Blue Jays, pitcher. **HONORS/ACHIEVEMENTS:** Voted MVP in baseball Tuskegee Inst 1974 & 1975; named to Appalachian All-Star Team.

JACKSON, RUDOLPH ELLSWORTH
Physician & educator. **PERSONAL:** Born May 31, 1935, Richmond, VA; married Janice Diane Ayer; children: Kimberley R, Kelley J, Rudolph E Jr, Alison D Ligon. **EDUCATION:** Morehouse Coll, BS 1957; Meharry Med Coll, MD 1961. **CAREER:** St Jude Childrens Rsch Hosp, asst mem in hematology 1969-72; Natl Heart Lung & Blood Inst, chief sickle cell disease branch 1972-77; Howard Univ Sch of Medicine, assoc prof dept of pediatrics 1977-79; Meharry Medical Coll, chmn dept of pediatrics 1979-83; Morehouse School of Medicine, act chr dept ofpediatrics 1984-. **ORGANIZATIONS:** Mem Amer Med Assn, Natl Med Assn, Amer Soc of Hematology, DHHS Secretary's Advisory Comm on lead, sickle cell disease & arthritis; mem Adv Ctme toSec DHEW sickle cell disease 1971-72; mem Natl Advisory Council Natl Inst Arthritis Diabetes Digestive Kidney Diseases NIH DHEW 1979-83; mem Adv Ctme to Sec DHEW lead poisoning 1984. **HONORS/ACHIEVEMENTS:** Mem Amer Acad of Pediatrics; mem Assoc of Med School Pediatric Dept Chmn Inc 1980; mem Sigma Xi Scientific Soc Howard Univ 1978-; mem Alpha Omega Alpha Med Soc Meharry Med Coll 1980-. **MILITARY SERVICE:** USN lt cmdr 5 1/2 yrs. **HOME ADDRESS:** 893 Woodmere Dr NW, Atlanta, GA 30318. **BUSINESS ADDRESS:** Acting Chmn Dept of Pediatrics, Morehouse School of Medicine, 720 Westview Dr SW, Atlanta, GA 30310.

JACKSON, RUSSELL A.
Educator. **PERSONAL:** Born Feb 26, 1934, Philadelphia; married Elois; children: Cheryll Renne, Charles Russell. **EDUCATION:** Cheyney State Coll, BA 1956; Temple U, MA 1962; Temple U, EdD 1970. **CAREER:** Philadelphia Schs, tchr prin; Chester PA, asst supt; E Orange NJ, supt 1968-72; Roosevelt Sch Dist #66, presently supt schs. **ORGANIZATIONS:** Mem Am Assn Sch Administr; Ariz Sch Admin Inc; Phi Delta Kappa Frat; pres Nat Alliance Black Sch Educ 1970-72; pres Greater Phoenix Supr Assn 1974-75; exec com Ariz Found for Blind. **MILITARY SERVICE:** USN 1958.

JACKSON, SAMUEL S., JR.
Educator. **PERSONAL:** Born Nov 08, 1934, Natchez, MS; married Margaret Atkins; children: Sharon, Orlando, Sheila, Samuel, III. **EDUCATION:** Okolona Jr Coll Okolona, MS, 1952; Alcorn A&M Coll Lorman MS, BS 1955; Antioch Coll Yellow Springs OH, MAT 1970. **CAREER:** HS teacher, guidance counselor, asst prin, 1957-68; Wilberforce Univ Coop Educ Cons, assoc dir coop educ 1968-69, dean of students & students personnel consult Co-op Educ, asst dir Univ Personnel Officer 1969-. **ORGANIZATIONS:** Mem Phi Delta Kappa; Omega Psi Phi; Am Personnel Guid Assn; Nat Assn Stud Personnel Adminstr. **HONORS/ACHIEVEMENTS:** Nom Outst Yng Man of Am 1970; Mega Man Yr 1972; cert achvmt Cntrb & Participation in 4th Nat Insti Narcotics & Dangerous Drugs; cert outst serv WilberforceUniv Student Govt 1973-74; recog Alpha Kappa Mu 1974. **MILITARY SERVICE:** AUS spl serv 1955-57. **BUSINESS ADDRESS:** WilberforceUniv, Wilberforce, OH 45384.

JACKSON, SEATON J.
Medical doctor. **PERSONAL:** Born Jun 13, 1914, Terrell, TX; married Kathryn Williams; children: Elaine J. **EDUCATION:** Bishop Coll, BS 1936; Meharry Med Coll, MD 1941. **CAREER:** Provident Hosp Chicago, intern; Homer Phillips Hosp St Louis, residency; Army Med Field Serv Sch Carlyle PA; Jackson Clnic Hosp, owner & staff mem. **ORGANIZATIONS:** Mem NMA; AMA; staff mem Terrell Comm Hosp; mem Renassance Civic Club; Kappa Alpha Psi Frat. **HONORS/ACHIEVEMENTS:** Serv award 1967; Bishop Coll Cit Award 1966; Beauticians Sor Chap Award 1968; 22 Marechal Niel Club Comm Serv Award 1971; Comm Award 1976. **MILITARY SERVICE:** Medical Corp ret maj. **BUSINESS ADDRESS:** Jackson Clinic Hospital, 612 S Rockwell, Terrell, TX.

JACKSON, SHIRLEY ANN
Theoretical physicist. **PERSONAL:** Born in Washington, DC. **EDUCATION:** MIT, SB Physics 1968, PhD Physics 1973. **CAREER:** Univ of CO Summer Inst for Theor Phys, participant 1971; Intl Schl of Subnuc Phys Erice, Sicily, part 1973; Natl Accel Lab Batavia, IL, res assoc1973-76; Europe Org for Nuclear Res Geneva, Switzerland, visit sci 1974-75; Stanford Linear Accel Ctr & Aspen Ctr for Phys, visit 1976-77; AT&T Bell Labs, mem tech staff-theoretical physics 1976-78; NATO Adv Study Inst Antwerp, Belgium, lecturer 1982; AT&T Bell Labs, mem tech staff scattering and low energy physics rsch 1978-. **ORGANIZATIONS:** Mem Corp of the MIT 1975-85; mem MIT Educ Coun 1976-; mem Lincoln Univ bd of trustees 1980-; dir NJ Resources Corp 1982-; consult NSF 1977; consult NRC-NAS 1977-80; pres Iota Chap Delta Sigma Theta Sor Inc 1966-68; fellow APS Soc of the Sigma X; AAAS; NY Acad of Sci; Natl Inst of Sci; Delta Sigma Theta Sor Inc 1966. **HONORS/ACHIEVEMENTS:** Valedict Roosevelt HS 1964; Scholar Martin Marietta Aircraft Corp 1964-68; Scholar Prince Hall Grand Masons 1964-68; Natl Sci Found Traineeship 1968-71; Adv Study Fellow Ford Found 1971-73; Grad Fellow Martin Marietta Corp 1972-73; Ford Found Grant 1974-75; CIBA-Geigy Except Black Scientists Poster Series 1981; Candace Award from Natl Coalition of 100 Black Women 1982; 1st Amer Black woman to receive PhD from MIT; Who's Who in the East 1981; Outstanding Young Woman of Amer Award 1976, 1981. **BUSINESS ADDRESS:** AT & T Bell Labs ID-337, 600 Mountain Avenue, Murray Hill, NJ 07974.

JACKSON, SPENCER
Clergyman. **PERSONAL:** Born Nov 18, 1910, Thomaston, AL; married Ella Pearl Davis; children: Spencer Jr, Cary, Elaine Arnold, Kenneth, William Davis, Ralphyel Adams. **EDUCATION:** Gregg Bus Sch, cert 1935; Midwestern Conservatory of Music, cert 1946-48; Chicago Conservatory of Music, cert 1948-51. **CAREER:** WI Steel Mill, blacksmith 1948-55; WI Steel Mill Chicago, second mill wright 1955-72; Good Shepherd Baptist Ch Chicago, pastor 1955-63; Afro Arts Theater Chicago, singer actor 1967-70; Black Heritage Theatrical Players, rev/dir. **ORGANIZATIONS:** Music tchr/choir dir Monumental Grant Meml & various Chicago Ch 1938-55; 32 Degree Mason; Natl United Architect Supreme Council of N & S Amer 1958; sponsor/organizer Bud Bilikin Parade Council. **HONORS/ACHIEVEMENTS:** In recog of book "Black Survival" Black Cultural Council Chicago 1970; Outstanding Achievement Intl Black Writers Conf 1974; 4th Annual Paul Robeson Awd Chicago Black Theater Alliance 1978; Outstanding Contrib to Black Theater Olive Harvey Black Studies Com 1979. **MILITARY SERVICE:** AUS sgt 1944-46. **BUSINESS ADDRESS:** Dir, Black Heritage Theat Players, 7023 S Eggleston Ave, Chicago, IL 60621.

JACKSON, THELMA CONLEY
Educator. **PERSONAL:** Born Oct 02, 1934, Huntsville, AL; divorced; children: Kathleen Ann, Keith Elliott. **EDUCATION:** Spalding Coll, BS Nursing 1956; Spalding Univ, MA 1972. **CAREER:** St Joseph Infirmary, staff nurse 1956-58; Evangelical & Reformed Deaconess Hosp, staff nurse & head nurse/instructor 1958-65; St Joseph Infirmary Sch of Nursing, instructor 1965-67; Sts Mary and Elizabeth Sch of Nursing, instructor 1967-69; Spalding Coll, asst instructor 1969-72; Jefferson Comm Coll, prof 1972-. **ORGANIZATIONS:** Mem Alpha Kappa Alpha Sor 1972-79, Amer Nurses Assoc 1972-, KY Nurses Assoc; volunteer spkr Amer Cancer Soc 1972-. **HOME ADDRESS:** 330 North 44th St, Louisville, KY 40212. **BUSINESS ADDRESS:** Professor of Nursing, Jefferson Comm Coll/Dwntn Cmps, 109 East Broadway, Louisville, KY 40202.

JACKSON, THOMAS MITCHELL
Judge. **PERSONAL:** Born Feb 05, 1932, Washington, DC; married Shirley Ann Lee. **EDUCATION:** CA State Univ of LA, BA 1958; Howard Univ Sch of Law, LLB 1962. **CAREER:** Jackson & Assos Macon, GA, atty 1976-; Law Office T M Jackson, atty 1965-76; Law Office CB King Albany, GA, atty 1963-64. **ORGANIZATIONS:** Mem Am Bar Assn; mem GA Conf of Criminal Def Lawyers; chmn Judicial Com GA Conf of Black Lawyers; sec Bibb Co Dem Exec Com; co-chmn Macon Chap Counc on Human Relations; dir Middle GA Counc on Drugs 1980. **HONORS/ACHIEVEMENTS:** Black georgian of the yr State Com on the Life & History of Black Georgians 1977; Martin Luther King Jr Humanitarian Award Walter F George Sch of Law 1978; outst achvmt award Lambda Phi Chap Omega Psi Phi 1978; outst serv rendered in law Macon Chap of Ft Valley State Coll Alumni 1980; Overseas Medal USMC. **MILITARY SERVICE:** USMC corpl 1952-55. **BUSINESS ADDRESS:** Macon City Hall, Macon, GA 31201.

JACKSON, TOM
Professional athlete. **PERSONAL:** Born Apr 04, 1951, Cleveland, OH. **EDUCATION:** Louisville U, Bus. **CAREER:** Denver Broncos, linebacker 1973-. **HONORS/ACHIEVEMENTS:** Named by teammates as Broncos' most inspirational player for 3 seasons 1983; 3 appearances in Pro Bowl 1977, 1978 & 1979; All-Pro 2 times 1977, 1978; named Denver's defensive most valuable player in 1974, 1976 & 1977; MO Vlly Conf Player of the Yr 1970, 1972; Am Bowl; Blue-Gray Game. **BUSINESS ADDRESS:** Denver Broncos, 5700 Logan St, Denver, CO 80216.

JACKSON, TOMI L.
Association executive. **PERSONAL:** Born Nov 28, 1923, Dallas, TX; daughter of Thomas Stephens and Ida Stephens; children: Joanne Ragan, Linda Marlane Craft. **EDUCATION:** Wayne State U, BA 1940. **CAREER:** Channel 2 (TV), 1950; Channel 7 (TV), 1965; Det Water & Sewerage Dept, 1979; Tomi Jackson & Assoc, public rel. **ORGANIZATIONS:** Area VP Amer Women in Radio & TV; bd mem Women's Advertising Club of Detroit; bd mem United Foundation. **HONORS/ACHIEVEMENTS:** Demmy Award United Found 1981. **BUSINESS ADDRESS:** Public Relations, Tomi Jackson & Assoc, 17300 Pontchartrain Dr, Detroit, MI 48203.

JACKSON, TOMMY L.
Law enforcement. **PERSONAL:** Born Apr 19, 1914, Livingston, AL; married Fonnie Mae Bolden; children: Shirley. **CAREER:** Sumter County Corlation, constable. **ORGANIZATIONS:** AL Democratic Conference 1985. **HOME ADDRESS:** Route 1 Box 60-A, Livingston, AL 35470.

JACKSON, VERA RUTH
Educator/photographer. **PERSONAL:** Born Jul 21, 1912, Wichita, KS; daughter of Otis Garland Ruth and Della Johnson Ruth; married Vernon Danforth Jackson, Aug 12, 1931 (deceased); children: Kerry Otis, Kendall Roger. **EDUCATION:** Univ of CA-Los Angeles, BA 1952, MA 1954; graduate courses, USC, UC-Irvine, UC-Riverside, UCLA in Educ and Art; doctoral candidate, USC, 1956. **CAREER:** CA Eagle (newspaper), staff photog, 1945-50; Los Angeles Unified School District, Los Angeles, CA, elementary school teacher, 1951-76, inservice demonstration, training and reading and resource teacher, 1970-76; Freelance, magazine articles; exhibits sculptor and photog, UCLA Gallery, Museum Science & Industry, Riverside Art Museum, Black Gallery Los Angeles, Public TV Channel 56 and Cable KDOC, LA Cinque Gallery New York and others 1948-87; Historical Enterprises, co-editor, 1980—. **ORGANIZATIONS:** Publicist Urban League Guild; overview Black Women Artists as Social Critics, Black Gallery Faces of Africa; mem, press representative, LA County Art Museum, Riverside Art Museum; exhib in Farnsworth Gallery; mem Urban League, NAACP, Poverty Law, CA Retired Teachers Assoc; mem Women in Photography, Friends of Photography, Pacific Coast Writers Group, Municipal Art Gallery; mem CA Museum of Afro-Amer Art & Culture in LA, Black Women's Forum. **HONORS/ACHIEVEMENTS:** Photographs "A Portrait in Black" Dorothy Dandridge by Earle Mills published by Holloway House 1970; articles published in art, photographic magazines and newspapers; one of the pioneer photographers in Jeanne Moutoussay-Ashe's book "Viewfinders, Black Women Photographers," 1986; twenty letters to LA Times on subject of combatting racism; contributor to museums, galleries, magazines, including CA Afro-American Museum, Black Angelenos, Travel and Art magazine, and Design magazine. **BUSINESS ADDRESS:** Educator/Photographer, Historical Enterprises, 1004 Railroad St, Corona, CA 91720.

JACKSON, W. SHERMAN
Educator. **PERSONAL:** Born May 21, 1939, Crowley, LA; married Frances P McIntyre; children: Sherlyn, Sherrese, W Sherman II. **EDUCATION:** So Univ, AB 1962; NC Central Univ, MA 1962-63; OH State Univ, PhD 1969. **CAREER:** Alcorn Coll Lorman MS, instr 1963-64; Central State Univ, instr 1966-68; Univ of Lagos Nigeria, sr fulbright lecturer 1972-73; Amer Constitutionalism Miami Univ, prof 1969-. **ORGANIZATIONS:** History ed NIP Mag 1969-71; assoc ed NIP Mag 1971-75; ed consult Pentagon Ed Testing Svc; pres, founder Assoc for Acad Advancement 1969-; pres OxfordNAACP 1979-; consult NEH. **BUSINESS ADDRESS:** Associate Professor, Amer Constitutionalism, MiamiUniv, 241 Irvin, Oxford, OH 45056.

JACKSON, WALTER K.
Clergyman. **PERSONAL:** Born Mar 28, 1914, Boley, OK; son of Eddie and Adelaide; married Eula Lee Wilhite; children: Waltine. **EDUCATION:** Bishop Coll, AB 1937; OK Sch of Rel, BTh 1947; Morris Booker Mem Coll, DD 1955; OK Sch of Rel, DD 1964; Union Theol Sem, 1960-66. **CAREER:** St John Mission Bapt Ch, minister 44 yrs. **ORGANIZATIONS:** Mem bd of trust Bishop Coll Dallas, TX; mem bd dir Med Cent State Bank; Gov Com on Rehab of State of OK; Coalition of Civic Ldrshp of OK City; bd dir Progressive Bapt Nat Conv; bd dir OK Mission Bapt State Conv. **HONORS/ACHIEVEMENTS:** Viola P

Cutler Award Urban Leag of OK Cty OK 1970; Dr of Humane Letters, Virginia Seminary, Lynchburg, VA. **BUSINESS ADDRESS:** 5700 N Kelley, Oklahoma City, OK 73111.

JACKSON, WARREN G.
Business executive. **PERSONAL:** Born Jun 18, 1929, Yonkers, NY; married Christina Victor; children: Tenley, Garrison, Terrance. **EDUCATION:** Manhattan Coll, Grad 1952. **CAREER:** NY Knickerbocker, circulation dir 1st Black circulation dir of a major NY newspaper; NY Times, asst circulation mgr 1952-63; Westchester Rockland Newspapers (mbrs of Gannett Group), syndicated columnist; Advertising Experti, president; Circulation Experti Ltd, founder and president. **ORGANIZATIONS:** Trustee Morehouse School of Medicine Atlanta GA; trustee Talladega College Talladega AL; trustee Jackie Robinson Foundation New York, NY. **HONORS/ACHIEVEMENTS:** Man of Year Empire State Woman's Club 1972; Man of Year Omega Psi Phi Westchester/Rockland Counties 1985. **BUSINESS ADDRESS:** President, Circulation Experti Ltd, 280 N Central Ave, Hartsdale, NY 10530.

JACKSON, WILLIAM E.
Educator. **PERSONAL:** Born Dec 01, 1936, Creedmoor, NC; married Janet. **EDUCATION:** NC Central U, BA 1958; NY U, MA 1961; Univ PA, PhD 1972. **CAREER:** Yale Univ, asst prof German; Univ PA, instructor 1967-70; City Coll NY, 1961-64. **ORGANIZATIONS:** Mem Am Assn Tchrs German; NC Central Alumni. **HONORS/ACHIEVEMENTS:** Scholarship Marburg, Germany 1958-59; publs in "Neophilologus" "Colloquia Germanica" & "Germanica Studies in Honor of Otto Springer"; pub book "Reinmar's Women" Amsterdambenjamins 1980. **BUSINESS ADDRESS:** Yale University, Dept of Germnic Languages, New Haven, CT 06520.

JACKSON, WILLIAM FRED
Publisher. **PERSONAL:** Born Jun 24, 1938, Sarasota, FL; children: Pamela, Miranda. **EDUCATION:** Bethune-Cookman Coll. **CAREER:** The Bulletin Newspapaer, publisher 1961-85. **ORGANIZATIONS:** Mem North Sarasota Bus & Prof Women Assn 1982-85; pres Norch County Cementary Assn 1984-85; pres Helen Payne Day Nursery 1985; pres Newtown Adv Bd 1984-85; pres Entertainment Ltd 1984-85; bd dir Sarasota TB Assn; bd dir First Step of Sarasota; bd dir Sarasota Perf Arts; Ft Myers dist coord for Edward Coll for the AME Church; mem Greater Hurst Chapel AME Church; mem Sarasota Br NAACP; mem North County Civic League; sponsor for the area'soldest Black Beauty Pageant which donates over $3,000 in scholarships and prizes per yr to young women from the Sarasota-Manatee area. **HONORS/ACHIEVEMENTS:** Journalism Award Bethune-Cookman Coll 1971; NAACP Freedom Award State of FL NAACP 1982; Martin L King Service Award Norch County Civic League 1983;Meritorious Serv Award United Negro Coll Fund 1973; Heritage Players of FL 1981; Community Father of the Yr 1971; Community Serv Kappa Alpha Psi 1985; Community Serv North County Civic League 1983; Community Bldg Educ Award Black Monitor 1985; Community Leaders Award from Bd of Amer Biographical Inst 1976-77. **BUSINESS ADDRESS:** Publisher, The Bulletin, 2003 Princeton St, Sarasota, FL 34237.

JACKSON, WILLIE LAVELLE
Professional athlete. **PERSONAL:** Born Jun 22, 1962, Heflin, LA. **EDUCATION:** Centenary Univ, 1980-84. **CAREER:** Houston Rockets, guard 1984-. **HONORS/ACHIEVEMENTS:** 3-time Trans Am Athletic Conf Plyr of Year; twice Coll Player of Year in LA.

JACKSON, WILLIS RANDELL, II
Educator, athletic director, coach. **PERSONAL:** Born Sep 11, 1945, Memphis, TN; son of Willis Randell Jackson and Louise Halbert Johnson; divorced; children: Ericka, Hasani, Jamila. **EDUCATION:** Rochester Jr Coll, certificate 1965; ND State Univ, BS 1967; SIU Edwardsville, MS & Admin Cert 1980. **CAREER:** Rochester Lourdes HS, head wrestling coach 1967-68; Soldan HS, head wrestling coach 1969-71; Lincoln Sr HS, athletic dir 1971-83; State Comm Coll, athletic dir 1985-; Hughes Quinn Jr HS, teacher. **ORGANIZATIONS:** Mem IL Wrestling Coaches & Officials Assoc 1974-, NWCOA Wrestling Coaches & Officials Assoc 1974-, Natl Basketball Coaches Assoc 1985-, Natl Athletic Directors Assoc 1974-. **HONORS/ACHIEVEMENTS:** IL State Athletic Dir of the Year Dist 15 1977,78; Coach of Year Wrestling East St Louis Journal 1975, ICBAA 1981. **BUSINESS ADDRESS:** Teacher, Hughes Quinn Jr High School, 1100 Broadway, East St Louis, IL 62201.

JACKSON, WILMA LITTLEJOHN See DEMILLE, DARCY

JACKSON, WINSTON BURLEIGH
Physician. **PERSONAL:** Born Apr 29, 1927, Fairfield, AL; married Alice Welch; children: Judith A, Linda L, Lillian A, Winston B. **EDUCATION:** Howard U, BS 1951, MD 1956. **CAREER:** Kirwood Gen Hosp, chief of staff; SW Detroit Hosp Kirwood Hosp, attend & consult Neurologist 1977; Clin Neur Wayne St U, instr 1962-; Allen Park VA Hosp, chief neur dept 1962-62; Wayne State U, resid 1960-62; Wayne Co Gen Hosp, resid internl med 1957-60, rotating intern 1956-57. **ORGANIZATIONS:** Mem Am Acad Neur; AMA; MI St Med Soc; Wayne Co Med Soc; Nat Med Assn; Det Med Soc; Omega Psi Phi Frat; MI Neur Assn. **BUSINESS ADDRESS:** 42720 W 7 Mile Rd, Detroit, MI 48235.

JACKSON, YVETTE P.
Publishing executive. **PERSONAL:** Born Dec 08, 1953, Chicago, IL; children: Rael Hashiem. **EDUCATION:** Eastern IL Univ, BS 1974. **CAREER:** Black United Fund, local convention coord 1976-77; Natl Publ Sales Agency, account exec 1977-79, sales mgr 1979-81, vp, dir of sales 1981-. **ORGANIZATIONS:** Life subscriber NAACP 1985; mem Oper PUSH 1987, League of Black Women 1987. **HONORS/ACHIEVEMENTS:** Black Achievers Awd YMCA 1983; Kizzy Awd Black Women's Hall of Fame 1985. **BUSINESS ADDRESS:** Vice President, Dir, Natl Publ Sales Agency, Inc, 1610 East 79th St, Chicago, IL 60649.

JACKSON-FOY, LUCY MAYE
Educator. **PERSONAL:** Born Sep 28, 1919, Texas; daughter of L J and Louise Jackson. **EDUCATION:** Attended, A&T Coll, OH State, Prairie View Coll, TX Woman's Univ; N TX State Coll, MS; Further study, KS State Tchrs Coll; KS Univ; KS Central MO State Univ, Univ MO. **CAREER:** Veteran Admin, employed 1946-50; A&T Coll, 1950-54; Hamilton Park HS, 1954-62; KC MO Sch Dist, vocational coord 1963-84 (retired). **ORGANIZATIONS:** Mem Natl Rehab Assn; Council for Exceptional Children; MO State Tchrs Assn; Disabled Amer Veterans; Natl Council Tchrs Math; NAACP; Natl Council Negro Women; mem Eta Phi Beta Sor; natl sec Eta Phi Beta 1968-74; sec KC Assn for Mentally Retarded Children past exec bd dirs; past mem Comm for Davis Brickle Report; Special Educ Adv Com; mem Community Serv for Greater KC; co-fndr Shelly Sch for Mentally Retarded; volunteer Adult Basic Education Program; Health Care AARP Bd of Kansas City; pres of Washington-Lincoln H.S. Club 1987-88; Women's Chamber of Commerce of Kansas City, MO. **HONORS/ACHIEVEMENTS:** Outstanding Sec Educ of Amer 1974-75; Certificate from National WLAA 1987-88. **MILITARY SERVICE:** WAC 1942-45. **HOME ADDRESS:** 1414 E 28 St, Kansas City, MO 64109.

JACKSON-TEAL, RITA F.
Educator. **PERSONAL:** Born Apr 26, 1949, Memphis, TN; children: Rashel, JanEtte, Teal. **EDUCATION:** TN State Univ, BS 1971; Univ of MI, MA 1973; Ed D Candidate, Memphis STUniv 1989. **CAREER:** Argonne Lab Argonne IL, student trainee 1971; Rust Coll Holly Springs MS, math instr, tutor 1973-75; Lincoln Lab Lexington MA, vstg scientist 1974; LeMoyne-Owen Coll Memphis, math instr 1975-78, dir Spec Serv Upward Bound & Learning Resource Ctr. **ORGANIZATIONS:** Coord Dual-Degree Engrg Prog 1977-80; chairperson Greek Letter Comm 1978-80; mem Cult & Ath Comm Rust Coll; mem Freshman Comm, Orientation Comm, Acad Standing Comm, Acad Task Force Cluster for Coop Ed Delta Sigma Theta; mem Delta Sigma Theta, Alpha Kappa Mu, Beta Kappa Chi, Kappa Delta Pi; vice pres TN Assoc of Spec Prog 1983-85; chairperson Delta Sigma Theta Scholarship Comm 1984-85; reg chairperson Southeastern Assoc for Ed Oppty Prog Personnel SAEOPPAnnual Conf 1985; pres TN Assn of Spec Prog 1985-87; chmn SAEOPP Scholarhsip Com 1986-87; chmn SAEOPP Constitution Com 1985-87; secy SAEOPP 1987. **HONORS/ACHIEVEMENTS:** Listed in Who's Who in Amer Coll & Univ 1969-71; Outstanding Young Women in Amer 1974,77. **BUSINESS ADDRESS:** Dir Spec Services/Upward Bnd, LeMoyne-Owen College, 807 Walker Ave, Memphis, TN 38126.

JACKSON-THOMPSON, MARIE O.
Judge. **PERSONAL:** Born Aug 14, 1947, Pittsburgh, PA; daughter of Warren Joseph Oliver and Nettie Marie Wall; married Henry Quentin Thompson Jr; children: Vincent, Al, Joshua. **EDUCATION:** Mt Holyoke Coll, BA 1969; Harvard Law Sch, JD 1972. **CAREER:** Cambridge and Somerville Legal Svcs, general trial work 1972-74; Tufts Univ, vstg lecturer 1973-74; MA Commn Against Discrimination, staff dir 1974-76; Exec Office of Admin & Finance, admin justice 1976-77, general counsel 1977-80; District Court Dept of the Trial Court Cambridge Div, justice 1980-. **ORGANIZATIONS:** Bd & Regional Director Natl Assn of Women Judges 1981-; mem Natl Council of Juvenile and Family Court Judges 1981-; Bd of dirs Adolescent Consultation Svcs, Greater Boston Youth Symphony Orchestra 1985-87; Natl Conf of Christians and Jews 1985-87; mem Natl Assoc of Negro and Professional Women Inc, MA Juvenile Justice Adv Comm 1983-, Judicial Admin Div Amer Bar Assoc, Alpha Kappa Alpha Sor Psi Omega Chapt, Middlesex Co Chap Links Inc, Judicial Conf Natl Bar Assoc, Middlesex Co Dist Attorney's Child Sexual Abuse Task Force 1985-86, Dist Court Standards Comm for Care & Protection and CHINS cases; mem Governor's Task Force Correction Alternatives 1985-86, Foster Care 1986-87; bd Judge Baker Guidance Center 1987-. **HONORS/ACHIEVEMENTS:** Outstanding Young Leader Boston Jaycees 1981; Leadership Massachusetts Black Lawyers 1981; "Use and Abuse of Certain Records in Custody Proceedings", Massachusetts Flaschner Judicial Institute 1984; "And They Do Not Live Happily Ever After: A Look at the Real Story of Family Violence", Mt. Holyoke Quarterly 1986; Sojourner Truth Natl Assn of Negro Business & Professional Women 1986; Community Justice Awd MA Justice Resource Inst 1985; Achievement Awd Cambridge YWCA 1985; numerous leadership achievement and serv awds; Sesquicentennial Alumnae Award Mt Holyoke Alumnae Assn 1988. **BUSINESS ADDRESS:** Judge, Cambridge District Court, 40 Thorndike St, Cambridge, MA 02141.

JACOB, JOHN EDWARD
Association executive. **PERSONAL:** Born Dec 16, 1934, Trout, LA; married Barbara May Singleton; children: Sheryl Rene. **EDUCATION:** Howard Univ, BA 1957, MSW 1963; Old Dominion Univ, LHD 1983; Fisk Univ, LHD 1984; Lafayette Coll, LLD 1985; Tuskegee Univ, LLD 1986; Central State Univ, LLD 1986. **CAREER:** US Post office, parcel post sorting mach oper 1958-60; Baltimore City Dept of Public Welfare, caseworker 1960-63, child welfare casework suprv 1963-65; Washington Urban League, dir ed & youth incentives 1965-66, branch office dir 1966-67, assoc exec dir for admin 1967-68, acting exec dir 1968-70, spec lecturer 1968-69; Howard Univ School of Social Work, spec lecturer 1968-69; Washington Urban League, dir soc work field work student unit 1968-70; Eastern Reg Natl Urban League, dir comm org training 1970-; San Diego Urban League, exec dir 1970-75; Washington Urban League, pres 1975-79; Natl Urban League, exec vice pres 1979-81, pres & CEO. **ORGANIZATIONS:** Life mem Kappa Alpha Psi 1954; mem Natl Assoc of Social Workers 1961-; consult Natl Council of Negro Women 1967-69, Natl Urban League 1968-69; vice chmn bd of trustees Howard Univ 1971-; consult Timely Investment Club 1972-75; mem Judicial Nominating Com DC 1976-79; dir Local Iniatives Support Corp 1980-; mem natl Advertisement Review Bd 1980-83; mem adv comm NY Hosp 1980-83; dir A Better Chance 1980-83; dir NY Found 1982-85; corp dir NY Telephone Co 1983-; dir Natl Conf of Christians & Jews 1983-88; mem Rockefeller Univ Council 1983-88; corp dir Churchill Trust Co 1984-; dir Eisenhower Found 1984-; vice chmn bd of trustees Howard Univ 1984-88; dir Independent Sector 1984-, Jr Achievement 1985; corp dir Continental Corp 1985-; corp dir Coca Cola Enterprises Inc 1986-; chrm Howard Univ 1988-. **HONORS/ACHIEVEMENTS:** Whitney M Young Awd Washington Urban League Inc 1979; Special Citation Atlanta Club Howard Univ Alumni Assoc 1980; Attny Hudson L Lavell Soc Action Awd Phi Beta Sigma 1982; Exemplary Serv Awd Alumni Club of Long Island Howard Univ 1983; Achievement Awd Zeta Phi Beta 1984, Cleveland Alumni Chap Kappa Alpha Psi 1984; Alumni Achievement Awd Alpha Psi Atlanta Club Howard Univ 1984; Natl Kappaman Achievement Durham Alumni Chapter Kappa 1984; Blackbook's Bus & Professional Awd Dollars & Sense Mag 1985; Achievement Awd Peoria Alumni Chap Kappa Alpha Psi 1985; Forrester B Washington Awd Atlanta Univ School of Social Work 1986; Presidential Scroll St Augustine's Coll 1987; receient of the United Way of America's National Professional Leadership Award 1989. **MILITARY SERVICE:** AUS Reserve capt 1957-65; Airborne Parachutist Badge 1958. **HOME ADDRESS:** 14 Barnaby Ln, Hartsdale, NY 10530. **BUSINESS ADDRESS:** President, Natl Urban League, 500 E 62nd St, New York, NY 10021.

JACOB, WILLIS HARVEY
Educator, scientist. **PERSONAL:** Born Jun 04, 1943, Lake Charles, LA. **EDUCATION:** So U, BS 1965;Univ KS, PhD 1971. **CAREER:** Southern Univ, asst prof 1970-71; Baylor

Univ, asst prof 1975-76, assoc prof 1976-77; Acad of Hlth Scis, chief basic sci br 1971-77; Dept of Clinical Investigation Madigan Army Med Ctr, physiologist 1978-83; US Army Medical Rsch and Develop Command, product mgr 1983-85; US Army Medical Matl Develop Activity, pharmaceutical systems project mgmt 1985-. **ORGANIZATIONS:** Mem Am Inst Biol Scis, Assn of Military Surgeons of the US, NY Acad of Sci, Phi Lambda Upsilon, Soc of Sigma Xi, Alpha Phi Alpha Frat, NAACP, Southern Univ Alumni Federation, Univ of KS Alumni Assoc. **HONORS/ACHIEVEMENTS:** NDEA Title IV Fellowship 1970. **MILITARY SERVICE:** AUS 2nd lt 1965-68, 1st lt 1968-71, capt 1971-79, maj 1979-85, lt col 1985-. **BUSINESS ADDRESS:** Lieutenant Colonel, AUS Med Matl Devel Activity, Fort Detrick, Frederick, MD 21701.

JACOBS, HAZEL A.
Legislative policy analyst. **PERSONAL:** Born Sep 25, 1948, Blakely, GA; daughter of Leamon Allen and Pearlia Jewell Allen; married Claude Jacobs, Jul 24, 1970. **EDUCATION:** GA State Univ, BS, 1982, MPA, 1986. **CAREER:** City of Atlanta GA, admin asst, 1970-71; Atlanta GA Charter Comm, admin asst, 1971-73; City of Atlanta GA, admin asst, 1973-74, office mgr, 1974-78, legislative policy analyst, 1978-. **ORGANIZATIONS:** Amer Assn of Public Admin, 1984-; Natl Assn of Professional Women, 1985-; Natl Forum for Black Public Admin, 1985-.

JACOBS, JACQUELINE MINETTE
Scientist, educator. **PERSONAL:** Born Oct 17, 1936, Camden, AL; married David Lee Jr; children: Madrid Vinessa Jacobs-Kees. **EDUCATION:** AL StateUniv Montgomery, BS Biology/Math 1957; FiskUniv Nashville TN, MA Sci Educ 1962;Univ of Wash Seattle WA, PhD Botany 1974. **CAREER:** CA Inst of Tech, sr mem of tch; Univ of WA Seattle, rsch assoc 1971-74; Bishop State Jr Coll Mobile AL, biology instructor 1968-71; Blount HS Prichard AL, sci teacher 1958-67. **ORGANIZATIONS:** Bd mem LA Women in Sci 1979-80; bd mem LA Chap of Black Engr 1980; adv bd S Outreach Proj 1978-80; bd of dir LA United Negrow Coll Fund 1980; adv bd NAACP; Career Women's Forum 1980. **HONORS/ACHIEVEMENTS:** Woman of yr Iota Phi Lambda Sorority Pasadena 1976-77; US Patent No 4160601 Biocontamination Particulate System NASA 1979.

JACOBS, LARRY BEN
Chemical engineer. **PERSONAL:** Born Dec 15, 1959, Arlington, GA; son of Tommy L Jacobs and Mattie C Jackson Jacobs; married Carolyn Laverne Malone; children: Matthew, Leah. **EDUCATION:** Tuskegee Inst, Certificate 1980, BSChE 1984. **CAREER:** International Paper Co, co-op engr 1980; Procter & Gamble, co-op engr 1982; Weyerhaeuser Co, professional intern 1984-86; Hercules Inc, process engr 1986-; Hercules Inc Radford VA Process Engineer 1986-88; General Electric Co Burkville AL Production Engineer 1989-. **ORGANIZATIONS:** Mem AIChE 1980-86; assoc mem Tech Assoc of Pulp & Paper Industry 1980-86; steward/choir president Turner Chapel AME Church 1984-86; educ chmn Columbus MS Coalition of Black Organizations 1985-86; correspondent The Jackson Advocate 1986; toastmaster Toastmaster's Intl 1986-; math tutor Asbury UM Church 1987. **HONORS/ACHIEVEMENTS:** Outstanding Young Men in Amer 1985; "Down Route 82" Manuscript "The Jackson Advocate" 1986; Best Speaker/Best Evaluator RAAP Toastmasters Club 1986-87. **MILITARY SERVICE:** USAF Reserves airman 1st class 3 yrs; Armed Forces Comm & Electronics Assoc Citation, Certificate of Merit. **HOME ADDRESS:** 2751 Norwich Drive, Montgomery, AL 36116.

JACOBS, PATRICIA DIANNE
Business executive. **PERSONAL:** Born Jan 27, 1950, Camden, AR; daughter of Felix H Jacobs and Helen M Tate Jacobs; divorced; children: Branden Kemiah. **EDUCATION:** Lincoln Univ, BA 1970; Harvard Law School, JD 1973. **CAREER:** Lincoln Univ, asst dir finan aid 1970; Exxon Corp, legal assoc 1973-75; US Senate Sm Business Comm, asst min counsel 1975-77; Amer Assoc of MESBICS Inc, pres 1977-83; K-Com Micrographics Inc, pres. **ORGANIZATIONS:** Asst prof John Jay Coll of Criminal Justice 1974-75; dir Wider Opportunities for Women 1983-; dir/trustee Lincoln Univ 1983-; dir Cooperative Assist Fund 1983-. **HONORS/ACHIEVEMENTS:** Regional Atty Advocate for Small Business DC Small Business Admin 1982; Lincoln Alumni Award Lincoln Univ 1981; Under 30 Achievement Award Black Enterprise 1978. **BUSINESS ADDRESS:** President, K-Com, 1353 H St NE, Washington, DC 20002.

JACOBS, SYLVIA MARIE
University professor. **PERSONAL:** Born Oct 27, 1946, Mansfield, OH; daughter of Love Jacobs and Murval Aletha Cansler Jabobs Porch; married Levell Exum, Jun 20, 1989; children: Levell Rickie Exum, Sylvia Agnes Jacobs Exum. **EDUCATION:** Wayne State Univ, Detroit MI, BS, 1969, MBA 1972; Howard Univ, Washington DC, PhD, 1975. **CAREER:** McKerrow Elementary School, Detroit MI, teacher, 1969-72; Federal City Coll, Washington DC, visiting lecturer, 1973; Univ of AR, Pine Bluff AR, asst prof, 1975-76; North Carolina Central Univ, Durham NC, assoc prof, 1976-82, professor 1982-; Univ of North Carolina, Chapel Hill, visiting prof, 1982; Univ of Florida,Gainesville, NEH seminar leader, 1988. **ORGANIZATIONS:** Mem, Delta Sigma Theta, 1968-; executive council, mem, Assn for the Study of Afro-Amer Life and History, 1983-; co-convener, Southeastern Regional Seminar in African Studies, 1983-87; natl dir, Assn of Black Women Historians, 1984-88; mem, Natl Council of Negro Women Inc, 1985-; mem, Southern Poverty Law Center, 1985-; mem, Committee on the Status of Minority Historians and Minority History, Organization of Amer Historians, 1987-; mem, NAACP 1987-; mem, Amer Historical Assn, 1987-. **HONORS/ACHIEVEMENTS:** Outstanding Young Women of America, 1977; Letitia Brown Memorial Publication Prize, Assn of Black Women Historians, 1984; Fellowship for Coll Teachers, Natl Endowment for the Humanities, 1984-85; Distinguished Achievement Award, Howard Univ Alumni Club, 1985; Fellowship for Minority-Group Scholars, Rockefeller Foundation, 1987-88; author of "The African Nexus: Black American Perspective on European Partitioning of Africa" 1981; author of "Black American and the Missionary Movement in Africa" 1982; 20 articles published 1975-89; 8 book reviews published 1975-88. **HOME ADDRESS:** 12 Cotswold Place, Durham, NC 27707. **BUSINESS ADDRESS:** Professor, North Carolina Central University, Department of History and Social Science, Durham, NC 27707.

JACOBS, THOMAS LINWOOD
Government official. **PERSONAL:** Born Feb 27, 1933, New York, NY; married Marcella Gilbert; children: Lauren. **EDUCATION:** St Joseph's Coll & Sem, BS 1961; NYU, MSW, 1969; Amer Mgmt Assn; Mgmt Certificate, 1979. **CAREER:** Fordham Univ, adj prof, 1973-74; Office of Borough Pres Manhattan, deputy, 1974-77; John Jay Coll of Criminal Justice, adj assoc prof 1980-; NY City Dept of Probation, 1st Black commissioner. **ORGANIZATIONS:** Bd of dir One Hundred Black Men 1977-, Brooklyn Childrens Museum 1982-; bd of dir Catholic Inter-racial council New York City 1980-; former chmn Boys Choir of harlem 1981-83. **HONORS/ACHIEVEMENTS:** Achievement Awd NY Fed of Negro Civil Serv Org 1983; Comm Outreach Awd Manhattan Cable TV 1984; Hon Dep Fire Chief New York City Fire Dept 1984; Dep Grand Marshall 17th Annual ML King Jr Parade, New York City 369th Vet Assoc 1984. **BUSINESS ADDRESS:** Commissioner, NY City Dept of Probation, 115 Leonard St, Room 2 E l, New York, NY 10013.

JACQUET, JEAN BAPTISTE ILLINOIS (ILLINOIS)
Musician. **PERSONAL:** Born Oct 31, 1922, Broussard, LA; married Barbara Potts; children: Michael Lane, Pamela Baptiste. **EDUCATION:** Percy H McDavid at Phillis Wheatley HS Houston TX, music training 1939. **CAREER:** Family orchestra led by father Gilbert until 1937; Milt Larking Band, 1938-39; Lionel Hampton Band, 1940-42; Cab Calloway Band, 1943; Stormey Weather 20th Century Fox, performer 1943; featured in jazz film classic Jammin' The Blues Warner Bros 1944; original mem of Jazz at the Philharmonic which created the historic1944 concert recording Philharmonic Blues Part II; Count Basie Band, 1946; led All-Star Band 1947-65; led Trio with Jo Jones & Milt Buckner 1970's; formed Quintet with Slam Stewart 1980-82; Harvard Univ, teacher jazz music 1982-; Tufts Univ, UC San Diego, Univ ofID, Crane Coll, Clark Coll, seminars; formed present 16 piece Big Band 1983-. **ORGANIZATIONS:** Created the immortal solo on the classic recording Flying Home with the Lionel Hampton Band; created Philharmonic Blues Part II on first recording of Jazz at the Philharmonic; compositions incl, Bottoms Up, You Left Me All Alone, Robbins nest, Black Velvet, Port of Rico, For Europeans Only, Blues for New Orleans, TheKing. **HONORS/ACHIEVEMENTS:** First Jazz Bassonist in the World; All Mem of Fam in Band; A Salute to Illinois Jacquet at Carnegie Hall Kool Jazz Festival; Commendation of Excellence Broadcast Music Inc; Cert of Apprec Smithsonian Inst.

JAGGERS, GEORGE HENRY, JR.
Educational administrator. **PERSONAL:** Born Feb 27, 1926, Dallas, NC; married Ida Hayes; children: George Henry III. **EDUCATION:** NC A&T State Univ, BS 1951, MS 1975; UNC Chapel Hill, cert 1978. **CAREER:** Pender Co NC, teacher 1951-59; Gaston Co Pleasant Ridge School, teacher 1959-66; Gaston Co Carr School, teacher (1st black) 1966-70; Gaston Co Ashley Jr HS, asst prin 1970-75; Gaston Co Hunter Huss HS, asst prin 1975-82; Gastonia Central Elementary School, principal 1982-. **ORGANIZATIONS:** Mem NCAE Prin Div; mem NEA; lt Gaston Co Police Aux; mayor pro tem (1st black) Town of Dallas NC 1978-80; alderman Town of Dallas NC 1980-82; governing body So Piedmont Health Systems Agency Inc 1980-83. **HONORS/ACHIEVEMENTS:** Outstanding Officer Gaston Co Police 1971 & 1977; Omega Man of the Yr Omega Psi Phi Frat Inc 1972; Human Relations Awd NC Assn of Educators Gaston Co 1980; Serv Awd ARC 1980; Serv Awd Dallas Police Dept 1980. **MILITARY SERVICE:** USN AOM 2/c 1944-46; Good Conduct Medal 1946. **BUSINESS ADDRESS:** Principal, Gastonia Central Elem School, 100 E Second Ave, Gastonia, NC 28052.

JAGNANDAN, WILFRED LILPERSAUD
Pastor. **PERSONAL:** Born Apr 19, 1920, Guyana; married Helen Mahadai Samaroo; children: Neville, Nora, Norris, Edward, Leonard. **EDUCATION:** Guyana, diploma in Theology; USA, BTh; Toronto, BA; Toronto, MA MS U, MEd 1973; London, DD; Cambridge, BSc, JD 1979. **CAREER:** Univ Hosp Augusta, asso chapl 1976-; Trinity Presb Ch MS, pastor 6 yrs; Guyana Presb Ch, pastor 24 yrs; Presbytery in Guyana, moderator twice; clerk of presbytery 1 yr; Commr of Oaths to Affidavits, Justice of the Peace 8 yrs; Christ Presbyterian Church, pastor. **ORGANIZATIONS:** Chmn League of Friends; chmn Improv of Port Mourant Hosp; chmn Tchr Parent Assn of Belvedere Govt Sch; chmn Adult Educ at Port Mourant Com Cntr; chmn Corentyne Minister's Assn; mem bd of Govr's Berbiee HS; 5 yrs Pastor at Trinity USA; chapl at Mary Holmes Coll 2 yrs mem bd Tombigbee Coun on human rel; mem head start bd; mem minister's frat in w point MS; ldr of Christian Student Assn; mem GA Presbytery 1975-; chrprsn ecumenical rel GA Presbytery of the UP USA Ch 1977-78; mem citzs adv com Title IV Richmond Co Bd of Educ Augusta 1980-81; vol math tchr Lucy Laney HS Augusta present; volunteer 1980-83, chmn feeding prog 1981-84 Help Line. **HONORS/ACHIEVEMENTS:** Rec plaque from Prairie Opport Inc 1974; cert from Personal of S 1972; Cert of Achiev of Educ Cambridge England 1974; recognition & appreciation Univ Hosp 1976,77,78-83; Chaplain of the Year for Faithfull & Loyal Serv Certs 1985,86. **BUSINESS ADDRESS:** Pastor, Christ Presbyterian Church, Augusta, GA 30901.

JAMAL, AHMAD
Jazz musician. **PERSONAL:** Born Jul 02, 1930, Pittsburgh, PA; married Laura A; children: Sumayanh. **CAREER:** George Hudson Orch touring in 1940's, jazz pianist; Four Strings, player 1950; The Caldwells, toured as accompanist 1951; formed own trio 1951; recording contract Cadet Records; performer at, Jazz Alley Downtown Seattle, George's Chicago, Voyager West St Louis, Ethyl's Place, Fairmont Hotel, Cricket Theater in Hennepin Center for the Arts, Apoloo Theatre Town Hall, Rainbow Grill (Waldorf Astoria), The Embers/Village Gate; Atlantic Records, under contract 3 new releases "Digital Works", "Rossiter Rd", "Live at the Montreal Jazz Festival"; performing at the Umbria Jazz Fesitval in Italy, also in Finland, Blues Alley in Georgetown; "Crystal"; performed 2 years with Philip Morris Tour around the world: Berne Jazz Festival 1989. **HONORS/ACHIEVEMENTS:** Only artist to have an LP album in the top ten of natl charts for 108 consec weeks "But Not For Me;" other albums incl, "All of You," "Jamal Plays Jamal," "At The Penthouse," "Extension," "Freelight," "Naked City Theme," "One.". **BUSINESS ADDRESS:** Shubra Productions, P O Box 295, Ashley Falls, MA 01222.

JAMALUDEEN, ABDUL HAMID (WILLIAM C. WADE JR.)
Physician. **PERSONAL:** Born Jun 26, 1945, Baltimore, MD; married Denese; children: Darryl, Efuru, Maryan, Idris, Arkia. **EDUCATION:** Univ Rochester, BA 1968; Howard U, MD 1968. **CAREER:** Self, physician; Whittaker Meml Hosp, emergency room phys 1975-77; Freedmen's Hosp, resd internal med 1973-75; Freedmen's Hosp, intern 1972-73. **ORGANIZATIONS:** Mem Muslin Stud Assn USA & Can 1976; Islamic Med Assn 1977; mem Peninsula Sickle Cell Anemia Assn 1975-. **HONORS/ACHIEVEMENTS:** Award for serv Graham Emerg Ste Whittaker Meml Hosp 1975-77. **BUSINESS ADDRESS:** 2000 Kecoughtan Rd, Hampton, VA 23661.

JAMERSON, JEROME DONNELL
Educator. **PERSONAL:** Born Nov 02, 1950, Memphis, TN; son of Rev. J. D. Jamerson and Rosalee Butler Jamerson; divorced; children: Jenielle Denise, Kendra Deon. **EDUCATION:** TN State Univ, BS 1973, MS 1972; Memphis State Univ, Nova Univ, EdD (pending). **CAREER:** Shelby State Comm Coll, instr of history 1973-78, asst prof of history 1979-80, assoc prof of history 1980-. **ORGANIZATIONS:** Past chmn Hollywood Day Care Center 1977; Life Mem, Omega Psi Phi Fraternity; Organizer, Council on Black Amer Affairs 1980; mem AAUP 1985, TN State Employees Assn 1985; co-chairperson Shelby State Professors Assn 1985; pres, Royal Gentlemens Social Club 1985; mem Greater St Luke MBC Church, Assn Study of Negro Life & History, Friends of Brooks Art Gallery, NAACP, Amer Assn of Univ Profs, Amer Assn of Community & Jr Colls, Assn of the Study of Afro-Amer Life & History, Org of Amer Historians, TN Assn of Community Action & Child Devel. **HONORS/ACHIEVEMENTS:** Outstanding Young Man of the Year Jaycees 1978; Master's Thesis Dr Arthur Melvin Townsend & the Natl Baptist Convention Inc; Certificate of Appreciation Memphis Shelby County Headstart & Telephone Pioneers of Amer; Certificate of Award Outstanding Volunteer Serv to the Headstart Program 1983; Hon Mem Congressional Staff of Harold Ford; Phi Theta Kappa Award for being 40 Instructor. **BUSINESS ADDRESS:** Associate Professor, Shelby State Community College, Dept of Social Sciences, Memphis, TN 38104.

JAMERSON, JOHN WILLIAM, JR.
Retired dentist. **PERSONAL:** Born Sep 22, 1910, Savannah, GA; son of John WIlliam Jamerson and Julia Aline Belcher Jamerson; married Dorothy Louise Breaux, Sep 28, 1940; children: Dorothy Anders MD, Kathleen O'Quinn, Patricia Manson, John W III DDS. **EDUCATION:** Lincoln Univ PA, AB 1933; Meharry Med Coll Sch of Dentistry, DDS 1941. **CAREER:** Private Practice, dentist (retired). **ORGANIZATIONS:** Pres Chatham Dental Soc 1971-; life Mem NDA, ADA, NY Omega Psi Phi Frat Mu Phi Chapt; life mem GA Dental Soc, NAACP; life mem GA Dental Assn; life mem SE Dist Dental Soc; life mem Lincoln Univ Alumni Assoc; mem Historic Review Bd Savannah GA. **HONORS/ACHIEVEMENTS:** Fellow Acad of General Dentistry 1983; fellow Acad of Dentistry Intl 1984; Annual Freedom Fund Honoree NAACP Savannah GA Branch 1986. **MILITARY SERVICE:** USAF capt 1951-52. **HOME ADDRESS:** 525 E Henry St, Savannah, GA 31401.

JAMES, ADVERGUS DELL, JR.
College administrator. **PERSONAL:** Born Sep 24, 1944, Garden City, KS; married Anna Flave Glenn; children: Anthony David, Adam Glen. **EDUCATION:** Langston Univ, BS 1966; OK State Univ, MS 1969. **CAREER:** Langston Univ, asst registrar 1966-69, dir admission & record 1969-70; Prairie View A&M Univ, dir 1970-85, dir admissions & financial aid 1986-. **ORGANIZATIONS:** Consultant State Student Financial Assistance Training 1979-80; pres TX Assn of Student Financial Aid Administrators 1981-82; mem Natl Council of Student Financial Aid Admin 1985-86; mem TX Guaranteed Student Loan Advisory Bd 1984-86; mem bd dirs Depelcin Center 1986; life mem Alpha Phi Alpha Fraternity; charter mem Prairie View Optimist Club. **HOME ADDRESS:** 7611 Hertfordshire Dr, Spring, TX 77379.

JAMES, ALEXANDER, JR.
Business executive. **PERSONAL:** Born Nov 02, 1933, Branchville, SC; married Dorothy Jones; children: Audrey D, Gregory A, Kevin ES. **EDUCATION:** City Coll NY, BEE 1961; NYU Grad Engrng, MSEE 1963; NYU Grad Business Admin, MBA 1986. **CAREER:** Bell Tele Lab, engr 1961-68; Market Monitor Data Inc, oper mgr 1968-69; EF Shelley & Co Mgmt Cons, sr vice pres 1969-75; Citibank NA, vice pres 1975-82; Group 88 Incorp, sr vp. **ORGANIZATIONS:** Mem Inst of Elec & Electronics Engr 1961-; mem Am Mgmt Assn 1975-; bd of dir Group 88 Inc Consult 1982-; bd of dir Urban Home Ownership Corp 1982-; chmn trustees Pilgrim Baptist Church 1978-; commnr Middletown Twp Human Rights Comm 1976-80; mem Natl Black MBA Assoc 1984. **HONORS/ACHIEVEMENTS:** Hon chmn Monmouth Co Collition Comm 1980; Commnty Achievemnt Award Natl Assn of Negro Business & Professinal Women's Clubs 1978; elected mem Eta Kappa Nu Elec Engr Hon Soc 1960; elected mem Tau Beta Pi Engr Hon Soc 1960. **MILITARY SERVICE:** AUS splist 2nd cl 1953-55. **HOME ADDRESS:** 10 Pineridge Ave, Middletown, NJ 07748. **BUSINESS ADDRESS:** Senior Vice President, Group 88 Incorp, One Penn Plaza, Floor 29, New York, NY 10119.

JAMES, ALLIX BLEDSOE
College president. **PERSONAL:** Born Dec 17, 1922, Marshall, TX; son of Samuel H and Tannie E; married Susie B Nickens; children: Alvan Bosworth, Portia J White. **EDUCATION:** VA Union Univ, AB 1944, M.Div. 1946; Union Theol Seminary, ThM 1949, ThD 1957. **CAREER:** VA Union Univ, instr Biblical studies 1947-50, dean of students 1950-56, dean of sch of theology 1956-70, vice pres 1960-70, pres 1970-79, pres emeritus; VA Union Univ, chancellor. **ORGANIZATIONS:** Bd trustees Richmond Meml Hosp; bd dir Natl Conf of Christians and Jews; president VA Region; mem adv cncl Robert E Lee Council Boy Scouts of Amer; chmn Black Adv Cncl Channel 6 WTVR; mem bd assoc St Paul's Coll; mem Kiwanis Intl; pres bd dir Richmond Gold Bowl Sponsors Inc; mem bd dir Richmond Renaissance Inc; pres bd dir Hathaway Assn; mem adv cncl Med Coll of VA Hospitality House; mem bd dir Shepherd's Center; pres Clergy Assn of Richmond Area; vice pres United Negro Coll Fund; bd gov United Way of Richmond; bd dir Amer Natl Red Cross; mem exec comm Central VA Educ TV Corp; mem exec com Dept of Ministry Natl Cncl of Churches; mem Richmond Downtown Dev Comm; mem Joint Subcommittee Studying Tchr Competency Exams; mem Richmond Dist Reg Planning Comm; bd dir VA Elec and Power Co; bd dirConsult Bank and Trust Co; Univ Adv Cncl Amer Cncl of Life Ins; consult Univ Assoc Inc; Governor's Virginia-Israel Commission, mem. **HONORS/ACHIEVEMENTS:** Citizen of the Year Award Astoria Benefic Club 1971; Disting Serv Award Links Inc 1971; Outstanding Educ of Amer 1971; Citizen of the Year Award Omega PsiPhi Frat 1972; Citizen of the Year Award Richmond Urban League 1974; Alpha Kappa Mu Natl Hon Soc 1974; Natl Brotherhood Award Natl Conf of Christians and Jews 1975; Churchman of the Year Moore St Bapt Ch 1980; Outstanding Educ Achievement Award Alpha Phi Alpha Frat Beta Gamma Lambda Chap 1981; Good Govt Award Richmond First Club 1985; Guest of the Govt of Rep of Taiwan to explore possib for educ cooperation 1976; conferences with European theolog educators from Germany, Switz, Italy, France and England 1969; Study of Higher Educ in the USSR 1973; Contributing Editor "The Continuing Quest"; Author "Calling A Pastor in a Baptist Church"; numerous articles local and natl publications and professional journals; Univ of Richmond, LLD honoris causa 1971; St Pauls Coll, DD honoris causa 1981. **HOME ADDRESS:** 2956 Hathaway Rd, Richmond, VA 23225. **BUSINESS ADDRESS:** Chancellor, Virginia UnionUniv, 1500 N Lombardyst, Richmond, VA 23220.

JAMES, ARMINTA SUSAN
Educator. **PERSONAL:** Born May 01, 1924, Erie, PA; daughter of Leonard Martin and Alice Bowers Martin; married Walter R Jr, Jun 30, 1951. **EDUCATION:** Fisk Univ, BA 1946; Roosevelt Univ, MA in Educ Admin 1965. **CAREER:** Erie Co TB Assn, health educ worker 1946-48; Chicago Welfare Dept, child placement worker 1948-52; N Chicago School Dist 64, teacher 1955-65, elementary principal 1965-1986. **ORGANIZATIONS:** Sec/treasurer, IL Principals Assn, 1965-; Natl Assn of Elementary School Principals, 1965-; Natl Alliance of Black School Educators, 1977-; life mem, past pres, Alpha Kappa Alpha Sorority Lake Co Chapter, 1944-; former bd mem, Lake Co Urban League; ASCD; NAACP; vestry mem, Christ Episcopal Church; vestry & Christian educ coordinator, St Timothy's Church, Aiea Hawaii; Amer Assn of Univ Women. **HONORS/ACHIEVEMENTS:** Educator of the Year, North Shore 12, 1975; Outstanding Woman of Lake County, Urban League, 1977; Outstanding Achievement Award, Omega Psi Phi Fraternity, 1978; Those Who Excell in Educ, Illinois State Bd of Educ, 1978; Outstanding Achievement in Educ, Waukegan YWCA, 1981. **HOME ADDRESS:** 95-201 Kahiku Place, Mililani, HI 96789.

JAMES, BETTY HARRIS
Educator. **PERSONAL:** Born Jun 21, 1932, Gadsden, AL; married Joseph E James (deceased); children: Cecilia Denise James Joyce, Tyrone Michael, Tyshaun Michele. **EDUCATION:** Univ of Pittsburgh, BS Educ, MEd (Magna Cum Laude) 1971, PhD 1974; Marshall Univ, MA 1976. **CAREER:** WV State Coll, prof of educ 1974-84, special asst to pres 1981-84; Livingstone Coll, assoc vice pres academic affairs 1984-86; Appalachia Educ Lab, dir regional liaison ctr 1986-. **ORGANIZATIONS:** Pres Charleston Branch NAACP 1979-81; mem Comm Council Job Corps 1979-; consultant WV Human Rights Commn 1980-; mem Phi Lambda Theta Hon Soc, Kappa Delta Phi. **HONORS/ACHIEVEMENTS:** Danforth Assoc 1976; Faculty Meritorious Serv WV State Coll 1977; Meritorious Serv Livingstone Coll Student Govt 1985. **HOME ADDRESS:** PO Box 143, Institute, WV 25112. **BUSINESS ADDRESS:** Dir Regional Liaison Ctr, Appalachia Educ Lab, PO Box 1348, 1031 Quarrier St, Charleston, WV 25325.

JAMES, BETTY NOWLIN
Administrator. **PERSONAL:** Born Feb 16, 1936, Athens, GA; married Lewis Francis James; children: Beth Marie Morris, Dewey Douglas Morris III. **EDUCATION:** Fisk University, BA1956; Univ of Houston, MEd 1969, EdD 1975. **CAREER:** Houston Ind School District, teacher and music specialist 1958-71, federal programs asst 1972-74, assoc dir research/evaluation 1975-76; Univ of Houston-Downtown, coord instr planning/evaluation 1976-80, dir of inst research 1980-83, dir of inst serv 1983-. **ORGANIZATIONS:** Phi Delta Kappa Rschng Frat 1976-; allocations review panel United Way 1983-; worksite coord Tenneci Inc Cities in Schools Pro 1984; top black achiever awd committee Human Enrichment of Life Prog 1985-;Black Achiever Selection Committee Chair-Riverside, Gen Hosp 1986; Executive Boards Houston YWCA/UNCF, Patterson Awards Committee UNCF. **HONORS/ACHIEVEMENTS:** Intellectual Dev Fund grantee Univ of Houston-Downtown 1982; Top Worksite Awd Tenneco, Inc 1984; Outstanding Woman of Univ Houston-Downtown Houston YWCA Bd 1985; HELP Outstanding Blk Achiever Awd Human Enrichment of Life 1985; Marquis Who's Who of Amer Women 1985. **HOME ADDRESS:** 3301 Oakdale, Houston, TX 77004. **BUSINESS ADDRESS:** Dir of Inst Services, Univ of Houston-Downtown, One Main St, Houston, TX 77002.

JAMES, BOBBY CHARLES
Educational administrator. **PERSONAL:** Born Aug 29, 1946, Andalusia, AL; married Jean; children: Steven M Ford, Shaun P Ford. **EDUCATION:** Mira Costa Community Coll, AS in PE 1968; Linfield Coll, BS in PE 1970, MEd 1972. **CAREER:** Crestview HS, teacher/coach 1971; Eglin AF Base, dir of recreation center 1977; Linfield College, dir of ethnic affairs. **ORGANIZATIONS:** Chm of board Okaloosa County CAP 1975; member of board McMinnville CAP 1980; member Yamhill County Econ Dev Comm 1981; member Yamhill County Soc Serv Comm 1982; vice president Oregon Multi-Cultural Ed Assn; member McMinnville Kiwanis Club. **HONORS/ACHIEVEMENTS:** Man of the Year Mira Costa CC AMS Oceanside, CA 1967; Contribution to Race Unity The Bahai of McMinnville 1979. **BUSINESS ADDRESS:** Dir of Ethnic Affairs, Linfield College, PO Box 411, McMinnville, OR 97128.

JAMES, CARLOS ADRIAN
Marketing manager. **PERSONAL:** Born Jun 01, 1946, Oyster Bay LI, NY; married Claudette Brown; children: Todd, Terrence, Carlos Jr. **EDUCATION:** Canton Coll StateUniv of NY at Canton, AAS 1967; LIUniv Brooklyn NY, BS 1970. **CAREER:** The Coca-Cola Co, mgr spl mkts planning 1979-; Atlanta Bus League, mgr 1978-79; Avon Prod Inc, budget Admn/div sales mgr 1972-78; NBC, budget adminstr 1970-72. **ORGANIZATIONS:** Mem Nat Assn of Market Developers 1980; mem Soc for Advancement of Mgmt; vice pres Zeta Alpha Phi; mem Urban League. **BUSINESS ADDRESS:** Coca Cola Co, 610 North Ave, Atlanta, GA 30301.

JAMES, CHARLES ALEXANDER
Retired ambassador. **PERSONAL:** Born Jun 06, 1922, Washington, DC; married L Jane Woodley; children: Donald, Dennis, Peter, Karen. **EDUCATION:** Middlebury Coll, BA 1949; Yale Law Sch, LLB 1952. **CAREER:** Niger, ambassador 1976-79; African Affairs, dep asst sec 1974-76; office of Near E Aff USAID, dir 1974-; Peace Corps, dir 1966-67; dep dir 1964-66; asst atty gen 1961-64; Pvt Pract, law 1954-61; Nathaniel S Colley, atty 1952-54. **ORGANIZATIONS:** Mem bd dir pres Family Serv Agency Stockton CA 1956-64; NAACP; Com of 100 Stockton; Stockton Redev Agy. **HONORS/ACHIEVEMENTS:** LLD hon Middlebury Coll 1977. **MILITARY SERVICE:** USN petty ofcr 1943-46.

JAMES, CHARLES FORD
Business executive. **PERSONAL:** Born Dec 21, 1935, Rochester, NY; married Jean Hunter; children: Catherine, Deborah. **EDUCATION:** Cornell U, BA 1957; HowardUniv Sch of Law, 1962-64; NYUniv Sch of Law, Dr of Jurisprudence 1966. **CAREER:** NY Tele, mgr 1964-. **ORGANIZATIONS:** Mem Nat Defense Exec Reserve 1966-; pres Millburn-Short Hills First Aid Squad 1985; mem Nat Ski Patrol Shawnee Mtn, PA; former mem Bd of Dir Urban League of Essex Co NJ 1966-74. **MILITARY SERVICE:** AUS capt 1957-62.

HOME ADDRESS: 151 Mohawk Rd, Short Hills, NJ 07078. **BUSINESS ADDRESS:** District Manager, NY Telephone, 1095 Ave of the Americas, New York, NY 10036.

JAMES, CHARLES HOWELL, II
Business executive. **PERSONAL:** Born Nov 22, 1930, Charleston; married Lucia Jeanette Bacote; children: Sheila, Stephanie, Charles III, Sarah. **EDUCATION:** Univ of Pennsylvania Wharton Sch of Finance & Commerce, BS 1953; WV State Coll, attended. **CAREER:** James Produce Co, salesman 1956-60; James Produce Co, sec treas 1961-63; James Produce Co, sec treas & gen mgr 1963-67; James Produce Co, pres & gen mgr 1967-72; C H James & Co, pres chmn 1972-. **ORGANIZATIONS:** Mem bd dir Charleston C of C Com of 100; dist adv coun Small Business Adminstrn 1971-; chmn Charleston C of C FFA Ham Bacon & Egg Show; mem US Cof C; Asso WV Assn of Retail Grocers; vice pres Mountain State Busienssmen's Assn of WV 1974-75; commr & sec of bd Kanawha Intl Airport Auth 1970-; bd trustees United Fund of Kanawha Valley 1967-75; bd dir Buckskin Coun BSA 1970-73; Rotary Club Charleston 1970-; chmn Mayor's Com on Interstate Understructure of Charleston 1973; bd dir Industrial adv coun OIC's of Am 1972-; bd dir Charston Progress Assn for Economic Devel; pres Alpha Iota Lambda Chap 1974-76; life mem Alpha Phi Alpha Frat; Sire Archon 1974 Upsilon Boule Sigma Pi Phi Frat; life mem NAACP; bd trustees First Bapt Ch. **HONORS/ACHIEVEMENTS:** Honorary soc Beta Gamma Sigma; top 100 businessmen Black Enterprise 1974 & 1975. **MILITARY SERVICE:** USAF capt 1953-56. **BUSINESS ADDRESS:** Chairman, The James Corporation, Lock Box 10170 Sta C, Charleston, WV 25357.

JAMES, CHARLES L.
Educator. **PERSONAL:** Born Apr 12, 1934, Poughkeepsie, NY; married Rose Jane Fisher; children: Sheila Ellen, Terri Lynn. **EDUCATION:** SUNY New Paltz, BS 1961; SUNY Albany, MA 1969. **CAREER:** Swarthmore Coll Swarthmore PA, assoc prof 1973-; SUNY Oneota NY, asst prof & assoc prof 1969-73; Dutchess Comm Coll Pughkeepsie NY, instructor in English 1967-69; Spackenkill School Poughkeepsie NY, elementary teacher English 1961-67. **ORGANIZATIONS:** Mem Am Assn ofUniv Prof; Modern Lang Assn; Coll Lang Assn. **HONORS/ACHIEVEMENTS:** Monograph "The Black Writer in Am" Albany SUNY 1969; "From the Roots short stories by black americans" dodd mead & co in 1970; post grad fellowship YaleUniv Danforth Found 1971-72; summer seminar Nat Endowment for the Humanities 1978. **MILITARY SERVICE:** AUS sgt 1955-57. **BUSINESS ADDRESS:** Dept of English Lit, Swarthmore Coll, Swarthmore, PA 19081.

JAMES, CLARENCE L., JR.
Business executive. **PERSONAL:** Born Oct 13, 1933, Los Angeles, CA; married Patricia Douglas; children: Clarence III, Craig. **EDUCATION:** John Muir Coll, AA 1952; OH State Univ, BS 1956; Cleveland State Univ, JD 1962; Case Western Reserve Univ, graduate program in public management science certificate 1968. **CAREER:** Cleveland Legal Aid Soc, civil dir 1964-68; City of Cleveland, Dir of Law/Dep Mayor 1968-71; James Moore & Douglas, attorney-at-law 1971-77; State of OH, atty general 1972-77; US Copyright Royality Tribunal, chmn/comm 1977-81; The Keefe Co, pres/chief operating officer. **ORGANIZATIONS:** Pres Law School Alumni Assoc 1970-71; mem bd of overseers Cleveland Marshall Coll of Law 1970-77; lst vice pres Legal Aid Soc of Cleveland 1972-73; memBd of Trustee Cleveland Bar Assoc 1972-75; dep state coord CA Carter/Mondale Pres Campaign 1976; state coord NJ DeRose for Governor campaign 1977. **HONORS/ACHIEVEMENTS:** Uniform Consumer Credit Code Georgetown Law Journal 1969; 1969 Chamber of Commerce Awd for one of Ten Outstanding Men; holder in Dug Course the Business Lawyer 1971; report of committee on Housing NIMLO Municipal Law Review 1972. **BUSINESS ADDRESS:** President/Chief Operating Ofcr, The Keefe Company, 444 North Capitol St, Washington, DC 20001.

JAMES, DAVA PAULETTE
Educational administrator. **PERSONAL:** Born Jul 16, Sharon, PA. **EDUCATION:** Westminster Coll, BA 1974; Hampton Inst, MA 1978; IA State Univ, PhD summer 1985. **CAREER:** Hampton Inst, grad asst women's div 1976-78; Slippery Rock State Coll, asst dir admissions 1978-79; Youngstown State Univ, academic advisor 1980-85. **ORGANIZATIONS:** Mem Natl Academic Advising Assoc; former 1st vice pres Natl Assoc of Negro Business & Prof Women's Clubs Ohio Valley Club; former bd mem Mercer Co NAACP; mem Urban League. **HONORS/ACHIEVEMENTS:** Listed in 1982 edition of Outstanding Young Women of Amer; certificate & trophy Meritorious Volunteer United Negro College Fund Youngstown Area Campaign 1982-85. **BUSINESS ADDRESS:** ACA Advisor Schl of Education, Youngstown State University, 410 Wick, Youngstown, OH 44555.

JAMES, DAVID PHILLIP
Educator. **PERSONAL:** Born Sep 02, 1940, Greenville, NC; son of John Oscar James and Lula Forbes James; married Janie Russell; children: Lauren Nicole, Joi Melissa. **EDUCATION:** Elizabeth City State Univ, NC, BS, 1962; Georgetown Univ, Washington, DC, MA, 1971; Nova Univ, Fort Lauderdale, FL, EdD 1978. **CAREER:** Pitt Co NC, teacher/coach, 1962-63; Clarke Co VA, social sci teacher/coach, 1963-67; Washington, DC Public Schools, Social Science teacher/coach, 1967-71; Prince George's Community Coll, educ admin, 1971-, assoc dean of extension centers & special programs. **ORGANIZATIONS:** Part-time consultant, self-employed, 1978-; Student Retention; mem, Natl Council Community Serv & Continued Educ, 1973-; mem, Adult Educ Assn, 1978-; mem, Amer Assn for Higher Educ, 1982. **HONORS/ACHIEVEMENTS:** Outstanding Teacher of the Year, Washington, DC Public Schools, 1971; Phi Alpha Theta Intl Award, History, Georgetown Univ, 1971; 1st Black Assoc Dean, Prince George's Community Coll, 1979; Honored Graduate, Elizabeth City State Coll, NC, 1962; Honored as the Outstanding Admin, Prince George Community Coll, 1988; Honorable Mention Recipient, Maryland Assn for Higher Educ as Outstanding Educator, 1989; Named Project Dir of the Black & Minority Student Retention Programs, Prince George's Community Coll, 1988; Authored, "Black Issues in Higher Education," 1988, "Increasing the Retention Rates of Black & Minority Students Through Mentoring & Tutorial Services at Prince George's Community College," 1989. **HOME ADDRESS:** 6238 Satan Wood Dr, Columbia, MD 21044. **BUSINESS ADDRESS:** Associate Dean, Prince George's Community Coll, 301 Largo Rd, Largo, MD 20772.

JAMES, DION
Professional athlete. **PERSONAL:** Born Nov 09, 1962, Philadelphia, PA. **CAREER:** Milwaukee Brewers, outfielder 1983-. **HONORS/ACHIEVEMENTS:** Named The Brewers Rookie of the Yr 1984; earned All-League, All-City & All-State Hon.

JAMES, DOROTHY MARIE
Certified financial planner. **PERSONAL:** Born Aug 19, 1936, Snow Lake, AR; married Lee Andrew James (divorced); children: Michelle Veronica, Rodney Michael. **EDUCATION:** TN A&I State Univ Nashville, BS 1959; San Francisco Law School, JD 1974; College for Financial Planning Denver Colorado CFP 1987. **CAREER:** Legal secretary, 1959-74; Private Practice, atty 1974-83; Operational Sentinel, lectr 1975-77; Lawyers Club of San Francisco, lecturer 1978; IDA/American Express, financial planner 1983-; The Phoenix Co Atlanta GA CFP Registered Representative 1988. **ORGANIZATIONS:** Bd dirs YWCA of San Francisco 1975-77; bd dirs San Francisco Council of Churches 1979-; bd dirs EOC of San Francisco 1980-; trustee Connectional bd of Personel Services CME Church 1986; bd of dir Societas Docta Inc 1987-. **HONORS/ACHIEVEMENTS:** Scholarship Lawyers Wives of San Francisco 1973; Mother of the Yr Knights of Honor Civic & Social Club 1976; nominee (professionl category) Black Enterprise 1978; Woman of the Yr (Oakland Dist) Christian Methodist Episcopal Church 1980; Lay Person of the Yr Christian Methodist Episcopal Church 1980; Pi Omega Pi Hon Soc TN A&I State Univ. **HOME ADDRESS:** 6223 Forest Hills Dr, Norcross, GA 30092. **BUSINESS ADDRESS:** Dorothy James JD CFP, The Phoenix Company, 223 Perimeter Center Parkway, Suite 100, Atlanta, GA 30346.

JAMES, ELRIDGE M.
Educator. **PERSONAL:** Born Mar 23, 1942, Eunice, LA; married Betty Lea Stewart; children: Rona La Ne, Heath Elridge Floront. **EDUCATION:** Grambling State U, BS 1966; Wayne State U, MEd 1969; MI State U, PhD 1973. **CAREER:** NE LA Univ, mem grad faculty, asst prof sec & coun educ 1975-76; Quachia Parish Bd of Educ, asst prof & clinical prof 1974-; Grambling State Univ, assoc prof 1973-74; MI State Univ, graduate asst 1972; Great Lakes Steel Corp, indus instructor 1969-70; Ecorse HS, teacher 1968-70; CJ Miller Elementary School; Great Lakes Steel Corp, dir educ 1968-70; Ford Motor Co, supvr 1966-68. **ORGANIZATIONS:** LA Indsl Arts Assn; Am Vocat Assn; LA Assn Pub Sch Adult Edn; So Assn for Counselor Educ & Supervision; LA State Reading Council; Assn Supr & Curriculum Devel; mem Phi Delta Kappa; Scottish Rite Mason King Solomon's Lodge; Omega Psi Phi. **HONORS/ACHIEVEMENTS:** Wrote several articles & books for Grambling Coll; dean's list of outstanding grads MI State U. **MILITARY SERVICE:** USN 1960-62. **BUSINESS ADDRESS:** NE LAUniv Sec Coun Educ, Monroe, LA 71202.

JAMES, FELIX
Educator. **PERSONAL:** Born Nov 17, 1937, Hurtsboro, AL; son of Leroy James, Sr. and Blanche Clark James; married Florence Bernard, Aug 07, 1985. **EDUCATION:** Fort Valley State Coll, Fort Valley, GA, BS, 1962; Howard Univ, Washington, DC, MA, 1967; Ohio State Univ, Columbus, PhD, 1972; attended New Orleans Baptist Theological Seminary, New Orleans, 1985. **CAREER:** Columbia Public Schools, Columbia, SC, instructor of social studies, 1962-64; Howard Univ, Washington, DC, reserve book librarian, 1965-67; Tuskegee Inst, Tuskegee, AL, instructor of history, 1967-70; Southern IL Univ, Carbondale, asst prof of history, 1972-74; Southern Univ at New Orleans, chairman of history dept, 1974-75, prof of history, 1979-. **ORGANIZATIONS:** Assn for the Study of Afro-Amer Life and History, state direc, 1973-, co-chair of program comm, 1979-80, member of exec bd; member, New Orleans Martin Luther King Steering Comm, 1977-; member, faculty coun, Southern Univ at New Orleans, 1980-85; vice-chair of arrangement comm, ASBS Annual Meeting in New Orleans, 1983; member of exec bd, Louisiana Historical Assn, 1984-86; member of advisory bd, Annual City-Wide Black Heritage Celebration, 1985-; commr, New Orleans Bicentennial Comm, 1987-91; consultant, Ethnic Minorities Cultural Center, Univ of N Iowa, 1988; senior warden, DeGruy Lodge, Prince Hall Free and Accepted Masons, 1989; member, bd of direcs, S Christian Leadership Conf, 1983-. **HONORS/ACHIEVEMENTS:** Author of The American Addition: History of a Black Community, Univ Press of Amer, 1978; contributor to Dict of Amer Negro Biography, 1982, Dict of Louisiana Biography, 1986, Black Leadership in the 20th Century, 1989, Edn of the Black Adult in the US, 1989, and Twentieth Century Black Leaders, 1989. **BUSINESS ADDRESS:** Dr Felix James, Southern University of New Orleans, 6400 Press Dr, New Orleans, LA 70126.

JAMES, FRANK SAMUEL, III
Attorney. **PERSONAL:** Born Aug 10, 1945, Mobile, AL; son of Mr and Mrs Frank S James, Jr; married Jothany Dianne Williams; children: David RF, Jothany Michelle, Julie Dianne. **EDUCATION:** Campbell Coll, BS 1973; Univ of AL, JD 1978. **CAREER:** Fed Judge Virgil Pittman, law clerk 1978-80; US Dept of Justice, asst us atty 1980-86; Univ of AL School of Law, prof, asst dean 1986. **ORGANIZATIONS:** Mem Amer Bar Assoc 1978-, AL State Bar 1978-, Birmingham Bar Assoc 1980-; bd of mgmt Downtown YMCA of Birmingham 1984-86; mem of council Synod of the Mid South 1985-86; moderator, mem of council Birmingham Presbytery 1986; pres of bd Alabama Capital Representation Resource Center 1988-. **HONORS/ACHIEVEMENTS:** Author Contingent Fees in Domestic Relations Actions 3 Jrnl of the Legal Prof 209 1978; elected to bench and bar Legal Hon Soc 1978; author with Charles W. Gamble, Perspectives on the Evidence Law of Alabama: A Decade of Evolution 1977-87, 40 ALabama Law Review 95, 1988. **MILITARY SERVICE:** US Army, Lt Col 23 years Bronze Star Medal, Air Medal, Purple Heart, Army Commendation Medal, Meritorious Service Medal, Army Achievement Medal, Combat Infantryman's Badge. **BUSINESS ADDRESS:** Professor of Law, Asst Dean, University of Alabama, School of Law, Box 870382, Tuscaloosa, AL 35487-0382.

JAMES, FREDERICK C.
Bishop. **PERSONAL:** Born Apr 07, 1922, Prosperity, SC; married Theressa Gregg. **EDUCATION:** Allen Univ, BA 1943; Howard Univ, MDiv 1947. **CAREER:** AME Episcopal Church, ordained to ministry; Friendship AME Church Irmo SC, pastor 1945; Meml AME Church Columbia SC, bishop 1946; Wayman AME Church Winnsboro SC, bishop 1947-50; Chappelle Meml AME Church Columbia SC, bishop 1950-53; Mt Pisgah AME Church Sumter SC, bishop 1953-72; AME Church Dallas, bishop 1972-. **ORGANIZATIONS:** Bd dir Greater Little Rock Urban League; chmn bd Shorter Coll; founder Mt Pisgah Apts, Sumter, James Centre, maseru, Lesotho, Mem Nat Interfaith Com Fund for Open Soc Dem Clubs; mem Odd Fellows, Masons, Shriners; dean Dickerson Theol Sem 1949-53; pres Sumter br NAACP 1959-72; mem World Conf Church &Soc Geneva 1966; chmn Wateree Community Actions Agency 1969-72; bishop in Botswana, Lesotho, Swaziland, Mozambique, South Africa, Namibia 1972-76; presiding bishop AR, OK 1976-; chmn Commnission on Missions AME Church 1976-; mem Natl Council Church Christ USA 1979-; hon consul-gen representing Lesotho in AR & OK 1979-; del World Meth Council Honolulu 1981; sec AME Council of Bishops 1981. **BUSINESS ADDRESS:** Bishop, African Meth Episcopal Church, 604 Locust St, North Little Rock, AR 72114.

JAMES, FREDERICK JOHN
Attorney. **PERSONAL:** Born Sep 01, 1938, Chicago, IL; married Barbara L Penny. **EDUCATION:** San Francisco State Coll, BA 1968; UC Berkeley Grad Sch Bus, MBA 1972; UC Berkeley Boalt Hall Sch of Law, JD 1973. **CAREER:** Law Offices of Frederick J James, atty 1974-; Law Offices of Hiawatha Roberts, law clerk, atty 1972-74; Del Monte Corp, mgmt trainee 1966-68; Wells Fargo Bank, field auditor 1964-66. **ORGANIZATIONS:** Treas Black MBA Asso Berkeley CA 1973; lectr CA StateUniv Hayward Sch of Bus Admin 1975-76; research asst Center for Real Estate & Urban Econmics 1970; bd mem Men of Tomorrow 1977; mem Charles Houston Bar Assn; Nat Bar Assn; ABA; ATLA; CTLA; bd, mem/legal counsel No CA Black C of C 1978-. **HONORS/ACHIEVEMENTS:** Academic scholarshipUniv of Chicago 1955-58. **MILITARY SERVICE:** AUS e-4 1962-64. **BUSINESS ADDRESS:** Law Offices of Frederick J Jam, Ste 206, Oakland, CA 94607.

JAMES, GILLETTE ORIEL
Clergyman. **PERSONAL:** Born May 05, 1935; married Rosa Vernita Ferguson; children: Jennifer. **EDUCATION:** God's Bible Sch & Coll Cincinnati, AB 1959; Univ of San Francisco, BA 1968; American Bapt Seminary of the West, MDiv 1970, DMin 1976. **CAREER:** Christian Union Church West Indies, pastor 1959-60; US Army, chaplain's asst 1961-62; Western Union, telephone recorder 1962-65; Grace Bapt Church San Francisco, organizer/pastor 1963-69; Beth Eden Bapt Church Oakland CA, minister of christian educ 1970-71, senior pastor 1971-. **ORGANIZATIONS:** Dean Baptist Ministers Union of Oakland 1971-85; pres bd of dirs Social Serv Bureau of Oakland 1976-79; vice pres Northern CA Credit Union 1976-79; pres Black Amer Baptists Northern CA 1977-84; vice pres Black Amer Baptists USA 1985-; exec sec CA State Baptist Convention 1985-86; vice pres Baptist Ministers Union of Oakland 1986-. **HONORS/ACHIEVEMENTS:** Caliborne Hill Awd for Acad Excellence Amer Bapt Seminary of the West 1970; Outstanding Immigrant Awd Intl Inst of East Bay 1977; Disting Serv Bapt Ministers Union of Oakland 1985. **MILITARY SERVICE:** AUS E-4 1961-62; Good Conduct Medal 1961, Rifle Marksman Medal 1962. **HOME ADDRESS:** 2400 Havenscourt Blvd, Oakland, CA 94605. **BUSINESS ADDRESS:** Senior Pastor, Beth Eden Baptist Church, 10th & Magnolia, Oakland, CA 94607.

JAMES, GRACE M.
Educator. **PERSONAL:** Born Aug 12, 1923, Charleston, WV; divorced; children: David Marshall. **EDUCATION:** WV St Clg Institute WV, BA 1944; Meharry Med Clg Nashville TN, MD 1950. **CAREER:** Camp Woodlands Phonecia NY, camp physician 1952; Louisville KY Gen Ped Practice, 1964-67;Univ of Louisville Sch of Med, instr in Child Hlth 1953-62; Louisville & Jefferson Co Dept of Hlth, child hlth physician 1953-55; public school physician 1962-63; Child Psychiatry, Kings Co Hosp Ctr Brooklyn NY, asst visiting psychiatrist 1965-66; St Hosp & Sch Frankfort KY, dir Diagnostic & Evaluation Div 1966, dir Diagnostic & Evaluation Serv Div of Mental Retardaltion 1966-67; Childrens Hosp, attending physician 1968-69; KY Kosair Crippled Chldrns Hosp ped 1968-81, 1983-. **ORGANIZATIONS:** Childrens Hosp 1955-81; Red Cross Hosp 1953-72; Jewish Hosp 1958; St Josephs Hosp 1958; Audubon Hosp 1974; Meth Evang Hosp 1961-81; Nortons Hosp 1967-83; Comm Hosp 1967-75; Kosair/Childrens 83-; all of Louisville KY; Am Med Asso 1953-; Natl Med Asso 1953-; KY Med Asso 1953-; Jefferson Co Med Soc 1953-; Falls City Med Soc 1953; Queens Clinical Soc 1964-66; KY Ped Soc 1956-; Louisville Ped Soc 1956-; Section II New York Am Academy of Pediatrics 1964-66; mem Action Rsrch TmUniv of Louisville Med Sch (Affiliate of Natl Planning Grp) Stdnt Am Med Asso 1971-72; Am Asso on Mental Deficiency 1965- Fellow; sec Falls City Med Soc 1960-64, 1972-74; pres Medical Staff Red Cross Hosp 1963; alternate del from Jefferson Co Med Soc; to House of Delegates of KY Med Asso 1959-60; pres Falls City Med Soc 1974; v chm Section on Pediatrics NMA 1962-66; chm Comm Hlth Serv Falls City Med Soc 1971; chm Comm Med Pediatric Section Natl Med Asso 1971-74; sec Pediatric Section Natl Med Asso 1971-74. **BUSINESS ADDRESS:** 2209 West Broadway, Louisville, KY 40211.

JAMES, GREGORY CREED
Educator. **PERSONAL:** Born Feb 29, 1956, Chicago, IL; son of Silas James, Jr and Dorothy Baker. **EDUCATION:** Southern IL Univ, BA 1977, MS 1983; Roosevelt Univ, Paralegal Degree 1981. **CAREER:** Goldblatt's Dept Store, oper supt 1977-79; CNA Ins Co, supvr 1979-81; Southern IL Univ, counselor 1981-83; Harrisburg Area Comm Coll, instructor counselor 1983-85; West Chester Univ, asst dir financial aid 1985-86; asst prof of counseling, Community Coll of Philadelphia, 1986-. **ORGANIZATIONS:** Consultant Southern IL Univ Office of Financial Aid 1982-83, Amer Assoc for Counseling & Devel 1983; consultant PA Assn of Minority Students 1984; bd of dir mem Amer Big Brothers/Big Sisters 1984, Amer Coll Personnel Assoc, Phi Delta Kappa Hon 1984; presenter Natl Assoc of Financial Admin 1985, PA Assn of Student Financial Aid Admin 1985; volunteer, Big Brother/Big Sister, 1988; mem, Alpha Phi Alpha Faternity, 1988. **HONORS/ACHIEVEMENTS:** Publications include The Survival of Black Colleges and Financing Your Coll Educ With Private Monies. **HOME ADDRESS:** 5817 Morris, Philadelphia, PA 19144.

JAMES, H. RHETT
Educator, clergyman. **PERSONAL:** Born Dec 01, 1928, Baltimore, MD. **EDUCATION:** VA Union U, AB 1950; Our Lady of the Lake Coll, MEd 1951; VA Union U, MDiv 1957; TX Christian U, MTh 1961; HarvardUniv Inst of Mgt, 1974;Univ ofIN, MemphisUniv Insts on on Mgt-Commun Servs 1974-75;Univ of TX at Arlington, PhD 1974. **CAREER:** Urban Affairs & Community Devel Center, asst prof of soc sci, assoc dir of devel, dir; New Careers for the Handicapped Program Bishop Coll TX, dir 1962-; New Hope Baptist Church TX, pastor 1958-; VA Union Univ, instructor 1955-58; San Antonio School System St Phillips Jr Coll, instructor 1950-55. **ORGANIZATIONS:** Educ com chmn Dallas NAACP 1961; pres Dallas NAACP 1962; bd of dir TX Counc of Chs; del Pres Com on Equal Employ Opportun; fdr, 1st pres DallasFrontiers Internat; pres Dallas Dem Men; bd mem Family Guid Ctr; bd mem Am Civ Lib Union; ret bd mem Dallas Urban Leag; bd mem TX Assn of Devlpng Colls 1970-74; bd mem City of Dallas; mem Am Mensa Soc; bd mem N Dallas Am Cancer Soc; mem So Histl Assn; mem Am Assn ofUniv Profs; bd mem Am Bapt Conv Chs of the S; mem Sigma Pi Phi & Kappa Alpha Psi Frat. **HONORS/ACHIEVEMENTS:** Listed in Who's Wo in the SW; Who's Who in Religion 1976-77 edtn; The Goals for Dallas Commun Serv Aw; OIC Commun Serv Aw; Urban Leag Disting Serv Aw; NKOK Radio Sta Commun Serv Aw; Big Bros Commun Serv Aw; Disting Serv Aw Urban Leag; Trail Blazers Aw; Dllas City Counc Serv Aw. **BUSINESS ADDRESS:** New Hope Baptist Church, 5002 S Central Expressway, Dallas, TX 75215.

JAMES, HAMICE R., JR.
Clergyman, educator. **PERSONAL:** Born Apr 19, 1929, La Grange, TX; married Carolyn. **EDUCATION:** St Mary's U, BBA 1961; St Mary's U, MA 1971. **CAREER:** Employment Counselor, state employment comm 1964-69; City Water Utility Co, dir human relations 1969-73; St Phillips Coll, instructor 1973-; Emmanuel Baptist Church, pastor 1971-. **ORGANIZATIONS:** Mem following San Antonio Economic & Business Assn; Personnel & Management Assn; TX Jr Coll Tchrs Assn; pres bd dir Am Cancer Society. **HONORS/ACHIEVEMENTS:** Hon business Fraternity; hon Economic Frat. **MILITARY SERVICE:** AUS sgar 1947-56. **BUSINESS ADDRESS:** St Philips Coll, 2111 Nevada St, San Antonio, TX.

JAMES, HENRY GRADY, III
Elected official. **PERSONAL:** Born Oct 24, 1945, Newark, NJ; married Jean Hunter; children: Christina, Grady IV. **EDUCATION:** Delaware State Coll, BA 1968; Kean Coll of NJ. **CAREER:** Essex Cty Park Comm, dir of athletics summers 1973, 1974; Essex Cty Jail, spec asst to warden summers 1975, 1976; Eastside HS Paterson, admin asst 1984-; Paterson Bd of Ed, teacher 1968-; City of East Orange; city council mbr, 1980-. **ORGANIZATIONS:** Life mem Oper PUSH 1979; bd of trustees Commun Day Nursury 1980-; trustee First Bethel Baptist Church 1980-; life mem F&AM PHA State & Jurisdiction of NJ 1982, NAACP, NJ Ed Assoc 1968-; co-founder H Grady James III Civic Assn; deacon First Bethel Baptist Church 1985; bd of dirs, Essex County Community Action; mbr, trustee, Community Day Nursery East Orange, NJ. **HONORS/ACHIEVEMENTS:** Christian Leadership Awd HGJ Civil Assn 1981; Outstanding Young Men of Amer 1982; Man of the Year Seventh Day Adventist Church 1983; Father of the Year Cub Pack 8 1984. **HOME ADDRESS:** 301 S Burnet St, East Orange, NJ 07018. **BUSINESS ADDRESS:** City Council Member, City of East Orange, 44 City Hall Plaza, East Orange, NJ 07019.

JAMES, HENRY NATHANIEL
City official. **PERSONAL:** Born Dec 28, 1908, East Point, GA; married Thelma Victoria Dudley. **EDUCATION:** Morris Brown Coll, AB; AtlantaUniv Sch of Social Work, attended 1934-35; Nat Cath Sch of Social Serv CathUniv of Am, 1955-56. **CAREER:** Atlanta Transient Bur, chief bursar 1933-36; Atlanta Urban Survey, investigator 1936-38; Atlanta Pub Sch, tchr 1938-41; Fed Agys, has worked for various since 1943; Glenarden MD, town mgr. **ORGANIZATIONS:** Chmn Physical Com Prince George's Co Model Neighborhood Action Bd 1972-74; mayor town of Glenarden 1975f state delegate Black Political Conv 1972; mem MD Black Caucus 1972; past pres DC Chap Assn for Study of Negro Life History; past asso chmn 2nd stewart bd Met AME Ch; sr stewart Met AME Ch; pres Wash Chap Morris Brown Coll Alumni Assn 1953-71; pres emeritus 1971; dir Eastern Regional Coun Morris Brown Coll Nat Alumni Assn 1968-74; mem Wash Inter-Alumni Coun; mem Omega Psi Phi Frat; past pres Fox Ridge Civic Assn 1969 & 1973; chmn Cit for Better Govt; councilman & vice chmn Town Coun Bd 1969-71; editor Glenarden Town Guardian 1971-72; prog chmn Fox Ridge Civil Assn 1971-72. **HONORS/ACHIEVEMENTS:** Listed in Who's Who in the East 1972-73, 1974-75; outstanding supervisory performance award Goddard Spcae Flight Cntr 1973; community achievement award MorrisBrown Coll Nat Alumni Assn; achievement award Wash Inter-alumni Coun 1972; mayor award for outstanding serv to Town of Glenarden 1971; citation award foroutstanding serv Morris Brown Coll Club 1971. **BUSINESS ADDRESS:** 8600 Glenarden Pkwy, Glenarden, MD 20801.

JAMES, HERBERT I.
Scientist/personnel manager. **PERSONAL:** Born Mar 30, 1933, St Thomas; married Christine M Stolz; children: Herbert Jr, Robyn. **EDUCATION:** Hampton Inst, BS; Clark Univ, MA, PhD; DB Hill Train Cs, insurance broker; DB Hill Train Cs, investment broker; LaSalle Ext Univ, bus mgmt. **CAREER:** DB Hill & Co, br mgr; DB Hill & Assoc, br mgr; Clark Univ, tchr asst; St Thomas HS, tchr; Exp Coll of the VI, tchr; Hampton Inst, tchr;ESB Inc, res sci 1965-76; Xerox Corp, scientist 1976-80; personnel manager 1980-. **ORGANIZATIONS:** Mem Electrochem Soc, Amer Assn for Adv of Sci, Instrument Soc of Amer, Beta Kappa Chi, Alpha Kappa Mu, NY Acad of Sci; pub sci works in various journ; presentations given at various mtgs of sci soc & presented sci papers at various coll; guest spkr & vocal at various mtgs; Episcopal Diocese of PA num comm and groups; exec bd Bucks Co Boy Scouts; bd dir Freedom Valley Coun Girl Scouts; NAACP Fellowship Clark Univ; scholarship Hampton Inst. **HONORS/ACHIEVEMENTS:** VI Pub Aff Awd 1965; Who's Who in the World; Who's Who in the E; Who's Who in Black Philadelphia; Who's Who in Amer; Amer Men of Sci; Natl Reg of Prominent Amer & Institutional Notables; Men of Achiev; Dict of Intl Biography; Who's Who in Black Amer 1975-76; Intl Who's Who in Comm Serv; Comm Lead & Noteworthy Amers; JFK Library Minority Awd, pres of the US Commendation Award. **BUSINESS ADDRESS:** Manager of Personnel, Xerox Research Centre of Canada, 2660 Speakman Drive, Mississauga, Ontario, Canada L5K 2L1.

JAMES, HERMAN DELANO
Educational administrator. **PERSONAL:** Born Feb 25, 1943, St Thomas, Virgin Islands of the United States;son of Henry James and Frances Smith James; married Marie Gray; children: Renee, Sybil, Sidney. **EDUCATION:** Tuskegee Inst, BS 1965; St Johns Univ, MA 1967; Univ of Pgh, PhD 1972. **CAREER:** Univ of Pgh, asst prof 1971-72; Univ of MA, asst prof 1972-78, assoc provost 1975-76, asst chancellor 1976-78; CA State Univ, vice provost 1978-82; Glassboro State Coll, vice pres 1982-84, pres 1984-. **ORGANIZATIONS:** Mem Cherry Hill Minority Civic Assoc 1982-84; bd mem NJ Educ Computer Network 1983-; chair-colleges Gloucester Co United Way 1985. **HONORS/ACHIEVEMENTS:** Fellowship Natl Inst of Health 1968-71; Young Black Achiever Boston YMCA 1977; Outstanding Educator Williamstown Civic Assoc 1984. **BUSINESS ADDRESS:** President, Glassboro State College, Glassboro, NJ 08028.

JAMES, HYTOLIA ROBERTS
Educator. **PERSONAL:** Born Oct 29, 1928, Salisbury, MD; married Samuel James Sr; children: Samuel Jr, Riley. **EDUCATION:** Bowie State Coll, BS 1950; Temple Univ, MEd 1967, Principalship Cert 1967; Nova Univ, EdD 1976. **CAREER:** Temple Univ, demo teacher; Philadelphia School Dist, instr in elem math 1963-65, curriculum writer 1965; MD School Dist, teacher 1950-61; Cleveland School Dist, teacher 1961-63; Stanton Schools, dist collaborator, asst to principal 1965-67; Philadelphia Schools, asst to dist supt 1967-70, principal 1970, exec dir of personnel oper 1983-85; Educational Consultant. **ORGANIZATIONS:** Consult Temple Univ, Univ of PA; chairperson Dist Six Performance Appraisal of Admin; mem Philadelphia Assoc of School Admin, Natl Assoc of Univ Women,Women in Ed; chairperson Dist Six Bicentennial; bd mem PUSH Philadelphia Chapt, Pride & Progress; mem Lambda Kappa Mu; vice pres Black Womens Ed All of Philadelphia; mem Educators

Roundtable Inc, Philadelphia Council of Admin Women in Educ. **HONORS/ACHIEVEMENTS:** Chapel of Four Chaplins Legion of Honor 1968; Alumni of the Year Bowie State 1969; LTBC Black Ed Awd 1972; Sor of the Year Lambda Kappa Mu 1973; Germantown Unied Comm Council Serv Awd 1974; Greater W Oaklane Coord Council Ed Awd 1974; Citation for Dedicated & Meaningful Ed Serv PA House of Rep 1974; Plaque for Loyal & Dedicated Serv to Ch & Comm Canaan Bapt Church 1975; Hon Mention Tribune-Greyhoudn Woman of the Year Contest; Awd of Recognition Philadelphia Councilof Admin Women in Ed; Spec Recog Cited in Philadelphia Daily News; 1 of 12 Top Black Ed in Philadelphia School Syst; Merit Citation Parents Union of Phila; Meritorious Awd PUSH Phila; Philadelphia Citizen of the Month The Philadelphia Tribune Newspaper and the Pepsi Cola Co; Disting Alumni Citation Natl Assoc for Equal Oppor in Higher Educ 1986; ERIC publications.

JAMES, ISAAC
Clergyman. **PERSONAL:** Born Jun 19, 1914, Grifton, NC. **EDUCATION:** VA Unoin U, AB 1950; VA State Coll; Univ MD; Unoin Theol Sem; Richmond Prolf Inst WA Sch Psychiatry. **CAREER:** Central State Hosp Petersburg VA, pastor; Unoin Branch Bapt Ch Chesterfield VA, pastor; 6th Mt Zion Bapt Ch Richmond; Fountain Bapt Ch. **ORGANIZATIONS:** Mem Nat & State Sunday Schs & BTU Cong; Lott Carey Foreign Mission Convention; exec bd Tuckahoe Assn; Bapt Minister's Conf; exec bd Goodwill Bapt Conv; hist bd Nat Bapt Conv USA; bd dirs Bapt Allied Bodies. **HONORS/ACHIEVEMENTS:** Author "The Sun Do Move".

JAMES, JOYCE L.
Advertising & public relations company executive. **PERSONAL:** Born Mar 05, 1950, Saginaw, MI; daughter of Andrew J Williams, Sr and Pearline Walker Wililams; divorced; children: Tanya L Donahue-Jackson. **EDUCATION:** Delta Coll, Univ Center MI, AA, 1981. **CAREER:** WWWS Radio, Saginaw MI, station manager, 1977-80; producer of "One-Up" shows, 1977-80; WUCM TV, Saginaw MI, producer and volunteer program coord, "Day by Day," 1978-82; Pride Inc, Saginaw MI, activity dir, 1980-82; YWCA, Saginaw MI, asst dir, 1982; Delta Coll, Univ Center MI, counseling specialist, 1983-87; Inland Area OIC, Riverside CA, specail projects dir, 1987-89. **ORGANIZATIONS:** Life mem, Opportunities Industrialization Center, 1978; chairperson, Intl Year of Child for City of Saginaw, 1979; public relations media consultant, committee to elect Dr Lawrence Crawford, 1981; mem, Assn of Junior League, 1982-; public relations media consultant, committee to elect Mildred Mason, 1983; mem, Junior League of Riverside, 1988-. **HONORS/ACHIEVEMENTS:** 1st Black Female Radio Station Manager in Midwest Market, 1977; Community Service Recognition Award, Zeta Omega Zeta Saginaw Chapter, Zeta Phi Beta Sorority, 1979; Community Service Award, Saginaw County Sickle Cell Anenia Council, 1981; Outstanding Community Service Award, City of Saginaw International Friendship Games, 1982; columnist, Model City Newspaper, Saginaw MI. **BUSINESS ADDRESS:** President, Chief Executive, JW Ellington and Associates, PO Box 7069, Moreno Valley, CA 92303.

JAMES, JUANITA T.
Publishing company executive. **PERSONAL:** Born Oct 01, 1952, Brooklyn, NY. **EDUCATION:** Princeton Univ, AB 1974; Columbia Univ Grad Sch of Business, MS 1982. **CAREER:** Time Life Books Inc, editorial rsch 1976-78, editorial admin 1978-81; Time Inc, financial analyst 1981-83; Time Life Books Inc, vice pres human resources1983-86; Time Life Libraries Inc, pres/ceo. **ORGANIZATIONS:** Mem Natl Black MBA Assoc 1982-, Natl Urban League 1982-; bd mem The Green Door 1984-88; trustee Princeton Univ 1984-; mem Natl Coalition of 100 Black Women 1986-. **HONORS/ACHIEVEMENTS:** Black Achievers in Industry Awd Harlem YMCA 1979; Outstanding Young Women of Amer 1982; Andrew Heiskell Awd for Comm Serv Time Inc 1982. **BUSINESS ADDRESS:** President/CEO, Time-Life Libraries Inc, 777 Duke St, Alexandria, VA 22314.

JAMES, JUNE, III
Educator. **PERSONAL:** Born Dec 27, 1934, Shreveport, LA; married Janie Spears; children: Kenneth, Michael, Kevin, June IV. **EDUCATION:** Univ Pittsburgh, PhD 1980;Univ Miami, spec in educ 1975; SoUniv Baton Rouge, MEd 1968; So U, BS 1962. **CAREER:** Rust College of Education, prof; Univ of Pittsburgh, graduate student asst 1976-77; Coll of Educ FL Atlantic Univ, asst prof 1970-75; Univ of Miami, teacher training models 1970; NSF TX Southern Univ, 1969; NSF Univ of MO, 1966; NSF Southern Univ, 1963; TX Southern Univ, admin asst; Planning & Devel Secondary Educ, instructor 1969; Univ of MO, instructor; Paseo Sr HS, instructor 1966-69; Bethune HS, instructor; Welsh LA, asst prin 1962-66; Multi-Culture Educ, consultant; Legal Problems in Educ; Human Behavior & Group Dynamics; admin & supervision; Secondary Educ Curriculum; Disadvantaged Children. **ORGANIZATIONS:** Am Assn ofUniv Profs; Assn ofr Supervision & Curriculum Devel; Council of Grad Students in Edn; NEA; FL Educ Assn; TX Assn of Coll Tchrs; LA Educ Assn; MO State Tchrs Assn; KS City Sci Tchrs Assn; Masonic Lodge Lone Star 131 3rd degree; Kappa Delta Pi Hon Soc; Alpha Phi Alpha; Alpha Phi Omega; vis team S Assn for Accredidation of Secondary Schs; FL Sch Desegregation Consult Team; FL Sch Plant Survey Team; FL Statewide Com on Common Course Designation; FL AtlanticUniv Com on Promotion & Tenure; Evaluation Team Tchr Corp Albany State Coll; faculty adv FL Atlantic U; black student union & grad adv Minority Students; faculty adv centrs & discover rsrch projs; dir Summer Enrichment Prgm; dir Crucial Issues in Educ Prgms for In-Serv Tchrs & Adminstrs; developed Tchr TrnG Prgms Humanizing Educ TX; consult Nat Urban League; co-chmn Coll of Educ FL Atlantic U; developed in-svc workshops for comm action council for Palm Beach Cty. **HONORS/ACHIEVEMENTS:** Wrote, prod, dir Financial Crisis of FL Schs; Is Every Tchr A Guidance Worker; Greet The Tchr; Shc Law; The Schs, Cts & Society; Students As Individuals; papers The Comm Sch Concept & Its Implications of Sch Plant Planning; Individualized Competency Based Instructional Modules on Criminal Justice for Sr HS Social Studies Curriculum; Organizational Norms & Their Implication on Staff-Personnel Admin-istr. **MILITARY SERVICE:** AUS 1956; USAF 1957. **BUSINESS ADDRESS:** College of Education, Rust College, PO Box 719, Holly Springs, MS 38635.

JAMES, LUTHER
Educator, writer, director. **PERSONAL:** Born Aug 08, 1928, New York, NY; married Marguerite Brisby; children: Robin, Julian. **EDUCATION:** Dramatic Workshop of the New Sch for Social Research, attended 1951; John Hay Whitney Fellow study in England France Germany Russia 1959-60; Ford Found Fellow, study of Broadway theatre 1962; Study of Brazilian Performance Art 1986; Study of film technique Russia, Hungary, Czechoslovakia 1986; study of performance in Jamaica Barbados Trinidad 1987; study/seminar with Brazillian actors and directors 1987; theatre devel in Zimbabwe 1988; study of performance in Cuba 1989. **CAREER:** NY, dir & tchr 1956-64; Luther James Theatre Workshop NY, LA, teacher 1958-68; Arena Prod MGM CA, asst to supervising & prod 1965-66; CBS TV Network LA CA, exec prod 1966-68; "On Being Black" Allston MA, prod 1968-70; Negro Ensemble Co NY, 1968-69; LA CA,TV writer and dir 1970-75; Drama Dept Univ CASan Diego, assoc prof; Portland State Univ, 1971; CA State Univ LA, 1971; CA State Univ Northridge, 1972-73; Univ of CA, prof. **ORGANIZATIONS:** Mem Acad of TV Arts & Sciences; dir Guild of Am; Writers Guild of Am; theatre editor Crisis Magazine 1986. **BUSINESS ADDRESS:** Professor, University of California-San Diego, Dept of DramaUniv of CA San D, La Jolla, CA 92093.

JAMES, MARQUITA L.
Educator. **PERSONAL:** Born Nov 09, 1932, Philadelphia. **EDUCATION:** WilberforceUniv Wilberforce OH, BA 1955; Seton AhllUniv S Orange NJ, MA 1966; Candidacy NY U, PhD 1974. **CAREER:** Nassau Comm Coll Garden City, Long Island NY, assoc prof History 1969-; Wyandanch Schools, Wydandanch NY, chmn 1964-68; Freeport NY, Afro-Amer History curr coor 1968-69. **ORGANIZATIONS:** Hist & ldr crea of estab of Afro-Am Hist Soc in Freeport & Long Island NY; activist leader in successful fight to deseg sch buses & discrim prac inFreeport Schls 1968-69; mem AssnUniv Prof Assn Afro-Am Edn; Am Hist Assn; Afro-Am Black Heritage Assn; Cong of Racial Equal; Coun on Interracial Books for Child; Alpha Kappa Alpha Sor; Nat Black Feminist Org; pres Nassau-Suffolk Br Assn for Study of Afro-Am Life & Hist. **HONORS/ACHIEVEMENTS:** Listed among black edrs in Black Hist Museum Hempstead LI NY; natl def educ award Tchrs Coll ColumbiaUniv NY UL,; inst intl educ awardUniv of Ghana Legon W Africa 1969; m l kingr jr grad fellow award NYUniv 1968-71. **BUSINESS ADDRESS:** History Dept Nassau Community, Garden City, NY 11530.

JAMES, NAOMI ELLEN
Health services, education administrator. **PERSONAL:** Born Jan 14, 1927, Inkster, MI; married Samuel M James Sr; children: Saundra Parsons, Marcia Allen, Samuel Jr, Carolyn G James. **EDUCATION:** WWCCC, Assoc Nursing 1979; Wayne State Univ, Nursing BSN 1983. **CAREER:** Wayne Cty Gen Hosp, hospital attend 1947-70, hosp attend supt I 1970-77; Hutzel Hosp, staff nurse 198-83; Vstg Nurse Assoc, public health nurse, rn1983-. **ORGANIZATIONS:** Pres St Clements Church Blessed Mothers Guild 1980-; sec Gamma Phi Delta Sor 1981-; past pres & sec Inkster School Bd 1981-84. **HONORS/ACHIEVEMENTS:** Woman Worth Watching Inkster Ledger Star 1983; Outstanding Volunteer City of Inkster 1983; Oustanding Women of the Year Delta Sigma Theta Sor 1984. **HOME ADDRESS:** 3051 Williams, Inkster, MI 48141.

JAMES, PEGGI C.
Association executive. **PERSONAL:** Born Dec 04, 1940, Dothan, AL; divorced; children: Rose, Roddy, Rolaunda. **EDUCATION:** AL State U, BS 1967. **CAREER:** Human Resource Devel Corp, exec dir; Grimsley HS Ashford AL, teacher, 1967-69. **ORGANIZATIONS:** Mem AL Assn Comm Action Agys; NEA; Les Vingts Socialietes Club; Dothan Asn Women's Clubs; NAACP; bd dirs Civic Cntr Opera House. **HONORS/ACHIEVEMENTS:** 4-yr scholarship AL Assn Women's Clubs 1957; HC Trenholm acad award 1958; Dothan woman of year 1974; AL woman achievement 1974;. **BUSINESS ADDRESS:** Executive Dir, Human Resource Dev Corp, 108 Main St, Enterprise, AL 36330.

JAMES, RAYMOND N.
Association executive. **PERSONAL:** Born Sep 03, 1933, Henderson, NC; married Sue Johnson; children: s Serv, Freeport, NY, 1965-66; dir, Neighborhood Youth Corps, Stamford, CT, 1968-70; probation officer, Juvenile Ct, First dist, 1971; proj. **EDUCATION:** Shaw Ud ba 1959; columbia ud msw 1963. **CAREER:** Family & Children Serv Freeport NY, social group worker 1965-66; Neighborhood Youth Corps Stamford CT, dir 1968-70; Juvenile Ct First dist, probation officer 1971; Planning Com Criminal Adminstrn, proj dir 1972-73; Minority Drug Abuse Control, dir 1972; Prog Planning & Dev W Main St Community Ctr Inc, dir. **MILITARY SERVICE:** AUS med corps corpl 1953-55.

JAMES, RICHARD L.
Educator. **PERSONAL:** Born Jul 31, 1926, Asheville, NC; married Velma A Kinsey. **EDUCATION:** Hampton Inst VA, BS 1949; Univ MI, MMus 1951; Univ MD, EdD 1968. **CAREER:** School of Educ Morgan State Univ, dean 1975-; Morgan State Univ Baltimore, assoc dean teacher educ 1973-75; Amer Assn Colleges Teacher Educ, assoc dir 1968-73; Prince George's County, teacher 1958-67. **ORGANIZATIONS:** Mem communications com Assn Tchr Educators; Assn Higher Edn; multicultural educ Com AACTE; Omega Psi Phi. **HONORS/ACHIEVEMENTS:** Author educ publs. **MILITARY SERVICE:** AUS 1945-46. **BUSINESS ADDRESS:** Dept of Educ, Morgan StateUniv, Baltimore, MD.

JAMES, RICK
Recording artist. **PERSONAL:** Born Feb 01, Buffalo, NY; son of James Johnson, Sr and Mable Johnson; children: 2 children. **CAREER:** Music, writing, arranging, producing, singing, movie producer. **ORGANIZATIONS:** Bd of directors, Buffalo Philharmonic Orchestra, 1987-. **HONORS/ACHIEVEMENTS:** 5 Gold Albums; 4 platinum albums; 1 triple platinum album; Juke Box Awds Top Male Artist of the Yr; R&B Awds Top Soul Artist, Intl Disco Awds Most Promising Artist, Black Coll Artist of the Year 1979; Most Promising Male Artist, NAACP Performance Awd, Authors & Publ Awd Amer Soc of Composers 1980; Grammy Awds Best Rock Vocal Performance Male Nominee "Super Freak", Best R&B Vocal Performance Male Nominee "St Songs" NARM Awd Best Selling R&B Album by a Male Artist "St Songs"; Amer Music Awds Winner Best Soul Album "St Songs", Best Soul Single Nominee "Super Freak", Best Soul Artist Nominee Male; Record World Mag #1 Crossover Male Artist Black Singles & Albums, #1 Male Vocalist Albums Black; Billboard Mag #1 R& B Singles Producer, Album, Artist; 25 Ampex Golden Reel Awds for producing The Mary Jame Girls album and Rick James "Reflections" album; Eddie Murphys "Party all the Time" 4 ampex awards; soundtrack for the movie "Colors," "Everywhere I Go" 5 ampex awards; ASCAP Award The Amer Society of Composers, authors & Publishers 1987 most played song "Party All the Time" pop Award. **BUSINESS ADDRESS:** Mary Jane Productions, 1289 Jewett Holmwood Rd, Orchard Park, NY 14127.

JAMES, ROBERT D.
Educational administrator. **PERSONAL:** Born Aug 24, 1950, New Rochelle, NY; son of Everett Lanier James and Shirley Arleen Clark; married Cheryl D Holley; children: Angela

Laura, Anika Laren, Jamaal Malik. **EDUCATION:** SUNY at Brockport, BS 1972, MS 1975; SUNY at Albany EdD in progress. **CAREER:** Baden St Settlement Cnslng Ctr, asst dir 1973-74; SUNY at Brockport, cnslr 1974-77; Educ Oppor Pgm, dir 1977-79; EOC, SUNY Brockport, exec dir 1979-87; SUNY Office of Spec Programs, acting senior assoc 1987; SUNY Office of Special Programs, sr dir; Public Employment Relations Bd, Albany, NY mediator/fact finder 1985-. **ORGANIZATIONS:** Consult Ctr for Urban Ethnic Affairs 1975-77; consultUniv of Roch Court Mntl Hlth Team 1974-79; mediator/fact finder NYS Pub Employment Rel Bd 1985-; bd mem YMCA of Rochester 1979-85; bd mem Urban League of Rochester 1984-88; bd mem Catholic Youth Organ 1979-87; bd mem Legal Aid Society 1984-86; bd mem Am Diabetes Asso 1984-86; Singer Lakes Occ ED Ctr, mem bd of governors. **HONORS/ACHIEVEMENTS:** Outstanding Alumni Award; Outstanding Service Award, SUNY Coll at Brockport 1988; Arthur A. Schomburg Distinguished Service Award/Assn for Equality & Excellence in Educ, Inc. 1989. **BUSINESS ADDRESS:** Sr Dir, Office of Special Programs, State Univ of New York, SUNY Plaza, #N-102, Albany, NY 12246.

JAMES, ROBERT EARL
Business executive. **PERSONAL:** Born Nov 21, 1946, Hattiesburg, MS; son of Mr and Mrs Jimmie James, Sr; married Shirley B; children: Robert III, Anne, Rachelle. **EDUCATION:** Morris Brown Coll, BA 1964-68; Harvard Univ, MBA 1968-70. **CAREER:** Armco Steel Corp Middletown, OH, accounting trainee 1967; C & S Natl Bank Atlanta, GA, mgmt trainee 1969; Savannah Tribune Savannah, GA, publisher; Carver State Bank Savannah, GA, pres. **ORGANIZATIONS:** Gen partner Atlantic Investors; dir Pilgrim Health & Life Ins Co; trustee mem Morris Brown Coll; mem White House Conf on Small Business; dir GA Telecommunications Commn. **HONORS/ACHIEVEMENTS:** Intl Bus Fellows 1983. **BUSINESS ADDRESS:** President, Carver State Bank, 701 W Broad St, Savannah, GA 31498.

JAMES, RONALD J.
Attorney. **PERSONAL:** Born Apr 08, 1937, Centerville, IA; son of Raymond B James and Jennie M Smith James; married Patraicia O'Donnell; children: Catlin, Kelly, Shannon, Ronald Jr, Kevin. **EDUCATION:** Univ of MO, AB 1959; AmUniv Wash Coll of Law, JD 1966; So IL U, MA 1972. **CAREER:** EEO Commn, regional att 1972-75; Waterloo IA Commn on Human Rights, exec dir 1967; Waterloo IA, asst Co atty 1967-69; OEO, spl asst to dir 1970-71; spl atty to con to pres 1971-72; Congressman James Bromwell, staff asst 1963-64; US Dept of Labor, admin wage & hour div 1975-77; Squire Sanders & Dempsey, partner 1977-. **ORGANIZATIONS:** Mem ABA; NBA; IA Bar Assn; Supreme Court Bar; mem Urban League; Ohio Bar Assn. **HONORS/ACHIEVEMENTS:** Nat speech honorary Delta Sigma Rho. **MILITARY SERVICE:** AUS 1st lt 1960-63; USAR capt. **BUSINESS ADDRESS:** Partner, Squire, Sanders & Dempsey, 1800 Huntington Bldg, Cleveland, OH 44115.

JAMES, SIDNEY J.
Educational officer. **PERSONAL:** Born Jun 25, 1935, Columbia, MS; married Margie Pope; children: Kenja. **EDUCATION:** Alcorn State Univ, BS Health & Phys Educ 1958; Univ of So MS, MS Coll Counseling 1972, Specialist's Ed Admin 1981; Marquette Univ, Certificate Management Training Inst 1980. **CAREER:** Prentiss Normal & Indus Inst, coach & teacher 1960-67, dean of students 1967-73, dir of special progs 1973-81, pres 1981-. **ORGANIZATIONS:** Past pres MS Assn Ed Oppor Prog Personnel 1979; mem bd of dir Amer Red Cross Marion Co 1975-80; mem of exec bd Southeastern Assoc Ed Oppor Prog Personnel 1977-81; mem Adv Bd First Federal Savings & Loan 1984; Phi Delta Kappa 1980-; vice pres City Planning Comm Columbia MS 1981-; mem MS State Job Training Coordinating Council 1983-; mem Shriner 33 Mason. **HONORS/ACHIEVEMENTS:** Coach of the Year Southern Intercollegiate Congress Co 1965; Personalities of the South Amer Biographical Inst 1975-76; Outstanding Service Awd SAEOPP 1981; Disting Service Awd Phi Delta Kappa 1983. **MILITARY SERVICE:** AUS specialist E4 2 yrs. **HOME ADDRESS:** 1200 Maxwell St, Columbia, MS 39429.

JAMES, THOMAS LESLIE
Dentist. **PERSONAL:** Born Nov 07, 1927, Pensacola; married Dora Lorene Adams. **EDUCATION:** Morehouse Coll; Fisk U; Meharry Med Coll, DDS 1951. **CAREER:** Pvt Pract, dentistry; Family Health Cntr HEW; Univ Miami Sch Medicine, asst prof oral biology 1968-72; N Dade Med Cntr & Hosp N Shore Hosp, staff. **ORGANIZATIONS:** Mem Am Nat FL & Dade Co Dental Socs; Dade Co Acad Med; Amvets; Elks; Kappa Alpha Psi. **MILITARY SERVICE:** USN (1st black reg comm offcr) 1951-58; USNR 1958-68.

JAMES, TROY LEE
Legislator. **PERSONAL:** Born in Texarkana, TX; married Betty; children: 1 daughter. **EDUCATION:** Fenn Coll, attnd; Bethany Coll; Western Reserve Coll. **CAREER:** 12th Dist Coyahoga Co OH Legislature, state rep. **ORGANIZATIONS:** Bd mem Margie Homes for Mentally Retarded; Eliza Bryant Home for Aged; dem exec com bd of OH State Legislators Soc; chmn Com on Aging; pres 5th WardDem Club; chmn Economic Develop Comm; mem NCSL Comm Economic Develop. **MILITARY SERVICE:** AUS 1943-46. **BUSINESS ADDRESS:** State Representative, State House, Columbus, OH 43215.

JAMES, WILLIAM
Educator. **PERSONAL:** Born May 10, 1945, Augusta, GA; son of Hinton James and Harriett James; married Maria Dawson; children: Kevyn, William. **EDUCATION:** Morehouse Coll, BA 1967; Howard U, JD 1972; Alanta U, MSLS 1973. **CAREER:** Federal City Coll, lectr 1972; Fed Trade Comm, law clerk, 1972; Atlanta Univ, grad asst 1972-73; Univ of TN, asst prof & asst librarian 1973-77; Univ of KY, asst prof of law/law librarian; assoc prof of law/law librarian Univ of KY 1977-82; prof of law/law lib 1982-88; Villanova Univ, prof of law/dir of law library, 1988-. **ORGANIZATIONS:** AALL Financial Advisory Comm 1989-92. **MILITARY SERVICE:** AUS e-5 1969-71. **BUSINESS ADDRESS:** Dir of the Law Library, Villanova Univ, School of Law, Villanova, PA 19085.

JAMES, WILLIAM M.
Religious adminstrator. **PERSONAL:** Born Jun 04, 1916, Meadville, MS; son of Warren James and Rosa Ann James; married Juanita; children: Edward. **EDUCATION:** Mt Beulah Coll, AA; Butler U, BS, B of Sacred Lit; Drew U, BD MA;Univ of Chgo, Drew Univ, grad courses. **CAREER:** Multi Ethnic Ctr for Ministry of the Northeastern Jurisdiction of the United Methodist Church, dir; Metro Comm United Methodist Ch NY, sr minister; Trinity United Meth Ch Bronx, formerly pastor; ordained deacon 1938; elder 1940; Drew Univ, dir. **ORGANIZATIONS:** Mem officer Natl Bd Of Educ of Methodist Church; organizer founder Ministerial Interfaith Assn which administers Halem Coll Assist Prog; Harlem Interfaith Harlem Counseling Assn; Found of Harlem; former pres New York City Br NAACP; chmn of bd Harlem Urban Develop Coop. **BUSINESS ADDRESS:** Dir, Drew University, Multi Ethnic Center, Madison, NJ 07940.

JAMISON, JUDITH
Dancer. **PERSONAL:** Born May 10, 1944, Philadelphia, PA. **EDUCATION:** Studied dance with private tecahers Marion Cuyjet, Nadia Chilkovsky, Joan Kerr, 1949-61; attended Fisk Univ; Philadelphia Dance Acad; Judimar Sch of The Dance. **CAREER:** Alvin Ailey Am Dance Theater, New York NY, lead dancer, 1965-80; dancer/ choreographer, 1980-; Amer Ballet Theatre/San Francisco Ballet/Dallas Ballet, guest appearances; "Joseph's Legend" Vienna Opera/"Le Spectre de la Rose" Brussels, leading roles; starred in Broadway show Sophisticated Ladies, 1980. **ORGANIZATIONS:** Former mem Am Ballet Theater; Harkness Ballet; bd mem Nat Council of the Arts; participated Harper Festival Chicago 1965; participated Festival of Negro Arts Dakar Senegal 1966; partic Edingburgh Festival 1968. **HONORS/ACHIEVEMENTS:** Dance Magazine annual citation 1972; key to City of New York, 1976; Distinguished Service Award, Harvard Univ, 1982; Distinguished Service Award, Mayor of New York City, 1982. **BUSINESS ADDRESS:** Alvin Ailey Am Dance Theater, 1515 Broadway, 8th Floor, New York, NY 10036. *

JAMISON, LAFAYETTE
Business executive. **PERSONAL:** Born Oct 08, 1926, Cleveland, OH; son of Lafayette Jamison, Sr and Estelle Jamison; married Elaine; children: Lynn, Dirk. **EDUCATION:** Virginia Union Univ, BA 1952; John Carroll Univ, grad work. **CAREER:** Joseph Schlitz Brewing Co, present mgr, YMCA, Salvation Army; teacher, asst prin; VA Union U, dean of students; Urban League, dir; St Dept Hertz, consultant; HUD; Bureau of Mint. **ORGANIZATIONS:** Pres Allentown Boys Club 1968-73; So MD Basketball Officials 1969-74; Toastmasters Inc; Khayyam Man of Yr; Citation Boys Clubs of Am; Big Bros. **HONORS/ACHIEVEMENTS:** Bask-Aerobics, designed for and dedicated to female athletes. **MILITARY SERVICE:** USAF corpl WW II. **BUSINESS ADDRESS:** President, Et Al Ltd, PO Box 23883, Milwaukee, WI 53223.

JAMISON, LEILA DUNCAN
Operations assistant. **PERSONAL:** Born Nov 06, 1932, Denmark, SC; divorced. **EDUCATION:** Voorhees Jr Coll, Diploma 1953; SC State Coll, BS 1955; AmUniv Washington DC, MPA 1979. **CAREER:** Voorhees Coll, assoc dir devel alumni affairs & public relations; business dept instructor 1966-77, alumni affairs sec 1967-70, alumni affairs 1970-72; Voorhees Coll, Denmark SC 1973-75; Howard Univ, operations asst Office of Vice Pres for Devel & Univ Relations; Special Economics Asst Program Office of Governor Div of Economic Devel & Transportation, program info coordinator; Office of the Gov Div of Rural Improvement, community consultant. **ORGANIZATIONS:** Mem Am Assn Univ Women; Voorhees Coll Alumni Assn; NAACP; Denmark Comm Rel Com-crowned Miss Alumni VCNAA 1961-62; Delta Sigma Theta. **HONORS/ACHIEVEMENTS:** Alumni Achievement Award 1963; Outstanding Young Woman Am 1968; Alumni Serv Award 1974; Certificate Appreciation NAC of UNCF 1975; Comm Ldrs & Noteworthy Ams 1975-76; rec'd Plaque for Unselfish & Outst Serv Voorhees Coll Nat Alumni Assn 1976; rec'd Faculty Staff Serv Award for 15 Yrs Serv & Voorhees 1976.

JANGDHARRIE, WYCLIFFE K.
Educator, pastor, business executive. **PERSONAL:** Born Dec 12, 1926; married Jewell; children: Rosalyn, Wycliffe II, Carolyn. **EDUCATION:** Oakwood Coll Huntsville, BA 1950; Amer Bapt Theol Sem Nashville, BRE 1955; Temple Univ Tchr Coll Philadelphia & Columbia Univ Tchr Coll NY, post grad; Norfolk State Coll, MA 1978; Jameson Bible Institute, Hon DD. **CAREER:** Trinidad, evang 1950-51; Louis Spilman & Co London England, docket clk 1952-53; Washington Hill Conv Home, business mgr 1954-; School Dist of Philadelphia, tchr 1959-65; Neighborhood Youth Corps, coord 1965-66; Philadelphia School Dist, teacher 1966-68; City of Philadelphia, asst to city managing dir. **ORGANIZATIONS:** Mem pub relat com 1964 Philadelphia Assn Nursing & Convlesc Homes; mem NW Comm Ambulance Corps; pres DE Valley Assn Family Serv 1968; mem bd Counc Black Clergy; So Christ Leadership Conf; State Ad Hoc Com on Nursing & convlsc Homes; mem Gr Philadelphia C of C; NAACP vice pres N Philadelphia 1968-70; pres W Philadelphia 1971-; chmn Prison Ref Com & mem State Bd; vice chmn Health & Welfare Counc W Phila; sec Parkside YMCA; mem Bldg Task Force; mem Fin Com Reg YMCA; served numerous other civic & professional groups; participation in panel discussions lectrs media appearances natl & intl confs & convs; pres/pastor The Reformed Seventh Day Adventist Church; pres Philadelphia Chap of the Natl Council for Church and Social Action. **HONORS/ACHIEVEMENTS:** Black Civic Awd Progress Plaze; Four Chaplains Leg Hon Awd 1964; Fellow of Amer Coll of Nursing Home Adminstrs 1970. **BUSINESS ADDRESS:** Asst to City Mng Dir, City of Philadelphia, 11 FL City Hall Annex, Philadelphia, PA 19107.

JARMON, JAMES HENRY, JR.
Educational admin. **PERSONAL:** Born Jan 09, 1942, Sheffield, AL; son of Mr and Mrs James Jarmon, Sr; married Lillie Watson; children: Elisa Ann, Monica Yvette, James Henry III. **EDUCATION:** Alabama State University, BS 1965; Troy State University, MS 1977. **CAREER:** DA Smith High School, teacher 1965-70; Mixon Elementary School, teacher 1970-77; DA Smith Jr High School, asst principal 1977-80; Flowers Elementary School, principal 1980-81; DA Smith Middle School, principal 1981-. **ORGANIZATIONS:** Member Alpha Phi Alpha 1963-; member OEA AEA NEA 1965-; member ACSAS 1977-; chairman Recreation Board City of Ozark 1978-; city councilman City of Ozark 1980-;member Natl Middle School Assn 1980-; bd of directors RSVP 1981-; bd of directors Parents Anonymous 1983-. **HONORS/ACHIEVEMENTS:** Appreciation award Ozark Voters League, President 1979; Man of the Year Ozark Voters League 1980; appreciation award Carroll High School Ozark 1983; member PhiDelta Kappa 1977-. **HOME ADDRESS:** 201 Don Ave, Ozark, AL 36360. **BUSINESS ADDRESS:** Principal, DA Smith Middle School, 159 Enterprise Rd, Ozark, AL 36360.

JARREAU, AL
Recording artist. **PERSONAL:** Born Mar 12, 1940, Milwaukee, WI. **EDUCATION:** Ripon Coll, BS Psychology 1962; Univ IA, MS Psychology 1964. **CAREER:** Jazz singer & writer; records on Warner Bros Label "We Got By" 1975, "Glow" 1976, "Look to the Rainbow" 1977; "All Fly Home" 1978, "This Time" 1980, "BreakingAway" 1981; solo recording

artist 1975-. **HONORS/ACHIEVEMENTS:** German Grammy Awd for Best New Intl Pop Vocalist; Number One Jazz Vocalist for Cashbox 1976; Italian Music Critics Awd Best Fgn Vocalist 1977; winner Readers' Poll Down Beat Mag 1977-78-79; Grammy Best Jazz Vocalist 1978-79. **BUSINESS ADDRESS:** c/o William Morris Agency, 1350 Avenue of the Americas, New York, NY 10019.

JARRETT, HOBART SIDNEY
Educator. **PERSONAL:** Born Nov 01, 1915, Arlington, TX; son of Wilson Hendrix Jarrett and Jo Pearl Nicholson Jarrett; married Gladys Janet Wynne, Aug 20, 1939. **EDUCATION:** Wiley Coll, BA 1936; Syracuse Univ, MA 1937; Harvard Univ, Grad Study 1939-41; Suracuse Univ, PhD 1953. **CAREER:** Langston Univ, instr, assoc prof, chmn of modern language dept, prof and dean of personnel 1937-49; Bennett Coll, prof and chmn humanities div 1949-61; Brooklyn Coll CUNY, prof English 1961-, prof PhD, prof emeritus 1985-. **ORGANIZATIONS:** Pres Greensboro NC Citizens Assoc 1959-61; bd of dir Coll Lang Assoc, Coll Engl Assoc; pres greater NY Reg Coll Engl Assoc; life mem MLA; mem MHRA-Shakespeare Soc of Amer; chmn Coll Sect Natl Council of Teachers of Eng 4 yrs; bd mem RR Moton Foundation 1984; life mem NAACP, UNCF Grand Boule Historian Sigma Pi Phi Fraternity 1987. **HONORS/ACHIEVEMENTS:** Fellowship General Education Board Rockefeller Foundation 1939; 1st black scholar to receive rank of prof of eng Brooklyn Coll 1965; Outstanding Teacher Awd CUNY 1973; Medal for Excellence in Teaching Brooklyn Coll 1973; First CUNY professor to conduct live seminar cable tv 1973; Award for Excellent Alumnus New York City Chap UNCF 1973; Man of the Year Alpha Phi Alpha 1978; ed book rev dept "Boule Journal" Sigma Pi Phi Frat; Distinguished Alumni Awd Natl Assn for Equal Opportunity in Higher Educ 1987; commencement address Wiley Coll 1983 and 1987; Hon degree Wiley Coll 1987; recipient of numerous awds for scholarship & civic accomplishments; Published numerous articles & reviews in learned jrnls. **HOME ADDRESS:** 315 W 70th St, Apt 15 J, New York, NY 10023.

JARRETT, THOMAS D.
Educator. **PERSONAL:** Born Aug 30, 1912; married Annabelle M Gunter; children: Paula Lynn. **EDUCATION:** Knoxville Coll, AB 1933; Fisk Univ, AM 1937; Univ of Chicago, PhD 1947. **CAREER:** Centrl High School, Paris TN, instr 1933-37; Knoxville Coll, asst prof English 1937-40; Louisville Muni Coll, assoc prof English 1941-43; Atlanta Univ, asst prof 1947-50, assoc prof 1950-55, prof English 1955-67, chmn dept of English 1957-67, acting dean school of arts & sci 1957-60, dean grad school of arts & sci 1960-67, chmn interim admin comm 1967-68, acting pres 1968, retired pres 1968-77; US Dept of State, consultant 1977-78. **ORGANIZATIONS:** Pres Natl Assn of Coll Deans & Registrars 1968-69; mem Commn on English Natl Council of Teachers of English 1968; chmn Natl Council of Teachers of English Nominating Comm 1962; chmn Res Comm Natl Council of Teachers of English 1951; book review poetry editor, Phylon, Atlanta Univ Journal of Race & Culture 1948-67; Comm on Ways & Means of Working With Public Natl Council of Teachers of English 1957-58; mem various other professional orgns; consultant Dept HEW 1966; appointed to adv comm for Natl Defense Language Devel Prog 1966-68; appointed to Georgia Sci & Tech Commn 1969; mem Natl Council of Teachers of English; Coll Language Assn; Assn of Amer Univ Professors; Conf of Deans of So Grad Schools; Natl Assn of Coll Deans & Registrars; Council of Grad Schools in US. **HONORS/ACHIEVEMENTS:** Gen Educ Bd Fellow 1939-40; Carnegie Grant for Rsch 1951-52; dir of Amer Scholars 1951; numerous publications to credit.

JARRETT, VERNON D.
Journalist. **PERSONAL:** Born Jun 19, 1921, Saulsbury, TN; married Fernetta; children: William, Thomas. **EDUCATION:** Knoxville Coll, BA; Northwestern Univ, studied journalism; Univ of Kansas City, studied TV writing & producing; Univ of Chicago, urban sociology. **CAREER:** Chicago Tribune Newspaper, editorial page columnist, Tribune column appears 3 times weekly; radio/TV producer; moderator; "Black on Black," weekly show interviews with outstanding Black people; WJPC, radio show "The Vernon Jarrett Report.". **ORGANIZATIONS:** Pres Nat Assn of Black Journalists 1977-79; mem bd govs Chicago Chap Nat Acad of TV Arts & Sci; chmn bd Dusable Mus of African-am Hist in Chgo; mem Sigma Delta Chi; vis assoc prof of history; Northwestern U; tchrTV Course Am History, City Coll of Chgo. **HONORS/ACHIEVEMENTS:** Nominated for Pulitzer Prize in journalism 1972-73; won numerous awards for his reporting. **BUSINESS ADDRESS:** Chicago Tribune, 435 N Michigan Ave, Chicago, IL 60611.

JASON, HENRY THOMAS
Retired police executive. **PERSONAL:** Born Aug 22, 1921, Detroit, MI; son of William Jason and Daisey Jason; married Lillian; children: Mark Owens Jason. **EDUCATION:** Wayne State U, Univ of MI; Henry Ford Comm Coll; Univ of MI. **CAREER:** Detroit Police Dept, retired dist commander 1947-74; City of Inkster, retired chief of police 1974-80. **ORGANIZATIONS:** Life mem NAACP; Detroit Police Lt & Sgts Assn; SE MI Assn of Chiefs of Police; Wayne Co Assn Chiefs of Police; mem Intl Assn Chiefs of Police IACP; Guardians MI Asso Black Law Enforcement Exec NOBLE; founding chmn Fabulous Floridians Social Club 1981; Palm Beach Paralyzed Vets Assn of Florida. **HONORS/ACHIEVEMENTS:** Relations awd Cotillion Club Police Community 1966; Military Excellence Awd Detroit Police 1973. **MILITARY SERVICE:** USAF 1942-46. **HOME ADDRESS:** 1064 Summerwood Circle, West Palm Beach, FL 33414.

JASON, HOWARD M.
Educator. **PERSONAL:** Born Feb 25, 1906, Santurce, PR; married Sadie Mae Davis. **EDUCATION:** Lincoln U, AB 1929; Columbia U, MA 1933; Universidad Interamericana Mixico, PhD 1962. **CAREER:** W KY Industrial Coll Paducah, instructor French & Biology 1933-38; KY State Coll Frankfort, asst prof of Spanish & English 1938-41; US Office of Censorship Miami & NYC, translator 1942-43; KY State Coll, asst prof 1946-47, 1949-57; Savannah State Coll, assoc prof of Spanish, prof of Spanish & dept head of modern languages 1963-73, chmn Div of Humanities; Emeritus, prof of Spanish 1973. **ORGANIZATIONS:** Mem Am Assn of Tchrs of Spanish & Portuguese; Coll Language Assn; Am Assn of Univ Prof; Alpha Phi Alpha Frat mem; Assn for the Study of Afro-am Life & His Inc; mem First Congregational Ch Savannah Ga; author of several pub. **MILITARY SERVICE:** AUS 1943-46.

JASON, JEANNE See WRIGHT, JEANNE JASON

JASPER, LAWRENCE E.
Business executive. **PERSONAL:** Born Oct 25, 1946, Philadelphia; married Diana Lundy; children: Laurette, Dawn. **EDUCATION:** ICA; LUTC. **CAREER:** Pilgrim Life Ins Co, 1st asst to vice pres 1974, vp; Debit Agt, 1968-69; Supr 1969-71; Serv Asst Spectrum Arena, supr 1971-74. **ORGANIZATIONS:** NAACP; Young Great Soc; 19 St Bapt Ch Youth Dept; Interest in Bus Training of Black & Youth. **HONORS/ACHIEVEMENTS:** Man of Year Pilgrim Life Ins 1970, 1972; 1st Black in mgmt Pilgrim Life; 1st man to rec Man of Year Award twice; youngest man & only black on bd of dir atPilgrim Life. **MILITARY SERVICE:** Sgt E-5 drill instr 1968. **BUSINESS ADDRESS:** Vice President, Pilgrim Life Ins Co, 1835 Delmar Dr, Folcroft, PA.

JAY, JAMES M.
Educator. **PERSONAL:** Born Sep 12, 1927, Fitzgerald, GA; married Patsie Phelps; children: Mark E, Alicia D, Byron R. **EDUCATION:** Paine Coll, AB 1950; OH State U, MSc 1953, PhD 1956. **CAREER:** OH State U, post doc fellow 1956-57; Southern U, asst prof 1957-61; Wayne State U, prof 1961. **ORGANIZATIONS:** Owner Balamp Publishing Co 1971-; consult Gaines Foods Inc 1984-85; former pres Detroit Cncl for Political Edn; chmn Food Microbiology Div Am Soc for Microbiology 1983-84. **HONORS/ACHIEVEMENTS:** Probus Award Wayne StateUniv 1969; Dist Alumni Award Paine Coll 1969. **MILITARY SERVICE:** AUS sgt 1946-47. **BUSINESS ADDRESS:** Professor of Microbiology, Wayne State Univ, Detroit, MI 48202.

JAYCOX, MARY IRINE
Public relations executive. **PERSONAL:** Born Aug 19, 1939, Camphill, AL; daughter of Eddie B Knight and Betty Busby; married James Curtis Jaycox; children: James Jr, Sharon, Mary, Thomas. **EDUCATION:** Univ of Northern IA, BA 1984, MA 1986. **CAREER:** Har-lin Pre-School Erie PA, parent coord 1966-67; Sears Roebuck & Co, div mgr 1973-80; KBBG-FM Waterloo IA, talk show host 1981-84; Dubuque City of Festivals, promotions dir. **ORGANIZATIONS:** Freelance feature writer Waterloo Courier, Telegraph Herald Dubuque; housing analyst Comm Housing Resource Bd; YMCA mem & publicity comm Waterloo 1985-86; commissioner Cable Comm Teleprogramming. **HONORS/ACHIEVEMENTS:** Poetry in Inner Weather library magazine 1983; Best Commercial Script 1984, Best Short Script Univ of Northern IA 1984. **HOME ADDRESS:** 1661 Donovan Dr, Dubuque, IA 52001. **BUSINESS ADDRESS:** Public Information Coordinator, City of Dubuque, 13th & Central, Dubuque, IA 52001.

JAYE, MILES
Recording artist. **HONORS/ACHIEVEMENTS:** Performer of song "Let's Start Love Over," Top Priority Records. **BUSINESS ADDRESS:** c/o Island Records, 444 Madison Ave, New York, NY 10022. *

JAYNES, GERALD DAVID
Educator. **PERSONAL:** Born Jan 30, 1947, Streator, IL; married Ann Shepherd; children: Vechel, Hillary. **EDUCATION:** Univ of IL-Urbana, BA (High Honors) 1971, MA 1974, PhD 1976; Yale Univ, MA 1984. **CAREER:** Univ of Pennsylvania, asst prof economics 1975-77; Yale Univ, asst prof of economics 1977-81, assoc prof economics 1981-84, prof economics 1984-; study dir Comm on the Status of Black Amers/Natl Rsch Council 1985-. **ORGANIZATIONS:** Bd of economists Black Enterprise Magazine 1984-88. **HONORS/ACHIEVEMENTS:** Adjunct Fellow Joint Ctr for Political Studies 1982-; book "Branches Without Roots, Genesis of the Black Working Class," Oxford Univ Press 1986; "A Common Destiny: Blacks and Amer Society" ed with R. Williams Jr, Natl Academy of Sciences Press 1989. **MILITARY SERVICE:** AUS spl 5th class 3 yrs. **BUSINESS ADDRESS:** Professor of Economics, Yale University, Dept of Economics, New Haven, CT 06520.

JEANBAPTISTE, CARL S.
Physician. **PERSONAL:** Born Feb 15, 1930, Hinche, Haiti;married Jo Ellen Lugenbeel. **EDUCATION:** Univ Haiti, 1951;Univ Haiti Med Schl, 1957; Meml Sloan-kettering Cancer Ctr, surg res 1966-68; Harlem Hosp Ctr, post-grad Training 1960-66; Surgery, Brooklyn Cumberland Med Ctr, asso atdng 1968-77; Brookdale & Brooklyn Jewish Hosp, asst atdng surgery 1970-77; StUniv NY, clinical instr. **CAREER:** Physician. **ORGANIZATIONS:** Provident Clinical Soc of Brooklyn; Kings Co Med Soc; NY St Med Assn; Nat Med Assn. **HONORS/ACHIEVEMENTS:** Fellow Am Coll of Surgeons; diplomate Am Bd of Surgery; Brooklyn Surgical Soc Publ NY St Jour of Med 1972. **BUSINESS ADDRESS:** 361 Eastern Parkway, Brooklyn, NY 11216.

JEFFERIES, CHARLOTTE S.
Educator. **PERSONAL:** Born Mar 08, 1944, McKeesport, PA. **EDUCATION:** Howard U, BS 1966; Rollins Coll, postgrad 1967; Duquesne Univ Sch of Law, JD 1980. **CAREER:** Seminole Co FL, teacher 1966-67; OIC of Erie, dir of couns 1967-70; Urban Coalition of RI, health planner 1970-71; Student Serv OIC of RI, dir 1971-72; Career Develop Brown Univ, assoc dir 1973-77; Neighborhood Legal Serv McKeesport, legal intern 1978-79; Office of US Attorney Dept of Justice, law clerk 1979-80; Honorable Donald E Ziegler Judge US Dist Ct Western Dist of PA, law clerk 1980-81; Horty Springer & Mattern PC, assoc 1981-. **ORGANIZATIONS:** Mem Delta Sigma Theta Inc; mem Amer Natl PA and Allegheny Bar Assocs; mem Homer S Brown Law Assoc, Soc of Hospital Attorneys; city councilperson Cityof Duquesne; mem YWCA of McKeesport; mem NAACP, Howard Univ Alumni Club; 1st vice pres Steel Valley Planning Commn. **HONORS/ACHIEVEMENTS:** Who's Who Among Women of the World 1978; apptmt law clerk Office of US Attorney 1979; appellate moot court bd Duquesne Univ 1979-80; Outstanding Student of the Year Black Amer Law Student Assoc Duquesne Univ Chap 1980; Richard Allen Awd Outstanding Civic contributions 1980; chmn Merit Selection Panel US Magistrates Western Dist of PA 1987. **BUSINESS ADDRESS:** Attorney at Law, Horty Springer & Mattern PC, 4614 Fifth Ave, Pittsburgh, PA 15213.

JEFFERS, BEN L.
Government employee. **PERSONAL:** Born Jun 18, 1944, Lake City, FL; married Salomia Lawson. **EDUCATION:** MT State U; A&T U; McNeese State U. **CAREER:** LA Hlth & Human Rsrcs Admnstrn, dir Div Mgmt; LA Hlth & Human Resources Admnstr, dir; LA Commn on Human Rltns Rights & Rspnsblities, dir; Gov Edwin Edwards, cong Aide. **ORGANIZATIONS:** Chmn LA Coalition for Social Serv Program; state adv bd Comprehensive Hlth Planning; mem Dvlpmntl Disabilities Cncl; Nat Rehabltatn Assn; LA Rehab Assn; Am Soc for Training & Devel; Am Pub Welfare Assn; LA Hlth Assn mem Kiwanis Club of Lake Charles; Am Legion; Prince Hall Masons; past mem bd dir Advertising & Press Clubg of SW LA; past bd mem Foreman-reynaud Br YMCA; gen mgr Lake Charles Newsleader; former

Exec asst to Pub of Newsleader Newspapers in LA & MS; editor Pub of Lake Charles Times; mem State Manpower Planning Cncl; mem NAACP. **MILITARY SERVICE:** USMC sgt 1963-67. **BUSINESS ADDRESS:** PO Box 44215, Baton Rouge, LA 70804.

JEFFERS, CLIFTON R.
Attorney. **PERSONAL:** Born Feb 08, 1934, Roxboro, NC; son of Theron Jeffers and Clara Jeffers; married Mary R Lloyd; children: Kwame. **EDUCATION:** TN State Univ, AB (magna cum laude) 1956; Hastings Coll Law Univ CA, JD 1964. **CAREER:** State of CA, state deputy atty 1964-69; US Dept HUD, reg admin 1969-76; State of CA, chief asst state pub defender 1976-84; James & Jeffers, sr partner. **ORGANIZATIONS:** Mem Natl, CA, San Francisco Bar Assns; Charles Houston Bar Assn; bd of dir Bar Assn of SF 1984-; bd dirs Lawyers Club of San Francisco 1981-82; mem Amer Judicature Soc; pres SF NAACP 1966-69; bd dir Amer Civil Liberties Union of No CA 1969-73; SF Coun of Chs 1967-72; SF Econ Oppt Coun 1967-68; founding president William Hastie Lawyers Assn; bd dir Frederick Douglas Haynes Gardens; gen counsel 3rd Baptist Ch; bd dir CA Rural Legal Assistance Found; founding mem San Francisco Black Leadership Forum; trustee 3rd Bapt Ch; bd dir NAACP; bd of dir First District Appellate Project; co-founder, State Bar Standing Comm on Legal Services to Criminal Defendants; mem, CA Assn of Black Lawyers; co-founder and dir Third Baptist Gardens, Inc.; mem Afro-Amer Agenda Council. **HONORS/ACHIEVEMENTS:** Outstanding Pres Awd NAACP 1967, 1969; Amer Jurisprudence Awd; US Dept HUD Equal empl Oppt Awd; US Dept HUD Cert of Fair Housing Achvmt; NAACP Meritorious Serv Awds; guest lectr in Criminology Univ of CA Berkeley; Outstanding Performance Awd HUD; commendations San Francisco bd of supervisors; certificate of Honor San Francisco bd of supervisors; guest lecturer Stanford Univ Law School; guest lecturer, Univ of Southern CA School of Law. **MILITARY SERVICE:** USAF lt 1956-59. **BUSINESS ADDRESS:** James & Jeffers, 870 Market St, Ste 1208, San Francisco, CA 94102.

JEFFERS, GRADY ROMMEL
Business executive. **PERSONAL:** Born Jul 11, 1943, New York, NY; married Maryann P; children: Anna, Debbie, Michael, Alberta. **EDUCATION:** Bernard Baruch Coll; Manhattan Comm Coll, AA 1973. **CAREER:** Bankers Trust Co, asst vice pres commercial loan grp; Franklin Nat Bank, mgr 1969-74. **ORGANIZATIONS:** Mem 100 Black Men; Nat Bnkrs Assn mem Masons; Minority Bus & Devel; Nat Assn of Accountants. **HONORS/ACHIEVEMENTS:** Nom Whitehouse Flwshp. **MILITARY SERVICE:** USAF 1961-65. **BUSINESS ADDRESS:** One Bankers Truse Plaza, New York, NY 10015.

JEFFERS, JACK
Professor of music. **PERSONAL:** Born Dec 10, 1928; son of George W Jeffers and Rose Bosfield Daly; children: Laura, Lee. **EDUCATION:** Northeastern Univ, BS 1951; New York Univ Sch of Law, JD 1982. **CAREER:** State Univ of NY, prof of music. **ORGANIZATIONS:** Chmn 7 Arts Chap CORE 1964-66. **MILITARY SERVICE:** AUS sp3 1956-58. **HOME ADDRESS:** 119 Manhattan Ave, New York, NY 10025.

JEFFERSON, ALPHINE WADE
Educator. **PERSONAL:** Born Dec 31, 1950, Caroline County, VA; son of Horace Douglas Jefferson and Ellie Mae Jefferson. **EDUCATION:** Univ of Chicago, AB 1973; Duke Univ, MA 1975, PhD 1979. **CAREER:** Duke Univ, instructor oral history inst 1974, inst for policy scis rsch assoc and coord of oral interviews 1974, instructor in social science 1976; Northern IL Univ, instructor dept of history 1978-79, faculty assoc ctr for black studies 1978-85, asst prof dept of history 1979-85; Southern Methodist Univ, vstg asst prof of history/interim dir of african-amer studies 1984-85, dir of african-amer studies/asst prof history 1984-; assoc prof History College of Wooster OH 1989-. **ORGANIZATIONS:** Mem Amer Historical Assoc, Assoc for the Study of Afro-Amer Life and History, The Oral History Assoc, The Org of Amer Historians, The Natl Cncl for Black Studies, The IL Cncl for Black Studies, The DuSable Museum of African Amer History; reader Natl Endowment for the Humanities 1980-; consultant Dwight Correctional Ctr Humanities Project 1980-81; reader The Newberry Library Inst Chicago 1984-; reader Scott Foresman and Co 1984-; mem adv bd Intl Journal of Oral History 1986-; mem bd of dir African Heritage Cultural Arts League 1986-; mem bd of dir The International Theatrical Arts Society 1988-; mem bd of dir Huang International, Inc. 1988-; mem Dallas Independent School District, African-American Advisory Board 1988-. **HONORS/ACHIEVEMENTS:** Alexander White Scholar The Univ of Chicago 1972-73; Fellow Duke Univ Oral History Prog 1973-76; Andrew W Mellon Postdoctoral Fellowship Harvard 1982-83; Natl Endowment for the Humanities Fellowship for Independent Rsch 1982-83; The Promise of World Peace Awd The Amer Baha'i Dallas TX 1986; Most Popular Professor Awd Southern Methodist Univ Student Body 1986; first recipient The Margareta Deschner Teaching Awd Southern Methodist Univ Women's Studies Cncl 1986; Publications, chapters in books, articles, reviews and numerous papers presented at professional conferences. **BUSINESS ADDRESS:** Assoc Prof of History, The College of Wooster, Dept of History, Wooster, OH 44691.

JEFFERSON, ANDREW L., JR.
Judge. **PERSONAL:** Born Aug 19, 1934, Dallas, TX; married Mary Brown; children: Andy, Martin. **EDUCATION:** TX SU, BA 1956;Univ TX Sch Law, JD 1959. **CAREER:** Washington & Jefferson, Attys at Law, prtnr 1960-61; Bexar Co, asst-crim dist atty 1961-62; US Atty, Western Dist TX, chief asst 1962-67; Humble Oil & Ref Co, cnsl 1968-71; Domestic Rel #2, Harris Co, judge 1970-74; 208th Dist Ct, Harris Co, judge 1974-75; Jefferson Sherman & Mims, pvt Pract 1975-. **ORGANIZATIONS:** Mem, numerous offices, coms, Houston Bar Assn; mem, Houston Lwyrs Assn; mem, St Bar TX; mem, Am Bar Assn; mem, Fed, Nat Bar Assns; Alpha Phi Alpha Frat, Inc; Phi Alpha Delta Legal Frat, Tom Greener Chpt; NAACP; Pilgrim Cong United Ch Christ; Dwntwn Rotary Clb, Houston; TX Brkfst Clb; bd dirs,pres, Houston Cncl on Hum rel 1974-75; Houston Area Urban League; treas, 1st vp, Houston Legal Found 1973-74; Houston Bus Growth Corp; Gov's Drug Abuse Cncl; bd mgrs, YMCA S Cntrl Br; Navigation Bk. **HONORS/ACHIEVEMENTS:** Numerous guest spkr engagmnts; Nat Torch Liberty Award, Anti-Defamation League 1974; Forward Times Comm Serv Award 1975; Charles A George Comm Serv Award1975; Nat Comm Serv Award, League United Latin Am Citizens 1975; Comm Serv Award, LaRaza 1974. **MILITARY SERVICE:** AUS res capt. **BUSINESS ADDRESS:** Senior Partner, Jefferson,Mims, Plummer & Rice, Attorneys at Law, 2100 Travis, Houston, TX 77002.

JEFFERSON, ARTHUR
Educational administrator. **PERSONAL:** Born Dec 01, 1938, Alabama; married Marion Martin; children: Mark, Michael. **EDUCATION:** Wayne State Univ, BS 1960, MA Pol Sci 1963, EdD 1973. **CAREER:** Detroit Public Schools, asst regional supt 1970-71, regional supt 1971-75, interim general supt 1975, general supt 1975-. **ORGANIZATIONS:** Mem Natl Polit Sci Hon Soc Pi Sigma Alpha; mem Natl & MI Councils Soc Studies; mem Assn for Supervision and Curr Devel; mem Amer/MI Assn of Sch Adminstr; mem Council for Basic Educ; mem Met Detroit Soc of Black Educ Adminstr; mem Natl Alliance of Black Sch Educators; mem Natl Review Panel on Study of Sch Desegregation; mem various other affiliations; bd of trustees Wayne State Univ Alumni Assn 1968-71; bd of gov Wayne State Univ Educ Alumni Assn 1968-71; bd of gov Wayne State Univ Educ Alumni Assn 1968-71 1979-82; mem Amer Civil Lib Union, NAACP; bd of dir Council of Great City Sch;bd of trustees Detroit Econ Growth Corp; bd dir Detroit Educ TV Found; bd of adv Detroit Pre-Employment Training Ctr; bd dir Detroit Tchrs Credit Union; mem Econ Club of Detroit; bd of dir United Found; mem Natl PTA Urban Adv Task Force; mem various other affiliations. **BUSINESS ADDRESS:** General Superintendent, Detroit Public Schs, 5057 Woodward Ave, Detroit, MI 48202.

JEFFERSON, AUSTIN, JR.
Clergyman. **PERSONAL:** Born in Aiken, SC; married Evelyn Griffin; children: Leonard A, Harry P, Evelyn L, Gene A. **EDUCATION:** Temple Sch of Theol, grad 1953; Moody Bible Inst, Attend; New Era Sem, Attend; E Sem, Attend; Universal Bible Inst, M, Bib Study 1974. **ORGANIZATIONS:** Mem, Bd of Fgn Miss; chmn, Bd St Home MS; Nat Bapt Conv; mem, Met Chris Coun, Phil; mem, Adv Bd, E Sem; vp, New Engl MS Conv 1971; mem, Past Conf, Phila, Vic; mem, Even Conf.

JEFFERSON, CLIFTON
Mayor. **PERSONAL:** Born Sep 10, 1927, Lynchburg, SC; married Gwendolyn; children: Carolyn, Chrishinda, Lamont, Latisha Lenora. **EDUCATION:** SC St Coll, BS 1946; Attended, Univ MD 1954; SC St Coll, MA 1968. **CAREER:** Fleming School, science teacher 1955-57; Mt Pleasant HS, asst prin 1957-77; Bishopville Middle School, prin; Lynchburg SC, mayor 1975-77, presently; Jefferson Funeral Home, owner. **ORGANIZATIONS:** Chmn admin bd Warren Chapel United Meth Sch; del SC Dem Conv; SC Morticians Assn; life mem NAACP; life mem Kappa Alpha Psi; United Meth Ch; Black Mayors of SC; NEA; SCEA; LCEA; SC Mun Assn. **HONORS/ACHIEVEMENTS:** Natl Funeral Dir & Embalmer Assn Man of Yr SC Mortician Assn 1976; Achievement Awd Kappa Alpha Psi 1977; Dedicated Serv Awd Mt Pleasant HS 1977. **BUSINESS ADDRESS:** Mayor, Jefferson Funeral Home, Town Hall, Lynchburg, SC 29080.

JEFFERSON, FREDRICK CARL, JR.
Educational administrator. **PERSONAL:** Born Dec 30, 1934, New Orleans, LA; married June Greene; children: Crystal, Frederick, Christian. **EDUCATION:** Hunter Coll NY, BS Music 1957, MA Music 1959, MA Guidance 1967; Univ of MA Amhurst, EdD 1981. **CAREER:** SUNY at Albany, prog assoc 1971-73; Univ of Rochester, dir educ oppor prog 1973-76, dir of minority student affairs & assoc dean of students 1976-85, asst to the pres 1985-. **ORGANIZATIONS:** Mem Action for a Better Comm 1976-, United Way 1978-; vice chmn bd of Dirs PRIS2M 1978-84; trainer Natl Training Labs 1978-; consultant New Perspectives Inc 1979-; mem William Warfield Scholarship Fund 1984-; mem bd of dirs Primary Mental Health Project 1985-; mem Austin Steward Professional Soc 1985-; mem Roundtable on Educ Change 1987-; mem Urban League of Rochester; asst prof Grad Sch of Educ & Human Develop at Univ of Rochester. **HONORS/ACHIEVEMENTS:** Volunteer Serv Awds United Way 1978-86; ABC Serv Awd Action for a Better Comm 1979-86; PRIS2M 1983; Hispanic Leadership Awd 1985; publication "Creating a Multicultural Perspective" Assoc of Coll Unions Intl Bulletin 1986. **BUSINESS ADDRESS:** Assistant to the President, University of Rochester, Administration 103, Rochester, NY 14627.

JEFFERSON, GARY SCOTT
Airline company executive. **PERSONAL:** Born Nov 04, 1945, Pittsburgh, PA; son of Willard M Jefferson; married Beverly J Allen, Dec 30, 1967; children: Gary S, Kelly J. **EDUCATION:** Indiana Univ of Pennsylvania, Indiana PA, BA, 1967. **BUSINESS ADDRESS:** Vice President-Northeast Region, United Airlines, PO Box 66100, Chicago, IL 60010.

JEFFERSON, HILDA HUTCHINSON
Elected government official, educator. **PERSONAL:** Born Jun 19, 1920, Charleston, SC; married James L Jefferson Jr; children: Marjorie, Leon, Charles, Herman, Edward, Jerome. **EDUCATION:** Avery Normal Inst, Cert 1940; Tuskegee Inst, BS Home Econ 1944; Allen Univ, Advance Studies 1954; SC State Coll, Advance Studies 1955. **CAREER:** Stark Gen Hosp, asst dietician 1944-45; 6 Mile Jr HS, sci teacher 1945-46; Macedonia HS, home econ teacher 1946-47; Avery HS, dietician 1948-50; Baptist Hill HS, home econ teacher 1950-53; Lincoln HS, sci teacher 1955-58; Wallace HS, home econ teacher 1958-69; St Andrews Parish HS, home econ teacher 1969-82; Charleston SC, councilmember 1975-. **ORGANIZATIONS:** Mrm New Israel RE Church 1920-, NAACP 1950-, Charleston Cty Democratic Women 1976, Charlestons Art & History Comm 1976-, Natl League of Cities 1976-; chmn Traffic & Transp Comm 1980-; mem Charleston Area Comm Relations Comm 1980, SC Governors Comm on Hwy Safety 1980; mdm bd Carolina Art Assoc 1980, Charleston Museum 1980-, Trident United Way 1982-; mem Council of Governments 1983-; chmn Black Portrait Study Comm 1984-85; pres Gamma Zeta Chap Zeta Phi Beta 1984-86; sec Charleston Cty Municipal Assoc 1985-; porgy & bess adv comm Catfish Row Co Inc 1985-; adv council Charleston Area Sr Citizens Serv 1985-. **HONORS/ACHIEVEMENTS:** Outstanding Contrib & Meritorious Serv as a Volunteer to the Community Charleston Fed of Womens & Girls Clubs 1972; Outstanding Serv & Dedication in the Fields of Ed 1976, Politics 1976, Serv 1979,84; 1st Black Woman City of Charleston selected Mayor Pro Tem 1976,84; Royal Light Awd Woman of the Year 1976; 1st Black Woman Home Econ of the Year for Charleston Cty & SC 1976; Recognized by Gamma Xi Omega Chap of Alpha Kappa Alpha 1977, Phi Beta Sigma, Omega Psi Phi; Contrib to Women Awd YWCA 1980; Safety Recognition of Dedicated & Outstanding Serv to the Citizens of SC-SC Governors Comm on Hwy 1982; Outstanding Serv to Community 1983. **HOME ADDRESS:** 11 Addison St, Charleston, SC 29403. **BUSINESS ADDRESS:** Councilmember, District 4, 80 Broad St, Charleston, SC 29401.

JEFFERSON, HORACE LEE
Dentist. **PERSONAL:** Born Oct 10, 1924, Detroit, MI; married Betty Lou Brown; children: Linda, Eric, Judith, Michael. **EDUCATION:** Highland Park Jr Coll, 1946-48;Univ of MI Dental Schl, DDS 1953. **CAREER:** Dentist 1953; Staff of Herman Kiefer, sr dentist 1954; City Hosp of Detroit MI 1971. **ORGANIZATIONS:** Mem Detroit Dist Dental Soc; MI Dental Assn; Am & Dental Assn 1953; pres Wolverine Dental Soc 1957; dir Cororate

Delta Dntl Plans of MI 1977; life mem Afro-am Museum of detroit 1975; life mem Alpha Phi Alpha Frat 1975; life mem NAACP 1979. **HONORS/ACHIEVEMENTS:** Meritorious Unit Award recipient;Clinical Presentation at 15th Review Detroit Dist Dental Soc 1957; clinical presentations Wolverine Dental Soc 1971; forum Presentation Gamma Lambda Chap AOA 1973; Cancer Seminar Participation MI Cancer Found 1976. **MILITARY SERVICE:** AUS 1944. **BUSINESS ADDRESS:** 10040 Puritan, Detroit, MI 48238.

JEFFERSON, JAMES E.
City government. **PERSONAL:** Born Jul 22, 1922, Redlands, CA; married Pearl. **CAREER:** Yuma City Council, mem 1973-. **ORGANIZATIONS:** Dir AZ Respiratory Disease Assoc 1971-75; ad hoc advisory comm AZ State Parks 1984. **HONORS/ACHIEVEMENTS:** Man of the Year Yuma 1973; Disting Serv Yuma Area Housing Opportunity 1981, City of Yuma 1984. **HOME ADDRESS:** 200 S 10th Ave, Yuma, AZ 85364.

JEFFERSON, JOHN
Professional athlete. **PERSONAL:** Born Feb 03, 1956, Dallas, TX; married DeWanda; children: Tiffany, John Larry II. **EDUCATION:** AZ State, attended. **CAREER:** San Diego Chargers, wide receiver 1978-81; Green Bay Packers, wide receiver 1981-. **HONORS/ACHIEVEMENTS:** Most Popular Player 1981; Named to Pro Bowl for 4th time & emerged as game's MVP 1984; Led NFL in TD Catches as a rookie 1978,80; All Amer selection at AZ State; Starter in both Hula & Japan Bowls. **BUSINESS ADDRESS:** Green Bay Packers, 1265 Lombardi Ave, Green Bay, WI 54307.

JEFFERSON, JOSEPH L.
Educator. **PERSONAL:** Born Nov 08, 1940, Pensacola, FL; married Ida C Wedgeworth; children: Eric, Clynita. **EDUCATION:** TX SoUniv 1968, BA 1968; TX So U, MA 1971; OH State U, Ph D 1974. **CAREER:** Vocational Guidance Houston, counselor 1971; TX Southern Univ, admin asst to dean coll of arts & sciences dir inst; TX Southern Univ, assoc dir Office of Inst Research, asst prof School of Educ. **ORGANIZATIONS:** Mem Am Educ & Research Assn; Phi Delta Kappa; Assn for Inst Research; Am Psychological Assn; TX Psychological Assn; Kappa Alpha Psi Frat; Houston JrC of C; Houston Lion's Club. **HONORS/ACHIEVEMENTS:** Recip Grad Fellow TX SoUniv 1970-71; Acad Year Inst Study Grant 1972-73 OH State U. **MILITARY SERVICE:** AUS sp E5 1962-65. **BUSINESS ADDRESS:** 3201 Wheeler Ave, Houston, TX 77004.

JEFFERSON, JUNE L., JR.
Chaplain. **PERSONAL:** Born Jun 25, 1924, Edgefield Co, SC; married Rosa L Lewis; children: Justin Lee, Jay Michael. **EDUCATION:** Howard U, Wash DC, BS 1954, BD 1959, MDiv 1971. **CAREER:** Hopkins House Settlemnt, Alex VA, grp soc wrkr 1957-59; Children's Cntr, Laurel MD, cnslr 1963-64; Grater Corr Inst, PA, chpln 1964-65; US PostalSrv, Wash DC, pstl clrk 1947-52; security guard, salesman, cab drvr 1950-63; Zion Bapt Ch, Alexandria VA, asst pastor 1957-; DC Dept Corr DetentionSrv Bd, retired chpln 1985. **ORGANIZATIONS:** Mem, Am Protestant Chplns Corr Assn 1972-73; Luther Rice Coll 1970-73; Cptl Cab Coop Assn 1959-64; ch, Crime & Dlnqncy Cntrl Unit, Hlth & Wlfr Cncl, Wash 1971; pres, Potomac HS Athl Assn 1976-77; charter mem, YMCA; mem, Am Corr Assn 1967; mem, Silver Hill Dads Clb; SW Planning Cncl, Wash 1969-71; spec asst Capital Centre Kiwanis Club Landover MD. **HONORS/ACHIEVEMENTS:** Cited, Recrtnl Dept, Wash 1970; chrmn, SW Recrtnl Cncl 1970-75; Academy Awareds Com, Wash 1974; grand prelate KP, Mason.

JEFFERSON, M. IVORY
Clergyman, attorney. **PERSONAL:** Born Sep 10, 1924, Logan, WV; married Reba N; children: Gwendolyn J Allen; Sygna J Little. **EDUCATION:** Attended, Univ of So CA, Univ of Manila; Emmanus Bible Sch, grad; Robert H Terrell Sch of Law, LLB LLD 1950. **CAREER:** Manpower Commn & Housing Div of Newport News Ofc of Human Affrs, consult in field of pastoral counseling; Sixth Mt Zion Bapt Temple, pastor. **ORGANIZATIONS:** Admitted to VA Bar 1951; admitted to US Supreme Ct Bar 1956; licensed & ordained in Gospel Ministry 1961 1963; authority in fields of Pastoral Counseling Taxation & Domestic Relations; moderator Tidewater Peninsula Bapt Assn; legal adv Progressive Natl Baptist Conv; mem validating Comm for the Fund of Renewal Amer Bapt Ch Inc; consult Office of Offender Aid & Restoration Newport News; past pres Ministers Conf; past sec treas York Co Ministers Assn; past sec VA State Delgation Progressive Natl Bapt Conv Inc; past corr sec Tidewater Peninsula Bapt Assn; past pres Peninsula Clergy Assn; past grand dist depIBPOE of W; past pres Pleasant Plains Civic Assn; past assoc legal counsel NAACP; past chmn Bd of Christian Educ Progressive Natl Bapt Conv; past chmn adv com to Newport News Redevel & Housing Auth; past historian Progressive Natl Bapt Conv Inc; reg vice pres Progressive Natl Bapt Convention. **MILITARY SERVICE:** WW II. **BUSINESS ADDRESS:** Pastor, Sixth Mt Zion Bapt Temple, 2003 Kecoughtan Rd, Hampton, VA 23661.

JEFFERSON, NANCY B.
Association executive. **PERSONAL:** Born Jul 20, 1923, Paris, TN; married Norvel Jefferson; children: Linda, Paul, Edwin, Erwin, Norvel. **EDUCATION:** Smith Coll Little Rock AR, Philander; Univ of Chicago, 1966-67; Univ of Chicago, 1969. **CAREER:** Midwest Comm, co exec dir 1963-; West Town-Med, Chicago, admin nurse, reg MMS 1949-63. **ORGANIZATIONS:** Gor bd, Garfield Park Community Mental Health; adv bd, Dist 8 Public Schools; exec bd, M L King Jr, Boys Club; bd dir, Citizen Info Serv; mem, League Women Voters; founder & organizer, Triple "C" Women Club, Helping Hand; mem, Steering Comm, 11th Dist Pol Dept; organizer, East Garfield Park-Joint Planning Comm 1970; professional forum, NWU; mem, Illinois Plan Bd Health-Fac, State of Illinois; Bd of High Ed, Community Serv; bd dir, Oper PUSH; mem, Health Educ Comm, State of Illinois. **HONORS/ACHIEVEMENTS:** Woman of the Year Award, Malcolm X Coll 1970; WBEE Outstanding Comm Serv Award 1973. **BUSINESS ADDRESS:** 9 South Kedzie, Room 200, Chicago, IL 60612.

JEFFERSON, OVERTON C.
Educator. **PERSONAL:** Born in Port Arthur, TX; married Marjorie; children: Robert, Olida. **EDUCATION:** Xavier U, New Orleans, AB 1949; NC Cntrl U, JD; NYUniv Sch Law, LLM. **CAREER:** Houston Legal Found, central office dir 1985; TX Southern Univ School of Law, asst prof 1953-58. **MILITARY SERVICE:** AUS 1942-45. **BUSINESS ADDRESS:** 609 Fannin Ave, Ste 1909, Houston, TX.

JEFFERSON, PATRICIA ANN
Administrator. **PERSONAL:** Born Nov 26, 1951, Richmond County. **EDUCATION:** Augusta Coll, BBA 1973. **CAREER:** Belk-Teen-A-Rama Fashion Bd, liasion coord 1968-69; GA Power Co, customer serv rep 1969-73; Black Student Union Augusta Coll, sec & organizer 1971-73; Augusta/Richmond Co Human Relations Commn, admin asst to dir 1974-81; Augusta Focus Newspaper, genl mgr 1982-. **ORGANIZATIONS:** Mem Epsilon Tau Epsilon Sor 1972-73; founder & dir Spiritualettes 1974-; adv bd mem Comm Action Agency 1975-77; mem Natl Assn of Human Rights Workers 1976-; vice pres Paine Coll Early Childhood Adv Bd 1976-78; mem CSRA Bus League 1978-; mem Amer Cancer Soc Educ Com 1975-77; mem Citizens Participation for Redistricting 1979; mem Spirit Creek Bapt Ch. **HONORS/ACHIEVEMENTS:** Shorthand Awd 1969; French Awd 1969; Typing Awd 1969; Intake Settlement Cert Equal Employment Oppor Comm 1978; Wilton Cake Decorating Awd 1979; Miss PBO2nd runner up 1970-71.

JEFFERSON, ROBERT R.
Association executive. **PERSONAL:** Born Sep 21, 1932, Lexington, KY; married Katie E Scott; children: Robert, Jr, Stanley. **EDUCATION:** KY State Coll, BA, History, Political Sci, Biology, 1967, MA, Public Affairs, 1974. **CAREER:** councilmember, Lexington-Fayette Urban County Govt, 1988-presennt; US Bureau of Prisons, sr case mgr, 1974-83 (retired); US Public Health Hospital, various positions, 1959-74; IBM, assembler, 1959; US Public Health Hospitals, file clerk, 1957-58. **ORGANIZATIONS:** committee organizer, Whitney Young Sickle Cell Center, 1973-74; acting exec dir, Urban Co Human Rights Commn, Lexington, 1974; mem, Omega Psi Phi; past dist rep & mem, Supreme-Council; mem, chmn, Human Rights Commn, 1969-70; Black & Williams Comm Center; mem, Natl Conf on Christians & Jews; mem, LFUC Urban League, CORE, Bluegrass Black Business Assn, Agency Exec Forum. **HONORS/ACHIEVEMENTS:** LFUCG Human Rights Commn Outstanding Serv Award, 1985; Micro-City Govt, Distinguished Service Award, 1985; Lima Dirve Seventh Day Adventist Church, Outstanding Serv Award, 1981; KY State Univ, Distinguished Serv Award, 1981; NCCJ Brotherhood Award, 1979; Micro-City Univ, Honorary Doctorate Degree, 1975; Minority Affairs Comm Distinguished Services, 1973; Several Omega Psi Phi Fraternal Awards. **MILITARY SERVICE:** USAF 1947-54; USAFR 1954-68. **BUSINESS ADDRESS:** Box 2000 FCI Lexington, Lexington, KY 40507.

JEFFERSON, ROLAND SPRATLIN
Physician. **PERSONAL:** Born May 16, 1939, Washington, DC; son of Bernard S Jefferson and Devonia H Spratlin; married Melanie L Moore; children: Roland Jr, Rodney Earl, Shannon Devonia, Royce Bernard. **EDUCATION:** Univ of S CA, BA Anthropology 1961; Howard U, MD 1965. **CAREER:** Martin L King, Jr Hosp, asso prof 1972-75; Dept of Rehabilitation, consult 1972-78; Social Security Admin, consult 1975-79; Watts Hlth Found, staff psychiatrist 1973-80; Assn of Black Motion Picture & TV Producers, pres/founding mem 1980-81; Private Prac, physician. **ORGANIZATIONS:** Mem Writers Guild of Am W 1981; mem Nat Medical Assn 1969; bd of dir Am Sickle Cell Found 1973-76; bd of advisors Brockman Gallery 1976-78. **HONORS/ACHIEVEMENTS:** Grassroots Award Sons of Watts 1977; Golden Quill Award Abffriham Found 1977; NAACP Image Award 13th Annual NAACP Image Awards 1980; 1st Place for Film Drama Black Filmmakers Hall of Fame 1980; author of 3 novels, The School on 103rd Street (1976), A Card for the Players (1978), 559 to Damascus (1985); Award of Merit by Black American Cinema Society 1989; Producer, Writer, Director of Feature Film "Perfume" 1989. **MILITARY SERVICE:** USAF capt 1969-71. **BUSINESS ADDRESS:** Physician, 3870 Crenshaw Blvd #215, Los Angeles, CA 90008.

JEFFERSON, ROY LEE, JR.
Manager. **PERSONAL:** Born Nov 09, 1943, Texarkana, TX. **EDUCATION:** Univ UT, BA 1965. **CAREER:** NFL Players Assoc, staff rep; Washington Redskins, wide receiver 1971-; Colonial Carpets Vienna VA, contract salesman 1979-; TV Program for Children-Washington, host 1978-; Interstate Carpet Inc Fairfax VA, contract salesman 1975-78; 5 Oh-Clock News Washington, sports announcer 1974-77; Roy Jefferson Learning Center Washington, researched, formed 1973-76; Continental Fore Products Washington, salesman 1975; Redskin Games Warner Wolf TV Prog Washington, co-host, reviewer 1974-75; Washington Met Transti Authority, youth specialist 1972-73; Coldwell Banker, mktg mgr new homes/condo 1986-; 1st Western Mrtg Corp of IL,vp builder serv 1987-. **ORGANIZATIONS:** Honorary chmn No Greater Love/DC Retarded Assn; mem DC Black Repertory Theatre; mem Redskin Alumni Assn; mem NFLPA Credit Union; bd mem Washington Redskin Alumni Assn Epilepsy Foundation; mem N VA Builders Assn; celebrity chmn, founder 65 Roses "Over The Hill Gang" Golf and Tennis Classic for the Systic Fibrosis Found 1986,86,87. **HONORS/ACHIEVEMENTS:** Runner up Dodge Man of Yr 1976; Honor for Community Service City of Alexander Parks named Roy Jefferson 1976; Community Service Award NFL Players Assn 1977; award involvement Special Olympics; lead NFL in 1968 in pass receiving yardage 1,074; Pro Bowls 1968, 1969, 1971; NVL Champ Games in 1970, 1972. **BUSINESS ADDRESS:** Vice President, 1st Western Mtg Corp of IL, 9603 Westwood Center Dr, Ste 200, Vienna, VA 22180.

JEFFERSON, SANDRA WILLIAMSON
Human rights investigator. **PERSONAL:** Born Jul 10, 1948, Chicago, IL; widowed. **EDUCATION:** Chicago State U, BA Sociology 1976. **CAREER:** Chicago Urban League, admin asst 1970-73; IL Commn on Human Rel, admin asst personnel/eeo ofcr 1974-80; IL Dept of Human Rights, human rights investigator 1980-. **ORGANIZATIONS:** Mem Delta Sigma Theta 1980-; mem Black Meth for Ch Renewal 1978; speakers bur Chicago Assn of Commerce & Ind 1974-; bd of dir S Austin Job Referral Serv 1979-. **HONORS/ACHIEVEMENTS:** Outstand Young Women of Am 1978; nominee White House Fellowship 1978; nominee Outstand Young Citizen of Chicago Jaycees 1980.

JEFFERSON, WILLIAM J.
Attorney. **PERSONAL:** Born Mar 14, 1947, Lake Providence, LA; married Andrea Green; children: Jamila Efuru, Jalila Eshe. **EDUCATION:** SU, BA 1969; HarvardUniv Law Sch, JD 1972. **CAREER:** Jefferson, Bryan & Gray, partner 1976-; Judge Alvin B Rubin, judicial clrk 1972-73; Sen J Bennett Johnston, leg Asst 1973-. **ORGANIZATIONS:** Mem LA Bar Assn; mem, Am & Bar Assn; mem, Natl Bar Assn; mem, DC Bar Assn; mem, Supreme Ct Bar; mem, S U, Found. **MILITARY SERVICE:** USAR capt 1969-.

JEFFERSON-MOSS, CAROLYN
Government official. **PERSONAL:** Born Sep 20, 1945, Washington, DC; married Alfred Jeffrey Moss. **EDUCATION:** Howard Univ, BA Pol Sci 1970, MA Pub Admin 1974. **CAREER:** Reps C Diggs & A Hawkins, congressional Black caucus legislative dir 1970-71; Exotech Systems Inc, sr asso/proj dir 1971-74; BLK Group Inc, sr asso/dir for survey rsch 1974-75; Mark Battle Asso Inc, sr asso dir of marketing/survey rsch div 1975-78; Dept of Commerce, dep to asst sec for congressional affairs 1978-. **ORGANIZATIONS:** Mem Alpha Kappa Alpha Inc 1968; mem Met Dem Women's Club 1974. **HONORS/ACHIEVEMENTS:** Fellowship for Advanced Studies in Polit Sci Ford Found Joint Ctr for Polit Studies 1970-71. **BUSINESS ADDRESS:** Deputy to Assistant Secretary, US Dept of Commerce, Congressional Affairs, 14th & Constitution Ave NW, Washington, DC 20230.

JEFFREY, CHARLES JAMES, JR.
Editor, clergyman. **PERSONAL:** Born Oct 27, 1925, Tulsa, OK; married Louise Simmons. **EDUCATION:** Amer Baptist Theological Seminary, Nashville, BTh 1948; Tulsa U, additional study. **CAREER:** Oklahoma Eagle Newspaper, editor 1985; Macedonia Baptist Church, pastor; Tulsa TV, commentator; minister, 1967; Gen Baptist Convention of Oklahoma, recording sec 1956-. **ORGANIZATIONS:** Mem, Enrolmnt & Com, Nat Bapt Conv of Am 1965; mem, Pub Rel Dept for Nat Conv; pres, Local NAACP; mem, Adv Bd, Okmulgee Pub Sch; Hum Rel Com, Okmulgee Sch for Retarded; bd for Comm Act Found; mem, bd OK Estrn Dev Corp; mem, Tulsa Press Clb. **HONORS/ACHIEVEMENTS:** Recip, Cert of Appreciation, US Jaycees 1972. **MILITARY SERVICE:** USN 1943-45. **BUSINESS ADDRESS:** PO Box 3667, Tulsa, OK 74106.

JEFFREY, RONNALD JAMES
Administrator, author, lecturer. **PERSONAL:** Born Mar 11, 1949, Cheyenne, WY; son of John Thomas Jeffrey and Lilliam Leola Jeffrey; married Marilyn Mansell, Dec 10, 1978; children: Keeya, Kaylee. **EDUCATION:** Chadron State Coll, BA 1972; Univ of Northern CO, MA 1976; Chadron State Coll Chadron, NE, BA 1968-72; Univ or Northern Colorado, Greely, CO MA 1974-76. **CAREER:** Laramie County Comm Coll, instr 1980; Univ of Wyoming, instr; Office of Youth Alternatives, dir. **ORGANIZATIONS:** Bd mem Juvenile Justice Adv Bd 1984-; bd mem Cheyenne Child Care Centers (NAACP) 1984; consultant 1975-; lecturer 1975-; dir Rocky Mountain Federal Bank 1988-89; pres Wy Assn of Marriage & Family Therapist 1986-88. **HONORS/ACHIEVEMENTS:** Author of book, "Guide to Family Therapists" 1985; article "Training Rural Workers" Journal of Cont Soc Work 1985; George Washington Medal of Honor Freedom Found 1977; Jaycees disting serv awd 1978; Jefferson Award Amer Inst of Publ Serv 1980; Who's Who of Contemporary Achievement 1985; recipient of Phi DeltaKappa awd for serv to education 1986. **BUSINESS ADDRESS:** Dir, Office of Youth Alternatives, City of Cheyenne, 1328 Talbot Ct, Cheyenne, WY 82001.

JEFFREYS, JOHN H.
Management consultant. **PERSONAL:** Born Mar 27, 1940, Youngsville, NC; married Constance Little; children: Gregory, Alvin. **EDUCATION:** Shaw Univ, AB Soc 1962; Univ of GA, M Public Admin 1975; Univ of GA, D PA 1985. **CAREER:** Rowan Cty Salisbury NC Anti Poverty Prog, dir neighborhood serv ctr 1964-67; City of Hickory, dir human resources 1967-70;; US Adv Commiss for Intergovt Relations, 1st black intern 1969-70; Univ of GA, mgmt consult assoc. **ORGANIZATIONS:** 1st black elected commiss Clarke Cty Govt 1982; consult Intl Assoc City Mgrs 1983, Public Safety Personnel St Croix 1984, Amer Soc for Training & Dev 1984; parliamentarian GA Assoc of Black Elected Officials 1984; public safety & criminal justice comm Natl Assoc Counties; charter mem Natl Assoc Blacks in Criminal Justice. **HONORS/ACHIEVEMENTS:** Man of the Year Phi Beta Sigma Delta Mu Sigma Chap 1977,81,83; 1st Black Clarke Cty GA Comm Elected 1982; Outstanding Mgmt Instr GA Clerks Assoc 1983. **HOME ADDRESS:** 140 Jones Dr, Athens, GA 30606. **BUSINESS ADDRESS:** Management Consultant Assoc, Univ of Georgia, 1260 S Lumpkin St, Athens, GA 30602.

JEFFRIES, LEROY WILLIAM
Business executive. **PERSONAL:** Born Aug 14, 1912, Greensboro, NC; married Vermont. **EDUCATION:** Wilberforce U, BA 1935, hon HHD 1966; Columbia U, MA 1944. **CAREER:** LeRoy W Jeffries & Asso, Mktg Cons, pres 1971-; Johnson Publ Co, sr vice pres 1950-71; Nat Off Urban League, Dept Indsl Rels, exec 1947-49; ARMA Corp, job analyst consult 1943-47; Urban League Grtr NY, dir indsl rels 1941-43; NY St Div Plcmnt & Unempl Ins, mgr 1936-40. **ORGANIZATIONS:** Mem, Pub Rel Soc Am; LA Advertising Clb; pres, LA Chpt, Nat Assn, Mkt Dev; mem, Nat Assn Mkt Dev; Town Hall; LAC of C; rep liberia, LA Co Oppt Ind Ctr Ind Adv Cncl Consult 1972-75; life mem, NAACP; Alpha Phi Alpha Frat; mem exec bd, SCLC/W; del, Nat Urban League; mem bd trustee, WilberforceUniv Male Decision Maker in Communications; Nat Assn Media Women 1974. **HONORS/ACHIEVEMENTS:** Publ, "Facts About Blacks" 1977; lectr, UCLA; lectr, USC. **BUSINESS ADDRESS:** 3540 Wilshire Blvd, Ste 816, Los Angeles, CA 90010.

JEFFRIES, ROSALIND R.
Artist. **PERSONAL:** Born Jun 24, 1938, New York, NY; married Dr Leonard, Jr. **EDUCATION:** Hunter Coll, NYC, BA 1963; Columbia U, MA 1968. **CAREER:** City Univ NY, art hist, artist, prof 1972-; San Jose St Univ, asst prof 1969-72; Brooklyn Museum, lectr 1969; Group Seminars, Africa, co-ldr 1966-72; US Govt USIS, Abidjan, & Ivory Cst, W Africa, dir exhib 1965-66. **ORGANIZATIONS:** Lectr, univs, colls & comm cntrs-num one-woman art shows; cat writer, Museums; mem, Coll Arts Assn; CA St Art Historians; Nat Conf Artists. **HONORS/ACHIEVEMENTS:** Listed, Black Artists On Art; Afro-am Artist; Negro in Music & Art 1969; African Arts Mag, UCLA 1974. **BUSINESS ADDRESS:** City Coll of the City of New York, 138 St & Convent Ave, New York, NY 10031.

JEMISON, MAE C.
Physician. **PERSONAL:** Born in Decatur, AL. **EDUCATION:** Stanford Univ CA, BChE 1977; Cornell Univ, MD 1981. **CAREER:** Peace Corps West Africa, staff doctor; CIGNA Health Plans of CA in Glendale, general practitioner; NASA, first Black female mem of astronaut program. **BUSINESS ADDRESS:** NASA Johnson Space Center, Houston, TX 77058.

JEMISON, THEODORE JUDSON
Clergyman. **PERSONAL:** Born Aug 01, 1918, Selma, AL; children: Bettye Jane, Dianne Frances, Theodore Judson. **EDUCATION:** AL St Coll, BS 1940; VA Union U, DM 1945, DD 1971; Natchez Coll, DD 1953. **CAREER:** Bapt Ch, ordained minister; Mt Zion Bapt Ch, Staunton, pastor 1945-49; Mt Zion 1st Bapt Ch, Baton Rouge, pastor 1949-. **ORGANIZATIONS:** Gen sec, Nat Bapt Conv USA, Inc 1953; mem bd cntrl, Nat Council Chs in US; mem, LA Rights Commn; Baton Rouge Comm Rels Com; NAACP; pres, Frontiers Intrnl, Baton Rouge Chpt; Alpha Phi Alpha; shriner, Mason. **HONORS/ACHIEVEMENTS:** Named Citizen of Yr For Outstndng Contbns in civics, recrtn, ed, religion, City of Baton Rouge; Minister of Yr, Nat Beta Clb 1973; Dstngshd Serv Award, E Rouge Ed Assn 1973. **BUSINESS ADDRESS:** 356 East Blvd, Baton Rouge, LA 70802.

JEMMOTT, HENSLEY B.
Manager business planning. **PERSONAL:** Born Mar 14, 1947, New York, NY; married Lynn Hooper; children: Hensley, Dara. **EDUCATION:** Syracuse U, BA 1968; Columbia U, MBA 1973. **CAREER:** Squibb Corp, financial analyst 1973-78; Am Standard, sr financial anal 1978-79; Am Cyanamid Co (Am Far East Div), mgr planning 1979-81; Am Cyanamid Co (Lederle Intl Med), product mgr; Lederle Intl, Mgr Marketing Research. **ORGANIZATIONS:** Bd of dir Am Lung Assn of NJ 1983-; bd of dir Urban League of Manhattan 1977-79; Dir Amer Lung Assn of NJ 1984-. **BUSINESS ADDRESS:** Mgr Marketing Research, Lederle Internat'l, One Cyanamid Plaza, Wayne, NJ 07470.

JENKINS, ADAM, JR.
College business manager. **PERSONAL:** Born Sep 09, 1942, N Carrollton, MS; married Margaree Gordon; children: Veronica, Randolph, Darryl. **EDUCATION:** Alcorn A&M Coll, BS 1967; Univ of Omaha, 1968; MS State Univ, 1968-69; MS Coll, MBA 1975. **CAREER:** Utica Jr Coll, cashier 1967-68, bus mgr 1969-; Hinds Jr Coll, vice pres bus svcs. **ORGANIZATIONS:** Consult Natchez Jr Coll; mem MS Jr Coll Bus Mgrs Assoc, Natl Assoc Colls & Univs Bus Officers, NEA, MS Teachers Assoc, NAACP; sec treas Phi Beta Sigma 1971-72. **BUSINESS ADDRESS:** Vice President Bus Services, Hinds Jr College, Raymond Campus, Raymond, MS 39154.

JENKINS, ADELBERT HOWARD
Educator. **PERSONAL:** Born Dec 10, 1934, St Louis, MO; married Betty Lanier; children: Christopher. **EDUCATION:** Antioch Coll, BA 1957; Univ of MI, MA 1958, PhD 1963. **CAREER:** A Einstein Med Coll, post doctoral fellow 1962-64, asst instr, instr 1964-67; NY Univ Medical Center, asst prof 1967-71; NY Univ, assoc prof, dir undergraduate studies psychology 1971-. **ORGANIZATIONS:** Training consult Veterans' Admin Med Centers Bronx, Manhattan, Brooklyn; mem Amer Psychological Assn 1964-, fellow 1985-; fellow Soc for Personality Assessment 1974-; mem Natl Assn of Black Psychol 1968-. **HONORS/ACHIEVEMENTS:** Scholar of the Yr Natl Assn of Black Psychologists 1983; Martin L King Jr Award NY Soc of Clin Psychologists 1984; author of book, "Psychol of Afro-American, A Humanistic Approach" 1982. **BUSINESS ADDRESS:** Dir Undergrad Studies Psychol, New York University, 6 Washington Place Room 151, New York, NY 10003.

JENKINS, ALONZO CLARK
Clergyman. **PERSONAL:** Born Mar 03, 1953, Greenville, SC; married Carolyn Pearson. **EDUCATION:** Claflin Coll Orangebrg SC, BA 1974; DukeUniv Div Sch, MDiv Cand. **CAREER:** Wesley Untd Meth Ch Aiken, SC, pastor 1972-74f Mt Olive & New Hope UM Chs Rock Hill, SC, Pastor. **ORGANIZATIONS:** Mem NAACP; Phi Beta Sigma. **HONORS/ACHIEVEMENTS:** Lstd Who's Who in SC 1974; mem Pi Gamma Mu Nat Hon Soc.

JENKINS, ALTHEA H.
Librarian. **PERSONAL:** Born Sep 11, 1941, Tallahassee, FL; daughter of Samuel Henry and Florence Brown Henry; divorced; children: James C II. **EDUCATION:** FL A&M Univ, BSLS 1963; FL Atlantic Univ, LD Certificate 19-70; FL State Univ, MSLS 1972; Nova Univ, EdD 1977. **CAREER:** Indian River School Bd, school media specialist 1963-71; FL State Univ, graduate asst 1971-72; Miami-Dade Comm Coll, library dir 1972-80; Univ of S FL Sarasota, library dir 1980-. **ORGANIZATIONS:** Mem Amer Library Assoc 1972-, Sarasota-Manatee NCCJ Ed Comm 1980-; pres Pine View School for Gifted PTO 1982-84; council mem Assoc Coll & Rsch Libraries 1983-87; vp, pres elect FL Assoc Coll & Rsch Library 1983-85; mem Eckerd Coll Bd of Trustees 1984-; pres, FL Library Assn, 1988-89; Sarasota Chamber of Commerce, 1989; Sarasota County Historical Commn, 1988-; Sarasota County United Way Bd, 1987-; Sarasota County Community Found, 1988-; "She Knows Where She is Going" Girls Clubs of Amer, 1989. **HONORS/ACHIEVEMENTS:** Certificate of Appreciation Newtown Library Planning Bd 1981; Certificate of Appreciation Sarasota-Manatee Phi Delta Kappa 1984. **BUSINESS ADDRESS:** Jane Bancraft Cook Library, Univ of South Florida, 5700 N Tamiami Trl, Sarasota, FL 34243.

JENKINS, ANDREW
Director, affirmative action and liaison activities. **PERSONAL:** Born Jul 20, 1936, Philadelphia, PA; son of William Jenkins and Madeline Green-Jenkins; married Patricia A Green Jenkins, Oct 25, 1958; children: Eric, Denise, Andrea, Andrew. **EDUCATION:** Antioch Univ, BA Human Services 1982. **CAREER:** Mantva Comm Planners, pres 1967-85; City of Philadelphia Liaison Officer Anti-Poverty Agency 1971-79; City of Philadelphia Chairman Mayor's Cittizen Advisory Committee 1977-79; Mt Vernon Manor Apts, pres 1978-85; Mantva Primary Health Ctr, pres 1984-85; First United Baptist Church Male Chorus, vice pres 1984-85; Mantva Comm Devel Corp, vice pres 1984-85; Philadelphia Redevel Authority, dir relocation & prop mgmt. **ORGANIZATIONS:** Pres Mantua Community Planners 1967-1979; Dir Univ of PA Commun Devel 1969-71; Community Organizer Univ of PA 1969-71; liaison officer Philadelphia Ant Pov Action Comm 1971-79; pres Mt Vernon Apartments 1978-; exec bd West Philadelphia Partnership Inc 1983-89; mem Amer Legion George J Cornish Post 1983-85, Natl Forum for Black Admin 1984-85; mem Mayor Wilson Goode's Labor Standard Bd 1985, Philadelphia Redevel Authority Labor-Mgmt Comm; real estate comm bd mem Martin Luther King Village Comm Assoc Inc; bd mem Stinger Square Corp. **HONORS/ACHIEVEMENTS:** Man of the Year Philadelphia Jaycees 1971; Outstanding Young Amer, Natl Jaycees 1972; Good Leadership Citations Mayor Bill Green City Council & Gov Thornburgh 1982; Outstanding Leadership West Philadelphia C of C 1984; City Council Citations 1983,84; Congressman Bill Gray Awd 1982; Young Great Soc Awd 1985; Mantua Comm Leadership Awd 1985. **MILITARY SERVICE:** US Air Force airman second class 4 yrs; Citation for Community Relation Basketball (in Italy), 1957. **HOME ADDRESS:** 3609 Spring Garden St, Philadelphia, PA 19104. **BUSINESS ADDRESS:** Director, Affirmative Action & Liaison Activities, Redevelopment Authority of the City of Philadelphia, 1234 Market St 8th Fl, Philadelphia, PA 19107.

JENKINS, ANDREW JAMES
Senator. **PERSONAL:** Born Jun 27, 1941, Brooklyn, NY; married Michelle Rios; children: Andrew Jr, Alexandra. **EDUCATION:** Fordham Univ, Soc Sci 1969; Fordham Univ Law School, JD 1972. **CAREER:** CUNY Coll, adjunct prof; Jenkins Aings & Johnson Law Firm, atty; NY State Senate, senator. **ORGANIZATIONS:** Parliamentarian Guy R Brewer Dem Club; mem Knights of Pythias. **HONORS/ACHIEVEMENTS:** Mem Natl Hon Soc. **BUSINESS ADDRESS:** Senator Dist 10, New York State Senate, 109-43 Farmers Blvd, St Albans, NY 11412.

JENKINS, AUGUSTUS G., JR.
Funeral director. **PERSONAL:** Born Aug 24, 1943, New York, NY; son of Augustus G Jenkins, Sr and W Louise Johnson Jenkins; married Nellie Kirkland, Jul 12, 1970; children: Natalie, Ashley. **EDUCATION:** Central State Univ, Wilberforce, OH, BS, 1965; Ohio State Univ, Columbus, OH, MS, 1966. **CAREER:** Jenkins Funeral Chapel, New York, NY, owner, 1970-; Black Tennis and Sports Found, New York, NY, founder and vice chair, 1977-; profl pilot flight instructor, 1985-. **MILITARY SERVICE:** US Army Signal Corps, 1966-68. **HOME ADDRESS:** Augustus G. Jenkins, Jr, 144 Lake St, Englewood, NJ 07631.

JENKINS, BARBARA WILLIAMS
Librarian. **PERSONAL:** Born Aug 17, 1934, Union, SC; daughter of Ernest N Williams and Johncie Sartor Williams; married Robert A Jenkins; children: Ronald, Pamela. **EDUCATION:** Bennett Coll, BA;Univ IL, MSLS; Rutgers U, PhD. **CAREER:** Circulation libr; ref & documents libr; SC State Coll, library dir & prof. **ORGANIZATIONS:** Mem SC Library Assn; SE Library Assn; Am Library Assn; Am Soc for Information Sci; Alpha Kappa Mu Hon Soc; Am AssnUniv & Profs Evaluator So Assn Coll & Schs; library consult instr; co-adj faculty Rutgers U; asso dir Inst for Libr in Corr Inst; mem NAACP; Delta Sigma Theta Inc S Atlantic Reg Dir 1968-70; mem Nat Com Constitution by-laws 1971-75; mem Links Inc; pres Orangeburg Chap 1975-77; consult WEEA Project "Contributions of Black Women to Am 1776-1977"; treas Blk Caucus of the Am Lib Assn 1976-78; adv com SC Museum Commin; contribtr/edtrl bd Publ SC Blks & Native Am 1977; vice area dir Southern Area The Links Inc 1979-83; mem Land Grant Library Directors' Assoc 1979-85; chmn ALA Black Caucus 1984-86; pres So Carolina Library Assoc 1986-87; bd of dir SOLINET Southeastern Library Network 1989-. **HONORS/ACHIEVEMENTS:** John Cotton Dana Award; Design & Planning Award MF Whittaker Library; Boss of the Yr Awd Orangeburg Chap Professional Secretaries Assoc 1980; Service Awd 1890 Land Grant Library Directors' Assoc 1984; President's Award South Carolina Library Assn 1987. **BUSINESS ADDRESS:** Library Dir, SC State College, Whittaker Library, Orangeburg, SC 29117.

JENKINS, BOBBY G.
Business executive. **PERSONAL:** Born Sep 30, 1939, Detroit; married Clara Gibson. **EDUCATION:** Wayne State Univ, BS 1966. **CAREER:** Ford Motor Co Lincoln-Mercury Div, gen field mr, mktg sales 1972-; Chicago, zone mgr 1969-71; Chicago, admin mgr, 1968-69. **HONORS/ACHIEVEMENTS:** Top mktg student of yr Sales Mktg Execs Detroit 1967; Beta Gamma hon soc 1967. **MILITARY SERVICE:** USN 1957-60. **BUSINESS ADDRESS:** Ford Motor Co Marketing Sales, 2010 Webster Ste 360, Oakland, CA 94612.

JENKINS, CARL SCARBOROUGH
Physician. **PERSONAL:** Born Jan 18, 1916, Wilberforce, OH; married Helen. **CAREER:** Springview Center OH State Hosp for the Mentally Retarded, co-medical dir 1978-79; Wright State Medical Sch Prog on Pain, co-chmn 1979-80; Springfield Bdof Health, pres 1980-81; Inst for Advanced Rsch in Asian Sci & Med New York, prof of acupuncture 1982; Wright State Univ Sch of Medicine, assoc prof fam practice/chmn acad of medicine 1984-. **ORGANIZATIONS:** Chmn elect of the Exec Committee of Wright State Univ Acad of Med; adv bd Center for Chinese Medicine. **HONORS/ACHIEVEMENTS:** Cert of Appreciation Wright State Univ Sch of Medicine; publications incl, "Transcutaneous Neural Stimulation" The Helping Hands Vol 20 1979; "How To Get Into Medical School" co-author John Nduaguba, PhD 1979; "TNS Relationship to Tryptophan Mechanism" 1982; "Indicator for Pain Rx" 1983. **BUSINESS ADDRESS:** 144 W Pleasant St, Springfield, OH 45506.

JENKINS, CAROL ANN
News correspondent. **PERSONAL:** Born Nov 30, 1944, Montgomery, AL; married Carlos Hines. **EDUCATION:** Boston U, BS 1966f NY U, MA 1968. **CAREER:** WNBC-TV, news corr 1973-; ABC-TVREASONOR/SMITH Report Eyewitness News, corr 1972-73; "Straight Talk" WOR- TV, moderator 1971-72f News Report with Bill RyanWOR-TV, co-anchor reporter 1970-71. **ORGANIZATIONS:** Mem Membership Com AFTRA; Writers Guild of Am E; Nat Acad of Arts & Scis; Intl Radio & TV Soc; Am Women in Radio & TV; Nat Assn of Media Women. **HONORS/ACHIEVEMENTS:** Recipient serv Award Harlem Prep Sch 1971; outstanding achievement Award Ophelia DeVore Sch 1972; outstanding achievement Award AL StateUniv 1972; outstanding achievement Award Journalism Alpha Wives 1974. **BUSINESS ADDRESS:** WNBC-TV, 30 Rockefeller Plaza, New York, NY 10020.

JENKINS, CHARLES E., SR.
Clergyman. **PERSONAL:** Born Aug 24, 1928, Paris, TN; married Lula Mae Reynolds; children: Chaliese Lunelle, Mary Louise, Charles, Jr, Frederick. **EDUCATION:** LeMoyne Coll, Attnd 1948; AL A&M Coll, Attnd; Union Bib Sem, Attnd; Billy Graham Sch of Evang, Attnd; S Theol Sem, Attnd; Monrovia Coll, DD 1963; Union Bapt Sem, LLD 1971. **CAREER:** Warren Chapel AME Ch, pastor 1971-79; Avery Chapel AME Ch Memphis TN, 1979-; St Paul AME Ch Fayetteville TN 1955-60; St Paul AME Ch Chattanooga, 1960-65; Asbury Chapel AME Ch Louisville, 1965-71. **ORGANIZATIONS:** Del, Gen Conf AME Ch 1960, 1964, 1964, 1968, 1972, 19768 1980; asst dir, Minimum Salary Dept AME Ch; holds25 yrs exp, FCC Brdcstng. **HONORS/ACHIEVEMENTS:** Exp, "Moments of Inspiration" WNOO Radio 1962; publ serv, rel works, Key to City of Chattanooga 1965; Key to City of Louisville 1966; commd, "Kentucky Colonel" 1970; apptd, TN Colonel adc, Gov Staff 1972; in %Biog, Dir of Negro Min Howard U, Sch of Rel Lib; Personalities in the S 1976; Men of Achvmt1976; Who's Who in Religion 1977. **BUSINESS ADDRESS:** 882 E Trigg Ave, Memphis, TN 38106.

JENKINS, CLARA BARNES
Educator. **PERSONAL:** Born in Franklinton, NC; daughter of Walter Barnes, Sr and Stella Griffin Barnes; divorced. **EDUCATION:** Winston-Salem State Univ, BS Educ 1940; NC Central Univ, MA 1947; Univ of Pittsburgh, EdD 1965; NYU; Univ of NC Chapel Hill; NC Agric and State Univ. **CAREER:** Fayetteville State Univ, instr 1945-50; Shaw Univ, asst prof 1954-64; NC Agric and Techn State Univ, visit prof 1965-84; St Paul's Coll, prof 1964-. **ORGANIZATIONS:** Class council Univ of Pittsburgh 1976-; adv St Paul's Student VA Educ Assn, 1966-; Natl Educ Assn; founder and adv Sigma Lambda Chptr of Zeta Phi Beta Sor 1982; Amer Assn of Univ Profs; Natl Soc for Study of Edn; Amer Hist Assn; NEA; AAUW; Assn of Teacher Educators; VA Educ Assn; Doctoral Assn of Educators; Amer Academy of Polit and Soc Sci; AAAS; Amer Assn of Higher Edn; Acad of Political Sci; Amer Psychol Assn; The Marquis Biograph Libr Soc; The Intl Platform Assn; Phi Eta Kappa Scholastic Soc; Soc for Rsch in Child Devel; Jean Piaget Soc; The Philos of Educ Soc; The Soc of Professors of Edn; Kappa Delta Pi Honor Soc; Phi Delta Kappa; Zeta Phi Beta Sorority Inc; mem The History of Educ Soc, Amer Soc of Notaries. **HONORS/ACHIEVEMENTS:** Citation First of Race to receive doctorate in Foundations of Education from Univ of Pgh; Plaque for Effective Class Instr NC Agr and Techn State Univ 1979; Dedicated and Humanistic Instr in Teaching NC Agr and Techn State Univ 1980; Outstanding Achievement Eastern Reg of Zeta Phi Beta Sor 1982; Who's Who in the So and So West; Who's Who of Amer Women; Who's Who in Amer Education; Natl Gold Book of Disting Women; Natl Soc Register of the US; Natl Register of Prominent Americans; The Intl Platform Assn Directory; Creative and Successful Pers of the World; The Intl Blue Book; The 2000 Women of Achievment; Leaders in Edn; Who's Who in Society; Personalities of the South; Dictionary of Intl Biography, Dir of Speakers by Langer; Who's Who in the World; Who's Who Among Human Serv Profls; Personalities of America; Directory of Educational Specialists; Teacher of the Year St. Paul's Coll 1988-89. **HOME ADDRESS:** 920 Bridges St, Henderson, NC 27536. **BUSINESS ADDRESS:** Prof Education & Psychology, Saint Paul's College, 406 Windsor Avenue, Lawrenceville, VA 23868.

JENKINS, CYNTHIA
Legislator & librarian. **PERSONAL:** Born Jul 21, 1924, Nashville, TN; married Joseph D Jenkins Sr; children: Joseph D Jr. **EDUCATION:** Univ of Louisville, BA History Political Science 1945; Pratt Institute, MLS Library Science 1966; Columbia Univ, Post Graduate. **CAREER:** Brooklyn Public Library, librarian 1960-62; Queens Borough Public Library, librarian 1962-82; New York Assembly, legislator. **ORGANIZATIONS:** Founder/chairperson Social Concern Comm of Springfield Gardens Inc 1969-82; Black Librarians 1970-75; founder/chairperson Social Concern Comm Develop Agency 1980-82; founder Caucus of Queens 1976-; mem of council Amer Library Assn governing body 1982-; founder/chairperson Social Concern Fed Credit Union1984-. **HONORS/ACHIEVEMENTS:** Community Service Awd Alpha Kappa Alpha Sor 1980; Distinguished Citizen Friends of Sr Citizens 1982; Political Leadership Awd Queens womens Political Caucus 1983; Outstanding Citizens Awd Omega Psi Phi Frat 1984. **HOME ADDRESS:** 226-18 Merrick Blvd, Laurelton, NY 11413.

JENKINS, DREWIE GUTRIMEZ
Retired educational administrator. **PERSONAL:** Born Apr 01, 1915, Logan Co; married Cornelia Watkins. **EDUCATION:** WV State Coll, BS 1940; WV U, MS 1951; Bradley U, further study 1952, 53, 54. **CAREER:** Kanawha Co Bd Educ, retired consultant industrial arts; taught in various elem Jr & Sr HS; Industrial Arts Kanawha Univ Co, supervisor. **ORGANIZATIONS:** Rep NEA; life mem AAIA; WV State Alumni Assn; Kanawha Co Alumni Assn; mem Kappa Alpha Psi Frat; Mayor's planning comm City of Charleston; Nat Educ Assn 1974f mem Am Ind Arts Assn NASCD WVASCD WVIA WVEA KCEA AVA; mem Phi Delta Kappa; charter mem Ebony Black Golf Tournament of Huntington, WV; pres elect of WV Indsl Arts Assn; mem NDEA Title XI Inst for Advance Study of Indsl Arts 1968-69; mem Am Legion Post 57; minister of Communion of Catholic Ch; WVAVA Cath lecturer. **HONORS/ACHIEVEMENTS:** Cit & Leadership Certificate from WV State Coll 1953; 1st black tchr WV sch 1954; 1st black tchr of WV honored as tchr of yr Am Ind Arts Assn 1965; 1st black supervisor ind arts Co & State; 1st black men of volunteer Fire Dept Bd of Malden; Improvement Coun of Malden; Boy Scout Ldrshp Certificate WVSC 1st & only black mem; com writing "Guide for Sch Adminstrs & Tchrs" Indsl Arts in Jr HS 1968. **MILITARY SERVICE:** AUS 1946-49.

JENKINS, EDMOND THOMAS
Educator. **PERSONAL:** Born Apr 04, 1930, Cleveland, OH. **EDUCATION:** Howard Univ, BA 1953; Western Reserve Univ, MA 1956, MSSA 1966; Moreno Academy of Sociodrama Psychodrama and Group Psychotherapy, Certificate 1968. **CAREER:** TN A&I State Univ, instructor 1956-60; Garden Valley Neighborhood House, teen group worker acting dir 1960-64; Ionia State Hosp for Criminally Insane, clinical sw supervisor 1966-69; Case Western Reserve Univ, asst prof assoc prof 1969-. **ORGANIZATIONS:** Certified mem Natl Assoc of Social Workers 1968-; life mem NAACP. **HONORS/ACHIEVEMENTS:** Appreciation Awd St Andrews Episcopal Church 1980; Outstanding Prof Awd Assoc of Black Student Social Workers 1980; Teacher of the Year Alumni Assoc 1982; Licensed Ind Social Worker State of OH 1986. **MILITARY SERVICE:** AUS corpl 2 yrs; Good Conduct Medal, Korean Serv Medal.

JENKINS, ELAINE B.
Consultant, business executive. **PERSONAL:** Born Apr 02, 1916, Butte, MT; married Howard Jenkins Jr; children: Judith E, Howard III, Lawrence. **EDUCATION:** Denver Univ, BA; OH State Univ, MA. **CAREER:** Publ School Admin, former teacher; Black Educ Consulting Serv, founder, dir; One Amer Inc, pres/founder 1969-. **ORGANIZATIONS:** Bd dir Min Cont Rsch Ctr for Washinton Metro Area Trans Authority Hon 1937; mem Urban League 1967, United Givers Fund 1970; founder DC Alpha Wives; past pres Howard Univ Faculty Wives; natl co-chmn Delta Sigma Theta; delegate Natl Convention; natl vice pres Womens Black Political Caucus; chmn Ed Task Force; appt Nelson Comm; mem Citizens Adv Council on European Affairs; trustee DC Inst of Mental Health; mem Panel for HEW Fellows; mem City Council Adv Comm on Indus & Commercial Devel; chairperson Council of 100 Black Republicans; dir Found for the Preservation of the Two-Party System; mem Natl Social Action Commn, Delta Sigma Theta; pres appt Natl Adv Council of Voluntary Action. **HONORS/ACHIEVEMENTS:** Comm Appreciation Awd Tri-Schools of SW Washington DC 1970; appt by pres US Comm on Org of DC 1973; Eartha MM White Awd Natl Business League; Awarded Cosmopolitan BPW Club; appt by Pres Natl Adv Council on Educ of Disadvantaged Children 1974; Woman of the Year Awd Natl Business League Bd Delta Sigma Theta; sel by Sec of Def 45th Annual Joint Civil Orientation Conf; Honored by Dollars and Sense Magazine as Woman of the Year 1985. **BUSINESS ADDRESS:** Founder, One Amer Inc, 1109 Spring St, Silver Spring, MD 20910.

JENKINS, ELIZABETH AMETA
Educator. **PERSONAL:** Born Mar 11, 1929, Brooklyn, NY; daughter of Lionel A Hunte

(deceased) and Ameta A Hackett-Hunte; divorced; children: Roland, Roderick, Howard, Rebecca, Leah. **EDUCATION:** Molloy Coll, BA Soc Psy 1977; Hofstra U, MA Cnsl Ed Family Therapy 1985. **CAREER:** Nassau Co Dept of Social Svcs, social work aid 1965-68; Econ Oppor Cncl Roosevelt, NY, summer youth dir commnty organizer 1970-72; Alliance for Minority Group Leaders Inc, activities planner/parent coord 1972-77; Molloy Coll, cnslr. **ORGANIZATIONS:** Mem Assn for Equality & Excell in Educ 1979; mem LI Cncl of Stdnt Pers Admin 1981-; mem Assn of Black Women in Higher Educ 1977-; mem HEOP Professnl Organ LI Region 1978; mem Am Assn ofUniv Women 1977; mem Am Bus Womens Assn 1984; pres Roosevelt Schlrshp Assn 1958-75; founding sec Nassau/Suffolk Hlth Sys Agency 1976-78; mem Nassau Co Task Force on the Status of Women 1977-79. **HONORS/ACHIEVEMENTS:** Cert of Commendation Nassau Co Dept Hlth 1964; Dedicated Serv Alliance of Min Group Leaders Inc 1978. **HOME ADDRESS:** 50 Holloway St, Freeport, NY 11520. **BUSINESS ADDRESS:** Counselor, Molloy Coll, 1000 Hempstead Ave, Rockville Centre, NY 11570.

JENKINS, ELLA LOUISE
Musician, singer, recording artist. **PERSONAL:** Born Aug 06, 1924, St Louis, MO. **EDUCATION:** Wilson Jr Coll, 1945-47; Roosevelt Coll, 1947-48; SF State Coll, 1949-51. **CAREER:** Free lance musician singer rec artist; conduted rhythm workshops & concerts around the US & other countries. **ORGANIZATIONS:** Mem Music Educ Nat Cofn; Intl Platform Assn; Am Soc of Composers. **HONORS/ACHIEVEMENTS:** Num Awards. **BUSINESS ADDRESS:** 1844 N Mohawk St, Chicago, IL 60614.

JENKINS, EMMANUEL LEE
Educational administrator. **PERSONAL:** Born Aug 07, 1934, Greenville, NC; widowed; children: Darel, Gregory, Jerome, Tamara. **EDUCATION:** Howard Univ, BA Pharmacy 1956; Long Island Univ, MS Educ 1974. **CAREER:** Rhodes Med, pharm 1956; Moore-Schley Cameron & Co, customers broker 1960-70; US Merchant Marine Acad, dir of admissions 1970-. **ORGANIZATIONS:** Ofcr Lakeview Educ Com 1968-73; rep Coll Bd 1973-; rep Natl Assn Coll Admissions Officers 1974-; mem Coll Bd Council 1982-83. **HONORS/ACHIEVEMENTS:** Special Achievement Awd for Performance USMM Acad 1975; Special Achievement Awd 1983. **MILITARY SERVICE:** USN cmdr served 23 yrs; Bronze Medal for Superior Fed Serv Maritime Admin 1978. **BUSINESS ADDRESS:** Dir of Admissions, US Merchant Marine Acad, Kings Point, NY 11024.

JENKINS, FERGUSON
Baseball player. **PERSONAL:** Born Dec 13, 1943, Chatham, Ontario, Canada. **CAREER:** Philadelphia Phillies Nat League, pitcher 1965-66; Chicago Cubs Nat League, 1966-73; TX Rangers Am League, 1973-. **HONORS/ACHIEVEMENTS:** Recipient Nat League Cy Young Meml Award 1971f named to Nat League All-Star Team Sporting News 1967, 71-72; Natl League pitcher of yr 1971. **BUSINESS ADDRESS:** C/O Pub Relations Dir TX Range, PO Box 1111, Arlington, TX 76004.

JENKINS, FRANK SHOCKLEY
Author, poet, publisher. **PERSONAL:** Born Apr 11, 1925, Seattle, WA; married Lynn Hamilton; children: Frank Alexander, Denise Shockley. **CAREER:** US Merchant marine, 1942-52; US Post Office, 1952-68; Time-DC Los Angeles, freight handler 1969-73; Hollywood, actor 1973-; Shockley Press, poet publisher. **ORGANIZATIONS:** Mem Screen Actors Guild; mem Teamsters 357; play "Last Man Out" LA 1975; play (poetic) "My World" coll 1979; publ "What It Is?" 1981; mem Screen Extras Guild, AFTRA. **HONORS/ACHIEVEMENTS:** Publ "I Didn't Start Out To Be A Poet" 1977,81, "Black Mac Say" 1981; works included in 1982 Emmy Awd Prog (KCET-LA) 1982 "Voices Of Our People, In Celebration Of Black Poetry". **BUSINESS ADDRESS:** Box 36012, Los Angeles, CA 90036.

JENKINS, GAYLE EXPOSE
Nurse. **PERSONAL:** Born Feb 12, 1927, Bogalusa, LA; married Monroe; children: Toni Harry, Don Expose, Willie E. **EDUCATION:** Booker T Washington LPN School, LPN 1968. **CAREER:** Highland Park Hospital, LPN; Richards Beauty School, beautician 1950. **ORGANIZATIONS:** Sec Bogalusa Voter's League Civil Rights Group 1964-; mem Emergency School Aid Act 1975-77; dir Washington Parish Children's Council 1978; advisory bd Comm Devel Block Grant 1979-; school bd Bogalusa School Bd 1978-; mem Natl Caucus of black school bd mem 1979-; mem Natl Citizen Participation Council 1979-80; advisory bd Adolescent Pregnancy Program 1980-; mem LA Sch Bd Assn 1980-; mem Nursing Alumni Assn 1979-80. **HONORS/ACHIEVEMENTS:** Ms Central, Central Memorial HS, 1946; Cert dep Gov Edwards LA 1973; Cert Dep Gov Treenla 1981. **BUSINESS ADDRESS:** Bogalusa City Schools, 331 Cumberland St, Bogalusa, LA 70427.

JENKINS, GEORGE ARTHUR, JR.
Marketing professional. **PERSONAL:** Born May 22, 1955, New York, NY; married Linda Ann Dawkins; children: Peter Anthony. **EDUCATION:** Univ of Rochester, BA 1977; Univ of Chicago Grad Sch of Business, MBA 1979. **CAREER:** Xerox Corp, market analyst 1979-83; Natl Data Corp Rapidata Div, acct rep 1983-84; Mead Data Central Inc, mgr corporate markets, 1984-86; Real Estate Data Inc, dir electronic publishing 1986-87; Lotus Devel Corp, Prod Mgr, 1988-. **ORGANIZATIONS:** Mem Alpha Phi Alpha Frat 1977-; mem CARI Inc 1980-83, Dayton Chap Natl Black MBA Assoc 1984-86; mem Information Industry Assoc 1984-, Assoc of MBA Execs 1984-; Assoc MBA Executives, 1984-87. **HOME ADDRESS:** 30 Brownlea Rd, Framingham, MA 01701. **BUSINESS ADDRESS:** Product Manager, Compact Disk Information Services, Lotus Development Corp Inc, 1 Cambridge Center, Cambridge, MA 02142.

JENKINS, HARRY LANCASTER
Dental surgeon. **PERSONAL:** Born Apr 22, 1932, Columbus, GA; married Janie R; children: Harry, Timothy, Anthony, Gary. **EDUCATION:** Morehouse Coll, AB 1955; Meharry Med Coll, DDS 1962; Tuskegee VA Hosp, internship 1962-63. **CAREER:** Self-employed, dental surgeon; Maryview Hosp Portsmouth VA, staff; Portsmouth Gen Hosp; Norfolk Comm Hosp, staff mem. **ORGANIZATIONS:** Am Cancer Soc mem Truxton Lodge 199 F&M; mem Am Youth Orgn; Eureka Bus & Professional Club; adv bd VA State Civil Rights Commn. **MILITARY SERVICE:** AUS corpl 1952. **BUSINESS ADDRESS:** 3335 Portsmouth Blvd, Portsmouth, VA 23701.

JENKINS, HERMAN LEE
Educational administrator. **PERSONAL:** Born May 07, 1940, Montgomery, AL; married Margaret Stephenson; children: Gloria, Herman Jr. **EDUCATION:** Assoc of Amer Geography, scholar 1976; Clark Univ, BA 1974, PhD 1983. **CAREER:** Southern Christian Leadership Conf, comm organizer civil rights activist 1965-69; Clark Univ, dir of comm rel 1972; Amer Intl Coll, lecturer 1976; Queens Coll, exec asst to pres 1978-80; HL Jenkins Geographic Analysis Inc, pres & ceo 1978-; Self-employed, artist mapmaker 1961-; Queens Coll, asst vice pres. **ORGANIZATIONS:** Mem NAACP 1971-; mem 100 Black Men Inc 1978-; mem Assoc of Amer Geographers. **HONORS/ACHIEVEMENTS:** Fellowship/president Metropolitan Applied Rsch Center 1967-68; Jonas Clark Scholar Clark Univ 1977. **MILITARY SERVICE:** AUS pfc 3 yrs. **HOME ADDRESS:** 241-20 Northern Blvd, Douglaston, NY 11363. **BUSINESS ADDRESS:** Asst Vice President, Queens College, 65-30 Kissena Blvd, Flushing, NY 11367.

JENKINS, HOWARD, JR.
Government official. **PERSONAL:** Born Jun 16, 1915, Denver; married Elaine; children: Judith, Howard, III, Lawrence. **EDUCATION:** Univ of Denver, AB, LLB. **CAREER:** Independent fed agency which administers nation's prin labor relations Laws 1963-; former law prof splst in Fields of Labor & Adminstrv & Law; aptd to NLRB by Pres John F Kennedy 1963 to Serve 5-yr term; re-apted to second term by Pres Lyndon Johnson 1968 reaptd to 3rd term by Pres Richard Nixon 1973f re-aptd to 4th term by Pres Jimmy Carter 1978; licensed to Prac in CO DC; served as atty for fed agencies in Rocky Mt area 1942-46; HowardUniv Law Sch, tchr labor adminstrv law 1946-56; US Dept of Labor, 1956-63; Ofc of Regulations, dir 1959-62. **BUSINESS ADDRESS:** Natl Labor Rel Bd, 1717 Pennsylvania Ave Ste 600, Washington, DC 20570.

JENKINS, JAMES E.
Clergyman. **PERSONAL:** Born Jan 14, 1939, Patterson, GA; married Lodine Pollock; children: James, Nerville, Tonji, Calvin. **EDUCATION:** Equiv BTh. **CAREER:** Seaboard Baptist Assn, asst dean & instr; Frndshp Miss Bapt Ch, # Minister-pstr; Seabd Bapt Assn Inc, fourth vice-moderator; Comm Devel Fund, 2nd vp; Haitian Refugee Info Cntr, founder exec dir. **ORGANIZATIONS:** Chmn Historical Commn Com Nat Bapt Conv USA Inc; mem Rotary Internat; appt to Gov Stop Crime Commn; org-chmn CRAC; mem Comm Rel Bd. **HONORS/ACHIEVEMENTS:** Recip man of the yr 1971 Front of Am; citzn of the yr 1972 Sigma Alpha Chap Omega Psi Phi; Nathan Collier Award FL Mem Coll 1972; cert of recog 1972 Nat Sor of Phi Delta Kappa; outstdg Comm Serv 1973 Blk Professional Nrses Assn; Qual of Life Award Jonathan Paul Turner Mem Found 1974; Humanitarian Award AEAON-MS Dau of Isi 1975. **BUSINESS ADDRESS:** 740 NW 58 St, Miami, FL 33127.

JENKINS, JIMMY RAYMOND
Educational administrator. **PERSONAL:** Born Mar 18, 1943, Selma, NC; married Faleese Moore; children: Lisa, Ginger, Jimmy Raymond Jr. **EDUCATION:** Elizabeth City State Univ, BS 1965; Purdue Univ, MS, PhD 1969-72. **CAREER:** Elizabeth City State Univ, asst prof biol 1972, asst acad dean 1972, assoc prof biol 1973, vice chancellor acad affairs 1977, chancellor 1983-. **ORGANIZATIONS:** Mem NC Humanities Comm 1980, Governor's Oversight Comm, Natl Caucus for Black Aged, Elizabeth City Chap Kiwanis Intl, NC Bd of Sci & Tech, Amer Assoc of Higher Ed. **HONORS/ACHIEVEMENTS:** Disting Alumni NAFEO; Outstanding Young Men in Amer; Boss of the Year Elizabeth City State Univ 1978. **HOME ADDRESS:** 1304 Parkview Dr, Elizabeth City, NC 27909. **BUSINESS ADDRESS:** Chancellor, Elizabeth City StateUniv, Box 790, Elizabeth City, NC 27909.

JENKINS, JOSEPH WALTER, JR.
Insurance executive. **PERSONAL:** Born Jan 28, 1941, East Orange, NJ; married Shirley G Hendricks; children: Khalil, Medinah. **EDUCATION:** TN State Univ, BS Bus Admin 1963; Farleigh Dickinson Univ, MBA Management 1976. **CAREER:** General Motors, prod control coord 1963; Ford Motor Co, engrg analyst 1966; Travelers Ins Co, asst mgr persl admin 1968; Chubb Corp, eeo mgr 1974, asst vice pres of human resources. **ORGANIZATIONS:** Pres Optimists Club Orange-East Orange 1976; pres Comm Day Nursery 1985; pres Spectrum Consultants Inc; vice pres Thelma McFall Found; pres J&J Ltd; mem Edges Group; mem League of Women Voters. **HONORS/ACHIEVEMENTS:** Black Achievers Awd Harlem Branch YMCA 1976; Outstanding Service Optimist Club Orange/East Orange 1979. **HOME ADDRESS:** 44 Madonna Place, East Orange, NJ 07018.

JENKINS, JULIUS
Educator. **CAREER:** Concordia College, Selma, AL, president/chancellor. **BUSINESS ADDRESS:** President, Concordia College, Selma, AL 36701. *

JENKINS, KENNETH VINCENT
Educator. **PERSONAL:** Born in Elizabeth, NJ; children: Roderick, Howard, Rebecca, Leah. **EDUCATION:** Columbia Coll NY, AB 1952; Columbia Univ NY, AM 1953; Columbia Univ, PhD candidate. **CAREER:** S Side HS Rockville Centre NY, chmn English dept 1965-72; Nassau Comm Coll, supvr adjunct faculty, prof English Afro-Amer Literature, chmn Afro-Amer studies dept 1974-. **ORGANIZATIONS:** Consult in Eng Convener chmn bd dir Target Youth Ctrs Inc NY 1973-75; mem Natl Bd Pacifica Found 1973-80, chmn 1975-76, pres 1976-79; chmn Nassau Co Youth Bd 1979-; Phi Delta Kappa; Assn Study Afro-Amer Life & Hist; Afro-Amer Inst NY; Unitarian Black Caucus 1968-69; Mensa 1968-70; Coun Black Amer Affairs; exec bd NY African Studies Assn; African Heritage Studies Assn; mem Governors New York State Council on Youth 1986-; mem Advisory Board Radio Station WBAI-FM NY 1972-85. **HONORS/ACHIEVEMENTS:** Cit of Merit B'nai Sholom Rockville Centre NY 1956; Baker Awd Columbia Univ 1953; pres Rockville Centre NY Tchrs Assn 1966-68; Cit State Consult Vassar Coll Engl Syllabus 1964; author of essays reviews "Last Day in Ch". **MILITARY SERVICE:** USNG. **BUSINESS ADDRESS:** Chmn Afro-Amer Studies Dept, Nassau Comm Coll, Garden City, NY 11530.

JENKINS, LOUIS E.
Clinical psychologist. **PERSONAL:** Born Dec 20, 1931, Staten Island, NY; married Althea L Jenkins; children: Le Toia M. **EDUCATION:** Union Coll, BA 1954;Univ NE, MA 1959; Pepperdine U, MA Psychol 1970; PA State U, PhD Clinical Psy 1973. **CAREER:** Pepperdine Univ, assoc prof of psychology 1970-75; LA Union SDA Sch, tchr 1959-64; LA City Schools, teacher 1964-65, counselor 1965-66, school psychologist 1966-69; Dept of Psychology & Human Behavior, Martin Luther King Jr General Hospital LA, staff psychologist; CA Fam Study Cent Downey, CA, private practice. **ORGANIZATIONS:** NAACP; USC

Comm Adv Bd; Am Psy Asso Comm Pilot; flight instr rating. **MILITARY SERVICE:** AUS Med Corp sp3 1954-56. **BUSINESS ADDRESS:** Augustus F Hawkins Mental Health Center, 1720 E 120th St, Los Angeles, CA 90059.

JENKINS, LOZELLE DELUZ
Business executive. **PERSONAL:** Born in Winston-Salem, NC; married Anthony; children: Michael, Patricia. **EDUCATION:** Winston-Salem State U, BS 1952; George Washington U, MA 1962. **CAREER:** JB Linppincott Co, vice pres editor-in-chief 1975-, exec editor 1973-75; Meyer Elem Sch, prin 1969-72; Grimke Elem Sch, prin 1967-69; Montgomery-Morse Elem Sch, asst prin 1966-67; DC Tchrs Coll, instr 1964-66; Kingsman Elem Sch, tchr 1957-64; EdwardUniv Taylor Sch, tchr 1953-57. **ORGANIZATIONS:** Mem WA Educ Assn 1959-69; NEA 1957-; Elem Classroom Tchrs Assn 1959-67; Metro Police Boy's Club 1964-72; Takoma Park Citz Assn 1958-66; Chillum-Ray Citz Assn 1965-72; Winston-Salem StateUniv Alumni Assn 1952-; pres WA Alumnae Chap 1964-; vice pres Delta Sigma Theta Sor 1965-72; Dept of Elem Sch Prin 1967-72; bd mem Children's Bur of DE 1976-; bd mem United Way of DE Allocations Com 1976-; mem Soroptimist Club of Philadelphia 1976-; Nat All of Black Sch Educs 1975-; chmn Model Sch Div 1969-70; mem Open House; DC Council of Sch Ofcrs; mem Supt Com on Reorgn; mem Adv Negotiating Com; Examng Panel forPrin & Asst Prin; consult PERT; consult Behavioral Resrch Lab; consult WV Dept of Edn; consult WI Dept of Instrn; consult Atlanta Pub Schs; consult Detroit Pub Schs Num Publ; life mem Nat Congress PTA; Nat Sci Found. **HONORS/ACHIEVEMENTS:** FlwshpUniv of IA; NEA Overseas Tchr Corps Flwshp Asis 1970; NEA Overseas Tchr Corps Flwshp Ethiopia 1969; outst serv award Delta Sigma Theta Sor 1968-69; alumni achvmt award Winston-Salem State Coll Alumni 1968; disting serv award Winston-Salem State Coll Alumni 1967. **BUSINESS ADDRESS:** E Washington Sq, Philadelphia, PA 19105.

JENKINS, LYNN See HAMILTON, LYNN

JENKINS, MARILYN JOYCE
Police officer. **PERSONAL:** Born Jun 17, 1943, Detroit, MI; daughter of Madison Martin, Sr and May Martin Mitchell; married Henry Jenkins, Jun 11, 1983; children: Simone Martin, Jamiil Brock Martin. **EDUCATION:** Wayne County Community Coll, Detroit MI, currently enrolled. **CAREER:** City of Detroit MI, police officer, 1975-. **ORGANIZATIONS:** Founder/pres, 7 Mile Schaefer Youth Assn, 1978-87; presenter, Career Day, Newberry Elementary School, 1984; pres, Ladies on the Move, 1984-; treasurer, Southwest Aging Coalition, 1984-86; moderator, Educational Training Seminar, 1985; moderator, Gerontology Program Workshop, 1985; presenter, Courtis Elementary-Child Molestation Prevention Program, 1986. **HONORS/ACHIEVEMENTS:** Officer of the Year, Detroit Police Dept, 1978, 1985; Spirit of Detroit Award, Detroit City Council, 1985, 1988; Distinguished Service Award, Wayne County Executive, 1985; Top Cop Award, Detroit Chamber of Commerce, 1985; Police Community Service Award, Detroit Police Dept, 1985; Women Police of MI Certificate of Appreciation; Certificate of Appreciation, Mayor Coleman Young. **HOME ADDRESS:** 19180 Ardmore, Detroit, MI 48235.

JENKINS, MELVIN E., JR.
Physician. **PERSONAL:** Born Jun 24, 1923, Kansas City, MO; son of Melvin and Marguerite; married Maria Parker; children: Janis, Carol, Lore, Frank, Ingrid, Colin. **EDUCATION:** Univ of KS, AB 1944; Univ of KS Coll of Med, MD 1946; Freedman's Hosp, internship 1946-47, pediatric residency 1947-50; pediatric endocrinology Johns Hopkins Hospital 1963-65. **CAREER:** Freedman's Hosp, asst pediatrician 1950-59, assoc pediatrician 1959-69; Howard Univ Coll Med, clinical instr 1951-54, clinical asst prof 1954-55, asst prof 1957-59, assoc prof 1959-69; Univ of NE Med Ctr, pediatrician 1969-73, dir pediatric endocrine clinic 1969-73, prof vice chmn dept of pediatrics 1971-73; George Washington Univ, professional lectr child health & devel 1973-; Hospital for Sick Children, attng staff 1973-; Childrens Hosp Natl Med Ctr of DC, sr attng pediatrician 1973-; Freedmen's Hosp, chief pediatrician 1973-; Johns Hopkins Univ, lectr dept of pediatrics 1974-; Howard Univ Coll of Med, prof chmn dept of pediatrics & child health 1973-. **ORGANIZATIONS:** Grad educ com admissions com Univ of NE Med Ctr 1969-73; policy adv com Ctr for Urban Affairs 1971-73; chmn Health Task Force; bd dirs Urban League of NE 1971-73; pres bd dirs Comprehensive Hlth Assn of Omaha Inc 1972-73; med dir Parent Ctr 1971-73; edtr in chief Pediatric Newsletter Natl Med Assn 1970-; adv bd Human Growth Inc 1971; chmn med records com Freedmen's Hosp 1966, Howard Univ Hosp 1974-; med sch rep Howard Univ Counc of Adm 1967, 1974; pres Freedmen's Hosp Med Dental Staff 1968-69; chmn ped sect Natl Med Assn 1966-69; consult Natl Inst of Health 1973-; campus rep Endocrine Soc 1974-; subcom on growth hormone 1974-; med adv com Nat Pituitary Agency 1975-; med adv com Natl Found March of Dimes 1974-; examiner Amer Bd of Pediatrics 1975-, bd mem 1983-; mem Natl Adv Rsch Resources Counc Natl I nst of Health 1975; mem Sigma Xi; Med Chirurgical Soc of DC; Amer Assn for Advancement of Sci; Black Child Devel Inst Inc; Alpha Omega Alpha; mem Pediatric Surgery Comm Amer Bd of Surgery 1984. **HONORS/ACHIEVEMENTS:** SAMA Golden Apple Awd 1963; Recog for Outstanding Contrib to Growth of Pediatric Sect Natl Med Assn 1966-69; Outstanding Achiev Awd So Christian Ldrshp Conf 1972; Outstanding Scholar-Teacher Awd Howard Univ 1984; Outstanding Contrib Citation City Council of DC 1984; Leadership in Medicine Award Univ of Kansas 1989. **BUSINESS ADDRESS:** Chmn Dept of Pediatrics, HowardUniv, College of Medicine, Washington, DC 20059.

JENKINS, MELVIN L.
Regional attorney. **PERSONAL:** Born Oct 15, 1947, Halifax, NC; son of Mr and Mrs S Jenkins; married Wanda Holly; children: Shelley, Melvin Jr, Dawn, Holly Rae-Ann. **EDUCATION:** NC A&T State Univ, BS 1969; Univ of KS School of Law, Juris Docorate 1972. **CAREER:** Legal Aid Soc Kansas City, MO, staff atty 1972; US Dept of Housing & Urban Devel, staff atty 1972-73; US Commn on Civil Rights, regional atty 1973-79; acting staff dir, US. **ORGANIZATIONS:** Bd of dir Joan Davis Special School 1984-; mem Natl Bar Assn; mem NE Bar Assn; mem Mayor's Human Rel Commn Kansas City, MO; mem Alpha Phi Omega Serv Frat. **HONORS/ACHIEVEMENTS:** Benton FellowshipUniv of KS Sch of Law; Smith Fellowship Legal Aid Soc; Civil Rights Award Blue Valley Lodge Masons. **HOME ADDRESS:** 8015 Sunset Cir, Grandview, MO 64030. **BUSINESS ADDRESS:** Regional Dir, US Comm on Civil Rights, 911 Walnut, Kansas City, MO 64106.

JENKINS, OZELLA
Convention manager. **PERSONAL:** Born Aug 13, 1945, Roanoke Rapids, NC. **EDUCATION:** NC Central Univ, attended 1962-64; Howard Univ, attended 1964-65; Cornell Univ, attended 1974. **CAREER:** C&P Telephone Co, customer serv rep 1964-71; Pitts Motor Hotel, restaurant mgr 1964-72; Sheraton Washington Hotel, convention mgr 1972-. **ORGANIZATIONS:** Mem Natl Cncl of Negro Women 1962-; mem Natl Assoc of Catering Execs 1976-; mem Natl Coalition of Black Mtg Planners 1984-; business mgr Washington Chap JUGS Inc 1984-; vice pres Bonaire Homes Assoc 1985-. **HONORS/ACHIEVEMENTS:** Certificate Daughters of the Amer Revolution 1979; Recognition of Excellence Successful Meeting Mag 1982,84,86; certificate/plaque Meeting Planners Intl 1984; plaque Natl Urban League 1985, US Marshall Service 1985, Metro Police Dept Washington DC 1985. **BUSINESS ADDRESS:** Convention Manager, Sheraton Washington Hotel, 2660 Woodley Rd, NW, Washington, DC 20008.

JENKINS, ROBERT KENNETH, JR.
Attorney. **PERSONAL:** Born Mar 11, 1947, Washington, DC; divorced; children: Robert K Jenkins III. **EDUCATION:** Howard Univ, BA 1970; George Washington Univ, JD 1974. **CAREER:** US Sec & Exch Comm, trial atty 1974-76; Direct Selling Assn, legisl counsel 1977; Natl YMCA, dep gen counsel real est operations 1978-80; Natl City Financial Serv Inc, pres. **ORGANIZATIONS:** Chmn bd Northwest Invest Group 1980-; dir Fall Invest Group 1979-83; chmn bd Sheperd Learning Center 1985-. **HOME ADDRESS:** 1406 Jonquil St NW, Washington, DC 20012. **BUSINESS ADDRESS:** President, Natl City Financial Serv, 1100 Wayne Avenue, Silver Spring, MD 20910.

JENKINS, ROGER J.
Association executive. **PERSONAL:** Born Oct 26, 1939, Fort Pierce, FL; married Rose Oliver; children: Roger, Jr, Courtney, Oren. **EDUCATION:** Clark Coll, BA 1962; Atlanta Sch of Soc Work;; MSW 1964fUniv of Cincinnati, MCP 1972;Univ of Cincinnati, PhD 1974. **CAREER:** Seven Hills Neighborhood Houses, exec dir 1968-71; Org Dev Consult for sev maj indsl org educ & rel systems; New Orleans Neighborhood Centers, group work 1964-65. **ORGANIZATIONS:** Adv com Neighborhood Tech Inf Serv Am Soc Plann Offs; Am Sociological Assn; Am Soc of Plann Off; Nat Assn of Soc Work; Am Assn ofUniv ProfUnited Black FacultyUniv of Cincinnati; Alpha Phi Alpha Frat Elec. **HONORS/ACHIEVEMENTS:** Outstndg young man in Am 1972; spl cit State of OH for Comm Serv; spl city Cty of Cincinnati for Comm dev. **BUSINESS ADDRESS:** 701 Lincoln Park Dr, Cincinnati, OH 45203.

JENKINS, SHIRLEY LYMONS
Educator. **PERSONAL:** Born Aug 09, 1936, Pine Apple, AL; married Henry J Jenkins. **EDUCATION:** Knoxville Coll, BS Educ 1958; Atlanta Univ, MA Educ 1969; Univ of AL, AA Educ 1974. **CAREER:** Boykin High School AL, teacher 1959-62; Camden Academy AL, teacher 1962-68; Leeds Elementary School, AL, teacher 1968-. **ORGANIZATIONS:** Southeastern regional dir Knoxville Coll Alumni Assoc 1978-84; chairperson Teen-Life Birmingham Alumnae Delta Sigma Theta Sorority Inc 1983-85; chairpersonScholarship Natl Sor of Phi Delta Kappa Inc 1983-; pres Knoxville College Natl Alumni Assoc Inc 1984-; mem bd trustees Knoxville Coll 1984-; mem Birmingham Alumnae Delta Sigma Theta Sorority Inc, Birmingham Chap Natl Sor Phi Delta Kappa Inc; mem Sixth Avenue Baptist Church Birmingham; mem Amer Fedeation of Teachers, Natl Council of Negro Women Inc. **HONORS/ACHIEVEMENTS:** Outstanding Young Woman of Amer 1971; Outstanding Regional Dir Knoxville Coll Alumni 1978-84; President's Disting Serv Awds Knoxville Coll 1979, 82; Hostess of Year Imperial Club Inc Debutante Ball 1983; Certificates Jefferson Co Bd of Health 1983-86; Certificate Outstanding Contribution Southern Region Delta Sigma Theta Sor 1984; Soror of the Month Phi Delta Kappa Sor Inc 1985; Disting Alumni of the Year Citation Natl Assoc for Equal Oppor in Higher Educ 1986; Citation Amer Federation of Teachers; life mem Knoxville College Natl Alumni Assoc Inc. **HOME ADDRESS:** 2692 20th St W, Birmingham, AL 35208.

JENKINS, THOMAS M.
President. **CAREER:** Lincoln Univ Jefferson City MO, pres.

JENKINS, THOMAS O.
Government employee. **PERSONAL:** Born Jun 13, 1926, Fairfield, AL; married Lucille Bell; children: Angela, Christopher. **EDUCATION:** Miles Coll Birmingham, BA (cum laude) 1949. **CAREER:** Fair Housing & Equal Oppor US Dept HUD, actg asst sec; acting dep asst sec 1972-75; Ofc Mgmt & Field Coord, dir; Contract Compliance Div, 1969-72; US Commn Civil Rights, reg dir 1968-69. **ORGANIZATIONS:** Mem Pub Personnel Assn; Nat Assn Inter-group Relation Ofcls. **HONORS/ACHIEVEMENTS:** Man of yr Award Omega Psi Phi; personalities of Sx; spl serv Award Civil Rights Commn 1968; dist serv Award HUD 1974. **MILITARY SERVICE:** AUS 1944-46. **BUSINESS ADDRESS:** 451 7 St SW, Washington, DC.

JENKINS, VAN
Retired educatioinal administrator. **PERSONAL:** Born Jan 23, 1911, Mobile, AL; son of Van Jenkins and Lillie Belle Jenkins; married Gloria M (Robinson). **EDUCATION:** Wilberforce Univ, BS 1936;Univ Mich, MA 1969f Wayne State Univ; Detroit Inst Tech; George William Coll Chicago. **CAREER:** Govt serv 1940-46; NY Public Schools, teacher; Edward Waters Coll Jacksonville FL; Detroit YMCA, dir health & phys educ; Detroit Public Schs, teacher, coach, athletic dir, dept head asst prin, principal Northwestern High School, Detroit, MI. **ORGANIZATIONS:** Mem Brown Bombers Pro Football Team; Renaissance Pro Basketball Team; NAACP; Detroit Varisty Club; Frontiers Mens Club; MI Sportsmen Club; MI Coaches Assn; MI Assn Secondary Sch Prin; Petro-Detroit Assn Black Administrators; Phi Delta Kappa; Prince Happ Mason; Kappa Alpha Psi Frat Detroit Polemarch 1972-; memUniv MI Alumni Club; Wilberforce Univ Alumni; Alumni Bd Trustee Wilferforce Univ. **HONORS/ACHIEVEMENTS:** Football coach of year 1965; Teacher serv Award MI State Univ 1970; Distinguished Serv Award Wilberforce Univ 1971; Church Track & Field State of Mich 1970-72.

JENKINS, WOODIE R., JR.
Engineer. **PERSONAL:** Born Jun 18, 1940, Washington, DC; son of Rev. Woodie R. Jenkins, Sr. (deceased) and Laura Berry Washington; married Ramona M Hernandez, Jun 21, 1968; children: Tammy Monique. **EDUCATION:** Howard U, BS Physics 1964; NM St U, MS Mech/Industrial Engrg 1972. **CAREER:** Natl Range Operations, WSMR, NM, physicist 1964-70; Quality Assurance Office, WSMR, genl engr 1970-77; Quality Evaluation Div, WSMR, chief 1977-82; US Army Training and Doctrine Command's Systems Analysis Activity, WSMR, spl staff asst to tech dir 1980; Las Cruces, NM, city councillor 1980-85, mayor protem 1982-85; High Energy Laser Program Office, WSMR, assoc program mgr plans and

opers 1982-84; High Energy Laser Systems Test Facility, White Sands Missile Range, chief test operations 1984-. **ORGANIZATIONS:** US Army Tech Liaison Rep to the Amer Defense Preparedness Assn 1975-; Registered Professional Engr 1979-; mem WSMR Speaker's Bureau 1979-; Political Action Comm Dona Ana County NAACP Branch 1979-85; mem WSMR Commander's Committee on Hispanic and Black Employment 1980-85; mem Transportation Communications and PublicSafety Policy Comm Natl League of Cities 1980-83; Deputy Activity Career Program Mgr for Engrs and Scientists at WSMR 1981-; mem lecture circuit New Mexico Junior College 1986; vice chmn bd of dirs Southern New Mexico Human Development, Inc 1985-; mem New Mexico Statewide Health Coordinating Council 1985-86; vice pres bd of directors, Las Cruces YMCA, 1988-; chairman, Las Cruces Extra Territorial Zoning Commn, 1987-. **HONORS/ACHIEVEMENTS:** WSMR Commander's Awd 1983; published over 40 technical articles, papers, and presentations; 8 Performance Awds from the US Dept of Army; Certificate of Nobility New Mexico Secretary of State 1982; American Scientific Registry, American Govermental Registry, Intl Registry of Profiles, Natl Roster of Black Elected Officials; Certificate of Apreciation for Public Service, State of New Mexico, 1989. **HOME ADDRESS:** 700 Turner Ave, Las Cruces, NM 88005.

JENKINS, YOLANDA L.
Educator. **PERSONAL:** Born Dec 31, 1945, Chicago, IL. **EDUCATION:** Univ of WI, BA 1967; Boston Univ, MEd 1971; Univ of CA Berkeley, PhD 1982. **CAREER:** SRI Intl, field supervisor 1971-72; Urban Inst for Human Serv and Westside Community Mental Health Center, rsch assoc 1973-80; Univ of California-Berkeley Teacher Corps Prog, rsch assoc 1980-82; Atari Inst, mgr of prog evaluation & rsch, acting dir 1982-84; Apple Computer Inc, mgr of educ market analysis, dir community affairs 1984-. **ORGANIZATIONS:** Bd mem, Bay Area Black Child Advocacy Coalition, 1977-80; founder, Bay Area Black Women's Forum, 1978-79; consultant, San Francisco Foundation, 1980; fund-raising comm mem, Parent Infant Neighborhood Center, 1984; bd of dir, San Jose Children's Discovery Museum, 1986-87; bd of advisors, Women's Resource Center, Palo Alto CA, 1987. **HONORS/ACHIEVEMENTS:** Commendation Award, Coro Foundation San Francisco, 1973; Outstanding Young Women of Amer, 1980; Outstanding Contribution & Appreciation Award, Los Angeles Student Film Inst, 1983. **BUSINESS ADDRESS:** Mgr, Education Market Analysis, Apple Computer, Inc, 20525 Mariani Ave, Cupertino, CA 95014.

JENKINS-SCOTT, JACKIE
Executive. **PERSONAL:** Born Aug 18, 1949, Damascus, AR; married James M Scott; children: Amal James, Amber Dawn. **EDUCATION:** Eastern MI Univ, BS 1971; Boston Univ School of Social Work, MSW 1973; Radcliffe Coll, Post Grad Rsch Prog 1975. **CAREER:** Commonwealth of MA Dept of Public Health, dir treatment serv reg mgr 1973-77; Roxbury Court Clinic, exec dir 1977-83; Dimock Community Health Ctr, pres 1983-. **ORGANIZATIONS:** Trustee Cousens Fund 1985-92; mem newton Chap of Jack & Jill of Amer 1985, Delta Sigma Theta; vice pres MA League of Health Ctrs 1987; sec Mass Public Health Assoc 1987-88, Consortium of Black Health Ctr Direct 1987; bd mem Blackstone Bank & Trust Co. **HONORS/ACHIEVEMENTS:** Outstanding Contribution of a Social Worker with Five Years or Less Experience Mass Chap of the Natl Assoc of Social Workers 1975; "Alcohol Abuse Among Black Women" Douglass Publ 1976; 1978 Lady of the Year Awd Project Understanding. **HOME ADDRESS:** 1063 Commonwealth Ave, Newton, MA 02159. **BUSINESS ADDRESS:** President, Dimock Community Health Center, 55 Dimock St, Roxbury, MA 02119.

JENNINGS, BENNIE ALFRED
Executive director. **PERSONAL:** Born Nov 21, 1933, Port Gibson, MS; married Mildred B Blackburn; children: Sharon, Marion, Brenda. **EDUCATION:** Alcorn Univ, attended 1956-57; Grambling State Univ, BS Secondary Educ 1957-60. **CAREER:** Chesebrough-Pond's Inc, machine adjustor 1960-63; Gen Dynamics/Electric Boat Div, draftsman/apprentice trang admin 1963-70; OIC of New London Co Inc CT,exec dir 1970-. **ORGANIZATIONS:** Life mem NAACP, Natl Council of Negro Women. **HONORS/ACHIEVEMENTS:** Mgmt Devel Inst Awd GE Corp NY 1976; Gold Key Awd OIC of Am Philadelphia 1979; 10 Yr Serv Awd OIC of Am Philadelphia 1980; Dr M L King Jr Comm Serv Awd; Club Cosmos New London CT 1980. **MILITARY SERVICE:** USAF A/3c 1951-55; Disting Serv Awd USAF 1951-55. **BUSINESS ADDRESS:** Executive Dir, OIC of New London County Inc, 106 Truman St, New London, CT 06320.

JENNINGS, JEANETTE
Educator. **PERSONAL:** Born Jan 21, 1945, Hattiesburg, MS. **EDUCATION:** Jackson StUniv MS, BA (cum laude) 1966; Tulane U, MSW 1969. **CAREER:** Univ of MS, asst prof Social Work 1971-; MS Dept of Public Welfare, social worker 1966-70; Jackson State Univ, instructor 1969. **ORGANIZATIONS:** Mem, Nat Assn Black Soc Wrkrs; Nat Assn Soc Wrkrs; MS Conf Soc Wel; Co Soc Wrk Ed; MS Co Hum Rel; N MS Rural Legal Srvs Inst, Comm Srv & Foster Grndprnt Prog; Oxford Dev Assn; Mntl Hlth Assn; adv xoun Oxford Daycare Cntr; Alcoholic Adv Cncl. **HONORS/ACHIEVEMENTS:** 1st black faculty mem,Univ MS; Who's Who Am Colls & Univs 1966; other Who's Who awards, plaques, comm Grps. **BUSINESS ADDRESS:** Hume HallUniv MS, University, MS 38677.

JENNINGS, LILLIAN PEGUES
Educator. **PERSONAL:** Born in Youngstown, OH; children: Dan, Kim. **EDUCATION:** Youngstown State Univ, BS 1954; Univ of Pittsburgh, MEd 1967, PhD 1971; Univ of MD, Post-Doctoral Study. **CAREER:** Publ school teacher 1954-66; ed consult 1966-67; Edinboro State Coll, coord of black studies, prof of ed & reading clinic 1968-71, affirm action officer 1972; Youngstown Publ School, head start prog dir, rsch staff assoc, multiple ed rsch teams; James Madison Univ School of Ed, assoc dean. **ORGANIZATIONS:** Mem Alpha Kappa Alpha, VA Assoc of School Psychol, Intl Reading Assoc; served on mayors comm of Human Resources Pittsburgh 1966-67; bd of dir Dr Barber's Ctr for Exceptional Children Erie; mem Phi Delta Kappa, Delta Kappa Gamma; chmn NCATE, Dept of Ed Accred Teams; mem Harrisonburg School Bd, VA Arts Commiss, Natl Alliance of Black School Ed; licensed Professional Counselor; vice chair Harrisonburg Sch Bd VA; Multiple Publications 1986,87; chaired multiple Accreditation teams. **HONORS/ACHIEVEMENTS:** Listed in World's Who's Who of Women; rsch grants Ford Found, Erie Found, NSF; author of multiple publs & monographs; listed in Outstanding Educators of Amer 1975, Dictionary of Intl Biography. **BUSINESS ADDRESS:** Associate Dean, James MadisonUniv, College of Education, Harrisonburg, VA 22801.

JENNINGS, ROBERT RAY
Educator. **PERSONAL:** Born Nov 15, 1950, Atlanta, GA; son of Forrest Jennings Sr and Mary Beeman Jennings. **EDUCATION:** Univ of Ghana Legon West Africa, Charles Merrill Scholar 1971; Morehouse Coll, BA, Sociology, 1972; Atlanta Univ, MA, Educ Psych, 1974; GA State Univ Sch of Educ, Certificate in Gifted Educ 1975; Univ of GA, Certificate in Adult Basic Educ, 1978; Atlanta Univ, Educ Specialist in Interrelated Learning, 1979; Doctorate, Admin, 1982. **CAREER:** Atlanta Univ, asst to dir of public relations, 1973; Atlanta Public School, Hoffman reading coord 1973-76; Literacy Action Inc Atlanta, reading consultant 1974-75; Reading Learning Ctr Inc East Point, dir 1975-79; Atlanta Public Schools, tchr of the gifted 1976-79; Atlanta Univ, consultant dean's grant proj 1979-80; Atlanta Area Tech Sch, part-time prof 1979-84; Equal Employ Comm US Govt, equal oppor specialist 1979-82; Morris Brown Coll Atlanta, assoc prof 1982-84; US Equal Employment Oppor Commn Atlanta Dist, official commn rep office of dir 1982-84; US Equal Employment Oppor Commn Washington, employee devel specialist 1984-85; asst vice pres, devel & placement, Norfolk State Univ, 1985-88; devel officer, Norfolk State Univ, 1988-present. **ORGANIZATIONS:** chmn, Human Relations Council, Student Natl Educ Assn, 1971-72; mem, Council for Exceptional Children, vice pres, Atlanta Area Chapter, 1978-79; pres, Atlanta Univ Natl Alumni Assn, 1979-81; mem, bd of dirs, Exodus Right-to-Read Program Adult Literacy Program, 1980; mem, bd of advisors, Volunteer Atlanta, 1980-84; parlimentarian Council for Exceptional Children Atlanta Area Chap 1980-81; bd of dirs, Parents Anonymous of GA, 1981-84; bd of trustees, Atlanta Univ 1981-85; founder and editor-in-chief Alumni Update of Leadership Atlanta 1982-; mem, Self-Study Evaluation Comm, Morris Brown Coll, 1983-84; bd of dirs, Planned Parenthood, 1983-; mem exec bd, Leadership Atlanta 1986-87; vice pres, Council for Advancement of Public Black Colleges & Universities, 1989-. **HONORS/ACHIEVEMENTS:** Outstanding Achievement Award, Economic Opportunity Atlanta 1972; President's Gold Cup Awd Morehouse Coll Student Govt Assoc 1972; Outstanding Serv Awd Atlanta Inquirer Newspaper 1972; Director's Award Frederick Douglass Tutorial Inst Morehouse Coll 1972; Outstanding Serv Award Student Natl Educ Assn, 1972; Awd ofExcellence Student Mississippi Teacher's Assn, 1972; WSB TV & Radio Fellow 1975; Teacher of the Year Home Park School Atlanta 1976; Award of Excellence Wm Finch Sch Parent Teacher's Assn, 1976; Appreciation Award for Outstanding Leadership SM Inman Sch Parent Teacher's Assn 1976; Outstanding Chapter Mem of the Yr Atlanta Univ 1979; Best of Service Award Frank Lebby Stanton Sch Atlanta 1979; Alumnus of the Yr Atlanta Univ 1980; Special Serv Award, Council for Exceptional Children, Atlanta, 1981; Special Serv Award, Natl Bd of Dirs, Atlanta Univ Alumni, 1981; Phi Delta Kappa Professional Fraternity in Educ, 1982; cited by Atlanta Journal & Constitution Newspaper as one of Atlanta's Most Outstanding Volunteers, 1982; Outstanding Serv Award, United Way of Metro Atlanta, 1984; First Recipient Leadership Award in Educ, Delta Sigma Theta Sor, 1986. **HOME ADDRESS:** 2005 King George Lane SW, Atlanta, GA 30331. **BUSINESS ADDRESS:** Development Officer, Norfolk State Univ, Norfolk, VA 23504.

JENNINGS, SYLVESTA LEE
Banking executive. **PERSONAL:** Born Jan 30, 1933, Halifax; son of Anthony Jennings and Luella Freeman Jennings; married Lillie Flippen, Jun 10, 1960; children: Mitchell. **EDUCATION:** North Carolina A&T State Univ, Greensboro NC, BS, 1958; Univ of Virginia, School of Consumer Banking, Diploma, 1968; Rutgers Univ, Stonier Graduate School of Banking, Diploma, 1972. **CAREER:** First State Bank, Danville VA, pres, 1988-. **ORGANIZATIONS:** Mem, Danville Chamber of Commerce, 1989; mem, Natl Bankers Assn, 1989; mem, Prince Hall Masons of Virginia. **HONORS/ACHIEVEMENTS:** Natl Assn for Equal Opportunity in Higher Educ Award, 1989; research selected for library at Rutgers Univ, Harvard Univ, and ABA, 1972. **MILITARY SERVICE:** US Army, cpl, 1953-55. **HOME ADDRESS:** 121 Lovelace Drive, Danville, VA 24540.

JENSEN, RENALDO MARIO
Automobile company executive. **PERSONAL:** Born Jun 29, 1934, New York, NY; son of Octive Jensen and Doris Davis Jensen; married Alicia Clark, Jan 26, 1959; children: Renaldo M, Malinda L. **EDUCATION:** Howard Univ, Washington DC, BS Mech Engrg, 1958; Air Force Inst of Tech, Dayton OH, MS Aerospace Engrg, 1966; Purdue Univ, West Lafayette IN, PhD Aerospace Engrg, 1970. **CAREER:** US Air Force, officer, 1958-78; Ford Motor Co, Dearborn MI, advanced concepts aerodynamics, 1978-86, mgr minority supplier devel, 1987-. **ORGANIZATIONS:** Mem, New Detroit, Inc, 1987-; mem, Greater Detroit Chamber of Commerce, 1987 -; Bd of Dir, Minority Business Dir, "Try Us," 1987-; Bd of Dir, Natl Minority Business Development Council, 1988-; Amer Society for Mechanical Engineers; Amer Institute for Aeronautics and Astronautics; The Combustion Institute; Military Operations Research Society; mem, Alpha Phi Alpha Fraternity. **HONORS/ACHIEVEMENTS:** Distinguished Service Award, Wisconsin Minority Purcchasing Council, 1988; Tau Beta Pi, Engineering Honor Society. **MILITARY SERVICE:** US Air Force, Lt Col, 1953-78; Missile Combat Crew Award, 1970, Air Force Commendation Medal. **HOME ADDRESS:** 26510 Rose Hill Drive, Farmington Hills, MI 48018.

JERKINS, JERRY GAINES
Clergyman. **PERSONAL:** Born in Loxley, AL; married Naomi Donald; children: Cntr, Gerald, Jennifer, Jacqueline. **EDUCATION:** Austin Peay U, BS 1972; N TN Bible Inst, D Evang. **CAREER:** St John Bapt Ch Clarksville, TN, pastor 1967-; Haynes Chapel Bapt Ch, pastor. **ORGANIZATIONS:** Mem, Clarksville Ministerial Assn; ministerial rep, C of C; corres sec, Pastor's Conf Nat & Bapt Conv Am; PTA; bd, Children Cntr Hilldale Meth Ch; pres, Missionary Bapt St Conv; bd, United Givers Fund; adv bd, Montgomery Co Wlfr Dept; adv bd, Youth Challenge Cntr; pres, Dist Pastor's Conf; bd, Salvation Army; NAACP; gospel Progmr, Radio Sta WJZM. **MILITARY SERVICE:** Mil serv sgt 14 yrs.

JERNIGAN, CURTIS DEAN
Counselor. **PERSONAL:** Born Jul 17, 1945, Bullock County, AL; married Rosia M Hughes; children: Valeria, Adero, Kwesi. **EDUCATION:** AL St Coll, BS 1967; AL St U, MEd 1974; AL St, AA Cert 1977. **CAREER:** Community Servs, specialist 1977-; Human Resource Devel Center, Tuskegee Inst, coordinator 1972-77; Bullock Co Bd of Educ, comm educ dir 1976-77, supvr 1976-77, teacher 1967-72. **ORGANIZATIONS:** Chmn, Bullock Co Bd of Ed 1974-76; mem bd of dir, SE AL Self Help Assn Inc 1976-78; mem bd of dir, Org Comm Act 1975-76; mem, Bullock Co Plng Com 1975-76; deacon, Union Hall Bapt Ch; mem, 32 Deg Mason; sec, orgnzr, Bullock Co Black Elctd Offl 1975-76; chmn, Bullock Co Coord Com; vp,Union Spgs NAACP Br; pres, Bullock Co Imprv Org Ford Found. **HONORS/ACHIEVEMENTS:** Fllwshp, Ldrshp Dev Prog 1969-70; Outst Young Men of Am 1974. **BUSINESS ADDRESS:** R R Moten Hall, Tuskegee Inst, Tuskegee Institute, AL 36088.

JEROME, NORGE WINEFRED
Educator. **PERSONAL:** Born Nov 03, 1930. **EDUCATION:** Howard Univ, BS (magna

cum laude) 1960; Univ of Wisconsin, Madison, MS 1962, PhD 1967. **CAREER:** Dept of Diet & Nutrition KSUniv Med Ctr, asst prof 1967-72; Dept of Commnty Hlth KSUniv Med Ctr, asso prof 1972-78; Dept of Preventive Med KSUniv Med Ctr, prof 1978-; Commnty Nutrition Div/KSUniv Med Ctr, dir 1981-; Nutritional Anthropology Communicator, ed 1974-77; Ed Resource Ctrs, dir 1974-77; Univ KS Med Ctr Coll of Health Sci, nutritionist, anthropologist, head comm nutr dir, prof of prev medicine. **ORGANIZATIONS:** Academic advisor Children's Advert Review Unit 1974-; media rep Bristol Myers Co 1981-82; research advisor Campbell Soup Co 1979-81; mem Mayor's Task Force on Food & Hunger 1983-; founder/chmn Comm on Nutritional Anthropology 1978-79; bd mem Urban League of Greater Kansas City 1969-77; adv bd Jrnl of NutrPlng 1977-; mem World Food & Nutrition Study Natl Acad of Sci 1976; fellow Amer Anthro Assoc; fellow Soc of Appl Anthro; mem Soc of Med Anthro, Amer Publ Health Assocc, Amer Dietetic Assoc; panelist White House Conf on Food Nutr & Health; mem US Assoc for the Club of Rome 1980-; fellow Amer Coll of Nutrition. **HONORS/ACHIEVEMENTS:** Higuchi Research Achievemnt AwardUniv of KS 1982; Citation for Service United Commnty Serv Kansas City, MO 1974; Matrix Award Women in Communications Inc 1976; Dairy Cncl Merit Award Greater Kansas City 1977. **HOME ADDRESS:** 14402 W 68th St, Shawnee Mission, KS 66216. **BUSINESS ADDRESS:** Professor & Dir, U of KS Sch of Med, 39th & Rainbow Blvd, Room 5030b, Kansas City, KS 66103.

JERVAY, MARION WHITE
Attorney. **PERSONAL:** Born Mar 26, 1948, Mt Olive, NC. **EDUCATION:** Univ of NC Wilmington, BA 1971; Nat Law Center, Geo WashUniv Wash, DC,1973-74; Sch of Law DukeUniv Durham, NC, JD 1976. **CAREER:** Liggett Group Inc Durham, NC, corp atty 1977-; Hon Earl W Vaughn, NC Ct of Appeals Raleigh, rsrch asst 1976-77; Wade & Roger Smith Attys at Law Raleigh, rsrch asst 1975; Norfolk City Schs, tchr 1972-73; New Hanover Co Bd of Educ Wilmington, engl tchr 1972. **ORGANIZATIONS:** Mem NC State Bar; mem NC Bar Assn; mem Wake Co Bar Assn; mem NC Assn of Black Lawyers; mem ABA; mem Am Bus Women's Assn.

JERVAY, PAUL REGINALD, JR.
Newspaperman. **PERSONAL:** Born Oct 25, 1949, Atlanta, GA; son of Paul Reginald Jervay, Sr. and Brenda Yancey Jervay; married Evelyn Harrison Jervay, Jul 24, 1988; children: Jeneea Jervay, Adria Jervay, Shenay Dunston, Kelvin Dunston. **EDUCATION:** NC Central Univ, Raleigh, NC, BS, 1971. **CAREER:** The Carolinian, Raleigh, NC, assoc publisher, 1971-; consultant, Advantage Advertising, 1987-. **ORGANIZATIONS:** Treasurer, Nay-Kel Educ Ctr and Girl's Club, 1984-. **HONORS/ACHIEVEMENTS:** Service Award, St. Augustine's Coll, 1983.

JERVAY, THOMAS CLARENCE, SR.
Business executive & journalist. **PERSONAL:** Born Nov 30, 1914, Wilmington, NC; son of Robert S Jervay and Mary A Jervay; married Wille E DeVane; children: Mary Alice Thatch, Katherine Jervay. **EDUCATION:** Hampton Inst; Howard Univ; Virginia State Coll, BS 1937. **CAREER:** Cape Fear Jrnl, ed 1938-45; Colored Shipbldrs NC Shipbuilding Co, publ 1943; Wilmington Jrnl, ed, publ 1945-89. **ORGANIZATIONS:** Founder, Hanover Bank 1975; mem, Family Service; United Fund; Chamber of Commerce former pres, NNPA Black Press of Amer, mem, Alpha Phi Alpha Frat Inc; Amalgamated Publ, Prince Hall Masons, others. **HONORS/ACHIEVEMENTS:** Omegas Citizen Yr 1954; Citizen of Yr Wilmington 1976; awards from NAACP; numerous other awards; awarded United Negro Coll Fund's Highest Award and awarded Kellogg's Celebrity Tribute Bronz Flame Award, 1988. **BUSINESS ADDRESS:** Editor/Publisher, Wilmington Journal, PO Box 1618, Wilmington, NC 28402.

JESSIE, RON RAY
Professional athlete. **PERSONAL:** Born Feb 04, 1948, Yuma, AZ; married Sharon; children: Ron, Brandon. **EDUCATION:** Imperial Valley Jr Coll;Univ of KS. **CAREER:** Los Angeles Rams, wide receiver 1975-; Detroit, 1971-75; Dallas, 1971; US Commerce Dept Bus Mgmt, employed off-season. **HONORS/ACHIEVEMENTS:** Named club's outst receiver Fellowship Prgm 1976, 1977; Pro Bowl 1976; NFC Championship Game 1975, 1976, 1978. **BUSINESS ADDRESS:** Los Angeles Rams, 10271 W Pico Blvd, Los Angeles, CA 90064.

JESSIE, WAYMON THOMAS
Educational administrator. **PERSONAL:** Born Oct 10, 1945, Newark, NJ; son of P Thomas Jessie and Alyce Mildred Mead Jessie; married Vanessa; children: Jarret Thomas, Nassor Nuru. **EDUCATION:** Essex Cty Coll, AS 1971; Rutgers Univ, BA 1974. **CAREER:** City of Newark, chief accountant 1975-76, chief of eval 1976-78; Comprehensive Empl & Training, dep dir 1978-81, dir 1981-82; City of Newark, asst to business admin; Assoc R. R. Brown & Co Inc Plainfield NJ 1986-. **ORGANIZATIONS:** Mem Kenneth A Gibson Civic Assoc 1974-; royal estate sales Dan Califri Inc 1980-; mem Natl Forum Black Public Admin 1982; charter mem Natl Black Child Development Inst 1982-; mem American Assn of Affimative Action Officers; licensed NJ State Realtor and Insurance Broker. **HONORS/ACHIEVEMENTS:** Outstanding Young Man Amer Natl Jaycees 1976; Achievement Awd United Way 1979; Good Citizenship Kenneth Gibson Civic Assoc 1980; Comm Serv Awd Ralph Grant Civic Assoc 1981. **MILITARY SERVICE:** AUS spec 4 1963-66. **HOME ADDRESS:** 650 So 19th St, Newark, NJ 07103. **BUSINESS ADDRESS:** Affirmative Action Officer, Newark Board of Education, 2 Cedar St, Suite 702, Newark, NJ 07102.

JESSUP, MARSHA EDWINA
Educator. **PERSONAL:** Born Nov 08, 1944, Washington, DC. **EDUCATION:** Howard U, BS 1967;Univ MI, MS 1971; Cath U, 1973; Temple Univ, 1978. **CAREER:** Dept of Media Resources, chf med illus, dir; Nat Inst of Health, med illus 1972-74; US Dept of Agr Grad Sch, faculty mem 1971-74; Armed Forces Inst of Pathology, med illus 1972; HowardUniv Coll of Med, asst med illus 1968-69; Smithsonian Inst, free-lance sci illus 1967-68; UMDNJ Robert Wood Johnson Medical School, dept & adj assoc prof surgery dept, dir of media resources. **ORGANIZATIONS:** Vchmn, bd of gov 1984-86, mem accreditation comm 1984-87, chmn, bd of giv 1986-87 Assoc of Medical Illustrators; ne region bd of gov rep Assoc of Biomedical Communications Directors 1982-84. **HONORS/ACHIEVEMENTS:** Cited Civic & Career Svc, Silver Spring MD Bus & Professional Womens Club 1973; US Civil Serv Task Force 1974. **BUSINESS ADDRESS:** Dir of Media Resources, UMDNJ, Robert Wood Johnson Med Sch, 675 Hoes Lane, Piscataway, NJ 08854.

JETER, CLIFTON B., JR.
Business executive. **PERSONAL:** Born Feb 22, 1944, Martinsville, VA; married Diane R Bates; children: Sheree, Amani, Aja. **EDUCATION:** Howard U, BA 1967; Am U, MBA 1970; MD, CPA 1972. **CAREER:** John F Kennedy Center for Performing Arts, controller; Wolf & Co, mgr 1975-77; Howard U, internal auditor 1974-75; Peoples Devel Corp, fin vice pres 1969-74; Peoples Involvement Corp, controller 1967-69. **ORGANIZATIONS:** Treas Quality Constrn Co 1974-77; Nat Inst for Tennis Devel 1975-77; Alpha Phi Alpha; Am Inst of CPA'S; MD Assn of CPA'S DC Inst of CPA'S; Nat Black MBA Assn; Nat Assn of Black Accts; Am Mgmt Assn; Assn of Practicing CPA'S; Am Accounting Assn. **BUSINESS ADDRESS:** Dir of Finance, John F Kennedy Center, Washington, DC 20566.

JETER, DELORES DEANN
Pharmacist. **PERSONAL:** Born Mar 11, 1949, Union, SC. **EDUCATION:** Univ SC Coll, Pharmacy 1973, Seeking PhD in Pharmacy Adminstrn. **CAREER:** Funderburks Drug, intern 1972; Moncrief Army Hosp, intern 1973; Richland Meml Hosp, clinical pharmacy 1973; Millers Pharmacy, reg pharmacist & mgr 1974. **ORGANIZATIONS:** Mem Am Pharmaceutical Assn; mem Palmetto & Med Dental Pharmaceutical Assn; mem Alcoholic & Drug Abuse Council; organist Calvary Bapt Ch. **HONORS/ACHIEVEMENTS:** Cit day Columbia SC; nominee Personalities S 1974; nominee to Who's Who Among Women of the World 1976. **BUSINESS ADDRESS:** 827 N Main St, Lancaster, SC.

JETER, FELICIA RENE
Journalist. **PERSONAL:** Born Dec 07, 1948, Atlanta, GA. **EDUCATION:** Mundelein Coll, BA 1970; Grad Sch of Broadcast Jour Columbia U, Spl M Equivalency Prgm 1972. **CAREER:** KHOU-TV; KHJ-TV LA, anchorwoman; NBC LA, reporter/anchorwoman/show Hostess 1974-80;WAOK Atlanta, radio broadcaster 1972-74; WAGA-TV Atlanta, producer/reporter 1972-74; Vince Cullers Adv Agency Chgo, asst broadcast dir 1970-72. **ORGANIZATIONS:** Mem Am Fedn of TV & Radio Artists; mem Nat Acad of TV Arts & Sci; mem Soc of Professional Journalists; mem Sigma Delta Chi; mem The Media Forum; mem The Greater LA Press Club; mem Nat Assn of Black Jour; mem Assn ofr Equal Representation of Minorities in Communications; mem Am Women in Radio & TV; memBlack Jour Assn of So CA; bd of dir Western States Black Research Cntr; bd of dir Brockman Art Gallery; bd mem Adv Counc USC Cancer Cntr. **HONORS/ACHIEVEMENTS:** First full-time black anchorwoman Los Angeles, CA; commendation, pres Jimmy Carter; Cit of Merit,Univ So CA; judge, 6th Ann Robt F Kennedy Jour Award; Image Award NAACP 1980; Award of Merit Outstdg Community Svc, Martin Luther King Legacy Assn. **BUSINESS ADDRESS:** Anchorwoman, KHOU-TV, 1945 Allen Parkway, Houston, TX 77001.

JETER, JOSEPH C., JR.
TV engineer. **PERSONAL:** Born Aug 16, 1961, Philadelphia, PA. **EDUCATION:** Taylor Univ, BA Comm 1983, BS System Analysis/Political Sci 1983. **CAREER:** Taylor Univ, minority recruitment coord 1980-83, minority fund raising/planner 1982-83; Applied Energy Svcs, intern 1982; Bell of PA, asst mgr network engrg. **ORGANIZATIONS:** Vice pres Black Cultural Soc 1980-82; editorial writer Taylor Univ 1982-83; Pres Adv Comm Minority Recruitment Taylor Univ 1982-83; mem Student & Economic Leadership Forum 1982-83; seminar writer on career planning self-employed 1983-; minority recruitment writer and consultant self-employed 1983-; career planning writer and consultant self-employed 1983-. **HONORS/ACHIEVEMENTS:** Outstanding Men in America 1983; Who's Who Among College Students 1983. **HOME ADDRESS:** 115 E Washington Ln, Philadelphia, PA 19144.

JETER, THOMAS ELLIOTT
Dentist, educator. **PERSONAL:** Born Jul 20, 1929, Washington, DC; married Tayloria. **EDUCATION:** HowardUniv Coll Dentistry, DDS 1967; NYUniv Sch Dentistry, cert oral surgery 1969; Harlem Hosp, Resd; Cath Med Ctr, Oral Surg Flwsp. **CAREER:** Oral Surgeon, prac; HowardUniv Coll Dentistry, asst oral surg. **ORGANIZATIONS:** Dir Anxiety & Pain Control Prgm; co-chmn Fed & Pyramid Sect Am Heart Assn; chmn Emergency Treatment Com HowardUniv Atdg Oral Surgon; Howard U; Mary Immaclate Hosp; HowardUniv Educ Devel Com; St Johns; St Mar's Hosp; HowardUniv Hosp Credentials Com; local Coord Nat High Blood Pressure Educ Prgm Howard U; mem Nat Dental Assn; Robert T Freeman Dental Assn; Basic Life Support Emergency Cardiac Com Am Heart Assn/Nat Capitol Affiliate; mem Am Assn Hosp Dentists Sigma Xi; Montgomery Co MD. **HONORS/ACHIEVEMENTS:** Am heart affl award Oral Surgery Outsdng Instr 1975; instr yr 1976; outsdng serv Am Heart Assn 1977; maj contrib "Comp Control of Pain & Anxiety"; "Plea to the Dental Prof & Hypertension Detection"; Jour Hosp Dental Prac; good conduct award. **MILITARY SERVICE:** USN Hm2. **BUSINESS ADDRESS:** 600 W St NW, Washington, DC 20059.

JETER, VELMA MARJORIE DREYFUS
Retired educator. **PERSONAL:** Born Jul 15, 1906, New Iberia, LA; daughter of Jules Dreyfus and Victoria Dreyfus; married Dr CE Jeter (deceased). **EDUCATION:** Prairie View Univ, AB 1932; Univ of NM Albuquerque, 1935-36; Univ of CA Berkeley, 1943-44; TX Southern Univ, MA 1952; Lamar Univ, Beaumont, TX. **CAREER:** TX Assoc of Teachers, pres 1961-62; Central Jurisdiction WSG, pres 1956-64; Natl Dental Aux, pres 1962; Grand Court Order of CA & Jurisdiction of TX, pres, bd of dir 1967-89; TX Employment Commission, 1983; retired educator. **ORGANIZATIONS:** Co-founder Orange Childhood Devel Ctr 1972-89, Thrift & Gift Shop for the Elderly 1975-89; pres NAACP 1980-89, Golden Heritage mem; bd dir Natl Fraternal Congress of America, 1986-89; TX Older Workers Task Force Commission; chmn exec bd TX Assoc of Women & Girls Clubs; bd dir Hughes School for Crippled Children; chmn Area Agency on Aging, Southeast TX; bd dir House of Refuge: A Home for the Homeless; pres Le Samedi Club, Top Ladies of Distinction, Sr Citizens Assoc, Orange Comm Action Assoc, NCNW. **HONORS/ACHIEVEMENTS:** Civil Rights Award NAACP 1950-87; TX Assoc of Teachers, Retired Teachers, TSTA, NEA 1960-87; columnist Forward Times 1962; Black Texans of Distinction 1970; Award of Distinction to Retired Educators, 1984; They Showed The Way Black Women of TX History 1987-; Sojourner Truth Award, Business and Professional Women; Woman of the Year, Zeta Phi Beta Sorority; TX Women of Couraage Award; TX Democratic Party Sustaining Supporter Award; Governor's Award for Public Service. **HOME ADDRESS:** 1202 N 3rd, Orange, TX 77630.

JETT, ARTHUR VICTOR, SR.
Business executive. **PERSONAL:** Born Dec 16, 1906, Union Springs, AL; married Katie; children: Kay Baker, A. **EDUCATION:** Morehouse Acad, grad 1928; Chicago Tech Sch. **CAREER:** Bankhead W Contractors & Devel Inc, pres; Atlanta Bd of Educ Estimating & Plan Reading, instr masonry trades 1948-51; Masonry Tredes & Utica Inst, instr 1932-34; Bricklayers Union Local #9 AFL, bus agt 1940-44; Masonary Trades, apprent com 1946-50; Dept of Labor, adv Com 1967-69; building contractor 1952-. **ORGANIZATIONS:** Past bd mem Atlanta Urban League 1944-74; mem YMCA; bd dir bd mem, past treas Atlanta Br NAACP; bd Nat Child Welfare Leag of Am; United Way; pres bd Gate City Day Nursery Assn; bd mem treas Consolidated Mortgage & Nvestment Co; mem Atlantic C of C; Nat Conf of Social Welfare; mem 1st Congregationsl Ch; UCC; v chmn Deacon Bd Morehouse Coll Alumni Assn. **HONORS/ACHIEVEMENTS:** Good nghbr award Nat Conf of Christians & Jews 1972; life mem NAACP; plaque NAACP 1974. **BUSINESS ADDRESS:** 825 Cascade Ave SW, Atlanta, GA 30311.

JEWELL, JERRY DONAL
Legislator, dentist. **PERSONAL:** Born Sep 16, 1930, Chatfield, AR; married Ometa; children: Eldin, Avelinda, Sharon, Jerrod, Kason. **EDUCATION:** AR AM&N Coll, grad; Meharry Med Coll Scho of Dentistry. **CAREER:** 3rd Dist AR, state sen first elected 1972; Pvt Prac Little Rock, dentistry. **ORGANIZATIONS:** Mem Am Dental Assn; Nat Dental Assn; pres All Inc; bd mem Eagle Life & Ins Co; life mem NACP; former pres St Conf of Br; pres Little Rock Br; Credential Comm 1972; Natl Dem Party Chrtr Comn Natl Dem Party 1973-75; mem Alpha Phi Alpha Vet Army Dental Corp. **BUSINESS ADDRESS:** 721 E 21st St, Little Rock, AR 72206.

JEWELL, PAULA L.
Attorney. **PERSONAL:** Born Aug 12, 1943, Indianapolis. **EDUCATION:** Howard U, BA (cum laude) 1964; ColumbiaUniv Law Sch, JD 1968; Howard U. **CAREER:** Howard Univ, special asst to pres, asst gen counsel; HUD, Atty; HUD, special asst to gen asst sec; Comm Plan & Mgmt HUD, sec 1968-72; Nat Corp for Housing Partnerships Assoc Coun, 1972-73; Nat Urban Coal Prog Off for Housing & Urban Growth & Trans, 1973-74; NEA Dushane Fund, atty; Intl House NY, foreign student advisor; DC Board of Zoning Adjustment, bd mem. **ORGANIZATIONS:** Mem Experiment in Intl Living Sweden 1962, Sperry-Hutchinson Fellow Columbia; asst to city council comm DC Bar Assn 1974; vchmn Younger Lawyer in PublicServ ABA 1974; chairperson DC Minimum Wage Indust Safety Comm 1976-80; assoc editor Survey of Human Rights Law Columbia. **HONORS/ACHIEVEMENTS:** Appt to US Commn on UNESCO ; served on Exec Com Nom Com & Chmn of Youth Com; Deans List Howard 1964; Liberal Arts Hon Prog.

JEWELL, TOMMY EDWARD
Attorney. **PERSONAL:** Born Jun 30, 1954, Tucson, AZ. **EDUCATION:** NM State U, bA 1976;Univ of NM, JD 1979. **CAREER:** Soc of Albuerque Inc, staff atty legal aid 1979-; Rocky Mountan, regional dir; Black Am Law Students Assn 1977-79. **ORGANIZATIONS:** Mem Juvenile Justice Adv Com 1978-; com mem Gov Juvenile Code Task Force 1979-. **HONORS/ACHIEVEMENTS:** Dean's awardUniv of NM Sch & of Law 1978-79; reginald heber smith fellow HowardUniv Sch of Law 198-81. **BUSINESS ADDRESS:** 401 Roma NW, Albuquerque, NM 87103.

JEWETT, CHARLIE RUTH
Educator. **PERSONAL:** Born May 25, 1936, Natchez, MS. **EDUCATION:** Tougaloo Coll, BA 1958; Univ of CA; Univ of Philippines; Michigan State Univ, MA 1975; Univ of Southern California (Overseas), additional educ 1981-. **CAREER:** Hill High School, teacher 1959-61; Dept of Defense Overseas School, teacher 1961-; Amer Educ Assn of Okinawa, pres, negotiator 1970-72; Dept of Defense Overseas Schools, EEO counselor 1980-. **ORGANIZATIONS:** Appt to adv comm by Sec of Ed Terrell Bell Dep Ed in DODDS 1981-85; mem, Dept of Defense Teacher Recruitment-Interview Team, 1972; rep, Overseas Educ Assn, 1970-; mem overseas bd of dir, Natl Educ Assn, 1974-77; mem exec comm, Overseas Educ Assn, 1974-77; newsletter ed, Overseas Educ Assn, 1974-76; vice pres, newsletter ed, Northeast Asia Teachers Assn, 1977. **BUSINESS ADDRESS:** EEO Counselor, Dept of Defense Overseas School, PSC Box 3492 APO, San Francisco, CA 96328.

JIGGETTS, DANNY MARCELLUS
Businessman/broadcaster. **PERSONAL:** Born Mar 10, 1954, Brooklyn, NY; son of Floyd Jiggetts and Hattie Jiggetts; married Karen; children: Lauren, Kristan. **EDUCATION:** Harvard, BS; MBA; Northwestern U, attndg. **CAREER:** Chicago Bears; Nat 1st Bank of Chicago; Proctor & Gamble, sales rep; Bd of Urban Affairs of NY, field rep; USFL, NBC-WMAQ TV; CBS Sports; ABN/LaSalle Bank, asst vp; CBS sports/WBBM-TV Chicago, sports broadcaster. **ORGANIZATIONS:** Mem Better Boys Found, Natl Hemophilia Found, Spec Olympics, Natl Sudden Infant Death Syndrome Found, Midwest Assoc for SickleCell Anemia, March of Dimes, Harvard Alumni Assoc. **HONORS/ACHIEVEMENTS:** BPO Elks Youth Ldrshp Awd; Football 3 times All Ivy New England; Track 2 times All Ivy; Football All American 1976. **BUSINESS ADDRESS:** Sports Broadcaster, CBS Sports, 51 West 52nd St, New York, NY 10019.

JOANS, TED
Writer, painter, musician. **PERSONAL:** Born Jul 04, 1928, Cairo, IL; married 1961; children: 10. **EDUCATION:** Indiana University, BFA, 1951. **CAREER:** Organization of African Unity, journalist, 1969-; Afro-American Ancestral Art Association, investigator; poet, travel writer, painter, and jazz musician. **HONORS/ACHIEVEMENTS:** Author of All of Ted Jones and No More: Poems and Collages, Excelsior Press, 1960; author and illustrator of Afrodisia: New Poems, Hill & Wang, 1971; author of Sure, Really I Is, Transformation, 1982; contributor to anthologies and periodicals. **BUSINESS ADDRESS:** c/o Rare Book Room, 125 Greenwich Ave, New York, NY 10014. *

JOBE, SHIRLEY A.
Library director. **PERSONAL:** Born Oct 10, 1946, San Bernadino, CA; daughter of Fines Jobe and Luejeannia Jobe; children: Robyn. **EDUCATION:** Texarkana Coll, AA 1966; East TX State Univ, AB 1968; Simmons Coll, MSLS 1971. **CAREER:** John F Kennedy Presidential Library, head librarian 1971-84; Boston Globe Newspaper Co, head librarian 1984-. **ORGANIZATIONS:** Vice pres, MA Black Librarians Network 1984-86; volunteer in Soup Kitchens to feed homeless; volunteer to visit incarcerated persons in MA prisons. **HONORS/ACHIEVEMENTS:** Education Professional Develop Act Grant 1970; Black Achiever's Awd Boston 1987. **HOME ADDRESS:** 54 Mt Pleasant, Cambridge, MA 02140. **BUSINESS ADDRESS:** Library Dir, The Boston Globe, 135 Morrissey Blvd, Boston, MA 02107.

JOELL, PAMELA S.
Career counselor/recruiter/sales manager. **PERSONAL:** Born Feb 01, 1961, Greenwich, CT; daughter of Willis Joell and Edith Marie Duncan. **EDUCATION:** Manhattanville Coll, BA 1982; Health Insurance Assoc of Amer, Certificate Group Ins 1986; St Louis Univ Metro College MBTI Certification 1988; Dun & Brdstreet Education Serv, Continuing Educ Unit. **CAREER:** NYS Bd of Educ, high school social studies teacher 1982-83; MONY Financial Svcs, group benefits special 1983-85; Equitable Life Assurance Soc, group contract analyst 1985-86; INROADS, manager 1986-. **ORGANIZATIONS:** Genl meetings comm Minority Interchange 1985-86; mem Player's Guild Theater Performance Soc, NBN Comm Theatre Players; general mtgs mem NY Chap Minority Interchange 1987; leader Troop 309 Girl Scouts of Amer 1988-89. **HONORS/ACHIEVEMENTS:** Merit Certificate Poetry World of Poetry Mag Jan 1988; poem title published "East Harlem". **BUSINESS ADDRESS:** Manager, INROADS/Fairfld Westchester Ctys, 111 Prospect St #510, Stamford, CT 06901.

JOHN-SANDY, RENE EMANUEL
Business executive. **PERSONAL:** Born Jul 22, 1945; son of Sydney Oliver Sandy and Miriam John (John-Hercules). **EDUCATION:** St Benedicts Coll Trinidad, diploma 1959; NY Business Sch, diploma 1970; NY Univ, BSc 1972. **CAREER:** Cahners Publishing NY, cost control analyst 1971-73; McGraw Hill NY, magazine mfg 1973-77; Time-Life Inc NY, magazine mfg/paper control 1977-79; Class Magazine, publisher 1979-. **ORGANIZATIONS:** Dir Harlem Soccer Club 1974-83; bd of dirs Emmbel Import & Export Inc 1980-84. **HONORS/ACHIEVEMENTS:** Awd for Excellence in Publishing Chap of the Trinidad & Tobago Alliance NY 1982; Honorary Image Award, Luster Products Inc-Chicago 1988. **MILITARY SERVICE:** Intelligence unit British Army Trinidad & Tobago Regiment 5 yrs. **BUSINESS ADDRESS:** Publisher, Class Magazine, 27 Union Square West, New York, NY 10003.

JOHNICAN, MINERVA JANE
Company executive. **PERSONAL:** Born Nov 16, 1939, Memphis, TN; daughter of John Bruce Johnican, Sr and Annie M Rounsoville Johnican. **EDUCATION:** Central State Coll, 1956-57; TN State Univ, BS 1960; Memphis State Univ, Graduate Study, 1965. **CAREER:** Memphis City Schools, elementary sch teacher 1960-65, elem school librarian 1965-79; Shelby County Govt, county commissioner 1975-82; Memphis City Govt, city councilwoman at large 1983-87 (first only black to win an at-large seat); 1987 candidate for mayor (first serious black women to run for mayor in the south.). **ORGANIZATIONS:** Chmn pro-tem Shelby Co Bd of Comm 1976-77; pres Gazell Public Relations & Adv Co 1976-78; mem Natl Assoc of Counties Natl Bd 1978-81; past pres TN County Commission Assoc 1980-81; mem Alpha Kappa Alpha Sor 1958-; budget chmn Memphis City Council 1984; pres Alpha Termite & Pest Control Inc 1982-88, pres, Gazelle Broadcasting, Coy Inc; pres & owner of Commonwealth Consultants, Ltd. **HONORS/ACHIEVEMENTS:** Distinguished History Makers Award Mallory Knights Org 1976; "A Salute to Minerva Johnican" Memphis Community Leaders 1977; Outstanding Women in Politics Alpha Kappa Alpha Sor 1978; Outstanding Leadership Award Coca Cola Co of Memphis 1979; Women of Achievement "COURAGE" Award Network Womens Org 1984; First Black to be elected to an At-Large Council the City of Memphis (received 40% of white votes cast); Person of Equality Award Memphis NOW Chapter; Citizen of the Yr Award Excelsior Grand Chapter of Order of the Eastern Star; 1986 NCCJ Govt Serv Award & TN Educ Assoc Humanitarian Award, 1986. **HOME ADDRESS:** 1265 Dunnavant St, Memphis, TN 38106. **BUSINESS ADDRESS:** President, CEO, 631 Madison Ave, Memphis, TN 38103.

JOHNS, JACKIE C.
Dentist. **PERSONAL:** Born Jul 14, 1953, Belle Glade, FL; son of Gonte Johns, I and Mattie M Johns. **EDUCATION:** Texas Coll, BS (Cum Laude) 1976; Prairie View A&M Univ, MS 1976-77; College of Medicine and Dentistry of NJ, DMD 1981. **CAREER:** Dr AS Ford, dentist 1981-82; Dr CJ Beck, dentist 1981; Dr RL Levine, dentist 1982-83; US Veterans Admin Outpatient, dentist 1983-84; Dr Thomas Scholpler, dentist 1983-84; Self Employed (2 offices), dentist. **ORGANIZATIONS:** Mem Amer FL Dental Assocs, North East Regional Bd Palm Beach County Dental Assoc; mem The Acad of General Dentistry, Alpha Omega Frat; mem Westboro Business and Professional Women Org; Family & Comprehensive Dentistry, Boynton Bch, FL; Family & Comprehensive Dentistry, Belle Glade, FL; mem of the Intl Congress of Oral Implantologist; Family & Comprehensive Dentistry of W.P.B., of Fort Pierce FL. **HONORS/ACHIEVEMENTS:** Nationally recognized in Journal of the Natl Dental Assoc for active participation in the 1978 Health Fair at NJ Dental School; Comm Serv Citations for work on voters registration drives; Pinacle Award by Being Single Magazine Chicago Ill, 1989; Dental Implantologist 1987. **MILITARY SERVICE:** AUS Reserve capt. **BUSINESS ADDRESS:** Dentist, 2600 N Australian Ave, Ste A, West Palm Beach, FL 33407.

JOHNS, MICHAEL EARL
Marketing consultant. **PERSONAL:** Born Jan 14, 1945, Alexandria, VA; children: Michael E Jr. **EDUCATION:** Howard Univ, BA, 1968; Wharton School of Finance, MBA 1972. **CAREER:** IBM Corp, systems engr 1968-71; Xerox Corp, financial mgr 1972-78; The Prism Corp, pres. **ORGANIZATIONS:** mem, Market Rsch Assn, 1980-, DC Chamber of Commerce 1984-. **BUSINESS ADDRESS:** President, The Prism Corporation, 4400 Jenifer St NW Ste 200, Washington, DC 20015.

JOHNS, PAUL V.
Professional athlete. **PERSONAL:** Born Nov 14, 1958, Waco, TX. **EDUCATION:** Tulsa. **CAREER:** Seattle Seahawks, wide receiver 1981; King-5 TV Seattle Seahawks Post-Game Show, co-host; AL Williams, div mgr. **HONORS/ACHIEVEMENTS:** Ranked AFC's leading punt returner 1984; Honored as the Seattle Miller/NFL Man of the Year 1983; one of five finalists for natl award. **BUSINESS ADDRESS:** Manager, AL Williams, 5305 Lake Washington Blvd, Kirkland, WA 98033.

JOHNS, SONJA MARIA
Physician. **PERSONAL:** Born May 13, 1953, Washington, DC; children: George Wheeler Jr, Ashante, Chiquita, Maria Wheeler. **EDUCATION:** Howard Univ Coll of Liberal Arts,

BS (Summa Cum Laude) 1976; Howard Univ Coll of Medicine, MD 1978; Howard Univ Hosp Family Practice Residency, Certificate of Completion 1978-81. **CAREER:** Natl Health Plan Inc, physician-in-attendance 1981-82; Women's Medical Ctr, family practitioner 1983; District of Columbia Air Natl Guard, chief hospital serv 1983-; Warsaw Medical Ctr, family physician 1983-. **ORGANIZATIONS:** Mem Amer Acad of Family Physicians 1979-, Natl Medical Assoc 1980-, Amer Medical Assoc 1980-, NAACP 1980-, Assoc of Military Surgeons of the US 1983-, Northern Neck Medical Soc 1984-; active medical staff Tidewater Memorial Hosp 1983-; co-founder Black Business & Professional Coalition 1985-; bd mem Richmond CoComm Serv Assoc Inc 1985-; soloist soprano Comm Chorus, Northern neck Convention Choir, Northern Neck Choral Soc; advisor 4-H Club Richmond Co. **HONORS/ACHIEVEMENTS:** Chief Resident Dept of Comm Health & Family Practice 1980-81; Physician's Recognition AwdAmer Medical Assoc 1981-88. **MILITARY SERVICE:** Air Natl Guard major 4 yrs; Perfect Attendance Ribbon. **BUSINESS ADDRESS:** Family Physician, Warsaw Medical Ctr, 404 Main St, Warsaw, VA 22572.

JOHNS, STEPHEN ARNOLD
Business executive. **PERSONAL:** Born Aug 21, 1920, Chicago, IL; married Tanis Fortier. **EDUCATION:** Roosevelt Coll, BA 1947; FLMI Life Office Mgmt Assn, 1959; CLU Am Coll of Life Underwriters, 1964. **CAREER:** Golden St Mutual Life Ins Co, vice pres agency dir 1974-; asso agency dir 1970; asso agency dir 1964; asst agency off 1962; dir & Of agency educ & tn 1960; methods analyst 1957; Jackson Mutual Life of Chgo, 1942-47. **ORGANIZATIONS:** Mem bd dir Golden St Mutual Life Ins Co; Life Underwriters' Assn of LA LA NAACP; Urban League; Kappa Alpha Psi. **MILITARY SERVICE:** AUS s/sgt 1943-45. **BUSINESS ADDRESS:** 1999 W Adams Blvd, Los Angeles, CA 90018.

JOHNSON, A. VISANIO
Attorney. **PERSONAL:** Born Mar 10, 1941, Chandler, OK; married Villetta M Bobo. **EDUCATION:** OK U, LlD 1965. **CAREER:** OK Legis, atty state rep 1975-. **ORGANIZATIONS:** Chmn Pub Health Comm; vchmn Com Health Care Delivery; mem Rules Common Educ Judiciary Pub Safety Penal Affairs Cms; mem OK Bar Assn; OK Trial Lawyers Assn; Delta Theta Phi; JJ Bruce & Law Soc; Alpha Phi Alpha NAACP; Urban League; Coalition Civic Ldrshp; 5th St Baptist Ch; bd Dirs Commun Action Prog; mem Darrel Bruce & Johnson Law Firm. **HONORS/ACHIEVEMENTS:** Outstanding legis gov's sp com Health Care; Gov's Rep State Confs. **BUSINESS ADDRESS:** Ste 410 Investors Capitol Bl, Oklahoma City, OK 73102.

JOHNSON, ADDIE COLLINS
Educator. **PERSONAL:** Born Feb 28, Evansville, IN; married John Q Johnson; children: Parker Collins. **EDUCATION:** Howrd Univ, BS 1956; Dietetic Internship PBB Hospital, RD 1957; Framingham State Coll, MEd 1968. **CAREER:** Boston Lying In Hospital, therapeutic dietitian 1957-61; Harvard School Public Health Rsch, dietitian 1963-64; Hour Glass Newspaper Kwajakin MI, editorial 1965-66; Foxborough Public School, teacher 1968-; Univ of MA Harbor Campus Dept of Nursing, nutritionist 1980-; Bridgewater State Coll, instructor 1982-. **ORGANIZATIONS:** Finance chmn, bd of dirs MA Home Economic Assoc; mem Amer Dietetics Assoc, Society Nutritional Ed, Amer Home Economics Assoc, Circle Lets Inc, Delta Sigma Theta Sor, MA Teachers Assoc; mem Links Inc; past pres Boston Chap Links Inc; mem nominating comm Natl Links Inc 1978-79; mem American Assoc University Women (AAUS). **HONORS/ACHIEVEMENTS:** Presenter Northeast Regional Social Studies Conference 1984-85. **BUSINESS ADDRESS:** Instructor, Bidgewater State College, Dept HEP, Bridgewater, MA 02324.

JOHNSON, AL
Bank executive. **CAREER:** Gulf Federal Bank, Mobile, AL, chief executive. **BUSINESS ADDRESS:** Chief Executive, Gulf Federal Bank, 901 Springhill Ave, Mobile, AL 36604. *

JOHNSON, ALBERT J.
Composer, musician. **PERSONAL:** Born Dec 14, 1910, Dallas, TX; married Bernice Milbrey. **EDUCATION:** New York Univ, studied with Prof Rudolf Schramm 1961. **CAREER:** Queens Coll, arranger, composer, musician, asst prof music; Constant Music Inc, pres; musician & arranger for Louis Armstrong, 1933, Benny Goodman, 1956-57, Dizzy Gillespie, Billy Eckstine, Sarah Vaughn, Count Basie; conducts workshops, concerts throughout the USA & Canada. **ORGANIZATIONS:** Mem NY Jazz Repertory Co; sec-treas JPJ Quartet; sec-treas Oliver Jackson & Budd Johnson's Inc. **HONORS/ACHIEVEMENTS:** Smithsonian Inst award 1975; USO shows in the US & Europe.

JOHNSON, ALBERT JAMES
Salesman. **PERSONAL:** Born Aug 20, 1943, Phoenix, AZ; married Beverly. **EDUCATION:** Univ of AZ, 1961-65. **CAREER:** Matthews Chev Co, 1977; Harlem Globletrotters, player 1965-67;Univ of AZ, asst coach 1968-72. **ORGANIZATIONS:** Mem Active 20-30 Serv Club 1970-72; mem Randolph Mens Golf Club 1976-; mem Desert Trails Mens Club 1969-74; memUniv of AZ & Alumni Club 1970-73; deacon & elder Trinity Presb Ch 1969-73. **BUSINESS ADDRESS:** 1000 E 22nd St, Tucson, AZ 85728.

JOHNSON, ALBERT LEE, SR.
Clergyman. **PERSONAL:** Born Sep 12, 1923, Hugo, OK; married Eddie Mae; children: Carl, Dessie Mae, Annie Jewel, Bernard, Horace Lee, Iralles Laverne, Albert, Terease Monee, Yolanda Denise, Erick Oneal. **EDUCATION:** Western Bapt Sem KC MO, attended; Western Baptist Bible Coll, D Humanities 1984; Gradalupe Coll Sequin TX, DD 1984. **CAREER:** Zion Grove Bapt Church KC MO, pastor. **ORGANIZATIONS:** Past pres Coun for United Action CUA; pres Cit for Ed Equality CEE; sec bd of dir Martin Luther King Jr Meml Hosp; 1st black pres Met Inner ChAgency; mem MICA; chmn bd of CUA Housing; past pres Bapt Ministers Union; past 1st vice pres Gen Bapt Conv of MO, KS, IA, NE & Co; mem Gen Bapt Conv MO, KS, NE; 1st vice moderator Sunshine Dist Assoc; co-admin Gen Bapt Nursing Home & Retirement Ctr; bd mem Black Political Org Freedom Inc; pres General Baptist Convention of MO, KS and NE 1980-85. **BUSINESS ADDRESS:** Pastor, Zion Grove Bapt Church, 2801 Swope Pkwy, Kansas City, MO 64130.

JOHNSON, ALBERT WILLIAM, SR.
Automobile dealer. **PERSONAL:** Born Feb 23, 1926, St. Louis, MO; son of Oscar William Johnson; married Marion, Feb 02, 1952; children: Albert W. Johnson, Jr., Donald King Johnson, Anthony Johnson. **EDUCATION:** Attended Lincoln Univ; Univ of IL, Champaign, IL, BS, 1942; Univ of Chicago, Chicago, IL, degree in hospital admin, 1955. **CAREER:** United Public Workers Union, former regional direc; Homer Phillips Hosp, St Louis, MO, former admitting supvr and asst to the admin and bus mgr; Al Johnson Cadillac-Saab-Avanti & Leasing Inc, Tinley Park, IL, pres, 1971-. **ORGANIZATIONS:** Member, citizens comm, Univ of IL; member, bd of direc, Better Business Bureau of Metro Chicago; vice pres, Variety Club of IL, Chicago chapter; bd member, Seaway Natl Bank; member, Execs Club of Chicago; member, Platformers Club; member, Metro club; member, Unicorn Club; life member, NAACP; member, Chicago United; sponsor, Chicago Berry-Johnson Business and Profl Person Recog Annual Award; founder, Messanger Found; founder, People United to Save Humanity Found; member, Orland Park Lions Club; hon member, Oaks Club; member, bd of direcs, Ingalls Memorial Hospital; pres, Pyramid Trotting Assn. **HONORS/ACHIEVEMENTS:** Fellow, Chicago Defender Roundtable of Commerce; certif of excellence, Cosmopolitan Chamber of Commerce; Partner in Progress Award, Chicago Assn of Commerce and Industry; Businessman's Award, Woodlawn Orgn; Black Excellence Award, Cultural Comm, PUSH; Top 100 Black Businessmen Award, Black Enterprise magazine; Man of the Year, Coalition for United Community Action; Humanitarian Award, Mayor Richard Hatcher, Gary, IN; certif of apprec, St Bernard's Hospital; certif of recog, Univ of Detroit; apprec award, CUS Natl Honor Soc; Black Businessman of the Year, Black Book NPSA; certif of merit, Adv Mgmt for Dealers, Oldsmobile; apprec award, Cosmopolitan Chamber of Commerce; certif of apprec, Chatham Business Assn; Time Magazine Quality Dealer Award, 1975; certif of apprec, General Motors Corp; IL Coun of Deliberation Award; Humanitarian of the Year Award, Coalition for United Community Action. **BUSINESS ADDRESS:** Albert William Johnson, Sr, Al Johnson Cadillac-Saab-Avanti & Leasing Inc, 8425 West 159th Street, Tinley Park, IL 60477.

JOHNSON, ALCEE LABRANCHE
Educator. **PERSONAL:** Born Jul 22, 1905, Fernwood, MS; married Thelma Wethers (deceased); children: Al, Joyce J Bolden. **EDUCATION:** Alcorn Coll, 1925; Fisk Univ, AB 1927; Columbia Univ, 1930-31, MA 1956; Univ of So CA, Further Study; Hon HHD Degrees, MS Bapt Sem 1972, Rust Coll 1974. **CAREER:** Prentiss Inst, instr 1927-30, dir of instruction 1931-36; Dept of Interior Washington DC Office of Educ Survey of Vocational Educ & Guidance, state supvr; Prentiss Inst, instr 1927-30, pres 1971-81, dir of instr 1973-, exec sec, bd of trustees 1981-. **ORGANIZATIONS:** Former pres 6th Dist Theacer Assoc, MS Teacher Assoc, MS Dist Teacher Assoc; mem Phelps-Stokes Fund Conf of Ed Leaders; life mem Amer Teacher Assoc, Natl Ed Assoc, MS Teacher Assoc; pres Prentiss Inst Jr Coll, MS Assoc of Developing Coll; chmn Western Div BSA; mem Alpha Phi Alpha, Phi Delta Kappa, 33rd Deg Mason, Voters League, NAACP, MS Reg Med Prog; past chmn bd 1st vice pres State Mutual Fed Savings & Loan, JDC Mutural Fed Credit Union; inst rep Heifer Proj Inc; only black pes So MS Plnng & Devel Dist Inc; mem MS Econ Council; ed comm, recorder, ed div White House Conf on Aging 1971; former vice pres Cty Council on Aging 1972; 1st black appt to the Probation & Parole Bd by Gov Wm Waller 1972. **HONORS/ACHIEVEMENTS:** Silver Beaver Awd BSA; MS Man of the Year 1973; Greene Awd Alpha Phi Alpha So Reg 1973.

JOHNSON, ALEXANDER HAMILTON, JR.
Vice president, manager, minority community relations. **PERSONAL:** Born Oct 03, 1924, Greensboro, AL; son of Rev Alexander Johnson and Erma Johnson; married Delores Mitzie Russel; children: Alexander III. **EDUCATION:** CA Pacific Univ, BA Public Admin 1978, MA Mgmt 1980. **CAREER:** Federal Aviation Admin, personnel staffing spec 1968-70, chief civil rights staff 1970-74; US Equal Empl Oppty Comm, compliance suprv 1974-81; The Arizona Bank, aa & equal em mgr, vp. **ORGANIZATIONS:** Pres Amer Fed of Govt Empl 1968; clerk of session Southminster Presbyterian Church 1980-84; chmn of bd Southminster Social Serv Agency 1981; pres Southwest Area Conf NAACP 1982-84; chmn Reg I NAACP 1984-85; keeper of records Phoenix Alumni Kappa Alpha Psi 1984-86; mem Sigma Pi Phi, Gamma Mu Boule 1988; mem Maricopa County Commission on Trial Court Appontments 1989. **HONORS/ACHIEVEMENTS:** Outstanding Citizen Maricopa Cty NAACP 1978; Awd for Caring Phoenix City Human Serv Comm 1980. **MILITARY SERVICE:** AUS corpl 1943-47. **BUSINESS ADDRESS:** Vice President/Manager, Minority Community Relations, Security Pacific Bank Arizona, AZ286, 101 N 1st Ave, Phoenix, AZ 85002.

JOHNSON, ALMETA ANN
Attorney. **PERSONAL:** Born Mar 11, 1947, Rockingham; daughter of Louise Johnson Brown; children: Cesseli A Cooke, Harry E Cooke IV. **EDUCATION:** OH State Univ, JD 1971; Johnson C Smith Univ, BA 1968. **CAREER:** Metzenbaum Gaines Finley & Stern, law clerk 1969-70; OH State Univ, rsch asst 1970-71; Benesch Friedlander Mendelson & Coplan, assoc atty 1971-75; City of Cleveland, chief police prosecutor, 1975-80; Private Practice, attorney; East Cleveland City Council, councilwoman, 1987-. **ORGANIZATIONS:** Chmn E Cleveland Citizens Adv Comm 1973-75, 1988-; chmn E Cleveland Charter Rev Commn 1976; bd mem sec treas OH Law Opportunity Fund; mem Amer Bar Assn, Bar Assn of Greater Cleveland, OH State Bar Assn, Black Women Lawyers Assn, Alpha Kappa Alpha; law dir Village of Woodmere 1983-86. **HONORS/ACHIEVEMENTS:** Lett Civil Liberties Award OSU Coll of Laws 1971; 1 of 10 Most Influential Women in greater Cleveland The Plain Dealer 1975; NAACP Outstanding Young Citizen Cleveland Jaycees 1976. **BUSINESS ADDRESS:** Attorney-at-Law, 13308 Euclid Ave, East Cleveland, OH 44112.

JOHNSON, ALVIN ROSCOE
Personnel administrator. **PERSONAL:** Born Oct 15, 1942, Alton, IL; married Thelma Marie Hart; children: Brent Alvin, Dirk Cyrus. **EDUCATION:** Souther IL Univ Edwardsville, BS Bus Admin 1972, MBA 1982. **CAREER:** Olin Corp, mgr train & dev 1962-77, mgr personnel 1977-80; Acco Babcock Inc, vice pres human resources 1980-. **ORGANIZATIONS:** Dir Amer Red Cross, Girl Scouts, Urban League, Acco Babcock Inc 1982-; treas & life mem NAACP, Alumni Assoc Ex BOD; deacon Immanuel Baptist Church; mem Sigma Pi Phi; hr council Machinery & Allied Prod Inst 1982-; life mem SIUE Alumni Assoc Ex BOD 1975-77. **MILITARY SERVICE:** AUS sgt E-5 1966-68. **BUSINESS ADDRESS:** Senior Vice Pres Human Resources, Acco Babcock Inc, 425 Post Road, Fairfield, CT 06430.

JOHNSON, ANDREW
Engineer. **PERSONAL:** Born Jun 03, 1946, Gould, AR; son of Andrew Johnson and Bertha Johnson; married Helen L Fleming; children: Andrew Raphel, Heather Louise. **EDUCATION:** Univ of AR at Pine Bluff, BS Chem 1968; Northeastern Univ, Certificate 1984. **CAREER:** IBM Corp, Endicott NY Eng/Mfg mgr 1976-80, Austin TX production control mgr 1980-82, Brooklyn NY functional mgr 1982-85, asst general mgr 1985-86, E Fishkill, NY, equipment engineering operations mgr, 1986-. **ORGANIZATIONS:** Baselius Omega Psi

Phi Fraternity Inc Kappa Nu 1972; adv bd mem George Westinghouse HS 1984-86; Sunday school teacher 1984-, deacon 1987-, Pilgrim Baptist Church Nyack NY; chairman Economic Develop NAACP Spring Valley 1986, mem, Affirmative Action Comm, Rockland Children's Psychiatric Center, Rockland County, NY. **HONORS/ACHIEVEMENTS:** Youth motivation table bd Natl Alliance of Business 1977-82; Presidential Citation NAFEO 1983. **HOME ADDRESS:** 12 Sandusky Road, New City, NY 10956. **BUSINESS ADDRESS:** Senior Engineer, International Business Machine, Z/56A Route 52, Hopewell Junction, NY 12533.

JOHNSON, ANDREW L.
Chaplain. **PERSONAL:** Born Sep 14, 1911, Memphis; married Dr Dora K. **EDUCATION:** John CarrollUniv Cleveland, AB 1933; Oberlin Coll Grad Sch of Theol, BD MA 1938; Payne Theol Sem Wilberforce U, DD 1952; Yale Divinity Sch, 1965. **CAREER:** Tuskegee Inst AL, chaplin 1966-; asso chpln 1965-68. **ORGANIZATIONS:** Mem Yale Div Assn; Armed Frcs Chplns & Assn; Alpha Phi Alpha; Nat Assn Coll &Univ Am Acdmies of Rel. **MILITARY SERVICE:** AUS /c 1938-64. **BUSINESS ADDRESS:** The Tuskegee Chapel Office, Tuskegee Institute, AL 36088.

JOHNSON, ANDREW L., JR.
Attorney. **PERSONAL:** Born Oct 04, 1931, Youngstown, OH; married Joan Carol Phillips; children: Andrew III, Paul. **EDUCATION:** Northwestern Univ, BS 1953; Cleveland State Univ Sch of Law, JD 1959. **CAREER:** Shaker Heights Municipal Ct, acting judge 1970-; Private Practice, atty 1960-. **ORGANIZATIONS:** Pres Bar Assn of Greater Cleveland 1978-79; trustee Bar Assn of Greater Cleveland 1970-73; labor arbitrator Major Steel Companies of NE OH; host of TV progKNOWLEDGE "Youth & the Law"; hearing examiner for OH Civil Rights Commn; chmn bd trustees Forest City Hosp Cleveland 1970-76; founding mem & first pres Cleveland Lawyers Assn Inc; mem Cleveland Council on Human Relations; former pres Home Owners Title Corp Cleveland; vice pres Northwestern Univ Alumni Club of Cleveland; life mem Alpha Phi Alpha Frat. **HONORS/ACHIEVEMENTS:** Merit Awd Northwestern Univ Coll of Arts & Sci 1979; Law Day Awd Cleveland Lawyers Assn 1969; listed in OH Lives 1969 edition; listed as preferred atty in Martindale Hubbell Law Directory 1974-80 editions; Who's Who in Amer Law 1976-77; Men of Achvmt Cambridge Press 1976; Meritorious Serv Awd Cleveland Bar Assn 1970; Trust Shaker Lakes Regional Native Ctr 1977-. **MILITARY SERVICE:** AUS specialist 4th class 1953-55. **BUSINESS ADDRESS:** Attorney, 33 Pub Sq, Ste 810, Cleveland, OH 44113.

JOHNSON, ANDREW L., SR.
Attorney. **PERSONAL:** Born Feb 05, 1905, Little Rock; married Henrietta Grinage; children: Kathryn Iona, Andrew L Jr. **EDUCATION:** Central State Univ Wilberforce OH, BS 1930; Youngstown State Univ Law School, LLB 1934, JD 1969. **CAREER:** Mahoning Cty Youngstown OH, asst cty prosecutor 1937-41; Private practice, attny 1936-. **ORGANIZATIONS:** Mem US Dist Ct, No Dist of OH 1954; ct apptd hearing attny for mentally ill patients Woodside Receiving Hosp; mem Bd of Cty Visitors, OH State Bar Asoc 1936-, Amer Bar Assoc, Alpha Phi Alpha, NAACP; past treas, mem, bd of dir Org of Prot Men Youngstown; mem Mahoning Cty OH Dem Org; bdmn Woodwrth Gar Club; mem, bd of trust, attny, leg adv St Andrew AME Church 1923-. **HONORS/ACHIEVEMENTS:** Listed in Personalities of the West & Midwest. **BUSINESS ADDRESS:** Attorney, 906 Metropolitan Tower Bldg, Youngstown, OH 44503.

JOHNSON, ANGEL PATRICIA
Educational administrator. **PERSONAL:** Born Oct 08, 1942, Elbert, WV; daughter of Cleo and Moncie Belcher; married Milton W Johnson; children: Brian, Marc, Erik. **EDUCATION:** Brooklyn Coll City Univ of NY, BA 1965; Rutgers Univ Grad Sch of Educ, MEd 1980; Rutgers Univ Grad Sch of Educ, EdD 1987. **CAREER:** Salvation Army Foster Home Svcs, social worker 1965-69; Georgian Court Coll, educ oppor fund asst dir 1977-78, upward bound project dir 1978-88; NJ Dept of Higher Education Trenton NJ Assistant Dir 1988-. **ORGANIZATIONS:** Vice pres Monmouth County Bus & Professional Women's Cncl 1977; bd dirs mem Assoc for Equality & Excellence in Educ 1981-82, 1984-89; mem Assoc of Black Educators 1983; bd of trustees mem Lakewood Prep School 1984-. **HONORS/ACHIEVEMENTS:** Dedication to Success of Upward Bound Project Georgian Court Coll Comm Adv Bd 1981; Special Citation Assoc for Equality & Excellence in Educ 1982; Outstanding Upward Bound Dir Students Class of 1984. **BUSINESS ADDRESS:** Assistant Director, New Jersey Deptartment of Higher Education, Office of College - School Collaboration, 20 W State Street, Trenton, NJ 08608.

JOHNSON, ANTHONY MICHAEL
Physicist. **PERSONAL:** Born May 23, 1954, Brooklyn, NY; son of James W. Johnson and Helen Weaver Johnson; married Dr Adrienne Steplight, Jun 02, 1975; children: Kimberly, Justin, Brandon. **EDUCATION:** Polytechnic Inst of NY, BS Physics Magna Cum Laude 1975; City Coll of the City Univ of NY, PhD Physics 1981. **CAREER:** AT&T Bell Laboratories, sr tech assoc 1974-77; doctoral can 1978-81; research in ultrafast optics & electronics; AT&T Bell Laboratories, mem tech staff 1981-, distinguished mem 1988-. **ORGANIZATIONS:** Mem Amer Physical Soc 1977-; mem Natl Soc of Black Physicists 1980-, tech prog co-char, 1989; mem Optical Soc of Amer 1982-; mem Inst of Elec & Electron Engrs 1982-; symposium organizer in "Ultrashort Pulses in Optical Fibers," 1985, vice-chmn on Tech Prog Com for "Ultrafast Optical Phenomena," 1985, symposium organizer in "Ultrashort Nonlinear Pulse Propagation in Optical Fibers," 1988, in Annual Mtg of Optical Society of Amer 1985; mem Amer Assoc for the Advance of Sci 1986-; mem tech council Optical Soc of Amer, chmn Tech Group on Ultrafast Optical Phenomena 1986-87; mem tech prog comm Annual Meeting of the Optical Soc of Amer 1986 (Seattle), 1987 (Rochester), 1988 (Santa Clara); mem tech prog comm Ultrafast Optics & Electronics for the Conf of Lasers & Electro-Optics 1986 (San Francisco), 1987 (Baltimore); chmn Tech Prog Subcom Conference on Lasers and Electro-Optics (CLEO) 1988 (Anaheim), 1989 (Baltimore), tech prog co-chair, 1990 (Anaheim); mem R W Wood Prize Comm, Optical Soc of Am, 1989, chair, 1990; topical editor, Optics Letters, 1989-91; mem Optics News advisory comm, 1989-91; mem science and tech advisory board, Journal of the Natl Tech Assoc, 1989-. **HONORS/ACHIEVEMENTS:** Undergraduate research award, Sigma Xi, 1975; Cooperative Research Fellowship, AT&T Bell Labs, 1975; chapters in books on laser usage, 1984, 1989; various patents in optics and electronics; guest editor, IEEE Journal of Quantum Electronics special issue, February 1988; AT&T Bell Labs Distinguished Technical Staff Award, 1988; Minds in Motion Award, Science Skills Center, Brooklyn, NY, 1989. **BUSINESS ADDRESS:** Distinguished Member Technical Staff, AT&T Bell Laboratories, Room 4D-321, Crawfords Corber Rd, Holmdel, NJ 07733.

JOHNSON, ARTHUR L.
Teacher/govt. official. **EDUCATION:** FL A&M Univ Tallahassee, BS Chem Math 1965; Pepperdine Univ, MS Admin 1974. **CAREER:** Inglewood CA School Dist, teacher, counselor; City of Gardena, Gardena planning comm. **ORGANIZATIONS:** Mem Amer Chem Soc 1969-71; mem Engrs Scientist Guild Lockheed Aircraft 1969-73; former mem Bicentennial Comm of Gardena 1976-77; mem Hollypark Homeowner Assn 1967-; chmn Dr Martin L King Jr Black Culture Comm of Gardena 1973-; dir S CA Planning Congress 1985. **HONORS/ACHIEVEMENTS:** Teacher of the Yr Inglewood School Dist 1983; Seal of the City-City of Gardena 1983. **MILITARY SERVICE:** AUS pvt 1st class 1944-45. **HOME ADDRESS:** 13116 Manhattan Pl, Gardena, CA 90249. **BUSINESS ADDRESS:** Gardenia Planning Comm, City of Gardena, 1700 West 162nd St, Gardena, CA 90247.

JOHNSON, ARTHUR LYMAN
Educator. **PERSONAL:** Born Aug 21, 1918, Hartford, CT; married Marie Love. **EDUCATION:** Johnson C Smith U, BA 1941;Univ of Hartford, MEd 1952. **CAREER:** Hartford Neighborhood Ctrs, group worker 1946-47; AFL-CIO, bus agent 1947-49; State of CT Civil Rights Commn, supr & dir 1950-62; Hartford Human Rel Commn, exec dir 1964-79; WFSB-TV, producer & host 1971-77; Hartford Star & Inquirer, columnist/editor 1972-85; Eastern CT State U, asso prof 1970-84, cons. **ORGANIZATIONS:** Consult Commnty Renewal Team 1983-; pres Hartford Chap NAACP; mem Omega Psi Phi Carpe Diem Frat High Noon Greater Htfd Comm Cncl. **HONORS/ACHIEVEMENTS:** Published, "Beyond Ourselves". **MILITARY SERVICE:** USAF 1941-45. **HOME ADDRESS:** 78 Warren Ave, PO Box 2026, Vernon-Rockville, CT 06066.

JOHNSON, ARTHUR T.
Elected official. **PERSONAL:** Born Oct 29, 1947, Earlington, KY; married Dorothy Radford; children: Belinda, Joy. **EDUCATION:** Earlington HS, 1967; Austin Peay State Coll, 1967-68. **CAREER:** City of Earlington, councilman 1972-83, mayor 1984-. **ORGANIZATIONS:** Memshp Earlington Civic Club 1972-, memshp Earlington Volunteer Fire & Rescue Sqd 1967-; pres Earlington Jaycees 1982; bd dir Pennyrile Area Development Dist for Pennyrile Housing Corp; Junior Advisor rep Goodyear Tire and Rubber Co 1983-84. **HONORS/ACHIEVEMENTS:** Citzen of the Year Hopkins Countains for Progress 1976; Hopkins Countians for Progress Man of the Yr 1985; Black Award Council Black Man of the Yr 1985. **BUSINESS ADDRESS:** Mayor, City of Earlington, City Building, Earlington, KY 42410.

JOHNSON, AUDREYE EARLE
Educator. **PERSONAL:** Born Aug 18, 1929, Memphis, TN; daughter of Dr Lyncha A Johnson, Sr and Mary Hairston Johnson. **EDUCATION:** Fisk Univ, Nashville, TN, BA, 1950; Univ of Chicago, MA, 1957; Univ of Denver, PhD, 1975. **CAREER:** Dept of Public Welfare, soc worker, 1950-54; Dept Public Welfare, Chattanooga, child welfare worker, 1955-56; Michael Reese Hospital-Med Center, social worker, 1957-67; MLK Neighborhood Center, Mt Sinai Hospital, dir, social serv, 1967-69; Meharry Med Coll, dir C & E, asst clinical prof, dept psychology, 1969-73; Univ of NC at Chapel Hill, School of Social Work, assoc prof 1975-. **ORGANIZATIONS:** mem, Natl Assn Social Workers Acad Cert Soc Workers, 1955-; founder, vice pres, Natl Assn Black Social Workers, 1978-82; program chmn, Amer Public Health Assn Social Work Section, 1979-80; sec, Natl Assn Black Social Workers, 1974-78; bd mem, Human Rights Comm Murdoch Center, 1976-; bd mem, Mental Health Rsch & Devel Bd, Howard Univ, 1976; mem, Assn Study Afro-Am Life & History, NC Assn of Black Educators; chairperson, Black Faculty/Staff Caucus at UNC-CH 1980-86; chairperson, Annual Black Experience Workshop UNC-CH 1980-; mem, Council on Social Work Educ & House of Delegates Rep to 1988; mem, Natl Conf Social Welfare, Assn of Black Women Historians; chairperson, Social Work Section of Amer Public Health Assn, 1986-87; mem, NAACP, Natl Urban League, Triangle Assn of Black Social Workers;. **HONORS/ACHIEVEMENTS:** NIMH Award Univ of Chicago, 1955, Univ of Denver, 1973-75; Founder's Award, Afro-Amer Fam & Comm Serv Chicago 1975; Recog Award Serv Triangle Assn Black Soc Workers, 1978; Cert Recog Faculty Grad Honors Com and Black Student Mov UNC CH 1979; Cert Apprec NC Senior Citizens Fedn 1979; First Bell Carter Awd as Most Valued Social Worker NC State Assn of Black Social Workers 1986; Human Serv Award NC State Assoc of Black Social Workers 1986; publications "Removing Cultural & Ethnic Barriers of Health Care," 1980; "The Black Experience, Social, Cultural & Economic Considerations," 1981; "The Black Experience, Considerations for Health and Human Services," 1983; author of several published articles on Black contributions to social work and welfare; Honored as a Distinguished Alumna, Univ of Chicago, 1988; Honored as a founder of the Natl Assn of Black Social Workers at the 20th anniversary celebration, 1988; Professional Social Worker of 1988, Alpha Delta Mu Natl Social Work Honor Society, inducted into NC A&T Univ, Hall of Fame, 1988. **HOME ADDRESS:** 4100 Five Oaks Dr, Townhouse #19, Durham, NC 27707. **BUSINESS ADDRESS:** Assoc Professor Social Work, Univ of NC at Chapel Hill, 223 E Franklin St, Box 3550, Chapel Hill, NC 27599-3550.

JOHNSON, AYUBU See JOHNSON, BENJAMIN EARL

JOHNSON, B. A.
Government official. **PERSONAL:** Born Mar 07, 1925, Swainsboro, GA; son of George E Johnson and Mozella J Givens; married Hattie T Thompson, Dec 27, 1957; children: Betty. **EDUCATION:** Atlanta Coll of Mortuary Science, BS, 1946; Savannah State Coll, BA, 1950; Tuskegee Inst, MEd and MA, 1960; Georgia Southern Coll, SpEd, 1964. **CAREER:** Emanuel Co Bd of Edn, Swainsboro, GA, teacher, 1943-44, 1947-48, principal, 1974-81; Jefferson Co Bd of Edn, Louisville, GA, eacher, 1950-58; Screuen Co Bd of Edn, Sylvania, GA, asst principal, 1958-61; Laurens Co Bd of Edn, Dublin, GA, principal, 1961-74; mayor of Wadley, GA. **ORGANIZATIONS:** Kappa Alpha Psi. **HONORS/ACHIEVEMENTS:** Deacon of the Year, Piney Grove Baptist Church, 1976; Man of the Year, NAACP, 1977; Principal of the Year, 1981. **HOME ADDRESS:** B A Johnson, 142 Bedingfield St, P O Box 572, Wadley, GA 30477.

JOHNSON, BARBARA C.
Educator, elected official. **PERSONAL:** Born Apr 11, 1931, New York, NY; married J David Johnson; children: Eleanore. **EDUCATION:** NY Univ School of Educ, BS 1953; NY Univ School of SW, MSW 1957; Natl Inst Mental Health, Fellow 1970-71; Columbia Univ Sch of Social Work, advancedcert social welfare 1974. **CAREER:** Comm Serv Bureau, dir foster care 1961-67; Columbia Univ School of Soc Work, asst prof 1967-70; Africana Studies Dept Brooklyn Coll, deputy chairperson 1972-78; Bridge to Medicine Prog CCNY, instructor

1980-81; CONNECT-Child Abuse Prevention, dir 1981-83; Harlem Comm for Intl Visitors, dir 1983-. **ORGANIZATIONS:** Post office mem alumni Oper Crossroads Africa 1967-; membership chairperson Black Task Force Child Abuse 1982-; vice chairperson Comm Sch Bd Five Harlem 1982-; bd mem Alma John Workshop 1984-; bd of directors Natl Caucus Black Sch Bd Members 1984-. **HONORS/ACHIEVEMENTS:** Comm Service Awds NABBPW Eastern Star 1968, 1982; Outstanding Teacher Brooklyn Coll Black Studies 1974-78; Intl Service 3rd World Trade Assn 1985; global contrivbutions AKA 1985. **BUSINESS ADDRESS:** Dir, Harlem Comm for Intl Visitor, 230 W 137th St, New York, NY 10030.

JOHNSON, BEN D.
Insurance executive. **CAREER:** Winnfield Life Insurance Company, Natchitoches, LA, chief executive. **BUSINESS ADDRESS:** Chief Executive, Winnfield Life Insurance Company, 315 North, Natchitoches, LA 71457. *

JOHNSON, BEN E.
City clerk. **PERSONAL:** Born Jan 31, 1937, Ashley County, AR; married Marlene; children: Jan, Paula, Jay. **EDUCATION:** Univ of WI Milwaukee, BS, MS 1977; numerous workshops & seminars. **CAREER:** 6th Alderman Dist, alderman 1971-; Milwaukee Common Coun, pres; City of Milwaukee, city clerk. **ORGANIZATIONS:** Black Caucus Natl League of Cities; 56th Dist vice pres WI League of Munic Exec Comm; joint congress state senat co supv & alderman; legis serv ctr Natl League of Cities Human Resources Comm; Milwaukee Area Manpower Council; Mil Urban Oserv; bd chmn Milwaukee Social Dev Commn 1974-; Milwaukee Econ Dev Comm; corp mem Milwaukee Urban League; bd dir CHPASW; adv com SE WI Reg Plan Commn; NAACP; bd of Greater Milwaukee Counc of Arts for Child; Milwaukee Rec Task Force; Sch Breakfast Coalition Bd; Milwaukee Pabst Theater Bd; Milwaukee Hear Soc Bd; Milwaukee Youth Serv Bureau Plan Com; Milwaukee House Task Force; adv bd SickleCell Anemia Found; adv bd Harambee Revit Proj; Milwaukee Repretory Theatre Bd; Milwaukee Perf Arts Ctr Bd; Milwaukee Caucus on Aging; Milwaukee Forum; N Side BusAssn Found mem; N Side Pol Action Ctr Found. **HONORS/ACHIEVEMENTS:** Cent City Bus Fed Civic Awd 1975; Walnut Improvement Coun Civic Awd 1975; Friend of ARts Milwaukee Comm Journ; Comm Serv Awd First Bapt Ch; Communication Awd CC Rider; Comm Serv Awd Milwaukee Little League; Comm Serv Awd Upper Third St Merchants; Legis Awd Comm Pride Expo; Comm Serv Awd Youth DevCtr; Comm Serv Awd Milwaukee Theol Inst; Bicen Awd Central City; Recog & Appreciation Milwaukee Sch of Engr Scholarships from Univ of WI Milwaukee 1955. **BUSINESS ADDRESS:** City Clerk, City of Milwaukee, City Hall, 200 E Wells St, Milwaukee, WI 53202.

JOHNSON, BENJAMIN EARL (AYUBU JOHNSON)
Art director. **PERSONAL:** Born Apr 23, 1943, Brooklyn, NY; children: Brian, Marilyn, Jerri, Nicole. **EDUCATION:** Housatonic Comm Coll, AA art 1974;Univ of Bridgeport, BS art 1979. **CAREER:** ABDC Inc, project dir; CABHUA New Haven CT, pres 1976-77. **ORGANIZATIONS:** Bd of dirs Art Resources New Haven CT 1976; bd of dirs Channel 8 Affirmative & Action New Haven CT 1974; lectr/art Bapt Correctional Cntr 1974-78; coord/art Harambee Festival 1975; commr CT Commn on the Arts 1976-80; mem Thirdstream 1974-79; visiting lectr Hosuatonic Comm Coll 1976-79; visiting lectr/artist Sacred HeartUniv Individual Artist Garrant CT Commr of the Arts 1974. **HONORS/ACHIEVEMENTS:** Best in show painting Barnum Festival 1976; 1st prize painting oils Barnum Festival 1977; 1st prize painting watercolor Barnum Festival 1979. **MILITARY SERVICE:** USAF E-4 served 8yrs.

JOHNSON, BENJAMIN WASHINGTON
Treasurer/retired army officer. **PERSONAL:** Born Jul 24, 1914, Hamilton, VA; son of Benjamin S Johnson and Ellen Washington Johnson; married Nannette Mack Palmer; children: Norbert Carl Benjamin. **EDUCATION:** Columbia Univ NY, AB 1938; Univ of MD, MA 1964. **CAREER:** NJ State Man Training & Industrial Sch, instructor 1938-42; US Army, pvt to colonel 1942-69; Commonwealth of PA, bureau dir 1970-80; Capital Area Regional Solid Waste Authority, treas 1986-. **ORGANIZATIONS:** Vice pres Urban League of Met Harrisburg 1978-84; vice pres YMCA Bd of Dirs 1984-; pres Presbyterian Mens Council 1985; life mem NAACP; mem Urban League, VFW. **HONORS/ACHIEVEMENTS:** Pennsylvania Sports Hall of Fame; Sigma Pi Phi; Alpha Phi Alpha; Two Yr Capt Track Team Columbia Univ; World Record Holder 60 Yds & 60 Meters. **MILITARY SERVICE:** AUS col 27 yrs; US Legion of Merit, Distinguished Military Service Medal Korea, Army Commendation Medal, Several Campaign Medals 1942-69. **HOME ADDRESS:** 3301 North 3rd St, Harrisburg, PA 17110.

JOHNSON, BERNARD
Designer, director, choreographer. **PERSONAL:** Born Dec 12, 1936, Detroit, MI; divorced. **EDUCATION:** Fashion Inst of Tech, aAS. **CAREER:** Plays All Negro Ensemble Co, Song of the Lusitanian Bogey, God is a Guess What, Man Better Man, Ballet Behing the Bridge; Broadway, Raisin, Guys & Dolls, Ain't Supposed & to Die a Naturl Death, Don't Play Us Cheap, Bubbling Brown Sugar, Eubi Eubie; num theatical acts, Ballets, Films, & TV. **HONORS/ACHIEVEMENTS:** Black filmmakers hall of fame 1977. **BUSINESS ADDRESS:** 176 W 87th St, New York, NY 10024.

JOHNSON, BETTY JO
Educator. **PERSONAL:** Born Aug 14, 1940, Rankin Cty, MS. **EDUCATION:** Piney Woods School MS, AA (Highest Rank) 1960; Tougaloo Coll MS, BA 1964; Jackson State Univ MS, MEd 1971; Memphis State Univ Memphis, EdD 1976. **CAREER:** Jackson Publ School System MS, teacher 1964-67; Lawyers Com for Civil Rights Under Law Jackson MS, legal sec 1967-69; Cty Health Improvement Proj Univ of MS Medical Center, fiscal spec 1970; MS Dept of Public Welfare Title IV, planning & eval specialist 1972-73; Comm Ed Ext Jackson MS, curriculum spec headstart 1972; Alcorn State Univ, visiting instructor 1973; Memphis State Univ, grad asst 1973-76; AR State Univ, assoc prof 1976-78; Shelby State Comm Coll, head dept of gen & early childhood educ, prof 1978-. **ORGANIZATIONS:** Mem Kappa Delta Pi 1976-, Natl Assoc for the Ed of Young Children 1976, Phi Delta Kappa 1978-, Assoc for Childhood Ed, TN Assoc for Young Children, Memphis Urban League, NAACP, AACJC/NCIA; Delta Sigma Theta, Memphis in May Ed Com; mem Child Care & Guidance Adv Comm Memphis City Schools; mem of the adv bd Comprehensive Day Care & Community Serv Assoc; mem Memphis Assoc for Young Children. **BUSINESS ADDRESS:** Professor, Shelby State Comm Coll, 737 Union Ave, PO Box 40568, Memphis, TN 38104.

JOHNSON, BEULAH C.
Retired educator. **PERSONAL:** Born Feb 25, 1909, Winston-Salem, NC; married James A Johnson; children: Jacquelyne J Jackson, Jeanne J Penn, Viola E. **EDUCATION:** Shaw Univ Raleigh, AB 1930; Tuskegee Inst Al, MEd 1957. **CAREER:** Tuskegee Inst AL, teacher 1938-65, 1968-74 retired. **ORGANIZATIONS:** Dir Macon Cty Comm Act Comm Inc 1964-68; pres Classroom Teachers Macon Cty, Macon Cty Ed Assoc 1971-73; treas ASTACT; mem Coalit for Imp Ed in AL; mem NEA, AEA; life mem, vice pres Tuskegee Civic Assoc; vice pres NAACP; sec AL State Chapt; chtr mem, sec AL Dem Conf Inc; sec, bd mem Stward Bd WashChpl AME Church; sec Lewis Adams Chap OES; chmn Pensions & Security Bd of Maccon Cty 1974-; mem Amer Assoc Univ Women, Kappa Sil, Phi Delta Kappa; bd dir Macon Cty Comm Act Comm Inc. **HONORS/ACHIEVEMENTS:** Plaque for Contribs in Community Serv Tuskegee Chap Links 1981; Serv Awd for Unselfish Contribs to Comm at the 50th Southeast Reg Conf of Alpha Kappa Alpha 1982; Cert of Honor for Outstanding Serv & Contribs to Comm Serv 1983; Citizens Awd in Recognition of the Acts of Public Serv to Humanity by Tuskegee Inst 1977; Cert of Merit & Appreciation for Meritorious & Faithful Serv to Your Comm County State & Nation by AL Dem Conf Inc 1977.

JOHNSON, BILL CALVIN
Professional athlete. **PERSONAL:** Born Oct 31, 1960, Millerton, NY. **EDUCATION:** Arkansas State, Marketing Major. **CAREER:** Denver Gold, running back 1984-. **HONORS/ACHIEVEMENTS:** Denver's fifth-leading rusher last year as a rookie.

JOHNSON, BILL WADE
Business executive. **PERSONAL:** Born May 09, 1943, Idabel, OK; married Barbara. **EDUCATION:** Central Oklahoma State Univ, BA 1965. **CAREER:** OIC Chicago IL, exec dir 1976-; OIC Pittsburgh PA, exec dir 1970-71; OIC Intl, field specialist 1970-71; Oklahoma City OIC, dir 1968-70; Night Training Oklahoma City OIC, supr 1965-68. **ORGANIZATIONS:** Chmn Frederick Douglass HA 1965-68; mem City of Chicago Manpower Planning Council; former convenor Region III OIC's of Amer; chmn bd dir Career Devel Inc; chmn bd Hill Dist Fed Credit Union 1975-76; mem bd dir Ozanam Strings; Kappa Alpha Psi Frat; Chicago Assembly; numerous other committees, boards and councils. **BUSINESS ADDRESS:** 7 E 73rd St, Chicago, IL 60619.

JOHNSON, BILLY (WHITE SHOES)
Professional athlete. **PERSONAL:** Born Jan 27, 1952, Marcus Hook, PA; married Barbara; children: Marcia, Kendra, Jared. **EDUCATION:** Attended, Widener. **CAREER:** Houston Oilers, wide receiver 1974-81; Montreal Alouettes, wide receiver 1981; Atlanta Falcons, wide receiver 1982-. **HONORS/ACHIEVEMENTS:** NFL's Comeback Player of the Yr 1983; Falcon's Top Punt Returner of All Time; led NFC in punt returns 1982; led NFL in punt returns 1975 1977; named to Pro Bowl 1975, 1977, 1983; MVP in 1975 Pro Bowl.

JOHNSON, BOBBIE GENE
Elected government official & business executive. **PERSONAL:** Born Jul 08, 1941, Bethpage, TN; son of Jim Carter Johnson; married Fenecia Wiggins, Jan 17, 1987; children: Sanjeanetta, Marty, Nichelle. **EDUCATION:** TN State Univ, 1962. **CAREER:** City of Gallatin, planning comm 1968-78, indus bd 1982-; Mid-Cumberland Council, bd of dirs at large PIC 1982-; Co Court of Sumner Co, school comm 1982-; County Court, county comm; owner Mattie Lou's Flowers 1981-; pres Springfield Ford-Linc-Merc 1982-; pres Ford-Linc-Merc of Logan Co 1984-. **ORGANIZATIONS:** Mem NAACP; deacon First Baptist Church; patron OES; mem 32 Mason; owner Mattie Lou's Flowers 1981-; pres Springfield Ford-Linc-Merc 1982-; pres Ford-Linc-Mercury of Logan Co 1984-. **HONORS/ACHIEVEMENTS:** Dollars & Sense 1989; Black Enterprise 1988. **HOME ADDRESS:** 1504 Pinkerton Rd, Brentwood, TN 37027.

JOHNSON, BOBBY JOJO
City official. **PERSONAL:** Born Jan 11, 1947, Pine Hill, AL; married Estory Mason; children: James W, Jolanda, Joe. **EDUCATION:** Booker T Washington Business College, diploma 1972. **CAREER:** Alabama Center for Higher Education, veteran counselor 1972-73; Wilcox County, commisioner 1973-81; Wilcox County Comm Camden, AL Comm Dist. 5; chmn of County Comm 1989. **ORGANIZATIONS:** Life member Disabled American Veterans; political adviser Wilcox County Branch NAACP; president Wilcox County Dem Conf 1976; bd of dir Alabama New South Coalition 1989; chmn of Political Action Comm Alabama New South Coalition 1989. **HONORS/ACHIEVEMENTS:** Outstanding Young Men of America US Jaycees 1980; Lyndon B Johnson Political Freedom Award Alabama Dem Conference 1981; Hall of Fame, Zeta Eta Omega Chapter of Alpha Kappa Alpha Sorority, Inc, 1988. **MILITARY SERVICE:** AUS sp-4 2 yrs; Purple Heart Vietnam Service Medal. **HOME ADDRESS:** PO Box 29, Pine Hill, AL 36769. **BUSINESS ADDRESS:** Chairman, Wilcox County Commission, PO Box 488, Camden, AL 36726.

JOHNSON, BRENT E.
Educational administrator. **PERSONAL:** Born Jan 17, 1947, Springfield, MA; married Karen G Winston; children: Jayce Arnee. **EDUCATION:** Hampton Inst, BS 1968; West GA Coll, MA 1975-77; Atlanta Univ, further study. **CAREER:** Presbyterian Church in US, personnel dir 1974-78; AMTAR Inc, vice pres 1977-80; Atlanta Univ, dir of recruiting 1980-. **ORGANIZATIONS:** Pres bd mem Northwest Y's Men 1975-78; consultant Grad Mgmt Adm Council 1984; mem Natl Hampton Alumni Assn 1972-; pres Atlanta Univ Staff Assembly 1981-; chmn & founder Minority Admissions Recruitment Network 1981-; owner/pres of E Nexus Inc a consult firm providing mgmt assist in recruitment, collegerelations, interviewing, job placement and minority career counseling. **HONORS/ACHIEVEMENTS:** Outstanding Young Man Natl Jaycees 1983; contributor Black Collegian Magazine 1980-. **MILITARY SERVICE:** USNG staff sgt 3 yrs. **BUSINESS ADDRESS:** Dir of Recruitment, AtlantaUniv, 223 James Brawley Dr SW, Atlanta, GA 30314.

JOHNSON, BUTCH
Professional athlete. **PERSONAL:** Born May 28, 1954; married Julie. **EDUCATION:** CA Riverside, attended. **CAREER:** Dallas Cowboys, professional football wide receiver 1976-; Record Store Plano TX, owner; Warner Amex Communications, mktg. **HONORS/ACHIEVEMENTS:** Second-leading punt returner in cowboys history; Holds club record for most punt return yardage & most punts returned in a season; all-am & honors.

JOHNSON, C. CHRISTINE
Educational administrator. **PERSONAL:** Born Jun 19, 1928, Jackson, MS; children: Ed-

ward. **EDUCATION:** Univ MD at Munich, MS 1960. **CAREER:** NY State Div Human Rights, field rep 1971; Hamilton Coll Clinton, NY, dir Higher Educ Opportunity Program 1972-. **ORGANIZATIONS:** Mem Air Force Assn; Retired Officers Assn; past pres NY State Higher Educ Oppor Professional Orgn; NY state pres of Amer Assn of Non-White Concerns (affiliate of Amer Assn for Counselling & Devel); NY State Health Sys Agency; Bd of Visitors of Central NY Psychiatric Cntr; NY State's only Forensic PsychiatricCenter; Professional Bus Women's Assn; NAACP; Natl & NY State Assn Human Rights Workers; mem Opera Guild; rep Urban Renewal Prog Dayton, OH 1958; Joint Prot/Cath Choir; City Plann (Rome, NY C of C); Tri-State mental Health Bd; pres Rome Day Care Cntr; mem Rome Sr Citz bd dir; Amer Assoc of Non-White Concerns is now The Amer Assoc of Multi-Cultural Cnseling & Development. **HONORS/ACHIEVEMENTS:** NOW Unsung Heroine Spl Award of Honor for Achievement in Working with Young Coll Women 1978; nom Female Heroine of Yr Pac Air Force 1969 (10th of 250 candidates). **MILITARY SERVICE:** USAF Maj 1950-70; Vietnam Hon Medal 1st Class; Outstanding Munitions Officer 1962; Recomm Viet People-To-People Prog Partic; Bronze Star; USAF Comm Medal. **BUSINESS ADDRESS:** Dir Higher Education, Hamilton College, College Hill, Clinton, NY 13323.

JOHNSON, CAGE SAUL
Educator, scientist. **PERSONAL:** Born Mar 31, 0941, New Orleans, LA; son of Cage Spooner Johnson and Esther Saul Johnson; married Shirley; children: Stephanie, Michelle. **EDUCATION:** Creighton Univ Coll of Med, MD 1965. **CAREER:** Univ So CA, instr in med 1971-74, asst prof med 1974-80, assoc prof medicine 1980-88, prof of medicine 1988-. **ORGANIZATIONS:** Chm Adv Comm Genetically Hndcpd Prsns Pgm, CA Dept Hlth Serv 1978-; vice-chm bd dir Sickle Cell Self-Help Asso Inc 1983-; sec bd of directors, Sickle Cell Disease Research Foundation, 1986-. **MILITARY SERVICE:** AUS mjr 1967-69; Air Medal with "V". **BUSINESS ADDRESS:** Professor of Medicine, University of Southern California, 2025 Zonal Avenue RMR 306, Los Angeles, CA 90033.

JOHNSON, CALIPH
Attorney, educator. **PERSONAL:** Born Oct 03, 1938, St Joseph, LA; married Cheryl Helena Chapman. **EDUCATION:** Univ of Maryland, BA 1964; San Jose State U, MA 1968; Univ of San Francisco Sch of Law, JD 1972; Georgetown Univ Law Ctr, LlM 1973. **CAREER:** Thurgood Marshall School of Law, Southwest Inst for Equal Employment, Thurgood Marshall School of Law TX Southern Univ, dir 1975-78; Office of Gen Counsel Equal Employment Opportunity Commn, appellate atty 1973-75; Inst for Public Interest Represent, atty 1972-73; Oakland Citizens Com for Urban Renewal, exec dir 1970-72; City of Oakland CA, admin analyst 1970-72; Univ of Miaduguri Nigeria, consultant 1978-80; Office of Lawyer Training Legal Serv Corp , advocacy trainer 1978-80; EEOC, hearing examiner 1979-80; Title VII Project Natl Bar Assn Bd of Dir Gulf Coast Legal Found, faculty. **ORGANIZATIONS:** Mem commn on law office exon Am Bar Assn; labor law sect Nat Bar Assn; civillitigation com Fed Bar Assn; civil procedure & clin sec assn of Am Law Sch; Grad Fellowship Inst for Pub Int Rep GeorgetownUniv Law Ctr 1972-73; a response to crises of enforcing fair employment Houston Lawyer 1975; coursematerial on fair empl lit TX SoUniv 1976; integrated clinical curr module TX SoUniv & HEW 1978-80; teamsters v US Impact on Seniority Relief TX SoNBA Law Rev 1979. **HONORS/ACHIEVEMENTS:** Book review Let Them Be Judges HowardUniv Law Jour 1980. **MILITARY SERVICE:** USN lt 3yrs. **BUSINESS ADDRESS:** 3201 Wheeler, Houston, TX 77004.

JOHNSON, CALVIN P.
Legislative assistant. **PERSONAL:** Born Aug 26, 1946, Tacoma, WA; married Lynne Morgan; children: Christian, Brooke, Damon. **EDUCATION:** Stanford Law Sch Stanford U, JD 1973;Univ of Satna Clara CA, BA 1968. **CAREER:** Senator Richard S Schwelker, sr legislative asst 1973-; Urbn Affrs Gov of MO, consult for 1971-73; St Louis Pub Sch Sys, gen consult 1971-73; Assocl Lashly Caruthers Thies Rava & Hamel. **ORGANIZATIONS:** Mem Moot Ct Bd; Leg Aid Soc; vice pres Law Sch Stdt Assn; pres Blk Am Law Stdt Assn; mem Pi Alpha Theta; pres Blk Stdts Union; mem bd dir St Louis Hlth & Wlfr Cncl; Hlth Del Sys; Bus Res Cent; Min Purcg Cncl; Early Chld Care Dev Corp; mem bd vis Stnford Law Schl HS Grad. **HONORS/ACHIEVEMENTS:** Cum laude 1964. **BUSINESS ADDRESS:** Old Senate Office Bldg, Rm 347, Washington, DC.

JOHNSON, CARL ELLIOTT
Mechanical engineer. **PERSONAL:** Born Oct 04, 1956, Houston, TX; married Mary Ann Jean; children: Patric, Cristina, Carren. **EDUCATION:** Prairie View A&M Univ, BSME 1979. **CAREER:** Union Carbide, maintenance engr 1979-83; Monsanto Chemical Co, sr process engr 1984-85, process supervisor 1985-, utilities supervisor. **ORGANIZATIONS:** Corp solicitor United Way 1985-; youth basketball YMCA 1987; Speakers Bureau. **BUSINESS ADDRESS:** Process Supervisor/Sr Engr, Monsanto Chemical Co, # 1 Monsanto Rd, Nitro, WV 25526.

JOHNSON, CARL J.
Social worker. **PERSONAL:** Born Aug 23, 1911, Houma, LA; married Narvella Moses; children: Carol Ann, Charlynne Diane. **EDUCATION:** CA State Univ of LA, AA Mus, BA Sociology, BS Soc Sci, LLB. **CAREER:** Dance band leader & vocalist 1932-70; LA Cty, soc worker 1934-37; News Guardian Weekly, publ 1940-42; CA State Correctional School, group suprv 1940-43; LA Cty Juvenile Hall, boys couns 1947-48; LA Cty, dep marshall, lt ret 1949-69; CA Ofc of Econ Oppty, comm prog analyst 1969-71; City of LA, manpower analyst 1971-73; SW Comprehensive Med Corp, sr alcoholic couns 1973-76. **ORGANIZATIONS:** Real estate broker 1935-77; instr Rio Hondo Jr Coll 1967-68; instr Fremont Adult School 1962; US customs officer 1943; asst sgt-at-arms CA State Senate 1942; ins salesman Golden State Life Ins 1935; mem Douglass Life Ins 1940-41, 23rd Dist Comdr 1964-65, LA Cty Comdr 1971-71; vcomdr Dept of CA AmerLeg 1974-75; pres So CA Area Conf of NAACP 1962-64; treas Waller Lodge F&AM No 49 1941-44; vice pres LA Cty Young Rep 1938; state treas CA Young Rep 1946; chmn Rep Cty Central Comm 53rd Dist 1948; life mem Alpha Phi Alpha, NAACP, Amer Legion, LA Cty Sheriffs Relief Assoc; mem CA Vet Bd 1968-69, Egyptian Temple No 5, Platform Comm Rep State Central Comm; consult Amer Legion Natl Membership Comm. **HONORS/ACHIEVEMENTS:** LA Cty Bd of Suprv Awd 1964; LA City Council Awd 1968; LA Human Rel Bur Awd 1968; LA Bd of Ed Awd 1964; LA Cty Marshal Awd 1968; VenturaCty Marshal Awd 1968; CA Vet Bd Awd 1969. **MILITARY SERVICE:** AUS 1944-46.

JOHNSON, CARL LEE
Oral surgeon, anesthesiologist. **PERSONAL:** Born Dec 23,1928, Greensboro, NC; married Percenia; children: Rensia, Dwain, Richard. **EDUCATION:** Hampton Inst, BS 1948; Meharry Med Coll, DDS 1953; PA Grad Sch Med, postgrad 1956. **CAREER:** Harlem Hosp, intern 1953-54; resident anesthesia 1954-55; Grassland Hosp Vahalla & NY, resident oral surgery 1956-57; Philadelphia, practice dentistry, specializing in oral surgery & anesthesiology 1957-; Mercy Douglass Hosp Philadelphia, chief anesthesiologist 1958-62; asst chief anesthesiology 196i-68; sr attending oral surgeon 1958-; John F Kennedy Hosp, sr oral surgeon 1960-; Grad Sch MedUniv of PA, instr 1960-. **ORGANIZATIONS:** Mem Am Del Socs of Oral Surgeons Med & Dntal Socs; mem NAACP; Alpha Phi Alphaa; Alpha Kappa Mu; Beta Kappa Chi. **HONORS/ACHIEVEMENTS:** James r cameron honor soc black doctors assn. **MILITARY SERVICE:** Major USAF 1965-68. **BUSINESS ADDRESS:** Claflin Coll, Box 19, Orangeburg, SC 29115.

JOHNSON, CARL THOMAS
Retired educator. **PERSONAL:** Born Nov 08, 1914, Bryn Mawr, PA; children: Marc, Heidi. **EDUCATION:** NC A&T Univ, BS 1939; Columbia Univ Tchrs Coll, MSW 1949; Post-Grad Ctr for Psychothrpy, Cert 1961; Alfred Adler Inst for Indiv Psych, cert 1964. **CAREER:** Domestic Peace Corps (ACT), exec dir 1964-67; Addicts Rehabilitation Center Harlem Hospital, clinical dir; Adolescent Clinic Harlem Hospital, founder & exec admin; Abbott House, special project dir; New York City Youth Bd, training consultant; Ittelson Center for Child Rsch, asst dir; Floyd Patterson House, exec dir; Hunter Coll CUNY, assoc prof of educ (retired). **ORGANIZATIONS:** Mem Am Asso Univ Prof; chrtr mem Natl Asso of Social Wrkrs; mem Am Orthogenic Asso; pres No Cntrl Bronx Hosp Comm Bd; pres Bd of Visitors Bronx State Hosp; exec bd mem Riverdale Mntl Hlth Assn; vice pres of bd Am Inst for Psychiatry & Psychoanalysis. **MILITARY SERVICE:** AUS sgt 1942-45; Bronze Star 1944. **HOME ADDRESS:** 5355 Henry Hudson Pkwy, Riverdale, NY 10471.

JOHNSON, CARRIE CLEMENTS
Educator. **PERSONAL:** Born Jan 02, 1931, Atlanta, GA; married Alfred James Johnson; children: Alfia Katherine. **EDUCATION:** Morris Brown Coll, Atl, GA, BS 1951; Columbia Univ NY, MA 1954; State Univ of NY at Buffalo, EdD 1978. **CAREER:** Fulton Co Bd of Ed Atlanta, GA, high sch tchr 1951-961; Morris Brown Coll, Atlanta, GA, dir of career plng & plcmnt asst prof 1961-67; State Univ Coll at Buffalo, cnslr 1967-71, dir of cnslng serv 1971-83, assoc dir 1977-78, asst prof bsns stds 1983-85; dir of classified staff development FultonCty Schools 1986-. **ORGANIZATIONS:** HEW fellow US Govt Dept HEW 1979-81; Natl Urban League So Reg 1966-67; assoc dir VISTA Training; Am Prsnl & Guidance Asso 1967-; bd dir Buffalo Area Engineering Awrness for Minorities 1982; bd dir Child Dev Inst Buffalo 1983; schlrshp comm Buffalo Urban League 1984; vice pres Jack & Jill of America Inc 1974; Zeta Phi Beta. **HONORS/ACHIEVEMENTS:** Life Long Learning Awrd Alpha Kappa Alpha Sor Buffalo, NY 1984; Publctn "Guide to Graduate Opportunities fo Minorities 1971; selected HEW Fellow US Govt Dept Of HEW 1979; elected local, cnty, regnl Tchr of Yr 1959. **BUSINESS ADDRESS:** Executive Director, Classified Staff Development/Affirmative Action/EEO, Fulton County Board of Education, 786 Cleveland Avenue, Atlanta, GA 30315.

JOHNSON, CARROLL JONES
Mayor, educational administrator. **PERSONAL:** Born Mar 01, 1948, Blackville, SC; daughter of Rufus Jones and Louise Felder Jones; divorced; children: F Kelvin Johnson, Herman N Johnson, Wayne Johnson. **EDUCATION:** Voorhees Coll, Denmark SC, BS, 1978; Univ of South Carolina. **CAREER:** Barnwell School Dist, Blackville SC, literacy coordinator, 1980-; mayor of Blackville SC. **ORGANIZATIONS:** Barnwell County Help Line, Barnwell County Community Improvement Board, NAACP. **HONORS/ACHIEVEMENTS:** Community Service Award, Delta Sigma Theta, 1987; Public Service Award, Alpha Kappa Alpha, 1988; Citizen of the Year, Omega Psi Phi, 1989; Woman of the Year, Barnwell County Chamber of Commerce, 1989. **HOME ADDRESS:** PO Box 305, Blackville, SC 29817.

JOHNSON, CARYN E. See GOLDBERG, WHOOPI

JOHNSON, CHARLES
Educator. **PERSONAL:** Born Jul 28, 1927, Acmar, AL; married Carol Ann; children: Carla, Charles. **EDUCATION:** Howard Univ, BS 1953, MD 1963; DC Gen Hosp, Internship in Med 1963-64. **CAREER:** Duke Univ Durham NC, athletic council; Private practice, 1967-70; Duke Univ, asst prof med 1970-74, assoc prof med 1974-. **ORGANIZATIONS:** Mem Durham Acad of Med; mem bd of admiss Duke Univ of Coll of Med 1976-81; mem Kappa Alpha Psi 1951-, Amer Soc of Intl Med, Amer Coll of Physicians, Amer Diabetes Assoc; med adv comm Area Health Ed Ctrs NC; adv comm Minority Students NC; chmn Reg III NMA 1975-78; sec House of Delegates NMA 1975-77; vspeaker House of Delegates NMA 1977-79; speaker House of Delegates NMA 1980-81; dir NMA Africa Health Proj 1975-80, Durham C of C, Durham Sports Club, Durham Outboard Motor Club, Doric Lodge 28, Durham Consistory 218, Shriner, Zafa Temple 176, St Titus Epis Ch, 33rd Deg Mason; exec sec bd trustee Natl Med Assoc 1981-82; mem, bd trustees 1982-84, sec bd of trustees 1984-85 Natl Med Assoc; sec bd of trustees 1985-87, chmn bd of trustees 1987-, NMA. **HONORS/ACHIEVEMENTS:** Disting Kappaman Achievement Awd Durham Alumni Chap 1978; Elected Outstanding Physician of the Year 1980. **MILITARY SERVICE:** USAF s/sgt 1946-49, capt 1953-57. **BUSINESS ADDRESS:** Associate Professor Medicine, DukeUniv, PO Box 3217, Durham, NC 27708.

JOHNSON, CHARLES BEVERLY
Attorney. **PERSONAL:** Married Quillard A Jonhson. **EDUCATION:** Sthwstn U, grad 1949. **CAREER:** State Bar of CA, atty mem; Passadena Bar Assn. **ORGANIZATIONS:** Pres So Area Conf NAACP. **MILITARY SERVICE:** USCG 1942-45. **BUSINESS ADDRESS:** 353 E Orange Grove, Pasadena, CA 91104.

JOHNSON, CHARLES E.
Administrator. **PERSONAL:** Born Jul 01, 1946, Woodville, MS; married Bessie M Hudson; children: Vanessa Lashea, Adrianne Monique, Andrea Melita. **EDUCATION:** Alcorn State U, BS 1968; So U, MEd 1971. **CAREER:** Wilkinson Co School Dist, supt of Educ 1976-; Amite Co School Dist, teacher 1974-75; Brookhaven School Dist, teacher 1972-73; Wilkinson Co School Dist, teacher 1969-71; Bay St Louis School Dist, teacher 1967-68. **ORGANIZATIONS:** Mem Nat Educ Assn MS Assn of Educ 1968; mem Am Assn of Sch Adminstr 1977; exec com mem MI Assn of Sch Supt 1978. **HONORS/ACHIEVEMENTS:** Charles

E Johnson Classroom Bldg Centreville MS 1980. **BUSINESS ADDRESS:** Wilkinson Co Sch Dist, PO Box 785, Woodville, MS 39669.

JOHNSON, CHARLES E. MEMUSI
Educator. **PERSONAL:** Born 1933, Chicago; married Marianne Kaufmann; children: Lawrence Tibor Alex, Claude Earl Hans, Claire Maria Carla, Christina Ardell Marianne, Charles Paul Michael. **EDUCATION:** RooseveltUniv Chgo, BA 1954; Univ Intl Commerce Vienna Autria, 1957-58; Economics Univ Vienna Austria, PhD 1961; Pvt Tutor & Coll Intl Commerce Vienna, 1961-62. **CAREER:** Arthur D Little Cambridge MA, consultant 1974-; Cabinet of the Commonwealth of MA, sec of educ 1979-80; Met Affaris Univ Cincinnati, vice pres 1972-74; Roxbury Inst Bus Mgmt Roxbury MA, dir 1970; HarvardUniv Grad Sch Bus Adminstrn, lectr 1969-72; Boston Coll, asso prof finance 1966-69; LovaniumUniv Kinshasa Rep Congo, asso prof econs 1964-66; consult mktg research; investment analysis; prog planning 1975-. **ORGANIZATIONS:** Mem bd dirs Gr Cincinnati Comm Chest 19725-; bd dirs Contemporary Arts Coun 1972-; Talbert House 1972-; bd dir St Scholastica Coll 1972-; bd trustees ADL Found 1975-; Am Econ Assn; Am Acad Religion & Mental Health; Am Coun Higher Edn; Cincinnatus Assn; Creative Educ Assn; Harvard Club; Royal Soc Health London England. **HONORS/ACHIEVEMENTS:** Two thousand men achievement 1969; outstandings young men am 1968; fellowhip Case Western Reserve UD. **MILITARY SERVICE:** Num publs. **BUSINESS ADDRESS:** Arthur D Little, Acorn Park, Cambridge, MA 02140.

JOHNSON, CHARLES EDWARD
Industrial scientist. **PERSONAL:** Born Feb 24, 1938, Dallas, NC; married Gladys E Hawkins; children: Nilolas, Andre, Sean, Markus, Karari. **EDUCATION:** Morgan State Univ, BS 1960; Univ of Cincinnati, PhD 1966. **CAREER:** Morgan State Univ, prof of biology 1973-74; Community Coll of Baltimore, lecturer 1974; The Union Cincinnati, adjunct prof 1980-81; Procter & Gamble Co, section head 1981-88; Clairol Inc, Stamford CT, mgr 1988-. **ORGANIZATIONS:** Mem AAAS 1980-83, Amer Soc for Microbiology; bd trustees West End Health Clinic 1980-82. **HONORS/ACHIEVEMENTS:** NDEA Fellowship; Patent detergent composition containing protealyton enzymes elaborated by thermactinomyces vulgaris 15734, 1972. **BUSINESS ADDRESS:** Manager, Manufacturing Quality Assurance, Clairol Inc, 1 Blachley Rd, Stamford, CT 06229.

JOHNSON, CHARLES FLOYD
Producer, attorney. **PERSONAL:** Born in Camden, NJ; son of Orange Johnson and Bertha Seagers Johnson; married Anne Burford; children: Kristin Suzanne. **EDUCATION:** Attended Univ of DE 1960-61; Howard Univ, BA 1962; Howard Univ Sch of Law, JD 1965. **CAREER:** Howard Berg Law Offices Wilmington, DE, attorney 1965; US Copyright Office Washington, DC, attorney 1967-70; Swedish Ministry of Justice Stockholm, Sweden, attorney 1970; Universal TV, prod coord 1971-74, assoc prod 1974-76, prod 1976-82, supvr prod 1982-, executive producer 1985-87; Universal TV CA Executive Producer "B L Stryker" 1988-89. **ORGANIZATIONS:** Mem Screen Actors Guild of Amer; mem Producers Guild of Amer 1974-84; mem Writers Guild of Amer W; mem Natl Acad of TV Arts & Scis 1974-84; mem Amer Film Inst; Omega Psi Phi. **HONORS/ACHIEVEMENTS:** Publ "The Origins of the Stockholm Protocol" US Copyright Soc 1970; Emmy Award (Rockford Files - Best TV Drama) Natl; Alumni Achvmnt Award Stony Brook Coll Prep Stony Brook, NY 1979; Outstanding Alumnus Howard Univ Alumni Club of So CA 1982; Outstanding Alumnus Howard Univ Wash, DC 1985; LA Area Emmy AwardWinner for producing and performing in a KCET/PBS Special "Voices of Our People, A Celebration of Black Poetry" 1981; 4 additional Emmy Nominations for, Rockford Files 1978-79, Rockford Files 1979-80, Magnum PI 1982-83, Magnum PI 1983-84; Commendation from City of LA 1982; Commendation from CA State Legislature 1982; Commendation from CA State Senate 1982. **BUSINESS ADDRESS:** TV Executive Producer, Universal TV, 100 Universal City Plaza, Universal City, CA 91608.

JOHNSON, CHARLES H.
Educator. **PERSONAL:** Born Mar 05, 1932, Conway, SC; married Vermelle J; children: Temple, Charles H. **EDUCATION:** SC State Coll, BS 1954; SC State Coll, MEd 1969; VA State Coll;Univ SC Columbia SC. **CAREER:** Claflin Coll Orangeburg SC, dean of students; educator & prin pub sch 1962-67; Claflin Coll, various advancing positions 1967-. **ORGANIZATIONS:** Mem SC Sutdent Personnel Assn; So Coll Personnel Assn; Nat Stud Pers Adminstrs; Nat Educ Assn; Professional Club Inc (life mem); bd dir Orangeburg Co Council on Aging; VFW; bd dir Orangeburg United Fund; bd trustees Trinity United Meth Ch; Omega Psi Phi; IBPO Elks of the World. **HONORS/ACHIEVEMENTS:** Cert of merit lifetime scholarships Peace Officers Training Svc; listed comm leaders of am 1969-70; outstanding personalities of s 1967; Who's Who Amg Blk Am 1976 (1st ed); recipient various Naval Awards & Citations. **MILITARY SERVICE:** USN petty officer.

JOHNSON, CHARLES HENRY
Attorney. **PERSONAL:** Born May 24, 1946, New Haven, CT; son of Charles H Johnson and Helen Taylor Johnson; married Bertha Brooks, Jun 26, 1979; children: Eric. **EDUCATION:** Yale Univ, BA 1968; Yale Univ Law Sch, JD 1972. **CAREER:** Montgomery McCracken Walker & Rhoads, attorney private practice 1972-75; US Food & Drug Admin, asst chief counsel 1975-79; US Equal Employ Oppor Commn, supervisory trial atty 1978-79; CT Gen Life Ins Co, atty 1979-82; New England Mutual Life Ins Co, counsel & asst sec, 1982-. **ORGANIZATIONS:** Mem Natl Bar Assn; bd of dirs Rhode Island Ins Guaranty Assoc, Maine Insurance Guaranty Assoc; mem Natl Hlth Care Anti-Fraud Assoc Inc; mem American Bar Assn, Massachusetts Bar Assn; Massachusetts Black Lawyers Assn; bd of dir NY Insurance Guaranty Corp; bd of dir Boys & Girls Clubs of Boston; bd of dir, Roxbury Youthworks Inc; mem Twelfth Baptist Church Roxbury MA. **HONORS/ACHIEVEMENTS:** Operations Crossroads Africa-Ethiopia 1964; Peace Corps Volunteer Senegal W Africa 1968-69. **MILITARY SERVICE:** AUS Hon Discharge 1976. **BUSINESS ADDRESS:** Counsel & Asst Secretary, New England Mutual Life Ins Co, 501 Boylston St, Boston, MA 02117.

JOHNSON, CHARLES LEE
Dentist. **PERSONAL:** Born Dec 18, 1941, Atlanta; son of Willie Johnson and Ollie Johnson; divorced; children: Nichole Denise Johnson, Charlena Natasha Johnson. **EDUCATION:** Morris Brown Coll, BS 1964; Meharry Med Coll, 1964-65; Howard Univ, DDS, 1969; Univ of MD Provident Hospital, certificate, 1970; Walter Reed Hospital Emory Univ Medical Coll of GA Intl Congr Oral Implantology (Paris), post doctoral studies 1972. **CAREER:** Private practice, dentist; Metro-Atlanta Doctor's Clinic; Ben Massell Char Dental Clinic, staff 1972-; Atlanta Coll for Med & Dental Assistance, consult 1972-; Atlanta Southside Comprehensive Health Crt, bd dir 1972-; Charles L Johnson Scholarship Award Morris Brown Coll, founder. **ORGANIZATIONS:** Mem Am Endodontic Soc; Am Soc of Clinical Hypnosis; Jamaica Dental Soc; Am Dental Assn; GA Dental Assn; N GA Dental Soc; vice pres Dist Dental Soc; Acad of Gen Dentistry; Morris Brown Coll Alumni Assn; American Cancer Soc; Atlanta C of C Phi Beta Sigma 1962; Dean of Probates & Pledgees Chi Delta Mu 1966; vice-pres Local Chpt; Butler St YMCA 1972; exec bd dir; Atlanta Urban League; St Anthony Catholic Church; Acad of General Dentistry. **HONORS/ACHIEVEMENTS:** Recipient football scholarship Morris Town Coll 1960; acad scholarship GA Higher Educ Assn, 1964-69; pres, Med Tech Class, Meharry Coll, 1964-65; vice pres, N Georgia Dental Soc, Chi Delta Mu Fraternity; mem, Phi Beta Sigma Fraternity; honorary mem, Beta Beta Beta Scientific Honor Soc. **BUSINESS ADDRESS:** Metro Atlanta Doctors Clinic, 649 Ashby St NW, Atlanta, GA 30318.

JOHNSON, CHARLES RICHARD
Educator, writer, cartoonist. **PERSONAL:** Born Apr 23, 1948, Evanston, IL; son of Benjamin Lee Johnson and Ruby Elizabeth Jackson Johnson; married Joan New, Jun 1970; children: Malik, Elizabeth. **EDUCATION:** Southern Illinois University, BA 1971, MA 1973; State University of New York at Stony Brook, 1973-76. **CAREER:** Chicago Tribune, Chicago, IL, cartoonist and reporter, 1969-70; St Louis Proud, St Louis, MO, member of art staff, 1971-72; University of Washington, Seattle, WA, asst prof, 1976-79, assoc prof, 1979-82, prof of English, 1982-. **HONORS/ACHIEVEMENTS:** Named journalism alumnus of the year by Southern Illinois Univ, 1981; Governors Award for Literature, State of Washington, 1983; Callaloo Creative Writing Award, 1983; citation in Pushcart Prize's Outstanding Writers section, 1984; Writers Guild Award for best children's show, 1986; nomination for PEN/Faulkner Award, PEN American Center, 1987; author of novel Oxherding Tale, Indiana Univ Press, 1982; author of television script "Booker," PBS, 1983; author of short story collection The Sorcerer's Apprentice, Atheneum, 1986; contributor of stories, essays, and cartoons to anthologies and periodicals; board member and former director of Associated Writing Programs Awards Series in Short Fiction. **BUSINESS ADDRESS:** Department of English, University of Washington, Seattle, WA 98105. *

JOHNSON, CHARLES RONALD, SR.
Legislator & attorney. **PERSONAL:** Born Feb 17, 1951, New York, NY; married Nancy Bradford; children: Jessica Ashley, Charles Ronald Jr. **EDUCATION:** Dartmouth Coll, AB 1971;Univ of CA Berkeley, JD 1974. **CAREER:** 76th Asmbly Dist NY, assmblymn 1978-80; Atty, pvt prac 1976-78; Sen Minority Ldr NY, criminal justice analyist 1975-76; Bronx Co NY, asst dist atty 1974-75. **ORGANIZATIONS:** Pres DeWitt Clinton Alumni Assn 1979-80. **HONORS/ACHIEVEMENTS:** Man of yr award New York City Housing Police Guardians Assn 1979; man of yr Bronx Lebanon Hosp Ctr; Comm Ldrshp Award 1980; legislator of yr Nat Urban Coalition 1980. **BUSINESS ADDRESS:** 1188 Grand Concourse, Bronx, NY 10451.

JOHNSON, CHARLES V.
Judge. **PERSONAL:** Born Jun 11, 1928, Malvern, AR; married Lazelle S; children: James W Brown, Tracy L, Terri Lynn. **EDUCATION:** AR AM&N Coll Pine Bluff, BA 1954; Univ of WA School of Law Seattle, 1957. **CAREER:** Municipal Court Seattle, presiding judge 1971-72, judge; State of WA King Cty Superior Court, judge 1981-. **ORGANIZATIONS:** Mem bd of dir WA State Mag Assoc; charter mem Judicial Council Natl Bar Assoc; mem Seattle-King Cty Bch-Bar Liaison Com; mem Amer Jud Soc, Phi Alpha Delta; treas MCT Inc, Cent Area Com for Civil Rights 1963-70, 1st AME Church 1960-; chmn bd mgmt E Madison Branch 1964-69, bd dir Met Br 1964-, pres Metro Branch 1972- YMCA; pres Seattle Br NAACP 1959-63; pres NW Area Conf 1965-71; mem natl bd dir 1968-, chmn 1973-79 Natl Legislative Comm; chmn Seattle Model Cities Adv Council 1968-72; mem Seattle Lawyers Com for Civil Rights 1968-69; mem Royal Esq Inc; Kiwanis; adv com US Comm on Civil Rights; pres Amer Judges Assoc 1981-82; natl pres Sigma Rho Hon Soc 1954-55; Board member Natl Center for State Courts 1985. **HONORS/ACHIEVEMENTS:** Distinguished Citizens Awd Model Cities Seattle 1973; 1st Citizens Awd Seattle 1973; Man of the Year Awd Alpha Phi Alpha 1973; Distinguished Community Awd for United Way, YMCA Service to Youth Award, Benefit Guilds Martin Luther King Community Services Award; Links Human Rights Award. **MILITARY SERVICE:** Univ S Army 1948-52.

JOHNSON, CHARLES W.
Educator, business executive. **PERSONAL:** Born Jun 29, 1929, San Antonio; married Josie W Robinson; children: Patrice Y, Norrene E, Josie I. **EDUCATION:** FiskUniv Nashville, BA magna cu laude math 1951; MA Inst of Tech Cambridge, grad study math 1951-52;Univ MN Minneapolis, grad study mat 1959-62. **CAREER:** Honeywell Inc, 1956-; Sys Dev Cent, dir 1970-73; Bus Dev & Eng, dir 1973-76; Bus Dev & Eng, vice pres general mgr 1976-;Univ MN, asst prof elec eng1959-60; MN A&M Coll Las Cruces, part-time instr math 1968; MA Inst of Tech Cambridge. **ORGANIZATIONS:** Mem Transonic Aircraft Cont Proj 1952-54; mem Am Mgmt Assn; bd trust Carleton Coll Northfield MI 1970; natl bd trust Nat Urban League 1970-; chmn New Skills Bank Nat Urban League 1973; bd dir Met Med Cent Minnea 1971-73; bd of dirs Denver C of C 1978-; bd dir Ault Inc Minnea 1970-; adv bd NW Nat Bank N Am Off Minnea 1971-73; bd & dir J W Robinson & Sons Houston 1968-; MN state gen chmn Uni Negro Coll Fund 1972; chmn Urban Affairs Com Uni Fund of Minnea 1969; mem Prior Determination Com Uni Fund Minnea; has held many off in various org in the past. **HONORS/ACHIEVEMENTS:** Has publ sev technical papers; distinguished serv awards 2 Minnea & St Paul Urban Leagues 1973; rockefeller fellow award 1951; distinguished serv award Un Fund Minnea Area 1969. **MILITARY SERVICE:** AUS spec 2nd class 1954-56. **BUSINESS ADDRESS:** Vice President, Honeywell Inc, Computers & Manufacturing, Honeywell Plaza MN12-5326, Minneapolis, MN 55408.

JOHNSON, CHARLES WILLIAM
Vice president. **PERSONAL:** Born Jan 25, 1922, Ennis, TX; married Mattie Shavers; children: Charles Jr, Phillip Noel, Livette Suzanne. **EDUCATION:** Prairie View A&M Univ, BS 1942; Univ of Southern CA, MS 1947; Meharry Medical Coll, MD 1953. **CAREER:** Rockefeller Inst for Medical Rsch, visiting investigator 1957-59; Meharry Medical Coll, instructor 1947-49, asst prof 1949-52, acting dept chmn/assoc prof 1953-59, dean school of grad studies 1967-81, vice pres for rsch 1978-81, vice pres and dean school of grad studies 1980-81, vice pres and interim dean school of medicine 1981-82, vice pres for academic affairs 1981-. **ORGANIZATIONS:** Mem bd of dirs and chmn bd of governors Cumberland Heights Fdn; mem Amer Soc of Microbiologists, AAAS, Amer Acad of Allergy; mem and vice pres Mid-Cumberland Council on Drug and Alcohol Abuse; mem Amer Assoc of Pathology, Amer

Assoc of Clinical Immunology and Allergy, Assoc for Gerontology in Educ,Soc of Rsch Administrators; mem Society of Sigma Xi, Alpha Omega Alpha Hon Soc, Kappa Pi Honorary Soc. **HONORS/ACHIEVEMENTS:** Listed in Who's Who in the South and Southwest 1985, Amer Men and Women of Sci 1985, Intl Who's Who in Educ 1985. **MILITARY SERVICE:** USCG signalman 1st class 3 yrs. **BUSINESS ADDRESS:** Vice Pres for Academic Affairs, Meharry Medical College, 1005 D B Todd Blvd, Nashville, TN 37208.

JOHNSON, CHERYL JEFFRIES
Educator. **PERSONAL:** Born Apr 30, 1948, Youngstown, OH; married Jimmie L; children: Chaka Malik, Rashid ?, Jamil. **EDUCATION:** Youngstown State U, BA (cum laude) 1972; Northwestern U, MA 1975; Nortestern U, PhD 1978. **CAREER:** Loyola Univ of Chicago, dir Afro-Amer studies 1978-, asst prof 1978-80; Northwestern Univ, asst dir African studies 1980. **ORGANIZATIONS:** Co-chairperson IL Council for Black Studies 1979-; co-chairperson for membership Assn of Black Women Historians 1979-; bd mem Chiaravalle Montessori Sch 1980. **HONORS/ACHIEVEMENTS:** Who's Who AmUniv & Coll 1971-72; Fulbright Hays Dissertation Year Fellow 1976; research affiliateUniv of Ibadan Nigeria 1976f co-editor "The Pan-Africanist" NorthwesternUniv 1975. **BUSINESS ADDRESS:** 6525 N Sheridan Rd, Chicago, IL 60626.

JOHNSON, CHRISTINE
Administrator. **PERSONAL:** Born Feb 01, 1946, Tyler, TX; children: Ralph Bessard, Roderic Bessard. **EDUCATION:** CA State U, BA 1967f CA State U, MA 1972;Univ of CA Berkeley, doctorate in progress. **CAREER:** Coll of Alameda, dean student serv 1978-; Coll of Alameda, asst dean 1976-78; Contra Costa Coll, chairperson of counseling-instr 1974-76; Fresno State Univ, asst prof 1971-74; Fresno State Univ, coordinator live & learn center 1969-70; Fresno Co Economic Opportunity Comm, counselor job develop 1968-69. **ORGANIZATIONS:** Consult Regional Ofc of Health & Welfare Head Start San Francisco; CA StateUniv Law Enforcement Training Prog; com on status of womenUniv of CA Berkeley; mem Am Personnel & Guidance Assn; mem Am Assn ofUniv Women; mem Council on Black Am Affaris. **HONORS/ACHIEVEMENTS:** Summer inst fellow Bryn Mawr Summer Inst 1979; outstanding young women of am Fresno 1976; golden educator's award Fresno state Coll 1973; white house fellows finalist Commn on White House Fellows 1972. **BUSINESS ADDRESS:** Coll of Alameda, 555 Atlantic Ave, Alameda, CA 94501.

JOHNSON, CLEMON LAVELLE
Professional athlete. **PERSONAL:** Born Sep 12, 1956, Monticello, FL; married Brenda. **EDUCATION:** Florida A & M, 1978. **CAREER:** Portland Trail Blazers, 1978-79; Indiana Pacers, 1979-83; Philadelphia 76ers, center-forward 1983-. **BUSINESS ADDRESS:** Philadelphia 76ers, Veterans Stadium, Ste 510, Philadelphia, PA 19141.

JOHNSON, CLEO M.
Business executive. **PERSONAL:** Born in Louin, MS; married Willie. **CAREER:** Cleo Johnson's Sch of Charm & Modeling Agency Chicago, pres. **ORGANIZATIONS:** Mem Civic Liberty League; PUSH; NAACP; C of C. **HONORS/ACHIEVEMENTS:** Great gal award WJPC 1974; Martin Luther King humanitarian award 1974; civic liberty league award 1970; outstanding volunteer serv award Chicago & Educ TV WTTW 1969; blue ribbon sch of yr award 1968-69; intl yr of woman award PUSH 1975; ideal womanhood award Providence Bapt Ch 1975; merit award in memory ofMcKie Fitzhugh 1975; num other awards. **BUSINESS ADDRESS:** 8445 S Cottage Grove, Chicago, IL 60619.

JOHNSON, CLEVELAND, JR.
Vice president. **PERSONAL:** Born Aug 17, 1934, Eufaula, AL; son of Cleveland Johnson, Sr and Arline Petty Johnson; married Joan B Maloney; children: Keith Michael, Genevieve Carolyn, Kelly Marie, Cleveland III. **EDUCATION:** Tri State Univ IN, BS 1955; NY Univ, M Public Admin 1975; Attended, Adelphi Univ; NY Police Acad Police Science Program, graduate 1959. **CAREER:** US PO, clerk & carrier 1956-57, 1959; New York City Police Dept, patrolman 1959-65; Investors Planning Corp of Amer 1960-65; Central Islip Public School System, substitute teacher, 1963-64; Islip Dept of Comm Affairs, dir 1965-70; Town of Islip Housing Authority, exec dir 1966-71; Town of Islip, dir of personnel 1969-70; Town of Islip, deputy town supervisor 1969-71; County of Suffolk Riverhead NY, deputy county exec 1972-79; SUNY at Farmingdale, exec asst to the pres 1979-81, vice pres prof of business, 1981; Johnson Diversified, Inc, Central Islip, NY, pres, 1969-; FCD Construction Corp, Central Islip, NY, pres, 1981-. **ORGANIZATIONS:** Mem bd dir Allstate Life Insurance Co of NY; former chmn mem comm Natl Black Republican Council 1984; chmn Credentials Comm Natl Black Rep Comm; chmn Economic Develop Comm Natl Black Rep Council; illustrious dep Orient of NY AASR Prince Hall Affiliation; mem and past master Master Lodge 99 NY F&AM; mem Eureka Chapter 17 RAM NY; King David Consistory 3 PHA NYC; United Supreme Council 33 degree AASR Prince Hall Affiliation; Medina Temple 19 AEAONMS; NY State Grand Lodge Education Com chmn; Most III Commander NY State Council of Deliberation PH; Southside Hosp Advisory Council; pres adv commn on Equal Opportunity State Univ of Farmingdale; pres adv council & assoc trustee Dowling Coll; former chmn Selective Serv System Local Bd 2; pres emeritus Urban League of Long Island; mem vice pres bd dir Te li Com Inc; Bay Shore Central Islip Branch NAACP; Acad of Political Science Columbia Univ; former vice pres bd trustees Long Island Health & Hospital Planning Council Inc; mem Suffolk Co Health Facilities Commn; mem 100 Black Men of Nassau-Suffolk; dir LI Area Devel Agency; bd of dir, Dental World, Inc. 1985-87; natl co-chmn, Natl Black Republican Council, 1988-; founding pres, NY State Black Republican Council, 1974-; bd of dir, WLIM-TV Channel 21, 1986-; pres, Central Islip Bd of Educ, 1972-80. **HONORS/ACHIEVEMENTS:** 1968 Award for Comm Relations Natl Council of Negro Women; 1969 Civic Achievement Award NY State Grand Lodge Prince Hall Masons; 1969 Distinguished Alumni Award Tri State Univ; 1966 Public Serv Award Islip Spanish Amer Council; 1966 Comm Serv Award Carleton Park Civic Assn; Sovereign Grand Inspector General 33rd Degree AASR Prince Hall Affiliation 1974; 1984 Presidential Award for Comm Svcs. **MILITARY SERVICE:** AUS spec E-4 1957-59; Army Reserve 1st sgt 1959-66. **BUSINESS ADDRESS:** Vice President, SUNY, Adm Bldg, Farmingdale, NY 11735.

JOHNSON, CLIFFORD, JR.
Professional athlete. **PERSONAL:** Born Jul 22, 1947, San Antonio, TX; married Pam Leonard; children: Antoinette, Dana, Clifford III. **CAREER:** Cleveland Indians, professional baseball player; NY, Houston, 1974-79; Oklahoma City, Columbus, Houston Denver, 1971-73; Cocoa, Covington, Penisula, Raleigh, Durh, 1967-70. **HONORS/ACHIEVEMENTS:** Am Assn Player of Yr 1973. **BUSINESS ADDRESS:** Cleveland Indians, Boudreau Blvd, Cleveland, OH 44114.

JOHNSON, CLIFTON E.
Judge. **PERSONAL:** Born in North Carolina. **EDUCATION:** NC Coll, law degree. **CAREER:** Resident superior ct judge; Mecklenburg Co Charlotted Dist, former dist ct judge.

JOHNSON, CLIFTON HERMAN
Executive director. **PERSONAL:** Born Sep 13, 1921, Griffin, GA; son of John Johnson and Pearl Parrish Johnson; married Rosemary Brunst; children: Charles, Robert, Virginia. **EDUCATION:** Univ of Connecticut, ASTP Certificate 1943-44; Univ of North Carolina, BA 1948; Univ of Chicago, MA 1949; Univ of North Carolina, PhD 1958. **CAREER:** LeMoyne Coll, asst prof 1950-56; East Carolina Univ, asst prof 1958-59; LeMoyne Coll, prof 1959-61; Fisk Univ, archivist 1961-63; LeMoyne Coll, prof 1963-66; Race Relations Dept, United Church Bd for Homeland Ministries, exec dir 1966-69; Amistad Research Center, exec dir 1966-; Tulane Univ, adjunct prof 1987-. **ORGANIZATIONS:** Dir United Nations Assn 1963-66; Race Relations Task Force, United Church Bd for Homeland Ministries 1971-73; dir Tennessee Council Human Relations 1967-69; dir Natl Comm Against Discrimination in Housing 1966-69; dir Friends of Archives of Louisiana 1978-. **HONORS/ACHIEVEMENTS:** Fellowship Southern Fellowships Found 1956-58; IBM Fellow, United Negro Coll Fund 1965; Man of Achievement, Intl Key Woman 1974; Chapital Award, NAACP New Orleans Branch 1976 ; Honorary Sec of State, State of Louisiana 1981. **MILITARY SERVICE:** AUS staff sergeant 5 yrs. **BUSINESS ADDRESS:** Executive Dir, Amistad Research Center, Tulane Univ, New Orleans, LA 70118.

JOHNSON, CLINISSON ANTHONY
Judge. **PERSONAL:** Born Nov 16, 1947, Memphis, TN; married Andrea Yvonne Morrow; children: Collin Anthony; Terrence GalonTiffany Gayle. **EDUCATION:** Fisk Univ Nashville, BA history 1969; Univ of TN Law Sch Knoxville, JD 1972. **CAREER:** Memphis Municipal Ct Sys, city ct judge div IV 1976-; Shelby Co Pub Defenders Ofc Memphis, asst pub defender 1974-75; City Atty's Ofc Memphis, part-time pub defender 1972-74; Ratner Sugarmon Lucas & Salky Law Ofc Memphi, asso assy 1972-76. **ORGANIZATIONS:** Mem, TN Bar Assn 1972-; mem, Memphis & Shelby Co Bar Assn 1972-; mem, Nat Bar Assn 1972-; mem, NAACP 1985. **BUSINESS ADDRESS:** City of Memphis Municipal Cour, 128 Adams Ave, Memphis, TN 38103.

JOHNSON, COLLIS, JR.
Dentist. **PERSONAL:** Born Nov 17, 1946, Oklahoma; married Marsha Michele Jones; children: Jonathan Ashley, Rachael Christine. **EDUCATION:** Langston Univ OK, BS 1969; Meharry Med Coll TN, DDS 1973; Martin Luther King General Hospital, general res 1974. **CAREER:** Denver, private general dentistry 1977-; Pilot City Health Center Minneapolis, general dentistry dept 1974-77. **ORGANIZATIONS:** Mem Am Dental Assn; Natl Dental Assn 1977-; asst treas Alpha Phi Alpha Inc Minneapolis Denver; mem Denver Urban League. **BUSINESS ADDRESS:** 2800 Race St, Denver, CO 80205.

JOHNSON, CONSTANCE W. VAN BRUNT
Business executive. **PERSONAL:** Born Jul 29, 1949, Los Angeles. **EDUCATION:** Sarah Lawrence Coll, AB 1971; Harvard U, MAT 1972. **CAREER:** Ebony Jr, Johnson Pub Co, mng ed; African Am Inst, prog asst 1969-71; Lincoln, MA Schools, reading tutor. **ORGANIZATIONS:** Trustee, WTTW; mem, Children's Rdng Roundtbl. **HONORS/ACHIEVEMENTS:** Fellow, John Hay Whitney, Harvard; fellow, Dwight D Eisenhower, Harvard.

JOHNSON, CYRUS EDWIN
Business executive. **PERSONAL:** Born Feb 18, 1929, Alton, IL; son of Cyrus L Johnson and Jennie Keen Johnson (deceased); married Charlotte E Kenniebrew; children: Judie, Rene. **EDUCATION:** Univ of IL, BS 1956, MA 1959; Harvard Business School, 1974. **CAREER:** Farmer 1946-50; Urbana Lincoln Hotel, asst mgr 1953-59; IL Bell Telephone Co, dist mgr 1959-72; Gen Mills Inc, vp; MGO Facilities & Svcs, dir. **ORGANIZATIONS:** Dir AULT Inc, Lifespan Inc; former trustee Gen Mills Found, Natl Minority Business Campaign; former dir Abbot-Northwestern Hospital; former deans adv council Purdue Univ, Business School, Harvard Business School Assoc; bd of dir W VA State College Foundation 1988-; Business Advisory Bethune-Cookman College Div of Business 1989-. **HONORS/ACHIEVEMENTS:** Amer Legion Scholarship Awd 1943; Portraits of Success Awd Purdue Univ, Old Masters 1975; Fellow Chicago Defender Roundtable of Commerce 1967. **MILITARY SERVICE:** AUS 1950-52. **BUSINESS ADDRESS:** Vice President and Dir, MGO Facilities & Serv, PO Box 1113, Minneapolis, MN 55440.

JOHNSON, DAVID FREEMAN
Biochemist. **PERSONAL:** Born Jan 28, 1925, Nashville, TN; married Gloria D Tapscott; children: Toni Y, David G. **EDUCATION:** Allegheny Coll, BS 1947, DSc 1972; Howard Univ, MS 1949; Georgetown Univ, PhD 1957. **CAREER:** Howard Univ, instr 1949-50; Freedmens Hosp, rsch chemist 1950-51; NIH, rsch biochemist 1952-; Grad School, instr 1960-; NIH Sect on Microanalytical Serv & Instr, chief 1972-82, chief lab of anal chem 1982-. **ORGANIZATIONS:** Mem Amer Governing Bd Univs & Coll 1972-; trustee Prince Georges Comm Coll Largo 1969-79; bd of regents Morgan State Univ 1979-85; bd of dirs Amer Assoc of Comm & Jr Coll 1975-79; mem Allegheny Coll Meadville PA 1972-76, Council for Inter Inst Leadership 1983-, Natl Ctr for Higher Ed Mgmt Serv 1984-; fellow Amer Soc Exptl Biology; mem ACS, AAA's Endoctrine Soc, Kappa Alpha Psi; contrib to professional jrnls. **BUSINESS ADDRESS:** Chief Lab of Anal Chem, Natl Inst of Health, NIH Bldg 8 Room B2A-17, Bethesda, MD 20892.

JOHNSON, DAVID HORACE
Educational administrator. **PERSONAL:** Born Dec 01, 1925, Crowley, LA; married Gladys Mae Allumns; children: Hortense, LaRose. **EDUCATION:** Lane Coll, Jackson TN, BA 1949; Univ of WI, Madison WI, MS 1954; Texas A&M Univ Coll, Station TX, PhD 1972. **CAREER:** TX Coll, Tyler TX, chmn dept of educ 1973-80, dean of students 1961-73, admin asst to pres 1965; dir coll prep clinics 1966-67, 1970-71; Carver Elementary School, Monroe LA, prin 1954-61; Swartz Elementary School, Monroe LA, prin 1950-54; Richwood HS, Monroe LA, instructor 1949-50. **ORGANIZATIONS:** Mem, Human Rels Cncl 1969-72; bd of dirs, Region VII Srv Cntr 1973-78; bd of dirs, Campfire Girls 1978-80. **HONORS/**

ACHIEVEMENTS: Recip of WW2 Victory Medal-Blue Ribbon with 2 Bronze Stars-Good Conduct Medal, AUS; cert of Appreciation, City of Tyler TX, Hum Rels Cncl 1972; Outstnding Ldrshp in Higher Ed, Lane Coll, Jackson TN 1973. **MILITARY SERVICE:** AUS tech sgt 1944-46. **BUSINESS ADDRESS:** Texas College, 2404 N Grand Ave, Tyler, TX 75702.

JOHNSON, DAVIS
Business executive. **PERSONAL:** Born Feb 23, 1934, Detroit, MI; married Alphia Bymun, Jun 21, 1958; children: Cheryl Rene Johnson. **EDUCATION:** Wayne St U, attend; Harvard U, attend MI St U, attend; Investment Seminar, attend; Notre Dame, attend. **CAREER:** Investors Divrsfd Srv, Inc, div sales mgr 1972-, dist sales mgr 1969-72, sales rep 1966-69. **ORGANIZATIONS:** Mem, Nat Assn, Securities Dealers; mem, NAACP; Booker T Wash Bus Assn; Cotillion Clb; Big 10 Alumni Assn; Metro Cntrctrs; Jugs African Med Assn. **MILITARY SERVICE:** AUS corpl 1952-54. **BUSINESS ADDRESS:** CEO, Update Diversified Financial Service, 15565 Northland Dr, Suite 502 E, Southfield, MI 48075.

JOHNSON, DENNIS
Professional athlete. **PERSONAL:** Born Sep 18, 1954, San Pedro, CA; married Donna; children: 1 son. **EDUCATION:** Pepperdine Univ, attended 1976. **CAREER:** Seattle Supersonics, player 1976-80; Phoenix Suns, player 1981-83; Boston Celtics, player 1983-. **HONORS/ACHIEVEMENTS:** Top Vote Getter NBA All Defensive Team 1978-80; MVP Championship Series 1978-79; player All Star Game 1979-82. **BUSINESS ADDRESS:** Boston Celtics, North Sta Boston Gardens, Boston, MA 02114.

JOHNSON, DIANE
Educator, author. **PERSONAL:** Born May 17, 1929, Milwaukee, WI; married Theodore H Johnson. **EDUCATION:** Univ WI, BS, PhD 1971. **CAREER:** Marquette Univ Med Sch, lab instr 1954-55; Inst for Enzyme Res, proj asst 1955-66; Univ WI Coll of Letters & Sci, asst dean 1968-78; WHA Radio Series "Educational Decision-making", panelist 1971-72; "The Undergraduate Student, A Case Study", panelist 1972-73; Univ of WI, asst dir of athletics 1978-. **ORGANIZATIONS:** Mem Amer Personnel & Guidance Assn; pres Natl Assn of Academic Advisors for Athletics 1982; WI Coll Personnel Assn; Natl Assn Women Deans Adminstrs & Couns; mem Alpha Kappa Alpha Sor; adminstr, counselor, vice pres 1973-75 WI Assn Women Deans; chmn WI Drug Quality Council 1976-69; several Univ WI coms srch screen coms; mem Madison Bd Zoning Appeals; chrpsn Coalition Minority Women of UW-Madison 1974-75; mem oral exam bds for state WI; NAACP. **HONORS/ACHIEVEMENTS:** Asbury United Meth Ch EB Fred Fellow 1964-71; Outstanding Serv Awd Delta Sigma Theta & Alpha Phi Alpha 1973-74; 1st Black valedictorian of non-black hs Milwaukee Lincoln 1946; Disting Serv Awd Wisconsin Alumni Assn 1981. **BUSINESS ADDRESS:** Asst Dir of Athletics, Univ of WI, 3040 StadiumUniv WI Madison, Madison, WI 53706.

JOHNSON, DONN S.
Journalist. **PERSONAL:** Born May 09, 1947, St Louis, MO; son of Clyde E Johnson, Sr and Ivory M Dodd Johnson (deeased); married Earlene Beverly Breedlove, Jun 01, 1969; children: Lauren Beverly Johnson. **EDUCATION:** St Louis Comm Coll Florissant Valley, AA 1976; Webster Coll, BA 1977. **CAREER:** KWK Radio St Louis, newsman/disc jockey 1970-72; WIL Radio St Louis, newsman/dir comm rel 1972-78; KTVI Channel 2 St Louis, anchor/reporter 1978-. **ORGANIZATIONS:** Mem advisory bd Mass Communications Forest Park Comm Coll 1972-; mem Greater St Louis Black Journalists Assoc 1979-; mem St Louis Press Club 1980. **HONORS/ACHIEVEMENTS:** Howard B Woods Memorial Award for Journalism Black Student Assoc Webster Coll 1977; Best News Story of the Year Award Greater St Louis Black Journalists Assoc 1978; Black Excellence in Journalism Award, Greater St Louis Black Journalism Assn, 1978, 1984, 1986, 1988-89; Unity Awards in Media, Lincoln Univ, 1985; Media Award, Gifted Assn of MO, 1987. **MILITARY SERVICE:** AUS corpl 1966-67. **BUSINESS ADDRESS:** Anchor/Reporter, KTVI Channel 2, 5915 Berthold Ave, St Louis, MO 63110.

JOHNSON, DONNA ALLIGOOD
Business executive. **PERSONAL:** Born Oct 25, 1956, Detroit, MI; married Curtis C Johnson. **EDUCATION:** Tufts Univ, BS 1978. **CAREER:** BBDO, acct coord 1978-79, asst account exec 1980-81, account exec 1982-85, senior account exec 1986. **ORGANIZATIONS:** Mem NAACP.

JOHNSON, DOUGLAS H.
Educator. **PERSONAL:** Born May 01, 1943, Bolivia, NC; married Shirley L. **EDUCATION:** Cheyney St Coll, Cheyne PA, BA 1969;Univ RI, Kingston, m comm planning 1971. **CAREER:** Univ of RI, asst prof Comm Planning; Wilmington Metro Area Plann Corr Council, Wilmington DE, sum intern 1970; Inst, comm planning 1974-; Comm Plann in CPAD, asst prof 1974-; State of RI, Providence, consultant to Office of Continuing Educ 1974. **ORGANIZATIONS:** Prin, vp, Comm Found 1973-; ed, Nat Assn of Planners, Nwsltr 1973-75; mem, Am Soc Plann Off; Nat Assn of Plann; Am AssnUniv Prof; mem, United Wrk-Study Fellow, US Dept of Hsg & Urban Dev 1969-71. **HONORS/ACHIEVEMENTS:** Std Award, Am Inst of Plann 1971; recevied, Natl Flwshp Fund Award, Academic Yr for PhD studies at MIT 1976-77. **BUSINESS ADDRESS:** Grad Curriculum Comm Planning, Kingston, RI 02881.

JOHNSON, EARL E.
Educational administrative assistant. **PERSONAL:** Born Sep 28, 1926, Atlantic City, NJ; married Juanita Hairston; children: Brett, Jeffrey. **EDUCATION:** WV State Coll, BS in Educ 1951; Galssboro State Coll, MA in Elem Adm 1964. **CAREER:** Penn Ave Sch Atlantic City, NJ, prin 1964-67; Mass Ave Sch, prin 1967; Atlantic City Pblc Sch, dir Title III 1967-68; Ind Ave Sch Atlantic City,NJ, prin 1968-84; Atlantic City, NJ Pblc Sch, adm asst/elem serv 1984. **ORGANIZATIONS:** Chm schlrshp comm Miss Am Bd of Dir 1964-; former vice pres Atlantic Co Adm Assn 1964-; mem Kiwanis Clb of Atlantic City 1964-; mem former bas Upsilon Alpha Chptr Omega Psi Phi Frat; mem former pres Atlantic City Chptr NAACP. **HONORS/ACHIEVEMENTS:** Outstndng Blck Ed Blck Atlantic City Mag 1982; Outstndng Ed Ind Ave Sch Parent Adv Cncl 1978; Outstndng Ctzn 4h Clb ofv Atlantic Co 1973-75; Outstndng Ed Kenneth Hawkins Am Legion No 61 1974. **MILITARY SERVICE:** US Fld Arty 2nd lt 1946; comm 1951. **HOME ADDRESS:** 658 New York Ave, Atlantic City, NJ 08401. **BUSINESS ADDRESS:** Administrative Assistant, Atlantic City, NJ Pub Sch, 1809 Pacific Ave, Atlantic City, NJ 08401.

JOHNSON, EARVIN, JR. (MAGIC JOHNSON)
Business executive/professional athlete. **PERSONAL:** Born Aug 14, 1959, Lansing, MI. **EDUCATION:** Attended, MI State. **CAREER:** Magic Johnson Enterprises Inc, owner; performer,TV endorsements; LA Lakers, guard 1980-. **HONORS/ACHIEVEMENTS:** Tallest point guard NBA hist; World Class Athlete MI State; 184 season scoring average; leads all NBA guards with 7 rebounds per game; NBA Player of the Week; 3 games 89 pts/35 rebounds/34 assists 1980; Schick Pivotal Player Awd; top vote getter on Sporting News All NBA Team; autobiography "Magic" published 1983; won 2 playoff MVP Awds; mem 36th and 37th NBA All Star teams; named NBA MVP 1987. **BUSINESS ADDRESS:** Los Angeles Lakers, PO Box 10, Inglewood, CA 90306.

JOHNSON, ED F.
Clergyman. **PERSONAL:** Born Mar 08, 1937, Swansea, SC; married Wilma Williams; children: Juanzena LaFanei, Edward Franklin Jr, LaFane. **EDUCATION:** Benedict Coll, AB 1965; Clemson Univ, attended 1970-71; Univ of SC, attended 1971-72; Benedict Coll, Doctor of Divinity 1984. **CAREER:** Zion Hill Baptist Church, pastor 1962-66; Bethlehem Baptist Church, pastor 1965-69; Morris Chapel Baptist Church, pastor 1969-; Greenwood-Ninety Six NAACP, pres 1971-76; Connie Maxwell Children's Home Greenwood, SC, social worker 1972-; Baptist E&M Convention, vp. **ORGANIZATIONS:** Life mem Natl Assoc for the Advancement of Colored People; chmn Bd of Dir GLEAAMS HRC; teacher John G Richards School for Boys 1969, Saluda Cty School Dist High School 1966-71; social worker Connie Maxwell Children's Home 1972; bd of visitors Piedmont Technical Coll; bd mem of the Natl Baptist Conv of Amer; moderator of Little River Baptist Union Num Two. **HONORS/ACHIEVEMENTS:** Cert of Appreciation Med Univ of SC 1983. **MILITARY SERVICE:** AUS spec 3 3 yrs. **BUSINESS ADDRESS:** Vice President, Bapt Educ & Missionary Conv, 1315 Bunche Ave, Greenwood, SC 29646.

JOHNSON, EDDIE C.
Judge. **PERSONAL:** Born Jun 01, 1920, Chicago, IL; married Olivia; children: Edward, Ella. **EDUCATION:** Roosevelt U, AB; John Marshall Law Sch, JD; Loyola U, attend. **CAREER:** Circuit Ct, Cook Co IL, judge 1965-; Pvt Pract, atty 1952-65; Ellis, Westbrook & Holman, sec, law clk. **ORGANIZATIONS:** Mem Cook Co & Nat Bar Asn, Judical Cncl of NBA. **BUSINESS ADDRESS:** Judge Circuit Court Cook Cty, State of Illinois, Richard J Daley Ctr #2600, Chicago, IL 60602.

JOHNSON, EDDIE C.
Professional athlete. **PERSONAL:** Born May 01, 1959, Chicago, IL. **EDUCATION:** Univ of IL, BA History 1981. **CAREER:** Kansas City Kings, 1981. **HONORS/ACHIEVEMENTS:** Set career marks for scoring, rebounding, field goals & field goal attempts; MVP 1979-80, 1980-81; Honorable Mention All Am AP 1980-81; 1st AP & UPI All Big Ten 1980-81; 2nd AP & UPI All Big Ten 1979-82; 2nd round draft choice KC Kings 1981; led team in 8 categories (minutes played, field goals made & attempted, total points, free throws made & attempted, & scoring avg) 1984-85; 16th in scoring NBA 1984-85; 70 consecutive double figure scoring games Kansas City Kings 1984-85; started 169 consecutive games 1982-85; NBA Player of Week.

JOHNSON, EDMOND R.
Attorney. **PERSONAL:** Born Jun 26, 1937, Plymouth, NC; married Thelma Crosby; children: Edrenna Renee, Erica Ronelle. **EDUCATION:** NC Centrl U, BA 1959; Howard U, JD 1968. **CAREER:** Pvt pract law 1970-; DE Tech Comm Coll, tchr law clk 1968-69. **ORGANIZATIONS:** Mem NC Acad Trial Lawyers; NC State Bar; Nat & Am Bar Assns; NC Black Lawyers Assn; NAACP; Alpha Phi Alpha. **BUSINESS ADDRESS:** 916 W 5th St, Charlotte, NC 28201.

JOHNSON, EDNA DECOURSEY
Educator. **PERSONAL:** Born Jun 01, 1922, Baltimore, MD; married Laurence Harry. **EDUCATION:** Coppin St Clg, BS 1944; Rutgers U, Cert Group Dynamic Human Relations 1950, 56; Johns Hopkins U, Post Grad Work Consumer & Law 1954;Univ of WI, Cert Fin Money Mgmt 1966. **CAREER:** Baltimore City Public Schools, elementary teacher 1944-63; Baltimore Urban League, dir consult serv 1963-78; Comm Clolgof Baltimore & other Comm Clgs, part-time instructor 1975-; Northwest Baltimore Corp, exec dir 1979-82; Maryland Food Bank, prog dir 1979-82; Natl Assoc Negro Business & Professional Womens Clubs Inc, prog dir 1979-82. **ORGANIZATIONS:** Consumer adv American Egg Bd 1979-; bd mem Consumers Union 1st Black Woman 1972-84; bd mem Natl Coalition for Consumer Ed 1982-; mem Zeta Phi Beta Sor Coppin Alumni ; past pres Baltimore Club Mid Alantic ABWA 1970-73; past Governor Dist Natl Asso Negro Bus & Prof Womens Clubs Balto Urban League 1967-71, 73-75; past Natl Corresp Sec Heritage United Church of Christ 1971-73. **HONORS/ACHIEVEMENTS:** Natl Meritorious Sojourner Truth Balto Club Natl Asso Negro Business & Prof Womens Club Inc 1974; Lambda Kappa Mj 1972; The Pilomathians 1982; 100 Otstndng Women Delta Sigma Theta Sor. **HOME ADDRESS:** 3655 Wabash Ave, Baltimore, MD 21215.

JOHNSON, EDWARD, JR. (FAST EDDIE)
Professional athlete. **PERSONAL:** Born Feb 24, 1955, Ocala, FL; married Diana Racisz. **EDUCATION:** Auburn U, attnd 30 hrs personne mgmt. **CAREER:** Atlanta Hawks, professional basketball player present; Eddie Johnson Enter Inc, pres & found. **ORGANIZATIONS:** Mem Muscular Dystrophy; mem NAACP; mem UNCF. **HONORS/ACHIEVEMENTS:** MVP 1979-80; 2nd All-Def 2 yrs. **BUSINESS ADDRESS:** Atlantic Hawks, 100 Techwood Dr NW, Atlanta, GA 30303.

JOHNSON, EDWARD A.
Educator. **PERSONAL:** Born Feb 25, 1940, New York, NY. **EDUCATION:** City Coll of NY, BS 1968, PhD 1978. **CAREER:** City Coll of NY, adjunct lecturer 1968-77; Medgar Evers Coll, asst prof 1977-78; New York City Tech Coll, adjunct lecturer 1982-; Pratt Inst, instructor 1978-. **ORGANIZATIONS:** Sec Natl Anti-Imperialist Movement in Solidarity with African Liberation 1975-; mem Metropolitan Council on Housing 1982-. **HOME ADDRESS:** 40 Morningside Ave, New York, NY 10026. **BUSINESS ADDRESS:** Instructor, Pratt Institute, Willoughby Ave, Brooklyn, NY 11205.

JOHNSON, EDWARD ELEMUEL
Educator. **PERSONAL:** Born in Crooked River, Jamaica;son of Rev Edward E Johnson and Elizabeth Blake Johnson; married Beverley Jean Morris; children: Edward E, Lawrence P, Robin Jeannine, Nathan J, Cyril U. **EDUCATION:** Howard Univ, BS 1947, MS 1948; Univ of CO, PhD 1952. **CAREER:** Southern Univ Baton Rouge LA, prof & assoc dean of univ 1955-72; LA State Univ Med Sch, clinical prof of psychiatry 1969-72; United Bd for Coll Development, dir 1972-74; Univ of Medicine & Dentistry of NJ Robt Wood Johnson Med Sch, prof of psychiatry 1974-. **ORGANIZATIONS:** Panelist Science Faculty Develop Natl Sci Foundation 1978-82; site visitor Natl Inst of Health 1978-; consultant Bell Laboratories Holmdel NJ 1982-85; bdof trustees Crossroads Theatre Co 1983-; bd of dirs PSI Assoc Inc 1984-. **HONORS/ACHIEVEMENTS:** Fellow Amer Assoc for Advancement of Science; life mem The Soc of the Sigma Xi; mem Pi Gamma Mu Natl Social Science Honor Soc, Psi Chi Natl Psychology Honor Soc; over 35 scientific publications including book chapt; Beta Beta Beta Biological Honor Society, Thirty-third Degree Mason, Prince Hall Affiliation. **MILITARY SERVICE:** AUS 1st lt 1951-53. **HOME ADDRESS:** PO Box 597, East Brunswick, NJ 08816. **BUSINESS ADDRESS:** Professor of Psychiatry, Robt Wood Johnson Medical Sch, Univ of Medicine & Dentistry of New Jersey, 675 Hoes Lane, Piscataway, NJ 08854.

JOHNSON, EDWARD M.
Business executive. **PERSONAL:** Born Jan 15, 1943, Washington. **EDUCATION:** BArch 1967; Master, City Planning 1970. **CAREER:** Edward M Johnson, AIA Asso, Architects & Urban Planners, pres; Roy Littlejohn Assn, Afro-Am Bicentennial Corp, Urban Sys & Dvrsfd Interprises, archit & urban planning cons; Architecture & Urban Planning at Wash Tech Inst, asst Prof. **ORGANIZATIONS:** Mem, DC Chpt, Am Inst of Architects, Am Inst of Planners 1974-; chmn, Housing Com for Mt Pleasant Nghbrs Assn 1974. **HONORS/ACHIEVEMENTS:** Recip, US Housing & Urban Dev Fellow; Doxiodus Fellow; Urban Transp Fellow. **BUSINESS ADDRESS:** 3610 12 St NE, Washington, DC 20017.

JOHNSON, ELAINE MCDOWELL
Federal government executive. **PERSONAL:** Born Jun 28, 1942, Baltimore, MD; daughter of McKinley McDowell and Lena McDowell; married Walter Johnson; children: Nathan Murphy Jr, Michael Murphy. **EDUCATION:** Morgan State Univ, BA 1965; Univ of MD, MSW 1971, Univ MD, Ph.D. 1988. **CAREER:** State of MD, acting regional dir 1971-72; Natl Inst on Drug Abuse, public health advisor 1972-76; Div of Comm Assistance, deputy dir/dir 1976-82; Div of Prevention & Communications, dir 1982-85; ADAMHA, exec asst to admin 1985; Natl Inst on Drug Abuse, deputy dir 1985-88; dir, Office for Substance Abuse Prevention 1988-. **ORGANIZATIONS:** Ordained officer Presbyterian Church 1981-84; natl dir drug abuse prevention prog Zeta Phi Beta Sor 1986-; consultant US Information Agency, US State Dept; mem Links Inc. **HONORS/ACHIEVEMENTS:** Public Serv Awd Natl Assoc State Alcohol & Drug Abuse Directors 1974; Administrator Meritorious Awd ADAMHA 1976; Natl Services to Youth Award, LINKS, Inc. 1986; DHHS Management Award 1984; Natl Award for Outstanding Leadership in Improving Health Care in the Black Comm, Natl Medical Assn, 1988; Outstanding Service Award in the Drug Abuse Field, Natl Assn of State Alcohol and Drug Abuse Directors (NASADAD) 1988; Prevention Award for Defining and Advancing the Science of Prevention, Natl Drug Information Center of Families in Action, 1988; F. Elwood Davis Award for Govt Official Responsive to the Needs of Youth, Boys and Girls Clubs, 1989; aurhor of: Cocaine: The Amer Experience, in: Allen, D. ed. "The Cocaine Crisis," NY Plenum Press, 1987; The Impact of Drug Abuse on Wom en's Health in "Public Health Reports," 1987; The Government's Response to Drug Abuse Problems Among Minority Populations, "Journal of the Black Nurses Assn.". **BUSINESS ADDRESS:** Director, Office for Substance Prevention, 5600 Fishers Lane, Rockville, MD 20857.

JOHNSON, ELIOSE See MCKINNEY, ELOISE VAUGHN

JOHNSON, ELMORE W.
Business executive. **PERSONAL:** Born Jul 12, 1944, Richmond, VA; married Lynne Saxon; children: Kendall, Elmore, Jr, Marc. **EDUCATION:** VA Union U, BA; Temple U, adv studies. **CAREER:** Hartranft Comm Corp, exec dir 1973-, comm serv coord 1972-73; Neighborhood Renewal Prog, comm splst 1971-72; Philadelphia, Dept of Licenses & Insps,comm splst 1971-72; US Dept of Housing & Urban Dev, comm splst 1971-72; Neighborhood Dev Prog, comm splst 1971; US Dept of HUD, comm splst 1971; Century Metalcraft Corp, rep 1970-71; St Empl Commn, unempl intrvwr 1969-70; Hanover Inst for Boys, supr 1967. **ORGANIZATIONS:** Mem, adv com, Urban Homesteading Comm Cncl; Urban Homesteading Task Force; Housing Assn of DE Valley; Nat Assn of Housing & Redevel Ofcls; PA Housing Imprvmnt Code Assn; Nat Conf of Soc Wlfr; Nat Assn of Black Soc Wrkrs; mem, City of Philadelphia Rodent Control Prog; ARC; Temple U, Comprhnsv Hlth Serv Prog; NORTH; Onwards, Inc; Holy Cross Luth Ch; Chapel of Four Chaplains; BSA Prvntv Med Splst. **HONORS/ACHIEVEMENTS:** Prtcpnt, Nat Black Caucus Legislative Think-Tank Sess; recip, & Award, Martin Luther King Cntr. **MILITARY SERVICE:** AUS 1967-69. **BUSINESS ADDRESS:** 2415-35 Germantown Ave, Philadelphia, PA 19133.

JOHNSON, ENID C.
Educator. **PERSONAL:** Born Oct 15, 1931, Miami; divorced. **EDUCATION:** Talladega Coll, AB 1953; Barry Coll, MS 1967. **CAREER:** Miami YWCA, adult prog dir; Chicago, grp wrkr; Dade Co Sch Sys, tch 1955, cnslr 1967, asst prin 1971, asst prin for guidance 1985. **ORGANIZATIONS:** Mem, NEA; mem, FEA; mem, Dade Co Adm Assn & Guidance Assn; mem, S FL Guidance Assn; mem, Am & Sch Cncl Assn; mem, Am Guidance & Prsnl Assn; mem, AAUW; mem, Hi Delta-Kappa; bd dir, Miami YWCA; bd dir, FL Conf United Ch of Christ; charter mem, Ch of Open Door; mem, UCC Fruits of the Sts; mem, Miami Inter Alumni Cncl, UNCf; mem, Sigma Gamma Rho Sor. **HONORS/ACHIEVEMENTS:** Listed, Personalities of South; cert of Apprec, Sigma Gamma Rho Sor. **BUSINESS ADDRESS:** 6750 SW 60th St S, Miami, FL 33143.

JOHNSON, ERMA CHANSLER
Educational administrator. **PERSONAL:** Born Jun 06, 1942, Leggett, TX; married Lawrence Eugene Johnson; children: Thelma Ardenia. **EDUCATION:** Prairie View A&M Univ, BS 1963; Bowling Green State Univ, MEd 1968. **CAREER:** Turner High School, teacher 1963-67; Bowling Green State Univ, grad asst 1967-68; Tarrant Cty Jr Coll Dist Ft Worth TX, assoc prof 1968-72, asst dir of personnel 1973-74, dir of personnel 1974-81, vice chancellor human resources. **ORGANIZATIONS:** Pres Fannie M Heath Cultural Club 1974-75, 1978-80; Ft Worth Amer Revolution Bicentennial Comm 1974-76; bd of dir 1974-78, treas 1977-78, Ft Worth-Tarrant Cty Supportive Outreach Svc; Task Force 100 1976; vice pres Ft Worth Minority Leaders & Citizens Council 1976-78; Ft Worth Public Transp Adv comm 1976-80;bd of dir Comm Devel Fund 1976-80; Ft Worth Girls Club 1976-81, pres 1979-81; Ft Worth Keep Amer Beautiful Task Force 1977-78; comm vice chairperson, bd of dir United Way of Metropolitan Tarrant Cty 1979; Ft Worth Central Bus Dist Planning Council 1979-81; seminar leader Coll & Univ Personnel Assoc 1980-; Ft Worth Citizens on the Move, 1983; Forum Ft Worth; sec Mt Rose Baptist Church; bd of dir Ft Worth Black Chamber of Comm; charter mem Tarrant Cty Black Historical & Genealogical Soc; vice pres Links Inc; sec bd of dir Mt Rose Child Care Ctr; chmn oper comm Dallas/Ft Worth Airport Bd; consult Coll& Univ US Civil Comm Serv 1972-; chmn Dallas/Ft Worth Intl Airport Bd 1987. **HONORS/ACHIEVEMENTS:** Grad Asstship Bowling Green State Univ 1967-68; One Week Ed & Professional Devel Act Grant in Vocational Ed 1969, four week 1970; Nominated Outstanding TeacherTarrant Cty Jr Coll 1971; Listed in Outstanding Ed of Amer 1972, Outstanding Young Women in Amer 1975; Ft Worth Black Female Achiever of the Year 1977. **HOME ADDRESS:** 2362 Faett Court, Fort Worth, TX 76119. **BUSINESS ADDRESS:** Vice Chancellor/Human Resrces, Tarrant County Junior College, 1500 Houston, Fort Worth, TX 76102.

JOHNSON, ERNEST KAYE, III
General surgeon. **PERSONAL:** Born Feb 07, 1950, Ocala, FL; married Clara Perry; children: ERnest IV, Clara Delores. **EDUCATION:** Univ of FL, Pre-Med 1971; Meharry Medical Coll, MD 1975; Hubbard Hosp Meharry Medical Coll, General Surgery 1980. **CAREER:** Student Natl Medical Assoc, vice pres 1973-74; Meharry House Staff Assoc, vice pres 1975-76; Infinity III Inc, vice pres 1983-85. **ORGANIZATIONS:** Mem Matthew Walker Surgical Soc 1975-87, RF Boyd Medical Soc 1975-87, Nashville Acad of Medicine 1980-83, TN Medical Assoc 1980-83; mem Alpha Phi Alpha. **HONORS/ACHIEVEMENTS:** Honorary mem US House of Representatives 1983; Honorary Deputy Sheriff Nashville Davidson Co 1984. **BUSINESS ADDRESS:** 3803 Hydes Ferry Pike, Nashville, TN 37218.

JOHNSON, EUNICE WALKER
Publishing executive. **PERSONAL:** Born in Selma, AL; married John H; children: John Harold, Linda. **EDUCATION:** Talladega Coll, BA; Loyola U, MA;Univ of Chicago, cmpltd courses in studies of the great books; Northwestern U, postgrad; Ray Vogue Sch of Interior Decorating, Attend. **CAREER:** Johnson Pub Co, Inc, sec-treas. **ORGANIZATIONS:** Mem, Women's Bd of Art & Inst of Chicago; mem, Nat Found for the Fashion Ind; mem, bd dir, Talladega Coll, found by maternal grndfthr; bd dir, Woman's Div, United Negro Coll Fund; mem, Midwest Ballet; trustee, Harvard St George Sch, Chicago; dir, Adoptive Info Citizenry Com; dir, Women's Bd,Univ of Chicago; bd mem, Hyde Pk-Kenwood Women's Aux of IL; aid soc pres, Children's Hm. **HONORS/ACHIEVEMENTS:** Named, by Pres Richard Nixon as a spl ambasador to accompany Mrs Nixon to Liberia for inauguration of country's new pres 1972; %Two models she selected forhaute couture-designer Emilio Pucci became first blacks to prtcpt in a showing of fashions at famed Pitti Palace, Florence, Italy 1964. **BUSINESS ADDRESS:** 820 S & Michigan Ave, Chicago, IL 60605.

JOHNSON, EVELYN F.
Attorney, executive assistant, judge. **PERSONAL:** Born Mar 23, 1925, Chicago, IL; married Glenn T; children: Evelyn A, Glenn T. **EDUCATION:** Univ of Chicago, BA 1946; John Marshall Law Sch, JD 1949, LLM 1950. **CAREER:** Pvt Prac, Chicago, atty 1950-73; St of IL, exec asst to sec 1973-; Cook County Circuit Court, judge. **ORGANIZATIONS:** Mem Cook Co Bar Assn; mem Am Bar Assn; mem Chicago Bar Assn; mem IL Bar Assn; mem Women's Bar Assn; mem World Peace Through Law; mem Conf of Conciliation Cts; mem YWCA; mem NAACP; mem Urban League; trustee Woodlawn African Meth Episcopal Ch 1960-. **HONORS/ACHIEVEMENTS:** Cook Co Bar Assn Award 1973; Citation of Merit, John Marshall Law Sch 1973. **BUSINESS ADDRESS:** Cook County Circut Court, 2600 Daley Center, Chicago, IL 60602.

JOHNSON, EZRA
Professional athlete. **PERSONAL:** Born Oct 02, 1955, Shreveport, LA; married Carmen. **EDUCATION:** Morris Brown, attended. **CAREER:** Green Bay Packers, defensive end 1977-. **HONORS/ACHIEVEMENTS:** Packers #2 sack artist with 7 for 55 yards in losses; Ranked among NFC leaders 1983 with 14 1/2 QB sacks; Led Packer defensive line in unassisted tackles with 86; Led defense in strike-shortened 1982 season with 5 sacks & shared tackle honors for defensive line; Led defensive line in solo tackles in 1980 with 53. **BUSINESS ADDRESS:** Green Bay Packers, 1265 Lombardi Ave, Green Bay, WI 54307.

JOHNSON, F. J., JR.
Association executive. **PERSONAL:** Born Jan 30, 1930, Marshall, TX; married May Joyce Wood; children: Teri, Valerie. **EDUCATION:** Univ of Washington, BA;Univ of OR, additional study. **CAREER:** Nat Educ Assn; mgr, tchr rights div; NEA, former coordinator of minority involvements prog; Shoreline Sch Sys Seattle WA, former tchr. **ORGANIZATIONS:** Former Mem exec bd Greater Seattle; Coun of Tchr of English; past pres Shoreline Educ Assn 1964-65; edited SEA Scope Assn newspaper; participant in NCTE Conv; mem SEA Scope Adv Bd; chmn Right ro Red Com; chmn Com on the Profession PSCTE; consult & speaker for Secondary Sch & Leadership Conf on Student Govt & Parliamentary Procedure; chmn bd Finance Mt Zion Bapt Ch; pres bd dir Mt Zion Bapt Ch Fed Credit Union; pres Beta Omicron Chpt; Phi Beta Sigma. **HONORS/ACHIEVEMENTS:** Author of several publications; recipient John Hay FellowUniv of OR 1964. **BUSINESS ADDRESS:** 1201 16 St NW, Washington, DC 20036.

JOHNSON, F. RAYMOND
Business executive. **PERSONAL:** Born May 10, 1920, Richmond, TX; children: Bernarde, Sheryl, Floyd. **EDUCATION:** So CA Coll Bus, attended 1953. **CAREER:** Self-Employed, pub acctnt 1955-65; Oppor Indslzn Ctrs of Amer, job develop specialist 1965-68; S Cent Improv Action Counc, dep dir 1968-70; Usina Comm Devel Corp, exec dir 1970-74; Barker Mgmt Inc, gen mgr 1974-78; CA Housing Finance Agency, state housing consultant 1978; Hjima Housing Corp, dir 1978-83. **ORGANIZATIONS:** Chmn bd of dirs Hjima Comm develop Corp 1978-83; mem NAACP, Urban League, YMCA, Brotherhood Crusade. **HONORS/ACHIEVEMENTS:** Cong Citation Asst of Minority Entrepreneurs Bus Devel LA Co. **MILITARY SERVICE:** AUS s/sgt 1941-45.

JOHNSON, FRANCIS EDWARD, JR.
Attorney. **PERSONAL:** Born Jan 26, 1948, Detroit, MI; son of Francis Edward Johnson, Sr and Jessie Mae Henry Johnson; divorced. **EDUCATION:** Wayne State Univ, Detroit MI, BA, 1971, JD, 1976. **CAREER:** Detroit Edison, Detroit MI, director EEO, 1979-84; F. Edward Johnson PL, Detroit MI, owner, 1984-87; Reynolds, Beeby & Magnuson, Detroit MI, partner, 1987-. **ORGANIZATIONS:** Mem, Natl Bar Assn; mem, Wolverine Bar Assn; Michigan Trial Lawyers Assn; Amer Bar Assn; Michigan State Bar Assn; chairman, Michigan Republican Mainstream Committee; chairman, The Young Professionals Inc; mem, State Central Republican Committee; bd mem, NAACP; mem, Urban League. **HONORS/ACHIEVEMENTS:** Alumni of the Year, Boysville of Michigan, 1982; Natl Outreach Committee, Republican Natl Committee, 1987; Natl Census Advisory Committee, Dept of Commerce, 1988-90; Leadership Commendation, Natl Mainstream Republican Comm, 1989; Leadership Award, Michigan Mainstream Republican Committee, 1989; Volunteer of the Year Award, Jones Elementary School, 1989. **BUSINESS ADDRESS:** Attorney, Partner, Reynolds Beeby & Magnuson, 400 Tower Renaissance Center, 15th Floor, Detroit, MI 48243.

JOHNSON, FRANK J.
Publisher. **PERSONAL:** Born Sep 01, 1939, Hope, AR; son of Odell Johnson and Irene Wingfield Johnson; married Betty J Logan; children: Troy, Frank Jr. **EDUCATION:** CA State Univ Fresno, BA Educ 1963. **CAREER:** Fresno Colony Sch Dist, teacher 1963-69; West Fresno Sch Dist, principal/counselor 1970-74, dist supt 1975-79; Grapevine Magazine, publisher/editor 1969-84; Who's Who of Black Millionaires Inc, ceo/publisher. **ORGANIZATIONS:** Mem Phi Beta Sigma Frat 1959-; mem West Coast Black Publishers Assn 1979-. **HONORS/ACHIEVEMENTS:** Author "Who's Who of Black Millionaires 1984 and 1990 2nd edition; First Black School Dist Supt in Central CA 1975-79; mem Civil Service Bd Fresno CA 1977-81; Alpha Phi Alpha Frat Outstanding Achievement Educ/Publ 1978; Outstanding Teacher West Fresno Sch Dist 1969, Admin 1977. **MILITARY SERVICE:** AUS; Comm Serv Awd 1974. **BUSINESS ADDRESS:** CEO/Publisher, Who's Who of Black Millionaires, PO Box 12092, Fresno, CA 93776.

JOHNSON, FRANK LAVELLE
Professional athlete. **PERSONAL:** Born Nov 23, 1958, Weirsdale, FL; married Amy. **EDUCATION:** Wake Forest, BS 1981. **CAREER:** Washington Bullets, guard 1981. **HONORS/ACHIEVEMENTS:** Career high with 15 assists; 1st round draft choice; Honorable Mention on 1982 All-Rookie Team; the top 10 NBA players in assists (4th) 1983; Honorable MentionAll-Am by AP & UPI; selected to the All-ACC Team; named outstndng player in Aloha Classic. **BUSINESS ADDRESS:** Washington Bullets, One Harry S Truman Dr, Ste 510, Landover, MD 20785.

JOHNSON, FRED D.
Educator. **PERSONAL:** Born Mar 07, 1933, Fayetteville, TN; married Cora S (deceased); children: Fredna, Sheraldine. **EDUCATION:** TN St U, BS; Memphis St U, MEd;Univ TN, EdD 1974. **CAREER:** Shelby Co Bd Ed, sci consult 1968-, supr, adult ed 1967-68; sci tchr 1954-67; Shelby Co Bd of Educ, asst supt for instr 1977-. **ORGANIZATIONS:** Mem, bd, BSCS; com, Nat Conv Prog 1972; chmn, Area Conv 1974; bd mem-at-large, NSTA 1985; NEA 1985; ASCD 1985; AAAS 1985; NASS1985; KDP 1985; AASA 1985; Optimist 1985; NAACP 1985; bd dir NAACP. **HONORS/ACHIEVEMENTS:** Outstndng Tchr Award, TN Acad Sci 1971. **MILITARY SERVICE:** AUS e-5 1955-57. **BUSINESS ADDRESS:** Asst Supt for Instr, Shelby Co Schools, 160 S Hollywood St, Memphis, TN 38112.

JOHNSON, FREDERICK, JR.
Educator. **PERSONAL:** Born Jul 14, 1940, Newberry, SC. **EDUCATION:** Howard U, BA 1963; Stanford U, MA 1971. **CAREER:** Rutgers U, instr; Clarion State Coll, asst prof of English 1971-72; Bell Telephone, tech writer; Philadelphia Public Sch, tchr 1963-70; Prentice -Hall Inc, manuscript reviewer 1975-; The PA Council on Arts, poet 1974-75. **HONORS/ACHIEVEMENTS:** Has & had numerous poems pub. **BUSINESS ADDRESS:** BOX 92, Armitage Hall, Camden, NJ.

JOHNSON, FREDERICK DOUGLASS
Educator. **PERSONAL:** Born Mar 28, 1946, Chattanooga, TN; married Jacqueline Faith Jones; children: Kyle. **EDUCATION:** Oakwood Coll Huntsville AL, 1965-66; Union Coll Lincoln NE, 1966-68; NE Weslyan Univ, BA 1972; Univ of NE, MA 1980. **CAREER:** Randolph School Lincoln NE, teacher 1972-75, team leader 1976-83; Belmont School Lincoln NE, asst principal curriculum coord 1983-86; asst principal, Park Elementary School Lincoln, NE. **ORGANIZATIONS:** Mem Phi Delta Kappa, Natl Ed Assoc, NE State Ed, Lincoln Ed Assoc Lincoln Public Schools Minority Connection, Guidance Study Comm, Personnel Recruitment Comm, Allan Chapel Seventh-Day-Adventist Church, Amer Legion, Kiwanis, Malone Community Ctr; bd mem Allan Chapel Church, Allon Chapel Church, Child GuidCtr of Lincoln; mem NE Weslyan Career Ctr. **MILITARY SERVICE:** AUS E-5 1 1/2 yrs; Good Conduct Medal, Asian Serv Medal. **HOME ADDRESS:** 7428 Ringneck Dr, Lincoln, NE 68506.

JOHNSON, FREDERICK E.
Engineer. **PERSONAL:** Born Jun 24, 1941, Detroit, MI; married Sandra A; children: Frederick II, Seth. **EDUCATION:** Wayne State Univ, BEE 1964; Syracuse Univ, MEE 1969. **CAREER:** IBM Endicott Lab, line printer test mgr, instrumentation & mech analysis, mgr of prod devel, engr mgr proj ofc. **ORGANIZATIONS:** Exec comm NY, PA Health Systems Agency; adv engr, tech asst, engr IBM; pres, bd dirs Broome Ct Urban League; pres Iota Theta Lambda Chap Alpha Phi Alpha 1977-79; treas bd of dir NY, PA Health Systems Agency; trustee Trinity AME Zion Church; publ chmn Broome Cty NAACP, Alpha Phi Alpha, Iota Theta Lambda, Buddy Camp Assoc 1970; chmn Minority Bus Adv Comm Broome Cty NY. **BUSINESS ADDRESS:** Engineer, Manager, IBM Endicott Lab, 1701 North St, Endicott, NY 13760.

JOHNSON, G. R. HOVEY
Judge. **PERSONAL:** Born Nov 13, 1930, Richmond, VA; married Joan J Crocker; children: Marjorie, Patricia, GR Hovey II. **EDUCATION:** Prairie View A&M Coll, BS 1951; George Washington Univ, MS 1974; Georgetown Univ, JD 1977. **CAREER:** Private Practice of Law, attorney 1977-82; Office of Public Defender, criminal defense lawyer 1979-82; 7th Judicial Circuit of MD, circuit court judge. **MILITARY SERVICE:** AUS col 23 yrs; (2) LM, DFC, (3) BSM, (2) MSM, (6) AM, (2) JSCM, ARCOM. **HOME ADDRESS:** 16014 Audubon Lane, Bowie, MD 20716. **BUSINESS ADDRESS:** Circuit Court Judge, 7th Judicial Circuit of MD, Court House, Upper Marlboro, MD 20772.

JOHNSON, GAGE
Physician. **PERSONAL:** Born Aug 19, 1924, Belzoni, MS; children: Shara, Gage Jr. **EDUCATION:** Bougaloo Coll, BA 1950; Howard U, MD 1955; Cleveland Metro Gen Hosp, resd ob-gyn 1960-64; Am Coll, flwOb-GYN. **CAREER:** Outer Dr Hosp, chf ob-gyn; Self, physician. **ORGANIZATIONS:** Mem AMA; mem Nat Med Assn; Wayne Co Med Soc; Detroit Med Soc; sec Fort & St Med Clinic; life mem NAACP. **HONORS/ACHIEVEMENTS:** Mem Alpha Phi Alpha Frat. **MILITARY SERVICE:** USN seaman 1st class 1943-46. **BUSINESS ADDRESS:** 2900 S Fort St, Detroit, MI 48217.

JOHNSON, GAREY A.
Sales engineer. **PERSONAL:** Born Sep 14, 1947, Benton Harbor, MI. **EDUCATION:** Lake MI Coll, AET 1968; MI Tech U, BSEE 1972; Am Grad Sch Of Intl Mgmt, MIM 1978. **CAREER:** Weitek, field sales engineer; Signetics Corp Mil Product Div, area marketing mgr 1979-; Signetics Copr Bipolar Memory Div, intl marketing mgr 1979;Sperry Flt Syst Mil & Aircraft, marketing rep 1978-79; USAF, pilot 1975-77. **ORGANIZATIONS:** Mem TMSA (Tech Marketing Soc Of Am); mem Nat Bus League; mem AIAA (Am Inst Aero & Astro); mem IEEE Published Bioengrng Project Neurophysiology & Electroencephlography 1971; pub book review Thunderbird Intl 1978. **MILITARY SERVICE:** USAF capt 4 1/2 yrs served. **BUSINESS ADDRESS:** Field Sales Engineer, Weitek, 1060 E Argues Ave, Sunnyvale, CA 94061.

JOHNSON, GENE C.
Association executive. **PERSONAL:** Born Mar 11, 1941, Parkin, AR. **EDUCATION:** Univ CA, BA 1964; Golden Gate Coll, MPA 1972. **CAREER:** Bay Area Urban League, employment coordinator 1967-69; Prof Upgrade Inc, asso dir 1969-72; Nat Assn Minority Contractors, reg dir; Housing Manpower Comm Devel, cons; G & O Assos, Owner. **ORGANIZATIONS:** Mem NAACP; vice pres NAACP 1969-71; Big Bro Inc Bay Area; former pres Opportunities Industrialization Center Oakland 1970-71. **HONORS/ACHIEVEMENTS:** Champion Pan Am Games Brazil 1963; alternate Olympic Team Tokyo 1964; track & field athlete of yr No CA 1964. **BUSINESS ADDRESS:** 722 Union St, Oakland, CA 94607.

JOHNSON, GENEVA B.
Company executive. **PERSONAL:** Born in Aiken County, SC; daughter of Pierce Bolton and Lillie Mae Bolton. **EDUCATION:** Albright Coll, BS 1951; Case Western Reserve Univ, MSSA 1957. **CAREER:** YWCA Houston, program dir; Wernersville State Hosp in PA, psychiatric social worker; Children's Aid Soc, supervisory positions; United Way of Berk's Co, asst exec dir; United Way of DE, dir; United Way of Greater Rochester, assoc exec dir, United Way of America, sr vice pres Family Serv Amer, pres/chief exec officer 1983-. **ORGANIZATIONS:** Consultant Council of Jewish Federations, the YWCA, Natl Fellowship Prog of the WK Kellogg Foundation, Natl Urban League, Big Brothers/Big Sisters of Amer, NAACP; trustee Wells Coll Aurora NY, Capitol Inst of Tech Kensington MD; mem bd of dirs Foundation for Children with Learning Disabilities; public advbd Amer Bd of Family Practitioners, Natl Foundation for Consumer Credit, Proposition One; bd mem Natl Assembly, Natl Council on the Aging, Natl Assoc for Sickle Cell Diseasel bd Mbr., Independent Sector; bd Mbr., Wisconsin Energy Corp and Wisconsin Electric & Power Co. **HONORS/ACHIEVEMENTS:** One of twenty women selected to attend the Jerusalem Women's Seminar held in Israel and Egypt; Hon Doctor of Humanities Albright Coll 1983; 1983 Disting Serv Awd Case Western Reserve Univ; 1984 Awd for Commitment to the Family Movement in USA; 1984 Awd for Outstanding Serv to Natl Urban League Movement; 1985 Awd for Efforts to Strengthen Family Life in Amer MA; one of the 1986 Top 100 Black Business and Professional Women in Amer by Dollars and Cents magazine; F Ritter and Hettie L Shumway Distinguished Serv Awd 1986. **BUSINESS ADDRESS:** President & Chief Exec Offr, Family Service America, 11700 West Lake Park Drive, Park Place, Milwaukee, WI 53224.

JOHNSON, GENEVIEVE N.
Planner/coordinator. **PERSONAL:** Born Jun 24, 1899, Washington, DC; children: Burton, Stanley, Carl, Sylvia Brown. **EDUCATION:** Armstrong High School, graduate. **ORGANIZATIONS:** Mem adv bd C&P Telephone Co; bd mem DC Dept of Recreation; mem Round Table on Human Svcs; trustee Family and Child Svcs; bd mem Natl Cncl of Senior Citizens; vice pres Regional Cncl of Sr Citizens; pres DC State Cncl of Senior Citizens; bd mem Zion Bapt Enterprises Inc; mem various auxiliaries with Zion Bapt Church; planner/coord Senior Citizens Prayer Breakfast, Senior Citizen Summer Festival, Senior Citizens Annual Fellowship Luncheon, Annual Senior Citizen Christmas Party; pres DC State Cncl of Senior Citizens. **HONORS/ACHIEVEMENTS:** Recipient of more than 30 awds including Meritorious Serv Awd from her majesty Queen of England presented by the British Ambassador (the BEM Medal); Awdsfor Disting Serv and Commitment presented by the District's two Mayors.

JOHNSON, GEORGE, JR.
Fireman. **PERSONAL:** Born Apr 15, 1934, Warrenton, GA; children: Inc. **EDUCATION:** Inst of Tech; GA Tech; Schell Sch of Marking & Mgmt. **CAREER:** E Richmond Co Fire Dept, capt 1970-; various positions 1968-70. **ORGANIZATIONS:** E Augusta Action Comm; Augusta-Richmond Co Hum Rel Task Force; GA Assn for Black Elected Officials; Dem Party of GA; Eureka Grand Lodge; NAACP; CSRA. **HONORS/ACHIEVEMENTS:** Involvement Council Award 1971-72; big bro cert appreciation GA Assn for Retarded Children Inc. **MILITARY SERVICE:** AUS sgt 1951-64. **HOME ADDRESS:** 401 Madison Ave, Oak Vill, Augusta, GA 30901.

JOHNSON, GEORGE ELLIS
Business executive. **PERSONAL:** Born Jun 16, 1927, Richton, MS; married Joan Henderson; children: Eric, John, George Jr, Joan Marie. **CAREER:** SB Fuller, employed during 1944; began own hair care company, self-empl 1954-; Johnson Products Co Inc (achieved listing on Amer Stock Exch in 1971 as first Black-owned company to be listed on a major stock exchange), pres, ceo 1954-. **ORGANIZATIONS:** Dir Independence Bank of Chicago; bd dir Commonwealth Edison Co; chmn of the bd Indecorp Inc; dir Amer Health & Beauty Aids Inst; pres George E Johnson Educ Fund, George E Johnson Found; mem Babson Coll; exec bd Boy Scouts of Amer; gov mem Chicago Orchestral Assoc; bd of trustees Chicago Sunday

Evening Club; bd of dir Chicago Urban League, Dearborn Park Corp, Intl African C of C Inc; natl adv comm Interracial Council of Bus Oppty; vice pres JrAchievement of Chicago; bd dir Lyric Opera of Chicago; principal Chicago United; bd dir Econ Club of Chicago; mem The Commercial Club; sponsoring comm NAACP Legal Defense Fund; bd dir Natl Asthma Ctr, Northwestern Memorial Hosp, Operation PUSH, Protestant Found of Greater Chicago; bd of trustees Northwestern Univ; mem The Hundred Club of Cook County, Leadership Greater Chicago. **HONORS/ACHIEVEMENTS:** Abraham Lincoln Ctr Humanitarian Serv Awd 1972; D of Bus Admin Xavier Univ 1973; D of Humanities Clark Coll 1974; D of Commercial Sci The Coll of the Holy Cross 1975; DL Babson Coll 1976; DHL Chicago State Univ 1977; DL Fisk Univ 1977; DL Tuskegee Inst 1978; Amer Black Achievement Awd Ebony Mag 1978; DHL Lemoyne-Owen Coll 1979; Harvard Club of Chicago Public Serv Awd 1979; DL Lake Forest Coll 1979; Horatio Alger Awd 1980; Babson Medal 1983. **HOME ADDRESS:** 95 Brentwood Dr, Glencoe, IL 60022. **BUSINESS ADDRESS:** President, CEO, Johnson Products Co Inc, 8522 S Lafayette, Chicago, IL 60620.

JOHNSON, GEORGE M.
Educator. **PERSONAL:** Born May 22, 1900, Albuquerque, NM; married Evelyn W. **EDUCATION:** Univ of CA, AB 1923, LLB 1929, JSD 1936; Univ Nigeria, Hon LLD 1964; Mi State Univ, Hon LLD 1974. **CAREER:** State of CA, state tax counsel 1933-39; Roosevelt's Wartime Fair Employment Practice Comm, dep chmn & acting gen counsel 1941-45; Howard Univ Sch of Law,dean 1946-58; US Commn on Civil Rights, head of legal div 1957-58, mem of commn 1958-60; MI State Univ Adv Group to Assist Nigeria, head 1960-64; Univof Nigeria, vice chancellor 1960-64; MI State Univ, vice pres equal oppor 1968-69, retired prof emeritus; Sch of Law Univ of HI, dir preadmission to lawsch prog 1974-75. **ORGANIZATIONS:** Adv staff NAACP 1945-60; mem World Affairs Forum of HI; mem Adventurers Club of Honolulu; author numerous publs in various fields. **HONORS/ACHIEVEMENTS:** Sheiffiel-Sanborne Scholarship 1930-31; Friendship House Achievement Awd 1954; Rockefeller Fellow 1958.

JOHNSON, GEORGIA ANNA
Physician-retired. **PERSONAL:** Born Feb 01, 1930, Chicago, IL; children: Barbara, Ruth, Mary. **EDUCATION:** West MI Univ, attended 1948-51; Univ of MI Med Sch, MD 1955. **CAREER:** Evanston IL, intern 1955-56; Ypsilanti St Hosp, phys 1960-65; Ingham Co Health Dept, phys 1967-69; Int Med Coll, asst prof 1969-75; MI State Univ, dir adoles serv 1973-; Olin Health Ctr, staff phys 1969-1987; retired. **ORGANIZATIONS:** Mem NAACP; AMA; MSMS; Ingham Co Med Soc; AKA sor; AEI Women's Med Frat; Kappa Rho Sigma Hon Sci Frat; MSU Black Women's Fac Assn; Black Fac & AdnAssn; Sickle Cell Anemia Found; bd of trust Capital Area Comp Health Plan Assn; chmn Adv Com Hlth Serv Agcy; bd of dir mem Comp Family Hlth Proj. **HONORS/ACHIEVEMENTS:** Dean's list West MI Univ 1948; Scholarship Jessie Smith Noyes Sch 1951-55; dist alumna awd West MI Univ 1972; Who's Who of No Amer Women; book "Children's Poems" 1958; article "The Interview Workshp" Jour Med Educ 1974; pub "Self Instruct Unit Black Skin" 1973; "The Black Female Her Image & Choice of Med Care" 1974; "The Black Patient-A Catal of Abuses" Med Dimension 1974; Persp on Afro-Amer Women 1975. **BUSINESS ADDRESS:** Retired Staff Physician, Olin Health Center, Michigan State University, East Lansing, MI 48824.

JOHNSON, GEORGIANNA
Labor union administrator. **PERSONAL:** Born Dec 13, 1930, Asheville, NC; daughter of William Fisher Johnson and Amelia Starks Johnson; married Eugene W Smith, Jul 30, 1950; children: Eugenia Smith Sykes. **EDUCATION:** Empire State, New York NY, 1976; Long Island Univ, New York NY, BA in Sociology, 1976; Hunter Coll, New York NY, Master in Sociology, currently attending. **CAREER:** New York State Employment Office, New York NY, claims examiner, 1950-63; Sherman Thursby, New York NY, insurance adjuster, 1963-68; Hospital for Joint Diseases, New York NY, case aide, 1968-79; Orthopaedic Institute, New York NY, social work asst, 1979-86; Drug, Hospital and Health Care Employees Union, Local 1199, New York NY, pres, 1986-. **ORGANIZATIONS:** Mem, Alpha Kappa Alpha Sorority, 1986-; mem, Black Trade Unionists, 1986-; mem, Coalition of Union Women, 1986-; mem, Natl Alliance Party, 1989-. **HONORS/ACHIEVEMENTS:** Equality for Social Justice Award, Health PAC, 1987; Supportive Spirit Award, 37 Women Committee, 1987; Outstanding Achievement Award, NY Urban League, 1987; Service/Action Beyond Call of Duty Award, Central Brooklyn, 1988; Labor Recognition Award, NAACP, 1988.

JOHNSON, GERALDINE R.
Business executive. **PERSONAL:** Married Robert Hudson Johnson; children: Robert, Mariea, Edward. **EDUCATION:** Canadian Sch & Univ. **CAREER:** LA Times Mirror, advertising 1950-55; Tool & Die Makers Intl Assn Of Maschinists, ofc mgr 1955-69; Longshoreman Union Local 10, ofc & bldg mgr; NAACP, region i field dir 1968; NAACP, natl & dir conv exhibits 1968; private investment real estate 1955-. **ORGANIZATIONS:** Mem Civilian Expeditor Signal Corps Washington WWII; mem Nat Assn Of Exposition Mgrs; Nat Assn Market Devel; mem Am Nat Red Cr; sec & bd dir Golden Gate chpt; Am Field Serv; volunteer Alta Bates Hosp; customers coun USPO; comm serv El Cerrito CA work with State Dept Foreign Visitors; mayors race relations com Wash. **HONORS/ACHIEVEMENTS:** Gold medal Winner Song Dance Division Scotch & Irish Festivals Canada; citaward Mayors Com Wash; co-cohmn award for first black float Rose Bowl Parade Pasadena; literace & charm sch classes award.

JOHNSON, GERALDINE ROSS
Attorney. **PERSONAL:** Born May 13, 1946, Moline, IL; married John T Johnson; children: Christine E, Glenda R, John T Jr. **EDUCATION:** Augustana Coll, BA 1968; Univ of PA Sch of Social Work, MSW 1974; Univ of IA Coll of Law, JD 1982. **CAREER:** Linn Co IA Dept of Soc Svcs, caseworker 1968-69; Children's Serv City of St Louis, intake case worker 1969-70; Get Set Day Care, preschool tchr 1970-72;Franciscan Mental Health Ctr, social worker 1974-78; Davenport Civil Rights Commn, attorney 1984-86; City of Davenport Legal Dept, atty 1986-. **ORGANIZATIONS:** Mem Iowa State Bar Assoc, Scott Co Bar Assoc; mem Sounds of Peace Choral Group 1981-86; mem Davenport Civil Rights Commn 1982-84; bd of dirs Family Resources Inc 1982-; mem Delta Sigma Theta Public Serv Sor Inc 1984-; volunteer United Way 1986; guest speaker Upward Bound, Marycrest Sociology Dept, MeritEmployment Council, Blackhawk Coll Alpha Ctr; mem Tabernacle Baptist Church Moline IL; mem Pulpit Comm 1986. **HONORS/ACHIEVEMENTS:** Survey of sex educ literature on file in the British Library by request 1984. **BUSINESS ADDRESS:** Staff Attorney, City of Davenport, City Hall 226 W Fourth St, Davenport, IA 52801.

JOHNSON, GLENN T.
Judge. **PERSONAL:** Born Jul 19, 1917, Washington, AR; son of Floyd Johnson and Reola Thompson Johnson; married Evelyn Freeman; children: Evelyn A, Glenn Jr. **EDUCATION:** Wilberforce Univ Xenia, OH, BS 1941; John Marshall Law School of Chicago, JD 1949, LLM 1950; Natl Coll of State Trial Judges Reno, NV, 1971; Appellate Court Judges Seminar, NYU, 1974. **CAREER:** State of IL, asst atty general 1957-63; Metro Sanitary Dist of Greater Chicago, sr atty 1963-66; Circuit Court of Cook County, IL, judge 1966-73; Appellate Court of IL 1st Dist, justice 1973-. **ORGANIZATIONS:** Mem Bench & Bar Section Council IL Bar Assn 1983; fellow Am Acad of Matrimonial Lawyers 1972-; trustee John Marshall Law School of Chicago 1976-; fellow IL Bar Found 1984-; mem Judicial Council Natl Bar Assn 1970-; mem NAACP; mem Urban League; mem YMCA; mem Chicago Boys & Girls Club; mem Judicial Council of African; trustee Methodist Epscopal Church Woodlawn AME Chrch 1976-; mem Cook County Bar Assn, mem Chicago Bar Assn; mem The Original Forty Club of Chicago. **HONORS/ACHIEVEMENTS:** Citation of Merit John Marshall Sch of Law 1970; Judge of Yr Cook County Bar Assn 1973; Certificate of Appreciation IL State Bar Assn 1975-76; Outstanding Serv Natl Bar Assn 1970; Workpaper (Madrid, Spain) Sentencing Procedures in the US of Amer 1979; Workpaper (San Paulo, Brazil) Recent Trends in Family Law in the US 1981; Workpaper (Cairo, Egypt) The Legal Response To Child Snatching In US 1983. **MILITARY SERVICE:** AUS chief warrant officer-3 1942-46; NG 1950-59; Reserve 1959-63. **HOME ADDRESS:** 6133 S Evans Ave, Chicago, IL 60637. **BUSINESS ADDRESS:** Justice, IL Appellate Court, 3000 Richard J Daley Ctr, Chicago, IL 60602.

JOHNSON, GLORIA DEAN
Librarian. **PERSONAL:** Born Jul 30, 1948, Morton, MS. **EDUCATION:** MS Valley State Univ, BS English Educ 1970; Univ of MS, MLS 1974; MS State Univ, attended; Jackson State Univ, attended. **CAREER:** Charleston Middle School, teacher/libr 1970-72; Morton Jr High School, teacher 1972-74; Meridian Jr Coll, circulation libr 1974-77; Allstate Ins Col, unit suprv 1977-78; East Central Jr Coll, asst librarian 1978-. **ORGANIZATIONS:** Mem MS Assoc of Ed, Natl Assoc of Ed; former mem MS Library Assoc; Alpha Kappa Alpha Sor Inc 1969-. **HOME ADDRESS:** Star Rte Box 83, Morton, MS 39117.

JOHNSON, GOLDEN ELIZABETH
Attorney, educator. **PERSONAL:** Born Mar 21, 1944, Newark, NJ. **EDUCATION:** Douglass Coll, AB 1961-65; Rutgers Newark Sch of Law, JD 1968-71. **CAREER:** Hoffman La Roche Inc, gen atty 1977-; Rutgers Law Sch, prof 1976-; Newark Muncpl Ct, judge 1974-77; Hoffmann-La Roche Inc, atty 1974; Comm Leagl Action Wrkshp, proj dir 1972-74; State of NJ, dep atty & gen 1971-72; US Atty Ofc, intern 1970; W Kinney Jr HS, tchr 1969; Newark Legal Serv, intern 1969; Spec Rsrch Lab, microblgst 1965-68. **ORGANIZATIONS:** Mem NJ State Bar Assn; Essex Co Bar Assn; Garden State Bar Assn; present mem bd of Gov & exec comm Nat Bar Assn; past pres bd mem Women's Div Nat Bar Assn; bd of tst NJ State Opera; bd of tst & past chmn Newark-Essex Co Legal Serv & Joint Law Reform; bd of dir Ctrl Ward Girls Club; mem NJ Adv Bd US Commn on Civil Rights 1973-77; bd of dir Leaguers Inc; mem NJ Coll of Med & Denistry's Bd of Concerned Citzs 1972-75; NAACP; life mem Nat Cncl of Negro Women; chtr mem Assn of Black Women Lwyrs; mem liaison City of Newark for Essex Co Fed of Dem Women 1977; 100 Women for Integ in Govt; mem Rutgers Newark Sch of Law Alumni Assn. **HONORS/ACHIEVEMENTS:** Comm serv awd Rutgers Law Sch 1972; comm serv awd Donald Tucker Civic Assn 1974; achvmt awd Essex Co Civic Assn 1975; black woman achvmt awd COM-BIN-NATION 1975; life mem Guild Legal Serv; awd Nat Cncl of Negro Women 1975; achvmt awd No Reg of Fedn of Colored Women's Club 1975; oust achvmt NJFedn of Colored Women's Club 1975; achvmt awd Delta Sigma Theta Inc 1975; comm serv awd Newark Title 1 Ctrl Parents Cncl 1975; achvmt awd Neward Sect Nat Cncl of Negro Women 1975; awd of excell Oper PUSH 1975; comm serv awd Roosevelt Homes Housing Proj 1975; achvmt awd Nat Assn of Negro Bus & Professional Women's Clubs 1975; comm serv awd Essex Co Legal Serv 1975; serv awd Newark Housing Cncl Comm 1976; disgshd serv awd Seton HallUniv 1976; certof apprctn Ctrl Ward Girls Club 1976; Oper PUSH Tidewater Women Achvmt Awd 1976; achvmt awd Dr Martin Luther King Jr Comm Ctr 1976; achiev awd Guyton-Callahan Post 152 1976; outsdng Woman of Yr NJ Jaycee-ETTES 1977; hon life mem Zeta Alpha Iota 1977; Alumni Roster of Superior Merit E Side HS 1977;Outstdg Young Woman of Am 1975, 77; gen Couns to Young Dems of NJ.

JOHNSON, GREGORY WAYNE
Educator. **PERSONAL:** Born Dec 06, 1953, Washington, DC; son of Sidney Johnson and Nita Jones; married Brenda Hayes, Dec 31, 1977. **EDUCATION:** Ohio State Univ, Columbus, BA Political Science, 1978. **CAREER:** Fellowship of Reconcilation, Nyack NY, director, 1987-89; Physicians for Social Responsibility, Washington DC, coordinator, 1989-. **ORGANIZATIONS:** Co-founder, Blacks Against Nukes, 1981-. **HONORS/ACHIEVEMENTS:** Certificate of Merit, Ohio State, 1976; newsletter 1981-; fellowship of reconciliation magazine-reviews, 1987-89. **HOME ADDRESS:** 3728 New Hampshire Ave, NW, Apt 202, Washington, DC 20010.

JOHNSON, GUY CHARLES
Systems analyst. **PERSONAL:** Born Dec 24, 1946, New York, NY; married Janet; children: Tracey Renee, Eric Ahmed. **EDUCATION:** Columbia U, BSEE 1968, MSEE 1972. **CAREER:** AT&T Technology, dept chf technology planning; Western Elec Co, dept chf 1978-; AT&T, sys analyst, staff splst 1976-78; Western Elec Co, sys staff mem 1974-76, devel engr 1971-74, 1968-71. **ORGANIZATIONS:** Co-fdr Co-op City Black Caucus; partic Nat Urban League's Block Exec Exchange Prgm; mem Tau Beta Pi; mem Columbia Track Team 1963-66; mem Nat Jogging Assn. **HONORS/ACHIEVEMENTS:** MVP Columbia Track 1963; Harlem YMCA's Black Achievers in Industry Awd 1983.

JOHNSON, HARLAN C.
Retired educator. **PERSONAL:** Born Jul 17, 1919, Eminence, KY; son of Joseph S Johnson and Elizabeth Helen Johnson. **EDUCATION:** New York Univ, BS 1950, MA 1952; Attended, Univ of WY, Univ of PR, Univ of Mexico, Harvard Univ, John Jay Coll of Criminal Justice 1986-. **CAREER:** New York Univ, teacher Business Ed 2 yrs; Southern Univ Baton Rouge, teacher Business Ed 1 yr; New York City Bd of Educ, retired teacher; participant in the pre-release program of Rehabilitation, Green Haven Prison; Peer Drug Counselor with Community Services Committee NY City. **ORGANIZATIONS:** Mem NBEA, UFT, Riverside Prison Ministry 1984-; mem/volunteer Riverside Shelter 1985-; Alpha Phi Alpha. **HONORS/ACHIEVEMENTS:** Humanitarian Service Plaque, Green Haven Prison, Stormville NY 1987. **MILITARY SERVICE:** AUS staff sgt 1943-46; Asiatic-Pacific Theater w/2

Bronze Stars, Philippine Liberation w/1 Bronze Star, Good Conduct Medal, World War II Victory Medal. **HOME ADDRESS:** 779 Concourse Vlge E 23-C, Bronx, NY 10451.

JOHNSON, HAROLD E.B.
Musician. **PERSONAL:** Born Feb 23, 1918, Tyler, TX; married Emma L Bishop. **CAREER:** Duke Ellington Inc Mason, first trumpet.

JOHNSON, HAROLD R.
Educator. **PERSONAL:** Born Jan 09, 1926, Windsor, Ontario, Canada;son of Lee Johnson and Catherine Johnson; married Marion; children: Robert Harold, Karen Elizabeth, Alan Douglas. **EDUCATION:** Attended, Patterson Collegiate Inst Windsor; Univ of Western ONT, BA; Wayne State Univ, MSW. **CAREER:** Windsor Labor Commn for Human Rights & Intl Union of United Brewery Soft Drink & Distillery Workers of Amer, exec dir 1951-57; United Comm Serv of Met Detroit, planning consult 1957-61; Neighborhood Serv Orgn Detroit, assoc dir 1961-69; Office of Youth Serv State of MI, dir 1970; Univ of MI Senate Assembly, 1st Black chmn; Univ of MI, prof dean sch of social work. **ORGANIZATIONS:** Consult Province of Alberta 1979 Univ of Regina 1978, Univ of Toronto 1978-84, Temple Univ 1978; consult MI Commn on Corrections 1972; US Dept of Justice 1972; Famiy Neighborhood Serv So Wayne Co 1972; City of Detroit-Charter Revision Commn 1971; Met Fund 1971; Center for Urban Studies Wayne State Univ 1969; Wayne Co Planning Commn 1968-69; Mayor's Devel Team Detroit 1967; pres Assn for Gerontology in Higher Educ 1979; past chmn Met Detroit Chap 1963-64; mem Natl Assn of Social Workers; fellow Gerontological Soc; mem Council on Social Work Edn; Acad of Certified Social Workers; Assn of Black Soc Workers; past chmn Blue Ribbon Cit Com Wayne Co Bd of Supvr; past vice pres chmn Prog Com Northeastern Wayne Co Child Guidance Clinic; past mem Detroit Public Sch Rsch Panel; past vice chmn MI mn on Criminal Justice; cmmr Amer Bar Assn, 1985-; consultant, Yeungnam Univ, Republic of Korea, 1984-; consultant, Univ of Iowa, 1987. **HONORS/ACHIEVEMENTS:** Hon PhD Yeungnam Univ Korea 1984; Alumni of the Year Awd Wayne State Univ 1985; author of numerous reports & papers. **MILITARY SERVICE:** Royal Canadian Armoured Corps sgt. **BUSINESS ADDRESS:** Dean, School of Social Work, Univ of MI, 2068 Frieze Bldg, Ann Arbor, MI 48109.

JOHNSON, HARRY A.
Educational administrator. **PERSONAL:** Born Nov 22, 1920, Norfolk, VA; married Mae Coleman; children: Sharon Lynne, Jeffrey Alan. **EDUCATION:** VA State Coll, BS 1942; Columbia Univ Tchr Coll, MA 1948, PhD 1952; Sorbonne Univ of Paris, post doctoral study 1958. **CAREER:** Visiting prof & consultancies at many colls & univs; VA State Coll, prof of educ dean summer sch. **ORGANIZATIONS:** Bd dir CINE Intl; bd dir Intl Journal of Instructional Media; adv bd Library & Educ Media Stanford Univ CA; bd dir Dept of Libr Sci & Educ Media NEA; mem Com Intl Pour Le Developpement Des Activities Educatives et Culturelles En Afrique Italy; mem Amer Assn of Univ Profs; Kappa Delta Pi Natl Hon Soc; Assn for Supervision & Curriculum Devel; Phi Delta Kappa Prof Educ Frat; VA Educ Assn; Natl Educ Assn; Kappa Alpha Psi Frat; Reserve Officers Assn. **HONORS/ACHIEVEMENTS:** Fulbright Rsch Scholar at Paris 1958-59; Amer Men of Sci 1963; Natl Register of Prominent Amers 1973; Awd Outstanding Media Educator of Yr VAECT 1970; Leaders in Educ 1975; author of numerous publications. **MILITARY SERVICE:** AUS WWII; AUS Reserve capt retired 1942-74. **BUSINESS ADDRESS:** Professor of Education, VA State College, Dept of Education, Petersburg, VA 23803.

JOHNSON, HENDERSON A., III
Business executive. **PERSONAL:** Born Dec 19, 1929, Nashville, TN; son of Henderson A. Johnson and Minerva Hatcher Johnson; married Gwendolyn Gregory; children: Gregory Paul, Andrea Lynn, H Andrew IV. **EDUCATION:** Fisk U, Hnrs, BS 1950; Springfield Coll, MA, MS 1951; Med Coll of VA, RPT 1952; Western Reserve Univ Sch of Dnstry, DDS 1959. **CAREER:** Western & Reserve Sch Dnstry, clin instr 1966-69; Highland View Hosp, staff 1985; Pvt Prct Dnstry, 1985; vice pres Management Office Design Inc 1981-; dir Dental Prgm Enhancement Project Cuyahoga Comm Coll 1985-; districtwide coordinator/director dental programs/health careers Cuyahoga Comm Coll 1987-. **ORGANIZATIONS:** Immediate past chmn Cuyahoga Comm Coll Fndtn 1971-84; dir Cleveland Pub Radio WCPN 1983-89; pres H Andrew Johnson DDS Inc 1973-89; vice pres Ctr for Human Rels 1984-; pres Shaker Hghts Pub Lbry 1978-83; vice pres Cleveland Public Radio WCPN 1986-89; Ohio Educational Broadcast Network Commn 1988-. **HONORS/ACHIEVEMENTS:** Ctzn of Yr Omega Psi Phi Frat Cleveland 1974; Dstngshd Alumni Awrd Fisk Univ 1976; elected to the International Coll of Dentists 1986. **MILITARY SERVICE:** USAF 1st lt 1953-54. **BUSINESS ADDRESS:** Cuyagola Community College, Metropolitan Campus, S & T 126, 2900 Community College Avenue, Cleveland, OH 44120.

JOHNSON, HENRY
Educator. **PERSONAL:** Born Mar 15, 1937, Atlanta, GA; children: Eric, Ian, Stephanie. **EDUCATION:** Univ Of MI, BA, MSW, Doctoral Student; Menniger Found, Post-grad Tng. **CAREER:** Ft Wayne State School, psychiatric social worker 1960-62; Menninger Clinic KS, trainee in post-grad psyciatric social work 1962-63; WJ Maxey Boys Training Sch MI, dir group care & counseling div 1964-70; Northville State Hosp Soc Serv Dept, conx group serv 1966-69; Opportunity School Of Educ Univ Of MI, assoc dir prog for educ 1970-72; Univ Of MI, vice pres student serv 1972-. **ORGANIZATIONS:** Trustee of Ann Arbor Sch Dist 1968-74; United Fund chmnUniv of MI 1973; mem trust adv bd for Charitable Trust; atty gen adv bd State of MI 1972; mem state bd of MI Assn for emotionally Disturbed Children. **HONORS/ACHIEVEMENTS:** Recipient Huron Valley Social Worker of Yr 1973. **BUSINESS ADDRESS:** Vice President of Student Serv, University of Michigan, 3000 Michigan Union, Ann Arbor, MI 48109.

JOHNSON, HERBERT M.
Advertising manager. **PERSONAL:** Born Aug 10, 1941, Syracuse, NY; married Barbara J Hale; children: Nicole Monique. **EDUCATION:** Citadel Bapt Theol Sem, BTheol 1983, M Rel Ed 1984; Triune Theological Seminary, D Min 1985, DD (hon) 1985, PhD 1986. **CAREER:** Johnson Publ Co, merch, market & rep 1962-66; Central Hard Co, commercial advertising artist 1966-73, adv dir 1973-; Realist & Surrealist Painter, prof; TheGreat Atlantic & Pacific Tea Co, advertising mgr 1975-77; Swank Motion Pict Inc, advertising mgr, prod mgr 1978-. **ORGANIZATIONS:** Pres Millar Park Neighborhood Assoc of Univ City MO; past pres Univ City Art Assoc 1970-72. **HONORS/ACHIEVEMENTS:** Disting Serv Awd Big Bros of St Louis 1971; Big Brothers of the Year Awd Bih Bros of St Louis 1973; Exh Art of Top 100 Black Artists Exhibit SIU Edwardsville 1972. **BUSINESS ADDRESS:** Advertising Manager, Prod Mgr, Swank Motion Pict Inc, 117-119 N 2nd St, Edwardsville, IL 62025.

JOHNSON, HERMEL
Attorney. **PERSONAL:** Born Aug 27, 1946, Jackson, MS; children: one. **EDUCATION:** Jackson State U, BA 1967; Harvard U, 1966;Univ Of MS, JD 1970; Billsaps Coll, 1970-71. **CAREER:** Johnson & Walker solo practicioner 1977, prtn 1973-77; n MS rural legal serv, law clerk 1968-70; equal empl opp commn, case analyst 1969-70; Educ Res Center of MS, dir 1971-72; Hall, Abram, Tucker & Johnson, prtn 1972-73; MS State Crts US Dist Crts for MS & 5th US Cir Crt of Appeals MS State Bar Assn, prac estens 1970-; Nat Conf Black Lawy, 1970-; Bar Assn, jackson jr 1970; Hinds Co Bar Assn, 1970-; Nat Bus League, jackson chap 1971-; Hinds Co Voter Proj, dir 1967. **ORGANIZATIONS:** Bd dir Comm Legal Serv 1971; commr Seminole Dist Boy Scouts 1971-; bd mem Jackson Met Boy's Clubs 1973-; Black Indep Political Club 1973-. **HONORS/ACHIEVEMENTS:** Outstndg Young Men of Am 1971; Personalities in the South 1975; Fellow of MS Inst of Politics 1971. **BUSINESS ADDRESS:** PO Box 2887, Jackson, MS 39207.

JOHNSON, HERMON M., SR.
Business executive, alderman. **PERSONAL:** Born May 05, 1929, Gilbert, LA; son of Samuel Vanora Johnson and Eamay Anderson Johnson; married Alfreta Thompson; children: Hermon, Jr, Cheryl Lynn, Darryl, Josef. **EDUCATION:** SU, Baton Rouge, LA, BS 1955; MS Valley St Coll, Elem Tchr Cert 1959. **CAREER:** Magnolia Mutual Life Ins Co, ofc mgr 1955-59; Myrtle Hall Sch, tchr 1964-66; comm & action splst 1966-68; Tufts Delta Hlth Ctr, ec dev splst 1967-73; Comm Hlth Ed, dir 1973; Dept of Patient Hlth Srv & Resource Coord, dir 1973-; Paul Revere Life Ins Co, sales rep. **ORGANIZATIONS:** Vice-mayor, alderman Mound Bayou 1961; pres Mound Bayou Dev Corp 1961-63; dir Mound Bayou Credit Union 1960-; asst ctr dir Delta Hlth Ctr; dir Delta Housing Dev Corp; dir S Legal Rights Assn Inc; vice pres S Assn of Minority Manufacturers Atlanta; mem Am Legion Post 220; Mound Bayour Civic Club; Mound Bayou Conversation & Rec League; trustee Bethel AME Ch. **MILITARY SERVICE:** AUS corpl 1951-53. **HOME ADDRESS:** PO Box 262, Mound Bayou, MS 38762.

JOHNSON, HERSCHEL LEE
Associate editor. **PERSONAL:** Born Feb 03, 1948, Birmingham, AL; married Mareta. **EDUCATION:** Dartmouth Coll, BA 1970. **CAREER:** Ebony Mag, asso editor; Black Enterprise Mag, freelance writer 1974-76, asst editor, asso editor 1972-74; Newsweek Mag, editorial asst 1971-72; ". **HONORS/ACHIEVEMENTS:** Publ "Young Black Poets"; anthology "The Bookers"; poetry anthology "Blackoout" Literary Mag. **BUSINESS ADDRESS:** 1270 Ave of the Ams, New York, NY 10020.

JOHNSON, HOWARD R.
Judge. **PERSONAL:** Born Aug 20, 1942, Atlanta, GA. **EDUCATION:** Morehouse Coll, BA 1970; Univ of Miami, JD 1973. **CAREER:** Private Practice, assoc lawyer 1973-75; City of Atlanta, public defender 1975-80, assoc judge 1980-82, chief judge 1982-. **ORGANIZATIONS:** Mem Gate City Bar Assoc 1973-, Atlanta Bar Assoc 1973-. **HONORS/ACHIEVEMENTS:** 1st Public Defender City of Atlanta 1975; 1st Black Chief Judge City of Atlanta 1982. **MILITARY SERVICE:** USAF airman 1st class 1962-66. **BUSINESS ADDRESS:** Chief Judge Municipal Court, 175 Decatur St SE, Atlanta, GA 30303.

JOHNSON, HYMON T., JR.
Business executive. **PERSONAL:** Born Nov 18, 1919, Chicago, IL; married Mary Ella Brogsdale; children: Karen, Gaye, Hymon, III, Judy. **EDUCATION:** Univ WI, attending; Univ IL; John Marshall Law School. **CAREER:** Marion Bus Coll, dir; The Woodlawn Orgn, manpower training dev; Affirmative Action, present dir; The Great Atlantic & Pacific Tea Co Inc, asst to vp. **ORGANIZATIONS:** Mem Am Mgmt Assn; Labor Educ Div Roosevelt U; pres Chicago Urban Affairs Counc; bd chmn Chicago Boys Club; mem PUSH; Urban League; NAACP Black Achiever of Ind; Breadbasket Commercial Assn. **HONORS/ACHIEVEMENTS:** Affirm Action Awd; hon deg No IL U. **MILITARY SERVICE:** USN Air Corps.

JOHNSON, I. S. LEEVY
Business executive. **PERSONAL:** Born May 16, 1942, Richland County, SC; married Doris. **EDUCATION:** Benedict Coll SC, BS 1965; Univ of SC, JD 1968; Univ of MN, Asso of Mortuary. **CAREER:** SC Gen Assembly, mem; Self, atty; Benedict Coll, former Instr; Funeral Dir, licensed embalmer. **HONORS/ACHIEVEMENTS:** One of three black legisl in SC since Reconstruction. **BUSINESS ADDRESS:** President, Johnson, Toal & Battiste, 1801 Gadsden St, Columbia, SC 29202.

JOHNSON, IOLA VIVIAN
Journalist. **PERSONAL:** Born Oct 10, 1947, Texarkana, AR. **EDUCATION:** Univ Of AZ, Pol Sci & Journalism 1971;Univ Of TX, M Pending. **CAREER:** WFAA TV Dallas, anchor reporter/talk show host 1973-; The Periscope Tucson, managing ed 1972-73; KVOA TV Tucson, reporter anchor/photographer 1971-73; AR Daily WildcatUniv Of AL, staff writer 1971; Wash Post DC, summer intern 1969. **ORGANIZATIONS:** Mem Wigma Delta Chi 1968; mem Am Women in Radio & TV 1972-; mem Nat Assn Of Black Journalist 1977-; chmn pub com Dallas Chap of Links Inc 1973-; mem Am Quarter Horse Assn 1979; mem TX Palimino Horse Breeders Assn 1979. **HONORS/ACHIEVEMENTS:** Outstanding Young Women of Am 1971; World Who's Who of Women 1972; Best Anchor Person in Dallas Ft Worth Dallas Morning News Readers Poll 1980; Braniff 727 Nicknamed "Iola". **BUSINESS ADDRESS:** WFAA TV, Communications Center, Dallas, TX 75202.

JOHNSON, IVORY
Educator. **PERSONAL:** Born Jun 11, 1938, Oakland, MS. **EDUCATION:** Harris Tchrs Coll St Louis, AA 1960; BA 1962; St Louis U, MEd 1969; PhD 1974. **CAREER:** Ferguson-Florissant Reorganized School Dist, Title I prog dir; Berkeley School Dist St Louis Co, elem sch prin 1969-; St Louis Univ, instructor 1973-; St Louis Bd of Educ, teacher 1962-69; Urban Rural Teacher Renewal Inst St Louis Public School System, consultant 1974. **ORGANIZATIONS:** Mem MO State Tchrs Assn; St Louis Suburban Principals Assn; MO Assn Elem Sch Prins; White House Conf Edn; Nat Assn Elem Sch Prins; Urban League; YMCA; MO PTA; bd dirs Metroplex; Kappa Alpha Psi NDEA Fellowship 1968. **HONORS/ACHIEVEMENTS:** J Jerome Peters Professionalism Award Kappa Alpha Psi 1975.

JOHNSON, JAMES A.
Government employee. **PERSONAL:** Born in Eudora, AR; married Beulah Naomi Crosby; children: Jacquelyne Johnson Jackson, Jeanne Johnson Penn, Viola Elizabeth. **EDUCATION:** NY U, BCS 1926; MCS 1931; further grad study. **CAREER:** Shaw U, prof 1929-30; Tuskegee Inst, dean sch business 1931-40; Tuskegee Inst, postmaster 1940-47; Veterans Hosp Tuskegee AL, chief educ therapy 1947-68. **ORGANIZATIONS:** # Mem Acad Political & Social Sci; Amer Accounting Assn; vice pres Nat Soc Accountants; 1st vice pres Amer Assn For Rehabilitation Therapy 1956-57, chmn natl membership com 1957-58, speaker Ho Delegates 1958-68; pres co-organizer Tuskegee Fed Credit Union 1957-; pres co-organizer Tuskegee Dev Corp 1970-; ch Trustee Bd Washington Chapel AME Ch; pres chmn bd dirs Washington Chapel Charitable Found Inc; pres chap 751 Nat Assn Retired Fed Employees; 33 deg Mason Shriner; life mem Tuskegee Civic Assn; mem NAACP; life mem Kappa Alpha Phsi Frat. **HONORS/ACHIEVEMENTS:** Community Leader Amer Award 1969; Cert & Honor Ala State Conf NAACP 1971; Cert Merit Shrine Mizraim Temple No 119 1973; Father of Yr Washington Chapel AME Ch 1974. **BUSINESS ADDRESS:** 310 Montgomery Rd, Tuskegee, AL 36083.

JOHNSON, JAMES EDWARD
Educational administrator. **PERSONAL:** Born Sep 01, 1931, Cuthbert, GA; married Mable Lumpkin; children: James Jr, Meryl, Joni. **EDUCATION:** Morehouse Coll, BS 1956; Atlanta Univ, MAEd Adm 1971, EdD EdAdm 1980. **CAREER:** DeKalb Co Schools, teacher 1956-57; Atlanta Public Schools, teacher 1957-60; Herff Jones Co, mfr rep 1961-69; Atlanta Public Schools, coordinator of personnel 1969-71, prin 1971-73, dir of personnel 1973-74, dir of employee relations & personnel 1976-. **ORGANIZATIONS:** Mem & del Natl Educ Assn Atlanta Tchr Assn & GA Assn of Educs 1956-; mem del Amer Assn of Sch Persnl Admins 1970-71; mem Assn of Educ Neg 1976-; consul GA Sch Bd Assn 1975; consul GA C of C 1976; consul MS Educ Serv Ctr 1976; consul GA Assn of Educ Leaders 1976; consul GA Assn of Educs 1976; consul Professional Assn of GA Educators 1977; mem bd of dir Grady Homes Boys Club 1965-; memshp worker YMCA 1961-; sec chmn Schlrshp Comm Alpha Phi Alpha Frat 1955-; committeeman Radcliffe Presby Ch 1956-; committeeman scoutmaster BSA 1957-; mem Ofcl Quarterback Club 1957-; mem Jr C of C 1962-64; mem Atlanta C of C 1963-64. **HONORS/ACHIEVEMENTS:** Deans List Morehouse Coll; mem Beta Kappa Chi Sci Hon Soc; Top Salesman Awd Herff Jones Co; Dist Serv Awd Morehouse Coll; EPDA; Fellowship Doctoral Cand Atlanta Univ. **MILITARY SERVICE:** USMC sgt 1951-54. **BUSINESS ADDRESS:** Asst Supt for Personnel, Atlanta Public Schools, 210 Pryor St SW, Atlanta, GA 30335.

JOHNSON, JAMES H.
District labor director. **PERSONAL:** Born Aug 05, 1932, Mohobe, MS; son of Eugene Johnson and Leesie Johnson; married Carrie B Miller; children: Carrie Arlena, Michele Francine, Yolanda Clarice, Vivian Jamie. **EDUCATION:** Wells HS Chgo, IL. **CAREER:** Kentile Flrs Inc Chgo, IL, prod wrkr 1956-69; URW Akron, OH, fld rep 1969-77, dist dir 1977-; Cntrl Church of God, assoc pstr 1973-84, pstr 1984-87; pastor Johnson Memorial Church of God 1987-. **ORGANIZATIONS:** Orgnzr & 1st pres Bellwood Comm 1976-79; bd of dir & adv A Philip Randolph 1980-83; mem NAACP 1980; sec-treas IPAC 1983-. **MILITARY SERVICE:** USMC pfc 1952-55; Nat Defense Svc; Korean Serv Medal w/2 stars; UN Serv Medal; Korean PUC. **BUSINESS ADDRESS:** District Dir URW #4, United Rubber Workers, 9930 Derby Ln #206, Westchester, IL 60153.

JOHNSON, JAMES KENNETH
Physician, surgeon. **PERSONAL:** Born Oct 09, 1942, Detroit, MI; son of William R Johnson and Frances C Brantley Johnson; married Jean E Hayes, Jul 11, 1965; children: Kalyn J Johnson, Kendell J Johnson. **EDUCATION:** Wayne State Univ, Detroit MI, BS, 1964; Meharry Medical Coll, Nashville TN, MD, 1969; Yale Univ, New Haven CT, 1973-76. **CAREER:** Strong & Johnson MD, PC, Detroit MI, physician, surgeon 1976-; Southwest Detroit Hospital, Detroit MI, medical director, vice pres of medical affairs, 1986-. **ORGANIZATIONS:** Pres, Detroit Medical Society, 1988-. **HONORS/ACHIEVEMENTS:** Distinguished teacher, Department of Family Practice, Wayne State Univ Medical School 1983. **MILITARY SERVICE:** US Army, major, 1971-73.

JOHNSON, JAMES R.
Educator, business executive. **PERSONAL:** Born Feb 19, 1934, Cory, MS; married Lottie Johnson; children: Tamaria, Jay, Thomas, Jamel. **EDUCATION:** Jackson State Univ, BS 1955, MS 1973. **CAREER:** MS Public School, teacher 1957-63; Bib Dist, pres; Jackson State Univ, resident counselor & dean of men, commissioner of camp sec 1963-68; Dynamic Photos & J & M Assoc Inc, partner 1968-75; Capital Studios Photos & Flowers, pres 1975-83; City of Jackson MS, proj dir sr aides prog 1983-. **ORGANIZATIONS:** Jackson StUniv Sen Mens' Counselor & Dean of Men 1963-68; chmn of Bd Nat Bus League Local 1971-; co-organizer MS State Bus Organ 1974; 1st Black Mem Jackson MS Sch Bd 1971; chmn Jackson St U's Dev Fund; chmn Seminole Dist BSA; chmn Finance Seminole Dist BSA; mem Hinds Co, St Ex Comm of MSRep Party. **HONORS/ACHIEVEMENTS:** In Outstanding Black Mississippian 1972; Omega Psi Phi Soc Serv Award 1972; Jackson State Coll Alumnus of Year in Politics 1972; Outstanding Leadership AwdNatl Bus League 1975; Dedicated Serv to Jackson Public School 1982; Outstanding Support of MS Headstart Assn 1985. **MILITARY SERVICE:** AUS MOS Food Serv 1955-57.

JOHNSON, JAMES S.
Physician. **PERSONAL:** Born Feb 22, 1918, Stull, KS; married Grace C; children: James, Nelson, Thomas. **EDUCATION:** Washburn Univ, BS, 1939; Howard Univ, MD, 1945. **CAREER:** Kansas City, MO, private practice, Ob/Gyn; Model Cities Health Center, Admin consultant; Univ MO, Kansas City Med Center, consulting Ob/Gyn; Menorah Med Center, teaching staff mem; St Joseph & Martin Luther King Memorial Hospitals, teaching staff mem; Lawrence Aviation, dir. **ORGANIZATIONS:** Mem Jackson Co & Kansas City Med Socs; Kansas City Gynecological Soc; YMCA; Sigma Pi Phi; Midwesterners Club; Heart of Am Golf Club; Negro Airman Internat; Paseo Bapt Ch State Champion MO Pan Med Soc. **HONORS/ACHIEVEMENTS:** Father of the Year Award, YMCA, 1962. **BUSINESS ADDRESS:** 4301 Cleveland, Kansas City, MO 64130.

JOHNSON, JAMES W., JR.
Automobile executive. **CAREER:** Barrington Dodge Inc, Barrington, IL, chief executive. **BUSINESS ADDRESS:** Barrington Dodge, Inc, 505 West Northwest Hwy, Barrington, IL 60010. *

JOHNSON, JAMES WALTER, JR.
Attorney. **PERSONAL:** Born May 12, 1941, Washington, DC; married Eva M Murdock; children: Kimberely, Stephanie, Christopher. **EDUCATION:** Howard Univ, BS 1963; George Washington Univ, MS 1969, JD 1971. **CAREER:** Lockheed Missile & Space Co, assoc engr 1963-64; US Patent Office, examiner 1965-66; Mitre Corp, staff 1968-71; Communication Satellite Corp, patent attny 1971-74; GE Co, div patent consult 1974-78; Intelsat, patent consult 1978-. **ORGANIZATIONS:** Mem DC Bar Assoc, PA Bar Assoc, Natl Bar Assoc, Amer Patent Lawyers Assoc; reg US Patent Attny; mem Kappa Alpha Psi. **MILITARY SERVICE:** AUS capt 1966-68. **BUSINESS ADDRESS:** Asst Legal Advisor, Intelsat, 490 L'Enfant Plaza SW, Room 7078, Washington, DC 20024.

JOHNSON, JANICE MARIE
Artist. **PERSONAL:** Born Jan 18, 1954, Los Angeles, CA. **EDUCATION:** SW Coll Los Angeles City Coll, 1973; Grants Music Center, 1973. **CAREER:** A Taste of Honey, bassist & vocalist & leader 1972; John Muir Jr High Sch, modern dance instr 1968-69; Gee Gee's Originals, designer seamstress 1967-69; Soul & Swingers/Quniques/Sound Stage # 1, vocalist 1966-71; Conducive Music Inc pres/Owner 1978-. **HONORS/ACHIEVEMENTS:** Best New Artist Grammy Award Nat Acad of Rec Arts & Sci 1978; Songwriters Award Broadcast Music Inc 1978; Pub Award Broadcast Music Inc 1978; Platinum &Gold Albums RIAA Sales Award 1978-79; Gold Prize 8th Annual Tokyo Song Festival 1979. **BUSINESS ADDRESS:** Conducive Music Inc, PO Box 78645, Los Angeles, CA 90016.

JOHNSON, JAY (SUPER JAY)
Radio manager/announcer. **PERSONAL:** Born Apr 02, 1947, Louisville, KY; married Arneda Moncure; children: Jason Troy, Tiffany Faye. **EDUCATION:** Attended, Triton Coll, Coll of Professional Broadcasting Chicago. **CAREER:** WGRT Radio, announcer 1968-71; WVON Radio, announcer 1971-75; WBBM-TV, announcer 1974-75; WISH-TV, reporter/host 1978-85; WTLC-FM, program dir 1975-. **ORGANIZATIONS:** Pres Jay Johnson Enterprises; bd mem Amer Lung Assoc Indy Chapt; consultant Indiana Black Expo, Ctr for Leadership Develop; comm mem PAXI 10th Pan Amer Games 1986-87. **HONORS/ACHIEVEMENTS:** Air Personality or Program Dir of the Year Billboard magazine 1974,80,82; Air Personality or Program Dir of the Year Black Radio Exclusive magazine 1977,78,79,85,86; Super Jay Johnson Day City of Indianapolis 1977; Outstanding Serv as Host UNCF 1978-85; Excellence Awd Operation PUSH 1981; Success Awd Black Woman Hall of Fame Foundation 1984. **MILITARY SERVICE:** AUS 3 yrs. **BUSINESS ADDRESS:** Program Dir, WTLC-FM, PO Box 697, Indianapolis, IN 46206.

JOHNSON, JEFFALYN BROWN
Business executive. **PERSONAL:** Born in Los Angeles, CA; married Alvin. **EDUCATION:** Univ So CA, PhD; CA StateUniv LA, MA, BA. **CAREER:** Jeffalyn Johnson Asso Inc, pres; Carter-Mondale Transition Planning Group, policy analyst; Fed Exec Inst, dean, prof;Univ So CUniv MA, instr; PasadenaCity Coll, Claremont Coll, Occidental Coll, asst prof; Pasadena & LA Sch Sys, tchr admin; LA Bur of Pub Assis Commr, Commn on Observance of Intl Women's Yr, soc case worker; Adv Counc for Women, pres. **ORGANIZATIONS:** Bd dir Nat Women's Educ Fund; Am Soc of Pub Adminstrs; Conf of Minority Pub Adminstrs; Am Polit Sci Assn; Nat Conf of Black Polit Scientists Alpha Kappa Alpha. **HONORS/ACHIEVEMENTS:** Pi Sigma Alpha Disting Scholar Ralph J Bunche Chair TX So U; Woman of Yr Comm Serv Awd.

JOHNSON, JEH VINCENT
Architect and lecturer. **PERSONAL:** Born Jul 08, 1931, Nashville, TN; son of Dr Charles Spurgeon Johnson and Marie Burgette Johnson; married Norma Edelin; children: Jeh Charles, Marguerite Marie. **EDUCATION:** Columbia Coll, AB 1953; Columbia Univ, March 1958. **CAREER:** Paul R Williams, Architect, designer/draftsman 1956; Adams & Woodbridge Architechts, designer 1958-62; Ginsdele & Johnson PC, architect pres 1962-80; LeGendre Johnson McNeil Architects, partner 1980-. **ORGANIZATIONS:** Lecturer Vassar Coll 1964-; consultant Dutchess County Planning Bd 1984-; dir Poughkeepsie Savings Bank 1977-; NY St Arch Registration Bd 1973-84; Am Inst of Arch 1963-; found mem Natl Org of Minority Arch 1972-; mem Sigma Pi Phi. **HONORS/ACHIEVEMENTS:** Students Medal AIA, NY 1958; William Kinne Fellows Traveaux Flwshp (Europe) 1959; elected to Fellowship Am Inst of Arch 1977; designed over 90 major projects & 4300 housing units 1963-89. **MILITARY SERVICE:** AUS sgt 1953-55. **HOME ADDRESS:** 14 Edge Hill Rd, Wappingers Falls, NY 12590. **BUSINESS ADDRESS:** Architect, LJM Architects, 175 W 125th St, New York, NY 10027.

JOHNSON, JERRY CALVIN
Educator. **PERSONAL:** Born Jun 20, 1920, Tulsa, OK; married Vaster M; children: Dr Jerry C Jr, Wandra Haywood, Oliver. **EDUCATION:** Fayetteville State Univ, BS 1950; Columbia Univ, MA 1951. **CAREER:** Ridgeview HS, teacher, coach 1951-58; LeMoyne Owen Coll, athletic dir, coach 1959-, prof health, phys ed, recreation. **ORGANIZATIONS:** Volunteer Amer Red Cross 1959-; consult Natl Youth Sports Prog 1972-82; bd of dir Memphis Shelby Cty Old Age 1975-80; adv council TN State Bd of Ed 1984-; vice pres Southern Intercollegiate Conf 1984-. **HONORS/ACHIEVEMENTS:** Coach of the Year NCAA 100% Wrong Club 1975; State Legislature Proclamation State of TN 1976; Faculty Mem of the Year LeMoyne Owen Coll 1980; Recreation AwdMemphis Park Commiss 1985. **BUSINESS ADDRESS:** Prof Health Phys Ed Rec, LeMoyne Owen Coll, 807 Walker Ave, Memphis, TN 38126.

JOHNSON, JESSE J.
Writer. **PERSONAL:** Born May 15, 1914, Hattiesburg, MS; married Elizabeth C. **EDUCATION:** Tougaloo Coll, AB 1939; Amer Ext School of Law, LLB 1950; Hampton Inst, MA 1964. **CAREER:** AUS, lt col retired 1942-62. **ORGANIZATIONS:** Guest speaker colls & univ. **HONORS/ACHIEVEMENTS:** Wrote "Ebony Brass", "Black Soldiers", Black Armed Forces Officers 1736-1971"; 3 other books about black men & women in mil serv in US. **MILITARY SERVICE:** AUS retired lt col 1942-62.

JOHNSON, JESSE J.
Psychological consultant. **PERSONAL:** Born Jul 14, 1921, New Madrid, MO; married Annie E Robinson; children: Jesse, Walter, Beverly. **EDUCATION:** Dillard U, BS 1946; Northwestern U, MS 1949; Northwestern U, PhD 1951; Center for Mental Health NYC, 4 yr Certificate in Psycoanalysis Post Grad 1967. **CAREER:** Jesse J & Johnson Asso, presently psychol cons; VA Tuskegee AL & Montrose, NY, supr Psychologist 1951-67; Briarcliff

Coll, lecturer; StateUniv of NY,asso prof; To Industry, cons; Graham Home for Children NY, cons; HEW, cons. **ORGANIZATIONS:** Mem Am Psychol Assn; pres Assn of Black Psychologists; travel agency Jayjay Travel White Plains NY; chmn Corporate Concerns Com Operations PUSH; mem Council of Concerned Black Executives; mem Soc of Sigma Xi. **MILITARY SERVICE:** Sgt 92 Infantry Div 1943-45. **BUSINESS ADDRESS:** Jay Jay Travel, 149 Grand St, White Plains, NY.

JOHNSON, JOE
Author, poet, educator, journalist. **PERSONAL:** Born Jan 18, 1940, New York, NY; son of Alonzo D Johnson Sr and Lillian Mae Young; married Harriet Nicole Luria, Aug 01, 1967; children: Jeremiah Joseph Johnson. **EDUCATION:** Columbia Univ, BA, 1970; Columbia Univ Teachers Coll, MA, 1973; Additional studies at New School for Social Research. **CAREER:** Reed Cannon & Johnson Publishing, editor-publisher, 1973-77; Crisis Magazine, contributing editor; Ramapo Coll of NJ, assoc prof, literature, 1971-; Co-charperson of the African-African American Inst of Ramapo Coll; teacher, City Univ City Coll, 1970-71. **ORGANIZATIONS:** chmn, Black Lit Panel NE Modern Language Assn, 1974. **HONORS/ACHIEVEMENTS:** Published poetry book, "At the Westend," 1976; published "Hot" Telephone Book, 1977; published, "Tight," Lee Lucas Press, 1978. **HOME ADDRESS:** 365 South End Ave, New York, NY 10280. **BUSINESS ADDRESS:** Assoc Prof, Literature, Ramapo Coll of New Jersey, 803 Ramapo Valley Rd, Mahwah, NJ 07430.

JOHNSON, JOHN H.
Business executive. **PERSONAL:** Born Jan 19, 1918, Arkansas City, AR; son of Gertrude Johnson Williams; married Eunice; children: Linda Johnson Rice. **EDUCATION:** Univ Chicago; Northwestern Univ; numerous honorary degrees. **CAREER:** Supreme Liberty Life Ins Co; WJPC Radio Sta Chicago, pres; WLOU Radio Sta, pres; Johnson Publ Co Chicago, IL, pres/publisher of Ebony, Jet and EM Magazines 1942-. **ORGANIZATIONS:** Chmn Supreme Life Ins Co; dir Marina Bank Chicago, Greyhound Corp, Zenith Radio Corp, Continental Bank, Chrysler Corp; trustee Art Inst Chicago; fellow Sigma Delta Chi; mem US Chamber of Commerce; dir Mag Pubs Assn; mem Pres Commn for Obsv of 25th Anniv of UN 1970. **HONORS/ACHIEVEMENTS:** Accompanied US Vice Pres to Russia and Poland 1959; appointed by Pres Special US Ambassador to Independence Ceremonies of Ivory Coast 1961; Spl US Ambassador to Independence Ceremonies of Kenya 1963; Natl Selec Serv Commn 1966; recip Horatio Alger Award 1966; John Russwurm Award Natl Newspaper Pubs Assn 1966; Spingarn medal NAACP 1966; Henry Johnson Fisher Award magazine Pubs Assn 1971; Communicator of the Year Award Univ Chicago Alumni Assn 1974; Columbia Journalism Award 1974; accompanied US Vice Pres on goodwill tour to nine African countries 1975; named to Acad Disting Entrepreneurs Babson Coll 1979; Chicago Boys Club Chicagoan of the Year 1983; Natl Press Foundation Award 1986; Black Enterprise No. I Black Business Award 1986; Black Enterprise No. I Black Business Award inducted into Black press Hall of Fame 1987; inducted into The Publishing Hall of Fame Folio Educ Trust, Inc 1987; Salute to Greatness Award Martin Luther King Center for Nonviolent Social Change Harold H. Hines, Jr. Benefactors' Award, United Negro Coll Fund 1988, Equal Opportunity Award, Natl Urban League 1988; inducted into Illinois Business Hall of Fame, EXCELL Award, Intl Assn of Business Communicators, inducted into Natl Sales Hall of Fame, Natl Conf of Christians and JEWS (NCCJ), NCCJ Founders Award, Natl NCCJ Mass Media Award, Special NCCJ Bd Award. **BUSINESS ADDRESS:** President, Johnson Publishing Co, Inc, 820 S Michigan Avenue, Chicago, IL 60605.

JOHNSON, JOHN J.
Business executive. **PERSONAL:** Divorced; children: Gloria, Don, Kavin, Felita. **EDUCATION:** Mid TN State Univ; Western KY Univ. **CAREER:** Louisvl-Jeff Co Comm Act Commn; Pk DuValle Neighborhood Serv Cntr, dir, adminstr fld opers 9/71-6/72, stf dev asso 5/71-9/71; Pinkett Brown Black Asso Inc, NYC, adminstrv dir 1970-71; So KY Ec Oppor & Concl, Bowling Grn, dir fld oper & training 12/69-10/70, dir cent opers 2/69-12/69; KYInst for Comm Dev, Lexington, trnr 9/68-2/69. **ORGANIZATIONS:** Mem NAACP 1963-, membrshp chmn Simpson Co Br 1963-64, pres 1967-69; mem KY State Exec Com 1967-70, 2nd vice pres 1969-70, yth adv 1971-72, pres 1972-; mem Nat Tsk Force on Membrshp 1974-; exec com S KY EOC 1967-68; persnl com 1966-67; Day Care Cent Strg Com 1967-68; Simpson Co Rep 1966-68; mem Alpha Bapt Ch, Franklin, KY; mem, bd dir KY Inst for Comm Dev 1967-68; Co of Louisvil Ec Dev Cncl 1972-; Louisvl-Jeff Co Hum Rel CommnAdv Bd 1972-; KY Educ TV Adv Com 1973-; chart mem W Louisvl JCs 1973-; Adv ComUniv of Louisvl W Campus 1974-; Adv Com Prob & Par Bd, KY Dept of Corr 1974-; fdr, treas Blk Scene Mag 1973-. **HONORS/ACHIEVEMENTS:** Nom, Outstdg Yng Man Award, Simpson Co JCs 1967; KY Coll 1968 & 1974; Dist Ctzn Award, Mayor of Louisvl 1972. **BUSINESS ADDRESS:** 1809 S 34 St, Louisville, KY 40211.

JOHNSON, JOHN THOMAS
Physician. **PERSONAL:** Born Feb 08, 1942, St Louis, MO; married Geraldine Ross; children: Christine E, Glenda R, John T Jr. **EDUCATION:** Parsons Coll, BS 1967; Philadelphia Coll of Osteopathic Medicine, DO 1974. **CAREER:** Davenport Medical Ctr, intern 1974-75, resident 19075-76; Private Practice, physician 1976-. **ORGANIZATIONS:** Mem Amer Osteopathic Assoc 1976-, Iowa Osteopathic Medicine Assoc 1976-, Scott County Medical Soc 1976-; bd of dirs Davenport Medical Ctr; volunteer physician Silver Gloves, Boy Scouts 1985. **HONORS/ACHIEVEMENTS:** Awd & Roast Sepia Guild 1977; Certificate of Appreciation The Honor Comm 1982; Recognition Awd Christian Comm Serv 1982, Calvary SDA Church 1983; Certificate of Appreciation Senior Citizens 1985; Recognition Awd Davenport Medical Ctr 1986. **MILITARY SERVICE:** AUS e4 1963-65. **BUSINESS ADDRESS:** 3801 No Marquette St, Davenport, IA 52806.

JOHNSON, JOHN W.
Attorney, law professor. **PERSONAL:** Born Nov 06, 1934, Summerfield, LA; children: John, Jr, Julian. **EDUCATION:** Georgetown Univ Law Center, LlM 1964; Howard Univ Sch of Law, JD 1962; So Univ Baton Rouge, BA 1957. **CAREER:** AT & T, atty 1972; NY Law Sch, law prof 1978-; US Dept of Just Wash, trial lawy 1964-68; OH Bell Tel & Co Cleveland Corp ABA, lawy 1968-72. **ORGANIZATIONS:** Nat Bar Assn; NY Bar Assn; OH Bar Assn; DC Bar Assn; LA Bar Assn; World Peace thru Law; Adm to Prac before Supreme Ct of US Sigma Delta Tau Legal Frat Part in LA first "sit in" demonstrn 1960 case reviewed by US Sup Ct Garner V LA. **MILITARY SERVICE:** Active military duty 1957-59. **BUSINESS ADDRESS:** AT&T 195 Broadway, Ste #1117, New York, NY 10007.

JOHNSON, JOHNNIE
Professional athlete. **PERSONAL:** Born Oct 08, 1956, La Grange, TX. **EDUCATION:** Texas. **CAREER:** L A Rams, safety 1983-. **HONORS/ACHIEVEMENTS:** 1983 named first-team All-nfl by the NEA; All Rookie selection in 1980; bd of dir Am Cancer Soc; Rams spokesman for this years United Way. **MILITARY SERVICE:** Won Carroll Rosenbloom Awd as the clubs Rookie of the Year. **BUSINESS ADDRESS:** Los Angeles Rams, 2327 Lincoln Ave, Anaheim, CA 92801.

JOHNSON, JOHNNIE L., JR.
Attorney. **PERSONAL:** Born Jan 01, 1946, Nesbitt, MS; daughter of Johnnie L Johnson, Sr and Beulah Merriweather; married Bethiness Theodocia Walker, Jun 07, 1970; children: Johnnie L III, Gregory Lloyd, Justice Millsaps, Ahmad Nakeill. **EDUCATION:** Morris Brown Coll, BA 1967; OH Northern Univ, JD 1970. **CAREER:** Dept of Justice, asst us atty 1970-73; Equal Employment Oppty Commission, asst reg atty 1973-75, spec asst to comm 1975-78, dir trial team II 1978-81, atty advisor 1981-; sr trail attorney. **ORGANIZATIONS:** Asst gen counsel EEOC 1981-83, dir legal & spec pol div 1981-85, dir spec proj 1985; pres Morris Brown Coll Alumni Assoc 1985-, mediator, DC Mediation Service 1989; bd of directors, Ohio Northern Univ Law Alumni Assoc 1988-; pres, Mediterranean Villas Cluster Assn 1986-. **HONORS/ACHIEVEMENTS:** Donnie Delaney Comm Defense Awd 1974; Outstanding Young Man of Amer 1979; participant in "Old Dominion 100 Mile Endurance Run" 1979, Empire State Run Up 1979,80, JFK 50 Miler 1980. **HOME ADDRESS:** 11644 Mediterranean Court, Reston, VA 22090. **BUSINESS ADDRESS:** Senior Trail Attorney, Equal Employment Opportunity Comm, 1801 "L" St, NW, Washington, DC 20507.

JOHNSON, JOHNNY B.
Educator. **PERSONAL:** Born Feb 17, 1920, Rison, AR; married Mildred Mazique; children: Johnny Jr, Mrs Patricia Berry, Revawn. **EDUCATION:** Agricultural Mechanical & Normal Coll, BS 1948; MI State Univ, MS 1948, MA 1955; Univ of AR, EdD 1963. **CAREER:** AM&N Coll, dean of men 1949-61; Univ of AR-Pine Bluff, prof 1963-73, interim chancellor 1973-74, vice chancellor academic affairs 1974-76, prof acting chancellor vice chancellor 1976-86, provost/vice chancellor. **ORGANIZATIONS:** Mem AR Educ Assoc, Natl Educ Assoc, Amer Assoc of Higher Educ 1949-86; mem Kiwanis Intl 1975-86. **HONORS/ACHIEVEMENTS:** Fellowship Southern Educ Foundation 1962; listed Outstanding Educators of Amer 1975; Outstanding Civilian Service Awd Army ROTC 1974. **MILITARY SERVICE:** AUS tech sgt 1942-45; Bronze Star. **HOME ADDRESS:** #67 Watson Blvd, Pine Bluff, AR 71601. **BUSINESS ADDRESS:** Provost/Vice Chancellor A A, Univ of Arkansas Pine Bluff, University Dr, Pine Bluff, AR 71601.

JOHNSON, JONDELLE H.
Executive director. **PERSONAL:** Born Mar 11, 1924, Charleston, SC; children: Carolyn, Jo Ann, Winfred, Edgar. **EDUCATION:** AllenUniv Columbia, SC, AB 1945; Atlanta U, MA 1953; EmoryUniv Atlanta. **CAREER:** Atlanta, GA Bd of Edn, tchr 1957-69; Dekalb Co GA Bd of Edn, tchr 1949-57; Cobb Co GA Bd of Edn, tchr 1946-47; Atlanta Inquirer Newspaper, soc editor 1961-67; Atlanta Inquirer Newspaper, mng editor 1966-67; Atlanta Voice Newspaper, soc editor 1967-74; Atlanta Voice Newspaper, news editor 1967-74; Bronze Am Mag, southeastern editor 1964-65; Atlanta Br NAACP, presently exec dir. **ORGANIZATIONS:** Mem Atlanta PTA Council; GA Educ Assn; NEA; GA PTA Congress; Atlanta Pub Sch Adv Council; Cit Trust Bank & Comm Adv Bd; WIGO Radio Adv Bd; Nat Bus & Professional Women's Club Mem Wheat St Bapt Ch; Met Assn for Blind Vol Com; #Exec #Bd NW Br YMCA; Maude Daniels Chap for Retarded; Atlanta Urban League Guild; Atlanta Theater Guild; Iota Phi Lambda Sorority; vote dep registrar; #Exec com Fulton & Co Rep Party; exec bd Atlanta Br NAACP; State Pub Relations Dir F&AA York Masons & Eastern Stars; YMCA; Atlanta Urban League Coalition on Census; exec com Fifth Dist Rep; Lincoln-Douglass Rep Club;Met Rep Women's Club; Metro Atlanta Summit Leadership Congress; Heroines of Jericho; Eastern Star Order of Nat Compact; USA-fAA Masons; All Cit Registration Com; precinct chmn 108 House Dist; bd mem Nat Clients Council; Consult Educ In-serv Workshops for Tchrs; Washington High Comm Sch Adv Com; coordinator Tutorial Prog in Poverty Areas; YMCA Membership Drives. **HONORS/ACHIEVEMENTS:** Recipient First Place Awards in Pub Serv Nat Newspaper Assn 1964, 65, 67; Woman of the Yr in Human & Relations Bronze Woman of the Yr Iota Phi Lambda Sorority 1967; Outstanding Educator's Award GA PTA Congress 1968; Fulton Co Rep Serv Awards 1969, 70, 73; Woman of Yr Award Metro Atlanta Summit Leadership Congress 1974; Citizenship Award Las Amigas Club 1968; YWCA-GAY Y Serv Club Award 1968; NAACP Leadership Award 1972; Fulton Co Rep Century Cluf Awards 1971-72; Dekalb Co Grad Scholarship for Outstanding Teaching summers 1952-53; Nat Continental Soc Bicentennial Distinguished Black Am Award 1975; YMCA Trophy for Leadership 1968; Nat Negro Women's Bus & Professional Leadership Award 1970; Freedom Award by Cit for Freedom 1971. **BUSINESS ADDRESS:** 859 1/2 Hunter St NW, Atlanta, GA 30314.

JOHNSON, JOSEPH A.
Educator. **PERSONAL:** Born Jun 09, 1925, Columbus, OH; married Olivia Scott. **EDUCATION:** Allen U, BS; Columbia U, MBA; NY U, MA. **CAREER:** Allen Univ, Columbia SC, dir gen studies 1973-; Federal Projects Allen Univ, dir 1973-; Special Servs, dir 1970-73; asst prof Business 1968-70; business mgr 1950-56. **ORGANIZATIONS:** Mem Phi Delta Kappa; mem Province Polemarch; Kappa Alpha Psi; chmn Jacks of Columbia Jack & Jill; Bethel AME Ch. **MILITARY SERVICE:** AUS 1943-45. **BUSINESS ADDRESS:** Allen Univ, Columbia, SC 29204.

JOHNSON, JOSEPH B.
Educational administrator. **PERSONAL:** Born Sep 16, 1934, New Orleans, LA; son of Sidney Johnson and Lillie Johnson; married Lula Young; children: Yolanda Dixson, Joseph III, Juliete, Julie. **EDUCATION:** Grambling State Univ, BS, 1957; Univ of CO, Boulder, MS, 1967, EdD, 1973; Harvard Univ, certificate, 1976. **CAREER:** Booker T Washington High School, Shreveport, teacher, 1962-63; Greenville Park High School, teacher, 1963-69; Univ of CO, Boulder, exec asst to the pres, 1975-77; Grambling State Univ, pres, 1977-. **ORGANIZATIONS:** Mem, NAFEO, Amer Council on Educ, Amer Assn of Univ Admins; Officer, YMCA, 1977; mem, Kappa Alpha Psi Fraternity, AME Church; bd trustees, State Colls & Univs for the State of LA, chmn, Pres' Council, 1982-83; Southwestern Athletic Conf, chmn Pres's Council 1982-84; mem, Gov's Economic Devel Comm 1984, commission on coll SACS, 1985; chmn, LA delegation SACS, 1985; mem, steering comm for historically black colleges; adv Office of Educational Rsch Improvement, US Dept of Educ, 1987; mem bd of advisors, Who's Who in South & Southwest; bd of dir, Univ of CO Alumni Assn, Boulder, 1989-92; Natl Collegiate Athletic Assn, Pres' Commn, 1989-93; Amer Assn of State Colleges & Universities' Comm on Humanities. **HONORS/ACHIEVEMENTS:** Scholarship, Grambling

State Univ, 1953-57; Teaching Assistantship, Univ of CO, Boulder, 1966; Fellowship, Harvard Univ, 1976; Distinguished Serv to Educ Awd, Harris-Stowe State Coll, 1987; Honorary Doctors of Law, Western MI Univ, Jewish Natl Fund Tree of Life Award, 1985; Natl Alliance of Business Leadership Award, 1984; Distinguished Alumni Achievement Award, Univ of CO; Thurgood Marshall Educ Achievement Award, 1988; Assn of Social & Behavioral Scientists Inc, WEB Dubois Award, 1988; Honorary Doctor of Philosophy, Gandhigram Rural Univ, India, 1988. **MILITARY SERVICE:** AUS sgt 1958-62. **BUSINESS ADDRESS:** President, Grambling State University, PO Drawer 607, Grambling, LA 71270.

JOHNSON, JOSEPH DAVID
Business executive. **PERSONAL:** Born Oct 26, 1945, Poplar Bluff, MO; son of Archie Johnson and Curley Johnson; married Julie Hamilton; children: Joy Laurice, Joelle Devon. **EDUCATION:** Lincoln Univ, BS Education 1968, MS Educ Admin 1969. **CAREER:** General Mills Inc, comp per mgmt 1969-72; Dayton Hudson Corp, sr comp specialist 1972-73; Intl Multifoods Corp, div per mgr 1973-75; Xerox Corp, various per mgmt pos 1975-83; vice-pres human resources 1983-88; pres, CEO The Telein Group, Inc, 1988-. **ORGANIZATIONS:** Co-founder Exchange Inc Professional Assoc 1973/74; bd of dir Eltrex Indus 1982-83; life mem Alpha Phi Alpha Fraternity 1965-; pres Advisory Bd Eltrex Ind 1984-;mem Amer Comp Assn, Natl Assoc of Corp Black Professionals, NAACP, SCLC, Urban League, PUSH, Lincoln Univ Alumni Assoc; bd of advisors Univ of So CA Center for Org Effectiveness; bd dirs United States Academic Decathalon 1986-; mem Exec Exchange Program Natl Urban League; mem Exec Leadership Council. **HONORS/ACHIEVEMENTS:** Community Serv Award Orange County Links 1985; Outstanding Alumni Achievement Award Lincoln Univ 1986/87; subject of case study on human resources at the Harvard Business School, 1985. **MILITARY SERVICE:** AUS (military intelligence) 1st lt 1970-72; Distinguished Military Graduate Lincoln Univ ROTC Program 1968. **BUSINESS ADDRESS:** Katella Corporate Center, 4281 Katella Center, Los Namitos, CA 90720.

JOHNSON, JOSEPH EDWARD
Educator. **PERSONAL:** Born Aug 07, 1934, Wilmington, DE; son of Joseph E Johnson, Sr. (deceased) and Dorothy Dean Johnson; married Ella B McAlister; children: Kevin. **EDUCATION:** Central State Univ, BS 1957; Seton Hall Univ, MA 1965; Univ of MA, EdD 1976. **CAREER:** Burnett JHS, teacher 1959-66; Wilm Pub Sch, v prin 1966-68, prin 1968-69, dir of presonnel & employee rel 1969-71, asst supt 1975-77, supt 1977-78; New Castle Co Sch, dep supt instr 1978-81; Red Clay Consol Sch Dist, supt 1981. **ORGANIZATIONS:** Mem Amer Assn of Sch Admin; Phi Delta Kappa Educ Frat; Natl Alliance of Black Sch Educs; Kappa Alpha Psi Frat; Sigma Pi Phi Boule; chairman bd of dir Delaware Div Amer Cancer Society 1987-89; mem bd of directors YMCA of Delaware 1980-89; mem bd of directors Boys Club of Delaware 1985-89. **HONORS/ACHIEVEMENTS:** Ford Fellowship Univ of MA; Rockefeller Fellowship; Sch Supt Nat Sci Found Fellow Brown Univ; Superintendent of Year, Delaware, Delaware Chief School Officers 1989. **MILITARY SERVICE:** AUS 1st Lt 1957-59; AUS Reserve Capt 1959-66. **BUSINESS ADDRESS:** Superintendent, Red Clay Consult Sch Dist, 1400 WashingtonSt, Wilmington, DE 19899.

JOHNSON, JOSEPH HARVEY
Attorney. **PERSONAL:** Born Dec 16, 1916, Cincinnati; married Hilda Payne; children: Pearl, Patricia. **EDUCATION:** Univ Cincinnati, Cert 1950; Salmon P Chase Coll of Law, LLB 1954, JD 1968. **CAREER:** Cty of Cincinnati Jr & Sr, acct clk 1947-53, & asst cty solctr & asst cty pros 1963-67; State of OH Exam State Aud Office, 1953-63; Render Black &Johnson Cincnti Bar Assn, atty 1967-. **ORGANIZATIONS:** Mem NAACP 1953; chmn leg red com Cincnti Br 1958-65. **HONORS/ACHIEVEMENTS:** Award Cincnti br NAACP 1962 & 1967; Dist Comm Ser Award Felwshp Hse of Cincnti 1963. **BUSINESS ADDRESS:** Ste 1029 31 138 E Ct St, Cincinnati, OH 45202.

JOHNSON, JOSHUA
Communications specialist. **PERSONAL:** Born Dec 30, 1949, Sumpter, SC; son of William Johnson and Marjorie Johnson; married Phyllis Graham; children: Terrence, Derrick. **EDUCATION:** Eastman Kodak Co Rochester NY, Photog Courses 1976; Rochester Inst of Tech, 1975 & 77; Rutgers Univ Coll, BS Mgmt; NY Microscopical Soc, attended 1981. **CAREER:** NJ Med Sch & CMDNJ, asst med photographer 1968-70; NJ Dental School, principal biomed dental photographer 1970-; Univ of Medicine & Dentistry of NJ, biomedical photographer/mgr of photographic serv 1984-. **ORGANIZATIONS:** Active mem Biology Photographer Assn 1973-; mem NY Microscopical Soc; illustrator of dental textbooks for dentists & assts "Four Handed Dentistry For Dentists & Asst" 1974; 2nd Book Clinical Mgmt of Head Neck & TMJ Pain & Dysfunctions 1977; Artical "Clinical Cameraman" Biomed Communications Journal 1980; Lecturer Dentists &Cental Students on Intra Oral Photography; illustrator of Many Articles of Highly Recognized Natl & Intl Dental Jour; co-founder & First Black Dental Photographer of Educ Communications Cntr NJ Dental Sch; mem Amer Business Mgmt Assoc 1987-. **BUSINESS ADDRESS:** Mgr Photographic Serv, Univ Med & Dentistry of NJ, 100 Bergen St, Newark, NJ 07103.

JOHNSON, JOY J.
Clergyman, government official. **PERSONAL:** Born Nov 02, 1921, Laurel Hill, NC; married Omega Foster. **EDUCATION:** Shaw U, AB LlD 1945 & 1972; Friendship Clg, Hon DD 1966. **CAREER:** First Bapt Ch Fairmont Nc, pastor; State Parole Commn, apptd 1978-; State Legistor, 1972-78. **ORGANIZATIONS:** Mem Fairmont City Cncl 1966-70; Robeson Co & Dem Exec Com 1968-71; So Region Pres Prog Natl Bapt Conv 1970-72; Pres Gen Bapt State Conv of NC Inc; life mem NAACP; Shriner; dir Town & Country Bnk; mem Alpha Phi Alpha; Mason; ShawUniv Theol Frat; NC Black Caucus; vice pres pres Fairmont Human Relations Cncl; chmn House Com on Human Resources 1975-79. **HONORS/ACHIEVEMENTS:** Author of "From Poverty to Power", "The Modern Dayt Prodigal"; recipient Fairmont Man of Yr Awrd 1971; State Bapt Dist Citizen Awrd 1972; State NAACP & Mason Awrd 1971; Shaw Uy Dist Awrd 1974; Robeson Co Human Relations Awrd 1972; Gen Bapt State Conv of NC Inc Statesman & Humanitarian Awrd 1975. **BUSINESS ADDRESS:** 831 W Morgan St, Raleigh, NC 27611.

JOHNSON, JOYCE COLLEEN
Govt. director. **PERSONAL:** Born Oct 24, 1939, Terre Haute, IN; married Ronald E Johnson. **EDUCATION:** IN State Univ, BS 1961. **CAREER:** US Dept of Housing & Urban Develop, equal oppor specialist 1973-78, multifamily housing rep 1978-83, dir fair housing and equal oppor 1983-. **ORGANIZATIONS:** Tutor Boy's Club 1968-71; education coord Intl Toastmistress 1980-83; botanical mgr Deco-Plants 1980-82; consultant American Cancer Soc 1982-; regional sec Alpha Pi Chi Sorority 1983-; housing advisor NAACP 1984-85. **HONORS/ACHIEVEMENTS:** Scholarship Alpha Pi Chi Sor 1965; co-author of book Certificate of Achievement US Dept of Army 1966; Recognition of Community Involvement NAACP 1984; Certificate of Excellence Alpha Pi Chi Sor 1985. **BUSINESS ADDRESS:** Dir, US Dept of Housing & Urban Dev, 151 North Delaware, Indianapolis, IN 46204.

JOHNSON, JUANITA B.
Retired educator. **PERSONAL:** Born Apr 25, 1927, St Louis, IL; married Roosevelt Jr. **EDUCATION:** Central StateUniv Xenia OH, BS 1950;Univ of TX Arlington TX, Grad Study 1962; East TXUniv Commerce, Grad Study 1965. **CAREER:** Wichita Falls Ind School Dist, teacher 1955-61; Dallas Ind School Dist, teacher 1952-55,61-77, institutional resource teacher 1977-; El Centro Jr Coll, retired teacher 1983. **ORGANIZATIONS:** Historian Dallas Urban League Guild 1970-; mem Basileus Alpha Xi Omega Chap Alpha Kappa Alpha 1970-; mem comm on admin YWCA Maria Morgan Br 1974-; mem Title I Task Force Dallas Ind School Dist 1977-; school book selection comm Dallas Ind School Dist 1978-80; coord testing Dallas Ind School Dist. **HONORS/ACHIEVEMENTS:** 25 yr recgtn Alpha Kappa Alpha Sor 1972; outst serv awrd Dallas Urban League Inc 1975; outst vol YWCA Maria Morgan Br 1978; most-outst serv awrd Alpha Kappa Alpha Sorority Inc 1979. **BUSINESS ADDRESS:** Dallas Ind School District, 3700 Ross AVe, Dallas, TX 75204.

JOHNSON, JULIANA CORNISH
International managing director. **PERSONAL:** Born Jun 26, 1957, Salisbury, MD; daughter of Jerome Cornish and Julia Cornish; married Douglas K Johnson, Feb 14, 1989. **EDUCATION:** Cornell Univ, BA (w/Honors) 1978; Harvard Grad Sch of Business, MBA 1982. **CAREER:** Chase Manhattan Bank, intern 1978; Huntington Natl Bank, sr analyst 1979-80; The World Bank, intern 1980; American Telephone & Telegraph Co, mgr 1982-89. **ORGANIZATIONS:** Mem Harvard Alumni Assoc 1982-89, Harvard Grad Sch of Business Black Alumni Assoc 1982-89, Natl Black MBA Assoc 1983-89; sponsor Oakland Ensemble Theatre 1984-89; bd of dirs Bay Area Black United Fund 1985-89. **HONORS/ACHIEVEMENTS:** Top 50 Fast Track Young Executives Business Week Magazine 1987; Woodford Memorial Public Speaking Awd. **BUSINESS ADDRESS:** District Manager, International Marketing, Rm N594, 412 Mt Kemble Ave, Morristown, NJ 07960.

JOHNSON, JUSTIN MORRIS
Intermediate appellate judge. **PERSONAL:** Born Aug 19, 1933, Wilkinsburg, PA; son of Oliver Livingstone Johnson and Irene Olive Morris Johnson; married Florence Elizabeth Lester Johnson, Jun 25, 1960; children: William Oliver, Justin Llewellyn, Elizabeth Irene. **EDUCATION:** Univ Chicago, AB, 1954, Law School, JD, 1962; attended Univ of VA, 1982-83. **CAREER:** Partner/sole proprietor, Johnson & Johnson, 1962-77; Board of Education, School District of Pittsburgh and Pittsburgh-Mt Oliver Intermediate Unit, assistant solicitor, 1964-70, solicitor and assistant secretary, 1970-78; Berkman Ruslander Pohl Lieber & Engel, partner, 1978-80; Superior Court of PA, judge, 1980—; adjunct professor, Duquesne Univ School of Law. **ORGANIZATIONS:** Ruling elder Bethesda United Presbyterian Church 1966-; apptd PA Supreme Court 1969; mem Natl Cong Bar Examiners 1969-; mem, PA Bd Law Examiners 1969-, vice chairman 1975-83, chairman 1983-; bd of trustees Mercy Hospital 1976-, Southside Hosp 1978-, United Way of Allegheny Co 1979-; hearing comm PA Supreme Court Disciplinary Bd. **HONORS/ACHIEVEMENTS:** Bond Medal, Univ Chicago, 1954; Dr Martin Luther King Jr Citizen's Medal, 1973; Top Hat Award, 1981, for distinguished judicial service; Homer S Brown Service Award, 1982; Man of the Year, Bethesda United Presbyterian Church, 1983; President's Award, Pennsylvania Trial Lawyers Association, 1983; award of merit, Pittsburgh Young Adult Club, 1983; St Thomas More Award, 1985; public service award, Pittsburgh chapter, ASPA, 1986. **MILITARY SERVICE:** USAF aircraft comdr 1956-59, USAFR maj 1963-73. **HOME ADDRESS:** 4915 Bayard St, Pittsburgh, PA 15213. **BUSINESS ADDRESS:** Judge, Superior Ct of Pennsylvania, 330 Grant St, Suite 2702 Grant Bldg, Pittsburgh, PA 15219.

JOHNSON, KAAREN PATRICIA
Management consultant. **PERSONAL:** Born Aug 01, 1946, Charleston, SC. **EDUCATION:** Hofstra U, BA Applied Psychol 1971; StateUniv NY, MA liberal studies 1974. **CAREER:** Kaaren Johnson Asso Inc, pres; NY State Urban Devel Corp, vice pres personnel 1971-76; Am Express Co, T/C Div, mgr; CBS-COLUMBIA Broadcasting System, unitsupr 1966-68. **ORGANIZATIONS:** Mem Met Assn of Applied Psychol; mem Am Soc for training & Devel; mem Intl Assn of Personnel Women; mem NY Assn of Women Bus Owners; bd dirs CSS-COMMUNITY Serv Soc NY 1979-80; bd of dirs PIC-PVT Industry Council 1980-; natl pres Black Professional Womens Network 1980-82; bd of dirs Nat Urban League-Black Exec Exchange Prgm 1980; bd of dirs Nat Hook-Up of Black Women 1980. **HONORS/ACHIEVEMENTS:** Author "Black Mgrs Survival Guide to Corp Life", Publr AMACOM; article "The Mentor Connection".

JOHNSON, KELLEY CALVIN
Professional athlete. **PERSONAL:** Born Jun 03, 1962, Carlsbad, NM. **EDUCATION:** Univ of Colorado, Busn Mgmt Major, Photography Minor. **CAREER:** Denver Gold, wide receiver 1985-. **HONORS/ACHIEVEMENTS:** Fastest player in the state of CA 1982.

JOHNSON, KEN
Professional athlete. **PERSONAL:** Born Nov 27, 1956, Miami, FL. **CAREER:** NY Giants, professional football fullback. **HONORS/ACHIEVEMENTS:** NFL Rokie of Yr 1979.

JOHNSON, KENNETH EUGENE
Professional athlete. **PERSONAL:** Born Mar 22, 1955, Nashville, TN. **EDUCATION:** Knoxville Coll. **CAREER:** San Fran 49'ers, 1979; Buffalo Bills, prof ath. **ORGANIZATIONS:** Collects old coins. **HONORS/ACHIEVEMENTS:** All-Amer choice as a Sr; twice chosen to the Southern Intercollegiate Ath Conf All-Star squad; Black Coll All-Star game.

JOHNSON, KENNETH LAVON
Judge. **PERSONAL:** Born Jul 26, 1937, Columbia, MS; son of Geylor Johnson and Minnie O Johnson; married Carolyn Elizabeth Dischert, Sep 05, 1970; children: Sara Elizabeth, Jennifer Lorraine. **EDUCATION:** Southern Univ & A&M Coll, BA 1955-59; Howard Univ School of Law, B of Law 1960-62. **CAREER:** Judge Advocate Gen Corps, capt US Army

1962-66; US Dept of Justice, trial attny 1967-69; Baltimore Lawyers Comm for Civil Rights Under Law, exec dir 1969-70. **ORGANIZATIONS:** Mem Natl Assoc for Advancement of Colored People 1969-; prof Univ of Baltimore School of Law 1988-; prof Villa Julia College 1988-. **HONORS/ACHIEVEMENTS:** Distinguished Comm Serv Baltimore Frontier Club 1974; MD 7th Congressional Dist Awd Congressman Parren J Mitchell 1981; Outstanding Comm Serv Vanguard Justice Soc 1982. **MILITARY SERVICE:** Judge Advocate Gen Corps capt, chief Military Justice Section 1964-66. **BUSINESS ADDRESS:** Judge Circuit Court, Circuit Court for Baltimore, 111 N Calvert St, Baltimore, MD 21202.

JOHNSON, KENNETH PETER
Association president. **PERSONAL:** Born May 27, 1930, Wichita Falls, TX; married Mae Doris Butler; children: Denice M Bain, Kenneth P Jr, Julie E, Jerome K, Martin T. **EDUCATION:** US Army Misle Sch/Ft Sill, OK, Fld Arty Ofcr 1965; Fayetteville Tech Inst, AAS Bsns Admn 1977; Redlands Bible Coll Redlands, CA, Diploma 1979;Hampton Inst, Continue Ed 1985. **CAREER:** SS Kreisge, retail sls mgr 1972-76; Jessup Realty, sls mgr 1974-; Council - Real Est, sls mgr 1974; Marlboro Improve Assn, fdr & pres 1974; Fayetteville Tech Inst, vet & couns 1975; Prince Hall Affiliate Masonic Crdt Un, treas; Co Dem Party Exec Com, v chmn; Eureka Masonic Lodge; Kindeh Temple #62 AEO; St John's Bapt Ch, pstr. **ORGANIZATIONS:** Commr Cnty Auditorium Cumberland, NC; sgt/mjr 92nd Fld Arty Gessen, Germany 1970-71; ownr/agnt Jessup Realty Fayetteville, NC 1976-80; vice pres Cape Fear Mnstr Inst 1977-; pres Seventy-First Civic Asso 1973-75; pres Marlbboro Imprvmnt Asso 1975-84; pstr St Anna FW Bapt Ch Raleigh, NC 1981-; pstr St John FW Bapt Ch Fayetteville, NC; mem County HS Adv Bd State Professional Review Bd Comm 1982. **HONORS/ACHIEVEMENTS:** Outstndng Comm Serv Seventy-First Twnshp 1975; Achvmnt Awrd Ft Bragg, NC Freedom Essay 1969; Pastor of Yr Cape Fear Region Conf 1981-82, 1984. **MILITARY SERVICE:** AUS sgt/mjr 23 yrs; Bronze Star Med Valor BSM for Mrtrs Serv 1969; Vietnamese Cross of Gallantry 1969; Army Cmndtn Med 1970. **HOME ADDRESS:** 6526 Lark Dr, Fayetteville, NC 28304.

JOHNSON, LAWRENCE E., SR.
Attorney. **PERSONAL:** Born Sep 22, 1948, Waco, TX; children: Daphne, Lawrence Jr, Demitria, LaShunia. **EDUCATION:** Prairie View A&M Univ, BS Elect Engineering 1971; George Washington Univ, JD 1975. **CAREER:** Insurance salesman, 1969; IBM, design engineer 1970; General Electric Corp, sales engineer 1971-72, patent engineer 1972-76; Private Practice, attorney. **ORGANIZATIONS:** Pres of bd Legal Serv Corp 1983; pres bd Mitchell Funeral Home 1982-85; dir HOT Legal Serv 1981-85; sec, McLennan Community Coll Bd of Trustees. **BUSINESS ADDRESS:** Attorney, 410 M Bank Tower, Waco, TX 76701.

JOHNSON, LAWRENCE WASHINGTON
Clergyman. **PERSONAL:** Born Feb 24, 1901, Clifton, TN; son of Frank Johnson and Ada Briggs Johnson Bracey; married Lucile Jackson Johnson, Jan 13, 1951; children: Camilla Sharon Cobb MD, Ralph Edward, Deborah Annett Mitchell, Roy Phillip. **EDUCATION:** TN State College, Nashville, BS 1937; Fisk Univ, Nashville, MA 1946. **CAREER:** St Luke AME Church, clergyman, 1955-; Wilcox Co Bd of Ed, Rochell, GA, high school principal, 1951-55; Burk Co Bd of Ed, Midville, GA, jr high school principal, 1946-51; City Bd of Ed, Princeton, KY, high school principal, 1935-43; Franklin Co Bd of Ed, Winchester, TN, teacher/coach/principal, 1930-35; Wilson Co Bd of Ed, Lebanon, TN, tchr/coach 1926-28. **ORGANIZATIONS:** Conf chmn, Negro HS Principals Association of KY, 1936-41; pres YMCA at TN Sate College, 1924-28; pres, Day Care Center, Gallatin, TN; mem, policy council, Mid-Cumberland Head Start Serv. **HONORS/ACHIEVEMENTS:** Recipient scholarship award, TN State College Club, 1929; ordained elder, AME Ch, 1959; vintagers cert, TN State Univ, 1979. **MILITARY SERVICE:** AUS pvt 1943-. **BUSINESS ADDRESS:** Pastor, Bethel African Methodist Episcopal Church, 1125 Glade St, Columbia, TN 38401.

JOHNSON, LEARDREW L.
Clergyman. **PERSONAL:** Born Apr 24, 1921, New York, NY; married Hanson Griffin; children: Leardrew, Ilona, LaNora, Karen. **EDUCATION:** VA Union Univ, AB, MDiv, DMin; Colgate Rochester, Div Sch. **CAREER:** 1st Baptist Ch Williamsburg, pastor 1950-57; Beth Bapt Ch Holyoke MA, 1957-59; Congdon St Bapt Prov RI, 1959-65; Fidel Bapt Ch Cleveland, 1965-67; MtOlivet Rochester, 1967-. **ORGANIZATIONS:** Mem Amer Assn Marr & Fam Cnslrs 1973; co-ldr Amer Bapt Retrt for Mil Persnl Berchtesgaden Germany 1973; mem City Pl Commn Rochester 1971, 1973; adj prof trustee Colgate Rochester Div Sch; preacher on "The Laymen's Hour" 1977-78 1983-84. **HONORS/ACHIEVEMENTS:** Who's Who in Religion. **BUSINESS ADDRESS:** Mt Olivet, 141 Adams St, Rochester, NY 14608.

JOHNSON, LECTOY TARLINGTON
Physician. **PERSONAL:** Born Nov 28, 1931, Tyler, TX; married Helen Collier; children: Lectoy Tarlington, III, Lynelle Teresa. **EDUCATION:** TX Coll Tyler, TX, BS Chemistry 1952; Howard Univ Coll of Med, MD 1956; Washington Univ St Louis, Anesthesiology 1960; Amer Bd Anesthesiology, Diplomate 1963-; Amer Coll of Anesthesiology, Fellow 1963-. **CAREER:** Riverside Gen Hosp Houston, chmn dept anesthesiology 1960-68; St Joseph Hosp Houston, chmn dept anesthesiology 1970-80; Univ TX Med Sch Houston, act chmn dept anesth 1973; St Joseph Hosp Houston, acad chf of anesth 1970-80; Private Practice, physician. **ORGANIZATIONS:** Mem, Harris Co Med Soc, TX Med Soc, Natl Med Soc, Intl Anesthesia Rsch Soc, Undersea Med Soc, Gulf Coast Anesthesia Soc, Houston Surgical Soc; chmn bd dir Assn Anesthes Houston 1970-80; bd dir Standard Sav & Loan Houston 1984-; med dir Ocean Corp Houston 1970-78; pres Gulf coast Anesth Soc Houston 1979-80; comm chmn Boy Scouts of Amer WL Davis Dist 1974-75; life mem Kappa Alpha Psi Frat. **HONORS/ACHIEVEMENTS:** Cert of Excellence Gulf Coast Chapter of Inhalation Therapists; Outstanding Instr Award St Joseph Hosp Surgical Dept. **BUSINESS ADDRESS:** 2301 McGowen, Houston, TX 77004.

JOHNSON, LEMUEL A.
Educator. **PERSONAL:** Born Dec 15, 1941, Nigeria; children: Yma, Yshelu. **EDUCATION:** Oberlin Clg, BA 1965; PA St U, MA 1966;Univ of MI, PhD 1969. **CAREER:** Dept of English Univ of MI, prof; English Univ of Sierra Leone Fourah Bay Clol, lecturer 1970-72; Radio Forum, host 1970-71. **ORGANIZATIONS:** Sierra Leone Broad Serv Freetown; Pres African Lit Assc 1977-78. **HONORS/ACHIEVEMENTS:** Recipient hopwood awds for Short Story & Essay Cont 1967-68; Bredvold Prize for Scholar Publ; citation for "The Devil, the Gargoyle & the Buffoon, The Negro as Metaphor in West Lit" 1971; Dept of EngUniv of MI awd 1972; pub num poems & translations; pub "Highlife for Caliban 1973, "Hand on the Navel" 1978. **BUSINESS ADDRESS:** Professor, University of Michigan, Ann Arbor, MI 48109.

JOHNSON, LEON
University executive. **PERSONAL:** Born Jul 14, 1930, Aiken, SC; married Janie L; children: Leon Jr, Lisa J. **EDUCATION:** SC State Coll, BS 1955, MS 1959; MI StateUniv MD State Coll,Univ MD. **CAREER:** Clemson Univ, asst count agent 1955-62; Univ of MD, extension agent Com & Resource Devel. **ORGANIZATIONS:** Mem MD Assn County Agricultural Agents; Teamwork Planning Com; charter founding mem Comm Dev Soc; Comm Resource Dev Task Force Com; SEMIS Work GroupCom; Task Force on Comm Dev Progs; govS com on Migratory Labor; pres Somerset County Comm Action Agency Inc; Tri-county Migrant Com Inc; 2nd vP Somerset County Civic AssnInc; mem Delmarva Adv Council Migrat Com; Princess Anne Area C of C; bd dirs Coston Recreation Council; mem Somerset County Civil Defense bd; comm orgn for Progress Inc; bd dirs Somerset County Head Start; mem for Propress Inc; mem Zion Hill Bapt Ch; Omega Psi Phi Frat; Epsilon Sigma Phi Frat; Delmarva Ecmenical Agency Rural Coalition; bd dir MD Chs United Board Recognitions Countys Head & Start Program; Migrant Programs; CommAction Agency. **BUSINESS ADDRESS:** U Maryland Civi Ctr, Crisfield Ln, Princess Anne, MD 21853.

JOHNSON, LEON, JR.
Business executive. **PERSONAL:** Born Nov 27, 1946, Washington, DC; married Cleo Figgures; children: Noel Alexander. **EDUCATION:** Howard Univ, BA 1969; Univ of PA Wharton Grad Div, MBA 1971; PA State Univ, DEd 1978. **CAREER:** Lincoln Univ PA, asst to the pres 1971-73; PA State Univ, staff asst 1973-75; Woodrow Wilson Natl Fellowship Found, dir ad internship prog 1975-78, vice pres planning & devel 1978-79; Natl Med Fellowships Inc, pres 1979-. **ORGANIZATIONS:** Rep White House briefing on minority group policies & programs 1972; negotiator Lincoln Univ Faculty Coll Bargaining 1973; mem Amer Assoc of Higher Ed 1974-; elected mem Phi Delta Kappa 1975; invited participant Aspen Inst for the Humanistic Studies Exec Seminar 1978; mem Amer Mgmt Assoc 1978-; consult Acad for Ed Devel 1979-; bd of dir Urban League of Met Trenton Inc 1979-83. **HONORS/ACHIEVEMENTS:** Paper publ "A Theoretical Rational, The Gen Ed Concept for Comm Devel" 1978; Paper presentation "Funding and Preparation for Minority Grad Studies" 1979.

JOHNSON, LEROY
Military. **PERSONAL:** Born Oct 13, 1928, Independence, LA; married Simmie Mae Deloney; children: Leana Marie, Darlene Arnell, Leroy Jr. **EDUCATION:** San Francisco State Univ, BA 1956; Golden Gate Theological Sem, Master of Divinity 1963; Chapman Coll, MA 1974; KS State Univ, Dr of Philosophy 1981. **CAREER:** St James CME Church, pastor 1954-58; Davis Chapel CME Church, pastor 1958-63; AUS, chaplain 1963-. **ORGANIZATIONS:** Instructor Lay Council Oakland Dist CME Church 1958-63; dean leadership training sch Oakland Dist CME Church 1961-63; mem Free Masonry 1951-; mem NAACP 1954-; coord Chaplain Services CME Church 1974-; chaplain Dist 8 OK Jurisdiction 1984-; mem Prince Hall Military Consistory 1984-. **HONORS/ACHIEVEMENTS:** Bronze Star Medal Saigon Vietnam 1967; Army Commendation Medal Kaiserslautern Germany 1970; Meritorious Svs Medal Fort Gillem GA 1982; Legion of Merit Darmstadt Germany 1985; Republic of Viet Nam Galantry Cross with Palm Unit Citation; Navy Unit Commendation Medal; Asiatic-Pacific Campaign Medal; Parachute Badge. **MILITARY SERVICE:** AUS-USN col 33 yrs; Natl Defense Serv Ribbon; Viet Name Serv Ribbon; Army Serv Ribbon; Overseas Serv Ribbon; Viet Nam Campaign Medal; WW II Victory Medal. **BUSINESS ADDRESS:** Colonel, U S Army, Office of the Center Chaplain, PO Box 22, Fort Rucker, AL 36362.

JOHNSON, LEROY
College president. **CAREER:** Miles College, Birmingham, AL, president/chancellor. **BUSINESS ADDRESS:** Miles College, Birmingham, AL 35208. *

JOHNSON, LEROY REGINALD
Attorney. **PERSONAL:** Married Cleopatra. **EDUCATION:** BA 1949; MS 1951; LlB 1957. **CAREER:** Leroy Johnson Law, attorney offices; Atlanta Pub Sch System, instr 1950-54; Solicitor Generals Staff Fifth Judical Dist Atlanta, crim investigator 1957-62; 38th Dist Fulton Co GA, elected state senator 1962. **ORGANIZATIONS:** Chm Senate & Judiciary Com vP Fourth Cir of Am Law Students Assn; mem exec Com Atlanta Negro Voters League; bd dir Atlanta Inquirer; bd dir Campfire Girls Inc; exec com Atlanta Com for Coop Action; pres GA Assn of Citizens Dem Clubs; mem GA Bar Assn; vP Gate City Bar Assn; mem bd dir YMCA; Phi Beta Sigm; 33 Deg Mason. **HONORS/ACHIEVEMENTS:** Recipient Russwurn Award Nat Publ Assn 1962; Citizen of Year Award Omega Psi Phi 1963; Freedom Award MAACP 1963; Scottish Rite Mason of Year; Lovejoy Award IBPOEW 1963; apptd by Pres Johnson as Spec Ambassador to Independence Ceremonies in Zanzibar 1963. **BUSINESS ADDRESS:** Executive Dir, Atlantic Fulton Co Stadium Aut, 521 Capital One SW, Atlanta, GA 30312.

JOHNSON, LEROY RONALD
Educator. **PERSONAL:** Born Jan 25, 1944, Smithville, GA; married Martina Flintrop; children: Sean, Stephen, Sydney. **EDUCATION:** Univ of Caen France, Licence-es Lettres Ancient & Medieval History 1966-69; The Sorbonne Univ of Paris, Maitrise-es Lettres Medieval History 1971; Univ of MI, PhD African History 1981. **CAREER:** Inst St Jean-Eudes France, dir & teacher 1969-70; Inst St Joseph Paris, dir & teacher 1970-72; MI State Univ, instructor 1973-77; Univ of FL, asst prof history 1977-78; Bryn Mawr Coll, lecturer African Hist. **ORGANIZATIONS:** Reg officer French Fed of Basketball Coaches 1964-72; hon mem African Students Assoc France 1966-72, West Indian Students Assoc France 1966-72; lecturer Ctr for Afro-Amer & African Studies Univ of MI 1978-79; sr lecturer history Univ of Lagos Nigeria 1982-83; lecturer history Bryn Mawr Coll 1983-86. **HONORS/ACHIEVEMENTS:** French govt scholarship Caen, Paris France 1967-68, 1971-72; Natl Defense Foreign Lang Fellowship MI State Univ 1972-73; Rackham Fellowship Univ of MI 1973-75. **BUSINESS ADDRESS:** Lecturer African History, Bryn Mawr College, Thomas 202, Dept of History, Bryn Mawr, PA 19010.

JOHNSON, LESTER
Personnel administrator. **PERSONAL:** Born May 16, 1947, New Orleans, LA; married Sherelle Denise; children: Risha Lauriann, Damone VonZell, Henry Jr. **EDUCATION:** Mt San Antonio Coll, AA Sociology 1973; CA State Polytech Univ, BA Behav Sci 1975, MA Publ

Admin 1980. **CAREER:** California Dept of Corrections, parole agent/center mgr 1970-77; Chaffey Coll, instructor/coordinator, correctional sci 1977-78, dir affirmative action/EEO 1978-82, asst supt personnes serv 1982-85; Cerritos Coll, dir employer, remployer relation 1985-86; Monterey Peninsula Coll, admin dean, chief negotiator 1986-. **ORGANIZATIONS:** Capt human aware/eo CA Army Natl Guard 1981-; facilitator/instr Defense Mgmt Inst FL 1982-; bd of dir Chaffey Employees Fed Cr Union 1983-. **HONORS/ACHIEVEMENTS:** Most Outstanding Vietnam Vet City of Ontario. **MILITARY SERVICE:** Army NG capt 9 yrs; Bronze Star with "V" Device, Army Com, Good Conduct, Natl Guard.

JOHNSON, LINDA C.
Commissioner. **PERSONAL:** Born Oct 18, 1945, Chicago, IL; children: Ricardo II, Nicole. **EDUCATION:** No IL Univ, BS 1967; Cntrl MI Univ, Masters 1971; We MI Univ, Doctorate 1974; Purdue, Univ of OK,Univ of MI, Postgrad Work 1975-79. **CAREER:** Michigan Vctnl Rehab Svc, asst dist supr 1974-75, state cnsltnt 1975-79; Professional Psychological Cons, pres 1979-82; Grand Valley State Coll, dean 1979-84; MN Dept of Human Rights, commr. **ORGANIZATIONS:** Sub ofc supr MI Vctnl Rehab Serv 1972-74, cnslr 1971-72; law enfrcmnt agncy prjct adm YWCA 1969-71; pres Grand Rapids Bd of Educ 1982-84; vicepres Grand Rapdis Bd of Educ 1980-81; chmn Am Assn Hghr Educ Blck Caucus 1984-86. **HONORS/ACHIEVEMENTS:** Treas Natl Caucus of Blck Schl Bds 1982-; chmn MI Recpnt Rghts Comm 1978-79; Dstngshd Alumni Awrd Cntrl MI Univ 1979; Scroll of Dstnctn We MI Univ 1980; Phi Delta Kappa St Paul Chptr;Univ S Off of Ed Fellowship for the Managem of Ed Change. **BUSINESS ADDRESS:** Commissioner, MN Dept of Human Rights, 500 Bremer Tower, 7th Pl & MN St, St Paul, MN 55101.

JOHNSON, LIVINGSTONE M.
Judge. **PERSONAL:** Born Dec 27, 1927, Wilkinsburg, PA; married Leeburn; children: Lee Carol, Oliver Morris, II, Judith Lee, Livingstone James, Patricia Lee. **EDUCATION:** Howard Univ Wasngtn DC, AB 1949; Univ MI Law Sch,JD 1957; Coll of St Judiciary, Grad Nat 1973. **CAREER:** Johnson & Johnson Law Firm, ptnr 1957-73; Cnty Solctr, asst 1962-73; Fifth Jud Dist PA, judge 1973-. **ORGANIZATIONS:** Mem Amer Bar Assn; Amer Bar Found; Amer Judicature Soc; PA Bar Assn; Allegheny County Bar Assn; bd gov 1967-74, Pub Ser Com 1965-; assn trial lwyres in crim; Crt Allegheny Cnty Bar Assn; mem PA Conf of St Trail Jdgs; bd Dir St Peters Chld Dev Ctrs Inc; ARC; Boys Club Wstrn PA; Ile Elegba Inc; Bus & Job Dev Corp Comnty Relse Agcy; Azanan Strgs Inc; mem Grtr Ptsbrg Civ Lgue; BS of Amer; Omega Psi Phi; NAACP; Panel of Jdgs; past bd mdm NAACP 1962-68; Urbn Lgue 1963-68. **HONORS/ACHIEVEMENTS:** Louis Caplan Hum Rel Award 1975; honors Dist Flyng Cross; commdtn Medal; oak leaf. **MILITARY SERVICE:** USAF 1st ltn 1949-54. **BUSINESS ADDRESS:** Judge, Ct of Common Pleas 5th Judicia, Pittsburgh, PA 15206.

JOHNSON, LLOYD A.
Government official. **PERSONAL:** Born Aug 05, 1932, Boston, MA; married Constance Riley; children: Scott A, Alison E. **EDUCATION:** Howard Univ, BA 1954; Aldephi Univ, MSS 1957; Georgetown Univ Law Ctr, JD 1984. **CAREER:** Worked with troubled ind & families under public & private auspices, 1954-66; Local Comm Corps, exec dir 1966-69; Comm Dev Agency, dir evalutation & rsch 1966-69; Urban Ctr of Columbia Univ, dir 1969-74; US House of Representatives, subcomm on postal opers & svcs, labor counsel subcomm on labor. **ORGANIZATIONS:** Mem Acad of Certified Social Workers; mem Natl Bar Assn; mem Natl Assn of Social Workers; consult lecturer at various colleges & univs; certified socialworker NY State; bd dir Amer Orthopsychiatric Assn; Natl Assn of Soc Workers; Acad of Cert Soc Works. **HONORS/ACHIEVEMENTS:** Listed Who's Who Among Students in Amer Colls & Univs 1954; Outstanding Alumni Awd nominee Howard Univ. **HOME ADDRESS:** 1121 Holton Lane, Takoma Park, MD 20912. **BUSINESS ADDRESS:** Labor Counsel, Subcommittee on Labor, US House of Representatives, Washington, DC 20515.

JOHNSON, LONNIE L.
National director. **PERSONAL:** Born Dec 23, 1932, Hickory, MS; children: Derian, Jocelyn, Andrea, Lonnie II. **EDUCATION:** Roosevelt Univ Chicago, 1957 attended. **CAREER:** Chicago PO, 1962; began labor actities in 1963, shop steward, local vp, local pres; Mail Handlers Union , natl educ dir 1965; central reg reg, 1967; Postal Union, first black natl AFL-CIO pres 1969; Mail Handlers Union, first natl dir 1970; Johnson Consultant Co, labor consultant. **ORGANIZATIONS:** Mem NAACP; mem Urban League. **HONORS/ACHIEVEMENTS:** Key to City of New Orleans 1970; Key to City of Kansas City 1975; honored by a host of affiliated labor locals. **MILITARY SERVICE:** AUS corpl 1952-54. **BUSINESS ADDRESS:** Labor Consultant, Johnson Consultant Co, Chicago, IL 60616.

JOHNSON, LORNA KAREN
Administrator. **PERSONAL:** Born Mar 12, 1958, Washington, DC; daughter of Malcolm Johnson and Evangeline Richardson Johnson. **EDUCATION:** Adelphi Univ, BA 1980; Rutgers Univ School of Law, JD 1983; Rutgers Univ School of Regional & Policy Planning, MA. **CAREER:** Urban Tech Dept of City Planning, urban tech 1984-85; Pres, Urban League of Essex Co, 1983-. **ORGANIZATIONS:** Vice chmn, bd dir Jubilations Dance Co 1984-; mem, bd dir Big Brothers Big Sisters 1986-; vice chair, Woodson Foundation. **HONORS/ACHIEVEMENTS:** New Jerseyan of the Year, Star Ledger Newspaper; NY Times, Academy of Women Achievers. **BUSINESS ADDRESS:** Pres, Urban League of Essex County, 3 William St, Suite 300, Newark, NJ 07102.

JOHNSON, LORRAINE JEFFERSON
Retired educator. **PERSONAL:** Born Dec 07, 1918, King George Cty, VA; daughter of Robert W Jefferson (deceased) and Sadie Corey Jefferson (deceased); married Samuel D Johnson (deceased); children: Samuel D Jr, Susanne J Watson, Stanley D. **EDUCATION:** Howard Univ, BS 1940, MS 1942; Marquette Univ, Cert 1948; Univ of PA, Univ of Berkeley, Montgomery Jr Coll, 1968. **CAREER:** Howard Univ, lab instr 1943-47; Livingstone Coll, sci teacher 1943-47; Howard Univ, sci teacher 1950-53; Publ School Dist of Columbia, sci teacher 1954-80; Mayors Office, steering committee. **ORGANIZATIONS:** Life mem Alpha Kappa Alpha 1938-, pres, chmn nominating comm DC Chap 1972-75, chmn nominating comm North Atlantic Region 1982-85; mem of bd, chmn comm Hillcrest Childrens Ctr 1980-86; life mem Natl Council Negro Women; mem Amer Assoc Univ Women, DC Retired Teachers Assoc; bd of dir Phyllis Wheatley YWCA 1982-; bd mgrs Anthony Bowen YMCA 1984-; mem United Black Christians UCC; vice pres Women's Intl Religious Fellowship 1985-86; mem NRTA Howard Univ Alumni DC; asst treas Church Women United; moderator Lincoln Congregational Temple UCC; Ward 2 Repre DC State Comm 1988-91; pres Women's Intl Religious Fellowship 1987-89; treasurer Church Women United 1988-89; sec DC Retired Teachers Assn 1988-89. **HONORS/ACHIEVEMENTS:** Outstanding Biology Teacher Awd DC School; Outstanding Teacher Awd Jr Citizens Corp 1981; 5 natl sci found grants 1948-68; community volunter AARP-DC 1989. **HOME ADDRESS:** 1010 S St NW, Washington, DC 20001.

JOHNSON, LORRETTA
Business executive. **PERSONAL:** Born Oct 29, 1938, Baltimore, MD; married Leonard; children: Leonard Jr, Jeffrey, Kevin. **EDUCATION:** Coppin State Univ Baltimore MD, BS 1976. **CAREER:** Baltimore Tchrs Union, pres paraprofessional chap 1978-; Baltimore Tchrs Union, paraprofessional chirperson 1970-76; Baltimore City Pub Schs, paraprofessional 1965-70; Am Fedn of Tchrs, vP 1978. **ORGANIZATIONS:** Exec bd Met AFL-CIO 1978; conS research of Better Schs 1980. **HONORS/ACHIEVEMENTS:** Community Serv Award United Way campaigh 1976; Vol Serv Award MD State AFL-CIO COPE 1977; Meritous Achievemnt Award United Tchrs of New Orleans 1977; Meritous Achievement Award A Phillip Randolph Inst 1978. **BUSINESS ADDRESS:** 2533 St Paul St, Baltimore, MD 21218.

JOHNSON, LOUIS
Choreographer, director. **PERSONAL:** Born Mar 19, 1933, Stateville, NC. **EDUCATION:** Sch of Am Balled; Ballet Theatre; Met Belled; Katherine Dunham Sch & Ballet Russe. **CAREER:** Louis Johnson Dance Theatre, founder/Dir; Howard U, head dance dept; has danced, directed & choreographed on Broadway; Opera & Ballet Co;TV & motion pictures. **HONORS/ACHIEVEMENTS:** Recipient Tony Award; nomination of Broadway show "Purlie"; A&M Shawfer Award for Purlie.

JOHNSON, LOUIS W.
Episcopal priest. **PERSONAL:** Born Sep 13, 1903, New Haven, CT; married Winonah. **EDUCATION:** Howard U, AB 1933; Phil Div Sch, ThB 1936. **CAREER:** Chaplain Training Sch for Boys Warwidk NY, asst chaplain; St Phillips Indianapolis, vicar; St Marys Chester, Vicar; St Pauls No PA & Ascension W Chester;St Thomas Epis Minneapolis, rector; Parochial Schs, res lctr, bd edn; NAACP, pres & vP interdenoml; Minst ALL; TCOIC in Twin Cities, co-fndr. **ORGANIZATIONS:** Bd mem Minneapolis Cncl of Chs; bd Urban League; bd Travelers Aid Soc; ed edn, chrmn Negro Ch Fund. **HONORS/ACHIEVEMENTS:** Ecumenical Soc Awards YMCA; Minstl Assn; Minneapls mayor; State Gov.

JOHNSON, LOUISE MASON
Educator. **PERSONAL:** Born Jun 20, 1917, Franklin, VA; married Tracy Owen Johnson. **EDUCATION:** NC Coll Durham, 1936-37; Shaw Univ, BA Elem Educ 1960-63; Kittrell Coll, night course. **CAREER:** Dr SM Beckford, secretary 1941-59; Franklin Co Schools, teacher 1963-67; Vance Co Schools, teacher 1967-82. **ORGANIZATIONS:** Charter former mem/pres/newspaper reporter/typist/sec of The Aster Garden Club over 40 yrs; mem of The Urban-Suburban Garden Club; deacon/pres Presbyterian Women-Cotton Meml Presbyterian Ch (mem 40 yrs); mem Retired Teachers Assn of NC; free-lance typist; typing teacher; donates time and knowledge of typing for churches and other organizations. **HONORS/ACHIEVEMENTS:** Cert of Appreciation from church and former schools; Cert of Merit from Vance Co Schls Henderson, NC; Hon Lt Gov to and for the Great State of NC to uphold good govt (appointed by Jimmy Green); Cert from the NC Assn of Educators (Retirement Cert); Silver-brass Plates from Eaton-Johnson Student Body Vance Co Schools for Dedicated Svc. **HOME ADDRESS:** 715 Powell St, Henderson, NC 27536.

JOHNSON, LUCIEN LOVE
Physician. **PERSONAL:** Born Dec 26, 1941, New Orleans, LA; children: Lucien III, Kimberly, Yewande. **EDUCATION:** Purdeu U, BS 1962; Howard U, MD 1966. **ORGANIZATIONS:** AMA; Nat Med Assn; CA Med Assn; Am Assn of Black. **HONORS/ACHIEVEMENTS:** Cardiologist publs 2 articles. **MILITARY SERVICE:** AUS capt 1966-67. **BUSINESS ADDRESS:** 3756 Santa Rosalia Dr, Los Angeles, CA 90008.

JOHNSON, LUTHER MASON, JR.
Educational administrator. **PERSONAL:** Born Nov 23, 1930, Brooklyn, NY; son of Luther Mason Johnson, Sr. and Constance Anglin Johnson; married Joan C Arrington; children: Lori H Luis, Luther III, Lance K. **EDUCATION:** Pratt Inst, city & regional planning; New York City Comm Coll, AAS Construction Tech 1959; NY Univ, BS Indus Arts Educ 1966, MA Higher Educ Adm in 1970. **CAREER:** St Univ of NY Urban Ctr, coord of business affairs 1966-69, dir 1968-70; New York City Comm Coll, dean 1970-84; New York City Tech Coll, prof 1973-86, vice pres of admin 1984-86 (retired); Facilities Mgmt Consultant, pres. **ORGANIZATIONS:** Trustee Episcopal Found for Educ 1976-; bd mem New York City Tech Coll Found 1980-; mem 100 Blk Men of NY 1978-; mem Am Soc of Cert Eng Tech 1972-; wrdn St Philips Episcopal Church Brooklyn 1975-. **HONORS/ACHIEVEMENTS:** Distinguished Alumnus Award New York City Comm Coll 1983; Professor Emeritus conferred February 1, 1986. **MILITARY SERVICE:** AUS Signal Corps cprl 1951-53. **HOME ADDRESS:** 1404 Union St, Brooklyn, NY 11213. **BUSINESS ADDRESS:** President, Facilities Mgmt Consultant, 1404 Union St, Brooklyn, NY 11213.

JOHNSON, MAL
Journalist. **PERSONAL:** Born Jul 04, 1924, Philadelphia, PA; daughter of Bishop Hooser and Johnnie Hooser; widowed. **EDUCATION:** Temple Univ; Brookings Inst, Economics in Journalism. **CAREER:** Cox Broadcasting Corp, dir comm affairs 1973-; Washington sr corr, 1972-; COX Broadcastinc Corp, 1st famale natl corr 1970; WKBS-TV; Coffee Break, host;Lets Talk About It; Dialing for Dollars Movie, 1966; traveled Africa served radio &TV coord consult 1974; produced documentaries Europe, Middle E, Israel; WAMU FM-TV, monthly guest reporter "Overseas Mission"; WA Workshops Congressional Sem, lectr communications; Mt Vernon Coll, guest lectr; Military Schools in England, Guam, teacher 1954-60; Cox Enterprises, dir community relations, sr correspondent. **ORGANIZATIONS:** Pres Task Force Minorities & Women; bd dir Am Women in Radio & TV ch of bd Educ Found; bd mem Urban Market Developers; past pres WA Chap Am Women in Radio & TV; chmn AWRT Study Tours; chmn AWRT Intl Broadcasters Prgm; mem US House of Reps US Senate Radio & TV Corr Asso; mem White House Corrs Assn; US Dept of State Corrs Assn; mem NAACP; Urban League; Philadelphia Fellow Somms; Mideast Areas Trustee AWRT; YWCA; bd dir Natl Womens Conf Comm; chmn Intl Broadcast Study Tours to China Far

East Europe Scandinavian Countries; commissioner UNESCO; bd of dir UNIFEM. **HONORS/ACHIEVEMENTS:** USN Comm Serv Award 1969; USN Recruiting Serv Award 1970; 2000 Outst Women of the World Award 1970; Dist Serv Award Dayton OH 1972; commend part in Presidential visit to Austria USSR, Iran, & Poland 1972; Outst Female Decision Maker of Yr 1974. **BUSINESS ADDRESS:** Dir Community Relations, Cox Enterprises, Broadcast Division, 400 N Capital St, Washington, DC 20001.

JOHNSON, MARGUERITE M.
Educational administrator. **PERSONAL:** Born Sep 23, 1948, Wilmington, DE; daughter of Norris R Milburn (deceased) and Elizabeth Milburn; married George Stephen Johnson, Aug 1971; children: Stephanie M, Stephen M. **EDUCATION:** Morgan State Univ, Baltimore, MD B.A., 1966-70; Indiana Univ of PA, Indiana, PA, M.Ed. 1976; Temple Univ, Philadelphia, PA Ed.D., 1987. **CAREER:** Delaware Technical & Comm Coll, Stanton-Wilmington Campuses, dir of continuing educ 1979-; Delaware Technical & Comm Coll, Stanton-Wilmington Campuses, acting dir of continuing educ 1979; Delaware Technical & Comm Coll, Stanton Camapus, asst dir of continuing educ 1975-79; Delaware Technical & Comm Coll, Stanton Campus, acting asst dir of continuing educ 1973-75; Delaware Technical & Comm Coll, Northern Branch, gen educ devel instructor/coordinator 1970-73. **ORGANIZATIONS:** Assn of Black Women in Higher Educ (ABWHE) Natl Bd Mem/Philadelphia Chapter Treasurer; Assn of Black Admin; Northeast Regional Council of Black Amer Affairs (NE/NCBAA) Bd Mem/Vice Pres for Programs (A Council of the AACJC); Neighborhood Youth Achievement Program, Bd Mem (Philadelphia). **HONORS/ACHIEVEMENTS:** Irene Diggs Award, Morgan State Univ 1970; The perceptions of Community Coll Admin and Industrial Mgrs Concerning Factors that Potentially Facilitate or Impede the Implementation of Exemplanary Partnerships, 1987. **BUSINESS ADDRESS:** Dir of Continuing Educ, Delaware Tech & Comm College, 400 Stanton-Christiana Rd, Newark, DE 19702.

JOHNSON, MARIE ELIZABETH
Educator & executive administrator. **PERSONAL:** Born Jun 03, 1948, New York City, NY; daughter of Wilmer T Johnson and Emily L Johnson; married Warren R Colbert; children: Warren Jr. **EDUCATION:** West VA State Coll, 1966; Howard Univ, BA Ed 1970. **CAREER:** Washington DC Public Schools, teacher 1969-70; Bonwit Teller/Retail, assoc buyer 1970-74; The Gap Stores, mgr 1974-76; Pierre Cardin/Gallant, sales rep 1977-79; Lester Hayatt, vice pres 1980-82; Special Concepts, pres, instructor; 1982-85; Articolo Inc, pres, 1986-87 LW Assoc, Inc NYC pres 1988-. **ORGANIZATIONS:** Volunteer NY School for the Blind 1965-66; mem NY Urban League, NAACP; interm Consumer Distribution Committee NY Urban League 1969; college bd B Altman & Co 1969; instructor/lecturer Lab Inst Merchandising 1977-; mem The Fashion Group Garment Mfg Org 1978-; coll summer intern program volunteer Urban League 1989-89. **HONORS/ACHIEVEMENTS:** Written articles US Mag, NY Daily News, NBC Dallas 1980, Black Enterprise 1981; Black Designer Awd L Hayatt 1980-81; Client of the Year Interacial Council Bus Opportunity 1983; guest appearance Fox Broadcasting Network NYC 1985. **BUSINESS ADDRESS:** President, LW Assoc, Inc, PO Box 391, New York, NY 10116.

JOHNSON, MARIE LOVE
Consultant. **PERSONAL:** Born Dec 18, 1925, South Bend, IN; married Arthur. **EDUCATION:** IN Univ, BS 1951; Univ of Hrtfrd, MEd 1953; Univ of CT, PhD 1978. **CAREER:** East Hrtfrd Bd of Educ, spch path 1949-60, supr 1960-77; Shadybrook Lang & Learning Ctr, clin dir 1971-76, exec dir 1977-78. **ORGANIZATIONS:** Pres JGM Corp 1971-78; mem clin & cert bd Am Spch & Hrng Assn 1969-75; vice pres Am Spch & Hrng Assn 1977-78; pres CT Spch & Hrng Assn 1971-75; pres Hrtfrd Alumnae Chptr Delta Sigma Theta 1954-56; bd of fin Town of Vernon 1963-65; chmn bd of mgrs YMCA 1976-78. **HONORS/ACHIEVEMENTS:** Comm serv Delta Sigma Theta 1966; fellow Am Spch & Hrng Assn 1972; honors CT Spch & Hrng Assn 1970; tribute lnchn CT Spch & Hrng Assn 1975 . **HOME ADDRESS:** 78 Warren Ave, P O Box 2026, Vernon-Rockville, CT 06066.

JOHNSON, MARION I.
Architect, business executive. **PERSONAL:** Born Oct 16, 1915, Longview, TX; married Crozet; children: Francis M, Carol Ann. **EDUCATION:** Prairie View A&M U, BS 1938;Univ of Md, 1959; Fed Exec Inst, 1972; Advanced Guided Missile Sch, 1960. **CAREER:** H & J Home Improvement Co, architect & pres; Div of Contracts US Atomic Energy Commn, asst dir 1971-74; Logistic US Atomic Engery Commn, dep asst dir 1969-71; AID US Dept of State, spl asst to the asso asst adminstr 1967-69; AID US Dept of State, asst to dir mgmt 1963-66; Air Defence Missile Battalion, commanding officer 1962; Nat Security Agy, dir mgmt & tech staff 1955-60; WV State Coll, asst prof of millitary sci & tactics 1951-53; Hurelco Land & Devel Corp, pres 1963-70. **ORGANIZATIONS:** Chmn bd Hurelco Land & Devel Corp 1971-; vP No VA Fair Housing Inc 1962-66; vice-chmn Urban League No VA Chap 1969-71; bd mem VA Council on Human Relations 1964-73; pres & alexandria VA Council on Human Relations 1970-73; chmn Minority Housing Com City of Alexandria 1966-73; mem spl com Planning& Zoning City of Alexandria 1965; mem planning adv commn City of Alexandria 1972-78; life mem NAACP. **HONORS/ACHIEVEMENTS:** NAACP Award Nat Capital Area Nat Conf Christian & Jews 1974; City of Alexandria Award 1973; Comm Leader of Am Award 1969; VA State Council on Human Relations Award 1973; Bronze Stat Medal for Valor 1945; Oak Leaf Cluster to Bronze Star Medal for Maritious Serv 1954; Army Commendation Medal 1962. **MILITARY SERVICE:** AUS lt col 1942-63.

JOHNSON, MARION T.
Business executive. **PERSONAL:** Born Jan 22, 1948, Chicago, IL. **EDUCATION:** Chicago State Univ, BS 1968; Kent State Univ, MA 1970; OH State Univ, PhD 1975. **CAREER:** OH Gen Assembly, leg analyst 1973-74; OH State Univ, asst prof, proj dir 1977-80; Dept of Health & Human Svcs, spec asst to reg dir 1980-81; Performance Systems Assoc, exec vice pres 1981-. **ORGANIZATIONS:** Consult Dept of Ed 1977-, Black Coll & Univ 1977-; bd of dir Youth Advocate Serv 1977-80, Natl Assn for Blacks in Vocational Ed 1977-80; consult Dept ofHealth & Human Serv 1981-; bd of dir Martin Luther King Ctr 1982-, Park South YMCA 1984-; consult Dept of Commerce 1985-. **HONORS/ACHIEVEMENTS:** Mayors Awd for Voluntary Serv 1978; Commendation from OH Gen Assembly for Voluntary Serv 1978; Listed in Who's Who in the Mid-West 1979; Dept of Health & Human Serv Fellow 1980-81; Outstanding Young Woman of Amer 1980. **HOME ADDRESS:** 3659 Stables Ln, Dallas, TX 75229. **BUSINESS ADDRESS:** Executive Vice President, Performance Systems Assoc, PO Box 29594, Dallas, TX 75229.

JOHNSON, MARLENE E.
Government official. **PERSONAL:** Born Jul 01, 1936, Milwaukee, WI; married Ben E Johnson; children: Jan, Paula, Jay. **EDUCATION:** Univ of WI Milwaukee, BS 1979. **CAREER:** Boston Store, saleswoman 1954-64; WXIX-TV Channel 18 Milwaukee,TV hostess 1962; Milwaukee Public Sch System, social improvement instr 1966-70; First WI Natl Bank, teller 1973-75; City of Milwaukee, alderman 1980-84. **ORGANIZATIONS:** Bd of dirs Bookfellows-Friends of the Milwaukee Pub Lib 1976-80; bd dir Milwaukee Symphony Orches 1977-80; pres Women's Aux of the Milwaukee Courier 1975-76; div leader YWCA Leader Luncheon 1977; lifetime mem NAACP 1980; century mem Boy Scouts of Amer Milwaukee Banner E Div 1974-75; bd dir vice chmn MECCA; vice pres bd dir Milwaukee United Way; mem Milwaukee Redevelop Auth; mem bd dir Milwaukee Convention & Visitors Bureau; mem OIC-GM; mem Pabst Theater Bd of Dirs; vice pres Milwaukee Area Tech Coll Bd Dirs; mem Natl League of Cities Comm & Economic Develop Steering Comm; vice pres WI League of Municipalities 6th Senate Dist. **HONORS/ACHIEVEMENTS:** Quota Buster Awd YMCA Milwaukee 1975; Women in Our Lives 1978; Milwaukee Women Today 1979; Mayoral Proclamation 1985; Milwaukee Realist Presidential Awd 1986. **BUSINESS ADDRESS:** Alderwoman, City of Milwaukee, 200 E Wells St, Room 205, Milwaukee, WI 53202.

JOHNSON, MARQUES LAVELLE
Professional athlete. **PERSONAL:** Born Feb 08, 1956, Nachitoches, LA; married Jocelyn; children: Kristaan, Josiah, Marques Kevin. **EDUCATION:** UCLA, 1977. **CAREER:** Milwaukee Bucks, 1977-84; Los Angeles Clippers, forward 1984-. **ORGANIZATIONS:** Honorary chmn City of Hope's annual Bike-a-Thon 1985. **HONORS/ACHIEVEMENTS:** 1st recipient John R Wooden Awd; 1st Team NBA All-Star in 1979 & earned Second Team honors 1980 & 1981; was mem of the NBA'S All-Rookie Team 1978; named Collegiate Player of Year 1977 at UCLA; also named Pac-Eight Player Of Year 1976-77; was named prep All-Am as well as All-State & All-Western League for 2 yrs atCrenshaw High Sch in Los Angeles; mem 36th NBA All Star Team. **BUSINESS ADDRESS:** Los Angeles Clippers, 3939 S Figueroa St, Ste 510, Los Angeles, CA 90037.

JOHNSON, MARTIN LEROY
Educator. **PERSONAL:** Born Dec 31, 1941, Westminster, SC; son of James C Johnson and Beatrice W Johnson; married Jo Ann Clinkscales; children: Yolandra, Martin II. **EDUCATION:** Morris Coll Sumter, SC, BS 1962; Univ of GA Athens, GA, MEd 1968, EdD 1971. **CAREER:** Anderson, SC, math tchr 1962-67; Univ of GA, grad asst 1967-71; Rutgers Univ New Brunswick, assist prof/math education 1971-72; Univ of MD-College Park, assist, assoc and full professor of education 1972-89. **ORGANIZATIONS:** Cnsltnt Natl Sci Fndtn 1984-85; vice pres Rsrch Cncl for Diagnstc & Prscrptv Math 1978-80; pres MD Cncl Tchrs of Math 1985-86; program dir Nat'lScience Found 1985-86, summer 1987; chair, Research Advisory Committee, Natl Council of Teachers of Mathematics 1988-89. **HONORS/ACHIEVEMENTS:** Fulbright Schlr Nigeria 1983-84; book - Guiding Each Child's Learning of Math - Char Merill 1983; articles- journal for research in mathematics education The Arithmetic Teacher and NCTM publications; Distinguished Minority Faculty Member , Univ of Maryland College Park 1985. **BUSINESS ADDRESS:** Professor, Univ of MD, College of Education, College Park, MD 20742.

JOHNSON, MARY BEATRICE
Government, civil service. **PERSONAL:** Born Jul 25, 1952, Edwards, MS; daughter of Robert J Johnson, Sr and E Lorean Marshall Johnson (deceased). **EDUCATION:** Utica Jr Coll MS, AA Business Admin 1972; Alcorn State Univ Lorman NJ, BA Business Admin 1974; Univ of MN, MBA 1977; Alcorn State Univ, MS Agr Economics 1983. **CAREER:** Agriculture Dept Alcorn State, rsch asst 1982-83; Dept of Defense, contract negotiator 1984-. **ORGANIZATIONS:** Mem NAACP, Heroines of Jericho, Amer Fed of Govt Employees, Intl Training in Commun; Natl Council of Negro Women, 1988. **HONORS/ACHIEVEMENTS:** Featured in April 1985 Ebony Magazine; appeared in Woman's World, Sunbelt & MS Farm Bureau Magazine; Natl Dean's List 1983; Presidents List 1982, 1983; Master's Thesis Topics Upward Mobility of Black Workers, "The Rise of the Black Manager" 1977, "The Economic Impact of Bechtel Power Corp 1983, Claiborne Cty MS, A Study of Change in Selected Factors 1973-83. **HOME ADDRESS:** 3B Richland Ln #205, Camp Hill, PA 17011.

JOHNSON, MATTIEDNA
Registered nurse. **PERSONAL:** Born Apr 07, 1918, Amite County, MS; daughter of Isaac Johnson and Minnie Johnson Ramsey; divorced; children: Bobby Lou, Robert Jr, Patricia E, Frances M Kelley. **EDUCATION:** Jane Terrell Memorial Hospital School of Nursing, RN 1940; Northwest Institute of Medical Technology, MT 1943; Ashland Theological Seminary, MA Divinity 1987. **CAREER:** Greater Cleveland-Ohio State ANA, private duty nursing 1959-87; Home Nursing, Church Nursing, teacher 1960-. **ORGANIZATIONS:** Consecrated Diocanal Minister United Methodist Church 1986. **HONORS/ACHIEVEMENTS:** Be Involved Nurse Award Greater Cleveland Nurses 1974; 50 Year Pin American Red Cross 1985; Pioneer Award NBNA 1986; Living Legacy Award NCCBA 1986; Merit Award presented by Congressman Oaker 1986.

JOHNSON, MELVIN RUSSELL
Physician, military. **PERSONAL:** Born Aug 26, 1946, Courtland, VA; married Joyce. **EDUCATION:** Hampton Inst, BA 1968; Meharry Med Coll, MD 1972. **CAREER:** Wm Beaumont Army Med Ctr, staff pulmonologist, asst ch pulmonary disease 1980; Womack Army Hosp, chf dept med 1977-80, chf pulmonary disease 1976-77,staff intern 1976; Brooke Army Med Ctr, resd intern med 1972-73; Cape Fear Valley Hosp, asso staff internist 1975-77. **ORGANIZATIONS:** Mem Omega Psi Phi Frat 1971; Nat Assn Resd & Interns 1972; asso mem Am Coll Phys 1973; mem CA Whittier Med Soc 1973; Nat Med Assn 1974; AMA 1975; Med Lincensure GA 1973; TX 1974; NC 1975; VA 1977. **HONORS/ACHIEVEMENTS:** Recpt Nat Defense Ribbon 1972; Flwshp Pulmonary Diseases Brooke AMC 1978-80. **MILITARY SERVICE:** AUS mc lt col 1975-.

JOHNSON, MERTHA RUTH
Educator. **PERSONAL:** Born in Jackson, MS; children: Victoria M. **EDUCATION:** Jackson State Univ, BS 1956; Univ of San Francisco, MEd 1977, MPA 1983. **CAREER:** Chicago School System, educator 1960-66; East Chicago School System, educator 1967-70; Manpower Training Program, administrator/teacher 1966; OICW, administrator/teacher; San Mateo School Dist, educator 1970-81; Neighborhood Housing Servs, exec dir 1982-83; Atlanta School System, instructor. **ORGANIZATIONS:** Parlimentarian Natl Council of Negro Women; mem Business & Professional Women's Club; mem Atlanta Federation of

Teachers, NAACP, SCIC; consultant, Literacy Project Black Cacus, GA State Legislature; Atlanta's Ministry to International Students. **HONORS/ACHIEVEMENTS:** Lecturer/consultant Multicultural Educ & Black History; author "Black History Study Manual"; publication "A Study of the Leadership Factors Involved in the Operation of a Successful Neighborhood Housing Program"; selected poetry; Oak Tree Award, Outstanding Teacher of the Year. **BUSINESS ADDRESS:** Instructor Humanities Magnet, Atlanta School System, 45 Whitehouse Dr SW, Atlanta, GA 30314.

JOHNSON, MERVIL V.
Business executive. **PERSONAL:** Born Dec 20, 1953, Fort Worth, TX. **EDUCATION:** TCU, BA Spanish/French 1976; Universite de Nice France, business school 1976-77; TX Christian Univ, M Pub Admin 1982. **CAREER:** City of Fort Worth, admin asst 1978-79; City of Fort Worth-Library, spanish/french instructor 1980-83; North Central TX Council of Govts, reg clearinghousecoord 1980-84; ICMA Retirement Corp, service rep 1984-. **ORGANIZATIONS:** Chmn univ liaison Urban Mgt Assts of N TX 1982-84; chmn newsletter Conf of Minority Public Admin 1983-84; mem Phi Sigma Iota Soc of Languages 1975-; mem Intl City Mgt Assn 1981-; mem Amer Soc for Public Admin 1981-. **HONORS/ACHIEVEMENTS:** ITT Fellow Intl Teleph & Teleg 1976-77; Clarence E Ridley Scholar TX City Mgt Assn 1980-81; ICMA scholarship Intl City Mgt Assn 1981; NCTCOG Urban Fellow N Central TX Council of Govts 1980-82. **BUSINESS ADDRESS:** Service Representative, 5116 Libbey Ave, Fort Worth, TX 76107.

JOHNSON, MICHAEL ANTHONY
Science educator. **PERSONAL:** Born Jan 15, 1951, New York, NY; children: Dieynaba. **EDUCATION:** New York City Tech Coll, AA 1971; City Coll of NY, Pre-Med 1973; Empire State Coll, BS Sci Educ 1985. **CAREER:** DMC Energy, consultant 1981-84; Energy Task Force, science writer 1982-83; New York City Tech Coll, rsch project 1983-84; Science Skills Ctr Inc, exec dir 1980-. **ORGANIZATIONS:** Pres Student Alumni Assoc Empire State Coll 1982-86; mem NY Acad of Scis, Amer Assoc for Advancement of Sciences. **HONORS/ACHIEVEMENTS:** Positive Father of the Year Awd 1984; Outstanding Young Amers 1985; Clark Fellow in Science & Math Educ Columbia Univ 1986-; Outstanding Achievements in Comm PHNC 1986; Professional Awd Natl Assoc Negro Bus & Professional Women 1987; Recognition Awd Women's League of Science & Medicine 1987. **BUSINESS ADDRESS:** Executive Dir, Science Skills Center Inc, PO Box 883, Brooklyn, NY 11238.

JOHNSON, MICHAEL KEVIN
Civil service engineer. **PERSONAL:** Born May 28, 1960, Frankfurt, Federal Republic of Germany;married Pamela Ann Jones. **EDUCATION:** NC State Univ, BSEE 1983. **CAREER:** Naval Mine Warfare Engrg Activity, electronics engr. **ORGANIZATIONS:** Mem bd of dirs Cooperating Hampton Roads Organ for Minorities in Engrg (CHROME) 1984-. **HOME ADDRESS:** 1326 Peabody Dr, Hampton, VA 23666.

JOHNSON, MICHELE
Sales representative. **PERSONAL:** Born Aug 12, 1959, Brooklyn, NY. **EDUCATION:** Boston Univ, BS 1981; Attending, Fordham Univ. **CAREER:** CBS Inc, clippings coord 1981-82, admin asst 1982-83, sr sales asst 1983-86; JP Martin Assoc Inc, exec asst 1986-87; Taylor Made Press, sales rep. **ORGANIZATIONS:** Mem CBS Black Employees Assoc 1981-86, Natl Assoc of Black MBA's 1986-, Assoc of MBA Execs 1986-, Advtg Club of NY 1986-; dir Union Bapt Church Youth Comm 1986-; volunteer Roosevelt Ctr for Comm Growth 1987-. **HOME ADDRESS:** 148 Elmwood Ave, Roosevelt, NY 11575.

JOHNSON, MICKEY E.
Professional athlete. **PERSONAL:** Born Aug 31, 1952, Chicago, IL; married Diana; children: Wallace Jr, Michelle. **EDUCATION:** Aurora Coll. **CAREER:** Portland Trail Blazers, forward; Chicago Bulls, forward; IN Pacers, forward; NJ Nets, forward; Warriors, forward. **HONORS/ACHIEVEMENTS:** NAIA All-Amer Squad Aurora Coll.

JOHNSON, MILTON D.
Business executive. **PERSONAL:** Born May 27, 1928, Sour Lake, TX; married Robbie Russell; children: Paula, Pamela. **EDUCATION:** Paul Quinn Coll, BBA 1951. **CAREER:** Union Carbide Corp, employee rel asso 1964-; Victoria TX, tchr 1956-64. **ORGANIZATIONS:** Mem bd educ LaMarque IN Schs 1972-; chmn adv bd First State Bank Hitchcock TX; pres C of C 1974. **MILITARY SERVICE:** AUS 1951-53. **BUSINESS ADDRESS:** PO Box 471, Texas City, TX 77590.

JOHNSON, MINNIE REDMOND
Retired educator. **PERSONAL:** Born Feb 27, 1910, Clarksville, TN; daughter of Dr Robert L Redmond and Julia Thomas Redmond; married Dr E Milton Johnson (deceased). **EDUCATION:** Fisk Univ, BA, 1932; Atlanta Univ, BLS, 1944; Univ of Chicago, MA, 1945. **CAREER:** Memphis Public School teacher, 1933-37; Atlanta Univ School of Library Serv, instructor, 1945-46; Fisk Univ, asst Librarian 1946-49, 1950-52, acting librarian, 1949-50; Hampton Inst, head librarian, 1952-58; Chicago State Univ, head catalog dept, head of library office campus center, Reference Librarian; acting dir, 1958-73; Chicago State Univ, head of library, Crane branch, 1958-65, reference librarian, Main Library 1965-66, head librarian West Center 1966-69, cataloger Main Library 1970-72, head of catalog dept 1972-73, acting dir of libraries 1973-74. **ORGANIZATIONS:** Dir, Hampton Book Fair, Sponsored by Children's Book Council of NY; AAUW Hampton Public School & Hampton Inst Library, 1956-58; work through retired Sr Volunteer Program (Hull House affiliate) with Amer Public Works Assn & Blind Serv Assn, 1985-. **HONORS/ACHIEVEMENTS:** Authored, "Standards for Coll Libraries", published in Coll & Rsch Libraries, 1959; Coll-Comm Book Fair, Publishers Weekly, 1956; Some Observations on Faculty/Library Relations, VA Librarian, 1958.

JOHNSON, MIRIAM B.
Businesswoman. **PERSONAL:** Born in Washington, DC; married Norman B. **EDUCATION:** Miner Tchrs Coll Wash DC; Brooklyn Coll, cum laude 1972. **CAREER:** Black Musicmakers Inc, exec dir; Husband's Law Office, office mgr. **ORGANIZATIONS:** Active comm worker for over 25 yrs; vol sec for Brooklyn Br NAACP; mem bd dir Brooklyn Assn for Mental Health; mem exec board of Brooklyn Nureau of Comm Serv for over 7 yrs; chrprsn Mental Health Com of Health Sys Agency Dist Bd; mem Urban Commn of Episcopal Diocese of Long Island; parliamentarian historian of Brooklyn Lawyers Wives; prog chairperson of Gr NY Links Inc; former mem Comm Relations Com of Central YWCA; exec board Stuyvesant Comm Cntr during era of gang wars in the 40's & 50's; gen chairman of City Wide Com of Looking Glass Ball a fund raising play ball for the construction & devel of Mac Donough St Comm Cntr in Bedford-Stuyvesant. **HONORS/ACHIEVEMENTS:** Recepient for comm serv from Berean Bapt Ch 1950's & 1974; NY Amsterdam News; Mac Donough St Comm Cntr in 1963; awarded baccalaureate degree in Sociologycum laude. **BUSINESS ADDRESS:** 79 Decatur St, Brooklyn, NY 11216.

JOHNSON, MONTE CHARLES
Professional athlete. **PERSONAL:** Born Oct 26, 1951, Denver, CO. **EDUCATION:** Oakland Raiders,Univ NE linebacker 2nd round draft pick 1973. **HONORS/ACHIEVEMENTS:** AFC Champ Game 1974-77; NFL Champ Game 1976.

JOHNSON, NATHAN
Evangelist/educator. **PERSONAL:** Born Dec 07, 1944, Lexington, MS; married Regina Bullock; children: Stanley, Darius. **EDUCATION:** Rust Coll, BS 1968; Univ So MS, grad studies 1971-72. **CAREER:** YMCA Campus Rust Coll, pres 1966-68; Pine County Business League, pres 1975-78; Networks Tutoring Inc, pres/founder 1985-; the Exodus Broadcast (radio prog), exec dir 1986-; Christian Rsch & Learning, pres. **ORGANIZATIONS:** Vice pres Southwest Times Inc (newspaper) 1978-81; church comm NAACP 1984; chmn We Care Prison Ministeries 1985-; bd mem Natl Conf for Pioneering BlackAmerica 1985-; founder/dir Vine & Branches Food Coop 1985-; exec dir Pike Co Business League. **HONORS/ACHIEVEMENTS:** Million Dollar Roundtable The Equitable Ins Co 1982-83. **HOME ADDRESS:** PO Box 1052, McComb, MS 39648.

JOHNSON, NORMA HOLLOWAY
Judge. **PERSONAL:** Born in Lake Charles, LA; married Julius A Johnson. **EDUCATION:** DC Teachers Coll, BS 1955; Georgetown Univ Law Ctr, JD 1962. **CAREER:** Dept of Justice, trial atty 1963-67; District of Col, asst corp counsel 1967-70; Superior Court of DC, judge 1970-80; US Dist Court for Dist of Col, district judge 1980-. **ORGANIZATIONS:** Fellow Amer Bar Fndn; dir Natl Assoc of Black Women Attorneys; dir Natl Childrens Center; mem Amer Judicature Soc; Ntl, Amer Washington Bar Associations; Natl Assoc of Women Judges. **BUSINESS ADDRESS:** District Judge, US Dist Court for Dist of Col, 2315 US Courthouse, Washington, DC 20001.

JOHNSON, NORMAN B.
Attorney. **PERSONAL:** Born in Lake Charles, LA; married Julius A. **EDUCATION:** GeorgetownUniv Law Ctr, JD 1962; DC Tchrs Coll, BS 1955. **CAREER:** Superior Ct of DC, judge 1970-; DC, asst corp counsel 1967-70; Dept of Justice, trial atty 1963-67. **ORGANIZATIONS:** Dir Am Judicature Soc; dir Nat Assn of Women Judges; Nat Assn of Black Women Attys; Nat Bar Assn; Wash Bar Assn; Am Bar Assn. **BUSINESS ADDRESS:** 79 Decatur St, Brooklyn, NY 11216.

JOHNSON, NORMAN J.
Educator. **PERSONAL:** Born Sep 08, 1919, Cape Girardeau, MO; married Helen Louise Watkins; children: Michael Oliver. **EDUCATION:** KY State Univ, AB 1941; Univ MI, MA 1947, EdD 1959. **CAREER:** Lancaster Public Sch, tchr 1941-42; Xavier Univ, chmn dept health & physical educ 1948-49; Bluefield State Coll, 1950-56; Prairie View A&M Coll, 1956-63; Lincoln Univ, chmn dept phys educ & athletics 1963-. **ORGANIZATIONS:** Mem Amer & MO Assns Health Phys Educ & Recreation; exec coun Black Educ Coun Human Svcs; asst dist commr BSA; personnel com GSA; ARC; NAACP. **HONORS/ACHIEVEMENTS:** Outstanding Leadership Awd Alpha Kappa Alpha; Merit Hon Awd BSA; Who's Who Poland; Who's Who Educ 1956; Outstanding Ldrs Educ; Ldrs Amer Edn. **MILITARY SERVICE:** AUS 1st lt 1942-46. **BUSINESS ADDRESS:** Chmn Dept Phys Educ & Ath, LincolnUniv, Jefferson City, MO 65101.

JOHNSON, NORRIS BROCK
Professor. **PERSONAL:** Born Apr 29, 1942, Chicago, IL; divorced. **EDUCATION:** MI State Univ, BA English 1965, MA English 1967; Univ of MI, MA Anthropology 1971, PhD Anthropology 1976. **CAREER:** Dept of Anthropology Univ of NC, asst prof 1980-85, assoc prof 1985-. **ORGANIZATIONS:** Rsch in Japan and China on Zen Buddhist temple architecture and landscape gardens; faculty assoc Natl Humanities Faculty 1980-; fellow Amer Anthropological Assoc 1980-; mem Assoc ofBlack Anthropologists; bd mem Soc for Humanistic Anthropology. **HONORS/ACHIEVEMENTS:** Spencer Foundation Grant 1980; book "West Haven"; 22 articles and chapters in books; Fulbright Lecturer 1985-86 Univ of Tokyo and Waseda Univ Tokyo Japan. **BUSINESS ADDRESS:** Assoc Prof of Anthropology, Univ of North Carolina, Chapel Hill, NC 27514.

JOHNSON, OLENDRUFF LEREY
Physician. **PERSONAL:** Born Oct 22, 1956, Los Angeles, CA. **EDUCATION:** Baylor Univ, BS 1977; Meharry Medical Coll, MD 1981. **CAREER:** Howard Univ Hosp, int med residency 1981-84; Nacogdoches Memorial Hosp, emergency room physician 1984-. **ORGANIZATIONS:** Assoc mem Amer College of Physicians 1981-; mem Amer Coll of Emergency Physicians 1981-. **BUSINESS ADDRESS:** Emergency Room Dir, Nacogdoches Memorial Hospital, PO Box 7350, Longview, TX 75607.

JOHNSON, ONETTE E.
College president. **CAREER:** Prentiss Institute Junior College, Prentiss, MS, president/chancellor. **BUSINESS ADDRESS:** Prentiss Institute Junior College, Prentiss, MS 39474. *

JOHNSON, OTIS SAMUEL
Educational administrator. **PERSONAL:** Born Mar 26, 1942, Savannah, GA; son of Otis Johnson and Lillian Brown Spencer; divorced. **EDUCATION:** Armstrong State Coll, AA 1964; Univ of GA, AB 1967; Atlanta Univ, MSW 1969; Brandeis Univ, PhD 1980. **CAREER:** City of Savannah Model Cities Program, deputy director, 1969-71; Simmons College of Scoial Work, special instructor, 1975-76; Savannah State College, assistant professor, 1976-80, associate professor, 1901-87, professor, 1987—, head department of social science, 1980-84, head department of social work, 1985-88, professor of social work and sociology, 1987—; City of Savannah, alderman 1982-88; commissioner, Housing Authority of Savannah, 1989—.

ORGANIZATIONS: Member, Acad of Certified Social Workers 1971-; secretary, Georgia Chapter, Natl Assn of Social Workers 1984-86; member, Assn for the Study of Afro-Amer Life & History, Central Baptist Church Trustees, Savannah Sickle Cell Committee, Alpha Kappa Delta Sociological Honor Soc, Pi Gamma Mu Social Sci Honor Frat; Georgia Cancer Advisory Comm; board of directors, Natl Council of Community Mental Health Centers; board member, NAACP, Girls Club of Savannah, Royce Center for Learning Disabilities; American Legion. **HONORS/ACHIEVEMENTS:** Social Worker of the Year SE GA Unit of NASW 1984. **MILITARY SERVICE:** US Navy, 1959-62, received honorable discharge; Naval Reserve, 1962-65. **BUSINESS ADDRESS:** Post Office Box 20537, Savannah State College, Savannah, GA 31404.

JOHNSON, PAM MCALLISTER
Business executive. **PERSONAL:** Born Apr 14, 1945, McAlester, OK; married Donald Johnson; children: Jason, Dawn. **EDUCATION:** Univ of WI-Madison, BS 1967, MA 1971, PhD 1977. **CAREER:** Chicago Tribune, news reporter 1967-68; WISM Radio Madison, reporter & interviewer 1969-71; WIMJ Milwaukee, news announcer 1969; Capital Times Madison, news reporter/feature writer/columnist 1972; WI State Journal Madison, freelance feature writer 1972; WISC Madison, reporter/announcer 1971-73; CBS Network News Chicago Bureau, rscher/reporter 1973; Univ of WI Telecomm Unit, dir of ethnic production unit 1977-79; WI Regional Magazine, editor 1979; The Ithaca Journal, asst to the publisher 1981, publisher. **ORGANIZATIONS:** Mem Natl Assn of Black Journalists; mem natl Assn for Educ in Journalism; mem NY State Publishers Assn; mem Amer Newspaper Publishers Assn; mem NYState Publishers Newspaper Found; mem Zonta's Intl Women's Organ; mem Downtown Prof Women's Organ; bd of dirs WCNY Public TV; mem Kingston Artists Group; bd of dirs Tompkins Co Chamber of Comm; bd of dirs Tompkins Co United Way; mem pres council St Bonaventure Univ; bd of dirs Security Trust Co; mem-adv bd Natl Youth Comm Bd; mem S Tier Regional Economic Develop Council; mem Assoc for Educ in Journalism; mem NY State Human Rights Advisory Council; mem Women in Communications; mem Soc of Prof Journalists; mem ASNE Minority Comm. **HONORS/ACHIEVEMENTS:** Judge Governor's Empire State Women of the Year Awd 1984; judge Pulitizer Prize Awds 1985. **BUSINESS ADDRESS:** Publisher, Ithaca Journal, 123 W State St, Ithaca, NY 14850.

JOHNSON, PARKER COLLINS
Educator. **PERSONAL:** Born Oct 17, 1961, Boston, MA; son of John Q Johnson and Addie Collins Johnson. **EDUCATION:** Williams College, BA 1984. **CAREER:** Fitchburg State Coll, asst dir of admissions 1984-85; Bentley Coll, asst dir of admissions 1985-87; asst dir of admisions Tufts Univ Medford MA 1987-89; graduate student Harvard Univ Cambridge MA 1989-90. **ORGANIZATIONS:** Mem Natl Assoc of College Admissions Counselors 1984-; mem Greater Boston Interuniversity Counsil 1985-; vice pres bd dirs Fitchburg Comm Action Ctr 1985; mem-at-large New England Consortium of Black Admissions Counselors 1985-; volunteer Boston Youth at Risk 1986-; external co-chair, on New England Consortium of Black Admissions Counselors Inc 1987-89; mem American Assn of Higher Education 1987-; bd mem Massachusetts Pre-Engineering Program 1988-; mem Trans Africa Inc Boston Chapter 1989-. **HONORS/ACHIEVEMENTS:** Outstanding Community Service Award, African Amer Center, Tufts Univ, 1989. **HOME ADDRESS:** PO Box 441239, Somerville, MA 02144.

JOHNSON, PATRICE DOREEN
Journalist. **PERSONAL:** Born Jul 17, 1952, New York, NY; daughter of Wilbourne Johnson and Irma Levy Johnson. **EDUCATION:** Barnard Coll, BA 1974; Columbia Univ Grad Schof Journalism, MSJ 1976. **CAREER:** Dauntless Books, asst editor 1974-75; Encore Am & Worldwide News, assoc editor 1976-80; Newsweek Magazine, researcher/reporter 1981-. **ORGANIZATIONS:** Panelist Am's Black Forum TV show 1978-79; mem Natl Alliance of Third World Journalists 1980-85. **BUSINESS ADDRESS:** Researcher/Reporter, Newsweek Magazine, 444 Madison Ave, New York, NY 10024.

JOHNSON, PATRICIA ANITA
Educational administrator, director. **PERSONAL:** Born Mar 17, 1944, Chicago, IL; children: David, Todd. **EDUCATION:** Oberlin Coll, BA 1961; Graduate School for Comm Devel, Fellowship 1982-83; US Intl Univ, MFA Candidate 1985. **CAREER:** Brockman Gallery Productions, curator 1976-78; New Visions Gallery, owner 1978-82; Multicultural Arts Inst, curator 1982-83; San Diego Comm Coll Dist, cultural affairs coord 1982-85; South Dallas Cultural Center City Arts Prog, dir 1985-. **ORGANIZATIONS:** Exhibition consultant Multicultural Arts Inst 1981-83; grant recipient CA Arts Council 1983-85; mem Catfish Club of San Diego 1983-85; adv comm San Diego Arts Festival Bd 1985; bd mem City of San Diego Public Arts Adv Bd 1985; founder INROADS an organ of Black Professional Singles 1985. **HONORS/ACHIEVEMENTS:** Achievement in Fine Arts Awd City of Los Angeles 1978; Achievement in Fine Arts San Diego Black Achievement Awds 1985; Comm Serv Awd San Diego Chap NAACP1985. **BUSINESS ADDRESS:** Dir, South Dallas Cultural Center, 1925 Elm St, City Arts Prog - Majestic Thea, Dallas, TX 75201.

JOHNSON, PATRICIA DUMAS
Educator & elected official. **PERSONAL:** Born Aug 12, 1950, Memphis, TN; married Lloyd G Johnson; children: Lloyd Timothy; Lila Victoria. **EDUCATION:** TN State Univ, BS Math 1973; Univ of IL Chicago, attending. **CAREER:** 3-M Co, indust engr 1973-78; Ford Motor Co, indust engr 1978-79; Sears Roebuck & Co, indust engr 1979-85; Bellwood School Dist #88, bd mem 1983-; Computerized Business Svcs, president. **ORGANIZATIONS:** Panelist Chicago Youth Motivation 1974-78; mem Delta Sigma Theta Sor 1979-; vice pres Parent Teachers Assoc 1981-83; Cosmopolitan C of C. **HONORS/ACHIEVEMENTS:** Image Awd Fred Hampton Scholarship 1982; Editor School Dist 88 Newsletter 1982; mem Black Caucus Natl School Bd Assoc 1984; Outstanding Woman of Amer 1985. **BUSINESS ADDRESS:** President, Computerized Business Services, Catfish Digby's West, 2135 S 17th Ave, Broadview, IL 60153.

JOHNSON, PATRICIA DUREN
Insurance company executive. **PERSONAL:** Born Oct 22, 1943, Columbus, OH; daughter of James Duren and Rosetta J Duren; married Harold H Johnson, Jr, Dec 25, 1965; children: Jill Johnson. **EDUCATION:** Ohio State Univ, Columbus, BS Educ, 1965; Univ of Michigan, Ann Arbor, Grad School Mgmt, 1984. **CAREER:** Teacher in Long Beach CA, San Bernardino CA, Cincinnati OH, Thetford Village UK, 1966-72; ITT Hartford, Portland OR, sales rep, 1972-73; Blue Cross of CA, Woodland Hills CA, sr vice pres, 1975-. **ORGANIZATIONS:** Bd dir, Amer Cancer Society, 1988-; mem, Amer Hosp Assn, 1976-; mem, Women in Health Admin, 1979-; mem, pres, Delta Sigma Theta Soroity (OSU), 1964-65. **HONORS/ACHIEVEMENTS:** Author of ABC's of Medicare, 1976; author of How Kids Earn Money, 1978; Women of Achievement, YWCA, 1979; NAACP/LDEF Black Woman of Achievement, 1987; One of 10 Corp Black Women, Essence Magazine, 1989. **BUSINESS ADDRESS:** Senior Vice President, Blue Cross of California, PO Box 70000, Van Nuys, CA 91470.

JOHNSON, PATRICIA L.
Lawyer. **PERSONAL:** Born Jan 29, 1956, New York, NY; daughter of Mamie Johnson. **EDUCATION:** John Jay Coll of Criminal Justice, BA 1977, MA 1979; Cornell Univ Sch of Law, pre-law prog 1978; Rutgers Sch of Law Newark, JD 1985; Office of Court Admin NY Frontline Leadership Certificate l988. **CAREER:** Bureau of Alcohol Tobacco & Firearms, student aide 1977; US Rsch Svcs, branch mgr 1979-82; Bronx Family Court, notifications supervisor 1982-83; Bronx Dist Attorney's Office, legal asst 1983-85; Judicial Friends, law intern 1985; Bronx District Attorney's Office, asst dist atty 1985-86; Bronx Public Admin Office, assoc counsel l986-88; Walter Kaitz Foundation Fellowship finalist l989. **ORGANIZATIONS:** Mem Black Women Attorneys 1981-; mem Natl Bar Assoc 1983-; mem Phi Alpha Delta Law Frat Intl 1983-; mem Professional and Business Women 1985-, NAACP 1985-, Natl Women's Political Caucus 1985-, Black Entertainment and Sports Lawyers Assoc 1986-; recording sec Black Bar Assoc of Bronx County 1986-; corresponding sec/chair program bd Black Bar of Bronx l987-89; exec dir & founder Black Entertainment & Sports Tribune l989-; Big Sister, The Big Sisters, Inc. l989. **HONORS/ACHIEVEMENTS:** Outstanding Achievement w/Distinction Rutgers Women's Rights Reporter 1985; Assoc of Black Law Students Serv to Black Comm 1985; moderator Entertainment & Sports Law Forum Black Bar Assoc of Bronx Cty 1987; battling the motion picture assoc of Amer movie rating of "The White Girl" published in NY Law Journal l988. **HOME ADDRESS:** GPO, Box 813, Bronx, NY 10451.

JOHNSON, PAUL EDWIN
Director. **PERSONAL:** Born Dec 27, 1933, Buffalo, NY; son of Maggie J Johnson; married Shirley Ann Williams; children: Paula Rene, Darryl Edwin. **EDUCATION:** Talladega Coll AL, AB (Psych) 1955; Harvard Univ, MA, MS (Psych) 1957; Hartford Semnry Fndtn, CT, Master-Dvnty 1958; Auburn Univ, MEd (Couns Psy) 1974, EdD (Counc Psy) 1980. **CAREER:** N Cngrgtnl Ch NYC, NY, asso mnstr 1958-62; US Army, chpln (ltc, ret) 1962-72; AL Dept MH & MR, cnsltnt III-MR div 1972-79, dir qlty assrnc-MR Div 1979-; Pvt Pract, psychlgst & mnstr; 1st Cngrgtnl-Chrstn Ch Montgomery, AL, 1980-. **ORGANIZATIONS:** Bd dir Montgomery Council on Aging 1982-84; chmn Lgsltv Strke Frc Am Mntl Hlth Cncl Assn 1983-84; pres AL Mntl Hlth Cnslrs Assn 1983-84; cnsltnt AL Dept of Pub Safety-Acad 1983-85; cnsltnt AL Cncl on Hghr Educ (HBC's) 1984-85; exec comm Montgomery Area United Way 1984-86; mem AL Bd of Examiners in Counseling 1986-90. **HONORS/ACHIEVEMENTS:** Delta Phi Kappa, Alpha Phi Alpha; Who's Who in South & Southwest 1980; Who's Who in Religion 1983. **MILITARY SERVICE:** AUS chpln (ltc, ret) 21 yrs; Silver Star; Bronze Star (3); Meritorious Svc; Army Comm Med (3) 1962-72; Air Medal (3), Vietnamese Cross of Gallantry; Master Parachutist Badge. **HOME ADDRESS:** 118 Elm Dr, Montgomery, AL 36117. **BUSINESS ADDRESS:** Dir Quality Assurance, AL Div of MR, Dept of MH & MR, 200 Interstate Pk Dr Box 3710, Montgomery, AL 361935001.

JOHNSON, PAUL L.
News photographer. **PERSONAL:** Born Oct 27, 1943, Savannah, GA; married Angelyne Russell; children: Monifa Ife, Ayeola Binta. **EDUCATION:** Matriculated Savannah State Coll; Univ of Ghana; Univ So IL; Univ of FL. **CAREER:** Acad Black Culture as dir Savannah Model Cities Cult Ctr 1969-72; prof three free TV pub serv progs 1971-72; Acad of Black Culture Inc, co-founder; KTUL-TV, news photographer. **ORGANIZATIONS:** Bd dir Inner City Comm Ctr 1970-72; art instr local cap agency EOA 1970; slide lectures Savannah State Coll, pub schs & libraries; mem PUSH, ASALH & NAACP. **HONORS/ACHIEVEMENTS:** Yr scholarship Omega Psi Phi 1961; One man show-paintings Savannah State Coll 1967; designed covers for Expression 1969 & Expression 1970; poems published Expression 1970; co-prod Black radio prog 1970-72; guest poet GA Poetry Soc 1971; one man show photo Savannah State Coll 1972; Outstanding Young Man of AmerAwd 1972. **MILITARY SERVICE:** AUS spl 5 1967-68. **BUSINESS ADDRESS:** KTUL-TV, PO Box 8, Tulsa, OK 74101.

JOHNSON, PAUL LAWRENCE
Elected official. **PERSONAL:** Born Sep 23, 1931, Coatesville, PA; married Dorothy Elizabeth Flowers; children: Bruce Michael, Darryl Lawrence. **EDUCATION:** St Paul's Coll, 1950-53. **CAREER:** Lukens Steel Co, shearman, 1957-63; estimator, 1963-70; Timestudy Tech, 1970-84; Coatesville City Council, pres 1980-85; Supreme Court of PA, district justice 1985-. **ORGANIZATIONS:** Bd mem Credit Union Lukens 1972-; pres Trustees of Hutchinson Church 1972-; pres Lancaster Co Chap Credit Unions 1984-; bd Coatesville Sr Citizens Ctr 1983-, United Way 1987. **HONORS/ACHIEVEMENTS:** Outstanding Comm Serv Award, J Frederic Wiese 1984. **MILITARY SERVICE:** AUS corpl 1954-56. **HOME ADDRESS:** 514 Elm St, Coatesville, PA 19320.

JOHNSON, PHYLLIS CAMPBELL
Government official, administrator. **PERSONAL:** Born Jul 21, 1954, Fort Worth, TX; daughter of Mira G Campbell and Ann Miller Campbell. **EDUCATION:** Univ of Texas, Arlington TX, BA Communication, 1979, MA Urban Affairs, 1984. **CAREER:** Texas Instruments, Dallas TX, manufacturing supervisor, 1979-82; City of Fort Worth TX, human services coordinator, 1984-87, administrative asst, 1987-88, fiscal services administrator, 1988-. **ORGANIZATIONS:** Mem, Neighborhood Advisory Council, 1983-; mem, Urban Management Asst of North Texas, 1984-; mem, Texas Municipal League, 1985-; mem, Network for Executive Women, 1985-; sec, North Texas Conference of Minority Public Administrators, 1986-87; vice pres ntc, Natl Forum for Black Public Administrators, 1987-88; mem, Tarrant County League of Women Voters, 1987-88; mem, NAACP; mem, Fort Worth Metropolitan Black Chamber of Commerce; mem, Minority Leaders and Citizens Council. **HONORS/ACHIEVEMENTS:** Kappa Delta Pi Honor Society, Univ of Texas at Arlington, 1979-; Urban Fellowship Recipient, North Central Texas Council of Governments, 1984; Notable Woman of Texas, Awards and Honor Society of America, 1984-85; Outstanding Young Women of America, OYWOA, 1986; Leadership Fort Worth Award, Fort Worth Chamber of Commerce, 1988. **BUSINESS ADDRESS:** Fiscal Services Administrator, City of Fort Worth, 2222 West Rosedale, Park and Recreation Bldg, Fort Worth, TX 76110.

JOHNSON, PHYLLIS MERCEDES (NEE SYDNOR)
Retired business executive. **PERSONAL:** Born Apr 17, 1919, Hutchinson, KS; married James P Johnson; children: Beverly. **EDUCATION:** Lincoln Univ, BS 1941; Washington Univ, MA 1965; So IL Univ, attended 1967-68. **CAREER:** Teacher home econ, 1942-46; MO Div of Empl Sec, dist mgr 1951-79. **ORGANIZATIONS:** Mem Alpha Kappa Alpha; past pres St Louis Personnel & Guid Assn; mem MO Personnel & Guid Assn; NAACP; Urban League; Intl Assn Personnel in Empl Sec; AAUW. **HONORS/ACHIEVEMENTS:** Merit Awd St Louis Personnel & Guid Assn 1973.

JOHNSON, POMPIE LOUIS, JR.
Business executive. **PERSONAL:** Born Dec 19, 1926, Pocatello, ID; son of Pompie L Johnson, Sr and Nellie B Johnson; married Marylynn T Hughes; children: Tamara, Karen. **EDUCATION:** ID St Univ, BA 1950; Boston Univ Sch of Law, JD 1952; Am Svngs & Loan Inst, Diploma 1967; Am Inst of Bnkng, Diploma 1971. **CAREER:** Boston MA, atty 1952-55; Mutual of Omaha Ins Co, sls & Clms 1956-60; Golden State Mutual Life Ins Co, plng spclst 1960-62; Safety Svngs & Loan Assn, vice pres-mgr 1963-66; Security Pacific Natl Bank, (1st blk mgr) vice pres-mgr 1967-72; CA Fed Svngs & Loan Assn, vice pres corp svngs 1973-. **ORGANIZATIONS:** Bd of dir Watts CA Econ Dev Comm 1973-76; bd of dir Inglewood CA Chmbr of Comm 1975-78; bd of dir Inglewood CA Mrchnts Assn 1975-78 ; bd of dir Gardena CA Econ Dev Comm 1983-; asst treas CA State Rep Cntrl Comm 1974-78; pres SW Los Angeles Rotry Clb 1979-80. **HONORS/ACHIEVEMENTS:** Delegate/mem Perm Org Comm Rep Natl Conv 1972; delegate Rotry Intl Conv Rome, Italy 1979; Unsung Hero Awrd LA Sntnl Nwspr 1972; Rotarian of Yr Los Angeles Rtry 1982. **MILITARY SERVICE:** USAF cprl 1945-46. **BUSINESS ADDRESS:** Vice President, CA Fed S & L Assn, PO Box 18934, Los Angeles, CA 90018.

JOHNSON, R. BENJAMIN
Administrator. **PERSONAL:** Born Aug 07, 1935, Marion, AR; son of Robert L Johnson and Willie B Clay Johnson; married Jacqueline Vassar Johnson, Dec 06, 1975; children: Rahman, Endesha, Jua, Sekon. **EDUCATION:** Attended, Indiana Univ, Antioch Coll, Tufts Univ, Prince George's Comm Coll Mgmt Inst. **CAREER:** WSBT TV South Bend IN, news reporter and host afternoon talk show; Action Inc, dir of employment; Manpower Assistance Program, manpower specialist; Youth Advocacy Program, dir 1971-73; St Joseph County Credit Union, mgr/treasurer 1975-77; Credit Union Inst Natl Center for Urban Ethnic Affairs, dir 1977-79; The White House Office of Consumer Affairs, dir of consumer programs/special asst to consumer advisor to the pres 1979-81; Natl Credit Union Admin, special asst to the chmn of the bd 1981-82; Black Resource Guide Inc, pres 1981-; Dept of Consumer & Regulatory Affairs Washington, administrator business regulation admin 1983-87, administrator housing & environmental regulation admin 1987-88; special asst to the mayor, 1988-89 (Washington, DC); Dept of Public and Assisted Housing, Washington, DC, deputy dir, 1989-. **ORGANIZATIONS:** Chmn The South bend Black Voters Assn; vice pres Valley Chapter of Credit Unions; chmn St Joseph County CETA Advisory Bd; has held elected positions in 20 professional civic and social orgs; publisher, The Black Resource Guide. **HONORS/ACHIEVEMENTS:** Distinguished Serv Award; Outstanding Professionals Award Business Exchange Network 1987; publications New Credit Union Mgmt Systems 1969, The Community Development Credit Union 1977,1979 editions, The Black Resource Guide 1981-89 editions. **MILITARY SERVICE:** AUS 2nd lt; Honorable Discharge. **BUSINESS ADDRESS:** Deputy Dir, DC Govt/Dept of Public & Assisted Housing, 1133 N Capitol, Washington, DC 20001.

JOHNSON, RAFER LEWIS
Athlete, actor, business executive. **PERSONAL:** Born Aug 18, 1935, Hillsboro, TX. **EDUCATION:** UCLA, AB 1959. **CAREER:** Rafer Johnson Enterprises, owner; Continental Tel Corp, vice pres com rel; NBC-TV, sportscaster. **ORGANIZATIONS:** Involved in Robt Kennedy's pres camp; active pres Council Physical Fitness Spcl Olympics. **HONORS/ACHIEVEMENTS:** Gold Medal, 1955 Pan Am Games; Silver Medal, 1956 Olympics in Australia; gold Medal, Olympic Decathalon Champion, Rome 1960; Athlete of Yr; Sullivan Trophy, AAU; films include "Sins of Rachel Cade", "Wild in the Country", A Global Affair", "The Games", "Soul Soldier"; sev TV appearances. **BUSINESS ADDRESS:** Rafer Johnson Enterprises, 8101 Orion Ave, Ste #6, Van Nuys, CA 91406.

JOHNSON, RALPH C.
Certified public accountant. **PERSONAL:** Born Dec 04, 1941, Pittsburg, TX; married Nadine; children: Stacie. **EDUCATION:** Oakwood Coll, BS 1964; Wichita State Univ, MS 1967. **CAREER:** Fox & Co Kansas City, staff accountant 1964-71; AL A&M Coll, assoc prof bus adminstr 1967-68; Ralph C Johnson & Co, founder 1971-. **ORGANIZATIONS:** Licensed CPA KS 1966, MO 1971; mem Amer Inst of CPA's. **BUSINESS ADDRESS:** Founder, Ralph C Johnson Co, 825 North 7th St, Kansas City, KS 66101.

JOHNSON, RALPH V.
Security service executive. **CAREER:** Lance Investigation Service Inc, Bronx, NY, chief executive. **BUSINESS ADDRESS:** Lance Investigation Service Inc, 1438 Boston Rd, Bronx, NY 10460. *

JOHNSON, RANDALL MORRIS
Educational administrator. **PERSONAL:** Born Nov 21, 1936, Chicago, IL; married Marva J Goldsmith; children: Terri A, Christopher L. **EDUCATION:** Northern IL Univ, BS 1958, MS 1959; Univ of Chicago, PhD (TTT Fellow) 1975. **CAREER:** Northwestern Med Sch, lab tech 1958; Phillips HS, teacher 1959-69; Kennedy King Coll, prof biology 1969-76, chmn natl sci math dept 1970-76, dean of arts & sci. **ORGANIZATIONS:** Super MAT Grad Stud in Sci 1970-72; super Student Teach N IL Univ 1971-72; consul Sci Dist #22 Chicago Bd of Educ; dir Cosmopolitan Comm Chuch Choir 1970-85; bd mem Gospel Arts Workshop Inc 1979-85; mem Chicago Council Fine Arts 1983, 1984; dir Voices of Melody Inc 1980-82; mem Alpha Phi Omega 1955-; mem Phi Mu Alpha 1956-; bd of dir ECC Music Workshop of Chicago 1988-89; dir Kennedy-King Community Chorus 1985-; dir St John Church-Baptist 1988-. **HONORS/ACHIEVEMENTS:** TTT Fellowship Univ of Chicago 1969; Guest Conductor Chicago Musician Assoc Messiah 1979; Outstanding Choir Dir Chicago Musicians Assoc 1979; Outstanding Educator Ora Higgins Foundation 1980; Hon mem Phi Theta Kappa Lambda Rho Chap 1983; Outstanding Achievement Awd Natl Assoc of Negro Musicians 1986; "Freedom Symphony"- a musical drama of the African American Experience 1986; Outstanding Achievement R N Dett Musicians Assoc 1989. **HOME ADDRESS:** 7342 S Euclid Ave, Chicago, IL 60649. **BUSINESS ADDRESS:** Dean of Arts & Sciences, Kennedy King College, 6800 S Wentworth Ave, Chicago, IL 60621.

JOHNSON, RAY
Business executive. **PERSONAL:** Born Dec 13, 1935, Port Gibson, MS; married Marcia Ann; children: Raymond Bradley, Fredrick Norman. **CAREER:** McDonald's Corporation, natl oper adv bd; McDonald's Restaurants, owner-operator of 9 stores; Ray Johnson Enterprises Inc, president & ceo. **ORGANIZATIONS:** AZ State Athletic Comm, chmn-commissioner 1981-83; Round-One Production, president 1983-86; AZ State Liquor Comm, chmn 1983-; City of Phoenix Civil Service Comm, commissioner 1986-; Chairman Regional Operator Advisory Board McDonald's Onwer/Operator 1989. **HONORS/ACHIEVEMENTS:** Phoenix AZ Human Resource Businessman of the Year 1980; AZ & US Small Businessman of the Year 1984. **MILITARY SERVICE:** USAF 4 years. **BUSINESS ADDRESS:** President & CEO, Ray Johnson Enterprises Inc, 6711 N Black Canyon Hwy, Phoenix, AZ 85105.

JOHNSON, RAYMOND L.
Attorney. **PERSONAL:** Born Jul 31, 1922, Providence, RI; married Evelyn Allen; children: Raymond L. **EDUCATION:** Univ WA DC, BS; HowardUniv Law, JD; Rochester Gen Hosp, med tech 1951. **CAREER:** Mathew C Long, gen prac law; All Cts of CA, admtd to prac 1964; Grp Hlth Assn, asst lab supr 1953-56; Cedars of Lebanon Hosp, med tech; Mt Sinai Hosp, med tech; Univ Hosp, chf med tech 1957-61; Advanced Bio-Chem Lab, asst med lab supr; US Congressman Edward R Roybal, spl asst 1962-68. **ORGANIZATIONS:** Chmn Hosp Hlth & Welfare Com Westside br NAACP; mem Hlth Cncl & Med-Legal Consult Watts-U So CA; gen counsel W Adams Comm Hosp; apptd by State Bar of CA to State Bar of CA Com to confer with CA Med Assn; licensed lab tech; Nat Adv Hlth Cncl; med-legal Coins CA Bar; arbitrator Am Arbitration Asszn; mem Judge Pro Tem panel of LA Mun Ct; adminstr Small Bus Devel Ctrs; AMA; LA Trial Layers Assn; State Bar of CA Jucicial Com; Am Arbitration Assn; Fed Ofc of Econ Oppty; mem Law Ofc Mgmt Com LA Co Bar Assn; LA Town Club; Am Soc of Hosp Attys. **HONORS/ACHIEVEMENTS:** Dem cand US Congressman 1968; alumni award HowardUniv 1961; guest spkr Pres's Nat Adv Commn 1967; attended White House Civil Rights Conf 1966; del AmBar Assn 1956; cand LA City Cncl. **MILITARY SERVICE:** USAF Air Force Cadet Pilot 1943-45. **BUSINESS ADDRESS:** 3756 Santa Rosalia Dr, Ste 315, Los Angeles, CA 90008.

JOHNSON, RAYMOND L.
Chief of police. **PERSONAL:** Born Apr 20, 1936, Arkansas; son of Grady Johnson and Lucy Johnson; children: Ava. **EDUCATION:** CA State Univ Sacramento, BA; State of CA, lifetime teaching credential. **CAREER:** Bakersfield CA, police dept; CA Highway Patrol, chief southern div; City of Inglewood Police Dept, chief of police. **ORGANIZATIONS:** Pres Peace Officers Assn of Los Angeles County; mem CA Peace Officers Assoc, CA Police Chiefs, Inter-Agency Chief Officers, Intl Assoc of Police Chiefs, Los Angeles County Police Chiefs Assn, South Bay Police Chiefs, Amer Mgmt Assoc, Natl Org of Black Law Enforcement Exec, Los Angeles-Lusaka Zambia Sister City Comm, Senate Task Force on Child Abuse, Natl Criminal Justice Assoc, Assoc of Black Law Enforcement Exec, CA Dist Atty Assoc; bd dir Oscar Joel Bryant Assoc; dir Homer Garrott Scholarship Found; bd of advisors Los Angeles Child Passenger Safety Assoc; honorary bd mem Amer Cancer Society; Assn of Black Law Enforcement Executives; Amer Mgt Assn; Automobile Club of South CA, Traffic Safety Advisors Program; past mem Boy Scouts of Amer Task Force; past member of State Task Force on Gangs and Drugs, CA Council on Criminal Justice; CA District Attorneys Assn; representative/accreditation task force CA Peace Officers Assn; CA Police Chiefs Assn Inc; Homer Garrott (retired judge) Scholarship Foundation, director; Independent Cities Assn of LA County; Inglewood Coalition on Alcohol and Drugs; Inter-Agency Chief Officers; Intl Assn of Police Chiefs mem of Narcotics and Dangerous Drugs Committee; Loved Ones of Homicide Victims, bd mem; LA Child Passenger Safety Assn bd mem; LA County Police Chiefs Assn; Natl Assn of Blacks in Criminal Justice; Natl Criminal Justice Assn; Natl Organization of Black Law Enforcement Executives chairman of Awards Committee 1989; Oscar Joel Bryant Assn bd of directors; Peace Officers Assn LA County past pres current bd mem, chairman Uniform Reporting Committee on Gangs; Police Foundation; Police Mgt Assn; Senate Task Force on Child Abuse past mem; South Bay Police Chiefs/Criminal Justice Admn Assn. **HONORS/ACHIEVEMENTS:** Hon mem Special People Involved in Community Endeavors. **MILITARY SERVICE:** USMC. **BUSINESS ADDRESS:** Chief of Police, City of Inglewood Police Dept, 1 Manchester Blvd, Inglewood, CA 90301.

JOHNSON, RAYMOND LEWIS
Educator. **PERSONAL:** Born Jun 25, 1943, Alice, TX; married Claudette Willa Smith; children: Malcolm Patrice. **EDUCATION:** Univ of TX (Phi Beta Kappa, Phi Kappa Phi), BA 1963; Rice Univ, PhD 1969. **CAREER:** Univ of MD, asst prof 1968-72, assoc prof 1972-80; Inst Mittag-Leffler, vstng mem 1974-75; Howard Univ, prof 1976-78; Univ of MD, prof of Math 1980. **ORGANIZATIONS:** Vstng prof McMaster Univ 1983-84; edtrl comm Am Math Soc 1982-86. **HONORS/ACHIEVEMENTS:** Wghtd estimates for frctnl pwrs of prtl dffrntl operator Trans Am Math Soc 1982; Application of Carleson measures to PDE 1983 Springer Lectr Notes #992, p16-72; distinguished Minority Faculty 1986. **HOME ADDRESS:** 6916 Woodstream Ln, Seabrook, MD 20706. **BUSINESS ADDRESS:** Professor of Mathematics, Univ of MD, Dept Math, College Park, MD 20742.

JOHNSON, REBECCA M.
Retired educator. **PERSONAL:** Born Jul 10, 1905, Springfield, MA; daughter of William D Johnson and Harriet B Johnson. **EDUCATION:** Fisk Univ, BA 1927; Attended, Northwestern Univ 1934, Springifeld Coll 1943; Columbia Univ, MA 1948. **CAREER:** Columbia SC Public School Dept, elem teacher 1927-35; Charleston SC Educ 24 Hr Camp for Unemployed, dir 1935; Columbia SC Public School Dept, jr high math teacher 1935-43; Springfield MA Public School Dept, jr high math teacher 1943-46, principal of 4 different elem schools 1947-75 (retired); Visiting Lecturer, Mount Holyoke College, Springfield College, American International College. **ORGANIZATIONS:** Life mem Springfield NAACP Bd 1960-89; bd of dirs Springfield Tech Comm Coll; bd mem Springfield Child Guidance Clinic Inc 1985-89; co-chair Scholarship and Educ Resource Network of Urban League 1985-89; mem Alpha Kappa Alpha Sor; mem Delta Kappa Gamma Hon Soc Women Educators; chmn scholarship comm St John's Congregational Church; mem Black-Jewish Dialogue Committee; mem John Brown Archives Committee, St John's Church. **HONORS/ACHIEVEMENTS:** Woman of the Year Harambee Holiday 1975; Black History Awd in Field of Educ Trailblazers US Post Office 1987; Woman of the Year B'Nai Brith Springfield Chapt; Educ Awd for First Black Public School Principal Springfield; Human and Comm Serv Awd Springfield Muslim

Mission; Dedicated Serv Awd as board mem Springfield Tech Comm Coll awarded by MA Bd of Regional Comm Colls; Award for Spirit and Dedication to Freedom 350 years of Black presence in MA, Museum of Afro-Amer History. **HOME ADDRESS:** 215 Ft Pleasant Ave, Springfield, MA 01108.

JOHNSON, RICHARD HOWARD
Social services. **PERSONAL:** Born Jan 07, 1931, Jersey City, NJ; married D Winona; children: Sandra Ellen Harris, Richard Nicholas. **EDUCATION:** VA Union Univ, AB Sociol (Cum Laude) 1953; Boston Univ Sch of Social Work, MA 1955. **CAREER:** Camp Downingtown, dir 1953-55; US Army Hospital, chief psychiatric sw 1955-57; Hawthornden State Hosp, psychiatric social worker 1957-59; Cuyahoga Co Court of Common Pleas, marriage counselor 1959-65; Maternal and Child Health, coord neighborhood serv 1965-68; Hough Parent-Child Ctr, dir 1968-72; Parent & Child Ctrs Head Start Bureau OCD-DHEW, chief 1972-87. **ORGANIZATIONS:** Chief social serv Parent Involvement Branch HSB, ACYF, DHHS 1975-87; mem Kappa Alpha Psi Frat; Boule-Sigma Pi Phi Frat Natl 30-Yr Oldtimers. **HONORS/ACHIEVEMENTS:** Departmental Awd for Chairing Task Force DHHS HSB 1986; Departmental Leadership Awd DHHS 1987; "Exploring Parenting" 1976, "Exploring Self-Sufficiency" 1982,"Looking at Life" 1986. **MILITARY SERVICE:** AUS specialist 3rd class 2 yrs. **BUSINESS ADDRESS:** Branch Chief US Government, Dept Health & Human Serv, PO Box 1182, Washington, DC 20013.

JOHNSON, RITA FALKENER
Interior designer. **PERSONAL:** Born in Arlington, VA; married Waldo C Falkener. **EDUCATION:** Academie Julien Paris, 1964-65; Grande Chaumi re Paris, 1964-67; Pratt Inst, BFA 1964. **CAREER:** Esq residential & commerical interior design; Essence Mag, home editor 1975-77. **ORGANIZATIONS:** Allied Bd Trade; mem Nat Home Fashions League Inc Professional showcase; YWCA Designers' Showhouse 1976; Designers' Showhouse 1977; YWCA Showhouse 1977. **BUSINESS ADDRESS:** 50 Pierrepont St, Brooklyn, NY 11201.

JOHNSON, ROBERT
Automobile dealer. **CAREER:** Bob Johnson Chevrolet Inc, Springfield, NY, chief executive. **BUSINESS ADDRESS:** Bob Johnson Chevrolet Inc, 195 West Main St, Springfield, NY 14141. *

JOHNSON, ROBERT B.
Educator. **PERSONAL:** Born Aug 19, 1928, Fair Bluff, NC; married Virginia J; children: Ronald Hal, Jacquelyn Foster. **EDUCATION:** A&T State Univ, BS 1950, MS 1959. **CAREER:** HS Loris SC, sci tchr 1955-63; Coastal Jr Coll, chem instr 1959-61; Pleasant Grove Elem Sch Rains SC, prin 1963-67; Mullins Sch Dist SC, elem sch prin 1968-; Lower Marion County, superintendent. **ORGANIZATIONS:** Mem Mullins City Coun 1970-82; Pee Dee Reg Devel Coun; Human Resource Devel Coun. **BUSINESS ADDRESS:** Superintendent, Lower Marion County, School Dist #3, Rains, SC 29589.

JOHNSON, ROBERT C.
Educator. **PERSONAL:** Born Aug 27, 1945, Richmond, VA. **EDUCATION:** Lincoln Univ, BA 1967; Institut D'Etudes Francaises France 1967; MAT 1969; MA 1974; Washington Univ, PhD 1976; Washington Univ, BS 1984. **CAREER:** Lincoln Univ Foreign Lang Lab, student dir 1964-67; Washington Univ, lectr 1969-71; Educ Cntr of E St Louis, dir 1969-72; Fontbonne Coll, lectr 1971; Inst Black Studies St Louis, dir educ 1971; Washington Univ, asst prof 1971-84; Grambling State Univ, assoc prof 1984-. **ORGANIZATIONS:** Numerous consultantships in field; mem Amer Assn for Higher Educ 1973-, Amer Assn Univ Profs 1971-, Assn for the Study of Afro-Am Life & Hist 1970-, Educators to Africa Assn 1972-, Natl & Reg Assn African-Am Educators 1969-72, Phi Delta Kappa 1969-; bd dirs Trainers Tchr Trainers Prog 1969-71; spl serv Washington Univ 1970-71; Inst Black Studies 1970-; Educ Center of E St Louis 1972-; mem So IL Univ Citizens Adv Com 1970-72; Comp Educ Comm 1970; E St Louis Model Cities Planning Com 1969-71; Afro-Am Studies Curriculum Adv Com 1972; St Louis Com on Africa 1970-; UN Assn 1973-. **HONORS/ACHIEVEMENTS:** Numerous publ appearances/addresses/publications in field; 1st Intl Black Merit Acad Award 1973; World Future Soc; Amer Assn for the Advancement of Sci;Eval Network; African Heritage Studies Assn; Outstanding Young Men in Amer 1974, 1977; Men of Achievement 1977; Comm Ldrs & Noteworthy Amer 1977; numerous scholarships/fellowships/grants. **BUSINESS ADDRESS:** Dept of Educ, The Master's Coll, PO Box 91322, Newhall, CA 91322.

JOHNSON, ROBERT EDWARD
Editor. **PERSONAL:** Born Aug 13, 1922, Montgomery, AL; married Naomi Cole; children: Bobbye LaVerne, Janet Bernice, Robert Edward III. **EDUCATION:** Morehouse Coll, BA 1948; Syracuse U, MA 1952; Miles Coll, LittD 1973. **CAREER:** Atlanta Daily World, reporter 1948-49; city editor 1949-50; Jet News Magazine Chicago, assoc editor 1953-54; asst mng editor 1954-56; mng editor 1956-63; exec editor 1963-. **ORGANIZATIONS:** Dir Project Upward Bound 1966-68 bd dirs duSable Mus Afro-Am Hist; Martin Luther King Jr Cntr Social Change; mem World Fed Scottish Socs; mem AlphaPhi Alpha, Alpha Kappa Delta, Sigma Delta Chi, Mason, Helms Athletic Found; dir Chicago Headline 1968-70. **MILITARY SERVICE:** USNR 1943-46. **BUSINESS ADDRESS:** Executive Editor, Jet Magazine, 820 S Michigan, Chicago, IL 60605.

JOHNSON, ROBERT H.
Educator. **PERSONAL:** Born Nov 24, 1938, NYC; divorced; children: Vietta. **EDUCATION:** Smith U, BS 1960; LIU, MS 1964; St John's U, PhD 1970. **CAREER:** Pharma-Verona Chem Co, chemist 1961-62; Hum Affairs Res Center, consultant 1970-72; R H Clark & Assoc, partner 1974-; LIU, teacher 1964-75; Medgar Evers Coll of CUNY, teacher 1975-76, dean of students 1977-. **ORGANIZATIONS:** Mem Am Chem Soc; Am Assn for Advance Sci; NY Acad Sci; Nat Assn Black Chemists & Engr; mem, bd trustee Nat Black Sci Stds Org 1972-; Fed Drug Addict Prog. **HONORS/ACHIEVEMENTS:** Outstndng Young Men of Am 1971; Outstndng Educators of Am 1973. **BUSINESS ADDRESS:** The Brooklyn Cntr, Long Island Univ, Brooklyn, NY 11201.

JOHNSON, ROBERT L.
Business executive. **PERSONAL:** Born in Hickory, MS; married Sheila; children: Paige. **EDUCATION:** Attended, Univ of IL; Princeton Univ, MA. **CAREER:** Corp for Public Broadcasting; Washington Urban League; Hon W E Fountroy, Congr Delegate frm DC, press secty; Nat'l Cable TV Assn, vice pres govtrel 1976-79; Black Entertainment Television, founder/pres 1980-. **ORGANIZATIONS:** Bd mem Cable TV Advertising Bureau, Black Entertinment TV, Black Coll Educ Network; vice pres for govt affairs NCTA 1978-79, bd of dirs 1982-84. **HONORS/ACHIEVEMENTS:** Pres Awd NCTA 1982; Image Awd NAACP 1982; Pioneer Awd Capital Press Club 1984; Business of the Year Awd DC Chamber of Commerce 1985. **BUSINESS ADDRESS:** President, Black Entertainment TV, 1232 31st St, NW, Washington, DC 20007.

JOHNSON, RONALD
Educator, dentist. **PERSONAL:** Born Jul 03, 1936, Cleveland, OH. **EDUCATION:** MiamiUniv Oxford OH, 1955; BradleyUniv Peoria IL, 1955-57;Univ of Pittsburgh, DDS 1957-61; Dental Ctr Boston, research fellow 1964; Harvard Sch of Dental Med Boston, postdoctoral fellow spclty cert 1964-67. **CAREER:** Univ of PA Sch of Dental Med, prof, chmn 1985; Charles R Drew Postgrad Med Sch LA CA, prof of ped dentistry 1977, asso prof of ped Dentistry 1972-77;Univ of CA LA, adj asso prof of ped dentistry 1972-77;Univ of IA IA City, asso prof of Pedodontics dir of grad pedodontics 1970-72, asst prof of pedodontics 1967-70; Children's Hosp Med Ctr Boston, intern & res 1967-67;Univ Hosp Sch IA City, staff 1970;Univ Hosp Sch IA City, dir grad pedodontics & Ped hosp dent 1970; M L King Jr Gen Hosp LA CA, chief of ped Dent 1972. **ORGANIZATIONS:** Mem Am Assn of Hosp & Dentists; mem Am Soc of Dentistry for Children; mem Am Acad of Pedodontics Res; com co-chmn Am Assn of Dental Schs Hosp Prog; mem Accreditaitons Com for Minority Recruitment, Internatl Assn for Dental Residents; mem NY Acad of Sci; mem LA Dental Soc; mem Assn of Pedodontic Diplomates; mem Am Soc of Preventive Dentistry; mem Nat Adv Dental Research Cncl NIH Cncl 1975; mem Sigma Xi 1970; mem Omicron Kappa Upsilon 1971. **HONORS/ACHIEVEMENTS:** Recip Grant & Prog Dir, Grad Training Prog in Care of Handicapped Children 1969-73; Prin Invstgtr Intrmrl Res Funding "Maximum Palatal Ht in Children with Good Occlussion" 1969-70; Grant for Grad Tng, Mott Found Flint MI 1970-73; Prin Invstgtr, Intrmrl Res Funding "Effects of Desensitization & Model Learning on Child Behavior" 1971-72; co-investigator CA Dental Assn "Vitreous Carbon Implants Used to Replace Permanent Teeth in Children" 1974; co-investigator Am Fund for Dental Ed "Vitereous Carbon Implants Used to Replace Permanent Teeth in Children" 1974; pub numerous articles on dentistry 1974-77. **MILITARY SERVICE:** USAF capt 1961-64. **BUSINESS ADDRESS:** U of PA Sch of Dental Med, 4001 Spruce A-1, Philadelphia, PA 19104.

JOHNSON, RONALD CORNELIUS
Public administrator. **PERSONAL:** Born Oct 02, 1946, Amelia County, VA; married Bessie; children: Aisha. **EDUCATION:** VA St Coll, BA 1969;Univ of Cincin, MA 1973; Xavier U, MEd 1977. **CAREER:** Ronson Mgmt Corp, pres; US Dept of HUD, specialist asst; Univ of DC, dir inst in comm & public serv; US Dept of Housing & Urban Dev, mgmt analyst; Model Cities Program, admin; The Jewish Hospital, 1st coord employee relations. **ORGANIZATIONS:** Pres Ronald C Johnson Asso Inc; bd dir Bushido Inc; srvs on natl panel Am Acad for Ed Dev; natl chmn Conf of Minor Pub Admin 1975-76; mem Nat Cncl Am Soc for Pub Adminstrn 1975-76; chmn Fairfax Cty Urban Leag; mem Rural Am Inc; Nat Assn Hous & Rehab Off; mem NAACP; mem Natl Com on Responsive Philantropy. **HONORS/ACHIEVEMENTS:** ASPA Apprec Award; Jewish War Vet Award; Urban Leag Serv Award; Conf of Min Pub Admin Award; Danforth Fellow. **MILITARY SERVICE:** AUSR 1st lt. **BUSINESS ADDRESS:** 1331 H St NW, Washington, DC 20005.

JOHNSON, ROOSEVELT, JR.
Executive director. **PERSONAL:** Born Feb 22, 1924, Conroe, TX; married Juanita; children: Melonee D. **EDUCATION:** Cntrl St Coll, BS;Univ NM, Grad Study; Geo Williams Coll Chgo. **CAREER:** US Post Ofc, empl 1950-51; YMCA of Dallas, prgm dir 1951-55; Wichita Falls, YMCA exec 1955-61; Dallas, YMCA br exec 1961-69; Dallas Urban Leag, exec dir 1969-. **ORGANIZATIONS:** Mem various coms offices; Bethel Meth Ch; Comm Counc of Gr Dallas; Alpha Phi Alpha Frat Inc; Lions Club Intl So Dallas Club; Frontiers Orgn; Knights of Pythias Grand Lodge; 32 deg Mason; Assn of YMCA Professional Secs; Tri Racial Com of Dallas Citiz Counc; Dallas Negro Chamber; Dallas Crime Commn; NAACP;Nat Conf of Chrstns & Jews Inc; Goals for Dallas; Channel 13 Spl Proj; Comm Relat Commn; Dallas Ind Sch Dist Network New Careers Proj; Dallas Assn for Safer Cities; past bd chmn Alpha Merit Grp Com Inc; past pres Regular Fellows Club; past pres bd chmn Dallas Pan Hellenic Counc Inc & Trust; exec dir Nat Pan Hellenic Counc Inc 1970-71; chmn St Fair of TX Bd dir & pres Task Force; past treas Nat Assn of Hum Rghts Wrks; incorp Dallas Assn for Minority Enterprise. **MILITARY SERVICE:** USAF. **BUSINESS ADDRESS:** Dallas Urban League, Inc, 2121 Main St, Dallas, TX 75201.

JOHNSON, ROOSEVELT YOUNG
Educator. **PERSONAL:** Born Jul 02, 1946, Spartanburg, SC; married Lina; children: David. **EDUCATION:** Howard U, BS 1968; IN U, PhD 1972. **CAREER:** Howard Univ Coll of Medicine, asst prof 1975-; Pacific Lutheran Univ, 1973-75. **ORGANIZATIONS:** Mem Am Soc for Microbiologists; Soc Sigma Xi; pres Langley-mcCormick PTA 1977-. **HONORS/ACHIEVEMENTS:** Postdoc flwUniv WA 1972-73; postdoc flwsp NIH 1972-73. **BUSINESS ADDRESS:** Asst Prof Dept of Botany, Howard University, Washington, DC 20059.

JOHNSON, ROY CALVIN
Professional athlete. **PERSONAL:** Born May 27, 1959, Parkin, AR. **EDUCATION:** TN State Univ. **CAREER:** Montreal Expos, outfielder 1984-. **ORGANIZATIONS:** Helped in building the Expos minor league complex at Lantana in the 1983-84 off-season. **HONORS/ACHIEVEMENTS:** Played Winter League ball in Mexican League with Hermosillo being named Most Valuable Player; made the A-New York-Penn League all-star squad in center field; captured Expos' minor league player of the month awards; named Southern League player of week; won the Am Assn batting title 1982 with 367 avg & figured in 135 runs in 102 games.

JOHNSON, ROY LEE
Corporate financial manager. **PERSONAL:** Born Jun 30, 1955, Charleston, MS; son of James Johnson and Viola Sayles Johnson; married Vicki Jo Williams, May 10, 1980. **EDUCATION:** Fisk Univ, Nashville TN, BS, 1977; Michigan State Univ, E Lansing, MBA, 1990. **CAREER:** Ford Motor Co, Detroit MI, financial analyst, 1977-83; The Stroh Brewery, Detroit MI, mgr of financial planning, 1983-. **HOME ADDRESS:** 18820 Jeanette, Southfield, MI 48075.

JOHNSON, ROY LYNN
Sales manager. **PERSONAL:** Born Mar 06, 1954, Buffalo, NY; children: Marcus. **EDUCATION:** Morris Brown Coll, attended 1972-75. **CAREER:** Electronic Data Systems, opers 1978-81, acct rep 1981-83, cost analyst 1983-85; East Chemical Co, sales mgr 1985-. **ORGANIZATIONS:** Wolverine charter mem Groove Phi Groove 1974-; mem NAACP 1977-80; Junior Black Acad Arts & Letters 1987. **HONORS/ACHIEVEMENTS:** Outstanding Young Men of Amer 1986. **BUSINESS ADDRESS:** Sales Manager, Case Chemical Co, 12770 Coit Rd #602, Dallas, TX 75251.

JOHNSON, RUTH M. (NEE MITCHELL)
Educator. **PERSONAL:** Born Jan 09, 1919, NYC, NY; children: Robin. **EDUCATION:** NY Univ, RN, BS, 1947; Columbia Univ, MA 1951. **CAREER:** Tchrs Coll Columbia Univ, instr 1951-53; Health & Hosp Corp NYC, assoc dir 1959-75; City Univ NY, rsch assoc specl in develop of gerontological curriculum, rsch assoc 1977, prof of nursing educ; J Stuartson Inc, chief operating officer. **ORGANIZATIONS:** Mem Chi Eta Phi Omicron Chapt; participant Harvard Univ exec progs Health Policy & Mgmt 1975; mem Amer Nurses Assn; Amer Assn of Univ Prof; NYU Bellevue Alumni Assn; mem NAACP; Kappa Delta Pi; N Manhattan Health Coalition 1974-; Cullen & Co & Riverside Day Care Ctrs; charter mem RENA Neighborhood Orgn 1960-; bd mem RENA 1969; supporter for Southern Poverty Law Center, Harlem Sch of the Arts, and Schomburg Center for Rsch in Black Culture. **HONORS/ACHIEVEMENTS:** Civic Awd RENA Scroll for Comm Work 1970; Kappa Delta Pi Hon Membership 1951.

JOHNSON, SAM
Automobile dealer. **CAREER:** Sam Johnson Lincoln-Mercury-Merkur Inc, Charlotte, NC, chief exec; Metro Lincoln-Mercury Inc, Charlotte, NC, chief exec. **BUSINESS ADDRESS:** Sam Johnson Lincoln-Mercury-Merkur Inc, 5201 East Independence Blvd, Charlotte, NC 28212. *

JOHNSON, SAMUEL HARRISON
Business executive. **PERSONAL:** Born Aug 31, 1916, Bowling Green, KY; married Edith; children: Cynthia, Pamela. **EDUCATION:** Lane Coll, 1935-37; IN U, AB 1955, MA 1957, MS 1959. **CAREER:** Natl Scholarship Serv & Fund for Negro Students, dir 1985; Natl Mission of The United Presbetary Church, dir, educ counseling serv bd; Marion Co Juvenile Court, probation officer; IN Med School Cons, HEW Office of Educ, staff. **ORGANIZATIONS:** Minority Engr Ed Proj; A Better Chance; Macy Found; Inst for Serv to Ed; Nat Assn of Coll Admissions Cnslrs; Acad of Certified Soc Wrkrs; Am Personnel & Guidance Assn; Nat Assn of Soc Wrkrs; Nat Assn of Std Fin Aid Assistance; orgnr, Fndr Assn of Non-White Concerns. **HONORS/ACHIEVEMENTS:** Publ "A Case for Structure" Am Jour of Orth. **BUSINESS ADDRESS:** 965 M L King Jr Dr NW, Atlanta, GA 30314.

JOHNSON, SANDRA VIRGINIA
Business executive. **PERSONAL:** Born in Hartford, CT. **EDUCATION:** Central State Univ OH, BS 1962; St Joseph Coll CT, MA 1968; Atlanta Univ, Post Grad 1968-69; Univ of MI, PhD 1972. **CAREER:** Assoc for Human Services Inc, pres, chief psychologist. **ORGANIZATIONS:** Mem Alpha Kappa Alpha, The Firl Friends; bd mem Planned Parenthood League; mem The Moles, NAACP, Assoc for Human Serv Inc; pres, bd mem Childrens Ctr; bd mem Epilepsy Ctr of MI, MI Metro Girl Scout Council, MI Protection & Advocacy for Developmentally Disabled Persons, Detroit Black Family Devel Inc, MI Psych Assoc, Amer Public health Assoc; pres Assoc of Black Psych; mem Amer Psych Assoc; chrpsn MI Bd of Psych 1981-. **HONORS/ACHIEVEMENTS:** Com Leaders & Noteworthy Amers 1978, Notable Amers 3rd ed, Personalities of the West & Midwest 6th ed Amer Biog Inst. **HOME ADDRESS:** 16300 North Park Dr #1205, Southfield, MI 48075. **BUSINESS ADDRESS:** President, Chief Psychologist, Assocs for Human Services Inc, Northland Medical Bldg, PO Box 2587, Southfield, MI 48037.

JOHNSON, SARAH H.
Councilwoman. **PERSONAL:** Born Mar 10, 1938, Charleston, SC; divorced. **EDUCATION:** Clark Coll, 1956-57; Elkins Inst, Grad 1974. **CAREER:** Greenville MS, councilwoman 1985; Headstart, area dir 1971-74. **ORGANIZATIONS:** Sec Delta Min Nat Cncl Ch 1968-71; xec sec Star Inc 1967; sec Weddington Wlm Sch 1964-65; bd dir Black Meth for Ch & Renewal 1971-73; gen bd ch soc UMC 1972-76; fellow MS Inst Politics 1972; Gov's Compreh Hlth Planning Adv Cncl 1974-75; radio lic course, rec FCC 1st Class Radio-tele Oprtrs Lic. **HONORS/ACHIEVEMENTS:** Elks Serene Lodge No 567, Civil Liberties Plaque; 1st black elected off of Greenville 1974; Tallahatchie Co Dev League, Silver Cup Outstndng Civic Achiev1974; Sunflower Co NAACP Plaque Outstndng Civic Achiev 1974; Elks Serene Lodge No 567, Civil Liberties Citation for Courageous Struggle Against Injustice 1973; Elite Civic & Soc Club Citation Outstndng Achiev Politics 1974; Queen City Lodge FM & AM, Woman Yr Award 1973; Woman Yr Award 1975, by the Utility Club Inc.

JOHNSON, SARAH YVONNE
Educational administrator. **PERSONAL:** Born Aug 17, 1950, Los Angeles, CA; married Frank Johnson Sr; children: Frank Jr, Ingrid Yvette. **EDUCATION:** Tuskegee Inst, BS 1972; Harvard Univ, EdM 1973. **CAREER:** PENN Cultural Ctr, assoc dir 1973-75; Beaufort Cty Bd of Ed, spec ed teacher 1975-76; Renaissance Wives Headstart Prog, ed dir 1976; Vacca Campus State School for Delinquent Youth, principal 1976-. **ORGANIZATIONS:** Mem AL Juvenile Justice Assoc 1979-, Harvard Club of Birmingham, Positive Maturity Adv Bd 1981-85. **HONORS/ACHIEVEMENTS:** Outstanding Young Women of Amer Nomination 1975,83; Outstanding Serv Awd Miles Coll Comm Sports Prog 1981; Outstanding Serv Awd Positive Maturity Foster Grandparent Prog 1981; 1st Black Principal of Vacca Campus. **BUSINESS ADDRESS:** Principal of Vacca Campus, Alabama Youth Services, 8950 Roebuck Blvd, Birmingham, AL 35206.

JOHNSON, SCOTT EDWIN
Educator. **PERSONAL:** Born Oct 14, 1894, Huntsville, TX; married Ethel Mae Downs; children: Ethel Ruth Daniels. **EDUCATION:** Hampton Inst, BS 1941, MA 1945. **CAREER:** E TX Teacher Assn, ret school prin, pres. **ORGANIZATIONS:** Pres E TX Sch Men's Club; co-chmn Day Care Ctr; bd dir Walker Co Tchr Fed Credit Union; vice -chmn St Tchr Assn; life mem TX Tchr Assn; memRetired Tchr Assn; pres C of C; deacon First Bapt Ch; mem City Cncl 1966-74; mem Aging Prog Adv Com; life mem NEA Mayor for a Day, City of Huntsville TX 1974. **HONORS/ACHIEVEMENTS:** Honored by pres & staff mem of Sam Houston U; honored by City Fire Dept; honored by City of Huntsville & others. **MILITARY SERVICE:** WWI pfc 1918-1919. **BUSINESS ADDRESS:** 10/ Phelps Dr, Huntsville, TX.

JOHNSON, SHARON REED
Educational administrator. **PERSONAL:** Born Aug 25, 1944, Wichita, KS; divorced; children: Michael. **EDUCATION:** Northern IL Univ, BA Sociol 1972; Roosevelt Univ, MA Urban Studies 1973; Univ of Manchester England, Cert Environ Design & Social Planning 1973. **CAREER:** Northeastern IL PLanning Comm, intern 1972-73; West NY Bd of Ed, teacher 1974, coord gifted ed & asst principal 1978-; Gifted & Bilingual Educ, Grants, affirmative Action & Special Events, principal assigned to supt's office. **ORGANIZATIONS:** Fin sec St Nicholas Tennis Club 1983-84; pres Mayor's Council for Youth/Sr; commun rep North Hudson Headstart; asst affirm action officer West NY Bd of Ed; bd mem Hudson Cty Coords Gifted Ed; mem State Coord Gifted Ed, West NY Ed Assoc, St James Episcopal Church; Natl Assoc of Elementary School Principals. **HONORS/ACHIEVEMENTS:** Internship/Tuition Northeastern IL Planning Comm 1972-73; 1st to institute Convocations for Gifted Students in West NY; Coord of the West NY Art Exposition; Coord of the West NY Sci Fair. **BUSINESS ADDRESS:** Principal/Supt's Office, West New York Bd of Educ, 100 51st St, West New York, NJ 07093.

JOHNSON, SOLOMON E.
Attorney. **PERSONAL:** Born Sep 25, 1920, Atlanta, GA; married Yoko Yamamoto; children: Barbara, Sandra, Andra, Richard, Michael. **EDUCATION:** Morehouse Coll, AB 1946 (honor student); Howard Univ Sch Law, JD 1949. **CAREER:** JB Blayton & Co, cpa 1944-46; City & Co of San Francisco, commr of housing 1961-64; Private Practice, attorney (retired 1979); State of HI, realtor assoc (part-time). **ORGANIZATIONS:** Commr of Scouting Atlanta 1944-46; bd mem Aid to Visually Handicapped San Francisco; bd mem Toastmasters Intl; Natl Housing Assn; Natl Assn of Housing & Redevel Officials; Charter Rev Com City & Co of San Francisco 1972-74; state adv com (apptd by Gov Reagan); bd gov CA Trial Lawyers Assn 1975; State Bar of CA; bd gov San Francisco Trial Lawyers Assn 1973-74; Chas O Houston Law Club; past mem Amer Assn Trial lawyers; past mem ABA; chmn Eisenhower-Nixon Club of N CA 1956; chmn 24th Dist Assy 1956; mem Repub Co Central Com 1956-64; Repub State Cen Com 1960-64; vice chmn United Negro Coll Fund 1963-64; bd of dirs Homeowners Assoc of Makaho Valley Towers Condominium 1984-86. **HONORS/ACHIEVEMENTS:** JB Blayton Accounting prize 1945; Law Review Howard Univ 1947-48, 1948-49; listed in Who's Who in Amer Law 1977-78, 1978-79, Community Leaders and NoteworthyAmers 1977-78. **MILITARY SERVICE:** AUS 1947-49. **BUSINESS ADDRESS:** Attorney, Tom Powers & Assocs Inc, 85-993 Farrington Hwy, Ste 201, Waianae, HI 96792.

JOHNSON, STAFFORD QUINCY
Educator. **PERSONAL:** Born Jan 02, 1948, Alameda, CA; son of Quincy and Rosa Mae Johnson; married Beverly Breaux Johnson; children: Jamaal, Rashaad. **EDUCATION:** Laney Coll, AA 1968; Univ of CA-Berkeley, BS 1970; CA State Univ, MS 1980. **CAREER:** Univ of CA-Berkeley, counselor. **ORGANIZATIONS:** Co-founder Black Staff and Faculty Organization (BSFO) UCB 1979-; chair George P Scotlan Endowment Fund 1986-; chair Black Staff and Faculty Org 1987-; founder of BSFO Recognition Awards, Ceremony and BSFO Gospel Program 1988. **HONORS/ACHIEVEMENTS:** Booklet "EOP Peer Counselor Program," Univ of CA-Berkeley 1980; articles "Achieving Success Through Self-Awareness," 1982, "Overcoming Academic Difficulty," African Perspectives 1985; recipient of BSFO Outstanding Staff Award 1988. **BUSINESS ADDRESS:** Counselor, University of CA-Berkeley, Student Learning Center, Bldg T-8, Berkeley, CA 94720.

JOHNSON, STEPHANYE
Consultant in business development. **PERSONAL:** Born Jul 27, 1959, Brooklyn, NY; daughter of Gene E. Johnson and Eartha L. Grant/Johnson. **EDUCATION:** Univ of PA Philadelphia, BA 1980; Univ of NC Chapel Hill, MBA 1984. **CAREER:** Univ of PA, admin asst 1976-80; Port Authority of NY & NJ, auditor 1980-82; The Pillsbury Co Green Giant Co, financial analyst 1984-86; The Pillsbury Co Burger King Corp, sr product analyst 1986-89; sr product/financial analyst, SYS Consultants, Ltd l989-; director of marketing Urban Development Corp of Greater Miami 1989-. **ORGANIZATIONS:** Consultant small business Business Student Assoc 1982-84; volunteer Big Brothers/Big Sisters 1984-; girl scout leader Minneapolis Cncl 1984-86; dir Greater Minneapolis Big Bros/Big Sisters 1985-86; recruitment/membership comm co-chair Natl Black MBA Assoc 1985-86; mem Natl Assoc of Black Accountants 1986-; pres South Florida Chapter, Natl Black MBA Assn l989-. **HONORS/ACHIEVEMENTS:** Consortium Fellowship Consortium Prog for Grad Study in Mgmt 1982-84; Service Awd Big Brothers/Big Sisters Minneapolis 1985; Service/Recognition Awd Outstanding Young Women of Amer 1985; Family Christian Assn of America Black Achiever l988.

JOHNSON, STEPHEN L.
Business executive. **PERSONAL:** Born Dec 14, 1944, Denver, CO; son of Mary Bess; children: Chemaine D, Scott S, Matthew. **EDUCATION:** Univ of Denver, 1963-66; Univ of San Francisco l978-80. **CAREER:** The Denver Post, reporter/editor 1968-72; Industrial Indemnity, asst mgr public relations 1972-74; Bank of America, sr public info ofcr 1975-79; First Interstate Bank, vice pres public relations 1979-83; First Nationwide Financial Corp, a subsidiary of Ford Motor Co vp/dir corp communications and appt 1st vice pres of subsidiory, 1987; appointed sr vice pres l988. **ORGANIZATIONS:** Trustee CA Neighborhood Housing Found 1980-85; dir Dance Gallery of Los Angeles 1984-; dir Communications Bridge (Los Angeles) 1984-87 finance chair mayor's Committee on Housing the Homeless; mem, conf bd, Public Affair Executive Comm l987-; Advisory Bd, San Jose State Univ l987-. **HONORS/ACHIEVEMENTS:** Directors Award for Public Service CA neighborhood Housing Foundation 1980; Honoree JFK School of Govt, Harvard Univ, for Housing Scholorships l988. **MILITARY SERVICE:** AUS Capt 1966-70; Bronze Star; Vietnam Serv Medals; Company Commander in Vietnam 1968. **BUSINESS ADDRESS:** Supt/Dir Public Affairs, First Nationwide Financial Cor, 700 Market St, San Francisco, CA 94102.

JOHNSON, STERLING
Narcotics prosecutor. **PERSONAL:** Born May 14, 1934, Brooklyn, NY; married Barbara; children: Sterling III, Alicia Daniels, Jennifer. **EDUCATION:** Brooklyn College, BA 1963; Brooklyn Law School, LLB 1966. **CAREER:** Southern Dist, asst US attorney 1967-70; Civil Complaint Review Bd, exec dir 1970-74; DEA, exec liason officer 1974-75; Special Narcotics Prosecutor's Office, special narcotics prosecutor 1975-. **ORGANIZATIONS:** Bd dir

Police Athletic League 1975-; chmn Drug Adv Task Force natl Adv Comm CDR USNR Annapolis 1975-. **HONORS/ACHIEVEMENTS:** Disting Serv Award Assn of Voluntary Agencies on Narcotic Treatment 1977; Disting Black Amer Drug Enforcement Adminstrn 1979. **MILITARY SERVICE:** USNR Captain. **BUSINESS ADDRESS:** Special Narcotics Prosecutor, Prosecutors Office, 80 Centre St, 6th Floor, New York, NY 10013.

JOHNSON, STEVE LAVELLE
Professional athlete. **PERSONAL:** Born Nov 03, 1957, San Bernadino, CA; married Janice; children: Marques; Christian; Michael. **EDUCATION:** Oregon State U, 1978-81. **CAREER:** Kansas City Kings, forward/center 1981-83; Chicago Bulls, forward/center 1984-. **HONORS/ACHIEVEMENTS:** Enters 4th pro season having played 1st two yeas with Kansas City & split time with Kings & Bulls last year; led Bulls in FG% hitting 559 on the season; has led his club in FG% every year which includes 4 years at Oregon State & 3 years in pros. **BUSINESS ADDRESS:** Chicago Bulls, 333 N Michigan Ave, Ste 510, Chicago, IL 60601.

JOHNSON, TAMMY ADELE
Promoter, advertising assistant. **PERSONAL:** Born Oct 26, 1965, Murfreesboro, TN; daughter of Mary J Johnson. **EDUCATION:** Middle TN State Univ, Murfreesboro TN, BS, 1988. **CAREER:** Minority Newsletter, Murfreesboro TN, reporter, 1986; WSMV TV, Nashville TN, intern, 1987; Freelance Producer, Murfreesboro TN, 1988; WTVF TV, Nashville TN, videotape editor, 1988-89; WRCB TV, Chattanooga TN, promotion advertising asst, 1989-. **ORGANIZATIONS:** Chairperson, NAACP Natl Youth Work Committee, 1986-89; ex-officio, Bd of Dir NAACP; Agnes Jones/Jackson Scholarship Committee NAACP; Alpha Kappa Alpha Sorority. **HONORS/ACHIEVEMENTS:** WW Law Award NAACP, 1987; Amer Business Women Scholarship, 1984-88; Chairperson of 1st Martin Luther King Jr March in Murfreesboro TN with nearly 2000 marchers, 1987. **HOME ADDRESS:** B-25 Normandy Apts, 3501 Dayton Blvd, Chattanooga, TN 37415.

JOHNSON, THEODORE, SR.
Retired army officer. **PERSONAL:** Born Aug 23, 1920, Ft Mitchell, KY; married Mattie E Butler; children: Theodore Jr, Winfred O, Frederick L, Larry E, Welton C, James C, Jeffrey M. **EDUCATION:** Univ of MD, attended; Brookdale Comm Coll, Degree Comm Mental Health; Stockton State Coll Pomona NJ, BS 1978, MA 1982; Kean College of NJ, Union NJ MA Counseling 1982. **CAREER:** AUS Field Artillery Brigade Battery, 829 Tank Destroyer Batallion, shipped Southampton England, basic training 1941; Le-Harve France Siefried Line Germany, 1944; SW Pacific, 1945, stateside 1946-50, Korea 1950; German Occupation duty, 1952-55; AUS Signal Corp & R&D Lab, 1955-64; VA Blind Ctr Hines Hosp, rehab 1965;AUS, retired 1964. **ORGANIZATIONS:** Mem Red Bank Comm Ctr Inc, Title I Adv Comm & ADv Comm Proj Seed; past mem, exec comm, past vp, chmn Vet Affairs; pres Red Bank Branch NAACP; mem VFW #438, Disabled Vet Org Prince Hall Masonic Lodge, Oswitchee Lodge 785; exec dir & natl pres NAACP Achievement Awd 1973;European African Mediterranean & Europe Theatre, Asiatic Pacific Theater Oper Medal; Motion Picture Photography. **HONORS/ACHIEVEMENTS:** Amer Theater Oper Medal; European African Mediterranean & Europe Theater; Asiatic Pacific Theater Oper Medal; Motion Picture Photography; Past Pres Awd in Appec of Untiring & Devoted Serv as pres for 6 Yrs The Greater Red Bank Br of NAACP 1980. **HOME ADDRESS:** 248 Leighton Ave, Red Bank, NJ 07701.

JOHNSON, THEODORE A.
Attorney. **PERSONAL:** Married Maureen Anette Foster; children: Christian. **EDUCATION:** Sherwood Music Sch, AB 1970; Western StUniv Coll Law, LLB 1972. **CAREER:** Co of Orange, deputy dist atty; WSU, instr of law 1973-; Santa Ana Coll, instr 1975-77. **ORGANIZATIONS:** Sec Orange Co Sel Srv Bd 1972-; chmn bd Orange Co Fair Housing Cnsl 1974-; pres NAACP Orange Co CA Br 1973-; mem Am Bar Assn; CA Bar Assn; Orange Co Bar Assn; Nu Beta Epsilon Nat Law Frat. **BUSINESS ADDRESS:** 700 Civic Ctr Dr, PO Box 808, Santa Ana, CA 92701.

JOHNSON, THEODORE L.
Educator. **PERSONAL:** Born May 27, 1929, Sanford, FL; married Gwendolyn B; children: Jawendo L, Angela Y Johson-Combs. **EDUCATION:** AZ State Coll Flagstaff, BS in Ed 1956; AZ State Univ Tempe, 1957; Bethune Cookman Coll, In-service; Northern AZ Univ, MAT in Engl 1969. **CAREER:** Crooms HS Sanford, FL, instr 1956-66; No AZ U, grad asst 1966-67; Cope Jr HS Redlands, CA, instr; No AZ U, instr 1969, dir, Upward Bound Prog 1971, asst prof of eng 1976-, asst dir for acad svcs. **ORGANIZATIONS:** Mem Natl Educ Assn 1956-; dir Upward Bound Pgm No AZ Univ 1970-71; coord Bilangual Pgm No AZ Univ 1973-78; mem Affrmtv Actn Coconino Co 1984-; mem Athltc Comm No AZ Univ 1981; mem Kappa Alpha Psi Frat 1959-. **HONORS/ACHIEVEMENTS:** Blue Key Hnr Frat No AZ Univ 1955; artcle Black Author Black Life Kappa Jrnl; Outstndng Fclty Mem No AZ Univ 1984. **HOME ADDRESS:** 2 E Silver Spruce, Flagstaff, AZ 86001. **BUSINESS ADDRESS:** Assistant Dir, MSRC Northern AZUniv, C Univ Box 5677, Flagstaff, AZ 86011.

JOHNSON, THEODORE THOMAS
Educational administrator. **PERSONAL:** Born Apr 26, 1949, Milwaukee, WI; married Marylyn P Lipman. **EDUCATION:** Univ of WI-Madison, BA History 1977. **CAREER:** Univ of WI-Milwaukee, affirmative action specialist 1975-76; Kemper & Assocs, asst mgr 1978-80; Univ of Houston, coord affirmative action 1980-83; NJ Inst of Technology, dir of affirmative action 1983-. **ORGANIZATIONS:** Treas Houston Citizens Chamber of Commerce 1981-82; mediator Houston Neighborhood Justice Prog 1981-83; mem Soc of Professional Dispute Resolution 1984-86; mem Kappa Alpha Psi 1968-86. **BUSINESS ADDRESS:** Affirmative Action Dir, NJ Institute of Technology, 323 Dr M L King Blvd, Newark, NJ 07102.

JOHNSON, THOMAS ALDRIGE
Business executive. **PERSONAL:** Born Oct 11, 1928, St Augustine, FL; married Josephine Holly; children: Thomas, Sondi, Jo Holly. **EDUCATION:** Long Island Univ, BA 1954; NY Univ, grad studies; Brooklyn Coll, grad studies. **CAREER:** NY Times, editor/reporter 1966-82; Thirdworld Trade Inst, dir 1981-82; Thomas A Johnson & Assoc, pres. **HONORS/ACHIEVEMENTS:** Dumont Awd Int'l Reporting UCLA 1968; Frontpage Awd Newspaper Guild 1968; Distinguished Alumni Awd Long Island Univ 1981. **MILITARY SERVICE:** Army Srgnt first class 1946-51. **HOME ADDRESS:** 135-20 Dennis St, Springfield Garden, NY 11434. **BUSINESS ADDRESS:** President, Thomas A Johnson & Associates, 461 Park Avenue South, Ste 921, New York, NY 10016.

JOHNSON, THOMAS H.
Evangelist. **PERSONAL:** Born Aug 05, 1932, Longview, TX; married Maggie L Stewart; children: Crystal Louise, Cathi Lynn. **EDUCATION:** Southwestern Christian Coll Terrill TX, BA 1955. **CAREER:** Madison Ave Ch Christ, evangelist 1955-. **HONORS/ACHIEVEMENTS:** Coord TV Spec "Cause for Christ" 1973; Christian Youths in Ac 1974; honored 25 yrs serv minister, & Madison Ave Ch of Christ Wichita 1980; Honored 32 year Madison Ave Church of Christ 1987; chmn Jamie Harris Livertransplant Fund 1987 (raise $100,000 by Aug 1987 for 6 yr old girl). **BUSINESS ADDRESS:** Evangelist, Madison Ave Church of Christ, 1740 N Madison Ave, Wichita, KS 67214.

JOHNSON, THOMAS O.
Dentist. **PERSONAL:** Born Jul 09, 1893, Jersey City, NJ; married Anna M Cecil; children: Thomas o Jr. **EDUCATION:** Columbia U, DDS 1914. **CAREER:** Priv Prac NYC, dentistry. **ORGANIZATIONS:** Life mem First Dist Dental Soc of NY & Affliated Orgn; mem Comm Ch of NY; mem Sigma Pi Phi Frat; Zeta Boule. **MILITARY SERVICE:** AUS 1st lt dental corps 1918; NY Nat Guard dental Corps capt 1919-38.

JOHNSON, TIMOTHY JULIUS, JR.
Artist. **PERSONAL:** Born Dec 30, 1935, Chester, SC; married Patricia B Hoye; children: Darryl Julius, Dianne Patrice. **EDUCATION:** MI State Univ, attended 1954-56. **CAREER:** Visual Display Arts Chanute AFB IL, supervisor 1979-82; US Govt Air Force, illustrator. **ORGANIZATIONS:** Leader/comm B mem Boy & Girl Scouts of Amer 1964-70; mem Alpha Phi Alpha 1955-; library bd mem Village of Rantoul IL 1979-82; mem The River Art Group 1983-84. **HONORS/ACHIEVEMENTS:** 1st place in the Chanute Fine Arts Festival; 2nd place in paintings & 3rd place in sculptures in Urbana St Fair; 1st place and Best of Show in the DanvilleFine Arts Festival; 1st and Best of Show in the Tech Exhibit Peoria; Best of Show 1982 Black Heritage week Chanote AFB. **BUSINESS ADDRESS:** Tech Illustrator, US Govt Air Force, 4Q ESC, San Antonio, TX 78243.

JOHNSON, TOBE
Educator. **PERSONAL:** Born Sep 16, 1929, Birmingham, AL; son of Tobe Johnson and Evelyn Johnson; married Goldie Culpepper; children: Tobie, Cheryl. **EDUCATION:** Morehouse BA 1954; Columbia Univ, PhD 1963. **CAREER:** Prairie View A&M, instr 1956-57; Morehouse Coll, asst prof 1958-59, asso prof 1962-66, prof 1967-; Prairie View, asst prof 1961-62; Univ Pittsburgh, visiting assoc prof 1956-66; Carleton Coll, prof 1968. **ORGANIZATIONS:** Dir Urban Studies Program, Frmr Cncl; mem Am Political Sci Assn; mem Bd Examiners Educ Testing Ser, Grad Rcrd Exam Political Sci 1972-76; mem Am Soc Public Admin; mem Conf Minstry Pub Admin Bd, United Way of Atlanta; S Ed Found; Natl Assn Reg Cncls; Atlanta Reg Comm Hons, Phi Beta Kappa; mem Natl Academy of Public Administration 1981-. **HONORS/ACHIEVEMENTS:** Awards, Columbia Univ Fellowship 1954-55; John Hay Whitney Fellowship 1959-60; Post-Doctoral Fellowship, Ealeton Inst of Politics & Natl Ctr Educ in politics faculty fellow to Dem Pres Nom Conv 1954; Post-Doctoral Rsrch Flw, Ford Found 1968-69; United Negro College Fund Distinguished Fellow 1981-82. **MILITARY SERVICE:** USAF s-sgt 1949-52. **BUSINESS ADDRESS:** Morehouse Coll, Box 43, Atlanta, GA 30314.

JOHNSON, TOMMIE ULMER
Educator. **PERSONAL:** Born Jun 23, 1925, Gary, IN; married Walter H Johnson. **EDUCATION:** Wayne State Univ, BS 1961, MEd 1964, EdD 1971. **CAREER:** Detroit Public Schools, teacher 1961-68; Wayne State Univ, asst prof 1971-76, assoc prof 1976-, assoc prof asst provost 1985-. **ORGANIZATIONS:** Vstg prof Norfolk State Univ 1978; sponsor Delta Pi Epsilon Wayne State Univ Grad Chap 1980-; mem MI Occupational Teacher Educ Assoc 1982-; consultant to public agencies, foundations, and professional assocs; mem Alpha Kappa Alpha Sor; life mem NAACP; asst treas/trustee Second Baptist Church of Detroit; memAmer Educ Rsch Assoc, Amer Vocational Assoc, MI Business Educ, Natl Business Educ Assoc, Women's Economic Club, Information Specialist Profls Assoc. **HONORS/ACHIEVEMENTS:** Ford Foundation Fellowship for Advanced Study 1971; publ "The Retail Community as a Classroom" Journal of Education for Business 1985. **BUSINESS ADDRESS:** Asst Provost for Affirm Action, Wayne StateUniv, 269 College of Educ, Detroit, MI 48202.

JOHNSON, TROY CALVIN
Professional athlete. **PERSONAL:** Born Oct 20, 1962, Houma, LA. **EDUCATION:** Southern Univ. **CAREER:** Denver Gold, slot back. **HONORS/ACHIEVEMENTS:** Will return kickoffs for the Gold in 1985.

JOHNSON, ULYSSES JOHANN, JR.
Educator. **PERSONAL:** Born Aug 11, 1929, Winter Haven, FL; married Thelma Mae Simmon; children: Marcus A, Melanie Aida. **EDUCATION:** Fisk Univ, BS 1951; Univ of Denver, MS 1955; TN Tech Univ, EdS 1973. **CAREER:** Rochelle Jr-Sr HS, teacher/counselor/coach 1951-69; Polk Jr Coll, counselor 1969-1971; Polk Cmmty Coll, DSS Spec dir 1971-73, counseling dir 1973-86. **ORGANIZATIONS:** Past pres Central Fl Guidance Assn 1972-73; past master Samson Lodge 142 F & A M Masons 1980-84; charter mem FSC Chapter Phi Delta Kappa 1983-86. **HONORS/ACHIEVEMENTS:** Keeper of records Kappa Alpha Psi 1980; clerk of voting Precinct 21-Polk Cty Voting Office 1976-86; Cameo Awd Winter Haven Little Theater 1986; Man of the Year Lakeland Alumni Chap 1985; Outstanding Boys St Chr Post 201 Amer Legion Dept FL 1984; SCABBA Adm of the Year AACJ Colleges 1986. **MILITARY SERVICE:** AUS corporal 1952-54; Good Conduct Medal, French Cord of War 1953. **BUSINESS ADDRESS:** Dir of Counseling, Polk Community College, 999 Avenue H NE, Winter Haven, FL 33881.

JOHNSON, VALRIE E.
Educator. **PERSONAL:** Born in Newton, TX; widowed; children: Michael G. **EDUCATION:** Tillotson Coll, BS, MEd; TX S U;Univ Houston, EdD, Admin & Supr. **CAREER:** HISD, tchr 1952-70, cons, hum rels 1970-73, curriculum coord, reading spclst 1973-75; Houston Comm Coll, part-time tchr 1972-77; Houston Ind Sch Dist, staff dev & Prog 1977-. **ORGANIZATIONS:** Mem Phi Delta Kappa Hon Soc; Houston Tchrs Assn; TX Classroom Tchrs Assn; TX St Tchrs Assn; Nat Ed Assn; mem Alpha Kappa Alpha Sor. **HONORS/**

ACHIEVEMENTS: Houston Jr C of C Award 1967; Houston Tillotson Alumni Award 1971; Hum Rels Award, Nat Ed Assn 1970.

JOHNSON, VANNETTE WILLIAM
Educational administrator. **PERSONAL:** Born May 27, 1930, Little Rock, AR; son of Charlie Johnson (deceased) and Laura Miller Johnson (deceased); married Delois V Davis, Aug 08, 1959; children: Juliette Laureen Lewis, Alberta Lynnette Shelton, Melanie Annette Dumas, Leontyne Delois Howard. **EDUCATION:** AK AM&N Coll, BS 1952; Univ of AR, MEd 1961; Univ of AR, DEd 1970. **CAREER:** Merrill HS, teacher/asst coach 1952-57; AR AM&N Coll, asst coach/instructor 1957-62, head football coach/AD 1962-74; Univ of AR Pine Bluff, athletic dir 1974-75, acting dept chair/athletic dir 1980-83, dept chair/athletic dir 1983-84, dept chair, prof 1984-. **ORGANIZATIONS:** Commiss AR Commission on Human Relations 1977-81; justice of the peace Jefferson County 1977-; corp bd Jefferson Comprehensive Care Center 1981-; educ comm Pine Bluff Chamber of Commerce 1982-; commiss Pine Bluff Transportation Commission 1982-; long range planning Pine Bluff Chamber of Commerce 1985; NAACP; Pine Bluff/Jefferson County Clean & Beautiful Comm 1982-85; Pine Bluff Convention Center Comm, finance comm 1977-; Literacy Council of Jefferson County, advisory board 1987. **HONORS/ACHIEVEMENTS:** Fellowship Southern Educ Found 1967-70; Pres Jefferson Cty Black Caucus 1978-; Vice Pres AR Black Caucus 1981-. **HOME ADDRESS:** 1905 Collegiate Dr, Pine Bluff, AR 71601. **BUSINESS ADDRESS:** Professor, Univ of Arkansas, Health, Phys Ed Dept, North Univ Dr, Pine Bluff, AR 71601.

JOHNSON, VAUGHN ARZAH
Minister. **PERSONAL:** Born Nov 22, 1951, Crisfield, MD; married Deborah Y Jarrett; children: Thomas, Kenneth, Jonathan. **EDUCATION:** Univ of MD Eastern Shore, BA 1973; Gammon-Interdenominational Theol Center, MDiv 1976; NY Theol Sem, grad study. **CAREER:** Metro UMC, sr minister 1976-84; Ebenezer UMC, sr minister 1976-84; Univ of MD, campus minister 1976-84; Peninsula Conf United Methodist Church, assoc council dir for ethnic minority minister 1984-. **ORGANIZATIONS:** Pres of bd Headstart 1977-79; bd mem Shore Up 1980-82; founder & pres Black Ministerial Fellowship 1982-84. **HONORS/ACHIEVEMENTS:** Crusade Scholar United Methodist Church 1973-75; Outstanding Achievement in Community Omega Psi Phi 1979; Chancellor's Awd Univ of MD 1980; Who's Who Among Young Amers Jaycees 1982; Evangelism Awd Whatcoat UMC 1986. **HOME ADDRESS:** 551 Westwood Dr, Dover, DE 19901. **BUSINESS ADDRESS:** Assoc Council Dir, United Methodist Church, 139 N State St, Dover, DE 19901.

JOHNSON, VERDIA EARLINE
Publisher/consultant. **PERSONAL:** Born Jul 14, 1950, Fort Worth, TX; married Everett N Johnson Jr. **EDUCATION:** Howard Univ, BA 1972; New York Univ, MBA 1974. **CAREER:** Colgate Palmolive NY, asst product mgr 1974-77; Standard Brands NY, sr product mgr 1977-81; Nabisco Brands NJ, sr product mgr 1981-84; BCI Mktg Inc NY,dir of marketing 1984-85; Black Enterprise Magazine NY, advertising dir 1985-86; The JEM Group Inc, pres. **ORGANIZATIONS:** Mem NAACP 1980-; sec Howard Univ Alumni Club 1985; mem Advertising Women of NY 1986-, Newark Collaboration Group/Small Business Council 1987. **HONORS/ACHIEVEMENTS:** Dean's Scholarship Howard Univ 1970-72; Consortium Scholarship NY Univ 1972-74. **HOME ADDRESS:** 7002 Blvd East #8I, Guttenberg, NJ 07093.

JOHNSON, VERMELLE JAMISON
Educator. **PERSONAL:** Born Aug 02, 1933, Islandton, SC; married Charles Harry; children: Charles H Jr, Temple Odessa. **EDUCATION:** SC St Coll, BS 1955, MEd 1969;Univ of SC, PhD 1976. **CAREER:** Claflin Coll, prof & chairperson dept of business admin 1985; SC State Coll, asst prof business educ 1969; Public Schools SC, teacher 1962-68; Federal Employee, 1957-62; AL State Coll, 1956-57; Univ of ND inst partic; Univ of RI. **ORGANIZATIONS:** Past st sec SC Bus Ed Assn; mem Alpha Kappa Mu Hon Soc; Delta Mu Delta Nat Bus Frat; Phi Delt Akappa Hon Soc; Iota Phi Lambda Bus Sor; Nat Bus Ed Assn; SC St Bus Ed Assn; Alpha Kappa Alpha Sor; Daughter Elk; IBPOE of W; sun sch tchr Trinity United Meth Ch. **HONORS/ACHIEVEMENTS:** Resrch An Analysis of Congruence Between Competencies, Requisite for Sec Sch Bus Ed Tchrs, & Prep Received in Tchr Ed Progs; author "A Look at Today's Increased Opptys for Adequately Prepared Bus Grad in SC" 1972, "Bus Educs Have A Tremendous Bill to Fill" 1970, "So You Think You're Ready to Teach" 1964, Bus Ed A Momentous Challenge in the 70hs"; listed in Dir of Outst Bus Educs in the Eastern Region; Who's Who Among Stds. **BUSINESS ADDRESS:** Dept Business Adm, Claflin Coll, Orangeburg, SC 29115.

JOHNSON, VINCENT L.
Attorney. **PERSONAL:** Born Aug 12, 1931, Brooklyn, NY; married Gertrude; children: Vincent Jr, Melissa. **EDUCATION:** Brooklyn Coll, BA 1958; St John's Univ, LLB 1960, JD 1963. **CAREER:** Fields & Rosen, asst atty 1960-61; Kings Co, asst dist atty 1968; Laufer & Johnson, prtnr 1968-. **ORGANIZATIONS:** Mem Brooklyn Bar Assn; mem Phi Alpha Delta Law Frat; bd of dir 100 Black Men of NY 1970-; past mem bd of dir NAACP 1956-75. **HONORS/ACHIEVEMENTS:** Subject of Police Athl League Post Police Athl League 1964. **MILITARY SERVICE:** USAF airmn 1st cls 1951-55. **BUSINESS ADDRESS:** Attorney, 26 Court St, Brooklyn, NY 11242.

JOHNSON, VIRGINIA ALMA FAIRFAX
Performer/dancer. **PERSONAL:** Born Jan 25, 1950, Washington, DC; daughter of James L Johnson and Madeline M Johnson. **EDUCATION:** Attended New York Univ, 1968-69, 1978-. **CAREER:** Guest artist Capitol Ballet, Chicago Opera Ballet, Washington Ballet, Baltimore Civic Youth Ballet, Stars of World Ballet in Australia, Detroit Symphony, Natl Symphony, Eugene Ballet; appeared in major film "A Piece of the Action"; TV includes Dance in Amer, Ancient Songs of Children, Night of 100 Stars; solo concert at Maymount Coll White House appearances for Pres Carter & Reagan; Blanche duBois in a Streetcar Named Desire for PBS Great Performances; Dance Theatre of Harlem, principal dancer 1969-; A Creole Giselle, NBC. **HONORS/ACHIEVEMENTS:** Young Women Achievers 1985; Outstanding Young Woman of America 1985; hon mem Alpha Kappa Alpha Sor. **BUSINESS ADDRESS:** Principal Dancer, Dance Theatre of Harlem, 466 W 152 St, New York, NY 10031.

JOHNSON, VIRGINIA O.
Business executive. **PERSONAL:** Born Jan 16, 1917, Oklahoma City; married Robert J; children: Denise, Renee. **EDUCATION:** LA School Physiotherapy & Massage, 1947; School Cosmetology, 1946. **CAREER:** Perc Westmore Warner Bros, hair dresser, masseuse; Johnsons Bath House, owner 1948; Beauty Salon & Barbar Shop, owner. **ORGANIZATIONS:** Mem Regalettes Charity Club; Holy Name Cath Ch; PTA; USC Med Ctr Cares Nat Best Dressed Wmn, NAFAD 1960. **HONORS/ACHIEVEMENTS:** Fashion recognition San Francisco Club; 10 Outstndng Bus Wmn 1972; 10 Best Dressed Bus Wmn 1974; Outstndng Bus Wmn 25 yrs 1973. **BUSINESS ADDRESS:** 4496 W Adams, Los Angeles, CA.

JOHNSON, WALDO EMERSON, JR.
Association executive. **PERSONAL:** Born Mar 13, 1955, Americus, GA. **EDUCATION:** Mercer Univ Sch of Social Work Macon, GA, AB 1977; Univ of MI Ann Arbor, MI, MSW 1979; School of Social Serv Admin Univ of Chicago, PhD candidate. **CAREER:** GA Sw Coll Upward Bound, proj coord 1979-82; Washtenaw Cty Comm Mental Health Ctr, staff assoc 1978-79; New Detroit Inc, comm organizer 1978; Alpha Phi Alpha Frat Inc, asst exec secr for programs 1982-85, develop consult 1985-. **ORGANIZATIONS:** Mem comm Chicago Chapter Nat'l Soc for Fund Raising Exec; charter mem vice pres Blacks in Development 1984; Chicago Chap of Black Social; bd of dir Chicagochapter IL Caucus on Teen Preg 1984; benefit chair Metropolitian bd of Chicago Urban League 1983; treas Southside Teen Preg Network 1983; community adv bd Proj IMAGE 1984; mem Southside Branch NAACP 1982; founding mem The Art Forum Urban Gateways of Chicago. **HONORS/ACHIEVEMENTS:** Doctoral flwshp cncl on soc work educ Wash, DC 1985-87; dist serv awd Alpha Phi Alpha Frat Inc 1984; grad flwshp Univ of MI Ann Arbor, MI 1978-79. **BUSINESS ADDRESS:** Asst Exec Sec for Programs, Alpha Phi Alpha Fraternity Inc, 4432 Dr ML King Jr Dr, Chicago, IL 60653.

JOHNSON, WALTER J.
Educational administrator, counselor. **PERSONAL:** Born Dec 31, 1957, Toledo, OH; son of Thomas Johnson and Maggie Johnson; married Elise Hood; children: David Walter. **EDUCATION:** N Central Coll, BA Speech/Comm Theater 1980; Natl Coll of Educ, MS Mgmt Develop of Human Resources 1986. **CAREER:** Proctor & Gamble, sales rep/mgmt training 1980-83; N Central Coll, admin counselor/minority rep 1983-87, dir of athletic development. **ORGANIZATIONS:** Consultant/adviser Minority Student Assoc N Central Coll; mem Harvey Chap Natl Jaycees; asst women's track coach Eisenhower HS 1982-83; mem IL Assoc of Mem Coll Admissions Counselors 1983-; mem, NCAA; mem, College Conference of IL & Wisconsin, Director Committee. **HONORS/ACHIEVEMENTS:** HL Richards HS First Black Vice Pres Student Counsel 1975, First Black Vice Pres Sr Govt 1976; Outstanding Alumnus Award Black Student Assoc NCC 1983; established the North Central Coll Minority Scholarship Fund 1984; publication "The Plight of Black Students on a Predominately White Campus" NCC Chronicle; Outstanding Student Serv Award N Central Coll; Handy Order Top Sales Award Procter & Gamble Chicago Dist. **HOME ADDRESS:** 356 S. Columbia St, Naperville, IL 60540-5416. **BUSINESS ADDRESS:** Dir of Athletic Development, North Central College, 30 N Brainard St, Naperville, IL 60566.

JOHNSON, WALTER LEE
Educator. **PERSONAL:** Born May 23, 1918, Greensboro, NC; son of Rev Fonce Johnson; married Rita Doss Johnson; children: Jennifer Rose, Tommye L Johnson. **EDUCATION:** NC AT&T State Univ, Greensboro NC, BS, 1942; Univ of IL, Urbana IL, MS Agronomy, 1947, PhD Agronomy, 1953. **CAREER:** Southern Univ, Baton Rouge LA, instructor 1947-50; Florida A&M Univ, Tallahassee FL, Dir Div Agricultural Sciences 1972-84, prof 1953-84. **ORGANIZATIONS:** Chairman Dept of Higher Educ, FL State Teachers Assn, 1955-64; Advisory Council, State Dept of Natural Resources, 1971-76; Natl Soil Conservation Committee, 1974; Southern Deans & Dir of Agriculture, 1972-84; Alpha Phi Alpha Fraternity. **MILITARY SERVICE:** US Army, Battalion Sergeant Major, 1942-46. **HOME ADDRESS:** 609 Gore Avenue, Tallahassee, FL 32310.

JOHNSON, WALTER THANIEL, JR.
Attorney at law. **PERSONAL:** Born May 18, 1940, Greensboro, NC; son of Walter T Johnson, Sr and Gertrude Alexander Johnson; married Yvonne Jeffries, Apr 20, 1985; children: Walter III, Vernon K, Lisa Yvonne, Shannon Tamara. **EDUCATION:** A&T State U, BS 1961; Duke Univ Sch of Law, JD 1964; Univ of North Carolina Chapel Hill Govt Executives Inst 198l; Univ of North Carolina Chapel Hill Justice Exec Program l984. **CAREER:** Frye & Johnson, atty; Guilford Co Superior Ct, asst dist atty 1968-69; USAF, judge adv 1965-68; Law Office of Elreta Alexander, asso 1964-65; Redevel Com Greensboro, relocation adv 1962-63; Public Storage & Warehousing Inc, sec, exec com 1971-76; Barjo Inc, sec, exec com 1973-; DukeUniv Law Sch, adjunct prof of law 1975-; Barbee & Johnson partner 1987-88; Barbee Johnson & Glenn partner 1988-. **ORGANIZATIONS:** Mem Greensboro Bd Dirs of NC Nat Bank 1976-; vice pres planning for United Way of Greensboro 1969-71; mem, chmn, Greensboro Cty Bd of Educ 1970-; mem Bdof Govs NC Bar Assn 1975-; chmn NC Inmate Grievance Co Com 1975-; chmn bd trusteeUniv NC 1974-; bd mem Eastern Music Festival 1972-76; chmn North Carolina Parole Comm l98l-85; Adjunct prof North Carolina Central School of Law l985-87; vice chmn Greensboro Vision l985-; bd mem Greensboro Economic Devel Council l988-. **HONORS/ACHIEVEMENTS:** Outstdng young men of NC NC Jaycees 1970; Freedom Guard Award NC Jaycees 1970-71; disting serv award Greensboro Jaycees 1970; Peacemaker Award Carolina Peacemaker Newspaper; vice pres Assn of Paroling Authorities l982-85; Citizens Comm on Alternatives to Inceration l98l-83. **MILITARY SERVICE:** USAF capt 1961-68. **BUSINESS ADDRESS:** Partner, Barbee Johnson & Glenn, 102 N Elm Street, 804 Southeastern Bldg, Greensboro, NC 27401.

JOHNSON, WALTON RICHARD
Retired physician. **PERSONAL:** Born Aug 16, 1909, Bessemer, AL; divorced; children: Walton Jr, Kristin D. **EDUCATION:** Morehouse Coll, BS 1934; Howard Univ, MD 1949; Univ PA. **CAREER:** Life Ins, salesman; Multinat Mktg Corp, instructor, HS Dir; Med Practice, physician (retired).

JOHNSON, WARREN S.
Business executive. **PERSONAL:** Born Apr 07, 1947, Philadelphia, PA; married Peggie A Parham; children: Warren S. **EDUCATION:** Hampton Inst, BA Ec1969; Temple U, (grad sch) 1973-75. **CAREER:** Fischer & Porter Co, mgr compensation & benefits 1973-; PA Hosp, training spclst prsnl, generalist 1970-73; PA Bell & Tele, mgmt dev trainee 1969-70. **ORGANIZATIONS:** MemAm Compensation Assn 1976; exec at large Philadelphia Survey

Grp 1976-; mem Am Soc Prsnl Admin 1977-; consult YMFT Wrkshp, Alliance of Bus. **BUSINESS ADDRESS:** 125 E County Line Rd, Warminster, PA 18974.

JOHNSON, WAYNE ALAN
Marketing programs manager. **PERSONAL:** Born May 22, 1961, Springfield, MA; son of Karl A. Johnson Sr. and Beverly M. Riley Johnson. **EDUCATION:** The George Washington Univ, BBA 1983; Univ of WI-Madison, MBA 1984; Georgetown Univ Washington, D.C. J.D. **CAREER:** Freedom Federal Savings, record dept mgr 1976-79; US House of Representatives Honorable Edw P Boland, staff asst 1980-83; IBM, marketing rep 1985-88. **ORGANIZATIONS:** Consultant/participant IBM Adopt-A-School 1985-86; mem Natl Black MBA Assoc 1986-88; mem NAACP 1989; mem Ebeneezer AME Church 1989. **HONORS/ACHIEVEMENTS:** College Scholarship Awd Emhart Corp 1979; MBA Fellowship Awd Consortium for Grad Study 1983; 100% Club Awd IBM 1986-87; IBM 100% Club 1986, 1987. **HOME ADDRESS:** 8524 Manchester Road, Silver Spring, MD 20901. **BUSINESS ADDRESS:** Marketing Program Mgr, IBM, 6705 Rockledge Drive, 9WB022, Bethesda, MD 20817.

JOHNSON, WAYNE LEE
Bank executive. **PERSONAL:** Born Oct 28, 1953, Hartford, CT; son of Hubert L Johnson (deceased) and Betty Hawthorne Johnson; married Bertha J; children: Jamaal Trumaine, Marquis Jawaan. **EDUCATION:** Grambling State Univ, BA 1975; Attended, Univ of Hartford's Grad Sch of Business. **CAREER:** The Hartford Ins Group, work measurement analyst 1975-77, sr work meas analyst 1977-79, mgmt consultant 1979-86; Citytrust, vice pres 1986-. **ORGANIZATIONS:** Mem Assoc of Internal Mgmt Consultants 1981-, Toastmasters Intl Org 1982-84; bd of dirs IMPACT 1985, Blue Hills Child Care Ctr Hartford 1986-. **HONORS/ACHIEVEMENTS:** Honor Grambling State Univ 1973; Dean List Grambling State Univ 1974,75; wrote article "Starting Up a New Internal Management Consulting Department" AIMC Forum 1988. **HOME ADDRESS:** 20 Donna Lane, Windsor, CT 06095. **BUSINESS ADDRESS:** Vice President, Citytrust Bank, 961 Main St, Bridgeport, CT 06601.

JOHNSON, WAYNE WRIGHT, III
Administrator. **PERSONAL:** Born Oct 26, 1953, Galveston, TX. **EDUCATION:** Univ of TX, BA 1976. **CAREER:** TX Dept of Labor & Stand, pers dir, EEO coord 1976-; St Sen AR Schwartz, legis aide 1973-75. **ORGANIZATIONS:** Mem Laborers' Intl Union of No Am 1972-; mem NAACP; mem Galveston Cnty Yg Dem; pres LaMarque HS student body 1972; pres TX AFL-CIO Youth Citizen Conf 1971; natl bd mem Am for Dem Action 1972-73; chmn Dem prec conv 1972, 1974, 1976; chmn cred comm Galveston Co Dem conv 1974. **HONORS/ACHIEVEMENTS:** Galveston Cnty NAACP outst supp awd 1976; del Dem Nat conv NY City 1976; alt-del Dem Nat conv Miami 1972; Who's Who Among Am HS Stud 1971-72. **BUSINESS ADDRESS:** PO Box 12157, Austin, TX 78711.

JOHNSON, WENDELL L., JR.
Business executive. **PERSONAL:** Born Dec 10, 1922, Lexington, KY; married Rose E Vaughn; children: Wendell III, Edith, Jeffrey, Brian. **EDUCATION:** Hampton Inst, BA 1947; Atlanta Univ, MSW 1949. **CAREER:** Chicago Housing Auth, asst dep dir of mgmt, dep exec dir 1956-; Psychopathic Hosp, psy soc worker 1952-56; Cook Co Hosp, med soc worker 1951-52; Chicago Welfare Dept, caseworker 1949-51. **ORGANIZATIONS:** Past mem S Side Cent Comm Work 1965-66; Grand Blvd Oakwood Comm Coun 1965-66; 2nd Dist Police Workshop 1965-66; bd mem Cit Adv Com Jnt Yth Dev Com 1967-69; pres Neigh Inst Adv Com; mem Comm Adv Bd Cabrini-Green Unit Cook Co Dept of Pub Assistance 1967-70; bd mem N Area Bd, Chicago Youth Ctrs 1968-71; mem 8th Dist Police Wkshp 1967-76; mem Chicago Chap Natl Assn Housing & Redev Ofcls 1968-76; mem Boy Scouts of Am; mem NAACP; mem, trustee Lilydale First Bapt Ch; mem Roseland Hts Comm Assn; mem Hampton Inst Alumni; mem AtlantaUniv Alumni; 1st Tee Golf Club. **HONORS/ACHIEVEMENTS:** Cert of Appreciation, Kiwanis Club of N Cent Chicago 1967; Superior Pub Serv Award, Chicago Assn of Commerce & Ind 1973; Great Guy Achvmt Award, WGRT-RADIO 1973; commend for ded to pub serv 1973; Cert of Appreciation, Chicago Youth Ctr 1976; award, appreciation of serv resid coun Cabrini-Green Homes 1966-76; Bronze Star; Purple Heart. **MILITARY SERVICE:** AUS tech/sgt 1943-45. **BUSINESS ADDRESS:** Region 3 Office, Chicago Housing Authority, 500 E 37th St, Chicago, IL 60653.

JOHNSON, WENDELL LOUIS
Business executive. **PERSONAL:** Born Mar 22, 1944, Atlanta, GA. **EDUCATION:** Howard U, BA 1966; Long Island U, MBA 1970. **CAREER:** Standard Oil Co, empl rels, consult 1985; Amoco Oil Co, urban affairs rep 1971-76; R Dixon Speas Asso, analyst 1968-71; Operations Rsrch Inc, rsrch asst 1967-68; Sys Analysis & Rsrch & Corp, analyst 1967; DC Pub Sch Sys, math instr 1966-67; US Dept of Commerce, jr economist 1966; GA St U, instr 1972-76. **ORGANIZATIONS:** Alpha Phi Alpha Frat; Hillside Invstmnt Club; Nat Soc for Perf & Instrn; Am Soc for Training & Dev NJ NG 1969-71. **MILITARY SERVICE:** GA Nat Guard staff sgt 1971-75.

JOHNSON, WENDELL NORMAN, SR.
Military official. **PERSONAL:** Born Dec 20, 1931, Boston, MA; son of Oscar A. Johnson and Ida M. Johnson; married Helen L. Underwood, Nov 15, 1958; children: Laura Lynn, Lois Underwood, Wendell Norman, Jr.. **EDUCATION:** New England Coll of Pharmacy, Boston, MA, BS, 1955; US Naval Postgrad School, Monterey, CA, certif, 1962; Natl War Coll, Washington, DC, certif, 1975; American Univ, Washington, DC, MA, 1976. **CAREER:** US Navy, USS Dahlgren, commanding officer, 1976-78, USS Jason, commanding officer, 1979-82, Destroyer Squadron 35, commodore, 1982-83, Pentagon, direc of research and devel, 1983-84, Pentagon, direc of planning and programming logistics, 1984-87, US Naval Base, Charlotte, SC, commander, 1987-89; Boston Univ, Boston, MA, dean of students, 1989-. **ORGANIZATIONS:** Member, US Naval Inst, 1980-; member, Govs Roundtable on Literacy, 1988-; consultant, Coun on Edn, 1988; lecturer, Coun for Higher Edn, 1988-; member, YMCA bd; member, Charleston Chamber of Commerce bd; member, United Way bd. d. **HONORS/ACHIEVEMENTS:** Author of US Navy Minority Recruiting Guide, 1968; Proclamation, City Council of Jacksonville, FL, for civic accomp, 1972; author of Communications Model for Integration of Blacks into the Navy, 1976; Disting Leadership Award, Omega Phi Psi, 1988; Doctor of Letters, Coll of Charleston, 1989; Disting Leadership Award, YMCA SE region, 1989; Distinguished Service Award, Commonwealth of MA, 1989; military awards inc, Legion of Merit, Meritorious Service Medal, Navy Commendation Medal, Navy Achievement Medal, Combat Action Medal, Order of Sikatura (Phili ppines). **BUSINESS ADDRESS:** Rear Admiral Wendell Norman Johnson Sr, Boston University, 775 Commonwealth Ave, Boston, MA 02115.

JOHNSON, WENDY ROBIN
Buyer. **PERSONAL:** Born Dec 26, 1956, New York; daughter of Clarence Woodson Johnson, Jr (deceased) and Dolores Elizabeth Dominguez Johnson. **EDUCATION:** Elizabeth Seton Coll, AAS Liberal Arts 1980; Marymount Manhattan Coll, BBA Finance 1983; Manhattan College Bronx NY MBA 1985-87. **CAREER:** RCA Records, buyer specialist 1976-83; PolyGram Records Inc, mgr of purchasing 1983-85; General Foods Corp, assoc buyer 1985-86; buyer 1986-. **ORGANIZATIONS:** Mem Delta Sigma Theta Sor Inc 1979-; troop leader Girl Scout Council of Greater NY 1983-; mem Natl Assoc of Female Execs 1984-; Founder We Buy 1988-; Asst Dean Learning Center Canaan Baptist Church 1988-; Instructor Junior Achievement Project Business 1989-. **HONORS/ACHIEVEMENTS:** Recipiant of 1984 Outstanding Young Women of America 1984. **BUSINESS ADDRESS:** Buyer, General Foods USA, 250 North Street, Suite EZ-2, White Plains, NY 10625.

JOHNSON, WILBUR EUGENE
Attorney. **PERSONAL:** Born Mar 01, 1954, Columbia, SC. **EDUCATION:** Univ of SC Aiken; Augusta Coll GA, BA History 1976;Univ of SC Law Ctr, JD 1979. **CAREER:** Palmetto Legal Srv, staff atty 1979-; Richland Co Pub Def Agy, law clk 1977-79. **ORGANIZATIONS:** Mem SC Bar Assn; Urban League Guild; Kwanza Com 1979-. **HONORS/ACHIEVEMENTS:** Outstndng Coll Athl of Am 1973-74; Who's Who in Am Jr Coll 1974; Who's Who Among Stds in Am Coll 1976; flwshp Earl Warren Legal Training Prog 1976-79. **BUSINESS ADDRESS:** 35 E Calhoun St, Sumter, SC 29150.

JOHNSON, WILHELMINA LASHAUN
Financial administrator. **PERSONAL:** Born Aug 13, 1950, Ft Worth, TX. **EDUCATION:** Tarrant Cty Jr Coll, AA 1970; TX Christian Univ, BS 1983; Univ of TX Arlington 1987. **CAREER:** City of Ft Worth, admin intern 1979, admin asst 1979-83, admin analyst 1983-. **ORGANIZATIONS:** Mem Conf of Minorities Assoc 1979-, Urban Mgmt Asst of North TX 1979-, Amer Soc of Public Admin 1980, Intl City Mgmt Assoc, 1980-, Natl Forum of Black Public Admin 1984-. **BUSINESS ADDRESS:** Admin Budget Analyst, City of Fort Worth, 1000 Throckmorton St, Fort Worth, TX 76104.

JOHNSON, WILLARD RAYMOND
Educator. **PERSONAL:** Born Nov 22, 1935, St Louis, MO; son of Willard Johnson and Dorothy Stovall; married Vivian; children: Karen L, Kimberly E. **EDUCATION:** Pasadena City Coll, AA 1955; UCLA, BA 1957; Johns Hopkins School of Advanced Intl Studies, MA 1961; Harvard Univ, PhD 1965. **CAREER:** MIT, asst prof 1964-69, assoc prof 1969-73; Circle Incorporated Boston, pres 1968-70; MIT, prof 1973-. **ORGANIZATIONS:** Vice pres African Heritage Studies Assn 1978; mem Amer Political Sci Assn 1965-; mem Natl Econ Assn 1971-82; Natl Conf of Black Political Scientists 1971-89; mem US Natl Comm for UNESCO 1960-66; bd mem Boston New Urban League 1967-72; bd mem Natl Scholarship Fund for Negro Students 1958-59; mem New England Political Sci Assn 1966-69; mem Council on Foreign Relations 1973-; mem Black Forum on Foreign Affairs 1976-78; mem Assn for Study of Afro-Amer Life & History 1968-72; bd mem Assn of Concerned African Scholars 1977; natl co-chr Assn of Concerned African Scholars 1983-; bd mem World Univ Serv 1958-60; bd mem Interfaith Housing corp, 1970; chmn bd The Circle Complex (Roxbury) 1970-72; chmn Africa Policy Task Force McGovern for Pres Campaign 1972; mem Democratic Party Adv Council Foreign Affairs Stud y 1976; pres TransAfrica Inc Boston Chap 1981-; bd mem TransAfrica Inc Natl 1977-; dir Business Management for Economic Develop Rsch Project; dir Communications Component of African American Issues Ctr MIT Ctr for Intl Studies 1982-. **HONORS/ACHIEVEMENTS:** Ford Found Foreign Area Training Fellowships 1959, 1960, 1963, 1964; John Hay Whitney Found Oppt Fellowship 1961; Research Grant Center for Intl Studies MIT 1971; Research Grant Technology Adaptation Project MIT 1973-74; resident fellow Rockefeller Center at Belagio Italy 1987; Fulbright Fellowship to West Africa 1987. **BUSINESS ADDRESS:** Professor of Political Science, MIT, E53-429, Cambridge, MA 02139.

JOHNSON, WILLIAM A.
Educator. **PERSONAL:** Born Aug 21, 1917, Norfolk, VA; married Louise Brown; children: William Jr, Dewitt. **EDUCATION:** Bluefield State Coll, BS 1940; Columbia Univ, MA 1949; Attended, Univ of Strasburg France 1952, Boston Univ, Univ of VA, Old Dominion Univ, Hampton Institute. **CAREER:** Norfolk County, principal 7 schools 1941-60; Title IV Program Emer School Assist Prog, dir 1969-74; Head Start (5 yrs Summers), dir 1965-69; Intergroup Education, dir 1969-73; Chesapeake Public Schools, asst supt for general admin. **ORGANIZATIONS:** Mem AASA, VASA, ASCD; past pres Tidewater Supervisors Group; CEA; NEA; past vice pres Tidewater Reg Suprs; past chmn Two So Assn of Coll & Schs; membd dir Local Amer Cancer Soc; Mental Health Assn 1957-70; United Comm Fund 1973-; Hunton YMCA; Tidewater Health Foundation; SE Lung Assn; Kirk Cone Rehabilitation Ctr; mem NAACP; mem trustee bd Queen St Baptist Ch; Omega Psi Phi; Chesterfield Club. **HONORS/ACHIEVEMENTS:** Alpha Phi Alpha Humanitarian Awd 1974; Nat Sor Phi Delta Kappa Inc Awd 1969; Amer Cancer Soc Awd 1966; Who's Who in Amer Education 1960-65; Who's Who in VA 1974. **MILITARY SERVICE:** AUS CIC 1st lt 1942-45 & 1952-53; Bronze Star Medal Awd; 4 US Commendations; sev battle stars. **BUSINESS ADDRESS:** 545 Fernwood Farms Road, Chesapeake, VA 23320.

JOHNSON, WILLIAM A., II
Business executive. **PERSONAL:** Born Dec 31, 1952, Columbia, SC. **EDUCATION:** CA State Univ LA, BS Civil Engrg 1975; Stanford Univ, MS Civil Engrg & Structural Engrg 1976, Degree of Engrg & Civil Engrg 1981; Harvard Univ Grad School, MBA 1986. **CAREER:** LA Cty Flood Control Dist, engrg aid 1973-75; Bechtel Inc San Francisco, civil/structural designer 1975-76; Pacific Soils Engrg Inc LA, civil/geotechnical engr 1976-77; Bechtel Inc San Fran, civil/structural engr 1978-79; Kercheval & Assoc Inc, 1980; WA Johnson & Associates, owner 1983. **ORGANIZATIONS:** Mem Amer Assoc of Univ Profs, ASCE, Amer Soc of Engrg Ed, CA Soc of Professional Engrs, Natl Soc of Black Engrs, NSPE, Structural Engrs Assoc of CA, Prestressed Concrete Inst, San Francisco Bldg Code Rev Comm-ASCE&SEAOC; vol asst ASCE; corr mem Comm on Minority Progs; mem Natl Rsch Council Common Minorities in Engrg, Minority Grad Engrg Ed Task Force, NAACP; vol chmn Summer Jobs Exposure Prog; mem San Fran Engrs Soc Comm on Manpower Trng, CA State Ofc of Emergency Svcs, Post Earthquake Inspection Prog Advocate, MInorities in Engrg; reg professional engr CA, KS, MO, NV; founding mem & 1st elected Natl Chairperson

Emeritus; founding mem Black Grad Students Org Stanford Univ; tech rsch Area of Soil-Structure-Interaction Analysis; pres Harvard Business Sch Black Alumnae Assoc 1987-89; mem Natl Black MBA. **HONORS/ACHIEVEMENTS:** Publ several articles in Natl Soc of Black Engrs Newsletters, papers in ASCE Civil Engrg Ed Conf 1979; workshop on Retention of Minority Undergrad Engrg Students sponsored by MIT & Natl Rsch Council; Leadership Awd NSBE as 1st Natl Chairperson Emeritus. **BUSINESS ADDRESS:** Consultant, Kercheval & Assoc Inc, PO Box 2022, Stanford, CA 94305.

JOHNSON, WILLIAM A., JR.
Association executive. **PERSONAL:** Born Aug 22, 1942, Lynchburg, VA; son of William A Johnson, Sr and Roberta Davis Johnson; married Mary A Griffin (divorced); children: Kelley M, Kristin R, Wynde A. **EDUCATION:** Howard Univ, BA 1965; Univ MI, postgraduate; Western Reserve Univ, case; Howard Univ, MA 1967. **CAREER:** Urban League Rochester, pres & chief exec off (formerly exec dir) 1972-; Urban League Flint MI, dep exec dir 1971-72; Genesee Comm Coll Flint, instructor political science 1967-71; Natl Hwy Users Conf Washington, legislative analyst 1966-67; US Supreme Ct, student aide 1966. **ORGANIZATIONS:** Mem NY State Coun Urban Leagues (pres 1975-79); 1st vice pres Eastern Reg Council Urban League Executives 1977-; regional vice pres Nat Urban League Council Exec Dirs 1976-; co-founder Com for a More Rep Govt; organist New Bethel ME Ch; co-founder Black Leadership Study group; trustee Monroe Community Coll Rochester NY 1976-; exec com NY St Employment & Training Council 1977-; v chmn 1978-79; chmn 1979-; pres Urban League of Rochester Economic Devel Corp 1985-; mediator Factfinder, NYS Public Employment Relations Bd 1985-; Sigma Pi Phi Fraternity, Gamma Iota Boule 1987-; Bd of Dir, Eltrex Industries, Inc. 1982-. **HONORS/ACHIEVEMENTS:** Fellowship Falk Found 1964-65; hon soc Pi Sigma Alpha 1967; Jefferson Award for Outstanding Public Service, Amer Inst for Public Service 1986; Vernon E. Jordon Jr. Fellowship, Natl Urban League 1986. **BUSINESS ADDRESS:** President and CEO, Urban League of Rochester, NY, Inc., 177 N Clinton Avnue, Rochester, NY 14604.

JOHNSON, WILLIAM C.
Mortgage banker. **PERSONAL:** Born Jul 01, 1930, New York, NY; children: William C Jr, Anthony C, Anita C, Robert W. **EDUCATION:** US Navy, 3 years college credits while serving. **CAREER:** First California Funding Inc, sr vice pres. **MILITARY SERVICE:** USN sr chief petty officer 30 yrs; Vietnam Service Medals, Good Conduct Medal, European Occupation Natl Defense. **BUSINESS ADDRESS:** Senior Vice President, First California Funding Inc, 6820 La Tijera Blvd Ste E15, Los Angeles, CA 90045.

JOHNSON, WILLIAM E.
Clergyman. **PERSONAL:** Born Apr 16, 1936, Centerville, AL; married Rosylyn E Pearson; children: Jamena, Lawrence, Jacquelyn, Louis, Janeen. **EDUCATION:** Aram&N, BS 1958; CA Western U, BA 1968; Sch of Theol Claremont CA, RelD. **CAREER:** SE United Presb Ch, minister; St Andrews Presb Ch UPUSA; Hollypark UM Ch, Gardina CA, asso pastor 1968-72. **ORGANIZATIONS:** Conducted numerous training grps on Hum Rels-Race Rels for HS & Chs; mem NAACP; Urban League; pres SE San Diego Lion's Club 1974-75; polemarch KappaAlpha Psi Frat San Diego Alumni Chap 1974-75; mem CA St Dem Cntrl Com 1977; bd dir Heartland Hum Rels Assn; various Citizens Adv Coms; Beta Kappa Chi Hon Soc. **HONORS/ACHIEVEMENTS:** Listed in Who's Who Among Std in Am Coll &Univ 1957-58; Comm Ldrs & Noteworthy Ams 1974-75; recip Man of Distinction Award, Heartland Hum Rel Assn 1973. **MILITARY SERVICE:** USMC 1958-67. **BUSINESS ADDRESS:** 210 S Euclid Ave, San Diego, CA 92114.

JOHNSON, WILLIAM JULIUS (JUDY)
Athlete. **PERSONAL:** Born Oct 26, 1900, Snow Hill, MD; married Anita; children: Loretta. **CAREER:** Pittsburgh Crawfords, bsbl plyr 1932-37; Homestead Grays, 1930; Darby PA, 1922-29, 1931. **HONORS/ACHIEVEMENTS:** 1st DE Hall of Famer; induction Bsbl Hall of Fame 1975.

JOHNSON, WILLIAM L.
Psychologist, psychoanalyst. **PERSONAL:** Born May 23, 1932, NYC; son of Richard johnson and Avtimeza Ward; children: Toni Ann, Hillary Sloan. **EDUCATION:** Inst Advanced Psychological, Postdoctoral Diploma Psychoanalysis 1968; Adelphi Univ; Yeshiva Univ, PhD Clinical Psychology 1964; City Coll, MS 1957; New Sch Soc Resrch, MA 1955; Queens Coll, BA 1953. **CAREER:** Private Practice, psychoanalyst 1964-; Orange Co Mental Health Clinics, chief psychologist 1962-64; NY St Training School Boys, consult psychologist; US Peace Corps Ankara Turkey; Falkirk Hosp Central Valley NY; NYS Rehab Hosp, psychologist 1959-62; Kings Pk St Hosp, clin Psychologist 1959; USAF, Mitchel AFB, prsnl psychologist prsnl lab 1957. **ORGANIZATIONS:** Am Psychol Assn 1957-74; St Psychol Assn 1959-74; pres Orange Co Psychol Assn 1963-64; Assn Black Psychologist 1972-74; AdelphiaUniv Postdoctoral Soc 1969-74. **HONORS/ACHIEVEMENTS:** Alvin Johnson Prize Scholarship New Sch for Soc Rsch 1953. **BUSINESS ADDRESS:** Psychologist-Psychoanalyst, 300 Mercer St, New York, NY 10003.

JOHNSON, WILLIAM LEE, JR.
Attorney. **PERSONAL:** Born Jun 22, 1927, Waco, TX; married Marvinell Winson. **EDUCATION:** Prairie View A&M Coll, BA 1950, grad study 1950; TX So Univ Law Sch, JD 1963. **CAREER:** Atlanta Life Ins Co, supr 1950-51; Sheppard Air Force Base, tech inst 1951-60; Private Practice, atty 1963-64; PHA, genl atty 1964-66; State of TX, asst US atty 1966-84; Johnson Vaughn & Heiskell, atty 1984-. **ORGANIZATIONS:** Mem TX Bar Assn, Ft Worth Tarrant Co Bar Assn; Amer Bar Assn; Fed Bar Assn; pres-elect Ft Worth Chap 1977-78; Natl Bar Assn; JL Turner Legal Soc; Fed Bus Assn; Ft Worth Black Lawyers Assn; Omega Psi Phi 1968-. **MILITARY SERVICE:** AUS t/3 1946-47.

JOHNSON, WILLIAM PAUL, JR. (SCOOGIE)
Educational consultant, computer consultant. **PERSONAL:** Born Jul 17, 1963, Washington, DC; son of William Paul Johnson Sr and Elizabeth Ann Johnson. **EDUCATION:** Univ of Washington DC, Washington DC, BBA, 1988; Syracuse Univ, Syracuse NY, attended, 1981-83. **CAREER:** Harry Diamond Labs (US DOD), Adelphi MD, computer specialist, 1981-87; US Treasury, Bureau of Engraving & Printing, Washington DC, computer specialist, 1987-89; Comp-U-Staff, Silver Springs MD, computer analyst/programmer, 1989-. **ORGANIZATIONS:** Certified lifeguard/pool operator/instructor, Amer Red Cross, 1982-; counselor, Boy Scout Swimming Merit Badge, 1985-87; pres, Univ of Washington DC Data Processing Mgmt Assoc, 1986-87; educ chairperson, Black Data Processing Assoc, 1987-; founder/pres, Univ of Washington DC Black Data Processing Assoc, 1987-88; coach, Natl High School Computer Competition Team (DC Chapter), 1988, 1989; chairperson, Univ of Washington DC Coll of Business Student Advisory Council, 1988. **HONORS/ACHIEVEMENTS:** Syracuse Univ Academic Scholarship Award, 1981-83; Athletic Scholarship Offer for Swimming, Howard Univ, 1981; Marion S Barry Scholarship Award, Univ of Washington DC, 1987; Mem of the Year, Washington DC Chapter of Black Data Processing Assoc, 1988-89; Graduated w/Honors (GPA 3.5), Univ of Washington DC, 1988; Devel of STAR Enterprises Youth Leadership & Devel Program, 1989; Devel of STAR Enterprises Youth Employment Program, 1989. **BUSINESS ADDRESS:** STAR Enterprises, Po Box 50099, Washington, DC 20004.

JOHNSON, WILLIAM RANDOLPH
Manager. **PERSONAL:** Born Jul 25, 1930, Oxford, NC; married Wendolyn; children: Wendolyn, Pamela, William III. **EDUCATION:** NC Central Univ, BS 1950; Univ of Notre Dame, MS 1952; Univ of PA, PhD 1958. **CAREER:** Philip Morris Rsch Ctr, mgr/asst mgr 1974-75; proj ldr 1966-74, chem 1963-66; W R Grace & Co, res chem 1961-63; FL A&M U, proj of chem 1958-61. **ORGANIZATIONS:** Past mem Air Poll Tch Advis Bd; mem City Plan Comm 1975-; past mem, advis bd mem Ed Ther Ctr; mem Focus Club; mem NOBCHE. **HONORS/ACHIEVEMENTS:** Publ J Polymer Sci 1960; 9 US pat, publ Jour of Org Chem 1971; 3 publ Tobac Sci 1973; 2 publ Nature 1973; 3 publ Chem & Ind 1973, 1975, 1979. **MILITARY SERVICE:** Army Chem Corps corpl 1953-55. **BUSINESS ADDRESS:** PO Box 26583, Richmond, VA 23261.

JOHNSON, WILLIAM SMITH
Systems specialist. **PERSONAL:** Born Apr 24, 1941, Salisbury, MD; son of Alonzo Johnson and Delcie Johnson; married Jacqueline Andrea Dennis; children: William Jr, Andrea. **EDUCATION:** Univ of MD Eastern Shore, BS 1963; Eastern Bible Inst, diploma in Pastoral Min 1985. **CAREER:** Wicomico Co Bd of Educ MD, teacher 1963-64; US Govt, computer programmer 1964-65; Sussex Co Bd of Educ DE, teacher 1965-66; Minister, 1981-; EI DuPont De Nemours Co Inc, systems specialist, 1966-. **ORGANIZATIONS:** Adv bd mem Wicomico Co Housing Authority 1983-84; adv bd mem Wicomico Co Sch Rezoning Comm; mem NAACP; Prince Hall Mason; asst pastor St James AME Zion Church; life mem Salisbury High Assn. **HONORS/ACHIEVEMENTS:** Univ of MD Eastern Shore Athletic Hall of Fame; Outstanding Service Awd for Church Serv Assistance; NAFEO Disting Alumni of Year 1983; Ordained Elder of AME Zion Church 1986. **HOME ADDRESS:** Rt 2 Box 27 West Road, Salisbury, MD 21801. **BUSINESS ADDRESS:** Senior Specialist, E I DuPont De Nemours Co Inc, 400 Woodland Lane, Seaford, DE 19973.

JOHNSON, WILLIAM T. M.
Educator. **PERSONAL:** Born Oct 22, 1921, Philadelphia, PA; children: 2 Children. **EDUCATION:** VA St Coll, BS 1943;Univ of PA, MS 1947, PhD 1950. **CAREER:** D I DuPont de Nemours & Co, resrch chem 1949-63; Lincoln Univ, prof of chem 1963-; Univ PA School of Medicine, rsch assoc 1971-; PA Hospital, non-clinical investigator 1971-. **ORGANIZATIONS:** Pres United & Political Act Com of Chester Co 1968-; pres Hum Rels Cncl of W Chester PA 1963-65; bd dir W Chester Comm Ctr 1975-. **HONORS/ACHIEVEMENTS:** Roon Award, Resrch First Pl 1961; Lindback Award for Distngshd Tchng 1965; John B Knecht Brthrhd Award 1965. **MILITARY SERVICE:** AUS eto 1943-46. **BUSINESS ADDRESS:** Chem Dept, Lincoln University, PA 19352.

JOHNSON, WILLIAM THEOLIOUS
Attorney. **PERSONAL:** Born Dec 24, 1943, Columbus, OH; married Gloria Kindle;; children: Michael, Michelle. **EDUCATION:** Capital Univ, AB 1968; Capital Univ, OH State Univ, JD 1972. **CAREER:** Dunbar Kienzle & Murphey Law Firm, atty 1972-75; Johnson & Ransier Co LPA, managing partner 1975-79; Private Practice, atty 1979-; KBLE OH Inc, pres 1979-. **ORGANIZATIONS:** Chmn Black Amer Law Student Assn; chmn Law Day; Phi Alpha Delta Law Frat; vice pres Student Bar Assn; natl chmn Elections Comm Amer Bar Assn Law Student Div; pres Franklin Co Legal Aid & Defender Soc; vice chmn Franklin Co Mental Health & Retardation Bd; bd mem spec cnsl Columbus Urban League; trustee Columbus Zoo; trustee OH Found for Independent Colls; natl chmn Minority Affairs Comm Natl Cable TV Assn; mem Legislative Comm NCTA; trustee Franklin Co Public Defender Comm; ruling elder Bethany Presbyterian Ch; mem Columbus, Amer, Natl Bar Assns; hearing officer OH Civil Rights Commn; hearing officer OH Dept of Educ; arbitrator United Steelworkers; Natl Cable TV Assn; OH Cable TV Assn; admitted to practice before, Supreme Ct of US, US Court of Appeals, US Dist Ct, US Tax Ct. **HONORS/ACHIEVEMENTS:** Outstanding Young Man in Columbus Columbus Jr C of C 1972; Outstanding Comm Serv Awd Columbus Bar Assn 1978; Gold Key Awd; Lutheran Brotherhood Scholarship; Hugh H Huntington Awd; Amer Jurisprudence Book Awd; West Publishing Co Constitutional Law Book Awd; selected Ten Outstanding Young Men in Columbus; Columbus Bar Assn Comm Serv Awd. **BUSINESS ADDRESS:** President, KBLE OH Inc, 1156 Alum Creek Dr, Columbus, OH 43209.

JOHNSON, WILLIAM THOMAS
Executive director. **PERSONAL:** Born Oct 24, 1930, New York, NY; married Lydia B; children: Milagros, Maria-Cristina. **EDUCATION:** St Joseph's Sem & Coll, bA 1952; NY Law Sch, JD 1961; Nrthwstrn Sch of Law, LLM 1971. **CAREER:** Civilian Complaint Rev Bd NYCPD, exec dir 1974-, asst dep commnr 1972; Gary IN, dir of pub sfty 1969; Neighbrhd Legal Serv Brooklyn, atty 1968. **ORGANIZATIONS:** Dir Cath Child Care Inst Brooklyn & Queens 1973; dir Cath Coll of Immaculate Concep 1974; dir Cath Med Ctr Brooklyn & Queens 1974; life mem NAACP 1971; past pres Macon B Allen, Black Bar Assn 1978; pres Queens Ec Dev Corp 1979. **HONORS/ACHIEVEMENTS:** "Police Legal Training Manual" AD-CRAFT Gary IN 1971. **BUSINESS ADDRESS:** New York City Police Civil Rev Bd, 200 Park Ave S, New York, NY 10003.

JOHNSON, WILLIE
City councilman. **PERSONAL:** Born May 26, 1925, Florence, SC; son of Luther Johnson and Evelener Richardson; married Fredericka Helen Gadsden, 1946; children: Franklin Lewis Johnson. **EDUCATION:** Wayne State Univ, 1970; Cass Tech HS, cert of accomplish 1971; MI Career Inst, cert of grad 1974. **CAREER:** Wayne Co Gen Hosp, Wayne Co guard 1951-78; Wayne Co, deputy sheriff 1961-68; Kaufman & Broad Homes, super 1961-69; State of MI, asst chief fire & safety officer 1978-; Personal Accomplishment, songwriter 1955-; City of Inkster, city councilman. **ORGANIZATIONS:** Mem Inkster NAACP 1974-; mem Central

Wayne Co Sanitation Auth 1975-77; mem Inkster Civil Defense Policy Bd 1975-; comm mem Nankin Transit Comm 1977-; mem Broadcast Music Inc 1984-; publ Wiljoe Music BMI 1984-; producer Inkster's New Sounds on "Inkster's New Sound" label 1984-; Nashville Songwriters Assoc International 1990; Broadcast Music Inc (BMI) 1984-. **HONORS/ACHIEVEMENTS:** Cert of appreciation Wayne Co Bd of Comm 1978; special tribute from State of MI Sen Plawecki & Rep Wm Keith 1978; won lawsuit as private citizen in state supreme ct to return money to citizens Home Owners' Org 1971-78; Disting Employee of the Yr Walter P Reuther Psych Hosp 1981; 1st Place Trophy at Sumpter Township Rodeo for compositions & vocalist 1988. **MILITARY SERVICE:** USN seaman 1st class 1943-46; Asia/Pacific Campaign Medal; Good Conduct Medal; personal letter from secy of Navy; WWII Victory Medal. **HOME ADDRESS:** 4066 Durand Ct, Inkster, MI 48141. **BUSINESS ADDRESS:** Councilmember, 2121 S Inkster Rd, Inkster, MI 48141.

JOHNSON, WILLIE F.
Commissioner. **PERSONAL:** Born Sep 27, 1939, Jacksonville, FL; married Bernice Lowery; children: Thandeka. **EDUCATION:** Allen U, BA 1961;Univ of PA, MSW 1970. **CAREER:** Commonwealth of PA Dept of Pub Wlfr, Sthestrn Reg, commr, ofc of yth serv 1974-; Yth Dev Ctr Philadelphia, exec dir 1972-74, cnslr 1961-64; Children's Hosp, soc serv dir 1970-72; Yth Dev Ctr S Philadelphia, cnslr 1966-68; Nat Biscuit Co, foreman 1965-66; SC Pub Sch, tchr 1961-64. **ORGANIZATIONS:** Mem Yth Serv Com for Philadelphia; Yth Serv Com for Philadelphia United Fund; adv bd of Minority Ed & Grp Training Labs; mem YMCA; Am Corr Assn; PA Assn of Parole Probtn & Corr. **BUSINESS ADDRESS:** RM 1303 STATE OFC BLDG, 1400 Spring Garden St, Philadelphia, PA 19130.

JOHNSON, WYNEVA
Attorney. **PERSONAL:** Born Oct 28, 1948, Greenwood, MS. **EDUCATION:** Georgetown Univ Law Ctr, LLM 1977; Univ of PA, JD 1974; Wheaton Coll, BA 1971. **CAREER:** Howard Jenkins Fr Nat Labor Rel Bd, counsel to bd mem 1974-. **ORGANIZATIONS:** Admitted PA Bar 1974; admitted MS Bar 1976; exec bd Wheaton Coll Alumnae Assn; former chmn Com of Black Alumnae. **HONORS/ACHIEVEMENTS:** Nom Outsdng Young Women of Am 1976. **BUSINESS ADDRESS:** 1717 Pennsylvania Ave NW, Room 745 A, Washington, DC 20570.

JOHNSON, ZODIE ANDERSON
Educator. **PERSONAL:** Born Nov 19, 1920, Muskogee, OK; married Robert; children: Robert, Dr Zonya, Dr Keith. **EDUCATION:** Wayne State U, BS 1948; Wayne State U, MEd 1964. **CAREER:** Reg V, supt 1978-; Reg I, asst supt; Sherrard Middle Sch Detroit Bd Edn, principal 1973-; Marxhausen Prim & Elem Schs, asst prin, adminstr 1970-71; various tchg positions 1950-; Civ Svc, supr, contracting officer 1941-50. **ORGANIZATIONS:** Mem Black Educ Adminstrs; Nat Alliance of Black Educators; Wayne StateUniv Women of Wyane; Tutoring Project; Delta Sigma Theta 1973; lecturer Inner City Educational Prog; consult Cornell U; Wayne State;Univ of Detroit; Oakland U; Wayne Comm Coll; various sch systems; mem Delta Sigma Theta; Women Asminstrs of Detroit; Concerned Women in Politics; Dir of Workshops - Desegreg Sch, Achvmt, Motivation IGE, Facilitator; Speakers Bureau MI Assn. **HONORS/ACHIEVEMENTS:** Supvn Women of Wayne Headliner of Year 1973; honored as Miracle Worker in Educ 1973; honored for Delta Sigma Theta sor; Phi Delta Kappa; Tutoring Proj, SatSch 1973. **BUSINESS ADDRESS:** Region V 10001 Puritan, Detroit, MI.

JOHNSON-BROWN, HAZEL WINFRED
Educator, nurse. **PERSONAL:** Born Oct 10, 1927, West Chester, PA; daughter of Clarence L. Johnson and Garnett Johnson; married David B Brown. **EDUCATION:** Harlem Hospital of Nursing, Diploma 1950; Villanova Univ, BS 1959; Columbia Univ Teacher's Coll, MS 1963; Catholic Univ, PhD 1978. **CAREER:** Letterman General Med Center, instructor, 1963-66; Valley Forge General, supvr, 1966-67; US Army, med rsch & devel command project dir, 1967-73; Univ of MD Sch of Nursing, dir, asst dean, 1976-78; US Army Hospital Seoul Korea, asst for nursing 1978-79; Georgetown Univ Sch of Nursing, asst prof 1983-84, adjunct prof 1985; George Mason Univ, commonwealth prof graduate program school of nursing, 1986-88; George Mason School of Nursing, prof, 1988. **ORGANIZATIONS:** Guest lecturer Georgetown Univ, Univ of Maryland, George Mason Univ Sch of Nursing; media participation TV & radio interviews for natl & local talk shows, 1979-82, Night Watch "Women's Issues and Professional Nursing" 1983, Public Broadcasting System Black History Month Programming "The Different Drummer Series," 1983-84; mem PA Nurses Assn, 1957-, Amer Nurses Assn, 1957-, Assn of Military Surgeons of US 1966-, Natl League for Nursing 1976-, Sigma Theta Tau 1977-, Assn of US Army 1978-, Retired Army Nurse Corps Assn, 1979-; lifetime mem, Nursing Educ Alumnae Assn Teacher's Coll Columbia Univ; honorary mem, Chi Eta Phi Alpha Chapter, Natl Black Nursing Sor, Delta Sigma Theta Black Professional Women's Org; Catholic Univ Alumnae Award. **HONORS/ACHIEVEMENTS:** Natl Freedom Day Assn Award, 1980; Recognition Award Tuskegee Inst Sch of Nursing 1981; Henry O Flipper Award Military Law Section Natl Bar Assn, 1981; Recognition Award, Syracuse Univ, 1981; Distinguished Prof of Nursing & Military Science, Prairie View A&M Univ, 1981; WK Kellogg lecturer AL State Univ, 1981; Bethune Tubman Truth Award Black Women Hall of Fame Found, 1981; Roy Wilkins Meritorious Serv Award, NAACP; Community Serv Award The Tuskegee Airmen Inc, 1983; Amer Black Achievement Award, Business & Professions Ebony Magazine 1983; Golden Heart Award, 1983; Alumni Achievement Award, Villanova Univ Coll of Nursing, 1983; Black Nurse of Year Greater Washington Area Black Nurses Assoc 1984; Fellow Amer Acad of Nursing 1984; Natl Inst for Women of Color Award, 1984; Natl Coalition of 100 Black Women's 1984 Candace Award; One of 100 Black Business & Professional Women in Amer, Dollars & Sense Magazine, 1985; numerous lectures & presentations; Catholic Univ Alumnae Award. **MILITARY SERVICE:** AUS Nurse Corps Brigadier General 28 1/2 yrs; First Black woman to reach rank of General in history of Military Services; Evangeline C Bovard Army Nurse of the Yr Award 1964; Army Commendation Medal 1966; Army Commendation Medal First Oak Leaf Cluster; Nurse of Yr Dr Anita Newcomb McGee Award Daughters of the Amer Revolution, 1971; Legion of Merit, 1973; Meritorious Serv Medal, 1979; Order of Military Med Merit, 1983; US Army ROTC Serv Award, 1983; Distinguished Serv Medal, 1983. **BUSINESS ADDRESS:** Professor of Nursing, George MasonUniv, 4400 University Dr, Fairfax, VA 22030.

JOHNSON-CARSON, LINDA D.
Department head of optometry. **PERSONAL:** Born Feb 05, 1954, Richland, MS; daughter of Adam Johnson and Gertrude Johnson; divorced; children: James III. **EDUCATION:** Jackson State Univ, BS 1974; Indiana State Univ School of Optometry, Doctor of Optometry 1978. **CAREER:** Jackson Hinds Comp Health Center, dept head, Optometry, 1978-. **ORGANIZATIONS:** Member, MS Optometric Assn 1978-, Southern Council of Optometrists 1974-; member & bd of dir Natl Optometric Assn 1974-; bd of dir, central MS chapter Amer Red Cross 1988-. **HONORS/ACHIEVEMENTS:** First black female optometrist in MS 1978; Professional Achievement Jackson State Univ Natl Alumni Assn 1980; Distinguished Serv Jackson Hinds Alumni Chapter Jackson State Natl Alumni Assn 1982; honorary member, Beta Beta Beta Biological Honor Soc, Jackson State Univ, 1984. **BUSINESS ADDRESS:** Department Head of Optometry, Jackson Hinds Comp Health Center, 4433 Medgar Evers Blvd, Jackson, MS 39213.

JOHNSON-CROCKETT, MARY ALICE
Physician. **PERSONAL:** Born May 06, 1937, Anderson, SC; daughter of William P Johnson and Bernice McAlister Johnson; married Edward D Crockett Jr (deceased); children: Edward D III, Alison V, Sharon P. **EDUCATION:** Howard Univ Coll of Liberal Arts, BS 1958; Howard Univ Coll of Medicine, MD 1962. **CAREER:** Freedman Hospital, intern 1963; DC General Hospital, Veterans Admin, Howard Univ, resident internal medicine 1963-66; Walter Reed Army Medical Center, medical officer 1966-67; Veterans Admin Hospital Downey IL, staff physician 1967-69; Community Group Health Found Inc, staff physician & acting medical dir 1969-72; Home Care Serv Bureau, medical officer, medical dir 1972-; Hospice Care of DC, medical dir 1979-82; private practice, internal medicine & geriatrics. **ORGANIZATIONS:** Consultant Income Maintenance Admin 1971-86; employee, health physician Law Enforcement Agency Admin & Consumer Products Safety Commn 1975, 1976-77; member exec comm Potomac PTA 1976-81; track physician Bowie Race Track 1977-81; professional adv comm Hospice Care of DC 1983-, UpJohn 1985-; steering comm Sidwell Friends School 1984-85; parent Support Group Youth Choir Plymouth Congregation UCC; consultant Natl Health Serv 1972-82; pres, W Henry Greene Friends of Music Soc 1988-. **HONORS/ACHIEVEMENTS:** Lucy Moten Fellowship Award for Foreign Travel Howard Univ 1957; Intern of the Year Howard Univ 1963; Hospice Award Hospice Care of DC 1983; Ronald C Newman Award Jackson-Newman Found Inc 1987. **BUSINESS ADDRESS:** Medical Dir, Home Care Services Bureau, DC General Hospital, Box 38, Washington, DC 20003.

JOHNSON-CROSBY, DEBORAH A.
Business executive. **PERSONAL:** Born Jan 15, 1951, Chicago; divorced; children: Malik Fanon. **EDUCATION:** Univ WI, BA 1974. **CAREER:** Mt Sinai Hosp, staff worker bus office 1969; Northside Comm Credit Union, loan clerk, comm relations 1970-71; Concentrated Employment Program, staff worker; Operation Breadbasket, pub relations dir 1972-73; Milwaukee Times, rptr 1973-74; Milwaukee Star Times, managing editor 1974-75; Milwaukee Bus Fedn, dir; free-lance journalist; communications consultant. **ORGANIZATIONS:** Mem Black Media Alliance WI; Pub Relations Comm; information officer Black Comm Student Alliance 1972-73; Milwaukee Assn; mem bd dirs Peckham Jr HS1974. **BUSINESS ADDRESS:** 3811 N 20 St, Milwaukee, WI 53206.

JOHNSON-SCOTT, JERODENE PATRICE
Physician. **PERSONAL:** Born Dec 15, 1952, Atlanta, GA; children: Lawrence Edward. **EDUCATION:** Spelman Coll, BS 1974; Meharry Medical Coll, MD 1978. **CAREER:** Atlanta Urban League, director-medical specialist program. **ORGANIZATIONS:** Mem Natl Assoc of Residents & Interns 1981-, Amer Medical Assoc 1983-; instructor Atlanta Urban League 1983-; vice pres Inner City Life Foundation 1984-;mem Natl Medical Assoc; mem Smithsonian Inst, Women's Health Network, Inner City Life Foundation. **HONORS/ACHIEVEMENTS:** Articles published Cascade Chronicle newspaper. **BUSINESS ADDRESS:** Dir Medical Speclst Prog, Atlanta Urban League, Career Opportunity Project, Atlanta, GA 30315.

JOHNSON-YOUNG, BARBARA JANEICE
Executive. **PERSONAL:** Born Oct 11, 1941, Mt Holly, NJ; married Benjamin H Young, Sr; children: Benjamin H Jr. **EDUCATION:** Wilberforce Univ, BA 1963; Springfield Coll, MEd 1978; American Internatl Coll, MA 1987. **CAREER:** Early Childhood Ctrs of Spfld, bd mem 1977-78; Amer Foundation for Negro Affairs, co-chairperson 1981-86; New England Consortium of Black Admissions Counselors, past external pres 1985-86; Mercy Coll, dir of admissions. **ORGANIZATIONS:** Mem Natl Assoc of Coll Admissions Counselors 1971-86; mem Alpha Kappa Alpha 1961-; liaison Young Services 1975-; volunteer Urban League 1984-; mem YWCA 1986-; mem New York Personnel & Guidance 1986-. **HONORS/ACHIEVEMENTS:** Licensed registered social worker for Commonwealth of MA 1983-. **BUSINESS ADDRESS:** Dir of Admissions, Mercy College, 555 Broadway, Dobbs Ferry, NY 10522.

JOHNSTON, HENRY BRUCE
Administrator. **PERSONAL:** Born Jul 04, 1927; married Cora Virginia Jackson; children: Geraldine, Mark, Lisa, Steven. **EDUCATION:** St John'sUniv Brooklyn, Attend;Univ Boston, natl grad; StUniv Farmingdale NY, AAS; StUniv Stoney Brook NY, MA, BS. **CAREER:** Suffolk Co Hum Rights Commn, exec dir 1985; StUniv Farmingdale, instr criminal justice; Suffolk Comm Coll, instr criminal justice; Police Acad Suffolk Co Police Dept, instr; Globe-Trotters Professional Bsktbl Org, former mem. **ORGANIZATIONS:** Bd of dir LI Sickle Cell Proj Nassau & Suffolk; bd dir Suffolk Rehab Ctr; bd of dir Suffolk Co Adv Bd Youth Srvs; bd of dir Diocesan Task Force for Poverty & Racism Nassau & Suffolk; adv bd of dir Crime Control Cncl Suffolk Co; bd of dir ed com NCCJ, Nassau & Suffolk; bd of dir Awards Com SCPD; bd of dir Boy Scouts of Am Suffolk Co; bd of dir Phi Beta Sigma Frat; bd of Dir Econ Opportunity Cncl Suffolk Co; bd of dir Urban League of LI Nassau & Suffolk Co; bd of dir Alcoholism Adv Commn Suffolk Co; mem NYCPD Youth Squad PAL Div; NAACP Nassau & Suffolk; Lions Club Hauppauge NY; bd of ed Grievance Com Hauppauge HS. **HONORS/ACHIEVEMENTS:** Purple Heart, AUS; Am Def Srv Medal, AUS; European-African Middle E Srv Medal AUS; Asiatic Pacific Srv Medal, AUS; Hunting PAL Award 1958; Top Bsktbl Ofcl 1960-61, 1969; Police Youth Award, SCPD 1961-62; Medal for Bravery, SCPD 1964; Outstndng Bsktbl Ofcl 1966; Meritorious Srv, SCPD 1967; Masons RecognitionAward, King Tyre Lodge 1967; Professionalization Award, SCPD 1969; Man of Yr NANBPW 1974; Black Std Union, SU Farmingdale 1975. **MILITARY SERVICE:** AUS 1st sgt 1942-45. **BUSINESS ADDRESS:** Co Center, Veterans Hwy, Hauppauge, NY 11787.

JOHNSTON, JULIA MAYO **See MAYO, JULIA A.**

JOHNSTON, PERCY EDWARD
Vice president. **PERSONAL:** Born May 18, 1930, New York, NY; children: 1 Child. **EDUCATION:** Howard U, AB 1960; Montclair St Clg, MA 1968; Long Island U, Cert SW 1967; New School, Film Prod 1969; Sltudio of Claire Heywood, Painting 1946-48. **CAREER:** Reliable Flower Shop, co-owner 1947-53; Dasein Quarterly Review, editor & publisher 1961-; Essex County Clg, adj prof speech 1968-69; Caldwell Adult Sch, adj prof philosophy 1968-69; Afro Am Studies Montclair St Clg Prof of Humanities, chm 1968-82; Studio Tangerine Theatre, artistic dir 1977-80; St Peters Clg, adj prof 1982-83; Afro Am Journal of Phil editor 1977-; Empire St Clg, adj prof drama 1984-85; Mohegan Comm Coll, prof of philosophy & lit 1985-; Richardson Foundation, vice pres. **ORGANIZATIONS:** Pres Afro Am Phil Asso Inc 1980-; coord NY Poets Coop 1974-76; partner Coffe & Confusion Gallery 1959-61; reporter Capital Times Newspaper 1959-61; partner Rinjohn Gallery 1974-76; auditor NY St Cncl on the Arts 1974-75; mem NJ St Cncl on the Arts 1981-83; pres Falasfa-frat & Sor in Philosphy 1982-; mem Pi Delta Epsilon Frat in Journalism 1969. **HONORS/ACHIEVEMENTS:** NDEA Flwshp in Humanities & Linguistics 1967-68; "Phenomenology of Space & Time 1975; "Dessalines, A Jazz Tragedy" New York City off of Bwy 1984; "Afro Am Philosophies" Editor 1970; Calliope Awd in Poetry 1975. **MILITARY SERVICE:** USAF 1949-51; Purple Heart, Air Medal 1951.

JOHNSTON, WALLACE O.
Business executive. **PERSONAL:** Born Nov 08, 1929, New York, NY; son of Wallace Johnston and Mary Smith Johnston; married Mildred Taylor; children: Arline, Wallace, Brenda, Kathryn, Asao, Toshio, Paige. **EDUCATION:** City Coll of NY, BMechEng 1963, Grad Study 1967; US Dept of Defense, Environ Eng 1968. **CAREER:** New York City Bd of Educ, eng 1959-68; Hannaham & Johnston, prtnr 1968-76; Wallace Johnston Engs, proprietor, chief engineer 1976-. **ORGANIZATIONS:** Bd of dir NY Assn Cnslt Engrs 1974-76; mem Nat Soc Professional Engr 1967-; mem Am Soc Mech Engr 1963-; tutorial dir Kappa Alpha Psi 1979; mem Natl Tech Assn 1982-; mem Math Assoc of Amer. **HONORS/ACHIEVEMENTS:** Tech Paper Bldng Systems Dsgns New York City 1976; Hnrbl Mntn Lincoln Wldng Inst OH 1961; Dsgn Awrd BSA Prgrsv Arch 1971; Lcnsd Engr NYS Bd ProfLcsng 1967; Who's Who in Engr 1982. **MILITARY SERVICE:** USAF airmn 1st cls 4 yrs; Good Cndct, Korean Theatre, Am Defense 1950-54. **BUSINESS ADDRESS:** Chief Engineer, Wallace Johnston Engineers, 363 7th Ave, New York, NY 10001.

JOINER, BURNETT
Educator. **PERSONAL:** Born Nov 10, 1941, Raymond, MS; son of Burnett and Arcine Joiner; married Inez Dixon; children: Michael, Christopher. **EDUCATION:** Utica Jr Coll, AA 1962; Alcorn State Univ, BS 1964; Bradley Univ, MA 1968; Univ of SC, PhD 1975. **CAREER:** Oliver School Clarksdale, MS, principal 1968-71; York School Dist #1, asst supt of schls 1971-73; SC Coll Orangeburg, SC, asst prof 1974-75; Atlanta Univ Atlanta, GA, exec dir/assoc prof 1975-80; Grambling State Univ, exec academic dean. **ORGANIZATIONS:** Mem Ouachita Valley Boy Scouts 1982-; charter mem Grambling Lion's Club 1983-; consultant US Dept Educ 1983-85; commr LA Learning Adv Commn 1984-85; commr LA Internship Commn 1984-85; mem Natl Inst of Education Study Group on Teacher Edn; chaired special comm in Coll of Educ Univ of SC on student advisement; past mem Curriculum Comm Sch of Educ at SC State Coll; mem Ruston-Lincoln C of C; vice chairperson Comm on Social Concerns Lewis Temple Church; conducted numerous workshops and seminars for more than 50 schools, agencies and community groups; mem of the bd of dir Teacher Ed Council for State Coll and Univ, American Assoc of Coll for Teacher Ed; mem of the Governor's Internship Commission and Learning Adv Commission. **HONORS/ACHIEVEMENTS:** Publications, "The Teacher Corps Policy Board; Three Perspectives on Role and Function" 1979; "A Documentation Primer; Some Perspectives from the Field" 1979; "New Perspectives on Black Education History" Book Review for the Journal of Negro History in progress; "Identifying Needs and Prioritizing Goals Through Collaboration" 1978; "Education That Is Multicultural; A Process of Curriculum Development" 1979; "The Design, Implementation and Evaluation of a Pre-Service Prototype Competency-Based Teacher Education Model" 1975; "Maximizing Opportunities for Professional Improvement" 1983; Improving Teacher Education: A Conscious Choice, co-author. **BUSINESS ADDRESS:** Executive Academic Dean, Grambling State University, PO Box 46, Grambling, LA 71245.

JOINER, CHARLES, JR.
Professional athlete. **PERSONAL:** Born Oct 14, 1947, Many, LA; married Dianne; children: Jynayna, Kori. **EDUCATION:** Grambling, BS 1969. **CAREER:** Gulf Oil Co, mgmt trainee 1971-; San Diego Chargers, tackle 1976-. **HONORS/ACHIEVEMENTS:** Pro Bowl 1976-77-80; 4 Varsity Letters Grambling; All Southwestern Athletic Conf 1968; named All Pro & All AFC second team AP & UPI 1980; MVP & Most Inspirational Player San Diego Chargers 1983; honored testimonial in Lake Charles on "Charlie Joiner Day" May 15, 1982 & Nov 20, 1986. **BUSINESS ADDRESS:** Assistant Coach, San Diego Chargers, 9449 Friars Road, San Diego, CA 92120.

JOLLY, MARVA LEE
Artist educator. **PERSONAL:** Born Sep 11, 1937, Crenshaw, MS; daughter of Floyd Pitchford, Sr and Mattie Louise Williams Pitchford; divorced. **EDUCATION:** Roosevelt Univ, BS 1961; Governors State Univ, MA 1974. **CAREER:** Univ of Chicago Lab Schools, teacher 1961-65; Chicago Youth Centers Head Start, teacher 1965, dir 1965-69; Chicago Commons Child Develop, program dir 1969-74; Chicago State Univ, prof of ceramics and practicing artist; Suburban Health Systems Agency, Chicago, IL, educator coord, l977-82; Chicago Youth Centers, Chicago, IL, dir headstart, l967-77. **ORGANIZATIONS:** Pres Artisan 21 Gallery 1981-85; self-taught ceramic/sculptor artist 1981-; bd mem African Amer Artist Roundtable 1985-, Exhibitions Comm Chicago Cultural Ctr; volunteer Southside Comm Art Center; curator Saphire and Crystals Black Women's Art Exhibition 1987; curator Earthstones and Rainbow Colors Clay & Textile by Black Chicago Artists; founder Mud Peoples Black Women's Resources Sharing Workshop; bd of dir, Urban Traditions, l984-; bd of dir, Chicago Cultural Center, l986-; sponsor, Children's Intl, l986-. **HONORS/ACHIEVEMENTS:** Best of Category Black Creativity Museum of Science & Industry 1984; Top Ten Emerging Black Chicago Artists 1986-87; Invitational Exhibition Changing Perceptions Columbia Coll Gallery; American Visions Afro-Amer Art 1986; Columbia Motion Pictures "Date Night" 7 art works by Marva Jolly for this movie; art work exhibited and sold Esther Saks Gallery Chicago; Today's Chicago Woman (profile,) l988; artist in Residence - Lakeside Group, l988. **HOME ADDRESS:** 5326 Hyde Park Blvd, Chicago, IL 60615.

JOLLY, MARY B.
Educational administrator. **PERSONAL:** Born Oct 23, 1940, New Orleans, LA; married Herbert Nicholas Jolly; children: Helaina, Nyla, Chanelle. **EDUCATION:** Loyola Univ, BS 1975; Univ of New Orleans, M 1982. **CAREER:** Jefferson Parish Sheriff's Office, personnel dir 1976-80; Loyola Univ, personnel dir 1980-. **ORGANIZATIONS:** Consultant Human Resources, EEO, Policies & Procedure 1980-; mem Coll and Univ Personnel Administration 1980-, LA Equal Oppor Assoc 1980-; exec bd mem Intl Information Assocs Personnel/Payroll System Users Group 1981-; regional conf program chair Amer Assoc for Affirmative Action 1986; pres of the bd Personnel Mgmt Assoc, New Orleans Metro Chap of Amer Soc of Personnel Administration 1986/87; mem Cross Keys Hon Serv Soc Loyola Univ; agency relationscomm United Way of Greater New Orleans. **HONORS/ACHIEVEMENTS:** Outstanding Serv to Community Urban League of New Orleans 1984; Outstanding Contribution to the City of New Orleans recognized by the Mayor of New Orleans 1984. **BUSINESS ADDRESS:** Dir of Personnel, Loyola University, 6363 St Charles Ave, New Orleans, LA 70118.

JONAS, ERNESTO A.
Physician. **PERSONAL:** Born Nov 13, 1939, Panama, PA; son of Harold L. Jonas and Laura Maria Anderson de Jonas; married Mary E. Cullen, Jan 15, 1965; children: Jorge A. Jonas, Clarissa M. Jonas. **EDUCATION:** Univ of Nueva Leon, Monterrey, Mexico, MD, 1966. **CAREER:** Nassau County Medical Ctr, E. Meadow, NY, chief, div of emergency medicine, 1973-76, direc, coronary care unit, 1976-79, chief, div of cardiology, 1979-, direc, cardiovascular training program, 1979-. SUNY at Stony Brook, asst prof of medicine, 1973-88, assoc prof of clinical medicine, 1988-. **ORGANIZATIONS:** Fellow, Amer Coll of Physicians, 1977-; fellow, Amer Coll of Cardiology, 1981-; treasurer, Assn of Black Cardiologists; member, exec comm, Dept of Medicine, SUNY at Stony Brook; member, bd of direcs, Amer Heart Assn, Nassau Chapter; member, Physician Edn Comm, Amer Heart Assn. **HONORS/ACHIEVEMENTS:** Excellence in Teachin Award, SUNY at Stony Brook, 1980; Disting Serv Award, Assn of Black Cardiologists, 1987; author of articles in medical journals. **HOME ADDRESS:** Dr. Ernesto A Jonas, Ten Orchard Drive, Woodbury, NY 11797.

JONES, ALBERT ALLEN
Clergyman. **PERSONAL:** Born Apr 02, 1913, New Orleans; married Beaulah Mae Houston. **EDUCATION:** Xavier U, PhB, AB 1952. **CAREER:** Pub Sch, tchr; Bapt Training Union Assn Ministers Alliance, tchr; Union Bapt Theol Sem LA, instr. **ORGANIZATIONS:** Asst dir Dept Christian Ed 1st Dist Missionary Bapt Assn; dir Bapt Training Union LA Bapt St Conv S & Region; mem bd trustees 1st Dist Missionary Bapt Assn; former pres, Mem Ponchartrain Pk Improvement Assn DD, conferred Inter-bapt Theol Ctr. **MILITARY SERVICE:** World War II vet, sgt. **BUSINESS ADDRESS:** Ephesian Bapt Ch, 4020 Melpomene Ave, New Orleans, LA 70125.

JONES, ALBERT J.
Educator. **PERSONAL:** Born Nov 25, 1928, Pittsburgh, PA; married Hattie E; children: Jeffrey L, Bertina M. **EDUCATION:** MD St Coll, BS; Univ Pittsburgh, MEd. **CAREER:** Somerset HS, sci tchr 1954-56; Wm C Jason HS, physics tchr 1956-66; Seaford HS, physics tchr 1966-71; DE Tech Comm Coll, cnslr 1971-74; DE Tech Comm Coll, adult ed coord 1974-87; DE Tech Comm Coll-South, Georgetown DE, test Coordinator 1988-89. **ORGANIZATIONS:** Omega Psi Phi 1958-87; Am Assn Physics Tchr 1966-71; DE Coll Cnslrs Assn 1971-74; Sussex Co Cnslrs Assn 1971-74; DE Foster Child Rev Bd 1979-80; Laurel DE Town Cncl 1971-75. **HONORS/ACHIEVEMENTS:** Nat Sci Found Grants Morgan St Coll 1958, Howard U, 1962, SC St Coll 1964,Univ Detroit 1965; St Laurence Univ 1968; Cnslrs In-Srv 1971, Training Inst OK St U; Univ of DE in-serv training inst 1981-84; Athletic Hall of Fame Univ of Maryland Eastern Shore 1975. **BUSINESS ADDRESS:** College Counselor, DE Tech & Comm College, PO Box 610 Rt 18, Georgetown, DE 19947.

JONES, ALEXANDER R.
Public relations manager. **PERSONAL:** Born Jan 21, 1952, Washington, DC. **EDUCATION:** MA Inst of Tech, BS 1970-74. **CAREER:** Nat Commn on Law Enforcement & Soc Justice Ch of Scientology, asso dir 1985. **ORGANIZATIONS:** Exec dir Citizens' Com for Comm Involvement 1985; ed "Unequal Justice-Under The Law" 1979-80. **HONORS/ACHIEVEMENTS:** Author nwspr column =Law & Social Justice" 1980-. **BUSINESS ADDRESS:** Ch of Scientology, 2125 S St NW, Washington, DC 20008.

JONES, ALFRED A.
Business executive. **PERSONAL:** Born Nov 07, New York, NY; married Lula; children: Lisa, Candice. **CAREER:** Al Jones Oil Corp, pres, founder 1970-; Grand Oil Co, vice pres 1961-69; Ebony Oil Corp, vice pres 1955-61; Concord Oil Corp, salesman 1954-55; Blackhills Oil Co, salesman 1951-53. **ORGANIZATIONS:** Dir Al Jones Fund & Pension Trust; pres Al Jones Trkg Corp; pres Nat Bus & League, Queens Chap 1973; mem Nat Bus League 1973; dir Jamaica Yth Org1971; dir Jamaica Trotters 1972; mem 8a-Contractors Achvmt, Phi Beta Sigma Frat 1973; Sevenday Adventist Choir, Rev Singleton 1971. **HONORS/ACHIEVEMENTS:** Man of Yr, St Albans Polit Act League 1972; rep Club Man of Yr Award, Geraldine Jones 1975. **MILITARY SERVICE:** AUS corpl 1948-50. **BUSINESS ADDRESS:** 110 14 Merrick Blvd, Jamaica, NY 11433.

JONES, ALFREDEAN
Educational administrator. **PERSONAL:** Born Sep 30, 1940, Jonesville, SC; married Betty Jean Smith; children: Pamela, Shelia, Dean. **EDUCATION:** SC State Coll, BS 1963; NC A&T State Univ, MS 1972; Lehigh Univ, Adm Cert 1975. **CAREER:** Chicago Cubs Minors, player 1963-67; NJ Correctional System, supervisor of recreation 1964-67; Easton Area School Dist, teacher 1967-75, administrator 1975-87. **ORGANIZATIONS:** Bd of dirs 1st vice pres Housing Authority 1976-; bd of dirs Educ Day Care Ctr, Children Home of Easton; 1st vice pres Easton Branch of NAACP. **HONORS/ACHIEVEMENTS:** Certificates of Appreciation Graduating Class of 1984, Children Home of Easton 1985, Easton Branch of NAACP 1986. **HOME ADDRESS:** 155 Reese St, Easton, PA 18042. **BUSINESS ADDRESS:** Assistant Principal, Easton Area School Dist, 25th & William Penn Hwy, Easton, PA 18042.

JONES, ALPHONZO JAMES
Physician. **PERSONAL:** Born Nov 13, 1946, Idabel, OK; son of B.J. Jones and Ada Jones; married Dorothy Ann Henderson; children: Dorothy Annette, Veronica Adele; Rose. **EDUCATION:** OK Baptist, BS (Cum Laude) 1968; Howard Univ, MD 1972. **CAREER:** US

Navy, medical officer (achieved rank Lt Commdr(incl residency fam med) 1973-77; Private Practice Memphis, TN, physician 1977-82; St Paul Hospital Dallas TX, medical staff 1983-; CIGNA Healthplan of TX Dallas, staff physician 1983-. **ORGANIZATIONS:** Chf of staff Garland Center CIGNA Healthplan 1983-84; bd of governors Memphis Health Center Inc 1979-81; mem Amer Acad of Family Physicians, Natl Medical Assoc, CV Roman Medical Soc Dallas. **HONORS/ACHIEVEMENTS:** Howard Univ Alumni Award for highest scholastic average over 4 yrs med sch; Alpha Omega Alpha Med Honor Soc 1971 induction; Physician of the Yr Bluff City Med Soc Memphis, TN 1981; Fellow Amer Acad of Fam Physicians 1978; certified, American Bd of Family Practice 1976, recertified 1982 and 1989. **MILITARY SERVICE:** USN Lt Cdr 1973-77. **HOME ADDRESS:** 1700 N Yale Blvd, Richardson, TX 75081.

JONES, AMMIA W.
Clergyman. **PERSONAL:** Born Jan 31, 1910, Mesic, NC; children: 4 Children. **ORGANIZATIONS:** Past pres, NAACP; commn, Mesic NC.

JONES, ANN R.
Educator. **PERSONAL:** Born Jul 05, 1921, New Castle, PA; married Paul L Jones; children: Connie E Rose. **EDUCATION:** Livingstone Coll, BA 1944; Univ of Pittsburgh, MSW 1964, PhD 1978. **CAREER:** Irene Kaufmann Ctr, prog dir 1952-60; Anna Heldman Ctr, prog dir 1960-64; Action Housing, dir of training 1964-66; Community Action, dir of training 1966-70;Univ of Pittsburgh, prof. **ORGANIZATIONS:** Provost adv comm Womens Concerns; dir Soc Work Field Educ; nom comm Natl Council Soc Work; site visitor Natl Council Social Educ Work; mem adv comm Allegheny Children Youth Svcs; pres Hazelwood Neighborhood Council; mem bd dir Three Rivers Adoption Council. **HONORS/ACHIEVEMENTS:** Post-Gazette Disting Woman 1969; Black Studies Univ of Pittsburgh Black Studies 1980; Disting Alumni Univ of Pittsburgh 1985; Task Force Recognition Cty Commissioners 1986. **BUSINESS ADDRESS:** Professor, University of Pittsburgh, 2217 Cathedral of Learning, Pittsburgh, PA 15260.

JONES, ANNETTE MERRITT **See MERRITT-CUMMINGS, ANNETTE**

JONES, ANTHONY, JR.
Business executive. **PERSONAL:** Born Sep 21, 1933, New York, NY; married Arnoline Whitten; children: Leslie Ann. **EDUCATION:** NY Univ, BS 1958, MS 1964. **CAREER:** Bd of Educ NYC, sci tchr 1959-69; Bedford Stuyvesant Restoration Corp, dir of emplymnt 1969-79; OIC of NY, div mgr 1979-81; So Bronx Dev Org Inc, proj dir 1981-84, dir of Emplymnt & Trng; NY City Police Dept, dir victim & volunteer serv 1987-. **ORGANIZATIONS:** Exec comm Manpower Plng Cncl New York City 1975-79; comm mem Mayors Comm on Adoption 1973-75; comm mem Alexander's Dept Store Affirmative Actn Comm 1973-75; mem Rotry Clb Bklyn, NY 1975-79; mem Kappa Alpa Psi New York Chptr 1956-65. **HONORS/ACHIEVEMENTS:** Natl Sci Alfred Univ, NY 1964; Fndtn Univ of Puerto Rico 1966. **HOME ADDRESS:** 114-65 222nd St, Cambria Heights, NY 11411. **BUSINESS ADDRESS:** Dir Victim & Volunteer Serv, New York City Police Dept, One Police Plaza, New York, NY 10038.

JONES, ARLENDER
Chief executive of bank. **CAREER:** Emerald City Bank, Seattle WA, chief executive, 1989. **BUSINESS ADDRESS:** Emerald City Bank, 1323 Second Ave, Seattle, WA 98101. *

JONES, ARNOLD PEARSON
Educational administrator. **PERSONAL:** Born in Chicago, IL; married Joan L; children: Victoria, Arnold, Douglas. **EDUCATION:** Western MI Univ, BS 1950; DePaul Univ, MEd 1955; Univ of IL Urbana, PhD 1972. **CAREER:** Chicago Public Schools, teacher, school psychologist, principal 1965, asst supt of schools 1967-69; Malcolm X Coll, vice pres acad 1969-70; Northeastern IL Univ, prof psychology, spec asst to pres 1971-78; City Colleges of Chicago, exec vice chancellor human resources & labor relations. **ORGANIZATIONS:** Comm Human Rights Commission 1981-83; bd of dirs ACLU; mem educ task force Chicago Urban League; life mem NAACP; mem educ core comm Chicago United; mem Alpha Phi Alpha; past natl pres Amer Bridge Assoc, Natl Assoc of Affirm Action; mem school bd nominating comm City of Chicago. **HONORS/ACHIEVEMENTS:** Phi Beta Kappa. **MILITARY SERVICE:** AUS capt 2 yrs. **BUSINESS ADDRESS:** Executive Vice Chancellor, City Colleges of Chicago, 226 West Jackson, Chicago, IL 60601.

JONES, ARTHUR L.
Engineer. **PERSONAL:** Born Apr 15, 1922, Sioux City, IA; married Annie Geneva Williams; children: Shirley, Joseph N, Ronald, Lester, Thomas, Nancy, Marcy. **EDUCATION:** Univ of MI, BS Civil Engineering 1955; MI State Univ, MS Civil Engineering 1973. **CAREER:** US Army Corp of Engineers, structural designer 1941-45; Doehler Jarvis-Electro Plating Div, solution maintainer 1945-55; Haven Busch Co Structural Steel Fabricators, structural engineer 1955-57; MI Dept of Transportation, bridge design engineer 1957-83, departmental administrator 1983-. **ORGANIZATIONS:** Pres Lansing-Jackson Branch ASCE (Amer Soc of Civil Engineers) 1968; pres MI Section ASCE 1974-75; chairperson Engineering Alumni Assn MSU 1979; mem Engineering Alumni Assn Univ of MI; mem MI Soc of State Highway Engineers; MI Licensed Professional Engr-Civil 1963-; mem trustee bd Trinity AME Church 1969-; mem NAACP; mem Big Brothers; mem Free and Accepted Mason (PHA) 1965-; mem Scottish Rites Masonry 1965-; mem AEAO Noble of the Mystic Shrine 1966-. **MILITARY SERVICE:** AUS M/Sgt 1941-45; Amer Defense Serv Ribbon; Euro-African-Middle East Theater Ribbon w/4 Bronze Battle Stars; 5 Overseas Serv Bars; Good Conduct Medal. **HOME ADDRESS:** 978 Crimson Court, East Lansing, MI 48823.

JONES, ASBURY PAUL
Clergyman. **PERSONAL:** Born Sep 23, 1914, Lynchburg, VA; married Annie Marie Holt; children: Annette, Paul Jr, Anita, Marion. **EDUCATION:** Conroe Normal Indsl Coll, BTh 1955, BD 1958; Linfield Coll, DD 1974. **CAREER:** Sacramento Br Conroe Coll, prof 1953-; New Hope Bapt Ch Sacramento CA, minister 1955-. **ORGANIZATIONS:** Dean of Christian Educ St John Dist BTU Sunday Sch Cong 1957-68; pres of cong St John Dist BTU Sunday Sch Cong 1968-77; first vice pres CA Baptist State Convention 1970-. **HONORS/ACHIEVEMENTS:** First Black Chaplain appointed CA Senate 1973. **MILITARY SERVICE:** AUS sgt t/4 3 yrs; Army Commendation Medal. **BUSINESS ADDRESS:** Minister, New Hope Baptist Church, 3700 32nd St, Sacramento, CA 95820.

JONES, AUDREY BOSWELL
Attorney. **PERSONAL:** Born in Dallas, TX; married Winfeld Jones (deceased); children: Ronald. **EDUCATION:** Univ of MN, Undergrad; TN St U, BS 1933; SW Law Sch, JD 1956; Univ of S CA, CA St, Grad Work. **CAREER:** Self-empoyed, atty at law 1958-; St of CA, welfare agt 1949-51; LA Dept Soc Srv, supvng soc wrkr 1937-52; LA Police Commn, hearing exam; Cal new car dealer board president. **ORGANIZATIONS:** Past pres, mem CA & New Motor Vehicle Bd 1969-; bd of dirs SE Symphony Assn, United Stroke Prog; Am Bar Assn; Langston Law Club; Black Women Lawyers; Wilshire Bar Assn; LA Co Bar Assn; arbtn panel LA Co Bar Assn; S CA Women Lawyers; mem Eastern Star; Heroine of Jericho; past Nat ofcr Alpha Kappa Alpha Sor; past pres LA Soc Wk Local AFL 1976; past ofcr Tiffany Guild Crippled Childrens Soc, Pres 12 Big Sisters; Oper of Faustine Home for Girls. **HONORS/ACHIEVEMENTS:** Cert for Comm Srv, LA Hum Rel Comm; num awards & recognitions;Anhauser Busch Comm Service Award, Phillys Temple.

JONES, BARBARA A. P. (NEE POSEY)
Educator. **PERSONAL:** Born Jun 23, 1943, Oklahoma City, OK; married Mack H; children: Lumumba. **EDUCATION:** Univ of OK, AB 1963;Univ of IL, AM 1966; GA St U, PhD 1973. **CAREER:** Clark Coll, prof, Economics 1971-; TX Southern Univ, instructor; Atlanta Univ, instructor 1968-69. **ORGANIZATIONS:** Sec-treas Nat Econ Assn 1975-80; papers del at meetings of Nat Econ & Assn, Am Econ Assn, Nat Conf of Blk Pol Sci, Ind Rel Res Assn; presOglethorpe Sch PTA 1976-78; bd of trst Clark Coll 1973-74, 1975-79. **HONORS/ACHIEVEMENTS:** Srv in civil rights Russell Bull Award 1963; S Felshp Fund 1969-71; Outstnd Indep Std,Univ of OK 1963; Ford Found Dissertation Award 1970-71; Mortar Bd. **BUSINESS ADDRESS:** Prairie View Univ, Prairie View, TX 77446.

JONES, BEN F.
Educator. **PERSONAL:** Born May 26, 1942, Paterson, NJ. **EDUCATION:** William Paterson Coll, BA 1963; NY Univ, MA 1967; Pratt Inst, MFA. **CAREER:** Natl Conf of Art, pres 1978-80, vice pres 1981-84; Sulaimoan Dance Co, chmn of bd 1981-83; Jersey City State, prof of art. **ORGANIZATIONS:** Mem NJ Printmkng Cncl 1979-; mem World Printmkng Cncl 1980-; mem Natl Conf Artists; bd mem Friends of Music & Art in Hudson Co 1985; exhibited at many galleries and museums throughout the country; mem bd of advisors Woodson Foundation of NJ. **HONORS/ACHIEVEMENTS:** Flwshp grant Natl Endowmnt for Arts 1974-75; flwshp grant NJ State Cncl the Arts 1977-78, 1983-84; 1st Pl & 2nd Pl in art comp Atlanta Life Ins 1982-83; Grant Jersey City State Coll 1982-83; Career Dev Awrd of Excel Passaic Cnty Coll Paterson, NJ 1984; Excellence in the Arts Delta Sigma Theta Sor 1985. **BUSINESS ADDRESS:** Professor of Art & Artist, Jersey City State, Kennedy Blvd, Jersey City, NJ 07305.

JONES, BENJAMIN E.
Business executive. **PERSONAL:** Born Sep 08, 1935, New York, NY; married Delcenia R; children: Leslie, Delcenia. **EDUCATION:** Brooklyn Coll, BA 1971; Pace U, MBA 1974. **CAREER:** Capital Formation Inc Econ Devel Found NYC, pres 1971-; Interracial Council for Business Opportunity NYS, program dir 1971; Gen Precision Inc, sr contract admin/negotiator/signer 1966-71; ESX Div Paal Corp, accountant 1962-66; Radio Recepter Co, admin 1959-60; MBA Mgmt Consult Ins, Columbia Univ, dir 1973-. **ORGANIZATIONS:** Mem, Minority Business Opportunity Comm Fed Exec Bd, 1972-; bd of dir, Upper Park Ave Comm Assn Day Care Center, 1974-; mem, Amer Mgmt Assn; mem, Natl Business League; mem, Council Concerned Black Execs; mem, Natl Assn Black Mfrs; mem, Assn MBA Execs; mem, NAACP; mem, One Hundred Black Men Inc; mem, Uptown Chamber of Commerce; mem, NY Urban League; mem, Amer Assn MESBICS. **MILITARY SERVICE:** USAF 1955-58. **BUSINESS ADDRESS:** President, Minority Business Exchange, One Madison Ave, New York, NY 10010.

JONES, BERNARD H., SR.
Administrator. **PERSONAL:** Born Feb 13, 1931, Pittsburgh, PA; married Geraldine C Johnson; children: Bernard H Jr, Hylene K, Cornell D. **EDUCATION:** Knoxville College, BA 1957; Duquesne University, Mgmt Inst Program. **CAREER:** Pittsburgh's Commission of Human Relations, co-worker 1963-64; Urban Redevelopment Authority, Pittsburgh, dir community improvement 1964-68; Allegheny Conf on Community Devel, assistant dir 1968-; POISE Foundation, president and dir 1980-. **ORGANIZATIONS:** Urban Youth Action, Inc, founder and honorary chairman 1966; The Misters, Inc & The Misters Investment Assoc, founder and president 1967; UMP Investment Club, founder and managing partner 1973; Pittsburgh Rotory Club, member 1974-; Pittsburgh Business Resource Center, board of dir 1979-; POISE Foundation, founder, president and dir 1980; West Penn Motor Club AA, board of dir 1984-; NAACP, life member. **HONORS/ACHIEVEMENTS:** Top Hat Award-New Pittsburgh Courier 1967; Natl Alliance of Business Award-NAB Washington, DC 1979; Pennsylvania NAACP State Award 1981; Man of The Year Award-Pittsburgh Gallat Ladies Club 1982. **MILITARY SERVICE:** USM Private 1951. **BUSINESS ADDRESS:** President, Poise Foundation, Allegheny Conf on Comm Dev, 600 Grant St, Stuie 4444, Pittsburgh, PA 15219.

JONES, BERTHA DIGGS
Writer, lecturer. **PERSONAL:** Born in Richland, GA; divorced; children: Betty Jean. **EDUCATION:** Cen School of Business Buffalo, 1968; Columbia, personnel; POHS NY, 1967. **CAREER:** Diggs Assoc Urban Affairs Cons, pres; NYS Or Nation, first black sec of labor 1944-55; FEPC, consultant 1945; EEA-WDP, Supr. **ORGANIZATIONS:** Mem & adv com NYS Div Housing 1961-69; bus consult NYS Dept of Commerce 1970-71; sec State Labor Dept 1973-75; mem Pres Adv Counc PaceUniv NY 1966-77; mem adv council Corsi Labor/Mgmt Inst PaceUniv 1966-77; exec NYS dir Crispus Attucks Rep Lge 1938-55; statewide orgnr & exec dir State Bapt Congress 1956-69; consult to chmn Buffalo Housing Auth 1942; org first Jr Club Nat Assn Negro Bus & Professional Women NYS 1945; designed Nat Empl Pool 1946; memUrban League; NAACP; bd dir Brooklyn Chap Am Red Cross; Am Acad Polit & Soc Sci Ctr for Study of Presidency. **HONORS/ACHIEVEMENTS:** Silver Cup Natl Rep Council 1948; Sojourner Truth Award 1964; Meritorious Serv Award State Amer Legion Unit; Serv Award Visiting Nurse Assn of Brooklyn 1967-69; cert of serv NYS Labor Dept 1975; Comm Serv Award, Woman of Year Philadelphia Church of Universal Brotherhood 1977; author Home & Family Seminars 1956; continuous publ newsletters 1935-77; natl hon mem Lambda Kappa Mu Sor.

JONES, BERTHA H.
Educator. **PERSONAL:** Born Oct 30, 1918, Earle, AR; married Joseph R children: Malcolm. **EDUCATION:** Illinois State Univ, BE; Ball State Univ, MA; Northwestern Univ; Michigan Univ; Loyola Univ; Indiana Univ; Northwest and Purdue Univ. **CAREER:** Gary Public Schools Educational Talent Search, dir 1969-; speech teacher 1951-56; English tchr 1956-59; counselor 1959-69. **ORGANIZATIONS:** IN Proj Dir & Assoc chrm v chrm; IN Pers and Guidance Assoc; Am Pers and Guidance Assoc Dele from IN; adv bd for INUniv Northwest Campus; spec serv Midwest Assoc Stu Fin Aid Admin; Upward Bound adv bd Metro Corps OEO Delegate Agcy bd dir; Delta Sigma Theta; YWCA Teen Comm bd dir; Van Buren Bapt Ch; Urban League Consumer Ed Task Force IN U. **HONORS/ACHIEVEMENTS:** Award of serv to students 1974; IN Pers and Guidance Assoc Merit Award in Guidance 1973; elected Supreme 1st Anti-basileus of Nat Sorority of Phi Delta Kappa 1969, 1971; Pi Lambda Theta; Hnr Soc for Women in Ed 1961. **BUSINESS ADDRESS:** 2131 Jackson St, Gary, IN 46407.

JONES, BETTY HARRIS
Educator. **PERSONAL:** Born May 25, 1937, St Louis, MO; married Calvin Walter; children: Christopher Walter, Calvin Walter Jr. **EDUCATION:** Rutgers Univ, AB (cum laude) 1967; Bryn Mawr Coll, MA 1968, PhD 1972. **CAREER:** Rutgers Univ, instr in English 1969-72, asst prof of English 1972-. **ORGANIZATIONS:** Mem Speakers Buireau Rutgers Univ 1972-; mem Scholar Comm Dist III of Bryn Mawr PA Coll Club 1973-; Danforth Found Fellow Danforth Found Assn 1972-. **HONORS/ACHIEVEMENTS:** Rutgers Univ Fac Fellow 1977; num Bryn Mawr Coll Tuition Scholarships; mem Athanaeum Adac Hon Soc 1966-; author "Moorhouse Revisited, Another Look at St John Rivers" The English Record Vol XXXII 1981; "Maidens and Magicians, Milton's "Comus" and Hawthorne's The House of the Seven Gables" Occasional Papers inLanguage Literature & Linguistics Series A 1983. **BUSINESS ADDRESS:** Asst Prof of English, Rutgers University, Camden, NJ 08102.

JONES, BETTY JEAN T.
Educator. **PERSONAL:** Born Jul 14, 1943, Charleston, SC; married Donald; children: Tracey Laverne. **EDUCATION:** Hampton Inst VA, BS 1965; FairfielsUniv CT, MA 1970;Univ of VA. **CAREER:** Charlottesville HS VA, biology tchr VA 1974-; Lane HS, tchr 1973-74; Charlottesville HS, tchr 1974-; Fairfield U, grad study 1968-69; Dolan Jr HS CT, sci & tchr 1965-68. **ORGANIZATIONS:** Mem Charlottesville Educ Assn bd dir 1974-; Environmental Sci Com Charlottesville Sch 1974-75; Am Assn of Univ Women 1970-; Nat Assn of Biology Tchr 1965-; Stanford Educ Assn 1965-68; CT Educ Assn 1973-; VA Assn 1973-; VA Assn of Sci Tchr 1973-; Nat Educ Assn; Exec Com Charlottesville HS Nat Honor Soc; participant Parent-edn ConfUniv of VA; sponsor Biol Experiments Club Charlottesville HS 1974-; mem Alpha Kappa Mu; Beta Kappa Chi Nat Honor Soc; Delta Sigma Theta Sorority; treas Barret Day Care Center bd 1973-; negotiating team Charlottesville Educ Assn 1975-76; supts Adv council & Charlottesville VA 1975-76; com for Gifted Charlottesville Sch System 1975-; man relations com Charlottesville Sch 1973-74; United Way of Charlottesville 1975-76; sec NY Hampton Alumni Club 1968-69; mem Jaycees Wives OHUniv 1970-72; Phi Delta Kappa Nat Honor Soc 1977; family life com Charlottesville Sch;Univ of VA Faculty Wives Club; First Bapt Ch Growth Com; Charlottesville Dem Womens Club Listed in Dictionar of Intl Biograph. **BUSINESS ADDRESS:** Charlottesville HS, 1400 Melbourne Rd, Charlottesville, VA.

JONES, BILLY EMANUEL
Physician. **PERSONAL:** Born Jun 11, 1938, Dayton, OH; children: Alexander. **EDUCATION:** Howard U, BS 1960; Meharry Med Coll, MD 1965. **CAREER:** Metropolitan Hospital CMHC, asst dir 1971-73; Coney Island Hosp Dept Psychiatry, assoc dir 1973-74; Fordham Hospital Dept Psychiatry, dir 1974-77; NYMC/Lincoln Hosp Dept of Psychiatry, dir 1977-. **ORGANIZATIONS:** Pres Black Psychiatrists of Amer 1978-80; prof Clin Psych NY Med Coll 1985-; fellow Amer Psychiatric Assn 1983-; diplomate Amer Bd of Psychiatry andNeurology 1977-; mem New York City Comm Serv Bd 1980-; mem NYS Alcohol Drug Abuse & Mental Health Block Grant Comm 1983-; mem 100 Black Men. **HONORS/ACHIEVEMENTS:** "Manic Depressive Illness Among Poor Urban Blacks" Amer Journ of Psych Vol 138#9 May, 1981; "Survey of Psychotherapy with Black Men" Amer Journ of PsychVol 139#9 Sept, 1982; author of book, "Treating the Homeless, Urban Psychiatry's Challange" Amer Psych Press (at press). **MILITARY SERVICE:** AUS Major served 2 yrs 1969-71. **BUSINESS ADDRESS:** Dir, NYMC/Lincoln Hosp, 234 E 149th St, Dept Psychiatry, Bronx, NY 10451.

JONES, BOBBY
Educator. **PERSONAL:** Born Feb 28, 1933, New York, NY; married Dolores; children: Lisa, Ivan. **EDUCATION:** Morehouse Coll, AB 1953; Columbia U, MA 1957;Univ of GA, EdD 1973. **CAREER:** Mercer Univ, chmn educ dept 1972-; Upward Bound Mercer Univ, dir 1970-72; Bib Cty School System, curriculum dir 1968-70; Ballard-Hudson Sr High, teacher 1963-68; Mercer Univ, dir math workshop 1975-79. **ORGANIZATIONS:** Mem GAE. **BUSINESS ADDRESS:** 1400 Coleman Ave, Macon, GA 31207.

JONES, BONNIE LOUISE
Lawyer. **PERSONAL:** Born Feb 03, 1952, Philadelphia, PA; daughter of William Smith Jones and Thelma Mills Jones. **EDUCATION:** Lincoln Univ, BA 1970; NC Central Univ School of Law, JD 1982. **CAREER:** VA Legal Aid Soc, law clerk 1982-83; Newport News Police Dept, permits examiner 1983-85; Hampton Roads Regional Acad of Criminal Justice, training/evaluation specialist 1985-; Blayton Allen & Assocs, assoc attorney 1986-; self-employed atty Hampton VA, 1988-. **ORGANIZATIONS:** Mem Phi Alpha Delta Law Fraternity 1982-; mem Big Brother/Big Sisters of Peninsula 1985; bd mem Natl Conf of Christians & Jews 1986-; pres Intl Training in Comm Odyssey Club 1986-; mem Amer & VA Bar Assocs 1986; mem Assoc of Trial Attorneys of Amer; mem PA Bar Assn 1987-; Hampton Bar Assn 1988-; council vice pres Intl Training in communication council II 1988-89; bd mem Hampton Youth Services 1989-. **HONORS/ACHIEVEMENTS:** Commendation for 5 city talent show from Committee for Educ of Gifted Students Hampton School System 1979; attorney for WVEC-Channel 13 Midday TV program 1987-; series of lectures to chines lawyers journalists and economnists at Hampton Univ on practicing law as a minority in Amer. **BUSINESS ADDRESS:** Attorney At Law, Harbour Centre, 2 Eaton Street, Suite 708, Hampton, VA 23669.

JONES, BOOKER TEE
Housing director. **PERSONAL:** Born Jun 30, 1939, Mesic, NC; married Loretta Johnson; children: Hilda Davis, Booker T Jr, Marietta, Coretta. **EDUCATION:** LaSalle Ext Univ, AA, Acct, 1959; Central Appraiser Soc, RE Appr Designation 1971; Natl Center for Housing Mgmt, Housing Mgmt Certificate 1981. **CAREER:** Kingsborough Realty Inc, real estate salesman 1963-67; One Stop Home Sales Co, owner, rebroker, appraiser 1967-74; Coastal Progress Inc, coordinator, admin 1977-80; Twin Rivers Opportunity Inc, housing dir 1980-85, exec dir 1985-. **ORGANIZATIONS:** Real estate broker Booker T Jones Real Estate Brokerage 1972-85; real estate appraiser, Dept of HUD 1972-73; pres United Communities Assn Net Inc 1975-85; bd of dir, mem Craven County Fed Credit Union 1979-82; vice chmn of bd Pamlico County Bd of Ed 1980-85; chmn of bd of dir NC Section 8 Housing Assn Inc 1984-85. **HONORS/ACHIEVEMENTS:** Outstanding Serv The United Way 1977; Leadership Training the Natl Citizen Participation Council Inc 1979; NC Governor's Appointment Pamlico Cty Transp Efficiency 1982; Exemplarary Serv NC Sect 8 Housing Assoc Inc 1984. **HOME ADDRESS:** PO Box 68, Grantsboro, NC 28529.

JONES, BRENT M.
Photographer, educator, journalist. **PERSONAL:** Born Feb 11, 1946, Chicago, IL; married Ingrid. **EDUCATION:** Columbia Coll, BA 1969. **CAREER:** Chicago Art Inst, tchr 1976-; freelance photographer & writer; Black Associated Enterprises, chief photographer 1970-73; Columbia Coll, instr creative writing; 1969-70; one-man exhibitions; US Rep; 2nd World Black & African Festival of Arts & Culture; photos from FESTAC Ebony; Opportunity Industrialization Training Cntr, English instr & asst dir pub relations 1969-70. **HONORS/ACHIEVEMENTS:** Management Mag contrib ed 1969-70; article Tribune Mag. **BUSINESS ADDRESS:** 540 N Lake Shore Dr, Chicago, IL.

JONES, BUCK
Clergyman. **PERSONAL:** Born Nov 18, 1940, Hernando, FL; married Ethel Mae; children: Diogenes, Jennifer, Careem. **EDUCATION:** MI State Univ, BA 1960; Yale Univ, BS MAR 1964; Eden Theol Sem, DD 1976. **CAREER:** NY State Council Chs, dir migrant prog 1964-66; United Ch Christ Neighborhood Houses, dir comm devel 1966-70. **ORGANIZATIONS:** Mem Yale Club; dir & founder Oper & Live Orgn; dir & founder E St Louis Tenant Rights Orgn; Comm Equal Justice bd dir; chm MO Task Force Walfare Reform Nat Assn. **HONORS/ACHIEVEMENTS:** Social Workers Citizen Yr; Ruth Porter Award; Jane Addams Medal; Geo Wash Carver Award Sigma Gamma Rho Sorority. **BUSINESS ADDRESS:** 1720 Chouteau Ave, St Louis, MO 63103.

JONES, BUTLER ALFONSO
Educator, sociologist. **PERSONAL:** Born Jul 22, 1916, Birmingham, AL; son of Jackson Jones and Nettie B Jones; married Lillian E Webster (deceased); married Mary M Martin, 1981. **EDUCATION:** Morehouse Coll, AB 1937; Atlanta Univ, AM 1938; NYU, PhD 1955. **CAREER:** Atlanta Univ Lab Schools, teacher 1938-42; Talladega Coll, prof Social Science 1943-52; OH Wesleyan Univ Delaware, assoc prof sociology 1952-69; Cleveland State Univ, prof dept sociology 1969-, chmn 1969-76; Oberlin Coll, visiting prof 1962-63; Hamline Univ, 1966-67. **ORGANIZATIONS:** Mem Ohio Valley Social Soc; Soc for Applied Anthropology; Amer Soc Assn; Soc for Study Social Problems; Assn for Study of Negro Life & History; conducted extension soc rsch on effectiveness of law in directing social change. **HONORS/ACHIEVEMENTS:** Phi Beta Kappa; Alpha Kappa Delta (sociology).

JONES, CALDWELL LAVELLE
Professional athlete. **PERSONAL:** Born Aug 04, 1950, Mc Gehee, AR. **EDUCATION:** Albany State Coll. **CAREER:** Philadelphia 76ers, center 1976-82; Houston Rockets, center 1982-83; Chicago Bulls, center 1984-. **HONORS/ACHIEVEMENTS:** Traded to Houston along with 1st round pick in exchange for Moses Malone in 1982; also set a new career high in free throw percentage hitting 837 from the Line. **BUSINESS ADDRESS:** Chicago Bulls, 333 N Michigan Ave, Ste 510, Chicago, IL 60601.

JONES, CALVIN BELL
Visual artist, painter. **PERSONAL:** Born Jan 07, 1934, Chicago, IL; son of Melvin Jones and Kathryn Elizebeth Bell; divorced; children: Bryon Eugene Jones. **EDUCATION:** Art Inst Univ of Chicago, BA drawing/paint/illus 1957. **CAREER:** AFAM Gallery Studio & Cultural Cntr, co-dir 1970-75; Tuesday Publs (Sunday Supplement), illustrator 1970-75; Black Book Bulletin-Third World Press, creative& art dir 1971-73; Chicago Mural Project Group, master muralist 1976-80; Chicago Tribune Magazine, illustrator 1977-78; C Jones Inc, painter/illustrator. **ORGANIZATIONS:** Creative & art dir Hallmark Card Inc adv sales promo 1960-62; painter/illust Coca Cola (famous Black Amer series) 1976; painter/artist Motorola (50th yrs); Natl Conf of Artist Coord of Regions 1983-85; mem Natl Conf of Artist 1970-80; visual artist/cons Ebony Talent Creative Arts Found 1977-80; US Rep/delegate Intl Arts & Cultural Festac 1977. **HONORS/ACHIEVEMENTS:** Builders Award Third World Press 1977; Natl Endowment (Mural Painting Grant) Natl Endowment of the Arts 1978-79; Aaron Douglas Muralist Award Natl Conf of Artist 1979 & 1983; Artist in Residence Univ of IL Urbana 1980; Achievement Award in the Arts Kappa Alpha Psi 1988; 24' X 125' Mural "Bright Moments-Memories of the Future" 1987.

JONES, CARL L.
Association executive. **PERSONAL:** Born Jan 21, 1933, Elmore City, OK; married Leontine. **EDUCATION:** Langston U, BS 1954; OK State U, grad study 1957; Washington U, 1967, 1970. **CAREER:** Langston U, accountant 1954-55, chief accountant, asst bus mgr 1956-61, dir pub relations 1961-66; IBM, adminstr Staff 1966-67; St Louis Human Devel Corp, asst comptroller 1967-73; Urban League St Louis, controller 1973-; Kingsway Merchants Assoc, exec dir 1981-86; St Louis Oppty Industrialization Ctr, exec dir 1987-. **ORGANIZATIONS:** Mem Nat Assn Black Accountants; Am Accounting Assn mem Union Memorial United Meth Ch; Omega Psi Phi Frat keeper of finance; Nat Budget Com 1973; Frontiers Club Internat; commr St Louis Area Council Boy Scouts Am; life mem NAACP. **HONORS/ACHIEVEMENTS:** Award of Excellence St Louis Human Devel Corp 1969; Cert for Outstanding Alumni for Lincoln HS Chickasha OK. **MILITARY SERVICE:** AUS reserves 1958-64.

JONES, CAROLINE ROBINSON
Advertising executive. **PERSONAL:** Born Feb 15, 1942, Benton Harbor, MI; children: Anthony. **EDUCATION:** Univ of MI, BA 1963. **CAREER:** Benton Harbor News Palladium, writer; J Walter Thompson, copywriter 1963-68; Zebra Assoc, vp, co-creat dir 1968-70;

Kenyon & Eckhardt Advt, sr copywriter 1970-72; Black Creative Group, creative dir 1972-75; Batten Barton Durstine Osborn Advt, vice pres creat suprv 1975-77; Mingo-Jones Advertising Inc, exec vp, creative dir; Caroline Jones Advertising Inc, pres 1987. **ORGANIZATIONS:** Mem Advertising Women of NY; bd of dir Amer Field Svc, YWCA City of NY, Edwin Gould Serv for Children, Interracial Council for Bus Oppty NY, bd of governors Natl Acad of TV Arts & Sci; mem Natl Urban League, Intl Radio & TV Soc Inc; found mem The Group; lecturer Advertising & Mktg Cons; bd mem Ad Cncl, United Way of NYC, Long Island Univ, NOW Legal Defense Fund, The One Club for Art and Copy; adv bd First Women's Bank; produced and moderated "Focus on the BlackWoman" for WNew York City Radio; host "In the Black, Keys to Success," WOR-TV New York. **HONORS/ACHIEVEMENTS:** 1st black female vice pres of major advertising agency; 100 Outstanding Creative People in Amer 1976; Foremost Women in Commun 1971; Matrix Awd 1982; Clio Awds for Creativity 1970,75; Numerous Anny Awds; WPIX Film Awd; Intl Radio & TV Soc Awd; Ford Motor Co Creative; Publ "Living Legends in Black" Bicen Trib 1977; Advertising Copywriter Kiplinger Press 1977; Contrib ed, num advertising trade publ & black mags; 100 Black Women Achievement Awd 1975; Links Inc of Westchester Awd 1975; Natl Assoc of Bus & Professional Women Awd 1975. **BUSINESS ADDRESS:** President, Caroline Jones Advertising Inc, 575 Madison Ave, New York, NY 10022.

JONES, CAROLYN G.
Business executive. **PERSONAL:** Born Aug 05, 1943, Chattanooga, TN; daughter of Clyde Goolsby and Paralee Johnson Goolsby; married Edward G Jones, Nov 26, 1980; children: Larketta, Harry Charles, Arthur, Edward Lee. **EDUCATION:** Emory Univ of Atlanta, BS 1976. **CAREER:** Metro Hosp West, dir of med records 1972-74; Erlanger Alton Park Hlth Cntr, administ asst 1974-76; Chattanooga State Comm Coll, prog dir 1976-81; CJ Health Record Consult Svcs, pres. **ORGANIZATIONS:** Chrpers Ed Comm Chatta Area Med Rec Cncl 1984-85; chrpers Publ Rel CAMRC 1983-84; mem By-Laws Comm TMRA 1983-84; co-dir Nursing Guild Hawkinsville Bapt Ch 1984-85; mem Chatt Minority Busn Dev 1984; mem Chamber of Commerce. **HONORS/ACHIEVEMENTS:** Woman of the Year Glenwood Busn & Professional Women's Club 1982; Outstanding Achievement Off of Minority Busn Devel 1983; Service Busn Award Chatt Minority Busn Busn 1984; Entp of the Year 1985; House Resolution No 1 TN House of Representatives 1986; Business of the Year, Urban League 1987. **HOME ADDRESS:** 8231 Cicero Trail, Chattanooga, TN 37421. **BUSINESS ADDRESS:** President, CJ Heath Record Consultant Services, Inc, 7010 Lee Highway, Suite 218, Chattanooga, TN 37421.

JONES, CASEY C.
Elected official. **PERSONAL:** Born Jun 15, 1915, Princeton, KY; son of Casey Jones; married Lovell; children: Casey, Jr, Leverne, Clarence, Sarah, Bill, Marsha, Curtis, George, Marilyn. **EDUCATION:** Graduate Knoxville Coll; attended Univ of Toledo. **CAREER:** Co Govt exp; Casey Jones Ins Agy, owner; Lucas Co, personnel dir 1966-68; Lucas Co Child Center, pupil personnel dir & dir Rec 1968-69; Lucas Co, sanitary engr insp 1949-66; IN YMCA, gen prog sec 1960-66; state representative 21 years; State appointed chmn Local Government; Rules Comm, Finance Comm. **ORGANIZATIONS:** Mem Public Pers Assn Am; Nat Soc State Legislators; Nat Council State Govt; exec bd mem A Philip Randolph Inst; bd mem equal opport planning assn Sec Black Elected Democrats OH; grand lodge officer IBPOE W Elks; mem Nat bd of Gov Cncl of State Governments; bd mem Black Clearing House Elected Officials; trustee Model Cities bd mem Comm Health Planning Council Northwestern OH; hon mem OH Dental Soc; sec Black Elected Democrats of Ohio 1974-; chmn Central Coordinating Committee Lucas County; vice chmn Lucas County Democratic Party; chmn House of Representatives Local Govt Comm. **HONORS/ACHIEVEMENTS:** Outstanding Legislator Award by OH Assn Public Sch employ; OH youth comm Cert Outstanding Leadership; amateur & professional basketball & softball player; Hall of Fame Scott High School; Harlem Globe Player; Black Legislator Year Award; Legislator of the Year Dental Society Education Dept. **BUSINESS ADDRESS:** State Representative, 1467 Avondale, Toledo, OH 43602.

JONES, CHARLES, JR.
Educator. **PERSONAL:** Born May 12, 1946, Bronx, NY; son of Mae; married Linda Marie Coggshall. **EDUCATION:** BS 1969; MS 1972; PhD candidate Columbia Univ. **CAREER:** Central CT State Univ, grad asst 1970-72, dir of educ opportunity program & asst basketball coach 1970-, dir educational support services. **ORGANIZATIONS:** Mem Hartford Bd of Approved Umpires 1969; mem Kappa Delta Pi 1970; coord Annual Thanksgiving Food Drive for Deprived Families in New Britain Area 1970-; mem Natl Assoc of Basketball Coaches 1970-; mem CT State Employees Assoc 1970-; bd trustees Catholic Family Serv Assoc 1971-; CT Commn for Higher Educ Accrediting Team 1972; coord the making of film demonstrating aspects of educ opport program 1973; faculty adv Ebony Choral Ensemble 1974-75; bd trustees CT Yankee Girl Scouts; pres (basic) Black Admin Staff Instr at Central; field reader govt grants; Phi Delta Kappa Sect Conn Assoc Educ Oppors Prog; coord Minority Youth Business Conference; FAC advisor Junior Class, PEP dancers; vice pres Connecticut Assn Educ Opportunity Personnel; faculty advisor Senior Class, bd directors CCSU Alumni Assn. **HONORS/ACHIEVEMENTS:** Co-host cable TV series "Pioneers"; Minority Alumni Awd; Afro-Amer Organization Student Awd; Puerto Rican Union Recognition Awd; Harrison J Kaiser Alumni Service Award, Central Connecticut State Univ, 1989. **BUSINESS ADDRESS:** Dir Educ Opportunity Program, Central Connecticut StateUniv, 1615 Stanley St, New Britain, CT 06050.

JONES, CHARLES A.
Educator. **PERSONAL:** Born Sep 25, 1934, Brooklyn; children: David, Kevin, Michael, Jason. **EDUCATION:** Coll Ozarks Clarksville AR, BA 1958; FordhamUniv NY, MSW 1964;Univ MI Ann Arbor, PhD 1977. **CAREER:** Univ TX, dir social work prog; Univ of MI, asst prof 1971-79; Antioch Coll, extramural assn 1970-71; Antioch Coll Yellow Springs OH, assoc dir 1969-71; Office of Economic Opportunity Chicago, reg admin 1969; Vista Chicago 1967-69; Office of Economic Opportunity Washington DC, program devel assoc 1966-69. **ORGANIZATIONS:** Vista Wash DC 1965-67; housing consult New York City Housing Authority 1965-66; NY Social Investigator 1958-60 Human Svcs; mem Acad Cert Social Workers; Nat Assn Comm Devel; chmn Continuing Ed Task Force; NABSW 1979; del NASW Del Asmbly Huron Valley 1979; mem Nat Conf Planning Com; NCSW 1979; mem NABSW/CSWE/AAUP/NACD/MLHS/AEA/USA/NASW/TABPHE. **HONORS/ACHIEVEMENTS:** Finalist Danforth Fellow; various local community citations for communioty serv. **MILITARY SERVICE:** AUS e-5 1955-56. **BUSINESS ADDRESS:** University of TX, Dept Soc Box 19599, Arlington, TX 76019.

JONES, CHARLES LAVELLE
Professional athlete. **PERSONAL:** Born Jan 12, 1962, Scooba, MS. **EDUCATION:** Louisville, 1980-84. **CAREER:** Phoenix Suns, forward-center 1984-. **HONORS/ACHIEVEMENTS:** All-Metro Conf second team; conf player of week twice. **BUSINESS ADDRESS:** Phoenix Suns, P O Box 1369, Ste 510, Phoenix, AZ 85001.

JONES, CHESTER RAY
Attorney. **PERSONAL:** Born Nov 09, 1946, Jackson, MS; son of William Jones, Sr (deceased) and River Lee Clark Jones (deceased); married Queen Jackson; children: Jaala, Heddie Rabekah. **EDUCATION:** Tougaloo Coll, BA Sociology 1968; MS Coll Sch of Law, JD 1978; Harvard Univ Grad Sch of Educ, Inst on Employment and Training Admin summer 1981. **CAREER:** Abbott House Irvinston-on-Hudson NY, child care worker 1968; Republic of Philippines, peace corps volunteer 1968-70; Governor's Office of Job Devel & Training, equal employment opportunity 1978-85; MS State Depot of Public Welfare staff attorney 1988-89; MS State Deot of Public Welfare sr attorney 1989. **ORGANIZATIONS:** Mem MS State Bar Assn 1979; mem Magnolia Bar Assn 1985-; mem Hinds County Bar Assn 1979; mem Amer Trial Lawyers Assn 1979; emm Alpha Phi Alpha Frat Inc 1965; mem natl Inst for Empl Equity 1982; mem Amer Legion (Post 214) 1984; mem The Natl Urban League 1984. **HONORS/ACHIEVEMENTS:** Harvard Univ's Institute on Employment and Training Admin summer 1981. **MILITARY SERVICE:** Univ S Coast Guard 3rd Class Petty Ofcr served 4 yrs; Good Conduct Award 1974. **HOME ADDRESS:** 548 Witsell Rd, Jackson, MS 39206. **BUSINESS ADDRESS:** Attorney, State Department of Public Welfare, 51 SE Amite Street, Jackson, MS 39205.

JONES, CHRISTINE MILLER
Educator, government official. **PERSONAL:** Daughter of Christine M Jones; married Robert E Jones, Sr; children: Robert E Jones Jr. **EDUCATION:** Huston Tillotson Coll Austin, TX, BA 1953; Univ TX, grad study; George Washington Univ Wash, DC, grad study. **CAREER:** MD State Govt, state delegate 1982-; Prince George's Co Bd of Edn, public sch teacher 1966-. **ORGANIZATIONS:** Mem Natl Educ Assn 1966-; mem MD State Teacher's Assn 1966-; mem Prince George's Educators Assn 1966-; mem MD Legisl Caucuses 1982-; mem Prince George Mental Hlth Assn 1980; mem Natl Conf of Christians & Jews 1976-. **HONORS/ACHIEVEMENTS:** Serv Award MD State Tchrs Assn 1984; Serv Award Prince George Coalition on Black Affairs 1983; Serv Award Links Inc 1983; Serv Award Delta Sigma Theta Sor 1982. **BUSINESS ADDRESS:** Teacher, Prince George's Co Bd Educ, 4518 Beech Rd, Temple Hills, MD 20748.

JONES, CLARANCE J.
Attorney. **PERSONAL:** Born Nov 08, 1943, Cleveland; divorced. **EDUCATION:** Tuskegee Inst, BA 1965; HowardUniv Sch Law, JD 1968. **CAREER:** Cntr Advocacy, Research & Planning New Haven, CT, asso dir, atty 1971-; New Haven Legal Assistance Assn, atty 1968-73. **ORGANIZATIONS:** Mem bd dirs CT Ec Revitalization Cncl; NAACP; CT Adv Com, US Civil Rights Comm; participant Operation Crossroads Africa 1963. **HONORS/ACHIEVEMENTS:** Reginald Heber-Smith Fellow 1968-70.

JONES, CLARANCE W.
Business executive. **PERSONAL:** Born Jun 16, 1938, South Carolina; married Lillie C Brown; children: 4 children. **EDUCATION:** Northeastern Univ, cert Govt Procurement. **CAREER:** Multi-Serv Maintenance Corp, pres 1973-; Preen Bldg Maintenance Serv, owner 1963-. **ORGANIZATIONS:** Pres, NAACP; bd dir, treas, Lynn Economic Oppor; charter mem, Proj COPE; candidate for Councilor-at-Large, Lynn MA 1975. **HONORS/ACHIEVEMENTS:** Serv Award, Lynn Econ Opportunity; Serv Award, COPE; Community Serv Award, NAACP, 1975; elected to Lynn City Democratic Comm. **BUSINESS ADDRESS:** 14 Mt Vernon St, Lynn, MA 01901.

JONES, CLARENCE J., JR. (JEEP JONES)
Government official. **PERSONAL:** Born Apr 17, 1933, Boston, MA; son of Clarence J Jones and Elizabeth Middleton; married Wanda Hale, Sep 03, 1983; children: Meta, Nadine, Mark, Michael, Melissa, Kenneth, Mark Duane. **EDUCATION:** Winston-Salem State OH, BS 1955; Goddard Coll, MS. **CAREER:** Boston Juvenile Ct, probation officer 1965-68; City of Boston, dir youth action 1968-72, dir human rights 1972-76, dep mayor 1976-81; Boston Redevelopment Auth, bd of dir. **ORGANIZATIONS:** 1st vice pres Winston-Salem State Univ 1984-; chmn trustees 12th Baptist Church; bd mem Girls & Boys Clubs. **HONORS/ACHIEVEMENTS:** Outstanding Citizen Afro-Amer Police 1980; Outstanding Alumnus Winston-Salem State Univ 1983; Martin Luther King Jr Drum Major for Peace 1986. **MILITARY SERVICE:** AUS Pfc 1955-57; Good Conduct Medal 2 yrs. **BUSINESS ADDRESS:** Chairman Bd of Dir, Boston Redevelopment Authority, 1 City Hall Square, Boston, MA 02201.

JONES, CLIFFORD ANTHONY, SR.
Clergyman. **PERSONAL:** Born Sep 01, 1943, Philadelphia, PA; married Carolyn Brenda Reynolds; children: Michelle A, Clifford A. **EDUCATION:** Univ Eastern Shore, BS 1967; SE Theol Sem, MDiv 1972; ThM cand 1978. **CAREER:** 1st Bapt Ch, pastor 1972-; Brookston Bapt Ch, pastor 1969-72; Bethlehem Apt Ch, pastor 1969. **ORGANIZATIONS:** Mem Alpha Phi Alpha Frat; Master Mason; chmn United Inisteries for Higher Edn, Am Bapt Ch of S; v moderator Western Union Assn; mem NC Counc of Chs; mem NC Consultation on Ministry in Higher Edn; mem NAACP; Voter's League; rep Sampson Co; Black Activist Com; 3rd Dist Who's Who in Religion ofAm. **BUSINESS ADDRESS:** 900 College St, Clinton, NC 28328.

JONES, CLIFTON PATRICK
Librarian. **PERSONAL:** Born May 11, 1927, Chapel Hill, NC; married Clara Baldwin; children: Michael, James, Twana, Allison. **EDUCATION:** Univ of NC, 1962-63; Brooklyn Inst, 1964-65; Durham Tech Coll, 1965-66. **CAREER:** Univ of NC, various positions to library asst past 27 yrs. **ORGANIZATIONS:** Suprv Durham Soil & Water Conservation 1972-; pres, bd mem Amer Arthritis Assoc 1973-, NC Hemophilia Found 1980-82, Amer Psoriasis Found. **HONORS/ACHIEVEMENTS:** Colonel Honorable Order of Kentucky Colonels 1976-; Listed in Personality of the South 1976. **HOME ADDRESS:** 3816 Pickett Rd, Durham, NC 27705.

JONES, CLIFTON RALPH
Educator. **PERSONAL:** Born Oct 02, 1910, Nanticoke, MD; married Susan Elizabeth Sut-

ton; children: Jo Ann B. **EDUCATION:** VA Union Univ Richmond, BA 1935; Univ of IA Iowa City, MA 1939, PhD 1943; Attended, London Sch of Economics London England 1952-53. **CAREER:** Fisk Univ Nashville, res fellow/instr 1943; Florida A&M Univ Tallahassee, prof of sociology 1945-46; Morgan State Univ Baltimore, prof of sociology 1946-63; Amer Univ, visiting prof 1956, 1961, 1963, 1964; Bryn Mawr Coll, 1969-70; College of Liberal Arts Howard Univ, assoc dean 1975-85; Howard Univ Washington, profof sociology 1963-. **ORGANIZATIONS:** Staff mem President's Commn on Rural Poverty 1966-67; consultant US Dept of Labor 1965-66; consultant & prog mgr Franklin Inst 1969-70; consultant US Dept of the Navy 1973-75, TechRep Div Philco Corp. **HONORS/ACHIEVEMENTS:** Rosenwalk Fellow Univ of Iowa; Amer Sociological Assoc Visiting Scholar Delaware State Coll 1972; Outstanding Scholar Delta Tau Kappa Intl Social Science Honor Soc 1975; Alpha Man of the Year Delta Lambda Chap Alpha Phi Alpha 1981; Outstanding Serv Coll of Lib Arts Howard Univ 1983. **MILITARY SERVICE:** AUS t/5 1943-45; Enlisted Men's Service Ribbon 1945. **HOME ADDRESS:** 1190 W Northern Pkwy #524, Baltimore, MD 21210. **BUSINESS ADDRESS:** Professor of Sociology, HowardUniv, 2600 6th St NW, Washington, DC 20059.

JONES, CLOYZELLE KARRELLE
Educator. **PERSONAL:** Born in Detroit, MI. **EDUCATION:** Wayne St U, EdD 1970. **CAREER:** Univ of MI, full prof 1970-; Wayne State Univ, instructor 1969-70; Detroit Public Schools, teacher 1961-68. **ORGANIZATIONS:** Asso Dir, treas Boys' Clubs MI Assn 1961-65; bd mem Ethnic Hertg Found 1972-; mem Chancellor's AdvUniv of MI 1970-77; fdr 1st adv Assn Black StdsUniv of MI 1970-71; chrmnUniv of MI Policy Bd Adv 1971; chrmn Spec Proj Adv Com,Univ of MI 1973-75; mem Admissions Policy ComUniv of MI 1974-75; cons, tchrcoord Det Bd of Ed 1968-77; mem, exec com Interdisciplinary Studies DivUniv of MI; mem, exec com Div of EdUniv of MI; mem Finan Aids BdUniv of MI 1974-77; mem Gov Inst on Talented-Gifted 1979-; mem ed com New Detroit Inc; mem Wayne StUniv Coll of Ed Alumni Bd Gov; pres Nat Urban Ed Assn 1979-81; dir Urban & Reg StudiesUniv MI; coord, Spcl Needs Grad ConcentrationUniv MI; mem MI Cncl for Arts; Nat Conf of Assoc Urban Ed 1977;symposium; bd mem Wayne Cnty 4h 1972-; mem Asso Children with Learn Disab 1972-; Asso Tchr Ed 1972-; MI Asso for Supv of Std Tchrs 1972-; exec bd mem Asso Urban Ed 1972-76; chmn Task Force 1972-; Phi Delta Kappa. **HONORS/ACHIEVEMENTS:** Nat Assn for Urban Ed Harvard Prize Book Award, (schlrshp); Miller HS Alumni Assn; listed in "Leaders in Am Ed", 70th Yrbk Nat Soc for Study of Ed1971; del address Nat Conf of Asso Urban Ed 1976-78; del 2 papers Ann Conf of Black Fam in AmUniv Louisville 1977-80. **MILITARY SERVICE:** AUS 1961. **BUSINESS ADDRESS:** 4901 Evergreen Rd, Dearborn, MI 48128.

JONES, CLYDE EUGENE
Attorney. **PERSONAL:** Born Dec 05, 1954, Birmingham, AL; married Julia Norment; children: Jakarra Jenise, Jasmine Jekesha. **EDUCATION:** Knoxville Coll, BA 1976; Univ of MS, Pre Law Cleo Fellow 1976; Samford Univ Cumberland School of Law, JD 1979. **CAREER:** Jefferson Cty Family Court, law clerk, baliff 1979-80; 10th Judicial Circuit AL, dep dist attny 1980; 5th Judicial Circuit AL, asst dist attny 1980-84; Penick, Williams & Jones, attny partner 1985-87; private practice 1987-. **ORGANIZATIONS:** Senator Jr Law Class Cumberland School of Law 1977-78; law clerk Shores & Larkin 1978; student prosecutor, law clerk Jefferson Cty DA Office 1978-79; pres Young Dem of Macon Cty 1981-84; mem AEAONMS 1984-, Shriner, Mizraim Temple #119 1984-; bd of dir Magic City Bar Assoc 1985-86; vice pres Magic City Bar Assoc 1987; Vestavia-Hoover Kiwanis Club, Magic City Jaycees, Alpha Phi Chapter, Omega Psi Phi Fraternity Inc. **HONORS/ACHIEVEMENTS:** Basileus Omega Psi Phi 1974-76; undergrad dist rep Omega Psi Phi 1975-76; undergrad vice pres Natl Pan Hellenic Council 1975-76; hon mem Attny Gen Staff State of AL 1979; Outstanding Young Men of Amer 1981,84; Proclamation 12/16/84 Clyde E Jones Day Mayor Tuskegee AL 1984; Leadership Birmingham 1989 Class. **BUSINESS ADDRESS:** Attorney, Pythian Temple Building, 310 18th St N, Suite 3006, Birmingham, AL 35203.

JONES, CODY
Professional football player. **PERSONAL:** Born 1951, San Francisco, CA; married Nina. **EDUCATION:** Trinidad St Jr Coll, Attd; San Jose St U, Attd. **CAREER:** Los Angeles Rams, 1973-. **HONORS/ACHIEVEMENTS:** NFC Championship Games 1974, 1976, 1978; Pro Bowl 1978. **BUSINESS ADDRESS:** Los Angeles Rams, 10271 W Pico Blvd, Los Angeles, CA.

JONES, CORNELL
Councilman. **PERSONAL:** Born Jan 06, 1923, Paris, TN; married Dorothy Lee Jones. **EDUCATION:** W Kentucky Trade Sch 1949. **CAREER:** Merit Clothing Co 1964-74; Mayfield, KY, councilman 1973-76; Ingrosoll Rand-Centac Co, 1976-. **ORGANIZATIONS:** Mem Christian Ch 1947-; organiz NAACP 1962 (pres 3 years); 32nd Degree Mason 1970; W Master Rising Star 17 1960; bd mem OEO 1967; DAV Chap 1971; Local 2523 IAMAW; bd mem Mayfield Planning Bd 1978-79; chmn Amer Legion Post 136. **MILITARY SERVICE:** AUS 1943-45; Recipient 2 Battle Stars, Normandy Beachhead 1944 & Rhine River, Germany 1945.

JONES, CURLEY C.
Librarian. **PERSONAL:** Born Feb 23, 1941, Rossville, TN; son of Cleve Jones and Susie Palmer Jones. **EDUCATION:** Saints Jr Coll, AA 1965; Tougaloo Coll, BA 1969; St Univ NY Geneseo, MLS 1971; Univ of UT, MEd 1975; Univ of IL, CAS 1977. **CAREER:** Rochester City Sch Dist Roch, NY, tchr intrn 1969-70, sub tchr 1970-72; Univ of IL, grad stdnt 1976-77; Univ of UT Marriott Libraries, assoc librarian. **ORGANIZATIONS:** Life mem Amer Library Assn 1972; Mtn Plns Lib Assn 1973; UT Hist Soc & ULA 1973; life mem NAACP 1984. **HONORS/ACHIEVEMENTS:** Contbd Chicano Bib Univ of UT 1973; contbd to Blk Bib Univ of UT 1974; Cmplr of Blk Bib Univ of UT 1977; Edtr of Splmnt to Blk Bib Univ of UT 1981. **BUSINESS ADDRESS:** Reference Librarian, Univ of Utah, Salt Lake City, UT 84112.

JONES, DAVID RUSSELL
Appointed official, educator. **PERSONAL:** Born Apr 30, 1948, Brooklyn, NY; son of Justice & Mrs Thomas R Jones; married Valerie King, PhD; children: Russell, Vanessa. **EDUCATION:** Wesleyan Univ, BA 1970; Yale Law School, JD 1974. **CAREER:** US Senator Robert Kennedy, senate intern 1967; Fed Dist Judge Constance Baker Motley, law clerk 1974-75; Cravath Swaine & Moore, litigation assoc 1975-79; NY City Mayor Koch, spec advisor 1979-83; NY City Youth Bureau, exec dir 1983-86; Community Service Society of NY, general dir 1986-. **ORGANIZATIONS:** Trustee Wesleyan Univ 1984-; NY Legal Services Corp, dir 1986; pres Black Agency Executives of NY 1988-; bd of Carver Federal Savings and Loan Association 1989-. **HONORS/ACHIEVEMENTS:** Thomas J Watson Fellow Thomas J Watson Found 1970; Honorary MA Wesleyan Univ 1982. **BUSINESS ADDRESS:** General Dir, Community Service Soc of NY, 105 E 22nd St, New York, NY 10010.

JONES, DEACON See JONES, GROVER

JONES, DELMOS J.
Educator. **PERSONAL:** Born Jul 12, 1936, Alabama; children: Valen, Adrian. **EDUCATION:** San Francisco State Coll, BA 1959; Univ of AZ, MA 1962; Cornell Univ, PhD 1967. **CAREER:** Univ of CO, asst prof 1967-70; CUNY, assoc prof, prof 1970-. **ORGANIZATIONS:** Fellow Am Anthropol Assn; fellow Soc for Applied Anthrop; program chmn 29th Annual Meeting of Soc for Applied Anthrop Boulder 1970; assoc ed Human Orgn 1970-73; mem program com 70th Annual Meeting of Am Anthrop Assn NY 1971; mem com on minorities in anthropology Am Anthrop Assn 1971-73; exec bd Soc for Applied Anthrop 1972-75; prelim review panel Foreign Area Fellowship Program of Social Sci Rsch Cncl & Am Cncl of Learned Soc 1972-73; co-chmnAnnual Meet of Soc for App Anthrop Amsterdam 1974; selection com Foreign Area Fellowship Program of Soc Sci Rsch Cncl 1974-75; mem Task Panel on Mental Health of Black Am; Pres Com on Mental Health 1977; mem Com on Ability Testing Natl Acad of Sci 1977-80; mem at large Cncl on Anthrop & Educ 1979-81; mem Soc Sci Training Review Com HEW PHS ADAMHA NIMH 1977-78. **HONORS/ACHIEVEMENTS:** Guest Editor Reviews in Anthropology Vol 4 No 5; SE Asian Program Fellowship Cornell Univ 1962-63; Foreign Area Fellowship Program 1964-66; SE Asian Program Fellowship Cornell Univ 1967; Fulbright Fellowship Thailand 1970-71; Participant in mumerous field rsch programs & grants 1964-82; Numerous publn 1961-80. **BUSINESS ADDRESS:** Professor, CUNY Graduate Center, 33 W 42 St, New York, NY 10036.

JONES, DEVERGES BOOKER
Marketing manager. **PERSONAL:** Born Mar 13, 1950, Brooklyn, NY; son of Booker T Jones and Elma DeVerges Jones; married Beverly Moss, Aug 29, 1981; children: Matthew DeVerges Jones. **EDUCATION:** Morehouse College, Atlanta GA, BA 1972; Columbia Univ, 1970; Cornell Univ, Ithaca NY, MBA 1974. **CAREER:** General Foods Corp, White Plains NY, assoc product mgr 1967-78, product mgr 1978-79; Clairol, Inc, New York City, product group mgr 1979-81; Pepsi-Cola USA, Purchase NY, marketing mgr of new products/bottler devel 1981, natl business planning mgr 1982-83, mgr of packaging 1983-84; sr marketing mgr 1984-86; Uniworld Group Inc, New York City, account supervisor 1986-88, vice pres/mgmt supvr 1988-. **ORGANIZATIONS:** Mem Assn of MBA Executives. **HOME ADDRESS:** PO Box 315A, Salem Rd, Pound Ridge, NY 10576.

JONES, DONALD W.
Business executive, educator. **PERSONAL:** Born Dec 07, 1939, Trenton, NC; married Betty Jean Tolbert; children: Tracey La Verne. **EDUCATION:** Hampton Inst VA, BS 1962; FairfieldUniv CT, MA 1969; OH U, PhD 1973. **CAREER:** Adv to Pres on Minority Affairs, asst to pres; Univ VA Charlottesville, asst prof 1972-; New Haven Redevel Agency, housing devel officer 1968-70; Norwalk Job Orientation Program, instructor 1967-68; Urban League of Westchester Co Inc, assoc dir in charge of economic devel & employment, training adv, field rep 1966; New York City Dept of Labor, labor-mgmt prac adj 1965-66. **ORGANIZATIONS:** Chmn Time & Pl Comm, Middle Atlantic Reg, Nat Hampton Alumni Assn; mod Panel Disc Nat Hampton Alumni Assn; part Invit Sem on Deseg in Pub HigherEd spons by HowardUniv Sch of Bus & Pub Admin; 1st vp, pres Nat Black Caucus; mem Speech Communication Assn; Intl Communication Assn S Assn of Black Admin Pers; Am Assn of High Ed; Nat Ed Assn of US; Intl Platform Assn; Lib Com OHUniv 1971-72; exec sec, Instnl Self-Study ProjUniv of VA 1972-; Comm Coll Adminstrv ComUniv of VA 1972-; Afro-Am Std Com-Univ of VA 1972-; exec sec Presidential Adminstrv Com on Comm CollUniv of VA 1972-74; chmn Presidential Adminstrv Com on Comm CollUniv of VA 1974; Presidential Adminstrv Com Ed & Employ Oppor, Oblig & RightsUniv of VA 1975; past pres NC 4-H Clubs; NY Hampton Alumni Club; pres Interfrat Cncl 1975-; Unit Negro Coll Fund 1973; chmn Plan ComUniv of VA, VA Comm Coll Artic Conf 1974-; VAComm Coll ConfUniv of VA 1974; Nat Hamp Alumni Assn, Mid Atlantic Prog 1975-. **HONORS/ACHIEVEMENTS:** Outst Srv toUniv in Area of Human Rel, Black Stds ofUniv of VA 1976; Awarded Queen Elizabeth of England Medal, Charlottesville Albermarle Bicent Commn 1976; United Negro Coll Fund Vol Ldrshp Award, United Negro Coll Fund 1977; UNCF Lapel Pin 1977; Thomas Jefferson Area United Way Award 1977; name put int timecapsule for srv as mem of Charlottesville Albemarle Bicent Comm, will Be opened during Tricennial Celeb July 4 2076.

JONES, DORINDA A.
Executive. **PERSONAL:** Born May 27, 1926, Trenton, KY; married John M; children: Dawna Lynn, John, Jr. **EDUCATION:** BA 1953; Wayne St U, MSW 1955. **CAREER:** Hum Resources Dept, exec asst to dir 1985; Mayor's Com, Hum Resources Dev Detroit, exec Dir 1971-73, dir office of prog plann-res & eval 1970; Wayne StUniv Sch Soc Work Detroit, asst prof 1969-70. **ORGANIZATIONS:** Dept hd Soc Serv for Head Start Detroit Pub Schs 1966-68; dir Oversees Proj, Nat Fed Settlements & Comm Ctrs New York City 1964-66; prog Supv, bd of dir Gleiss Meml Ctr, Protest Comm Serv 1959-64; soc grp worker & supv Neighborhood Serv Org 1955-58; princ soc planning & dev consult City of Detroit; mem Nat Assn Soc Workers; Nat Assn Black Soc Workers, Acad Cert Soc Workers; Am Socl Pub Admin; Cncl Minority Pub Admin; mem Delta Sigma Theta Sor; Bethune Sect, Nat Cncl of Negro Woman. **BUSINESS ADDRESS:** 801 City Co Bldg, Detroit, MI 48221.

JONES, DUANE L.
Business executive. **PERSONAL:** Born Mar 11, 1937, Duquesne, PA. **EDUCATION:** Univ Pittsburgh, BS 1959;Univ Oslo, Sorbonne U, Paris, adv study 1962-63; NY U, MA 1970. **CAREER:** Black Theatre Alliance, exec dir 1976-; Antioch Coll, Dept of Literature assoc prof 1971-76; NY Univ, Opportunities Program English program coordinator 1967-71; Harlem Prep, English dept 1965-67; Prince Edward Co Farmville VA, English dept 1965; TV Film Negro Ensemble Co Natl Black Theatre, actor; Opera Ebony Richard Allen Center, stage dir; Caribe Magazine, guest editor. **ORGANIZATIONS:** Mem New York City Mayor's Commn on Culture, Art 1979-81; mem Alpha Phi Alpha Actors Equity Negro Actors Guild; bd of dirs PRIDE on TV 1980. **HONORS/ACHIEVEMENTS:** Phyllis Wheatley SchlrshpUniv of Pittsburgh 1955; PA St SchlrshpUniv of Pittsburgh 1955-59; Phelps-Stokes Flwshp,

LectrUniv of Niamey Niger 1975. **BUSINESS ADDRESS:** 410 W 42nd St, New York, NY 10036.

JONES, EARL FREDERICK
Elected government official. **PERSONAL:** Born Jul 20, 1949, Yanceyville, NC; married Adri-Anne Donnell. **EDUCATION:** NC Central Univ, BA Pol Sci 1967-71; TX Southern Univ School of Law, JD 1973-76. **CAREER:** Greensboro Legal Aid Found, assoc attorney 1976-81; Offender Aid & Restoration, dir 1981-; City of Greensboro, councilmember. **ORGANIZATIONS:** Co-founder NC Black Caucus of Legal Serv Employees 1979; mem Guilford Co Assoc of Black Lawyers 1982-; bd mem Shiloh Baptist Church Housing Bd 1983-; exec bd mem NC Black Municipal Elected Officials Bd 1984. **HONORS/ACHIEVEMENTS:** Comm Serv Awd NAACP Greensboro 1983; received appointment as Honorary Atty Gen to and for the State of NC 1983. **BUSINESS ADDRESS:** Councilmember, City of Greensboro, 301 S Elm St Ste 210, Greensboro, NC 27402.

JONES, EDGAR LAVELLE
Professional athlete. **PERSONAL:** Born Jun 17, 1956, Newark, NJ. **EDUCATION:** Nevada Reno, Phys Ed Major 1979. **CAREER:** New Jersey Nets, 1980-81; Detroit Pistons, 1981-83; San Antonio Spurs, forward 1982-. **ORGANIZATIONS:** Trade with Detroit 1983; came to San Antonio from Detroit 1983; drafted by Milwaukee 1979; went to Detroit for 1981-82 season. **HONORS/ACHIEVEMENTS:** Had double pts 44 times with 20 or more 6 times; led in steals 12 times rebounds 9 times & pts twice; season high 5 blocks 1984; season high 22 pts 1984; career high 25 rebounds 1984; 107 blocks & 826 pts on the year were career highs 1983-84; all-CBA & rookie of year. **BUSINESS ADDRESS:** San Antonio Spurs, HemisFair Arena, Ste 510, San Antonio, TX 78292.

JONES, EDITH IRBY
Physician. **PERSONAL:** Born Dec 23, 1927, Conway, AR; daughter of Robert Irby and Mattie Irby; married James Beauregard; children: Gary Ivan, Myra Jones Romain, Keith Irby. **EDUCATION:** Knoxville Coll, Knoxville TN, BS, MChem, Bio, Physics; NorthwesternUniv Chgo, IL Clinical Psych 1948;Univ of AR Sch of Med; WV Coll of Med, Postgraduate, 1965; Cook Co Graduate School, Postgraduate, 1966; Methodist Hosp, Post Grad Self Assessment Course Internal Med, 1974; Baylor Coll of Med, Continuing Ed; Univ of TX Internal Med Review, Fundamentals of Practical Therapeutrics 1977; Baylor Coll of Med, Practical Therapeutics 1977; Univ of TX Houston Med Sch, Int Med Rev; Hermann Hosp, Carldipulmonary Course 1978; Amer Heart Assn, Houston, Adv Cardipulmonary Life Support Course 1978. **CAREER:** Univ Hosp, Little Rock AR, intern 1952-53; Hot Springs, AR, general practice of med, 1953-59; Baylor Affiliated Hosps, res in int med 1959-62; Houston, TX, private practice, internal med, 1962-; Baylor Coll, clinical asst prof in med;Univ of TX; clinical asst prof of med; Riverside Hosp Med Staff Houston TX, exec comm; Prospect Med Lab, dir Riverside Hosp;; sec of staff; Houston Council on Alcoholism, adv bd; Comm for Revising Justice Code Harris Co; Mercy Hosp Comp Hlth Care Grp, bd of dir, sec; Jones, Coleman & Whitfield; partner. **ORGANIZATIONS:** mem, admin comm, Univ of TX School of Med; pres, former exec sec Natl Med Asso; chm Utilization Comm Meth Hosp; Houston Amer Revolution Bi-centennial Comm; Pres of AR Med, Dental & Pharmaceutical Asso; chmn, Internal Med Comm St Eliz Hosp; med adv Selective Bd #60 Houston TX; bd of dir & chmn, comm for Homemakers Serv Family Service Ctr; chm Bd of Delta Rsch & Educ Found; mem bd of dir Houston Council on Human Relations; candidate for Houston Independent Sch Bd 1975; mem of comm on Hypertension, Natl Med Asso; chmn, Scientific Council, Natl Med Asso; bd of Third Bank Control Grp; bd of dir Natl Med Asso; mem of TX Health Assn; comm on Drug Abuse Houston Independent School Dist; adv med bd Visiting Nurses Asso; bd of dir Sudan Corp; bd of dir Afro Amer Book Distributors; Med Adv Bd Planned Parenthood of Houston Inc; chmn, Southwest Volunteers Delta-one Amer; Health Care Comm for Schools, Harris Co Med Soc; Questions & Answers in Health Car, KCOH Monthly Radio. **HONORS/ACHIEVEMENTS:** Houston Med Forum for Outstanding Achievement in Religious/Civic Affairs & Scientific Literature 1965; Woman of Year by Charmettes 1965; Y-Teen Award for Servs To Blue Triangle YWCA 1968; Eta Phi Beta Sor Meritorious Comm Serv 1967; Woman of Yr Theta Sigma Phi Houston TX 1969; commended by Senate CA Legislature Reg Session 1969; Woman of Year, Jack Yates Fed Girls Club, 1969; Golden Anniversary Award, Zeta Phi Beta Sorority Inc, 1970; Dist serv award, Houston Section of Natl Council of Negro Women Inc 1972; service to promote the Efficient Adm of Justice by the Amer Judicatgure Soc, 1973; Kato Models Woman of Year Award, 1974; Certificate of Recognition for Contribution in field of Med; Anyioch Baptist Church, 1975; Kato Models Lois Allen Humanitarian Award, 1975; life mem, Natl Council of Negro Women; Houston League of Business & Prof Women Achievement Award, 1977; Award for Contribution in Educ Antioch Missionary Baptist Church, 1977; Citation for Volunteer Serv, Eta Phi Beta Sor, 1978; Certificate for Participation in 3rd Annual Fulbright Intl Seminar; TX Southern Univ, 1978; Edith Irby Jones Award Day, State of AR, 1979; Pres' Dist Ser Award, Knoxville Coll, Natl Alumni Assoc Inc, 1979; Exemplary Serv to and Support of Prof Educ, 1979. **HOME ADDRESS:** 3402 S Parkwood Dr, Houston, TX 77021. **BUSINESS ADDRESS:** 2601 Prospect St, Houston, TX 77004.

JONES, EDWARD HENRY
Business executive. **PERSONAL:** Born Aug 29, 1936, Richmond, VA; divorced; children: Anthony R. **EDUCATION:** VA UnionUniv Richmond, BS 1960; NYUniv Grad Sch of Bus, MBA 1972; Alliance Francaise/French Inst New York, 1974-80. **CAREER:** Intl Commercial Resources Ltd, pres 1978; Office of Econ Devel of NYC, commr of manpower 1974-78; consult financial mgmt & self-employed consult to private firms 1972-74; Interracial Council for Bus Opportunity of NY, exec dir 1970-72; Marine Midland Bank of NY, commercial banking officer 1969-70; US Small Bus Adminstrn NYC, commercial loan officer branch mgr 1964-67; New York City Housein & Devel Adminstrn, financial consult 1968-69; Ford Found NYC, consult minority econ devel 1969-72; lectr minority bus devel various univ in US 1971-73. **ORGANIZATIONS:** Mem Alpha Phi Alpha Frat 1957-; mem 100 Black Men Inc NY 1965-80; Martin Luther King Fellowship NYUniv Grad Sch of Bus 1968-72. **HONORS/ACHIEVEMENTS:** Auth "Blacks in Business" Grosset & Dunlap 1971. **MILITARY SERVICE:** USN S & A 1954-55. **BUSINESS ADDRESS:** Intl Commercial Resources, 200 Park Avenue, Ste 303E, New York, NY 10166.

JONES, EDWARD LEE (TOO TALL)
Professional athlete. **PERSONAL:** Born Feb 23, 1951, Jackson, TN. **EDUCATION:** TN State, Health & Phys Educ. **CAREER:** Made guest appearance on TV's "Different Strokes"; Imperial Investors, partner, Professional Boxer, 1979; Dallas Cowboys, defensive end 1974-78 1980-. **ORGANIZATIONS:** Active in promoting Special Olympics. **HONORS/ACHIEVEMENTS:** MVP 1982; All Pro 1981 NEA, 1982 by AP; Pro Bowl three yrs.

JONES, EDWARD LOUIS
Educational administrator, author. **PERSONAL:** Born Jan 15, 1922, Georgetown, TX; married Lynne; children: Cynthia, Frances, Edward Lawrence, Christopher, Teresa. **EDUCATION:** Univ of WA, BA (2) 1952, BA 1955; Univ of Gonzaga, JD 1967. **CAREER:** Hollywood Players Theatre, prod, dir 1956-58; Roycroft Leg Theatre, prod, dir 1958-59; WA State Dept of Publ Asst, soc worker 1958; Seattle Water Dept, cost acctg clerk 1960-61; State of WA, attny gen office 1963-66; Seattle Oppty Indust Ctr, suprv 1966-68; Univ of WA, asst dean a&s 1968-, lecturer. **ORGANIZATIONS:** Lecturer Univ of WA; consult State Attny Gen Adv Comm on Crime, State Supr of Counseling; vice pres WA Comm on Consumer Interests, Natl Council on Crime & Delinquency; bd mem Natl Acad Adv & Assoc; ed NACADA Jrnl; mem Natl Assoc of Student Personnel Admin, The Amer Acad of Pol & Soc Sci, The Smithsonian Assoc; historical advisor, Anheuser Busch. **HONORS/ACHIEVEMENTS:** 1st Pl Moot Court Contest 1953; author of, "Profiles in African Heritage", "Black Zeus" 1972, "Tutankhamon, King of Upper & Lower Egypt" 1978, "Orator's Workbook" 1982, "The Black Diaspora: Colonization of Colored People," 1989; co-author "Money Exchange Flashcards", currency converters 1976. **MILITARY SERVICE:** AUS 1940-45. **BUSINESS ADDRESS:** Lecturer, Univ of Washington, B-507 Padelford, Seattle, WA 98105.

JONES, EDWARD N.
Retired educator. **PERSONAL:** Born Jul 25, 1914, Hampton, VA; son of Edward Jones and Alberta Jones; married Agnes Phillips. **EDUCATION:** Hampton U, BS 1936; Hampton Inst, MA 1973. **CAREER:** Hampton Inst, acting assoc dean of student affairs 1974-, dormitory dir 1972-74; Jr HS Hampton VA, teacher 1974-72; USPO Hampton, supr, foreman of del 1957-69, letter carrier 1938-57; Rosenwald HS Madisonville KY, teacher 1936-38. **ORGANIZATIONS:** past Pres Bachelor Benedict Club; past pres Alpha Phi Alpha Frat; Nat Assn of Letter Carriers; Natl Assn of Postal Supr; past chmn exec bd VA St Assn of Letter Carriers; mem Nat Ed Assn; VA Ed Assn; Hampton Ed Assn; past pres Men's Club, First Baptist Church; asst dir Tidewater N VA Assn of Chpts, Alpha Phi Alpha; Kappa Delta Pi; past mem, bd dir ARC Hampton VA. **HONORS/ACHIEVEMENTS:** Certificate of Merit, Alpha Phi Alpha 1975. **MILITARY SERVICE:** AUS corpl 1943-46.

JONES, EFFIE HALL
Associate executive director. **PERSONAL:** Born Jan 13, 1928, Washington, DC; married Edward William Jones, Sr; children: Edward W Jr, Franz Emil, Kevin Dennis;. **EDUCATION:** Morgan State U, BS 1949; Cath U, MA 1966; George Washington U, EdD 1985. **CAREER:** Dist of Columbia Public Schools, teacher, counselor 1952-67, vice prin 1967-70; Montgomery Co Md Publuc Schools, vice prin, prin 1970-76; Amer Assn of School Admn, assoc exec dir 1976-. **ORGANIZATIONS:** Cnslt Ford Found 1979, A B & Assc Cambridge MS 1980; mem AKA Theta Omega Omega Chptr 1983-; life mem Natl Alcn Blck Sch Ed 1983; advsry bd Am EdRsrch Assc 1984. **HONORS/ACHIEVEMENTS:** Women at the top film Dept of Ed Womens Equity 1980; hon by Mc Graw Hill Pblshr Otstndg & Cntrbtr To Women & Memories in Ed Admn 1985; speakg of people Ebony Mag 1982. **BUSINESS ADDRESS:** Associate Executive Dir, Am Assc of Sch Admn, 1801 N Moore St, Arlington, VA 22209.

JONES, ELAINE R.
Attorney. **PERSONAL:** Born Mar 02, 1944, Norfolk, VA. **EDUCATION:** Howard U, AB 1965;Univ of VA, LlB 1970. **CAREER:** NAACP Legal Def & Ed Fund, asst cncl 1970-. **ORGANIZATIONS:** Mem Nat Bar Assn 1971; Old Dominion Bar Assn 1970; VA Trial Lawyers Assn 1971; Intrntl Fed of Women Lawyers 1973. **HONORS/ACHIEVEMENTS:** Panel of arbitration Am Stock Exchange; Delta & Sigma Theta Sor; Recognition Award, Black Am Law Students' Assn for Outstndng Legal Serv to the Comm 1974; Spl Achievement Award, Nat Assn of Black Women Attys 1975. **BUSINESS ADDRESS:** 10 Columbus Circle, Ste 2030, New York, NY 10019.

JONES, ELNETTA GRIFFIN
Educator. **PERSONAL:** Born Jul 07, 1934, Mullins, SC; married Aaron Mullins Jones; children: Aaron Daryl. **EDUCATION:** SC St Coll, BS 1957; Shippensburg State Coll, ME 1972; American Univ, DEd 1979. **CAREER:** Rosenwald High School, teacher 1957-59; AUS/Air Force, Educational Dev Cntr, Wiesbaden, Germany 1960-63; AUS Infantry Cntr, Ft Benning, GA, teacher 1964-66,1969-70;Shippensburg Univ, asst dir of Act 101 Program 1972-76, dir Act 101 Program 1976-78, asst vice president for acad affairs 1979-80, assoc dean ofspecial academic programs 1980-82, dean special academic programs 1982-. **ORGANIZATIONS:** Numerous consultantships; mem PA Assoc of Developmental Educators, The PA Black Conference on Higher Educ, Phi Delta Kappa, Natl Academic Advising Assoc, The Natl Political Congress of Black Women, The Shippensburg Civic Club, Delta Sigma Theta, Inc; Natl Assoc of Developmental Educators. **HONORS/ACHIEVEMENTS:** Who's Who of American Women 1981-82; Outstanding Humanist Awd Shippensburg Univ Black Alumni 1985; 5 publications including contributor to "Research in Higher Education," 1983, The Amer University Press Washington, DC. **BUSINESS ADDRESS:** Dean Special Academic Programs, Shippensburg University, DHC #112, Shippensburg, PA 17257.

JONES, EMIL, JR.
Politician. **PERSONAL:** Born Oct 18, 1935, Chicago, IL; son of Emil Jones, Sr. (deceased) and Marilla Mims Jones (deceased); married Patricia; children: Debra Ann, Renee L, John M, Emil III. **EDUCATION:** Chicago City Loop Clg, AA Liberal Arts; Roosevelt U, 1953-55. **CAREER:** Licensed Stantionary Eng; US Post Office, frmrly emplyd; Dem Org, precinct capt 21st ward rglr 1962-70; Young Dems, sec 1963-67; So Dist Water Filtrtn Plant, mem exec bd orgn & chlorine eng 1964-67; Chicago City Cncl, sec to alderman 1967-73; 34th Ward Regular Dem Orgn, pub rltns 1972, precinct capt 1971, exec sec 1971; State of IL, rep. **ORGANIZATIONS:** Clorine eng South Dist Water Filtration Plant 1964-67; sec to alderman Chicago City Cncl 1967-73; pblc rltns precinct capt 34th Ward Reg Demo Orgn 1971; exec sec 34th Ward Regular Demo Orgn 1971; mem Morgan Park Savs & Loan; 32nd degree mason Shriner; mem Sheldon Heights Comm Cncl, Lions Clb Intrntl. **HONORS/ACHIEVEMENTS:** Friend of ed IL State Bd of Ed; IL Delta Kapp Appreciation; Coalition to Save Chicago Sch Ldrshp; IL Assc Blck Am Voc Ed; civil rights IL Dept of Human Rights & Human Rltns Ofcr 1984. **BUSINESS ADDRESS:** State Senator, IL Senate, 329 A Capitol Building, Springfield, IL 62706.

JONES, EMMA PETTWAY
Educator. **PERSONAL:** Born Jul 29, 1945, Boykin, AL; daughter of John B. Pettway and Allie Pettway; married J Jones (divorced); children: James, John, Tracy, Malik. **EDUCATION:** Albertus Magnus Coll, 1978-80; NH Coll, Manchester, BS 1981, MBA 1985; CUNY Law School Queens, JD 1988. **CAREER:** New Haven Fed Credit Union, organizer/mgr 1979-81; EMA Assoc, pres 1980-86; Jones Turner & Wright, legal asst 1986-87; Williams & Wise, legal intern 1987; independent consultant. **ORGANIZATIONS:** Exec dir People Acting for Change New Haven CT; researcher Yale Univ Provost Dept; consultant, trainer Legal Assistance New Haven CT, Public Housing Prog Tenant Representative Council, NH Coll, Organizational Development Inst Cheyney State Coll, Fair Haven Mediation Prog; exec dir CT Afro-American Historical Society; chairperson Natl Econ Devel & Law Ctr; vice pres New Haven YWCA. **HONORS/ACHIEVEMENTS:** Received numerous Certificates of Excellence & Outstanding Service Awards. **HOME ADDRESS:** 286 James St, New Haven, CT 06513.

JONES, ENOCH
Clergyman. **PERSONAL:** Born Aug 19, 1922, Biloxi, MS; children: Stephen, Enoch Lee, Janet. **EDUCATION:** Am Bapt Sem, BTh 1954; Fisk U, BA 1956; MA 1957; Scarrit Coll, additional study; Houston Tillotson Coll, hon doctorate deg. **CAREER:** Friendship Bapt Ch, pastor 1952-61; ABT Sem, tchr & dean of chapel 3 yrs; 15th Ave Bapt Ch, pastor. **ORGANIZATIONS:** Mem Nat Bapt Conv USA Inc 1956; mem TN BM&E Conv; trustee of ABT Sem; minister for prisoners at state prison; conducts joint worship serv with Woodmonat Bapt Ch White Ch; viewes yearly by 50,000 on TV; mem Deta Epsion Hon Soc; mem Pres CarterS CLUB oF tHE DEM Natl Com Wash DC. **HONORS/ACHIEVEMENTS:** Winner of outstdng sermon of yr award Natl Batp Convention Inc; listed in men of achvmt; named for ldrsp Nashville 1977-78; hon dep sheriff of Davidson Cnty 1977; invited to wash to partcip in Inauguration of Pres Carter; a judge of the best sermon of the yr of Natl Bapt Pulpit of NB Con Inc; guestprch John B Falconer Lect & Monrovia Liberia 1978; col aide de camp Gov Staff 1978; hon sgt-at-arms TN St Ho of Reps; hon del US House of Rep 1980; recipient 3 battle stars for serv in Italy 92nd Inf Div 3yrs. **BUSINESS ADDRESS:** 1203 9 Ave N, Nashville, TN 37208.

JONES, ERIC LOUIS
Attorney. **PERSONAL:** Born Apr 05, 1948, Los Angeles, CA; married Elizabeth Parker; children: Rakiya. **EDUCATION:** Harvard U, BA 1970; UCLA Sch of Law, 1974. **CAREER:** Lemaire Faunce & Katznelson, atty; Hall & Bayliff, bus mgr 1974-75; Central City Investors, corp sec 1974; Tax Shelter Prgms, fin consult 1971-74; Econ Sect, The Brookings Inst, rsch asst 1970. **ORGANIZATIONS:** Mem CA, LA Bar Assn; Langston Bar Assn; Am Bar Assn; sec, steward bd # 1, usher, tchr Phillips Temple CME Ch; chmn adv subcom on crime, State Sen Nate Holden 1976-77; mem Harvard Club of So CA & Schs Com; asst sec, bd of dir Harvard Club of So CA; Town Hall Assn 1976-77; com on prgms Coro Assn. **HONORS/ACHIEVEMENTS:** Serv Award NS Curry Schlshp Club 1976.

JONES, ERNEST
Business executive. **PERSONAL:** Born Jul 20, 1923, Suffolk, VA; married Mary Ann Mckoy; children: Brenda, Ernest, Wanda, Cheryl, Marc. **EDUCATION:** St Paul's Coll Lawrenceville VA. **CAREER:** Rite-way Cleaners & Tailors, owner 1956-; tailor 1947-56. **ORGANIZATIONS:** Mem St Luke's Epis Ch 1949-; mem bd dir Businessmen's Assn; Dixwell Comm House; Dixwell Plaza Merchants Assn; 32 Deg Past Master Prince Hall Masons;past pres Craftsmans Club; instr, tailoring Opportunities Industrialization Ctr New Haven CT; mem New Haven Black Elected Officials. **MILITARY SERVICE:** AUS bandsman 1943-46. **BUSINESS ADDRESS:** Rite-Way Cleaners & Tailors, 190 Dixwell Avenue, New Haven, CT 06511.

JONES, ERNEST EDWARD
Lawyer. **PERSONAL:** Born Nov 21, 1944, Savannah, GA; son of Orlando Jones and Luella Williams; married Denise Rae Scott, Feb 14, 1981; children: Jamal Jones, Kahlil Jones. **EDUCATION:** Dickinson Coll, Carlisle PA, AB Economics, 1966; Temple Univ School of Law, Philadelphia PA, JD, 1972. **CAREER:** District Attorney's Office, Philadelphia PA, asst district atty, 1972-74; Temple Univ School of Law, Philadelphia PA, general counsel 1974-77; Community Legal Services, Philadelphia PA, deputy director 1977-79, executive dir, 1979-83; Philadelphia Urban coalition, executive dir, 1983-. **ORGANIZATIONS:** Corporate Dir, Philadelphia Natl Bank, 1987-; mem, Natl Bar Assn, 1988; mem, Philadelphia Bar Assn; mem, Urban Affairs Partnership; mem, Greater Philadelphia Economic Devel Corp; mem, Mayor's Commission on Puerto Rican/Latino Affairs; mem, Center for Literacy. **MILITARY SERVICE:** US Army, Korea, company commander, 1967-69. **BUSINESS ADDRESS:** Executive Director, The Phildelphia Urban Coalition, 121 N Broad Street, 6th Floor, Philadelphia, PA 19107.

JONES, ERVIN EDWARD
Medical technologist. **PERSONAL:** Born Oct 04, 1938, Lake City, SC; married Pauline; children: Vincent, Yvette, Michael. **EDUCATION:** Franklin Sch Sci & Arts, 1959; Montg Cnty Comm Coll; Morris Coll, 1957. **CAREER:** Philadelphia Coll of Osteo Med, med Tech 1973-; Norristown PA, coun bd 1974-. **ORGANIZATIONS:** Chmn Opport Coun 1968-69; Shmn Pub Safety PA Police & Dept 1974-; chmn negot comm Boro 1976-77; chmn Norristown House Comm 1977; 1st black chmn pub safety Boro 1974-; 2nd black elected coun Boro 1974-; past mem Norristown Advis Comm 1968-70; past mem Norristown Jaycees 1970-72; mem MT Zion AMC Ch. **HONORS/ACHIEVEMENTS:** Won state supreme ct dec subpoena power of Boro Coun 1976; hon mem young Dem of Montg Cnty 1976. **BUSINESS ADDRESS:** 1030 Walnut, Norristown, PA 19401.

JONES, EVA
Manager. **PERSONAL:** Born Mar 15, 1931, Frenchman's Bayou, AR; married James A B; children: 6. **EDUCATION:** CP Bus Coll, attended 1950. **CAREER:** Firestone Tire & Rubber Co, traffic mgr 1968-; Gen Tel, supr/traffic 1963-68. **ORGANIZATIONS:** Sch bd mem Dist 87th Bloomington IL 1971-79; pres sch bd & Bloomington 1977-78; city council Bloomington 1979-; pres Normal Champaing Chap of Links Inc 1979-81; mem Delta Nu Alpha 1979-; hairperson adv bd Sunnyside Neighborhood Center Bloomington IL; mem admission & priorities com United Way; mem Assn of Commerce & Industry of Mclean Co; mem Bloomington's Transportation Club; clerk Mt Pisgah Bapt Ch; mem NAACP; coordinator Minority Voters Coalition. **BUSINESS ADDRESS:** 66 Veteran Pkwy, Bloomington, IL 61701.

JONES, FARRELL
Health insurance executive. **PERSONAL:** Born May 06, 1926, Chicago, IL; married Audrey E Howard; children: Joanne Kathryn, Jacqueline Elinor. **EDUCATION:** Lincoln Univ, BA 1950; NYU, JD 1957. **CAREER:** New York City Dept Soc Svc, soc investigator 1957-58; Gov Harriman's Com to Rev NY State Parole Syst, asst cncl 1958; NY St Comm for Human Rights, field rep1958-60, sr field rep 1960-61, reg dir LI Region 1961-63; Nassau Co Comm on Human Rights, exec dir 1963-70; Nassau Co, dep co exec 1970-71; StateUniv of NY Downstate Med Ctr, assoc dir, clin asst prof 1971; New York City Human Resources Adm, 1st dep adminstr 1971-74; Blue Cross & Blue Shield of GreaterNY, asst vice pres spec operations 1974-81, asst vice pres govt & comm rel 1981-86, asst vice pres comm develop 1986-. **ORGANIZATIONS:** Consult NY St Dept Educ on Intergroup Rel; consult LI Sch Dist; pres Nassau Co Law Serv com 1970-71; chmn Nassau Co Econ Oppor Commn 1970-71; vice pres Hlth & Welf Coun of Nassau Co 1968-69; sec Am Comm on Africa 1965-72; bd of dir Fam Serv Assn of Nassau Co; mem bd of gov N Shore Hosp 1970-74; bd of trust Adelphi Univ 1971-; Hofstra Univ Adv Coun 1968-71; chmn Adv Bd of Adelphi Univ Sch of Soc Work 1972-; Nassau Co Youth Bd 1965-71; Nassau Co Crime Coun 1964-71; Nassau Co Bar Assn; life mem NAACP; founder Nassau Co Black Hist Museum 1966; bd of dir New York City Comp Hlth Plng Agency 1971-74; Mayor's Narc Contr Coun 1971-74; bd of trust Port WA Pub Libr 1976-; v chmn Comm Econ Dev Corp of Nassau Co 1976-; mem bd dir Cow Bay Housing Port WA, NY 1975-; mem Gov Carey's Com on Human Rights 1974-75; pres North Shore Br NAACP 1983-; pres Science Mus of Long Island 1984-; mem 3rd Congr Dist NY Serv Acad Screening Acad 1977-81; bd dirs Inst for Child Mental Health 1980-; Comm Hlth Plan of Suffolk County NY 1981-; Health Watch 1986-. **HONORS/ACHIEVEMENTS:** Brotherhood Awd Natl Conference of Christians & Jews 1982. **MILITARY SERVICE:** AUS 1951-53. **BUSINESS ADDRESS:** Asst Vice Pres Community Development, Empire Blue Cross/Blue Shield, 622 Third Ave, New York, NY 10017.

JONES, FERDINAND TAYLOR, JR.
Health service director, educator. **PERSONAL:** Born May 15, 1932, New York, NY; married Myra Rogers; children: Joanne E Jones-Rizzi, Terrie L. **EDUCATION:** Drew U, AB 1953;Univ of Vienna, PhD 1959. **CAREER:** Riverside Hospital NY, staff psychologist 1959-62; Westchester County Community Mental Health Bd, chief psychologist 1962-67; Lincoln Hospital Mental Health Serv NY, training consultant 1967-69; Sarah Lawrence Coll Bronxville NY, psycholpgy faculty 1968-72; Brown Univ, dir pschology serv, prof of psychology & lecturer psychtry human behavior. **ORGANIZATIONS:** Pres Westchester Cnty Psychol Assc 1967-69; bd dir Am Orthopsychiatric Assc 1984-87, Women & Infants Hosp 1983-; mem Am Psychol Assc, Assc BlackPsychlgst, Am AsscUniv Profs Soc for Psych Study of Racial Issues; scholar-in-residence Schomburg Center for Rsch in Black Culture 1987. **HONORS/ACHIEVEMENTS:** Dstngshd serv awrd West Cnty Psychol Assc 1972; Charles H Nichols Awrd BrownUniv Afro Am Studies Dept 1980. **MILITARY SERVICE:** AUS sp3 1953-56. **BUSINESS ADDRESS:** Dir Psych Serv & Prof, Brown Univ, Box 1960 BrownUniv, Providence, RI 02912.

JONES, FLORESTA DELORIS
Educator. **PERSONAL:** Born Dec 14, 1950, Hopewell, VA. **EDUCATION:** Barry Coll, BA (Magna Cum Laude) 1972; MI State Univ, MA 1975. **CAREER:** State Journal Lansing MI, Detroit Free Press, staff writer intern 1974; Richmond Afro-Amer, staff writer, reporter 1975-76; State Office of Min Bus Enterprise, prog info office, ed spec 1976-78; VA State Univ, adj faculty 1977-78; Georgian Court Coll, dir & adj faculty ed oppty fund prog 1978-82; Brookdale Comm Coll, writing team faculty 1982-. **ORGANIZATIONS:** Mem NJ Ed Oppty Fund Professional Assoc, AAUW, Women in Commun, Intl Comm Assoc, NAACP, Soc of Professional Jrnl, Assoc for Equality & Excellence in Ed, YWCA, Annual Womens Conf Comm, Goodwill Chorus of Petersburg VA. **HONORS/ACHIEVEMENTS:** Scholarship Awd Natl Scholarship Serv & Fund for Negro Studies 1969; Sigma Tau Delta English Hon Frat Berry Coll 1970-72; Alpha Chi Beta of GA Coll Hon Berry Coll 1971-72; Grad Fellowships & Grad Assistantships MI State Univ 1972-74; Articles Publ in Detroit Free Press, Lansing State Jrnl, Richmond AFRO, US Info Agency & other newspapers. **BUSINESS ADDRESS:** Writing Team Faculty, Brookdale Comm College, Applied Humanities Inst, Lincroft, NJ 07738.

JONES, FRANK
Security guard, mayor, chief of police. **PERSONAL:** Born Oct 25, 1950, Sellers, SC; son of John Jones and Pearlena Melton Jones; married Sylvia G Jones, Apr 1974; children: Dennis, Tyrone, Deon Jones. **EDUCATION:** Marion-Mullins Voc, Agriculture Mechanics, 1967-70; State of SC Law Enforcement, Basic Law Enforcement, 1974; Francis Marion Coll, Science and Law, 1976; SC Criminal Justice Academy, Columbia SC, First Line Supervisor, 1983-85, Traffic Radar Operator, 1987-88; Florence Darlington Tech, Jail Removal Initiative 1983. **CAREER:** Hargrove Groceries, Sellers SC, clerk; Latta Police Dept, Latta SC, policeman, 1971-73; Marion Police Dept, Marion SC, lt policeman, 1973-87; Jones Groceries, Marion SC, owner; Mcleod Hospital, Florence SC, security guard; Town of Sellers SC, mayor and chief policeman. **ORGANIZATIONS:** Adviser, Sellers Junior Policeman Department. **HONORS/ACHIEVEMENTS:** Hazardous Material Training, Familiy Line System, 1981; Guest Relation Program, Mcleod Hospital, 1988; Outstanding Policeman of the Year, Marion Jaycees, 1977-88; Law Enforcement Torch Run, SC Law Enforcement, 1989; Outstanding Community Worker, Baptist Educ and Missonary, 1989. **MILITARY SERVICE:** Coordinator Military Police, private. **BUSINESS ADDRESS:** Mayor & Chief Policeman, Town of Sellers, Sellers Town Hall, PO Box 116, Sellers, SC 29592.

JONES, FRANK BENSON
Pilot. **PERSONAL:** Born Aug 21, 1938, Kansas City, MO; son of Benson Jones and Frankie Helen Boyd Jones; married Marie Janivar Hicks; children: Eleanor, Angela, Gregory, Mia. **CAREER:** Jones Computer Systems, pres 1983-; United Air Lines, pilot 1966-. **ORGANIZATIONS:** Editor Black Panther Newspaper 1969; dir Contra Costa County Emerg Food & Med Serv 1972-73; pres PPCP Fed Credit Union 1971-72; editor Richmond Crusader Newspaper 1973-75; sec/treas Comm Developers Inc 1973-76; ecumenical dir Church of Acts 1977-78; pastor Church of Acts 1977-83. **MILITARY SERVICE:** USAF Cpt 1957-66; Air Medal with 8 Clusters; Air Force Commendation Medal. **BUSINESS ADDRESS:** United Air Lines, PO Box 5505, Carson, CA 90749.

JONES, FRANK S.
Professor. **PERSONAL:** Born Nov 09, 1928, Greensboro, NC; married Judith B Griffin; children: David D, Christopher W. **EDUCATION:** Harvard Coll, AB 1950; Harvard Business School, MBA 1957; Trinity College, LHD 1976. **CAREER:** Harvard Business School,

asst dean 1957-62; Scott Paper Co, group product mgr 1962-68; MA Institute of Technology, prof 1968-, bd prof of urban affairs 1970-. **ORGANIZATIONS:** Mem bd of dirs Polaroid Corp 1973-, Burlington Industries 1977-, Greater Roxbury Comm Develop Corp 1977-83; mem bd of trustees Mount Holyoke Coll 1977-83; mem bd of govs Ctr for Creative Leadership 1978-; mem Charles Stark Draper Lab 1980-; consultant A Better Chance Inc 1982-84; mem bd of dirs Cigna Corp 1982-, Corporation for Boston 1983-85, American Broadcasting Companies Inc 1984-85; mem exec comm The Partnership 1985-. **BUSINESS ADDRESS:** Board Prof of Urban Affairs, MA Institute of Technology, Room 3-401 MIT, Cambridge, MA 02139.

JONES, FRANKLIN D.
Educator. **PERSONAL:** Born Aug 18, 1939, Eastman, GA. **EDUCATION:** Millersville State Coll, BS 1964; Millersville State Coll, MEd 1971; Lehigh U, EdD 1975. **CAREER:** Biological Sci & Gen Sci Avon Grove Area Sch W Grove PA, tchr 1964-66; Medium Tower Tube Mfr RCA Lancaster PA, asst supt 1966-69; Kutztown State Coll PA, asst dir of admissions 1969-; PA Dept of Educ, special programs adv com 1970, special programs evaluation team 1971. **ORGANIZATIONS:** Mem Reading Berks Mental Health Assn 1940-72. **HONORS/ACHIEVEMENTS:** Reading martin luther king scholarship found 1969-; lancast king clements scholarship found 1971. **MILITARY SERVICE:** USMC corpl 1957-59. **BUSINESS ADDRESS:** State Coll, Kutztown, PA 19530.

JONES, FRANKLIN D.
Educator. **PERSONAL:** Born Dec 07, 1935, Oakland, MS; married Allene; children: Cedric D, Tamekia L. **EDUCATION:** Mississippi Industrial Coll, BS 1961; MS Univ, further studies 1970's; Delta State, further studies 1984. **CAREER:** Charleston Elementary, teacher 1961-80; Oakland Elementary, teacher 1980-; Town of Oakland, mayor. **HOME ADDRESS:** Route 1 Box 200, Oakland, MS 38948. **BUSINESS ADDRESS:** Teacher, Oakland Elementary, Gen Del, Oakland, MS 38948.

JONES, FREDERICK DOUGLASS, JR.
Assistant city attorney. **PERSONAL:** Born Oct 08, 1955, Albuquerque, NM; son of Frederick Jones, Sr and Ruth Carey Jones. **EDUCATION:** Earlham Coll, Richmond IN, BA, 1980; University of New Mexico, Albuquerque NM, School of Law, JD, 1984. **CAREER:** State of New Mexico, Albuquerque NM, asst district attorney 1984-87; City of Albuquerque, NM, asst city attorney, 1987-. **ORGANIZATIONS:** Pres, New Mexico Black Laywers Assn, 1986-88; mem, NAACP, 1986-; mem, Natl Bar Assn, 1986-; bd of dir, New Futures Inc, 1988-. **HONORS/ACHIEVEMENTS:** Honorarium, Amer Bd of Trial Advocates, 1984, NAACP, 1989; Pappy Seed Award, Univ of New Mexico School of Law 1984. **HOME ADDRESS:** 1313 Alamo SE, Albuquerque, NM 87106.

JONES, FREDRICK E.
Auto dealer. **CAREER:** Fred Jones Pontiac-GMC Truck, Inc, Brookfield, WI, chief executive officer, 1984—. **BUSINESS ADDRESS:** Fred Jones Pontiac-GMC Truck, Inc, 13000 Capital Dr, Brookfield, WI 53008. *

JONES, FURMAN MADISON, JR.
Physician. **PERSONAL:** Born Nov 01, 1927, New York, NY; married Patricia; children: Phillip, Jol, Furman III. **EDUCATION:** Tufts Univ, BS 1948; Meharry Medical Coll, MD 1953. **CAREER:** Private Practice, physician. **ORGANIZATIONS:** Mem Omega Psi Phi 1948-87, Natl Negro Coll Assoc 1969-87; dir Home Health Serv Harlem Hosp 1976-. **MILITARY SERVICE:** AUS capt 3 yrs. **BUSINESS ADDRESS:** 470 Lenox, New York, NY 10037.

JONES, G. DANIEL
Clergyman. **PERSONAL:** Born in Norfolk, VA; son of George R Jones (deceased) and Estelle Campbell Jones (deceased); married Geraldine S Saunders; children: Bryant Daniel. **EDUCATION:** VA Union Univ, BS 1962; Andover Newton Theological School, MDiv 1966; Howard University's Divinity School, DMin 1978. **CAREER:** Ministry St John Baptist Church Woburn, MA, pastor 1965-67; Messiah Baptist Church Brockton, MA, pastor 1967-73; Zion Baptist Church Portsmouth, VA, pastor 1973-82; Grace Baptist Church of Germantown, Philadelphia, PA sr pastor 1982-; graduate adjunct, School of Theology, Virginia Union Univ 1979-82; undergraduate instructor Philosophy of Religion Norfolk State Univ, Norfolk, VA 1973-82. **ORGANIZATIONS:** Coll instructor Norfolk State Univ 1974-82; second instructor Hanson Public Schools Hanson, MA 1969-73; pres bd dir Family Serv Personal Couns Brockton, MA 1969-73;sch bd mem Sch Dist Portsmouth, VA 1974-80 (chairing business comm); bd mem YMCA Portsmouth, VA 1975-82; bd mem YMCA Philadelphia, PA 1984-; 2nd vice pres Amer Bapt Churches of the South 1981-82; Hampton Inst Minister's Conf 1986-; mem general bd Amer Baptist Churches USA chairing the Natl Comm on the Ministry 1987-; bd mem, Lutheran Home at Germantown 1986-; Executive Comm Bd, Lott Carey Baptist Foreign Mission Conv; Executive Comm Bd, Philadelphia Baptist Assn. **HONORS/ACHIEVEMENTS:** Human Relations Award Omega Psi Phi Frat Inc Portsmouth, VA 1979 & 1982; 1st Place Sermon Contest Amer Bapt Churches of PA and DE 1984; Key to City of Brockton, MA 1983; Citations from City of Portsmouth, VA and Sch Bd 1980 & 1982; Doctoral Thesis, "Educational Ministries in the Black Baptist Churches of Norfolk and Portsmouth, VA"; "Man of the Year" Grace Baptist Church of Germantown 1989. **BUSINESS ADDRESS:** Senior Pastor, Grace Baptist Ch of Germantown, 25 W Johnson St, Philadelphia, PA 19144.

JONES, GARY
Theater director. **PERSONAL:** Born Jun 29, 1942, Chicago, IL; son of Leonard Jones and Jessie Tolbert Jones. **EDUCATION:** IL Inst of Tech Inst of Design, 1963-64. **CAREER:** Kungsholm Min Grand Opera of Chicago, senic designer & principal puppeteer 1969-71; Blackstreet USA Puppet Theatre, dir, founder 1975-. **HONORS/ACHIEVEMENTS:** Designed exec prods Porgy & Bess, Carmen, The King & I, My Fair Lady, Gypsy 1969-71; 5 week sold out engagement at the Smithsonian Inst Div of Performing Arts 1980,82; 3 month tour of Iceland, West Germany, Holland, Portugal 1984; The Brody Arts Foundation Fellowship Program Los Angeles 1987. **BUSINESS ADDRESS:** Dir, Blackstreet USA Puppet Theatre, 4619 W Washington Blvd, Los Angeles, CA 90016.

JONES, GAYL
Author, educator. **PERSONAL:** Born Nov 23, 1949, Lexington, KY; daughter of Franklin Jones and Lucille Wilson Jones. **EDUCATION:** CT Coll, BA, 1971; Brown Univ, MA, 1973, DA, 1975. **CAREER:** Univ of MI, Ann Arbor, MI, prof of English, 1975-83. **HONORS/ACHIEVEMENTS:** Author of Corregidora, Random House, 1975, Eva's Man, Random House, 1976, White Rate, Random House, 1977, Song for Animals, Lotus Press, 1981, The Hermit-Woman, Lotus Press, 1983, Xarque and Other Poems, Lotus Press, 1985. **BUSINESS ADDRESS:** Gayl Jones, c/o Beacon Press, 25 Beacon St, Boston, MA 02108. *

JONES, GEORGE ALBERT
Retired public health executive. **PERSONAL:** Born Dec 20, 1904, Ithica, NY; married Helen P Brandt; children: George, James, Shirley Carter, Suzanne Smith. **EDUCATION:** Lincoln Univ, BA 1929; Howard Univ, MD 1935. **CAREER:** Private Practice, 1937-72; PA Dept of Health, dir kidney dis prog 1972-81 retired. **ORGANIZATIONS:** Exec bd State Conf NAACP 1954-60; pres Harrisburg Br NAACP 1953-60; Natl Med Assn; AMA; Dauphin Co Med Soc; Amer Acad of Family Physicians; PA Allergy Assn; bd mem Tri-Co Welfare Council of Harrisburg 1961-65; Planned Parenthood Assn 1950-60. **HONORS/ACHIEVEMENTS:** Omega Man of Yr 1963. **HOME ADDRESS:** 326 N Front, Steelton, PA 17113.

JONES, GEORGE H.
Educator. **PERSONAL:** Born Feb 21, 1942, Muskogee, OK; son of George H Jones and Bernice Weaver Jones. **EDUCATION:** Harvard Coll, BA 1963; Univ of CA Berkeley, PhD 1968. **CAREER:** Univ of MI, asso prof of bio 1975-, asst prof of Zoology 1971-75; Inst of Health Univ of Geneva, Switzerland 1968-71; prof of Biology Univ of MI 1986-89; prof of Biology Emory Univ, GA 1989. **ORGANIZATIONS:** Mem NY Acad of Sci. **HONORS/ACHIEVEMENTS:** Helen Hay Whitney Found Postdoctoral Fellowship; Ford Foundation postdoctoral fellowship 1982; Univ Teaching Award Univ of MI 1989; over 40 publications in scientific journals. **BUSINESS ADDRESS:** Graduate Dean, Vice President for Research & Professor of Biology, Emorty University, Atlanta, GA 30322.

JONES, GEORGE W.
Education association executive. **PERSONAL:** Born May 15, 1924, Camden, SC; married Rose Martin; children: Lawrence G, George W, Jr. **EDUCATION:** Benedict Coll, AB 1948; Univ of Chicago, MA, 1951. **CAREER:** NEA, asso dir; Hum Rel NEA, dir 1970-74; Miles Coll Birmingham, dean 1963-66; Am Tchr Assn Montgomery, exec dir 1961-63; AL State & Tchrs Assn Montgomery, exec dir 1958-61; AL State U, instr 1951-58. **ORGANIZATIONS:** Mem bd dir YFM Assn Consulting Firm; mem NAACP; SCLC; NAHRW; elder Presb Ch. **MILITARY SERVICE:** USN seaman 1942-46. **BUSINESS ADDRESS:** 1201 16 St NW, Washington, DC 20036.

JONES, GEORGE WILLIAMS
Surgeon/urology. **PERSONAL:** Born Jul 13, 1931, Mobile, AL; married Edna Robinson; children: Randall, Carleton, Janet, George B, Adria T. **EDUCATION:** NC Coll, BS 1953; Howard Univ, MD 1960. **CAREER:** Freedman's Hospital, intern 1960-61, resident 1961-62, asst resident urology 1962-64, chief resident urology 1964-65; Howard Univ Coll of Medicine, assoc prof of urology 1972-76, prof of urology 1976-; Urologic Assocs, surgeon. **ORGANIZATIONS:** Bd of dirs Natl Kidney Foundation of Natl Capitol Area 1981-; bd mem DC Div, Amer Cancer Soc 1984-; mem The Amer Assoc of Clinical Urologists, The Amer Coll of Surgeons, Assn for Acad Surgery, Amer Tissue Culture Assn, Soc of Univ Urologists, Assn of Amer Med Colls, Washington Urologic Assoc, Mid-Atlantic Section, Amer Urological Assn, The Soc of Surgical Oncology, Amer Med Assn, Amer Assn of Clinical Urologists, Amer Assn of Cancer Educ; chmn Bd of the Capital Area Health Plan. **HONORS/ACHIEVEMENTS:** Charles R Drew Award, Most Worthy Scientific Contribution at the Natl Medical Assoc Convention Cincinnati, OH 1965; Thomas Jefferson Award, Fox Productions WTTG Channel 5 TV Washington, DC 1986; numerous presentation, lectures; 29 publications including contributing editor in "American Cancer Society's Book on Cancer," the chapter Urinary Tract Cancer published by DoubleDay 1986; "Idiopathic Renal Arteriovenous Fistual, Spontaneous Closure," Urology Vol XXIX No 1 pp 86-89, 1987. **MILITARY SERVICE:** AUS specialist 1955; DC Natl Guard 1st lt Medical Corps 1961, capt Medical Corps 1962. **BUSINESS ADDRESS:** Urologic Associates PC, 2139 Georgia Ave NW #4A, Washington, DC 20001.

JONES, GERALD E.
City employee, educator. **PERSONAL:** Born Nov 02, 1937, Chicago; married Barbara; children: Gerald III. **EDUCATION:** Loyola U, M 1970; IL Tchrs Coll, 1965-66; Malcolm X Coll, aA 1963-; Chicagostate Coll, deg bus educ 1963-65. **CAREER:** City Council 7 Ward, first black mem 1973; Behavioral Science Dept Trinton Coll, 1972-74; GE Jones & Assoc, pres 1967-71; Kennedy King Coll, instructor1970-71; Malcolm X Coll, coordinator 1970; Malcolm X Comm Coll, 1969-70; Chicago City Coll, Tchr 1968; Chicago City Coll, dir bus 1967-69; Chicago Bd Edn, Tchr 1965-67; Concerned Minority Businessmen, spokesman. **ORGANIZATIONS:** Mem Am Bus & Economis Soc Chicago; assoc sec am Mgmt Assn; Assn Sch Bus Officials US & Can; IL Retailing & Marketing Found; NAACP; afroamHictory Club; Operation PUSH; C of C; S Shore Community Center; YMCA; Kiwanis. **MILITARY SERVICE:** AUS med splst. **BUSINESS ADDRESS:** 2554 E 79 St, Chicago, IL 60649.

JONES, GERALD WINFIELD
Government official. **PERSONAL:** Born Jun 27, 1931, Jetersville, VA; son of Emmett Jones, Jr; married Ann H; children: Crenshaw, Cassandra Coleman, Lessie, Eric. **EDUCATION:** VA State Coll, AB 1952; Howard Univ, LLB 1960. **CAREER:** Postal clerk, 1956-57; Dept of Justice, atty 1960-65; Dept of Justice Civil Rights Div, super atty chief voting sect 1965-. **ORGANIZATIONS:** Mem bd dirs Melwood Hort Training Ctr; mem Natl Bar Assn; mem Govt Lawyers Sect Natl Bar Assn. **HONORS/ACHIEVEMENTS:** Superior Performance Awd Dept of Justice 1964; Spec Commendation Awd Dept of Justice 1972; Atty Gen Disting Serv Awd 1973 1983; Atty Gen's Awd forUpward Mobility 1978; Sr Exec Serv Meritorious Awd 1982, 1985-87. **MILITARY SERVICE:** AUS 1st lt 1952-55. **BUSINESS ADDRESS:** Supv Atty Chief Voting Sect, Dept of Justice, 9th & Constitution Ave NW, Washington, DC 20530.

JONES, GERALDINE J.
Educator. **PERSONAL:** Born Jul 30, 1939, Seaford, DE; divorced; children: Monica.

EDUCATION: DE State Coll, BS 1961; Central MI, MA Business Admin 1977; Temple Univ, 1986. **CAREER:** Div Social Services, social worker 1962-64; Head Start Camden Summer, social worker 1965, dir 1971; Migrant Prog Summer, home coord 1974; Capital Sch Dist Dover, visiting teacher, educator. **ORGANIZATIONS:** Mem NEA, DSEA, Assoc Visiting Teachers, Capital Assoc, Tri-Co Investment & Savings Assoc, Intl Assoc Pupil Personnel Workers; mem Adv Council DE Adolescent Program; Delta Sigma Theta; Nat Coun Negro Women; Whatcoat United Meth Ch; DE State Coll Alumni Assn; Kent Co Alumni Assn; vol tchr Black StudiesDE Youth Servs Initiated; pres UM Women, Whatcoac Church Dover; pres Kent County Chap DE State Coll Alumni; treas Wm C Jason Alumni; secty/treas Delaware Assoc of Certified Vstg Teachers; lay leader Whatcoat UM Church; vice pres UMW Peninsula Conf; Miss Alumni 1986-87 DE State Coll; consultant. **HONORS/ACHIEVEMENTS:** Scholarship fund blacks John WesleyUniv M Ch; James R Webb; scholarships; poem pub IAPPW Jornal 1974; Sigma Iota Epsilon Central MI 1979; Youth Serv Awd Whatcoac UM Church 1984; Alumnus of the Year DE State Coll 1985; Certificate of Appreciation NAACP Central Delaware Branch 1985; Serv Awd Peninsula ConfUnited Methodist Women. **BUSINESS ADDRESS:** Educator, Capital School District, 945 Forest St, Dover, DE 19001.

JONES, GROVER (DEACON JONES)
Professional athlete. **PERSONAL:** Born Apr 18, 1934, White Plains, NY; married Tiki; children: Monica. **EDUCATION:** Ithaca Coll, BS. **CAREER:** Chicago White Sox, scout/instr/minor league mgr 1962-63 & 1966; Houston Astros, coach 1976-82; NY Yankees, scout 1983; San Diego Padres, batting coach 1984-, professional athlete. **HONORS/ACHIEVEMENTS:** Mem Westchester Co & Ithaca Coll Hall of Fame; 1st Black Man Recog Hall of Fame Cooperstown; Honored Nations Top Am Legion Player 1951; Silver Bat Award Winner 1956. **MILITARY SERVICE:** Military 1957-58. **BUSINESS ADDRESS:** San Diego Padres, PO Box 2000, San Diego, CA 92102.

JONES, HARDI LIDDELL
Government administrator. **PERSONAL:** Born Nov 02, 1942, St Louis, MO; son of T H E and Jamesetta Jones; married Yvonne A Thompson; children: Miriam Yvette, Sandra Lynnette. **EDUCATION:** St Paul's Coll, BS (Cum Laude) 1962; Attended, Univ of MD-College Park 1963, George Washington Univ 1965. **CAREER:** US Naval Oceanographic Office, physical oceanographer 1962-63; US Fish & Wildlife Svcs, physical oceanographer 1963-65; US Naval Oceanographic Office, physical oceanographer 1965-67; Underwater Systems Inc, oceanographer 1967-71; US Naval Oceanographic Office, equal opportunity officer 1971-74; Bureau of Reclamation US Dept of Interior, dir office of equal opportunity 1974-81; US Dept of Treasury IRS, asst to the commissioner 1981-. **ORGANIZATIONS:** Pres Prince George's County Club Frontiers Intl 1980-82; chmn bd of dirs Combined Comms in Action Prince George's County MD 1981-; mem Sigma Pi Phi Frat Beta Mu Boule 1981-; chmn labor and industry comm Prince George's Co MD NAACP 1983-; chmn bd of trustees St Paul's Coll Lawrenceville VA 1985-88; life mem Kappa Alpha Psi Frat Inc. **HONORS/ACHIEVEMENTS:** Citation Oceanographer of the Navy 1974; Community Serv Awd Combined Communities in Action 1981; Distinguished Alumnus St Paul's College 1985. **HOME ADDRESS:** 10215 Buena Vista, Seabrook, MD 20706. **BUSINESS ADDRESS:** Asst to the Commissioner, Internal Revenue Service, 1111 Constitution Ave NW, Washington, DC 20224.

JONES, HARLEY M.
Educator. **PERSONAL:** Born Jun 12, 1936, Brooklyn, NY. **EDUCATION:** Brooklyn Coll, BA 1956; Yale Sch of Arch, MA 1960. **CAREER:** Environmental Design Porat Inst Brooklyn, assoc prof resigned as chmn 1975; NY State Counc on the Arts, cons; Interior Desing Mag, juror comp held by 1975; Bedford Stuyvesant Restoration Corp, supr architect; Westerman & Miller, project designer; ARCH Architect's Research Com in Harlem Gowanusboerum Hill Asso, consult to; Edgar Rafel William Lescaze, designer; Archit Practice in NYC, Specializing in Comm oriented projects. **ORGANIZATIONS:** Bd mem Soc of Preservation of Weeksville & Bedford Stuyvesant History; mem Interior Design Educ Counc; mem Studio Museum in Harlem; mem Nat Preservation Hotel. **HONORS/ACHIEVEMENTS:** Project chosen for show of Am Students Abroad 1959; exhibited in "Black Architects" show NY AIA 1972.

JONES, HAROLD M.
Flutist. **PERSONAL:** Born Mar 25, 1934, Chicago, IL; son of William Henry Jones and Rosetta Jones; married Wanda J Hudson, Jul 10, 1953; children: Ernest Milton, Louis Eugene, Antar Patrice. **EDUCATION:** Sherwood Music School, certificate; Juilliard Sch of Music, diploma 1959. **CAREER:** Soloist Symphony of the New World, Gordon Jacob Flute Concerto, Mozart Flute & Harp Concerto; Municipal Concerts Orchestra & the Amer Symphony Orchestra; Brooklyn Philharmonia; Riverside Symphony Orchestra; Principal Flutist, Chicago Civic Orchestra, Natl Orchestral Assn; Bach Aria Orchestra, Festival Symphony Orchestra, Symphony of the New World; Yachacts Music Festival, Yachacts, OR; numerous recordings shows & productions; Teaching, Metro Music Sch, Bronx House Music Sch, Julliard Sch of Music, Westchester Sch of Music, Manhattanville Coll, Brooklyn Coll Conservatory of Music; Manhattan Sch of Music, CUNY; freelance musician; China Daily Press, Tainan, Taiwan, soloist/instructor 1988; Antara Records, NY,NY soloist/recital 1989; Mozart Society Orchestra, Cambridge, MA artist in residence 1989. **ORGANIZATIONS:** NY Flute Club, pres 1976-79, mem 1965-, bd of dir 1961-; mem Natl Flute Assn, 1979. **HONORS/ACHIEVEMENTS:** Arion Awd for Outstanding Instrumentalist DuSable HS 1951; Outstanding Woodwind Player Julliard Sch of Music 1959; recording, Harold Jones Cespico Records 1981; recording, From Bach to Bazzini Antara Records 1985; Afternoon Fantasies, Antara Records, 1987; Outstanding Woodwind Award Juilliard School of Music 1958-59. **HOME ADDRESS:** 100 W 94 St, New York, NY 10025.

JONES, HERBERT C.
Otolaryngologist. **PERSONAL:** Born Aug 01, 1936, Demopolis, AL; son of Tom Allen Jones, Jr and Bettie Mae Young Jones; married Bessie Chapman Jones, Jun 13, 1958; children: Sandra Jo Jones, Nancy Gayle Jones, Herbert Chapman Jones, Lisa Carol Jones. **EDUCATION:** Talladega Coll, Talladega AL, 1953-56; Indiana Univ, Bloomington IN, AB 1957, MD 1961; Univ of IL Medical Center, Chicago IL, Residency in Otolaryngology, 1965-68. **CAREER:** Self-employed Surgeon, Atlanta GA, 1968-. **ORGANIZATIONS:** Mem, chairman Otolaryngology section, Natl Medical Assn, 1969-; mem & fellow, Amer Academy of Otolaryngology, 1969-; mem, Amer Coll of Surgeons, 1972-; GA State Medical Assn; mem, NAACP. **HONORS/ACHIEVEMENTS:** Alpha Omega Alpha Honor Society, 1961; Father of the Year in medicine, Concerned Black Clergy of Atlanta, 1987; Outstanding Physician in Otolaryngology, Black Enterprise Magazine, 1988. **MILITARY SERVICE:** US Air Force, Captain, 1961-65. **BUSINESS ADDRESS:** Herbert C Jones MD, PA, 2600 ML King Jr Drive SW, Suite 302, Atlanta, GA 30311.

JONES, HERMAN HARVEY, JR.
Physician. **PERSONAL:** Born May 13, 1925, Nashville, TN; married Barbara; children: Dr Herman III. **EDUCATION:** Fist U, BA 1950; Meharry Med Coll, MD 1954. **CAREER:** Gen surgeon, self; KSUniv Med Ctr, asst clinical prof; Wyandotte Co, dep coroner; Wadsworth KS VA Hosp, resd gen surgery 1959-63; KC Gen Hosp,1955-58; Comm Gen Hosp, intern 1954-55; Providence Hosp Staff, pres 1971; Providence St Margaret Hosp, chf surg 1972-76. **ORGANIZATIONS:** Mem KS State Bd Healing Arts; diplomate Am Bd Surgery; flw Am Coll Surgeons; vice pres SW Clinical Soc 1973; mem Wyandotte Co Med Soc; pres 1976-77;mem Kaw Valley Med Soc; KC Surg Soc ; Pan-Pacific Med Soc; AMA; Nat Med Assn; Fed Med Exnrs; Am Coll Emergency Physicians; pres bd adv Donnelly Coll 1972-73; bd dir Wyandotte Co Guidance Ctr; Boys Club KC KS; Wyandotte Co Cancer Assn; mem Nat Hlth Com; Nat BD NAACP; Sigma Pi Phi Frat; Kappa Alpha Psi Frat. **MILITARY SERVICE:** USN 1943-43. **BUSINESS ADDRESS:** 600 Nebraska, Kansas City, KS 66101.

JONES, HORTENSE
Consultant. **PERSONAL:** Born Jan 10, 1918, Franklin, VA; married Theodore T Jones; children: Theodore Jr, Theodora Blackmon, Lawrence. **EDUCATION:** Hampton Inst, BS 1947; NYU, MA 1950. **CAREER:** Newport News, tchr 1936-41; Cadman Cntr, tchr 1948; Day Care Cntr, educ dir 1948-50; City Day Care Ctrs, dir 1950-56; tchr 1956-63; More Effective Schs, dir & asst dir 1964-72; Childhood Edn, asst dir 1963-64, 1972-75; Ctr for Sch Dev New York City Bd of Edn, dir 1975-83; La Guardia Comm Coll, CUNY, adjunct prof; consultant in early childhood/elementary education. **ORGANIZATIONS:** Tech Inst Peach Corp 1966-72; adj instr Queens Coll, Medgar Evers Coll 1972-75; dir early childhood educ 1979-80; mem NJ Day Care Council; mem Detroit Tchrs Assn; conducted workshops in, Akron, OH; Gary, IN; Indianapolis, IN; Canton, OH; Glen Falls, NY; Rochester, NY; consult Migrant Educ Conf 1970-72; Child Care Worker Training Prog Rutgers Univ 1971-72; lectr for num organizations. **HONORS/ACHIEVEMENTS:** Mother of the Year Que Ives 1968; Sojourner Truth Award Natl Negro Bus & Professional Women's Club 1968; Comm Serv Award Preschool 1974; Day Care Award Newark, NJ1977. **BUSINESS ADDRESS:** Consultant, 131 Livingston St, Brooklyn, NY 11201.

JONES, I. GENE
Educational administrator. **EDUCATION:** Jarvis Christian Coll, BA 1951; Ball State Univ, MA 1963; Univ of MI, PhD 1974. **CAREER:** Denver Public Schls, tchr and tchrs asst 1954-62; Ball State Univ, asst prof 1962-64; Central Comm Coll, instruct 1964-66; Unified School Dist, reading resource and curriculum devel spec 1966-68; Eastern MI Univ, asst prof of education 1969-73; GA State Univ, adjunct faculty 1975-78; Albany State College, asst dean-academic affairs 1973-78; St Paul's Coll, vice pres for academic affairs 1978-. **ORGANIZATIONS:** Bd of directors YWCA Denver 1960-62; bd of directors United Way of Dougherty Cty 1975-78; team capt GA Heart Fund Assn 1977-78; mem New Mexico First. **HONORS/ACHIEVEMENTS:** Amer Book Co textbooks published 1967; Exxon Fellow Amer Council of Educ Educl Leadership Devel 1975; Distinguished Alumni Award, Jarvis Christian College 1985; Presidential Citation, National Assn for Equal Opportunity in Higher Education 1986. **HOME ADDRESS:** 1601 Pennsylvania, NE, Winrock Villas H-10, Albuquerque, NM 87110.

JONES, IDA KILPATRICK See WHITE, IDA MARGARET

JONES, IDUS, JR.
Clergyman. **PERSONAL:** Born Apr 18, 1927, Philadelphia, PA; married Cora F Coleman; children: 12 children. **EDUCATION:** IN Univ PA, continuing educ Black studies 1970, BA Sociology Anthropology 1972; Pgh Theological Seminary, MDiv 1975. **CAREER:** Cornerstone Baptist Church, minister 1958-60; Church of the Living God, minister 1960-70; Pleasant Hills Baptist Church, asst pastor 1970-72; John Wesley United Methodist Church, pastor 1973-74; Brushton United Methodist Church, pastor 1974-80; John Stewart United Meth Church, pastor 1980-81; Ebenezer United Methodist Church, pastor/chmn; Ebenezer Comm Outreach Bd, 1981-. **ORGANIZATIONS:** Visitation minister at various Correctional Inst throughout Eastern PA and NJ area; super Ebenezer Comm Outreach Ctr Inc; mem Huntington Food Bank Inc; mem Tri-State Evangelistic Assn; mem NAACP; charter mem Psi Beta Beta Chap Omega Psi Phi Frat Inc; mem Kiwanis Club Intl; chairperson Emphasis Comm; mem Tri State Area Council No 672 Boy Scouts of Amer; mem Mt Moriah Lodge No 36 F&AM; consistory St Cyprian No 4 Sahara Temple No 2 AEAO NMS Inc; mem Gov's Commn on Crime Correction Delinquency Subcomm Juvenile; bd of dirs Salvation Army; bd ordained minister WV Dist; chaplain in charge Cabell County Jail WV. **HONORS/ACHIEVEMENTS:** Minister of the Yr Awd Hand-in-Hand 1977; Scottish Rite Mason of the Yr Awd AASR F AM (PHA) 1978; Human Serv Awd Teen Challenge Western PA; Black PastorsMinisterial Comm Awd 1987. **MILITARY SERVICE:** USN seaman 1st class 4 yrs; Amer Campaign Medal; Asiatic-Pacific Campaign Medal; Good Conduct Medal; WWII Victory Medal; Korean Medal; USCG Boatsw 13 yrs. **BUSINESS ADDRESS:** Pastor-Chairman, Ebenezer United Methodist Chrc, 1651 8th Ave, Huntington, WV 25701.

JONES, ISAAC, JR.
Business executive. **PERSONAL:** Born Jun 19, 1933, Opelika, AL; son of Isaac Jones Sr and Katie Chisolm; married Zerelene E White. **EDUCATION:** AL State Univ, BS, Educ, 1954; State Univ of NY, Binghamton, MS, Mgmt, 1971. **CAREER:** IBM, Boulder, CO, mgr, 2nd level, 1980-81; IBM, Brooklyn, mgr, 3rd level, 1984; IBM Division Headquarters, sr business planner, 1984-. **HOME ADDRESS:** Rd 6, Maplewood Dr, Brewster, NY 10509-9806.

JONES, JACQUELINE
Educator and author. **PERSONAL:** Born Jun 17, 1948, Wilmington, DE; daughter of Albert H. Jones and Sylvia Phelps Jones; married Jeffrey B. Abramson, May 18, 1980; children: Sarah, Anna. **EDUCATION:** University of Delaware, BA, 1970; University of Wisconsin—Madison, MA, 1972, PhD, 1976. **CAREER:** Wellesley College, Wellesley MA, associate professor of American history, 1981—, chair of history department, 1985—. **ORGANIZA-**

TIONS: Organization of American Historians, National Women's Studies Association. **HONORS/ACHIEVEMENTS:** ACLS grant in aid, 1977; National Endowment for Humanities research fellowship, 1979-80; Bancroft Prize, Columbia University, 1986, for Labor of Love, Labor of Sorror: Black Women, Work, and the Family from Slavery to the Present. **BUSINESS ADDRESS:** Department of History, Wellesley College, Wellesley, MA 02181. *

JONES, JAMES
Retired professional basketball player. **PERSONAL:** Born Jan 01, 1945, Tallulah, LA; children: Michael, Kimako. **EDUCATION:** Grambling Coll, BS 1967. **CAREER:** New Orleans Buccaneers, played guard; Mmphis Pros; UT stars 1971-74; washington bullets, 1974-77. **HONORS/ACHIEVEMENTS:** Mem All-rookie Team 1967-68; all-star team 1968-69; all-star team 1968-71.

JONES, JAMES
Professional football player. **PERSONAL:** Born Mar 21, 1961; married Sheila; children: Jasmine. **EDUCATION:** Univ of FL. **CAREER:** Detroit Lions, professional football player (fullback). **HONORS/ACHIEVEMENTS:** Coll, fourth all-time leading rusher in FL Gators' hist with 2,026 yards on 468 carries (43 ave); also caught 68 passes for 593 yds; profl,broke the 1967record set by Pat Studstill for single-season receiving mark of 67 receptions; 77 receptions in 1984; Lions' Most Valuable Player in 1984; led the Lions with 46 receptions his first yr; registered 942 yds of total offense in 1983. **BUSINESS ADDRESS:** Detroit Lions, Pontiac Silverdome, 1200 Featherstone Rd Box 4200, Pontiac, MI 48057.

JONES, JAMES A.
Educator. **PERSONAL:** Born Mar 07, 1932, Boston, MA; son of James H Jones and Alice R Jones; married T Louise Lawrence; children: Karen Williams, Lawrence Jones, Gail Smith, Bruce Jones. **EDUCATION:** Boston Univ, AA 1951; Harvard Univ, AB 1953; Columbia Univ, MA 1955, PhD 1965. **CAREER:** Lab Soc Relations, stat clerk 1952-53; Bur Applied Soc Rsch, rsch asst 1953-58; Columbia Univ, tchr asst 1955, lecturer 1956-58; NY Sch Soc Work, rsch asst 1958-61; Mobilization Youth 1961-62; Harlem Youth Opport Unlimited, rsch dir 1962-66; NYU, assoc prof 1965-70, rsch assoc 1966-68; Clark, Phipps & Harris, sr rsch consult 1980-; New Jersey St Bd of Educ, mem 1981-; Columbia Univ Sch Social Work, assoc prof 1970-. **ORGANIZATIONS:** Consult US Dept Labor; Ocean-Hill Brownsville Comm Educ Cntr 1969; Ofc Econ Opportunity; Met Applied Rsch Cntr; Child Welfare League Amer; Dept HUD; Natl Fedn Settlements & Neighborhood Cntrs; Allegheny Co Mental Hlth & Mental Retardation Program; mem Amer Social Assn; Amer Acad Political Soc Sci; Council Soc Work Educ AAAS Com mem following, Coll Entrance Exam Bd Study NY State Prog Financial Aid for Coll Students; Human Resources Admin; ERIC; Strycker's Bay Neighborhood Council; Urban Edn; Comm Council Greater NY; Adolescent Health Proj; Family Serv Assn; Comm Serv Soc Study. **HONORS/ACHIEVEMENTS:** Many papers published. **BUSINESS ADDRESS:** Associate Professor, ColumbiaUniv Sch Soc Work, 622 W 113 St, New York, NY 10025.

JONES, JAMES BENNETT
Government official. **PERSONAL:** Born Jun 02, 1931, Wilson, AR; son of Will Jones and Marie Jones; married Mary Frances Bynum; children: Theresa, Gwendolyn. **EDUCATION:** Lawrence Inst of Tech, BS 1963; Wayne State U, 1972. **CAREER:** Detroit Bldg Authority, gen mgr 1976-; Detroit Gen Hosp, dir of planning 1973-76; dir 1971-73; proj mgr 1968-71; sr asso 1965-68; Lawrence & of Tech, instr 1973-; Detroit Water & Sewer, architect 1976-82; Saudi Arabia, senior construction mgr 1982-85; Ford Motor Co architect/engineer 1985-87; City of Milwaukee, asst supt 1987-. **ORGANIZATIONS:** Bd dir, treas Friends of Econ Devel 1972-75; Am Inst of Architects; MI Soc of Architects; Nat Assn of Minority Architects; Nat Fire Prevension Assn; Fire Safety Adv Com MI Phi Beta Sigma; Optimist Internat; pres Kingsmen Soc Club 1966-76; NAACP; Urban Alliance; Am Mgrs Assn; Amer Public Works Assn; Natl Assn Housing Redevelopment Officials. **HONORS/ACHIEVEMENTS:** Nat award Nat Urban League 1973; natl march of dimes 1974; career guidance award Detroit Housin Com 1972. **MILITARY SERVICE:** AUS corpl 1951-53. **HOME ADDRESS:** 3220 North Sherman Blvd, Apt 2, Milwaukee, WI 53202. **BUSINESS ADDRESS:** DPW/Bureau of Bridges, 841 N Broadway, Suite 3ll, Milwaukee, WI 53202.

JONES, JAMES C.
Business executive. **PERSONAL:** Born Feb 14, 1913, Westmoreland Co, VA; married Gertrude Robb; children: Beverly, Collis, Sheila. **EDUCATION:** Howard Univ; Catholic Univ. **CAREER:** James C Jones Builders Inc, pres 1947-; Construction Supr Cassell Contruction, 1943-47; Phelps Vocational Sch, tchr blueprint reading & woodworking 1938-43; Oliver B Cassell & Construction Co, construction supr 1936-38; Morrison Bros Construction Co, foreman 1935-36. **ORGANIZATIONS:** Mem bd of trustees Minority Contractors Assn of DC; historian Natl Tech Assn; mem Mayors Task Force NAACP; Urban League; past pres Holy Name Soc; past treas Archidiocesan Holy Name Union; past treas, vice pres & mem of bd dir Sierra Club of Washington; mem Archbishops Annual Comm on Appeal for Execs Gifts; Omega Psi Phi. **HONORS/ACHIEVEMENTS:** Plaque for outstanding business leadership Washington Minority Contractors; plaque for outstanding serv Natl Tech Assn; past pres outstanding award from Holy Name Soc of St Anthony's Catholic Church. **BUSINESS ADDRESS:** 5331 Georgia Ave NW, Washington, DC.

JONES, JAMES EARL
Actor. **PERSONAL:** Born Jan 17, 1931, Tate County, MS; married Cecilia Hart. **EDUCATION:** Univ of MI, BA 1953; Amer Theatre Wing, diploma 1957. **CAREER:** Appeared in plays: Romeo and Juliet, Wedding in Japan, Sunrise in Campobello, The Pretender, The Cool World, King Henry V, Measure for Measure, The Blacks, A Midsummer Nights Dream, The Apple, Moon on a Rainbow Shawl, Infidel Caesar, The Merchant of Venice, The Tempest, Toys in the Attic, PS 193, Macbeth, The Love Nest, The Last Minstrel, Othello, The Winter's Tale, Mr Johnson, Next Time I'll Sing to You, Bloodknot, King Lear, Of Mice and Men, Paul Robeson, Master Harold and The Boys. **ORGANIZATIONS:** Mem Natl Council of Arts. **HONORS/ACHIEVEMENTS:** Appeared in movies, Dr Strangelove; The Man; Claudine; The River Niger; Swashbuckler; Bingo Long Traveling All-Stars and Motor Kings; Exorcist II, The Heretic; The Greatest; The Last Remake of Beau Geste; A Piece of the Action; The Bushido Blade; Conan the Barbarian; Blood Tide; TV appearances incl, The Defenders; East Side/West Side; Camera 3; Look Up and Live; The Cay; King Lear; Big Joe and Kansas; UFO Incident; TV appearances, Jesus of Nazareth; The Greatest Thinks That Almost Happened; Guyana Tragedy, The Story of Jim Jones; The Golden Movement, An Olympic Love Story; narrated Malcolm X; Sojourner; A Day Without Sunshine; Recip The Village Voice Off-Broadway Awards 1962; Theatre World Award 1962; Tony Award for Best Actor in Great White Hope 1969; Grammy Award 1976; Medal for Spoken Lang Amer Acad Arts and Letters 1981; Tony Award for Best Actor in Fences. **BUSINESS ADDRESS:** Actor, c/o Jack Fields & Assocs, 9255 Sunset Blvd, Suite 1105, Los Angeles, CA 90069.

JONES, JAMES EDWARD
Physician. **PERSONAL:** Born Aug 14, 1896, Elizabeth City, NC; married Elaine; children: Elma. **EDUCATION:** Meharry Med Sch, MD 1926; Bowman Grey Sch Med. **CAREER:** Self, physician. **ORGANIZATIONS:** Mem Hedel OB Clinic; State Med Dir Elks State NC 32 Yrs; past grand exaltry ruler Elks; mem State Med Soc; Nat Med Assn; AMA; chaplain Old N State Med & Pharm Soc; Alumnus Elizabeth City State U; minister bd dir chmn fin com Quial Alumni Assn Hon Hlth Dept Elizabeth City; Bowmann Grey Med Sch; Gleliror Leaf Lodge U; Omega Frat.

JONES, JAMES EDWARD, JR.
Educator. **PERSONAL:** Born Jun 04, 1924, Little Rock, AR; married Joan Cottrell Turner; children: Evan, Peter. **EDUCATION:** Lincoln Univ, BA 1950; Univ IL Inst Labor and Indus Relations, MA 1951; Univ WI, JD 1956. **CAREER:** Univ WI-Madison, vistg prof law and indus relations 1969-70; Inst for Rsch on Poverty, assoc 1970-; Inst Relations, Rsch Inst, dir 1971-73; Ctr for Equal Employment and Affirmative Action, Indus Relations Rsch Inst, dir 1974-; Univ WI, prof of law 1970-, Bascom prof law 1982-87. **ORGANIZATIONS:** Mem rsch and educ staff Pulp, Sulphite and Paper Mill Workers AFL-CIO; mem pub rev bd Intl Union UAW 1970-; dir Ctr for Equal Employ and AffirmativeAction Indsl Relations Rsch Inst 1974-; mem Fed Mediation and Conciliation Arbitration Panel 1975-; special arbitrator US Steel and United Steel Workers 1976-; mem Fed Service Impasses Panel 1978-82; mem Labor Law Group Trust, Indus Relations Rsch Assoc; mem Fed, WI State, Natl Bar Assocs; mem Natl Acad Arbitrators. **HONORS/ACHIEVEMENTS:** Sec Labor Career Service Awd Dept Labor 1963; John Hay Whitney Fellow; contributor articles, chapters to professional publs. **BUSINESS ADDRESS:** Professor of Law, Univeristy of Wisconsin, University Law School, Madison, WI 53706.

JONES, JAMES G.
Engineer. **PERSONAL:** Born May 21, 1936, Jefferson County, GA; married Novelene Sanders; children: Jeffery P, Jennifer L. **EDUCATION:** BS 1960; graduate student. **CAREER:** Johns Hopkins Univ Applied Physics Lab, asst, math 1962-64; Pratt-Whitney Aircraft, W Palm Beach, sr computing engr, 1974; Riviera Beach City, Councilman, chmn, 1971-; Palm Beach & County Area Planning Bd, chmn, 1973-. **ORGANIZATIONS:** Mem, Kappa Upsilon Chapter, Omega Psi Phi Fraternity Inc. **HONORS/ACHIEVEMENTS:** Man of year Kappa Upsilon Omega 1975. **MILITARY SERVICE:** AUS 1960-62. **BUSINESS ADDRESS:** Pratt & Whitney Aircraft, West Palm Beach, FL 33401.

JONES, JAMES MCCOY
Educator. **PERSONAL:** Born Apr 05, 1941, Detroit; son of Arthur McCoy Jones and Eliza Marcella Hayes-Jones; married Olaive Burrowes; children: Shelly, Lovelle, Itenash. **EDUCATION:** Oberlin Coll, BA 1963; Temple U, MA 1967; Yale U, PhD 1970. **CAREER:** Minority Fellowship Program Amychol Assn, dir 1977; Natl Inst for Adv Studies, staff dir 1976-77; HarvardUniv Asso Prof Soc Psychology, 1974-76; Asst Prof Soc Psychology, 1970-74; The Franklin Institute Philadelphia Research Psychology, 1964-66; Boston Office Lawrence Johnson & Assocs, dir 1974-76; Exploring Childhool Proj Educ Dev Cent, sr scholar 1973-74. **ORGANIZATIONS:** Mem Am Psychology Assn; Assn of Black Psychologists; Soc for the Psychol Study of Study fo Social Issues; Educ Consult Journal of Personality & Social Psychology; Journal of Clin Psy; Psychology Bulletin; mem NIMH Small Grant Review Com; assembly of Behavioral Sci 1973-77; Adv Bd WEB Dubois Research Inst; mem Comm Research Review Com Roxbury MA 1970-74; executive dir of Public Interest Amer Psychology Assn. **HONORS/ACHIEVEMENTS:** Glen Grey mem scholar Oberlin Coll 1959-63; Hon Sterling Fellow Yale Univ 1968-69; NIMH predoctoral Fellow 1967-70; John Simon Guggenheim Fellow 1973-74; published "Prejudice & racism"; "The Black Experience.". **MILITARY SERVICE:** Glen grey mem schol Oberlin Coll 1959-63; hon sterling fellow YaleUniv. **BUSINESS ADDRESS:** Professor of Psychology, University of Delaware, Newark, DE 19716.

JONES, JAMES P.
Dentist. **PERSONAL:** Born Mar 28, 1914, New York, NY; married Ada Celeste. **EDUCATION:** HowardUniv Dental Coll, DDS 1941; New York U, BS chemistry. **CAREER:** Private Practice, dentist; Dept of Oral Surg Harlem Hosp, attending dentist 1946-; Dept of Dentistry Sydehham Hosp, attending dentist; Dept of Social Serv, investigator; Dept of Probation, probation officer. **ORGANIZATIONS:** Bd of dirs/delegate First District Dental Soc; bd mem New York City USO; bd chmn Amistad Housing Devel; asso dir Sydenham Hosp Model Cities Facilities. **HONORS/ACHIEVEMENTS:** Fellow Am Coll of Dentist; fellow Intl Coll of Dentist; fellow New York Acad of Dentist; fellow Am Acad of Dentist Internatl. **MILITARY SERVICE:** AUS major 1941-46. **BUSINESS ADDRESS:** 219 W 138 St, New York, NY 10030.

JONES, JAMES RANDALL
Physician. **PERSONAL:** Born Oct 28, 1925, Americus, GA. **EDUCATION:** Morehouse Coll, BS 1947; Meharry Med Coll, MD 1951; Coll Physician Ft Valley St Coll, 1961-. **CAREER:** Pvt Prac, 1959; Fordham Hosp, residency 1952-54; intern 1951; GA St Med Assn; Reach Co Hosp, med staff. **ORGANIZATIONS:** Mem NAACP Frontiers Internat; gamma Sigma Lombda; Alpha & Phi Alpha; Man in the Comm Trinity Bapt Ch 1974. **HONORS/ACHIEVEMENTS:** Frat serv award Alpha Phi Alpha 1975-76. **MILITARY SERVICE:** USAF 1st lt 1955-56.

JONES, JAMES V.
Automobile dealer. **PERSONAL:** Born May 16, 1942, Jackson, NC; son of James Jones and Viola M Brown-Jones; divorced; children: James III. **EDUCATION:** North Carolina Central Univ, Durham NC, law degree, 1976. **CAREER:** Ozone Ford, Ltd, Ozone Park NY, pres, 1987-. **BUSINESS ADDRESS:** President, Ozone Ford Ltd, 81-20 Atlantic Ave, Ozone Park, NY 11416.

JONES, JAMES WESLEY
Clergyman. **PERSONAL:** Born Oct 30, 1935, Lake Commerant, MS; married Annie Cath-

erine Proctor; children: James Jr. **EDUCATION:** Detroit Bible Coll, attended 1959-61; Am Bapt Sem, attended 1964-65. **CAREER:** Mt Moriah Bapt Cincinnati, pastor 1965-; New Liberty Bapt Detroit, asso minister 1959-65; Electronic Media Cincinnati, 1972; increased black employment; increased black on-air personalities; increased black oriented programming, all netword affilliated TV stations; created comm access to TV & radio through progson all stations; independently produced over 60 spls on 3 network affiliates 1973-; James Wesley Housing; operator creator of thousands of job opportunities; working on minority participation cable TV. **ORGANIZATIONS:** Mem World Bapt Alliance 1965-80; mem Bapt & Conv USA Inc 1965-80; chmn social action Missionary Bapt Dist Assn Cincinnati 1980-; pres/exec producer Black Cultural Prodn Inc 1971-80; chmn Coalition of Blacks Concerned for Justice & Equality Media 1971-80; bd mem So Leadership Conf 1973-;chmn Hunger Coalition; expanding free feeding progs to thousands; pres M M Devel Corp. **HONORS/ACHIEVEMENTS:** Golden Mick Award WCIN Radio-wlw Radio Cincinnati 1975 & 1977; Giant Among Men Award Women In Communications 1976; Outstanding Contrib Media to Community WLW-TV 5 Cincinnati 1977; Contrib Histo Soc 1979. **BUSINESS ADDRESS:** 1169 Simmons St, Cincinnati, OH 45215.

JONES, JENNIE Y.
Educator. **PERSONAL:** Born May 26, 1921, Woodlawn, IL; widowed; children: Johnetta, Harry, Jerry, Danny. **EDUCATION:** SIU Carbondale IL, BEd, BEd 1942; Univ IL, MA 1949. **CAREER:** Child Devel Lab SIU Carbondale , asst prof & dir; Head Start SIU, regional training ofcr 1970-74; prog dir 1973; Carbonate Sch Dist #95, tchr 1948-70. **ORGANIZATIONS:** Mem bd dirs IL assn for Educ of Young Children Children; Delta Kappa Gamma; adv com Training & Technical Assistancemodel Citied; bd dirs State Comm Coordinated Child Care; adv com Lincolnland Comm Coll. **HONORS/ACHIEVEMENTS:** Hon advisory consult award Jackson Co Mental Halth Bd IL Assn Head Start Dirs 1975. **BUSINESS ADDRESS:** Dept of Child & Family, 1168 SIU, Carbondale, IL 62901.

JONES, JENNIFER
Opera singer. **PERSONAL:** Born in Wilmington, DE; children: Three Children. **EDUCATION:** Curtis Inst of Music, BM 1975; Houston Grand Opera, alto soloist 1980; New York Philharmonic, soloist 1979; Montreal Symphony, soloist 1980; Los Angeles Philharmonic, soloist 1980/78/76; Israeli Philharmonic, Soloist 1980/76; Philadelphia Orch, soloist 1973; Grant Martha Baird Rockefeller & Found Philadelphia Orchestria Competition, soloist 1973.

JONES, JEROME B.
Educational administrator. **PERSONAL:** Born Jul 01, 1947, Baltimore, MD; divorced; children: Merrill, Allison. **EDUCATION:** St Augustine's Coll, BA Acctg 1959; Trenton State Coll, MA History 1970; Rutgers Univ, MA Reg Plnng 1973, PhD Ed Plnng 1974. **CAREER:** Essex Cty, acctg cty supt 1975-76; NJ Dept of Ed, acctg asst comm ed 1975-76; Providence School Dept, supt 1976-81; Stamford Public Schools, supt 1981-83; St Louis Public Schools, supt. **ORGANIZATIONS:** Mem Amer Assoc of School Admin 1983, Council of Great City Schools 1983-, Civic Progress 1983-; mem Backstoppers Firemen 1984-. **HONORS/ACHIEVEMENTS:** Sammy Davis Jr Award St Louis Sentinel Newspaper 1984. **BUSINESS ADDRESS:** Superintendent of Schools, St Louis Board of Education, 911 Locust, St Louis, MO 63101.

JONES, JERRY T.
President. **PERSONAL:** Born Mar 25, 1936; divorced; children: three. **EDUCATION:** IIT, BS 1964. **CAREER:** Argonne Nat Lab, Western Elec, IIT Res Inst, asst physicist 1956-66; IITRI Samoa as Civilian Contractor with Defense Atomic Supplor Agcy testing High Altitude Nuclear devices & anal data; he went to Quebec to measure the effects of solar-sphere projects relating to Apollo Earth Orbital Flights, 1963 Sonicraft Inc, pres chmn of bd fndr est 1967-. **ORGANIZATIONS:** Chmn bd of dir Nat Assn of Black Manu; bd mem Chicago Min Purch Coun; treas Black Affairs Coun; pres BAC Invest Corp; Selma March; dele Coordinating Counc for Comm Org; fndr dir Black Unitarian Universalist Caucus IL. **HONORS/ACHIEVEMENTS:** Small businessman of year award 1970; Chicago award for Sonicraft from Osmopolitan C of C 1971. **BUSINESS ADDRESS:** President, Sonicraft, Inc, 8859 S Greenwood Avenue, Chicago, IL 60619.

JONES, JESSE J., JR.
Auto dealer. **CAREER:** Northwestern Dodge, Ferndale MI, chief executive, 1980-85; Maumee Ford Inc, Maumee OH, chief executive, 1985-87; Capital Chrysler-Plymouth Inc, Lansing MI, chief executive, 1987—. **BUSINESS ADDRESS:** Capital Chrysler-Plymouth Inc, 6525 Saginaw Highway, W, Lansing, MI 48917. *

JONES, JESSE W.
College educator/administrator. **PERSONAL:** Born Jan 16, 1931, Troup, TX; married LaBelle; children: Penola Washington, Tacora Ballums, Phelisha, Jesse Jr, David, Stephen, Lilla. **EDUCATION:** TX Coll, BS 1954; Univ of UT, Advanced Work 1956; Highlands Univ, MS 1956; AZ State Univ, PhD 1963. **CAREER:** TX Coll, instructor of chem 1956-58; AZ State, rsch assoc 1958-63; TX Coll, chmn/prof 1963-68; Bishop Coll, chmn/prof 1968-. **ORGANIZATIONS:** Pres Bishop Coll Fed Credit Union 1969-85; vice chmn City of Dallas Bd of Adjustment 1977-82; pres Dallas Cty Democratic Progressive Voters League 1977-85; vice chmn Dallas Environ Health Commiss 1983-; mem Amer Chem Soc; fellow Amer Scientific Soc; sec Searcy's Youth Found; fellow Amer Inst of Chemists. **HONORS/ACHIEVEMENTS:** Salutatorium EJ Scott High School 1950; Outstanding Citizenship Mu Gamma Chap Omega Psi Phi 1976; Silver Beaver Awd Boys Scouts of Amer 1983; Craft Awd in Politics Dalls Chap NAACP 1984; UNCF Disting Scholar 1986; TX Black Legislator's Citizenship Awd 1987. **HOME ADDRESS:** 6139 Moonglow, Dallas, TX 75241.

JONES, JIMMIE DENE
Business consultant. **PERSONAL:** Born Feb 26, 1939, Childress, TX; married Thelma Wilkerson; children: Vickie Harris, Jimmie D Jr, Amanda Lene Scott, Darryl Bryan. **EDUCATION:** St Marys Coll, BS, BA 1973; George Washington Univ, MBA 1978; College of Financial Planning, Certificate 1984. **CAREER:** Law Engineering, personnel dir 1979-86; J&L Financial Svcs, owner 1986-; New Visions Consulting, business consultant 1985-. **ORGANIZATIONS:** Mem Northern VA Minority & Professional Business Assoc 1984. **HONORS/ACHIEVEMENTS:** Proclamation for Volunteer as Financial Counselor County Extension Office 1986. **MILITARY SERVICE:** AUS cmd sgt major E9 22 yrs; Army Commendation Medal, Bronze Star. **HOME ADDRESS:** 14760 Independent Lane, Manassas, VA 22111.

JONES, JOHN L.
Director. **PERSONAL:** Born Jan 18, 1939, Delray Beach, FL; son of James and Willie Mac; married Betty Jones; children: Jonathan Vance Jones. **EDUCATION:** Butler U, B Psych & Span 1960; Temple U, M Psych 1964; Boston U, EdD Human Rel 1970. **CAREER:** Project Follow Through, NTL-IABS, dir 1970-71; Mgmt Consultant firm, Vice Pres owner 1968-71;General Electric Co, Mgr personnel devl 1966-67; empl mgr 1966-67;General Foods, communications specialist 1965-66; Dept of Defense supply inventory mgr; Xerox Corp, mgr human resources planning, dir corporate affirmative action 1974-77; mgr corporate person devl 1972-77; mgr region training & orig 1971-72; Xerox of Canada, mgr mgmt & org dev 1975-77; Xerox Stamford, mgr corp human resources 1977-80; Xerox; personnel mgr 1880-81; Dir Corp Employer Resources 1987. **ORGANIZATIONS:** Chrmn business policy review counsel;chrmn, natl consortium for educational access; audit committee, Boys choir of Harlem; executive comm, Program to increase minnorities in bussiness. **HONORS/ACHIEVEMENTS:** Martin Luther King fellow, Boston U; Outst Young Men of Am 1974. **BUSINESS ADDRESS:** Director/Personnel, Americas Operations, Xerox Corporation, PO Box 1600, Stamford, CT 06904.

JONES, JOHN P.
Retired educational administrator. **PERSONAL:** Born Mar 01, 1915, Tyler, TX; married Nollie V; children: Rhoda, John. **EDUCATION:** TX Coll, AB; Univ of Chicago, AM. **CAREER:** Jarvis Christian Coll Hawkins TX, head of english dept, chmn of humanities & Asst to pres 1962-72, pres 1972-76; Texas Coll, academic dean 1976-81, deandir of institutional advancement 1981-85, interim pres 1985-86, dean/dir of institutional advancement 1986-. **ORGANIZATIONS:** Dir, Institutional Self-Study TX Coll, 1982-84; Coordinator, Isatim Program, TX Coll 1982-87. **HONORS/ACHIEVEMENTS:** Hon degrees LD Texas Coll 1972; Hum D, LLD Texas Christian Univ 1972. **MILITARY SERVICE:** AUS staff sgt 1942-45. **BUSINESS ADDRESS:** Dean of Inst Advancement, Texas College, 2404 N Grand Ave, Tyler, TX 75702.

JONES, JOHNNIE ANDERSON
Senior lawyer. **PERSONAL:** Born Nov 30, 1919, Laurel Hill, LA; married Sebell Elizabeth Chase; children: Johnnie Jr, Adair Darnell, Adal Dalcho, Ann Sarah Bythelda. **EDUCATION:** Southern U, BS in Psychology 1949; SouthernUniv Law Sch, JD in Law 1953. **CAREER:** Universal Life Ins Co, ins agcy 1947-48; US Post Office, ltr carrier 1948-50; SouthernUniv Law Sch, law sch stdnt 1950-53; LA State Bar Assc, lwyr 1953-; Jones & Jones, sr lwyr. **ORGANIZATIONS:** Asst parish atty City Parish Govt 1969-72; state rep LA House of Rep 1972-76; sr lwyr Jones & Jones Atty at Law 1975-; mem Frontiers Clb Intnl 1962-, Alpha Phi Alpha Frat 1972-, NAACP 1936-. **HONORS/ACHIEVEMENTS:** Cert of aprctn LB Johnson & HH Humphrey 1964; frontierman/yr Frontiers Clg Intrntl 1962; plaque Alpha Kappa Alpha Sorority 1972; most otsndng Mount Zion First Bapt Ch 1970. **MILITARY SERVICE:** AUS warrant ofcr 1942-46; Good Conduct Medal 1942-46. **HOME ADDRESS:** 1438 N 32nd St, Baton Rouge, LA 70802. **BUSINESS ADDRESS:** Attorney, Jones & Jones, 251 Florida St #215, Baton Rouge, LA 70801.

JONES, JOHNNY (LAM JONES)
Professional athlete. **PERSONAL:** Born Apr 04, 1958, Lawton, OK. **CAREER:** NY Jets, wide receiver 1980-. **HONORS/ACHIEVEMENTS:** All Amer; All SW Conf; MVP Longhorns 1978; won Gold Medal 400 meter US Relay Team Olympics 1976. **BUSINESS ADDRESS:** New York Jets, 1000 Fulton Ave, Hempstead, NY 11550.

JONES, JOHNNY L.
Educator. **PERSONAL:** Born Jul 26, 1933, Greenville, NC; married Mattye; children: Joni. **EDUCATION:** Bethuen-Cookman Coll, BA 1955;Univ ID, MEd 1964;Univ ID. **CAREER:** Dade County Public Schools, supt of schools, deputy supt 1973-77, area supt 1971-73, dir of sec schools 1969-71, prin 1967-69, coord of rsch evaluation 1966-67, asst prin 1965-66; Univ of ID, professorial asst; USA, consulting editor educ 1972-75. **ORGANIZATIONS:** Consult Rockefeller Found Supt Training Prgm 1972-; educ dir Labor Educ Advncmt Prgm Urban League 1969-77; bd dir Miami Dade C of C; YMCA; Boy Scouts of Am; Nat Educ Adv Bd; Nat Urban League; Jackson Meml Hosp; FL Comm So Assn of Colls & Schs; bd trustees Bethune-Cookman CollUniv Miami; Am Assn ofSch Adminstrn; Kappa Delta Pi Nat Educ Frat; Phi Delta Kappa; Sigma Pi Phi Frat; Nat Alliance of Black Sch Educators; NAACP; Big Bros; life mem Kappa Alpha Psi Frat; 32nd degree Free & Accepted Mason; Nat Order of Shriners; Nat Sch Pub Rels Assn; Nat Comm Sch Educ Assn; Am Vocational Assn; Assn of Suprvn & Curriculum Devel; bd trustees Ch of Open Door; fellow Christian Athletes; bd dir James E Scott Comm Assn. **HONORS/ACHIEVEMENTS:** Publ "Decentralization as a Mgmt Tool", NASSP Bull; "Sensitivity Training An Approach to Improved Ldrshp"; "Perfromacne Contracting the wrong solution to a RealProblem"; "A Layman's View of Pragmatism"; "Assessing the Academic Achvmt of Negro Students" 1964. **MILITARY SERVICE:** USAF; SAC 1955-58. **BUSINESS ADDRESS:** 1410 NE 2nd Ave, Miami, FL 33132.

JONES, JONI LOU
City official. **PERSONAL:** Born Aug 24, 1932, Ellisville, MS; divorced; children: Andre, Stepfon, Valerie. **EDUCATION:** Benson Voc HS, 1951. **ORGANIZATIONS:** Mem, comm org Roosevelt Comm Serv Committee 1983; temp pres for org Natl Council Negro Women 1984; mem NAACP. **HONORS/ACHIEVEMENTS:** Natl Drug Inst Aldelphia Univ Training Course 1972; Courts of Common Pleas Volunteers in Probation 1973; Alderman Ward III City Municipality Ellisville 1981; Notary Public State of MS Exec Dept 1982; Appreciation Awd Asst Cub Scout Prog 1983. **HOME ADDRESS:** 203 Roosevelt St, Ellisville, MS 39437.

JONES, JOSEPH
Educator. **PERSONAL:** Born Jun 03, 1928, Albany, GA; married Etta M; children: Josetta I, Robyn M Thomas. **EDUCATION:** Morris Brown Coll, BS 1950; Northwestern Univ, MSc 1952; OH State U, PhD 1960. **CAREER:** TX Southern Univ, dean of grad sch; Univ of Sci & Tech Ghana W Africa, Fulbright-Hays prof 1972-73; Acad Affairs St Augustine's Coll, vice pres 1969-72; St Augustine's Coll, acad dean 1966-69; St Augustine's Coll, head dept of biology 1952-57; Title III Proj St Augustine's Coll, coordinator; duties abroad in several

countries; consultant on strategic planning and education. **ORGANIZATIONS:** Dir Natl Sci Found & Atomic Energy Commn Inst for Teacher of Sci; mem Visitation Teams to evaluate instr in various coll in southeastern states Danforth Asso; Fellow of OH Acad of Sci; mem Sigma Xi Sci Honor Soc; Alpha Mu Honor Soc; OH Acad of Sci; Am Soc of Parasitologists; Nat Sci Tchr Assn; Am Museum of Natural History; Alpha Phi Alpha Frat. **HONORS/ACHIEVEMENTS:** Recipient Sr Fulbright-Hays Professorship, Ghana W Africa 1972; United Negro Coll Fund Fellowship 1959; Special Danfoth Grad Fellowship 1958; BA awarded cum laude 1950. **BUSINESS ADDRESS:** Dean of Graduate School, Texas SouthernUniv, 3100 Cleburne St, Houston, TX 77004.

JONES, K. C.
Coach. **EDUCATION:** Attended, Univ of San Francisco. **CAREER:** Los Angeles Rams, defensive specialist 1958; Brandeis Univ Waltham MA, 1968-71; Los Angeles Lakers, asst to head coach 1971-72; Capital Bullets, head coach 1973-74; Milwaukee Bucks, asst, 1976-77; Boston Celtics, asst 1978, head coach. **HONORS/ACHIEVEMENTS:** Represented USA in the 1956 Olympics team won Gold Medal; Mem, Ceremonies, Bay Area Hall of Fame 1986; mentor Eastern Conference All-Stars (3 seasons).

JONES, KELSEY A.
Educator. **PERSONAL:** Born Jul 15, 1933, Holly Springs, MD; married Virginia Bethel Ford; children: Kelsey Jr, Cheryl Darlene Campbell, Eric Andre, Claude Anthony. **EDUCATION:** MS Industrial Coll, AB (Summa Cum Laude) 1955; Garrett Theol Seminary NW Univ, MDiv 1959; MS Industrial Coll, DD 1969. **CAREER:** Walls Meml Ch Chicago, pastor 1956; Lane Meml Ch Jackson, MS, pastor 1959-62; Cleaves Temple Omaha, NE, pastor 1962-65; St Matthew Ch Wichita, KS, pastor1965-70; Wash, DC Min of Celebration & Human Resources, natl pulpit 1970-72; Fed City Coll (UDC Mt Vernon Campus), vis lectr in Black history 1973-75; INTER/MET, dir of Bacc & Liason consult 1973-77; Univ of DC Van Ness Campus, prof social sci 1972-77; UDC (Van Ness Campus), chmn dept soc/behavioral sci 1977-78; Dept Criminal Justice, prof 1978-79; The President of the US, special asst for Environmental Health, Occupational Safety & Instit Security 1984-; Univ of DC Dept of Criminal Justice, professor & chairman 1979-. **ORGANIZATIONS:** Dean Leadership Educ ea of 3 confs of 3rd Episcopal Dist; sec KS/MO Annual Conf 1962-70; delegate Gen Conf of Christ Meth Epis Ch 1966; delegate Centennial Session Gen Conf 1970; sec NY/WA Ann Conf Vis Chpl Meth Pop Cook Cnty Jail 1956-58; aptd staff Recep-Diag Cntr MI Correct Commn 1961; mem Acad of Criminal Justice Scis, North Atlan Conf of Criminal Just Educators, Inst for Criminal Justice Ethics, Natl Criminal Justice Assn, NortheasternAssn of Criminal Justice Educators, Amer Soc for Indust Security, Natl Assn of Chiefs of Police, Amer Soc for Publ Admin, ASHE (Amer Assn for Higher Edn); chmn State Bd of Probation & Parole 1967; mem Phi Alpha Frat Mu Lamda Chap DC; 1st vice pres Wichita Urban League; bd dirs Bros Inc; mem LEAP com for deseg of pub schools in Wichita. **HONORS/ACHIEVEMENTS:** Included in Men of Achievement; Comm Ldrs of Amer; Who's Who in Black Amer 1974-76; Men & Women of Distinction 1979; awarded Presidential Citation the Natl Assn for Equal Opportunities in Higher Edn; Alumnus of the Year; The Directory of Disting Americans 1st Ed The Amer Biographical Inst; Marquis Who's Whoin the East; Disting Serv Award Howard Univ Univ Without Walls; Received Disting Serv Award Univ of DC Lorton Student Govt Assn for contribution to the Lorton Prison Project; nationally in demand as public speaker & lecturer; written and published many papers and articles. **BUSINESS ADDRESS:** Professor & Chairman, Univ of DC Dept Criminal Just, 4200 Connecticut Ave NW, Washington, DC 20008.

JONES, KEN
Newsman, publisher. **PERSONAL:** Born Jun 09, 1938, Los Angeles, CA; married Regina Nickerson; children: Ken, Kevin, Keith, Kory, Karen. **CAREER:** KNXT LA, reporter 1976-; KTTV LA, anchorman, reporter 1967-76; KRLA Pasadena, newcaster 1965-67; NBC News LA, prod asst 1963-65; Soul Magazine (natl), editor & publisher; Soul Illus Magazine, publisher 1966-. **ORGANIZATIONS:** Sigma Delta Chi. **BUSINESS ADDRESS:** 6121 Sunset Blvd, (KNXT), Los Angeles, CA.

JONES, KENNETH LEROY
Surgeon. **PERSONAL:** Born May 06, Kinston, NC; children: Kathryn, Amber, Jonathan. **EDUCATION:** Amherst Coll, BS 1973; Howard Univ Coll of Medicine, MD 1978. **CAREER:** US Public Health Serv Johns Hopkins Hosp, general surgery resident 1978-83; Advanced Industrial Medicine Inc, vice pres/medical dir; East Coast Health Org Inc, pres med dir.

JONES, KING SOLOMON
Physician/surgeon. **PERSONAL:** Born Jan 29, Florida; married Grace Watkins; children: Charles E. **EDUCATION:** Howard Univ, BS 1922, MD 1925. **CAREER:** St Anthony Hosp, pres medical staff; Laporte Co Medical Soc, pres; Laporte Co Bd of Health, pres; private practice, physician. **ORGANIZATIONS:** Mem bd, trustee Natl Medical Assoc; mem Amer Acad Family Practice, Amer Medical Assoc, 1000 Club Howard Univ Medical Alumni, Rotary, United Way, NAACP, ML King Comm Ctr, Omega Psi Phi; assoc pastor Bethel AME Church 1980-86. **HONORS/ACHIEVEMENTS:** Dr King S Jones Medical Scholarship Fund Inc 1975; Comm Serv Awd IN State Medical Assoc 1981; Dist Serv Awd Coll Medicine Howard Univ 1984; Physician of the Year NW IN Natl Medical Assoc 1985. **MILITARY SERVICE:** ROTC lt 3 yrs. **BUSINESS ADDRESS:** Physician, 723 Franklin Square, Michigan City, IN 46360.

JONES, KIRKLAND C.
Educator. **PERSONAL:** Born Oct 16, 1938, Beaumont, TX; son of Charles Alcott Jones, Sr. and Margaret Lee Jones. **EDUCATION:** Univ of WA, Seattle, BA, 1959; Texas S Univ, Houston, MA, 1966; Univ of WI, Madison, PhD, 1970; Austin Presbyterian Theological Seminary, Austin, TX, Master of Divinity, 1988. **CAREER:** Teacher in Texas schools, 1961-65; Texas S Univ, Houston, TX, adjunct instructor, 1965-70; Johnson C. Smith Univ, Charlotte, NC, assoc prof and head of English dept, 1970-73; Lamar Univ, Beaumont, TX, assoc prof and direc, freshman studies, 1973-77, prof of English, 1985-. **ORGANIZATIONS:** Member, Coll Language Assn, 1962-; life member, Alpha Phi Alpha, 1972-; member, Sigma Tau Delta, 1972-; member, S Central Modern Language Assn, 1973-; member, steering comm, OOIC, 1976-80; member, Coll Conf of Teachers of English, 1978-; member, Black Presbyterians United, 1980-; member, Amer Studies Assn of Texas, 1985-; charter member, Zora Neale Hurston Soc, 1985-; member, Mid-Atlantic Writers Assn, 1987-; panelist, Texas Academic Skills Program, 1987-; member, Jefferson County Historical Commn, 1989. **HONORS/ACHIEVEMENTS:** Outstanding Educator of the Year, Natl Coun of Teachers of English, 1972; author of Anna Wendell Bontemps: A Biography, and two dozen articles. **BUSINESS ADDRESS:** Dr. Kirkland C. Jones, Dept of English, Box 10023, Lamar Univ, Beaumont, TX 77710.

JONES, LAFAYETTE GLENN
Marketing executive. **PERSONAL:** Born Feb 17, 1944, Cincinnati, OH; married Wanda S Harriel; children: Kevin, Keith, Melanie, Glenn, Tara. **EDUCATION:** Fisk U, BA 1965; Howard U, grad study 1965-66; Stanford U, cert Mktg Mgmt 1976. **CAREER:** American Health & Beauty Aids Institute, exec dir; Johnson Prod Co Chgo, vice pres mktg & sales 1979-; Hunt-Wesson Foods Div, Norton Simon Inc, mktg mgr Hunts Manwich & Tomato Paste 1974-79; Pillsbury Co, Refrig Foods Div, prod mgr Hungry Jack; Birds Eye Div, Gen Foods Corp, asso prod mgr Orange Plus 1970-72; Imperial Margs Food Div, Lever Bros Co, prod mdse asst Golden Glow 1969-70; Sta WOL, Sonderling Brdcst Co, dir mdse, pub rel 1967-69; Job Corps, ABT Asso, Westinghouse Learning Corp YMCA, dir prgm act 1965-67; Supreme Beauty Products, Chicago IL, vice pres & gen mgr, 1988-. **ORGANIZATIONS:** Bd dir hon Am Youth Fedn 1972-74; vp, bd of trst Mardan Educ Ctr; mem Nat Assn of Mkt Dev; Urban League. **HONORS/ACHIEVEMENTS:** Author articles on mktg; Natl Business League's Frederick Douglas Patterson Award, 1987. **BUSINESS ADDRESS:** Vice President & General Manager, Supreme Beauty Products, 820 S Michigan Ave, Chicago, IL 60605. *

JONES, LAM See JONES, JOHNNY

JONES, LARRY EARL
City employee. **PERSONAL:** Born Aug 04, 1946, Seattle; divorced; children: Karen. **EDUCATION:** Univ WA, BFA 1971;Univ WA, MUP 1973. **CAREER:** Dept of Pks & Rec Seattle, environ plnr 1973-; Seattle Pub Schs, consult in fine arts 1970-71; Bon Marche, retl salesman 1970-71; Sears Roebuck & Co, retl salesman 1969. **ORGANIZATIONS:** Mem ASPO; PSAUniv WA; Blk Org of Plnrs; mem Trans ComUniv of WA; past vice pres Comm Hlth Bd; mem WA State Land Plng Commn; EIRC; HAB; res grt ASPO.

JONES, LAURA MAE (NEE GREEN)
Attorney. **PERSONAL:** Born Apr 17, 1949, Louisville; divorced; children: Mitchell Lindsay Holman. **EDUCATION:** Univ Louisvl, BA 1971; JD 1974. **CAREER:** City of Louisvl Law Dept, law clk 1973-74; Gittleman Charney & Michels, paralegal 1973-74; Comm Act Commn, dist supr sum 1969; Univ of Louisville Office of Blk Affr, tut 1970-71; Chevron USA Inc, corp atty. **ORGANIZATIONS:** Mem KY Bary Assn 1974-; Louisville Blk Lawyers' Assn 1974-; Women's Law Caucus 1972-74; Blk Law Stud Assn; presUniv of Louisville Chap 1972-73; bd dir Louisville Br NAACP; bd dir Louisville YWCA; v chpsn KY Internatl Women's Yr Commn; KY Del 1977; IWY Natl Conf; hearing officer Louisville& Jefferson Cnty Human Rel Comn; KY Econ Devel Comn; adv to subcom On Energy; Legal Serv Adv Council; mem CWENS; Pi Sigma Alpha; Mortar Bd;Univ ofLouisville Law Sch Nat Moot Ct Team 1972-74. **HONORS/ACHIEVEMENTS:** Who's Who Amng Am Coll & U's 1970-71; Flexnor Scholar; Maude Ainsle Schlrshps. **BUSINESS ADDRESS:** Standrar Oil Co, Box 1446, Louisville, KY 40208.

JONES, LAWRENCE N.
Educational administrator. **PERSONAL:** Born Apr 24, 1921, Moundsville, WV; married Mary Ellen Cooley; children: Mary Lynn Walker, Rodney Bruce. **EDUCATION:** WV State Coll, BS in Educ 1942; Univ of Chicago, MA in Hist 1948; Oberlin Grad Schl of Theology, BD 1956; Yale Univ Grad Schl, PhD in Religion 1957, 1961. **CAREER:** Fisk Univ, dean of chapel 1960-64; Union Theological Seminary NY, dean prof 1965-75; Howard Univ Divinity Schl, dean prof 1975-. **ORGANIZATIONS:** Mem United Church Pod for World Ministries 1975-81; consult Lilly Endowment Inc, Congress of Natl Black Churches, Grad Theological Union 1983; chrmn Civil Rights Coord Comm Nashville 1962-64; pres Soc for Study of Black Religion 1974-77; secr Assc Theological Schls 1981-82; bd mem WHMM TV Public Advisory Board 1984-. **HONORS/ACHIEVEMENTS:** Lucy Monroe Flwshp Oberlin Grad Schl 1956; Rosenwald Schlrshp Rosenwald Fund 1942; Rockefeller Doctoral Flwshp Rockefeller Brothers 1959-61; LLD West Virginia State College 1965; DHL Jewish Theological Seminary 1971; DD Chicago Theological Seminary 1975. **MILITARY SERVICE:** Quartermaster capt 1943, 1946, 1947, 1953. **HOME ADDRESS:** 1206 Devere Dr, Silver Spring, MD 20903. **BUSINESS ADDRESS:** Dean-Howard University School of Divinity, Howard University, 1400 Shepherd St, NE, Washington, DC 20903.

JONES, LAWRENCE W.
Educator. **PERSONAL:** Born Feb 06, 1942, Newport News, VA; married Lolita Diane Grey; children: Lawrence W Jr, Leonard W. **EDUCATION:** Hampton Inst VA, 1960-64; Bowie State Tchr MD, BS in Educ 1965-67;Univ of MA Amherst, EdD 1970-73. **CAREER:** Bd of Educ NYC, tchr reading specialist 1977-; Univ of City of NY Medgar Evers Coll, asst prof educ 1974-77; Univ of MA Brooklyn COP Program, supvr student teaching 1971-73; Univ of MA, teaching asst 1970-73; Bd of Educ NYC, tchr 1967-73; Youth-in Action Neighborhood Youth Corp, remedial coordinator 1973; DeSign Team Sprinfield Ave Comm Sch Newark, consult educ 1978; Mayor Newark, spl asst educ program 1979-. **ORGANIZATIONS:** Mem Omega Psi Phi Frat 1972-; consult wedn program Day Care Centers Pvt Sch in New York City 1975-; mem One Hundered Black Men 1978-. **HONORS/ACHIEVEMENTS:** Degree with high honors, Bowie State Tchr 1967; Innovation in Teaching Dissertation,Univ of MA 1973; publ Classroom Mgmt Ind of Instruction 1973-74; Comm Serv Awards, Brooklyn COP & Comm Life Center 1974-78; Measuring Children's Growth in Reading Expanding Reading Experience 1978. **BUSINESS ADDRESS:** Electrical Engineer, AT&T Bell Laboratories, 20 Shatuck Rd, Rm 2Q-242, Andover, MA 01810.

JONES, LEANDER CORBIN
Educator. **PERSONAL:** Born Jul 16, 1934, Vincent, AR; son of L C Jones and Una Bell Jones; married Lethonee Angela Hendricks; children: Angela Lynne, Leander Corbin. **EDUCATION:** Univ of AR at Pine Bluff, AB 1956; Univ of IL, MS 1968; Union Graduate School, PhD 1973. **CAREER:** Chicago Public Schools, English teacher 1956-68; Peace Corps Volunteer, English teacher 1964-66; City Colls of Chicago,TV producer 1968-73; Meharry Medical Coll, media specialist 1973-75; Western Michigan Univ, assoc prof Black Amer studies, 1975-89, prof 1989-. **ORGANIZATIONS:** Mem Kappa Alpha Psi 1953-; mem exec comm DuSable Mus African Amer History 1970-; designer of programs in theatre andTV for

hard-to-educate; pres TABS Ctr 1972-; mem AAUP 1973-; mem Natl Council of Black Studies 1977-, MI Council of Black Studies 1977-, Popular Culture Assoc 1978-; chmn Comm Against Apartheid 1977-; mem South African Solidarity Org 1978-; mem MI Org African Studies 1980-; commander Vets for Peace Kalamazoo 1980-; pres Black Theatre Group of the Kalamazoo Civic Players 1980-83; bd of dirs Kalamazoo Civic Players 1981-83, MI Commn on Crime and Delinquency 1981-83; pres Corbin 22 Ltd 1986. **HONORS/ACHIEVEMENTS:** "Roof Over My Head" TV Series WDCN Nashville 1975; acted in and directed several plays Kalamazoo 1979-86; authored "Africa is for Reel," Kalamazoo 1983; exec producer & host for TV series "Fade to Black" 1986. **MILITARY SERVICE:** AUS pfc 1956-58. **HOME ADDRESS:** 2226 So Westnedge Ave, Kalamazoo, MI 49008. **BUSINESS ADDRESS:** Prof Black Amer Studies, Western Michigan University, Kalamazoo, MI 49008.

JONES, LEELAND NEWTON, JR.
Retired educational administrator. **PERSONAL:** Born Jun 15, 1921, Buffalo, NY; son of Leeland N Jones, Sr and Julia M Anthony Jones; married Carlita Murphy, May 05, 1945; children: Dr Leeland Anthony Murphy Jones, Dr J Aaron Murphy Jones, Carlita C M J Perkins. **EDUCATION:** Univ of Buffalo, BA 1947; UB Law School 1948-51; Univ of Wisconsin Law School 1953. **CAREER:** State Educ Dept, consult 1948; county legislator 1949; Met Serv Accnt, owner; Buffalo City, councl 1952; City Councl Buffalo, pres pro tem 1953-56; NYS Com vs Discrimination, rep 1957-60; Buffalo Urban League, assoc dir 1964-67; Comm Coll State Univ of NY, consult proj dir; OJT Prgm Chamber of Commerce, dir 1967; Erie Comm Coll, retired asst vp. **ORGANIZATIONS:** Organizer & lst Treas US Natl Student Assn 1946; past mem bd trustees Univ of Buffalo; Buffalo & Erie Co Planning Assn; USO; Camp Fire Girls; IBPOE Elite Lodge; pres Leukemia Found of Western NY; mem DAV; Amvets; 32nd Prince Hall Mason; Shrine; pres Black Hist Found; Press correspondent Amer Legion; pres-Intl Veteran's Assoc Intl. **HONORS/ACHIEVEMENTS:** Man of the Year Jr Chamber of Commerce; Civil Liberties Award Elks, NY; Natl Oratorical Scholarship Winner; City of Buffalo Man of the Year 1988; UB Football Scholarship 1940; Bison Head Honor Society 1942. **MILITARY SERVICE:** AUS Lt. **HOME ADDRESS:** 89 E Depew Ave, Buffalo, NY 14214.

JONES, LEMUEL B.
Personnel assistant. **PERSONAL:** Born Mar 03, 1929, Norway, SC; married Mary Jamison; children: Mark, Karla, Jarret, Eric Jamison. **EDUCATION:** BS 1952. **CAREER:** EI DuPont Co, operator chemical 1952-65; Production & Quality Assurance, foreman 1965-72; EEO, personnel asst 1972-. **ORGANIZATIONS:** Pres chap NAACP; vice pres PTA; vice pres Sunday Sch Conv; mem Kappa Alpha Psi Frat Inc. **HONORS/ACHIEVEMENTS:** US Army Achievement Award. **MILITARY SERVICE:** USN 1946-48; AUSR maj 1952-. **BUSINESS ADDRESS:** E I du Pont Co, Savannah River Plant, Aiken, SC 29801.

JONES, LEON C.
Clergyman. **PERSONAL:** Born Apr 16, 1919, Laurel, MS; married Rubye L Brown; children: Kathryn. **EDUCATION:** BA 1962; MSW 1968. **CAREER:** Second Bapt Ch Everett WA, pastor 1960-69; State Dept Pub Assistance, social caseworker 1963-66; supr caseworkers & soc workers 1968-69; Wash Bapt Conv, area minister 1969-; Seattle Pacific Coll, inst Black Am history & culture 1968-; Bellevue Coll, 1969; Seattle Comm Coll, 1971; Seattle U. **ORGANIZATIONS:** SOIC 1967-68; mem Nat Acad Soc Workers 1970-; WA Assn Soc Workers 1973-; chmn Black Am Bapt 1969-; chmn Nat Council Black 1970-; Convener Black-United Clergy PAC NW 1973-. **MILITARY SERVICE:** USN cook 1st class 1938-46. **BUSINESS ADDRESS:** 321 1 Ave W, Seattle, WA 98119.

JONES, LEON P.
Resource officer. **PERSONAL:** Born Dec 07, 1940, Birmingham, AL; divorced; children: La Tony Colita. **EDUCATION:** Miles Coll, BA 1969;Univ of Montevallo; AL State U, MEd 1975. **CAREER:** Jefferson Co Plng & Comm Devel, comm resource ofcr; Criminal Justice Prgm, adm asst; Miles Coll, track coach 1976, sports info dir, track coach, recruiter 1974-76, pub rel dir, sports info dir 1971-74, asst to pres 1970-71, dir pub rel 1969. **ORGANIZATIONS:** Mem Pub Relat Counc of AL; Am Coll Pub Relat Assn; 2nd vice pres Nat Alumni Counc Exec Bd, UNCF; mem NAACP; Birmingham Urban League & AL Inter-Alumni Counc, UNCF. **HONORS/ACHIEVEMENTS:** Outst Young Men of Am 1971; cit for pub relat, visit of Robert Brown, Spec Asst to Pres of US 1972; Outst Educ of Am 1974; Grid Forecasters Hall of Fame 1974; Achvmt Award, United Negro Coll Fund Pre-Alumni Counc, Miles Coll 1975. **MILITARY SERVICE:** USAF 1963-67. **BUSINESS ADDRESS:** EEOC, 2121 Eighth Ave North, Birmingham, AL 35203.

JONES, LEONADE DIANE
Media financial executive. **PERSONAL:** Born Nov 27, 1947, Bethesda, MD; daughter of Leon Adger Jones and Landonia Madden Jones. **EDUCATION:** Univ of Pittsburgh, PA, 1965-67; Simmons Coll, Boston MA, BA, 1969; Stanford Law School & Graduate School of Business, JD, MBA, 1973. **CAREER:** Capital Research Co, Los Angeles CA, research analyst, 1973-75; The Washington Post Co, Washington DC, asst sec & asst treasurer, 1975-79; Post-Newsweek Stations, Washington DC, dir of financial services, 1979-84, vice pres business affairs, 1984-86; The Washington Post Co, asst treasurer, 1986-87, treasurer, 1987-. **ORGANIZATIONS:** Mem, California Bar 1973-; mem, DC Bar, 1979-; mem, Amer Women in Radio & TV, 1979-84; treasurer and mem bd of dir, Big Sisters of Washington Metro Area, 1984-85; pres, 1948-85, mem bd of dir, 1986-88, Stanford Business School Alumni Assn; bd of dir, DC Contemporary Dance Theatre, 1987-88; corp co-chair, Duke Ellington Fundraiser, mem of advisory council, Charlin Jazz Society 1988-; mem, Natl Assn of Corp Treasurers, 1989-. **HONORS/ACHIEVEMENTS:** Outstanding Young Women of Amer Award, 1982. **BUSINESS ADDRESS:** Treasurer, The Washington Post Co, 1150 15th Street, NW, Washington, DC 20071.

JONES, LEONARD VIRGIL
Auditor. **PERSONAL:** Born Aug 25, 1921, Kansas City, MO; married Effie Lee Morris. **EDUCATION:** Univ of CA, BA 1950. **CAREER:** Trans Bay Fed Svgs & Loan, branch mgr 1953-66; Fidelity Svgs & Loan, branch mgr 1966-82; Citicorp Savings, auditor 1982-. **ORGANIZATIONS:** Mem Alpha Phi Alpha; founding mem UCB Black Alumni Club 1974; Financial Vice Pres CA Alumni Assn 1979-81; pres N CA Chap of the Internal Auditors Div of the Fin Mgrs Soc 1984-85. **HONORS/ACHIEVEMENTS:** Alumni citation CA Alumni Assn; Achievement Awd Alpha Phi Alpha 1950. **MILITARY SERVICE:** ACE s/sgt 1942-46. **BUSINESS ADDRESS:** Auditor, Citicorp Savings, 180 Grant Ave, Oakland, CA 94602.

JONES, LEROI See BARAKA, IMAMU AMIRA

JONES, LISA PAYNE
Public housing administrator. **PERSONAL:** Born Dec 30, 1958, Camp Zama, Japan;daughter of Charles Benjamin Payne, Jr and Eleanor Towns Hamilton Payne; married Peter Lawson Jones, Oct 12, 1985; children: Ryan Charles Jones. **EDUCATION:** Eastern MI Univ, BBA 1980. **CAREER:** AmeriTrust Co NA, general analyst I 1980-82, II 1982-85, III 1985-86; Cuyahoga Metro Housing Authority, marketing mgr 1986-88; Leasing Marketing Mgr 1989. **ORGANIZATIONS:** Mem Delta Sigma Theta Sor Inc 1978-; project business consultant Junior Achievement 1982-83; mem Cleveland Branch NAACP 1982-; chairperson 1983, treas 1984-85 Operation Greater Cleveland Big Vote 1983-85; mem Urban League of Greater Cleveland 1985-; mem Natl Black MBA Assoc Inc 1986; mem League of Women Voters 1987; mem of Amer Marketing Assn 1987-; mem Shaker Hts Alumni Assn; 1988-. **HONORS/ACHIEVEMENTS:** EMU Coll of Business Academic Achievement Awd 1978; Honors Awd Delta Sigma Theta Inc EMU 1979. **HOME ADDRESS:** 13800 Fairhill Rd #520, Shaker Heights, OH 44120. **BUSINESS ADDRESS:** Marketing/Leasing Manager, Cuyahoga Metro Housing Authority, 1435 West 25th St, Cleveland, OH 44113.

JONES, LLOYD O.
County treasurer. **PERSONAL:** Born Aug 06, 1944, Charles City, VA; married Terri. **EDUCATION:** Morehouse Coll, BA 1964;Univ of So CA, MBA 1971; Coll of William & Mary, JD 1975. **CAREER:** Eastman Kodak Co, accountant, cost engr 1964-65; Charles City Co, co treas; SEDFRE Inc, part-time cons. **ORGANIZATIONS:** First vice pres Local Br NAACP; adv, bd mem Colonial Bank Providence Forge VA; bd mem Charles City New Kent Comm Action Aby; mem Local PTA; Local Civic League. **MILITARY SERVICE:** AUS payee disbursement specialist 1965-67. **BUSINESS ADDRESS:** PO Box 38, Charles City, VA 23030.

JONES, LOIS MAILOU
Professor emerita of design and watercolor painting. **PERSONAL:** Born Nov 03, 1905, Boston, MA; daughter of Thomas Vreiland Jones and Caroline D Jones; married Vergniaud. **EDUCATION:** Museum Sch Fine Arts, diploma 1927; Designers Art Sch, 1928; Academie Julian, Cert 1938; Howard Univ, AB 1945; Academie de la Grande Chaumiere, Paris, Cert 1962. **CAREER:** Grace Ripley Studios, costume designer 1920-25; Palmer Mem Inst, art dept head 1928-30; free lance textile designer 1928-31; Assn Study Negro Life & Hist, illustrator 1930-53; Howard Univ, professor Emerita design & watercolor 1930-77. **ORGANIZATIONS:** Intl exhibits; 35 - 1 man exhibits; paintings in many museums & colls incl Boston Mus of Fine Arts, Brooklyn Mus, Corcoran Gallery of Art, Phillips Collection Hirshhorn Mus, Atlanta Univ, Howard Univ, Natl Portrait Gallery; Caribbean & Afro-Amer Women Artists-Budek Slide Inc 1983; film "50 Years of Painting Lois Mailou Jones," by Prof Abiyi Ford, Howard Univ Film Dir. **HONORS/ACHIEVEMENTS:** Diplome Honneur et Merite Haiti Govt; Robert Woods Bliss Oil Painting Landscape Award; 3 Howard Univ Research Grants - Comtemp African Art, Contemp Haitian Art & Afro-Amer Art; Author "Peintures Lois Mailou Jones," hon PhD CO State Christian Coll 1973; hon PhD Suffolk Univ 1981; Candice Award Met Mus 1982; Alumni Awd Howrard Univ; Hon PhD MA Coll of Art 1986; Women's Caucus for Art Honor Awd for Outstanding Achievement in the Visual Arts Cooper Union 1986; Howard Univ Hon PhD in the Hamanities 1987; honorary PhD in Fine Arts received 1989, The Atlanta Coll of Art, Atlanta Univ; oil painting "Chou-Fleur et Citroville" installed in the Lila Acheson Wallace Wing of Amer Paintings at the Metropolitan Museum of Art in NY City; Howard Univ Gallery of Art named Gallery No. 3: The Lois Mailou Jones and James L Wells/Gallery 1989. **BUSINESS ADDRESS:** Art Dept, Howard Univ, Washington, DC 20001.

JONES, LONZIE L.
Retired foundation executive. **PERSONAL:** Born Mar 06, 1912, Starksville, MS; married Alma Roach; children: Romeile R (Greer), Rhonda (Lavender). **EDUCATION:** Long Beach City Coll; California Univ, Southern CA. **CAREER:** Sickle Cell Disease Research Found, exec dir, retired 1977; Personnel & Comm Serv, dir 1969; Public Serv, officer 1967; Agency Serv, officer 1964; Agys, asst officer 1960; Agys, jr officer & asst supt 1956; Agys, asst supt 1955; Special Agency Dept, asst 1954; So CA, regional supr 1950; LA Dist, supr 1946; LA Dist, assoc supr 1944; LA Dist, supt staff 1942; Golden State Mutual Life Ins Co, agt 1934. **ORGANIZATIONS:** Mem Dist Atty's Adv Council; Atty Gen's Adv Council-Whilshire Comm; Plocie Council Inc; mem, former chmn Bd of Mgrs 28th St YMCA; former mem SW Pacific Area Bd YMCA Natl Council; YMCA of Amer; mem Urban League NAACP; past master, mem William Nickerson Jr Masonic Lodge; bd dir Dollars for Scholars; pres emeritus, mem, bd dir Sickle Cell Disease Research Found; treas, mem bd dir Natl Assn for Sickle Cell Disease; mem bd of trustees Pacific & SW Annual Conf of the United Methodist Church. **BUSINESS ADDRESS:** 4401 So Crenshaw Blvd, Ste #208, Los Angeles, CA 90043.

JONES, LOREAN ELECTA
Government official. **PERSONAL:** Born Jun 29, 1938, Arlington, TN; married Jimmie (deceased); children: Gale Carson, Dale Justin, Elna C, Ervin C, Denise F, Dennis R, Teresa Y, Terry O (dec). **EDUCATION:** Owen Coll, AA 1968; LeMoyne-Owen Coll, BA 1970; Memphis State Univ, MS 1977. **CAREER:** State of TN Dept of Mental Health, social worker 1970-76; State of TN Dept of Corrections, parole officer 1976-78; US Dist Cts Western Dist of TN, probation officer; Western Dist of TN, fed drug treatment specialist 1984-. **ORGANIZATIONS:** Comm mem Black on Black Crime Task Force 1979-; mem Fed Probation Officers Assoc; mem PUSH 1980, NAACP 1980; apptd to bd of trustees Gov of TN Arlington Devel Ctr 1972-73; sec, treas Southeast Region Federal Probation Officers Assoc 1983-85; historian Natl Council of Negro Women 1983; mem TN Selective Service Local Bd 38; sec LeMoyne Owen Alumni Assoc; Natl Certified Counselor; mem Amer Probation & Parole Assoc, Amer Assoc of Counseling & Develop;mem Natl Alliance of Business Youth Motivating Task Force 1982-83. **HONORS/ACHIEVEMENTS:** Citizen of the Week Awd WLOK Radio Station 1978; 1st Female Probation/Parole Officer WD/TN 1978; Who's Who in the South and Southwest 20th ed 1986-87; Who's Who Among Human Serv Profls 1986-87; Personalities of Amer for Contributions to Human Serv 1987; Disting Leadership Awd Outstanding Serv to the Human Serv Profession 1987. **BUSINESS ADDRESS:** Fed Drug Treatment Specialist, Western District of TN, US Cts 921 Fed Bldg, Memphis, TN 38103.

JONES, LOUIS CLAYTON
Attorney. **PERSONAL:** Born Nov 13, 1935, Lawrenceburg, KY; married Barbara Ann Griffin. **EDUCATION:** Howard Univ, BA (Summa Cum Laude) 1953-57; Univ de Bordeaux Fulbright 1957-58; Yale Law School, LLB 1958-61. **CAREER:** New School for Social Rsch, lecturer 1977; New York Law School, assoc prof 1976-78; SUNY, lecturer 1969-72; KY Comm on Human Rights, asst dir 1962-63; CBS News, asst to dir of bus affairs 1963-64; Louis Clayton Jones PC, attny. **ORGANIZATIONS:** Mem Phi Beta Kappa Howard Univ 1956; Natl Emergency Civil Liberties Comm, exec comm 1972; bd of dir Fund for New Priorities in Amer 1974-. **HONORS/ACHIEVEMENTS:** Fulbright & John Hay Whitney Fellowships Univ de Bordeaux 1957-58; Listed in Who's Who in the East 1975. **BUSINESS ADDRESS:** Attorney, Louis, Clayton, Jones PC, 75 Maple St, Brooklyn, NY 11225.

JONES, LUCIUS
Educator. **PERSONAL:** Born Jun 16, 1918, Birmingham, AL; married Vivian D; children: Vivian Eilene. **EDUCATION:** AL A&M, cert in Printing 1936; Lincoln U, BS1973; San Jose State, additional study 1973. **CAREER:** Flashlight Herald Knoxville, linotype operator 1937; Tulsa Art Printer Tulsa, shop foreman 1939-48; OK Eagle Tulsa; Modern Litho-Print Co Jefferson City MO,linotype operator 1973; Lincoln Univ, instr. **ORGANIZATIONS:** Mem Danforth Assoc 1963-; seminar leader Typographers Union 1972-74; mem Intl Graphic Arts Educ Assn; Am Vocational Assn; deacon & minister of music Second Bapt Ch Jefferson City; chmn Midwest Reg Selection Comm Danforth Assoc 1973; intl comm to nominate First Albert Schweitzer Prize 1975; dir Jefferson City Comm Male Chorus; mem NAACP; Omega Psi Frat Inc; United Investment Club; mem Jefferson City Industrial Development Commission. **HONORS/ACHIEVEMENTS:** LincolnUniv Bd of Curators Award for Serv 1973. **BUSINESS ADDRESS:** Instructor, LincolnUniv, PO Box 29, Jefferson City, MO 65101.

JONES, MACK H.
Educator. **PERSONAL:** Born Jan 13, 1937, Oakdale, LA; married Barbara Posey; children: Maxine, Lumumba, Tayari. **EDUCATION:** TX So U, BA 1962;Univ IL, PhD 1968. **CAREER:** Univ of IL, teaching asst 1963-64; Southern Univ, instructor summer 1965; TX Southern Univ, asst prof 1966-67; Atlanta Univ, assoc prof 1967-, prof 1971; Emory Univ, lecturer summer 1969; Dept of Political Science Atlant Univ, prof, chmn. **ORGANIZATIONS:** Mem Am Assn of Soc & Behavioral Sci; pres Nat Conf of Blk Pol Sci; Assn for African Edctrs; Assn sec 1973-74; edtr Jrnl of Pol & Repress; adv edtr Soc Sci Quart Edtrl Bd Phylon; chmn adv bd GA Ser Cent for Elctd Officials; Edtrl Bd Rev of Blk Pol Econ. **HONORS/ACHIEVEMENTS:** Magna cum laude, TX SoUniv 1962; Woodrow Wilson Fellow 1962-63; John A Fairlie Fellow,Univ IL 1964-65; Kendric C Babcock Fellow,Univ IL 1965-66; Russell Bull Award 1964; Ford Found Post-Doc Flwshp 1968-69. **MILITARY SERVICE:** AUS 1954-57.

JONES, MARCUS EARL
Educator. **PERSONAL:** Born Jan 07, 1943, Decatur, IL; married Valerie Daniel; children: Anthony, Malik, Omar, Taisha, Samira, Malaika, Na'el, Amina, Jamia. **EDUCATION:** Southern IL Univ Carbondale, BA Geog 1965; Chicago State Univ, MA Geog 1969; Univ of Ghana, Certificate 1968; Southern IL Univ, PhD Geog 1978. **CAREER:** Southern IL Univ Carbondale, ombudsman 1972-73; FL A&M Univ, asst prof geog 1973-76; Univ of So FL Tampa, vstg prof geog 1976-77; Morris Brown Coll,chair & prof geog 1978-85; Valdosta State Coll, prof of geog 1986-87; Chicago Public Schools, Social Studies Instructor 1988-89. **ORGANIZATIONS:** Mem Assoc of Amer Geographers, Southeastern Assoc of Geographers, Assoc of Social and Behavioral Scientists inc, African Studies Assoc. **HONORS/ACHIEVEMENTS:** Book "Black Migration in the United States with Emphasis on Selected Central Cities," Century Twenty One Publishing 1980; article "Black Counterstream Migration, New and Return Migrants to the South, 1965-78," Natl Council of Black Studies 1982. **HOME ADDRESS:** 379 Hillside Dr SW, Atlanta, GA 30310. **BUSINESS ADDRESS:** Teacher, Chicago Public Schools, 1819 West Pershing Road, Chicago, IL 60609.

JONES, MARILYN ELAINE
Govt. field representative. **PERSONAL:** Born Dec 17, Waco, TX; children: Spencer. **EDUCATION:** TX Woman's Univ, MA 1970, BS 1972, PhD 1978. **CAREER:** Early Childhood Educ TX Woman's Univ, consultant 1970-74; TX Woman's Univ, prof/lab instructor 1972-74; Paul Quinn Coll, counselor/placement dir 1974-83; Prairie View A&M Univ, instructor 1980-84; General Land Office State of TX, field rep. **ORGANIZATIONS:** Licensed by the TX State Bd of Examiners of Prof Counselors; mem Delta Sigma Theta Sor; mem NAACP; mem Natl Assoc for Young Children; mem APGA; mem TX Coalition of Black Democrats; mem Eastern Star; city councilmember first female elected 1980-84; vice pres Heart of TX Council of Govs 1982-84; mayor Pro-Tem Waco City Council 1983. **HONORS/ACHIEVEMENTS:** Serv Awds Phi Delta Kappa Inc Gamma Upsilon Chapt, Citizens of Waco, Waco City Council, Heart TX Council of Governors; Quality of Life Awd NTSU/TWU Alumni1981; Women of the Yr Progressive Women of Wichita KS 1982. **HOME ADDRESS:** 1604 Harrison Ave, Waco, TX 76704.

JONES, MARK E.
Lawyer. **PERSONAL:** Born Oct 15, 1920, Indianapolis, IN; son of Mark E Jones, Sr and Pearl Campbeck Jones; married Anita LLorens, Sep 04, 1988; children: 4 Children. **EDUCATION:** Roosevelt Univ, AB 1948; Loyola Univ, JD 1950. **CAREER:** Jones Ware & Grenard, atty, partner; Chicago TV Commission, commissioner; Cook Co IL, circuit ct judge 1963-80; atty pvt practice 1957-63; Cook Co, asst state atty 1951-57. **ORGANIZATIONS:** Founding mem, treas Judicial Council; mem Nat Bar Assn; Am Bar Assn; Cook Co Bar Assn; bd trustee Roosevelt Univ; bd dir Better Boys Found; life mem NAACP; pres bd dir Southside Community Art Center. **HONORS/ACHIEVEMENTS:** Recipient 1st prize, Chicago Bar Assn Art Show for Painting 1965-66; 1st prize Englewood & Lake Meadows Art Fairs 1970, 1973. **MILITARY SERVICE:** USN 1942-45. **BUSINESS ADDRESS:** Attorney at Law, Jones Ware & Grenard, 180 N LaSalle St, Ste 801, Chicago, IL 60601.

JONES, MARSHA REGINA
Journalist. **PERSONAL:** Born Jan 26, 1962, Brooklyn, NY; daughter of Eudolphin Jones and Iona L. Williams Jones. **EDUCATION:** Nazareth College, Advanced Placement Courses Spanish 1978-80; Purdue Univ, BA Journalism 1980-84. **CAREER:** Purdue Exponent Newspaper, reporter 1981-83; Purdue Reports Magazine, reporter 1983-84; Black Cultural Ctr Newspaper, reporter 1983-84; About Time Magazine, editorial asst/reporter 1984-88, assistant editor, 1988—. **ORGANIZATIONS:** Mem Soc of Professional Journalists 1980-, National Association of Black Journalists, 1988-, East HS Ebony Culture Club; Black Scholars Mentor Program Urban League of Rochester NY Inc 1985-; Black Scholars Alumni Comm Urban League of Rochester Inc 1985-; mem Amer Red Cross Minority Screening Campaign Comm 1985-; mem Village Gate Theater 1985-; mem Rochester Assoc of Black Communicators 1986-; mem Rochester Purdue Alumni Assoc. **HONORS/ACHIEVEMENTS:** Black Scholar Award Urban League of Rochester NY Inc 1980; Purdue Reamer Honorary Soc Purdue Univ 1983 (first black student to be inducted in honor society, to hold office in honor society, to be elected to exec council); Howard G McCall Award Purdue Univ Black Cultural Ctr 1984; Grand Prix Award Purdue Univ 1984; Matrix Award nominee, Women in Communications, 1988; published A People's Pledge, 1989. **HOME ADDRESS:** 24 Bradford Hill Road, Fairport, NY 14450. **BUSINESS ADDRESS:** Assistant Editor, About Time Magazine Inc, 283 Genesee St, Rochester, NY 14611.

JONES, MARTHA E.
Retired educator. **PERSONAL:** Born Feb 14, 1926, Lumberton, NC; daughter of Rev & Mrs H C Jones. **EDUCATION:** Winston-Salem State Univ, BS 1946; A&T Univ, M 1954; Attended, Ohio State Univ, NC Central Univ. **CAREER:** Wardell Chapel AME Church, organist 1953-82; Cleveland Co Teachers Fed Credit Union, mgmt consultant. **ORGANIZATIONS:** Mem NEA, NCAE; life mem NAACP, Alumni Assoc Winston-Salem State Univ. **HONORS/ACHIEVEMENTS:** Certificate of Appreciation Today's Ebonites Womens Club 1984; Community Civic Educ Work NAACP Cleveland Co Chap 1984; Plaque-Wardell Chapel AME Zion Church.

JONES, MAVIS N.
Dental surgeon. **PERSONAL:** Born Mar 07, 1918, Canton, MS; married Bernard; children: Bernard C jr, Thelma (shepherd). **EDUCATION:** Meharry Med Coll, DDS 1948, RDH 1938. **CAREER:** MS State Bd Health, itinerant dental hygienist; Ft Jackson SC, dental hygienist; Meharry Med Coll, inst dental hygiene; Jackson Hinds Comp Health Cntr, dental surgeon, pvt pract. **ORGANIZATIONS:** Mem MS Am & Nat Dental Assns; MS Dental Soc; life mem NAACP; mem Business Women's League. **HONORS/ACHIEVEMENTS:** WYCA Merit Award 1973; 1st female dentist; 1st & only black female dentist in MS. **BUSINESS ADDRESS:** 1102 Woodrow Wilson, Jackson, MS.

JONES, MELTON RODNEY
Educational administrator. **PERSONAL:** Born Jan 13, 1945, Virginia; married Energelia Guillen Uzeta; children: Mavel U, Christina V. **EDUCATION:** AmUniv Wash, DC, BS 1966; HowardUniv Wash, DC, MS 1968, PhD 1972. **CAREER:** Comm Coll of Baltimore, chairperson sci dept 1978-; OH Univ Coll of Osteopathic Med, asst to dean 1977-78. **ORGANIZATIONS:** Chmn blk studiesUniv of CO Boulder 1975-77; asst prof biologyUniv of CO Boulder 1975-77; chmn div of sci ShawUniv Raleigh 1974-75; asst prof biology ShawUniv 1972-75. **HONORS/ACHIEVEMENTS:** NDEA Flwsp HowardUniv 1968-71. **BUSINESS ADDRESS:** 2901 Liberty Heights Ave, Baltimore, MD 21215.

JONES, MICHAEL ANDREA
Clergyman, psychologist. **PERSONAL:** Born Aug 06, 1937, Atlanta, GA; married Linda; children: Gattie. **EDUCATION:** GA State U, BA; Atlanta U, MA; Am U, ED. **CAREER:** Morris Brown Coll, dir; Mitchell Chapel, pastor. **ORGANIZATIONS:** AME Ch Atlanta Ass of Educators; GA Assn of Educators; GA Cncl Of Chs 1977-; So Christian Leadership Conf; United Youth Adult Conf; mem NAACP; So Christian Leadership 1959-; Atlanta Christian Cncl 1975-. **BUSINESS ADDRESS:** Fayetteville Parish AME, PO Box 430, Fayetteville, GA 30314.

JONES, MICHAEL PERRIN
Engineer. **PERSONAL:** Born May 31, 1959, Greenwood, SC. **EDUCATION:** Duke Univ, BSEE 1981; Attended, Rutgers Univ 1983-84, George Washington Univ 1984-85. **CAREER:** WVSP-FM Radio, chief engr 1982; Teledyne Brown Engrg, systems analyst 1982-84; Potomac Systems Engrg, systems analyst 1984; BTG Inc, sr systems analyst 1984-. **ORGANIZATIONS:** Tutor Duke Univ 1979-82; mem Big Brother Program Durham NC 1979-82; tutor NTA NJ 1983,84; vice pres SMART Pty 1984; coach City of Alex Rec Dept 1985,86;mem IEEE, NSBE, AFCEA. **HONORS/ACHIEVEMENTS:** Natl Ach Scholarship Natl Merit School Duke 1977. **BUSINESS ADDRESS:** Sr Systems Analyst, BTG Inc, 1945 Old Gallows Rd, Vienna, VA 22180.

JONES, MICHELE WOODS
Educational administrator. **PERSONAL:** Born Oct 03, 1945, Los Angeles, CA; daughter of David A Francis and Mary Ellen Harris; children (previous marriage): Sjaun, Leasa; married Reginald L Jones, Jan 03, 1988. **EDUCATION:** Phoenix College, Phoenix, AZ, AA, 1965; University of California, Berkeley, CA, BA in history, 1969, grad study in history, 1969-70; California State University, Hayward, CA, MS in educational psychology, 1979. **CAREER:** University of California, Berkeley, CA, co-director, special summer project, 1968, Educational Opportunities Program, counselor, 1968-70, tutorial staff coordinator, 1970-72, counselor coordinator, 1972-73, Student Information Center, assistant director, 1973-77, Student Learning Center, assistant director, 1977-81, principal student affairs officer, 1981-83, director of student activities and services, 1983-89, assistant to the vice chancellor and staff ombudsperson, 1989—. **ORGANIZATIONS:** Member & past president, Alpha Kappa Alpha sorority, 1967—; campus liaison, Black Alumni Club, University of California, Berkeley, 1969—; board of directors, California Alumni Association, University of California; member, Order of the Golden Bear, 1975—; member, Association of Black Psychologists; member, Educational Resource Council, 1979—; member of advisory board, Center for the Study, Education & Advancement of Women, University of California, Berkeley; honorary member, Golden Key National Honor Society, 1985; honorary member, Delta Delta Delta sorority, 1986; National Association of Student Personnel Administrators; National Orientation Directors Association; Soroptomist International. **HONORS/ACHIEVEMENTS:** Outstanding Black Women of California, 1981-82; Recognition Award, African Students' Association, University of California, Berkeley, 1982; Michelle Woods Scholarship established in her honor by Alpha Kappa Alpha sorority, University of California, Berkeley, 1983; Rosalie M Stern Award, California Alumni Association, 1984; Citizen of the Year awd from Basileus-Epsilon Mu/Omega Psi Phi fraternity, 1986; Black Alumnae of the Year, Black Alumni Club, University of California, Berkeley, 1987; Outstanding Service Award, University of California, Berkeley, 1988. **BUSINESS ADDRESS:** Assistant to the Vice Cahncellor, Staff Ombudsperson, University of California, 490 Crowell Hospital, Berkeley, CA 94720.

JONES, MILES JAMES
Pathologist. **PERSONAL:** Born Nov 22, 1952, Abington, PA; married Linda D Ableitner; children: Dominick, Jessica. **EDUCATION:** Princeton Univ, attended 1970-73; Howard Univ Medical School, MD 1977; post grad work at Cleveland Clinic, 1977-78, Mayo Clinic, Mayo Graduate School of Medicine, 1978-82. **CAREER:** Armed Forces Inst of Pathology, pathologist 1982-84; Herring Hosp, pathologist & lab director 1985—; Southern IL Univ Med School, clinical asst prof of pathology. **ORGANIZATIONS:** Mem editorial bd Minnesota Medicine 1980-; med adv comm American Red Cross; coroner's physician Saline Co, Franklin Co, White Co, Alexander Co, Johnson Co, Polaski Co 1984-; bd mem community affairs Herrin Rotary 1985-; clinical asst prof of pathology So IL Univ Carbondale Medical Sch 1986-; mem Amer, IL State, Williamson County Medical Socs; mem Intl Acad of Pathology, Intl Soc of Gynecologic Pathologists, AMA, Amer Acad Forensic Sciences; fellow Coll of Amer Pathologists, Amer Soc of Clinical Pathologists; alternate house of delegates Coll of Amer Pathologists. **HONORS/ACHIEVEMENTS:** Natl Science Found fellowships 1968-70; Natl Sudden Infant Death fellowship, 1975; Stowell-Orbison Award for Pathologist in Training, US-Canadian Division, Intl Acad of Pathology, 1982; 5 publications including "Verrucous Squamous Cell Carcinoma of the Vagina," w/LA Ballard and HS Levin, Cleveland Clinic Quarterly 48; 6 abstract presentations; 3 book reviews published. **HOME ADDRESS:** RR1 Box 573 West Brewster Rd, Herrin, IL 62948. **BUSINESS ADDRESS:** Pathologist/Lab Dir, Herrin Hospital, 201 S 14th St, Herrin, IL 62948.

JONES, NAPOLEON A., JR.
Judge. **PERSONAL:** Born Aug 25, 1940, Hodge, LA; children: Lena L. **EDUCATION:** San Diego State Univ, BA 1962, MSW 1967; Univ of San Diego School of Law, JD 1971. **CAREER:** CA Rural Legal Asst Modesto, attny 1972-73; Defenders Inc of San Diego, attny 1973-75; Jones & Adler San Diego, attny 1975-77; San Diego Municipal Court, judge 1977-82; San Diego Superior Court, judge 1982-. **ORGANIZATIONS:** Chairperson Citizens Adv Comm; mem San Diego Integration Task Force; faculty mem Continuing Judicial Studies Prog; mem Indigent Defense Policy Bd, Law in a Free Soc, Black Comm Ctr, San Diego Law Review. **HONORS/ACHIEVEMENTS:** Listed in Who's Who in Amer Coll & Univ 1970-71; Reginald Herber Smith Fellowship 1971-73; Disting Alumni School of Social Work Merit; USD Law School & SDSU Coll of Human Svcs. **BUSINESS ADDRESS:** Judge, San Diego Superior Court, 220 W Broadway, San Diego, CA 92101.

JONES, NATHAN WILLIAM
Minister. **PERSONAL:** Born Feb 28, 1952, Indianapolis, IN. **EDUCATION:** Univ WI, BA 1975; VA Theol Sem, MDiv 1977; Mundelein Coll, post-grad Studies; Notre Dame Sch of Theol; Union Grad Sch, PhD candidate. **CAREER:** Our Lady of Charity RC Ch, minister of educ 1976-; Black Religiuos Exp Inst, co-founder 1976-; City Univ of NY, campus minister 1976-. **ORGANIZATIONS:** Consult Urban Religious Edn; dir Survival & Faith Inst for Lifelong Adult Learning; co-dir Black Religious Exp Inst; mem Coalition of Concerned Black Educators; Council of Independent Black Insts; Interfaith Alliance of Ministers of Brooklyn; Educ Task Force for Positive Direction; Central Brooklyn Youth FamilySvcs; Brooklyn Coalition for Afrikan Liberation Day; parish bd Our Lady of Charity Cath Ch. **HONORS/ACHIEVEMENTS:** Guidling Light Award 1977; Lilly Found Grant, Notre Dam Sch of Theo 1977; listed, Black World; Black News; Religion; Tchr's Jour; Contemplative Review, NY Amsterdam News; Freeing the Spirit. **BUSINESS ADDRESS:** 1669 Dean St, Brooklyn, NY 11213.

JONES, NATHANIEL, SR.
Elected official. **PERSONAL:** Born Oct 03, 1948, New Orleans, LA; married Brenda; children: Natalie, Nathaniel, Natash. **EDUCATION:** Southern Univ, attended 1968-73. **CAREER:** King Triumph BC, member 1969; Southern Univ Recreation Club, vice president 1970-72; Prince Hall Masons, member 1973; Lutcher and Gramercy Jaycees, member 1984. **ORGANIZATIONS:** Member Rive Parishes Improvement League 1972; chairman Building & Planning Comm 1975 & 1981; board of directors LA Black Municipal Assn Caucus 1982 & 1983; member USWA 1973-; member LA Municipal Assn 1981-; member Natl League of Cities 1983; member Lutcher-Gramercy Jaycees 1984; dist coordinator Natl Black Caucus of LEO 1984-; member NAACP. **HONORS/ACHIEVEMENTS:** Worked Summer Youth in Drug Program 1985. **MILITARY SERVICE:** ROTC Southern Univ Baton Rouge, LA. **BUSINESS ADDRESS:** Alderman, Town of Lutcher, Box 456, Lutcher, LA 70071.

JONES, NATHANIEL R.
Judge, attorney, administrator. **PERSONAL:** Born May 13, 1926, Youngstown, OH. **EDUCATION:** Youngstown Univ, BA 1951, LLB (Honorary) 1956. **CAREER:** NAACP, gen counsel 1969-79; Fair Employment Practices Comm City of Youngstown, exec dir 1966-69; Private practice, attny; US Attny No Dist of OH, former asst attny; US Court of Appeals 6th Circuit, judge. **ORGANIZATIONS:** Dep gen counsel Pres Comm on Civil Disorders 1967; co-chmn Civilian-Mil Task Force on Mil Justice 1972. **HONORS/ACHIEVEMENTS:** Headed three-man team which investigated grievances of black servicemen in W Germany. **BUSINESS ADDRESS:** Judge, US Court of Appeals 6th Crct, 541 US Court House, Cincinnati, OH 45226.

JONES, NELLIE L.
Elected official. **PERSONAL:** Born Apr 11, 1933, Minter City, MS; children: James Jr, Sandra, Jerry, Michael, Audrey Jones Kenner, Jennifer Jones Witherspoon, McDaniels. **EDUCATION:** MS Vocational Coll, 1955. **CAREER:** Metro Sanitary Dist of Greater Chicago, commissioner. **ORGANIZATIONS:** Steering Police Comm Mayor's Task Force; beat rep pres of 2nd Ward Women; LAC Comm Aux Democratic Org. **HONORS/ACHIEVEMENTS:** Affirmative Action 1978; Black Contractors United 1982; Robert Taylor Homes 4 Star Assn 1983; Outstanding Awd United Comm Action 1984. **BUSINESS ADDRESS:** Commissioner, Cook Co Metro Sanitary Ds, 100 E Erie St, Chicago, IL 60611.

JONES, NETTIE PEARL
Educator, author. **PERSONAL:** Born Jan 01, 1941, Arlington, GA; daughter of Benjamin Jones and Delonia Mears Jones Whorton; divorced; children: Lynne Cheryl Harris. **EDUCATION:** Wayne State Univ, Detroit, MI, BS, Secondary Educ, 1963; Marygrove Coll, Detroit, MI, MEd, Reading, 1971; Fashion Inst of Technology, New York, NY, Advertising, Communications, 1973-76. **CAREER:** Detroit Bd of Educ, Detroit, MI, teacher of secondary social studies, English, and reading, 1963-72; Royal George School, Greenfield Park, Quebec, teacher of secondary English, 1966-68; Martin Luther King School, New York, NY, teacher of reading, 1971-72; Wayne State Univ, Detroit, MI, lecturer, visiting writer, 1986-87; Chmn Wayne County Commr, Detroit, MI, writer, 1988; Wayne County Community Coll, Detroit, MI, teacher of devel reading, 1988; Michigan Technological Univ, Houghton, MI, asst prof, writer in residence, 1988-89, minority affairs asst to the vice pres, 1989-. **ORGANIZATIONS:** Detroit Women Writers, 1985; Amer Assn of Univ Prof, 1986; adjudicator, 1989 Michigan Governor's Artist Awards. **HONORS/ACHIEVEMENTS:** Yaddo Fellow Writer, 1985; one of the Most Promising Novelists, New York Times Book Review, March 17, 1985; Notable New Artist, Contemporary Literary Criticism Yearbook, 1985; Individual Artist, Michigan Council of the Arts Award, 1986; second runner-up, DH Lawrence Competition, 1987; Grant for Fiction, Natl Endowment of the Arts, 1989; author, Fish Tales, 1984, Mischief Makers, 1989, "When Crack Comes Home," non-fiction short story, Detroit Free Press Magazine, Feb 5, 1989; featured in Detroit Monthly, Feb 1989; readings, 1984-.

JONES, NINA F.
Educational administrator. **PERSONAL:** Born Jul 30, 1918, Madison, GA; married Dr William M Jones; children: William M Jr, Steven L. **EDUCATION:** Central YMCA Clge, AB 1938; Chicago Tchrs Clge, MEd 1942; Loyola Univ Chicago, EdD 1975. **CAREER:** Chicago Public Schools, teacher 1942, prin 1965, dist supt 1969, asst supt personnel 1975, sec bd of examiners 1983-. **ORGANIZATIONS:** Mem Alpha Kappa Alpha Sor 1940, Alpha Gamma Pi Sor 1967; Pi Lambda Theta. **HOME ADDRESS:** 9156 S Constance, Chicago, IL 60617.

JONES, O. MARION
Business executive. **PERSONAL:** Born Jul 14, 1946, St Louis; married Dorothy Wilkerson; children: Kito Dawn, Kwanza, Meta, Mahiri. **EDUCATION:** LlB, JD 1948. **CAREER:** Natl Equal Opportunity Coun, gen counsel, Black Adv Multi-Purpose Legal Serv Center, gen counsel; private practice lawyer, NY State; Natl Bar Found, gen counsel & dir; OEO & The Comm Serv Admin, compliance officer; Natl Bar Found Newsletter, publisher, editor; W Center Law & Poverty, dir comm affairs & econ devel; Natl Bar Assn, special consultant; Amsterdam Employment Agency, owner. **ORGANIZATIONS:** Wrote NY State & Fed Govt Minimum Wage Law for Domestic Workers; established Seminar of APH Enterprises for Hispanic People & Natl Group Legal Serv Prog; civil rights worker, Titles VI, VII & VIL; pres & polemarch Kappa Alpha Psi Frat; published several articles on compliance procedures. **HONORS/ACHIEVEMENTS:** Outstanding trial work pioneered in negligence & damage work, NY Lawyers Assn 1958; Achievement Award, NY Chap Kappa Alpha Psi 1963; Provincial Award, Kappa Alpha Psi. **MILITARY SERVICE:** AUS 1943-45.

JONES, OLGA UNITA See THOMPSON-CLEMMONS, OLGA UNITA

JONES, ORIS PINCKNEY
Embalmer/funeral director. **PERSONAL:** Born Jan 01, 1903, Florence County, SC; married Alva Victoria Robinson. **EDUCATION:** Worsham Training School, Diploma Mortuary Science 1930; St Augustine's Coll, DCL 1979. **CAREER:** Oris P Jones Funeral Homes, owner 1930-. **ORGANIZATIONS:** Mem Virginia Morticians Assoc 1950-, Natl Funeral Directors Assoc 1950-; mem President's Council Saint Paul's Coll 1985. **HONORS/ACHIEVEMENTS:** Citation Phi Beta Lambda 1978; Citation Southside Funeral Directors 1978-82; Citation Southside Senior Citizens 1979; Meritorious Serv Awd United Negro Coll-Fund 1979; Certificate of Appreciation Brunswick NAACP 1979,81,86; Certificate of Appreciation Saint Paul's Coll 1983; Certificate of Recognition Brunswick Co VA 4H 1986; Sponsorship Certificate Anti-Drug Prog WKLV 1987; Saint Paul's Coll Dormitory named "Jones Hall". **HOME ADDRESS:** 418 North Main St, Lawrenceville, VA 23868. **BUSINESS ADDRESS:** Owner, Oris P Jones Funeral Homes, 400 North Court St, Lawrenceville, VA 23868.

JONES, OSCAR C., JR.
Clergyman. **PERSONAL:** Born Sep 01, 1932, San Antonio, TX; married Helm; children: Dennis. **EDUCATION:** Attended City Coll 1962; Univ of Eastern FL, BA 1965; Symbol of Salvation Bible Sch, AB 1965; attended Amer Bapt Theol Sem 1968-70; Am Divinity Sch, ThD ThNT; Rosemead Grad Sch of Psychol, PhD (summa cum laude) 1976; Trinity Theol Seminary, DMin (magna cum laude) 1981 & 1982. **CAREER:** Mt Olive Baptist Ch, pastor 1959-64; St John's Baptist Church, pastor 1965-69; CA State Coll, prof of Black Church in Amer; Shiloh Baptist Church, pastor. **ORGANIZATIONS:** Sweet Hour of Prayer Broadcast Narrator 1953-59; dir Christian Ed LA 1955-59; release time tchr for LA Coun of Ch 1965-69; LA Bapt City Mission Soc 1969-71; editor "The Reconciler" 1969-72; LA Minister to Comm Affairs Zion Bapt Ch 1969-73; mem NAACP 1969-74; Zion Hill Bapt Ch Tchr World ChristianTraining Ctr 1970-73; bd mem LA Coun of Chs 1970-73; Sugar Ray Robinson's Youth Found 1970-71; Minister of Comm Affairs Sr Cit 1972-73; Natl ChaplainsAssn 1972-74; Ministers & Missionaries Benefit Bd Amer Bapt Ch USA; exec dir Mutual Asst Team Endeavors of Amer Bapt Ch Pacific SW. **HONORS/ACHIEVEMENTS:** Alpha Theta Omega Sor 1962; cert Probate Ct of LA Co 1967; Sr Cit Comm Serv Awd 1973; BSA Cert of Recog 1973.

JONES, OZRO T., JR.
Clergyman. **EDUCATION:** Temple U, BS 1945; Temple U, MA 1946; TempleUniv Sch of Theol, STB; Temple U, STM 1953; TempleUniv Sch of Religion & Philosophy, STD 1962. **CAREER:** Holy Temple Ch of God in Christ, pastor; Commonwealth of PA Ch of God in Christ, juris bishop 1973-; Holy Temple Ch of God in Christ, asso pastor 1963; Meml Ch of God in Christ, pastor 1953; Ch of God in Christ to Liberia W Coast Africa, missionary 1949; Young People's Ch of Holy Temple, leader 1941; Holy Temple Ch of God in Christ, asso minister. **ORGANIZATIONS:** Organized Tuesday Night Young People's Ch Svc; Sons of Gideon; Dau of Ruth; Young People's Choral of Holy Temple; Upper Room Fellowship; Pentecostal StudentYouth Conf; Big Bros & Big Sisters Fellowship; bd mem Oppty Indsln Ctr Inc; mem Cncl of Christian Missionaries in Liberia; asso editor YPWW Quarterly Topics; coeditor The Christian View of Life; pres Intl Youth Congress Of Ch of God in Christ; began Christ Seeks You youth rallies; writer of 3 hymns. **BUSINESS ADDRESS:** Jurisdictional Bishop, Church of God in Christ, 336 N 60th St, Philadelphia, PA 19139.

JONES, PATRICIA YVONNE
Nurse & elected official. **PERSONAL:** Born Oct 22, 1956, Muskegon, MI; daughter of Theo Jones and Juanita Henry Jones; children: Dwayne. **EDUCATION:** Muskegon Comm Coll, Practical Nursing diploma 1978, AS 1978. **CAREER:** Hackley Hosp & Medical Ctr, licensed prac nurse II 1978-; City of Muskegon Hts, councilwoman. **ORGANIZATIONS:**

Mem MI Licensed Practical Nurse Assn 1978; mem NAACP 1981; bd mem Muskegon Comm Coll Adv Bd 1982; mem Harriet J Cole Order of Eastern Stars 1983; gen mem Natl Black Caucus Local Elected Official 1983; gen mem Muskegon Hts Bd of Commerce 1984; mem Muskegon Black Women Political Caucus. **HOME ADDRESS:** 222 East Hackley Ave, Muskegon Heights, MI 49444. **BUSINESS ADDRESS:** Councilwoman, City of Muskegon Hts, 2724 Peck St, Muskegon Heights, MI 49444.

JONES, PATRICK P.
Association executive. **PERSONAL:** Born Apr 08, 1928, Bulloch County, GA; children: Andre Jones. **EDUCATION:** Certificate civil rights. **CAREER:** Gen builder; farmer; lumber checker; crop reporter & landscaping; plant machine operator; Devel Unique Services Ourselves, chmn bd dir; Jones & Jones Homeground Improvement Serv; operator; Blending-Aires Singers, mgr. **ORGANIZATIONS:** Pres NAACP 1965-; mem PAC; Church Trustee Bd; mem Church Programing Comm; Group Song Leader. **HONORS/ACHIEVEMENTS:** Man of Yr Award; William M Boyd Award; Citizenship Award; NAACP Award for Branch Programming; Certificate for Voter Registration.

JONES, PAUL R.
Business executive, political consultant. **PERSONAL:** Born Jun 01, 1928, Bessemer, AL; children: Paul R Jones Jr. **EDUCATION:** AL State Univ Jr Coll, 1947; Howard Univ, BA 1949, MA 1950; Governors State Univ, MA 1975; Yale Univ, Univ of CA, attended. **CAREER:** Interracial Comm Birmingham AL, exec dir; Johnson Publishing Co, public relations field rep; US Govt Atlanta, Charlotte, dir model cities prog; Peace Corps Thailand, dep dir; Action Atlanta, southeastern region dir; Model Cities Prog, US community relations expert justice dept; PJ Enterprises, CEO. **ORGANIZATIONS:** Bd mem High Museum; founded The Paul Jones Collection (fine art); past/present mem of natl housing, art, and community groups. **HONORS/ACHIEVEMENTS:** Sustained Superior Performance Awd US Atty Gen; Fellowship Yale Univ; writer of articles published in journal of Intl City Mgrs Assn & other natl journals; owns largest most significant collection of black art privately held. **HOME ADDRESS:** 1790 Willis Mill Rd SW, Atlanta, GA 30311.

JONES, PEARL PULLINS
Retired association executive, court clerk. **PERSONAL:** Born Jun 29, 1915, Birmingham, AL; daughter of Charles Pullins and Willie Harris Pullins; married Thomas O Jones, Feb 13, 1936 (deceased); children: Constance Gilliard, Thomas O, III, Michael T Jones. **EDUCATION:** NYUniv Sch of Mdse & Bus Mgmt, AA 1954. **CAREER:** Louis Harris & Assocs New York NY, natl field supr 1966-73; Louis Harris & Assocs NY, field interviewer 1963-66; New York City Health Dept Jamaica, sr clerk 1960-63; AUS, sr clerk; Ordinance Dept Raritan NJ, 1942-43; Alexander Dept Stores NYC, mgr price change dept 1939-42, 1945-48, 1951-55; Rio Rancho, NM, deputy court clerk, 1982-85. **ORGANIZATIONS:** Pres NAACP NW Mesa NM Branch; founder, pres Natl Key Women of Amer Queens Branch 1956-74; co-founder, pres NW Mesa NM NAACP 1978-80; first vice pres NM State Conf of Branch NAACP 1978-80; chaplain Amer Assn of Retired Persons Unit 78 Rio Rancho 1976-79; chaplian Disabled Amer Vet Aux 1976-78; first vice pres Lutheran Church Women All Saints Lutheran NM 1977-78; vice chairperson, Democratic County Org, Sandoval City, NM, 1985-89. **HONORS/ACHIEVEMENTS:** Juez Comisionado Comm Award, Lt Gov Robert Ferguson NM 1978; Certificate of Appreciation Award, NM State Conf of Branch NAACP 1979; Certificate of Recognition Serv,Lt Gov Roberto Mongragon 1979; Colonial & Aide de Camp, Gov Bruce King 1979; Certificate of Appreciation, Shirley Hooper Sec of State 1980; NM Mesa NAACP Award: first pres 1979-81; state conf of NM NAACP; Outstanding Service Award, 1983-84; City of Rio Rancho, NM Municipal Ct 1982-85; Faithful Service Award.

JONES, PERCY ELWOOD
Physician. **PERSONAL:** Born Jun 25, 1940, Richmond, VA; married Nora; children: Sabrina, Christopher. **EDUCATION:** VA Union Univ, 1961; Meharry Med Coll, MD 1968. **CAREER:** Med Coll VA, pathology resd, pathology intern 1968-73; L Richardson Meml Hosp, chf staff, pathologist 1975-. **ORGANIZATIONS:** Pathologist Amer Soc Clinical Pathologists; mem Old N State Med Soc; Natl Med Assn; mem Kappa Alpha Psi Frat; Greensboro Med Soc; Guilford Co Med Soc; Hayes-Taylor YMCA; fellow of College of Amer Pathologists; fellow of Amer Soc of Clinical Pathologists; diplomate Amer Bd of Pathology; life mem NAACP. **MILITARY SERVICE:** USAF Maj 1973-75.

JONES, PETER LAWSON
Attorney, elected official. **PERSONAL:** Born Dec 23, 1952, Cleveland, OH; son of Charles W Jones and Margaret H Jones; married Lisa Payne Jones; children: Ryan Charles Jones. **EDUCATION:** Harvard Coll, BA 1975; Harvard Law School, JD 1980. **CAREER:** Hon Yvonne B Burke US House of Rep, pres & leg aide 1975-76; Carter-Mondale Pres Campaign, writer & spokesman 1976; Carter-Mondale Transition Planning Group, transition officer 1976-77; Office of Intergovt Relations & Congressional Affairs HUD, liaison officer 1977; Dyke Coll Cleveland OH, instructor 1980, 1983; Supreme Court of OH, law clerk 1982-83; Attorney 1980-; Ohio Works Co, pres 1984-85. **ORGANIZATIONS:** Mem exec committee Cleveland Branch NAACP 1983-88; volunteer A Better Chance Inc 1984-; volunteer United Negro Coll Fund 1984; chmn Operation Greater Cleveland Big Vote 1985; mem Leadership Cleveland Alumni Assoc Steering Comm 1986-; mem bd of trustees United Black Fund 1986-; volunteer Case Western Reserve Univ Career Beginnings Prog 1986-; mem Cuyahoga County Bar Assn 1988; mem Natl League of Cities Human Devel Policy Comm 1988; treasurer Harvard Law School Assn of Cleveland 1986; mem Executive Comm Cuyahoga County Democratic Party 1986-; mem Advisory Bd Cuyahoga County Minority Business Devel Program 1987; mem bd of trustees Univ for Young Americans 1987. **HONORS/ACHIEVEMENTS:** Magna Cum Laude, Govt Harvard Coll; Harvard Rhodes Scholarship Nom; Harvard John F Kennedy Inst of Politics Summer Fellowship; Harvard Natl Scholarship; Paul Revere Frothingham Scholarship; Currier House Sr Creativity Awd; Meritorious Achievement Awd US Dept of HUD 1977, PUSH-Excel Program 1981; Outstanding Young Men of Amer Jaycees 1984; The Eastside Coalition Comm Serv Awd 1986; Inductee, Shaker Heights Alumni Assn Hall of Fame 1987; Outstanding young Cleveland Award for Public Service Jaycees 1989; "The Family Live" a full length play produced at Harvard Coll, Ohio Univ, 1975, Ohio Univ 1976 and given a staged reading at the E Cleveland, Ohio Theatre 1985. **HOME ADDRESS:** 13800 Fairhill Rd #520, Shaker Heights, OH 44120. **BUSINESS ADDRESS:** Attorney, 3705 Lee Rd, Suite 200, Shaker Heights, OH 44120.

JONES, PHILLIP ERSKINE
Educator. **PERSONAL:** Born Oct 26, 1940, Chicago, IL; married Jo Lavera Kennedy; children: Phyllis, Joel. **EDUCATION:** Univ of IL, BS 1963; Univ of IA, MA 1967, PhD 1975. **CAREER:** Chicago Youth Ctrs, group work counselor 1963-64; Flint Comm Schs, secondary tchr phys ed 1967-68; Univ of IA, dir special support serv 1970-75, asstvice pres & dir affirmative action asst prof of counselor educ 1975-78, assoc dean of student serv & asst prof of counselor educ 1978-83, dean of student serv & asst prof of counselor educ 1983-. **ORGANIZATIONS:** Mem IA City Human Relations Comm 1972-74; chair IA City Human Relations Comm 1974-75; human relations training sessions IA City Fire Dept 1985; field reader for spec serv prog US Office of Educ 1980-87; human relations workshop Dept of Correction Serv Session 1981; re-entry workshop for tchrs IA City Sch Dist; consul redevelopment of training prog for educators in USOE; field reader for grad & professional oppor progs US Office of Educ 1978; consul HUD. **HONORS/ACHIEVEMENTS:** Rep US Ethnic Professional Exchange Prog to W Germany; Sister Cities Intl; Carl Duisberg-Gesellschaft; and Instut fur Auslandsbeziehungen; numerous publications including "Special Educ & Socioeconomic Retardation" Journal for Spec Educators Vol 19 No 4 1983; Commentary "Student Decision Making, When and How"; College/Career Choice, Right Student Right Time Right Place; proceedings of the 1972 ACT Invitational Conf Iowa City. **BUSINESS ADDRESS:** Dean of Student Services, Univ of IA, Rm 105 Jessup Hall, Iowa City, IA 52242.

JONES, QUINCY
Producer, composer, arranger. **PERSONAL:** Born Mar 14, 1933, Chicago, IL; son of Quincy Delight and Sarah J Jones; divorced; children: Quincy III, Martina-Lisa, Jolie, Kidada, Rashida. **EDUCATION:** Berklee Coll of Music, Boston. **CAREER:** Formed rock band at age 15 with friend Ray Charles playing throughout Seattle area; traveled with Lionel Hampton band to Europe at age 18; arranged, composed and produced for Billie Holiday, Dinah Washington, Count Basie, Duke Ellington, Sammy Davis Jr, Sarah Vaughn, Dizzy Gillespie, Frank Sinatra, Johnny Mathis, Lena Horne, George Benson, Brothers Johnson, Michael Jackson, Chaka Khan, others; first black vice pres at Mercury Record Co; scored over 33 major motion pictures including "The Wiz" and "In Cold Blood"; produced Michael Jackson's first solo album "Off the Wall"; produced Michael Jackson's "Thriller" album with Michael Jackson; owner, Q West Records; served as exec producer & wrote score for movie "The Color Purple.". **HONORS/ACHIEVEMENTS:** Nominated for Oscar Awards for four film scores; received 20 Grammy Awards and over 50 Grammy nominations; 1979 production of "Off the Wall" sold over 8 million copies and at that time a record-breaking four Top 10 singles; album "The Dude" received an unprecendented 12 Grammy nominations in 1981 and won five Grammy Awards; received 8 Grammy nominations in 1983 (the most ever received by one person in one year); received several more Grammys in 1984 including one for Producer of the Year for "Thriller" album, co-produced with Michael Jackson (album has sold over 30 million copies worldwide); received 1985 ABAA Music Award for efforts to aid African famine victims, and for conceiving and giving leadership to USA for Africa, producing the album and video, "We Are the World". **BUSINESS ADDRESS:** Producer, Composer, Arranger, c/o Q West Records, 7250 Beverly, Los Angeles, CA 90036.

JONES, RANDY KANE
Attorney. **PERSONAL:** Born Oct 25, 1957, Jacksonville, NC; son of Henry Jones and Julia Mae Saunders Jones; children: Randy. **EDUCATION:** Univ of NC, BA 1979, Sch of Law JD 1982. **CAREER:** Judge Advocate General's Corps, attorney 1983-86; United States Attorney, asst. **ORGANIZATIONS:** Mem Federal Bar Assoc 1984-, Amer Bar Assoc 1985-, Christian Fellowship Cong Church 1985, BE SLA 1986-; Parlimentarian Earl B Gulliam Bar Assn 1988-; mem of the bd California Assn of Black Lawyers 1989-; Chairman Veterns Affairs NAACP San Diego Branch 1989-. **MILITARY SERVICE:** USN lt 3 yrs; Defense Counsel of Quarter 1983-86; USNR, LCDR 1987-. **BUSINESS ADDRESS:** Assistant, United States Attorney, 940 Front St 5-N-19, San Diego, CA 92189.

JONES, RAYMOND, SR.
Businessman. **PERSONAL:** Born Jan 06, 1925, Norfolk, VA; married Edris W. **EDUCATION:** Norfolk Naval Air Sta Apprentice Sch, 1948-52. **CAREER:** Jones Auto Sales & Serv, pres, owner; Maurice E Collette Real Estate Co, pres; licensed real est brkr 1957; City of Norfolk, comm notary public. **ORGANIZATIONS:** Mem Nat'l Assn Real Est Brokers Inc; area adv bd Tidewater Group Inc; mem Tidewater Area Bus League; Alpha Omega; Nat'l Fed Indep Bus; Consistory #9; Arabia Temple #12. **HONORS/ACHIEVEMENTS:** Five-yr serv award, Humble Oil & Refing Co; Cert of Commendation, Com of 100 Women 1968; businessman of yr, Tidewater Area Bus League 1970. **MILITARY SERVICE:** AUS 1943-47. **BUSINESS ADDRESS:** 727 E 26 St, Norfolk, VA 23504.

JONES, RAYMOND DEAN
Judge. **PERSONAL:** Born Nov 30, 1945, Pueblo, CO; married Carolyn S; children: Latoya Bryant, Ruth Marie, Raymond Dean II. **EDUCATION:** CO Coll, BA 1967; Harvard Law, JD 1971. **CAREER:** CO Supreme Court, clerk to chief justice, 1971-72; Holme Roberts & Owen, atty 1972-74; Met Denver Dist Atty Consumer Office Prosec of Consumer Defrauders,chief counsel 1974-77; Denver County Court, judge 1977-78; Denvery District Court, judge 1979-. **ORGANIZATIONS:** Mem bd dir New Dance Theatre Inc 1972-, CO State Bd of Law Exam 1973-; mem, vp, bd dir Denver Oppty Inc 1974-; mem St Bd CO Humanities Prog 1977, Gov Task Force Labor Legis 1976, Gov Task Force on Employ Agencies 1976; pres Sam Cary Bar Assoc; mem Denver Bar Assoc, CO Bar Assoc, Amer Bar Assoc, natl Bar Assoc; sec CO Dem Party; chmn CO Black Caucus 1973-74; del Dem natl Conv 1976; mem Amer Judges Assoc, CO Assoc of District Judges, Bar of State of CO, Fed Dist of CO, 10th Fed Circuit, US Supreme Court; faculty Natl Judicial Coll Reno NV; bd of trustees Colorado Coll Colorado Springs; mem Colorado Council on the Arts; numerous community bds. **HONORS/ACHIEVEMENTS:** Marshal of the Class Harvard Univ Law School 1971; Barney Ford Comm Awd for Law & Justice 1977; listed in Who's Who in Amer Law 1977, The Amer Bench 1977;author "A Search for Better Police Serv & An End to Police-Comm Tensions in Black Urban Neighborhoods & An Examination of Comm Control of Police" 1971; numerous community awds Denver and Colorado.

JONES, RAYMOND MORRIS
Professional engineer, retired professor. **PERSONAL:** Born Nov 29, 1922, St Louis, MO; married Frances; children: Michael, Byron, Sandra, Patricia. **EDUCATION:** Howard Univ, BSCE 1947; Univ of MI, MSSE 1954. **CAREER:** Howard Univ, instr to prof 1947-84; RM Jones & Assoc, consultant 1965-; Howard Univ, retired prof civil engineering. **ORGANIZATIONS:** Mem NTA, ASCE, ASEE, APHA, NABCE, EABCE, AIDIS; former mem

Reg III GSA Adv Panel, DC Bd of Appeals & Rev, Joint Conf Comm, World Wide, Water Resources,AID. **MILITARY SERVICE:** USN seaman 1/c 1945-47.

JONES, REGINA NICKERSON
Publisher. **PERSONAL:** Born Sep 23, 1942, Los Angeles, CA; married Ken; children: Kenneth Jr, Kevin, Keith, Kory, Karen. **EDUCATION:** Los Angeles Cty Coll. **CAREER:** Soul Publ Inc, publisher. **ORGANIZATIONS:** Mem Nat Asso Media Women; mem United Way Ment Hlth & Devel 1974-.

JONES, REGINALD L.
Educator. **PERSONAL:** Born Jan 21, 1931, Clearwater, FL; married Johnette Turner; children: Juliette, Angela, Cynthia. **EDUCATION:** Morehouse Coll, AB 1952; Wayne State Univ, MA 1954; OH State Univ, PhD 1959. **CAREER:** Miami Univ, asst prof 1959-63; Fisk Univ, assoc prof 1963-64; UCLA, asst prof 1964-66; OH State Univ, prof vice chmn dept of psychol 1966-69; Univ of CA Riverside, chmn & prof dept of educ 1969-72; Haile Selassie Univ Addis Adaba Ethiopia, prof & dir testing ctr 1972-74; Univ of CA Berkeley, prof 1973-75; Univ of CA Berkeley, chmn dept of afro-amer studies prof of educ 1975-. **ORGANIZATIONS:** Natl chmn Assn of Black Psychol 1971-72; fellow Amer Psychol Assn; mem Council for Exceptional Children; guest ed Journal of Black Psychology; assoc ed Amer Journal of Mental Deficiency; editor Mental Retardation 1979-83. **MILITARY SERVICE:** AUS med corps 1954-56. **BUSINESS ADDRESS:** Chairman, Univ of CA Berkeley, Dept of Afro Am Studies, Berkeley, CA 94720.

JONES, RENA TALLEY
Educator. **PERSONAL:** Born Aug 03, 1937, Pine Mountain, GA. **EDUCATION:** Morris Brown Coll, BA 1960; Atlanta U, MS 1967; Wayne State U, PhD 1974. **CAREER:** Spelman Coll, asst prof of biology, chairperson 1973-; Wayne State Univ, graduate asst 1967-73; Fulton County Bd of Educ, instructor 1961-66; Lee County Bd of Educ, instructor 1960-61; Washington DC, partic, pre-med health careers advs & conf; Columbia MD; Pinehurts NC; Tulane Medical Coll; Univ of FL School of Med; Argonne Natl Lab on Air Pollution, course; Macy Summer Inst in Premed Educ, 1977; Chautauqua-type Prgram for Rnat Sci Found, reviewer Health Careers Office, dir. **ORGANIZATIONS:** Mem hlth careers com; adv AtlantaUniv Ctr Viol Hon Soc; mem Am Assn for Advcmt of Sci; Am Soc for Microbiol; GA Acad of Sci; asso mem Socof Sigma Xi; Beta Kappa Chi Nat Sci Hon Soc; sci fair judge, sec sch. **HONORS/ACHIEVEMENTS:** Nat Sci Found Grant 1966-67; Spec Hlth Careers Opport Grant-dir; tchng Asstshp Wayne StateUniv 1967-73; biol publ 1968-74. **BUSINESS ADDRESS:** Associate Professor, Spellman College, 350 Spelman Lane SW, Atlanta, GA 30314.

JONES, RICHMOND ADDISON
Business executive/graphic designer. **PERSONAL:** Born Jul 09, 1937, Chicago, IL; son of Dr Silas Jones and Mabel Jones; married Christine Ann Osada; children: Philip Frederick. **EDUCATION:** Univ of IL, 1956-57; Amer Acad of Art, AA 1957-59; School of Visual Arts 1959-61. **CAREER:** Batten Barton Durstine & Osborn, asst/assoc art dir 1961-66; J Walter Thompson Co, art dir 1966-68; Jones James & Jameson Inc, pres 1968-69; Fuller Smith & Ross, art dir 1969-70; Richmond A Jones Graphics, owner/designer 1970-. **ORGANIZATIONS:** Mem Intl House Assoc 1959-62; dir/mem Sponsors for Ed Opportunities 1965-70; founder/vp/mem Group for Advertising Progress (Devel Minority Opportunities) 1966-70; dir/mem IL Epilepsy League 1972-74; dir/mem Soc of Typographic Arts 1972-; mem Amer Inst of Graphic Arts 1975-; mem Chicago Press Club 1980, Chicago Assoc of Commerce & Industry 1986. **HONORS/ACHIEVEMENTS:** Highest Readership (2 awds) Design News 1966; Published Art Direction Mag 1968; Selected Top Creative Visual Talent Amer Showcase 1978-; winner of Max Awd for brochure produced for Underwriters Labs Inc from TCR Graphics 1985; judge for Typographers Intl Awd Prog 1985; judge for awards program Acad for HealthServ Mktg of Amer Mktg Assoc 1986. **MILITARY SERVICE:** AUS Sergeant 1962-68; Marksmanship, Good Conduct Medal, Cert of Achievement 1963-64. **HOME ADDRESS:** 2530 W Eastwood Ave, Chicago, IL 60625.

JONES, ROBBIE NEELY
Librarian. **PERSONAL:** Born Jun 25, 1940, W Point, MS; married Eddie Charles; children: Christopher Charles, Amy Michelle. **EDUCATION:** TN StateUniv Nashville, BS 1962;Univ of MS, MLS 1970; MS State U, doctoral studies. **CAREER:** MS State Univ, asst prof, documents librarian; Starkville Public Schs, librarian 1965-68; W Point Public Schools, English teacher 1962-65. **ORGANIZATIONS:** Pres MS Library Asn GODORT 1977-78; vice pres MS Library Assn NE Section 1978-79; chmn Women's Week Activities; Today's Black Woman MS StateUniv 1978; presOverstreet PTA 1978-79; vice pres PTA Council Starkville Public Schs 1979-80; mem Starkville C of C Educ Com 1980; mem Adv Bd The United Way Starkville MS 1980; mem Adv Bd The Gifted & Talented Starkville Public Schs 1980; librarian Second Bapt Ch. **HONORS/ACHIEVEMENTS:** First black mem Faculty Council MS StateUniv 1976-77; listed, "Personalities of the S" 1975-76; "Outstanding Young Women of Am" 1976; named Outstanding Woman at MS State U, Women's Week Status of Women MS StateUniv 1978. **BUSINESS ADDRESS:** MS State Univ, Box 5408, Mississippi State, MS 39762.

JONES, ROBERT ALTON
Attorney. **PERSONAL:** Born Jan 30, 1944, Houston, TX; married Velma Chester; children: Jessica. **EDUCATION:** TX So U, JD 1972; TX SoUniv Sch of Law, BA. **CAREER:** Anderson Hodge Jones & Hoyt Inc, Houston, TX, stockholder & vice pres 1974-;Univ Houston, part-time professor; Teamster's Local 968, official 1969-73; Private Practice, atty. **ORGANIZATIONS:** Mem Houston Lawyer's Assn; State Bar of TX; ABA; TX Crim Defense Lawyer's Assn; Bus & Professional Mens Orgn; Phi Alpha Delta; US Dist Ct, So & Eastern Dist of TX; participant Am Bar Assn Seminar of Criminal Defense Litigation. **HONORS/ACHIEVEMENTS:** Recipient achvmnt awards from Student Govt & Student Bar Assn; Am Jurisprudence awards for Debtors & Creditors Rights & Oil & Gas; listed Who's Who in Black America 1974-75. **BUSINESS ADDRESS:** Attorney, Robert A Jones, 3000 Post Oak Blvd, Ste 1400, Houston, TX 77056.

JONES, ROBERT EARL
Clergyman. **PERSONAL:** Born Feb 11, 1942, Franklinton, NC; married Karen; children: Darrell Amani. **EDUCATION:** Houston-Tillotson Coll, BA 1965; Yale Univ, MDiv 1969, STM 1970. **CAREER:** Coll Hill Comm Ch (UP), asst pastor, sr pastor; Grand Ave United Ch of Christ, asst pastor 1974-77; New Haven Anti-Poverty Agy, dep dir 1974-75; Yale Div Sch, asst prof 1970-74; Fair Haven Parents Ministry, exec dir 1967-74; So CT State Coll, adjunct prof 1974-75; Quinnipiac Coll, sem instr 1968-69. **ORGANIZATIONS:** Adv bd CT Mental Health Center 1974-77; bd pres Black Coalition of New Haven 1970-75; vp, bd pres Natl Coalition for Econ Justice; consultant Natl Acad for Churches in transition 1970-75; Natl Alliance of Businessmen of New Haven 1970-72. **HONORS/ACHIEVEMENTS:** Richard Allen Achievement Award 1970; Albert B Beebe Award 1970. **BUSINESS ADDRESS:** Senior Pastor, College Hill Community Church, 1547 Philadelphia Dr, Dayton, OH 45406.

JONES, ROBERT G.
Business executive. **PERSONAL:** Born Jul 04, 1936, Ft Worth, TX; son of Ocie Jones (deceased) and Ruby F Jones. **EDUCATION:** USC, 1953-58. **CAREER:** LA Herald Dispatch, entertainment editor 1957-68; Rogers & Cowan, acct exec 1968-70; Motown Records, publ mgr 1970-75, exec dir press & art rel 1975-87; MJJ Productions, vice pres, communications & media relations, 1987-. **ORGANIZATIONS:** Bd dir USO 1977-83, vice pres 1983-84; bd dir Hollywood C of C; chmn bd dir Beverly Hills NAACP 1971-83; pres Black Public Rel Soc of Southern CA 1985-87. **HONORS/ACHIEVEMENTS:** Image Awards 1973-74 responsible for raising over $180,000 for br with those 2 award shows; Men of Distinct 1976; Who's Who in Public Relations 1976; recipient of the Natl Black Showcases 1986; Par Excellence Awd in Oakland CA; Pioneer of Excellence NY 1989. **BUSINESS ADDRESS:** Vice President, Communications & Media Relations, MJJ Productions, 10880 Wilshire Blvd, Suite 2003, Los Angeles, CA 90024.

JONES, ROBERT WESLEY
Business executive. **PERSONAL:** Born Jul 24, 1929, Boston, MA; married Gudrun Heider-Jones; children: Todd, Stacy. **EDUCATION:** Howard Univ, 1950; NY Univ, BS 1956; NY Law Schl, Cert NY Bar 1960. **CAREER:** Pianta Dosi and Assc, vice pres 1966-1968; Ctiy of NY, deputy comm 1966-68; Burnett Constr Co, ex vice pres 1968-1970; Robert W Jones and Assc Inc, pres. **ORGANIZATIONS:** Pres Independent Fee Appraisers (NYC) 1984-, Citizens Housing and Planning Council 1974-; chrmn Tougaloo Clge Bd of Trustees 1980-; mem bd adv NY Univ Real Est Inst 1974-; exec comm Assc for Better NY 1975-; mem bd adv Federal Natl Mtg Assc 1985-. **HONORS/ACHIEVEMENTS:** Articles on housing and planning 1970; Adj Prof NY Univ Real Est Planning 1972-. **MILITARY SERVICE:** USMC sgt 1950-54; Purple Heart 1952. **BUSINESS ADDRESS:** President, Robert W Jones & Assc Inc, 80 Fifth Ave, New York, NY 10011.

JONES, ROSCOE T., JR.
Dentist. **PERSONAL:** Born Jan 25, 1935, Washington, DC; married Marva A J; children: Nancy Ellen. **EDUCATION:** Howard U, BS 1958; Howard U, DDS 1965. **CAREER:** Self-employed, dentist 1968-; Dental Clinic Ft Belvoir AUS Dental Corp, acting chief 1966. **ORGANIZATIONS:** Mem Robert T Freeman Dental Soc 1970; mem Acad of Gen Dentistry 1973-; treas Metro Dental Assoc Chartered 1978-; Sunday sch tchr All Souls UnitarianCh 1970-77. **HONORS/ACHIEVEMENTS:** Outstanding Cadet, Howard U. **MILITARY SERVICE:** AUS ROTC 1959; AUS cpt served 2 1/2 yrs. **BUSINESS ADDRESS:** 1238 Monroe St NE, Washington, DC 20017.

JONES, ROY JUNIOS
Educator. **PERSONAL:** Born Nov 15, 1925, Longview, TX; married Pauline Carol Finley; children: Roderick, Arlyss, Valerie. **EDUCATION:** Morgan State U, BS psychology 1951; HowardUniv ms 1954; am u;; phd soc-psychology 1961. **CAREER:** Crownsville State Hospital, chief psychology servs, dir research 1961-62; Washington Action for Youth, dir training 1963-64; Howard Univ, mem faculty & admin 1964, asst clinical prof psychiatry 1967-69, prof urban studies 1969-77, dir Center Comm Studies 1967-72, urban studies program 1967-72, asst dean Graduate School 1967-71. **ORGANIZATIONS:** Chmn bd examiners psychol, Wash, 1972-78; mem Am Soc Training Devel, natl chmn professional standards, ethics com 1969; Am, Eastern, DC, MD Psychol Assns; AAAS; soc psychol pres Social Systems Intervention Inc, Wash, 1967-; bd chmn Soc Systems Devel Inst Inc 1980-; consult govt pub & pvt agys; mem DC adv com US Commn Civil Rights 1968-78; govt rev bd Mayor's Youth Oppor Serv 1969; bd overseers Dag Hammarskjold Coll, Columbia, MD 1967-71; bd dirs Wash Heart Assn 1969-72; chmn gov Bd councilUniv Instr Urban Affairs 1970-76; dir Nat Assn Minority Group Urbanologists; Psi Chi; Alpha Kappa Mu; consult editor Jour of Professional Psychology 1969-76. **MILITARY SERVICE:** Decorated Bronze Star Medal; AUS 1944-46. **BUSINESS ADDRESS:** 3603 14 St NW, Washington, DC 20010.

JONES, RUTH BRASWELL
Business executive. **PERSONAL:** Born Nov 24, 1914, Rocky Mount, NC; married Eddie J Jones (deceased) (deceased). **EDUCATION:** Brick Jr Clge, Salutatorian 1933; Elizabeth City State Clge, BS Educ 1938; A&T State Univ, MSc Educ (Hnr Stdnt) 1959. **CAREER:** Halifax Cty School, elementary teacher 1933-62; Rocky Mount City School, elementary teacher 1962-80; Hammocks Beach Corp, pres. **ORGANIZATIONS:** Pres NC Tchrs Assc 1968-70, NC Assc of Educ 1971-72; dir Natl Educ Assc 1975-80; parliamentarian Natl Educ Assc 1968-73, SW regional dir NEA classroom teachers 1972-76; NC Chptr Zeta Phi Beta Sor 1975-80, Gaylor Chptr Order of Eastern Star 1982-84; NEA-R advisory council; Rocky Mount Human RelationsCouncil; pres Brown-Pearson Federated Clb. **HONORS/ACHIEVEMENTS:** Terry Sanford Award for Ldrshp and Creativity in Educ 1972; NEA'S Trenholm Award for fostering intercultural understanding 1982; NC Distg Women's Award ForOutstanding Educ 1984; article pub Blacks in Amer History from 1492 to the Present. **HOME ADDRESS:** 509 Myrtle Ave, Rocky Mount, NC 27801.

JONES, SADIE WATERFORD
Business executive. **PERSONAL:** Born Aug 13, 1889, Memphis, TN; widowed. **EDUCATION:** Univ Chicago, AB; attended, Tuskegee Inst, Langston Univ. **CAREER:** Muskogee OK High School, Latin teacher; Illinois Commn on Delinquency Prevention, consultant. **ORGANIZATIONS:** Natl staff, Playground & Recreation Assn of Amer; supr, Dept of Correction Chicago; organizer/founder, Beatrice Caffrey Youth Serv; dir/founder, Halfway House Comm. **BUSINESS ADDRESS:** Consultant, Illinois Commission on Delinquency Prevention, 213 E 50th St, Chicago, IL 60615.

JONES, SAM H., SR.
Business executive. **PERSONAL:** Born Jun 29, 1938, Denver, CO; married Carolyn Ruth Spain; children: Marya, Sam, Michael. **EDUCATION:** Regis Coll Denver, CO, BA sociolo-

gy (cum laude) 1966;Univ of NM Sch of Law, JD 1969. **CAREER:** US Equal Employ Oppor Comm, regional atty;Univ of NM Sch of Law, dir title Vii law clinic lectr in law 1975-76; US Equal Employ Oppor Commn, sr trial atty 1973-75; Boise Cascade Corp Diversified Mfg, compliance mgr 1971-73; Reginald Herber Smith Comm Lawyer Flwhp Prog Albuquerque Legal Aid Soc, atty 1970-71. **ORGANIZATIONS:** Prog dir CO Civil Rights Commn 1969-70; mem 10th Circuit Ct of Appeals 1969; mem State Bar of NM 1969-; mem Nat Bar Assn 1971-; mem US 5th Circuit 1978-. **HONORS/ACHIEVEMENTS:** Margaret Keiper Daley AwdUniv of NM Sch of Law. **MILITARY SERVICE:** USN petty ofcr 2 1957-62. **BUSINESS ADDRESS:** President, Indianapolis Urban League, 850 N Meridian St, Indianapolis, IN 46204.

JONES, SAMUEL
Athletic director. **PERSONAL:** Born Jun 24, 1933, Laurinburg, NC; married Gladys Chavis; children: Aubre, Phyllis, Michael, Terri, Ashley. **EDUCATION:** North Carolina Coll, BS. **CAREER:** Boston Celtics, professional basketball player 1957-69; North Carolina Central Univ, former head basktball coach; New Orleans Jazz Basketball Team, LA, former asst coach; Fed City Coll, Washington, former dir athletics 1969-77; Blue Ribbon Sports, NIKE Shoe Div, head of promotions. **ORGANIZATIONS:** Mem Kappa Alpha Psi. **MILITARY SERVICE:** AUS.

JONES, SHIRLEY JOAN
Educational administrator. **PERSONAL:** Born Nov 26, 1931, New York, NY; married Sande R Jones, Sr; children: Susan, Sande Jr. **EDUCATION:** NY Univ, BA 1954, MA 1956, MSW 1964; Columbia Univ, Doctorate of Soc Work 1977. **CAREER:** NY Univ Schl of Social Wrk, asst prof 1967-70; State Univ NY at Stony Brook, assc prof 1972-78; NY Univ Metro Studies, adj prof 1973-77; Univ of Southern MS, dean prof 1978-. **ORGANIZATIONS:** Comm Commission of Child Support Enforcement 1985; bd dir Gov Office of Vol Citizen Participation 1985; bd dir Natl Alliance of Bus 1982-85; mem Natl Assc of Black Soc Wrkrs, Natl Assc of Social Wrkrs, Council on Social Work Educ, Intl Assc of Social Work; bd of dir Amer Humane Assoc; mem State Constitutional Change Comm 1986-87, Intl Comm of NASW; commr on accrediation Council on Social Work Educ. **HONORS/ACHIEVEMENTS:** Waldoff's Ach 1983; Soc Wrkr of the Year NABSW MS Chptr 1983; Distg Srv Award Gov Office of Vol Citizen Part 1983; Woman of the Year Hattiesbg City Businessmen's Club 1981; Dedicated Serv Awd NABSW Natl 1986; Certificate of Appreciation DHHS/OHDS/AFCYF 1986. **BUSINESS ADDRESS:** Dean, Univ of Southern Mississippi, Southern Station Box 5114, Hattiesburg, MS 39406.

JONES, SIDNEY A., JR.
Retired judge/attorney. **PERSONAL:** Born Jul 02, 1909, Sandersville, GA; son of Sidney A Jones and Mary Hollis Jones; married Roma Lawson, Aug 10, 1935; children: Roma Jones-Stewart, Laurel Jones-Boyd, Sidney A Jones, III. **EDUCATION:** Atlanta U, BA 1928; Northwestern U, JD 1931. **CAREER:** Circuit Ct of Cook Co, judge 1964-80; US Dept of Labor, legal staff 1939-46; Municipal Ct of Chicago, judge 1960-64. **ORGANIZATIONS:** Mem Chicago City Council 1955-59; mem, bd dir, past pres Cook County Bar Assn; life mem NAACP; Alpha Phi Alpha; vp, bd dir Chicago Boys Club; trustee emeritus Atlanta U; trustee Coppin Memorial AME Church. **HOME ADDRESS:** 2851 King Drive, Suite 1202, Chicago, IL 60616.

JONES, SIDNEY ALEXANDER
Physician. **PERSONAL:** Born Sep 25, 1934; son of Herbert A Jones and Ann E Jones; married Vuriley Maria Harris; children: Raquel, Erika. **EDUCATION:** Univ W Indies, MB, BS 1963; Freedmens Hosp, intern 1964-65; Howard Univ Hosp, residency 1965-69. **CAREER:** Howard Univ, asst instr 1967, asst prof 1971, dir 1976; Parkside Neighborhood Health Clinic, chief 1969-71; DC General Hosp, med officer 1971-76, chairman Ob/Gyn. **ORGANIZATIONS:** Mem Am Fertility Soc; Am Coll Ob-Gyn; Royal Soc of Med; Intl Coll of Surgeons; DC Med Soc. **HONORS/ACHIEVEMENTS:** Daniel Hale Williams Award 1966. **BUSINESS ADDRESS:** Chairman Ob/Gyn, DC General Hospital, 19th & Massachusetts Ave SE, Washington, DC 20003.

JONES, SIDNEY EUGENE
Urban social service administrator. **PERSONAL:** Born Jul 11, 1936, New York, NY; married Yolande Goodison; children: Cydnie, Stephen. **EDUCATION:** Columbia College, BA 1959; Columbia Univ Sch of Social Work, MS 1968. **CAREER:** New York City Dept of Social Svcs, field dir 1968-70; Mayor's Office NYC, dist mgr 1970-76; State Communities Aid Assoc, project dir 1976-78; Comm Serv Soc, administrator 1978-. **ORGANIZATIONS:** Mem Alpha Phi Alpha Frat 1956-; mem Mt Vernon Human Rights Commn 1982-84, Mt Vernon Youth Board 1984-86. **HONORS/ACHIEVEMENTS:** Blanche Ittleson Awd Social Serv Career Ctr 1973. **MILITARY SERVICE:** Army Natl Guard capt 1953-65. **BUSINESS ADDRESS:** Administrator, Community Service Society, 105 East 22nd St, New York, NY 10010.

JONES, SONDRA MICHELLE
Educator. **PERSONAL:** Born Sep 07, 1948, Norfolk, VA. **EDUCATION:** Morgan State, BA 1970;Univ of PA Sch of Edn, grad work; HarvardUniv Grad Sch of Edn;Temple U, grad study Master's Cand 1977. **CAREER:** Buck Lane Memorial Community Day Care Center, Haverford, PA, dir 1976-; Devel Disabilities Day Care Center PA; educ dir comm coord teacher 1972-73; St Martin's Day Care Center Baltimore, teacher 1971-72; Health & Welfare Council of Baltimore, social work trainee 1968; STOP Program Norfolk, VA, rec counselor 1967; Health & Welfare Council, social work trainee 1966. **ORGANIZATIONS:** Mem Alliance of Blk Soc Workers; Ivy Club of Alpha Kappa Sor; Nat Assn for the Educ of Young Children; Phil Assn for Retarded Children; Child Welfare League of Am; Phil Coord Child Care Counc 4 C'S; Nat Counc of Blk Child Devel; Black Child Devel Inst. **HONORS/ACHIEVEMENTS:** Particptd in HarvardUniv Early Childhood Educ Prog unde Schlrshp from Harvard U.

JONES, SPENCER
Clergyman. **PERSONAL:** Born Mar 24, 1946, Poplar Bluff, MO; married Kathy AE Drake; children: Daliz E, Trayon D, Shemen A, Melinet MB. **EDUCATION:** North Central Bible Coll, BA Religion 1972. **ORGANIZATIONS:** Alternate presbytery Assemblies of God; vice pres of Student Govt; exec dir Natl Inner-City Workers of Amer; mem Natl Inner-City Workers Conference; mem of the bd of Chicago Teen Challenge; mem of the Decade of Harvest Committee; (to be) one of the speakers at the 1989 General Council. **HONORS/ACHIEVEMENTS:** Article in The Pentecostal Evangel 1984, The Pentecostal Minister. **MILITARY SERVICE:** AUS sp5. **BUSINESS ADDRESS:** Pastor, Southside Tabernacle, 7742 S Racine, Chicago, IL 60620.

JONES, STANLEY BERNARD
Higher education administrator. **PERSONAL:** Born Mar 18, 1961, Greenwwod, SC; son of Herbert C Jones, Jr and Maggie P Jones. **EDUCATION:** Radford Univ, BS 1984, MS Educ 1987. **CAREER:** Radford Univ, asst dir of admissions, dir, special student services. **ORGANIZATIONS:** VA Admin Council on Black Concerns 1984-; Treasurer 1988-; EEO, mem 1985-; NAACP, mem 1985-; National Association of Student Personnel Administrators 1987-; Assoc of Handicapped Student Service Programs in Post-secondary Education 1987-; Omega Psi Phi Fraternity 1988-. **HONORS/ACHIEVEMENTS:** Outstanding Young Man of American 1985; Outstanding Service Award Radford Univ Chapter NAACP 1988. **BUSINESS ADDRESS:** Director, Special Student Services, Radford University, PO Box 5705, Radford, VA 24141-5705.

JONES, STEPHANIE TUBBS
Judge. **PERSONAL:** Born Sep 10, 1949, Cleveland, OH; daughter of Andrew Tubbs and Mary Tubbs; married Mervyn L Jones; children: Mervyn L II. **EDUCATION:** Case Western Reserve Univ, BA 1971, Law Sch JD 1974. **CAREER:** Case Western Reserve Univ, Cleveland, OH, resident director, 1971-74, research instructor, part time instructor in Afro-American Studies program, 1974; Northeast Ohio Regional Sewer District, asst gen counsel 1974-76; Cuyahoga County Prosecutor's Office, asst co prosecutor 1976-79; Equal Employment Opportunities Commission, trial attorney 1979-81; Cleveland Municipal Ct, judge 1982-83; Common Pleas Court of Cuyahoga Co, judge 1983—. **ORGANIZATIONS:** Trustee, Cleveland Hearing & Speech Ctr; past trustee, Legal Aid Soc of Cleveland, Bethany Baptist Church; trustee, Regional Council on Alcoholism; trustee, Federation for Community Planning; mem, Greater Cleveland Alumnae chapter, Delta Sigma Theta Sorority Inc; mem, Cleveland Bar Assn; mem, Natl Bar Assn; mem, past treas, Norman S Minor Bar Assn; bd of trustees, Cleveland Public Library; trustee, Community Reentry Prog, Leadership, Cleveland 1983-84. **HONORS/ACHIEVEMENTS:** Martin Luther King Jr Award recipient, Case Western Reserve Univ, Law School, 1974; Outstanding Young Woman of America, 1982; featured in Ebony magazine, 1983, 1984; Young Alumnus Award, Case Western Reserve Univ, 1984; Panhellenic Council Action Award, 1984; Urban League of Greater Cleveland award for volunteer service in law and justice, 1986; Woman of the Year award, Cleveland Chapter, Natl Association of Negro Business and Professional Women's Clubs, 1987; Outstanding Citizens Award, Minority Construction Coalition, 1987; Pacesetter Award, Directory of Greater Cleveland's Enterprising Women, 1987; Valued Alumnus Award, Collinwood High School, 1988; Centennial Citation, Flora Stone Mather College, Case Western Reserve Univ, 1988. **BUSINESS ADDRESS:** Judge Common Pleas Court, Cuyahoga Co, 1200 Ontario St, Cleveland, OH 44113.

JONES, SUSAN SUTTON
High school principal. **PERSONAL:** Born in Nanticoke, MD; daughter of Douglass J. Sutton and Emma Evans Sutton; married Dr Clifton Ralph Jones; children: George Henry Miles Jr. **EDUCATION:** Fisk Univ, BS 1946; Johns Hopkins Univ, Master of Educ 1965; Temple Univ, Doctor of Educ 1984. **CAREER:** Dept Publ Asst Philadelphia PA, caseworker 1946-49; Baltimore City Publ Schl, biology tchr 1949-63, guidance cnslr 1963-67, schl admin 1967-84; Edmondson Sr HS, principal 1975-84; Morgan State Univ, visiting prof 1986-. **ORGANIZATIONS:** Historian Baltimore Alumna Delta Sigma Theta; pres Baltimore Chptr Continental Soc 1983-; historian, pres, mem Alpha Wives 1983-85; pres Alpha Phi Alpha 1986; bd of dir Delta Foundation, Baltimore Alumnae; charter mem The Societas Docta, Inc. Feb. 1987; mem Foster Care Review Bd 1987-91; commr Department Social Services Commn Advisory 1988-91. **HONORS/ACHIEVEMENTS:** Awardee Natl Science Fnd 1958; prin Ford Fnd High Schl Grant 1982-83; Publ Srv Award Miles W Connor Chptr VA Union Univ 1983; citation for excellence in maintaining discipline Phi Delta Kappa 1980; panelist MD Humanities Council 1984, Natl Assoc of Secondary Sch Admin 1984; Mayor's Citation for public service 1987; founders day service award Delta Sigma Theta 1987. **HOME ADDRESS:** 1190 W Northern Pkwy 524, Baltimore, MD 21210.

JONES, SYLVESTER
Educator. **PERSONAL:** Born Mar 11, 1942, Tulsa; married Carole; children: Nicole Lane. **EDUCATION:** Grand Rapids Jr Coll, AA 1962; Wichita State U, BA 1966; MI State U, MA 1972, presently doctoral candidate. **CAREER:** William C Little Elementary, teacher 1966-67; Jefferson School, 1967-70; Neighborhood Health Servs, admin 1970-71; Sigsbee Elementary School, comm school dir 1968, teacher 1969-70; prin 1972-. **ORGANIZATIONS:** Past polemarch Kappa Alpha Psi, Grand Rapids Alumni; mem GR Elem Admn Assn; Ta-wa-si Athletic Assn; Sheldon Complex Adv Com; MI StateUniv Alumni Assn; bd dirs Neighborhood Hlth Svcs; adv Eastown Comm Assn; mem Grand Rapids br NAACP; first orgn Sickle Cell Program 1971; coord New Bldg Prgm,Grand Rapids Pub Sch Sys. **BUSINESS ADDRESS:** 1250 Sigsbee SE, Grand Rapids, MI 49506.

JONES, TERRY (BIG T)
Professional athlete. **PERSONAL:** Born Nov 08, 1956; married Willie Mays; children: Terry Jr, Teresha Maya. **EDUCATION:** AL Univ, BS Ed, Indust Arts. **CAREER:** Green Bay Packers, nose tackle 1978-. **HONORS/ACHIEVEMENTS:** Shared tackle honors for defensive line 1982. **BUSINESS ADDRESS:** Green Bay Packers, 1265 Lombardi Ave, Green Bay, WI 54307.

JONES, THEODORE
Educator, elected official. **PERSONAL:** Born Dec 23, 1923, Menifee, AR; married Laura Mattison; children: Linda Paxton, Theodore Jr. **EDUCATION:** UAPB, BS 1949; attended UCA Conway, AR. **CAREER:** Pine St HS, principal 1966-70; Faulkner Cty Dist 11, 1st black justice of the peace 1981-86; Conway Jr HS, teacher. **ORGANIZATIONS:** Bd mem Falkner Cty Selective Serv 1975-78; 1st black elected justice of the peace Faulkner Cty 1981-86; pres AR Voc Teachers Assoc 1983-84; bd mem AR Vocational Assoc 1983-84; Notary Public. **HONORS/ACHIEVEMENTS:** Cert of Appreciation for Service of Selective Serv Bd Mem by Pres Gerald Ford 1976. **MILITARY SERVICE:** AUS corpl 1944-46; Service in South Pacific, Good Conduct. **HOME ADDRESS:** 1258 Lincoln St, Conway, AR 72032. **BUSINESS ADDRESS:** Teacher, Justice of the Peace, Conway Jr High School, Prince & Davis Sts, Conway, AR 72032.

JONES, THEODORE A.
Certified public accountant. **PERSONAL:** Born in Pueblo, CO; married B Mae Howard; children: Janice, Lynn. **EDUCATION:** Univ of IL, BS 1933, CPA 1940. **CAREER:** Jones Anderson & Co, partner 1940-; Nat Bd NAACP-SCF 1976-; Chicago Pk Dist, commr 1977-; King Tercq Mcdonalds Franchises, chmn; Chicago Burr Oak Cemetary Assn, sec treas & dir; Serv Federal Savings & Loan Assn, sec treas & dir; WJPC Radio, pres 1970-74; Dept of Revenue, State of IL, dir 1967-69; OEO, reg dir 1966-67; Supreme Life Ins Co, sr vp, gen mgr 1955-67. **ORGANIZATIONS:** Mem Am Inst of CPAs; IL Soc of CPAs; Nat Assn of Tax Adminstr; bd trusteesUniv of IL; bd trustees Talladega Coll; bd mem Economic Club of Chicago; mem Chicago br NAACP; adv commn Cook Co Personnel; Chicago Commn on Human Relations; Cosmopolitan C of C; People United to Save Humanity; mem Chicago Yacht Club; Burnham Park Yacht Club; Royal Coterie of Snakes; The Forty Club; The Chicagoans; Beta Boule, Sigma Pi Phi. **HONORS/ACHIEVEMENTS:** Recipient Thomas J Crowe Award, Cath Interracial Couns 1958; Beta Gamma Sigma, Scholastic Honors; NAACP Outstanding Serv Award 1971. **BUSINESS ADDRESS:** 471 E 31st St, Chicago, IL 60616.

JONES, THEODORE CORNELIUS
Educator, dentist. **PERSONAL:** Born Sep 29, 1941, Jackson, MS; married Clintoria Inge; children: Dana, Vann, Margo, Kristen, Karrin. **EDUCATION:** Tougaloo Coll, BS 1962; Howard U, DDS 1966; Walter Reed, cert 1969; cert 1970; Tufts U, 1973. **CAREER:** Univ of MS School of Dentistry, asst prof 1974-; Private Practice, 1974-; Howard Univ, extramural practice 1975; Jackson Hindscompr Health Center, staff dentist 1972-73; MS private practice 1970-71. **ORGANIZATIONS:** Am Den Assn; Nat Den Assn; Am Assn of Orthodontists; MS Den Assn; MS Den Soc; Jackson-Tougaloo Alumni Club; pres Tufts Assn of Orthodon; AlphaPhi Alpha; Musica Sacra Singers; New Stage Theatre. **HONORS/ACHIEVEMENTS:** Who's Who in S & SW 1972; Outst Young Men of Am 1974; Who's Who in Am Colls & U'S 1962. **MILITARY SERVICE:** USAF capt 1966-68. **BUSINESS ADDRESS:** PO Box 9606, Jackson, MS 39206.

JONES, THERESA DIANE
Government administrator. **PERSONAL:** Born Jun 07, 1953, Erie, PA; daughter of Robert P Jones and Mable R Jones. **EDUCATION:** Edinboro State Coll, BA 1976. **CAREER:** Pinellas Oppor Council Inc, sr outreach worker 1976-77; Information & Referral, suicide intervention spec 1977; City of St Petersburg, relocation officer 1977-80, administrative serv officer 1980-86, MBE coord 1986-. **ORGANIZATIONS:** Bd dirs Pinellas Oppor Council Inc 1984-; bd govs St Petersburg Area Chamber of Commerce 1985; co-chair Community Alliance 1985; real estate assoc LouBrown Realty & Mortgage Inc 1985-88; sec Natl Forum Black Public Administrators, Tampa Bay Chap 1986-. **HONORS/ACHIEVEMENTS:** Graduate Presidential Classroom for Young Americans 1971; graduate Leadership St Petersburg 1984; Up & Comers Award, Price Waterhouse 1988. **HOME ADDRESS:** PO Box 3986, St Petersburg, FL 33731. **BUSINESS ADDRESS:** Minority Bus Enterprise Coord, City of St Petersburg, PO Box 2842, St Petersburg, FL 33731.

JONES, THERESA MITCHELL
Business executive. **PERSONAL:** Born May 12, 1917, Denison, TX; married Artis Jones; children: Leroy, Pat, Michael, Anthony. **EDUCATION:** Compton Coll CA, AA 1951; Univ of Pacific, BS 1973. **CAREER:** LA County Bureau of Public Assistance, clerk-typist 1951-55; Beauty Salons, propr 3 1956-66; Real Estate, part-time salesman 1961-74; Elementary Sch, teacher 1971-74; City of Stockton Comm Devel Renewal Redevel Agency, relocation/real estate asst 1974-. **ORGANIZATIONS:** Mem Natl Beauty Culturist League 1959-66; dir SE Ctr 1968-70; dir WICS San Joaquin Co 1970-; assoc mem Stockton Real Estate Bd 1972-75; organizer dir Progressive Youth of Compton; supr Jr Ch. **HONORS/ACHIEVEMENTS:** Woman of the Yr Awd LA Alpha Lambda Chap of Theta Nu Sigma Sor 1966; Awd UOP Comm Involvement Prog 1973. **BUSINESS ADDRESS:** Relo/Real Estate Asst, Comm Devel Renewal Redevel Agency, City of Stockton, 742 E Charter Way, Stockton, CA 95206.

JONES, THOMAS L.
Attorney. **PERSONAL:** Born Jan 12, 1941, Greenwood, MS; married Nettie Byrd; children: Martilla R, Nicole L, LaTanya Dionne, Thomas II. **EDUCATION:** Tougaloo Coll, BS 1963; HowardUniv Law Sch, 1971. **CAREER:** Continental Tel Corp, asst vp, legal atty 1972-; Fed Hwy Adminstrn, Wash, spl asst chief counsel 1971-72; Neighborhood Consumer Info Ctr, Wash, prog dir 1970-71; Cook Co Circuit Ct, probation officer 1965-66; US Peace Corps, Philippines, 1963-64. **ORGANIZATIONS:** Mem Am, Nat, DC Bar Assns; Practicing Law Instr; Phi Alpha Delta; adv couns Fed City Coll Psychology Dept; mem Urban League. **MILITARY SERVICE:** AUS sp/5 1966-68. **BUSINESS ADDRESS:** Partner, McFadden, Evans & Sill, 2000 M St NW, Ste 260, Washington, DC 20036.

JONES, THOMAS RUSSELL
Retired judge, attorney. **PERSONAL:** Born Aug 05, 1913, Brooklyn, NY; married Bertha; children: Margaret, David. **EDUCATION:** St John's Univ, LLD; NYU, LLM (Intl Law). **CAREER:** General Practice, atty; Civil Ct NYC, judge; Supreme Ct State of NY, justice. **ORGANIZATIONS:** Pres Supreme Ct Justices Assn NYC; mem NY State Constl Conv; mem NY State Assembly; founder/chmn Bedford Stuyvesant Restoration Corp 1966-72; founder Unity Democratic Club 1959-64. **MILITARY SERVICE:** ETO mem Gen Ct Martial Bd 1st Lt. **BUSINESS ADDRESS:** Attorney-At-Law, 160 Montague St, Brooklyn, NY 11201.

JONES, TIMOTHY EARL
Administrator. **PERSONAL:** Born Sep 21, 1948, Atlanta, GA; married Lennie B Warner; children: Alvin Henderson, Andrea, Andriette, Timothy E, II. **EDUCATION:** GA State U, BA 1974; Woodrow Wilson Sch of Law, attended 1975-76; GA State U, MEd 1977. **CAREER:** GA Bd of Pardons & Paroles, hearing examiner (1st black) 1977-; GA Dept of Offender Rehabiliation, chief parole officer 1976-77, parole officer 1974-76; Pat Jarvis Counselor Center Halfway House, counselor, 1972-74. **ORGANIZATIONS:** Mem, Amer Parole Assn, 1977, GA Parole Assn 1979, NAACP 1976-, Butler St YMCA 1978-; first vice pres Y's Men Intl 1978-. **HONORS/ACHIEVEMENTS:** Appreciation Plaque award, Butler St YMCA 1978. **MILITARY SERVICE:** AUS sgt E-5 1968-70; recipient Purple Heart/Bronze Star/Air Medal/Vietnam Campaign Ribbon AUS 1969. **BUSINESS ADDRESS:** GA Bd of Pardons & Paroles, 800 Peachtree St Ste 610, Atlanta, GA 30308.

JONES, VANN KINCKLE
Physician. **PERSONAL:** Born Nov 20, 1940, Flushing, NY; married Judith; children: Karen, Glenn. **EDUCATION:** Cornell U, BA 1962; HowardUniv Coll Med, MD 1966. **CAREER:** Jewish Hosp & Med Ctr of Brooklyn, dir med clinic 1974-; Downstate Med Ctr, asso attdng physician, asst clinical prof med 1976-; Kings Co Hosp, Resd 1967-70, intern 1966-67. **ORGANIZATIONS:** Mem NY State Med Soc; Kings Co Med Soc; Am Coll Physicians; NY Assn Ambulatory Care; diplomate Am Bd Intl Med; mem Alpha Omega Alpha Hon Med Soc 1966. **HONORS/ACHIEVEMENTS:** Hon mention All Am Lacrosse, CornellUniv 1962. **MILITARY SERVICE:** USAF maj 1970-72. **BUSINESS ADDRESS:** 555 Prospct Pl, Brooklyn, NY.

JONES, VELMA LOIS
Instructor. **EDUCATION:** Lemoyne-Owen Coll, BA; Columbia Univ, MA; Memphis State Univ, MI State Univ, grad study. **CAREER:** Hyde Park Elem Sch Memphis, instr; LeMoyne Owen Coll, MI Coll & Memphis Univ, master tchr for student tchrs; Cypress Jr HS Memphis, instr math. **ORGANIZATIONS:** Memphis Educ Assn; exec bd Memphis Educ Assn; parliamentarian co-fdr mem chrpsn Memphis chap Natl Educ Assn Black Caucus; del TN Educ Assn Rep Assembly 1970-79; del Natl Educ Assn Rep Assembly 1971-79; past pres W TN Educ Assn; bd dirs TN Educ Assn; Natl Cncl of Tchrs of Math; TN Cncl of Teachers of Math; Memphis area Teachers of Math; NEA concerns Com; TN Educ Assn; vice pres Memphis Dist Laymen's Cncl CME Ch; sec Soc Rel Missionary Soc ofW TN Ann Conf CME Ch; asst sec W TN Ann Conf & chpsn of com on soc concerns; parliamentarian TN Conf of NAACP Branches; Women's Missionary Cncl of CME Ch; mem Compilation com to revise the Ch Discipline; mem Staff for Leadership Fellows Prog & Pre-Boule Workshop of Alpha Kappa Alpha Sor; pastS Eastern Regional Dir; chtr mem Memphis Chaptr Amer Inst of Parliamentarians; N Memphis Area Adv Cncl; Natl Cncl of Negro Women; mem TN State Educ Assn; v chrpsn Shelby Co Housing Auth; Am Inst of Parliamentarians; dir Christian Educ Trinity Christian Meth Epis Ch. **HONORS/ACHIEVEMENTS:** First woman pres Memphis Br NAACP; Excellent Leadership & Outstanding Serv Awds Alpha Kappa Alpha 1966-70; Women of Yr 1974; Missionary of Yr 1975; TwentyMost Prominent Memphians 1975; Women Making History 1976; Brotherhood Awd 1977; listed 1976 editions, Who's Who Among Black Americans, Who's Who Among Amer Women 1977-78; Outstanding Woman in S Eastern Region; Women of Yr 1970; Comm Serv Awd 1958 1978; Certificate of Merit Awd NAACP 1972; numerous other civic awds; Outstanding Woman of the Yr Awd NAACP Women's Natl Conf 1980. **BUSINESS ADDRESS:** Math Instructor, Cypress Jr High School, 2109 Howell, Memphis, TN 38108.

JONES, VERNON A., JR.
Clergyman. **PERSONAL:** Born Sep 19, 1924, Brunswick Co, VA; married Lillian Clark; children: Cecilia, Harriett, Vernelle. **EDUCATION:** VA Union U, AB 1945; Bishop Payne Div Sch, BD 1948; VA Theol Sem, MDiv. **CAREER:** St Andrew's Episcopal Ch Tuskegee Inst, rector 1960-; vicar 1957-60; St Stephen's Ch Petersburg VA, rector 1953-57. **ORGANIZATIONS:** Sec Coun Episcopal Diocese AL 1975-78; mem Diocesan Liturgical Comm 1973-; Dept Ministry Higher Educ 1957-67; Lions Club; bd dirs Tuskegee Fed Credit Union; chmn Model Cities Commn. **BUSINESS ADDRESS:** Rector, St Andrew's Episcopal Church, 701 Montgomery Rd, Tuskegee Institute, AL 36088.

JONES, VIRGINIA LACY
Librarian. **PERSONAL:** Born Jun 25, 1912, Cinn, OH; married Edward Allen. **EDUCATION:** Sch Educ Hampton Inst, BS 1936, BS in LS 1933;Univ IL, MS in LS 1938 (Gen Educ Bd fellow 1937-38), PhD 1945 (Gen Educ Bd fellow 1943-45); Bishop Coll, Hon Doctor of Humane Letters 1979;Univ of MI, Hon Doctor of Letters 1979. **CAREER:** Louisville Municipal Coll, asst librarian 1934-35, librarian 1936-37; Hampton Inst Library, asst circ Dept 1935-36; Prairie View State Coll, dir dept Library Sci summers 1936-39; Atlanta U, catalog librarian 1939-41, instr Sch Library Serv 1941-43, dean 1945-. **ORGANIZATIONS:** Mem Assn Am Library Schs, pres 1967-68, exec bd 1971; mem ALA; mem NAACP; Delta Sigma Theta; Beta Phi Mu. **HONORS/ACHIEVEMENTS:** Recipient Melvil Dewey ALA award 1973; Joseph W Lippincott Award 1977; Beta Phi Mu Award 1980.

JONES, WALTER L.
Editor. **PERSONAL:** Born Nov 30, 1928, Bloomington, IL; married Cleo E Brooks; children: Walter, Jr, Stephen, Joy. **EDUCATION:** Illinois State Univ; Tennessee A&I State Univ; Univ of Illinois. **CAREER:** The Milwaukee Courier Newspaper, editor, asst publisher; Milwaukee Star, editor 1964-71; Info Newspaper Gary, managing editor 1959-63. **ORGANIZATIONS:** Mem Milwaukee Advertising Club; Alpha Phi Alpha; Sigma Delta Chi; pres Northside & Businessmen's Assn; mem NAACP. **HONORS/ACHIEVEMENTS:** Var awards for newspaper writings. **MILITARY SERVICE:** USAF airman third class 193-55. **BUSINESS ADDRESS:** Milwaukee Community Journal, 3612 N Green Bay, Milwaukee, WI 53212.

JONES, WILLIAM
Alderman. **PERSONAL:** Born Sep 14, 1934, Youngstown, OH; married Eunice L Rogers; children: Lowell, Diane Marie, Sherri Lynne. **EDUCATION:** Houston-Tillotson Coll, BA 1961; Trinity U, CT State Coll, grad study 1967-69;Univ MA. **CAREER:** City of New Haven, dir of organizational devel 1980-, city town clerk 1978-80, chmn Dem Tow 1976-78, alderman 1970-78, dir of com 1975-77; New Haven Health Care Inc, dir health educ & comm relations 1972-75; IBM Corp, sales rep 1965-67; Xerox Corp, 1969; Services Inc, pres 1968-72; S Central Comm Coll, lectr 1969-72. **ORGANIZATIONS:** Adv Tri-State Transp Comm 1971; vice-chmn New Haven Black Coalition 1972; fdr New Haven Black Arts Theatre 1967; vice-chmn bd New Haven Opportunities Industrialization Cntr 1967-69; mem CT Dem Central Comm 1968-70; mem Nat Urban League 1970; mem Alpha Fi Alpha; exec vice-chmn Caucus CT Dems 1967-71;Am Cancer Soc; Quinnipiac Council of Boy Scouts; Dixwell Neighborhood Corp; chmn New Haven Reg Com on Hypertension; cmmr COMMN on Higher Edn; pres New Haven Midget Football League; mem New Haven Human Serv Com; CT Assn of Local Legislators; Nat Black Caucus of Local Elected Officials; mem Urban Lealgue; NAACP. **HONORS/ACHIEVEMENTS:** Recipient Man of the Yr Award, Human Relations Council 1970. **MILITARY SERVICE:** USAF 1954-58. **BUSINESS ADDRESS:** 200 Orange Hall of Records, New Haven, CT 06503.

JONES, WILLIAM A., JR.
Clergyman. **PERSONAL:** Born Feb 24, 1934, Louisville, KY; married Natalie Barkley Brown; children: William III, Elsa, Lesley, Jennifer. **EDUCATION:** Univ of KY, BA 1958;

Crozer Theol Sem, BD 1961; Benedict Coll, SC, Hon DD 1969; Colgate Rochester-Bexley Hall-Crozer Theol Sem, PhD 1975. **CAREER:** 1st Baptist Church Phila, pastor 1959-62; Bethany Baptist Church Brooklyn, pastor 1962-. **ORGANIZATIONS:** Preacher at churches, conventions, conferences univs & colls in Amer, England, Israel, India, Australia, W Africa; pres Prog Nat Bapt Conv 1968-70; prof Black Ch Studies Colgate Rochester Bexley Hall Crozer 1972-76; preacher for NBC's "Art of Living" 1977; frequently featured Conf Echoes Family Radio Network; mem Martin Luther King Jr Fellow Inc; mem Genl Council Bapt World Alliance; trustee Colgate Rochester Div Sch; vis prof Princeton Theol Sem; vis prof Colgate Rochester Div Sch; coord Min's Com on Job Oppors for Brooklyn 1963-64; bd chmn Bedford Stuyvesant Youth in Action 1965-67; founder/chmn Greater NY SCLC Operation Breadbasket 1967-72; chmn Natl SCLC Operation Breadbasket 1972-73; vis prof Practical Tehol Union Theol Sem 1975-76; chmn combd Kings Co Hosp Ctr 1970-77; adj prof romiletics Wesley Tehol Sem Wash DC 1976-77. **HONORS/ACHIEVEMENTS:** Editor Missions Outlook 1961-62; cited "Man in the News" NY Times; Man of the Yr Brooklyn Jaycees 1967; Outstanding Young Men of Amer 1968; Outstanding Brooklynite NY Recorder Poll 1970; Ophelia Devore Achievement Awd 1970; The Black Heritage Assn Awd 1971; Capital Formation Comm Leader Awd 1971; Comm Serv Awd Brooklyn Chap Phi Beta Sigma 1972; Frederick Douglass Awd NY Urban League 1972; Natl Assn of Health Serv Exec Awd 1975; Disting Serv Awd Colony Club First AME Zion Ch Brooklyn 1977; Freedom Awd Comm Mus of Brooklyn Inc 1978; listed in One Hundred Most Influential Black Amers Ebony Magazine 1979; co-author "The Black Ch Looks at the Bicentennial" PNB Pub House Elgin IL 1976; author "Freedom of Conscience, The Black Experience in Amer" Religious Liberty inthe Crossfire of Creeds-Ecumenical Press Philadelphia 1978; author "God in the Ghetto" PNB Pub House Elgin IL 1979; Who's Who in Amer 1984; One of America's Fifteen Outstanding Black Preachers Ebony Mag 1984; article contribs Bapt Progress-Black Monitor-Founds-Freeing The Spirit-The NY Recorder-The Amsterdam News; doctoral thesis The Gospel & the Ghetto. **MILITARY SERVICE:** AUS 1st lt 1954-56. **BUSINESS ADDRESS:** Pastor, Bethany Baptist Church, 460 Sumner Ave, Brooklyn, NY 11216.

JONES, WILLIAM ALLEN
Business executive. **PERSONAL:** Born Dec 13, 1941, Philadelphia, PA; son of Roland E Jones and Gloria T Jones; married Dorothea S Whitson; children: Darlene, Rebecca, Gloria, David. **EDUCATION:** Temple Univ, BA (Magna Cum Laude) 1967; Harvard Business School, MBA 1972; Harvard Law School, JD 1972. **CAREER:** Walt Disney Prod, attny 1973-77, asst treas 1977-79, treas 1979-81; Wyman Bautzer Rothman Kuchel Silbert, attny 1981-83; MGM/UA Entertainment Co, vp, gen counsel corp & sec; United Artists Corp, sr. vp, corp gen counsel 1986-. **ORGANIZATIONS:** Bus mgr Los Angeles Bar Jrnl 1974-76; mem Amer Bar Assoc 1974-, State Bar of CA 1974-, Los Angeles Cty Bar Assn 1974-; bd dir Harvard Bus School Assoc of So CA 1985-88; bd of trustees Marlborough School. **HONORS/ACHIEVEMENTS:** Pres Scholar Temple Univ 1967; mem History Honor Soc 1967, German Honor Soc 1967, Political Sci Hon Soc 1967. **MILITARY SERVICE:** USAF airman 1st class 4 yrs. **BUSINESS ADDRESS:** Senior Vice Pres & General Counsel, United Artists Corp, 450 North Roxbury, 5th Floor, Beverly Hills, CA 90210.

JONES, WILLIAM BOWDOIN
Consultant, lecturer, lawyer. **PERSONAL:** Born May 02, 1928, Los Angeles, CA; son of William T Jones and LaVelle Bowdoin Jones; married Joanne F Garland, Jun 27, 1953; children: Lisa Jamison, Dr Stephanie A Marioneaux, Walter C. **EDUCATION:** Univ of CA-Los Angeles, AB 1949; Univ Southern CA, JD 1952. **CAREER:** Private Practice, attorney-at-law 1952-62; US Foreign Service Officer, diplomat 1962-84; US Dept of State, ambassador to Haiti 1977-80; Univ of VA, ambassador in residence 1984-85; House of Representatives Subcommittee on Western Hemisphere Affairs, staff dir, 1987; private law practice consulting 1988-. **ORGANIZATIONS:** Diplomat-in-residence Hampton Univ 1980-81; fellow Woodrow Wilson Foundation Princeton NJ 1986-87; mem Sigma Pi Phi-Boule, Kappa Alpha Psi, Washington Intl Club; mem CA Bar, Dist of Columbia, US Supreme Court; fellow Woodrow Wilson Foundation, Princeton NJ; mem of Bar of the US Court of Intl Trade 1988. **HONORS/ACHIEVEMENTS:** Outstanding Public Serv CA Legislature 1972; Professional Achievement UCLA Alumni 1980; Merit Awd Alumni Univ So CA 1981; Key to City Los Angeles 1981. **BUSINESS ADDRESS:** Partner, The Intl Business Law Firm, 1025 Connecticut Ave NW, Washington, DC.

JONES, WILLIAM C.
Obstetrician, gynecologist. **PERSONAL:** Born Oct 22, 1933, Richmond, VA; married Evora Williams; children: Lisa, Mark, Lori, Michael, David, Lydia. **EDUCATION:** VA State Coll, BS 1953; Howard U, 1957-59; Meharry Med Coll, MD 1963; DukeUniv Med Cntr, 1967-68. **CAREER:** Physician Ob/Gyn pvt practice Richmond, VA 1968-; DukeUniv & affiliated hosps, Durham, NC, fellow, Endocrinology 1967-68; Hubbard Hosp, Meharry Med Coll, residency & internship 1963-67. **ORGANIZATIONS:** Mem Am Coll Ob/Gyn; mem Richmond Acad of Medicine; mem Richmond Med Soc; Old Dominion Med Soc; cert Am Bd of Observ & Gyn; Kappa Alpha Psi Frat. **MILITARY SERVICE:** AUS 1st lt 1954-56. **BUSINESS ADDRESS:** 2809 N Ave, Richmond, VA 23222.

JONES, WILLIAM DONNELL
Government official. **PERSONAL:** Born Jun 23, 1955, Dallas, TX; children: Lia. **EDUCATION:** Univ of San Diego, BA Economics 1980. **CAREER:** San Diego City Councilman Leon Williams, student intern, staff aide, chief asst; City of San Diego 4th District, city councilman, deputy mayor. **ORGANIZATIONS:** Mem Metro Transit Develop Bd; alternate Regional Employment Training Consortium; mem San Diego Sports Aena Adv Bd; mem bd of dirs San Diego Conventionand Visitors Bureau; chairperson San Diego Alcohol and Drug Abuse Presention Task Force; apptd by County Bd of Supervisors as chmn County Charter Review Panel; bd of dirs Big Brtothers of San Diego County; honorary chair Friends of Contemporary Blacks Arts Prog sponsored by Univ of CA San Diego Drama Dept; hon mem San Diego Jr C of C; mem League of Women Voters, NAACP; sponsor mem Boy Scouts of Amer. **HONORS/ACHIEVEMENTS:** Selected as one of thirty-five minority students nationwide to attend Amer Economic Assoc summer prog at Northwestern Univ 1976; named by Ebony Magazine asone of fifty Black Future Leaders 1980; Outstanding Young Man of Amer 1980; one of five Outstanding Young Citizens of CA by CA Junior Chamber of Commerce 1984; Distinguished Leadership Awd for Elected Officials Amer Planning Assoc CA Chap and San Diego Chapt. **BUSINESS ADDRESS:** Councilman, 4th District City of San Diego, 202 "C" St MS 10A, San Diego, CA 92101.

JONES, WILLIAM EDWARD
Educator. **PERSONAL:** Born Jul 04, 1930, Indianapolis, IN; married Janet; children: Leslye. **EDUCATION:** Butler U, BS 1956; IN U, MS 1960. **CAREER:** Broad Ripple HS, prin 1970-; IN State Univ, counselor, instructor, vice prin, dean 1964-68; Crispus Attucks HS, teacher 1957-61. **ORGANIZATIONS:** Consult HEW; Urban Sch Affairs, OH State U; Midwest Equal Oppt Cntr;Univ Psgh; Gen Asst Cntr; Desegregation Nat Assn; mem Secondary Sch Prin; Phi Delta Kappa; IN Secondary Sch Adminstr; adv cncl Danforth Found; elder Witherspoon United Presb Ch; mem Grtr Indianapolis Progress Com; Kappa Alp Psi; NAACP; Urban League flw Danforth Sch Adminstr 1975-76; John Hay flw Humanities 1964. **MILITARY SERVICE:** USAF 1952-55. **BUSINESS ADDRESS:** 1115 E Broad Ripple Ave, Indianapolis, IN 46220.

JONES, WILLIAM HENRY, JR.
Educator. **PERSONAL:** Born Mar 03, 1916, Brooklyn, NY; married Virginia; children: Wilma. **EDUCATION:** Shaw Univ, AB 1937; Columbia Univ, MA 1947; William & Mary Univ, 1950; Univ Virginia, 1952; Shaw Univ, hon dr degree 1972. **CAREER:** PW Moore Jr High School, principal 1970-; Pasquotank Co Elementary School, 1950-70; Rosenwald High School, 1948-50; PW Moore High School, teacher 1945-48; Frederick Douglass Jr High School, vice principal 1944-45; PW Moore High School, teacher 1942-44; Central High School, teacher 1937-42; Walson Funeral Home, owner, operator. **ORGANIZATIONS:** Mem North Carolina Natl Funderal Dir Assn; North Carolina Merchants Assn; C of C; life mem NEA; mem North Carolina Assn Educators; past chmn, bd trustee Shaw Univ; mem NE North Carolina Schoolmasters Club; bd dir Emille Educ Found; exec bd Roanoke Inst Org; Boys & Girls Club for Black Youth 1942; Boy Scout Master; mem North Carolina State Migrant Labor Adv Comm; White House Conf under Pres Kennedy & Pres Johnson; deacon bd Cornerstone Missionary Bapt Church; past teacher, supt Sunday Sch Cornerstone Missionary Baptist Church; organizer, past dir Jr Choir Cornerstone; life mem Omega Psi Phi Frat; mem Elk Lodge; past finance sec Roanoke Missionary Baptist Assn; mem Elizabeth City Chap NAACP; Natl Urban League; Southern Christian Leadership Conf; Urban Adv Comm; Dist Health Bd NE North Carolina. **HONORS/ACHIEVEMENTS:** Outstanding Black Mal, Elizabeth City Chap Jack & Jill 1972; Distinguished Serv Rendered as Principal, Pasquotank Elem Sch; Savings Club Distinguished Serv Award, Elizabeth City; Golden Anniversary Award, PW Moore; Distinguished Serv Award, Pasquotank Co NAACP; 40 yr Omega Psi Phi Frat 57th Grand Conclave Award; Cit Appreciation, Shaw Univ. **BUSINESS ADDRESS:** 504 South Rd St, Elizabeth City, NC 27909.

JONES, WILLIAM J.
Engineer. **PERSONAL:** Born Mar 23, 1915, New York City, NY; married Dorothy; children: 3. **EDUCATION:** BS 1941; MS 1951. **CAREER:** US Army, chief test equipment & meas, Signal Corps Lab; Lincoln Lab, MA Inst Tech, staff mem; Harvard Univ, lecturer 1960-75; MA Inst Tech, sr staff engr 1975-. **ORGANIZATIONS:** Sr mem Inst Elec Engr Commr, Civil Rights & Human Relations 1965-70; trustee SE MA Univ 1971-; dir Garden City Bank. **BUSINESS ADDRESS:** MIT, Cambridge, MA.

JONES, WILLIAM JENIPHER
Clergyman. **PERSONAL:** Born Oct 27, 1912, Spring Hill, MD; married Pauline Payne; children: William Edward, William David. **EDUCATION:** Attended, Cordoza Business Sch 1929; TN Christian Univ, BDiv 1977; YMCA Local Comm Coll, BS Real Estate; Moraine Valley Comm Coll, real estate broker/appraiser; Biblical Studies, certificate; Univ of IL Commissioners Training Inst, 1985. **CAREER:** Chicago Transit Authority, station transportation clerk 1953-77; Village of Robbins, village trustee 1969-77; IL Police & Fire Commn Bd, commnr chaplain 1984; St John Comm Ch, pastor 1985-. **ORGANIZATIONS:** Gen ins broker Universal Ins Agency 1970; agent United Ins Co of Amer 1953; debit mgr Supreme Life Ins Co 1978; special deputy Pape Security Serv 1977; sec Village of Robbins Fire & Police Commnr 1983; village trustee Village of Robbins 1969-77; chaplain IL Fire & Police Commnrs Assn 1983-85; vice presSouth Suburan Legal Aid Harvey IL 1970; chmn South Suburban Mayors Planning Group 1969-77; past comdr Robbins Memorial Post 1281 Amer Legion 1975; past master Alpha Omega Masonic Lodge #121 Robbins 1979; pres Concedrned Citizen Party Robbins IL 1981. **MILITARY SERVICE:** Quarter master staff sgt 1943-46; Good Conduct Medal; 3 Battle Stars; Medal of Honor. **HOME ADDRESS:** 3702 W 135th St, Robbins, IL 60472. **BUSINESS ADDRESS:** Pastor, St John Community Church, 13430 South Harding Ave, Robbins, IL 60472.

JONES, WILLIAM LAWLESS
Editor. **PERSONAL:** Born Oct 20, 1914, Frankfort, KY; son of Paul W L Jones and Ada Anderson Jones; married Helen Elizabeth Lewis; children: Paul W L II, Robert L, Terence L. **EDUCATION:** Fisk Univ, BA 1938; Univ of MI, MA 1939; Univ of Cincinnati, MEd 1973. **CAREER:** AUS, various intell & admin pos 1941-66; Job Corps NJ, ed spec 1966-69; Univ of Cinti, coord min recruiting 1969-73, asst prof 1973-79; NIP Magazine, entertainment editor. **ORGANIZATIONS:** Writer jazz music columnist NIP Magazine 1969-; tchr history and appreciation of jazz Univ of Cinti 1973-75; mem bd dir Cinti BR NAACP 1981-; TV News Commentator For NAACP Presents; mem bd trustees Greater Cinti Council Performing Arts 1981-; writer and lecturer Jazz Prog of the Council. **HONORS/ACHIEVEMENTS:** Writer 3-Hour Documentary Video Prod The Evolution of Black Music IN Cinti 1980-82; prepared curriculum Jazz Studies for the Union for Expermenting Clges and Univ in Cinti 1984. **MILITARY SERVICE:** AUS lt col; Bronze Star ; Army Commendation Medal. **BUSINESS ADDRESS:** Entertainment Editor, NIP Magazine, 617 Vine St, Ste 1428, Cincinnati, OH 45202.

JONES, WILLIAM MOSES
Physician. **PERSONAL:** Born Nov 12, 1898, Earle, AR; married Geneva May; children: Jean. **EDUCATION:** Fisk U, AB 1922;Univ of Chicago, MD 1932; Wayne U, 1922-24. **CAREER:** Physician, self-employed;Univ of Chicago, mem Med Sch Fac 23 yrs, in charge of student health serv 19 yrs; Jackson Park Hosp, Woodlawn & Provident Hosps,Sturgis Meml Hosp, consult Ophthalmology; license to practice In MI. **ORGANIZATIONS:** Consult Ophthal, Chicago Bd of Edn; trustee Chicago Temple United Meth Ch; mem Alpha Phi Alpha; NAACP - FACS; Am Coll of Surgeons 1950; fellow Am Acad Ophthal & Otolary; NY Acad of Sci; Chicago Ophthal Soc; AMA; SATC FiskUniv 1918. **HONORS/ACHIEVEMENTS:** Honored byUniv of Chicago, pub services, 1979. **BUSINESS ADDRESS:** Physician, 7531 Stony Island, Chicago, IL.

JONES, WILLIAM O.
Clergyman. **PERSONAL:** Born Feb 16, Covington, TN; married Helen Crombie; children:

4 Children. **EDUCATION:** Moody Bible Inst; KY State, BS; Gammon Theol Sem, BD; Murry's Theol Sem, DD. **CAREER:** Chattanooga Bible Center, dean & dir; Home Mission Bd So Bapt Conv 1975-; pastorates TN, KY. **ORGANIZATIONS:** Asst sec Nat BYPU Bd 1947-54; editor Intermed Nat BYPU Qrtly; precinct chmn 12-5 Dist 8 yrs; chaplain CCC Camp 1935-37. **HONORS/ACHIEVEMENTS:** AUS 1941-45. **MILITARY SERVICE:** AUS 1941-45. **BUSINESS ADDRESS:** 805 E 9 St, Chattanooga, TN.

JONES, WILLIAM RONALD
Educator. **PERSONAL:** Born Jul 17, 1933, Louisville, KY; married Lauretta; children: Jeffrey, Darrell. **EDUCATION:** Howard U, AB 1955; Harvard U, BD 1958; Brown U, PhD 1969. **CAREER:** FL State Univ, dir; Howard Univ, lecturer 1964-69; Yale Div School, assoc prof 1969-77; FL State Univ, dir Black Studies; First Unitarian Church, dir Rel Educ 1958-60. **ORGANIZATIONS:** Mem Am Acad Relg; Am Humanist Assn; Am Phil Assn; Educ to Africa Assn; Relg Educ Assn; Soc for Study of Black Relig; Soc for Study of Christian Eth; Unitarian-Universalist Min Assn; mem, asso fellow Unitarian His Soc Danforth; ed bd Nat Unitarian-Univ Jrnl; bd of dir Gr New Haven Mem Soc; chmn, coun on educ Prof Relg Ldrshp; mem Unitarian-Univ Assn; Phi Beta Kappa; Nat Compet Sch 1951-55. **HONORS/ACHIEVEMENTS:** Rockefeller Theo Fellowship 1955-56; NDEA fell 1960-3; Rockefeller Doct Fell 1964; Urban League Fam of Yr 1963; Richard Allen Award 1972; A Whitney Griswold Award 1974. **BUSINESS ADDRESS:** Florida StateUniv, Afro Am Prog Black Stud, Tallahassee, FL 32306.

JONES, WILLIAM W.
Educator. **PERSONAL:** Born Apr 08, 1928, Pageton, WV; children: Valerie Jones Hairston, - 1968-74; bd. **EDUCATION:** Mercer Co Barber Sch, Bluefield, WV, diploma 1947-48; Bluefield State Coll, BS building-constr 1954-58; WV U, MSW 1970-72. **CAREER:** Parkersburg Community Coll, asst prof 1978-, instr 1974-78; Hall Acres Child Care Cntr & Wood Co Juvenile Detention Cntr, Parkerburg, WV, dir 1974-78;Concord Coll, Athens, WV, instr 1974; WV Dept of Welfare Juvenile Delinquency Serv, soc worker/state coord 1972-74; Fed Reformatory for Women, Alderson, WV, consult 1971; WV Dept of Welfare, social worker 1962-70; gen contractor, building trades 1958-62; barber, Bluefield & Princeton WV 1953-68; Norfolk & Western Railway Co, mail handler 1949-62. **ORGANIZATIONS:** Mem Mercer Co Steering Com for the Est of Juvenile Facilaities 1972-74; mem Mercer Co Bd of educ Adv Council 1973-74; pres City Economic Oppor Office, Bluefield, WV 1966; pres HS Athletic Boosters Club 1967-69; bd of dir Mercer Co Oppor Workshop for Retarded Children 1968-74; bd of dir WV Div ofRehab Serv 1967-74; bd of dir Easter Seal So 1968-70; mem NAACP; mem Nat Assn of Social Workers; chmn educ com local branch NAACP, Parkersburg, WV; sec-treas WV Undergrad Social Work Educators Assn; lic minister Zion Bapt Ch Parkersburg, WV 1977-; mem & past dist chmn VFW; mem Civitan Club; mem Midtown Kiwanis Club; bd dir Commn on Race & Relgn; bd dir Logan Job Training & Info Cntr; exec bd Boy Scouts of Am; bd dir WV Assnon Crime & Delinquency; bd dir West-Central Regnl Juv Detention Cntr; youth dir Zion Bapt Ch; co-founder of first 3 small group homes in WV, WV ChildCare Assn, 1976. **HONORS/ACHIEVEMENTS:** Public Service Award, WV Dept of Welfare 1973; Recognition for Loyalty & Dedication, VFW, 1968-69; article pub in the Nat Juvenile Det Assn Newsletter, "Communication Skills Is A Two-Way Street"; attended numerous conferences & workshops; radio-tv appearance, In Regard to Juv Delinquency Activities; guest spkrnumerous organizations; counselor/advisor/volunteer worker many organizations & groups. **MILITARY SERVICE:** AUS corpl 1951-52. **BUSINESS ADDRESS:** Parkersburg Comm Coll, Rt 5 Box 167 A, Parkersburg, WV 26101.

JONES, WILLIE
Business executive. **PERSONAL:** Born Oct 16, 1932, Seaboard, NC; married Jacqueline; children: Sharon, Kurtis. **EDUCATION:** Long Island Univ, BA 1964; Pace Univ 1974. **CAREER:** EEO, Supermarkets Gen Corp, dir 1985. **ORGANIZATIONS:** Mem Natl C of C; Natl Assn Mfrs; Natl Business League; Corp Urban Affairs Adv Comm; Public Affairs Coun; Natl Minority Purchasing Coun; Econ Devel Coun; mem numerous offices, committees, NE region; Natl Urban Affairs Coun; Natl Urban League; bd of dir, life mem NAACP; Natl Urban Coalition; EDGES Group, Food Markets Inst; bd of adv Fleican Coll; Artist Family Theater Proj; Natl Assn Marketing Devel; Congressman Andrew Maguire Military Acad Selection Comm; Toastmaster Intl; past mem, USAF Speakers Bureau; Gen "Hap" Arnold Air Soc; Ancient Free & Accepted Masons; Ed Adv Eastern Dist. **HONORS/ACHIEVEMENTS:** High School Red Hot Scouting Award; Natl Hon Soc Pi Gamma Mu; Merit Award, Black Media. **MILITARY SERVICE:** USAF ret 20 yrs. **BUSINESS ADDRESS:** Dir of Human Resources, Supermarkets General Corp, 301 Blair Road, Woodbridge, NJ 07095.

JONES, WILLIE C.
Educator. **PERSONAL:** Born Sep 13, 1941, Birmingham; married Kay Rice; children: Errol, Clyde, Harriett. **EDUCATION:** Miles Coll, BA Interdenominational Theol Ctr, MDiv 1967;Univ AL, MA 1967, EdD 1974. **CAREER:** Stillman Coll, instructor 1968, acting dean 1968-69, asst dean 1969-70, asst to pres 1970; dean of students 1973. **ORGANIZATIONS:** Mem Phi Delta Kappa; Rotary Interntl; Boy Scouts; UMCA; Cntrl Club; Miles Coll Alumni; Kappa Alpha Psi Frat. **HONORS/ACHIEVEMENTS:** Man of Yr, Kappa Alpha Psi Frat 1972; Outstndng Young Man of Am 1973. **BUSINESS ADDRESS:** Stillman Coll, PO Box 1430, Tuscaloosa, AL 35401.

JONES, WINTON DENNIS, JR.
Chemist. **PERSONAL:** Born Jun 23, 1941, Terre Haute, IN; son of Katherine Jones and Winton Jones; married Sandra Murdock; children: Winton III, Kimberly L. **EDUCATION:** Butler Univ, BS Pharm 1963, MS Pharm Chem 1966; Univ of KS, PhD Med Chem 1970. **CAREER:** Merrell Dow Rsch Inst, sr rsch chemist 1970-. **ORGANIZATIONS:** Mem Big Brothers of Hamilton County 1972-82; assoc advisor Boy Scouts of Amer #494 1973-; chairperson Forest Park Housing Comm 1976-78; comgressional sci couns OH 1st Dist 1978-; treas Tech Sci Soc of Cincinnati 1979; bd of dir Amer Chem Soc 1979; charter mem Natl Org of Black Chemists & Chem Engrs Cincinnati Chapter. **HONORS/ACHIEVEMENTS:** Fellowship Natl Inst of Health 1969-70; Citation City of Forest Park OH 1979; 11 publications, 16 patents, 5 presentations. **HOME ADDRESS:** 1464 Longacre Dr, Cincinnati, OH 45240. **BUSINESS ADDRESS:** Senior Research Chemist, Merrell Dow Research Inst, 2115 Galbraith Rd, Cincinnati, OH 45215.

JONES, WOODROW HAROLD
Educator. **PERSONAL:** Born May 29, 1913, Wewoka, OK; married Lucille White; children: Ethel. **EDUCATION:** Langston U, BS 1937; Columbia, MA 1947;Univ of OK, PhD 1954. **CAREER:** OK Public Schools, teacher 1939-46; Langston Univ, instructor Biology 1948-50; Fisk Univ, assoc prof 1953-56; Southern Univ, prof Biology 1956-60; Univ of Pacific, postdoctoral fellow 1960-61; NASA, rsch sci 1962-69; San Francisco State Coll, prof 1969-; NSF, postdoctoral Fellow 1960-61. **ORGANIZATIONS:** Mem Am Soc Limnology & Oceanography; AASS; Ecol Soc Am; mem Sigma Xi; NAACP; Urban League; Beta Beta Beta; Phi Sigma; Omega Psi Phi. **BUSINESS ADDRESS:** 1600 Halloway, San Francisco, CA 94132.

JONES, YVONNE DE MARR
Civil rights leader. **PERSONAL:** Born in Dayton, OH; divorced; children: Diane R-Singh, Bercenia, Shelley Smith. **EDUCATION:** Hunter Clge, BA 1947, MA 1955. **CAREER:** WP Urban League, comm org 1947-49; Blythedale Chidlren's Rehabilitation, psych Group Worker 1950-54; Elmsford Public Schools, 1955-84. **ORGANIZATIONS:** Consult Fed City Clge DC 1970; wrkshp Org tchr Black History 1960-; bd chrmn Greenburgh Elmsford CAP 1980-; Westchester Comm Opport Ctr Bd 1981-; ed chr Christian Educ St Francis Episcopal Church; pres Westchester Association for the Study of Afro-Amer Life and History; branch pres White Plains Greensburgh NAACP. **HONORS/ACHIEVEMENTS:** Recognition, Assn Study, Afro-Amer Life & History 1976; 1976 Comm Merit Award Operation PUSH Westchester 1976; Achievement Award Westchester Co Club BPW 1978; Recogniton Westchester Black Women's Political Caucus 1984; Key Women of Westchester Award 1987. **HOME ADDRESS:** 118 N Evarts Ave, Elmsford, NY 10523.

JONES, YVONNE HARRIS
Business executive. **PERSONAL:** Born Sep 15, West Palm Beach, FL; daughter of Albert Thomas and Mary Lightfoot Thomas; married Alan C Jones, May 04, 1988. **EDUCATION:** City Coll of NY, BA 1970; New School for Social Rsch, MA 1977. **CAREER:** NY Life Insurance Co, training asst 1970-72; Fed Reserve Bank of NY, sr training specialist 1972-76; Amer Stock Exchange, asst vice pres. **ORGANIZATIONS:** Pres Zeta Delta Phi Graduate Chapter 1970-76; visiting prof Urban League Black Exec Exchange Program 1976; Coalition of 100 Black Women 1977-; mem advisory bd Murry Bergtraum HS 1979-; mem bd of dirs Battery Dance Co 1983-; mem advisory bd NCNW Women's Center 1983-; mem Displaced Homemakers Task Force 1984-; mem SEC Sec Indus Comm on EEO 1981-, Amer Soc for Personnel Admin 1976-; mem adv bd Private Indus Council 1980- ; mem advisory board, OIC High Tech Center, mem bd of dir United Neighborhood Houses 1987-. **HONORS/ACHIEVEMENTS:** Black Achievers in Indus Award, YMCA Harlem Branch 1979; contributed article to professional magazines, 1984; Corporate Achievement Award Negro Business & Professional Women's Clubs Inc 1985; Salute to Black Business & Professional Women, Dollars & Sense Magazine 1989. **HOME ADDRESS:** 29 Winthrop Dr, Peekskill, NY 10566. **BUSINESS ADDRESS:** Asst Vice Pres, Amer Stock Exchange, 86 Trinity Place, New York, NY 10006.

JONES, YVONNE VIVIAN
Educator. **PERSONAL:** Born Jul 29, 1946, New York, NY; children: Michael Kenneth. **EDUCATION:** Amer Univ, BA 1971, PhD 1976. **CAREER:** Eugene & Agnes E Meyer Found, assoc dir 1971-74; Univ of Louisville, asst prof 1975-81, assoc prof anthropology 1981-. **ORGANIZATIONS:** Pres of bd Planned Parenthood of Louisville Inc 1977-81; chair, Minority Group Mental Health Prog Review Comm Natl Inst of Mental Health 1979-82. **HONORS/ACHIEVEMENTS:** Outstanding Scholarship Grad Level Amer Univ 1976; Outstanding Young Woman of Amer 1978. **BUSINESS ADDRESS:** Associate Professor Anthropol, University of Louisville, Dept of Pan-African Studies, Louisville, KY 40292.

JONES, ZOIA L.
Educator. **PERSONAL:** Born Oct 02, 1926, Iota, LA; daughter of Joseph Lemelle and Elena Laws-Lemelle; married Everett; children: Zola. **EDUCATION:** Certificate, Special Educ, Prairie View A&M Univ, 1981; MEd, Guidance, TX Southern Univ, 1976; Certification in Elementary Education, 1963; BS, Home Econ, TX Southern Univ, 1960. **CAREER:** Wharton Elementary School Teacher, 1976-; Houston Ind Sch Dist, 16 yrs; Houston-Harris Co "Proj" (anti-riot), coordinator volunteer, summer 1967; Del Teacher Task Force, 1974. **ORGANIZATIONS:** Advisory Comm VISTA; mem comm Houston Chamber of Commerce; pres, Natl Council Negro Women, 1968-78; Women in Community Serv, 1968-70; mem NAACP; Black Art Center, Black Art Museum, RGM Rose Mary Grand Chapter OES TX; United Negro Coll Fund; Delta Sigma Theta; founder, bd mem, Adopt Black Children Comm; mem, Eta Phi Beta Sor Inc; Assn study Negro Life & History; Houston Teachers Assn; TX Classroom Teachers Assn; TX State Teachers Assn; NEA; All Nations Rescue Mission; columnist, Globe Advocate; past columnist, Houston Informer; Forward Times; KCOH Radio Station moderator. **HONORS/ACHIEVEMENTS:** Distinguished Serv Award, Houston Classroom Teachers Assn; Delta Sigma Theta Sor; 3rd vice pres, supreme general, Grand Chapter OES of USA; Human Relations Comm Bd of Educ, HISD; Houston Teachers Assn; Natl Council Negro Women; Christian Rescue Mission. **HOME ADDRESS:** 3417 Charleston, Houston, TX 77021.

JONES-GRIMES, MABLE CHRISTINE
Educator, home economist. **PERSONAL:** Born Dec 06, 1943, Malden, MO; daughter of Albert Jones and Anna Mae Turner Jones; married James Robert Grimes, Dec 21, 1969; children: Ori Brandon Jones Grimes. **EDUCATION:** Univ of MO-Columbia, BS 1965, MS 1968, PhD 1976. **CAREER:** Univ of MO Coop Extension Svcs, home economist 1965-68; Delta Headstart Program, home economist 1968-69; Univ of MO 4-H Program, youth specialist & asst prof child & family 1969-. **ORGANIZATIONS:** Bd mem Planned Parenthood Inc 1985-; pres Kappa Chi Omega Chap of Alpha Kappa Alpha Sor Inc 1986-87; mem Chamber of Commerce, Women's Network 1986; mem Amer Home Economics Assn 1965-; mem Natl Council of Family Relations 1980-; pres, bd of directors, Planned Parenthood of Central MO 1988-90; Faculty Advisor Delta Tau Chapter of Alpha Kappa Alpha Sorority 1983-. **HONORS/ACHIEVEMENTS:** Meritorious Serv Awd State 4-H Office 1983; Institute for Management of Life Long Learning Harvard Univ 1984; Fellow, Natl Inst In Adult & Continuing Educ, Univ of Georgia, 1989-90; Univ of MO South African Faculty Exchange Program with Univ of Western Cape 1989; Presentation & Article "Race and Leadership Styles of Women" 1988. **BUSINESS ADDRESS:** Asst Prof Child & Family Dev, Univ of Missouri-Columbia, 209 Whitten Hall, Columbia, MO 65211.

JONES-YOUNG, TERRI ANITA
Educator. **PERSONAL:** Born May 11, 1957, Laurel, MS; daughter of Heywood Jones and Betty Jean Jones; married James Keith Young, Sep 06, 1986. **EDUCATION:** Eastern IL Univ, BS 1979; IL Inst of Tech, MBA 1989. **CAREER:** Knutson Mortgage Co, insurance claims spec 1979-80; IL Inst of Tech, asst dir pre-univ 1980-85, dir pre-univ 1985-88; Chicago State University, dir, Pre-engineering 1988-. **ORGANIZATIONS:** Mem Phi Gamma Nu 1979-, NACME 1981-, Toastmasters intl 1984-; mem Phi Beta Lambda, Natl Black MBA Assoc, NAACP; NAMEPA, bd of dir, natl chair-membership. **HONORS/ACHIEVEMENTS:** Service Awd UNCF 1984; Outstanding Serv NSBE 1985; Outstanding Young Women in Amer 1985; Ronald McNair President's Awd NTA Chicago Chap 1986. **BUSINESS ADDRESS:** Chicago State Univ, Office of Engineering Studies, 95 Street at King Dr, Chicago, IL 60628-1598.

JORDAN, ABBIE H. (NEE WILLIAMS)
Educator. **PERSONAL:** Born in Wilcox County, GA; daughter of Samuel Williams and Leah Jones Williams; married Dr J Wesley Jordan; children: W Kenneth. **EDUCATION:** Albany State Coll, BS 1949; Atlanta Univ, MA 1953; Univ of GA, Doctorate Degree Reading. **CAREER:** Tuskegee Inst, instr; Atlanta Univ Complex, instr of reading; Jr HS Ben Hill Cty, principal; Veterans School, principal, instr; GA-SC Read Conf, org & dir; Savannah Morning News, ed-op columnist; Savannah State Coll Reading Inst, founder; US Office of Education (EPDA). **ORGANIZATIONS:** Consultant in reading for the Southeastern ARea of the US; mem adv comm IRA Resol Comm 1974-; exec sec/treasurer Savannah Hospital Authority 1975-; mem adv comm GA Hist Found 1974-80, Telfair Art Acad 1975-80, Basic Ed & Reading 1977-78; mem, exec bd NAACP 1977-83; coord/founder of the Society of Doctors Inc 1986-. **HONORS/ACHIEVEMENTS:** Outstanding Teacher of the Year 1973; featured in Essence Mag 1976; Novelet "Ms Lily" 1977; authored numerous articles; featured in Atlanta Constitution Journal June 1988. **BUSINESS ADDRESS:** Founder, Reading Inst, Savanna State Coll, Savannah, GA 31404.

JORDAN, ANNE KNIGHT
Civic worker. **PERSONAL:** Born Jul 08, Tampa, FL; married Dr Carl R Jordan; children: Dr Carmen A Jordan Cox, Dr Karen T, Harold K. **EDUCATION:** Howard Univ, AB 1949, postgrad 1955; Savannah State Coll, attended 1957; Catholic Univ, attended 1958; Univ GA, continuing educ 1967-68; Armstrong State Coll, attended 1971-72. **CAREER:** Soc Sec Agency Baltimore, clerical 1941-42; Dept Pub Welfare Wash, staff foster care serv 1943; Dept of Anatomy & Pharmacology Howard Univ Wash, sec 1948-49; US Civil Serv Commn Investigations Wash, clerical 1953; Savannah, tchr spl educ 1956-57; Tots & Teens Savannah Chapt, 1965; Grasshoppers Socio-Civic Club 1973; Adopt-A-Family MS Delta Poverty Area, 1970; Jr Nat Med Assn, 1970; Happy Homemaker, editor 1970. **ORGANIZATIONS:** Pres Woman's Aux Natl Med Assn 1969-70; chmn adv bd 1970-71; pres Woman's Aux GA State Med Assn 1961-62; basileus Sigma Gamma Rho 1961-62; mem NAACP; life mem ex bd 1960 March of Dimes; Natl Found Savannah Chap League of Women Voters; GA Council Human Relations; ex bd Speech & Hearing; delegate Natl Counc Cath Women 1964; White House Conf Health Nutrition & Food 1969; NAACP Natl Conv NY 1959, MN 1960. **HONORS/ACHIEVEMENTS:** Sigma of Yr Awd Sigma Gamma Rho 1962; listed in Who's Who in S & SW 1973, 74; Intl Platform Assn 1976; Historical Preservations of Amer 1976; Dict of Intl Biog 1975; cert State GA, Univ GA, GA Defense Dept teach Civil Defense Courses; certified season color analyst & fitness consultant 1984. **MILITARY SERVICE:** AUS WAC.

JORDAN, BARBARA C.
Professor, former government official. **PERSONAL:** Born Feb 21, 1936, Houston, TX. **EDUCATION:** Boston U, LlB 1959; TX So U, BA Pol Sci & Hist 1956; honorary doctorate degrees,27 including Harvard, Princeton, Notre Dame, Brandeis, William and Mary, Wake Forest and Tuskegee Inst. **CAREER:** Private Legal Practice Houston; admin asst to County Judge of Harris Co 1960-66; TX Senate, 1966-72; US House of Reps; Congresswoman from 18th Dist of TX 1972-78; Lyndon B Johnson School of Public Affairs Univ of TX at Austin, professorship 1979-82;, holder of Lyndon B Johnson Centennial Chair in Natl Policy 1982-. **ORGANIZATIONS:** Amer Bar Assoc; Fellow of Am Bar Foundaton; St Bar of TX; MA Bar; Dist of Columbia Bar; publications, Barbara Jordan a Self-Portrait (with Shelby Hearon, Doubleday 1979), "Individual Rights, Social Responsibility" Rights & Responsibilities (Nov 1978 pp 9-17), The Great Society-A Twenty Year Critique (edited with Elspeth Rostow 1986); mem bd of dir Mead Corp; mem bd of dir TX Commerce Bancshares Inc; Trilaterla Commission, advisory bd; bdof dir Public Broadcasting Sys; mem of Pres Adv Bd on Ambassadorial Appointments 1979-81; hearings officer for Natl Inst of Educ Hearings on Minimum Testing; People for the Amer Way, founder & bd of trustees; Henry J Kaiser Family Found, bd of trustees; mem, House Comm on the Judiciary, House Comm on Governmnt Operations, Steering & Policy Comm of Dem Caucus. **HONORS/ACHIEVEMENTS:** Recipient of Eleanor Roosevelt Humanities Awd St of Israel Bonds 1984; voted "Best Living Orator" by Intl Platform Asso 1984; elected to TX Womens Hall ofFame Public Serv Category 1984; selected by World Almanac 1984 as "One of 25 Most Influential Women in Am" for 10th Cnsctv yr; hosted TV series on PBS "Crisis to Crisis with Barbara Jordan" 1982; selected by editors of Ladies Home Journal as among the "100 Most Influential Women in Am"; selected as 1st choice in poll conducted by Redbook Magazine on "Women Who Could Be Appointed to Supreme Ct" 1979; presented Keynote Address at Natl Conv 1976; selected by Time Magazine as one of 10 Women of Yr 1976; appointed by Secretary-General of the UN to serve on an 11 mem panel to conduct hearings on the role of transnat'l corps in South Africa & Namibia 1985; various major legislative achievments enacted into law. **BUSINESS ADDRESS:** Professor, LBJ School of Publ, University of TX at Austin, Drawer Y, University Station, Austin, TX 78713.

JORDAN, BETTYE DAVIS
President/owner. **PERSONAL:** Born Sep 14, 1946, Tampa, FL; daughter of Lee Davis and Ethel Davis; children: Lisa Darlene Walker, Christopher Charles White II. **EDUCATION:** Univ of Tampa, BS Medical Tech 1968. **CAREER:** B Davis Enterprises, owner; Harambee Enterprises, president. **ORGANIZATIONS:** Bd mem FL Med Tech Assoc 1979-; exec bd mem 1980-86, vice pres 1986-, NAACP Tampa; bd mem Women's Survival Ctr 1981-83; vice pres Pride of Joy Enterprises 1982-85; mem Movie Guild 1984-86; mem Tampa Urban League 1987, Civic Review Bd 1987; bd mem College Hill Dev & Comm Cv Org 1987; vice pres NAACP 1989-91. **HONORS/ACHIEVEMENTS:** Life mem NAACP; Medical Technologist Awd Univ Comm Hosp 1982; Natl Assoc for Female Exec Inc 1984. **HOME ADDRESS:** 3702 E Osborne Ave, Tampa, FL 33610. **BUSINESS ADDRESS:** President, Harambee Enterprises, 3525 No 22nd St, Tampa, FL 33605.

JORDAN, CARL RANKIN
Physician. **PERSONAL:** Born Jul 24, 1924, Savannah, GA; married Anne; children: Carmen, Karen, Harold. **EDUCATION:** Howard Univ Coll of Arts, BS 1946; Howard Univ Coll Med, MD 1948. **CAREER:** Self, physician; Charity Hosp, prgm training prgm, gen pelvic surgery, 1949-51, 1953-57; Freedman's Hosp, intern 1948-49; Harvard, postgrad surg edn; MayoClinic; Cook Co Grad Sch & Med;Univ Vienna; Emmoryu; UCinc;Univ MD; Johns Hopkins; Med Coll GA;Univ MS Med Ctr; MedUniv SC; Charity Hosp, chf surgery 1960-64. **ORGANIZATIONS:** Past pres Cath Laymen's League GA 1957-59; pres HowardUniv Alumni Club 1971-; past pres S Atlantic Med Soc 1956; GA State Med Assn 1959; chmn bd 1960; ofcr Nat Med Assn; organized & established Jordan Clinic 1979; mem, bd tst 1968-75; sec Exec Com 1972-74; chmn Time & Place Com 1973-75; life mem NAACP 1959; ofcr NAACP; chmn, treas 1959-60; regional vice pres Cath Holy Name Soc 1970-71; flw Am Soc Abdominal Surgeons 1961; Intl Acad Proctology 1975; diplomate Intl Bd Proctlogy 1976; mem AMA. **HONORS/ACHIEVEMENTS:** Physician Reg Award 1976-79; Cert Apprt, Nat Med Assn 1976; Master Surgeon's Cert 1958; recertified Intl Bd of Proctology 1980; hon citz, Louisville KY 1974. **MILITARY SERVICE:** AUS MC capt 1951-53. **BUSINESS ADDRESS:** 818 Waters Ave, PO Box 3567, Savannah, GA 31404.

JORDAN, CAROLYN D.
Attorney. **PERSONAL:** Born Mar 07, 1941, Ft Worth, TX. **EDUCATION:** Fisk U, BA 1963; Howard U, JD 1966. **CAREER:** Herman A English, atty 1971-72; Compton CA, dep city atty 1970-71; Economic & Youth Opportunities Agency Los Angeles, prog mgmt splst 1969-70; VA Regional Ofc Los Angeles, veterans claims adjudicator 1968-69; Library of Congress, copyright examiner 1966-68. **ORGANIZATIONS:** Asst counsel Banking, Housing & Urban Affairs Com 1973-; legislative asst 1972-73; mem State Bar of CA; Los Angeles Co Bar Assn; Comm Resources Council; Nat Bar Assn; Bar of the Dist of Columbia; Kappa Beta Pi Intl Legal Sorority; Copyright Lawyers Assn; Intl Law Soc; Delta Sigma Theta Sorority; Am Bar Assn; bd dir Progressive Black Asso Publishing Co; bd dir Parent-Child Guidance Center; bd dir A Better Chance for Educ Washington; bd dir SOME Washington; vice pres Economic Opportunities Credit Union 1969; Active on Moot Ct Team; mem Law Students Civil Rights Council; mem Law Students Bar Assn. **HONORS/ACHIEVEMENTS:** Received highest grade in Admiralty. **BUSINESS ADDRESS:** US Senate Rm 5300, Washington, DC.

JORDAN, CAROLYNE LAMAR
Educational administrator. **PERSONAL:** Born in Augusta, GA; married Lawrence M Jordan; children: Lara Gayle, Samuel Lamar. **EDUCATION:** Fisk Univ, BA 1960; New England Univ, MMus 1970; Harvard Univ, EEd 1977. **CAREER:** Hamilton Central School, dir of music 1962-67; Lexington Public Schools, supervisor of music 1967-70; Salem St Coll, prof of psychology & music 1971-83;Suffolk Univ, asst to the president 1983-. **ORGANIZATIONS:** Board mem Friends Nat'l Center of Afro-American 1971-73; mem American Psychological Assoc 1977-; trustee Cambridge Friends School 1980-; exec bd Natl Amer Friends Serv Comm 1983-; chairperson long range plng comm Suffolk Univ; renway consortium Retention Comm; pres Human Resources Cons; pres Alpha Kappa; exec bd mem ACE/NIP 1985; exec bd Freedom House 1985. **HONORS/ACHIEVEMENTS:** Ford Found Grant Harvard Univ 1975-77; Radcliffe Grant to Grad Women 1975; Disting Serv Awd Salem St Coll 1980; Natl Endowment for the Humanities Harvard 1982; Outstanding Young Men of Jaycees 1982; Who's Who in the East 1982; Humanities Post Doct Grant Harvard Univ; Amer Council on Ed Forum Participant; presidential Fellow Smith Coll 1986-87; American Council on Ed. **HOME ADDRESS:** 2826 Central Ave, Memphis, TN 36111.

JORDAN, CASPER LEROY
Retired educator, librarian. **PERSONAL:** Born Mar 05, 1924, Cleveland, OH; son of John Jordan and Leola Lloyd Jordan. **EDUCATION:** Case-Western Reserve Univ, AB 1947; Atlanta Univ, MS in LS 1951. **CAREER:** Wilberforce Univ, chief librarian 1951-61; Nioga Library Syst, asst dir 1961-68; Atlanta Univ, prof library serv 1968-79, univ librarian 1974-79; Atlanta-Fulton Pub Libr, acting dir 1986-87, deputy dir 1979-; adjunct prof, Atlanta, GA, 1979-. **ORGANIZATIONS:** Active mem various professional organizations in OH, NY, GA; editor "Free Lance" 1950-80; contributor to professional journals; mem NAACP (br pres 1967-68, reg officer 1966-68); officer CORE 1963-66; Beta Phi Mu Hon Libr Sci Frat; book editor AME Church Review 1984-; African-Amer Family History Assoc 1986. **HONORS/ACHIEVEMENTS:** Alumni Resident Lecturer Atlanta Univ Library School 1987; Outstanding Black Librarian, Black Caucus of Amer Library Assoc, 1981. **HOME ADDRESS:** 2041 Fairburn Rd, SW, Atlanta, GA 30331.

JORDAN, CHARLES R.
City commissioner. **PERSONAL:** Born Sep 01, 1937, Longview, TX; married Esther Gauff; children: Patricia Renee, Dion Christopher. **EDUCATION:** Gonzaga U, BS 1961; Loma Linda U, graduate studies;Univ So CA. **CAREER:** Portland OR, city commr 1974-; Div of Career Educ Programs NW Regional Educ Lab, dir 1973-74; Bur of Human Resources City of Portland, dir 1972-73; Model Cities Agency City of Portland, dir 1970-72; Palm Springs CA, asst city mgr 1968-70; Youth Outpost, dir 1966-68; Recreation & Spl Events Palm Springs, asst dir 1964-66; State of OR, apptd to educ coordinating council 1972-73; State of OR, apptd to Gov's Manpower Plng Council 1972. **ORGANIZATIONS:** Mem Am Assn for Pub Adminstrs; mem Kiwanis Club. **HONORS/ACHIEVEMENTS:** Recipient Boss of Year Award, Am Bus Professional Women's Club 1972; Official Order of the Palms, Palm Springs 1970; Gavel Award, Palm Springs Sch Dist 1968; Distinguished Military Grad 1964; Military Olympic Basketball Team, Greece 1963. **MILITARY SERVICE:** AUS 1st lt 1962-64.

JORDAN, CHARLES WESLEY
Clergyman. **PERSONAL:** Born May 28, 1933, Dayton, OH; son of David Morris Jordan and Noami Harper Jordan; married Margaret Crawford, Aug 02, 1959; children: Diana, Susan. **EDUCATION:** Roosevelt Univ, BA 1956; Garrett-Evangelical Theological Seminary, MDiv 1960. **CAREER:** Woodlawn United Methodist Church, pastor 1960-66; Rockford IL Urban Ministries, dir 1966-71; Northern IL Conference Council, program staff 1971-82; Chicago Southern Dist, supt 1982-; St Mark United Methodist Church; Chicago, IL; senior pastor 1987-. **ORGANIZATIONS:** Delegate UM General Conference 1976,80,84; chairperson UM Natl Strategy on New Church Develop 1980-84; dir UM General Council on Ministries 1980-; bd of trustees Garrett-Evangelical Theol Seminary 1982-; life mem Kappa Alpha Psi Frat; dir, United Methodist General Council on Ministries, 1980-88; Delegate, United Methodist General Conf 1976, 1980, 1984, 1988. **HONORS/ACHIEVEMENTS:** Achievement Awd in Religion from the Chicago Alumni of Kappa Alpha Psi Frat 1986; Hall of Fame, Wendell Phillips High School 1989. **MILITARY SERVICE:** AUS pfc 1953-55.

BUSINESS ADDRESS: Sr Pastor, St Mark United Methodist Church, 8441 St Lawrence Ave, Chicago, IL 60619.

JORDAN, DAVID LEE
Educator. **PERSONAL:** Born Apr 03, 1933, Greenwood, MS; married Christine Bell; children: David Jr, Joyce Jordan Dugar, Donald, Darryl. **EDUCATION:** MS Valley State U, BS 1959;Univ of WY, MS 1969. **CAREER:** Greenwood Voters League, pres 1965-; The Greenwood Pub Sch System, sci tchr 1970-. **ORGANIZATIONS:** Mem Leflore Co Br of the NAACP 1960-; mem Leflore Co & Democratic Exec Com1976-; mem Nat Democratic Platform Civil Righst Adv Com 1978; chmn MS Valley StateUniv Nat Alumni Assn Legislative Commn 1980; assisted Black in getting elected to pub Office in Leflore Co govt 1970-; Demanded That Blacks be Appointed to bds & commns 1970-. **HONORS/ACHIEVEMENTS:** Gov Merit Award, Gov Office 1974; JH White Meml Award, MVSU Nat Slumni Assn 1977; Comm Serv Award, Omega Psi Phi Frat 1977-79; invited White House meet Pres Carter, White House Staff 1978-79. **MILITARY SERVICE:** AUSR pfc 1960-62. **BUSINESS ADDRESS:** 1103 Jordan St, Greenwood, MS 38930.

JORDAN, EDDIE JACK, SR.
Artist, educator. **PERSONAL:** Born Jul 29, 1927, Wichita Falls, TX; son of Oscar and Arnetas; married Gladys McDaniel; children: Eddie Jack, Jr, Gregory Keith, La Kara Jovarn. **EDUCATION:** Langston Univ, BA 1948; IA Univ, MA 1949; State Univ of IA, MFA 1956; IN Univ, MS 1973, DEd 1975. **CAREER:** Claflin Univ, chmn dept of art 1950-Army; Allen Univ, chmn dept of art 1954-56; Langston Univ, chmn dept of art 1956-61; Southern Univ in NO, chmn dept of art 1961-. **ORGANIZATIONS:** Natl co chmn Comm for Devel of Art in Negro Colls 1962-; pres, adm bd Bethany United Ch 1968-80; mem comm Phi Delta Kappa Inc 1980-81; pres bd of dirs Natl Conf of Artists 1983-; sec treas New Orleans Ctr of Creative Arts 1983-; life mem NAACP; life mem Alpha Phi Frat Inc. **HONORS/ACHIEVEMENTS:** Rec'd 41 awds in local regional & natl competition; Sculpture Awd Rhode Island Natl, Philbrook Museum in OK, Walker ARt Ctr MN, Gibbs Art Museum SC, Carnegie Inst Pgh; 2 sculptures as a first of Blacks purchased for IN Museum 1974; Delta Phi Delta Natl Hon Art Frat; Dissertation "Past Present and Future of NCA" 1973; foreign exhibition Africa Germany Russia Caribbean, Africa 1973-77. **MILITARY SERVICE:** AUS corpl S-3 draftsman 1951-52; Inf Btn; Formal Btn Salute & Citation. **HOME ADDRESS:** 5545 Congress Dr, New Orleans, LA 70126. **BUSINESS ADDRESS:** Professor, SouthernUniv of NO, Art Dept, 6400 Press Dr, New Orleans, LA 70126.

JORDAN, EMMA COLEMAN
Educator, attorney. **PERSONAL:** Born Nov 29, 1946, Berkeley, CA; married Don; children: Kristen Elena. **EDUCATION:** CA State U, BA 1969; Howard U, JD 1973. **CAREER:** Stanford Law School, tching fellow 1973-74; Univ of Santa Clara, asst prof 1974-75; Univ of CA Sch of Law, acting prof 1975-80, prof 1980-87; Georgetown Univ Law Ctr, prof 1987-. **ORGANIZATIONS:** Mem Nat Conf of Black Lawyers; Nat Bar Assn; Am Soc of Intl Law; pub mem CA State Bd of Dental & Exmnrs; Am Assn of Law Schs Sects on Commercial Law & Contracts, Minority Grps; mem Charles Houston Bar Assn; bd of dir CA Assn of Black Lawyers; pres Soc of Amer Law Teachers 1986-88; chr CA St Bar Financial Inst Comm; chr AALS Financial Inst & Consumer Fin Serv Sect; bd mem Consumer Action; adv comm Natl Consumer Union Northern CA; mem Amer Law Inst. **HONORS/ACHIEVEMENTS:** Publs litigation without representation; "The Need for Intervention to Affirm Affirmative Action, Harvard Civil Liberties Civil Rights Law Rev 1979, "After the Merger of Contribution & Indemnity, What are the Limits of Comparative Loss Allocation" AR St Law Rev 1980; "Problems & Proscpects of Participation in Affirmative Action Litigation" UC Davis Law Rev 1980; Limitations of the Intl Lega Mech Namibia 1972; outstdng acad achvmt award Phi Alpha Delta 1973;grad 1st in class Howard Law Sch 1973. **BUSINESS ADDRESS:** Professor of Law, University of CA, School of Law, Davis, CA 95616.

JORDAN, ERIC CALVIN
Professional athlete. **PERSONAL:** Born Nov 17, 1961, Pineville, LA. **EDUCATION:** Purdue. **CAREER:** Oakland Invaders, halfback 1984-. **HONORS/ACHIEVEMENTS:** Named USFL Player of Week after win over Denver.

JORDAN, FREDERICK DOUGLASS
Clergyman. **PERSONAL:** Born Aug 08, 1901, Atlanta; widowed. **EDUCATION:** Howard U, 1918-21; Garret Sem Evanston IL, BD 1923; Northwestern U, BA 1924;Univ Chgo, grad studies 1939. **CAREER:** Urban Ministries & Ecumenical Relations AME Ch, bishop 1968-76; retired 1976; TN & KY, bishop 1964-68; LA & MS 1957-62; W US 1956-57; S & Cent Africa 1952-56; clergyman-minister 1924-52. **ORGANIZATIONS:** Mem, chmn Consultation Ch Union 1973-76; vice pres World Meth Hist Cox 1970-75; gov & exec bds Nat Coun Chs; del World Coun Chs 1954, 1961, 1968, 1975,; NAACP; ACLU; 32 deg Mason; Alpha Phi Alpha; Sigma Pi Phi; ambassador Goodwill Commonwealth KY 1968. **HONORS/ACHIEVEMENTS:** Hon LLD & PhD, Monrovia Coll; Morris Brown Coll; Allen U; PhD Shorter Coll; LLD Wilberforce U.

JORDAN, FREDERICK E.
Associate executive, consulting engineer. **PERSONAL:** Born Apr 27, 1937, Loveville, MD. **EDUCATION:** Howard U, BSCE; Civ Engr Cntr, grad. **CAREER:** FE Jordan Assoc, president; Nat Counc of Minority Consul Engn, pres 1976-77; Inst Tech; NortheasternUniv MSCE Stanford U, grad study; Bonelli, Young , Wong & Biggs, San & Fran, div civ-struct engr; Echtel Corp San Fran & Charles T Main Consult Engrs, Boston, struct engr; Riverside Dept Pub Works Riverside CA, civ engr; LA Air Def Command, dir civ engr; Sandrestrom Air Force Base Greenland, asst chf engr pvt pract, 1968; West Assn Minority Consult Engr, pres 1974; Am Soc Civ Engr SF Sect, sec dir 1974-. **ORGANIZATIONS:** Mem Nat Soc Prof Engr; consult Engrs Assn US; Struct Engrs Assn CA; Soc Am Mil Engrs; Met Assn Urban Designers & Environ Planners; fnd mem,past pres, chmn bd dir Engr Soc Com Manpower Training Inc; fnd mem 1st chmn No CA Counc Black Prof Engrs; past vice pres San Fran Forum Am Soc Civ Engrs; mem engr adv & bd CA StateUniv San Fran; past mem San Fran Engr Counc; pres bd dir Bay Area Urban League Inc 1972-73. **HONORS/ACHIEVEMENTS:** Bay Area & State of CA outstanding civ engr in comm activity Am Soc Civ Eng 1967-68; distinguished alumni award Bay Area HowardUniv Alumni Club 1972; Distinguished Black in Sci & Engineering in US Oakland Mus Assn 1973; several Publs. **MILITARY SERVICE:** USAF 1 lt. **BUSINESS ADDRESS:** FE Jordan Associates, 111 New Montgomery St, Ste 209, San Francisco, CA 94105.

JORDAN, GEORGE LEE
Dentist. **PERSONAL:** Born Nov 02, 1935, Norfolk Co, VA; married Marguerite W; children: George III, Bernard. **EDUCATION:** Cen St U, BS 1957; Fisk U, MA 1963; Meharry Med Coll, DDS 1971. **CAREER:** MI St U, asst prof 1972-76; Meharry Med Coll, instr 1971-72; Phoenix, sci tchr 1964-67; WA DC, tchr 1963-64; Protsmouth VA, tchr 1958-62; Pontiac Sch Dist, consult 1974-77; Olin Health Ctr, dir 1975-76; Lakeside Health Ctr, dir 1972-75. **ORGANIZATIONS:** NAACP; Pontiac Area Urban League. **HONORS/ACHIEVEMENTS:** Citation, Pontiac Schs 1977; outst citizen, Omega Psi Phi 1967; outst tchr Jaycees WA DC 1962. **MILITARY SERVICE:** AUSR 2nd lt 1957-58. **BUSINESS ADDRESS:** 490 Liberty St, Chesapeake, VA 23324.

JORDAN, GEORGE WASHINGTON, JR.
Engineering executive. **PERSONAL:** Born Mar 11, 1938, Chattanooga, TN; son of George Jordan and Omega Jordan; married Fredine Sims; children: George Washington III. **EDUCATION:** Tuskegee Univ, BSEE 1961; GA Inst of Tech, MSIM 1978; Emory Univ, management inst 1976. **CAREER:** Boeing Co, engr 1961-65; Gen Elec Co, engr 1965-66; Lockheed-Georgia Co, engr/mgr 1966-. **ORGANIZATIONS:** Chmn/mem Atlanta Zoning Bd 1978-84; mem Natl Mgmt Assn 1966-; mem Merit Employees Assn 1975-; mem Assn of MBA Execs 1978-; mem Inst of Management Science 1978-; sr mem Amer Inst of Aero/Astro 1973-; life mem Alpha Phi Alpha Frat 1957-; mem NAACP 1985-; bd of deacons, council on christian ed, youth leadership council, Sunday school teacher, royal ambassador counselor, fin comm, asst treas, vchmn march bd mem bd of trustees Union Baptist Church. **HONORS/ACHIEVEMENTS:** Natl Mem of Flt Sim Tech Comm AIAA 1984-. **HOME ADDRESS:** 3609 Rolling Green Ridge SW, Atlanta, GA 30331. **BUSINESS ADDRESS:** Engineering Dept Manager, Lockheed-Georgia Co, 86 So Cobb Dr SE, Marietta, GA 30063.

JORDAN, HAROLD WILLOUGHBY
Physician. **PERSONAL:** Born May 24, 1937, Newnan, GA; son of Edward P. Jordan and Dorothy W. Jordan; married Geraldine Crawford; children: Harold II, Vincent, Karen, Kristie. **EDUCATION:** Morehouse College, BS, 1958; Meharry Medical College, MD, 1962; G W Hubbard Hospital, rotating internship, 1963, medical residency, 1964; Vanderbilt University Hospital, psychiatric residency, 1967. **CAREER:** Meharry Medical College, Department of Psychology, clinical instructor, 1965-67, instructor, acting director of outpatient department, 1967-68, assistant professor, director of psychiatric outpatient clinic, 1968-71, professor, chairman of department of psychology, 1979—; Vanderbilt Univerissity Hospital, courtesy staff member, 1967—, clinical instructor, 1968-72, clinical assistant professor, 1972—; Florence Crittendon Home, psychiatric consultant, 1967; State Divisional Vocational Rehabilitation, Intensive Treatment Center, psychiatric consultant, 1967-71; Fisk University Student Counseling Center, psychiatric consultant, 1969-71; Tennessee Department of Mental Health/Mental Retardation, assistant commissioner, 1971-75, commissioner, 1975-79; Tennessee State University, psychiatric consultant, 1984—; Cumberland Hall Hospital, attending physician, 1985—. **ORGANIZATIONS:** Member, NAACP, 1957, American Psychological Association, 1967, American Association of University Professors, 1967, R F Boyd Medical Society, 1968, National Medical Association, 1970, Black Psychiatrists of America, 1973, Tennessee Medical Associationn, 1975, Nashville Academy of Medicine, 1975, American Association of Chairmen of Psychiatry 1979, Alpha Omega Alpha Honorary Medical Society, 1980, Sigma Pi Phi. **HONORS/ACHIEVEMENTS:** Certificate of Recognition, Nashville Chapter, Association of Black Psychologists, 1976; certificate of appreciation, Joseph P Kennedy Jr Foundation, 1976; certificate of recognition, Metro Atlanta Chapter of National Association of Human Rights Workers, 1976; awarded plaque, National Association of Black & Social Workers, 1977; plaque, Harriet Cohn Mental Health Center, 1979; plaque, Meharry Medical College Class of 1980; President's Award, Meharry Medical College, 1987. **MILITARY SERVICE:** US Army Reserve, captain, 1963-69; Tennessee Army National Guard, lieutenant colonel, 1974-81. **BUSINESS ADDRESS:** Professor and Chairman, Meharry Medical College, 1005 D B Todd Blvd, Nashville, TN 37208.

JORDAN, J. ST. GIRARD
Attorney. **PERSONAL:** Born Feb 29, 1944, Philadelphia, PA; married L Elaine Bullock; children: Daniel, Mark, Chonda, Kijsa. **EDUCATION:** Temple Univ, ABS 1969, BS 1970; Univ of PA Law Sch, JD 1973. **CAREER:** SmithKline Corp, finan analyst 1967-69, sr mkt rsch analyst 1960-70; Black Book TV Prod, vice pres treas 1969-72; Norden Labs Lincoln & VPO Inc Omaha, corp officer; Goodis Greenfield Henry Shaiman & Levin, assoc 1973-74; SmithKline Corp, group general counsel 1974-, asst general counsel 1986; asst sec 1987; gen counsel, director & sec Consumer Products Inc 1987. **ORGANIZATIONS:** Pres Barristers Assn of Philadelphia Inc 1976-77; mem Natl, Amer, PA, Phila, NJ, Camden Co Bar Assns; legal com United Negro College Fund Dr 1977; vice chmn AHI Law Com Washington DC; pres Philadelphia Fed of Black Bus & Professional Orgs; mem NAACP, Mt Zion Baptist Church, United Fund/Way; Neighborhood Servs Comm adv bd Christian St YWCA; bd of dirs United Comm United Way Agency 1982-84; chmn AHI Law Comm 1982; exec comm Barristes Assn of Philadelphia 1986-87; Govt Affairs Comm Proprietry Assn. **HONORS/ACHIEVEMENTS:** Outstanding Student Award Temple Univ 1968; Tibune Outstanding Citizen Centennel Awd 1984. **MILITARY SERVICE:** USAF A/1C 1962. **BUSINESS ADDRESS:** Group Genl Counsel, SmithKline Corp, One Franklin Plaza, P O Box 7929, Philadelphia, PA 19101.

JORDAN, JANICE MARIE
Health services. **PERSONAL:** Born Mar 29, 1947, Lexington, NC; married Jesse Coleman, Apr 22, 1989. **EDUCATION:** Antioch College, BA 1970; Univ of Delaware, MEd 1975; Univ of MD College Park, PhD 1985. **CAREER:** City of Hampton, VA Public Schools, substitute teacher 1970-71; Special Services Program,Univ of DE, staff advisor 1971-72, co-director 1972-76, Ctr for Counseling & Student Dev UD, counseling psychologist 1976-85, assistant dir 1985-88, associate dir 1988-. **ORGANIZATIONS:** Assoc Muticultural Cslg & Dev, no atlantic regional rep 1982-86, president elect 1986-87, pres 1987-88; Del Valley Assoc Black Psych, Professional Affairs Chair 1985-86, Secretary 1986-87; Black Alumni Organization of Univ of DE, president 1986-87. **BUSINESS ADDRESS:** Associate Dir, University of Delaware, 1750 Danube Street, Aurora, CO 80011.

JORDAN, JOHN EDWARD
Dentist, business executive. **PERSONAL:** Born Nov 17, 1930, Nashville, TN; son of Captain John E Jordan and Mary Richardson Jordan; divorced; children: John E III. **EDUCATION:** Lincoln University, PA, BA, 1952; Meharry Medical College, Dental School, DDS, 1957; attended Fisk University, Wayne State University, Lincoln University; post grad courses, University of Tennessee Dental School, University of Arkansas, Meharry Medical

College School of Dentistry. **CAREER:** Jordan Copy Svc, owner, 1960-87; Shirts Unlimited Clothing Store, partner, 1972-79; dentist in private practice, 1958—. **ORGANIZATIONS:** Vice pres bd dir Northeast Mental Health Ctr 1978-85; pres Laymen Middle Baptist Ch 1983-85; corresponding sec Baptist City Laymen Memphis TN 1984-89; chmn dental health Shelby Co Dental Soc Pen TN Dental Assoc 1965-89; participant dentist Memphis Health Fair 1984-86; comm rep Memphis Shelby Co Headstart Policy Council 1985-87; trustee Middle Baptist Church 1983-89; chmn, contact rep Memphis Br Afro-Amer Historical Assn 1980-89; pres Hyde Park Hollywood Comm Develop Block Club 1980-85; bd of dir PMA; chmn Headstart Policy Council 1986-87; chmn Dental Health Month for Shelby City Dental Soc NDA; participant Dentist Memphis Health Fair w/Memphis Dental Soc ADA 1985-89; fin sec Memphis City Baptist Laymen 1986-87. **HONORS/ACHIEVEMENTS:** Certificate of Achievement Middle Baptist Church 1984; Dental Health Week Achiev Awd ADA Shelby Co Dental Soc Pan TN Dental Assn 1983-84; Certificate Northeast Mental Health Ctr Bd Dirs 1984; Plaques from Shelby Cty Dental Soc for dedication to Dentistry for 28 yrs, North Memphis Tennis Club-Thanks 1986, NE CMTY Mental Health Cntr in appreciation for Outstanding Contributions 1978-85; Meharry Medical College Presidents Awd 1957-82; certificates from Douglass Optimist Club chartermem, Natl Childrens Dental Health Month 1985-87, Middle Baptist Church in appreciation 1984, Gov Lamar Alexander appreciation for helping senior citizens; Positive Mental Attitude Association Dr Martin Luther King Awd 1985; honorary mem Hyde Park Alumni Assoc 1983; Proclamation St of TN Rep Larry Turner Pride-de-Camp 1985. **BUSINESS ADDRESS:** 2154 Chelsea Ave, Memphis, TN 38108.

JORDAN, JOHN WESLEY
Clergyman. **PERSONAL:** Born Sep 10, 1941, Edenton, NC; son of Earl Holley and Annie L. Jordan Holley; divorced; children: Johann Earle. **EDUCATION:** Elizabeth City State Univ, BS English 1963; Teachers Coll Columbia Univ, MA English 1964; A Phillip Randolph Inst, 2 courses 1973; Columbia Univ, advance study 1974; NC State Univ, 1 course 1976. **CAREER:** Savannah State Coll, instr in humanities 1964-66; Eliz City State Coll, instr in humanities 1965; Claflin College SC, instr in humanities 1966; Hampton Inst, instr in humanities 1966-67; New York City Bd of Education, English teacher 1967-74; HQ USAG Ft Bragg, NC, personnel actions spec 1975-77; Camp Casey, Korea, awards and decorations spec 1977-78; Ft Bragg, NC, ID card sgt NCOIC 1978-81; Ft Shafter, HI, NCOIC of personnel actions 1982-84; Fort Drum NY, personnel actions sgt 1984-86, personnel admin ctr supervisor HQ 7th FA 1986-89; Watertown Correctional Facility, Watertown, NY, English teacher 1988; Watertown Urban Mission, Watertown, NY, director Operation Breakthrough 1988-89; City of Refuge Christian Church, Great Bend, NY, pastor. **ORGANIZATIONS:** NCOIC Separations HQ USAG Ft Drum NY 1984-; active with Non-denominational Pentecostal Religion (Full Gospel); editor Refuge Flame City of Refuge Christian Church of HI 1982-84; volunteer minister Watertown Correctional Facility Watertown, NY 1984-, Cape Vincent Correctional Facility 1988-; mem religious advisory bd Watertown Correctional Facility 1988-; volunteer lay religious leader Ft Drum Prayer/Bible Study/Fellowship 1984-; 1st vice pres 1985, pres 1986 Full Gospel Business Men's Fellowship Intl (Ft Drum/Charthage Chpt); mem Watertown/Jefferson County NAACP 1988-; chmn worship comm Ft Drum Gospel Svcs; speaker for FGBMFI; bd mem New Gate Prison Ministry. **HONORS/ACHIEVEMENTS:** Bearer of Mace/Top Grad Class of 1963 Eliz City State Univ 1963; American Spirit Honor Award (Aug 1975) Ft Jackson, SC; Omega Psi Phi Fraternity Undergrad Scholarship 1962; Grad Scholarship 1963; academic graduate of Advance Non-Commissioned Officer Course class 1985-86 Administration Ft Ben Harrison IN; first Annual Freedom Fund Award, Watertown/Jefferson County NAACP, 1989. **MILITARY SERVICE:** AUS, sgt 1st class, 1975-88; Army Commendation Medal (1st Oak Leaf Cluster); Army Achievement Medal; Certificate of Appreciation; Meritorious Service Medal, 1988. **HOME ADDRESS:** PO Box 321, Great Bend, NY 13643. **BUSINESS ADDRESS:** Supervisor, Transition Center, United States Army, 10th Mountain Division, Fort Drum, NY 13602.

JORDAN, JOSEPHINE E.C.
Organization official. **PERSONAL:** Born Dec 13, 1935, Philadelphia, PA; married Rev Harry A Jordan Sr (deceased). **EDUCATION:** Allied Corporation, Business Certificate 1971. **CAREER:** Order of Eastern Star PHA of PA, worthy matron. **ORGANIZATIONS:** Mem Daughter of Isis 1983-, Heroines of Jericho 1983-; worthy matron Hadassah Chap #91 OES 1985-87; mem Court of Cyrenes 1987-. **HOME ADDRESS:** 2202 Airacobra St, Levittown, PA 19057.

JORDAN, JUNE M. (NEE MEYER)
Educator, author. **PERSONAL:** Born Jul 09, 1936, Harlem, NY; daughter of Granville Ivanhoe Jordan and Mildred Maud Fisher; divorced; children: Christopher D Meyer. **EDUCATION:** Barnard Coll, attended 1953-57; Univ Chicago, attended 1955-56. **CAREER:** CCNY, asst prof 1968; Sarah Lawrence Coll, writing faculty 1968-71; Yale Univ, visiting lectr 1974-75; Loft Mentor Series Minneapolis, vstg mentor poet 1983; SUNY at Stony Brook, assoc prof of english 1978-82, dir The Poetry Ctr 1986-, dir the creative writing prog 1986-89; prof of english 1982-89; Univ of California, Berkeley, prof of Afro-American Studies and Women's Studies 1989-. **ORGANIZATIONS:** Bd dirs Poets & Writers 1979-87; exec bd PEN Amer Ctr 1980-84; exec bd Amer Writers Congress 1981-83; judge Lamont Prize Acad of Amer Poets 1981,82,83; judge The Massachusetts Cncl on the Arts Awds in Poetry 1984; bd dirs Center for Constitutional Rights 1984-; mem Authors Guild Council 1986-; bd of governors The NY Foundation of the Arts 1986-; bd of dir The Nicaraguan Culture Alliance 1986-. **HONORS/ACHIEVEMENTS:** Rockefeller Grant in Creative Writing 1969; Prix de Rome in Environmental Design 1970; CAPS Grant in Poetry 1978; NEA Fellowship in Poetry 1982; Fellowship Awd in Poetry NY Foundation for the Arts 1985; Massachusetts Cncl on the Arts Awd in Contemporary Arts 1985; 19 books published to date; poetry readings; keynote lectures, playwright, regular political columnist for The Progressive Magazine. **BUSINESS ADDRESS:** Poet & Professor of Afro-American Studies, Univ of California, Berkeley, 3335 Dwinelle Hall, Berkeley, CA 94720.

JORDAN, KENNETH ULYS
Educator. **PERSONAL:** Born Apr 10, 1944, South Pittsburg, TN; married Constance Elaine Walker; children: Kenneth II. **EDUCATION:** Univ of TN, BS 1966; Vanderbilt Law Sch, JD 1974. **CAREER:** Vanderbilt Law School, asst dean, instructor 1975-77; Vanderbilt Law School, assoc dir 1974-75; General Foods Corp, corporate personnel specialist 1970-71; Urban Affairs Inst, instructor 1975-. **ORGANIZATIONS:** Mem Am Bar Assn; TN Bar Assn; pres, bd of dir Grace M Eaton Day Home; bd mem Family & Children's Svcs; Crisis Call Ctr; Martin Luther King Jr Fellow; Woodrow Wilson Found 1971-74. **HONORS/ACHIEVEMENTS:** US Law Week Award, VanderbiltUniv Law Sch 1974. **MILITARY SERVICE:** USAF capt 1966-70. **BUSINESS ADDRESS:** Box 1809, Sta B VanderbiltUniv, Nashville, TN 37235.

JORDAN, LEROY A.
Administrator. **PERSONAL:** Born Dec 27, 1941, Murphysboro, IL; married Johnetta Williams; children: Laura, Loralean, Jennifer. **EDUCATION:** So IL Univ, BS Elem Educ 1964; Sangamon State Univ, MA Educ Admin 1972. **CAREER:** Hopkins Park Pembroke Township Sch, teacher 1964-65; Sch Dist 186 Springfield IL, tchr adult educ/prin 1965-69; State Bd of Educ Div of Vocational Tech Educ, consult rsch & devel 1969-72; Sangamon State Univ, asst dir applied studies 1972-75, dir applied studies & experimental learning 1975-81, dean innovative & experimental studies 1982-85. **ORGANIZATIONS:** Mem IL Assn of Sch Bd 1976-; educ adv com Springfield Jr League 1978-80; corp bd of dir Meml Hosp Springfield Jr League 1978-80; corp bd of dir Meml Hosp Springfield IL 1979-84; pres bd of educ Springfield IL 1976-77, 1980-81; mem Natl Sch Bd Assn 1976-82; pres bd dir Statesmen Drum & Bugle Corps 1978-81; mem Natl Com Campaign for Human Devel Natl Cath Conf 1979-82. **HONORS/ACHIEVEMENTS:** Outstanding Leadership Awd Black Caucus Sangamon State Univ 1979-80; Cert of Appreciation Bd of Control Springfield Area Voc Ctr 1979-80; Outstanding Citizen Springfield IL Urban League 1980. **BUSINESS ADDRESS:** Dean, Innovat & Exp Studies, Sangamon StateUniv, Sheppard Rd, Springfield, IL 62708.

JORDAN, MABEL B.
Retired educator. **PERSONAL:** Born Mar 17, 1912, Raleigh, NC; married Anthony Jordan. **EDUCATION:** Shaw Univ, AB 1933; NC Central Univ, Grad Study. **CAREER:** Nash Cty, prin 1933-46; Middlesex Elem, principal 1946-56; South Nash, 8th Grade 1956-69; Middlesex, spec math 1969-75. **ORGANIZATIONS:** Pres Nash Co Tchr 1963-65; dept chrmn Intermediate Dept 1965-68; ACT Pub Chrmn ACT 1972-73, bldg rep 1970-74; pres Franklin Bd Union Women 1964-66, Raleigh Sect Negro Women 1973-77, South Park Comm Floral 1973-77. **HONORS/ACHIEVEMENTS:** NC Resource Use NC Central Univ 1967; Tchr of the Year South Nash 1969, PTA Award 1969; NCNW Comm Srv Award Raleigh Sect of NCNW 1973, 1985. **HOME ADDRESS:** 211 Bledsoe Ave, Raleigh, NC 27601.

JORDAN, MARILYN E.
Financial administrator. **PERSONAL:** Born Aug 31, 1944, Yonkers, NY; married Limuary Alja Jordan Jr. **EDUCATION:** Central State U, BS 1966; City Coll NY, MA, MA Advanced Cert grad hon 1974, 1972-74, 1976; Columbia U, doctoral candidate (pending) 1978-80. **CAREER:** New York City Bd of Edn, dir of finance; New York City Bd of Edn, acting prin 1976-77; New York City Bd of Edn, asst prin 1972-76; New York City Bd of Edn, tchr in charge 1970-72; New York City Bd of Edn, tchr 1967-70; IBM, programmer 1966-67. **ORGANIZATIONS:** Treas CCNY Black Alumni Assn 1980; mem Am Assn of Sch Admin 1980; mem Assn of Sch Bus Officials 1980; mem Nat Educ Assn 1980; publicity dir Teaneck & Englewood Vicinity Ass of Negro Bus & Professional Women Club 1980; mem NY Urban League 1980; mem NAACP 1980; mem Alpha Kappa Alpha Sorority1980. **HONORS/ACHIEVEMENTS:** Grad Student Award, City Coll Grad Student Council 1971, 1972, 1974; Nat Tchng Award; Outstanding Tchr of Am 1972; Who's Who Women of the World, Internatl Chap 1978; Who's Who in Am, Nat Chap 1980. **BUSINESS ADDRESS:** 1377 Jerome Ave, Bronx, NY 10452.

JORDAN, MARJORIE W.
Multiservices coordinator. **PERSONAL:** Born Jan 12, 1924, New Orleans; widowed; children: Cornelius, Emmett. **EDUCATION:** Dillard U, BA magna cum laude 1944;Univ of Chgo;Univ of Cincinnati; Coll of Comm Serv Comm Health Adminstrn. **CAREER:** Cincinnati Health Dept, coordinator of health programs; Housing Opportunities Made Equal, dir. **ORGANIZATIONS:** Mem Nat Assn Black Soc Workers; mem OH Pub Health Assn; mem Professional Soc of Pub Health Workers of OH; mem Nat Conf on Soc Welfare; mem Bd Nat Non-Profit Housing Corp; bd mem, sec, exec com mem 7 Hills Neighborhood Houses Inc; exec com Easy Riders Inc; bd Urban League; ARC; Am Cancer Soc; co-chmn Consumer Affairs Commn of Fed; exec bd, chmn Consumer Forum; exec com Hosusing Opportunities Made Equal Inc; Unitarian Universalist Serv Com Bd (Nat); Womans City Club; Social Serv Assn; other ciic orgns. **HONORS/ACHIEVEMENTS:** Recip Serv Award, Am Cancer Society 1972. **BUSINESS ADDRESS:** 614 Provident Bank Bldg, 7 & Vine Sts, Cincinnati, OH 45202.

JORDAN, MICHAEL
Professional athlete. **PERSONAL:** Born Feb 17, 1963, Wilmington, NC; son of James Jordan and Deloris Peoples Jordan. **EDUCATION:** NC Univ, 1985. **CAREER:** Chicago Bulls, basketball player guard. **HONORS/ACHIEVEMENTS:** NBA Most Valuable Player, 1988; Coll Player of the Year 1983,84; Bulls 1st round pick (3rd overall) in 1984 NBA; unanimous selection 1st team All-Amer 1982-83,83-84; ACC Rookie of the Year as freshman; named to all-tournament team at Final Four & ACC tourney; leading scorer on US Pan Amer team which won the Gold Medal in Caracus Venezuela five-time NBA; All Star Guard and 1984-85 Rookie of the Year; Set an all-time NBA Playoff Record for the Most points in a three game serie; Was the only player in the NBA to score in double figures in all 82 games played in his rookie year. **BUSINESS ADDRESS:** The Chicago Bulls, 980 N Michigan Ave, Chicago, IL 60611.

JORDAN, MICHELLE DENISE
Attorney. **PERSONAL:** Born Oct 29, 1954, Chicago, IL; daughter of John A Jordan and Margaret O'Dood Jordan; divorced. **EDUCATION:** Loyola Univ, BA (magna cum laude) 1974; Univ of MI Law School, JD 1977. **CAREER:** States Atty Office of Cook County, atty 1977-82; Chicago State Univ, teach political science 1985-; Attorney Generals Office, atty; IL Attorney General's Office, Chicago, IL, chief environmental control div, 1988-, deputy chief, 1987-88; Chicago City Counsel, Chicago, IL, legal counsel license comm, 1986-. **ORGANIZATIONS:** Mem Chicago Bar Assn 1977-, Cook County Bar Assn 1977-, Natl Bar Assn 1980-, IL State Bar Assn 1978-, bd mem Loyola Univ Alumni Assn 1984-87; mem Prof Women's Auxiliary of Provident Hospital 1981-82; subcommittee co-chmn, Chicago Bar Assn, Young Bar Assn, 1986-87; mem, Child Witness Project, Task Force, 1987-88; mem, Hearing Div, Chicago Bar Assn, Judicial Evaluation Comm, 1987-88; investigator, investigations, Chicago Bar Assn, Judicial Evaluation Comm, 1986-87. **HONORS/ACHIEVEMENTS:** Operation PUSH Womens Day Award 1978; America's Top 100 Business & Professional Woman, editorial bd Dollars & Sense Magazine, 1988; instructor, IL Attorney General's Training Program, 1988; instructor, Chicago Bar Association's Young Lawyers Intensive Trail Practice Program, 1986. **HOME ADDRESS:** 7750 S Hoyne, Chi-

cago, IL 60620. **BUSINESS ADDRESS:** Attorney, Attorney Generals Office, 100 W Randolph, Chicago, IL 60601.

JORDAN, MILTON C.
Editor. **PERSONAL:** Born May 23, Durham, NC; married Sadie Smith; children: Edward Lee, Milton C II. **CAREER:** The Carolinian Newspaper, staff writer; The Carolina Times, staff writer; The Carolina Peacemaker Newspaper, staff writer; Wilmington Star Newspaper, staff writer 1970-72; WWIL Radio, station mgr 1972-73; WIDU Radio, acct exec 1973-74; The Charlotte Observer, urban affairs specialist 1974-79; The Carolina Times, exec editor. **HONORS/ACHIEVEMENTS:** School Bell Awd NC Assn of Educators 1983; Unity Awd for Excellence in Journalism Lincoln Univ 1983. **BUSINESS ADDRESS:** Exec Editor, Carolina Times, PO Box 3825, Durham, NC 27702.

JORDAN, ORCHID I.
Legislator. **PERSONAL:** Born Aug 15, 1910, Clay Center, KS; married Leon M. **EDUCATION:** WilberforceUniv OH, grad. **CAREER:** MO 25th Dist, state rep 1970-; Pan Am World Airways Monrovia Livera, former travel agt, ofc mgr. **ORGANIZATIONS:** Cofounder Freedom Inc Kansas City. **BUSINESS ADDRESS:** 2745 Garfield Ave, Kansas City, MO 64109.

JORDAN, PATRICIA CARTER
Government official. **PERSONAL:** Born Jan 23, 1941, Mobile, AL; daughter of Nelver S. Carter and Olivette Glaude Carter; married Richard O. Jordan, Jr., Aug 21, 1965; children: Orisha Katrina Jordan. **EDUCATION:** Howard Univ, Washington, DC, degree in sociology; Top 40 Mgmt Training Program, City of NY, graduate. **CAREER:** City of NY Housing Preservation and Devel/Office of Property Mgmt, admin mgr; direc of research and devel, Black Citizens for a Fair Media, 1971-. **ORGANIZATIONS:** Asst to deputy chancellor, City of NY Bd of Edn; mgmt consultant, City of NY High Div; communication supvr, Communications Inst, NY; consultant and instructor, Found for Change in Inter-Racial Books for Children; consultant, Public Edn Assn, NY; community rels speclst and trainer, Community Rels Serv, US Dept of Justice; research asst/adjunct lecturer, Hunter College Dept of Urban Affairs; research assoc, HARYOU-ACT Assoc, NY; research/training asst, Columbia Univ Grad School of Arts and Sciences, NY. **HONORS/ACHIEVEMENTS:** Author of Youth in the Ghetto—A Study of the Consequences of Powerlessness and a Blueprint for Change, HARYOU-ACT, 1964. **HOME ADDRESS:** Patricia Carter Jordan, 50 West 97th Street #4R, New York, NY 10025.

JORDAN, R. D.
Educational administrator. **PERSONAL:** Born Sep 18, 1930, Texas. **EDUCATION:** Reed Christian Coll, BA 1955; St Stephens Educ Bible Coll, BS 1965; Antioch Coll, MS 1975; St Stephens Educ Bible Coll, PhD 1979. **CAREER:** St Stephen's Baptist Church & Coll, founder & natl pres 1952-; St Stephen's Baptist Church, pastor 1952-. **ORGANIZATIONS:** 1st vice pres PBSC of CA 1979; pres of christian educ United Bapt Assn 1979-. **HONORS/ACHIEVEMENTS:** Minister of the Year, St Stephen's Na Youth Counsel 1975; Image Award, NAACP Hollywood Chap 1977; Outstanding Pres, Black Women's Nat Counsel 1978. **BUSINESS ADDRESS:** 330 W 61st St, Los Angeles, CA 90003.

JORDAN, RALPH
Educational administrator. **PERSONAL:** Born Sep 05, 1926, Mooresville, NC; married Juanita T Jones; children: Ronald Anthony. **EDUCATION:** NC CentralUniv Durham, BS 1952; Springfield Coll MA, MS 1961; GW U, Howard U, NCCU,Univ of DC, Cath U, adv studies. **CAREER:** Spingarn STAY High School, prin 1969-; Office of Programs & Serv DCPS, special assignment 1978; Office of Instructional Serv DCPS, acting dir alternative educ 1976; Spingarn STAY High School, asst prin 1967-69; Anacostia HS, counselor 1966-67; Terrell Jr HS, summer school asst prin 1967; Stuart Jr HS, summer school asst prin 1966; Gordon Jr HS, counselor 1966; Public Schools of DC, teacher 1958-66; Public Schools of Charles County MD, teacher 1956-58; Public Schools of NC, teacher 1952-56. **ORGANIZATIONS:** Consult HEW Conf on Sch Age Parenthood 1978; consult Educ Dept DC Tchr Coll; consult Educ Dept Coppin State Coll; mem Omega Psi Phi Frat 1951-; mem Free & Accepted Masons 1954-; mem Nat Assn of Secondary Sch Prin; mem Stonegate Citizens Assn Mont Co MD 1973-; mem Assn for Supervision Curriculum Devel; mem Am Assn of Sch Adminstr Grad Fellowship Springfield Coll MA 1961. **HONORS/ACHIEVEMENTS:** Outstanding Serv to Youth, YMCA 1965; Award of Merit-Contribution in Area of Edn, Faculty Spingarn STAY 1974. **MILITARY SERVICE:** USN 1943-46. **BUSINESS ADDRESS:** Spingarn Sch To Aid Youth, Washington, DC 20002.

JORDAN, ROBERT
Concert pianist. **EDUCATION:** Eastman Sch, BA; Julliard Sch, MA; studied under Cecile Genhart, Edward Steuermann & Rosina Lhevinne; as Fulbright Scholar spent 3 yrs studying & performing in Germany. **CAREER:** Major Capitals, including New York City at teh Avery Fischer & Alice Tully Halls of Lincoln Center, the John F Kennedy Center in Washington, appearances in recitals;Prague Philharmonic in Czechoslovakia, the Bayerisches Rundfunk Orch Munich, soloist; Chattanooga Symphony; Symphony of the New Wolrd; Buffalo Philharmonic; Baltimore Symphony; Second Wolrd Black & African Festival, recitalist 1977; toured Brazil 1978; Triad Presentations Inc, bd of dir mem of adv council; Morgan St U, artist-in-residence 1976-78;Univ of DE, artist-in-residence 1979. **ORGANIZATIONS:** Inaugurated Minority Schlrshp FundUniv of DE 1979. **HONORS/ACHIEVEMENTS:** Recipient four different awards during 1975; one of 12 pianists chosen nationally ot commn a new composition from an Am composer & give its world premiere atKennedy Center; recipeint Outstanding Young Men of Am Award; Comm Leaders & Noteworthy Am Award; listed in Who's Who in Am.

JORDAN, ROBERT A.
Social worker. **PERSONAL:** Born Dec 04, 1932, Atlanta; married Edna Fraley. **EDUCATION:** Clark Coll, AB 1958; Atla U, MA 1969;Univ of GA, post grad 1972-73. **CAREER:** Atlanta Public School System, reading teacher 1972-, social worker 1972, teacher 1966-72; Fulton County School System, teacher 1961-66. **ORGANIZATIONS:** Bd Dir Atlanta Assn of Educ (past vp); mem GA Educ Assn; NEA; Professional Rights Comm, AAE mem, Educ Chmn, Forward GA Assembly; pres Jazz Disciples Club; mem State Dem Party; Phi Beta Sigma; bd of trustees Ebenezer Bapt Ch; articles written "Parent Input In Publ Schs" & "Why SAT Scores Are Low"; appeared on Radio (WRNG) & TV (ch 5, 2, 11, 30); co-host Jazz Radio Prog, Stat WYZE; collector of Jazz Records five thousand albums; interviewed for article "State of Jazz in Atlanta", Constitution Nwspaper; aauthor article "Profile of a VIP"; article "What's Wrong with Education". **MILITARY SERVICE:** AUS pfc 1953-55. **BUSINESS ADDRESS:** 1890 Bankhead Hwy, Atlanta, GA 30318.

JORDAN, ROBERT HOWARD, JR.
Televison news anchor, reporter. **PERSONAL:** Born Aug 31, 1943, Atlanta, GA; son of Robert H Jordan and Millicent Dobbs Jordan; married Sharon Lundy, Dec 20, 1970; children: Karen Millicent Jordan. **EDUCATION:** Attended Morehouse Coll, Atlanta GA, and Fisk Univ, Nashville TN; Roosevelt Univ, Chicago IL, BA, 1975. **CAREER:** WSM TV, Nashville TN, reporter/announcer, 1970-73; WGN TV, Chicago IL, reporter, 1973-78; CBS News, Chicago IL, reporter, 1978-80; WGN TV, anchor/reporter, 1980-. **ORGANIZATIONS:** Mem, Amer Federation of Radio & Television Artists, 1972-; mem, Chicago Assn of Black Journalists, 1983-; mem bd of dir, John G Shedd Aquarium, 1987-; mem bd of dir, Evanston Hospital, 1987-. **HONORS/ACHIEVEMENTS:** Black Achievers of Industry, YMCA of Metropolitan Chicago, 1975; Appreciation Award, Chicago Dental Society, 1976; co-host, UNCF Telethon, 1981-; co-host, MS Telethon, 1983-; master of ceremony, Black and Hispanic Achievers Industry, 1985-89; Article/Scuba Diving, Chicago Tribune Newspaper, 1988. **MILITARY SERVICE:** US Army, spc 4th class, outstanding trainee, company D, 9th BN USATCI, 1965-68. **BUSINESS ADDRESS:** WGN TV, 2501 Bradley Place, Chicago, IL 60618.

JORDAN, ROBERT L.
Clergyman. **PERSONAL:** Born May 20, 1906, Knoxville, TN; married Maisie Norman; children: Robert Lee Jr, Emma Goldie, Kenneth Samuel. **EDUCATION:** Chapman Coll, AB 1936; Univ of MI, MA 1945; Bethany Coll, DD 1969. **CAREER:** West Challenger LA, bus mgr newspaper 1932; Young Men's Civic Assn, field rep 1933-35; E Side Comm Ctr LA, asst supt 1933-35; Committee of Friendly Relations LA, chmn 1934-36; City of LA, ordained minister 1936, asst minister 1935-36; United Christian Ch, pastor 1936-74. **ORGANIZATIONS:** Primary organizer Inter-Denom Ministers Alliance Detroit 1937; chmn Social Action Comm Natl Conv Christian Chs 1954-56; vice pres state conv ChristianChs MI 1959; mem Soc Serv Dept Detroit Council Chs 1960, bd dir 1968; bd dir Campas Christian Fellowship Wayne State Univ 1960-70; vice pres Natl Christian Missionary Conv 1954-56; pres Natl Christian Missionary Conv 1956-58; delegate 3 world conv Ch of Christ Scotland 1960, PuertoRico 1965, S Australia 1970; mem Inter-Denom Ministers All Detroit; mem Kappa Alpha Psi; pres W Side Pastors Alliance; exec bd Triangel Assoc; mem Grass Roots Orgn; pres Inter-Denom All Detroit 1970-72; mem MI State Fair Bd 1965-70; mem NAACP; mem Detroit Comm Relations Com Police Commn 1970-72; mem Mayors Ministers Adv Com 1972-74; mem Planned Parenthood Ministers Adv Com. **HONORS/ACHIEVEMENTS:** Longevity Awd Disciple Ministers Detroit 1962; Biographies & Negro Preachers of Amer; auth "Two Races in One Fellowship" 1944; Colored Disciples in MI 1942; auth "Black Theology Exposed" 1983.

JORDAN, STEVE
Professional athlete. **PERSONAL:** Born Jan 10, 1961, Phoenix, AZ; married Anita. **EDUCATION:** Attended, Brown Univ. **CAREER:** Minnesota Vikings, tight end 1982-. **HONORS/ACHIEVEMENTS:** In coll set school record for most receiving yds in a game w/188; mem 1987 Pro Bowl team. **BUSINESS ADDRESS:** Minnesota Vikings, 9520 Viking Dr, Eden Prairie, MN 55344.

JORDAN, THURMAN
Certified public accountant. **PERSONAL:** Born Dec 02, 1936, Harrisburg, IL; married Teiko Ann; children: Eric, Neal, Philip. **EDUCATION:** Roosevelt U, BSBA 1966; Univ of Chicago, MBA 1982; IL, CPA 1972. **CAREER:** Signode Corp, controller 1976-; Arthur Andersen & Co, audit mgr 1966-76. **ORGANIZATIONS:** Mem IL Soc CPA's Am Inst CPA's; Alumni Chicago Forum; mem Chicago United; vchmn Operatin & Effectiveness Com; mem Agency Serv Com Comm Fund; bd mem United Way of Chicago, Evanston Art Center. **HONORS/ACHIEVEMENTS:** Black achiever award YMCA 1974. **MILITARY SERVICE:** AUS PFC 1961; Outstanding Trainee Awd. **BUSINESS ADDRESS:** Vice President, Signode Industries, Inc, 8501 W Higgins Rd, Chicago, IL 60631.

JORDAN, VERNON E., JR.
Attorney. **PERSONAL:** Born Aug 15, 1935, Fulton City, GA; married Ann Dibble; children: Vickee, Antionette Cook, Mercer Cook, Janice Cook. **EDUCATION:** DePaw Univ, BA, 1957; Howard Univ Law Sch, JD, 1960; Fellow Inst Pol John F Kennedy Sch Govt, Harvard Univ, 1969. **CAREER:** Natl Urban League Inc, pres; United Negro Clg Fund, exec dir; Voter Education Project Southern Reg Council, dir; US Office Economic Opportunity, atty-consultant; NAACP GA field dir; GA & AR, prvt legal practice; partner, Akin, Gump, Strauss, Hauer & Feld. **ORGANIZATIONS:** Mem AR Bar; mem Dist of Columbia Bar; mem GA Bar; mem US Supreme Ct Bar; mem Am Bar Assc; mem natl Bar Assc; memUniv Clb; mem Century Assc;mem Bd Room; mem Cncl Foreign Reltations; dirctrshp Am Express Co; dirctrshp AtlantaUniv Cntr Corp; dirctrshp Bankers Trust Co; dirctrshp Bankers Trust NY Corp; dirctrshp Celanese Corp; dirctrshp Clark Clg; dirctrshp Corning Glass Works; dirctrshp Dow Jones & Co Inc; dirctrshp JC Penney Co Inc; dirctrshp RJ Reynolds Inds Inc; dirctrshp Taconic Found; dirctrshp White House Preservation Fund; dirctrshp United Way Am; dirctrshp Xerox Corp; fed apptmt Cncl of the White House Conf "To Fulfill These Rights" 1966; fed apptmt Natl Advsry Cmsn on Selective Serv 1966-67; fed apptmt Am Revolution Bi-centennial Cmsn 1972; fed apptmt Presdential Clemency Bd 1974; fed apptmt Advsry Cncl on Soc Sec 1974; Secretary of State's Advisory Com on South Africa; dir RJR/ Nabisco, Inc; mem bd dirs, Revlon Group Inc, 1989-. **HONORS/ACHIEVEMENTS:** Hon degrees Baldwin-Wallace Clg, Benedict Clg, Bloomfield Clg, Boston Clg, Brandeis U, Brooklyn Ctr Long Island U, Brown U, CityUniv NY, Dartmouth Clg, Davidson Clg, DePauw U, Dillard U, Duke U,Univ Evansville, Fordham U, Hamilton Clg, Harvard U, Clg Holy Cross, Howard U, Knoxville Clg, Lafayette Clg,Univ MA, MI State U, Morehouse Clg, Morris Brown Clg, NY U, NC A&T U, Notre Dame U,Univ PA, Princeton U, Rutgers U, SuffolkUniv Law Sch, Tougaloo Clg, Tuskegee Inst, Wesleyan U, Wilberforce U, Williams Clg, Winston-Salem State U, Xavier U, Yale U; Rhodes Coll, Tulane U,Univ West FL,Univ of Chgo,U of TX at Austin. **BUSINESS ADDRESS:** Revlon Group Inc, 757 Fifth Ave, New York, NY 10022. *

JORDAN, WESLEY LEE
Educator. **PERSONAL:** Born Jan 06, 1941, Petersburg, VA; married Alice Barber; children: Wesley. **EDUCATION:** State Coll, BS 1963; Fordham U, MS 1965 columbia u, edd 1976. **CAREER:** Pace Univ, asst prof of math 1969-; Belmont Abbey Coll, 1964-67. **ORGANIZATIONS:** Mem Nat Counc of Tchrs of Math Math Assn of Am; Am Assn ofUniv Profs Trustee, Shiloh Bapt Ch; J. **HONORS/ACHIEVEMENTS:** 1st black & full-time faculty mem of So white coll, Belmont Abbey Coll 1964. **BUSINESS ADDRESS:** 78 N Broadway, White Plains, NY 10663.

JORDAN, WILBERT CORNELIOUS
Physician. **PERSONAL:** Born Sep 11, 1944, Wheatley, AR. **EDUCATION:** Harvard Coll, AB 1966; Case Western Reserve, MD 1971; UCLA, MPH 1978. **CAREER:** Center for Disease Control, epidemiologist 1973-76; US Public Health Svcs, lt commander 1973-78; Los Angeles County, area public health chief 1979-83; Drew Medical School, assoc prof 1979-87; King-Drew Medical Ctr, dir grad education. **ORGANIZATIONS:** Life mem NAACP 1978-; sec of bd PSRO Area XXIII 1980-84; chmn of bd Minority AIDS Project LA Cty 1984-87; bd mem NAMME 1984-87; mem Coalition Against Black Exploitation 1985-87; chmn of bd Sallie Martin Foundation 1986-87; med dir Natl Convention of Gospel Choirs & Choruses Inc; mem Undersea Medical Soc; mem Amer Venereal Disease Assn, Assoc Amer Med Colls, Natl Med Assn; pres Inglewood Physicians Assoc; grad liaison Natl Assoc of Minority med Educators. **HONORS/ACHIEVEMENTS:** Outstanding Physician of Year SNMA 1973; Recognition Awd NAMME 1984; also numerous articles. **BUSINESS ADDRESS:** Dir Graduate Education, King-Drew Medical Center, 12021 So Wilmington, Los Angeles, CA 90059.

JORDAN, WILLIAM ALFRED, III
Educator. **PERSONAL:** Born Feb 01, 1934, Durham, NC; divorced; children: Vanessa, Alexander DuBois. **EDUCATION:** Georgetown U, BS 1955; Northwestern U, MA 1960; Columbia U, MS 1962. **CAREER:** CA State Polytech Univ, currently lecturer; Dept of Ethnic & Womens Studies; Assoc Negro Press, correspondent 1961-63; Zambia Star Lusaka Zambia, asst editor 1964-65; NY Times, fgn corr 1964-65; Wash Post, reporter 1965-66; Govtl Affairs Inst Washington, program officer 1966-67; Howard U, instr journalism 1966-67; Metro Applied Rsch Ctr, jr fellow 1968-69; Pratt Inst, asst prof social sci 1968-73; Nat Commis Critical Choices for Am Africa, consul 1974-76; Sonoma St U, assoc prof anthropology 1971-82; City Councilman City of Cotati CA, 1974-80. **HONORS/ACHIEVEMENTS:** Martin Luther King Fellow NYUniv 18970-71; Ford Found Fellowship 1972-73; Kenya E Africa; chmn Faculty Council Pratt Inst 1971; Natl Endowment of the Humanities Museum of African Art Wash DC 1979. **BUSINESS ADDRESS:** Lecturer, CA State PolytechUniv, 3801 W Temple Ave, Dept Ethnic & Womens Studies, Pomona, CA 91768.

JORDON, SAMUEL F.
Editor. **PERSONAL:** Born Oct 18, 1936, Shannon, MS; married Doretha C Wilder; children: Samuel F, III, Tamara Ruth, David Mark. **EDUCATION:** Tuskegee Inst, attnd; Weavers Sch Real Est, attnd; Finley Eng Coll, attnd;Univ MI, attnd; Nrthwstnr U, Sch of Mortgage-Banking. **CAREER:** Empire Mort & Invstmnt Co, exec vp, sec-treas; Comm Fin Co Inc; Modern Am Realty Co Inc; LIFT Inc; NE Bus Assn; Empire Protest Movement forEcon & Civil Justice, exec dir. **ORGANIZATIONS:** Mem, Mortgage Bkrs Assn Am; United Mortgage Bkrs Am; NAACP; Operation PUSH; mem, Greater KCC of C; NeE Bus Assn; YMCA; Rltrs Assn; United Comm Fund & Cncl; Consumer Credit Cncl; vice pres Empire Land Dev; SCLC; United Minority-Media Assn. **HONORS/ACHIEVEMENTS:** Okalana Jr Coll Trade Sch Award 1957; Mayors-Beautification Award 1970. **MILITARY SERVICE:** AUS pfc 1962-64. **BUSINESS ADDRESS:** 1304 N S St, Kansas City, KS 66101.

JOSEPH, ANTOINE L.
Attorney. **PERSONAL:** Born Jul 04, 1923, St Croix, VI; married Lorraine F; children: Antoine, Jr. **EDUCATION:** Dillard U, BA 1947; NrthwstrnUniv Law Sch, JD 1950. **CAREER:** Private practice, atty 1983-; Legislature of Virgin Island, dep chief counsel 1980-83; Territorial Ct of VI, judge 1965-80; Legislature of VI, leg cnsl 1962-65; Law Chicago, priv prac 1950-62. **ORGANIZATIONS:** Mem, VI Bar Assn. **MILITARY SERVICE:** AUS 1943-46. **BUSINESS ADDRESS:** Attorney, 71 E Two Brothers, Frederiksted, Virgin Islands of the United States 00840.

JOSEPH, FRANK DOUGLAS
Psychologist. **PERSONAL:** Born Oct 24, 1937. **EDUCATION:** CA St U, BA 1971; AZ St U, PhD 1975. **CAREER:** Children's Preventive Srvs, dir 1974-; Maricopa Tech Coll, vis faculty 1972-; CD Boags & Assoc, rsrch consult 1972-; Mntl Hlth Tech Prog, Mesa Comm-Coll, instr 1972-74. **ORGANIZATIONS:** Mem, Am & Black Stds Psychological & Assns; Am & AZ Prsnl & Guidance Assns; Assn Black Psychologists; Assn Black Soc Wrkrs; Black Stds Psychol Assn; mem, AZ Gov Juvenile Justice Planning Adv Com 1975-; bd dir on numerous Comm. **MILITARY SERVICE:** USAF com 1955-59. **HOME ADDRESS:** 2610 S Rita Ln, Tempe, AZ 85282.

JOSEPH, JAMES ALFRED
Chief executive officer. **PERSONAL:** Born Mar 12, 1935, Opelousas, LA; married Doris Taylor; children: Jeffrey, Denise. **EDUCATION:** Southern Univ, BA 1956; Yale Univ, BD, MA 1963; Southeastern Univ, LLD 1982; Univ of MD, DPS 1984. **CAREER:** Claremont Coll, chaplain and prof 1969-70; Irwin-Sweeney-Miller Fnd, exec dir 1970-72; Cummins Engine Co, vice pres 1972-77; US Dept of Interior, undersec 1977-81; Yale Divinity Sch, visiting prof 1981-82; Council on Foundations, pres. **ORGANIZATIONS:** Chmn US Comm on Northern Marianas 80-86; bd dir Cummins Engine Fnd 1981-87, Colonial Williamsburg 1981-87, Pitzer Coll 1972-77; mem Council on Foreign Rel 1981-85, The Hague Club 1983-87, Adv Com US Dept of State 1982-84, Bd of Visitors Duke Univ 1981-83; bd of dir Brooking Inst 1985-, Salzbert seminar 1985-; Atlantic Council 1985-, United Nations Assoc 1986-; mem adv comm Natl Academy of Sci 1982-83; bd dir Children Defense Fund 1983-, Africare 1982-. **HONORS/ACHIEVEMENTS:** Public Serv Award, Yale Afro Amer Alumni 1976; Visiting Fellow Oxford Univ 1985; Business Person of the Year, Natl Assn of Concerned Business Students 1974; co-editor, Three Perspectives on Ethnicity 1972; chmn US Gov Del 1977, UN Conf in Kenya 1977. **MILITARY SERVICE:** Med Serv Corps 1st lt 1956-58. **BUSINESS ADDRESS:** President, Council on Foundations, 1828 L Street, NW, Washington, DC 20036.

JOSEPH, RAYMOND ALCIDE
Reporter. **PERSONAL:** Born Aug 31, 1931, San Pedro de Maco, Dominican Republic. **EDUCATION:** Univ of Chgo, MA 1964; Wheaton Coll, BA 1960; Moody Bible Inst, dipl 1957. **CAREER:** Wall St Journal, Div Dow Jones, staff reporter; "Haiti-Observateur," co-publ. **ORGANIZATIONS:** Found 1st printshop for WI Mission in Haiti 1950; ed, Creole Mmthly "Reyon & Lumie"; translated, edited, publ, New Testament in Creole for Am Bible Soc1960; sec gen of "Haitian Coalition" NY opposition to regime of Duvalier; organizer, daily pol broad cast to Haiti in French; edited "Le Combattant Haitien" in French & Eng. **BUSINESS ADDRESS:** 22 Cortlandt St, New York, NY 10007.

JOSEPH-MCINTYRE, MARY
Director. **PERSONAL:** Born Jan 12, 1942, Shreveport, LA; married Jethro; children: Jarrett. **EDUCATION:** Contra Costa Jr Coll, 1962; Willis Coll of Bus, 1963;Univ CA, 1966; Univ of San Francisco, continuing education - business admin 1983. **CAREER:** UC Berkeley, coord sec pool 1968-71, sec 1963-78; N Peralta Jr Coll, sec to pres 1971-72; UC Berkeley, pscy dept 1972-74; Oakland Met Enterprises, adminstrv asst 1975-76, exec dir 1976-79; Dukes, Dukes & Assoc, project admin 1979-83; "Sweet Touch", owner 1984-. **ORGANIZATIONS:** Mem Nat Frat of Student & Tchrs 1958-60; NAACP 1961-65, League of Women Voters 1964-70; vol Kilmanjaro House 1968; Black Caucus 1968-69; Nat Contract & Mgmt Assn 1977-; Negro Women Bus & Professional Inc 1977-. **HONORS/ACHIEVEMENTS:** Pres TAPS Prgm; mem Albany Youth Cncl 1959-60; award Alameda Co March of Dimes 1960; No CA Adoption Agy;Univ CA outst merit increase 1968. **HOME ADDRESS:** 3922 Turnley Ave, Oakland, CA 94605.

JOSEY, E. J.
Educator. **PERSONAL:** Born Jan 20, 1924, Norfolk, VA; son of Willie Josey and Frances Josey; married Dorothy Johnson (divorced); children: Elaine Jacqueline. **EDUCATION:** Howard Univ, AB 1949; Columbia Univ, MA 1950; State Univ of NY Albany, MSLS 1953; Shaw Univ, LHD 1973; Univ of Wisconsin-Milwaukee, DPS 1987. **CAREER:** Columbia Univ, desk asst 1950-52; NY Public Library Central Branch, tech asst grade 1 1952; NY State Libr, part-time asst 1952-53; Free Library of Philadelphia, librarian 1953-54; Savannah State Coll, instructor social science 1954-55; DE State Coll, librarian & asst prof 1955-59; Savannah State Coll, librarian & assoc prof Savannah State Coll 1959-66; NY State Educ Dept, assoc in acad & rsch libraries 1966-68; NY State Educ Dept, chief bureau of acad & rsch librarys 1968-76; NY State Educ Dept, chief bureau of specialist library serv 1976-86; University of Pittsburgh, prof school of library & info science. **ORGANIZATIONS:** Mem, pres Albany Branch Assoc for Study of Afro-Amer Life & History; mem Amer Assoc of Univ Prof, Amer Acad of Political & Social Science, NY Library Assn, Freedom to Read Found, NY Library Assoc Comm on Intellectual Freedom 1972, NY Library Club; chmn Assoc of Coop Library Org 1974-75; chmn ALA Black Caucus Task Force on Librarians for Africa 1972; founder & 1st chmn ALA Black Caucus; various positions incl pres Amer Library Assn 1984-85; mem bd dirs Amer Library Assn 1985-; exec bd Savannah Branch NAACP 1960-66; exec branch 1968-, pres 1982-, bd of trustees 1969-, treas 1970-72, chmn program comm 1972- Albany Branch NAACP; bd trustees Minority Educ & Devel Agency 1973; ed bd Dictionary of Amer Library History; bd advisors Childrens Book Review Svc; state youth adv GA Conf NAACP 1962-66; bd mgr Savannah Public Library, 1962-66; bd dir Coretta Scott King Award; mem tech Task Force EOA of Savannah; life mem NAACP 1971-; mem Amer Civil Liberties Union 1966-, Albany Interracial Council. **HONORS/ACHIEVEMENTS:** Savannah State Coll Debating Soc Award 1965; NAACP Natl Ofc Award 1965; GA State Conf NAACP Award for Youth Work 1966; Savannah Chatham County Merit Award for Work on Econ Opptunityy Task Force 1966; Savannah State Coll Library Award for Distinguished Serv to Librarianship 1967; Journal of Library History Award 1970; Certificate of Appreciation for Distinguished Serv as Council ALA 1978; ALA Black Caucus Award for Distinguished Serv to Librarianship 1979; NY Black Librarians Caucus Award for Excellence 1979; author of numerous publications; Distinguished Alumni Award for Contributions to Librarianship from School of Library & Info Science SUNY 1981; Distinguished Serv Award Library Assn of City Univ NY 1982; Award for Distinguished Comm Leadership as Pres of Albany NAACP SUNY 1984; DC Assoc of School Librarians Award for Contributor to Librarianship 1 Assoc of School Librarians Award for Contributor to Librarianship 1984; Award from NJ Black Librarians Network 1984; Africa Librarianship Award Kenya Library Assn 1984; Award for Contributions to Intl Librarianship Afro-Caribbean Library Assn of England 1984; Outstanding Leadership & Serv as Pres of Albany NAAC, NY State Conf of NAACP Branch Award 1984; NY Library Assoc Award 1985; NAACP President's Award 1986. **MILITARY SERVICE:** Military serv 1943-46. **BUSINESS ADDRESS:** Professor, Bureau of Acad & Rsch Library, School of Library & Info Science, University of Pittsburgh, Pittsburgh, PA 15260.

JOSEY, LERONIA ARNETTA
Government official. **PERSONAL:** Born in Norfolk, VA; children: Quenton C. **EDUCATION:** Spelman Coll, BA 1965; Univ of Maryland Sch of Soik & Comm Planning, MSW 1973; Syracuse Univ Coll of Law, JD (cum laude) 1977; Maxwell Sch of Citizenship Public Affairs Syracuse Univ, MPA 1977. **CAREER:** US Dept of Housing & Urban Devel, Washington DC, atty 1977-81; Maryland Parole Commission, commr 1981-. **ORGANIZATIONS:** Pres Natl Assc Blck Women Atty 1983-; dir Echo House Found 1978-82, Med Eye Black Bd 1981-82, Luic Carroll Jackson Museum 1982-. **HONORS/ACHIEVEMENTS:** 3rd hon grad Spilman Clg; Who's Who in the East 1984-85, 85-86; Who's Who Blck Am 80-81; Who's Who Am Women's 1983-84; law sch senate awd 1977; nominated outstndg young woman 1978; white house flwshp finlst 1977. **HOME ADDRESS:** 3700 Locheam Dr, Baltimore, MD 21207. **BUSINESS ADDRESS:** Commissioner, MD Parole Commsn, Ste 601 1 Investment Pl, Towson, MD 21204.

JOSHUA, VON E.
Professional athlete. **PERSONAL:** Born May 01, 1948, Oakland, CA; married Deborah Franklin; children: Vanessa, Dawne. **EDUCATION:** AA. **CAREER:** Milwaukee Brewers, maj league bsbl plyr 1976-77; San Francisco Giants, 1975-76; Los Angeles Dodgers, 1970-71, 1973-74, 1979. **ORGANIZATIONS:** Practitioner, Buddhism. **HONORS/ACHIEVEMENTS:** 3 batting titles, Tri-Cities 1967, Albuquerque 1972, Dominican Rep 1972; hit 318 with San Fran Giants 1975; Plyr of Month 1967; Plyr of Wk 1972; World Series 1974. **MILITARY SERVICE:** AUSR med splst 4 1969-74. **BUSINESS ADDRESS:** San Diego Padres, PO Box 2000, San Diego, CA 92120.

JOURNEY, LULA MAE
Appointed official. **PERSONAL:** Born May 08, 1934, Doddsville, MS; divorced; children: Larry, Callie Sanders, Linda, Ronnie, Marilyn Kirk, Blondina. **EDUCATION:** Delta In-

dust Inst Bus School Doddsville MS, 1954; Market Training Inst Indianapolis IN, 1958; IN/Purdue Univ, 1979. **CAREER:** Center Twp Trustees Office, investigator of Marion Cty Home, asst suprv, suprv of investigators, asst chief suprv of oper 1965-. **ORGANIZATIONS:** Former pres Indianapolis Pre School 1972; bd of dir Citizens Neighborhood Coaltion 1976-; city-cty councilor 10th dist City-Cty Council 1976-; bd of dir Mapleton/Fall Creek Assoc 1977-; past chmn of mem comm Amer Bus Women Assoc 1981; state coord of municipal women in govt Natl League of Cities 1982-;minority leader dem caucus City-Cty Council 1985. **HONORS/ACHIEVEMENTS:** Key to the City City-Cty Council 1976; Cert for Coop Beyond the Call of Duty Ctr Twp Trustees Office 1978; Cert of Appreciation Indianapolis Pre-school 1978; Two Certs for Suprv of the Month Ctr Twp Trustees Office 1979; Cert for Serv Rendered IN Assoc of Motorcycle Clubs 1983. **HOME ADDRESS:** 2020 N New Jersey St, Indianapolis, IN 46205.

JOY, DANIEL WEBSTER
Judge. **PERSONAL:** Born Apr 15, 1931, Middleton, NC; son of Andrew Joy and Mattie Joy; married Ruby M Collins; children: Darryl, Kathry. **EDUCATION:** State Univ of NY at Albany, BA 1952; Brooklyn Law Sch, JD 1957. **CAREER:** Rent & Rehab Admin, chief counsel 1967-70, commr 1970-73; Housing Preservation & Devel Dept, commr 1973-83; Queens County Civil Court, judge 1984-85; Justice Supreme Court, 1985-. **ORGANIZATIONS:** Mem Assn of the Bar City of NY 1976-83; chairman bd of dir Edwin Gould Foundation 1980-; mem Queens County Bar Assn 1981-; mem Macon B Allen Black Bar Assn 1982-; mem Natl Bar Assn 1983-. **MILITARY SERVICE:** AUS pfc 1952-54. **BUSINESS ADDRESS:** Judge Supreme Court, Queens County, 88-11 Sutphin Blvd, New York, NY 11435.

JOY, JAMES BERNARD, JR.
Clergyman. **PERSONAL:** Born Jan 16, 1937, Washington, DC. **EDUCATION:** St Mary'sUniv Balto MD, BA 1958; GregorianUniv Rome Italy, STB (summa cum laude) 1962; CathUniv Wash DC, MA 1970. **CAREER:** Holy Name Ch, asst pastor 1962-65; Holy Comforter Ch, asst pastor 1965-66; St Thomas More Ch, asst pastor 1966-1969; Sacred Heart Ch, asst pastor 1969-74; Holy Redeemer Ch, asst pastor 1974-76; St Gabriel's Ch, pastor 1976-85; Ft Sill OK, church pastor 1985-. **ORGANIZATIONS:** Bd dir Carroll Pblshg Co 1985-, Washington Cath Histrorical Soc 1978-; mem DC Citizens Traffic Bd 1965-70, chrmn 1968-70. **MILITARY SERVICE:** AUSR maj 1969-; ASR 1975; CSR 1969; AUS 1985-. **HOME ADDRESS:** 26 Grant Cir N W, Washington, DC 20011. **BUSINESS ADDRESS:** Pastor, St Gabriels Ch, Fort Sill, OK 73503.

JOYCE, DONALD FRANKLIN
Coordinator, educator. **PERSONAL:** Born Nov 04, 1938, Chicago, IL. **EDUCATION:** Fisk Univ, BA 1957;Univ of IL, MS 1960; Univ of Chicago, PhD 1978. **CAREER:** Chicago Public Library, branch librarian 1960-69; Harsh Collection, Chicago Public Library, curator 1969-81; Downtown Library, Tenn State Univ, coordinator/assoc professor 1981-87; director, library, Austin Peay Stat Univ. **ORGANIZATIONS:** Mem 2 committees Amer Librarians Asn 1970-; IL Librarians Assn; ALA Black Caucus; consultant Natl Endowment for the Humanities 1979-84; book reviewer Nashville Tennessean 1981-; College Land Assoc 1982-. **HONORS/ACHIEVEMENTS:** CIC Doctoral Fellowship Univ of Chicago 1973-78; Gatekeepers of Black Culture, black-owned book publishing in the US, 1817-1981 (Greenwood Press 1983); Blacks in the Humanities, 1750-1984, A Selected Annotated Bibliography (Greenwood Press, 1986); Numerous articles in professional journals. **BUSINESS ADDRESS:** Felix G Woodward Library, Austin Peay State Univ, Clarksville, TN 37043.

JOYNER, ARTHENIA LEE
Attorney. **PERSONAL:** Born Feb 03, 1943, Lakeland, FL; married Delano S Stewart. **EDUCATION:** FL A&M Univ, BS 1964, Coll of Law JD 1968. **CAREER:** Booker T Washington Jr HS, teacher 1964-65; FL House of Reps, admin asst to Rep Jose Lang Kershaw, 1969; Attorney at Law, genl practice 1969-. **ORGANIZATIONS:** Mem of following organs Hillsborough Comm Housing Resource Bd; Citizen Adv Comm Hillsborough Co Sch Bd; League of Women Voters; PUSH; Allen Temple AMEChurch; NAACP; Tampa Urban League; Tampa Alumnae Chap Delta Sigma Theta Inc; bd mem Helding Hand Day Nursery 1978-84; bd mem Travelers Aid Soc Inc 1980-84; pres Bay Area Legal Serv 1983; life mem & held various positions in Natl Bar Assn; mem Amer, FL, Hillsborough Co Bar Assns; mem FL Assn of Women Lawyers; mem Natl Assoc of Women Lawyers; mem George E Edgecomb Bar Assn; mem Hillsborough Co Assn of Women Lawyers; participant Lawyers Against Apartheid 1985. **HONORS/ACHIEVEMENTS:** 1st Black female atty in Tampa; 2nd female pres in 60 yr history of the Natl Bar Assn; Outstanding Leadership Awd FL Chap NBA 1977; NBA Pres Awd NatlBar Assn 1982; Outstanding Leadership Awd Bay Area Legal Serv Inc 1983; 100 Most Influential Blacks in Amer Ebony Mag 1985. **BUSINESS ADDRESS:** Attorney, 400 E Buffalo Ave Ste 106, Tampa, FL 33603.

JOYNER, CLAUDE C.
Management, systems analyst. **PERSONAL:** Born Nov 08, 1950, New Haven, CT; son of Claude Joyner (deceased) and Minnie Joyner (deceased). **EDUCATION:** Central State Univ, BS 1974; Pepperdine Univ, MBA 1983. **CAREER:** Lincoln Natl Life Insurache Co, system designer 1974-76; First Interstate Bank, operations officer 1977-79; Aerospace Corp, programmer 1979-80; Transaction Tech Inc, systems analyst 1980-84; Electronic Data Systems, sr systems analyst 1984-85; Booz Allen & Hamilton, associate 1985-86; Contel ASC, sr system analyst 1986-87; Computer Based Systems Inc, staff analyst 1987-. **ORGANIZATIONS:** Mem Deaf Pride Inc 1980-86; mem student outreach comm Natl Black MBA Assn 1984-87; educ chairperson Black Data Processing Assoc 1985-87; Sunday school teacher Mt Sinai Baptist 1986-; staff volunteer Mt Sinai Outreach Center 1987-. **HOME ADDRESS:** 2210 Dawn Lane, Temple Hills, MD 20748-4213.

JOYNER, GORDON L.
County commissioner, judge. **CAREER:** Fulton County, GA, Atlanta GA, Board of Commissioners, District 6. **BUSINESS ADDRESS:** 165 Central Ave S W, Atlanta, GA 30303.
*

JOYNER, IRVING L.
Attorney, educator. **PERSONAL:** Born Jun 11, 1944, Brooklyn, NY; son of Dorothy Joyner; married Maola Jones, Jul 1987; children: Lauren, Kwame, Tuere. **EDUCATION:** Long Island Univ, Brooklyn NY, BS, 1970; Rutgers Univ School of Law, Newark NJ, JD. **CAREER:** United Church of Christ Comm for Racial Justice, New York NY, dir of criminal justice, 1968-78; Currie & Joyner, Raleigh NC, attorney at law, 1978-80; Natl Prison Project of ACLU, Washington DC, staff attorney, 1980-81; Currie, Pugh & Joyner, Raleigh NC, attorney at law, 1981-85; NC Central Univ School of Law, Durham NC, assoc dean and assoc prof of law, 1985-. **ORGANIZATIONS:** Mem/former pres, NC Assn of Black Lawyers, 1977-; mem, NC State Bar, 1977-; mem, Natl Bar Assn, 1977-; mem, NC Academy of Trial Lawyers, 1977-. **HONORS/ACHIEVEMENTS:** Outstanding Contribution to Racial Justice, Assn of Black Law Students, 1977; Paul Robeson Award, Black Amer Law Student Assn, 1977; Professor of the Year, NCCU Student Bar Assn, 1985; Living Legacy Award OA Dupress Scholarship Foundation, 1987; Outstanding Contribution to Civil Rights, Wake Forest Black Law Student Assn 1987; author of The Black Lawyer in NC (article), 1988; Conflicts of Interest (article), 1988; Police Misconduct Litigation (CLE manuscript), 1988; Preparation and Use of Requests for Jury Instructions (CLE manuscript), 1988; Criminal Procedure in NC (book), 1989. **BUSINESS ADDRESS:** Associate Dean, North Carolina Central University School of Law, 1801 Fayetteville Street, Durham, NC 27707.

JOYNER, JOHN ERWIN
Medical doctor. **PERSONAL:** Born Feb 07, 1935, Grambling, LA; son of John E Joyner and Mary Rist Joyner; married Joyce N Sterling; children: Sheryl, John III, Monica. **EDUCATION:** Albion Coll, BS 1955; IN Univ Sch of Medicine, MD 1959, Straight Surg Internship/Neurosurgery Residency 1959-67. **CAREER:** Winona Mem Hosp, dept chmn of neurology & neurosurgery 1980-; IN Univ Sch of Medicine, assoc prof of neurosurgery 1983-; Winona Hosp Medical Staff & Exec Council, secty-treas 1985; RehabCare, med dir 1986-; Natl Med Assoc IN, pres-elect. **ORGANIZATIONS:** Mem Fellow Amer Coll of Surgeons; mem Royal Soc of Med London England; mem Amer Assoc of Physicians & Surgeons; mem Neurosurgical Soc of IN; mem Indianapolis Urban League; mem IN Conservation Council; mem American Legion; chmn bd of dirs CT Scanner Assocs 1977-84; life mem NAACP 1979-; mem NIH Tech Merit Review Comm 1981, 1982; mem AMA Health Policy Agenda for the Amer People 1982, 1983, 1984; sec chmn of Regional Constituent Socs Natl Med Assoc 1983-1984, 1980-84; mem Congress of Neurological Surgeons 1967-; chmn of bd 100 Black Men of Indianapolis Inc 1984-87; chmn bd of dirs Meridan Scanner Assoc Inc 1984-89; mem IN State Health Coordinating Council 1985; mem, World Medical Assoc, The Soc of Prospective Medicine; patrons comm 10th Pan American Games Indianapolis 1986-87; mem medical evaluation comm IN Univ Sch of Med; pres Natl Med Assn 1987-88; Amer Medical Assn 1967-; Marion County Medical Soc 1967-; Amer Academy of Neurological & Ortho Surgeons 1985-; past pres, Natl Medical Assn 1988-89; Natl Black Health Conf Steering Comm 1988-; Minority AIDS Advisory Comm 1988-; Alpha Eta Sigma Pi Phi (Boule). **HONORS/ACHIEVEMENTS:** Martin Luther King Freedom Awd SCLC Indianapolis 1972; Sickle Cell Anemia Found Awd 1973; Friend of Youth Awd YMCA Kokomo IN 1976; AMA Physician's Achievement Awd Natl Med Assoc 1980; AMA Physicians Recognition Awd Amer Med Assoc 1983; Dr of Humane Letters, Martin Center Coll; Distinguished Public Service Award for NMA, US Dept of Health & Human Serv; Scroll of Merit Natl Medical Assn; Benjamin Hooks Award, Gary in NAACP; Outstanding Serv Award, Scott United Methodist Church, Indianapolis. **MILITARY SERVICE:** AUS med serv grp capt 1961-64. **BUSINESS ADDRESS:** 3202 North Meridian, East Building Ste 201, Indianapolis, IN 46208.

JOYNER, LEMUEL MARTIN
Director. **PERSONAL:** Born Jun 20, 1928, Nashville, TN; married Barbara; children: Lemuel Jr, John M, Christopher A, Dennis L, Victor P, Lonnie. **EDUCATION:** Univ Notre Dame, BFA 1957, MFA 1969. **CAREER:** Mntl Hlth Ctr of St Joseph City Inc, art therapist 1985; Day Treatment Ctr, co-devel 1972-; Ofc of Inter-Cultural Dev, spl asst to pres 1970; St Mary's Coll Notre Dame, asst prof of art 1965-71; Liturgical Artist 1958-65. **ORGANIZATIONS:** Am Art Therapists Assn; S Bend Art Assn; S Bend St Acad; Nat Cncl of Artist; Alpha Phi Alpha. **HONORS/ACHIEVEMENTS:** Excellence in Tchng Award, St Mary's Coll 1969; Outst Contrib to Std Life Award; Model Upward Bound Prog 1966; pringint in Black Dimensions In Am Art 1969. **BUSINESS ADDRESS:** Center for Creative Orchestrtn, 18067 State Road 23, South Bend, IN 46637.

JOYNER, MARJORIE STEWART
Civic leader. **PERSONAL:** Born 1996. **CAREER:** United Bty Sch Owners & Tchrs Assn, fdr, natl supr. **ORGANIZATIONS:** Dir, Chicago Defender Charities. **HONORS/ACHIEVEMENTS:** Bud Billiken Parade; Cosmopolitan Comm Ctr; num hons including Sr Citizen of Yr Chicago 1975. **BUSINESS ADDRESS:** 5607 S Wabash Avenue, Chicago, IL 60637.

JOYNER, RUBIN E.
Educational administration. **PERSONAL:** Born Dec 05, 1949, Trenton, NJ; married Phyllis A; children: Zanada, Ciarra. **EDUCATION:** Rider Coll, BA 1970-73; Trenton State Coll, MEd 1975-77. **CAREER:** Ocean County Coll, dir educ opportunity fund 1986. **ORGANIZATIONS:** NJ Ed Opp Assoc, 1978; American Assoc Counseling Dept 1979; Soc for Special & Ethnic Studies 1979; Monmouth Coll, dir black student Union 1979-85; Acceleration Computer Sci Prog, co-founder 1983-85; Organization Black Unity, dir 1985; Access Prog, founder 1986; Student Leadership Ed Opp, co-chairperson1986. **HONORS/ACHIEVEMENTS:** Monmouth Coll, appreciation awrd black student union 1984; Outstanding Young Men of the Year 1985. **BUSINESS ADDRESS:** Director, Educ Oppy Fund, Ocean County College, College Drive, Toms River, NJ 08753.

JOYNER, WILLIAM A.
Finance manager. **PERSONAL:** Born May 19, 1933, Brooklyn, NY; married Barbara J Westphal; children: Beverly, Kelli, Regina. **EDUCATION:** City, Univ Baruch, BBA 1965. **CAREER:** Crane Co New York NY, internal audit mgr 1975; Masonite Corp Chicago IL, sr finance analyst 1982; Woodland Serv Co, mgr internal audit & taxes. **ORGANIZATIONS:** Officer dir Civic Assn Westbury LI NY 1959-75; comm zone leader Westbury Demo Club 1968-75; officer mem Inst Internal Auditors NY & Chicago Chap 1968-80. **MILITARY SERVICE:** AUS sgt 1st cls; Hon Discharge 1959. **HOME ADDRESS:** 815 Gaffield Pl, Evanston, IL 60201.

JOYNER-KERSEE, JACQUELINE
Athlete. **PERSONAL:** Born Mar 03, 1962, East St. Louis, IL; married Bob Kersee. **EDUCATION:** University of California, Los Angeles, CA, BA. **ORGANIZATIONS:** Jackie Joyner-Kersee Community Foundation; UCLA Alumni Association; Athletic Congress Athletics Advisory Board; member, board of directors, St Louis Girl's Club. **HONORS/ACHIEVEMENTS:** James E Sullivan Award for Most Outstanding Amateur Athlete; Los

Angeles Olympics, silver medalist, American record holder in Heptathlon, 1984; American Outdoor record holder in long jump, 1985; UCLA Scholar Athlete, 1985; Broderick Cup Winner, for Collegiate Woman Athlete of the Year, 1986; most valuable player, UCLA Basketball and Track and Field, 1986; American Indoor Nationals champion, long jump, 1986; saluted as one of the top ten athletes in the world, Beijing, PRC; world record in Heptathlon, Goodwill Games, Moscow, US Olympic Festival, 1986; Outstanding Athlete of the Goodwill Games, Soviet Life magazine, 1986; Olympia Award, for outstanding athlete in sports, scholarship and leadership, 1986; City of Hope Victor Award, 1986, 1987; Woman Athlete of the Year, Track & Field News, 1986, 1987; St Louis Athlete of the Year, 1986; Amateur Sportswoman of the Year, 1986, 1987; Jesse Owens Memorial Award, 1986, 1987; tied world record in long jump, Pan American Games, Indianapolis, IN, 1987; gold medalist, Heptathlon, Long Jump, World Championship, Rome, 1987; broke records in shot put, and Heptathlon, US Olympic Trials, 1988; US record in 100 m hurdle, 1988; gold medalist in long jump, Seoul Olympics, 1988; Essence Award winner, 1988; AAF's World Trophy recipient, 1989; honorary doctorate, University of Missouri, 1989.

JUDSON, HORACE AUGUSTUS
Educator. **PERSONAL:** Born Aug 07, 1941, Miami, FL; married Beatrice Gail; children: Tamara Renee, Sonya Anita, Sojourner Maria. **EDUCATION:** Lincoln U, BA 1963; Cornell U, PhD 1970. **CAREER:** Morgan State Univ, vice pres acad affairs 1974-, prof 1974; Morgan State Coll, assoc dean 1973-74, assoc prof 1972-74, asst prof 1969-72; Bethune-Cookman Coll, asst prof 1969. **ORGANIZATIONS:** Mem, Am Chem Soc; md, Section of Am Chem Soc; Beta Kappa Chi; Estrn Assn of Coll Deans; Soc for Coll &Univ Planner; Omega Psi Phi; Elks; IBPOEW; acad adv bd, St Mary's Sem. **HONORS/ACHIEVEMENTS:** Several articles in the Jour of Am Chem Soc 1970; rsrch, flwshp, CornelUniv 1965-69. **MILITARY SERVICE:** AUS md civ aide to sec 1975. **BUSINESS ADDRESS:** Cold Spring & Hillen, Baltimore, MD 21239.

JULIAN, ANNA JOHNSON
Sociologist & retired business exec. **PERSONAL:** Born in Baltimore, MD; married Dr Percy L Julian; children: Percy L Jr, Faith R, Leon R Ellis. **EDUCATION:** Univ of PA, BS (Phi Beta Kappa), MA in Sociology, PhD in Sociology; Columbia Univ and Univ of Chicago, Summer Grad Studies. **CAREER:** Public Schools, Washington DC, research asst 1935-39; Julian Labs Inc, and Julian Research Inst, vice pres and treas 1952-. **ORGANIZATIONS:** Mgr trustee The Julian Fnd 1964-; bd trustees MacMurray Coll, Rosary Coll, Erikson Inst, 1970-; Natl Bd of NAACP Legal Defense and Educ Fund; Delta Research and Educ Fnd; past natl pres Delta Sigma Theta; mem The Links Inc; hon mem United Nations Assn; mem Amer Acad of Political & Social Sci; co-chair Delta Sigma Theta Sor Inc; mem Sigma Pi Phi Boule Foundation Bd; adv bd Chicago Foundation for Women. **HONORS/ACHIEVEMENTS:** Phi Beta Kappa; Brotherhood Award, Natl Conf of Christians and Jews 1959; Distinguished Serv Award Comm Renewal Soc of Chicago 1972, NAACP Legal Defense and Educ Fnd 1973, Recognition Awd The Links Inc 1978; Award of Distinction Delta Sigma Theta 1979; "This is Your Life" Founders Day Celebration by Chicago Alumnae Chap Delta Sigma Theta; Distinguished Serv Awd in Field of Human Relations Natl Assn of Colored Women; Awd of Merit NAACP Women's Auxiliary of Chicago.

JULIAN, JOHN TYRONE
Educational administrator. **PERSONAL:** Born Sep 03, 1947, Rayne, LA; married Evelyn West; children: Karen, Shellie. **EDUCATION:** Grambling State Univ, BS 1969; LA State Univ, MEd 1975, EdS 1978. **CAREER:** Rayne HS, teacher 1969-70; USAF Sheppard AF Base Wichita Falls, med instructor 1970-73; Armstrong Elementary, teacher 1973-77; Ross Elementary, principal 1977-. **ORGANIZATIONS:** Mem Acadia Parish Police Jury 1984-88; mem Natl Assn of Elementary Sch Principals 1985; mem LA Assn of Principals 1985; mem LA Assn of Sch Executives1985; mem Knights of Peter Claver 1984-; mem Rayne Chamber of Commerce 1984-; mem Amer Legion 1984-; Acadia Admins Assn, pres 1985-86; A&O 21st Century Club, sec 1987-. **HONORS/ACHIEVEMENTS:** Merit Scholar Grambling State Univ 1966-69; Alpha Phi Alpha Frat Grambling State Univ 1967; Who's Who in Amer Colls & Univs 1968-69. **MILITARY SERVICE:** USAF sgt 1970-73; Master Instructor Certificate; Honorable Discharge. **HOME ADDRESS:** 909 Chappuis Ave, Rayne, LA 70578. **BUSINESS ADDRESS:** Principal, Ross Elementary, 1809 West Hutchinson Ave, Crowley, LA 70526.

JULIAN, PERCY L., JR.
Attorney. **PERSONAL:** Born Aug 31, 1940, Chicago, IL. **EDUCATION:** Oberlin Coll, BA 1962; Univ WI, JD 1966. **CAREER:** Julian & Olson, sr partner; Private Practice, attorney 1966-. **ORGANIZATIONS:** Coop atty & spl counsel NAACP-LDF, Amer Civil Liberties Union, Ctr Constl Rights; rep many civil rights groups; lectr Univ WI 1970-77, 1979-80; proflphotographer 1960-66, 1978-; mem WI State Bar, Fed Bar Western Dist WI, Eastern Dist WI, So Dist IL, Cent Dist IL, 5th 7th 8th 9th & 11th Circuit Ct Appeals; US Ct Appeals; DC/US Supreme Ct; ABA, Dane Co Bar Assn; Natl Assn Criminal Defense Lawyers; Bar Assn 7th Fed Circuit; mem Amer Soc of Magazine Photographers; Natl Press Photographers Assn; Professional Photographers of Amer; chmn WI State Personnel Bd 1972-76; chmn WI State Com US Commn Civil Rights 1970-80; mem WI Council Criminal Justice 1972-80; Cit Study Com Judicial Orgn 1971-72; Employment Rel Study Commn 1975-77; NAACP; Amer Civil Liberties Union; state bd Amer Civil Liberties Union 1969-74. **HONORS/ACHIEVEMENTS:** Mem of the Yr Awd WI Civil Liberties Union 1972; many speaking & debate awds. **BUSINESS ADDRESS:** Attorney, 330 E Wilson St, Madison, WI 53703.

JUNIOR, E. J.
Professional athlete. **PERSONAL:** Married Jacquelyn; children: Adam. **EDUCATION:** Alabama, degree in Public Relations. **CAREER:** St Louis Cardinals, linebacker 1981-. **ORGANIZATIONS:** Counselor (off-season) Hyland Medical Ctr; involved w/Matthews-Dickey Boys Club in St Louis. **HONORS/ACHIEVEMENTS:** Voted to Alabama's Team of the Decade for the '70's; named to the Strength Coaches All-Amer team; Outstanding Defensive Performer in 1981 Senior Bowl; 1981 named to several All-Rookie teams; mem Pro Bowl teams 1984-86. **BUSINESS ADDRESS:** St Louis Cardinals, PO Box 888, Phoenix, AZ 85001.

JUNIOR, ESTER JAMES, JR.
College business administrator. **PERSONAL:** Born Feb 11, 1932, Claxton, GA; married Eva G Westbrook Burton; children: Avis, EJ III, Keith, Lori M Burton, Lesli M Burton. **EDUCATION:** Morehouse Coll, BA 1952; Atlanta Univ, MBA 1954. **CAREER:** Tuskegee Inst, intern for coll fiscal & bus mgmt 1954-55; Southern Univ, mgr of aux enterprises 1955-57; Jarvis Christian Coll, business mgr 1957-59; Livingston Coll, business mgr 1959-61; Albany State Coll, dir of business & finance 1961-68; Fisk Univ, asst vice pres for business & finance 1968-73; Meharry Medical Coll, dir of budget & purchasing 1973-76; Univ of AR, vice chancellor for fiscal affairs 1976-78; TN State Univ, vice pres for business affairs 1978-80; Meharry Medical Coll, asst vice pres for bus & finance 1980-82; Fort Valley State Coll, vice pres for business & finance 1982-. **ORGANIZATIONS:** Mem past basileus Omega Psi Phi Frat 1950-; mem accreditation comm Southern Assoc of Schools 1968-84; mem exec comm Middle TN Cncl of Boy Scouts 1973-80; mem Phi Delta Kappa 1976-; comm mem on porject review Southern Assoc of Colls 1978-79; mem Financial Exec Inst 1978-; mem dir Peach Co Chamber of Commerce 1982-; chmn Scholarship Comm Southern Assoc of Coll & Univ Business Officers 1982-83; mem Sigma Pi Phi Frat 1983-; mem bd of deacons Trinity Baptist Church 1986-; mem exec comm on business affairs Natl Assoc of State Univ & Land Grant Colls 1986-87. **HOME ADDRESS:** 103 Cochran Court, Byron, GA 31008. **BUSINESS ADDRESS:** Vice Pres Business and Finance, Fort Valley State College, 805 State College Drive, Fort Valley, GA 31030.

JUNIOR, SAMELLA E. (NEE WALTON)
Educator, musician. **PERSONAL:** Born Dec 15, 1931, Chattanooga, TN; married Ester James; children: Avis, EJ. **EDUCATION:** Spelman Coll, AB 1953; LA St U, m Music Ed 1957; George Peabody Coll, PhD 1977. **CAREER:** East HS, prin 1978; Whites Creek Comprehensive HS, asso prin; Pearl HS, Cumberland Jr HS, prin 1975-78; Joelton HS, asst prin 1974-75; Isaac Litton Jr HS, 1971-74; Highland Hts Jr HS, tchr 1969-71; Carver Jr HS, tchr dir, chmn 1963-68; E Baker HS & Elem Sch, tchr 1961-63; Livingstone Coll, prof 1959-60; Jarvis Christian Coll, 1957-59; Leland Coll, instr, dir 1956-57; HS, tchr 1953-57. **ORGANIZATIONS:** Choir dir, minist, Mt Zion Bapt Ch; First Bapt Ch; Disciples of Christ Ch; asst organist, First Bapt Ch; choir dir, minister of music, current pres, Spelman Clb; pres, vp, sec, com chmn, mem, Delta Sigma Theta Inc; treas, Nat Cncl of Negro Women; treas, Black Expo; sec, Albany St Coll Wives; com chmn, mem, NEA, MNEA, TEA, NASSP, TASSP, ASCD, ATE, Phi Delta Kappa, AAUW, Nashville Pin; pres-elect, Middle Region TEA; chmn, Metro Cncl of Tchr Ed; mem, Nat Flwshp of Ch Muscns; NAACP; vice-chmn bd, Operation PUSH. **BUSINESS ADDRESS:** E Nashville Sr H S, Nashville, TN 37206.

JUPITER, CLYDE PETER
Nuclear science and engineering company executive. **PERSONAL:** Born Oct 31, 1928, New Orleans, LA; married Pat (Schofield) Jupiter, Nov 27, 1987; children: Carol A, Lisa A Byles, Joan C, Deanne S, Matthews, Mike Schank, Steve Schank, Chris Schank, Erika Schank. **EDUCATION:** Xavier Univ New Orleans, BS Physics 1949; Univ of Notre Dame S Bend, MS Physics 1951. **CAREER:** Gen Atomic Co San Diego, staff sci 1964-69; EG&G Inc Santa Barbara, mgr radiation physics dept 1969-70; EG&G Inc Albuquerque, dir of applied sci 1970-71; EG&G Inc Las Vegas, mgr radiation & environmental sci dept 1971-75; US Nuclear Reg Commn, tech asst to dir of rsch 1975-78, program mgr waste mgmt 1978-82; US Nuclear Regulatory Comm, sr policy analyst office of policy eval 1982-86; Howard Univ Sch of Engineering, adjunct prof nuclear engineering program 1981-86; Jupiter Corporation president 1986-. **ORGANIZATIONS:** Mem Amer Nuclear Soc 1965-; bd dir Amer Nuclear Soc 1976-79; mem Alpha Phi Alpha Frat 1947-; mem NAACP. **HONORS/ACHIEVEMENTS:** Teaching Fellowship Univ of Notre Dame S Bend IN 1949-50; elected to Grade of Fellow Amer Nuclear Soc 1980. **MILITARY SERVICE:** AUS sp-3 1954-56. **BUSINESS ADDRESS:** President, Jupiter Corporation, 2730 University Blvd, West, Wheaton, MD 20902.

JUSTICE, NORMAN E.
Business executive. **PERSONAL:** Born Nov 01, 1925, Kansas City, KS; married Kathryn Flanagan; children: Patricia, Pierson. **EDUCATION:** Fayetteville State Teachers Coll, attended; North Carolina Weaverhs Sch of Sales & Real Estate; Dale Carnegie Inst. **CAREER:** Kansas City, KS, Police Dept, 1955. **ORGANIZATIONS:** Recording sec, vice pres, pres, Construction & Gen Laborers Local 1290 1961; elected, St Rep 1972; delegate, Western MO & KS Laborers Dist Council, KS State Fedn of Labor, Tri-County Central Labor Council, Greater Kansas City Bldg Trades Council; pres, Wyandotte Co Chap of the A Phillip Randolph Inst; bd mem, EOF; United Way; chmn Priorities Comm of KS, KS Model's City, all since 1968; Optimist Intl, Masons; 1st vice pres, Dem Inc Black Ind Dem, NAACP. **HONORS/ACHIEVEMENTS:** Awards of Appreciation, Bd of Trustees Econ Opportunity Found; Proj Head Start; Optimist Club of NE Kansas City, KS; Comm Act Prog; Men of First AME Church Kansas City, KS. **MILITARY SERVICE:** USN stw mate 1st class 1943-45. **BUSINESS ADDRESS:** 2600 Merriam Ln, Kansas City, KS 66106.

K

KAISER, ERNEST DANIEL
Retired librarian. **PERSONAL:** Born Dec 05, 1915, Petersburg, VA; son of Ernest Kaiser and Elnora Ellis Kaiser; married Mary G Orford, 1949; children: Eric, Joan. **EDUCATION:** CCNY, attended 1935-38. **CAREER:** Advisor, author 10 intro's for Arno Press series The Amer Negro, His History & Literature 145 vols; McGraw Hill Pub Co New York R R Bowker Co New York, Chelsea House Publ, Univ Massachusetts Press Amherst, reviewer consultant editor; co-editor & contrib editor, The Negro Almanac 1971, 1976, 1983, 1989; Black Titan, WEB DuBois: An Anthology 1970; Paul Roseson, The Great Forerunner 1978, 2nd ed 1985; Encyclopedia of Black Amer, 1981; Freedomways Reader, editor; Science & Soc, contrib editor; Freedomways Magazine, co-fndr & assoc editor1961-85; Schomburg Ct, admin assoc staff mem 1945-86 retired. **HONORS/ACHIEVEMENTS:** Author "In Defense of the People's Blk & White Hist & Cult 1970; co-author "Harlem, A Hist of Broken Dreams 1974; contributor EJ Josey & Ann A Shockley Handbook of Black Librarianship 1977; RW Logan & M R Winston Diction of Amer Negro Biography 1982; numerous essays bk reviews introductions & bibl pub in many books, mags & newspapers; Plaque Kappa Sigma Chap Sigma Gamma Rho 1982; Humanitarian Awd Harlem School of the Arts 1985; Ernest D Kaiser Index to Black Resources named in 1985 at Schomburg Center; has bibliographies of his work in Richard Newman's Black Access: A Bibliography of Afro Amer Bibliographies, 1984, and in Betty K Gubert and Richard Newman's Nine Decades of Scholarship: A Bibliography of the Writings 1892-1983 of the Staff of the Schomburg Center for Research in Black Culture, 1986. **HOME ADDRESS:** 31-37 95 St, East Elmhurst, NY 11369.

KAISER, INEZ YEARGAN
Business executive. **PERSONAL:** Born Apr 22, 1918, Kansas City, KS; married Richard S Sr; children: Richard, Jr. **EDUCATION:** KS St Tchrs Coll, B Home Ec 1940; Columbia U, M Home Ec 1958. **CAREER:** Teacher, 1940-61; US Dept Comm, 1972-73; EEOC, consult 1975; Inez Kaiser & Assocs Inc, owner/pres 1961-. **ORGANIZATIONS:** Am Hm Ec Assn; Hm Econts in Bus; Am Women in Radio & TV; Nat Assn of Mrkt Dev; Am Assn of Media Women; Am Assn ofUniv Women; Sales & Mkt Exec Clb; Advertising Clb of NY; Am Mkt Assn; Advertising & Sales Exec Clb; Wash DC Press Clb; Pub Rel Soc of KC; Am Soc for Hosp Pub Rel; plbcty, Clb of NY; Am Fed of TV & Radio Anncrs; Intrntl Platform Spkrs; Phi Lambda Theta Sor; pres, Nat Assn of Minor Women in Bus; natl treas, Delta Sigma Theta Sor Womens's C of C; Men's C of C; spnsr Del Sprites; Friends of Art; Flwshp House; Proj Equal; Task Force of Plnd Prnthod; conv, vstrs, Bur of Grtr KC;co-chmn, United Negro Coll Fund Dr; Nat Urban League; pres, Nat Urban League Guild; Episcopal Bd of Dir; NAACP; bd mem OIC. **HONORS/ACHIEVEMENTS:** Biograph of Outstndng Am; Top Award, Am Assn ofUniv Women; Golden Mike, Am Women in Radio & TV 1968; Foremost Women in Communicat 1969-73; article Time Mag 1969; Alumn Award KS St Tchrs Coll 1969; Betty Jayne Everett Awd; Outstndng Black Woman in Mkt PR; Ertha M White Award, Outstndng Black Bus Woman in Country; Nat Assn of Mkt Develprs; citation, Nat Med Assn, Delta Sigma Theta Sor, Alpha Phi Alpah Frat; NNY Person, Mang Assn Awd 1972; Businesswoman of Yr, Eta Phi Beta; Awd Nat Assn of Media Women; Awd Tallahassee Links; Nat Assn of Negro & Prof Women's Clb; NY Pers Mgmt Assn; Sales & MktgExec Clb; AR Travler Award; Hon Citz of KY, AR, AL; Personalities of W & Midwest 1970-71; Award Dau of ISIS Aux; Hon PhD in Laws Lincoln Univ 1986; 100 Most Outstanding Black Business and Professional Women by Dollars & Sense Mag; Black Archives Outstanding Citizen Awd. **BUSINESS ADDRESS:** President, Inez Kaiser & Associates Inc, 906 Grand Ste 500, Kansas City, MO 64106.

KAISER, JAMES GORDON
Executive. **PERSONAL:** Born Feb 28, 1943, St Louis, MO; married Kathryn Juanita Mounday; children: Lauren Elizabeth. **EDUCATION:** Univ of CA at Los Angeles, BA 1966; MA Inst of Tech, MS 1973. **CAREER:** Corning Glass Works Corning NY, sales rep 1968-70, sales promotion specialist 1970-72, product line mgr 1973-75, business planning mgr 1975-76, general mgrsales & marketing 1976-79, mgr new business develop 1979-81, business mgr 1981-84, vice pres and general mgr 1984-86. **ORGANIZATIONS:** Mem bd of dirs Corning Hospital 1980-, Soc of Black Professionals 1981-; mem SBI Roundtable Advisory Bd to Natl Entrepreneur Devel Center FL A&M Univ 1985-; mem bd of dirs Corning Enterprises 1985-, Natl Black MBA Assn, 1986-; mem bd of dirs, Exec Leadership Council 1986-. **MILITARY SERVICE:** USNR lt 2 yrs; Navy Achievement Medal, Natl Defense Medal, 2 Bronze Stars Vietnam Svcs, Republic of Vietnam Campaign Medal. **HOME ADDRESS:** 42 Overbrook Rd, Painted Post, NY 14870.

KAMAU, MOSI (ANTHONY CHARLES GUNN WHITE)
Educator. **PERSONAL:** Born May 05, 1955, Chicago, IL. **EDUCATION:** Univ of Minnesota, BFA 1979; Florida State Univ, MFA 1983; Temple Univ, PhD candidate, African-Amer Studies, 1989-. **CAREER:** Talbot Supply Co Inc, welder 1979-80; Florida State Univ, asst preparator 1980-81; Williams Foundry, foundryman 1981-82; St Pauls Coll, asst prof of art 1984-89. **ORGANIZATIONS:** Pottery instructor, Tutle Contemporary Elem School 1977-78. **HONORS/ACHIEVEMENTS:** Intl Exchange Scholarship from Univ of Minnesota to Univ of Ife Ile, Ife Nigeria 1976-77; Sculpture/$5000 Natl Endowment of the Arts, Visual Arts, Washington DC 1984-85. **MILITARY SERVICE:** USN Reserve E-3 1984-90; grad with honors 1984. **HOME ADDRESS:** 9502 Glenway, Fort Washington, MD 20744.

KAMOCHE, JIDLAPH GITAU
Educator. **PERSONAL:** Born Dec 01, 1942, Kabete, Kenya;married Charity Njambi; children: Nyakio, Kamoche Gitau. **EDUCATION:** Amherst Col, BA 1967;Univ of MA, MA 1969; StateUniv of NY at Buffalo, PhD 1977. **CAREER:** African & Afro-Amer Studies Univ of OK, asst prof of History dir 1977-; State Univ Coll Buffalo, asst prof History 1972-77; African & Afro-Amer, dir; State Univ Coll Buffalo, stud 1970-72. **ORGANIZATIONS:** Mem Several African & Afro-am Studies Orgns 1970-80; past vice pres Assn of Black PersonnelUniv of OK 1978-79. **HONORS/ACHIEVEMENTS:** Recipeint ins of intl Educ Fellowship NY 1968-69; author Afro-am Life & Hist 1977; author articles & book reviews in several scholarly journs 1977-;recipient coll of arts research fellowshipUniv of OK 1979-80; author "Umoja" 1980. **BUSINESS ADDRESS:** Associate Prof, Department of History, University of Oklahoma, 455 W Lindsey, Norman, OK 73019.

KANE, JACQUELINE ANNE
Educator. **PERSONAL:** Born Aug 27, 1946, New York City, NY; daughter of Phillip Gough Kane and Jacqueline Jones Kane. **EDUCATION:** Morgan State Univ, AB 1968; State Univ New York Coll Onconta MS, 1974; State Univ of New York at Albany, PhD (In Progress). **CAREER:** New York City Dept of Soc Srvs, caseworker 1968-70; State Univ of New York Clge At Onconta, coord of cnslng & acad adv 1970-75; New York State Educ Dept, assc in higher educ opport 1975-; State Univ of New York at Albany, adjunct instr 1984-88. **ORGANIZATIONS:** Conf comm chair newsletter editor, bd mem Assc of Black Women in Higher Educ 1978-88; mem New York State Planning Comm Amer Council of Educ Natl Ident Proj 1980-; pres 1983-85, chmn fin comm 1985-87; Financial Secretary, 1987-, Albany New York Alumnae Chptr Delta Sigma Theta Sor Inc 1983-; bd mem 1984-, chmn youth serv comm 1986- Albany Area Chptr Amer Red Cross 1984-. **HONORS/ACHIEVEMENTS:** Schrlshp award Delta Sigma Theta Sor Inc 1981; Outstanding Young Woman of Amer 1978-81; Hilda H Davis Award for Distinguished Leadership and Service by a Professional; SAGE, a scholarly journal of black women 1988. **BUSINESS ADDRESS:** Assc Higher Educ Opportunity, NY State Educ Dept, CEC5a55 Empire State Plz, Albany, NY 12230.

KARIM, WALI J. (WENDELL D. KINCEY)
Artistic director. **PERSONAL:** Born Jul 14, 1951, Philadelphia, PA; divorced; children: Rabiyah Karim, Sabur Karim. **EDUCATION:** CA StUniv Long Beach, 1969-72; Compton Comm Coll, 1975-76; Los Angeles SW Comm Coll, 1979-. **CAREER:** Solartist Prod, artistic dir 1985; City of Inglewood Pub Lib, lib clrk 1979-; City of Compton, manpower anlyst 1977-78; City of Compton Pub Wrks Dept,engring aide 1974-77; Los Angeles Pub Lib, lib aide 1973-74, lib page 1972-73. **ORGANIZATIONS:** Writers workshop motivator, Compton Communicative Arts Acad 1972-74; theatre arts spec, Paul Robeson Plyrs 1976-78; art inst, City of Los Angeles Watts Towers Art Cntr 1978-; sec Community Unity Block Club 1979-; Biographical Sketch Black Am Writers Past & Present 1975. **HONORS/ACHIEVEMENTS:** Author/Pub Songs of a Wandering Poet 1976.

KASHIF, GHAYTH NUR (LONNIE KASHIF)
Executive editor, consultant, author, TV producer/director. **PERSONAL:** Born Sep 09, 1933, Raeford, NC; son of L Smith (deceased) and Annie Mae Dale; married Hafeeza N A; children: Alif-Ahmed, Rul-Aref, Shazada Latifa, Sadara Barrow. **EDUCATION:** Keesler Comm Chenute USAF, Dip (Tech Mass Comm) 1953; Univ MD Grant Tech (CA), 1953; NY Schl of Writing, Dip 1955. **CAREER:** Muhammad Speaks Bilalian News, Wash Bur chief 1968-78; Bilalian News AM Journal, editor 1978-81; Intl Graphics Kashif News Svc, consult writer 1981-85; Internatl Inst of Islamic Thought, editor 1987; American Journal Muslim Social Scientists, consultant 1986-87; Jornal Iqraa and Open Magazines and Metropolitan Magazines, exec editor 1982-84, 1985; TV director, producer, Islam in Focus, Warner Cable TV, Virginia. **ORGANIZATIONS:** Pres chmn Bilalian News Inc 1978-81; dir secr treas Metro Magazine Inc 1982-83; dir Shaw Bus Inc 1985; consult Intl Graphics/IQraa Magazine 1981-1987; mem Natl Red Cross 1985, Capital Press Club 1985, Org 3rd World Journal NNPA 1987; rep Black Media Inc 1982-83; dir comm Majdush Shura; mem Internatl platform; comm Bilalian Economic Devel Corp 1985-87; dir, The Roundtable for strategic studies 1989. **HONORS/ACHIEVEMENTS:** 1st Annual Freedom Jour Award Univ of DC 1979; Fred R Doug Award HU (Muhammad Speaks) 1977; Excel in Jour CM Fnd 1979; "Sacred Journey" author 1986. **MILITARY SERVICE:** USAF s/sgt; Distinguished Natl Defense Srvc Medal; Good Conduct Medal 1955. **HOME ADDRESS:** 3506 Varnum St, Brentwood, MD 20722.

KASHIF, LONNIE See KASHIF, GHAYTH NUR

KAY, ULYSSES
Composer, reitred educator. **PERSONAL:** Born Jan 07, 1917, Tucson, AZ; son of Ulysses Kay and Elizabeth Kay; married Barbara J; children: Virginia, Melinda, Hillary. **EDUCATION:** Univ of AZ, B Music 1938; Eastman School of Music of the Univ of Rochester, M Music 1940; Yale Univ, 1941-42; Columbia Univ, 1946-49. **CAREER:** Broadcast Music Inc, music consultant 1953-; Boston Univ, visiting prof summer 1965; UCLA, visiting prof 1966-67; Lehman Coll, prof of music 1968-, distinguished prof 1972-1988. **ORGANIZATIONS:** Composer mem Broadcast Music Inc 1947-; bd mem Corp of Yaddo Saratoga Springs, NY; bd mem Amer Music Center; mem Natl Inst of Arts & Letters New York City 1979-; mem, American Composers Alliance. **HONORS/ACHIEVEMENTS:** Julius Rosenwald Fellow 1947-48; Prix de Rome Amer Acad in Rome 1949-52; Fulbright Fellow to Italy 1950-51; Guggenheim Fellow New York City 1964-65; Resident Fellow Bellagio Study & Conf Center Como, Italy August 1982; Hon Doctorates from, Lincoln Coll 1963; Bucknell Univ 1966; Univ of AZ 1969; IL Wesleyan Univ 1969; Dickinson Coll 1978; Univ of MO/Kansas City 1981. **MILITARY SERVICE:** USN Reserve Mus 2C WWII served 3 1/2 yrs. **HOME ADDRESS:** 1271 Alicia Ave, Teaneck, NJ 07666.

KAZI-FERROUILLET, KUUMBA
Editor. **PERSONAL:** Born Dec 15, 1951, New Orleans, LA; son of Wilbur F Ferrouillet and Yvonne Gavion Ferrouillet; married Sandra Pierre; children: Shujaa, Zijazo, Ambata. **EDUCATION:** Tulane Univ, attended 1969-71; Univ of New Orleans, attended 1985-86. **CAREER:** Moret Press, printer 1971-80; Figaro Newspaper, production Associate 1980-81; Black Collegiate Serv Inc, copy editor 1981-83, assoc editor 1983-86, managing editor 1986-. **ORGANIZATIONS:** Founder/mem Black Runners Organization 1980-; contributing writer New Orleans Tribune 1985-87; guest lecturer Univ of New Orleans 1985, Dillard Univ 1986; mem National Assn of Black Journalists 1988-89; mem American Society of Magazine Editors 1988-89. **HONORS/ACHIEVEMENTS:** Unity Awd in Media Lincoln Univ of MO 1985, 1989; Keynote Speaker/Black History US Dept Agriculture 1986; keynote speaker, Black Students on White Campuses Conference 1989; guest panelist, Print Journalism Seminar, Southern Univ at New Orleans 1989; keynote speaker, Black Students Conference, Georgia State Univ 1989. **BUSINESS ADDRESS:** Managing Editor, Black Collegiate Services Inc, 1240 South Broad St, New Orleans, LA 70125.

KEANE, HORACE JAMES BASIL
Dentist. **PERSONAL:** Born Mar 21, 1926, Boston, MA; children: Karen, Mark. **EDUCATION:** Howard Univ, BS 1948; Howard Univ Coll of Dentistry, DDS 1952. **CAREER:** Howard Univ Coll of Dentistry, clin instr 1954-57; Jamaica WI, Govt Dental Officer 1957-59; private practice 1957-; first Jamaican Full Length Film, "Harder They Come" played role of "Preacher"; many radio and TV appearances in Jamaica and Britain. **ORGANIZATIONS:** Pres, Jamaica Dental Assn, 1965-68; mem, Illinois, District of Columbia & Jamaica WI Dental Bds; rep, Dental Conf in England, 1968; rep, NDA Conv, 1970-72; dental adv, Minister of Health Re-Establishment Dental Aux School; mem, JDA; ADA; mem, Omega Asi Phi; Jamaica Labour Party; Calabar Old Boys Assn; Lions Club; Melbourne, Lucas, Kensington Cricket Clubs; toured UK as guest of British govt. **HONORS/ACHIEVEMENTS:** Published various articles in Daily Gleaner; recipient, Order of Distinction, Jamaican Govt, 1978. **MILITARY SERVICE:** USNR lt comm 1952-57.

KEARSE, AMALYA LYLE
Judge. **PERSONAL:** Born Jun 11, 1937, Vauxhall, NJ. **EDUCATION:** Wellesley Coll, BA 1959; Univ Michigan Law Sch Ann Arbor, JD 1962. **CAREER:** Hughes Hubbard & Reed, assoc 1962-69; NY Univ Law Sch Washington Sq, adjunct lectr 1968-69; US Court of Appeals, circuit judge. **ORGANIZATIONS:** Exec com Lawyers Com for Civil Rights Under Law 1970-79; mem Amer Law Inst 1977-; fellow Amer Coll of Trial Lawyers 1979-; mem Pres's Comm for Selection of Judges 1977-78; bd dirs NAACP LD&E Fund 1977-79; bd dir Natl Urban League 1978-79. **HONORS/ACHIEVEMENTS:** Cum Laude; Order of the Coif; Jason L Honigman Awd for Outstanding Contribution to Law Review Edit Bd. **BUSINESS ADDRESS:** Circuit Judge, US Court of Appeals, Foley Square, Rm 1006, New York, NY 10007.

KEARSE, GREGORY SASHI
Editor. **PERSONAL:** Born Feb 13, 1949, Brooklyn, NY; married Erica; children: Nina Monique. **EDUCATION:** Howard U, BA English 1974. **CAREER:** HowardUniv Press, editor 1978-; Mutual Black Radio Network, editor/Writer 197-78; Etcetera Mag, assoc editor 1971-72; WABC-TV NY, desk asst/ writer 1970-71. **ORGANIZATIONS:** Mem Sigma Delta Chi Soc of Prof & Journalists 1976-; assoc mem Authors League & Authors Guild of

Am 1978-; mem Assn Am ofUniv Presses 1978-; mem WashArea Publ Assoc 1978-; Big Brothers of Greater Wash 1980-; mem Black Belt Karate Guide; past mem AFTRA. **HONORS/ACHIEVEMENTS:** Creative Writing Award Writers Digest 1970; Pub Serv Award Sec of Labor 1977; commentary award Gay Activists Alliance 1976; Various Articles Pub. **BUSINESS ADDRESS:** 2900 Van Ness St NW, Washington, DC 20008.

KEATON, WILLIAM T.
College president/chancellor. **CAREER:** Arkansas Baptist College, Little Rock AK, president/chancellor. **BUSINESS ADDRESS:** Arkansas Baptist College, Little Rock, AR 72202. *

KEE, MARSHA GOODWIN
Government equal opportunity, affirmative action director. **PERSONAL:** Born Oct 03, 1942, Durham, NC; daughter of Lewis Marshall Goodwin and Margaret Kennedy Goodwin; divorced. **EDUCATION:** Spelman Coll, Atlanta GA, BA, 1964; Atlanta Univ, Atlanta GA, MA, 1969. **CAREER:** NC Central Univ, Durham NC, instructor of sociology, 1966-72; NC State Univ, Raleigh NC, instructor of sociology, 1973-74; Durham Coll, Durham NC, counselor/director, 1974-80; NC Office of State Personnel, Raleigh NC, personnel analyst, 1980-89; County of Durham, Durham NC, dir equal opportunity/affirmative action, 1989-. **ORGANIZATIONS:** Mem, Delta Sigma Theta Sorority Inc, 1967-; mem, Intl Personnel Mgmt Assn, 1985-; mem, NAACP, 1987-; mem, Nat Forum for Black Pub Admin, 1989-; mem, NC Minority Women's Business Enterprise, 1989-. **HONORS/ACHIEVEMENTS:** Alpha Kappa Delta, Natl Sociological Honor Society, 1965; Outstanding Young Women in Amer, 1975; Outstanding Soloist, White Rock Baptist Church, 1985; Outstanding Soloist, St Joseph's AME Church Lay Organization, 1988. **BUSINESS ADDRESS:** Equal Opporuni-ty/Affirmative Action Director, County of Durham North Carolina, 201 N Roxboro Street, Commerce Building, Durham, NC 27701.

KEELER, VEMES
Construction company executive. **CAREER:** V Keeler & Co Inc, New Orleans LA, chief executive, 1971—. **BUSINESS ADDRESS:** V Keeler & Co Inc, 2920 Earhart Blvd, New Orleans, LA 70125. *

KEELING, LAURA C.
Administrator. **PERSONAL:** Born Oct 28, 1949, New York, NY; married Clint Carter; children: LeShaun Carol, Shelan Crystal. **EDUCATION:** Bronx Comm Coll, AAS 1969; New York Univ, BS 1974; Washington Univ, MA Educ 1975. **CAREER:** NFL Players Assoc, asst dir 1980-81; NY Urban League, program dir 1981-84; Natl Urban League; asst dir 1985-86; Broome County Urban League, pres/ceo 1986-. **ORGANIZATIONS:** Mem Broome/Tioga Private Industry Cncl, Binghamton Local Develop Cncl, Broome Co Martin Luther King Comm, Urban Women's Shelter Adv Bd, Broome Legal Assistance Corp Bd of Dirs, NYSEG Consumer Panel, WBNG Comm Cncl all 1986-; mem Broome Co Economic Develop Corp 1987-. **HONORS/ACHIEVEMENTS:** Outstanding Young Women of Amer 1983. **BUSINESS ADDRESS:** President, Broome County Urban League Inc, 43-45 Carroll St, Binghamton, NY 13901.

KEELS, JAMES DEWEY
Mayor. **PERSONAL:** Born Jan 12, 1930, Blackfork, OH; son of G Dewey Keels and Hulda Howell Kells; married Dorothy M Wilmore; children: James Jr, Tawana. **EDUCATION:** Univ of Cincinnati Ev Coll, attended 1971. **CAREER:** US Post Office, postal clk 1953-78; Village of Woodlawn, counc 1969-71, mayor 1972-79; US Post Office, supr del & collection 1979-80; Address Information Systems, mgr 1981-85, retired 1986. **ORGANIZATIONS:** Exec officer treas OH Mayors Assn; cr comm mem Cincinnati Postal Empl Cr Union 1969-; mem Hamilton Co Mun League 1972-79; mem Woodlawn Action Club;mem Valley YMCA Cincinnati; cmdr John R Fox #631 Amer Leg 1960-64; mem First Baptist Church Comm; mem Cincinnati Postal Empl Cr Union 1969-; past exec vice pres Natl All Fed Empl 1969-72; trustee, Gallia Economic Devel Assn 1988-; finance chmn, Gross Branch YMCA 1980-88. **HONORS/ACHIEVEMENTS:** First black mayor Vill of Woodlawn 1972; first black chmn Post Office Cr Union 1974-75; KY Colonel Hon Or KY Col Commonw 1971; Award of Merit, Pride Magazine 1979; Outstanding Community Service, Gen Assembly Ohio Senate, 1979; First Black elected officer treasure of Ohio Mayor Assn, 1978. **MILITARY SERVICE:** AUS corpl 1951-53.

KEELS, PAUL C.
Auto dealer. **CAREER:** Kemper Dodge, Inc, Cincinnati OH, chief executive, 1988. **BUSINESS ADDRESS:** Kemper Dodge, Inc, 1280 E Kemper Rd, Cincinnati, OH 45246. *

KEEMER, EDGAR B.
Medical doctor. **PERSONAL:** Born May 18, 1913, Washington, DC; children: 6 Children. **EDUCATION:** IN U, BS; Meharry Med Coll, MD 1936; Freedmens Hosp, residency 1937-38. **CAREER:** Detroit Inner City, gynecology 1939-. **ORGANIZATIONS:** Active militant civil rights struggle & Women's right abortion; forced USN accept black Drs 1943; mem Nat Assn Repeal Abortion Laws; Kappa & Alpha Psi; pres Surf Club; mem MI Pub Health Assn; Big Game Hunting Safaris Africa; med adv Clergy Counseling Problem Pregnancy; publ many articles Therapeutic Abortion Pub. **HONORS/ACHIEVEMENTS:** Cit Yr 1974; Feminist Yr nomination Nat Assn Soc Workers 1974. **BUSINESS ADDRESS:** 1111 David Whitney Bldg, Detroit, MI 48226.

KEENE, SHARON C.
Business executive. **PERSONAL:** Born Feb 27, 1948, Philadelphia, PA. **EDUCATION:** Morgan State Univ, BS 1970; Univ of PA, MLA 1976. **CAREER:** Natl Park Svc, chief planning & fed prog 1980-. **BUSINESS ADDRESS:** Division Chief, Natl Park Service, 75 Spring St, Atlanta, GA 30303.

KEITH, DAMON J.
Judge. **PERSONAL:** Born Jul 04, 1922, Detroit, MI; married Rachel Boone; children: Cecile Keith, Debbie, Gilda. **EDUCATION:** WV State Coll, SB 1943; Howard Univ, LLB 1949; Wayne State Univ, LLM 1956; Hon Degrees, Univ MI, Howard Univ, Wayne St Univ, MI State Univ, NY Law Sch, Det Coll Law, WV State Coll, Univ Detroit, Atlanta Univ, Lincoln Univ. **CAREER:** Friend of Ct Detroit, office 1952-56; Keith, Conyers Anderson, Brown & Wahls Detroit, sr partner 1964-67; Wayne Co Bd Suprs, mem 1958-63; Eastern Dist MI, chief US judge 1967-77; US Ct Appeals for 6th Circuit Detroit, judge 1977-. **ORGANIZATIONS:** Chmn MI Civil Rights Commn 1964-67; pres Detroit Housing Commn 1958-64; commr State Bar MI 1960-67; mem MI Com Manpower Devel and Vocat Training 1964; Detroit Mayor's Health Adv Com 1969; trustee Med Corp Detroit; trustee Interlochen Arts Acad; trustee Cranbrook Sch; mem Citizen's Adv Com Equal Educ Opportunity Detroit Bd Edn; vice pres United Negro Coll Fund Detroit; 1st vice pres emeritus Detroit Chap NAACP; mem com mgmt Detroit YMCA; Detroit Cncl Boy Scouts of Amer; Detroit Arts Commn; mem Amer (council sect legal educ and admission to bar) Bar Assn; mem Natl Bar Assn; mem MI Bar Assn; Detroit Bar Assn; Natl Lawyers Guild; Amer Judicature Soc; Alpha Phi Alpha; Baptist (deacon) Club; Detroit Cotillion. **HONORS/ACHIEVEMENTS:** Recip Alumni Citation Wayne State Univ 1968; Citizen Award MI State Univ; Spingarn Medalist 1974; named 1 of 100 Most Influential Black Americans Ebony Mag1971, 1977. **BUSINESS ADDRESS:** Judge, US Court of Appeals, 240 Federal Bldg, Detroit, MI 48226.

KEITH, DORIS T.
Business executive. **PERSONAL:** Born May 28, 1924, District of Columbia; daughter of Rev Dr Julian A Taylor and Viola M Taylor; married DeWitt Keith Jr (deceased); children: DeWitt Keith III. **CAREER:** DC Assn Women Hwy Safety Leaders Inc, pres; DC Assn Women Highway Safety Leaders, Inc, pres 82-; DC Govt, Washington DC, chmn Traffic Adjudication Appeals Bd. **ORGANIZATIONS:** Chmn DC Citizens Traffic Bd; past fin secy DC Fed of Civ Assn; mem Bus & Prof Assn of Far NE; NE Council Amer Cancer Soc; mem Our Lady of Mercy Church; past mem DC Hlth & Welfare Council; co-founder 14th Prec Adv Council; past mem Commrs Youth Council; mem Hacker's Lic Review Bd; past pres River Terr Comm Org, River Terr PTA; mem Natl Captl Area Boy Scouts; past mem Automotive Consumer Action Panel; mem Traffic Adjud Appeals Bd 1979-; mem AAA Adv Bd 1977-; bd trustees Amer Cancer Soc; mem Natl Assn Women Hwy Safety Leaders Inc 1982-; past mem DC bd of zoning St Luke's Church; chmn, Traffic Adjudicution Appeals Bd; pres DC Assoc Women Highway Safety Leaders, Inc, 1982-. **HONORS/ACHIEVEMENTS:** Awd Woman of the Yr Dist Hlth & Welf Cncl 1966; Afro Woman of Yr 1952, 1966; Awds Cancer Soc, Heart Assn, Comm Chest, BSA; UCF Crime Council; D C Dept Public Works 1986; Citizents Traffic bd 1985; AAA Advisroy bd 1987; mem Mayor's Advisory Council Alcohol, Drug Traffic 1985. **HOME ADDRESS:** 3453 Eads St, NE, Washington, DC 20019. **BUSINESS ADDRESS:** President, DC Assn Women Hwy Safety, 2000 14th Street, NW, Frank Reeves Bldg 7th Floor, Washington, DC 20009.

KEITH, KAREN C.
Track & field coach. **PERSONAL:** Born Apr 16, 1957, Boston, MA; daughter of Albert Keith and Margaret Stokes Keith. **EDUCATION:** Florida State Univ, Tallahassee Fl, BS Educ, 1978; Boston Coll, Chestnut Hill MA, M Ed Admin/Supervision, 1989. **CAREER:** Beth Israel Hospital, Brookline MA, phlebotimist, 1978-83; US Youth Games Team, coach, 1980-81; Newton South High School, coach, 1981-83; Brown Jr High School, Newton MA science/pysical educ teacher, sports coach team leader, administrator, 1981-87; Boston College, head coach track & field, 1989. **HONORS/ACHIEVEMENTS:** mem, New England Select Side Rugby Team, 1985-86; Division I Region I Coach of the Year, 1987; Brookline High School Hall of Fame Sagamore Award, 1988. **BUSINESS ADDRESS:** Head Track & Field Coach, Boston College, Conte Forum, Chestnut Hill, MA 02167.

KEITH, LEROY
Educational administrator. **PERSONAL:** Born Feb 14, 1939, Chattanooga, TN; son of Roy Keith and Lula Keith; married Anita Halsey; children: Lori, Susan, Kelli, Kimberly. **EDUCATION:** Morehouse Coll, BA 1961; Indiana Univ, MA 1969, PhD 1970. **CAREER:** Chattanooga Publ School, science teacher 1961-66; Neighborhood Serv Ctr Chattanooga TN, dir 1966-68; Indiana Univ Exec Sec Human Relations Comm 1968-70; Dartmouth Coll, assoc dean/asst prof of educ & urban studies 1970-73; Univ of MA System, assoc vice pres 1973-78; MA Bd of Higher Ed, chancellor 1975-78; Univ of the Dist of Columbia, exec vice pres 1978-82; Univ of MD, vice pres for policy & planning 1982-87; Morehouse Coll Atlanta, pres. **ORGANIZATIONS:** New England Morehouse Alumni Assn, pres 1975; United Way of MA Bay, chair 1977-78; St Andrews Episcopal School, trustee 1984-87; Westminister School, trustee 1989-; Rotary Club of Atlanta 1987-. **HONORS/ACHIEVEMENTS:** Alvin & Peggy Brown Fellowship Aspen Inst for Humanistic Studies 1980; 100 Top Young Leaders in Amer Acad Amer Council on Educ 1978; Dist Alumni Serv Indiana Univ Bloomington 1977; Resolution for Outstanding Achievement Tennessee House of Representatives 1976; Phi Beta Kappa. **BUSINESS ADDRESS:** President, Morehouse College, 830 Westview Dr SW, Atlanta, GA 30314.

KEITT, L. (LIZ ZIMMERMAN)
Advisor, purchasing agent. **PERSONAL:** Born Nov 28, 1938, Calhoun County; married Joseph L; children: Vincent Lewis, Marvin. **EDUCATION:** Claflin Coll, BS Phys Educ 1970; SC State Coll MEd Guidance 1974. **CAREER:** Claflin Coll, purchasing agt present; NAACP State of SC, adv 1975-; Student Govt Assn, adv 1975; Claflin Coll Gospel & Choir, adv 1974-78; Alpha Kappa Sor, adv 1973-; NAACP Claflin Coll, #Adv 1972-; Mt Carmel Bapt Ch Cameron SC, supt 1971-. **ORGANIZATIONS:** Chairperson Lower Savannah Grassroots Adv Com 1976-; sec Claflin Coll Nat Alumni Assn 1976-; sec Dem Women's Club 1977-79; coordinator Ward III Voters 1978; reg dir Miss Black Universe Pageant in Orangeburg Co 1979. **HONORS/ACHIEVEMENTS:** Outstanding Comm Leader Bd of Dir (Newspaper) 1975; Outstanding NAACP Adv NAACP Ms 1976-77; Outstanding Serv NAACP Claflin Coll 1978; Adv Award NAACP Portland OR 1978; Outstanding Adv NAACP Charlotte NC 1980. **BUSINESS ADDRESS:** Purchasing Agent, Claflin College, College Ave, NE, Orangeburg, SC 29115.

KELLAR, ARTHUR H.
Dentist. **PERSONAL:** Born Jul 04, 1921, Abbeville, SC; married Dorothy Carr. **EDUCATION:** Morehouse Clge, BS 1947; Howard Univ Dental Schl, DDS 1954. **CAREER:** Bowman, GA, h s princ 1946-48; Augusta, GA, hosp dentist 1956-. **ORGANIZATIONS:** Mem ADA, GDA Stoney Med Dent, Omega Psi Phi; Sportsman Boat Club. **MILITARY SERVICE:** AUS 1st sgt; Good Conduct Medal N Africa, Italy, Phillipines 1942-1945. **HOME ADDRESS:** Rt 1 Box 171a, Graniteville, SC 29829. **BUSINESS ADDRESS:** 833 Spruce St, Augusta, GA 30901.

KELLER, EDMOND JOSEPH
Education administration. **PERSONAL:** Born Aug 22, 1942, New Orleans, LA; married

Genevieve Favorite; children: Vern A, Erika V. **EDUCATION:** LA State Univ New Orleans, BA 1969; Univ of WI Madison, MA 1970, PhD 1974. **CAREER:** IN Univ Bloomington, asst-assoc prof 1974-83; Comm on Inst Cooperation, dir cic minority fellowships prog 1982-83; Univ of CA Santa Barbara, chmn black studies 1983-84, assoc prof 1983-, assoc dean grad div. **ORGANIZATIONS:** Chmn Current Issues Comm African Studies Assn 1981-84; editor African Studies Assoc, A Jrnl of Africanist Opinion 1982-; bd mem Oxfam Amer 1985. **HONORS/ACHIEVEMENTS:** Dissertation Rsch Fellowship Ford Found 1972-73; African-Amer Scholars Council Post-Doctorate 1976-77; Post Doctorate Natl Fellowship Fund 1980-82; Ford Found Post Doctorate Ford Found 1981-82. **MILITARY SERVICE:** AUS E-5 3 yrs. **BUSINESS ADDRESS:** Associate Dean, Grad Div, Univ of California, Chedele 3117, Santa Barbara, CA 93106.

KELLER, MARY BARNETT
Controller. **PERSONAL:** Born Nov 06, 1938, Mt Vernon, NY; daughter of Raymond Mizell and Grace McNair; married Thomas Keller, Dec 18, 1971; children: Ericka. **EDUCATION:** New York Univ School Commerce, BS 1960; Columbia Univ, MS 1978. **CAREER:** Bedford Stuyvesant Restoration Corp, asst treas/dir fin; Hoffbert & Oberfest CPA's; Foreign Policy Study Found, Inc; Lisc, Inc controller. **ORGANIZATIONS:** Bd of Trustees, St Paul Christian School. **BUSINESS ADDRESS:** 666 Third Avenue, New York, NY 10017.

KELLER-BRINSON, CHARLOTTE JARVIS
Retired nurse, educator. **PERSONAL:** Born Jun 24, 1913, New York, NY. **EDUCATION:** Lincoln Sch for Nurses NYC, 1941-44; ColumbiaUniv NYC, BS 1946-50; Columbia U, MA 1954; NYU NYC, EdD 1966. **CAREER:** Skidmore Coll Dept of Nursing, assoc prof 1973-retired, dir mental health proj 1968-73; Joint Commn on Mental Health of Children, researcher 1967-68; Yonkers Dept of Public Health, supvr pub health nurse 1954-55; New York City Dept of Health & Visiting Nurse Serv of NY, public health nurse 1946-53. **ORGANIZATIONS:** Past pres Nursing Bur of Manhattan & Bronx 1968-75; adv com NY State Nurses Assn 1972-74; pres NY Co RN Assn 1972-74; mem League of Women Voters 1963-75; mem Met Opera Guild 1963-; mem The Studio Mus in Harlem; Nat Council of Negro Women 1970-; bd of dirs 1270 Fifth Ave Coop Inc 1971-73; life memSigma Theta Tau Upsilon Chap NYU. **HONORS/ACHIEVEMENTS:** Am Campaign Medal & WWII Victory Medal, AUSNC 1945-46; Commendatory Letter for gen excellence of doctoral research design, Com on Doctoral Research Design NYU 1964; Founders Day Award, NYU 1966. **MILITARY SERVICE:** AUSNC 2nd lt 1645-46.

KELLEY, DANIEL, JR.
Association executive. **PERSONAL:** Born Nov 19, 1922, Muncie, IN; married Zelma M Fisk; children: Stephanie C, James E. **EDUCATION:** Indiana U, 1964. **CAREER:** Ind Steel & Wire Co, electrician 1945-1968; United Steelworkers of Am, staff rep 1968-; Muncie City Councilman, pres & budget-finance com chmn 1967. **ORGANIZATIONS:** Mem bd dir United Fund 1967; adv council & mem Gateway Health Clinic 1970; citizen adv bd mem Ball State Univ IN Univ Medical Prog. **MILITARY SERVICE:** AUS 1940-45. **BUSINESS ADDRESS:** 206 1/2 E Willard St, Muncie, TN 47302.

KELLEY, DELORES G.
Educational administrator. **PERSONAL:** Born May 01, 1936, Norfolk, VA; daughter of Stephen Goodwin and Helen Goodwin; married Russell Victor Jr; children: Norma, Russell III, Brian. **EDUCATION:** VA State Coll, AB Philos 1956; New York Univ, MA Educ 1958; Purdue Univ MA Comm (grad tchg fellow) 1972; Univ of MD, PhD Am Studies 1977. **CAREER:** New York City Protestant Council, dir christian educ 1958-60; Plainview JHS, tchr of English 1965-66; Morgan State Univ, instr of English 1966-70; Purdue Univ, grad teaching fellow in speech 1971-72; Coppin State Coll, dept chmn lang lit & philos 1976-79, dean of lower div. **ORGANIZATIONS:** Mem Alpha Kappa Alpha 1955-; vol host family Baltimore Council Intl Visitors 1976-; Roots Forum project grant MD Com on Humanities & Pub Policy 1977; mem evaluation team Hood Coll MD State Dept of Educ 1978; reviewer & panelist Natl Endowment for the Humanities 1979-80; chairperson adv council Gifted & Talented Educ Baltimore City Sch 1979-; bd mem Harbor Bank of MD 1982-; exec bd Baltimore Urban League; sec MD Dem Party 1986-90. **HONORS/ACHIEVEMENTS:** PhD Thesis "Rhetorical Analysis of 1884-1888 Controversy, Response of Presbyterian Ch in US to Evolution" 1977; Gov's apptmt State Com on Values Educ 1980; fellow Amer Council on Educ 1982-83; mem Baltimore Jewish Council Fact-Finding Mission to Israel 1987. **BUSINESS ADDRESS:** Dean of Lower Div, Coppin State Coll, 2500 W North Ave, Baltimore, MD 21216.

KELLEY, JACK ALBERT
Museum curator, educator. **PERSONAL:** Born Aug 23, 1920, Edmonton, Alberta, Canada;son of Frank A Kelley and Fannie Cobbs Kelley; married Rose Lee Conley, Apr 26, 1946; children: Jacqueline K Waters, Pamela K Lamar, Keith A Kelley, Elizabeth R Kelley. **EDUCATION:** California State University, Fresno California, BA (Physical Educ) 1946. **CAREER:** Fresno City Police Department, (Detective), 1949-71; Boys Group Sur; CA State Univ Fresno, coordinator law enforcement training proj, 1972-80; Fresno City Coll, curator, Fresno County African Amer Cultural Museum. **ORGANIZATIONS:** Lifetime mem Varsity Ftball; trust Carter Meml AME Ch; YMCA mem; Gamma Xi Chap Phi Beta Sigma Frat; past pres Past Potentate Saphar Temple #117; past v chmn Model City Bd; mem Shriners; Black Educators of Fresno. **HONORS/ACHIEVEMENTS:** All-City team in basketball, football, baseball; All-Valley Football Team 1941; CSUF 1942 All-Western Basketball; hon mention Little Am Football 1942; One of Fresno's Fabulous "100" Citizens, 1985; Community service Awards, City of Fresno 1971, Phi Beta Sigma Fraternity 1980, United Black Men 1988, NAACP 1989. **MILITARY SERVICE:** AUS tank corps, sergeant, 1942-44. **HOME ADDRESS:** 5295 E Tulare, Fresno, CA 93727.

KELLEY, ROBERT W.
Advertising specialist. **PERSONAL:** Born Nov 25, 1940, Nashville, TN; divorced; children: Robert, Jr, Lanedria, Christopher Shea. **EDUCATION:** TN State U, BS 1963; Syracuse U, 1963; Foreign Serv Inst, 1966; US Intl Univ Steamboat Springs CO, 1970. **CAREER:** Nashville Urban League, asso dir 1969-70; Met Nashville Educ Assn, dir field serv 1970-72; Meharry Med Coll, prog ofcr, materials mgr hosp & hlth svc; S St Comm Ctr, dir; OIC Inc, 1978-80; TN State Univ, proj dir, instr Div of Cont Educ 1982-83; advertising specialist 1983-. **ORGANIZATIONS:** Mem Alpha Phi Alpha Frat 1960-; mem NAACP; Urban League; Psi Delta Kappa Educ Frat; Nat Educ Assn vice pres Civitan Intl NW Nasville 1974-75; NashvilleChap Nat Assn of Human Rights Workers Nat Bd 1974; mem Transformed Liberty Inc 1987. **HONORS/ACHIEVEMENTS:** Honorary Sgt At Arms TN State Senate 1971; publ, writer, volunteer, summer issue Peace Corps Vol Mag 1971; publ Tenth Anniversary Issue US Peace Corps Magazine " A Plan for Future Peace".

KELLEY, ROBERT WILLIAM
Clergyman. **PERSONAL:** Born Feb 26, 1913, Springfield, OH; married Mattiedna; children: Bobby Lou, Patricia E, Robert Jr, Frances M. **EDUCATION:** OH Wesleyan U, 1938; Union Theol Sem, 1941. **CAREER:** Cory United Meth Ch, minister; New York City Springfield MO St Louis, Nashville, Cleveland, and Liberia, West Africa, pastor. **ORGANIZATIONS:** Mem of United Meth Ch and E OH Conf for 41 yrs; mem NAACP, CORE; trustee OH WesleyanUniv Missionary United Meth Bd Liberia. **BUSINESS ADDRESS:** 1117 E 105, Cleveland, OH 44108.

KELLEY, WILBOURNE ANDERSON, III
Government official. **PERSONAL:** Born Jun 07, 1935, Montgomery, AL; son of Wilbourne A. Kelley II and Carrie Lee Samuels; married Barbara Jean Anthony, Jun 29, 1980; children: Caron Yvonne Hawkins, Wilbourne A. Kelley IV, Krystal Arden Kelley. **EDUCATION:** Wayne State University, Detroit, MI, 1952-53, 1954-55; University of Michigan, Ann Arbor, MI, 1953-54; United States Military Academy, West Point, NY, BS, 1959; Iowa State University, Ames, IA, MS, 1964; US Army Management School, Fort Belvoir, VA, certificate, 1965; Harvard University, Cambridge, MA, certificate, 1967. **CAREER:** US Army Corps of Engineers, began as 2nd lieutenant, became major, 1959-70; Michigan Consolidated Gas Company, Detroit, MI, became vice president of gas operations, 1970-83; Charter County of Wayne, Detroit, MI, director of engineering and county highway engineer, 1985-86, deputy director in office of public services, 1987-. **ORGANIZATIONS:** Director, American Society for Personnel Administration, 1972-76; member of business advisory committee, Greater Opportunites Industrialization Center, 1972-75; member, New Detroit, Inc, Detroit, MI, 1972-75; director, Greater Detroit Safety Council, Detroit, MI, 1972-75; member, Task Force 100, City of Detroit, 1973; member, Business Office Career Education Task Force, US Government, 1975; Major Gifts chairman, Boy Scouts of America, Detroit Council Central Section, Detroit, MI, 1977-79; president of board of directors, 1978-, chairman of board of directors, 1986-88, Wayne County Easter Seal Society, Detroit, MI; director, Michigan Easter Seal Society, 1980-; chairman of board of trustees, Peoples Community Church, 1987-. **HONORS/ACHIEVEMENTS:** Author of X-Ray Diffraction Analysis of Lateritic Soils, Iowa Academy of Sciences, 1964; author of Revision of Personnel Policies and Reorganization of the City of Detroit under the New City Charter, Office of the Mayor of Detroit, 1974; distinguished service award, American Society for Personnel Administration, 1976; award of excellence, Boy Scout of America, Detroit, MI, 1977, 1978, 1979; Trail Blazer Award, Association of Business Engineering and Science Students and Professionals, 1977; Minority Achiever in Industry award, YMCA, 1980; Volunteer of the Year Award, Wayne County Easter Seal Society, 1981, 1988, and Michigan Easter Seal Society, 1988. **MILITARY SERVICE:** US Army, Corps of Engineers, 1959-70; received Purple Heart, Air Medal, Bronze Star, Legion of Merit, Special Certificate of Achievement from Government of Liberia. **HOME ADDRESS:** 16400 North Park Place, Apt 516, Southfield, MI 48075. **BUSINESS ADDRESS:** Deputy Director, Wayne County Office of Public Services, Wayne County Office of Public Services, 415 Clifford Avenue, Detroit, MI 48226.

KELLEY, WILL GENE
Optometrist. **PERSONAL:** Born Aug 14, Dekalb, TX; children: Cybl, Kelley. **EDUCATION:** Univ of CA Berkeley, BS 1961, OD 1963; CA StateUniv Hayward, MPA 1976. **CAREER:** Pvt Prac, optometrist 1969-; Merritt Coll, instr 1970-; AUS, optometry ofcr 1964-68; Alameda-Contra Costa Cos Optom Soc, pres 1972; Nat Optom Assn,pres 1976; CA State Bd of Optom, pres 1977-80. **ORGANIZATIONS:** Bd dir Childrens Home Soc 1972-76; bd of Dir CA Pub Hlth Assn 1972-76; bd of dir Am Cancer Soc 1976-80. **HONORS/ACHIEVEMENTS:** Cert of merit AUS 1967; Young Man of the Yr Berkeley Jaycees 1972; Optometrist of the Yr Nat Optometric Assn 1974; Optometrist of the Yr Alameda-Contra Costa Cos Optometric Soc 1979. **MILITARY SERVICE:** AUS capt 4 yrs served. **BUSINESS ADDRESS:** 414 15th St, Oakland, CA 94612.

KELLEY, WILLIAM MELVIN
Author, photographer, sign maker. **PERSONAL:** Born Nov 01, 1937, New York, NY; married Karen Isabelle Gibson; children: Jessica, Tikaiji. **EDUCATION:** Harvard Univ, attended 1956-61. **CAREER:** Author; photographer; sign maker; books, "A Different Drummer" 1962; "Dancers on the Shore" 1964; "A Drop of Patience" 1965; "dem" 1967; "Dunfords Travels Everywheres" 1970; periodical publns, "If You're Woke You Dig It" New York Times Mag May 20, 1962; "The Ivy League Negro" Esquire August 1963; "An American in Rome" Mademoiselle March 1965; "On Racism, Exploitation, and the White Liberal" Negro Digest Jan 1967; "On Africa in the United States" Negro Digest May 1968; Playboy, Quilt, River Stix, Eagle and Swan; numerous anthologies; Dancers on the Shore Reissued by Howard Univ Press 1983. **HONORS/ACHIEVEMENTS:** Dana Reed Prize Harvard Univ 1960; Bread Loaf Scholar 1962; John Jay Whitney Found Award 1963; Rosenthal Found Award 1963; Black Acad of Arts & Letters Prize for Fiction 1970. **BUSINESS ADDRESS:** The Wisdom Shop, P O Box 2658, New York, NY 10027.

KELLMAN, DENIS ELLIOTT
Company executive. **PERSONAL:** Born Jul 06, 1948, New York, NY. **EDUCATION:** Yale Coll, BA 1970; Harvard Law Sch, JD 1975; Harvard Business Sch, MBA 1975. **CAREER:** Le Boeuf Lamb Leiby & Macrae, assoc attorney; Columbia Pictures Industries Inc, counsel; Bertelsmann Music Group, dir legal and business affairs. **ORGANIZATIONS:** Mem Intl Federation of Phonogram and Videogram Producers, British Phonograpic Industry, Black Music Assoc, Harvard Business Sch Black Alumni Assoc, Harvard Law Sch Black Alumni Assoc. **BUSINESS ADDRESS:** Dir Legal & Business Affairs, Bertelsmann Music Group, One Bedford Ave, London WC1B 3DT, England.

KELLOGG, CLARK LAVELLE
Professional athlete. **PERSONAL:** Born Jul 02, 1961, Cleveland, OH; married Rosy. **EDUCATION:** Ohio State, 1983. **CAREER:** Indiana Pacers, forward 1982-. **ORGANIZATIONS:** Hon head coach of IN Special Olympics. **HONORS/ACHIEVEMENTS:** Runner up to San Diego's Terry Cummings for Rookie of Year honors 1982-83; finished 3rd in league in offensive rebounds (340); Big Ten's MVP 1981-82; the only unanimous 1st team AP & UPI Big-Ten selection in 1981-82; named second team All-Big Ten by both AP & UPI.

BUSINESS ADDRESS: Indiana Pacers, Two West Washington St, Ste 510, Indianapolis, IN 46204.

KELLOGG, REGINALD J.
Clergyman. **PERSONAL:** Born Jul 02, 1933, Ann Arbor, MI. **EDUCATION:** Assumptn Sem & Coll, BA 1961fUniv Laval PQ, MA 1965;Univ Bordeaux France, lic lit 1967. **CAREER:** Cent Cath High Sch Toledo OH, tchr 1961-65; Holy Trin Milwaukee, 1966; St Francis Coll Kitwe Zambia, tchr hd lang dept 1967-70; Cent Cath High &Ft Wayne IN, tchr, asst princ 1970-72; Bishop Luers High Sch Ft Wayne IN, tchr; Cat Ch Dioc of El Paso, priest, asso pastor. **ORGANIZATIONS:** Secy Amer Assn Tchrs of Fr & Sp N IN Chptr 1970-72; mem Nat Blk Cath Clrgy Caucus 1970-. **BUSINESS ADDRESS:** Our Lady of Perpetual Help, PO Box 1331, Jennings, LA 70546.

KELLY, A. PAUL
Physician. **PERSONAL:** Born Nov 23, 1938, Asheville, NC; son of Dr J Paul Kelly and Amanda Walker-Kelly; married Dr Beverly Baker; children: Traci, Kara. **EDUCATION:** Brown Univ, BA 1960; Howard Univ School of medicine, MD 1965. **CAREER:** Harper Hospital, intern 1965-66; Henry Ford Hosp Detroit, dermatology residency 1968-71; Brown Univ, teaching & rsch fellow 1971-72, instructor & dir of medical educ 1972-73; King/Drew Medical Ctr, chief div of dermatology 1975-, asst dean & dir of grad med educ 1979-82, prof of medicine 1983-, interim chmndept of internal med 1985-86; UCLA, assoc prof of medicine 1979-; Martin Luther King Hospital, chmn of dept of dermatology. **ORGANIZATIONS:** Admission Interviewer Brown Univ 1974-; Annual participant in several public school career day programs 1975-; dermatology consultant annual "Week of the Child, Health Fair" 1978-80; Natl Medical Assn; Amer Medical Assn; Amer Acad Dermatology, Amer Dermatology Assn; Soc Invest Derm; Metro LA Derm; Amer Soc Derm Surgery. **HONORS/ACHIEVEMENTS:** Published 33 papers, 17 book chapters, 9 abstracts, 11 exhibits, 101 invited lectures 1973-. **MILITARY SERVICE:** AUS capt 1966-68; Medal of Accommodation Vietnam 1967. **BUSINESS ADDRESS:** Chmn Dept of Dermatology, Martin Luther King Hospital, 12021 S Wilmington Ave, Los Angeles, CA 90059.

KELLY, DAVID A.
Business executive. **PERSONAL:** Born May 07, 1938, Chicago; married Sandra McKendrick; children: Denise, Michele, Renee, David. **EDUCATION:** Roosevelt Univ Chicago, BS, BA 1960; CPA 1962; Loyola Univ Sch Law, JD 1967. **CAREER:** Arthur Andersen & Co Chicago, partner 1967-; IRS Chicago, agt 1960-67. **ORGANIZATIONS:** Mem, Natl Soc CPA's; Amer Inst CPA's; IL Soc CPA's; Chicago Bar Assn; Amer Mgmt Assn; treas, John Howard Assn 1975; trustee, IL Childrens's Home Aid Soc 1977; hearing bd Univ Civil Serv Sys IL 1974 Bd S Shore Commn; treas, Merit Employment Counselor; Assn Commerce & Industry; Loyola Univ Alumni Assn guest speaker, tax seminars; accounting consultant, Black Businessman's Seminar, Malcolm X Coll 1970. **BUSINESS ADDRESS:** 69 W Washington, Chicago, IL 60602.

KELLY, EARL LEE
Educator. **PERSONAL:** Born Mar 13, 1956, Prentiss, MS; children: Earl L Jr, Eric N, Adrianne C. **EDUCATION:** Jackson State Univ, BS 1977, MS 1979; Meharry Medical Coll, MD 1983. **CAREER:** Jackson Area COGIC Youth, vice pres 1977-79; Martin Luther King Jr General Hospital, intern 1983-84, resident 1984-86; Meharry Medical Coll, instructor/fellow. **ORGANIZATIONS:** Mem Amer Medical Student Assoc 1980-86, Amer Acad of Family Physicians 1983-85; provider/supervisor Saturday Clinic Manchester Medical Group 1985-86. **HONORS/ACHIEVEMENTS:** Water Pollution Control Tech IV MS Air and Water Pollution Central Commn 1979; Honor Student Biochem Meharry Med Coll 1980. **BUSINESS ADDRESS:** Instructor/Fellow, Meharry Medical College, 1005 DB Todd Blvd, Nashville, TN 37208.

KELLY, FLORIDA L.
Educator. **PERSONAL:** Born Oct 13, 1920, Chesterfield, SC; married George; children: Joyce Kelly Moore. **EDUCATION:** Howard U, BA 1938-44; NY U, MA 1953-54; CW Post, 1974. **CAREER:** Bd of Educ NY City, reading specialist 1975-; Libr Bd of Educ of New York City, teacher 1962-75; Elementary Bd of Educ of New York City, teacher 1954-55. **ORGANIZATIONS:** Bd of dir porg chmn "Big Sisters"; Educ Action of Beta Omicron Chap 1970-; fund raising chmn Nat Sorority of Phi Delta Kappa 1970-; leadership com Black Trade Unionists AFL CIO 1970-; mem Jamaica Br NAACP; chap leader PS 160 Queens 1969-79; pres Social Serv Club Calvarty Bapt 1975-; mem Delta Sigma Theta Inc Queens Alumnae. **HONORS/ACHIEVEMENTS:** Chap Leader Award United Fedn of Tchrs 1979; Article Pub Education Black Youth to Live in a Multi Racial Soc 1977; Article Pub "Bibliography of Black History-ednl Perspectives" 1975; Outstanding Serv Award Nat Sorrority of Phi Delta Kappa Inc Beta Onicron Chap 1975; Community Serv Award & Negro Bus & Professional Women Jamaica Club 1968. **BUSINESS ADDRESS:** Board of Educ, P S 160 109 59 Inwood St, Jamaica, NY 11435.

KELLY, JACK ARTHUR
Dentist. **PERSONAL:** Born Oct 28, 1916, Covington, GA; married Marian cameron; children: Carla, Gaines. **EDUCATION:** Morehouse Coll, BS 1939; Meharry Medical Coll, DDS 1955. **CAREER:** Kelly's Cleaners, owner 1948-49; LO Kelly, Jeweler, partner/mgr 1950-53; J Arthur Kelly, dentist 1955-. **ORGANIZATIONS:** Chairman and vice pres NDA Bd of Trustees 1986; pres Natl Dental Assoc 1987; life mem Alpha Phi Alpha Chi & Lamda Chapt; mem Atlanta C of C; mem Amer and GA Dental Assocs, Northern Dist Dental Soc. **HONORS/ACHIEVEMENTS:** Dentist of the Year N GA Dental Soc 1976; President's Awd NDA 1975; Serv Awd GA Dental Soc 1979,80; Serv Awd NDA 1979,82. **BUSINESS ADDRESS:** 210 Auburn Ave Ste 1, Atlanta, GA 30303.

KELLY, JAMES CLEMENT
Clergyman. **PERSONAL:** Born Sep 29, 1928, Bethlehem, PA; married Loretta; children: Lynne, James Jr, Susan. **EDUCATION:** VA Union U, BA 1964; VA Union Sch Rel, MDiv 1967. **CAREER:** Calvary Bapt Ch, Clergyman. **ORGANIZATIONS:** Mem at Large BSA; mem Queens Fedn Chs; Rotary Club Jamaica; mem Prog Nat Bapt NY; life mem NAACP; mem NY Mission Soc; vP Home Mission bd; PNBC; mem Admin bd of Am Bapt Chs of Metro NY pres Calvary Bapt Fed Credit Union. **HONORS/ACHIEVEMENTS:** Recpt CIB Badge. **BUSINESS ADDRESS:** 111 10 New York Blvd, Jamaica, NY 11433.

KELLY, JAMES JOHNSON
Retired military officer. **PERSONAL:** Born Mar 29, 1928, High Point, NC; son of Nathan Kelly and Elsie Johnson Kelly; married Sallie Mae Williams; children: Eva Mae Jones, Thomas Edward, Cheryl Yvonne. **EDUCATION:** Univ of MD, 1957; Our Lady of the Lake Univ, BA 1971, MEd 1973. **CAREER:** USAF, opers ofcr, sqdrn comdr, remote air base comdr, sr pilot & expert weapons controller, instr pilot, maj 1971 retired; city of San Antonio TX Planning Commissioner 1988-. **ORGANIZATIONS:** Mem NAACP, So Poverty Assoc, Retired Officers Assoc, Disabled Officers Assoc, Community Workers Council of San Antonio, San Antonio Club of OLLU of San Antonio, Lackland AF Base Officers Club, Chap #5 DAV; lifetime mem TX Congress of PTA; mem Star of the West Masonic Lodge 24, New Mark Street Bapt Church of San Antonio; 1st black cand for city counc Dist 6 San Antonio TX 1977; 1st black budget officer Edgewood Urban-Rural Council 1977; former mem bd of trustees Our Lady of the Lake Univ; former pres OLLU Alumni Assoc; adv Brentwood Jr H PTA; chmn Brentwood Athletic Booster Club; mem St John Bosco PTC; treas John F Kennedy H Athletic Booster Assoc; pres Bethel Neighborhood Council 1987; pres Community Workers Council San Antonio TX 1987-. **HONORS/ACHIEVEMENTS:** UN Serv Medal; Natl Def Medal; USAF Outstanding Unit Awd; USAF Good Conduct Medal w/3 OLC; ROKPUCE; WW II Occupation Medal Japan. **MILITARY SERVICE:** USAF maj 1946-71; Legion of Merit; Meritorious Serv Medal; WW II Victory Medal; Korean Serv Medal; AUS Commendation Medal; USAF Commendation Medal w/2 OLC.

KELLY, JOHN P.
Business executive. **PERSONAL:** Born Mar 08, 1941, New Orleans; married Laura; children: John, Lauren. **EDUCATION:** Manhattan Coll, BS 1963; City Coll of NY, MA 1965. **CAREER:** Nidwest Nat Bank, pres chief exec ofcr; First Nat City Bank of NY, asst vP; First Nat City Bak of NY, corp lending ofcr; New York City Sch Sys & Chapman & Allen Hancock Coll, tchr; Indianapolis Clearing Hse, vp. **ORGANIZATIONS:** Mem New York City Urban Bankers Coalition; mem Indianapolis Kiwanis Club; Columbia Club; Athletic Club; Kappa Alpha Psi. **MILITARY SERVICE:** USAF capt 1965-70.

KELLY, JOHN PAUL, JR.
Banking, government affairs consultant. **PERSONAL:** Born Mar 08, 1941, New Orleans, LA; son of John P Kelly, Sr (deceased) and Dorothy M Jones Kelly; married Lethia A Robinson, Sep 19, 1981; children: John P Kelly, III, Byron M Smith, Phillip L Smith, Kelli C Smith, Lauren E Kelly. **EDUCATION:** Manhattan Coll, Bronx NY, BS, 1963; City Univ of NY, New York NY, MS, 1965. **CAREER:** Citicorp, New York NY, asst vice pres, 1970-74; Midwest Natl Bank, Indianapolis IN, pres, 1974-83; Natl Bankers Assn, Washington DC pres, 1984-; Castine Financial Inc, Washington DC chairman, 1983-; Unibind of Washington DC, managing partner, 1987-; MMB & Associates, Washington DC, partner, 1988-. **ORGANIZATIONS:** Life mem, Kappa Alpha Psi, 1965-; bd mem, Indianapolis Chamber of Commerce, 1979-85; mem & state treasurer, Air Force Assn, 1979-81; bd mem, Citizens Gas & Coke Utility, 1980-85; bd mem & sec, Indianapolis Airport Authority, 1981-85; mem, Governor (IN) Fiscal Policy Advisory Council, 1981-85; chairman, Capital Fund Drive, 1982; bd mem, Natl Business League, 1987-; bd mem, Amer Society of Assn Executives, 1988-. **HONORS/ACHIEVEMENTS:** Four-Year Academic Scholarship, Manhattan Coll, 1959; Dean's List, Manhattan Coll, 1963; Academic Scholarship, City Univ of NY, 1964; Top Performing Bank in US, Bank Admin Institute, 1981, 1982. **MILITARY SERVICE:** US Air Force, captain, received US Air Commendation Award, 1963-70. **BUSINESS ADDRESS:** President, National Bankers Association, 122 C Street NW, Suite 580, Washington, DC 20001.

KELLY, JOHN RUSSELL
Government official. **PERSONAL:** Born Nov 18, 1947, Utica, MS; son of Mr and Mrs John H Kelly; married Bernell Topp; children: Jon Felice, Kristi Bernell. **EDUCATION:** Alcorn State Univ, BS 1970; Wayne State Univ, MEd 1972; Univ Southern MS, PhD 1979. **CAREER:** US Army, education specialist 1971-72; MS Cooperative Ext Svcs, youth develop specialist 1973-79; Sea Grant Adv Svcs, marine specialist 1979-83; US Navy Family Serv Ctr, dir. **ORGANIZATIONS:** Pres Resources Mgmt Inc 1981-; deputy dir Navy Family Serv Ctr 1983-; pres governing bd Phillips Coll 1985-; pres MS div Amer Cancer Soc 1986-; general vice pres Alpha Phi Alpha Frat 1987-; pres Harrison Co United Way 1987-; pres J & B Printing, Inc DBA Print Shack 1987-. **HONORS/ACHIEVEMENTS:** Outstanding Young Man in Amer Natl Jaycees 1979,82. **MILITARY SERVICE:** AUS sgt 2 yrs. **BUSINESS ADDRESS:** Dir, US Navy Family Service Ctr, Construction Battalion Ctr, Bldg 29, Gulfport, MS 39501.

KELLY, LEONTINE T. C.
Bishop. **PERSONAL:** Born in Washington, DC; daughter of David D Turpeau and Ila M Turpeau; married Gloster Current (deceased); children: Angela, Gloster Jr; married James David Kelly; children: John David, Pamela. **EDUCATION:** Attended West Virginia State Coll; Virginia Union Univ, graduated, 1960; Union Theological Seminary, Richmond, VA, MDiv, 1969. **CAREER:** Schoolteacher; Galilee United Methodist Church, Edwardsville, VA, pastor; Virginia Conf Council on Ministries, staff mem; Asbury United Methodist Church, Richmond, VA, pastor, 1976-83; United Methodist Church, Nashville, TN, mem of natl staff, 1983-84; California-Nevada Conf, San Francisco, CA, bishop, 1984-. **HONORS/ACHIEVEMENTS:** First black female bishop in a major religious denomination. **BUSINESS ADDRESS:** 330 Ellis, San Francisco, CA 94102. *

KELLY, MARION GREENUP
Organization executive. **PERSONAL:** Born Nov 28, 1947, Baton Rouge; married Harlan H; children: Ingrid, Ian. **EDUCATION:** H Sophie Newcomb Coll Tulane U, BA 1969; Tulane U, MEd 1970. **CAREER:** Mayors Ofc New Orleans, cit partic coord 1975-; Headstart, tchr 1970-71; Neighborhood Coord, asst exec dir 1971-73. **ORGANIZATIONS:** Mem Nat Assn Planners 1971-73; Am Soc & Planning Ofcls 1971-74; Honors Educ Soc 1970-73; Gr New Orleans Presch Assn 1970-74; Childrens Bur New Orleans 1973-74. **HONORS/ACHIEVEMENTS:** Civic Orgn awards pub schs Baton Rouge 1963-64. **BUSINESS ADDRESS:** City Hall BE10, New Orleans, LA 70112.

KELLY, MILTON LEO
Business executive. **PERSONAL:** Born Sep 30, 1935, Houston, TX; married Shirley Mary Triche; children: Arnold Lee, Stephen. **EDUCATION:** San Francisco State, AB 1958, MA 1968. **CAREER:** Oakland Recreation Dept, head dir 1962-64; City of Richmond, dir job upgrading proj 1964-68; Crown Zellerbach, corp mgr emloy rel 1968-. **ORGANIZA-**

TIONS: Mem Amer Soc for Personnel Admin 1984-, Equal Employ Adv Comm 1970-, Federated Employ of the Bay Area 1970-; bd dir Natl Black United Fund 1980-, Western Addition Sr Citizens Serv Ctr 1980-, Oakland Athletics Comm Adv Bd 1981-.

KELLY, THOMAS, JR.
Financial administrator. **PERSONAL:** Born Apr 02, 1951, Augusta, GA; married Geraldine; children: Thomas III, Tiffany Nicole. **EDUCATION:** Augusta Coll Schof Bus, BBA 1973; Augusta Coll;; MBA 1978. **CAREER:** Med Coll of GA Talmadge Meml Hosp, asso hosp adminstr 1978-; Med Coll of GA Talmadge Meml Hosp, asst hosp adminstr 1976-78; Med Coll of GA Talmadge Meml Hosp, fiscal & affairs analyst 1975-76; Med Coll of GA Talmadge Meml Hosp, cost Accountant 1974-75; Med Coll of GA Talmadge Meml Hosp;; gen assountant 1973-74. **ORGANIZATIONS:** Mem Hosp Financial Mgmt Assn 1975-; chmn Internal Audit Com Health Center Credit 1977-79; loan exec United Way Agency 1978-79. **BUSINESS ADDRESS:** Med Coll of GA Eugene, Talmade Meml Hosp 1120 15th St, Augusta, GA 30912.

KELLY, THOMAS MAURICE, III
Manager, purchasing. **PERSONAL:** Born May 26, 1950, Des Moines, IA; married Gwendolyn Faye Howard; children: Thomas IV, Patrick. **EDUCATION:** Luther Coll, BA acctg 1968; Luther Coll, BA economics 1972. **CAREER:** John Deere Component Works, magr, Cost Acctg & Auditing 1979; Deere & Company, 1980. **ORGANIZATIONS:** Past chrmn brd dir Jesse Cosby Neighborhood Ctr; mem, brd dir Jesse Cosby Neighborhood Ctr; brd of trustees mem YWCA; div ldr United Way Campaign 1982; campaign worker Jr Achvmnt 1982; pres Superv Club; allocation panel mem United Way Campaign 1984; mem brd dir Peoples Health Clinic; mem brddir Waterloo Chmbr Comm; mem brd dir Amer Red Cross, Hawkeye Chptr; mem brd dir Black Hawk Cnty Economic Develop Ment Cncl; brd dir & mem Waterloo Seratoma Serv Club; mem Waterloo Optimist Serv Club; mem Natl Assoc of Accountants. **HONORS/ACHIEVEMENTS:** CPA IA 1977. **BUSINESS ADDRESS:** Manager of Purchasing, John Deere Tractor Works, P O Box 3500, Waterloo, IA 50704.

KELSEY, GARY MATTHEW
Administrator/educator. **PERSONAL:** Born Jun 30, 1954, Washington, DC. **EDUCATION:** Allegheny College, BA 1976; Howard University, MEd 1987. **CAREER:** US Treasury Dept, student intern 1971-72; Alleghany College, asst dir of admin 1975-78; University of Pennsylvania, dir of minority rec 1978-83; Copper State College, assoc dean of students 1983-85; The College Board, assoc dir admissions and guidance services 1985-. **HONORS/ACHIEVEMENTS:** William Bentley Prize-Allegheny College 1976; Outstanding Young Men of America 1981 and 1986; Natl Association of College Admissions Counselors; Natl Alliance of Black School Educators; Natl Scholorship Service Fund for Negro Students. **BUSINESS ADDRESS:** Associate Dir, The College Board, 3440 Market St Ste 410, Philadelphia, PA 19104.

KELSEY, GEORGE DENNIS SALE
Educator. **PERSONAL:** Born Jul 24, 1910, Columbus, GA; married Leola; children: George, Everett (dec). **EDUCATION:** Morehouse Coll, AB 1934; Andover Newton Theol Sch, BD 1937; Yale U, PhD 1946; Harvard U, 1958-59; Sch of Econ & Polit Sci, 1965-66; Morehouse Coll, DD 1970. **CAREER:** Drew Univ Madison NJ, Henry Anson Butts prof of Christian Ethics ; Morehouse Coll, prof of religion & philosophy 1938-45; School of Religion Morehouse Coll, dir 1945-48; Field Dept Natl Council of Ch, assoc dir 1948-52; Christian Ethics Drew Univ, assoc prof 1952-57. **ORGANIZATIONS:** Author "Racism & the Christian Understanding of Man" 1965; "Social Ethics Among So Bapts" 1917-1965. **BUSINESS ADDRESS:** Drew Univ, Madison, NJ 07940.

KEMP, C. ROBERT
Business executive. **PERSONAL:** Born May 26, 1934, Detroit, MI; married Wilbertean Yvonne Bowser; children: Ronald Brown, Andrea Beaubien, Roderick Kemp, Jenine Hunter. **EDUCATION:** Univ of Wash EEE Studies, 1962; Carnegie Fellowship, Cert 1968; Alexander Hamilton Inst, BA 1971; UCLA Exec Prog, Cert 1972; UCLA Grad Schl of Mgmt, MBA 1977; MIT Exec Prog, Cert 1984; Stanford Grad Bus Sch, Cert 1986. **CAREER:** TRW Systems Inc (Aerospace/Engr), mem tech staff 1963-69; Interracial Council for Bus Opportunity, vice pres 1969-73; Economic Resources Corp, pres CEO 1973-78; Interagency Council for Minority Bus Enterprise US Dept of Commerce, exec dir sp asst to secr 1978-79; Opportunity Funding Corp, pres CEO 1979. **ORGANIZATIONS:** Dir Safeway Stores Inc, Sovrany DC Natl Bank, Freedom Natl Bank; dir chrmn Syndicated Comm Inc, Fulcrum Venture Capital Corp; dir Natl Urban Coalition, Natl Black United Fund. **HONORS/ACHIEVEMENTS:** Flwshp Carnegie Inst 1968 Urban; Exec Ldrshp Outstanding Citizen City of Los Angeles; Outstanding Comm Srv State of CA; Recognition Articles Living Legends in Black Amer Black Enterprises. **MILITARY SERVICE:** USAF airman 1st class 1953-57. **BUSINESS ADDRESS:** President/Chief Executive Ofcr, Opportunity Funding Corp, 2021 K St NW 701, Washington, DC 20006.

KEMP, EMMERLYNE J.
Musician. **PERSONAL:** Born May 06, 1935, Chicago, IL. **EDUCATION:** NY U, Mus Educ 1973; Monterey CA Sptings, MPC 1960; Sch of Boston, jazz subjects 1965; NY U, communications 1973; NY U, MPC 1960; Northwestern U, piano 1952-54. **CAREER:** Private piano 1939; Beth Eden Bapt Ch, Concert; performed in mid/West & so cities 1940; Berkeley Little Theater CA, West Coast Concert 1950; played with jazz groups with military men 1956-59; supperclub performing 1959; appeared solo & with groups in HI, OR, NV, & AZ; Santa Clara Coll, concert with jazz group1961; based in New York City 1965; San Francisco, TV appearance 1961; Radio & TV commercial voice overs 1966; ASCAP writer; Audubon Mus, original music pub 1969; Emme Kemp Mus formed 1974; Ballad of Box Brown Mus; George WashingtonUniv St Louis MO,. **HONORS/ACHIEVEMENTS:** 1st place Nat Talent Competition Bapt Ushers Washington 1953; 2nd place Young & Artists Soc Competition San Francisco 1954; 3rd Amry Area Choruses Competition dir/Records div CA 1957. **MILITARY SERVICE:** WAC sp4 1956-59.

KENDALL, LETTIE M.
Educator, government official. **PERSONAL:** Born May 02, 1930, Magnolia, AR; married Robert B; children: Yvonne, Sharon, Donald, Ronald. **EDUCATION:** AR Bapt Coll, BS 1951; Bishop Coll 1951; TN State U; Austin Peay State U, MA 1974; Austin Peay State U, EdS 1979. **CAREER:** Woodruff County Sch Sys, tchr 1951-52; Clarksville & Mont City Sch 1961; Byrns L Darden Sch 1966; Moore Elem & Cohn Schs, prin 1977-; Clarksville Sch. **ORGANIZATIONS:** Mem Clarksville Mont City Educ Assn; past mem TEA, MTEA, NEA; Kappa Delta Pi; Dept Byrns L Darden Sch; Middle TN Council IRA; attended numerous workshops; mem Co Commrs Assn of TN; Adv Com EEO bd Ft Campbell KY; Sch Com of County Ct; NAACP; Clarksville Comm Devel Com; v chmn Recreational & Historical bd of the County Com; past dir St John Bapt Ch Sunday Sch.

KENDALL, MARK ACTON ROBERTSON
Physician. **PERSONAL:** Born Nov 27, 1938, New Amsterdam, Guyana;children: 3 children. **EDUCATION:** Howard Univ, BS 1961, MD 1965. **CAREER:** Methodist Hospital Grad Med Ctr, radiology resident 1971; Univ of CA Davis, asst prof of radiology 1972-74; Whittaker Memorial Hospital, dir of radiology 1975-85; Newport News General Hosp, dir of diag imaging 1985-. **ORGANIZATIONS:** Mem Amer Coll of Radiology 1980, Natl Medical Assoc 1984-; mem bd of dirs Sickle Cell Asoc 1986. **HONORS/ACHIEVEMENTS:** Bd Certification Amer Bd of Radiology, Amer Bd of Nuclear Medicine. **BUSINESS ADDRESS:** Dir of Diagnostic Imaging, Newport News General Hospital, 5100 Marshall Ave, Newport News, VA 23607.

KENDALL, ROBERT, JR.
Attorney. **PERSONAL:** Born Feb 11, 1947, Thomaston, GA; married Lolita Marie Toles; children: Yolanda Yvette, Robert III. **EDUCATION:** Ft Valley State Coll, BS Educ 1969; TX So Univ Sch of Law, JD 1973. **CAREER:** US Dept of Justice, asst dir civil division. **ORGANIZATIONS:** Mem Phi Beta Sigma Frat 1968; mem Phi Alpha Delta Law Frat 1969. **HONORS/ACHIEVEMENTS:** Spl Achievement Awds for Sustained Superior Performance of Duty US Dept of Justice Washington DC 1977 and 1985. **MILITARY SERVICE:** AUS E-5 2 yrs; Bronze Star. **BUSINESS ADDRESS:** Assistant Dir, US Dept of Justice, 10th & PA Ave NW, Washington, DC 20530.

KENDALL, SHIRLEY I.
Education administrator. **PERSONAL:** Born Jun 26, 1954, Manhattan, NY; married Victor Parris; children: Victor Kendall. **EDUCATION:** Morrisville Ag & Tech Coll, AA 1974; SUNY Oneonta, BS Early Secondary Ed 1976; SUNY State Ed Dept, Public School Teacher Cert 1981; SUNY Oneonta, MS Counseling 1984. **CAREER:** Ed Oppty Program SUNY Oneonta, counselor 1977-79, instr peer counseling 1977-79, admissions counselor 1979-80, asst dir 1980-82, asst to pres. **ORGANIZATIONS:** Mem Amer Assoc for Affirm Action 1982-85, Assoc of Black Women in Higher Ed 1984-85; vice pres bd of dir State Univ Coll at Oneonta Childrens Ctr 1984-85. **HONORS/ACHIEVEMENTS:** Excellence in Academic Achievement SUNY Oneonta Ed Oppty Prog 1976; Serv to Third World Assoc Students Third World Assoc 1985. **BUSINESS ADDRESS:** Assistant to the President, State University College, Oneonta, NY 13820.

KENDRICK, ARTIS G.
Clergyman. **PERSONAL:** Born May 11, 1914, Stamps, AR; married Eddie E; children: Barbara Ann. **EDUCATION:** Am Bapt Coll of the Bible Nashville, BTh 1965;Univ of AZ, AB 1956; Seter Bapt Cntrs Houston, DD 1976; Providence Theol Sem LA CA, DD. **CAREER:** Various locations, Pastor 1940-65; Pilgrim Bapt Ch, Pastor 1965-. **ORGANIZATIONS:** Mod Providence Dist Assn; assn exec Bapt Ministers Conf of LA; pres Paradise Bapt State Convention 1944-49 & 1957-63; chaplain State Legislature of AZ 1960-65; mem bd dir ARC 1960-62; pres AZ Narcotics Educ Assn 1959-60; moderator Providence Missionary Assn of Los Angeles; mem trst bd Am BaptColl of the Bible; mem corporate bd Natl Bapt Sunday Sch publ bd Organizer & leader in church construction in AZ. **BUSINESS ADDRESS:** 950 E 45 St, Los Angeles, CA 90011.

KENDRICK, CURTIS
Physician. **PERSONAL:** Born Feb 12, 1921, Atlanta, AR; married Marguerite S Holloway; children: Carol Y, Janet L, Curtis L, Elizabeth A. **EDUCATION:** Meharry Medical Coll, MD 1949. **CAREER:** Brooklyn VA Hosp, staff psychiatrist 1953-55; Ct Spl Sessions NY City, dir psychiat clinic 1958-59; Hillside Hosp, clinical psychiat 1960-61; self-employed psychiatrist; NYU Medical Sch, asst clinical prof psychiatry 1980-. **ORGANIZATIONS:** Lectr Downstate Med Ctr 1969-; supr Hillside Hosp 1961-; clinical asst prof NY Med Coll 1973-75; vice pres Great Neck br NAACP 1968-70; v chmn Roslyn Urban Renewal 1967-74; treas Psychoanalytic Assn NY 1970-72; sec Long Island Psychoanalytic Soc 1974-75; mem Natl Med Assn Amer Psychiat Assn; fndg mem Prgm for Biomed Careers 1966. **HONORS/ACHIEVEMENTS:** Publ "On the Autobiography of Malcolmy" Jour Natl Med Assn 1970. **HOME ADDRESS:** 24 Hillside Ave, Great Neck, NY 11021.

KENDRICK, GRIFF WILLIAM
Financial administrator. **PERSONAL:** Born Mar 05, 1927, Clifton, TN; married Irma L; children: Karen Elsie, Genora Ann. **EDUCATION:** LincolnUniv Jefferson City MO, BS bus admin 1954; Prairie View A&MUniv Prairie View TX, grad work 1965-66;Univ of NE at Omaha, cert 1974. **CAREER:** Prairie View A&M Univ, vice pres Fiscal 1977-, business mgr 1976, assoc business mgr 1969, accountant 1957, accounting asst 1954. **ORGANIZATIONS:** Mem Nat Asso of Coll &Univ Bus Officers; mem So Asso of Coll &Univ Bus Officers; mem TX State Asso of Coll &Univ Bus Officer; Ch treas Bethlehem United Methodist Ch 1959-80; chap pres Alpha Phi Alpha Frat Inc 1968-69; chap financial sec Alpha Phi Alpha Frat Inc 1974-80. **HONORS/ACHIEVEMENTS:** Recipient World War Ii Victory Medal AUS 1947; Distinguished Serv Award Prairie View A&MUniv 1970. **MILITARY SERVICE:** AUS tech 4th gr 18mo. **BUSINESS ADDRESS:** PO Box 2818, Prairie View, TX 77445.

KENDRICK, TOMMY L.
Educational administrator. **PERSONAL:** Born May 29, 1923, Sycamore, GA; married Geneva Bhanton; children: Deborah Elane, Welchel, Diane H, Denise. **EDUCATION:** Fort Valley State Coll, BSA 1948; Tuskegee Inst MS Educ 1958, MAdm & Sup 1969. **CAREER:** Ft Baptist Church, supt sunday school 1955-85, clerk 1961-85; Masonic Lodge, wishful master 1968-85; elem school principal. **ORGANIZATIONS:** Worshipful master Prince Hall Masons 1950-85; mem Co Bd of Commission 1976-84; mem State Assn of Co Comm 1976-84; mem Order of Consery 32 Maston 1979-85; asst deputy grand master Prince Hall Masons 1984-85; mem GTA 1970-85; mem Natl Assoc of Educators 1970-85; mem Page Prof Org 1983-85. **HOME ADDRESS:** Kaiglen Rd, Georgetown, GA 31754.

KENDRIX, MOSS H., SR.
Business owner, executive. **PERSONAL:** Born Mar 08, 1917, Atlanta; divorced; children: Moss, Jr, Alan Lofton. **EDUCATION:** Morehouse Coll, AB 1939; Allen Univ, LlD 1959. **CAREER:** Moss H Kendrix Public Relations Organization, owner 1948-; Negro Affairs SE Region Natl Youth Admin, admin asst 1939-43; A Monthly Summary of Events & Trends in Race & Relations, Fisk Univ, mng editor 1943-44; YMCA Veterans Rehab Prog, dir 1945. **ORGANIZATIONS:** Mem, NNPA; rep, US Treasury 6th War Loan Drive 1945; public relations officer, Liberian Centennial Commn 1945-47; Natl Educ Assn 1948-52; co-founder, Delta Phi Delta Journalists Soc 1937; originator, D Phi D sponsored Natl Negro Newspaper Week 1938; founder, Natl Assn Market Developers 1953; mem, Assn Study Afro-Amer Life & Hist; life mem, Alpha Phi Alpha; Amer Teachers Assn; LMNEA; Capital Press Club; C of C; Natl Assn Colored Women's Club; Natl Assn Market Developers; Natl Assn Negro Business & Professional Women's Clubs; Natl Business League; Natl Council Negro Women; NEA; Natl Public Relations Roundtable; Public Relations Soc; natl pres, Morehouse Coll Alumni Assn 1959-61; pres emeritus, NAMD 1978, Pub Assn 1972. **HONORS/ACHIEVEMENTS:** Published articles in magazines and professional journals; Founders Award, Natl Assn Market Developers 1973; awarded NAMD-DC lifetime membership 1977; Key to City of Birmingham AL 1955; founders day speaker, Morehouse Coll. **MILITARY SERVICE:** AUS 1944. **BUSINESS ADDRESS:** 2112 New Hampshire Ave, NW, Suite 712, Washington, DC 20009.

KENNARD, PATRICIA A. (NEE BYRD)
Newscaster, reporter. **PERSONAL:** Born Jun 26, 1949, Canton, OH; married Dino M; children: Maya Khalla. **EDUCATION:** Central StateUniv Wilberforce OH, BS 1972;Univ of Akron Sch of Grad Studies, 1975-76. **CAREER:** Harford Jr HS, lang arts teacher 1972-73; Canton Urban League; educ specialist (counselor) 1973-79; WHBC, newscaster 1976-79; Summit Radio Corp WAKR, newscaster, reporter. **ORGANIZATIONS:** Mbr Women in Communications, Zeta Phi Beta Sorority Inc, Assn of Black Professional Business Women, NAACP Historical Society, American Cancer Society, UrbanLeague; local co-host Natl Children's Miracle Network Telethon for Children's Hospital. **BUSINESS ADDRESS:** TV 23 / WAKR, PO Box 1590, Akron, OH 44309.

KENNEDY, ADRIENNE L.
Playwright. **PERSONAL:** Born Sep 13, 1931, Pittsburgh, PA; divorced; children: Joseph, Jr, Adam. **EDUCATION:** OH State Univ, BS, 1953. **CAREER:** Author of numerous plays; Brnun Univ, visiting asst prof 1979-80. **ORGANIZATIONS:** Mem, PEN Natl Soc of Literacy & Arts 1975; Yale Lecturer 1972-74; Actors Studio 1962-64. **HONORS/ACHIEVEMENTS:** Yale Fellow 1974-75; CBS Fellow; Chancellor's Distinguished Lecturer Berkeley, Univ CA 1980; Natl Reg of Prominent Amer, 1975; recipient Rockefeller Grant 1965, 1968, 1974; Obie Winner 1964; Guggenheim Grant 1968; Natl Endowment of Arts Grant 1972.

KENNEDY, ANNE GAMBLE
Retired educator, musician. **PERSONAL:** Born Sep 25, 1920, Charleston, WV; married Matthew W Kennedy; children: Nina Gamble. **EDUCATION:** Fisk Univ, AB (Cum Laude) 1941; Oberlin Coll, BM 1943; Juilliard School of Music, 1951; George Peabody Coll, 1970; private study with concert artist RayLev 1945-50. **CAREER:** Tuskegee Inst, instr 1943-45; Talladega Coll, assoc prof 1945-48; Concertized throughout US, Haiti, Jamaica, VI; concerts on coll campus; Fisk Jubilee Singers, accompanist 20 yrs, incl European Tour in 1956; many duo-piano recitals with Matthew Kennedy; Fisk Univ, assoc prof of piano 1950-81 retired. **ORGANIZATIONS:** Mem Womans Adv Bd of the TN Performing Arts Found; music consult Nashville C of C; mem John W Work III Mem Found; mem Middle TN Music Teachers Assoc, Nashville Chap of Links, Nashville Fine Arts Club; music comm 1st Bapt Church Capitol Hill; mem Alpha Kappa Alpha. **HONORS/ACHIEVEMENTS:** Cum Laude & Dept Honors from Fisk; Scgholarship at Oberlin Conserv of Music; listed in Who's Who in the East 1950-, Who's Who of World Musicians.

KENNEDY, CAIN JAMES
Circuit judge. **PERSONAL:** Born Apr 02, 1937, Thomaston, AL; married Brenda J; children: Celestine Carry. **EDUCATION:** Los Angeles Cty Coll, AA 1964; CA St U, BA 1966; George Washington U, JD 1971. **CAREER:** 13th Jud Circuit AL, circuit judge; St of AL, st rep; Kennedy, Wilson & Davis Law Firm, partner. **ORGANIZATIONS:** Mem of, Mobile County Urban League, Governor's Commission on Crime 1979-80, Law Enforcement and Justice Leadership Mobile, Amer Friends Service Committee Southeast Region; bd of dir Penelope House of South Alabama 1981-82; bd of dir Sickle Cell Disease Assoc Inc Gulf Coast AL. **HONORS/ACHIEVEMENTS:** Outst Young Man in Am 1965; Outst Young Man in Am 1974. **MILITARY SERVICE:** USNR CDR, Judge Advocate Generals Corps. **BUSINESS ADDRESS:** 13th Judicial Circuit, Mobile County Courthouse, Mobile, AL 36602.

KENNEDY, CALLAS FAYE
Educator. **PERSONAL:** Born Oct 13, 1954, Lisman, AL; married Wynathen Ketchum. **EDUCATION:** Sacramento City Coll, AA (w/Honors) 1975; CA State Univ of Sacramento, BA 1978. **CAREER:** Sacramento County Headstart Programs, teacher/dir 1978-83; Children's Home Soc of CA, prog specialist 1983-84; Pacific Oaks Coll, instructor 1984; Yuba Comm Coll, instructor 1985; Child Action Inc, resource specialist. **ORGANIZATIONS:** Chairperson Natl Black Child Develop Inst 1978-; chairperson Sacramento Area Black Caucus Inc 1983-85; treas CA Child Passenger Safety Assoc 1983-; consultant/speaker Child Develop Inc 1985, Marriage and Family Counselors Inc 1986; conference speaker Sacramento VAlley Assoc for Educ of Young Children. **HONORS/ACHIEVEMENTS:** Lewis Lamtier Awd Pacific Bell 1984; Black Female Educator Black Educators for Action 1985; Human Rights Awds Sacramento City/Cty 1985-86. **HOME ADDRESS:** 5930 Mclaren Ave, Sacramento, CA 95822.

KENNEDY, FLORYNCE
Attorney. **PERSONAL:** Born Feb 11, 1916, St Louis, MO. **EDUCATION:** Columbia U, BA 1948; LlD 1951. **CAREER:** Media Workshop & Comsumer Info Svc, lawyer, polit activist, dir; Feminist Party Co-author Abortin Rap Avortement Droit Des Femmes, fdr. **HONORS/ACHIEVEMENTS:** Contrb articles to various publs. **BUSINESS ADDRESS:** 699 Rhode Island St, San Francisco, CA 94107.

KENNEDY, FLOYD C.
Psychologist, educator. **PERSONAL:** Born Jun 14, 1925, Wheeling, WV; married Geraldine C Broussard; children: Lisa Marie, Kevin Eugene. **EDUCATION:** Howard U, BS 1950; CA State Coll, MA 1957. **CAREER:** USAF, personnel psychologist 1952-55; USAF, Personnel officer 1956; USAF, research & devel officer 1957-62; USAF, behavioral scientist 1963-70; Met State Coll, counseling & psychologiszt 1970-75; Counseling & Career Devel, asso dir; Met State Coll, asst prof psychology. **ORGANIZATIONS:** Mem Am Correctional Assn 1966-71; mem Am Personnel & Guidance Assn; Nat Council of Family Relations; volunteer probation counselor Denver Co Ct; mem Psi Chi Nat Psychol Honorary Soc 1951-52; Omega Psi Phi Frat. **HONORS/ACHIEVEMENTS:** Recipient USAF Merit Serv Medal 1970. **MILITARY SERVICE:** USAF major 1970. **BUSINESS ADDRESS:** Met State Coll, 1006 11th St Ave, Denver, CO 80204.

KENNEDY, FREDERICK A.
Educator. **PERSONAL:** Born Jun 17, 1925; married Audrey; children: Kathryn, Michael, Roderick, Karen. **EDUCATION:** UCLA, BS; CA State U, MS; USC, EdD. **CAREER:** Fred Kennedy Associates, pres; instructor 1953-66; Compton Community Coll, instructor, coordinator 1961-66; Compton Area Admin, 1970-73; asst supt 1973-; SF State Coll, instructor 1973-74. **ORGANIZATIONS:** Assn CA School Admin; bd dir Assn of CA School Adm; rep Reg 14 Am Assn Sch Personnel Adminstrs; Phi Delta Kappa Prof Educ Frat; CTA; So CA Assn of Sch Prs Adminstrs; So CA Basketball Coaches & Off Assn; Cont to educ journals Compton Council Hum Rel; pres Optimist Club of Compton; Welfare Planning Council; bd dir So Area Boys Club; chmn Annual Brotherhood Contest; San Fran Black Leadership Forum; SF Human Rights Commn; Ed Com Bayview-Hunter's Pt Coord Council. **MILITARY SERVICE:** AUS warrant ofcr 1943-46. **BUSINESS ADDRESS:** Fred Kennedy Associates, 302 W 5th St, San Pedro, CA 90731.

KENNEDY, HAYS
Foundation executive. **PERSONAL:** Born Mar 01, 1893, Louisville, KY; widowed. **ORGANIZATIONS:** Founder of various centers for children in Harrods Creek KY & Hays Kennedy Community Center; treas of bldg fund Harrods Creek Bapt Ch. **HONORS/ACHIEVEMENTS:** Awarded Kentucky Colonel 1973.

KENNEDY, HENRY HAROLD, JR.
Judge. **PERSONAL:** Born Feb 22, 1948, Columbia, SC; married Altomease Rucker; children: Morgan Rucker. **EDUCATION:** Princeton U, AB1966-70; Harvard Law Sch, JD 1970-73. **CAREER:** Neighborhood Dev Yth Prog, consult 1967-69; Time Inc, corres 1969-70; Office of Genl Couns GSA, 1971; Reavis Poque Neal & Rose, law clerk 1972, assoc 1973; US Attorney's Office, asst US attorney 1973-76; US Dist Court, magistrate; Superior Court of DC, assoc judge. **ORGANIZATIONS:** Dist of Columbia Bar; Bar Assn of DC; Wash Bar Assn; asst US Atty Assn; Lawyers Study Grp. **HONORS/ACHIEVEMENTS:** Outstanding Young Men of Am. **BUSINESS ADDRESS:** DC Superior Court, 500 Indiana Ave, NW, Washington, DC 20001.

KENNEDY, HOWARD E.
Perfumer. **PERSONAL:** Born Nov 30, 1941, Fernandina Beach, FL; son of Charles E Kennedy and Cecil D Watson-Kennedy-Williams; divorced. **EDUCATION:** St Petersburg Jr Coll, St Petersburg FL, Assoc, 1962; NY Inst of Tech, New York NY, 1977-80. **CAREER:** Revlon, Bronx NY, apprentice perfumer, 1965-70; Pfizer Consumer Products, chief perfumer, 1970-87; Royal Essence Ltd, New York New York, pres, 1987-. **ORGANIZATIONS:** Pres, NAACP Youth Coucil, 1961-62; mem, Society of Cosmetics Chemists, 1970-; dir, Amer Society of Perfumers, 1975-. **HONORS/ACHIEVEMENTS:** Sweet Earth & Wild Musk Fragrances, 1971, 1973; Sophia Fragrance, 1984; Stetson Fragrance, 1984; Black Achievers in Industry, New Chapter of the Greater YMCA, 1985; Lady Stetson Fragrance & De Kuyper Peachtree Schnapps Scent, 1987; Iron Fragrance & Grand Marnier Scent, 1988; Seagrams EXTRA Wine Cooler Flavor & Billy Dee Williams Fragrance, 1988, 1989; Outstanding Entrepreneur of the Year, Natl Black MBA Assn, 1989. **MILITARY SERVICE:** US Army, pfc, 1962-65. **BUSINESS ADDRESS:** President, Royal Essence Ltd, 1290 Avenue of the Americas, New York, NY 10104.

KENNEDY, JAMES E.
Educator. **PERSONAL:** Born Sep 30, 1933, Jackson, MS; divorced; children: Jia Lynette, Jason Edward. **EDUCATION:** AL State U, BS 1954; IN U, MAT 1964. **CAREER:** Mobile Co Pub Sch, instr 1958-67; Mobile Co Public Sch, admin 1967-68; Univ of So AL, instr asst prof, prof of art 1968-. **ORGANIZATIONS:** Mem The Coll Art Assn; mem reg membership chmn Nat Conf of Artist; mem Kappa Alpha Psi; Adv Eta Nu ChapUniv So AL; mem bd dir YMCA Mobile mem culture in black & white mobile; bd mem Fine Arts Museum of the South; bd mem Cornerstone Halfway Home; dir, curator Amer Ethnic Slide Library. **HONORS/ACHIEVEMENTS:** Exhibitor in innumerable shows & recipient of 19 awards. **MILITARY SERVICE:** USAF s/Sgt 1954-58. **BUSINESS ADDRESS:** Professor of Art, Univ of Southern Alabama, 307 University Blvd, Mobile, AL 36688.

KENNEDY, JAMES E.
Pastor, retired auto company supervisor. **PERSONAL:** Born Jun 21, 1938, Weir, MS; son of Ethel Kennedy and Girtha Kennedy; married Thelma Brown, Sep 18, 1960; children: Sandra Kennedy, Sheri Kennedy, Stephan Kennedy. **EDUCATION:** John Wesley Coll, Owosso MI, BA, 1976; Southern Seminary, Louisville KY, Graduate. **CAREER:** General Motors Corp, Flint MI, supervisor, 1956-87, retired; Mount Carmel Baptist Church, Flint MI, pastor, 1981-. **ORGANIZATIONS:** Bd of dir, Genesee Baptist Assn; bd of dir, Baptist State Convention; family ministry consultant, Genesee Baptist Assn; family ministry consultant, Baptist State Convention of MI; executive committee, Baptist State Convention of MI; bd of dir, Genesee County Commission on Substance Abuse; bd of dir, Advisory Council GCCSA; national chairperson, Pro-Minority Action Committee. **HONORS/ACHIEVEMENTS:** Frederick Douglas Award, Natl Assn of Business & Professional Women Inc, 1989.

KENNEDY, JAYNE See KENNEDY-OVERTON, JAYNE

KENNEDY, JIMMIE VERNON
Educational administrator. **PERSONAL:** Born Oct 06, 1925, Mexia, TX; married Lois Betha Hobbs; children: Demetra James, Brenda Picola. **EDUCATION:** Prairie View A&M Colld bs 1948; u of TX, med 1963. **CAREER:** Temple High School, vice prin 1975-80; Bon Hdm Jr High, asst prin 1971-75; Meridith Jr High Temple, prin 1969-71; Dunbas High School

Temple, prin 1967-69; Dunbar High Sch Temple, asst prin 1964-67; Temple High, vocational agr teacher 1956-64; Cold Springs ISD, vocational agr teacher 1948-56. **ORGANIZATIONS:** Mem TX Assn of Secondary Sch Prin; mem Nat Educ Assn; mem TX State Tchrs Assn; bd of dirs Temple Fed Credit Unoin; chmn Bd Sr Citizens Inc; chmn Bd of Salisbury Day Care Center; chmn City Bd of Housing; mem Temple City Planning Commn. **HONORS/ACHIEVEMENTS:** Recipient plaques & achievement awards from all Orgns Servec. **BUSINESS ADDRESS:** Temple Independent Sch Dist, 415 N 31st, Temple, TX 76501.

KENNEDY, JOSEPH J., JR.
Educator, violinist, arrranger, composer. **PERSONAL:** Born Nov 17, 1923, Pittsburgh, PA; married Thelma Marion Copeland; children: Joseph J III, Victoria Lynn. **EDUCATION:** VA State Univ, BS 1953; Duquesne Univ, MMus 1960; Carnegie Mellon Univ, applied music. **CAREER:** Broadcast Music Inc, arranger/composer; VA Polytechnic Inst & State Univ, prof dept of music. **ORGANIZATIONS:** Mem Amer Fed of Musicians, Music Educ Natl Conf, Phi Mu Alpha Sinfonia, Phi Delta Kappa; guest conductor Cleveland Summer Symphony 1965; Encyclopedia of Jazzin the Sixties & Seventies Leonard Feather Horizon Press New York City 1966, 1976; guest conductor All American Dir Orch Chi 1968; Black American Music, Past & Present Hildred Roach Crescendo Publishers Boston 1973; natl bd mem Amer Youth Sym & Chorus 1973; bd dir Richmond Symphony 1974; bd dir Rotary Club Richmond 1981; guest conductor Kentucky All State Orchestra Cincinnati OH 1982; guest soloist Natl Assn of Jazz Educators Columbus OH 1984; adv bd Richmond Jazz Soc. **MILITARY SERVICE:** AUS WW II. **BUSINESS ADDRESS:** Professor, VA Polytech Inst & StateUniv, Department of Music, Blacksburg, VA 24061.

KENNEDY, JOYCE S.
Educator. **PERSONAL:** Born Jun 15, 1943, St Louis, MO; divorced. **EDUCATION:** Harris Tchr Coll, AB 1965; St Louis U, MEd 1968; MI State U, PhD 1975. **CAREER:** Coll of Arts & Sciences Governors State Univ, occupational educ coordinator, prof 1975-; Meramec Jr Coll, counselor 1971-74; Forest Park Jr Coll, counselor 1969-71; St Louis Job Corps Center for Women, counselor 1968-69; Carver Elementary School, teacher 1966-68. **ORGANIZATIONS:** Mem Am Personnel and Guidance assn; mem IL Assn of Non-White Concerns; mem IL Guidance and Personnel Assn; keynote speaker Roseland Community Sch Graduation 1978; facilitator Career Awareness Workshop 1978; speaker Harvey Pub Library 1978; Urban Counseling Fellowship Nat Mental Health Inst MI StateUniv 1972-74. **HONORS/ACHIEVEMENTS:** Cert of Recognition for Outstanding Serv IL Guidance adn Personnel Assn 1977; Distinguished Prof Governors StateUniv 1977; Outstanding Young Woman of Am Award 1978. **BUSINESS ADDRESS:** College of Arts & Sciences, Governors State University, University Park, IL 60466.

KENNEDY, KAREL R.
Internal medicine. **PERSONAL:** Born May 06, 1946, Greeleyville, SC; daughter of Ben Kennedy and Susie Kennedy. **EDUCATION:** Howard Univ, BS 1967, MD 1971. **BUSINESS ADDRESS:** Clinical Instructor, Mount Sinai College of Med, 464 W 145th St, New York, NY 10031.

KENNEDY, LINDA CHERYL
Journalist. **PERSONAL:** Born Oct 07, 1950, Brooklyn, NY. **EDUCATION:** Univ of NE, 1968-69; Macalester Coll, BA 1972. **CAREER:** KING-TV Seattle, news reporter, anchor 1976-; KGW AM Portland, news reporter, anchor 1974-76; WOW AM Radio Omaha, news reporter 1973-74; KOWH AM Radio Omaha, pub affairs mgr 1972-73; KOLN/KGIN TV Lincoln, intern 1968; KMTV Omaha, news intern 1968. **ORGANIZATIONS:** Mem Women in Communications 1976-; mem, shop steward AFTRA 1976-; mem bd Wash Chap Nat Com for Prevention of Child Abuse 1979; mem NAACP 1980. **HONORS/ACHIEVEMENTS:** Recipient First Place Spot News Reporting Award Sigma Delta Chi NW 1979. **BUSINESS ADDRESS:** c/o KING-TV, PO Box 24545, Seattle, WA 98124.

KENNEDY, MARVIN JAMES
Corporate director. **PERSONAL:** Born Apr 18, 1931, Ben Wheeler, TX; married Linzel Harmon; children: Wendolyn K Walker, Patrick A, Marva C, Angela M. **EDUCATION:** Prairie View A&M U, BS 1952;Univ of TX San Antonio, MA 1975. **CAREER:** Bexar Co OIC, exec dir 1974-; HQ 5th Army Ft Sam Houston race rela officer 1972-73; HQ 5th Army Ft Sam Houston, chief readiness oper officer 1969-72; Army Rep of Vietnam, inspector gen adv dir 1968-69; Prairie View A&M Coll, ROTC prof 1966-69. **ORGANIZATIONS:** Mem exec dir Assn of OIC's 1975-; mem past vice pres San Antonio Personnell & Mgmt Assn 1976-; mem Am Soc of Training Devel 1979-; exec com mem United Negro Coll Fund 1976-; review com mem Metro Youth Orgn 1978-; fund review com United Way 1979-. **HONORS/ACHIEVEMENTS:** Recipient of bronze star air & commendation medals AUS 1960-66; appreciation award San Antonio Personnel & Mgmt Assn 1978; comm serv award Nat Counc of Negro Women Inc 19790; outstanding performance award Kappa Alpha Psi 1979. **MILITARY SERVICE:** AUS maj served 21 yrs. **BUSINESS ADDRESS:** Bexar Co OIC, 1931 E Houston St, San Antonio, TX 78202.

KENNEDY, MATTHEW W.
Educator, musician. **PERSONAL:** Born Mar 10, 1921, Americus, GA; son of Royal C Kennedy and Mary Dowdell Kennedy; married Anne Lucille Gamble; children: Nina Gamble Kennedy. **EDUCATION:** Fisk Univ, AB 1946 (cum laude); Juilliard School of Music, MS 1950. **CAREER:** Fisk Univ, assoc prof 1947-48, 1954-84, acting dean music dept 1975-78; Fisk Jubilee Singers, piano soloist natl & intl dir 1957-67, 1971-73, 1975-83 (retired 1984). **ORGANIZATIONS:** Mem Music Teachers Natl Assn; mem Sigma Upsilon Pi; Omega Psi Phi; deacon Baptist; mem Nashville Fine Arts Club; First Baptist Church; Omega Psi Phi; TN Arts Comm 1968-82; bd mem John W Work Mem Found 1973-; program chmn Nashville Fine Arts Club 1967-69; Gabriel Scholorship Fisk Univ; Sigma Upsilon Pi Honor Soc Fisk Univ 1946; United Negro Coll Fund IBM Faculty Fellowship 1969; bd mem Nashville Symphony Assn 1975-78. **HONORS/ACHIEVEMENTS:** Outstanding Educator of Amer 1973; Omega Man of Yr 1974; Distinguished Negro Georgians; Special Achievements solo recitals, Carnegie Hall recital; Natl Galry of Art; Town Hall Philadelphia 1958-60; Spirituals published Abingdon Press Nashville 1974. **MILITARY SERVICE:** AUS m/sgt 1943-46. **HOME ADDRESS:** 2417 Gardner Lane, Nashville, TN 37207.

KENNEDY, NATHELYNE ARCHIE
Civil/structural engineer. **PERSONAL:** Born Jun 01, 1938, Richards, TX; married James D Kennedy; children: Tracey A, David J. **EDUCATION:** Prairie View A&M Univ, BS Arch Engr 1959. **CAREER:** Alfred Benesch & Co, engr 1960-72; Bernard Johnson Inc, engr 1978-81; Nathelyne A Kennedy & Assoc Inc, pres, engr 1981-. **ORGANIZATIONS:** Mem Amer Soc of Civil Engrs, Natl Soc of Professional Engrs, TX Good Roads Transportation Assn. **BUSINESS ADDRESS:** President, Nathelyne A Kennedy & Assoc Inc, 6100 Hillcroft, Ste 710, Houston, TX 77081.

KENNEDY, OLA B.
Association executive. **PERSONAL:** Born Feb 26, 1932, Madison, AR; widowed; children: Ola Kennedy Smith, Brenda Gail Kennedy Grey, Diane Denise Kennedy Smith, Tonya Marie Kennedy Harrison. **EDUCATION:** Indiana U; Labor InstUniv Illinois. **CAREER:** Loc 1273 USWA, past fin sec; Local 1273 USWA, rec sec; Loc 1273 USWA, chrmn civil rights com; Lake Co Park & Recreation Dept Crown Point IN, pres. **ORGANIZATIONS:** Past fin sec Loc 1273 USWA; rec sec Local 1273 USWA chrmn civil rights com Loc 1273 USWA; sec Sub Dist 2 Compensation Counc; rep Central Labor Coun; neg com Lobal 1273; sec treas Nat Ad-Hoc Com Concerned Steelworkers; labor com for Mayor Richard Hatcher; treas Local 1273 USWA; Hammond Valve CorpSteering Com Coalition of Labor Unoin Women Nat; exec com Coalition of Black Trade Unionists Nat; treas Midwest Coalition of Labor Unoin Women; Gary Com Status of Women; Manpower Comm Gary; chrmn Dist 31 Ad-Hoc Com Concerned Steelworkers; grievance com person Local 1273 USWA; labor com for Mayor of Gary;life mem NAACP. **HONORS/ACHIEVEMENTS:** One of 15 Most Outstanding Black Women in Organized Labor; Female Partaicipation in Am Trade Union Movement Smithsonian Inst Traveling Exhib.

KENNEDY, SANDRA DENISE
State representative. **PERSONAL:** Born Dec 25, 1957, Oklahoma City, OK; daughter of Leland W Kennedy and Doll Alford Kennedy; children: Mahogany. **EDUCATION:** Coursework at Phoenix Coll, Phoenix AZ, 1975; Maricopa Technical Coll, Phoenix AZ, 1975-86; South Mountain Comm Coll, Phoenix AZ, 1975-86; Mesa Comm Coll, Mesa AZ, 1975-86; Arizona State University, Tempe AZ, 1975-86. **ORGANIZATIONS:** Office aide, Natl Youth Corps, 1974-75; tutor, Valle del Sol City of Phoenix performer, Black Theatre Troupe, 1981; mem, Natl Assn for Executive Women, 1983-; volunteer, Valley Christian Center, 1983-1984; consultant, Kennedy & Associates, 1984-; bd mem, Arizona Cactus Pine Girls Scout Council, 1987-; exofficio mem, Phoenix Community Alliance, 1987. **HONORS/ACHIEVEMENTS:** Outstanding Young Woman of America, 1984.

KENNEDY, THEODORE REGINALD
Educator. **PERSONAL:** Born Jan 04, 1936, Winter Haven, FL. **EDUCATION:** Univ of WA Seattle, BA 1970; PrincetonUniv NJ, MA 1972; PrincetonUniv NJ, PhD 1974. **CAREER:** SUNY Stony Brook, assoc prof Antrhopology 1980-; SUNY Stony Brook, asst prof anthropology 1974-80; The Boeing Co Seattle, employee 1961-69. **ORGANIZATIONS:** Consult HowardUniv Press 1980; mem adv group Nat Endowment for the Humanities 1980; mem NAACP 1967; mem Nat Hist Soc 1974-; mem Assn of Am Anthropologists 1970-. **HONORS/ACHIEVEMENTS:** Recipient numerous fellowships & grants Afro-Am, Study ProfUniv of WA; Princeton U;Univ of PA; Ford Found; HEW; Research Found of NY 1969-75; numerous research experiences Seattle New York City Philadelphia NJ Spain So US W & E Coasts US Virgin Islands; "Relations in a So Comm" Oxford Press 1979; pub "Black Argot asociolanguistic analysis of black lyfestyle through verbal & non-Verbal communication" oxford u press; dissertation "you gotta deal With It the relationship in the black domestic unit"; lectr u of WA u of CA stanstudents. **MILITARY SERVICE:** AUS pfc 1959-60. **BUSINESS ADDRESS:** St Univ of NY at Stony Brook, Anthropology Dept, Stony Brook, NY 11794.

KENNEDY, WILLIAM J., III
Business executive. **PERSONAL:** Born Oct 24, 1922, Durham, NC; son of William J Kennedy Jr and Margaret Spaulding Kennedy; married Alice C Copeland; children: William J IV. **EDUCATION:** VA State Coll, BS 1942; Univ of PA, MBA 1946; NY Univ, MBA Finance & Investments 1948; NY Univ, grad studies 1948-50; Stanford Univ, executive program 1971. **CAREER:** NC Mutual Life Ins Co, pres, ceo, chmn bd dirs. **ORGANIZATIONS:** Bd dir Investors Title Co Chapel Hill NC; bd dir The Quaker Oats Co Chicago; bd visitors NC Central Univ Durham NC; charter mem NC Soc of Financial Analysts; Conf Bd NY; bd dir and vice chair Mechanics & Farmers Bank; UNC Ventures Inc; NC Order of the Tar Heel One Hundred; bd visitors Duke Univ, The Fuqua School of Bus; bd dir NC 4-H Devel Fund Inc; bd dirs Mobil Corp NY; bd dir Jones Group Inc Charlotte; bd dir Pfizer Inc NY; chair, President Carter's Advisory Committee on Small and Minority Business Ownership, 1980-81; mem various other business, cultural and civic organizations. **HONORS/ACHIEVEMENTS:** Selected by Ebony Magazine as on of the 100 most influential Black Americans, 1973—; annual award for professional achievement, Tribune Charities, 1974; annual achievement award, Black Enterprise magazine, 1975; Pathfinder Award, Opportunities Industrialization Centers of America, 1976; C C Spaulding Insurance Award, Natl Business League, 1976; Twenty First Century Foundation Achievement Award, 1977; VA State College Alumnus of the Year, 1977; inducted into National Minority Business Hall of Fame, 1977; NY Univ Grad School of Business Admin Alumni Association Achievement Award, 1980-81; 1985 Business and Professions Award Honoree for achievements as pres of NC Mutual Life Insurance Company, the largest Black-managed insurance company in the US; Ebony Magazine American Black Achievement Award, 1985; honorary Doctor of Laws, NC Central Univ, 1986; J E Walker Humanitarian Award, Natl Business League, 1987. **MILITARY SERVICE:** AUS lieutenant 1943-45. **BUSINESS ADDRESS:** President/Chairman Board Dirs, NC Mutual Life Ins Co, 411 West Chapel Hill St, Durham, NC 27701.

KENNEDY, WILLIAM THOMAS, JR.
Theologian. **PERSONAL:** Born Mar 18, 1928, Washington, DC; son of Rev. William T. Kennedy and Hattie T. Kennedy; children: Stephanie. **EDUCATION:** Dist Columbia Tchrs, BS 1953; Wesley Theol/Drew Theol, STB/BD 1955-60; Wesley Theol, STM 1968. **CAREER:** Yale Divty Schl, assoc prof 1969-78; Wesley AME Zion Chrh Phila, pastor homeo/pratl theol 1971-83; Eastern Bpt Semy adj prof preaching 1978-85; Tioga United Methd Chrh, pastor 1983-85; Drew Theol Seminary, adj prof preaching 1985-; Grace UM Church, pastor 1985-. **ORGANIZATIONS:** Prsdg elder Barbados Dist/AME Zion 1980-; prof socio/rel Eastern Coll 1977-79; prof soc Mattatuck Coll 1964-68; prest Waterbury Conn NAACP 1964-68; chrmn Waterbury Hmn Rel Comm 1964-68; town Comm Waterbury Conn 1964-70. **HONORS/ACHIEVEMENTS:** Dr divty Livinstone Coll 1980; professional cas-

sette Lyman Beecher Series Yale 1969. **MILITARY SERVICE:** AUS pers admn tech 2. **HOME ADDRESS:** 2228 Georges Ln, Philadelphia, PA 19131.

KENNEDY, WILLIE B.
City & county official. **PERSONAL:** Born Nov 05, 1923, Terrell, TX; daughter of A C Williams and Isabell Lois Borders; married Judge Jos G Kennedy (deceased); children: Paulette Marie Fobbs. **EDUCATION:** San Francisco State Univ, BA 1975. **CAREER:** San Francisco Human Rights Commn, commissioner 1979-80; San Francisco Redevelopment Commn, commissioner 1980-81; Gamma Phi Delta Sorority Far Western Region, regional dir 1974-82; City & County San Francisco, supervisor. **ORGANIZATIONS:** Mem, Univ of CA Volunteer Aux 1978-; mem Natl Assoc of Colored People 1979-; pres Methodist Federation of Social Concern 1979-; mem Natl Council of Negro Women Golden Gate Section 1981-; natl pres Gamma Phi Delta Sorority; bd of supvrs City and County of San Francisco 1981-; delegate Assn of Bay Area Govts 1981-; mem Natl Assn of Black Co Officials 1981-; mem Natl Forum of Black Public Admins 1982-; mem Natl Black Caucus of Local Elected Officials 1982-;mem North Coastal Co Supvrs Assn, 1984-; bd of dirs Co Supervisors Assn of CA 1986-; exec comm Co Supervisors Assn of CA 1986-; mem City Democratic Club of San Francisco, Chinese Amer Democratic Club, Democratic Women's Forum, CA Democratic Black Caucus. **HONORS/ACHIEVEMENTS:** Woman of the Year TX Coll Alumni 1976, 1981, 1984; Distinguished Serv San Francisco Black Chamber of Commerce 1982; Comm Serv San Fran Business & Prof Women Inc 1982; Outstanding Serv Natl Council Negro Women Golden Gate Section 1983; Certificate of Merit SF Mayor's Summer Youth Prog 1983; Outstanding Contributions to Minority Business Develop US Dept Commerce 1984; Hon DL Urban Bible Coll School of Religious Studies Detroit MI. **BUSINESS ADDRESS:** Supervisor, City & County San Francisco, 235 City Hall, San Francisco, CA 94102.

KENNEDY, YVONNE
Educational administrator. **PERSONAL:** Born Jan 08, 1945, Mobile, AL. **EDUCATION:** Bishop State Jr Coll, AA 1964; Alabama State Univ, BS 1966; Morgan State Coll, MA 1968; Columbia Univ, advanced study, summers of 1972 & 1973. **CAREER:** Southern Assn of Colleges & Schools, assoc dir, cooperative prog educ improvement prog; Bishop State Jr Coll, coord, higher educ achievement prog 1971-74; Bishop State Jr Coll, English instr 1968-71; Morgan State Coll Baltimore, asst, English dept 1966-68. **ORGANIZATIONS:** Mem, English & Verbal Skills Comm, Educ Testing Serv, Princeton NJ, 1972; mem, Human Relations Commn, Alabama Educ Assn, 1972; advisory committee mem, Southeastern Conf on English in 2-Year Coll, 1972-74; dir, Southern Region, Delta Sigma Theta Inc; bd dir, YMCA 1973-; bd dir, Opportunities Industrialization Ctr, IOC, 1973-; mem, Women's Missionary Connectional Coun, Christian Methodist Episcopal Church. **HONORS/ACHIEVEMENTS:** Eected "Miss Alabama State Univ," 1965; recipient of Outstanding Community Serv Awd, Mobile AL, 1973; Queen of Mobile Area Mardi Gras Assn, 1973; awarded grad fellowship, Columbia Univ, NY, summers of 1972 & 1973; recipient of President's Award, Alabama State Univ, 1964 & 1966. **BUSINESS ADDRESS:** President, Bishop State Junior College, 351 N Broad St, Mobile, AL 36690.

KENNEDY-OVERTON, JAYNE (JAYNE KENNEDY)
Actress, model, sports caster, TV host. **PERSONAL:** Born Oct 27, 1951, Washington, DC; married Bill Overton; children: Savannah Re. **CAREER:** Laugh-In, Dean Martin Show, Mysterious Island of Beautiful Women, Death Force, Big Time, Cover Girls, Wonder Woman, Police Story, Trapper John MD, Hollywood Squares, Dance Fever, actress; Greatest Sports Legend, 1st female host; CBS NFL Today, anchorwoman; Pan Am Games, AAU Indoor Track & Field Championship, features;Body & Soul, actress; Jayne Kennedy's Complete Exercise Prog Beginner thru Advanced, Love Your Body exercise albums; Radiorobics, syndicated radio prog host;Coca Cola, rep; Butterick's patterns, helped design line of exercise and active sportswear 1984; Jayne Kennedy Enterprises, owner, actress. **ORGANIZATIONS:** Finale speaker Great Amer Talk Festival 1982; public services The Lose-Natl Toll Free Number for finding lost children, Health Hotline Natl Cncl of Negro Women, Help to find our MIA's, Black Women Portrait of Dignity Black History Month, host summer program for children Communication Bridge. **HONORS/ACHIEVEMENTS:** Emmy Award for coverage of 1982 Rose Bowl Parade; Belding Award 1985. **BUSINESS ADDRESS:** Dan Pitragello, William Morris Agency, Inc, 151 El Camino Dr, Beverly Hills, CA 90212.

KENNEY, VIRGIL COOPER
Educator. **PERSONAL:** Born Feb 23, 1926, Shreveport, LA; married Locellous. **EDUCATION:** Grambling Coll, BS 1946; TX So U, MED 1961; Atlanta U, 1963; UCLA, 1968; TX A&M, 1969. **CAREER:** School of Educ TSU, asst prof; Spelman Coll, dorm dir 1963; Coddo Parish School, prin 1958-63; Alsalom Jones Jr HS, teacher 1949-54. **ORGANIZATIONS:** Dir testing TSU 1964; asst prof & educ 1971; asst prof educ coord of elementary student tchg prgm 1974; mem NAACP; Zeta Phi Beta Sor Inc; Am Personnel & Guidance Assn; TX Assn of Coll Tchrs; Am Psychol Assn. **HONORS/ACHIEVEMENTS:** Recpt NDEA Flwsp 1959; Crounzellerbach Award.

KENNON, DANIEL, JR.
Business executive. **PERSONAL:** Born Aug 01, 1910, Pensacola, FL; married Verna Herron; children: Rozmond, Dannetta. **EDUCATION:** Talladega Coll, AB 1932. **CAREER:** Teacher, 1932-37; US Postal Svcs, 1937-67; Bradford's Funeral System, vice pres 1967-73; Bradford's Ind Ins Co, vice pres 1967-73; Bradford's Funeral System Inc, pres treas 1974-; Bradford's Ind Ins Co, pres treas 1974-. **ORGANIZATIONS:** Bd dir Urban League 1974; Fellowship House 1970-76; mem NAACP; YMCA; BSA; Metro AME Zion Ch; Omega Psi Phi Frat; B'Ham Housing Bd of Appeals; Downtown Action Com. **HONORS/ACHIEVEMENTS:** C of C Disting Serv Awd Talladega Coll Alumni 1965; pres Talladega Coll Alumni Assn 1959-67; Herman H Long Awd United Negro Coll Fund 1976. **BUSINESS ADDRESS:** President/Treasurer, Bradford's Ind Ins Co, PO Box 11091, Birmingham, AL 35202.

KENNON, LARRY K.
Professional athlete. **PERSONAL:** Born Dec 13, 1952. **EDUCATION:** Memphis State, attended 1973. **CAREER:** Chicago Bulls, professional basketball forward; San Antonio Spurs, professional basketball player 1979-80; NY Nets, professional basketball player 1973-74. **HONORS/ACHIEVEMENTS:** Two-Time NBA All-Star; Three-Time ABA All-Star.

KENNON, ROZMOND H.
Physical therapist. **PERSONAL:** Born Dec 12, 1935, Birmingham, AL; married Marion Jones; children: Shawn, Rozmond Jr, Jr. **EDUCATION:** Talladega Coll AL, BA 1956;Univ CO, Cert 1957;". **CAREER:** St John's Hosp St Paul, asst chf physc thrpst 1957-58; Creighton Mem St Joseph's Hosp Omaha, Asst chf physc thrpst 1958-61; Sis Kenny Inst Minnea, asst chf & physc thrpst 1962; Sis Kenny Instr Minnea, chf physcl thrpy 1962-64; Mt Sinai Hosp Minnea, consltnt in physcl thrpy 1963-70; Rozmond H Kennon RPT Inc, 1964; Physician's Physical Therapy Serv, self-empl; Ebenezer Nurs Home Minnea, chf physcl thrpst; Texa-tonka Nurs Home, consltnt in physc thrpy; Cedar Pines Nurs Home; Villa Maria Nurs Home; all of Minnea; Samaritan Hosp St Paul. **ORGANIZATIONS:** Mem Amer Physcl Thrpy Assn; Amer Reg of Physc Thrpsts; mem Soc-ec Com; past chrmn Prof Prac Com; bd mem past secy MN Chap Amer Physcl Thrpy Assn; ptnr Physcl Thrpy ptnr RKR Assocts; past mem MN Long-Term Care Physcl Thrpy Int & Grp Intntl Cong Physcl Thrpy; mem bd dir Southdale YMCA; Edina Humn Rghts. **HONORS/ACHIEVEMENTS:** Author various artls on phycl thrpy.

KENNY, ALFREIDA B.
Attorney. **PERSONAL:** Born Mar 12, 1950, Richmond, VA. **EDUCATION:** Syracuse U, AB 1968-72; ColumbiaUniv Sch of Law, JD 1972-75. **CAREER:** Federal Reserve Bank of NY, staff atty 1975-76; Harper & Row Publ Inc, asst gen counsel 1976-80; Weil Gotshal & Manges, assoc 1980-84; Cooper & Kenny, partner 1984-. **ORGANIZATIONS:** Mem Phi Delta Phi Legal Frat 1973-; mem Nat Assn of Black Women Atty 1977-; mem Am Bar Assn 1977-; mem Assn of the Bar of the City of NY 1977-; pres Assn of Black Women Atty NY 1978-80; mem Com on Labor & Employ of the assn of the Bar of the City of NY; bd of dir Nat Bar Assn Women's Div 1980-82; treas 1975-80, mem bd of dirs 1975-, vice pres Alumni Assn Columbia Law Sch Class of 1975, 1980-85; vice pres Friends of Syracuse (Black Alumni Assn) 1979-80; admitted to the bar of Dist Ct for Southern Dist of NY, Dist Ct Eastern Dist for the Dist of NY, US Supreme Court 1981, Ct of Appeals for the 6th Circuit; mem Zeta Phi Beta Sor Inc 1980-; mem Paul Robeson Scholarship Comm Columbia Univ Sch of Law 1980-; Civil Court Comm of Assoc of Bar of the City of NY1986-. **HONORS/ACHIEVEMENTS:** Publications, "The Voting Rights Act of 1965 & Minority Access to th Polit Process" Columbia Human Rights Law Review Vol 6 No 1 1974; Charles Evans Hughes Fellowship Columbia Law Sch 1976; Outstanding Young Women of Am US Jaycees 1978; Who's Who of Am Women Marquis Publ 1980; Who's Who in the East 19th ed 1982-84; Professional Awd for Outstanding Serv Natl Assoc of Negro Business & Professional Women's Club; Columbia Univ Chap Outstanding Alumnus Awd Black Law StudentsAssoc. **BUSINESS ADDRESS:** Partner, Cooper & Kenny, 71 Broadway, New York, NY 10006.

KENT, ERNEST
Manufacturing administrator. **PERSONAL:** Born Jan 22, 1955, Rockford, IL; married Dianna Lynn; children: Marcus, Jordan. **EDUCATION:** Univ of OR, BS 1977. **CAREER:** KEZI TV Sports, commentator 1978; Disco Club, owner/mgr 1978; Univ of OR; asst basketball coach 1979-80; Alkleege Club Saudi Arabia, head coach 1980-82; Arabian Amer Oil Co, athletic coord. **ORGANIZATIONS:** Mem Crime Prevention Mayors Office 1977; head coach Eastern Providence Natl Team Saudi Arabia 1982. **HONORS/ACHIEVEMENTS:** Natl Hon Soc HS 1971-72, 1972-73; Amer Legion Awd & Athlete of the Year Awd 1973; Basketball Scholarship Univ of OR 1973; Community Serv Awd 1977. **HOME ADDRESS:** c/o Aramco, Box 10796, Dhahran, Saudi Arabia. **BUSINESS ADDRESS:** Athletic Coordinator, Arabian American Oil Co, c/o Aramco, Box 117, Dhahran 31311, Saudi Arabia.

KENT, MELVIN FLOYD
Supervisor. **PERSONAL:** Born Oct 22, 1953, Panama City, FL; son of Floyd M Kent, Jr and Viletta McIntyre Kent. **EDUCATION:** Gulf Coast Community Coll, AA 1974; University of South FL, BA 1977. **CAREER:** Domestic Laundry and Cleaners, crew supervisor 1970-74; International Paper Co, shop keeper 1975; Sears Roebuck & Co, credit interviewer 1978; Bay County Juvenile Detention Ctr, detention supervisor 1978-. **ORGANIZATIONS:** Vice pres/secty Xi Sigma Lambda Sphinx Club 1985; sec Xi Sigma Lambda Chap Alpha Phi Alpha 1986. **HONORS/ACHIEVEMENTS:** Outstanding Young Man of America 1986, 1988. **HOME ADDRESS:** 909 Bay Avenue, Panama City, FL 32401. **BUSINESS ADDRESS:** Supervisor, FL Dept of HRS, Bureau of Detention, 450 East 11th Street, Panama City, FL 32401.

KERN-FOXWORTH, MARILYN L
Educator. **PERSONAL:** Born Mar 04, 1954, Kosciusko, MS; daughter of Jimmie Kern (deceased) and Marella Dickens Kern (deceased); married Gregory L Foxworth, Jul 03, 1982; children: Gregory LaMar II. **EDUCATION:** Jackson State Univ, BS Speech 1974; FL State Univ, MS Mass Communications 1976; Univ of WI-Madison, PhD Mass Community 1982. **CAREER:** FL State Univ, comm specialist 1974-76; General Telephone, personnel rep 1976-78; Univ of TN, asst prof 1980-87; Univ of TN, prof of mass communications 1987-89; Texas A&M Univ, assoc prof, 1989-. **ORGANIZATIONS:** Exec comm Assn for Educ in Journalism 1980-; mem Natl Council of Negro Women 1980-; mem Assn of Black Communicators 1980-; mem Natl Comm Assn 1982-; mem Intl Platform Assn 1982-; advisor Campus Practitioners 1982; mem Public Relations Soc of Amer 1982-; consultant/assoc editor Nashville Banner 1983; minister of educ Mt Calvary Baptist Church 1983; staff mem Graduate Teaching Seminary 1983-; adviser Public Relations Student Soc of Amer 1983-; mem Natl Fed of Press Women 1983-; mem Natl Assn of Media Women 1983-; mem Natl Fed of Exec Women 1983-; advisory comm Phyllis Wheatly YWCA 1983-; mem Black Media Assn; Black Faculty & Staff Assn newsletter editor; regional corres Still Here. **HONORS/ACHIEVEMENTS:** Valedictorian of graduate class 1974; Readers Digest travel grant 1979; 1st prize Alan Bussel Rsch Competition 1980; Leadership Award Assn of Black Comm 1980; Kizzy Award Black Women Hall of Fame Found 1981; PR Fellow Aloca Professional 1981; Amon Carter Evans Awd Scholar 1983; Outstanding Personalities of Amer 1983; Women of Achievement Univ of TN 1983; Unity Awards in Media 2nd Place Lincoln Univ 1984; num publs & presentations incl, "Helping Minorities, Student Organizations Can Fill Gaps in Minority Programs" Journalism Editor 1982, "Advertising More Than a Black Face" Black Journalism Review 1981, "A Challenge to Your FutureGTE Automatic Electric" 1977, "All Minority Grads-Opportunity is Knocking" 1982; 1st & only black in the nation to receive a PhD in mass communications with a concentration in advertising & public relations Special Award Recognition of Excellence PRSA Chap Knoxville TN 1985; author Alex Haley's bio for Dictionary of Literary Biography, Afro-Amer Writers After 1955 published 1985; PRSA, advisor of the year 1985; Poynter Institute Fellow, 1988; Amer Press Institute Fellow, 1988; Pathfinder Award, Public Relation Institute, 1988. **BUSINESS ADDRESS:** Associate Professor, Texas A&M University, 230 Reed Mcdonald Building, College Station, TX 77843-4111.

KERNISANT, LESLY
Obstetrician/gynecologist. **PERSONAL:** Born Aug 15, 1949, Port-au-Prince, Haiti;son of Rene Kernisant and Claire Albert; married Danielle Duclos; children: Lesly Jr, Natalie. **EDUCATION:** Howard Univ Liberal Arts, BS 1971; Howard Univ School of Medicine, MD 1975. **CAREER:** Harlem Hospital, exec chief resident in Ob/Gyn 1978-79; Natl Health Serv Corps, physician 1979-81; Mid-Brooklyn Health Assn, clinic dir 1981-86; Interfaith Hospital, clinical instructor 1980-; Brookdale Hospital, assoc attending 1981-; Central Medical Group of Brooklyn, Ob/Gyn partner 1983-. **ORGANIZATIONS:** Exec comm mem Haitian Biomedical Foundation 1987, Central Medical Group 1987. **HONORS/ACHIEVEMENTS:** Best Chief Resident Certificate Harlem Hosp Dept of Ob/Gyn 1979. **BUSINESS ADDRESS:** Partner, Central Med Group of Brooklyn, 345 Schermerhorn St, Brooklyn, NY 11217.

KERNODLE, OBRA SERVESTA, III
Attorney. **PERSONAL:** Born Dec 11, 1947, Philadelphia, PA; daughter of Aubrey S and Mary S; divorced; children: Whytni, Raigan, Obra, IV. **EDUCATION:** Temple Univ, BBA 1969; Columbia Univ Sch of Law, JD 1974. **CAREER:** Sun Co Inc, atty; IBM Corp, rep 1970-71; Philadelphia Black Date Processing Assn, counsel; Attorney at Law, private practice. **ORGANIZATIONS:** Pres Black Amer Law Students Assn 1972-74; mem Philadelphia Urban Coalition Comm Task Force 1974-; NAACP 1974-; Barrister's Assn of Phil 1974-; AFNA 1975-; general counsel Philadelphia Urban League 1983-85. **HONORS/ACHIEVEMENTS:** Charles Evans Hughes Fellow Columbia Univ School of Law 1972-74. **MILITARY SERVICE:** AUS 1969-70. **BUSINESS ADDRESS:** 260 S Broad St # 1000, Philadelphia, PA 19102.

KERR, FRANCES MILLS
Educator. **PERSONAL:** Born Oct 21, 1919, Atlanta, GA; married Oliver Wendell Sr; children: Judith Nina, Oliver Wendell Jr. **EDUCATION:** Livingstone Coll Salisbury NC, AB 1939; StateUniv of IO, AM 1943. **CAREER:** Mount Holyoke Coll, assoc prof psychology & educ; Tokyo Japan, coordinator early childhood programs 1953-56; Tuskegee Inst, instructor child devel and dir of the center for young children 1943-46. **ORGANIZATIONS:** Consult Headstart Program Holyoke MA 1966-69; Danforth Asso Mount Holyoke Coll 1971-; bd of trustees Concord Acad 1975-77; bd of dirs Holyoke Chicopee Mental Health Center 1966-; bd of trustees Vanguard Svings Bank Holyoke MA 1972-; bd of trustees Holyoke Hosp 1978-. **HONORS/ACHIEVEMENTS:** Honorary trustee Concord Acad. **BUSINESS ADDRESS:** Mt Holyoke Coll, South Hadley, MA 01075.

KERR, HORTENSE R.
Music educator, pianist. **PERSONAL:** Born Apr 03, 1926, Detroit, MI; daughter of Lorenzo E Reid and Helen G Reid; married Thomas H Kerr Jr (died 1988); children: Thomas H III, Judy E (stepchildren). **EDUCATION:** School of Music The Univ Michigan, BMus 1947, MMus 1951; Catholic Univ of Amer, Washington, DC, Doctor of Musical Arts candidate, 1984-89. **CAREER:** W Charlotte Sr High School Charlotte, NC, dir vocal music, 1951-70; Dept Perf Arts Charlotte-Mecklenburg Schools, asst dir, 1970-73; Univ of North Carolina, Charlotte, assoc prof 1973-77; Howard Univ, Washington, DC, assoc prof 1977-. **ORGANIZATIONS:** Recording sec Natl Black Mus Caucus 1984-88; bd mem, Garth Newel Mus Center, Hot Springs, VA, 1984-; resch chmn, Dist of Columbia Mus Assoc, 1980-84; student mem chmn, Dist Columbia Mus Educators Assoc, 1977-80; pres, North Carolina Mus Educ Assoc, 1970-72; pres, North Carolina State Mus Teacher Assoc, 1961-70; prcs elect, Natl Black Music Caucus, 1988-. **HONORS/ACHIEVEMENTS:** Mem Pi Kappa Lambda Honorary Music Fraternity, 1980-; mem Sigma Alpha Iota Intl Music Fraternity, 1983; Piano chamber of music Perf, 1970-; Duo piano performances, 1980-;. **BUSINESS ADDRESS:** Assoc Professor of Music, Howard Univ, 2400 Sixth St NW, Washington, DC 20059.

KERR, WALTER L.
Attorney at law. **PERSONAL:** Born Mar 26, 1928, Cleveland, OH; son of George H Keer, Sr; married Ruby Cowan Kerr; children: Diane. **EDUCATION:** Kent State Univ, BBA 1957; Cleveland Marshall Law School, JD 1962. **CAREER:** Yellow Cab Co, taxicab driver 1953-55; Postal Clerk, 1955-57; Internal Revenue Service Cleveland, agent 1957-83; Attorney at Law. **ORGANIZATIONS:** Admitted OH Bar 1963; mem Cleveland Bar Assn 1963, Cuyahoga Co Bar Assn 1963, OH Bar Assn 1963; mem John Harlan Law Club 1963; EEO counselor Cleveland Dist Internal Revenue Serv 1973-77; exec bd mem Chap 37 Natl Treas Emp Union 1974-83; assn exec E 147 St Club 1969-71; trustee Shiloh Baptist Church 1968-80; business mgr Shiloh Baptist Church Gospel Chor & Shiloh Male Church 1968-76; assn exec Shiloh Educ Bd 1971-72; chmn Supv Audit Comm Shiloh Credit Union 1973-86; assn exec The Metro Chorus 1974-89; pres Cleveland Chapter Amer Jr Bowling Cong 1974-78; trustee Forest City Hosp 1974-76. **HONORS/ACHIEVEMENTS:** Fed Comm Serv Award Cleveland Program Exec Bd 1976; Cleveland Dist Equal Opportunity Program Commendation IRS 1976; Award Tax Inst Cleveland Public School System. **MILITARY SERVICE:** AUS sgt 1st class 1947-53; Good Conduct Medal 1950.

KERSEE, BOBBY
Track coach. **PERSONAL:** Married Jackie Joyner-Kersee, 1985. **CAREER:** University of California, Los Angeles, coach, women's track and field, 1980—. **BUSINESS ADDRESS:** University of California, Los Angeles, 405 Hilgard Avenue, Los Angeles, CA 90024. *

KERSEY, B. FRANKLIN, IV
Attorney. **PERSONAL:** Born Oct 28, 1942, Richmond, VA. **EDUCATION:** TN State U, BS 1964; Howad Univ Sch of Law Washington, JD 1968; George WashingtonUniv Nat Law Cntr Washington, 1971. **CAREER:** Atty Gen Ofc, legal intern 1966; US Dept of Justice Washington; Congressman Robert NC Nix D PA, legislative analyst 1968; US Dept of Justice, admins of justice spec comm relations serv 1969-71; Match Institutiond sr legislative analyst 1971-72; Fed City Coll Washington, Washington lecturer 1973-; Commissioner Colston A Lewis EEO Comm Washington, spec asst 1973-. **ORGANIZATIONS:** Mem Nat Bar Assn; mem Am Civil Lebierties Unoin; mem Dist of Columbia Bar Assn; bd of dir Dist of Columbia ACLU bd of gov MD ACLU consultant to Nat Bar Found Wash; Urban Law Institute Wash; The Urban Institute Wash; Dist of Columbia Bd of Ed & Intensive Ed Devel ProgUniv of MD; regional dir Young Lawyers; sec Nt Bar Assn; mem NAACP; mem Nat Urban League; legal counsel TN State Alumni Assoc Washington; mem Nat Conf of Black Lawyers; Big Brother Nat Capitol Big Brothers Inc. **HONORS/ACHIEVEMENTS:** Ford found fellowship HowardUniv Sch of Law Wash 1964-68; urban fellowship George WashingtonUniv Nat Law Cntr 1969-71; athletic scholarship TN State U; citation of apprecitationUniv of MD Intensive Ed Devel Prog 1972. **BUSINESS ADDRESS:** Chairman, The Fazzor Group, 800 4th St, SW, Ste 820, Washington, DC 20024.

KERSEY, BERTHA BRINNETT
Educator. **PERSONAL:** Born Jul 21, 1954, Morven, NC. **EDUCATION:** Bennett Coll, BA 1977, cooperative educ certificate 1977; Anson Tech Coll, 1982, computer sci 1985; working on Masters in Adult Educ for 1988. **CAREER:** Anson Tech Coll, job-related educ instructor 1978; NC Adult Probation-Parole, clerk-typist 1978-79; Sandhills Comm Action, spec oppor serv counselor 1979-80; Anson Tech Coll, instructor human resources develop 1980-82, instructor adult basic educ. **ORGANIZATIONS:** Mem NAACP; asst recording sec 1980-82, recording sec 1982-84, 2nd vice pres 1984-86 Natl Assn of Univ Women 1986-88; pres Natl Assoc of Univ Women - Wadesboro Branch; mem Streater Grove AME Zion Church; chrprsn Student Aid Committee Rockingham Dist of AME Zion Church; financial sec Streater Grove AME Zion Church. **HONORS/ACHIEVEMENTS:** Inclusion in 1983 Edition of Outstanding Young Women of Amer 1983. **HOME ADDRESS:** Rte 4 Box 313, Wadesboro, NC 28170.

KERSEY, ELIZABETH T.
Administrator. **PERSONAL:** Born Oct 30, 1956, Wadesboro, NC; married Marion W Kersey; children: Mario, Kinyotta, Fateana. **EDUCATION:** Anson Tech Coll, AAS 1977. **CAREER:** Anson Tech Coll, secretary to dean of instruction 1977-. **ORGANIZATIONS:** Mem Professional Secretary Intl 1983-; chairperson Anson Cty Social Serv Adolescent Parenting Program 1984-; secretary Parent Teacher Org 1984-; pres Anson Tech Coll Alumni Assoc. **HONORS/ACHIEVEMENTS:** Outstanding Woman Young Women of Amer 1983; Notary 1983; Employee of Quarter Anson Tech Coll 1983; Anson Cty's Sec of the Year 1985. **HOME ADDRESS:** Rt 1, Box 199, Polkton, NC 28135.

KEY, ADDIE J.
Social worker. **PERSONAL:** Born Jan 01, 1933, Suffolk, VA; daughter of Woodrow Wilson Myrick and Bertha Walters Myrick; married Leon E Key, Nov 30, 1959; children: Angela N, Lynn E, Leon A, Leroy N, Leonard H, Larry M, Lennell W. **EDUCATION:** Morgan State Coll, AB 1954; Univ of PA Sch of Social Work, attended 1958-59. **CAREER:** Baltimore Dept Soc Servs, caseworker 1956-59; Barrett Sch Girls & Montrose Sch Girls, soc wkr 1960-65; Baltimore Bd Election Suprs, registrar 1965-71;Anne Arundel Co Dept Soc Servs, day care soc wrkr 1971-80; Baltimore City Dept of Soc Servs, comm resources coord 1980-85; Anne Arundel County Executive's Drug and Alcohol Program, asst coord 1985-87; US Depart of Health and Human Servs, ADAMHA, Office for Substance Abuse Prevention (OSAP) Public Health Advisor 1987-. **ORGANIZATIONS:** Co-founder/dir Neighborhood Action Coalition for Substance Abuse Prevention 1982-; chmn East Baltimore Chem People Task Force 1983-; bd mem MD Federation of Parents for Drug Free Youth 1984-; mem bd advisors Fed Reformatory Women 1970-78; pres Benj Banneker Elem Sch PTA 1975-77; pres Cecil Comm Sch Cncl 1970-71; mem adv bd Baltimore Urban League 1968-76; pres Metro Child Devel Council 1966-70; mem Rep State Central Com; del Constl Conv MD 1967-68;asst dir youth prog St Paul Bapt Ch 1961-63; coord E Baltimore Comm Info Ctr 1965-67. **HONORS/ACHIEVEMENTS:** Mayor's Citation 1983; Outstanding Contribution in Community Substance Abuse Prevention, Coppin State Coll 1989; publication in preparation, "Substance Abuse Prevention Within Inner City Communities". **BUSINESS ADDRESS:** Public Health Advisor, US Dept of Health and Human Services, Alcohol, Drug Abuse, and Mental Health Admin, Office for Substance Abuse Prevention, 5600 Fishers Lane, Room 9A-40, Rockville, MD 20857.

KEY, JUAN ALFRED
Personnel administrator. **PERSONAL:** Born Mar 08, 1951, Orange, NJ; married Joyce Yvonne Heard; children: Juan II, Rahim, Joy. **EDUCATION:** Rutgers Univ, BA Personnel Admin. **CAREER:** RCA/SSD, personnel admin 1976-79; Planned Parenthood of Essex Cty, personnel mgr 1980-83; Power Authority of NY, employee rel spec 1984; GHQ Fed Cred Union, personnel admin. **ORGANIZATIONS:** Mem EDGES Group Inc 1976-, Silver Bow Lodge # 58 AF & AM 1979-. **BUSINESS ADDRESS:** Personnel Administrator, GHQ Federal Credit Union, 219 South St, New Providence, NJ 07974.

KEY, JUNE ROE
Retired educator. **PERSONAL:** Born Jul 03, 1917, Paris, TX; divorced. **EDUCATION:** Wiley Coll, BA 1938; Reed Coll, 1945; OR State Univ, MA 1971; Grad Work, Univ of CA Berkeley 1951, NM Western Silver City NM 1962, Eastern NM PortalesNM 1963, TX State Univ Houston 1964, Pacific Univ Forest Grove OR 1967. **CAREER:** Lamar Cty TX School, educator 1938-40; Douglas HS Sherman TX, educ 1940-41; Lamar Cty HS, educator 1941-44; Pentagon Overseas Div of Educ Amer Schools, educ 1954-56; Roswell City Schools, educator 1949-67; Urban League of Portland OR, staff dir 1967-69; Tongue Pt Job Corps, counselor 1969; OR State Univ, teacher corps 1969-71, assoc dir supvr 1971-73; OR State Univ, asst prof 1974; Adams HS, vice pres 1973-79; OH State Univ, honorary prof 1974-75; Cleveland HS Protland OR, admin vice pres 1979-80 retired. **ORGANIZATIONS:** Soc worker Cory Meth Church Cleveland OH 1947-48; sec Portland Urban League 1962; mem exec bd Youth Activities YMCA 1966; mem Natl Ed Assoc, NM Ed Assoc, Roswell Ed Assoc, YMCA, NAACP, Orderof the Eastern Star, League of Womens Voters, Roswell Comm Chorus, Comm Action Prog; co-chmn Roswell Youth Advisors, NM Gov Comm-Bar Assoc, Council of Churches of Roswell, Neighborhood Assoc of Roswell, Cleveland Assoc of Soc Workers, OR Soc Welfare Assoc, Urban League Guild, Portland Univ Upward Bound Comm; chmn Albina Neighborhood Council; mem YUWCA Bd, Ad Hoc Review Com State of OR; pub rel com YWCA, Urban League of Portland, Delta Sigma Theta, Freemont United Meth Church, NAACP Portland, OR Black Caucus, Irving Com Assoc; adv bd Early Childhood Ed Proj; co-chprsn Black Coll Comm; chprsn to adv bd Montessori Teacher Training Ctr; mem adv bd Loaves & Fishes Nutrition Ctr, Piedmont Steering Comm; mem City Commiss Housing Comm on Aging; Fremont UM Church chrprsn Mission Commission; mem OR StateUniv Board of Visitors; advisory board Beaumont Millde School; Police advisory board; representative payee for the elderly (limited).

KEYES, ALFRED LEE
Retired military officer. **PERSONAL:** Born Sep 08, 1937, Oriental, NC; married Ossie Johnson; children: Desmond T, Kenneth S. **EDUCATION:** A&T Coll, BS Indus Arts 1959; Ft Leavenworth KS, diploma Mil Command and Gen Staff Coll; Central MI Univ, MA Mgmt 1974; Industrial Coll of the Armed Forces, diploma Mil 1974. **CAREER:** AUS, comdr engr

equipt co Vietnam 1967, personnel officer ordnance cent & sch Aberdeen proving ground 1967-68; staff officer mgr maintenance & repair opns Vietnam 1969, staff officer devel & reviewing orgns 1970-74, staff officer comptroller functions joint AUS/USAF/USN hdqrs Bangkok Thailand 1974-76, execofficer/operations officer logistics support group (maint & supply opers) 1976-78; AUS ROTC Instr Group, prof of mil sci 1978-85; AC Spart Plugs Div of General Motors, manager 1985. **ORGANIZATIONS:** Mem Amer Mgmt Assn 1978-; chmn Acad Policy Com Central State Univ 1979-; leader Boy Scouts of Amer 1970-74; mem Fed Exec Assn (Civil Service) 1979-. **HONORS/ACHIEVEMENTS:** AUS Commendation Medal (2); Vietnam Serv Medal; Bronze Star (2); Meritorious Serv Medal 1960-; Defense Meritorious Serv Medal Dept of Defense 1978; Humanitarian Serv Medal Dept of Defense 1978. **MILITARY SERVICE:** AUS Ft Bragg NC 1978; AUS lt col 1960-85. **BUSINESS ADDRESS:** Mgr, General Motors, AC Div, Flint, MI 48556.

KEYES, ANDREW J.
Engineer. **PERSONAL:** Born Oct 18, 1918, Newark, NJ; married Ursula; children: Debbie, Gwendolyn, Andy Jr, Carlton. **EDUCATION:** BS Mech eng 1957. **CAREER:** Mun Base Prof & Exp, proj mgr 1968-; Picatinny Arsenal, proj engr 1957-68; NY Naval Shipyd, draftsman 1942-57. **ORGANIZATIONS:** Mem Am Def Pres Asso; former pres Roxbury Twshp bd of educ. **MILITARY SERVICE:** USAAF 1944-46.

KEYES, LEROY
Football statistician. **PERSONAL:** Born Feb 18, 1947, Newport News, VA. **EDUCATION:** Purdue Univ, BPE 1969. **CAREER:** George Washington Carver HS, football, basketball & track all-state 1963-65; Philadelphia Eagles, player 1969-72; Kans City Chiefs, 1972-; Camack-Alston Racing Team Atlanta Ga, chief statistician. **ORGANIZATIONS:** Mem Omega Psi Phi. **HONORS/ACHIEVEMENTS:** Played in East-West Shine Game Hula Bowl; second in Heisman Trophy balloting 1969. **BUSINESS ADDRESS:** School Dist of Philadelphia, Parkway at 21st St, Philadelphia, PA 19153.

KEYS, BRADY, JR.
Business executive. **PERSONAL:** Born May 19, 1937, Austin, TX; married Anna M; children: Brady Tyrone, Brady III, Yvette, Rodney M, Jamie A. **EDUCATION:** East LA Jr Coll, 1955-56; CO State Univ, 1956-61. **CAREER:** Pittsburgh Steelers, professional football player 1961-68; Keys Group Co, pres. **ORGANIZATIONS:** Pres Minoirty Franchise Assoc KY Fried Chicken; appt by Pres Richard Nixon to natl adv council for Minority Bus Enterprise, NFL Players Assoc. **HONORS/ACHIEVEMENTS:** Numerous honors & awards. **BUSINESS ADDRESS:** President, Keys Group Company, 23828 W Seven Mile, Detroit, MI 48219.

KEYS, DORIS TURNER See TURNER, DORIS

KEYSER, GEORGE F.
Engineer, educator. **PERSONAL:** Born Sep 27, 1932, Washington, DC. **EDUCATION:** San Jose State Coll, BS 1965; Univ of MD, MS 1968; Washington Univ St Louis, DSc 1973. **CAREER:** US Army Ord Sch, philco field engr 1957-60; Philco W Dev Labs, tech writer 1960-65; Univ of MD, grad teaching asst 1966-68; McDonnell Astronautics St Louis, electronics design engr 1968-70; Washington Univ, asst prof 1973-74; Howard Univ, assoc prof elec engrg dept 1974-. **ORGANIZATIONS:** Mem Sigma Xi; Amer Asso Adv Sci; Inst Elect & Electronic Engrs; Amer Assn Artit Intl, Assoc for Computational Linguistics. **HONORS/ACHIEVEMENTS:** Owens-Corning Fiberglas Scholarship 1965. **MILITARY SERVICE:** USN electronics tech 1st class 1953-57. **BUSINESS ADDRESS:** Associate Professor, HowardUniv, Dept of Electrical Engrg, Washington, DC 20059.

KHAN, AKBAR See ELLIS, ERNEST W.

KHAN, CHAKA
Singer. **PERSONAL:** Born Mar 23, 1954, Chicago, IL; children: Milini. **CAREER:** Rufus, featured singer recorded num albums; Europe; tour; Japan, tour; SAm, tour. **HONORS/ACHIEVEMENTS:** Recipient platinum LP for Rufus Featuring Chaka Khan. **BUSINESS ADDRESS:** c/o Triad Artists, 10100 Santa Monica Blvd, Los Angeles, CA 90067.

KHATIB, SYED MALIK
Educator. **PERSONAL:** Born May 07, 1940, Trenton, NJ; children: Koren Clark. **EDUCATION:** Trenton State Coll, BA 1962; UCLA, diploma African Studies 1962; MI State Univ, MA 1966, PhD 1968. **CAREER:** Stanford Univ, asst prof 1969-75; SF State Univ, assoc prof 1978-82; Princeton Univ, visiting lecturer 1984; Trenton State Prison MCC, instructor 1985; Rahway State Prison MCC, instructor 1985; Mercer Coll, adjunct assoc prof. **ORGANIZATIONS:** Mem editorial bd Assn of Black Psychologists 1970; consultant SRI 1970; SSRC 1971; HEW 1972; 10 publications in the areas of methodology philosophy & psychology. **HONORS/ACHIEVEMENTS:** Dean's Honor List Trenton State Univ 1960; NDEA Fellow MI State Univ 1965-67; Postdoctoral Fellow Univ of PA 1968; Issue Editor Journal of Social Issues vo l 29, 1973; mem editorial bd Journal of Black Psychology, 1974-76; recipient, Comm Serv Award Bay Area, 1975. **MILITARY SERVICE:** Peace Corps Vol Nigeria 1962-64. **HOME ADDRESS:** 50 Dublin Rd, Pennington, NJ 08534.

KIDD, FOSTER
Dentist. **PERSONAL:** Born Feb 02, 1924, Lake Charles, LA; son of Sylvester Kidd and Louvenia Levy Kidd; married Pearl Coleman; children: Foster Jr, Cheryl, Jocelyn. **EDUCATION:** Fisk U, BA 1949; Meharry Coll of Dentristy, DDS 1953. **CAREER:** Pvt Prac, dentist 1953. **ORGANIZATIONS:** Mem ADA; NDA; TX Dental Assn; Gulf State Dental Assn; Dallas Co Dental Soc; MC Cooper Dental Soc; TX State Bd of Dental Examiners 1973; Flw Acad ofGen dentistry 1973; vis clinical asso prof Pedodontics 1975-; pres GSDA 1966; bd dir Dallas Co Dental Soc 1973; pres elec TX State Bd Dental Examiners 1977; pres chmn bd Soc for Rsrch & Study of Negro in Dentistry 1969; v chmn Acad of Dentistry for Children of Nat Dental Assn 1968-77; vice pres TX Soc of Dentistry for Children 1977; charter mem YMCA 1969; life mem NAACP 1977; treas Concerned Voters Cncl 1977; mem New Hope Bapt Ch; mem Sigma Pi Phi;Omega Psi Phi Club; Rotary Internat. **HONORS/ACHIEVEMENTS:** Recpt outsdng achvmt award in dentistry Com of 100 of Dallas Black C of C 1976; publ "Pediatric Dentistry Provided by TX Negr & Dentists" TX Dent Jour 1968;

"Role of Dentist & Dental Assn in These Changing Times" NDA 1967; "Selection & Appointment of Black Dentists to State Bd of Dental Examiners" NDA 1976; "Profile of Negro in Am Dentistry" HowardUniv Press 1978; Am Thtr Campaign Medal; Asiatic Pacific Campaign Medal; 1 Bronze Star; Good Conduct Medal; Victory Ribbon; 2 Overseas Serv Bars. **MILITARY SERVICE:** AUS sgt 1943-45. **BUSINESS ADDRESS:** 1420 Martin Luther King Blvd, PO Box 15763, Dallas, TX 75215.

KIDD, HERBERT, JR.
Association executive. **PERSONAL:** Married Grace Erby; children: Five Children. **ORGANIZATIONS:** Pres NAACP Bessemer Br Bristol Steel Corp; mem New Zion No 2 Choir; past pres New Zion No 1 Choir; vice pres Choir Unoin; mem of Bessemer Voters League; Bessemer Civic League; Bessemer Progress Assn; Citizens Committee Bessemer; Candidate of Order of Elks. **HONORS/ACHIEVEMENTS:** P. **MILITARY SERVICE:** USN. **BUSINESS ADDRESS:** PO Box 884, Bessemer, AL.

KIDD, WILLIE MAE See ROBINSON, KITTY

KILCREASE, IRVIN HUGH, JR.
Judge. **PERSONAL:** Born Nov 21, 1931, Nashville, TN; son of Irvin H Kilcrease Sr and Carrie E Kilcrease; married Kathleen Lacy; children: Irvin Hugh III. **EDUCATION:** Nashville School of Law, JD 1966; Tennessee State Univ, 3 3/4 yrs; Natl Judicial Coll, Certificate 1983. **CAREER:** US Vet Admin Reg Office, claims examiner 1966-68; Private practice of Law, attny 1968-72; City of Nashville,; 1st asst public defender 1969-72; US Attny Office, asst attny 1972-80; State of Tennessee Judiciary Dept, chancery court judge. **ORGANIZATIONS:** Dist commander Amer Legion Dept of Tennessee 1961-62; dir Nashville Chap of Urban League 1971-72; pres Fed Bar Assoc 1975-; mem Phi Beta Sigma 1976-; pres Frontiers 1979; dir Nashville Bar Assoc 1982-85, Napier-Looby Assoc 1984-89. **HONORS/ACHIEVEMENTS:** Fed Employee of the Year Fed Exec Assoc 1973; Vice Chmn Governors Commiss on Status of Women 1973; Grand Master Masonic Grand Lodge AF&AM Tennessee 1974-75; Presiding Judge Trial Judges of Nashville-Davidson Cty 1984-85. **MILITARY SERVICE:** AUS corpl 1952-54; Good Conduct Medal. **HOME ADDRESS:** 945 Inverness Avenue, Nashville, TN 37204. **BUSINESS ADDRESS:** Chancery Court Judge, State of TN Judiciary Dept, 402 Davidson County Courthouse, Nashville, TN 37201.

KILDARE, MICHEL WALTER ANDRE
Neurological surgeon. **PERSONAL:** Born Jan 15, 1935, Tunis, Tunisia;son of George Walter Kildare and Louise Andree Kildare; married Paula S Calahan, Aug 23, 1983. **EDUCATION:** Univ of MA, BS 1957; Meharry Medical Coll, MD 1961. **CAREER:** Minneapolis Hennepin General Hospital, intern 1961; Univ of IA-VA Med Center, general surgery resident 1966; New York Univ, resident neurological surgery 1969-74; Iowa Methodist Hospital, attending neurosurgeon 1977-84; Robert Packer Hospital, attending neurosurgeon 1984-85; United Communities Hosps, attending neurosurgeon. **ORGANIZATIONS:** Medical serv comm IA Medical Soc 1977-84; mem Amer Medical Assn 1976-, Iowa Midwest Neurosurgical Soc 1977-, Congress of Neurological Surgeons 1978-, Amer Assn of Neurological Surgeons 1983-, CA Assn of Neurological Surgeons 1987. **HONORS/ACHIEVEMENTS:** Alpha Omega Alpha 1960; Certification Amer Bd of Surgery 1969; "Annals of Neurology" Journal of Neurosurgery 1980; Certification Amer Bd of Neurological Surgery 1982. **MILITARY SERVICE:** US Medical Corps capt general surgeon, 1966-68 Vietnam; National Service, Vietnam Valor-Clusters. **BUSINESS ADDRESS:** Neurosurgeon, 710 Fourth Street Suite A, Marysville, CA 95901.

KILGORE, THOMAS, JR.
Clergyman. **PERSONAL:** Born Feb 20, 1913, Woodruff, SC; married Jeanetta; children: Lynn Elda, Jini Medina. **EDUCATION:** Morehouse Coll, AB 1935; Unoin Theol Sem, BD 1957. **CAREER:** Second Bapt Ch Los Angeles the oldest black Bapt Ch in Los Angeles, sr pastor. **ORGANIZATIONS:** First black pres Am Bapt Conv 1971. **HONORS/ACHIEVEMENTS:** Recipient honorary degrees from ShawUniv 1956; & Morehouse Coll 1963; &Univ of So CA & VA UnoinUniv 1972. **BUSINESS ADDRESS:** Second Baptist Church, 2412 Griffith Ave, Los Angeles, CA 90011.

KILGORE, TWANNA DEBBIE
Model, former Ms Black America. **PERSONAL:** Born 1954. **CAREER:** Immanuel Prod Inc, exec dir. **HONORS/ACHIEVEMENTS:** Won Miss Black Washington DC 1976; Miss Black America 1976-77; as title holder traveled US & Europe; contracted with Avon as beauty consultant spokeswoman.

KILIMANJARO, JOHN MARSHALL
Business executive, educator. **PERSONAL:** Born Jun 06, 1930, Little Rock, AR; married Culey Mae Vick. **EDUCATION:** Univ of AR, BA 1952;Univ of AR, MA Ed D 1965; NC A&T State U, attended. **CAREER:** Carolina Newspapers Inc, publisher, pres; NC A&T State Univ, prof speech & theatre 1969-, instructor English 1955-58, 1962-69; AR A M & N Coll, prof English 1959-61; State Univ of IA, teaching fellow 1958-59. **ORGANIZATIONS:** Exec dir Richard B Harrison Players 1969-; pres NC Balck Pubs Assn; bd dir Children's Home Soc Greensboro Arts Soc; mem NADSA ATA; former 2nd vice pres NAACP; consult Civil Rights; Comm Action Programs NC Fund; mem Guilford Co Young Dem. **HONORS/ACHIEVEMENTS:** Recipient O Henry award for artistic excellence Greensboro C of C 1973. **MILITARY SERVICE:** USN 1949-50; USMC 1952-54. **BUSINESS ADDRESS:** Dept of Theatre Arts, A&T State Univ, Greensboro, NC.

KILKENNY, JAMES H.
Assistant to dean. **PERSONAL:** Born May 05, 1923, Georgetown; widowed; children: Rosemary, Allyson, Andrew. **EDUCATION:** Univ MI, PhD 1977; KSUniv MA 1964; UK France Holland, comparative ednn Cert 1960; Reading UK, BS 1960; London UK, BA 1948. **CAREER:** Prin secondary sch 1952-59; educ supt 1960-63; KS U, prof 1964-66; Canton OH Cap, exec dir 1967-73;Univ Of MI Sch of Natural Resources Ann Arbor MI, asst dean 1973-; Domestic Sci & Handicraft Center & Housing Accommodation for tchr, Built; OH State Assn of CAA's, exec sec; OH Municipal League Coordinated interagy seminars, consult adv; Guyana Tchr Assn, pres 1956-59; Black Faculty & Staff AssnUniv of MI, co-chmn. **ORGANIZATIONS:** Mem OH Bur of Employment Svc; Nat Assn ACP'S; Urban League; v chmn Delta Omega Phi Si Kappa Tau. **HONORS/ACHIEVEMENTS:** Recipient Kent StateUniv Meritorious Acad Achievement Award 1964; Bain Gray Gold Medal of Merit for

Outstanding Work in Sch & Comm; Tchr's Scholarship Award For Outstanding Serv to Sch & Comm to pursue postgrad studies in Comparative educ in the United Kingdom & Europe 1959-60. **BUSINESS ADDRESS:** Coll of Natural Resources, U of MI, Ann Arbor, MI 48104.

KILLIAN, IRIS LOUISE
Educator. **PERSONAL:** Born Aug 28, 1962, Hickory, NC; daughter of James C Killian and Dorothy Booker Killian. **EDUCATION:** Univ of NC at Chapel Hill, BSPH (Summa Cum Laude) 1984; Duke Univ, MBA 1986. **CAREER:** Amer Medical Intl, summer associate 1985; Siecor Corp, training specialist 1986-89; Siecor Corp, Supervisor Training Dept Telephone Cable Plant 1989-. **ORGANIZATIONS:** Church organist Clinton Tabernacle AME Zion Church 1978-; mem Natl Black MBA Assoc 1986-; speaker LEAD program Speaker's Forum 1986-; tutorial adv council mem Hickory High School Tutorial Program 1986-; mem NC Black Women's Task Force 1986-; mem Community Relations Council Hickory NC 1987-; mem Manpower Committee, Chamber of Commerce 1989. **HONORS/ACHIEVEMENTS:** Graduate Fellowship Duke Univ Fuqua Sch of Business 1984-86; Outstanding Young Women of Amer 1986. **HOME ADDRESS:** 315 14th Ave Dr SW, Hickory, NC 28601.

KILLION, THEO M.
Personnel executive. **PERSONAL:** Born Apr 13, 1951, Montgomery, WV; son of Omega Killion and Maggie Lewis Killion; divorced; children: Aliya Killion, Niyama Killion. **EDUCATION:** Tufts Univ, Medford MA, BA, 1973, MEd, 1975. **CAREER:** Concord Public Schools, Concord MA, teacher, 1973-75; Harvard Univ, Cambridge MA, asst dir Upward Bound, 1971-75; RH Macys, New York NY, vice pres executive personnel, 1975-. **ORGANIZATIONS:** Black Retail Action Group, 1975-; Simmons Coll Advisory Board, 1988-. **HONORS/ACHIEVEMENTS:** Gold Pencil Award, Black Retail Action Group, 1982; Business Achievement Award, Black Retail Action Group, 1987. **BUSINESS ADDRESS:** Vice President, Executive Personnel, R H Macy's, 151 W 34th Street, 17th Floor, New York, NY 10001.

KILPATRICK, CAROLYN CHEEKS
Politican. **PERSONAL:** Born Jun 25, 1945, Detroit, MI; daughter of Marvel Cheeks and Willa Cheeks; divorced; children: Kwame, Ayanna. **EDUCATION:** Ferris State College, AS 1965; Western MI Univ, BS 1972; Univ of MI, MS 1977. **CAREER:** REA Express, sec 1962-63; Detroit Public Schools, teacher 1971-78; MI House of Representatives, state rep, 1978—, mem Appropriations Committee, chair Black Caucus, 1983-84. **ORGANIZATIONS:** Mem Brd Trustees New Detroit 1983; mem Brd Trustees Henry Ford Hosp 1984; mem Resource Committee Your Children Our Children (documentary) 1984; Natl Org 100 Black Women; Natl Order Women Legisl; chair Women's Caucus of Natl Black Caucus of Black Legislators; chair Intl Affairs Comm of the Natl Black Caucus of State Legislators. **HONORS/ACHIEVEMENTS:** Anthony Wayne Award for Leadership, Wayne State U; distinguished legisl award, Univ of MI; Burton Abercrombie Award; appointed by Gov James Blanchard to represent MI in first African Trade Mission, 1984. **BUSINESS ADDRESS:** State Representative, House of Representatives, Room 105 Capitol Bldg, Lansing, MI 48909.

KILPATRICK, GEORGE ROOSEVELT
Physician. **PERSONAL:** Born Dec 09, 1938, New Bern, NC; married Lillian Farrington; children: Michaux, Gregory, La Tonya. **CAREER:** NC Textile Occupational Lung Dis Panel, physician; Private Practice, pulmonary diseases & internal med. **ORGANIZATIONS:** Mem Amer Thoracic Soc, Greensboro Med Soc, Natl Med Soc, Amer Med Assn, mem Amer Bd of Internal Med #43697 1973; licensure NC #18881 GA #12504. **MILITARY SERVICE:** Ltc 1970-76. **BUSINESS ADDRESS:** 107 Murrow Bldg, Greensboro, NC 27401.

KILSON, MARTIN LUTHER, JR.
Educator. **PERSONAL:** Born Feb 14, 1931, E Rutherford, NJ; married Marion Dusser de Barenne; children: Jennifer Greene, Peter Dusser de Barenne, Hannah Laws. **EDUCATION:** Lincoln Univ, BA 1953 (valedictorian magna cum laude); Harvard Univ, MA Polit Sci 1958, PhD Polit Sci 1959. **CAREER:** Harvard Univ Dept Govt, tchng fellow 1957-59; Harvard Ctr for Intl Affairs, res fellow 1961-72; Harvard Univ, tutor govt 1962-67; Univ of Ghana, visiting prof 1964-65; Harvard Univ, asst prof govt 1967-69; Ford Found, consultant 1973-74; Harvard Univ, prof govt 1969-. **ORGANIZATIONS:** Res fellow Ford Found Foreign Area Training Prog 1959-61 W Africa; has authored many articles & books on Polit Devel Africa, Urban Politics, Intl Politics, Afro-Amer Politics, Ethnic Studies; mem NAACP; fellow Amer Acad of Arts & Sci; Founding fellow of Black Acad of Arts & Letters; bd dir Amer AfricanStudies Assn 1967-69. **HONORS/ACHIEVEMENTS:** Harvard Grad Fellowship 1953-55; John Hay Whitney Opp Fellowship 1955-56, 1958-59; Fellow Black Acad of Arts & Letters; Fellow Amer Acad of Arts & Sci; Fellow Guggenehim Found 1975-76; visiting scholar Un Chpts of Phi Beta Kappa 1974-75; consult Fulbright-Hayes Intl Exchange Prog 1972-; consult Ford Found 1972-73. **BUSINESS ADDRESS:** Professor of Government, HarvardUniv, Dept of Littauer Cntr, Cambridge, MA 02138.

KIMBER, LESLY H.
Business executive. **PERSONAL:** Born Aug 13, 1934, Boonville, NC; married Pauline Johnson; children: Duane, Terri, Mark. **EDUCATION:** Morehouse Coll Atlanta, bus admin major; George Washington U. **CAREER:** City of Fresnod council member; CA advocate newspaper, publsiher; central valley printing co inc, pres; fresno co pub defender's ofc, criminal investigator; CA StateUniv Fresno, formerly taught, lectures throughout city and state. **ORGANIZATIONS:** Mem West Coast Publishers Assn; pres of bd of dir King of Kings Housing Corp; pres West Fresno Optimist Club; co-chmn KFSN-TV Minority Advisory Committee; vice pres Fresno Free Coll Found; mem and steward Carter Memorial African Methodist Ch; serves on ad committe Greater Fresno Area Plan; bd mem West Fresno Boys Club; mem King of Kings Community Cntr Bd; mem Centarl CA Criminal Justice Planning Bd; served on Fresno Co Reorganization Committee Kimber; throughhis paper has initiated action to promote justice & equality for the minority community of Fresno. **BUSINESS ADDRESS:** City Hall Council Office, 2326 Fresno St, Fresno, CA 93721.

KIMBLE, BETTYE DORRIS
Educator. **PERSONAL:** Born Jun 21, 1936, Tulsa, OK; daughter of JC Kimble and Ethel Kimble; divorced; children: Jay Charles, Cheleste Kimble-Botts. **EDUCATION:** Tulsa Univ, BME 1959; Pepperdine Univ, MA 1979, MS 1980. **CAREER:** Sapulpa OK Bd of Educ, music instructor 1959-61; Hamlin KS School Dist, coordinator of Music 1961-62; Kansas City MO School Dist, music instructor 1963-67; Willowbrook Jr High, choral dir & vocal music educ 1967-79; Compton Unified School Dist, chairperson performing & visual arts, teacher/choral dir 1967-; Centennial HS instructor 1979-. **ORGANIZATIONS:** Mem Phi Delta Kappa Pepperdine Chapter 1983-; scholarship chairperson (EHP) NA of NM 1983-; composer/music publisher for Broadcast Music Inc 1983-; lecturer and choral consultant 1984-; dist missionary dir Southern CA Conf 1985-; commissioned to write choral arrangement to "Inner City Blues" Rod McGrew Scholarship Inc; mem Performing Arts Council, NEA, MENC Educ, NARAS, NAS Recording; Amer Choral Dir Assn. **HONORS/ACHIEVEMENTS:** Teacher of the Year Centennial Sr High School 1982; Honored for Music Serv City of Inglewood CA 1983; Commendation for Music Serv to Church & Comm County of Los Angeles; Musical Tribute for Contributions to Music Industry Kimble Comm Choir; founder/dir internationally known "Kimble Community Choir"; Religious Musical Called "Revelation". **BUSINESS ADDRESS:** Choral Dir & Chairperson, Centennial High School, 2606 N Central Ave, Compton, CA 90222.

KIMBREW, JOSEPH D.
City government official. **PERSONAL:** Born May 31, 1929, Indianapolis, IN; married Carolyn; children: Joseph D Jr, Tracey. **EDUCATION:** Crispus Attucks High School graduate. **CAREER:** Indianapolis Fire Dept, mem 32 years, deputy chief of admin, 1985-87, appointed first Black chief of fire dept 1987. **ORGANIZATIONS:** Bd of dirs Greater Indianapolis Federal Firefighters Credit Union 10 yrs; mem NAACP 1968-. **HONORS/ACHIEVEMENTS:** Firefighter of the Year 1968; Overall Achievement Award Center for Leadership Develop 1987; mem Red Cross Hall of Fame; designated Distinguished Hoosier by Governor of IN. **MILITARY SERVICE:** AUS corpl 2 yrs. **BUSINESS ADDRESS:** Fire Chief, Indianapolis Fire Department, 555 N New Jersey, Indianapolis, IN 46204.

KIMBROUGH, CHARLES E.
Veterinarian, clergyman. **EDUCATION:** TN State U, BS 1956; Tuskegee Inst, DVM 1960; So IL Coll Bible, cert 1965. **CAREER:** Sparta, area veterinarian 1960-69; Meat & Poultry Inspection Program, supr veterinary med officer 1969-75; New Hope Missionary Bapt Ch, pastor 1964-69; MtZion Missionary Bapt Ch, 1970-74. **ORGANIZATIONS:** Mem Middle TN Veterinary Med Assn; past pres Nashville Chap Nat Assn Fed Veterinarians; mem Local offices NAACP; Phi Beta Sigma Frat; TN StateUniv Alumni Assn; TN Voters Council; Phi Beta Sigma Eta Beta Chpt. **HONORS/ACHIEVEMENTS:** Man of Yr 1974; cert, cash award, supr vet med officer 1972.

KIMBROUGH, CLARENCE B.
Physician, educator. **PERSONAL:** Born Jun 01, 1922, Elkton, KY; married Catherine L Murray; children: Clarence II, Colette, Candance. **EDUCATION:** TN State U, BS 1948; Meharry Med Coll, MD 1952. **CAREER:** Hurley Hosp & Mclaren Gen Hosp Flint, MI, hosp training 1952-53; Flint, MI, private practice 1953-; MI St Coll of Human Med, assoc clinical prof; Dept of Family Hurley Hosp, dir 1965-67; Hurley Hosp, vice-chief of staff 1967-71; St Joseph Mclaren Genesee Meml & Hurley Hosp, med staffs. **ORGANIZATIONS:** Mem Am Geriatric Soc; bd dir Genesee Co Outpatient Assn; mem AMA; NMA; MSMS; World Med Soc; Vienna Med Assn; Am Acad of Family Practice; diplomat of Am Bd of Family Practice; fellow Am Bd of Family Practice; Fellow Am Coll of Emergency Physicians Bd dir Cit Commercial & Sav Bank Flint; bd dir Urban League of Flint 1966-68; dir YMCA of Flint; dir Mus Performing Arts Assn; Flint bd educ 1967-72 pres bd dir 1968-69 sec 1967-68 vice pres 1971-72; life mem NAACP; chmn of the bd Flint Metro Mass Media & Inc Parent Co of Radio Station WDZZ (One of only Two Black Owned Radio Stations in the Stateof MI) 1979; trustee Mott Children's Health Cntr 1979; bd of dir Flint Coll & Cultural Develop 1979; bd of dir Flint Institute of Arts 1980; mem KappaPh Honor (Med) Soc; Alpha Kappa Mu Honor Soc. **HONORS/ACHIEVEMENTS:** Recipient Martin Luther King Drummer Boy Award 1974; Liberty Bell Award Gen Co Bar Assn for Comm Svc; cited by Meharry Med Coll for Continous support since 1952 1972; Physician's Recognition Award Am Med Assn 1974-77. **MILITARY SERVICE:** AUS 1943-46. **BUSINESS ADDRESS:** 1402 S Saginaw St, Flint, MI 48503.

KIMBROUGH, FRED H.
Urban League executive. **PERSONAL:** Born Jul 24, 1931, Chicago, IL; married Willa B Gaitor; children: Angelia D, Fred II. **EDUCATION:** So IL U, BA 1965; So IL U, MS 1969; St Louis U, Ph D 1972. **CAREER:** Metro-east Conf of Black Mayors, consult 19789-80; St Louis Metro Urban League, educ consult 1979-84; Howard & Assoc, pres; The Thacker Org, proj mgr 1985-. **ORGANIZATIONS:** Mem American Assn Univ Admin; Phi Delta Kappa Inc; life mem Kappa Alpha Psi Inc; American Assn Higher Educ; Black River Writers Inc; Black Consultants Inc; mem Econ Devel Commission; commiss E St Louis; adv bd Alcorn Univ Alcorn MS. **HONORS/ACHIEVEMENTS:** Merit award East St Louis Urban Academy; recognition award East St Louis Model City Agency; merit award East St Louis Comm Sch; merit award Monitor Newspaper; meritorious service award Phi Delta Kappa; outstanding achievement award Black Merit Academy; achievement award Kappa Alpha Psi; distinguished comm serv award City of East St Louis. **MILITARY SERVICE:** AUS 1951-53. **BUSINESS ADDRESS:** Project Manager, The Thacker Organization, 5400 Truman Dr, Decatur, GA 30035.

KIMBROUGH, ROBERT L.
Dentist. **PERSONAL:** Born Aug 20, 1922, Birmingham, AL; married Luequster Murphy; children: Kernelia, Donna Lynn. **EDUCATION:** Univ of IL Coll of Dentistry, DDS 1951. **CAREER:** Chicago, dentist pvt practice. **ORGANIZATIONS:** Program chmn Chicago Dental Soc 1975-76; pres Kenwood Hyde Park Dental Soc; vice pres Med Assn Chicago; fellow Acad of Gen Dentistry; treas Legis InterestCom IL Dentist; chrmn Peer Review Com IL St Dental Soc; dir Highland Community Bk Chicago; mem Am Dental Assn; Nat Dental Assn; Lincoln Dental Soc; IL State Dental Soc; Am Soc for Practice of Childrens Dentistry; pres Southside Comm Arts Center; past exec com Chicago Br; life mem NAACP; mem Urban League. **HONORS/ACHIEVEMENTS:** 1st lt AUS Dental Corps 1951-53. **MILITARY SERVICE:** 1st lt AUS Dental Corps 1951-53. **BUSINESS ADDRESS:** 3233 King St, Chicago, IL 60616.

KIMBROUGH, ROOSEVELT
Dentist. **PERSONAL:** Born Oct 04, 1932, Birmingham, AL; children: Lisa A, Keith A, Fritz. **EDUCATION:** Roosevelt Univ, BS 1958; Univ of IL, BS 1961, DDS 1962. **CA-**

REER: Self-Employed, dentist 1962-. **ORGANIZATIONS:** Mem Chicago Dental Soc; mem IL State Dental Soc; mem Lincoln Dental Soc. **MILITARY SERVICE:** AUS Sp 2 1955-57. **BUSINESS ADDRESS:** 2026 W 95th St, Chicago, IL 60643.

KIMBROUGH, THOMAS J.
Educator. **PERSONAL:** Born Apr 24, 1934, Morristown, NJ; married Eva Harden; children: Jerome Joseph. **EDUCATION:** Wilberforce U, BS 1956; Xavier U, MEd 1969. **CAREER:** Sch for Creative & Performing Arts, tchr presently; Student Servs Laurel Oaks Career Devel Ctr, supvr 1976-79; Educ OH Youth Comm, asst supt 1974-76; Princeton City Schools, asst prin 1972-73; Princeton Schools, advisor staff on race rel 1970-72; guid couns 1969-70; Middletown, OH, educator 1963-68. **ORGANIZATIONS:** Consultant Nat Equal Educ Inst Hartford, CN; consultant Equal Educ Office Ind; treas Interracial Interaction Inc pres Funds for Legal Defense; pres Dayton Chap Wilberforce Alumni; past chmn Ohio Ed Assn Human Rel Comm; past vice pres Butler Co CAC 1972; chmn Educ Com Middletown Coun for Human Dignity;exec comm Middletown Br NAACP; chmn Educ Comm NAACP; co-fdr Anti-Klan Network. **MILITARY SERVICE:** AUS sp3 1956-58.

KIMBROUGH-JOHNSON, DONNA L.
Manager of personnel, government official. **PERSONAL:** Born Aug 26, 1948, Oklahoma City, OK; daughter of Irvin Roger Kimbrough and Irene Betty Jones; divorced; children: Dawn Marie, Jason Leigh. **EDUCATION:** Univ of WA, BA (with Distinction) 1977, MBA 1980. **CAREER:** Dept of Human Resources Washington DC, social service caseworker 1971-75; City of Seattle Water Dept, personnel specialist 1978-80; Seattle Public Schools, classification admin 1980-86; Pierce Transit, mgr of personnel 1986-. **ORGANIZATIONS:** Mem Four Seasons NW Ski Club 1985-; assoc mem Benefit Guild 1986-; bd of dirs Inst for Business and Industry Tacoma Comm Coll 1987; mem Delta Sigma Theta Sorority 1988-. **HOME ADDRESS:** 6201 47th Ave So, Seattle, WA 98118. **BUSINESS ADDRESS:** Manager of Personnel, Pierce County Transit System, PO Box 99070, Tacoma, WA 98499.

KIMMONS, CARL EUGENE
Educator. **PERSONAL:** Born Apr 10, 1920, Hamilton, OH; son of Posey M Kimmons and Mary V Whitaker; married Thelma Jean Lewis; children: Karen Toni West, Larry Carlton, Kimberly Ann Kimmons-Gilbert. **EDUCATION:** CT Coll, BA (magna cum laude) 1973; Univ CT, MA 1976; S CT State Univ, Sixth Year Certificate 1986. **CAREER:** USN, mess attendant third class 1940, master chief yeoman 1960, lt 1963; Bd of Educ Waterford CT, tchr 1973; Waterford HS, teacher. **ORGANIZATIONS:** Top secret control officer USN 1961-70; navy liason officer to bi-racial com City of New London CT 1965-66; private airplane pilot 1965-89; fitness leader YMCA New London CT 1978-89. **HONORS/ACHIEVEMENTS:** WW II Victory Medal; Phillipine Liberation Ribbon; Submarine Combat Insignia w/5 Bronze Stars; enlisted Submarine Qualification Insignia; Navy Commendation Medal w/Combat Distinguished Device; Presidential Unit Citation; Navy Unit Commendation; Meritorious Unit Commendation; Good Conduct Medal w/1 Silver Star; Asiatic-Pacific Campaign medal w/1 Silver & 4 Bronze Stars; Amer Campaign Medal; Amer Defense Serv Medal w/Fleet Clasp; Navy Occupational Medal with Europe Clasp; Natl Defense Serv medal w/Bronze Star; first Black to become a commissioned officer from mess attendant rating. **MILITARY SERVICE:** USN retired lt 1940-70. **BUSINESS ADDRESS:** Teacher, Waterford High School, 20 Rope Ferry Rd, Waterford, CT 06385.

KIMMONS, WILLIE JAMES
Educator, administrator. **PERSONAL:** Born Apr 04, 1944, Hernando, MS; children: Tonia. **EDUCATION:** Lincoln U, BS 1966; No IL U, MS 1970; No IL U, PhD 1974. **CAREER:** Downtown Campus Wayne Comm Coll, dean 1979-; St Francis Coll, dean 1977-79; Central State Univ, dir 1976-77; NC Central Univ, asst vice chancellor 1973-76; No IL Univ, instructor 1969-73; Sikeston HS, instructor 1966-67; Antioch Coll adjunct prof 1976-; Univ of Dayton Graduate School, lecturer 1976; Shaw Univ, adjunct prof 1974-76; Natl Lab for Higher Educ, consultant 1973-74. **ORGANIZATIONS:** Mem Cncl on Black Am Afrs; Nat Alliance of Black Educs; Kappa Alpha Psi Frat; Am Assn for Hghr Edn; NatUniv Extensions Assn; Adult Educ Assn of USA; Soc of Ethnic & Spec Studies; Am Assn of Jr & Comm Coll; Phi Delta Kappa; Profnl Educ Frat; Am Persnl Guid Assn; NEA Athletic schlrsp 1962-66; tchng flshp 1969-70; Educ of Yr 1975-76; post doc flwshp Am Mgmt Assn 1975-76; publ Cont Educ for the Elderly OH Dominican Coll 1976; Black Adminstrs in Pub Comm & Coll Carlton Press Inc 1977. **MILITARY SERVICE:** AUS 1st lt 1967-69. **BUSINESS ADDRESS:** 1001 Fort St, Detroit, MI 48226.

KINARD, HELEN MADISON MARIE PAWNE
Educator. **PERSONAL:** Born Jul 07, Washington, DC; daughter of David Madison and Helen Madison; children: Lenise Sharon, Monique Sherine. **EDUCATION:** Washington Univ, BMT 1963; Howard Univ, BA 1971, MA 1973; Univ of So CA, Public Admin; Howard Univ, PhD candidate. **CAREER:** Univ of West Indies, distinguished visiting prof 1971-72; Howard Univ, liaison for pres 1971; Dr Joyce Ladner Carrington, res asst 1972-74; Dept of Comm Plan, asst prof 1973-74; Howard Univ Sch of Social Work, adj prof 1973-74; TV, writer/co-star 1973; Howard Univ Sch of Communications, asst for admin/prof; Howard Univ, ad asst to mgr Cramton Aud; Travel Way Foundation, prof soc plan & policy; RLA Inc, sr assoc/dir of the Zambia (HIRD) Project Lusaka, Zambia; Liscensure Real Estate, Washington DC; LICSW Social Work, Washington DC. **ORGANIZATIONS:** Coord 7th World Law Conf 1975; consult in soc planning Congress Black Caucus 1973; State of CA Child Care Conf 1973; Intl Manpwr Dev Sem 1972, 1974; com on Human Settlements 1976; State Organizer Natl Council of Negro Women 1973; mem Amer Ded of Radio & TV Artists, Amer Planning Assn, Amer Soc for Plan Ofcls, Delta Sigma Theta Sor, Natl Acad of Sci, Natl Assn of Black Soc Workers, Natl Assn of Soc Workers, Natl Assn of Coll & Univ Concern Mgmts, NAACP, Natl Council of Negro Women, Southern Christian Leadership Conf, Natl Assn of Black Educators; natl vice pres Natl Assn for the Educ of Young Children, Councl for Exceptional Children, Intl City Mgmt Assn, HU Alumni Assoc; bd of dirs Freedom Bowl Alumni Comm, Assoc of Black Psychologists, Caribbean Amer Intercultural Org Inc, Caribbean Festivals Inc. **HONORS/ACHIEVEMENTS:** Phi Delta Kappa; Phi Betta Kappa 1973; Southern CA Film Inst Award 1973; Emmy Award for TV Show 1973; Rockefeller Found Award 1973; Natl Inst for Mental Health Maint & Tuition 1973; full scholarship for con study 1972; Natl Inst for Mental Health Howard Univ Scholarship 1972; Natl Endowment for Arts Scholarship 1971; partial scholarship for continued study 1971; Outstanding Human Serv Howard Univ MS Proj 1971; Chi Lambda Phi; Bureau of Std Award for Outstanding HS Student in Math & Sci. **BUSINESS ADDRESS:** Senior Associate, RLA Inc, 1101 14th St NW, 10th Floor, Washington, DC 20005.

KINCEY, WENDELL D. See KARIM, WALI J.

KINDALL, LUTHER MARTIN
Educator. **PERSONAL:** Born Nov 01, 1942, Nashville, TN; son of Bruce Kindall and Lucy Moore Kindall; married Dr Alpha J Simmons; children: Kimberly, Katrina. **EDUCATION:** TN State Univ, BS 1967, MS 1968, EdD 1973. **CAREER:** TN State Univ, asst prof of psychology 1968-70; Brushy Mountain State Prison, instr of psychology 1972; Roane State Comm Coll, asst prof of psychology 1972-73; Univ of TN, prof of educ psychology 1973-. **ORGANIZATIONS:** Chmn UT Commn for Blacks; asst prof NIMA Summer Inst UT-K Sch of Social Work 1979; state coord Project to Utilize Educ Talents 1968; pres TN Alliance of Black Voters 1979-; mem Omega Psi Phi Frat 1973-; unsuccessful candidate for gov of State of TN 1982; pres Comm Relations Council of Knoxville Job 1986; Commissioner Tennessee Human Rights Commission 1985-; pres Elk Development Co 1988-89. **HONORS/ACHIEVEMENTS:** Alpha Kappa Mu Honor Soc 1966-; Phi Delta Kappa 1973; Outstanding Teacher of the Yr UT Panhellenic and Intrafraternity Councils 1978-79; various publ; Phi Kappa Phi 1978; Phi Lamda Theta 1985-. **BUSINESS ADDRESS:** Assoc Prof of Educ Psychol, Univ of TN, 108 CEB, Knoxville, TN 37916.

KINDER, RANDOLPH SAMUEL, JR.
Financial services executive. **PERSONAL:** Born Dec 12, 1944, Chester, PA; son of Randolph Samuel Kinder and Mildred White Ricks; married Joan Logue, Dec 13, 1986; children: Lowell Henry, Catherine Henry, Christopher Henry, Randolph Samuel Kinder III. **EDUCATION:** Howard Univ, Washington DC, BA, 1967; Univ of VA, Charlottesville VA, executive program, 1986. **CAREER:** Dept of Housing & Urban Devel, Washington DC, exeutive asst to secretary, 1977-79; Dept of Health & Human Services, Washington DC, chief of staff to secretary, 1979-81; The Equitable, New York, vice pres, 1981-82, Milford Conn, vice pres, 1982-84, New York, NY, vice pres, 1984-86, Secaucus NJ, sr vice pres, 1986-. **ORGANIZATIONS:** Bd of dir, The Coro Foundation, 1987-; bd of trustees, Lincoln Univ, 1988-; bd mem, NY City Health & Hospitals Corp, 1989-. **HONORS/ACHIEVEMENTS:** Black Achievers in Industry, Harlem YMCA, 1982. **BUSINESS ADDRESS:** Sr Vice Pres, Pension Fin Mgmt Group, The Equitable Financial Companies, 200 Plaza Drive, Secaucus, NJ 07094.

KING, ALBERT
Professional athlete. **PERSONAL:** Born Dec 17, 1959, Brooklyn, NY. **EDUCATION:** Univ of MD College Park MD, attended. **CAREER:** NJ Nets, basketball player 1981-. **HONORS/ACHIEVEMENTS:** Named to The Sporting News All-Amer First Team 1981. **BUSINESS ADDRESS:** Basketball Player, New Jersey Nets, Byrne Meadowlands Arena, East Rutherford, NJ 07073.

KING, ANITA
Writer, editor, researcher. **PERSONAL:** Born Feb 03, 1931, Detroit, MI. **EDUCATION:** Univ Detroit, B Mus 1956. **CAREER:** PBS/NET In Search of Hart Crane; History of the Negro People Series; The Sun & Richard Lippold, prod asst; FM Guide, assoc editor/writer 1966-69; Essence Mag, copy-editor 1969-71; Family Tree Black History Series, contributing editor/creator 1973-78; Quotations in Black, author 1981; United Nations Gen Assembly 39th Session, editor/proofreader/word-processor/trnscriptionist 1984; free-lance editor copy-editor proofreader writer/reasercher transcriptionist/word-processor 1972-. **ORGANIZATIONS:** Bd dir, vice pres Roots of Brazil, Dance Company. **HONORS/ACHIEVEMENTS:** Author, An Introduction to Candomble, 1987; author, Samba! And Other Afro-Brazilian Dance Expressions, 1989. **HOME ADDRESS:** 10 E 138th St 8e, New York, NY 10037.

KING, ARTHUR THOMAS
Educator. **PERSONAL:** Born Feb 10, 1938, Greensboro, AL; son of Harvey King and Elizabeth Williams King; married Rosa Marie Bryant, Jun 24, 1962; children: Donald, Kevin. **EDUCATION:** Tuskegee Univ, BS 1962; SD State Univ, MS 1971; Univ of CO, PhD 1977. **CAREER:** USAF Acad, asst prof of economics 1970-74; Air Force Inst of Tech, assoc prof of economics 1979-82; Baylor Univ, assoc prof of economics 1982-, coord of minority affairs 1984-. **ORGANIZATIONS:** Mem bd dirs EOAC (community action prog) 1984-; mem bd dirs Heart of Texas Goodwill 1985-; mem Natl Economic Assoc of Govt Economists, Amer Econ Assoc; mem bd of dir Goodwill Industries of Amer, Inc. **HONORS/ACHIEVEMENTS:** Numerous articles published on economics 1978-86. **MILITARY SERVICE:** USAF lt col 20 yrs; 2 Air Force Commendation Medals; 2 Meritorious Serv Medals. **BUSINESS ADDRESS:** Associate Professor of Economics, Baylor University, Dept of Economics, Box 8003, Waco, TX 76798.

KING, B. B. See KING, RILEY B.

KING, BARBARA LEWIS
Clergy. **PERSONAL:** Born Aug 26, 1930, Houston, TX; children: Michael Lewis. **EDUCATION:** Texas Southern Univ, BA 1955; Atlanta Univ, MSW 1957, course work completed EdD; Univ of Metaphysics, DD 1978; Christian Church of Universal Philosophy, DD 1984. **CAREER:** South Chicago Comm Serv Assn, exec dir, 1966-68; Chicago City Coll Malcolm X Campus, dean, community relations, 1967-69; Atlanta Univ Sch of Social Work, instructor 1970-71; South Central comm Mental Health Ctr, dir 1971-73; Spelman Coll Atlanta, dean of students 1973-74; Barbara King School of Ministry, founder/president 1977-; Hillside Intl (Church), founder/minister 1971-; National/Intl speaker, preacher, teacher. **ORGANIZATIONS:** Rules committee Democratic Natl Committee 1984; board member Christian Council of Metro Atlanta; board vice president Intl New Thought Alliance; chaplain Atlanta Bureau of Police Services; NAACP bd dir Atlanta Chapter. **HONORS/ACHIEVEMENTS:** Achievement in Religion (numerous awards) local, state, natl & intl organizations 1974-; author of six books, several monographs, sermons & messages on tape;television show hostess "A New Thought, A New Life" weekly half-hour program, aired regionally; Zeta of the Yr Award Zeta Phi Beta Sorority Inc; presented keys to cities of Roanoke, VA; Tuskegee, AL and Macon, GA. **BUSINESS ADDRESS:** Minister & Chief Executive, Hillside Intl Truth Center, 2450 Cascade Rd Sw, Atlanta, GA 30311.

KING, BERNARD
Professional athlete. **PERSONAL:** Born Dec 04, 1956, Brooklyn, NY; married Collette Caeser. **EDUCATION:** Attended, Univ of TN. **CAREER:** NJ Nets, player 1977-79;

Utah Jazz, player 1979-80; Golden State Warriors, player 1980-82; NY Knickerbockers, player 1982-. **HONORS/ACHIEVEMENTS:** NBA Player of the Year Sporting News; Player of the Month for Feb; Player of the Week for Feb 6th; 1st time since 1967 that anyone in the NBA had scored 50 or more points in consecutive games on consecutive nights; Named to NBA All-Rookie Team 1978; 1st-ever winner of NBA Comeback Player of the Year Awd 1980-81 while with Warriors; All-Amer 1976; named 3 times to Southeast Conf All-Star team.

KING, CALVIN E.
Retired educator. **PERSONAL:** Born Jun 05, 1928, Chicago, IL; son of David King and Florence King. **EDUCATION:** Morehouse Coll, AB 1949; Atlanta Univ, MA 1950; Ohio State Univ, Ph D 1959. **CAREER:** Tennessee State Univ, prof math & head dept physics & math 1964-74; Head Dept Math Fed Adv Teachers Coll Lagos Nigeria, spec math 1962-64; Tennessee State Univ, prof math 1958-62. **ORGANIZATIONS:** Mem Mathematical Assn of America; Natl Council of & Teachers of Math; mem Beta Kappa Chi Hon Scientific Soc; mem Omega Psi Phi; mem Alpha Kappa Mu Natl Hon Soc. **MILITARY SERVICE:** AUS corpl 1951-53; Counter Intelligence Corps.

KING, CELES, III
Business executive. **PERSONAL:** Born Sep 18, 1923, Chicago, IL; married Anita Givens; children: Tobi, Teri, Toni, Mike. **EDUCATION:** Pacific CoastUniv CA, LLB 1951; Pepperdine U, MBA 1972; Laurence U, PhD 1977. **CAREER:** King Bail Bond Agy, bondsman 1951-; ins broker & real estate agt 1951-. **ORGANIZATIONS:** Chrm LA Col Bail Agents Assn Pres CA Bail Agents Assn 1979-80; CA State Chmn CORE, Congress of Racial Equality 1979-80; asst prof CA StateUniv of LA Pan African Studies; Master of Bus Adminstrn; PepperdineUniv Grad Sch Adminstr 1973-75; past pres LA City Human Relations Commn; past pres LA NAACP; exec dir LA Rumor Ocntrol & Info Cntr; co-founder LA Unifed Sch Bd Black Educ Commn 1969-; LA Brotherhood Crusade 1968; pres bd of trustees LaurenceUniv Santa Barbara, CA 1975-; vice pres Natl Assn of Private Nontraditional Schls & Colls. **HONORS/ACHIEVEMENTS:** LA Langston Bar Assoc Outstanding Comm Serv Award 1965, 1973; CORE Award for Significant Contrib to Cause of Freedom & Human Dignity 1964; CA State Assembly Resolution Commending Credit to Comm & State 1965, 1970; LA NAACP Award for Outstanding Contrib to NAACP Movement 1963; Outstanding Bus Leadership LA Bus Assn 1965; Outstanding Comm Serv Award Com for Rep Govt 1965; LA Comm Achievement Award 1968; LA Martins Award 1970, 1973. **MILITARY SERVICE:** USAF lt. **BUSINESS ADDRESS:** King Bail Bond Agency, 1530 W King Blvd, Los Angeles, CA 90062.

KING, CEOLA
City official. **PERSONAL:** Born Jun 10, 1927, Macon, MS; children: Terasa. **CAREER:** Town of Old Memphis, council mem. **HOME ADDRESS:** Rt 1 Box M 158C, Aliceville, AL 35442.

KING, CHARLES ABRAHAM
Attorney. **PERSONAL:** Born Feb 27, 1924, New York, NY; married Nellie Alexander; children: Alexandra, Victoria. **EDUCATION:** NY Univ Sch of Bus, BS 1949; Fordham Univ Sch of Law, LLD 1952. **CAREER:** Deluxe Lab, sr acct 1951-59; King & Jones Esqs, 1960-63; Nat Bur of Casualty Underwriters, asst cnsl 1964-68; Ins Rating Bd, cnsl 1968-70; Ins SvcOfc, cnsl 1970-72; Metro Property & Liability Ins Co, vice pres & genl counsel. **ORGANIZATIONS:** Bd dir NY Motor Vehicle Accident Indemnification Corp; trustee Barbar-Scotia Coll; mem Amer Bar Assn; NY Co Lawyers Assn; RI Bar Assn; Natl Bar Assn; Ind adv com Recodification for NY State Ins Law; Ins Com Amer Arbitration Assn; past mem Ind Adv Com implementation of state no-fault auto ins law; mem Urban League of RI; vis prof Natl Urban League's Black Exec Exchange Program. **MILITARY SERVICE:** AUS 2nd lt 1943-46. **BUSINESS ADDRESS:** Vice Pres General Counsel, Metro Prop & Liab Ins Co, 700 Quaker Ln, Warwick, RI 02887.

KING, CHARLES E.
Singer. **PERSONAL:** Born Jul 06, 1920, Cleveland, OH; married Helen Grieb; children: Dolissa, Darla. **EDUCATION:** Heidelberg Coll OH, 1938-39; Julliard School of Music, NY, 1948. **CAREER:** Baritone singer/minister present; Karamu Theater Cleveland OH, mgr/actor/voice tchr 1950-53; The Charles King Choir NY, dir/founder 1948-50; Wings Over Jordan Choir on CBS, dir/singer 1941-48. **ORGANIZATIONS:** Pres Charles King Orgn 1971-; pres/owner King Worm Ranch 1975-79; pres/owner King Tree Nursery 1979-; songleader/speaker/leader CFO Internatl 1952-; minister/founder The Awareness Center 1965-; songleader-retreat dir Unity Sch of Practical Christianity 1968-; toured USA/Europe/Far East/ Australia/Jamaica/Trindad/Mexico/Tahiti/Fiji Island 1941-; singer appeared on all major concert stages of USA 1941-; invited by the Pentagon to entertain servicemen in Vietnam& Korea 1970-71; numerous recordings; actor/singer in Porgy & Bess/Showboat/The Medium/Kiss Me Kate/Lost in the Stars/ Mikado/Carmen Jones/The Maid in & Mistress. **BUSINESS ADDRESS:** Reverend, The Awareness Center, Rt 3 Box 600, Walla Walla, WA 99362.

KING, CHARLES E.
Educator. **PERSONAL:** Born Oct 08, 1911, Waynesboro, GA; married Edythe Louise McInver, Jun 04, 1938. **EDUCATION:** Paine Coll Augusta GA, BA 1937; Univ of MI Ann Arbor, MA 1940; Univ of Chicago, Chicago, PhD 1951. **CAREER:** NC Central Univ, prof emeritus/sociologist 1977-; St Augustine's Coll, visiting prof 1984-85; NC Central Univ, research constlt 1984-85. **ORGANIZATIONS:** Pres Hble Elders/Kiwanis Club 1984; dir Hnble Elders/Kiwanis Club 1981-85; vice pres Univ of Chicago Club/NC 1981-; Arbitrator Natl Consumer Arbitration Panel/Better Business Bureaus. **HOME ADDRESS:** 1008 Chalmers St, Durham, NC 27707. **BUSINESS ADDRESS:** Prof Emeritus/Sociology, NC Central Univ, 1008 Chalmers St, Durham, NC 27707.

KING, CLARENCE MAURICE, JR.
Retired government executive. **PERSONAL:** Born Jul 25, 1934, Greenwood, MS; son of C Maurice King and Eddie Mae King; divorced; children: Mark, Michael, Jeffrey, Cierra. **EDUCATION:** Detroit Institute of Commerce, Accounting Certificate 1961; Wayne State Univ, BS 1974; Central MI Univ, MS 1981. **CAREER:** Internal Revenue Servcs, tax auditor 1961-65, group mgr 1965-68, branch and div chief 1968-76, asst dist dir 1976-81, district dir 1981-89; retired 1989. **ORGANIZATIONS:** Also saxophonist Jack Morgan Quartet; lecturer Wichita State Univ; archon Alpha Nu Boule Sigma Pi Phi 1986-; life mem NAACP; bd of directors natl Business League; mem 32 degree Prince Hall Mason, IRS campus exec for Langston Univ & Wichita State Univ; mem Wichita Rotary. **HONORS/ACHIEVEMENTS:** Outstanding Comm Activity Sigma Gamma Rho 1986; Corporate Achiever Award, Urban League Guild of Wichita, 1988. **MILITARY SERVICE:** AUS sgt E-5 5 yrs; Good Conduct Medal, European Occupation, Natl Defense and Marksman 1954-59. **HOME ADDRESS:** 6526 O'Neil, Wichita, KS 67212. **BUSINESS ADDRESS:** District Dir, Internal Revenue Service, 412 South Main St, Wichita, KS 67202.

KING, COLBERT I.
Banking executive. **PERSONAL:** Born Sep 20, 1939, Washington, DC; son of Isaiah King and Amelia Colbert King; married Gwendolyn Stewart, Jul 03, 1961; children: Robert, Stephen, Allison. **EDUCATION:** Howard Univ, BA 1961, grad studies. **CAREER:** Exec Vice Pres, 1981-present, Riggs Natl Bank; Exec Dir, World Bank, 1979-81; Treasury Dept, asst sec, legislative affairs, 1977; Govt Relations, Potomac Electric Power Co, dir 1976-77; Comm on DC, senator, staff dir 1972-76; Senator Mathias of MD, legislative dir 1975-; re-election & campaign aid 1974; VISTA, dir program & political analyst, 1970-71; HEW, special asst under sec, 1964-70; US Dept St Foreign Serv Attache, 1964-70. **ORGANIZATIONS:** Mem, Natl Capital Planning Comm, 1974; mem, Capital Bull Advisory Comm; Randolph Civic Assn, Montgomery Co Branch, NAACP; bd of dir, Africare, 1987-present; trustee, Arena Stage Theatre, 1986-present. **HONORS/ACHIEVEMENTS:** HEW Fellowship Prog 1970-71; NAACP 1969; Distinguished Serv Award, US Sec of Treasury, 1980; lecturer, JFK Inst of Politics, Harvard Univ 1983; lecturer, Foreign Serv Inst 1982-86; Distinguished Graduate Award in Business, Bd of Trustees, Howard Univ, 1987. **MILITARY SERVICE:** AUS 1 lt 1961-63. **HOME ADDRESS:** 1506 Hamilton Street, NW, Washington, DC 20011.

KING, CORETTA SCOTT (MRS. MARTIN LUTHER KING JR.)
Business executive/civil rights activist. **PERSONAL:** Born Apr 27, 1927, Marion, AL; daughter of Obidiah Scott and Bernice McMurry Scott; married Dr Martin L King Jr, Jun 18, 1953 (died 1968); children: Yolanda Denise, Martin Luther III, Dexter Scott, Bernice Albertine. **EDUCATION:** Antioch Coll, AB, 1951; New England Conservatory of Music, Mus B, 1954, MusD, 1971. **CAREER:** Martin Luther King, Jr Ctr for Nonviolent Social Change Inc, Atlanta, GA, pres, 1968-; Cable News Network, commentator 1980-. **ORGANIZATIONS:** Delegate to White House Conf on Children and Youth, 1960; sponsor, Comm for Sane Employment; mem, exec bd, Natl Health Insurance Comm; mem, bd of direc, S Christian Leadership Conf; mem, bd direc, Martin Luther King Jr Found, Grt Britain; trustee, Robt F Kennedy Meml Found; mem, Ebenezer Baptist Church; mem, Women's Intl League for Peace and Freedom; mem, NAACP; mem, bd of mgrs, United Church Women; mem, Alpha Kappa Alpha (hon); mem, Choir & guild adv, Baptist Club; Links. **HONORS/ACHIEVEMENTS:** Outstanding Citizenship Award, Montgomery Improvement Assn, 1959; Merit Award, St Louis Argus, 1960; Disting Achievement Award, Natl Orgn of Colored Women's Clubs, 1962; Louise Waterman Wise Award, Amer Jewish Cong Women's Aux, 1963; Myrtle Wreath Award, Clevel Hadassah, 1965; Award for Excell in field of human relations, Soc Fam of May, 1968; Univ Love Award, Premio San Valentine Comm, 1968; Wateler Peace Prize, 1968; Dag Hammarskjold Award, 1969; Pacem in Terris Award, Intl Overseas Serv Found, 1969; Leadership for Freedom Award, Roosevelt Univ, 1971; Martin Luther King Meml Medal, Coll City of NY, 1971; Intl Viareggio Award, 1971; named Woman of the Year, Natl Assn Radio and TV Announc 1968; Ann Brotherhood Award, Natl Coun of Negro Women; delegate to disarmament conf, Geneva, Switzerland. Honorary degrees: Boston Univ, Marymount Manhattan Coll, Brandeis Univ, all 1969, Morehouse Coll, Wilburforce Univ, Univ of Bridgeport, Morgan State Coll, Bethune-Cookman Coll, Keuka Coll, Princeton Univ, all 1970, Northeastern Univ and Bates Coll, both 1971. **BUSINESS ADDRESS:** President, MLK Center for Nonviolent, Social Change Inc, 449 Auburn Ave NE, Atlanta, GA 30313. *

KING, DELUTHA HAROLD
Physician. **PERSONAL:** Born Jan 17, 1924, Weir, KS; married Lois; children: Michael, Ronald. **EDUCATION:** Western Res, BS 1962; HowardUniv Coll Med, 1956; Freedmen's Hosp, intern 1956-57; Freedmen's Hosp, res urology 1957-61. **CAREER:** Physician pvt prac 1965-; VA Hosp, chf urology 1961-65; VA Hosp, consult 1966-72; SW Comm Hosp, chief of staff 1979; Hughes Spalding Pavilion, staff& mem; SW Comm Hosp; GA Bapt Hosp; Crawford W Long Meml Hosp; Physician & Surgeons Hosp; St Joseph's Infirmary; Atlanta W Hosp. **ORGANIZATIONS:** Mem Am Urol Assn; flw Am Coll Surgeons; mem Atlanta Urol Soc; bd of trustees Nat Med Assn 1979-; GA State Med Assn; Med Assn GA; AMA; mem Metro-Atlanta Med Assn; bd of trustees SW Comm Hosp 1979-80; pres Atlanta Hlth Care Found 1973-; chmn bd Metro Atlanta Hlth Plan; sec co-fndr chmn bd Sickle Cell Found GA; pres Atlanta Med Assn 1974; bd of trustees Atlanta Med Assn; bd mem Cancer Network GA State Com; bd mem chmn physicians com GA Partners 1976; mem Kappa Alpha Psi Frat; Gov Task Force HSA Devel 1975; pres N Ctr GA Hlth Systems Agency; bd mem Metro Atlanta CounselAlcohol & Drug Abuse; 2nd vice pres Nat Assn Sickle Cell Disease; bd mem/pres-elect GA State Med Assn; bd mem Am Cancer Soc; natl pres HowardUniv AlumniAssn 1978-80; apptd Nat Council on Hlth Planning & Devel; past pres Atlanta Club HowardUniv Slumni Assn Publ "Hyperparathyroidism" Jour of Med Assn of GA 1966. **HONORS/ACHIEVEMENTS:** Outst achvmt as Chf Resd in Urology Assn of Former Interns & Resd Freedmen's Hosp 1961; spec award for serv to Atlanta Med Assn; mem Alpha Omega Alpha Med Hon Soc. **MILITARY SERVICE:** AUS tech 1943-45. **BUSINESS ADDRESS:** 2600 Martin Luther King Dr SW, Atlanta, GA 30311.

KING, DEREK BARBER
Clergyman. **PERSONAL:** Born Apr 12, 1915, Atlanta, GA; married Janice Withers; children: Derek B II. **EDUCATION:** Morehouse Coll, BA Religious Studies/Political Sci 1976; Colgate Rochester Divinity Sch, Master of Divinity 1979. **CAREER:** Pleasant Grove Bapt Church, pastor 1980; New Life Baptist Church of Christ, pastor 1982-83; Christian Council of Metro Atlanta, staff assoc 1983-84; Concerned Black Clergy, exec dir 1984; Tabernacle Baptist Church, pastor. **ORGANIZATIONS:** Dir martin Luther King Jr Center for Non-Violent Social Change; mem Sun Coast Chamber of Commerce; mem Natl Assn of Ecumenical Staffs. **HONORS/ACHIEVEMENTS:** Inductee Outstanding Young Men of America 1978; published article USA Today 1983; public service NAACP Rome GA Branch. **BUSINESS ADDRESS:** Pastor, Tabernacle Baptist Church, 801 8th St, West Palm Beach, FL 33401.

KING, DON
Boxing promoter. **PERSONAL:** Born Aug 20, 1931, Cleveland, OH; married Henrietta; children: Debbie King Lee, Carl, Eric. **CAREER:** Ernie Shavers, Larry Holmes, boxing mgr; George Foreman-Ken Norton, Ali-Foreman, Ali-Frazier, promoted prize fights; Don King Sports Entertainment Network, owner, pres; King Training Camp, owner; Don King Prod, pres, chmn & ceo. **ORGANIZATIONS:** Supports United Negro Coll Fund; mem Oper Push, The Martin Luther King Center for Social Change, Trans-Africa, The Anti-Apartheid Assoc; bd mem President's Physical Fitness Council; has promoted over 200 championship fights throughout the world-more than any other promoter; responsible for the heavyweight unification series to unify the heavyweight title currently in progress Time Mag described him as "the most powerful promoter in sports" and People Mag described him as "one of America's most influential individuals". **HONORS/ACHIEVEMENTS:** Helped mastermind the Jacksons Victory Tour; Man of the Year Awd Natl Black Hall of Fame 1975; Urban Justice Awd Antioch School of Law 1976; Heritage Awd Edwin Gould Serv for Children 1976; Minority Businessman of the Year Gr WA Bus Ctr; Man of the Year NAACP; World Boxing Council Promoter of the Decade 1974-84; US Olympic Comm for Outstanding Support & Serv 1980; The Presidential Inaugural Comm George Herbert Walker Bush Awd 1981; Natl Black Caucus Awardee of theYear 1981; North Amer Boxing Fed Promoter of the Year 1983-84; Natl Police Athletic League for Unselfish dedication & generous contribs 1983; World Boxing Council Humanitarian Awd 1984; Black Entertainment & Sports Lawyers Assoc Merit Awd 1986; IN Black Expo Freedom Awd 1986; The Pigskin Club of WA Only in Amer Can a Don King Happen Awd 1986; Dr Martin Luther King Jr Humanitarian Awd The Jamaica Amer Soc in Assoc with the US Info Serv 1987; Natl Youth Movement Crack Buster of the Year Awd 1986; Guantes Mag Promoter of the Year Awd; A True Champion of Humanitarian Causes IN State Branch NAACP 1987; East Chicago Chap IN Black Expo Martin Luther King Humanitarian Awd 1987; Minority Oppty for Racial Equality More Inc in Appreciation on Don King's Devotion to His Fellow Man 1987. **BUSINESS ADDRESS:** Chairman, Chief Exec Officer, Don King Productions, Inc, 32 E 69th St, New York, NY 10021.

KING, DONALD E.
Judge. **PERSONAL:** Born Mar 24, 1934, Atlantic City, NJ; children: 1 Child. **EDUCATION:** Lafayette Coll, AB 1956; St John's Univ Law Sch, LIB 1960; St John's Univ Law Sch, JD 1964. **CAREER:** Zashin & King, partner 1962-70; Juv & Dom Rel Court Essex Co NJ, judge; Newark, corp counsel 1973-74; Newark, asst corp 1970-73; Rutgers Inst for Cont Legal Educ Rutgers Law Sch, instructor; Garden State Bar Assn, pres. **ORGANIZATIONS:** Mem Pi Lambda Phi; PAD Legal Fraternity; Essex Co Bar Assoc; NJ Bar Assoc; American Bar Assoc; Nat Bar Assoc; Urban League; NAACP Appointed to Essex Co Ethics Comm by NJ Supreme Ct. **MILITARY SERVICE:** AUS 1st lt. **BUSINESS ADDRESS:** State of New Jersey, Essex County Courts Bldg, Newark, NJ 07102.

KING, EDGAR LEE
Hospital executive. **PERSONAL:** Born in Shellman, GA; married Georgia Roberta Chester; children: Laura Smith, Edgar Jr. **EDUCATION:** Northwestern Univ; Georgia State Coll; Univ of IL, CPA 1980. **CAREER:** S Buchsbaum & Co, acct supvr 1951-56; Am Whlsle Co, acct mgr 1956-58; Allier Rdo Corp, sr accountant 1958-61; Schwab Rehabilitation Hosp, business 1961-63; central 1963-73, assoc admin 1973-79; Hospital of Englewood, chief finance officer 1980-88. **ORGANIZATIONS:** Mem Amer Inst of CPA's; mem IL Soc of CPA's; mem Health Care Financial Mgmt Assn; mem Amer Hospital Assn; mem IL Hospital Assn; mem Natl Assn of Hotel Serv Exec; mem Chicago Urban League. **HONORS/ACHIEVEMENTS:** Delta Mu Delta Beta Chap, Northwestern Univ.

KING, ESTELLE HOLLOWAY
Retired educator. **PERSONAL:** Born Dec 11, 1927, Greensboro, NC; married Roy King; children: Roy Jr, Michael. **EDUCATION:** Univ of MI, MA 1946; Pittsburgh Univ, PhD 1972. **CAREER:** Fisk Univ, instr 1946-49; Meharry Med Coll, asst prof 1949-52; Behrend Coll of Penn State Univ, instr 1963-64; Edinboro State Coll, retired prof 1965-84. **ORGANIZATIONS:** Mem Task Force on Educ & Training of State Adv Com on Aging 1976-78; mem Bd of assoc Mercyhurst Coll 1976-; mem Delta Sigma Theta Sor, NAACP, Erie Cty Womens Med Aux, AAUW, Doctoral Assn of Educ; sec Jones PTA 1958-59; pres McKean PTA 1961-62. **HONORS/ACHIEVEMENTS:** Sarah McKim Maloney Awd Fisk Univ 1942; Scholarship Awd Delta Sigma Theta 1945; Civic Awd Outstanding Contributor to the Erie Comm 1976; Contr Improv Coll & Univ Tchng 1977; author of textgs med statistics 1950; rsch in math educ 1977.

KING, GWENDOLYN
Elected government official. **PERSONAL:** Born in E Orange, NJ; married Colbert I King; children: Robert, Stephen, Allison. **EDUCATION:** Howard Univ, BA (Cum Laude) 1958-62; George Washington Univ, 1972-74. **CAREER:** US Dept of HEW, health desk officer, HEW mgmt intern 1971-76; US Dept of HUD, dir div of consumer complaints 1976-78; US Sen John Heinz, sr legislativeasst 1978-79; Commonwealth of PA, dir 1979-. **HONORS/ACHIEVEMENTS:** Ex officio bd mem PA Soc of Washington DC 1983-; found mem Women Exec in State Government 1984-. **BUSINESS ADDRESS:** Dir of Washington Office, Commonwealth of Pennsylvania, 400 N Capitol St, Ste 285, Washington, DC 20001.

KING, HODGE
Educator. **PERSONAL:** Born Nov 10, 1914, Dooly County, GA; married Hattie F Burson. **EDUCATION:** Morris Brown Coll, AB 1940; New York U, MA 1952; New York U, 1959; cert 1959. **CAREER:** Turner Co Jr High, principal 1970-80; Uereka High Sch, prin 1946-70; Turner Cty Bd of Edn, tchr 1940-41. **ORGANIZATIONS:** Regional dir GA Tchr & Educ Assn 1949-54; dist exec sec GA Interscholastic Assn 1949-64; pres GA Interscholastic Assn 1968-70; vice pres Morris Brown Coll Nat Alumni southeastern reg 1977- Shriner Mason 1957-; stewart-trustee Emmery Chapel AME Ch 1959-; pres Alpha Phi Alpha Frat Gamma Omricrom Chap 1960-62. **HONORS/ACHIEVEMENTS:** Meritorius serv award Am Cancer Soc 1967; meritorius serv award GA Interscholastic Assn 1970; meritorius serv award Boy Scout of Am 1974; meritorius serv award Morris Brown Coll Nat Alumni Assn 1979. **MILITARY SERVICE:** AUS msgt 1941-45. **BUSINESS ADDRESS:** Turner City Jr High, Ashburn, GA 31714.

KING, HOWARD A. T.
Physician. **PERSONAL:** Born Jun 26, 1922, St Croix, Virgin Islands of the United States;children: Howard, Jr, Yvonne. **EDUCATION:** FiskUniv 1940-43; Fisk U, BA 1946; Meharry Med Coll, MD 1946; ColumbiaUniv Sch Pub Hlth & Admin Med, MS 1970. **CAREER:** Govt VI, physician 1977; City Newark, hlth dept 1976-77; Western Elec Co NE Region, asso med dir 1974-76; River Region Mental Hlth Mental Retardation Ctr, physician 1973-74; VI Govt, med dir 1970-72; VI Govt, 1966-70; self 1947-66. **ORGANIZATIONS:** Mem AMA; NMA; AHA; APHA; mem NAACP; Rotary Intl 1966-68. **MILITARY SERVICE:** AUS capt 1949-52. **BUSINESS ADDRESS:** Dir, St Croix Hospital, PO Box 520, Christiansted, St Croix, Virgin Islands of the United States 00820.

KING, HOWARD O.
Government official. **PERSONAL:** Born Aug 24, 1925, Pensacola, FL; married Lillie Marie Pollard; children: Howard O. **EDUCATION:** Florida A&M Univ, BS 1956; Fed Exec Inst 1979. **CAREER:** Office of Civil Rights, FAA, Washington DC, dep dir 1972-; FAA, Atlanta, regional civil rights officer 1970-72; US Forest Serv Atlanta, regional intergroup relations specialist 1967-70; Dept of Defense, Atlanta, contract compliance officer 1965-67; Naval Air Sta Pensacola, various titles 1941-65; Washington Adult Sch Pensacola, adult educ 1957-65; HO King Sales & Serv Pensacola, proprietor 1958-65. **ORGANIZATIONS:** Bd of dirs, MDTA Pensacola, 1963-65; sec, Bi-Racial Comm Pensacola, 1963-65; officer, Ebenezer Baptist Church, Atlanta, 1985-. **HONORS/ACHIEVEMENTS:** Good Conduct Medal, USN, 1945; award, SNEAD, 1956; citizenship award, NAACP, 1965; citizenship plaque, City of Pensacola, 1965; certificate of achievement, Dept of Transportation, FAA, 1972; outstanding achievement award, Natl Black Coalition of FAA Employees, 1978. **MILITARY SERVICE:** USN petty officer 1st class 40 months.

KING, JAMES, JR.
Technical manager. **PERSONAL:** Born Apr 23, 1933, Columbus, GA; son of James King and Lucille Jameson Williams; divorced; children: Jennifer King Slickbern, Jeffrey King. **EDUCATION:** Morehouse Coll, Atlanta GA, BS, 1953; CA Institute of Technology, Pasadena CA, MS, 1955, PhD, 1958. **CAREER:** Jet Propulsion Lab, manager, Pasadena CA, 1969-74; NASA, Washington DC, spaceshuttle environmental effects, 1974-75, dir upper atmospheric research office, 1975-76; JPL, Pasadena CA, program manager for atmospheric sciences, 1976-79, technical manager for Space Science and Applications, 1981-88, asst lab dir Technical Division, 1988-. **ORGANIZATIONS:** Mem, Sigma Xi, 1958-; mem, Amer Physical Society, 1960-; mem, Amer Chemical Society, 1960-; bd of dir, Pasadena Child Guidance Clinic, 1969-72, 1980-86; mem, LA Air Pollution Control, 1971-74; mem, Caltech YMCA Bd of Dir, 1972-74; mem, Amer Assn for the Advancement of Science, 1976-; dir, Caltech Alumni Assn, 1977-80; mem, Amer Geophysical Union, 1977-80; chairman, Pasadena Community Devel Committee, 1982-83. **HONORS/ACHIEVEMENTS:** Danforth Fellowship, Danforth Foundation, 1953; Scholarship, General Educ Board, 1953; Certificate of Merit, Natl Council of Negro Women, 1968; nominee for the US Jaycee's Distinguished Service Award, 1966; Phi Beta Kappa, 1975; author of 13 articles in professional journals. **HOME ADDRESS:** 1720 La Cresta Drive, Pasadena, CA 91103.

KING, JAMES B., JR.
Wholesale salesman. **PERSONAL:** Born Mar 09, 1914, Cuthbert, GA; married Amanda Hammond; children: 1 Child. **EDUCATION:** Albany State Coll Albany, GA, BS 1947; AtlantaUniv Atlanta, GA, MA 1957. **CAREER:** Woodland High & Elem Sch, principal 1947-57; Ruth Carter High & Elem Sch, principal 1957-70; Central HS Tablton GA, principal 1971-74; Talbot Co Sch GA, supt 1977-81; King's Mail Order Svcs, owner/manager. **ORGANIZATIONS:** Past pres Talbot Co Tchrs Assn GA 1948-70; mem adv counc Upson Voc Tech Sch Thomaston GA 1960-80; past pres Columbus Dist GA Congress Colored PTA 1965-70; mem Am Assn of Sch Adminstr 1977-81; mem GA Assn of Sch Supt 1977-81; mem adv council Tchr Educ Columbus Coll GA 1977-80. **HONORS/ACHIEVEMENTS:** Awards Personalities of the South & Notable Am, Am Biog Inst Raleigh, NC 1976-79; Hon D of Humane Letters Faith Coll Birmingham 1977; listed in Intl Who's Who in Comm Serv Intl Biog Centre Caimbridge, Eng 1979; listed in Who's Who in Educ Admin, Am Assn of Sch Adminstr Arlington, VA 1980-81. **MILITARY SERVICE:** AUS t-5 spec 1943-46; Asiatic-Pacific Ribbon, Bronze Star, Victory Medal. **BUSINESS ADDRESS:** King's Mail Order Service, PO Box 147, Woodland, GA 31836.

KING, JEANNE FAITH
Marriage, family, child counselor. **PERSONAL:** Born Sep 20, 1934, Philadelphia, PA; daughter of Julian Frederick King and Minnie Hines King; divorced; children: Heather O. Bond. **EDUCATION:** Antioch Univ LA, BA 1977, MA Clinical Psychology 1987; Antioch Univ, Los Angeles, CA, MA, 1985-87; Antioch Univ, Los Angeles, CA, BA 1973-77. **CAREER:** Performing Arts Soc of LA,TV producer 1969-70; Watts Media Ctr, pr instr 1972-74; WTTW-Chicago Pub TV, TV production 1975; Self Employed, free lance comm pr 1976-78; Central City Comm Health Ctr, dir of pub relations 1978; Jeanne King Enterprises, consultant firm 1984-; Valley Cable LA, producer cable TV show "Jazz 'n U" 1984; Local Jazz Clubs, free lance entertainment specialist 1984; Julia Ann singer Ctr in Family Stress Prog, intern 1985-86, intern family therapy prog 1986-87; Rosa Parks Sexual Assault Crisis Center LA, counselor 1987-; Play It Safe with SASA, consult & trainer for focus consult teaching 1987; Marriage Family Child Counselor, intern; In the Beginning Corp, pres 1978-; self employed, 1988-89. **ORGANIZATIONS:** Exec dir Performing Arts Soc of LA 1973-74; cons, contrib Black Art, An Intl Quarterly 1976-79; mem Black Womens Forum 1978-80; bd dir Ureaus Quarterly Magazine 1976-80; mem LA, Salvador Sister Cities Com 1978-80; volunteer for New Horizons; MFCC private practice; mem California Assn of Marriage, Family, Child Therapists, 1987-89; mem bd of dirs Centinela Child Guidance Clinic 1988-89. **HONORS/ACHIEVEMENTS:** Public Serv Awd; Watts Summer Festival Awd 1969; Comm Contribution Head Start Awd 1970; Outstanding Serv Awd Compton Comm ARts Acad 1971; Outstanding Serv Awd Natl Conf of Artists Awd 1975; Day of the Drum Festival Mistress of Ceremonies 1984 Watts Tower Art Ctr LA CA; co-editor "Day of the Drum Festival Book"; Marla Gibbs Comm Award, Marlas Memory Lane 1987. **HOME ADDRESS:** 5811 Bowcraft Street, #1, Los Angeles, CA 90016.

KING, JOHN B.
Business executive, educator. **PERSONAL:** Born Sep 17, 1908, New York, NY; married Adalinda Garcia; children: John Jr, Gil, Lynne, Joan. **EDUCATION:** NY Univ, BS 1931, MA 1936; St Johns Univ, D of Pedagogy 1962. **CAREER:** New York City Schools, elem teacher 1928-37; Brooklyn Jr HS, teacher 1938; Brooklyn Tech HS, teacher 1939-40; Brooklyn, asst principal 1940-45, principal 1945-50, asst supt of schools 1951-59; New York City School, assoc supt of schools 1959-63, dep supt of schools 1963-65, exec dep supt of schools 1965-67; Fordham Univ, prof 1967-74; New York City Assoc, exec dep supt of school 1967-74; Equitable Fed Savings & Loan Assoc, chmn, bd of dir. **ORGANIZATIONS:** Consult

various ed rsch groups 1940-; org, chmn Bushwick School Comm League 1945-51; pres NY Acad of Publ Ed 1968-70; officer Amsterdam News Brooklyn Citizen Comm 1942-51; dir Brooklyn Counc for Soc Plnng 1948-56, Natl Scholarship Serv & Fund for Negro Stud 1957-67. **HONORS/ACHIEVEMENTS:** Medalist NY Acad of Publ Ed 1967; 1st & only black principal in Brooklyn NY Publ School; devel training prog black & PR school officials Fordham Univ 1966-74; Leading Citizen Amsterdam News 1946,49; Awd Youth United 1951; Hoey Awd NY Cath Interracial Conc 1953.

KING, JOHN L.
Human resources executive. **PERSONAL:** Born Apr 29, 1952, Detroit, MI; son of Johnnie L King and Lillie Mae Hannah King; divorced. **EDUCATION:** Oakland Univ, Rochester MI, BA Human Resources, 1975. **CAREER:** County of Oakland, Pontiac MI, employment coordinator, 1972-78; Visiting Nurses Assn, Detroit MI, sr personnel representative, 1978-80; Rehabilitation Institute, Detroit MI, dir human resources, 1980-88; The Detroit Medical Center, Detroit MI, compensation admin, 1988-89, manager equal employment plan, 1989. **ORGANIZATIONS:** Mem, NAACP, 1980-; mem, Michigan Devel Disabilities Council, 1983-; mem, Mayor's Handicapper Advisory Council, 1987-; treasurer, SW Detroit Community Mental Health Services Group, 1987-; mem, Natl Assn for the Advancement of Blacks in Health, 1988-; program devel chairperson, Healthcare Personnel Admin Assn of SE Michigan, 1988-90; special projects chairperson, Healthcare Personnel Admin Assn of SE Michigan, 1989-90. **HONORS/ACHIEVEMENTS:** Testimonial Resolution, Detroit City Council, 1983, State of Michigan Senate, 1984. **BUSINESS ADDRESS:** Manager, Equal Employment Planning, The Detroit Medical Center, 4201 St Antoine, 9C/UHC, Detroit, MI 48201.

KING, JOHN Q. TAYLOR, SR.
President. **PERSONAL:** Born Sep 25, 1921, Memphis, TN; son of Dr John Q Taylor and Alice Woodson Taylor King; married Dr Marcet Alice Hines, Jun 28, 1942; children: John Q Jr MD, Clinton Allen MD, Mrs Marjon King Christopher, Stuart H ines. **EDUCATION:** Fisk Univ, BA 1941; Landig Coll of Mortuary Sci, Diploma 1942; Huston-Tillotson Coll, BS 1947; DePaul Univ, MS 1950; Univ of TX at Austin, PhD 1957. **CAREER:** US Army, pvt to capt 1942-46; King Funeral Home, Austin TX, mortician, 1946-55; Kings-Tears Mortuary, Inc, funeral dir & embalmer (part-time) 1955—, pres, 1984—; Huston-Tillotson Coll, instr, 1947-52, asst prof, 1952-54, prof of math, 1954-88, dean 1960-65, pres 1965-88, chancellor 1987-88, chancellor and pres emeritus, 1988—, director and chair, Center for the Advancement of Science, Engineering and Technology, 1985—. **ORGANIZATIONS:** General secretary, Natl Protestant Brotherhood, 1966-80; pres, Union Welfare and Burial Assn, 1941-85; senior vice pres, Amer Underwriters Life Insur Co, 1986-89; Dir TX Comm Bank-Austin; trust Austin Coll Sherman TX; pres King-Tears Mortuary Inc; life mem NAACP & Natl Urban League; Phi Beta Kappa; Alpha Phi Alpha Frat; Sigma Pi Phi Frat; Phi Delta Kappa; Philosophical Soc of TX; mem Austin Greater E KiwanisClub 1966-; mem, past chmn Austin Civil Serv Comm; founder Union Natl Bank; church lay leader, United Methodist Church. **HONORS/ACHIEVEMENTS:** LLD, Southwestern U, 1970, St Edward's U, 1976; LHD, Austin Coll, 1978, Fisk U, 1980; DSc, Huston-Tillotson Coll, 1988; Alumni Awds Houston-Tillotson Coll & Fisk Univ; Roy Wilkins Meritorious Award NAACP; Disting Serv Awd TX Lutheran Coll; Arthur B DeWitty Awd Austin Branch NAACP; Martin Luther King Humanitarian Awd; Frederick D Patterson Award, Alpha Phi Alpha; Minority Advocate of the Year, Austin Chamber of Commerce; Military/Education Award, San Antonio League, Natl Assn of Business and Professional Women's Clubs; Brotherhood Award, Natl Conf of Christians and Jews; co-author of math texts; co-author of Stories of Twenty-Three Famous Negro Americans, Steck-Vaughan, 1967, and Famous Black Americans, Steck-Vaughan, 1975. **MILITARY SERVICE:** AUS maj gen (WWII, 1942-46; USAR 1946-83); TX State Guard lt gen 1985; received many combat & other military ribbons, decorations & awds. **HOME ADDRESS:** 2400 Givens Ave, Austin, TX 78722-2105. **BUSINESS ADDRESS:** Director and Chair, Center fo the Advancement of Science, Engineering and Technology, Huston-Tillotson College, 1820 East 8th St, Austin, TX 78702-2793.

KING, JOSEPH PRATHER
Child psychiatrist. **PERSONAL:** Born Jul 15, 1927, Cuthbert, GA; son of William King Jr and MaeBelle Prather King. **EDUCATION:** Univ of Chicago, 1943-46; Northside Cntr for Child Devel, Child Psychiatry 1957-61; IN Univ, BS, Pre-Med 1946-48 IN Univ, md 1947-51; Manhattan VA Hosp, NYC, Psychiatry Residency 1955-57; City Hosp, Cleveland, OH, Rotating Internship 1951-52; Hines VA Hosp, Chgo, IL, Psychiatry Res 1952-53. **CAREER:** IN State Dept of Mental Health, assoc dir Child Mental Health Div 1972-74; IN Med Schl, asst prof Psychiatry 1972-82; Midtown Mental Health Clinic, med dir 1974-85; Buchanan Counseling Cntr of Methodist Hosp, consultant 1976-85; Westinghouse Head Start, mental health consultant 1979-80; Quinco CMHC, consultant 1983-84; S Central Mental Health Cntrs, child psychiatrist 1983-84; Indiana State Sch for the Deaf, consultant 1985-; Mood Swing Clinic, psychiatrist; Humana Hospital Adolescent Psych Ward, child psychiatrist 1989-. **ORGANIZATIONS:** Mem NY Cnty Med Soc 1956-, Amer Med Assn 1956-, IN State Med Assn, Amer Psychiatric Assn 1956-; chmn Harlem Neighborhood Assn, Mental Health Comm 1959-66, bd mem 1965-72; New York City Council on Child Psychiatry 1962-72; vice chmn Courts Comm 1962-63; mem Comm on Integration 1965-66; Interracial Group Therapists Workshop 1965-66; mem Aesculapian Med Soc 1973-; mem Black Psychiatrists of Amer 1974-; bd mem Marion County Guidance Clinic 1976-78, vice pres 1978-79; bd mem IN Council Family Relations 1977-79; mem Mental Health Delivery Sys Comm IN Univ Schl of Soc Work 1978-79; mem advisory comm Central IN Health Sys Agency 1979-80; mem Marion Cnty Med Soc 1972-, IN Psychiatric Soc 1972-; brd mem Diagnostic Presscriptive Learning Cntr 1982-83. **HONORS/ACHIEVEMENTS:** Papers; "Traps in Comm Psychiatry" 1968, "Identity Changes in the Amer Negro" 1969, "Issues in the Devel of Comm Mental Health Serv in the Inner City" 1970, "Therapeutic Comm in Ghetto Facilities" 1970, "Recovery, Inc" 1970, "Changing Attidues Towards Homosexuals" 1972, "Audiovisual Alternatives , A Way Around the Reading Problem" 1973. **HOME ADDRESS:** 2303 E 2nd St Apt 8, Bloomington, IN 47401. **BUSINESS ADDRESS:** Psychiatrist, Mood Swing Clinic, 740 East 52nd St, Ste #6, Indianapolis, IN 46205.

KING, JULIAN F.
Judge. **PERSONAL:** Born May 20, 1931, Philadelphia, PA; married Shirley A Mackey; children: Andra Victoria. **EDUCATION:** Lincoln Univ PA, BA (cum laude) 1953; Temple Univ Schl Of Law, DL 1956. **CAREER:** Office of Philadelphia Dist Atty, assis dist atty 1963-66; PA Const Conv, delegate 1967-68; Commonwealth of PA, judge court of common pleas. **ORGANIZATIONS:** Chrmn Brd of Dir Blue Cross of Greater PA 1981-; lectur in law TempleUniv Schl of Law 1985-86; Sigma Pi Phi Fraty; Kappa Alpha Psi Fraty; brd of mgrs Christian St YMCA; brd of mgrs Assoc Alumni of Ctrl High Schl of PA. **HONORS/ACHIEVEMENTS:** Man of yr S Philadelphia Brch of NAACP 1973; govr citation Serv to Commonwlth 1973; cou Recog Awd United Auto Workers Fair Govt Pract 1981; black Aerospace Workers Awd 1983. **MILITARY SERVICE:** USNAC sergeant 1956-58.

KING, LAWRENCE C.
Business executive. **PERSONAL:** Born in Washington, DC; married Beulah; children: Larry, Craig. **EDUCATION:** Howard Univ, BA 1951. **CAREER:** Gen Foods Corp NY, regional sales mgr; Gen Foods Corp, former assoc market research mgr, dist sales mgr & sales devel mgr. **ORGANIZATIONS:** Mem Urban League; Kappa Alpha Psi. **BUSINESS ADDRESS:** 250 North St, White Plains, NY 10605.

KING, LAWRENCE P.
Energy sources executive, marketing specialist. **PERSONAL:** Born Feb 03, 1949, Detroit, MI; son of Samuel King and Vivian Jenkins Henry; children: Alexandria E. **EDUCATION:** Cleveland State Univ, Cleveland OH, BSME, 1974. **CAREER:** General Electric, customer service specialist in Cleveland OH, 1972-74, application specialist in Fort Wayne IN, 1974-76; General Electric, Worthington OH, engineer, 1976-79, mgr of marketing, 1979-80; Babcock & Wilcox, Alliance OH, sr marketing specialist, 1980—; consultant to Natl Council of Black Mayors, 1985-87; engineering consultant to Morgan State Univ, 1986. **ORGANIZATIONS:** Natl Technical Assn, regional dir, 1981-84, pres, 1987; mem, Amer Assn of Blacks in Energy, 1986—. **HONORS/ACHIEVEMENTS:** Samuel R Cheevers Award, Natl Technical Assn; community service award, Frontiers Intl, 1984; articles published in technical publications in the US and abroad. **HOME ADDRESS:** 1460 Commonwealth Dr, Akron, OH 44313-5714.

KING, LEROY J.
Educational administrator. **PERSONAL:** Born Jul 28, 1920, Mobile, AL; married Arminta Alma Norfleet; children: Juanita E, LeRoy J. **EDUCATION:** Military Sch career guidance/command/staff/mgmt engineering various;Univ of NE Omaha, BE psychol major 1963;Univ of HI Manoa, MEd 1968;Univ Of So CA Present. **CAREER:** Kauai Comm Coll, provost 1979-; Windward Community Coll, provost 1973-79; Univ Of HI Manoa, dir student financial aids 1969-73; Juvenile Delinquency & Youth Devel Center School of Social Work Univ of HI Manao, program specialist 1967-69; USAF, commn officer 1944-66. **ORGANIZATIONS:** Past treas/pres-elect/mem HI Personnel & Guidance Assn; mem Am Personnel & Guidance Assn; mem Rotary Internat; past pres Kaneohe Rotary Club; past pres Ret Officers Assn HI Chpt; past mem HI Chap Nat Crime & Delinquency Council/Pacific & Asian Affairs Council/Windward Health Planning Council; past pres windward Reg Council; consult Winward KEY Project USAF & AUS Commendations 1944-66; campaign ribbons. **HONORS/ACHIEVEMENTS:** Publications "Application of Behavior Mod Techniques in HI"/"DECISIONS '69"/"Designing An Information Sys for Student Financial Aid". **MILITARY SERVICE:** USAF maj 20 yrs served. **BUSINESS ADDRESS:** RR 1 Box 216, Lihue, HI 96766.

KING, LEWIS M.
Scientist, professor. **PERSONAL:** Born Oct 05, 1942, Trinidad; son of Henry King and Gladys King; children: Eric. **EDUCATION:** Howard Univ, BS 1967; UCLA, MA 1968; UCLA, PhD 1971. **CAREER:** UCLA, psychology lecturer 1967-71; Martin Luther King Jr Hosp, chief psychologist 1971-73; Drew Med Sch, dir research 1972-74; Drew Med Sch, prof psychiatry 1972-74; Dir Fanon Res & Devel Center, Drew Med Sch; Drew Medical School, Dean. **ORGANIZATIONS:** Bd dir Behavior Res & Dev 1970-74; chmn Comm Res Review Com LA 1972-74; dir Trinidad Drama Guild 1960-63. **HONORS/ACHIEVEMENTS:** Howard Univ Scholarship 1964-67; outstanding contribution to student life Howard Univ 1966; Dean's honor role 1964-67; UN Institute of Intl Educ Fellowship 1965-67; Physcics Honor Soc Howard Univ 1965; Distinguished Teaching Award UCLA 1969-70; first black PhD in Psychology from UCLA. **BUSINESS ADDRESS:** Charles R Drew, University of Medicine, 1621 E 120th St, Los Angeles, CA 90059.

KING, LLOYD
Educator. **PERSONAL:** Born Sep 13, 1936, Zinnerman, LA; married Ann Adkins; children: Vicki, Eric. **EDUCATION:** Grambling State Univ, BS 1960; LA Tech Univ, MS 1971; LA Tech Univ, post grad study 1975. **CAREER:** Pinecrest HS, teacher vice pres coach 1961-68; Winnfield Sr HS, tchr 1968-75; Winnfield Middle School, teacher 1985-. **ORGANIZATIONS:** Past pres Winn Educ Assn; adv com Title I prog Winn Parish; mem Natl Educ Assn; mem LA Tech Alumni Assn; dir Indoor Recreation for Blacks; past program dir Local Radio Prog Hobdy's Soul Sauce; past publicity dir Math Dept LA Educ Assn; mem Natl Aerospace Educ Assn; past pres Grambling Alumni Assn; mem Winn Parish Voters League; counselor Job Training Participation Act Summer Youth. **HONORS/ACHIEVEMENTS:** Winn Educ Assn Teacher of the Yr 1971; cited for Outstanding Serv to Educ & Comm 1972 Winn Educ Assn; nominee for Tchr of Yr 1973, 74, 75; Honorary Sec of State 1974; cited for Outstanding Serv Winn Parish Voters League 1975; Outstanding Serv Citation LA Educ Assn 1976; Voters League Teacher of the Year1985. **MILITARY SERVICE:** Sgt 1960-62 reserves 5yrs.

KING, MARCELLUS, JR.
Marketing director. **PERSONAL:** Born Jun 14, 1943, Tampa, FL; married Romaine C Ruffin; children: Marcellus III. **EDUCATION:** Hampton Inst VA, BS (dean's list) 1965; RutgersUniv NJ, MBA 1976; The Am Coll, CLU 1978. **CAREER:** The Prudential Ins Co, dir group pension servs 1974-, mgr group pensions 1971-74, asso mgr group pensions 1970-71. **ORGANIZATIONS:** Guest speaker Minority Interchange 1978-80; pres Omega Phi Epsilon 1961; mem allocations com United Way of Morris Co NJ 1975-80; vice pres Urban League of Essex Co NJ 1976-80. **HONORS/ACHIEVEMENTS:** Medic of the Year Award AUS 1971; designation CLU The Am Coll 1978; exec mgmt prog Prudential Ins Co 1980. **MILITARY SERVICE:** AUS sp 6th class 1966-72. **BUSINESS ADDRESS:** Hanover Rd, Florham Park, NJ 07040.

KING, MARY BOOKER
Educator. **PERSONAL:** Born Jul 14, 1937, Quitman, GA; married Grady J; children: Felicia, Adriene, Karon. **EDUCATION:** Morris Brown Coll, BA 1959; Atlanta U, MA 1961; Nova U, Ed D 1975. **CAREER:** Miami Dade Comm Coll, prof of language arts 1975-; Miami Dade Comm Coll, dept chmn of reading 1973-75; Miami Dade Comm Coll, assoc prof

of English 1970-72. **ORGANIZATIONS:** Commr Dade Co Com on the Status of Women 1978-80; consult Devel of Coll Programs in Reading & Writing; chairperson Women Involved in Comm Affairs 1979-80; mem Educ Task Force Com 1979-80. **HONORS/ACHIEVEMENTS:** Outstanding Young Women of Am 1971; comm leadership award Kappa Theta Delta 1972. **BUSINESS ADDRESS:** Miami Dade Comm Coll, 300 N E 2nd Ave, Miami, FL 33132.

KING, MATTIE M.
Association executive. **PERSONAL:** Born Sep 04, 1919, Savannah, GA; daughter of Lemuel Latimer and Hattie Latimer; married Robert V. **EDUCATION:** Brooklyn Coll, BA 1974. **CAREER:** Bedford Stuyvesant Comm Legal Serv Corp, adminstr; fiscal ofcr 1970-71; adminstrv Sec 1968-70; Fleary Gibson & Thompson, exec sec 1956-68; William H Staves & Judge & Lewis S Flagg Jr, legal sec; Port Embarkation, purchasing clk 1949-50; Mail & Records, supr 1947-49; asst supr 1946-47; Spl Mail & Records Div, supr; USAF, Special Mail and Records 1943-45. **ORGANIZATIONS:** Mem bd of dirs Bedford-Stuyvesant Restoration Corp; 2nd vice pres Brooklyn Br NAACP; mem Bedford-Stuyvesant Restoration Constrn Corp & RDC Commercial Ctr Inc; Comm Plng Bd #3 Borough of Brooklyn NYC; mem Concord Bapt Ch; Sisterhood Concord Ch; Unity Dem Club 55 AD; Com Elect John F Kennedy. **HONORS/ACHIEVEMENTS:** Distinguished serv award OES; Grand Ct Daug Sphinx Serv award; award Rebecca Chap 23 OES; leading cit award Brooklyn Recorder; supreme grand financial sec Nat Order Eastern Star; 11 yr serv award Com Action for Legal Serv Inc 1968-79; 10 Yrs Serv Bd of Dir Award Bedford-Stuyvesant Restoration Corp 1967-77; Freedom Fund Award, Brooklyn Branch NAACP 1981.

KING, NETTIE (NEE SCOTT)
Business executive. **PERSONAL:** Born Dec 05, 1891, Media, PA; widowed. **CAREER:** King & King Funeral Home, sec-treas & funrl dir. **ORGANIZATIONS:** Mem Ordr of Leah of Estrn Star 1913; YWCA; NAACP Nat Cncl Negro Wmn; Ordr of Elks 1932; Alpha Home for Aged Col 1929. **HONORS/ACHIEVEMENTS:** Hon Nat Cncl of Neg Wmn 1961; award Funrl Dir of Yr 1970; hon YMCA 1967; hon NAACP.

KING, PATRICIA ANN
Educator. **PERSONAL:** Born Jun 12, 1942, Norfolk, VA; daughter of Addison King and Grayce King; married Roger Wilkins, 1981; children: Elizabeth Wilkins. **EDUCATION:** Wheaton Coll, BA 1963; Harvard Law School, JD 1969. **CAREER:** Dept of State, budget analyst 1964-66; Equal Employment Opportunity Commn, special asst to chmn 1969-71; Dept of Health Educ & Welfare, dept dir office of civil rights 1971-73; Civil Div Dept of Justice, dep asst atty general 1980-81; Georgetown Univ, assoc prof of law 1974-88; Georgetown Univ, Law Center, prof of law, 1988-. **ORGANIZATIONS:** Mem Natl Commn for Protection of Human Subjects 1974-78; sr rsch scholar Kennedy Inst of Ethics 1977-; fellow Hastings Inst NY 1977-; mem Recombinant DNA Adv Com 1979-82; mem pres Commn for the Study of Ethical Problems in Med & Rsch 1980-81; chmn Redevelopment Land Agency DC 1976-79; mem US Circuit Judge Nominating Com 1977-79; vice chmn, Russell Sage Foundation 1981-; mem, Amer Law Institute 1988-; bd, Women's Legal Defense Fund, 1987-; bd of trustees, Wheaton Coll, 1989-. **HONORS/ACHIEVEMENTS:** Distinguished Serv Award HEW 1973; Secretary's Special Citation HEW 1973; John Hay Whitney Fellowship John Hay Whitney Found 1968; "The Juridicial Status of the Fetus"77 MI Law Review 1647, 1979; co-author "Law Science and Medicine" 1984. **BUSINESS ADDRESS:** Professor of Law, GeorgetownUniv, 600 New Jersey Ave NW, Washington, DC 20001.

KING, PATRICIA E.
Attorney. **PERSONAL:** Born Jan 16, 1943, Chester, SC. **EDUCATION:** John C SmithUniv Charlotte, NC, BS 1965; NC Central U, JD; Durham, NC, honor in Constitutional Law & Pleadings. **CAREER:** Bell & King, atty; Jenkin Perry Pride, researcher 1969-70; Pearson Malone Johnson & Dejermon, researcher 1967-69; Chester, SC, sch tchr 1965-66; Funeral, Directress & Atty. **ORGANIZATIONS:** Mem NC Bar Assn; Black Lawyers Assn; Am Bar Assn; NC Bar Found; NC State Bar Assn. **HONORS/ACHIEVEMENTS:** OIC Award 1972. **BUSINESS ADDRESS:** Attorney at Law, 623 East Trade St, Charlotte, NC 28202.

KING, PERRY F.
Actor. **PERSONAL:** Born Apr 30, 1948, Alliance, OH; married Karen; children: Louise. **EDUCATION:** Yale U, BA 1970; Juilliard Drama Div. **CAREER:** "The Possession of Joel Delany", actor films; "Lords of Flatbush, "Mandingo", "Slaughterhouse 5", "Wild Party", "Bigg Truck & Poor Clare", TV, stage, off-broadway, stock.

KING, REATHA CLARK
University president. **PERSONAL:** Born Apr 11, 1938, Pavo, GA; married Dr N Judge King Jr; children: N Judge III, Scott Clark. **EDUCATION:** Clark Coll, BS 1968; Univ of Chicago, MS 1960, PhD 1963; Columbia Univ, MBA 1977; Aspen Exec Seminars 1984,85. **CAREER:** Natural Bureau of Standards DC, rsch chemist 1963-68; York College of CUNY, prof of chemistry 1968-77; York Coll of CUNY, assoc dean for natural sciences and math 1970-74, assoc dean for academic affairs 1974-77; Metropolitan State Univ, pres 1977-. **ORGANIZATIONS:** Mem Delta Sigma Theta Sor 1957-; corp dir HB Fuller Co St Paul 1978-; mem NAACP, Urban League; mem bd & vice pres St Paul United Way 1978-; corp dir Norwest Minneapolis Bank 1979-, Minnesota Mutual Insurance Co 1984-; mem of bd educ Testing Serv 1984-; presidential adv comm Assoc of Governing Bds 1984-; corp dir Norwest Corporation (Bank Holding Co) 1986-; chairperson of bd St Paul United Way 1987; chair-elect of the bd Amer Assoc of Higher Educ 1987; bd mem St Paul Foundation St Paul MN, Carnegie Foundation for the Advancement of Teaching Princeton NJ. **HONORS/ACHIEVEMENTS:** Hon DL Carleton Coll 1982; Paul Harris Fellow St Paul Rotary Club 1983; Educational Leadership Awd YWCA of St Paul 1984; Exceptional Black Scientist Awd CIBA-GEIGY Corp 1984; Spurgeon Awd for Comm Work Indianhead Cncl Boy Scouts of Amer 1985; Outstanding Publication Awd Natl Bureau of STandards; Honorary Doctor of Letter Empire State College of SUNY 1985; Drum Major for Justice Awd SCLC Atlanta 1986. **BUSINESS ADDRESS:** President, Metropolitan StateUniv, 7th & Robert Sts, St Paul, MN 55101.

KING, REGINALD F.
Engineer. **PERSONAL:** Born Mar 11, 1935, Powellton, WV; son of Isaiah King and Marie Fairfax King; married Grace V Tipper; children: Reginald T, Thaxton E. **EDUCATION:** Youngstown State Univ, BE 1961; San Jose State Univ, grad study. **CAREER:** Reynolds Electronics, co-owner dir engr 1968-70; NASA, rsch engr 1961-. **ORGANIZATIONS:** Mem IEEE; NAACP, KAY Frat; publs in field; ISA. **HONORS/ACHIEVEMENTS:** NASA Tech Brief Awd; Patent in Field; Registered Professional Engineer-Electrical Engineering, State of California 1975; Registered Professional Engineer-Control System, State of California, 1978. **MILITARY SERVICE:** USAF 1954-58. **BUSINESS ADDRESS:** Research Engineer, NASA Ames Res Center, N213-4, Moffett Field, CA 94035.

KING, RICHARD DEVOID
Psychiatrist. **PERSONAL:** Born Nov 19, 1946, New Orleans, LA; children: Khent. **EDUCATION:** Whittier Coll, BA 1968;Univ CA San Francisco Med Ctr, MD 1968;Univ So CA Med Ctr, intern 1973;Univ CA Med Ctr, resd 1976. **CAREER:** Fanon Mental Hlth Rsrch & Devel Ctr, develmt schlr 1976-; San Francisco, psychotherapy rsrch 1974-; Goddard Coll, faculty adv 1975-76;Univ CA, asst tchr 1970; Nghbrhd Yth Cor, educ aide 1969; lab tech 1968; factory wrkr 1967; Lose Angeles, tchr aide 1965; UCLA, lab asst 1964; Palm Springs, lectr 1977; School of Ethnic Studies Dept of Black Studies SF State U, lectr 19780; Aquman Spiritual Ctr, prin 1976-77. **ORGANIZATIONS:** Pres Black Psychiatrists of No CA 1978-80; pres Black Psychiatrists of CA 1980; mem Am Coll of Surgery; Fanon Adv Cncl; Atlanta Med Assn; Nat MedAssn; Assn of Black Psychologist 1977; lectr Martin Luther King Hosp 1977; Black Hlth Ldrsp Conf 1977; Pan-Am Conf 1977; mem Nat of Islam 1969-71; Black Psychiatrist of Am 1975-; Am Psychiat Assn 1975-; mem Nat Inst of Mental Hlth Ctr Devel Prgm 1973-; US Pub Hlth Serv. **HONORS/ACHIEVEMENTS:** Bibliographymelannin 1977; Pineal Gland Rev 1977; Uracus 1977-79. **MILITARY SERVICE:** Lt com 1973-78.

KING, RILEY B. (B. B. KING)
Guitarist, singer. **PERSONAL:** Born Sep 16, 1925, Indianola, MS; divorced. **EDUCATION:** Tougaloo Coll, LHD (hon) 1976; Yale Univ, D Mus 1977. **CAREER:** Memphis radio stas, past disc jockey/singer; intl appearances throughout the world; records on RPM, Crown, Bullet, Kent, ABC Records, ABC/Dunhill Records; toured Russia 1979. **ORGANIZATIONS:** Founding mem John F Kennedy Performing Arts Center 1971. **HONORS/ACHIEVEMENTS:** Subject/collaborator, BB King 1970; BB King Blues Guitar 1970; BB King Songbook 1971; BB King The World's Greatest Living Blues Artist; Blues Guitar A Method by BB King; Humanitarian Award Fed Bur Prisons 1972; B'nai B'rith Music and Performance Lodge New York City 1973; Gallery of Greats and Best Blues Guitarist 1974; Artist of the Decade and Humanitarian Award Record World Mag 1974; Best Blues Singer Natl Assn TV and Radio Announcers 1974; Hall of Fame and Best Blues Vocalist and Guitarist Ebony Mag 1974; Recip of more than 25 awards as best singer and/or guitarist incl Grammy Award 1970; King's hits incl, Three O'Clock Blues, You Know I Love You, Woke Up This Morning, Please Love Me, Rock Me Baby, You Upset Me Baby, Whole Lotta Love, Every Day I Have the Blues, Sweet Little Angel, Partin' Time, Peace of Mind, Paying the Cost to be the Boss, The Thrill Is Gone, Ask Me No Questions, To Know You Is To Love You, I Like to Live the Love, Ain't Nobody Home. **BUSINESS ADDRESS:** c/o Sidney A Seidenberg, 1414 Ave of the Americas, New York, NY 10019.

KING, ROBERT SAMUEL
Educational administrator. **PERSONAL:** Born Oct 16, 1921, Philadelphia, PA; married Rosalie Ernestine Ilivier; children: Gwendolyn Susan, Nancy Gail. **EDUCATION:** WV State Coll, 1943-44;Univ of PA, AB (Physics) 1956; Temple U, grad 1959. **CAREER:** Philadelphia Coll of Pharmacy & Sci, dir of planning, affirmative action officer 1975-80, dir student affairs 1974-75; Naval Air Engineering Ceter Philadelphia, supr mechanical engineer 1961-74, physicist 1956-61; Veterans Admin, insurance underwriter 1950-55. **ORGANIZATIONS:** Mem bd of dirs Magee Meml Hosp 1975-80; mem bd of dirs Berean Savings Assn 1978-80; chmn west sub area cuncil Health Systems Agency Southeast PA 1979-80; mem bd of dirs West Philadelphia Corp 1964-80; mem bd of dirsUniv City Sci Center 1970-80; bd of trustees Comm Coll of Philadelphia 1972-80. **HONORS/ACHIEVEMENTS:** ETO Central Phinel & Asia-pac Award AUS; Quality of Life Award W Philadelphia Corp 1965; winner area dist speech contests Toastmasters Intl 1972-73; panelist, presenter reg annual conf, Assn Comm Coll Trustees 1978-80; article "Identifying Urban Community Coll Needs" ACCT Trustee Quarterly 1978-79. **MILITARY SERVICE:** AUS tech sgt 1943-46. **BUSINESS ADDRESS:** Phil Coll of Pharm & Sci, 43rd St & Kingsessing Mall, Philadelphia, PA 19104.

KING, ROSALYN CAIN
Pharmacist. **PERSONAL:** Born Sep 10, 1938, New York, NY; daughter of Samuel Cain and Ethel Davis; married Dr Sterling King, Jr; children: Kristin, Aaron. **EDUCATION:** Duquesne Univ, BS 1962; Univ of CA-Los Angeles, MPH 1972; Univ of Southern CA, PharmD 1976. **CAREER:** SECON Inc, vice pres 1977-80; Agency for Intl Develop Charles R Drew Univ of Medicine and Science, public health advisor/pharmacy & expert consultant 1980-85, assoc dir office of intl health 1985-86, dir office of intl health 1986-87; dir, International Health Institute, 1987. **ORGANIZATIONS:** Guest lecturer Health Serv Howard Univ 1977-; chairperson Ambulatory Care Comm Amer Public Health Assoc 1979-; instructor Dept of Family Practice King/Drew Medical Ctr 1984-87; adjunct assoc prof College of Pharmacy & Pharm Sciences, Florida A&M Univ 1985-; adjunct assoc prof, Florida A&M Univ 1985, Coll of Pharmacy Xavier Univ 1987-; associate professor, Dept of Family Practice King/Drew, 1988-; mem Amer Public Health Assoc, Amer Pharmaceutical Assoc, Natl Pharmaceutical Foundation; deaconess Mt Calvary Baptist Church Rockville MD. **HONORS/ACHIEVEMENTS:** Mem Rho Chi Natl Pharmaceutical Honor Soc 1961; The Hildrus A Poindexter Award Black Caucus of Health Workers 1976; Certificate of Appreciation presented by Sec of USDHEW 1978; Distinguished Serv Award Natl Pharmaceutical Foundation 1982.

KING, RUBY E.
Consultant. **PERSONAL:** Born Mar 03, 1931; children: Cynthia, Paul, Gayle, Carol. **EDUCATION:** W Mich U, MA 1968; Mich U, BA 1963. **CAREER:** Natl Education Assoc, assistant executive dir for public affairs; Minority Affairs Div MI Educ Assn, consultant 1971-; Mich U, educator 1968-71;MichUniv Campus Sch, supv 1967; elementary sch educator 1961-67. **ORGANIZATIONS:** Mem, bd dir ASCD 1971-74; mem MEA Prof Staff Assn; mem Lansing Urban League; mem Gen Educ Adv Com; mem State Advisory Bd Migrant Education 1971; mem Governor's Task Force Improving Education 1970; group leader NEA Urban Educ Conf 1969; chrmn Personnel Com Grand Rapids YWCA 1971; mem Mayor's Adv Bd on Housing 1971; mem Bd Dir Grand Rapids Legal Aid Soc 1971; bd dir YWCA 1970-71; chmn Educ Com Grand Rapids Model Cities Prog 1969-71. **HONORS/ACHIEVEMENTS:** Nom Teacher of Yr Grand Rapids 1965. **BUSINESS ADDRESS:** Asst Exec Dir for Pub Affs, Natl Education Assoc, 1201 16th St NW, Washington, DC 20036.

KING, RUBY RYAN
Educator. **PERSONAL:** Born Jan 26, 1934, Oktaha, OK; married Clifford King; children: Diane, Gerald, LaDonna. **EDUCATION:** BS 1957; MS 1975; OK St U, fthr study 1975. **CAREER:** Home Economics Coop Extention Program, area program agent 1976-; Langston Univ, Family Living Specialist Cooperative Extention Serv 1972-; Morningside Hospital LA, supvr 1961-63; OK Medical Center, supvr 1957-60. **ORGANIZATIONS:** Chmn Parafessional Training Conf LangstonUniv 1973-74; Sec Ext Homemakers Group Kingfisher, OK 1971-72; prog chmn Western Dist Bapt Convention 1968; mem Am Home Econ Assn; Okla Home Econ Assn (Sec 1974-75); Am Assn ofUniv Women; Nat Counc on Family Relations; Phi Delta Kappa; Phi Upsilon Omicron; LangstonUniv Alumni Assn Inspector, Election Bd Kingfisher, OK 1971; mem Young Mens Christian Assn; mem NAACP; mem Intl Fed for Home Econ; mem Kingfisher Lioness Club; mem Alpha Kappa Alpha Sor Inc (Beta Omicron Omega Chpt); mem Am Home Econ Assn World Food Supply Comm Home Mgmt Sec 1975-. **HONORS/ACHIEVEMENTS:** Worlds Who's Who of Women 1976. **BUSINESS ADDRESS:** Box 970, Langston, OK 7305.

KING, RUTH ALLEN
Consultant. **PERSONAL:** Born Oct 08, 1910, Providence, RI; daughter of Arthur S Allen and Wilhelmina H Allen; children: Phyllis King Dunham. **EDUCATION:** Commercial High School, graduate; Tefft Business Inst Providence RI, Diploma (Hnr Grad) 1929. **CAREER:** Law Office of Joseph LeCount, Esq, legal secretary 1929; New York Urban League NYC, stenographer 1929; Natl Urban League NYC, secy admin secy, assist/plcmnt officer, admin asst 1929-75; Natl Urban League Skills Bank, asst dir; founder/secy, consultant The Edges Group Inc 1969-; Equal Employment Opportunity Commission (EEOC), consultant/assistant to chmn, Lowell Perry 1976; Hazeltine Corporationm Greenlawn L I, personnel department, consultant, 1976-; Sony Corporation of America, Park Ridge NJ, consultant 1980-. **ORGANIZATIONS:** Mem NY Personnel Management Assn 1970; consultant to chairman EEOC Wash DC 1976; Minority Relations Consultant Hazeltine Corp NY 1976-; life mem NAACP 1977-; chart mem Julius A Thomas Soc Natl Urban League 1979; consult to executive vice pres Sony Corp of Amer NJ 1980-; mem NY City Commission on Status of Women 1982. **HONORS/ACHIEVEMENTS:** First black member of the Rhode Island Honor Society; recipient two testimonials at Waldorf-Astroia 1970 & 1975; one year "Ruth Allen King Scholarship Fund"; named "Affirmative Action Pioneer" Metro NY Project Equality 1975; recip Natl Urban League Ann Tanneyhill awd 1975; citation from NY Gov Hugh L Carey 1975; proclamation by borough of Manhattan pres Percy Sutton "Sept 18, 1975 Ruth Allen King Day in NY"; "EDGES Ruth Allen King Annual Excalibur Award" established 1978; proclamation by the Gov, the Mayor, the RI Legislature and Urban League of RI declared "March 9, 1981 Ruth Allen King Appreciation Day in Providence"; "Woman of the Yr" awd Suffolk Cnty Chap of Jack & Jill of Amer 1982; recognition awd by Affirm Action & Equal Oppy Inst of Natl Conf of Christians & Jews 1982; citationby Medgar Evers Coll 1983; recip of "Special Tribute" and gift from EDGES members 1985; cited in 2nd edition of "Black Executive List 1986; The USA Directory of Human Resources Officials"; "saluted" in Chicago as one of Amer 1986 Top 100 Black Business & Professional Women -Dollars & Sense Magazine 1986; cited in "EXCEL volume III's book-Excellence in Black Organizations & Black Achievers" 1986; full pg biog salute/feature "The King Who Is A Queen" 1987; recip of "Professional Awd" of Brookln Club of the Natl Assn of Negro Business & Prof Women's Clubs Inc 1987; recipient of 1987 Whitney M Young, Jr Medallion "For outstanding service to the Urban League. **HOME ADDRESS:** Willoughby Walk Coop. Apts, 185 Hall Street, Apartment 1715, Brooklyn, NY 11205. **BUSINESS ADDRESS:** Willoughby Walk Coop. Apts, 185 Hall Street, Apartment 1715, Brooklyn, NY 11205.

KING, RUTH G.
Educator. **PERSONAL:** Born Jan 28, 1933, Mt Holly, NJ; divorced; children: Mary Esther, Donna Marie. **EDUCATION:** Temple U, EdD 1972; Temple U, MA 1970; Trenton State Coll, BA 1952. **CAREER:** Federal City School of Graduate Studies, assoc prof of comm psychology 1972-75; Bureau of Business & Govt Serv Temple Univ, program coordinator 1968-72; Keystone Job Corps Cener, counselor 1967-68; Philadelphia School Bd, health & physicale instrutor1962-68; NJ School, health & physical education instructor; Office of Equal Opportunity Natl Guard Bureau of Educ, chief; Educ Devel Center, consult 1967-70; Polaroid Corp, 1971; Amer Assn of R & Comm Coll, 1971-72; Office of Black Cath, 1972-73; Dept of Defense Race Relations Inst, 1973-74; Natl Guard Bureau, 1974; Philadelphia Public Schools, part-time cons; Philadelphia Catholic Archdiocese. **ORGANIZATIONS:** Mem Educ Com DC NAACP 1974-75; mem HowardUniv Research Task Force. **HONORS/ACHIEVEMENTS:** Recipient Blue Chips Award outstanding educ serv to comm 1974; Minuteman Award outstanding consult serv Nat Guard Bur 1974; publ "I Am Somebody" Social Change vol 4 Nov 1974; "A Workshop Model for Improving Self-Concept of Black Youth" Journal of Black Psychology vol 2 #1 1975.

KING, RUTH J. See PRATT, RUTH JONES

KING, TALMADGE EVERETT, JR.
Physician, educator. **PERSONAL:** Born Feb 24, 1948, Sumter, SC; married Mozelle Davis; children: Consuelo, Makaika M. **EDUCATION:** Gustavus Adolphus Coll, BA 1970; Harvard Med School, MD 1974. **CAREER:** Harvard Univ, teaching fellow 1972; Health Career Summer Prog for Minority Students Harvard Univ, asst coord 1973; Emory Univ Affiliated Hosp, resd in med 1974-77; Univ of CO Health Sci Ctr, pulmonary fellowship 1977-79; Univ of CO Health Sci Ctr, assoc prof of med; Natl Jewish Center for Immunology& Respiratory Med, dir of Cohen Clinic. **ORGANIZATIONS:** Mem civil rights comm St Peter MN 1969; diplomate Internal Med & Pulmonary Diseases Amer Coll of Physicans 1977; assoc ed Seminars in Respiratory Med;pres Mile High med Soc 1982-83; pres CO Trudeau Soc 1986-87; fellow Amer Coll of Chest Physicians 1984; partic Pulmonary Physicians of the Future Amer-Coll of Chest Physicians 1983; fellow Amer Coll Physic; sec Council of Chapter Representatives Amer Lung Assoc 1986-87. **HONORS/ACHIEVEMENTS:** Guild of St Ansgar Hon Soc Gustavus Adolphus Coll 1970; Fellowship Awd Amer Lung Assoc NY 1977-79; Cecile Lehman Mayer Rsch Awd Amer Coll of Chest Physicians 1979; 1st Decade Awd for Outstanding Achievement Gustavus Adolphus Coll 1980; numerous publs. **BUSINESS ADDRESS:** Dir, Natl Jewish Ctr for Immunology, 1400 Jackson St, Denver, CO 80206.

KING, WARREN EARL
Controls engineer. **PERSONAL:** Born Jul 09, 1947, Durham, NC; married Hiawatha Mechall Jackson; children: Justin Christopher. **EDUCATION:** Purdue Univ, BSE 1976; Indiana Univ, MBA 1987. **CAREER:** US Postal Svcs, distrib clerk 1970-72; Delco Remy Div of GMC, project engr 1976-87; Hewlett Packard Co, prod mgr 1987-. **ORGANIZATIONS:** Subscribing life mem NAACP 1984; chmn rules & bylaws comm CASA/SME 1984; mem Natl Black MBA Assoc 1985. **HONORS/ACHIEVEMENTS:** Consortium Fellow Grad Study in Mgmt Indiana Univ 1985-87. **MILITARY SERVICE:** USMC staff sgt 1966-70; Avionics Communications/Navigation Meritorious Commandetions; Vietnam Combat Air Crewman. **HOME ADDRESS:** 7934 No Richard St, Indianapolis, IN 46256.

KING, WESLEY A.
Surgeon. **PERSONAL:** Born Sep 25, 1923, Napoleonville, LA; son of Dr & Mrs Wesley King Sr; married Barbara Johnson; children: Robin, Wesley, Jan, Erik. **EDUCATION:** Dillard Univ, AB 1943; Howard Univ, MD 1956. **CAREER:** Meharry Med Coll Inst of Surgery, surgeon 1955-57; USC Med School, assoc prof clin surgery 1974; LA Cty USC Med Ctr, attending surgeon 1967-. **ORGANIZATIONS:** Mem LA County Med Assn, Amer Med Assn; mem bd mgrs Crenshaw YMCA 1972; past junior warden Christ the Good Shepherd Episcopal Church; founding bd mem The Good Shepherd Manor; mem Phi Beta Sigma; fellow Amer Coll Surgeons. **HONORS/ACHIEVEMENTS:** Better Businessman's Awd 1962; Certified by Amer Bd of Surgery 1958. **MILITARY SERVICE:** AUS sgt 1943-46. **BUSINESS ADDRESS:** 5260 S Figueroa St, Ste 208, Los Angeles, CA 90037.

KING, WILLIAM CARL
Dentist. **PERSONAL:** Born Nov 29, 1930, Albany, GA; married Rosaria Thomas; children: Sarita, Sarmora. **EDUCATION:** Paine Coll, BA; Meharry Med Coll, DT, DDS. **CAREER:** Val Comm Coll, adv dentl hyg 1977; Private Practice, dentist. **ORGANIZATIONS:** Mem Central Dist Dental Soc, ADA, NDA, FL Med Dental Phar Assoc, FL Dental Assoc; bd of trustees Valencia Comm Coll 1971-75; treas Goodwill Ind of FL; Handicap advis bd FL; pres Handicap Wrkshp; KC first clncl dentist in Health Dept 1966-67. **HONORS/ACHIEVEMENTS:** Acad of Dentstry Aw Am Soc of children 1966; Excell Schlrshp Alpha Omega Frat 1966; Schlrshp Aw Chi Delta Mu Frat 1966; Certificate of Appreciation Awd FL Dept of Educ 1977. **MILITARY SERVICE:** AUS capt 1960. **BUSINESS ADDRESS:** 809 Goldwyn, Orlando, FL 32805.

KING, WILLIAM J.
Clergyman. **PERSONAL:** Born Jul 21, 1921, Selma, AL; son of Joseph King and Lillian King; children: 3. **EDUCATION:** Talladega Coll, AB 1943; Howard Univ School of Religion, MDiv 1946; Eden Theological Seminary, exchange student from Howard Univ 1946. **CAREER:** Shiloh Baptist Church, pastor; private practice, licensed counselor; USAF, chaplain 1951-73; Third Baptist Church, pastor 1946-51; interim pastor, Antioch Progressive Church Trinity Missionary Baptist Church. **ORGANIZATIONS:** Natl Baptist Convention Inc Chicago; Amer Assn of Marriage & Family Counselors; CA State Assn of Marriage Counselors; mem Natl Alliance for Family Life Inc; Alpha Phi Alpha Fraterity. **MILITARY SERVICE:** USAF chaplain 1951-73; retired colonel 1973.

KING, WILLIAM L.
Minister. **PERSONAL:** Born Jun 15, 1933, Jacksonville, FL; son of Theodore King, Jr and Ellawese Jackson King Robinson; divorced; children: Kendall, Theodore, III, Kyleen. **EDUCATION:** Rutgers Univ, New Brunswick NJ, AB, 1972; Lutheran Theological Seminary, Philadelphia PA, MA, 1984, MA Div, 1985; Lancaster Theological Seminary, Lancaster PA, DMin, 1989. **CAREER:** Mt Calvary Baptist Church, Camden NJ, asst minister, 1963-64; Shiloh Baptist Church, Bordentown NJ, minister, 1965-73; NJ Dept of Labor, Camden NJ, counselor, 1967-89; Calvary United Church of Christ, Philadelphia PA, minister, 1974-. **ORGANIZATIONS:** Pres, Young Peoples Dept, pres, parent body, New Light Missionary Baptist Union; pres Baptist Training Union, Bethany Baptist Assoc; sec/treasurer, United Black Christian United Church of Christ; pres, Camden County Branch NAACP; sec, NJ State Conference NAACP Branches; mem, bd of dir, Urban League of PA; mem, bd of dir, UNCF bd of dir; chairman, bd of dir, OIC, Southern NJ. **HONORS/ACHIEVEMENTS:** US Wiggins Presidential Award, NAACP, 1984; Outstanding Membership Award, NAACP, 1988; Award of Appreciation, NAACP, 1989; Citation NJ State Senate, 1989; Citation NJ General Assembly, 1989; Distinguished Leadership Award, UNCF, 1989. **MILITARY SERVICE:** US Army, pfc, 1953-56. **HOME ADDRESS:** 3041 Mickle Street, Camden, NJ 08105.

KING, WILLIAM MOSES
Physician. **PERSONAL:** Born Jul 13, 1927, Philadelphia, PA; children: William Michael, Eric William. **EDUCATION:** Univ of MI, BS1952; PA Coll Osteopathic Med, DO 1962. **CAREER:** Gemedco Family Med Ctr, physician; Nat Heart, biochemist. **ORGANIZATIONS:** Mem AOA 1964-; mem PA Osteo Assn 1964-; mem Philadelphia Osteo Assn 1964-; mem NAACP; mem Alpha Phi Alpha. **HONORS/ACHIEVEMENTS:** Army Commendation Ribbon AUS 1947-48; Honor Soc Phi Eta Sigma MIUniv 1949; Honor Soc Phi Kappa Phi MIUniv 1952; Honor Soc Phi Beta Kappa MIUniv 1952. **MILITARY SERVICE:** AUS tech 4 3yrs. **BUSINESS ADDRESS:** Gemedco Family Med Center, 5801 Chew Avenue, Philadelphia, PA 19138.

KING, WOODIE, JR.
Film/play producer & director. **PERSONAL:** Born Jul 27, 1937, Alabama; son of Woodie King and Ruby; married Willie Mae, Nov 04, 1959; children: Michelle, Woodie Geoffrey, Michael. **EDUCATION:** Will-O-Way Sch of Theater, grad. **CAREER:** Concept-E Theatre Detroit, founded & mgr 1960-63; Detroit Tribune, drama critic 1959-62; Concept E Theatre Detroit, dir plays 1960-63; Mobiliz for Youth, cultural arts dir 1965-70; Henry Street's New Federal Theatre of NY, founder/dir, 1970-; Woodie King Assoc, pres; Natl Black Touring Circuit, producer & founder. **ORGANIZATIONS:** Natl Theatre Conf; Soc of Stage Dirs & Choreographers; Audelco; Theatre Communications Group; Assn for Study of Negro Life & History; Black Filmmakers Found. **HONORS/ACHIEVEMENTS:** John Hay Whitney Fellowship for directing 1965-66; Ford Found Grant for filmmaking; Theatre Award, NAACP; Audelco Award for best dir; dir of 17 plays; producer of more than 20 plays; dir & co-producer of film, The Long Night, 1976; author or co-author of 6 screenplays; author, Black Theatre: Present Condition, 1982; author of feature articles in magazines; editor of 5 books of plays, short stories & poems. **HOME ADDRESS:** 417 Convent Ave, New York, NY 10031.

KING, YOLANDA D.
Actress/producer/lecturer. **CAREER:** Nucleus (performing arts company), co-director w/ Attallah Shabazz; King Center, dir of cultural affairs. **ORGANIZATIONS:** Lecturer on

civil rights, politics, and the arts before various organizations. **HOME ADDRESS:** 14 Washington Pl #9E, New York, NY 10003.

KING-HAMMOND, LESLIE
Educational administrator, lecturer, curator, consultant. **PERSONAL:** Born Aug 04, 1944, Bronx, NY; divorced; children: Rassaan-Jamil. **EDUCATION:** Seek Grant Queens College, 1966-69; Queens College CUNY, BA 1969; Horizon Fellowship, 1969-73; Kress Fellowship, 1974-75; The Johns Hopkins Univ, MA 1973, PhD 1975. **CAREER:** Performing Arts Workshops of Queens, New York, NY, chair dept of art, 1969-71; HARYOU-ACT, Inc, Harlem, NY, program writer, 1971; MD Institute, College of Art, lecturer 1973-, dean of grad studies 1976-; Corcoran School of Art, lecturer 1977, visiting faculty 1982; Howard Univ, Dept of African Studies, doctoral supervisor, 1977-81; Civic Design Commission Baltimore City, commissioner 1983-. **ORGANIZATIONS:** Panelist, Natl Endowment for the Humanities 1978-80; panelist Natl Endowment for the Arts 1980-82; mem bd Baltimore School for the Arts 1984-; mem Natl Conf of Artist, College Art Association; mem bd Community Foundation of Greater Baltimore 1984-; consult MD Arts Council 1985-; mem bd Art Commission, Baltimore City, Office of the Mayor, 1988. **HONORS/ACHIEVEMENTS:** Guest curator, awarded Mellon Grant, Vantage of Dreams Deferred, Baltimore Museum of Art 1979; published Celebrations: Myth & Ritual in Afro-American Art, Studio Museum in Harlem, 1982; Wellon Grant for Faculty Research, MD Institute, College of Art, 1984; guest curator, The Intuitive Eye, MD Art Place 1985; Trustee Award for Excellence in Teaching 1986; co curator, Woman of the Year 1986, Women's Art Caucus, 1986; Mellon Grant for faculty research, 1987; curator, 18 Visions/Divisions, Eubie Blake Cultural Center and Museum, 1988; co curator, Art as a Verb: The Evolving Continuum, 1988; curator, Black Printmakers and the WPA, Lehman Gallery of Art, 1989; exhibited Hale Woodruff Biennial, Studio Museum in Harlem, 1989. **BUSINESS ADDRESS:** Dean of Graduate Studies, Maryland Inst Coll of Art, 1300 W Mt Royal Ave, Baltimore, MD 21217.

KINGI, HENRY MASAO
Stunt man. **PERSONAL:** Born Dec 02, 1943, Los Angeles, CA; married Eilene; children: Henry, Jr, Deanne. **EDUCATION:** Motion Pictures, stunt coordinator, "Bionic Woman, stuntman, actor, model. **CAREER:** Mem bd dirs founder Black Fashion Mag "Elegant" 1963; mgr 1st major Black Pvt Key Club Maverick's Flat, CA; #Organizer mem The Coalition of Black Stuntman's Assn Hollywood; sec mem Soc 10th Cavalry Buffalo Soldiers; NAACP chmn Labor & Industry Com co-chmn Motion Picture Com; PUSH; CORE Worked with Image. **HONORS/ACHIEVEMENTS:** Awards to get Blacks in motion pictures; Image Award 10th Cavalry Cowboy Hall Fame; Image Award Black Stuntman's Assn.

KINLOCH, JEROME
Community developer. **PERSONAL:** Born Mar 28, 1943, Charleston, SC. **EDUCATION:** Coll of Charleston, brdcsting Sch. **ORGANIZATIONS:** Mem Chrlston Counc Shaws Boy Club; Grassroot Coalit; Nat Blck Soc Wrkr; Chrlstn Indsl Educ Bd; Comm Agnst Racm and Polit Repress; Chrlstn LibPty. **HONORS/ACHIEVEMENTS:** Outstanding Yg Man of Am 1975; award for Polit Action Mu Alpha 1976; Outstanding Yg Man CIEC. **BUSINESS ADDRESS:** 86 Drake St, Charleston, SC.

KINNAIRD, MICHAEL LEON
Educational administrator. **PERSONAL:** Born Jul 12, 1945, Indiana; married Kathryn Gaertner; children: Eric Michael. **EDUCATION:** ScottsbluffColl, AA 1967; Chadron State Coll, BS Educ 1969; No AZ U, MA 1973. **CAREER:** Opportunity Sch Clark Co Sch Dist, prin 1978-; Jim Bridger Jr H Clark Co Sch Dist, asst prin 1973-78, admin asst 1972-73, dean 1971-72, tchr 1970-71. **ORGANIZATIONS:** Treas PDK Chap 1113 1979-80; pres Clark Co Assn of Sch Adminstrn 1977-78; treas Clark Co Secondary Prin Assn 1976-77; mem Phi Delta Kappa Chap 1113 1974; mem Nat Assn of Secondary Prin 1973. **HONORS/ACHIEVEMENTS:** Appreciation for Continued Support Am Afro Unity Festival Las Vegas, NV 1978. **BUSINESS ADDRESS:** Clark Co Sch Dist, 2832 E Flamingo Rd, Las Vegas, NV 89121.

KINNEY, EDNA M.
Public employee. **PERSONAL:** Born Dec 09, 1905, Savannah, GA; divorced; children: Jacqueline M (hodge). **EDUCATION:** Hunter Coll; NY U; Miller U, grad 1968. **CAREER:** Mt Olivet Bapt Ch, sec 1933-48; Henry W Payne Funeral Home, mgr 1948-49; Dept Health Adminstr, employee 1949-72; Prince Hall Sentinel, women's editor 1938-65. **ORGANIZATIONS:** Mem numerous coms offices Mt Olivet Bapt Ch; William Stanley J Ones Tabernalce of Moses; Iota Phi Lambda Sor; Vocational Guidane & Workshop Center; Orderof Cyrenes PHA; Nat Council Negro Women; Bapt Educ Center; Harlem Teams for Self Help; Commn for Status of Black Women; ARC; Omicron Chap Iota Phi Lambda Sor IBPOE of W; NAACP. **HONORS/ACHIEVEMENTS:** Numerous certificates, awards, honors.

KINNIEBREW, ROBERT LEE
Real estate company executive. **PERSONAL:** Born Feb 13, 1942, Manhattan, NY; son of Covton Kinniebrew and Daisy Crawford Cobb; married Raymona D Radford, Nov 30, 1963; children: Robertina, Rolanzo. **EDUCATION:** Acad of Aeron NY; Commun School AUS; Non-Commiss Officers Acad Bad Toelz West Germany; Officers Candidate School Commiss Second Lt Artillery Ft Sill OK; Ins Underwriter's School PA; MW Funk Sales Inst Real Estate NJ; South Jersey Realty Abstract Sales Schooll NJ; Grad Realtors Inst NJ; Natl Assoc of Independent Fee Appraisers NJ; Mgmt Devel Course Washington DC. **CAREER:** Veterans Admin, mgmt broker; Fed Housing Admin, mgmt broker; Vet Admin, appraiser; Mututal of NY Ins Co, dir sales underwriter; Protect A Life Burglar Alarm Co, dir sales; jewelry store chain, dir sales; Gen Sound in Philadelphia, customer relations mgr; Westinghouse, mgr lighting dept; Fort Dix NJ, post signal, oper & commanding officer; Fort Bliss TX & Viet-Nam, battalion commun officer; AUS West Germany, pole lineman, fixed station transmitter repairman 1963-65; Lockheed Aircraft Co Idlewild Airport, flight line mechanic; Century 21 Candid Realty Inc, pres 1972-. **ORGANIZATIONS:** Mem Edgewater Park Jaycees, Burlington Cty Draft Bd, Burlington Cty Chamber of Commerce, Masonic Lodge, Century 21 Brokers' Council of South Jersey, Beverly Rotary Club, Boy Scouts of Amer, Make Amer Better Comm, Natl Assoc of Realtors; bd mem Burlington Cty Red Cross; chap chmn Burlington Cty Red Cross; exec comm Burlington Cty Red Cross; chmn Burlington Cty Red Cross Blood Program, Blood Drive Edgewater Park & Beverly Comm; rep Century 21 Natl Brokers' Commun Congress; pres, dir Burlington Cty Bd of Realtors; dir NJ State Bd of Realtors; dir, Natl Assn of Realtors; legal action comm, Natl Assn of Realtors; nominating comm, equal opportunity comm, library comm, legal action comm, New Jersey Assn of Realtors. **HONORS/ACHIEVEMENTS:** Community Serv Awd Burlington Cty Bd of Realtors 1983; Realtor of the Year Awd NJ State Assoc of Realtors 1983. **MILITARY SERVICE:** Comm Chf 101st Airbn Div 327th Battle Grp; 10th Spec Forces Bad Toelz, Germ 1962; Comm 2nd Lt Battal Comm Ofcr 1st Battal 44th Artillery Ft Bliss. **BUSINESS ADDRESS:** Pres, Century 21 Candid Realty Inc, Route 130, South Edgewater Park, PO Box 567, Edgewater Park, NJ 08046.

KIRBY, JACQUELINE
Physician. **PERSONAL:** Born Dec 17, 1946, Atlanta, GA; married Edward G Helm; children: Lisa. **EDUCATION:** Spelman Coll, BA 1968; Meharry Med Coll, MD 1973. **CAREER:** EmoryUniv Affiliated Hosps, fellow rheumatology 1977-, internal med 1974-76, med internship 1973-74; externship 1972; Harvard U, rsrch & fellow 1971; Crawford W Long Hosp, emergency room physician 1976-77. **ORGANIZATIONS:** Mem YWCA 1973; asso mem Am Coll of Physicians. **HONORS/ACHIEVEMENTS:** Research Fellow HarvardUniv 1971; honor Dept of Pharmcacology 1971; fellow EmoryUniv 1977.

KIRBY, MONEY ALIAN
Social services consultant. **PERSONAL:** Born Aug 08, 1914, Biscoe, AR; married Ann Ida Wall; children: Mattye Jo Willis, Ollie L, Scott. **EDUCATION:** Philander Smith Coll, BA Mus 1950; SoUniv Baton Rouge, La, Spec-Std-M Us 1953; UAPB Pine Bluff, AR Spec Std-Media 1968; SAU Magnolia AR 1965-84. **CAREER:** S AR-Conf CME Chch, exec-secty 1974-84; Foster High Schl Lewisville AR, bnd dir 1960-64; Walker High Schl Magnolia AR, bnd-soc stds 1965-84. **ORGANIZATIONS:** Pres Columbia-cty Techers Assoc 1966; dir Evangelism CME Church So-conf 1980-82; Special Edu Teachers AEA 1983-84; dir Socials-Concern-CME Ch-So-AR Conf 1983-85; pres Walker Schl Dist "AEA Techr" 1982-84; pres Philander Smith Coll "Magnolia Alumni" 1980-85; pres Columbia Cty NAACP 1985-. **HONORS/ACHIEVEMENTS:** Spl recgt awd NEA-PAC Fundg 1981-82; outstndg cont ed Aug 4 1984 awd Peake High Schl Classes 1957-59; outstndg tchg serv awd Walker Schl Brd andAdmin May 22, 1984. **MILITARY SERVICE:** USNA duty corp T-5 4-7 mo; Good-Conduct, Sharp Shooter, Service Strips 1941-45. **HOME ADDRESS:** 615 Gantt St, Magnolia, AR 71753. **BUSINESS ADDRESS:** Social Services Consultant, S Conf CME Ch, 615 Gantt St, Magnolia, AR 71753.

KIRBY, NANCY J.
Educational administrator. **PERSONAL:** Born Apr 20, 1940, Haddonfield, NJ. **EDUCATION:** Bennett Coll, BA Psych 1960; Bryn Mawr Coll, MSS 1965. **CAREER:** Temple Univ Med Ctr, chief social worker outpatient medicine 1966-69; Planned Parenthood of SE PA, dir of soc serv 1969-71; Beaver Coll, asst prof 1971-79; Bryn Mawr Coll, asst dean, dir of admissions 1979-. **ORGANIZATIONS:** Bd of dirs Planned Parenthood of SEPA 1974-78; bd of dirs Family Planning Council of SEPA 1979-85; bd of dirs Spectrum Health Serv 1978-; bd of dir Natl Assn of Social Workers (PA Chapt) 1986-. **BUSINESS ADDRESS:** Asst Dean & Dir of Admission, Bryn Mawr College, Graduate School Of Social Work, & Social Research, Bryn Mawr, PA 19010.

KIRK, LEROY W.
Government official. **PERSONAL:** Born Apr 12, 1924, Tulsa, OK; son of Leroy W Kirk Sr and Mary Payne; married Annie M Brown; children: Leroy W III, Annette. **EDUCATION:** Langston Univ, BS 1948; Univ IL, MS 1949. **CAREER:** Moton HS, principal 1949-50; Ponca City, math dept head 1950-53; Dunbar Jr HS, principal 1953-56; Tinker AFB, computer programmer/system analyst 1956-67, discrimination complaints officer 1967-85; State Bd Corrections, sec 1971-79, pres 1985-87, member 1971-; Real Estate Rentals 1982-. **ORGANIZATIONS:** Pres OK City Urban League 1978-81; active Local Boy Scouts of Amer; deacon St John Baptist Church; life mem NAACP; mem Langston Univ Alumni Assn, YMCA, Langston Univ Boosters Club. **HONORS/ACHIEVEMENTS:** Outstanding Performance Awards 1967, 1976; Achievement Awards Kappa Alpha Psi Fraternity; chief EEO couns Dept Air Force 1979-; OK Fed Employee of the Year 1982. **MILITARY SERVICE:** USN 1943-46. **BUSINESS ADDRESS:** President, State Bd of Corrections, 3400 N Martin Luther King Bl, Oklahoma City, OK 73117.

KIRK, ORVILLE
Educator. **PERSONAL:** Born Mar 05, 1936, St Louis, MO; married Joyce; children: Orville Jr, Gerald, Ronald. **EDUCATION:** Wiley Coll, BA 1953-57; Harris Tchrs Coll, MO elem cert 1965; St Louis U, MO Spl Educ Cert 1967, MEd 1970, post masters work educ splst degree 1972, resident student 1973, supt cert 1973-. **CAREER:** MO Dept of Elementary & Secondary Educ, supvr Title I ESEA 1976-, speciall educ consult 1972-76; Univ of MO, rsch tech 1971-72; St Louis Baby Study Project CEMREL, resch tech 1968-71; St Louis Public School Sys, tchr 1961-72; Urban Behav Rsch Asso, consult 1973-77; Acad of Urban Serv, consultant 1973-77. **ORGANIZATIONS:** Pres Chap 103 Counc for Except Children 1975-76; mem Counc of Admnstr of Spl Edn; mem Counc of Children with Behav Disorders; mem Counc for Execpt Children; bd of dir The Annie Malone Children's Home; mem Counc of Mental Retardation CEC-MR. **MILITARY SERVICE:** AUS spec 4 c 1959-61. **BUSINESS ADDRESS:** PO Box 480, Jefferson City, MO.

KIRK, PHYLLIS O. (NEE WILLIAMS)
Caseworker. **PERSONAL:** Born Feb 27, 1943, Milwaukee, WI; divorced; children: Jacqualine, Michael, Kevin. **EDUCATION:** Univ of WI, BA 1974, working on masters. **CAREER:** Baker House, case worker 1977; Self Help Coalition, case worker 1975; Comm Rel, Soc Devel Agy, CAP Agy, planner 1973; Corp for Corrections, tchr 1972-74; HEW, 1970; Epworth Ch, comm orgnzer 1969; Concentrated Emplmt Prog, 1967. **ORGANIZATIONS:** Dir Oper Breadbasket 1973-74; consult Delaney & Asso 1970-77; consult YWCA 1977; pres Parent Act Grp Headstart Prog 1965; mem Bd on Govtl Oper 1966-68; tchr Our House Comm Ctr 1970; mem bd Epworth Meth Ch 1964-71; mem bd Youth Serv Bur 1974-76; Dem Party ran for 4th Aldermanic Ward 1972; ran for 26thAsmby of State 1976; affirmative Act ofcr 26th Assby Dist 1974-; affmtv act ofcr Milwaukee Co Counc 1976-; del State Conv 1974-77; 5th Congr Caucus 1975-77; Nat Conv 1976; exec bd Milwaukee Co Dem Party Co Counc; mem 513 com 1975. **HONORS/ACHIEVEMENTS:** Del Women's & Intl Yr 1977; Comm Serv Awd 1976; HUD fellshp 1975; Outstd People of Comm 1975; Concern Consumers cert; Fcert Women of Colored Mgmt Conf 1974; Gov Comm Awd 1967; wrote black women column Milwaukee Star Times Newspaper 1976; mastes flwhpUniv of Milwaukee 1975.

KIRK, SARAH VIRGO
Educator, social worker. **PERSONAL:** Born Oct 19, 1934, Kingston, Jamaica;daughter of David Virgo and Velmon Virgo; married Dr Wyatt Douglass Kirk. **EDUCATION:** St Augustines Coll Raleigh NC, BA 1955; Atlanta Univ School of Social Work, MSW 1957; Univ of Pittsburgh School of Public Health, MS Public Health 1972; Univ of Pittsburgh School of Social Work, PhD Social Work 1975. **CAREER:** Meml Hospital Univ of North Carolina, med soc worker 1957-60; Johns Hopkins Hosp, med soc worker 1960-63; Public Health Grant, rsch team mem 1964-66; Dept of Public Welfare Work Training Ctr, soc work supv 1967, soc work supv public health adolescent program 1967, chief soc worker orthopedic prog 1968; Howard Univ School of Soc Work, asst prof 1969-71; School of Work Univ of Pennsylvania instr 1972-74; Three Rivers Youth, rsch asst 1975; School of Soc Work Virginia Commonwealth Univ, asst prof 1975-77; Western Michigan Univ School of Soc Work, asst prof 1977-78; North Carolina A&T State Univ, assoc prof, field coord 1978-79, assoc prof social work, chairperson Dept of Sociology & Social Work 1982-. **ORGANIZATIONS:** Treasure Triad Assoc of Human Serv 1978-84; chairperson North Carolina Council on Social Work Education 1983-84; mem Womens Professional Forum 1986-; bd mem Family Life Council Greensboro North Carolina 1986-87; bd mem Commiss on the States of Women 1987. **HONORS/ACHIEVEMENTS:** Co-author "Counseling, Black Family Involvement" Journal of Elementary School Guidance and Counseling 1981; inducted into Departments Hall of Fame 1989. **HOME ADDRESS:** 5303 Broadmoor Pl, Greensboro, NC 27410. **BUSINESS ADDRESS:** Chairperson, NC A&T StateUniv, Dept of Sociology, Social Wrk, Greensboro, NC 27411.

KIRK, WYATT D.
Educator. **PERSONAL:** Born May 10, 1935, Elgin, IL; married Dr Sarah Virgo Kirk. **EDUCATION:** Western MI U, BA 1963; Western MI U, MA 1969; Western MI U, EdD 1973; Licensed Psycologist 1978; NBCC 1984. **CAREER:** NC A&T State Univ Dept of Human Development & Services, chairperson; Benton Harbor HS, tchr 1963-67; Ft Custer Job Corps, counselor 1967-68; Kalamazoo Pub Sch, counselor 1967-68; Western MI U, counselor 1968-70; Kalamazoo Resources Devel Council, assistance to founder, dir 1968-69; Experimental Program toEmploy Ex-Consult & Drug Users Ford Motor Co Dearborn, consult 1969-71; In-Serv Training Program for Tchr Grand Rapids Pub Sch, consult 1970; Western MI U; assoc prof 1970-78; Staff Relations Kalamazoo Planned Parenthood, consult 1972; Basic Treatment Counseling Techniques for Minorities MI Probate Ct, consult 1975; NC A&T St Univ, professor/chairperson. **ORGANIZATIONS:** Pres elect Amer Assoc for Counseling Dev; Assn Counselor Educ & Sprvsn; MI Personnel & Guidance Assn; MI Coll Personnel Assn; MI and NC Assn for Non-White Concerns; NC Assn Counselor Educ & Supervision; NC Personnel & Guidance Assn; Assn of Black Psychologists; charter mem MI and mem Natl Alliance of Black School Educ; Kappa Alpha Psi Inc; vice pres NAACP; bd mem, treas Churches United Effort; Equal Empl for the Disadvantaged & Minority chrmn; bd of trustees for the Lift Fdn; Inter-Faith Housing Council bd of dir; Greater Kalamazoo Cncl vice chairperson; Kalamazoo Cnty Substance Abuse bd mem; Greater Kalamazoo United Way Allocation & Budget Committeel editorial bd Journal of Multicultural Counseling and Develop; chairperson NC Assoc for Counseling and Develop; mem AMCD Comm. **HONORS/ACHIEVEMENTS:** Listed in Outstanding Young Men of Amer 1973, Who's Who Among Black Amer 1975, Who's Who In The Midwest 1977, Men of Achievement 1978, Personalitites of the West and Midwest 1978, Community Leaders & Noteworth Americans 1978, Notable Americans 1978; MI Personnel & Guidance Assn serv awd 1976; Faculty Research Grant for Scholarly & Creative Research 1977; Presidents Citation, the Natl Assn of Nonwhite Concerns in Personnel & Guidance 1977 & 1978; Assn Counselor Educ& Spvsn recognition awd for successful completion of the Accreditation Workshop Training 1979; grants awds Kalamazoo Fdn Doctoral Research, Grand Rapids Fnd, Title IV Desegregation Inst, Intern, Cmty-Based Alternatives, State of NC, Dept of Human Resources, Managerial Schlrshp Center for Creative Leadership, Greensboro, NC; several publications published & non-published. **BUSINESS ADDRESS:** Professor/Chairperson, Nort Carolina A&T StateUniv, 212 Hodgin Hall, Greensboro, NC 27411.

KIRK-DUGGAN, CHERYL ANN
Minister. **PERSONAL:** Born Jul 24, 1951, Lake Charles, LA; daughter of Rudolph V Krik (deceased) and Naomi R Kirk; married Dr Michael Allan Kirk-Duggan, Jan 01, 1983. **EDUCATION:** Univ of Southwestern Louisiana, BA 1973; Univ of Texas at Austin, MM 1977; Austin Presbyterian Theological Seminary, MDiv 1987. **CAREER:** Univ of Texas at Austin, music of black amers coach accomp 1974-77; Austin Community Coll, music of black amers 1976-77; Prairie View A&M Univ, teacher 1977-78; The Actor's Inst, teacher 1982-83; Williams Inst CME Church, organist/choir dir 1979-83; Self-employed, professional singer, voice teacher, coach 1980-85; Christian Methodist Church, ordained minister, deacons orders 1984, elders orders 1986. **ORGANIZATIONS:** Mem Pi Kappa Lambda Music Honor Soc 1976-; mem Omicron Delta Kappa Leadership Honor Soc 1977-; assoc pastor Trinity CME Church Austin 1985-86; pres Racial Ethnic Faith Comm Austin Seminary 1986-87. **HONORS/ACHIEVEMENTS:** Univ Fellowship, Univ of Texas at Austin 1975-77; Carnegie Hall debut 1981; featured in Life, Black Tress, Das Goldene Blatte, Bunte 1981,82; Third Duke Ellington Sacred Concert recorded with EMI & on Virgil Thompson's Four Saints in Three Acts 1981-82; recipient Fund for Theological Educ Fellowship for Doctoral Studies 1987-88, 1988-89; Graduate Asst, Baylor Univ Inst of Oral History 1987-89; Teaching Asst, Baylor Univ Dept of Religion 1989-90. **HOME ADDRESS:** 117A Romana Circle, Hewitt, TX 76643.

KIRKENDOLL, CHESTER ARTHUR, II
Clergyman. **PERSONAL:** Born Jun 03, 1914, Searcy, AR; married Alice Elizabeth Singleton; children: Chester Arhtur III, Loretta Jean, Leland Kapel. **EDUCATION:** Lane Coll, BA 1938; Northwestern Univ Evanston IL, MA 1941; TX Coll Tyler, LittD 1957; St Andrews Seminary London England, DD 1962; MS Industrial Coll, DD 1971; Lane Coll Jackson, LHD 1972; Interdenominational Theol Ctr, DD 1982; Miles Coll, Hon Doctorate 1984. **CAREER:** Natl Youth Work CME Church, dir 1935-40; Natl Leadership Training School, dir, assoc ed church school publ 1940-50; Lane Coll, pres 1950-70; Christian Methodist Episcopal Church, bishop; Christian Methodist Episcopal Church, retired sr bishop 1970-86. **ORGANIZATIONS:** Mem, bd of dir United Negro Coll Fund Inc 1950-70; mem TN Council of Human Relations 1961-70, Jackson Comm Relations Bd 1964-70, Natl Advisory Councilon Student Aid to the US Dept of Health Ed & Welfare 1966-70, TN Higher Ed Comm 1966-70; delegate World Methodist Conf 1966,71,76,81; chmn bd of trustees Miles Coll 1970-82; delegate 5th Assembly World Council of Churches 1975; recording sec Governing Bd Natl Council of Churches 1978-81; mem 33 Degree Masonic Order 1983; mem Christian Meth Episcopal Church, Natl Assoc for the Advancement for Colored People; bd of trustees Phillips School of Theol Interdenom Theol Ctr; Natl Advisory Council Amer Bible Soc, Natl Council Birm Area Boy Scout of Amer; recording sec Natl Council of Churches of Christ; mem Central Comm World Council of Churches; chmn v chmn Gen Bd of Evangelism CME Church; mem Governing Bd Natl Council of Churches of Christ in Amer; mem bdof dir Birm Big Brothers of Greater Birmg Inc,Travelers Aid Soc, Volunteer Bureau of Greater Birmingham Inc. **HONORS/ACHIEVEMENTS:** Community Chest Campaign Awd 1951; Man of the Year Awd Omega Psi Phi Frat 1953; Citation by Amer LFW 1953; Award of Merit The Clara Maas Found 1962, Citation by West TN Teachers Conf 1964; Col-Aide-De Camp Governor's Staff TN 1967; author of, "The Obligation of the Church in the Field of Higher Ed During the Current Revolution" 1967; Citation by City of Jackson TN 1970; Citation by State of TN as Disting Citizen 1970; Disting Serv Awd Booker T Washington BusinessColl 1971; Isaac Lane Awds Lane Coll Alumni Assoc 1971; Disting Serv Awd Boy Scouts of Amer 1975; B Julian Smith Awd for Disting Serv in Christian Ed 1976; Beaver Awd Boy Scouts of Amer 1980. **HOME ADDRESS:** 10 Hurtland, Jackson, TN 38305.

KIRKLAND, CORNELL R.
Chief executive of bank. **CAREER:** Enterprise Savings & Loan Association, Long Beach CA, chief executive, 1989. **BUSINESS ADDRESS:** Enterprise Savings & Loan Association, 304 East Pacific Coast Highway, Long Beach, CA 90806. *

KIRKLAND, GAIL ALICIA
Orthodontist. **PERSONAL:** Born Apr 12, 1960, Tuskegee, AL; daughter of Dr Levi S Kirkland Sr and Mrs Mary L Pratt Kirkland. **EDUCATION:** Vanderbilt Univ, BS (Cum Laude) 1982; Howard Univ Coll of Dentistry, DDS (class rank # 1) 1986, Certificate in Orthodontics 1986-88. **CAREER:** Orthodontist. **ORGANIZATIONS:** Mem Alpha Kappa Alpha Sor 1979-; mem Alumni Assn of Student Clinicians of Amer Dental Assn 1985; mem Omicron Kappa Upsilon 1986-, Natl Dental Assn 1986-; American Assn of Orthodontics 1986-. **HONORS/ACHIEVEMENTS:** Deans Award Alpha Omega Natl Soc 1986; Scholarship Award for #1 Class Rank 1986; Intl Coll of Dentists Award 1986; Harold S Fleming Memorial Award for Dental Rsch 1986; Orthodontic Award for Superior Performance in Research, Howard Univ 1988; author of Forensic Dentistry: Solving the mysteries of identification, General Dentistry, 35:120, 1987; Changing Anatomical Developments in Permanent 1st Bicuspid Teeth, Journal of Dental Research, 65 (Abstracts):188, 1986. **HOME ADDRESS:** 8201 16th St #110, Silver Spring, MD 20910. **BUSINESS ADDRESS:** 65 Michigan Avenue, NE, Washington, DC 20002.

KIRKLAND, GLORIA
Educator. **PERSONAL:** Born Aug 29, 1952, Charleston, SC. **EDUCATION:** Fisk U, BA 1974; IN State U, MS 1975, PhD 1978. **CAREER:** Univ of No IA, asst prof early childhood educ & dept of tching 1978-; Rose Southside Child Care Cntr, dir 1976-78; IN State U, adj asst prof 1976-78; IN State Lab Sch, nursery tchr 1978; Maehling Terrace Day Care Cntr, dir tchr 1976; Margaret Ave Child Care Center, asst dir parent coord 1975-76. **ORGANIZATIONS:** Mem Nat Assn for the Educ of Young Children 1975-; mem IA Assn ofr the Educ of Young Children 1975-; chairperson sec IA NE State Conf NAACP 1979-; chairperson program com Proj headstart 1979-; mem Black Child Devel Inst 1977; bd mem Logandale Urban Housing Corp 1979-; youth adv Black Hawk Co NAACP Youth Group 1979-. **HONORS/ACHIEVEMENTS:** Who's Who Among Students in Am Coll & U, IN StateUniv 1976; Achievement of Knowledge Afro-Am Cultural Cntr & Black Student Union IN StateUniv 1977; Outstanding Yng Women of Am, Outstanding Yng Women 1977; 10 Top Min Women in IA appointed by Gov Ray 1980; Alpha Kappa Alpha Sor Pi Chap FiskUniv 1971. **BUSINESS ADDRESS:** Associate Professor, Univeristy of Northern Iowa, Price Lab School, 19th & Campus Streets, Cedar Falls, IA 50613.

KIRKLAND, JACK A.
Educator, consultant. **PERSONAL:** Born Oct 28, 1931, Blythedale, PA; son of Aaron and Anna; married Iris; children: Jack, Jr, Adrianne, Kelly. **EDUCATION:** Syracuse Univ, BA 1959; Syracuse Univ, MSS 1961. **CAREER:** Washington Univ, counselor of social work, professor; Washington Univ St Louis, former asso prof & dir of black studies, social work 1970-74; St Louis Univ, asst prof social work 1964-70; consult to bd of edn, children's homes, neighborhood self help groups, state dept of pub welfare & many others; serves on several bds of dirs and is a natl and intl consultant in economic devel. **ORGANIZATIONS:** Former mem bd educ Univ City MO 1967-70; Phi Delta Kappa End Honorary Soc; mem editorials bd Child Care Quarterly Spring Valley NY 1970; Focus/MidwestJournal St Louis 1971. **BUSINESS ADDRESS:** Assoc Prof of Social Work, Washington University, Box 1196, St Louis, MO 63136.

KIRKLAND, THEODORE
Commissioner. **PERSONAL:** Born Jan 01, 1934, Camden, SC; married Winona; children: Sharon, Adrianne, Cynthia. **EDUCATION:** State Univ of NY, BA 1976; State Univ of NY at Buffalo, MS 1984. **CAREER:** NY Police Dept, police Ofcr 1962-78; WKBW-TV, Buffalo,TV host & producer of "Kirkland & Co" 1974-78; NY State Parole Brd, comm 1978-85; Hunter College &Cora P Maloney Coll Buffalo, prof. **ORGANIZATIONS:** Edtrl wrtr Buffalo Black Newspaper (Challenger 1985; brd mem Harlem Restoration Proj 1985; brd mem NY State Civil Liberties Union 1985; mem Natl Assn of Blacks in Criminal Justice 1985; pres & fndr Afro-Amer Police Assn of Buffalo 1969-71; chrtr mem Natl Black Police Assoc 1972; fellow Buffalo State Coll Comm 1984. **HONORS/ACHIEVEMENTS:** Testimonal dinner by Concern Citizens in 1973 & 1983; published article A Black Policemans Perspective on Law Enfrcmnt 1977; more than 30 Awards & Citations between 1970 & present; Presidential Citation for Exceptional Service 1972. **MILITARY SERVICE:** USAAF airman first class 1952-56; United Nations Service Medal, Natl Defense Medal, Good Conduct Medal, Korean Service Medal 1952-56. **HOME ADDRESS:** 352 Pratt St, Buffalo, NY 14204. **BUSINESS ADDRESS:** Professor, Hunter Coll/Cora Maloney Coll, 68th & Lexington, Room 1111 West Building, New York, NY 10021.

KIRKLIN, PERRY WILLIAM
Scientist. **PERSONAL:** Born Feb 28, 1935, Ellwood City, PA; son of Perry Kirklin and Martha Peek Kirklin; married Betty Jean Lampkins; children: Cheryl Hawkins, Perry W III, Pamela. **EDUCATION:** Westminster Coll, BS. **CAREER:** Rohm & Haas Co, analyst group leader 1964-70; Mobil research & Dev Corp, sr Research chemist 1970-78, assoc chemist 1978-; Aviation Fuels Research Leader, 1978-. **ORGANIZATIONS:** Adjunct Prof Bucks County Comm Coll 1976-77; chmn Amer Soc for Testing and Materials Aviation Fuel Stability 1984-; chmn Buckes County Health Planning 1968-72; bd of dir Ph Regional Comprehensive Health Planning 1968-74; mem PA State Health Planning Council 1970-74; vice

pres Salem Fed Credit Union 1972-; bd of dirs Bucks County Comm Center 1965-; mem Salem Baptist Church Jenkingtown PA 1968-; Natl Org Black Chemists & Chem Engineers, 1979-; pres, Salem Federal Credit Union, 1986-. **HONORS/ACHIEVEMENTS:** Numerous technical articles published; numerous technical journals 1964-; PA Regional Introduction of Minorities to Engineering Award, 1988. **HOME ADDRESS:** 1860 Hillside Rd, Southampton, PA 18966. **BUSINESS ADDRESS:** Associate Chemistry, Mobil Res & Dev Corp, Billingsport Rd, Paulsboro, NJ 08066.

KIRKPATRICK, GARLAND PENN
Physician. **PERSONAL:** Born Aug 23, 1932, Chicago, IL; married Dorothy; children: Garland Jr, Dawn. **EDUCATION:** Talladega Coll, AB 1954; Univ of IL Coll of Med, BS 1956, MD 1958; Cook Cty Hosp, intern 1959; Univ IL Rsch & Ed Hosp, resd 1959-61. **CAREER:** Kirkpatrick & Germain SC, pres; Northwestern Univ Med School, pediatrician; Childrens Mem Hosp, pediatrician; Michael Reese Med Ctr, pediatrician; Private practice, 1963-; Chicago Bd of Health, medical serv provider 1984-; Northwestern Univ Med Sch, asst clinical prof. **ORGANIZATIONS:** Mem Amer Acad Peds, Chicago Ped Soc, Natl Med Assoc, Cook Cty Physician Assoc, Chicago Urban League, Comm Recruitment Minority Stud Northwestern Med School 1969-70; bd of dir Erikson Inst for Adv Child Devel 1982-83, Siegel Inst Michael Reese Hosp 1984-; mem People to People Group to USSR & Europe for Med Care of Children 1983; chmn Preschool Comm IL Chap of Amer Acad of Ped 1984-; reactivation of mem AMA, IL State Med Soc, Chicago Med Soc 1987-. **HONORS/ACHIEVEMENTS:** Publ "Treatment of Various Childhood Tumors with Actinomyein D & X-Ray" IL Med Jrnl 1961, "Emergeny Prob in Pediatrics", "The Critical First Hours", "Ross Round Table" 1976, "Relapsing Pneumococceal Meningitis" Jrnl Ped 1974; "Principles of Developmental Pediatrics in Private Practice, They Work", "A Pediatricians Perspective on the Black Child and His Family", "Beating the Odds," WABC TV Channel 7. **MILITARY SERVICE:** USAF capt 1961-63.

KIRKSEY, PETER J.
Farmer, clergyman. **PERSONAL:** Born Nov 11, 1904, Eutaw, AL; married Florence Mccalpine; children: 5 Children. **EDUCATION:** Greene Co Training Sch; Miles Coll. **CAREER:** Greene Co Bd of Edn, pres; farmer; Greene Co Chap SCLC, minister vp. **ORGANIZATIONS:** Mem AL Assn of Sch Bd Mem; N Central AL Minsteral Conf of CME Chs. **BUSINESS ADDRESS:** PO Box 569, Eutaw, AL 35462.

KIRTON, EDWIN EGGLESTON
Retired Episcopal priest. **PERSONAL:** Born Dec 13, 1907, Port of Spain, Trinidad and Tobago;married Eunice Odessa Brathwaite; children: Eunice Kirton Davis, Edwin, Elsie. **EDUCATION:** Coll City of NY, BS 1932; NY Law Schl, 1938; Gen Theological Seminary, 1949. **CAREER:** St Michael's & All Angles, vicar 1949-51; St Mark's Episcopal, rector 1951-76; Oceanside Episcopal Camp, dir 1953-75; Provincal Synod, delegate 1954-55, 1963-65; General Convention Episcopal Church of the USA, deputy 1961-73; Bishop Coadjutor, nom 1968; Diocese of E Carolina Episcopal Church of The USA, retired Episcopal Priest. **ORGANIZATIONS:** First black pres New Hanover Ministerial Ass 1966; mem Gov's Comm Jnvl Delncy & Youth Crime 1962-75; mem brd Family Serv; mem br Mental Health Advsry Comm; chptr dir New Hanover Blood Assurance Plan; brd mem Phyllis Wheatly YWCA; mem comm promo bond issue New General Hosp 1961; chrmn Dept ofMissions Diocese of E Carolina 1963-65; mem Exec Cncl Diocese of E Carolina, Dept Chrstn Ed Diocese of E Carolina, St Augustine's Summer Schl Religious Ed 1955-60, Christian Soc Rel Standing Comm on Program Budger & Fin 1973-75, Camps & Conf Comm Diocese of E Carolinda 1969-74; pos chrmn Orgniation Welfare Comm PTA; chrtr mem & dir Opportunities Inc; mem Wilmington Youth Cncl Advsry Brd; chrmn & Mem Biracial Comm Cty & Cnty 1963-72; mem & chrmn Govnrs Comm for the Employmnt of the Hndcp 1967-76; chrmn Rgnl 0 Family Resources Inc 1973-75; mem Pres Comm for Emplymnt of the Hndcp 1967-76; chrmn Region 4 Pres Comm for Eplymnt of the Hndcp 1975-77. **HONORS/ACHIEVEMENTS:** Outstanding Citizen Omega Psi Phi Frat 1958; Citizen of the Year Wilmington Star News 1970; Distinguished Citizen Governor of NC 1980; distinguished Serv Pres of USA for serv Presidents Comm for Emplymnt of the Hndcp 1981. **HOME ADDRESS:** 3007 Ivy Bridge Rd, Ft Washington, MD 20744-2142.

KIRVEN, JOE W.
Business executive. **PERSONAL:** Born Jun 05, 1932, Wortham, TX; married Gloria Foster; children: Lili Josette. **EDUCATION:** Wiley Coll Marshall, TX, BS 1953. **CAREER:** ABCO Bldg Maintenance Co Inc, pres/founder; Venture Advisers Inc, founder apptd by Pres Nixon Adv Council Minority Enterprise, 1969. **ORGANIZATIONS:** Past mem Dallas Proprietary Sch Bd; past mem Dallas Indep Sch Bd & chmn, bd trustees St John Bapt Ch; trustee Wiley Coll, YMCA; trustee & past pres Dallas Negro C of C; trustee Boys Club Dallas. **HONORS/ACHIEVEMENTS:** One of outstanding black businessmen in the US, Ebony Mag, 1969 & 1971; one of Five Young Outstanding Texans, Jaycess 1968; featured in Getting It Together, a book on 15 outstanding black men in Amer; Business Enterprise Award, Alpha Phi Alpha, 1974; Bigger & Better Business Award, Phi Beta Sigma, 1973; award for outstanding leadership, DAME, 1971. **BUSINESS ADDRESS:** 2828 Forest Ave, Dallas, TX 75215.

KIRVEN, MYTHE YUVETTE
Govt. administrator. **PERSONAL:** Born Jun 12, 1956, Dallas, TX. **EDUCATION:** TX Tech Univ, BS 1977; Atlanta Univ, MPA 1980. **CAREER:** City of Dallas, admin asst. **ORGANIZATIONS:** Mem NAACP; recording sec Delta Sigma Theta Dallas Chap 1980-84; mem Conf of Minority Public Admin 1978-; vice pres South Dallas Club Natl Assn of Negro Bus & Professional Women's Clubs 1985-; mem Urban Mgmt Assistants of N TX 1983-; mem TX City Mgmt Assn 1983-; mem Intl City Mgmt Assn 1983-. **BUSINESS ADDRESS:** Administrative Assistant, City of Dallas, 1500 Marilla St 2BS, Dallas, TX 75201.

KISNER, ROBERT GARLAND
Physician. **PERSONAL:** Born Jun 15, 1940, Lexington, KY; married Gloria Hinmon; children: Robert, Angela. **EDUCATION:** Morgan State Coll, BS 1964; Meharry Med Coll, MD 1969. **CAREER:** Univ of Pittsburgh, asst prof 1973-; Magee Womens Hosp, resd 1973-; Family Planning Cncl of Western PA, med dir 1973-77. **ORGANIZATIONS:** Mem Gateway Me Grp pres 1976-; mem Keystone Med Soc; Nat Med Assn; Allegheny Co Med Soc; AMA; fellow Am Coll of Ob Gyn Civic Ser mem NAACP. **HONORS/ACHIEVEMENTS:** Recpt Cultural Critique Award World Comm of Islam in the W 1977; Upjohn Achvmt Award Meharry Med Coll 1969. **MILITARY SERVICE:** AUSR capt 1970-76. **BUSINESS ADDRESS:** 211 N Whitfield St, Pittsburgh, PA 15206.

KISPERT, DOROTHY LEE
Organization executive. **PERSONAL:** Born Dec 10, 1928, Detroit, MI; daughter of Leo Priestley and Pearl Priestley; married Wilson G Kispert; children: Kimberly A, Cynthia L Kispert. **EDUCATION:** Univ of MI, BA 1950; Wayne State Univ, MA 1971. **CAREER:** Merrill-Palmer Inst, faculty 1975-80; Parent Child Devel Center, dir 1975-80; Parent Child Center, dir 1980-81; Parents and Children Together, dir 1981-. **ORGANIZATIONS:** Lay rep Children's Hospital of MI 1978-88; consultant Spelman College 1979; mem/tech review panel CDA Bank St Coll 1981; pres Metro Detroit Day Care Assn. **HONORS/ACHIEVEMENTS:** Publications, "PACT, A Partnership with Parents," Contemporary Parenting 1983, co-author "Teaming Social Services with Education Cooperative," Journal of Cooperative Educ 1986. **BUSINESS ADDRESS:** Dir/Parents & Children Together, PACT/ Wayne StateUniv, Knopp Bldg FIE Ferry, Detroit, MI 48202.

KITCHEN, WAYNE LEROY
Educational administrator. **PERSONAL:** Born Sep 07, 1948, Sedalia, MO; son of Edgar Roy Kitchen and Imogene Nurse-Kitchen. **EDUCATION:** Lincoln Univ, BS Business Educ 1970; Univ of MO, MEd Coll Admin 1977. **CAREER:** Admissions Dept Cogswell Coll, asst dir 1978-80; Marketing Division St Mary's Coll, program coord 1980-82; Marketing Div Univ of San Francisco, assoc dir 1982-84; Bay Area Urban League Training Ctr, dir 1984-85; Peralta Comm Coll Dist, educ consultant; Mills Coll, upward bound asst dir 1986-. **ORGANIZATIONS:** Mem Phi Delta Kappa Educ Frat 1983-; bd of dirs Lincoln Univ Natl Alumni Assn 1984-88; pres Lincoln Univ of MO Alumni Assn 1984-88; vice pres Phi Beta Sigma Frat Inc 1984-86; chmn Comm to elect Lloyd Vann for School Bd 1985; bd of directors, Oakland Ensemble Theatre; UNCF Inter-Alumni Council. **HONORS/ACHIEVEMENTS:** President's Serv Awd Phi Beta Sigma Frat Alpha Nu Sigma Chap Oakland 1984; Distinguished Lincoln Univ Alumni Awd 1987; Distinguished Alumni Award, Local Chapter, Lincoln Univ 1989. **MILITARY SERVICE:** AUS E-4 1970-72; Good Conduct Medal; Natl Defense Serv Medal; M-16SS Medal 1972. **HOME ADDRESS:** 44 Oak Hill Circle, Oakland, CA 94605.

KITCHENS, ASHTON C.
Businessman, youth counselor. **PERSONAL:** Born Dec 06, 1902, Georgia; married Rosetta Kallas; children: Ashton C, Jr. **EDUCATION:** Tuskegee Inst, 1927; Columbia U, BS 1936; New York City U, MA 1937. **CAREER:** Bennezet House Assn, boys work dir 1928; Wissahickson Boys Club, Philadelphia PA, asst boys club dir 1929-30; Columbus Hill Comm Center Children's Aid Soc, Germantown, PA, boys work dir 1930-36; Work Progress Admin, New York City recreation supr 1936-47; YMCA, New York City USO dir 1941-46; Glover & Sons Inst Design & Tailoring, Alexandria LA, Ft Huachuca AR, Los Angeles CA, Bremerton WA, admin officer 1947-51; grocery store owner/operator 1952-60; retail package stores, Los Angeles CA, 1960-73. **ORGANIZATIONS:** Life mem NAACP; life mem Omega Psi Phi Frat; mem LA Tuskege Club; Tuskegee Nat Alumni Assn; mem Urban League; Common Cause; Half Century Tuskegee Alumni Club; elected Tuskegee Athletic Hall of Fame 1974; admitted Pres Assoc Tuskegee Inst 1976; Distinguished Person Assn 1980; Omega Psi Phi Frat Lambda Omicron Chap 1976; mem The Southern Poverty Law Center; mem YMCA. **HONORS/ACHIEVEMENTS:** Citizen of Yr 1976; numerous honors & awards.

KITHCART, LARRY E.
Legislator. **PERSONAL:** Born Jul 25, 1939, Glasco, NY; married Audrey; children: Larry, Jr. **CAREER:** Ulster Co, 1st Black legislator 1975; Co Legislator, elected 4th consecutive term. **ORGANIZATIONS:** Mem & pres Kingston City Recreation Com 1968-77; comnr recreation 1977; past pres Kingston Dem Men's Club, mem Sheriff's comm; pub health- Indus devel; taxbase & study; bridge & hwy; program for aged; conser Vation com Chmn Mayor's policy making bd Kingston Rondout Neighborhood Center; ward chmn; YMCA; United Way; Cancer com; Jaycees; NAACP; com pres Ulster Cnty Community Action Adv Bd; Finance Com Co Legis; Audit & Ins Com, Legis, Finance Com of Co Legis, Municipal Power Study Commn of Co Legis. **MILITARY SERVICE:** USAF 4 yrs.

KITT, EARTHA MAE
Actress, singer. **PERSONAL:** Born Jan 26, 1928, North, SC; divorced; children: 1 daughter. **CAREER:** Katherine Dunham Dance Group, soloist 1948; Night Clubs France, Turkey, Greece, Egypt, New York City, Hollywood, Las Vegas, London, Stockholm, singer 1949-; Stage play Dr Faust Paris 1951, New Faces of 1952, Mrs Patterson 1954, Shinbone Alley 1957, Timbuktu 1978, performer; Motion pictures New Faces 1953, Accused 1957, Anna Lucasta 1958, Mark of the Hawk, St Louis Blues, Synanon 1965, Up the Chastity Belt 1971; RCA, Victor, recording artist. **HONORS/ACHIEVEMENTS:** Author "Thursday's Child" 1956, "A Tart Is Not A Sweet", "Alone With Me"; Woman of the Year Natl Assoc Negro Musicians 1968; Several command performances before the Queen of England; 1 Grammy Awd; 2 Tony Nominations. **BUSINESS ADDRESS:** c/o Intl Creative Mgmt, 40 W 57th St, New York, NY 10019.

KITTRELS, ALONZO WILLIAM
Educational administrator. **PERSONAL:** Born Dec 27, 1939, Philadelphia, PA; married Gloria Swigett; children: Yahnar. **EDUCATION:** DE State Coll Dover, BA1962; TempleUniv Philadelphia, MA 1969. **CAREER:** Dept of Public Welfare Philadelphia, interviewer 1962-66; Opportunities Indus Center Inc, personnel dir, asst personnel mgr, personnel specialist 1966-70; Mgtm Training School Philadelphia, dir 1970-72; City Hall Office of Business Mgmt, dir of personnel devel 1972-73; City of Newark Dept of Admin, personnel dir 1973-75; Bd of Educ Newark, exec dir of personnel 1975-77; Bd of Educ Newark, exec supt 1977-81; Kittrells Educ & Training Systems, pres. **ORGANIZATIONS:** Mem Kappa Alpha Psi. **MILITARY SERVICE:** AUSR 1962-63. **BUSINESS ADDRESS:** President, Kittrells Educ & Training Sys, 374 Clifton Ave, Clifton, NJ 07011.

KLAUSNER, WILLETTE MURPHY
Theatrical and film producer. **PERSONAL:** Born Jun 21, 1939, Omaha, NE; son of William Murphy and Gertrude Murphy; married Manuel S. **EDUCATION:** UCLA, BA economics 1957-61; Tobe-Coburn Sch for Fashion Careers NY, honors cert 1961-62. **CAREER:** Universal Studios Inc CA, vice pres marketing research & marketing 1974-81; Audience Studies Inc, research 1972-74, research unit dir 1968-72, proj dir 1966-68, research

analyst 1965-66; Carnation Co, research analyst 1965; Edgework Productions, pres. **ORGANIZATIONS:** Mem Womens' Trusteeship 1980; mem Gold Shield UCLA Alumni Assn 1974-; founder, mem bd of dir Amer Inst of Wine & Food; mem bd dir Constitutional Rights Found, Wonder Woman Found; mem, Los Angeles County Music Center Operating Company Board of Directors. **HONORS/ACHIEVEMENTS:** Recipient Mehitabel Award for outstanding Professional Achievement, Tob-Coburn Sch for Fashion Careers 1978. **BUSINESS ADDRESS:** President, Edgework Productions, 5538 Red Oak Drive, Los Angeles, CA 90068.

KLINE, EDDIE
Magistrate, carpenter. **PERSONAL:** Born May 31, 1917, Dale, SC; married Frances Jones; children: 6 Children. **EDUCATION:** Certificate of judicial edn. **CAREER:** Independent Contractor, carpenter; Sheldon Beaufort Co, magistrate twp 1956-. **ORGANIZATIONS:** Mem NAACP; Dale-Lobeco Comm Cntr; bd dirs Ofc of Economic Opportunites; Douglas Lodge #277; Prince Hall FAM. **HONORS/ACHIEVEMENTS:** Recipient Cert of Serv Award, Serv to Beaufort Co.

KLINE, WILLIAM M.
Educational administrator. **PERSONAL:** Born Feb 24, 1933, Paterson, NJ; married Lillian Thomas; children: Wayne, Michelle, William Jr, Wesley. **EDUCATION:** William Paterson Coll, BS 1954, MS 1959. **CAREER:** Paterson Bd of Educ, teacher 1957-65, dir neighborhood youth corp 1965-68, vice prin sch #6 1968-71, prin Eastside hs 1971-79, dir curriculum & spl educ proj 1979, asst supt. **ORGANIZATIONS:** F & AM commr Bd of Recreation City of Paterson 1962-64; alderman City of Paterson 1965-67; mem NAACP; Omega Psi Phi; Phi Delta Kappa; IBPOE of W Integrity Lodge; 4th Ward County Committeeman; Paterson Rotary Club. **HONORS/ACHIEVEMENTS:** Freedom Campaign Awd NAACP Paterson 1963; Cert of Merit Passaic Co Med Soc 1964; White House Conf Pres Lyndon Johnson 1965; Comm Serv Awd NAACP Paterson 1967; Educ Leadership Awd Lambda Kappa Mu Passaic Co 1971; DECA Serv Awd Distributive Educ Club Paterson 1973; Educ Awd New Polit Alliance Paterson 1976; Sci of Creative Intelligence Educ Awd NY 1976; Unity Serv Awd 1982; Hinton Comm Serv Awd 1983; Comm Bettermant Awd SECA Inc 1983; Morris Co Serv Awd NJ State Elks 1984; PH Grand Lodge Awd 1985; Amer Lodge Education Awd 1985; Passaic Cty Coll Awd 1985. **MILITARY SERVICE:** AUS pfc 1955-57; Good Conduct Medal. **BUSINESS ADDRESS:** Assistant Superintendent, Patterson Bd of Education, 33 Church St, Paterson, NJ 07501.

KLUGE, PAMELA HOLLIE
Economics and business journalism educator. **PERSONAL:** Born Apr 17, 1948, Topeka, KS; daughter of Maurice Hollie and Frances Hollie; married P F Kluge, Feb 14, 1977. **EDUCATION:** Washburn Univ, Topeka KS, BA English, 1970; Columbia Univ, New York NY, MS Journalism, 1971; Univ of Hawaii, Honolulu HA, Asain Studies, 1977; Columbia Univ, American Studies, 1987-. **CAREER:** Wall Street Journal, 1969-75; Honolulu Advertiser, Pacific correspondent, Saipan, 1975-76; Trust Territory of the Pacific Island, economics dept Micronesia, 1976; New York Times, natl correspondent in Los Angeles, foreign correspondent in Manilla, financial columnist in NY, 1977-87; NY Stock Exchange, New York NY, media consultant, 1987-, Knight Bagenot Fellowship in Economics & Business Journalism, Columbia Univ Graduate school of Journlism, dir, currently. **ORGANIZATIONS:** Dir, The Newspaper Foundation, 1973-75; contributor, Encyclopdeia Americana, 1985-; advisory board, The Kansas Center for the Book, 1988-; consultant, The Paragon Group, 1989-; visiting faculty, Poynter Institute, 1989-. **HONORS/ACHIEVEMENTS:** Distinguished Service Award, Washburn Univ, 1981; Topeka High School Hall of Fame, 1988; Fulbright Fellow to Malaysia, 1988; Best in the Business, Washington Journalism Review, 1985; Editor, The Knight-Bagehot Guide to Business and Economics Journalism, Columbia Univ Press, 1990. **BUSINESS ADDRESS:** Director, The Knight-Bagehot Fellowship in Economics and Business, Columbia University, Graduate School of Journalism, 116th and Broadway, New York, NY 10027.

KNABLE, BOBBIE MARGARET BROWN
Educator. **PERSONAL:** Born May 20, 1936, Knoxville, TN; daughter of Isaac Brown and Jacqueline Jordan Brown (deceased); married Norman Knable, Dec 21, 1963; children: Jacob. **EDUCATION:** Oberlin Conservatory, Oberlin OH, BMus, 1958. **CAREER:** Tufts Univ, Medford MA, asst prof of English, 1970-76, dir of continuing educ, 1974-78, dean of freshmen, 1978-79, dean of students, 1979-. **ORGANIZATIONS:** Mem, New England Deans, 1978-; mem steering comm, New England Coll Alcohol Network, 1980-; trustee, Vermont Academy, 1983-85; mem 1986-, recording sec 1988-89, Massachusetts Assn of Women Deans, Administrators and Counselors; mem, Deans of the Round Table, 1988-; mem, Student Affairs Think Tank, 1988-; trustee, Pine Manor Coll, 1989-; commr, New England Assn of Schools and Colleges, 1989-. **BUSINESS ADDRESS:** Dean of Students, Tufts Univ, Ballou Hall, Medford, MA 02155.

KNAIVE, HENRY LOUIS
Physician. **PERSONAL:** Born Oct 26, 1902, Scooba, MS; married Henrine Simpkins. **EDUCATION:** Alcorn AM Coll, BS 1926; Meharry Med Coll, MD 1930. **CAREER:** Physycian, gen pvt pract 1930-77. **ORGANIZATIONS:** Mem MS Med Den Assn; Nat Med Assn; Kappa Alpha Psi Frat; pres trste bd St Elmo Bapt Ch; owner DH Hair Real Estate; Notary Pub; co-partner Southeastern Benevolent Hosp; chtr mem 1st black Boy Scout Troop; orgnd Laurel Citizens League; promoted bldg Oak Park swimming pool 1st black; past pres MS Med Den Pharm Assn; 1st Chap Laurel Prog Voters League; Jones Cnty Alcorn Alumni Club; Laurel Med Den Pharm Soc; Laurel Citizens League; mem Masonic Lodge 33rd Degree; col on staff Gov Cliff Finch; mem staff S MS State Hosp; staff Jones Co Comm Hosp; mem Jones Co Selective Serv Bd; bd mem JonesCo Home Hlth Rehab Bd served civic coms; co-chmn United Givers Fund; Red Cross; March of Dimes. **HONORS/ACHIEVEMENTS:** Recip merit & appreciation Plaque Boy Scouts of Am; pres Richard Nixon for serv on Selective Serv Bd; Alpha Kappa Alpha Sor; man of yr Alcorn Alumni Clubpf Jones Co 1966.

KNIGH, BILLY EARL, I.
Educator. **PERSONAL:** Born Aug 14, 1939, Hattiesburg, MS; married Lois B McIntyre; children: Billy E II. **EDUCATION:** MS Valley State U, BS 1963;Univ of S MS. **CAREER:** Gulf Coast Jr Coll, math instr 1979-; MS Gulf Coast Jr Coll Gautier, math tech 1979; Photos by BK's Moss Point MS, owner mgr 1978-; WLOX-TV Biloxi "The Ebony Experience", prod host 1976-; BK's Mens Shop Moss Point, owner mgr 1974-80; Ingalls Ship Yard Pascagoula, mgr inventory control 1971-74; Gulf Coast Dist Boy Scouts, exec 1969-71; Neighborhood Youth Corp Dept of Labor, couns 1968-69; Public Sch System MS Gulf Coast, tchr coach 1963-68. **ORGANIZATIONS:** Pres Pas-Pt Devel Co 1974-; pres Drug Bd Singing River Mental Hlth 1978-79; commr Mosquito Control Jackson Co Bd of Suprs 1979-; bd mem Our Lady of Victories Central HS; mem Mens Wear Assn; mem NAACP 1973-; mem Nat Bus League 1974-; mem MS Cancer Soc 1978-; mem & past pres MS Valley State UGulf Coast Alumni Assn; exec bd Jackson Co Boys Club; mem & past pres S Peters Parish Council; mem State Cancer Soc; mem Pas-pt C of C; mem Dem Party; sponser various athl teams; Pres Sophomore Jr & Sr Classes MS Valley State; capt Ftbll & Bsbll Teams Jr & Sr Yrs. **HONORS/ACHIEVEMENTS:** Named All-conf Quarterback Sr Yr. **BUSINESS ADDRESS:** MS Gulf Coast Jr Coll, Jackson Co Campus, Gautier, MS 39553.

KNIGHT, BILLY
Professional athlete. **PERSONAL:** Born Jun 09, 1952, Pittsburgh, PA. **EDUCATION:** Pittsubrgh, 1972-74. **CAREER:** Indiana Pacers; Buffalo Braves (now San Diego Clippers), 1977-78; Boston Celtics, 1978-79; Kansas City Kings, professional basketball player; 1983-. **HONORS/ACHIEVEMENTS:** Tied pacer record for field goal prcntg (533) 1979; scored 44 pts in one game a team high 1979; 3 yrs varsity bb atUniv of Pittsburgh; set 6 Panther records 4 of which still stand; Sporting News 2nd All-Amer Team 1974; 1st round draft choice ABA IN 1974; led in free throw prcntg KC Kings 1984-85; 6th in free throw in league NBA 1984-85; scored in double figures 49 times; played on All-Star Team 1977.

KNIGHT, BUBBA
Singer. **CAREER:** Singer with Gladys Knight and the Pips, 1952—; member of entertainment firm Shakeji, Inc. **BUSINESS ADDRESS:** c/o MCA Record, 70 Universal City Plaza, Universal City, CA 91608. *

KNIGHT, DEWEY W., JR.
Government official. **PERSONAL:** Born Apr 07, 1930, Daytona Beach, FL; married Clara Brown; children: Dewey III, Patrick. **EDUCATION:** Bethune Cookman Clg, BS 1947-51; Atlanta U, MSW 1955-57; MA Inst Tech, Urban Exec Pgm 1970. **CAREER:** Dade Cty Childrens Hm, dir prfsnl serv case spvr casewrkr 1960-64; Dade Cty Dept Pblc Welfare, dir 1967-70; Dade Cty Dept Housing & Urban Dev, dir 1970; Metropolitan Dade Cty, asst cty mgr & dir dept human resources 1970-75, interim cty mgr 1976-, deputy county mgr 1970-. **ORGANIZATIONS:** Natl Acad Pblc Admn; Acad Cert Soc Wrkrs; pres Am Soc Pblc Admn; mem C of C Advsry Bd Natl Assc Businessmen; bd dir James E Scott Comm Assc; bd dir Am Red Cross; bd dir United Way; bd dir Kappa Alpha Psi Frat; sire archon-pres Sigma Pi Phi Frat; prof advsry cmt Barry Clg Grad Sch Soc Work; chtr mem Miami Vrsty Clb; bd trustee FL Memrl Clg; bd trustee Stillman Clg; mem Who's Who in Blck Am 1975-; bd dir Chase Fed & Loan Assc; mem Natl Forum Black Admn. **HONORS/ACHIEVEMENTS:** Natl pblc serv awrd; natl acad pblc admn & am soc pblc admn 1983; natl ldrshp awrd Natl Forum Blck Pblc Admn 1984; man of the yr Miami Chptr Rinky Dinks 1967; prod of a dream awrd Miami-Dade Chptr Bethune Cookman Alumni Assc 1975; comm serv awrd James E Scott Assc 1975; comm serv awrd Dade-Monroe Manpower Area Plng Cncl 1974; man of the yr Iota Phi Lambda 1976; dstgshd serv awrd Miami-Dade C of C 1975; awrd serv rendered to frat Kappa Alpha Psi Frat; comm serv awrd Minrty Cntrctrs Assc 1972; otstndg comm serv awrd Frontier Intrl Miami Clb; dstgshd comm serv awrd Natl Conf of Christians & Jews 1977; man of the yr Zeta Phi Beta; dstgshd serv awrd Natl Assc of Soc Wrkrs 1977; kappa of the month natl; pblc admn of the yr Am Soc Pblc Admn S FL 1982; natl pblc serv awrd Natl Acad Pblc Admn & ASPA 1983; natl forum Black Admn Ldrshp Awrd 1984. **MILITARY SERVICE:** USAF stf sgt. **BUSINESS ADDRESS:** Deputy County Manager, Metropolitan Dade Cty Govt, 111 NW 1st, Ste 2910, Miami, FL 331281994.

KNIGHT, ETHERIDGE
Poet. **PERSONAL:** Born Apr 19, 1931, Corinth, MS; son of Bushie Knight and Belzora Cozart Knight Taylor; married Mary McAnally, May 25, 1975; children: Etheridge Bombata, Mary Tandiwe, Isaac Bushie Blackburn. **ORGANIZATIONS:** Conference on the Great Mother & The New Father; "Free Peoples" poetry workshops, founder & general counselor. **HONORS/ACHIEVEMENTS:** Guggenhiem Fellowship, 1975; NEA Fellowship, 1980; Shelley Memorial Award, 1986; The American Book Award, 1987; Author of: Poems from Prison, Broadside Press, 1968; Belly Song & Other Poems, Broadside Press, 1975; Black Voices from Prison Pathfinder Press, 1971; Born of a Woman, Houghton Mifflin, Boston 1980; The Essential Etheridge Knight, Univ of Pittsburgh Press, 1986. **MILITARY SERVICE:** US Army, pfc, good conduct, 1947-51.

KNIGHT, FRANK W., JR.
Business executive. **PERSONAL:** Born Jan 03, 1923, Birmingham, AL; married Lucretia E Hill; children: Francine, Patricia. **EDUCATION:** AL State U; Chicago City Coll; DePaul U. **CAREER:** Frank Knight Realty & Bldg Co Chgo, real estate operator & gen bldg contractor 1954-66; Dept Housing & Urban Devel, chief real property br Housing Assist Div, real estate appraiser Urban Renewal Div; HUD Region V, regional real property ofcr. **ORGANIZATIONS:** Mem Dearborn Real Estate Bd; treas v chmn nom com Assn Fed Appraisers Mid-West Chap 1971-72; mem Chatham Lions Club; hon mem Am Soc Appraisers Minneapolis Chpt. **HONORS/ACHIEVEMENTS:** Cert of Merit 1972; Four Battle Stars. **MILITARY SERVICE:** AUS sgt 1943-45.

KNIGHT, FRANKLIN W.
Educator. **PERSONAL:** Born Jan 10, 1942; son of Willis J Knight and Irick M Knight; married Ingeborg Bauer; children: Michael, Brian, Nadine. **EDUCATION:** Univ Coll of WI London, BA (honors) 1964; Univ of WI Madison, MA 1965, PhD 1969. **CAREER:** SUNY at Stony Brook, asst/assoc prof 1968-73; Johns Hopkins Univ, assoc prof 1973-77, prof 1977-. **ORGANIZATIONS:** Visit prof Univ of TX at Austin 1980; bd dirs Social Sci Rsch Council 1976-79; consultant NEH 1977-85; comm mem Inter-American Found 1984-86; rsch comm Amer Historical Assn 1984-86; chmn Intl Scholarly Relations Comm Conf of Latin Amer Historians 1983-86; exec comm Assn of Caribbean Hist 1982-85. **HONORS/ACHIEVEMENTS:** Fellow Natl Endowment for Humanities 1976-77; Fellow Center for Adv Study in Behav Sciences 1977-78; author, "Slave Society in Cuba During 19th Century" 1970; "The Caribbean, Genesis of a Fragmented Nationalism" 1978; Fellow Natl Humanites Center 1986-87. **HOME ADDRESS:** 2902 W Strathmore Ave, Baltimore, MD 21209. **BUSINESS ADDRESS:** Professor of History, Johns HopkinsUniv, 3400 N Charles St, Baltimore, MD 21218.

KNIGHT, GLADYS MARIA
Singer. **PERSONAL:** Born May 28, 1944, Atlanta, GA; married Barry Hankerson; children: Kenya, Jimmy, Shanga-Ali. **CAREER:** Morris Brown Choir, singer 1950-53; concert appearances in England 1967,72,73,76, Australia, Japan, Hong Kong, Manila 1976; Pipe Dreams movie, performer; Gladys Knight & The Pips, singer 1953-; TV show "Charlie & Company", co-starring role as elementary school teacher. **HONORS/ACHIEVEMENTS:** Winner Grand Prize Ted Mack Amateur Hour 1952; 1 Gold Album; 1 Platinum Album; 2 Grammy Awds 1974; Top Female Vocalist, Blues & Soul Mag 1972; Spec Awd forInspiration to Youth WA City Council; Rolling Stone Awd; Ladies Home Jrnl Awd; author "I Don't Want To Do Wrong", "Do You Love Me Just a Little Honey", "Daddy Could Swear I Declare", "Me & My Family", "Way Back Home"; Winner 6 Gold Budda Records; NAACP Image, Ebony Music, Cashbox, Billboard, Record World Awds 1975; American Music Awd (with Pips) 1984; 1989 Grammy Award for best group. **BUSINESS ADDRESS:** c/o Network Talent Intl, Box 82 Ste 342A, 98 Cuttermill Rd, Great Neck, NY 11021. *

KNIGHT, JOHN F., JR.
Educational administrator. **PERSONAL:** Born Jun 07, 1945, Montgomery, AL. **EDUCATION:** AL State U, BS 1974. **CAREER:** AL State Univ, dir public relations 1976; AL PSC, exec asst to pres; Postal Serv, clerk 1969-74. **ORGANIZATIONS:** Pres adv council AL Dem Conf Young Dem 1973; Students Affairs Com 1973; pres AL StateUniv Student Govt Assn 1972-73; mem St Dem Exec Com 1975. **HONORS/ACHIEVEMENTS:** Highest ranking black in AL State Govt 1974; Silver Star 1964; Vietnam Serv Medal, Natl Defense Medal; Vietnam Campaign Medal; Combat Infantryman Badge. **MILITARY SERVICE:** AUS 1967-69. **BUSINESS ADDRESS:** P O Box 271, Montgomery, AL 36101.

KNIGHT, LYNNON JACOB
Electronics engineer. **PERSONAL:** Born Jan 13, 1920, Ernul, NC; married Louise Dixon. **EDUCATION:** Lincoln U, BS 1941; Univ of PA, Postgrad 1942-44; Univ of AZ, 1959-61; Univ of CA at Los Angeles, 1968-72. **CAREER:** Radar/Electronics Defense Dept SE Asia, staff engr 1946-58; Army Dept Ft Huachuca, AZ, supv electronics engr 1958-62; Navy Dept Los Angeles, staff engr electronics 1962-65; Def Supply Agency Pasadena, tech mgr chief engr 1965-; Knight-dixon Co Los Angeles, pres 1971-. **ORGANIZATIONS:** Mem Power Source Com Army Dept 1961-62; AASS; IEEE; Armed Forces Communications & Elec Assn; mem Omega Psi Phi. **BUSINESS ADDRESS:** 125 S Grand, Pasadena, CA 91105.

KNIGHT, MURIEL B.
Instructor. **PERSONAL:** Born Apr 21, 1922, Hartford, CT; children: Muriel V Bullard, William A, Sheila E King. **EDUCATION:** AS Northeastern Univ, AS 1970; Northeastern Univ, BS 1972; Harvard Grad Schl of Ed, Ed M 1973; Northeastern Univ Boston Bouue', Doctoral Student 1979-85. **CAREER:** Northeastern Alumni, mem 1973-; Harvard Grad Alumni, mem 1974-; Harvard Chap Phi Delta Kappa, histrn-elect 1985-86; New England Woman's Press Assoc, pres-elect 1985-86; Ecumenical Social Action Comm, instructor ged. **ORGANIZATIONS:** Vice pres New England Woman's Press Assoc 1983-85; brd mem S End Neighborhood Action Prog 1985; brd mem Dimock St Health Cntr 1983-85; warden Election Dept City of Boston 1983-. **HONORS/ACHIEVEMENTS:** Awarded Kennedy Fdn Schlrshp; Northeastern Univ Martin Luther King Schlrshp; Professional Award; Merit Media Award; Comm Serv Award; Who's Who Among BlackAmer; World's Who's Who of Women; Citation for Civic Endeavors, Comm Work, Media Work, Comm Endeavors, Public Relations Work. **HOME ADDRESS:** 31-C Village Court, P O 18366, Boston, MA 02118.

KNIGHT, PERRY VERTRUM
Educator. **PERSONAL:** Born Dec 30, 1928, Dublin, GA; married Washington; children: Perry David. **EDUCATION:** Morehouse Coll Math, AB; NYUniv Grad Sch Arts & Sci Soc & Econ, MA; NYUniv Sch of Educ Soc Sci, mAEd; Manhattan Coll Bronx NY, MA; ColumbiaUniv Urban Edn, EdM; New Sch of Soc Res & Econ Pol Sci, PhD; ColumbiaUniv Urban Affairs, EdD; Econs & Polit Sci, Fordham Univ, MA. **CAREER:** Fordham Univ, assoc prof Economicss; Manhattan Coll NYC, prof; Winston-Salem NC Teachers Coll; Hampton Inst, assoc prof; Pairie View State Coll TX; Bluefield State Coll WV; Public School Greenville SC, teacher; Acme Educ & Psychology Serv NYC, pres; Yonkers School System Yonkers NY, counselor; Edwards, Edwards, & Edwards Intl Invest Co NYC, cons. **ORGANIZATIONS:** Mem Am Assn of Coll Prof; Phi Delta Kappa; Am Social Assn; NY State Social Assn; Kappa Alpha Psi. **HONORS/ACHIEVEMENTS:** Recip coll honors Morehouse Coll; Ford Found Fellowship; graduate fellowships. **MILITARY SERVICE:** WW II. **BUSINESS ADDRESS:** Professor of Economics, Fordham University, Urban Studies Program Rm 414D, New York, NY 10023.

KNIGHT, RICHARD, JR.
City official. **PERSONAL:** Born May 31, 1945, Fort Valley, GA; married Mavis Best; children: Richard L, Marcus E, Nolan C. **EDUCATION:** Fort Valley State Coll, BA 1968; Univ of NC, MPA 1976. **CAREER:** Carrboro NC, town mgr 1976-80; Gainesville FL, deputy city mgr 1980-82; City of Dallas, asst city mgr 1982-; city manager, 1986-. **ORGANIZATIONS:** Mem Rotary Intl; mem Free and Accepted Mason (3rd) Degree; past comm Cub Scout MAWAT Durham Dist Boy Scouts; mem Intl City Mgmt Assn; chmn Dallas Regional Minority Purchasing Council 1984-85; vice chair Dallas Alliance 1985; mem, Natl Forum Black Public Admin; mem, Salesmanship Club of Dallas, 1989. **HONORS/ACHIEVEMENTS:** Perspectives of a Black City Mgr published in Popular Govt 1979; Observations from a Mgr in Local Govt published in Public Management 1982; vice pres Intl City Mgmt Assn 1982. **MILITARY SERVICE:** AUS staff sgt 1969-71; Honors/Commendations. **BUSINESS ADDRESS:** City Manager, City of Dallas, 150 Marilla St 4CN, Dallas, TX 75201.

KNIGHT, ROBERT S.
Dentist, educator. **PERSONAL:** Born Aug 10, 1929, Montgomery, AL; married Patricia Tyler; children: Lynn, Robert, Joan, Stephen. **EDUCATION:** Talladega Coll, BA 1949; Meharry Med Coll, DDS 1954. **CAREER:** Bridgeport, CT, private practice 1964; Howard Univ Coll of Dentistry, asst prof 1965-71, asso prof 1972-, asso dean for Student Affairs 1975-, professor 1978-. **ORGANIZATIONS:** Mem Amer Dental Assn; Natl Dental Assn; DC Dental Soc; Robert T Freeman Dental Assn; Amer Acad of Oral Pathology; Amer Assn of Dental Sch; Soc of Tchr of Oral Pathology; Capitol Order of Oral Pathologist; mem Natl Urban League; com chmn Explorer Scouts, BSA; Howard Univ Coll of Med Post; mem Sigma Xi 1971; mem Omicron Kappa Upsilon Honorary Dental Soc 1974. **HONORS/ACHIEVEMENTS:** Recip Amer Cancer Soc Fellow in Oral Pathology New York Univ 1963; Fellow, Amer College of Dentist 1981. **MILITARY SERVICE:** AUS dental corps 1954-61; USAR col. **BUSINESS ADDRESS:** Howard Univ, College of Dentristy, Office of the Dean, Washington, DC 20059.

KNIGHT, W. H., JR. (JOE)
Educator. **PERSONAL:** Born Dec 05, 1954, Beckley, WV; son of W H Knight and Frances Knight; married Susan L Mask, Jun 06, 1981; children: Michael Joseph Mask Knight, Lauren Louise Mask Knight. **EDUCATION:** Univ of NC at Chapel Hill, BA 1976; Columbia Univ Sch of Law, JD 1979. **CAREER:** Colonial Bancorp, assoc counsel and asst sec 1979-83; Univ of IA Coll of Law, assoc prof 1983-88, prof 1988-. **ORGANIZATIONS:** Bd adv mem CT Economic Development Authority 1982-83; consultant Knight Financial Consulting 1982-; mem Lawyers Alliance for Nuclear Arms Control 1983-, Amer & Iowa Civil Liberties Union 1983-; pres Iowa City NAACP 1986-; mem Natl Conference of Black Lawyers, IA Natl Bar Assoc; mem Society of American Law Teachers 1988-. **HONORS/ACHIEVEMENTS:** Woodrow Wilson Administrative Fellowship 1979; Univ of IA Old Gold Fellowship Grants 1984, 1985-87; author Iowa Bar Review Materials on Contracts 1985-89; author bookreview "In Banks We Trust," P Lernoux Vol 10 IA Journal Corp Law 1095, 1985; International Debt and the Act of State Doctrine: Judicial Abstention Reconsidered, 13 North Carolina Journal of International Law & Commercial Regulation 35-72 (1988); book brief, Black Robes, White Justice, Bruce Wright 10 UCLA National Black Law Journal 366-369 (1988); Loan Participation Agreements; Catching Up With Contract Law, 1987 Columbia Business Law Review 587-631. **HOME ADDRESS:** 10 Brickwood Knoll, Iowa City, IA 52240. **BUSINESS ADDRESS:** Prof of Law, Univ of IA, College of Law, Iowa City, IA 52242.

KNIGHT, WALTER R.
City official, association executive. **PERSONAL:** Born Aug 16, 1933, Camden, AR; married Sadie M Brown; children: Harriet, Vicki, Sabrena, Michelle. **EDUCATION:** Univ WI;Univ MN. **CAREER:** City Councilman; Un Steelworkers Am Local 1533, pres 1975-; USWA, vice pres 1969. **ORGANIZATIONS:** Bd dirs Gr Beloit Assn Commerce; mem City Ambassadors Club; exec com Black Res Personnel; Beloit Improv Coalition; bd dirs WI Equal Employ Oppor Assn 1967-; Rock Co Manpower Plng Council 1974. **HONORS/ACHIEVEMENTS:** Serv award Salvation Army 1966; Soul Fest 1972; Beloit Coll Pres Counc. **BUSINESS ADDRESS:** 614 Broad St, PO Box 1219, Beloit, WI 53511.

KNIGHT, WILLIAM ROGERS
City official. **PERSONAL:** Born Jan 08, 1945, Halifax Co, NC; married Nelma Kaye; children: Lisa, Kimberely, Ida Michelle. **EDUCATION:** Wilberforce U, BA 1968. **CAREER:** Raleigh City Dist C, councilman; St Augustines Coll, dir pub relat; Raleigh Comm Relat Com, asso dir 1969-73; Wake Co Oppor Inc, manpower coord 1968-69. **ORGANIZATIONS:** Mem Assn of Am Colls; Nat Assn of Fed Relat Ofcls; mem Shriners Masonic Lodges; NAACP; Un Ways of Wake Co; LQC Lamar Soc; Raleigh Cits Assn; Black Dem Caucus of Wake Co; Team for Progress; NC Comm Action Assn; Omega Psi Phi Frat; Nat Black Caucus of Local Elected Ofcls. **HONORS/ACHIEVEMENTS:** Recip cert of merit US Jaycees; speak-up award Raleigh Jaycees; outst cit in field of pub relat 6th Dist Omega Psi Phi; outst cit award Jack & Jill Inc 1974; outst cir award Phi Beta Sigma. **BUSINESS ADDRESS:** 1315 Oakwood Ave, Raleigh, NC.

KNIGHT-PULLIAM, KESHIA
Actress. **PERSONAL:** Born in Newark, NJ. **CAREER:** First show business job appeared in ad for baby care products (8 months old); appeared in several TV commercials; semi-regular on children's program Sesame St 1982; film, The Last Dragon; plays role of "Rudy" in the Cosby Show. **HONORS/ACHIEVEMENTS:** Emmy nomination for Outstanding Supporting Actress in a Comedy Series.

KNOTT, ALBERT PAUL, JR.
Physician, business, consulting. **PERSONAL:** Born Mar 23, 1935, Pittsburgh, PA; son of Albert Paul Knott Sr MD and Fannie Merideth Scott Knott; married Lynda Steenberg; children: Albert Paul Knott III, Olivia Merrideth Knott. **EDUCATION:** Yale Coll, AB 1956; NJ Coll of Medicine, MD 1960; DC Gen Hosp, Internship 1961; Micheal Rece Hosp Chicago, Cardoiology Fellowship 1961-63; VA Hosp Hines IL, Med Res 1961-65. **CAREER:** Statevl Cortl Inst, med dir 1981-83; Metpl Corlt Pk Hosp, med dir 1984-85; Bethany/Garfield Pk Hsp, med dir 1977-81; Tabernacle Com Hosp, assoc med dir 1972-77; CHA Ltd. Chicago Illinois, president 1985-; Communication Equipment Consultants, president, 1987-; Marine Cellular Specialists Chicago and Fort Lauderdale,vice pres; Knott Lock Corporation, president. **ORGANIZATIONS:** Am Coll of Phys 1968-; dir Inner Cty Ind 1967-; dir Lux Yachts LTD 1980-; dir Reg Ind 1980-; dir St Johns Entp 1970-; dir Kings Bay LTD 1972-. **MILITARY SERVICE:** USN lieut commander 2yr1965-75. **BUSINESS ADDRESS:** c/o CHA LTD, Suite 1506, 53 West Jackson Blvd, Chicago, IL 60604.

KNOWLES, CLAIRE EM
Higher education administrator. **PERSONAL:** Born Jun 06, 1952, Sacramento, CA; daughter of Sidney S Knowles and Almeana Early Knowles. **EDUCATION:** Univ of CA, Davis CA, BA, 1973, Univ of CA, Berkeley CA, MLS, 1974, Certificate/Mgt, 1975; CA State Univ, Sacramento CA, MPA, 1986; Simmons Coll, Boston MA,Doctor of Arts, 1988. **CAREER:** Univ of CA, Davis CA, reference librarian, 1975-82;, soc science librarian, 1982-85; Wentworth Inst of Tech, Boston MA, archives librarian, 1982; Simmons Coll, Boston MA, circulation librarian, 1982; Univ of CA, Davis CA, coordinator of bib instr, 1985-88; Simmons Coll, Boston MA, asst dean, 1988-, freelance proofreader, reviewer, 1988-. **ORGANIZATIONS:** Life mem, Amer Library Assn, 1984-; councillor, 1978-90, mem, 1975-88, CA Library Assn, mem, MA Black Librarians Network, 1988-; chairman, Librarians' Assn of the Univ of CA, Davis CA, 1985-86. **HONORS/ACHIEVEMENTS:** Fellow, Wentworth Institute of Tech, 1982; Outstanding Black Staff, Sacramento Observer, 1981; Outstanding Service, Ethnic Monority Students Delta Sigma Theta, Lambda Xi, 1980; Outstanding Young Woman of America, 1984; mem, CA Governor's Conference on Library and Information Science, 1979; author of Fulbright Scholars offered a Glimpse of American Academic Libraries," CA Clearinghouse of Library Instruction Newsletter, 7(2):1-2 May 1987; Dual Career Couple Relationships: An Annotated Bibliography. University of CA, Women's Resources and Research Center. Working paper series No 7, April 20, 1980; Black Women in Science and Medicine: A Bio- Bibliography, with Mattie T Evans, Affirmative Action Council, 1977. **BUSINESS ADDRESS:** Assistant Dean, Graduate School of Library and Information Science, Simmons College, 300 The Fenway, Boston, MA 02115.

KNOWLES, EDDIE (ADENOLA)
Educational administrator. **PERSONAL:** Born May 03, 1946, New York City, NY; married Druis; children: Alisa, Themba, Citalala. **EDUCATION:** LincolnUniv PA, BA 1970; ColumbiaUniv Tchr Coll, MA 1973. **CAREER:** Bronx Comm Coll Bronx NY, dir 1972-74; Hostos Comm Coll Bronx NY, assit prof 1974-75; Rensselaer Ldr Poly Inst, dean of miniority affairs 1977-82; Rens Poly Inst, dean of stud 1982-. **ORGANIZATIONS:** Consult Exxon Ed Found 1984; consult NY Edtl Oppty Ctrs 1984; writer consult Blk Coll Mag 1980-; vice pres brd of dir Sponsors for Ed Opp 1970-. **HONORS/ACHIEVEMENTS:** Martin Luther King awd Ren Poly Inst 1983; sevc awd Minty Stud Ldr RPI 1982; unity awd in media LincolnUniv MO Ntl Media Comp 1981. **HOME ADDRESS:** 2115 Burdett Ave, Troy, NY 12180. **BUSINESS ADDRESS:** Dean of Students, Rensselaer Polytechnic Inst, Troy Building RPI, Troy, NY 12180.

KNOWLES, MALACHI
Association executive. **PERSONAL:** Born Jul 25, 1941, W Palm Beach; married Genevieve O Day. **EDUCATION:** Morgan State Coll Baltimore, BA 1963;Univ of OK, MA (1st black) 1965; Urban Travel Forecasting US Dept Commerce, Cert 1967; Metro Chicago StudiesUniv of Chicago, Cert 1967; US Army Finance Sch, Diploma 1968; HUD Mgmt & Plng Seminar for Minority Professional in State & Local Govt, Cert 1974; Inst for Govt SC Council for Human Rights, Cert 1974; Community Plng & Dev Inst US Dept HUD, Cert 1974. **CAREER:** The President, spl asst 1974-; Chicago, urban plnr 1965-69; Wash DC, 1969-70; Washington, sp projs urban plnr 1970-71, sr desk ofcr urban plnr 1971-74;Univ of OK, tchng fellow 1963-64, rsrch asst 1964-65; Am Geog Soc NY, student fellow 1965;Univ of OK, plng sch lib 1964-65; Morgan State Coll, vis lctr 1971;Univ of Miami, vis lctr 1973; Fed City Coll Washington, assoc prof 1971-; Black Voices Mag & Photo Newspaper, vis ed 1975-. **ORGANIZATIONS:** Mem White House Small Towns Task Force Wash DC; vice pres & natl mbrshp chmn Natl Assn Plnrs 1973-; bd dirs Natl Minority Leg Educ Training Prgm Inc 1974-; Operation PUSH Inc; Am Soc Plng Ofcls; ASPO Ford Found Sch Scholarship Selection Commn; S FL Chap FL Plng & Zoning Assn Inc 1973-; Omega Psi Phi; Gamma Theta Upsilon; Met Wash Plng & Housing Assn; plng adv to Capital View Devel Corp Inc; Task Force on Black Colls; NAACP; Varsity M Golf Club; Morgan State Coll; Metro Wash Urban Leag; Jaycees; SW Nghbrhd Asmbly. **MILITARY SERVICE:** AUSR 1967-73.

KNOWLES, WILLIAM W.
Engineer. **PERSONAL:** Born Oct 01, 1941, New York City, NY. **EDUCATION:** Stevens Inst of Tech, BS 1963; NC State Univ Nuclear Engrng, MS; San Jose State Univ Mech Engrng, MS 1972. **CAREER:** GE Nuclear Enrgy Prod Div, reliability engr nuclear engr; Oakridge Nat Lab, nuclear engr 1967-70; Grumman Aircraft, mech engr 1964-66. **ORGANIZATIONS:** Com mem Nuclear Engineering Educ for Disadvantaged Am Nuclear Soc; bd dirs N CA Counc of Black Professional Engrs; co-founder "Co-Kno Asso"; past pres Local-Chap Regional Ofcr Nat Com; mem Omega Psi Phi Frat; co-founder "Collaga Mag"; CA Sunday Sch Supt, Layman Youth Worker St Paul Missionary Bapt Ch; mem Fahamu. **HONORS/ACHIEVEMENTS:** Candidate Omega Man of Yr 1975. **BUSINESS ADDRESS:** 175 Curtner Ave, San Jose, CA 95125.

KNOX, ANNIE BELL
Educator. **PERSONAL:** Born Oct 30, 1894, Lisbon, LA; widowed; children: Ruby Hebert. **EDUCATION:** So U, Tchrs Cert 1922, AB 1936; Tuskegee Inst, Addtl Study 1924; Wayne State U, 1951-52. **CAREER:** E Baton Rouge Parish, ret elem sch prin 1922-57. **ORGANIZATIONS:** Mem E Baton Rouge Parish Prin Assn 1922-57; mem Ret Tchrs Assn; mem bd of dirs Human Relat Counc of Baton Rouge; treas Zeta Phi Beta Sor; mem Coll Women of So U; life mem YWCA; charter mem, past pres Am Legion Aux Unit 502, 6th Dist LA; treas Comm Assn for Welfare of Sch Children; mem Mt Pilgrim Bapt Ch; Educ of Yesteryr Club; Flower Lover's Garden Guild; Custodian of Voting Machines; Personal Preparedness for Survival. **HONORS/ACHIEVEMENTS:** Established 1st sch lunch prgm, 1st lib for black elem sch children in E Baton Rouge Parish; woman of yr Zeta Phi Beta Sor 1964; Annie B Knox Hon Soc for Comm Serv Scotlandville Sr HS; cert Scotlandville Coop of Prog Entrepreneur.

KNOX, GEORGE F.
Attorney. **EDUCATION:** MI State Univ, BS Zoology 1966; Univ of Miami School of Law, JD 1973. **CAREER:** Univ of Miami School of Business Admin, lecturer 1973-74; City of Miami, FL, asst city attorney 1974-75; Univ of AR Fayetteville, asst prof of law 1975-76; Univ of Miami School of Law, lecturer 1978-80; Nova Univ Center for the Study of Law, lecturer 1980-82; City of Miami, FL, city attorney and dir of law dept 1976-82; Paul, Landy Beiley & Harper PA, partner 1982-84; Long & Knox, partner 1984-. **ORGANIZATIONS:** Mem FL, Natl, Amer, DC Bar Assns; mem, Natl Inst of Municipal Law Officers; mem Assn of Amer Law Schools, Black Lawyers Assn, FL League of Cities, Assn of Amer Trial Lawyers, Acad of FL Trial Lawyers; mem US Dist Court Southern Dist of FL, US Court of Appeals for Fifth Circuit, United States Supreme Court; mem NAACP; bd dirs Miami-Dade Community College Foundation Inc; chmn, Miami Sports and Exhibition Authority; mem Greater Miami Chamber of Commerce; mem FL Memorial College Ctr of Excellence; bd dirs YMCA of Greater Miami. **HONORS/ACHIEVEMENTS:** Jaycees Outstanding Young Men of Amer 1976; Miami-Dade Chamber of Commerce Awd of Outstanding Contribution to Social and Economic Development 1977; Black Lawyers' Assn Virgil Hawkins Achievement Award 1977; Alpha Phi Alpha Fraternity Achievement Award 1977; participant "Law and Justice in Today's Society" seminar sponsored by Natl Endowment for the Humanities Harvard Univ 1978; FL Jr Coll at Jacksonville Community Awareness Award; Beta Beta Lambda Chap Alpha Phi Alpha Fraternity Community Service Award 1981; NAACP Appreciation Award 1981; Northwest Council of Jacksonville Chamber of Commerce Jacksonville Achiever Award 1986; numerous publications. **BUSINESS ADDRESS:** Attorney at Law, Long & Knox, PA, 4770 Biscayne Blvd, Ste 1460, Miami, FL 33137.

KNOX, GEORGE L., III
Corporate executive. **PERSONAL:** Born Sep 06, 1943, Indianapolis, IN; son of George L. Knox II and Yvonne M. Wright; married B. Gail Knox, Jan 01, 1979; children: Reed, Gillian. **EDUCATION:** Tuskegee Univ, Tuskegee AL, BS, 1967; Harvard Business School, Boston MA, MBA, 1975; attended American Univ, Washington DC. **CAREER:** US Dept of State, Washington DC, member of foreign service office, Tokyo, 1968-73; McKinsey & Co, New York NY, associate, 1975-77; Philip Morris, New York NY, mgr internal mgmt consultant, 1977-79, mgr financial relations, 1979-83, dir financial relations and administration, 1983-85, dir corp communications, 1985-87. **MILITARY SERVICE:** US Air Force, 2nd Lt., 1967.

KNOX, WAYNE D. P.
Community developer. **PERSONAL:** Born Jun 19, 1947, West Reading, PA; children: Latina Marie. **EDUCATION:** Cheyney State Coll, BA 1970; Pennsylvania State Univ, M 1984. **CAREER:** City of Reading, dir of orientation & training USAC project 1974-75; Bureau of Planning City of Reading, urban planner 1973-78; Neighborhood Housing Serv of Reading, assoc dir 1978-80, exec dir 1980-82; Neighborhood Reinvestment Corp, field serv officer 1982-. **ORGANIZATIONS:** Committee mem Reading Downtown Adv Comm 1980-; dir Old Bethel Cultural Serv Ctr 1985-. **HONORS/ACHIEVEMENTS:** Elected to Natl Coll Poetry Publications 1969,70; pres Youth Employment Serv 1970; Outstanding Serv Awd Cheyney State Coll 1970. **MILITARY SERVICE:** AUS E-5 2 yrs; Letter of Commendation, 1st Infantry Div 1971. **BUSINESS ADDRESS:** Field Services Officer, Neighborhood Reinvestment Corp, 427 Woodward St, Reading, PA 19601.

KNOX, WILBUR BENJAMIN
Director, clergyman. **PERSONAL:** Born Nov 25, 1912, Smith, SC; married Susie Boulwere; children: Paul, Kathleen. **EDUCATION:** Johnson C Smith U, AB, BD 1950, DD. **CAREER:** Friendship Coll, dir public relations; Many Baptist Churches, pastor 1946-65. **ORGANIZATIONS:** Pres Rock Hill SC Br NAACP 1963-65; pres York Co Educ Proj 1968-; mem Sons of Light Lodge Masons 61; mem Christian Ministers Assn; mem Political Action Group; mem Intl Poetry Soc. **HONORS/ACHIEVEMENTS:** Listed Who's Who in S & SE 1959; listed Nat Soc Reg 1960; author of pub poems & plays; creator of greeting cards.

KNOX, WILLIAM ROBERT
Business executive. **PERSONAL:** Born Jun 19, 1951, Alba, AL; son of Henry Knox and Johnnie Knox; children: Rashad, Rachelle, Jerret. **EDUCATION:** Purdue Univ, BS 1974. **CAREER:** Chicago Bears, corner back; estimator; W R Knox Corp, president. **HONORS/ACHIEVEMENTS:** Mem of East Chicago Sports Hall of Fame. **BUSINESS ADDRESS:** President, W R Knox Corp, P O Box 6351, Gary, IN 46406.

KOGER, LINWOOD GRAVES, III
Physician. **PERSONAL:** Born Feb 21, 1951, Baltimore, MD; son of Linwood G Koger Jr Esq and Margaret Pigott Koger; married Iantha Angela Hill Koger, Jul 04, 1987; children: Brian Anthony Koger. **EDUCATION:** Howard Univ, Coll of Liberal Arts BS 1974, Coll of Medicine MD 1978. **CAREER:** Howard Univ, Dept of General Surgery, resident 1983; private practice Baltimore, physician 1983-85; Meharry Medical Coll, asst prof of surgery 1986-; Alvin C York VA Med Center, asst chief of surgery, 1985-. **ORGANIZATIONS:** Fellow, American College of Surgeons 1988-; mem, Assn of Academic Surgeons 1988-. **HONORS/ACHIEVEMENTS:** Diplomate Amer Bd of Surgery 1984; Clinical Sciences Faculty Member of the Year Meharry Med Coll Pre-Alumni Council, 1985-86; Mesenteric Ischemia; The York VA Experience, presented at the NMA Convention, 1989. **BUSINESS ADDRESS:** Asst Chief Surgical Service, Alvin C York VA Medical Ctr, Murfreesboro, TN 37130.

KOGER, MICHAEL PIGOTT, SR.
Physician. **PERSONAL:** Born Jan 20, 1953, Baltimore, MD; divorced; children: Michael Pigott, Jr. **EDUCATION:** Fisk Univ; MIT; Meharry Medical Coll, MD 1979. **CAREER:** Franklin Square Hospital resident physician 1979-82; Provident Hospital, medical staff 1982-85; North Charles General Hospital, medical staff 1982-85; Jai Medical Center, internist 1982-84; Constant Care Medical Center, internist 1984; Basil Health Systems, internist 1985; St Joseph Hospital, physician 1985; Lutheran Hospital, house physician 1985; Hancock Memorial Hospital, internist 1985-86; Sparta Health Care Center, internist 1986; Veterans Administration Medical Center, internist 1986-88; Central State Hospital, medical staff, 1988-. **ORGANIZATIONS:** Certified in Basic Cardiac Life Support 1981, 1985,& 1986; certified in Advanced Cardiac Life Support 1981,& 1985; mem Baltimore City Medical Soc 1983-, Medical and Chirurgical Faculty of MD 1983-; chmn Hancock Co Bd of Health Sparta GA 1985-86; mem Medical Assn of GA 1985-86; chmn Dept of Utilization Hancock Memorial Hosp Review and Quality Assurance 1985-86; chmn physician's peer Utilization Review Comm Hancock Memorial Hospital 1985-86; vice pres of medical staff Hancock Memorial Hosp 1986; mem, Amer Society of Internal Medicine 1988-. **HONORS/ACHIEVEMENTS:** Physician's Recognition Award Amer Medical Assn for Continuing Medical Educ 1985; publication "Your Health," a weekly column in The Sparta Ishmaelite newspaper 1985-86; Physician's Recognition Award, Amer Medical Assn for Continuing Medical Educ 1988. **HOME ADDRESS:** 141 Frank Bone Rd, #61, Milledgeville, GA 31061. **BUSINESS ADDRESS:** Attending Physician, Central State Hospital, Medical Surgical Division, Milledgeville, GA 31062.

KONDWANI, KOFI ANUM
Consultant. **PERSONAL:** Born Mar 11, 1955, Dayton, OH. **EDUCATION:** Maharishi Intl Univ Fairfield IA, attended 1976-77; Canada Coll Redwood City CA, attended 1978-79; Univ of CA Dvais, attended 1979-80. **CAREER:** AUS, admin asst Korea 1972-75; Canada Coll Redwood City CA, recruitment consult 1976-78; TMC Inc San Francisco, transcendental meditation tchr 1977-; Univ of CA Davis, recruitment consult 1979-80; James E Tolleson, public relation rep for home study training course; Dayton & CA, syndicated columnist; Univ of CA, affirmative action officer. **ORGANIZATIONS:** Mem NAACP 1978-; vice pres Black Health Sci 1979-80. **HONORS/ACHIEVEMENTS:** Awd of Gratitude Maharishi Intl Univ 1977; Eula Dyer Awd E Palo Alto CA 1979; Citizens Against Racism Scholarship

Redwood City CA 1979. **MILITARY SERVICE:** AUS E-4 1972-75. **BUSINESS ADDRESS:** Affirmative Action Officer, Univ of CA, Davis, CA 95616.

KORNEGAY, FRANCIS A.
Social agency official. **PERSONAL:** Born Sep 14, 1913, MtOlive, NC; married Geraldine; children: Francis Jr, John Dancy. **EDUCATION:** NC State Univ, BS 1935; Wilberforce Univ, MA 1941, PhD 1972. **CAREER:** Downington Indsl Sch, commandant of boys head of sci; US Treasury Dept, employee; Urban League, vocational sec 1944-56, asst exec dir 1956-60, exec dir 1960-. **ORGANIZATIONS:** Toured Europe lecturing on problems of youth 1952, 55; participant Intl Conf on Social Welfare & Human Rights Helsinki Finland 1968; trustee VA Union Univ; FL Memorial Coll; mem Econ Club of Detroit. **HONORS/ACHIEVEMENTS:** Recipient Hon Degrees from Wilberforce Univ 1965, Grand Valley State Coll 1970, Eastern MI Univ. **BUSINESS ADDRESS:** Michigan HMO Plans, Inc, 7650 Second Ave, Detroit, MI 48202.

KORNEGAY, HOBERT
Dentist. **PERSONAL:** Born Aug 28, 1923, Meridian, MS; married Ernestine Price; children: Carmon Kateena, X, Donna, James. **EDUCATION:** Morehouse Coll, BS 1945; Meharry Med Coll, DDS 1948; Walter Reed Inst Rsrch, Post Grad. **CAREER:** Dr of Dental Surgery, Dentist, pvt prac 1948-53; Myricks Meridian Nursing Home, dental cons; Volt Tech Corp, dental surgeon 1970-72; Westinghouse Learning Corp, 1971-72; Riley's & St Joseph's Hosp, mem staff; MS Head StartUniv PR Dental Sch, consult preventive dentistry 1970-71; MS UI Prgm, cons. **ORGANIZATIONS:** Mem Gov Com Hlth Needs of Children in MS 1971-72; mem Task Force MS Counc Child Devel 1971; chmn Chetan Area Counc BSA 1955-65; chmn Lauderdale Econ Oppor Prgm 1971-75; dir Maridian Redevel Authority Urban Renewal 1971-75; bd dir St Francis Homes 1971-; mem Acad of Gen Dentistry; Nat Am Dental Assn; NAACP; mem Intl Platform Assn Com; TV & Radio Appearances; mem City Adv Counc on City Plng; 4-H Adv Counc; Cits Adv Com for City Plng; pres Cloverleaf Chap Toastmasters Internat; v mayor City Councilman Precinct IV; bd dir Lauderdale Co Red Cross; bd dir Grp Foster Home Lauderdale Co; Cancer Soc Bd Lauderdale Co; mem Hlth Com C of C. **HONORS/ACHIEVEMENTS:** Listed in Who's Who in S & SW; Men of Achvmt 1975. **MILITARY SERVICE:** AUS capt 1953-55. **BUSINESS ADDRESS:** 1428 39 Ave, Meridian, MS 39301.

KORNEGAY, WADE M.
Chemical physicist. **PERSONAL:** Born Jan 09, 1934, Mt Olive, NC; son of Gilbert Kornegay and Estelle Williams Kornegay; married Bettie Joyce Hunter; children: Melvin, Cynthia, Laura. **EDUCATION:** NC Central Univ, BS (Summa Cum Laude) 1956; Bonn Univ Germany, 1957; Univ of CA Berkeley, PhD 1961; MIT Sloan School of Mgmt, 1979. **CAREER:** Univ of CA, postdoctoral fellow 1961-62, rsch assoc 1962; MIT, tech staff mem 1962-71; MIT Radar Signature Studies, tech group leader 1971-86; MIT, assoc div head 1986-. **ORGANIZATIONS:** Mem Amer Physical Soc 1959-, Sigma Xi Sci Rsch Soc 1960-, vice pres Humphrey's Task Force on Youth Motivation 1964-68; mem Exec Council of United Church of Christ 1971-77; mem bd dir Natl Consortium for Black Professional Devel 1976-, Boston City Missionary Soc 1977-; mem YMCA MA & RI Camp Comm 1977-, YMCA Black Achievers Assn 1979, NYAS 1984, AAAS, Alpha Phi Alpha. **HONORS/ACHIEVEMENTS:** Fulbright Fellowship US State Dept 1956-57; Grad Fellowship Danforth Found 1956-61; Natl Sci Found Postdoctoral Fellowship 1961-62; Hon ScD Lowell Univ 1969. **BUSINESS ADDRESS:** Assoc Division Head, Massachusetts Inst of Tech, 244 Wood St, Lexington, MA 02173.

KORNEGAY, WILLIAM F.
Director, administrator. **PERSONAL:** Born Mar 09, 1933, Apalachicola, FL; married Dorothy L Little; children: Bill, Jr. **EDUCATION:** Bethune-Cookman Coll, BS 1954; FL A&M U, MEd 1961;Univ of IL, PhD 1970. **CAREER:** Fisher Body Div, dir Quality of Work Life 1979-; Gen Motors Inst, dean of student affairs 1974-79; Bethune-Cookman Coll FL, acad dean of instr 1970-74;Univ of IL, coord of math tchrs 1967-70; Bethune-Cookman Coll FL, asst prof math 1966-67; Hampton Jr Coll, instr sci & math 1961-66; Rosenwald HS FL, head of sci dept 1957-58;Univ HS FL, head sci dept 1958-61. **ORGANIZATIONS:** Bd of trustees Jr Achvmt 1975-80; bd of trustees Flint Urban Leag 1977-79; bd of trustees United Way Chpn Allocations Com 1978-80; life mem Alpha Phi Alpha Frat. **HONORS/ACHIEVEMENTS:** Who's Who in Am Educ 1965; Ford Fellow 1967; Outst Educator in Am 1972; Phi Delta Kappa Educ Frat 1965. **MILITARY SERVICE:** AUS corpl 1954-56. **BUSINESS ADDRESS:** Fisher Body Div, Gen Offices Rm 109-12, Warren, MI 48090.

KOTTO, YAPHET FREDRICK
Actor, director, producer. **PERSONAL:** Born Nov 15, 1944, Harlem, NY; married Antoinette Pettyjohn; children: Natascha, Frederick, Robert, Sarada, Mirabai, Salina. **CAREER:** Appeared in Off-Broadway and Broadway productions including Great White Hope, Blood Knot, Black Monday, In White America, A Good Place to Raise a Boy; film appearances include Nothing But a Man 1963, Liberation of Lord Byron Jones 1964, Across 110th St 1973, Report to the Commissioner 1974, Sharks Treasure 1974, Liveand Let Die 1974, Monkey Hustle 1975, Drum 1976, Blue Collar 1977, Alien 1978, Brubaker 1979, Hey Good Looking 1982, Fighting Back 1982, Star Chamber 1983; TV movies include Raid on Entebbe 1977, Rage 1980, Women of San Quentin 1983.

KOUNTZE, MABRAY (DOC)
Retired government employee. **PERSONAL:** Born Mar 22, 1910, Medford, MA. **EDUCATION:** Univ Ext (Harvard) Night School Jour, Certificate 1930-40; Natl Tech School (Hts) Home Study Correspondence Course Elec; since 1970's FCC Comm Lic 2nd Class 1930-40; ICS 2nd other radio home studies (Inst Boys Radio Class Roxbury YMCA and West Medford Ctr). **CAREER:** Assoc Negro Press (ANP), sports gen news reporter 1929-50; Boston Chronicle, sports assoc editor newspaper 1930-40; Natl Negro Newspaper All Amer Assn, founder and dir sports editors 1930-40; Family Comm City Medford Historic Soc, hist 1930-; Boston Guardian, sports & assoc editor 1940-58; freelance writer 1929-. **ORGANIZATIONS:** Mem Shiloh Bapt Church (West Medford) 1920; mem NAACP Natl, Local 1930; West Medford comm ctr mem since founding 1930; mem Carter Woodson Assoc, Smithsonian Inst Assoc, Boston Museum Afro-Amer History, Monroe Trotter Natl Equal Rights League, charter mem New England Sports Museum, Medford Historic Soc; amateur radio oper 1954-87; author of This Is Your Heritage, 50 Sports Years Along Memory Lane, special papers in colleges including Harvard & Howard—History of Colored Press in Massachusetts, A Second Sketch of the Boston Guardian, Monroe Mason & Monroe Trotter; history tapes in Medford Public Library, on in Tuskegee. **HONORS/ACHIEVEMENTS:** Comm serv of journalism awd, West Medford Comm Ctr 1978; Dr Martin Luther King Jr Awd, Medford NAACP 1982; Greater Boston Black Historian Griot Award, Boston Coll 1984; life mem Natl Baseball Hall of Fame Museum 1984; Life Mem Award, Soc Radio Operators, New England, 1985; Negro Natl OMIK group of radio hams 1985 at OMIK convention.

KRAFT, BENJAMIN F.
Higher education administrator. **PERSONAL:** Born Jan 15, 1948, Baton Rouge, LA; married Yanick Douyon; children: Benjamin Robeson, Phillip Fouchard, Guileine Frances. **EDUCATION:** Rutgers Coll, AB 1970; Northeastern Univ, JD 1973; Amer Univ, MBA 1978. **CAREER:** Natl Labor Relations Bd, staff attorney 1973-77; Caribsun Export-Import Inc, pres 1977-79; Big Ben Hardware Haiti, owner/general mgr 1979-86; Florida Memorial College, assoc dir ctr for comm change 1986-, chairperson, Division of Business and Economics, 1988-. **ORGANIZATIONS:** Mem DC Bar Assoc 1974-; credit comm mem NLRB Fed Credit Union 1975-77, Haitian Foundation for Aid to Women 1985-86; bd mem treas Haitian Amer Chamber of Commerce 1984-86; bd mem Carib America Enterprises of Florida Inc 1986-; assoc editor, sphinx, Alpha Phi Alpha Fraternity Inc, Beta Beta Lambda 1989-; NAACP. **HONORS/ACHIEVEMENTS:** Outstanding Young Men in Amer US Jaycees 1977. **MILITARY SERVICE:** USAF Reserves capt 4 yrs. **BUSINESS ADDRESS:** Assoc Dir Ctr for Comm Change, Florida Memorial College, 15800 NW 42nd Ave, Miami, FL 33054.

KRESY-POREE, R. JEAN
Administrative director. **PERSONAL:** Born May 06, 1931, Maywood, IL; married Gerald Kresy; children: Lynne, Scott, Lee, Tsan. **EDUCATION:** San Francisco State Univ, BA 1963, MA 1978. **CAREER:** San Francisco State Univ, serv to minority students; Ford Found, proj dir; Office for Civil Rights, chief of oper; US Dept of Educ, acting dir higher educ div, dir elementary & secondary educ div regional office for civil rights. **ORGANIZATIONS:** Dir Sapphire Publ Co Inc; dir Advocates of Women 1973-77; dir, treas Consumers Coop of Berkeley 1977-83; dir, pres Consumers Group Legal Serv 1973-76; adv bd Women Org for Employment; founding mem Black Women Org for Action; mem Assn of Fed Women Execs Speaking Engagements, Higher Educ Branch, Office for Civil Rights, HEW. **HONORS/ACHIEVEMENTS:** Published "70 Soul Secrets of Sapphire," "Toward Viable Directions in Postsecondary Education.". **BUSINESS ADDRESS:** Dir, US Dept of Education, Elementary & Secondary Educ Div, 1275 Market St 14th Fl, San Francisco, CA 94102.

KRIGGER, MARILYN FRANCIS
Educator. **PERSONAL:** Born Mar 27, 1940, St Thomas, Virgin Islands of the United States;married Rudolph E Sr; children: Rudolph E Jr. **EDUCATION:** Spelman Coll Atlanta GA, BA Social Sci 1959; ColumbiaUniv NY, NY, MA History 1960;Univ of DE, Newark, DE, PhD-History 1983. **CAREER:** Charlotte Amalie High Schl St Thomas, soc stud tchr 1960-66; Coll of the Virgin Islands St Thomas, history prof 1967-. **ORGANIZATIONS:** Mem Virgin Islds Histl Soc mem Assoc of Caribbean Histn; mem Phi Alpha Theat; consult Virginia Islds Dept of Ed; mem Virgin Islds, Hum Coun; mem VI State Rev Brd for hist Pres Founder Virgin Island 2000; mem VI Brd of Ed 1974-76. **HONORS/ACHIEVEMENTS:** Elec for incl Who's Who Amg Stud in Am Unts and Coll 1957-59; grd flw John Hay Whitney Found Flwshp 1959-60; study-travel flw African Am Inst Ed-to-Africa Prog 1972. **HOME ADDRESS:** Crown Mountain Rd, PO Box 4099, St Thomas, Virgin Islands of the United States 00801. **BUSINESS ADDRESS:** Professor of History, Coll of the Virgin Islands, St Thomas, Virgin Islands of the United States 00801.

KUGBLENU, GEORGE OFOE
Educational administrator. **EDUCATION:** Shaw Univ, BA 1973; NC State Univ, MPA 1975; Atlanta Univ, PhD 1983. **CAREER:** Shaw Univ, lecturer 1975-76; Atlanta Univ, asst prof 1979; Dept of Publ Admin Atlanta Univ, chairperson 1983-. **ORGANIZATIONS:** Co-chair/program com COMPA-Atlanta Chap 1982-84; vice pres arts & sci AU Natl Alumni Assoc Atlanta Chap 1984; asst vp, mem SID Atlanta Chap 1985; mem Amer Soc for Public Admin, Natl Forum for Black Publ Admin. **HONORS/ACHIEVEMENTS:** Mem Alpha Chi Honor Soc 1973; Outstanding Facility Awd Dept of Publ Admin Atlanta Univ 1983; Outstanding Svd Awd Natl Forum for Black Publ Admin 1984. **BUSINESS ADDRESS:** Chairperson, Atlanta Univ - Dept of Pub Admin, 223 James P Brawley Dr, Atlanta, GA 30314.

KUMANYIKA, SHIRIKI K.
Dietician, educator. **PERSONAL:** Born Mar 16, 1945, Baltimore, MD; daughter of Maurice L Adams (deceased) and Catherine Williams Adams; married Christiaan Morssink; children: Chenjerai. **EDUCATION:** Syracuse Univ Coll Arts & Scis, BA Psychology 1965; Columbia Univ, MS Social Work 1969; Cornell Univ, PhD Human Nutrition 1978; The Johns Hopkins Univ Sch of Hygiene & Publ Health, MPH Epidemiology 1984. **CAREER:** James Weldon Johnson Mental Health Clinic/Bird S Coler Hospital/Windham Child Serv, caseworker 1965-69; Natl Urban League, dir family planning proj 1969-70; Addiction Rsch and Treatment Corp Dept Educ & Prevention, community organizer 1970-71; Naomi Gray Assoc NY, proj dir 1971-72; Cornell Univ Ujamaa Residential Coll, resident dir 1973-74; Cornell Univ Div Nutritional Sciences, asst prof 1977-84; The Johns Hopkins Univ School of Hygiene & Public Health, asst prof 1984-89, assoc prof, 1989-. **ORGANIZATIONS:** Assn of Black Cardiologists; Black Caucus of Health Workers; Society for Nutrition Educ; Soc for Epidemiologic Rsch; Fellow, Amer Coll of Nutrition;Amer Public Health Assn, 1976-; Amer Dietetic Assn, 1979-. **HONORS/ACHIEVEMENTS:** Delta Omega Natl Public Health Honor Soc elected 1984; Natl Rsch Serv Award Cardiovascular Epidemiology Trainee The Johns Hopkins Univ 1983-84; Quaker Oats Fellowship Cornell Univ Div of Nutritional Sciences 1976-77; General Mills Fellowship Cornell Univ Div of Nutritional Sciences 1974-76; numerous publications and abstracts, including "Towards a Lower Sodium Lifestyle in Black Communities", Journal of the Natl Medical Assn, 1985; "Ischemic Heart Disease Risk Factors Among Amer Indians and Alaska Natives", background paper for Dept of Health and Human Serv Task Force on Black and Minority Health, 1985, "Obesity in Black Women", Epidemiologic Reviews, 1987, "Beliefs about High Blood Pressure Prevention in a Sample of Black and Hispanic Adults", Amer Journal of Preventive Medicine, "Designing Sodium Reduction Strategies: Problems and Solutions", Clinical Nutrition 1989. **HOME ADDRESS:** 4400 Roland Springs Drive, Baltimore, MD 21210. **BUSINESS ADDRESS:** Associate Professor, The Johns Hopkins University, Dept of Epidemiology, 615 North Wolfe St, Baltimore, MD 21205.

KUNES, KEN R.
Assessor. **PERSONAL:** Born Feb 07, 1932, Maywood, IL; divorced; children: Ken, Leigh

Ann, Jeff. **EDUCATION:** Univ of AZ, Undergrad 1949; NE U, BSBA 1955. **CAREER:** Maricopa Co, assessor 1968-81; Phoenix-Am Ins Agy, fdr 1965-85; Mid-City Glass & Mirror, owner 1986-. **ORGANIZATIONS:** Indep Ins Agents Assn; Phoenix Jaycees; past pres C of C; vice pres Kiwanis; N Phoenix Bapt Ch; state rep Intl Assn of Assessing Ofcrs; past pres AZ Assn of Assessing Ofcrs; Maricopa Cty Sheriff's Religious Comm, chmn; Phoenix Baptist Church, licensed preacher; Alpha Tau Omega frat. **HONORS/ACHIEVEMENTS:** Boss of yr Phoenix Midtowners Bus & Professional Women's Club 1975; rec Cert Appraisal Evaluator (CAE) professional desig for Intl Assn of Assessing Ofcrs the only assessor in AZ to chieve this professional designation. **MILITARY SERVICE:** AUS sgt. **BUSINESS ADDRESS:** owner, Mid-City Glass & Mirror Co, 2934 N 16th St, Phoenix, AZ 85016.

KUYKENDALL, CRYSTAL ARLENE
Educator, attorney. **PERSONAL:** Born Dec 11, 1949, Chicago, IL; daughter of Cleophus Campbell and Ellen Logan (deceased); married Roosevelt Kuykendall Jr, Apr 10, 1969 (deceased); children: Keisha, Rasheki. **EDUCATION:** So IL Univ, BA 1970; Montclair State Coll, MA 1972; Atlanta Univ, EdD 1975; Georgetown Univ Law Ctr, JD 1982. **CAREER:** Seton Hall US Orange NJ, Montclair State Coll, instr 1971-73; DC Publ School, admin intern plnng rsch & eval 1974-75; Natl Comm for Citizens in Ed, dir 1975-77; Natl School Bds Assoc Wash DC, dir urban & minority rel dept 1978-79; PSI Assoc Inc Wash DC, dir ed devel 1979-80; Natl Alliance of Black School Ed, exec dir 1980-81; Roy Littlejohn Assoc Inc, sr assoc 1982-. **ORGANIZATIONS:** Chpsn Natl Adv Council Continuing Ed 1978-; consult Natl Teachers Corp Proj 1978-79; cons, mem Natl Transition Team for the Office of Elem Secondary Ed 1980; mem Amer Assn of School Admin 1974-; mem ed task force Martin Luther King Jr Ctr for Soc Change 1977-; mem Black Amer Law Students Assn 1978-; mem, Amer Bar Assn, Natl Bar Assn, DC Bar Assn, 1988. **HONORS/ACHIEVEMENTS:** Awd for Outstanding Comm Serv to Women & Minorities, Natl Coalition of Esea Title I Parents 1979; "50 Leaders of the Future" Ebony Mag 1978; Hon Citizen New Orleans State of LA, Outstanding Serv Natl Caucus of Black School Bd Mems 1979; "Comm Serv & School Bd" Publ Cross Reference Journal of Multicultural Ed 1979; Presidential Appointment to The Natl Advisory Council on Continuing Educ, US Pres, Jimmy Carter 1978-81, chairperson 1979-81; Black Excellence Award, Black Alumni Association of Southern IL Univ 1981; You*Yours: Making the Most of this School Year, motivational calendar, 1987; booklet published by Amer Univ Mid-Atlantic Equity Center, "Improving Black Student Achievement Through Enhancing Self-Image 1989. **BUSINESS ADDRESS:** Director of Marketing, Roy Littlejohn Assoc, Inc, 1101 14th Street NW, Suite 1000, Washington, DC 20005.

KUYKENDALL, LAWRENCE P.
Publisher. **PERSONAL:** Born Oct 05, 1919, Okeene, OK; married Lee Belle; children: Mack L, Don P, Kathleen K. **EDUCATION:** Langston U. **CAREER:** Ft Sill, driver instr 1944, athl dir 1966, EEO counselor 1953-63; Community Guide, fdr editor pblshr. **HONORS/ACHIEVEMENTS:** Outst handicap yr from Gov OK. **MILITARY SERVICE:** AUS Civil Serv Dir undersecretary.

KYLE, AARON
Professional athlete. **PERSONAL:** Born Apr 06, 1954; married Judy; children: Ashley. **EDUCATION:** Univ of WY, deg journ. **CAREER:** Dallas Cowboys, professional footbl cornerback 1976-; owner of record store Dallas. **HONORS/ACHIEVEMENTS:** Played in E W Bowl; All-Western Conf 1975; Shared Club Lead, Fumble Recoveries (2) 1978; intercepted 3 passes reg season & another in playoffs 1978. **BUSINESS ADDRESS:** c/o Dee Rauch, NFL Players Association, 1300 Connecticut NW Ste 407, Washington, DC 20036.

KYLE, GENGHIS
Organist, bandleader. **PERSONAL:** Born Jun 07, 1923, Los Angeles, CA; married Dorothy F; children: Alfred C, Marie J. **EDUCATION:** Los Angeles City Coll; USC Ext. **CAREER:** Vultee Aircraft Co, sub assembler 1942; City of Los Angeles CA Dept of Water & Power, storekeeper 1954-82 (retired); Genghis Kyle Enterprises, band leader, personal manager. **ORGANIZATIONS:** Mem Broadcast Music Inc; mem Local 47 Musicians Union; mem shop co-dirSignature Music Pub Co Imperial Youth Theater Work; mem Coaches & Mgr Assoc LA. **HONORS/ACHIEVEMENTS:** Salute to Stars Award 1963; Recorded For Many Record Co 1963-73. **MILITARY SERVICE:** AUS pfc 1943-46; AUS sgt ES 1950. **BUSINESS ADDRESS:** Genghis Kyle Enterprises, 1544 W 93 St, Los Angeles, CA 90047.

KYLE, MARY J.
Free lance writer. **PERSONAL:** Born in St Paul, MN; daughter of Ernest B James (deceased) and Edith Burnett James (deceased); married Earl F Kyle Sr, Nov 12, 1927 (deceased); children: Shirley Kyle Heaton, Robert C, Earlene Kyle Walker, Earle F. **EDUCATION:** Univ Minnesota; Univ of M Estension Div; Palmer Inst of Writng California; Croydon Inst of Writing-Illinois; Writers Digest School Ohio. **CAREER:** WLOL AM/FM, talk show host 1969-79; KMSP-TV, edtrl commentator 1969-79; Minnesota Sentiel Publishing Co, pres. **ORGANIZATIONS:** Pres Minnesota Press Club 1975-76; Minnesota Newspaper Assc; Natl Newspaper Assc; Natl Newspaper Pblshr Assc; Press Women of Minnesota; Minnesota Business League; Natl Business League; Sigma Delta Chi Soc Professional Journalists SDX; Greater Minnesota C of C; life mem NAACP; Minnesota Cncl Ec Ed; Minnesota State Bd Law Examiners 1981; SBA Regnl Cncl; Amer Rhbltn Found; Metropolitan YMCA Greater Mpls; Norwest Bank/N Amer Officec; trustee Minnesota Soc Fine Arts; Natl Advsry Cncl/Status Women 1975; public broadcasting dir KTCA-TV; bd dir Minneapolis NAACP; Minneapolis Urban League; Minnesota Press Club; Natl Conf of Christians & Jews. **HONORS/ACHIEVEMENTS:** Foremost Women Commnctns; MN Historical Soc Women of Minnesota; Black Women of Minnesota; Minnesota Black Comm; Minnesota Women's Yearbook 1984; Herman Roe Memrl Award Editorial Writing MNA First Woman; Frank Murrary Award Journalism St Thomas Coll; human rights award Jewish Labor Com; alpha phi alpha Journalism award; NAACP journalism/human rights award; Bishop Allen Journalism Award; Urban League civic & serv awrd; Afrcn Am cultural arts ctr comm serv awrd; city of Mpls dstngshd serv awrd; mn govnr citation of hon; Alpha Kappa Alpha comm Serv Award; Minnesota state bar assc meritorious serv awrd; norwest bnk comm serv awrd; nab spec commendation; YWCA outstanding achievement award; published "View From a Window," (memoir) 1989. **HOME ADDRESS:** 3637 4th Avenue S, Minneapolis, MN 55409.

KYLE, ODES J., JR.
Engineer. **PERSONAL:** Born Jan 30, 1931, Toledo, OH; married Bobbie Mcclelland; children: Odes, Lewis, Vickie, Lora, George. **EDUCATION:** Mech Engr IN Inst of Tech, BS 1962. **CAREER:** Timken Co, ind eng 1962, mgmt trainee 1964, foreman 1965, gen foreman 1967, manager of admin 1982, supervisor of trainging & education & safety-canten dist 1986. **ORGANIZATIONS:** Past pres Camton Bd of Educ 1974; mem Recreation Bd; Draft & Bd # 109; trustee St Paul AME Canton OH; grand orator of PH Grand Lodge of OH; grand master Prince Hall Grand Lodge. **HONORS/ACHIEVEMENTS:** Recip Camton Man of Yr 1967; utstanding Man of Am 1967-68; 33 Deg Mason 1975. **MILITARY SERVICE:** USMC 1951-53. **BUSINESS ADDRESS:** Timken Co, Canton, OH.

KYLES, DWAIN JOHANN
Lawyer. **PERSONAL:** Born Aug 25, 1954, Chicago, IL; son of Rev Samuel Billy Kyles and Gwendolyn Kyles Griffin; married Theresa Cropper Kyles, Jun 19, 1988; children: Chad Joseph Kyles. **EDUCATION:** Lake Forest Coll, BA Econ Urban Study 1976; Georgetown Univ Law Center, JD 1979. **CAREER:** Congressman Harold Ford 9th Dist TN, staff aide 1976-78; Office for Civil Rights Dept Health Educ & Welfare, law clerk 1978-79; Johnson Products Co, staff attny 1979-83; Office of Mayor Harold Washington, special counsel for minority bus devel 1983-84; McCormick Place Convention Center, house counsel, mgmt & intergovt liaison 1984-88; Dept of Economic Devel, special counsel to commissioner 1989-; Heroes A Sports Bar: Grill, Inc, owner, 1987-. **ORGANIZATIONS:** Mem Amer Bar Assoc 1979-, Natl Bar Assoc 1979-, Cook Cty Bar Assoc 1979-; bd mem Forum for Evolution of Progressive Arts 1983-; found & 1st pres mem New Chicago Comm; mem Operation PUSH, NAACP. **HONORS/ACHIEVEMENTS:** Dean's List Jr & Sr Years; 1st recipient of Mentor of the Year Urban Focus 1984.

KYLES, JOSEPHINE H.
Educator. **PERSONAL:** Born Sep 06, 1900, Lynchburg, VA; married Bishop Lynwood W Kyles (deceased); children: 2 children. **EDUCATION:** Oberlin Coll, MA; Columbia Univ, MA; Union Theol Seminary, MRE; D Adult Educ. **CAREER:** Lynchburg VA, teacher; VA State Coll and Hampton Inst, instructor; Dept of Christian Educ for the Cncl of Churches of Greater Washington Area, dir; GradSch of Religion of Howard Univ, instructor; Metro Detroit MI Cncl of Churches, dir of christian educ, dir serv dept; Arthritis Foundation Project at Washington Hospital Ctr, social health educator. **ORGANIZATIONS:** Trainer/consultant Covenant for the Natl Ctr on Ministry with the Aging; mem Natl Adv Comm Interfaith Volunteer Caregivers Prog; vstg lecturer in Religious Educ Seminary for Black Ministries in Philadelphia PA; five certificates from the Psychiatric Inst on Stress, Crisis Prevention, Values and Ethics, Alcoholism; mem adv bd DC Village, adv bd Robert Wood Johnson Foundation; delegate Conf of the Soc for Intl Develop in Abijon West Africa; staff mem White House Conf on Aging. **HONORS/ACHIEVEMENTS:** Sojourner Truth Awd.

KYLES, SHARRON FAYE
Police officer. **PERSONAL:** Born Jan 03, 1950, Jackson, MS; daughter of Willie Lee Catchings and Bennie Lee Lewis Catchings; married James Tyrone Kyles, Aug 09, 1978; children: Darrell Augustues Kyles, La Keista Renee Kyles. **EDUCATION:** Jackson State Coll, Jackson MS, 1968-69; Jackson Police Training Academy, Jackson MS, 1975. **CAREER:** Jackson Police Department, patrol sergeant, 1975-. **ORGANIZATIONS:** Pres, Smith Chapel Freewill Baptist Church Choir, 1975-85; pres, Jackson Concerned Officers for Progress, 1980-88; Committee on Administration, YWCA, 1984-; mem, Natl Black Police Assn, 1986-; mem, New Mount Zion Inspirtional Choir, mem, NAACP; mem, Mississippi Mass Choir. **HONORS/ACHIEVEMENTS:** Outstanding Bravery, North Jackson Kiwanis Club, 1983; Lawman of the Year, LA/MS/West Tenn Dist of Kiwanis, 1983-84; Distinguished Service Award, Jackson Police Dept, 1984; Police Officer of the Month, Jackson Assn of Life Underwriters, 1984; J-Cop Silver Shield Community Service, Jackson Concerned Officers for Progress, 1985; Outstanding Heroic Performance Award, Lanier Class of 1965, 1985; The Mississippi Mass Choir Live Gospel Recording, 1988. **BUSINESS ADDRESS:** Sergeant, Jackson Police Dept, City of Jackson, 327 East Pascagoula Street, Jackson, MS 39205.

L

LABELLE, PATTI
Singer/actress. **PERSONAL:** Born Oct 04, 1944, Philadelphia, PA; married Armstead Edwards; children: Stanley, Dodd, Zuri. **CAREER:** Began career as lead singer of Patti LaBelle & the Bluebelles 1950; Sang in choir growing up; Sang with group Ordettes; Formed new group Bluebelles 1961; Went solo 1977; appeared in hit move Beverly Hills Cop, 2 hits from movie were at the top of the charts; participant Live AID Benefit Rock Concert; TV Special "Sisters in the Name of Love" 1986. **HONORS/ACHIEVEMENTS:** First single w/ Bluebelles went Gold group made Top 40; Gold LP "Winner in You" album went Gold; was in Billboard's Top 10. **BUSINESS ADDRESS:** MCA Records Inc, 100 Universal City Plaza, Universal City, CA 91608.

LABRIE, HARRINGTON
Elected official. **PERSONAL:** Born Oct 06, 1909, Lebeau, LA; married Ernestine (deceased); children: Dolores Fischer, Ann Marie McCune, Theron, Kenneth J, Willard, Doris Matthew, Janice Domechet. **EDUCATION:** Immaculate Conception High School 1927. **CAREER:** St Landry Parish School Bd, school bus driver 1952-75; Cattle, Cotton, farmer 1932-; Williams Progressive Life Ins Co, insurance agent 1951-; St Landry Parish Ward 4, justice of peace 1972-; Labrie Realty, chmn of bd 1979-. **ORGANIZATIONS:** Grand knight Knights of Peter Claver 1932-; mem NAACP 1956-, LA Justice of Peace Assoc 1972-; advisory bd mem First Natl Bank 1978-. **HOME ADDRESS:** PO Box 395, Lebeau, LA 71345.

LABRIE, PETER, JR.
City planner, educator. **PERSONAL:** Born Mar 13, 1940, Palmetto, LA; married Rita Y Montgomery; children: Jalilah Alisha, Cesaire Patrice. **EDUCATION:** Univ of CA, B Pol Sci 1962, M City Plan 1965. **CAREER:** Oakland Ofc of Comm Devel, city planner educ consult asst dir; Early Warning Sys Assn of Bay Area Govts, consult 1974; San Mateo Co, design of rapid transit sys; Parsons-Brinkerhoff, tudor & bechtel 1972-73; Atlanta, rapid transit station area devel 1972;Univ of C, lecturer 1969-73; Soc Sci Hampton Inst, 1966-67; Planning Dept Atlanta, planner 1967-69. **ORGANIZATIONS:** Adv Nat Assn of Planners; bd chmn Govt Reforms in Planning; has written various articles. **BUSINESS ADDRESS:** Oakland Ofc of Comm Devel, Oakland, CA 94612.

LACAILLE, RUPERT ANDREW
Physician. **PERSONAL:** Born Nov 30, 1917, Port of Spain; married Marjorie; children: Terri. **EDUCATION:** WV St Coll, BS 1939; Meharrymed Coll, MD 1943; intrnshp 1943-44; Harlem Hosp, res 1944-45; Montifiore Hosp, 1945-46; Harlem Hosp, 1953-58; NYU Post Grad Sch of Med, Grad Courses basic scis in surg 1956-57; am coll of orthopeds, symposium on trauma & orthopeds 1966; HarvardUniv Sch of Med, PostGrad Course Surg 1967; Cook Co Post Grad Sch of Med, Trauma & Fractures 1968. **CAREER:** W Adams Hosp, surg srv 1974-; VA Hosp Long Bch, spinal %Cord injury serv 1973-74; Meth Maint Prog Lincoln Hosp CPD, unit dir 1972-73; BrookdaleHosp & Med Ctr, emerg serv 1970-73; Kings Co Med Ctr, asst att surg 1967-73; Jewish Hosp & Med Ctr Brooklyn, asst att surg 1966-73; Greepoint Hosp, dir %Emerg svc, Asso chief surg 1966-70; Italian Hosp, att Surg 1958-61; Manhattan Gen Hosp, asso att surg 1958-65; Harlem Hosp, asst att Surg 1958-65. **ORGANIZATIONS:** Am Soc of Med Examiners; Intrntl Coll of Surgs. **HONORS/ACHIEVEMENTS:** Numerous rsrch pblctns. **MILITARY SERVICE:** AUS capt 1951-53.

LACEY, DIANE E.
Administrator. **PERSONAL:** Born in New York, NY. **EDUCATION:** Univ of CT, BA. **CAREER:** Radio Station WWRL AM, dir pub affairs 1978-; Sydenham Hosp, dir patient relations & vol serv 1977-78; New York City Health Hosp Corp, asst to pres 1974-76; John Hay Whitney Ford Found, grantee 1971-73; City of New York, spl asst to mayor 1970-71; Hunts Point Multi-Serv Compre Health Cntr, dir 1968-70. **ORGANIZATIONS:** Dir New York City Health & Hosp Corp; natl bd mem Girls Clubs of Am; bd mem Am Cancer Soc; founding mem Asn of Black Social Workers; founding mem Nat Black Feminists; mem Nat Council of Negro Women; bd mem Conf on Alternative State & Local Policies; organizer 1st Nat Conf on Drug Abuse Policy for Third World Leaders 1972; candidate State Leg. **HONORS/ACHIEVEMENTS:** Twice Elected Dem Dist Leader; Paul Robeson Contributor Awardee Nat Coalition of Black Trade Unionists. **BUSINESS ADDRESS:** 41-30 58th St, New York, NY 11377.

LACEY, SAM
Athlete. **PERSONAL:** Born Mar 28, 1948, Indianola, MS. **EDUCATION:** NM State U, 1970. **CAREER:** KS City Kings, player. **ORGANIZATIONS:** All Star Team 1975. **HONORS/ACHIEVEMENTS:** Holds num team defensive records; Team Leader/Defensive Rebounds 7 Straight Yrs/Blocked Shot Leader 7 Straight Yrs/Blocked Shot Season Record 1 Yr 2 SingleGame Records For Most Steals & Most Blocked Shots Kings.

LACEY, WILBERT, JR.
Psychiatrist. **PERSONAL:** Born Dec 01, 1936, Washington, DC; married Bernardine Jackson; children: 4 Children. **EDUCATION:** Howard U, BS 1959; HowardUniv Coll of Med, MD 1968. **CAREER:** HowardUniv Coll of Med, clinical asst prof 1975-; HowardUniv Hlth Serv,Univ psychiatrist 1973-. **ORGANIZATIONS:** Mem DC Me Soc; Nat Med Assn; Am Inst of Hypnosis; Am Coll Hlth Assn; Metro WA Soc for Adolescent Psychiatry; Joint Cncl of WA Psyc Soc; life mem Kappa Alpha Psi Frat; mem Fox Ridge Civic Assn 1977. **HONORS/ACHIEVEMENTS:** Cert Am Bd of Psychiatry & Neurology Inc 1977. **MILITARY SERVICE:** AUS 1st lt 1960-62. **BUSINESS ADDRESS:** HowardUniv, Washington, DC 20059.

LACHMAN, RALPH STEVEN
Physician, educator. **PERSONAL:** Born May 12, 1935; married Rose Katz; children: Nicole, Monette. **EDUCATION:** Temple Univ, BA 1957; Meharry Med Coll, MD 1961; Bronx-Lebanon Med Cntr NYC, rotating intern 1961-62; Mt Sinai Hosp NYC, ped resident 1962-64, radiology 1966-68; Children's Hosp Boston, ped radiology 1969-70. **CAREER:** US Army Hosp Bad Kremznach, Germany, Cpt USMC 1964-66; UCLA, asst prof radiology & ped 1970-73, assoc prof 1973-79, prof 1979-. **ORGANIZATIONS:** Chmn Equal Opp/Academic Affirm Action Comm UCLA 1981-83; mem Soc Pediatric Radiol; Am Coll Radiology; LA Pediatric Soc; AAAS; Western Soc for Pediatric Rsrch; Am Fedn Clinical Rsrch. **HONORS/ACHIEVEMENTS:** Fellowship Am Coll of Radiology 1983; to date 103 scientific articles published. **MILITARY SERVICE:** AUS Capt Med Corps 1964-66. **BUSINESS ADDRESS:** Prof Radiology & Pediatrics, UCLA, HGH/UCLA Med Center, Torrance, CA 90509.

LACKEY, EDGAR F.
Executive officer. **PERSONAL:** Born Mar 09, 1930, Ennis, TX; children: Anglyn, Anita, James, Mia, Ronald, Tammy. **EDUCATION:** Texas Coll, BA 1963; Ball State Univ, MBA; Univ of Oklahoma, MLS. **CAREER:** Hamilton Pk High School, educator & coach; Dallas Industrial School, educator; USAF, criminal investigator; Lynn's Enterprises Private Investigators, owner. **ORGANIZATIONS:** Asst dir OIC; dir Law Enforce Minority Manpower Proj; mem Fed Exec Assn; NAACP; Urban League; Negro C of C Dallas. **MILITARY SERVICE:** USAF Special Investigator 1947-60. **BUSINESS ADDRESS:** Executive Officer, Natl Conf Christians & Jews, 43 W 57th St, New York, NY 10019.

LACOUR, LOUIS BERNARD
Attorney. **PERSONAL:** Born Aug 12, 1926, Columbus, OH; son of Louis LaCour and Cleo Carter LaCour; married Jane McFarland; children: Lynne Denise, Avril R LaCour-Hartnagel, Cheryl Celeste. **EDUCATION:** OH State Univ, BA 1952; Franklin Univ Law School, LLB 1961; Capital Univ, JD 1969. **CAREER:** City of Columbus, OH, land acquisition ofcr 1959-62; Capital Univ Law Sch, adjunct prof 1975-80; Private Practice, attorney; USDistrict Court, special master 1981-87; GreenBern Mgmt, Inc, president. **ORGANIZATIONS:** Past vp, devel code adv comm United Comm Council; mem Columbus Bar Assoc, past pres Columbus Urban League; past sec Mid-OH Reg Planning Commission; past vice pres, Columbus Area Intl Prog; mem Columbus Leadership Conf, Selective Serv Appeals Bd, Fed Bar Exam Comm, So Dist, E Div; past vice chmn Columbus Civic Ctr Comm; steering comm Devel Com Greater Columbus; adv bd Bishop Hartley HS; mem Univ Area Civic Assn, Eastland Area Civic Assn, Kensington Park Area Civic Assn, Blendon Meadows Civic Assn, Model Cities Neighborhood Rev Bd, Bethany Homes Devel Corp, Bide-A-Wee Pk Civic Assn; spec master US Dist Ct 1975-80; fed bar examiner US Dist Ct 1980-84; spec counsel Columbus City Atty 1984-85; trustee Jazz Arts Group 1984-85; trustee, Greater Columbus Arts Council; trustee, Ohio Citizens Com for the Arts. **HONORS/ACHIEVEMENTS:** Most Influential Men in Columbus 1972. **MILITARY SERVICE:** US Air Corps 1944-45. **HOME ADDRESS:** 1809 N Cassady Ave, Columbus, OH 43219. **BUSINESS ADDRESS:** Attorney, Cox, Cox & LaCour, 50 W Broad St, Columbus, OH 43215.

LACOUR, NATHANIEL HAWTHORNE
Educational administrator. **PERSONAL:** Born Feb 11, 1938, New Orleans, LA; married Josie Brown; children: Carey Renee, Carla Cenee, Charlette Jene. **EDUCATION:** SoUniv A&M Coll Baton Rouge, BS 1960; SoUniv A&M Coll Baton Rouge, MSTB 1965. **CAREER:** United Teachres of New Orleans, pres 1970-; Carver Sr HS, biology teacher 1961-70. **ORGANIZATIONS:** Officer various tchr assns; chmn New Orleans Manpower Adv Planning Council; mem Am Inst of Biologists; mem exec bd Greater New Orleans AFL-CIO; mem YMCA; mem NAACP; exec bd New Orleans Urban League; bd of dirs New Orleans Pub Library. **BUSINESS ADDRESS:** President, United Teachers of New Orleans, 4370 Louisa Dr, New Orleans, LA 70126.

LACOUR, VANUE B.
Retired attorney. **PERSONAL:** Born Sep 10, 1915, Natchez, LA; son of Ernest Lacour and Ernestine Prudhomme; married Arthemise Wilson; children: Vanue B Jr, Leonard J, Cynthia Marie, Bernard L, Elaine Theresa, Michael M, Anthony G. **EDUCATION:** Xavier Univ New Orleans, AB 1938; Howard Univ, JD 1941. **CAREER:** Private Practice Kansas City, MO, attorney 1942-47; Southern Univ Law School Baton Rouge, LA, educator 1947-70, dean law school 1970-71; Lacour & Calloway, retired atty. **ORGANIZATIONS:** Past chmn LA Commn Govtl Ethics; advisory mem Istrouma Area Boy Scout Council; mem Alpha Phi Alpha; mem LA Commission of Ethics for Public Employees. **HONORS/ACHIEVEMENTS:** Alpha Eta Honor Soc; Silver Beaver Boy Scouts Amer; past vice pres Natl Bar Assn; past sec MO Conf of Branches-NAACP; Baton Rouge Legal Secretaries Assn, boss of the yr 1980-81; past bd mem Blundon Home-Family Counseling Serv; Branch Chapter American Red Cross.

LACY, EDWARD J.
Educator. **PERSONAL:** Born Sep 13, 1922, Dallas, TX; married Freddie J Slusher; children: Charles M. **EDUCATION:** A&T Coll, BS 1947; Columbia Univ, MA 1952; Springfield Coll, further study 1953; Indiana Univ, further study 1954-55. **CAREER:** Voorhees Jr Coll Denmark, SC, teacher & coach 1947-50; Bladen Cnty Schools Elizabethtown, NC, teacher & coach 1950-56; St Paul's Coll Lawrenceville, VA, teacher & coach 1956-57; Booker T Washington HS Tulsa, OK, teacher & coach 1957-74; Tulsa Publ Schools, dir of athletics/phys ed. **ORGANIZATIONS:** Bd mgmt Hutcherson YMCA Tulsa 1960-; adv bd St John's Hospital Tulsa 1981-; mem Kappa Alpha Psi Frat 1946-; consult Am Football Coaches Assn 1971; OK Coaches Assn 1970; NE Dist HS Coaches Miami, OK 1972; mem Natl HS Coaches Assn; Am All Health Phys Educ & Rec; mem N Tulsa Optimist Club; Tulsa Pk & Rec Bd; St Monica Cath Par Counc. **HONORS/ACHIEVEMENTS:** Physical Fitness Award Southeast Tulsa Jaycees 1968; Coach of the Year Dist 5 Natl HS School Coaches Assn 1972; Coach of the Year OK Coaches Assn 1968, 1971, 1973; OK Hall of Fame OK Coaches Assn 1979. **MILITARY SERVICE:** AUS Sgt served 10 months. **HOME ADDRESS:** 21 E Woodrow Pl, Tulsa, OK 74106.

LACY, LESLIE ALEXANDER
Author, lecturer. **PERSONAL:** Born Aug 08, 1937, Franklin, LA. **EDUCATION:** Univ So CA, MA 1959;Univ Ghana, MA 1964. **CAREER:** New Sch Social Rsrch, lectr 1969-70; Howard U, lectr 1968-70; NY U, lectr 1968-70; Univ Ghana, tutor dept polit sci 1964-66. **ORGANIZATIONS:** Author Black Africa on The Move 1969; The Rise & Fall of a Proper Negro 1970; Cheer the Lonesome; Traveller 1970. **BUSINESS ADDRESS:** c/o Tom Feelings, 31 West 31st St, New York, NY 10001.

LACY, VERSIA LINDSAY
Educator. **PERSONAL:** Born Mar 15, 1929, Houston, TX; married JW; children: Lindsay Keith, Elizabeth Juliene. **EDUCATION:** Huston-Tillotson Coll, BS 1944-48; Atlanta Univ, MS 1948-50; Univ of TX, 1952,55-56; Univ of OR, 1958; TX Womans Univ, PhD 1966-73. **CAREER:** Paul Quinn Coll, instr, dean of women 1950-55; Tyler Jr Coll, asst prof 1956-66; TX Womans Univ, grad rsh asst 1966-69; Bishop Coll, assoc prof 1969-77; TX So Univ, guest prof 1971; Dallas ISD, sci/health coord 1977-82; Dallas ISD Sci/Engrg Magnet, prof 1977-. **ORGANIZATIONS:** Mem Radiation Rsch Soc, AAAS, AIBS, NIS, SW Photobiol Group, TARR, TAS, NTBS, BBB Biol Soc, BKX Sci Hon Soc, TWU Club of Sigma Xi Soc, Third Natl Anti-Basileus Zeta Phi Beta Sor Inc 1952-54; gov S Central Dist Natl Assoc of Negro Bus & Professional Womens Clubs Inc; 2nd natl vice pres NANB & PH Clubs Inc 1979-81; chpsn Amer Heart Assoc Spec Task Force; bd dir Amer Heart Assoc Dallas Chapt; bd dir YMCA Moorland Br; natl ed of Crown; mem SME Comm Mustang Dist, Circle 10 Counc, BSA, PTA, David W Carter & DA Huley Schools. **HONORS/ACHIEVEMENTS:** Top Ladies of Distinction Inc; Woman of the Year Psi Chap Iota Phi Lambda Sor So Reg 1976; 1st Runner-up Natl Liola P Parker Awd; Woman of the Year United for Action Dallas Black C of C 1976; Outstanding Achievement Awd Zeta Phi Beta 1974; Outstanding Achievement Awd, Top Ladies of Distinction 1973; Sojourner Truth Natl Meritorious Awd 1982; Total Images Awd Mountain View C 1983. **BUSINESS ADDRESS:** Professor, Dallas ISD, Science/Engineering Magnet, 3434 So RL Thornton Fwy, Dallas, TX 75224.

LADAY, KERNEY
Office equipment executive. **PERSONAL:** Born Mar 14, 1942, Ville Platte, LA; son of Sampson and Lillius Laday; married Floradese Thomas; children: Marucs K, Kerney Jr, Anthony D. **EDUCATION:** Southern Univ, BS 1965; Louisiana State Univ, MS 1970; Southern Methodist Univ, MBA 1982. **CAREER:** Southern Univ, asst placement dir 1968-71; Xerox Corp, vice pres 1971-, vice pres/region general mgr. **ORGANIZATIONS:** Bd of dir Eltrex Corp 1982-86, United Way of Dallas 1987-; bd of dir North TX Commn; trustee Shiloh Bapt Church Plano TX; assoc bd of dirs SMU; bd of dir African American Museum; mem Dallas Transportation "Thing Tank"; bd of dir Dallas Chamber of Commerce; bd of dir Dallas Citizens Council; bd of dir North Carolina Natl Bank of Texas. **HONORS/ACHIEVEMENTS:** Renowned Graduate Southern Univ; Presidential Citation Natl Educ for Equal Opportunities. **MILITARY SERVICE:** Signal Corp capt 1965-68. **HOME ADDRESS:** 6001 Jericho Court, Dallas, TX 75248. **BUSINESS ADDRESS:** Vice Pres/Regional Genl Mgr, Xerox Corporation, 222 W Las Colinas Blvd, Irving, TX 75039.

LADD, FLORENCE CAWTHORNE
Educator, psychologist. **PERSONAL:** Born Jun 16, 1932, Washington, DC; daughter of William Cawthorne and Eleanor Willis Cawthorne; children: Michael Cawthorne Ladd. **EDUCATION:** Howard Univ, BS 1953; Univ of Rochester, PhD 1958. **CAREER:** Age Center of New England, rsch assoc 1958-60; Simmons Coll, asst prof 1960-61; Robert College (Istanbul), asst prof 1962-63; Harvard Graduate School of Educ, lecturer & rsch assoc 1965-

70; Radcliffe Inst, fellow 1970-72; Harvard Graduate School of Design, assoc prof 1972-77; School of Architecture & Planning MIT, assoc dean 1977-79; Wellesley Coll, dean of students 1979-84; S African Educ Program, consultant 1984-85; WEB DuBois Inst, visiting scholar; Oxfam Amer, dir of educ & outreach 1985-87; Oxford America Assoc Executive Director, 1987-. **ORGANIZATIONS:** Mem Black Women for Policy Action; mem TransAfrica; bd mem Overseas Development Network, United Natl Intl Rsch & Training Inst for the Advancement of Women; Natl Council of South African Programs; Association of Women in Development. **HONORS/ACHIEVEMENTS:** Hon mem Amer Inst of Architects, Wellesley Alumnae Assn, Phi Beta Kappa, Sigma Xi. **HOME ADDRESS:** 82 Larch Rd, Cambridge, MA 02138. **BUSINESS ADDRESS:** Dir Educ & Outreach, Oxfam America, 115 Broadway, Boston, MA 02138.

LADSON, LOUIS FITZGERALD
Pharmacist. **PERSONAL:** Born Jan 03, 1951, Georgetown, SC; son of Henry Ladson and Susan Smith Ladson; married Sharon Harris; children: Eric, Tisha. **EDUCATION:** St Olaf Coll, BA History 1978; Central Michigan Univ, MA Business 1982; Creighton Univ, BS Pharmacy 1981. **CAREER:** James A Haley VA Hosp, resident pharmacy 1982-83; SuperX Univ Sq Mall, pharmacy mgr 1983-84; Lincourt Pharmacy, pharmacy mgr 1984-. **ORGANIZATIONS:** Mem Amer Soc of Hosp Pharm 1979-, Kappa Psi Frat 1980-, Natl Assoc of Retail Druggists 1982-, FL Pharmacy Assoc 1982-; pharmacy consultant Adult Care Living Facilities 1984-; mem Chamber of Commerce Clearwater 1985-, NAACP clearwater Chap 1985-; mem, Alpha Phi Alpha Frat 1988-. **HONORS/ACHIEVEMENTS:** Outstanding Leadership Certificate Creighton Univ 1981; Outstanding Serv Awd Creighton Univ Black Faculty 1982; Pharmacy Consultant Bd of Pharmacy 1982; Lincourt Pharmacy Newsletter 1984-. **MILITARY SERVICE:** AUS 1st Lt 3 yrs; Captain; Certificates of Appreciation 1977,80, Commission 1981. **BUSINESS ADDRESS:** Dir of Pharmacy, Lincourt Professional Pharmacy, 501 Lincoln Ave South, Clearwater, FL 34616.

LAFAYETTE, BERNARD, JR.
Educational administrator. **PERSONAL:** Born Jul 29, 1940, Tampa, FL; married Kate Bulls; children: 2 Children. **EDUCATION:** Am Bapt Theol Sem, BA 1958-61; Harvard U, EdM 1972, EdD 1974. **CAREER:** Lindenwood Coll Four, dir; Exce Inst, adm chief prog ofc dep dir PUSH 1979-80; Gustavus Adolphus Coll, dir prof 1974-76; So Christian Leadership Conf, natl prog admin 1976; SNCC AL Voters Regist Project, dir 1962-63. **ORGANIZATIONS:** Nat coor Poor People's Campaign 1968; founder chmn of exec bd Inst of Human Rights & Resp 1979-; natl chmn Founder Nat Black Christian Student Leadership Consult 1979-; chmn Consortium on Peace Research Educ & Devel 1975; bd mem Ministries to Blacks in Higher Educ 1977; treas & past pres Phi Delta Kappa. **HONORS/ACHIEVEMENTS:** Hon Prof Frat Harvard Chpt; Underwood Fellowship Danforth Found; Full Fellowship Nat Council of Negro Women; Award for Settling Sch Strikes The Group ofConcerned Students St Louis; Fact-finding Visit to Panama with Congressman Andrew Young 1973. **BUSINESS ADDRESS:** Lindenwood College, Four 100 S Hanley, Clayton, MD 63105.

LAFAYETTE, KATE BULLS
Educator. **PERSONAL:** Born Dec 26, 1935, Tuskegee Inst, AL; married Dr Bernard LaFayette Jr. **EDUCATION:** Eliot-Pearson Sch Medford MA, early childhood educ cert 1957; Tufts Univ Medford MA, bS Educ 1957, MEd early childhood educ 1965. **CAREER:** Webster Coll Webster Groves MO, prof child study 1976-; MN Region IX Council for Child Care, child devel specialist 1975-76; MN Family Day Care Training Proj, family day care consultant 1974-75; Assoc Day Care Serv of Boston, educ consult 1971-73; Wheelock Coll Boston, instructor 1971; KLH Child Devel Center Cambridge, exec dir 1967-71. **ORGANIZATIONS:** Dir Orchard Park Day Care Ctr Boston 1965-67; tchr kindergarten Chambliss Children's House Tuskegee 1961-62; corr secr St Louis Links 1965-; bd mem DayCare & Child Dev Council of Amer 1970-; bd mem Edgewood Children's Ctr Webster Groves MO 1977-. **HONORS/ACHIEVEMENTS:** Recipient Outstanding Young Women of Amer Award 1965; mem Danforth Assc Prog; Natl Adv Council of Danforth Assc Prog. **BUSINESS ADDRESS:** Webster Coll &, 470 E Lockwood Ave, Webster Groves, MO 63119.

LAFONTANT, JEWEL STRADFORD
Attorney, government official. **PERSONAL:** Born Dec 03, Chicago, IL; widowed; children: John Rogers. **EDUCATION:** Oberlin Coll, BA 1943; Univ of Chicago Law, JD 1946. **CAREER:** US Attorney's Office, asst attny 1955-58; Stradford Lafontant Law Firm, partner 1961-72, 1975-; United Nations, rep 1972; US Dept of Justice, dep solicitor gen 1973-75; Vedder Price Kaufman Kammholz, sr partner 1983-. **ORGANIZATIONS:** Chmn Fed Womens Prog, Dept of Justice 1973-75; former dir Jewel Co Inc, Hanes Inc, Foote Cone & Belding; dir TWC-TWA, Continental IL Bank & Trust Co,Pantry Pride Inc; former dir Bendix Corp, Harte Hanks Commun; commiss Natl Coun on Ed Rsch 1976-80; vchmn US Adv Comm Intl Ed & Cultural Affairs1969-73; pres Council on Minority Bus Enterprise 1970-73; sec Natl Bar Assoc 1956-61; bd mgr Chicago Bar Assoc 1962-64; bd trustees Lake Forest Coll; alumni bd Univ of Chicago Law School; dir Mobil Corp, Equitable Life Assurance Soc; mem Pres Exec Exchange Commiss, Pres Private Sector Commiss on Cost Control; mem Pres Reagan's Library Foundation; bd of dirs Revlon Group Inc, TBG Broadcasting Corp, Capital Mgmt Inc. **HONORS/ACHIEVEMENTS:** Howard Univ Doctor of Humane Letters 1973; Providence Coll Doctor of Humanitarian Letters 1973; Hon LLD, Cedar Crest Coll, Providence Coll, Eastern MI Univ, Heidelberg Coll, Lake Forest Coll, Marymount Coll, Oberlin Coll, Loyola Univ of Chgo, Governors State Univ; LLD Chicago Medical Univ 1984. **BUSINESS ADDRESS:** Senior Partner, Vedder Price Kaufman Kammholz, 115 So LaSalle, Chicago, IL 60603.

LAFONTANT, JULIEN J.
Educator. **PERSONAL:** Born in Port-au-Prince, Haiti;married Blandine. **EDUCATION:** SUNY Binghamton, MA (distinction) 1974, PhD 1976. **CAREER:** Exec Mansion Morovia Liberia, translator 1961-63; Ivory Coast Embassy Monrovia Liberia, translator 1963-66; Cuttington Coll Suakoko Liberia, asst prof 1966-72; SUNY Binghamton, teaching asst 1972-76; Univ of NE Lincoln, asst prof 1976-77; Acting Chair Black Studies UNO, asst prof 1977-78; Univ of NE, assoc prof 1978-82, full prof French Chair Black Studies UNO 1983-85; full prof French and Black Studies 1986-. **ORGANIZATIONS:** Bd mem NE Comm for the Humanities 1983-; mem Humanities Adv Panel to NE ETV 1984. **HONORS/ACHIEVEMENTS:** Great Teacher Awd Univ of NE Omaha 1982; book on Montesquieu book entitled Understanding A Culture and several articles dealing with the Black exper in general and the French encounter with Blacks. **HOME ADDRESS:** 5301 Ida St, Omaha, NE 68152. **BUSINESS ADDRESS:** Prof of French & Black Studies, Univ of Nebraska-Omaha, Foreign Language Dept, Omaha, NE 68182.

LAGARDE, FREDERICK H.
Clergyman. **PERSONAL:** Born Apr 10, 1928, Teaneck, NJ; married Frances Frye; children: Frederica, Francine, Francella, Frederick Jr. **EDUCATION:** Grand Music Acad, 1948; VA Union Univ & Sem, AB, MDiv 1953-59. **CAREER:** 1st Bapt Church, pastor 1956-58; Providence Bapt Church, pastor 1958-66; Community Bapt Church of Love, pastor 1966-; president & founder of come-unity & the annual greater Youth Crusade of Paterson vicinity 1980. **ORGANIZATIONS:** Founder United Neighborhood for Indust Training & Econ Devel 1967, Housing Oppty Provided for Everyone 1969, House of Action 1970, Paterson Community Schools 1983; co-writer Official Song of Paterson 1983; mem NAACP, Reg Rep SCLC; mem ASCAP; mem Alpha Phi Alpha; active in civil rights movement; co-writer & producer of the Martin Luther King video/song 1986. **HONORS/ACHIEVEMENTS:** Awd IBPO Elks of the World 1965; Black & Poor Citizens Awd 1966; Citizens of Paterson Awd 1967; NJ Council Churches Social Ed & Action Awd 1969; Paterson pastors workshop award 1986. **MILITARY SERVICE:** AUS 1950-52. **BUSINESS ADDRESS:** Pastor, Comm Bapt Church of Love, 6 Auburn St, Paterson, NJ 07501.

LAGRONE, CLARENCE OLIVER
Artist. **PERSONAL:** Born Dec 09, 1906, McAlester, OK; married Lillian G; children: Lotus J Johnson. **EDUCATION:** Howard Univ, 1928-29; Univ of NM, BA 1938; Cranbrook Art Acad 1940-42; Wayne State Univ, Masters Equiv plus 30 hrs 1956-60. **CAREER:** UAW Educ Dept, intl rep 1948-53; Teacher Detroit Public Schools, Social Studies, 1956-57; PA State Univ, instructor, Afro-Amer History, Art, 1970-72, special asst, vice pres educ 1972-74; Sculptor, poet, lecturer. **ORGANIZATIONS:** Life mem NAACP 1964-; mem MI, PA Councils of Artists 1966-68; lecture exhibits Over 60 Coll, Univ 1968-85; appt spec assist to vice pres of undergrad ed PAState Univ 1972-73; bd dir Oliver LaGrone Scholarship Fund 1974-85; mem Kappa Alpha Psi 1981-, Harrisburg Human Relations Comm 1983-; mem bd of dir Neighborhood Ctr United methodist Church of Harrisburg 1983. **HONORS/ACHIEVEMENTS:** McGregor Fund Grant Detroit MI for Study Cranbrook Art Acad 1940-42; Det Howard Univ Alumni of the Year Awd Local Chapter Detroit 1965; Sculpted life-sizedbust of the late Langston Hughes 1965; Scholarship Fund Named in Honor Unitarian Univ 1974-; Memorial Plaque Awd Ethelen Jones Crockett Amer Lung Assoc 1981-82; Feb 3, 1983 declared "Oliver LaGrone Day" City Hall Ceremony 1983.

LAHR, CHARLES DWIGHT
Educator, mathematician. **PERSONAL:** Born Feb 06, 1945, Philadelphia, PA; married Beatriz Pastor; children: Elena, Maria, Emilio. **EDUCATION:** Temple Univ, AB (Magna Cum Laude, Math) 1966; Syracuse Univ, MA 1968, PhD 1971. **CAREER:** Bell Labs, mathematician 1971-73; Savannah State Coll, visiting prof/math 1973-74; Amherst Coll, visiting prof/math 1974-75; Dartmouth Coll, asst prof/math1975-79, assoc prof/math 1979-84, assoc dean sciences, dean of Grad Studies 1981-84, prof math GCS 1984-, dean of faculty 1984-. **ORGANIZATIONS:** Consultant Alfred P Sloan Fndtn 1982-; reviewer Mathematical Reviews; mem AmerMathematical Soc; mem Mathematical Assoc of Amer; mem Amer Assoc for Advancement of Sci. **BUSINESS ADDRESS:** Dean of Faculty, Dartmouth Coll, 301 Wentworth Hall, Hanover, NH 03755.

LAINE, CLEO
Singer. **PERSONAL:** Born Oct 27, 1927, South Hill, Middlesex, England;married John Dankworth; children: Alex, Jacqueline. **CAREER:** Singer, John Dankworth's Jazz Band, popularized Gimme a Pigfoot & It's a Pity to Say Goodnight, 1952; recorded on RCA A Beautiful Theme, Pierrot Lunaire All About Me, Born on a Friday, Day by Day & many others; made Amer debut at Lincoln Ctr, actress, England State Prod, The Roman Spring of Mrs Stone, 1961; guest singer, One Man's Music, Marvelous Party, Talk of the Town, Not So Much a Programme, The Sammy Davis Show, Merv Griffin Show 1974, Cotton Club 1975, and Dinah. **BUSINESS ADDRESS:** The Old Rectory, Wavendon, Bletchley, Bucks, England.

LAING, EDWARD A.
Ambassador, attorney, educator. **PERSONAL:** Born Feb 27, 1942; married Margery V Fairweather; children: Obi Uchenna, Nyasha Rufaro. **EDUCATION:** Cambridge, BA 1964; Cambridge, LLB 1966; Columbia, LLM 1968; Barrister at Law 1966; Atty at Law IL 1969. **CAREER:** Belize, magistrate & crown counsel 1966-67; Baker & McKenzie, assoc 1968-69; Univ of West Indies, Barbados & Jamaica, sr lectr 1970-74; expertise & prac commercial law, int law, intl trade law, civil law 1974; Notre Dame Law Sch, asst Prof 1974-76; Howard Univ Schl of Law, Univ of Maryland, law prof; Embassy of Belize, ambassador. **ORGANIZATIONS:** Prof dir Jamaica Legal Servs for Inter-Am Found. **HONORS/ACHIEVEMENTS:** Publ Intro to Sources & Sys of the Common Law Caribbean 1974; numerous articles on law & devel countries, trade law & electoral law. **BUSINESS ADDRESS:** Ambassador, Embassy of Belize, 1575 I St NW, Ste 695, Washington, DC 20005.

LAIRET, DOLORES PERSON
Educator. **PERSONAL:** Born Dec 27, 1935, Cleveland; widowed; children: Christine, Evin. **EDUCATION:** Wheaton Coll, AB 1957; Middlebury Coll, AM 1958;Univ of Paris; Case Western Reserve U, PhD 1972. **CAREER:** Cleveland State Univ, assoc prof 1972-77, instructor 1971-72, lecturer 1969-71; City of Cleveland, sr personnel asst 1969-71; Western Reserve Univ, teaching fellow lecturer 1965-67; John Marshall HS, French teacher 1963-65; Fox Lane Sch Bedford NY, educator 1960-62; Southern Univ Baton Rouge, instructor 1959. **ORGANIZATIONS:** Mem Am Assn of Tchrs of French 1971-; Am Assn ofUniv Prof 1971; Am Council on Tching of Foreign Lang 1972-; NE Modern Lang Assn 1974-; African Lit Assn; Music Critics Assn; OH Mod Lang Tchrs Assn; past sec & pres Cleveland Chap Tots & Teens Inc 1963-73; mem of bd Glenville Health Assn 1974-; mem Champs Inc 1964-; Am Spec Lctr for US Dept of State in Niger Mali Upper Volta Senegal & Togo. **HONORS/ACHIEVEMENTS:** Publ The Francophone African Novel Perspectives for Critical Eval Presence Africaine; Various Art on Jazz Cleveland Press Showtime; Recipient of various Fellowships. **BUSINESS ADDRESS:** E 24 St & Euclid Ave, Cleveland, OH 44115.

LAISURE, SHARON EMILY GOODE
Personnel administrator. **PERSONAL:** Born Sep 03, 1954, Wiesbaden; daughter of Mr & Mrs Robert A Goode; married W Floyd Laisure. **EDUCATION:** Univ of NC Chapel Hill, BA 1976, MPA 1979. **CAREER:** City of Winston-Salem, admin asst to dep city mgr 1977-78, admin asst to asst city mgr 1978-79, personnel analyst 1979-80; City of Petersburg VA, personnel dir 1980-85; dir, human resources and employee relations, city of Richmond VA, 1986-89; personnel director, county of Durham NC, 1985-86. **ORGANIZATIONS:** Mem

Amer Soc of Publ Admin 1979; mem bd of dir Southside Chap Amer Red Cross 1980, United Way of Southside VA 1982; 70001 1983; pres elect SouthernReg IPMA 1984. **HONORS/ACHIEVEMENTS:** Natl Assoc of Schools of PA Fellowship UNC At Chapel Hill 1980. **BUSINESS ADDRESS:** Dept of Human Resources & Employee Relations, City of Richmond, 900 E Broad St, Richmond, VA 23219.

LAKE, ALFREEDA ELIZABETH
Educator. **PERSONAL:** Born Jan 07, 1923, Hickory Valley, TN; divorced; children: Neeley Jr. **EDUCATION:** LeMoyne Coll, BA 1943;Univ of TN, MS 1967; Memphis State U; Grambling State U, Pre-serv Trng; Lane Coll. **CAREER:** Hardeman Co Schs, supr of instructor 1964-; Bolivar Indsl School, primary teacher 1950-64; Prospect School, elementary school prin 1945-50; Washington School, primary teacher 1943-45. **ORGANIZATIONS:** Mem St Paul Christian Meth Epis Ch; past pres Delta Sigma Theta Sor Inc; NAACP; Nat Counc of Negro Women; exec bd of dirs W TN Hlth Improve Assn; Bolivar Housing Auth Bd; contrib to the pub Toward the Prep of Elem Sch Tchrs 1969; consult lectr Num Colls Univ & Pub Sch Sys Civic & ReligiousGroups. **HONORS/ACHIEVEMENTS:** Publ A Study of 15 Black Students Enrolled in Formerly All White Schs in Hardeman Co 1965-66; Author Handbook for Parents of Pre-Sch Children 1974. **BUSINESS ADDRESS:** Courthouse 2nd Floor, Bolivar, TN 38008.

LAMAR, CLEVELAND JAMES
Association executive. **PERSONAL:** Born Apr 21, 1924, Atmore, AL; married Annie Ruth Wilkerson; children: Cleveland James, Mona Lisa, Torlorf Pinzo, Ave Maria, Arturo Laertes, Alvino Degoge, Caruso Noel. **EDUCATION:** AL State U, BS 1949, MEduc 1954. **CAREER:** Eutaw, instr 1949-58; GW Carver Br YMCA Shreveport, sec boys work 1959; Samuel F Harris Br YMCA, %Exec dir 1962-63; YMCA Mobile Dearborn St, exec dir 1964; Mobile Area Com for Training & Devel, vice pres bd of dirs 1965-70. **ORGANIZATIONS:** Mem AL Tchrs Assn Bd of Dirs; NAACP; Manna House YMCA Blue Ridge Assembly; mem Phi Beta Sigma; Century Mobile Club. **HONORS/ACHIEVEMENTS:** Recipient Cert of Achvmnt in Phys Educ SE Region YMCA 1960; Cert of AchvmnNat Bd YMCA 1965; YMCA Cert Springfield Coll 1965. **MILITARY SERVICE:** AUS 1943-46. **BUSINESS ADDRESS:** 309 Washington, Mobile, AL 36603.

LAMAR, WILLIAM, JR.
Restaurant executive. **PERSONAL:** Born Apr 25, 1952, Chicago, IL; son of William Lamar Sr and Jeanette Jarrett Lamar; married Kathy Amos Lamar, Aug 28, 1976; children: Brian William, Andrew Marcus. **EDUCATION:** Univ of Illinois, Chicago IL, BS, 1973; Northwestern Univ, Kellogg School of Mgmt, Evanston IL, MBA, 1976. **CAREER:** Quaker Oats Co, Chicago IL, brand mgr, 1976-81; Burrell Advertising Co, Chicago IL, vice pres, account supvr, 1981-82; United Airlines, Elk Grove Village IL, market mgr, 1982-84; McDonald's Corp, Oakbrook IL, dir of mktg, Bloomfield NJ, dir of operations, 1984-. **ORGANIZATIONS:** Mem, 100 Black Men of New York, 1986-; bd mem, New York Ronald McDonald House, 1986-88, Harlem Boys Choir, 1987-; trustee, bd mem, New Hope Baptist Church, 1988-. **BUSINESS ADDRESS:** Director of Operations, McDonald's Corporation, One McDonald Plaza, Oak Brook, IL 60521.

LAMAUTE, DENISE
Tax attorney. **PERSONAL:** Born Mar 14, 1952, St Louis, MO; daughter of Frederick Washington, Sr and Josephine Carroll; married Daniel Lamaute, May 14, 1980. **EDUCATION:** Brandeis Univ, Waltham, MA, BA, (Magna cum Laude) 1973; Washington Univ, St Louis, MO, JD, 1977, LL.M. (tax) 1980. **CAREER:** Teachers Insurance & Annuity Assn, sr tax attorney, 1978-82; Ernst & Whinney, New York, NY, supvr, 1982-85; Lamaute Tax & Financial Servs, New York, NY, owner, 1985-. **ORGANIZATIONS:** Mem, US Tax Ct, 1981-; mem, Nzingha Soc, 1987-88; co-chmn, Natl Bar Assn, 1988-89; mem volunteer, Jr Achievement, 1989. **HONORS/ACHIEVEMENTS:** Author "Tax Loopholes for Investors" to be published by Tab Books NY, 1989; natl speaker for "Black Enterprise" networking Forum; frequent speaker on tax & financial matters at confs around the country; frequent contributing writer to magazines, newspapers on financial issues. **BUSINESS ADDRESS:** Principal, Lamaute Tax & Financial Serv, 4727 Wilshire Blvd, Suite 500, Los Angeles, CA 90010.

LAMBERT, BENJAMIN FRANKLIN
Patent attorney. **PERSONAL:** Born Mar 06, 1933, Lowell, MA. **EDUCATION:** Boston Univ, BA 1955; Brandeis Univ, MA 1959; Seton Hall Univ Sch of Law, JD 1968. **CAREER:** Ciba Phar Co Inc, rsch chem 1957-66; Ciba Ltd, rsch asst 1962-63; Merck & Co Inc, atty 1966-70; Fitzpatrick, Cella, Harper & Scinto, atty 1970-72; Johnson & Johnson, patent atty 1973-. **ORGANIZATIONS:** Mem NJ Bar Assn; Reg US Patent Ofc 1968; admtd NY Bar 1972; admtd US Ct of Customs & Patent Appeals 1977; admtd US Dist Ct Dist of JN 1969; admtd Dist Ct So Dist NY 1972; admtd Dist Ct Eastern Dist NY 1972; NJ Patent Law Assn; Amer Patent Law Assn; NAACP 1977. **HONORS/ACHIEVEMENTS:** Who's Who in the E 1975; Who's Who Among Students in Amer Univ & Coll; Delta Hon Soc; Scarlet Key Hon Soc; Student Fac Asmbl; Augustus Howe Buck Schlr; Tchng Fellow Brandeis Univ; num publ. **MILITARY SERVICE:** AUS Sgt 1962. **BUSINESS ADDRESS:** Patent Attorney, Johnson & Johnson, One Johnson & Johnson Plaza, New Brunswick, NJ 08933.

LAMBERT, BENJAMIN J., III
Optometrist. **PERSONAL:** Born Jan 29, 1937, Richmond, VA; son of Benjamin S Lambert Jr and Mary Frances Warden Lambert; married Carolyn L Morris, May 14, 1966; children: Benjamin IV, David, Charles Justin, Ann Frances. **EDUCATION:** Virginia Union Univ, BS 1959; MA College of Optometry, OB 1962. **CAREER:** Private Practice, optometrist 1963-87; VA General Assembly, senator; director consolidated bank & trust co. **ORGANIZATIONS:** Mem general assembly House of Delegates 1977-85; sec bd of trustees VA Union Univ 1977-87. **HOME ADDRESS:** 3109 Noble Ave, Richmond, VA 23222. **BUSINESS ADDRESS:** Senator, VA General Assembly, 904 No First St, Richmond, VA 23219.

LAMBERT, CHARLES H.
Educational administrator. **PERSONAL:** Born May 14, 1948, Mobile, AL. **EDUCATION:** Kentucky State Univ, BS 1970; Miss State Univ, Mgmt Training Cert 1971; Eastern Kentucky Univ, MPA 1972; Michigan State Univ, Natl Assn of Reg Utility Comm Cert 1979; Univ of Arizona, Cert in Reg Economics 1979. **CAREER:** KY Dept of Economic Security, technical service rep, 1970-72; Whitney M Young Jr Job Corps Center, asst dir of programs, 1972-74; KY Legislative Research Comm, legislative fiscal analyst, 1974-75; KY Dept of Finance/Policy & Budget, senior policy advisor, 1975; Kentucky Dept of Finance & Admin, executive assist 1975-76, deputy secretary 1976-79; Energy Regulatory Comm State of Kentucky, commissioner/vice chairman 1979-81; Kentucky State Univ, asst, 1981-82, Vice President for University Relations, 1982—. **ORGANIZATIONS:** member of board of directors, The Lincoln Foundation, 1982—; exec secretary, KSU Foundation, Inc, 1982—. **BUSINESS ADDRESS:** Vice PresidentUniv Relations, Kentucky State University, E Main St, Frankfort, KY 40601.

LAMBERT, JOSEPH C.
Business executive. **PERSONAL:** Born Jul 04, 1936, Vaux Hall, NJ; married Joan E Cross; children: Kim, George, Joseph Jr. **EDUCATION:** VA State Coll. **CAREER:** St Bank of Plainfield NJ, teller trainee 1961-64; Security Nat'l Bank Newark NJ, chief clerk 1964-66; Nat'l State Bank Linden NJ, adminstrv asst 1966-68; Nat'l State Bank Elizabeth NJ, asst br mgr 1968-70; Nat'l State Bank Plainfield NJ, asst chashier & br mgr 1970-72; East Orange Comm Bank, vice pres & treas 1972-; Deryfos Consumer Bank, sr vice pres & treas. **ORGANIZATIONS:** Mem Plainfield Area Urban Coalition; Plainfield Kiwanis; bd dir So Second St Youth Cntr YMCA; finance chmn Plainfield Bd of Edn. **HONORS/ACHIEVEMENTS:** Apptd first Black Jury Commr Union Co 1974. **MILITARY SERVICE:** AUS 1958-60; AUSR 1960-62; discharge 1966. **BUSINESS ADDRESS:** Sr Vice President & Treasurer, Dreyfus Consumer Bank, 554 Central Ave, East Orange, NJ 07018.

LAMBERT, LECLAIR GRIER
Director, writer, lecturer. **PERSONAL:** Born in Miami, FL; son of George F Lambert (deceased) and Maggie Grier Lambert-Scott (deceased). **EDUCATION:** Hampton Univ, BA 1959; Harvard Univ, further study communications 1958-59; Univ Munich, Germany, art history 1966; Grantsmanship Cntr-Pgrm Planning & Mgmt, Cert 1981; coursework People Management of MD 1985. **CAREER:** Holt Rinehart and Winston, biology editor 1966-68; Faraday Press, editor trans Russian and biology monographs 1971-72; Natl Found March of Dimes, publ relations writer 1972; St Paul Urban League, asst to dir/comm officer 1972-80; African Am Museum of Art and Hist, dir 1980-85; MN State House of Representatives, dir educ programs; Minnesota House of Representatives, Educational Programs, coordinator/sergeant-at-arms. **ORGANIZATIONS:** Tchr US Dependent's Schls Overseas 1964-65; writer/researcher Time-Life Books 1961-63; co-founder Summit Univ Free Press St Paul MN 1974; bd mem HEART 1978-88; lecturer Black History 1982-; mem Dr Martin L King Jr Bust Comm Minn State Capitol 1983; consultant/writer/designer Black History Exhibits 1984-; bd mem Twin Cities Cable Arts Consortium 1984-; bd mem City of Golden Valley Human Rights Commn Black History Month Celebration 1984-87; Natl African Amer Museums Assoc Exec Cncl and Midwest Regional Rep 1984-87; mem City of St Paul Roy Wilkins Aud Dedication Commn 1984; mem St Paul Urban League/Urban League Volunteers 1972-; Cable Arts 1984-86; Natl African-American Musuems regional rep 1984-; bd mem, St Paul Civic Center Authority; representative, City Public Arts, Operations and Personnel Committee. **HONORS/ACHIEVEMENTS:** St Paul NAACP Awd 1974; Certificate of Appreciation Univ of MN Black Students 1981; Minneapolis St Acad Appreciation Awd 1983; Special Apprec Award Cultural Awareness Roosevelt HS Minneapolis 1985; Natl African Amer Museums Assoc Appreciation Awd 1985; 50th Anniversary Guest Speaker and Awardee Liberty Square Tenant's Assoc Miami FL 1986; author/editor Minnesota's Black Comm; editor Art in Development A Nigerian Perspective 1984; various articles/speeches Twin Cities Courier, Summit Univ Free Press, Miami Herald 1986; Volunteer Service Award, St Paul Urban League 1988; A learning Journey Through Black History 1982. **MILITARY SERVICE:** AUS 1st Lt served 2 years Honorable Discharge 1959-61. **HOME ADDRESS:** 590 Simpson, St Paul, MN 55104. **BUSINESS ADDRESS:** Dir Educational Programs, MN State House of Reps, 120 D State Capitol, St Paul, MN 55155.

LAMBERT, LEONARD W.
Attorney. **PERSONAL:** Born Oct 27, 1938, Henrico Co, VA; married Sylvia Jeter; children: Leonard Jr, Ralph, Linda, Brice, Mark. **EDUCATION:** VA Union Univ, BA 1960; Howard Univ Sch of Law, JD 1963. **CAREER:** Private Practice, attorney. **ORGANIZATIONS:** Vice pres bd Metro YMCA; Jewish Comm Ctr; Children's Home Soc; Travelers Aid Soc; Richmond Chap Amer Red Cross; Neighborhood Legal Aid Soc; Old Dominion Bar Assn; VA Adv Council Com on Youthful Offenders; VA State, Richmond Criminal Bar Assns; VA Trial Lawyers Assn; Natl Assn of Defense Lawyers; Natl Bar Assn; Richmond Trial Lawyers Assn; Focus Club; Club 533; substitute Judge of Juvenile & Domestic Relations Ct of City of Richmond VA; mem Omega Psi Phi Frat; selective appeal bd Eastern Dist of VA; chmn trustee bd Westwood Baptist Church; Natl Bd YMCA; Natl Prog Chmn YMCA; vice pres VA Ctr for thePerforming Arts; vice pres Federated Arts Council. **BUSINESS ADDRESS:** Attorney, 2025 E Main St, Richmond, VA 23223.

LAMBERT, ROLLINS EDWARD
Clergyman. **PERSONAL:** Born Mar 03, 1922, Chicago. **EDUCATION:** Univ of Chicago, AB 1942; St Mary of the Lake Sem, STL 1949. **CAREER:** US Catholic Conf, priest; Parish Ministry Chicago, 1949-61, 1968-70;Univ of Chicago, campus Ministry 1961-68, 1970-75. **ORGANIZATIONS:** Pres Comprehensive Health Planning Inc 1974-75. **BUSINESS ADDRESS:** 1312 Massachusetts Ave NW, Washington, DC 20005.

LAMBERT, SAMUEL FREDRICK
Engineer. **PERSONAL:** Born Jul 08, 1928, Monroville, AL; son of Frederick Lambert and Nannie Howard Lambert; married Florence Mickings; children: Carla, Pamela Roberts, Samuel II, Michele, Wanda. **EDUCATION:** Armstrong School of Engrg, Marine Engrs License 1953; Pace Univ, Bachelor 1978. **CAREER:** 1st Army Headquarters AUS, SP 3/C 1954-56; Military Sea Transport Service, marine engr 1956-60; New York City Bd of Educ, custodian engr 1962-74, supervisor of custodian/engrs 1974-. **ORGANIZATIONS:** Engr-consultant WEBB & Brooker Inc; past natl pres Natl Assoc of Power Eng 1982; elected mem Comm School Bd 11 1980-. **MILITARY SERVICE:** AUS spec 2nd class 1954-56; USN Reserve lt sgt while serving as merchant marine engrg officer. **HOME ADDRESS:** 4071 Edson Ave, Bronx, NY 10466. **BUSINESS ADDRESS:** Custodian/Engineer, John Jay High School, 237 7th Avenue, Brooklyn, NY 11215.

LAMBERT, WILFRED LEE
Clergyman. **PERSONAL:** Born Feb 08, 1926, Iowa, LA. **CAREER:** Cottrell Chapel Christian Meth Episcopal Ch New Iberia, LA, pastor. **ORGANIZATIONS:** Sec So LA Annual Conf Christ Meth Epis Ch; pres New Iberia Br NAACP; mem Zoning Review Bd

New Iberia; sec/treas New Iberia Interdenom Ministerial Fedn; treas SNAP Battered Women Iberia Parish; bd dir Bacmonila Housing Proj pres Iberia Alliance for Prog (leader in court fight for reapportionment of Iberia Parish); successful with subsequent elect of 3 Blacks to sch bd, 3 to parish council & 2 to city council; elec del 1978 Gen Conf Christian Meth Episcopal Ch; bd dir Iberia Red Cross chpt; bd dir New Iberia Bi-Centen Commn; delegate to Gen Conf of Conf of Christian Meth Epis Ch 1970 & 1974; elec del to Triennial Sess Natl Cncl of Ch of Am 1966; serves as worship leader for LA Sch for Christian Workers held annually in Grambling Coll. **HONORS/ACHIEVEMENTS:** 1st Black to serve on Iberia Parish School Board.

LAMONT, BARBARA
Company executive, journalist. **PERSONAL:** Born Nov 09, 1939, Hamilton, Bermuda;married Ludwig Gelobter; children: Michel, David, Elisabeth. **EDUCATION:** Sarah Lawrence Coll, BA 1960; Harvard Univ Sch of Business Admin, MPA 1985; Attended, Kennedy Sch of Govt, Harvard Business School. **CAREER:** WINS Radio NY, reporter 1970-73; WNEW TV NY, reporter/anchor 1973-76; CBS News NY, reporter/writer 1976-82; Columbia Sch of Journalism, assoc prof 1980-84; Nigerian TV Authority, sr producer 1982-83; ABC News, 1985-86; WCCL-TV New Orleans, 1987-; Crescent City Comms, pres; New Orleans Teleport, pres 1987-. **ORGANIZATIONS:** Dem dist leader Democratic Party 1970; bd mem NARAL 1975; bd mem Planned Parenthood 1975; editorial bd, Amsterdam News 1986-. **HONORS/ACHIEVEMENTS:** Author "Journey to Nigeria" 1984; Associated Press Awd NY State 1974; Front Page Awd News Women's Guild 1975; Reporter of the Yr New York City Retired Detectives Assn 1976; book "City People" Macmillan 1975. **BUSINESS ADDRESS:** President, Crescent City Communications, 620 Desire St, New Orleans, LA 70117.

LAMOTHE, ISIDORE J.
Physician. **PERSONAL:** Born Feb 12, 1924, New Orleans; married Grace Cooper; children: Michelle Alicia, Isidore J. **EDUCATION:** Xavier U, BS 1944; Howard U, MD 1947. **CAREER:** HG Phillips Hosp St Louis, internship 1947-48; VA Hosp Tuskegee, jr staff physician 1948-49; Marshall TX, gen practice med 1949-53, 1955-; Webb AFB,chief med serv 1953-55. **ORGANIZATIONS:** Mem Hosp Med Staff Chief Gen Prac Sect; mem Nat Med Assn; mem past pres East TX Med Dental & Pharm Assn; vice pres Lone Star State Med Assn;mem adv com TX Heart Assn; pres Harrison Ct Med Soc; mem TX Med Assn; mem Amer Heart Assn; mem St Joseph Parish Council; pres Parish Sch Bd; past pres St Joseph Home; past pres Sch Assn; bd dir NE TX Hlth Sys Agcy; mem at large Nat Coun Boy Scouts of Am; adv bd So Central Reg Boy Scouts of Am; consumer rep Food & Drug Admin; mem past pres Marshall Reg Fellow Club; mem past natl comptrllr Alpha Phi Alpha Frat Inc; mem Mrshll Human Rels Comm; life mem Ch Educ Com Harrison Co Br NAACP; mem Harrison Ct Progrssv Vot League; bd of trsts Wiley Coll; Ch Finance & Fiscal Affairs Com; dir Mrshl Allli for Justice. **MILITARY SERVICE:** AUS pfc 1944-46; USAF capt 1935-55. **BUSINESS ADDRESS:** PO Box 1558, 1407 Uiversity, Marshall, TX 75670.

LAMOTTE, JEAN MOORE
Director. **PERSONAL:** Born Sep 02, 1938, Shreveport, LA; divorced. **EDUCATION:** CA State Univ Sacramento, attended; Amer River Clge Sacramento, attended; Central State Univ Wilberforce OH, attended. **CAREER:** KXTV-10 Corinthian Broadcasting, host moderator daily pub srv talk show 1973-; Human Rights Comm, proj dir/Affirmative action prog 1970-73; Affirm Act Prog for underutilizing employers, writer; Campbell Soup Co, voc spec 1966-70. **HONORS/ACHIEVEMENTS:** Comm Serv Award Golden Empire Chap Amer Heart Assc 1977-80; Woman of Year Sacramento Observer Newspaper 1977; Sacramento's Most Influential Black Woman Sacramento Observer 1978; Outstanding Comm Serv Award Women's Civic Improvement Ctr 1980. **BUSINESS ADDRESS:** KXTV 10, 400 Broadway, Sacramento, CA 95818.

LAMPKIN, CHERYL LYVETTE
City government middle manager. **PERSONAL:** Born May 16, 1961, Brunswick, GA; daughter of William T. Lampkin, Sr. and Cynthia L. Lampkin. **EDUCATION:** Attended Intl School of Kenya, 1976-78; Univ of Maryland, BA, 1983; Carnegie Mellon Univ School of Urban and Public Affairs, certificate of participation, summer, 1982; Harvard Univ School of Govt, certificate of participation, summer, 1983; State Univ of New York at Stony Brook, Harriman Coll, MPA, 1985. **CAREER:** Waxler Sr Center, Baltimore, MD, social work intern, summer, 1980; City of Brookhaven, Brookhaven, NY, consultant, 1984; City of New York Department of Correction, New York, NY, management intern, summer, 1984; City of Kansas City, Kansas City, MO, management intern, 1985-86; Montgomery County Govt, Rockville, MD, personnel specialist, 1986-88; City of Rockville, Rockville, MD, asst to city m gr, 1988—. **ORGANIZATIONS:** Mem 1985—, Natl Forum for Black Public Admin; mem 1988—, Natl Accoc of Female Exec; mem 1989—, Intl City Mgr Assoc. **HONORS/ACHIEVEMENTS:** Scholastic achievement cash award, Links Inc, 1980; Outstanding Young Woman of America, 1983 and 1984. **HOME ADDRESS:** 20301 Grazing Way, Gaithersburg, MD 20879.

LAMPLEY, CALVIN D.
Educator. **PERSONAL:** Born in Dunn, NC. **EDUCATION:** NC A&T State U; Juilliard Sch of Music, Dip; Peabody Conservatory, MusM. **CAREER:** Morgan State Univ, prof of music; Columbia Records, producer; RCA Victor Records, producer; Warner Brothers, producer; Prestige Records, producer; WCBM-AM Baltimore, classical/Jazz disc jockey; Peabody Conservatory of Music, composition faculty; Concert Pianist. **ORGANIZATIONS:** Mem Am Soc of Univ Composers; Broadcast Mus Inc; Met Opera Guild; mus critic for Public Television.

LAMPLEY, EDWARD CHARLES
Physician. **PERSONAL:** Born Jun 21, 1931, Hattiesburg, MS; son of Willie Lee Lampley Sr and Elma Wilson Lampley; married Norma Jean Mosley; children: Edward, Marguerite, Karl. **EDUCATION:** Alcorn Coll, 1953-54; Wayne Univ, AB 1956; Howard Univ, MD 1960. **CAREER:** Detroit Receiving Hosp, intern 1960-61; Provident Hosp Chicago, resident 1961-63; Harlem Hosp New York, resident 1963-66; Private Practice Oakland, CA, physician spec in obstetrics & gynecology 1966-; Memorial Hosp, sr md, chmn dept ob/gyn. **ORGANIZATIONS:** Mem staff Highland Hosp; mem Herrick Meml Hosp; mem Providence Hosp; mem Merrick Hosp; mem Meml Hosp; former clin med dir E Oakland Planned Parenthood Clinic; diplomate Amer Bd Observ & Gyne; fellow Amer Coll Obst & Gynecol ACS; mem AMA; mem CA, Alameda Cnty & Natl Med Assns; Golden State Med Assn; Sinkler-Miller Med Soc; Alameda Cnty Gynecol Soc; Amer Fertility Soc; re-cert Amer Bd Obs-Gyn 1978; Am Assn Planned Parenthood Physicians; mem Alpha Psi; co-founder E Oakland Med Cntr Oakland, CA; chmn bd dir Comm Devel Inst E Palo Alto, CA 1984-85; chmn bd dir Community Devel Inst East Palo Alto CA 1984-86; mem Kappa Alpha Psi; chmn scholarship comm Downs Memorial Church; chmn Boy Scout Troup 33; councilman Alameda Contra Costa Med Soc,1985-; mem, House of delegates Calif Med Assn, 198 5-. **HONORS/ACHIEVEMENTS:** Man of the Year Awd Ravenswood School Dist; Soloist Downs Memorial Church Chapel Choir. **MILITARY SERVICE:** USAF s/sgt 1949-52. **BUSINESS ADDRESS:** President, East Oakland Obs Gyn Med Grp Inc, 9925 E 14th St, #1, Oakland, CA 94603-0097.

LAMPLEY, HANDY ELLIS
Manager. **PERSONAL:** Born Apr 19, 1949, Akron, OH; married Jo A. **EDUCATION:** Kent State U, BS 1972, MA 1975. **CAREER:** OH Bell Tele Co, mgr distrib serv legislative contact with State legislator 1973-; Goodrich Tire & Rubber Co, mkt mgr 1972. **ORGANIZATIONS:** Mem Summit Athletic Club; adv bd mem Sch of Commun Kent StateUniv 1978-; exec bd treas Kent StateUniv Alumni Assn 1979-80. **BUSINESS ADDRESS:** Ohio Bell Telephone, 2525 State Rd, Cuyahoga Falls, OH 44223.

LAMPLEY, PAUL CLARENCE
Educator. **PERSONAL:** Born Dec 12, 1945, Louisville, MS; married Fannie; children: Samantha. **EDUCATION:** Tougaloo Coll, BS 1967; Atlanta U, MS 1971, NSF Grad Trainee; Howard Univ; Memphis St Univ; Univ of MS, PhD 1981. **CAREER:** Rust Coll, asst develop dir; Harris Jr Coll, instr; Rust Coll, div of social sciences chair, academic dean. **ORGANIZATIONS:** Mem NAACP; Yacona Area Council BSA; Omega Psi Phi; Nat Assn of Fed Rel Officers; Phi Delta Kappa; Sigma Pi Phi. **HONORS/ACHIEVEMENTS:** Outstanding Young Man in Am 1972; UNCF distinguished professor 1985-86. **BUSINESS ADDRESS:** Academic Dean, Rust College, Develop Office, Holly Springs, MS.

LANCASTER, HERMAN BURTRAM
Legal counsel. **PERSONAL:** Born Mar 06, 1942, Chicago, IL; son of Eddie Lancaster and Louise Lancaster; married Kathleen E Murton; children: Lauren E, Rachel J, Meredith E; married Patricia L Malucci; children: Meredith E. **EDUCATION:** Chicago State Univ, BS 1965; Rosary Coll, MA 1968; DePaul Univ, JD 1972. **CAREER:** Chicago Bd of Ed, teacher 1965-66; DePaul Univ Law School, asst dir law library 1966-70; Univ of Chicago, psychiatric dept dir of info 1970-72, legal counsel 1972-73; Glendale Univ Law School, prof, dir of research 1973-; The Legal Inst, legal counsel 1976-. **ORGANIZATIONS:** Adv The Subcontractors Inst 1984-; consultant White House 1972-, Ford Found 1972-; consultant McCoy Ming & Black 1973-; consultant Kennedy-King Coll 1973-, Glendale Law Review 1976-; advisory bd mem, Altadena Trustee Bd Friends 1974; NAACP 1975-, Altadena YMCA 1976-. **HONORS/ACHIEVEMENTS:** Omega Psi Phi Scholarship 1963; Grad Fellowship 1966; DePaul Law School Scholarship 1968; DePaul Law Review Scholarship 1969-72; Blue Key Law Hon Soc 1968; Man of the Year Omega Psi Phi 1966; has published numerous articles. **BUSINESS ADDRESS:** Legal Counsel, The Legal Inst, 1214 E Colorado Blvd, Ste 207, Pasadena, CA 91106.

LANCASTER, JOHN GRAHAM
County commissioner. **PERSONAL:** Born Jan 31, 1918, Farmville, VA; married Albertine Thomas; children: John G Jr, Shirley Lancaster Gholston. **EDUCATION:** Hampton Univ, BS 1940; George Washington Univ, MA 1964; Univ of MD, AGS 1974. **CAREER:** VA Coop Extension Svcs, extension agent 1940-55; NC Mutual Life Ins Co, salesman 1956-57; Univ of MD Coop Extension Serv, state 4H prog 1957-79; St Marys Co MD Govt, county commissioner 1986-. **ORGANIZATIONS:** Dir MD 4H Foundation 1981-86; mem Bd of Educ St Marys Co 1984-87; pres LOTT Enterprises Inc 1986-; dir So MD Business League of NBL 1986-; mem IBOEN, NAACP, Masons, Toastmasters; chmn St Marys Co Housing Authority. **HOME ADDRESS:** PO Box 26, California, MD 20619. **BUSINESS ADDRESS:** County Commissioner, St Mary's Co MD Government, PO Box 653, Leonardtown, MD 20650.

LAND, CHESTER LASALLE
Recreational therapy administrator. **PERSONAL:** Born Apr 29, 1938, Jacksonville, TX; son of Mrs George Ann Price Land; married Shirley Walker; children: Celeste, Chrystal. **EDUCATION:** CA State Univ LA, BS 1972; CA State Univ Northridge, MS 1980. **CAREER:** Olive View Med Center, supervisor recreational therapy 1964-81; Rancho Los Amigos Med Ctr, dir recreational therapy 1981-. **ORGANIZATIONS:** Chair recreational commn Los Angeles City Council on the Disabled 1977-; dir CA Park & Recreation Soc 1979-81; vice chair Los Angeles City Council on the Disabled 1981; chair Certification Review Board Natl Council for Therapeutic Recreation 1987-89; President - National Therapeutic Recreation Society 1988-90. **HONORS/ACHIEVEMENTS:** Citation Award CA Park & Recreation Society 1984; Employee of the Month Los Angeles County 1985; Employee of the Year Rancho Los Amigos Medical Center 1985; Outstanding Therapeutic Recreation CA Park & Recreation Society 1987. **HOME ADDRESS:** 7726 S Hobart Blvd, Los Angeles, CA 90047. **BUSINESS ADDRESS:** Dir Recreation Therapy, Rancho Los Amigos Med Ctr, 7601 E Imperial Hwy, Downey, CA 90242.

LAND, GEORGIANNA ANDERSON
Executive director. **PERSONAL:** Born Nov 12, 1940, Cross, SC. **EDUCATION:** Allen Univ, BS 1962; Pace Univ, MA 1973; Univ of MD, PhD 1980. **CAREER:** Mt Sinai & Elmhurst Hosps, supvr microbiology 1963-66; Catonsville Comm Coll, adminstrv intern 1968-70; New York City Bd of Educ, tchr & guidance counselor 1966-68; NY City Central Bd of Educ, staff recruiter 1968-70; Sch Dist 5 New York City Bd of Educ, personnel dir 1970-76; Amer Public Transit Assn, proj dir 1978-80; Cong Caucus for Sci & Tech, exec dir. **ORGANIZATIONS:** Washington liaison Alpha Kappa Alpha Sor Inc 1982-; Natl Nominating Comm Natl Women's Polit Caucus 1983-; pres Capital City Chap of Natl Coalition of100 Black Women 1984. **HONORS/ACHIEVEMENTS:** Fellowship MD State Bd for Higher Educ 1978; Fellowship Natl Sci Found 1978; nom Outstanding Young Women of Amer 1983; Outstanding Mem Alpha Kappa Alpha 1984; Speaking of People Ebony Mag 1980. **BUSINESS ADDRESS:** Executive Dir, Cong Caucus for Sci & Tech, H2-583 House Annex #2, Washington, DC 20515.

LANDER, CRESSWORTH CALEB
Public administrator. **PERSONAL:** Born May 15, 1925, Tucson, AZ; son of James Frank-

lin Lander and Julia B Watson Lander; married Linda Chyrl Hill, Mar 03, 1979; children: Melodie Lynette, Rochelle Elaine. **EDUCATION:** Univ of Arizona Los Angeles State Coll, BS Business Admin 1958; MIT Sloan Business School, summer course 1975; Harvard Business School & Kennedy School of Govt, 1979. **CAREER:** City of Tucson's Dept Human & Comm Dev, dir 1974-78; Univ of AZ Urban Planning Dept, lectr 1976-78; Civil Aeronautics Bd, managing dir 1979-81; Comm Dev Training Inst, consultant 1983-; Dept Housing City of Tucson, dir. **ORGANIZATIONS:** Dir City of Tucson's Dept Urban Resource Coord (Model Cities) 1969-74; dep dir Pima-Santa Cruz Co CEO 1968-69; real estate business 1959; dep assessor LA Co Assessor's Office Business Div 1958-59; bd trustees Public Housing Authority Directors Assn; bd mem Pima Council on Aging; bd mem Tucson Airport Authority; vice pres bd mem Tucson Urban League. **HONORS/ACHIEVEMENTS:** Comm Leadership Award Jack & Jill of Amer Tucson Chap 1985; Par Excellence Award AZ Black C of C 1984; US Govt Charter Sr Exec Serv 1979; Meritorious Serv Civil Aeronautics Bd 1981. **MILITARY SERVICE:** USMC Gunnery Sgt served 3 yrs. **HOME ADDRESS:** 7440 N Juniper Dr, Tucson, AZ 85741. **BUSINESS ADDRESS:** Dir, City of Tucson Dept of Housing, PO Box 27210, Tucson, AZ 85726.

LANDERS, NAAMAN GARNETT
Project director. **PERSONAL:** Born Oct 23, 1938, Anderson, IN; married Stephanie E Cox; children: Naaman III. **EDUCATION:** Purdue Univ, BSCE 1966; Univ of Chicago, MBA 1969. **CAREER:** Amoco Oil Co, engr 1966-69; Esso Chem Co, trans analyst 1969-71; Amoco Oil Co, material mgr 1972-76; Standard Oil Co, coord inventory contr 1977-79; Amoco Technology Corp, proj dir. **HONORS/ACHIEVEMENTS:** Presidential Citation Reconnaissance over Cuba. **MILITARY SERVICE:** USN 1959-63. **BUSINESS ADDRESS:** Project Dir, Amoco Technology Corp, 200 E Randolph Dr, Chicago, IL 60601.

LANDREAUX, KENNETH FRANCIS
Professional athlete. **PERSONAL:** Born Dec 22, 1954, Los Angeles, CA; married Clissy; children: Kenneth Antoine. **EDUCATION:** AZ State Univ. **CAREER:** CA Angels, outfielder 1977-78; MN Twins, outfielder 1979-80; Los Angeles Dodgers, outfielder 1981-. **HONORS/ACHIEVEMENTS:** Led team in triples (5) 1984; tied for club in triples with Steve Sax (7), errorless streak snapped at 142 games 1982; longest hitting streak in majors in 1980 (31 games); selected to Amer league All-Star team; 1980 tied mark for tripless in a game (3); 1979 tied a mark with two doubles in same inning; tied league fielding 1981, entire season without making an error in 244 chances; 1980 played Aguilas in the Dom Rebublic winter league, capturing most val plyr honors; selected Minor League Plyr of the Year by The Sporting News in 1977. **BUSINESS ADDRESS:** Los Angeles Dodgers, 1000 Elsyian Park Ave, Los Angeles, CA 90012.

LANDRUM, TERRY LEE
Professional athlete. **PERSONAL:** Born Oct 25, 1954, Joplin, MO; married Theresa; children: Melissa, Julie. **EDUCATION:** Eastern OK St Jr Coll. **CAREER:** Baltimore Orioles, outfielder; Cardinals outfielder 1980. **HONORS/ACHIEVEMENTS:** Committed only 3 errors in 5 yr big league career; led Am Asso with career high 12 triples; established lifetime Milestones in Runs (79); on Orioles 25 manchampionship roster; earned 2nd Consec World Series Ring; 4 League Championship Series Games; state batting champ in NM Babe Ruth League. **BUSINESS ADDRESS:** St Louis Cardinals, 250 Stadium Plaza, St Louis, MO 63102.

LANDRY, DOLORES BRANCHE
Business executive. **PERSONAL:** Born in Philadelphia, PA; married Lawrence A Landry; children: Jennifer E, Michael H. **EDUCATION:** Fisk Univ, BA 1950; Den Intl Hojskole Elsinore Denmark, diploma 1950-51; Univ of Chicago, MA 1960. **CAREER:** Sci Rsch Assocs, editor/guidance dir 1954-60, proj dir rsch & devel 1960-61; Chicago Commn on Youth Welfare, acting dir city-wide youth serv 1961-63; Joint Youth Develop Comm, youth employment consul 1963-64; Horizons Employment Counselors Inc, founder/pres 1964-66; Chicago Commn on Urban Oppor, chief planner 1964-65; private consultant, 1965-71; Associate Consultants Inc, co-founder/vice pres 1971-. **ORGANIZATIONS:** Mem Chicago Guidance & Personnel Assn 1955-66; mem bd dirs Elliott Donnelly Youth Ctr 1961-63; mem Assn of Women Business Owners 1971-; chmn child guidance comm vice pres Murch Home & Sch Assn 1973-78; vice pres Howard Univ Faculty Wives Assn 1974-75; vice pres mem bd dirs DC assn for Children w/Learning Disabilities 1974-; bd dirs Glenbrook Found for Exceptional Children Bethesda MD 1980-; mem Alpha Kappa Alpha. **HONORS/ACHIEVEMENTS:** Woman of the Year Award, Sigma Gamma Rho Sorority, Chicago, 1960; Outstanding Volunteer Award, DC Public Schools, Washington DC, 1979; author of over 200 articles & pamphlets in field of vocational guidance for Sci Rsch Assocs Chicago; author/editor of Handbook of Job Facts. **BUSINESS ADDRESS:** Vice President, Associate Consultants, Inc, 1726 M St NW, Washington, DC 20036.

LANDRY, L. BARTHOLOMEW
Sociologist, educator. **PERSONAL:** Born Apr 28, 1936, Milton, LA. **EDUCATION:** St Mary's, BA 1961; Xavier U, BA 1966; Columbia U, PhD 1971. **CAREER:** Purdue Univ, asst prof 1971-73; Univ of MD, asst prof 1973-. **ORGANIZATIONS:** Mem African Studies Assn; Am Soc Assn; Caucus of Black Sociologists; Law Soc Assn; Population Assn of Am Publs in field ColumbiaUniv & Faculty Flw 1966-67. **HONORS/ACHIEVEMENTS:** IMH Flw 1967-69; NIH Dissertation Flw 1969-71; Rsrch Contract 20th Century Fund 1975-77. **BUSINESS ADDRESS:** University of Maryland, Dept of Sociology, College Park, MD 20742.

LANDRY, LAWRENCE ALOYSIUS
Research sociologist. **PERSONAL:** Born Jun 21, 1935, Chicago, IL; married S Dolores Branche; children: Jennifer E, Michael H. **EDUCATION:** Univ of Chicago, BA 1958, MA 1960. **CAREER:** ACT, chmn 1964-68; The BLK Group, vice pres 1969-71; Howard Univ, lecturer 1971-79; Associate Consultants Inc, pres 1971-. **ORGANIZATIONS:** Co-chmn Chicago Friends of SNCC 1962-64; co-chmn Chicago Comm March on Washington 1963; chmn Chicago Sch Boycott Comm 1963-64; mem bd of dirs PUSH Intl Trade Bureau 1984-, Natl Rainbow Coalition 1986-. **HONORS/ACHIEVEMENTS:** Chmn Coord Cncl of Civil Orgns School Boycott Comm 1963-64; listee Who's Who in Amer 1964-; Ford Found Fellow The Univ of Chicago 1959-60. **BUSINESS ADDRESS:** President, Associate Consultants, Inc, 1726 M St NW Ste 600, Washington, DC 20036.

LANDSMARK, THEODORE CARLISLE
Association executive. **PERSONAL:** Born May 17, 1946, Kansas City, MO; married Karen Rheinlander. **EDUCATION:** St Paul's Sch Concord NH, 1964; Yale Coll, BA 1969; Yale Architecture Sch, 1973; Yale Law Sch, JD 1973. **CAREER:** Contractors' Assn Boston, exec dir; Hill & Barlow Law Firm Boston, asso; Yale Coll Polit Sci Dept New Haven CT, tchng asst; Quinnipiac Coll PolitSci Dept Hamden CT, instr; 540 Chester Park Limited, gen partner; Yale Law Sch New Haven CT, dir media wrkshp, film soc 1970-73; Hill Cinema Wrkshp,dir. **ORGANIZATIONS:** Mem New England Soc Assn Execs; mem Yale Alumni Bd; governing bd Episcopal Ch Yale; dir Yale Civil Rights Council. **HONORS/ACHIEVEMENTS:** John Hay Whitney Opportunity Fellow; Nat Sci Found Res Fellow. **BUSINESS ADDRESS:** 227 Roxbury St, Roxbury, MA 02119.

LANE, ALLAN C.
Urban planner. **PERSONAL:** Born Dec 21, 1948, Akron, OH; son of Sanford Lane and Mable Farrior Lane (deceased); married Nancy McClendon. **EDUCATION:** Hiram Coll, BA 1971; Univ of Cincinnati, MCP 1973. **CAREER:** City of Cincinnati, city planner 1972-73; Cincinnati Comm Action Agency, asst project dir 1972; Model Cities Housing Corp, deputy planning dir 1973-75; City of Dayton, sr city planner 1975-89; City of Atlanta, urban planner 1989-. **ORGANIZATIONS:** Founder/artistic advisor The Creekside Players 1978-; bd mem Dayton Contemporary Dance Co 1984-; bd mem OH Theatre Alliance 1984-; presenting/touring panelist OH Arts Council 1984-86. **HONORS/ACHIEVEMENTS:** Employee of the Year Dayton Dept of Planning 1981; Outstanding Serv to Project Alpha, Alpha Phi Alpha Frat 1985-86; Service to Gifted Children Dayton PublicSchools 1986. **HOME ADDRESS:** 3655 Habersham Rd NE, Atlanta, GA 30305.

LANE, CECELIA ROSE (CECE)
Business executive. **PERSONAL:** Born Jan 29, 1942, New York, NY; married Dr John Clifton Harris; children: Layne Cydney Harris. **EDUCATION:** State Univ of NY at Buffalo, BS 1959-63; New School of Social Rsch, attended 1974-76; NYU, grad sch of business 1976-77. **CAREER:** Human Resources Bankers Trust Co, AVice Pres 1970-76, AVice Pres govt security sales 1976-78; Lane & Rudd, partner 1978-80; Lane-Harris Enterprises, pres 1980-83. **ORGANIZATIONS:** Past vice pres Corporate Women's Network 1972-; mem The Edges Group Inc 1973-; adv bd Grad Prog for Women Pace Univ 1974-76; treas 1986-87, spec events NY Girlfriends 1975-; adv bd Fashion Inst of Tech-Aff Action Council 1980-83; mem Jack n' Jills of Amer 1982-. **HONORS/ACHIEVEMENTS:** Black Exec Exchange Prog Cert of Appreciation Natl Urban League NY 1974-78; Black Achiever in Industry Harlem Branch YMCA 1975; Industry Outlook Bazaar Mag interviewed for article 1976; Women in Banking Essence Mag interviewed for article 1977.

LANE, DAVID PULASKI, SR.
Dentist. **PERSONAL:** Born Nov 05, 1912, Raleigh, NC; married Vivian Tate; children: Deborah, David Jr, Victor. **EDUCATION:** St Augustine's Coll, BS 1935; Howard Univ Dental School, DDS 1942. **CAREER:** Private practice, dentist 1946-. **ORGANIZATIONS:** Mem Chi Delta Mu Med Frat; Old N State Dental Soc; Natl Dental Soc; mem Raleigh Citizens Assn; NAACP; St Embrose Episcopal Church; St Augustine's Alumni Assn; adv comm, The Raleigh Downtown Mall; Howard Univ Alumni Assn; charter mem Meadowbrook Country Club. **HONORS/ACHIEVEMENTS:** Distinguished Alumni Award, Natl Alumni Assn of St Augustine's College, 1975; Humanitarian Award, Gen Baptist State Convention, 1977. **MILITARY SERVICE:** AUS capt 1942-45.

LANE, EDDIE BURGYONE
Educational administrator, clergyman. **PERSONAL:** Born Aug 08, 1939, Providence, LA; married Betty Jo Washington; children: Felicia, Carla, Eddie II. **EDUCATION:** GW Griffin High Sch; Barber Coll, M, 1960; So Bible Inst Dallas Theol Sem, ThM Bible Diploma 1974;Univ of TX at Dallas, BA 1980. **CAREER:** Dallas Theol Sem, asst to pres 1977-, adminstrv asst to vice pres 1975-77; Dallas Bible Coll, prof 1975-76; So Bible Inst, prof 1975-76; Bibleway Bible Ch, founder pastor 1969-. **ORGANIZATIONS:** Co-founder vice pres Black Evangelistic Enterprise Dallas 1974-; bd mem chmn Dallas Nat Black Evangelical Assn 1974-; dir Black Chr Lit Am Tract Soc 1978-. **BUSINESS ADDRESS:** Dallas Theol Sem, 3909 Swiss Ave, Dallas, TX 75204.

LANE, ELEANOR TYSON
Educator. **PERSONAL:** Born Feb 14, 1938, Hartford, CT; married James Perry Lane, Jr; children: Randall P, Hollye Cherise. **EDUCATION:** St Joseph Coll, BA 1960; Univ of Hartford, MEd 1975. **CAREER:** Hartford Bd of Educ, teacher 1960-72; Amistad House, acting dir 1973-75; Univ of CT, asst dir 1966-. **ORGANIZATIONS:** Mem New England Minority Women Administrators Annual Conf Wellesley Coll 1985; panelist Assoc of Social & Behavorial Scientists Inc 1985; participant Successful Enrollment Management Seminar sponsored by Consultants for Educational Resource & Rsch Inc 1986; mem New England Minority Women Administrators, Assocof Social and Behavorial Scientists, Urban League of Greater Hartford, Natl League of Business and Professional Women, Delta Sigma Theta Sor Inc, Univ of CT Professional Employees Assoc, CT Assoc of College Admissions Officers, Natl Assoc for Women Deans Administrators and Counselors, Natl Assoc for College Admissions Counselors, New England Assoc of Collegiate Registrars and Admissions Officers. **HOME ADDRESS:** 113 Vernwood Dr, Vernon, CT 06066. **BUSINESS ADDRESS:** Asst Dir of Admissions, University of Connecticut, 28 North Eagleville Rd, Storrs, CT 06268.

LANE, GEORGE HENRY
Physician. **PERSONAL:** Born Jul 02, 1902, Jonestown, MS; married Laura. **EDUCATION:** Alcorn Coll, BS 1927; Meharry Med Coll, MD 1931. **CAREER:** Internal Med Cardiovascular Disease, 1957-; Greenwood MS, internal med 1952-57; Pvt Pract, physician 1932-52; WI Med Coll, physician asso. **ORGANIZATIONS:** Mem Omega Phi Psi; chf Sickle Cell Clinic Deaconess Hosp; Am Soc of Internal Med; AMA; WI State Med Soc; Milwaukee Co Med Soc; Nat Med Assn; Cream City Med Soc; past pres MS Black Med Dental & Pharmcy Soc; chmn Internal Med Sect Nat Med Assn 1964, 1971; 1st black vice pres Nat Med Assn 1970; alumni mem AOA 1972. **HONORS/ACHIEVEMENTS:** Hon mem Kappa Pi Med Soc 1930; Commendation NAACP 1971; fight against sickle cell anemia award Calvary Bapt Ch 1972; Presidential Recg for Ldrsp Pres Nixon1973; award for accompl Congressional Cert of Acvmt 1973; recg of outsdng serv Cert of Appreciation Milwaukee Co Comm 1973; personal contrib to various comm activs Cert of Appreciation Milwaukee Co Comm 1974; outsdng ldrsp in Sickle Cell Anemia Prgm & Professional Serv Epsilon Kappa Omega 1976; shield for ldrsp Educ Soc Devel Rust Coll 1976; in appreciation Serv Award Sickle Cell Ctr 1977; Super

Am Award Dr Martin Luther King Jr 1977; Physician of Distinction Award Cream City Med Soc 1977; num publ.

LANE, GEORGE S., JR.
Dental surgeon. **PERSONAL:** Born Dec 28, 1932, Norfolk, VA. **EDUCATION:** BS Biology 1958; BS Chem 1959; MS Endocrinology 1960; DDS 1963; Cert in Oral Surgery 1969; post grad training in oral surgery, First Dist Dental Socof NYC; Albert Einstein Sch of Med; Northwestern U; Roosevelt Hosp of NYC; Walter Reed Army Hosp; Walter Reed Inst of Dental Research. **CAREER:** VA State Dental Health Prog, dental clinician. **ORGANIZATIONS:** Mem Am Dental Assn; Royal Soc of Health of London; Acad of Gen Dentistry; VA State Dental Soc; Virginia-Tidewater Dental Assn; bd mem YMCA; life mem NAACP; mem Alpha Phi Alpha; Shiloh Bapt Ch; Norfolk C of C; diplomate Nat Bd of Dental Examiners; elected for fellowship confirmation Acad of Gen Dentistry. **MILITARY SERVICE:** USAF capt. **BUSINESS ADDRESS:** 1419 E Brambleton Ave, Norfolk, VA.

LANE, JOHN HENRY
Minister. **PERSONAL:** Born Apr 07, 1924, Brookfield, GA; married Donneter Elizabeth Dean; children: DeEtta P, Gwendolyn T. **EDUCATION:** Albany State Coll, attended; Univ of San Francisco, 1954; SF State Coll, 1963; Univ CA Ext, 1965; SF Theo Sem, Grad Theo Union 1972; SF Theo Sem, MAV Cand 1977. **CAREER:** Bayview Br Dept of Emp, asst mgr 1960-71; US Dept of Housing & Urban Devel, suprv spec 1971-; Grace Bapt Church, pastor 1973-; Self-Employed, ins broker; Golden State Life Ins Co, life underwriter; State of CA, toll-collector; US Post Office SF, clerk; Hunters Point Ecumenical Ministries, pres 1976-. **ORGANIZATIONS:** Mem gen bd Amer Bapt Church 1970-79; chaplin Natl Civil Rts Assoc 1976-80; mem bd of mgrs Amer Bapt Ch W 1968-81; past pres Amer Bapt Ch W 1968, SF Afro-Amer Historical & Cultural Soc 1968,83, No CA Ecumenical Council 1970-71, CA Church Council 1971; mem NAACP, Commonwealth Club of CA, APGA, Franklin Mint, Smithsonian Inst, Assoc of Fed Invest, Ecumenical Inst, Republican Residential Task Force. **HONORS/ACHIEVEMENTS:** Roger Williams Fellowship Cert of Accomplishment "The Black Break", Black Urban Studies, Grad Theo Union; Cert of Apprec Amer Bapt Ch of W; Cert of Apprec Outstanding Citizenship City of LA CA, Cert of Apprec 5 Yrs Serv to the Nation Pres Nixon 1973; Cert of Commendation Efficiency in State Govt Gov R Regan 1967. **MILITARY SERVICE:** USN hon disc 1941-47. **BUSINESS ADDRESS:** President, Hunters Point Ecumenical Min, 450 Golden Gate Ave, San Francisco, CA 94102.

LANE, JULIUS FORBES
Retired army officer, fashion museum director. **PERSONAL:** Born Sep 09, 1918, Portsmouth, VA; son of Julius Lane and Lillian Forbes Lane; married Lois Kindle Alexander, Nov 17, 1971; children: Juliette Lane Stanback, Julius Lane, Jr, Sylvia Adel, Lawrence Lane, Nichola Martin. **EDUCATION:** Univ of Omaha, Omaha, NE, AB, 1962; Temple Univ, Philadelphia, PA; Art Students League, New York, NY; Natl Academy School, New York, NY; Natl Academy School of Fine Arts, New York, NY. **CAREER:** US Army, Camp Craft, SC, enlisted army, 1942-44; US Army, Ft Benning, officer-candidate 1944; US Army, Ft Dix, NJ, retired lieutenant Colonel, 1962; Bd of Educ of New York City, New York, NY, teacher; admin, Harlem Inst of Fashion, 1970-; deputy dir, Black Fashion Museum, 1979-. **ORGANIZATIONS:** Mem, Riverside Church NYC, 1980-; mem, 555 Parachute Infantry Assn, 1984-. **HONORS/ACHIEVEMENTS:** "White Vase with Apples and Oranges" oil on canvas, 1962; "Our Little Girl" oil on canvas, 1988. **MILITARY SERVICE:** US Army, Lieutenant Colonel, 1942-62; received master parachutist badge, 1948. **BUSINESS ADDRESS:** Deputy Dir, Black Fashion Museum & Harlem Inst of Fashion, 157 W 126th St Bldg, New York, NY 10027.

LANE, MACARTHUR
Professional athlete. **PERSONAL:** Born Mar 17, 1942, Perote, AL; married Edna; children: Rhonda; Cassandra. **EDUCATION:** Laney Coll; Utah State. **CAREER:** Oakland Invaders, running backs coach 1984-. **ORGANIZATIONS:** Co-owner of Nautilus of Alameda Physical Fitnesss Ctr. **HONORS/ACHIEVEMENTS:** 1st round draft choice St Louis Cardinals 1968; played 4 seasons; led NFL in 1970 with 11 rushing touchdowns; played from 1975-1978 with Chiefs, leading NFL with 66 catches in 1976; for his efforts, was voted to the NFC Pro Bowl squad & was named All-NFC by The Sporting News.

LANE, NANCY L.
Personnel director. **PERSONAL:** Born Sep 03, 1938, Boston, MA. **EDUCATION:** Boston Univ, BS Public Relations 1962; Univ of Pittsburgh Grad School of Public & Intl Affairs, Master of Public Admin 1967; Univ of Oslow, Norway, undergrad studies; Harvard Univ Grad School of Business Admin Prog for Mgmt Devel, certificate 1975. **CAREER:** Chase Manhattan Bank, second vice pres 1972-73; Off-Track Betting Corp, NYC, vice pres 1973-75; Johnson & Johnson Corp, corporate personnel staff 1975-76; Ortho Diagnostic Systems Inc Div of Johnson & Johnson, dir of personnel 1976-78, vice pres personnel & admin and mem bd of dirs 1978-. **ORGANIZATIONS:** Adv bd Black Executive Exchange Prog 1970-87; trustee Benedict Coll 1974-87; chair bd of trustees Studio Museum in Harlem 1987; officer Harvard Business Sch Club of NYC; mem Women's Forum. **HONORS/ACHIEVEMENTS:** Living Legends in Black, JE Bailey III, 1976; Distinguished Award, Harvard Business School, 1985; Distinguished Alumni Award, Boston Univ School of Public Communications, 1987; published numerous articles. **BUSINESS ADDRESS:** Vice Pres Personnel & Admin, Ortho Diagnostic Systems Inc, Rt 202, Raritan, NJ 08869.

LANE, PINKIE GORDON
Professor emerita. **PERSONAL:** Born Jan 13, 1923, Philadelphia, PA; daughter of William A Gordon (deceased) and Inez Addie West Gordon (deceased); married Ulysses Simpson Lane, May 1948 (deceased); children: Gordon Edward. **EDUCATION:** Spelman Coll, Atlanta GA, BA 1949; Atlanta Univ, Atlanta GA, MA 1956; Louisiana State Univ, Baton Rouge LA, PhD 1967. **CAREER:** Southern Univ, Baton Rouge LA, instructor, asst prof, assoc prof 1959-86, prof 1967-86, chairperson dept of English 1974-86. **ORGANIZATIONS:** Poetry Society of Amer; Natl Council for Teachers of English; Modern Language Assn; Coll Language Assn; contributing & advisory editor, The Black Scholar; poetry editor, Black American Literature Forum; Delta Sigma Theta Sorority; Capita Area (Baton Rouge) Network of Executive and Professional Women; YWCA; Early Risers Kiwanis Organization, Baton Rouge Chapter. **HONORS/ACHIEVEMENTS:** Natl Award, Achievement in Arts & Humanities, Spelman Coll, Washington DC Alumnae Chapter 1983; among 57 LA Women included in the Women's Pavilion, World Exposition held in New Orleans LA 1984; Tribute to Black Women Writers at the Inaugural Celebration of Johnetta Cole, Spelman Coll, Atlanta GA 1988; Natl Award for Achievement in Poetry, Coll Language Assn 1988; Louisiana State Poet Laureate, State Governor Roemer 1989; published books: Wind Thoughts, South & West Inc 1972; The Mystic Female, South & West Inc 1975; I Never Scream, Lotus Press Inc 1978; works published in many magazines, including Callaloo, Negro Amer Literature Forum (now Black ALF); The Southern Review, Nimrod, Obsidian, The Black Scholar, Ms. **HOME ADDRESS:** 2738 77th Ave, Baton Rouge, LA 70807.

LANE, RICHARD (DICK NIGHT-TRAIN)
Director, athlete. **PERSONAL:** Born Apr 16, 1928, Austin, TX; divorced; children: Richard Ladimir, Richard Walker. **EDUCATION:** Southern U, 1972-73; Central State U. **CAREER:** Pol Athl Leag, exec dir 1975-; Det Lions, staff asst 1965-72, pro football player 1960-65; Chicago Cardinals, 1954-59; LA Rams, 1952-53; Southern U,coach 1972-73; Central U, 1973-74; Redd Foxx, consult 1974-75; Police Athletic League, exec dir. **ORGANIZATIONS:** Dir Mayor Daley's youth prgms 1954-57; dir Youth Opp Detroit 1963-65; Armed Forces Draft Bd; mem NFL Alumni Assn; past pres Detroit Varsity Club; fdr MI Yth Devel Found; mem Mason Cotillion Club; bd Boy's Club of Metro Detroit; Foursome Golf Club; Booker T Washington Bus Men's Assn; Detroit Optimist Club; Ring 32 Vet Boxing Assn. **HONORS/ACHIEVEMENTS:** All-Time Player of the Century 1968; Football Hall of Fame 1974; Cert of Recognition West Lake JCC; Man of Yr Metro Boy's Clubs; Black Athl Hall of Fame 1977; One of the Best Ever Played in LA Colosseum voted by fans 1985. **MILITARY SERVICE:** AUS corpl 1948-52. **BUSINESS ADDRESS:** Executive Dir, Police Athletic League, PO Box 21013, Detroit, MI 48235.

LANE, RUSSELL A.
Educator. **PERSONAL:** Born Sep 12, 1897, Baltimore, MD; married Marie Clarke; children: 1 Adopted Dau. **EDUCATION:** Brown U, PhB 1921; Dayton U, LlB 1927; IN U, AM 1930, JD 1941; Heidelberg U, Germany, grad student 1923-24. **CAREER:** Retired, present; Supt of Sch, Indianapolis, asst admin 1957-68; HS, Indianapolis, prin 1930-57, English teacher 1927-30; Wilberforce HS, prin 1924-27; Frederick Douglas HS, Baltimore, substitute teacher 1921-23. **ORGANIZATIONS:** Author of numerous articles on Negro education; mem various bds & org. **HONORS/ACHIEVEMENTS:** Numerous awards & honors.

LANE, WILLIAM CLAY
Editor, publisher. **PERSONAL:** Born Jan 27, 1922, Rosedale, MS; son of Rogers Lane and Ruth Lane; married Nancy Petchersky; children: Carol Evelyn McCoo, David, William, Philippa, Laurie Anne James, Linda Sue, Clayton. **EDUCATION:** Univ of IA, Journalism 1947; Univ of MI, Special Study 1949. **CAREER:** Michigan Chronicle, feature/ent ed 1949-61; Assureds Adjusters of Amer, owner ins adjusters/appraisers 1955-; LA Sentinel, feature/end ed 1962-80; Natl Newspapers/Mags, natl synd writer 1965-; World News Synd Ltd, publisher 1970-. **ORGANIZATIONS:** Pres Hollywood NAACP 1973-74; editor Sepia Magazine 1980-81; publisher World Press Ltd 1981-. **HONORS/ACHIEVEMENTS:** Writer/editor "How To Keep Your Face Looking Young" author, Nancy Lane 1980; writer/editor "Saving Face" author, Nancy Lane 1985. **BUSINESS ADDRESS:** Publisher, World News Synd Ltd, P O Box 419, Hollywood, CA 90078.

LANEY, ROBERT LOUIS, JR.
Educator. **PERSONAL:** Born Sep 23, 1956, Conway, SC; son of Robert L Laney Sr and Thillian Moore Laney. **EDUCATION:** SC State Coll, BA 1976; Atlanta Univ, MPA 1979; Clark-Atlanta Univ, Atlanta GA, EdD expected 1989. **CAREER:** Morris Coll, dir career planning placement & coop educ & instructor 1982-84; GA Institute of Tech, admissions officer. **ORGANIZATIONS:** Mem Kappa Alpha Psi Frat 1976-; mem Amer Assoc of Coll Registrars & Admission Officers 1984-; mem Phi Delta Kappa Educ Frat 1986-. **HOME ADDRESS:** 524-A Beckwith Ave, Atlanta, GA 30314. **BUSINESS ADDRESS:** Admissions Officer, Georgia Institute of Tech, 225 North Ave, Atlanta, GA 30332.

LANG, CHARLES J.
Educator. **PERSONAL:** Married Agatha Daniel; children: Angele, Lori, Keith, Twyla. **EDUCATION:** Tuskegee Inst, BA; Xavier U; Citrus Comm Coll; UCLA, MEd, EdD. **CAREER:** W Los Angeles Coll, dir educ prgm; Watts Skill Ctr, assoc dir; LA City Sch, tchr, prin; NASA Space Shuttle Prgm, recruiter, black astronauts & women. **ORGANIZATIONS:** Bd mem Our Authors Study Club; Mayor's African Sister City Com; vp, dir educ tutorial prgm Lang's Learning Lab; cert Scuba Diver & Underwater Photographer; consult Fgn Travel; adv French Lycee Sch of LA; hon mem PTA. **HONORS/ACHIEVEMENTS:** Recip Audio Visual Grant; prod pioneer black sound filmstrip, Equal Oppor in Space Flight; rsrch gifted in Can, Mexicao, US; commd Motivating Black Yth to Achieve, LA City Council; Black Hist Week Award. **MILITARY SERVICE:** AUS infantry offr 1948-51. **BUSINESS ADDRESS:** Director, Dept of Education, West Los Angeles College, 4800 Freshman Dr, Culver City, CA 90230.

LANG, MARVEL
Educator. **PERSONAL:** Born Apr 02, 1949, Bay Springs, MS; son of Rev & Mrs Otha Lang Sr; married Mozell Pentecost, Sep 15, 1973; children: Martin, Maya. **EDUCATION:** Jackson State Univ, BA, 1970; Univ of Pittsburgh, MA, 1975; Michigan State Univ, PhD, 1979. **CAREER:** Jackson State Univ, instructor, 1973-78; Lansing Community Coll, instructor, 1976-78; Jackson State Univ, assoc prof, 1978-84; US Census Bureau, research goegrapher, 1984-86; Michigan State Univ, center of urban affairs dir, 1986-. **ORGANIZATIONS:** bd mem, Urban League of Jackson, 1979-81; steering comm mem, Southeastern Assoc of Amer Geographers, 1980-81; consultant, Mississippi Institute for Small Towns, 1980-84; co-owner, Capital Energy Consultants of Jackson, 1981-83; bd mem, Catholic Social Services-St Vincent's Children's Home, 1986-, Boys and Girls Clubs of Lansing, 1986-; advisory bd mem, Michigan Legislative Black Caucus Found, 1987-. **HONORS/ACHIEVEMENTS:** Candidate, US Air Force Acad, 1966; Governor's Council on Selective Service (MS), mem, 1969-70; Natl Youth Advisory Council on Selective Ser, mem, 1969-70; Meritorious Serv Award, Michigan Legislative Black Caucus, 1988; Black Student Retention in Higher Educ (book) co-editor w/Clinita Ford, 1988. **BUSINESS ADDRESS:** Dir, Cntr for Urban Affairs, Michigan State University, W-104 Owen Hall, East Lansing, MI 48824.

LANG, WINSTON E.
Administrator. **PERSONAL:** Born Dec 20, 1929, Detroit, MI; married Annie Lois Lee; children: Mark, Andrea, Paul. **EDUCATION:** Wayne State U, BA 1952, MSW 1968.

CAREER: Det Cntrl Br NAACP, exec sec, Present; Detroit Urban League, dep dir 1970-79; Neighborhood Serv Orgn, soc serv Admin 1967-70; City of Det, psychiatric soc worker 1962-67. **ORGANIZATIONS:** Consult Detroit Mayor's Comm on Human Resources Devel 1968-70; adv Det Employment Prgm 1971; Mem Kappa Alpha Psi Frat 1950; bd of deacons 2nd Bapt Ch; ch sch supt 2nd Bapt Ch of Det 1970-; mem Detroit Urban League. **HONORS/ACHIEVEMENTS:** Good Conduct Medal AUS 1954; Father of Yr Second Bapt Ch 1964; Outstanding Serv Award, Am Cancer Soc 1974; Man of yr Second Bapt Ch 1975; Spirit of Det Award, Det City Council 1979. **MILITARY SERVICE:** AUS corpl 1952-54. **BUSINESS ADDRESS:** Executive Secretary, Detroit Central - WAACP, 2990 E Grand Blvd, Detroit, MI 48202.

LANG-JETER, LULA L.
Government administrator. **PERSONAL:** Born May 19, Pickens Co, AL. **EDUCATION:** Central State Univ, BS 1951; Wright State Univ Grad Sch, 1968-69; Central State Univ Grad Sch 1969-70. **CAREER:** Central State Univ, super of acctg 1968; Internal Revenue Svcs, auditor & super 1963-71, branch chief 1971-78, sr exec 1979-. **ORGANIZATIONS:** Co-chairperson N VA Minority Task Force for the Amer Cancer Soc; mem Amer Inst of Parliamentarians; participant Natl Urban League's Black Exec ExchangeProg; mem Soc of Women Accountants; local pres Alpha Kappa Alpha Sor Inc; mem League of Women Voters; life mem Natl Council of Negro Women; bd of dir YM-YWCA 1962-83; Natl Adv Bd Assn for Improvement of Minorities 1981-; natl treas Alpha Kappa Alpha Educ Advancement Found 1982-; natl treas Alpha Kappa Alpha Sor Inc 1982-; Natl Adv Bd Federally Employed Women 1983-; public relations Arlington Chap of Links Inc 1984-. **HONORS/ACHIEVEMENTS:** Top Ten Women Dayton Daily newspaper 1969; Fed Employee of the Yr Fed Exec Bd Cincinnati 1971, Detroit 1974, Indianapolis 1982; Grad Leadership Awd Alpha Kappa Alpha 1981; Who's Who Among Blacks 1983; IRS Comm EEO Awd IRS Washington 1982; Outstanding Black Women in State of IN. **HOME ADDRESS:** 1001 S Queen St, Arlington, VA 22204. **BUSINESS ADDRESS:** Asst Director/Sr Exec, US Treasury-IRS, 1111 Constitution Ave NW, Washington, DC 20224.

LANGE, GERALDINE BERNICE
Educator, journalist. **PERSONAL:** Born Jan 03, 1925, Oakland, CA; divorced; children: Theodore W III, Michael F, James C. **EDUCATION:** Merritt Comm Coll, attended 1959-60; San Francisco State Univ, attended 1964-65. **CAREER:** CA State Legislature, legislative aide 1951-53; San Francisco Chronicle, editorial asst 1964-67; KBHK-TV San Fran, news anchor/pub affairs dir 1970-73; San Francisco State Univ, instr 1973-77; Amber Star Prods, pres. **ORGANIZATIONS:** First vice pres Natl Acad of TV Arts & Scis 1973; mem amer Women of Radio & TV 1977-78; mem Amer Fed of TV Arts & Scis 1970-79; mem bd dir OaklandSymphony 1971-81; mem bd dir KQED-TV Public Broadcasting 1976-79; pres Amer Lung Assn of SF 1980-81. **HONORS/ACHIEVEMENTS:** Outstanding Broadcaster of the Yr AWRT 1978; Broadcast Preceptor Awd SF State Univ 1978; Blacks in the West Hall of Fame African-Amer Hist 1980; Broadcast Media Awd SF State Univ 1972.

LANGE, TED W., III
Actor/director. **PERSONAL:** Born Jan 05, Oakland, CA; married Sherryl Thompson; children: Ted IV, Turner Wallace. **EDUCATION:** Attended, San Francisco City College, Merritt Junior College. **CAREER:** Made Broadway debut in the hit musical "Hair"; For the past nine seasons has portrayed Isaac Washington on ABC-TV's "The Love Boat"; film credits include "Wattstax", "Trick Baby", "Blade", "Larry"; has written screenplays, plays and Love Boat segment "Starmaker" 1981; taught at San Francisco City College, Univ of CA,George Washington Univ. **ORGANIZATIONS:** Mem Amer Film Institute. **HONORS/ACHIEVEMENTS:** Donated an annual cash prize to each winning actor/actress in the adult division of the Ira Aldridge Acting Competitions; Bartender of the Year 1983; accepted at Royal Acad of Dramatic Art in London sponsored by Lynn Redgrave 1984. **BUSINESS ADDRESS:** Artist Group, 1930 Sentry Park West, Ste 303, Los Angeles, CA 90067.

LANGFORD, ANNA RIGGS
Attorney. **PERSONAL:** Born Oct 27, Springfield, OH; divorced; children: Lawrence W Jr. **EDUCATION:** Roosevelt U, attended 1946-48; John Marshall Law Sch, LlB, JD 1956. **CAREER:** Robinson Farmer & Langford, atty 1959-69; atty pvt practice, present. **ORGANIZATIONS:** Bd dir Cook Co Bar Assn 1973-75; mem Nat Bar Assn 1958-75; mem NAACP; Chicago Urban League; Chicago Chap SCLC; fdr Pride Comm Cntr Inc; bd mem Am Civil Liberties Union 1970-71; bd mem Operation Breadbasket & PUSH; chmn, bd dir IMPACT drug abuse prgm; one of first two women elected to Chicago City Council 1971; delegate -at-large Nat Dem Conv 1972; mem Sparling Commn; del Pres Johnson's Conf "To Fulfill These Rights" 1968; mem IL Gov Olgilvie's Com for Sr Citizens; del to Pres Nixon's Conf on Aging 1971; del World Congress of Peace Forces, Moscow 1973; mem Commn of Inquiry into conditions in Chili 1974; invitee to Intl Commn of Inquiry into Crimes of Military Junta in Chili, Helsinki, Finland 1974. **HONORS/ACHIEVEMENTS:** Written about in many articles; citation Cath Interracial Council; Interracial Justice & Brotherhood Award 1970; Civil Rights Award, Cook Co Bar Assn; SplAchvmnt Award, Cook Co Bar Assn 1971; Mahatma Ghandi Centennial of Greater Chicago Award 1969; IOTA Bus Week Award, Alpha Chpt, Iota Phi Lambda 1969; James B Anderson Award for Outstanding Achvmt in field of politics, Montford Point Marine Assn 1971; Achievement Award, 7th Ward Ind Polit Orgn 1971; Outstanding Serv in Govt for human outstanding & equal justicew in performance as Alderman, SCLS's Operation Breadbasket 1971; Certificate Award Intl Travellers Assn 1971; Woman of Distiction, Etta Moten Civic & Educ Club 1970; Am Friendship Club Award of Distinction 1971; Afro-am Patrolmen's Assn Testimonial Award 1971; WBEE Radio Comm Aard 1971; Operation Bootstrap Award 1971; hon mem Chicago Police Capt Assn 1974; & numerous others.

LANGFORD, ARTHUR, JR.
City councilman, minister. **PERSONAL:** Born Oct 03, 1949, Atlanta, GA; married Susan Elaine Pease; children: Sarah Elizabeth. **EDUCATION:** Morris Brown Coll, Political Sci 1971. **CAREER:** United Youth-Adult Conf, pres 1972; Atlanta City Council, councilman 2 - 4 yr terms; Rush Memorial Congr Church, pastor 1981; GA State Senate, state senator 1984-. **ORGANIZATIONS:** Lecturer; mem/pres United Youth-Adult Conf (UYAC) 1972-; mem NAACP; mem Southern Christian Leadership Conf (SCLC); mem Phi Beta Sigma Fraternity. **HONORS/ACHIEVEMENTS:** Author of play "Life of a King" drama on the life of Martin Luther King 1969. **BUSINESS ADDRESS:** State Senator, State of Georgia, 123-B State Capitol, Atlanta, GA 30334.

LANGFORD, CHARLES D.
Attorney. **PERSONAL:** Born Dec 09, 1922, Montgomery, AL. **EDUCATION:** TN State A&I Univ, BS; Cath Univ of Am, LLB 1952, JD 1967. **CAREER:** State of AL, legal advisor; Gray, Langford, Sapp & McGowan, partner/attorney. **ORGANIZATIONS:** Mem Senate State of AL; Elks; IBPOE of W. **HONORS/ACHIEVEMENTS:** Recipient Cert of Appreciation Ofc of Econ Opportunity Montgomery Comm Action Agency. **BUSINESS ADDRESS:** Attorney, Gray, Langford, Sapp & McGowan, 352 Dexter Ave, Montgomery, AL 36104.

LANGFORD, JOHN W.
Attorney. **PERSONAL:** Born Mar 20, 1914, Montgomery, AL. **EDUCATION:** Clark Coll Atlanta GA, AB 1936; NC Central Law School, LLB 1947. **CAREER:** Private practice, attny. **ORGANIZATIONS:** Mem, High Point Bar Assn, NC Assn of Black Lawyers, Amer Civil Liberties Union, So Poverty Law Ctr, St Marys United Methodist Church; NC State Bar Nat'l Assoc of Civilian Conservation Corps Alumni; Nat'l Assoc against discrimination in housing; Africare; North Carolinians Against Racist and Religious Violence; mem, High Point N.C. City Council; mem, TransAfrica. **MILITARY SERVICE:** USAAF s/sgt 1942-46. **BUSINESS ADDRESS:** Attorney, 414 Cedar St, High Point, NC 27260.

LANGFORD, VICTOR C., III
Clergyman. **PERSONAL:** Born Aug 06, 1939, Detroit, MI; son of Victor Langord, Jr and Charlotte langord; married Luana Calvert; children: Tanya, Natalie, Kineta, Victor IV. **EDUCATION:** Seattle Pacific Coll, BA 1970; Concordia Sem, BD 1970, MDiv 1975. **CAREER:** Bethel Lutheran Church New Orleans, founder/pastor 1962-64; Holy Cross Lutheran Church Houston, pastor 1965-68; Good Shepherd Lutheran Church Seattle, pastor 1968-76; Nu-Life Enterprises, pres 1979-86; St Mark's Lutheran Church Seattle, minister 1976-. **ORGANIZATIONS:** Treas Black United Clergy for Action 1969-76; chmn exec com Emerg Feeding Prgm Seattle 1977-86; chmn Proj People of Seattle 1970-72; bd dir Seattle Opportunities Industrial Center 1969-86; mem NAACP 1969-; exec bd Assn for Black Lutherans 1983-87; instr Seattle Pacific Univ 1978; instr Seattle Univ 1978, 1980; exec comm bd dir Church Council of Greater Seattle 1983-86; organizer & chmn Filling the Gap Conf March 26 & 27, 1982; ed assoc Lutheran Partners magazine 1985-; exec bd PNW Synod Lutheran Church in Amer 1986-87 Northwest Washington Synod Council 1988-89; founding bd chairman Emerald City Bank Seattle WA 1988-. **HONORS/ACHIEVEMENTS:** Juneteenth Fathers Day Awd Future Production of Seattle 1977. **MILITARY SERVICE:** Washington Army NG LTC, chaplain 1972-; STARC Chaplain. **BUSINESS ADDRESS:** Minister, St Mark's Lutheran Church, 6020 Beacon Ave So, Seattle, WA 98108.

LANGHAM, JOHN M.
Business executive. **PERSONAL:** Married Carvine; children: John Jr, Jimmy. **EDUCATION:** Alabama State Coll, Alabama A&M, Univ of Southern Alabama, attended & received certificates; Univ of Southern Alabama, further studies in physical science. **CAREER:** Prichard Trading Post, self-employed, present. **ORGANIZATIONS:** Pres, PTA Mobile Co; pres, Toulminville Recreation Ctr; mem, 8 yrs, pres, 3 yrs, Prichard City Council; mem, Alabama & Amer Teachers Assns; bd dir Commonwealth Natl Bank; mem adv bd, Bishop State Jr Coll; pres, Prichard NAACP; mem, Supervisory Comm, Mobile Co Personnel Bd; mem, Mobile United, Natl League of Cities, Joint Ctr Political Action; mem, Southern Black Caucus of Elected Officials; mem, Natl Democratic Party. **HONORS/ACHIEVEMENTS:** Prichard C of C Citizen of Week; Kappa Citizen of the Year; The John M Langham Auditorium, Prichard, AL; Prichard Senior Citizen Org; ACT Educ Prog. **MILITARY SERVICE:** AUS. **BUSINESS ADDRESS:** Prichard City Hall, PO Box 10427, Prichard, AL 36610.

LANGHART, JANET FLOYD
Model, journalist. **PERSONAL:** Born Dec 22, 1941, Indianapolis, IN; divorced. **EDUCATION:** Attended coll 2 yrs. **CAREER:** Sunday Open House WCVB Needham, MA, hostess, present; WCVB-TV Boston; WISH-TV Indpls, IN, hostess interview talk show Controversial Issues; WBBM-TV Chicago,weather reporter; Ebony Fashion Fair, former model. **ORGANIZATIONS:** Mem Am Women in Radio & TV; Chicago Women in Broadcasting. **HONORS/ACHIEVEMENTS:** Chosen "Miss Sepia, 1966", "Miss Chicagoland, 1967", "Miss Intl Auto Show, 1968". **BUSINESS ADDRESS:** WCVB, 5 TV Place, Needham, MA 02192.

LANGSTON, ANDREW A.
Salesman. **PERSONAL:** Born May 12, 1929, Coleman, GA; married Gloria Muir; children: Andre M. **EDUCATION:** Morris Brown Coll, attended 1947; Morehouse Coll, attended 1948; City Coll NY, BA 1949; NY Univ, MBA 1954. **CAREER:** CBS, continuity/copywriter 1950; Aglaw Corp, efficiency/comptroller 1953-56; Chase Manhattan Bank, mgmt trainee 1956-60; Prudential Ins Co, spl agent 1960-; Genesee Funeral Home Inc, owner/treas 1973-; Radio Station WDKX-FM, owner/gen mgr/sales mgr 1974-. **ORGANIZATIONS:** Trustee Rochester C of C; bd of dir Otetiana Council Boy Scouts of Amer; bd of dir William G Crimm Inst of Music; bd dir Eltrex Industries; bd dirDavid Hochstein Memorial Sch of Music; bd dir Natl Assn of Broadcasters Medium Markets; founder/past pres current chmn of bd Natl Assn Black Owned Broadcasters; pres Club Honor Guard. **HONORS/ACHIEVEMENTS:** Comm Serv Awds, Pres Citations, Acad of Honor Prudential Ins Co of America; life & qualifying mem Million Dollar Round Table. **BUSINESS ADDRESS:** General Manager/Sales Manager, WDKX-FM Radio, 160 Allen's Creek Rd, Ste 103, Rochester, NY 14618.

LANGSTON, ESTHER R.
Educator. **PERSONAL:** Born Jun 20, 1939, Shreveport, LA; daughter of Frank Jones and Daisy Jones. **EDUCATION:** Wiley Coll, BA 1963; San Diego State Univ, MSW 1970; Univ of S CA, 3rd Yr Cert Social Work/Gerontology 1974; Univ of TX, PhD 1982. **CAREER:** Univ of Nevada Las Vegas, assoc prof 1970-. **ORGANIZATIONS:** Pres Undergrad Faculty Cncl of Social Work Educ 1984-85; pres LV Chap Natl Assn of Black Social Workers 1983-84; chairperson Debutante Adv Comm Les Femmes Douze 1982; mem Faculty Senate UNLV 1984-85; chrpsn Dept Faculty Recruitment Comm 1983-84-85; mem Grievance Comm UNLV 1983-85; chairpsn Psychological Counseling & Eval Ctr Recruitment Comm 1983-84; bd mem Oper Life Comm Develop Corp 1977-79; proj dir Minorities Public Policies & Laws & their Effect on Serv Delivery 1977; oral exam bd NV State Div Personnel 1976; vice pres, bd of directors, Aids for AIDS of Nevada 1988-; vice chair, Governor's Commission on Mental Health M/R 1985-. **HONORS/ACHIEVEMENTS:** Co-recipient Univ Rsch Cncl Grant for Cross Cultural Comparison of Informal Support Systems for the Elderly 1983; "The

Family & Other Informal Supports" Campanile Press 1983; "Care of the Terminally Ill, A Look at the Hospice Movement" Indian Journal of Social Services 1986. **HOME ADDRESS:** 3618 Anthony, Las Vegas, NV 89121. **BUSINESS ADDRESS:** Associate Professor, Univ of NV Las Vegas, 4505 Maryland Pkwy, Dept of Social Work, Las Vegas, NV 89154.

LANGSTON, JOSEPHINE DAVIDNELL
Nurse. **PERSONAL:** Born Jun 02, 1948, Philadelphia, PA. **EDUCATION:** Winston-Salem State U, BS 1969; Temple U, BA 1974. **CAREER:** Phila-vA Med Cntr, head nurse 1974-; Hosp of theUniv of PA, head nurse 1969-74; Phila-vA Med Cntr, staff nurse 1969. **ORGANIZATIONS:** Chpsn Health-Hygiene Comm Grand Household of Ruth 1978; educ com Frances E Edwards #20 OES PHA; instr first aid, Boy Scout Troop 161, 1976; mem procedural com Phila-vA Med Cntr; mem Alpha Kappa Alpha Sor; mem Black Women's Collective; mem St Valentine Royal Court of Cyrene #25. **HONORS/ACHIEVEMENTS:** Miss Alumni Award, Winston-sal StateUniv Alumni Assn 1976; Recognition Award, Boy Scout Troup 161, 1976; Recognition Award - Outstanding Young Women in Am 1977; Pub Service Award, Chapel of Four Chaplin 1978. **BUSINESS ADDRESS:** Philadelphia V A Med Center, Univ & Woodland Ave, Philadelphia, PA 19104.

LANIER, BOB
Advertising and promotion executive. **PERSONAL:** Born Sep 10, 1948, Buffalo, NY; son of Robert Lanier, Sr and Nanette Lanier; married Shirley Neville; children: Tiffany, Kimberly, Jack, Robert. **EDUCATION:** St Bonaventure, BBA 1970. **CAREER:** Bob Lanier Enterprises, Milwaukee WI, president, 1984—; Milwaukee Bucks, professional basketball player 1980-84; Detroit Pistons, professional basketball player 1970-80. **ORGANIZATIONS:** Mem Boys Club of Met Detroit; trustee, Boys and Girls Clubs of Greater Milwaukee; bd of dir, Milwaukee Council on Alcoholism; Miller Lite All-Stars; former sec-treas, former pres, NBA Player Assn. **HONORS/ACHIEVEMENTS:** College All-American, St Bonaventure, 1970; Most Valuable Player, NBA All-Star Game, 1974; Basketball Writers Kennedy Award 1977-78; NBA Walter Kennedy Citizenship Award, Pro Basketball WRiters, 1978; Jackie Robinson Award, YMCA, 1981; Milwaukee Distinguished Athlete of the Year, Milwaukee Council on Alcoholism, 1984; NBA All-Star Team 8 times; 12th all-time NBA scorer; tenth all-time NBA field goal scorer; tenth leading all-time Milwaukee Bucks scorer; holds Detroit Piston career, season, and game rebound records; honorary chairman, Thurgood Marshall Scholarship Fund; honorary doctorate, St Bonaventure Univ. **BUSINESS ADDRESS:** Bob Lanier Enterprises, 8989 North Deerwood Dr, Suite 190, Milwaukee, WI 53223.

LANIER, DOROTHY COPELAND
Educator. **PERSONAL:** Born Aug 19, 1922, Pine City, AR; married Marshall Alee; children: Frederick Delano, Adrien Copeland, Vanessa King. **EDUCATION:** Henderson State Tchr Coll, BSE 1965; E TX State U, MS 1968, EdD 1974. **CAREER:** Jarvis Christian Coll, chmn div of humanities, prof of English 1977-; E AR Comm Coll, instr of English 1975-77; Jarvis Christian Coll, asst prof English, public relations assoc 1960-75; Sparkman Training School, elementary teacher 1957-60; Universal Life Insurance Co, sec-cashier 1952-54. **ORGANIZATIONS:** Mem Zeta Phi Beta Sor Inc 1941-; exec com mem Linguistic Assn of the SW 1974-77; talent file Nat Council of Tchr of Engl 1974-; mem AR Philol Assn 1976. **HONORS/ACHIEVEMENTS:** Zeta of the Year, Zeta Phi Beta Sor Inc 1973; Outstanding Tchr, Jarvis Christian Coll 1974; publ "Selected Grammar Patterns in the Lang of Jarvis Students", Sociolinguistics in the SW 1974; Outstanding Professional Serv, Jarvis Christian Coll 1975; publ "Black Dialect grammar in fact & fiction", AR Philol Assn Publ 1976; Outstanding Contributor to Edn, Zeta Phi Beta Sor Inc 1977; publ "Textual Puzzle Technique", ERIC 1977. **BUSINESS ADDRESS:** Jarvis Christian Collee, Hawkins, TX 75765.

LANIER, FRAN See STRONG, HELEN FRANCINE

LANIER, HORATIO AXEL
Education association executive. **PERSONAL:** Born Feb 07, 1955, Augusta, GA. **EDUCATION:** Univ of GA, AB Journalism 1977; Georgetown Univ Law Center, JD 1987. **CAREER:** Southern Bell Telephone Co, business office mgr 1977-79; Xerox Corp, marketing rep 1980-82; Sears Business Systems Ctgr, marketing rep 1982-84; US Justice Dept Office of Legal Counsel, legal editorial asst 1984-85; H Lanier Small Business Develop Consultant, pres 1985-86; Natl Black Alumni Assoc, natl president 1986-. **ORGANIZATIONS:** Pres Univ of GA Black Alumni Assoc 1980-82; mem Univ of GA Bicentennial Planning Comm 1984-85; exec producer UHURU Performing Arts Ensemble Georgetown Law Ctr 1985-87; vice chair Black Law Students Assoc Georgetown Law Ctr 1985-86; mem Amer Bar Assoc 1986-, Natl Bar Assoc 1987-. **HONORS/ACHIEVEMENTS:** Disting Serv Awd Black Law Students Assoc 1985; WEB DuBois Awd Georgetown Law Ctr 1987. **BUSINESS ADDRESS:** Natl President, Natl Black Alumni Assoc, 3531 16th St NW, Washington, DC 20010.

LANIER, MARSHALL L.
Retired educator. **PERSONAL:** Born Jan 12, 1920, Halifax Co, VA; son of Parish L Lanier and Mary S Lanier; married Dorothy Copeland; children: Frederick D, Adrien C, Vanessa C. **EDUCATION:** Tuskegee Univ AL, BSA 1948, MSA 1950; E TX StateUniv Commerce TX, PhD 1971. **CAREER:** Marvell Independent Sch Dist, instr of vets 1950-51; Sparkman Training Sch Sparkman AR, prin & teacher 1957-60; E AR Community Coll, dir spec serv 1976-77; Jarvis Christian Coll Hawkins City AR, dir student teaching 1977-85. **ORGANIZATIONS:** Mem Assn of Tchr Educators; mem TX State Tchrs Assn; mem Phi Delta Kappa; mem Assn for Supervision & Curriculum Devel; mem Kappa Delta Pi; mem Omega Psi Phi Frat. **HONORS/ACHIEVEMENTS:** Recipient plaque for Outstanding Advisor, Jarvis Christian Coll 1975; Blue & Gold Plaque, Jarvis Christian Coll 1978. **MILITARY SERVICE:** AUS sgt 1941-45.

LANIER, WILLIE
Former professional athlete. **PERSONAL:** Born Aug 21, 1945, Clover, VA. **EDUCATION:** Attended, Morgan State. **CAREER:** Kansas City Chiefs, linebacker 1967-77. **HONORS/ACHIEVEMENTS:** All-Pro, All-AFL, All-AFC every yr from 1968-76; Defensive MVP 1971; elected Pro Football Hall of Fame.

LANSDEN, WILLIE F.
Emergency medical physician. **PERSONAL:** Born Jan 19, 1953, St Louis, MO; married Cynthia D Ware; children: Akeesha. **EDUCATION:** St Louis Univ, BA 1976; Meharry Medical Coll 1980. **CAREER:** Natl Council on Alcoholism, bd of dirs 1984-87; US Public Health Svcs, lt commander 3 yrs; Broadway Family Practice Ctr, dir. **ORGANIZATIONS:** Mem NAACP 1976-, Amer Coll of Emergency Physicians 1981-. **HONORS/ACHIEVEMENTS:** Outstanding Young Men of Amer 1984. **BUSINESS ADDRESS:** Dir, Broadway Family Practice Ctr, 2216 E Broadway Rd, Phoenix, AZ 85040.

LANSEY, E. GAINES
Bank executive. **CAREER:** Ideal Federal Savings Bank, Baltimore MD, chief executive, 1988—. **BUSINESS ADDRESS:** Ideal Federal Savings Bank, 1629 Druid Hill Ave, Baltimore, MD 21217. *

LANSEY, YVONNE F.
Bank executive. **PERSONAL:** Born Sep 09, 1946, Baltimore, MD; daughter of E Gaines Lansey, Sr and Priscilla Phillips-Lansey. **EDUCATION:** Morgan State Univ, Baltimore, MD, BS, 1969; Long Island Univ, Brooklyn, NY, MBA, 1974. **CAREER:** Fed Reserve Bank of NY, New York, NY, credit analyst, 1969-74; Xerox Corp, Rochestr, NY, financial analyst, 1974-76; Westinghouse Electric Rorp, Hunt Valley, MD, financial analyst, 1976-79, project dir, 1979-85; Ideal Fed Savings Bank Baltimore, MD, vice pres, 1985-88, pres, 1988-. **ORGANIZATIONS:** Trustee, Florence Crittenton Servs, 1986; trustee, Girl Scouts of Central MD, 1987; trustee, Combined Health Agencies, Inc. 1987; Governor's Task Force to Study & Revise the Inheritance & Estate Tax Law of the State of MD, 1987; financial sec, The Links, Inc,Harbor City Chapter, 1987-89; bd of dir & sec, Amer League of Financial Insts, Washington DC, 1988; trustee, Baltimore Museum of Art, 1989; Alpha Kappa Alpha Sorority. **HONORS/ACHIEVEMENTS:** Women on the Move, Sigma Gamma Rho, 1986; Booker T Washington, Business League of Baltimore, 1989. **HOME ADDRESS:** 3303 Glen Ave, Baltimore, MD 21215.

LAPEYROLERIE, FRANK M.
Dentist. **PERSONAL:** Born May 04, 1929, Reserve, LA; son of Frank Lapeyrolerie and Marguerite Lapeyrolerie; married Delia; children: Jacques, Michele, Daryl, Donna, Crystall. **EDUCATION:** Xavier Univ, BS 1949; Howard Univ, DDS 1953. **CAREER:** Harlem Hospital, oral surgery rsd, 1958-61; Seton Hall, assoc prof, 1961-65; CMDNJ New Jersey Dental School, chmn, prof, oral surgery, anesth & hospital dent, 1965-70; act chmn oral surgery, anesth & hospital dental, 1976-; Univ of Med & Dentistry of New Jersey, New Jersey Dental School, dean, 1979-86 retired. **ORGANIZATIONS:** Pres, founder, Crossroads Health Maint Org, 1973-; diplomate Amer Bd of Oral Med, 1979, Amer Bd Oral Surgery; fellow Amer Acad Oral Pathology, Amer Coll of Dentists, Amer Soc Oral Surg, Amer Dental Soc Anesth; mem, Essex Cty Dental Soc, Commonwealth Dent Soc, Amer Dent Soc of Anesth, NJ Soc Oral Surg, Natl Dent Assoc, Amer Soc Oral Surg, Amer Dental Soc; pres, founder, Center Parkway Professional Org, 1970; 1st black adv bd mem, Midlantic Bank Essex Brs, 1980; mem, NAACP, E Orange Model Cities Dent Planning; dental dir, E Orange Nursing Home, bd dir, Dental Manpower Devel Corp; comm adv comm, Dental Med; fellow Amer Soc of Anesthesiology, Intl Coll of Dentists; founding mem, Amer Coll of Oral & Maxillofacial Surgeons. **HONORS/ACHIEVEMENTS:** Numerous publs. **MILITARY SERVICE:** USAF DC capt 1952-55. **BUSINESS ADDRESS:** Retired Dean, Univ of Med & Dentistry, NJ Dental School, 100 Bergen St, Newark, NJ 07103.

LARA, EDISON R., SR.
Company executive. **CAREER:** Westside Distributors, South Gate CA, chief executive, 1988—. **BUSINESS ADDRESS:** Westside Distributors, 2405 Southern Ave, South Gate, CA 90280. *

LARK, RAYMOND
Artist, lecturer. **PERSONAL:** Born Jun 16, 1939, Philadelphia, PA. **EDUCATION:** Philadelphia Museum School of Art, attended 1948-51; Los Angeles Trade Tech Coll, attended 1961-62; Temple Univ Phila, BS 1961; Univ of CO Boulder, LHD 1985. **CAREER:** Exhibitions, Library of Congress Wash DC; Guggenheim Museum NY; Smithsonian Inst Wash; Metro Museum NY; Ava Dorog Galleries Los Angeles & Munich; LaGalerieMouffe Paris; Nader's Art Gallery Port-au-Prince Haiti; Galleria d'Arte Caglairi Naples Italy; Centre Intl D-Art Contemporain Paris France; Accademia Italia Parma Italy; Honolulu Acad of Arts Hawaii; PA State Museum Harrisburg; Museum of African and African-Amer Art & Antiquities Buffalo NY; Portsmouth Museum VA; CA Museum of Sci & Industry Los Angeles; NJ State Museum Trenton; The UCLA Ctr for Afro-Amer Studies LA; Stanford Univ Museum CA; Exec Mansion Vice Pres NelsonA Rockefeller NY; Santa Barbara Museum CA; Univ of Colorado Museum Boulder. **ORGANIZATIONS:** CA Museum of African Historical & Cultural Soc San Fran; San Diego Museum CA; The Museum of African Amer Art Santa Monica in conjunction w/ 1982 Natl Urban League Annual Conference; Gallery Vallombreuse Biarritz France; Smith-Mason Gallery of Art Wash DC; Phillip E Freed Gallery of Art Chicago; Playboy Club Century City CA; Beverly Wilshire Hotel Beverly Hills CA; Dalzell Hatfield Galleries Ambassador Hotel LA; Diplomat Hotel FL; Sheraton Park Hotel Wash DC; Griffon's Light Gallery Denver CO; Phoenix Art Gallery Atlanta GA; The Multi-Cultural Arts Inst San Diego CA; Lyzon Galleries Nashville TN; Ames Art Galleries & Auctioneers Beverly Hills; and over 60 other exhibitions; lectured, various educational institutions throughout the US; Art Commissions, did art work "All in the Family", "The Carol Burnett Show", "Sonny & Cher Show", "Maude", "Young and the Restless", Univ City Studios Movie Land Wax Museum, Blue Cross Insurance Company,among others; Previous Endorsements, Dewar's Profile Schenley Affiliated Brands Corp NY 1980; Founders Savings & Loan Assn CA 1979. **HONORS/ACHIEVEMENTS:** Listed in no less than 600 history books, directories & periodicals; rec'd a succession of citations, honors, salutes, commissions, advertising endorsements, headlined billings, and Best-of-the-Show Cash Awds and Gold Medals; Citations from Pres Jimmy Carter, Gerald R Ford, Richard M Nixon, Gov Jerry Brown of CA, and mayor Tom Bradley of LA among others; recipient of over 50 "first" accomplishments; Grants, Natl Endowment for the Arts, ARCO, Coors Beer Company, Colorado Humanities Prog, the Students at the Univ of Colorado, among others; authored and contributed to over 50 scholarly treatises on art, education, historical development of Black amers, which are used as textbooks translated and subscribed to by institutions and individuals in nearly every country of the world. **BUSINESS ADDRESS:** The Art of Raymond Lark, PO Box 8990, Los Angeles, CA 90008.

LARKINS, E. PAT
Mayor-commissioner. **CAREER:** Mayor-commissioner of Pompano Beach, FL. **BUSINESS ADDRESS:** PO Drawer 1300, Pompano Beach, FL 33061. *

LARKINS, JOHN RODMAN
Director. **PERSONAL:** Born Dec 24, 1913, Wilmington, NC; married Marian; children: Sandra. **EDUCATION:** Shaw U, AB; AtlantaUniv Sch of Soc Work, MSW; Sch of Serv AdminstrnUniv of Chgo, adv study. **CAREER:** Div of Youth Dev, dir 1973-; NC Probation Commn, asso dir 1968-73; Dept Soc Svc, coord of civil rights 1942-68. **ORGANIZATIONS:** Mem bd trustees Shaw U; NC Cntrl U; mem bd adv Raleigh Bus Coll; mem NC Adv Coun on Librs; mem NC Bd Juv Correc; adv bd, vice pres NC Coun on Human Rels; bd dirs So Regional Coun, Atlanta; aptd NC Recreation Commn, Adv Com of Thirty, Steering Com, Cit Com 1961; first vice pres Family Life Coun of NC Exec Com 1962; aptd Govs Com on Juv Delin & Youth Crime 1962; aptd Cit Adv Coun of Pres Com on Juv Delin & Youth Crime 1962; aptd NCGood Neighbor Council 1963; Gov Com on Demon Proj for Youth 1963; Family Svc, Travelers Aid Assn of Raleigh 1965-66; mem Nat Adv Coun of Upward BoundProj; Gov Law & Order Com 1973-; Juv Jus Adv Com of Gov & Order Com 1973-; Criminal Just Educ & Training Sys Coun 1973-. **HONORS/ACHIEVEMENTS:** Recip Cert of Merit for pub svc, Bus & Professional Mens Club 1957; Man of Year, Negro Progess 1958; Cert for Merit Christ & Civic Serv to people of state, NC Fed of Negro Wom Club. **BUSINESS ADDRESS:** Div of Youth Devel, 116 W Hargett St, Raleigh, NC 27602.

LARKINS, WILLIAM CONYERS
Appointed government official. **PERSONAL:** Born May 11, 1934, Washington, DC; married Delores M; children: William Jr, Renee, Frederick, Marisa Spriggs, Marcellus Spriggs, Tina, Rosey, Anthony. **EDUCATION:** Crordoza Sr HS, hs diploma 1948-51. **CAREER:** Blind Liberation Into New Dimension; BLIND; public recreation ofcr; Nia-Umoja, 1973-78; Fareast Comm Organiz; Advisory Neighborhood Council 8A01; Area D Comm Mental Health Organiz 1979-82. **ORGANIZATIONS:** Councilperson W Jackson Rolak 1976-82; bd of dirs Area D Comm Help Hos 1982-83; volunteer CIO-Comm Improvement Organ 1980-; mem comm to re-elect W Rolak 1976-80. **HONORS/ACHIEVEMENTS:** Cert of Appreciation Barry Farms 1980; Barry Farms Comm Awd 1980; Fisher Awd Best Community 1981; Mayor Comm of Blind 1982; ANC Comm Awd 1983; Fab Fisher Award 1981; Mayor Commr of Handicapped Persons 1980-84; Cert of Apprec from Recreation Dept of Wash, DC 1983. **MILITARY SERVICE:** AUS 2nd Lt from OCS 1952-54. **HOME ADDRESS:** 1223 Sumner Rd SE, Washington, DC 20020.

LAROCHE, GERARD A.
Educator. **PERSONAL:** Born Oct 03, 1927, Cap Haitien, Haiti;married Carolyn Mae Seese; children: 2 Children. **EDUCATION:** SD State Coll, BS 1955; Bethel Sem, 1960; Roosevelt U, MA 1967;Univ of Strasbourg, Doc 1971; Tchr Coll, 1968;Univ of MN, 1961-63, 69, 72; Sioux FallsColl, 1950-53. **CAREER:** Bethel Coll & Seminary, prof 1969; SW HS, teacher 1968-69; Oaklawn HS, teacher 1967-68; Dusable Jr HS, teacher 1966-67; Zion Baptist Church, assoc minister 1961-64; Haiti, miss 1956-57; Shiloh Baptist Church, assoc minister 1973- 75; Amer Baptist Conv, ministry 1961; Family Tie Daily Dev Guide, 1974. **ORGANIZATIONS:** Chmn Minorities & Intl Com 1973-76; vice pres Spanish Evang Educ Crusade 1971-75; found Black French Club in St Paul 1973-74; mem Alln Francaise of TwinCities; Am Tchrs of French; rep MN Cncl of Chs 1963-64. **BUSINESS ADDRESS:** 3900 Bethel Dr, Arden Hills, MN 55112.

LARRIE, REGINALD REESE
Educator and author. **PERSONAL:** Born Sep 05, 1928, Detroit, MI; son of Robert Reese Larrie, Jr and Dora Reese; married Margaret Price; children: Debra, Reginald, Jr, Raymond. **EDUCATION:** Upper Iowa Univ, BA, 1979; Maryglove Coll, MeD, 1982, Pacific Western Univ, PhD, 1988. **CAREER:** Michigan Chronicle, auto writer, 1964—; Wayne County Community Coll, Detroit, MI, instructor, 1969—; Black Sports Magazine, auto editor, 1973-75; Wayne State Univ, Detroit, MI, prof, 1976. **ORGANIZATIONS:** Comm mem 1969—, New Detroit; mem 1969—, Museum of African Amer History; mem 1970—, Assoc for the Study of African Amer History; mem, 1975—, Detroit Historical Soc; mem, Detroit Triumph Club, Detroit Auto Writers Group. **HONORS/ACHIEVEMENTS:** 15 years award, Boy Scouts of Amer, 1970; New Detroit Dedicated Service Award, 1971; City of Detroit Distinguished Service Award, 1976; Montgomery Ward Bicentennial Award, 1979; Wayne County Community Coll Recognition Award, 1988; author of Corners of Black History, 1971, "Swing Low, Sweet Chariot," WXYZ-TV, February, 1973, Black Experiences in Michigan History, 1975, Makin' Free, 1981. **BUSINESS ADDRESS:** Wayne County Community College, 801 Fort St., Detroit, MI 48226.

LARRY, JERALD HENRY
State representative. **PERSONAL:** Born Jul 29, 1944, Dallas, TX; children: Jerald Andre, Jerrod Enrique. **EDUCATION:** Attended, NTSU, Denton, TX, 1962-64, El Centro, Dallas, TX, 1969-71, Bishop Coll, Dallas, TX, 1972-77. **CAREER:** Regional Admin of Natl Bank Office of Comptroller of the Currency, US Treasury, asst natl bank exec, 1974-75; Interracial Council for Business, Dallas, loan serv officer, 1975-76; Jessie's Nursing Facility, business mgr, 1976; Larry's 4-J's/Professional Business, owner/mgr, 1977-83; Texas State Treasury, supvr, investigator, 1983-86; State of Texas, representative. **ORGANIZATIONS:** Bd mem, Dallas Black Chamber of Commerce, 1976-; bd mem, VNA, 1979-83; chmn, budget & finance, Texas Coalition of Black Democrats, 1983-. **HOME ADDRESS:** 2430 Marfa Ave, Dallas, TX 75216. **BUSINESS ADDRESS:** State Representative, TX House of Representatives, PO Box 2910, Austin, TX 78769.

LARUE, KARL MCLAINE
Program manager. **PERSONAL:** Born Jan 30, 1940, Bryn Mawr, PA; married Deborah Overton; children: Karl Jr, Anthony, Cheryl, Craig, Scott, Yevette. **EDUCATION:** Drexel Univ Phil, 1968; Rutgers U, 1975; Univ of CA Berkeley, 1979. **CAREER:** Mansken Engrg, design asst prod engr 1963-65; Scott Paper Co, engrg assoc 1965-68; Allstate Design & Devel Co, supr designer 1968-71; United Engrg Phil, design leader eng 1971-73; United Engrs & Constr Inc, lead sys engr 1973-76; Daniel Intl, construction mgr 1976-79; Rockwell Intl, prog mgr design & const 1979-. **ORGANIZATIONS:** Mem ASTM/ASME/AM Soc of Elec Engr.

LASANE, JOANNA EMMA
Theatrical director. **PERSONAL:** Born Jul 24, 1935, Atlantic City, NJ; daughter of John Westly Foreman and Viona Marie Foreman; married Karlos Robert LaSane, Aug 29, 1955; children: Karlos Robert LaSane Jr. **EDUCATION:** Katherine Dunham School of Dance NY, 1953-55; Martha Graham School of Modern Dance NY, 1953-55; Amer School of Ballet & Intl School of Dance, 1957; Montclair State Coll for Theatre Arts & Speech 1970; Negro Ensemble Co NY, 1971; New Lafayette Theatre NY, 1972-73. **CAREER:** Ebony Fashion Fair Johnson Publishing, Chicago, high fashion model 1965-66; Atlantic City Bd of Ed, comm agent 1972-75; Atlantic Human Resources, consultant 1973-85; Stockton Performing Arts Ctr, rep to the arts & lecture series 1983-85; Atlantic City Childrens Theatre, dir 1973-. **ORGANIZATIONS:** Drama consultant Altantic City Bd of Ed 1983-; mem Allied Arts, NAACP, Urban League; mem NJ Educ Assoc, Natl Educ Assoc, Stockton State Coll Friends Assoc, Atlantic City Education Foundation; advisory council Westside School Complex; drama consultant Center for Early Childhood Educ; mem NJ State Council on the Arts; mem NJ Speech and Theatre Assoc; bd of directors Atlantic City Education Foundation 1987-89; committee chairman Boy Scouts of America 1988-89. **HONORS/ACHIEVEMENTS:** 1st Black model to do an intl ad for Pepsi Cola 1967; NJ Senate Citation for Excellence in the Cultural Arts 1981; Creating New Pathways for Youth Distinguished Award Gentlemen of Sports NJ 1981; Cultural Arts Award Atlantic City Magazine 1981; Leadership in the Arts 101 Women Plus NJ 1983; Delta Sigma Theta Appreciation Awd for Serv at 37th Natl Convention Detroit MI 1983; Outstanding Citizen NAACP & Civic Betterment Assoc 1984; member of the NJ State Council on the Arts (1st Black woman); Theta Kappa Omega Arts Award 1986; Alpha Kappa Alpha Comm Serv Award 1986; Omega Psi Phi Fraternity Upsilon Alpha Chapter Inspiration & Leadership Award 1986; apptd to serve as a commissioner of the Atlantic City US Constitution Bicentennial Commn 1987; role model award Sun Newspaper 1989; achievement award National Conference of Christians and Jews 1988-89; people to watch award Atlantic City Magazine 1989. **BUSINESS ADDRESS:** Dir, Atlantic City Children's Theater, Westside School Complex, Illinois & Mamora Aves, Atlantic City, NJ 08401.

LASHLEY, BARBARA ANN
Realtor. **PERSONAL:** Born Aug 20, 1942, Biloxi, MS; children: Stacy, Patricia. **EDUCATION:** San Francisco State Coll, BFA 1967; Occidental Coll, MA. **CAREER:** Program Planning Housing & Devel Dept, div chief 1975-76; Berkeley House Auth, dir 1976-77; The Fiber Studio, sole proprietor 1979-84; So Berkeley Local Dvel Corp, consultant 1981-83; Brooks Realty Co. **ORGANIZATIONS:** Pres bd mem S Berkeley Local Devel Corp 1981-83; city councilwoman Berkeley City Council 1982; chairwoman Loan Admin Bd 1983-84; life mem Natl Council of Negro Women. **HONORS/ACHIEVEMENTS:** Fellowship Natl Urban Fellows 1971-72. **HOME ADDRESS:** 3110 Ellis St, Berkeley, CA 94703. **BUSINESS ADDRESS:** Brooks Realty Co, 1734 Alcatraz Ave, Berkeley, CA 94703.

LASSITER, JAMES EDWARD, JR.
Dentist. **PERSONAL:** Born Feb 12, 1934, Newport News, VA; children: Teri, Tina, James III, Judi. **EDUCATION:** Howard Univ, B Music Ed 1957, DDS 1963. **CAREER:** Overlook Hosp Summit NJ, assoc attendant 1967-; Martland Hosp, assoc attendant 1972; Coll of Medicine & Dentistry, assoc prof 1972-73; Coll of Dentistry Fairleigh Dickenson, asst prof 1974-78; Coll of Medicine & Dentistry, asst prof 1982-84; Private Practice, dentist 1965-. **ORGANIZATIONS:** Numerous lectures; consul Union Co Vocational Sch 1975-; adv comm Coll of Medicine & Dentistry 1977-79; consul Piedmont Rsch Ctr 1979; consul Dept of Health Educ & Welfare 1979; adv comm Natl Health Professional Placement Network WK Kellogg Found 1979; adv comm to Review Coll of Med & Dentistry Dental Sch 1979; bd mem Group Health Ins of NY 1981-; mem Amer Dental Assn 1965-; mem Natl Dental Assn 1965-; mem NJ Dental Assn 1965-; mem Commonwealth Dental Soc 1965-; mem Amer Analgesia Soc 1976-; mem Acad of Medicine of NJ 1969-; mem NJ Dental Group PA 1970-; mem Morristown Dental Assocs 1973-78; mem Paterson Dental assocs 1974-; mem Acad of Genl Dentistry 1976-; mem Amer Soc of Dentistry for Children 1977-; Fellow Acad of Dentistry Intl 1977-; Fellow Amer Coll of Dentists 1978-; acting exec dir Natl Dental Assn 1981-; sr consul Natl Dental Assn 1981-; mem ADAîs Special Comm of "The Future of Dentistry" 1982; chmn & pres Natl Dental Assn Found 1982-; life mem Golden Heritage mem NAACP; Kappa Alpha Psi Frat; Wallace AME Chapel. **HONORS/ACHIEVEMENTS:** Citation Head Start Prog 1969; Citation Children's Dental Health Prog Summit NJ Bd of Heath 1972; Comm Serv Awd Greater Newark Urban Coalition 1975; Who's Who in Northeast Amer 1975; Outstanding Serv Awd Natl Dental Assn 1976; President's Awd Natl Dental Assn 1977; Citation Giant of Excellence in the Health Care Arena 1979; Alumni Achievement Awd Howard Univ Coll of Dentistry 1981; Bergan/Passaic Howard Univ Alumni Awd 1981; President's Awd Natl Dental Assn 1982; Outstanding Achievement Awd Commonwealth Dental Soc of NJ 1983; Outstanding & Valuable Contrib to 70th Scientific Session Natl Dental Assn Baltimore MD 1983. **BUSINESS ADDRESS:** President, James E Lassiter DDS PA, 475 Springfield Ave, Summit, NJ 07901.

LASSITER, JOHN
President. **PERSONAL:** Born Apr 18, 1937, Chicago, IL; son of John Sr and Ethel; married Rosielyn Utley; children: John Randall, Eric Winston. **EDUCATION:** Univ of IL, BS Econ 1959; Am Coll of Life Underwriters, CLU 1969. **CAREER:** Prudential Insurance Co, agent 1963-66, sales mgr 1966-69, district mgr 1969-81, div mgr 1981-84. **ORGANIZATIONS:** Pres Chicago Assn of Life Underwriters; bd mem Chicago General Agents & Mgrs Assn; bd mem Chicago Chap Amer Soc of CLU; bd mem, bd dirs South Chicago Comm Hosp; bd mem, bd dirs Operation PUSH. **HONORS/ACHIEVEMENTS:** Pres's Citation Prudential Ins Co of Amer 1964-74; Pres' Trophy Prud Ins Co of Am 1968; Mid-Am Trophy Prudential Ins Co of Amer 1970; Nat Mgmt Awd General Agents & Mgrs Conf 1976-80. **MILITARY SERVICE:** AUS 2nd lt 1960-65. **HOME ADDRESS:** 555 W Madison, Apt 3610, Chicago, IL 60606. **BUSINESS ADDRESS:** President, Financial Designs Inc, One Prudential Plaza # 2222, Chicago, IL 60601.

LASSITER, WRIGHT LOWENSTEIN, JR.
Educational administrator. **PERSONAL:** Born Mar 24, 1934, Vicksburg, MS; married Bessie Loretta Ryan; children: Michele Denise, Wright Lowenstein III. **EDUCATION:** Alcorn State U, BS 1955; Tuskegee Inst, Certf Institutional Bus Mgmt 1956; IN U, MBA 1962; Auburn U, EdD 1975; CA Western U, PhD 1977. **CAREER:** Hampton Inst, investments accountant 1956; Tuskegee Inst, sr accountant 1958-61; Tuskegee Inst, dir aux Enterprises 1962-76; asst prof mgmt 1962; IN Univ Bloomington, research assoc 1961-62; Morgan State Univ, vice pres business & finance 1976-80; Schenectady County Community Coll, pres 1980-83; Bishop Coll, pres 1983-86; El Centro Coll, pres. **ORGANIZATIONS:** Mem Counil Educ Facility Planner, Soc for Advancement Mgmt; bd dir, treas Howard Co Commun Action Council Inc; bd dir, sec, treas Deville InvestCorp; bd dir Baltimore Urban Coalition; sec, treas MD Assn of Coll Bus Officers; dir First Republic Bank, Dallas Opera, YMCA of Metro Dallas, Dallas Urban League, United Way of Metro Dallas, Dallas Black C of C, Dallas Symphony Assoc, Oak Cluff C of C. **HONORS/ACHIEVEMENTS:** Martin Luther King Disting Leadership Awd SUNY 1981; NAACP Leadership Awd 1982; Outstanding Conribs in Educ

Awd Alpha Phi Alpha 1983; Disting Serv Awd Hamilton Hill Neighborhood Assoc 1983; Appreciation Awd State of NY 1983; Apprec Awd Alpha Phi Alpha 1984; Disting Achievement & Serv Awd 1984; Meritorious Serv Awd United Way of Metro Dallas 1984,85; Disting Serv Awd in Christian Educ TX Baptist Conv 1984; Disting Serv Awd InterFirst Bank 1984; Disting Serv Awd Interdenominational Ministerial Alliance 1984; Man of the Year Awd So Dallas Bus & Professional Women's Club Inc 1984; Brotherhood Awd New Jersulaem Bapt Church 1984; Cert of Appreciation Vet Admin Reg Med Ctr 1985; Cert of Special Congressional Recognition US Congressman James Armey 1985; Cert of Appreciation Dallas Reg Office US Dept of Ag 1985; Appreciation Awd in Educ Office of Civil Rights Dallas Reg 1985; Cert of Recognition Natl Republican Congressional Comm 1985; Black Portfolio Excellence Awd in Educ 1985; Disting Serv Awd New Birth Baptist Church 1985; Disting Serv Awd in Educ Arlington Assoc of Concerned Citizens 1985; Outstanding Serv Awd in Educ Most Worshipful St Joseph Grand Lodge 1985. **MILITARY SERVICE:** AUS 1956-62 lt col USAR. **BUSINESS ADDRESS:** President, El Centro College, Lamar & Main St, Dallas, TX 75202.

LATCHOLIA, KENNETH EDWARD
Administrator. **PERSONAL:** Born Jun 17, 1922, Beaumont, TX; married Ruth Johannetta Weber; children: 2 Children. **EDUCATION:** Prarie ViewUniv Prairie View TX, Cert 1941-42;Univ of Wash, BA 1952-56. **CAREER:** Rural Development USDA, dep admin 1969; US Peace Corps Nigeria, dir 1967-69; Econ Devel Adminstrn Dept of Commerce & Seattle, project officer 1966-67; Jackson St Community Council Seattle, exec dir 1963-66; Wash State Bur of Rehab Seattle, asst supt 1960-63; King Co Juvenile Ct Seattle, asst supt 1954-60; EDA US Dept of Commerce Seattle, econ devel spec 1969-72; EDA US Dept of Comm, dep reg dir 1972-77; FMHA US Dept of Agr Wash DC, dep adminstr 1977. **ORGANIZATIONS:** Bd mem Seattle Urban League 1972-74; area council mem Greenbelt Cooperative Greenbelt MD 1978. **HONORS/ACHIEVEMENTS:** Silver medal US Dept of Commerce 1973; cert fed employee of year Region 10 Seattle 1973; cert natl urban league Nat Mfg Atlanga GA 1975; commendation letter Pres Carter 1978. **MILITARY SERVICE:** AUS PFC 1942-43. **BUSINESS ADDRESS:** 14th at Independence SW, Washington, DC 20250.

LATEEF, YUSEF
Jazz artist. **PERSONAL:** Born Oct 09, 1920, Chattanooga, TN. **EDUCATION:** Manhattan School of Music, BM & MM; Univ of Massachusetts, PhD 1975. **CAREER:** Borough of Manhattan Community Coll, assoc prof, 1971-76; musical compositions include Nocturne (Ballet), 1974, & Yusef's Mood; numerous TV & theater appearances; quartet leader, New York City, 1960; featured with Charles Mingus, 1960-61; Babatundi Olatunji, 1961-62; featured with Cannonball Adderley Combo on European tour, two yrs; combo leader; saxaphone teacher, Stan Kenton Summer Jazz Clinics, 1963; lecturer at various colleges; recordings on Impulse Prestige and other labels. **HONORS/ACHIEVEMENTS:** Author, Yusef Lateef's Flute Book of the Blues. **BUSINESS ADDRESS:** Nigerian Culture Studies Ctr, Ahmadu Bello University, Zaria, Kaduna, Nigeria.

LATHAM, BERNICE GRANT
Physician. **PERSONAL:** Born Jan 22, 1945, Richmond, VA; married Wiley; children: Ruth, Vicki, Wiley IV. **EDUCATION:** VA Union U, 1964; CathUniv Am, AB 1966; Meharry Med Coll, MD 1971; Med Coll VA, intern; HowardUniv Hosp, resd 1976. **CAREER:** Physician, partner with husband; Alex Hlth Dept Med Clinic, 1976-77. **ORGANIZATIONS:** Mem Alpha Kappa Alpha Sor; Jack & Jill Am Inc; bd dir YWCA Richmond, VA; diplomate Am Bd of Family Prac 1977; Richmond Med Soc. **HONORS/ACHIEVEMENTS:** Nomin Outstdg Young Women Am 1977. **BUSINESS ADDRESS:** 1400 Westwood AveSte 310, Professional Bldg, Richmond, VA 23227.

LATHAM, WELDON HURD
Attorney. **PERSONAL:** Born Jan 02, 1947, Brooklyn, NY; son of Aubrey Latham and Avril Latham; married Constantia Beecher; children: Nicole Marie, Brett Weldon. **EDUCATION:** Howard Univ, BA Business Admin 1968; Georgetown Univ Law Ctr, JD 1971; George Washington Univ Natl Law Ctr, advanced legal courses 1975-76; Brookings Inst, exec educ prog 1981. **CAREER:** Cecchi & Co, mgmt consultant 1968-71; Covington & Burling, atty 1971-73; Howard Univ Sch of Law, adj prof 1972-82; Exec Ofc of Pres Ofc of Mgmt & Budget The White House, asst genl counsel 1974-76; Hogan & Hartson, atty 1976-79; Univ of VA Law Sch, guest prof 1976-; US Dept of Housing & Urban Develop, genl deputy asst sec 1979-81; Sterling Systems Inc, vice pres genl cnsl1981-83; Planning Research Corp; Executive Asst Counsel to the Chrmn & CEO; 1983-86 Reed Smith Shaw & Mc Clay Natl Law Firm managing partner, McLean VA office 1986. **ORGANIZATIONS:** Bd dirs Univ of the District of Columbia foundation Inc 1982-; mem Amer District of Columbia Natl Fed VA & Washington Bar Assns 1972-; mem Natl Contract Mgmt Assn 1982-; legal counsel MD Mondale/Ferraro Campaign Com 1984; apptee VA Gov's Business Adv Comm on Crime Prevention 1983-86; apptee VA Gov's Regulatory Adv Bd 1982-84; mem US Small Business Admin Task Force 1982; Washington steering comm NAACP Legal Defense & Educ Fund 1976-; Professional Services Council, Bd of Dir 1984-88; Editorial Advisory Brd Wash Business Jrnl 1985-88; Brd of Dir, VA Comm Univ & Hospital 1986-88; Democratic Natl Business Councl 1986-; Bd of Dir Wash Urban League 1986-; bd of directors, Fairfax County Chamber of Commerce 1987-88. **HONORS/ACHIEVEMENTS:** Outstanding Performance Awd US Dept of HUD Sr Exec Serv Washington DC 1980; listed in Inaugural Edition Who's Who in Amer Law 1977-;Who's Who in the East 1985-; Who's Who in Business and Finance 1986-; Nat'l Assoc of Equal Opp in Higher Education Achievement Awd 1987. **MILITARY SERVICE:** Capt/atty adv 1 1/2 yrs; Honors Prog Ofc of the Sec of the Air Force; Genl Counsel's Office 1973-74. **BUSINESS ADDRESS:** Partner, Reed, Smith, Shaw & Mc Clay, 8201 Greensboro Drive, McLean, VA 22102.

LATHEN, JOHN WILLIAM
Psychiatrist. **PERSONAL:** Born Jul 06, 1916, Hackensack, NJ; married Almeta Virginia Crockett; children: John B, Mahasin Abdal Sabur nee Karen. **EDUCATION:** VA State Coll, BS 1938; attended Columbia Univ 1938-39; Howard Univ Med Sch, MD 1949. **CAREER:** Manassas Ind Sch, dean of men-instr latin & english 1939-41; Progressive Life Ins, salesman 1941-43; Bendix Corp, metallurgical chemist 1943-45; private practice, psychiatrist 1949-80; Bd of Educ Hackensack, psychiatric consult 1950-; Berger Co Justice Dept, psychiatric sons 1978-; Essex Co Adolescent Psychiatry 1980-84; Greystone State Hosp, asst med dir 1977-. **ORGANIZATIONS:** Mem Amer, Natl, World Medical Assn 1950-; mem Amer Ortho Psychiatric Assn 1960-. **HONORS/ACHIEVEMENTS:** 1st Black Chemist for Bendix Corp 1945; 1st Black intern of the Hackensack Hosp 1949; 1st Black med dir of Greystone State Hosp 1977. **BUSINESS ADDRESS:** Assistant Medical Dir, Greystone State Hosp, Greystone Park, NJ 07950.

LATIMER, ALLIE B. (ALICE LATIMER WEEDEN)
Attorney. **PERSONAL:** Born in Coraopolis, PA. **EDUCATION:** Hampton Inst Hampton VA, BS; HowardUniv Washington DC, JD; CathUniv Washington DC, LlM; Am U, Study Towards Doctorate. **CAREER:** Chief counsel atty 1960-71; Gen Serv Adminstrn Asst gen counsel 1971-76; Gen serv adminstrn; counsel 1976-77; Gen Serv Adminstrn, asst gen counsel 1971-76; Natl Aeronautics & Space Adminstrn; asst gen counsel 1976-77; General Srvc Administratn 1977. **ORGANIZATIONS:** Vol work Am Friends Serv Com in Europe; sec Nat Bar Assn 1966-76; co-chmn bd of dirs Presbyterian Economic Devel Corp 1974-80; pres Nat Bar Found1974-75; pres DC Memtal Health Assn 1977-79; mem Supreme C of US US Ct of Appeals DC NC St Ct of Appeals; mem Am Bar Assn Fed Bar; Nat Bar, NC Bar, DC Bar, Washington Bar Asso; fndr 1st pres Federally Employed Women 1968-69; vice pres Links Ind 1976-80; mem bd of gov Nat Cncl of Ch USA 1978; mem NAACP & NAACP Legal Def Dund DC Steering Com. **HONORS/ACHIEVEMENTS:** Pub Serv Award & GSA 1971; GSA Exceptional Serv Awards 1976-79; Humanitarian Award Sigma Delta Tau Legal Frat 1978; Outstanding Achievement Award; Kiwanis Club Award DC 1978; various others. **BUSINESS ADDRESS:** General Counsel, General Services Admini, 18th & F St NW, Washington, DC 20405.

LATIMER, INA PEARL
Educator. **PERSONAL:** Born Oct 19, 1934, Okeechobee, FL; married Harold A Latimer; children: Cynthia L. **EDUCATION:** Tuskegee Inst, BS Nursing 1956; N IL Univ, MS Education 1979. **CAREER:** Univ of IL, staff nurse charge 1958-60; St Mary of Nazareth Sch of Nursing, instruc medical-surgical nursing 1960-70; Triton Coll, instruc 1970-73, chairperson prac nursing prog 1973-. **ORGANIZATIONS:** Mem Homemaker-Home Health Aide Comm IL Council of Home Health Svcs; mem Natl League for Nursing; mem IL Voc Assn; mem Bd of Review Natl League for Nursing Council of Prac Nursing Progs 1979-84; eval Dept of Voc & Tech Educ 1981; accreditation site visitor Natl League for Nursing 1978-. **HONORS/ACHIEVEMENTS:** Undergrad mem Delta Sigma Theta Sor; undergrad mem Alpha Kappa Mu Natl Honor Soc. **BUSINESS ADDRESS:** Dept Chrprsn Practical Nrsg, Triton College, 2000 5th Ave, River Grove, IL 60171.

LATIMER, STEVE B.
Research director. **PERSONAL:** Born Nov 04, 1927, Okla City; married Louise Cunningham; children: Steve, Jr, Ronald, Gail. **EDUCATION:** Tuskegee Inst, BS Chem 1953; Tuskegee Inst, MS 1955; NC State U, PhD 1967; Fed Exec Inst, 1972. **CAREER:** Langston Univ 1966, chmn physical science dir div of arts & sciences, res & coord CSRS progs, USDA, marc visiting faculty, OK med res found; NC State Univ, chief control chem, res Asst 1962-66; Fries & Fries Chem Co, 1956; Shaw Univ, chmn chem 1955-62. **ORGANIZATIONS:** Fellow Am Inst Chem; Sigma Xi; Nat Inst of Sci; Am Chem Soc; OK Acad of Sci; Nat Geographic; Am Assn Advancement of Sci; Pre-med Adv 1968-72;prog dir MBS Lic Lay Reader; charter mem Langston Lions Club 1973; Guthrie Kiwanis Club 1975; Mason Shriner; Alpha Phi Alpha Frat. **HONORS/ACHIEVEMENTS:** First black to receive Doctoral Degree from NC StateUniv 1967; listed in Am Men of Sci; Who's Who S & SW; Pers of S; recip Outstanding Educator 1972; Fed Exec Inst; XXII Cert; 3 NSF Scholarships; PHS Trainee 1962; NIH Marc Faculty Fellowship 1975-77; Carver Found Fellow 1953; Alpha Phi Omega, Alpha Mu Gamma; Sigma Xi; Beta Kappa Chi.

LATNEY, HARVEY, JR.
Attorney. **PERSONAL:** Born May 26, 1944, Caroline Co, VA. **EDUCATION:** VA Union U, BA 1966; HowardUniv Sch Law, JD 1969. **CAREER:** US Dept Transp, legal intern June 1969-July 1969 & Aug 1971-Sept 1972; Richmond Comm Sr Cntr, dir Oct 1972-July 1973; Greene & Poindexter Inc, atty 1973. **ORGANIZATIONS:** Mem Nat Bar Assn; Am Bar Assn; VA Bar & Assn; VA Trial Lawyer's Assn; Old Dominion Bar Assn. **MILITARY SERVICE:** AUS sgt 1969-71. **BUSINESS ADDRESS:** 10 S 10 St, Ste 613, Richmond, VA 23219.

LATTA, GREGORY EDWIN (G-MAN)
Athlete. **PERSONAL:** Born Oct 13, 1952, Newark, NJ; married Diane Gethers. **EDUCATION:** Morgan State, BBA. **CAREER:** Chicago Bears, tight end; Tommy Reamon Football Camp, instr (off season). **ORGANIZATIONS:** Varsity "M" Club Morgan State; Boy's Club of Newark Inc; donated time to Hampton Scholarship Fund; quarter host, Chicago Area Christmas Parties at Childrens' Rehab Inst, Childrens' Meml Hosp; Carmelite Home for Abused & Abandoned & Children; participant, Ford PPK Program; YMCA of Newyork; mem AMEZ Church. **HONORS/ACHIEVEMENTS:** 1st team All-state Football & Basketball 1970; 2 time goldmedalist in track, shot put, javlin, MX Shabazz HS; 2 time first team, all MD Football, Morgan State U; 1st team all-MEAC 1972-73; all-pro world football 1974; recip CYO Award, NY Daily News All Star 1970. **BUSINESS ADDRESS:** 55 E Jackson Blvd, Chicago, IL 60604.

LATTIMER, AGNES DOLORES
Physician. **PERSONAL:** Born May 13, 1928, Memphis, TN; married Frank D Bethel (deceased); children: Bernard Goss. **EDUCATION:** Risk Univ, BS (Magna Cum Laude) 1949; Chicago Medical School, MD 1954. **CAREER:** Michael Reese Hosp, dir amb peds 1966-71; Cook County Hosp, dir amb peds 1971-84, dir Fantus Clinic 1984-85; Cook Co Hosp, med dir 1986-. **ORGANIZATIONS:** Mem Ambulatory Ped Assoc 1974-; pres IL Chap Amer Acad of Pediatrics 1983-86; mem Physician's Task Force on Hunger 1984-; mem Amer Assoc Public Health. **HONORS/ACHIEVEMENTS:** Pediatrician of the Year Awd IL Chap AAP 1985. **HOME ADDRESS:** 746 E 79th St #426, Chicago, IL 60619.

LATTIMORE, CAROLINE LOUISE
Educational administrator, youth motivator, women's leader. **PERSONAL:** Born May 12, 1945, Winston-Salem, NC; daughter of Earl R Lattimore Sr and Mary Rhodes Lattimore. **EDUCATION:** Hampton Inst, BS 1967, MA 1973; Duke Univ, PhD 1978. **CAREER:** Richmond Public School, Virginia, secondary english teacher, 1967-74; State Univ, coord sr citizens program Winston-Salem, 1974; Duke Univ, psychological testing intern, 1974-75, educ consult & spec couns, 1978; NTS Research Corp Washington, coord, 1978; Duke Univ, dean of minority affairs; asst provost, 1978-83; academic dean, 1987-. **ORGANIZATIONS:** Mem, pres, Council on Black Affairs, 1984; mem, Reggie B Howard Scholarship Selection Comm, 1985; mem, Amer Educ Research Assn, 1980; mem, NAACP, 1985; mem, Natl Council of Negro Women, 1985; pres, Durham Chapter Alpha Kappa Alpha Sor Inc, 1984; natl chair, AKA Connection, 1982-86. **HONORS/ACHIEVEMENTS:** Award of Merit for Outstanding Achievement Winston Salem Jr C of C 1963; Who's Who Among Students in

Coll & Univs Hampton Inst VA 1966; Kappa Delta Pi Honor Soc Educ Hampton Inst VA 1973; Kappa Delta Pi Hon Soc Duke Univ 1975; Natl Fellow Ford Found, 1976-78; Outstanding Young Woman of Amer State Winner for North Carolina, 1979; C Eric Lincoln Award, 1984; Regional Graduate Leadership Award A.K.A. 1986; MLK Award Durham, 1987. **BUSINESS ADDRESS:** Academic Dean, DukeUniv, 107 Union West, Durham, NC 27706.

LATTIMORE, EVERETT CARRIGAN
Educator. **PERSONAL:** Born May 17, 1927, Winston-Salem, NC; married Rosetta Norwood; children: Karen Goffin, Keith, Dawn Edwards, Derek, Karl, Kraig, Kirk. **EDUCATION:** Shaw Univ, BS 1949; Seton Hall Univ, MA48 credits 1968; Shaw Univ, LLD Hon 1982. **CAREER:** Rose of Sharon Church, dir of christian educ 1961-65; Plainfield Pub Schs, sci english tchr 1961-68; Plainfield Public Schs, vice prin Hubbard Middle Sch 1968, prin Hubbard Middle Sch 1970, asst supt personnel 1974, asst supt operations 1981, acting supt of schs 1984; City of Plainfield, mayor 1982-84; City of Plainfield, mayor 1982-86; Plainfield Bd of Educ, asst supt of schs 1974-. **ORGANIZATIONS:** Host Mayor's Corner Storer Cable TV Plainfield NJ 1982-84; mem NJ State League of Municipalities 1982; mem US Conf of Mayors 1982; Natl Summit Conf on Black Economic Survival Gary IN 1982; New Mayors' Assn 1982; Natl Conf of Black Mayors 1982; Plainfield City Councilman 1961-70; Union Co Freeholder 1971-79; dir Bd of Union Co Freeholders 1972; chmn Bd of Union Co Freeholders 1979. **HONORS/ACHIEVEMENTS:** Letters of Commendations, US Senator Harrison Williams, US Senator Clifford Case, Congresswoman Florence Dwyer, various mayors of Union Co; Who's Who in Educ; Who's Who in Govt; Intl Who's Who in Comm Svcs; Who's Who in Colls & Univs; Who's Who in Amer Politics; Notable Amers; Dict of Intl Biographies; Comm Leaders of Amer; numerous awds, plaques, certificates and citations. **BUSINESS ADDRESS:** Asst Supt of Schools, Plainfield Bd of Educ, 504 Madison Avenue, Plainfield, NJ 07060.

LATTIMORE, OLIVER LOUIS, SR.
Dentist. **PERSONAL:** Born Oct 04, 1893, Rusk, TX; son of Jacob Lattimore and Lucy Lattimore; married Charlie Lee Robinson, Mar 30, 1948 (deceased); children: Jacquelyn L Knox, Tanya C Lattimore. **EDUCATION:** Prairie View A&M Univ, BS 1913; Howard Univ Sch of Dentistry, DDS 1917. **CAREER:** Dentist, 70 yrs; businessman; restaurant mgr; Lattimore's Funeral Home, owner; Prairie View A&M Univ, specialist; Rusk & Lufkin TX, educator; professional singer. **ORGANIZATIONS:** Founder Charles A George Dental Soc; Gulf State Dental Assn of TX; National Dental Assn; regnl vice pres Zone 6; Alpha Phi Alpha Frat 50 yrs; mem Mt Vernon Methodist Church 57 yrs; Steward Chancel Choir; pres Methodist Men; master mason of Ionic Lodge 469; Elk's Club; life mem NAACP; YMCA; pres Path-Finders Club; Lamb's Club; Am Legion. **HONORS/ACHIEVEMENTS:** Houston Howard Alumni Assn Centennial Award 1967; 59th Annual Conv Gulf State Dental Anns Inc. **MILITARY SERVICE:** 10th vol 1st lt 1918. **HOME ADDRESS:** 3441 N Parkwood, Houston, TX 77021.

LAVAN, ALTON
Football coach. **PERSONAL:** Born Sep 13, 1946, Pierce, FL; married Bessie Lavonia Jewell; children: Travis Alton, Douglas Milo, Maeleeke. **EDUCATION:** CO State Univ Ft Collins, BS Sociology 1966-68; GA St U, 1971. **CAREER:** Philadelphia Eagles, def back 1968; Atlanta Falcons, def back 1969-70; CO State Univ, offensive rec coach 1972; Univ of LA, def backfield coach 1973; IA State Univ, offensive receivers coach 1974; Atlanta Falcons, def backfield coach 1975-76; GA Tech, offensive receiver coach 1977, offensive backfield coach 1978; Stanford Univ, offensive backfield coach 1979-80; Dallas Cowboys, offensive backfield coach 1980-. **ORGANIZATIONS:** Mem Nat Ftbl Coaches of Am 1971-. **HONORS/ACHIEVEMENTS:** 1st Black Coach Dallas Cowboys & Atlanta Falcons. **MILITARY SERVICE:** AUS sp 4 1969-71.

LAVELLE, ROBERT R.
Banking executive. **CAREER:** Dwelling House Savings & Loan Association, Pittsburg PA, chief executive, 1988—. **BUSINESS ADDRESS:** Dwelling House Savings & Loan Association, 501 Herron Ave, Pittsburgh, PA 15219. *

LAVENDER, JOE
Professional athlete. **PERSONAL:** Born Feb 10, 1949, Rayville, LA; married Shirley Ann Davis; children: Danielle. **EDUCATION:** San Diego State, M crim Justice. **CAREER:** Wash Redskins, professional ftbl cornerback 1976-; Phil Eagles, professional ftbl player 1973-76. **HONORS/ACHIEVEMENTS:** Pro Bowl 1979. **BUSINESS ADDRESS:** c/o Dee Rauch, NFL Players Association, 1300 Connecticut NW Ste 407, Washington, DC 20036.

LAVERGNEAU, RENE L.
Administrator. **PERSONAL:** Born Nov 04, 1933, New York, NY; son of Armando Lavergneau and Myrtle Lavergneau. **EDUCATION:** CCNY, BA 1958, MS 1963, MA 1974. **CAREER:** WNYE-TV, NY Ed TV, TV instr 1965-67; Bureau of Audio-visual Instr NYC, writer & voice-over 1966-68; New York City Bd of Ed, bd of examiners 1968; Hackensack Public Schools, dir bureau of foreign languagues, bilingual ed and English as a second language, 1986—; Fairleigh Dickinson Univ in PR, grad instr 1969; Univ of PR, Bayamon, instr, 1974. **ORGANIZATIONS:** Consult, Princeton Conf for Foreign Language Curriculum Devel 1967; chair NE Conf on the Teaching of Foreign Languages 1974; chair Statewide Committee on Bilingual & Teaching English as a Second Language Ed Cert NJ 1974; keynoter Amer Assoc of Teachers 1974; chair NJ Bilingual Minimum Standards 1978; com mem Bergen City Health & Welfare Council 1980; chmn bd of dirs Teatro Duo 1986-87; bd dir Hackensack Public School Historical Society, 1986—; mem selection committee, American Council on the Teaching of Foreign Languages/National Textbook Company Award for Building Community Interest in Foreign Language Education, 1987—. **HONORS/ACHIEVEMENTS:** Careers Comm & Publ Awareness Awd NE Conf Rept Publ 1974; actor "The Wiz" 1977; Natl Awd for Bldg Comm Interest in Fgn Lang Ed Amer Council on Teaching of Fgn Langs & Natl Textbook Co 1983. **BUSINESS ADDRESS:** Dir, Hackensack Public Schools, Bur of Fgn Lang & Biling Ed, 355 State St, Hackensack, NJ 07601.

LAW, ELLEN T.
Educator. **PERSONAL:** Born Jul 10, 1918, Stephens, AR; married William Jefferson. **EDUCATION:** Univ OR, BS 1941, MEd 1962, Secondary Admin Cert 1974. **CAREER:** Bennett Coll for Women, teacher 1941-42; Seattle Port-Embarkation, clerk 1942-43; Comm Center, dir 1943-44; Better Housing Assn, sec; Roch Brance NAACP, acting dir; Amer Natl Red Cross, 1944-46; Providence Hospital School of Nursing, register instr 1950-54; George Elementary School, teacher 1954-56; Jefferson, 1956-61; counselor 1956-61; vice pres 1968-71; Thomas Jefferson HS, prin 1971-74; Franklin HS, vice prin. **ORGANIZATIONS:** Mem numerous offices, coms, numerous professional civic orgns. **HONORS/ACHIEVEMENTS:** Woman of Yr Beta Psi 1968; 10 of achievement portland 1964. **BUSINESS ADDRESS:** 5405 SE Woodward, Portland, OR 97206.

LAW, M. EPREVEL
Educator, businessman. **PERSONAL:** Born Aug 19, 1943, Chicago, IL; married Marlene Ann; children: Martin Peter, Michelle Allison. **EDUCATION:** NSF Fellow, BS; NSF FellowUniv of MN, mS 1969;Univ of MN, PhD 1970. **CAREER:** Law & Assoc, in V analyst & tax consultant 1974-; Minneapolis Public Schools & Univ of MN, teacherr & research 1966-; Kenney Kenney Real, real est 1971-74; H&R Block, tax consultant 1970-71; Pact Real Inc, pres 1974-77; Archer & Law Inc, pres 1976-; Twin City Property Mgmt Maintenance & Improvement Co, 1978-; The Three "M" Realty Co, broker/mgr 1977-. **ORGANIZATIONS:** Bd mem Southside Comm Enter; co-owner Law Assoc Southside Comm Ctr Inc; MN Assn for Retard Child; MN Hist Soc; Mayor's Appt to City Wide City-wide Adv Com; co-chmn CW-CAC Phys Imp & Hous Asst Task Force; cap Long-range Imp Comm Hum Dev Task Force; proj acct St of MN Coun on Qual Educ; Cit Unit for Resp Educ Steer Comm; MN Urban Leag; Citizen League; NAACP; natl Women's Polit Caucus; MN DFL Feminist Causus; MI Environmental Educ Bd; So MN Comunity Fed Credit Union; chpsn 60th Sen Dist 1976; assoc chmn 60th Sen Dist 1974-76; prec chmn 8th Wd 14th Prec 1975-77; mem atlarge 60th Sen Dist Exec Comm 1972-74; 5th Ist Cent Comm 1972-76; St Cent Comm 1974-76; 8th Wd, Conv Chair 1975, prec coord For Mcgovern 1972; dist lawn-sign coord for Fraser 1972; wd & prec coord for Hofsteds 1973-75; prec work for Humphrey 1968-70,76; prec work for Mondale 1974; work for Carter-mondale 1976 & 80; natl del to Nat Dem Onv from NY City 1976; sev Nat Science Found Fellowshps. **BUSINESS ADDRESS:** 4307 E 50th St, Minneapolis, MN 55417.

LAW, RUDY KARL
Professional athlete. **PERSONAL:** Born Oct 07, 1956, Waco, TX; married Evelyn Silva; children: Randy. **CAREER:** Los Angeles Dodgers, 1978, 1980; Chicago White Sox, outfielder 1982-84. **ORGANIZATIONS:** Despite hitting 300 and stealing 24 bases in senior year at Ravenswood HS in East Palo Alto, CA was bypassed in June free agent draft of 1 975. **HONORS/ACHIEVEMENTS:** Led AL outfielders with A 994 fielding percentage committing only two errors in 309 total chances thus became first White Sox outfielder to lead the league in defense since Pat Kelly in 1975 (991); best fielding percentage by a Pale Hose outfielder since Ken Berry set the team rec ord in 1969 when he was errorlessin 222 total chances; set a Dodger rookie record for stolen bases 40 that was broken by Steve Sax. **BUSINESS ADDRESS:** Chicago White Sox, Dan Ryan & 35th St, Chicago, IL 60616.

LAW, THOMAS MELVIN
Educator, business executive. **PERSONAL:** Born Sep 23, 1925, Bristol, VA; son of Thomas K and Rebecca; married Katherine Tillar; children: Thomas Fenimore. **EDUCATION:** St Pauls Coll, BS (Summa Cum Laude) 1950; NY Univ, MA 1953; Cornell Univ, EdD 1962; St Pauls Coll, Hon Degree 1982. **CAREER:** James Solomon Russell High School, instructor, 1950-54; Hampton Inst, dir div of business 1965-67; St Pauls Coll, dean of coll & prof of business 1967-69; WA Tech Inst, vice pres acad affairs 1969-71; Penn Valley Community Coll, pres 1971-76; VA State Univ, pres 1976-82; SUNY, dep to the chancellor for special progs 1982-86, deputy to chancellor for Community Colleges 1986-87, associate vice chancellor for contracts & purchasing 1987-. **ORGANIZATIONS:** Mem univ council Cornell Univ 1983-87; mem adv council School of Human Ecology Cornell Univ 1984-85; mem bd of trustees St Pauls Coll 1984-; bd of dir Laurel Bank Kansas City MO; sire archon elect Alpha Beta Boule Sigma Pi Phi Frat; licensed lay reader St Stephens Eipscopal Church; mem Rotary Intl; mem Inspection Team to Sierra Leone W Africa, Hampton Inst, AID; coord Hampton Cornell Exchange Prog Title III; vice chmn, bd dir Amer Assn of Community & Jr Colls; bd dir KS City Gen Hosp, Truman Med Ctr; mem adv bd St Marys Hosp; bd gov KS City Art Inst, Community Serv Broadcasting of Mid-Amer; exec comm North Central Comm of Higher Ed; mem Amer Tech Ed Assoc, Amer Assn for Higher Ed, Amer Voc Coop Ed Assn, Intl Assn of Approved Basketball Officials; bd dir Petersburg C of C; adv com State Bd for Teacher Ed; bd of dir Natl Ctr for Higher Ed Mgmt Syst, VA State Fair; sire archon elect Beta Psi Boule Sigma Pi Phi 1985-; life mem NAACP; mem Rotary Intl; board dir Living Resources Corp, Albany NY; board dir Child's Nursing Home, Albany NY. **HONORS/ACHIEVEMENTS:** Distinguished Alumni Award St Pauls Coll Natl Alumni Assn 1978; Martin Luther King Community Serv Awd Southern Christian Leadership Council 1980; 1st 4 yr degree grad St Pauls to receive an earned doctorate degree; Distinguished Trustee Awd; Alpha Phi Alpha Fellow; United Negro Coll Fund Grad Fellow; Alpha Kappa Mu, Phi Delta Kappa, Sigma Gamma Rho Community Serv Award; Distinguished Alumni Award St Pauls Coll 1974; Civilian Distinguished Service Award, US Army, 1979. **MILITARY SERVICE:** AUS s/sgt 2 1/2 yrs. **HOME ADDRESS:** 6119 Nott Rd, Guilderland, NY 12084.

LAWERNCE, LONNIE R.
Law enforcement. **PERSONAL:** Born Jun 11, 1946, Miami, FL; children: Derek Lawrence. **EDUCATION:** Miami-Dade Comm Coll, 1972; St Thomas Univ 1979. **CAREER:** Metro-Dade Police Dept, patrolman 1968-80, sgt 1980, commander 1981-83, maj, dist commander 1983-. **ORGANIZATIONS:** Bd of dir Leadership Miami Alumni Assn, Big Brothers/Big Sisters, Informed Families of Dade; bd of dir/treas Miami-Dade Chamber of Comm. **HONORS/ACHIEVEMENTS:** Officer of the Year Richmon-Porrine Jaycees 1982; Public Serv US Dept of Justice 1984; Officer of the Year MIK Devel Corp 1985. **MILITARY SERVICE:** USMC corpl 3 1/2 yrs. **BUSINESS ADDRESS:** District Commander, Metro-Dade Police Dept, 2950 NW 83rd St, Miami, FL 33147.

LAWES, VERNA
Executive secretary. **PERSONAL:** Born Sep 07, 1927, Philadelphia, PA; married Sylvester; children: Anthony, David. **EDUCATION:** Temple Univ, BS. **CAREER:** US Treasury Dept, data coord; IBM, librarian; Sperry Univac Corp, rsch mgr; Certified Data Serv Inc, pres; Natl Political Congress of Black Women, exec secty. **HOME ADDRESS:** 5505 Harper Farm Rd, Columbia, MD 21044.

LAWHORN, JOHN B.
Educator. **PERSONAL:** Born Apr 02, 1925, Youngstown, OH; married Phyllis Jane; children: Michael John. **EDUCATION:** Youngstown U, BS 1950; Columbia U, MA 1953.

CAREER: Allen U, dept chmn band dir 1950-57; Albany State Coll, acting chmn, dept music, band dir 1957-62; Atlanta Pub Schs, band dir tchr 1961-66; GA StateDept Edn, consult 1966-73; Metro Cooperative Educ Serv Agy, music coodinator 1973-74; Newton Co Schs, 1974-75; Basic Instructional Concepts Inst Nat, concert pianist founder dir; The Child & Leisure Com White House Conf on Children, chmn 1970. ORGANIZATIONS: Mem Leadership Atlanta; Govs Adv Council for the Arts; Atlanta Symphonyd Bd; State Adv Commn on Correctional Recr%Eation Publs in Field. HONORS/ACHIEVEMENTS: Mrs Fred W, petterson award. MILITARY SERVICE: USN 1943-46. BUSINESS ADDRESS: Newton County Bd Educ, 2109 Newton Dr, Covington, GA 30209.

LAWHORN, ROBERT MARTIN
Military officer. PERSONAL: Born Jan 08, 1943, Camden, SC; married Jacqueline Carter; children: Bridgett Tiffany, Brandon Tilman. EDUCATION: NC A&T State Univ, BS 1965; Natl Univ, M Bus Admin 1985. CAREER: Aviation Officer Candidate Sch, officer cand 1966; Basic Naval Aviation Trng, aviation trnee 1966; Advanced NFO Trng, student 1967; VF-101 NAS Oceana VA & Key West FL, student 1967; VF-41 Oceana VA, power plants div off & asst admin off 1967-70; Navy Recruiting Dist St Louis, exec officer minor recruitingofficer 1970-72; VF-124 Miramar CA, student 1972-73; VF1 NAS Miramar, nfo training officer administrative officer 1973-77; VF 124 Miramar, asst operations ofcr instr 1977-79; VF 1 NAS Miramar CA, maintenance ofcr safety ofcr 1980-81; USS Range CV 61 San Diego, weapons officer co-dept head 1981-83; Commander Naval Base San Diego, asst chief of staff for admin 1983-. ORGANIZATIONS: Mem Natl Naval Officers Assn 1972-. MILITARY SERVICE: USN commander 18 yrs; Natl Def Medal; Navy Expiditionary Medal; Meritorious Unit Commen; Humanatrian Serv Medal; Sea Serv Ribbon; Armed Forces Exp Medal. BUSINESS ADDRESS: Asst Chief of Staff for Admin, US Navy, Commander, Naval Base, (Code N1), San Diego, CA 92132.

LAWING, RAYMOND QUINTON
Educator. PERSONAL: Born Mar 03, 1910, Chesterfield Co, VA; married Florence Jones; children: 6 Children. EDUCATION: VA State Coll, BS 1932; VSC & VPI Blacksburg VA, adavance study; Moody Bible Inst Chicago. CAREER: Appomattox Co, tchr of agriculture educ 1932-; Appomattox VA, mnister of O local churches 1946-. ORGANIZATIONS: Pres Appomattox Tchrs Assn 15 Yrs; pres E & W Bound SS Union; past moderator Hasadiah Bapt Assn; prs Appomattox Improvement Assn 1939-; pres elect & pres Appomattox Educ 1971-72; mem Appomattox Educ Assn; mem VA Voc Assn; mem NVATA; mem NEA; mem NEA; pres Appomattox Assembly 1972; mem Appomatox Chap NAACP 1940-; mem C of C 1970; mem Cancer Society; Hasadiah; Cornrstone Assn; PM Long Mt Lodge 204 F&A Masons; mem Phi Beta Sigma Frat. HONORS/ACHIEVEMENTS: Recipient distinguished serv award Local Group 1948; 35-yr plaque VA Voc Agriculture Assn 1967; revere bowl Appomattox Educ Assn 1975.

LAWLAH, GLORIA GARY
Educator. PERSONAL: Born Mar 12, 1939, Newberry, SC; married John Wesley Lawlah III; children: John Wesley IV, Gloria Gene, Gary McCarrell. EDUCATION: Hampton Univ, BS 1960; Trinity Coll, MA 1970. CAREER: Washington DC Public Schools, administrator; Maryland General Assembly, delegate. ORGANIZATIONS: Mem bd of dirs Natl Hook-up of Black Women 1980-81; 3rd vice pres PG Cty Chap NAACP 1980-82; mem bd dirs Coalition of Black Affairs 1980-; life mem Natl Council of Negro Women; mem Oxon Hill Democrats; co-chair PG Govt Review Task Force Public Safety 1982; co-chair PG Cty Execs 7th Councilmanic Dist Campaign 1982; mem Democratic State Central Comm 1982-86; mem bd of dirs Hillcrest-Marlow Planning Bd 1982-; bd dirs Family Crisis Ctr 1982-84; mem Alpha Kappa Alpha Sor 1982-; delegate Democratic Natl Convention 1984; mem bd of dirs Natl Political Congress of Black Women 1984-; mem Black Democratic Cncl 1985-; mem John Hanson Women's Democratic Club 1985-; mem bd Ctr for the Aging Greater SE Comm Hosp 1985-. HOME ADDRESS: 3801 24th Ave, Hillcrest Heights, MD 20748. BUSINESS ADDRESS: Delegate, Maryland General Assembly, House of Delegates, Lowe House Office Bldg, Annapolis, MD 21401.

LAWRENCE, ANNIE L.
Nurse, educator. PERSONAL: Born Feb 14, 1926, Virginia; widowed. EDUCATION: Freedman's Hosp of Nursing; Loyola U, cert of pub hlth nursing; Depaul U, MSNEd. CAREER: Gov's State Univ, prof nursing; nursing educ coord; St of IL Dept of Registration & Educ, asst nursing educ coord; Evangelical School of Nursing, asst dir; Mt Sinai Hospital School of Nursing, nursing educ; Provident Hospital School of Nursing, sup instr dir of nursing educ. ORGANIZATIONS: Treas Depaul Nursing Sch Alumni Assn; Northeastern League for Nursing; chmn Adv Student Sect Am Nurses Assn; Nat League ofr Nursing; parliamentarian N Assn of Lawyers Wives; aux vice pres immediate past pres N Assn of Lawyers Wives; N Ethical Guideline Com; United Ch of Christ; bd dir Park Manor Congregational Ch; pres Women's Fellowship Park Manor Congressional Ch; Am Inst of Parliamentarians; consult educ & civic coms; cororate mem bd of Homeland Ministries; past pres Sigma Gamma Rho Sor; bd dir Evangelical Hosp Assn Publ. HONORS/ACHIEVEMENTS: Publ "Adminstrn & Its Effectiveness; "Can an Evaluation Tool be meaningful to Studies & Tchrs?"; "Professional Leadership"; "The Scope of Nursing Prac" listed The Emony Sucess Library; Successful Blacks; Who's Who in Am 1976.

LAWRENCE, AZAR MALCOLM
Jazz musician. PERSONAL: Born Nov 03, 1952, Los Angeles; children: Daneka, Azar Malcolm III, Aisha. EDUCATION: W LA Jr Coll; CA State U; USC. CAREER: Mccoy Tyner's Quintet, jazz musician. ORGANIZATIONS: Mem of various prominent quarters & bands; currently recording on Prestige Label Serv. HONORS/ACHIEVEMENTS: Currently recording on Prestige Label Serv to Sickle Cedd Fdn; Urban League Guild; Black Awareness Programs; featured in Downbeat Mag 1973; Esq Mag 1975; Montreaux Jazz Festival 1973.

LAWRENCE, CHARLES B.
Judge. PERSONAL: Born Jan 12, 1920, Brooklyn, NY; son of George L Lawrence and Carrie E Brown Lawrence; widowed; children: Charles, Paula. EDUCATION: City Coll of NY, BSS 1941; Brooklyn Law School, LLB (cum laude) 1950. CAREER: Attorney, 1951-70; Carver Federal Savings & Loan Assn, general counsel 1968-70; Civil Court of City of NY, judge 1971; Supreme Court of NY, justice 1979; Appellate Div of Supreme Court of State of NY 2nd Judicial Dept, justice 1984-. MILITARY SERVICE: AUS s/sgt 1942-45. BUSINESS ADDRESS: Justice Appellate Division, Supreme Ct of State of NY, 2nd Judicial Dept, 45 Monroe Place, Brooklyn, NY 11201.

LAWRENCE, EDWARD
Association executive. PERSONAL: Born Jan 08, 1935, Gasden, AL; married Marion Winn; children: Rita, Edward Jr, Jill, Lawrence. EDUCATION: Empire State Coll, BA 1957; Studio Theatre Sch. CAREER: African-am Cultural Ctr, prof actor, exec dir 1968-. ORGANIZATIONS: Mem Actors Equity; Studio Arena Theatre 1966-68; Buffalo Urban League; Community Action Orgn; Buffalo & Build Orgn. HONORS/ACHIEVEMENTS: Community serv award Black Harmony. BUSINESS ADDRESS: 350 Masten Ave, Buffalo, NY 14209.

LAWRENCE, EILEEN B.
Branch librarian. PERSONAL: Born Apr 11, 1919, Centralia, IL. EDUCATION: Loyola U, PHB 1950; Wilson State Coll L & A Chicago T Chr Coll, attended 1964-65. CAREER: Fredrick A Douglass Br Library, br librarian Iii 1964-75; Oakland Br Washington Park Sub-br, librarian; Dusable HS & Englewood HS, 1st asst; library asst ch pianist & choir & dir 1939-62; St Mark Amez Ch & Kelly Meth Ch. ORGANIZATIONS: Bd dir Lawndale Homemakers 1971-75; mem Model Cities Educ Task Force; mem Intl Platform Assn; mem Old Friends of Greater Chicago Recipient Mayoral Citation Model Cities Sub-com; Chicago Commn on Human Relations 1971-74. HONORS/ACHIEVEMENTS: Who's Who of Am Women & Other Notables 1970. BUSINESS ADDRESS: 4801 S Michigan Ave, Chicago, IL.

LAWRENCE, ERMA JEAN
Business executive. PERSONAL: Born Jul 12, 1926, Arkansas; married Joseph; children: Ronald, Gloristene, Imogene, Michelle, Valerie. EDUCATION: Nat Inst of Prac Nurs, 1953; WA U, com dev training 1967-68; Urban Training Cent HDC, 2yrs trng; WA U, cert in mngmt 1971; MO U, soc minority stud;MOUniv WA U, org training sem; dev training sem econ 1970; MO U, econ dev sem 1970; GEO Grant CAP, 1970. CAREER: West Educ Cong, 3rd vp; Block Unit, chmn 10 yrs; Urban League, leadership trng; precinct capt 13 yrs; Main Post Office, mail clerk 1950-62; Firmin Deslodge Hosp, prac nurse 1953-63; Coll of Rev, tax collector, auditor processor 1963-66; HDC, com dev 1966; West End Gateway Cent Sub Station, com dev 1966-; West End Dev Corp, dir 1972-79; Northside preservation Commn Inc, exec dir 1979-. ORGANIZATIONS: Mem Urban League; Police Comm Rel Commn; YMCA; coorgan of Poor People Camp; coord Mat Blk Health Causus; Mental Health Task Force; bd mem ARCH; col People Guide; bd mem West End Dev Corp; Met Ten Orgn; West End Com Conf; Blk Women of Unity; Blk Women Com Dev Found; consult Youth Adv Coun; St Louis City Bd of Dn 1975; mem Baptist Ch of Good Shephard; org Blk People Coun; mem Kinder Cottage Women for City Living; pers comm Freedom of Resident; Mayors Coun on Aging; mem Educ Com to Study Dropouts; PTA; adv com OfUniv Year in ActionUniv ofUniv of MO; treas WAUniv Com Action Alumni; bd mem West End Comm Conf; past chmn West End Neighborhood Adv Comm; bd mem Dignity Reading Clinic; found pres Operation Challenge; mem appointed by Gov Teasdale The Neighborhood Commn; mem St Louis Round Table Housing & Brain Thrust of St Louis Round Label St Louis Black Leadership; charter mem Scott Joplin Soc Constr Emp Prgm. HONORS/ACHIEVEMENTS: Outstanding Supv; Aid of Delinq; Beautification Blocks Awd; Spec Awd Dinner West End Adv Comm; Spec Awd Bd of Educ Svc; Awd for Vol Serv on Coms Mayor James F Conway St Louis; Awd for Training 200 Youth & Adults in Work Experience Progs Operation Challenge Inc; Awd for Active Block Unit Chairmanship & Vol Serv St Louis League. BUSINESS ADDRESS: Executive Dir, Northside Preservation Commiss, 5647 Delmar, St Louis, MO 63112.

LAWRENCE, GEORGE CALVIN
Physician. PERSONAL: Born Apr 11, 1918, Greene County, GA; son of Noel Lawrence and Lozie Ann Favors Lawrence; married Pauline Blockshear (deceased); children: Brenda Jean Lawrence Harris, Montrois, George Calvin Jr; married Helenda Ann Simmons, Oct 20, 1987. EDUCATION: Meharry Med Coll, MD 1944; FACOG, 1972. CAREER: Private practice, obstetrics/gynecology. ORGANIZATIONS: Pres Atlanta Med Assn; sec GA State Med Assn; pres Atlanta Guardsmen; mem & 32nd degree Mason; Omega Psi Phi Frat; Ebenezer Baptist Church. HONORS/ACHIEVEMENTS: Recpt recog awrd 25 yrs med serv Morehouse Coll & Meharry Med Coll; fellow, Amer Coll of Obstetrics-Gynecology. MILITARY SERVICE: USNR MC comdr 1953-56. BUSINESS ADDRESS: 550 Fairburn Rd SW, #A-5, Atlanta, GA 30331.

LAWRENCE, HENRY
Athlete. PERSONAL: Born Sep 25, 1951, Danville, PA; children: Dina, Starlin, Juliet. EDUCATION: FL A&M Univ, BS 1974; Travelers Financial Planning Sch, attended 1975. CAREER: Manatee Growers Packing Co Inc, pres; Henry Lawrence Productions Inc, pres; L & S Farms, vice pres; LA Raiders, football player; Solid Rock Realty, vice pres; Solo Vocal Entertainer and Recording Artist. ORGANIZATIONS: Mem Manatee Co Sickle Cell 1976-78; bd dir Amer Cancer Soc 1976-80; mem NAACP; chmn of bd Manatee Growers Produce Packing Inc; life mem Alpha Phi Alpha Frat 1973-; mem Masonic Lodge Prentice Hall 1971-; founder/producer Miss Black Manatee Co Scholarship Beauty Pageant Inc 1978-; Henry Lawrence Youth Football Camps; fund raiser United Negro Coll Fund, The Sonance Ear Inst. HONORS/ACHIEVEMENTS: Comm Contrib Awd FL State Women's Assn 1978; Comm Image & Serv Awd NAACP 1979; 3 Super Bowls 1976, 1980, 1983; Who's Who Among Students in Amer Univ & Colls 1974; All American Teams 1973-74; NFL (AFC-NFC) Pro Bowls Hawaii 1984 and 1985; NFL All Pro; nominated for Humanitarian Awd by The Southern CA Alm Inst1987. BUSINESS ADDRESS: Los Angeles Raiders, 332 Center St, El Segundo, CA 90245.

LAWRENCE, JACOB A.
Artist, educator. PERSONAL: Born Sep 07, 1917, Atlantic City, NJ; married Gwendolyn Knight. EDUCATION: Harlem Art Workshop NYC, attended 1934-48; Amer Artists Sch NYC, attended 1938-39. CAREER: Harlem YMCA, Columbia Univ, Baltimore Museum, work shown 1938-40; work Migration of the Negro reproduced 26 of the paintings in Fortune Magazine in 1941; started work on "Struggle, From the History of the American People" 1955; taught at Pratt Institute starting in 1955 for 15 years; 1967 Simon & Schuster published a children's book, Harriet and the Promised Land, and did a series of 17 paintings based on the life of Harriet Tubman; 1972 designed posters for Olympic Games in Munich; 1973 produced a series of paintings for the Washington State Capital Museum; commissioned by Limit-

ed Edition Books to illustrate a special edition of John Hersey's Hiroshima 1982; Univ of Washington, full prof 1970-. **ORGANIZATIONS:** Elected to Amer Acad of Arts & Letters 1984; mem Natl Inst Arts & Letters; Washington State Arts Commn; mem Natl Acad Design 1971. **HONORS/ACHIEVEMENTS:** Rosenwald Fellowship 1940-42; Guggenheim Fellowship 1946; Spingarn Med 1970; exhibition sponsored by Ford Found 1960; retrospective exhibition Whitney Museumof Amer Art sponsored by IBM 1974; Washington State Governor's Awd of Special Commendation 1981; Washington State Governor's Arts Awd 1984; Citation by Washington State Senate 1985. **MILITARY SERVICE:** USCG 1943-45. **BUSINESS ADDRESS:** Professional Artist, Seattle Art Museum, Volunteer Park, Seattle, WA 98112.

LAWRENCE, JAMES T.
Business executive. **PERSONAL:** Born Nov 20, 1921, Madison, GA; married Carrie B Dorsey; children: Sylvia L. **EDUCATION:** Morris Brown Coll, attended; LUTC Grad. **CAREER:** Pilgrim Health & Life Ins Co, agent, mgr, state supr, state mgr, special claims controller, special ordinary supr, asst dean training school, asst vice pres chief acct 1947-. **ORGANIZATIONS:** Mem, Natl Accountants Assn, 1961-; SE Trainers Dir Assn, 1971-; mem, YMCA; NAACP; Urban League; bd dir, Pilgrim Employees Fed Credit Union; bd mem Amer Cancer Soc, 1973-. **HONORS/ACHIEVEMENTS:** Cancer crusade chairman awards 1967; mgmt idea award 1969; 6 NIA certificates. **MILITARY SERVICE:** AUS 1 lt 1942-45. **BUSINESS ADDRESS:** Vice Pres, Chief Accountant, The Pilgrim Life & Health Insurance Co, 1143 Laney-Wolkey Blvd, Augusta, GA 30901.

LAWRENCE, JOHN E.
Educator. **PERSONAL:** Born May 11, 1941, Durham, NC; married Virginia Landers; children: John II, Jason. **EDUCATION:** NC Central Univ, BS; FL A&M Univ, M. **CAREER:** Lincoln HS, 1963-67; Godby HS, tchr 1967-69, asst prin 1969-73, prin 1973-78; FL Dept of Educ, bureau chief adult & comm educ 1979-. **ORGANIZATIONS:** Mem Comm Educators; Natl Comm Educ Assn NAPCAE; FAEA; Leon Dist Adv Com; mem Kappa Delta Pi; Phi Delta Kappa; Frontiers Intl; bd dir Capital City Tiger Bay Club; Tallahassee Urban League; mem NAACP. **HONORS/ACHIEVEMENTS:** Frontiersman of the Ur Awd 1975. **BUSINESS ADDRESS:** Bureau Chief Adult & Comm Educ, FL Dept of Educ, Knott Bldg, Tallahassee, FL 32301.

LAWRENCE, LEONARD E.
Physician, educator. **PERSONAL:** Born Jun 27, 1937, Indianapolis, IN; married Barbara Ann Price; children: Courtney, L Michael, David. **EDUCATION:** IN Univ, BA 1959; IN Univ School of Med, MD 1962. **CAREER:** IN Univ School of Med, psych resident 1965-68, chief psych res 1967-68, child psych fellow 1967-69; Child Psych Serv Wilford Hall USAF Med Ctr, chief 1969-72; San Antonio Childrens Ctr, assoc med dir; Univ of TX Health Sci Ctr, prof of psych pediatrics & fam practice, assoc dean student affairs. **ORGANIZATIONS:** Cert Amer Bd Psych & Neurology 1970-71; TX Juvenile Corrections Master Plan Adv Council, mem 1974-75; Council on Children Adolesc & Their Families AmerPsych Assoc 1976, 1978-83; Natl Med Assoc; Amer Acad of Child Psych; Amer Ortho Psych Assoc; Amer Psych Assoc; Kappa Alpha Psi; ed bd Jrnl Amer Acad Child Psych; McGavin Awd Selection Comm Amer Psych Assoc; mem of, Nat'l Med Assoc Bd of Trustees, Nat'l Advisory Council on Drug Abuse. **HONORS/ACHIEVEMENTS:** Co-authored with J Spurlock "The Black Child" Basic Handbook of Child Psych vol 1 JB Noshpitz Ed-in-Chief Basic Books Inc NY 1979. **MILITARY SERVICE:** Lt col 1963-72. **BUSINESS ADDRESS:** Associate Dean Student Affairs, Univ of Texas, Health Science Center, 7703 Floyd Curl Dr, San Antonio, TX 78284.

LAWRENCE, MARGARET MORGAN
Physician. **PERSONAL:** Born Aug 19, 1914, New York, NY; married Prof Charles R Ii (deceased); children: Prof Charles R, III, Prof Sara Lightfoot, Paula Wehmiller. **EDUCATION:** Cornell U, AB 1936; Coll of Physicians & Surgeons Columbis U, MD/MS pub health 1940-43, cert in psychoanalytic med 1951. **CAREER:** Harlem Hosp Center, supervising child psychiatrist & psychoanalyst 1963-84; Nyack Hosp, consult in pediatric psychiatry 1970-; Coll of P&S Columbia, assoc clinical prof of psychiatry 1963-84; Pomona NY, practicing child psychiatrist psychoanalyst 1951-; Child Devel Center, dir 1969-74; Sch Mental Health Unit, dir 1957-63; Children's Therapy Rockland Co Center for Mental Health, assoc dir 1954-57; Northside Child Devel Center City Coll Educ Clinic, psychiatrist 1951-57; Pediatrics Meharry Med Coll, asso prof 1943-47. **ORGANIZATIONS:** Life fellow Am Psychoanalytic Assn, life fellow Am Psychiatric Assn, Am Acad of Psychoanalysis, Am Orthopsychiatric Assn; life mem Nat Med Assn/Black & Psychiatrists Of Am; life mem Med Soc Co of Rockland Rosenwald Fellow 1942-43; Nta Research Council Fellow 1947-48; US Pub Health Serv Fellow 1948-50; Licentiate Am Bd of Pediatrics 1948. **HONORS/ACHIEVEMENTS:** Publ "Mental Health Team in the Schools" Human Sci Press 1971; publ "Young Inner City Families the development of ego strength under stress" human Sci Press 1975; Joseph R Bernstein mental health award Rockland Co NY 1975; EY Williams MD Clinical Scholars of Distinction Awd 1984; Outstanding Women Practioners in Medicine Awd of the Susan Smith McKinney Steward Med Soc 1984. **BUSINESS ADDRESS:** 34 Dogwood Lane, Pomona, NY 10970.

LAWRENCE, MONTAGUE SCHIELE
Surgeon. **PERSONAL:** Born Apr 22, 1923, Laurel, MS; married Melbahue Green; children: Michael, Julie. **EDUCATION:** Alcorn A&M Coll, BS 1943; Meharry Med Coll, MD 1946; Homer Phillips Hosp, intern 1946-47, resd 1947-51. **CAREER:** Homer Phillips Hosp, supr sur 1953-54; Univ IA, chest surg resd instr assoc 1954-56, rsch asst prof 1956-57, asst prof 1957-59, assoc prof surgery 1959-65, prof surgery 1965-71; VA Hosp, vis surgeon 1962-71; Univ of IA, chmn div vascular surg 1970-71; Private Practice, surgeon. **ORGANIZATIONS:** Mem AMA; Natl Med Assn; fellow Amer Coll of Surgeons; Amer Coll of Chest Physicians; mem Amer Assn for Thoracic Surgery; Soc of Thoracic Surgeons; Western Surg Assn; Central Surg Assn; Amer Heart Assn; Amer Thoracic Socl; IA Thoracic Soc; IA Acad of Surgery; IA State Med Soc; Linn Co Med Soc; Alpha Omega Alpha; Kappa Pi Med Soc; Sigma Xi; diplomate Amer Bd of Surgery; Amer Bd of Thoracic Surgery; mem NINDB Prog Proj Comm; consult Thoracic &Cardiovascular Surgery; mem Joint Com for Stroke Facilities; gov Amer Coll of Chest Physicians; mem Central Adv Com Cncl on Cardiovascular Surgery; pres IA Acad of Surgery; IA Thoracic Soc; bd mem Human Experimentation & Rsch; mem House Staff Affairs Com; Med Sch Admission Comm. **MILITARY SERVICE:** AUS capt 1951-53. **BUSINESS ADDRESS:** Surgeon, 1030 5th Ave SE, Cedar Rapids, IA 52403.

LAWRENCE, PAUL FREDERIC
Private consultant. **PERSONAL:** Born Mar 20, Paterson, NJ; son of Joshua Lawrence and Louise Lawrence; married Vivian Ann Hall; children: Katherine Louise, Robin Ann. **EDUCATION:** Newark State Tchrs Coll, BS Educ 1935; Stanford Univ, MA Educ 1946, EdD 1947; Kean Coll, DHL 1965. **CAREER:** Howard Univ, assoc dir counseling 1948-56; Willowbrook Sch Dist, supt of schs 1956-60; CA State Coll, assoc dean counseling 1960-63; CA State Dept ofEduc, assoc state supt 1963-67; US Office of Educ, regional comm of ed 1967-73, dept asst comm regional off 1973-79, dir postsecondary liaison 1979-82; Consultants in Educational Policy and Admin, chief exec officer 85-; Self-Employed, private consultant; settlement team mem, federal court monitor in case of NAACP vs San Francisco School District & California State Department of Education. **ORGANIZATIONS:** Mem Phi Delta Kappa 1946-; bd mem Fair Play Council Palo Alto CA 1946-48; dir Southern Field Proj Natl Scholarship Serv Found 1949-54; bd mem Natl Conf Christians & Jews LA Region 1956-60; bd mem Scholastics Mag Adv Bd 1964-68; bd mem Coll Placement Bureau 1966-70; chmn pre-coll Council Natl Acad Sci Engrg Council 1975-80; bd mem Stanford Univ Alumni Assn 1984-; fed court monitar in case of NAACP vs SF Sch Dist & CA State Dept of Ed. **HONORS/ACHIEVEMENTS:** Hon Doctorate NJ St Univ NJ 1965; Keys to City Riverside CA 1966-70; Citations (2) CA State Legislator (Senate & Assembly) 1967-68; Serv Awd US office of Ed Washington 1970; Distinguished Educator Natl Alliance Black Sch Educators 1974; Publications, College Primer for Negro Youth 1946; co-author, Negro American Heritage (textbook) 1964; Primer for Compliance Monitoring 1989. **MILITARY SERVICE:** AUS, USAF lt col 22 yrs; numerous medals. **HOME ADDRESS:** 4837 Crestwood Way, Sacramento, CA 95822.

LAWRENCE, PHILIP MARTIN
Company executive. **PERSONAL:** Born Nov 12, 1950, Evansville, IN; son of William H Lawrence and Pilar Lawrence; married Cheryl Darlene Moore, Jun 06, 1971; children: DeVonna Marcel Lawrence, Philip M Lawrence, II, Shane Kiwan Lawrence. **EDUCATION:** ISUE, Evansville, IN. **CAREER:** People's Voice, Evansville, IN, editor, Black Newspaper, 1969-71; WJPS, Evansville, IN, radio announcer; City of Evansville, Evansville, IN, contract compliance officer (business devel supvr); Tomorrow's Treasures, CA, regional mgr; Heritage, New Jersey, regional/mgr; Community Action of Evansville, Evansville, IN, senior aide dir; ATSCO Inc, Evansville, IN, chief exec. **ORGANIZATIONS:** Bd mem, Council on Aging, 1984-87; Steering Comm Head, 1986-89, treasurer, 1987-89, Evansville Area Minority Supplies Devel Council; mem, State Chamber of Commerce, 1986-89; mem, Rotary Intl, 1987-89; mem, bd of dir, Private Industry Council, 1987-89. **HONORS/ACHIEVEMENTS:** Played the beast in "Beauty & the Beast" on local TV station, 1982; Master of Ceremonies for Black History Talent, 1978-88. **BUSINESS ADDRESS:** Pres, ATSCO, Inc, PO Box 3912, Evansville, IN 47737.

LAWRENCE, RODELL
Company executive. **PERSONAL:** Born Feb 19, 1946, Apopka, FL; married Cedar Lavern Evans; children: Christopher, Debora, Biram, Raegena. **EDUCATION:** South Carolina State Coll, BSEE 1970. **CAREER:** North Amer Rockwell Missile System Div, mem tech staff 1970-73; Xerox Corp, test engr, sr engr field engr, regional product serv mgr midwest region headquarters, project mgr I II III, multinatl serv opers mgr, product support mgr, product serv mgr; Xerox Corp, Mgr, Multinational Configuration Mgmt, 1988-. **ORGANIZATIONS:** Bd of dirs CARI 1980-85; dean of educ Omega Psi Phi Frat 1984, 1985, 1987; athletic dir, Irondequoit Football League 1985-86; bd of dir Lewis St Settlement 1986-87; Bd of Visitor, Claflin Coll, 1988-present; Advisory Council, SC State Coll, 1988-present. **HONORS/ACHIEVEMENTS:** Distinguished Corporate Alumni Citation NAFEO 1983; Houston Engrs Soc Awd SC State Coll 1986; 1989 Benjamin E Mays Most Distinguished Grauate Award, SC State Coll, 1989; Outstanding Performance Award, Xerox, 1989; Leadership through Quality Award, Xerox, 1989. **MILITARY SERVICE:** AUS; staff sgt E-6 2 yrs; Bronze Star, Silver Star, Purple Heart, Army Accomodations. **HOME ADDRESS:** 75 Ellinwood Dr, Rochester, NY 14622.

LAWRENCE, THERESA A. B.
Physician. **PERSONAL:** Born Dec 17, 1953, Aiken, SC; married Jimmy R Ford; children: Kito Ford, Nyesha Ford, Jaamal Ford. **EDUCATION:** Manhattanville Coll, BS 1974; Tufts Univ Sch of Medicine, MD 1978. **CAREER:** Morehouse Sch of Medicine, faculty Develop 1983-85; Dept of Human Resources, medical consultant 1984-; Arthritis Foundation, bd of dirs 1984-; Gwinnett Hosp System, med dir phy therapy dept 1984-. **HOME ADDRESS:** 741 Stratford Green, Avondale Estates, GA 30002. **BUSINESS ADDRESS:** Physician, Gwinnet Arthritis Center, 449 Pleasant Hill Rd Ste 101, Lilburn, GA 30247.

LAWRENCE, THOMAS R., JR.
Employment recruiter. **PERSONAL:** Born Sep 02, 1929, Waycross, GA; son of Tom Reid Lawrence and Thelma Sue Williams Lawrence; married Caroline Barbosa, Nov 16, 1952; children: Lisa Frazier, Dwayne, Damon, Rene. **EDUCATION:** Suffolk Univ, BA, 1960, MA, 1962; further graduate study at American Univ, Washington, DC, 1963-64. **CAREER:** Office of Economic Opportunity, Washington, DC, educ specialist, 1963-6 5; Urban League of Springfield, Springfield, MA, exec dir, 1965-68; Information Systems, NAO Relations, Waltham, MA, mgr of EEO, N Amer Operations, 1970-1973; Honeywell Inc, Corporate Employee Relations, Minneapolis, MN, mgr of corporate EEO programs, 1973-75; Information Systems—Field Engineering Division, Newton, MA, mgr of Distribution and Priority Control, 1975-77, mgr of natl accounts, 1977-79; Avionics Division—Product Support Logistics, Minneapolis, MN, mgr of systems and procedures, 1979-80; Controls Systems—Honeywell Plaza, Minneapolis, MN, staff asst, 1980-82; Honeywell Inc, Corporate Employee Relations, Minneapolis, MN, mgr of univ relations and minority recruitment, 1983—. **ORGANIZATIONS:** Mem, Minneapolis NAACP, 1972—; mem, Minneapolis Urban League, 1972—; bd mem, Industry Advisory Council NAACP ACT-SO, 1985—; bd mem, Natl Consortium for Minority Engineers, 1985—; bd mem, Natl Soc of Black Engineers, 1988—. **HONORS/ACHIEVEMENTS:** Meritorious Service Award, Florida A & M Univ, 1988; Honeywell Focus Award, 1988; Black Engineer of the Year Award, Affirmative Action, 1989. **MILITARY SERVICE:** U.S. Army, master sgt, 1948-52; received Bronze Star. **HOME ADDRESS:** 1054 Wyoming Ave. S., Bloomington, MN 55438.

LAWRENCE, WILLIAM WESLEY
Educator. **PERSONAL:** Born Jan 27, 1939, Whiteville, NC; son of Horace Lawrence and Mary Lawrence; married Queen E Wooten; children: William Wesley Jr, Lori Elecia. **EDUCATION:** NC Coll, BS Chem 1962; St Josephs School of Med Tech Tacoma WA, Cert Med Tech 1967; NC Central Univ Durham, MA Counseling 1971; Univ of NC ChapelHill, PhD

Counseling Psych 1974. **CAREER:** Liggett & Myers Inc, rsch chem 1969-71; Univ of NC Chapel Hill, counselor 1972-73; NC Central Univ Durham, assoc dir inst rsch & eval 1973-74; NC A&TState Univ Greensboro, chmn educ psych & guidance 1974-78; Natl Inst of Environ Health Sci, counseling psych/dir human resource devel; Fayetteville State Univ, prof of education 1978-87. **ORGANIZATIONS:** Med lab consult Hospitals & Scientific Labs 1967-72; consult Bus Educ Government 1975-85; public notary Durham Cty 198-85; real estate broker & instr Century21 NC Comm Coll 1982-85. **HONORS/ACHIEVEMENTS:** Ray Thompson Humanitarian Awd NC Personnel & Guidance Assoc 1973; Ed Leadership Awd Afro-Amer Soc of Transit Employees NY 1978; Outstanding Work Performance Awd US Dept of Health & Human Serv 1983. **MILITARY SERVICE:** AUS E-4 lab spec 2 yrs; Outstanding Recruit Awd, Platoon Leader 1963-65. **HOME ADDRESS:** 308 Wayne Circle, Durham, NC 27707.

LAWRENCE-EVANS, SANDRA
Interior designer. **PERSONAL:** Born Jan 28, 1938, New York, NY; married Paul Evans Jr. **EDUCATION:** NY School of Interior Design, BFA; Parsons, attended 1983-84. **CAREER:** Batakari Ltd NY, pres int designer 1973-81; Sandra Lawrence Assocs Inc, pres/director. **ORGANIZATIONS:** Mem Allied Bd of Trade 1980-85. **BUSINESS ADDRESS:** President, Sandra Lawrence Assocs Inc, 337 Convent Ave, New York, NY 10031.

LAWS, CLARENCE A.
Business executive. **PERSONAL:** Born Mar 23, 1911, Opelousas, LA; married Ann L Parnell German; children: Dawn, Artist, Jann. **EDUCATION:** Dillard Univ, AB; Dillard Univ & Loyola Univ, additional study. **CAREER:** Insurance salesman 1934-36; research specialist in black history 1936-38; New Orleans Urban League, exec sec 1938-42; The LA Weekly, pub relations dir & feature & editorial writer; SW Regional Dir NAACP, field dir 1955-65; Office for Civil Rights US Dept of HEW, dep regional dir 1965-; Organized Black Painters & Paper Hangers & Decorators Union; established a welding school where blacks were trained for jobs on liberty ships in 1941; Black Housing Project Mgr, organized Com 1937; headed citizens comm on re-election of Pres Harry S Truman. **ORGANIZATIONS:** Mem, Health, Educ & Welfare Employees Assn; Dallas-Ft Worth TX Federal Exec Bd; pres, Black United Dallas Fed Govt Employees Assn; exec bd mem & chmn, Housing Comm, Greater Dallas Community Relations Commn; life mem, NAACP; mem, Natl Life Membership Comm, NAACP; mem, Men's Dialogue, Natl Conf of Christians & Jews, Dallas Chap; treas, John F Kennedy Branch, NAACP; mem, YMCA; Omega Psi Phi Frat; Knights of Pythias Fraternity; Dallas Tri-Racial Comm. **HONORS/ACHIEVEMENTS:** Omega Man of Year, 1957-70; Father John LaFarge Award, Dallas Chap, Catholic Interracial Council, 1969; Licensed Vocational Nurses Assn, Distinguished Citizen Award, 1970; NAACP branch awards, 1966 & 1970; Dallas Fed Business Assn; Fed Career Man of Year, 1970-71; Natl Office for Black Catholics, Commendation for Serv Citation, 1973; Founder's Citation Award, Natl Catholic Conf for Interracial Justice, 1973; Golden Plate Award, SW Region, NAACP, 1974; Commanding Gen Citation, 8th Army, Bronze Star Medal, 1945; YMCA award; BSA award; New Orleans Tuberculosis Assn Award; New Orleans Community Chest Award. **MILITARY SERVICE:** AUS, major. **BUSINESS ADDRESS:** 1114 Commerce St, Dallas, TX 75201.

LAWS, RUTH M.
Educator. **PERSONAL:** Born Jul 25, 1912, Gatesville, NC; married William J Laws; children: Cherritta Matthews. **EDUCATION:** Hampton Inst, BS 1933; Cornell Univ, MS 1943; NY Univ, EdD 1956. **CAREER:** Peabody Acad, teacher 1933-34; Rural Soc, caseworker 1934-36; Wilmington, adult educ supr 1936-37; Smyrna, teacher 1937-41; State Dept Pub Instr Home Econ, dir asst supr 1942-56, supr 1956-68; Adult & Continuing Educ, state dir 1968-71; DE Tech & Comm Coll, asst to pres 1971-77, vice pres 1977-78; L & M Educ Resources Ltd. **ORGANIZATIONS:** Mem numerous offices consult numerous professional civic orgns; mem Natl Bd YMCA 1979-83. **HONORS/ACHIEVEMENTS:** Merit Awd Natl Bd New Homemakers Amer 1954; Merit Awd DE Assn New Homemakers Amer 1961; Woman of Yr Dover Alumni Chap Delta Sigma Theta 1964; Commendation Cert Vet Admin Serv 1970; Outstanding Voc Educ Awd DE Dept Pub Instr 1972; recognition Adult Educ Assn USA 1974; Diamond State Awd Gov DE 1974; YMCA Citizen of the Yr 1980; Del Council of Women Hall of Fame 1981; Philadelphia Freedom Day Awd (Ed) 1981; Del Coll Personnel Assn Leadership in Educ Awd1981; Brandywine Professional Assn Outstanding Achievers Awd (Educ) 1982; DE State Bar Assn Law Day Liberty Bell Awd 1983; Delaware Mother of the Year 1986; Delaware Ecumenical Awd 1986. **BUSINESS ADDRESS:** L&M Educ Resources Ltd, 844 Forest St, Dover, DE 19901.

LAWSON, CASSELL AVON
Educator. **PERSONAL:** Born Mar 29, 1937, Little Rock, AR; married Amy Davison; children: Cassell, Cassandra, Roderick, Nikki, Joi. **EDUCATION:** Langston U, BA 1959; IN U, MSED 1970;Univ of Notre Dame, PhD 1974; IN State U, postdoctoral 1975-76. **CAREER:** Erie Comm Coll, vice pres cty campus; Coppin State Coll, vice pres acad affairs; Coppin State Coll, former dean of educ; Morgan State Univ, asst to vice pres dir 1976-77; IN State Univ, rockefeller fellow 1975-76; Univ of MA, asst prof & dir 1974-75; Off Campus Student Activities & Min Student Affairs Univ of Notre Dame, dir 1973-74; S Bend Urban League, exec dir 1968-70; Grand Rapids Urban Leag, dir 1956-68. **ORGANIZATIONS:** Pres Toxbur Es Roxbury Comm Coll 1974; staff asso Inst for Urban StudiesUniv of Notre Dame 1974; postdoctoral fellow Lab Comm Psychiatry Harvard Med Sch 1972-73; internUniv of MA 1972-73; mem Kappa Alpha Psi Frat; Phi Delta Kappa; chpsn Black Student Afrs 1973-74; chpsn S Bend Black Caucus 1973-74; NatEduc Assn 1965; Am Personnel & Guid Assn 1974-75; Am Assn for Higher Educ 1975-76; chpsn IN Counc of Urban Leag Exec 1967-68; chpsn Midwestern RepUrban Leag Exec 1968-69; Jaycees 1966-67; Area Plan Commn 1968-69; Black Ldrshp Counc. **HONORS/ACHIEVEMENTS:** Nat urban leag schlrshp 1968; rockefeller fellow IN StateUniv 1975-76; comm serv award Suburban Club 1967; comm serv award Lamba Kappa Mu 1968; outst yng man of yr award 1968; publ Quality Educ a view from the top notre dame jour of educ 1971; instnl power a view from the top Contemp Educ Jour 1976. **MILITARY SERVICE:** USAF a/1c 1959-63. **BUSINESS ADDRESS:** VP City Campus, Erie Community College, 121 Ellicott St, Buffalo, NY 14203.

LAWSON, CHARLES H., III
Association executive. **PERSONAL:** Born Nov 20, 1931; married Marie; children: Kim, Linda. **EDUCATION:** Tuskegee Inst, BS 1954, advanced study in Industrial Educ 1955, secondary Tchr Certificate Holder in IL 1974. **CAREER:** Manual Arts & Indus Therapy at VA Hospital, Jefferson Barracks & John Cochran Div, St Louis MO, chief 1967-; E St Louis NAACP Br, pres 1969-; IL State NAACP Conf of Br, regional dir 1971-. **ORGANIZATIONS:** Mem Kappa Alpha Psi Frat; Elks; past canister chmn March of Dimes in E St Louis & St Clair Co; mem Greater New Hope Bapt Ch of E St Louis; mem Reserve Officers Assn of US; Am Federation of Govt Employees; life mem Nat NAACP Recipient of Awards for Comm Serv & Leadership from E St Louis Model Cities Agy, Sigma Gamma Rho Sorority, NAACP Nat Ofc St Luke AME Ch & others. **MILITARY SERVICE:** USAFR lt col. **BUSINESS ADDRESS:** PO Box 301, East St Louis, IL 62202.

LAWSON, DANNY
Business executive. **PERSONAL:** Born in Louisville, KY. **EDUCATION:** Oklahoma State Univ, attended. **CAREER:** Washington Redskins, defensive back; Fed Dept Store, mgr trainee; Gulf Oil Co; Metro Transit Authority, transit admin; Lawson Natl Distrib Co, founder & pres. **ORGANIZATIONS:** Vchmn Conf of Minority Transit Official; mem adv bd Transp Rsch Ctr TX So Univ.

LAWSON, ELIZABETH HARRIS
Educator. **PERSONAL:** Married Harris Lawson; children: Dr Clyde H, Carol H Cuyjet, Dr Leonard J. **EDUCATION:** IIT Chicago, BS; Chicago State Univ, MS 1961; Univ Chicago, post grad work, Hon PhD 1974. **CAREER:** City of Chicago, hs & univ counselor, teacher 20 yrs; Chicago State Univ, dir intensive educ prog 1968-72, asst dir admiss & foreign student adv 1974-. **ORGANIZATIONS:** Mem NAFSA, Natl Assn of Women Deans Couns & Admins; Natl Guidance & Personnel Assn; mem & sec Master Plan Com for Chicago State Univ; chmn CSU's 5th Div Univ Senator 1968-74; mem Amer Assn Sch Educators; IL Guidance & Personnel Assn; mem & rsch ch Delta Kappa Gamma Intl Soc; Alpha Kappa Alpha Sor; consult SC Desegregation Ctr 1968-69; served N Cntrl Bd for accreditation of HS's 1970-80; served as IL del & co-chair White House Conf on Lib & Inf Serv Washington DC 1979; bd gov's ICOLA 1983-84; vol coord for Natl Conf of Christians & Jews 1980-84. **MILITARY SERVICE:** USAF; Citation 1965.

LAWSON, HERMAN A.
Business executive. **PERSONAL:** Born Dec 25, 1920, Fowler, CA; married Pearl Lee Johnson; children: Betty, Patricia, Gloria, Yvonne, Thomas, Tracey. **EDUCATION:** Fresno State Univ CA, attended; Univ of the Pacific; Sacramento State Univ; Chapman Coll. **CAREER:** State Employment Devel Dept, minority employment rep, manpower consultant 1963-; Sacramento, councilman 2nd dist 1973-75. **ORGANIZATIONS:** Mem, Del Paso Heights Library Comm; Coll Awareness Bd, Amer River Coll; mem, adv to the president on programs for the disadvantaged at Amer River Coll; City Amendments Study Comm; Sacramento Businessman's Adv Coun; 99th Fighter Squad Flight Leader Frt Pilot; bd dir, Tuskegee Airmen Inc 1974-75 & 1978-80; mem, NAACP; commodore Port of Sacramento. **HONORS/ACHIEVEMENTS:** Awarded Distinguished Flying Cross Air Medal, Commendation Medal, Unit Cit Medal, Award of Valor; campaign medals. **MILITARY SERVICE:** USAF major 1942-63. **BUSINESS ADDRESS:** State Manpower Planning Ofc, 800 Capitol Mall, Sacramento, CA 95814.

LAWSON, J. RANALDO
Educator. **PERSONAL:** Born Sep 13, 1943, Cleveland, OH; married Desadre Denise Skinner; children: Curtis, Derrick, Querida. **EDUCATION:** OHUniv Athens, BS 1965; NC CentralUniv Durham, MA 1969; Kent StateUniv Kent OH, phD 1976. **CAREER:** Case Western Reserve Univ, admissions dir health career opportunity 1979-; Cuyahoga Community Coll, counselor & assoc prof 1976-79; Developmental Assistance Kent State Univ, coordinator 1970-76; Career Planning and Placement Elizabeth City State Univ, dir 1968-70; Cleveland Public School System, history & govt teacher 1965-67. **ORGANIZATIONS:** Chmn bd of trustees Portage Co Community Actioncouncil 1975-76; Pres OH of Non-white Concerns in Personnel and Guidance 1977-79; exec committe mem OH Personnel & Guidance Assn 1977-79; mem finance committe Black Professional Assn 1978; keeper of records and seals Omega Psi Phi Frat 1979-; mem natl bd of dirs OHUniv Alumni Assn 1979-. **HONORS/ACHIEVEMENTS:** Social sci hon Pi Gamma Mu 1968; endl hons Phi Delta Kappa & Kappa & Delta Pi 1971-72. **BUSINESS ADDRESS:** 423 Pardee Hall, Cleveland, OH 44106.

LAWSON, JAMES M., JR.
Clergyman. **PERSONAL:** Born Sep 22, 1928, Uniontown, PA; married Dorothy Wood; children: John, Morris, Seth. **EDUCATION:** Baldwin-Wallace Coll, 1952; Boston Univ, STB 1960; Vanderbilt Univ Nashville, grad work 1960. **CAREER:** Centenary United Meth Ch Memphis, pastor 1962-74; Nonviolent Educ So Christian Leadership Conf, dir 1960-67; Student Nonviolent Coordinating Com, advisor 1960-64; Fellowship of Reconciliation So Region, field sec 1957-69; Hislop Coll Hagpur India, chmn dept of physical educ 1953-56. **ORGANIZATIONS:** Mem working com of ch and soc World Coun of Ch 1966-; mem Theological Comm of Nat Com of Black Churchmen 1969-; adv com aclu Amnesty Prof 1972-; chmn Black Meth for Ch Renewal 1968-71; bd mem SCLC 1973-; bd NAACP Memphis Br 1964-74; chmn educ com NAACP Memphis 1963-65 1974-; Nat Coun 1960-66; A Phil Randolph Inst bd 1971-; West TN ACLU bd 1969-74. **HONORS/ACHIEVEMENTS:** Distinguished Alumnus Award Boston 1970; Russwurm Award 1969; Elk Award 1960; civic award Mallory Knights of Memphis 1974; Man of the Yr Cath Interracial Coun Memphis 1969; Cit of the Yr Prince Hall Lodge of TN 1969; NAACP award Memphis 1965 & 1974; Outstanding Witness to Christ award AME Nat Laymen's Assn 1971; Spec award AFSCME Intl 1968. **BUSINESS ADDRESS:** 3320 W Adams Blvd, Los Angeles, CA 90018.

LAWSON, LAWYER
City official. **PERSONAL:** Born Aug 29, 1941, Cincinnati, OH. **EDUCATION:** Ohio Coll of Applied Sci, Associate; Pre-Med Xavier Univ; Univ of Cincinnati. **CAREER:** Villae of Woodlawn, mayor. **ORGANIZATIONS:** Trustee Amer Red Cross; trustee Hamilton Co Development Co; mem OH Mayors Assn 1980-; mem Natl League of Cities 1980-; bd of dirs Natl Conf of BlackMayors 1984-; pres OH Chap of Black Mayors 1985. **BUSINESS ADDRESS:** Mayor, Village of Woodlawn, 10141 Woodlawn Blvd, Cincinnati, OH 45215.

LAWSON, MARJORIE MCKENZIE
Attorney. **PERSONAL:** Born 1912, Pittsburgh, PA; married Belford V Jr; children: Belford, III. **EDUCATION:** Univ of MI, BA; Univ of MI, cert in social work; Columbia Univ Sch of Law, JD. **CAREER:** Lawson & Lawson Law Firm Washington, atty; DC Juvenile Ct, asso judge 1962-65. **ORGANIZATIONS:** Mem Pres's Commn on Equal Employment Opport 1962; pres vP Com on Crime DC 1965; UN Commn for Social Devel 1965-69; Pres's

Task Force on Urban Renewal 1969; Commn on Orgn of Govt of DC 1970; dir Nat Bk of Washington DC Tax Revision Com; Fed City Counc; Mayor's Com on Econ Devel Washington Urban Leag Housing Opport Counc of Met Washington; found trust Educ Found of Nat Council of Negro Women; founder Model Inner-City Comm Orgn. **BUSINESS ADDRESS:** 2101 "L" St NW, Ste 210, Washington, DC 20037.

LAWSON, QUENTIN ROOSEVELT
Government official, educator. **PERSONAL:** Born Jan 07, 1933; married Helen Louis Betts; children: Rosilend, Quentin II. **EDUCATION:** Wv State Coll, BA;Univ MD, MEd; Morgan State Coll, MSc; Inst, NSF; Morgan State, 1958; Vassar Coll, 1960; StateUniv Coll, 1962. **CAREER:** City of Baltimore, human devel dir present; Baltimore, former mayor; Baltimore City Schs MD State Dept of Edn, tchr unit head, unit prin, dir, dropout prevention program 1958-71; Accountability in the Inner City, cons; am psychol assn conf 1971; OH, FL, AL, cons, dropout prevention programs; Public Tech Inc, exec vice pres. **ORGANIZATIONS:** Pres PTA; Phi Delta Kappa; Gov Task Force State Sch Constrn; Mental Health Support System; mayor's rep Nat League of Cities; Cen MD Health Systems Agy; retail study Soc Serv Commn; John F Kennedy Inst for Handicapped Children; Med Eye Bank; United Fund CICHA; Bay Coll of MD; Dept of HEW; steering comMet Communications System Study; YMCA; pres Comm Orgn Notable Ams 1976-77; developed dropout prevention proposal 1st 10 funded by US Office of Edn. **BUSINESS ADDRESS:** Executive Vice President, Public Technology Inc, 1301 Pennsylvania Ave NW, Washington, DC 20004.

LAWSON, ROBERT L.
Educational administrator. **PERSONAL:** Born Feb 24, 1950, Gallipolis, OH; children: Robert L Jr. **EDUCATION:** Rio Grande Coll, BS 1973; Marshall Univ, MA 1978; Nova Univ, DEd expected 1988. **CAREER:** Gallia Acad HS, teacher 1973-76; Marshall Univ, admin asst 1977-83, dir of continuing ed 1984-. **ORGANIZATIONS:** Consult Continuing Ed/SUCCESS 1978-; speaker SUCCESS 1980-; mem Com Coll Council 1982-, Com Serv Roundtable 1983-; mem bd of dir Opportunity Indust Ctr1983-; chmn Affirmative Action Advisory Com 1984-; co-authur of "The Black Pursuit Study Guide"; tape published "The Power of Creative Genius"; authur of "The Cutting Edge, A Study Guide for Achievers". **HONORS/ACHIEVEMENTS:** Trophy for Oral Interpretation of Poetry OH Univ 1969; Outstanding Coll Athletes of Amer Rio Grande Coll 1970; Who's Who Among Students Rio Grande Coll 1973; Affirmative Action Plaque President's Cabinet/Marshall Univ 1984. **HOME ADDRESS:** PO Box 5524, Huntington, WV 25703. **BUSINESS ADDRESS:** Dir of Continuing Ed, Marshall University, Huntington, WV 25701.

LAWSON, WALTER I., JR.
Business executive. **PERSONAL:** Born May 30, 1950, Biloxi, MS; married Olive E Cason; children: Andrea, Maria, Denise. **EDUCATION:** Hampton Inst, BS 1972. **CAREER:** VA Nat Bank, vice pres present; Pontiac Motor Div GMC, supr production 1972. **ORGANIZATIONS:** Mem Norfolk Manpower Planning Council 1976-79; mem Citizens Adv Council Norfolk 1976-78; mem Alpha Phi Alpha Frat & Inc 1970; commodore club Norfolk C of C 1980 Sec Class of 1981 VA Banker's Sch of Bank MgmtUniv of VA Charlottesville 1979.

LAWSON, WILLIAM DANIEL
Educator. **PERSONAL:** Born Nov 05, 1948, Alpine, AL; married Nora Davenport; children: Sonya Danette, Nicole Danielle. **EDUCATION:** Knoxville Coll, BA 1964-68; Atlanta Univ, MA 1968-70; IA State Univ, PhD 1975-78. **CAREER:** AL State Univ instructor of soc 1971-74; USAF, race relations spec 1974-75; NC A&T State Univ, asst prof rural sociology 1978-79; AL State Univ, assoc prof of sociology 1979-85, chmn dept of sociology. **ORGANIZATIONS:** Consultant AL Center for Higher Educ 1982-83; licensure monitor Amer Sociological Assoc 1984-; polemarch Montgomery Alumni Chap Kappa Alpha Psi 1984-; pres Tuskegee Area Knoxville Coll Alumni Assoc 1984-; bd of dirs Montgomery Area Council on Aging 1985. **HONORS/ACHIEVEMENTS:** Amer Sociological Assn Fellow 1977-78; Kappa Man of the Year Kappa Alpha Psi Frat Inc 1985. **HOME ADDRESS:** 142 Elm Dr, Montgomery, AL 36117. **BUSINESS ADDRESS:** Chmn Dept of Sociology, Alabama State University, 915 S Jackson St, Montgomery, AL 36195.

LAWSON, WILLIAM EMMETT
Optometrist. **PERSONAL:** Born Nov 24, 1922, Detroit, MI; son of Dr William H Lawson (deceased) and Mrs Florence A Lewis-Lawson; children: Diane C Lawson-Taylor, William W. **EDUCATION:** IL College of Optometry, graduated 1943; Wayne State Univ, attended 1947. **CAREER:** Optometric Inst & Clinic of Detroit, co-fndr/bd mem/former pres 1965-; Ferris State Coll of Optometry, clinical assoc instr 1980; Private Practice, drof optometry. **ORGANIZATIONS:** Life mem Amer Optometric Assoc, MI Optometric Assoc charter mem contact lens section; mem Metro Detroit Optometric Soc; clinical assoc Optometric Extension Prog 1963 special section on children vision; mem White House Conference on children and youth 1970; charter mem 1979, honorary mem 1986 Lafayette Clinic Adv Council; mem Alpha Phi Alpha Frat, Detroit Bd of Commerce and Sports Comm; co-founder, charter mem, chmn, Debutante Ball Committee Cotillion Club 1949-50. **HONORS/ACHIEVEMENTS:** Detroit Public School Comm Serv & Human Relations Awd Region 8 1968; Comm Serv Awd Wayne Co Comm Coll 1979; Awd of Merit for Disting Serv Greater Christ Baptist Church 1981,84; Griffith Award, Optometric Institute and Clinic of Detroit 1988; Honorary Clan Chief, Kpella Tribe, West Africa 1974; Certificate, Diagnostic Pharmaceutical Aids 1984; World Contact Lens Conference, Tokyo. **MILITARY SERVICE:** USAF 1944. **BUSINESS ADDRESS:** Optometrist, 1450 Broadway, Detroit, MI 48226.

LAWSON-THOMAS, ALTHEAN SHANNON
Educator. **PERSONAL:** Born Jan 16, 1953, Ft Gaines, GA; married Eddie Walden Thomas; children: Shadrin, Jasil. **EDUCATION:** Hampton Univ, BA 1973; Univ of TN, MS 1975; Attended, Troy State Univ 1983-84. **CAREER:** Wallace State Comm Coll, counselor/instructor 1975-82, instructor 1982-. **ORGANIZATIONS:** Mem AL Personnel & Guidance Assoc 1975-82; pres Young Women's Serv Club 1977-79; chair Henry Co Bd of Educ Bi-racial Comm 1978-80; mem Natl Council of Negro Women 1979-; Delta Sigma Theta Sor Inc; sec Wallace Coll Educ Assoc 1986-. **HONORS/ACHIEVEMENTS:** Outstanding Young Women of America 1979-81. **BUSINESS ADDRESS:** Instructor in Psychology, Wallace State Community Coll, Napier Field, Dothan, AL 36303.

LAWSTON, MARJORIE GRAY
Clergyman. **PERSONAL:** Born Aug 26, 1928, Weakley Co Martin, TN; married Sylvester Ralph Gray; children: Michael. **EDUCATION:** Univ of TN at Martin, BS 1975. **CAREER:** Burdette Chapel United Meth Ch Memphis, pastor 1980-; Andrews United Meth Ch Memphis, pastor 1978-79; Union City Sch TN, tchr 1978-79; Key's Chapel Circuit Lexington TN, pastor 1975-78; Beaver Elem Schl Lexington TN, tchr 1975-78. **ORGANIZATIONS:** Sem Schlrshp Bd of Global Ministries United Meth Ch New York City 1979-80. **BUSINESS ADDRESS:** United Meth Church, 4953 Malone Rd, Memphis, TN 38118.

LAWYER, CYRUS J., III
Educator. **PERSONAL:** Born Sep 21, 1943, Vicksburg, MS; married Vivian Moore; children: Lenaye Lynne, Sonya Denise. **EDUCATION:** Tougaloo Clge, BS 1966; Bowling Green Univ, MS 1969; Univ Toledo, PhD 1974. **CAREER:** SBowling Green Univ, grad asst & tchr asst 1967-69; Univ Toledo, 1969-71; Univ Toledo, admin intern 1971-72, asst dean adj instr 1972-73, asst dean & housing dir 1973-75, sr prog assoc Inst for Srvs to Educ. **ORGANIZATIONS:** Mem Amer Chem Soc; Orgn Black Scientists; Amer Assc Univ Profs; Phi Delta Kappa; Assc Clge & Univ Housing Officers; mem Alpha Phi Alpha Frat; NAACP. **HONORS/ACHIEVEMENTS:** Outstanding Young Men Amer 1975. **BUSINESS ADDRESS:** 2001 S St NW, Washington, DC 20009.

LAWYER, VIVIAN (NEE MOORE)
Educational coordinator. **PERSONAL:** Born Jan 06, 1946, Cleveland; married Cyrus J Lawyer III; children: Lenaye Lynne, Sonya Alyse. **EDUCATION:** Bowling Green State Univ, BS 1967; Green State Univ, MEd 1968. **CAREER:** Natl Council Teachres Eng, coord human resources 1967-68; OH Assn Women Deans & Counselors 1968-; Bowling Green Sate Univ, asst dean students 1968-72. **ORGANIZATIONS:** OH Affirmative Action Officers Assc 1973-; Natl Assc Womens Deans, Admin & Cnslrs 1972-; Natl Council Negro Women 1972-; Delta Sigma Theta Sor Toledo Alumnae 1973-; bd trustees Toledo YWCA 1974-77; Lucas Ct Health Srv Comm NW OH Health Planning Assc 1971-72. **HONORS/ACHIEVEMENTS:** Dist Srv to Univ Award BGSU 1967; Delta Sigma Theta Midwest Region's Adv Award 1972; Who's Who Among Amer Women 1975. **BUSINESS ADDRESS:** Bowling Green StateUniv, 231 Administration Bldg, 901 Rye Beach Road, Huron, OH 44839.

LAYMON, HEATHER R.
Banker. **PERSONAL:** Born Nov 10, 1948; daughter of Ellis W Sealy and Beryl O Harris Sealy; married John Laymon, Dec 22, 1973; children: Shawn M Laymon, Nasya H Laymon. **EDUCATION:** Northeastern Univ, MA, BA, 1968-72; Natl School of Savings Banking, CT, 1978-80; Cambridge Coll, MA, MED, 1981-83. **CAREER:** Suffolk Franklin Savings Bank, Boston, MA, mgr, 1972-80; Mutual Bank for Savings, Boston, MA, asst treasurer, 1980-82; Bank of Boston, Boston, MA, asst vice pres, 1982-87; Boston Bank of Commerce, Boston, MA, vice pres, 1987-. **ORGANIZATIONS:** Mem, Boston Bankers Urban Forum, 1980-; trustee, Cambridge YWCA, 1983-87; pres, Boston & Vicinity Club of the Natl Assn of Negro Business & Professional Women, 1986-89; mem, Plan Giving Comm, Andover Newton Theological Seminary, 1988-; mem, Roxbury Multi Serv Center, 1988-;. **HONORS/ACHIEVEMENTS:** Pres Award, Natl Assn of Negro Business & Professional Women, 1988; Prof Award, Women Serv Club of Boston, 1988, Black Achiever's Award, YMCA, 1981. **BUSINESS ADDRESS:** Vice Pres, Dir of Business Devel, Boston Bank of Commerce, 110 Tremont St, Boston, MA 02108.

LAYMON, JOHN W.
Attorney. **PERSONAL:** Born Apr 26, 1945, Boston; married Heather Sealy; children: Shawn M M, Nasya H. **EDUCATION:** Howard Univ & Howard Univ Sch of Law, 1968 & 1971. **CAREER:** Proj Boston, legal asst 1971-73; Peter Dowd Esq Boston, supr atty 1973-; MA Defenders Comm, supr atty 1973-; Boston St Coll, asst prof 1975-; US Atty Dist of MA, asst atty 1977-82; Kressler Kressler & Pitnof, partner 1982-84; Dept of Elder Affairs Boston, hearing officer; private practice, atty 1984-. **ORGANIZATIONS:** Pres MA Black Lawyers Assn Boston; mem MA Bar Assn, US Dist Ct Dist of MA, US Court of Appeals for First Circuit, US Supreme Court; exec comm MA Legal Svcs; mem Plan for Action, Criminal Justice Sect Council of MBA; fellow MA Bar Found Boston MA. **BUSINESS ADDRESS:** 65 Franklin St, Ste 403, Boston, MA 02110.

LAYTON, WILLIAM W.
Director. **PERSONAL:** Born Jul 17, 1915, Hanover, VA; son of William Brown and Mary Sully Layton; married Phoebe Anderson; children: Andree, Mary, Serena. **EDUCATION:** Lincoln Univ, grad 1937; Fisk Univ, MI State Univ, post-grad study. **CAREER:** Columbus Urban League, indus relations dir 1943-51; Greater Muskegon Urban League, exec dir 1951-59; Lansing Fair Employment Practices Commn, reg dir 1959-64; MI OEO, assoc dir 1965; US Dept Agri, dir contract compliance 1965-71; EEO Bd Govs Fed Reserve System, dir 1971-78 (retired); Americana Originals, proprietor, lecturer, exhibitor, retail sales of framed original letters & documents. **ORGANIZATIONS:** Collector original abolitionist & civil war documents over 1500 items; collection on microfilm at Natl Archives; mem Muskegon Bd Social Welfare 1955-59; Mayor's Human Relations Comm 1962-64; founder 1st vice pres Greater Lansing Urban League 1964-65; pres Lansing Torch Club 1964; pres Muskegon Co Council Chs 1955; chap chmn Washington NAIRO 1969; mem Sigma Pi Phi; mem bd chmn Tri County VA 1984-86; mem bd Grafton School 1984-; bd mem, US Capitol Historical Society 1987-; bd mem, Shenandoah Arts Council 1987-. **HONORS/ACHIEVEMENTS:** Comm Serv Citation Lansing 1965; lectr & exhibitor including TV presentations US Abolitionist Movement & Mil Serv of Blacks in the Civil War; Awd of Merit Natl Afro-Amer Museum & Cultural Center 1982; Poet-Author of A Paul Robeson Retrospective and My Bridge. **BUSINESS ADDRESS:** Proprietor, American Originals, 1311 Delaware Ave SW, Washington, DC 20024.

LEA, JEANNE EVANS
Educational administrator. **PERSONAL:** Born Jul 02, 1931, Washington, DC; daughter of John Evans and Edna Jenkins Evans; divorced; children: Anne Richele Wharton, Jewa Maria. **EDUCATION:** Miner Teachers College, BS 1953; Trinity College, MAT 1970; Virginia Tech, EdD 1975. **CAREER:** Federal City College, curriculum specialist 1969-71, associate prof 1971-76, acting dean, continuing ed 1976-78; University of DC, prof 1976-, vice pres student affairs 1984-88; Edward Waters College, Academic Affairs, dean 1989-. **ORGANIZATIONS:** President Adult Ed Assn Metropolitan Wash 1976-77; co-founder Wash Women's Forum 1977; member Network on Female Offenders, Women's Bureau 1979-; vice president, Region II Amer Assn for Adult/Cont Ed 1983-85; board member Met Wash Assn

for Adult/Cont Ed 1983-85; bd mem/mem Wash Correctional Fdn; Potomac Chapter, LINKS, Inc 1984. **HONORS/ACHIEVEMENTS:** Outstanding Young Educators DC Jaycees 1968; Outstanding Educator Black Men's Salute to Black Women 1977; Co-host, Knowledge Series NBC-TV "Man to Woman" 1977 5 28 min segments 1977; "Continuing Ed for Women" 1981. **BUSINESS ADDRESS:** Edward Waters College, 1658 Kings Rd, Jacksonville, FL 32209.

LEACE, DONAL RICHARD
Educator. **PERSONAL:** Born May 06, 1939, Huntington, WV; married Jakki Hazel Browner. **EDUCATION:** Howard Univ, BFA 1966; George Washington Univ, MFA 1978; Georgetown Univ, MA, 1984. **CAREER:** The Howard Univ Players, pres 1965-66; Roanoke VA Total Action Against Poverty, dram/music consult 1966-67; Duke Ellington School of the Arts, chair theatre dept 1979-86; Duke Ellington School of Arts, teacher. **ORGANIZATIONS:** Mem Amer Fed of Music 161-710 1960-; mem Amer Fed of TV & Radio Artists 1979-; bd dir Tokama Theatre WA DC 1983-85. **HONORS/ACHIEVEMENTS:** Presidential Scholars Program Cert of Excellence, Presidential Scholars Prog Commission 1983; judge Helen Hayse Awds The Washington Theatre Awds Soc 1986-; solo recording artists Atlantic Records Co, Gateway Records, Franc Records Co. **HOME ADDRESS:** 3022 Porter St NW, Washington, DC 20008. **BUSINESS ADDRESS:** Teacher, Duke Ellington School of Arts, 3500 R St NW, Washington, DC 20007.

LEACOCK, FERDINAND S.
Physician. **PERSONAL:** Born Aug 08, 1934, New York, NY; children: 4 children. **EDUCATION:** Columbia Coll, BA 1956; Howard Medical Coll, MD 1960. **CAREER:** San Joaquin Hosp, rotating internship 1961; Ft Howard VA Hosp, residency 1961-65; Univ of MD Hosp, thoracic surgery residency 1967-69; UCLA Sch of Med, asst prof of surgery 1972-76; Martin Luther King Jr Gen Hosp, chief div thoracic & cardiovascular surgery 1973-74; Charles R Drew Postgrad Med Sch, asst prof of surgery 1972-76, v chmn dept of surgery 1974-75; CMA/CHA Educ Patient Care Audit Workshop Prog 1974-76; private practice, thoracic & cardiovascular surgery 1975-; Bon Secours Hosp, chief thoracic & cardiovascular surg 1987-; MD Gen Hosp, chief thoracic surg 1987-. **ORGANIZATIONS:** Mem Univ of MD Surgical Soc, Baltimore City Medical Soc, Amer Coll of Surgeons, Amer Coll of Chest Physicians, The Soc of Thoracic surgeons, The Baltimore Acad of Surgery. **HONORS/ACHIEVEMENTS:** 3 publications; 1 abstract. **MILITARY SERVICE:** AUS 2 yrs. **BUSINESS ADDRESS:** Chief Thoracic Surgery, Maryland Gen Hosp, 3502 West Rogers Ave, Baltimore, MD 21215.

LEACOCK, STEPHEN JEROME
Educator. **PERSONAL:** Born Oct 28, 1943; married Phyllis Otway; children: Natasha, Talitha, Baron. **EDUCATION:** CNAA, BA 1970; Garnett Coll, grad cert educ 1971; Council for Natl Acad Awds London, MA 1971; King's Coll, LLM 1971; Barrister Middle Temple 1972. **CAREER:** City Univ, visting lecturer 1971-72; SW London Coll, 1971-72; Hugh Wooding Law Sch, assoc turor 1974; Coll of Law DePaul Univ prof law. **ORGANIZATIONS:** Assoc mem British Inst of Mgmt; Inst of Export; hon mem British Inst of Securities Laws. **HONORS/ACHIEVEMENTS:** Publications include "Public Utility Regulation in a Developing Country"; "Lawyer of the Americas"; "Fundamental Breach of Contract & Exemption Clauses in the Commonwealth Caribbean"; Anglo-Amer Law Review; "Essentials of Investor Protection in Commonwealth Caribbean & US". **BUSINESS ADDRESS:** Professor of Law, DePaul University Law School, 25 E Jackson Blvd, Chicago, IL 60604.

LEAGUE, CHERYL PERRY
Equal opportunity manager. **PERSONAL:** Born Nov 29, 1945, New York, NY; daughter of Charles Smith and Freida Dean Smith; married Arthur League, Dec 27, 1983; children: Anthony, Robeson, Assata. **EDUCATION:** Merritt Coll, Oak, CA, AS, 1977; San Francisco State Univ, BA, 1979. **CAREER:** Legal Aid Soc, Alameda County, CA, contract compliance officer, beginning in 1975; US Dept of Commerce, Minority Business Development Agency, minority business program specialist, beginning in 1980; Management Professional Services, Oakland, CA, principle partner, beginning in 1982; Port of Oakland, CA, contract compliance officer, beginning in 1983, equal opportunity manager, beginning in 1986; founding mem of California Affirmative Action Council. **ORGANIZATIONS:** mem, Personal Mgmt Assoc of Aztlan, Natl Assoc for Female Exec Equal Right Advocates, Coalition on Civil Rights, Natl Council of Negro Women, Natl Assoc for the Advancement of Colored People, United Negro Coll Fund, Planning Committee for Maxwell Park Neighborhood Assoc, Claremont Middle Schools Parent Teachers Assoc, Coalition of Civil Rights, Amer Civil Liberties Union, National Forum of Black Public Admin, California Assoc of Affirmative Action Officers; pres, Bay Area Contract Compliance Officers Assoc. **HONORS/ACHIEVEMENTS:** Minority Advocate of the Year Award, US Dept of Commerce, San Francisco, CA, 1988; Special Recognition Award for the Port of Oakland for outstanding contribution to the minority business community, Minority Business Devel Agency, San Francisco, CA, 1988; Outstanding Achievement Award on Behalf of Minority Entrepreneurs, Minority Enterprise Devel Week Committee, Oakland, CA, 1988; Community Service Award for outstanding service to the city of Oakland and for valuable service to the profession of public admin, Oakland/San Francisco Bay Area Chapter of the Natl Forum for Black Public Admin, 1989. **BUSINESS ADDRESS:** Port of Oakland, 160 Franklin St, Oakland, CA 94607.

LEAK, LEE VIRN
Educator. **PERSONAL:** Born Jul 22, 1932, Chesterfield, SC; son of Robert L Leak and Lucille E Moore Leak; married Eleanor C Merrick; children: Alice Elizabeth, Lee Virn Jr. **EDUCATION:** SC State Coll, BS 1954; MI State U, MS 1959, PhD 1962. **CAREER:** MI State Univ, teaching asst cytology electron microscopist div biol sci; Brookhaven Natl Lab, rsch asst dept biol 1960; MI State Univ, rsch assoc biol sci 1961, asst prof biol sci 1962; Harvard Med School MA Gen Hosp, rsch fellow surgery 1962-64, asst surgery 1964, asst biol, asst surgery 1964, instr anatomy 1965-67; MA Gen Hosp, Shriners Burns Inst, dir lab biol structure 1967-70; Brookhaven Natl Lab, collabor biol 1968; Harvard Med School, asst prof anatomy 1968-70; Howard U, prof chmn rsrch prof; Howard Univ, rsch prof 1982-, dir cellular and molecular biology 1985-. **ORGANIZATIONS:** Asst prof 1968-71, prof, chmn anatomy 1971-81 Harvard U; sr investigator NIH 1982; mem biol dir to exec council Electron Microscopy Soc of Amer 1968-70; mem DC Anatomical Bd 1971-81; mem exec cncl WA Soc of Electron Microscopy 1971-74; mem Anatomical Training Comm Natl Inst of Gen Med Sci NIH 1972-73; mem biol & agr Natl Rsch Cncl Natl Acad of Sci 1972-75; mem anatomy test comm Ntl Bd of Med Examiners 1973-76; vice pres Howard Univ Chap Sigma Xi 1974-75; mem exec comm Assoc of Anatomy Chmn 1976-78; mem cancer biol & diagnosis bd sci couns Natl Cancer Inst NIH 1979-82; mem exec comm Amer Assoc of Anatomists 1980-84; mem panel on basic biomed sci Natl Rsch Cncl Ntl Acad of Sci 1980-85; mem adv bd lung diseases Natl Heart Lung & Blood Inst NIH 1982-86; mem Amer Assoc of Anatomists, Amer Physiol Sci, Amer Soc for Cell Biol, Amer Soc of Zoologists, Intl Soc of Lymphology, Marine Biol Lab, NYAS, NY Soc for Electron Microscopy, Tissue Culture Assoc, Microcirculatory Soc Inc, Soc for Devel Biology; ed bd Jrnl of Microvascular Rsch 1975-, Jrnl of Microcirculation 1980-; exec com NA Soc Lympholgy. **HONORS/ACHIEVEMENTS:** Cert for Scientific Exhibit 23rd Annual Meeting of the Electron Microscopy Soc of Am 1965; Medal Sci Exhib 23rd Annual Meeting of Electron Microscopy Socof Am 1968; Outstanding Eductors of Amer 1971, 1973; Outstanding Fac Rsch Awd Howard Univ 1976; Outstanding Faculty Awd Grad School of Arts & Sci Howard Univ 1979-80; Outstanding Faculty Rsch Awd Howard Univ, 1981; rsch grant support, Lymphatic Capillaries During Early Inflammation NIAID 1966-74, The Lymphatic Syst in Health & in Inflammation NIAID 1974-78, The Role of the Lymphatic System in Health & in Inflammation NIAID 1979-84, A Comparative Ultrastructural & Cytochem Study of Vertebrate Heart Tissue Amer Heart Assn 1967-70, Lymphatic Capillaries During Early Inflammation NIH Natl Heart Lung & Blood Inst 1970-75, Ontegeny, Ultrastructure & Function in the Lymphatic Syst Natl Heart Lung & Blood Inst NIH 1976-86; training grant support, Grad Training in the Anatomical Sci Natl Inst of Gen Med Sci Dept of Anatomy Coll of Med 1974-79, Multi-Disciplinary Biomed Rsch Training Natl Inst of Gen Med Sci Dept of Anatomy & Microbiology Coll of Med 1979-84; Adelle Melbourne Award, American Med Assn 1989. **MILITARY SERVICE:** AUS 1st lt 1954-56. **BUSINESS ADDRESS:** Research Professor, Howard University, College of Medicine, Anatomy Dept 520 "W" St NW, Washington, DC 20059.

LEAKE, WILLIE MAE JAMES
City official. **PERSONAL:** Born Mar 13, 1932, Philadelphia, PA; married Willie Ralph Leake. **EDUCATION:** Ekels Coll of Mortuary Science; Univ of Pittsburgh. **CAREER:** City Treasurer, City of Chester 1982; City Council, City of Chester 1983; Mayor City of Chester 1986. **ORGANIZATIONS:** Nat'l Funeral Dir & Embalmers Assoc,. **HONORS/ACHIEVEMENTS:** Delaware Cnty Womens Commission, Distinguished Leadership Awd 1986; Chester Scholarship Fund, Comm Service Awd 1983. **HOME ADDRESS:** 10th & Pusey St, Chester, PA 19013. **BUSINESS ADDRESS:** Mayor, Municipal Building, 5th and Welsh Sts, Chester, PA 19013.

LEAKS, ROOSEVELT (ROSEY)
Professional athlete. **PERSONAL:** Born Jan 31, 1953, Washington County. **EDUCATION:** School of Communications, Univ of TX, BS. **CAREER:** Baltimore Colts, football player 1975-79; Buffalo Bills. **ORGANIZATIONS:** Mem Friar SocUniv of TX. **HONORS/ACHIEVEMENTS:** Hon mem Big Bros of Austin Back of the year NCAA 1973; Amateur Athlete of the Year TX 1973; All Am at TX; 3rd Heisman Trophy Voting in jr yr; 2nd leading rusher in TX history; set SW conf rushing record jr season; set SWC record yards gained in one game 1973; All SWC sophomore & jr years; team co-capt sr yr. **BUSINESS ADDRESS:** 1 Bills Dr, Orchard Park, NY 14127.

LEAKS, SYLVESTER
Business executive. **PERSONAL:** Born Aug 11, 1927, Macon, GA; divorced; children: Gideon. **EDUCATION:** City Univ NY; Cambridge School of Radio Broadcasting; Dramatic Workshop. **CAREER:** Bedford Stuyvesant Restoration Corp Brooklyn, dir pub information 1969-73; Muhammad Speeks Newspaper Chicago, NY editor 1960-65; Afro-Amer Hist & Culture Brooklyn, dir 1965-68; dir, writer, dancer, specialist, biographer, playwright & screenwriter; Sylvester Leaks Associates Inc, pres. **HONORS/ACHIEVEMENTS:** Published numerous articles, poems, essays, short stories. **MILITARY SERVICE:** AUS 1946-47.

LEAL, CAROL ANN
Physician, psychiatrist. **PERSONAL:** Born Sep 17, 1941, New Orleans, LA. **EDUCATION:** LA State Univ, BS 1963; Howard Univ Coll of Med, MD 1967; Harlem Hosp Ctr, intern 1967-68. **CAREER:** Harlem Hosp Ctr, gen psychiatry resident 1968-71; Bellevue Psychiatric Hosp, child psychiatry resident 1971-73; Harlem Hosp Div of Child Psychiatry, staff psychist & dep chief 1973-83; NY Hosp Cornell Med Ctr, asst unit chief to unit chief; Psychiatry Coll of Physicians & Surgeons of Columbia Univ, asstclinical prof 1979-83; NY Hosp Cornell Med Ctr Westchester Div, asst unit chief; Cornell Univ Coll of Medicine Dept of Psychiatry, asst prof of psychiatry. **ORGANIZATIONS:** Diplomate Amer Bd of Psychiatry & Neurology in Gen Psychiatry 1973, 1974; candidate Columbia Univ Ctr for Psychoanalytic Training & Rsch 1971-79; mem AmerPsychiatric Assn 1971-. **HONORS/ACHIEVEMENTS:** Fellow Amer Acad of Child Psychiatry 1974-. **BUSINESS ADDRESS:** Asst Prof of Psychiatry, Cornell Univ, Coll of Med, Westchester Div 21, Bloomingdale Rd, White Plains, NY 10605.

LEAPHART, ELDRIDGE
Engineer. **PERSONAL:** Born Sep 02, 1927, Sims, NC; married Audra Lane; children: Eldridge, Jr, Eldon Gerrald. **EDUCATION:** Howard U, BS 1953; OH State U, 1964; UCLA, 1967; Air U, 1965, 1966, 1973. **CAREER:** TN Valley Authority, electrical engr 1953-55; Air Force Logistics Command 1955-58; Air Force Systems Command, electronics engr 1958-. **ORGANIZATIONS:** Mem Assn Old Crows 1962-; treas Kittyhawk Toastmasters Club 1108-40 1974-; cmn, supr com Bethel Bapt Fed Credit Union 1972-; supr Bethel Bapt Ch Sch 1969-70. **HONORS/ACHIEVEMENTS:** Air Force Systems Command Certificate Merit Award 1974. **MILITARY SERVICE:** USN 1945-47; USAR 2nd lt 1953-55. **BUSINESS ADDRESS:** Air Force Avionics Lab, Wright Patterson AFB, Dayton, OH 45433.

LEARY, JAMES E.
Clergyman. **PERSONAL:** Born Mar 08, 1935, Ashburn, GA; married Shirley E Fitzpatrick; children: Tamar, Tracy, Teresa. **EDUCATION:** Morris Brown Coll Atlanta, BA 1965; Andover Newton Theol Sch Newton Cntr, MDiv 1968. **CAREER:** First Bapt Ch Appomatox VA, pastorages 1960; Shilo Bapt Ch Milledgeville GA, 1961-63; Central Bapt Ch Norcross GA, 1963-65; Calvaray Bapt Ch Haverhill MA, 1965-67; Pond St Bapt Ch Providence RI, 1967-69; St Paul's Bapt Ch Richmond VA, 1969-; Sch of Theol VA Union U, asst to dean 1972-74. **ORGANIZATIONS:** Vp Am Bapt Black Churchmen 1970-71; pres Richmond Com of Black Churchmen 1973-76; bd mem Richmond Progress Assn for Econ Devel 1970-73; NeighborhoodLegal Aid Soc Inc 1973-; mem Minister's Conf of Richmond & Vicinity 1969-; Richmond Clergy Area Assn 1969-; Nat Com of Black Churchmen 1969-; pres St Paul's Housing Devel Corp 1970-; mem Alpha Kappa Mu Honor Soc. **HONORS/ACHIEVEMENTS:** Grad cum laude from coll; Outstanding Young Men of Am Award 1970

ed Tion; Who's Who in Religion 1974 edition. **MILITARY SERVICE:** USAF 1954-58. **BUSINESS ADDRESS:** 2600 E Marshall St, Richmond, VA 23223.

LEATHERMAN, OMAR S., JR.
Automobile dealerf automotive dealership. **CAREER:** South Boulevard Chrysler-Plymouth, Inc, Charlotte NC, chief executive, 1988—. **BUSINESS ADDRESS:** South Boulevard Chrysler-Plymouth, Inc, 7725 South Blvd, Charlotte, NC 28217. *

LEATHERWOOD, LARRY LEE
Appointed official. **PERSONAL:** Born Sep 07, 1939, Peoria, IL; married Martha; children: Jeffrey, Stacy. **EDUCATION:** Kellogg Comm Coll, AA 1967; Western MI Univ, BS 1969, Masters of Publ Admin 1982. **CAREER:** Battle Creek Area Urban League, exec dir 1970-73; MI Dept of Commerce, spec asst 1973-77; MI State Minority Bus Office, dir 1977-83; MI Dept of Transportation, liaison officer 1983-85, deputy dir for admin 1985-. **ORGANIZATIONS:** Vice-chmn Lansing Urban League 1982-83; chmn Minority Tech Council of MI 1983-; vice-chmn State Advisory Council for Voc Ed; mem Conf of Minority Trans Officials, Amer Public Works Assoc; Board of Lansing Opportunities Industralization Center. **HONORS/ACHIEVEMENTS:** Listed in Who's Who in Voc Ed 1980; Man of the Year Natl Assoc of Black Women Entrepreneur 1980; Presidential Small Business Recognition 1980; MI Small Business Advocate 1985; wall of distinction Selected Western Univ and Alumni Assoc 1986; Recognition by the MI Council of NAACP Branches for Contributions to Black Economic Development 1986. **MILITARY SERVICE:** USAF sgt 4 yrs. **BUSINESS ADDRESS:** Deputy Dir, Michigan Dept of Transport, PO Box 30050, 425 W Ottawa, Lansing, MI 48909.

LEATHERWOOD, ROBERT P.
Advertising executive. **PERSONAL:** Born Jun 10, 1920, Forrest City, AR; married Pauline; children: 1 Stepdaughter. **EDUCATION:** FiskUniv Nashville, BA 1942; Wayne StateUniv Detroit, marketing courses 1957-58. **CAREER:** MI Chronicl Pub Co Detroit, advertising exec 1945-59; Seymour Leatherwood Cleveland Detroit 1959-64; aide ot Congressman Diggs; Leatherwood Co, 1964-. **ORGANIZATIONS:** Founder Detroit Chapter Nat Asso Market Dev; consult Negro Manufacturers Dist Br Asso Detroit; consult MI State Senator Arthur Cartwight 1975. **HONORS/ACHIEVEMENTS:** Pub numerous articles; NAMD honor 1974. **BUSINESS ADDRESS:** PO Box 608, Detroit, MI 48206.

LEAVELL, ALLEN LAVELLE
Professional athlete. **PERSONAL:** Born May 27, 1957, Muncie, IN. **EDUCATION:** Okla City Univ, 1975-79. **CAREER:** Houston Rockets, guard 1979-. **HONORS/ACHIEVEMENTS:** Chosen to 2nd All-Rookie team; 1st team by Bsktbl Digest. **BUSINESS ADDRESS:** Houston Rockets, The Summit, Ste 510, Houston, TX 77046.

LEAVELL, DOROTHY R.
Publisher, editor. **PERSONAL:** Born Oct 23, 1944, Pine Bluff, AR; widowed; children: Antonio, Genice. **EDUCATION:** RooseveltUniv IL, 1962. **CAREER:** Crusader Newspaper, publisher ed; Holy Name of Mary Sch Bd, pres. **ORGANIZATIONS:** Past bd dir mem Washington park YMCA 1974; past asst sec Nat Newspaper Pub Assn 1976; sec PUSH; comm div bd mem Directions Schlshp Found. **HONORS/ACHIEVEMENTS:** YMCA Aw; PUSH Aw; Holy Name of Mary Awd. **BUSINESS ADDRESS:** Gary Crusader, 1549 Broadway, Gary, IN 46407.

LEAVELL, WALTER F.
Educator. **PERSONAL:** Born May 19, 1934; married Vivian; children: Pierce, Pierre. **EDUCATION:** Univ of Cincinnati College of Pharmacy, BS 1957; Meharry Medical Coll, MD 1964; Univ of Cincinnati Coll of Law, Scholar-in-Residence 1981. **CAREER:** Cincinnati General Hosp, assoc chief of staff 1977-79, assoc administrator for professional affairs 1977-79; SUNY Upstate Medical Ctr Coll of Medicine, assoc dean 1971-75, vice dean and tenured assoc prof of medicine 1975-82; Meharry Medical Coll, dean school of medicine and dir medical affairs Hubbard Hosp 1982-. **ORGANIZATIONS:** Consultant AAMC on Minority Affairs 1972-; mem AAMC/GSA Steering Comm 1974-; natl chairperson AAMC/GSA Minority Affairs Section 1976-; consultant EDUCOM 1979-; mem Hubbard Hospital Attending Staff 1982-; mem Council of Deans 1982-; mem adv bd Natl Fund for Medical Educ 1983-; mem AAMC Ad Hoc MCAT Review Comm 1985-; mem AAMC Spring Meeting Program Comm 1985-; mem LCME Accreditation Review Team Council of Free Standing Medical Schools 1985-; mem Amer, Natl, Cincinnati Medical Assocs; mem Natl Assoc of Medical Minority Educators; mem Amer Assoc of Medical Colleges. **HONORS/ACHIEVEMENTS:** AAMC Service Recognition Awd 1979; listed in Who's Who in Amer 1984; NAMME Presidential Citation 1985. **MILITARY SERVICE:** USAF major.

LEBER, MARIANN C.
Nursing administrator. **PERSONAL:** Born Oct 01, 1921, Hamtramck, MI; divorced. **EDUCATION:** Wayne State U, BS 1951; Harlem Sch of Nursing NYC, grad 1943. **CAREER:** Detroit Gen Hosp, gen staff nrse 1944; hd hosp nrse 1949; nrsng supr 1955; asst dir of nrses 1963; Detroit Gen Hosp, dir of nurses; Wayne St UColl Nrsng, adj instr 1970. **ORGANIZATIONS:** Advsry Com Wayne Co Comm Coll Dept Nrsng; vol tutrng serv nrsng schl grads; Advis Com Highland Park Comm Coll Dept of Nurs. **HONORS/ACHIEVEMENTS:** Elected to Hamtramck Hall of Hon 1977. **BUSINESS ADDRESS:** Detroit Gen Hosp, 1326 St Antoine, Detroit, MI 48226.

LECESNE, TERREL M.
Councilman. **PERSONAL:** Born Apr 13, 1939, New Orleans; married Gale H; children: Terrel, Jr, Haydel. **EDUCATION:** Xavier U, BA 1961; Eastern MI U, MA 1967, EdS 1973. **CAREER:** City of Inkster, MI, former mayor, counclmn; Elem Sch Prin, 1968-; Fr HS, couns 1966-68; Tchr, 1961-66. **ORGANIZATIONS:** Pres Romulus Assn of Sch Bldg Adminstrs; past pres Inkster Jaycees; Dearborn-Inkster Human Relat Counc. **HONORS/ACHIEVEMENTS:** Named outst yng man of yr Inkster Jaycees 1970. **BUSINESS ADDRESS:** 35408 Beverly Rd, Inkster, MI 48141.

LECHEBO, SEMIE
Educational administrator. **PERSONAL:** Born Apr 05, 1935, Addis Ababa, Ethiopia;married Sandra Nettles-Lechebo; children: Monique Thomas, Shena Thomas, Meskeram. **EDUCATION:** Univ of WI, BS 1964, MS 1967; SUNY at Albany, EdS 1975, EdD 1975; Harvard Univ, Higher Educ Mgmt diploma summer 1982. **CAREER:** Haile Selassie I Day School (Addis Ababa), School admin 1956-60; Ministry of Educ (Addis Ababa), dir 1964-66; Milwaukee Public School, teacher 1967-68; Jimma Teacher Training, dir 1968-69; College of Teacher Educ (Addis Ababa), vice principal 1969-71; Comm Agency in Albany, rsch fellowship 1975; NY State Educ Dept, rsch assoc 1976-77; SUNY at Albany, coord of tutorial prog 1976; SUNY Coll at Brockport, coord of academic affairs 1977-. **ORGANIZATIONS:** Consultant NY Educ Dept 1975-76, Rochester City School Dist 1978-82; mentoring doctoral students SUNY Albany, Buffalo, Brockport 1976-86; mem Faculty Senate SUNY Brockport 1980-86; mem Coll Affirmative Action Bd SUNY Brockport 1982-83; chair Rochester Inst of Tech Adv Bd on Minority and Female Recruitment 1984-86; mem Educ Task Force County of Monroe Human Relations Commn 1985-; supervising interns SUNY Brockport 1986; chair mentoring programs Urban League of Rochester 1986; mem Coll Academic Council SUNY Brockport 1986-. **HONORS/ACHIEVEMENTS:** UNESCO Fellowship 1967-68; AFGRAD Fellowship 1971-75; Outstanding Award for Service 1984-85; Black Scholars Sponsor Award, Urban League of Rochester, 1985; Naturalized United States Citizen 1985. **HOME ADDRESS:** 14 Teakwood Lane, Fairport, NY 14450. **BUSINESS ADDRESS:** Dir/Coord Acad Affairs, SUNY Brocksport, Educational Opportunity Ctr, 305 Andrews St, Rochester, NY 14604.

LECOMPTE, PEGGY J. (NEE LEWIS)
Education, TV host. **PERSONAL:** Born Oct 07, 1938, St Louis, MO; daughter of Obadiah Lewis, Sr and Winnie Penguite Lewis; married Larry Ferdinand LeCompte Sr, Nov 22, 1962; children: Larry F Jr. **EDUCATION:** Lincoln Univ, BS 1960; Sangamon State, MS 1985; Natl Coll of Educ, Evanston IL, MS 1989. **CAREER:** E St Louis School Dist 189, educator 1962-67; USAF, librarian 1968; E St Louis School Dist 1889, educator 1970-; Channel 10 E St Louis, TV host 1983-; Alpha Kappa Alpha Sor, natl sec; Natl Educ TV Network, vice-president academic prod. **ORGANIZATIONS:** Sec Ed Adv Found 1982-; mem Boys Club of Amer Planning Commission 1985-; bd pres Boys Club of E St Louis 1978-; pres/ organizer Jopladies of Distinction;Natl Workshop Chmn Top Ladies of Distinction, Inc; Language Arts Dept Head, District 189, 1988-; Natl Parliamentarian, Top Ladies of Distinction, Inc 1987-91; chairman Nominating Committee, bd of dir Girl Scouts of Amer 1990. **HONORS/ACHIEVEMENTS:** Boys Club Medallion Boys Clubs of Amer 1984; Youth Awd YMCA 1984; Media Awd Shriners Aahmes Temple 112 1983; Leadership Alpha Kappa Alpha Sor 1983; Teacher of the Year Awd Zeta Phi Beta Sor 1977; Outstanding Serv Awd NAACP E St Lous 1978; Key to the City E St Louis 1978-79; Most Outstanding Jill Past Pres Awd Jack & Jill of Amer In E St Louis 1980; YMCA Communications Awd 1986; Boys Clubs of America Natl Serv Medallion; Metro St Louis Most Outstanding Speaker Toastmasters 1982; Top Lady of Distinction of Area III 1986; Master Teacher School District 189, 1988; Protocol: A Guide. **HOME ADDRESS:** 212 Bunker Hill Rd, Belleville, IL 62221.

LEDAY, JOHN AUSTIN
Business executive. **PERSONAL:** Born Sep 11, 1931, Basile, LA; married Christine Sandoval; children: Anna, Angela. **CAREER:** Southend Janitorial Supply Inc, owner/pres 1961-; People Chem Co, sales mgr 1954-61, warehouseman 1948-52. **ORGANIZATIONS:** Pres, Amer Enterprises Inc; pres, MTM Corp; mem, Natl Assn of Black Mfrs; Sanitary Supply Assn of Southern California; Los Angeles C of C; bd of dir Black Businessmen's Assn of Los Angeles; exec comm, Los Angeles Office Urban Devel; commissioned by Gov Brown Adv Council on Econ Business Devel State of California, 1978; dir, Equip Bank; bd dir, Pickett Enterprises; Natl Community Business Devel. **HONORS/ACHIEVEMENTS:** Businessman of Year Award, BBA, 1977; Top 100 Black Businesses in US, Black Enterprise, 1974. **MILITARY SERVICE:** AUS 1952-54. **BUSINESS ADDRESS:** 11422 S Broadway, Los Angeles, CA 90061.

LEDBETTER, ROBERT L.
Football coach. **PERSONAL:** Born Sep 24, 1934, Tupelo, MS; married Delores Singletary; children: Donnie. **EDUCATION:** Geo Wash Carver, 1952; MS Indsl Coll, BS 1960; S IL U, MS 1970; So IL U, 50 hrs toward doctorate. **CAREER:** Booker T Wash High Memphis, offensive line coach 1960-61; Corry Jr High Memphis, head football & trach coach & athletic dir 1961-63; Hamilton H S Memphis, head football & track coach & Athletic dir 1963-68; So ILUniv Carbondale IL, head freshman coach & WR varsity 1968-72; Norfolk State Coll Norfolk, head football coach 1972-74; New Orleans Saints, offiensive backfield coach. **ORGANIZATIONS:** Am Football Coaches Assn 1965-; AAHPER 1961-74; Lifetime Sports 1961-74; Nat Black Sports Found; All-Army 1956; All Conf Tackle 1957-60; chmn phys ed dept Memphis City Sch 1963-65. **MILITARY SERVICE:** AUS master sgt 1952-57. **BUSINESS ADDRESS:** 6928 Saints Dr, Metairie, LA 70003.

LEDBETTER, RUTH POPE
Health services consultant, nurse. **PERSONAL:** Born in Indianapolis, IN; married Wilbur E Ledbetter (deceased); children: Mark F (deceased). **EDUCATION:** Indiana Univ, Bloomington, pre-nursing, 1939-41; Amer Univ, Washington, BSNE, 1958; Marion County Gen Hospital, RN, 1958; Catholic Univ UDC, grad studies, 1974-80. **CAREER:** St Elizabeth Hospital, supvr training instructor, 1950-69; Area B Alcoholism Center, mental health nurse specialist, 1969-70; Congress Heights Health Center, community mental health specialist, 1970-73; Employee Counseling Serv, sr comm mental health specialist, 1973-76; Dept of Human Resources, trans analysis instr 1975-77; DHR Bureau of Alcohol RX, state prevention coord, 1976-80; Woodson Sr High, sex educ, alcohol, drug abuse, 1978-80; Trifax Corp, dir research & devel. **ORGANIZATIONS:** Speakers bureau Chi Eta Phi Sor Inc; 2nd vice pres, Amer Assn Black Women Entrepreneurs; certified sex educ; past pres, Hughes Mem Toastmistress Club. **HONORS/ACHIEVEMENTS:** Incentive Serv Award, DHR, 1971; Mayors Serv Award, Dist of Columbia, 1980; Outstanding Achievement Award CIC Alcoholism Program, 1980; Dedicated Serv Award, Dist of Columbia Task Force on Alcoholism, 1981; Outstanding Comm Serv, Woodson Sr High, 1981; Cert of Recognition for Outstanding Serv to the Ward 7 Community from Councilmen HR Crawford, 1984; Spirit of Business Award Amer Assn of Black Women Entrepreneurs Inc, 1985. **HOME ADDRESS:** 72-54th St SE, Washington, DC 20019. **BUSINESS ADDRESS:** Vice President Clinical Services, Trifax Corp, 4121 Minnesota Ave NE, Washington, DC 20019.

LEDE, NAOMI W.
Educator. **PERSONAL:** Born Mar 22, 1934, Huntsville, TX; children: Susan, Paul. **EDUCATION:** Bradley U, BA, MA; Mary Allen Coll; TX So U;Univ TX, EdD 1979. **CAREER:** Lifson Wilson & Ferguson Houston; Survey Research Ctr Ann Arbor; Juvenile Delinquency Survey Univ Houston; Race Relations Inst Survey Fisk Univ Nashville; Reg Transportation Study Arlington TX; Consumer Opinion Inst NY; SRDS DATA Inc NY;

Batten Barton Drustine & Orborne NY; Louis Harris & Asso; Inst for Social Research Univ SC; Natl Urban League St Louis; St Louis Urban Leauge, dir research; St Louis Univ; lecturer; Washington Univ; Urban Intern Arlington TX; City of St Louis, program analyst & research cons; Bishop Coll Dallas TX, asst prof & dir reseach. **ORGANIZATIONS:** Mem Amer AssoUniv Prof; Nat Council ofUniv Research Administrators; Asso Study Negro Life & Hist; TX Asso Coll Tchrs; Nat Asso Social Science Tchrs;Am Sociological Soc; Research & Consult Dalls Urban League & Dallas Negro C of C; Soc Study Negro in Dentistry; Delta Sigma Theta Sor; Iota Phi Lambda BusSor; World Future Soc; Soc Research Administrators; Council ofUniv Inst Urban Affairs; bd mem Urban Affairs Corp; Transportation Research Bd; Nat Acad Political & Social Sci; Smithsonian Inst; asso mem AIP; State Educ Comm AIP; mem Mayor's Manpower Adv Council. **HONORS/ACHIEVEMENTS:** Who's Who Among Am Coll Student Leaders 1953; one of outstanding personalities of S; received special recognition for participation in program Operation Champ from Vice Pres Hubert Humphrey; publ "Extensive Research in Trans Planning & Citizen Participation/mental Hlth Services/ feasibility of Housing". **BUSINESS ADDRESS:** Urban Resources Ctr, TX So Univ 3201 Wheeler, Houston, TX 77004.

LEDEE, ROBERT
Deputy chief. **PERSONAL:** Born Aug 20, 1927, Brooklyn, NY; married Victoria Marzan; children: Yvonne Alvarez, Robert Jr, Reginald, Anthony. **EDUCATION:** John Jay Coll of Criminal Justice, AS 1971; BA 1973; MPA 1976; Fed Bur of Narcotics Training Sch, grad 1967; BBI Nat Acad 1968. **CAREER:** Sea Gate NY Harbor Police Dept, chief 1979-; New York City Housing Police Dept, dep chief 1970-78; insp 1970; dep insp 1967-70; capt 1964-67; lt 1960-64; sgt 1958-60; apptd 1955;Fed Funded Comm Serv Ofcr Prgm, adminstr; Hispanic Law Enforcement Training Inst of Justice, cons; New York City Dept of Personnel, cons. **ORGANIZATIONS:** Guest lctr FBI Nat Acad; rep Housing Pol Dept; 1st Nat Symposium on Law Enforcement Tech 1967; 13th Annueal Inst on Polic & Comm MI StaeUniv 1967; Crive Prevention Sem 1968; Insterst Conf on Delinq Control 1965; adminstr Model Cities Comm Serv Ofcr Prgm. **HONORS/ACHIEVEMENTS:** 1st black mem to hold rank of lt, capt, dep insp, dep chief New York City Housing Police Dept; 3 dept commendations for outst police work; awards from, Upper Pk Ave Bapt Ch 1963; Fedn of Negro Civil Serv Orgns 1964; Bronx Dective Unite 1965; Counc of Police Orgns 1966; Hispanic Soc 1966, 1970; Anti-Crime Com 1969; Grand Counc of Hispanci Soc 1971; Nat Police Ofcrs Assn 1972; Comm Relat Unit 1973; NY Club 1974; John Jay Coll Alumni Assn 1976; Nat Conf of Christians & Jews 1977; autor article FBI Bull 1975; manual High Rise Policing Tech US Merchant Marine 1945-55. **BUSINESS ADDRESS:** 216 E 99th St, New York, NY 10029.

LEDOUX, JEROME G.
Theologian. **PERSONAL:** Born Feb 26, 1930, Lake Charles, LA. **EDUCATION:** Divine Word Sem, Ordained 1957; Ponitifical Gregorian Univ Rome, Italy, MST 1961, Dr of Ch Law 1961. **CAREER:** Divine Word Theol Bay St Louis MS, prof of Moral Theol & Canon Law 1961-67; MS History Divine Word HS Sem, instr English civics 1967-69; Xavier UnivNew Orleans, 1st black chpln the only predominantly black Cath Univ in the US 1969-71; Xavier Univ, assoc prof of Theol 1971-; Author, weekly synd colmn carried in 6 cath diocesan papers & 3 black weeklies; Author, montly clmn in natl cath paper. **ORGANIZATIONS:** Bd mem of Ministries to Blacks in Higher Edn. **BUSINESS ADDRESS:** XavierUniv, 7325 Palmetto St, New Orleans, LA 70125.

LEDUFF, STEPHANIE CARMEL
Marketing director publishing company. **PERSONAL:** Born Apr 30, 1953, Columbus, OH; daughter of Dallas Winkfield and Esther Winkfield; children: Eric Jason Wallace. **EDUCATION:** Ohio State Univ, BS 1975; Attended, Harvard Univ 1981-82, MIT 1981-82. **CAREER:** Community Action Agency New Orleans, dir of program planning & develop; Real Estate Publication, managing editor 1984-86; News-Press Publishing Co, marketing dir. **ORGANIZATIONS:** Mem FL Public Relations Assoc 1986-87, Evaluation Rsch Soc 1986-87, Intl Newspaper Mktg Assoc 1986-87; bd mem Barbara Mann Performing Arts Ctr 1986-87, Abuse Counseling & Treatment Ctr 1987; bd of directors, Lee Mental Health. **BUSINESS ADDRESS:** Marketing Dir, News-Press Publishing Co, 2442 Anderson Ave, Fort Myers, FL 33901.

LEE, AARON
Business executive. **PERSONAL:** Born Aug 29, 1948, Hinds Co, MS; married Frances Jackson; children: Aaron Brennan. **EDUCATION:** Utica Jr Coll, AA 1970; Jackson State Univ, BS 1975, MS 1976. **CAREER:** Major Associates Construction Co, estimator 1975-77; Natl Business League, construction mgr 1977-80; Town of Edwards, alderman 1977-, fed prog coord 1982-; Jackson State Univ, super building serv 1981-83; asst dir physical plant 1983-. **ORGANIZATIONS:** Mem Phi Beta Sigma Frat 1976-; mem bd of dirs NAACP Bolton-Edwards Branch 1981-; mem Amer Mgmt Assn 1984-. **HONORS/ACHIEVEMENTS:** Outstanding Achievement in Public Serv MS Valley State Univ Social Sci Dept 1977; Outstanding Dedicated Serv Natl Business League 1980; Outstanding YoungMan of Amer-Outstanding Young Men of Amer 1984. **MILITARY SERVICE:** AUS sgt 1st class 14 yrs; Meritorial Serv Awd USAR 1978. **HOME ADDRESS:** PO Box 88, Edwards, MS 39066.

LEE, AFTON M., SR.
Businessman. **PERSONAL:** Born Jun 19, 1898, Eufaula, AL; widowed; children: Afton M, Jr, Arhodia (johnson), Myrtle (tinsley), Thelma (clark), Reginald Damon, Loretta (jones), Robert Melvin. **CAREER:** Real estate; Afton M Lee Grocery Store, merchatn. **ORGANIZATIONS:** Dir, vice pres Citizens Fed Savs & Loan Assn 1957; bd dirs Lake Shore Hosp; mem Homewood City Council. **BUSINESS ADDRESS:** 2562 S 18, Birmingham, AL.

LEE, ALLEN FRANCIS, JR.
Educator, scientist. **PERSONAL:** Born Apr 12, 1943, Notasulga, AL; married Lula M Wheat; children: Allen F III, Aryanna F. **EDUCATION:** Tuskegee Inst AL, DVM 1967; Univ of GA Athens, PhD 1978. **CAREER:** Univ of GA, post-doctoral rsch asst 1967-69, rsch assoc 1969-71; Emory Univ, NIH spl post-doctoral fellow 1971-72; Univ of GA, instr 1972-73; LA StateUniv, assoc prof 1973-. **ORGANIZATIONS:** Mem Amer Vet Med Assn 1967-; mem Amer Soc of Vet Physiologists & Pharmacologists 1969-; mem AAAS; mem Kappa Alpha Psi Frat 1965-; mem Amer Radio Relay League 1977-; bd dir Campus Fed Credit Union 1978-; bd of dir Kenilworth Civic Assn 1980-. **HONORS/ACHIEVEMENTS:** Schol in Vet Medicine Tuskegee Inst 1965; Outstanding Sr Vet Student Womens Aux AVMA 1967; NIH Post Doctoral Fellowship Emory Univ 1971; disertation "Evaluation of Ulnar Nerve Conductio Velocity in the Dog" Univ of GA 1978; researcher nerve/muscle physiology electromyography. **BUSINESS ADDRESS:** Associate Professor, LA StateUniv, School Vet Med, Dept Physiology Pharm & Tox, Baton Rouge, LA 70803.

LEE, ANDRE L.
Educational administrator. **PERSONAL:** Born Aug 14, 1943, Detroit, MI; children: Andre, Bryan, Tracey, Robin. **EDUCATION:** MI State Univ, BS 1966; Cornell Univ, MPA 1972; Nova Univ, DPA 1978. **CAREER:** Highland Park Gen Hosp MI, dir 1972-76; Sidney Sumby Hosp MI, dir 1976-78; St Joseph Hosp Ft Wayne IN, asst dir 1978-81; Hubbard Hosp TN, dir 1981-. **ORGANIZATIONS:** Pres Natl Assoc of Health Serv Exec 1985-87; state dir Amer Acad Med Admin IN & TN 1983-85; chmn Mgmt Housing Scholarship Comm; mem Alpha Phi Alpha, NAACP; tech Sinai Hosp Detroit 1966-67; propr Health Care Fin Sys; mem Amer Professional Mgmt Ltd, Amer Coll of Hosp Admin, Amer Publ Health Assoc, Amer Acad of Med Admin, MI Publ Health Assoc; bd mem Comprehensive Health Ctr, Model Neighborhood Health Ctr, Resd Manpower Ctr,, MI C of C Ed Sub-Com, Reg Emergency Room Task Force, Cty Emergency Room Task Force. **HONORS/ACHIEVEMENTS:** Publ over 60 articles; COGME Fellowship Awd 1970-72. **MILITARY SERVICE:** AUS capt 2 yrs active, 4 yrs reserve. **BUSINESS ADDRESS:** President, Budget Medical Inc, 1201 Division St, Nashville, TN 37203.

LEE, ANDREA
Writer. **PERSONAL:** Born 1953, Philadelphia, PA. **EDUCATION:** Harvard University, MA. **CAREER:** Writer; staff writer for New Yorker magazine, New York NY. **HONORS/ACHIEVEMENTS:** American Book Award nomination, 1981, for Russian Journal; Jean Stein Award, American Academy and Institute of Arts and Letters, 1984. **BUSINESS ADDRESS:** New Yorker, 25 West 43rd St, New York, NY 10036. *

LEE, AUBREY W.
Banking officer. **PERSONAL:** Born Oct 26, 1934, Huntington, WV; married Jeane Hill; children: Aubrey Jr, David, Mark. **EDUCATION:** WV State Coll, BA 1955; Marshall U, MA 1956;Univ Wis Grad Sch Banking, Diploma 1969. **CAREER:** GM Bldg Office Nat Bank of Detroit, teller br mgr reg mr officer in charge of minority commercial lending group vice pres commercial lending officer 1957-. **ORGANIZATIONS:** Asso mem Nat Bankers Asso; mem Urban Bankers Forum; Booker T Washington Businessmen's Asso; mem Detroit Bd Commerce; NAACP; friends of AMISTAD; adv bd MI Inter-Asso Black Business & Eng Students. **HONORS/ACHIEVEMENTS:** Who's Who in Midwest; distinguished serv award WilberforceUniv Detroit Alumni Chpt; Professional Men's distinguished serv award Huntington WV; Nat Honor Soc; Pi Sigma Alpha Honor Frat. **MILITARY SERVICE:** AUS capt 1956-64. **BUSINESS ADDRESS:** Troy Chamber of Commerce, 4555 Corporate Drive #300, Troy, MI 48098.

LEE, BERNARD SCOTT
Government administrator. **PERSONAL:** Born Oct 02, 1935, Norfolk, VA; children: Kincherlow S, Chiquita V, Bernadette L, Toinette D, Bertha T. **EDUCATION:** Howard Univ Divinity Sch, MDiv 1985. **CAREER:** SCLC, exec vice pres 1973-77; US Environmental Protection Agency, spec assist 1977-79; Gethsemane Baptist Church Washington, assoc minister 1978-82; US Comm Serv Admin, spec assist 1980-81; DC Govt, special assist to the mayor. **ORGANIZATIONS:** Asst pastor Trinity Baptist Church NE 1982-. **HONORS/ACHIEVEMENTS:** Rosa Parks Award SCLC 1976. **MILITARY SERVICE:** USAF A/2C served 4 years; Service Medal 1953. **BUSINESS ADDRESS:** Special Assistant to the Mayor, Dist Columbia Government, 1350 E St NW, Washington, DC 20004.

LEE, BERTRAM M.
Business executive. **PERSONAL:** Born Jan 21, 1939, Lynchburg, VA; son of William T Lee Sr and Helen Harris Lee; married Laura Murphy; children: Paula, Elaine. **EDUCATION:** North Central Coll, BA 1961; Roosevelt Univ, graduate studies 1963-65. **CAREER:** Various city agencies in Chicago, dir 1961-67; OIC of Greater Boston, exec dir 1967-68; EG & G of Roxburgy, Inc, gen mgr & vice pres 1968-69; Dudley Station Corp, president 1969-81; BML Assoc, Inc, president 1969-; New England TV Corp, president 1982-86; Albimar Mgmt Inc, treas 1983-; Mountaintop Ventures Inc, treas 1984-; Kellee Communications Group Inc, pres 1986-; BML Associates Inc, pres. **ORGANIZATIONS:** Boston Bank of Commerce, chairman; Natl Assoc of Broadcasters, copyright committee; Sportsmens Tennis Club, advisory board; Martin Luther King, Jr Center for Non-Violent Social Change, Inc, board of trustees; Convention and Tourist Bureau of Greater Boston, director; Jackie Robinson Foundation, director; Jobs Clearing House, mem; Natl Assn of Sickle Cell Inc, dir 1987-; Congressional Black Caucus Foundation 1987-. **HONORS/ACHIEVEMENTS:** NAACP, Image Award 1982; American Heritage & Freedom Award 1983; New England Telephone/ Minority Management Assoc, Recognition Award 1983. **MILITARY SERVICE:** US Army, 1963-65. **BUSINESS ADDRESS:** Chairman, BML Associates Inc, 60 State St, Ste 550, Boston, MA 02109. *

LEE, CHANDLER BANCROFT
Automobile dealer. **CAREER:** Chandler Lee Motors, Inc, Southern Pines, NC, chief executive officer, 1986—. **BUSINESS ADDRESS:** Chandler Lee Motors, Inc, 1590 US Hwy 1, Southern Pines, NC 28387. *

LEE, CHARLES GARY, SR.
General contractor. **PERSONAL:** Born Sep 29, 1948, Jacksonville, FL; married Claudia Pittman; children: Charles, Marcus, Cedric. **EDUCATION:** H Council Trenholm Jr Coll, A Masonry 1969; Westfield State Coll, Certificate Occ Ed 1974; Univ of MA, BA Occupational Educ 1984. **CAREER:** Springfield Sch System, adult educ instructor 1973-80; Lee-Hamilton Construction Co, pres/genl mgr 1974-78; Neighborhood Housing Svcs, asst dir 1978-80; Charles Gary Lee Inc, owner/president 1980-. **ORGANIZATIONS:** 3rd Degree Master Mason FAM of AL Prince Hall 1967-; dir Corporate Mem Springfield Girl's Club Family Ctr Inc 1979-; pres Big Will Express Athletic Club 1983-; certified mem Minority Business Enterprise 1983-; affiliate mem Western MA Contractor's Assoc 1985-; consultant shareholder Lee-Brantley Inc 1986-. **HONORS/ACHIEVEMENTS:** Man of the Year Awd Big Will Express AA 1984; Outstanding Citizen Awd MA Black Caucus 1986; Letter of Recognition Mayor City of Boston 1986. **HOME ADDRESS:** 32 Briarwood Ave, Springfield, MA 01118. **BUSINESS ADDRESS:** President, Charles Gary Lee Inc, PO Box 90953, Springfield, MA 01139.

LEE, CHARLOTTE O.
Educator. **PERSONAL:** Born Jul 13, 1930, Boligee, AL; married Ralph Hewitt Lee; children: Krystal, Karla, Rachel, Rosalind. **EDUCATION:** Knoxville College, BS 1953; Tuskegee Institute, MS 1955; The University of Kansas, PhD 1959. **CAREER:** Nassau Community College, asst prof chemistry 1970-71; St Louis Univ, rs assoc 1971-72; Southern IL Univ at Edwardsville, assoc prof 1972-78; Triton College, instructor 1979-. **ORGANIZATIONS:** Asst prof nutrition Univ of Kansas 1963; prof chemistry Alabama A&M Univ 1964-69; parks commissioner City of University City, MO 1976-78; community chest dir Oak Park River Forest Community Chest 1982. **HONORS/ACHIEVEMENTS:** AAUW Research Fellowship Amer Assn of Univ Women 1958-59; American Men & Women of Science 1960; research grant Natl Institute of Health 1964-67; research grant NASA 1965-68; Women in Science Project NSF 1977-78; proposal review panelist Natl Science Foundation 1978, 1979. **HOME ADDRESS:** 333 N Cuyler, Oak Park, IL 60302.

LEE, CLARA MARSHALL
Educator. **PERSONAL:** Born Feb 14, 1946, Mobile, AL; daughter of Edward J Marshall Sr and Clara Mae Marshall; married Marion Sidney Lee, Jr, Jul 10, 1971; children: LaToia Ejuan Marius Sidward. **EDUCATION:** Bishop State Jr Coll, 1963-65; AL State Univ, Montgomery Al, BS 1967; Natl Coll of Educ, Chicago IL, MA 1983. **CAREER:** Harvey Park Dist, commissioner 1981; Delta Sigma Theta Sor Inc Joliet Area Alumni Chapter, finance sec 1984; Harvey Publ Schools Dist 152, history teacher. **ORGANIZATIONS:** Bd mem People Organized to Secure Election Equalities 1982; mem IEA, NEA, NPRA, IPRA, The Natl Sor of Phi Delta Kappa Inc.

LEE, CLIFTON VALJEAN
Physician. **PERSONAL:** Born Jan 21, 1929, New York, NY; married Irene Warner; children: Marquetta C, Michele C, Jeanine C. **EDUCATION:** HowardUniv Washington DC, BS 1951; Howard U, MD 1955. **CAREER:** Univ of So CA Med Sch LA, physician/asst clinical prof ob-gyn 1968-; CA Coll of Med LA, clinical instr ob-gyn 1963-; Western Res Med Sch Cleveland OH, demonstrator ob-gyn 1962-63. **ORGANIZATIONS:** Mem numerous ob-gyn socs; consult Numerous Ob-gyn Dept Hosps; Nat Med Fellowship 1960-63; diplomate Am Bd of Ob-gyn. **MILITARY SERVICE:** USAF capt 1956-58.

LEE, CODY M.
Clergyman. **PERSONAL:** Born Aug 03, 1910, Sparkman, AR; married Amanda; children: Cody, Maeola, Ada C. **EDUCATION:** AR Bapt Coll, AA 1948; Rust Coll, AB 1957; AR Bapt Coll, DD 1958. **CAREER:** AR & TN, barber 1929-45; Pilgrim Rest Bapt Ch Memphis, minister 1948-. **ORGANIZATIONS:** Pres TN Bapt Sch of Religion Memphis, TN; mem bd dir Nat Bapt Conv USA Inc; state dir TN BM & E State Congress; co-chmn Shelby Rep Party Shelby Co TN 1965-66. **HONORS/ACHIEVEMENTS:** Sermon writer; publisher of Poem Book for all occasions; publisher of Chair Handbook.

LEE, DALE GEORGE
Chief executive officer. **PERSONAL:** Born Feb 19, 1937, Pittsburgh, PA; married Ethel Robinson; children: Dale G Jr, Douglas Ashville. **EDUCATION:** Muskingum Coll New Concord OH, BA 1960; AUS Info School, 1961; Univ of MD, 1968. **CAREER:** The AMOCO Oil Co Baltimore, mktg trainee, dealer recruiting rep 1964-65, mktg & rep 1965-67, asst dist mgr 1967-69, employee rel & urban affairs 1969;Amoco Intl Oil Co, sr staff employee rel rep retired; DDMD Corp of Fantastic Sam's Hair Saloons, pres, owner. **ORGANIZATIONS:** Bd of dir Houston NW C of C 1982-86; intl pres Frontiers Intl Club 1982-87; vice pres Sam Houston Area Boy Scouts 1983-85; mem Personnel Assoc 1980; charter mem Amer Assoc of Blacks in Energy, Urban League Black Exec Exchange Prog; pres Phi Kappa Tau Muskingum Coll 1959; pres N Houston Frontier Club 1980; mem Olde Oaks Racquet Club 1980; bd dir Julia C Hester House 1980; mem Greensport Exch Club 1980, Houston Boy Scouts Counc 1980. **HONORS/ACHIEVEMENTS:** Black Achievers Awd 1976; Awd United Negro Coll Fund 1974. **MILITARY SERVICE:** AUS 1960-63. **BUSINESS ADDRESS:** President, Fantastic Sams Haircutters, 6731 Arline Dr, Houston, TX 77076.

LEE, DANIEL
Physician. **PERSONAL:** Born Apr 28, 1918, Pinehurst, GA; son of Amos Lee, Jr and Leila; married Thelma Ragin (deceased); children: Daniel Jr, Kenneth, Sharon. **EDUCATION:** Lincoln Univ, BA 1940; Howard Univ Coll of Med, MD 1945; Harlem Hosp, internship 1946. **CAREER:** Lincoln Univ Coll Hygiene, sch physician/asst prof 1946-48; Pine Forge Inst, sch physician 1948-55; Coatesville Hosp, med staff 1960-; Coatesville Area Schools, sch physician 1968-; Coatesville Sr High Varsity Ftbl 1968-; physician private practice. **ORGANIZATIONS:** Grand asst med dir IBPOE of W 1983-; coord cncl Southeastern PA High Blood Pressure Control Program 1983-; charter mem US Defense Comm 1983-; pres Club XV 1972-; pres Western Chester Cnty C of C; bd dir Western Chester County Indus Devel Corp & Auth; Coatesville Red Cross; mem AMA; sust mem YMCA Coatesville area; mem Fellowship Comm Philadelphia, PA; com on admissions & allocations United Way of Chester Cnty; bd dir Chester County OIC Inc; mem Mount Vernon Lodge #151; IBPOE of W; NMA; Boy Scout Council Chester Cnty; NAACP 1976; mem Philadelphia Urban League; mem Coatesville Area Hall of Fame Selection Comm; mem bd of dirs United Cerebral Palsy Assoc of Chester Co 1985-; mem Health & Welfare Council Chester Co PA; dir Health Dept, Improved Development Protective Order 1988; bd of dir Atkinson Memorial Comm unity Center 1989. **HONORS/ACHIEVEMENTS:** Diplomate Natl Bd of Medical Examiners; Honoree Coatesville Hall of Fame 1976; fellow Amer Acad of Family Physicians 1975; Honoree Chapel of Four Chaplains 1970; Laura S Greenwood Outstanding Serv Award 1970, 1975; Man of Year Award S Eastern Bus & Professional Women of Chester Cnty, PA 1979; fellow Amer Geriatrics Soc 1969; life mem Kappa Alpha Psi Frat 1969; Paul Harris Fellow, Rotary Intl 1989; Community Services Award Veterans of Foreign Wars 1989; 50 Year Membership Award Kappa Alpha Psi Fraternity 1989; life mem American Academy of Family Practice 1989. **MILITARY SERVICE:** AUS Maj 1959. **BUSINESS ADDRESS:** 723 Merchant St, Coatesville, PA 19320.

LEE, DEBRA LOUISE
Attorney. **PERSONAL:** Born Aug 08, 1954, Columbia, SC; married Randall Spencer Coleman. **EDUCATION:** Brown Univ, AB 1976; Harvard Law School, JD 1980; Harvard Kennedy School of Govt, MPP 1980. **CAREER:** US Dist Ct Judge Barrington Parker, law clerk 1980-81; Steptoe & Johnson, attorney 1981-86; Black Entertainment Television, vice pres/general counsel 1986-. **ORGANIZATIONS:** Mem Minority Recruitment Comm Federal Comm Bar Assoc 1982-; mem Public Service Activities Comm DC Bar 1983-; bd of dirs Legal Aid Soc of DC 1986-. **HONORS/ACHIEVEMENTS:** Eva A Mooar Awd Brown Univ 1976. **BUSINESS ADDRESS:** Vice Pres/General Counsel, Black Entertainment TV, 1232 31st St NW, Washington, DC 20007.

LEE, DETROIT
Retired business executive. **PERSONAL:** Born Aug 22, 1916, Daingerfield, TX; son of Jessie lee (deceased) and Lou Ella Rivers Lee (deceased); children: Detroit Jr, David M, Mary E Davis, Anthony T, Henry A. **EDUCATION:** Tuskegee Inst Coll, 1936-42. **CAREER:** Civilian Conservation Corps, asst clerk & sr leader 1937-42; Tuskegee Army Air Field, clerk-typist II & III 1942-44; VA Hosp AL, clerk typist II & admin clerk 1944-65; Tuskegee Inst Comm Educ Program, admin asst & comm organizer 1965-67; Tuskegee Inst, res dir 1967-72; Pardon & Parole Bd, clerk typist III 1973; ABC Bd, store clerk & cashier 1974-78; AL Ind Relations, clerk typist III super 1980-81; Lee & Sons Enterprises Inc, pres, 1971-85. **ORGANIZATIONS:** Organizer & 1st pres Tuskegee Br NAACP 1944; vice-pres Tuskegee Civic Assn 1940's; organizer & promoter school desegregation 1956, 1963. **HONORS/ACHIEVEMENTS:** Americanism Awd for Voter Registration Amer Vet Comm 1964; Serv to Fellow Alabamians AL Sec of State 1983; Awd for Outstanding Leadership Westminster Presbyterian Church 1983; author "Christianity Democracy or Communism" 1985, "Lee v Macon" Cty & State of AL 1985; won job discrimination suits: Lee v State of Alabama Personnel Dept, 1984, 1989; Lee v Robert White, 1985; Lee v ABC Board, 1987; Lee v Dept of Health and Human Services 1988; Lee v Darris, 1988; Lee v SCADC and City of Tuskegee, 1989. **MILITARY SERVICE:** AUS pvt 1945. **HOME ADDRESS:** H-109 Sojourner Apts, Tuskegee, AL 36083.

LEE, DON L. See **MADHUBUTI, HAKI R.**

LEE, DOROTHEA
Association executive. **PERSONAL:** Born Dec 13, 1930, Yonkers, NY. **EDUCATION:** Seton Hall U, BS 1956; Seton Hall U, MA 1964. **CAREER:** Planned Prnthd Wrld Pop NY, dir fld dept 1972-; Nat Urban Lgue Inc NY, proj dir 1972; NJ St Hosp Marlboro, asst dir nrses 1969-70; NJ St Hosp Marlboro, proj spec 1964-69; NJ Rehab Comm, voc rehab cnslr 1964; St Barnabas Med Ctr, stf nrse 1962-64; Chaumont Air Frce Bse, nrse 1961-62; Neward Bd Ed, sch nrse 1960-61; NJ St Hosp Marlboro, instr 1957-60; Newark Cty Hosp, surg clin instr 1955-57; Newark Cty Hosp, asst supr nrses 1953-55; Newark Cty Hosp, stf nrse 1951-53. **ORGANIZATIONS:** Mem Am Persnnl & Guidnc Assn; Nat Rehab Assn; Newark Cty Hosp Sch of Nrsng alum Assn; Am Nrs Assn; Nat Lgue for Nrsng; Amer Pub Hlth Assn; Am Mngmt Assn; chmn NJ St Nrs Assn; pres Club Cicuso Inc 1965-67; fin secy Nat Assn Neg B & PW Club Inc 1970-74; mem NAACP; Nat Pol Caucus; Womns Po Caucus Essex Cnty NJ. **HONORS/ACHIEVEMENTS:** NJ Med of Merit 1958; prof whmn of yr 1971; hon Who's Who Amer Womn 1972; The World's Who's Who of Wmn 1973; Two Thous Wmn of Achvmnt 1972; achvmnt Pubctn in Jrnl Psychtrc Nrsng & Mntl Hlth Serv 1968. **MILITARY SERVICE:** USAF captn 1961-62; NJ Air Nat Gd 1957-68; USAFR mjr 1957-69. **BUSINESS ADDRESS:** 810 7 Ave, New York, NY 10019.

LEE, EDWARD S.
Former city official. **PERSONAL:** Born May 12, 1935, Phila; married Fay E Jones; children: Michael, Eric. **EDUCATION:** Cheyney State Coll, BS 1968;Univ PA Fels Inst & State Govt 1969-70. **CAREER:** US PO; HELP Inc, exec dir 1967-69; Philadelphia Urban Coalition, exec staff mem task force coordinator & chmn 1969-71; City Phila, elected clerk quarter sessions 1971-; Nat Assn Postal & Fed Employees, former union rep; Regional & Community Treatment Centers Women, appointed attys 1967; elected ward leader 1970; Black Political Forum, exec dir 1968-70; Cheyney State Coll, adjunct prof 1974; appointed PA Gov's Justice Com. **ORGANIZATIONS:** Bd mem Nat Assn Court Adminstrs; Ile-Fe Black Humanitarian Center; Greater Germantown Youth Corps; mem bd trustees Canaan Bapt Ch; Ralph Bunche Club Phila; NAACP; Urban League Phila; elected delegate Dem Nat Mini Conv 1974; exec asst chmn Second World & Conf Arts & Culture; bd dir Police Athletic League; bd dir Community Services & Development Corp. **HONORS/ACHIEVEMENTS:** Who's Who Among Students AmUniv & Coll 1968; outstanding achievement award Inter Urban League PA; chmn bd trustees Cheyney State Coll 1974; light weight boxing champion 1956. **MILITARY SERVICE:** USAF 1952-56. **BUSINESS ADDRESS:** 673 City Hall, Philadelphia, PA 19107.

LEE, EDWIN ARCHIBALD
Physician. **PERSONAL:** Born Jan 12, 1914, Indianola, MS; married Geraldine Elizabeth Dobisson; children: Edwin, Jr, Harold, Edith, Rhandie. **EDUCATION:** Morehouse Coll Atlanta, GA, BA 1937; Meharry Med Coll Nashville, TN, MD 1941. **CAREER:** Pvt Practice St John's Hosp Springfield, IL, med staff; Meml Med Center, med staff; Comm Hosp, med staff 1949-; So ILUniv Med Sch, clinical asso1949-; St Mary's Infirmary, resident 1945-49; Homer Phillips Hosp St Louis, MO, intern 1941-42. **ORGANIZATIONS:** Pres Sangamon StateUniv Found; mem NAACP; mem Alpha Omega Alpha Nat Med Hon Soc; bd of dir Peoples Nat Bank 1969-; pres St John's Hosp Staff 1969-; organizer/co-chmn Springfield Citizens for Effective Voter Participation & Communication 1978; mem Springfield Bd of Educ 1965-71; pres Springfield Bd ofEduc 1969-70; trustee chmn Zion Bapt Ch 1979-. **HONORS/ACHIEVEMENTS:** Springfield merit award Springfield Bd of Educ 1969-70; hon life membership IL Congress of PTA's 1971; copley first citizens award Copley Press 1972; external serv award Frontiers of Am Intl 1976; hon cert Morehouse Coll 1977; man of the year Omega Nu Chap Omega Psi Phi Frat 1979. **MILITARY SERVICE:** AUS maj 1941-45. **BUSINESS ADDRESS:** 501 S 13th St, Springfield, IL 62703.

LEE, FORREST A., SR.
Business executive. **PERSONAL:** Born Nov 19, 1937, Boley, OK; son of Maurice W Lee Sr and Harriett Anderson Lee; married Joyce A Kirksey; children: Forrest, Carole, Catherine, Brian, Gregory, Michael, Rachael, Reginald, Crystal, Lee Otis. **EDUCATION:** OK City Univ, BA 1961. **CAREER:** Liberty Tower Co OK City, draftsman 1959; Central State Hospital Norman, OK, psychiatric aide 1960-61; MW Lee Mfg Co, plant supvr 1961-68; Leefac Inc Boley, OK, pres 1963-70; Smokaroma Inc, vice pres 1974-; Farmers Home Adm Okemah, FHA loan committeeman 1970-73, chmn 1973; Smokaroma, Inc, vice president. **ORGANIZATIONS:** Exec com mem Central OK Criminal Comm 1970-73; public Chapter Boley Chamber of Commerce 1962-; councilman Town of Boley 1961-73; mem Natl Assn Black Mfgrs 1972-, bd of dir 1972-76; comm State of OK Human Rights Comm 1973-; bd trustees, treas Ward Chapel AME Church Boley; Wewoka Alumni Chapter Kappa Alpha Psi Fraternity; national assoc of food equipment mfgrs 1980-; national restaurant assoc 1977-. **HOME**

ADDRESS: Drawer 7, Boley, OK 74829. **BUSINESS ADDRESS:** Vice President, Smokaroma, Inc, Drawer 25, Boley, OK 74829.

LEE, FRED D., JR.
Automobile dealer. **PERSONAL:** Born Apr 26, 1947, Tallahassee, FL; son of Fred Mosley Lee and Maude Sneed Lee; married Patricia Mosley Lee, Aug 26, 1971; children: Adrienne Dionne Lee, Fred Douglas Lee, III. **EDUCATION:** FL A&M Univ, Tallahassee, FL, BS Music, 1964-69, extensive study toward Master's Degree in Guidance Counseling, 1970-71; Ford Motor Co, Detroit, MI, dealer training program, 1984-85. **CAREER:** Ford Motor Co, Jacksonville, FL, market analyst, 1971-74; Ford Motor Co, Memphis, TN, dist sales representative, 1974-78, business mgmt mgr, 1978-79, truck merchandising, 1979, fleet/leasing/rental mgr, 1979-82, vehicle dist mgr, 1982-84; Shoals Ford, Inc, Muscle Shoals, AL, pres/owner, 1986-. **ORGANIZATIONS:** Mem, Black Ford Lincoln Mercury Dealer Assn, 1986-; vice-chmn, Area Ford Dealer Council, 1988-89; bd of dir, Amer Heart Assn, 1988-; exec comm, United Way of the Shoals, 1988-; mem, Sheffield, Alabama, Rotary Club, 1988-; mem, Alabama Commn on Higher Educ, 1988-. **HONORS/ACHIEVEMENTS:** Distinguished Achievement Award for Quality, Ford Motor Co, 1988. **BUSINESS ADDRESS:** Automobile Dealer, Shoals Ford, Inc, 2800 Woodward Ave, PO Drawer 3060, Muscle Shoals, AL 35660.

LEE, GABRIEL S., JR.
Clergyman. **PERSONAL:** Born Jul 06, 1922, Junction City, AR; son of Gabriel S Lee, Sr (deceased) and Mollie Elder Lee (deceased); married Leona Jean Williams. **EDUCATION:** Bishop Coll Marshall TX, AB 1949; Howard Univ, MDiv 1954; St Andrews Univ St Andrews Scotland, special certificate 1970; McCormick Theological Seminary, DMin, 1987. **CAREER:** Fellowship New Land Baptist Churchs Lillie LA, pastor 1948-51; Westminster House Buffalo, dir boys' work 1954-55; Hollywood Heights Presbyterian Church Shreveport, stated supply minis 1955-60; Beacon Reformed Church Beacon NY, co-pastor 1960-61; pastor 1961-62; Erie Ct Dept Public Welfare Buffalo, caseworker 1963-65; Nazareth Baptist Church Washington PA, pastor 1965-71; Fellowship Baptist Church Christ Cleveland OH, pastor 1971-. **ORGANIZATIONS:** Treas UABA Con Christ Educ Pittsburgh 1969-71; vice moderator Allegheny Union Baptist Assn Pittsburgh 1969-71; instructor Penna Con Christ Educ 1968-71; pres Washington PA Council Churches 1970-71; pres Washington PA Ministerial Asso 1971; staff mem Natl SS & BT Univ Cong 1970-; instructor Cleveland Ext Unit American-Baptist Theological Seminary Nashville; sec Greater Clevland Ministerial Assn Cleveland 1974-; mem Mayor's Comm Human Relations Washington PA 1966; advisory bd Washington Ct Dept Child Welfare; mem Washington Ct Mental Health Assn 1966-71; exec bd Bldg Com Washington YMCA 1970-71; life mem NAACP; exec com Clevleand Branch; Phi Beta Sigma Rat 1960-; Ions Intl Serv Org 1962-; mem, Executive Board Cleveland Baptist Assn, 1989-93; mem, Executive Board Greater Cleveland Interchurch Council, 1989-93; pres, Cleveland Host Lions Intl, 1989-91. **HONORS/ACHIEVEMENTS:** McKinley Theological Seminary, Doctor of Divinity, 1980. **MILITARY SERVICE:** AUS staff sgt 1942-46. **BUSINESS ADDRESS:** 1754 E 55th St, Cleveland, OH 44103.

LEE, GERALD E.
Educational administrator. **PERSONAL:** Born Jan 11, 1958, Los Angeles, CA; son of Eugene Lee and Erma W Lee; married Tonya Marie Durley, Jul 22, 1978; children: Dawn Racquel, Gerald Eugene II, Darryl Eugene, Dennis Edward. **EDUCATION:** Southwestern Christian Coll, AS 1978; Oklahoma Christian Coll, BS 1980. **CAREER:** First & Euclid Church of Christ, minister 1976-78; Eastside Church of Christ, minister 1978-81; Florence St Church of Christ, minister 1981-84; Metropolitan Church of Christ, minister 1984-87. **HONORS/ACHIEVEMENTS:** GP Bowser Bible Awd Southwestern Christian Coll 1978; Outstanding Young Men in Amer 1981,82,83. **BUSINESS ADDRESS:** Dir of Admissions/Recruitment, Southwestern Christian College, 200 Bowser Circle, Terrell, TX 75160.

LEE, GLORIA A.
Entrepreneur. **PERSONAL:** Born Mar 10, 1940, Cumberland, VA; divorced; children: Rhonda Michelle, Leroy E Jr. **EDUCATION:** Univ of MD, BS 1978; Johns Hopkins Univ, MBA 1984. **CAREER:** Social Security Admin, supervisor 1976-80; Equal Employ Oppor Commn, eeo specialist 1980-86; Ward AME Church, admin/consultant 1987-; Easy Transitions, pres 1986-. **ORGANIZATIONS:** Presenter Black Family in Amer Conf 1985-; mem Natl Black MBA Assoc 1985-; non-affiliated pres Amer Assoc Black Women Entrepreneurs 1986-. **BUSINESS ADDRESS:** President, Easy Transitions, 3022 Valle Vista Dr Ste 2, Los Angeles, CA 90065.

LEE, GUY MILICON, JR.
Educator. **PERSONAL:** Born May 24, 1928, E Chicago, IN; married Trevor J Lee; children: Kim Valerie, Rodney, L Smith. **EDUCATION:** Roosevelt Univ, BA, 1954; Inidana Univ, MS, 1959; Ball State Univ, EdD, 1969. **CAREER:** Gary Comm Schools IN, public school teacher 1956-64, administrator 1964-70; Saginaw Valley State Coll, dir of student teaching 1970-73, assoc dean sch of educ prof 1973-75, admin asst to the pres 1975-78, asst to the pres 1978-82, dean sch of educ 1982-86, prof of educ 1986-. **ORGANIZATIONS:** Mem, Assn Supervison & Curriculum Devel; mem, Natl Org on Legal Problems in Educ; mem, Amer Assn of School Admin; rep, United Way of Saginaw Co; mem, Assn teach educ; mem, Amer Asoc Higher Educ; mem, Assn of Super and Curr devel; bd of dir League of United Latin Amer Citizens, 1982-. **HONORS/ACHIEVEMENTS:** High Scholastic Achievement Award INUniv Bloomington 1953; Doctoral Fellowship Ball StateUniv Muncie IN 1968-69; Citizen of the Age of Enlightement Award for Educ Am Found for the Sci of Creative Intelligence 1976; Keyman Award for community Serv United Way of Saginaw Co MI 1979. **MILITARY SERVICE:** AUS technician 1946-48. **BUSINESS ADDRESS:** Professor of Education, Saginaw Valley State University, College of Education, Room 232 Brown Hall, University Center, MI 48710.

LEE, HELEN JACKSON
Retired social worker. **PERSONAL:** Born Jul 23, 1908, Richmond, VA; widowed; children: Barbara Nan, Robert Edward, Jr. **EDUCATION:** VA State U, BA 1930. **CAREER:** NJ Dept of Human Svc, social worker 1971-73; NJ Dept of Human Svc, pub information asst 1967-71, asst supr stenog pool 1965-67, sec fire marshal 1962-65, sr clerk stenog 1947-62; Philadelphia Ed Chicago Defender, feature writer 1936-37; Philadelphia Ind, newspaper reporter 1937-38; Philadelphia Ed Pittsburgh Courier, newspaper reprtr 1938-40. **ORGANIZATIONS:** Historian Epsilon Upsilon Omega Alpha Kappa Alpha Soroity Inc 1985; charter mem Trenton Alumae Chap Epsilon Upsilon Omega; bd mem Central YWCA Trenton NJ; mem Trenton Mus Soc 1985; mem NJ Hist Soc Prescious Pearl Award. **HONORS/ACHIEVEMENTS:** Epsilon Upsilon Omega Chap Alpha Kappa Alpha Sorority Inc 1975; Citation for Literary Work Fire II Mag Trenton State Coll 1978; Comm Serv Award Metro Civic League & Bronzettes Inc 1978; Golden Sorority Cert; Alpha Kappa & Alpha Sorority Inc 1978; Author of Autobiography "Nigger in the Window" Doubleday & Co NY 1978; Comm Serv Award; Top Ladies of Distinction 1979.

LEE, HOWARD N.
City official. **PERSONAL:** Born Jul 28, 1934, Lithonia, GA; married Lillian Wesley; children: Angela, Ricky, Karin Alexis Lou Tempie. **EDUCATION:** Clark Coll, 1953-56; St Coll Ft Valley, BA 1959;Univ NC, MSW 1966; Acad of Cert Social Workers, ACSW 1968; Shaw U, LLD 1971. **CAREER:** Juvenile Comestic Rel Ct Savannah, prob off 1961-64; Yth Prog Duke U, dir 1966-68; NC Central U, vis asst prof 1967-68; Employee Rel Duke U, dir 1968-69; Lark Cinemas Inc, pres; Lee Dist & Mfg Co; Lark Entertainment Enter, pres chmn bd; Plastiwood Prod Inc, pres; ShawUniv adj prof; office of human devel duke u, dir; chapel hill NC, mayor 1969-75. **ORGANIZATIONS:** Numerous professional mem. **HONORS/ACHIEVEMENTS:** Recip GA St Tchrs Hon Student's Awd; honor student's awd St Coll; hunt fellow awd Ft Valley St Coll; achmnt awd Atlanta Br NAACP; achmnt awd Phi Beta Sigma Frat 1969; Nat Urban Leag Equal Oppor Day Awd 1970; publs in field. **MILITARY SERVICE:** AUS 1959-61. **BUSINESS ADDRESS:** UNC School of Social Work, 223 E Franklin St, Chapel Hill, NC 27514.

LEE, J. KENNETH
Chief executive. **CAREER:** American Federal Savings and Loan Assn, Greensboro, NC, chief exec. **BUSINESS ADDRESS:** American Federal Savings and Loan Assn, 701 E Market St, Greensboro, NC 27401. *

LEE, JAMES E.
Dentist. **PERSONAL:** Born Mar 05, 1940, Conway, SC; son of Richard A Lee and Ophelia B Lee; married Patricia Ponds; children: James E Lee Jr, Allen Earlington Lee, Arrington Patrick Lee. **EDUCATION:** SC State Coll, 1963; HowardUniv Coll of Dentistry 1971. **CAREER:** Private Practice, dentist 1973-; Franklin C Fetter Comprehensive Health Care Clinic Charleston, staff dentist 1971-73; Appalachian Reg Health Policy & Planning Council Anderson, SC, staff dentist 1970-71; Dental Serv Howard Univ Upward Bound Program Sum, dir 1971; private practice, dentist. **ORGANIZATIONS:** Chmn Salvation Army Adv Bd 1980; Palmetto Med Dental & Pharm Assn; Pee Dee Dist Dental Soc; SC Dental Soc; Am Dental Assn; Conway C of C; Nat Dental Assn Conway Alumni Chap Kappa Alpha Psi; chmn Conway Housing Authority 1980-81; mem Bethel AME Ch Young Adult Choir; mem exec & com Palmetto Med Dental & Pharm Assn; Grans Strand Dental Soc; pres Dee Dee Medical Dental & Pharmaceutical Assn; chmn Palmetto Medical Dental & Pharmaceutical Assn; past pres council Pres Palmetto Medical Dental & Pharmaceutical Assn 1983-84; mem health adv commm Waccamaw Econ Oppty Council; mem Mental Health Assn of Horry County; mem Steward Board, Bethel AME Church; mem SC State Board of Dentistry. **HONORS/ACHIEVEMENTS:** Howard Univ Dental Award 1958; Doctor of the Year, Palmetto Medical Dental and Pharmaceutical Assn 1989. **MILITARY SERVICE:** AUS sp5 1964-67. **BUSINESS ADDRESS:** Dentist, 611 Hwy 501, Conway, SC 29526.

LEE, JOHN C., III
Chief executive. **CAREER:** J C Lee Construction and Supply Co, Butler, PA, chief exec, 1977-. **BUSINESS ADDRESS:** J C Lee Construction and Supply Co, Inc, 2346 N Main St Extension, Butler, PA 16001. *

LEE, JOHN ROBERT E.
Business executive. **PERSONAL:** Born Jul 11, 1935, Tallahassee, FL; children: John Robert E Lee IV. **EDUCATION:** FL A&M Univ, BA 1959; Boston Univ, MA 1961; Univ of KS, Doctorate 1973. **CAREER:** Communications Transportation & Real Estate Devel, pres, owner, entrepreneur; Silver Star Commun Corp, pres. **ORGANIZATIONS:** Dir of athletics TN State Univ 1985; mem Natl Assoc of Broadcasters 1985; pres Natl Assoc of Black Owned Broadcasters; chmn fund raising YMCA 1985; committee mem Boy Scouts of Amer 1985; mem Natl Coll Athletic Assoc 1985, ford Mercury Lincoln Minority Auto Assoc 1985. **HONORS/ACHIEVEMENTS:** Outstanding Serv Awd Albany State 1970; Humanitarian of the Year NAACP 1977; Broadcaster of the Year HABOB 1983; Outstanding Comm Serv Hella Temple #105 1984. **BUSINESS ADDRESS:** President, Silver Star Commun Corp, 1945 S Martin L King Dr, Tallahassee, FL 32301.

LEE, KATHERINE I.
Educator, government official. **PERSONAL:** Born Jul 04, 1942, Lexington, KY. **EDUCATION:** Fisk U, BA (summa cum laude) 1963; Stanford U, MA 1966; Stanford U, PhD 1971; Colby Coll, addl study; Scandinavian Intl Inst;Univ of Munich;Univ of Hamburg. **CAREER:** OH State Univ, asst prof of German 1970-76; Washington DC & Mexico City, foreign serv officer 1976-; Amer Inst of Music Graz, Austria, prof of german 1976; Miami Univ, instructor 1968-70; OH State Univ, honors adviser 1971-. **ORGANIZATIONS:** Mem Am Assn of Tchrs of German 1971; Modern Language Assn 1971-; mem adv Bd Office of Minority Affairs OH StateUniv 1974-; chairperson recruitment Com;vol Columbus Pub Sch Sys; mem Delta Sigma Theta 1962-; Phi Beta Kappa. **HONORS/ACHIEVEMENTS:** Scandinavian Intl Inst Scholarship 1961; Deutscher Akademischer Austauschdienst Fellowship form German Govt 1963-64 & 1968; Woodrow Wilson Fellowship 1964-65; StanfordUniv Fellowship 1966 & 1968; Grant-in-Aid OH State 1972; OH StateUniv Devel Fund Summer Fellowship 1973; Am Philosophical Soc Grant 1973-74.

LEE, KERMIT J., JR.
Educator, architect. **PERSONAL:** Born Mar 27, 1934, Springfield, MA; son of Kermit J Lee Sr and Lillian Lee; married Lore Leipelt; children: Karin Justine, Jason Anthony. **EDUCATION:** Syracuse Univ, BArch (Magna Cum Laude) 1952-57; Technische Hochschule Braunschweig Germany, Fulbright 1958, 1959. **CAREER:** Technische Hochschule Braunschweig W Germany, Fulbright fellow 1958-59; Amer Inst of Arch, medary fellow 1959-60; Afex, Wiesbaden Germany, chief arch hq 7480th sup gp 1960-63; P Zoelly Arch Zurich Switzerland, assoc arch 1963-66; Syracuse Univ, prof of arch 1973-; SU Institute for Energy Research, faculty assoc 1978-; Syracuse Univ Pre-College Prog, appoint dir 1986-; Enenergesis Development Corp, vice pres 1983-; Kermit J Lee Jr, AIA architect, principal 1989-. **ORGANIZATIONS:** Vice pres arch Skoler & Lee Arch 1969-; principal, CEO Chimaera Energy

Tech Corp 1979-; mem NY Bd for Arch 1979-, Gov Cultural Adv Comm for Time Square, Natl Council Arch Regional Bd ARE 1985; mem NY Coalition of Black Arch 1977; adj assoc prof urban design Columbia Univ 1974; consultant Urban Designer Model Cities Springfield MA 1969-75; dir Campus Plan Group Syracuse Univ 1970; mem Amer Inst of Arch; mayors comm Revise City Charter 1972-74; bldg code bd of appeal 1970-; graphic exhibit Proj for Energy Syracuse Univ School of Arch 1979; technical consultant Onondaga County Citizens Energy Comm 1979-; Syracuse Univ, mem steering comm for accreditation 1987, Advisory Board for Human Development 1987; chmn, New York Board for Architecture, 1986-87; mem Citizen's Cultural Advisory Comm, Times Square Development 1985-. **HONORS/ ACHIEVEMENTS:** Honor Diploma Swiss Natl Exposition 1964; Fulbright Fellowship US State Dept 1958; Medary Fellowship Amer Inst of Arch 1959; Rsch Grant Natl Endowment for the Arts 1980; Civ/Non-Appropriated Funds; School Medal AIA 1957; Luther Gifford Prize Design 1967; Class Marshall 1957; Phi Kappa Phi Hon 1957; Alpha Rho Chi Medal 1957; NY State Soc of Arch Medal 1957; Appt AIA Natl Comm on Design; Syracuse Black Leadership Council, Black Pioneer Award 1986; invitation to publish manuscript, International Forum for Design ULM, Germany 1989. **MILITARY SERVICE:** AF Exchange gs12 2 yrs. **HOME ADDRESS:** 104 Berkeley Dr, Syracuse, NY 13210. **BUSINESS ADDRESS:** Professor of Architecture, SyracuseUniv, Syracuse, NY 13210.

LEE, KERMIT L.
Business executive. **PERSONAL:** Born Aug 09, 1938, Atlantic City, NJ. **EDUCATION:** Howard Univ, BA 1959; Univ MD Sch Social Work, attended 1968. **CAREER:** Pres, Youth Opportunity Prog, team chief 1968-69; Continental Bank, dir urban affairs 1969-74, vice pres 1974-; White House, consultant on policies' affect minority groups 1971; Univ Chicago, assoc prof 1973. **ORGANIZATIONS:** Co-founder/natl chmn Natl Urban Affairs Cncl 1973-74; mem adv com Urban Devel MI State Univ 1974-78; Gov's Task Force on Univ-State Relations & Comm Serv Prog 1975; bd dir Planned Parenthood 1970-78; pres Ernie Banks Golf Classic for Sickle Cell Anemia 1972-73; co-chmn Natl Football League's Players Assn Awards Dinner 1972; treas Better Boys Found 1974-; conducted fact finding tour of Israel May, 1974, as guest of Israeli Govt. **HONORS/ACHIEVEMENTS:** Chicago Urban League Beautiful Person Award 1974. **MILITARY SERVICE:** AUS maj 1960-69; Meritorious Serv Medal; Bronze Star.

LEE, LAVERNE C.
Educator. **PERSONAL:** Born Dec 19, 1933, Bayonne, NJ; daughter of Hugo W; widowed; children: Juvia A. **EDUCATION:** Morgan St Coll, BS 1955; Loyola Coll, MEd 1969; Johns Hopkins U, advanced study. **CAREER:** Baltimore Co Bd of Educ, instr reading spl; tchr of physically handicapped for 19 yrs; Battle Monumental School Eastwood Ctr, principal. **ORGANIZATIONS:** Treas 1970-74, vice pres 1974-75 CEC; sec Teacher Assn Baltimore Co 1973-; pres Baltimore Co Chap Council for Excep Children 1974-76; del NEA Conv; del CEC Conv; mem Orton Soc; hon life mem PTA; exec bd TABCO; Phi Delta Kappa; Delta Kappa Gamma. **HONORS/ACHIEVEMENTS:** Recip Tchr of the Year Awd. **BUSINESS ADDRESS:** Principal, Battle Monument School, 7801 E Collingham Drive, Dundalk, MD 21222.

LEE, LENA S. KING
Lawyer, educator, business executive. **PERSONAL:** Born Jul 14, Pennsylvania; widowed. **EDUCATION:** Morgan State Coll, BA 1939; NY U, MA 1947; MDUniv of Law, LLB 1951, JD. **CAREER:** Citizens Commn on Recreation 1956; Urban Renewal and Housing Com 1955-61; Redevel Com 1955; Kennedy's Civil Rights Conf, pres 1961; Pres's Com on Govt-Contractors & Conf 1958; Commn on Mfg Tax 1958; Justice of the Peace 1959-61. **ORGANIZATIONS:** Mem MD Gen Assembly House of Dels 1966-; mem Am Judicature Soc, Monumental, Baltimore Bar Assns, Center for Dispute Settlement, Nat Assn of Parliamentarians; coms Herbert M Frisby Hist Soc, Intl Platform Assn, Lambda Kappa, Sigma Gamma Rho, Bus & Professional Women's Club, Du Bois Circle, MD League of Women's Clubs, Cheyney Alumni Assn; alumni Univ MD Law School; univ club mem Univ of MD; gov comm on Criminal Justice 1968; gov comm on Juvenile Justice 1970; joint comm on Corrections 1973; comm Family Court & Domestic Relations 1973; comm on Chesapeake Bay Affairs 1980-83. **HONORS/ACHIEVEMENTS:** Numerous Awards and Honors.

LEE, LUCIUS E.
Journalist. **PERSONAL:** Born Mar 05, 1906, Chicago, IL. **EDUCATION:** BA, MA. **CAREER:** Wilberforce Univ, freelance journalist, prof, hist & pol sci; Black Newspapers, editor. **MILITARY SERVICE:** AUS 1932, 1943.

LEE, MARK
Professional athlete. **PERSONAL:** Born Mar 20, 1958, Hanford, CA. **EDUCATION:** WA Univ, attended. **CAREER:** Green Bay Packers, corner back 1980-. **HONORS/ ACHIEVEMENTS:** 4th consecutive season he has either led Packer secondary or shared the lead in knocking down opponent passes; Packers leading punt returner running one back 94 yards for a TD against Giants longest such return in the league & second longest in Green Bays Natl Football League history 1981. **BUSINESS ADDRESS:** Green Bay Packers, 1265 Lombardi Ave, Green Bay, WI 54307.

LEE, MICHAEL WARING
Judge. **PERSONAL:** Born Jan 16, 1953, Baltimore, MD; son of Thomas M Lee and Frances W Lee. **EDUCATION:** Johns Hopkins Univ, 1973; Macalester Coll, BA, 1975; Univ of Maryland, JD, 1978. **CAREER:** Univ of Maryland Law School, teaching & research asst, 1976-78; Circuit Court for Baltimore City, law clerk baliff, 1978-79; Baltimore City Law Dept, asst solicitor, 1979-81; Mitchell Mitchell & Mitchell PA, managing atty, 1981-83; Orphans Court of Baltimore City, chief judge. **ORGANIZATIONS:** Double bassist St Paul Civil Symphony Orchestra, 1971-75; bd mem, Univ of Maryland Law School Alumni Assoc, 1979-84; pres, Northwestern HS Alumni Assoc, 1980-84; asst prof of mgt science Coppin State Coll, 1985. **HONORS/ACHIEVEMENTS:** Outstanding Young Man Jaycees, 1978; distinguished serv, Northwestern High School Alumni Assn, 1982; distinguished alumnus, Black Law Students Assn, Univ of Maryland Chapter, 1985-; lecturer, Univ of Baltimore School of Law, 1986-87; asst prof, Univ of Maryland School of Law, 1987. **BUSINESS ADDRESS:** Chief Judge, Orphans Court of Baltimore Cty, 311 Courthouse East, Baltimore, MD 21202.

LEE, MILDRED KIMBLE
Educator. **PERSONAL:** Born Jan 02, 1919, New York, NY; daughter of Ural Kimble and Ernestine Scott Kimble; married Granville Wheeler, Sr., Nov 09, 1940; children: Granville Wheeler, Jr.. **EDUCATION:** Hunter Coll, New York, NY, AB, 1938; City College, (Baruch), New York, NY, MBA, 1943; further graduate study at Hunter Coll, 1943-60, City College of New York, 1960-64, State Univ Humanistic Educ Center, Albany, NY, 1971-72; Fordham Univ, New York, NY, EdD, 1977. **CAREER:** Morris High School Bd of Educ, New York, NY, teacher, guidance counselor, AP in guidance, 1949-66; District 8 Bd of Educ, New York, NY, supervisor of guidance, 1966-77; Fordham Univ, Lincoln Center Campus, New York, NY, asst and assoc prof, 1977-84; City Univ of New York Graduate Center, Center for Advanced Study Educ (CASE), New York, NY, project dir, 1984—; worked as adjunct prof, 1966-77, at Adelphi Univ Urban Center, City Coll of New York, and Teachers Coll at Columbia Univ; mem of Retired School Supervisors and Admin (RSSA), NYC Bd of Educ, 1977—; advisory council mem of Assoc of Black Women in Higher Educ (ABWHE), 1979—; partner of Lee & Lee Financial Mgmt, 1982—; evaluator for Fordham Univ, Day Care Council, 1984—; consultant for Adult Basic Educ, NYC Bd of Educ, 1984—. **ORGANIZATIONS:** Mem, Natl Urban Educ Assoc, 1981-85; mem, contributor, NAACP; mem, contributor, Natl Urban League; contributor, United Negro Coll Fund. **HONORS/ ACHIEVEMENTS:** Sarah Ollesheimer Scholarship, Hunter Coll, 1939; plaque for "outstanding achievements in education," Natl Council Negro Women, 1978; plaque for "outstand ing guidance supervisor," Morrisania Community Council, 1978; author of articles published in periodicals, including Forum, Educ Technology, Journal of Black Studies, and Educ Forum. **HOME ADDRESS:** 2 Fordham Hill Oval, #8EF, Bronx, NY 10468. **BUSINESS ADDRESS:** Graduate School and University Center of the City University of New York, Center for Advanced Study in Education (CASE), 25 West 43 St, Rm 620, New York, NY 10036.

LEE, NORVEL L. R.
Educator. **PERSONAL:** Born Sep 22, 1924, Eagle Rock, VA; married Leslie Jackson; children: Deborah Ricks, Denise Anderson. **EDUCATION:** Howard U, BS 1953; Fed City Coll, MA 1969; Cath Univ Am, PhD Candidate. **CAREER:** Dept Justice, tchr couselor bur prisons 1952-62; DC Dept Corrections, dir educ 1962-65; DC Welfare Dept, supr work experience counselor 1965-68; Inst Computer Tech, asso dir 1968-69; Adult & Continuing Educ Fed City Coll, dir 1969-74; Adult & Comm Educ Baltimore City Pub Schs, coord 1974-79; Equal Opport Fed Emergency Mgmnt Agency Washington DC, dir 1979-. **ORGANIZATIONS:** Mem AssnUniv Profs Adult Edn; adv bd mem Am Soc for Pub Adminstrn 1973-74; bd dirs DC Police Boys Clubs; sec DC Dept Correction's Toastmasters Club 1964-65; pres Nat Child Day Care Assn 1970-72; pres Diplomat Cab Assn 1965-; DC Pre-Sch Council 1960-61; Lamond-Riggs Citizens Assn 1961-63; chmn DC Boxing Commn 1964-68; Exec com World Boxing Assn 1973-. **HONORS/ACHIEVEMENTS:** Numerous Boxing Championships. **MILITARY SERVICE:** USAF Reserves lt col. **BUSINESS ADDRESS:** 1725 I St NW, Washington, DC 20472.

LEE, OLIVER B.
Educator. **PERSONAL:** Born Sep 27, 1926, Cleveland, OH; married Isis Edna; children: Brenda, Linda, Jacquelyn, John. **EDUCATION:** Springfield Coll Springfield MA, BS 1953; Springfield Coll Springfield MA, MS 1957. **CAREER:** Cleveland YMCA, dir pe 1954-59; Cleveland, Vocational Rehab Cleveland, counselor supr 1959-64; OH Bur of Vocational Rehab Cleveland 1964-66; Rehab Serv Cleveland Soc for Blind Cleveland, dir 1966-67; Counseling & Placement Aim-Jobs Cleveland, dir 1967-69; Comm Extension Program Cleveland State U, dir 1969-73; Cleveland State U, asso dean 1973-; Youth Program Dir, Salvation Army, Superior Corps, Cleveland 1963-. **HONORS/ACHIEVEMENTS:** United Area Citizens Agency Leadership Devel Award 1972; Kiwanis Club Serv to Youth Award 1973; Lincoln HS Football Hall of Fame Hinton WV 1972. **MILITARY SERVICE:** USAF sgt 1946-48. **BUSINESS ADDRESS:** Div of Continuing Ed, Cleveland State Univ, Cleveland, OH.

LEE, RICHARD THOMAS
Educator. **PERSONAL:** Born Oct 17, 1944, Waco, TX; married Emily A; children: Richard II, Rodrick, Rendall. **EDUCATION:** So U, BS sec educ 1968; Mankato St U, MSc educ 1975;Univ of KS, PhD cand educ 1980. **CAREER:** Supp Educ Serv Univ of KS, dir 1975-; Min Groups Stud Central Mankata State Univ, asst dir 1970-75; Minneapolis Public Sch, instrcutor U969-70; Twin Cities Oppor Ind Cent, couns, instructor 1969-70; East Baton Rouge Parish School Sys, instructor 1968-69; Placement Cood Manpower Training Cent, instructor, counselor 1968-69; African Studies Dept Univ of KS, consult 1976; Univ of KS, 27th annual prin couns, student conf; Univ of KS, career guidance counselor sys tech 1976; Mankato State Coll, 1972-75. **ORGANIZATIONS:** Pres Black Faculty & Staff Council 1979-; Com on Analysis & Advancement of Instruction AAUP 1979-; faculty senate Com on Faculty Rights Privileges & Responsblts 1978-79; Black Host Family Program Com African Student Assn 1979;Mem Pearson Tr Com KSUniv 1975-76; minor Prof Adv Prog Comm 1975-; mem Blk Fac Staff Coun KSUniv 1976-; mem E & Cen KS Comm Act Agency 1976-; pres app chmn Affirmative Act Prog Mankato St Coll 1973-75; chmn Minority Women Salary Equity Adj Com Mankato Sta Coll 1974-75; fac sen appointee Stud Fin Aid Adv Comm 1972-75; Stud Conduct Bd 1973-75; Lib Adv Comm 1973-75; hon mem Black Stud Un Native Am Assn; Chicano Stud Organ 1970-75; Mankato Area Human Rights Comm 1973-75; Mankato Chamber of Com; Human Rel Com 1972-75; Assn for Study of Negro Life & Hist 1972-; Am Assn of Higher Educ 1971-; Voca Rehab Couns Assn 1973-; MN Assn of Fin Aid Admn 1972-74; MN Personnel Guid Assn 1972-75; MN Coll Personnel Assn 1971-75; MN Fed of Teachers 1969-74. **HONORS/ACHIEVEMENTS:** Ath scholarship SoUniv 1964-68; fellowship RSA 1973-75. **BUSINESS ADDRESS:** 202 Carruth O Leary Hall, Lawrence, KS 66045.

LEE, RITTEN EDWARD
Business administrator. **PERSONAL:** Born Jun 25, 1925, Brighton, AL; son of Ritten Lee and Mattie Hoque Lee; married Betty Allen; children: Anthony Edward, Juliana Hogue. **EDUCATION:** Earlham Coll, BA 1950; Univ of CT School of Soc Work, MA 1953. **CAREER:** Hudson Guild NYC, exec dir 1972-77; United Neighborhood House NYC, dir manpower 1977-80; Natl Charities Info Bur NYC, asst dir 1980-81; Seneca Ctr, exec dir. **ORGANIZATIONS:** Publ BLACFAX Mag 1982-85; jazz disc jockey WCVI, WENY, WHRC 1981-84; consult New York City Dept of Law 1981-82; adj prof Rutgers Univ Coll 1965-80; trustee Comm Church of NY 1973-77; bd mem RENA-COA Multi-Serv Ctr; trustee Earlham Coll 1970-79; adj lecturer sociology Rutgers Univ Coll 1966-80, Hunter Coll School of Soc Work 1977-78; publisher, BLACFAX Calendar 1988-89. **HONORS/ACHIEVEMENTS:** Sarah Addington Awd Earlham Coll 1950; Hon Mention Poetry Mag 1950-51; Poetry Publ

Span, Botteghe Oscure Crisis, Flame, Crucible & others; Commiss NCNCR Appt Newark Comm for Neighborhood Conserv 1968; Cert of Apprec RENA-COA Multi Serv Ctr 1979. **MILITARY SERVICE:** AAF sgt 2 yrs 4 mo; Good Conduct; Amer Theatre Victory 1943-46. **HOME ADDRESS:** 214 W 138th St, New York, NY 10030.

LEE, ROBERT E.
Attorney. **PERSONAL:** Born Nov 23, 1924, Cleveland, OH; children: 3 Children. **EDUCATION:** Adelbert Coll, 1950; Cleveland State Law Sch, 1961. **CAREER:** Atty private practice 1961. **MILITARY SERVICE:** USAF 2nd lt 1943-46. **BUSINESS ADDRESS:** 1405 Superior Bldg, Cleveland, OH 44114.

LEE, ROBERT EMILE
Oil company executive. **PERSONAL:** Born Aug 19, 1948, New Orleans, LA; son of Robert Emile Lee Sr and Mae Louise Lee; married Glendarene Beck; children: Joseph. **EDUCATION:** Tulane Univ, BS 1970; Univ of Chicago, MBA 1973. **CAREER:** Martin Marietta Aerospace, engineering admin specialist 1973-75; Tenneco Oil, planning analyst 1976-78, supply coord 1978-80, mgr product distribution 1980-84, mgr mktg & planning 1984-86; sr crude oil representative 1986-87. **ORGANIZATIONS:** Mem NBMBA Assn Houston Chapter 1986-. **HOME ADDRESS:** 2318 Sugarline Dr, Sugarland, TX 77479. **BUSINESS ADDRESS:** Sr Crude Oil Rep, Tenneco Oil Co, PO Box 2511, Houston, TX 77001.

LEE, ROBERT H.C.
Clergyman. **PERSONAL:** Born Oct 12, 1897, Greensboro, NC; married Lillian; children: Betty. **EDUCATION:** Livingston Coll, DD 1959; Livingston Coll, 1920. **CAREER:** AME Zion Dept of Recs & Rsrch, gen sec auditor; AME Zion Ch, pastor 53 yrs. **ORGANIZATIONS:** Past grand chaplain Elks; past qchaplain Am Legion. **HONORS/ACHIEVEMENTS:** Prayer offered House of Reps 1975; recpt Purple Heart. **MILITARY SERVICE:** USAF maj. **BUSINESS ADDRESS:** PO Box 1401, Charlotte, NC 28213.

LEE, RON
Athlete. **PERSONAL:** Born Nov 02, 1952, Boston, MA. **EDUCATION:** Univ of OR, BS 1976. **CAREER:** Detroit Pistons, professional basketball player 1980-; Atlanta Hawks, professional player 1979; New Orleans Utah Jazz, professional player 1979; Phoenix Suns, professional player 1976-79. **HONORS/ACHIEVEMENTS:** MVP Natl Invitational Tournament 1975; holds Univ of OR records for points scored/assists/field goals/free throws; Pac 8 Conf Player of Yr 1976; 1st conf player named All Pac 8, 4 straight seasons; Piston Rep Player's Assn; All Rookie Team 1976-77; led league in steals (274) 1977-78; tied Piston team record, steals in single game; set team record by sinking 6 out of 12 3-pt field goal tries; currently only NBA player to be drafted by teams in 3 different professional sports. **BUSINESS ADDRESS:** Detroit Pistons Pont Silverdo, 1200 Featherstone Rd, Pontiac, MI 48057.

LEE, RONALD B.
Business executive. **PERSONAL:** Born May 26, 1932, New York; son of Kermit J Lee and Lillian B (Jackson) Lee; married Nancy Jean (Knowalk), Oct 10, 1985; children: Dean E, Brett M. **EDUCATION:** US Military Acad West Point, BS 1954; US Defense Language Inst, attended 1962; Indsl Coll Armed Forces, attended 1962; Syracuse Univ, MBA 1964; Syracuse Univ, Army Comptrollership School 1964; Western New England Coll, LLD (Hon) 1969; American Univ, PhD (ABD) 1971, MA 1977; Center for Urban Affairs, dir; Lawrence F O'Brien, asst provost. **CAREER:** White House Fellow, staff 1965-66; US Postal Serv, dir planning & syst analysis 1966-68; Michigan State Univ, prof 1968-69; US, asst postmaster gen 1969-72; Xerox Corp, dir mktg analysis 1972-73, region manager tech serv NE reg 1973-75, reg mgr branch operations 1975-78, mgr govt/educ & med mktg Rochester 1978-79, mgr bus & comm affairs Arlington VA 1979-82; Energy Intl Corp, pres; Marc London Ltd, chmn; Phoenix Group Intl Ltd, pres 1982-89; Development Management Group Inc, Chicago IL, exec vice pres 1989-. **ORGANIZATIONS:** Mem Assn West Point Grads; mem Assn of Syracuse Army Comptrolles; mem Amer Soc Public Admin; mem Alpha Phi Alpha; mem White House Fellows Assn; life mem NAACP; life mem Natl Urban League; mem Amer Acad Pol & Soc Sci; bd trustees Western New England Coll; bd trustees Natl Acad Public Admin; bd trustees Natl Inst Public Admin; bd advisors Natl Assn Sickle Cell Diseases; mem Natl Alliance of Business DC; mem Natl Inst of Public Affairs; mem Greater Washington Bd of Trade; mem DC Private Indus Counc; chmn bd of trustees Capital Children's Mus; bd dir United Way Inc Rochester; bd dir Jr Achievement of Greater Washington; bd dir Natl Conf of Christians & Jews Washington; bd dir Comm Found of Greater Washington DC; bd dir Metro Washington Min Purchasing Council; 1st pres Okinawa Coll Club 1958-59; 1st pres White House Fellows Assn 1966. **HONORS/ACHIEVEMENTS:** Arthur S Fleming Awd 1 of 10 Most Outstanding Young Men in Govt 1968; Dept Army Outstanding Civilian Serv Med 1968; Miles Kimball Awd Contrib Bus Mailers 1971; numerous publications & speaking appearances; elected Beta Gamma Sigma (Bus Hon); pres Universal Postal Union Special Study Group Berne Switzerland; 20-25 publications & chapters of books. **MILITARY SERVICE:** AUS 1954-67, Vietnam Veteran, major. **BUSINESS ADDRESS:** Executive Vice President, Development Management Group Inc, 3660 N Lakeshore Dr #4700, Chicago, IL 60613.

LEE, ROTAN
Retired physician. **PERSONAL:** Born Nov 06, 1906, Bushkill, PA; married Bessie; children: Terry, Rotan. **EDUCATION:** PA State U, BA 1928; Howard U, MD 1938; Columbia U, post grad 1932-33. **CAREER:** Med Audit Com, chmn; Utilization Rev Com, co-chmn; Ctr City Hosp, co-chmn 1976-; Diamond Family Med Ctr, dir 1974-75; Dist Health Ctr City of Phila, adminstr 1947-73; sch physician 1941-42; surg resd 1939-40; Mercy Hosp, med internship 1938-39; pvt med prac gen surgeon 1946-75; Center City Hosp, med staff 1960-77; Bushkill Water Co. **ORGANIZATIONS:** Mem HM Club of Am 1972-; Philadelphia Co Med Soc PA State Med Soc; AMA; Nat Med Assn; Chi Delta Mu; Omega Psi Phi. **HONORS/ACHIEVEMENTS:** Articles on "Twins & Twinning"; human Mastoid Process". **MILITARY SERVICE:** AUS med corps capt 1942-46.

LEE, SHEILA JACKSON
Judge. **PERSONAL:** Born Jan 12, 1950, Queens, NY; married Elwyn Cornelius; children: Erica Shelwyn, Jason Cornelius Bennett. **EDUCATION:** Yale U, BA polit sci (honors) 1969-72;Univ of VA Sch of Law, JD 1972-75. **CAREER:** Mudge Rose Guthrie & Alexander, summer assoc 1974; Wld Harkrader & Ross, atty 1975-78; US House of Reps & Select Comm on Assasinations, staff counsel 1977-78; Fulbright & Jaworski, atty 1978-80; United Energy Resources, atty 1980-87; Brodsky & Ketchand, partner 1987-; City of Houston, assoc judge 1987-. **ORGANIZATIONS:** Bd dirs John Courtney Murray Found Yale Univ New Haven 1972-73, John Courtney Murray Traveling & Rsch Fellowship, Houston Area Urban League 1979-, Episcopal Ctr for Children 1976-78, WA Council of Lawyers 1976-78; mem State Bar of TX Bar Jour Com 1980; bd dir Amer Assn of Blacks in Energy 1980; chairperson-Black Women Lawyers Assn 1980; pres Houston Lawyers Assoc 1983-84; dir TX Young Lawyers Assoc 198-86; pres Houston Metro Ministries 1984-85; dir Children's Museum 1985-; dir Sam Houston Area Council Boy Scouts of Amer 1987-. **HONORS/ACHIEVEMENTS:** Outstanding Young Lawyer Pampered Lady Botique Awards Luncheon NY 1977; Women's Day Spearker Award Linden Blvd Seventh-Day Adven Ch NY 1978; Outstanding Young Woman of Am 1979,80,81; Rising Star of TX Awd TX Bus Mag 1983; Outstanding Young Houstonian Awd C of C 1984; Houston Lawyers Assoc Outstanding Serv Awd 1984; nominated Outstanding Young Lawyer of Houston 1985; Named one of Houston's 20 Most Influential Black Women 1984; Named Outstanding History Maker (Legal) Riverside General Hosp Awds Prog 1987; selected as fellow TX Bar Found for Outstanding Legal and Community Serv 1986. **BUSINESS ADDRESS:** Judge, City of Houston, Municipal Court, 2800 One Allen Ctr, Houston, TX 77002.

LEE, SHELTON JACKSON See LEE, SPIKE

LEE, SHIRLEY FREEMAN
Administrator. **PERSONAL:** Born May 06, 1928, Cleveland, OH; married Douglas F Lee (deceased); children: Vivian, Durriyya. **EDUCATION:** Notre Dame Coll, BA, 1950; Boston Coll, School of Social Work, MSW, 1952; Case Western Reserve, 1980-; Baldwin-Wallace, 1986. **CAREER:** Com of Massachusetts Div of Child Guardianship, foster home, 1954-58; Head Start, supvr, 1965; Boston Redevel Authority, relocation spec, 1968-71; De Paul Infant Home, admin, 1981-83; Ohio Licensed Independent Social Worker, 1986; Cahtolic Soc Serv of Cuyahoga City, supvr foster home dept, admin day care. **ORGANIZATIONS:** Mem, Delta Sigma Theta; bd of dir, Long Beach & Van Nuys School of Business,, 1977-. **HOME ADDRESS:** 14221 Kingsford Ave, Cleveland, OH 44128. **BUSINESS ADDRESS:** Administrator School Service, Catholic Social Services, 3409 Woodland Ave, Cleveland, OH 44115.

LEE, SILAS, III
Public opinion pollster, educator. **PERSONAL:** Born Jul 24, 1954, New Orleans, LA; son of Silas and Henrietta Lee; married Marcell Williams (divorced). **EDUCATION:** Loyola Univ, BA 1972-76; Univ of New Orleans, MS 1976-79. **CAREER:** Loyola Univ, sociology instructor 1979-; Silas Lee & Assoc, pres 1982-. **ORGANIZATIONS:** pres Silas Lee & Assoc first Black Opinion Pollster 1982-; consultant Ed Found 1984-; Published, The Econ Profile of Blacks & Whites in New Orleans; vice chairman Natl Black Tourism Assn 1989. **HONORS/ACHIEVEMENTS:** Inventor of educational/amusement game Flight 701 1983; honorary secretary of state for LA 1984; Court Certified Expert on the Social and Economic status of blacks and public opinion research-eastern district of Louisiana court and federal district court.

LEE, SPIKE (SHELTON JACKSON LEE)
Film director. **PERSONAL:** Born 1957, Atlanta, GA; son of William Lee and Jacqueline Shelton Lee. **EDUCATION:** Morehouse Coll, BA 1979; New York Univ, MA filmmaking 1983. **CAREER:** Producer/writer/director. **HONORS/ACHIEVEMENTS:** Writer and director of films "She's Gotta Have It," 1986, "School Daze," 1988, and "Do the Right Thing," 1989; author of Spike Lee's Gotta Have It: Inside Guerilla Filmmaking, Simon & Schuster, 1987, and Uplift the Race, Simon & Schuster, 1988. Student director's award from Academy of Motion Picture Arts and Sciences for "Joe's Bed-Stuy Barber Shop: We Cut Heads," 1982; New Generation Award, LA Film Critics, for "She's Gotta Have It"; Prix de Jeunesse, Cannes Film Festival, for "She's Gotta Have It," 1986. *

LEE, STRATTON CREIGHTON
Retired educational administrator. **PERSONAL:** Born Apr 17, 1920, Tarrytown, NY; married Yvonne Holder; children: Stratton C, Jr. **EDUCATION:** Coll of the City of NY, BS 1942, MBA 1952. **CAREER:** Licensed real estate broker NY State 1955-; Adelphi Univ & Queens Coll, instr Afro-Am History 1967-70; Urban Home Ownership, vice pres 1970-71; Natl Corp for Housing Partnerships, dir of mgmt 1971-72; Natl Center for Housing Mgmt, exec assoc 1972; Inst of Real Estate Mgmt, prop mgr 1974-; Creighton Housing Mgmt, pres 1974-77; Pratt Inst vice pres campus mgmt 1977-82; Arco/Metro Prop Mgmt corp, pres 1982-. **ORGANIZATIONS:** Mem Natl Assn of Housing & Redevel Ofcrs 1950-; mem Nassau Cnty Econ Opportunity Commn 1969-70; mem Assn of Phys Plant Adminstrs 1980; Ny State Legislative Aide 32nd AD Congr Dist 1974-76. **HONORS/ACHIEVEMENTS:** CPM of the Year Inst of Real Estate Mgmt 1976; mem HUD-IREM natl Com Natl Assn of Realtors 1976-78. **MILITARY SERVICE:** ROTC Sgt 1938-39. **BUSINESS ADDRESS:** Real Estate Manager & Devel, 113 Bon Aire Circle, Suffern, NY 10901.

LEE, THEODOSIA L. CRAWFORD
Investment representative. **PERSONAL:** Born Nov 23, 1919, Payson, OK; married Archie Crawford. **EDUCATION:** Langston Univ OK. **CAREER:** Westamerica Finance Corp, reg rep; stocks; bonds; mut funds; ins; Lawton Community Guide, adv agt. **ORGANIZATIONS:** Pres Okla City NAACP 1975-76; 2d vice pres OK Conf NAACP; chmn task force Black Political Assembly; mem & Ok Urban League Metro Lib Comm; exec bd OKCity Bd NAACP; bd mem OK Co Cancer Soc; mem Criteria Study Club Versatile Club; 1st black fin chmn OK Co Dem Party; co-chmn Precinct 5 Ward 7; past chmn Politican Womens Caucus; lobbyist NAACP and Politacal Womens Caucus; Zeta Phi Beta; mem 5th St Bapt Ch Certif. **HONORS/ACHIEVEMENTS:** Merit YMCA 1959-60; certif apprec Urban League 1958; 1963-64; certif apprec OK State Fed Colores Womens Club 1969; cert honor CREO 1974. **MILITARY SERVICE:** WAC pfc 1942-45. **BUSINESS ADDRESS:** 3201 NW 63rd St, Oklahoma City, OK 73116.

LEE, THOMAS F.
Clergyman. **PERSONAL:** Born Feb 06, 1925, Tuscaloosa, AL; married Willie Nell; children: Clifford, Michael, Franchon, Eric. **EDUCATION:** Crane Jr Coll; Shield Bus Coll; Chicago State Coll; Chicago Bapt Inst Theol Sem, grad. **CAREER:** Emmanuel Bapt Ch Chicago, pastor; Cook County Dept of Corrections, dept sheriff. **ORGANIZATIONS:** Mem Am Bapt Conv; Progressive Nat Bapt Conv; bd dir Ch Fedn of Chicago; Chicago Bapt

Assn; chaplain, bd mem Fraternal Order of Police; mem Prince Hall Mason. **BUSINESS ADDRESS:** 6820 S Emerald Ave, Chicago, IL 60621.

LEE, TYRONNE T.
Business administrator. **PERSONAL:** Born Aug 18, 1949, Pittsburgh, PA; married DeBorah Rozier; children: Tyronne Jr, Charela Nani Aja. **EDUCATION:** Univ of Pittsburgh, BA (magna cum laude) 1973; Duquesne Law Sch. **CAREER:** Selma Burke Art Ctr, exec dir 1977-; Bidwell Inc, program dir 1973-77; Urban League Pittsburgh, media specialist 1972; Intl Third World Design Ltd, pres. **ORGANIZATIONS:** Mem NAACP Kiwansis; Health & Educ Com; Urban League; mem Nat Conf Artists. **HONORS/ACHIEVEMENTS:** Young Writers Award Writers Forum 1976; Film-maker Award Pittsburgh Film-makers 1977; Outstanding Young Men of Am US Jaycees 1979. **BUSINESS ADDRESS:** 6118 Penn Cir S, Pittsburgh, PA 15206.

LEE, VAN SPENCER
Government official. **PERSONAL:** Born Mar 02, 1942, Morristown, TN; married Beulah Annette Arnett; children: Eric M, Melissa R, Steven M. **EDUCATION:** Knoxville Coll Knoxville TN, 1961-63; TVA Pub Safety Serv Sch, cert 1971; Walters State Coll, AS (cum laude) 1972. **CAREER:** City of Morristown TN, vice mayor; TVA, pub safety officer 1971-77, equal employment investigator 1973-77, lt unit supv 1977-84, asst chief. **ORGANIZATIONS:** Mem TN Law Enforcement Officers Assn 1967; mem Fraternal Order of Police 1967; life mem Nat Rifle Assn 1970; elder Lawrence United Presb Ch 1968; mem Morristown Area C of C 1972; mem, past pres W Elem PTA 1973-74; mem, sec Morristown City Council PTA 1973-74; mem bd of dir Morristown-Hamblen Day Care Ctr 1972-76; mem adv com Morristown City Schs 1973-77; mem Lincoln Heights Middle Sch PTA 1977-; mem Morristown-Hamblen HS W Band Boosters 1977-; speaker Emeritus TVA Pub Safety Serv Sch 1971. **HONORS/ACHIEVEMENTS:** 1st black patrolman Morristown Police Dept 1967-71; 1st black operator Am Enka 1965-67; 1st black commr Morristown Housing Authority 1975-77; 1st black councilmember Ward 1 City of Morristown 1977; 1st black commr Hamblen Co Work Release Program 1978-79; 1st black chmn Hamblen Co Am Cancer Soc 1980; 1st black-mem Morristown Kiwanis Club 1976; 1st black mem bd of trustees Morristown-Hamblen Hosp 1977-; Outstanding Young Man of Am 1973; Charter Pres Award Lincoln Heights Middle Sch PTA Morristown 1974; Outstanding Defensive Course Instr Award TVA Nat Safety Council 1977; Meritorious Serv Award TVA Pub Safety Serv Knoxville TN 1978; Outstanding Comm Serv Award Morristown Coll 1978; award Morristown Honor Club 1980. **BUSINESS ADDRESS:** Asst Chief, US TVA, 700 Chestnut St Tower II, Chattanooga, TN 37411.

LEE, VIVIAN BOOKER
Federal government administrator. **PERSONAL:** Born Jan 28, 1938, Spring, TX; children: Anthony. **EDUCATION:** Univ of WA, BS; Univ of Puget Sound, M Pub Admin. **CAREER:** VA Hosp Seattle, psychiatric nurse 1959-60; Group Health Corp Puget Sound, outpatient clinic nurse 1961-66; Seattle Public Sch, sch nurse 1966-68; Renton Sch, supr group health hosp & title I health supr 1968-72; Pub Health Serv HEW, prog mgmt officer 1972-77; Family Planning Serv, reg prog consult 1977-. **ORGANIZATIONS:** Mem Natl Black Nurses Assn, Univ of WA Nurses Alumnae Assn; pres visiting com Univ of WA; host family for World Affairs Coun; mem Found for Intl Understanding through Students; mem NAACP; mem Urban League; United Way Panel on Natl Agencies & Special Projects; mem Delta Sigma Theta; mem Girls Club of Puget Sound; participant White House Conf on Civil Rights 1966; Food Nutrition Health & Children 1969-70; mem Natl Family Planning and Reproductive Health Assoc, Washington State Family Planning Cncl. **HONORS/ACHIEVEMENTS:** Dept HEW Outstanding Performance Awd for Promoting Women's Equality 1975; HEW Sustained Superior Performance Awds 1973,77,78,79,80,81,87; HHS Secty's Awd for Excellence 1982; Washington Sch Nurse of Yr 1972; invited to Matrix Table held for honoring Women of Achievement 1970-87; Outstanding Young Womanof Amer Awd 1971; Outstanding Dedication Awd Washington State Cncl on Family Planning 1978; Annual Awd of Family Planning Advocates of Oregon State 1983,87; Region X Nurse Practitioner Awd is named "The Vivian O Lee Nurse Practitioner of the Year Awd" in her honor 1987. **MILITARY SERVICE:** 50th Gen Hosp Reserve Corps 1959-63. **BUSINESS ADDRESS:** Regional Program Consultant, DHHS PHS DHSD CSB, 2901 Third Ave MS 405, Seattle, WA 98121.

LEE, WILLIAM H.
Business executive. **PERSONAL:** Born May 29, 1936, Austin, TX; married Kathryn Charles; children: Roderick Joseph, William Hanford, Jr, Lawrence Charles. **EDUCATION:** Univ of CA, AB 1957; Sacramento State Coll, 1953-55. **CAREER:** Lee Sacramento Observer, pres, publisher; Lee Publishing Co, pres. **ORGANIZATIONS:** Pres, West Coast Black Publishers Assn, 1974-; sec, bd dir, Natl Newspaper Publishers Assn, 1970-73; mem, Delta Sigma Chi Journalism Frat; commr, Sacramento County Welfare Commn; founder, past pres, Men's Civil League of Sacramento; bd dir, Sacramento NAACP Credit Union; United Christian Center; dir, Sacramento Central YMCA; Sacramento Urban League; United Way; Sacramento County, Amer Cancer Soc; bd chmn, Sacramento Business Coordinating Council; co-founder, Sacramento Area Black Caucus; vice-chmn, Cancer Fund Drive; life mem, NAACP; mem, Sacramento Comm for Urban Renewal; Statewide Comm on Voter Registration. **HONORS/ACHIEVEMENTS:** Sacramento's Outstanding Young Man of Year, 1965; received Sacramento C of C Distinguished Serv Award twice; Carl Murphy Plaque for community serv, 1974; John B Russwurm Trophy, 1973, 1975; Media Award, Western Regional Conf of Black Elected Officials, 1973; United Negro Coll Fund, 1975; Natl Media Appreciation Award; numerous natl & local newspaper awards; other civic leadership citations. **MILITARY SERVICE:** USAFR 1959-65. **BUSINESS ADDRESS:** PO Box 209, Sacramento, CA 95801.

LEE, WILLIAM J.
Clergyman. **PERSONAL:** Born May 19, 1936, Charlotte Mecklenb, NC. **EDUCATION:** Johnson C Smith Univ, 1952-57. **CAREER:** Silver Mt Bapt Ch, pastor 1966-; JB Ivey Co Charlotte NC, slesman 1968-74; St John's Bapt Ch Newell, builder 1965-. **ORGANIZATIONS:** Sec Mecklenburg Gen Bapt Asso 1958-; NAACP; YMC; mem Nat Bapt Conv. **HONORS/ACHIEVEMENTS:** 1st black mgr Harris Teeter Supermarket 1965-; master mason honored for civil rights leadership radio ministry; top men's clothing salesman JB Ivey 1974. **BUSINESS ADDRESS:** Ivey's, 127 N Tryon St, Charlotte, NC 28202.

LEE, WILLIAM RONNELL
Athlete. **PERSONAL:** Born Sep 17, 1953, Martins Ferry, OH; married Toni Ramele Chavis; children: William Ronnell, II, Chrystal Chavis. **EDUCATION:** WV U, BS social work 1976. **CAREER:** Baltimore Colts, running back 1976-80. **ORGANIZATIONS:** Vol Spl Olympics 1974-79; civic spkr Baltimore Colts Pub Rel 1976-78; mem Nat Football Players Assn 1976-80; player US Chess Fed 1979-80; spkr Human Rel Yth Employment Sem 1979; master mason Masons 1979-80. **HONORS/ACHIEVEMENTS:** Selected to all e team WVUniv 1979; appre dinner Baltimore Colts Corral #2 1977; Ron Lee Day Dity of Bellaire 1978. **BUSINESS ADDRESS:** NFL Players Association, 1300 Connecticut Ave NW, Ste 407, Washington, DC 20036.

LEE-MILLER, STEPHANIE
Government official. **PERSONAL:** Born Mar 07, 1950, Los Angeles, CA; daughter of Robert W Lee and Betty Lee; divorced. **EDUCATION:** Occidental Coll, MA 1975; CA St Coll Dominguez Hills, BA 1971; Coro Fellowship Prog, cert of comp 1973. **CAREER:** US Dept of Transportation, Washington DC, director of office of commercial space transportation, 1989—; US Dept of Health and Human Services, Washington DC, asst secretary for public affairs, 1983-89; US Dept of Commerce, Washington DC, special asst of public affairs, 1981-83; Contact California, Beverly Hills CA, owner, partner, 1979-81; Coro Found, fellow in public affairs, 1972-73, dir of comm prgm 1974-79; Cent City Men Hlth Centr, comm wkr 1971-72; Cmpgn to Elect Congresswoman Burke Cons, off mgr; Laison Cit Training Prgm, cons; LA Comm Coll Dist, cons; Now Wow Prod, pt owner; freelance songwriter, scriptwriter. **ORGANIZATIONS:** Bd dir, mem UnWay Urban Coalition; cand LA City Council 1975; Natl Council of Negro Women; act mem Soroptimist Intrnat; Delta Sigma Theta Pub Serv Sor; mem Rep St Cent Com; mem Nat Coun Negro Women; bd of dir, Natl Council; Natl Links, Inc; mem Town Hall LA Nom. **HONORS/ACHIEVEMENTS:** Ach award Soroptimist Intrnat, 1977; who's Who in Am Coll &Univ 1970; Coro Found Felshp 1972; del Rep Nat Conv 1977; del Rep Conv 1980; listed Outstanding Yng Women in Am 1979-80; named outstanding young woman of America, 1981; outstanding performance certificate, Secretary of Commerce, 1983; US delegate, Internatl Women's Conference, 1985; Scroll of Merit, Natl Medical Assn, 1988. **HOME ADDRESS:** 116 G St SW, Washington, DC 20024.

LEE-SMITH, HUGHIE
Artist. **PERSONAL:** Born Sep 20, 1915, Eustis, FL; son of Luther Lee-Smith and Alice Lee-Smith; married Patricia Ann Thomas; children: Christina. **EDUCATION:** Cleveland Inst of Art, Cert of Grad 1938; Wayne State Univ, BS Art Edn. **CAREER:** Artist; Art Students League, instr of painting. **ORGANIZATIONS:** Council member, Natl Acad of Design, 1986-89; council mem, 1983—, vice president, 1985-88, Artists Fellowship Inc; pres, 1980-82, vice pres, 1984—, Audubon Artists Inc; bd dir Artists Equity Assn 1982-84; Natl Adv Cncl Studio Museum Harlem, NYC; mem Grand Central Art Galleries 1967-80; Adv Commn High Sch of Art & Design New York City 1976-80; MI Assn of Pub Sch Adult Educators; MI Acad of Sci, Arts & Letters; The Century Assn NYC; The Lotos Club NYC; lectures & panel discussions at, Princeton Univ, Univ of Chgo, Coll Art AssnWash,DC, Montclair State Coll, NC Central Univ, Voorhees Coll, Morgan State Coll, The Walden Sch, Pub TV Channel 13 1979, Cleveland Inst of Art, Cleveland State Univ. **HONORS/ACHIEVEMENTS:** Audubon Artists Inc The Ralph Fabri Award 1982, The Binny and Smith Award 1983, The Emily Lowe Award 1985; Bronze Plaque MD Commn on Afro-Amer Hist & Culture 1981; Art Achievement Award Wayne St Univ 1983; Key to the City of Hartford 1984; "Hughie Lee-Smith Day," Cleveland OH, Oct 19, 1984; numerous collections incl, The Natl Mus of Amer Art Wash, DC; Chase Manhatten Bank NYC; Univ of MI; Howard Univ; Barnet-Aden Coll Wash, DC; Alain Locke Soc Princeton Univ; US Post Office NYC; Schomburg Coll NYC; numerous one man shows incl, Snowden Gallery Chicago 1945; Janet Nessler Gallery New York City 1960, 1962, 1964; Western MI Univ Kalamazoo 1977; CRT's Craftery Gallery Hartford, CT 1984; Malcolm Brown Gallery Cleveland 1984; Century Assn of NY 1984; Malcolm Brown Galler, 1984-88; Butler Inst of American Art, 1989; VA Polytechnical Univ, 1989; publications incl, Newsweek Mag June 22, 1 970; Art Galler y Mag 1968, 1970; Beyond Black or white Vernon J Dixon & Baldi Foster 1971; Crisis Mag 1970, 1983; Amer Artist Mag Oct 1978; Scholastic Mag HS Art Exhib Catalogue 1981; Represented in Cleveland Inst Art "The First Hundred Years" 1983; num other exhib; The Len Everette Memorial Prize Audubon Artists Inc 1986. **MILITARY SERVICE:** USN Seaman 1st Class 1943-45; Cert of Commendation 1974. **HOME ADDRESS:** 52-16 Gardenview Terrace, East Windsor, NJ 08520.

LEEK, EVERETT PAUL
Attorney. **PERSONAL:** Born Jun 08, 1929, Canton, IL; married Doreen A Dale; children: Everett Craig, Jennifer Ann, Paul Scott. **EDUCATION:** MI State Univ, BS 1957, MS 1964; Univ of Detroit Law Sch, JD 1976. **CAREER:** US Treas Dept, agent 1957-60; Chevrolet Div Gen Motors, labor relations rep 1960-67; polygraph examiner/private consultant 1973-; Delta Coll, prof; Printross Corp, pres. **ORGANIZATIONS:** Mem NAACP, Alpha Phi Alpha, MI Assn of Polygraph Examiners; mem Amer, MI, Bar Assns; mem MI Trial Lawyers Assn. **HONORS/ACHIEVEMENTS:** Professional Man of the Year, Negro Business & Professional Women's Assn 1970; Outstanding Educators of Amer 1972. **MILITARY SERVICE:** USN 1949-53. **BUSINESS ADDRESS:** President, Printross Corp, 330 S Washington, Saginaw, MI 48604.

LEEK, SANDRA D.
Lawyer. **PERSONAL:** Born Oct 08, 1954, Durham, NC; daughter of J Donald Leek and Inez Rempson Anderson. **EDUCATION:** Tufts Univ, Medford, MA, BA Political Science, 1976; Indiana Univ, Bloomington, IN, JD, 1979. **CAREER:** Legal Services Org of Indiana, Inc (LSOI,) Indianapolis, IN, staff atty, 1979-81, managing atty, 1986-; Indiana Legal Serv Support Center (ILSSC,) dir, 1981-86. **ORGANIZATIONS:** Mem, Delta Sigma Theta Sorority, Inc, 1979-; mem, Amer Bar Assn, 1979-; mem, Indiana State Bar Assn, 1979-; mem, Indianapolis Bar Assn, 1979-; Civil Cmt Representative, Natl Legal Aid & Defender Assn, 1981-; mem, Natl Bar Assn, 1982-; chmn, Public Affairs/Indy YWCA, 1983-86; chmn, Political Action/Coalition of 100 Black Women, 1986-88; 2nd vice pres/bd of mgrs, Fall Creek YMCA, 1987-88; pres, Marion City Bar Assn, 1987-88; exec comm, NAACP, Indianapolis Branch, 1988-; mem, Links, Inc, 1988-; corp atty, Indiana Black Expo, Inc, 1988-. **HONORS/ACHIEVEMENTS:** Exec editor, "You and the Law," 1983, 1985; moderator, Law for Laymen TV series, 1983, 1984, 1985; Woman of Achievement, Indy YWCA, 1985; Outstanding Contribution, Legal Services Org of Indiana, Inc, 1986, Outstanding Communnity Serv, Marion County Bar Assn, 1989. **BUSINESS ADDRESS:** Mng atty, Indianapolis Regional Offices, Legal Servs Org of Indiana, Inc, 107 N Penn St, Suite 300, Indianapolis, IN 46204.

LEEKE, JOHN F.
Educator, organizational development. **PERSONAL:** Born May 19, 1939, Indianapolis, IN; married Thetese Gartin; children: Michael, Madelyn, Mark, Matthew. **EDUCATION:** IN St U, BS 1961;Univ MI, MS 1966; Union Grad Sch, PhD 1977. **CAREER:** NEA, instrtn & prof devel spec 1968-; Flint Comm Schools, teacher 1963-68; DC Public Schls, teacher 1962-63; IN State & Penal Frm, counselor 1962; Natl Training Lab of App Behavoral Science, consultant; US Dept Agriculture Grad School; Natl School Bds Assn; Natl Inst Drug Abuse; Consumer Product Safety Comm; Bell Labs; GSUSA; IN State Dept Instruction; numerous school systems. **ORGANIZATIONS:** Mem St Joseph Ch Landover MD; Neighborhood Civic Orgnzn; Pi Lambda Phi. **HONORS/ACHIEVEMENTS:** Hons Who's Who in Amer Coll &Univ 1962; achvmnt recgntn Pi Lambda Phi. **BUSINESS ADDRESS:** 1201 16 St NW, Washington, DC.

LEEPER, LEMUEL CLEVELAND
Company executive. **PERSONAL:** Born Jul 08, 1927, Balitmore, MD; married Martha Johnson; children: Lynn Tilghman. **EDUCATION:** Morgan State Univ, BS 1949; Howard Univ, MS 1953; Georgetown Univ, PhD 1958. **CAREER:** Morgan State Coll, instructor 1949-51; Natl Insts of Health, chemist 1951-58; Riverton Labs, Inc, vice pres tech dir 1958-66; Redoc Labs, Inc, pres owner 1966-80; USV Pharmaceuticals Inc, dir of ac 1966-71; Hope Che Corp, pres 1976-80; Lynn Cosmetics Inc, pres owner 1981-. **ORGANIZATIONS:** Pres mem Urban League of Union County NJ 1962-66; mem Housing Authority City of Summit NJ 1970-76; pres/mem Summit Bd of Educ 1977-85; steward Phillips Metro CME Church 1982-86. **HONORS/ACHIEVEMENTS:** Pioneer in automated analytical procedures; numerous articles published in the field of biochemistry; contributor to determination of cause of phenyketonuria; numerous publications on biosynthesis of adrenaline and noradrenaline; developer of special shave cream (Easy Shave) for shaving problems. **MILITARY SERVICE:** AUS corpl 1953-55. **BUSINESS ADDRESS:** President/CEO, Lynn Cosmetics Inc, 12 Bank St, Summit, NJ 07901.

LEEPER, LUCIUS WALTER
Physician. **PERSONAL:** Born Jan 09, 1922, Baltimore, MD; married Shirley Jenkins; children: Yvette, Fern, Frederick. **EDUCATION:** Morgan State Univ, BS 1945; Howard Univ, MD 1948. **CAREER:** Resident Trng, 1948-52; Private Practice, physician 1954-66; MD State Helth Dept Div Voc Rehab, med adv comm 1960-66; State of MD Bd Mental Health, mental hygiene rev bd 1960-63; Occupational Medicine, 1977-79; Social Security Administration, dir employee health and occupational safety 1974-79. **ORGANIZATIONS:** Bd dir Amer Diabetes Assn 1974-; mem Cncl of Fed Med Dir 1969-; mem AEAONMS; tb & cancer bd Imp Cncl AEAONMS 1969-71; bd of dirs Lynn Cosmetics. **HONORS/ACHIEVEMENTS:** First person operating iron lung via USAF plane 1953. **MILITARY SERVICE:** AUS pvt 1943-46; USAF capt 1952-54. **BUSINESS ADDRESS:** PO Box 27241, Baltimore, MD 21216.

LEEPER, RONALD JAMES
City government. **PERSONAL:** Born Dec 14, 1944, Charlotte, NC; married Phyllis Mack; children: Rhonda, Atiba. **CAREER:** Charlotte City Council, council mem 10 yrs. **ORGANIZATIONS:** Chmn city council Community Devel Committee 1979-; pres NC Black Elected Municipal Official Assoc 1982-; mem of bd of dir Urban League 1983-; chmn Charlotte-Meck Lenburg Black Elected Office 1984-85; pres Westpark Youth Athletic Assoc; pres Colony Acres Home Owners Assoc; mem of bd of dir Natl Conf Christians & Jews; bd mem Visitors of Boys Town NC; organizer/past pres of Vote Task Force; pres LRT & Assoc Consultant Firm; pres L&S Housing Corp. **HONORS/ACHIEVEMENTS:** Cert of Appreciation St Mark United Meth Church 1978, Sr Citizen United for Serv Christian Social Concern 1980; Certificate of Appreciation Black PoliticalAwareness League Winston-Salem NC 1984; Meritorious Awd NAACP Outstanding Comm Serv 1984. **HOME ADDRESS:** 417 Colony Acres Dr, Charlotte, NC 28210.

LEEVY, CARROLL M.
Educator, physician. **PERSONAL:** Born Oct 13, 1920, Columbia, SC; married Ruth S Barboza; children: Carroll B Leevy MD, Maria S Leevy. **EDUCATION:** Fisk Univ, AB 1941; Univ of MI, MD 1944; NJ Inst of Techn, ScD 1973; Fisk Univ, DHon 1981. **CAREER:** Jersey City Med Cntr, dir clinical invest 1947-56; Harvard Med Sch, assoc in med 1959-60; NJ Med School, assoc prof/prof med 1960-; Sammy Davis Jr Natl Liver Inst, med dir & chm bd 1984-; NJ Med Sch, prof/chmn dept med 1975-. **ORGANIZATIONS:** Consult Food & Drug Admin 1970-; consult Natl Inst Health 1966-; consult VA 1966-; pres Am Assn for Study of Liver Disease; pres Intl Assn for Study of the Liver; Natl Commn on Digestive Disease 1977-79; NIH Alcohol & Addiction Found; chmn faculty Conf on Stand of Diagnostic Criteria & Methodol in Liver Disease; Soc for Experimental Biol; Amer Coll of Phys; editorial bd Amer Jour of Med; chmn Faculty Orgn 1970-72; bd Concerned Citizens 1971-75. **HONORS/ACHIEVEMENTS:** Author and co-author of 10 books and over 500 scientific articles 1946-; mem Phi Beta Kappa; mem Alpha Omega Alpha; natl Comm on Digestive Diseases; Visiting Prof over 50 Universities; Recip of numerous awards. **MILITARY SERVICE:** USNR Commander served 6 years. **HOME ADDRESS:** 35 Robert Dr, Short Hills, NJ 07078. **BUSINESS ADDRESS:** Chmn Dept Med/Phys in Chief, Univ Med & Dent of NJ, 100 Bergan St, Newark, NJ 07103.

LEFFALL, LASALLE DOHENY, JR.
Surgeon oncologist medical educator. **PERSONAL:** Born May 22, 1930, Tallahassee, FL; married Ruth Mc Williams; children: La Salle III. **EDUCATION:** FL A&M Univ, BS 1948; Howard Univ, MD 1952. **CAREER:** Howard Univ Coll Med, asst dean 1964-70, acting dean 1970, prof chmn dept surgery 1970-. **ORGANIZATIONS:** Natl Med Assn 1962; mem SE Surg Congress 1970; Soc of Surg Chmn 1970; mem Alpha Omega Alpha 1972; Inst of Med Natl Acad of Sci 1973; Mem Amer Surg Assn 1976; pres Amer Cancer Soc 1979; Mem Natl Urban League, NAACP; YMCA; Alpha Phi Alpha; Sigma Pi Phi; mem Natl Cancer Adv Bd 1980; mem Amer Bd of Surgery 1981; mem Cosmos Club; Comm on CA; sec Amer Coll Surgeons 1983. **HONORS/ACHIEVEMENTS:** 1st prize Charles R Drew Fundamental Forum 1954; Outstanding Young Man of Yr 1965; Outstanding Educator in Am FL A&M 1971, 1974; William H Sinkler Meml Awd 1972; Star Surgeon Newsletter of NMA 1973; Who's Who in Black Amer 1976; St George Medal & Citation Amer Cancer Soc 1977. **MILITARY SERVICE:** AUS capt 1960-61. **BUSINESS ADDRESS:** Prof Chmn Dept Surgery, HowardUniv Hosp, 2041 Georgia Ave, NW, Washington, DC 20060.

LEFLORE, LARRY
Educator. **PERSONAL:** Born Oct 01, 1949, Cuba, AL; married Amanda L Collins. **EDUCATION:** William Carey Clge, BA 1971; Univ So MS, IMS 1974; Univ of So MS, MS 1980; FL State Univ, PhD 1984. **CAREER:** Columbia Training Sch, inst soc worker 1971-72; MS Dept Youth Serv Forrest Cty Youth Court, youth ct cnslr 1972-74, intake cnslr 1974-76, reg supr 1976-77; Univ of So MS, instr 1977-; private practice, marriage & family therapist 1982-; Univ of So MS, asst prof 1982-. **ORGANIZATIONS:** Mem Natl Clge Juvenile Ct Judges; commnr Gov's Commn For Standards & Goals in Crim Justice; bd dir Spl Serv Prog William Carey Clge; Opport House; consult Jackson County Dept of Public Welfare 1987-; curriculum comm mem MS Judicial Coll 1984-; adv comm Gov's MS Juvenile Justice 1984-; bd dir Hattiesburg MS Main St Project 1987-88; adv bd mem Grad School of Social Work Univ of So MS 1987-89.

LEFLORE, OBIE LAURENCE, JR.
Marketing research manager. **PERSONAL:** Born Jan 02, 1951, Chicago, IL; married Joyce Diane Kimbrough; children: Ericka, Obie III. **EDUCATION:** Univ of IL Chicago, BS Mgmt Econ 1973; Northwestern Univ Kellogg Sch of Mgmt, MM Finance-Marketing 1975; City Coll of Chicago/Northwestern Mutual Life Training Prog, cert to sell ins & real estate 1974-79. **CAREER:** Continental IL Natl Bank & Trust Co of Chicago, asst mkting rsch analyst 1975-76, mktg rsch analyst 1976-77, sr mkting analyst 1977-78; Chicago State Univ, instr 1979-; Continental IL Natl Bank & Trust Co of Chicago, mgmt serv officer 1978-. **ORGANIZATIONS:** Chmn policy comm JT O'Neal & Assoc realtor 1977-; dir of communication Urban Bankers Forum of Chicago 1978; mem Amer Marketing Assn; mem Bank Mkting Assoc; brother & pres Omega Psi Phi Frat Iota Chap 1972-78; mem Graduate Mgmt Assn Northwestern Univ 1973; mem Urban League 1977; adv bd mem Mt Zion Church of Universal Awareness 1978-. **HONORS/ACHIEVEMENTS:** 10th Dist Scholar of the Yr Omega Psi Phi Frat Inc 1972; Minority Fellow Northwestern Univ 1973-74. **BUSINESS ADDRESS:** Management Services Officer, Continental IL Natl Bank & Tst, 231 S LaSalle, Chicago, IL 60693.

LEFLORE, WILLIAM B.
Educator, research scientist. **PERSONAL:** Born Feb 22, 1930, Mobile, AL. **EDUCATION:** St Augustine's Coll, BS 1950; Atlanta Univ, MS 1952; Univ of Southern California, MSc 1961, PhD 1965. **CAREER:** Bennett Coll, instructor in biology 1952-57; Spelman Coll, asst to prof biology 1964-; North Carolina A&T Univ, visiting prof of biology 1966; College of St Teresa, exchange prof of biology 1968-69; Spelman Coll, prof & chmn biology dept. **ORGANIZATIONS:** Consul Office of Educ USPHS 1968 1970-74; ad hoc consul MBS Prog USPHS 1975; consul Kellogg Found Univ of AR Pine Bluff 1981; consul Biol Dept Savannah State Coll 1984; mem Helminthological Soc of Washington, Amer Soc of Parasitologists, Amer Microscopical Soc, Amer Soc of Zoologists, Amer Physiological Soc. **HONORS/ACHIEVEMENTS:** United Negro College Fund, Distinguished Scholar Award, 1982-83; Missouri Beale Scroll of Merit, Mobile Press Register, 1978; MARC Research Fellowship, Univ of Leeds, England, 1978; published over 30 scientific articles in Journal of Parasitol and other journals. **MILITARY SERVICE:** AUS e-5 2 yrs. **HOME ADDRESS:** 864 Victoria Place, Atlanta, GA 30310. **BUSINESS ADDRESS:** Prof & Chmn, Biology Dept, Spelman College, 350 Spelman Lane, SW, Atlanta, GA 30314.

LEFLORES, GEORGE O., JR.
Educational administrator. **PERSONAL:** Born Jul 02, 1921, Mobile, AL; children: Victoria Gray, Willie J, George Jr, Claira. **EDUCATION:** Vernon Sch of Real Estate, AA 1962. **CAREER:** Sacramento Black Alcohol Center, bd mem 1979-82; Project Area Comm, elected bd mem 1974-82; Delpaso Heights School Dist, elected bd mem 1981-; Faith Deliverance Center, bd mem 1972-; Delpaso Hts School Dist, clerk school bd. **ORGANIZATIONS:** Trustee bd mem Co-op Group 1977-81; trustee bd mem Elks Lodge #587 1948-85; bd mem Faith Deliverance Serv 1972-85. **HONORS/ACHIEVEMENTS:** Recog & Outstanding Valuable Serv to the Young People Search for Solution Awd 1973; Comm Serv Awd Delpaso Heights Project Area Comm 1974; Outstanding Serv & Bd Mem Awd SCARE 1973; Comm Involvement Awd City of Sacramento Parks & Recreation Dept 1981. **HOME ADDRESS:** 3925 Alder St, Sacramento, CA 95838. **BUSINESS ADDRESS:** Clerk School Board, Del Paso Elem Sch Dist, 575 Kesner Ave, Sacramento, CA 95838.

LEFTRIDGE, WILLIAM K.
Social worker. **PERSONAL:** Born Nov 10, 1904, Pittsburgh, PA. **EDUCATION:** Lincoln U, AB 1930;Univ Pittsburgh, Grad Sch 1955. **CAREER:** NYA, head, ass't proj head; Dept Welfare, social worker 22 yrs; Gov's Branch Office. **ORGANIZATIONS:** Mem Urban League; NAACP; Grubstake Frogs Club; Boys Club; Alpha Phi Alpha; Alpha Kappa Delta; Nat Scholastic Sociological Society; Signed Book Knowledge; Signed Book of ScholarsUniv of PA; Book Scholars Nat Sociological Society. **MILITARY SERVICE:** USAF 1942-45.

LEFTWICH, NORMA BOGUES
Government official. **PERSONAL:** Born Aug 08, 1948, New York, NY; married Willie L Leftwich Jr; children: Curtis. **EDUCATION:** Univ of Pittsburgh, BA 1969; Harvard-Kennedy Sch of Govt, Sr Govt Mgrs Prog 1982. **CAREER:** Boone Young & Assoc, sr consultant 1977; Dept of Commerce, special asst 1978-79; Dept of Defense, dir 1979-. **ORGANIZATIONS:** Mem Delta Sigma Theta Sor 1968. **HONORS/ACHIEVEMENTS:** Black Business Asoc of LA Outstanding Achievement 1982,86; SBA Awd of Excellence 1984; Dept of Defense Special Achievement Awd 1985; The Roy Wilkins Meritorious Serv Awd NAACP 1985; Governor's Awd Commonwealth of Puerto Rico 1985. **BUSINESS ADDRESS:** Dir, Ofc of Small & Disadv Business, 2A340 The Pentagon, Washington, DC 20301.

LEFTWICH, WILLIE L.
Attorney. **PERSONAL:** Born Jun 28, 1937, Washington, DC; married Paula. **EDUCATION:** Howard U, BSEE 1960; GWU Sch of Law, JD 1967; GWU Sch of Law, LLM 1972. **CAREER:** Hudson Leftwich & Davenport, atty; George WashingtonUniv Sch of Law, prof; Tech Media Sys Inc, vp/gen counsel; Dept of Transportation FAA, patent atty; Naval Air Systems Command, adv & research engring; research electro-optical engr; NASA, research aero instrumentatn engr; Engr. **ORGANIZATIONS:** Mem DC Bar Assn; dir PA Ave Devel Corp; DC Redevel Land Agy; mem Commerce Tech Adv Bd DC Judicial Nomination Commn; mem numerous political affiliations. **MILITARY SERVICE:** 1st lt 1960-62. **BUSINESS ADDRESS:** 1101 15 St NW, Washington, DC.

LEGENDRE, HENRI A.
Business executive. **PERSONAL:** Born Jul 11, 1924, New York, NY; married Ruth E

Mills; children: Renee, Laurette, Jacques. **EDUCATION:** Howard Univ, Civ Engrg ASTP 1943; CCNY, Liberal Arts 1949; Pratt Inst, Deploma Arch 1952. **CAREER:** Designs for Business, designer 1962; Ifill & Johnson Arch, partner 1963-67; Henri A LeGendre & Assoc, 1967-; LeGendre Johnson McNeil Arch & Planners, private arch pract 1978. **ORGANIZATIONS:** Mem Amer Inst of Arch, NY State Assn of Arch, NY Soc of Arch, Natl Orgn of Minority Arch, Amer Arbitration Assn, US Gen Serv Admin Adv Panel onA/E Selections 1977, 100 Black men Inc, Bd of Educ Valhalla, Alpha Phi Alpha, 369th VA, US Powerboat Squadron, The Promeatheans Inc, Rotary Intl, St George Assn B&P Chap DAV, Order of St Vincent, Euclid Lodge 70 F&AM; reg Arch State of NY; mem NAACP, Westchester Coalition. **HONORS/ACHIEVEMENTS:** Concrete Ind Awd of Merit Riverside Park Com & IS #95 1977; World Serv Awd YMCA Housing Devel 1979; Bldrs Inst Mr Vernon Nghbrhd Fac & Theatre Westchester/Putnam Co 1979; Honorable Mention Grant Park Housing Proj Mnpls Chap AIA; Certificate of Merit 139th St Playground NY Assn of Arch. **MILITARY SERVICE:** AUS 9th Calvary WW II. **BUSINESS ADDRESS:** Architect, LeGendre/Johnson/McNeil Arch, 96 Haarlem Ave, White Plains, NY 10603.

LEGGETT, RENEE
Communications marketing manager. **PERSONAL:** Born Oct 07, 1949, Cleveland, OH. **EDUCATION:** Fisk Univ, BA (Magna Cum Laude) 1972; Northwestern Univ, MA 1973; New York Univ, MBA 1980. **CAREER:** Cleveland State Univ, instructor (summer) 1973; Lincoln First Bank, mktg analyst 1973-76; Fortune Magazine, reporter 1976-79; Mobil Corp, mktg analyst 1979-81; The New York Times, mktg analyst 1981-82, planning mgr 1982-83, circulation marketing mgr 1983-86, advertising mktg & promo mgr. **ORGANIZATIONS:** Mem NY Univ Black Alumni Assoc, Natl Black MBA Assoc, Black Reps in Adv of NY; tutor First World Alliance Childrens Ctr; volunteer fund raiser Boy Choir of Harlem; speaker New Alliance of Public Schools; speaker Urban League's Black Exec Exchange Prog 1983. **HONORS/ACHIEVEMENTS:** Wall St Journal Student Achievement Awd 1972; numerous articles published at Fortune Magazine 1976-79. **BUSINESS ADDRESS:** Marketing Manager, The New York Times, 229 West 43rd St, New York, NY 10036.

LEGGETT, VINCENT OMAR
Government official. **PERSONAL:** Born Jun 26, 1953, Baltimore, MD; married Aldena Pinkney; children: Reginald, Clayton, Lamarr, Akil. **EDUCATION:** Univ of MD, 1971-73; Morgan State Univ, BS 1973-75; Univ of Baltimore, 1978. **CAREER:** Baltimore City Public Schools, planning assoc 1973-80; Anne Arundel Cty Public Schools, school planner 1980-83, supv plng student demographics 1983-86; Anne Arundel County Housing Authority, exec dir 1986-. **ORGANIZATIONS:** Pres Vol & Assoc Master Planners 1975-; bd dir Baltimore Jr Assoc Comm 1978, MD Inst of Planning & Public Policy 1984-, Council of Educ Facilities Planners Intl 1985-; vice pres Arundel-on-the-Bay Property Owners Assoc 1986; mem Alpha Phi Alpha Frat, Frontiers Intl, Annapolis Club, Young Profls Ann Arundel County. **HONORS/ACHIEVEMENTS:** Key Man Awd Baltimore Jr Assoc Comm 1978; Gold Cert Bd Mem Baltimore NAACP 1978; Outstanding Young Amer US Jaycees 1985. **HOME ADDRESS:** 3436 Cohasset Ave, Annapolis, MD 21403. **BUSINESS ADDRESS:** Executive Dir, Anne Arundel Cty Housing Auth, 7885 Gordon Court, Glen Burnie, MD 21601.

LEGGETTE, LEMIRE
Military officer. **PERSONAL:** Born Jan 04, 1949, Hemingway, SC. **EDUCATION:** Lincoln U, 1971; NorthwesternUniv Sch of Law, 1974. **CAREER:** USNR Judge Advocate Ge Corps, lt. **ORGANIZATIONS:** Mem IL State Bar Assn; Am Bar Assn; Chicago Bar Assn; Cook Co Bar Assn; Cook Co Bar Assn; scholarship com pres Thurgood Marshall Law Soc 1970; chmn Judicial Council of Northwestern Jr Bar Assn; pres NU Chap Alpha Phi Alpha 1971; mem Black Law Students Assn. **HONORS/ACHIEVEMENTS:** Listed in Who's Who in Am Coll & Univ 1971; Outstanding Coll Athlete of Am 1971; Women Auxiliary Club Award 1971; Class of 1915 Award; Dean's List; Nat Clearinghouse Review; Harrison A Cain Award 1970. **MILITARY SERVICE:** USNR lt (jg) 1975-.

LEGGETTE, SEBETHA JENKINS
Educational administration. **PERSONAL:** Born Sep 29, 1939, Learned, MS; married Clyde Leggette; children: Jennifer. **EDUCATION:** Jackson State Coll, BA English 1956-60; Delta State Coll MEd English 1968-70; MS State Univ, EdD Admin 1975-78. **CAREER:** Coahoma Jr Coll, English instr 1968-75; MS Ed Svcs, consult 1975-78; Coahoma Jr Coll, title III coord 1978-79; MS State Univ, asst to vice pres 1979-84, asst to pres. **ORGANIZATIONS:** Mem Delta Sigma Theta Sor 1959-; state title IX contact person MS Ed Serv 1975-78; mem Comm on Status of Women 1979-, Natl Assoc of Women Deans Adm Counselors 1980-; vice pres of bd Big Brothers/Big Sisters Reg 1980-; mem Southern Reg Advisory Comm Black Women 1981. **HONORS/ACHIEVEMENTS:** Most Outstanding Women in Higher Ed MS Univ for Women 1980; Outstanding Leadership MS State Univ 1982,84; Starkville Leadership Starkville MS Chamber of Commerce 1984-85; Most Outstanding Administrative Woman MSU 1985. **BUSINESS ADDRESS:** Asst To President, Mississippi StateUniv, Box J, Mississippi State, MS 39762.

LEGGETTE, VIOLET OLEVIA BROWN
Mayor. **PERSONAL:** Born in Tallula, MS; daughter of Alfred Brown and Theresa Brown; divorced; children: Clyde, Melanye, Eric, Terrell. **EDUCATION:** Natchez Jr Coll, AA 1955; Tougaloo Coll, BS Elem Educ 1957; Univ of IL, MLS 1974. **CAREER:** Bob Woods Elem Sch, teacher 1957-74; Bolivar Co Sit, elementary library supr 1974-78; Delta Pace Preschool, dir 1978-79; Bolivar Co Headstart, educ dir 1979-; Town of Gunnison, mayor 1977-. **ORGANIZATIONS:** Vice chairperson MS Democratic Party; chairperson Bolivar Co Democratic Comm; pres Bolivar Co Sch Dist I Tch Assn 1977; vice pres mS Conf Black Mayors 1978-; mem NAACP; bd dir Amer Assn of Small Cities 1979-; chmn Legislative Com MCBM 1978-; bd dir MS Inst of Small Cities 1980-; mem MS Assn of Educators; mem NEA, Alpha Kappa Alpha Sor; mem Natl Council of Negro Women; mem Natl Democratic Committee. **HONORS/ACHIEVEMENTS:** Outstanding Achievement Award Alcorn Coll Chapter/Negro Business & Professional Women Club 1978; Community Service Awd MS Valley St Univ 1978; Leadership Awd Black Genesis Found 1979; Mother of the Year 1988, First Baptist Church. **BUSINESS ADDRESS:** Mayor, Town of Gunnison, PO Box 278, Gunnison, MS 38746.

LEGGON, HERMAN W.
Systems analyst, mathematician. **PERSONAL:** Born Sep 20, 1930, Cleveland, OH; married Zara M. **EDUCATION:** BS Chemistry 1953; MS Chemistry 1966. **CAREER:** Union Carbide Corp, systems analyst & mathematician; Dyke Coll, part-time instr, bus math, computer sci & applied quantitative techniques; Systems & Computer Techology Corp, supervisor of tech support for micro computers. **ORGANIZATIONS:** Life mem Alpha Phi Alpha Frat; mem Juvenile Delinquency of the ACLD; bd chmn Am Sickle Cell Anemia Assn; chmn ASTM Com E31-01; scoutmstr Troop 370; Ada; NAACP; Urban League; former serv dir, councilman, pres Council of Oakwood Village. **HOME ADDRESS:** 3470 Belvoir, Beachwood, OH 44122.

LEGRAND, BOB (SNAKE)
Educator. **PERSONAL:** Born Aug 28, 1943, Nashville, TN; son of Sarah H Joyner; married Gloria Jean Young; children: Lisa, Robert III, Christopher, Brianna, Brian. **EDUCATION:** St Mary's Univ TX, BA 1970; Southwest TX State Univ, MA 1973, Professional Certificate in Guidance & Counseling 1974. **CAREER:** Jefferson HS San Antonio, TX, head coach 1970-75; Univ of TX Arlington, asst coach 1975-76, head coach 1976-87, Irving High School, Irving TX 1988-. **ORGANIZATIONS:** Chmn Dist 6 Editorial Comm Natl Assn of Basketball Coaches; chmn Dist 6 Membership Comm Natl Assn of Basketball Coaches; chmn United Way Campaign Univ TX Arlington 1980; mem bd dir Arlington Boys Club 1978-82; Arlington Noon Optimist Club; Texas Assn of Basketball Coaches. **HONORS/ACHIEVEMENTS:** Man of the Year Omega Psi Phi 1980; Award for Outstanding Achievement Omega Psi Phi 1977; Coach of the Year Southland Conf 1981; News Maker of the Year Fort Worth Press Club 1981; Honorary Commissioner Tarrant Cnty Commissioners 1980. **MILITARY SERVICE:** USAF E-4 served 4 years. **HOME ADDRESS:** 4901 Rockford Ct, Arlington, TX 76017. **BUSINESS ADDRESS:** Head Basketball Coach, Irving High Schoolon, 900 N O'Connor Rd, Irving, TX 75061.

LEGRAND, ETIENNE RANDALL
Executive. **PERSONAL:** Born Sep 01, 1956, Philadelphia, PA; children: Justin Alan. **EDUCATION:** Boston Univ, BS 1978; Northeastern Univ, MBA 1981. **CAREER:** United Mine Workers of Amer, asst cash mgr 1981-82; Finalco Inc, cash mgr 1982-86; Children's Defense Fund, dir of finance 1986-87; Howard Univ Small Business Develop Ctr, deputy dir 1987-. **ORGANIZATIONS:** Pres, vice pres Delta Sigma Theta Inc 1976-; mem Big Sister Assoc 1978-80; prog co-chair NBMBAA Natl Conf 1985; fund develop chair Washington DC NBMBAA 1986; mem DC Coalition of Black Professional Org 1986-; sponsor Jr Achievement 1986-; pres Washington DC Natl Black MBA Assoc 1987; bd mem Owl School 1987-. **HONORS/ACHIEVEMENTS:** Dr Martin Luther King Jr Fellowship Northeastern Univ 1979-81; Disting Serv Awd Natl Black MBA Assoc 1985-87. **BUSINESS ADDRESS:** Deputy Dir, HowardUniv SBDC, 2600 6th St, Washington, DC 20059.

LEGRAND, YVETTE MARIE
Management consultant. **PERSONAL:** Born Nov 08, 1950, Chicago, IL. **EDUCATION:** Loyola Univ Chicago, bA History 1971; Univ of Chicago, MBA 1975. **CAREER:** Intl Mgmt Asst United Way of Met Chicago, dir 1977-; First Natl Bank Chicago, loan ofc 1977; First Natl Bank, acct mgr 1975-77, first schlr mgmt trainee 1972-75. **ORGANIZATIONS:** Mem Natl Black MBA Assc Chicago Chap 1974-77; vice pres Chicago Jr Assc of Commerce & Industry Found 1979-80; first black pres Chicago Jaycees 1980-81 Vol; Lois R Lowe Women's Div United Negro Clge Fund 1972-79; vice pres pub rel Chicago Jaycees 1977-78; dir Chicago Jazz Gallery 1978-80. **HONORS/ACHIEVEMENTS:** Pres Award of Honor Chicago Jaycees 1975-76; Outst Chap Ofc Chicago Jaycees 1978; Outst Young Woman of Amer 1979. **BUSINESS ADDRESS:** 72 W Adams, Chicago, IL 60603.

LEHMAN, HARVEY J.
Retired clergyman. **PERSONAL:** Born Oct 10, 1905, Mansura, LA; son of Mr and Mrs Paul M Lehman; married Lillian B Evans; children: Harvey Jr, Lillian, Philip. **EDUCATION:** Immanuel Lutheran Coll & Seminary, attended 1930; Concordia Lutheran Theological Seminary, Hon DD 1975. **CAREER:** Ordained, 1930; Trinity & St Timothy Congregations Selma, 1930-34; St Paul's & Christ Congregations Oakhill Rosebud, pastor teacher parochial school 1934-46; St Matthews Lutheran Church Baltimore, pastor 1946-49; Our Savior Lutheran School Buffalo, bd missions 1949-65; St Paul's Lutheran Church, pastor chmn Urban Ministry Dept 1965-; So CA Dist Lutheran Church, MO Synod; Morningside Hospital, protestant chaplain 1969-; retired June 30, 1980. **ORGANIZATIONS:** Mem Coll of Chaplains, Amer Protestant Hosp Assn; clergy Police League Comm Relations. **HONORS/ACHIEVEMENTS:** Congregation celebrated 50th yr in the ministry June 15, 1980.

LEHMAN, PAUL ROBERT
Educator. **PERSONAL:** Born Apr 18, 1941, Mansura, LA; son of Mr & Mrs K W Lehman; married Marion W White; children: Christopher Paul, Karlyn Elizabeth, Jeffrey Robert. **EDUCATION:** LA City Coll, AA 1966; Central State Coll, BA 1969; Central State U, ME 1971; Lehigh U, PhD 1976. **CAREER:** Central State U, dean of grad coll 1985-88, prof dept of English 1984, 1988-, assoc prof dept of eng 1976-; NCACC, adjunct prof 1974-76; CSU, instr 1971-73;CSU, lecturer 1969-71; KWTV, newsman reporter writer editor photographer producer & weekend anchorman 1968-70; KOFM radio, music newsman 1968-69; Standard Oil of CA, credit dept 1966-67; Western Electric Co, tester insptct 1963-66; Northampton Co Area Community Coll, dev co-ordinated coll orientation wkshp for minority stud 1975; Blk Am Lit, vol lecturer coll pub private sch (Jr & Sr) churches on Radio/TV News 1974-75. **ORGANIZATIONS:** Natl Jay-Cees; NAACP; Urban League; Heart Assn Natl Assn of Press Photographers; stud exec officer LACC 1966; mem NEA, OEA, CSEA, NCTE; vice chmn, Oklahoma Foundation for the Humanities 1988-89; treasurer, Oklahoma Alliance for Arts Education 1988-; Oklahoma Folklife Council; Edmond Community Housing Resource Board; Afro-American Southern Assn. **HONORS/ACHIEVEMENTS:** Best actor in minor roll CSC 1968; dean's honor roll CSC 1968; 1st blk Am to rec PhD in Eng from Lehigh 1976; 1st blk Am to teach at CSU 1969; 1st blk in OK to anchor weekendTV news 1969; listed in Contemporary Authors for 1977-78; LehighUniv Fellowship 1973-76; 1st dissertation on John Oliver Killens 1976; 2nd place all-coll speech contest 1965; Awd for Serv to Urban League of Greater Okla City 1984; Awd for Serv to Boy Scouts of Amer 1985. **MILITARY SERVICE:** USN 3rd cl petty off 1959-63. **BUSINESS ADDRESS:** Dept of English, Central State University, 100 University Drive, Edmond, OK 73034.

LEIGH, JAMES W., JR.
Educator. **PERSONAL:** Born Jun 01, 1927, Detroit, MI. **EDUCATION:** Wayne State Univ, BA 1952; Wayne State Univ Sch of Social Work, MSW 1954; Smith Coll Sch for Social Work, third yr cert 1961. **CAREER:** Dept Pub Welfare Detroit, social worker 1952-54; Wayne Co Juvenile Court Detroit, probation officer 1954-60; Family Serv of the Cincinnati

area, social worker 1960-67; Sch of Social Work Univ of WA, asst prof 1967-70, assoc prof 1970-. **ORGANIZATIONS:** Vice pres Natl Assn Black Soc Worker WA State Chap 1975-77; bd mem Smith Coll Sch for Social Work 1979-; mem NAACP; mem Urban League; mem Council on Social Work Educ. **BUSINESS ADDRESS:** Associate Professor, Univof Washington, School of Social Work, Seattle, WA 98105.

LEIGH, WILLIAM ALVIN
Contractor, developer. **PERSONAL:** Born Sep 12, 1929, Dayton, OH; children: William, Cornell, Bernard. **EDUCATION:** Attended, Miami-Jacobs Business Coll, Sinclair Comm Coll. **CAREER:** Fleetline Cab Co, owner 1950-61; Main Auto Parts & Glass Co, sales rep 1960-68; Madden Inc, pres. **ORGANIZATIONS:** Bd mem Newfield Comm Authority; treasurer, Amer Business Council; chmn Black Contractors & Business Assn; Dayton Housing Advisory Bd; bd mem Miami Valley Cncl of BoyScouts; United Fund Agency; Miami Valley Child Devel; vice pres, Dayton Fund for Home Rehab; bd mem SCLC. **HONORS/ACHIEVEMENTS:** Frontiersman of the Year, 1972; Listed as 1 of top 100 Black Business', Black Enterprise Magazine; Recognized by Professional Builders Magazine for Outstanding Land Use & Design, 1972. **BUSINESS ADDRESS:** President, Madden Co Inc, 2305 Heartsoul Ave, Dayton, OH 45408.

LEIGHTON, GEORGE NEVES
Judge. **PERSONAL:** Born Oct 22, 1912, New Bedford, MA; married Virginia Berry Quivers; children: Virginia Anne, Barbara Elaine. **EDUCATION:** Howard U, AB 1940; Harvard, LLB 1946; Elmhurst Coll, LLD 1964; John Marshall Law Sch, 1973. **CAREER:** MA Bar, 1946; IL Bar, 1947; Moore Ming & Leighton Chicago, partner 1951-59; US Supreme Court, 1958; McCoy Ming & Leighton Chicago, partner 1959-64; Circuit CtCook County IL Appellate Ct 1st Dist, judge 1969-76; US District Court Northern Dist of IL, district judge 1976-. **ORGANIZATIONS:** Mem council sect legal educ & admissions to bar Am Bar Assn; commr as mem character & fitness com for 1st Appellate Dist Supreme Ct IL 1955-63; chmn character & fitness com 1961-62; mem joint com for revision IL Criminal Code 1959-63; chmn IL adv com US Commn on Civil Rights 1964; mem pub rev bd UAW AFL-CIO 1961-70; bd dirs United Ch Bd for Homeland Ministries, United Ch of Christ, Grant Hosp, Chicago Fellow, Am Bar Found; mem HowardUniv Chicago Alumni Club, Chicago & IL Bar Assns; NAACP (chmn legal redress com Chicago br); council Nat Harvard Law Sch Assn; Phi Beta Kappa; contrib articles to legal jours; trustee Univ Notre Dame 1979-83, trustee emeritus 1983-; bd overseers Harvard Coll 1983-. **HONORS/ACHIEVEMENTS:** Recip Civil Liberties Award IL Div Am Civil Liberties Union 1961; named Chicagoan of Yr in Law & Judiciary Jr Assn Commerce & Industry 1964. **MILITARY SERVICE:** AUS inf 2nd lt to capt 1942-45; Bronze Star. **BUSINESS ADDRESS:** US District Judge, Northern District of IL, Dirksen Federal Building, 219 South Dearborn St, Chicago, IL 60604.

LELAND, JOYCE F.
Deputy chief of police. **PERSONAL:** Born Sep 08, 1941, Washington, DC; married John Watkins. **EDUCATION:** Howard Univ, BA Sociology 1965. **CAREER:** Metropolitan Police Dept, lieutenant 1975-78, capt 1978-83, eeo inspector 1983-85, deputy chief 1985. **ORGANIZATIONS:** Bd dirs MPDC Boys and Girls Club, Police Mgmt Assoc; consultant Police Foundation, Ctr for Youth Svcs. **HONORS/ACHIEVEMENTS:** Crime Reduction Awds; numerous awds from citizens, law enforcement agencies, churches, business establishments. **BUSINESS ADDRESS:** Deputy Chief of Police, Metropolitan Police Department, 1324 Mississippi Ave, SE, Washington, DC 20032.

LEMEH, DOROTHA HILL
Dentist, educator. **PERSONAL:** Born in Knoxville, TN; daughter of William Edward Hill and Mary Lucille Evans Hill; married Dr. Charles N. Lemeh, Jun 15, 1956 (deceased); children: Wayne, Dorotha, Eva, Carol. **EDUCATION:** Fisk Univ, BA 1947; Morgan State Coll & Howard Univ, postgrad 1948-50; Howard Univ Coll of Dentistry, DDS 1950-54; Univ of MI School of Dentistry, MS Pediatric Dentistry 1955-58; Univ of MI School of Public Health, MPH 1970. **CAREER:** Forsyth Dental Infantry for Child, intern 1954-55; Mott Found Dental Clinic, res 1957-58; Enugu Nigeria, minister of health dentistry div 1965-67; Meharry Med Coll School of Dental, assoc prof 1970-79, vice chmn 1971-76, act chmn dept of preventive dentistry & comm health 1976-79, prof 1979-, chmn dept of preventive dentistry & comm health 1979-. **ORGANIZATIONS:** Amer Acad Oral Med; Amer Assn of Dental School; Amer Assn of Public Health Dental; TN Assn of Public Health Dentistry; Natl Dental Assn; Pan TN Dental Assn; Cap City Dental Soc; Delta Sigma Theta; rec sec Cap City Dental Soc; exec sec, Pan TN Dental Assn; Intl Assn of Dental Rsch, Amer Assn of Dental Research. **HONORS/ACHIEVEMENTS:** Louise C Ball Scholarship; CS Mott Found Scholarship; US Pub Health Serv Special Traineeship; Published numerous articles. **BUSINESS ADDRESS:** Prof/Chairperson, Meharry Med Coll, School of Dentistry, 1005 D. B. Todd Blvd, Nashville, TN 37208.

LEMELLE, TILDEN J.
Educational administrator. **PERSONAL:** Born Feb 06, 1929, New Iberia, LA; married Margaret Guillion; children: Joyce Marie, Stephanie Marie, Therese Marie. **EDUCATION:** Xavier Univ New Orleans, AB 1953, MA 1957; Univ of Denver, PhD 1965. **CAREER:** Grambling Coll LA, asst prof 1957-63; Fordham Univ NY, assoc prof 1966-69; Ctr Intl Race Rel Univ Denver, prof, dir 1969-71; Hunter Clge NY, prof & acting dean 1971-; Amer Com on Africa, treas 1973-; Hunter Coll CUNY, provost, vp. **ORGANIZATIONS:** Trustee Africa Today Assoc Inc 1967-; editor/publ Africa Today 1967-; bd office pres Amer Comm on Africa 1973-; trustee New Rochelle Bd of Educ 1976-;mem Cncl on Foreign Rel 1978-; trustee Social Sci Found 1979-; trustee Africa Fund 1979-; trustee Intl League for Human Rights 1980-; trustee Nurses Educ Fund 1984-. **HONORS/ACHIEVEMENTS:** John Hay Whitney Fellow NY 1963-65; The Black Coll Praeger NY 1969; Hon Consul-Senegal Denver CO 1969-71; Race Among Nations Heath-Lexington MA 1971. **MILITARY SERVICE:** AUS sp4 1953-56; Special Agent Counterintelligence. **BUSINESS ADDRESS:** Provost, Vice President, Hunter College CUNY, 695 Park Ave, New York, NY 10021.

LEMELLE, WILBERT JOHN
Educator. **PERSONAL:** Born Nov 11, 1931, New Iberia, LA; son of Eloi LeMelle and Theresa Francis LeMelle; married Yvonne Tauriac; children: Patrice DiCioccio, Wilbert Jr, Gerald, Edward. **EDUCATION:** Notre Dame Seminary, BA 1955, MA 1956; Univ of Denver Grad Sch of Intl Studies, PhD 1963. **CAREER:** Ford Foundation, held various positions 1965-77; United States Dept of State, ambassador to Kenya and the Seychelles 1977-80; State Univ of New York, system assoc vice chancellor 1981-85; Mercy Coll, president 1985-. **ORGANIZATIONS:** Dir Council of Amer Ambassadors 1983-; dir Westchester Coalition 1985-; dir Chase NBW's Regional Bd 1986-; trustee Phelps-Stokes Fund 1986-; dir Dropout Prevention Fund 1986-; mem Council on Foreign Relations; dir, Borden Inc, 1987-; trustee, Carnegie Endowment for Intl Peace, 1989-; trustee, Amer Health Found, 1989-. **HONORS/ACHIEVEMENTS:** Honorary Doctor of Laws (LLD) Cuttington Univ Liberia 1978; Gold Medallion Awd Black Catholic Ministeries and Laymen's Council 1978. **MILITARY SERVICE:** Army 1957-59. **BUSINESS ADDRESS:** President, Mercy College, 555Broadway, Dobbs Ferry, NY 10522.

LEMMONS, HERBERT MICHAEL
Clergyman. **PERSONAL:** Born Sep 25, 1952, Little Rock, AR; son of Herbert G Lemmons and Deliah A Herron-Lemmons; married Karenga Rashida Hill, Aug 31, 1974; children: H Michael Lemmons, II. **EDUCATION:** Univ of Detroit, Detroit, MI, BA, 1973; Interdenominational Theological Center, Atlanta, GA, Master of Divinity, 1976; Howard Univ School of Law, Washington, DC, Juris Doctor, 1979. **CAREER:** Seaton Memorial AME Church, Lanham, MD, pastor, 1977-84; US Small Business Admin, Washington, DC, attorney advisor, 1979-81; Univ of MD, College Park, MD, chaplain, 1982-84; Congress of Natl Black Churches, Washington, DC, deputy dir, 1984-85; Mount Moriah AME Church, Annapolis, MD, pastor, 1984-89; Congress of Natl Black Churches, Washington, DC, exec dir, 1989. **ORGANIZATIONS:** Mem, Human Relations Commn Annapolis, MD, 1986-88; mem, Mayor's Task Force on Substance Abuse, 1987-89; mem, Bd of Commrs, Annapolis Housing Authority, 1988-. **HONORS/ACHIEVEMENTS:** Walder G Mueller Student Lectureship in Social Ethics, Interdenominational Theological Center, 1976. **BUSINESS ADDRESS:** Exec Dir, The Congress of Natl Black Churches, Inc, 600 New Hampshire Ave, NW, Suite 650, Washington, DC 20037-2403.

LEMON, CHESTER EARL
Professional athlete. **PERSONAL:** Born Feb 12, 1955, Jackson, MS; married Valerie Jones; children: Geneva, Chester Jr, David. **EDUCATION:** Pepperdine Univ, attended. **CAREER:** Chicago White Sox, 1975-81; Detroit Tigers, outfielder 1982-84. **HONORS/ACHIEVEMENTS:** Played finest centerfield by a Tiger player in years; earned numerous standing ovations both at home and on the road; voted to starting lineup on AL All-Star Team for first time as a Tiger; voted Best Def Outfldr by AL mgrs; tied AL rec with 4th season of 400-ir-more putouts in the outfield; All-Star team 9th in AL batting (318), AL Player of Wk April 9, 1979; Set AL records for centerfielders with 524 chances & 512 putouts 1977. **BUSINESS ADDRESS:** Detroit Tigers, 2121 Trumbull Ave, Detroit, MI 48216.

LEMON, MEADOWLARK
Professional athlete. **PERSONAL:** Born Apr 25, 1932, Wilmington, NC; married Willie Maultsby (divorced); children: George, Beverly, Donna, Robin, Jonathan. **EDUCATION:** High School Graduate. **CAREER:** Harlem Globetrotters, 1954-78; The Bucketeers, basketball group 1978-; appeared inTV series Hello Larry 1979; films, The Fish That Saved Pittsburgh, Sweepstakes. **MILITARY SERVICE:** AUS 1952-54.

LEMON, MICHAEL WAYNE, SR.
Police officer. **PERSONAL:** Born Nov 02, 1953, Detroit, MI; son of Primus Lemon and Mary Strong Lemon; married Valerie Lemon, Apr 02, 1978; children: Michael Wayne Lemon, Jr, Ashlee Michelle Lemon. **EDUCATION:** Wayne County Community Coll, associate, 1988; Wayne State Univ. **CAREER:** Detroit Police Dept, Narcotics Div, police officer, currently; Michigan Bell Telephone, consultant, 1987-. **ORGANIZATIONS:** Bd mem, Community volunteer, 1986-; mem, Task Force on Drug Abuse, Detroit Strategic Plan, 1987-. **HONORS/ACHIEVEMENTS:** Appreciation Award, Michigan Bell Telephone, 1986; Community Serv Award, Detroit Chamber of Commerce, 1988; Man of the Year Award, Minority Women Network, 1988; Spirit of Detroit, Detroit Common Council, 1989, Heart of Gold Award, United Found, 1989. **BUSINESS ADDRESS:** Police Officer,, Detroit Police Dept, Narcotic Div, 1300 Beaubien, Detroit, MI.

LENIX-HOOKER, CATHERINE JEANETTE
Business administrator. **PERSONAL:** Born May 10, 1947, Camden, SC; daughter of Frank and Annie Lenix; divorced; children: Frank R Jr. **EDUCATION:** Univ of MD, MLS 1970; Howard Univ, BA 1968. **CAREER:** Washington DC Public Library, chief, black studies div 1970-77; Anaheim CA Public Library, dir of public servs 1977-81. **ORGANIZATIONS:** Mem Harlem Tourism Assn; chairperson S CA Chap Howard Univ Alumni Scholarships 1980-81; mem Amer Library Assn 1970-; mem Black Caucus 1970-; 2nd vicechmn Harlem Hosp Ctr Comm Adv Bd 1981-. **HONORS/ACHIEVEMENTS:** HEW Title II Fellowship Univ of MD 1969-70; Comm Serv Awd NY Chap of Negro Business and Prof Women's Club 1985. **HOME ADDRESS:** 940 St Nicholas AveApt II, New York, NY 10032. **BUSINESS ADDRESS:** Assistant Chief, Schomburg Ctr for Research, 515 Lenox Ave, New York, NY 10037.

LENOIR, HENRY
Association executive. **PERSONAL:** Born Sep 25, 1912, Philadelphia, TN; married Teri; children: Michael, Kip, Barry, Keith. **EDUCATION:** Knoxville Coll, BA 1936;Univ WI, post grad work;Univ Cincinnati. **CAREER:** Ninth St YMCA, youth work dir 1945-51; exec dir 1951-57; Moreland YMCA, 1957-61; Page Park YMCA, 1961-68; St Louis YMCA, asst metro dir 1968-70; HarlemYMCA, exec dir 1970-75; YMCA of Greater NY, vice pres 1975-. **ORGANIZATIONS:** Mem Omega Psi Phi Frat; Dallas Comm Council; St Louis Council for Black People; NAACP; Ethical Practices Commn; Assn Professional Employees of YMCA; Banwys. **HONORS/ACHIEVEMENTS:** Hon Citizen Dallas; Omega Man of Yr Dallas Chap 1961; Jack & Jill Award St Louis; Awards in Black Harlem. **BUSINESS ADDRESS:** 422 9 Ave, New York, NY 10001.

LENOIRE, ROSETTA
Business executive, performer. **PERSONAL:** Born Aug 08, 1911, New York City, NY; widowed; children: William M. **EDUCATION:** Attended, Hunter Coll Amer Theatre Wing. **CAREER:** ABC TV Ryan's Hope, role; John F Kennedy Ctr for Performing Arts & Brooklyn Acad of Mus, toured with "The Royal Family"; AMAS Repertory Theatre, artistic dir and co-founder, 1968-. **ORGANIZATIONS:** Mem Screen Actors Guild; Amer Fedn of TV & Radio Artists; Actor's Equity Assc; nom com SAG, AFTRA, AEA; chmn Welfare Dance Com Negro Actors' Guild; adv bd Off Off Broadway Alliance; vice chrmn Concerned Cit for the Arts; bd trustees The Actors Fund of Amer; bd dir The Cath Acts Guild of Amer;

Natl Endowment For The Arts Policy & Small Grants Panel; life mem Cath Actors' Guild Com Woman NY State Re Party; Theatre Communications Group. **HONORS/ACHIEVEMENTS:** Spl Citation Tribute to Greatness Award Cermony 1975; Harold Jackman Award; appeared film version "The Sunshine Boys"; broadway credits, "God's Favorite"; "A Streetcar Named Desire"; "I Had A Ball" plus many more;TV appearances, The Nurses, The Doctors & the Nurses; Kraft Theatre; Studio One; Lamp Unto My Feet; Calucci Dept; Guess Who's Coming To Dinner; conceived "Bubbling Brown Sugar" first prod at AMAS Repertory Theatre currently on Broadway; "Thank You Ma'am" docum on Langston Hughes; founder of AMAS 1968; Bd of Directors Awd Frank Silvera Writer's Workshop 1977; Tribute to Greatness Awd 1980; Hoey Awd Catholic Interracial Cncl 1985; City Cncl Citation 1985; Richard Coe Awd New Playwrights 1986; Cecilia Cabiness Saunders Awd YWCA 1986; Woman of the Year Carribean Cultural Assoc 1986 ; Mayor's Awd of Honor for Art and Culture 1986; Sojourner Truth Awd Negro Professional Women 1986. **BUSINESS ADDRESS:** Dir, AMAS Repertory Theatre, Inc, 1 East 104th St, New York, NY 10029.

LEON, WILMER J., JR.
Consultant. **PERSONAL:** Born Mar 06, 1920, Louisiana; married Edwina T Devore; children: Valerie, Wilmer III. **EDUCATION:** So Univ, BS 1949; Univ of CA Berkeley, MA 1954. **CAREER:** CA Adult Auth, admin officer; CA Dept of Educ, Bureau of Intergroup Relations, Sacramento, consultant; CA Dept of Corrections, parole agent; asst dist parole supr; State Dir of Corrections, consultant; CA State Univ Sacramento, lecturer in Criminal Justice. **ORGANIZATIONS:** Mem CA Probation & Parole Assn; Proj Safer CA Ofc of Criminal Justice Planning; Sacramento Reg Area Planning Comm CA Coun on Criminal Justice; mem Am Sociological Soc; bd dir Cath Welfare Bureau; exec bd CYO; Golden Gate Psychotherapy Soc; NAACP; Sacramento Com for Fair Housing; Sacramento Unified Sch Dist Adult Educ Group; educ coordinator Urban League Formation Com.

LEONARD, BYRDIE A. LARKIN
Politcal scientist, educator. **PERSONAL:** Born in Tuskegee Inst, AL; daughter of Rev Charles Haile Lakin and Lula Berry Lakin; divorced; children: Seve, Mwangi, Leonard. **EDUCATION:** AL State Univ, BS 1973; Atlanta Univ, MA 1975; Atlanta Univ, PhD 1982. **CAREER:** Atlanta Jr Coll, part time instructor 1975-77; Atlanta Public School System, assigned supply teacher 1977; AL State Univ, Dept of Political Sci asst professor 1977-87, acting chairperson, assoc prof, currently. **ORGANIZATIONS:** Alpha Kappa Mu Natl Honor Soc; Beta Nu Omega Grad Chapter Alpha Kappa Alpha Sorority; Phi Delta Kappa Educ Fraternity; appointed to steering comm to plan annual Conf on the Advancement of Women in Public Admin; mem NAACP; bd mem Montgomery Habitat for Humanity; charter mem Black Women Academicians; Pi Gamma Nu Intl Social Science Honorary Soc. **HONORS/ACHIEVEMENTS:** 4 year Valedictorian Scholarship AL State Univ 1969; Grad Scholarships & Fellowships Atlanta Univ, Notre Dame & OH State Univs 1973; Outstanding Grad Student Awd Atlanta Univ Dept of Political Sci 1975; Awd AL State Univ Study Grant 1979; Dept of State Scholar Diplomat Conf on Europe 1981; Summer Inst on the Amer Judicial System sponsored by the Amer Judicial Soc in Chicago IL, 1984; Fulbright Scholar to Israel 1985; Leadership Montgomery Participant 1986-87; Ford Found Fellowship for seminars on Southern studies at the Univ of Mississippi, 1989. **HOME ADDRESS:** 3213 McGhee Rd, Montgomery, AL 36111. **BUSINESS ADDRESS:** Assoc Prof of Political Science, Alabama State Univ, 915 S Jackson St, Montgomery, AL 36195.

LEONARD, CAROLYN MARIE
Educational administrator. **PERSONAL:** Born Nov 20, 1943, Portland, OR; daughter of Kelly Miller Probasco and Grace Ruth Searcie Probasco; married Benjamin M Leonard, Dec 08, 1962; children: Cherice M, Chandra M. **EDUCATION:** Portland State Univ, BS 1976, MS Educ 1979. **CAREER:** Oregon Assembly for Black Affairs, vice pres 1979-86; Alpha Kappa Alpha, treasurer 1982-; Oregon Commn for Black Affairs, vice chmn 1986-; Oregon Council for Excellence in Educ, sec 1987-; Portland Public Schools, Portland OR, evaluator 1979-85, coordinator of multicultural educ 1985-. **ORGANIZATIONS:** Mem Natl Alliance of Black School Educ; mem City Club of Portland 1984-; sec Black United Fund of Oregon 1987-; bd mem Oregon Commn on Black Affairs 1984-, Natl Council of Black Studies 1986-, Metro Human Relations Commn 1987-. **HONORS/ACHIEVEMENTS:** President's Award, Oregon Assembly for Black Affairs 1984; Community Leadership Award, Skanner Newspaper 1987; Merit Award, Skanner Newspaper 1987; Cheik Anta Diop Award, Outstanding Scholarly Achievement in Multicultural Educ 1988; Education Award, Delta Sigma Theta Sorority 1988; editor African-Amer Baselive Essays 1987; editor, Hispanic-Amer Women 1988; chair Martin Luther King Street Renaming Committee 1989. **HOME ADDRESS:** 2015 NE Ainsworth, Portland, OR 97211.

LEONARD, CATHERINE W.
Business executive. **PERSONAL:** Born Aug 26, 1909, Greensburg, LA. **EDUCATION:** Leland Coll, BA 1943; Tuskegee Inst, MEd 1958. **CAREER:** St Helena Parish Greensburg LA, tchr; Day Care Center Union Bethel AME Ch, dir; Elementary Principals Assn, pres 1952-54; Sixth Dist Educ Assn in St Helena Parish, two terms pres. **ORGANIZATIONS:** Mem Natl Educ Assn; mem Parish Educ Assn; mem JB Poew Crescent City Temple No 185 New Orleans LA GWM; Queen Elizabeth Grand No 11 OES; State of Louisiana F&AA York Masons; Natl Compact; Alpha Gamma Zeta Chap, Zeta Phi Beta Sorority Inc; Union Bethel AME Ch; asst SS Sunday Sch; tchr pres Missionary Soc; class leader, mem Steward Bd; chmn Natl Council of Negro Women Inc. **HONORS/ACHIEVEMENTS:** Tchr of Yr 1969; Mayoralty of New Orleans Certif of Merit for Outstanding Comm Serv 1973; Moon Landrieu Mayor Outstanding Layman of AME Ch LA Conf; PTA Award Helena HS 1969; honor award Union Bethel AME Ch for Outstanding Chairmanship of Women's Div of United Effort 1973; trophy award for Speaker of Yr for Women's Day Program Bethel AME Ch 1973. **BUSINESS ADDRESS:** 2310 Peniston St, New Orleans, LA 70115.

LEONARD, JEFF
Professional athlete. **PERSONAL:** Born Sep 22, 1955, Philadelphia, PA. **CAREER:** Los Angeles Dodgers, outfielder 1977; Houston Astros, outfielder 1978-80; San Francisco Giants, outfielder 1981-. **HONORS/ACHIEVEMENTS:** Tied career high with 21 homers; team leading 86 RBIs 1984; 1974 Northwest League All-Star 7th in the league in Batting 324; 1976 2nd in CA League with nine triples; 7th in Batting 330 1976; 1977 Major League debut with Dodgers hitting 300 in 11 games; 1978 Pacific Coast League Player o f the Year; 1979 Sporting News Natl League Rookie of the Year; set record for Giants left fielders with 17 assists 1983; set career-highs for ga mes 139, at-bats 516, triples 7, RBIs 87,stolen bases 26. **BUSINESS ADDRESS:** San Francisco Giants, Candlestick Park, San Francisco, CA 94124.

LEONARD, LEON LANK, SR.
Educator. **PERSONAL:** Born Jun 18, 1922, Waco, TX; married Vandoly O Leonard; children: Leon Jr. **EDUCATION:** TX Coll, AB 1946; Univ of Denver Art School, BFA 1948. **CAREER:** LA Independent School Dist, art teacher 1960-; AJ Moore Waco, 1956-66; Prairie View A&M Coll, asst art chmn 1955, 1963, 1966; Booker T Washington High School, art teacher, 1948-54. **ORGANIZATIONS:** Mem Waco Art Forum 1957-66; TX Fine Art Assn 1957-66; TX Watercolor Soc 1958-74; CA Nat Watercolor Soc 1969; Art West Assn 1968; mem Black Artist Assn 1971-; Art Teachers of LA 1967-74; Am Printmakers 1974. **HONORS/ACHIEVEMENTS:** Artists Paintings Mexico Mil Watercolor USA; recip Winslow Homer Cash Awd Requiem For Pablo Picasso; Distinc Award of Merit Nat Conf of Artists 27 ribbons, 3 tri-colors, ceramics TX, LA, OK 1958; repre in Johnson Pub Co of Chicago Art Work Painting Pride of Eight Prod Ebony, Tan, Jet, Black Stars; LA all City Art Fest Art Works; Watercolor USA Ptng, Blue Vase, Springfield Art Mus 1977; Nat &Watercolor Soc Mt San Jacinto Coll 1977; Dr Regina Perry's Book, Black Artists 1972; photo with art work NCA Conv 1972, Johnson Pub for Art Brochure; Recipient of over 68 awards. **MILITARY SERVICE:** AUS field artillery 1943. **BUSINESS ADDRESS:** Audubon Jr High, 4120 11 Ave, Los Angeles, CA 20008.

LEONARD, RAY CHARLES (SUGAR RAY)
Professional boxer, business executive. **PERSONAL:** Born 1957, Rocky Mount; married Juanita Wilkinson; children: Ray Jr, Jerrel. **CAREER:** Amateur Fights Olympics, team capt, boxer 1976; professional boxer; Sugar Ray Leonard Inc, pres; professional fighter, commentator. **HONORS/ACHIEVEMENTS:** Won Light Welterweight Gold Medal Olympics Montreal 1976; regained WBC Welterweight Champion Title 1980; won fight against Marvin Hagler 1987.

LEONARD, WALTER FENNER (BUCK)
Broker. **PERSONAL:** Born Sep 08, 1907, Rocky Mount, NC. **EDUCATION:** La Salle Extension U, real estate 1965. **CAREER:** Real estate broker; truant officer, asst in physical educ elem schs of Rocky Mount 1958-70. **ORGANIZATIONS:** Mem Natl Baseball Hall of Fame 1972-, NC Sport Hall of Fame 1974-; vice pres Rocky Mount Leafs Baseball team, Class A league; mem Comm Redevel Commn 1977; mem St James Bapt Ch of Rocky Mount, 32 degree Mason & Shriner. **HONORS/ACHIEVEMENTS:** Mem Baseball Hall of Fame 1972; honored by OIC Rocky Mount 1972; "Good Will" Ambassador of NC 1972; "Boy Scouts Hall of Fame 1973; Tar Heel of the Week" 1975; Who's Who in NC 1975. **BUSINESS ADDRESS:** 605 Atlantic Ave, Rocky Mount, NC 27801.

LEONARD, WALTER J.
Educator. **PERSONAL:** Born Oct 03, 1929, Alma, GA; married Betty E Singleton; children: Anthony Carlton, Angela Michele. **EDUCATION:** Savannah State Coll, 1947; Morehouse Coll Atlanta, 1959-60; Atlanta Univ Grad Schl of Business, 1961-62; Howard Univ Sch of Law, JD 1968; Harvard Univ Inst of Educ Mgmt, 1974; Harvard Univ, AMP 1977. **CAREER:** Ivan Allen Jr Atlanta, asst campaign mgr 1961; The Leonard Land Co Atlanta, owner/operator 1962-65; Sam Phillips McKenzie, campaign asst 1963; Dean Clarence Clyde Ferguson Jr Sch of Law Howard Univ, legal rsch asst 1966-67; Washington Tech Inst, admin asst to pres 1967-68; Howard Univ Sch of Law, asst dean & lectr 1968-69; Harvard Univ Law Sch, asst dean/asst dir admiss & finan aid 1969-; US Office of Econ Oppty, hearing examiner 1969-70; Univ of CA/Univ of VA, visit prof summers 1969-72; Harvard Univ, asst to pres 1971-77; Fisk Univ, pres 1977-84; Howard Univ, disting sr fellow 1984-. **ORGANIZATIONS:** Mem Assn of Amer Law Schs; Council on Legal Educ Oppty; Law Sch Admissions Council; Amer Assn of Univ Prof; Howard Univ Law Sch Alumni Assn; bd of visitors USN Acad; bd trustees Natl Urban League; bd trustees Natl Pub Radio; Intl Assn of Y's Men's Club Inc; NAACP; num other civic and ednlorgns; pres Natl Bar Assn; consult The Ford Found NY 1969-71. **HONORS/ACHIEVEMENTS:** Award for Disting Serv to Assn & Office of Pres 1972; Apprec Award Harvard Black Students' Assn 1971; Walter J Leonard Day and key to city of Savannah, GA 1969; 1st Annual Melnea A Cass Comm Award Boston YWCA 1977; New England Tribute Dinner to Walter J Leonard spons by Hon Thomas P O'Neill Jr, Hon Edw M Kennedy, Hon Edw W Brooke, Pres Derek Bok of Harvard Univ 1977; Paul Robeston Award Black Amer Law Students Assn 1977; Frederick Douglass Pub Serv Award Greater Boston YMCA 1977; Special Orator Celebration of 50th Birthday of Martin Luther King Jr Boston, MA 1979; Alumni Achievement Award Morehouse Alumni Club of New England 1977; Apprec Dinner and Award Urban League of Eastern MA 1977; Exemplary Achieve Award Faculty Resolution Grad Sch Educ Harvard Univ 1976; numerous published works incl, "Our Struggle Continues-Our Cause is Just" The Crisis May 1978; "Reflecting on Black Admissions in White Colleges" The Morning After A Retrospective View 1974; articles in, The Boston Globe, USA Today, The Harvard Law School Bulletin; featured in, The Harvard Gazette, The Boston Evening Globe, The Wall St Journal; listed in Who's Who in America. **MILITARY SERVICE:** USCG 1945-46. **BUSINESS ADDRESS:** Distinguished Senior Fellow, Howard University, 2400 Sixth St NW, Washington, DC 20059.

LESLIE, MARCIA LOUISE
Videotape editor. **PERSONAL:** Born Mar 24, 1952, Cincinnati, OH; divorced; children: Nissan Leslie-Thomas. **EDUCATION:** Northwestern Univ, BA Speech 1974. **CAREER:** Kamlager & Assocs, producer/director 1980-86; Tangerine Dream West, video/commercial music production; CBS-TV Network, video-tape editor 1978-. **ORGANIZATIONS:** Mem Urban League 1970-, NAACP 1978-, CBS Black Employees Assoc 1978-, Black Amers Against Famine in Africa 1984-; mem Women in Theatre 1986; mem BASE 1986-. **BUSINESS ADDRESS:** Video-Tape Editor, CBS-TV Network, 7800 Beverly Blvd, Los Angeles, CA 90036.

LESTER, BETTY J.
Judge. **PERSONAL:** Born Oct 14, 1945, Bristol, PA; daughter of John Johnson and Ollie Kimbrough Johnson; married Althear; children: Alyse Renee. **EDUCATION:** Howard Univ, BBA 1968; Rutgers Univ, JD 1971; Marymount Manhattan, LLD (Honors) 1983. **CAREER:** Public Defenders Office, asst dep public def 1972-74; Public Advocates Office, asst dep public advocate 1974-76; Supermarkets Gen, staff attny 1976-77; Newark Municipal Court, judge 1977-80, presiding judge 198-85; Superior Court of NJ, superior court judge 1985-. **ORGANIZATIONS:** Mem EC Bar Assoc 1971-, Natl Bar Assoc 1971-; mem Natl Assoc of Negro Business & Professional Women's Club 1977; bd of dir The Joint Connection 1978; bd of dir, gov NJ State Bar Assoc 1978-80; mem, treas EC Mun Ct Judges Assoc 1982-; mem Natl Assoc of Women Judges 1982-, NJ Coalition of 100 Black Women 1983-. **HONORS/ACHIEVEMENTS:** Outstanding Achievement Assoc of Black Women Lawyers 1980;

mary Philbrook Awd Rutgers Law School 1986; Woman of the Year Zonta Club Intl 1986. **BUSINESS ADDRESS:** Superior Court Judge, Superior Court of NJ, Essex County Courts Bldg, Room 1016, Newark, NJ 07102.

LESTER, DONALD
Educator. **PERSONAL:** Born Sep 20, 1944, Detroit, MI; children: Tarik. **EDUCATION:** Wayne State Univ, BS 1967; Western MI Univ, EdM 1972. **CAREER:** Detroit Public School System, teacher; Wayne County Community Coll, instructor; Univ of Detroit, instructor; Western MI Univ, instructor; Shaw Coll, assoc prof. **ORGANIZATIONS:** Natl dir Basic Trng, Black Christian Nationalist Church; vchmn Reg #1; bd ed Detroit Schools; southern reg bishop Shrines of the Black Madonna of the Pan-African Orthodox Christian Church; chmn Atlanta Housing Auth. **BUSINESS ADDRESS:** Associate Professor, Shaw College, 944 Gordon St SW, Atlanta, GA 30310.

LESTER, ELTON J.
Attorney. **PERSONAL:** Born Sep 28, 1944, Bronx, NY; married Sandra Hight; children: Eric, Shawne. **EDUCATION:** Atlantic Union Coll, BA 1966; Howard Univ, JD 1969. **CAREER:** US Dept of Housing & Urban Devel, atty & adv; Ofc of Mgmt & Budget, examiner. **ORGANIZATIONS:** Mem Fed Bar Assn; DC Bar Assn; Nat Bar Assn; mem Omega Psi Phi; Urban League; Concerned Black Fathers. **HONORS/ACHIEVEMENTS:** Recip Ford Foundation Scholarship 1966; guest speaker at annual conv for Urban Econ Devel.

LESTER, JULIUS
Writer, educator. **PERSONAL:** Born Jan 27, 1939, St Louis, MO; son of Woodie Daniel Lester and Julia Smith Lester; married Alida C. Fechner, Apr 21, 79; children: Jody, Malcolm, Elena Grohmann (step-daughter), David. **EDUCATION:** Fisk Univ, Nashville, TN, BA, 1960. **CAREER:** Univ of Massachusetts, Amherst, MA, prof, 1971—. **HONORS/ACHIEVEMENTS:** Newbery Honor Award, Amer Library Assoc, 1969; Natl Book Award finalist, Amer Publishing Assoc, 1972; author of Look Out, Whitey! Black Power's Gon' Get Your Mama, Dial Press, 1968, To Be A Slave, Dial Press, 1968, The Seventh Son: The Thought and Writings of W. E. B. Dubois, 2 vols, Random House, 1971, All Is Well: An Autobiography, Morrow, 1976, Lovesong: Becoming a Jew, Holt, 1988; author of fiction, including Long Journey Home: Stories From Black History, Dial Press, 1972, This Strange New Feeling, Dial Press, 1982, The Tales of Uncle Remus: The Adventures of Brer Rabbit, Dial Press, 1987, More Tales of Uncle Remus: The Further Adventures of Brer Rabbit, Dial Press, 1988; author of poems, Who I Am, Dial Press, 1974. **BUSINESS ADDRESS:** P.O. Box 333, North Amherst, MA 01059-0333.

LESTER, NINA MACK
Journalist, consultant. **PERSONAL:** Born Oct 16, Fort Davis, AL; married Eugene A; children: Adlai, Valinda Regina. **CAREER:** WGPR-TV, variety show hostess 1976; Consumer Garden Newspaper, organizer 1972; Detroit Courier, adv & gen mgr. **ORGANIZATIONS:** Mem Consumer Educ Consultant; trustee bd mem RAYA; bd mem Estsd C of C 1963; Samaritan Hosp Divisional Bd Quality Assurance; mem Women Comm United Negro Coll Fund; League of Women Voters; Adv Comm Expl of Negro Hist & Educ; mem Deaconess Plymouth United Church of Christ natl & area publicist; past pres Top Ladies of Distinction; trustee Met Assn United Church of Christ; co-editor E Area News of the United Church of Christ; Booker T Washington Business Assoc Noonday Luncheon Chrmn; Specialty Advertising Assoc of Michigan; Urban League Guild; Chamber of Commerce; Eta Phi Beta; NAACP Life Member; Women's Assn Detroit Symphony Orchestra. **HONORS/ACHIEVEMENTS:** Hon Un Comm Svcs; Serv Awd March of Dimes 1966; Recog Cert Un Comm Negro Hist 1967; Town Crier Bell Awd & Citizen of Yr Awd Ford Motor Co; 1983 Honorary Doctorate Journ Humanities Shaw College; Women of the Year 1971; Top Lady of the Year 1983; Highland Park YMCA Outstanding Mother of the Year 1983; Detroit Urban League Guild Initiative awd 1985; Michigan Legis House Concurrent Resolution for distinguished contrib of service to community; Detroit City Council Testimonial Resolution 1985. **BUSINESS ADDRESS:** Owner, L & T Adv Specialities Gifts, 16834 Princeton St, Detroit, MI 48221.

LESTER, RONNIE
Professional athlete. **PERSONAL:** Born Jul 30, 1959, Chicago, IL. **EDUCATION:** Univ of IA, attended 1976-80. **CAREER:** Chicago Bulls, professional basketball guard. **HONORS/ACHIEVEMENTS:** First Team All Big Ten IA Univ 1978-79; All Amer Teams AP & UPI; MVP IA Univ; US Gold Medal Winner US Pan Amer Games Team 1979; had 2 games of double figures points & assists.

LESTER, THEODORE
Educator. **PERSONAL:** Born Apr 29, 1909, Marion, SC; married Louise Rainey; children: Ada, Theodore II, Tanya. **EDUCATION:** Morehouse Coll, BS 1930; Temple Univ, MA 1952; Columbia Univ, further study. **CAREER:** Mayo HS, teacher 1930-31; Vox Sch, prin coach 1932-39; High Hill Sch, 1939-41; Holmes Sch, tchr coach 1945-62 (retired). **ORGANIZATIONS:** Mem Sch Bd 1970-; Nat Pee Dee Palmetto Educ Assns; Coastal Palmetto Athletic Assns; So Eastern Coastal Official; mem NAACP; Omega Psi Phi; Florence Boys Club; pres Wilson High PTA; commr Pee Dee Little League; mem Cumberland Meth Ch Boys Club. **HONORS/ACHIEVEMENTS:** Man of Yr 1970; Disting Serv Awd Natl Little League 1973; Wilson HS Hon Soc Awd 1972; Theodore Lester Comm Ballfield Citizens of Comm; Theodore Lester Swimming Pool authorized City-Council Florence; Theodore Lester Elem Sch Florence Distr #1 Bd of Trustees 1980. **MILITARY SERVICE:** AUS cap 1942-45.

LESTER, WILLIAM ALEXANDER, JR.
Educator. **PERSONAL:** Born Apr 24, 1937, Chicago, IL; son of William A Lester and Elizabeth Clark Lester; married Rochelle Diane Reed; children: William Alexander III, Allison Kimberleigh. **EDUCATION:** Univ of Chicago, BA/BS 1958, MS 1959; Catholic Univ of Amer, PhD 1964. **CAREER:** Theoretical Chem Inst Univ WI, research assoc/asst dir 1964-68; Univ of WI Dept Chem, lecturer 1966-68; IBM San Jose Research Lab, research staff mem/mgr 1968-81; IBM TJ Watson Research Lab, techn planning staff 1975-76; Lawrence Berkeley Lab, assoc dir 1978-81; Natl Resource for Computation in Chem, dir 1978-81; Univ of CA Berkeley, prof chem. **ORGANIZATIONS:** Volunteer instr Project SEED (Spec Elem Educ for the Disadvantaged) 1970-72; chmn Black Liason Comm San Jose Unified Sch Dist 1971-72; mem Chem Eval Panel Air Force Off Sci Research 1974-78; chmn Div Phys

Chem Amer Physical Soc 1979; mem US Natl Comm of Internatl Union of Pure and Applied Chemistry, 1976-79; mem Natl Research Council Panel for Chemical Physics of Natl Bureau of Standards, 1980-83; mem Chem Adv Panel Natl Science Found 1980-83; mem Comm to Survey Chem Sciences Natl Acad Sciences 1982-84; bd mem Marcus Foster Educ Inst 1982-86; Comm on Recommendations for US Army Basic Research, 1984-87; Chmn Div of Chemical Physics, Amer Physical Society, 1986-87; committee on nominations American Assn for the Advancement of Science 1988-. **HONORS/ACHIEVEMENTS:** Outstanding Contrib Award IBM Corp 1974; Chmn Gordon Conf on Atomic and Molecular Interactions 1978; Percy L Julian Awd Natl Organization of Black Chemists and Chemical Engineers 1979; Alumni Award in Sci Catholic Univ of Amer 1983; Elected Fellow Amer Phys Soc 1984; mem editorial brd, Journal of Physical Chemistry, 1979-81, Journal of Computational Chemistry 1980-87, International Journal of Quantum Chemistry 1979-87, Computer Physics Communications 1981-86; Outstanding Teacher Awd, Natl Organization of Black Chemists and Chemical Engineers 1986; Prof Achievement Award Northern CA Council of Black Prof Engineers 1989. **BUSINESS ADDRESS:** Professor of Chemistry, Univ of CA Berkeley, Dept of Chemistry, Berkeley, CA 94720.

LETT, GERALD WILLIAM
Entrepreneur. **PERSONAL:** Born Sep 28, 1926, Lansing, MI; married Ruby Truitt; children: William, Gerald, Debra. **CAREER:** Letts Fashions Inc, owner 1952-; Lansing C of C, bd dir. **ORGANIZATIONS:** Mem MI Retailers Assn Bd; dir YWCA; mem Lansing Econ Devel Corp; past pres Lansing Sexton HS PTA; mem NAACP; mem Urban League. **HONORS/ACHIEVEMENTS:** Sales & Idea Book Citation Award Intl Newspaper Advertising Exec; Boss of Yr Professional Women's Club; Man of Yr Negro Professional & Bus Women's Club; 1st black retail owner to have story written on him Women's Wear Daily. **BUSINESS ADDRESS:** 119 N Butler, Lansing, MI 48915.

LEVELL, EDWARD, JR.
Airport commissioner, retired air force commander. **PERSONAL:** Born Apr 02, 1931, Jacksonville, AL; son of Edward A Levell, Sr and Gabrella Williams Levell (deceased); married Rosa M Casellas, Aug 03, 1951; children: Edward A Levell, III, Ruben C Levell, Kenneth W. LevellRaymond C. Levell, Randy C. Clark, Cheryl D. Levell Rivera, Michael K Levell. **EDUCATION:** Tuskegee Inst, Tuskegee, AL, Bachelor of Science, 1953; US Air Force, Bryand AFB, TX, USAF Pilot Training, 1953-54; Univ of Northern CO, Greeley, CO, MA Urban Sociology, 1972; Industrial Coll of the Armed Forces, Washington, DC, MA Mgmt, 1973; Air War Coll, Maxwell AFB, AL, Leadership/Mgmt, 1973-74. **CAREER:** US Air Force, USAF Academy Commander, CO Springs Cadet Group 1, 1970-72, deputy commander of Cadets, 1972-73; US Air Force, Hurlburt AFB, FL, commander Sr Special Operations SOWG Wing, 1973-82; US Air Force, Luke, AFB, AZ, commander 58 Ttwg Tactical Training Wing, 1977-78; US Air Force, Langley AFB, VA, commander 20th Air Div, 1978-84; Commr of Aviation, Chicago, IL, deputy commr of Aviation, 1984. **ORGANIZATIONS:** Life mem, Kappa Alpha Psi Fraternity; life mem, The Retired Officers Assn (TROA); life mem, The Daedalian Found; life mem, The Tuskegee Airman, Inc (TAI). **HONORS/ACHIEVEMENTS:** Winner of USAFE "Top Gun" Award, 1961; Tactical Air Command (TAC) "Top Gun" (F-100 Super Sabre) 1961, 1965, 1969; Distinguished Service Award, Jacksonville, AL, 1974; Air Force Assn Special Citation of Merit, State of FL, 1977; State of FL Commn of Human Relations Award for Special Recognition, 1977; over 5500 hours of flying time as a command pilot. **MILITARY SERVICE:** US Air Force, Colonel, 1953-84; received Legion of Merit Award, 1983, Distinguished Flying Cross, 1969, Meritorious Serv Medal, 1970, Air Force Commendation Medal, 1966, Air Medal (eight awards) 1970, Vietnam Campaign Medals, 1965-69. **BUSINESS ADDRESS:** Deputy Commr, Chicago O'Hare Intl Airport, PO Box 66142, Chicago, IL 60666.

LEVERMORE, CLAUDETTE MADGE
Educational administrator. **PERSONAL:** Born Feb 28, 1939, St Andrew, Jamaica;daughter of Herbert Willacy; married Oswald Burchell Levermore; children: Monique Althea, Jacqueline Maureen. **EDUCATION:** McGill Univ, Certificate 1968; Univ of Miami, BBA 1978; Wharton Univ, Certificate 1981; Nova Univ, MBA 1984. **CAREER:** Government of Jamaica, civil servant 1958-64; Geigy Pharmaceuticals, admin asst 1964-68; McGill Univ, admin asst 1968-71; Univ of Miami, dir admin serv 1971-. **ORGANIZATIONS:** Mem Natl Black MBA Assoc; bd mem Black Cultural Art Ctr, Black South Florida Coalition for Economic Develop; Nursing School Business Officers Assoc; mem Woodson Williams Marshall Assoc 1978-; instructor Miami-Dade Comm Coll 1984-; bd mem & treas United Nations Florida Chapter. **HONORS/ACHIEVEMENTS:** Outstanding Achievement in Accounting Univ of Miami; Outstanding Achievement in Business Consulting Univ of Miami. **HOME ADDRESS:** 14865 116th St, SW, Miami, FL 33187. **BUSINESS ADDRESS:** Dir Admin Serv, University of Miami, 1755 NW 12th Ave, Rm 412, Miami, FL 33101.

LEVERT, FRANCIS E.
Engineer. **PERSONAL:** Born Mar 28, 1940, Tusculoosa, AL; married Faye Burnett; children: Francis, Gerald, Lisa. **EDUCATION:** Tuskegee Inst, BS 1964; Univ MI, MS 1966; PA State Univ, PhD 1971. **CAREER:** Tuskegee Inst Schl Engr, acting head mech engr 1972-73; Commonwealth Edison Co, prin engr 1973-74; Argonne Natl Lab, nuclear engr applied physics div 1974. **ORGANIZATIONS:** Mem Amer Nuclear Soc; amer Soc Mech Engrs; mem Phi Kappa Phi; mem Pi Tau Sigma; mem Beta Kappa Chi; Amer Soc for Engr Educ Ford Found Fellow. **HONORS/ACHIEVEMENTS:** Author more than 17 tech jrnl articles; Atomic Energy Commn Fellow Univ MI; DNEA Fellow PA State Univ.

LEVISTER, ERNEST CLAYTON, JR.
Physician. **PERSONAL:** Born Feb 04, 1936, New York, NY; son of Ernest C Levister and Ruth Amos Levister; divorced; children: E Clay, Michelle Nicole. **EDUCATION:** Lincoln Univ, AB 1958; Lafayette Coll, BS Chem Eng 1958; Howard Univ Coll of Med, MD 1964. **CAREER:** Norfolk VA, internal medicine/cardiology private practice 1974-78; Embassy of USA Lagos Nigeria, medical attache 1978-79; Private Practice, internal/occupational med San Bernardino CA 1979-; Univ of California-Irvine, asst clinical prof of occupational and environmental medicine 1987-. **ORGANIZATIONS:** Asst prof Inst Sch of Engr Tuskegee Inst 1958-59; asst prof medicine George Washington Medical Sch 1973-74; asst prof medicine Eastern VA Medical Sch 1974-81; radio host Medical Talk Show Norfolk 1980-81; mem Los Angeles Council of Black Professional Engrs 1982-; columnist (medicine) Voice News Riverside CA 1986-; commissioner, Environmental Protection Commission, Riverside CA 1989. **HONORS/ACHIEVEMENTS:** Fellow Amer Coll of Physicians 1977. **MILITARY SERVICE:** AUS Medical Corps major 1969-72; Vietnam, Unit Citation. **BUSINESS ADDRESS:** 1738 N Waterman Ave, San Bernardino, CA 92404.

LEVISTER, ROBERT L.
Judge. **PERSONAL:** Born Oct 25, 1918, Rocky Mount, NC; married Lerlaine Mitchell. **EDUCATION:** Johnson C Smith Univ Charlotte NC; Howard Univ Wash; Boston Univ Sch of Law, LLB. **CAREER:** Stamford CN bd of Finance, (elected) practicing atty recodification comm MA 1949-51; MA Dept of Corps & Taxation, counsel 1951-54; Fairfield Co CT, asst admin judge; Superior Ct State of CT, judge. **ORGANIZATIONS:** Mem bd of dir, exec com CT Blue Cross-Blue Shield; dir Const Fed Savings & Loan; lecturer NY Univ Grad Sch of Pub Admin; adv bd to US CivilRights Comm; chmn CT Coun on Human Rights; Am Soc of Judicature; mem Alpha Phi Alpha Frat; mem Guardsmen Inc; Am Trial Judges Assn; MA CT & Fed Bars. **HONORS/ACHIEVEMENTS:** NAACP Achievement Award 1966; Johnson C Smith Univ Legal Achievement Award 1967; Father McNerney Social Justice Award 1965-66; Comm Coun Serv Award 1969. **MILITARY SERVICE:** AUS m/sgt 1942-46. **BUSINESS ADDRESS:** Hoyt St, Stamford, CT.

LEVISTER, WENDELL P.
Judge. **PERSONAL:** Born May 14, 1928, Rocky Mount, NC; divorced; children: Degna P, Drew F. **EDUCATION:** Hampton Inst, BS 1950; NY Univ, MBA 1951; NY Univ Law Sch, JD 1958; Stanford Univ, certificate Stanford Exec Prog 1973. **CAREER:** Greenup Golar & Levister Esqs, co-founder 1960-63; New York City Law Dept, asst corp counsel 1963-67; Borough of Brooklyn NYC, dir office of spec proj city planning comm 1970-74; Dept of Parks & Recreation, deputy commr revenue devel & park policy 1979-; Civil Court NYC, judge. **ORGANIZATIONS:** Chief Internal Review DAC HQ Ft Wadsworth USARADCOM SI NY; assoc Amer Inst of Planners 1973-; Bedford Stuyvesant Lawyers Assn 1960-; Brooklyn Bar Assn 1964-65; Omega Psi Phi 1949-; bd dir Stuyvesant Comm Ctr Brooklyn 1964-65; NAACP NY 1958-; exec bd United People's Com of Brooklyn UPC 1973-. **HONORS/ACHIEVEMENTS:** Merrill Foundation Fellowship. **MILITARY SERVICE:** USAF 1946-47. **BUSINESS ADDRESS:** Judge, Civil Court, City of New York, 111 Centre St, New York, NY 10007.

LEVY, VALERIE LOWE
Government employee. **PERSONAL:** Born in New York, NY; married Edward J Levy, Jr; children: Vanessa Lynn, Edward Joseph III. **EDUCATION:** NY Univ, BA; CCNY, grad studies; New Sch for Social Research, masters candidate. **CAREER:** New York City Dept for the Aging, dir Manhatten field office 1969-79, dir minority affairs 1979-. **ORGANIZATIONS:** Bd mem Natl Caucus and Center on the Black Aged Wash, DC 1974-; mem Gerontological Soc of Amer 1973-; mem Amer Pub Health Assn 1979-; Delta Sigma Theta Sor; one of orig organizers & coord of the Harlem Interagency Coun on Aging. **HONORS/ACHIEVEMENTS:** Has written and pres many papers on aging and the elderly in the US; Is a recognized authority on the minority elderly. **BUSINESS ADDRESS:** Dir of Minority Affairs, New York City Dept for the Aging, 2 Lafayette St, New York, NY 10007.

LEVY, VICTOR MILES, JR. (VIC MILES)
TV anchorman. **PERSONAL:** Born Nov 07, 1931, Philadelphia, PA; divorced; children: 3 Children. **CAREER:** WCBS-TV rptr anchorman; KDKA-TV, corr; NBC monitor-Radio press internat, voice of am 1966-71; WHOA radio, prgm news dir. **ORGANIZATIONS:** Mem The Inner Circle. **HONORS/ACHIEVEMENTS:** Comm Serv Award; Pittsburgh Guardian Soc 1970; Responsive Environ Found & Awd; "Serv to Children" 1970; Black Achiever Award; Harlem YMCA 1972; Ministerial Interfaith Assn Media Award 1977; 1st Black to Anchor Sched News Prgrm in Pittsburgh. **MILITARY SERVICE:** USAF 1950-54. **BUSINESS ADDRESS:** 524 W 57th St, New York, NY 10019.

LEWIS, ALEXANDER L.
Rehabilitation counselor. **PERSONAL:** Born Dec 10, 1910, St Paul, NC; children: Alexander Lewis, Jr, Gertrude Francoise. **EDUCATION:** Johnson C Smith U, AB 1935; Johnson C Smith U, BD 1942; Johnson C Smith U, MD 1973; US Chaplain Sch, Columbia U, Hunter Coll, Additional Studies. **CAREER:** Hs prin 1935-40; Presb Ch, minister 1943-44; Boy Scout Exec 1943-44; AUS, chaplain 1944-64; Hawaiian Clergy Counseling Service, coordinator & counselor1965; Dept of Corrections NYC, rehab counselor 1966-69. **ORGANIZATIONS:** Pres bd dirs Leahi Hosp Fed Credit Union 1971-; mgr Civil Defense Shelter Leahi Hosp Honolulu 1970-74; chmn membership com Rhab Assn Hawaii; vice-chmn membership com Mental Health; commander-in-chief HI; Cosmopolitan Consistory #291; w master Cosmopolitan Lodge #82; worthy patron Cosmopolitan Chap #72 OES; mem ROA Assn; chmn Advancement Com Oahu Co BSA; pres PTA Leilehua HS 1961-63; mem Kiwanis Club, Phi Beta Sigma; Shriner. **HONORS/ACHIEVEMENTS:** Two Bronze Stars One Silver Star; Goodwill Korean Medal; Citiations for Outstanding Military Serv; Rehab & Comm Activities. **MILITARY SERVICE:** AUS chaplain major 1944-64. **BUSINESS ADDRESS:** Leahi Hosp, Wahiawa, HI 96786.

LEWIS, ALMERA P.
Educator. **PERSONAL:** Born Oct 23, 1935, Chicago; married Thomas P Lewis; children: Tracy, Todd. **EDUCATION:** Univ of WI, BS 1957; Loyola Univ, MSW 1959. **CAREER:** Day Care Cntrs & Sch, cons; Mental Hlth Cntr, psychiatric & sco worker 1959-65; Crittenton Comprehensive Care Cntr supr of professional staff 1966-68; Park Forest Sch Sys, social worker 1968-69; Chicago Circle-jane Adams Sch of Soc, work prest; Univ of IL, prof/dean of students, social work. **ORGANIZATIONS:** Mem, natl bd od dir Nat Assn of Soc Workers; Il Assn of Sch Soc Workers; Academy of Certified Soc Workers; Am Assn ofUniv Prof Bd; mem Women's Com of United Cerebral Palsy of Greater Chicago; Chicago Urban League PUSH; The Art Inst of Chicago. **BUSINESS ADDRESS:** Associate Dean, Univ of IL-Chicago, PO Box 4348, Chicago, IL 60680.

LEWIS, ALVIN
Church agency executive. **PERSONAL:** Born Oct 01, 1935, Chicago, IL; married Dr Juanita L; children: Alvin, Lydia, Lystrelle. **EDUCATION:** Northern Bapt Seminary, theological studies 1959-62; KS State Univ, MS 1970, PhD 1975. **CAREER:** First Ch of God, pastor prof dir minorities resources ctr family consult 1966-74; KS State Univ, instr 1970-74, asst prof 1975; Minor Resources & Rsch Ctr, dir 1973-75; Bd Christian Educ Ch of God, assoc sec 1975-. **ORGANIZATIONS:** Mem Natl Coun Family Rel; dir Natl Met Black Family Conf; Amer Assn Univ Profs; vice chmn & commr Family Life Nat Council of Ch; supervisor & clinical mem Natl Acad of Counselors & Family Therapists Inc; cert leader marriage enrichment Assn Couples for Marriage Enrichment; former pres Junction Manhattan NAACP 1967-71; vice chmn Madison Co Urban League 1985-86; mem Phi Alpha Theta 1969-71; served as ed consult in Africa Carribean & Europe. **HONORS/ACHIEVEMENTS:** Omicron Hon Soc 1968. **BUSINESS ADDRESS:** Associate Secretary, Bd Christian Educ Ch of God, PO Box 2458, Anderson, IN 46011.

LEWIS, ANDRE
Banking executive. **CAREER:** Victory Savings Bank, Columbia SC, chief executive, 1989. **BUSINESS ADDRESS:** Victory Savings Bank, 1545 Sumter St, Columbia, SC 29201. *

LEWIS, ANNE A.
Retired educator. **PERSONAL:** Born Apr 06, 1905, Cleveland, OH; married Kenneth Lewis. **EDUCATION:** Univ MI, AB 1930, grad study. **CAREER:** Juvenile Ct Detroit Pub Welfare US Employment Serv, social worker 1930-45; elem teacher, 1950-62; Detroit Urban League, adminstr asst dir rsch 1962-71 (retired). **ORGANIZATIONS:** Mem Tucson Chap Hospitality Intl; mem Detroit Urban League Guild; memUniv of MI Alumni Assn; Tucson Art Ctr Leag & Tucson Museum of Art; AZ Sonora Desert Museum; Amer Assn Social Workers; Social Workers' Club of Detroit; mem Alpha Kappa Alpha Sor; YWCA; Original Willing Workers of Detroit; Amer Assn Retired Persons; speaker's bur United Found Torch Dr. **HONORS/ACHIEVEMENTS:** Golden Soror 50 Year Mem Alpha Kappa Alpha.

LEWIS, ANTHONY HAROLD, JR.
Computer company executive. **PERSONAL:** Born Aug 31, 1953, Baton Rouge, LA; married Sonja Marie Newkirk; children: Kirsten Sonja, Kira Antoinette. **EDUCATION:** Harvard Coll, AB (Cum Laude) 1975; Harvard Grad Sch of Business Admin, MBA 1977. **CAREER:** Touche Ross & Co, mgmt consultant 1977-79; Raychem Corp, business planner 1979-83; Headquarters Companies, mgr new business 1983-84; Bank of Amer, vice pres 1984-86; Tandem Computers, mgr corporate financial planning. **ORGANIZATIONS:** Treas trustee Katherine Delmar Burke Sch 1984-. **BUSINESS ADDRESS:** Tandem Computers Inc, 5300 Stevens Creek Blvd, LOC 219-30, San Jose, CA 95129-1033.

LEWIS, ARTHUR A.
Auditor. **PERSONAL:** Born Nov 04, 1925, Los Angeles, CA; married Elizabeth; children: Ivy, Derek, Cornell, Arthur III, Jeffrey, Jason. **EDUCATION:** UCLA, BS 1947. **CAREER:** Fed Energy Adminstrn, presently audit investigator; Defense Contract Audit Agy, former supr auditor; Caltech's Jet Propulsion Lab Pasadena CA, former resident auditor for DCAA; Vending Machine Bus Los Angeles, owns & operates cigarette 1954; Income Tax Ofc Los Angeles, Presently; Golden State Mutual Life Ins Co 1947-52. **ORGANIZATIONS:** Pres Visionaries of the Blind Children Ctr; mem Fed Govt Accountants Assn; mem NAACP; Urban League; Alpha Phi Alpha Frat; Trustee for Lincoln Memorial Congregational Ch of Los Angeles; CA Eagle (black newspaper), former sports editor 1951. **HONORS/ACHIEVEMENTS:** Certificate Certified Internal Auditor (CIA). **MILITARY SERVICE:** AUS e-5 1952-54. **BUSINESS ADDRESS:** Lewis Tax Serv, 2315 W Santa Barbara Ave, Los Angeles, CA 90008.

LEWIS, ARTHUR W.
Government official. **PERSONAL:** Born Jul 01, 1926, New York, NY. **EDUCATION:** Dartmouth Coll, AB 1966, AM 1969; Foreign Serv Inst, Postgrad 1969-70. **CAREER:** USIA, fgn serv 1943-45,50-53,54-68,68-; US Embassy, cultural affairs officer Bucharest 1970-72, counselor for pub affairs Lusaka 1972-74, Addis Ababa 1974-77, Lagos 1977-79, dir African Affairs 1979-.

LEWIS, AUBREY C.
Business executive. **PERSONAL:** Born 1935, Montclair, NJ; married Ann; children: Lauren, Aubrey, Jr, Lisa, John, Gary. **EDUCATION:** Notre Dame Univ, BS; FBI Acad; Cornell Univ; New York Univ. **CAREER:** F W Woolworth Co, NYC, vice pres, exec personnel rep 1967-; FBI, special agt; Chicago Bears, scout; football & track coach. **ORGANIZATIONS:** Bd mem NJ Sports & Exposition Auth; Naval Acad Found; United Cerebral Palsy Fairleigh Dickinson U. **BUSINESS ADDRESS:** F W Woolworth Company, 233 Broadway, New York, NY 10007.

LEWIS, BILLIE
Physician. **PERSONAL:** Born Oct 24, 1929, Longdale, OK; married Vivian P Moon; children: Vivian Sanford, William, Beverly. **EDUCATION:** Langston Univ, BS 1951; Univ of OK, MD 1959; Hurley Hosp, Surgery Residency 1959-64; Amer Coll of Surgeons, FACS 1972. **CAREER:** Genessee Meml Hosp, chmn surgery dept 1971-77; MI State Univ, asst clinical prof surg 1975-85; Lewis Medical Services, pres. **ORGANIZATIONS:** Delegate Natl Med Assn 1965-84; mem bd dir Genessee Cnty Med Soc 1978-80; mem MI State Med Soc, AMA, Flint Acad Surg 1964-; chmn Hurley Hosp Med Records Comm 1980-; teaching staff Hurley and St Joseph Hosp 1964-83; active staff at Hurley, St Joseph, Mclaren, Genessee Meml 1964-; vice pres United Way 1975-82; pres Family Serv Agency 1978-79; pres Amer Cancer Soc-Genessee 1981-83; exec bd Amer Cancer Soc-MI Div 1984-85. **HONORS/ACHIEVEMENTS:** Natl Honor Soc AED 1956; Outstanding Physician in Community Flint, MI 1977. **MILITARY SERVICE:** AUS Corpl 1952-54. **HOME ADDRESS:** 1618 Kensington, Flint, MI 48503. **BUSINESS ADDRESS:** President, Lewis Medical Services, 1910 Robert T Longway, Flint, MI 48503.

LEWIS, BYRON E.
Business executive. **PERSONAL:** Born Dec 25, 1931, Newark, NJ; son of Thomas Eugene Lewis and Myrtle Evelyn Allen; divorced; children: Byron Eugene Lewis Jr. **EDUCATION:** Long Island U, BA 1953; NY U, Grad Study; City Coll NY; King Meml Coll, hon DHL. **CAREER:** Uniworld Group Inc, chmn/ceo; Afro Mkt Co, pres, publ 1968-69; Tuesday Publs, vice pres 1964-68; Amalgamated Publs, asst ad mgr 1963-64; Urbanite Mag, co-fdr 1961-62. **ORGANIZATIONS:** Lectr Black Coll; Black Exec Exch Prgm Nat Urban League. **HONORS/ACHIEVEMENTS:** Creator "This Far by Faith" 1977; exec Prodcr "Sounds of the City" 1974-75; Minority Bus Man of the Yr ICBO New York City 1980; exec producer, Americas Black Forum Television Show 1989. **MILITARY SERVICE:** AUS pfc 1953-55. **BUSINESS ADDRESS:** 1250 Broadway, New York, NY 10034.

LEWIS, CARL
Track and field athlete. **PERSONAL:** Born Jul 01, 1961, Birmingham, AL. **EDUCATION:** Univ of Houston, Communications major 1979-. **CAREER:** Began running at age 8; Won long jump at Jesse Owens Youth Prog Meet 1973; Ran track in high school; Continued

running in college. **HONORS/ACHIEVEMENTS:** Top ranked HS track athlete in US; All Amer in 200 meters & long jump 1978; Natl HS long jump/100 yd record 1978; Ranks #1 in the world in the 100 meterrace & long jump, #2 in the world in 200 meters; Third fastest time ever in 100 meters; Long jump indoor world record; Duplicated Jesse Owens feat at 1936 Berlin Olympics; 1984 Olympics won 4 Gold medals, 100 meters, 200 meters, long jump, 4x400 meter relay. **BUSINESS ADDRESS:** c/o Tom Tellez, U of Houston/Athletic Dept, 4800 Calhoun Blvd, Houston, TX 77004.

LEWIS, CARY B., JR.
Educator, attorney. **PERSONAL:** Born Sep 13, 1921, Chicago, IL; married Mary S; children: Cheryl, Cary B III. **EDUCATION:** Univ of IL, AB 1942; Univ of Chicago, MBA 1947; Univ of IL, CPA 1950; DePaul Univ, JD 1966; Harvard Univ, AMP 1971; Teaching Certificates & Licenses, HS 1951, Jr Coll 1967, Coll 1958, Supervisory 1967. **CAREER:** KY State Univ, asst prof 1947-50; So Univ, assoc prof 1950-; CPA, 1950-75; MT Washington & Co CPA's Chicago, sr auditor 1951-53; Chicago Pub Sch, 1951-57; Collier-Lewis Realty Co, auditor 1953-71; Chicago Tchrs Coll, 1957-65; AA Rayner & Sons, auditor 1960-72; Budget Coord, 1966-67; Atty at Law, 1966-; Chicago State Univ, spec asst to vice pres 1967, prof law & acctg 1957-,. **ORGANIZATIONS:** Budgetary consult office of econ oppor 1967-69; educ consult to dept hlth educ & welfare 1968-69; auditing consult to dept of labor 1967-69; mgmt consult to Black Econ Union 1969; chmn educ adv comm Chicago NAACP; mem Amer Bar Assn, IL Bar Assn; Chicago Bar Assn; Cook Co Bar Assn; Amer Judicare Soc; Amer Bus Law Assn; Amer Inst CPA's; IL Soc CPA's; Natl Soc CPA's; Amer Acct's Assn; Amer Assn of Univ Prof's; City Club of Chicago. **HONORS/ACHIEVEMENTS:** Wisdon Hall of Fame, 1972; Worldwide Acad of Scholars 1975; Natl Hon Soc 1938; Sachem 1941; First Black to practice as CPA LA 1951; First Black Atty & CPA State of IL 1966. **MILITARY SERVICE:** USEAC bombardier & navigator 1942-45. **BUSINESS ADDRESS:** 95 St at King Dr, Chicago, IL 60628.

LEWIS, CHARLES BADY
Educator, missionary. **PERSONAL:** Born Sep 20, 1913, Paincour Ville, LA. **EDUCATION:** Leland Coll, AB 1945; ABT Seminary, BD 1947, ThM 1948; Mississippi Bapt Seminary, DMin Candidate 1982. **CAREER:** Natchez Coll, dean of religion 1948-74, dean of chapel 1948-77; Mississippi Bapt Seminary, dean of Natchez Center, 1962-. **ORGANIZATIONS:** Mem Natl Assn of Profs of Religion 1970-; pastor/advisor Natl BSU 1970-73; pastor/advisor State BSU 1974-85; social sci tchr 1948-68; mem NatchezCivic Business League 1957-65. **HONORS/ACHIEVEMENTS:** Who's Who Natl BSU 1988; Who's Who State BSU 1971; Who's Who Home Mission Bd 1981; Outstanding Personalities 1984; Who's Who in Religion's Outstanding Educators 1968; Who's Who Sunday Schl Studnts Dept 1985. **BUSINESS ADDRESS:** Dean of Natchez Center, Mississippi Baptist Seminary, 1006 N Union St, Natchez, MS 39120.

LEWIS, CHARLES GRANT
Designer. **PERSONAL:** Born Mar 12, 1948, Los Angeles, CA. **EDUCATION:** ELA Coll, AA 1973;Univ So CA, BS 1977. **CAREER:** Edward C Barker & Asso, proj designer 1977-; AIA, asst vice pres 1977-; Benito Sinclair PE, engr 1974-77; John D Williams, draftsman 1971-74; Charles Grant Orgn, prin 1974-77. **ORGANIZATIONS:** Alpha Phi Alpha Building Found 1972-74; assoc Urban Workshop 1967-77; Alpha Phi Alpha Frat 1971-73; stu rep Nat Orgn of Minority Architects 1974-77; comm Design Ctr Planning & Arch for Urban grps. **HONORS/ACHIEVEMENTS:** Leadership Award Am Soc of Engrs & Arch 1973; outst serv to sch; comm Order of Omega Hon Frat; num articles publ by local & natl jours. **BUSINESS ADDRESS:** 3123 W 8th St, Los Angeles, CA 90005.

LEWIS, CHARLES H.
Dentist. **PERSONAL:** Born Dec 31, 1923, Vicksburg, MS; married Dorothy Foote; children: Stephen A, Brenda A, Phyllis G. **EDUCATION:** HowardUniv Wash DC, BS Chem 1949; Meharry Med Coll Nashville, DDS 1955. **CAREER:** Alpha Phi Alpha Frat Inc, SW regional vp; Dentistry, priv pract 1955-70, 1973-; Morton-neighborhood Health & Ctr, dir 1970-73. **ORGANIZATIONS:** Mem Am Dental Assn 1955-; sec-tres Moton Meml Hosp 1958-; pres Oil Capital SW Reg Golf Assn 1958-; mem NAACP; YMCA 1958-; pres Greenwood C of C1977-79. **HONORS/ACHIEVEMENTS:** Ribbon for campaigns "Invasion of Borneo & China Coast" 1944; Honorary Dental Soc; hon mem Omicron Kappa Upsilon Honor Dent Soc 1955-; twice rec "Serviceto Humanity" Award LangstonUniv 1978-79; Tourn named "Charles H Lewis Classic" Oil Capital Golf Club 1979. **MILITARY SERVICE:** USN signalman/2/c 1942-45. **BUSINESS ADDRESS:** 5050 N Peoria, Tulsa, OK 74126.

LEWIS, CHARLES MCARTHUR
Information systems planner. **PERSONAL:** Born May 29, 1949, Fitzgerald, GA; married Katrinda McQueen. **EDUCATION:** Fort Valley State Coll, BS Math 1971; Univ of GA, MA Math 1973; GA State Univ, MBA 1984. **CAREER:** Southern Bell Telephone & Telegraph, engr 1973-78, management skills assessor 1978-80, staff engr 1980-86; Bell South Services Inc, information systems planner 1986-. **ORGANIZATIONS:** Mem Church Affiliated Orgs 1983-87; mem Natl Black MBA Assoc 1986-87. **HONORS/ACHIEVEMENTS:** Alpha Kappa Mu Honor Soc Fort Valley State Coll 1970; Speakers Awd 1986. **HOME ADDRESS:** 3424 Boring Rd, Decatur, GA 30034. **BUSINESS ADDRESS:** Staff Manager, BellSouth Services, 37F57 SBC, 675 W Peachtree St NE, Atlanta, GA 30375.

LEWIS, CLEVELAND ARTHUR
Engineer. **PERSONAL:** Born Apr 21, 1942, Selma, AL; son of Levi Lewis and Elsie Lewis; married Betty Faye Harris; children: Aisha, Jahmilla. **EDUCATION:** Purdue Univ, AAS 1972, BS 1976. **CAREER:** Chrysler Corp, industrial engr 1972-76; Allison Transmission Div, senior product engineer. **ORGANIZATIONS:** Mem Inst of Industrial Eng 1970-; pres Clevetech Work Systems Inc 1975-; bd of regents Concordia College 1986-. **HONORS/ACHIEVEMENTS:** Outstanding Achievement General Motors 1984; Distinguished Alumni Purdue Univ 1986. **MILITARY SERVICE:** USAF airman 2nd class 4 yrs; Outstanding Performance Awd. **HOME ADDRESS:** 5085 Knollton Rd, Indianapolis, IN 46208. **BUSINESS ADDRESS:** Product Engineer, Allison Transmission, 4700 West 10th St, Indianapolis, IN 46206.

LEWIS, CLIFF
Professional athlete. **PERSONAL:** Born Nov 09, 1959, Brewton, AL. **EDUCATION:** So MS Univ, Radio-TV Major. **CAREER:** Green Bay Packers, linebacker 1981-. **HONORS/ACHIEVEMENTS:** Special Teams standout 1984; Finished as runnerup in unassisted tackles with 17 & led kamikazes in fumble recoveries with 3; Has not missed a game & enters the1985 season with a consecutive game streak of 57.

LEWIS, COLSTON A.
Lawyer, employment recruiter. **PERSONAL:** Born Jan 23, 1914, Lynchburg, VA; married Glenyce Davis; children: Colston A, Jr. **EDUCATION:** VA Union U, AB 1939; HowardUniv Law Sch, JD 1948. **CAREER:** Atty, gen pract 1949-70; Equal Employment Opport Commn, commr 1970-. **ORGANIZATIONS:** Mem VA St Bar Assn; Old Dominion Bar Assn; Nat Bar Assn; VA Trial Lawyers; World Asson of Lawyers of the World; Peace Through Law Center. **HONORS/ACHIEVEMENTS:** Rep NAACP Urban League; bd dir United Way Washington DC Bicenntenial Commn for Black Am; Hon LlD 1973; Hon Colonel 1974; Cit of the Yr 1957; AchievAward Old Dominion Bar & Nat Bar Assns 1975. **MILITARY SERVICE:** AUS 1942-46. **BUSINESS ADDRESS:** 2401 E St NW, Washington, DC.

LEWIS, DANIEL
Attorney. **PERSONAL:** Born Apr 22, 1946, New York City, NY. **EDUCATION:** New Lincoln Sch, Acad Deg 1963; BrownUniv , BA 1967; PA Law Sch, JD 1970. **CAREER:** Harlem Br Off NYC, asst dist atty in charge 1974-; Dist Atty Off Sup Ct Bur, trial asst da 1970-74; Harlem Commonweatlh Coun NYC, writer; Nat CORE, researcher 1968; Am Emb Rome, intern 1967; State Dept Bur of African Affairs Wash DC, intern 1966. **ORGANIZATIONS:** Vol SCLC SCOPE Project AL 1966; mem One Hundred Black Men; Am Civil Lib Union; Nat Dist AttyHs Assn; mem CORE; former trustee Professional Children's Sch. **BUSINESS ADDRESS:** DA's Harlem Br Office, 55 W 125 St, New York, NY.

LEWIS, DAVID BAKER
Attorney. **PERSONAL:** Born Jun 09, 1944, Detroit, MI; married Kathleen Louise McCree; children: Aaron McCree, Sarah Susan. **EDUCATION:** Oakland Univ, BA 1965; Univ of Chicago, MBA 1967; Univ of MI, JD 1970. **CAREER:** Miller Canfield Paddock & Stone, summer law clerk 1969; Univ of MI, lectr Afro-Am and African Studies Dept 1970; Hon Theodore Levin US Dist Ct, law clerk 1970-71; Patmon Young & Kirk, assoc atty 1971-72; David Baker Lewis Atty at Law, sole practitioner 1972; Lewis, White & Clay, senior partner 1972-. **ORGANIZATIONS:** Charter mem bd trustees Oakland Univ 1970-81, chmn bd trustees 1978-81; trustee emeritus; trustee Oakland Univ Found 1985-; pres bd trustees Franklin-Wright Settlements Inc 1975-76; vice pres MI Assn of Governing Bds of Colls & Univs 1977-78; mem bd trustees Exec Comm HGH Health Syst; mem bd dir Harper-Grace Hospitals; mem exec com bd dir Greater Detroit Area Hosp Cncl 1976-79, mem Credentials Comm 1983-; mem bd dir Center for Creative Studies Coll of Art and Design 1983-; life mem Judicial Conf of the US Ct of Appeals for the Sixth Circuit; mem bd dir Exec Comm Metro Center for High Techn 1983-; life mem Comm of Visitors Univ of MI Law Sch; mem Amer Bar Assn; mem Natl Bar Assn; mem State Bar of MI; mem Wolverine Bar Assn; mem Detroit Bar Assn; mem steering com Bond Attorneys Workshop 1979. **BUSINESS ADDRESS:** Senior Partner, Lewis, White & Clay, PC, 1300 First Natl Building, Detroit, MI 48226.

LEWIS, DELANO EUGENE
Administrator. **PERSONAL:** Born Nov 12, 1938, Arkansas City, KS; son of Raymond E Lewis; married Gayle Jones; children: Delano Jr, Geoffrey, Brian, Phillip. **EDUCATION:** Univ of KS, BA 1960; Washburn Sch of Law Topeka KS, JD 1963. **CAREER:** US Dept of Justice, genl atty 1963-65; US Equal Employment Oppor Commn, staff analysis & advice 1965-66; US Peace Corps Nigeria/Uganda, assoc dir/country dir 1966-69; Office of Sen Edward W Brooke, legislative asst 1969-71; Office of Rep Walter E Fauntroy, admin asst 1971-73; C & P Telephone Co, vice pres 1973-; C & P Telephone of Washington DC, pres 1988-. **ORGANIZATIONS:** Bd dirs Comm Found of Greater Washington 1978-; bd dir Psychiatric Inst of DC 1979-; bd dirs Natl Bank of Wash 1982-; past pres bd Friendship House 1971-; mem Arena Stage 1977-; president elect The Greater Washington Bd of Trade 1987; Military Order of the Knights of Malta 1987-. **HONORS/ACHIEVEMENTS:** Comm Serv Awd Foxtrappe Club 1977; Washingtonian of the Yr Washington Mag 1978; comm Serv-Pres Medal Catholic Univ of Amer 1978; chmn Mayor's Transition Commn mayor Marion Barry Jr 1978-79; Distinguished Community service Award, Washburn Univ 1989; Honorary Degree, Marymount Univ 1988. **BUSINESS ADDRESS:** Vice President, C & P Telephone Co, 2055 L St NW, Room 700, Washington, DC 20036.

LEWIS, DIANE CLAIRE
Government official. **PERSONAL:** Born Jul 14, 1945, Bronx, NY; married Julius Wilson. **EDUCATION:** Econ City Coll of NY, BA Econ 1968; Princeton U, MA 1971; GeorgetownUniv Law Cntr, 1971-74. **CAREER:** Educ Office of the Mayor Wash DC, spl asst to the Mayor 1979-; Inter Govt Rel Bd of Educ DC, dir 1975-79; Bd of Educ DC, spl & asst to the pres 1974-75; Dept of Labor Ofc of Policy Eval & Resch,research analyst 1972-73; Ford Found Tanzania E Africa, cons-research 1970. **ORGANIZATIONS:** Fld supr grad work Incentives Exper Princeton 1968-69; Task Force chair DC Coalition for the Appointment of Women; chair-judiciary com DC Women's Polit Caucus. **BUSINESS ADDRESS:** 1350 E St NW, Washington, DC 20004.

LEWIS, DICK EDGAR
Educator. **PERSONAL:** Born Dec 23, 1938, Freeport, Bahamas;divorced; children: Anthony, Roshaun. **EDUCATION:** San Diego City Coll, AA 1970; Cabrillo Pacific Univ Coll Law, BS 1975, JD 1976. **CAREER:** San Diego PD, spec asst to chief of police; San Diego Chargers, spec asst to gen mgr; San diego Comm Coll Dist, prof at law. **ORGANIZATIONS:** Bd mem Encanto Boys Club; bd mem House of Metamorphasis. **HONORS/ACHIEVEMENTS:** Adult Scouter of the Year Boy Scouts of Amer 1977; Scout Order of Merit Boy Scouts of Amer 1978; Comm Conscience Award Action Ent Dev Inc 1983. **MILITARY SERVICE:** USN Hml served 13 1/2 years; Purple Heart 1965. **BUSINESS ADDRESS:** 801 W Market St, San Diego, CA 92101.

LEWIS, EDWARD T.
Publisher. **PERSONAL:** Born May 15, 1940, Bronx, NY. **EDUCATION:** Univ NM, BA 1964, MA 1966; NY Univ, postgrad 1966-69. **CAREER:** Peace Corps Univ NM, lecturer 1963; City Mgr's Office Albuquerque,admin analyst 1964-65; First Natl City Bank NYC, fin

analyst 1966-69; Essence Mag NYC, publisher 1969-. **ORGANIZATIONS:** Bd dir Vol Urban Consult Group, Black Counil on Africa, Fund for New Horizons for Retarded Inc, 21st Century Found, Rheeland Found, Negro Ensemble NYC, School Vol Prog; trustee Coty; mem 100 Black Men, Inc, Uptown C of C, New York City Commerce & Industry. **HONORS/ACHIEVEMENTS:** Recipient Decision Maker Awd Natl Assn Media Women 1974; Natl IGBO Awd for Minority Businessman of the Year 1979; Named Businessman of the Year Blackafrica Promotions Inc 1974. **BUSINESS ADDRESS:** Publisher, Essence Communications, Inc, 1500 Broadway, New York, NY 10036.

LEWIS, ELMA I.
Educator. **PERSONAL:** Born Sep 15, 1921, Boston. **EDUCATION:** Emerson Coll, BLI 1943; Boston U, MEd 1944. **CAREER:** Elma Lewis Sch Fine Arts, founder/dir 1950-; Robert Gould Shaw House Chorus, staged dir chorgrpd 21 Operas & Operettas; Harriet Tubman House, fine arts wrkr; MA Mental Health Habit Clinics Boston/Woodward Sch Quincy, teacher; Doris Jones Sch of Dance Boston, teacher; Roxbury Memorial HS for Girls, speech therapist; Natl Educ Assoc, consultant; Natl Endowment of the Arts, consultant; Natl Ctr Afro-Amer Artist, founder/dir 1968-. **ORGANIZATIONS:** Overseer Museum of Fine Arts; fellow Black Acad of Arts & Letters; trustee WGBH; mem Corp of Northeastern U; fellow Am Acad of Arts & Sci; Black Professional &Bus Women Arts Commn; bd mem Theater Commn Group; bd mem 2nd World Festival of Black Art in Nigeria; mem Meco Cultural Alliance; mem numerous offices,coms numerous civic orgns groups & councils; trustee MA College of Art, Boston Zoological Soc; mem Joslin Diabetes Foundation. **HONORS/ACHIEVEMENTS:** Samuel Adams Bicentennial Comm Awd; NAACP Gold Cert Awd; Lambda Kappa Mu Cit; NE Theatre Conf Awd; Woman of Yr Awd; Zeta Phi Beta Sor 1969; Mayor'sCitation City Boston 1970; Omega Psi Phi Frat Awd; Negro Bus & Professional Women's Awd Boston & Vic; Black Womanhood Awd Black Big Bro Assn 1970; Hon degrees Boston Coll 1971, Anna Maria Coll 1974; Dr of Fine Arts Colby Coll 1972; many other hon degrees from various colls & univs; listed Contemporary Black Amers vol 1, Living Legends in Black; several other listings; MacArthur Prize Fellow Awd 1981; Presidential Citation and Medal President's Comm on the Arts & Humanities Washington DC 1983; Alumni Awd for Disting Public Serv to the Comm Boston Univ Alumni Assoc 1984; induction into Acad of Disting Bostonians Greater Boston Chamber of Commerce 1985; author "Let Minorities Interpret Their Own Culture" Baystate Feb 1978; author "Celebrating Little People" Boston Review of the Arts 1972; various newspaper art written about her. **BUSINESS ADDRESS:** Artistic Dir, Natl Ctr Afro-American Artists, 122 Elm Hill Ave, Boston, MA 02121.

LEWIS, ELSIE MAKEL
Educator. **PERSONAL:** Born May 02, 1914, Little Rock, AR; married Joseph. **EDUCATION:** Fisk U, BA 1932;Univ of So CA, MA 1933;Univ of Chicago, PhD 1946. **CAREER:** Hunter Coll NY, prof Amer History; Sweet Briar Coll VA, teacher; Emory Univ, teacher; Earlham Coll, teacher. **ORGANIZATIONS:** Visited univ in Kenya, Uganda, Tanzania, Ethiopia, Egypt 1971; mem Am Hist Assn; mem Phi Beta Kappa; Assn for Study of Afro-am Life & History. **HONORS/ACHIEVEMENTS:** Author of numerous articles & scholarly papers. **BUSINESS ADDRESS:** Hunter Coll, 695 Park Ave, New York, NY 10017.

LEWIS, EMANUEL
Actor. **PERSONAL:** Born in New York. **CAREER:** TV Movie, Lost in London 1985; TV Special, My Very Own Special 1987; TV, Bob Hope in Sweden, Bloops & Bleepers; variousTV commercials; Webster, actor. **HONORS/ACHIEVEMENTS:** Many guest appearances & specials; People Choice Awds 1985,86. **BUSINESS ADDRESS:** Schuller Talent Inc, 276 Fifth Ave, Room 1001, New York, NY 10001.

LEWIS, EPHRON H.
Farmer. **PERSONAL:** Son of Jasper Lewis (deceased) and Adline Mathis Lewis (deceased); married Doris; children: Ephron Lewis Jr. **EDUCATION:** Arkansas AM&N Coll, Graduate. **CAREER:** Lewis and Son Rice Processing Co, owner. **ORGANIZATIONS:** Former mem Natl Rice Advisory Comm; pres, AK Land & Farm Devel Corp, 1980-. **HONORS/ACHIEVEMENTS:** Persistence of the Spirit, Univ of AK Pine Bluff, 1987.

LEWIS, ERMA (NEE DUFFY)
Association executive. **PERSONAL:** Born Feb 07, 1926, Ft Worth, TX; married James Edward Jr. **EDUCATION:** DillardUniv TX. **CAREER:** Sojourner Truth Players Inc, exec prod 1972-75; HEW-ESAA, proj dir; HEW-ESAA, camp dir 1960-71; YWCA, dir num proj 1958-71; Highland Park YWCA, only prof staff 1971-72; Greater St James Bapt Ch, sec 1951-58. **ORGANIZATIONS:** NAACP Nom comm 1955; supv Youth Coun 1957-59; Voter Regis 1969; Life mem YWCA Assn 1959; Life mem Nat Coun of Negro Women 1976; mem numerous ofcs,coms, civic, poltl, rel orgns. **HONORS/ACHIEVEMENTS:** Woman of Yr Awd F Brooks & Gray Literary Art Charity Club 1973; Gold Star Awd Better Infl Assn 1973; Image Awd Mayor's Coun on Youth Opport 1973; Outst Cit Awd Jack & Jill 1973; 15th Ann Celeb Plaque Jr Debutants 1973; plaque Nolan Robert Monseigneur HS Black Awareness Club 1973; Woman of Yr Mildred M Anderson 1974; nominee Sojourner Truth Awd 1974; Dist Serv Awd Com of 100 1974; Hidden Heroines Hall of Fame Girl Scouts 1975; Merit Comm Serv Am Revol Bicentennial Comm 1976; cert of Recogn Am Revol Bicentennial Comm 1976; Personalities of South Honoring Am Leaders 1976; Comm Awd Cert TX Ministers & Cit Leadership Coun 1976; Nat Cult Arts Fest Awd Sojourner Truth Players Inc 1976; chmn Ft Worth Black Cit for Fest 1976; Mary McLeod Bethune Bicent Achiev Awd Nat Coun of Negro Women 1976. **BUSINESS ADDRESS:** 1060 E Terrell Ave, Fort Worth, TX 76104.

LEWIS, ERMA JEAN
Financial manager. **PERSONAL:** Born Nov 17, 1943, Star City, AR; married Richard D Lewis; children: Eric Stewart, Darin Stewart, Jeanine. **EDUCATION:** Univ of San Francisco, BA 1984; Attended, Los Angeles Trade Tech Coll 1982, Loyola Univ 1981; Univ of CA Los Angeles, Certificate 1973. **CAREER:** Title Insurance & Trust, admin asst 1969-73; Central Medical Group, personnel mgr 1973-74; Central City Comm Mental Health, personnel mgr 1974-78; Home Savings of Amer, asst vice pres 1978-. **ORGANIZATIONS:** Mem Personnel Industrial Relations Assoc 1983-85; adv bd Summit Youth House 1983-84, People Who Care Youth Ctr 1986; group leader YMCA 1985-86. **HONORS/ACHIEVEMENTS:** Participant Youth Motivation Task Force 1982-84; Five Year Service Awd Home Savings 1983. **HOME ADDRESS:** 2642 S Normandie Ave, Los Angeles, CA 90007.

LEWIS, FELTON EDWIN
Educational administrator. **PERSONAL:** Born Oct 02, 1923, New Orleans, LA; children: Ronald, Anthony, Felton III, Marita, Karen. **EDUCATION:** Xavier Univ, BA (cum laude) 1955; Univ WI-Madison, MA 1956; Universite d'Aix-Marseille France, diplome 1956-58; Fordham Univ, professional diploma 1968-69; Universidad Interamericana Mexico, PhD 1970. **CAREER:** New York City Bd of Educ, teacher 1958-66; Foreign Language Dept JHS, acting chmn 1963-66; Jr High Spec Serv Sch, acting asst prin 1966-67; Title I New York City Bd of Educ, ESEA coord 1967-68; New York City Bd of Educ, student & intern of educ admin & super prin intern 1968-69, dep dist supt dist 12 1969-71, acting comm supt dist 12 1971-72, comm supt dist 12 1972-78; comm supt dist 16 1978-. **ORGANIZATIONS:** Consult Verona NJ Sch Bd, Portsmouth VA Sch Bd, Huntington LI NY Sch Bd, Copiage NY Sch Bd; mem Al;pha Kappa Mu; pres Council of Parents Assn. **HONORS/ACHIEVEMENTS:** Alpha Epsilon Partial Grad Scholarship Middlebury Coll 1955; French Teaching Assistantship WI Univ 1955-56; Maison Francaise Scholarship WI 1956; Fulbright Scholar 1956-57; Fulbright Grant 1957-58; Ford Found Fellowship Fordham Univ 1968-69; numerous awds & testimonials S Bronx NAACP, WIN Adult Council, JFK Library for Minorities, Bronx NAACP, Fairmount Sch, Prin of Dist 12, CSA of Dist 12, Bronx Boys Club, Behaviorial Rsch Lab, Drug Abuse Prevention Project, Dr Martin Luther King Com, numerous certifications in teaching & admin. **MILITARY SERVICE:** AUS sgt 1942-45; Bronze Arrowhead. **BUSINESS ADDRESS:** Comm Supt Dist 16, Bd of Education, 1010 Lafayette Ave, Brooklyn, NY 11221.

LEWIS, FLOYD EDWARD
Corporate director. **PERSONAL:** Born Nov 23, 1938; married Ruth M Lewis. **EDUCATION:** S IL U, BS 1961; M Urban Affairs Bus St Univ 1972. **CAREER:** Anheuser-Busch Co Inc, dir equal oppor affairs 1975-; Monsanto Co, mgr equal oppor 1974-75; Urban League of St Louis, dir personnel 1972-74; United Way of St Louis, agency relations assn 1970-72. **ORGANIZATIONS:** Bd mem Carver House Assn 1977; bd mem Assn of Black Psychologist 1977; bd mem Annie Malone Children's Home 1978. **BUSINESS ADDRESS:** Anheuser Busch Co Inc, One Busch Plaza, St Louis, MO 63118.

LEWIS, FRANK ROSS
Librarian. **PERSONAL:** Born Jul 13, 1931, Seale, AL; son of Mr & Mrs Willie Lewis Sr; married Laura Scott, Aug 17, 1958; children: Jason. **EDUCATION:** NC Central Univ, AB Pol Sci 1957; Atlanta Univ, MLS 1969. **CAREER:** LaGrange Sr HS, librarian 1969-73; LaGrange Coll, asst librarian 1973-74, library dir 1974-. **ORGANIZATIONS:** Treas GA Library Assn 1980; past dir bd of dirs Council on Aging 1978; mem adv bd West Central GA Regional Hosp Adv Council three year term ending in1990; past pres Alpha Phi Alpha Frat Theta Nu Lambda Chap 1979. **HONORS/ACHIEVEMENTS:** Mem Georgia Council for the Arts; reapptd to second term by Gov Joe Frank Harris for term ending in 1989, 3 yr appts. **MILITARY SERVICE:** AUS pvt 1952-54. **BUSINESS ADDRESS:** Library Dir, La Grange College, Wm & Evelyn Banks Library, La Grange, GA 30240.

LEWIS, FREDDIE
Athlete. **PERSONAL:** Born Jul 01, 1943, Huntington, WV. **EDUCATION:** AZ St, 1966. **CAREER:** IN Pacers, ret professional basketball player 1980. **HONORS/ACHIEVEMENTS:** Holds team record for most free throws in one game-17 1970; holds team record of most free throws in career-2999 1967-74 & 77; holds team record of most assists in career-2711 1967-74 & 77; leading team scorer-1565 Pts 1967-68; team best freethrow percentage-799 & 822 1967-68 & 1968-69; led team in assists-346 1968-69; led team in assists-362 1971-72; led team in assist-322 1973-74; Pacersh 2nd highest point scorer career-11036; lead team in number of games played-672; was 2nd in total # of minutes played-23282.

LEWIS, FREDERICK CARLTON
Administrator. **PERSONAL:** Born Jul 01, 1961, Birmingham, AL. **EDUCATION:** Univ of Houston, 1979-82. **CAREER:** American Heart Assn, honorary chairman 1984-; Carl Lewis Foundation, chairman. **ORGANIZATIONS:** Peoples Workshop 1984-.

LEWIS, GEORGE RALPH
Business executive. **PERSONAL:** Born Mar 07, 1941, Burgess, VA; son of Spencer Harcum Lewis and Edith Pauline Toulson Lewis; married Lillian Glenn; children: Tonya, Tracey. **EDUCATION:** Hampton Inst, BS 1963; Iona Coll, MBA 1968. **CAREER:** Gen Foods Corp, sales analyst 1963-64, profit planning analyst 1964-65, product analyst 1965-66; WR Grace Co, financial analyst 1966-67; Philip Morris Inc, corp analyst 1967-68, sr planning analyst 1968-70, mgr investor relations 1970-72, mgr financial serv 1972-73, asst treas 1973-74, vice pres financial & planning & treas 1975-82; Seven-Up Co, vice pres financial 1982-84; Philip Morris Inc, vice pres, treas. **ORGANIZATIONS:** Bd mem Meharry Med Coll 1983, Central Fidelity Bank 1984, Natl Urban League 1986, Hampton Univ 1985. **HONORS/ACHIEVEMENTS:** Arthur A Loftus Achievement Awd Iona Coll 1980; Outstanding Twenty Year Alumnus Awd Hampton Inst 1982. **BUSINESS ADDRESS:** Vice President & Treasurer, Philip Morris Companies Inc, 120 Park Ave, New York, NY 10017.

LEWIS, GUS EDWARD
Broadcast executive. **PERSONAL:** Born Oct 12, 1932, New Orleans, LA; divorced; children: Deidra Sutton, Dawn, Lamont, Shannon, Sherman, Sharon, Scarlette. **EDUCATION:** Medical Technologist Certificate, 1950; Surgical Technician Certificate, 1951; Dillard Univ, BA Ed 1958. **CAREER:** New Orleans Public School System, teacher 1958-59; WYLD, sales/prog dir 1959-70; WHAT, WXEL, WNNR, WYLD, operations mgr/news dir/sales mgr 1970-81; KBCE-FM, general mgr/pres 1981-. **ORGANIZATIONS:** Mem Phi Beta Sigma Frat 1979-; founding vice pres Central LA Minority Business Cncl 1982-; mem Mayor's Adv Commn 1986-; mem bd of dirs Chamber Political Action Comm 1986-89; mem Rapide's Parish Sch Bd Comm 1987; vice pres Central LA Chamber of Commerce 1987. **HONORS/ACHIEVEMENTS:** Affiliate of the Year Sheridan Broadcasting News Network 1986. **MILITARY SERVICE:** USN petty officer 4 yrs; Korean Svc, Good Conduct, European Occupation, United Nations 1950-53. **BUSINESS ADDRESS:** President/General Manager, Trinity Broadcasting/KBCE FM, PO Box 69, Boyce, LA 71409.

LEWIS, H. RALPH
Physicist. **PERSONAL:** Born Jun 07, 1931, Chicago, IL; married Renate J. **EDUCATION:** Univ of Chicago, AB 1951, SB 1953; Univ of IL, MS 1955, PhD 1958. **CAREER:** Univ of Heidelberg, rsch assoc 1958-60; Princeton Univ, instr 1960-63; Los Alamos Natl Lab, rsch physicist 1963-, Laboratory Fellow 1983-. **ORGANIZATIONS:** Mem Amer Physical

oc; pres Student Concerts Inc 1973-75; mem Los Alamos Sinfonietta 1963-84. **HONORS/ CHIEVEMENTS:** Univ Fellow Univ of IL 2 yrs during 1953-58; Fellow of American Physal Society. **BUSINESS ADDRESS:** Los Alamos Natl Lab, MS-F642, Los Alamos, NM 7545.

EWIS, HELEN MIDDLETON
lergyman. **PERSONAL:** Born Apr 25, 1905, Crystal River, FL; married Felix Early; chilren: 9 Children. **CAREER:** The Ch of the Living God the Pillar & Ground of the Truth ic, chief overseer & pres 1968-; The Ch of the Living God W Palm Beach FL, pastor & predingbishop 1952-68; The Ch of the Living God Nashville TN, pastor 1940-50; The Ch of e Living God, sec/treas 1937; The Ch of the Living God Sanford FL, asst chief overseer 937; The Ch of the Living God KY IN, dist bishop 1935; The Ch of the Living God Sanford L, ordained to bishopric 1932; The Ch of theLiving God Daytona Beach FL, pastor 1930. **IONORS/ACHIEVEMENTS:** Outstanding leadership award The Ch of the Living God 973; publications award "75th Anniversary Year Book" 1978. **BUSINESS ADDRESS:** he Church of the Living God, Hydes Ferry Pike, Nashville, TN.

EWIS, HENRY
rchestra conductor. **PERSONAL:** Born 1932, Los Angeles, CA; married Mailyn Horne; hildren: Angela. **EDUCATION:** Univ of So CA. **CAREER:** NJ Symphony Orch New-k, dir 1968-; guest conductor numerous orchs; NY Philharmonic, debut 1972; Met Opera rch, first black to conduct 1972; LA Philharmonic Orch, youngest double bass player; LA hilharmonic Orch, former asso conductor; LA Opera Co, mus dir 1965-68. **ORGANIZA-IONS:** Founder LA Chamber Orch 1958; founder Black Acad of Arts & Letters; mem Cal rts Commn; Young Mus Found; commentator condr Los Angeles Philharmonic Yth Con-erts Radio Series; conducted Gershwiniana La Scala Opera House Milan Italy 1965; bassist onductor Seventh Army Symphony Orch Stuttgard Germany 1955-57. **MILITARY SER-ICE:** AUS 1955-56. **BUSINESS ADDRESS:** NJ Symphony, 1020 Broad St, Newark, NJ 7102.

EWIS, HENRY S., JR.
mployee assistance counselor, marital & family therapist. **PERSONAL:** Born Sep 26, 935, Chester County, SC; son of Henry S Sr and Marie Lewis; married Savannah D Winsad; children: Robin Anita, Kenneth W, Jonathan H, Karen E. **EDUCATION:** Winston-alem State Univ, BS 1957; Andover Newton Theol School, MDiv 1961; Wake Forest Univ, irther Study; School of Pastoral Care Boston City Hosp, 1959; School of Pastoral Care North arolina Baptist Hospital, 1977; Univ of Kentucky Coll of Med RBT Ctr, 1977. **CAREER:** hiloh Bapt Church, student asst 1957-59; Wentz memorial United Church of Christ, summer inister 1958-; James A Gray, asst prof religion & sociology 1960-77; Winston-Salem State niv Winston-Salem NC, univ chaplain 1960-77; Mt Pleasant Bapt Church, pastor 1966-77; Vinston-Salem Forsyth Cty Schools Urban Affairs Inst, human relations consultant 1967, 969; Zion Bapt Church, 1969; Wake Forest Univ, part-time instr dept religion 1970-72; RJ eynolds Tabacco Co, Winston-Salem NC, senior employee counselor 1977. **ORGANIZA-IONS:** Mem Baptist Ministers Conf & Assoc; bd dir Ministries to Blacks in Higher Educ 975-77; clinical mem Amer Assn for Marriage & Family Therapy, Natl Inst of Business & ndustrial Chaplains, North Carolina Chaplains Assn; mem Phi Beta Sigma, Winston- Salem hap NAACP; North Carolina Bd Cert Marital & Family Therapist; bd of dir, Council of lder Adults; bd dir, Experiment in Self Reliance; mem, North Carolina Assn for Marital & amily Therapy. **BUSINESS ADDRESS:** Department of Employee Counseling, R.J. eynolds Tabacco Company, Plaza Building, First Floor, Winston-Salem, NC 27102.

EWIS, HENRY W.
usiness administration. **PERSONAL:** Born Nov 10, 1927, Meridian, MS; married Sarah ; children: Henry W Jr, Deborah, Barry, Deshawn. **EDUCATION:** Jackson State Univ, 949-52; Univ Ctr of Harrisburg, 1964. **CAREER:** Carpen's Fed Credit Union, vice pres 973-85; NAACP Harrisburgh Cty Tri-Cty Affirm Action, pres, coord. **ORGANIZA-IONS:** Trustee St Paul Baptist Church 1961-75, Carpenter's Local Union #287 1968-, Delgate to Council 1968-; vice pres Dauphin Cty Dem Party 1977-83; mem Harrisburg School dv Bd 1977-85, Harrisburg Incinerator Authority 1978-80; chmn Harrisburg Parking Auth 980-82; mem P Hall Masonic Families 1977-83; mem HarrisburgAdv Bd, Harrisburg Down-wn Devel Comm 1983-85; vice pres Himyar Temple Partrol #17 PHA 1983; affirm action fficer Harrisburg School Dist 1984-; mem Harrisburg Comm Coll Bd 1984-85; trustee Car-enters Local Union #287; vice pres Harrisburg Br of NAACP 1987-88; pres Himyar Temple 17 Patrol Drill Team 1987. **HONORS/ACHIEVEMENTS:** Man of the Year AASR of ree Masonry NJ USA Corp PHA 1983; Awd Himyar Temple 17 AEAONMS Patrol PHA 984; Awd Life Mem NAACP, Golden Heritage 1984; Awd for 30 yrs Caprenters Local nion 30 Yr Pin 1985; received 33 Final Degree United Supreme Council Ancient and Ac-epted Scottish Rite of Free Masonry PrinceHall Affiliation 1987. **MILITARY SERVICE:** nfantry pfc military policeman 1946-47; Awd for Outstanding Military Policeman 1947. **USINESS ADDRESS:** President, NAACP-Harrisburg Branch, 1824 N 4th St, Harrisburg, A 17102.

EWIS, HOUSTON A.
entist. **PERSONAL:** Born May 04, 1920, Bonham, TX; married Clara Houston; children: uth Ann Collins, Pamela Brinkley. **EDUCATION:** XavierUniv 1941-42; FishUniv 1946-7; Meharry Med Coll Sch of Dentistry, DDS 1951. **CAREER:** Self employed gen dentistry resent; Girl Scouts, dir 1958-67; Gtr Wheeling Cncl of Chs, dir 1955-64; Children & Fam erv Assn, dir 1956-62 ; United Way, dir 1967-60. **ORGANIZATIONS:** Mem Nat Den ssn; Am Den Assn; pres WV Med Soc Inc 1977-78; mem Am Soc of Endodntics; Acad of en Den Mem Civitan Club of Wheeling 1963-; dir Moundsville Wheeling Chap Am Red ross 1963-66; dir Urban Renewal Auth 1966-71; ran for WV House of Del 1968; dir wheeling rea Blue Cross-Blue Shield1969-. **HONORS/ACHIEVEMENTS:** One of outst W Vir-nians 1965-66; %Mem Intl Plat form Assn. **MILITARY SERVICE:** Mil Serv enlisted an 1942-45; commnd duty Den Corps 1951-53; 1951-53; col active res. **BUSINESS AD-RESS:** Ste 402, Med Tower, Wheeling, WV 26003.

EWIS, HYLAN GARNET
ociologist, educator. **PERSONAL:** Born Apr 04, 1911, Washington, DC; son of Harry Vythe Lewis and Ella Wells Lewis; children: Carole Ione Bovoso, Guy Edward. **EDUCA-ION:** VA Union Univ, AB 1932; Univ of Chicago, AM 1936, PhD 1951. **CAREER:** How-rd Univ Washington, instr sociology 1935-41; Talladega Coll, prof soc sci 1941-42; OWI, info pec 1942-45; Hampton Inst, assoc prof 1945-48; Inst for Rsch in Social Sci Univ of NC, research assoc 1947-48; Atlanta Univ, assoc prof sociology 1948-56, prof 1956-57; Unitarian Serv Com Inc, assoc dir comm serv 1957-59; Health & Welfare Council Washington, dir child rearing study 1959-64; Brooklyn Coll, prof sociology 1967-77; Met Applied Rsch Center, sr vice pres 1968-75; City Univ NYC, prof grad cntr 1977-; Brooklyn Coll, prof emeritus 1977-; CUNY Grad Center, prof. **ORGANIZATIONS:** Mem delinq grants review comm Natl Inst Mental Hlth 1963-67; mem Soc Problems Rsch Review Comm 1969-73; mem Dev Behavioral Sci Study Sect Natl Inst of Health 1974-76; sr consult Clark Phipps Clark & Harris Inc 1975-86, RBC & Assoc 1986-; consult Volta River Proj Prep Commn Gold Coast 1954; Ashmore Project Fund for Advance of Educ 1953; So Regional Cncl 1955-57; Commn on Race & Housing 1956-57; consult Disaster Study Comm NRC 1955; mem adv com grants prog US Children's Bur 1962; mem adv panel small grants prog US Dept Labor 1963-83; chief consult family panel White House Conf Civil Rights Planning 1965; mem review panel US Office Educ 1965-67; mem head start research adv com Office Econ Opport 1965-67; mem grants adv com natl Endowment for the Humanities Natl Found Arts & Humanities 1967-68; mem Amer Social Soc; mem, fellow AAAS; Soc Applied Anthropology; Alpha Phi Alpha. **HONORS/ ACHIEVEMENTS:** Rosenwald Fellow 1939-41; author Blackways of Kent 1955; Fund for Advancement of Educ Fellow 1956; DuBois-Johnson-Frazier Award 1976; Merit Award Eastern Sociological Soc 1979; visiting scholar Russell Sage Found 1974-75. **BUSINESS ADDRESS:** Professor, CUNY Graduate Center, 33 W 42nd St, New York, NY 10036.

LEWIS, IDA ELIZABETH
Publisher, editor. **PERSONAL:** Born Sep 22, 1935, Malverne, PA. **EDUCATION:** Sch Public Communications Boston U, BS 1956. **CAREER:** Tanner Publs Co Inc, pres 1972-; Encore Am & Worldwide News Mag; pub editor; Teil House Inc, pres; Encore Communications Inc, publ & editor 1971-72;Essence Mag, editor chief 1970-71; Jeune Afrique Mag, correspondent 1968-71; British Broadcasting Corp, writer broadcaster 1967; Life Mag, writer 1964-65;NY Age, finicial editor 1960-63. **ORGANIZATIONS:** Trustee Tougaloo Coll; bd dir Am Com Africa; mem Commn Inquiry Into HS Journalism; mem Nat Council Negro Women; mem Alpha Kappa Alpha Soc; mem Am Mgmt Assn Scarlet Key BostonUniv 1956. **HONORS/ACHIEVEMENTS:** Citz of Yr award Omega Psi Phi 1975; Intl Benih award for contrbn to black people throughout world 1975; numerous other awards. **BUSINESS ADDRESS:** 515 Madison Ave, New York, NY 10022.

LEWIS, J. B., JR.
Funeral service business executive. **PERSONAL:** Born Oct 22, 1929, Clifton Forge, VA; son of J B Lewis Sr (deceased) and Mattie Douglas Lewis; married Mary Louise Colbert; children: Aaron. **EDUCATION:** Eckels Coll of Mortuary Sci, grad 1957. **CAREER:** Insurance underwriter 1958-63; Greyhound Lines, optr 1964-65; Mt View Terr Apts, mgr/agent 1970-; JB Lewis Funeral Service, owner. **ORGANIZATIONS:** Adv bd Coreast Savings Bank 1972; VA Funeral Dir Assn 1976; Natl Funeral Dir Assn 1976; VA Mortic Assn 1959; councilman City of Lexington 1969; v mayor City of Lexington 1976; vice pres Rockbridge Area Housing Corp 1967-70; vice pres Human Relat Counc 1968; pres Lylburn Downing PTA 1962-63; treas sec Cub Scouts 1963; mem NAACP; Amer Legislative Post 291. **HONORS/ACHIEVEMENTS:** Eye Enucleat Cert 1976. **MILITARY SERVICE:** AUS 1954-56. **BUSINESS ADDRESS:** JB Lewis Funeral Service, 112 N Randolph St, Lexington, VA 24450.

LEWIS, JAMES, JR.
Educator, author. **PERSONAL:** Born Mar 07, 1930, Newark; married Valdmir M; children: Michael, Patricia, Terrence. **EDUCATION:** Hampton Inst, BS 1953; Columbia U, MS 1957; Harvard U, Alfred North Whitehead Flwshp for Adv Study in Educ 1970; Union Grad Sch, phD 1972. **CAREER:** Wyandanch School Dist, teacher act asst, HS prin 1957-66; Elem prin 1966-67; Dist prin 1967-72; Villanova Univ, assoc prof 1972-73; City Univ of NY, prof of educ, chmn of div of teacher educ 1972-74; Central Berkshire Regional School Dist, supt of schools 1974-; Educ Improvement Center NE, exec dir 1974-. **ORGANIZATIONS:** Mem Am AssnUniv Profs; Am Assn Sch Adminstrs; Nat Educ Assn; Nat Alli Black Sch Educators; Mass Assn Sch Supr; Assn for Suprvsn & CurriculumDevel; NJ Assn of Sch Adminstr; Am Soc of Training & Devel; Am Mgmt Assn; Nat Soc of Corp Plnrs. **HONORS/ACHIEVEMENTS:** Outst ldrshp award Sch Dist 1968; Who's Who in Comm Serv 1977; Who's Who in US 1977; Man of Achvmt; Who's Who in E 1970; Dictnry of Intl Biography; author of 14 Professional Books. **MILITARY SERVICE:** AUSR maj 1955-67. **BUSINESS ADDRESS:** EIC/NE 2 Babcock Pl, West Orange, NJ 07052.

LEWIS, JAMES B.
Government official. **PERSONAL:** Born Nov 30, 1947, Roswell, NM; son of William Reagor and Dorris Lewis; married Armandie Lillie Johnson; children: Teri Seaton, James Jr, Shedra, LaRon. **EDUCATION:** Bishop Coll, BS Educ 1970; Univ of NM, M Public Admin 1977; Natl Coll Business, AS Business 1980, BS Business (Magna Cum Laude) 1981. **CAREER:** Univ of Albuquerque, afro-studies adminis/instr 1974-77; District Attorney's Office, investigator/purchasing dir 1977-83; Bernalillo Co, treasurer 1983-85; New Mexico State Govt, state treasurer 1985-. **ORGANIZATIONS:** Past state housing chair, mem NAACP 1980-; bd mem finance comm Victims of Domestic Violence 1983-; past treas mem Amer Soc for Public Admin 1983-; mem Natl State Treasurers 1985-; mem bd State Investment Council NM 1985, Public Employee Retirement Bd 1985, Educ Retirement Bd 1985; mem Amer Legion PO 99 1985; mem Kiwanis Club of Albuquerque, Masons, NAACP, American GI Forum, Intl Alumni Assoc Bishop Coll, Taylor Ranch Neighborhood Assoc; life mem Omega Psi Phi Frat; pres-elect New Mexico Chapter Amer Society for Public Admin 1989; mem New Mexico State Bd of Finance, mem Educ Foundation Assistance Board, mem Ad-Hoc Committee (Oil & Gas) State Investment Council 1989. **HONORS/ACHIEVEMENTS:** Outstanding Young Men in Amer Natl Jaycees 1980; Citizen of the Year Omega Psi Phi Frat 1983; Outstanding County Treasurer Co Treasurer's Assoc 1984; Hon mem Beta Alpha Psi CPA Hon Societ 1989; commencement speaker Zuni High School Zuni NM 1989. **MILITARY SERVICE:** AUS E-4 2 yrs. **HOME ADDRESS:** 5313 Sooner Tr NW, Albuquerque, NM 87120. **BUSINESS ADDRESS:** State Treasuer, New Mexico State Government, 224 E Palace Ave, LaVilla Riviera, Santa Fe, NM 87501.

LEWIS, JAMES EARL
Engineer. **PERSONAL:** Born Jun 02, 1931, Jackson, MS; son of Martin L Lewis, Sr and Willie Mae; married Annette Moody, Jun 20, 1959; children: Janice, Tamara, Jacquannette. **EDUCATION:** Howard U, BSEE 1955; Physics Howard Univ, MS 1976. **CAREER:** Bendix Communication Div, sr staff engineer; "A" Westinghouse Elect Co, sr engineer 1969-75; Lockheed Electronics Co, sr elec engr 1966-69; US Naval Research Lab, elec scientist 1957-66; Raytheon Corp, principal engineer. **ORGANIZATIONS:** Mem IEEE Co-founder

Naylor-Dupont Community Assembly 1973; neighborhood commr Boy Scouts 1969-71; bd of dir Jr Citizen Corp, pres of DC Striders. **HONORS/ACHIEVEMENTS:** US patent holder "Microwave Antenna Feed for Two Coordinate Radars" 1968; pub paper "Automatic Electronic Polarization Control for Satellites" Intl Conf on Communications 1972; invention award "Technique for Reduced Sidelobes on Radar Antennas" Westinghouse 1972. **HOME ADDRESS:** 3504 Sugar Tree Ct, Johnson City, TN 37603.

LEWIS, JAMES EDWARD
Artist, educator. **PERSONAL:** Born Aug 04, 1923, Phenix, VA; married Jacqueline; children: James E Jr, Cathleen Susan. **EDUCATION:** Philadelphia Coll of Art, BFAE 1949; Temple Univ, MFA 1950, Ford Found Faculty Fellow 1954; Syracuse Univ, Ford Found Faculty Fellow 1964; Yale Univ, Ford Found Faculty Fellow 1955. **CAREER:** Morgan State Univ, dir gallery of art, Henry O Tanner prof of fine arts 1950-. **ORGANIZATIONS:** Bd mem MD Artists Equity, Balto Council of Foreign Affairs, Orchard St Museum, School #33; pres Lillie Carroll Jackson Museum; chmn Baltimore City Comm for Hist & Archit Presvtn; bd mem Baltimore Counc on Intl visitors; alumni bd Phiadelphia Coll of Art. **HONORS/ACHIEVEMENTS:** Commiss Clarence M Mittchell Sculpture Courthouse Bldg Balto MD 1985; Black Amer Serviceperson Bronze 9 1/2' Balto MD 1974. **MILITARY SERVICE:** USMC corpl 3 yrs. **HOME ADDRESS:** 5011 Herring Run Dr, Baltimore, MD 21214. **BUSINESS ADDRESS:** Dir, Morgan StateUniv, Coldspring Lane & Hillen Rd, Baltimore, MD 21239.

LEWIS, JAMES R.
Dentist. **PERSONAL:** Born Aug 03, 1938, Asheboro, NC; married Barbara Walker; children: Krista, Erica. **EDUCATION:** Chem NC Central U, BS 1963 howard u, dds 1968; rotating dent internship mcgill u, montreal, can, & va hosp, albany 1968-69. **CAREER:** Lincoln Health Cent Durham NC, dental dir 1971-75;Univ NC Sch Dent, asst prof dep ecology 1969-71. **ORGANIZATIONS:** Mem Am Dent Assn; Acad Cent Dent; NC Dent Soc; Am Endodontic Soc; Chi Delta Mu Med & Dent Frat Bd Mem NC Health Plan Agcy; mem Highest Order Mystic Shrine 32nd deg Mason; health prof coun for Black Stud int in dent First black as mem Adm Comm for Sch of Dent UNC 1969-71. **MILITARY SERVICE:** USN HM3 3rd class hospitalman 1956-59. **BUSINESS ADDRESS:** P O Box 427, Lincoln Health Center, Durham, NC 27707.

LEWIS, JESSE CORNELIUS
Educator. **PERSONAL:** Born Jun 26, 1929, Vaughan, MS; married Emma Goldman; children: Valerie. **EDUCATION:** Tougaloo Coll, BS 1949; Univ of IL, MS 1955, MA 1959; Syrause Univ, PhD 1966. **CAREER:** Southern Univ Baton Rouge, instructor math 1955-57; Prairie View Coll, 1957-58; Syracuse Univ, rsch asst computer center 1963-66; Jackson State Coll, prof math, dir computer center 1966-. **ORGANIZATIONS:** Cons, lectr Amer Amth Assoc 1971; proj dir NSF Computing Network 1973-, NSF Sci Faculty Fellow 1958,61; mem Math Assoc, Amer Assoc Computing Mach, mem Math Soc; sec dir State Mut Savs & Loan Jackson 1969-75; chmn Faculty Senate Jackson State Coll 1970-73; mem Alpha Phi Alpha.

LEWIS, JESSE J.
Business executive. **PERSONAL:** Born Jan 03, 1925, Tuscaloosa, AL; married Helen Merriweather; children: James, Jesse Jr. **EDUCATION:** Miles Coll Birmingham AL, BA 1951-55; Troy State Univ Montgomery AL, MS 1976-77. **CAREER:** The Birmingham Times Newspaper, pres 1963-64; Office of Hwy Traffic Safety Montgomery, dir 1974-78; Lawson State Comm Coll, pres 1978-. **ORGANIZATIONS:** Mem Law Enforcement Plnng Agency, Birmingham Urban League; life mem Alpha Phi Alpha. **HONORS/ACHIEVEMENTS:** Citation for Outstanding Serv Gov of AL 1975; Outstanding Acad Excellence Awd Miles Coll 1975, Ctr to Promote Safety in AL State of AL 1978. **BUSINESS ADDRESS:** President, Lawson State Community Coll, 3060 Wilson Rd SW, Birmingham, AL 35221.

LEWIS, JOHN ROBERT
Government official. **PERSONAL:** Born Feb 21, 1940, Troy, AL; son of Eddie Lewis; married Lillian Miles. **EDUCATION:** Am Bapt Theol Sem, BA 1961; Fisk U, BA 1967. **CAREER:** Voter Educ Project Inc, exec dir 1970-; So Regional Council, comm orgn proj dir 1967-70; Field Found, assoc dir 1966-67; Nonviolent Coord Com Chmn, student 1963-66; Atlanta City Councilman-At-Large; elected Congressman, 1986—. **ORGANIZATIONS:** Mem Am Civil Liberties Union; Afro-Am Inst; Adv Com Biracial Com Atlanta Bd Edn; Adv Bd Black Enterprises; mem Martin Luther King Jr Ctr for Social Change; Life mem NAACP; SCLC; various others; mem Leadership Atlanta 1974-75; leading speaker organizer and worker in the Civil Rights Movement; apptd by Pres Johnson to White House Conference "To Fulfill These Rights" 1966; mem Speaker's Bureau during Sen Robert Kennedy's campaign. **HONORS/ACHIEVEMENTS:** Named "One of Nation's Most Influential Black" Ebony Mag 1971-72; "One of America's 200 Rising Leaders" by Time Mag 1974. **BUSINESS ADDRESS:** 501 Cannon House Office Bldg, Washington, DC 20515.

LEWIS, LAURETTA F
Educator. **PERSONAL:** Born in Chattanooga, TN. **EDUCATION:** Univ of TN Chattanooga BSW 1971; Univ of TN, MSSW 1974; Univ of MI Inst of Geron, Cert Aging 1982-; North Carolina A&T State Univ, Summer Inst on Aging 1986. **CAREER:** Family Serv Agency, social worker aide 1966-68; Community Action Program TN, out reach soc worker 1968-70; Neighborhood Youth Corp, youth counselor 1972; Clover Bottom Dev Ctr Nashville TN, social worker 1973; Florence Crittenton Home TN, social worker aide 1973-74; East Carolina Univ, assoc prof social work; East Carolina Univ School of Social Work, coord of aging component for grad studies. **ORGANIZATIONS:** Consult Long Term Care 1976-; vice chmn, treas, 1980-82, chmn 1983 NC Council on Social Work Ed; past pres, exec bd Pitt Co Mental Health Assoc 1983-; chmn bd Pitt Cty Council on Aging 1983-85; mem exec comm & chap rep to state bd Pitt Co Mental Health Assoc 1987; mem exec bd Creative Living Ctra Day Prog for Geriatric Patients. **HONORS/ACHIEVEMENTS:** Received Alumni Upper Classman Awd 1971; Danforth Assoc Danforth Found 1980; Awds of Appreciaiton NC Dept Human Serv MR 1981; Teacher of the Year Student Assoc Social Work Dept 1983; Outstanding Service Mental Health Assoc 1984-85; Appointee Reg Faculty Liaison Natl Assoc Soc Works; Minority Leadership Devel Fellowship Awd School of Public Health Univ of NC Chapel Hill 1985; Certificate of Appreciation from Undergrad Student Org 1987; Training Assistantship in Geriatric Educ & Leadership Dev from the Univ of NC at Chapel Hill Sch of Social Work & Geriatric Educ Ctr Summer Inst 1987; Merit Awd Mental Health Assoc Pitt Co 1987; inducted into "The Carolinas Associates" ofr Excellence in Higher Educ as Charter Mem 1987. **BUSINESS ADDRESS:** Assoc Prof Social Work, East CarolinaUni School of Allied Health & SW, Div of Social Work, Greenville, NC 278344353.

LEWIS, LEROY C.
Podiatrist. **PERSONAL:** Born Jun 23, 1917, Mason City, IA; married Elizabeth L Harri children: Ronald. **EDUCATION:** Buena Vista Coll; IL Coll Podiatric Med 1946. **OR-GANIZATIONS:** Mem Am Podiatry Assn; MO Podiatry Anns; KC Podiatry Soc; Marti Luther King staff bd dir Urban League; YMCA; BSA 1958-62; Midwesterners Inc StAndre Meth Ch; Sigma Ph Phi. **HONORS/ACHIEVEMENTS:** Man Yr; Distinguished Se award. **MILITARY SERVICE:** AUS 1943-46. **BUSINESS ADDRESS:** 2713 E 31 S Kansas City, MO.

LEWIS, LILLIAN J.
Social services. **PERSONAL:** Born Apr 20, 1926, Chicago, IL; widowed; children: Rober Gloria, Benjamin, Vivian. **CAREER:** US Naval Hosp, 1955-63; DeWitt Army Hosp, nu div 1963-65; Group Health Assoc, clinical asst 1966-70; Manpower Admin, chief support se 1971-. **ORGANIZATIONS:** Mem Natl Org for Women, Natl Polit Womens Caucus, M State Dem Steering Comm 1976, NWPC Affirm Action Task Force; vice pres NAACP; me Comm Rel Deseg Task Force; adv bd Model Cities Fellowship, League of Women Voter Prince Georges Pol Womens Caucus & Affirm Action Coord, Prince George Cty Publ Scho ESAP 1971, Prince George Ment Health Assoc; comm to elect Marvin Mandel; chmn Com Affairs 1970-72; bd of dir So Christian Leadership Conf MD Chapt, Prince Georges Cty M Black Dem Council. **HONORS/ACHIEVEMENTS:** Cert of Apprec for Meritiroius As US Dept of Commerce 1970; Cert of Merit NAACP 1973; deleg at large Dem Conv State MD 1976.

LEWIS, LLOYD E., JR.
Business executive. **PERSONAL:** Born Nov 17, 1926, Xenia, OH; son of Lloyd Edwar Lewis and Ruth Hamilton Lewis; married Edythe Mulzac; children: James D, Crystal M **EDUCATION:** Univ of Dayton, BS Business Admin 1948; Central MI Univ, MA Publ Admin 1976. **CAREER:** Lloyd Lewis Sales & Serv Inc, vice pres 1950-66; SCOPE, progra developer 1966; Rikes, general mgr 1966-75; City of Dayton, asst city mgr 1975-80; The Day ton Power & Light Co, asst vp. **ORGANIZATIONS:** Pres Dayton City Plan Bd 1967-7 dir Dayton Area Chamber of Comm 1978-84; treas Montgomery Cty Devel Corp 1980-8 trustee Miami Valley Auto Club 1980-85; chmn St Elizabeth Med Ctr 1984-85; trustee, Fra ciscan Health System of Dayton 1987-; secretary, Citywide Development Corp 1985- **HONORS/ACHIEVEMENTS:** Outstanding Civic Achievement Univ of Dayton Alum Assn 1971; Outstanding Public Affairs Citizens Amer Soc of Public Admin 1973; Outstandin Achievement Awd OH Planning Conf 1978; Marketeer of the Year Amer Mktg Assn 198 Citizens Legion of Honor, President's Club of Dayton 1988; Archon of the Year, Sigma Bo & Sigma Phi Frat 1988. **MILITARY SERVICE:** AUS capt 2 yrs active, 14 yrs reserve **HOME ADDRESS:** 800 Oak Leaf Dr, Dayton, OH 45408. **BUSINESS ADDRESS:** Assi tant Vice President, Dayton Power & Light Company, PO Box 1247, Dayton, OH 45401

LEWIS, MARC CALVIN
Professional athlete. **PERSONAL:** Born May 15, 1960, Columbia, MO. **EDUCATIO** Missouri Western. **CAREER:** Oakland Invaders, wide receiver 1983-; Denver Gold, wi receiver 1984-. **HONORS/ACHIEVEMENTS:** Voted honorable mention All-Centr States Intercoll Conf.

LEWIS, MARTHA S.
Administrator. **PERSONAL:** Born Feb 24, 1924, Kensett, AR; divorced. **EDUCA-TION:** Univ of AR, BA 1944; Atlanta Univ Sch of Soc Work, MSW 1947. **CAREER:** M NY Dept of Soc Srv, dep commr 1976-; NYS Dept of Soc Srv, dep commr 1975-76; Dept Soc & Comm Srv New York City Housing Auth, dir 1972-76, 1972-75; Maternity Ctr Ass mgmt consult spl asst to dir 1971-72; Maurice W Perreault & Assc, consult 1971; Marth Lewis & Assc Mgmt Consult Firm, established 1970; Operation Better Block, dir 1968-7 Dept of Soc & Comm Srv New York City Housing Auth, dep dir 1964-68; New York Ci Housing Auth, chief tenant org tenant educ div 1961-64; New York City Youth Bd 1954-6 New York City Bd of Educ, soc wrkr 1951-54. **ORGANIZATIONS:** Soc Welfare Foru Natl Assc of Soc Workers; Natl Assc of Housing & Redev Officials; mem Zonta Intl; N Urban League Guild; NAACP; mem Women Unitedfor NY Steering Comm; found mem ex bd Coalition of 100 Black Women; Black Women's Communications Hookup; mem Con Black Caucus Dinner Plnng Comm 1976. **HONORS/ACHIEVEMENTS:** Woman of Y Phi Beta Sigma Sor 1961; Founders Day speaker AM&N Clge 1962; nom Incentive Awa New York City Housing Auth 1962; hnrd by Women's Advertising Counc of NY 1964; Re Com of Pres Com on Consumer Afrs 1964; Comm Leaders of Amer Award 1972, publ Comm Ldrs of Amer 1972; Night Owl Mayor City of NY1974. **BUSINESS ADDRES** 40 N Pearl St, Albany, NY 12243.

LEWIS, MARTIN RICHARD, JR.
Corporate secretary. **PERSONAL:** Born Aug 12, 1938, Anniston, AL; married Bess Gilkey; children: Marni, Nicole. **EDUCATION:** KS St Coll, BS 1960;Univ of (Mn, J 1966. **CAREER:** United Tech Corp, corp sec; IOS Leas Corp, vice pres & gen coun 1971-7 Inves Diver Serv Inc, asst coun 1968-71; Lgl Asst of Ramsey City, asst lgldir 1966-68. **OR-GANIZATIONS:** MN St Bar; OH St Bar; Am Bar Assn 1968-; dir Gr Hartford C of C; d Guthrie Theatre 1971-74; Hartford Stage Co; dir Gr Hartford Arts Coun; dir The Amista House; corp Hartford Hosp. **MILITARY SERVICE:** AUS 1st lt 1960-62. **BUSINES ADDRESS:** 1 Financial Plaza, Hartford, CT 06101.

LEWIS, MATTHEW, JR.
Editor. **PERSONAL:** Born Mar 08, 1930, McDonald, PA; married Jeannine Wells; ch dren: Charlene, Matthew, Kevin. **CAREER:** The Wash Post Newspaper, asst mgr, edito & photogrphr; Morgan State Coll, inst 1957-65. **ORGANIZATIONS:** White House Ne Photograph Assn; Nat Press Photograph Assn. **HONORS/ACHIEVEMENTS:** Pulitz Prize for Feature Photograph 1975; 1st prize Nat Newspaper Publs Assn 1964; White Hou News Photograph Assn 1968 & 71; Wash-Baltim Newspaper Guild 1971-72; Bill Pry Award Wash-baltim Newspaper Guild 1971-72. **MILITARY SERVICE:** USN 1949-52 **BUSINESS ADDRESS:** The Washington Post, 1150 L St NW, Washington, DC 20071.

LEWIS, MAURICE
Journalist. **PERSONAL:** Born Aug 23, 1943, Chicago, IL; children: Stephanie, Kevin

CAREER: WBZ-TV 4, news anchrmn rprtr 1976-; WHYY, guest journ 1976-77; WNAC-TV, co-anchrmn 1975-76; WNAC-TV, anchrmn rprtr 1974-76; WBZ Radio News, rprtr 1969-74; CNL Radio, mgr 1965-67; AF Radio, rprtr commentator. **ORGANIZATIONS:** Chmn & co-fdr The Afro Am Media Assn 1975-; bd of dir Elma Lewis Sch of Fine Art 1977; bd of dir Family Serv Ctr 1976; bd dir Urban League 1976; bd trustees Graham Jr Coll 1977. **HONORS/ACHIEVEMENTS:** Outst serv to comm award Jan Matzlinger 1974; news rprtr of yr MA Afro Am Patrolman's Assn 1977; Who's Who Boston's 100 Influential Black Citizens 1976-77; outst achvmt MA Sec of State Paul Guzzi 1976; outst citizen of yr MA State Senate 1976; outst citizen Congrsnsl Record 1976; outst contbns City of Bonston 1976; outst min broadcaster MA House of Rep 1976; black achvr in bus award Grtr Boston YMCA 1976; man of yr Nat Assn of Negro Bus & Professional Women's Club Inc; black achvr of yr Boston 200's Victorian Exhib & Gilette Co; outst commun serv award area of media Boston Chptr NAACP; 10 outst yg ldrs Boston Jaycees 1975. **MILITARY SERVICE:** USNR seaman 1960-62, 65-67. **BUSINESS ADDRESS:** 1170 Soldiers Field Rd, Boston, MA 02134.

LEWIS, MEHARRY HUBBARD
Educator. **PERSONAL:** Born Aug 02, 1936, Nashville, TN; son of Felix E Lewis and Helen M Lewis; married Floretta I Williams; children: Karen Anita, Arlan David. **EDUCATION:** TN State Univ, BA 1959; TN State Univ, MS 1961; IN Univ, PhD 1971. **CAREER:** IN Univ, NDEA fellow 1966-67; Student Activities Office IN Univ, frat affairs adv 1967-69, lecturer 1970, visiting asst prof 1970-72; Macon Cty Bd Ed, coord rsch & eval 1972-73; Natl Alliance of Black School Educators, dir rsch proj 1973-74; School of Educ, prof of educ, asst dean Tuskegee Inst, dir institutional rsch & planning 1974-84; MGMT Inc, pres, dir 1984-. **ORGANIZATIONS:** Mem natl Alliance Black School Ed, Kappa Delta Pi, Phi Delta Kappa Intl, Alpha Kappa Mu Natl Honor Soc, Amer Personnel & Guid Assoc, ACES Div & Assoc for Non-White Concerns; general sec, trust Church of the Living God, Pillar & Ground of the Truth Inc; mem youth comm YMCA 1963-66; mem Beta Kappa Chi. **HONORS/ACHIEVEMENTS:** Publisher of several poems & articles; Presidents Awd Natl Alliance of Black School Educators 1974. **BUSINESS ADDRESS:** Dir, MGMT, Inc, 404 N Elm, Tuskegee, AL 36083.

LEWIS, ORA LEE (NEE MCQUILLER)
Business executive. **PERSONAL:** Born Apr 27, 1930, Port Huron, MI; married Cornelius W; children: 5 Children. **EDUCATION:** Erie Comm Coll. **CAREER:** Langston Hughes Ctr for Visual & Performing Arts, exec dir 1971-; NY State Div for Yth, super couns 1975-; Westminster Comm House, admnstrv asst 1967-71; Comm Yths Boys Town, couns 1968-; YWCA, chaperone 1956-67; United Mutual Life Ins Co, sec 1947-51; Mrs Sims, sec atty 1951-54; Friendship House, prgm asst 1947-49; Buffalo Criterion Press, rptr clmnst 1947-65; Ora-Lee's Sec Svc, owner 1955-. **ORGANIZATIONS:** Human Serv Assn 1974-; E Side Coalition 1975-; Review & Referral Bd 1972-74; Consortium of Human Serv 1975-77; Westminster Comm House 1972-74; Buffalo Sister City to Ghana 1974-77; rep City of Buffalo meet Ghanian Ambassdr 1975; vice pres Embassy Educ Culture Com Model Cities 1972-74. **HONORS/ACHIEVEMENTS:** Cert of completion Erie Comm Coll 1976; outst achvmt in the Arts CommUniv 1976; cert of award Victoria Sch of Sch Reporting 1976; comm serv award Westminster Comm House 1975; hon mem award vol serv Friendship House 1949; picture exhib Top Blacks in Buffalo for Comm Serv in Photography 1976; exhib Buffalo Savings Bank 1976; dev Langston Hughes Educ Coloring Book for Children 1975. **BUSINESS ADDRESS:** 25 High St, Buffalo, NY 14203.

LEWIS, PERCY LEE
Clergyman, educator. **PERSONAL:** Born May 11, 1937, Monterey, LA; married John Evelyn Hilleard; children: Twila. **EDUCATION:** Bay Ridge Christian Coll, Ministry D 1966, BTh 1973. **CAREER:** Bay Ridge Christian Coll, exec vice pres 1975-80, dean of students 1971-80; Austin Pl Church of God, pastor 1969-70; Maple Grove Church of God, pastor 1965-68. **ORGANIZATIONS:** Chmn Southern Assn of Churches 1970-76; Head Coach Bay Ridge Christian Coll 1978-80; mem soc concerns Church of God Anderson, IN 1973-80; mem business comm Church of God Anderson, IN 1974-79; mem School Bd Kendleton ISD 1977-80. **HONORS/ACHIEVEMENTS:** Southwest Region Coach of the year, Bay Ridge Coll Kendleton, TX 1978-79. **HOME ADDRESS:** 509 N Kossuth, Rockport, TX 78382.

LEWIS, POLLY MERIWETHER
Appointed official. **PERSONAL:** Born Aug 16, 1949, Clarksville, TN; married Joseph B Lewis; children: Barry, Justin. **EDUCATION:** Austin Peay State Univ, 1967-69; GA State Univ, BS 1973, MPA attending. **CAREER:** DeKalb Cty Comm Devel Dept, program monitor 1975-79; GA Dept of Comm Affairs, prog mgmt consult 1979-80; DeKalb Comm Relations Comm, exec dir 1981-. **ORGANIZATIONS:** Former chap basileus Alpha Kappa Alpha 1973-; chairperson, bd of dir DeKalb EOA Inc 1980-; mem Leadership Atlanta 1981-82; bd of dir YWCA of Greater Atlanta 1984-; provisional Jr League 1984-85. **HONORS/ACHIEVEMENTS:** Outstanding Young Women of Amer 1979; Personalities of the South 1979; Woman of the Week DeKalb News Sun 1984. **BUSINESS ADDRESS:** Executive Dir Commun Relat, DeKalb County Government, 556 N McDonough St #900, Decatur, GA 30030.

LEWIS, PRINIC HERBERT, SR.
Clergyman. **PERSONAL:** Born Mar 13, 1930, Camden, AL; married Alice Grady; children: Prinic H, Jr, Kenneth H. **EDUCATION:** Daniel Payne Coll & Payne Theol Sem Birmingham AL, BA, BTh, DD 1957. **CAREER:** Bethel AME Ch, minister; Social Act Com Tuscaloosa, orgn 1962; Brown Chapel AME Ch, pastor 1963-70; Dallas Co & Voter Leag, vice pres 1963-70; March from Salem to Montgomery by Dr Martin L King, host. **ORGANIZATIONS:** Mem NAACP; Black Causeus; Master Mason; trust Daniel Payne Coll; mem Bd dir B&P Supermarket; pres AME Ministerial Alliance; candidate for Bishopric in Atlanta GA 1976; mem bd dir Good Samaritan Hosp 1968; mem bd dir Commonwealth Bank 1974.

LEWIS, RAMSEY EMANUEL, JR.
Pianist, composer. **PERSONAL:** Born May 27, 1935, Chicago, IL; married Geraldine Taylor; children: Vita Denise, Ramsey Emanuel III, Marcus Kevin, Dawn, Kendall, Frayne, Robert. **EDUCATION:** Chicago Music Coll, student 1947-54; Univ of IL, 1953-54; DePaul Univ, 1954-55; priv music study. **CAREER:** Hudson-Ross Inc Chicago, mgr record dept 1954-56; Ramsey Lewis Trio, organizer/mem 1956-; 1st professional appearance 1957; Randalls' Island Jazz Fest New York City 1959;Saugatuck, MI Jazz Fest 1960; Newport Jazz Fest 1961 & 1963; jazz concerts at numerous univs; toured with Free Sounds of 1963; numerousTV appearances; rec artist Argo-Cadet reocrds; CBS Records, 1971-. **ORGANIZATIONS:** Organizer Ramsey Lewis Productions Inc Chicago 1966; Ramsey Lewis Pub Co Chicago 1966; Ramsey Lewis and Sons Chicago 1978; Ramsey Lewis Music Co 1978 Chicago. **HONORS/ACHIEVEMENTS:** Recordings incl, In Crowd, Look-a-Here, Hang On Sloopy, Hard Day's Night, Wade in the Water; compositions incl, Fantasia for Drums, Look-a-Here, Sound of Christmas, Sound of Spring; recorded with James Mack conducting the London Philharmonic 1987; received 8 RIAA Gold Records; received Grammys for "The In Crowd", "Hold It Right There", "Hang on Sloopy". **BUSINESS ADDRESS:** Ramsey Lewis and Sons, 180 No LaSalle St, Chicago, IL 606011538.

LEWIS, REGGIE
Professional football player. **PERSONAL:** Born Jan 20, 1954, New Orleans, LA; married Nisha; children: Reggie Jr, Dhati, Amisho, Vanja. **EDUCATION:** Univ of OR. **CAREER:** CFL Toronto; New Orleans Saints, defensive end 1982-. **ORGANIZATIONS:** Works in off seasons at local radio station learning broadcasting. **HONORS/ACHIEVEMENTS:** Coll, Honorable Mention All-America at Univ of OR; All-Pac Eight jr yr; lettered four times in football; profl, selected All-Pro in CFL three times 1978-80.

LEWIS, REGINALD F.
Attorney, business executive. **PERSONAL:** Born Dec 07, 1942, Baltimore, MD; married Loida Nicolas; children: Leslie Nicolas, Christina Savilla Nicolas. **EDUCATION:** VA State Coll, AB 1965; Harvard Law Sch, LLB 1968. **CAREER:** Paul, Weiss, Rifkind, Wharton & Garrison, atty 1968-70; Murphy, Thorpe & Lewis, partner 1970-73 (1st Black firm on Wall St); Lewis & Clarkson, pvt prac corporate lawyer 1973-. **ORGANIZATIONS:** Mem ABA, NBA, Nat Conf of Black Lawyers; dir North St Capital Corp; bd of trustees Antioch Univ; former mem bd dir New York City Off-Track Betting Corp; former mem bd dir Central Park Conservancy. **HONORS/ACHIEVEMENTS:** Distinguished Serv Awd Amer Assn of MESBIC 1974; Black Enterprise Achievement Awd for the Professions. **BUSINESS ADDRESS:** Chairman of the Board, TLC Group, Inc, 99 Wall St 16th Floor, New York, NY 10005.

LEWIS, RICHARD U.
Government official. **PERSONAL:** Born Oct 03, 1926, W Field, AL; married Avial; children: 3 Children. **EDUCATION:** Morehouse Coll. **CAREER:** Brighton, AL, mayor 1972-; Brighton, cnclmn 1968-72. **ORGANIZATIONS:** Mem Dem Com Jefferson Co; mem Ust Bapt Ch. **MILITARY SERVICE:** AUS WW II. **BUSINESS ADDRESS:** 3700 Main St, Brighton, AL 35020.

LEWIS, ROBERT EDWARD
Retired district superintendent. **PERSONAL:** Born Apr 27, 1903, Sturgis, KY; son of George G Lewis and Mary Ann Wynn Lewis; married Virginia F Lewis, Nov 29, 1929. **EDUCATION:** Fisk Univ, AB 1926; Chicago State Univ, Teaching Certificate 1927; Northwestern Univ, MA 1939; Harvard Univ, EdD 1960. **CAREER:** Chicago Public Elementary Schools, teacher 1927-35, teacher/counselor 1935-45, asst principal 1945-48, elementary school principal 1948-61, high school principal 1961-65, dist 13 supt 1965-68; General Learning Corp, Womens Job Corps Center, consultant, 1968-69; Encyclopaedia Britannica, associate, 1968-78. **ORGANIZATIONS:** First black male administrator in Chicago Public Schools 1948; educ consultant Job Corps Ctr Clinton IA; supervisor M degree candidates Harvard Univ; consultant for develop of Middle Schools Chicago Bd of Educ; principal of adult evening schools (Carver, Dunbar & Phillips HS Chicago); vice pres Property Owners Assoc Madison Park Chicago; mem Kappa Alpha Psi Frat, Sigma Pi Phi, Phi Delta Kappa; life mem Natl Educ Assoc; mem AASA, Chicago 40 Club, Druids, Nomads Golf Club, Good Shepherd Church, NAACP, Urban League, Fisk Club, Tee Birds, Scufflers; lecturer, DePaul Univ Grad School of Educ, 1969-72. **HONORS/ACHIEVEMENTS:** Alumni Commencement Week Speaker Fisk Univ; Jubilee Day Speaker Fisk Univ; speaker Intl Reading Assoc Natl Conf on English Educ NDEA Inst of Western ILUniv and Tuskegee Inst. **HOME ADDRESS:** 4650-54 Ave South #308 W, St Petersburg, FL 33711.

LEWIS, ROBERT LOUIS
Pastor, city official. **PERSONAL:** Born Mar 10, 1936, Gilbert, LA; married Lendy Mae Neal; children: Gregory B, Keith A, Steven J, Christine M, Gerald W, Pamela V. **EDUCATION:** SIU, BA 1980. **CAREER:** USAF tsgt E-6 1955-75; Sears, salesman 1978-83; Pulaski Cty Spec School Dist, sub teacher 1975-; Mt Pisgah Baptist Church, asst pastor 1980-; City of Jacksonville, alderman. **ORGANIZATIONS:** Scout master Boy Scouts of Amer 1956-60; short order cook Grand Forks AFB Exchange 1967-70; eoa rep USAF 1972-74; minister Base Chapel 1973-74; childrens church minister Mt Pisgah Baptist Church 1982-. **MILITARY SERVICE:** USAF tsgt E-6 20 yrs; AFM 900-3; AF/SA W/4; AFM 900-3; AFGCM W/40LC 1973. **HOME ADDRESS:** 401 Stevenson St, Jacksonville, AR 72076.

LEWIS, RONALD C.
Chief executive officer. **PERSONAL:** Born Jun 15, 1934, Philadelphia, PA; married Leslie Annette Williams; children: Terri Anne, Anita Marie Lewis, Audrey Yvonne. **CAREER:** Philadelphia Fire Dept, fire fighter, fire lt, fire capt 1956-78, fire battalion chief 1974-78; Valiants Inc IABPFF Local, pres 1970-74; Intl Assoc of Black Prof Firefighters, reg vice pres 1974-77, affirm action officer 1978-82; City of Richmond, chief bureau of fire. **ORGANIZATIONS:** Bd of dir Offenders Aid & Restoration 1979-81, Muscular Dystrophy Assoc 1979-81, Alcohol & Drug Abuse Prevention & Treatment Serv 1984-; life mem NAACP 1960-; mem IABPFF 1970-, Intl Assoc of Fire Chiefs 1978-, Bldg Officials & Code Admin 1979-. **HONORS/ACHIEVEMENTS:** S Singleton Awd of Excellence Valiants IABPFF Philadelphia 1977; Outstanding Serv Awd NE Reg IABPFF 1978; Outstanding Achievement Awd NAACP Richmond Chap 1978; Outstanding Firefighter Pheonix Soc Hartford CT 1979. **BUSINESS ADDRESS:** Chief Bureau of Fire, City of Richmond, 501 N 9th St, Room 134, Richmond, VA 23219.

LEWIS, SAMELLA (NEE SANDERS)
Art historian, artist, editor. **PERSONAL:** Born Feb 27, 1924, New Orleans, LA; daughter of Samuel Sanders and Rachel Taylor; married Paul G Lewis, Dec 22, 1948; children: Alan, Claude. **EDUCATION:** Hampton Inst, BS 1945; OH State Univ, MA 1948, PhD 1951; Postdoctoral studies, Tung Hai Univ, NYU, Univ of Southern CA. **CAREER:** Art Hist Scripps Coll, prof; LA Co Museum of Art; Coordinator of Educ, CA State Univ; Univ State of NY; FL A&M Univ; Morgan State Univ; Hampton Inst. **ORGANIZATIONS:** Mem,

Expansion Arts Panel, NEA 1975-78; pres Contemp Crafts Inc; bd mem Museum African Amer Art; Art Educ Black Art Intl Quarterly Natl Conf of Artists; Coll Art Assn of Amer; Pres, Oxum Intl, 1988-; Dir/founder, Museum of African Amer Art, 1976-80. **HONORS/ACHIEVEMENTS:** Published, Art African Amer" 1978; "black artst on art" volumes I & II, 1969-71; Permanent collections, Baltimore Museum Art, VA museum fine arts, palm springs museum, high Mus Atlanta; Delta Sigma Theta Scholarship, Dillard Univ; Art Scholarship Hampton Inst; Amer Univ Fellowship OH State; Fulbright Fellowship Chinese Studies; NDEA Fellowship; NY Ford Found Grant; Honorary Doctorate, Chapman Coll, 1976; Fellowships, Fulbright Found, Ford Found; Published, "Art: African Amer", 1978. **BUSINESS ADDRESS:** The Intl Review of African American Art, 3000 Biscayne Blvd, Suite 505, Miami, FL 33137.

LEWIS, SAMUEL, JR.
Transportation services analyst. **PERSONAL:** Born Jul 19, 1953, Philadelphia, PA; son of Samuel Lewis Sr and Georgianna Johnson. **EDUCATION:** Penn State Univ, BA 1976; Community Coll of Phila, AS Mgmt 1986. **CAREER:** WPHL-TV Phila, broadcast dir 1976-77; Consolidated Rail Corp, operations mgr 1977-83; New Jersey Transit Rail Operations, revenue analyst 1983-85 sr operations planner 1985-. **ORGANIZATIONS:** Mem Conf of Minority Transportation Officials, Amer Public Transit Assn Minority Affairs Comm, Omega Psi Phi Frat, F&AM, The Brain Trust, Penn State Alumni Assn, Concerned Black Men of Philadelphia, Natl Assn of Watch and Clock Collectors, Direct Mail Marketers Assn, Black Music Assn; panelist One Minute Manager Seminar, Financial Strategies for the Eighties; mem HBCU Transportation Consortium; transportation research bd Natl Acad of Sciences; mem Columbia Univ MBA Conf; Wharton Schoo Black MBA Conf. **HONORS/ACHIEVEMENTS:** Outstanding Young Men of Amer 1984, 1986, 1987. **HOME ADDRESS:** 1643 Cobbs Creek Pkwy, Philadelphia, PA 19143. **BUSINESS ADDRESS:** Sr Operations Planner, New Jersey Transit Rail Opers, 1160 Raymond Blvd, Newark, NJ 07102.

LEWIS, SHERMAN
Coach. **PERSONAL:** Born Jun 29, 1942, Louisville, KY; married Toni; children: Kip, Eric. **EDUCATION:** Michigan State Univ, M Educ Admin 1974. **CAREER:** MSU, assistant head coach/defensive coord 1969-82; San Francisco 49ers', running back coach. **HONORS/ACHIEVEMENTS:** Football News College Player of the Year 1963.

LEWIS, STEPHEN CHRISTOPHER
Business executive. **PERSONAL:** Born Aug 19, 1950, Chicago, IL; married Stefanie Woolridge. **EDUCATION:** Bradley Univ, BSIE 1972; Marquette Univ, MBA 1975. **CAREER:** Jos Schlitz Brewing Co, superintendent for production scheduling 1974-78; Ford Motor Co, escort/lynx plng analyst 1978-82, taurus/sable plng analyst 1982-83, small car import mgr 1983-86. **ORGANIZATIONS:** Omega Psi Phi, baselius 1971-72; NAACP, mem 1978-; Nat'l Technical Assoc, mem 1983-85; Nat'l Black MBA, detroit chapter pres 1984, nat'l scholarship chairperson 1984-, nat'l vice president 1985-; Assoc of MBA Executives. **HONORS/ACHIEVEMENTS:** Omega Psi Phi, omega man of the year 1971; YMCA of Greater New York, black achievers in industry 1976; Nat'l Black MBA-Detroit Chapter, president's award 1984; Nat'l Black MBA, outstanding MBA of the year. **HOME ADDRESS:** 5944 Naneva Ct, West Bloomfield, MI 48322.

LEWIS, SYLVIA AUSTIN
Retired educational administrator. **PERSONAL:** Born Apr 08, 1921, Meredian, OK; daughter of Joseph H Austin and Viola A Lewis Austin; married Davis C Lewis Sr; children: David C Jr, Sanestelle. **EDUCATION:** Langston Univ, BA 1942; Univ of Omaha, Grad Study 1974; Univ of OK, MEd 1959. **CAREER:** Ponca City, teacher 1942-51; Oklahoma City Schools, spec ed teacher 1954-67; OK City Schools, principal, curriculum spec 1954-67; Oppty Indust Ctrs, training adv 1967-74; Langston Univ, dean for student devel 1974-82; 1982-85 Dir Langston Univ Okla City Urban Ctr. **ORGANIZATIONS:** Vchmn State Conf Intl Womens Year Conf 1977; del-at-large Intl Womens Year Conf Houston 1977; mem ACLU State Bd OK Humanities Com 1979; consult Manpower Trng; mem NAACP, Urban League, United Nations Conf of Women 1979; 1986 Brd of Regents, Univ of Oklahoma. **HONORS/ACHIEVEMENTS:** Citation of Congratulations OK State Senate for Comm Serv 1971; Meritorious Awd YWCA 1979;1986 Distinguished Zeta Awd; Natl office Zeta Phi Beta; Afro-American Hall of Fame, Oklahoma NTU Art Assn 1988.

LEWIS, THERTHENIA W.
Educator. **PERSONAL:** Born Mar 01, 1947, Dayton, OH; married Dr Jerry J Lewis. **EDUCATION:** Sinclair Comm Coll, A Liberal Arts, A Early Childhood Educ 1974; Univ of Dayton, BS 1975; Ohio State Univ, MS 1978; Atlanta Univ, MSW 1986. **CAREER:** Ohio State Univ, grad admin asst 1976-78; Wernle Residential Ctr, adolescent therapist 1978-81; Georgia State Univ, asst to the dir 1982-84; Bureau of Planning City of Atlanta Coll of Arts & Sci, HUD fellow intern 1984-85; Univ of Pittsburgh, grad student asst 1986-87. **ORGANIZATIONS:** Adv comm mem Big Sisters/Big Brothers Adv Bd 1977-78; mem Amer Soc of Public Admin 1984-; mem Natl Assoc of Black Social Workers 1987, Amer Home Economics Assoc 1987, Black Child Develop Inst 1987. **HONORS/ACHIEVEMENTS:** Outstanding Young Women of Amer 1978; HUD Fellowship Atlanta Univ 1984-86; Honor Soc Alpha Kappa Delta Intl Soc 1985. **HOME ADDRESS:** 1515 Snapfinger Rd, Decatur, GA 30032.

LEWIS, THOMAS P.
Business executive, educator. **PERSONAL:** Born Mar 17, 1936, Chicago, IL; married Almera P; children: Tracy, Todd. **EDUCATION:** Kentucky State Coll, BS Business Admin 1959. **CAREER:** South Side Bank Chicago, pres & chief exec officer 1973-; Independence Bank of Chicago, sr vice pres 1972, vice pres 1970-72; Professional Opportunity Inc, pres 1969-70; Mgmt Opportunity Inc Northfield, pres 1968-69; Commonwealth Edison Co, market rsch & sales rep 1963-65; Chicago Housing Authority, 1961-63; Horner School Chicago, teacher 1959-61. **ORGANIZATIONS:** Chmn Commrcl Div Operation PUSH; mem Bd dir YMCA Hotel; Chicago Urban League; bSA; Chicago Forum; Chicago Assn of Commerce & industry. **BUSINESS ADDRESS:** South Side Bank, 4659 S Cottage Grove Ave, Chicago, IL 60653.

LEWIS, TIM JAY
Retired football player. **PERSONAL:** Born Dec 18, 1961. **EDUCATION:** Univ of Pittsburgh. **CAREER:** Green Bay Packers, cornerback 1983-86. **HONORS/ACHIEVEMENTS:** Coll, named to NEA second All-Amer as senior; chosen to play in Senior and Hula Bowls; Packer's no 1 draft choice in 1983; knocked 13 passes and made 52 unassisted tackles; 218 yard average for 12 career interception returns to date. **BUSINESS ADDRESS:** Retired Football Player, Green Bay Packers, 1265 Lombardi Ave, Green Bay, WI 54303.

LEWIS, VIOLA GAMBRILL
Educator. **PERSONAL:** Born Feb 05, 1939, Baltimore, MD; divorced; children: Robin, Van Allen. **EDUCATION:** Morgan State Coll, BS 1959; Loyola Coll, MA 1978. **CAREER:** Psychohormonal Unit Johns Hopkins School of Medicine, rsch asst 1960-62, asst med psychol 1962-74; instructor 1974-. **BUSINESS ADDRESS:** Asst Prof Med Psych, Johns Hopkins Medical Inst, Baltimore, MD 21205.

LEWIS, VIRGINIA HILL
Senior chemist. **PERSONAL:** Born Feb 13, 1948, Berria Co, GA; married Robert Lewis; children: Michael, Roslyn. **EDUCATION:** Albany State Coll GA, BS Chemistry 1970; UOP Stockton CA, MS 1972. **CAREER:** Grad Sch Univ of Pacific, lab asst 1972; Albany State Coll, advanced chemist; 3M Co, sr chemist & quality assurance 1973-. **ORGANIZATIONS:** Summer training prog Argonne Natl Lab Argonne IL 1969; Sunday Sch Tchr Mt Olivet Bapt Ch St Paul MN 1973 & 1975-76; active in social affairs 3M & community. **HONORS/ACHIEVEMENTS:** Who's Who in Black Colls Albany State Coll 1967-68; mem Alpha Kappa Mu Honor Soc Albany State Coll GA 1967-70; Affiliate ACS 1968-70; "This is Your Life" Awd & mem Delta Sigma Theat Sor 1969. **BUSINESS ADDRESS:** Sr Chemist in Quality Assuran, 3M Center, 236-EC, Commercial Chemical Div, St Paul, MN 55144.

LEWIS, VIVIAN M.
Physician. **PERSONAL:** Born in Pensacola, FL; married Billie Lewis MD; children: Vivian V Sanford MD, William P, Beverly Gooden. **EDUCATION:** Fisk Univ, BA 1952; Univ of OK Sch of Medicine, MD 1959; Hurley Hosp, rotating intern 1959-60, pediatric residency 1961-63. **CAREER:** Mott Childrens Health Ctr, pediatric staff 1963-69; Dept of Maternal & Infant Health Mott Childrens Health Ctr, chairperson 1967-69; Hurley Med Ctr & St Joseph Hosp, mem teaching staff; McLaren Hosp, courtesy staff; MI State Univ Dept of Human Medicine, asst prof clinical pediatrics; Univ of MI Medical Sch, preceptor for the interflex prog; Lewis Medical Svcs, pediatric practice 1970-. **ORGANIZATIONS:** Life mem Alpha Kappa Alpha Sor Inc; mem bd of dirs Girl Scouts of Amer; mem bd of dirs Flint Inst of Arts; mem Flint Women Business Owners' Council; mem MI State Med Soc; mem Amer Med Assn; mem Natl Med Assn; mem Amer Acad of Pediatrics; mem Genesee Valley March of Dimes Med Adv Comm; med advisor Flint Easter Seal Soc; bd mem Genesee Valley Chap Amer Lung Assn 1969-78; chairperson Genesee Co March of Dimes Campaign 1971; mem Flint Acad of Medicine; co-chair of the 1975 Flint United Negro College Fund Dr; adv comm Univ of MI-Flint; pres Flint Chap Links Inc 1983-; citizens adv comm Univ of MI-Flint. **HONORS/ACHIEVEMENTS:** Comm Serv Awd Flint Chap Negro Bus & Prof Women's Club 1973; Liberty Bell Awd Genesee Co Bar Assn 1975; listed in 1975-76 Who's Who in Govt; Pan Hellenic Woman of the Yr 1978; Woman of the Yr Zeta Beta Omega Chap Alpha Kappa Alpha Sor Inc 1978.

LEWIS, W. ARTHUR
Clergy/administrator. **PERSONAL:** Born Dec 13, 1930, Princeton, NJ; son of George P Lewis Sr and Blanche Taylor Chase; married Rose Marie Dais, Jun 20, 1970; children: Adrienne Richardson, Andrea Lewis. **EDUCATION:** Trenton Jr Coll, AA 1957; Rider Coll, BS 1959, MA 1977; Harvard Univ JF Kennedy School, Cert 1982; Lutheran Theol Sem MA Religion 1985. **CAREER:** United Progress Inc, personnel dir 1966-68; OIL Intl, prog advisor 1968-69; Economic & Manpower Corp, project mgr 1969-71; NJ Dept of Comm Affairs, div dir & asst commiss 1972-82; Philadelphia OIC, exec dir 1982-85; Lutheran Children & Family Svcs, clergy/administrator 1985-; Evangelical Lutheran Church in America 1988. **ORGANIZATIONS:** Consult Natl Urban Coalition 1974; chmn Natl State Econ Oppty Office Dir Assoc 1976-77; bd of trustee Glassboro State Coll 1979-; vice pres NJ Chap of ASPA1980-82; bd mem Evesham Twp School Dist 1981-; mem Alpha Phi Alpha 1983-; consult NJ Synod Lutheran Church in Amer 1985. **HONORS/ACHIEVEMENTS:** Man of the Year Somerset Cty Comm Action 1976; Man of the Year Burlington Cty NAACP 1977; Philadelphia Liberty Bell City of Philadelphia 1984. **MILITARY SERVICE:** USAF airman 2nd class 1951-54; Natl Defense Good Conduct European Defense Korean Conflict 1951-54. **HOME ADDRESS:** 41 Country Club Lane, Marlton, NJ 08053.

LEWIS, WALTER (FURRY)
Musician. **PERSONAL:** Born Mar 06, 1893, Greenwood, MS. **CAREER:** Memphis, city worker 1966; Vocalian Records, singer musican 1927, 29; Victor Records, 1928; Folkways, 1959; Prestige, 1959; numerous others; now recs on Fantasy Records. **ORGANIZATIONS:** Mem Cast film The Blues; mem Memphis Blues Carsoan. **HONORS/ACHIEVEMENTS:** Named KY Col.

LEWIS, WALTON A.
Insurance executive. **PERSONAL:** Born Nov 28, 1910, Clearwater, FL; married Dorothy Baker; children: Robert P, David B. **EDUCATION:** Univ of No IA, BS 1973; Howard U, 1935-36. **CAREER:** Victory Loan & Invest Co, pres; Lewis & Thompson Agy; Ford Motor Co. **ORGANIZATIONS:** Orgnzr & mem of Interim Bd Dir First Indpndnc Nat Bank 1st black bank in Detroit; bd mem & past pres Ind Ins Agts of Greater Detroit; bd dir Nat Bank of Detroit; Greater Detroit C of C; mem Econ Club of Detroit; Detroit Press Club; Engineering Soc of Detroit; bd dir United Hosp of Detroit; vice pres exec com United Found; Detroit Hist Commn; Detroit Symp Orch; life mem NAACP; corp mem Detroit Sci Ctr; vchmn Randolph W Wallace Jr Kidney Rsrch Found; mem past pres Booker T Wash Bus Assn; trustee & chmn Fin Com Bethel AME Ch; exec bd OaklandUniv Found Proclamation City of Detroit 1975; Resol City of Detroit Common Coun 1975. **BUSINESS ADDRESS:** 2617 W Grand Blvd, Detroit, MI.

LEWIS, WENDELL J.
Government administrator. **PERSONAL:** Born Mar 22, 1949, Topeka, KS; son of Bryon Lewis and Bonnie Lewis. **EDUCATION:** KS State Teachers Coll, BS Ed 1972, MS 1973. **CAREER:** Disability Determination Servcs, disability examiner I 1974-80, disability examiner II 1980-85, quality assurance speciality 1985-88; unit manager 1989-. **ORGANIZATIONS:** Exec sec Great Plan Wheelchair Athletic Conf 1974-76; advisory bd Vocational Rehabilitation 1978-79, Shawnee County Affirmative Action Program 1979-80, KS Council on Devel

Disabilities 1982-. **HONORS/ACHIEVEMENTS:** Inductee Natl Student Reg 1970-72; 2nd Place 100 yard dash Rocky Mountain Wheelchair Games 1975; 1st Place table tennis Rocky Mountain Wheelchair Games 1975;Delegate White House Conf Handicapped 1977; Leadership Award KS Advocacy & Protective Serv 1980. **HOME ADDRESS:** 1811 W 7th, Topeka, KS 66606. **BUSINESS ADDRESS:** Unit Manager, Disability Determination Serv, 2036 SE 30th St, Topeka, KS 66605.

LEWIS, WILLIAM A., JR.
Attorney. **PERSONAL:** Born Aug 15, 1946, Philadelphia, PA; son of William and Constance; married Deborah Cover; children: Ryan. **EDUCATION:** Amer Univ, 1967-68; Susquehanna Univ, BA 1968; Boston Univ Law School, JD 1972. **CAREER:** City of Philadelphia PA, asst dist attorney 1972-75; US Civil Rights Commission, attorney 1975-80, dir cong lia div 1980-84, dir congressional & community relations div 1984-86, acting asst staff dir for congressional & public affairs 1987, counsel senate judiciary committee 1987-. **ORGANIZATIONS:** Pres, Blacks in Govt US Civil Rights Comm 1977-80; exec comm Susquekanna Univ Alumni Assoc 1980-83, 2nd vice pres 1987; mem PA Bar Assoc 1972-, Eastern Dist Court PA 1974-; del Legal Rights & Justice Task Force White House Conf on Youth Estes Park Co 1970; pres Susquehanna Univ Alumni Assoc 1988-91. **HONORS/ACHIEVEMENTS:** Legal Defense Fund Scholarship NAACP 1971-72; publ "Black Lawyer in Private Practice" Harvard Law School Bulletin 1971. **MILITARY SERVICE:** AUSR sgt e-5 1968-75. **BUSINESS ADDRESS:** Counsel, Senate Judiciary Committee, 224 Dirksen Senate Bldg, Washington, DC 20510.

LEWIS, WILLIAM ARTHUR
Educator. **PERSONAL:** Born Jan 23, 1915, St Lucia; married Gladys Isabel Jacobs; children: Elizabeth Anne, Barbara Jean. **EDUCATION:** St Marys Coll St Lucia, attended 1924-29; London Sch of B Econ, BCom 1937; London Sch of Econ, PhD 1940. **CAREER:** London School of Economics, lecturer 1938-48; Univ of Machester, prof of polit econ 1948-59; Univ of West Indies, vice-chancellor 1959-63; Princeton Univ, prof of polit econ. **ORGANIZATIONS:** Deputy managing dir United Nations Special Fund 1959-60; pres Caribbean Devel Bank 1970-73. **HONORS/ACHIEVEMENTS:** Shared Nobel Prize in Econ Nobel Found 1979; 27 Hon Degrees; 11 books. **BUSINESS ADDRESS:** Professor Political Economy, PrincetonUniv, Woodrow Wilson School, Princeton, NJ 08540.

LEWIS, WILLIAM SYLVESTER
Editor. **PERSONAL:** Born Aug 31, 1952, Manhattan, NY. **EDUCATION:** Columbia Univ Coll, BA Sociology 1974; Columbia Graduate School of Journalism, MS Journalism 1975-76. **CAREER:** Black Sports Magazine, contributing editor 1977-78; Encore Magazine, sports ed 1979-80; Good Living Magazine, sr editor 1979-80; Black Agenda Reports, producer, writer 1979-81; Touro Coll SGS, adjunct prof English. **ORGANIZATIONS:** Consulting Comm School Bd 9, 1978-; consulting coordinator, Bronx Area Policy Bd, 4 1982-87; sec, Legacy Intl Inc 1982-; chairperson Morrisania Ed Council Jrnl Comm 1978-; mem bd of dir, Columbia Coll Class of 1974, 1979-; founding mem, Columbia Univ Club of NY 1980-; mem Amer Athletic Union Distance Running Div 1978-; co-chairperson Morrisania Educ Council Journal Comm 1978-. **HONORS/ACHIEVEMENTS:** Pulitzer Scholarship, Columbia Univ 1970; Bennett Certificate Award Writing Columbia Univ 1974; CBS Fellowship Columbia Univ Graduate School of Journalism 1976; Presidential Citation for Excellence Dist 9 Comm School Bd 1983, 1984; Loyal & Outstanding Serv Award Morrisania Educ Council, Bronx NY 1978. **HOME ADDRESS:** 348 West 123rd St, New York, NY 10027. **BUSINESS ADDRESS:** Adjunct Professor of English, Touro College SGS, 1178 Washington Avenue, New York, NY 10456.

LEWIS, WILLIE MAE
Educator & psychologist. **PERSONAL:** Born Nov 04, 1943, Lee Co, TX; married Harlem Harold Lewis; children: Herease, Harlem Jr. **EDUCATION:** TX Southern Univ, BS Psychology/Biology 1967, MA Counseling 1972; Temple Univ, PhD Counseling Psychology 1978. **CAREER:** Kennecott Chem Co, analyst 1967-72; Delaware State Coll, counselor/instructor 1972-76; Prairie View A&M Univ, counselor/educator 1976-80; Center for Counseling, therapist 1978-80. **ORGANIZATIONS:** Chair public relations Southwest Charity Organ 1972; chair ethics comm Lower Shore Personnel & Guidance Assn 1983; treas MD Assn for Counseling & Develop1984; trainer Elderhostel Progs 1984, 1985; mem planning bd Upward Bound Prog 1984, 1985; pres elect MD Assn for Multicultural Counseling 1985. **HONORS/ACHIEVEMENTS:** Leadership Awd MD Assn for Non-White Concerns 1981; Presidential Citation MD Personnel & Guidance Assn 1983; article Advising Minority Students-Natl Assn of Academic Advising Journal 1984; article Behavioral Parent Training 1984. **BUSINESS ADDRESS:** Coord Guidance & Counseling, Univ of Maryland Eastern Shore, PO Box 1086, Princess Anne, MD 21856.

LEWIS, WOODROW
Government official. **PERSONAL:** Born in Brooklyn, NY; married Ruth; children: 2 Sons. **EDUCATION:** Brooklyn Coll, BA; Brooklyn Law Sch, LLD. **CAREER:** Bklyn, state assmblymn 1972-; City NY Dept Transp, admin atty; Pvt Prac. **ORGANIZATIONS:** Chmn Election Law Com; mem Brown Meml Bapt; Bedford Sty Lawyers Assn. **BUSINESS ADDRESS:** 1293 Dean St, Brooklyn, NY 11216.

LEWTER, ANDY C., SR.
Clergyman. **PERSONAL:** Born Oct 06, 1929, Sebring, FL; son of Rufus Cleveland and Maryh Lee; married Ruth Fuller; children: Rita Olivia Davis, Cleo Yvette, Veda Ann Pennyman, Andy C Jr, Rosalyn Aaron, Tonya Marie. **EDUCATION:** Morris Brown Coll, BA 1954; Atlanta U, Addl Stud; Biblical Seminary NY; James Teamer's School of Religion, BD 1964; NY Theol Seminary, MDiv 1985. **CAREER:** St John Bapt Ch Ft Myers, asst minister 1951-52; Morris Brown Coll, asst to coll pastor 1953-54; Zion Grove Baptist Church Atlanta, asst minister 1953-54; Stitt Jr HS, teacher 1954-60; First Bapt Ch Rockaway, asst minister 1954-59; AC Lewter Interdenom Sch of Religion, founder pres 1975; Pilgrim State Psychiatric Hosp, chaplain; Suffolk Co Office for the Aging, adv bd; Hollywood Bapt Church of Christ Amityville, pastor 1959-. **ORGANIZATIONS:** Mem past vice pres NAACP; past chmn mem Interfaith Hlth Assn; mem Bd Gov Interfaith Hosp of Queens; pres Interdenominational Ministerial Fellowship of Amityville; trustee of Long Island Health & Hosp Planning Council; vice pres Lewter-Scott Travel Assn; supr Ushers Nat Bapt Conv USA; adv bd Suffolk Co Office for the Aging; mem Amityville Taxpayers Assoc. **HONORS/ACHIEVEMENTS:** Hon DD Friendship Coll 1962; Hon LLD T School of Religion 1975. **BUSINESS ADDRESS:** Pastor, Hollywood Baptist Church of Christ, 3504 Great Neck Road, Amityville, NY 11701.

LIETEAU, HALVAN JOSEPH
Business executive. **PERSONAL:** Born Oct 26, 1931, New Orleans; married Theyon Doucette; children: Hallene, Lawrence. **EDUCATION:** Xavier Univ, BS 1953; Brooklyn Boro, BSA 1972. **CAREER:** IBM Brooklyn Plant, gen mgr sys products div; Corp Accounting Colt Ind Inc, NYC, asst mgr 1960-67; Roto-Broil Corp of Am Long Island, credit mgr 1955-60; Brooklyn C of C, vice pres 1971-. **ORGANIZATIONS:** Bd of gov XavierUniv of LA 1972-; trustee Poly Prep Co Day Sch 1973-; exec bd Brooklyn Boro 1972-. **BUSINESS ADDRESS:** 390 Nostrand Ave, Brooklyn, NY 11216.

LIGHTFOOT, CLAUDE M.
Retired author. **PERSONAL:** Born Jan 19, 1910, Lake Village, AR; married Joyce; children: Earl. **EDUCATION:** Rostock U, PhD. **CAREER:** Black Liberation Commn Communist Party USA, chmn 1959-73; GP USA, vice chmn 1959. **ORGANIZATIONS:** Chicago League of Struggle for Negro Rights 1931; business agent Young Mem's Democratic Club 1930; Consolidated Trades Council 1933. **HONORS/ACHIEVEMENTS:** Outstanding Scholarship Achievement, Dr WEB Dubois Comm Ctr 1973; plaque Bulgarian Govt 1973; author Ghetto Rebellion to Black Liberation 1968; author Racism & Human Survival 1972; author Human Rights US Style 1977; recognition of 40 yrs of contrib in struggle for black rep in govt Salute to Black History Award Chicago 1979; Hon PhD Rostock Univ; author Chicago Slums to World Politics.

LIGHTFOOT, JEAN DREW
Government official, association executive. **PERSONAL:** Born in Hartford, CT; divorced. **EDUCATION:** Howard Univ, BA 1947; Univ of MI, MPA 1950. **CAREER:** Coca Cola WA, publ relations 1954-55, asst dir 1959-61; Comm Rel Conf So CA LA, dir 1961-62; Dept of State, fgn serv reserve ofcr 1962-69; Consumer Protection & Environ Health Serv HEW, chief consumer spec sect 1969-70, asst dir publ affairs 1970-71; EPA intl affairs ofcr 1971, spec asst Training &Upward Mobility, dep dir eeo 1978-. **ORGANIZATIONS:** Women's aux bd Northwest Settlement House; former bd mem West Coast Reg Natl Negro Coll Fund, NAACP, Urban Laeague, Fred Douglass Mus African Art, Legal Def Fund, Intl Club Wash Inc, Women's Intl Religious Fellowship, Univ of MI Club, Common Cause, Publ Citizen, Circle-Lets Inc, Neighbors Inc, Carroll Valley Cit Assoc, Crestwood Cit Assoc. **HONORS/ACHIEVEMENTS:** NAACP Comm Serv Awd 1975; Natl Council Negro Women Mary McLeod Bethune Awd 1962; Comm Relations Conf So CA Comm Serv Awd 1962; Natl Assoc IntergroupRelations Fellowship 1958; Daughters of the Amer Revolution Good Citizenship Awd 1940; Hartford Publ HS Ideal Girl Awd 1940. **BUSINESS ADDRESS:** Special Assistant, Training & Upward Mobility, 401 M St SW, Washington, DC 20460.

LIGHTFOOT, JEAN HARVEY
Educator. **PERSONAL:** Born Nov 29, 1935, Chicago, IL; divorced; children: Jaronda. **EDUCATION:** Fisk Univ, BA 1957; Univ of Chgo, MA 1969; Northwestern Univ Evanston IL, PhD 1974. **CAREER:** Chicago Public Schools, English teacher 1957-69; Kennedy King Campus Chicago City Coll, prof English 1969-; Citizens Comm on Public Educ, exec dir 1975-76; Comm on Urban Affair Spec Projects AME Church, exec dir 1978-80; The Neighborhood Inst, educ coordinator 1979-. **ORGANIZATIONS:** Counselor Hillcrest Ctr for Children NY 1958-61; asst prof ed Northeastern Univ Chicago 1974-76; consult Prescription Learning Inc 1977-; featured soloist Park Manor Cong Church 1958-, John W Work Chorale 1959-; staff dir, convener The S Shore Schools Alliance 1979-80. **HONORS/ACHIEVEMENTS:** Outstanding Young Women of Amer 1968; Ford Fellowship Univ of Chicago 1968-69; TTT Fellowship Northwestern Univ 1972-73; listed in Who's Who of Amer Women1977. **BUSINESS ADDRESS:** Education Coordinator, The Neighborhood Inst, 1950 E 71st St, Chicago, IL 60649.

LIGHTFOOT, MOSES
Educator. **PERSONAL:** Born Jun 11, 1915, Ft Valley, GA; married Cartie; children: Moses Jr, Agnes Ozell (Fletcher), Willie Benjamin, Isaac George. **EDUCATION:** Savannah State Coll, BS 1952; Tuskegee Inst, MEd 1959; Union Sem, D Humanities 1970. **CAREER:** Lee Co Elementary School, retired prin 1970-77; Lee County Training School, prin 1962-70; NC Mutual Life Insurance Co, insurance agent; Pilgrim Life Insurance Co, asst mgr; Guaranty Life Insurance Co, mgr; Macon Telegraph News, solicitor circ dept; Negro Sect, trouble shooter editor; GA Baptist Coll, teacher; Crawford County Training School, educator; Flint Rivers Farms Elementary & HS, prin 1955-62. **ORGANIZATIONS:** Mem Gov Maddox Temperance Comm; scout commdr AME Ch; Ad Hoc Comm GA Assn Edn; chmn St Audit Comm; Macon County Teach Assn; vice pres Middle GA Dem Club; mem Woodmen of the World. **HONORS/ACHIEVEMENTS:** Listed in Personalities of the South 1970; part in 1st Inst for Promotion of Non Violence in a Violent Soc ; ctr for social change Martin Luther King Jr; contrbn to the educ comm Cert of Thanks Lee Co Bd of Edn.

LIGHTFOOT, WILLIAM P.
Physician. **PERSONAL:** Born Sep 12, 1920, Pittsburgh, PA; married Edith Wingate; children: William, Philip. **EDUCATION:** Lincoln Univ, AB 1943; Howard Univ Med Coll, MD 1946. **CAREER:** John F Kennedy Memorial Hospital, Philadelphia, attending surgeon; Temple Univ Hospital & Med School Faculty, prof of surgery. **ORGANIZATIONS:** Mem, Amer Coll of Surgeons, Philadelphia Acad of Surgery, Philadelphia Coll of Physicians; mem, AMA, Natl Med Assn, Philadelphia Co Med Soc; mem, Amer Soc of Abdominal Surgeons. **HONORS/ACHIEVEMENTS:** Amer Bd of Surgey; Amer Bd of Utilization Review and Quality Assurance. **MILITARY SERVICE:** AUS cpat 1953-55. **BUSINESS ADDRESS:** Prof of Surgery, TempleUniv, 3401 N Broad St, Philadelphia, PA 19140.

LIGHTFOOTE, WILLIAM EDWARD, II
Physician, neurologist. **PERSONAL:** Born Oct 06, 1942, Tuskegee, AL; son of William Edward Lightfoote and Mary Johson Lightfoote; married Marilyn Frances Madry; children: Lynne Jan-Maria. **EDUCATION:** Grinnell Coll, AB 1963; Howard Univ, MD 1967. **CAREER:** Natl Inst of Health, rsch officer 1975-77; FDA Neurologic & Analgesic Drugs, group leader 1977-79; United States Public Health Svcs, lt commander; PrivatePractice, self-employed neurology 1979-. **ORGANIZATIONS:** Mem Alpha Phi Alpha Frat 1965-, Medical Soc of District of Columbia 1969-, Amer Acad of Neurology 1972-, Assoc for Research in Nervous and Mental Diseases 1976-, Foundation for Advanced Educ in the Sciences 1977-,

medical consultant to law firms in metro DC area 1979-, Natl Medical Assoc 1980-, Medical-Chirurgical Soc of the District of Columbia 1980-, Amer Medical Assoc 1981-, Dist of Columbia Assoc for Retarded Citizens Inc 1981-, Amer Soc of Internal Medicine 1982-; assoc mem Eastern Assoc of Electroencephalographiers Inc 1983-; mem Amer Soc of Law and Medicine 1983-, Southern medical Assoc 1983-, New York Acad of Sciences 1985-; mem bd of trustees of Office Serv corp 1985-. **HONORS/ACHIEVEMENTS:** Mem, Alpha Omega Alpha Honor Medical Soc; publ 11 bibliographies, 12 abstracts/presentations; fellow, Amer Acad of Neurology, 1988. **MILITARY SERVICE:** USAF major 4 yrs. **HOME ADDRESS:** 827 Swinks Mill Rd, McLean, VA 22108. **BUSINESS ADDRESS:** 1328 Southrn Ave SE, Washington, DC 20032.

LIGHTNER, CLARENCE E.
Mortician. **PERSONAL:** Born Aug 15, 1921, Raleigh, NC; married Marguerite Massey; children: Bruce, Lawrence, Debra, Claire. **EDUCATION:** Echols Coll, Mortuary Sci; Shaw U, LLD 1972; NC Central U, Grad 1975. **CAREER:** Lightner Funeral Home & Ins Agency, pres gen mgr; Raleigh City Council, 1967-71; Mayor Pro-Tem, 1971-73; Mayor, 1973-75. **ORGANIZATIONS:** Past pres Nat Funeral Dirs & Morticians Assn; past mem US Conf Mayors' Bicentennial Com; bd of dirs Nat League Cities; steering com Public SafetyNat League Cities; exec bd Occoneechee Council Boy Scouts Am; natl mem com NAACP; chmn NC Black Ldrsp Dem Caucus; mem N Raleigh Exchange Club; memOmega Psi Phi Frat; Shriners; Nat Business League; Masonic Elk Lodges. **HONORS/ACHIEVEMENTS:** Raleigh C of C Hon; man of yr award Mid-Atlantic Region Alpha Kappa Alpha Sor 1975. **MILITARY SERVICE:** AUS. **BUSINESS ADDRESS:** Lightner Funeral Home, 312 Smithfield St, Raleigh, NC 27601.

LIGON, CLAUDE M.
Commissioner. **PERSONAL:** Born Jun 28, 1935, Baltimore, MD; married Doris Hillian; children: Capt Claude M, Carole Ann. **EDUCATION:** Morgan State Univ, BS Math 1957; Univ of IL, BS Civil Engrg 1965; Univ of MD, MS Civil Engrg 1971, PhD Civil Engrg 1984. **CAREER:** US Army Corps of Engrs, Lt Col 1957-79; AMAF Industries Inc, mgr civil engrg and transp sys div 1979-85; MD Pub Serv Comm, commissioner 1985-. **ORGANIZATIONS:** Regist prof engr VA/MD/DC; fellow Inst of Transportation Engrs Washington, DC Sect (pres 1982); mem Amer Soc of Civil Engrs; indiv assoc Transportation Research Bd; mem NAACP, Baltimore Urban League, Kappa Alpha Psi Frat, Morgan State Univ Alumni Assn, Univ of IL Alumni Assn; Univ of MD Alumni Assoc; bd dir Howard Arts United; mem Howard Co Arts Grants Comm 1983-85; mem Columbia, MD Resident's Transportation Comm; mem Howard Co Public Transportation Bd 1976-79; mem Baltimore City Public Schools Industrial Arts Adv Comm 1983-85; co-founder (1980)/mem MD Museum of African Art; mem bd of dir Columbia Festival Inc. **HONORS/ACHIEVEMENTS:** Chi Epsilon Natl Civil Engrg Hon Frat; Publications include, Arrow Panel Placement at Urban and Freeway Work Zones slide tape presentation Fed Highway Adm 1985; Development of the Highway Safety Improvement Decision Model doctoral dissertation 1984; Pedestrian Accommodation in Highway Work Zones report 1982; "Pedestrian and Bicycle Issues and Answers" FHWA 1981. **MILITARY SERVICE:** RA Corps of Engineers Lt Col served 23 years. **HOME ADDRESS:** 9560 Highwind Ct, Columbia, MD 21045. **BUSINESS ADDRESS:** Commissioner, Maryland Public Serv Commission, 231 E Baltimore St, American Bldg, Baltimore, MD 21202.

LIGON, DORIS HILLIAN
Museum executive. **PERSONAL:** Born Apr 28, 1936, Baltimore, MD; married Dr Claude M Ligon; children: Claude M Jr, Carole Ann. **EDUCATION:** Morgan State Univ, BA Sociology (Summa Cum Laude) 1978, MA Art Hist/Museology 1979; Howard Univ, PhD courses African Hist. **CAREER:** Natl Museum of African Art Smithsonian Inst, docent (tour guide) 1976-88; Morgan State Univ, art gallery rsch asst 1978-79; Howard Cty MD School Syst, consult African art & culture 1980-; MD Museum of African Art, founder/exec dir 1980. **ORGANIZATIONS:** Mem Assn Black Women Historians, African-American Museums Assn; charter mem Eubie Blake Cultural Center 1984; charter mem Columbia (MD) Chap Pierians Inc 1983; mem Morgan State Univ Alumni; mem NAACP; mem Urban League; mem Arts Council of the African Studies Assn. **HONORS/ACHIEVEMENTS:** Goldseeker Fellowship for Graduate Studies MSU 1978-79; Phi Alpha Theta (Natl History Hon Soc); Alpha Kappa Mu; Nirmaj K Sinha Award for highest honors in Sociology 1978. **HOME ADDRESS:** 9560 Highwind Court, Columbia, MD 21045. **BUSINESS ADDRESS:** Executive Director, Founder, Maryland Museum of African Art, PO Box 1105, Columbia, MD 21044.

LILLARD, ROBERT EMMITT
Attorney. **PERSONAL:** Born Mar 23, 1907, Nashville, TN; married Ozella E; children: Gladys, Sandra, Robert. **EDUCATION:** Biggins Commercial Coll; Kent Coll of Law. **CAREER:** Pvt Pract, atty. **ORGANIZATIONS:** Fndr past pres TN Fedn of the Dem Leagues Inc; Davidson Co Dem League; past mem TN Bd of Paroles & Pardons; mem World Peace Through Law; past bd mem United Givers Fund; mem Nashville TN Am Bar Assn; past pres JC Napier Bar Assn; past pres life mem Nat Bar Assn; mem Prince Hall 32nd Degree F& AM Pride of TN Lodge Elks; AFL; past mem Nashville City Metro Cncl 1951-71. **HONORS/ACHIEVEMENTS:** C Francis Stratford Award Nashville Bar Assn 1963; outstdg citzsp award Davidson Co Dem League; outstdg serv award Pearl HS; pub Who's Who Nat Bar Assn; Distgd Citz Award Metro Gov; Distgd Serv Citz Frontier's Internat; Cert of Apprctn Middle TN Bus Assn 1976; Col on Gov Staff; Col Antlerd Guard. **BUSINESS ADDRESS:** 1031 Stahlman Bldg, Nashville, TN 37201.

LILLARD, W. LOVELL
Business executive. **PERSONAL:** Born Dec 10, 1936, Memphis, TN; divorced; children: Arnett, Charlotte, Ella, Bernidette. **EDUCATION:** Sussex Coll England, PhD 1972. **CAREER:** Police Dept, various postions 1957-67; W L Lillard Bureau of Investigation, dir 1967-; W L Lillard Stars of Tomorrow WCIU, host of TV show 1973. **ORGANIZATIONS:** Bd mem Operation PUSH; former precinct capt 24th Dem Orgn; former mem IL Policemen Assn; bd mem Midwest Comm Council; founder of Met Bus Comm Young Found. **HONORS/ACHIEVEMENTS:** Outstanding Black Businessman 1973, 1974; Businessman of Yr 1974; Best Dressed Man of Yr 19738 1974. **BUSINESS ADDRESS:** 5824 W Madison St, Chicago, IL.

LILLIE, VERNELL A. (NEE WATSON)
Educator. **PERSONAL:** Born May 11, 1931, Hempstead, TX; married Richard L Lillie Jr (deceased); children: Charisse Lillie McGill, Hisani Lillie Blanton. **EDUCATION:** Dillard Univ, BA (Cum Laude) 1952; Carnegie-Mellon Univ, MA 1970, DA 1972. **CAREER:** Julius C Hester House, group work spec 1952-56; Houston Indep School Dist Phillis Wheatley HS, chmn & teacher speech, drama & debate 1956-59; TX So Univ Project Upward Bound, english coord, dir drama workshop 1965-69; Carnegie-Mellon Univ Proj Upward Bound, dir student affairs 1969-71; Univ of Pittsburgh , assoc prof black studies. **ORGANIZATIONS:** Mem Amer Soc Group Psychotherapy & Psychodrama, Natl & PA Counc Teachers of Engl, Speech Assoc of Amer, NADSA, ATA Black Theatre Prog, Afro-Amer Educators; bd dir Julius C Hester House Houston 1965-69, Earnest T Williams Meml Ctr, Pittsburgh Ctr Alterntive Ed 1972-78; Women in Urban Crisis 1973-80; coord curriculum & staff devel mem Hope Devel Houston; dir, founder The Hester House Exper Theatre, The Black Theatre, Scenario Theatre Concept, The Kuntu Repertory Theatre; Black Theatre Network. **HONORS/ACHIEVEMENTS:** Awd for Outstanding Contrib to Arts Delta Sigma Theta 1969; Awd for Ed Achievements Carnegie-Mellon Univ Proj Upward Bound 1972; Pittsburgh Outstanding Ed Black Cath Ministeries 1973; Spec Achievements include curriculum & staff devel models for various schools & comms; Univ of Pittsburgh, Distinguish Teacher Awd 1986; Arts and Letter Awd, Alpha Kappa Alpha Sorority, 1987; Women of Color Caucus, 1985. **BUSINESS ADDRESS:** Associate Professor, Univ of Pittsburgh, Dept of Black Studies, 230 S Bouquet St, Pittsburgh, PA 15260.

LIMA, GEORGE SILVA
Government official. **PERSONAL:** Born Apr 04, 1919, Fall River, MA; married Selma Elizabeth Boone; children: Anna Maria Lima Bowling, George II, Robert. **EDUCATION:** Brown Univ, AB 1948; Harvard Business Sch, Trade Union Labor Relations Mgmt 1958. **CAREER:** Amer Federation of State County & Municipal Employees New England, regional dir 1950-64; US Govt Action Dept of Vista, Older Amer Volunteer Progs, dir 1979-84; State of Rhode Island, state rep; 1986-87. **ORGANIZATIONS:** Vice chairman East Providence Comm Develop Corp 1978-82; natl bd mem Natl Blacks in Govt 1980-84; chmn Steering Comm New England Gerontology 1984-85;bd mem RI AFL-CIO; chmn East Providence Coalition for Human Rights; mem RI State Employees Retirement Commn; mem Amer Assoc of Retired Persons; mem Intl Sr Citizens Org; chmn of steering comm of SENE Gerontology Ctr at Brown Univ; mem RI Black Caucus of State Legislators; mem Comm to Study State of RI Affirmative Action; vchmn RI Commission of Needs of Cape Verdean Community; mem House Labor Comm. **HONORS/ACHIEVEMENTS:** NAACP Membership Enrollment Awd 1961; Delta Sigma Theta Comm Serv Awd 1978; Achievement Awd 274 Business Club 1986; Omega Man of the Year Sigma Nu Chap 1987. **MILITARY SERVICE:** AUS Air Corps 1st lt 4 1/2 yrs; Tuskegee Army Air Base 477th Bom B Gp.

LINCOLN, ABBEY See MOSEKA, AMINATA

LINCOLN, C. ERIC
Educator. **PERSONAL:** Born Jul 23, 1924, Athens, AL; married Lucy Cook; children: Cecil, Joyce Godfrey, Hilary, Less II. **EDUCATION:** LeMoyne Coll, AB 1947; Fisk Univ, AM 1954; Univ of Chicago, BD 1956; Boston U, MEd, PhD 1960; Carleton Coll, LLD 1968; St Michael's Coll, LHD 1970. **CAREER:** Duke Univ, prof of religion 1976-; Fisk Univ, prof & chmn 1973-76; Union Theol Sem, prof 1967-73; Portland State Univ, prof 1965-67; Clark Coll, prof 1954-65; Dartmouth Coll, lectr 1962-63; Vassar Coll, adj prof 1969-70; State Univ of NY, visiting prof 1970-72; Queens Coll, visiting prof 1972; Vanderbilt Univ, adj prof 1973-76; Change Magazine, consultant; Rev of Religious Research Soc, assoc editor for scientific study of religion. **ORGANIZATIONS:** Amer Sociol Assn; Authors League of Amer; Black Acad of Arts & Letters; NY Acad of Arts & Scis; Soc for Study of Black Religion. **HONORS/ACHIEVEMENTS:** Fellow Amer Acad of Arts & Sciences; Lilly Ednowment Grant; author of The Black Church Since Frazier 1974, The Black Experience in Religion 1974, A Profile of Martin Luther King Jr 1969, The Black Americans 1969, Is Anybody Listening? 1968, Sounds of the Struggle 1967, The Negro Pilgrimage in America 1967, My Face is Black 1964, The Black Muslims in America 1961; co-author of A Pictorial History of the Negro in America 1968; Lillian Smith Book Award, 1989, for first novel, The Avenue, Clayton City. **MILITARY SERVICE:** USN hosp corp 1944-45. **BUSINESS ADDRESS:** Prof of Religion & Culture, Duke University, Dept of Religion, Durham, NC 27706. *

LINCOLN, LILLIAN H.
Business executive. **PERSONAL:** Born May 12, 1940, Ballsville, VA; divorced; children: Darnetha, Tasha. **EDUCATION:** Howard Univ, BA (Cum Laude) 1966; Harvard Univ, MBA 1969. **CAREER:** Sterling Inst, assoc 1969-72; Ferris & Co, stockbroker 1972-73; Bowie State Coll, instructor 1973-74; Unified Serv Inc, exec vice pres 1973-76; Centennial One, Inc, president 1976-. **ORGANIZATIONS:** Bd dirs Universal Bank; mem MD Small Business Financing Authority; bd dirs Natl Business League of So MD; bd Minority Business Legal Defense and Educ Fund; chairperson Minority Business Enterprise Comm Anne Arundel County, MD;bd dirs Building Service Contractors Assoc Intl; mem bd dirs Capitol Assoc of Building Serv Contractors; bd dirs Prince George's County Chamber of Commerce 1983-85; chairperson Referral Aide Program United Way 1984; mem Anne ArundelCo and Prince George Co Minority Business Enterprise Task forces 1985. **HONORS/ACHIEVEMENTS:** MD Small Business Person of the Yr 1981; Who's Who in the East 1981-82; US Dept of Commerce Cert of Appreciation 1981; MD Cert of Distinguished Citizenship1981; Bigger and Better Business Awd Phi Beta Sigma Frat 1982; Business and Entrepreneurship Awd Spelman Coll 1983; Leadership in the Business Arena Awd Delta Sigma Theta Sor 1983; Minority Female Contractor of the Yr Dept of Commerce 1984; Harvard Business Sch Black Alumni Entrepreneurship Awd 1986; HUB Organization Entrepreneurship Awd 1986; Minority Business Directory Awd 1986; America's Top 100 Black Business and Professional Women Awd by Dollars & Sense magazine 1986.

LINDO, J. TREVOR
Psychiatrist. **PERSONAL:** Born Feb 12, 1925, Boston, MA; married Dr Thelma Thompson. **EDUCATION:** Boston Latin Sch; Boston Coll; NY Univ, AB 1946; Columbia Univ; Univ of Freibourg Switzerland, certificate 1953; Univ of Lausanne, MD 1957; attended Univ of Paris, State Univ of NY-Kings County Hosp Ctr 1957-61; Yale Univ, Neuropathology seminars. **CAREER:** St John's Episcopal Hosp, assoc attending psychiatrist; Columbia Univ NY, clinical instructor psychiatry; Brooklyn Bureau of Comm Svcs, psychiatric consultant; Ct Valley Hosp, supr psychiatrist 1961-64; Harlem Hosp, asst visiting psychiatrist 1964-66; Bedford Stuyvestant Comm Mental Health Ctr, psychiatrist 1976-; Columbia Univ, asst clinical prof of psychiatry 1981-,assoc clinical prof of psychiatry 1983-85; Marcus Garvey Manor,

psychiatric consultant 1983; Bedford Stuyvestant Comm Mental Health Ctr, med dir 1986; Harlem Hosp Ctr, sr psychiatrist 1966-. **ORGANIZATIONS:** Mem Natl Med Assn, Provident Clinical Soc; bd of dir Lyndon B Johnson Health Ctr; mem Amer Psychiatric Assn, World Federation for Mental Health; co-chmn Com for Dr Thomas Matthew Crown Heights Civic Assn; mem Black Psychiatrist of Amer, Carribean Fed for Mental health; chmn NAACP Freedom Fund Dinner; mem Amer Assoc of French Speaking Health Profls, Amer Assoc of Comm Mental Health Ctr Psychiatrists, Adv in Psychiatry Medical Soc County of Kings, Brooklyn Psychiatric Soc; mem educ comm NAACP; mem NY Acad of Scis, Amer Assoc for Advancement of Science. **HONORS/ACHIEVEMENTS:** Fellow Amer College of Intl Physicians 1983. **MILITARY SERVICE:** US Merchant Marine 1948-51. **BUSINESS ADDRESS:** 1265 President St, Brooklyn, NY 11213.

LINDSAY, BEVERLY
Educator, business executive. **PERSONAL:** Born Dec 21, 1947, San Antonio, TX. **EDUCATION:** St Marys Univ, BA (Magna Cum Laude) 1969; Univ of MA, MA 1971, EdD 1974; Amer Univ, PhD 1986. **CAREER:** PA State Univ, asst prof 1974-79; Natl Inst Ed Amer Council on Ed, fellow 1979-81, sr rsch & mgr 1981-83; US Info Agency, dir teacher text tech 1983-86; PA State Univ, spec asst vice pres 1983-86; Univ of Georgia, assoc dean for academic affairs and professor 1986-. **ORGANIZATIONS:** Bus mgr, sec Compar Ed Soc 1976-79; faculty council, senate PA State Univ 1976-79; prog reviewer Amer Ed Rsch Assoc 1976-; bd mem Fairfax Comm Assoc 1982-84; treas Winston-Beers Comm School 1980-83; pres elect Comparative Ed Soc 1987-88; pres Compar Ed Soc 1988-89. **HONORS/ACHIEVEMENTS:** Co-author & ed of books "Comparative Perspectives of Third World Women", "Migration & Natl Development in Africa"; listed in Who's Who Among Amer Women 1982,85, World's Who's Who Among Women 1980,84, Outstanding Young Women of Amer 1980,82,84, Disting Doctoral Student Amer Univ 1984,85; published over 45 articles, chapters and reviews. **BUSINESS ADDRESS:** Assoc Dean for Academic Affairs, The University of Georgia, G-3 Aderhold Hall, Athens, GA 30602.

LINDSAY, CRAWFORD B.
Educator. **PERSONAL:** Born Oct 19, 1905, Birmingham, AL; married Rachel M Darden; children: Crawford B Jr, Henry H, Hettie (McCants). **EDUCATION:** Talladega Coll, AB (Cum Laude) 1927; Univ of MI, AM 1931; Cornell Univ, PhD 1950; TN Law School, LLB. **CAREER:** Morchonse Coll, instr English 1931-41; FL A&M Univ, prof 1943-46; TN State Univ, chmn dept, prof English 1946-73; TN State Univ, retired English prof, visiting prof 1975-. **ORGANIZATIONS:** Mem Amer & TN Barr Assoc; pres Coll Lang Assoc 1953-55; gen ed bd; admitted to TN Bar 1958. **HONORS/ACHIEVEMENTS:** Fellowships 1936-37,48-49.

LINDSAY, EDDIE H. S.
Business executive. **PERSONAL:** Born Oct 23, 1931; married Joyce McCrae; children: Paul, Lisa. **EDUCATION:** Attended, London Polytechnic Coll London, Quens Coll NY, Am Inst of Banking NY, Hofstra Univ. **CAREER:** Ins Salesman, 1968; Manufacturers Hanover Trust Co, credit officer; Broadway Bank & Trust Co, dir urban affairs, loan officer commercial minority economic devel, br mgr main ofc, asst vp. **ORGANIZATIONS:** Mem Nat Bankers Assn; New Jersey Bankers Urban Affairs Com; EDGES NY Professional Assn; dir Cath Diocese Com for Human Devel; dir Planned Parenthood of Passaic Co; finance chmn mem Boys Club of Paterson-Passaic; mem Legal Aid Soc; YMCA; United Way. **BUSINESS ADDRESS:** President, Priority Chemical Co, Inc, 285 Fourth Ave, Paterson, NJ 07514.

LINDSAY, GILBERT W.
City councilman. **PERSONAL:** Born Nov 29, 1900, Jasper Co, MS; married Theresa Willis (deceased); children: Herbert Howard, Sylvia Thornton, Melvin Lindsay. **EDUCATION:** Attended Univ of AZ Sch of Bus Admin; Civic Ctr Div of USC. **CAREER:** Co of LA, deputy supvr 1952-63; City of LA, city councilman. **ORGANIZATIONS:** Vice chmn City Council's Charter & Elections; chmn Recreation & Parks Comm; mem Ind & Transp Comm; Rules Comm Sister Cities Comm; past pres LA Coliseum Commn; mem LA Co & Cities Disaster & Civil Defense Commn; Watershed Commn; LA Civic Ctr Auth; chmn LA Parking Authority; alternate Bd of Grants; CO River Assn; alternate Adv Group CA Water Resources Assn; mem Amer Legion, Rotary, Urban League; So CA Minority Capital Corp; past exec vice pres Physically Handicapped Indus Inc; Phi Beta Sigma; dir Wilshire State Bank; mem CA Bankers Trust Co. **HONORS/ACHIEVEMENTS:** Citizen of Yr LA Co 1956; Boss of Yr Women City Employees 1965; Elk of Yr Natl Conv of Elks 1965. **MILITARY SERVICE:** US Calvary 1920-21; US Infantry 1921-23. **BUSINESS ADDRESS:** City Councilman, City of Los Angeles, Room 375 City Hall, 200 N Spring St, Los Angeles, CA 90012.

LINDSAY, HORACE AUGUSTIN
Business executive. **PERSONAL:** Born Mar 01, 1938, New York, NY; son of Horace A Lindsay, Sr and Cecelia T Mitchell; married Donna McDade; children: Gloria, Horace. **EDUCATION:** Prairie View A&M Univ, BS 1959; CA State Univ, MS 1969. **CAREER:** Boeing Co, rsch engr 1961-63; Martin Co, syst engr 1963-64; Bunker Ramo, proj engr 1964-66, program mgr 1966-68, mktg dir 1968-72, program dir 1973-75, mktg vice pres 1975-; Eaton Corp, plans & bus devel vice pres; Contel Corp, vice pres & gen mgr, 1989-. **ORGANIZATIONS:** mem, Amer Management Assn, Armed Forces Communications & Electronics Assn. **MILITARY SERVICE:** AUS 1st lt 1959-61.

LINDSAY, REGINALD C.
Attorney, government official. **PERSONAL:** Born Mar 19, 1945, Birmingham, AL; son of Richard Lindsay and Louise Lindsay; married Cheryl Elizabeth Hartgrove. **EDUCATION:** Univ of Valencia Spain, Certificate 1966; Morehouse Coll, BA (Hon) 1967; Harvard Law School, JD 1970. **CAREER:** MA Dept of Public Utilities, commn 1975-77; Hill & Barlow, atty, partner. **ORGANIZATIONS:** Mem MA Commiss on Judicial Conduct 1983-89; mem bd of trustees First Mutual of Boston; mem bd of dirs Natl Consumer Law Center, United Way of MA Bay 1981-85; mem bd of trustees Thompson Island Ed Center 1975-86; mem advisory bd Museum Natl Center of Afro-Amer Artists; mem Commercial Arbitration Panel, Amer Arbitration Assn; mem bd of dirs Disability Law Center 1989-. **BUSINESS ADDRESS:** Attorney, Hill & Barlow, One Intl Place, Boston, MA 02110.

LINDSEY, JEROME W.
Educator. **PERSONAL:** Born Apr 07, 1932, Phoenix City, AL. **EDUCATION:** Howard U, BArch 1956; MIT, MArch 1960, MCity Planning 1961. **CAREER:** Howard Univ, dean 1971-, assoc dean 1970-71, chmn 1969-70, assoc prof 1962-68; Yale Univ, visiting prof 1967-68; Washington DC, dir planning 1964-68; Providence Redevelopment Agency, sr planner 1961-62; Jose Luis Sert, planner 1959-61; Samuel Glaser, planner 1958-59; John Hans Graham, planner 1956-58; Harold M Lewis, planner1955-56. **ORGANIZATIONS:** Reg architect MA/WASH DC/VA/MD/PA/MI; mem AIB; mem Bd of Edn; consult World Bank Urban Development Proj. **HONORS/ACHIEVEMENTS:** NCARB Certificate. **BUSINESS ADDRESS:** 390 Cedar St NW, Washington, DC 20012.

LINDSEY, OUIDA
Columnist. **PERSONAL:** Born Sep 10, 1927, Chicago, IL; married Paul C; children: Paul Kevin, Kathryn Karen. **EDUCATION:** Herzl Jr Coll Chicago, 1948; Roosevelt Coll, 1952; DePaul Univ; Daniel Hale Univ Chicago, BA 1977; Governor's State Univ Chicago, MA 1979. **CAREER:** Chicago Sun-Times, columnist; WFLD-TV, host "Soul Searching"; Columbia Coll, instr race & human relations; high sch & grammar sch, tchr; Univ of Chicago MA Tchr Prog, tchr 1968-72; Bur of Quida Lindsey Inst for Career Relations, contem forum lectr 1974-. **ORGANIZATIONS:** Mem Nat Acad of TV Arts & Sci; adv council to dir of community affairs of Chicago City Coll; consult WTTWUniv of Chicago HEW Joint Proj on Human Rel SpotCommercials 1973; consult Gov State of IL Human & Race Rel 1971; mem AFTRA 1975; Chicago Women in Broadcasting; PUSH; Chicago Press Club. **HONORS/ACHIEVEMENTS:** Family Affair Award PUSH Found 1975; Nat Assn of Media Women Inc Award; Female Decision Maker Communications Award 1974; NANW Chicago Chpt; Parker House Pioneer Award 1975; Cert of Merit for Outstdng Accompl & Gen Excell 1974; Chicago Merit Employment Commn Award 1973-74; given by residents Royal Plaza Retirement Hotel Award 1972-73; Chelsea House Sr Cit Award 1973-74; Nomination for Emmy Award Chicago Chap Nat Acad of TV Arts & Sci; author of num publ on Race & Human Relations; co-authored with husband now on approved textbook list of Chicago Pub Schs Breaking the Bonds of Racism publ Apr 1974. **BUSINESS ADDRESS:** Sun Times, 400 N Wabash, Chicago, IL 60610.

LINDSEY, S. L.
City official, clergyman. **PERSONAL:** Born Aug 23, 1909, Swiftwater, MS; widowed. **EDUCATION:** MS Baptist Seminary Jackson MS, B Theol. **CAREER:** Ordained Minister 37 yrs; Town of Metcalfe, mayor. **ORGANIZATIONS:** Pres Metcalfe Devel Assoc 1975-; mem South Delta Planning 1977-; bd mem Washington Cty Oppty 1978-; mem Black Mayors Conf 1978-; pres Metcalfe Indust Dev Found 1981-; pastor at 4 churches. **HONORS/ACHIEVEMENTS:** Outstanding Achievements Delta Council on Aging 60 1980. **BUSINESS ADDRESS:** Mayor, Town of Metcalfe, PO Box 250, Metcalfe, MS 38760.

LINDSEY, TERRY LAMAR
Attorney. **PERSONAL:** Born Jul 16, 1950, Gainesville, GA; children: Kevin. **EDUCATION:** Clark Coll, BA 1972; SoUniv Sch of Law, JD 1975. **CAREER:** Atty Gen State of LA, staff atty 1976-77, legal rsrch asst 1973-75; Gov Office of Consumer Protection, consumer protection mediator 1972-73; Shreveport LA, asst dist atty 1977-86; Miami FL, asst US atty 1986-. **ORGANIZATIONS:** Mem LA State Bar Assn 1976; Am Bar Assn; Nat Bar Assn; LA Dist Atty Assn; mem Fed Bar Assoc, So Dist of FL. **HONORS/ACHIEVEMENTS:** Alpha Kappa Delta Hon Soc. **BUSINESS ADDRESS:** Asst US Attorney, US Attorney So Dist of FL, 155 S Miami Ave, Miami, FL 33130.

LINNETTE, VALLETA H.
Educator. **PERSONAL:** Born Sep 25, 1924, Cincinnati; widowed. **EDUCATION:** Tchrs Coll Columbia U, BS MA 1944;Univ London, Grad Study 1950; SD State U, 1958, 1961-. **CAREER:** VA State Coll, dean of women 1945-57; SD HS, tchr 1957-64; San Diego City Coll, coord tchr 1970-71, dean 1972-74; San Diego Miramar & Coll, dean instrnl svc. **ORGANIZATIONS:** Mem bd dirs Pacific Coast Bank; San Diego Co Cit Scholarship Found; reg bd NCCJ; past pres San Diego Br AAUW; mem City Adv Bd Status Women; Acad Consortium & Dist Bicentennial Com; Delta Kappa Gamma; Nat Council Adminstr Women in Edn; mem Women Inc; pres San Diego Chap Links Inc ; bd mem Proj YES; life mem Nat Council Negro Women; mem Urban League; NAACP; pres San Diego Co Cit Sch Found 1971-73; San Diego Ch AKA Sor 1969-71. **HONORS/ACHIEVEMENTS:** Woman of Achievement 1973; award Pres Council 1974; Sojourner Truth Natl Meritorious Serv Award NANBPW 1972; Woman of Valor in Educ Sisterhood Temple Beth Israel 1970; ISA Appreciation Cert 1970. **BUSINESS ADDRESS:** 10440 Black Mountain, San Diego, CA 92126.

LINSEY, NATHANIEL L.
Clergyman. **PERSONAL:** Born Jul 24, Atlanta, GA; married Mae C Mills; children: Nathaniel Jr, Ricarldo Mills, Julius Wayne, Angela Elise. **EDUCATION:** Paine Coll, BS 1949; Howard Univ Sch of Religion, BD 1951; Scarritt Coll, Masters degree with distinction 1974; Miles Coll, hon doctorate; Texas Coll, hon doctorate. **CAREER:** CME Church, natl youth dir 1951-52; Rock of Ages CME Church Walterboro, SC, natl youth dir 1952-53; Columbia Dist Columbia, SC, presiding elder 1953-55; Vanderhorst CMECh, pastor 1955-56; Mattie E Coleman CME, pastor 1956-62; Thirgood CME Church, pastor 1962-66; CME Ch, gen sec of evangelism 1966-74; CME Church, elected the 39th Bishop May 1978; Christian Meth Episcopal Ch, presiding bishop 9th district. **ORGANIZATIONS:** Pres K'ville branch NAACP 1957; chmn Bd of Lay Activities CME Ch 1974-82; pres Southern CA Ecumenical Council of Churches 1984; chmn Bd of Finance CME Church 1982-; chmn College of Bishops CME Ch 1984-; mem World Meth Council. **HONORS/ACHIEVEMENTS:** Presidential citation Natl Assoc for Equal Oppor in Higher Educ 1979; Alumni Achievement Awd Paine Coll Natl Alumni Assn 1983; Disting Serv Awd Govt of the District of Columbia 1984; Public Serv Awd TX Coll 1984. **HOME ADDRESS:** PO Box 170127, Atlanta, GA 30317.

LINTON, GORDON J.
Elected official. **PERSONAL:** Born Mar 26, 1948, Philadelphia, PA; married Jacqueline Flynn; children: Sharifah, Sabriya. **EDUCATION:** Pierce Jr Coll, AS 1967; Lincoln Univ, BA 1970; Antioch Univ, MEd 1977. **CAREER:** School Dist of Philadelphia, comm consult 1971-74; Baptist Childrens House, educ dir 1974-78; Philadelphia Child Guidance Ctr, psyched spec 1978-80; Dept of Auditor General, reg dir 1980-82; PA House of Representatives, state rep. **ORGANIZATIONS:** Mem Natl Black Caucus State of Legislators 1982-, Minority Bus Enterprise Council 1982-; Trustee Lincoln Univ 1982-; mem Philadelphia Economic Roundtable 1983-; pres reg II Conf of Minority Transportation Officials 1984; chmn Sub-

comm on Public Transportation; chmn PA Legislative Black Caucus. **HONORS/ACHIEVEMENTS:** Listed in Outstanding Young Men of Amer 1981; Com Serv Awd Ivy Hill Youth Assn 1982; Com Serv Awd Leeds Middle School 1982; Com Serv Awd Crisis Intervention Network 1984; Appreciation Awd New Penn Del Minority Purchasing Cncl 1985; Independent Minority Businessmen of Central PA Appreciation Awd 1985; Outstanding Civic Leadership Awd Entrepreneurial Club-Business and Technology Ctr 1985; Dedicated Service to Higher Educ Lincoln Univ 1986. **BUSINESS ADDRESS:** Representative Dist 200, PA House of Representatives, 1521 E Wadsworth Ave, Philadelphia, PA 19150.

LINTON, SHEILA LORRAINE
Educator. **PERSONAL:** Born Dec 19, 1950, Philadelphia, PA; daughter of Harold Linton (deceased) and Elvera Linton Boyd. **EDUCATION:** Pennsylvania State Univ, BS 1972; Drexel Univ, MS 1976. **CAREER:** School Dist of Philadelphia, teacher 1972-78; The Pew Charitable Trusts, program officer 1979-87; School District of Philadelphia, teacher 1988-. **ORGANIZATIONS:** Mem Alpha Kappa Alpha 1970-; natl sec Bullock Family Reunions 1978-85; adv comm Jack & Jill of Amer Found 1981-87; volunteer United Negro Coll Fund 1982-; mem Women in Philanthropy 1983-87; bd of dir Assoc of Black Found Execs 1984-87; bd of dir Jack & Jill of Amer Foundation 1989-. **HONORS/ACHIEVEMENTS:** Presidential Award for Distinguished Serv Jack & Jill of Amer Found 1984. **HOME ADDRESS:** 14 S Ruby St, Philadelphia, PA 19139.

LINYARD, RICHARD
Banker. **PERSONAL:** Born Nov 16, 1930, Maywood, IL; married Maggie; children: Linda, Lance, Timothy. **EDUCATION:** Northwestern Univ, attnd; Amer Inst of Banking standard & advance cert; grad schl of banking univ of wI, diploma. **CAREER:** Seaway Natl Bank Chicago, exec vice pres bd dir cashier 1964-; Oak Park Trust & Savs Bank, janitor, elevator Oper, savs bookkeeper, teller, gen bookkeeper, savs dept, asst mgr, asst cashier; 1950-64. **ORGANIZATIONS:** Pres Chicago Chap Amer Inst of Banking. **BUSINESS ADDRESS:** 645 E 87 St, Chicago, IL 60619.

LIPPMAN, LOIS H.
Retired government employee. **PERSONAL:** Born Jan 13, 1925, Boston, MA; married Romeyn V Lippman Jr; children: Marc R. **EDUCATION:** Harvard Univ Extension School, attended. **CAREER:** NY State, asst to state senate, senate 1977; Gilbert A Robinson Inc Special Project, public relations consultant, 1979; Public Relations Bd Inc, vice pres; Intercontinental leisure Inc, vp; Alaska Airlines Inc, sales mgr; The White House, secretarial asst, sec; State of AK, consultant; Political Consultant. **ORGANIZATIONS:** Active in political and civic activities; volunteer in arts and cultural affairs. **HONORS/ACHIEVEMENTS:** 1st black person assigned to White House above level of messenger or domestic served under Pres Dwight D Eisenhower 1953-59; one of the 1st women in a managerial position at a scheduled airline.

LIPPS, LOUIS ADAM, JR.
Professional athlete. **PERSONAL:** Born Aug 09, 1962, New Orleans, LA. **EDUCATION:** Attended, Univ of So MS. **CAREER:** Pittsburgh Steelers, wide receiver 1984-. **ORGANIZATIONS:** Hon chairman Big Brothers & Sisters Bowl for Kids; chmn MS Read-a-thon; chmn Variety Club Golf Tournament, Ronald McDonald House; owner Halls Mortuary Hattiesburg MS; drug and alcohol educ prog Blue Cross of Western Pennsylvania 1986-. **HONORS/ACHIEVEMENTS:** 1984 NFL Rookie of the Yr; 1st Steeler rookie since Franco Harris to be named to AFC Pro Bowl; Great Performance Award; Professional Athlete of the Yr; MS Professional Athlete of the Year 1984; Joe Greene Great Performance Awd 1984; voted to AFC Pro Bowl 1985-86; MS Professional Athlete of the Year; Steeler MVP 1985; Pittsburgh's Man of the Year in Sports; LA Professional Athlete of the Year by Sugar Bowl's Sports Awds Comm 1985; mem 1986 NFL Pro Bowl Team. **BUSINESS ADDRESS:** Pittsburgh Steelers, Three Rivers Stadium, 300 Stadium Circle, Pittsburgh, PA 15212.

LIPSCOMB, DARRYL L.
Marketing manager, compliance officer, civil rights commission. **PERSONAL:** Born Jan 18, 1953, Chicago, IL; son of Mary C Lipscomb; married Kathryn Gregor. **EDUCATION:** Univ of WI-LaCrosse, BS 1977, MS 1979. **CAREER:** Univ of WI, admissions counselor 1979-82; COE Coll, asst dir admissions 1982-83, assoc dean of admissions 1983-86; Cedar Ridge Publishing, dir of marketing 1986-89; City of Cedar Rapids, civil rights compliance officer 1989-. **ORGANIZATIONS:** Mem TX and IL Assoc of College Admissions Counselors 1984-87; mem Iowa Assoc of College Admissions Counselors 1984-86; mem Mid Amer Assoc Equal Opportunity Prog Personnel 1985-86; mem Amer Assoc of Collegiate Registrars and Admission Officers 1985-87; mem Kappa Alpha Psi Frat 1985-; mem Natl Assoc of Coll Admission Counselors 1986-87; mem, IC/CR Alumni Chapter Kappa Alpha Psi. **HONORS/ACHIEVEMENTS:** Keeper of Records, Kappa Alpha Psi IC/CR Alumni Chapter 1988-. **HOME ADDRESS:** 1713 7th Ave SE, Cedar Rapids, IA 52403. **BUSINESS ADDRESS:** Cedar Rapids City Hall, Civil Rights Commission 2nd Floor, Cedar Rapids, IA 52401.

LIPSCOMB, EMANUEL A.
Business executive. **PERSONAL:** Born Oct 01, 1926, Crewe, VA; married Norma Wimp; children: Pamela Renee, Emanuel A. **EDUCATION:** Amer Univ, JD 1956; Howard Univ; Terrell Law Schl. **CAREER:** Fgn Trade Div Census Bur Census Bureau Commerce Dept, chief 1949-57; pvt law prac 1957-58; Trad Analysis Div Office of Textiles, dir 1964-73; Office ofTextiles US Dept Commerce, asst dir 1973-76; Commerce Fed Credit Union, pres; Hampton Univ, visiting prof; US Delegation to GATT, advisor; BilateralTrade Agreements, negotiator; Tech Adv to Foreign Govts on Export Control Proc. **ORGANIZATIONS:** Mem Wash Bar Assc; pres Woodridge Civic Assc 1968-70; chmn Mayor's Adv Com; chmn DC Rent Commin; vice pres Mt Airy Housing Corp; pres Ward 5 Educ Com; mem Model Cities Appeals Bd Silver medal Dept of Commerce 1969. **MILITARY SERVICE:** AUS 1944-47. **BUSINESS ADDRESS:** 3510-18 St NE, Washington, DC 20018.

LIPSCOMB, WANDA DEAN
Administrator. **PERSONAL:** Born Jan 29, 1953, Richmond, VA; married Keith N Lipscomb; children: Nicholas K. **EDUCATION:** Lincoln Univ, BA 1974; Washington Univ, MA 1975; Michigan State Univ, PhD 1978. **CAREER:** MI State Univ Coll of Human Medicine, assoc dean of admissions. **ORGANIZATIONS:** Mem bd dirs Assoc for Multiculture Counseling and Development 1980-87; mem bd dirs Amer Assoc for Counseling and Develop 1982-85; mem Assoc of Black Psychologists 1984-; mem bd dirs Natl Bd of Certified Counselors 1985-88; pres Lansing Alumnae Chap Delta Sigma Theta Sor Inc; mem Natl Program Planning Comm Delta Sigma Theta Sor Inc; mem bd dirs MSU Black Alumni Assoc. **HONORS/ACHIEVEMENTS:** John L Lennon Awd for Disting Professional Service Assoc for Multicultural Counseling 1984; Sisterwood Awd Delta Sigma Theta 1985. **HOME ADDRESS:** 3422 Penrose Dr, Lansing, MI 48911. **BUSINESS ADDRESS:** Assoc Dean of Admissions, Michigan State University, College Of Human Medicine, A239 Life Science Bldg, East Lansing, MI 48824.

LIPSCOMB, WENDELL R.
Physician, association executive. **PERSONAL:** Born Jun 09, 1920, Berkeley, CA; divorced. **EDUCATION:** San Diego State Clge, AB 1947; Univ CA, MD 1951; Univ MI, MPH 1953. **CAREER:** Bur Chronic Diseases State CA Dept Pub Health, supr 1955-57; Div Alcoholic Rehab, sect chief 1957-59, asst chief 1959-61; Mendocino State Hosp, resident psychiat 1961-64; Cowell Mem Hosp, psychiat resident 1964-65; Mendocino State Hosp, chief research 1965-72; Gen Research Corp, prin cons/Study dir1972-73; Westside Comm Mental Health Ctr, chief research 1972-74; Drug Abuse Prog Berkeley Health Dept, chief clin serv 1973-75; W Oakland Health Ctr, staff psychiat 1974-; E Oakland Mental Health Ctr, consult med clin dir 1975-; Source Inc Cons, exec dir, physician. **ORGANIZATIONS:** Mem N CA Psychiat Soc; pacific Sociological Soc; Amer Assc for Advancement of Sci; Pan Amer Med Assc; Amer Acad Polit & Social Sci; Amer Med Soc on Alcoholism; Amer Therapeutic Soc; Amer Social Health Assc; Acad Psychosomatic Med; Biofeedback Research Soc; Intl Council on Alcohol & Addictions; Amer Soc Clin Pharmacology & Therapeutics; Black Psychiatrists of N CA; CA Soc for Treatment of Alcoholism & Other Dependencies. **HONORS/ACHIEVEMENTS:** Prin investigator "An Assessment of Alcoholism Serv Needs & Alcoholism Serv Utilization of CA Black Population". **MILITARY SERVICE:** USAF 1953-55. **BUSINESS ADDRESS:** Physician, Source Inc, 1713 Martin Luther King Jr Way, Berkeley, CA 94709.

LIPSCOMBE, MARGARET ANN
Educator. **PERSONAL:** Born Dec 12, 1939, Alabama. **EDUCATION:** NY Univ, MA 1960; Univ MN, BS 1957; Columbia Univ 1968; CT Clge, 1967; Juilliard, 1970; New York City Studios 1975. **CAREER:** Instr of Dance W CT State Clge, professional dance wrkshps 1967-; City Clge of NY, instr 1964-67; Spelman Clge, instr 1959-64; Hunter Clge HS, instr 1959-60; Vassar NY, choreography performance under Mary Jean Corvele 1965-68; Dancers of Faith, performer 1971-72; Valmar Dance Co, performer 1958-59; Women's Dance Proj Henry St Playhouse NY, performer 1960. **ORGANIZATIONS:** Mem Assc for Mental Health; Amer Assc for Health Physical Educ & Recreation; Natl Tchrs Assc; Univ Professional Women; Music Fedn Inc.

LISTER, ALTON LAVELLE
Professional athlete. **PERSONAL:** Born Oct 01, 1958, Dallas, TX; married Bobby Jo. **EDUCATION:** AZ State Univ, 1978-81. **CAREER:** Milwaukee Bucks, center 1981-. **ORGANIZATIONS:** Named to 1980 Olympic team that played a series of games vs NBA All-Stars called the Gold Medal games. **HONORS/ACHIEVEMENTS:** Saw action in all 16 playoff games & started in 12. **BUSINESS ADDRESS:** Milwaukee Bucks, 1001 N r St, Milwaukee, WI 53203.

LISTER, DAVID ALFRED
Educational administrator. **PERSONAL:** Born Oct 19, 1939, Somerset; son of James Lister and Etoile Johnson Lister; married Anita Louise Browne, Dec 29, 1962; children: Mimi, Gigi. **EDUCATION:** Central State Univ, BA 1962; Stetson Univ Coll of Law, JD 1977. **CAREER:** Johns Hopkins Medical Institutions, dir affirmative action 1978-79; Univ of MA Medical Center, assoc vice chancellor 1979-82; Inst of Intl Educ, dir of personnel 1982-86; Fairleigh Dickinson Univ, univ dir/human resources 1986-87, asst vice pres for admin 1987-88; Univ of Medicine and Dentistry of New Jersey, vice pres for human resources 1988-. **ORGANIZATIONS:** Mem President's Advisory Comm Morgan State Univ 1978; mem NAACP, Amer Soc for Personnel Administration, Coll & Univ Personnel Assoc, Alpha Phi Alpha Fraternity Inc; past mem Advisory Comm to the Commn on the Blind and Visually Impaired (state of NJ); bd mem, chmn Program Comm, mem Exec Comm, Comm of the Newark Private Industry Council; Amer Assn of Affirmative Action; Intl Personnel Mgmt Assn; Amer Mgmt Assn; Amer Hospital Assn; Amer Compensation Assn; Assn of Hospital Personnel Administrators; New Jersey Coll and Univ Personnel Assn; New Jersey Assn of Hospital Personnel Administrators; Greater Newark Chamber of Commerce; Urban League; Central State Univ Alumni Assn. **BUSINESS ADDRESS:** Vice President for Human Resources, Univ of Medicine and Dentistry of New Jersey, 30 Bergen St, Newark, NJ 07107.

LISTER, WILLA M.
Human services specialist. **PERSONAL:** Born Jan 16, 1940, Charleston, SC; married L Venice. **EDUCATION:** Dillard Univ, BA 1962; N TX State Univ, grad studies, MEd 1978, Doctoral Candidate; East Texas State Univ Commerce TX, attended. **CAREER:** New Orelans Sch, phys educ tchr 1962-63; Ft Worth Sch, tchr 1964-73; Highland Park YWCA, ballet & modern dance instr 1964-71; Community Action Agency, activities dir 1967-70; Episcopal Found for Youth, dir Top Teens Tune In 1968-70; City of Fort Worth, personnel analyst training div HRD 1986-. **ORGANIZATIONS:** Mem Astro Rangers Riding Club 1980-; mem Ft Worth Classroom Tchr Assn 1964-75; TX State Tchr Assn 1964-75; Natl Educ assn 1964-75; Nat Council of Tchr of Social Studies 1964-70; mem Ft Worth Comm Devel Fund 100 Com; Horizon Club Sponsor Camp Fire Girls Texas Dist 1964-66; Y Teen Sponsor Morningside Area 1969-71; Planning Com for Teen Activities 1966-68; bd dir Highland Park YWCA 1966-68; pres Delta Sigma Theta Sor Ft Worth Chapt. **HONORS/ACHIEVEMENTS:** Henry Armstrong Awd for Coll Sr Dillard Univ 1962. **BUSINESS ADDRESS:** Assistant to the City Manager, City of Fort Worth, 1000 Throckmorton, Fort Worth, TX 76102.

LISTON, HARDY, JR.
Educational administrator. **CAREER:** Knoxville College, Knoxville TN, president/chancellor. **BUSINESS ADDRESS:** Knoxville College, Knoxville, TN 37921. *

LISTON, HUGH H.
Business executive. **PERSONAL:** Born Oct 12, 1917, Charlotte, NC; married Louise Walls. **EDUCATION:** Knoxville Coll of TN, BS 1938. **CAREER:** Human Devel Corp, chief, neighborhood action prog 1965-68; Volt Info Sci Inc, consult 1967-74; Human Devel Corp,

dep neighborhood devel 1968-69, dep gen mgr 1969-74; Tower Village Inc, exec dir 1974-. **ORGANIZATIONS:** Futures comm Amer Assoc of Homes for the Aged 1978-80; bd mem MO Assoc of Homes for the Aged 1979-80, Gov Adv Council on Aging 1979-80; past treas, bd dir Near N Side Team Ministry; mem Natl Assoc of Community Developers, Natl Assoc Intergroup Relations Ofcl. **BUSINESS ADDRESS:** Executive Dir, Tower Village Inc, 4518 Blair Ave, St Louis, MO 63107.

LITTLE, BRIAN KEITH
Workplace diversity coordinator, human resources. **PERSONAL:** Born Apr 05, 1959, Peoria, IL; son of James A Little and Georgia Gordon Little; married Anise D Wiley Little, Jun 23, 1984. **EDUCATION:** IL State Univ, BS 1981, MS 1983. **CAREER:** IL State Univ, teaching asst 1981-82; Eastern Broadcasting, adv consultant 1982-83; Public Serv Co of CO, specialist career planning/training. **ORGANIZATIONS:** Educ chmn PSC Black Employees Council 1986-; promotions chmn PSC Employee Volunteer Comm 1987-; safety chmn PSC Human Resource Div 1987-. **HONORS/ACHIEVEMENTS:** Outstanding Achievement in Pluralism (an effort by PSC to help people of different cultures & races understand each other). **BUSINESS ADDRESS:** Workplace Diversity Coordinator, 1400 Glenarm #100A, Denver, CO 80202.

LITTLE, CHESTER H.
Appraiser. **PERSONAL:** Born Oct 12, 1907, Paducah, KY; married Leone Bryson; children: Michael Armistead. **EDUCATION:** Wilberforce Univ, attnd 1927; IN Christian Univ, hon degrees 1971. **CAREER:** Eli Lilly Pharm Co, tech biols 1949-72; Malleable Foundry Indpls, 1926-45. **ORGANIZATIONS:** First vice pres Employees Credit Union Malleable Foundry; capt aux police Indpls; WWII chmn adv Com Marion Co Foster Grandparent Prog 1974-80; mem Central IN Council On Aging; chrmn Personnel Com/Evaluation Com 1979-80; pres Marion Co Council on Aging 1980-81; first vice pres Fedn of Assc Clubs 1956-78; bd dir Indianapolis Urban League 1972-78; bd dir Operation Late Start 1975-. **HONORS/ACHIEVEMENTS:** TSP Award Women in Communications; Best Regards Award Urban League; SRE PAC Com 1979. **BUSINESS ADDRESS:** Indianapolis, IN.

LITTLE, CLARENCE E.
Auto dealer. **CAREER:** Little Chevrolet, Inc, Roslyn Heights, NY, chief executive officer, 1984—. **BUSINESS ADDRESS:** Little Chevrolet, Inc, 22 Mineola Ave, Roslyn Heights, NY 11577. *

LITTLE, CLEAVON JAKE
Actor, executive. **PERSONAL:** Born Jun 01, 1939, Chickasha, OK. **EDUCATION:** San Diego Clge, BA 1965; Amer Acad Dramatic Arts, postgrad 1967. **CAREER:** MacBird, actor in play 1967; Hamlet, actor in play 1967; Scuba Duba, actor in play 1967-68; Jimmy Shine, actor in play 1968-69; Someone's Comin' Hungry, actor in play 1969; Ofay Watcher, actor in play 1969; Purlie, actor in play 1970; Temperature's Rising,TV appearence 1972; Blazing Saddles, film aapearence 1974; ThePoison Tree, actor in play; Same Time Next Year, actor in play; Malchi Little, Ltd, pres; Movies of the Week, The Homecoming, Don't Look Back, The Day the Earth Moved, Denmark Vesey (for PBS); appeared in Man is Man in the Summerfare, as Oberon in A Midsummer Night's Dream at Los Angeles Shakespeare Festival. **HONORS/ACHIEVEMENTS:** Recip Tony Award best actor in Musical 1969-70; NY Critic Poll Award 1970; Drama Disk Award 1970; F&M Schaefer Brewing Co Award 1970. **BUSINESS ADDRESS:** President, Malchi Littl, Ltd, 9200 Sunset Boulevard, Ste 607, Los Angeles, CA 90069.

LITTLE, GENERAL T.
Physician. **PERSONAL:** Born Sep 10, 1946, Wadesboro, NC; married Barbara McConnell; children: Christopher, Adrienne, Kimberly. **EDUCATION:** NC A&T State Univ, BS 1967; Meharry Med Clge, MD 1969-71; Walter Reed Gen Hosp, attnd 1975. **CAREER:** Cardio-Pulmonary Assc Charelston, md; Kimbrough AUS Hosp, chief internal medicine 1975-76; Am Bd of Internal Medicine, diplomate 1975. **ORGANIZATIONS:** Mem Natl Med Assc 1971-; consult internal med Sea Island Health Care Corp 1976-77; mem Amer Soc of Internal Medicine 1978-; bd trustees Charleston Co Hosp 1979-; bd trustees Charleston Area Mental Health Bd 1979-; mem Omega Psi Phi Frat Inc. **MILITARY SERVICE:** USMC maj 1971-76. **BUSINESS ADDRESS:** 696 Rutledge Ave, Charleston, SC 29403.

LITTLE, HERMAN KERNEL
Education administration. **PERSONAL:** Born Jan 25, 1951, Wadesboro, NC; son of Bryant Little and Margie Little; married H Patricia; children: Kernell, Karlton. **EDUCATION:** Anson Tech Coll, AAS Acctg 1980, AAS Retailing & Mktg 1980; Wingate Coll, BA Bus Admin Mgmt 1984. **CAREER:** Anson Tech Coll, asst proj dir 1977-83, proj dir 1983-, ed admin. **ORGANIZATIONS:** Bd of dir Morven Area Med Ctr 1978-, Anson Cty Red Cross 1978-; mem NC Comm Coll Adult Ed Assoc 1978-; bd of dir Anson Cty Bd of Adjustment 1980,Anson Cty Waste Mgmt Bd 1981-, Savannah AME Zion Church 1982-; mem Amer Soc for Personnel Admin 1982-; pres Political Action Comm for Concerned Citizens 1982-, Anson Cty Young Democratic Party 1982-83; mem Phi Beta Lambda Wingate Coll 1982-; Grace Sr Center Advisory Council 1983-; mem Anson Cty Personnel Assoc 1983-; bd of dir Anson Cty Art's Council 1984-, PDCOG Emergency Med Serv Advisory 1984-; elected first black Anson Cnty Commissioner 1986; Anson Cnty Health Bd 1987. **HONORS/ACHIEVEMENTS:** Outstanding Young Men of Amer 1981,82; Governor's Volunteer Awd State of NC 1983. **MILITARY SERVICE:** USAF E-4 1972-77; NDSM, AFOUA, AFLSA, AFGCM, AFM 900-3. **HOME ADDRESS:** Rt 1 Box 325, Wadesboro, NC 28170. **BUSINESS ADDRESS:** Educational Administrator, Anson Community College, 117 S Greene St, Wadesboro, NC 28170.

LITTLE, JAMES KELLY, JR.
Consultant. **PERSONAL:** Born Feb 23, 1925, Memphis, TN. **EDUCATION:** Hampton Inst, 1943; Northwestern U, 1946; Roosevelt U, 1947; IL Inst, 1947. **CAREER:** Met Boys Clubs Chicago, founder dir 1944-55; Chicago, policeman juvenile officer 1947-56; Fuller Products Co Chicago, dir pub relations 1956-60; NY Courier, pub editor 1960-66. **ORGANIZATIONS:** Mem adv council NY Urban League Harlem Hosp Center 1966-72; consult in field former unit supr OTC Merrill Lynch & supr commodity operations; exec asst conf asst to asst sec Equal Opport 1974; consult Info & Referral NY City Dept for the Aging 1975-; bd dir Vocational Guidance & Workshop Center NYC; mem Alpha Phi Alpha; mem Nat Urban League Guild; NY Urban League; Nat Council Negro Women. **HONORS/ACHIEVEMENTS:** Hon recipient distinguished comm serv award Alpha Kappa Alpha; outstanding cit award F & M Schaefer Brewing Co 1967; apptd hon Lt Colonel Aide de CampAL State Militia. **BUSINESS ADDRESS:** 250 Broadway, New York, NY 10007.

LITTLE, JEAN PERKINS
Management consultant. **PERSONAL:** Born Sep 21, 1951, Mt Olive, NC; divorced; children: Sonja. **EDUCATION:** Cornell Univ School of Industrial Rel, Cert EEO Spec 1976; Pace Univ White Plains NY, BS Liberal Studies 1981. **CAREER:** Ciba-Geigy Corp NY, corp eeo coord 1975-76, sr personnel admin 1976-78; Amer Cyanamid Lederle Labs, equal oppty affairs mgr 1978-80; Amer Home Products Corp, personnel manager 1980-83; Goodyear Tire & Rubber Co, employment manager. **ORGANIZATIONS:** Mem Amer Bus Womens Assoc 1982-, Corp Womens Network 1976-80; bd of dir Union Child Day Care Ctr White Plains NY 1976-77; bd mem Central NC School for Deaf 1980-83; task force mem Equal Employment Oppty Commiss WA 1975-76, NAACP 1977-79;Search Committee member of Executive Dir of YWCA-Greensnboro 1986. **HONORS/ACHIEVEMENTS:** Keynote speaker Amer Mgmt Assoc 1979; speaker Natl Bus & Professional Womens Club 1979. **HOME ADDRESS:** 1000 Woodlark Ln, Greensboro, NC 27406. **BUSINESS ADDRESS:** Employment Manager, Goodyear Tire & Rubber Co, 800 Pineview St, Randleman, NC 27317.

LITTLE, LEONE BRYSON
Educator. **PERSONAL:** Born Aug 04, 1924, Indianapolis, IN; married Chester H Bryson; children: Michael Armistead. **EDUCATION:** Butler Univ Indpls, BS 1972, MA 1972; IN Univ Purdue Univ, grad work Social Studies 1972, 76, 77, 79; Notre Dame Univ, grad work admin 1977; Boston State, attnd 1980. **CAREER:** Thomas Carr Howe HS, chmn social studies dept 1979-; Forest Manor Schl Indpls, dept chmn soc studies 1976-79; Robert Browning Jr HS, tchr 1968-73;US Civil Srv Army Finance Ctr, examiner 1952-67. **ORGANIZATIONS:** Mem Natl Council for Soc Studies Com Sexism & Social Justice 1974-78; chmn IN Council for Soc Studies Jr High Comm 1975-78; pres IN Council for SocStudies 1979-80; pres Central IN Council for Soc Studies 1979-80; chmn League of Women Voters Gov Comm 1975-80; first vice pres Amer Assc Univ Women 1976-78; pres Indianapolis Br Amer Assc of Univ Women 1978-80; pres life mem Guild Natl Council Negro Women 1970-74; Outst Soc Studies Educ IN Council Soc Studies Supt of Pub Instr 1976; mem Indianapolis Pub Schs Black History Com 1977-79; mem Natl Sci Found Team of Soc Studies Educators who worked on proj atIN Univ 1978. **BUSINESS ADDRESS:** Thomas Carr Howe HS, 4900 Julian Ave, Indianapolis, IN 46219.

LITTLE, MONROE HENRY
Educator. **PERSONAL:** Born Jun 30, 1950, St Louis, MO; married Shelia Maria Josephine Parks; children: Alexander. **EDUCATION:** Denison Univ, BA 1971 (magna cum laude); Princeton Univ, MA 1973, PhD 1977. **CAREER:** MIT, instructor 1976-77, asst prof 1977-80; Indiana Univ-Purdue Univ, Indianapolis, asst prof 1980-81, asst prof dir afro-amer studies 1981-. **ORGANIZATIONS:** Mem Amer Historical Assn; mem Organization of American Historians; mem Natl Urban League; mem Assoc for Study of Afro-Amer Life & History; consultant Educ Develop Ctr 1980; consultant CSR Inc US Dept of Labor 1981; consultant Black Women in the Mid-West Project Purdue Univ 1983. **HONORS/ACHIEVEMENTS:** Elected Omicron Delta Kappa Men's Leadership Honorary 1971; Fellowship Rockefeller Fellowship in Afro-Amer Studies 1972-75; nominee Amer Studies Who's Who Among Black Amers 1980; Awardee Outstanding Young Men in Amer 1981-82. **BUSINESS ADDRESS:** Asst Prof History, Indiana University, Purdue University-Indianapolis, History Dept, Indianapolis, IN 46206.

LITTLE, REUBEN R.
Operations supervisor. **PERSONAL:** Born Sep 01, 1933; married Margaret Jean Davis. **EDUCATION:** Alabama A&M, BS 1975; Univ of Texas, grad study 1963; Kansas State Univ, 1964; Western Illinois Univ, 1965; Indiana Univ, MSS 1966. **CAREER:** DHEW/SSA, Newton MS, oper supvr; DHEW/SSA, Tuscaloosa AL, mgmt trainee 1974-75; teacher admin at jr high school level; Neighborhood Youth Corp Prog, dir. **ORGANIZATIONS:** Mem Natl Bus League 1970; NAACP 1968; Natl Council for Geography Tchrs 1964; Natl Assc of New York City Dirs 1970; vol Youth Court Couns 1972; EEO Assc 1970; lay minister trustee chmn Bd of Elders Good Shepherd Luthern Ch Meridan MS; mem Kappa Alpha Psi 1954; Rescue Lodge 439 3rd Deg Mason 1958; IBPO Elk of W 1960; charter mem Cloverleaf Toastmaster Club 1967; past pres & area gov Toastmasters Intl 1973-74; Choctaw Area Council BSA 1965; div chmn Lauderdale Co March of Dimes 1968-70. **HONORS/ACHIEVEMENTS:** Recipt Ldrshp Award Outst Achievement Toastmasters 1969; Hall of Fame Award 1973 Keyman 1974 Toastmasters; Able Toastmaster 1974; listed Outst Young Men ofAmer 1974; Who's Who in S & SW 1975. **BUSINESS ADDRESS:** PO Box 518, 103 Banks St, Newton, MS 39345.

LITTLE RICHARD See PENNIMAN, RICHARD

LITTLE, ROBERT BENJAMIN
Medical doctor. **PERSONAL:** Born Apr 25, 1955, Dublin, GA; son of Mr William Albert Little and Mrs Druzy P Little. **EDUCATION:** Morehouse Coll, BS (received dept honors) 1977; Meharry Medical Coll, MD 1982. **CAREER:** Harlem Hospital, internship and residency 1983-85; US Navy, general medical officer; Morehouse Medical School, Atlanta, GA, family medicine intern and resident, 1989-. **MILITARY SERVICE:** US Navy, lt commander 1986-89; Sharp Shooters Medal 1988. **HOME ADDRESS:** 2709 Shannon Lake Drive, Union City, GA 30291.

LITTLE, RONALD EUGENE
Surgeon. **PERSONAL:** Born Jun 29, 1937, Chicago, IL; married Jane Mclemore; children: Ronald Jr, Kevin, Bryan, Jennifer. **EDUCATION:** Wayne State U, BS 1965; HowardUniv Coll Med, MD 1970. **CAREER:** Wayne State U, orthopedic Surgeon clinical instr 1975-. **ORGANIZATIONS:** Mem Am Acad of Orthopedic Surgeons 1977; AMA; Nat Med Assn; MI State Med Soc; Wayne Co Med Soc; Detroit Med Soc; diplomat Am Bd of Orthopedic Surgeon; Detroit Acad of Orthopedic Surgeons; mem Alpha Omega Alpha Hon Med Frat 1970. **MILITARY SERVICE:** AUS spec 4 1955-58. **BUSINESS ADDRESS:** 3750 Woodward, Detroit, MI 48201.

LITTLE, WILLIE HOWARD
Educator, coach. **PERSONAL:** Born Aug 20, 1949, Greenwood, MS; married Janice Lynn

Franklin. **EDUCATION:** IA Wesleyan Coll, BA 1972. **CAREER:** Hugh Manley HS Chicago Bd of Educ, teacher, basketball coach 1975-; Calhoun N Elementary School Chicago, teacher 1972-75. **ORGANIZATIONS:** Mem Operation PUSH Chicago. **HONORS/ACHIEVEMENTS:** Chicago City coach of the yr Chicago Pub League Coaches Assn 1977-78; coach of the yr Com on Urban Athletics & Educ 1978; IL State coach of the yr DistOne IL Basketball Coaches Assn 1978-79; basketball coach of the yr Chicago PUSH ofr Excellance 1979; IL State Basketball Champs IL State Basketball Class AA 1980. **BUSINESS ADDRESS:** Head Coach, University of IL - Chicago, PO Box 4348, Chicago, IL 60680.

LITTLEJOHN, BILL C.
Attorney. **PERSONAL:** Born Jan 25, 1944, Gaffney, SC; married Gail A Hodge; children: Erica A, Shai A. **EDUCATION:** Central State Univ, BS Acctg 1969; Ohio Northern Law Univ, JD 1972. **CAREER:** Montgomery Co Public Defender, criminal defense atty 1974-75; City of Dayton, prosecutor 1975-76, traffic court referee 1978-80, acting judge 1978-; Austin Jones Littlejohn & Owens, trial atty 1980-85; Littlejohn & Littlehohn, pres. **ORGANIZATIONS:** Bd mem Natl Business League 1985; bd mem Private Industry Cncl 1985; vice pres regional Natl Business League 1986; chmn of bd Gleksto Inc 1986; pres Neighborhoods USA 1986; 32 degree Prince Hall mason; disting pres Optimist Intl; bd mem United Cerebral Palsy. **HONORS/ACHIEVEMENTS:** Wrote a column for media on entertainment law; Young Republican of the Year State of Ohio 1975; over 100 awards & certs. **MILITARY SERVICE:** AUS 1st lt 1966-75. **BUSINESS ADDRESS:** President, Littlejohn & Littlejohn Co LPA, 323 Salem Ave, Dayton, OH 45406.

LITTLEJOHN, EDWARD J.
Attorney, educator. **PERSONAL:** Born May 05, 1935, Pittsburgh, PA; son of Chester W Littlejohn and Crystal Hudson-Littlejohn; divorced; children: Martin, Victor. **EDUCATION:** Wayne State Univ, BA 1965; Detroit Coll of Law, JD (cum laude) 1970; Columbia Univ Law Sch, LLM 1974, JSD 1982. **CAREER:** City of Detroit, varied Gov serv 1959-70; Detroit Coll of Law, prof 1970-72; Wayne State Law Sch, assoc prof & assistant dean 1972-76, assoc dean & prof of law 1976-78, prof of law 1972-; Univ of Utrecht Netherlands, visiting prof, 1974; Wayne State Center for Black Studies, faculty research assoc. **ORGANIZATIONS:** Apptd to Bd Police Commrs Detroit 1974-78, chmn 1977-78; mem MI Bar Assn, NBA, ABA, Wolverine Bar Assn, Alpha Phi Alpha; ed bd The Urban Educator; hearing officer MI Dept of Civil Rights; consult Police Civil Liability and Citizen Complaints; reporter Amer Bar Assoc; task force on Minorities in the Legal Profession. **HONORS/ACHIEVEMENTS:** Charles Evans Hughes Fellow Columbia Univ Law School 1973-74; WEB Dubois Scholarship Awd Phylon Soc Wayn State Univ 1986; Special Alumni Awd Wolverine Student Bar Assoc Detroit Coll of Law 1986; Trailblazer Award, Wolverine Bar Assn 1988; publications in various legal journals. **MILITARY SERVICE:** USA 1957-59.

LITTLEJOHN, J. B.
Business executive. **PERSONAL:** Born Mar 17, 1942, Paris, TX; divorced; children: C Ann, J B Jr. **EDUCATION:** Dodge City Coll, AA 1958f Kansas State Univ, BS 1961; Kansas Univ, MSW Cand. **CAREER:** Marin Tractor Co, dir public affairs; urban renewal negotiator 1972-74; Topeka Corrugated Container Corp, owner, vice pres, gen mgr 1970-73; Greater Topeka C of C, div mgr 1969-70; Juvenile Ct, chief couns 1964-69; Topeka Upward Bound, guidance dir 1968-69; State Banking Bd, dir 1976-81; Blue Cross/Blue Shield, adv bd; Mental Health Prog for Kansas, adv council; Topeka Club, dir; Greenbay Packers, player 1961; 52nd Dist, state rep 1976. **ORGANIZATIONS:** Chmn of bd topeka Boy's Club 1976-; dir YMCA; co-fdr Big Bro/Big Sister; co-fdr The Villages Inc; dir Topeka United Way. **HONORS/ACHIEVEMENTS:** Football All-Am 1957-58; all big 8 hon mention 1959; outst young man of Am 1970-71. **MILITARY SERVICE:** AUS sp 5 1961-64.

LITTLEJOHN, JOSEPH PHILLIP
Educational administrator. **PERSONAL:** Born Aug 31, 1937, Hackensack, NJ; divorced; children: Mavis, Marc. **EDUCATION:** Rutgers Univ, BS Sociology 1960; NY Univ, MPA 1972. **CAREER:** Steward AFB NY, eeo officer & fed women's progs coord 1968-70; NAACP NY, asst dir housing prog 1970; Inter-religious Found for Comm Organ Amilcar Cabral Inst, asst dir for admins 1972-73; Natl Council of Churches, coord 1973; New York City Human Resources Admin, prog mgr 1973-75; Jersey City State Coll, dir of affirmative action 1975-78; Fairleigh Dickinson Univ, dir of affirmative action 1978-. **ORGANIZATIONS:** US Army Signal Corps 1960-68; bd of dirs Orange Co United Fund 1968-71; EEO Officer Region II Genl Serv Admin 1970-71; bd of dirs Jersey City Branch NAACP 1977-83; bd of dirs Hudson Co Opportunities Ind Ctr 1978-82; 1st vice pres Amer Assoc for Affirmative Action 1984-. **HONORS/ACHIEVEMENTS:** Student Council Rutgers Univ 1958-60; Who's Who in Amer Univs & Colls 1958-69; Martin Luther King Scholarship NY Univ 1969. **MILITARY SERVICE:** AUS Signal Corps major 8 yrs. **HOME ADDRESS:** 66 Madison Ave, Jersey City, NJ 07034. **BUSINESS ADDRESS:** Dir of Affirmative Action, Fairleigh DickinsonUniv, 1000 River Rd, Teaneck, NJ 07666.

LITTLEJOHN, SAMUEL GLEASON
Retired administrator. **PERSONAL:** Born Sep 04, 1921, Gaffney, SC; son of Cleo Littlejohn and Mamie G Littlejohn; married Juanita Price, Aug 06, 1946; children: Samuel G, Jr. **EDUCATION:** A&T State Univ Greensboro, NC, BS MS 1942; Appalachian State Univ, Educ Specialist Degree 1974. **CAREER:** Richmond County School, retired school prin; city council 1972-77; pro-tem, mayor 1973-74. **ORGANIZATIONS:** Past master Masonic Order; NAACP; past dir NC Teachers Assn; NC Educ Assn; pres NC Principals Assn; dir Scotland Meml Hosp; dir Lauringburg-Maxton Airport; dir United Way; NEA; past chmn Schtland Co Br NAACP 1959-69; dist pres Dist 8 NC Educ Assn 1972-74; past pres Richmond County Teachers Assn 1959-65, 1967-69. **HOME ADDRESS:** 218 Center, Laurinburg, NC 28352.

LITTLEJOHN, WALTER L.
Educator. **PERSONAL:** Born Mar 05, 1932, Pine Bluff, AR; married Virginia Lowery. **EDUCATION:** BS 1954; MEd 1957; EdD 1966. **CAREER:** Magnolia, AR, teacher 1954; Magnolia AR, principal 1965-58; Magnolia, AR, public school supt 1958-64; AM&N, prof 1966-74; dean of educ 1975-. **ORGANIZATIONS:** Mem Phi Delta Kappa; Alpha Kappa Mu; life mem Omega Psi Phi Frat; Natl Educ Assn; past pres State Tchrn Assn. **BUSINESS ADDRESS:** Dean, School of Education, Univ of AR at Pine Bluff, University Dr, Pine Bluff, AR 71601.

LITTLETON, ARTHUR C.
Research psychologist. **PERSONAL:** Born Sep 25, 1942, St Louis, MO; married Paula; children: Stephen, David, Jeffrey, Dennis. **EDUCATION:** Univ of MO, BA 1962, MEd 1963; St Louis Univ, PhD 1969. **CAREER:** Univ of MO St Louis, instr 1968-69, asst prof of ed, research psych 1969-71; Urban Behavioral Rsch Assoc, pres. **ORGANIZATIONS:** Former cons, rschr, youth counselor, publ school teacher; lecturer, numerous natl conf of professional orgs. **HONORS/ACHIEVEMENTS:** Co-author "Black Viewpoints"; contrib articles in various scholarly jrnl; chmn black caucus Amer Ed Rsch Assoc 1972; bd mem Bi State Transit Agency. **BUSINESS ADDRESS:** President, Urban Behavioral Rsch Assoc, 1210 Washington Ste 100, St Louis, MO 63101.

LITTLETON, RALPH DOUGLASS
Retired educational administrator. **PERSONAL:** Born Nov 24, 1908, Bryan, TX; married Vergie Daizolu Hinton. **EDUCATION:** Bishop Coll, BA 1930; Univ of No CO, MA 1948; Univ of CA, Post Grad 1960; Univ of USC, Post Grad 1964. **CAREER:** Bralos Cty Schools TX, principal 1934-43; John M Moore Elem School, principal 1943-48; Booker T Washington School, principal 1948-74. **ORGANIZATIONS:** Pres Hobbs Teachers Assoc 1965; employment counselor NM State Employment Hobbs 1975-81; pres Chaporral Kiwanis Club 1978; lt gov Kiwanis Southwest Dist Div III 1985; vice pres Hobbs School Bd 1985. **HONORS/ACHIEVEMENTS:** Hall of Fame Southeastern Ed Assoc of NM 1975; Hall of Fame Bishop Coll Dallas TX 1976.

LITTLETON, RUPERT, JR.
Auto dealer. **PERSONAL:** Born Jul 26, 1950, Fort Gaines, GA; son of Rupert Littleton, Sr and Trava L Reynolds; married Carolyn Dixon, Aug 29, 1981; children: Shaeyna, Zogko, Maceo, stepchildren: Michael, Duane. **CAREER:** Sunbelt Ford-Mercury Inc, Quincy, FL, owner/gen mgr, currently. **ORGANIZATIONS:** Black Ford-Lincoln-Mercury Dealers Assn; Natl Auto Dealers Assn. **BUSINESS ADDRESS:** Owner/Gen Mgr, Sunbelt Ford-Mercury Inc, 916 W Jefferson St, PO Box 410, Quincy, FL 32351.

LIVELY, IRA J.
Realtor. **PERSONAL:** Born Apr 18, 1926, Memphis, TN; children: Illona D Threadgill Jones. **EDUCATION:** Monterey Peninsula Coll, AS 1970; Golden Gate Univ, Bachelor degree 1974, MA 1978. **CAREER:** Seaside Police Dept, juvenile officer 1956-82; MPC & Gavilan Coll, instructor 1972-; Bell's Real Estate, realtor assoc 1984-; Seaside City Council, seaside council mem; Monterey Peninsula USD, school bd mem; Seaside City Council, mayor pro-tem 1986-88; Monterey Peninsula USD, realtor assoc. **ORGANIZATIONS:** Pres MPUSD 1982-84; notary public Bell's Real Estate 1984-. **HONORS/ACHIEVEMENTS:** Officer of the Year Seaside Amer Legion 1971. **BUSINESS ADDRESS:** Realtor Assoc, Monterey Peninsula Univ S D, 1351 Fremont Blvd, Seaside, CA 93955.

LIVERPOOL, CHARLES ERIC
Budget analyst. **PERSONAL:** Born Mar 14, 1946, Ann's Grove Village, Guyana;married Joan Ann Paddy; children: Charles Jr, Dionne, Euisi, Jamal. **EDUCATION:** Bronx Comm Coll, AA 1978; Bernard M Baruch Coll, BBA 1982; Long Island Univ, attending. **CAREER:** Navy Resale Serv Spt Office, acctg/liab ins asst 1974-83, programmer/analyst 1983-86; HQ 77th US Army Reserve Cmd, budget analyst 1986-; state of New York, notary public, comm expires 7/90. **ORGANIZATIONS:** Educ vp/secty Navresso Toastmasters #2285 1978-82; vice chmn supv comm 1980-85, mem bd of dirs 1985-, CGA Federal Credit Union Brooklyn NY; literacy volunteer tutor Queens Boro Public Library 1984-; mem New York Urban League 1985-; mem Natl Black MBA Assoc 1986-. **MILITARY SERVICE:** AUS Reserve sgt 1st class (sfc)/E-7 8 yrs; Army Achievement Medal, Army Reserve Comp Achm Medal 1979-. **BUSINESS ADDRESS:** Budget Analy Reserve Pgm Army, HQ 77th US Army Reserve Cmd, Ernie Pyle USAR Ctr, Fort Totten, Flushing, NY 11359.

LIVERS, VIRGIL CHESTER, JR.
Athlete. **PERSONAL:** Born Mar 26, 1952, Nelson County, KY; married Linda Lou Alexander; children: Alexander Gerard. **EDUCATION:** W KY U, BS 1975. **CAREER:** Chicago Bears, ath 1975-. **HONORS/ACHIEVEMENTS:** Who's Who amg Coll & U; little All-Am in Ftbl; OUC def plyr of yr 1974f all conf tr & ftbl; athlete of yr aw 1975.

LIVINGSTON, JEWEL P.
Educator, association executive. **PERSONAL:** Born Jan 05, 1922, St Louis; divorced. **EDUCATION:** AB 1942; MA 1964. **CAREER:** St Louis Sch Sys, tchr 1942-71; St Louis OIC, exec dir. **ORGANIZATIONS:** Mem MO State Tchrs Assn; Intl Reading Assn; NEA; NAACP; YWCA; Citizens for Non-Partisan Voter Registration; League of Women Voters; Nat Citizens & Redevel Corp; vol Citizens for Goins; life mem Zeta Phi Beta Sor Inc; Kappa Delta Pi Hon Soc Edn; Top Ladies of Distinction; ABWA; mem exec bd Urban League of St Louis; Ferrier Harris Home for the Aged; Carver House Youth Center; Page Park YMCA; Educ Assistance Fund for Radio Station KATZ; Nat Citizen's Redevel Corp; HELP Inc; Central City Foods; Jolly Jesters Inc; League of Women Voters; vol Citizens for Goins; Aunts & Uncles Inc; mem All Saints EpiscopalCh; Kappa Delta Pi. **HONORS/ACHIEVEMENTS:** St Louis Argus Pub Serv Award; distinguished laymans award All Saints Episcopal Ch; serv award Radio Station KATZ; Xi Zeta Chap Woman of Yr 1972; boss of yr award Louis IX Chap Am Bus Women's Assn. **BUSINESS ADDRESS:** 5671 Delmar Blvd, St Louis, MO 63112.

LIVINGSTON, L. BENJAMIN
Psychologist. **PERSONAL:** Born Jul 01, 1931, Eufaula, OK; married Margaret Juanita Johnson; children: David, Harvey, Lawrence. **EDUCATION:** Univ of AZ, BA 1958; AZ State U, MA 1968; AZ State U, PhD 1971. **CAREER:** Univ of CA Riverside, psychologist; AZ State U, couns psychol 1969-71; Booker T Washington Sch, Instr 1967-69; Youth Oppor Ctr AZ State, supv couns; Employment Svc, 1965-66; St Mary's HS, dir music 1963-65; Maricopa Co Detention Home, home couns 1961-63; Whiteriver Pub Sch, supr 1959-61. **ORGANIZATIONS:** Couns to many schools private & govtl agencies; workshops & group facilitator; Mental Health Affirmative Action Com; consult Prof Sch of Psychology LA; adj facultyUniv of Redlands CA; dist rep Omega Psi Phi 1974-; western reg rep Assn of Black Psychologists 1973-; mem NAACP; MENC western reg bd dir Migrant Programs; Urban League; OIC; APGA; Omega Head Start; Phi Mu Alpha 1957; Phi Delta Kappa 1968. **HONORS/ACHIEVEMENTS:** 12th dist Omega man of the year 1967; jaycee recognition & award 1968. **MILITARY SERVICE:** AUS e-3 1954-56. **BUSINESS ADDRESS:** 201 E Big Springs Rd, Riverside, CA 92507.

LIVINGSTON, RUDOLPH
Government official. **PERSONAL:** Born May 08, 1928, Decatur, IL; married Dorothy Louise Krushall; children: Mark Douglas, Julie Ann, Cathy Lynn Barnbwall, John Christopher. **EDUCATION:** Millikin Univ, BS Bus Admin 1957; Denver Univ, MPA 1960. **CAREER:** CO State Dept of Personnel, dep dir 1970-76, exec dir 1976-80; US Office of Personnel Mgmt, asst dir 1980-81; CO State Dept of Personnel, dep dir 1981-. **ORGANIZATIONS:** Pres, exec bd CO Chap Intl Pers Mgmt Assoc 1965-; mem human rights comm IPMA 1977-78; officer, dir Summa Inc 1965-; adj prof Univ of CO Denver;pres Black United Denver Govt Employees 1983-85, Kingsman Club; mem KAY. **HONORS/ACHIEVEMENTS:** Govs Scholastic Achievements Awd Univ of Denver 1970; Alumni Achievement Awd Millikin Univ Decatur IL 1978; Disting State Serv Awd State of CO 1971. **MILITARY SERVICE:** AUS Infantry sgt 2 yrs. **HOME ADDRESS:** 22 S Holly St, Denver, CO 80222. **BUSINESS ADDRESS:** Deputy Dir Personnel, State of Colorado, 1313 Sherman St, Room 123, Denver, CO 80203.

LIVINGSTON-WHITE, DEBORAH J. H. (DEBI STARR-WHITE)
Business executive. **PERSONAL:** Born Nov 21, 1947, DuQuoin, IL; daughter of Jetson Edgar Livingston and Tressie Me Gaston-Livingston; married Dr William Tyrone White. **EDUCATION:** Southern IL Univ, BS Ed 1968, MS Ed 1971; Northern IL Univ, EdD Admin 1975; MI State Univ, Post-Doctoral Studies 1980-82; Univ of MI, Post-Doctoral Studies 1981-84. **CAREER:** Affiliated Models & Talent Agency, Full-Figure Model, 1987-present; Talent Shop, Model, Actress, 1987-present; Oak Park School Dist, Dir of Special Educ, 1987-present; MI State Univ, asst prof 1980-; Yale Univ, guest lecturer, 1984; Dansville Ag Schools, teacher consultant 1976-78; Mgmt Recruiters, account exec 1976-78; MI Dept of Educ, special educ consultant 1978-; Intl Consultants, Public Relations & Marketing Consultant; Private Pilot; management trainer. **ORGANIZATIONS:** Sales Rep, United Natl Life Insurance Co 1976-79; consultant, evaluator, US Dept of Educ 1979-; fellow Ed Policy Fellowship Program 1979-80; adv comm mem Black Notes MSUMedia Prod 1980-83; pres, exec dir Intl Consultant 1981-; vocational chairperson Altrusa Intl 1982-83; reg coord Volunteers in Special Educ 1982-; trainer Project Outreach MDE 1984;Habitat for Humanity fund raising comm greater Detroit; Mental Health Educ Exhibit Treasurer; Alternative Living for Physically Handicapped Adults; Pres; The Tressie Found, Founder & Pres. **HONORS/ACHIEVEMENTS:** IL Congress of Parents & Teachers Scholarship 1968; Natl Ford Found Fellowship 1970-75; Phi Kappa Phi Honor Soc 1971; Self Magazine-Chrysler "Fresh Start Award" 1986; Publ "The Vicky Caruso Story, A Miracle in Process" 1979, "Use of the Optacon by Visually Impaired Persons in MI", 1980; Follow-up Study of Visually Impaired Students of the MI School for the Blind "Journal of Visual Impairment & Blindness" 1985; poem "Black Glass" in World's Most Cherished Poems 1985; poem "White Pearl Satin, Pink Orchid Lace" in World's Best Poets 1985; Intl Model & Talent Award, 1987. **BUSINESS ADDRESS:** Executive Director, President, International Consultants, 24041 Geneva, Oak Park, MI 48237.

LLEWELLYN, JAMES BRUCE
Company chairman. **PERSONAL:** Born Jul 16, 1927, New York City, NY; married Shahara; children: Kristen Lisa, Alexandra, JayLaan. **EDUCATION:** CCNY, BS; Columbia Grad School of Business; NYU School of Public Admin; NY Law School, LLB, JD. **CAREER:** Coca Cola Bottler of Philadelphia, chmn; Overseas Private Investment Corp, pres 1977-81; Fedco Food Stores NY, pres 1969-82; New York City Housing & Devel Admin, dep commr 1968-69; Small Business Devel Corp, exec dir 1967-68, dir mgmt training 1966-67, prog officer 1965-66; Small Business Admin, regional dir 1965; Upper Manhattan Office of Small Business Devel Corp, exec dir 1965; Housing Div Housing & Redevel Bd, asst dir 1964-65; Evans Berger & Llewellyn, atty 1962-65; NY Co Dist Atty Office, student asst 1958-60; Retail Liquor Store, proprietor, 1952-56. **ORGANIZATIONS:** Mem Harlem Lawyers Assn; NY State Food Merchants; pres 100 Black Men Inc; past pres bd of Riverpoint Towers Coop; chmn of bd Freedom Nat Bank; pastco-chmn NY Interracial Council for Bus Opportunity; vice pres bd mem Bd of Fedn of Protestant Welfare Agencies; chmn Bd of NY Urban Coalition Venture Capital Corp; mem Bd of NY Urban Coalition; bd dir Flower 5th Ave Hosp; bd trustees City Coll; bd trustees Grad Center CityUniv of NY; mem Bd of Nat Interracial Council for Bus Opportunity; dir Amer Can Co, Amer Capital Mgmt Rsch. **HONORS/ACHIEVEMENTS:** Wagner Coll Staten Island Hon PhD; City Univ of NY Hon PhD; Atlanta Univ Hon PhD. **MILITARY SERVICE:** US Corp of Engrs, 1st lt 1944-48.

LLOYD, DAVID
Chief executive. **CAREER:** Bay City Marine, Inc, San Diego, CA, chief exec. **BUSINESS ADDRESS:** Bay City Marine, Inc, 3040 Terminal Ave, National City, CA 92050. *

LLOYD, GEORGE LUSSINGTON
Clergyman. **PERSONAL:** Born Aug 09, 1931, Valley. **EDUCATION:** Alma White Coll, BA 1959; Moravian Theological Seminary, MDiv 1962; Iona Coll, MSEd 1969; San Francisco Theological Seminary, DMin 1984. **CAREER:** Moravian Church, Guyana, S America, minister 1962-65; United Moravian Church, minister 1965-; Pastorial Counselor; Licensed Marriage Counselor 1986 State of NJ. **ORGANIZATIONS:** Board president Harlem Interfaith Counseling Service 1966-70; fellow Amer Assn of Pastoral Counselors 1967-; president dept Pastoral Care Council of Churches City of NY 1983-; member board of directors Council of Churches City of NY 1983-; member Christian Assn for Psychological Studies 1984. **HONORS/ACHIEVEMENTS:** Special Contribution NYVA Med Center 23 St at 1st Ave 1983; Performance Award NYVA Med Center 23rd at 1st Ave NY 1984; Recognition Award NY Healing Community, NY 1984. **MILITARY SERVICE:** AUS PFC 1953-55. **BUSINESS ADDRESS:** Minister, United Moravian Church, 200 E 127th St, New York, NY 10035.

LLOYD, JAMES
Business executive. **PERSONAL:** Born Jul 13, 1932, Hensley, WV; son of James Llyod and Evangeline Lloyd; divorced. **EDUCATION:** WV State Coll Inst, attended 1950, graduate. **CAREER:** James Lloyd Ins Agency Inc, owner; CLM Development & Consturction Co, pres; CLM Trucking Inc, vice pres. **ORGANIZATIONS:** Bd dir Rochester-Genesee Reg Transportation Auth; mem NAACP; Urban League; chmn Adv Bd for PUSH Excel; bd mem Genesee Health Care Assn. **HONORS/ACHIEVEMENTS:** Black Student's Awd St John Fisher Coll 1975; Outstanding Man in the Comm Rochester NY. **BUSINESS ADDRESS:** President, James Lloyd Insurance Agency, 440 Genessee, Rochester, NY 14611.

LLOYD, LEONA LORETTA
Attorney. **PERSONAL:** Born Aug 06, 1949, Detroit, MI; daughter of Leon and Naomi; married David Anderson, Apr 02, 1989. **EDUCATION:** Wayne State Univ, BS 1971, JD 1979. **CAREER:** Lloyd & Lloyd Law Firm, senior law partner. **ORGANIZATIONS:** Mem Amer Bar Assoc, Wolverine Bar Assoc, Mary McLeod Bethune Assoc of MI; past mem Natl Conf of Black Lawyers, Natl Assoc of Negro Business & Prof Women; Admitted to US District Court 1983, Michigan Supreme Court 1985, US Supreme Court 1988; National Assn of Recording Artists. **HONORS/ACHIEVEMENTS:** Scholarship Bd of Governors Wayne State Univ, 1970,75; Fred Hampton Image Awd 1984; Black Women Hall of Fame Found 1985; Kizzy Image Awd 1985; Black Women in MI Exhibit 1985; Nat'l Coalition of 100 Black Women Achievement Awd 1986; comm serv awd presented by Wayne Cnty Exec 1986; Univ of Detroit Black Law Students Assn, cert of merit 1986; Wayne St Univ Assn of Black Business Students, minority business of the year awd 1986. **BUSINESS ADDRESS:** Senior Law Partner, Lloyd & Lloyd, 600 Renaissance Ctr Ste 1400, Detroit, MI 48243.

LLOYD, LEONIA JANNETTA
Attorney, performing artist manager. **PERSONAL:** Born Aug 06, 1949, Detroit, MI; daughter of Leon Lloyd and Naomi Lloyd. **EDUCATION:** Wayne State Univ, BS 1971, JD 1979. **CAREER:** Lloyd & Lloyd, sr law partner; Double L Management, partner. **ORGANIZATIONS:** Past mem Natl Conference of Black Lawyers 1975-79; mem Friends of the Afro-American Museum 1983-; mem Amer Bar Assn; mem Wolverine Bar Assn; mem Mary McLeod Bethune Assn; past mem Natl Assn of Negro Business and Professional Women; mem, State Senator Smith's Cabinet, 1989. **HONORS/ACHIEVEMENTS:** Scholarship Bd of Governors Scholarship/Wayne State Univ 1970, 1975; Certificate of Appreciation bestowed by Mayor Coleman Young 1977; Kizzy Image Award 1985; Fred Hampton Image Award 1984; IL Black Woman's Hall of Fame; Black Women in MI Exhibit 1985; Natl Coalition of 100 Black Women Award 1986; ABBS Minority Business of the Year 1986; Wayne County Exec Community Serv Award bestowed by William Lucas 1986; negotiated recording contracts for, Arista's recording artist, "KIARA" and MCA's recording artist, "Ready for the World" and RCA's recording artists, "David Ruffin" and "Eddie Kendricks". **BUSINESS ADDRESS:** Senior Law Partner, Lloyd & Lloyd, 600 Renaissance Center, Ste 1400, Detroit, MI 48243.

LLOYD, LEWIS JOEL
Professional athlete. **PERSONAL:** Born Feb 22, 1959, Philadelphia, PA. **EDUCATION:** Drake Univ, 1979-81; New Mexico Military Jr Coll, 1977-79. **CAREER:** Golden State Warriors, guard 1981-83; Houston Rockets, 1983-. **BUSINESS ADDRESS:** Houston Rockets, The Summit, Ste 510, Houston, TX 77046.

LLOYD, PHIL ANDREW
Automobile dealer. **PERSONAL:** Born Jun 24, 1952, Buffalo, NY; son of Otis Lloyd and Mable Spivey Lloyd; divorced; children: Phil A Lloyd, Jr. **EDUCATION:** Erie Community, Buffalo, NY, AAS, 1972; Buffalo State, Buffalo, NY, BS, 1975. **CAREER:** Manufacture Trader Trusts, Buffalo, NY, collector, 1975; Wicks Lumber, Orchard Pk, NY, sales mgr, 1976-80; Ed Mullinax Ford, Amherst, OH, salesman, 1981-86; Western Ford-Mercury, Clyde, OH, pres, 1987-. **ORGANIZATIONS:** Mem, Phi Beta-Lamba, 1971-73; mem, Environmental Pollution Control, 1972-73; mem, Clyde Business Assn, 1987-; pres, Twin City Kiwanis, 1980-81; trustee, Clyde Kiwanis, 1988-89. **HONORS/ACHIEVEMENTS:** Distinguished Service, Ford Motor, 1981-86; Salesman of the Year, Mullinas Ford, 1985; Sales Quality and Service, Lincoln-Mercury Div, 1988; Marketshare Pacesetter, Black Ford-Lincoln Mercury Assn, 1988; Quality Commitment, Black Ford-Lincoln Mercury Assn, 1988. **BUSINESS ADDRESS:** Pres, Western Ford-Mercury Inc, 1036 W McPherson Hwy, Clyde, OH 43410.

LLOYD, RAYMOND ANTHONY
Physician, educator. **PERSONAL:** Born Nov 25, 1941; married Eveline Moore; children: Raymond, Rhea, Ryan. **EDUCATION:** Jamaica Coll, 1958; Howard Univ, BS 1962; Howard Univ Coll Med, MD 1966; Freedmen's Hosp, resident 1967-68; VA Hosp, Children's Hosp & NIH, fellow 1969-71. **CAREER:** Howard Univ Coll Med, asst prof of med 1971-; Comm Group Health Found, consultant 1971-76; Narcotics Treatment Admin, assoc admin treatment 1972-73; Div of Prevention, Natl Inst of Alcoholism & Alcohol Abuse, initial rev comm 1972. **ORGANIZATIONS:** Mem DC Med Soc; Caribbean Am Intercultural Orgn; Nat Assn of Intern & Residents; AMA; Nat Capital Med Found Inc; DC C of C; Am Heart Assn; AmFedn of Clinical Rsrch; Am Professional Practice Assn; flw Intl Coll of Angiology; mem WA Heart Assn; sub-com for CPR; Nat Capital Med Found; sub-com on Cardiovascular Diseases; pres L&L Hlth Care Assn; adv bd Hemisphere Nat Bank; mem Bata Kappa Chi 1962; Phi Beta Kappa 1962. **HONORS/ACHIEVEMENTS:** Hon in chem 1962; hon pediatrics 1966; Daniel Hale & Williams Award; intern of yr 1967; BKX Award in Chem 1961. **BUSINESS ADDRESS:** 1613a Rhode Island Ave NE, Washington, DC 20018.

LLOYD, WANDA (NEE SMALLS)
Editor. **PERSONAL:** Born Jul 12, 1949, Columbus, OH; married Willie Burk; children: Shelby Renee. **EDUCATION:** Spelman Coll, BA 1971. **CAREER:** The Providence Evening Bulletin, copy editor 1971-73; Columbia Univ, instr 1972; The Miami Herald, copy editor 1973-74; The Atlanta Jrnl, copy editor 1974-75; The Washington Post, copy editor 1975-76; Univ of MD, instr 1978; Los Angeles Times-WA Post News Svc, dep editor. **ORGANIZATIONS:** Mem WA Assoc of Black Journalists, Natl Assoc of Black Jrnlst, Amer Assoc of Sunday & Feature Editors; bd mem, consult Howard Univ Urban Jrnl Workshop; vice pres WA Spelman Alumnae Assoc 1984-86; mem Delta Sigma Theta; guest lecturer Univ of MD 1977, Booker T Washington Jr HS 1974; mem So Reg Press Inst. **HONORS/ACHIEVEMENTS:** Listed in Who's Who Among Young Women in Amer 1976. **BUSINESS ADDRESS:** Deputy Editor, Los Angeles Times, WA Post, 1150 15th St NW, Washington, DC 20071.

LOCHE, LEE EDWARD
Business executive. **PERSONAL:** Born Feb 17, 1926, Collinston, LA; married Opeary Mae Hill; children: Veronica Tappin, Howard D, Edward C. **EDUCATION:** Univ of Sipan, 1943-45; Atlanta Coll of Mortuary Science, 1949; Spaulding Business Coll, 1952. **CAREER:** Loche's Mortuary, Inc, mortician 1964; Purple Shielf Life Ins Co, manager 1966; Loche's Mortuary, Inc, president. **ORGANIZATIONS:** Treasurer S Louisiana Conf EME 1962-; pres Loche's Mortuary, Inc 1965-; mem Fidelity Lodge No 53 1966-; Police Jury mem 1972-, vice pres 1983-; vice pres Morehouse Police Jury 1983-. **HONORS/ACHIEVEMENTS:** Cert of Merit Natl Insurance Assn 1981. **MILITARY SERVICE:**

Transportation pfc 2 yrs. **HOME ADDRESS:** 126 Cyrstal St, Bastrop, LA 71220. **BUSINESS ADDRESS:** President, Loche's Mortuary, Inc, 412 W Hickory, Bastrop, LA 71220.

LOCKARD, JON ONYE
Artist, educator, lecturer. **PERSONAL:** Born Jan 25, 1932, Detroit, MI; divorced; children: John C, Carlton E. **EDUCATION:** Wayne Univ, 1949-50; Fields' Sch of Art, Cert 1951-52; Meinzinger Art Sch, Cert 1951-52. **CAREER:** Natl Conf of Artists, exec bd 1972-83; Washtenaw Comm Coll, faculty 1979-; Acad of Creative Thought, dir; Natl Conf of Artists, pres; Univ of MI Center for Afro-American & African Studies, artist & asst prof art & Afro-Amer Hist. **ORGANIZATIONS:** Intl coord First World Cultural Feltival Bahia, Brazil 1980; exhibiting artist Suriname Festival of the Diaspora 1980-81; artist/curator Asubuhi Cultural CenterUniv M 1984; numerous art exhibitions throughout country & abroad - Africa, Brazil, Suriname; sponsor Sandy Sanders Basketball League Ann Arbor 1983-85; consult "The State of Black America" channel 56 PBS Detroit 1983-84; consult "Suriname" a documentary channel 56 PBS Detroit 1984 (won 3 Emmys). **HONORS/ACHIEVEMENTS:** NCA Disting Award of Honor Natl Conf of Artists Dakar, Seneyal 1985; Af Am mural "Continium" Wayne State Univ Detroit 1979; mural "Tallest Tree in the Forest" Central State Univ Wilberforce, OH 1981; City of Detroit Proclamation Detroit City Cncl 1980. **HOME ADDRESS:** 2649 Wayside Dr, Ann Arbor, MI 48103.

LOCKE, DON C.
Educator. **PERSONAL:** Born Apr 30, 1943, Macon, MS; son of Willie Locke and Carlene Locke; married Marjorie P Myles; children: Tonya E, Regina C. **EDUCATION:** TN A&I State Univ, BS 1963, MEd 1964; Ball State Univ, EdD 1974. **CAREER:** South Side HS, Social Studies teacher 1964-70; Wayne HS, school counselor 1971-73; Ball State Univ European Program, asst prof 1974-75; NC State Univ, asst/assoc prof/prof 1975-89, dept head 1987-. **ORGANIZATIONS:** Mem Alpha Phi Alpha Fraternity Inc; mem New Bern Ave Day Care Center Bd 1978-86; pres NC Personnel & Guidance Assoc 1979-80; chairperson S Region Branch AACD 1983-84; mem Carroll Comm Schools Advisory Council 1984-87; chairperson NC Bd of Registered Practicing Counselors 1984-87; sec Assn for Counselor Educ & Supervision 1985-86; pres Southern Association for counselor Educ and Supervision 1988-89. **HONORS/ACHIEVEMENTS:** Summer Fellow Center for Advisory Study in Behaviorial Sciences 1979; co-author "Psychological Techniques for Teachers"; author or co-author of more than 40 articles in professional journals. **HOME ADDRESS:** 1509 Shelley Rd, Raleigh, NC 27612. **BUSINESS ADDRESS:** Prof Counselor Educ, North Carolina StateUniv, Box 7801, Raleigh, NC 27695.

LOCKE, HENRY DANIEL, JR.
Journalist. **PERSONAL:** Born Nov 16, 1936, Greenville, SC; married Audrey Marie Harris; children: Daniel Leroy, Tara Yvonne, Henry III. **EDUCATION:** Univ of MD, attended 1955-58; Univ of Buffalo NY, attended 1958-61; Associated Press Inst Reston VA, completed editing sch 1979. **CAREER:** MI Ave YMCA Buffalo, weekend exec 1959-63; Buffalo Courier-Express, dist mgr 1960-72; Buffalo, youth counselor 1964-78; Black Enterprise Mag NYC, contrib (corr) 1979-; Courier-Express Buffalo, columnist/reporter 1972-82; The Natl Leader Phila, columnist/reporter 1982-83; Chicago Defender, natl reporter 1983-. **ORGANIZATIONS:** Mem Comm Assn of Black Journalists; bd dir MI Ave YMCA 1960-64; bd trustees Lloyd's Meml United Ch of Christ 1962-63; state pr dir NAACP Conf of Br 1976-77; mem Alpha Phi Alpha Frat, NAACP, Urban League, Operation PUSH, Black Communicators Assn, Black Social Workers/No Region Black Polit Caucus; mem NY State Affirmative Action Com; mem BUILD; vice chmn Local 26 Amer Newspaper Guild 1975-. **HONORS/ACHIEVEMENTS:** Nominee Pulitzer Prize 1977; 6 awds page one competition newspaper articles; 1st place On the Spot Newspaper Reporting AP Wire Serv 1977; 38 Awds Outstanding Comm Serv various orgns. **MILITARY SERVICE:** USAF A/1c 1954-58; Good Conduct Medal; Occupation of France; Germany Occupation; Natl Defense Medal. **BUSINESS ADDRESS:** Natl Reporter, International Reporter, 2400 S Michigan Ave, Chicago, IL 60616.

LOCKE, HUBERT G.
Educator. **PERSONAL:** Born Apr 30, 1934, Detroit, MI; married Linda K Christian; children: Gayle, Lauren. **EDUCATION:** Wayne Univ, BA 1955; Univ of Chgo, BD 1959; Univ of MI, MA 1961. **CAREER:** Wayne State Univ, asst prof, ed soc 1967-72; Univ of NE Omaha, dean public affairs 1972-76; Univ of WA, assoc dean arts & sci 1976-77, vice pres acad affairs, dean, prof public affairs. **ORGANIZATIONS:** Admin asst to commiss Detroit Police Dept 1966-67; exec dir Citizens Comm for Equal Oppty 1962-65; bd of dir Police Found 1970-71; dir Wm O Douglas Int 1972-; exec vice pres Inst for the Study of Contemp Soc Problems 1972-; bd dir Publ Admin Serv DDiv, Payne Theol Sem 1968. **HONORS/ACHIEVEMENTS:** Liberty Bell Awd MI Bar Assoc 1966; publ "The Detroit Riot of 1967" Wayne State Univ press 1969, "The Care & Feeding of White Liberals" Paulist Press 1970,"The CHurch Confronts the Nuzis" 1984, "Exile in the Futherland" 1986; DDiv Payne Theological Sem 1968; DDivChC Chicago Theol Sem 1971; Doctor of Human Letters Univ of Akron 1971. **BUSINESS ADDRESS:** Professor, Univ of Washington, Grad School of Public Affairs, DP-30, Seattle, WA 98195.

LOCKERMAN, GENEVA LORENE REUBEN
Educator. **PERSONAL:** Born Nov 04, 1928, Silverstreet, SC; married Joseph H Lockerman; children: Joseph H Jr. **EDUCATION:** Benedict Coll, BA 1949; Columbia Univ, MA 1950; NY Univ, Columbia Unvi, post-grad study. **CAREER:** FL A&M Univ, counselor freshmen women 1951-53; NY Telephone Co, serv rep 1954-55; Jersey City Bd of Educ, hist tchr 1959-64; Jersey City Comm & Neighborhood Devel Orgn, educ specialist 1965-68; Dartmouth Coll Educ Ctr, lectr in educ/adjunt 1971-74; Jersey City State Coll, counselor counseling & psychol svc. **ORGANIZATIONS:** Mem Alpha Kappa Mu Hon Soc; mem Phi Delta Kappa; mem Amer Personnel & Guid Assn; chairperson/hon soc mem Jersey City Educ Ctr; bd dir I Jersey City Bd of Personnel Practices; mem Natl Cncl of Negro Women; bd dir Sr Companion Prog Alpha Kappa Alpha Sor; past mem Jersey Cty Br NAACP; mem Bayview Ave Black Assn; mem Jersey City Planning Bd; mem NJ Assn for Affirmative Action; mem Assn for Non-White Concerns. **HONORS/ACHIEVEMENTS:** Jersey Journal Woman of Achievement 1967; NJ Outstanding Citizen 1969; Sr Companion Awd Action Agy; World Who's Who for Women 1978; Who's Who in the E 1979-80; Who's Who of Amer Women 1980-81; Sojourner Truth Awd 1984 Action for Sickle Cell Anemia of Hudson Co Inc; Mary McLeod Bethune Awd for Black Women Achievers 1983 Com-Bi-Nations; listing in Who's Who in Amer. **BUSINESS ADDRESS:** Counselor I, Jersey City State Coll, 2039 Kennedy Blvd, Jersey City, NJ 07305.

LOCKET, ARNOLD, JR.
Clergyman. **PERSONAL:** Born Oct 06, 1929, Bethel, NC; married Jeffie Bernadine; children: Gwendolyn E. **EDUCATION:** No AZUniv Flagstaff, BA 1971f No AZ U, MA 1975. **CAREER:** Coconino Co & Flagstaff NAACP Br, reverend 1977-; Coconino Comm Guidance Cntr Inc, prog dir 1974-77; AZ State Dept of Econ Security, vocat rehab couns 1973-74; AZ State Dept of Econ Security, correctional rehab couns 1971-73. **ORGANIZATIONS:** Mem Nat Assn of Vocational Couns 1971-; adv counc mem AZ State Dept of Econ security 1977-; chmn plan devel com No AZ Health Systems Agency 1979;br pres Flagstaff NAACP Br 1976-; chmn of Mayor's Human Rel Com City of Flagstaff 1976-80. **HONORS/ACHIEVEMENTS:** 1st Worshipful Master F&AM Prince Hall Lodge Killeen TX 1963; Ust Black Dept Head Coconion Co Flagstaff AZ 1977; recipient of Bronze Star & Army Commendation Medal AUS. **MILITARY SERVICE:** AUS sfc-e7 1948-68. **BUSINESS ADDRESS:** County Courthouse, San Francisco Birch, Flagstaff, AZ 86001.

LOCKETT, BRADFORD R.
Designer, tailor. **PERSONAL:** Born Sep 26, 1945, Norfolk, VA; married Brendale Joyce; children: Belinda Joyce. **EDUCATION:** TX Southern Univ, BS 1968; Natl School of Dress Design, 1966. **CAREER:** JC Penney Co Tucson, AZ, head tailor 1970-71; Brotherhood Assn of Military Airmen Tucson, vice pres 1971-72; Tucson, master mason 1971-72; Research & AnalysisDMAFB Tucson, AZ, clothing counselor for USAF 1970-72; Joe Frank of Houston, Asst fashion designer 1973; Mr Creations Inc & Battlesteins, fashion designer & master tailor. **ORGANIZATIONS:** Mem Gulf Coast Fashion Assn; Small Bus Administrn; Basilus of Omega Psi Phi Frat 1966-67; master mason 11th Degree Pima Lodge #10 Tucson. **HONORS/ACHIEVEMENTS:** Spl air force Documentary (AFN Series #38-ON Preparatory Mgmt) Film of the Fashion Entertainment of Brad Lockett 1972; man of yr award Ohega Psi Phi 1967; outstanding clothing design award The Yardley Co 1969; award to study fashion design under Italian Designer Emilio Pucci 1966; outstanding Military Achievements 1972. **MILITARY SERVICE:** USAF e-5 staff sgt. **BUSINESS ADDRESS:** Mr Creation Inc, Pima Co, Tucson, AZ.

LOCKETT, BROOKER THOMAS
Educational administrator. **PERSONAL:** Born Aug 28, 1925, Albany, GA. **EDUCATION:** Fisk Univ, bA 1948; Atlanta Univ, MA 1958; Peabody Coll for Teachers, Post Grad 1960; Emory Univ, 1964; Atlanta Univ, PhD Ed Admin 1984. **CAREER:** DM Therrell HS Atlanta, instr, chmn dept english 1968; W GA Coll Carrollton, instr english 1972-73. **ORGANIZATIONS:** Mem NEA, Natl Soc Secondary Ed, Natl Council Teachers English, GA Assoc Ed, Atlanta Area English Assoc, Natl Soc Study Ed Soc, Negro History & Life, NAACP, Alpha Phi Alpha; chmn constl com Fisk Univ, Emblem YMCA; past exec sec Met Atlanta Assoc for Blind So Ed Found; grantee Ed Admin Seminar Peabody Coll for Teacher 1960; mem Natl Def Lang Inst, Vanderbilt Univ 1962, Knoxville Coll 1962, Inst Humanities Knoxville Coll 1965.

LOCKETT, HAROLD JAMES
Physician, assistant director. **PERSONAL:** Born Jul 17, 1924, Wilmington, DE; widowed; children: Cherie. **EDUCATION:** IN Univ, AB 1948; Meharry Med Coll, MD 1952; Univ of MI Med Ctr, Psych 1956; Hawthorn Ctr, Child Psych 1958; LA County Gen Hosp internship. **CAREER:** Univ of MI, asst prof psych; Hawthorn Ctr, staff psych 1958-71, asst dir 1971-. **ORGANIZATIONS:** Clinical asst prof Univ of MI Med School; psych consult Ferndale Sch Dist, St Peter's Home, St Francis Home for Boys; bd dir Spaulding for Children 1968-, mem Amer Psych Assoc; fellow Amer Acad of Child & Adolescent Psych; fellow Amer Ortho Psych Assoc; Black Psychiatric Assn. **HONORS/ACHIEVEMENTS:** Several articles in professional jrnls & books. **MILITARY SERVICE:** Infantry s/sgt 1943-45; Med Corp 2nd lt 1950. **HOME ADDRESS:** 319 Brookside Dr, Ann Arbor, MI 48105.

LOCKETT, JAMES D.
Educator. **EDUCATION:** Morehouse Coll, BA Political Science; Atlanta Univ, MA Library Svcs, DA History/Humanities; Case Western Reserve Univ, MA Political Science. **CAREER:** Allen Univ, natl teaching fellow 1966-67; TN State Univ, asst prof political sci and history 1967-69; Tuskegee Inst, asst prof 1969-70; St Augustine Coll, acting chmn dept of history political sci black studies social scis 1970-72; MS Valley State Univ, asst prof in the TCCP 1972-74; Opportunities Industrialization Ctr, staff; Stillman Coll, assoc prof history political sci and geography 1977-. **ORGANIZATIONS:** Pres West AL Chap Assn for the Study of Afro-Amer Life and History 1983; apptd mem economic adv council AL Conf of Black Mayors Inc 1984; chmn of the bd AL Afro-Amer/Black Hall of Fame 1985; appointed mem economic develop comm AL Conf of Black Mayors Inc 1985; appointed mem advisory bd AL Historical Commn 1985; mem NEA, Amer Library Assoc, Assoc of Higher Educ, Amer Historical Assoc, Southern Historical Assoc, Org of Amer Historians, Assoc for the Study of Afro-Amer Life and History, Birmingham Astronomical Soc; mem, Advisory Bd AL History Com; associate commissioner, AL Election Comm; mem Executive Comm W AL Oral History Assn; campus coordinator of Kettering Public Leadership; coordinator of SREB. **HONORS/ACHIEVEMENTS:** Certificate of Appreciation Atlanta-Fulton Co Dist Social Sci Fair 1983; one of principal founders and first pres West AL Chap Assoc for the Study of Afro-Amer Life and History; one of principal founders AL Afro-Amer/Black Hall of Fame; first chmn of bd of dirs AL Afro-Amer Hall of Fame; articles published in US Black and the News, Negro History Bulletin, Presbyterian Survey, Aerospace Historian; compiled bibliography of all works by and about Dr Martin Luther King Jr and the Civil Rights Movement for Dr Martin Luther King Jr Ctr for Social Change Atlanta GA; nominated for NAFEO Achievement Awd; articles published in US Black and the News, Negro History Bulletin, Presbyterian Survey, Aerospace Historian; books James A Garfield and Chester A Arthur in vol 1 and 2 of a five volume work, edited by Frank N Magill, Great Lives from History, A Biographical Survey Pasadena CA, Salem Press Inc 1987; saluted as Great Black Alabamian by Govenor's AL Reunion; nominated as best teacher. **BUSINESS ADDRESS:** Associate Professor, Stillman College, PO Box 1430, Tuscaloosa, AL 35403.

LOCKETTE, AGNES LOUISE
Educator. **PERSONAL:** Born Apr 21, 1927, Albany, GA; daughter of Fred Pollard (deceased) and Wessie McIntee (deceased); married Emory W Sr; children: Sharon Anita, Emory W Jr. **EDUCATION:** Albany State Coll, Albany, GA, BS, 1948; Univ of Nevada, Las Vegas, MEd, 1967; Univ of Arizonia, Tucson, EdD, 1972. **CAREER:** Carver HS Dawson, GA, teacher, 1948-49; Clark County School Dist, Las Vegas, NV, teacher, 1952-70; Univ of Nevada ,Las Vegas, prof of educ, 1972-84, prof, 1971-. **ORGANIZATIONS:** Kappa Delta Pi; Delta Kappa Gamma Soc; Natl Concil of Teachers of English; Amer Assn Univ Women; mem, Phi Kappa Phi; Assn of Childhood Educ Intl; Natl Soc of Profs; Natl Educ Assn; mem,

Grace Community Church, Boulder City, NV; chairperson, Clark Co Air Pollution Hearing Bd, Las Vegas, NV; financial secretary, Grace Community Church, 1989-. **HONORS/ACHIEVEMENTS:** Honors Hazard Training School, Albany State Coll, GA; diploma, Albany State Coll HS Albany State Coll, GA; class valedictorian; first woman appointed to Clark County Air Pollution Hearing Bd, 1972-; Comm Leaders & Noteworthy Amers, 1976-77; The World Who's Who of Women, 1977; Personalities of the W & Midwest 1978; Intl Who's Who of Intellectuals, 1978; Keynote speaker Annual Honor Convocation Univ of NV Las Vegas 1984; Disting Teaching Awd Coll of Educ Univ of NV Las Vegas 1984; Intl Register of Biographies, 1985; Outstanding Service Award, Westside School Alumni Assoc, 1988. **BUSINESS ADDRESS:** Emeritus Prof of Education, University of Nevada Las Vegas, 4505 Maryland Parkway, Las Vegas, NV 89005.

LOCKETTE, NICOLE MERCEDES
Entertainment management executive. **PERSONAL:** Born Mar 08, 1958, Cincinnati, OH. **EDUCATION:** Hampton Univ, BA 1980; Howard Univ Sch of Law, JD 1988. **CAREER:** Design Concepts Washington DC, partner 1982-84; The Thomas "Fats" Waller Entertainment Law Archives, prog coord 1985-86; Keinman & Krasilovsky PC, legal asst 1986-87; ITC Entertainment Inc, legal clerk 1986-87; Earthling Mgmt, pres 1986-. **HONORS/ACHIEVEMENTS:** Design Awd Soft Sculpture Exhibit entitled "Working for the Government" Natl Archives Smithsonian Inst Washington DC 1980-81.

LOCKHART, JAMES B.
Attorney, insurance executive. **PERSONAL:** Born May 27, 1936, NYC, NY; married Ruth; children: Marc. **EDUCATION:** Palmer Meml Inst, 1954; Boston Univ Coll of Bus Adminstrn, ES 1957; Boston Univ Sch of Law, JD 1959. **CAREER:** Transamerica Corp, vice pres pub affairs, 1979—; Budget Rent A Car Corp, sr vice pres 1971-79; Rivers Lockhart Clayter & Lawrence attys at law Chicago, partner 1967-71; City of Chicago, asst corp counsel 1965-67; Office of Chief Counsel US Treas Dept, atty adv 1963-65. **ORGANIZATIONS:** Bd of dirs Pub Affairs Council; deputy CA Business Roundtable; deputy Industry & Educ Counc; mem Commonwealth Club of CA; mem World Affairs Council; mem World Trade Club; mem Moraga Country Club; mem SC Bar Assn; mem Kappa Alpha Psi Frat; Episcopalian; former mem bd dir & v chmn of Legal Legislative Com Intl Franchise Assn; Car & Truck Rental & Leasing Assn; mem Gen Practice Antitrust Trademark & Corp Com; Am Bar Assn; Corp Antitrust & Real Estate Com; IL Bar Assn; Corp Law Dept Com; Chicago Bar Assn former mem bd trustees & exec com Episcopal Charities Diocese of Chicago; mem Standing Com Episcopal Diocese of Chicago; mem Com on Legislation of the Conv of the Episcopal Diocese of Chicago; vice pres & exec com Lawrence Hall Sch for Boys; pres, Downtown Assn of San Francisco; past chair, Bay Area Urban League; dir and vice chair, Public Broadcasting Service; dir, Oakland Private Industry Council; Bohemian Club; dir and vice chair, City Club of San Francisco. **HONORS/ACHIEVEMENTS:** Outstanding contbns to the comm WBEE (Radio) Comm Serv Citation 1973; San Francisco Planning and Urban Research Associeate Award for creative corporate community leadership, 1988. **MILITARY SERVICE:** AUS asst army staff judge advocate 1960-63. **BUSINESS ADDRESS:** Vice President-Public Affairs, Transamerica Corp, 600 Montgomery St, San Francisco, CA 94111.

LOCKHART, LILLIE MARIE
Educational administration. **PERSONAL:** Born Feb 08, 1943, Houston, TX; daughter of Lucian Lucellus Lockhart, Jr (deceased) and Lillian Lee Lockhart (deceased); married Marc Riedel, Jan 02, 1982. **EDUCATION:** Univ of Denver, BA 1962; Carnegie-Mellon Univ, MA 1971; Univ of Pittsburgh, PhD 1972. **CAREER:** Allegheny County Communtiy Coll, dir oper hi-support 1971-73; Temple Univ English Language Enrichment Ctr, asst prof, coord acad support 1973-75; Univ of Houston Downtown Campus, dean student serv 1975-76; Southern IL Univ, dir Center for basic skills 1977-83; Southern IL Univ, dir Undergraduate Academic Services 1983-; Southern IL project dir Career Preparation Program 1987-88. **ORGANIZATIONS:** Consultant IL State Bd of Ed 1980-84; in-svc consultant Reg Supt of Schools 1982; book reviewer Little Brown & Co Publs 1982; prog vice pres Phi Delta Kappa Ed Frat SIUC 1984-85; memshp vice pres Phi Delta Kappa Ed Frat SIUC 1983-84; natl prog chmn Amer Soc of Criminology 1984-85; consult US Office of Ed Maj Nat Univ IL State Bd of Ed/Dept of Corrections 1971-; reaffirm/accred teams So Assoc of Schools & Colls Atlanta 1978-; Editorial Board, Journal of Equal Opportunity Assn; principal investigator Project Upward Bound. **HONORS/ACHIEVEMENTS:** US Dept of Ed Grad Fellowships 1969-71; Legion of Honor Chapel of Four Chaplains Philadelphia PA 1974; Acad Grant Univ of Denver 1960-62; 1st black yearbook queen Univ of Denver 1962; created and developed The Southern IL Career Preparation Program for Rural Minority Youth; writing and developing grants Women and Minorities. **BUSINESS ADDRESS:** Dir Undergraduate Academic Service, Southern Illinois Univ at Carbondale, Woody Hall, Room 104, Carbondale, IL 62901.

LOCKHART, ROBERT W.
Dental surgeon. **PERSONAL:** Born Jul 19, 1941, Houston, TX; married Betty J Moore; children: Robert III, Chris, Lisa. **EDUCATION:** Univ of TX, BA 1962, DDS 1966, MPH 1973. **CAREER:** Harris Co Hosp Sunnyside Clinic, dir dept serv 1973-74; CA George Dental Soc, vice pres 1974-; Private practice, dentist 1968-. **ORGANIZATIONS:** Mem Amer & Natl Dental Assoc, Acad Gen Dentistry, Amer Assoc Publ Health Dentists, Alpha Phi Alpha, NAACP, Urban League. **MILITARY SERVICE:** AUS Dental Corps capt 1966-68.

LOCKHART, VERDREE
Educator. **PERSONAL:** Born Oct 21, 1924, Louisville, GA; son of Fred D Lockhart and Minnie B Roberson Lockhart; married Louise Howard, Aug 05, 1950; children: Verdree II, Vera Louise, Cargile, Fernandez, Abigail Williams. **EDUCATION:** Tuskegee Inst, BS 1949; Atlanta Univ, MA 1957; George Peabody Coll, 1960; Atlanta Univ, PhD 1975. **CAREER:** Jefferson County HS, teacher 1949-58, counselor 1958-63; GA Dept of Edn, education consultant 1963-80; Atlanta Univ, vice pres 1981-82; Phillips College, dean of educ 1984-85; Regional Asbestos Inspector 1985-86; North Fulton High School, counselor 1986-. **ORGANIZATIONS:** Alpha Phi Alpha Fraternity 1949-; Former state pres Assn of Counseling & Devel 1963-; mem exec, bd, Atlanta Area Cncl Boy Scouts of Amer 1965-; GA Governor's Medallions Gov State of GA 1967-68; Silver Beaver Awd Atlanta Area Council Boy Scouts 1968; treas Atlanta Br NAACP 1972-; Alumni Merit Awd Atlanta Univ Alumni Assn 1972; trustee Atlanta Univ 1975-81; mem Tuskegee Univ Forest Resource Cncl 1978; Alumni Brother of the year Alpha Phi Alpha 1980; vice pres Tuskegee Univ Natl Alumni Assn 1980-84; Parlimentarian, Eta Lambda Chapter Alpha Phi Alpha 1980-88; Amer Coll Personnel Assn 1981-; Phi Delta Kappa 1981; mem Bd of Dir Economic Opportunity Atlanta Inc 1985-; spec asst toGen Pres; Amer Vocational Assoc; GA Adult Educ Assn; GA Educ Artic Com; GA Assn of Educators; former mem Youth Employment & Planning Cncl Atlanta CETA Office; mem Mayor's Task Force on Public Education 1986-; pres Atlanta Univ Consortion Chapter Phi Delta Kappa 1988-89; chairperson Constitution and Procedures Committee Eta Lambda Chapter Alpha Phi Alpha Fraternity 1988-. **HONORS/ACHIEVEMENTS:** Alumni Merit Award Atlanta Univ Alumni Assn 1972; Silver Beaver Award Atlanta Area Council Boy Scouts Amer 1968; GA Governor's Medallions Gov State of GA 1967-68; Alumni Brother of the Year Alpha Phi Alpha Frat 1980; Presidential Award Atlanta Univ Consortium Chater of Phi Delta Kappa 1989. **MILITARY SERVICE:** AUS retired M/Sgt 22 years; WW II Victory Medal; Good Conduct Medal 1943-45; Amer Serv Medal; Asiatic Pacific Service Medal; 2 Bronze Stars. **HOME ADDRESS:** 2964 Peek Rd NW, Atlanta, GA 30318.

LOCKHART-MOSS, EUNICE JEAN
Business executive. **PERSONAL:** Born Nov 28, 1942, Mt Olive, MS; daughter of Ernest L Lockhart and Eunice O Lockhart; divorced; children: Tracy, Cory. **EDUCATION:** Univ of WI Milwaukee, BS 1963;Univ of WI Milwaukee, Ms 1975. **CAREER:** E Inc Milwaukee, pres 1977-; CS Mott Found Flint, prog off 1976-77; The Johnson Found Racine, program assoc 1972-76; Dominican Coll Racine, instr 1971-72; Racine Eviron Com Educ Trust, admin 1969-71. **ORGANIZATIONS:** Bd of dirs Council on Founds 1974-80; pres, E Incorporated, 1977-; bd of dirs Found Cntr 1979-82; pension & annuity bd City of Milwaukee 1979-82; bd of dirs United Way of Greater Milwaukee 1978-82; personnel bd st of WI 1979-82; mem pres Commn on US Liberian Relations 1980; bd dir Maryville Coll TN 1984-; author In Seach of Parnterships; publisher, E Publications, 1988-; mem DC Commission on the Arts, 1988-; mem, Mayor's Advisory Board for the Howard Theater, 1989-. **BUSINESS ADDRESS:** President, E Inc, 1201 Pennsylvania Ave NW, Ste 720, Washington, DC 20004.

LOCKLEY, CLYDE WILLIAM
Law enforcement. **PERSONAL:** Born Jul 14, 1938, Jacksonville, FL; married Mary Frances Jordan; children: Rhonda M, Karen P, Larry K, Brian K, Darrell W, Rodney A. **EDUCATION:** Liberal Arts LA SW Coll, AA 1971; CA State U, BA Pol Sci 1974; USC, Masters of Pub Adminstrn 1976; CA Highway Patrol Academy, Completion 1965; CA Specialized Inst, Completion Certificate 1976;Univ of VA, Cert of Completion Criminal Justice 1978; FBI Academy Quantico VA, Completion 1978. **CAREER:** CA Highway Patrol, lieutenant; Compton Comm Coll, part-time instr criminal justice. **ORGANIZATIONS:** V chmn Environmental Commn City of Cars on CA; mem FBI Nat Academy Asso; mem CA Assn of Hwy Patrolman LA Co Peace Officers Assn; life mem USC Alumni Assn; mem CA State Employees Assn. **HONORS/ACHIEVEMENTS:** Outstanding Airman-Special Honor Guard VIP Guard March AFB CA 1959; %Certificates basic training, intermediate, advance, supervision, administrative CA State Commn of Peace Office Standards & Training; full-time Comm Coll Tching; credentials in Police Science, Political Science, Public Adminstr, Administrative-Supervision. **MILITARY SERVICE:** USAF airman second 1956-60. **BUSINESS ADDRESS:** California Highway Patrol, 4520 S Sepulveda Blvd, Culver City, CA 90230.

LOCKLIN, JAMES R.
Business manager. **PERSONAL:** Born Jan 20, 1958, Monroe, GA; married Sherry Jackson; children: Jacques. **EDUCATION:** Clark Coll, BA 1980. **CAREER:** WCLK-FM, announcer/reporter/promo mgr 1978-80; WAOK-AM, admin asst 1979-80; WORL-AM, news, public affairs dir 1980; Clarke Cty GA, probation officer 1980-82, WXAG-AM, gen mgr 1982-83; First Class Mktg Ltd, pres 1984-; Leon Farmer & Co, vice pres marketing 1983-. **ORGANIZATIONS:** Mem Citizens for Better Govt 1981-, Athens Bus & Professional League 1981-, Athens Ad Club 1983-; bd mem Morton Theatre Corp 1984, Hope Haven School 1985-, Athens Tutorial Prog 1985; exec comm Athens Area Human Rel Cncl, Clarke Co Partnership with Business & Edn, Alcohol Countermeasures Prog; mem Zeta Beta Beta Chap of Omega Psi Phi Frat Inc. **HONORS/ACHIEVEMENTS:** Participant Class of Leadership Athens 1985; Steering Comm Finance C0-Chairperson Leadership Athens 1985-86. **HOME ADDRESS:** 151 Chesterfield Rd, Bogart, GA 30622. **BUSINESS ADDRESS:** Vice President Marketing, Leon Farmer & Co, PO Box 249, Athens, GA 30603.

LOCKMAN, NORMAN ALTON
Journalist. **PERSONAL:** Born Jul 11, 1938, Kennett Square, PA; married Virginia Trainer; children: Holly Beth, Carey Paige, Sarah Elizabeth. **EDUCATION:** Kenneth Consolidated Sch, 1956; Penn State, 1957-58; Dept of Defense Sch of Journalism, 1963. **CAREER:** Edwards AFB, spts edtr/co-edtr 1962-64; WCOJ Coatesville, PA, announcer 1965-66; Kennett News, columnist 1965-68; DE Dept Mental Health, therapist/social worker 1967-69; Wilm News-Jour, reporter/WA Corresp 1969-75; WILM Wilmington, DE, talk show host 1972-73; The Boston Globe, state house bur chief 1975-84; The News-Journal Papers, managing editor. **ORGANIZATIONS:** Bd mem UUA Mass Bay Dist 1979; trustee Unitarian-Univ Assn 1983-84; mem natl Press Club 1972-73; mem Capitol Press Club 1974; mem The Monday Club 1985; MA St House Press Assn; NAACP. **HONORS/ACHIEVEMENTS:** MD/DE/DC Press Assn Awards for Loc Col 1968-69; Pulitzer Special Local Reporting The Boston Globe 1984. **MILITARY SERVICE:** USAF 1961-65. **BUSINESS ADDRESS:** Managing Editor, The New-Journal Papers/Gannett, 831 Orange St, Box 1111, Wilmington, DE 19899.

LOCKMAN-BROOKS, LINDA
Advertising manager. **PERSONAL:** Born Jan 21, 1953, St Louis, MO; married W E Brooks; children: Morgan;Garrett. **EDUCATION:** Univ of MO, BA 1973. **CAREER:** Trans World Airlines, mgr personnel 1974-77, mgr marketing 1977-80; J Walter Thompson, acct exec 1980-83; American Express Co, mgr advertising;1983-85, Director-FSA Marketing 1985-86, Dir Advertising & Public Relations 1986. **ORGANIZATIONS:** Mem The Edges Group 1975-85; charter mem Corporate Women's Network Inc 1976-85; mem Delta Sigma Theta Sorority 1970-85; Junior League of the Oranges & SHort Hills 1986. **HONORS/ACHIEVEMENTS:** Award of Merit Black Media Inc 1975. **BUSINESS ADDRESS:** Dir Advertising & PR, American Express Co, 610 Fairview Rd, Charlotte, NC.

LOCKWOOD, JAMES CLINTON
Educator. **PERSONAL:** Born May 22, 1946, Philadelphia, PA; son of William and Signora; married Carolyn Francina McGowan; children: Jason. **EDUCATION:** West Chester State Coll, BS 1968; Salisbury State Coll, attended 1972-76. **CAREER:** Oxford Area School Dist PA, fifth grade teacher 1968-70; Lincoln Univ PA, asst in financial aid 1970-71; Salisbury State MD, dir of financial aid 1971-77; Coppin State Coll MD, dir of financial aid 1977-78; Univ of MD Eastern Shore, dir of financial aid 1979-. **ORGANIZATIONS:** Mem Natl Appeals Panel US Dept of Educ 1981; USMD chairperson 1985-86, pres1982-84, vice pres 1982

DE, DC, MD Assoc of Student Financial Aid Admin Inc; MD trainer College Bd 1983-84; instructor Sociology Univ of MD Eastern Shore 1983, 1985-89 (part time); mem Natl Assoc of Student Financial Aid Admin Task Force on Minority Concerns 1982-83; exec cncl Eastern Assoc of Student Financial Aid Admin 1982-84; instructor Moton Consortium on Admissions and Financial Aid 1986; life mem US Chess Federation. **BUSINESS ADDRESS:** Dir of Financial Aid, Univ of MD Eastern Shore, Backbone Rd, Princess Anne, MD 21853.

LOCKWOOD, LEE JONATHAN
Photographer, author. **PERSONAL:** Born May 04, 1932, NYC; married Joyce Greenfield; children: Andrew William, Gillian. **EDUCATION:** Boston U, BA 1954; Columbia U, post-grad 1956-59. **CAREER:** Bunte Illustrierte, US corr 1959-61; Black Star Agy, staff photographer 1961-; Contemporary Photographer Quar, editor 1963-66; WGBH-TV Boston, Rockefeller artist-in-residence 1967-68. **ORGANIZATIONS:** Mem Author's Guild; Assn Heliographers. **HONORS/ACHIEVEMENTS:** Recip awd for best fgn reporting Oversears Press Club 1967; author Castro's Cuba Cuba's Fidel 1967; conversation with Eldridge Cleaver Algiers Modest Hopes 1972; producer TV documentary The Holy Outlaw 1970; photographs & arts in natl mags.

LODGE, HERMAN
City official. **PERSONAL:** Born Nov 08, 1928, Midville, GA; married Anna Roberts; children: Terri Patrice. **EDUCATION:** Ft Valley State Coll, BS 1951; Med Field Serv School, Cert 1952. **CAREER:** Corry HS, teacher, coach 1953-54; VA Hosp, corrective therapist 1953-84; Burke Cty Bd of Commissioner, vice chmn. **ORGANIZATIONS:** Exec sec Burke Cty Improvement Assoc Inc 1961-; pres bd of dir Burke Cty Housing Improvement Inc 1979-; bd mem GA Housing Coaltion 1980-; pres of bd of dir GA Legal Serv 1981-; past pres Burke Cty Black Coalition Inc 1982-83. **HONORS/ACHIEVEMENTS:** Econ Devel Phi Beta Sigma 1982; Bill of Rights Awd Amer Civil Liberties Union of GA 1982; Outstanding Comm Service Mt Olive AME Church 1983; Pres Citation NAEOHE 1984. **MILITARY SERVICE:** AUS corpl 1951-53. **HOME ADDRESS:** 1139 Quaker Rd, Waynesboro, GA 30830. **BUSINESS ADDRESS:** Vice Chairman, Burke County Bd of Commiss, Burke County Courthouse, Waynesboro, GA 30830.

LOEB, CHARLES P., JR.
Educator. **PERSONAL:** Born Dec 06, 1927, Eunice, LA. **EDUCATION:** Leland Coll, BA 1954; So U, MEd 1960;Univ TX, LSU;Univ SW LA, Further Study;Univ OK; Xavier U; Nicholls U. **CAREER:** St Landry Parish Sch Bd, supr 1954-67; Carter G Woodson HS prin 1966-68; st landry parish sch bd, supr 1966; asst supt; emergency sch Aid, dir. **ORGANIZATIONS:** Act chmn LA State Dept Educ Adult Educ Adv Council; chmn LA Educ Assn Adult Educ Sect; mem Adv Com Spl Serv LSU; bd dirs United Progressive Investment Corp; ARC; LA State Dept Edn; Am Legion Post #519; Satellite Civic & Social Club; Frontiers Intl Opelousas Club. **HONORS/ACHIEVEMENTS:** Citizen of yr award 1965; frontiers Intl distinguish award 1973. **MILITARY SERVICE:** AUS pfc 1946-47. **BUSINESS ADDRESS:** PO Box 310, Opelousas, LA 70570.

LOFTON, ANDREW JAMES
Government official. **PERSONAL:** Born Oct 16, 1950, Longstreet, LA; son of Junius E Lofton and Ethel M Peyton Lofton; married Veroa J Minnix, May 30, 1970; children: Junius, Lamar. **EDUCATION:** Univ of Puget Sound, Tacoma, WA, BA, 1972; Univ of Washington, Seattle, WA, MUP, 1974. **CAREER:** Office of Policy Planning, Seattle WA, human resource planner, 1974-76; capital improvement planner, 1976-78; Dept of Comm Devel, Seattle, WA, block grant advisor, 1978-80; deputy dir, 1980-87; Dept of License & Consumer Affairs, Seattle WA, 1987-. **ORGANIZATIONS:** Mem, Natl Forum for Black Public Admins, 1983-88; Region X Council mem, Blacks in Govt, 1983-87; pres, Seattle Chapter, Blacks in Govt, 1983-86; bd mem, Seattle Mgmt Assn, 1986-87, bd mem, Rainier High Boys & Girls Club, 1987-; Region IX Representative, Conf of Minority Public Administrators, 1989-. **BUSINESS ADDRESS:** Dir,, Dept of Licenses & Consumer Affairs, 102 Municipal Bldg, Seattle, WA 98104.

LOFTON, DOROTHY W.
Educator. **PERSONAL:** Born Jun 22, 1925, Marlin, TX; married Donald D; children: Ronald, Deanne Michelle. **EDUCATION:** Baylor U, BA 1971. **CAREER:** Marlin Independent Sch Dist, tchr. **ORGANIZATIONS:** Mem TX Classroom Tchrs Assn; Falls County Tchrs Assn; TX State Tchrs Assn; pres City Fedn Women's Clubs; vice pres Strivette Club; sec Falconer- stampsComm Center; sec-treas Marlin Parents Orgn; treas Carrie Adams Dist TX Women & Girls' Clubs. **HONORS/ACHIEVEMENTS:** Adult leader certificate 4-H Council 1974.

LOFTON, JAMES
Professional athlete. **PERSONAL:** Born Jul 05, 1956, Fort Ord, CA; married Beverly; children: David James. **EDUCATION:** Stanford Univ, BS 1978. **CAREER:** Real Estate & Investment Firm, employed off-season; Green Bay Packers, professional football wide receiver 1978-. **ORGANIZATIONS:** Served as state chmn Mental Health Assoc of WI; state chmn March of Dimes Superwalk Walk America; chmn Greater Green Bay Jog-A-Thon 1981-84; chmn March ofDimes Golf Tournament 1983-84; Packer United Way Spokesman 1983; volunteer Special Olympics; bd mem Athletes for Youth; speaker Boys Club of Milwaukee; volunteer Urban League; mem bd of dirs Milwaukee Ballet; serves as team player rep and is officer-at-large mem of the NFL Players Assoc Exec Comm. **HONORS/ACHIEVEMENTS:** First Green Bay Packer Receiver to catch 100 passes in first two seasons 1978-79; posted second best average per catch among NFC's Top Ten Receivers 1979; consensus NFL & All Rookie Selection; NFC's Offensive Rookie of the Year by NFL Players Assoc; led NFL in average yards per reception in both 1983 and 1984; named to Pro Football Writers of Amer all-NFL team 1983; NEA all-pro team 1984; player NFL Pro Bowl 1980,82,83,84,85,86. **BUSINESS ADDRESS:** Green Bay Packers, 1265 Lombardi Ave, Green Bay, WI 54303.

LOFTON, MELLANESE (NEE SLAUGHTER)
Attorney. **PERSONAL:** Born Aug 24, 1941, Houston, TX; married Jimmy Dale; children: Frederick Douglas, Robin Mellanese. **EDUCATION:** Univ of TX, BA 1962; Univ of CA Boalt Hall Sch of Law, JD 1974. **CAREER:** Law Offices of Mellanese S Lofton, atty; US Steel Corp, atty 1974-82; Jacobs Sills & Coblentz, law clerk 1973-74; Contra Costa Co, social worker 1969-73; Alameda & Co, social worker employ couns 1963-69; Univ Of TX, photographic tech 1961-62. **ORGANIZATIONS:** Mem PA Bar; CA State Bar; Am Bar Assn; Alameda Cty Bar Assn; mem Alpha Kappa Alpha Sor; Publ Project Future. **BUSINESS ADDRESS:** Attorney, Law Office of Mellanese Lofton, 4464 A Willow Rd, Pleasanton, CA 94106.

LOGAN, ALPHONSO
Elected official. **PERSONAL:** Born Aug 15, 1908, Hot Springs, AR; married Dorothy Lynne Lockhart; children: Sybil Buford, Rachael Top, Mildred Summerville, Eloise Natl. **EDUCATION:** Knoxville Coll, BS, 1933; Univ of Oklahoma, Counseling, 1966; Henderson State, Hrs on Masters, 1967. **CAREER:** Hot Springs School System, math teacher, coach, 1934-42; Employment Security Div, counselor, 1966-79; Justice of the Peace, Garland County. **ORGANIZATIONS:** Pres, NAACP, 1938; secretary, NAACP, 1942; secretary, Lamplighters Black Caucus, 1948, 1984; pres, Business & Professional Men's Club, 1980. **HONORS/ACHIEVEMENTS:** Plaque Sangston Alumni Assn 1983; plaque Sharon Seventh Day Adventist Church 1984. **MILITARY SERVICE:** USAF Sgt 3; Good Conduct Amer Theatre 1942. **BUSINESS ADDRESS:** Justice of the Peace, Gardland Co Dist 3, Hot Springs, AR 71901.

LOGAN, BERTIE HAWTHORNE
Clergyman, journalist. **PERSONAL:** Born Sep 13, 1897, Richmond, VA; married Beatrice M; children: Bertie Hawthorne, Jr, Roper Lee, Sue Eloise. **EDUCATION:** VA Union, AB 1920; Grad Comm Sch of Religion 1942;Univ Pittsburgh, BS 1948. **CAREER:** Waiter cook 1916-19; Westinghouse Air Brake Co, stationery & publicity dept 1918-1926; Keystone Singers, mgr 1917-47; retired journalist; Bapt Temple Ch, minister. **ORGANIZATIONS:** Author of two books on religious educ 1943 & 1955; numerous citations awards honors. **HONORS/ACHIEVEMENTS:** Author of two books on religious educ 1943 & 1955; numerous citations awards honors. **BUSINESS ADDRESS:** American Bapt Theol Seminary, Pres Pittsburgh Ext, Nashville, TN.

LOGAN, DAVID
Professional football player. **PERSONAL:** Born Oct 25, 1956, Pittsburgh, PA. **EDUCATION:** Univ of Pittsburgh, BA, BS Urban & Black Studies 1979. **CAREER:** Tampa Bay Buccaneers, nose tackle 1979-85. **HONORS/ACHIEVEMENTS:** Named to The Sporting News NFL All-Star Team 1984. **BUSINESS ADDRESS:** Nose Tackle, Tampa Bay Buccaneers, One Buccaneer Place, Tampa, FL 33607.

LOGAN, FRENISE A.
Educator. **PERSONAL:** Born Sep 30, 1920, Albany, GA; married Mary Esther Whitfield; children: Jewel, Frenise II. **EDUCATION:** Fisk Univ, BA 1943; Case Western Reserve Univ, MA 1957, PhD 1953; Univ of Bombay India, Post-doctoral study 1954. **CAREER:** Univ of Zambia, visiting prof 1968-70; Amer Embassy Lusaka Zambia, 1st sec Cultural Affairs 1968-70; Bur of Educ & Cultural Affairs US Dept of State Wash DC, chief East Central & So Africa 1970-73; Amer Embassy Nairobi Kenya, 1st sec cultural affairs 1973-77; Museum of African Art WA DC, assoc dir 1977-78; Amer Consulate Kaduna Nigeria, 1st consultant & br public affairs officer 1978-80; NC A&T State Univ, prof of history 1980-. **ORGANIZATIONS:** Mem Amer Hist Assoc, So Hist Assoc, Assoc for Study of Afro-Amer Life & Hist, Alpha Phi Alpha, East African Acad, Indian Hist Congress; mem Carolinas Symposium on British Studies. **HONORS/ACHIEVEMENTS:** Author "Negro in NC 1876-1894"; num articles in scholarly publs in US & India; num hons, awds, fellowships & grants including Commendation for Outstanding Achievements in Intl & Educ/Cultural Exchanges from the United States Dept of State, Bureau of Educ and Cultural Affairs 1977. **MILITARY SERVICE:** USAAF 1943-45. **BUSINESS ADDRESS:** Professor, NC A&T State Univeristy, Department of Histroy, Greensboro, NC 27411.

LOGAN, GEORGE, III
Attorney. **PERSONAL:** Born Dec 23, 1942, Elizabeth, NJ; married Sheila Jacqueline Miller; children: Natalie, Camille, George Spencer. **EDUCATION:** Rutgers Coll, BA 1964; Rutgers Sch of Law, JD 1967. **CAREER:** Logan Marton Halladay & Hall, atty 1978-; atty self-emp 1976-78; Lindauer & Logan, 1975-76; Lindauer & Goldberg, asso atty 1975; Karl & N Stewart, 1973-74; Deprima Aranda & de Leon, 1972-73; USAF, asst staff judge advoc 1968-72; Ctr for Constl Rights, staff atty 1967-68. **ORGANIZATIONS:** Pres AZ Black Lawyers Assn; mem Phoenix Urban League; Nat Bat Assn; Am Civil Liberties Union; bd of dir Casa Linda Lodge; former pres Comm Legal Serv; City of Phoenix Com on Aging; Joint Legis Comm Conflict of Interest. **MILITARY SERVICE:** USAF cpt 1968-72. **BUSINESS ADDRESS:** Asst Dir, Management Review, AZ Dept of Econ Sec, 1140 E Washington, Phoenix, AZ 85034.

LOGAN, JOSEPH LEROY
Physician. **PERSONAL:** Born Feb 24, 1922, Mansfield, OH; children: Leanora, JoAnn. **EDUCATION:** OH State Univ, BA 1947; Howard Univ Med Sch, 1951; special training Montefiore Hosp; post-grad Columbia Univ, Univ Chicago, OH State Univ, Harvard Univ; Civil Aero Med Inst. **CAREER:** Staff mem, Trumbull Memorial Hosp; St Joseph's Del Ohio State Medical Assn; Trumbull Co, dep coroner; Warren School Dist, athletic physician; Ohio State Univ, mem athletic medical team; Miami Dolphins, Cleveland Browns, asst med physician; private practice, physician 1952-. **ORGANIZATIONS:** Lifetime mem NAACP; mem Piltos Intl Assn; mem Air Force Assn; sponsor of Paul Warfield through high school, college, and professional career to Hall of Fame; physician in charge of Sickle Cell Testing in Warren OH 1973; appeared on the Dorothy Fuldheim TV show, Cleveland OH, to discuss veneral disease; sponsored a building & recreation prog for children in Warren OH; past interviewer for Northeastern Ohio Coll of Medicine & advisor for minority students; mem Med Intl Assistance; mem Med Staff, Ohio State Univ Athletics; mem Pilots Intl Assn; mem Air Force Assn; mem Buckeye Medical Assn; mem Amer Coll of Gen Practice; mem Science Group of Natl Inst of Health; mem Trumbull Co Metro Housing Authority; bd dir Planned Parenthood Assn; mem OSU Med Assn, NMA, AMA, Aerospace Med Assn, Civil Med Assn, Amer Acad Gen Practice, NY Acad Sci; fellow Amer Geriatric Soc; mem Intl Coll Angiology, Flying Physicians Assn, British Med Assn; author "Venereal Disease: Problems in Schools, Rural Areas & Among Juveniles," Archives of Environmental Health. **HONORS/ACHIEVEMENTS:** Civic Award for Man of the Year, Urban League, 1973; Volunteer Serv Award, 1973; Outstanding American, 1976; United Negro College Fund Award, 1985; Award of Merit, Ohio Planning Comm; Trumbull Memorial Hospital delegete to the Amer Med Assn; elected to Amer Coll of Physicians. **MILITARY SERVICE:** AUS s/sgt 1943-46; WW II Victory Ribbon; Good Conduct Medal; Amer Theater Ribbon; Three Bronze Stars. **BUSINESS ADDRESS:** 1129 Youngstown Rd, Warren, OH 44484.

LOGAN, JUAN LEON
Artist. **PERSONAL:** Born Aug 16, 1946, Nashville, TN; married Geraldine Johnson; children: Kim, Sidney, Jonathan. **EDUCATION:** Howard Univ; Clark Coll. **CAREER:** Selected One-Man Exhibitions, Rowe Gallery Univ of NC at Charlotte 1983; Natl Museum of African Art Wash,DC 1980; Winston-Salem Univ Art Gallery 1979; SC State Coll 1976; Winthrop Gallery Winthrop Coll 1974; Davidson Coll Art Gallery 1973; Charlotte Arts and Cultural Soc 1970; Jefferson Gallery 1969; Selected Juried and Invit Exhibitions, Drawing Invitational Somerhill Gallery 1984; Six North Carolina Artists Pfeiffer Coll Gallery 1984; Afro-Amer Artists of NC Center/Gallery 1984; LA Watercolor Soc's 14th Annual Intl Exhibit 1984; 1984 Invitational/Black and White Spirit Square Arts Center 1984. **HONORS/ACHIEVEMENTS:** 1st Place Award LA Watercolor Society's 14 Ann Intl Exhibit New Orleans 1984; The Romare Bearden Award for Creativity/Innovation of Medium Carnegie Inst 1972; Honorable Mention-PIC Award/Nonprocess Educ Posters Assoc Printing Co Charlotte, NC 1974. **MILITARY SERVICE:** USAF. **HOME ADDRESS:** 305 Henry's Chapel Rd, Belmont, NC 28012.

LOGAN, LINDA ANN
Consumer goods manufacturer. **PERSONAL:** Born Aug 07, 1950, Cincinnati, OH. **EDUCATION:** Fisk Univ, BA 1972; Xavier Univ, MBA 1975. **CAREER:** Frigidaire/General Motors, mktg analyst 1972-75; IBM, mktg trainee 1975-76; Drackett Co/Bristol Myers, project dir 1977-82, mgr consumer rsch 1982-84, sr mgr consumer rsch 1984-. **ORGANIZATIONS:** Mem Alpha Kappa Alpha Sorority 1970-; visiting prof Natl Urban League Black Exec Exchange Program 1978-; mem Natl Assoc of Female Execs 1982-; youth prog chairperson YMCA Black Achievers Program 1983-84; bd mem Gross Branch YMCA 1984-85; vice pres membership bd of dirs Amer Mktg Assoc 1985-86; exec sec bd of dirs Cincinnati Scholarship Found 1986-88; exec adv bd Amer Mktg Assoc 1986-89; mem Natl Black MBA Assoc 1986-; account mgr United Way Campaign 1987. **HONORS/ACHIEVEMENTS:** YMCA Black Achiever Award 1981; Outstanding Alumni Black Achiever YMCA 1982. **HOME ADDRESS:** 7624 Castleton Place, Cincinnati, OH 45237. **BUSINESS ADDRESS:** Sr Manager Consumer Research, The Drackett Company, 201 E 4th St, Cincinnati, OH 45202.

LOGAN, LLOYD
Pharmacist. **PERSONAL:** Born Dec 27, 1932, Columbia, MO; married Lottie A Pecot; children: Terri, Connie, Gerald, Michael, Kevin. **EDUCATION:** PurdueUniv 1951-52; Belleville Jr Coll 1953-54; St Louis Coll of Pharmacy, BS 1958. **CAREER:** Dau of Charity Shared Servs Assn, asst dir of purchasing servs 1972-; Rhodes Med Supply Inc, sec 1968-72; Mound City Pharmacy, owner 1962-; Dome Pharmacy, owner 1980-; dir pharmacy & purchasing 1966-69; chief pharmacist 1959-67; St LouisUniv Hosp, staff pharmacist 1958-59. **ORGANIZATIONS:** Mem Shared Servs Adv Panel Am Hosp Assn; pres People Inc 1967-68; sec 1967-69, pres 1973-74 hi Delta Mu Med Frat; mem YMCA; adv com Help Inc; treas Page Comm Devel Corp 1971-77; trustee Lindell Hosp 1974-78; mem Am Pharmaceutical Assn; Nat Pharm Assn; pres Mound City Pharm Assn 1964; Nat Assn of Retail Druggists Patentee; mem St Engelbert Sch Bd 1969-76; pres 1973-76; pres St Louis Archdiocesan Sch Bd 1977-79; mem bd St Louis Urban League 1980-. **HONORS/ACHIEVEMENTS:** Marquis' & Who's Who in Am; Who's Who in Midwest 1969-. **MILITARY SERVICE:** USAF 1952-56. **BUSINESS ADDRESS:** 7806 Natural Bridge Rd, St Louis, MO 63121.

LOGAN, THOMAS W. S., SR.
Episcopal minister. **PERSONAL:** Born Mar 19, 1912, Philadelphia, PA; son of John Richard Logan and Mary Harbison Logan; married Hermione Hill, Sep 03, 1938; children: Thomas, Jr. **EDUCATION:** Johnson C Smith Univ 1930-33; Lincoln U, AB 1935; Gen Theol Sem, cert 1935-38; Philadelphia Div Sch, STM 1941. **CAREER:** Calvary Epis Ch, Philadelphia PA, rector & canon 1945-84, rector emeritus, 1984—; St Michaels, vicar 1940-45, rector, 1945; St Augustine, NY, vicar 1938-39; St Philips, New York NY, curate 1938-39. **ORGANIZATIONS:** Past pres Tribune Chrtrs 1945-69; past pres Nat Ch Wrkrs conf 1951-61; chpln Philadelphia police 1968-; trustee Haverford St Hosp 1970-; fndr Parkside YMCA1945; past pres Philadelphia YMCA 1946-47; life mem Central HS; life mem Lincoln U; life mem NAACP; bd mem Darby NAACP; past pres Hampton Min conf 1960-61; dean smr sch St Paul; pub dir Blk Cler Dir Epis Ch; past grnd mstr Prince Hall Masons 1968-69; life mem Alphia Phi Alpha; past grnd chpln 1973-74; past imp chpln Inperial Coun Shrinedon 1970-71; 1st asst grnd chpln IBPOEW 1968-; past grnd chpln Frontiers Int 1971; fndr/past & pres/chpln Philadelphia Chptr of Frontier 1945 65-67. **HONORS/ACHIEVEMENTS:** Afro-Am aw 1944; Philadelphia Tribune Char aw 1968; Demolay consult aw 1966; hon mem Cornish Post 292 1944; bd Eme Philadelphia USO 1944; LHL, St Augustine's College, 1982; LLD, Lincoln Univ, 1985, VA Seminary, 1989. **HOME ADDRESS:** 46 Lincoln Ave, Yeadon, PA 19050.

LOGAN, WILLIS HUBERT
Executive director. **PERSONAL:** Born Nov 23, 1943, Springfield, IL; married Joyce A Day; children: Gennea, Andre. **EDUCATION:** Western ILUniv 1943; Sangamon State U, BA 1972. **CAREER:** Dept of Community Devel & Programs Springfield IL, exec dir present; Dept of Conservation, employ coord 1979; IL Nat Bank, bank teller 1967; Allis Chalmers, machine operator 1963; Springfield Recreation Commn, youth supr 1962. **ORGANIZATIONS:** Mem Frontiers Intl 1976; v chmn Spfld Planning Commn 1979; chmn Spfld Sangamon Co Reg Planning Commn 1980; bd mem United Fund 1976; pres Springfield E Assn 1977; sec Alpha Phi Alpha Mu Delta Lambda 1980. **HONORS/ACHIEVEMENTS:** Community serv award NAACP 1977; community serv award United Way 1978. **MILITARY SERVICE:** AUS sgt e-4 1965-67. **BUSINESS ADDRESS:** Dept of Community Devel Progs, 601 E Jefferson St second floo, Springfield, IL 62701.

LOGUE-KINDER, JOAN
Business executive. **PERSONAL:** Born Oct 26, 1943, Richmond, VA; daughter of John Thomas Logue and Helen Harvey Logue; married Lowell A Henry Jr, 1963 (divorced 1983); children: Lowell A Henry III, Catherine Dionne Henry, Christopher Logue Henry; married Randolph S Kinder, Dec 1987. **EDUCATION:** Wheaton Coll, attended 1959-62; Adelphi Univ, BA 1964; Mercy Coll, Certificate in Educ 1971; New York Univ. **CAREER:** TWA NYC, ticket agent 1964-65; US Census Bureau, admin asst to dist mgr 1970; Bd of Educ Yonkers, social studies tchr/admin 1971-75; Natl Black Network, dir public relations 1976-83; NBN Broadcasting Inc, vice pres 1983-; The World Inst of Black Communication Inc, co-dir, co-founder, 1978-. **ORGANIZATIONS:** Bd dirs Girl Scout Council of Greater NY 1985-; bd dirs Natl PUSH 1985; bd dirs NY Chap PUSH 1983; consultand KLM Royal Dutch Airlines 1976; consultant Kentucky Fried Chicken 1976; consultant ATESTA Spanish Natl Tourist Bd 1977; asst coord Howard Samuels for Gov NY 1974; advance pers Rep Morris Udall 1976; bd dirs Nigerian-Amer Friendship Soc; mem 100 Black Women; del White House Conf on Small Business; coord Natl Assn of Black Owned Broadcasters 1977-; counsultant, The Sony Corporation; sr black media advisor, Dukakis-Bentsen. **HONORS/ACHIEVEMENTS:** Excellence in Media Award Inst of New Cinema Artists Inc 1984; co-pub "Communications Excellence to Black Audiences" CEBA Exhibit Awards Journ 1978-; creator and developer The Action Woman Radio Prog 1979-. **BUSINESS ADDRESS:** Vice President, NBN Broadcasting Inc, 10 Columbus Circle, New York, NY 10019.

LOKEMAN, JOSEPH R.
Accountant. **PERSONAL:** Born Jul 24, 1935, Baltimore; son of Joseph Miles Lokeman and Beulah V Lokeman; married Shirley M Morse; children: Pamela, Kimberly, Sherre, Shereen. **EDUCATION:** AS 1967; BS 1969. **CAREER:** Bureau Public Debt Treasury, auditor 1968-70; Bureau Accounts Treasury, staff accountant 1971-73; Bureau Govt Financial Operations Treasury, systems accountant 1973-, chief general ledger branch, treasury 1984; public accountant, enrolled agent, private practice 1967-. **ORGANIZATIONS:** Mem Fed Govt Accountants Assn; Nat Soc Public Accountants; Nat Soc Black Accountants; Nat Soc Enrolled Agts; MD Soc Accountants, Notary Public; Mem White Oak Civic Assn Silver Spring. **MILITARY SERVICE:** AUS 1957-59. **BUSINESS ADDRESS:** Public Accountant, J Royce Lokeman PA, 4022 Edmondson Ave, Baltimore, MD 21229.

LOMAS, RONALD LEROY
Educator. **PERSONAL:** Born May 21, 1942, Rock Island, IL. **EDUCATION:** Western IL Univ, BA 1965, MA 1967; Bowling Green State Univ, PhD 1976. **CAREER:** Western IL Univ, grad asst dept of speech 1965-66; Bowling Green State Univ, grad asst dept of speech 1969-70; Lorain Cty Comm Coll instr speech & dir forensics, reg adv 1969; Bowling Green State Univ, instr speech & ethnic studies 1970-, asst to dir of ethenic studies 1970-75; Univ of Cincinnati Med School, coord of supportive serv 1975-76; TX So Univ Houston, assoc prof speech comm. **ORGANIZATIONS:** Chmn faculty eval comm Lorain Cty Comm Coll 1968-69; chmn Minority Affairs Comm 1968-69; adv Black Progressives 1968-69; consult & lectr Black Culture St Pauls Episcopal Church Maumee OH 1972-73; leadership consult B'nai B'rith Youth Org S Euclid OH 1972-73, Lorain Council 1970-71, MI Council 1973; communication consult Title I Grant Toledo Minority Businessmen 1974-75; mem Intl Commun Assoc, Speech Commun Assoc; producer Black Perspectives WBGU Channel 70 1971;producer, host & writer of prog WBGU Channel 57 1973. **HONORS/ACHIEVEMENTS:** Foreign Serv Scholar 1964; Omicron Delta Kappa 1973; Disting Faculty Awd 1974; Outstanding Instr TSU 1980. **BUSINESS ADDRESS:** Assoc Professor Speech Comm, Texas SouthernUniv, 3201 Wheeler St, Houston, TX 77004.

LOMAX, DERVEY A.
Electronic specialist, mayor. **CAREER:** Naval Electronic Systems Command, electronic splst; City Council of Coll Park, elected 1957-65; City Council, re-elected 1967-73; Coll Park MD, elected mayor 1973. **ORGANIZATIONS:** Mem Mat Washington Council of Gov't Policy Com on Pub Safety; mem City Univ Liason Com; founder Lakeland Civic Assn; founder Lakeland Boy Scout Troop; former mem Am Legion; former mem bd dir Coll Park Boys Club; former vice pres Coll Park Boys Club; former mem Prince George's Boys Club; basketball coach forBoys Club of Coll Park 7 yrs; founded Local Civil Air Patrol Unit. **BUSINESS ADDRESS:** Ofc of the Mayor, 4500 Knox Rd, College Park, MD 20740.

LOMAX, FRANK, III
Executive director. **PERSONAL:** Born Jun 30, 1937, Akron, OH; married Margaret Louise Satterwhite; children: Dawn, Kelly, Frank, Dionne. **EDUCATION:** BS 1962; MA. **CAREER:** Columbus Urban League, exec dir; Akron Mod Cities, dir 1969-73; Summit Co United Comm Counc, plng asso 1968-69; Nghbrhd Ctr, dir 1965-68; Akron Pub Sch, tchr coach 1962-65. **ORGANIZATIONS:** Pres OH Counc Urban League; dir v chmn Columbus Metro Sch Com; bd mem Friends in Action; Columbus Metro Club; Columbus Area Ldrshp Prog; deleg Columbus PTA Counc. **HONORS/ACHIEVEMENTS:** Achiev award Akron Comm Serv Commin & Urban League 1971; Columbus Pub Sch 1976. **MILITARY SERVICE:** USMC reserv 8 yrs. **BUSINESS ADDRESS:** 700 Bryden Rd, Columbus, OH 43215.

LOMAX, MICHAEL WILKINS
Business executive. **PERSONAL:** Born in Philadelphia, PA; married Dr A Faye Rogers; children: Lauren. **EDUCATION:** St Josephs Univ, BS Soc 1973; Ins Inst of Amer. **CAREER:** Allstate Insurance Co, dist claim mgr 1977, div claim mgr 1978-79, asst reg claim mgr 1979-83, reg claim mgr 1983-84. **ORGANIZATIONS:** Mem Insurance Ed Dir Soc 1982-; Black Exec Exchange Prog Urban League 1982; bd of dir Brockport Found 1983-84. **BUSINESS ADDRESS:** Regional Claim Manger, Allstate Insurance Company, 1111 Old Eagle School Rd, Valley Forge, PA 19482.

LOMAX, PEARL CLEAGE
Association executive. **PERSONAL:** Born Dec 07, 1948, Springfield, MA; married Michael. **EDUCATION:** Spelman Coll, BA 1971; Howard U; Yale U; Atlanta U;Univ Of WI. **CAREER:** City of Atlanta, dir of communications 1974-; Dept of Pub Affairs WQXI-TV, exec producer 1972-73; So Educ Program Inc, asst dir 1971-72; Martin Luther King Jr Memorial Library, archival staff 1970-71; author of Poetry plays & various other articles. **ORGANIZATIONS:** Mem bd dir Atlanta Cntr for Black Art 1970-71. **BUSINESS ADDRESS:** City Hall, 68 Mitchell St SW, Atlanta, GA 30303.

LOMAX, WALTER P.
Physician. **PERSONAL:** Born Jul 31, 1932, Philadelphia; children: 3 girls, 3 ?, boys. **EDUCATION:** Lasalle Coll, AB 1953; Hahnemann Med Coll 1957. **CAREER:** Pvt practice 1958. **ORGANIZATIONS:** Mem Med Soc E PA; AMA; Philadelphia Co Med Soc. **BUSINESS ADDRESS:** 1300 S 18 St, Philadelphia, PA 19146.

LOMOTEY, KOFI
Associate executive, educator. **PERSONAL:** Born Jul 13, 1950, New York, NY; married Aama Nahuja; children: Faida, Juba, Mbeja. **EDUCATION:** Oberlin Coll, BA 1970-74-; Cleveland State Univ, MEd 1976-78; Stanford Univ, MA 1979-81; Stanford Univ, PhD 1985. **CAREER:** Shule Ya Kujitambua School, dir 1973-77; Oberlin Coll, instr 1977-79; Stanford Univ, instr 1979-82; Shule Ya Taifa School, dir 1981-84; Canada Coll, instr 1983-84; Univ CA Santa Cruz, lecturer 1985-; Santa Clara Univ, lecturer 1987-; Council of Independent

Black Inst, natl exec officer. **ORGANIZATIONS:** Convenor Nairobi Secretariat 1979-82; exec comm mem Pan Afrikan Secretariat 1982-84; treas Nairobi Secretariat 1983-. **HONORS/ACHIEVEMENTS:** Nation Bldg Awd The Council of Independent Black Inst 1977; Black Physical Fitness The Inst of Positive Ed 1978.

LONDON, CLEMENT B.G.
Educator. **PERSONAL:** Born Sep 12, 1928; son of John London and Henrietta Myrtle Simmons-London; married Pearl Cynthia Knight; children: Tony, Chet, Sharon, Shawn, Tamika. **EDUCATION:** City Clg CityUniv of NY, BA 1967, MA 1969; Tchr Clg ColumbiaUniv NY, EdM 1973, EdD 1974; Doctoral Dissertation, "A Strategy for the Organization Soc Stds for the Jr Scndry Schls Trinidad-Tobago, Implications for Curriculum Design". **CAREER:** Toco & Morvant EC Elem Sch Trinidad-Tobago Sch Systm Trinidad, W Indies, asst prncpl 1953-60; St Augustine Parochial Sch Brooklyn, NY, tchr 1960-61; Harlem Hosp Sch of Nrsng New York City, sec/registrar 1963-66; Development & Training Ctr Distrbtv Trades Inc NYC, instr math & engl 1967-70; Crossroads Alternative HS East 105th St NYC, assc prncl dean stdnt 1970-71; Tchr Clg ColumbiaUniv NYC, grad asst & instrctnl asst 1971-73; Intermediate Sch136 Manhattan NYC, substitute tchr math 1974; Fordham Univ at Lincoln Center, Graduate School of Educ, asst prof of educ 1974-82, assoc prof of educ 1982-. **ORGANIZATIONS:** Mem Natl Alliance Black Sch Educators 1975; bd dir Alumni Assn City College City Univ of NY 1976; mem Editorial Bd College Student Journal, editor Curriculum for a Career Ed & Dev Demonstration Proj for Youth 1978; editorial consultant Natl Council Negro Women 1978; mem Assn Teacher Educators 1979; summer chmn Div Curriculum & Teaching 1979; bd elders Council of Mwamko Wa Siasa Educ Institute 1980; mem Natl Sch Bd Assn 1980-; mem Organization American Historians 1980; mem Assn Caribbean Studies 1980-; mem American Assn for Advancement of Humanities 1980; mem American Academy Political & Social Science 1980-; mem rprtr bd dir Kappa Alpha Psi 1980-; faculty secretary Sch of Educ Fordham Univ 1981; mem Journal of Curiculum Theorizing 1982-; dir Project Real 1984; bd dir Solidaridad Humana 1984; faculty adv, exec comm mem Phi Delta Kappa; mem Kappa Delta Pi; adv bd, curriculum consultant La Nueva Raza Halfway House program; coordinator Curriculum Studies program div of Curriculum & Teaching; bd mem African Heritage Studies Assn; coordinator Social Studies Educ. **HONORS/ACHIEVEMENTS:** Author of numerous rsrch pblctns & profsnl actvts including, "Afro-Am Cath Sch NYC", Black Educator in theUniv Role as Moral Authority Clg Stdnt Jrnl Monograph 18(1 Pt 2), Career Ed for Educational Ldrs, A Focus on Decision Making 1983, "Crucibles of Caribbean Conditions, Factors of Understanding for Tchg & Lrng Carribbean Stdnts Am Ed Settings" Jrnl of Carribbean Studies 2,2&3 Autumn/Winter 1982 pp 182-188, "Career & Emplymnt, Critical Factors in Ed Plng" Am-Afrcn Jrnl Rsrch & Ed 1981, Black Women of Valor Afrcn Heritage Studies Assc Nwsltr p 9 1976, WABC Radio Brdcst "Conf Call, The Carribbean & Latin Am" 3 Hr Brdcst 1979-80; Position Paper "The Toco Composite School, An Experiment in Progress" 1977; 2 Video-taped TV Apprnc Natl TV Trinidad, W Indies Featuring Edctnly Oriented Issues 1976-77; recipient of notable am awrd Am Biographical Inst 1976-77; recpnt cert of aprctn Vol Serv Salem Comm Serv Cncl New York City 1981; cited celebration of Clement Lonfon day Toco Anglican Elem Sch 1977; spec rcgntn & awrd for outstndg qltys Project Real 1983; author of "On Wings of Change," 1989,"Through Caribbean Eyes," 1989, "Test-taking Skills: Guidelines for Curricular and Instructional Practices," 1989, "A Piagetian Constructivist Perspective on Curriculum," 1989. **BUSINESS ADDRESS:** Associate Professor of Educ, Fordham Univ Grad Sch of Educ, 113 W 60th St, New York, NY 10023.

LONDON, EDDIE
Analyst. **PERSONAL:** Born Nov 25, 1934, Morgan City, LA; married Doris J; children: Lori B. **EDUCATION:** AA; BA; MBA. **CAREER:** Pacific Missile Range, supr mgmt analyst present; Navy, operations research analyst 1971-73; Navy, mgmt analyst 1970-71; design technician 1965-70. **ORGANIZATIONS:** Pres Oxnard-Ventura NAACP; bd of Professional Employees; past chmn Grass Roots Poverty Program. **MILITARY SERVICE:** AUS sgt e-5 1953-56. **BUSINESS ADDRESS:** Pacific Missile Range, Point Mugu, CA 93042.

LONDON, EDWARD CHARLES
Real estate educator. **PERSONAL:** Born Aug 18, 1944, Memphis, TN; son of Mr & Ms James London Sr; divorced; children: Edwin C. **EDUCATION:** LeMoyne-Owen Coll, BA 1967; Atlanta Univ, MBA 1972; John Marshall Law School, JD 1975. **CAREER:** Metropolitan Atlanta Rapid Transit Authority, federal grants/sr accountant 1973-75, sr contracts admin 1975-79, mgr of contracts 1979-81; Edward C London & Assocs Real Estate Appraisers, Mgmt Consultants, pres 1981-; Real Estate Mgmt Brokers Inst/Natl Assoc of Real Estate Brokers, natl dir 1984-; Empire Real Estate Board Inc, pres/ceo 1989-. **ORGANIZATIONS:** Chmn bd of dirs Reach-Out Inc 1979-84; comm mem GA Real Estate Commn Educ Adv Comm 1983-87; coord Pastor's Higher Ground Task Force Antioch Baptist Church 1984-86; bd mem GA Chapter Natl Soc of Real Estate Appraisers 1986-87; mem Real Estate Educators Assoc 1987; mem bd of dirs 1st vice pres Empire Real Estate Bd Inc 1987; mem Alpha Phi Alpha, NAACP, The Atlanta Business League, The Atlanta Exchange, The Progressive Alliance, The Minority Purchasing Council of the Atlanta Chamber of Commerce; sr mem & certified real estate appraiser Natl Assoc of Real Estate Appraisers 1987; certified senior mem, National Society of Real Estate Appraisers 1989-; mem, Board of Zoning Appeals, Fulton County GA 1987-; mem, Bd of Dirctors, Community Housing Resources Board of Atlanta 1987-. **HONORS/ACHIEVEMENTS:** Outstanding Leadership Awd Reach-Out Inc 1981; Assoc Partner Awd, Century Club Awd Butler St YMCA 1986; Outstanding & Dedicated Serv Awd Empire Real Estate Bd Inc 1986; publications Principles of Apartment Management, 1983, Basic Budgeting & Accounting for Property Management, 1986; Real Estate Broker of the Year, Empire Real Estate Board Inc 1988. **MILITARY SERVICE:** AUS E-5 2 yrs; Superior Cadet Awd, Expert Rifleman Badge, Bronze Star, USRVN Serv Medal, Good Conduct Medal 1968-70. **BUSINESS ADDRESS:** Natl Dir, Real Est Mgmt Brokers Inst, 136 Marietta St NW, Atlanta, GA 30301.

LONDON, ROBERTA LEVY
Construction company executive. **PERSONAL:** Born in New York, NY; daughter of Henry Edward Levy and Carrie Belle Calier Levy; married Lester London, Jr, Jul 30, 1955. **EDUCATION:** Nassau Community Coll, Garden City, NY, AA, 1972; Hunter Coll, New York, NY, BA, 1977; Queens Coll, Flushing, NY, educl credits, 1978; Adelphi Univ, Garden City, NY, Graduate Certificate, 1988. **CAREER:** Presbyterian Church, New York NY, mgr Human Resources, Program Agency, 1981-89; Turner/Santa Fe Construction Co., Brooklyn NY, coordinator of Local Laws 49/50, 1989-. **ORGANIZATIONS:** Dist Clerk, Lakeview Public Library; mem, One Hundred Black Women of Long Island, 1979-83; Governor, Northeast Dist, Natl Assn of Negro Business and Professional Women's Clubs, Inc, 1987-; mem, Delta Sigma Theta Sorority, Inc; mem, bd of trustees, Union Baptist Church, Hempstead, NY. **HONORS/ACHIEVEMENTS:** Community Service Award, Long Island Black History Comm, 1981; Finalist, Long Island Woman of the Year, 1986; Sojourner Truth Award for Meritorious Serv, Brooklyn Club, Natl Assn of Negro Business and Professional Women's Clubs, Inc, 1989. **HOME ADDRESS:** 425 Columbia Ave, Rockville Centre, NY 11570.

LONEY, CAROLYN PATRICIA
Business executive. **PERSONAL:** Born Jun 16, 1944, New York, NY; daughter of Daniel Loney and Edna Loney. **EDUCATION:** Morgan State Univ, BS 1969; Columbia Univ, MBA 1971. **CAREER:** Royal Globe Ins Co, rater 1962-65; NY NAACP, br mgr 1965; Human Resources Admin, field auditor 1967; NY State Senate, rsch worker 1967; Citibank, corp lending officer 1969-77; Federal Research Bank of NY, special asst; Citibank, vice pres. **ORGANIZATIONS:** Bd dir New Harlem YWCA 1975-76; mem 100 Black Women 1977-; adv bd Columbia Univ Alumni 1971-; mem Urban Bankers Coalition 1973-80; mem Natl Assn of Accountants 1973; mem Natl Credit & Financial Women's Org 1972-74; founder Carolyn P Lonely Schlrsp Awd Morgan State Univ; mem Amer Mgmt Assn 1977-; Uptown C of C 1977-. **HONORS/ACHIEVEMENTS:** Outstanding Instr of Yr ICBO 1974; Black Achiever Awd Harlem YMCA 1973.

LONG, ANDU TRISA
Fundraising. **PERSONAL:** Born May 13, 1958, Akron, OH; daughter of George W Long Jr and Pauline Long. **EDUCATION:** Univ of Akron, BS 1981, MS 1987. **CAREER:** Delta Sigma Theta Zeta Alpha Chapt, faculty advisor; Delta Sigma Theta AkronChapt, pres; Univ of Akron, asst dir alumni relations 1983-85, associate dir 1985-88, assoc dir development & dir annual giving 1988-. **ORGANIZATIONS:** Mem Council for the Advancement & Support of Ed; 3 vice pres Delta Sigma Theta 1984-86; 1st vice pres 1986-88, pres 1988-.; mem Ohio Assoc of Women Deans, Admin and Counselors, Youth Motivational Task, Force Team; UA Martin Luther King Jr Scholarship Fund Committee; Univ of Akron, contract professional advisory committee to the president. **HONORS/ACHIEVEMENTS:** Outstanding Employee, Univ of Akron Board of Trustees 1985; Woman of the Year, Akron Women's History Project 1988; Raised over $300,000 in private support fo Univ of Akron 1988-89. **BUSINESS ADDRESS:** Assoc Dir of Development, Dir of Annual Giving Programs, The Univ of Akron, Development Foundation, Akron, OH 44325.

LONG, BARBARA COLLIER See BRIDGEFORTH, BARBARA

LONG, CHARLES H.
Educator. **PERSONAL:** Born Aug 23, 1926, Little Rock, AR; son of Samuel Preston Long and Geneva Diamond Thompson; married Alice M Freeman; children: John, Carolyn, Christopher, David. **EDUCATION:** Dunbar Jr Coll, Diploma 1946; Univ of Chicago, BD 1953, PhD 1961; Dickinson Coll, LHD 1971. **CAREER:** Univ of Chicago, instr 1956-60, asst prof 1960-64, assoc prof 1964-70, prof 1970-74; Duke Univ, prof history of religion 1974-; Univ of NC Chapel Hill, Wm Rand Keenan jr prof 1974-88; Jeanette K Watson prof, history of religions, Syracuse Univ. **ORGANIZATIONS:** Past pres Amer Acad of Religion; mem Soc for Religion in Higher Edn; Intl Assn of Historians of Religion; Soc for Study of Black Religion; American Society for Study of Religion. **HONORS/ACHIEVEMENTS:** Guggenheim Fellowship 1971; mem bd of govs Univ of NC Press Natl Humanities Faclty; consult Encyclopaedia Brittanica. **MILITARY SERVICE:** USAAF Sgt 1944-46. **BUSINESS ADDRESS:** Jeanette K Watson Prof, History of Religions Dept of Religion, 501 Hall of Languages, Syracuse Univ, Syracuse, NY 13244.

LONG, HENRY ANDREW
Physician. **PERSONAL:** Born Aug 16, 1910, Elmore Co, AL; married Vennie Smiley; children: Walter, Henry Jr, Sherida. **EDUCATION:** OH State Univ, BA 1935, MD 1939. **CAREER:** Homer G Phillips Hosp, intern 1939-40; Hamilton OH, physician 1940-74. **ORGANIZATIONS:** Mem Natl Med Assoc, AMA, Butler Cty Med Soc, Amer Acad of Gen Physicians, Buckeye State Med, Dental & Pharm Assoc, Cincinnati Med Assoc, OH State Med Assoc; pres, mem Butler Metro Housing Auth 1945-74; deacon Pilgrim Bapt Church 1945-77; mem Amer Legion, Mason, Shriner, Eastern Stars, Elks; mgr Long Bros Cab Co 1947-50; pres Booker T Washington Comm Ctr; mem C of C; bd dir Butler Cty AAA; dr HA Long Health Ctr, Butler Cty Comm Action 1974. **HONORS/ACHIEVEMENTS:** Hon Girl Scout; Hon Plaque Awd Pilgrim Bapt Church for outstanding work in church & comm.

LONG, IRENE
Physician. **PERSONAL:** Born in Cleveland, OH. **EDUCATION:** Northwestern Univ Evanston IL, attended; St Louis Univ School of Med, attended. **CAREER:** Cleveland Clinic, internship gen surgery; Mt Sinai Hosp, resd; Wright State Univ, Dayton OH, resd aerospace med; NASA, chief of med oper 1982-. **HONORS/ACHIEVEMENTS:** 1st black woman chief of med at NASA. **BUSINESS ADDRESS:** Chief of Medical Operations, NASA, Kennedy Space Center Office, MD-MED, Orlando, FL 32899.

LONG, JAMES, JR.
Company executive. **PERSONAL:** Born Apr 26, 1931, St Francis County, AR; son of James Long, Sr and Almamie Gray Long; married Patricia Hardiman, Apr 18, 1954; children: Karen R Long, Kathryn C Long, Kaye Patrice H Long Allen, James, III. **EDUCATION:** Lincoln Univ of MO, BS Educ/Commn ROTC Corp Engineers, 1954; attened MO at Kansas City, MO, 1965-66; Northeastern Univ, Boston, MA, Graduate School MBA, 1976. **CAREER:** US Govt Army, Ft Belvoir, officer/US Army, 1954-57, Ft Riley, KS, officer/US Army Corp Engineers, 1954-57; Lincoln Univ of Jefferson City, MO, asst instructor & dir student union, 1957-61; Lincoln Sr High School, Kansas City, MO, teacher/coach, 1961-64; Western Elec Co, Lee's Summit, MO, supv mfg & safety dir, 1964-69; Gen Electric Co, Lynn MA, mgr mfg manpower devel, mgr personnel practices, 1970-74, mgr employee relations LUO, 1974-81, mgr EO & compliance, 1982-. **ORGANIZATIONS:** Chmn, Lynn Corp Advisory Bd Salvation Army, 1982-86; dir, Private Industry Council, 1983-; dir, Private Industry Council, 1983-; dir, Action for Boston Community Devel, 1984-; dir, vice pres, Industrial Relations MA Pre-Engineering Program, 1985-; dir, Lynn, MA Historical Soc, 1986-. **HONORS/ACHIEVEMENTS:** Developed a group of black square dancers for TV, 1957; No 1 Safety Program, Western Electric's Parent Body, 1964; Omega Man of the Year, Beta Omega Graduate Chapters, 1967; Past Basileus Award, Beta Omega Chapter Omega Psi Phi Fraternity, Inc, 1988; co-founder, The Henry Buckner School, St Paul AME Church Cambridge, MA, 1973;

Hall of Fame ROTC, Lincoln Univ of MO, 1975; Others Award, Salvation Army, 1986; organized "The Soulful Squares" during black history month, 1988; Gen Electric Managerial Award, 1989; co-organized Minority Mentor's Program at Gen Electric, 1989. **MILITARY SERVICE:** US Army Corp Engineers, lst Lieutenant, 1954-57; No l Student, Ft Riley, KS, Fifty Army Physical Training Instructors Academy, 1955.

LONG, JAMES ALEXANDER
Communications executive. **PERSONAL:** Born Dec 26, 1926, Jacksonville, FL; son of Willie Long and Ruby Long; married Ruth Beatrice Mitchell; children: John Alexander. **EDUCATION:** North Carolina A&T State Univ, BS 1950; Univ of MI, MA 1962; Wayne State Univ, post grad study. **CAREER:** North Carolina A&T State Coll, instructor of English and journalism 1950-52; St Paul's College, instructor of English and journalism 1952-57; Foch Jr High School, teacher of English & social studies 1957-62, English dept head 1962-65; Cooley High School, guidance counselor 1965-67, asst principal 1967-70; Northwestern High School, principal 1970-72; Storer Broadcasting Co, general exec and coord of training programs 1972-74, mgr of personnel development 1974-80; Storer Communications Inc, corp vice pres of personnel development 1980-87; executive director, American Civil Liberties Union of Florida, 1987-. **ORGANIZATIONS:** Mem Amer Mgmt Assn 1973-; mem Amer Soc of Personnel Admin 1975-; mem Administrative Mgmt Soc, Phi Delta Kappa Educ Frat; mem Industry Labor Council Human Resources Ctr Albertson NY; mem Dade's Employ the Handicapped Comm Miami; exec bd Goodwill Industries Miami; mem Lafayette Park Kiwanis Club; mem Church of the Open Door United Church of Christ; mem Alpha Phi Alpha Frat Inc; mem Alpha Rho Boule Sigma Pi Phi Frat Inc; bd dirs Family Counseling Serv Miami; chairperson employment comm Private Industry Council Miami. **HONORS/ACHIEVEMENTS:** North Carolina A&T State Univ Gate City Alumni Chap Awd; Achiever's Awd Family Christian Assoc of Amer Inc Miami 1986; Presidential Citation Natl Assn for Equal Opportunity in Higher Educ Washington DC 1986. **MILITARY SERVICE:** AAF pfc 1 yr 7 mths. **BUSINESS ADDRESS:** Exec Dir, Amer Civil Liberties Union, 225 NE 34th St, Suite 208, Miami, FL 33137.

LONG, JAMES L.
Superior court judge. **PERSONAL:** Born Dec 07, 1937, Wintergarden, FL; son of James J Long and Susie L Long. **EDUCATION:** San Jose State Coll, BA, 1960; Howard Univ Law School, JD, 1967. **CAREER:** Legislative Counsel Bureau CA State Legislature, grad legal asst; Legal Aid Soc of Sacramento Co, grad legal asst; NAACP Western Region, special counsel;Private Practice, atty; Superior Court Bar Assn Liaison Comm, mem; Superior Court, judge; California State Univ, Sacremento, CA, asst prof, criminal justice. **ORGANIZATIONS:** Hon mem, Wiley W Manual Bar Assn, Sacramento, CA; mem, Appellate Dept Superior Court of Sacramento Co, 1987; mem, Sacramento City/County Commn of the Bicentennial of the US Constitution. **HONORS/ACHIEVEMENTS:** The Law and Justice Award Sacramento Branch NAACP; Outstanding Contribution Award in the Field of Civil Rights Riverside Branch NAACP; sat as Pro Tem Justice of the Supreme Court Dec 9, 1985; assigned Justice Pro Tem to the Court of Appeal Third Appellate Dist 1987; co-author "Amer Minorities, The Justice Issue," Prentice Hall Inc, 1975. **MILITARY SERVICE:** AUS Reserve Corps 2nd lt. **BUSINESS ADDRESS:** Judge, Sacramento Co Superior Court, 720 9th St, Sacramento, CA 95814.

LONG, JAMES S.
Director. **PERSONAL:** Born Apr 03, 1936, Philadelphia, PA; married Betty Harrison; children: James Stanford Jr, Bruce Anthony, Mary Elizabeth. **EDUCATION:** Morgan St Coll, AB econ 1958; Temple U, post grad 1959-61;Univ of DE, post grad 1961-63. **CAREER:** Employee Rel Personnel CBS Inc, dir 1979-; Insl Rel CBS Inc, asst dir 1972-79. **ORGANIZATIONS:** Bd sec S Brunswick Comm Devel Corp NJ 1976-; bd mem consult SEP Prodns Variety Mags 1979-; founer pres Mid-State Unoin Track Club 1976-.

LONG, JOHN BENNIE
Retired educator. **PERSONAL:** Born Apr 04, 1923, Landis, NC; married Esther Clark; children: Sheila Long Hunt, Robert A, Glenn E. **EDUCATION:** Livingstone Coll, BS (Honors) 1949; North Carolina A&T State Univ, MS 1957. **CAREER:** Army 93rd Infantry Div, 1942-46; North Warren High School, teacher coach & athletic dir 1946-50, 1954-66; Salisbury Rowan Comm Serv Council, ctr coord 1966-69; Kannapolis City Schools, classroom teacher 1969-82 (retired). **ORGANIZATIONS:** Post commander 1970-79, veterans serv officer 1984-87 Amer Legion Post 413 1970-79; pres Rowan Veterans Council 1982; life mem The Retired Officers Assoc;life mem Reserve Officers Assoc of the US; comm chmn BSA Troop 373 Sandy Ridge AME Zion Church Landis NC; mem Kappa Alpha Psi Frat; supt church schoolSandy Ridge AME Zion Church. **HONORS/ACHIEVEMENTS:** Beta Kappa Chi Natl Hon Scientific Soc Inc; Dist Awd of Merit BSA Rowan Dist 1976; Veterans Serv Office of the Yr Rowan Veterans Council 1985. **MILITARY SERVICE:** AUS col 37 yrs Commissioned Serv 1950-54, Reserves 1954-83 (retired); Meritorious Serv Medal, Asiatic-Pacific Campaign Medal, Army Reserve Components Achievement Medal; Educ, Ord Co Officers Course, QM Co Officers Course, QM Adv Officers Course Command and Genl Staff Coll; Assoc Logistics Exec Develop Course, Industrial Coll of the Armed Forces. **HOME ADDRESS:** PO Box 771, Kannapolis, NC 28081.

LONG, JOHN EDWARD
Educator. **PERSONAL:** Born Mar 16, 1941, Philadelphia, PA; married Carolyn Yvonne Wakefield. **EDUCATION:** Temple U, BA 1963; Theol Sem of the Reformed Episcopal Ch, BD 1966; Westminister Theol Sem, Th M 1970; Brandeis U, MA PhD 1978. **CAREER:** Western KY Univ, assoc prof of religious studies present. **ORGANIZATIONS:** Mem Am Assn of Tchrs of Arabic 1979; mem Middle East & Studies Assn 1975; mem Middle East Inst 1975; Dissertation Research Fellowship Fulbright-Hays Research Fellow in Algeria 1974-75; Grad Study Fellowship Ford Found Advanced Study Fellowship for Black Am 1972-73; Fellowship to Study Arabic in Tunisia N African Cntr for Arabic Studies 1972. **HONORS/ACHIEVEMENTS:** Dissertation Research Fellowship Fulbright-Hays Research Fellow in Algeria 1974-75; Grad Study Fellowship Ford Found Advanced Study Fellowship for Black Am 1972-73; Fellowship to Study Arabic in Tunisia N African Cntr for Arabic Studies 1972. **BUSINESS ADDRESS:** Western KY Univ, Dept of Philosophy & Religion, Bowling Green, KY 42101.

LONG, JUANITA OUTLAW
Educator. **PERSONAL:** Born in Philadelpha, PA; divorced; children: Thomas Marshall Jr. **EDUCATION:** Boston City Hosp, Nursing Diploma 1943; Washington Univ St Louis, BS Nurs 1956, MS Nurs 1958; Northeastern Univ, Cert of Advanced Grad Studies 1974; Harvard Univ, Grad Study 1975; Boston Univ, EdD 1981. **CAREER:** Boston City Hosp, private duty 1943-44, head nurse 1944-46; Norfolk Comm Hosp, dir of nursing 1944-46; Homer G Phillips School of Nursing, instr 1958-59,clinical coord 1958-59, dir nurs ed 1961-65; Beth Israel Hosp School of Nurs, assoc dir 1965-67; Northeastern Univ, asst prof coord 1967-68; Coll of Nursing Northeastern Univ, acting dean 1968-69, dean & prof 1969-. **ORGANIZATIONS:** Bd of dirs MA Nurses Assoc 1975-77; corporator Lawrence Meml Hosp Medford 1976-78; bd of dirs Med Found Boston 1978-; chmn serv comm Zonta Intl Medford Club 1975-. **HONORS/ACHIEVEMENTS:** Achievement Awd Dept of Health & Hosp Boston 1970; Black Achievers Awd YMCA 1977. **MILITARY SERVICE:** ANC 1st lt 1948-52. **BUSINESS ADDRESS:** Dean, Professor, NortheasternUniv, Coll of Nursing 102 RB, 360 Huntington Ave, Boston, MA 02115.

LONG, NATE
Business executive. **PERSONAL:** Born Apr 18, 1930, Phila; married Gigi; children: Patricia. **EDUCATION:** Univ of MD 1964-66; Wash StateUniv 1974-75. **CAREER:** VPC (Viewer Promotion Center), exec dir 1979-; TvAC (TV for All Children), exec dir 1977-; S by NW (I & II), exec producer 1974-; Oscar Productions Inc, exec dir 1968-; Presidents Council on Youth Opportunity, adminstrv asst 1968-69. **ORGANIZATIONS:** Mem Screen Actors Guild 1973-; mem Directors Guild of Am 1977-; mem activities com Nat Acad of TV Arts & Sci 1979-; mem NAACP 1975-; adv bd mem Nat Black Media Coalition 1977-; chmn childrensTV (sub com) Brain Thrust-Congressional Black Caucus-Arts Com. **HONORS/ACHIEVEMENTS:** USAF commendation USAF 1948-69; Citizen of the Day KIXI Seattle 1969; Profile In Black Core's NY 1970; media award KOMO-TV Seattle 1971; award excellence KBLEColumbus OH 1979. **MILITARY SERVICE:** USAF e-6 1948-69. **BUSINESS ADDRESS:** TvAC, TV for All Children, Hollywood, CA.

LONG, OPHELIA
Hospital administrator. **PERSONAL:** Born Dec 05, 1940; married Henry Long; children: Donald, Celeste, Camille. **EDUCATION:** Los Angeles City Coll, AA 1962; California State Univ, BS 1971; Univ of Southern California, MA in progress. **CAREER:** Kaiser Foundation Hospital, nursing care coord 1966, supervisor ICU 1966, asst dir of CCU 1972-81, dir of nursing 1981-84, hospital admin 1984-. **ORGANIZATIONS:** Mem CA Nurses Assoc 1970-71; pres Council of Black Nurses Inc 1974-75; mem Black Congress on Health & Law 1979, Congressional Black Caucas Health Brain Trust 1979, Adv Com WLACC, CA State LA 1979-; bd of dir Natl Black Nurses Assoc 1982-83; pres Natl Black Nurses Assoc 1983-. **HONORS/ACHIEVEMENTS:** Outstanding Awd Council of Black Nurses 1973; Merit Employees Assoc Kaiser Found Hosp 1974-75; Outstanding Nurse of the Year Awd Council of Black Nurses 1983; Outstanding Alumna Los Angeles City Coll 1984. **BUSINESS ADDRESS:** Hospital Administrator, Kaiser Foundation Hospital, 6041 Cadillac Ave, Los Angeles, CA 90034.

LONG, RICHARD A.
Educator. **PERSONAL:** Born Feb 09, 1927, Philadelphia, PA. **EDUCATION:** Temple Univ, AB 1947, MA 1948; Univ of PA, Grad Study 1948-49; Oxford, 1950; Paris, 1954; Univ of Paris, Fulbright Scholar 1957-58; Univ Poitiers, D 1965. **CAREER:** Morgan State Coll, instr, assoc prof 1951-66; Univ Poitiers, lectr 1964-65; Hampton Inst, prof, mus dir 1966-68; Atlanta Univ, prof, 1968-87; Harvard Univ, lectr 1969-71; Attius Haygood Prof of Interdisciplinary Studies, Emory University, 1987-. **ORGANIZATIONS:** Conducted numerous symposiums, exhibitions, confs; past pres Coll Language Assoc, SE Conf Linguistics; ed bd Phylon. **HONORS/ACHIEVEMENTS:** "Bulletin of Research in the Humanities"; Black Americana (cultural history) 1985; Afro-American Writing (anthology) 1985. **BUSINESS ADDRESS:** Attius Haygood Prof of Interdisciplinary Studies, Emory University, Atlanta, GA 30322.

LONG, STEFFAN
Business executive. **PERSONAL:** Born Oct 06, 1929, Philadelphia, PA. **EDUCATION:** Hward U;Univ of Mex;Univ of Bridgeport; Am Inst of Banking. **CAREER:** CT Nat Bank, vice pres & mgr present. **ORGANIZATIONS:** Past treas Family Serv of SE Fairfield Co; Gtr Bridgeport Heart Assn; bd mgrs YMCA; present exec bd mem Gtr Bridgeport-Stratford NAACP; treas Hall Neighborhood House; bd mem St Marks Day Care Cntr; mem UNA; Nat Negro Coll Fund; 2nd pres UNA of Fairfield Co; pres Japanese Schlrshp ComUniv of Bridgeport; treas Gr Bridgeport Opera Co; treas Gr Bridgeport Vis Nurses Assn; bd mem Italian Comm Cntr Guild. **HONORS/ACHIEVEMENTS:** Barnum Festival Soc Award 1968; Rotary Cluf of Newtown 1952; Bureau of Naval Personnel Award 1946; Spec Guest & Soloist Ch of England; formal invitation toWhite House; citations Mayor of Bridgeport NAACP & Nat Negro Business Women. **BUSINESS ADDRESS:** Vice President, Connecticut Natl Bank, 777 Main St, Hartford, CT 06607.

LONG, WILLIAM H., JR.
Associate judge. **PERSONAL:** Born Jun 07, 1947, Daytona Beach, FL; married Diann C; children: William, III, Cherylen. **EDUCATION:** Univ Of Miami, BA 1968 u of miami law sch, jd 1971. **CAREER:** Opa Locka Mun Ct, apptd assoc judge 1972; Long & Smith PA, partner; Counc on Legal Educ OpporUniv of Miami Law Sch, instr 1970. **ORGANIZATIONS:** Founder United Black StudentsUniv of Miami 1968; pres Black American Law Students Assn 1971; chmn adv com Dade Co Comprehensive Offender Rehab Program Inc; Phi Alpha Delta. **HONORS/ACHIEVEMENTS:** Recipient James E Scott Comm Serv Award 1973. **BUSINESS ADDRESS:** 1 Biscayne Tower, Miami, FL 33131.

LOPES, DAVEY
Professional athlete. **PERSONAL:** Born May 03, 1946, East Providence, RI; married Linda Bandover. **EDUCATION:** Washburn Univ Topeka KS, BS Educ; IA Wesleyan Clge. **CAREER:** Los Angeles Dodgers, infielder/outfielder 1972-81; Oakland Athletics, infielder/outfielder designated hitter 1982-84; Chicago Cubs, infielder/outfiel der 1984-. **HONORS/ACHIEVEMENTS:** Fourth consecutive All-Star appearances with the Dodgers in 1981; top number of fan votes for the 1980 All-Star team; named to The Sporting News AP And UPI All-Star squads in 1979; 1978 named to The Sporting News AP And UPI All-Star teams at second base; Gold Glove; 1978 Dodgers team Cpt; 1976 led the NL in stolen bases 63 for second consecutive year; stole 77 bases a career high in 1975; led Pacific Coast League AAA in steals with 48 in 1972. **BUSINESS ADDRESS:** Chicago Cubs, 1060 W Addison St, Chicago, IL 60613.

LOPES, WILLIAM H.
Educator. **PERSONAL:** Born Oct 25, 1946, Providence, RI; married Sandra Gaines; children: William, Mitchell. **EDUCATION:** Providence Coll, BA 1967; Univ of CT, MA 1972; Univ of RI, MBA; Univ of CT, PhD Educ Admin 1976. **CAREER:** McAlister Middle Sch, vice principal 1972-74; RI College, instr 1974-, exec asst to pres 1977-. **ORGANIZATIONS:** Pub ASCD Annual Bulletin 1970; trustee Providence Public Library; bd dir OIC RI; bd dir RI Grp Health Assn; EPDA Fellow 1970-72; sev art in prof journals; doctoral dis felshp Univ of CT. **HONORS/ACHIEVEMENTS:** RI Educator of the Yr; IBA of RI; Phi Kappa Phi Hon Soc; other grants awds. **BUSINESS ADDRESS:** Executive Asst to President, Rhode Island College, 600 Mount Pleasant Ave, Providence, RI 02908.

LOPEZ, MARY GARDNER
Director, educator. **PERSONAL:** Born Apr 30, 1920, Nashville, TN; daughter of Kossie Gardner Sr and Jean Chandler; married George; children: Sharon, Adrienne. **EDUCATION:** TN State Univ BS; Univ MI MBIA; Fisk Univ; MA degree Newark State Teachers Coll; Columbia Univ; Yeshiva Univ. **CAREER:** Natl Bus Coll Meharry Med Coll, inst; New York City School System, inst 1962-64; NY State Consumer Protection Td, dir consumer educ & rsch; Queens Div NY State Div of Human Rights, dir 1964-84, reg mgr. **ORGANIZATIONS:** Mem Natl Media Women; Alpha Kappa Alpha Sorority; NAACP; Negro Business & Professional Womens Clubs Inc; NAIRO; Notary Public; mem East Elmhurst Civic Assn; Ditmars Blvd Block Assn; Doll League Inc. **HONORS/ACHIEVEMENTS:** Special Cutty Sark Editorial Award; Good Neighbor Award; Journalism Award; radio sta WWRL award in Communications. **BUSINESS ADDRESS:** Regional Manager, State Div Human Rights, 105-11 Ditmars Blvd, East Elmhurst, NY 11369.

LORD, CLYDE ORMOND
Physician. **PERSONAL:** Born Aug 10, 1937, Brooklyn, NY; married Barbara; children: Sharon, Clyde Jr, David. **EDUCATION:** Univ of VT, BA 1959; Meharry Med Coll, MD 1963. **CAREER:** Kings County Hospital, internship 1963-64; Columbia Presbyterian Med Mtr, resd 1964-66, fellow pharmacology 1966-67; AUS Hosp, chief of anesthesia 1967-69, asst prof dept of anesthesia 1969-70; SW Comm Hosp, staff physician 1970-; Westside Anesthesia Assoc, anesthesiologist. **ORGANIZATIONS:** Elder Westend Presbyterian Church 1973-; mem AMA, Natl Med Assoc, Amer Soc of Anesthesiologist; fellow pharmacology 1966-67; Alpha Omega Alpha Hon Med Soc; mem Amer Bd Anesthesiology; fellow Amer Coll of Anesthesiology. **HONORS/ACHIEVEMENTS:** AUS maj 1967-69. **BUSINESS ADDRESS:** Westside Anesthesia Assoc, 510 Fairburn Rd SW, Atlanta, GA 30331.

LORDE, AUDRE GERALDINE
Poet, educator. **PERSONAL:** Born Feb 18, 1934, New York, NY; divorced; children: Beth Lorde-Rollins, Jonathan Lorde-Rollins. **EDUCATION:** Hunter Coll, BA 1959; Columbia Univ, MLS 1961. **CAREER:** Mt Vernon Public Library, young adult librarian 1966-68; St Clare's Hosp Sch of Nursing, librarian 1965-66; Town Sch, head librarian 1966-68; City Coll Lehman Coll, lectr 1968-70; Tougaloo Coll, poet in residence 1968; John Jay Coll of Criminal Justice, assoc prof 1974-; Hunter Coll of CUNY, prof of english. **ORGANIZATIONS:** Founder/mem Kitchen Table, Women of Color Press. **HONORS/ACHIEVEMENTS:** Public Serv Awds grant Creative Artists 1972, 1976; hon commn of Col staff of Gov of LA 1973; Woman of the Yr Staten Island Comm Coll 1975; Broadside Poets Awd Detroit 1975; numerous publications including "Cables to Rage" 1970; "Between Ourselves" 1976; "The Black Unicorn" 1978; "Chosen Poems Old & New" 1982; "ZAMI, A New Spelling of My Name" 1983; "Sister Outsider" 1984; "Our Dead Behind Us" 1986; "A Burst of Light" 1988; Natl Book Awd nominee Poetry 1974; Amer Library Assn Gay Book of the Yr 1980; NEA Writing Grant 1981; ThomasHunter Professorship 1987. **BUSINESS ADDRESS:** Professor of English, Hunter College of CUNY, 695 Park Avenue, New York, NY 10021.

LORIS, JOSEPH JAMES
Business executive. **PERSONAL:** Born Mar 19, 1943, Philadelphia, PA; married Cathleen; children: 2 Children. **EDUCATION:** TempleUniv 1960-62. **CAREER:** Impact (Nat Black Trade Mag), pres/co-owner 1977-; Power Play (Regional Tip Sheet), pres/owner 1972-; Record Mus, gen mgr 1965-. **ORGANIZATIONS:** Bd mem Black Mus Assn 1978-. **BUSINESS ADDRESS:** 1525 Clearview Dr, Norristown, PA 19401.

LORTHRIDGE, JAMES E.
Education administration. **EDUCATION:** Prairie View A&M Univ, BS 1964; CA State Univ Long Beach, MA 1970; Claremont Grad School, PhD 1974; Rockefeller Found, Post Doctoral 1978. **CAREER:** Mt Pleasant School Dist, asst supt 1978, supt 1978-79; West Valley Comm Coll, dir, personnel 1979-83; Stockton Unified School Dist, supt 1983-. **ORGANIZATIONS:** Bd mem Mt Pleasant School Bd; mem CA Assn of Secondary School Admin, Amer Assn of Secondary School Admin, Assoc of CA School Admin, Phi Delta Kappa, Natl Assn for Advance of Colored People; hon life mem PTA. **HONORS/ACHIEVEMENTS:** Hon Serv PTA; Listed in Who's Who in the West, Who's Who in Ed Admin; Panel Mem Amer Arbitration Assoc. **BUSINESS ADDRESS:** Superintendent, Stockton Unified School Dist, 701 N Madison St, Stockton, CA 95202.

LOTT, GAY LLOYD
Attorney. **PERSONAL:** Born Mar 12, 1937, Chicago; children: Gay Lloyd, Jr. **EDUCATION:** Univ IL; RooseveltUniv 1962; John Marshall Law Sch 1964. **CAREER:** IRS, 1960-65; Peterson Johnson & Harris, 1965; Chicago, asst corp counsel 1965-67. **ORGANIZATIONS:** Pres chmn Civil Service Commn Met Sanitary Distr 1967; Weston Lott & William Ltd 1969-70; atty Lott, Powell & Williams Ltd 1970-78; Alpha Phi Alpha Inc; Phi Alpha Delta Law Frat; Am Bar Assn; regional dir Nat Bar Assn; mem bd of governors IL State Bar Assn; past pres Cook County Bar Assn; spkrs bureau Chicago Bar Assn; Defense Lawyers Assn; Trial Lawyers Assn. **BUSINESS ADDRESS:** 33 N Bearborn St, Chicago, IL.

LOTT, RONNIE
Professional athlete. **PERSONAL:** Born May 08, 1959, Albuquerque, NM. **EDUCATION:** Univ of Southern CA, Public Admin 1981. **CAREER:** San Francisco 49ers, cornerback 1981-. **HONORS/ACHIEVEMENTS:** Named all-pro 1983; hnrd NFL Alumni Assoc as Defensive Back of the Year 1983; estbl team record Most Career TDs on Interceptions; runner-up for NFL Rookie of the Year; 1981 made every conceivable all-star team from rookie to all-pro; All-Pc 10 performer; USC's 1980 MVP & Most Inspirational Player; mem NFL 1987 ProBowl team. **BUSINESS ADDRESS:** San Francisco 49ers, 711 Nevada St, Redwood City, CA 94061.

LOUARD, AGNES A.
Educator. **PERSONAL:** Born Mar 10, 1922, Savannah, GA; daughter of Joseph Anthony and Agnes Anthony; married V Benjamin, Sep 02, 1950 (deceased); children: Rita, Diane, Kenneth. **EDUCATION:** Univ of PA, BA 1944; Fisk Univ, MA 1945; Columbia Univ, MS 1948; NY Univ Add Studies. **CAREER:** The Manhattanville Neighborhood Ctr, suprv childrens div 1948-52; Union Settlement Assoc, dir rec & ed 1952-57; The E Harlem Proj, dir 1958-59; Speedwell Serv for Children NYC, sr caseworker 1959-61; Leake & Watts Children's Home, sr caseworker 1962-63; Patterson Home for Aged, suprv 1964-65; Columbia Univ, asst prof 1965-72, assoc prof 1972-. **ORGANIZATIONS:** Bd mem Harriet Tubman Comm Ctr 1965-; mem, vice pres Pleasant Ave Day Care Ctr 1971-; bd mem 1972-, pres 1985-88 Peninsula Counciling Ctr; consultant Spence Chapin Service for Families & Children 1974-; exec comm State Manpower Services Council 1977; mem NY State Employment & Training Council 1977-82; consultant Harlem Teams 1979-82; mem Alumni Assn Columbia Univ; adv bd JW Jr Comm Mental Health Bd 1982-84; panel chmn staff mediation comm Columbia Univ 1984-89; consultant Brooklyn Bureau of Community Services 1988-; bd mem Schomburg Corp 1988-; mem NY Coalition of 100 Black Women 1988-; mem ACLU, NAACP, Common Cause, Urban League, The Cottagers; trustee Union Chapel Marthas Vineyard; mem NASW. **HONORS/ACHIEVEMENTS:** Award for dedicated service, Peninsula Counseling Center and Town of Hempstead, NY, 1988. **HOME ADDRESS:** 560 Riverside Drive #62, New York, NY 10027.

LOUDEN, HENDERSON NATHANIEL, SR.
Clergyman. **PERSONAL:** Born May 25, 1928, Greenwood, SC; married Johnnie Mae Pompey; children: Henderson Jr, Coris, Darnell. **EDUCATION:** Allen Univ, DD. **CAREER:** Warrenton Circuit, pastor; Factory Furniture Outlet, vp; Self Memorial Hospital, clergyman staff; Greenwood Cty Dist #52, bd mem. **MILITARY SERVICE:** AUS Sergeant 4 years. **HOME ADDRESS:** Rt 1, Box 485-B, Ninety Six, SC 29666.

LOUIS, JOSEPH
Chemical operator. **PERSONAL:** Born Apr 04, 1948, Vacherie, LA; son of Marshal Louis and Albertha Louis (Davis); married Linda Ann Isaac; children: Crystal Michelle, Jeremy Allen. **EDUCATION:** Southern Univ, 30 aver overall 1966-70. **CAREER:** CJ's Ins Agency, mgr & owner 1985; Justice of Peace & Constables Assoc, constable. **ORGANIZATIONS:** Mem NAACP 1964-; mem Health & Phys Ed Club 1966-70; mem Southern Univ Alumni Federation 1970-; mem Hiram Lodge #12 of Free & Accepted Masons 1974-; memLA Underwriters Assn 1983-. **MILITARY SERVICE:** ROTC E-5 1966-68. **HOME ADDRESS:** Rt 2 Lot 51 Pecan Acres, Iberville, LA 70776.

LOUISTALL-MONROE, VICTORINE AUGUSTA
Retired educator. **PERSONAL:** Born Aug 19, 1912, Cumberland, MD; daughter of Campbell McRae Louistall and Malinda Waller Smith Louistall; married Ernest E Monroe, Oct 21, 1981. **EDUCATION:** WV State Coll, BS 1936, MA 1945; West Virginia Univ, MALS 1963; Univ Pittsburgh, adv work. **CAREER:** Kelly Miller HS, teacher 1937-66; Roosevelt-Wilson HS, librarian 1956-66; WV Univ, asst prof 1966-74, assoc prof 1974-78, assoc prof Emerita Dept Library Sci 1978-. **ORGANIZATIONS:** Consultant & instructor WV Univ 1964-66; consultant WV St Dept Libr Workshop at Morris Harvey Coll 1970; treas Harrison County Citizens Comm for Educ 1962-66; mem Pres Advisory Comm on Civil Rights 1960; vice pres WV Young Republicans 1953-55; bd dir Harrison County United Fund 1963-66; life mem NEA; mem Amer Library Assn; AAUW; NAACP; Alpha Kappa Alpha; WV Library Assn; treas Harrison County Citizens Comm 1960-64; Assn for Educ Communication & Technology; advisory comm; WV Library Commn 1971; chmn Certification Comm WV State Dept of Educ; mem Clarksburg-Harrison Public Library 1978-; bd mem Clarksburg Human Rights Commn 1978-; hon mem Delta Kappa Gamma Intl Soc 1980; appointed to WV Library Comm 1980; re-appointed 1984; appointed to Pres Adv Bd WV Univ 1982; mem Phi Delta Kappa WV Univ 1973-; re-appointed to Clarksburg-Harrison Public Library Trustee Bd 1984, reappointed pres adv bd West Virginia Univ 1986; trustee emerita, Clarksburgh Harrisonn Public Library, 1985. **HONORS/ACHIEVEMENTS:** 1st black woman to receive MA from WV Univ 1945; 1st black to receive acad appointment in Coll of Arts & Sci 1966; Citation Harrison County Bd of Educ 1960; Woman of the Year 1958; Achievement Award, Woman's Club 1981; Achievement Award, Library Skills Institute 1989. **BUSINESS ADDRESS:** Associate Professor Emerita, WVUniv Dept Library Sci, Rm 101 Main Library, Morgantown, WV 26506.

LOURY, GLENN CARTMAN
Educator. **PERSONAL:** Born Sep 03, 1948, Chicago, IL; married Linda Datcher; children: Lisa, Tamara, Glenn II. **EDUCATION:** Northwestern Univ, BA Mathematics 1972, Outstanding Graduate Dept of Mathematics 1972; MA Inst of Tech, PhD Economics 1976. **CAREER:** Northwestern Univ, asst prof dept of economics 1976-79; Univ of MI, assoc prof dept of economics 1980-82, prof 1980; Harvard Univ John F Kennedy Sch of Government, prof1982. **ORGANIZATIONS:** Mem rsch adv bd Joint Center for Political Studies Washington; mem rsch adv bd Southern Center for Policy Studies Clark Coll; mem rsch adv bd DuBois Inst Harvard Univ; assoc editor Journal of Urban Economics; referee for various journals; Publication Comm,"The Public Interest". **HONORS/ACHIEVEMENTS:** Books and articles "From Children to Citizens" 1987; The Family, The Nation and Senator Moynihan", commentary, 1986; "Matters of Color Blacks and the Constitutional Order" Public Interest 1987; "Who Speaks for American Blacks?", commentary 1987; "Why Should We Care About Group Inequality?" Social Philosophy and Policy, 1987; A New American Dilemma The New Republic 1984; A Theory of 'Oil'igopolicy Cournot Equilibrium in Exhaustible Resource Markets Intl Market Review; Embargo Threats and the Management of Emergency Reserves Journal of political Economy 1985; On the Need for Moral Leadership in the Black Community New Perspectives 1984; Responsibility and Race Vital Speeches of the Day 1983; Is Equal Opportunity Enough Amer Economic Review 1981; Intergenerational Transfers and the Distrib ution of Earnings Econometrica 1981; Ford Found Doc Fellow 1972-76; Guggenheim Fellow 1985-86, Winner Leavy Awd for Excellence in Free Enterprise Education 1987. **BUSINESS ADDRESS:** Prof of Public Policy, HarvardUniv, 79 Kennedy St, Cambridge, MA 02138.

LOVE, BARBARA
Educator. **PERSONAL:** Born Apr 13, 1946, Dumas, AR. **EDUCATION:** AR AM & N, BA 1965;Univ of AR, MA 1967;Univ of MA, PhD, EdD 1972. **CAREER:** Univ of MA Amherst Campus, assoc prof; Fellowship House, exec dir; Kansas City, teacher 1969-70; Center for Urban Educ, Univ of MA, grad asst 1970-71, instructor 1971-72, asso prof, chmn. **ORGANIZATIONS:** Mem Phi Delta Kappa 1974; Nat Alliance Black Sch Educators 1973;

Am Educ Studies Assn 1974; Panel Am Women 1968-70; Urban Coalition Task Force on Educ 1968-70; comm rep Nat Tchrs Corps 1969-70; tast force Nat Alternative Schs Prgm 1971-73. **HONORS/ACHIEVEMENTS:** Leadership Found Scholarship 1965-66; Jr League Award 1967. **BUSINESS ADDRESS:** Professor, University of Massachusetts, Furcolo Hall, Amherst, MA 01002.

LOVE, CLARENCE C.
Retired state representative. **PERSONAL:** Born Feb 24, 1922, Weir, KS; married Travestine Myers; children: Marva C Roberson, Cheryl C Thompson, Travestine, Terri Collier, Clarence Jr. **CAREER:** State of Kansas 35th Dist, rep, 1966-88, (retired). **ORGANIZATIONS:** Mem, Allen Chapel AME Church, St James Masonic Lodge 59, Orient Consistory 19, 33 Degree Mason, 1971. **MILITARY SERVICE:** AUS sgt 1944-45. **BUSINESS ADDRESS:** State Representative, State of Kansas 35th Dist, State House, Topeka, KS 66612.

LOVE, EDWARD M., JR.
Entertainer. **PERSONAL:** Born Jun 29, 1952, Toledo, OH. **EDUCATION:** OH Univ, BA; NYU School of the Arts, work/study certificate. **CAREER:** "Dancin", actor/dancer 1978; "A Piece of the Action", actor 1977; " A Chorus Line", dancer 1976; Alvin Ailey Dance Theatre, dancer 1974; Workshop for Careers in the Arts GWU, Consult 1972; Walt Disney & World-coll Prog Orlando, consult 1979; Janis Ian/Miguel Bose/Amanda Ambrose, choreographer 1980. **ORGANIZATIONS:** Mem Alpha Phi Alpha Fraternity Inc; mem AEA; SAG; AFTRA; mem Blk Music Assn. **HONORS/ACHIEVEMENTS:** Outstanding achievement in the arts award Alpha Phi Alhpa/Alpha XI Lambda Chap 1978; outstanding achvmnt in the arts Ebony Mag 1978.

LOVE, ELEANOR YOUNG
Educator. **PERSONAL:** Born Oct 10, Lincoln Ridge, KY; daughter of Whitney M Young, Sr and Laura R Young; children: Laura, David Whitney. **EDUCATION:** KY State Univ AB 1944; Atlanta Univ, BLS 1946; Univ Louisville, med 1965; Univ IL, DED 1970. **CAREER:** FL A&M Univ, library 1946-51; Bergen Jr Coll, head librarian 1951-53; Lincoln Inst, librarian, prin, counselor 1953-66; Univ Coll Univ Louisville, asst dean, prof of educ psychology & counseling 1966-70, asst prof assoc prof 1970-78; fall prof 1978-. **ORGANIZATIONS:** Mem Presbyterian Ch; Urban League; YMCA; AKA; Moles Inc; Les Belles; consult Head Start & Sickle Cell Anemia; pres Adult Student Personnel Assn 1974-75; mem bd Vis Nurses; JADD; Health Licensure & Needs; Lincoln Found; Red Cross; Educ Commn of States; pres Lincoln Foundation 1987-; counselor Human Development EAP consultant 1987-. **HONORS/ACHIEVEMENTS:** Numerous scholarships, fellows. **BUSINESS ADDRESS:** Professor, University of Louisville, School of Education, Belknap Campus, Louisville, KY 40292.

LOVE, EZEKIEL
Government official. **PERSONAL:** Born Jun 18, 1944, Augusta, SC; married Regina C Miller. **EDUCATION:** Benedict Coll Columbia SC, BS 1966; Bowie State Coll Bowier MD 1975. **CAREER:** USDA Dept of Agr, confidential asst to adminstr present; Task Force Organizer of Black Religious Leaders for Carter/Mondale Campaign, polit coordinator 1976; 4-H Co ActivitiesUniv of GA, dir 1975-76; Dekalb Co Atlanta, tchr 1974-75; Franklin Life Ins Co, dist mgr 1974; DC Pub Sch, tchr 1966-72. **ORGANIZATIONS:** Qualifying mem Million Dollar Round Table Franklin Life 1979; asso mem Wash Ind Writers Assn 1980; mem NEA 1966-72; mem Black Spl Asst Carter Adminstrn 1977-; co-troop leader Boy Scouts of Am 1979-. **HONORS/ACHIEVEMENTS:** "Grain Exchanges & the Am Farmer" US Dept of Agr 1978.

LOVE, GEORGE HAYWARD
Educator. **PERSONAL:** Born Oct 15, 1924, Philadelphia, PA; son of Samuel H Love and Daisy G Love; married Hettie Simmons; children: George Hayward Jr, Karen Love Alford. **EDUCATION:** Univ of Pennsylvania, BA 1948, MS Educ 1950, EdD 1973. **CAREER:** Philadelphia Sch Dist, teacher/admin 1952-71; Pennsylvania Dept of Educ, asst commissioner 1971-75; Appalachia Educ Lab, assoc dir 1975-81; Harrisburg Sch Dist, biology teacher, 1981-84; dir of personnel 1984-88; dir, division of special projects, 1988-. **ORGANIZATIONS:** Consultant PA Dept of Educ 1981-; bd mem Camp Curtin YMCA 1981-; founder/past sire archon Beta Pi Boule, Sigma Pi Phi 1983; bd mem/exec comm Dauphin Co Children & Youth 1983-; chmn Dept of Christian Educ Diocese of PA 1984-; pres Greater Harrisburg Area Branch NAACP 1986-; president Harrisburg Bridge Club 1989; lay reader and vestryman, St Paul Episcopal Church. **HONORS/ACHIEVEMENTS:** Service Awd Frontiers Intl 1973; Outstanding Citizenship Awd Omega Psi Phi Frat 1981; Judge Awd Pennsylvania Junior Acad of Science 1987; YMCA Award 1988. **MILITARY SERVICE:** USAF pvt 1943-45. **HOME ADDRESS:** 3757 Chambers Hill Rd, Harrisburg, PA 17111.

LOVE, JAMES RALPH
Business executive. **PERSONAL:** Born Apr 02, 1937, Hahira, GA; married Bernice Grant; children: Rhita V, James R II, Gerald K, Reginald. **EDUCATION:** KY State Coll, BS 1958; Tuskegee Inst, MS 1968. **CAREER:** Project MARK Jackson MS, job developer 1968; Natl Alliance of Bus Denver C of C, mgr 1968-71; Mt Bell, public relations 1971-74; Mutual Benefit Life, ths agt 1974-79; James R Love & Assocs Inc, pres 1980-. **ORGANIZATIONS:** Pres Delta Psi Lambda 1971-74; treas Denver Bd Mentally Retarded & Physically Handicapped 1972-78; vice pres Park Hill Br NAACP 1979-80; advisor to Gov Love Govt CO 1969-71; dir UNCF CO 1971-72; mem ethics comm Denver Area Life Underwriters 1978-79. **HONORS/ACHIEVEMENTS:** Agent of the Yr Mutual Benefit 1974-75; Man of the Yr AA 1975-76; article pub "Prospecting Through My Board of Directors" Life Insurance Selling vol 52 1978. **BUSINESS ADDRESS:** President, James R Love & Assocs Inc, 240 Josephine St, Ste 204, Denver, CO 80206.

LOVE, JOE W.
Business executive, government official. **PERSONAL:** Born Aug 20, 1937; married Wilma; children: Bryon, Carol. **EDUCATION:** Bethume Cookman Coll BA; Continuing Ctr of Jacksonville MA. **CAREER:** Bank of Green Cove Springs', vice pres pub rels present; Green Cove, mayor 1977-; commr 1975-; Green Cove Springs Police Dept, 1967-68 clay co sch Bd, tchr 1961-62; Johnson & Johnson Inc, sales & rep; Love Inc Contractors, pres gen mgr. **ORGANIZATIONS:** Mem Masonic Lodge; Yng Dem Club; C of C; dir FL League Voters; chmn Clay Co Voters Registration; mem Black Mayors Assn; Pres's 1600 Club; St JohnsBapt Ch. **BUSINESS ADDRESS:** 229 Walnut St, Green Cove Springs, FL 32043.

LOVE, MABEL R.
Educator. **PERSONAL:** Born Jun 27, 1908, Hampton, VA; married Dr T A. **EDUCATION:** Hampton Inst, BS 1929; Columbia U, MA 1933; Syracuse U, summer work; CT Coll for Women, summer work. **CAREER:** Fisk Univ, prof health physical educ; AL State Teachers Coll; Leynoyne Coll; Fisk Univ, dance prof; Dance Eductors of Amer, summer work for 15 yrs. **ORGANIZATIONS:** Bd mem Friends of Chamber Mus City of Nashville; sec TN Arts Commn 2 terms; mem AAUP; AAUW; TN St Dance Assn; life mem Am Tchr Assn; pres Delta Sigma Theta Sor three terms; golden life mem Girl Friends Inc. **HONORS/ACHIEVEMENTS:** Spl awd Lieg for dedication in field of performing arts; orgn of "Orchesis" Coll Dance Group Fisk U.

LOVE, MILDRED L.
Administrator. **PERSONAL:** Born Oct 25, 1941, Ringgold, LA. **EDUCATION:** So U, BA 1963;Univ of Pittsburgh, MA 1969; Columbia U, MBA 24 credits 1979. **CAREER:** Nat Urban League Inc, dir career training & econ resources 1979-; Nat Urban League Inc, dir Eastern reg ofc 1976-79; Nat Urban League Inc, asst dir eastern reg ofc 1973-76; Harlem Teams for Self Help, instr & counselor 1965-72; New York City Dept of Social Svc, case worker 1964-65; Manhattan State Hosp, rehab counselor 1970; Cowles Publ Co, editorial consult 1971-72. **ORGANIZATIONS:** Volunteer ATC Domestic Peace Corps 1963-64; commr Nat Commn on Unemployment Compensation 1980-82. **HONORS/ACHIEVEMENTS:** Who's Who in Am Coll &Univ 1963; Ford Found Fellowship Award 1968-69. **BUSINESS ADDRESS:** Vice Pres Programs & Field Service, Natl Urban League, Inc, 500 East 62nd St, New York, NY 10021.

LOVE, ROOSEVELT SAM
Business executive. **PERSONAL:** Born Jun 11, 1933, Bulloch Co, GA; widowed; children: Katheleen, Patricia, Bonnie, Julia, Sandra. **CAREER:** Love's Fina Serv Sta, operator; JP Stevens, cement mixer; Gulf Inc, serv sta atdnt. **ORGANIZATIONS:** Mem Comm Rels Cncl 1975-77; DUSO Devel Uique Serv Ourselves; Comm Action Club; SCWC; mem Negotiations Com Textiles Wrkrs Unoin 1974; rep JP Stevens Empl Twisting Dept 1971; pres Bulloch Co Br NAACP 1973-; mem Bethel Primitive Bapt Ch. **HONORS/ACHIEVEMENTS:** Outsndg serv awd NAACP 1977. **BUSINESS ADDRESS:** 219 S Main St, Statesboro, GA 30458.

LOVE, RUTH B.
Educator. **PERSONAL:** Born Apr 22, 1935, Lawton, OK. **EDUCATION:** San Jose State Univ, BA Elem Ed; San Francisco State Univ, MA Guid & Couns; US Intl Univ, PhD Human Behavior. **CAREER:** Oakland Unified School Dist, teacher 1954-59, couns, consult 1960-62, instr 1961-65, supt 1971-75; Girls Correctional Inst, proj coord 1958; Cheshire Engla, Fulbright exchange teacher 1960; Oper Crossroads Ghana West Africa, proj dir 1962; Bureau of Pupil Personnel Serv GA State Dept of Ed, consult 1963-65; Buru of Compensatory Ed Prog Devel CA State Dept of Ed, chief 1965-71; Chicago IL School Dist, gen supt 1981; WLS-TV, commentator. **ORGANIZATIONS:** Mem Assoc for Suprv & Curriculum Devel, Guidance & Counseling Assoc, Assoc for Childhood Ed Intl, World Council of Teachers, Intl Reading Assoc, AmerPersonnel & Guidance Assoc, Natl Ed Assoc, Delta Kappa Gamma Hon Soc, CA Teachers Assoc, Afro-Negro Intl Travel Club, Amer Acad Pol & Soc Sci, Women's Forum West, People-to-People Prog, World Org of Early Childhood Ed, Alpha Kappa Alpha, Amer Assoc of School Admin, CA Assoc of School Admin, ProflWomen's Assoc, Phi Delta Kappa, Natl Assoc of Black School Ed, Black Amer Pol Assoc of CA, Commonwealth Club of CA, Natl School Bd Assoc, E Bay Areaub of the Natl Assoc of Negro Bus & Professional Women's Clubs Inc, State Tech Adv Comm on Testing CA; mem bd dir Oper Crossroads Africa Inc NY; mem United Cerebral Palsy Found; ex bd Boy Scouts of Amer, Girls Scouts of Amer Chgo; mem adv bd Natl Hispanic Univ; mem Statue of Liberty-Ellis Island Centenial Commiss; mem Sec of the Navy's Adv Bd of Ed & Trng; mem UNESCO, Amer Bar Assoc Adv Comm on Juvenile Delinquency & Reading. **HONORS/ACHIEVEMENTS:** In honor of Ruth Love Holloway The Holloway-Gonzalez Library Bakersfield CA; listed in Who's Who in Amer Ed 1969, Outstanding Young Women of Amer Publ 1967;Pres Awd Assoc of CA Admin in Compensation Ed; Life Mem Awd Assoc of School Admin Compensatory Ed; Woman of the Year Awd Zeta Phi Beta Sor 1967,77;Outstanding Woman Awd 1976; Ruth Love Scholarship Awd Univ of San Francisco 1977; Disting Serv Awd Natl Alliance of Black School Ed 1983; Role Model in Ed Awd Alpha Kappa Alpha 1984; num publs inc, "Strenghtening Counseling Serv for Disadvantaged Youth" CA State Dept of Ed 1966, "Bold Plng Required to Shore Up Ailing Schools" The Review of Ed 1983, "Focusing on Reading & Math" The Supt As Instrl Leader 1984, "The Paideia Proposal, Problems & Possibilities"w/Mortimer Adler 1984; Commun Serv Awd Negro Bus & Professional Women's Club 1977; MORE Handbook of Outstanding Black Amer 1980; Exec Ed 100 No Amer Top School Exec 1980; Outstanding Serv Awd Natl Urban League 1978; Dist Serv Awd Lincoln Univ Alumni Assoc 1977; Achievement Awd Commun Streetwork Ctr Annual Unity Day 1977; 3rd Annual Martin Luther King Jr Humanitarian Awd Glide Meml Church 1976. **BUSINESS ADDRESS:** Commentator, WLS-TV, 190 N State St, Chicago, IL 60610.

LOVE, THOMAS CLIFFORD
Editorial director. **PERSONAL:** Born Jul 23, 1947, New Rochelle, NY. **EDUCATION:** Howard Univ, BA 1969. **CAREER:** WRC-TV AM-FM Washington, employment spec, publ serv dir 1969-71; WABC-AM Rdio New York City publ serv dir 1971-72, dir comm affairs 1972-73; WABC AM-Radio NY, ed, community affairs dir 1973-79; St Johns Univ, adj prof 1976-78; Montclair State Coll, vstg spec 1978-; WABC-TV, ed dir 1979-. **ORGANIZATIONS:** Mem Natl & Intl Radio & TV Soc, Natl Broadcast Ed Assoc, Alpha Phi Alpha. **HONORS/ACHIEVEMENTS:** NY Emmy Awd 1980; Andy Awd of Merit Ad Club of NY 1978; NY State Broadcasters Awd 1979,84; UPI & AP Awd 1974; YMCA Black Achievers in Indust Awd 1974. **BUSINESS ADDRESS:** Editorial Dir, WABC-TV, 7 Lincoln St, New York, NY 10023.

LOVELACE, DEAN ALAN
Government administrator. **PERSONAL:** Born Jan 31, 1946, Kittaning, PA; married Phyllis Jean Rutland; children: Leslie Denise, Laeina Deandra, Dean Nyerere. **EDUCATION:** Sinclair Comm Coll, Asso of Sci Bus 1971;Univ of Dayton, BS Bus Adminstrn 1972; Wright State U, MS Economics 1981. **CAREER:** Univ of Dayton, dir of neighborhood dev; City of Dayton NW Office of Neighborhood Affairs, coordinator/dir 1979-80; City of Dayton NW Office of Neighborhood Affairs, comm serv adv 1977-79; City of Dayton Dept of Planning, neighborhood planner 1973-79; Nat Cash Register, lathe operator 1965-71. **ORGANIZATIONS:** Mem Citizens Avd Council Model Neighborhood Comm Center 1977-; mem

Econ Resources Com Miami Valley Regional Planning Council 1977-; chmn Dayton OH Black Polit Assembly 1977-; trustee Housing Justice Fund Inc 1978-; pres Edgemont Neighborhood Coalition Inc 1980-; 1st vice pres Dayton Urban League 1982-; adv bdDayton Found Neighbor to Neighbor 1983-; council mem Montgomery County Human Serv Levy 1984-; chmnDayton-Montgomery County Rainbow Coaltion 1984-, Dayton Anti-Apartheid Comm 1985-. **HONORS/ACHIEVEMENTS:** Comm Serv Awd Concerned Citizens of Dayton View 1977; Employee of the Year City of Dayton Div of Neighborhood Affairs 1978; Disting Serv Awd OH State Leg1979; Outstanding Young Man of Amer US Jaycees 1979; NAACP Freedom Fund Dinner Civil Rights Awd 1985. **BUSINESS ADDRESS:** Dir of Neighborhood Dev, University of Dayton, 300 College Park Ave, Dayton, OH 45408.

LOVELACE, GLORIA ELAINE
Business executive. **PERSONAL:** Born Jan 24, 1945, Danville, VA; daughter of Dr Theodore R Lovelace and Sara Thomas Lovelace; children: Jabrie Daverand. **EDUCATION:** VA State Univ, BS Health/Phys Ed/Biology 1968; Univ of IL, MS Kinesiotherapy 1971. **CAREER:** Scovill Mfg Co, employ asst 1974, asst to the dir of marketing 1974-75, coord of marketing systems 1975-76; Xerox Corp Info Systems Group, br internal control mgr 1976, mid-atlantic reg personnel admin 1976-77, affirm action/personnel relations 1977-78, personnel relations mgr 1978-79; Office Prod Div, midwest region personnel mgr 1979-81, mgr compensation affirm action safety/security & health serv 1981-83, mgr of human resources 1983; Old Stone Bank,sr vice pres Human resources 1983-85; owner and business counselor General Business Service 1985-88; National Captioning Institute, Falls Church VA, dir personnel 1988-89; US Sprint, Reston VA, dir human resources 1989-. **ORGANIZATIONS:** Bd of dirs Family Svcs, Urban League, Council for Aging, Visiting Nurses; personnel comm YWCA Rochester; mem Prof Women's Network; participant Chicago Forum 1980-81; mem Black Career Women Inc; corp advisor Bishop Coll; bd mem YMCA Providence 1984-; comm mem Providence Chamber of Commerce 1984-85; mem of, Natl Assn of Bank Women 1984-; Personnel Executives Club 1984-; Natl Assn of Urban Bankers 1984-85; Washington DC Chamber of Commerce, Nat'l Federation of Independent Businesses, Small Business Federation. **HONORS/ACHIEVEMENTS:** Selected as one of the Outstanding Young Women of America; Guest Faculty Williams Coll Sch of Banking. **HOME ADDRESS:** 1531 Hemlock St NW, Washington, DC 20012.

LOVELACE, JOHN C.
Business executive. **PERSONAL:** Born Mar 04, 1926, West Point, GA; married Mary Jean Roebuck; children: Juan Carlos, Carlita Joy. **CAREER:** Pittsburgh Plate Glass Industrial Inc, employee. **ORGANIZATIONS:** Mem Drug & Alcoholic Comm; numerous offices local NAACP; bd dirs Kiski Valley Med Facilities Inc 1974-75; planning comm Gilpin Township 1973-75; mem Youth Comm 1968; mgr Valley Choraliers Leechburg 1960-75. **HONORS/ACHIEVEMENTS:** Thalheimer Award, NAACP, 1970; citation, Pennsylvania House of Rep, 1970; 1st place, Pennsylvania State Conf Brs 1974. **MILITARY SERVICE:** USN 1944-46.

LOVELACE, ONZALO ROBERT
Business executive. **PERSONAL:** Born Mar 20, 1940, Homestead, PA; son of Onzalo Lovelace and Dorothy Lovelace; divorced; children: Caroline. **EDUCATION:** Univ of Pittsburgh, BS Indus Engrg 1964. **CAREER:** IBM, indus engr 1966-67; Trans World Airlines, mgr quality assurance 1967-72; Pan Am World Airways, dir corporate indus engrg 1972-77; Pan Am World Airways, dir corporate budgets 1977-78, system dir indus engrg 1978-82, division controller 1982-86, corporate budget dir 1986-87; First Nationwide Bank, vice pres/div controller 1987-89. **ORGANIZATIONS:** Mem Amer Inst for Indus Engrs 1966-80; mem Assn for Systems Mgmt 1972-80; "Mgmt System for Maintenance" Plant Engrg Magazine 1975. **MILITARY SERVICE:** AUS spec 5 1964-66. **HOME ADDRESS:** 451 Rich St, Oakland, CA 94609. **BUSINESS ADDRESS:** Vice President/Division Controller, First Nationwide Bank, 33 New Montgomery St, San Francisco, CA 94105.

LOVELADY, RUEBEN LEON
Corporation executive. **PERSONAL:** Born Mar 28, 1958, West Helena, AR; children: Larissa, Angel, Christopher. **EDUCATION:** Regis Coll, AAS 1982; Southern IL Univ, BS 1987. **CAREER:** Helena Chemical Co, mill supervisor 1974-75; AUS, biomedical equipt tech 1975-83; Southeastern Scientific Corp, vice president 1983-. **ORGANIZATIONS:** Mem Amer Legion 1986-87; pres Carolina Scientific Corp, Triangle Academic Svcs. **MILITARY SERVICE:** AUS staff sgt 8 1/2 yrs; Expert Infantry, Overseas, Good Conduct, Army Commendation. **HOME ADDRESS:** 8315 Kestrel Dr, Raleigh, NC 27615.

LOVETT, EDWARD P.
Attorney. **PERSONAL:** Born Dec 17, 1902, Fayetteville, NC; married Louise Kathleen Johnson; children: Lanna Lou Lovett Love. **EDUCATION:** Hampton Inst, post-grad ork 1922, 26; Howard U, AB LLB 1926, 32; Harvard U, LLM 1936. **CAREER:** US Dept of HUD, 1972; Office of EOE, 1969; HHFA, asst gen counsel 1965; Pres Com on EO in Housing, gen counsel of com 1963-65; Office of Gen Counsel HHFAD asst gen counsel legal opinions & adminstrn law br 1963; office of gen counsel, head of legal opinoins & rsrch sect 1957; Office of Gen Counsel, head of briefs & opinions & rsrch sect 1957; Office of Gen Counsel, chief of gen prgms & housing plans sect 1946; Office of Gen Counsel, head of briefs & opinoins unit 1943; Dept of HUD, 1965; Housing & Home Finance Agency, 1947-65. **ORGANIZATIONS:** Mem Nat Legal Com of NAACP; chief warden Civil Def; pres PTA; pres Neighborhood Citizens Assn; supt Summer Camp for underpriviledged Mothers & Children; mem several civil rights & EOE natl & local orgns or groups; Kappa Alpha Psi Frat. **HONORS/ACHIEVEMENTS:** AUS 2nd lt. **MILITARY SERVICE:** AUS 2nd lt.

LOVETT, LEONARD
Clergyman. **PERSONAL:** Born Dec 05, 1939, Pompano Beach, FL; son of Charles Lovett and Cassie Lovett; married Phyllis Bush; children: Laion, Lamont, Lamar, Mandon. **EDUCATION:** Saints Jr Coll, AA 1959; Morehouse Coll, BA 1962; Crozer Theological Seminary, MDiv 1965; Emory Univ Candler's Grad Sch of Theology, PhD 1979. **CAREER:** Meml COGIC, pastor 1962-70; Health & Welfare Council Philadelphia New York City Proj, coord 1965-67; Stephen Smith Towers 202 Senior Citizens, proj mgr 1967-70; Ch Mason Theological Seminary, pioneer pres 1970-74; Fuller Theological Seminary, assoc dir Black Ministries 1977-81. **ORGANIZATIONS:** Pres Soc for Pentecostal Studies 1975; mem Soc for the Study of Black Religion 1972-; reactor Vatican-Pentecostal Dialogue W Germany 1974; visit prof Grad Theological Union Berkeley 1975; prof of Ethics & Theology Ecumenical Cntr for Black Church Studies 1978-; prof of Ethics & Theology Amer Bapt Seminary of the West 1984; visiting fellow Human Behavior Amer Inst of Family Relations 1982-85; bd mem, Watts Health Foundation, United Health Plan 1985-; columnist, Black Church, Ministries Today Magazine 1988-. **HONORS/ACHIEVEMENTS:** Conditional Liberation Spirit Journal 1977; What Charismatics Can Learn from Black Pentecostals Logos Journal 1980; Tribute to Martin Luther King in Outstanding Black Sermons Vol 2 Judson Press 1982; contrib Aspects of the Spiritual Legacy of the Church of God in Christ in Mid-Stream An Ecumenical Journal Vol XXIV No 4 1985, Black Witness to the Apostolic Faith Eardmans 1988; Black Holiness-Pentecostalism, Black Theology, Positive Confession Theology, Dictionary of the Pentecostal Charismatic Movement, Zondervan 1988. **BUSINESS ADDRESS:** Senior Pastor/Prof Soc Ethics, Church at the Crossroads COGIC, 9216 Parmelee Ave, Los Angeles, CA 90002.

LOVETT, MACK, JR.
Educator. **PERSONAL:** Born Aug 31, 1931, Shreveport, LA; married Marlene; children: Alice, Pamela, Michelle, Albert. **EDUCATION:** Oakland City Coll, AA 1959; CA State Univ, BA 1965, MPA 1970. **CAREER:** Municipal Court, court clerk 1956-65; Litton Indus, instr 1965-66, admin 1966-68; CA State Univ, asst to pres 1968-72, dir instruct serv 1972, asst vice pres 1978-. **ORGANIZATIONS:** Consult Hayward Uni Sch Dist 1966-73; consult Chabot Comm Coll 1969; consult CA Employ Serv 1968; dir & treas Ebony Constr Co 1972-73; dir Plnd & Appl Rescrs Inc 1967-68; Gr Hayward Kiwanis Serv Club; bd dir So Alameda Co Econ Oppor Orgn 1965-67; chmn Polit Actn Com NAACP So Alameda Co Chap 1958-64; pres NAACP 1964-68; bd dir New Lady mag 1965-70; Reg Adult Voca Educ Advis Com; bd mgrs YMCA Eden area. **HONORS/ACHIEVEMENTS:** Publ "How to File Your Income Tax" Litton Indus Educ Sys Div. **MILITARY SERVICE:** AUS 1954-56. **BUSINESS ADDRESS:** Asst Vice President, CA StateUniv, 25800 Carlos Bee Blvd, Hayward, CA 94542.

LOVING, ALBERT A., JR.
Retired accountant. **PERSONAL:** Born Mar 16, 1920, Chgo; divorced; children: Karyn L, Alan H. **EDUCATION:** De-Paul U, BSC 1950; grad sch 1950-51, 1971. **CAREER:** US Atomic Energy Commn, accountant auditor asst br chief budget examiner 1957-66; Chicago Land Clearance Commn; asst comptroller 1951-57; Chicago Bd Edn, tchr 1950-51; Parkway Sec & Accounting Svc, proprietor 1948-51; G Stevens Marchman & Co, asst to pres 1947-48; Audit US Dept Labor, special asst to inspector genl-audit 1966-80; Executive Service Corps of Chicago, exec consultant 1980-. **ORGANIZATIONS:** Mem Army Finance Assn 1953-73; exec sec Jr Assn Commerce & Industry 1955-57; sec Jaycee Senate Toastmasters 1955-57; Fed Govt Accountants Assn 1959-;So Shore Commn 1961-71; Reserve Officers Assn US 1969-; Am Accounting Assn 1970-; Inst of Internal Auditors 1973-; Fed Exec League 1974-; bd trusteesJackson Towers Condo Assn 1974-78; bd of trustees Hyde Park Hosp 1983-. **HONORS/ACHIEVEMENTS:** Certified Internal Auditor 1983-; Natl Assn of Minority CPA Firms Outstanding Serv Awd 1975; US Dept of Labor Office of the Reg Dir Commendable Serv Awd 1976; Chicago St Univ President's Awd 1979; Jones Commerical High Sch Afro American Hist Cert of Appreciation 1981. **MILITARY SERVICE:** AUS lt col 1939-46; Reserve 1946-70.

LOVING, JAMES LESLIE
Business executive. **PERSONAL:** Born Aug 14, 1944, Boston, MA; son of James Leslie Loving and Wauneta Barbour Loving; married Leebertha Beauford; children: Robyn Leslie. **EDUCATION:** Boston Bus School, Diploma 1964; Harvard Univ, EdM 1974, CAS 1975; Univ of S CA, DPA. **CAREER:** City of Boston, spec asst to mayor 1972-77; US Dept of HHS, spec asst 1977-81; Student Natl Med Assoc, exec admin 1981-83; Data Processing Inst, vice pres 1983-86; The Career Business Academy, pres 1986-. **ORGANIZATIONS:** Natl coord Dr King 51st Celebration 1980; chmn Roxbury Cancer Crusade 1974; treas Boston Br NAACP 1972; dir Boston Legal Asst Proj 1972; hew fellowUS Dept of Health Ed & Welfare 1977; trustee Emmanuel Temple Church 1977. **HONORS/ACHIEVEMENTS:** Finalist White House Fellows Prog 1977; Outstanding Leader JC's Boston Chap 1978; Outstanding Young Men of Amer 1976; 100 Black Influentials 1976; United Student Oakwood Coll Huntsville 1975. **HOME ADDRESS:** 8717 Baskerville Place, Upper Marlboro, MD 20772. **BUSINESS ADDRESS:** President, The Career Business Academy, Inc, 1411 K Street, N W, Ste 600, Washington, DC 20005.

LOVING, PAMELA YVONNE
Educational administrator, personnel administrator. **PERSONAL:** Born Sep 28, 1943, Detroit, MI; married William Copeland; children: Gregory McKay, Michelle McKay. **EDUCATION:** Mott Comm Coll, Associate Degree (honors) Registered Nurse 1967; Univ of Detroit, BA 1978; Univ of MI Flint, MBA prog. **CAREER:** GMI Eng & Mgmt Inst, coord health serv 1972-80, salaried personnel rep 1980-81, mgr personnel serv 1981-82, personnel admin 1982-. **ORGANIZATIONS:** Appointed Project Self-Reliance by Gov Blanchard 1984; mem Prison Ministry & Huron Valley Women's Facility Milan FCI 1982-; historian Hist Chap Top Ladiesof Distinct 1982-; consult Flint Bd of Educ Vocational Adv Comm 1982-; mem at large Flint Environ Action Team 1984-86; asst treas Flint Area Personnel Assn 1985-87. **HONORS/ACHIEVEMENTS:** Author/editor GMI Employee Handbook 1st edition 1985; Except Volunteer Serv Award State Correct Facilities. **BUSINESS ADDRESS:** Personnel Administrator, GMI Engineering & Mgmt Inst, 1700 W 3rd Ave, Flint, MI 48502.

LOVING, ROSE (NEE BILLUPS)
Educator. **PERSONAL:** Born Nov 15, 1927, Kenner, LA; married Parker A Jr; children: Ronald, Janice, Robin, Robert. **EDUCATION:** YMCA Ch of Commerce, dip 1946; So U, 1965; Tulane U, 1966. **ORGANIZATIONS:** Mem Orleans Praish School Bd; US Office of Educ & Evaluation Adv Comm 1974-77; public health educator LA Family Planning Program 1970-76; chairperson Tatle I Adv Com 1965-74; receptionist comm worker Comm Serv Center 1966-70; gen chairperson New Orleans Sickle Cell Anemia Found Telethon; bd mem Bayou River Health Sys Agencyy; bd mem Nat Coalition of Title I Parents; mem Human Relations Com; bd mem Mental Health Assn; co-founder Emergency Fund United Churches of Algiers; mem St Stephen Baptist Church. **HONORS/ACHIEVEMENTS:** Outst civic award Zeta Phi Beta Sor 1975; 1st annual friend of educ award United Tchrs of New Orleans 1976; 11 yrs of execptional serv New Orleans Title IAdv Com 1976; Award of Merit New Orleans Levee Bd; 1st black woman on Orleans Parish Sch Bd; only black to serve on US Ofc of Educ Rsrch & Eval Adv Com; 1st parent chpsn Title I Adv Com. **BUSINESS ADDRESS:** 4100 Touro St, New Orleans, LA 70122.

LOW, PATRICIA ENID ROSE
Educator. **PERSONAL:** Born Jun 04, 1932, Somerset, Bermuda;daughter of Arnim Smith and Nina Smith; divorced; children: Doris, Sharon, William, Jacquelyn. **EDUCATION:** Morgan State Coll Baltimore, BS 1956; Bryn Mawr Coll, Bryn Mawr PA, MA 1958; Univ of MD School of Medicine, attended 1964-67. **CAREER:** Morgan State Univ, asst prof in physicial science 1968-, instructor in chemistry 1961-64; MD State Coll Div of Univ of MD, instructor in chemistry & math 1958-60. **ORGANIZATIONS:** Consulting Instructor for Serv to Educ Inc 1975; 1st presiding officer Faculty Advisory Com to State Bd for Higher Educ in MD 1977-80; bd of Trustees Graduate School of Innovative Studies 1979-; Spiritual Frontiers Fellowship Conf 1979; intuitive perceptor Integrated Awareness 1980; trained in NLP neurolinguistic programming Soc of NLP 1980, contextual therapy, spiritual therapy. **HONORS/ACHIEVEMENTS:** NSF research fellow PrincetonUniv 1960; research fellow in biochemistry Nat Inst of Mental Health 1964-67; coll research fellow NASA Goddard Space Flight Center 1970; a personalized system of instruction Workshop Published by Inst for Serv to Educ Inc 1975. **BUSINESS ADDRESS:** Morgan State Univ, Hillen Rd & Coldspring Ln, Baltimore, MD 21239.

LOWE, AUBREY F.
Financial analyst. **PERSONAL:** Born Jul 07, 1940, Suffolk, VA; married Anne L Pulley; children: Gary, Brandon. **EDUCATION:** NC Central U, BS Accounting 1960; NC Central U, LLB 1963. **CAREER:** Eli Lilly & Co, marketing financial analyst 1973-; Indianapolis Bus Investment Corpd pres 1971-73; eli lilly co, financial analyst 1967-71; fed Housing &Adminstrn, staff atty 1963-67. **ORGANIZATIONS:** Mem NAACP; Omega Psi Phi. **BUSINESS ADDRESS:** 307 E Mc Carty St, Indianapolis, IN 46204.

LOWE, EUGENE YERBY, JR.
Clergyman, educator. **PERSONAL:** Born Aug 18, 1949, Staten Island, NY; son of Eugene Y Lowe and Minam V Lowe; divorced; children: Benjamin, Sarah. **EDUCATION:** Princeton Univ, AB 1971; Union Theol Sem, MDiv 1978, PhD 1987. **CAREER:** Princeton U, dean of students; Union Theol Sem, tutor 1979-; Gen Theol Sem, tutor 1978-80; Parish of Calvary & St George's, asst minister 1978-; Chase Manhattan Bank, 2nd vice pres 1973-76; St Agatha Home for Children, soc work asst 1971-73. **ORGANIZATIONS:** Dir Forum for Corp Responsibility 1976-80; mem Com on Soc Responsibility & Investments, Exec Council of the Episcopal Ch 1976-; mem Council on Fgn Relations 1977-81; trustee Princeton Univ 1971-83; trustee Elizabeth Seton Coll 1972-83. **HONORS/ACHIEVEMENTS:** The Harold Willis Dodds Prize, PrincetonUniv 1971; Phi Beta Kappa, PrincetonUniv 1971; fellow, Fund for Theol Educ 1976-77; fellow, Episcopal Ch Found 1978-80. **BUSINESS ADDRESS:** Dean of Students, Princeton University, 308 West College, Princeton, NJ 08544.

LOWE, HAZEL MARIE
Secretary. **PERSONAL:** Born Aug 04, 1936, La Grange, NC; daughter of George Rouse (deceased) and Musetter Gardner Rouse (deceased); married Earl C Lowe; children: Katrina E Lombre, Cassandra Eileen. **EDUCATION:** Barnes Business Coll, diploma 1955; Attended, US Agriculture Dept School of Business 1963-64, Univ of the District of Columbia 1982-83. **CAREER:** Interstate Commerce Commn, secty/stenographer 1977-78, secty/admin asst 1978-79, secty/admin officer 1982-84, confidential asst. **ORGANIZATIONS:** Mem Fairlawn Civic Assoc 1978-; mem Frink HS Alumna 1982-. **HONORS/ACHIEVEMENTS:** Outstanding Performance Awd Interstate Commerce Commn 1965, 1977, 1978, 1981, 1983-88. **BUSINESS ADDRESS:** Confidential Assistant, Interstate Commerce Commission, 12th & Constitution Ave NW, Washington, DC 20423.

LOWE, JACKIE
Actress. **PERSONAL:** Born Dec 14, Bamberg, SC. **EDUCATION:** Rider Coll, 1973. **CAREER:** Film, The Wiz; TV, The Guiding Light, Edge of Night, Ryan's Hope, The Merv Griffin Show, Easter Seals Telethon; Theatre, Daddy Daddy, The First, Ain't Misbehavin, Eubie, Best Little Whorehouse in TX, Storyville, Selma, West Side Story, Sweet Charity, Pippin, Daddy Daddy; J Walter Thompson Advertising, prod asst 1973-76; The Tap Dance Kid, actress. **ORGANIZATIONS:** Coord Mothers March March of Dimes 1972; mem AFTRA, SAG, AGVA, Equity Unions. **HONORS/ACHIEVEMENTS:** Nominated Best Supporting Actress Santa Monica Theatre Guild 1977; 1st recipient of Capitol City Dance Awd in Recog for accomplishments in dance and/or fine arts Trenton NJ 1985. **BUSINESS ADDRESS:** The Tap Dance Kid, 200 W 45th St, New York, NY 10036.

LOWE, JAMES EDWARD, JR.
Plastic surgeon. **PERSONAL:** Born Dec 05, 1950, Warsaw, NC; children: James Edward III. **EDUCATION:** Harvard Univ, Health Careers Program 1970; Livingstone Coll, BS 1971; Univ of NC Chapel Hill, Health Careers Program 1971; Meharry Medical Coll, MD 1975. **CAREER:** Downstate Medical Ctr, resident in surgery 1975-78; Lutheran Medical Ctr, resident & chief resident 1978-81; Lutheran Medical Ctr, teaching fellow general surgery 1981-82; Maple Medical Ctr, co-director; Long Island College Hosp, asst attending plastic & reconstructive surgery; Lutheran Medical Ctr, asst attending plastic & reconstructive surgery; Cabrini Medical Ctr, asst attending plastic & reconstructive surgery; Lenox Hill Hospital, plastic surgery residency 1982-84, asst attending plastic and reconstructive surgery. **ORGANIZATIONS:** Mem Phi Beta Sigma Frat 1968-, NAACP 1985, CORE 1985, New York County Medical Soc 1985-, Natl Medical Assoc 1986-; vice pres Brooklyn Medical Surgical Inst 1987-. **HONORS/ACHIEVEMENTS:** Physician Recognition Awd AMA 1986; publications "Adriamycin Extravasation Ulcers," Amer Soc of Plastic & Recons 1983; "Non-Caucasian Rhinoplasty," Plastic and ENT Surgical Group Lutheran Medical Ctr 1986; "Common Pressure Ulcers and Treatment," Natl Medical Assoc Convention New Orleans, LA 1987; History of the Carter-Morestin Soc presented at Natl Medical Assoc Convention New Orleans LA 1987. **BUSINESS ADDRESS:** Asst Atndg Plastic/Reconstruc, Lenox Hill Hospital, 103 East 75th St, New York, NY 10021.

LOWE, RICHARD BRYANT, III
Government official. **PERSONAL:** Born Jul 26, 1941, New York, NY. **EDUCATION:** Univ of WI, BS 1964; St John'sUniv Law Sch, JD 1967. **CAREER:** Dept of HEW, acting insp gen 1979-; Dept of HEW, dep insp gen 1979; NY Co Dist Atty's Office, asst dist atty 1967-79. **ORGANIZATIONS:** Mem 100 Black Men NY 1977; mem NY State DA Assn; mem NY State Bar Assn; mem NAACP; mem Big Brothers Orgn Nat Capital Area. **BUSINESS ADDRESS:** 330 Independence Ave SW, Washington, DC 20201.

LOWE, SAMUEL M.
Musical composer, arranger, producer. **PERSONAL:** Born May 14, 1918, Birmingham, AL; married Betty Haynes. **EDUCATION:** TN State U, 1 yr. **CAREER:** Erskine Hawkins Orchestra, musical dir trumpeter arranger 22 yrs; recording studios of NY working with various well-known stars, freelance conductor & arranger1958-70. **HONORS/ACHIEVEMENTS:** Inducted into the Jazz Club of Switz in Zurich 1962; inducted into Birmingham AL Arts Festival Hall of Fame Mar 1974; inducted into the Nat Black Cultur Soc Jazz Hall of Fame 1978; key to city of Birmingham by Mayor Geo G Siebels Fr City of Birmingham Mar 1974; keys to city of Birmingham Mayor David Vann 1978.

LOWE, SCOTT MILLER
Physician. **PERSONAL:** Born Sep 02, 1942, Charlottesville, VA; married Sharon Brewer. **EDUCATION:** VA Unoin U, BS 1964; Meharry Med Coll, MD 1970. **CAREER:** Ob-gyn chf resd physician 1974-75; Albany Med Ctr, ob-gyn sr resd 1973-74; ob-gyn jr resd 1971-73; Harlem Hosp Ctr, intern 1970-71; Richmond Dept of Hlth, insp 1964-66. **ORGANIZATIONS:** Bd dir Tidewater Area Bus & Contractors Assn 1975; attdb physician Norforlk Comm Hosp; Norfolk Gen Hosp; Bayside Hosp; Leigh Meml Hosp; mem Norfolk Med Soc; Norfolk Acad of Med; VA Ob-gyn Soc; jr fellow Am Coll of Ob-gyn; mem Med Soc of VA Omega Psi Phi; Zeta Chap Busileus 1963-64; Delta Chap Basileus 1969-70; VA UnoinUniv Alumni Assn 1970-; Meharry Med Coll Alumni Assn 19720. **HONORS/ACHIEVEMENTS:** Who's Who Among Studenst in Am U's & Coll's 1964; Outst Young Men of Am 1976. **BUSINESS ADDRESS:** 555 Fenchurch St, Norfolk, VA 23510.

LOWE, SYLVIA ONEICE
Engineer. **PERSONAL:** Born Nov 01, 1946, Detroit, MI. **EDUCATION:** Wayne St U, BS 1972; Cent MI U, MA 1977; Dale Carnegie Human Rela & Efective Speaking Course, 1979; Dale Carnegie Sales Course, 1980. **CAREER:** General Motors Assmbly Div Central Office GM Corp, sr ins enr 1978; Ford Motor Co, product design engr 1977-78; Ford Motor Co, sys engr 1976-77; NI-GAS, dev engr 1976; NI-GAS, aquifer engr 1975; Catepillar Tractor Co, ind engr 1975; Ford Motor Co, auto body desgn 1968-74; Fruehauf Corp, sales engr 1967-68; USATACOM, draftsman 1966-67. **ORGANIZATIONS:** Sec Soc of Ind & Voc Educ Wayne StUniv 1971-72; SAE Jr Chptr Wayne StUniv 1964-68; Soc Mech Engr Wayne StUniv 1965; sec instr grp leader coord Gen Educ Wkshp 1968-77; sec Thompson Court Area Block Club 1964; Dale Carnegie Graduate Asst 1980; mem Engineering Soc of Detroit; mem Ind Ambassador Com 1978-80. **BUSINESS ADDRESS:** GM Assem Div Cent Offc Gmc I, Dept 30009 Van Dyke, Warren, MI 48090.

LOWERY, JOSEPH E.
Clergyman. **PERSONAL:** Born Oct 06, 1924, Huntsville, AL; married Evelyn Gibson; children: Yvonne, Karen, Cheryl. **EDUCATION:** Clark Coll, AB, BD, DO, DD 1975; Chicago Ecumenical Inst, Garrett Theological Seminary, Payne Theological Seminary, Knoxville Coll, AL A&M, Payne Coll, Wayne Univ, attended; Morehouse Univ, DD; Atlanta Univ, LLD; Dillard Univ, LittD. **CAREER:** Warren St Church Birmingham AL, pastor 1952-61; Bishop Golden, admin asst 1961-64; St Paul Church, pastor 1964-68; Emory Univ Candler School of Theology & Nursery School, instructor 1970-71; Enterprises Now Inc, pres; Central United Methodist Church, minister 1968-86; Cascade United Methodist Church, minister 1986-. **ORGANIZATIONS:** Founder, vice pres SCLC 1967; natl chmn, bd dir SCLC Mobile AL 1967-77; natl pres SCLC 1977; mem Comm on Race Relations of United Methodist Church 1968-76, United Methodist Comm on Relief of United Methodist; bd dir Global Ministry 1976; mem, bd dir MARTA 1975-78; past vice chmn Atlanta Comm Relations Comm; mem General Bd of Publ United Methodist Public Housing 1960-72; mem Mayors Comm on Human Relations; chmn Civil Rights Coord Comm; past pres Interdenominational Ministry All Nashville TN; pres OEO Comm Act Agency; del, general conf United Methodist Church World Methodist Council Birmingham AL; mem, bd dir United Way, Martin Luther King Jr Center for Social Change; mem bd dir Urban Act Inc; mem Natl Leadership Council on Civil Rights; mem bd trustees Paine Coll; founder, pres Cascade Forest Comm Asson. **HONORS/ACHIEVEMENTS:** Awards from Natl Conf Black Mayors, Ebony; Medal of Honor Moscow Theological Seminary 1971; twice named Citizen of the Year OEO Award Atlanta Urban League 1975; Outstanding Comm Serv Contr; Honoree 1985 Religion Award for accomplishments as pastor of Central United Methodist Church in Atlanta, and for leadership as Natl Pres of SCLC. **BUSINESS ADDRESS:** Minister, Cascade United Methodist Church, Atlanta, GA 30311.

LOWERY, ROBERT O.
Retired city official. **PERSONAL:** Born Apr 20, 1916, Buffalo, NY; widowed; children: Lesie Ann Strickland, Gertrude Erwin. **EDUCATION:** Attended, Coll of City of NY, MI State Univ, Natl Inst on Police & Comm Relations. **CAREER:** New York City Fire Dept, fireman 1942, lt fire marshall, fire commr retired. **ORGANIZATIONS:** 1st black apptd adminstr of a fire dept in a major city; founder of progs to educate people about fires & encourage better relations between the dept & the pub; attempting to recruit more blacks into dept. **HONORS/ACHIEVEMENTS:** Received numerous awds & citations from various civic orgns.

LOWMAN, ISOM
Physician. **PERSONAL:** Born Jun 03, 1946, Hopkins, SC; married Irma Jean Smith; children: Joye Katrese, Isom Batrone, Robin Patrese. **EDUCATION:** SC State Coll, BS Prof Chem 1968; Meharry Med Coll, MD 1972; Wm Beaumont Army Med Center, Bd Internship 1972-75, Bd Residency 1978-80. **CAREER:** Ft Benning, chief of medicine 1975-78; Wm Beaumont Army Med Center, nuclear fellowship 1978-80; Moncrief Army Hospital Ft Jackson SC, chief of nuclear med 1980-82, deputy commander, chief of nuclear med & med 1983-. **ORGANIZATIONS:** Mem Alpha Phi Alpha Fraternity 1965-, Palmetto Med Soc; pres Cong Med Soc; fellow Amer Coll of Physicians; mem Soc of Nuclear Med, Amer Med Assoc. **HONORS/ACHIEVEMENTS:** Outstanding Alpha Alpha Phi Alpha Fraternity; Distinguished Grad Hopkins High School 1984. **MILITARY SERVICE:** AUS col; military medal of merit award. **HOME ADDRESS:** 51 Running Fox Rd, Columbia, SC 29223.

LOWRY, A. LEON, SR.
Chief executive. **CAREER:** Community Federal Savings and Loan Assn of Tampa, Tampa, FL, chief exec. **BUSINESS ADDRESS:** Community Federal Savings and Loan Assn of Tampa, PO Box 75303, Tampa, FL 33675. *

LOWRY, JAMES E.
Manager. **PERSONAL:** Born Jul 08, 1942, Wyoming, OH. **EDUCATION:** Xavier Univ Cincinnati, BS Bus Admin 1975. **CAREER:** General Electric Co, adminstr equal oppor minority relations 1970-71; Lincoln Heights OH, mayor 1972-74; General Elec Co, mgmt trainee 1975-78, buyer machined parts 1978-79, mgr long term agreements; materials administrator. **ORGANIZATIONS:** Bd dir Comm Action Commn Cincinnati 1972-74; bd dir Lincoln Heights Health Clinic 1972-74; consult Comm Chest Cincinnati 1972-74; bd dir People United to Save Humanity 1972-74; bd dir Freedom Farm Ruleville MS 1972-74; bd dir OH Black Polit Assembly 1972-74. **HONORS/ACHIEVEMENTS:** Key to City Cincinnati 1972; KY Col State of KY 1972; Awd of Appreciation City of Fayette MS 1973; Extra Step Awd Gen Elec Co 1980. **BUSINESS ADDRESS:** Materials Administrator, General Electric Co, Interstate 75, Evendale, OH 45215.

LOWRY, JAMES HAMILTON
Company executive. **PERSONAL:** Born May 28, 1939, Chicago, IL; children: Aisha. **EDUCATION:** Grinnell Coll, BA 1961; Univ of Pittsburgh, MPIA 1965; Harvard Univ, Prog for Mgmt Development (PMD) 1973. **CAREER:** Bedford-Stuyvesant Restoration Corp Brooklyn, spl asst to pres proj mgr 1967-68; Peace Corps Lima, Peru, assoc dir 1965-67; McKinsey & Co Chicago, sr assoc 1968-75; James H Lowry & Assoc, pres 1975-. **ORGANIZATIONS:** Mem Inst of Mgmt Consult 1980-85; mem Natl Black MBA Assn 1981-85; prinicpal Chicago United 1982-85; mem Harvard Alumni Assn 1980-85; pres Chicago PublLibrary Bd 1981-85; bd trustees Northwestern Meml Hosp 1980-85; bd trustees Grinnell Coll 1971-85; bd dir Independence Bank/Chicago 1983-85; bd of dirs Johnson Product. **HONORS/ACHIEVEMENTS:** John Hay-Whitney Fellow Univ Pittsburgh 1963-65; pres of class Harvard Business Sch 1973; Travel Fellowship Grinnell Coll 1961-62; Honor Scholarship Grinnell Coll 1958-61. **BUSINESS ADDRESS:** President, James H Lowry & Associates, 218 No Jefferson St, Chicago, IL 60606.

LOWRY, WILLIAM E., JR.
Business executive, TV host. **PERSONAL:** Born Feb 16, 1935, Chicago, IL; married Lillie T Lowry; children: Kim Maria, William Andre. **EDUCATION:** Kenyon Coll, AB 1956; Loyola Univ of Chgo, MSIR 1969. **CAREER:** Francis W Parker School, athletic dir, coach 1960-62; Inland Steel Co, suprv 1962-65; Inland Steel Container Co, personnel mgr 1965; Inland Steel Co, personnel mgr 1968-76; Opportunity Line WBBM TV, host TV series 1967-82; Objective Jobs WBBM TV, host TV series 1982-; Jos T Ryerson & Son Inc, mgr human resources 1976-86; Personnel Administration, dir 1986-88; Inland Steel Industries 1988-. **ORGANIZATIONS:** Mem Human Resource Assoc Chicago 1965-; sec Midwest Coll Placement Assoc 1967-; comm chmn Chicago Assoc Commerce Indust 1967-; vp, bd of dir Chicago Boys & Girls Clubs 1967-, Training Inc 1963-; mem bd of dir, trustees Lake Forest Coll 1984-88; mem bd of dir United Charities of Chicago 1967-87; mem bd of dir, Rehabilitation Institute of Chicago 1988-; mem bd of dir, Neighborhood Housing Services of Chicago 1985-; mem bd of dir, Trustees Kenyon College. **HONORS/ACHIEVEMENTS:** Distinguished Journalism Awd 1984; George Foster Peabody Awd 1968; TV Emmy Natl Acad TV Arts & Sci 1968-69; Human Relations Mass Media Awd Amer Jewish Comm 1968; 10 Outstanding Men of Chicago 1969; Blackbook's Black Bus Man of the Year 1981; Distinguished Journalism Award, AICS 1984. **MILITARY SERVICE:** USAF 1st lt 3 yrs. **BUSINESS ADDRESS:** Director, Personnel and Recruitment, Inland Steel Industries Inc, 30 W Monroe St, Chicago, IL 60603.

LOYD, WALTER, JR.
Utility company manager. **PERSONAL:** Born Dec 23, 1951, Tampa, FL; married Raye Evelyn Smith; children: Stacey, Tracey. **EDUCATION:** Univ of AR-Pine Bluff, BS 1974. **CAREER:** Arkansas Power & Light, sales rep 1974-77, adm rate analyst 1977-78, procedures analyst 1974-78, contracts administrator 1979-84, mgr 1984-. **ORGANIZATIONS:** Mem & treas Amer Assoc of Blacks in Energy; century club and leadership mem Quapaw Area Boy Scouts of Amer; mem ad hoc comm on Business Dev AR Develop Comm; bd of dirs Arkansas Regional Minority Purchasing Council. **BUSINESS ADDRESS:** Mgr, Minority Business Prog, Arkansas Power & Light Co, Capitol Tower 2311, Box 551, Little Rock, AR 72203.

LUCAS, C. PAYNE
Executive director. **PERSONAL:** Born Sep 14, 1933, Spring Hope, NC; married Freddie Hill; children: Therese Raymonde, C Payne Jr, Hillary Hendricks. **EDUCATION:** MD State Coll, BA Govt (summa cum laude) 1959; The Amer Univ, MA Govt 1961. **CAREER:** Peace Corps, top official Uganda & Kenya 1964, dir Niger 1964-66, dep dir/Africa region 1966-67, dir of the Africa region 1967-69; Africare, exec dir. **ORGANIZATIONS:** Mem bd of dirs Oversead Dev Council; mem bd of dirs Interaction; New Directions Educ Fund; Intl Develop Conf; bd of dirs Intl Voluntary Svcs; bd of dirs Carribeana Council; bd of dirs DC Inst of Mental Hygiene; bd of dirs Washington/Metro Jr Citizen Police Corps. **HONORS/ACHIEVEMENTS:** Disting Fed Serv Awd for Peace Corps 1967; Honorary Doctorate of Law Univ of MD 1975; Capitol Press Club's Humanitarian of the Yr 1980; Presidential Hunger Awd Outstanding Achievement 1984.

LUCAS, CHARLES C.
Production supervisor. **PERSONAL:** Born Apr 15, 1927, Brackenridge, PA; married Melverna Dumas; children: Cosetta, Zorita, Darenda, Ranotta, Richardo, Veleta. **EDUCATION:** Comm Business Coll. **CAREER:** Allegheny Ludlum Steel Corp, prod supvr. **ORGANIZATIONS:** Pres Allegheny Kiski Valley Br NAACP; con Coord Office Econ Oppor; Stewart AME Ch Tarntum; past pres Highlands OEO-CAC; mem Steering Com Allegheny-Kiski Valley Citizens for Peace; bd mem Umberalla Drug Program; bd mem YMCA; past pres mem Allegheny Valley Assn for Racial Equality; chmn Direct Action Com PA State NAACP; bd mem Allegheny Valley C of C 1974-77. **HONORS/ACHIEVEMENTS:** Cert of merit NAACP 1967; cert of achievement Allegheny Ludlum Steel Inc 1968; comm participation recognition Allegheny Valley C of C 1969; plaque Comm Leaders of Am 1970, 1971 & 1972; citation PA House of Rep 1970; recog cert of achvmt Allegheny Valley C of C 1976; recog plaque for outst leadership in Civil Rights Struggle Allegheny Kiski Valley Br NAACP 1975; apptd to serve on Anti-Poverty Coun Bd 1976; apptd mgmt chmn Anti-Poverty Coun Bd 1977; del Dem Conv 1972; letter of recogn 1976 election of Carter; Who's Who In Am 1973. **MILITARY SERVICE:** AUS t/Sgr 1946-48.

LUCAS, DAVID EUGENE
State representative. **PERSONAL:** Born Apr 23, 1950, Byron, GA; married Elaine Huckabee; children: David Jr, Leonard, Aris. **EDUCATION:** Tuskegee Inst, BS 1972. **CAREER:** State of Georgia, rep; Bibb Co School, teacher coach; NAACP, franchr judge exterm. **ORGANIZATIONS:** Vice pres, Macon Chfs Amtr football team; mem Black Eagles Motorcycle Club; C of C Macon; Fellowship of Christian Athletes. **BUSINESS ADDRESS:** 448 Woolfolk St, Macon, GA 31201.

LUCAS, DOROTHY J.
Physician. **PERSONAL:** Born Nov 27, 1949, Lambert, MS; daughter of Garvie Lucas Sr and Elizabeth Killebrew Lucas; divorced 1981. **EDUCATION:** Kennedy-King Coll, AA (w/Honors) 1971; Roosevelt Univ, BS 1973; UHS/The Chicago Medical Sch, MD 1977. **CAREER:** Mercy Hosp Medical Ctr, asst atten 1986-87; Columbus Cuneo Cabrini, resident 1977-81, assoc attending 1981-; senior attending 1986-. **ORGANIZATIONS:** Mem Natl Council Negro 1983-, Alpha Kappa Alpha 1986-; mem CMC, AMA, ISMA; diplomate Amer Bd Ob-Gyn; fellow Amer Coll of Ob-Gyn; instructor Roosevelt Univ; American Medical Assn. **HONORS/ACHIEVEMENTS:** ACOG Amer Coll of Ob-Gyn 1985; AMA Physician recognition Amer Medical Assoc 1985; Chicago Jaycees Ten Outstanding Young Citizens 1987; Distinguished Alumni City Colleges Trustee Award 1987; Push-Andrew Thomas Health Award 1987. **BUSINESS ADDRESS:** Sr Attending Physician, Columbus Cuneo Cabrini, 2600 So Michigan, Chicago, IL 60616.

LUCAS, EARL S.
City official. **PERSONAL:** Born Jan 01, 1938, Renova, MS; married Marilee Lewis; children: Eric, Vicki, Carla, Tina, Mark, Kendric. **EDUCATION:** Dillard Univ, BA 1957; further study DePauw Univ & Beloit Coll. **CAREER:** Bolivar County Sch System, teacher 1958-65; Star Inc, exec dir 1965-73; City of Mound Bayou, mayor 1969-. **ORGANIZATIONS:** Treas So Conf of Black Mayors; dir Mound Bayou Devel Corp; dir Fund for Educ & Comm Devel; mem Com Delta Ministry Natl Council Chs; dir Delta Found; mem Alpha Phi Alpha Frat; mem Conf Black Mayors. **BUSINESS ADDRESS:** Mayor, City Mound Bayou, PO Drawer H, Mound Bayou, MS 38762.

LUCAS, FLORENCE V.
Attorney. **PERSONAL:** Born Oct 10, 1915, New York, NY; married David Rex Edwards. **EDUCATION:** Hunter Coll, BA 1936; Brooklyn Law Sch, JD 1939. **CAREER:** Office Price Admin, enforcement atty 1942-46; Jamaica NY, private practice 1946-66; NY State Div Human Rights, asst commnr spl counsel 1966-71, dep commnr 1972-75; EEO Compliance Serv Inc, exec dir 1975-82; Consulting Firm, specializing in the preparation and monitoring of affirmative action prog owner. **ORGANIZATIONS:** Consul in Affirmative Action; vice pres of Judicial Council of United Methodist Church; mem NY, Queens Co Bar Assns; mem Queens Co Women's Bar Assn; mem NAACP, Natl Assn Negro Bus & Professional Women's Clubs, Jamaica Club, Natl Council Women of US; chmn Human Rights Comm; bd trustees Marymount Manhattan Coll. **HONORS/ACHIEVEMENTS:** Bronze plaque Natl NAACP; Natl Appreciation Awd 1974; Sojourner Truth Awd Natl Assn negro Bus & Professional Women's Clubs; Certificate of Merit Natl CouncilNegro Women. **BUSINESS ADDRESS:** Owner/Counsultant, Affirmative Action, 144-07 228 St, Rosedale, NY 11413.

LUCAS, GERALD ROBERT
Federal senior executive. **PERSONAL:** Born Sep 18, 1942, Washington, DC; son of Mack Lucas and Sylvia Coats Lucas-Jiles; married Patricia Selena Jones, Jan 19, 1975; children: Gerald R Jr, Kenya, Kimberlee. **EDUCATION:** Brandeis U, 1968-71; StateUniv of NY Stoney Brook, MSW 1973;Univ of MN, PhD 1976. **CAREER:** US Dept of Commerce, special assistance to the asst sec for adminstrn 1978-;Univ of Cincinnati, assoc prof 1976-78; Minneapolis Urban League, proj dir 1974-76; US Dept HEW, personnel mgmt specialist 1969-71; Waszh Urban League, program Dir 1967-69; US Dept of Commerce, dir office of civil rights 1982-. **ORGANIZATIONS:** Mem bd of dirs Minneapolis Zion Group Home 1975-76; mem Nat Assn of Black Social Workers Minneapolis Chap 1973-76; mem Am Soc for Pub Adminstrs Nat Capital Area Chap 1979-80; mem Cincinnati Title XX Adv Comm 1975-76; mem Barnaby Manor Civic Assn 1978-80; mem Conference of Minority in Pub Adminstrn 1979-80. **HONORS/ACHIEVEMENTS:** DHEW secretary's special citation Dept of HEW 1969; urban coalitation fellowship Minneapolis Urban Coalition 1976; article pub 1977; commendation award AUS. **MILITARY SERVICE:** AUS specialist 1964-66. **HOME ADDRESS:** 12006 Hazem Court, Fort Washington, MD 20744.

LUCAS, JAMES L.
Educator. **PERSONAL:** Born Oct 20, 1923, Canton, OH; divorced; children: Carol Bryne. **EDUCATION:** Boston Univ, AB 1947; Cornell Univ Law School, LLB 1950; Univ of Chgo, MA English 1965; Univ of Chicago Divinity School, MA 1970; No IL Univ, PhD 1980. **CAREER:** OH Indust Commiss, atty examiner 1953-57; Wittenberg Univ Springfield OH, instr english & humanites 1957-60; Harper Coll Palatine IL, instr english 1967-; TV Coll Chicago City Coll,TV instr 1970-74,84-; Chicago City Coll Wilbur Wright Coll, prof english 1965-. **ORGANIZATIONS:** Mem Bar of US Supreme Court 1955-, US Court of Military Appeals 1955-, Supreme Court of OH 1952-; lecturer fine arts, lit, humanites Chgo-Area Orgs 1965-; mem United Lutheran Church of Amer 1960, Sigma Tau Delta Natl English Honors Soc; Modern Lang Assoc 1975-, Natl Council of Teachers of English 1980-. **HONORS/ACHIEVEMENTS:** Listed in Directory of Amer Scholars 1982; Martin Luther Fellow United Lutheran Church of Amer 1950; author 2 manuals in Amer Literature for televised college courses publ by Chicago Ed TV Assoc 1970-,71; author The Religious Dimension of Twentieth-Century & Amer Lit publ by Univ Press of Amer 1982-; listed in Men of Acheivement 1977; author Executive Seizure Power Constitutional Power of the President to Seize Private Industry publ JAG Bulletin USAF 1959. **MILITARY SERVICE:** AUS sgt 1943-45; USAFR capt, judge advocate gen 1951-53. **HOME ADDRESS:** 6033 No Sheridan Rd, 36C Malibu East, Chicago, IL 60660. **BUSINESS ADDRESS:** Professor, Wilbur Wright College, Chicago City Colleges, 3400 N Austin Ave, Chicago, IL 60634.

LUCAS, JOHN (COOL HAND LUKE)
Professional athlete. **PERSONAL:** Born Oct 31, 1953, Durham, NC; married DeEdgra; children: Tarria, John. **EDUCATION:** Univ of MD, BBus 1976; Univ of San Francisco, M Second Educ. **CAREER:** Houston Rockets, player 1976-78; Golden Gaters, World Tennis Team 1977; Golden State Warriors, player 1978-81; New Orleans Nets, World Team Tennis 1978; GoldenState Warriors, player 1978-81; Washington Bullets, player 1981-83; San Antonio Spurs, guard 1983-. **HONORS/ACHIEVEMENTS:** NBA All Rookie Team 1977; All-Amer Tennis Player; won Atlantic Coastal Conf Singles Title Twice (Tennis). **BUSINESS ADDRESS:** San Antonio Spurs, Hemis Fair Arena, San Antonio, TX 78292.

LUCAS, JOHN H.
Educator. **PERSONAL:** Born Nov 07, 1920, Rocky Mount, NC; married Blondola O Powell; children: Cheryl, John Harding, Jr. **EDUCATION:** ShawUniv NC, BS 1940; NC Central U, MA 1951; NY U, certificat of advanced study in edn; NY U,Univ of NC, Duke U, additional study. **CAREER:** Adkin HS NC, sci tchr guidance dir coordinator of diversified occupations coack admin asst 1940-44, 1946-52; Orange St Elementary School Oxford NC, prin 1952-57; Mary Potter HS Oxford NC, prin 1957-62; Hillside Sr HS Durham NC, prin 1962-. **ORGANIZATIONS:** Pres NC Assn of Educators 1974-75; pres Kinston Tchr Assn 1942-44, 1948-50; adv com Gov Commn on Study of Pub Sch in NC 1967-68; bd dir NC Assn of Educators 1970-72; dir for NC Nat Educ Assn 1961-72; Liaison Com NC Tchr Assn NC EdnAssn; US Delegate to World Assembly of World Confederation ofOrgn of Tchr Profession in Africa, Asia British Columbia & Ireland 1965-73; consult Race Relations; contr Educational & Professional Journals; chmn NC Delegationsto Annual Conv NC Assn of Educators at Nat Educ Assn Nat Rep Assemblies; editor Beta Phi Chap Omega Psi Phi Frat Inc; deacon trustee White Rock Bapt Ch Durham NC; Task Force on NC Mental Health Cntr 1970; Nat Commn for TX Educ Assn Evaluation 1970; adv com White House Conf on Children & Youth 1970; chmn Durham Human Relations Commn 19730; bd dir Learning Inst of NC 1971-; bd dir Nat Found for Improvement of Educ 1970-; NC Cit Com on Sch; Durham Civic Conv Cntr Commn 1972-; honorary mem bd dir NEA 1973; Boy's Adv Council Salvat. **HONORS/ACHIEVEMENTS:** Man of yr award Cit Welfare Legue NC 1951; Who's Who in the S & SW; Who's Who in Am Edn; Outstanding Personalities of the S; distinguished serv award NC TchrA Ssn 1968; meritorious awad NC Resource Use Educ 1969; honor award NC State Fair 1969; distinguished serv awrd Durham City Assn of Educators 1971-72; Durham's Father of Yr 1972; honorary cit Durham NC 1974. **MILITARY SERVICE:** WWII veteran 1944-46. **BUSINESS ADDRESS:** Hillsid Sr HS, Durham, NC 27707.

LUCAS, LEO ALEXANDER
Business executive. **PERSONAL:** Born Sep 29, 1912, Woodbine, GA; son of Davis Lucas and Lidia Belle Lucas; married Alyce Downing; children: Lea Ann. **EDUCATION:** Fl A&M Univ,(FAMU) BS 1937; Miami Univ (Oxford, OH), MA 1951, LLD 1979. **CAREER:** Dayton, OH, teacher 1944-57; Dade Co FL Public Schools, tchr 1937-39; LALucas & Co, Inc, pres/chmn 1944-; Dayton Mesbic, Inc, pres, CEO 1973-81; Public School Governance, consultant 1973-; LA Lucas & Co Inc, sr accountant. **ORGANIZATIONS:** American Assoc of Mesbics, Inc, past ntl pres 1976-78; Natl Assoc of SBICS past mem/bd of dir 1976-78; Greater Dayton, OH Public Television, Inc, secy-treasurer 1980-88; Greater Dayton, OH Private Industry Counsel, vice pres 1981-; mem Accredication Council of Accountancy 1974-, Natl Soc of Public Accountants, Inc 1956- Natl Assoc of Black Accountants 1972 OH Schl Bds Assoc-Trustees 1972-88; co-chair Dayton Elected Officals, Inc 1973-, mem & past pres Dayton Bd of Educ 1965-88; founder & past natl pres Natl Caucus of Black School Bd Members 1967-; American Assn of Mesibs Inc; mem, NAACP Dayton 1989; mem, Dayton Urban League 1989; treasurer, bd of trustees, Creekside Players Inc 1987-. **HONORS/ACHIEVEMENTS:** Mem Dayton Community Affairs Council 1967-; member Ohio Council for the Aging 1985-; past chair of Large City Commision of OH 1972-; life mem Alpha Phi Alpha1934-; mem/sire archon Sigma Pi Phi 1980-; Man of the Year Frontiers International & Alpha Phi Alpha; Natl Award Outstanding Service in Education Governance NABSE 1974; 33 degree Prince Hall Mason/trustee-Bethel Baptist Church; Distinguished Daytonian Award, Miami Jacobs College 1989; Distinguished Elected Official, Dayton School Board past 22 years,1988; Dr Leo A Lucas Day, Ohio General Assembly and Mayor of Dayton Ohio, 1988 (March 11). **HOME ADDRESS:** 736 Argonne Dr, Dayton, OH 454081502. **BUSINESS ADDRESS:** Senior Accountant, LALucas & Co, Inc, 2243 Germantown St, Dayton, OH 454081623.

LUCAS, LINDA GAIL
Guidance counselor. **PERSONAL:** Born Jul 18, 1947, Charleston, SC; married Henry Lucas, Jr (deceased); children: Ayoka L. **EDUCATION:** Herbert Lehman Coll, BA 1969; The Citadel, MEd 1984. **CAREER:** Rockland Children Psych Ctr, sr speech pathologist 1972-80; Dorchester Co Schools III, speech correctionist 1980; Chas Co Sch Dist, speech correctionist 1980-84; Hunley Park Elem, guidance counselor 1984-85; Buist Acad, guidance counselor 1985-. **ORGANIZATIONS:** Sec Tri-County Foster Parents Assoc 1982; adjunct staff mem Dorchester Mental Health Ctr 1984; guardian ad litem GAL Program 1985-; delegate Alice BirneySchool Bd 1986-87. **HONORS/ACHIEVEMENTS:** News & courier article on single parent survival 1985; Licensed professional counselor State of SC 1986. **BUSINESS ADDRESS:** Guidance Counselor, Buist Acad for Adv Studies, 103 Calhoun St, Charleston, SC 29403.

LUCAS, MAURICE
Professional athlete. **PERSONAL:** Born Feb 18, 1952, Pittsburgh, PA; married Rita Lyles; children: Maurice II, David. **EDUCATION:** Marquette Univ, 1970-74. **CAREER:** Basketball player, Carolina-St Louis ABA 1974-75; Kentucky Colonels ABA 1975; Portland Trailblazers 1976-80; New Jersey Nets 1980-81; New York Knicks 1981-82; Phoenix Suns 1982. **HONORS/ACHIEVEMENTS:** Member of Portland's World Championship Team in 1977; NBA All-Star Performer all 3 years while a Portland Trail Blazer and was named to the NBA's All-DefensiveTeam in 1977-78 and the All-Defensive Second Team in 1978-79; Named to the All-NBA Second Team in 1978; Voted to starting position on West All-Star Team in 1983; Has 8,572 NBA points and needs 1,428 to hit 10,000. **BUSINESS ADDRESS:** Phoenix Suns, PO Box 1369, Phoenix, AZ 85001.

LUCAS, MAURICE F.
Government official. **PERSONAL:** Born Oct 10, 1944, Mound Bayou, MS; son of Julius Lucas and Glady Collins Lucas; married Carolyn Cousin Lucas, Feb 03, 1968; children: Maurice F Lucas, Jr. **EDUCATION:** Delta State Univ, Cleveland, MS, BBA, 1971. **CAREER:** Cleveland School Dist, sec & trustee, 1987-; Town of Renova, Renova, MS, mayor, 1978-; Renova Enterprises, Cleveland, MS, pres, 1988-. **ORGANIZATIONS:** Deputy grand master, PH Masons of MS, 1984-; dir, Industrial Devel Found, 1985-; dir, Chamber of Commerce, 1985-; dir, United Way, 1985-. **MILITARY SERVICE:** US Army, sergeant, 1962-65.

LUCAS, RENDELLA (NEE WISE)
Social worker. **PERSONAL:** Born Oct 30, 1910, Cheriton, VA; widowed. **EDUCATION:** VA Unoin U, BA 1932; Hampton Inst, MA 1943. **CAREER:** PA Dept of Public Welfare, retired caseworker supvr admin asst 1945-73; Fauquier HS, teacher 1932-36. **ORGANIZATIONS:** Youth ldr Salem Bapt Ch 1937-55; supr yth dept No Bapt Missionary Unoin 1940-55; vice pres Woman's Aux Easternbapt Keystone Assn 1945-48; vice pres Woman's Aux Sub Bapt Ch Assn 1951-53; pres Bapt Ministers' Wives Unoin 1943-45; corrs sec Nat Assn of Ministers Wives Inc 1943-55; pres Nat Assn of Ministers' Wives Inc 1957-70; fdr 1st edtr Newsette 1965; mem Philadelpha NAACP; exec sec Nat Assn of Ministers' Wives Inc 1970-74; mem Salem Bapt Ch; mem Ch Women United; life mem Nat Assn of Ministers' Wives Inc; mem exec bd No Bapt Missionary Unoin & Woman's Aux to Suburban Bapt Chs Assn; schlrshp sec No Bapt Missionary Unoin; recording sec Interdenom Ministers' Wives Flwshp of Philadelphia; vice pres PA Bapt Bus & Professional Women; vice pres Bapt & Women's Ctr of Philadelphia; comunist Ministers' Wives Herald; mem ML Chepard Chap VA UnoinUniv Alumni; mem Commn Disadvantaged Students Eastern Sem & Coll;vol Leukemia Soc of Am; mem adv counc Rose Butler Brown Fund RI Coll of Edn; coord Ministe. **HONORS/ACHIEVEMENTS:** Testimonial & disting achvmt award Philadelphia Ch Comm 1957; cert of merit VA UnoinUniv 1958; disting service award Philadelphia NAACP 1961; disting serv award Bapt Ministers' Wives of Philadelphia 1961; natl achvmnt award Salem Bapt Ch 1965; cert of achvmnt Bapt Ministers' Wives Unoin 1967; cert of award PA Batp Assn 1968; comm serv award Chapel of 4 Chaplains 1968; cert of hon life membership VA Assn of Ministers' Wives 1966; Elizabeth Coles Beueymeml ldrshp trophy Nat Assn of Ministers' Wives 1962; ousts natl chwmn plaque Bapt Ministers' Philadelphia Conf 1967; outst serv award plaques NY &Rose City Portland Ministers' Wives 1969; outstn serv cit PA Dept of Welfare 1973; Shrinre's Woman of the Yr Award 1970.

LUCAS, VICTORIA
Public relations executive. **PERSONAL:** Born Feb 02, Chicago, IL. **EDUCATION:** Malcolm-King Clg; Chicago, IL, Liberal Arts; Clg of theUniv NY, Bus Admn. **CAREER:** Amer Museum of Immigration, public relations asst 1955-57; Natl Council on Alcoholism, mgr publications dept 1957-63; Norman Craig & Kummel, copywriter/acct exec 1964-66; Cannon Advertising, public relations dir/copywrtr 1966-67; Victoria Lucas Assc, pres/owner. **ORGANIZATIONS:** Former mem bd of dir Publicity Clb NY; mem Pblc Rel Soc of Am; Natl Assc Media Women; conduct workshop Understanding The Basics of Public Relations,new school for Social Research, New York City 1977-. **HONORS/ACHIEVEMENTS:** Natl assc of media women Media Woman of Yr awrd; among women honored achvmnt bus Intrl Womens Year Com Operation PUSH Chicago, IL 1975; D Parke Gibson Outstanding Mentor awd; NY chap Committee on Minorities; Public Relations Society of Amer 1985. **BUSINESS ADDRESS:** President, Victoria Lucas Asso, 888 7th Ave, Ste 401, New York, NY 10019.

LUCAS, VIRGIL HILRY
Judge, attorney. **PERSONAL:** Born Jul 30, 1907, Buechel, KY; married Luella McIntyre; children: Virgil Jr, Robert, Katherine. **EDUCATION:** Howard U, BS 1931f Howard U, JD 1934. **CAREER:** State of MO, asso circuit judge; St Louis, atty 1956-74; 42-48; 34-39; LincolnUniv Sch of Law, law libr instr 1939-42; Loyal Automobile Ins, bd dir vice pres 1951-56. **ORGANIZATIONS:** Past bd mem St Louis NAACP; atty NAACP; past spl atty St Louis Urban League; life mem Kappa Alpha Psi Frat; past pres Mound City Bar Assn; Howard UAlumni Assn of St Louis. **HONORS/ACHIEVEMENTS:** Hugh Jones schlrsp award HowardUniv Sch of Law. **BUSINESS ADDRESS:** Civil Cts Bldg, 12 N 12th St, St Louis, MO 63101.

LUCAS, WILLIAM
Assistant attorney general. **CAREER:** Has worked as teacher, social worker, policeman, civil rights investigator, and FBI agent; lawyer; Wayne County Michigan, Detroit MI, county executive; US Govt, Washington DC, asst attorney general, 1989-. **BUSINESS ADDRESS:** Assistant Attorney General, Department of Justice, Civil Rights Division, 10th & Constitution Ave N W, Washington, DC 20530. *

LUCAS, WILLIAM S.
Educator. **PERSONAL:** Born Oct 31, 1917, Hampton, GA; married Doris Anderson; children: Yolande, Deborah, William. **EDUCATION:** Morris Brown Coll, AB 1942; Univ Pittsburgh, MEd 1951. **CAREER:** Thomaston Training School, teacher 1946-47, prin 1947; A Leo Weil School, teacher 1949-50; So Fulton HS, teacher coach 1963-64; Fairburn HS, prin 1964-70; admin asst 1970-73; Fed Programs, Fulton County Schools, dir 1973. **ORGANIZATIONS:** Mem NEA; AFT; AASA; Natl Alliance Black Sch Educators; Phi Beta Sigma Frat; vice pres Morris Brown's Tay Club; recorder Knights of Columbus, pursuer; mem Summer Youth Employment Planning Comm; Title I Parents Adv Council; mem YWCA; Official Black Caucus of NEA. **HONORS/ACHIEVEMENTS:** Tchr of Yr 1963; PTA Council Award 1963; Fulton County Tchrs Assn Pres's Award 1966-67. **MILITARY SERVICE:** S/sgt 1942-46. **BUSINESS ADDRESS:** 580 College St, Hapeville, GA 30354.

LUCAS, WILMER FRANCIS, JR.
Playwright, writer, journalist, producer-director, educator. **PERSONAL:** Born Sep 01, 1927, Brooklyn, NY; son of Wilmer Francis and Inez Williams; married Cleo Melissa Martin, Feb 18, 1969 (deceased); children: Alain Francis. **EDUCATION:** New York Univ, 1945-48. **CAREER:** Playwright, 1965-; writer, 1973-; New School for Social Research, New York City, lecturer in comparative Afro-American literature, 1962-68; University of Tennesse, Knoxville, instructor in humanities, 1971-; founder of Carpetbag Theater, Knoxville, 1971-, producer and director of "Carpetbag Theater Presents," 1972-. **HONORS/ACHIEVEMENTS:** Natl Endowment for the Arts award and grant, 1973, for perpetuation of the Carpetbag Theater; author of Bottom Fishing: A Novella and Other Stories, Carpetbag Press, 1974, Patent Leather Sunday: And S'More One Act Plays, Carpetbag Press, 1975. **HOME ADDRESS:** 1936 Prospect Pl, Knoxville, TN 37915. *

LUCK, CLYDE ALEXANDER, JR.
Surgeon. **PERSONAL:** Born Mar 03, 1929, Danville, VA; son of Dr & Mrs Clyde Luck Sr; children: Kelli. **EDUCATION:** Howard Univ, BS 1950; NY Univ, MA 1952; Howard Univ, MD 1959. **CAREER:** St Joseph Mercy Hospital & Detroit Receiving Hospital, resident in general surgery 1960-64; Kaiser Found Hospital LA, 1 yr fellowship 1964-65; Crenshaw Hospital, chmn dept of surgery 1974-78. **ORGANIZATIONS:** Mem Omega Psi Phi, NAACP, Urban League, LA Cty Med Soc; fellow Amer Coll of Surgeons, Intl Coll of Surgeons. **MILITARY SERVICE:** USAF 1st lt 1952-54. **BUSINESS ADDRESS:** 6200 Wilshire Blvd, Los Angeles, CA 90048.

LUCK, ETTA ROBENA
Educator. **PERSONAL:** Born Dec 24, Danville, VA; divorced. **EDUCATION:** Howard U, BS 1941;Univ IA, MS 1942;Univ Toronto, MA 1956, PhD 1958. **CAREER:** Univ DC,

asso prof;Univ Toronto, asso prof 1961-76; TX So U, asst prof, Diversified Sci Devel Corp sr consult 1977. **ORGANIZATIONS:** Phi Sigma Biol Soc; Delta Sigma Epsilon; Delta Sigma Theta; Brit Mycol Soc; Mycol Soc of Am; Can Bot Assn; Smithsonian Asso Who's Who Among Students in Am U'S & Colls 1940-41; Am Men of Sci; Women in Sci; Comm Leaders & Noteworthy Ams. **HONORS/ACHIEVEMENTS:** Grant Nat Rsrch Council Operating Grant in Aid of Rsrch 1974-75, 75-78; publ Resupinate Tremellaceae of Ontario, Intl Bot Congress Abstracts; "The Genus Heterochaetella" 1960; "The Genus Basidiodendron" 1963; "Semidelitschia" 1969; "Iodophanus", The Pezizeae Sergregate of Ascophanus 1969; "A New Species of Trichodelitscchia" 1970; "N Am Species of Coprotus" 1972; "Lasiothelebolus A New Genus of the Thelebolaceae" 1974. **BUSINESS ADDRESS:** 425 2nd St NW, Washington, DC.

LUCKEY, EVELYN F.
Educator, educational administrator. **PERSONAL:** Born Apr 30, 1926, Bellefonte, PA; daughter of Arthur R Foreman and Agnes Haywood Foreman; divorced; children: Jennifer, Carolyn. **EDUCATION:** Central State Univ, 1945; OH State Univ, BA, BsEd, English, Psych 1947, MA English 1950, PhD Ed 1970. **CAREER:** Columbus Public Schools, teacher 1957-66, evaluation asst 1965-67; OH State Univ, asst prof 1971-72; Columbus Public Schools, exec dir 1972-77, asst supt 1977-. **ORGANIZATIONS:** Mem Amer Assoc of School Admin 1977-, Adv Bd of Urban Network of No Central Reg Ed Lab 1985-, Assoc for Suprv & Curriculum Devel 1972-, Natl Alliance of Black School Ed 1978-, Central OH Mktg Council 1984-, Bd of Planned Parenthood of Central OH 1984-87; trustee, pres Bd of Public Libr of Columbus & Franklin Cty 1973-89. **HONORS/ACHIEVEMENTS:** Outstanding Educator Awd Alpha Kappa Alpha 1978; Woman on the Move Moles 1978; Woman of the Year Omega Psi Phi 1980; Distinguished Kappan Awd Phi Delta Kappa 1981; Disting Alumnae Awd OH State Univ 1982; Certificate of Honor City of Columbus 1984; YWCA Woman of Achievement Award 1987. **HOME ADDRESS:** 2747 Bryden Road, Columbus, OH 43209.

LUCKEY, IRENE
Educator. **PERSONAL:** Born May 29, 1949, New York, NY. **EDUCATION:** North Carolina Agric & Tech State Univ, BA 1971; Univ of Chicago,Schl of Soc Serv Administration MA 1973; City Univ of New York, The Graduate Schl, DSW1982. **CAREER:** Metropolitan Hosp New York City, medical social worker 1973-76; NC Agric & Tech State Univ, asst prof social work 1976-78; Brookdale Ctr of Aging-Hunter Coll, dir of educ prgms 1979-81; LeMoyne Owen Coll, visiting prof 1981-82; Clark College, asst prof 1982-84; Univ of West Florida, asst prof of social work, assocdir ctr on aging 1985-. **ORGANIZATIONS:** Consultant; Admin on Aging 1981; Atlanta Reg Comm on Aging 1984; Clark Coll Soc Work Prgrm 1985-86; Natl Assoc of Black Social Workers, Chair Educ Prgm 1985- ; Mental Health Assoc of Escambia Cnty, Advisory Member 1985-;State of Florida Long Term Care Council, Governor Appointed 1986-; Board of Directors, Northwest Florida Area Agency on Aging 1986; Geriatric Residential & Treatment of NW Florida 1986-; Phi ALpha, Kappa Alpha Kappa; Alpha Kappa Mu. **HONORS/ACHIEVEMENTS:** Impact of Race on Student Evaluations of Faculty, Article Published 1986. **HOME ADDRESS:** 1601 Texar Dr, Pensacola, FL 32503. **BUSINESS ADDRESS:** Asst Prof Social Work, University of West Florida, 11000 University Pkwy, Pensacola, FL 325145751.

LUCUS, EMMA TURNER
Educational administrator. **PERSONAL:** Born Feb 05, 1949, Meridian, MS; children: Kamilah Aisha. **EDUCATION:** Tougaloo Coll, BA 1970; Purdue Univ, MA 1972; Univ of Pgh, MSW 1978, AB 1985. **CAREER:** Planned Parenthood, counselor 1973-75; St Francis Hosp, rehab specialist 1975-76; Chatham Coll, dir of Black studies 1976-79, asst vice pres for academic affairs 1979-. **ORGANIZATIONS:** Pres Pgh Chap Assn for the Study of Afro-Amer Life and History 1983; consultant Presbyterian Home for Children 1982-; bd of dirs YWCA Pgh 1982-; bd of dirs Training Wheels Childrens Ctr 1984-. **HONORS/ACHIEVEMENTS:** Pgh Professional Awd Talk Mag 1982;TV prod Career Trends for the 80's 1983; grant HJ Heinz Foundation 1983; faculty develop grant Chatham Coll 1983-84-85. **BUSINESS ADDRESS:** Asst Vice Pres of Academic Affairs, Chatham College, Woodland Rd, Pittsburgh, PA 15232.

LUCY, WILLIAM
Administrator. **PERSONAL:** Born Nov 26, 1933, Memphis, TN; married Dorotheria; children: Benita Ann, Phyllis Kay. **EDUCATION:** Univ of CA Berkeley; Comton Costa Jr Coll Richmond. **CAREER:** Am Fedn State Co Municipal Employees, intern sec treas; AFSCME AFL-CIO, exec asst to pres; Contra Costa Co CA, asst mat & research eng. **ORGANIZATIONS:** Bd of trustees Nat Bank of Wash; bd of trustees African Am Inst; bd of trustees Transafrica; vice pres Indsl Union Dept AFL-CIO; vice pres Maritime Trades DeptAFL-CIO bd of dir Am for Dem Action; bd of dir Nat Laws of Black Aged; pres Coalition of Black Trade; mem Judicial Nomination Commn Wash DC; bd oftrustee Martin Luther King Center for Social Change. **HONORS/ACHIEVEMENTS:** Hon Doctorate of Humane Letters Bowie State Coll. **BUSINESS ADDRESS:** Coalition of Black Trade Union, P O Box 13055, Washington, DC 20009.

LUDLAM, VALERIE POPE
Business executive. **PERSONAL:** Born Aug 11, 1932, Detroit, MI; children: Marshal, Michelle, George. **EDUCATION:** Northfield State Hospital, psychiatric tech 1954-55; Lafayette State Clinic, pshchiatric tech 1964-66;Univ of CA Riverside, human relations 1967. **CAREER:** San Bernardino W Side CDC, pres; Lady Michelle's, owner mgr 1969-72; Operaton Second Chance, pub relations 1968-70; Patton State Hosp, psychiatric tech 1963-66. **ORGANIZATIONS:** Chairwoman Welfare Rights Orgn 1972; mem CDC Energy Tech Center 1979; mem Indsl Park Facility 1979; bd mem NAACP; bd of dir Comprehensive Health Planning; mem of Solar Cal Council State of CA 1978-; bd mem of Energy Extension Serv Dept of Energy 1979. **HONORS/ACHIEVEMENTS:** TV Documentary of Solar Energy Jane Fonda 1978; certificate of Spl Congressional Recognition Gov Brown 1979; commendation City of San Bernardino 1980; Ambassador of Goodwill Mayor's Office City of San Bernardino 1980; mem of CETA Adv Council apptd by Gov Brown 1980. **BUSINESS ADDRESS:** 1736 W Highland, San Bernardino, CA 92411.

LUDLEY, RICHARD
Educator. **PERSONAL:** Born Oct 18, 1931, Grambling, LA; married Sadie Pearl Allen; children: Gregory, Karen, Valerie, Patrick. **EDUCATION:** BS 1957; MS 1974. **CAREER:** Pinevew HS Lisbon, LA, public school teacher 1960-64; Hopewell HS Dubach, LA, 1964-68; Dubach HS, 1968-69; Ruston HS Ruston, LA, 1969-; Town of Grambling, alderman, mayor. **ORGANIZATIONS:** Mem LA Educ Assn, Nat Educ Assn, Grambling Voters League, Phi Delta Kappa, Optemist Intl, NAACP, Grambling State Univ Alumni Assoc, Prince Hall Mason 33degree, Lewis R Price Consistory No 173, Jomadi Temple No 171, bd of dir Grambling Federal Credit Union; mem Grambling Chamber of Commerce. **HONORS/ACHIEVEMENTS:** Teacher of the Year Hopewell High School 1965; Thunderbird Dist Awd Boy Scouts of Amer 1984; Romeo of the Year Sigma Gamma Rho Sor Intl 1986; Top Scouter of the Year Boy Scouts of Amer 1986.

LUE-HING, CECIL
Environmental engineer. **PERSONAL:** Born Nov 03, 1930; children: Cecil Barrington, Robert James. **EDUCATION:** Marquette U, BS civil engineering 1961; Case Western Reserve U, MS sanitary engineering 1963; WashUniv St Louis, doctorate environmental & san engineering 1966. **CAREER:** Met Sanitary Dist of Greater Chicago, dir Research & Devel; Ryckman Edgerley Tomlinson & Assoc Consult Engrs St Louis, vp; Wash U, asst prof; Huron Rd Hosp Cleveland, research technician; Milwaukee Sewerage Commn, field engr; Histopathology Lab Mt Sinai Hosp Milwaukee, supr; Human AnatomyUniv WI Reg, chief, professional engr; consult engr; corp dir & partner consult engr firm. **ORGANIZATIONS:** Mem Am Soc Civil Engrs, mem Nat Acad Scis Task Force; mem Water Pollution Control Fedn; mem Am Water Works Assn; mem Am Public Works Assn; mem Sigma Si. **HONORS/ACHIEVEMENTS:** Recipient Fellowship Wash U; pub 30 tech articles; pub chpts in 6 books. **BUSINESS ADDRESS:** Metro San Dist of Greater Chic, 100 E Erie St, Chicago, IL 60611.

LUIS, WILLIAM
Educator. **PERSONAL:** Born Jul 12, 1948, New York, NY; married Linda Garceau; children: Gabriel, Stephanie. **EDUCATION:** SUNY at Binghamton, BA 1971; Univ of WI Madison, MA 1973; Cornell Univ, MA 1979, PhD 1980. **CAREER:** Bd of Educ NYC, tchr 1971-72, tchr 1973-74; Handbook of Latin Amer Studies, contrib editor 1981-, consul 1981-; Latin Amer Literary Review, mem editorial bd 1985-; Natl Endowment for the Humanities, reader 1985; Natl Research Cncl/Ford Fndtn Fellowship Panel, 1986; Dartmouth Coll, asst prof of latin amer & caribbean, assoc prof 1985-. **ORGANIZATIONS:** Mem Modern Lang Assn; Assn of Caribbean Studies; Amer Assn of Tchrs of Spanish & Portuguese; mem adv bd Comm on Spec Educ Projects; mem Ad Hoc Comm to Study Hispanic Admissions & Recruitment; mem Minority Educ Council; mem Black Caucus; mem African Afro-Amer Studies Steering Comm; mem Literary Criticism Seminar; mem Latin Amer Literary Seminar; co-dir Latin Amer Literary Seminar; faculty advisor Phi Sigma Psi; mem African & Afro-Amer Studies Seminar; mem exec comm Assn of Caribbean Studies; mem Screening Comm for the Dir & Adjunct Curator of Film DC; mem Native Amer Studies Steering Comm; mem exec comm of the Faculty of DC; mem Agenda Subcomm of the Exec Comm of the Faculty of DC; mem Library Search Comm for the Humanities Bibliographer. **HONORS/ACHIEVEMENTS:** Deans List SUNY at Binghamton 1968-71; Vilas Fellowship UW 1972; Grad Sch Fellowship UW 1973; Grad Sch Fellowship CU 1974-76; Berkowitz Travel & Rsch Fellowship CU 1974-76; Sigma Delta Pi 1975; Latin Amer Studies Prog Travel Grant CU 1977; Edwin Gould Awd Aspira 1974-76-78; Tchng Asst CU 1976-78; Summer Rsch Fellowships CU 1975-79; Special Grad School Fellowships CU 1975-79; Directory of Amer Scholars 1982; ed Voices from Under, Black Narrative inLatin Amer & the Caribbean 1984 and numerous lectures, publications, articles. **BUSINESS ADDRESS:** Assoc Prof Latin Am & Caribb, Dartmouth Coll, Dept of Spanish & Portuguese, Hanover, NH 03755.

LUKE, SHERRILL DAVID
Judge. **PERSONAL:** Born Sep 19, 1928, Los Angeles, CA; son of Mordecia Luke and Venye Richards Corporal; married Anne Bradford, Aug 22, 1959; children: David, Melana. **EDUCATION:** Univ of CA at Los Angeles, BA 1950; Univ of CA at Berkeley, MA 1954; Golden Gate Univ, JD 1960. **CAREER:** District of Columbia Govt, dir prog dev 1967-69; Aetna Life & Casualty, dir urban affairs 1969-71; ConnVal Dev Corp, pres/dir 1971-73; Jacobs Kane Luke, attorney/partner 1973-78; Los Angeles County, chief deputy assessor 1978-81; Los Angeles Municipal Court, judge 1981-88; Los Angeles Superior Court judge 1989-. **ORGANIZATIONS:** Cabinet sec CA Governor's Office 1964-65; consultant Ford Foundation 1966-67; pres LA City Planning Commn 1975-76; bd of trustees UCLA Foundation 1976-; adjunct prof Loyola Law Sch 1979-81; pres (first black) UCLA Alumni Assoc 1980-88; regent Univ of CA 1988-90. **HONORS/ACHIEVEMENTS:** Outstanding Senior Award UCLA Alumni Assn 1950; Outstanding Achievement Awd Kappa Alpha Psi; CA Historical Soc 1981-83; Justice Pro Tem CA Court of Appeal 1985-86. **MILITARY SERVICE:** USAF 1st lt 1954-56. **BUSINESS ADDRESS:** Judge, Los Angeles Superior Court, 1601 East Lake Ave, Los Angeles, CA 90033.

LUKE, STEVE NORMAN
Athlete. **PERSONAL:** Born Sep 04, 1953, Massillon, OH. **EDUCATION:** OH St U, BA 1975. **CAREER:** Green Bay Packers, strong safety; WHLQ, spt anncr. **ORGANIZATIONS:** OH Yth Commin Found Boy Scouts of Am; Big Brths Assn; pres Flwshp Christian Athl; OH St Alumni Boy Clubs. **HONORS/ACHIEVEMENTS:** Athl in Actn Side Liners Aw; all Am OSU; Plyr of Yr OMA; Boby Watkins aw; aw Outstdng Pub Serv; Citznsdhp aw; outstdng sr athl 1971; Lkng Glass aw BS of Am; started 3 Rose Bowl Games for OH State; capt prep football & track teams; co-capt Packer Def 1979. **BUSINESS ADDRESS:** Green Bay Packers, 1265 Lombardi Ave, Green Bay, WI 54303.

LUMSBY, GEORGE N.
Business executive. **PERSONAL:** Born Dec 20, 1935, New York, NY; married Jean; children: Colette, Genieve. **EDUCATION:** Hunter Coll, BA 1957; City U, MBA 1973. **CAREER:** Aff Act Hum Res Philip Morris Inc, dir; Urban Affairs, mgr; Div Dir Pers Merrill Lynch, Pierce, Fenner, Smith Inc, adm asst; Richard Clarke Assoc, gen mgr; Corporate Recruiting IBM Corp, Fprog mgr. **ORGANIZATIONS:** Mem bd dir Inwood Mental Health Counc; mem bd dir Episcopal Miss Soc of NY; mem bd dir Manhattanville Comm Cen NY; mem Nat Urban Aff Coun NY. **MILITARY SERVICE:** AUS qu mst corps 1957-58, trans corps 1961-62. **BUSINESS ADDRESS:** c/o Margaret Hennes, Phillip Morris, Inc, 100 Park Avenue, New York, NY 10017.

LUPER, CLARA M.
Educator. **PERSONAL:** Born May 03, 1923, Okfuskee Co; married Charles P Wilson; children: Calvin, Marilyn Luper Hildreth, Chelle Marie. **EDUCATION:** LangstonUniv Langston, OK, BA 1944; OKUniv Norman, MA 1951. **CAREER:** Talent USA, pres dir 1974-80; consult various coll u 1959-80; OK City Bd of Edn, tchr history 1959-79; Choctaw Bd of Edn, tchr history 1961-78; Radio, commentator Clara Luper Radio Show 1960-80; Soul Bazaar,

founder 1970-80; Miss Black Am, state promoter 1968-80; Amigos Club Grayhoff & Woods Neighborhood Club, co-founded 1949-70. **ORGANIZATIONS:** Youth adv NAACP 1957-80; past basileus Zeta Phi Beta Sor Chi Zeta Chap 1962-; pres Freedom Center Inc 1968-80. **HONORS/ACHIEVEMENTS:** Alumni Award LangstonUniv 1969; Woman of Year Zeta Phi Beta Chi Zeta Chap 1970; nominee Nat Award Delta Sigma Sor 1975; Serv to Manking Award Sigma Gamma Rho1980; winner of 154 awards; author "Behold the Walls"; writer/director/producer "Brother President" a movie about Rev Martin Luther King Jr.

LUTCHER, NELLIE
Pianist, vocalist. **PERSONAL:** Born Oct 15, 1915, Lake Charles, LA. **CAREER:** Self Employed, pianist vocalitst jazz; "He A Real Gone Guy", recorded; TV Ed Sullivan Show; Town Hall, Paramount Theater, Apollo Theater, appeared at. **ORGANIZATIONS:** Mem local 67 Musicians Union; ASCAP, AFTRA, AGAC; Pioneer Club; NAACP.

LUTHER, LUCIUS CALVIN
Pastor. **PERSONAL:** Born Feb 19, 1929, Mound Bayou, MS; divorced; children: Shirl Taylor, Elaine Taylor, Carol K, Lucius C Jr, Jacqueline F, Rev Byron E. **EDUCATION:** Boliver County Training Sch, JL Campbell Sch of Religion, Religious Law; Brewster Sch of Theology, TN Reg Bapt Sch of Rel, B Theol, LLD, M Theol. **CAREER:** Brewster's School of Theol, teacher, assoc dean; Natl Bapt Convention USA Inc Dept of Christian Educ, instr of stewardship; EC Morris Inst of AR Bapt Coll, instr of christian educ; Thomas Chapel MB Church, pastor 1963-65; New Wrights Chapel MB Church, pastor 1963-65; Mt Zion MB Church, pastor 1965-68; Greater First Baptist MB Church, pastor 1967-68; First Baptist Church, pastor 1968-87. **ORGANIZATIONS:** V chmn Stewardship Bd 1976-, Natl Bapt Conv USA Inc; bd of dirs Chicago Baptist Inst; moderator New Fellowship Baptist Dist Assoc; mem of bd of evangelism Natl Bapt Convention USA Inc; vice pres United Baptist State Convention IL; vchmn of the bd EC Morris Inst at AR Baptist Coll Little Rock; chmn of loan dept, chmn of fed housing dept Natl Bapt Convention USA Inc; bd mem Natl Bapt Convention USA Inc. **HONORS/ACHIEVEMENTS:** Mayor's Key to the City for Soul Saving Citywide Revival Tacoma WA; Mayor's Key to the City Gary IN, Baton Rouge LA; Hon Dist Atty of Baton Rouge LA; Hon Council Mem of Baton Rouge, Hon Mayor of Baton Rouge; Hon Degrees Brewster's School of Theology DD, JL Campbell School of Religion DD, TN Regular Baptist School of Religion DL. **MILITARY SERVICE:** AUS 1954-56. **HOME ADDRESS:** 1829 Greenfield Ave, North Chicago, IL 60064. **BUSINESS ADDRESS:** Pastor, First Baptist Church, 2219 14th St, North Chicago, IL 60064.

LYDA, WESLEY JOHN
Educator. **PERSONAL:** Born Apr 10, 1914, Terre Haute, IN; married Minnie V Davis; children: Meredith, Kimberly. **EDUCATION:** DepauwUniv Greencastle, IN, AB 1935; INSTATEUniv Terre Haute, AM 1936; INUniv Bloomington, PhD. **CAREER:** Center for Afro-Am Studies & IN State Univ, dir & prof of educ 1968-; Central State Univ OH, dean graduate studies acting pres 1966-68; Ft Valley State Coll GA, dean grad div prof of educ 1957-66; Atlanta Univ GA, dean grad sch dir summer school 1950-57; TX State Univ, dean coll of arts & sci, prof of educ & math 1948-50; Morgan State Coll MD, head dept of educ dir curriculum study 1945-48; Phelps Stokes Found NYC, natl consult on curriculum & evaluation 1952-57; Cleveland Job Corps Center for Women, educ dir 1966; EOA Bd of Dir, mayor's rep 1980-. **ORGANIZATIONS:** Mem Omega Psi Phi Social Frat; mem Kiwanis Club Terre Haute 1974-; pres Terre Haute Br of the NAACP 1979-. **HONORS/ACHIEVEMENTS:** Recipient Outstanding Educator of Am Award 1972-73; recipient Distinguished Alumni Award DepauwUniv 1973; recip IN Black Expo Dist Serv Award & Plaque in Educ 1978; Scholastic Hon Societys Kappa Delta Pi Phi Delta Kappa Pi Mu Epsilon. **BUSINESS ADDRESS:** Stalker Hall, Room 203, Terre Haute, IN 47809.

LYELLS, RUBY E. STUTTS
Educator, business & civic leader. **PERSONAL:** Born in Anding, MS; daughter of Thomas F Stutts and Rossie A Cowan Stutts; married Meredith Jerry Lyells, Sep 10, 1932 (deceased). **EDUCATION:** Alcorn State U, BS 1929; Hampton Univ, BS (LS) 1930; Chicago U, MA 1942. **CAREER:** Alcorn State Univ High Sch, Lorman MS, instr 1929; Auburn Br Atlanta Pub Library, Atlanta GA, acting librarian 1930; Inspector Julius Rosenwald Sch Librs, librarian 1930-32; Alcorn State Univ, Lorman MS, head librarian 1930-45; IA State U, Ames IA, spec libr asst 1945; Jackson State U, Jackson MS, head librn 1945-47; Negro Coll YM-YWCA's of MS, dir 1947-50; Jackson Municipal Libr, Jackson MS, br librarian 1951-55; MS State Council on Human Relat, exec dir 1955-59; MLS Serv Co Drug Store, co-owner mgr 1959-69; US District Court, Southern District, Jackson MS, jury commissioner, 1970-74. **ORGANIZATIONS:** Mem Alpha Kappa Alpha Sor, Beta Delta Omega Chpt; Alumni Assns; past pres Alcorn State U; Hampton Univ; Univ of Chicago; Am Assn of Univ Women; Aux to Goodwill Inds; mem Blacks in Govt; Capitol Area Rep Club; MS Econ Council; Ch Women United; Hinds Co Rep Woman's Club; past bd mem Hinds Co Chap Am Red Cross; Intl Friends; past pres Jackson Area Counc on Human Relat; pres Jacksonians for Pub Edn; League of Women Voters; past moderator LWV Public Affairs TV Prog "Learn with the League"; State Negro Libr Assn; Urban League; bd mem Jackson YWCA; Co Blossom Counc of Black Ldrs of State Organ of MS; Common Cause of MS; MS Art Assn; bd mem MS Consumers Assn; MS Econ Counc; MS Libr Assn; past pres MS State Fedn of Colored Women's Clubs; MS Women's Cabinet; LQC Lamar Soc; chmn bd of trustees Pren tiss Inst Jr Coll; bd dirs WMPR radio Tougaloo, MS; mem Jackson, MS Mayor's Adv Comm, Chamber of Commerce; mem Symphony Encore Club; mem MS Museum of Art Rembrandt Society; mem Common Cause of MS; mem MS Economic Council; life mem NAACP; life mem Natl Cncl of Negro Women; International Platform Assn, Washington DC; Women in Community Service; past pres, SE Assn of Colored Women's Clubs. **HONORS/ACHIEVEMENTS:** Who's Who in Comm Serv 1976-77; Intl Register of Profiles N Am & World Edit 1976; World's Who's Who of Women 1977; MS Black Women 1976; Notable Ams of Becent Era 1976; Personalities of the S 1972, 74; Who's Who in Am Educ 1945-48; Who's Who in Colored Am 1950; Who's Who in Library Sci; bd of trst Prentiss Inst Jr Coll; DHL, Prentiss Inst Jr Coll, World Univ; author "New Voices in American Poetry Lectures"; Chicago U Alumni Assn citation; Hampton U award for "pioneers in education"; Alcorn State Univ Alumni Assn "Alcornite of the Year".

LYKE, JAMES P.
Clergyman. **PERSONAL:** Born Feb 18, 1939, Chicago, IL. **EDUCATION:** St Joseph Sem Coll Oak Brook IL, 1957-59; St Francis Novitiate Teutopolis IL, 1959-60; Our Lady of Angels House of Philosophy; Quincy Coll Philosophy Quincy IL, AB 1960-63; St Joseph Theol Sem, MDiv 1963-67; Union Grad School Cincinnati, PhD 1981; Coll of New Rochelle NY, honorary DHL 1980; Grambling St Univ, honorary DL 1980. **CAREER:** Padua Franciscan HS Parma OH, religion teacher 1966-67; St Thomas Church, pastor 1969-77; Church of St Benedict the Black, pastor 1977-79; Diocese of Cleveland, aux bishop 1979-; Grambling St Univ, dir of campus ministry. **ORGANIZATIONS:** Chmn Memphis Area Project South; bd dir SCLC; bd dir Memphis Girls Club Inc;, Amer Civil Liberties Union; mem Natl Conf Cath Bishops; pres Natl Black Cath Clergy Caucus; mem Natl Urban League; mem So Poverty Law Ctr; founding mem Assoc for the Study of Afro-Amer Life & History; mem Knights of Columbus 4th Degree; mem USCC Comm Campaign for Human devel; mem Natl Black Evangelist Assoc, Bread for the World, Pax Christi USA, NAACP. **HONORS/ACHIEVEMENTS:** Ordained Priest 1966, ordained Bishop 1979. **BUSINESS ADDRESS:** Diocese of Cleveland, 1031 Superior Ave, Cleveland, OH 44114.

LYLE, PERCY H., JR.
Sales representative. **PERSONAL:** Born Oct 15, 1937, Detroit; married Glenda Wilhelma; children: Kipp E, Jennifer B, Anthony S. **EDUCATION:** Communications Univ Colo, BA 1970; MA 1972. **CAREER:** Intl Business Machines, systems marketing rep. **ORGANIZATIONS:** Mem Park Hill Businessmens Assn; Optimist Club; Blessed Sacrament Ch; Com to Elect George Brown for Lt Gov; exec bd Malcolm X Mental Health Ctr; mem YMCA; Park Hill Improvement Assn. **BUSINESS ADDRESS:** 2490 W 26 Ave, Denver, CO 80217.

LYLE, ROBERTA BRANCHE BLACKE
Educator. **PERSONAL:** Born Jul 20, 1929, Glasgow, VA; divorced; children: Valerie, Robert Jr, Carl. **EDUCATION:** VA State Coll, BS 1966; Univ of VA, MEd 1972. **CAREER:** Town of Glasgow, councilperson 1972-75, 1972-; Rockbridge Cty School Bd, teacher. **ORGANIZATIONS:** Mem, bd of dir Stonewall Jackson Hosp 1972-78; scholarship comm Burlington Indust Glasgow 1976-77; endowment bd Grand Chap OES VA 1976; mem REA, VEA,NEA 1958, Order of Eastern Star 1952, NAACP, PTA, Ann Ellen Early #209 OEA; usher bd, sr choir, teacher Sunday School, Union Bapt Church; sec Mt Olivet Cemetary Comm. **HONORS/ACHIEVEMENTS:** Teacher of the Year Awd 1975.

LYLE, RON
Athlete. **PERSONAL:** Born 1943, Denver, CO. **CAREER:** Boxer. **ORGANIZATIONS:** Mem US Boxing Team. **HONORS/ACHIEVEMENTS:** 7 1/2 yrs CO prison & became outsdng athlete; Nat AAU Title; N Am Title Intl Boxing League.

LYLES, DEWAYNE
Educational administration. **PERSONAL:** Born Mar 08, 1947, Clanton, AL; married Michelle Billups; children: Raquel Lynn, Ryan Milton, Roderic. **EDUCATION:** Miles Coll, Sociology & Ed 1969; Univ of AL Birmingham, Counseling & Guidance 1975; Marshall Univ, Mgmt 1981. **CAREER:** Miles Coll Special Prog, counselor 1971-75, instr 1975; Emergency School Aide Act Prog Miles Coll, asst dir 1975-76; Miles Coll, dir admissions 1976-77; Marshall Univ, dir minority student affairs. **ORGANIZATIONS:** Test suprv 1973-75, principal suprv 1975-76, Natl Assessment of Students; consult WV School of Osteopathic Med 1983; prog comm Fairfield West Comm Ctr Jobs 1983-84; mem Progressive Black Men's Assoc 1983-; treas Omega Psi Phi; vice pres Men's Assoc Church. **HONORS/ACHIEVEMENTS:** Volunteer Serv Awd Joint Action in Community Serv 1973; Cert of Appreciation for Outstanding & Dedicated Serv Miles Coll Student Govt Assoc 1974-77; 1st Place Winner, 1st Awd Miles Coll Alumni Tennis Tournament 1977; Cert of Apprec OIC Help Our Youth Week Tri-State Oppty Indust Ctr 1979; Cert of Apprec for Outstanding Serv Student Activities; 1st Place Publ Spec Student Svcs. **MILITARY SERVICE:** AUS E-4 1969-71; Commendation Medal w/2 OLC 1970-71. **HOME ADDRESS:** 6 Samson Place, Granville, OH 43023. **BUSINESS ADDRESS:** Asst Dean for Educ Services, Dentson University, Granville, OH 43023.

LYLES, LEONARD E.
Executive. **PERSONAL:** Born Jan 01, 1936, Nashville, TN; married Faith Wilson; children: Leonard, Jr, Michael, Christopher. **EDUCATION:** Univ of Louisville, BS 1958. **CAREER:** Brown & Williamson Tobacco Corp, dir of Equal Opportunity Affairs, factory personnel mgr 1969-72, training coordinator 1967-69, asst to Nat Sales Mgr 1966-67, line supr 1963-66; Baltimore Colts & San Francisco 49'ers, 1958-69. **ORGANIZATIONS:** Mem Louisville Alcoholism Council; State Crime Commn; Jefferson Co Police Merit Bd; Jefferson Co Improvement Commn; Louisville Assn of Concerned Businessmen Youth Motivation; Lenny Lyles Inner City Football League. **HONORS/ACHIEVEMENTS:** Award of merit Louisville Jefferson Co Human Relations Commn 1971; one of ten Outstanding Young Men US Jaycee's 1972; Man of Yr Louisville Quarterback Club;Stoic Achievement Award; Frontiers of Amer Achievement Award. **BUSINESS ADDRESS:** 1600 W Hill St, Louisville, KY 40201.

LYLES, MADELINE LOLITA
Association executive. **PERSONAL:** Born Sep 27, 1953, New York, NY; daughter of Gilbert H Lyles and Mable Penergrass Lyles. **EDUCATION:** Morris Brown College, BA 1971-75; Howard Univ, Master of Social Work 1979-81. **CAREER:** Kennedy Institute, program coordinator 1981-83; PSI Associates, program dir 1983; Roy Littlejohn Associates, consultant 1979-; Urban Shelters & Health Care Systems, Inc, dir of admin 1983-89, vice pres Residential Treatment Services, 1989-. **ORGANIZATIONS:** Consultant Roy Littlejohn Associates 1979-; member Natl Assoc of Black Socialworkers 1980-; member Group Health Assoc Advisory Council 1984-; volunteer Center for Youth Services; member NAACP; consultant, Multi-Therapeutic Services, 1987-; practicum instructor, Howard Univ School of Social Work, 1988-; bd sec, DC Institute of Mental Hygiene, 1988-. **HONORS/ACHIEVEMENTS:** Merit Scholar; Natl Dean's List 1971-81; Scholarship Award Howard University School of Social Work 1980; volunteer appreciation Center for Youth Services 1984.

LYLES, MARIE CLARK
Educator, city official. **PERSONAL:** Born Oct 12, 1952, Sledge, MS; daughter of Dave Clark and Mary McCoy Clark; married Eugene D Lyles, Oct 1977; children: Jamaal Ventral Lyles, Justin Eugene Lyles, Jessica Marie Lyles. **EDUCATION:** Coahoma Jr Coll, AA, 1972; MS Valley St Univ, BS, 1974. **CAREER:** Quitman Caenties School, Marks, MS, teacher, 1970-89; Town of Crenshaw, Crenshaw, MS, mayor 1987-. **ORGANIZATIONS:** Natl Teacher Org, 1970-89; Crenshaw Community Builders, treasurer, 1985; Troop Leader, Brownie Troop (Girl Scouts,) 1986; vice pres, Ebonette, 1988. **HONORS/**

ACHIEVEMENTS: Outstanding Religion Leader, Quitman County, 1978; Outstanding Young Women, 1988.

LYLES, WILLIAM K.
Psychologist, educational administrator. **PERSONAL:** Born in Winston-Salem, NC; children: Don L. **EDUCATION:** Univ of NC, BS 1939; New York Univ, MS 1947, PhD 1958. **CAREER:** Queens Coll, assoc dean of students 1972-73; West Harlem-Inwood Mental Health Ctr, exec dir 1973-74; Childrens Aid Soc, coord of mental health 1974-79; Bronx-Lebanon Hosp, assoc chief psychologist 1978-83; Harlem-Dowling Childrens Services, coord mental health servs 1984-. **ORGANIZATIONS:** Pres Richmond Co Psychological Assoc 1974; mem NY Urban League Adv Bd 1980-83; pres Natl Assoc of Black Psychol 1983; pres NY Assoc of Black Psychol 1983; mem Natl Black Leadership Round Table 1983; mem Natl Task Force on Black Race Homicide 1984. **HONORS/ACHIEVEMENTS:** President's Awd Natl Assoc of Black Psychol 1984; President's Awd NY Assoc of Black Psychol 1984. **BUSINESS ADDRESS:** Coordinator, Mental Health Services, PO Box 257, Staten Island, NY 10301.

LYMAN, WEBSTER S.
Attorney, chairman. **PERSONAL:** Born Sep 24, 1922, Columbus, OH; married Marion E Newman; children: Bonita L Logan, Alisa K Blair. **EDUCATION:** OH State Univ, BS 1944, LLB 1949, JD 1949. **CAREER:** OH Civil Rights Comm, hearing examiner 1970-78; Common Pleas Ct, chmn/med arbitration 1982-; private practice attorney 1950-. **ORGANIZATIONS:** Parliamentarian OH Assn of Black Attorneys 1975; pres Lawyers Christian Fellowship 1981; pres Robert B Elliott Law Club 1955-56; nominating comm Natl BarAssn 1977-78; commander Amer Legion 690 before 1956; legal advisor Franklin Lodge of Elks 203; legal advisor Past Exalted Rulers Council Elks 1978-; pres Inner City Lions Club 1984-85; treas Columbus Urban League before 1960; pres Isabelle Ridgway Home for Aged before 1970; vice pres Project Linden 1980; pres Mu IotaChapter Omega Psi Phi Frat 1954-55; charter mem Good Shepherd Baptist Church 1976; vice pres Franklin County Forum 1985-87; past pres Buckeye Bridge Club 1982-84; past pres Second Community Bowling League 1981-82. **HONORS/ACHIEVEMENTS:** 40 Year Pin Omega Psi Phi Frat Inc 1982; Family Award Second Baptist Ch before 1970; Charter Mem OH Assn of Black Attorneys 1975; Charter Mem Lawyers Christian Fellowship 1966; Humanitarian Award Gamma Phi Delta Sorority Inc 1984. **MILITARY SERVICE:** AUS S/Sgt 1944-46. **BUSINESS ADDRESS:** Attorney, Lyman and Lyman, 1313 E Broad St, Columbus, OH 43205.

LYNCH, GEORGE K.
Business executive. **PERSONAL:** Born Oct 28, 1913, Enfield, NC; married Louise Mae Hinton; children: Joycelyn, Jewelle, Myrna, Carol. **EDUCATION:** Shaw Univ, BS 1940; Poh's Inst of Real Estate & Insurance, 1948; Long Island Univ, grad work 1957; Eastern School of Housing, NYC, business admin 1967. **CAREER:** Halifax County NC Bd of Educ, high school teacher, head of science dept, dir of athletes 1940-45; Warden's Real Estate Firm, dir of sales & property mgmt 1945-48; The Vogue Home Realty Co, owner/operator, real estate mgmt, insurance, public accounting & tax consultant specialist; Equitable Life Assurance Soc of USA, rep. **ORGANIZATIONS:** Mem NAACP; past basileus Omega Psi Phi Frat 9 yrs; past chmn bd trustees Janes Meth Ch; charter mem Bedford-Stuyvesant Area C of C; mem Central Brooklyn Coordinating Council. **HONORS/ACHIEVEMENTS:** Honor Club Award Agency Leaders Corps Equitable Life Assurance Co; Top Ten Brooklynite Award 1973; Honored Alpha Upsilon Chapter Omega Psi Phi Frat for over four decades of service and financial commitment to the frat as local and district keeper of finance and community involvement 1986. **BUSINESS ADDRESS:** The Vogue Home Realty Co, 704 Decatur St, Brooklyn, NY 11233.

LYNCH, HOLLIS R.
Educator. **PERSONAL:** Born Apr 21, 1935, Port-of-Spain, Trinidad and Tobago;divorced; children: Shola Ayn, Nnenna Jean, Ashale Herman. **EDUCATION:** British Columbia, BA 1960;Univ of London, PhD 1964. **CAREER:** Univ of IFE Nigeria, lecturer 1964-66; Roosevelt Univ Chicago, assoc prof 1966-68; State Univ of NY at Buffalo, assoc prof 1968-69; Columbia Univ, prof 1969-; Inst of African Studies Columbia Univ, dir 1971-74. **ORGANIZATIONS:** Fmem African Studies Assn; Assn for Study of Afro-Am Life & History; Am Historical Assn. **HONORS/ACHIEVEMENTS:** Recipient Commonwealth Fellow LondonUniv 1961-64; Hoover Nat Fellow StanfordUniv 1973-74; fellow Woodrow Wilson Intl Ctr for Scholars 1976; ACLS (Am Council of Learned Soc) Fellowship 1978-79; author Edward Wilmot Blyden Pan Negro Patriot 1967 & The Black Urban Condition 1973; Black Africa 1973; "Black Am Radicals & Liberaton of Africa" 1978; "Black Spokesman" 1970; "Selected Letters of Edward W Blyden" (with a foreword by Pres Leopold Sedar Senghor) 1978. **BUSINESS ADDRESS:** Inst of African Studies Columb, New York, NY 10027.

LYNCH, LEON
Union executive. **PERSONAL:** Born Jun 04, 1935, Edwards, MS; married Dr Estella Smith; children: Tina, Sheila, Tammy. **EDUCATION:** IN Univ, attended; Purdue Univ, attended; Roosevelt Univ Chgo, BS 1967. **CAREER:** Younstown Sheet & Tube Co, loader 1956; United Steelworkers of Amer, staff rep 1968; United Steelworkers of Amer, intl rep 1973, intl vice pres human affairs1976-. **ORGANIZATIONS:** Chmn of bd Memphis AFL-CIO Labor Council; vice pres Memphis Health & Welfare Plnng Council; bd mem Memphis Urban league, United Way, Southern Reg Council; trustee Natl Comm for Coop Ed, Negro Ed Emergency Dr; mem USWA Intl Civil Rights Comm, AFL-CIO Civil Rights & Housing Coms Founding; chmn Memphis A Philip Randolph Inst; exec com mem Natl A Philip Randolph Inst, Natl Steelworkers Oldtimers Found, Natl Urban League, Workers Defense League, Blue Cross of West PA, Natl Comm Against Discrimination in Housing, WQED; review comm City of Pgh's Job Training Partnership Act; Gov Relations Council of United Way, Labor Partic Com of SW United Way, Steel Adv Comm, PA Adv Comm of US Com on Civil Rights; life mem NAACP 1981; budget & fin comm Dem Natl Comm; Dem Party Commiss on Pres Nominations; dir Natl Dem Inst for Intl Affairs; mem natl exec comm Amers for Dem Action. **HONORS/ACHIEVEMENTS:** 1st A Philip Randolph Achievement Awd A Philip Randolph Inst 1977; A Philip Randolph Labor Awd Negro Trade Union Leadership Council 1977; Chicago Conf forBrotherhood Awd 1979; Apprec Awds APRI Chattanooga Chapt, NAACP Perth Amboy Br 1980; Declaration as Hon Mem in Good Standing of Local Union 5298 Dist 9;Local Union 1011 Awd of Gratitude & APRI Calumet Chap Grateful Recog Awd 1981; APRI Chicago Chap Henry Harrison Awd, Cert of Apprec from the VocationalRehab Ctr, NAACP IN State Awd for Outstanding Contribs to the Labor Movement 1982; ADA 35th Annual Roosevelt Day Dinner Awd & Dist 29 Cert of Apprec Awd for Outstanding & Dedicated Serv in Saving Jobs at McLouth Steel 1983; APRI Youngstown Chap Awd for Dedicated Serv to Mankind Careers Inc; Humanitarian Awd Local Union 1011 Awd in Reocg for Outstanding Serv & Achievements in USWA. **MILITARY SERVICE:** AUS sgt 1 yr. **BUSINESS ADDRESS:** International Vice President, United Steelworkers of America, 5 Gateway Center, Pittsburgh, PA 15222.

LYNCH, LILLIE RIDDICK
Educator. **PERSONAL:** Born in Gatesville, NC; divorced. **EDUCATION:** Hampton Inst VA, BS 1941; Univ of MI Ann Arbor, MPH 1949; NY Univ, PhD 1971. **CAREER:** NC Public Schools, tchr of sci & social studies 1944-46; VA Public Schools, tchr of elem grades 1947, tchr biology & chem 1947-48; Portsmouth VA Public Schs, tchng high sch & elem sch levels 1951-57; New York City Public Schs, health educ & testing 1957-64 1964-67; Jersey City State Coll, asst prof of health educ 1964-69, assoc prof & coord of comm health educ 1969-76; Univ of MA, assoc prof of pub health 1972-73; Jersey City State Coll, prof health scis 1976-. **ORGANIZATIONS:** Fellow Amer Sch Health Assn; Amer Alliance for Health Physical Educ & Recreation; Royal Soc & Health London; Amer Fed of Tchrs AFL-CIO 1974-76; Amer Public Health Assn; Amer Assn of Univ Profs; Natl Soc of Public Health Educators; Tri State Soc of Public Health Educators; mem Constitution & Bylaws Comm Amer Sch Health Assn 1968-72; dept rep Amer Fed of Tchrs AFL-CIO 1974-78; mem SOPHE Ad Hoc Comm. **HONORS/ACHIEVEMENTS:** Alpha Kappa Alpha; Kappa Delta Pi Betta Pi Chapt; Pi Lambda Theta Rho Chapt; Alpha Kappa Delta Mu Chap NY Univ Founder's Day Awd 1972; Zonta Club; Intl Inst of Jersey City & Bayonne NJ; Natl Found for Infantile Paralysis for study in Health Educ at Univ of MI Fellowship 1948-49; Fellowship Found Field Study Public Health Educ in MI Kellogg Found; Leaders in Educ 5th Ed 1974; The World Who's Who of Women; The World Who's Who of Women in Educ; Who's Who AmongBlack Amers 1975-76 Ed; Dictionary of Intl Biography; Comm Leaders & Noteworthy Amers 9th ed 10th ed; Notable Amers of 1976-1977; auth of many books &articles. **HOME ADDRESS:** P O Box 2177, Teaneck, NJ 07666. **BUSINESS ADDRESS:** Professor Health Education, Jersey City State Coll, 2039 Kennedy Blvd, Jersey City, NJ 07666.

LYNCH, LORENZO A., SR.
Clergyman. **PERSONAL:** Born Apr 21, 1932, Oak City, NC; married Lorine Harris; children: Lorenzo, Jr, Loretta, Leonzo. **EDUCATION:** Shaw U, BA 1955, BD 1957; Boston U, grad student 1957-58 & 1967-68;Univ NC Chapel Hill, 1957, 1962-65; DukeUniv Div Sch; Southeastern Theol Sem, 1958-59. **CAREER:** White Rock Bapt Ch Durham, NC, pastor; Davis Chapel Washington, former pastor; Endstreet Bapt Ch Scotland Nec; Mt Zion Arapahoe; St Delight Nashville; Reid's Chapel Fountain; Mt Olive Ayden; Bazzel Creek Fuquay Springs; Providence Bapt Ch Greensboro; Jones Chapel Palmyra, past asst pastor; Pittman Chapel Oak City; Peoples Bapt Ch Boston; Religious Educ Program (sponsored by Boston Council of Week-day Religous Edn), former tchr; Bapt Student Union at A&T Coll, former pastor-adv; Palmer Meml Inst Sedalia; preacher counselor. **ORGANIZATIONS:** Pres Durham Minister's Assn 1967-68; mem Durham's Clergy Hosp Chaplain's Assn chmn, Greensboro Br NAACP; bd dir United So Christiaowship & Found A &T Coll;bd dir Cumberland Ct Inc; bd dir Edgemont Comm Center 1968-71; bd dir Coordinating Council Sr Cit Durham 1968-71; adv bd Durham Co Mental Health Center 1968-74; mem bd dir Triangle Kidney Found 1975-; vis instr Duke Divinity Sch bd missions Gen Bapt Conv of NC Inc; mem Guilford CoYDC Club; critic of Interdenominational Minister's Alliance Durham 1975; chmn Precinct #8 Curham Co Dem Party; mem exec com Durham Co Dem Party; bd dir Triangle Housing Corp; exec bd Durham NAACP; chmn Com on Econ Devel Durham's Com on Affairs of Black People; unsuccessful candidate Durham's Mayor 1973. **BUSINESS ADDRESS:** White Rock Baptist Church, 3400 Fayetteville St, Durham, NC 27707.

LYNCH, ROBERT D.
Educator. **PERSONAL:** Born Sep 04, 1933, Greensburg, PA; married Dolores C. **EDUCATION:** Indiana Univ of Pennsylvania, BS, 1956, MEd, 1965; Duquesne Univ, MME, 1966; Pennsylvania State Univ, DEd candidate. **CAREER:** Hempfield Area Sch Sys, dept head 1958-65; Duquesne Sch of Music, instr 1965-66; PA State Univ, grad asst to dept chmn 1966-67; Fine Arts Component, asst proj dir coord; PA Reg J Title III, 1967-69; Upward Bound, proj dir; Lock Haven Univ, assoc prof 1969-71, dir supr coord 1971-, dir of development & special programs 1974-83, asst to vice pres for admin & development, affirmative action officer 1983-. **ORGANIZATIONS:** Life mem, Music Educ Natl Conf; mem, PA Music Educ Assn; Natl Sch Orchestra Assn; PA Black Higher Educ Conf; Assn for Inst Rsch; Natl Council Univ Rsch Admin; Amer Assn Univ Admin; Amer Coll Pub Relations Assn; PA Assn Trio Program Admin; Phi Beta Mu; Phi Delta Kappa; Phi Mu Alpha; pres, PA Black Conf on Higher Educ, 1984-88; gov, Rotary Intl Dist 737, 1985-86; pres, PA Black Conf on Higher Educ, 1984-90; pres, Phi Beta Mu, 1980-82; pres, Phi Delta Kappa, 1973-81; conductor Lock Haven Univ Symphony Orchestra and Chorus. **HONORS/ACHIEVEMENTS:** Lock Haven Citizen of the Year; TV Station WFBG "People Are Great Awd" Rotary Intl Paul Harris Fellow; Mary Davis Baltimore Awd by PA BCOHE for State & Community Svc; Hon Lt Colonel Aide-De-Camp to the Gov State of AL. **MILITARY SERVICE:** AUS 1956-58; reserve army 1954-62. **BUSINESS ADDRESS:** Asst to Vice Pres Admin & Devel, Lock Haven University, Office Devel, Lock Haven, PA 17745.

LYNCH, RUFUS SYLVESTER
Court administrator. **PERSONAL:** Born Nov 30, 1946, Baltimore, MD; son of Rufus Lynch and Marie Lynch; children: Marie Rachel, Kirkland Alexander. **EDUCATION:** Morgan State Univ, BA 1968; Univ of Pittsburgh School of Social Work, MSW 1970; Univ of PA School of Social Work, adv cert soc work admin, 1971, DSW, 1973. **CAREER:** Westinghouse Defense & Space Ctr, urban soc scientist 1967-68; Catholic Diocese of Pittsburgh, prog dir & consult 1969; Ford Motor Co, staff coord 1969; Philadelphia Health Mgmt Corp, res dev & outreach specialist 1973-74; Comm Coll of Phila, dir serv for aging 1975-76; Office of Lt Gov of PA, sr human svcspolicy adviser 1975-76; Office of Majority Leader PA H of R, ex asst chief of staff 1976-77; Office of Speaker of PA H of R, ex asst chief of staff 1977-78; MLB Inc, pres 1978-84; Temple Univ, sen exec mgmt cons, spec asst to exec vice pres for univ admin 1984-85; Admin Off of Supreme Court of PA, asst court admin 1986-87, director of court management, 1987—. **ORGANIZATIONS:** Founder Ctr for Studying Social Welfare & Comm Dev 1979; mem PA Bicentennial Comm of the US Const 1985-. **HONORS/ACHIEVEMENTS:** Social Worker of the Year NASW PA 1978; Outstanding Young Man Jaycee & Outstanding Young Men of Amer 1978-80; Cert of Appreciation City of Philadelphia Personnel Dept 1980; Alumni of Year Awd Univ of Pittsburgh School of Soc Work 1981; PA Assn of Special Courts special award, 1988; President's Friendship Award, PA State Constable's Assn, 1988; Distinguished Service Award, Natl Constable's Assn, 1989. **MILI-**

TARY SERVICE: AUS pvt 6 months; Honorable Discharge. **HOME ADDRESS:** 1013 S St Bernard St, Philadelphia, PA 19143.

LYNN, JAMES ELVIS
Government official. **PERSONAL:** Born Feb 16, 1920, Highbank, TX; married Zona Mae Hunnicutt; children: Wanda E. **EDUCATION:** Paul Quinn Coll Waco, TX, BS 1950; Prairie View Coll Prairie View, TX, MS 1957. **CAREER:** Falls Co Marlin, TX, commr pct 2 1978-; Hubbard Sch Hubbard, TX, counselor 1976-; Marlin Pub Sch Dist, principal 1955, tchr 1950. **ORGANIZATIONS:** Pres Marlin Falls Co Br NAACP 1974;scout master troop 320 Marlin, TX 1950-65; deacon & ss supt Zion Rock Bapt Ch 1960; mem Marlin C of C 1978; Sci Inst (2) Prairie View Coll 1958-59. **MILITARY SERVICE:** AUS spc 5 1942-45. **BUSINESS ADDRESS:** Falls County, Marlin, TX 76661.

LYNN, LOUIS B.
Research scientist. **PERSONAL:** Born Mar 08, 1949, Bishopville, SC; son of Lawton Lynn and Dorothy Evans; married Audrey Johnson; children: Adrienne, Krystal, Bryan. **EDUCATION:** Clemson Univ, BS (Honors) 1970, MS 1971; Univ of Maryland, PhD 1974. **CAREER:** Elanco Product Co, field scientist 1976-80; Ebony Agricultural Associates Inc, product mgr 1980-83, sr scientist 1983-; Ebony Agricultural Associates Inc, pres 1985-. **ORGANIZATIONS:** Mem Clemson Univ Alumni Assoc, Weed Science Soc of Amer; pres, South Carolina Horticultural Society 1987-88; Amer Soc for Horticulture Sci; South Carolina Agricultural Study Committee. **MILITARY SERVICE:** AUS Capt 5 years. **HOME ADDRESS:** 85 Olde Springs Rd, Columbia, SC 29223.

LYONS, A. BATES
Government official. **PERSONAL:** Born Nov 20, 1944, Philadelphia, PA; son of Archie Lyons and Irma Bates Lyons; divorced; children: Joanna, Daniel, Ashley. **EDUCATION:** Central State Univ, Wilberforce, OH, BS, 1966; Columbia Univ, New York, NY, MBA, 1972. **CAREER:** US Army, captain, 1966-69; Atlantic Richfield, Philadelphia, PA, mgr, 1969-72; Philip Morris, New York, NY, mgr, 1972-77; Heublein, Farmington, CT, mgr, 1977-78; Office of Policy Mgmt, Hartford, CT, under sec, 1978-87; State Technical Colls, Hartford, CT, deputy exec dir, 1987-. **ORGANIZATIONS:** Pres, Fed of Black Democrats, 1982-84; polemarch, Kappa Alpha Psi Fraternity, 1982-84; mem, State Retirement Commn, 1985-. **MILITARY SERVICE:** US Army, captain, 1966-69. **HOME ADDRESS:** 212 Carriage Ln, Torrington, CT 06790.

LYONS, CHARLES A., JR.
Educational administrator. **PERSONAL:** Born Apr 05, 1926, Conetoe, NC; married Rosa Lee Dance; children: Sheila Yvonne, Brenda Marie, Charles Herbert. **EDUCATION:** Shaw Univ, BA History (w/highest honors) 1949; OH State Univ, MA Polit Sci 1954, PhD Polit Sci 1957. **CAREER:** Raleigh Public Schs, tchr of english & soc studies 1949-50; OH State Univ, tchng grad asst 1951-54 1955-56; Grambling Univ, assoc prof 1956-59; Elizabeth City State Coll, prof of polit sci history & dean of coll 1959-62; NC Tchrs Assn, exec sec 1962-64; Howard Univ, dir of admissions 1964-69; Fayetteville State Univ, pres 1969-72, chancellor 1972-. **ORGANIZATIONS:** Pres Natl Assoc for Equal Oppor in Higher Educ 1973-81; pres NC Assoc of Colleges & Univs 1982-83; pres CIAA Council of Presidents/Chancellors 1982; mem Amer Middle States Assocs Collegiate Registrars and Admissions Officers, Assoc Coll Admissions Counselors, Amer Polit Science Assoc, NEA, Assoc for Study Negro Life and History, Amer Assoc State Colls & Univs, Fayetteville Area C of C, Alpha Kappa Mu, Sigma Rho Sigma, Pi Sigma Alpha, Phi Alpha Theta, Baptist Club. **HONORS/ACHIEVEMENTS:** Natl Leadership Awd in Higher Educ Natl Assoc for Equal Oppor in Higher Educ 1979; Hon Dr of Humane Letters Shaw Univ Raleigh NC 1980; Outstanding Citizenship Appreciation Awd NC Council on Deliberation 1980; Disting Alumnus OH State Univ Columbus 1974 1980. **MILITARY SERVICE:** AUS 1944-46. **BUSINESS ADDRESS:** Chancellor, Fayetteville StateUniv, Newbold Station, Fayetteville, NC 28301.

LYONS, CHARLES H.S., JR.
Educator. **PERSONAL:** Born May 03, 1917, Athens, GA; son of C H S Lyons Sr and Ophelia Lyons; children: Lottie, Charles III, Charlotte, Collins, Beatrice, Faye. **EDUCATION:** Savannah State Coll, BSE 1939; Attended, Univ of Hawaii 1944-45, Hampton Inst 1948, Univ of CA 1978-79. **ORGANIZATIONS:** Mem VFW 3910. **HONORS/ACHIEVEMENTS:** Teacher of the Year Oglethorpe Co 1960. **MILITARY SERVICE:** AUS corpl 3 1/2 yrs; Army Medal. **HOME ADDRESS:** 232 Rhodes Dr, Athens, GA 30606.

LYONS, DONALD WALLACE
Librarian. **PERSONAL:** Born Dec 11, 1945, Lexington, KY; married Myra Briggs. **EDUCATION:** KY St U, AB 1968;Univ of KY, MSLS 1971. **CAREER:** KY State Univ, dir of library, asst librarian, teacher, supvr Adult Educ; Am Libr Assn, tchr; Amer Assn of Univ Prof; KY Library Assn. **ORGANIZATIONS:** NEA Alpha Phi Alpha frat. **HONORS/ACHIEVEMENTS:** Who's Who in KY; publ "Afr & Afr Am Hsty & Cult a biblio"; "follow-up on the job training plcmnts"; "blazer bugle". **BUSINESS ADDRESS:** Blazer Lib, KY St Univ, Frankfort, KY 40601.

LYONS, GEORGE W.C., SR.
Director. **PERSONAL:** Born Aug 20, 1923, New Orleans, LA; married Delores Scott; children: George WC Jr, Joanne C. **EDUCATION:** Bishop Coll, AB 1948; TX S Univ, ME Voc Educ Guidance; Bapt Theol Sem, DD 1963. **CAREER:** Certified public school teacher & vocational guidance for several states; Lyons Mail Order House; Evang Ambassadors for Christ Inc of LA, pres founder; Lyons Religion Clinic, teacher, minister. **ORGANIZATIONS:** Mem LA Police Clergy Cncl; Comm Police Cncl; Holand Lodge Mason; dir Lyons Religious Clinic; mem S Ministers Conf; CA Tchr Assn; mem Omega Frat, Urban League; past bd mem Com for Rights of Disabled; YMCA; Amer Legion; Disabled Amer Vets; teacher handicapped students; Mason; NEA. **HONORS/ACHIEVEMENTS:** Head Start Cncl Univ of TX at Austin 1966; Hon in Men of Achievement Comm Worldwide 9th ed; Leaders & Noteworthy Amers; Honorary Mem Ins Comm State ofLA 1984; Key to the City of New Orleans LA 1984. **MILITARY SERVICE:** USAAF WW II chaplain 2 yrs; Good Conduct Medal. **BUSINESS ADDRESS:** Teacher & Minister, Lyons Relig Clinic, 1206 W 89th St, Los Angeles, CA 90044.

LYONS, JAMES E., SR.

University president. **CAREER:** Bowie State Univ, Bowie, MD, pres. **BUSINESS ADDRESS:** Bowie State Univ, Jericho Park Rd, Bowie, MD 20715. *

LYONS, LLOYD CARSON
Business executive. **PERSONAL:** Born Aug 01, 1942, New Castle, PA; children: Lloyd Jr, Shannon, Christopher. **EDUCATION:** IN U, AB 1966; IN Central U, MBA. **CAREER:** IN Nat Bank, sr vp, dir personnel 1966-. **ORGANIZATIONS:** Mem Am Soc of Personnel Adminstrs; mem United Negro Coll Fund; bd mem Day Nursery Assn of Indpls; United Way Allocations & Admissions Com. **BUSINESS ADDRESS:** Sr Vice President, Indiana Natl Corporation, One Indiana Square, Ste 2580, Indianapolis, IN 46266.

LYONS, ROBERT P.
Business executive. **PERSONAL:** Born Nov 18, 1912, Kansas City, MO; married Claudia Mae Hopkins. **EDUCATION:** Attended, Univ of KS. **CAREER:** Universal Life Ins, dist mgr Kansas City 1949-55; Crusader Life Ins Co, agency dir 1957-69; Amer Woodmen's Life Ins Co, bd chmn. **ORGANIZATIONS:** Past pres Millionaires Club Natl Ins Assn; Beta Lambda chap Alpha Phi Alpha; past chmn Agency Sect Natl Ins Assn; past chmn pro-tem, Bethel AME Trustee Bd; mem Bethel AME Ch; co-incorporator Bethel AME Ch Not-For-Profit Found; pres & founder Soft & Sweet Music Club; past dir Region 2 Natl Ins Assn;past mem Bd Mgmt Paseo-Linwood YMCA; mem KS City Area C of C; life mem Alpha Phi Alpha. **HONORS/ACHIEVEMENTS:** Certificate of Achievement Millionaires Club Natl Ins Assn 1958-71; elected to Midwestern Hall of Fame. **BUSINESS ADDRESS:** Board Chairman, Amer Woodmen's Life Ins Co, 853 Minnesota Ave, Kansas City, KS 66101.

LYONS, WILLIAM B.
Clergyman. **PERSONAL:** Born Aug 27, 1924, Burnwell, AL; married Gracie Mae Pendleton; children: Harvey, Kathy Powell, Elaine Graham, Wilford, Carl, Gary, Kevin, William Jr. **EDUCATION:** Golden Gate Sem, evangelism 1969; MI Bapt Sem, DDiv 1974; Anchorage Interdenominational Inst of Practical Theol, grad. **CAREER:** New Hope Bapt Ch, pastor. **ORGANIZATIONS:** Pres NAACP; moderator Chugach Bapt Assn; citizens adv educ concerns Anchorage Sch Dist; chmn AK State Bd of Parole; pres So Bapt Convention AK; health bd mem City of Anchorage; career educ bd mem Anchorage Sch Dist; pres PTA Fairbanks & Anchorage, AK; pres Ministerial Alliance. **BUSINESS ADDRESS:** New Hope Bapt Ch, 333 N Price St, Anchorage, AK 99504.

LYTLE, ALICE A.
Judge. **PERSONAL:** Born in Jersey City, NJ. **EDUCATION:** Hunter Coll, AB; Hastings Coll of Law, JD 1973. **CAREER:** Albert Einstein Coll of Medicine, medical rsch tech 1961-70; Univ of CA San Francisco Cardiovascular Rsch Inst; Gov Edmund G Brown Jr, dep legal affairs sec 1975-77; Dept Indus Relations Div Fair Employee Practices, chief 1977-79; State & Consumer Serv Agency (Cabinet Office in admin of Gov Brown), sec 1979-82; Sacramento Municipal Court, judge. **HONORS/ACHIEVEMENTS:** Hall of Fame Hunter Coll NYC. **BUSINESS ADDRESS:** Judge Municipal Court, Sacramento Municipal Court, 720 9th St, Sacramento, CA 95814.

LYTLE, WILLIAM F.
Business executive. **PERSONAL:** Born Oct 23, 1940, Boston, MA; married Veronica; children: Monica, Shawn. **EDUCATION:** Northeastern U, BS 1963, MBA 1969. **CAREER:** Waterbury Scroll Pen Corp, pres 1972-; business consultant, 1968-72; GE Co, mfg engr 1967-68, design engr 1963-64; Artisan Ind 1959-63. **MILITARY SERVICE:** AUS capt 1964-67.

M

MABEN, HAYWARD C., JR.
Physician. **PERSONAL:** Born Jun 03, 1922, Augusta, GA; married Carrie M harris; children: Hayward III, Burton, Michael. **EDUCATION:** Wayne State Univ, BS 1942; Meharry Med Coll, MD 1945. **CAREER:** Wayne State Univ School of Med, clinical asst prof; Private practice, cardiovascular & thoracic surgeon. **ORGANIZATIONS:** Bd cert Amer Coll of Surgeons, Amer Bd of Surgery, Amer Bd of Thoracic Surgery; fellow Amer Coll of Chest Physicians; mem Soc of Thoracic Surgeons;life mem NAACP; mem Natl Med Assoc. **HONORS/ACHIEVEMENTS:** 1st black thoracic surgeon in state of MI. **MILITARY SERVICE:** AUS 1943-45. **BUSINESS ADDRESS:** Cardiovasc & Thoracic Surgeon, 868 Fisher Bldg, Detroit, MI 48202.

MABIN, JOSEPH E.
Chief executive. **CAREER:** Mabin Construction Co, Inc, Kansas City, MO, chief exec, 1980-. **BUSINESS ADDRESS:** Mabin Construction Co, Inc, 8640 E 63rd St, Kansas City, MO 64133. *

MABREY, HAROLD LEON
Director of procurement and production. **PERSONAL:** Born May 24, 1933, Pittsburg, TX; son of Horace L Mabrey and Ethelyn E Peoples; married Barbara Johnson; children: Vicki Lynn, Lesley Harold, Kevin Frank. **EDUCATION:** Lincoln Univ MO, BS Business Admin 1955; George Washington Univ, MBA 1971; Indus Coll of the Armed Forces, Grad 1978; Harvard Univ, diploma in National & International Security Affairs 1987. **CAREER:** AUS Avn Res & Dev Cmd, suprv contract specialist/chief proc div 1977-; AUS, GS-14 supv contr spec 1973-77, GS-13 supv contr spec 1969-73, GS-12 supv contr spec 1966-69, GS-11 supv contr spec 1964-66. **ORGANIZATIONS:** Mem Natl Contract Mgmt Assn 1975-; mem Minority Bus Oppor Comm 1979-; vice chmn EEO Working Group AUS 1980; mem Omega Psi Phi Frat 1953-; mem Lincoln Univ Alumni Assn 1955-; Berea Presbyterian Church 1978-. **HONORS/ACHIEVEMENTS:** Marksman, Good Conduct Medal AUS 1955-57; sustained superior performance award AUS Transp Command 1962; meritorious civilian serv award AUS 1970, 76, 77; outstanding performance award AUS 1971, 1977 & 1980; honor grad def adv proc mgmt AUS 1973; cert of achievement AUS 1977; Distinguished Alumni Award 1986; Secretary of Defense Superior Management Award 1989. **MILITARY SERVICE:** AUS corpl 1955-57. **BUSINESS ADDRESS:** US Army Troop Support Command, 4300 Goodfellow Blvd, St Louis, MO 63120.

MABREY, MARSHA EVE
Educator. **PERSONAL:** Born Nov 07, 1949, Pittsburgh, PA. **EDUCATION:** Univ of MI School of Music, BM 1971, MM 1972; Univ of Cincinnati Coll Conservatory of Music, DMA Orchestral Conducting attending. **CAREER:** Univ of Cincinnati Coll Conservatory of Music Orch, asst conductor 1973-76; Winona State Univ Symphony Orch, instr of music 1978-80; Grand Rapids Symphony Orch, asst conductor 1980-81; Grand Valley State Coll Symphony Orch, asst prof of music 1980-82; Interlochen All State Music Prog, conductor for All State Orchestra Concer Prog 1982; Eugene Chamber Orch, music dir, conductor comm orchestra 1984-; Univ of OR Symphony Orch, asst prof of music 1982-. **ORGANIZATIONS:** Guest conducting MI Youth Symphony Orch 1977; coord, dir West Coast Women Conductor/Composer Symposium 1984-85; orchestra chmn OR Music Ed Assoc 1984-86;keynote speaker OR String Teacher Assoc 1984; guest conducting PA Music Ed Assoc Conf Symphony; mem Natl School Band & Orchestra Assoc, Coll Music Soc;mem Amer Symphony Orchestra League, The Conductors Guild, MENC, OMEA. **HONORS/ACHIEVEMENTS:** $10,000 Grant for West Coast Women Conductor/Composer Symposium Ctr for the Study of Women in Soc 1974; Grant for Amer Women Conductor/Composer Symposium Ctr the Study of Women in Soc. **HOME ADDRESS:** 1593 Jefferson, Eugene, OR 97402. **BUSINESS ADDRESS:** Professor, Music Conductor, Univ of Oregon, School of Music, Eugene, OR 97403.

MABRIE, HERMAN JAMES, III
Physician. **PERSONAL:** Born Jul 10, 1948, Houston, TX; married Linda; children: David, Herman IV, Brent. **EDUCATION:** Howard U, BS 1969; Meharry Med Coll, MD 1973. **CAREER:** Otorhinolaryngologist, pvt prac; Baylor Affiliated Hosp, otorhino resd 1975-78, gen surg resd 1973-75. **ORGANIZATIONS:** Mem Houston Med Forum; Alpha Phi Omega Serv Frat; The Deafness Rsrch Found; AMA; Nat Medc Assn; Harris Co Med Assn; TX Med Assn; Am Cncl Otolaryn; Houston Otolaryn Assn. **HONORS/ACHIEVEMENTS:** 1st black otolaryn resd Baylor Affiliated Hosp 1975-78, Houston 1978; publ Archives of Otolaryn; 1 of 1st 10 Nat Achvmt Schlrsp 1965. **BUSINESS ADDRESS:** 1412 Med Arts Professional Bldg, Houston, TX 77002.

MABRY, EDWARD L.
Educational administrator. **PERSONAL:** Born Nov 21, 1936, Brownsville, TN. **EDUCATION:** Millikin Univ, BA 1966; Princeton Theol Sem, MDiv 1969; Princeton Theol Sem, PhD 1982. **CAREER:** Millikin Univ, dir relgious activity 1969-70; Princeton Theol Sem, master in resd 1970-73; NJ State Home for Girls, chaplain 1971-72; Talladega Coll, dir of religious action & asst prof of religion 1973-75; OK School of Religion, dean. **ORGANIZATIONS:** Dir Christian Ed OK Bapt State Conv 1975-; mem AAUP 1973-; minister of ed Morning Star Bapt Church Tulsa 1975-; organist Morning Star Bapt Church 1975. **HONORS/ACHIEVEMENTS:** Student Senate Apprec Awd Talladega Coll 1974. **MILITARY SERVICE:** AUS sp4 1960-63. **BUSINESS ADDRESS:** Dean, Oklahoma School of Religion, 1405 N Cincinnati Ave, Tulsa, OK 74106.

MACBETH, ROBERT
Director, educator. **PERSONAL:** Born Mar 25, 1934, Charleston, SC; married Helen Pearl Ellis; children: Rob Douglas, Jamie Cecil. **EDUCATION:** Morehouse Coll, 1951-52; Newark Coll of Engineering, 1952-53; City Coll of NY, 1958-61; Curt Conway/Lonnie Chapman Studio, NYC; Actors' Studio, NYC. **CAREER:** The New Lafayette Theatre Harlem, founder 1967-73; NYU School of the Arts, prof 1977-79; The Leonard Davis Center CCNY, asst prof 1979-83; Professional Acting Experience, understudy to Billy Dee Williams in Broadway product of "A Taste of Honey" 1961; off Broadway production of "The Merchant of Venice" 1962; "The Blacks" St Marks Playhouse 1962; "The Living Premise" 1963; "The Living Theatre" perf in Brecht's "Jungle of Cities"; "The Apple and the Connection"; "Tiger Tiger Burning Bright" perf at Booth Theatre Broadway; "Daddy" perf at the American Place Theatre 1976; "So Nice They Named It Twice" NY Shakespeare Fest 1977. **HONORS/ACHIEVEMENTS:** "The Electronic Nigger, A Son Come Home, Clara's Ole Man" for the Amer Place Theatre Clarence Derwent Award 1968; "Clara's Ole Man" a revival pres by La Mama Experimental Theatre Club videotaped for NYC TV 1981.

MACCLANE, EDWARD JAMES
Retired archives technician. **PERSONAL:** Born Aug 09, 1907, Cambridge, MA; married Frances Dolliver Conrad; children: Elizabeth E Soverall. **EDUCATION:** NY Univ, attended 1944-50. **CAREER:** Adjutant Genl Office, corres clerk 1951-54; Natl Archives, archives tech 1954-71; asst state dir, New Jersey, Cape May & Atlantic Counties, 1987-. **ORGANIZATIONS:** Pres DC Federation of Civic Assns 1968-70; state legislative comm, natl adv comm 1980-82 Amer Assns Retired Persons; pres Midway Civic Assn 9 yrs;pres 1500 Block T St NW 3 yrs; 1st vice pres Model Inner City Comm Organ and mem bd of dirs; mem comm chmn District Officials & Citizens promotingtraffic safety in the District of Columbia; adv comm DC Mayor's Ft Lincoln Proj 1971; pres Ocean City Chap 1062 AARP. **HONORS/ACHIEVEMENTS:** Outstanding Contribution Promoting Traffic Safety Metro Washington Council of Govts 1965; Public Serv Awd Genl Serv Admin 1969; Outstanding Serv Awd DC Federation of Civic Assns 1970; Outstanding Serv to all People Chapel of Four Chaplains 1977; People's Drugstore Awd for Disting Public Serv 1963. **MILITARY SERVICE:** AUS warrant officer jg 32 mos. **HOME ADDRESS:** 119 Bay Ave, Ocean City, NJ 08226.

MACDONALD, RALPH
Musician, publisher. **PERSONAL:** Born Mar 15, 1944, New York, NY; married Geraldine Houlder; children: Anthony Shawn, Jovonni Tanesia. **CAREER:** Bullet Instrument Rentals Inc, pres 1975-; Rosebud Rec Inc, pres 1975-; Antisia Music Inc, 1970-; Roberta Flack Enterprises, producer songwriter musician 1971-75; Harry Belafonte Enterprises, musician songwriter 1961-70; various TV & Radio Commercials; Recording Studio Work. **HONORS/ACHIEVEMENTS:** ASCAP Award achvmt in songwriting; 3 Gold 45 RPM Recs; 2 Gold 33 1/3 Recs.

MACK, ALLY FAYE
Educator. **PERSONAL:** Born Apr 06, 1943, Marthaville, LA; married Dr Robert Mack; children: Robert III, Ryan, Renfred, Jessica. **EDUCATION:** Grambling State Univ, BA 1963; Atlanta Univ, MA 1964; TX A&M Univ, further study 1971; Univ of So MS, PhD 1979. **CAREER:** Prarie View A&M Univ, asst prof 1968-69; TX A&M Univ, instr 1969-71; Langston Univ, asst prof 1971-74; Jackson State Univ, prof, acting chpsn 1974-. **ORGANIZATIONS:** Consult TN Valley Auth 1979-; trainer Natl Womens Ed Fund 1980-; mem Hinds Co Dem Exec Domm 1975-; distr chair Dem Women 1982-; mem MS Council on Human Rel 1976-, MS Health Systems Agency State Bd 1978-79, MS R&D Bd 1980-. **HONORS/ACHIEVEMENTS:** Cert & Listing Outstanding Educators in Amer 1975; Plaque NAACP Citizen Participation Awd 1977; Publ Serv Awd Fannie Lou Hamer Awd 1980. **BUSINESS ADDRESS:** Professor, Acting Chairperson, Jackson StateUniv, Dept of Pol Sci, 1400 J R Lynch St, Jackson, MS 39217.

MACK, ASTRID KARONA
Educator. **PERSONAL:** Born Aug 21, 1935, Daytona Beach, FL; son of Meta M Mack; children: Astrid Kyle, Kristen Nichole. **EDUCATION:** Bethune-Cookman Coll, BS (Magna Cum Laude) 1960; Univ of MN, MS (Zoology) 1965; MI State Univ, PhD (Human Genetics) 1974. **CAREER:** Dade Co FL Public Schls, tchr Biol & Chem 1960-66; Miami-Dade Comm Coll, instr asst prof 1966-73; Univ Miami Schl of Med, asst assoc prof 1973-; UMSM Associate Dean for Minority Affairs 1988-. **ORGANIZATIONS:** Mem Amer Soc of Human Genetics 1969-; mem Amer Assn for the Advancement of Sci 1974-; mem Amer Genetics Assn 1978-; exec dir Dade County Sickle Cell Fdn 1978-; 1st v dist rep Omega Psi Phi Frat Inc 1982-85; district rep Omega Psi Phi Frat Inc 1985-. **HONORS/ACHIEVEMENTS:** NSF Fellowship Earlham Coll 1962, Bowdin Coll 1964; acad yr fellowship Univ of MN (MSF) 1964-65; EO fellowship MI State Univ 1974-72; pres citation Natl Assn for Equal Opportunity in Higher Educ 1979. **MILITARY SERVICE:** AUS sp5 1955-58. **BUSINESS ADDRESS:** Research Associate Prof Med, Univ of Miami Sch of Med, 794 NW 18th St, Miami, FL 33136.

MACK, CHARLES RICHARD
Educator. **PERSONAL:** Born Oct 02, 1942, Clarke Co, GA; married Joan Jacqueline Thomas. **EDUCATION:** Univ GA, BS, MEd. **CAREER:** Clarke County School System, teacher, asst prin; Macedonia Baptist Church Athens, GA, Baptist minister; City of Athens, ward 1 alderman. **ORGANIZATIONS:** Vp Clarke Chap NAACP; mem CCAE; GEA; NEA; sec NE GA Bapt Ministerial Union; 2nd vice pres 8 Dist Gen Missionary Bapt Conv of GA Inc; sec 8th Dist Layman Group; pres-elect Clarke Co Assn of Educators; mem Phi Beta Kappa.

MACK, CLEVELAND J., SR.
Chief executive officer. **PERSONAL:** Born Dec 05, 1912, Alabama; married Mary Holly; children: Cleveland Jr, Mary, Clarence. **CAREER:** Detroit, MI, contractor. **ORGANIZATIONS:** Mem Asso Gen Contractors of Am; mem Met Contract Assn; mem BTWBA; mem Urban League; mem Prince Hall Masons. **HONORS/ACHIEVEMENTS:** Recip MCA Award for Contractor of Yr 1973; laid out & poured found The Renaissance Ctr (worlds larges hotel & related bldgs) 1974; businessman of yr BTWBA 1975; man of yr award State of MI Dept of Commerce 1976; listed Top 100 Businesses of Nation 1977. **BUSINESS ADDRESS:** 14555 Wyoming, Detroit, MI 48238.

MACK, DANIEL J.
Chief executive. **CAREER:** Virginia Mutual Benefit Life Insurance Co, Inc, Richmond, VA, chief exec. **BUSINESS ADDRESS:** Virginia Mutual Benefit Life Insurance Co, Inc, 112 E Clay St, Richmond, VA 23219. *

MACK, DONALD J.
Publisher. **PERSONAL:** Born Jun 01, 1937, Port Arthor, TX; married Gussie L Vinson. **EDUCATION:** BS 1963. **CAREER:** TX So U, tchr 1964-66; Galveston Co CAA, asst dir 1966-67; Nghbrhd Action Inc, dir 1967-72; Comm Action Agy, dir 1972-74; Ft Worth Ctr for Ex-offenders, dir; Ebony Mart, publshr. **ORGANIZATIONS:** Chmn Nghbrhd Action Apts 1973-; bd mem Conf of Christians & Jews 1974-; mem Ldrshp Ft Worth 1974-. **HONORS/ACHIEVEMENTS:** Cert of merit from Comm Action Agy; cert of accmplshmt Criminal Justice Sys; cert of completion Ldrshp Inst for Comm Devel. **MILITARY SERVICE:** USN.

MACK, FAITE
Military officer. **PERSONAL:** Born Jan 08, 1919, Stratham, GA; married Katie; children: Faite, Jr, Phillip, Gregory. **EDUCATION:** Wilson Jr Coll, 1951; Aircraft & Engine Mech Course, Grad 1942 & 48; Army Helicopter Mech Course, 1956; Multi-engine Single-rotor Helicopter Mech Course, 1966; Air Frame Repair Extension Course, 1962; Shop-Foreman Sch, 1971; Ldrshp & Pers Mgmt Extensions Course, 1971; UH1 Extension Course, 1971; Radiological Monitoring Course, 1971; Command & Gen Staff Coll, 1973; num other military courses. **CAREER:** AUS, master sgt 1942-; IL Army Nat Guard, 1947; Sr Aircraft Mech; Communications Chief; Sec Ldr; Platoon Sgt; Tech Inspector; Sr Flight Ops Chief; Battalion Sgt Major; Command Sgt Major, current assign Nov 1975; Gov Dan Walker, selected as aide promoted to Bird Col; Gov James R Thompson Gov IL Military Aide, personal staff 1977; Army Aviation Maintenance Shop, civilian aircraft maintenance supvry 25 yrs; IL & Army Aviation Support Facility; Midway Airport; IL Army Nat Guard, racial relat recruiting & retention splst. **ORGANIZATIONS:** Pres IL Nat Guard Non-Command Ofcr Assn; mem Bd Elimination of Racial Imbalance in IL Nat Guard. **HONORS/ACHIEVEMENTS:** Recip Am Theatre Ribbon; European, African, Middle Eastern Theatre Ribbon with 4 Bronze Stars; Good Conduct Medal; Victory Medal WW II; Rome-Arno Campaign; N Appennines Campaign; PO Valley Campaign; State of IL Long & Hon Serv Medal; State Active Duty Ribbon 9th Award; Sr Air Crewman Badge. **BUSINESS ADDRESS:** Colonel, Military & Naval Dept, 234 East Chicago Ave, Chicago, IL 60611.

MACK, FRED CLARENCE
Financial administrator. **PERSONAL:** Born Sep 01, 1940, Elloree, SC; married Mildred Elaine Oliver; children: Lennie B, Keith O, Erika L, Fred S. **EDUCATION:** South Carolina State College, BS 1973. **CAREER:** Utica Tool Co, leadman 1968-72; NC Mutual Insurance Co, debit manager 1970-73; Family Health Center, Inc, assoc dir 1973-85; Orangeburg County Council, vice-chairman 1976-. **ORGANIZATIONS:** Member Chamber of Commerce 1980; member OCAAB Community Service Agency 1983-85. **HONORS/ACHIEVEMENTS:** Executive Board NAACP Bowman Branch 1960-85; Treasurer Antioch Baptist Church 1970-85; Political Action Concerned Citizen Dist #94 1972-85; Chairman/Deacon Antioch Baptist Church 1983-85; Advisor Board Orangeburg-Calhoun Tec College 1983-85. **BUSINESS ADDRESS:** Vice Chairman, Orangeburg County Council, PO Box 1125, Orangeburg, SC 29115.

MACK, GLADYS WALKER
Government official. **PERSONAL:** Born Feb 26, 1934, Rock Hill, SC; daughter of Zenith

Walker and Henrietta Alexander Walker; married Julius Mack, Jan 25, 1958; children: Geofrey, Kenneth, Johnathan. **EDUCATION:** Morgan State Univ, Baltimore MD, BS, 1955; graduate study at Catholic Univ of America, Washington DC, 1956-58. **CAREER:** Urban Renewal Admin Housing and Home Finance Agency, Washington DC, budget analyst, 1955-65; Office of Economic Opportunity, VISTA Program, Washington DC, budget analyst, 1965-67, program analysis officer, 1967-69; Exec Office of the Mayor, Washington DC, senior budget analyst, 1969-72; Washington Technical Inst, Washington DC, dir of budget and finance, 1972-75; Exec Office of the Mayor, Was hington DC, deputy budget dir, 1975-78, acting dir, 1978-79, asst city admin, 1979-82, dir of Office of Policy and Program Evaluation, 1983-85, gen asst to the mayor, 1985-86; DC Board of Parole, Washington DC, chairperson, 1986-. **ORGANIZATIONS:** Mem, Assn of Paroling Authorities International; mem, Urban Planning Org; mem, Amer Public Transportation Assn; mem, Amer Correctional Assn; mem, Middle Atlantic States Correctional Assn; mem, Delta Sigma Theta. **BUSINESS ADDRESS:** Chairperson, D C Board of Parole, 1111 E St NW, Suite 600, Washington, DC 20004.

MACK, GORDON H.
Educator. **PERSONAL:** Born Jul 01, 1927, Chicago, IL; married Kay Bell; children: Melissa, Michael, Margot, Matthew. **EDUCATION:** Southern Univ, BA; New York Univ, MA. **CAREER:** Bank St College Field Serv Div, chmn 1970-; Ldrshp Resour Inc, sr asso 1970-; Nat Bd of YMCA, dir 1967-69; Ctrl Atlantic Area Counc of YMCA, asst dir 1964-67. **ORGANIZATIONS:** YMCA Chicago Metro Assn 1953-63; Ctrl Atlantic Area Nat Counc; unit supr JOBS YMCA; yth dir Hyde Park; spec advs Tuckagee MIOTA Proj; inst & field supr George Williams Coll; Am Soc for Training & Dev; Am Counc on Educ 1970-; Assn of Prof YMCA & Whats New in Recrtng; bd of dirs Amer Montessori Society. **HONORS/ACHIEVEMENTS:** Human relat award Nat Conf of Christians & Jews. **MILITARY SERVICE:** AUS 1st lt 1952-54. **BUSINESS ADDRESS:** Personnel Services Dir, YMCA of USA, 101 N Wacker Dr, Chicago, IL 60606.

MACK, JAMES E.
Business executive. **PERSONAL:** Born Apr 25, 1941, Winston-Salem, NC; married Doris White; children: Kimberly, Courtney, Wesley. **EDUCATION:** Winston-Salem St U, BA 1963. **CAREER:** B&C Asso Incd pres chief operating off 1968-80; HRC inc (human resorces consult inc), pres chief exec off; media ventures inc, pres; Wachovia Bank &Trust Co, exec mgmt trainee; Journal & Sentinel Newspapers, journalist. **ORGANIZATIONS:** Mem SE Reg Bd of BSA 1969-71; at-large mem Nat Bd of BSA; trust Winston-Salem St U; dir NC Symphony; mem High Point C of C Bd 1972. **BUSINESS ADDRESS:** Human Resource Consultants, PO Box 11864, Winston-Salem, NC 27106.

MACK, JAMES KEVIN See MACK, KEVIN

MACK, JOAN
News media professional. **PERSONAL:** Born Nov 23, 1943, Charleston, SC; daughter of Alonzo Gladden (deceased) and Harriet Robinson Gladden (deceased); married Charles Henry; children: Dandria, Charles, Kashauna. **EDUCATION:** SC State Coll, BS Biology 1964; Ccity Coll of NY, Cert 1965. **CAREER:** Manpower Training & Devel Ctr, teacher 1970-72; WCSC TV-5 Charleston SC, public serv dir/TV hostess 1972-77; WCBD-TV Charleston SC, news reporter 1977-1985; College of Charleston, media resources coord adjunct prof. **ORGANIZATIONS:** Mem Amer Women in Radio & TV 1972-80; bd mem Mayor's Comm on the Handicapped 1976-80; bd mem March of Dimes 1976-80; bd mem Charles Webb Ctr for Crippled Children 1977-80; Gov Comm on Physical Fitness 1980; mem Natl Federation of Press Women 1983-85, ITVA 1986-87; bd mem Charleston County Heart Assn 1986-87; mem speakers bureau YWCA; bd mem, Charleston County Substance Abuse Commn, 1987-; public relations comm, YMCA Auxiliary, 1988-. **HONORS/ACHIEVEMENTS:** Communications award Omega Psi Phi Frat 1974; vol serv award United Negro Coll Fund 1974; Sch Bell Awards for reporting SC Educ Assn 1975-76 & 79; Outstanding Young Woman of Amer 1977,1978; YWCA Tribute to Women in Industry Awd 1981; SC Commn on Women Broadcast Awd 1981; Natl Federation of Press Women Awd 1983; 2 Silver Reel Awds Intl TV Assoc 1986; Merit Award, Intl Television Assn, 1988; Communicators Award, Carolina Assn of Businesses, 1987. **BUSINESS ADDRESS:** Media Resources Coordinator, College of Charleston, 25 St Philip St, Charleston, SC 29424.

MACK, JOHN L.
Educator. **PERSONAL:** Born Jul 25, 1942, Philadelphia, PA; son of Norman Mack and Catherine Mack; married Bettie Taylor; children: Monica, Michael, Mark, Gwendolyn. **EDUCATION:** MIT, BS 1973; Suffolk Univ, MBA 1978. **CAREER:** MIT, assoc dir admin 1975-78, personel staff rec 1974-75; Brown Univ Providence RI, assoc dir of admissions 1978-79; Univ of TX Austin TX, post-grad course in intl finance 1979-80; Sonicraft Chicago IL, dep program mgr for control 1980-82; US State Dept Wash DC, admin officer 1982-83; US Embassy Abidjan Invory Coast, admin officer 1983-85; US Embassy Paris France, mgmt officer 1985-87, US State Dept, Washington DC; coordinator Regional Administrative Management Centers 1987-. **ORGANIZATIONS:** Elec consult fdr Dearborn Proj; mem bd dir Cambridge Comm Ctr; pres bd dir Cambridge Comm Ctr; mem MIT Comm Serv Fund; chmn MIT Urban Act Comm; mem MIT Rech Training Adv Com; mem bd dir Hope for Housing; co-chmn MIT Blk Stud Un; mem MIT Task Force on Educ Oppor; real est broker; mem Intl Assoc of Financial Planners; Intl Association of Black Professionals in Foreign Affairs. **HONORS/ACHIEVEMENTS:** Amer Spirit Medal of Hon; Marron W Fort fellowship MIT; MENSA; assoc dir admin MIT 1977; selected as Outstanding Young Amer Jaycees 1977; US Patent #4596041 electronic device. **MILITARY SERVICE:** USN elec petty off 1961-66. **BUSINESS ADDRESS:** U S State Dept, A/ISO Room 1916, Washington, DC 20520.

MACK, JOHN W.
Civil rights administrator. **PERSONAL:** Born Jan 06, 1937, Kingstree, SC; married Harriett Johnson; children: Anthony, Deborah, Andria. **EDUCATION:** Agr & Tech, Coll of NC, BS; Atlanta Univ, MSW. **CAREER:** Camarillo St Hosp, P SW 1960-64; UL of Flint, MI, exec dir 1964-69; Los Angeles Urban League, pres 1969-. **ORGANIZATIONS:** Ldr Atlanta Student Civil Rights Protest 1960; co-fndr/v chrm Comm on Appeal for Human Rights 1960; co-fndr & Co-chrp LA Black Ldrshp Coalt on educ 1977; bd mem KCET-TV-CHANNEL 28 1975-; v pres United Way Corp Cncl of Exects 1984; brd mem LA Cty & Cnty Priv Ind Cncl 1983. **HONORS/ACHIEVEMENTS:** Annual Roving Mbrshp Trophy Comm Rel Conf of S CA 1984; Mary McCleod Bethune Nat'l Cncl of Negro Women 1984; outstanding pub serv award Assn of Blk Law Enfrcmnt Exec 1984; civil rights LA Basin Equal Oppor Leag Ue 1984; commsnr LA Brd of Zoning Appls 1984; mem CA's Atty Gen John Van DeCamp's Racila, Ethnic, Rel, & Minority Violence Comm. **BUSINESS ADDRESS:** President, Los Angeles Urban League, 3450 Mount Vernon Drive, Los Angeles, CA 90008.

MACK, JULIA COOPER
Judge. **PERSONAL:** Born in Fayetteville, NC; widowed; children: Cheryl. **EDUCATION:** Hampton Inst, BS 1940; Howard Univ, LLB 1951. **CAREER:** Dept of Justice, trial atty appellate sect criminal div 1954-58; EEO Comm, assoc gen cnsl 1968-73, dep gen cnsl 1973-75; DC Ct of Appeals, assoc judge. **HONORS/ACHIEVEMENTS:** Nominee Fed Women's Awd 1969; EEOC Awd for Disting Serv 1971; Outstanding Fed Career Lawyer Justice Tom C Clark Awd 1974; Alumnus of Yr Howard Univ Law Alumni Assn 1975; Disting Alumnus Awd Hampton Inst 1976; Hon Mem AKA Sor; Natl Bar Assn Disting Jurist Awd 1980; Howard Univ Awd for Disting Postgraduate Achievement 1981. **BUSINESS ADDRESS:** Associate Judge, DC Court of Appeals, 500 Indiana Ave NW, Washington, DC 20001.

MACK, KEVIN (JAMES KEVIN MACK)
Professional athlete. **PERSONAL:** Born Aug 09, 1962, Kings Mountain, NC; son of Calvin Mack and Mary Francis; married Ava Bassett, May 31, 1986. **EDUCATION:** Attended, Clemson. **CAREER:** Los Angeles Express, USFL team, LA Calif, professional running back 1983-84; Cleveland Browns, running back 1985-. **HONORS/ACHIEVEMENTS:** Co-Most Valuable Player of Year by Akron Browns' Backers; honored by Hometown of Kings Mountain with "Kevin Mack Day"; named NFL Offensive Rookie of Year by Football Digest; named UPI AFC Rookie of Year; first team UPI NFL All-Rookie squad; first team Football Digest All-Star team; Most Valuable Player on offense by Cleveland TD Club; PFWA All Rookie team; AFC Offensive Player of the Week 10/6/85; broke Jim Brown's rookie rushing record; mem 1986 Pro Bowl team; mem 1988 Pro Bowl team. **BUSINESS ADDRESS:** Cleveland Browns, Cleveland Stadium, Cleveland, OH 44114.

MACK, LURENE KIRKLAND
Educational administrator. **PERSONAL:** Born May 20, 1948, Graceville, FL; married Robert Eastmon Mack; children: Uhura Jamal, Niesha Rochet. **EDUCATION:** Miami Dade Com Coll, AA 1970; Barry Coll, BS 1982. **CAREER:** Dade Cty, 1st Black female consumer protection agent 1970-74; Dade Cty Schools, 1st Black female investigator 1974-79, 1st Black female area supervisor 1980-; Early Advantage Kindergarden Inc, Miami, FL, president 1980-. **ORGANIZATIONS:** 1st black female student at Miami Dade Com Coll to join a sorority Gamma Delta Sor 1966; mem NAACP 1979-, Black Public Admin Assoc 1983-, Youth Crime Watch Advisory Bd 1982-, Exec Bd YEW 1984-; vice pres NOBLE-FL Chap Sect 6 1984-. **MILITARY SERVICE:** AUS sp4 4 years. **HOME ADDRESS:** 18635 NW 38th Ave, Opa-Locka, FL 33055. **BUSINESS ADDRESS:** Area Supervisor, Dade County School Board, 2210 SW 3rd St, Miami, FL 33135.

MACK, MIRANDA
Community relations regional manager. **PERSONAL:** Born Jun 21, 1955, Atlanta, GA; daughter of Dennis Mack and Jewel Hillman. **EDUCATION:** Morris Brown Coll, BA 1977. **CAREER:** WAOK Radio, acct exec 1977-80; City Beverage Co, brand dir 1980-84; Adolph Coors Co, asst mgr special mkts 1984, field mgr 1984-86, comm realtions regional mgr 1986-. **ORGANIZATIONS:** President-elect Natl Assn of Market Developers 1989-; bd mem NAACP 1983-; board member, Atlanta Urban League 1984-; board member, Atlanta Business League 1988-; board member, Georgia Association of Minority Entrepreneurs 1988-. **HONORS/ACHIEVEMENTS:** Named 1 of 10 Outstanding Atlantans Outstanding Young People of Atlanta 1986; Media Woman of the Year Natl Assn of Media Women 1986; Bettye Jane Everett Awd Natl Assn of Mkt Developers 1986; Leadership Awd Council of Natl Alumni 1986; Leadership America, 1989; Leadership Atlanta, 1986. **BUSINESS ADDRESS:** Community Relations Regional Mgr, Coors Brewing Company, One CNN, South Tower, Suite 790, Atlanta, GA 30303.

MACK, PEARL WILLIE (NEE GILMER)
Educator. **PERSONAL:** Born Aug 16, 1941, Laurel, MS; daughter of Sammie Gilmer and Delia Ann Jones Moncrief; married Tommie Lee; children: Dwayne Mack. **EDUCATION:** Illinois State Univ, BA 1962; Roosevelt Univ, Graduate Work; Governor's State Univ, MA 1975. **CAREER:** Harvey Educ Assn, teacher 1962-; treasurer 1971-75, chair grievance comm 1987-; Illinois Educ Assn, resolutions comm 1972-74; IEZ/NEA Women's Caucus, planning comm 1974-; Minority Caucus, chairperson 1974-75; Natl Educ Assn, exec comm 1987-87, chair elections comm 1987-89, chairperson special comm on black concerns. **ORGANIZATIONS:** Mem Political Action Comm Natl Educ Assn 1976-, Political Action Comm Illinois Educ Assn 1975-; bd mem Natl Educ Assn 1975-; Grievance Com Harvey Educ Assn 1977-; mem PUSH, NAACP, Governers State Univ Alumni Assn 1977; del rep NEA; bd dir World Confederation Org of Teaching Profession 1976,78,84,86; delegate to Democratic Natl Convention 1980; mem Coalition of Labor Union Women 1980-, Women in Arts 1984-, Citizens Utility Bd 1984-. **HONORS/ACHIEVEMENTS:** 1 of 100 Outstanding Women in Educ NEA 1975; co-writer Mini-grant Proposal for Cultural Studies Program 1974-75; Intl Business and Professional Women, Dollars & Sense Magazine 1987.

MACK, RODERICK O'NEAL
Managing owner. **PERSONAL:** Born Jul 30, 1955, Birmingham, AL; son of Edward Mack and Irene Mack; married Votura E Hendeson; children: Amrette, Shanta, Roderick Jr, Tamarka. **EDUCATION:** Miles Coll Birmingham, BS 1977; Jefferson St Jr Coll Birmingham, AAS 1981; Sanford Univ Birmingham, MBA 1981. **CAREER:** Liberty Natl Life Insurance Co, accounting intern 1975-76; Emergency Sch Aid Act, tutor 1976-77; Amer Inst of Banking, instructor 1982-83; Amer South Bank NA Birmingham, corporate accounting officer 1977-85; Mack & Associates, managing owner. **ORGANIZATIONS:** Treas Natl Black MBA Assoc 1985-; treas Family & Child Services A United Way Agency 1985-87; pres Birmingham Minority Business Adv Comm 1986-87; assoc dir Natl Assoc of Accountants; mem Inst of Mgmt Accountants, Birmingham Inter Professional Assoc; assoc dir Birmingham Vulcan Chap Natl Assoc. **HONORS/ACHIEVEMENTS:** Natl Assoc of Accountants Outstanding Member Awd 1983,1985; Outstanding Young Man of Amer 1985. **HOME ADDRESS:** 809 6th Ave West, Birmingham, AL 35204. **BUSINESS ADDRESS:** Managing Owner, Mack & Associates, PO Box 11308, Birmingham, AL 35202.

MACK, RUDY EUGENE, SR.
Business executive. **PERSONAL:** Born Feb 09, 1941, Miami, FL; son of Flossie M Mack; divorced; children: Rudy Jr, Derek, Maurice, Jason. **EDUCATION:** TN A&I, BS 1967. **CAREER:** Rep Airlines, capt; Prudential, ins agt 1967-71; Burnside OTT, flight instr 1968-71. **ORGANIZATIONS:** Mem Airline Pilot Assn; Orgn Black Airline Pilot; co-chmn com Rel com The Airline Pilot Union; aeromed chmn OBAP. **BUSINESS ADDRESS:** Captain, Northwest Airline, Minneapolis-St Paul Airport, Minneapolis, MN 55406.

MACK, SYLVIA JENKINS
Educational administrator. **PERSONAL:** Born Dec 22, 1931, Deal Island, MD; children: Alphonso L DDS, Lt Comm Michael L USSN, Don Frederick, Thomas E Anthony C. **EDUCATION:** Newmaan Coll, BS Prof Ed; Certified Trade & Indus Inst DE State Board of Ed; DE State Board of Cosmetology, licensed cosmetologist licensed cosmetologyinstructor; St Joseph Univ Philadelphia PA, Masters Prof Educ. **CAREER:** Del Castle Tech HS Wilmington, DE, instr cosmetology & science 17 yrs. **ORGANIZATIONS:** Mem Brnadywine Professional Assoc; elected school bd member Brandywine Sch Dist DE 1981-84, re-elected to same position 1984-89; pres Progressive Black Cosmetologist Assn of DE; mem Natl Assoc of Black School Bd Mem. **HOME ADDRESS:** 2121 Jessup St, Wilmington, DE 19802.

MACK, VOYCE J.
Government official. **PERSONAL:** Born Aug 10, 1921, Ocala, FL; married Margaret Rogers (deceased) (deceased); children: Ronald J. **EDUCATION:** Hampton Inst, BS 1948; Cornel U, MS 1951, PhD 1953; John HopkinsUniv Sch for Adv Internatl Studies, Postgrad Work. **CAREER:** Ofc of the Sec of Trans Ofc of Internatl Progs, deputy dir 1969-; Agency for Intl Devel Wash, economist 1967-69; US AID Mission Ceylon, dir 1965-67; Agency for Intl Devel, intl economist 1963-65; Intl Coop Adminstrn, prog ofcr 1958-63; VA State Coll, asso prof 1953-58. **ORGANIZATIONS:** Mem bd dirs Capital Area Div The United Nat Assn of USA 1972-. **HONORS/ACHIEVEMENTS:** Recip Clinton-DeWitt-Smith Fellowship CornellUniv 1952; num letters of commendation; nom selected to attnd Fed Exec Inst Educ Prog 1973; US Rep to United Nat Econ Comm for Asia & Far East Bangkok 1973, 74, 76, 77. **MILITARY SERVICE:** AUS s/sgt 1943-46. **BUSINESS ADDRESS:** Ofc of the Secretary, Dept of Transportation, Washington, DC 20590.

MACK, WILBUR OLLIO
Educator. **PERSONAL:** Born Aug 11, 1919, Seward, OK; married Martha Margaret Mayo; children: Ronald Wilbur, Waymond Ollio, Larry Wayne, Wilma Denise. **EDUCATION:** Langston Univ, BS 1947; OK State Univ, MS 1954. **CAREER:** Prairie View coll, teacher 1953-57; So Univ Baton Rouge, 1957-62; FL A&M Univ Tallahassee, asst prof engrg 1962-. **ORGANIZATIONS:** Registered professional engr TX LA; mem Amer Soc Engrs; mem Natl Safety Council; Kappa Alpha Psi; Mason 32 degree. **MILITARY SERVICE:** AUS 1st lt 1941-45.

MACKEL, AUDLEY MAURICE
Dentist. **PERSONAL:** Born Oct 01, 1904, Natchez, MS; married Rosetta Liblan Lloyd; children: Audrose, Charles Banks, Audley Maurice, Harriett Gatlin, Lyvonne, Wilbert Washington, Gwendolyn, Marilyn. **EDUCATION:** Natchez Coll, 1921; Atlanta U, 1921-22; Meharry Dental Coll, DDS 1927. **CAREER:** Dentist Chicago, pvt prac 1956-; Monroe, 1930-48; Natchez, 1927-30. **ORGANIZATIONS:** Vp Tri-State Med Dental Pharm Assn 1929; pres MS Dental Soc 1940; commr Joint Commn Accrediation Dental Labs 1962-71; founder exec sec Natchez BrNAACP 1951, mem Nat Bd 1953-57; pres Nat Parents Counc Bennett Coll 1955; mem Gen Bd Educ AME Ch 1956-60; pres Layman 8th Episcopal Dist 1954; fdr pres Monroe Civic League 1933; chmn educ com Natchez Bus & Civic League 1954; bd dirs exec com Southtown Br Met YMCA Chicago 1962-72; dist commr Adams Co Dist BSA 1942, Englewood Dist Chicago 1958; trustee Campbell Coll Jackson; Interdenominational Minister Civic League 1964; mem Am Nat IL Dental Assn; Lincoln Dental Soc; Kappa Alpha Psi; trustee AME Ch; Mason 32 Degree; dir S Shore Valley Comm Assn. **HONORS/ACHIEVEMENTS:** Recip award cert Pres Roosevelt 1940. **BUSINESS ADDRESS:** 1025 W 63 St, Chicago, IL 60621.

MACKEL, AUDLEY MAURICE, III
Orthopaedic surgeon. **PERSONAL:** Born Dec 03, 1955, Natchez, MS; son of Audley M Machel Jr and Nannie Love Blassingame; married Sharon White, Aug 14, 1982; children: Ashley Monique. **EDUCATION:** Morehouse Coll, BS 1977; Meharry Medical Coll, MD 1981. **CAREER:** Northwestern Univ Medical Center, intern 1981-82, orthopaedic resident 1982-86; Kerlan Jobe Orthopaedic Clinic, orthopaedic surgeon, arthritis/joint implant fellow 1986-87; Charles Drew Medical School, Los Angeles, CA orthopaedic surgeon 1987-88. **ORGANIZATIONS:** Mem Alpha Phi Alpha Frat Inc 1974-81; mem Cook Co Physicians Assoc 1982-86, Natl Medical Assoc 1982-. **HONORS/ACHIEVEMENTS:** The Natl Dean's List 1981; Alpha Omega Alpha Medical Honor Soc 1981; Outstanding Young Men of Amer 1983; Anatomy Awd Dept of Orthopaedic Surgery 1984. **HOME ADDRESS:** 3715 Warrensville Center Road #206, Shaker Heights, OH 44122. **BUSINESS ADDRESS:** Orthopaedic Surgeon, Associates in Orthopaedics, Inc., 11201 Shaker Blvd, Cleveland, OH 44104.

MACKEY, ANDREW, JR.
Clergyman. **PERSONAL:** Born Dec 10, 1939, Lancaster, SC; married Cora Lee; children: Sandra Lorraine, Andrea Benita, Andrew, III. **EDUCATION:** Livingstone Coll Salisbury NC, BA 1961; Hood Theol Sem Salisbury NC, MDiv 1964; NY Theol Sem NYC, student. **CAREER:** Oak St AME Zion Ch, pastor; Shrewsbury Ave AME Zion Ch Red Bank NJ, minister; St Mark's AME Zion Ch Dallas, 1965-70; Dallas, oppor ind cntr 1966-70; St Simon Epos Cntr Dallas, 1965-66; First AME Zion Ch Brooklyn, 1964-65; Protestant Council Brooklyn, group worker 1964-65. **ORGANIZATIONS:** Bd educ Titon Falls New Schrewsbury NJ 1973-; pres NJ Conf AME Zion Ministers Alliance; pres West Side Alliance Red Bank NJ; vice pres NAACP Red Bank Chpt; fin com mem NJ Coun Chs; mem Celestial Lodge F & A Masons; Elks; Kiwanis Internat; chmn Spritirual Emphasis Com; bd dir Red Bank Comm Cntr; bd dir Yth Employment Svc. **HONORS/ACHIEVEMENTS:** Outstnd citz awd NAACP 1973; lelcted del AME Zion Gen Conf 1968. **BUSINESS ADDRESS:** Pastor, Oak St AME Zion Church, P O Box 2154, Petersburg, VA 23804.

MACKEY, HOWARD H., III
Business executive. **PERSONAL:** Born Sep 17, 1947, Washington, DC; married Marsha V Townes; children: Kristin, Stanford. **EDUCATION:** HowardUniv Wash DC, BS 1969; ColumbiaUniv Grad Sch of Bus, MBA 1971. **CAREER:** Prepac Inc Bronx, chmn & chief exec ofcr 1978-; Equico Capital Corp NY, pres & chief exec ofcr 1972-78; Chemical Bank of NY, finan analyst 1971-72. **ORGANIZATIONS:** Mem Nat Urban League; mem So Conf of Black Mayors; mem Spclty Advertising Counc of DE Valley. **HONORS/ACHIEVEMENTS:** Recip Outst Yng Men of Am Award 1975; annual achvmt award for bus Black Enterprise 1976; minority econ devel award Equitable Life Assurance 1978; listed Who's Who in Finan 1979; appeared in articles NY Times, NY Post, Black Enterprise Mag, Jet Mag, Amsterdam News, US Review Mag, Atlanta Jour, The Couns Mag.

MACKLIN, ANDERSON D.
Educator. **PERSONAL:** Married Georgia Day. **EDUCATION:** BS 1954; MS 1956; EdD 1969. **CAREER:** Dept Fine Arts VA State Coll, prof chmn 1962-; MS Valley State Coll, 1960-62; Wiley Coll, 1958-60; Lincoln U, instr art 1954-58. **ORGANIZATIONS:** Vp VA Art Educ Assn; past polemarch Petersburg Alumni Chpt; Kappa Alpha Psi FratInc; Delta Phi Delta Art Frat; Phi Delta Kappa Educ Frat; Nat Conf of Artists; AAUP; NAACP; pres Men's Fellowship Gillfield Bapt Ch; chmn Spl Frat Com for AP Hill Comm Ctr. **HONORS/ACHIEVEMENTS:** Listed Who's Who in Intl Arts & Antiques 1971; Who's Who in SE Dictionary of Intl Biography 1975; So Found Fellowship Recip 1967; Syracuse Fellowship for Faculty Devel 1969-70; num awards for paintings incl AtlantaUniv Annum.

MACKLIN, JOHN W.
Educator. **PERSONAL:** Born Dec 11, 1939, Ft Worth, TX; children: Marcus E. **EDUCATION:** Linfield Coll McMinnville, OR, BA 1962; Cornell Univ, PhD 1968. **CAREER:** Univ of WA, asst prof of chemistry 1968-, assoc prof 1987. **ORGANIZATIONS:** Mem Amer Chem Soc 1966-; mem AAAS 1978-; NOBCCHE 1986-. **BUSINESS ADDRESS:** Associate Professor, University of Washington, Dept of Chemistry, BG-10, Seattle, WA 98195.

MACKLIN, RUDY JOEL
Professional athlete. **PERSONAL:** Born Feb 19, 1958, Louisville, KY. **EDUCATION:** Louisiana State, Business 1981. **CAREER:** Atlanta Hawks, 1981-83; New York Knicks, 1983-84; Los Angeles Clippers, forward-guard 1984-. **BUSINESS ADDRESS:** Los Angeles Clippers, 3939 S Figueroa St, Ste 510, Los Angeles, CA 90037.

MACLACHLAN, JANET A.
Actress. **PERSONAL:** Born Aug 27, NYC, NY; daughter of Dr James M MacLachan and Ruby I MacLachan; children: Samantha. **EDUCATION:** Hunter Coll, BA. **CAREER:** Media Forum Inc, treasurer 1984-88; MagaLink Inc, sec bd dirs 1982-88. **ORGANIZATIONS:** Mem bd dirs Screen Actors Guild 1976-81; Academy of TV Arts & Sciences, bd of governors 1986-88. **HONORS/ACHIEVEMENTS:** Emmy Awd for Best Performance Los Angeles area Academy of TV Arts & Sciences 1982.

MACLIN, MELVIN M.
Dentist. **PERSONAL:** Born Feb 07, 1929, Mason, TN; divorced; children: Richard, David, Melanye, Melvin, II. **EDUCATION:** BD; DDS. **CAREER:** Dentist, pvt prac. **ORGANIZATIONS:** Mem treas Com IL Dentists 1973-; Kenwood Hyde Park Dent Soc; Com 100 Univ IL; adv Com Recruitment Disadv Students Univ IL; Nat & Am Dent Assns; Chicago & IL Dental Socs; Am Inst Oral Biology; bd dir Merit Real Est Invest Trust; NAACP; YMCA; Urban League; TN State Alumni Assn. **HONORS/ACHIEVEMENTS:** Yth serv award Washington Park YMCA 1970; great guy for day Rad Sta WGRT. **MILITARY SERVICE:** AUS sgt maj 1951-53. **BUSINESS ADDRESS:** 243 W 95 St, Chicago, IL 60628.

MACON, NORMAN
Chief executive. **CAREER:** Highland Corp, Cincinnati, OH, chief exec, 1983-. **BUSINESS ADDRESS:** Highland Corp, 300 Murray Rd, St Bernard, OH 45217. *

MADDOX, ELLIOTT
Professional baseball player. **PERSONAL:** Born Dec 21, 1948, E Orange, NJ; married Valerie Don Scott. **EDUCATION:** Univ of MI, BS 1971. **CAREER:** Detroit Tigers, 1970; Wash Senators, 1971; TX Rangers, 1971-74; NY Yankees, 1974-. **ORGANIZATIONS:** During off seasons drug adv New York City Bd of Educ Spark Prog. **HONORS/ACHIEVEMENTS:** Tied Carolina Leag in double plays by a 3rd baseman 1969; played in championship & world series 1976. **BUSINESS ADDRESS:** Mercer Meidinger HA, 1375 E Ninth St, #2600, Cleveland, OH 44114.

MADDOX, ELTON PRESTON, JR.
Dentist, educator. **PERSONAL:** Born Nov 17, 1946, Kingston, MD; son of Elton Maddox and Virginia Maddox. **EDUCATION:** Morgan State Coll, BS 1968;Univ of MD Dental Sch, DDS 1972. **CAREER:** Team Clinic, clinical dir, acting dir 1976-77; Univ of MD Dental Sch, asst prof 1975-77, instr 1973-75, clinical asst prof 1977-82; private practice 1977-. **ORGANIZATIONS:** Chmm Minority Recruitment Comm 1974-77; admissions comm Univ of MD Dental Sch 1974-77; clinical competency comm 1975-76; mem Alpha Phi Alpha Frat Inc.; Jr C of C; MD State Dental Assn, Eastern Shore Dental Assn; pres Community Awareness Committee. **HONORS/ACHIEVEMENTS:** Publ "A Guide to Clinical Competency," Jour of Dental Educ 1976; "Why Not?" Univ MD 1976. **BUSINESS ADDRESS:** 1229 Mt Hermon Rd, Salisbury, MD 21801.

MADDOX, GARRY LEE
Athlete. **PERSONAL:** Born Sep 01, 1949, Cincinnati, OH; married sondra; children: Garry, Derrick. **EDUCATION:** Attended, Temple Univ. **CAREER:** San Francisco Giants, outfielder 1972-75; Philadelphia Phillies, retired outfielder 1975-86, broadcasting games, outfield instructor, helping in community relations. **ORGANIZATIONS:** Mem bd dirs Philadelphia Child Guidance Clinic. **HONORS/ACHIEVEMENTS:** NL All-Star Fielding Team 1975-79; played in Championship Series 1976-77-78; 1984 Young Leaders of Philadelphia Awd; shares LCS record for most consecutive games with one or more RBI's total series w/4; led NL in sacrifice flys with 8 in 1981; 8 Gold Glove Awds. **MILITARY SERVICE:** AUS 1968-70. **BUSINESS ADDRESS:** Philadelphia Phillies, PO Box 7575, Philadelphia, PA 19101.

MADDOX, JACK H.
Real estate broker, realtor. **PERSONAL:** Born Jul 17, 1927, Detroit, MI; son of Wylma; married Anna Geck, Feb 17, 1988; children: 1 daughter. **EDUCATION:** Wayne State Univ, BS; Univ of MI, Cert; MI State Univ, Cert. **CAREER:** Detroit School System Adult Ed, real estate & rel subj teacher; Assoc Ins Agency, pres & gen agent; Past Brokers Invest Co, past vp; JH Maddox & Co, proprietor real estate, currently. **ORGANIZATIONS:** Past sec & dir Ebony Dist Cty; mem Real Estate Alumni MI; chmn fund raising comm for local state natl pol candidates; chaired comm Alpha Phi alpha; guardsman Jaycees; mem NAACP Freedom Fund Dinner Comm; past dir Detroit NAACP; chmn Housing Comm; mem Detroit Real Estate Brokers Assoc, Pol Action Comm; dir Housing Owners of US Exchange; mem natl life membership comm NAACP; chmn 1300 Lafayette E Co-op Bd of Dir; mem, Detroit Bd of Realtors, chmn, Govt Affairs Comm 1988-90. **HONORS/ACHIEVEMENTS:** Past chmn 1300 Lafayette E Co-op Bd of Dir, which negotiated purchase of 9 million dollar luxury apt overlooking Detroit River from HUD; contracted erection 1st black individually owned medical office bldg Detroit; co-chaired, 1970 NAACP Freedom Fund Dinner; Million Dollar Club, NAACP 1975-88. **MILITARY SERVICE:** USN & USNR 3rd class P O 1948-55, Victory Medal.

MADDOX, MARGARET JOHNNETTA SIMMS
Public relations counselor. **PERSONAL:** Born Aug 31, 1952, Clio, SC; married Rev Odinga Lawrence Maddox. **EDUCATION:** Livingstone Coll, BA 1973; The OH State Univ, MA 1975. **CAREER:** TRW Marlin-Rockwell Div, systems analyst 1977-78; FL A&M Univ, prof 1978-80; Senator Wm F Bowen OH, admin asst 1980-83; MJ Simms and Assocs Inc, ceo/pres 1983-. **ORGANIZATIONS:** Benefits comm Columbus Area C of C 1983-; mem Amer Mktg Assoc Central OH 1984-; develop comm OSU Coll of Nursing 1985-; pr counselor Interdenominational Ministerial Alliance of Central OH 1985-; mem Public Relations Soc of Amer 1986-. **HONORS/ACHIEVEMENTS:** Outstanding Young Women of Amer 1983; Certificate of Commendation The Ohio Senate 1983. **BUSINESS ADDRESS:** President and CEO, M J Simms and Associates Inc, 815 E Mound St 1st Floor, Redwood Bldg, Columbus, OH 43205.

MADDOX, MARION THELMA
Educator. **PERSONAL:** Born Oct 01, 1923, Norfolk, VA; married Claude Maddox. **EDUCATION:** Norfolk State U, BS 1960, Kindergarten Endorsement 1968. **CAREER:** Norfolk Pub Sch, tchr elem & basic adult edn; JJ Smallwood Elem Sch Norfolk, 1st grade tchr 10 yrs, custodian 13 yrs. **ORGANIZATIONS:** Recording sec Tidewater Alli of Black Sch Educators 1979-80; Nat vice pres Auxiliary 1976-80, pres 2 Dist 1969-80, Auxiliary Nat Alli of Postal & Fed Employees; life mem Nat Alli of Black Sch Educators; mem Norfolk Educ Assn; VA Educ Assn 1961-; mem Nat Educ Assn; WHTaylor PTA; mem Negro Coll Fund & Intl Reading Counc; mem 1st Bapt Ch Lamberts Point 1929-; exec bd mem Ldrshp Conf on Civil Rights 1976; asst sec Sunday Sch & Finan Com; mem NAACP; mem Hunton YMCA; mem Chrysler Mus Class of 42 BTW; chmn David D & Irene J Alston Libr Trust Fund Lib of 1st Bapt Ch Lamberts Point. **HONORS/ACHIEVEMENTS:** Silver tray for serv 1st Bapt Ch Lamberts Point 1979; cert for serv Nat Alli of Postal & Fed Employees; cert for serv Dist 2 & Nat Auxiliary NAPFE. **BUSINESS ADDRESS:** W H Taylor Elementary School, 1129 W Princess Anne Rd, Norfolk, VA 23507.

MADDOX, ODINGA LAWRENCE
Minister. **PERSONAL:** Born Mar 06, 1939, Akron, OH; married Margaret "MJ" Simms; children: Sharon, Lawrence, Stephen, Christopher. **EDUCATION:** Akron Univ, 1963-65; Livingstone Coll, BA 1974; Hood Theol Sem, MDiv 1977; Trinity Theol Sem. **CAREER:** Gaston Cty School System, teacher 1975-77; Cuyahoga Cty School System, teacher 1978-82; Cleveland Hts OH School System, teacher 1983-85. **ORGANIZATIONS:** Pres student body, trustee Livingstone Coll Hood Theol Sem 1976-77; trustee Coaltion of Concerned Clergy 1985-; pres Interdenominational Ministerial Alliance 1985-. **HONORS/ACHIEVEMENTS:** The ID Blumenthall Awd 1977; The Reverend JM Hoggard Mem Prize 1977; The WD Carrington Awd 1977; The William & Ella Lawrence Awd 1977. **HOME ADDRESS:** 1295 EGates Str, Columbus, OH 43206. **BUSINESS ADDRESS:** Minister, African Meth Episcopal Zion Ch, 873 Bryden Rd, Columbus, OH 43206.

MADGETT, NAOMI LONG
Poet, professor, publisher, editor. **PERSONAL:** Born Jul 05, 1923, Norfolk, VA; daughter of Clarence M Long Sr and Maude S Hilton Long; married Leonard P Andrews, Sr, Mar 31, 1972; children: Jill Witherspoon Boyer. **EDUCATION:** VA State Coll, BA 1945; Wayne State Univ, MEd 1955; Intl Inst for Advanced Studies, PhD 1980. **CAREER:** Poet and Author, 1941-; MI Chronicle, staff writer 1946-47; MI Bell Tel Co, serv rep 1948-54; Detroit Pub Sch, teacher 1955-65; Public Speaker, poetry readings only 1956-; Oakland Univ, res assoc 1965-66; East MI Univ, assoc prof English 1968-73; Univ of MI, lectr 1970; East MI Univ, prof 1973-84, prof Emeritus 1984-; Lotus Press, publ & editor 1974-. **ORGANIZATIONS:** Coll Language Assn; Alpha Kappa Alpha Sor; Amer Assn Univ Profs; historian Plymouth United Ch Christ; mem NAACP, Detroit Women Writers. **HONORS/ACHIEVEMENTS:** Seven books published including "Star by Star"; "Pink Ladies in the Afternoon"; "Exits & Entrances"; poems widely anthologized & translated; Distinguished English Teacher of the Year Met Detroit English Club 1967; 1st recipient Mott Fellowship in English 1965; Disting Soror Award Alpha Rho Omega Chap Alpha Kappa Alpha Sor 1969; papers being collected in Special Collections Libr Fisk Univ; Resolutions from Detroit Cty Cncl 1982 and MI State Legisl 1982 & 1984; Key tothe City of Detroit 1980; Recognition by Black Caucus of Natl Cncl of Teachers of English 1984; Natl Coalition of 100 Black Women 1984; Induction into Stylus Club Howard Univ 1984; Disting Artist Awd Wayne State Univ 1985; Robert Hayden Runagate Awd 1985; Creative Artist Awd MI Council for the Arts 1987; Creative Achievement Award, College Language Assn, 1988; "In Her Lifetime" Award, Afrikan Poets Theatre, Inc 1989; Octavia and Other Poems (book), 1988. **HOME ADDRESS:** 16886 Inverness Ave, Detroit, MI 48221.

MADHUBUTI, HAKI R. (DON L. LEE)
Editor. **PERSONAL:** Born Feb 23, 1942, Little Rock, AR; son of Jimmy L Lee and Maxine Graves Lee; married Johari Amini; children: 2. **EDUCATION:** Attended Wilson Jr Coll, Roosevelt Univ, and Univ of Illinois, Chicago Circle; Univ of Iowa, MFA, 1984. **CAREER:** DuSable Museum of African Amer History, Chicago IL, apprentice curator, 1963-67; Montgomery Ward, Chicago IL, stock dept clerk, 1963-64; US Post Office, Chicago IL, clerk, 1964-65; Spiegels, Chicago IL, jr exec, 1965-66; Cornell Univ, Ithaca NY, writer-in-residence, 1968-69; Northeastern Illinois State Coll, Chicago IL, poet-in-residence, 1969-70; Univ of Illinois, Chicago IL, lecturer, 1969-71; Howard Univ, Washington DC, writer-in-residence, 1970-78; Morgan State Coll, Baltimore MD, 1972-73; Chicago State Univ, Chicago IL, assoc prof of English, 1984-; Third World Press, Chicago IL, publisher and editor, 1967-; Inst of Positive Educ, Chicago IL, dir, 1969-. **ORGANIZATIONS:** Founding mem, Org of Black Amer Culture, Writers Workshop, 1967-75; past exec council, Congress of African People; vice-chmn, African Liberation Day Support Comm 1972-73. **HONORS/ACHIEVEMENTS:** Published works include Think Black, Broadside Press, 1967; Black Pride, Broadside Press, 1967; For Black People (and Negroes Too), Third World Press, 1968; Don't Cry, Scream, Broadside Press, 1969; We Walk the Way of the New World, Broadside Press, 1970; Dynamite Voices I: Black Poets of the 1960s, Broadside Press, 1971; Directionscore: Selected and New Poems, Broadside Press, 1971; From Plan to Planet—Life Studies: The Need for Afrikan Minds & Institutions, Broadside Press, 1973; Book of Life, Broadside Press, 1973; Earthquakes and Sunrise Missions: Poetry and Essays of Black Renewal, 1793-1983, Third World Press, 1984; Say That the River Turns: The Impact of Gwendolyn Brooks, Third World Press, 1987. **BUSINESS ADDRESS:** Editor, Third World Press, 7524 S Cottage Grove, Chicago, IL 60619. *

MADISON, ALFREDA LOUISE
Columnist. **PERSONAL:** Born Apr 05, 1911, McKenney, VA. **EDUCATION:** Howard U, AB. **CAREER:** Washington Informer, clmnst; Capitol Hill, clmnst 1975-; NY Cty Sch, tchr 1953-74; Pub Sch VA, tchr 1943-53. **ORGANIZATIONS:** NAACP; Blk Joursts; White House Press; Capitol Hill Press Club; brf brp Riverside Bapt Ch; cvl rghts wrkr VA & NY 1945-53, 60-72. **HONORS/ACHIEVEMENTS:** Lucy Moten Flwshp Howard U; accom rptr; Pres Carter London Trip 1977. **BUSINESS ADDRESS:** 700 7th St SW, Washington, DC 20024.

MADISON, EDDIE L., JR.
Writer/editor/public affairs coordinator. **PERSONAL:** Born Sep 08, 1930, Tulsa, OK; son of Eddie L Madison Sr and Laverta Pyle Madison; married Davetta Jayn Cooksey, Nov 17, 1956; children: Eddie III, Karyn Devette, David. **EDUCATION:** Lincoln Univ of MO Jefferson City, MO, BJ 1952; Univ of Tulsa, MA Mass Communications (1st Black) 1959. **CAREER:** The Chicago Tribune, sect editor (1st Black full-time editorial staff mem) 1963-65; Info Div US Dept of Commerce, info spec (1st Black profl) 1965; Office of Publ & Info for Domestic & Intl Bus, dept dir publ div 1965-69; Wash Star Station Group, mgr comm serv (1st Black mgr) 1969-77; Wash Star Comm Inc Broadcast Div, mgr admin serv 1977-78; US Indsl Outlook-1979, chief editor 1978-79; US Dept of Commerce Bus Amer Mag, asst editor 1979-81; Congressman Gus Savage of IL, chief press asst 1981-82; Three Elms & Assocs, founder/pres; US Dept of Health & Human Svcs, writer/editor/public affairs coord 1982-. **ORGANIZATIONS:** Public relations/management consultant; founding pres Natl Broadcast Assn for Community Affairs 1974-76; public relations dir, Alpha Phi Alpha Fraternity; consult Ofield Dukes & Assoc; Intl Bus Serv; USDept of Commerce; Natl Assn of Educ Broadcasters 1978-79; dir Opportunities Industrialization Cntr 1971-; mem Commn on Human Rights DC 1970-75; dir DCUnited Way 1970-78; bd trustees Children's Hosp Natl Med Center 1975-78; mem & officer numerous organizations & committees; public relations dir, vice pres Natl Black yellow Pages 1988-. **HONORS/ACHIEVEMENTS:** Outstanding Young Men of Amer 1966; Citation of Merit for Outstanding Performance in Journalism Lincoln Univ of MO 1971; Spl Citation Presidential Classroom for Young Amer 1973; Plaque/Appreciation/Thanks Natl Broadcast Assn for Community Affairs Columbus, OH 1977. **MILITARY SERVICE:** AUS 1952-54; UN Defense Medal, Good Conduct Medal. **BUSINESS ADDRESS:** President/CEO, Three Elms & Associates, Public Relations/Management Consultant, PO Box 90835, Washington, DC 20090.

MADISON, JOSEPH EDWARD
Radio talkshow host. **PERSONAL:** Born Jun 16, 1949, Dayton, OH; married Sharon; children: Shawna, Jason, Monesha, Michelle. **EDUCATION:** WA Univ, BA 1971; Wayne State Univ, Graduate School 1972; Univ of Dayton. **CAREER:** General Motors Corp, public relations 1969-70; St Louis Cardinal Football, statistician 1970-71; Seymour & Lundy Assoc, urban affairs 1971-74; Detroit Branch NAACP, exec dir 1974-77; Natl Political Dir, NAACP; Political Dir of SEIU; Dir of COTE; Talkshow host WWDB & WXYT. **ORGANIZATIONS:** Bd of dir Operation Big Vote 1978-; bd of advisors US Census Bureau 1985; newstalk host WXYT-AM 1983-; life mem NAACP 1984-; mem Intl Platform Assoc 1985; leader NAACP Overground RR/Bury Voter Apathy March 1983-84; Natl Board, NAACP, 1986. **HONORS/ACHIEVEMENTS:** 50 Leaders of Future Ebony/Johnson Publication, Amer noteworthy community leaders; Leadership Award, Michigan Leadership Conference, 1986; 1st Cross Country March, LA to Baltimore MD, 1986.

MADISON, LEATRICE BRANCH
Educator. **PERSONAL:** Born Sep 05, 1922, Washington, DC; married Robert P Madison; children: Jeanne M Anderson, Juliette M Little. **EDUCATION:** Miner Teachers Coll, BA 1943; Univ of Chicago, MA 1947. **CAREER:** Syphax Elementary Sch, teacher 1943-48; Miles Standish Elem Sch, teacher 1949-51; George Washington Carver Sch, teacher 1954-57; Case Elem Sch, teacher 1957-60. **ORGANIZATIONS:** Board member Federation of Community Planning 1967-85; United Way Services 1970-76; Blue Cross of Northeast Ohio 1974-84;Greater Cleveland Girl Scouts; Shaker Lake Regional Nature Center; Cleveland Child Guidance Center; Western Reserve Historical Society; YWCA; Planned Parenthood; University of Chicago Alumni Board of Directors; Case Western Reserve University Board of Overseers and Visiting Committees 1973-86; Cleveland Symphony Orchestra Advisory Council; president/founding member Harambee: Services to Black Families 1979-85; chairman NAACP Freedom Fund Dinner; chairman Youth Services Advisory Board Cuyahoga Commissioners and Juvenile Court; chairman Cleveland Heights Advisory Commission HUD Block Grants. **HONORS/ACHIEVEMENTS:** Distinguished Serv Awd Blue Cross 1984; Citation City of Cleveland 1984; Distinguished Serv Awd Harambee 1985; President's Awd Federation of Community Planning; Pi Lambda Theta Honorary Education Sorority; first black woman to serve as vice president, Federation of Community Planning 1977, as vice chairman of United Way Services Capital Campaign, 1974; first black person to serve as chairman of Federation of Community Planning Annual Health and Human Services Institute, 1981. **HOME ADDRESS:** 2339 North Park Blvd, Cleveland Heights, OH 44106.

MADISON, RICHARD
Government official. **PERSONAL:** Born Dec 06, 1932, Camden, AL; married Edith Sauhing Ho. **EDUCATION:** Morehouse Coll, BA 1953;Univ of PA, MGA 1958;Univ of Pittsburgh, PhD. **CAREER:** Gov's Ofc of Adminstr PA, dir of personnel 1972-; Inst for Minority Bus Educ Howard U, exec dir 1970-71; Nat Urban League Entrepreneurial Devel, natl dir 1969-70; Nat Urban League Field Operations, asst dir 1968-69; CARE E Pakistan, dir 1968;

CARE Malaysia, acting dir 1967; CARE Hong Kong, asst dir 1965-68; CARE Honduras, asst dir 1963-65; Peace Corps Colombia, asso dir 1962-63; CARE Turkey, field rep 1961-62; Gov's Ofc Harrisburg PA, adminstr asst to dir of personnel 1960-61; Budget Bur Gov's Ofc Harrisburg, bdgt analyst 1958-60. **ORGANIZATIONS:** Mem Am Soc for Pub Adminstr; Intl Personnel Mgmt Assn; mem NAACP; Frgn Policy Assn; Omega Psi Phi Frat; Black Polit Assmbly. **MILITARY SERVICE:** AUS 1953-55. **BUSINESS ADDRESS:** Gov's Ofc of Adminstrn, 517 Finance Bldg, Harrisburg, PA 17120.

MADISON, ROBERT P.
Architect. **PERSONAL:** Born Jul 28, 1923, Cleveland, OH; son of Robert James Madison and Nettie Josephine Brown; married Leatrice Lucille Branch, Apr 16, 1949; children: Jeanne M Anderson, Juliette M Little. **EDUCATION:** Western Reserve Univ, BA rch 1948; Harvard Univ, MA rch 1952; Ecole Des Beaux Arts Paris, attended 1953; Howard Univ, HHD 1987. **CAREER:** Robert A Little Architects, designer 1948-51; Howard Univ, asst prof 1952-54; Robert P Madison Intl, pres 1954-. **ORGANIZATIONS:** Trustee Case Western Reserve Univ 1969-81; dir Industrial Bank of Washington 1975-81; trustee Cuyahoga Metropolitan General Hospital 1982-; mem Ohio Bd of Building Standards State of Ohio 1984-; chairman Jury of Fellows Natl AIA 1985; trustee Cleveland Chap Amer Red Cross 1986-; trustee Ohio Motorists Assoc 1986-; mem Cleveland Downtown Plan Steering Comm 1986; mem City Planning Commn Cleveland Heights OH 1987-; mem Alpha Phi Alpha, Sigma Pi Phi. **HONORS/ACHIEVEMENTS:** Architect US Embassy Dakar Senegal 1965-77; Architect's delegation Peoples Republic of China 1974; Fellow Amer Inst of Architects 1974; Disting Serv Award BEDO State of Ohio; President's Award Cleveland Chap AIA; Distinguished Firm Award, Howard Univ, 1989; Distinguished Serv Award, Case Western Reserve Univ, 1989. **MILITARY SERVICE:** AUS Infantry 1st lt 4 yrs. **HOME ADDRESS:** 2339 N Park Blvd, Cleveland Heights, OH 44106. **BUSINESS ADDRESS:** President, Robert P Madison Intl, 2930 Euclid Ave, Cleveland, OH 44115.

MADISON, RONALD L.
Electrical engineer. **PERSONAL:** Born Feb 03, 1942, Detroit, MI; married Mamie; children: Monica, Jeffrey. **EDUCATION:** Univ of MI, BSEE 1964; Univ of MI Dearborn, MSEE 1972. **CAREER:** Ford Motor Co, sr design engr, body & elec prod engr 1976-, serv proj devel engr 1974, prod design engr 1973-74; Ford Motor Co Serv Rsrch Ctr, serv opr coord 1974-76; GM Tech Ctr, sr proj engr 1969-73; Delco Elec Div GM, proj engr 1966-69; GM Proving Ground, jr engr 1964-66. **ORGANIZATIONS:** Vp Alpha Phi Alpha FratUniv of MI 1961-63; memUniv of MI Dearborn Assn of Black Students 1972; Engineering Soc of Detroit 1972-74; NAACP 1974-75. **HONORS/ACHIEVEMENTS:** Fellowship Chapel Lay Rdrs; Fellowship Chapel Men's Club; hon grad Cass Tech HS 1959; Grant-in-Aid Schlrshp Sr YrUniv of MI 1964. **BUSINESS ADDRESS:** Body & Elec Prod Engr Ford Mot, 21500 Oakwood Blvd, Dearborn, MI 48121.

MADISON, SHANNON L.
Engineer. **PERSONAL:** Born Jun 21, 1927, Texas; married Ruth Jean; children: Earl Wayne, Michael Denard, Stephanie Annett, Sharon, Maria. **EDUCATION:** Howard U, BS. **CAREER:** York Div Borg Warner Corp, devel engr 1954-59; Emerson Radio & Phonograph Co, chief test engr 1959-61; Whirlpool Corp, sr mfg rsrch engr 1965-; Delco Appliance Div GM, sr proj engr 1961-65. **ORGANIZATIONS:** Human Resources Counc 1965-68; Tri-Co Comm Action Commn 1965-71; mem SME; NTA; ASHRAE; Sigma Xi; SPE; written many articles; subj of many articles; Relat Adv Bd; pres Homes Berrien Co Families Inc 1968-; mem State Adv Bd Gov MI 1972-; Comprehen State Hlth Plng Adv Counc 1971-74; Commnty Twin City Area Human Relat Counc; Twin Cities Comm Forum; Model Cities; mem NAACP; Self Devel Com Chmn. **BUSINESS ADDRESS:** Sr Mfg Res Engr, Whirlpool Corp, Monte Rd, Rm 2050, Benton Harbor, MI 49022.

MADISON, STANLEY D.
Physician. **PERSONAL:** Born Aug 10, 1932, Columbia, SC; married Vivian Banks; children: Laura Elaine, Leslie Karen. **EDUCATION:** HowardUniv Coll of Pharm, BS Pharm 1951; Western ResrvUniv Med Sch, MD 1960. **CAREER:** MD, pvt prac of family med 1960-; Johns Hopkins Hosp, Baltimore, & Rovident Hosp, staff;Univ of PA, lctr family med. **ORGANIZATIONS:** Mem AMA; Med & Chirurgical Faculty of MD; Am Heart Soc; Am Acad of Family Physicians. **BUSINESS ADDRESS:** 5821 Moravia Rd, Baltimore, MD 21206.

MADISON, WILLIAM L.
Manufacturer. **PERSONAL:** Born Apr 03, 1933, Columbus, OH; children: Michael Phillip, Melissa Ann. **EDUCATION:** Attended, Case Western Reserve Univ, Columbia Univ; Indiana Univ, BA 1954. **CAREER:** American Health & Beauty Aids, president/owner. **ORGANIZATIONS:** Mem NAACP, Urban League, PUSH Inc, Woodlawn Associates. **HONORS/ACHIEVEMENTS:** Man of the Year Natl Hairdressers; Black Achiever New York YMCA 1974; Businessman of the Year Ohio Hairdressers 1973,74; Great Achievements Revlon Inc 1976-78.

MADLOCK, BILL
Professional athlete. **PERSONAL:** Born Jan 12, 1951, Memphis, TN; married Cynthia; children: Sarah, Stephen, William Douglas, Jeremy Joseph. **EDUCATION:** Southwestern IA Comm Coll. **CAREER:** Houston Astros, infielder 1973; Chicago Cubs, infielder 1974-76; San Fran Giants, infielder 1977-79; Pittsburgh Pirates, infielder 1980-. **ORGANIZATIONS:** Cystic Fibrosis "65 Roses" Campaign. **HONORS/ACHIEVEMENTS:** 4th NL Batting Title, becoming 11th player in Major League hist to win the crown 4 times 1983; mem NL All-Star Team 1983; tied for 10th in GWRBI 1982; helped lead the Pirates to the World Championship 1979; mem The Sporting News All-Star Team 1975; led the PCL in runs scored & total bases/2nd in avg & hits 1973; had a perfect 6 for 6 night 1973.

MADRY, MAUDE HOLT
Health services administrator. **PERSONAL:** Born Aug 03, 1949, Thomaston, AL; daughter of Henry J Holt and Naomi Holt Levert; divorced; children: Andre, DeNeal, Madry. **EDUCATION:** AL A&M Univ, BS 1976; Univ of Miami, MBA/HA 1983. **CAREER:** Rochester Telephone, acct clerk 1972-76; Allstate Insurance, supervisor 1976-77; Jackson Memorial Hosp, asst administrator 1978-86; Metro-Dade, administrator. **ORGANIZATIONS:** Mem Delta Sigma Theta Sor, Eta Phi Beta Sor, NAACP, Urban League, Coalition for the Homeless, Black Public Administrators, Natl Assoc of Counties Business& Professional Women, Amer Business Women, FL Voters League; pres Greater Miami Chap AL A&M Univ Metro-Action Plan. **HOME ADDRESS:** 10090 NW 80th Ct, Unit 1237, Hialeah Gardens, FL 33016. **BUSINESS ADDRESS:** Division Director, Central Intake & Detox, Metro Dade County, 2500 NW 22nd Ave, Miami, FL 33142.

MAGEE, ROBERT WALTER
Family practitioner. **PERSONAL:** Born Apr 23, 1951, New Orleans, LA; married Deborah Ketcheus. **EDUCATION:** Southern Univ, BS 1973; Meharry Medical Coll, MD 1977. **CAREER:** Plasma Alliance, staff physician 1979-82; Mathew Walker Health Ctr, staff physician 1980-82; Meharry FP Program, asst prof 1980-82; New Orleans Health Corp, medical dir 1982-85; HMO, staff physician. **ORGANIZATIONS:** Staff physician Health America 1985-. **HOME ADDRESS:** 13933 Explorers Ave, New Orleans, LA 70129.

MAGEE, SADIE E.
Educator, coach. **PERSONAL:** Born Oct 27, 1932, Mt Olive, MS. **EDUCATION:** Alcorn State Univ, BS 1954; Jackson State Univ, MS Ed 1975. **CAREER:** Lanier HS Jackson Publ School, teacher, coach 1954-69; Central HS Jackson Publ School, teacher 1969-75; City of Jackson Allied Svcs, counselor 1971-73; Jackson State Univ, instructor of physical educ, head basketball coach for women 1975-. **ORGANIZATIONS:** Mem NAACP 1950-, YWCA 1954-. **HONORS/ACHIEVEMENTS:** Alumnus of the Month Natl Alumni Assoc 1978; Coach of the Year Natl Sports Found 1978-, Natl Assoc of Womens Sports 1978; Beverly Saulcy Awd Natl Sports Found 1978; Natl Alumni Awd in Sports JSU Natl Alumni Assoc 1978; Outstanding Achievement Awd Dept of HPER JSU 1978-79; Outstanding Coaching Awd NatlAssoc of Women Sports 1979; Leadership Awd Dept of Athletics JSU 1979; Achievements in Coaching & Serv Dept of HPER JSU 1980; Coach of the Year Natl Assoc of Womens Sports 1980; Coach of the Year Jackson Daily News 1980; Activist Awd Women for Progress 1981; Winning Coach Awd Jackson State 1981; Notable Achievements Awd Nine Iron Golf Club 1981; Outstanding Accomplishmnets in Coaching & Serv HPER Dept JSU 1981; Outstanding Achievements in the Field of Ed & Sports Mbel Carney Chap Students NEA JSU 1981; Resolution Miss Leg 1981; Nominated for the Jackie Robinson Awd in Sports 1981; Resolution State Bd of Ed Inst of Higher Learning State of MS 1981; Winning Coach Jackson State 1982; Coach of the Year SWAC 1982-83, Miller Brewer Co 1983; Outstanding & Meritorious Serv HPER Dept JSU 1983; Devotion & Dedicated Serv JSU HPER Majors Club 1983; Winning Coach Roundball Club 1984; Resolution MS Leg 1984; Spec in Ed JSU 1981. **BUSINESS ADDRESS:** Instructor of PE, Head Coach, Jackson StateUniv, 1325 Lynch St, Jackson, MS 39217.

MAHAN-POWELL, LENA
Mayor, teacher. **PERSONAL:** Born Dec 03, 1951, Myrlewood, AL; daughter of Buster Mahan and Anna Givan Mahamn; married Willie Powell, Nov 22, 1978; children: Donyale Jones, Ricky Leyvahn Powell. **EDUCATION:** Univ of South Alabama, Mobile AL, attended, 1970-71; Alabama State Univ, Montgomery, AL, BS, 1974, MEd, 1977; Univ of Alabama Tuscaloosa, Tuscalossa AL, attended, 1978; Auburn Univ Montgomery, Montgomery AL, attended, 1984-86. **CAREER:** Wilcox County Bd of Educ, Camden AL, teacher, 1974-89; Talladega Deaf and Blind, Montgomery AL, teacher, 1984-86; Town of Yellow Bluff, Yellow Bluff AL, councilmember, 1984-88, mayor, 1988-. **ORGANIZATIONS:** Church sec, Arkadelphia Baptist Church, 1978-; pres, Universal Brotherhood, 1980-; mem, Lewis Delight #598 OES, 1982-; bd of dir, Wilcox Human Resources Dept, 1984-; mem, Prepared Cities Org, 1986-; bd of dir, Wilcox Educ Assn, 1987-89; mem, Alabama Conf of Black Mayors, 1988-, Natl Conf of Black Mayors, 1988-; by laws comm, Central High School PTO, 1988-; mem, Volunteer Fire Dept Assn, 1988-, vice pres, Wilcox Educ Assn, 1989-. **HOME ADDRESS:** Rte 1, Box 198, Pine Hill, AL 36769.

MAHIN, GEORGE E.
Business executive. **PERSONAL:** Born Oct 18, 1914, Franklin, KY; married Marjorie J Hines; children: George Frederick, Jerome, Daniel, Philip, David. **EDUCATION:** Municipal Coll; Simmons Univ. **CAREER:** Mammoth Life & Accident Insurance Co, assoc agency dir, admin asst dir, agency sec, supt agencies, asst agency dir, mgr Gary & Cleveland Districts, home rep; Herald-Post, district mgr; Courier-Journal & Times, dist mgr. **ORGANIZATIONS:** Mem NAACP bd; served coms for YMCA; Boy Scouts; American Legion; commnity orgns; active chr groups; Ordained Elder AME Zion Ch. **HONORS/ACHIEVEMENTS:** Recip numerous awards Mammoth & Nat Ins Assoc. **MILITARY SERVICE:** AUS. **BUSINESS ADDRESS:** 606-608 W Walnut St, Louisville, KY 40203.

MAHONEY, KEITH WESTON
Health services. **PERSONAL:** Born Jan 12, 1939, Montego Bay, Jamaica. **EDUCATION:** Brooklyn Coll, BA Sociology 1960-68, MA Political Sci 1972-75, MSc Ed 1979-82. **CAREER:** Dept of Welfare, caseworker 1968-72; Sch Dist 22 Drug Prevention Prog, specialist 1972-. **ORGANIZATIONS:** Comm org Vanderveer Park Actions Council 1973-79; bd of dirs Amersfort Flatlands Dev Corp 1980-; mediator Childrens Aid Soc 1982-; mediator Brooklyn Coll Dispute Resolution Centre 1982-; health coord Caribbean Action Lobby 1983-; comm org Amersfort Junction Anti Drug Task Force 1983-; comm bd mem Comm Bd 14 1985-; mem Natl Assn of Black Counselors 1985-. **HONORS/ACHIEVEMENTS:** Service to Comm Amersfort Flatlands Dev Corp 1980-83; Excellence & Serv to Comm Brooklyn Coll Grad Guidance & Counseling Student Orgs 1982-83; Prof Friend Brooklyn Coll Grad Guidance & Comm Serv Org 1982-84; Outstanding Effort to Prevent Drug Abuse Sch Dist 22 Drug Prev Prog 1972-. **MILITARY SERVICE:** AUS med corps pfc 2 yrs; Honorable Discharge. **BUSINESS ADDRESS:** Drug Abuse Prev/Interv Spec II, Sch Dist 22 Drug Program, 2525 Haring St, Brooklyn, NY 11235.

MAHORN, RICK JOEL
Professional athlete. **PERSONAL:** Born Sep 21, 1958, Hartford, CT. **EDUCATION:** Hampton Inst, BS Bus Admin 1980. **CAREER:** Washington Bullets, center 1980. **ORGANIZATIONS:** Active in num charities; spent week at Special Olympics Intl Games 1983. **HONORS/ACHIEVEMENTS:** Career high rebounds 19 against Sixers; set career playoff high with 15 rebounds against Celtics 1984; 1st smart coll player taken in 1980 NBA draft (35th overall); 3-time NAIA All-Am at Hampton Inst; played in 4 postseason all star games including the Aloha Classic where he became 3rd small coll player to be invited. **BUSINESS ADDRESS:** Washington Bullets, One Harry S Truman Dr, Ste 510, Landover, MD 20785.

MAITLAND, LEO C.
Physician. **PERSONAL:** Born Jan 12, 1928, New York, NY. **EDUCATION:** Coll of City of NY, BS 1949; Meharry Med Coll, MD 1953; Morrisania Hosp, rotating internship 1953-54; Harlem Hosp, resd in surgery 1954-59. **CAREER:** Private practice, physician 1962-; Harlem Hosp, asst attending surgery 1962-65; Sydenham Hosp, attending surgery 1965-78; Carbini Hosp, assoc attending surgery 1972-; Health Ins Prog, contract surgeon 1973-78; NY Med Coll, assoc prof surgery 1972-. **ORGANIZATIONS:** Chmn dept of surgery Sydenham Hosp 1973-74; assoc dir dept of surgery Sydenham Hosp 1974-78; consult surgery Prospect Hosp 1977-; consult surgery Sydenham Hosp 1978; co-chmn Fund Dr to build new Mt Morris Park Hosp 1962-63; co-chmn bd of dirs Fredrick Douglass Creative Arts Ctr; mem Dep Mayor Herman Bedillo Adv Comm on Rehab of the S Bronx 1978-79; diplomate Natl Bd of Med Examiners 1954, Amer Bd of Surgery 1962. **BUSINESS ADDRESS:** Associate Professor Surgery, New York Medical College, 49 W 96 St, New York, NY 10025.

MAJETE, CLAYTON AARON
Educator. **PERSONAL:** Born Apr 19, 1941, Woodland, NC; son of Barnabas Majete (deceased) and Doreather Jefferson Majete; children: Lisa. **EDUCATION:** Morgan State Univ, BA 1964; New York Univ, MA 1965, PhD 1984. **CAREER:** CUNY John Jay Coll, instructor 1970-72; CUNY Baruch Coll, instr 1972-75, lecturer 1975-84, asst prof 1984-. **ORGANIZATIONS:** Mem Amer Assoc of Univ Profs 1975-, Soc for Field Experience Educ 1978-; chmn bd dirs Inst for Urban Affairs 1978-; mem Natl Assoc of Black Social Workers 1980-, Amer Sociological Assoc 1981-; consultant and researcher NY Times and WCBS-TV 1985; consultant Governor of State of MD 1986. **HONORS/ACHIEVEMENTS:** Mem Alpha Kappa Delta; Fellowship Johns Hopkins Sch of Medicine; published "Black Voting Behavior: The Effect of Locus of Control and Socio-economic Status", The Western Journal of Black Studies Vol II, No 3, 1987. **HOME ADDRESS:** 2500 W Forest Park Ave, Baltimore, MD 21215. **BUSINESS ADDRESS:** Professor of Sociology, CityUniv of NY Baruch Coll, 17 Lexington Ave, New York, NY 10010.

MAJOR, CLARENCE
Novelist, lecturer. **PERSONAL:** Born Dec 31, 1936, Atlanta, GA. **EDUCATION:** Art Inst of Chicago, 1953; New School for Social Research, 1972; State Univ of New York at Albany, BS; Union for Experimenting Coll and Univ, PhD. **CAREER:** Various colls, univs, churches, radio, visiting writer 1967-74; Sarah Lawrence Coll, lecturer, creative writing, lit, 1967-; Journal Black Poetry, ed 1972-; Prof, English, Univ of Colorado. **ORGANIZATIONS:** mem, Author's Guild, Author's League of Amer, PEN Amer Ctr, Bantam Lecture Bur, Wm Morris Agency, Assoc Amer Univ Profs, Intl Platform Assoc, Jas Nelson Raymond Scholarship Art Inst, Chicago, 1951. **HONORS/ACHIEVEMENTS:** Natl Council Arts Award, 1970; NY Cult Found Grant, 1971; Numerous publication awards, newspapers; Published seven books, numerous poems & essays; lectured/traveled to several countries; Western States Book Award for Fiction (My Amputations); The Pushcart Prize; Fulbright Fellowship. **MILITARY SERVICE:** USAF airman 1955-57. **BUSINESS ADDRESS:** Department of English, Box 226, Univ of Colorado, Boulder, CO 80309. *

MAJOR, HENRYMAE M.
Guidance counselor, department head. **PERSONAL:** Born Mar 09, 1935, Earle, AR; daughter of Andrew McCoy and Clara McCoy; married Isadore; children: Kelly Dianne. **EDUCATION:** Lincoln U, BS 1956; Wayne State U, MA Guidance & Counseling 1963. **CAREER:** Central High School Detroit, guidance dept head 1970-, guidance counselor 1965-70, health, phys educ tchr, bd of & educ tchr, bd of educ 1958-65; State of ILinois, recreational therapist 1957. **ORGANIZATIONS:** Mem Girls Work Council; Detroit Counselor's Assn; Guild Assn of Metro Detroit; Orgn of Sch Admin & Supvrs; Assn of Black Admin; Future Tchrs of Amer Sponsor; mem Lincoln Univ Alumni Assn; Delta Sigma Theta Alum Chap; Women of Wayne State Univ Alumni Chap Established Coord Health Clinic, Spain Middle School health counseling socio-econ areas; mem NAACP, Hartford Memorial Baptist Church; mem Amer Assn of Counseling Development 1980-; mem Michigan Assn of Counseling Development 1980-; mem Michigan Assn of College Admissions Counselors; mem Natl Board of Certified Counselors 1979-. **HONORS/ACHIEVEMENTS:** Outstanding Young Woman of Amer 1967; co-author, Role of the Counselor. **BUSINESS ADDRESS:** Dept Head Guidance & Counseling, Central High School, 2425 Tuxedo, Detroit, MI 48206.

MAJOR, PAUL CHARLES
Chief executive officer. **PERSONAL:** Born Jan 02, 1947, Chicago, IL. **EDUCATION:** IN Univ 1965-67; OH State Univ 1978-80. **CAREER:** WGEE/Indianapolis, announcer/programmer, WCAR WJLB/Detroit, announcer/programmer 1966-82, WKLR/Toledo, gen mgr, WVNS/Tuskegee, gen mgr, WTUN-TV Columbus,TV acct exec 1966-82; WTMP/Tampa, pres gen mgr 1982-. **ORGANIZATIONS:** Bd mem Hillsborough Comm Coll Tampa FL 1985; gubernatorial appointment Alafia Riner Basin Bd Southwest Water Mgmt Dist State of FL. **HONORS/ACHIEVEMENTS:** Outstanding Comm Serv FL Employment Project 1984; Outstanding Business Awd NAACP 1985. **BUSINESS ADDRESS:** President, Westerville Comm Inc, 5207 Washington Blvd, Tampa, FL 33610.

MAJORS, EDITH SARA
Association executive, statistician. **PERSONAL:** Born Jun 08, 1920, Columbia, SC; widowed; children: Major Charles Wesley Simmons, Dr Reginald Leigh Simmons. **EDUCATION:** Allen Univ, BS 1939-42; Howard Univ, 1943; Univ of MI, 1944; Amer Univ, 1954-56; USDA, 1964-65. **CAREER:** Carver Jr High School, math teacher 1942-45; Fed Government, stat clk 1953-59; stat super 1959-62; stat MED 1962-74. **ORGANIZATIONS:** Pres Justamere Club 1957; exec sec Lambda Kappa Mu 1981-85; sec Northwest Boundary Civic Assn 1983; organizer Nieghborhood Block Club 1984; Basileus Theta Chap Laubda Kappa Mu Sor 1984-; ward coord Older Adult Learning Ctr DC Office on Aging. **HONORS/ACHIEVEMENTS:** Sustained Superior Awd Dept of Army Office of Surgeon Gen; Comm Awd Fourth Dist of Wash DC 1984. **HOME ADDRESS:** 433 Ingraham St NW, Washington, DC 20011.

MAJORS, MARY E.
Caterer, delicatessan. **PERSONAL:** Born Mar 16, 1912, Keokuk, IA; married Carl. **CAREER:** Self-employed, catering/delicatessan operation. **ORGANIZATIONS:** Legis chmn, Business & Professional Women; past pres, NAACP; past pres, Lee Co Rep Women's Club; past pres, Self Culture Club; 2nd vice pres, League of Women Voters; bd mem, Lee Co Historical Soc; former bd mem, Mental Health Bd; planning commn, bd of human relations, Keokuk; comm rep, Head Start; committeewoman of 3rd ward 12 yrs; mem, Lee Co School Bd; treas, Keokuk Soroptimist Intl; 1st Dist IA Fedn of Rep Club Treas; delegate, Natl Rep Conv 1972; mem, MS Parkway Commn; chmn, Heritage & Americanism, IA Fedn of Rep Women State; former mem, Status of Women Commn; mem, Church Women United. **HONORS/ACHIEVEMENTS:** BP&W Woman of Achievement Award.

MAJORS, MATTIE CAROLYN
Journalist. **PERSONAL:** Born Jan 16, 1945, Waynesboro, GA; children: Brandon Matthew Quentin Van Majors. **EDUCATION:** Central St U, chemistry 1970. **CAREER:** CWRU Cleveland, rsch lab tech 1970-72; WABQ Radio Cleveland, news reporter 1970; WJMO Radio Cleveland, news reporter acting news dir 1970-72; WKBN Radio-TV Youngstown OH, minority affairs coord 1972-77; STorer Broadcasting WJKW-TV, reporter coanchor 1977-; WJBK-TV, co-host PM Mag Detroit, general assignment reporter, special reporter for "For Kid's Sake". **ORGANIZATIONS:** Pres mem Younstown Sickle Cell Anemi Found 1973-76; MENSA Cleveland Press Club 1980; Negro Business & Professional Women's Club 1980; Young Black Businessmen 1979;Youngstown Fedn Woman' Clubs; Freedom Inc; United Negro Improvement Assn; Omega Psi Phi Frat; hon co-chmn 1986, hon chair 1987 Black United Fund Campaign 1986; bd mem local AFTRA Chap. **HONORS/ACHIEVEMENTS:** Outstanding Achievement in Broadcasting Youngstown Comm Action Council; Proclamation Mattie Majors' Day Youngstown City Council Mayor of Youngstown 1977; BestSpot News Story Cleveland Press Club 1980; nom as Outstanding Female on Air Talent 1984-85. **BUSINESS ADDRESS:** WJBK-TV, News Dept, PO Box 2000, Southfield, MI 48037.

MAKLE, VIVIAN B.
Educator. **PERSONAL:** Born in East Orange, NJ; children: Judith V Banks, Adelbert W. **EDUCATION:** NY Univ, BS 1940; Seton Hall Univ, MA 1973. **CAREER:** Busy Bee Nursery East Orange, owner, dir 1946-55; Quitman St School, Title I Proj Coord 1967-. **ORGANIZATIONS:** Mem Boys Club of Amer; Cong Vivian Makle Mem E Orange Bd Ed 1970; pres Chr-Homemaker Ill Serv 1984-85; pres Newark Presbyterial 1984-85. **HONORS/ACHIEVEMENTS:** Civic Awd Recog Outstanding Civ Contrib Cosmopolitan Womens Club 1970; Outstanding Contribs Quitman St School PTA 1974; Cert Appr Outs & Dedicated Serv NJ St Fed Colored Womens Clubs 1971; Outstanding Contrib to Quitman St School & Comm 1970-71; Outstanding Serv to Comm Civic Action League E Orange 1968; Grateful Apprec Ded Comm Serv E Orange 1968; Grateful Apprec Ded Comm Serv E Orange C of C 1969; Recog Unselfish Serv Field of Furthering Quality Ed 5th Ward Civic Assoc 1969; Outstanding Comm Serv Citizens Com E Orange 1969; Serv E Orange Model Cities Council 1974; Bamberger Comm Gallery Comm Leaders 962; Woman of Year Worrall Publ. **BUSINESS ADDRESS:** Title I Proj Coordinator, Quitman St School, 21 Quitman St, Newark, NJ 07013.

MAKUPSON, WALTER H.
Attorney. **PERSONAL:** Born Sep 27, 1946, Gaffney, SC; married Amyre. **EDUCATION:** Miami U, BA 1968;Univ of Cincinnati, JD 1972. **CAREER:** Gen Mtrs Corp, gen counsel 1972; Gen Mtrs Corp, buyer delco products div 1968-69; Dayton-walther Corp, personnel supr 1968. **ORGANIZATIONS:** Mem Nat Bar Assn; Wolverine Bar Assn; MI Bar Assn; OH Bar Assn; Am Bar & Assn; Am Arbitration Assn. **BUSINESS ADDRESS:** Gen Mtrs Corp, 3044 W Grand Blvd, Detroit, MI 48202.

MALBROUE, JOSEPH, JR.
Manager. **PERSONAL:** Born Aug 24, 1949, LaFayette, LA; married Joretta Leauntine Tyson. **EDUCATION:** Univ of Southwest LA, BSChE 1966-70. **CAREER:** Union Carbide Corp, prod engr 1970-73, tech sales rep 1973-76, asst customer serv mgr 1976-78, dist planner 1978-84, LPG supply mgr 1984-. **HONORS/ACHIEVEMENTS:** Dir cncl Union Carbide Corp 1975; EI Dupont schlrshp Univ of SW LA 1968. **MILITARY SERVICE:** USMCR sgt 1970-76. **BUSINESS ADDRESS:** LPG Supply Manager, Union Carbide Corp, 11111 Katy Freeway, Ste 900, Houston, TX 77079.

MALEKEBU, DANIEL SHARP
Physician, clergyman. **PERSONAL:** Born Mar 01, 1889; widowed. **EDUCATION:** Nat Training Sch, BS 1913; Meharry Med Coll, MD 1917;Univ PA, Tropical Micine 1918; Selma U, hon DD 1935. **CAREER:** Malawi Inc, chmn african bapt assembly 1945; Providence Indsl Mission, dir 1926-71; Union Coll of Malawi, physician, educator, lectr, theologian, humanitarian, pres Estbl coll ready to open 1979. **HONORS/ACHIEVEMENTS:** Fdr Flora Malekebu Scholarship Fund; Pres's Award Meharry Med Coll 50 yrs of serv to humanity; gov's award State of TN; red carpet award C of C Nashville TN; letter of commendation Pres Lyndon B Johnson; hon citizen award City of Nashville TN.

MALLETT, CONRAD L.
County official. **PERSONAL:** Born Feb 22, 1928, Ames, TX; married Claudia Gwendolyn; children: Conrad, Jr, Lydia Gwendolyn, Veronica ?, Thierry. **EDUCATION:** Wayne State U, BS 1957;Univ of MI, MA 1962; Wayne State U, EdD 1972. **CAREER:** Detroit Dept of Transportation, dir 1977; Wayne County Comm College, vice pres 1973-77; Wayne State U, dir 1970-73; Detroit Housing Commn, dir 1969-70; City of Detroit, asst to mayor 1966-68; City of Detroit, tchr 1957-64; Detroit, patrolman 1952-57. **ORGANIZATIONS:** Chmn SE MI Council of Governments. **MILITARY SERVICE:** USAF 1945-47. **BUSINESS ADDRESS:** 726 City County Bldg, Detroit, MI 48226.

MALLETTE, JOHN M.
Biologist, educator. **PERSONAL:** Born Aug 06, 1932, Houston, TX; son of Jules Mallette and Lydia Myers Mallette; married Pazetta Berryman; children: John Michael Jr, Adelaide Veronica, Pazetta Ann. **EDUCATION:** Xavier Univ, BS 1954; TX Southern Univ, MS 1958; PA State Univ, PhD 1962; Univ of TN, Executive Development 1977. **CAREER:** TX Southern Univ, instr; PA State Univ, instr; Univ of TN at Nashville, vice chancellor; TN State Univ, vice pres research & dev/prof biological sci. **ORGANIZATIONS:** Mem Amer Assn of Univ Professors, Amer Zoological Soc; past pres TN Acad Sci 1976-77; pres bd of dir Catholic Charities of TN 1974-76; trustee Leadership Nashville 1977-; mem bd dir Council of Comm Serv 1980-; mem bd dir Middle TN Soc Action Comm; mem Urban Observator; past clubmaster St Vincent Sch; Religious Heritage of Amer; mem bd dir Natl Conf Christians and Jews 1973-74; mem bd dir People United for the Restoration of the Environ; pres Nashville Reg Cncl of the Laity 1972-73; mem bd dir Samaritan's Inc; mem steering comm Leadership Nashville 1976; mem selection comm Leadership Nashville 1976; mem bd dir Operations

Come-Back; mem bd dir First Step Found; mem assoc bd dir St Thomas Hospital Nashville, TN; UN Nashville Chapter; Amer Assn of Univ Professors past pres TN State Chapter 19 67-68; Amer Zoological Soc; Amer Assn for Advance of Sci; TN Acad of Sci; fellow NY Acad of Sci; Amer Inst of Biolog Sciences; Sigma Xi; Natl Inst of Science. **HONORS/ACHIEVEMENTS:** Pre-Doctoral Fellow Natl Foundation Penn State 1960-61; nominee for Teacher of the Year TN State Univ 1964-65 and 1966-67; paper chosen as one of the most outstanding and newsworthy presented at the Amer Assn for the Advancement of Sci 1965; Fellow TN Acad of Sci 1967; Fellow NY Acad of Sci 1968; Knight of St Gregory Papal Honor 1971; Standard Oil Found Award Teacher of the Year TN State Univ 1971; Keynote Speaker of the 50th Anniversary Banquet Xavier Univ 1975; Judge Miss Teenage Amer 1979; Recip of the Human Relations Award in honor of Dr Martin Luther King Nashville Metro Govt 1980; named one of the l5 finalists in the reg 1981 Jefferson Awards; received grants from Natl Sci Found, Gulf Oil Grant, Natl Insts Health. **MILITARY SERVICE:** AUS Sp 3 1954-56. **BUSINESS ADDRESS:** Professor of Biology, TN State University, 3500 John A Merritt Blvd, Nashville, TN 37203.

MALLISHAM, JOSEPH W.
Business executive. **PERSONAL:** Born Jun 14, 1928, Tuscaloosa, AL; married Sadie B Townsend; children: Sheila, Ivy, Darlene. **EDUCATION:** Tuscaloosa County Tech Trade Sch, 1954. **CAREER:** Gulf Serv Station, owner. **ORGANIZATIONS:** Pres Druid HS PTSA 1974; chmn bd dirs Tuscaloosa Opportunity Program 1968-71; 1st chmn Tuscaloosa Community Relations Adv Bd 1969; mem bd mgmt Benjamin Barnes Br YMCA 1969; mem Human Rights Com for Bryce Hosp 1972; NAACP; hon mem ODK; pres Tuscaloosa Citizens for Action. **HONORS/ACHIEVEMENTS:** Citizen of Year, W Alabama Unit, Natl Assn (Soc Work); Man of Year, Tuscaloosa Community Alpha Phi Alpha Frat, 1974; hon staff, Atty Gen, State of Alabama, 1972. **MILITARY SERVICE:** Corpl AUS 1950-51. **BUSINESS ADDRESS:** 3135 20th St, Tuscaloosa, AL.

MALLORY, WILLIAM HENRY
Supply supervisor. **PERSONAL:** Born Mar 30, 1919, Monroe City, MO; married Mary Taylor; children: Wanda Florence, R. **EDUCATION:** Gem City Bus Coll Quincy IL; MO U, Equip Tech & Oxygen Therapy. **CAREER:** Mallory Trucking Serv, self-employed for 20 yrs; St Mary's Hosp Quincy, IL, equip tech 1964-74; Levering Hosp Hannibal MO, central supply supr. **ORGANIZATIONS:** Chmn NE & Comm Action Coalition; Personnel Com for 11 Co on Comm Aff; chmn Marion Co Advisory Bd; chmn MO Comm-coord Child Care; vice pres Hannibal BrNBAACP pres 1975; vice pres St Con; elected auditor 1975, chmn Deacons & Laymen Union North MO Bapt Assn; aptd mem Affirm Action Com. **HONORS/ACHIEVEMENTS:** Hannibal Sp Award for aid in Head-start Schls 1972; Men Among Achvmt Award, London, England 1975; Comm Ldrs & Noteworthy Am Am Biog Inst of Raleigh NC 1976; life membership award in St 4-C's of MO for outs accomp 1973. **BUSINESS ADDRESS:** 1734 Market, Hannibal, MO 63401.

MALLORY, WILLIAM L.
Government official. **PERSONAL:** Married Fannie; children: 5 children. **EDUCATION:** Xavier Univ, grad; Univ of Cincinnati; Central State, LLD (Hon). **CAREER:** Cinn Publ School, teacher; Univ of Cinn, assoc prof; State of OH, state rep 1967-. **ORGANIZATIONS:** Maj flr ldr, vchmn Dem Exec Com Hamilton Co. **HONORS/ACHIEVEMENTS:** Pioneer Awd Hamilton OH Comm on Aging; Outstanding Citizen Awd City Cinn. **BUSINESS ADDRESS:** State Representative, State of Ohio, State House, Columbus, OH 43215.

MALLOY, H. REMBERT
Physician, director. **PERSONAL:** Born Jul 19, 1913, Hamlet, NC. **EDUCATION:** Johnson C Smuth U, BS 1934;Univ Chicago, MS 1935; Spartanburg Methodist Coll; Howard U, MD 1939; Reynolds Meml Hosp, MD 19639; Freedmen's Hosp, Resd; NY, postgrad. **CAREER:** Mt Zion UM Ch, pastor 4 yrs; Yellow Freight System, truck driver; Howard U, instr; Winston-salem State U, dir student hlth svcs; Bowman Grey Sch ofMed, clinical instr; Med Park Hosp, attending surgeon; Forsyth Meml Hosp, attending surgeon; Jour of Nat Med Assn, edt staff; John Hale Surg Soc, former pres; Reynolds Hosp, chf 13; Area Civil Def Hosp, chf of surgery. **ORGANIZATIONS:** Bd of dir 1st Union Nat Bank 1974; Old N State Med Soc; Forsyth Co Med Soc; NC Med Assn; Nat Med Assn; chmn AMA Chmn Hlth & Safty Com; Boy Scouts 1948-58; Scout Master 1956-60; Com of Mgmt YMCA 1945-58; bd trste United Met Bapt Ch 1945-77; bd dir Am Cancer Soc; Outst Citizen of Yr Urban League 1950; Brotherhood Award Urban League 1975. **HONORS/ACHIEVEMENTS:** Author, Coauthor 13 Med Publs Am Jour 1942, 45, 49; Jour Of Nat Med Assn 1946, 47-51, 54; Jour of Old N State Med Soc 1957. **BUSINESS ADDRESS:** 801 Camel Ave NE, Winston-Salem, NC 27101.

MALLOY, HELEN G.
Salesperson. **PERSONAL:** Born Oct 07, 1898, Huntsville, AL; married LD. **EDUCATION:** AL St Tchr Coll. **CAREER:** Malloy's Shoe Ser Shop, co-worker with husband; Chene St & Brewster Proj, 15 yrs; Voice of Negro Bus Journal Booker T Washington Trade Assn Detroit, Editor; Slater & Lincoln Elem Schs Birmingham, tchr 13 yrs. **ORGANIZATIONS:** Nat historian fin & sec past pres Housewives Leag of Detroit; supt Primary Dept Bethel AME Ch Detroit; past pres Ruth Missionary Sco Bethel Ch; mem & past Chaplan Detroit Sec Council Negro Women; Fin Sec 100-300 Block Club Detroit. **HONORS/ACHIEVEMENTS:** Plaque for comm ser to businesses in Detroit; Detroit Sec Coun Nego Women & Davis Mtrs Sales; awd for outst serv Housewives Leag of Detroit; Humanitarian Serv Award Rosa L Gragg Educ & Civic Club of Detroit.

MALONE, AMANDA ELLA
Elected official. **PERSONAL:** Born May 30, 1929, Lafayette Cty, MS; daughter of Jerry Malone and Leona Ingrom Malone; married James Malone; children: Lawrence, Malcolm L, Kenneth Leon, Kelsey Lee, Sheila Elaine, Cheryl Leona, Travis, James Roland (deceased). **EDUCATION:** Rust Coll Holly Springs MS, AS. **CAREER:** Elementary School, sub teacher; Head Start, teacher, parent involvement coord, soc serv dir; Marshall & Lafayette Cty Soc Serv Org, pres; Marshall Cty Bd of Ed, chmn. **ORGANIZATIONS:** Mem NAACP, Sunrise Chap Order of Eastern Star; mem, sunday school teacher New Hope MB Church; mem Marshall Cty Bd of Ed. **HONORS/ACHIEVEMENTS:** Effort and Proficience as county bd mem MS Indust Coll 1979; Outstanding Community Serv Galena Elementary School 1980; Citation Inst of Community Serv Head Start Agency 1980; Cert of Recognition as Outstanding Black Elected Official Chulahoma MB Church.

MALONE, CHARLES A.
Attorney. **PERSONAL:** Children: Tony, Charles, Vicki, Keith, Kevin, Julian. **EDUCATION:** Detroit Coll, JD Law. **CAREER:** Sura & Malone, Inkster MI, atty at law; Mobil Oil, analytical chemist 1966-72. **ORGANIZATIONS:** Mem MI & Detroit Bar Assns; charter mem MI State Bar Crim Law Sect NAACP; chmn Inkster & Elected Officers Compensation Bd; co-chmn Westwood Comm SchDist Ad Hoc Com; Elks; Golden Gate Lodge; IBPOE of W; Lions. **BUSINESS ADDRESS:** 2228 Inkster Rd, Inkster, MI 48141.

MALONE, CLAUDINE BERKELEY
Business executive. **PERSONAL:** Born May 09, Louisville, KY. **EDUCATION:** Wellesley Coll, BA; Harvard Business School, MBA (High Distinction). **CAREER:** IBM Corp, systems engr 1963-65; Raleigh Stores, controller, mgr dp 1966-70; Crane Co, sr systems engr 1966; Harvard Bus School, assoc prof 1972-81; Fin & Mgmt Consulting Inc, pres 1982-. **ORGANIZATIONS:** Trustee Dana Hall School 1974-77; treas Wellesley Coll Alumni Assoc 1977-80; trustee Wellesley Coll 1982-; dir Scott Paper Co, Campbell Soup Co, MTV Networks, The Limited, Dart Drug, Supermarkets Gen Corp, Houghton Mifflin Corp, Penn Mutual Life, The Boston Co. **HONORS/ACHIEVEMENTS:** Candace Awd Natl Coalition of Black Women 1982. **BUSINESS ADDRESS:** President, Financial Mgmt Consulting Inc, 7570 Potomoc Fall Road, McLean, VA 22102.

MALONE, CLEO
Executive director. **PERSONAL:** Born Mar 02, 1934, Athens, AL; married Judy Sue; children: Pamela McKinley, Daniel, Karen, Donald. **EDUCATION:** Case Western Res Univ, Psychology/Sociology 1965-66; Urban Training Inst Chgo, Theological Training 1967; Cleveland State Univ, Grp Dynamics 1971; Union of Experimenting Coll & Univ, Health Plng PhD 1981. **CAREER:** United Appeal/United Area Citizens Agncy, consultant & expeditor 1969-71; UCSD Muir Coll LaJolla, CA, assc dean of stdnts 1971-75; Off of the Dir Univ Hosp, comm liaison 1975-80; S San Diego Health Ed Cntr, exec dir 1980-. **ORGANIZATIONS:** Campus mnstr Case Western Res Univ 1969-71; mem CA Cncl on Alchol Problems; mem San Diego Cnty Alcohol Adv Bd; bd mem Natl Blk Alcoholism Cncl; sec San Diego Assoc of Black Health Ser Exec; orgnzr Protestant Ministry to Poverty 1961-64; assoc mnstr E Cleveland Cong Church 1961-64; v pres SE Interdnmntnl Minstrl Alliance 1985; mem San Diego Urban League. **HONORS/ACHIEVEMENTS:** Publication "Minority Participation in Health Planning" 1981; Black Fellowship Award; UCSD Black Faculty & Staff. **BUSINESS ADDRESS:** Executive Dir, Alcoholism Cnslng & Ed Ctr, 1212 S 43rd St Ste D, San Diego, CA 92113.

MALONE, EUGENE WILLIAM
Educator. **PERSONAL:** Born Aug 08, 1930, Washington, PA; married Roberta Joanne Miller; children: Gina Dawn. **EDUCATION:** Central State U, Sociology AB 1957, BS Educ 1958; Kent State U, MEd Guid & Counseling 1962; Nova U, EdD 1976. **CAREER:** Cuyahoga Comm Coll, dean student services 1975-; Cuyahoga Com Coll, dir counseling adm & records 1972-75; Cleveland State Univ, dir student devel program 1970-72; Cleveland State Univ, coord stud devel proj 1968-70; Central State U, dean of men 1967-68; Cleveland Pub Schs, guidance cnslr 1965-67; Com Action for Youth, guidance counselor 1964-65; Cleveland Pub Schs, tchr 1959-64; Canton Pub Schs, tchr 1958-59; Cleveland Pub Sch, group discussion leader 1966-67; Curber Assoc, consult 1968-71; Shaker Heights Pub Schs, consult 1969-70. **ORGANIZATIONS:** Mem Vocational Educ Adv Bd 1979; mem OH Assn Staff Program & Organizational Devel 1979; mem Nat & Assn Student Pers Adminstr; mem Am Pers & Guidance Assn; mem OH Pers & Guidance Assn. **HONORS/ACHIEVEMENTS:** Good Conduct Medal. **MILITARY SERVICE:** USAF airman 1949-53. **BUSINESS ADDRESS:** Dean, Cuyahoga Community College, 25444 Harvard Rd, Cleveland, OH 44122.

MALONE, GLORIA S.
Educator. **PERSONAL:** Born May 12, 1928, Pittsburgh, PA; daughter of John Snodgrass and Doris Harris Snodgrass; married Arthur A; children: Merrick, Deanna, Myrna. **EDUCATION:** Central State Wilberforce OH, BS 1949; Kent State, ME 1956, MA 1969, PHD 1979. **CAREER:** Alliance OH Public Schools, elementary teacher, 1949-53, high school teacher, 1953-69; Mt Union Coll, prof of English 1969-. **ORGANIZATIONS:** Member, NAACP, Modern Language Assn, Natl Educ Assn, Amer Assn of Univ Prof, Delta Kappa Gamma Soc; grand worthy matron, Amaranth Graduate Chapter OES PHA 1972-74; bd of dir, YWCA; goodwill advisory bd, Family Counseling Serv, Alliance Red Cross, Stark Cty Bd of Mental Health; table leader, ETS essay readings, 1985-; consultant, evaluator, North Central Assn of Schools & Coll, 1987-. **HONORS/ACHIEVEMENTS:** State Scholarship Awards, Delta Kappa Gamma, 1967, 1974; Teacher of the Year, Alliance High School, 1969; outstanding member, Al Kaf Court Dts of Isis Akron, 1970; frequent speaker, Religious Civic Fraternity Groups; Citizen of the Year, 1986. **BUSINESS ADDRESS:** Prof of English Dept Chairmn, Mount Union College, 1972 Clark Ave, Alliance, OH 44601.

MALONE, J. DEOTHA
Vice mayor, educator. **PERSONAL:** Born May 27, 1932, Sumner County, TN; daughter of Harvey Malone and Sadie Malone. **EDUCATION:** Fisk Univ Nashville, BA/MA 1950 and 1955; TN State Univ, MA Adult Educ 1973; AL State Univ, Montgomery, AL, EdD 1974; Univ of AL Tuscaloosa, PhD 1981. **CAREER:** Sumner Cnty School System, teacher/librarain 1950-70; City of Gallatin, TN, vice-mayor 1969-; State Comm Coll, instr 1976-80; TN State Univ, instr 1982-83; Sumner County Schools, instruct supvr 1970-; of intl students, English as a second language, supervisor 1986. **ORGANIZATIONS:** Mem NAACP, Gallatin Voter's League, Beacon Civic Club, Econ Dev Program; vice pres Democratic Women's Club Sumner Cnty; former chmn Retired Senior Vol Progrm Sumner Cnty; notary public; mem NEA, TN Educ Assn Adv Bd, Middle TN Educ Assn, Sumner Cnty Educ Assn, TN Assn for Publ Sch Adult Edn; past pres Middle TN Assn for Pub Sch Adult Edn; mem Austin Peay Area Supvrs Council, TN Assn of Adult Educators, Natl Teacher's Sor of Phi Delta Kappa, TN Assn for Supvrs and Admin; past pres RSVP Pres Program; former chmn Human Relations Comm with Sumner Cnty Educ Assn; former pres Sumner Cnty Teacher's Assn; first Black dir of Sumner Cnty Headstart Program 1966-70; adv mem Gallatin Day Care Center; mem Human Serv Career Educ Adv Comm for Volunteer State Comm Coll; adv bd for TN Assn of Licensed P ractical Nurses; mem bd dir TN Educ Assn; former adv bd mem Cont Educ for Women at Volunteer State Comm Coll; adv bd First & Peoples Bank Gallatin; mem Governor's Mgmt Team for TN Master Teacher Program; mem First Baptist Ch Gallatin, TN. **HONORS/ACHIEVEMENTS:** HS Class Valedictorian; four-year scholarship to any college in US or Canada from Pepsi-Cola Co for highest score on exam given to 14,500 students; Outstanding Member Award in Alpha Beta Chapter of Phi Delta Kappa Sor 1972; Outstanding Woman of the Year by Masonic Lodge 1972; Honorary Citizen of Fayette, MS

Charles Evers Mayor; Selected to be in Ebony Dec 1973 "The Distaff Side of Politics"; Invited to serve on US Comm for Civil Rights; mem Kappa Delta Pi Natl Honor Soc; mem Phi Delta Kappa Honor Soc; selected by the US Office of Educ and TN State Dept of Educ to travel and study in 17 foreign countries; Honorary Citizen of Indianapolis Richard Lugar Mayor; selected by former Pres Jimmy Carter to serve as adv for Comm Dev 1978-79; Appreciation Day by citizens of Gallatin and Sumner Cnty with people from forty-four states present 1973; Deotha's Day sponsored by State Rep Jack Burnett 1979; The Adult Education Handbook, Montgomery AL 1976; Descriptive Study of Formal Training and Career Patterns of Secondary Principals in a Southeastern State in the US 1981. **HOME ADDRESS:** 1000 Woodmont Drive, Gallatin, TN 37066. **BUSINESS ADDRESS:** Supvr Secondary Education, Summer County Board Education, PO Box 1199, Gallatin, TN 37066.

MALONE, JEFF JOEL
Professional athlete. **PERSONAL:** Born Jun 28, 1961, Mobile, AL. **EDUCATION:** MS State, Educ Major 1983. **CAREER:** Washington Bullets, guard 1983-. **HONORS/ACHIEVEMENTS:** 3rd leading rookie scorer; led Bullets in scoring 10 times; a first team All-Rookie selection; Coaches All-Southeastern Conf team; SEC Player of the Year; named a first team All-Am by The Sporting News; mem 36th NBA All Star Team. **BUSINESS ADDRESS:** Washington Bullets, One Harry S Truman Dr, Ste 510, Landover, MD 20785.

MALONE, MICHAEL GREGORY
Administrator. **PERSONAL:** Born Oct 27, 1942, Evansville, IN; children: Malik LeRoi, Stephanie Nicole. **EDUCATION:** Butler Univ, 1960-61; IN State Univ Evansville, 1967-71; Univ of Evansville, BS Pol Sci 1971-74. **CAREER:** Iglehart Opers, quality control tech 1966-68; CAPE, dir youth prog 1968-71, dir commun serv 1971-72, exec dir 1972-; Malone Assoc Inc, pres, mgr. **ORGANIZATIONS:** Mem Natl Assoc of Social Workers 1971-; charter mem bd of dirs Natl Council for the Transportation Disadvantaged 1975-; bd mem Govs Council on Addictions 1976-; mem Downtown Civitans 1976-; mem Lakeview Optimist 1976-; exec bd mem Boy Scouts of Amer Buffalo Trace Council 1976-; mem Southern IN Soccer Officials Assoc 1977-. **HONORS/ACHIEVEMENTS:** Community Serv Awd Gov of IN 1976; Outstanding Man Awd for Commun Affairs Evansville Black Expo 1978; listed in Who's Who in Fin & Indust 1979-83. **BUSINESS ADDRESS:** President, Manager, Malone Associates Inc, 906 Main St, Evansville, IN 47708.

MALONE, MOSES EUGENE
Professional athlete. **PERSONAL:** Born Mar 23, 1955, Petersburg, VA; married Alfreda; children: Moses, Michael. **CAREER:** Utah Stars ABA, player 1974-76; Buffalo Braves, player; St Louis Spirits, player; Houston Rockets, player 1976-82; Philadelphia 76ers, player 1982-; Washington Bullets, player. **HONORS/ACHIEVEMENTS:** Mem NBA Championship team 1973; named to ABA All-Rookie Team 1975; led NBA in rebounding 1979, 1981, 1982, 1983, 1984, 1985; NBA Most Valuable Player 1979, 1982, 1983; All NBA First Team 1979, 1982, 1983, 1985; All NBA Second Team 1980,81, 1984; NBA All Defensive First Team 1983; NBA All Defensive Second Team 1979; NBA Playoff MVP 1983; mem 36th & 37th NBA All Star Teams. **BUSINESS ADDRESS:** Washington Bullets, Capital Centre, Landover, MD 20785.

MALONE, SANDRA DORSEY
Educator. **PERSONAL:** Born Oct 05, Mexia, TX; married Joseph L. **EDUCATION:** MEd 1972; BS. **CAREER:** Dallas Independent Sch Dist, asst dir 1974-75; Accountability, asst dir 1972-74; Guaranteed Performance Proj Dallas, educ analyst 1970-71; Team Teaching-Sch Chattanooga, team ldr 1961-65. **ORGANIZATIONS:** Mem Dallas Sch Adminstr & Assn; Am Asn of Sch Adminstrs; Am Educ Research Assn State; orgainzer Nat Council of Negro Women 1973-75; pres Dallas Alumnae Chap Delta Sigma Theta 1973-75; pres RL Thornton PTA 1973-74; vice pres Hulcy Middle Sch PTA 1975-76. **HONORS/ACHIEVEMENTS:** Pres's award Pan Hellenic Council 1973; Comm Serv Award; United for Action Dallas Negro C of C 1975; serv award Delta Omega Chap Delta Sigma Theta 1975; pres's award RL Thornton PTA 1974. **BUSINESS ADDRESS:** 3801 Herschell Ave, Dallas, TX.

MALONE, STANLEY R.
Judge. **PERSONAL:** Born Jun 16, 1924, Wash, DC. **EDUCATION:** Southwestern U, JD 1951. **CAREER:** Judge; Tolbert, Wooden & Malone, atty 1965; LA Co CA, superior ct bench 1975; Miller & Malone, atty 1960-65; Lang, Malone & Hall, atty 1960-65. **ORGANIZATIONS:** Pres Langston Law Club 1964-69; mem State Bar Unauthorized Practice of Law; bd mem Western & Cntr Law & Poverty; LA Trial Lawyers Assn; Am Judicature Soc; mem Nat Adv Bd Nat Bar Assn 1969-72; bd trustees LA Co Bar Assn; founder & First V Chmn LA Co Bar Human Rights Section; pres bd mem LANeighborhood Legal Services Inc; adv Bd Black Law Journal. **HONORS/ACHIEVEMENTS:** Recip LA Co Resltn Comm 1972; Assembly Rules Com; CA Legislature Resl CommDtn 1971. **BUSINESS ADDRESS:** Judge, Superior Ct Criminal Dept Los, Dept 114, Los Angeles, CA 90012.

MALONE, THOMAS ELLIS
Scientist. **PERSONAL:** Born Jun 03, 1926, Henderson, NC; married Dolores; children: Shana, Thomas Jr. **EDUCATION:** NC Coll, BS 1948; Harvard U, PhD 1953; NC Coll, MS 1949. **CAREER:** Nat Inst of Health, deputy dir 1977; Extramural Research & Training, asso dir 1972-77; Extramural Prog NIDR, assoc dir 1969-72. **ORGANIZATIONS:** Chmn Dept of Biology AmUniv of Beirut 1967-69; chief Periodontal Diseases & Soft Tissue Studies NIDR NIH 1966-67; dep chief Extramural Prgms NIDR NIH 1962-66; asst prof LoyolaUniv 1960; research assoc Argonne Nat Lab 1958-60; asst prof NC Coll 1952-58; teaching fellow HarvardUniv 1950-52; mem Am Asso for the Advn of Sci; Am Asso for Lab Animal Sci; Am Soc of Zoologists; Histochemical Soc; Am Soc for Cell Biol; Intl Asso of Dental Research; SigmaXi; Soc of Research Adminstr Harvard Fellow 1950-52. **HONORS/ACHIEVEMENTS:** Distg serv 1974; NAS NRC Fellow 1958-59; supr serv. **MILITARY SERVICE:** AUS 1945-46. **BUSINESS ADDRESS:** 9000 Rockville Pike, Bethesda, MD 20014.

MALONEY, CHARLES CALVIN
Medical technologist. **PERSONAL:** Born May 24, 1930, W Palm Beach, FL; married Ethel Pearl Covington; children: Charda Corrie, Charles Calvin, III. **EDUCATION:** FL A&M U, BS 1951;Franklin Sch, Med Tec 1956. **CAREER:** N Dist Hosp Inc, chief med tech; Christian Hosp Miami, Chief Tech 1956-58; Provident Hospital, 1958-62; Broward Gen Med Cntr, 1962-75; Gen Diagnostics Sci Prod, clinical spec. **ORGANIZATIONS:** Mem Am Med Tech; Omega Psi Phi; Boys Club; Jacs Inc; vice pres & sec Broward Med Cntr CredituUniv 1971; mem Jack & Jill of Am Inc; sec Omega Psi Phi 1962-65; Connecting Link; All Am Tackle FL Agr & MechUniv 1950-55; Basilus 1970-71. **HONORS/ACHIEVEMENTS:** Man of Yr Omega Psi Phi 1960-61 & 1961-62. **MILITARY SERVICE:** USAF sgt 1951-54.

MALRY, LENTON
Legislator, educator. **PERSONAL:** Born Sep 30, 1931, Shreveport, LA; married Joy. **EDUCATION:** Grambling Coll, BS 1952; TX Coll, MEd 1957;Univ of NM, PhD 1968. **CAREER:** NM Legislature, rep Bernalillo County; Albuquerque Pub Schs, equal opportunity ofcr 1975; Albuquerque, co-commisioner; Albuquerque Schl System, jr highschl tchr & principal; Albuquerque Publ Schl, dir Cltrl Awareness. **HONORS/ACHIEVEMENTS:** Legislative Achievements include passage of a drug abuse bill & an anti-bias bill. **BUSINESS ADDRESS:** PO Box 25704, Albuquerque, NM 87125.

MALVEAUX, FLOYD
Immunologist. **EDUCATION:** Creighton University, Omaha, NE, BS, 1961; Loyola University, New Orleans, MS, 1964; Michigan State University, East Lansing, MI, PhD, 1968; Howard University College of Medicine, MD, 1974. **CAREER:** Johns Hopkins University, Baltimore, MD, associate professor and staff member; Howard University Hospital, Washington, DC, professor. **HONORS/ACHIEVEMENTS:** Medical Service Award, National Medical Association, 1986. **BUSINESS ADDRESS:** Howard University, Department of Medicine/Microbiology, 2400 Sixth Street, NW, Washington, DC 20059. *

MALVIN, REUBEN L.
Psychotherapist. **PERSONAL:** Born Aug 10, 1942, Cotton Plant, AR; married Johnnie; children: Dimitri, Adrienne, Tiffani. **EDUCATION:** Univ of AR, BA; Loyola U, MSW 1971; Progress Chicago Sch of Professional Psychology, PsyD. **CAREER:** Coll of Human Learning & Devel Gov State Univ IL, psychotherapist pri pcomm prof; Tinley Park Mental Health & Cntr Tinley Park IL, mental health administr. **ORGANIZATIONS:** Mem Exec Council of the Hosp; mem Nat Assn of Social Workers 1971; Assn of Black Soc Workers; Academy of Certified Soc Workers 1973; Consult Therapist to IL State Dov of Voc Rehab; mem Am Jr C of C. **HONORS/ACHIEVEMENTS:** Outstanding Achievement with minority clients.

MANCE, JOHN J.
Business executive. **PERSONAL:** Born Mar 18, 1926, Chicago, IL; married Eleanore Edson, Sep 09, 1949; children: Richard, David. **EDUCATION:** CA-aERO Tech Inst, AeroE 1949;Univ of CA LA, Indl Rel 1969;Univ of So CA 1972. **CAREER:** Lockheed CA Co, asst to indsl rel dir 1972; Lockheed Watts-willow-brook, indsl rel dept mgr 1970-72; San Fernando Valley Lutheran Hosp Assn Credit Union, rep personnel prog 1969; employment & interviewer 1968; engineering planning asst 1966-68; asst treas & mgr; Don Baxter Inc, engineering 1959-63; Marquardt Corp, test engr 1956-59; So CA Coop Wind Tunnel, techn 1953-56; Frank Mayer Engineering Co, tool designer 1950-53; Lockheed Aeronautical Systems Co, Burbank CA, retired, now self employed, consultant 1988. **ORGANIZATIONS:** Mem Natl Management Assn; Lockheed Management Club; life mem NAACP; exec com mem of San Fernando Vlly NAACP; Br NAACP So CA Area Cnf; Br pres 1959-62; So CAArea pres 1966-67; pres CA Credit Union League San Fernando Vlly Chap 1968; Golden Heritage Life Member, NAACP 1981-; vice pres NAACP, Los Angeles 1989-. **HONORS/ACHIEVEMENTS:** Man of Month Lockheed Mgmt Club Nov 1970; cert of appreciation, Indsl Coll of Armed Forces 1972; several citations from various hum rel & civil rights groups between 1959 & 1968; Roy Wilkins Award, San Fernando Valley NAACP 1985; elected to NAACP Bd of Dirs 1976-84, 1988-. **MILITARY SERVICE:** USN aviation metalsmith 3rd class 1944-46. **HOME ADDRESS:** 16257 Marilyn Dr, Granada Hills, CA 91344.

MANESS, DONALD B.
Associate director. **PERSONAL:** Born Aug 24, 1939, Greensburg, PA; married Emily; children: 2 children. **EDUCATION:** Wilberforce Univ, BS 1961; DT Watson Sch of Physiatrics Univ of Pgh, Physical Therapy Training; LaSalle Univ, MPA 1986. **CAREER:** Home Health Care of Cleveland, coord rehab serv 1969-; Margaret Wagner House of the Benjamin Rose Inst, dir of physical therapy dept 1970-77; Vstg NurseAssoc of Greater Cleveland, consultant physical therapist 1975; Margaret Wagner House of the Benjamin Rose Inst, asst admin 1978-79, administrator 1979-; The Benjamin Rose Inst, assoc dir for resiential & rehab serv 1980-. **ORGANIZATIONS:** Mem Amer Physical Therapy Assoc, Amer Registry of Physical Therapists, Ludlow Assoc Shaker Heights OH; mem Citizens League of Greater Cleveland, Omega Psi Phi Frat; mem resident life comm Amer Assoc of Homes for Aging; mem Gerontological Soc; mem Commn on Aging City of Cleveland Heights; mem exec commWestern Reserve Ctr for Long Term Care of the Elderly; mem House of Delegates Amer Assoc of Homes for the Aging; bd of trustees Eliza Bryant Ctr; mem Natl Assoc of Human Rights Workers Comm, Sigma Pi Phi Frat; mem house of delegates Amer Assoc of Homes for the Aging 1984-; membership comm Assoc of OH Philanthropic Homes for the Aging; bd of advisors April Assoc Inc; mem exec bd Amer Assoc of Homes for the Aging. **HONORS/ACHIEVEMENTS:** Publications "Physical Therapy for the Geriatric Patient" Journal of the Amer Geriatrics Soc 1969.

MANGUM, CHARLES M. L.
Attorney. **PERSONAL:** Born Nov 13, 1933, Salisbury, NC; married Lovella W Brown; children: Rhia, Mark, Travis. **EDUCATION:** NC A&T State Univ, BS 1956; Howard Univ, JD 1966. **CAREER:** Peterson & Mangum Funeral Home, funeral dir 1956-62; Private Practice, attorney. **ORGANIZATIONS:** Mem VA, Old Dominion & Natl Bar Assns; adv bd Law Ctr Constl Rights 1968-76; co-operating atty, legal staff VA, Golden Heritage mem NAACP; co-operating atty Legal Defense Fund; VA Trial Lawyers Assn; chmn of bd Hunton YMCA; pres & life mem Gamma Nu Lambda Chap of Alpha Phi Alpha Frat; pres LynchburgChap NAACP; mem bd of dir Lynchburg Chap OIC; vice chmn bd dir VA Legal Aid Soc; pres Old Dominion Bar Assn; pres Lynchburg VA Chap NCA&T Aggie Club; bd dir Lynchburg Comm Action; mem Central VA Criminal Justice Adv Com; mem Masonic Lodge; mem Amer Civil Liberties Union; pres Virginia State Conf NAACP; mem bd of dirs Lynchburg Chap Natl Conf of Christians and Jews; publisher Lynchburg Area Journal Newspaper. **HONORS/ACHIEVEMENTS:** Recipient of numerous state, local and natl awds and certificates. **MILITARY SERVICE:** AUS 1957-58. **BUSINESS ADDRESS:** Attorney, 915 Main St Ste 310, Lynchburg, VA 24504.

MANGUM, ROBERT J.
Judge. **PERSONAL:** Born Jun 15, 1921, Petersburgh, VA; children: one. **EDUCATION:** City Coll of NY, BS 1942; Brooklyn Law, LLB 1949; Brooklyn Law Sch, JD 1967; NY U, MPA 1957; Adm Med Columbia, MS 1964; St John U, dr humane letters 1969; City Coll of NY, DL 1977. **CAREER:** Beth Israel Med Cntr, legal counc 1978-; Ct of Claims NY, st judge 1971-78; New York City Pol Dept 1942-54; 7th Dept Pol Commr, patrolman; Licensing Yth, deputy commr 1954-58; Dept of Hosp NYC, 1st deputy commr 1958-66; OEO, NE reg dir 1966-67; NY St Div of Human Rights, commr 1967-71. **ORGANIZATIONS:** Mem spl study group Dept of Correct 1956; parole commn pol commn rep New York City 1958; mem of com to revise Prin & Prac of NY St Parole Syst 1957; chmnof steering com Interdept Hlthl Coun New York City 1964; lctr in pub hlth Columbia U; bd of trust past NY U; chmn bd of trust Harlem Preparatory Sch; bd trust legal couns Beth Israel Med Cent; found Guardians Assn Police Dept NYC; 100 Blackmen NY City. **HONORS/ACHIEVEMENTS:** Frederick Douglass awd NY Urban Leg cit masonic group; dept of corr; man of yr New York City bd of trade; cert of merit hosp admin assn dept of hosp NYC; charter mem Prof Assn of Publ Exec. **MILITARY SERVICE:** AUS 1st lt 1946.

MANIGAULT, WALTER WILLIAM
Business executive, elected official. **PERSONAL:** Born Sep 26, 1939, Georgetown, SC; married Earlyne Derious Rand; children: Terrence, Troy, Tiffany. **EDUCATION:** Howard Univ, BS 1960; Atlanta Univ, MS 1968; Univ of OR Med School, Post-Grad Study 1969-71. **CAREER:** Manigault & Son Morticians, Inc, mortician 1961-85. **ORGANIZATIONS:** Mem Georgetown Cty Bd of Ed 1976-84, Natl Bd of Funeral Svc, SC Morticians Assoc, 6th Dist Progressive Morticians, Natl Funeral Dir & Morticians Assoc; past mem bd of dir Georgetown Cty Chamber of Comm; trustee Bethel AME Church; mem bd of dir Georgetown Breakfast Rotary Club, Bakservill Housing Development Corp. **HONORS/ACHIEVEMENTS:** Public Serv Awd 6th Dist Omega Psi Phi 1976; 8 Yrs Serv Awd Georgetown Cty Bd of Ed 1984. **MILITARY SERVICE:** AUS capt 1961-63. **HOME ADDRESS:** Martin Luther King PO Box 822, Pawleys Island, SC 29585.

MANIGO, GEORGE F., JR.
Clergyman. **PERSONAL:** Born Nov 10, 1934, Bamberg, SC; son of George F Manigo Sr and Ertha M Ramsey; married Rosa L Lewis; children: Marcia B, George F, III. **EDUCATION:** Claflin Coll, BS 1959; Gammon Theol Sem, BD 1962. **CAREER:** Trinity United Methodist Church, pastor; St Mark & St Matthew Chs Taylors SC, minister 1970-; Wesley Church St James, 1965-70; Market St United Methodist Church, 1962-65; Hurst Memorial United Methodist Church, 1960-62; United Methodist Church, Walterboro District,district superintendant, 1986-. **ORGANIZATIONS:** Mem SC Conf Merger Com 1973-; chmn bd dirs Greenville CAP Agy; NAACP; sec Greenville Urban Ministry; Phi Beta Sigma; Trustee of Columbia Coll, Columbia SC, 1978-. **MILITARY SERVICE:** AUS sp/3 1953-56. **BUSINESS ADDRESS:** District Superintendent, Walterboro District United Methodist Church, PO Box 829, Walterboro, SC 29488.

MANLEY, ALBERT
Former college president. **PERSONAL:** Born Jan 03, 1908, San Pedro Sula, Honduras;married Audrey Elaine Forbes. **EDUCATION:** Johnson C Smith Univ, BS 1930; Columbia Univ Teachers Coll, MA 1938; Univ Chicago, student 1942; Stanford Univ, EdD 1946; Johnson C Smith Univ, LLD 1966; Spelman Coll, LHD 1981. **CAREER:** Stephens-Lee High School Asheville NC, teacher 1931-34, principle 1935-41; Negro High Schools NC, supr 1941-45; Coll Arts & Sci, dean; NC Coll Durham, prof educ 1946-53; School Bus Mgmt Harvard Univ, guest lectr summers 1970-75, Univ WA 1976, Center Urban Educ Univ No IA 1980; Spelman Coll Atlanta, pres 1953-76, pres emeritus 1976-. **ORGANIZATIONS:** Mem NC Commn Interracial Coop 1941-49; mem GA Commn Interracial Coop; pres NC Coll Conf 1950; chmn council of pres Atlanta Univ Center, Univ Center in GA; mem natl adv comm on black higher educ Dept of Educ 1979-87; bd dir United Negro Coll Fund, Atlanta High Mus Art; bd dir, trustee MartinLuther King Jr Center Non-Violent Social Change 1968-; trustee Atlanta Univ; chmn comm Disting Calloway Profs; mem NEA, Amer Teachers Assn, Intl Platform Assn, Phi Delta Kappa, Omega Psi Phi. **HONORS/ACHIEVEMENTS:** Contrib articles to educ journals; Recipient Alumni Citation Johnson C Smith Univ 1950. **HOME ADDRESS:** 2807 18th St NW, Washington, DC 20009.

MANLEY, AUDREY FORBES
Physician, administrator. **PERSONAL:** Born Mar 25, 1934, Jackson, MS; daughter of Jesse Lee and Ora Buckhalter Lee; married Albert E Manley, Apr 03, 1970. **EDUCATION:** Spelman Coll, AB 1955; Meharry Med Coll, MD 1959; Cook County Hosp, resident pediatrics 1963; Abraham Lincoln Sch Med, fellow 1965. **CAREER:** Spelman Coll, med dir family planning program/chmn health careers advisory com 1972-76, org/program consultant family planning program & inst 1972-76; Emory Univ Family Planning Program Grady Memorial Hospital, chief of med services 1972-76; USPHS, comm officer/med dir/chief family health & preventive serv 1976-78; USPHS, comm officer/chief sickle cell diseases/ 1978-83; Howard Univ Dept Pediatrics, clinical asst prof 1981; Natl Navel Med Center, Dept Peds, Court Clinical attend, 1981; NIH Inter-Inst Genetics Clinic, guest attending 1981; USPHS, capt 06/med dir assoc admin for clinical affairs 1983-85; dir, Natl Health Serv Corps, 1987-89; asst surgeon general, 1988; deputy asst, Sec for Health, 1989-. **ORGANIZATIONS:** Mem, Advisory Council Headstart Chicago Comm on Urban Opportunity 1966-69; Amer Acad of Pediatrics 1967-; Natl Med Assn 1968-; mem Soviet-Amer Clinic Ped Conf USSR & Austria 1968; mem comm for Recruitment of Minority Students Pritzker School Med 1968-69; consultant Governor's Comm on Hunger & Malnutrition in IL 1969; mem consultant Amer Acad, of Pediatrics IL Headstart Prgm 1969; mem Health Manpower Task Force 1971-74; mem European Educ Exchange Program London/Paris/Madrid/Vienna; Amer Public Health Assn 1972-; Amer Assn of Univ Women 1972-; commr Atlanta Reg Comm 1974-76; mem bd dir Atlanta Southside Comp Neighborhood Health Center, 1974-76; mem Liason Comm for Health & Soc Serv Planning 1974-76; mem bd dir Atlanta Univ Center Health Serv Project 1974-76; mem visit fac comm Harvard Univ & Radcliffe Coll 1974-80; Inst of Med/Natl Acad of Sci, 1976-; AAAS, 1978-; Comm Officers Assn, 1978-; Amer Soc of Human Genetics, 1981-; Natl Soc of Genetic Counselors, 1981-. **HONORS/ACHIEVEMENTS:** Zeta Phi Beta Sor Scholarship 1951; Selected Woman of the Year Zeta Phi Beta Sorority in recognition as first Black woman and youngest person to be appointed Chief Resident of Cook County's 500 bed Children's Hospital; NIH Fellowship 1963-65; Selected for Outstanding Young Women of America 1965; Mary McLeod Bethune Achievement in Govt Award of the Natl Council of Negro Women 1979; Meritorious Serv Medal for Sustained Leadership and Prof Excellence in Implement of the Genetics Serv Program 1981; Invited for launch of Space Shuttle Challenger Mission #7 1983; Keynote Speaker VA State Sickle Cell Assn Annual Meeting 1978; Keynote Speaker SC State Sickle Cell Assn 1978. **HOME ADDRESS:** 2807 18th St NW, Washington, DC 20009. **BUSINESS ADDRESS:** Assoc Admin Clinical Affairs, HRSA/HSPHS/DHHS, 5600 Fishers Lane, Rm 7-49, Rockville, MD 20857.

MANLEY, DEXTER
Professional athlete. **PERSONAL:** Born Feb 02, 1959; married Glinda Joy; children: Dexter Keith II, Dalis Joy, Derrick Keith. **EDUCATION:** Attended, Oklahoma State. **CAREER:** Washington Redskins, defensive end 1981-. **ORGANIZATIONS:** Hon mem Comptex Assoc; owner Mr D Enterprises; filmed commercial for The Washington Post; contributed time/money Easter Seals, Epilepsy Foundation; owner professional automobile detailing co Auto-Brite. **HONORS/ACHIEVEMENTS:** Defensive Player of the Game honors twice 1984, five times 1985; mem Pro Bowl team 1987. **BUSINESS ADDRESS:** Washington Redskins, PO Box 17247, Dulles Intl Airport, Washington, DC 20041.

MANLEY, JOHN RUFFIN
Clergyman. **PERSONAL:** Born Oct 15, 1925, Murfreesboro, NC; married Gloria Roysler. **EDUCATION:** Shaw U, AB BD 1949; DukeUniv Durham NC, ThM 1967; Shaw U, DA 1955. **CAREER:** First Bapt Ch Chapel Hill NC, pastor 27 yrs; Hickory Bapt Ch, 23 yrs; New Hope Assn, moderator. **ORGANIZATIONS:** Vp & chmn of Political Action Com Gen Bapt Conv of & NC Inc; mem Chapel Hill-caraboro Sch Bd; mem Chapel Hill Planning Bd; mem NAACP; 2nd Masonic Lodge; vice chmn Governor's Coun on Sickle Cell Syndrone; chmn Proj Area Com of Redevel Comm; mem Task Force for Community Devel Act for Chapel Hill. **HONORS/ACHIEVEMENTS:** Man of Yr Shaws Theol Alumni; delegate to World Bapt Alliance. **BUSINESS ADDRESS:** First Baptist Church, Chapel Hill, NC.

MANN, GEORGE LEVIER
Attorney. **PERSONAL:** Born Dec 18, 1901, Harriman, TN; son of Jacob Mann and Lucy Mann; married Susie Haire; children: Doris Elise, Lucia Carol. **EDUCATION:** OH State Univ, AB 1930, AM 1931; IN Univ, EdD 1949; St Louis Univ, JD 1955. **CAREER:** W KY Coll, prof 1931-32; US Consvtn Corps, educ adv 1934-37; Dunbar High & Grade Schs Madison IL, prin 1937-40; St Louis Public Sch Sys, prin 1940-71; retired 1971. **ORGANIZATIONS:** Mem MO Bar Assn; Natl Bar Assn; Mound City Bar; mem Samaritan United Meth Ch; Omega Psi Phi Frat; bd mem N Side YMCA; Union Sarah Comm Corp; Anniversary Club; Creve Coeur Demo Coalition; life mem NAACP. **HONORS/ACHIEVEMENTS:** Omega Man of Yr in St Louis 1952; Unique Grad St Louis Law Coll 1955; Certificate Sr Counsellor MO Bar 1976; Awd for Serv to St Louis pupils Omega PsiPhi Frat 1972; Awd for Serv to Boy Scouts; author poetry; Elijah P Lovejoy Award 1989; Natl Assn of Univ Award 1989.

MANN, JOSEPH B.
Executive director. **PERSONAL:** Born Nov 05, 1939, Tarrytown, NY; divorced; children: Jocelyn. **EDUCATION:** Shaw Univ Raleigh, BA 1961; Columbia Univ, MS Hosp Adminstrn; NY Univ, doct prog in pub admin; Union Grad Sch, PhD 1977. **CAREER:** Cumberland Hosp Brooklyn, admin 1965-71; New York City Dept of Hosps, asst commr 1966; New York City Health & Hosps Corp, sr vice pres 1971-74; Provident Hosp, exec dir 1974-. **ORGANIZATIONS:** Mem Amer Coll of Hosp Admins 1969-; mem 100 Black Men Inc; chmn Health Comm 1967-; pres Natl Assn of Health Serv Exec 1972-; mem & various offices held in num other orgs; lecturer Columbia Univ Sch of Pub Hlth & Admin Med NY, Columbia Univ Sch of Pharm, Cornell Univ Ithaca NY, Shaw Univ Raleigh NC; consult to Narcotic Inst NY, Neighborhood Med Care Demonstrtn, OEO Bronx. **HONORS/ACHIEVEMENTS:** Numerous scholastic awds & other honors; publ sev art & docum on med problems. **BUSINESS ADDRESS:** Executive Dir, Provident Hosp, 500 E 51st St, Chicago, IL 60615.

MANN, MARION
Educator. **PERSONAL:** Born Mar 29, 1920, Atlanta, GA; married Ruth R; children: Marion Jr, Judith R. **EDUCATION:** Tuskegee Inst, BS 1940; Howard Univ Coll of Med, MD 1954; Georgetown Univ Med Ctr, PhD 1961. **CAREER:** Howard Univ, coll of med dean 1970-79, asst through full prof dept of pathology; associate vice pres, research, 1988-. **ORGANIZATIONS:** Mem AMA, Natl Med Assn, Inst of Med, Natl Acad of Sciences. **MILITARY SERVICE:** AUS 1942-50; USAR 1950-54 1958-80; USAR brigade general 1975-80 retired 1980. **BUSINESS ADDRESS:** Associate Vice President for Research, HowardUniv, 520 W St NW, Washington, DC 20059.

MANN, PHILIP MELVIN
Business executive, clergyman. **PERSONAL:** Born May 31, 1940, Richmond, VA; married Hazel Smith. **EDUCATION:** Lincoln Univ, BA 1960; Union Theol Sem, Pace Univ, Grad Studies. **CAREER:** The Kahali Modeling Prog, founder 1971; Blessed Trinity Bapt Church, pastor; The Helping Hand Comm Ctr, exec dir. **ORGANIZATIONS:** Bd mem Crispus Attucks Found, Urban Crisis Task Force, Ctr for Youth Devel, Mt Hope Bapt Church; expert org & civil rights activist; bd mem Ecclesiastical Soc, Harlem Planning Bd #10, Area Policy Bd #10. **HONORS/ACHIEVEMENTS:** Man of the Year Awd NY Civic Assoc 1975. **BUSINESS ADDRESS:** Executive Dir, Helping Hand Comm Ctr, 131 W 129th St, New York, NY 10030.

MANN, RICHARD
Assistant coach. **PERSONAL:** Born in Aliquippa, PA; married Karen; children: Deven, Richard, Mario. **EDUCATION:** Arizona State, BS Elem Educ. **CAREER:** Arizona State, coach 1974-82; Indianapolis Colts, receiver coach; Cleveland Browns, wide receiver coach. **HONORS/ACHIEVEMENTS:** Inducted Aliquippa Sports Hall of Fame 1982.

MANN, THOMAS J., JR.
Senator/attorney. **EDUCATION:** TN State Univ, BS Polit Sci 1971; Univ of IA Law Sch, JD 1974. **CAREER:** State of Iowa, asst attorney genl 1974-76; Iowa Civil Rights Commn, exec dir 1976-79; State of Iowa, asst attorney genl 1980-82, senator. **ORGANIZATIONS:** Mem IA State Bar Assn, Polk Co Bar Assn; bd mem Des Moines Br NAACP; former bd mem IA State Dem Party Centrl Comm; former bd mem Central IA Chap Amer Red Cross; mem Omega Psi Phi. **HONORS/ACHIEVEMENTS:** Comm Appreciation Awd Omega Psi Phi 1978; Outstanding Young Iowan IA Jaycees 1979. **BUSINESS ADDRESS:** Senator, State of Iowa, 4921 Douglas Ave, Ste 4, Des Moines, IA 50310.

MANNEY, WILLIAM A.
Broadcast executive. **PERSONAL:** Born Jul 12, 1931, Springfield, AR; married Alice. **EDUCATION:** Philander Smith Coll, Little Rock, BA. **CAREER:** WENN Radio, gen mgr; WBEE Radio, Chicago, gen mgr 1970-, acct exec 1966-70. **ORGANIZATIONS:** Mem Nat Assn of Market Developers; black media rep, bd dir Cosmopolitan C of C Chicago; second vice pres Jane Dent Home for the Aged. **BUSINESS ADDRESS:** General Manager, WAGG-AM, 424 16 St N, Birmingham, AL 35203.

MANNIE, WILLIAM EDWARD
Government employee. **PERSONAL:** Born Jan 19, 1931, Helena, AR; son of Tony Manney and Sylvia Manney; married Jessie A; children: Regina D, Lynnette A, Gregory A, Reginald K. **EDUCATION:** Wilson Jr Coll, AA 1951; Roosevelt Univ, BSC Acctg 1957; Kent Coll of Law, attended 1967-68. **CAREER:** US Treas Dept IRS Criminal Investigation Div, supervisory criminal investigator 30 yrs retired 1984; City of Chicago Law Dept, first Black dir of legal investigations. **ORGANIZATIONS:** Mem Fed Criminal Investigators Assn, IL Chief's of Police Assn, IL Police Assn, Natl Assn of Treasury Agents. **HONORS/ACHIEVEMENTS:** Received following awds from US Treas Dept, Superior Perf Awd 1964, Finalist Fed Employee of the Yr 1967; Spl Achievement Awd 1974, 1975, High Quality Step Increase 1973, Meritorious Serv Awd Criminal Investigation Div 1983, Albert Gallatin Awd 1984. **MILITARY SERVICE:** USAF 1952-56. **BUSINESS ADDRESS:** Dir of Legal Investigations, City of Chicago Law Dept, 180 N LaSalleSt, Chicago, IL 60601.

MANNING, BLANCHE MARIE (NEE PORTER)
Judge, educator. **PERSONAL:** Born Dec 12, 1934, Chicago, IL; daughter of Julius L Porter (deceased) and Marguerite Anderson Porter; married William Manning. **EDUCATION:** Chicago Tchrs Coll, BE 1961; John Marshall Law Sch Chicago, JD 1967; Roosevelt Univ Chicago, MA 1972. **CAREER:** Chicago Bd of Educ, teacher 1961-68; Cook Co State's Attys Office, asst states atty 1968-73; Equal Employment Oppor Commn, supervisory trial atty 1973-77; United Airlines, gen atty 1977-78; US Attys Office, asst US atty 1978-79; Circuit Ct of Cook Co, assoc judge; 1st Municipal Dist Circuit Ct of Cook Co, supervising judge 1979-86, supervising circuit judge 1986-87; Justice of the Illinois Appellate Court, 1st District 1987-. **ORGANIZATIONS:** Professional lectr Malcolm X Comm Coll 1969-70; prof of law NCBL Coll of Law 1978-79; adj faculty mem Department of Justice, Atty Gen Adv Inst 1979; mem Natl Bar Assn; IL Judges Assn; mem Women's Chicago Bar Assns; mem Natl Assn of Women Judges; lecturer IL Judicial Conf New Judges Seminar, Professional Devel Prog for New Assoc Judges, IL Judicial Conf Assoc Judges Sem 1982-86; Illinois Judicial Conference Annual Meeting, 1987-89; chmn Illinois Judicial Council 1988-89; mem of bd of dirs of The Cook County Bar Assn 1988-89; mem Chicago Bar Assn Symphony Orchestra. **HONORS/ACHIEVEMENTS:** Jud Awd Cook Co Bar Assn 1979; Black Judiciary Awd We Can Found Inc 1980; Comm Recognition Awd Natl Assn of Negro Bus & Professional Women's Clubs Inc 1980; WBAI Honoree 1984; Young Lawyers Cert of Appreciation Chicago Bar Assn 1985; Edith Sampson Meml Awd 1985; Awd of Appreciation The Intl Assoc of Pupil Personnel Workers 1985; IL Judicial Council; Kenneth E Wilson Judge of the Year Awd Cook County Bar Assn; Disting Alumna Awd Chicago State Univ 1986; Awd of Excellence in Judicial Admin Women's Bar Assn 1986; Black Rose Award, League of Black Women 1987; Thurgood Marshall Award, IIT Kent Law School BALSA 1988; Professional Achievement Award, Roosevelt Univ 1988; We Care Role Model Award, Chicago Police Department 1987-89; Distinguished Service Award, John Marshall Law School 1989. **BUSINESS ADDRESS:** Justice Illinois Appellate Court, Suite 2800, Richard J Daley Civic Center, Chicago, IL 60602.

MANNING, EDDIE JAMES
Administrator. **PERSONAL:** Born Mar 19, 1952, Philadelphia, PA; married Carolyn; children: Eddie Jr, C Jamal. **EDUCATION:** Cheyney State Coll, BS 1974; Temple Univ, MEd 1976, DEd 1985. **CAREER:** Chester Upland School Dist, teacher/guidance counselor; Ashbourne School, teacher; Temple Univ Special Recruitment & Admissions Program, counselor/academic advisor 1977-79; Act 101 Program Temple Univ, coord 1979-80, dir 1980-. **ORGANIZATIONS:** Mem Amer Assoc of Counseling and Develop, PA Counseling Assoc, Amer Assoc of Multi-Cultural Counseling and Develop, PA Assoc of Multi-Cultural Counseling and Develop; treas PA Chap of the Amer Assoc for Non-White Concerns in Personnel and Guidance 1982-; chmn Act 101 Eastern Regional Exec Comm 1982-83; chmn State Chapts Div of Amer Assoc of Multi-Cultural Counseling and Develop 1983-85; mem Temple Univ Sub-Comm for Academic Excellence in Athletics 1985-; mem Temple Univ Residency Review Bd 1985-. **HOME ADDRESS:** 7834 Williams Ave, Philadelphia, PA 19150.

MANNING, EVELYN See HALL, EVELYN ALICE

MANNING, GLENN M.
Business executive. **PERSONAL:** Born Aug 12, 1935, Baltimore; married Inez C; children: Glenda La Verne, Glenn M, Jr, Donald C. **EDUCATION:** Howard U, AB 1957; CityUniv of NY, Grad Studies. **CAREER:** Comm Bank of NE, pres 19720; First Nat City Bank NY, asst mgr 1967-72; Bowery Saving Bank NY, asst supr 1960-67. **ORGANIZATIONS:** Bd dir Comm Bank of NE; adv bd Urban Bus Develop; bd dir YMCA; N Branch YMCA; Comprehensive Health Assn of Omaha; Woodson Cntr; United Com Serv of the Midlands; bd of trustees Morning Star Bapt Ch; mem pres adv bd C of C; Riverfront Minority Bus Oppor Task Force. **MILITARY SERVICE:** AUS spec 4th class 1957-59.

MANNING, HOWARD NICK, JR.
Attorney. **PERSONAL:** Born Jan 07, 1943, Montgomery, AL; married Lois. **EDUCATION:** Univ of MO Sch of Mines & Metallurgy, BSCE 1967; UCLA Sch of Law, JD 1974. **CAREER:** Manning Reynolds & Roberts LA, sr partner 1976-; Fed Trade Commn LA, staff atty 1974-75; Mobil Oil Corp LA, proj engr 1969-71; Army Corps of Engrs, commd ofcr; Army of Thaild, constrn advr 1968-69; Engrng Div Proctor & Gamble Co, civil tech engr 1967. **ORGANIZATIONS:** Mem Am Soc of Civil Engrs; mem Am Bar Assn; LA Co Bar Assn; CA State Bar Assn; Langston Bar Assn; Nat Bar Assn; Beverly Hills Bar Assn; lectrCA Luth Coll Sem; bd of dirs Beverly Hills Bar Assn Schlrshp Found 1974; vice pres bd of dirs Beverly Hills Bar Assn Schlrshp Found 1976; mem LA Br NAACP; mem Alpha Phi Alpha Frat. **HONORS/ACHIEVEMENTS:** Mem Midwestern Hall of Fame Alpha Phi Alpha Frat 1966f fdr Epsilon Psi Chap Alpha Phi Alpha Frat 1965; outst advocate mem sec bd of judges Moot Ct Honors Prgm UCLA Sch of Law 1973; schlrshp recipient Beverly Hills Bar Assn Schlrshp Found. **BUSINESS ADDRESS:** 1900 Ave of the Stars, Ste 2840, Los Angeles, CA 90067.

MANNING, HUBERT VERNON
Clergyman, college president. **PERSONAL:** Born Aug 02, 1918, Cheraw, SC; married Ethel Braynon; children: June, Michelle. **EDUCATION:** Claflin Coll, AB 1940; Grammon Theol Sem, BD 1945; DD 1957; Boston U, MA 1947; Bethune-Cookman Coll, LLD 1971;Univ MI, Postgrad. **CAREER:** Pub Schs SC, tchr 1940-43; Meth Ch, ordained to ministry 1944; Home Mission Council N Am, minister to migrants 1945-47; Rural & Urban Chs, pastor 1947-48; Claflin Coll, prof hist chaplain 1948-51; pres 1956-; Wesley Meth Ch Charleston, pastor 1951-56; Missions Meth Bd Edn, dean sch 1948-49. **ORGANIZATIONS:** Chmn bd educ SC Conf 1947-57; del World MI Conf 1960; chmn comm ecumenical Qaffairs SC Ann Conf; mem bd higher educ & ministry United Meth Ch; mem exec com higher educ & ministry exec com ordained ministry rep Southeastern Jurisdiction; dir newspaper Palmetto Leader; bd dirs Orangeburg Co United Fund; mem adv counci SC Higher Edn; Facilities Commn; chmn bd dirs Triangle Assn Colls; mem Orangeburg C of C; Phi Beta Sigma; Alpha Kappa Mu. **HONORS/ACHIEVEMENTS:** Contrib articles to professional jours; recipient Alumni Merit Award BostonUniv 1969. **BUSINESS ADDRESS:** Claflin Coll, Orangeburg, SC 29115.

MANNING, JANE A.
Educational administration. **PERSONAL:** Born Mar 22, 1947, Wichita Falls, TX. **EDUCATION:** TX Southern Univ Houston, BA Journalism 1969; Columbia Univ NY, MA Journalism 1970. **CAREER:** Press Enterprise, city reporter 1971-74; TX Southern Univ, instr of journalism 1974-79; Riverside City Coll, dir info serv 1979-84; Media Methods, owner &gen mgr 1981-; Truckee Meadows Comm Coll, part-time journalism inst 1985-; Univ of NV Reno, dir office of public info 1984-. **ORGANIZATIONS:** Mem Assn of CA Coll Admin 1979-85, Natl Council for Community Relations 1980-84; dir Oppty Indust Ctr of Inland Counties 1980-82, Friends of Inland Counties Legal Serv 1981-83; bd mem Publ Relations Soc of Amer 1982-83; mem Soc of Prof Journalists Sigma Delta Chi, Council for the Advancement & Supportof Ed, Silver State Chap Intl Assoc of Business Comm; NV State Press Assoc; WIN; AAHE; bd mem and UNR Rep, AAUW; bd of dir Nevada Women's Fund; mem Nat'l Assoc for the Advancement of Colored people; mem Alliance of Racial Minorities; mem Reno/Sparks Negro Bus and Prof Women's Club; bd ofdir American Red Cross. **HONORS/ACHIEVEMENTS:** City Resolution for Outstanding Contrib to Centennial Celebration 1983; Valuable & Disting Serv Awd City of Riverside 1983; Listed in Who's Who in the West 1984-85; Inspirational Awd UNR Black Student Org 1985. **HOME ADDRESS:** PO Box 8478, University Station, Reno, NV 89507. **BUSINESS ADDRESS:** Dir Office of Pub Informn, Univ Nevada at Reno, Jones Visitor Center, Reno, NV 89557.

MANNING, JEAN BELL
Educator. **PERSONAL:** Born Aug 14, 1937, LaMarque, TX; married Dr Reuben D Manning. **EDUCATION:** Bishop Coll, BA (hon student Valedictoria Scholarship) 1958; N TX State Univ, MEd 1964, EEd 1970. **CAREER:** Douglas HS Ardmore OK, instr 1958-60; Reading Lab Jarvis Coll Hawkins TX; instr & dir 1961-64; TX So Univ Houston, vis prof 1964-65; Douglas HS OK, instr 1964-65, 1965-67; Univ of Liberia Liberia W Africa, prof of English 1973-74; Paul Quinn Coll Waco TX, chmn dept educ 1970-73, 1974-78; Langston Univ OK, assoc prof/dir resources 1978-86, vice pres for academic affairs 1986-. **ORGANIZATIONS:** Educ for Leadership in Black Ch Lilly Found Sponsored Houston TX 1975-77; curriculum devel Wiley Coll Marshall TX 1978; competency based educ Dallas Independent S Dist 1979; mem Alpha Kappa Alpha Sor 1956-; mem Links Inc 1974-; mem Phi Delta Kappa Sor 1956-. **HONORS/ACHIEVEMENTS:** Ford Found Doctoral Grant 1969; Personalities of the Southwest; Who's Who in Black America 1973; Outstanding Sor of SW Phi Delta Kappa Sor 1978. **BUSINESS ADDRESS:** Assoc Prof Dir Resources, LangstonUniv, PO Box 907, Langston, OK 73050.

MANNING, RANDOLPH H.
Educator. **PERSONAL:** Born Dec 18, 1947, New York, NY; son of Ruthfoy Manning and Gertrude Manning; married Monica S McEvilley; children: Randolph, Craig C, Corey A. **EDUCATION:** Suffolk Co Comm Coll, AA 1969; SUNY at Stony Brook, BA 1971, MA 1975. **CAREER:** R H Manning Enterprises, owner/operator 1973-; Suffolk Co Comm Coll, counselor 1971-80, prof of psy & sociology 1980-85, dean of instruction 1985-. **ORGANIZATIONS:** Educational consultant BOCES 1980-; adv bd mem Re-Rout Dept of Labor BOCES, SOCC, SC Correction 1980-; bd dirs LI Sickle Cell Inc 1981-; bd of dir Gordon Heights Federal Credit Union; Past President New York State Special Programs Personnel Assn. **HONORS/ACHIEVEMENTS:** Outstanding Young Men of Amer 1981; SUNY Distinguished Alumni Chancellor Awd State Univ of NY 1983; Proclamation for Service County of Suffolk 1986. **BUSINESS ADDRESS:** Dean of Instruction, Suffolk Co Community College, Speonk-Riverhead Rd, Riverhead, NY 11901.

MANNING, REUBEN D.
Educator. **PERSONAL:** Born Mar 18, 1931, Waco, TX; married Jean Bell. **EDUCATION:** Paul Quinn Coll, BS; TX So U, MS; N TX State U, EdD; UCLA;Univ of TX;Univ of OK. **CAREER:** Paul Quinn Coll, pres;Univ of Liberia, vis lectr 1976, vis prof 1973-74; Paul Quinn Coll, dean of instr 1970-; N TX State U, grad asst 1967-68; Langston U, asso prof, chmn, research prof 1966-69; TX Coll, vis prof 1962; Wiley Coll, vis prof 1961; Jarvis Christian Coll, asst prof, chmn 1959-64; Bishop Coll, instr 1965-58. **ORGANIZATIONS:** Am Assn of Sci; Nat Assn of Sci Tchrs; Nat Inst of Sci; Am Counc of Edn; Nat Educ Assn; TX Educ Assn; Nat Asst of Coll Deans & Registrars; Edwards Chapel AME Ch; Alpha Phi Alpha Frat Inc; Phi Delta Kappa Frat, Beta Kappa Chi Sci Soc; Rotary Internat; BSA; YMCA; NAACP; bd dirs Heart O'TX Boy Scout Counc; chmn training div, bd dir ALIVE; bd dir, vice pres McLennan Co Heart Assn; co-chmn E Waco Heart Fund Campgn; bd dir Caritas; steering com Waco Environtl Task Force; bd dir Waco Manpower Plng Counc; bd dir Grtr Waco United Fund; bd dir Waco Urban League; bd dir Waco Econ Oppty Advncmt Coop; bd chmn Waco Min Afrs Clearing House; tast force Goals for Waco Edn; bd mem Waco Creative Art Ctr; consult E Waco Merchants Assn; Minority Forum; Ministry of Edn, Rep of Liberia; Waco Classroom Tchrs Assn; E TX Sch Men Assn. **HONORS/ACHIEVEMENTS:** Acad cit Jarvis Christian Coll 1960; NSF Acad Yr Flwshp,Univ of OK 1964; NSF Rsrch Grant,Univ of OK 1965; Outst Tchr Award, LangstonUniv 1966; NSF SumFlwshp, AmUniv 1967; Title III Grant 1967; Ford Found Study Grant, N TX StateUniv 1968; Tchng Asstshp, TX StateUniv 1969; Rsrch Grant, LangstonUniv 1969; Personalities of the S; num publs. **MILITARY SERVICE:** AUS 1952. **BUSINESS ADDRESS:** Research Professor, Langston University, PO Box 730, Langston, OK 73050.

MANSELL, BUFORD H. L.
Clergyman. **PERSONAL:** Born Mar 10, 1938, Dacusville, SC; married Ruby Smith. **EDUCATION:** SEUniv Greenville, SC, ThD; EmoryUniv Atlanta, GA, Certificate of Attainment (Theology). **CAREER:** Chesnee Circuit Chrg, pastor 4 yrs; Duncan Landrum Chrg, 1 yr; Mt Zion UM Ch 6 yrs; Yellow Freight System, truck driver. **ORGANIZATIONS:** F&AAYM Mtn City Masonic Lodge; Blue Ridge Royal Arch Chptr; Voorhees Commandery Knights Templar; Islam Temple AAONMS; OES patron; heroine of Jericho; Crusader & Daughter of Isis. **MILITARY SERVICE:** USAF A1c 1956-64; Good Conduct Medal, Marksmanship Ribbon, Longevity Serv Awd.

MANSFIELD, ANDREW K.
Government official. **PERSONAL:** Born Feb 17, 1931, Morehouse Parish, LA; married Mae. **EDUCATION:** Grambling State, BS; Atlanta U, MEd; So U. **CAREER:** Grambling, LA, mayor 1977-. **ORGANIZATIONS:** Mem Lincoln Parish Police Jury 1972-; mem Am Personnell & Guidance Assn; NEA; LEA. **BUSINESS ADDRESS:** PO Box 183, Grambling, LA 71245-0183.

MANSFIELD, CARL MAJOR
Physician, educator. **PERSONAL:** Born Dec 24, 1928, Philadelphia, PA; married Sarah Lynne; children: Joel, Kara. **EDUCATION:** Lincoln Univ, AB 1951; Temple Univ, 1952; Howard Univ, MD 1956. **CAREER:** Episcopal Hospital, resident intern 1956-58; USAF, radiologist 1958-60; Epis Hosp, resident 1960; Jefferson Med Coll Hosp, assoc radiologist, chief div, Chernicoff Fellow, instr radiologist, NIH post doct fellow, resident 1960-67; Jefferson Med Coll, adv clinical fellowship 1965-68, asst prof 1967-69; Univ of PA Sch Med, lectr 1967-73; Thomas Jefferson Univ Hosp, assoc prof 1970-74; Hahnemann Med Coll Hosp, visiting prof 1971; Thomas Jefferson Univ Hosp, prof, chief div 1974-76;Univ of KS Med Center, prof chmn dept radiation 1976-83; Jeff Med Coll & Thomas Jefferson Univ Hosp, prof & chmn dept radiation thermo & nuclear med 1983-. **ORGANIZATIONS:** Mem Amer Bd of Radiology 1962; Amer Bd of Nuc Med 1972; Amer Coll of Nuc Med; Amer Coll of Radiology; AMA; Amer Soc of Therapeutic Radiologists; Assn Univ Radiologists; British Inst Radiology; Amer Coll Nuclear Physicians; Natl Med Assn; Radiol Soc N Amer; Royal Soc Med; Soc Nuc Med Gardens Bd Mt Carmel Bapt Ch 1965-73; adv bd BSA 1965-66; Hall-Mercer Comm Mental Hlth & Mental Retardation Ctr of PA Hosp 1973-74; mem PAC Philadelphia Redevel Authority 1973-75; bd tsts St Peter's Sch 1975-76; mem Pharmacy Com 1965-66; Admiss Com 1968-72; Student Affairs Com 1968-71; Alt Judiciary Com 1971-72; Student Promotion Com 1973-75; Pharmacy & Therapeutic Com 1974-76; Radiation Safety Com 1974-76; Computer Com 1974-76; natl bd of Amer Cancer Soc. **HONORS/ACHIEVEMENTS:** Over 150 publications, exhibits, presentations; Natl & Intl meetings. **MILITARY SERVICE:** USAF Capt 1958-60. **BUSINESS ADDRESS:** Chmn Dept Radiation Therapy, Jefferson University Hospital, 111 S 11th St, Philadelphia, PA 19107.

MANSFIELD, W. ED
Administration consultant. **PERSONAL:** Born May 07, 1937, Clifton Forge, VA; married Maxine L; children: Amy, Yolanda. **EDUCATION:** Dept of Def Info School, 1964; Univ of Denver, 1969-70. **CAREER:** Equal Employment Opportunities Commn, St Louis Dist Office, dist dir; Minority Affairs Corp for Public Broadcasting, dir 1976; Alternative Mgmt, consultant 1975-76; Affirmative Action Programs Dept, leader 1972-75; Gen Mills Inc, consultant to chmn of bd & pres 1972; marketing & enrollment, dir 1971-72; Natl Urban Coalition, asst dir field operations 1971; Univ of Denver, asst to chancellor 1969-71; CO Assn of Industrial Colleges & Universities, exec dir 1969-71; Public Relations, dir 1967-68; Radio Station KTLN, moderator, commentator, newscaster 1966-67; Lincoln Natl Life Insurance Co, special agent 1966-69. **ORGANIZATIONS:** Consult EEO Laws Affirmative Action; Gn Mills Inc; Nat Assn of Cos; Nat Civil Serv League; Intl Personnel Mgmt Assn; MN League of Cities; ND League of Cities; Am Compliance Soc & Inc; Intl Assn of Official Human Rights Orgns; City & Co of Denver; fdr past chmn of bd MN Affirmative Action Assn; chmn Hennepin Co Bicentennial Planning Commn; Affirmative Action Adv Com; Intl Personnel Mgmt Assn; 1st v chmn Minneapolis Urban Coalition; mem MN State Bd of Nursing; Abbott-Northwestern Hosp Copr; Minneapolis Citizens Concerned for Pub Edn; Am Soc of Personnel Adminstrn; Nat Orgn for Women; NAACP; Nat Urban League; Exchange of Minneapolis. **MILITARY SERVICE:** USAF 1954-66. **BUSINESS ADDRESS:** 1601 Olive St, St Louis, MO 63103.

MANUEL, JOHN N.
Dentist. **PERSONAL:** Born Sep 12, 1921, Shepherdstown, WV; married Gertrude Henderson; children: Melanie Manuel Evans. **EDUCATION:** Lincoln Univ PA (cum laude) 1944; Howard Univ Coll of Dentistry, 1952. **CAREER:** Private practice, dentist. **ORGANIZATIONS:** Mem Amer Dental Assn; Natl Dental Assn; WV Dental Assn; WV Med Dental & Pharm Soc; courtesy staff Williamson Mem Hosp; Charles B Payne Study Club; Huntington Dental Soc; Kappa Alpha Psi; Beta Kappa Chi; mem NAACP; Methodist Episcopal Church. **MILITARY SERVICE:** AUS s/sgt 1944-46. **BUSINESS ADDRESS:** Cinderella Bldg, Suite 25, Williamson, WV 25661.

MANUEL, LOUIS CALVIN
Physician. **PERSONAL:** Born Jun 13, 1937, Cleveland, OH; married Idabelle Todd; children: Donna L, April D, Erika L, Louis C. **EDUCATION:** Bowling Green State U, BA 1960; Meharry Med Coll, MD 1965. **CAREER:** Louis C Manuel MD Eye Serv Inc, ophthalmologist 1971-. **ORGANIZATIONS:** Sec & mem Kansas City Med Soc 1971-; past pres & current sec MO Pan Med 1971-; mem House of Delegates; mem Nat Med Soc 1971-; mem AMA; MO StateMed; Jackson Co Med; SW Med Assn; APPA KC Oph & Otol; Roman Barnes Soc; Castroviejo Soc; Am Soc of Con Oph 1971-; life mem NAACP; consult ophthal Model Cities Health Orgn KC MO 1971-80; deacon Covenant Presbyterian Ch KC MO 1977-; youth council career devel United Presbyterian Ch; bd of dir Civic Plaza Nat Bk KC MO 1979-; mem Alpha Phi Alpha; YMCA;Univ of MO Asso; Midwesterners of Greater KC Med Svc. **HONORS/ACHIEVEMENTS:** Combat Citation; commendation Medal; vietnamese serv ribbon AUS; Morgagmi Soc Meharry Med Pathology 1963f spl citation Med Consult City of St Louis Boxing Tourn 1969; Bowling Green State Rep St LouisUniv 200th Anniversary 1970; fellow Royal Soc of Medicine 1973. **MILITARY SERVICE:** AUS capt 1966-68. **BUSINESS ADDRESS:** Louis C Manuel MD Eye Services, 1734 E 63rd St Ste 601, Kansas City, MO 64110.

MAPLE, GOLDIE M.
Educational administration. **PERSONAL:** Born Nov 21, 1937, Neptune, NJ; married Jesse Maple; children: Yolanda, Desiree, Jomo. **EDUCATION:** Brooklyn Coll, 1955-56; New York City Comm Coll, 1956-58. **CAREER:** New York City Board of Education, asst accountant 1968-78, educ admin 1978-83, principal admin assoc 1983-, mem bd of ed 1980-. **ORGANIZATIONS:** Life mem NAACP 1966-; sec Rockaway Day Care Coalition 1976-80; mem Comm School Bd 1980-; pres Rockaway Democratic Coalition 1982-; asst clerk Comm Church of God in Christ 1983-; mem bd of dir Far Rockaway Revitalization Corp 1984-. **HOME ADDRESS:** 3226 Mott Ave, Far Rockaway, NY 11691.

MAPLE, VETRELLE
Nurse. **PERSONAL:** Born Sep 07, 1915, Ocala, FL. **EDUCATION:** FL Agr & Mech U, Nrs Deg. **CAREER:** FL East Coast Hosp, nurse; Gen Hosp Monchscorner, SC, 1st negro nurse; Coulter Academy Cheraw, SC, scl nrs & health ed inspector; Mt Sinai Hosp, operating room supr; Metro Oste Hosp Phil, night & OB supr; Phil Gen Hosp, emer room graduate; Atkinson Mem Hosp Coatesville, PA, night supr; pvt duty nurse asst; Devereux Foundation Bryn Mawr Hosp, retired nurse. **ORGANIZATIONS:** St Educator SC TB Assn; mem Nat Fed Women's Club; charter mem Chester Co Med Asst Assn; supr NE Fedn of Girls Club; mem MOD Chester; mem OIC Coatesville; mem Red Cross Chester; Lovers Club of Coatesville, PA; pres Epsilon Omega Zeta Ch Zeta Phi Beta; chairperson Zeta Nat Proj "Stark's Nest"; sponsor Archonetty (Zetas Jr); Epislon Omega Zeta Chap Coatesville; adm chmn Coatesville Housing Mini Serv Center for Adults; stewardess at St Pual AME Ch Coatesville; mem Phil Chap FAMU Alumni; past senior matron Coatesville-West Chester Negro Bus & Prof Women's Club Southeastern Fed Negro Women; Penn St organizer Nat Negro Bus & Prof Women's Club; mem The Nat Am Red Cross; mem Reg Comprehensiv Hlth Plng Counc; mem The Child Devel Assn Consortium; mem Coalesville, PA Adult Citize Bd. **HONORS/ACHIEVEMENTS:** Appreciation Aw Narristown B & PWC 1976; appreciation Aw SE Chester Co; Appreciation Aw W Chester PA 1976; commun serv Aw Mid-Atlantic Dist; achiev Aw mgt training certif 1976; sojurner truth Award from W Chester Negro Bus & Prof Women's Club 1974; Zeta of the Yr 1979.

MAPP, CALVIN R.
Attorney. **PERSONAL:** Born Sep 10, 1924, Miami, FL; son of Herschel Mapp and Edna Mapp; married Catherine Nelson Mapp; children: Calvin Jr, Corey Ramon. **EDUCATION:** Morris Brown Coll, BA; Howard Law School, LLB; Attended, North Dade Jr Coll, Bethune Cookman Coll, Natl Judicial Coll, Univ of FL, Alcohol Abuse Seminar, Harvard Univ. **CAREER:** Teacher, Math, Chemistry, 1951-52; City of Miami, police officer, 1952-60; Community Relations Bd, 1963-66; All State Courts, State of FL, attorney, 1965; State Attorney's Office, 1966-68; Matthews Braynon & Mapp, attorney, 1968-73; County of Dade, county court judge. **ORGANIZATIONS:** Dir 11th Judicial Circuit of FL Co Ct Judges Conf; mem FL, Amer, Natl Bar Assns; mem Amer Judicature Soc; admitted to bar State of FL, FL Supreme Ct, US Supreme Ct S Dist of FL 1965; mem Miami Varsity Club; life mem Kappa Alpha Psi Frat; bd mem Advocate Prog; 1st vice pres Advocate Prog; mem Milton Littman Memorial Found. **HONORS/ACHIEVEMENTS:** Morris Brown Coll Hon Dr Laws degree 1974; included in the Black Archives photo section of Dade Co 1976; Certificate of Appreciation Supreme Ct 1980; selected as a delegate by People to People Org, 1981; Judge of the Month Awd Spotlight Club 1983; City of Opa Locka Commendation 1983; Commendation City of Hialeah Gardens FL 1983; Gwen Cherry Political Award Sigma Gamma Rho Sor 1983-84; Outstanding Commitment to Mankind & Continuous Support of Shrine Progs Award, 1984; Certificate of Appreciation Black History Month Lillie C Evens Elem Sch 1984; Disting Leadership Awd Conf of the Co Court Judges of FL; Certificate for participation in 1981 FL Judicial Coll as Instructor FL Supreme Ct; inventor, holds patents on disposable syringe 1977, electra hoop 1978, sliding glass door dustpan; written 4 books entitled, Traffic, A Compilation of Florida Case Law; pres, The Advocate Program; vice pres, The Conf of the County Court Judges; mem, Rotary Intl. **MILITARY SERVICE:** AUS s/sgt 1943-46. **BUSINESS ADDRESS:** County Court Judge, Dade Co, 1351 NW 12th St, Miami, FL 33125.

MAPP, DAVID KENNETH, JR.
Law enforcement. **PERSONAL:** Born Nov 15, 1951, Norfolk, VA; married Cynthia Gaines; children: Shomarr, Patrice. **EDUCATION:** Norfolk State Univ, BA Sociology 1973. **CAREER:** Norfolk Sheriff's Dept, recreation dir 1973-75, clafficiation officer 1975-78, dir of classification & rehabilitative progs 1978-80, sheriff 1981-. **ORGANIZATIONS:** Officer Norfolk State Univ Alumni Assoc 1973-; officer Eureka Lodge 1973-; officer Norfolk Jaycees; mem Natl Sheriff's Assn 1981-; mem VA State Sheriff'sAssn 1981-; mem VA Assoc of Law Enforce Const Officers 1981-. **HONORS/ACHIEVEMENTS:** Citizen of the Year Alpha Phi Omega Frat 1983; chmn Norfolk United Way campaign 1983; Cardiac Arrest Awd Norfolk Heart Assn 1983-84; mem JJDP State Advisory Council 1982-. **BUSINESS ADDRESS:** Sheriff, Norfolk Sheriff's Dept, 811 East City Hall Ave, Norfolk, VA 23510.

MAPP, EDWARD C.
Educator. **PERSONAL:** Born Aug 17, New York, NY; son of Edward Mapp and Estelle Sampson Mapp; children: Andrew, Elmer, Everett. **EDUCATION:** City Coll of NY, BA 1953; Columbia Univ, MS 1956; NY Univ, PhD 1970. **CAREER:** NY City Bd of Educ, tchr 1957-64; NY City Tech Coll, dir of Library Learning Resources Center 1964-77; Borough of Manhattan Community Coll, dean of faculty 1977-82; City Colleges of Chicago, vice chancellor 1982-83; Borough of Manhattan Community Coll, prof 1983-. **ORGANIZATIONS:** Dir Natl Serv Corp 1984-87; bd of dir United Nations Assoc of NY 1975-78; bd of trustees NY Metro Ref & Rsch Agency 1980-81; Feature Columnist Movie/TV Mktg 1979-; mem 100 Black Men Inc 1975-85; bd mem (Brooklyn Region) Natl Conf of Chritians & Jews 1975-81; treas City Univ of NY Fac Senate 1972-77; Brooklyn Borough Pres Ed Adv Panel 1981; commissioner, New York City Human Rights Commission, 1988-. **HONORS/ACHIEVEMENTS:** Founders Day Award for Outstanding Scholarship NY Univ 1970; Distinguished Serv Award Borough of Manhattan Community Coll The City Univ of NY 1982; elected to NY Acad of Pub Educ 1978; author Blacks in Amer Films 1972, Puerto Rican Perspectives 1974, Blacks in the Performing Arts 1978, 2nd edition 1989. **BUSINESS ADDRESS:** Professor of Speech & Comm, Manhattan Comm Coll City UNY, 199 Chambers St, New York, NY 10007.

MAPP, FREDERICK EVERETT
Educator. **PERSONAL:** Born Oct 12, 1910, Atlanta, GA; married Betty Lewis; children: Wm M Boyd, Robert A Boyd. **EDUCATION:** Morehouse Coll, BS 1932; Atlanta Univ, MS 1934; Harvard Univ, MA 1942; Univ of Chicago, PhD 1950; Gen Ed Brd Flwshp 1946-48. **CAREER:** BT Washington HS (Atlanta), instr 1933-43; Knoxville Coll, prof of biology-

chrmn 1944-46; TN State Univ, prof of biology-chrmn 1951-52; Morehouse Coll, prof of Biology-chrmn 1952-. **HONORS/ACHIEVEMENTS:** Gen Educa Bd Flwshp 1946-48; the David Packard Prof of Biology 1973-82. **HOME ADDRESS:** 703 Waterford Rd NW, Atlanta, GA 30318. **BUSINESS ADDRESS:** Professor of Biology, Morehouse Coll, Morehouse Coll, Atlanta, GA 30314.

MAPP, JOHN ROBERT
Physician, neonatology. **PERSONAL:** Born Jan 26, 1950, Springfield, MA; son of Alexander B Mapp, Sr and Edna Royster Mapp; married Maria Mejia, Nov 13, 1981; children: Alexandra, Lorean. **EDUCATION:** Hillsdale Coll Hillsdale, MI, BA 1971; Meharry Med Coll Nashville TN, MD 1975; Med Coll of PA Philadelphia, Residence in Pediatrics 1975-77; California State Univ, San Diego, Master in Public Health 1986-87. **CAREER:** Univ Southern California, Los Angeles County Medical School, neonatal pathologist 1979-80; Univ Southern California Medical School, clinical instr in pediatrics 1977-79; Pediatrics Los Angeles, CA, symposuim re neonatology AA 1978; Hosp Italiano Rosario South Amer, guest lectr neonatologist, consultant in neonatology, 1979; Glendale Hospital Los Angeles co-chief of neonatology dept, 1979-. **ORGANIZATIONS:** Co-founder pres Blacks United at Hillsdale Coll 1969-71; mem Amer Assn of Pediatrics 1976-. **HONORS/ACHIEVEMENTS:** Natl TV Program "Lifeline" segment filmed at USC newborn/neonatology unit of Med Center at Los Angeles 1978. **HOME ADDRESS:** 135 Thompson St, Springfield, MA 01109.

MAPP, YOLANDA I.
Physician. **PERSONAL:** Born Jun 26, 1930, New York, NY; children: Donald, David, Douglas, Daniel, Dorothy, Darryl. **EDUCATION:** Monmouth Jr Coll, AA 1951; NJ Coll for Women Rutgers Univ 1953; Howard Univ Coll of Med, MD 1957; DC Genl Hosp, internship 1957-58; Freedman's Hosp Washington DC, residency 1958-60; DC Genl Hosp, residency 1960-61; Hahnemann Med Coll & Hosp, fellowship clinical pharmacology; Temple Univ Hosp, fellowship hermatology-oncology 1964-66. **CAREER:** Hanemann Med Coll & Hosp Philadelphia, instr of med & dir of alcoholic ctr 1961-64; Emory Univ Coll of Med Atlanta, prof of med & internist 1969-70; Temple Univ Hosp, physician 1967-; Temple Univ Coll of Med, assoc prof; Temple Univ, acting dir univ health serv. **ORGANIZATIONS:** Med adv Leukemia Soc of Amer Greater Atlanta Chap 1970; vol physician Thaler Meml Hosp Bilwaskarma Nicaragua 1972; med adv Amer Cancer Soc Philadelphia 1976-; licensure MD 1959, PA 1961, GA 1969. **HONORS/ACHIEVEMENTS:** Howard Whitfield Found Med Scholarship 1952-57; Schering Pharm Corp Hon Awd 1957; speaker "Honors & Awds Day" Howard Univ Coll of Med 1965; Certificate Amer Bd of Internal Medicine 1969; Certificate Amer Coll of Physicians 1970; Disting Achievement at Douglass Coll Douglass Soc Rutgers Univ New Brunswick NJ 1973; The Four Chaplains Legion of Hon Membership for Humanitarian Serv Chapel of Four Chaplains Philadelphia 1973; 6th Place in Nation Awd for Free Flight Soaring Entry Nordic A-2 Glider Aero Crafts Exhibit Civic Ctr Philadelphia 1974. **BUSINESS ADDRESS:** Acting Dir, Univ Health Serv, Temple University, Philadelphia, PA 19122.

MARABLE, JUNE MOREHEAD
Educator. **PERSONAL:** Born Jun 08, 1924, Columbus, OH; married James Palmer; children: Dr. **EDUCATION:** Central StateUniv Wilberforce, OH, BS Educ 1948;Univ of Dayton, MS Educ 1965; MiamiUniv Oxford, OH, PhD Educ 1974. **CAREER:** Miami Univ Oxford, OH, assoc prof 1977-; Wright State Univ Dayton, asst prof 1972-77; Dayton Bd of Educ, reading consultant 1954-72; KS City Bd of Educ KS City, MO, teacher 1952-54; Wright Patterson AFB Dayton, cartiographic draftsman & clerk-typist 1948-52. **ORGANIZATIONS:** Educ dir Marable Early Childhood Educ Center Dayton 1960-77; admin asst Black Research Asso Dayton 1979-; mem OH State Right to Read Commn State Dept Educ for OH 1970-; educ consult & lectr Pub Schools Universities Comm Civic Orgns Churches 1970-; coordinator Reading Improvement Prog Alpha Kappa Alpha Sor 1974-78; Sen Mer Rek Honor Soc WilberforceUniv Wilberforce, OH 1974; Alpha Kappa Mu WilberforceUniv Wilberforce, OH 1948. **HONORS/ACHIEVEMENTS:** Outstanding citizen award Optimist Club Dayton 1978; listed Who's Who in Am 1975-; Who's Who in Nursery Sch Educators 1975-; Who's Who in Women of World 1975-; outstanding citizens in Bicentennial of Am 1975-. **BUSINESS ADDRESS:** Vice President, Black Research Associates, PO Box 208, Dunbar Station, Dayton, OH 45417.

MARBURY, CARL HARRIS
Educator. **PERSONAL:** Born Mar 24, 1935, Leeds, AL; divorced. **EDUCATION:** AL A&M, BS (magna cum laude) 1957; Oberlin, MA 1961; Oberlin, BD (summa cum laude) 1962; Harvard, PhD 1968. **CAREER:** Garrett-Evang Theol Sem, vice pres acad affairs dean of faculty; Ctr for Resrch, dir; Inst for Serv to Edn, info & tech asst 1971-75; Ctr of Inst Resrch AL A, dir 1974-75; AL A&M, prof 1974; AL A&M, prof dean 1970-72;Univ of AL, vis prof 1968-70; AL A&M, asso prof chmn 1968-70. **ORGANIZATIONS:** Bd of dir AL League for the Adv of Edn; ombudsman AL A&M U; asst dir pub relat Intl Assn of Educs for World Peace; fdr exec sec Assn for Educ & Professional Opport Found; consult EW CtrUniv of HI; consult Huntsville VISTA Prgm; charter mem Intl Assn of Educs for World Peace 1970; mem Intl Secretariat; mem AL Acad of Sci; AL Counc on Human Relat; regnl adv group AL Regnl Med Prgm Bd of Dir Harris Home for Children; Kappa Alpha Psi Frat;Univ of AL Sch of Med Com Recruiting Blacks to Study Med; NEA; ALA; AAUP; SSR; Phi Delta Kappa Educ Frat; SSBR; Chicago Soc of Bibl Resrch; SBL; Alpha Phi Omega; AAHE; AL EA. **BUSINESS ADDRESS:** 2121 Sheridan Rd, Evanston, IL 60201.

MARBURY, DONALD LEE
Writer. **PERSONAL:** Born Nov 26, 1949, Pittsburgh, PA; son of Sherrill Marbury and Susie Burroughs Marbury; married Sheila JoAnn King, Mar 24, 1973; children: Cara Jean, Evan Lee. **EDUCATION:** Univ of Pittsburgh, BA English 1971. **CAREER:** Pittsburgh Post Gazette, general assignment reporter 1969-71; WQED-TV, news anchorman, producer/host, executive producer/ dir local programming, special asst 1971-80; Chatham College, instructor communications 1977-80; Corp for Public Broadcasting, assoc dir cultural & general programs, childrens programs 1980-; Univ District of Columbia, instructor screen playwriting 1984-85; freelance writer non-fiction, publishes articles, Pittsburgh Magazine, current magazines, Public Broadcasting Review 1973-,. **ORGANIZATIONS:** Bd dirs Intercultural House 1971-; mem bd dirs Pittsburgh Black Media Coalition 1971-74; bd dirs WYEP-FM 1974-75; mem Steering Comm of Producer's Council 1976-80; mem bd dirs Natl Black Program Consortium 1978-80; mem exec steering comm Producers Council Natl Assoc Education Broadcasters 1978-80; mem Task Force on Public Participation 1978; bd dirs Louise Child Care Center; poet, featured in nationally syndicated radio series, "The Poet Another Poem"; bd of dir, Children's Advocacy Newspaper, 1989. **HONORS/ACHIEVEMENTS:** Golden Quill (2) Western PA Journalism Honorary 1973; Pittsburgh Goodwill Ambassador Pittsburgh Goodwill 1975; Black Achiever of the Year Talk Magazine 1975; Founders Award Natl Black Programming Consortium 1983; US delegate public broadcasting to the European Broadcasting Unions working party on programs for children & youth, 1984-86; featured poet in perforamce, WPFW-FM, 1985-88; Certificate of Appreciation, Natl Black Programming Consortium, 1988; English speaking moderator, Poix Jeunesse, Intl, Munich (Intl Children's Program Festival,) 1988. **HOME ADDRESS:** One Tupelo Court, Rockville, MD 20855. **BUSINESS ADDRESS:** Associate Dir, The Program Fund, Corp for Public Broadcasting, 1111 16th St NW, Washington, DC 20036.

MARBURY, HOWARD W.
Officer/corporate. **PERSONAL:** Born Mar 24, 1924, Dayton, OH; married Wessie M Willis; children: Cheryl, Howard W. **EDUCATION:** Medgar Evers Coll Brooklyn, BA 1973; FordhamUniv NY, ME 1975; Gadsden State Jr Coll AL, Cert 1978. **CAREER:** Town of Ridgeville, AL, mayor; Town of Ridgeville, supt of utilities 1979-80; Etowah Co AL, dep voter registrar 1980; John Paul Jones Sch Bronx, tchr 1974-75; NY City Fire Dept, fireman 1960-77. **ORGANIZATIONS:** Mem bd of dir Etowah Co Voters League 1977-80; mem exec com Nat Conf of Black Mayors 1979-80; chmn of the bd Etowah Co Mayor's Assn 1979-80; mem bd of dir So Christian Leadership Conf AL 1978-80; mem bd of dir E AL Reg Planning Commn 1978-80; town councilman Ridgeville Town Bd 1977; mem NAACP 1977-80; mem State Chap AL Black Mayors Assn 1977-80; mem bd of dir Jacksonville Sr Citizens Assn 1979-80; mem Black Caucus AL Dem Conf 1979-80; mem Bd of dir Gadsden Met C of C 1980. **HONORS/ACHIEVEMENTS:** Five battlestars AUS 1943-45, 53-58. **MILITARY SERVICE:** AUS capt 8 yrs. **BUSINESS ADDRESS:** Town of Ridgeville, Route 1 Box 413, Ridgeville, AL 35954.

MARCEE, EMERSON
Clergyman, business executive. **PERSONAL:** Born Jun 27, 1918, Gonzales Co, TX; married Cynthia. **EDUCATION:** St Phillips Coll, Grad; St Mary's U, Grad 1957; Guadalupe Coll Tehol Sem, Grad; Dyer Real Estate Sch, Grad; Trinity U, Grad Studies. **CAREER:** Mt Carmel Baptist Ch, pastor 1963-; Eastside Printing Co, owner 1971-; US Govt, 1946-70, 1941-42; licensed real estate broker. **ORGANIZATIONS:** Mem NAACP Nat Bd of Dirs 1963-; life mem com Nat NAACP; pres San Antonio Br NAACP 1953-59, 1968-77; mason; past chmn Region VI NAACP; mem NAPFE; Bapt Ministers Union. **HONORS/ACHIEVEMENTS:** Recip San Antonio Br Achievement Award 1960; TX State Conf Achievement Award 1968; while pres of San Antonio Br Br awarded NAACP Nat Thalheimer Award 1956; award 1st prize State Conf 1954; Sammie Davis Nat Life Mem Award 1974; NAACP Nat publication award NAACP State Conf 1963-66. **MILITARY SERVICE:** AUS s/sgt 1942-46. **BUSINESS ADDRESS:** 2308 E Commerce St, San Antonio, TX 78203.

MARCERE, NORMA SNIPES
Educator. **PERSONAL:** Born Oct 21, 1908, Canton, OH; daughter of Norman Sherwood Snipes and Ida Rosella Evans Snipes; married Percy Alluren Marcere (deceased); children: Norma Jean, Alluren Leonard. **EDUCATION:** Kent State Univ, MA 1957; Walsh Coll, Doctorate (hon) 1980. **CAREER:** Stark Co Welfare Dept Canton, soc caseworker 1938-42; Stark Co TB & Health Assn Canton, health educator 1944-56; EA Jones Jr HS, tchr/counselor 1957-66; Human Engrg Inst, voc counselor 1962-66; Garfield HS Akron, guidance counselor 1966-71; Kent OH City Sch, sch psychologist 1971-72; Stoydale-Brunnerdale Summer Projects, dir 1972-73; Hilltop House, psychologist 1972-74; Prog for Academic Excellence: A Saturday Sch, 1979-84; Stark Tech Coll, founder & dir 1974-84; Stark Technical College, Canton OH consultant/minority affairs 1984-86. **ORGANIZATIONS:** Mem OH Educ Assn; OH Sch Counselors Assn; OH Sch Psychologists; mem Natl Council Cath Women 1940-; mem Natl Assn Colored Women's Clubs 1940-80; mem Panel of Amer Women 1965-; sec Canton City Charter Comm 1961-62; mem Youngstown Diocesan Catholic Sch bd 1964-70; bd dir Urban League 1964-66; mem Youngstown Diocesan Sch Bd 1969-75; sec Stark Co Bd Mental Retardation 1970-76; mem Phi Delta Kappa Frat 1970; mem adv bd Cath Charities 1970-76; mem Alpha Kappa Alpha Sor 1972; mem Adv Bd Walsh Coll 1974-; Kent State Campus Ministries 1974-79; sec YWCA Bd 1978-82; mem Alpha Kappa Alpha Sor 1972-; mem Phi Delta Kappa Frat 1970-; life mem NAACP; bd mem Black United Fund 1980-83; bd mem Big Bros & Sisters 1980-82; mem Cath Charities Adv Bd 1970-76. **HONORS/ACHIEVEMENTS:** Woman of the Yr Jr League 1973; "Bridging the Gap Between the Races" Urban League; Mayor of Canton; Oldtimers & others; rec'd at White House for positive contributions toward race relations, 40 Panel of Amer Women 1979; author "Genteel Violence" Good Housekeeping May 1970; author Round the Dining Room Table, a childhood autobiography, 1984, Daring Press Canton Ohio; Ohio Women's Hall of Fame, State of Ohio, Governor Celeste, 1987; Honorary bd mem Walsh College 1989; author The Fences Between - Autobiography (young adult) 1989; author How to Start a Saturday School for Academic Excellence 1989. **BUSINESS ADDRESS:** Psychologist and Admin Counselor, Stark Tech Coll, 6200 Frank Ave NW, North Canton, OH 44720.

MARCH, ANTHONY
Automobile dealer. **PERSONAL:** Born Feb 25, 1951, Brooklyn, NY; married Gail, Dec 21, 1974; children: Crystal. **EDUCATION:** Howard Univ, Washington DC, BS Electrical Engineering, 1973; General Motors Dealer Academy, Flint MI, graduate, 1985. **CAREER:** Fisher Body Div of General Motors, Warren MI, engineering group man 1971-84; Tony March Buick, Hartford CT, pres, 1985-89. **ORGANIZATIONS:** Mem, NAACP, 1985-; founder, dir, Sentinel Bank, 1986-; dir, Univ of Hartford Assn, 1987-, Greater Hartford Better Business Bureau, 1987-, Greater Hartford YMCA, 1988-, Mount Sinai Hospital, 1988-. **HONORS/ACHIEVEMENTS:** America's Best & Brightest, Dollars & Sense Magazine, 1987; Meritorious Award, United Negro Coll Fund; Best-In-Class, Buick Motor Div, 1987, 1988; Business Man of the Year, Univ of Hartford, 1987; Business Man of the Year, Upper Albany Merchants, 1987.

MARCHAND, MELANIE ANNETTE
Chemical engineer. **PERSONAL:** Born Mar 12, 1962, New Orleans, LA; daughter of Mr Edward Janvier Marchand and Mrs Sandra Baker Marchand. **EDUCATION:** Tulane Univ, New Orleans, LA, Bachelor of Science in Chemical Engineering, 1980-84. **CAREER:** Union Carbide Corp, Taft, LA, production eng, 1984-86; Air Products and Chemicals, Inc, New Orleans, LA, process eng, 1986-87; Air Products and Chemicals, Inc, Allentown, PA, process eng, 1988-. **ORGANIZATIONS:** Mem, LA Engineering Soc, 1984-; mem, Soc of Women Engineers, 1988-90; mem, Assn for Integrated Mgmt, 1988-; mem, Minority Community Advisory Bd-Muhlenberg Coll, 1989. **HONORS/ACHIEVEMENTS:** Appreciation

Award for Leadership and Dedication to the UCC Aerobics Class, Union Carbide Corp Family Safety & Health Comm, 1985; Quality Recognition Variable Compensation Award, Air Products and Chemicals Inc, 1989. **HOME ADDRESS:** 7416 Scottsdale Dr, New Orleans, LA 70127.

MARCHMAN, ROBERT ANTHONY
Attorney. **PERSONAL:** Born Jan 21, 1958, Brooklyn, NY; married Fay Pamela Chin. **EDUCATION:** Allegheny Coll, BA (Magna Cum Laude) 1980; Univ of PA, JD 1983. **CAREER:** Office of the Deputy Mayor for Criminal Justice, intern 1979; Dept of Corrections New York, intern 1980; NAACP Legal Defense Fund Inc, intern 1981; US Attorney for the Southern Dist of NY, intern 1982; US Securities and Exchange Commn, staff attorney 1983-. **ORGANIZATIONS:** Mem NY State Bar Assoc; pres Concerned Black Men Inc Washington DC 1986-. **HOME ADDRESS:** 8750 Georgia Ave, #1209B, Silver Spring, MD 20910. **BUSINESS ADDRESS:** Attorney, U S Securities/Exchange Commsn, 450 Fifth St NW, Washington, DC 20549.

MARDENBOROUGH, LESLIE A.
Human resources executive. **PERSONAL:** Born Mar 25, 1948, Bronx, NY; daughter of Victor E Mardenborough (deceased) and Dorothy Richards Mardenborough. **EDUCATION:** Albright Coll, Reading PA, AB, 1968. **CAREER:** Brooklyn Coll, career counselor, 1969-73; Wildcat Serv Corp, vice pres, Operations, 1978, other positions 1973-78; New Life Group Inc, exec dir, Career Center, 1979-81; The New York Times Co Magazine Group, project mgr, Human Resources, 1981-84, dir, Employee Relations, 1984-86, dir, Personnel, 1986-87, dir, Corporate Personnel, 1987-. **ORGANIZATIONS:** Mem, Human Resource Planners Assn, 1982-; bd mem, membership officer, New York Human Resource Planners, 1986-88; mem, President's Advisory Council, Albright College, 1987-, ANPA Human Resources Comm, 1988-, Newspaper Personnel Relations Assn, 1988-, African-Amer Advisory Bd for County Exec (Westchester County), 1988-; bd of dir, New York Bd of Trade, 1989-. **HONORS/ACHIEVEMENTS:** Black Achievers in Industry, Harlem YMCA, 1986. **BUSINESS ADDRESS:** Director, Corporate Personnel, The New York Times Company, 229 W 43rd St, New York, NY 10036.

MARGERUM, ROGER WILLIAMS
Architect, designer. **PERSONAL:** Born May 14, 1930, Chicago, IL; married Frances L Esnault; children: Michael B, Kim. **EDUCATION:** Univ of IL, BArch 1956. **CAREER:** Skidmore Ownings & Merril Assoc, designer 1959; Perkins & Will Partnership, designer 1961; Morrison & Margerum Assoc Inc, partner 1965; Smith Hinchanan & Gryles Assoc, assoc & asst to bd chmn 1973; Roger Margerum Inc Arch, pres. **ORGANIZATIONS:** Pres MI Soc of Arch 1983; charter dir vice pres 1972 and vice pres Natl Orgn of Minority Arch 1985. **HONORS/ACHIEVEMENTS:** Founding dir & charter mem Natl Org of Minority Arch 1972; mem of coll of fellows Amer Inst of Arch 1984; Design Awards, Engrg Soc of Detroit 1982; Masonry Inst of MI; Natl Orgn of Minority Architects 1983; Two Awards Detroit Chap of Amer Inst of Architects. **HOME ADDRESS:** 401 S LaSalle St #608, Chicago, IL 60605. **BUSINESS ADDRESS:** President, Roger Margerum Inc, Archit, 47 E Adams, Detroit, MI 48226.

MARINO, EUGENE ANTONIO
Clergyman. **PERSONAL:** Born May 29, 1934, Biloxi, MS; son of Jesus Maria Marino and Irnen Bradford Marino. **EDUCATION:** Epiphany Apostolic Coll, Sem Edn; St Joseph Sem; Fordham Univ, MA, 1967. **CAREER:** Ordained to priesthood 1962; St. Joseph's Sem, dir, 1963; Auxiliary bishop of Washington DC; Josephites, vicar general, 1971; Archbishop Baum, ordained to episcopate by 1974; St Gabriel's Parish, res; Walla Walla WA, titular Bishop; ordained archbishop, Atlanta Arch Diocese, 1988; Epiphany, teacher of science and religion. **ORGANIZATIONS:** Mem, Josephite Gen Counc; dir, Spiritual & Educ Form Josephites; Bishop's Comm on Per Diaconate; US Cath Conf; bd trustees, Cath Univ of Am; episcopal bd, Word of God Inst Rsrch Found at Chldrn's Hosp; chmn, Bishops' Comm for Liaison with Natl Office Black Catholics; trustee, Cath Univ Amer; mem, Devel Comm Natl Shrine of Immaculate Conception; mem, Natl Conf Catholic Bishops. **HONORS/ACHIEVEMENTS:** Hon DD 1974; appointed first black Catholic archbishop, 1988. **BUSINESS ADDRESS:** Most Rev. Eugene Marino, Archbishop of Atlanta, 680 West Peachtree StN W, Atlanta, GA 30308. *

MARION, CLAUD COLLIER
Retired educator. **PERSONAL:** Born in Fort Pierce, FL; son of James Marion and Hattie Marion. **EDUCATION:** FL A&M Univ, BS 1936; Univ of MN, MS 1941; Cornell Univ, PhD 1948. **CAREER:** TN A&I Univ, guest prof of educ 1951-52, 1956-70; Univ of MD Eastern Shore, asst dir and coordinator of 1890 extension programs 1972-77, prof agricultural educ and teacher training 1948-, administrator of 1890 extension programs 1977-80. **ORGANIZATIONS:** Mem UMES Extension Comm, Administrative Conf Comm, Personnel Coord Comm, Publications Comm; mem Foreign Relations Comm Amer Vocational Assoc; commissioner of Higher Educ Peninsula Conf United Methodist Church Dover DE 1970-; advisor Alpha Tau Alpha; mem Masonic Lodge, Elks Lodge, Alpha Phi Alpha Frat. **HONORS/ACHIEVEMENTS:** Certificate of Appreciation for Serv to the Office of Admin by Pres Harry S Truman 1946; Honorary American Farmer degree Natl Org of FFA 1975; Teacher of Teachers Gold Award Natl Vocational Agriculture Teachers Assoc Inc 1976; Certificate of Award for Outstanding Citizenship Princess Anne Chapter of Links Inc 1976.

MARIUS, KENNETH ANTHONY
Physician. **PERSONAL:** Born Feb 22, 1937, New York, NY; married Esther Bailey; children: Kenneth Jr, Robert. **EDUCATION:** Howard Univ, BSEE 1960; NEW JERSEY Inst of Technology, MS 1965; Howard Univ Coll of Med, MD, 1970. **CAREER:** Comm Coop Corp, pres 1972; Tricities Progress for Women, consult 1972; New Jersey Coll of Medicine & Dentistry, clinical instr 1976-. **ORGANIZATIONS:** Treasurer NJ Med Soc; NJ Med Soc; mem Essex Co Med Soc; Consult City of Newark; team physician Weeguanic HS; spkr Essex Co Heart Assn; mem Alpha Omega Alpha Med Hon Soc; Tau Beta Pi Eng Hon Soc; pres North Jersey Med Soc, NJ Med Soc 1984; Natl Med Assn delegate 1981-; Sickle Cell Found Advisory Bd 1983-;. **HONORS/ACHIEVEMENTS:** Bd of Concerned Citizens Awd 1986; Distinguished Serv Award, Tricities chamber of Commerce 1985; Distinguished Serv Award, Sports Physician, Weeguanic 1983-86. **MILITARY SERVICE:** USAF 1952-56; USAR med ofcr 1984-86. **BUSINESS ADDRESS:** NJ Coll Medicine & Dentistry, 198 Clinton Ave, Newark, NJ 07108.

MARK, FREEMON A.
Attorney. **PERSONAL:** Born Nov 30, 1948, Caswell Co, NC. **EDUCATION:** Wake Forest U, BA 1971;Univ of FL Coll of Law, JD 1974. **ORGANIZATIONS:** Mem State of FL Bar; US Dist Ct Bar; So Dist FL; US Ct of Appeals for the 5th Circuit; trustee Grtr Antioch Bapt Ch. **HONORS/ACHIEVEMENTS:** Listed Who's Who; man of yr; book award. **BUSINESS ADDRESS:** Law Office Mark Chennault, 1577 N Dixie Hghwy &, Pompano Beach, FL 33060.

MARKETTE-MALONE, SHARON
Legislative liaison. **PERSONAL:** Born Feb 05, 1956, Montgomery, AL; married Columbus Malone Jr, Feb 25, 1989. **EDUCATION:** Chicago State Univ, BS Corrections 1978. **CAREER:** 28th Ward Young Democrats, sec 1981-83; 28th Ward Reg Democratic Org, precinct capt 1981-83; 28th Ward Women on the Move, recording sec 1982-83; IL House of Rep, state legislator 1983-85; IL Dept of Employment Sec, legislative liaison. **ORGANIZATIONS:** Choir dir Original Providence Young Adult Choir 1971-81; mem Young Democrats of Cook Cty 1980-83; state rep IL House of Rep 1983-85; mem Natl Black Caucus of State Leg 1983-; sec Ray Hudson Scholarship Club 1982-84; pres Women's Aux Original Prov Bapt Church 1984-86; advisory council State of IL 1985; mem Sigma Gamma Rho Sorority Inc 1989. **HONORS/ACHIEVEMENTS:** Cert Outstanding Young Women of Amer 1984; Plaque Concerned Black Exec 1984. **HOME ADDRESS:** 208 N Kolin Ave, Chicago, IL 60624.

MARKEY, BEATRICE (NEE GREENE)
Educator. **PERSONAL:** Born Jul 15, 1913, Kansas City, KS; married John. **EDUCATION:** Univ of Chicago, PhB 1935;Univ of So CA, MPA 1952;Univ of So CA, DPA 1956. **CAREER:** Hilo Coll Univ of HI, prof polit sci. **ORGANIZATIONS:** Am Polit Sic Assn; Am Soc for Publ Adminstrn; Ctr for Study of Dem Instrn; Common Cause Acad of Polit Sci; Am Assn ofUniv Women; Haynes Found Felshp 1955. **BUSINESS ADDRESS:** Hilo Coll, Hilo, HI 96720.

MARKS, LEE OTIS
Educator. **PERSONAL:** Born Nov 17, 1944, Carthage, AR; married Karen Vaughn; children: Cynthia Lynne, Valerie Jeanne, Allison Marie. **EDUCATION:** Sioux Falls Coll, BA 1966; Univ of IL Champaign-Urbana, MS 1974. **CAREER:** Rockford Guilford HS, Physical Educ teacher, head track coach asst football coach, 1967-; Lincoln Park Elementary School, teacher, 1966-67; Madison Mustang, football player, 1966-67; Rockford Rams, football player, 1969-70. **ORGANIZATIONS:** SFC Letterman Club Sioux Falls Coll Alumni Assn 1966; mem Rockford Educ Assn; IL Educ Assn; mem Natl Educ Assn; IL Health Physical Educ & Recreation Assn; IL Coaches Assn; Rockford Coaches Assn; exec bd of dir Rockford Educ Assn 1971-73; Natl Educ Assn Black Caucus; IL Human Relations Commn 1971-73; Natl Letterman Assn; bd dir Rockford Black Educators Assn 1971-73; program dir BT Washington Comm Cent 1966-70; Allen Chapel AME Church; bd dir Centeral Terrace Co-op 1972. **HONORS/ACHIEVEMENTS:** Teacher of year Guilford HS Student Body 1971; delegate to Natl Educ Assn Conv 1971; co-captain MVP football Sioux Falls Coll 1965. **BUSINESS ADDRESS:** Guilford HS, 5620 Springcreek Rd, Rockford, IL 61111.

MARKS, ROSE M.
Library technician. **PERSONAL:** Born Mar 17, 1938, Chicago; children: Deborah, Charles. **EDUCATION:** Sacramento City Coll, 1958; Sacramento State U. **CAREER:** Oak Park Branch Library, branch supr; Sacramento City-Co Library, libr clk 1961-77. **ORGANIZATIONS:** Past bd dir KVIE Educ TV; past bd dir Sacramento Reg Arts Council; past sec Oak Park Comm Theatre; Sacramento Black Women's United Front; mgr of Band & co-mgr of singing group; past vice pres Sacramento City Employees Assn; past pres Sacramento City Library Assn. **BUSINESS ADDRESS:** Oak Park Branch Library 3301 5, Sacramento, CA 95817R.

MARQUEZ, CAMILO RAOUL
Physician/child psychiatry. **PERSONAL:** Born Feb 25, 1942, New York, NY; son of Cecil Marquez and Gloria Marquez. **EDUCATION:** Colby Coll, AB 1963; Howard Univ Sch of Medicine, MD 1976. **CAREER:** St Vincent's Hosp, resident in psychiatry 1977-79, chief resident 1978-79; Manhattan Psychiatric Ctr, rsch psychiatrist 1979-80; Harlem Hosp, staff psychiatrist 1980-82; North General Hosp, dir in-patient psychiatry 1982-84; Health Sci Ctr of Brooklyn SUNY, asst instructor; Harlem Hospital, attending physician div of child and adolescent psychiatry 1988-; Columbia University, College of Physicians & Surgeons asst clinical professor psychiatry 1988-. **ORGANIZATIONS:** Mem Amer Psychiatric Assoc 1978-, Black Psychiatrists of Amer 1979-; bd of trustees Wooster Sch 1986-; mem Amer Acad Child and Adolescent Psychiatry 1986-; co-chmn Black Health Professionals for School Based Health and Sex Educ Programs 1986-. **HONORS/ACHIEVEMENTS:** Falk Fellow Amer Psychiatric Assoc 1978-79; "Diagnosis of Manic Depressive Illness in Blacks", in Comprehensive Psychiatry, Vol 26, No 4 1985. **MILITARY SERVICE:** Sp 4 1963-70. **HOME ADDRESS:** 35 East 10th St #8C, New York, NY 10003.

MARR, CARMEL CARRINGTON
Attorney. **PERSONAL:** Born Jun 23, Brooklyn, NY; daughter of William P Carrington (deceased) and Gertrude C Lewis Carrington (deceased); married Warren Marr II; children: Charles, Warren III. **EDUCATION:** Hunter Coll, BA (Cum Laude) 1945; Columbia Univ Law School, JD 1948. **CAREER:** Dyer & Stevens Esqs, law asst 1948-49; Private Practice, attorney at law 1949-53; US Mission to the United Nations, advisor on legal affrs 1953-67; United Nations Secretariat, sr legal officer 1967-68; New York State Human Rights Appeal Bd, mem 1968-71; New York State Public Serv Comm, commr 1971-86 (retired); Consultant, energy 1987. **ORGANIZATIONS:** Chairperson adv council Gas Rsch Inst 1979-86; chairperson US Dept of Trans Tech Pipeline Safety Standards Comm 1979-85; chairperson Natl Assoc of Regulatory Utility Commnrs Gas Comm; pres NARUC's Great Lakes Conf of Public Utility Commn; chmn Amistad Rsch Center; bd mem Natl Arts Stabilization Fund; mem Natl Cncl of UN Assn of the USA; mem bd Helen Keller Serv for the Blind, Brooklyn Soc for the Prevention of Cruely to Children, Natl Council to Hampshire Coll; mem bd Prospect Park Alliance. **HONORS/ACHIEVEMENTS:** Outstanding Community Serv Brooklyn Urban League; plaques and other citations from Friends of Amistad, Brooklyn Home for the Aged, Barbados Nurses Assoc, Amer Caribbean Scholarship Fund, Gas Rsch Inst, NYS Public Serv Commn, Amer Red Cross, Natl Council of Churches, Mademoiselle Magazine, The Links; mem Phi Beta Kappa, Alpha Chi Alpha Honorary Societies; elected to Hunter Coll Hall of Fame.

MARR, WARREN, II
Editor. **PERSONAL:** Born Jul 31, 1916, Pittsburgh, PA; son of Warren Quincy Marr and Cecelia Antoinette McGee Marr; married Carmel Carrington, Apr 11, 1948; children: Charles Carrington, Warren Quincy III. **EDUCATION:** Wilberforce Univ, Journalism, Printing. **CAREER:** St Louis Argus, linotype oper 1938-39; The Plaindealer KC KS, linotype oper, shop foreman, asst ed 1939-42; Concert Mgmt, 1942-48; James Lassiter & Sons Madison NJ, drapery maker & asst to decorator 1948-52; House of Marr Inc, proprietor 1952-60; United Church Bd for Homeland Ministries NY Div of Higher Ed & Amer Missionary Assoc, AMA Coll Centennials Amistad Awds, founder & dir 1961-. **ORGANIZATIONS:** Mem NAACP; ed "The Crisis Mag" 1968-80; founder & exec dir Friends of Amistad; bd mem So NY Div UN Assn USA, Brooklyn Arts & Cultural Assn, Brooklyn Boys Club, Medgar Evers Coll Comm Council; past hon Natl Chmn Pan-African Found Art Shows, photography exhibits, private art collections; commiss Art Commiss of NYC; chmn Comm Art Comm York Coll; co-founder with Clifton H Johnson, Amistad Research Center, New Orleans, 1966; member, New York City Community Board #9. **HONORS/ACHIEVEMENTS:** Awds, Amer Assn for United Nations Eleanor Roosevelt 1955, Testimonial Luncheon Waltann School for Creative Arts 1967, JFK Awd JFK Library for Minorities 1972; Intl Key Women of Amer 1974; Pan-African Found 1974; Frederick Douglass Awd Afro-Amer Hist Assn 1975; Third Army ROTC Reg 1974; Black Heritage Assn 1974; Achievement Awd Detroit Friends of Amistad 1976; co-editor w/Maybelle Ward "Minorities & Amer Dream, A Bicentennial Perspective" NY Arno Press 1977; co-editor w/Harry Ploski "Negro Almanac" 3rd ed NY Bellwether Publ Co 1977.

MARRETT, CORA B.
Educator. **PERSONAL:** Born Jun 15, 1942, Richmond, VA; daughter of Horace S Bagley and Clorann Boswell Bagley; married Louis E. **EDUCATION:** VA Union Univ, BA 1963; Univ of WI, MA 1965, PhD 1968. **CAREER:** Univ of NC-Chapel Hill, asst prof 1968-69; Western MI Univ, asst to assoc 1969-74; Univ of WI-Madison, assoc to full 1974-. **ORGANIZATIONS:** Bd of governors, Argonne Natl Lab 1982-; bd of trustees Cntr for Adv Study in the Behavioral Sciences 1983-89. **HONORS/ACHIEVEMENTS:** Fellowship, Center for Advanced Study 1976-77, Natl Acad of Sci 1973-74; edtr Research in Race & Ethnic Relation (JAI Press) 1985; Distinguished Teaching Award, University of Wisconsin 1989. **BUSINESS ADDRESS:** Professor of Sociology, Univ of WI-Madison, Madison, WI 53706.

MARRIOTT, SALIMA SILER
Educator. **PERSONAL:** Born Dec 05, 1940, Baltimore, MD; daughter of Jesse James Siler and Cordie Ayers Siler; divorced; children: Terrez Siler-Merriott Morris, Patrice Kenyatta Siler-Marriott. **EDUCATION:** Morgan State Univ, BS 1964; Univ of MD, MSW 1972; Howard Univ, DSW 1988. **CAREER:** Dept of Social Services New York City, social worker 1965-68; Dept of Social Service, city of Baltimore, social worker 1968-72; Morgan State Univ, instructor 1972-87, chairperson 1981-87. **ORGANIZATIONS:** Chairperson 1986-87, corporate sec Park Heights Develop Corp 1976-86; founding mem/vice pres African-Amer Women Caucus 1982-85; organizer Natl Conf Women of African Diaspora 1984; consultant President's Domestic Council 1986; Public Schools, Baltimore Md; deputy state dir, Dykakis/Bentsen Campaign, 1988; mem Delta Sigma Theta Sorority Inc 1989; vice chmn Maryland Chapter Natl Rainbow Coalition1988-89; NAACP; Natl Black Women's Health Project; Natl Women's Studies Assn; AFSCME. **HONORS/ACHIEVEMENTS:** Editor Behold the Woman Journal 1981, US Policy Toward Southern Africa 1984; Community Service Awd Morgan State Univ 1984,86; workshop convener United Nation's Decade for Women Conference 1985; Outstanding Teacher, Dept of Social Work & Mental Health Morgan State Univ 1988; Baltimore's Black Women of Courage Exhibit 1988; Jesse Jackson Delegate, Democratic Natl Convention, 1988; Maryland Democratic Central Committee. **HOME ADDRESS:** 4515 Homer Ave, Baltimore, MD 21215.

MARROW-MOORING, BARBARA A.
Government official. **PERSONAL:** Born May 04, 1945, Trenton, NJ; married Kelly Daniel Mooring, Oct 29, 1988; children: Carla, Paula, Connie; stepchildren: Venessa Culbreth, Kelly D Mooring, Jr, Anthony Mooring, Shawn Mooring. **EDUCATION:** Mercer County Community Coll, AA (cum laude) Social Science & Humanities, 1973; Trenton State Coll, BS (magna cum laude) Elementary Educ, 1975. **CAREER:** Educational Testing Serv, Princeton NJ, division mgr, 1982-83, asst to vice pres, 1983-86, field serv representative, 1982-89; Trenton Bd of Educ, teacher, 1983-88; New Jersey General Assembly, Trenton NJ, clerk, 1986-87; New Jersey Lottery, Trenton NJ, exec dir, 1987-. **ORGANIZATIONS:** Pres, Natl Assn of Univ Women, 1977-79; vice pres, mem, Lawrence Township School Bd, 1978-87; founder, past pres, Coalition of 100 Black Republicans; treasurer, mem, Mercer County Improvement Authority, 1983-88; trustee, Rider Coll, 1987-; mem, Capital City Redevelopment Corp, 1987-, New Jersey Job Training Coordinating Council, 1987-89; trustee, Urban League of Metropolitan Trenton Inc, 1988-. **HONORS/ACHIEVEMENTS:** Outstanding Achievement, NJ State Fedn of Colored Women's Clubs Inc, 1986; Community Service Award, BAC Publishing Co, 1988; Women of Achievement Award, NJ Fedn of Business & Professional Women Inc, 1989. **BUSINESS ADDRESS:** Executive Director, New Jersey Lottery, CN 041, Trenton, NJ 08625.

MARRS, STELLA
Actress, vocalist, writer, painter, counselor, activist. **PERSONAL:** Born Mar 22, 1932; daughter of Stella Marrs; divorced; children: Lynda, Joseph, Walter, Tita, Joseph III, Shawn, Cortez, Freddie. **EDUCATION:** Attended, CCNY, RCC, Hunter Coll. **CAREER:** Lional Hampton Orchestra, vocalist 1969-70,72-73;TV special with Toots Thielmans 1977; recorded album Belgium Dicovers Stella Marrs 1977; toured US, Australia, Europe, jazz artist; Stella Marrs Cable TV Show, hosted; WRVR Radio, jazz DJ; WNJR, bright moments in jazz; Jazz Festivals Belgium, France, Amsterdam, Holland; Martin Luther King Multi-Purpose Center Inc, exec dir. **ORGANIZATIONS:** Intl Jazz Fed; contributing editor African-Amer Classical Music/Jazz Publication; mem Jazz at Home Club 1972, Westchester Jazz Soc 1975, Bi-Centennial Jazz Citation Manhattan Boro Pres 1976; mem Rockland County on Womens Issues 1986; mem adv comm Cooperative Extension 4H Club 1986; mem Crystal Run Environmental Center Adv Bd 1986; mem Spring Valley NAACP Educ Comm 1987; mem adv council Village of Spring Valley Comm Develop Advisory Council 1987; Rotary Intl, 1989; Ramapo Housing Authority, bd mem, 1988. **HONORS/ACHIEVEMENTS:** Philadelphia Jazz Honor Soc 1971; Woman of the Year Kennedy Center in Harlem 1976; Consortium of Jazz Artists Award of Excellence 1981; wrote, produced, dir, performed "I A Black Woman" New Heritage Repertory Theatre; researching Amer Indian, African Amer, Hispanic, Asian Cultures for publ called "History Not To Be Denied"; Certificate of Excellence, A proud Heritage; St Paul Honorary Black Belt; Certificate of Appreciation, 1989; Workshops and lectures on Human Race Relations, with families the primary source, along with School Districts, Prisons, Community; Certificate of Appreciation, Rockland County Dept of Social Services, 1989. **BUSINESS ADDRESS:** Executive Dir, M L King Multi-Purpose Ctr Inc, 26 No Bethune Blvd, Spring Valley, NY 10977.

MARSALIS, BRANFORD
Musician. **PERSONAL:** Born Aug 26, 1960, New Orleans, LA; son of Ellis Marsalis II and Dolores Ferdinand Marsalis; married Teresa Reese, May 31, 1985; children: Reese Ellis. **EDUCATION:** Southern Univ, 1978-79; Berkeley Coll of Music, 1979-81. **CAREER:** Musician with Lionel Hampton Orchestra, 1980, Clark Terry Band, 1981, Art Blakey and the Jazz Messengers, 1981, Herbie Hancock Quartet, 1981, 1986, Wynton Marsalis Quintet, 1982-85, Sting, 1985-86, English Chamber Orchestra, 1986; recording artist, has appeared in motion pictures, including "Bring on the Night," 1985, "School Daze," 1987, "Throw Momma from the Train," 1987. **HONORS/ACHIEVEMENTS:** Grammy Award nominations, 1987, "Royal Garden Blues," 1988, for best jazz instrumental solo performance on Duke Ellington album "Digital Duke": own recordings incl "Scenes in the City," "Royal Garden Blues," "Renaissance," "Random Abstract.". **BUSINESS ADDRESS:** 3 Hastings Square, Cambridge, MA 02139. *

MARSALIS, WYNTON
Recording artist, trombonist. **EDUCATION:** Studied with John Longo; Student, New Orleans Ctr for Performing Arts, Berkshire Music Ctr, Julliard Sch Music 1979-81. **CAREER:** Trumpet soloist with New Orleans Philharmonic Orch 1975; recitalist with New Orleans orchs; with Art Blakey's Jazz Messengers from 1980; Herbie Hancock's VSOP quartet; formed own group 1981; albums include Father and Sons 1982, Wynton Marsalis (best jazz record Downbeat readers poll 1982), Think of One 1983, TrumpetConcertos 1983, Hot House Flowers 1984, Black Codes from the Underground 1985. **HONORS/ACHIEVEMENTS:** Named Jazz Musician of the Year Downbeat readers' poll 1982,84,85; best trumpet player Downbeat critics' poll 1984; Acoustic Jazz Group of Year Awd 1984; Grammy Awds for solo jazz instrumental 1984,86, for classical soloist with orchestra 1984, best trumpet player 1985, for group awd 1986.

MARSH, ALPHONSO HOWARD
Engineering manager. **PERSONAL:** Born Sep 22, 1938, Mobile, AL; son of Alphonso H Marsh and Augusta B Marsh; married June E Peterson (deceased); children: Preston, Howard, Alphonso, Van. **EDUCATION:** Howard Univ, BSEE 1961. **CAREER:** Radio Corp of Amer, electrical engineer 1961-63; General Dynamics, electrical engineer 1963-66; Rochester Inst Syst, electrical engineer 1966-67; Raytheon Co, sr engineer 1967-73; Digital Equipment Corp, project engineer 1973-77; LFE Corp, engineering mgr 1977-87; Honeywell-EOD, engr supvr 1987-. **ORGANIZATIONS:** Mem Inst of Electrical & Electronic Engrs 1960-; mem Tau Beta Pi Honor Soc 1960-; elected Town of Medway Planning Bd 1979-, chmn 1986-87; membership comm Natl Soc of Professional Engrs 1984-86; natl dir, Natl Soc of Professional Engrs 1984-; state pres MA Soc of Professional Engrs 1983-84; st PEI chmn MA Soc of Professional Engrs 1984-86; chapter pres MSPE Western Middlesex Chapter 1978-79; elected Town of Medway School Comm 1984-89; chmn MA Engrs Week Comm Proclamation 1984-; mem Constitution and Bylaws Comm Natl Soc of Professional Engrs 1986-88. **HONORS/ACHIEVEMENTS:** Reg Professional Engr State of MA 1972-; Pres Award MA Soc of Professional Engrs 1984; Serv Award MA Soc of Professional Engrs 1982, 1984; Design Awards Professional Journals, Raytheon Co 1969-; 12 articles published professional journals 1968-; Govt Citations Governor of MA & House of Representatives 1983. **BUSINESS ADDRESS:** Engineering Supervisor, Honeywell-EOD, 2 Forbes Rd, Lexington, MA 02173.

MARSH, DONALD GENE
Medical administrator. **PERSONAL:** Born Oct 12, 1936, Ft Madison, IA; married Rose E Guy; children: David, Dianne, Donna. **EDUCATION:** Parsons Coll, BS 1958; Univ of MN, Radiology 1968; Univ of IA, MD 1962. **CAREER:** Univ of MN, asst prof radiology 1968-78; St Croix Vly Hosp, chief of Radiology 1978—; NW WI Med Imaging (Mobile Nuclear Medicine & Ultrasound), pres1980-. **HONORS/ACHIEVEMENTS:** Publication Traumatic Rupture of the Aorta 1977. **HOME ADDRESS:** 6810 Kingston Cir, Golden Valley, MN 55427.

MARSH, DOUG
Professional football player. **PERSONAL:** Born Jun 18, 1958, Akron, OH. **EDUCATION:** Attended Univ of MI. **CAREER:** St Louis Cardinals, tight end 1980-.

MARSH, HENRY L., III
Attorney, government official. **PERSONAL:** Born Dec 10, 1933, Richmond, VA; married Diane Harris; children: Nadine, Sonya, Dwayne. **EDUCATION:** VA Union Univ, BS 1956; Howard Univ, LD 1959; VA Union Univ, Hon LD. **CAREER:** City of Richmond, former mayor; City of Richmond VA, councilman present; Hill Tucker & Marsh, partner, atty. **ORGANIZATIONS:** Mem US Conf of Mayors Spec Com on Decennial Census; chmn subcom on urban hwy syst US Conf of Mayors; adv bd Natl League of Cities; past pres NatlBlack Caucus of Local Elected Officials; mem Youth Task Force Natl League of Cities; chmn Income Security Com Natl League of Cities; mem Human Resources Steering Policy Com US Conf of Mayors; chmn Effective Govt Policy Com VA Municipal League; mem Judicial Council of Natl Dem Party; mem adv com State Dem party; mem Judicial Selection Comm US Court of Appeals for 4th Circuit, Alpha Phi Alpha; bd dir Voter Ed Project, Lawyers Com for Civil Rights Under Law. **HONORS/ACHIEVEMENTS:** Selected a Laureate of VA Laureate Ctr of VA 1979-80; del US Conf of Mayors to People's Repub of China 1979; hon mem US China Peoples Friendship Assoc; Outstanding Man of the Year Kappa Alpha Psi; Outstanding Mason of the Year VA; Man of the Year Alpha Phi Alpha; bldg addition named in hon of Mr Marsh GeorgeMason Elem School 1980. **BUSINESS ADDRESS:** Attorney, Hill, Tucker & Marsh, PO Box 27363, Richmond, VA 23261.

MARSH, MCAFEE
Insurance broker. **PERSONAL:** Born Aug 29, 1939, Meridian, MS; married Ruby Putmon; children: Marcellus G. **EDUCATION:** Wilson Coll; Life Underwriters Training Course, Grad; LIAMA Mgrs Sch, Grad. **CAREER:** Chicago Metropolitan Mutual Assurance Co, 1960-72; Supreme Life Ins Co, assoc agency dir vice pres 1972-79; Cosmopolitan Chamber of Commerce School of Business Mgmt, instr; Al Johnson Cadillac, 1979-80; United Ins Co, 1980-82; McAfee Marsh Ins Agency, pres, owner (represents 18 of the largest ins com-

panies in US) 1982-. **ORGANIZATIONS:** Past sec Chicago Ins Assn 1975; pres grad class LUTC 1969; asst agency dir dist mgr Natl Ins Assn; every position from salesman to vice pres Natl Ins Assn; Operation PUSH; mem Christ Universal Temple; pres Men of C.U.C. of Christ Universal Temple, Chicago IL, 1987-89. **HONORS/ACHIEVEMENTS:** Cert of Merit Chicago Assn of Commerce; The Excellence Award, Time Ins Co 1989; Pres Award & trip winner to Hawaii, Hong Kong & Tokyo 1987. **MILITARY SERVICE:** AUS 1962-64. **BUSINESS ADDRESS:** President, McAfee Marsh Insurance Agency, 2952 Polly Lane, Flossmoor, IL 60422.

MARSH, TAMRA GWENDOLYN
Insurance sales/social work. **PERSONAL:** Born Oct 08, 1946, Philadelphia, PA. **EDUCATION:** Temple Univ, BA Sociology 1972, MSW Admin 1976; Charles Morris Price School, journalism & advertising 1980. **CAREER:** Dept Public Welfare, caseworker/applications interviewer 1969-74; Delaware Co, asst comm serv coord 1975-76; YWCA Southwest Belmont Branch, branch admin1976-79; Horizon House, mgr/training consultation coord 1979-82; Arbor Inc, job develop 1984-85; Natl Liberty Corp, ins sales licensed ins sales agent1984-. **ORGANIZATIONS:** Natl promotion dir Delaware Valley Defender Newspaper; mem Amer Women in Radio & TV; publ relations chair Philadelphia Club NANBPINC Inc; finance sec Mid-Atlantic Dist Women's Clubs Inc; natl dir for youth Natl Assn of Negro Business & Professional Women 1983-85; Natl Assn of Female Executives 1985. **HONORS/ACHIEVEMENTS:** Assistantship for Graduate Study-Administration 1974-76; Comm Serv Awd Tau Gamma Delta Sor Inc 1978; State-wide and City-wide Awd for Excellence in Mental Health & Mental Retardation Serv Delivery 1981; Listed in Who's Who of Amer Women 12th & 13th editions; numerous awds for progs implementation and leadership in volunteer organizations 1979-; listed Who's Who in the East. **HOME ADDRESS:** 1225 N 53rd St, Philadelphia, PA 19131. **BUSINESS ADDRESS:** Insurance Sales/Social Work, Natl Liberty Corp, Valley Forge, PA 19493.

MARSH, WILLIAM A., JR.
Attorney. **PERSONAL:** Born Jan 31, 1927, Durham, NC; married Bernice Sawyer; children: William A, Jewel Lynn. **EDUCATION:** NC Central U, BS 1949; NC Central U, LLB 1953; NC Central U, JD 1970. **CAREER:** Self-employed, attorney; Mechanics & Farmers Bank, gen counsel; UDI-CDC Garrett Sullivan Davenport Bowie & Grant CPA's, atty. **ORGANIZATIONS:** UDI Comm Devel Corp; Found for Comm Devel; Durham Opportunities Found Inc; chmn Legal Redress Com; mem ABA; NBA; mem Durham Com on Negro Affairs; Durham Chap NAACP; Beta Phi Chpt; Omega Psi Phi; Durham C of C; NC Central Alumni Assn; Masonic Lodge; Shriners; historian NC Assn of Black Lawyers; mem NC State Bd of Elections; mem 33 degree Mason. **MILITARY SERVICE:** WWII veteran. **BUSINESS ADDRESS:** Attorney, Garrett, Sullivan, Davenport,, 203 1/2 E Chapel Hill St, PO Box 125, Durham, NC 27702.

MARSH-LOTT, FREDDIE ALEXANDER
Medical investigator. **PERSONAL:** Born Jun 15, 1949, Enterprise, MS. **EDUCATION:** Univ of WI, BA 1973; Inst of Certified Photography, COA 1975. **CAREER:** WI Dept Health & Soc Serv, asst affirmative action office 1978-80; WI Dept Natl Resources, equal oppor office 1980-82; Univ of WI, instructor 1986-; WI Dept Reg & Licensing, medical investigator 1982-. **ORGANIZATIONS:** Pres Dane County 4H 1983; exec officer State Aff Act Assm 1983; mem State Training & Devel Comm 1985; Medical Examining Bd Discipline Comm 1986. **HONORS/ACHIEVEMENTS:** Governors Orchid Awd WI State Govt 1981; Governors Proclamation WI State Govt 1984; Legislative Citation State Senate 1984; Outstanding Young American 1984;author of "Le Quartier Francais" 1986; Outstanding Young American 1986. **HOME ADDRESS:** 1624 Fordem Ave #301, Madison, WI 53704.

MARSHALL, ALBERT PRINCE
Publisher, writer, speaker. **PERSONAL:** Born Sep 05, 1914, Texarkana, TX; son of Early Marshall (deceased) and Mary L Bland Marshall (deceased); married Ruthe Helena Langley; children: Satia Yvette Marshall Orange. **EDUCATION:** Lincoln Univ MO, AB 1938; Univ of IL, BSLS 1939, MA 1953. **CAREER:** Lincoln Univ (MO), asst Librarian 1939-41; Winston-Salem State Univ, librarian 1941-50; Lincoln Univ MO, univ librarian 1950-69; Eastern MI Univ, dir of libry 1969-72; Eastern MI Univ, acting dir of library 1979-80; Eastern MI Univ, dean of academic serv 1973-77; EMU, prof emeritus 1980-; Marlan Publishers, Inc (specializing in black historical subjects), organizer and pres. **ORGANIZATIONS:** Pres Missouri State Conference of Branches, NAACP, 1953-55; Consultant Library Serv, US Off of Educ 1965-80; Consultant on Library Resources N Central Assoc 1973-80; Natl Endowment for Humanities, 1975-80; dist gov, Rotary Intl, 1977-78; state pres, NAACP, 1953-55; pres Missouri Library Assn, 1959-60; vice pres Amer Library Assn, 1971-72; Speaker and consultant in Black History; Author of Martin Luther King Jr: A Synopsis and Molders of Black Thought, 1780-1980. **HONORS/ACHIEVEMENTS:** Distinguished Alumnus, Lincoln Univ MO 1956; distinguished librarian Black Caucus, Amer Library Assn 1978, MO Library Assn 1970; Hon Griot Washtenaw Community Coll 1984; Martin Luther King Jr Award Ann Arbor Public Schools 1985; Distinguished Career Citation, Assn of College & Research Libraries 1989; The Real McCoy of Ypsilanti, Marlan Publishers 1989. **MILITARY SERVICE:** USCG seaman first class 1943-45; 5 Area Ribbons, 1 Battle Star. **HOME ADDRESS:** 1616 Gregory St, Ypsilanti, MI 48197.

MARSHALL, CALVIN BROMLEY, III
Clergyman. **PERSONAL:** Born Jun 13, 1932, Brooklyn, NY; son of Evans and Edith; married Delma Mann; children: Sharon Wallinger, Monica, Edythe, Chad. **EDUCATION:** Anderson Coll, Anderson, IN, BA 1955; Anderson Theological Sem, BD 1958; Teamer School of Religion, NC, DD 1972, LHD 1973; Grasslands Hospital, Valhalla, NY, CPC 1963-65. **CAREER:** Park St AME Zion Church, Peekskill, NY, pastor 1960-68; Cumberland Hospital, dir of Pastoral care 1972-83; Varick Mem AME Zion Church, pastor 1968-; Woodhull Medical & Mental Health Center, dir of Pastoral Care 1983-. **ORGANIZATIONS:** Adjunct prof NY Theological Sem; chrtr mem & v chmn of bd Natl Conf of Black Church Men; chief of protocol NY Conf AME Zion Church; mem of bd AME Zion Church Publishing House; mem, bd of trustees Brooklyn Public Lib; bd of trustees, New York Theological Seminary. **HONORS/ACHIEVEMENTS:** Article "Living on the Left Hand of God" Theology Today 1968, "The Black Church-It's Mission is Liberation", Black Scholar 1970. **MILITARY SERVICE:** USAF 1st lt 1951-53. **HOME ADDRESS:** 125 Fairway, Hempstead, NY 11550. **BUSINESS ADDRESS:** Pastor/Dir of Pastoral Care, Varick Mem AME Zion Ch, 806 Quincy St, Brooklyn, NY 11221.

MARSHALL, CARL LEROY
Educator. **PERSONAL:** Born Aug 23, 1914, Dayton, OH; son of M C Marshall and Lora Marshall; married Mary Ellen Jenkins; children: Betty Lewis, Donna McIntosh, Carl L Jr, Lora Marshall. **EDUCATION:** Wilberforce Univ, BS in Ed 1935; OH State Univ, MA (English) 1947, PhD (English) 1954. **CAREER:** AR AM&N Coll, asst prof & chmn English 1947-51, prof & chmn English 1954-55; Southern Univ, prof of Engl 1955-69, chmn dept 1962-69, OH State Univ, prof of English 1969-82, prof emeritus 1982-. **ORGANIZATIONS:** Life mem Modern Lang Assn; mem Coll Lang Assn; life mem Alpha Phi Alpha Frat; officer OH State Univ Retirees Assn 1983-86; mem, American Legion, 1978-. **HONORS/ACHIEVEMENTS:** Author "American Critical Attitudes toward the Fiction of W D Howells," CLAJ 1955, "Eliot's 'Sweeney Erect,'" Southern Univ Bull 1956, "Two Protest Poems by Albery Whitman," CLAJ 1975; "Albery A Whitman, a Rebellious Romantic," included in the ERIC system of the Clearinghouse on Reading & Communication Skills 1975; "In Defense of Huck Finn", Sphinx, 1986. **MILITARY SERVICE:** Army Infantry 1st lt 1941-46; Commendation 366th Inf Reg 1945. **HOME ADDRESS:** 3296 Colchester Rd, Columbus, OH 43221.

MARSHALL, CARTER LEE
Educator. **PERSONAL:** Born Mar 31, 1936, New Haven, CT; married Carol Paul; children: Wendy, Holly, Com. **EDUCATION:** Harvard, BA 1958; Yale, MD 1962; Yale, MPh 1964. **CAREER:** Coll Hospital, dir ambulatory care 1977-; NJ Medical School Coll of Medicine & Dentistry, dir ofc PRICARE prof of medicine & prev medicine 1977-; Dept Comm Med Morehouse Coll School of Medicine, prof chmn 1976-77; Mt Sinai School Medicine, prof comm med 1975-76; Mt Sinai, assoc dean 1973-76; City Univ of NY, dean for health affairs 1973-75; Mt Sinai School of Medicine, assoc prof 1969-75; Univ KS Medical School, asst prof 1967-69; New Haven Health Dept, fellow 1965; Yale Univ, 1964. **ORGANIZATIONS:** Mem Intl Med Care Com 1967-70; vis asst profUniv Antioquia Sch Med 1968; consult Hlth Serv Adminstrn 1970-71; mem Com on Minorities in Sci 1971-72; Panel on Black Sci 1972-75; consult Children's TV Workshop 1973-75; chmn Com of Helth Educ of Pub Am Coll of Preventive Med 1974; mem Hlth Adv Com 1974-76; Editorial Bd Jour of Comm Hlth Assn of Tchrs of Preventive Med 1974; Task Force on Hlth Educ of the Pub Fogarty Intl Ctr 1974-75; TaskForce on Minority Student Opprt 1976-; Hlth Care Technology Study Sect Nat Ctr for Hlth Serv Rsrch 1975-; Minority Recruitment Team Nat Ctr Hlth Serv Rsrch 1975-; Nat Air Quality Criteria Adv Com 1975; Expert Panel Hlth Educ Fogarty Ctr 1975-76; bd dir Assn of Tchrs of Preventive Med 1976-; pres Hew Haven, CT Br NAACP 1964-65; New Haven City Planning Commn 1964-65; New Haven Redevel Adv Com 1964-65; bd tsts Williston-Northampton Sch 1970-73; bd dir Am Cncl for Emigres in the Professions 1972-73. **HONORS/ACHIEVEMENTS:** Publ "Dynamics of Hlth & Disease" 1972; "Toward An Educated Hlth Consumer 1978; 43 sci publ; listed Who's Who in Am 1976-; commendation medal AUS 1967; flw Am Coll of Prev Med 1973. **MILITARY SERVICE:** AUS capt 1965-67. **BUSINESS ADDRESS:** Coll Med & Dept of New Jersey, New Jersey Med Sch, Newark, NJ 07103.

MARSHALL, CHARLENE JENNINGS
State inspector. **PERSONAL:** Born Sep 17, 1933; married Roger Leon; children: Gwendolyn, Roger Jr, Larry. **CAREER:** WV Dept of Labor, state insp 1978-; Rockwell Internat, stores attendant 1975-78; Rockwell Internat, machine operator 1963-75; United Steelworkers of Am Local 6214, recording sec 1976; Mon-Preston Labor & Council 1968-78. **ORGANIZATIONS:** Dir WV Women's Bowling Assn 1971-; chairperson Morgantown Human Rights Commn 1974-79; past vice pres NAACP Morgantown Br 1973-76. **BUSINESS ADDRESS:** WV Dept of Labor, 1900 Washington St E, Charleston, WV 25305.

MARSHALL, CHARLES H.
Physician. **PERSONAL:** Born Jun 26, 1898, Washington, DC; married Esther Tibbs; children: Charles H. **EDUCATION:** Howard U, BS 1921; MD 1924. **CAREER:** Pvt Prac, 1925-; Dept of Med Howard U, asst instr 1928-32. **ORGANIZATIONS:** Pres DC Fedn of Civic Assn 1952-54; pres Nat Med Assn 1949-50; bd dir Citiz Assn of Georgetown 1969-72; mem Jr Police & Citz Corp; bd Whipper Maternity Home; mem Mayors Com for Employment of Handicapped; met Police Boys' Club; NAACP; Rock Creek Civic Assn; mem Commr's Youth Counc; bd dir Met Police Club; bd mem Nat Capital Area Boy Scouts; v chrmn Commr's Youth Coun. **HONORS/ACHIEVEMENTS:** Kiwanian of the year Award 1974. **BUSINESS ADDRESS:** 2712 P St NW, Washington, DC 20007.

MARSHALL, CONSUELO B. (NEE ARNOLD)
Judge. **PERSONAL:** Born Sep 28, 1936, Knoxville, TN; married George E Marshall Jr; children: Michael, Laurie. **EDUCATION:** Howard Univ, BA 1958, LLB 1961. **CAREER:** City of LA, dep city attny 1962-67; Cochran & Atkins, pvt practice 1968-70; City of LA, superior ct commiss 1972-76, municipal cout judge 1976-77, superior court judge 1977-80; US Dist Court Central Dist CA, judge 1980-. **ORGANIZATIONS:** Mem Black Women Laywers Assoc, CA Women Lawyers Assoc, CA Judges Assoc; mem State Bar CA, Los Angeles Cty Bar Assoc, NAACP, Urban League, Beta Phi Sigma, Ch Religious Sci, Los Angeles Women Lawyers' Assn, Assn of Black Lawyers, Natl Assn of Women Judges; bd mem Legal Aid Found, YMCA, Beverly Hills WestLinks Inc; mem, bd dir Antioch School of Law Wash DC; mem 9th Circuit Court of Appeals Educ Comm 1984-86; faculty mem Trial Advocacy Workshop Harvard Law Sch 1984-85; mem 9th Circuit Court of Appeals Library Comm 1985-86; lecturer Continuing Legal Educ of the Bar "Discovery in Federal Court" 1986. **HONORS/ACHIEVEMENTS:** Honoree Black Women Laywers Assoc 1976; Woman of the Year Zeta Phi Beta 1977; Honoree Angeles Mesa YWCA 1977; Honoree Natl Bus & Professional Women's Club of Los Angeles 1978; Grad of the Year Howard Univ 1981; Woman of the Year for Contribs to the Improvement of Soc, The Los Angeles Sentinal 1983; Presidential Awd in Recognition for Serv and Contribs in Improving Quality of Life for Mankind, Alpha Phi Alpha 1984; Honoree, Black Amer Law Students Assn, UCLA 1985; Honoree Verbum Dei Catholic Boys High School Los Angeles 1986; Honoree Econ Equal Oppty Prog for Black History Month 1986; Ernestine Stahlhut Awd Women Lawyers Assoc of Los Angeles; Certificate Dept of Treasury Economic Equal Oppor Prog for Black History Month 1986. **BUSINESS ADDRESS:** Judge, US Dist Court Central Dist, 312 N Spring St, 155 US Courthouse, Los Angeles, CA 90012.

MARSHALL, DON A.
Physician. **PERSONAL:** Born Mar 04, 1929, Frankfort, KY; married Roumania Mason; children: Donna Marya (dec), JD; Don A Jr MD, C Angela RN. **EDUCATION:** KY St U, BS 1951, MA 1954; Meharry Med Coll, MD 1967. **CAREER:** Delco Prods (GM), med dir 1974-; KY St U, phys ed instr 1961-63; USPHS (Narcotic Farm Lexton KY), physchtrc aide 1950-56. **ORGANIZATIONS:** Mem Alpha Kappa Mu KY StUniv 1948; mem Phi

Delta KappaUniv of KY 1955; pres Gem City Med Dntl & Phrmcy Soc 1976. **BUSINESS ADDRESS:** Medical Dir, Delco Products, 2000 Forrer Blvd, Kettering, OH 45420.

MARSHALL, DONALD JAMES
Performer. **PERSONAL:** Born May 02, 1934, San Diego, CA; divorced. **EDUCATION:** San Diego City Coll, 1956-57; LA City Coll, 1958-60. **CAREER:** DJM Productions Inc, past actor/prodr pres; Bob Gist Group, Frank Silvera Thtr of Being, Thtr E Workshop, Richard Boone Repertory Co, 1960-67; Land of the Giants ABC-TV, co-star 1967-79; performed in num TV shows, features, stage shows, motion pictures. **ORGANIZATIONS:** Mem Equity, Am Fedn of TV & Radio Artists, Screen Actors Guild, Nat Acad of TV Arts & Sci; natl mem Am Film Inst; charter mem fdr Negro Actors for Action; vice pres natl mem NAACP; num cons. **HONORS/ACHIEVEMENTS:** Actor's Achvmt Award African Meth Epis Ch 1970; ABC Movie of the Week Award The Egghead on Hill 656 Aaron Spelling Prodns 1971; Black Achiever in US CA Mus of Sci & Indus 1976; num others. **MILITARY SERVICE:** AUS 1954-56.

MARSHALL, EDWIN COCHRAN
Optometrist, educational administrator. **PERSONAL:** Born Mar 31, 1946, Albany, GA; married Robin A Howlette; children: Erin C, Erika H. **EDUCATION:** IN Univ, BA/BS 1968/1970, OD 1971, MS 1979; Univ of NC, MPH 1982. **CAREER:** Natl Optometric Assn, pres 1979-81; InterAmer Univ of Puerto Rico, consultant 1982; IU Sch of Optometry, assoc prof 1977-; Cebu Drs Coll of Optometry Phillippines 1980-; Natl Optometric Assn, exec dir 1981-; Natl HBP Educ Prog, coordinating comm mem 1984-; IN Sch of Optometry, chmn dept of clinical sciences 1983-. **ORGANIZATIONS:** Life mem Kappa Alpha Psi Frat; public health exam comm Natl Bd of Examiners in Optometry 1983-; coun of academic affairs Assn of Schools and Colls of Optometry 1983-; sec Black Congress on Health Law & Economics 1985-; mem, Natl Advisory Council on Health Professions Education 1987-91; chmn, Vision Care Section, American Public Health Assn 1988-90; vice chmn, Black Congress on Health, Law & Economics 1987-89; pres, Eye Ski Inc 1986-. **HONORS/ACHIEVEMENTS:** Optometrist of the Year Natl Optometric Assn 1976; Delta Omega Natl Public Health Honor Soc 1982; Diplomate in Public Health, American Academy of Optometry 1987; Founders Award, National Optometric Assn 1987; Co-Editor: Public Health and Community Optometry, Second Edition 1989. **BUSINESS ADDRESS:** Chmn Dept of Clin Science, School of Optometry, IndianaUniv, Bloomington, IN 47405.

MARSHALL, ETTA MARIE-IMES
Educator. **PERSONAL:** Born Jul 16, 1932, Goldsboro, NC; married Lt Col Michael J Marshall; children: Cheryl S. **EDUCATION:** Bowie State Coll, BS (45 credits) 1954; Minor Fed City Coll; MD Univ, Amer Univ, George Washington Univ of DC, attended workshop seminars. **CAREER:** Math tchr 1954-84; Lamond-Riggs Civic Assoc Block Two, lt 1964; PGC Tr Assn of MD, faculty rep 1968-84; Advisory Neighborhood Commission, recording sec 1981, vice chairperson 1984, commissioner, chr gov operations 1985; ANCSA treas 1986; Orientation of New Com Committee Member 1987 MCTerrell Elem Tr. **ORGANIZATIONS:** Mem PGC Ed Assoc Inc 1954-84, NEA 1954-84, MSTA 1954-84, CEC 1964-84; leader Girl Scout Brownie Troop 107 1967; faculty rep PGC of MD 1968-84; treas Longfields Elem School PTA 1974; lt Lamond-Riggs Civic Assoc Block Two 1981-85; treas 1983, pres 1984-85 DC Chap Bowie Alumni 1983; mem NEA-R 1984, CEC-R 1985; DC Chptr Alumni membership chrmn 1986-87. **HONORS/ACHIEVEMENTS:** Plaque PGC Ed Assoc Interpersonal Com Relations 1972-84; Letter PG Bd of Ed 1984; Plaques PG Bd of Ed 1984; Plaque Family-Kings of PA 1984; Gold Watch &Chain Longfields Elem School 1984; King Family Mem 50th Reunion Shirt Lakeland, MD HS 35th Class Reunion Member of 1985 Yearbook; recd class cup letters from Mayor Barry 1986 election; congradulatory letters from city cncl members. **HOME ADDRESS:** 1014 Galloway St NE, Washington, DC 20011. **BUSINESS ADDRESS:** Commissioner 5A-02, Advisory Neighborhd Comm of 5A, Slowe School Demountable, 14th & Irving St NE, Washington, DC 20011.

MARSHALL, FRANK BRITT, III
Graphic designer, company executive. **PERSONAL:** Born Jan 18, 1943, Bronx, NY; married Katie Wynn; children: Sean, Stacey, Travis. **EDUCATION:** Newark Sch of Fine & Indsl Arts, 1962-65. **CAREER:** Park Advertising Agy, asst art dir 1969-70; Silver Burdett Textbook Pub, asso book designer 1965-69; Park Advrt Agy, asst art dir 1969-70; Chem Bank of NY,graphic designer 1970-73; GAF Corp, supr & sr graphic designer 1973-; Frank Marshall Graphic design, president. **ORGANIZATIONS:** Bd of trustees Black Art Dir Group of NY 1978-; mem Soc of Illustrators; mem Art Dir Club of NY. **HONORS/ACHIEVEMENTS:** 5 creativity awards Art Direction Mag 1977-79; 7 awards for excellence in Design Graphic USA/NY "Desi" Awards 1978; gold medal & bronze medal excellence of design Art Dir Club of NJ 1979; 3 awards for excellence in Design Advertising Club of North Jersey 1979. **MILITARY SERVICE:** AUS sp-5 1966-68. **BUSINESS ADDRESS:** President, Frank Marshall Graphic Design, 270 Park Ave So, Ste 2D, New York, NY 10010.

MARSHALL, GLORIA A. See SUDARKASA, NIARA

MARSHALL, HENRY H.
Professional football player. **PERSONAL:** Born Aug 09, 1954, Broxton, GA. **EDUCATION:** Attended Univ of MO. **CAREER:** Kansas City Chiefs, wide receiver 1976-85. **BUSINESS ADDRESS:** Wide Receiver, Kansas City Chiefs, One Arrowhead Drive, Kansas City, MO 64129.

MARSHALL, HERBERT A.
Educator. **PERSONAL:** Born Feb 17, 1916, Cleveland; married Hattie N Harrison. **EDUCATION:** VA Union U, AB 1938; Case-Western Reserve U, MA 1939; The VA Coll, DA; Carnegie-Mellon U;Univ Ghana;Univ of So CA. **CAREER:** Norfolk Unit VA U, acting dir 1940-42; Norfolk Polytechnic Coll, dept head 1945-45; Case-Western Reserve U, research assoc 1946-48; VA Union U, visiting prof 1940-45; Hampton Inst, tchr corps 1969; instruction, dir 1956-68; Norfolk State Coll, dir & prof. **ORGANIZATIONS:** Pres VA Tchrs Assn 1960-62; co-chmn VA United Negro Coll Fund 1964-65; consultant Black Studies; mem Adult Educ Assn US & VA; YMCA; NEA; VA StateCouncil Higher Edn; evaluator So Assn 1972-; Assn Higher Edn; mem Pub Library Bd; Mayor's Youth Commn; Nat Achievement Week Proj; OIC. **HONORS/ACHIEVEMENTS:** Distinguished serv award VA Tchrs Assn 1966f outstanding educator award 1969; leadership Award Lambda Omega; serv youth Award UMCA 1970; Omega man yr 1972; meritorious serv Award; silver beaver Award BSA; cit Award NCIE 1973; hon Award Student Govt Assn 1975; certificate appreciation Award AUS 1975; host & coordinator TV proj PRIDE 1972-. **BUSINESS ADDRESS:** 2401 Corprew Ave, Norfolk, VA 23504.

MARSHALL, JAMES ANDREW
Director. **PERSONAL:** Born Jun 11, 1934, Chicago, IL. **EDUCATION:** Chicago Cty Jr Coll, 1952-54; Indstrl Coll of Armed Forces, 1970; Univ of Chgo, 1955; Northwestern Univ, 1955. **CAREER:** US Army Sub Ctr, sys anlys ofcr 1960-66; Hqs Defns Subsistence Sply Ctr, chief, sys off 1961-65; Def Contract Admin Reg, Chgo, chief, sys mgmnt 1965-78; Def Sys Automation Cntr, chief, contract mgmnt 1978-81. **ORGANIZATIONS:** Mem Amer Acad of Pol & Soc Sci 1974-; mem Acad of Pol Sci 1974-75; mem brd of dir Woodlawn Comm Cntr 1972. **MILITARY SERVICE:** AUS sp4 1957-59. **BUSINESS ADDRESS:** Dir Contract Administration, Defense Systems Automation Ctr, P O Box 1605, Columbus, OH 43216.

MARSHALL, JOHN DENT
Physician. **PERSONAL:** Born Jun 13, 1946, Savannah, GA. **EDUCATION:** Savannah State Coll, BS (Cum Laude) 1968; Meharry Medical Coll, MD 1982. **CAREER:** Pfizer Labs NY, professional sales rep 1972-78; Morehouse Family Practice, resident in training 1984-86; GA Regional Mental Hospital, consultant 1984-86; Plains Health and Dental Ctr, medical dir. **ORGANIZATIONS:** Consultant Middle TN Mental Health 1983-84, Homeless Mothers & Children of Atlanta 1986; mem Amer Acad of Family Practice 1986. **HONORS/ACHIEVEMENTS:** Honoree Beta Kappa Chi Scientific Hon Soc 1967. **MILITARY SERVICE:** USAF E4 non-commissioned officer 4 yrs; Good Conduct Medal. **HOME ADDRESS:** 120 Lonnie Ln, Americus, GA 31709.

MARSHALL, JOHN DONALD
Physician. **PERSONAL:** Born Nov 23, 1921, Chicago, IL; children: John Donald, Robert Eugene, Steven Allen, Paul Andrew, Michael Bruce, Margaret Lucille. **EDUCATION:** Univ of Chicago, BS 1942; Meharry Med Coll Nashville, MD 1946. **CAREER:** Portland State U, sch bd 1965; St Vincents Hosp, Emanuel Hosp, Good Samaritan Hosp, Provident Hosp, staff 1947-70; Kansas City Gen Hosp KC, MO, residency 1947; Harlem Hosp NYC, Internship 1946. **ORGANIZATIONS:** Mem Portland Med Soc; Multnomah Co Med Soc; OR Soc 1974-; bd of med examiner State of Oregon 1978; mem NAACP; mem Urban League Portland, OR 1949; med dir Princeton Educ Testing Serv 1966; med dir CEP & CETA Portland Br 1967; med dir Nero Assos 1970; mem CAPA Frat 1940; mem NAACP Urban Laegue 1947; bd of dir Portland StateUniv United Negro Coll Fund 1965-. **MILITARY SERVICE:** AUS 1st lt 1942-47.

MARSHALL, JONNIE CLANTON
Social worker. **PERSONAL:** Born Jul 24, 1932, Memphis, TN; married Kenneth Evans Marshall (deceased); children: James Kwame. **EDUCATION:** Morgan State Coll, BA 1956; Columbia Univ Sch of Social Work, MSW 1963; Fashion Inst of Tech, attended 1974-86. **CAREER:** Retreat for Living Hartford, psych aide 1958-59; YWCA New York City, group leader 1959-61; Grant Houses Comm Ctr, supervisor & dir 1964-67; Designer of Fine Millinery, 1980-; Bd of Educ Comm on Special Educ New York City, school social worker 1967-. **ORGANIZATIONS:** Mem Alpha Kappa Alpha Sor Inc Tau Omega Chap 1954-; bd Friend of Children's Art Carnival 1968-; bd of dirs Harlem Comm Council Inc 1971-, Commonwealth Holding Co Inc 1971-; vice pres Natl Assoc of Milliners Dressmakers 1983-; instructor Harlem Fashipn Inst New York 1983-; mem fashion show coord Cottagers of Martha's Vineyard MA 1985,86. **HONORS/ACHIEVEMENTS:** Fashions have appeared in numerous fashion shows at the Black Fashion Museum, Howard Univ Alumni Fashion Show, Cottagers, Salem United Methodist Church Affairs. **HOME ADDRESS:** 470 Lenox Ave #17P, New York, NY 10037.

MARSHALL, LEONARD
Professional athlete. **PERSONAL:** Born Oct 22, 1961, Franklin, LA; son of Mr.& Mrs. Leonard Marshall, Sr.; married Annette DiNapoli. **EDUCATION:** LA State Univ, Sociology, Business Commun w/emphasis on Finance; now attending Fairleigh Dickerson Univ of Teaneck. **CAREER:** New York Giants, second round draft choice defensive end 1983-. **ORGANIZATIONS:** Natl sports chmn The Leukemia Soc in Westchester & Putnam Valley NY; work with Gary Carter on NY City Bd; work with March of Dimes, NAACP & Cystic Fibrosis. **HONORS/ACHIEVEMENTS:** Three years as a starter, an all-Amer from LSU; MVP at LSU 1983; led Giants Ded Lines 8 1/2 1984, 15 1/2 1985, 12 1/2 1986; first team All-NFL 1985, first team NFC 1985; first team All-NFC 1986; second team All-NFL 1986; NFC Defensive Lineman of the Year by NFLPA 1985; mem Pro Bowl teams 1986, 1987; finished tied for tackles each season w/55. 57/ 51 consecutively; voted as a leader among defensive lines; co-author, The End of the Line. **BUSINESS ADDRESS:** New York Giants, Giants Stadium, East Rutherford, NJ 07073.

MARSHALL, LEWIS WEST, JR.
Physician. **PERSONAL:** Born Sep 21, 1958, Washington, DC. **EDUCATION:** Morehouse Coll, BS 1979; Howard Univ Coll of Medicine, MD 1979-83. **CAREER:** Columbia Univ Coll of P&S Harlem Hosp, resident in int medicine 1983-86; Montefiore Medical Ctr, attending physician 1985-; Drs Marshall & Raymore, partner 1987-; Long Island Jewish Queens Affiliation, attending physician 1986-. **ORGANIZATIONS:** Diplomate Natl Bd of Medical Examiners 1984-; mem Amer Medical Assoc; scholarship recipient US Public Health Serv 1986-89; physician Physician Homestead New York City Health & Hospital Corp 1986-89; assoc Amer College of Physicians. **HONORS/ACHIEVEMENTS:** John B Johnson Awd in Cardiology Howard Univ 1983. **BUSINESS ADDRESS:** Attending Physician, Long Island Jewish Medical Ctr, 82-68 164th St, Jamaica, NY 11432.

MARSHALL, PAUL M.
Clergyman. **PERSONAL:** Born Aug 17, 1947, Cleveland, OH. **EDUCATION:** Univ of Dayton, BA 1969; Univ of St Michael's Coll, Toronto, ON, Canada. **CAREER:** Soc of Mary, religious bro; Formation Prog, Cincinnati Province, Soc of Mary, regional coord, 1972-74; Dayton Urban Corps City of Dayton, dir, 1970-73; Natl Urban Corps Assn, regional coord, 1972-73. **ORGANIZATIONS:** Bd dir, Natl Urban Corps Assn, 1971-73; bd dir Pub Serv Internship Programs, 1972-73; dir, bd of youth, Screen Printing Co, 1972-73; Social Action Commn, Archdiocese of Cincinnati, mem 1971-73, vice chmn 1973; chmn, Dayton Black

Catholic Caucus, 1971-73; vice chmn, Archdiocese of Cincinnati Black Catholic Caucus, 1972-73; Natl Black Catholic Clergy Caucus, mem 1970-75, bd dir 1972; Natl Comm on Urban Ministry, Notre Dame. **HONORS/ACHIEVEMENTS:** Listed in Who's Who Among Coll Students 1969. **BUSINESS ADDRESS:** 95 St Joseph St, Toronto, Ontario, Canada.

MARSHALL, PAULE BURKE
Author. **PERSONAL:** Born Apr 09, 1929, Brooklyn, NY; daughter of Samuel Burke and Ada Clement Burke; divorced 1963; children (previous marriage): Evan; married Nourry Menard, Jul 30, 1970. **EDUCATION:** Brooklyn Coll (now of City Univ of New York), BA, 1953; Hunter Coll, 1955. **CAREER:** Our World magazine, staff writer, 1953-56; Yale Univ, lecturer in creative writing, 1970—. **HONORS/ACHIEVEMENTS:** Guugenheim fellow, 1960; Rosen Award, Natl Inst Arts and Letters, 1962; Before Columbus Foundn Amer Book Award, 1984; author of Brown Girl,Brownstones, Random House, 1959, Soul Clap Hands and Sing, Atheneum, 1961, The Chosen Place, The Timeless People, Harcourt, 1969, Praisesong for the Widow, Putnam, 1983, Reena and Other STories, Feminist Press, 1983; author of teleplay based on Brown Girl, Brownstones, 1960. **BUSINESS ADDRESS:** Feminist Press, c/o Gerrie Nuccio, PO Box 334, Old Westbury, NY 11568. *

MARSHALL, PLURIA W., SR.
Professional photographer. **PERSONAL:** Born Oct 19, 1937, Houston; married Corbin Carmen; children: Pluria, Jr, Mishka Lin, Jason. **EDUCATION:** TX So U. **CAREER:** Self Employed, professional photographer; Nat Black Media Coalition, natl organizer; Operation Breadbasket of TX, exec dir 5 years; responsible for proj which produced nations First Black Franchise in Burger King Corp. **ORGANIZATIONS:** Mem TX State Adv Com US Commn on Civil Rights; treas Nat Black Media Coalition; elected chmn Nat Black Media Coalition 1975. **HONORS/ACHIEVEMENTS:** Recip outstanding ex-student Award TX SoUniv 1974; comm serv Award Nat Assn of Mkt Developers 1973f marketeer of yr Award Houston Chap NAMD 1974; commsvc award Omega Psi Phi Houston Chap 1973; others. **MILITARY SERVICE:** USAF E-3 1956-60. **BUSINESS ADDRESS:** Chairman of the Board, Natl Black Media Coalition, 38 New York Ave NE, Washington, DC 20002.

MARSHALL, PLURIA WILLIAM, JR.
Broadcasting executive. **PERSONAL:** Born Jan 17, 1962. **EDUCATION:** Clark Coll, Atlanta, GA, BS, 1984. **CAREER:** KTRE-TV, Lufkin, TX, sales/marketing, 1982, sales/accounting exec, 1983; WTBS/Turner Broadcasting, Atlanta, GA, research, 1982-83; WLBT-TV, Jackson, MS, Mgmt devel/sales, 1983-84; WLBM-TV30, Meridan, MS, station mgr/sales mgr, 1985-86, vice pres/gen mgr, 1986-. **ORGANIZATIONS:** Natl Black Media Coalition; Natl Assn of Broadcaster; Natl Assn of TV Programming Execs.

MARSHALL, REESE
Attorney. **PERSONAL:** Born Sep 03, 1942, Ft Lauderdale, FL; married Leonora Griffin; children: Dara Isabelle, Kemba Lee, Reese Evans. **EDUCATION:** Morgan State Coll, BA 1963; Howard Univ-Law, LLB 1966. **CAREER:** Jacksonville Urban League, chrmn; FL Comm on Human Relations, chrmn; FL Chapter NBA, pres; Regnl Brd of Dir-MBA, mem; Johnson & Marshall, prtnr 1971-. **ORGANIZATIONS:** Mem Kappa Alpha Psi Frat, Inc. **HOME ADDRESS:** 9100 Westlake Circle, Jacksonville, FL 32208. **BUSINESS ADDRESS:** Attorney, Law Office, 201 W Union St, Jacksonville, FL 32202.

MARSHALL, RICHARD DOUGLASS
Educator. **PERSONAL:** Born May 24, 1931; married M Bernadine Johnson. **EDUCATION:** Lincoln U, AB; Howard U, LLB; Northwestern U, Grad Sch. **CAREER:** Rutgers U, prof; Gov Nat Mortgage Assn Dept of HUD, assoc dir loans; Prudential Ins Co, sr investment analyst. **ORGANIZATIONS:** Chmn bd dir Newark Housing Devel & Rehabilitation Corp; mem Educ Com Mortgage Bankers Assn; mem Am Real Estate & Urban Economics Assn; mem Mayor's Educ Task Force; mem Am Personnel Guidance Assn; faculty adv Rho Epsilon Real Estate Fraternity; consult Urban Inst Washington, DC; consult Educ Testing SvcPrinceton, NJ; mem Beta Gamma Sigma Frat. **HONORS/ACHIEVEMENTS:** Publ numerous articles on housing & land use; author various prof publications; listed Who's Who in America 1974-75; Who's Who in East 1974-75; Who's Who in Finance & Industry. **BUSINESS ADDRESS:** Rutgers Univ, 92 New St, Newark, NJ 07102.

MARSHALL, RUSSELL LEON
Retired educator. **PERSONAL:** Born Jun 16, 1905, Topeka, KS; son of Jesse Marshall and Bessie Green Marshall. **EDUCATION:** Univ of Chicago, PhB, 1931. **CAREER:** US Post Office Chicago, postal employee 1923-60; Chicago Public Schools, teacher 1964-74; RC Church, deacon. **ORGANIZATIONS:** Volunteer & bd of dir, Friendship House, 1942-; Volunteer, Rehabilitation of Chicago 1975-80; volunteer chaplain, Cook County, Dept of Corrections, 1976-. **HONORS/ACHIEVEMENTS:** Tutor Salem House Chicago 4 Awards 1976-81; chaplain Cook Co Dept of Corr 1980; St Stephen Award, Permanent Diaconate of Chicago Archdiocese 1987. **HOME ADDRESS:** 1012 E 47th St, Chicago, IL 60653.

MARSHALL, THURGOOD
Associate justice supreme court. **PERSONAL:** Born Jul 02, 1908, Baltimore, OH; married Cecelia S Suyat; children: Thurgood, John. **EDUCATION:** Lincoln Univ, AB 1930; Howard Univ, LLD 1947, LLB 1933, LLD 1954; VA State Coll, 1948; Morgan State Coll, 1952; Grinell Coll, 1954; Syracuse Univ, 1956; NY School Social Rsch, 1956; Univ Liberia, 1960; Brandeis Univ, 1960; Univ of MA, 1962; Jewish Theol Sem, 1962; Wayne Univ, 1963; Princeton Univ, 1963; Univ of MI, 1964; Johns Hopkins Univ, 1966; Far Eastern Univ Manila, Hon Degree 1968; Victoria Univ of Wellington, 1968; Univ of CA, 1968; Univ Otago, Dunedin, New Zealand 1968. **CAREER:** Baltimore Private practice, 1933-37; NAACP, asst spec counsel 1936-38, spec counsel 1938-50, dir counsel legal def & endl fund 1940-61; US 2nd Jud Circuit, circuit judge 1961-65; US Circuit Court, solicitor gen 1965-67; US Supreme Court, justice 1967-. **ORGANIZATIONS:** Consult Constl Conf on Kenya, London 1960; rep White House Conf Youth & Children; mem Natl Bar Assoc, New York City Cty Lawyers Assoc, Amer Bar Assoc, Bar Assoc DC, Alpha Phi Alpha, Masson 33 Deg, Episcopalian Club. **HONORS/ACHIEVEMENTS:** Argued num civil rights cases; Spingarn Medal 1946; Living History Awd Rsch Inst. **BUSINESS ADDRESS:** Justice, US Supreme Court, Washington, DC 20543.

MARSHALL, THURGOOD, JR.
Legislative assistant. **PERSONAL:** Born Aug 12, 1956, New York, NY; son of Thurgood Marshall and Cecilia S Marshall; married Colleen P Mahoney, Sep 24, 1983; children: Thurgood William Marshall III. **EDUCATION:** Univ of Virginia, BA, 1978; Univ of Virginia School of Law, JD, 1981. **CAREER:** Judge Barrington D Parker, Washington DC, law clerk, 1981-83; Kaye Scholer Fierman Hays & Handler, Washington DC, attorney, 1983-85; Senator Albert Gore Jr, Washington DC, counsel & staff dir, 1985-87, deputy campaign mgr, 1987-88; Senate Judiciary Committee, Senator Edward M Kennedy, counsel, 1988-. **ORGANIZATIONS:** Amer Bar Assn; District of Columbia Bar; Bars of the US District Court for the District of Columbia and the Second Circuit Court of Appeals; mem, Commn for the Advancement of Policy Affecting the Disadvantaed, 1978-80; bd mem, Fed Bar Assn, DC Chapter, 1984-86. **HONORS/ACHIEVEMENTS:** Pres, Univ of Virginia Student Legal Forum, 1980-81; semifinalist, Lile Moot Court Competition, 1981; co-author, The Sony Betamax Case, Computers & The Law, 1984; contributing editor, The Nicaragua Elections: A Challenge of Democracy, 1989. **BUSINESS ADDRESS:** Counsel, US Senate Judiciary Committee, 520 Dirksen Senate Office Building, Washington, DC 20510-6275.

MARSHALL, TIMOTHY H.
Consultant, ethnomusicologist. **PERSONAL:** Born Dec 08, 1949, Aiken Co, SC. **EDUCATION:** Lone Mtn Coll San Francisco, BA 1974; Lone Mtn Coll San Francisco, Grad Studies. **CAREER:** Nat United Com to free Angela Davis & all Pol Prisoners Communications Fund raising, natl staff mem 1971-72; The Black Scholar Speakers Bureau, natl dir; Black World Foundation The Black Scholar, promotional dir 1973-74; Comm Lieson Cinema Lone Mountain Coll San Francisco, promotional coord 1974-. **ORGANIZATIONS:** Creator-director "In Concert for Angela 1972; mem Black Expo Concert Prod Staff 1972; prof musician Episcopal Diocese Augusta, GA 1970-71; musical dir "Jr League Follies" Extravaganza 1970; mem Black World Foundation; Afro-Am Music Opportunites Assn; Nat Alliance Against Racist & Pol Repression; Inst BlackWorld; African-Am Historical & Cultural Soc; founder & pres Black Students Union Agusta Coll 1968-69; Nat Coordinator Elayne Jones Defense Com; founding mem pres & min affairs Progressive Black Organization 1967-70. **HONORS/ACHIEVEMENTS:** Exclusive interview with James Baldwin France 1973; published The Blak Scholar Black History Issue 1974; Investigative Research Berlin 1973; silver ring presented by Loatian Delegation; fraternal pin deleg Guinea Bissau Africa 1973; outstanding service trophy Laney HS Agusta, GA 1968; Omega Psi Phi Scholarship 1967; Augusta Chronical Newspaper Gold Plaque 1966-67. **BUSINESS ADDRESS:** Box 6285, C/o KEAL, San Francisco, CA 94101.

MARSHALL, WARREN
Association executive. **PERSONAL:** Born Mar 07, 1922, Mobile City, AL; married Genevieve L Garner; children: Braden, Cynthia, Verda. **EDUCATION:** Psychol Long IslUniv Brooklyn, BS 1952; Columbia U, MA 1963; ColumbiaUniv Tchrs Coll, Attending. **CAREER:** City School Dist of NY; bd of edn; Bureau for child with retarded mental devel, supvr; USAF Rome & NY, civ 1943; US Maritime Serv, 1943-46; Natl Maritime Union CIO, 1942-65; US Post Office, 1948, 1959-62; Bd of Educ Newark, teacher 1956-58; Bd of Educ Englewood, NJ, teacher 1958-59; Bd of NY, teacher 1959-66; Methodist Church Manokin, MD, pastor 1956; E Shore Chs of Meth Ch, other. **ORGANIZATIONS:** Prof mem Assn for CRMD; Assn for Help of Retarded Child; United Fedn of Tchrs; NY United Tchrs; NEA; AFT; AFL-CIO 1947-57; educ consult pres Borough of Manhattan; St John #29 F & AM; pres Caribbean Voca Educ Fudn Inc; reg dir reg 2 Assn for Study of Afro-am Life & Hist; educ consult West Educ Sym Orch. **HONORS/ACHIEVEMENTS:** Eli Tractenberg Award UFT 1964; Smallheiser Award UFT 1966; spl hon Award NY Br Assn for Study of Afro-am Life & Hist; spl serv Award SW Harlem Addict Serv Agcy; sev Award Dist 20k1 Kings & Queens of Emp State Lions. **MILITARY SERVICE:** AUS pfc psy tech 1946-47. **BUSINESS ADDRESS:** 65 Court St, Brooklyn, NY.

MARSHALL, WILBER
Professional athlete. **PERSONAL:** Born Apr 18, 1962, Titusville, FL. **EDUCATION:** FL Univ, attended. **CAREER:** Chicago Bears, professional linebacker 1984-. **HONORS/ACHIEVEMENTS:** Lombardi Awd Finalist; honors incl, AP, UPI, NEA, Football Coaches, Walter Camp 1stTeam All-Amer; was only jr among 12 finalists for Lombardi Awd; selected 1st team All-Amer by Parade Mag & Natl HS Athletic Coaches; All-Southern Player-of-the-Year & Acad All-Amer as sr; mem 1987 NFL Pro Bowl team. **BUSINESS ADDRESS:** Chicago Bears, Halas Hall, Lake Forest, IL 60045.

MARSHALL, WILLIAM HORACE
Actor. **PERSONAL:** Born Aug 1924, Gary, IN; son of Vereen Marion Marshall, DDS and Thelma Edwards. **EDUCATION:** Chicago Art Inst; Art Students League NY; Amer Theatre Wing NY; Observer Actors Studio NY; Master Class Lee Strasberg UCLA; studied mime with Etienne Descroux; studied voice with J Scott Kennedy, Abby Mitchell, Emma Otero, Gladys Lee & Alan Greene in NY, Jeanne Filon in Paris, & Robert Sellon in Los Angeles; studied French language & civilization at the Alliance Francaise in Paris; studied blues with Hazel Scott; Governors State Univ IL, BA 1978; Golden State Univ CA, PhD Theatre Arts 1983. **CAREER:** Busboy; steelworker; commercial artist; longshoreman; Harlem YMCA, prog dir; appeared in numerous stages plays including Carmen Jones, Lost in the Stars, Peter Pan, The Green Pastures, Oedipus Rex, Othello, Time To Go, Toys In the Attic, The Bear & the Marriage Proposal, When We Dead Awaken; numerous motion pictures including Lydia Bailey, Demetrius & the Gladiators, Shelia; TV guest star include Bonanza, Rawhide, Ben Casey, Star Trek, Tarzan; in London The Green Pastures, Interpol, the Magic Ring; dir 1st English Language production of The Tragedy of King Christophe 1970; CA State Northridge Smithsonian Inst, A Ballad for Americans as a tribute to Paul Robeson 1986; Enter Frederick Douglass, Smithsonian Inst (one man 2 act play with spirituals). **HONORS/ACHIEVEMENTS:** Composer Gospel & Poetry; US Tour with Mahalia Jackson 1966; Poetry & Prose of Black Writers with UGMAA Watts Music Group at Univ CA LA 1968; Benjamin J Hooks Distinguished Achievement Award NAACP 1983; Roy Wilkins Award NAACP 1983; Hon Degree of Doctor of Human Serv Univ Without Walls 1984. **BUSINESS ADDRESS:** Actor, Teacher, Lecturer, Devel of Black Heritage Drama, 11351 Dronfield Ave, Pacoima, CA 91331.

MARSHALL, WILLIAM T.
Corporate director. **PERSONAL:** Born Jul 17, 1935, Beloit, WI; children: Cynthia, Christopher, Dawn, William. **EDUCATION:** Gov StUniv Forest Park S IL, BA human serv 1976; Fielding Inst Santa Barbara, MA cinical psychol 1980; Fielding Inst Santa Barbara, PhD pendind 1981. **CAREER:** Inst for Advancement In Human Serv Inc, exec dir found 1978-; Central City Comm Mental Health Center, dir substance abuse serv 1976-78; Westland

Health Serv Inc, dir substance abuse training 1974-78; Westland Health Serv Inc, dir marketing 1972-74; Watts Writers Workshop, founder dir 1966-68. **ORGANIZATIONS:** Vchmn LA Co Narcotic & Dangerous Drugs Commn 1976-; consult Nat Inst on Drugs Abuse HEW 1979-; mem Assn Balck Spychol; founder bd Of dir Mafundi Inst 1966-76; sec bd of dir Frederick Douglass Child Devel Ctr 1964-; pres bd of dir Watts Cable Communication Assn 1972-76. **HONORS/ACHIEVEMENTS:** Commendation for the film prodn "Johnny Gigs Out" & "Angry Voices of Watts" 1967-68; publ "Prgm Graduates in a Quandry" 1977; fundamental considerations forTraining Substance Abuse Profls 1978; Who's Who in Am Coll &Univ 1979-80; various serv awds.

MARTIN, AMON ACHILLES, JR.
Dentist. **PERSONAL:** Born May 21, 1940, Anderson, SC; married Brenda Watts; children: Jocelyn, Amon III, Theodore. **EDUCATION:** Fisk Univ, BA; Howard Univ, DDS. **CAREER:** USAF, dentist; BMH Devel Real Estate. **ORGANIZATIONS:** Member, Amer Dental Assn, Natl Dental Assn, Palmetto Medical Dental & Pharmaceutical Assn, Omega Psi Phi Inc; past pres, Anderson Dental Soc; member advisory bd, Amer Federal Bank; member bd of visitors, Clemson Univ 1984-86. **MILITARY SERVICE:** USARF ltc. **BUSINESS ADDRESS:** Dentist, 208 N Walnut, Seneca, SC 29678.

MARTIN, ANGELA M. COKER
Government professional. **PERSONAL:** Born Jun 02, 1953, Baltimore, MD. **EDUCATION:** Morgan State Univ, BS 1975; The OH State Univ, MS 1976; Univ of Dayton, MBA 1984. **CAREER:** Enoch Pratt Library, traveling info/retrieval agent 1977-78; Rehab Serv Commn, vocational rehab counselor 1979-80, personnel officer 1980-83, EEO Supvr, 1983-85; Mass Transit Admin, EEO officer 1986-. **ORGANIZATIONS:** Acting pres 1982-83, vice pres programs 1983-84 Amer Soc for Personnel Admin (Franklin Univ Chapt) 1980-86; mem Assoc of MBA Execs 1984-86; asst sec Conf of Minority Transportation Officials 1986-87; mem Natl Black MBA Assoc 1986-87, NAACP 1986-87. **HONORS/ACHIEVEMENTS:** Departmental Honor Scholar Morgan State Univ 1974-75; Minority Master's Fellowship OH State Univ 1975-76. **BUSINESS ADDRESS:** EEO Officer, Mass Transit Administration, 300 W Lexington St, Baltimore, MD 21201.

MARTIN, ANNIE B.
Association executive. **PERSONAL:** Born Dec 20, 1925, South Carolina. **EDUCATION:** AllenUniv Columbia, SC, BA; NY U, MSW; Cornell Rutgers PA State U, Cert Labor Edn. **CAREER:** NY State Dept Labor, asst indsl commr 1972-; Cornell U, sr extension asso; Fordham U, asst adjunct prof; ER Squibb & Sons Brooklyn, chem. **ORGANIZATIONS:** Mem Intl Assn Personnel Employment Security; New York City Guidance Adv Coun; Am Assn Univ Women; chmn NY State Advisory Coun Voc Edn; Soroptimist; charter mem 1st vice pres Black Trade Unionists Ldrship Com New York City Cent Labor Coun AFL-CIO; bd dirs NY Lung Assn; exec bd New York City Cent Labor Council AFL-CIO; life mem Nat Coun Negro Women; NAACP; Bethel AME Ch. **HONORS/ACHIEVEMENTS:** Comm serv award New York City Cent Labor Coun 1961; dist serv award 1971; woman of yr NY Brn NAACP 1976; award of merit Black Trade Unionists Ldrshp Com 1977; NY City Central Labor Cncl AFL-CIO; awards in Black 1973; woman of yr award Priv Voc Schs 1973. **BUSINESS ADDRESS:** Rm 7384, 2 World Trade Cntr, New York, NY 10047.

MARTIN, ARNOLD LEE, JR.
Health services administrator. **PERSONAL:** Born Jan 10, 1939, Hartford, CT; married Mary Remona Garner; children: Zena Monique, Arnold Lee III. **EDUCATION:** Attended, FBI Natl Acad 1981; New Hampshire Coll, BS 1983. **CAREER:** Hartford Police Dept, chief's advisor 1962-83; WTIC 1080 Corp, chmn adv comm 1974-82; American Red Cross Hartford, bd of dirs 1975-84, exec dir 1986-. **ORGANIZATIONS:** Chmn Project 90 US Navy Recruiting Team 1974-75; bd dir NAACP 1975; 1st vice pres CT Assoc Police Comm Rel Off 1979-81; mem Hartford Hosp Public Relations Bd 1981-83; 1st vice pres West Hartford Lions Club 1982; mem Urban League 1982; rhetoricos Sigma Pi Phi Frat 1985-; pres Alpha Phi Alpha Frat 1986-. **HONORS/ACHIEVEMENTS:** Hartford Man of the Month CT Mutual Life Ins Co 1974; Outstanding Serv Awd march of Dimes 1977; US Air Force Commendation Medal Westover AFB 1980; Lions Intl Dist Gov Serv Awd 1980; Director's Awd FBI Natl Academy 1981; Chairman's Awd Amer Red Cross 1984; Hartford Guardians Outstanding Community Serv Awd 1985. **MILITARY SERVICE:** AUS Reserve sgt 1st class 3 yrs; Non-Commissioned Officers Achievement Ribbon 1987. **HOME ADDRESS:** 626 Park Rd, West Hartford, CT 06107.

MARTIN, BARON H.
Judge, attorney. **PERSONAL:** Born Sep 14, 1926, Boston. **EDUCATION:** Suffolk U, AA BA JD;Univ of Chicago Exec Mgmt Training, 1972. **CAREER:** Wareham Dist Ct, judge; Comm of MA, former spl justice; Comm of MA, spl asst atty gen 1972; asst gen counsel 1973; sr atty; 1970; MA Bay Transp Authority, clerk 1951; MA Bay Transp Authority, atty 1958. **ORGANIZATIONS:** Mem MA Bar Assn; Am Bar Assn; MA Trial Lawyers; Am Judges Assn; Admitted to US Dist Ct 1959; US Supreme Ct 1966f Am Jud Soc; Intl Acad Law & Sci; mem Urban League; NAACP; chmn Dem Ward Com 1950-64; alternate delegate Dem Nat Conv 1968. **HONORS/ACHIEVEMENTS:** Recip Alpha Phi Alpha Sigma Chtp Outstanding Achievement 1948. **BUSINESS ADDRESS:** Wareham Dist Court, West Wareham, MA 02756.

MARTIN, BASIL DOUGLAS
Doctor of dental surgery. **PERSONAL:** Born Oct 18, 1941, Roanoke, VA; son of Basil Martin and Amanda Martin; married Geneva Gail Allen; children: Basil D Jr, Shoan Beaufort Orell. **EDUCATION:** Central State Univ, BS 1963; Meharry Medical Coll, DDS 1969; Baltimore City Hospitals, Johns Hopkins Univ, Univ of MD, Certificate Oral Surgery; New York Univ, Certificate Orthodontics. **CAREER:** Private Practice, doctor of dental surgery. **ORGANIZATIONS:** Worshipful master Mason 32nd F&AM of PA 1979-87; bd mem YMCA 1979-86; consistory 32nd Position Sublime Prince Pitsburgh St Cyprian #4 1982-87; shriner Pittsburgh Sahara #2 1982-87; mem Chamber of Commerce 1987; Omega Psi Phi Fraternity 1961. **HONORS/ACHIEVEMENTS:** Publication "The Canadian Geese - Spirocete-Patuxent," Dept of Int 1963-65; clinical instructor, Pittsburgh Univ School of Dental Medicine 1974-75. **BUSINESS ADDRESS:** Doctor of Dental Surgery, Ofcs of Dr Basil D Martin, 625 Washington Trust Bldg, Washington, PA 15301.

MARTIN, BERTHA M.
Pediatric dentist. **PERSONAL:** Born Apr 05, 1928, Pulaski, TN; divorced; children: Beryl. **EDUCATION:** Howard Univ, BS 1947, DDS 1951; Holyoke Hosp, Internship 1951-52; Univ of MI, Cert, Pediatric Dentistry 1955-56. **CAREER:** Berkley, CA, private practice 1959-62; Los Angeles, CA, dental consultant 1963-66; Washington, DC, pediatric dentist 1966-. **ORGANIZATIONS:** Amer Dental Assn; Amer Acad of Pediatric Dentistry; Alpha Kappa Alpha Sor; DC Dental Society; Robert T Freeman Dental Society; Amer Society of Dentistry for Children; St Mark's Church; bd of trustees, Dean Junior College, Franklin Massachusetts 1988-91; bd of advisors, Burgundy Farm Country Day School, Alexandria, Virginia, 1987-93. **BUSINESS ADDRESS:** Dentist, Private Prac HowardUniv, 3230 Pennsylvania Ave SE, Washington, DC 20020.

MARTIN, BLANCHE
Dentist. **PERSONAL:** Born Jan 16, 1937, Millhaven, GA; divorced; children: Gary, Steven, Michael. **EDUCATION:** MI St U, BS 1959;Univ of Detroit, DDS 1967. **CAREER:** Self Emp, dentist. **ORGANIZATIONS:** Mem MI StUniv bd of trsts 1969-76, 77-84; chmn bd 1975-76; mem Am Den Assn; MI Den Assn; Cen Dist Den Asso 1969-76 & 77-84; past mem River Rouge Youth Commn; mem bd of deacons Pentecostal Miss Baptist Ch; Omicron Kappa Upsilon Nat Den Hon 1967. **HONORS/ACHIEVEMENTS:** Recpt award for excel in Gen Dent. **BUSINESS ADDRESS:** 201 1/2 E Grand River, East Lansing, MI 48823.

MARTIN, CARL E.
Government official. **PERSONAL:** Born Feb 14, 1931, Birmingham, AL; married Patricia; children: Ennis, Joel, Carla, Dana. **EDUCATION:** Miles Coll, BA 1953; Pepperdine U, MPA 1973; LA Coll of Law, JD 1978. **CAREER:** LA Co Human Relat Commn, exec dir; CA Youth Auth, grp supr; CA Youth Auth, parole agt; LA Co Probation Dept, sr dep prof ofcr; LA Inglewood Culver City Duarte Sch Dist, cons;Univ of So CA UCLA CA State Univ Sys, cons. **ORGANIZATIONS:** Bd of dirs Econ & Youth Opptys Agy; pres Fedn of Black History & Arts Inc; bd of dir HELM Schlrshp Found; bd of dir RAKESTRAW Educ & Comm Ctr Wesley United Meth Ch; mem Employ Devel Com LA Urban League; bd of dir Westminster Neighborhood Assn. **HONORS/ACHIEVEMENTS:** Num awards from orgns in Grtr LA areas. **MILITARY SERVICE:** AUS sp-4 1953-55. **BUSINESS ADDRESS:** 320 W Temple St, 1184 Hall of Records, Los Angeles, CA 90012.

MARTIN, CAROL (FRANCES MARTIN)
Reporter. **PERSONAL:** Born Jul 15, 1948, Detroit, MI. **EDUCATION:** Wayne State U, BA 1970. **CAREER:** WCBS-TV, NY, gen assignment news correspondent 1975-; WMAL-TV, Washington, DC, gen assignment reporter 1973-75; Detroit Free Press, ed features dept, feature writer 1971-73; WWJ-TV, Detroit, dept asst public affairs 1970-71. **ORGANIZATIONS:** Mem Amer Fed of TV & Radio Artists; US Sen & House of Representatives Radio/TV Gallery; mem adv bd Natl Child Day Care Assn 1974-75. **HONORS/ACHIEVEMENTS:** Wayne State Univ Scholarship for Academic Achievement 1966-70. **BUSINESS ADDRESS:** C/O WCBS-TV, 524 W 57th St, New York, NY 10019.

MARTIN, CAROLYN ANN
Educator. **PERSONAL:** Born Aug 14, 1943, Versailles, MO. **EDUCATION:** Lincoln Univ of MO, BS Phys Ed, Psych 1968; CA State Polytech Univ Pomona, MS 1974; Univ of CA Riverside, Grad Courses 1969-72. **CAREER:** Lincoln Univ of MO Dept of Phys Ed, teaching asst 1964-68; Perris High School Dist, instructor phys ed 1968-78, phys ed teacher, nursing women's athletic dir 1968-74; Perris Jr HS, chmn phys ed 1970-74; CA State Univ Summer Upward Bound, recreation coord 1976; San Bernardino HS head coach women's varsity softball 1981-84; CA State Univ Univ, associate prof phys ed 1974-. **ORGANIZATIONS:** Mem Amer Alliance of Health, CA Teachers Assoc, CA Faculty Assoc, Natl Bowling Council, Natl Assoc for Sport & Phys Ed, Natl Assoc of Girls & WomensSports, CA Assoc of Black Faculty & Staff, Natl Strength Training Assoc; pres CA Assoc Health Phys Ed Recreation & Dance 1973-74, 1979-80; rsch "The Personality Characteristics of Black Female HS Athletes"; sec Delta Kappa Gamma; selected by State School Supt Wilson Riles to serva as mem of State Task Force on Athletic Inuries 1976-77; arbitrator BBB; pres 3 Sports Inc 1977-; proj ace coord for Amer Alliance for Health Phys Ed Rec & Dance 1979; pres CA Faculty Assoc; mem Natl Girls & Womens Speedball Guide Comm 1980-82; "Teaching Blind Students to Bow" 1981-83; "Playing the Net Aggressively" 1979; chmn Natl Girls & Womens Sports Speedball Guide Comm 1982-84; editor Natl Girls & Womens Sports Speedball Rules Publ 1982-84; bd mem San Bernardino Sexual AssaultServ Ctr 1983-84; mem Joint Comm of Amer Assoc of Leisure & Rec, Amer Alliance for Health Phys Ed Rec & Dance Natl Assessment of Elem School Playgrounds 1985. **HONORS/ACHIEVEMENTS:** Publ Workbook, Fundamentals of Basketball Officiating 1978, Games Contests & Relays 1981, Teaching Softball 1985; Softball Coach of the Year Perris HS 1970;Teacher of the Year 1973; Perris Jr HS Teacher of the Year 1973; Teacher's Advocate Awd San Bernardino Teachers Assoc 1974; Kiwanis Intl of San Bernardino Cert of Appreciation 1976; Mini Grant Awd CA State Univ Comm on Improvement of & Innovations in Ed 1978,80; San Bernardino Affirm Action Fac Devel Awd State Univ 1981. **BUSINESS ADDRESS:** Professor of Physical Ed, California StateUniv, 5500 University Pkwy, San Bernardino, CA 92407.

MARTIN, CHARLES EDWARD, SR.
Association executive. **PERSONAL:** Born Aug 03, 1943, Jackson, TN; married Paricia Ann Johnson; children: Charles Jr, Jenell, Rodrick. **EDUCATION:** Ball State Univ Muncie, BS Social Science, 1967; Bin Univ South Bend, 30 hrs towards MS. **CAREER:** YMCA Met S Bend, exec dir 1972-; YMCA Met S Bend, youth dir 1970-72; S Bend Com Sch Corp, teacher coach 1967-70. **ORGANIZATIONS:** Pres IN Chap YMCA Assn of Professional Dir 1978f pres Big Bros/Big Sisters 1975-76; chmn CETA Adv Coun 1979; bd of dir Urban League of St Joseph Co 1979-. **HONORS/ACHIEVEMENTS:** Outst young men of Am 1974; outst achvmt Kappa Alpha Psi 1975; com serv award Urban League 1975; prince hall freedom award Most Worshipful Prince Hall Grand Lodge Juris of IN 1976. **BUSINESS ADDRESS:** Executive Dir, YMCA Community Service Branch, 1201 Northside Blvd, South Bend, IN 46615.

MARTIN, CLARENCE L.
Attorney. **PERSONAL:** Born Sep 05, Baxley, GA; married Annie D; children: Anthony L, Bernard E. **EDUCATION:** Savannah St Coll, BS (cum laude) 1970; Emory U,; Notre Dame Law Sch, 1973. **CAREER:** City of Savannah, asst city atty, judge pro temporo recorders court; C & S Bank,; SS Kresge Co,; Hill, Jones & Farrington,; Whitcomb & Keller

Mortgage Co,; Martin, Thomas & Bass PC, attorney. **ORGANIZATIONS:** Mem Savannah, Georgia & Amer Bar Assocs; mem NAACP; Operation Push. **HONORS/ACHIEVEMENTS:** Martin Luther King Fellow Woodrow Wilson Fnd. **MILITARY SERVICE:** USAF staff sgt 1962-67. **BUSINESS ADDRESS:** Attorney, Martin, Thomas & Bass PC, 109 W Liberty St, Savannah, GA 31402.

MARTIN, CORNELIUS A.
Chief executive. **CAREER:** Martin Olsmobile-Cadillac-Subaru-Isuzu, Bowling Green, KY, chief exec, 1985-. **BUSINESS ADDRESS:** Martin Oldsmobile-Cadillac-Subaru-Isuzu, 2201 Scottsville Rd, Bowling Green, KY 42101. *

MARTIN, CORTEZ HEZEKIAH
Educator. **PERSONAL:** Born Jul 25, 1935, Jacksonville, FL; married John Timothy Martin; children: Sonijia, Latacha. **EDUCATION:** Tenn A&I Univ, BS 1955, MS 1957; Howard Univ, MSW 1980, Doctor of Social Work 1984. **CAREER:** 18th Ave Comm Center, program dir 1955-57; Tenn A&I State Univ, instructor, social work 1956-57; Edward Waters Coll, instructor, soc sci; Memphis City Schools, teacher, counselor, school social worker 1959-78; Comm Action Agency, eval coord, program dir 1967-70; US Dept of Agriculture, student intern, co-project mgr 1978-81; Howard Univ Sch of Soc Work, grad assist 1981-82; Congressman Harold E Ford, staff assist 1982-83; US Dept Health & Human Svcs, evaluator/reviewer 1984; Lemoyne-Owen Coll, assoc prof of rsch social sci dept. **ORGANIZATIONS:** Member Memphis Ed Assn 1960-78; member Natl Ed Assn 1960-78; member Tenn Ed Assn 1960-78; member Alpha Kappa Alpha Sorority 1972-; treasurer (Grad Chapter Tenn A&I Univ) 1972-74; Natl Assn of Social Workers 1978-; Natl Assn of Black Social Workers 1978-; Ford's Foundation Assn 1983-; bd of dirs, Porter Leath Children's Center, 1984-; res team, Free-the-Children. **HONORS/ACHIEVEMENTS:** Trustee Scholarship Award Howard Univ 1978-82; The Dean's List Honor Society Howard Univ 1978-82; Natl Institute of Mental Health Doctoral Training Grant 1981-82; Alumni Student Doctoral Rep Committee, Howard Univ 1981; Community Services Award, St Joseph's Hospital, 1988; editorial bd, Social Science Assn, 1988; author, "The Lack of Communication within the Office of Safety & Health, DA," 1980, "The Relationship Between the Level of Self Concept and Drinking Patterns of Black Youth" Dec 1984; co-author, "The Role of Top Management in the Implementation of the US Dept of Agriculture Employee Assistance Program," 1979; author, "Mary Had a Baby and Don't Know How She Got It," 1989; author, "Family Violence: Please Tell She Hit Me: Husband Abuse," 1989. **BUSINESS ADDRESS:** Lemoyne-Owen College, 807 Walker Ave, Memphis, TN 38126.

MARTIN, CURTIS JEROME
Educator. **PERSONAL:** Born Nov 16, 1949, Kansas City, MO; married Valerie Joy Smith. **EDUCATION:** USAF Acad, BS Humanities 1967-71; MI St U, MA Eng 1975-76. **CAREER:** USAF Acad Activties Grp, chief congr liaison br 1980-; USAF Acad, asst prof of Eng 1976-80; Lowry Air Force Base Denver, dir drug/alcohol abuse prgm1972-75; USAF Acad CO, asst ftbll coach 1971-72. **ORGANIZATIONS:** Mem Nat Counc of Tchrs of Eng 1975-; course dir Blk Lit, Minority Lit, African Lit USAF Acad Eng Dept 1978-80; acad liaison ofcr mem USAF AcadWay of Life Com 1976-80; alcohol abuse rehab couns SW Denver Mntl Hlth Ctr 1973-74; parliamentarian Lowry AFB Chap Brthrhd Assn for Blk Svcmn & Svcwmn 1973-75; mem Aurora CO Drug Alcohol Abuse Counc 1973-75; Spkrs Bur Lowry AFB 1973-75; Spkrs Bur USAF Acad 1976-80. **HONORS/ACHIEVEMENTS:** Outst yng man of Am US Jaycees 1977; dist grad Squadron Ofcr Sch Maxwell AFB 1978; jr ofcr of yr USAF Acad Faculty 1979; recip Clements award "MilEducator of Yr" USAF Acad 1980; recip of Cmmndtn Medal USAF 1975. **MILITARY SERVICE:** USAF capt 1971-. **BUSINESS ADDRESS:** HQ USAF/MPPA Pentagon, Washington, DC 20330.

MARTIN, DANIEL E.
Attorney. **PERSONAL:** Born Apr 14, 1932, Bluffton, SC; married Ruby N; children: Daniel Jr, Max Maurice. **EDUCATION:** Allen Univ, BS Health & Phys Educ 1954; SC State Coll, JD 1966. **CAREER:** Wallace HS, phys educ dept 1959-62; Gresham Meggett HS, math tchr 1962-63; Neighborhood Legal Asst Prog, dir 1968-72; 9th Jud Circuit, asst solicitor First Black; SC House of Rep, mem judicial committee. **ORGANIZATIONS:** Mem ABA, SC Bar Assn, Charleston Co Bar Assn, Judges Selection Com for sTate of SC only Black lawyer; mem Gov Energy Commn; mem State Bd of Voc REhab US Tax Ct; US Ct Customs & Patent Appeals; Fed Dist Ct Dist of SC; US Supreme Ct Trustee Emanuel AME Ch; mem turst bd Allen Univ; mem Neimiah Lodge #51 Free & Accepted Masons; charter mem Choraliers Music Club. **HONORS/ACHIEVEMENTS:** Alpha Phi Alpha Frat Scroll of Honor Omega Psi Phi frat 1969; Cert of Achieve Alpha Phi Alpha Frat 1970; Cert of Apprec Charleston Sym Assn 1970; Dist Serv Awd Alpha Phi Alpha Frat 1973; Apprec Awd Clara D Hill Mission Club 1974; Apprec Awd BSA 1974; Juris Prudence Achieve Awd Omega Psi Phi Frat 1974. **MILITARY SERVICE:** AUS corpl 1955-57. **BUSINESS ADDRESS:** Attorney, 61 Morris St, Charleston, SC 29403.

MARTIN, DAVID CALVIN
Professional athlete. **PERSONAL:** Born Mar 15, 1959, Philadelphia, PA. **EDUCATION:** Villanova, BA Communications 1981. **CAREER:** Denver Gold, cornerback 1982-. **HONORS/ACHIEVEMENTS:** Number one punt returner in USFL 1983; named to first team All-USFL as both cornerback & punt returner; Pro Football Weekly first team cornerback & punt returner; Sporting News first team selection as cornerback; voted first team All-USFL punt returner; second team selection as cornerback; Pro Football Weekly All-USFLcornerback & punt returner; Sporting News All-USFL choice as a cornerback and punt returner; All-USFL punt returner by College & Pro Football Newsweekly; Assoc Press All-Am.

MARTIN, DERRICK
Professional athlete. **PERSONAL:** Born May 31, 1957, Los Angeles, CA. **EDUCATION:** San Jose State. **CAREER:** Oakland Invaders, cornerback. **HONORS/ACHIEVEMENTS:** Named 2nd team All-PCAA as cornerback.

MARTIN, DOUG
Professional athlete. **PERSONAL:** Born May 22, 1957, Fairfield, CA; married Audrey. **CAREER:** MN Vikings, defensive end/tackle 1980-.

MARTIN, D'URVILLE
Performer. **PERSONAL:** Born Feb 11, 1939, New York, NY; married Lillian Ferguson; children: Jacques, Kala. **CAREER:** Producer dir actor over 36 Maj TV shows 16 Films; most recent The Omen, The System Shady Lady Disco 9000. **ORGANIZATIONS:** Mem Black Businessman's Assn of Atlanta; chmn Am Cancer Soc; bd of dir DiscO 9000. **HONORS/ACHIEVEMENTS:** Hon citizen of Tusckeke. **BUSINESS ADDRESS:** 1101 S Alfred St, Los Angeles, CA 90035.

MARTIN, EDWARD
Clergyman. **PERSONAL:** Born Jun 30, 1936, Grove Hill, AL; divorced. **EDUCATION:** AL State U, BS 1969; Carver Bible Inst, BTh; Interdenom Theological Cntr and Horehouse Sch of Rel Atlanta, mDiv (honor roll) 1973. **CAREER:** Bethel Bapt Ch Montgomery, AL, pastor 1967-; Union Acad Bapt Ch; SelmaUniv Sch of Rel, instr. **ORGANIZATIONS:** Pres Montgomery-Antioch Dist SS and Bapt Training Union Congress 1970; mem Natl Bapt Conv USA Inc; Am Beatury Lodge 858; Charlie Garrett Chapter Royal Arch No 78a; United Supreme Council 32; Prince Hall Affil Grand Orient Wash, DC; NAACP 1958-; YMCA 1966-; Montgomery Improvement Assn Inc 1967-; Phi Beta Sigma 1969-. **HONORS/ACHIEVEMENTS:** Nat Fndtn March of Dimes awd 1971. **BUSINESS ADDRESS:** 1110 Mobile Rd, Montgomery, AL 36108.

MARTIN, EDWARD ANTHONY
Podiatrist. **PERSONAL:** Born Dec 25, 1935, Mason City, IA; married Barbara C Payne; children: Gail Ingrid, Edward Brian, Stephen Vincent. **EDUCATION:** Mason City Jr Coll, 1953054; IL Coll of Podiatric Medicine, DPM 1958. **CAREER:** Dr E A Martin , podiatrist 1958-. **ORGANIZATIONS:** First natl pres Acad of Ambulatory Foot Surgery 1973-74; diplomate Am Bd of Amubulatory Foot Surgery 1976; past pres Nat Podiatry Assn 1977-78; mem AmPodiatry Assn 1960-80; pvt pilot Single Engine-land 1974-; podiatry examiner IL Dept of Registration/Educ 1978. **HONORS/ACHIEVEMENTS:** Henri L DuVries Award Proficiency in Clinical Surgery 1958; pectr foot surgery Nationally & Canada 1973-80; "Podiatry A Step Toward Healthy Happy Feet" EbonyArticl 1978; instr in surger-instructional movie on ambulatory surgery 1979. **BUSINESS ADDRESS:** 2301 Lincoln Ave, San Jose, CA 95125.

MARTIN, EDWARD WILLIFORD
Administrator. **PERSONAL:** Born Nov 29, 1929, Sumter, SC; son of Eddie Martin and Frances Martin; married Pearl Evelyn Sewell; children: Andrea Michelle, Debra Yvette, Christopher Edward. **EDUCATION:** Fisk Univ, BA 1950; Univ of IN, MA 1952; Univ of IA, PhD 1962. **CAREER:** Prairie View A&M Univ, instr of biology 1952-56, asst prof of biology 1956-59, chmn div of natl sci/prof of biology 1968-81, dean college of arts & scis 1981-. **ORGANIZATIONS:** Mem Amer Soc of Zoologists, Soc of Sigma Xi, Amer Men of Science; adv bd Baylor Coll of Medicine; mem Omega Psi Phi Frat, Sigma Pi Phi Frat Nu Boule. **HONORS/ACHIEVEMENTS:** Natl Sci Faculty Fellowship Natl Sci Found 1961-62; Beta Kappa Chi Distinguished Awd Beta Kappa Chi Sci Hon Soc 1965; Piper Prof for Teaching Excellence Minnie Stevens Piper Foundation 1979. **BUSINESS ADDRESS:** Dean, Coll of Arts & Sciences, Prairie View A&MUniv, PO Box 878, Prairie View, TX 77446.

MARTIN, ELMER P.
Educator. **PERSONAL:** Born Oct 31, 1946, Kansas City, MO; son of Elmer P Martin (deceased) and Harriet Cason Martin (deceased); married Joanne Mitchell Martin, Jul 29, 1972. **EDUCATION:** Lincoln Univ, Jefferson City MO, BA Sociology, 1968; Atlanta Univ, Atlanta GA, MA Sociology, 1971; Case Western Reserve Univ, Cleveland OH, PhD Social Welfare, 1975. **CAREER:** St Louis Dept of Welfare, caseworker, 1968-69; Cleveland State Univ, asst prof, 1975-76; Morgan State Univ, Baltimore MD, professor, 1976-, chairperson Dept of Social Work and Mental Health, 1985-. **ORGANIZATIONS:** Mem, Natl Assn of Social Workers, 1980-; founder, "For Our People" Food Program, 1983-; mem, Natl Assn of Black Social Workers, 1984-; mem, Sandtown-Winchester Neighborhood Improvement Assn, 1984-85; bd pres, The Great Blacks in Wax Museum, 1988-. **HONORS/ACHIEVEMENTS:** Co-author, The Black Extended Family, Univ of Chicago Press, 1978; co-author, Perspectives of the Black Family (in Family in Transition), Little Brown and Co, 1980; co-author, The Helping Tradition in the Black Family and Community, Nation Assn of Social Workers, 1985; Outstanding Achievement City of Baltimore, 1985; co-author, The Black Woman: Perspectives on Her Role in the Family in Ethnicity and Women, Univ of Wisconsin, 1986; Teacher of the Year, Morgan State Univ, 1986. **BUSINESS ADDRESS:** Co-Founder, The Great Blacks in Wax Museum, Inc, 1601 East North Avenue, Baltimore, MD 21213.

MARTIN, ERNEST DOUGLASS
Physician, educator. **PERSONAL:** Born Oct 26, 1928, Petersburg, VA; married Aurelia Joyce Dent; children: Shellye, Erika, Tia. **EDUCATION:** Lincoln Univ PA, AB 1951; Howard Univ Med School Wash DC, MD. **CAREER:** VA Hospital, Washington DC, consultant 1964-74; Dist of Columbia General Hospital, medical officer; Howard Univ Medical School, clerical asst prof 1964-. **ORGANIZATIONS:** Bd of dir Community Group Health Found Wash DC 1979-80; mem Omega Psi Phi Frat Fellow, Amer Acad of Orthopedic Surgeons 1973. **MILITARY SERVICE:** USN lt 1957-59.

MARTIN, EVELYN B.
Educator, educational administator. **PERSONAL:** Born Oct 12, 1908, Concord, NH; married Anatole Emile. **EDUCATION:** Hampton Inst, BS; Columbia Univ, MA, EdD. **CAREER:** USOE Dept HEW, panelist 1974-77; Coll of Educ FL A&M Univ, acting dean 1978; FL A&M Univ, prof dept chmn 1947-, dir center for comm educ. **ORGANIZATIONS:** Gov bd Natl Assn Admin; AASA Adv Com on Higher Educ 1977-79; appointed by gov of FL Leon Co Sch Bd 1979; appointed by governor of FL Regional Adv Council Dept of Corrections; elected first vice pres Leon Co United Way 1980; mem Kappa Delta Pi; Delta Kappa Gamma; Phi Delta Kappa; Pi Gamma Mu. **HONORS/ACHIEVEMENTS:** Distinguished Serv Award Amer Assoc of School Administrators 1983; Distinguished Serv Award Florida A&M Univ 1986. **BUSINESS ADDRESS:** Dir, Florida A&MUniv, Ctr for Community Education, Box 513, Tallahassee, FL 32307.

MARTIN, FRANCES **See MARTIN, CAROL**

MARTIN, FRANKLIN FARNARWANCE
Printing chief executive officer. **PERSONAL:** Born Jun 22, 1950, Cleveland, OH; son of Rev General Martin and Mozelle Martin; married Barbara Joyce Branic (deceased); children:

Tiona Camille. **EDUCATION:** Cuyahoga Comm Coll, AA 1968-69; Cleveland Plain Dealer Publ Co, journeyman printer degree 1968-75; Cleveland State Univ, attended 1969-70. **CAREER:** Parkview Fed S/L Assoc, printing systems dir 1976-85; Cleveland Plain Dealer Publ Co, asst composing room foreman 1980-85; Frandon Printing Inc, pres, CEO 1983-. **ORGANIZATIONS:** Vp Disabled Amer Vets 1974-, Urban League of Cleveland 1983-, Shaker Towne Ctr 1984-; bd mem Shaker Towne Ctr Adv Bd for the Mayor of Shaker Hts 1986-; bd mem Black Profls of Amer 1986-; bd of directors Rotary Intl 1987-; bd mem Shaker Heights Youth Center 1987-. **HONORS/ACHIEVEMENTS:** Bus Person of the Year C of C Eastern Suburbs 1988-89; one half page story in Cleveland Plain Dealer on Successful Entrepreneurship 1986; Making It Black Enterprise 1987; nominated Black Professional of the Year, Cleveland Growth Assn; Regional Minority Purchasing Council, 1989. **MILITARY SERVICE:** USAF staff sgt 1969-72; Two Commendation Medals, Vietnam Vet Citation, Disabled Amer Vet. **BUSINESS ADDRESS:** President, CEO, Frandon Printing Inc, 3486 Lee Road, Shaker Heights, OH 44120.

MARTIN, FRED
Educational administrator. **PERSONAL:** Born Oct 21, 1926, Detroit, MI; married Ernestine; children: Robin, Keith. **EDUCATION:** Wayne State U, BA 1952, MA 1954. **CAREER:** Detroit Public Schools, exec dir personnel office 1973-, asst to supt 1967-73, personnel admin 1963-37, asst prin 1961-63, teacher 1953-61; Wayne State Univ, instructor soc; MI State Univ & Univ of MI, curr seminar educ research. **ORGANIZATIONS:** Mem Supts Com of Achvmnt; vice pres Det Council Campfire Girls 1968-74; past pres Det Soc Black Educ Adms; NAACP. **HONORS/ACHIEVEMENTS:** Outstanding Achvmnt Award, McKerrow Sch PTA 1960; Black Educ Admin 1974; Natl Campfire Girls Inc 1974. **MILITARY SERVICE:** AUS 1944-46, ETO, PTO. **BUSINESS ADDRESS:** Schools Center Bldg, 5057 Woodward, Detroit, MI 48202.

MARTIN, GEORGE ALEXANDER, JR.
Administrator. **PERSONAL:** Born May 04, 1943, New York, NY. **EDUCATION:** Parsons Coll, BS 1966; City Univ of NY, MPA 1977. **CAREER:** Bedford-Stuyvesant Alcoholism Treatment Ctr, special asst to admin; Marlin Enterprises, pres 1973-; New York Univ Grad School of Public Admin, clinical asst prof of public admin 1972-73; Univ Year for ACTION Proj, New York City & Urban Corps, dir 1972-73; Herald-Bridge House, admin 1970-72. **ORGANIZATIONS:** Amer Soc for Public Admin; Amer Soc for Political Science; Conf of Minority Public Admin; dir, Public Mgmt Sys Inc; consultant, VISTA Region III, 1971; ATAC Inc 1972; Williamsbridge NAACP; Williamsburg Taxpayers Assn; Citizens Comm for Children; Brooklyn Comm on Alcholism; co-chmn, Achievement Week Comm, Omega Psi Phi Frat; adv bd, New York City Urban Corps/Acad Credit Internship Prog 1973; dir, Independent House Inc, Publ Professional Studies in Public Mgmt NYC/Compa Forum 1975. **BUSINESS ADDRESS:** 1121 Bedford Ave, New York, NY 11216.

MARTIN, GEORGE DWIGHT
Professional athlete. **PERSONAL:** Born Feb 16, 1953, Greenville, SC; married Diane; children: Teresa Michelle, George Dwight II, Benjmain Dean, Aaron. **EDUCATION:** Oregon, Art Ed. **CAREER:** New York Giants, defensive end 1975-. **ORGANIZATIONS:** Former rep United Way Pblc Serv TV Commercial. **HONORS/ACHIEVEMENTS:** 5 career touchdowns most ever clb history by defensive lineman; 5 time winner Byron "Whizzer" White Awd Tm Cntrbutn; elected defnsv capt 198 1. **BUSINESS ADDRESS:** New York Giants, Giants Stadium, East Rutherford, NJ 07073.

MARTIN, GWENDOLYN ROSE
State official. **PERSONAL:** Born Dec 12, 1926, Cleveland, OH; daughter of Monroe Fuller (deceased) and Rosa M Johnson Fuller (deceased); married Aaron Martin; children: Jeffrey A. **EDUCATION:** OH State Univ, 1946-48; Case Western Reserve Univ, real estate 1952; George Washington Univ, Ext Course 1976. **CAREER:** Commun Workers of Amer, CWA rep 1972, dir 1975, admin asst to vice pres 1976-87; Illinois Department of Labor, dir 1987-. **ORGANIZATIONS:** Delegate Dem Natl Conv 1976, 1978, 1982, 1984; vice pres Leadership Council Comm 1978-81; vice pres IL AFL-CIO 1978-87; chmn United Way New Appl 1980-81; mem Dem Natl Comm; vice chmn Dem Natl Comm Women's Caucus 1980-84; bd dir Amer Red Cross 1982-84; exec bd member Natl Assn Govt Labor Officials 1988; exec bd mem Women Executing in State -Govt 1987-88. **HONORS/ACHIEVEMENTS:** Sojourner Truth Awd MI Women Trial Lawyers Assoc 1974; Harriet Tubman Awd Coalition of Black Trade Unionist 1975; Resolution #1161 IL House of Rep 1978; Florence Criley Awd Coalition of Labor Union Women 1980. **BUSINESS ADDRESS:** Dir, Illinois Department of Labor, 310 S Michigan, Chicago, IL 60604.

MARTIN, HAROLD B.
Dentist. **PERSONAL:** Born Oct 26, 1928, Petersburg, VA; married Dolores H; children: Harold, Lisa, Gregory. **EDUCATION:** Lincoln U, AB 1950; Howard U, DDS 1957; John Hopkins U, MPH 1971. **CAREER:** HowardUniv Coll of Dentistry, chmn dept of comm dentistry 1959-; pvt prac 1959-; Dept of Corrections, DC 1960-70. **ORGANIZATIONS:** Vp Nat Dental Assn; Century Ltd Inc; bd dir E of River Health Assn; mdm Am Dental Assn; Nat Dental Assn; DC Med Care Adv Com; Nat Review Com for Guidelines for the Expanded Function Training Prgm, HEW; mem Midway Civic Assn, US Youth Games Comm; NAACP; Urban League; Omega Psi Phi; past pres Huntsmen Inc; bd dir Ionia Whipper Home for Unwed Mothers; bd dir Pigskin Club of WA. **MILITARY SERVICE:** AUS Med Corp, Dental Sec 1951-53. **BUSINESS ADDRESS:** Howard Univ Coll of Dentistry, 600 W St NW, Washington, DC.

MARTIN, HARVEY BANKS
Athlete. **PERSONAL:** Born Nov 16, 1950, Dallas, TX. **EDUCATION:** E TX State U. **CAREER:** Dallas Cowboys, def end 1973-; partner, 2 Dallas Barbeque Restaurants; ABC, commentator, Superteams Comp in Hawaii 1980; 7-11 Stores, natl radio voice. **HONORS/ACHIEVEMENTS:** NAIA/FOOTBALL News/AP All-Am honors 1972; NFC Champ Game 1973; NFL Champ Game 1975; Pro Bowl 1976; Line Star Conf Def Player of Decade 1980; Consensus All-Pro/NFL Defensive Player of the Yr; MVP, Superbowl.

MARTIN, HERMAN HENRY, JR.
Investment banker. **PERSONAL:** Born Dec 29, 1961, Dayton, OH. **EDUCATION:** Florida A&M Univ, BS 1984; The Wharton Sch Univ of PA, MBA 1986. **CAREER:** Hoffman LaRoche, pharmaceutical sales rep 1981-82; Cabot Corp, intl audit intern 1982; Chase Manhattan Bank, credit analyst intern 1983; Johnson & Johnson Products, mktg intern 1984-85; Salomon Bros Inc, fixed income rep. **ORGANIZATIONS:** Mem Kappa Alpha Psi Frat 1982-, Natl Black MBA Assoc 1986-, Natl Florida A&M Univ Alumni Assoc 1987-; mem The Wharton Business School Club of NY 1987-. **HONORS/ACHIEVEMENTS:** Leadership Fellowship Johnson & Johnson 1985-86; Wharton Intl Exchange Student (Institut Superieur Des Affaires) Paris France 1985. **BUSINESS ADDRESS:** Fixed Income Representative, Salomon Brothers Inc, One New York Plaza, New York, NY 10004.

MARTIN, I. MAXIMILLIAN
Chief executive. **CAREER:** Berean Savings Assn, Philadelphia, PA, chief exec. **BUSINESS ADDRESS:** Berean Savings Assn, 5228 Chestnut St, Philadelphia, PA 19139. *

MARTIN, IONIS BRACY
Artist, educator. **PERSONAL:** Born Aug 27, 1936, Chicago, IL; daughter of Francis Wright Bracy and Hattie O Robinson Bracy; married Allyn A Martin; children: Allyn B, Martin. **EDUCATION:** Fisk Univ, BA, 1957; Hartford Univ, MEd, 1968; Pratt Inst, MFA, 1987. **CAREER:** Artist's Collective Inc, artist/educator, 1971-, founder/visual arts dir; WFSB-TV, Wadsworth Atheneum, produced art & craft segments for children's programs; Central CT State Univ, Northwestern CT Community Coll, lecturer 1985; The Hartford Courant, illustrator 1986-; Hartford, Bloomfield Public Schools, art teacher 1961-. **ORGANIZATIONS:** Trustee, Burr Memanus Found, 1985-; Commissioner, Hartford Fine Arts Comm; dir, Greater Hartford Arts Council; dir Hartford Stage Co; co-founder & dir, Artists Collective Inc; corporator, Renbrook School; state rep, Natl Conf Artists; mem bd electors Wadsworth Atheneum; Delta Kappa Gamma Intl Educ Sor; Natl Asso Art Educators; CT Art Assn; Delta Sigma Theta; trustee, Wadsworth Atheneum 1977-85,86-; mem adv comm CT Bd of Educ 1986-87; pres Artworks Gallery 1986-87; Romane Bearden/Jackie McLean "Sound Collages & Visual Improvizations" 1986; curator/producer Cotra Gallery "Five From CT" exhibit 1987; dir Charter Oak Temple Restoration Assn; exhibitor many group shows. **HONORS/ACHIEVEMENTS:** CT State Comm on Arts Grant 1970; Outstanding Community Serv Award, Hartford Univ, BPU, 1974; Honored by CT Historial Soc, 1984; 200 Years of Achievement Against the Odds Black Women of CT; Getty Found; Curriculum Devel Inst, 1988-; Skidmore Coll, Art Fellow, 1987. **BUSINESS ADDRESS:** Artist, Teacher, Bloomfield High School, 7 Huckleberry Lane, Bloomfield, CT 06105.

MARTIN, JAMES C.
Attorney. **PERSONAL:** Born Apr 07, 1938, Sledge, MS; married Barbara Jo; children: Angela Rhae. **EDUCATION:** Attended Univ of MO Columbia 1961; Westminster Coll, BA 1965; Univ of AR Fayetteville Sch of Law, JD 1971; 15 hrs on MA Lincoln Univ 1973-74. **CAREER:** MO Public Serv Comm, hearing examiner/atty 1971-73; Barbara Black & Assoc Inc, dir/sec 1973-; MO Div of Finance, asst dep commr 1973-74; MO Div of Corrections, gen couns 1974-79; State of MO Dept of Soc Serv, atty 1978-. **ORGANIZATIONS:** Mem Mayor's Comm on Fair Housing 1966; mem MO & Am Bar Assn 1971-; dir Lincoln Univ Found 1972-74; mem United Way Bd of Dir 1973; dir/chmn Jefferson City Day Car Ctr Inc 1974-79; mem Second Baptist Ch/Sunday Sch Supt; mem NAACP. **MILITARY SERVICE:** MANG MOANG capt 1977-; Good Conduct Medal. **BUSINESS ADDRESS:** Attorney, State of MO Dept Social Serv, PO Box 1527, Broadway State Office Building, Jefferson City, MO 65101.

MARTIN, JAMES LARENCE
Dentist. **PERSONAL:** Born Sep 03, 1940, Dubuque, IA; son of James Martin and Ada Martin; married Willie Mae; children: Linda, James Larence III, John Lance. **EDUCATION:** Loras Coll, BS 1954; Marquette Univ, 1954-55; IA State Tchrs Coll, 1958-59; TN State Univ, MS 1959; Meharry Med Coll Sch of Den, DDS 1966; Univ MI, MPH 1975. **CAREER:** Meharry Med Coll, prof 1977-, assoc prof 1977-, coord 1975-, asst prof, dept pediatrics 1972-, asst prof, dept of operative 1974-75, dir 1973-75; Comprehensive Health Care Program for Children & Youth Promotion, proj dir 1972-73; Meharry Med Coll, assoc prof 1969-72, dental dir 1967-72, instr 1967-69,instr 1960-62; TN State Univ, grad asst, lab instr 1959-60; Sacred Heart HS, chmn sci dept 1957-59; Marquette Univ, lab instr 1954-55. **ORGANIZATIONS:** Mem Amer Dental Assn; Natl Dental Assn; Amer Pub Hlth Assn; Intl Assn for Dental Rsrch, 1973; Amer Assn for Dental Rsrch; Amer Acad of Oral Med; Amer Acad of Gold Foil Operators; AAAS; Amer Assn of Dental Schs; Amer Assn of Med Schs; TN Pub Hlth Assn; Capitol City Dental Soc; Human Rights Commn; Alpha Phi Alpha; St Vincent DePaul Men's Club; Boy Scouts of Amer; Meharry Century Club; Nashville Area C of C; 50 Critics Orgn; Civitan Intl St Vincent DePaul Church Council. **HONORS/ACHIEVEMENTS:** Numerous awards honors & recognitions; numerous manuscripts & publications. **BUSINESS ADDRESS:** Professor, Meharry Medical Coll, 1005 18th Ave N, Nashville, TN 37208.

MARTIN, JAMES TYRONE
Physician, clergyman. **PERSONAL:** Born Aug 17, 1942, Elkhorn, WV; son of Mr & Mrs Henry Martin. **EDUCATION:** Bluefield St Coll Bluefield WV, BS 1960-66; Meharry Med Coll Nashville TN, MD 1969-73. **CAREER:** Tri-Dist Comm Hlth Serv; med dir; McDowell Co, teacher, 1966-69; US Army, 1980-88; staff physician, Comm Health Serv, Raleigh County, Beckley, WV, 1988-present. **ORGANIZATIONS:** Mem Beta Kappa Chi Hon Sci Frat; mem IBPOOE of WV; F&AAY; Royal Arch Masons; bd dir Highlands Educ Proj; asst pastor Emmanuel Tabernacle Bapt Ch 1965-88; mem Amer Acad of Family Physicians; WV Acad of Family Physicians. **MILITARY SERVICE:** AUS major, 1980-; Army Serv Medal, 1980; Army Commendation Medal 1986; Army Achievement Medal, 1988. **HOME ADDRESS:** 108 Springwood Lane, Stanaford Acres, Beckley, WV 25801-9242. **BUSINESS ADDRESS:** Staff Physician, Community Health Serv, Raleigh County, Beckley, WV.

MARTIN, JAMES W.
Administrator. **PERSONAL:** Born Nov 01, 1932, Cleveland, NC; married Marie Sanders; children: Dawn Martin. **EDUCATION:** Claflin Coll, BS Biology 1954; SC State Coll Orangeburg, BS Ed 1960; Univ of SC Columbia, MS biology 1969; Univ of SC Columbia, PhD Biology 1971. **CAREER:** Emmett Scott HS Rock Hill SC, sci teacher, coach 1956-61; Voorhees Coll Denmark SC, acting pres, exec vice pres, dean of acad affairs 1961-76; Area Health Ed Center Med Univ of SC, dir of minority affairs state coor of minority affairs 1976-80; Affirmative Action & Minority Affairs Med Univ of SC, exec asst to pres 1980-. **ORGANIZATIONS:** Mem Mycological Soc, Mycrobiology Soc of Amer, Central Assoc of Sci & Math Teachers, So Assoc of Biologist, AAAS, Amer Assoc of Higher Ed, Amer Council on Higher Ed, Natl Assoc of Deans Registrars & Admiss Off, SC Ed Assoc, Alpha Kappa Mu Natl Hon Soc, Alpha Chi Natl Hon Soc, Sigma Xi Natl Rsch Hon Soc; off Univ Affirm Action

1978; elected chmn of bd Affirm Action 1978; elected chmn exec comm Affirm Action Bd 1978; bd mem Carolina Youth Devel 1982-; consult United Negro Coll fund 1979-; coord Morris Brown AME HS Tutorial Prog; consult United Negro Coll Fund ISATIM 1979-; dir Smal Bus Enterprise prog 1980-; consult Natl Sci Found Summer Inst; bd mem Equal Employment Oppty Commiss. **HONORS/ACHIEVEMENTS:** Publ "Devel Morphology of Apothecium of Trichophawa Abundans Karst An Epigean Operaculate Discomycete" Mycrobiological Rschr Jour 1969; publ "Structure &Function of Hardwood Litter & Soil Subsystems After Chronic Gamma Irradiation" Third Nat Symposium on Radioecology 1970; Outstanding Educators 1971; Outstanding Alumni Awd Claflin Coll 1971; Achievement Awd Alpha Phi Alpha Frat 1971; Palmetto Awd State of SC 1985; Alpha Chi Natl Honor Soc, Sigma Xi Natl RschHonor Soc, Alpha Phi Alpha Frat Acheivement Awd. **MILITARY SERVICE:** AUS Med Corp spec 4 1954-56. **BUSINESS ADDRESS:** Exec Assistant to President, MedicalUniv of So Carolina, 171 Ashley Ave, Charleston, SC 29425.

MARTIN, JOANNE MITCHELL
Educator. **PERSONAL:** Born Jun 12, 1947, Yulee, FL; daughter of Jeremiah Mitchell and Bessie Russell Mitchell; married Elmer P Martin, Jul 29, 1972. **EDUCATION:** Florida A&M, Tallahassee FL, BA French, 1969; Atlanta Univ, Atlanta GA, MA French, 1971; Case Western Reserve Univ, Cleveland OH, MA Reading, 1976; Howard Univ, Washington DC, PhD Educational Psych, 1985. **CAREER:** Nassau County Bd of Educ, Fernandina Beach FL, teacher, 1969-70; Coppin State Coll, Baltimore MD, dir learning skills center, 1977-. **ORGANIZATIONS:** Mem bd of dir, The Great Blacks in Wax Museum, 1985-; mem, African American Heritage Tour Assn, 1987-. **HONORS/ACHIEVEMENTS:** Co-author, The Black Extended Family, Univ of Chicago Press, 1978, Perspectives of the Black Family (in Family in Transition), Little Brown and Co, 1980; Teacher of the Year, Coppin State Coll, 1984; Co-author, The Helping Tradition in the Black Family and Community, Natl Assn of Social Workers, 1985; Author, The Effects of a Cooperative, Competitive and Combination Goal Structure on the Math Performance of Black Children from Extended Families, 1985; Co-author, The Black Woman: Perspectives on Her Role in the Family in Ethnicity and Women, Univ of Wisconsin, 1986; Pace Setter Award, Balto City Urban Services, 1988. **BUSINESS ADDRESS:** Executive Director, Co-Founder, The Great Blacks in Wax Museum, Inc, 1601 East North Avenue, Baltimore, MD 21213.

MARTIN, JOEL P.
Business executive. **PERSONAL:** Born in New York, NY. **EDUCATION:** OH State Univ, BFA. **CAREER:** IBM, av specialist; Fulton & Partners, industrial designer; McCaffrey & McCall, art director; JP Martin Assocs, president. **ORGANIZATIONS:** Mem bd dirs Council of Concerned Black Execs; natl pres elect, pres Natl Assoc Market Developers; co-chair United Negro College Fund Walkathon.

MARTIN, JOHN GORDON
Business executive. **PERSONAL:** Born Jul 14, 1937, Boston, MA; married Paula S Rickson; children: Kenneth Gordon, Lauren Elisabeth. **EDUCATION:** Harvard U, BA 1959; Babson Coll, MBA 1971; SuffolkUniv Law Sch, JD cum laude 1975;Ions 1968-75; New Eng Tel Co, mgmt Positions 1963-68. **CAREER:** Indsl Accident Bd, Commonwealth of MA, chmn; Honeywell Inf Systems Inc, mgmt positions 1968-75; New Eng Tel Co, mgmt positions 1963-68. **ORGANIZATIONS:** MA Bar Assn; Alpha Phi Alpha; football coach Central MA Youth Athletic Assn. **MILITARY SERVICE:** AUS 1st lt 1959-62. **BUSINESS ADDRESS:** 100 Cambridge St, Boston, MA 02202.

MARTIN, JOHN THOMAS
Retired military officer. **PERSONAL:** Born Apr 29, 1920, NYC, NY; son of John T Martin and Bertha H Martin; married Hestlene Lee Brooks; children: Joan M Teaiwa, John Thomas, III (dec), Alan, Theresa M Roberson, Charles. **EDUCATION:** Howard Univ, AB 1940; Sch Law, student 1940-41; Univ WI Sch Jour, student 1962. **CAREER:** Sec Defense Washington, exec to counselor's office 1952-53, 1956-62, 1965-66 ret 1968; AUS, commd 2nd lt 1940 advanced through grades to Col 1966-68; Selective Serv Washington, dir 1966-79; Met Capital Corp, dir; US Army, retired col. **ORGANIZATIONS:** Mem Retired Officers Assn, Assn US Army, Reserve Officers Assn, Capital Health & Welfare Council 1969; dir Capitol USO 1967-70; dir Natl Capitol Area Council BSA 1968-69; Met Capital Corp; Greater Southeast Comm Hosp Found; mem Kappa Alpha Psi. **MILITARY SERVICE:** AUS col retired; Legion of Merit; Bronze Star Medal w/one Oak Leaf Cluster; Combat Infantryman's Badge.

MARTIN, JOHN W.
Educator. **PERSONAL:** Born Feb 15, 1924, Johnson City, TN; widowed. **EDUCATION:** Knoxville Coll, BA 1948; Atlanta U, MA 1949; IN U, PhD 1959. **CAREER:** Univ of IL, asso prof of soc; IL Inst of Tech, Chicago, 1964-65; IL Wesleyan U, 1961-64; Dillard U, New Orleans, 1957-61; Miles Coll, 1949-57. **ORGANIZATIONS:** Mem IL Sociological Assn; Am Sociological Assn; Midwest Sociological Soc; Soc for Study of Soc Problems; mem Comm Fund of Chicago Inc, Operation PUSH; NAACP. **MILITARY SERVICE:** USN 1944-46. **BUSINESS ADDRESS:** Assoc Prof of Sociology, Univ of Illinois at Chicago, Sociology Department, Chicago, IL 60680.

MARTIN, JOSHUA WESLEY, III
Judge. **PERSONAL:** Born Sep 14, 1944, Columbia, SC; son of Joshua W Martin Jr and Bernice Baxter Martin; married Lloyd E Overton; children: Victoria, Alexis. **EDUCATION:** Case Inst of Tech, BS 1966; Drexel Univ, 1971-73; Rutgers Schl of Law-Camden, JD 1974. **CAREER:** EI DuPont DeNemours & Co, sr physicist 1966-71; Hercules Inc, sr patent atty 1974-82; DE Pub Serv Comm, chmn 1978-82. **ORGANIZATIONS:** Mem DE Bar Assn 1975-; Natl Bar Assn 1975-; Philadelphia Patent Law Assn 1976-82; trustee Goldey Beacom Coll 1982-; Better Business Bureau of DE 1978-82; advisory comm Univ of DE Legal Asst Program 1982; trustee, Delaware Community Foundation 1988-. **HONORS/ACHIEVEMENTS:** Alpha Man of Year Alphi Phi Alpha Frat Wilmington, DE 1978; Citizen of Year Omega Psi Phi Frat Wilmington, DE 1982; Outstanding Achievement Sigma Pi Phi Wilmington, DE 1983; Comm Serv Award Rutgers Univ-Camden BLSU Camden, NJ 1974; Adjunct Professor, Delaware Law School, 1988-89; Adjunct Professor, Wilmington Coll, 1984-89. **BUSINESS ADDRESS:** Resident Associate Judge, Superior Court of Delaware, Public Building, Wilmington, DE 19801.

MARTIN, JULIA M.
Educator. **PERSONAL:** Born Nov 09, 1924, Snow Hill, MD. **EDUCATION:** Tuskegee Inst, BS 1946, MS Chem 1948; PA State Univ, PhD Biochemistry 1963. **CAREER:** Tuskegee Inst, instr of chem 1948-49; FL A&M Univ, asst prof of chem 1949-59; Tuskegee Inst, assoc prof of chem 1963-66; So Univ, prof of chem 1966-, spec asst to the dean 1973-74, acting dean of grad sch 1974-76, dean coll of sci 1978-. **ORGANIZATIONS:** Mem Amer Chem Soc; Amer Assn for Advancement of Science; Amer Inst of Chemists; LA Acad of Scis; NY Acad of Scis; Natl Assn of Coll Women; AmerAssn of Univ Women; Alpha Kappa Alpha; YWCA; NAACP; mem Alpha Kappa Mu, Beta Kappa Chi, Iota Sigma Pi, Sigma Delta Epsilon, Gamma Sigma Delta; lectr UnitedNegro Coll Fund Disting Lecutre Series in Chemistry 1976, 1984; cncl mem LAUniv Marine Consortium (LUMCON); mem LA Cncl of Deans of Arts Science & Humanities 1978-, mem exec comm 1979-85, chmn 1983-84; mem exec comm Cncl of Colls of Arts & Scis 1982-85; Marine Div NANGUSC. **HONORS/ACHIEVEMENTS:** Citation Outstanding Educ of Amer 1974-75; Urban League Fellow Union Carbide 1968; Fellow Hoffmann-LaRoche 1969; listing Amer Men & Women of Sci, Personalities of the S. **BUSINESS ADDRESS:** Dean, College of Science, SoUniv, Box 9608, So Univ, Baton Rouge, LA 70813.

MARTIN, LAWRENCE RAYMOND
Clergyman. **PERSONAL:** Born Sep 04, 1935, Archie, LA; married Barbara Thompson; children: Lawrence II, Perry, Chantel. **EDUCATION:** Grambling State U, BS 1959; United Theo Seminary, BTh 1973; Interdenom Theo Cntr & Morehouse Sch of Religion, MDiv 1973. **CAREER:** Monroe City Edu Assn, pres 1971-; NAACP Monroe, LA, pres 1973-74; Tenth Dist Assn, Bible Instr 1970-; United Theo Sem Am Bapt Exten Classes, tchr. **ORGANIZATIONS:** Mem Monroe City Educ Assn; LA Educ Assn; Nat Educ Assn; LA Bapt Conv; Nat Bapt Conv USA Inc; mem LA Bicentennial Comm; mem bd on Drug Abuse & Alcoholism Co hon col on staff, Gov Edwin Edwards.

MARTIN, LEE
Educator. **PERSONAL:** Born Aug 04, 1938, Birmingham, AL; married Nora White; children: Lee, Jr, Kristi, Dia. **EDUCATION:** Eastern MI U, BS, MA;Univ of MI, PhD. **CAREER:** Romulus Sch, dir 1974-; Metro Learning & Mental Health Clinic, co-dir 1974-;Univ of Detroit, instr 1973-74. **ORGANIZATIONS:** Mem Task Force 1977; mem MI Dept of Mental Health 1976; mem Cncl for Exceptional Children 1975-; mem MI Soc of Mental Health 1976-; mgmt bd Western Wayne Cnty YMCA; trustee Peoples Comm 1975; bd of dir Northwest Guidance Clinic 1975-; trustee Inkster Sch Bd 1973-; pres Annapolis Park Homeowner's Asso 1965-67; aiding fellow-minorities MI Asso for Retarded Citizens. **HONORS/ACHIEVEMENTS:** Achvmt Spec Educ. **BUSINESS ADDRESS:** 36540 Grant Rd, Romulus, MI 48174.

MARTIN, LOUIS E.
University administrator. **PERSONAL:** Born Nov 18, 1912, Shelbyville, TN; married Gertrude Scott; children: Trudy Hatter, Anita, Toni Darey, Linda, Lisa Baumbaugh. **EDUCATION:** Univ of MI, BA 1934; Harvard Univ, LLD Honors 1970; Howard Univ, LLD 1979; Wesleyan Univ, LLD 1980. **CAREER:** MI Chronicle, editor/publisher 1936-47; Chicago Defender, editor-in-chief 1947-59, editor 1969-78; Democratic Natl Comm, deputy chmn 1960-69; White House, special asst to pres 1978-81; Howard Univ, asst vice pres communications 1981-. **ORGANIZATIONS:** Former mem bd dir Chicago City Bank & Trust Co; bd dir Service Fed Savings & Loan Assn; dir advisory bd, Amalgamated Bank & Trust; Overseas Press CLub; Federal City Club; Chicago Press Club chmn of bd Joint Center for Political Studies; bd trustees DePaul Univ; bd dir Overseas Devel Council; bd United Way of Am; bd dir Metro YMCA; bd dir Chicago Comm Ventures, Inc; Chicago Boys Club; Community Fund of Chicago; steering comm Natl Urban Coalition. **HONORS/ACHIEVEMENTS:** Equal Oppor Awd Natl Urban League 1979; Russwurm Natl Newspaper Publ Assoc 1980; Communications Awd Howard Univ 1987; bd dir Opera/South Recipient John B Russwurm Awd. **BUSINESS ADDRESS:** Asst Vice Pres Communications, Howard University, 2900 Van Nes, Washington, DC 20088.

MARTIN, MARY E. HOWELL
Educator. **PERSONAL:** Born Apr 05, 1941, Terre Haute; married Laurence A. **EDUCATION:** IN State U, BS 1961, MS 1969. **CAREER:** IN State Univ, asst dir Univ High School Relations 1973-; Vigo Co Schools, asst dir Admissions 1973-73, teacher 1964-70. **ORGANIZATIONS:** Mem Vigo Co IN State Tchrs Assns; IN Assn Coll Admissions Couns; adv bd Afro Am Studies; adv bd Blue & Berets; Black Affairs Coun; bd Center AvComm Cntr; bd Hyte Comm Cntr; YWCA; selection com Martin Luther King Scholarship; 2d Mission Bapt Ch; Alpha Kappa Alpha; mem cotillion com Negro Bus& Professional Women. **HONORS/ACHIEVEMENTS:** Cert appreciation & trophy Black Student Union 1973-75. **BUSINESS ADDRESS:** Office of Admissions, Univ High School Relations, IN State Univ, Terre Haute, IN 47809.

MARTIN, MAXINE SMITH
Educational administrator. **PERSONAL:** Born Aug 09, 1944, Charleston, SC; daughter of Henry W Smith and Emily Simmons Smith; married Montez C Jr, Mar 08, 1974; children: Emily Elise; Montez C III. **EDUCATION:** Hampton Inst Hampton, VA, BS 1966; Atlanta U, MA 1973. **CAREER:** Coll of Charleston, student prog coord/advisor Center for Continuing Educ 1985-; Charleston County School Dist & Trident Tech Coll, English instr 1980-85; Coll of Charleston, dir of coll relations 1979-80, public inf specialist 1973-79; Morehouse Coll, fed relations coord 1972-73; Atlanta U, pub relations asst 1971-72; Supplementary Educ Cntr, publ specialist 1970-71; Charleston County School District, reading consultant II 1988-89. **ORGANIZATIONS:** Mem Charleston Chap Hampton Univ Alumni Assoc 1966-, Delta Sigma Theta 1969-, YWCA 1971-, Council for the Advancement & Support of Educ 1973-80, Coll News Assoc 1973-80; mem, comm chmn Charleston Chap of Links Inc 1974-; bd mem Charleston Area Mental Health Assoc 1976-80; mem Univ & Coll Designers1977-80; bd mem Charleston Civic Ballet 1983-85, Florence Crittenton Home 1983-85, SC Assoc of Higher Continuing Educ 1985-; bd of dirs, Young Charleston Theatre Company 1988-. **HONORS/ACHIEVEMENTS:** Cert for Pub Relations Serv, Delta Sigma Theta 1975; Cert for Pub Relations Serv, YWCA 1975; Cert for Pub Relations Serv, Am Freedom Train Found 1977; YWCA Public Relations Awd 1984, YWCA Twin Women Awd 1985; WPAL Radio Community Serv Awd 1986. **BUSINESS ADDRESS:** Student Prog Advisor/Coord, College of Charleston, 25 St Philip St, Charleston, SC 29424.

MARTIN, MCKINLEY C.
Educational administrator. **PERSONAL:** Born Dec 02, 1936, Clarksdale, MS; married

Willie Beatrice Burns; children: McKinley C II, Myron Craig, Marcia Corteze. **EDUCATION:** Coahoma Jr Coll, AA (Magna Cum Laude); Jackson State Univ, BS (Cum Laude) 1961; Delta State Univ, ME 1967; FL State Univ, PhD (Summa Cum Laude) 1972. **CAREER:** Sandy Bayou Elementary School, principal 1962-65; Coahoma Jr Coll, registrar 1965-66; FL State Univ, instructor/admin asst 1970-72; Coahoma Jr Coll, dir continuing educ, 1973-80, pres 1980-. **ORGANIZATIONS:** Exec bd mem Coahoma Cty Chamber of Commerce; planning com Governor's Office of Job Devel & Training; spec steering com US Dept of the Interior-Historically Black Coll & Univ; state chmn Child Devel Assoc, Delta Agency for Progress; mem Coahoma Cty Port Com, Hira #131 Shrine Temple, HW Nichols Lodge #556-Elk, Prince Hall Mason, Alpha Phi Alpha Fraternity; Mem, Planning Committee of the US Dept of Educ, Office of Student Financial Assistance; US Dept of the Interior's Natl Parks Services; Coahoma County Committee on the Lower Mississippi Delta Development Act; Leadership Clarksdale Bd of Dir; Mississippi Junior & Community coll Economic Council, Vice Pres of the Mississippi Assn of Community & Junior Colleges; vice chmn, Mississippi Assn of Community & Junior Coll Legislative Committee; Mem, Univ of Mississippi Minority Advisory Bd. **MILITARY SERVICE:** AUS 1955-58. **HOME ADDRESS:** PO Box 1013, Clarksdale, MS 38614. **BUSINESS ADDRESS:** President, Coahoma Junior College, Route 1 Box 616, Clarksdale, MS 38614.

MARTIN, MONTEZ CORNELIUS, JR.
Construction engineer. **PERSONAL:** Born Jun 11, 1940, Columbia, SC; married E Maxine Smith; children: Tanya, Elayne, Terrie, Lanita. **EDUCATION:** Hampton Inst, BS 1963; Polytech Inst Brooklyn, grad studies 1967. **CAREER:** WSOK Radio, dir of operations 1973-74; Coll of Charleston, dir constrn 1974-; Montez Real Estate, broker-in-charge 1976-. **ORGANIZATIONS:** Mem SC Chap Natl Assn Real Estate Brokers 1977-; mem Greater Charleston Bd of REaltors 1979-; constrn consult Franklin C Fetter Health Care Ctr; financial sec Avery Inst of Afro-Amer History & Culture 1980. **HONORS/ACHIEVEMENTS:** Marketeer of the Yr Atlanta Chap Natl Assn Market Developers 1972; Certificate Am Freedom Train Found 1977; Cert of Achievement Beta Kappa Lambda Chap Alpha Phi Alpha Frat Inc 1978; Living the Legacy Awd Columbia Sect Natl Council of Negro Women 1980. **MILITARY SERVICE:** AUS maj 1963-70; Army Commendation; Army Commendatin w/Oak Leaf Cluster; Meritorious Svcs. **BUSINESS ADDRESS:** Montez Real Estate, 218 Coming St, Charleston, SC 29401.

MARTIN, PAUL W.
Dentist. **PERSONAL:** Born Dec 04, 1940, Columbus, OH; married Barbara Burts; children: Todd Christopher Emmeal. **EDUCATION:** Indiana Univ Sch of Dentistry, BS, DDS 1958-62; IN State Teachers Coll, 1955-58; NY Univ Coll of Dentistry, 1978. **CAREER:** Royal Society of Health, fellow 1962-; Prison Health Serv, dir 1973-75; private practice, oral surgery 1976; North Gen Hospital, acting chief of oral surg 1985; Harlem Hospital Ctr, assoc attending surgery 1986-; Gov Hospital, staff oral surgeon; 223 W 80th St Corp, pres 1983-. **ORGANIZATIONS:** Mem Frontiers Intl 1963-; co-founder/mem exec comm Natl Dental Acupuncture Soc 1984-; acting chief of oral surgery N General Hosp 1985. **HONORS/ACHIEVEMENTS:** Topical Antibiotic Maintenance of Oral Health 1968; Supraorbital Emphysema 1972; Phencyclidine (PCP) Abuse 1986; Crack (an extra potent form of cocaine) Abuse 1987. **MILITARY SERVICE:** USNR lt 1963-69. **BUSINESS ADDRESS:** President, 223 W 80th St Corp, 145 W 86th St, New York, NY 10024.

MARTIN, RAYFUS
Educator. **PERSONAL:** Born Jan 12, 1930, Franklinton, LA; married Elnora Lowe; children: Mechelle Denise. **EDUCATION:** Leland College, BA 1956; Southern Univ, 1973; Southeastern LA Univ, MEd 1974. **CAREER:** St Tammary HS, teacher, English, 1957; Washington Parish HS, History teacher, 1962; Franklinton HS, English teacher 1969-. **ORGANIZATIONS:** First Black council member Town of Franklinton 1975-. **MILITARY SERVICE:** AUS corpl 1951-54. **HOME ADDRESS:** 2020 Williams St, Franklinton, LA 70438.

MARTIN, REDDRICK LINWOOD
Business executive. **PERSONAL:** Born Jul 20, 1934, Anderson, SC; son of Reddrick B Martin and Mamie Lee Martin; married Ernestine Heath. **EDUCATION:** Allen Univ, BS 1962. **CAREER:** Winnsboro SC Pub Schs, tchr 1962-63; Lancaster SC Public Schs, tchr 1963; Columbia Coca-Cola Bottling Co Columbia SC, sales & Mktg rep 1963-73; Miami Coca-Cola Bottling Co, regional market mgr 1973-76; Coca Cola USA, area mktg mgr 1976-82, asst market develop mgr 1982-83; Martin Real Estate Investment Co, pres; Century 21, James Gray Assocs, agent, 1989-; A L Williams Insurance Co, agent, 1987-. **ORGANIZATIONS:** Bd mem Palmetta Businessmen Assn 1970-73; bd mem OIC Columbia, SC 1972-73; adv bd mem Bus Dept FL Val State Coll 1980; mem Industry Cluster A&T State Univ 1980; mem NAACP; mem Urban League; bd mem Natl Assoc of Market Developers 1983-. **HONORS/ACHIEVEMENTS:** Outstanding Serv Award in Community Affairs, Save Our Community Club Columbia, SC 1970; Meritorious Serv Award in Pub Affairs, So Regional Press Inst Savannah State Coll 1980. **MILITARY SERVICE:** USAF airman 1st class 1954-57. **BUSINESS ADDRESS:** President, Martin's Real Estate Inv Co, 1123 Braemar Ave SW, Atlanta, GA 30311.

MARTIN, RICHARD CORNISH
Clergyman. **PERSONAL:** Born Oct 15, 1936, Philadelphia, PA; son of Leon Freeman Martin and Virginia Lonette Bullock Martin. **EDUCATION:** Pennsylvania State Univ, BA in Science 1958; Episcopal Theolgical Seminary in VA, Master of Divinity 1961; St Augustine's Coll, Canterbury; Howard Univ, Washington DC, DMin 1988. **CAREER:** PA State Univ, chaplain 1961-64; St Andrew's Church State Coll PA, assoc rector 1961-64; George Washington Univ, Washington DC, chaplain 1964-66; St Paul's Parish, Washington DC, assoc rector 1966-73, rector 1989-; St George's Parish, Washington DC, rector 1973-89. **ORGANIZATIONS:** Supreme gen Soc of Mary Amer Region 1966-; pres Prevention of Blindness Soc 1982-84; mem Research Found Children's Hospital Natl Medical Center 1976-; mem Studia Liturgica; dir Comm Outreach Ministry; mem Inter-Church Club. **HONORS/ACHIEVEMENTS:** Editor Studies & Commentaries I & II; editor The Dragon; composer Liturgical Music. **HOME ADDRESS:** 957 25th St, NW, Washington, DC 20037.

MARTIN, ROBERT EDWARD
Producer, reporter. **PERSONAL:** Born Dec 17, 1948, Bronx, NY; son of Robert Martin and Mary Martin; divorced; children: LeRonne. **EDUCATION:** RCA Inst, graduated 1973. **CAREER:** WABC-TV, assoc producer 1971-72; Capital Formation Inc, dir of comm 1972-75; WNEW-TV, producer 1976-83; WNBC-TV, producer 1983-88; WNYW-TV, reporter/producer. **ORGANIZATIONS:** Mem Writers Guild of Amer East; former mem Council of Concerned Black Exec; mem YMCA; former dir Male Echoes 1st Union Bapt Ch; AFTRA. **HONORS/ACHIEVEMENTS:** Emmy Awd "Like It Is" spl on Attica NY 1972; Spl Awd for Promotion of Orgn NY Jaycees 1973; Serv Awd Salvation Army 1977; CEBA Award 1988. **MILITARY SERVICE:** AUS sgt-E5 1969-71. **BUSINESS ADDRESS:** Reporter, A Current Affair, Fox-TV WNYW, 205 E 67th St, 4th Fl, New York, NY 10021.

MARTIN, ROD
Professional football player. **PERSONAL:** Born Apr 07, 1954, Welch, WV. **EDUCATION:** Attended Los Angeles City Coll, Univ of So CA. **CAREER:** Oakland, 1977-81; LA Raiders, 1982-85. **HONORS/ACHIEVEMENTS:** Named to The Sporting News NFL All-Star Team 1983. **BUSINESS ADDRESS:** Linebacker, Los Angeles Raiders, 332 Center St, El Segundo, CA 90245.

MARTIN, ROSETTA P.
Librarian. **PERSONAL:** Born Jun 20, 1930, Charleston; married George E Sr. **EDUCATION:** Morgan State Coll, BA 1953; Boston U, adv grad work in Educ 1957; Simmon Coll, MS 1962. **CAREER:** Ident Tech Coll Palmer Campus, Charleston, SC, librarian 1978-; Tufts U, ref Librarian 1970-78, supr curriculum lab 1965-, asst ref librarian 1963-70; Manning HS, tchr 1954-55; Boston Public Lib, children's librarian 1958-63. **ORGANIZATIONS:** Mem Am Library Assn; Special Library Assn; New England Library Assn; Am Assn ofUniv Profs; Librarians in Educ & Research in The NE; mem NAACP; CivicAssn; Black Bibliographer; Assn for Study of Negro Life & Hist. **BUSINESS ADDRESS:** Palmer Campus Library, Trident Tech Coll, Charleston, SC 29407.

MARTIN, RUBY JULENE WHEELER
Administrator. **PERSONAL:** Born Jan 24, 1931, Charleston, SC; daughter of Coleman James Wheeler and Pearl Gladys Dunn; children: Angela Zora, Edward Alfred Jr. **EDUCATION:** Bennett Coll, BA 1952; SC State Coll, MS 1959; Syracus Univ, EdD. **CAREER:** Bonds Wilson High School Charleston, instructor of English & French 1953-55; SC State Coll, asst prof of English 1959-64; SC State Coll, asst prof of Reading 1964-68; professor of Reading 1969-; Learning Resources Reading Center TN State Univ, dir; TN State Univ, head dept Teaching and Learning 1986-, head dept Reading & Special Educ 1979-. **ORGANIZATIONS:** Consultant Inst for Serv to Educ Washington DC 1972-74; mem ed adv bd Intl Reading Assoc 1973-77, Natl Reading Conf Yearbook 1973-74; consultant State of MS First Annual Reading Conf 1975; consultant Dr Mary F Berry Asst Sec for Dept of HEW 1978; chmn TSU First & Second Natl Basic Skills Conf TN State Univ 1978-79; field reader Tech Serv Dept of HEW Office of Educ 1980; consultant Southern Assn of Coll & Schools Atlanta GA 1980-; mem public comm Intl Reading Assoc 1984-85. **HONORS/ACHIEVEMENTS:** Published "Current Issues-The Public Coll" Journal of Reading vol 16 #3 1972, "Realities & Fallacies of Tea Rea to Black High School Students" Journal of Reading vol. 18 #61975; reviewer of books for young people Journal of Reading 1977. **BUSINESS ADDRESS:** Head Teaching & Learning, Tennessee StateUniv, PO Box 850, Nashville, TN 37203.

MARTIN, RUDOLPH G. (RUDY)
Salesman. **PERSONAL:** Born Nov 02, 1916, Benton, LA; married Ruth L. **EDUCATION:** Lincoln U; New York Sch Med Dentistry. **CAREER:** New & Used Cars, salesman 1955-. **ORGANIZATIONS:** Longest Service of Black Authorized Salesman in Tulsa Area; mem Master Sale Smans Guild; Kappa Alpha Psi; Tulsa Urban League ; NAACP; Optimist Club; Esquire Club; 1st Bapt Ch N Tulsa. **HONORS/ACHIEVEMENTS:** Salesman of Month numerous times. **MILITARY SERVICE:** USAF corpl sp serv 1942-46. **BUSINESS ADDRESS:** 2111 E 11th, Tulsa, OK 74104.

MARTIN, RUSSELL F.
Dental consultant, dentist. **PERSONAL:** Born Aug 18, 1929, Hartford; married Jean E Procope. **EDUCATION:** Howard U, BS 1950, DDS 1955; Yale U;; MPH 1970. **CAREER:** Pvt Practice Hartford, 1957-58; St Dept of Hlth, operated Mobile Dental Trailer Unit in Rural CT 1957-58; Hartford Dispensary;; staff dentist 1958-68;Univ of CT Hlth Cntr, staff dentist 1968-69;Univ of CT Hlth Cntr research assoc 1969-70; Hlth Action Survey proj dir 1969-70; Cit Hlth Action Coun HEW, proj dir 1971-72; Hlth Planning Coun Inc assoc dir 1972-74; Pvt Practice; Dept of Corrections, staff dentist; Aetna Ins Co, dental cons; Dept of Comm DentistryUniv of CT, clinical assoc 1974-. **ORGANIZATIONS:** Mem Am Dental Assn; CT St Dental Assn; Hartford Dental Soc; Am Pub Hlth Assn; CT St Pub Hlth Assn; bd dir Comm Hlth Serv Inc Hartford, pres bd; mem pub hlth & welfare comm Urban League of Greater Hartford; Sickle Cell Anemia & Com Bloomfield CT; adv com on Occupational Therapy, Manchester Comm Coll; Ambulatory Hlth Care Coun Inc; chp NW Hartford Hlth Care Task Force ; bd dir Urban League of Greater Hartford; Minority Involvement in Higher Educ Com Hew Haven CT Co-author "Health & Health Care in Hartfords N End; 1974. **MILITARY SERVICE:** AUS Dental Corps capt 1955-57. **BUSINESS ADDRESS:** Aetna Life & Casualty Dntl Cla, 151 Farmington Ave, Hartford, CT 06105.

MARTIN, SALLIE
Chairman. **PERSONAL:** Born Nov 20, 1895, Penfield, GA; married Wallace Martin. **CAREER:** Began singing with Dr Thomas A Dorsey, Father of Gospel Music 1929; Martin/Dorsey collaboration formed the Natl Convention of Gospel Choirs & Choruses 54 yr old org; Discovered pianist named Ruth Jones who later gained fame as Ms Dinah Washington; Began travelling gospel circuit in 1940 as a solo artist later forming the Sallie Martin Singers; Formed Martin/Morris Publishing Co with Kenneth Morris; Recently featured as one of the principal subjects in the acclaimed gospel documentary "Say Amen, Somebody". **ORGANIZATIONS:** Established many private scholarships; involved in the formation of the Sallie Martin Foundation. **HONORS/ACHIEVEMENTS:** Baptist Missionary School in Nigeria West Africa named one of its buildings in honor of Sallie Martin; referred to as the "Mother of Gospel Music". **HOME ADDRESS:** 5050 S Lakeshore Dr, #3201, Chicago, IL 60615.

MARTIN, SAMUEL
Business executive. **PERSONAL:** Born Sep 20, 1918, Newport, AR. **EDUCATION:** Prairie View St Coll 1938-39; KCK Jr Coll. **CAREER:** Atlanta Life Ins Co KC KS, staff mgr; hd stockman & union ldr AFL-CIO; Nat Bellas Hess KC MO; rec dir KC Recreastion

Dept; vice pres Atlanta Life Agency Group 1972-74; vP Greater & KC Underwriters 1971-72; pres Greater KC Underwriters 1973-74. **ORGANIZATIONS:** Introduced Boys Club of Am Prog KC KS 1972-74. **HONORS/ACHIEVEMENTS:** Recpt Sales & Serv Awd Atlanta Life Ins Co 1972; Sales & Serv Awd Nat Ins Assn 1971-73; grad Agency Mgmt Assn 1973; Silver Tray Otstndng Sales 1973; Staff Mgr Cert 1974. **MILITARY SERVICE:** AUS 1943-45. **BUSINESS ADDRESS:** 4725 Paseo, Kansas City, MO.

MARTIN, SHEDRICK M., JR.
Government employee. **PERSONAL:** Born Jan 05, 1927, Savannah, GA; married Laura B Randolph; children: Beverly Anne, Brenda Annette. **EDUCATION:** Savannah St Coll, BS 1951; FBI Nat Acad 1970. **CAREER:** Dept of Pub Serv City of Saavvannah GA, adminstr 1972-; Savannah, personnel asst training 1971-72; Savannah GA Police Dept, detective 1957-70; Chatham Co Bd of Educ Savannah, tchr 1952-57; PO Atlanta Ga, clk 1951-52. **ORGANIZATIONS:** Mem Am Public Works Assn; Fraternal Order of Police; NAACP; Cath Holy Name Soc; Wolves Social Club. **HONORS/ACHIEVEMENTS:** Listed In whos Who In S & SW. **MILITARY SERVICE:** AUS 1945-46. **BUSINESS ADDRESS:** PO Box 1027, Savannah, GA 31402.

MARTIN, SYLVIA COOKE
Human resource manager. **PERSONAL:** Born May 02, 1938, Baltimore, MD; daughter of Emanuel Levi Cook and Clara Evans Cook; divorced; children: Donald E K Martin, Marcia Lauren Martin. **EDUCATION:** Univ of Maryland, College Park MD, BA, 1972, MPS, 1978; Univ of Virginia, Charlottesville VA, cert, 1975. **CAREER:** Social Security Admin, Baltimore MD, file clerk, 1963-66, health insurance analyst, 1966, mgmt intern, 1967-68; Social Security Admin and Health Care Financing Admin, Baltimore MD, career devel specialist, 1968-70; Library of Congress, Washington DC, chief of staff training and devel, 1978-; Bowie State College, Bowie MD, instructor, 1986-89; self-employed mgmt consultant, 1989-; lecturer. **ORGANIZATIONS:** Historian, Natl Assn of Negro Business and Professional Women's Clubs, Inc, 1978-89; historian, 1984-85, parlimentarian, 1985-88, pres, 1988-89, Amer Historical and Genealogical Soc; mem, Maryland Historical Soc, 1980-89; mem, Oral History Assn, 1984-89; mem, Natl Council of Negro Women; life mem, NAACP. **HONORS/ACHIEVEMENTS:** Commissioner's citation, Social Security Admin, 1972; distinguished achievement award, Conference of Minority Public Administrators, 1980; distinguished service award, 1983, Sojourner Truth Award, 1985, Natl Assoc of Negro Business and Professional Women's Clubs Inc; special achievement awards, Library of Congress, 1987, 1988; dedication and leadership award, Afro-Amer Historical and Genealogical Soc, 1989; editor and author of Just For You Cook Book, 1986; author of Another Cook Book, A Family History, 1989; developer and designer of black history month exhibits. **HOME ADDRESS:** 6375 Shadowshape Place, Columbia, MD 21045. **BUSINESS ADDRESS:** Chief, Staff Training and Development, Library of Congress, Washington, DC 20540.

MARTIN, TONY
Educator. **PERSONAL:** Born Feb 21, 1942, Port-of-Spain, Trinidad and Tobago. **EDUCATION:** Hon Soc of Gray's Inn, Barrister-at-Law 1965; Univ of Hull England, BSc Economics (honors) 1968; MI State Univ, MA History 1970, PhD History 1973. **CAREER:** St Mary's Coll Trinidad, teacher 1962-63; Univ of MI Flint, asst prof 1971-73; Wellesley Coll, assoc prof 1973-79, full prof 1979-. **ORGANIZATIONS:** Mem Negro Historical Assn of Colorado Springs; vice pres Natl Council for Black Studies New England 1984-86; exec bd mem African Heritage Studies Assn 1982-88; exec bd Assn of Caribbean Historians; mem Assn for the Study of Afro-Amer Life History. **HONORS/ACHIEVEMENTS:** Numerous publicationss including "Race First, The Ideological and Organizational Struggles of Marcus Garvey and the Universal Negro Improvement Assn" 1976; "Rare Afro-Americana" co-author 1981; "Amy Ashwood Garvey, Pan-Africanist Feminist and Wife No1" 1989. **BUSINESS ADDRESS:** Prof, Black Studies, Wellesley College, Dept of Black Studies, Wellesley, MA 02181.

MARTIN, WALTER L.
Operational manager. **PERSONAL:** Born Apr 15, 1951, New York, NY; son of Robert Martin and Elizabeth Martin; married Regina Marvel Montgomery; children: Shalya Mekeela Kelly, Merissa Tarla Mekeshia. **EDUCATION:** Northeastern Univ, BS 1975; Atlanta Univ, MBA 1977. **CAREER:** Pyramidwest Develop Corp, financial analyst/accountant 1979-82; Mobil Chem Co, financial analyst 1982-83; Federal Express Corp, sr financial analyst 1983-86, station oper mgt 1986-. **ORGANIZATIONS:** Dir Changes the Full Arts Production Co 1977-82; allocation comm Youth Services United Way Atlanta 1985-; dir membership Natl Black MBA Assoc Atlanta 1985-86; dir student affairs Natl Black MBA Assoc Atlanta 1987; partner East Coast mgmt Group. **HOME ADDRESS:** 5264 Golfcrest Circle, Stone Mountain, GA 30088.

MARTIN, WILLIAM R.
Chemist. **PERSONAL:** Born Dec 19, 1926, Washington, DC; married Mildred Dixon; children: William R, Jr, Janice Y. **EDUCATION:** Morgan St Coll, BS 1951; PA Southeastern U, MBA 1976. **CAREER:** Food & Drug Adminstrn, chemist drug mfg controls 1963-; Howard U, reseasrch proj 1962-63; Nat Inst Mntl Hlth research neurochem 1960-62; Walter Reed Ins, reseasrch biochem 1955-60; NIH, biologist 1952-55. **ORGANIZATIONS:** Mem Am Soc Qual Control 1972-; Plymouth Cong United Ch Christ; past chmn Bowie St Coll Bd Of Visitors 1973-78; mem exec bd Prince George Co; NAACP 1979; Chillum-ray Citizens Assn; imed past pres Morgan StUniv Nat Alumni Assn; mem DC Metro Chptr NCCJ; Org Black Sci; mem Omega Psi Phi Frat; Dem. **MILITARY SERVICE:** USN 1944-46. **BUSINESS ADDRESS:** 5600 Fishers Ln, Rockville, MD 20852.

MARTINEZ, RALPH
Chief executive. **CAREER:** Town and Country Chrysler-Plymouth Inc, Milwaukie, OR, chief exec. **BUSINESS ADDRESS:** Town and Country Chrysler-Plymouth Inc, 16803 SE McLoughlin Blvd, Milwaukie, OR 97267. *

MARVE, EUGENE
Professional athlete. **PERSONAL:** Born Jun 14, 1960, Flint, MI. **EDUCATION:** Saginaw Valley State Coll, BA. **CAREER:** Automobile assembly line worker; Buffalo Bills, linebacker 1982-. **HONORS/ACHIEVEMENTS:** Named to Football Digest and Pro Football Weekly All-Rookie teams and was fourth in balloting for AP Defensive Rookie-of-the-Year; two-time NAIA All-Amer at Saginaw Valley State Coll playing for coaches Muddy Waters and Jim Larkin; twice his team's MVP; three-time All-Great Lakes conf pick; named to the Amer Football Coaches Assn All-Amer Team 1981; Bills' candidate for Lite/NFL Man of the Year 1984-85. **BUSINESS ADDRESS:** Buffalo BIlls, One Bills Drive, Orchard Park, NY 14127.

MASCOLL, EDWARD G.
Business executive. **PERSONAL:** Born Jun 21, 1935, Boston; married Helen C Sayles; children: Dawn Helene. **EDUCATION:** LincolnUniv PA, Adv Ins Courses in Bus Pension & Tax Sheltered Plans. **CAREER:** Mutual Life Ins Co of NY Agcy, mbr; IBM, data proc eqpt spec 1958-63; began in Life Ins Bus 1964 as prof field underwri; 1968 moved into mngmt as asst agcy mgr. **ORGANIZATIONS:** Apptd 1st black agcy mgr for (Mony bd of dirs 100 Black Men; bd dirs Urban Home Ownership Corp; Nat Assn of Security Dlrs; Life Mgrs Assn Nat Assn Life Underw mem; NAACP; Urban League of Greater NY; NYh Coalition. **BUSINESS ADDRESS:** Ste 3700, 150 E 58 St, New York, NY 10022.

MASON, B. J.
Writer. **PERSONAL:** Born Oct 31, 1945. **EDUCATION:** Grambling St Univ, BS 1963; Colorado State Univ, MA 1965. **CAREER:** The Chicago Sun Times, features writer & novelist. **ORGANIZATIONS:** Writers Guild of Am W; Chicago Newspaper Guild. **HONORS/ACHIEVEMENTS:** 1st place Unity Awd for Minority Journalism, Operation PUSH, 1975; Black Film Critics Awd 1973. **BUSINESS ADDRESS:** c/o Ebony Magazine, 820 S Michigan Avenue, Chicago, IL 60605.

MASON, BRENDA DIANE
Counselor. **PERSONAL:** Born Nov 06, 1947, Paris, TX. **EDUCATION:** Chapman Coll, (Honors Sem) 1969;Univ of NV, BA 1974, MS 1977; McGeorge Sch of Law Sacramento; Stdnt. **CAREER:** N V Indust Commin, indus rehab coun 1975-77; St of NV,Univ regent 1974-76; Tchrs Corp, coord 1971-75; GED Stlud, lab Instr 1971; Westinghouse Cred, cred clk; VISTA Vol Trustee Higher Educ Commin NV; Mntl Hlth Tech Children 1975; Child Dvlp Ctr, tchrs aide 1967-68; Friendly Ctr for Span Am, tutor 1966-67; Op Indep, tutor 1965-66. **ORGANIZATIONS:** Nat Hnr Soc 1960-66; NAACP 1962-66; Fr Soc 1963-64; Std of Serv Abrd 1968; Blk Voters Assn 1975-76; NLV Dem Club 1974-; trustee Act Refrl Serv 1975-77;Univ regent 1974-82; hghr Educ Com L1974-82; Ebony shwcse Lthtr for Actng 1965; Guy Ctr Actors Wrkshp 1971. **HONORS/ACHIEVEMENTS:** Whos Who Amg AmUniv & Coll Stud 1974-75; Nat Mer Sch Fin 1965-66; schlrshp Chapman Coll & World Campus Afloat 1966-69; 6 Cert in Mus 1959-64. **BUSINESS ADDRESS:** 2601 E Sahara, Las Vegas, NV 89105.

MASON, CHERYL ANNETTE
Physician. **PERSONAL:** Born Jul 02, 1954, McAlester, OK; daughter of Lucious C Mason, III and Helen M Stuart; married Mack Henderson, Feb 14, 1988; children: Alisha Dixon; Samuel Dixon. **EDUCATION:** Univ of CA-San Diego, BA 1977; Howard Univ Coll Med, MD 1981. **CAREER:** San Pedro & Peninsula Hospital, family practice intern 1983; Georgetown Univ Hosp, resident Ob-Gyn 1983-87; The Memorial Hospital Danville VA Staff Physician 1987-89. **ORGANIZATIONS:** Mem Amer Business Women's Assn 1988-1990; mem Pittsylvania County Medical Society 1988-; bd mem American Cancer Society. **BUSINESS ADDRESS:** Medical Doctor, The Memorial Hospital, 326 Taylor Drive, Danville, VA 24541.

MASON, CLIFFORD L.
Playwright. **PERSONAL:** Born Mar 05, 1932, Brooklyn. **EDUCATION:** BA 1958. **CAREER:** Freelance writer; playwright; Manhattanville Clge, tchr; Rutgers Univ NEH Grant Theatre Res 1978; Grant for Playwriting NEH Grant 1979. **HONORS/ACHIEVEMENTS:** Pub article on Black Theatre NY Times Mag 1979; authored novel "When Love Was Not Enough" Playboy Press 1980.

MASON, DACOSTA V.
Administrator. **PERSONAL:** Born Jul 26, 1916, Brooklyn, NY; married Cynthia Rousseau; children: DaCosta Rousseau. **EDUCATION:** Howard Univ, AB 1942, JD 1947. **CAREER:** Legal Aid Soc of DC, exec dir 1974-; Neighborhood Legal Srv, mgng atty 1970-74; United Planning Org, gen couns 1964-70; dept of Army, statistician 1942-64. **ORGANIZATIONS:** Pres Far NE Civic Assc 1972; gen couns E of River Health Assc 1970-76; pres Ft DuPont Civic Assc 1964-70; pres E of River Health Assc 1977-; memFed Bar Assoc DC Chapt, Dist of Columbia Bar, WA Bar Assoc. **BUSINESS ADDRESS:** Executive Dir, Legal Aid Society of DC, 666 11th St NW, Washington, DC 20001.

MASON, EDWARD JAMES
Surgeon. **PERSONAL:** Born Jul 31, 1923, Greenville, AL; married Rae; children: James, III. **EDUCATION:** Youngstown Univ; Howard Univ; Clge of Med 1949. **CAREER:** DC General, surgeon self-emp, 1st black internship 1949-50; VA Hosp Tuskegee; Homer Phillips St Louis, residencies in gen surg; VA Hosp Pittsburg, 1st Black chief res 1959-60. **ORGANIZATIONS:** Diplomate Amer Bd of Gen & Abdominal Surgery; bd dir Forest Ave Hosp Dallas; BSA. **HONORS/ACHIEVEMENTS:** Natl Hon Soc 1942; Undergrad Hon Soc 1944; AOA Kappa Pi Med Hon Soc 1949; Trailblazer Award 1974. **BUSINESS ADDRESS:** 2516 Forest Ave, Dallas, TX 75221.

MASON, GILBERT RUTLEDGE
Physician. **PERSONAL:** Born Oct 07, 1928, Jackson, MS; married Natalie Lorraine Hamlar. **EDUCATION:** TN State Univ, BS 1947; Howard Univ, MD 1954. **CAREER:** Homer G Phillips Hosp St Louis, intern 1954-55; Biloxi, gen prac med 1955-; Harrison Co Head Start, med dir 1969. **ORGANIZATIONS:** Mem tissue & drug consult Howard Meml Hosp Biloxi 1967; chief family prac sect 1971; Fellow NY Research Found; diplomate Amer Bd Family Prac; fellow Amer Acad Family Phys; mem AMA; Natl Med Assc v chmn bd Greater Gulf Coast Sand Devel Corp 1970-; dir MS Indsl Spl Serv Inc; pres NAACP Biloxi 1960-; chmn USO 1959-60, 1970-; chmn Comm Action Prog 1966-69; mem city planning commn 1969-; mem state adv com Cabinet Com on Pub Educ 1970; mem state adv com Div Comprehensive Health Planning 1969-; v chrmn Harrison Co Regl Econ Commn 1973; Scoutmaster BSA 1959-72; pres Biloxi Civil League 1960-69; mem Harrison Co Dem Exec Com 1968-72; mem Alpha Phi Alpha; Elk Mason 32 Deg. **HONORS/ACHIEVEMENTS:** Recip Sivler Beaver Award BSA 1963; outst Alumnus citation Semi-Centennial Celebration TN State Univ 1962; Citizen of Year 1959, 64; Outst Citizen 1970. **BUSINESS ADDRESS:** 433 E Division St, Biloxi, MS 39530.

MASON, HILDA HOWLAND M.
City official. **PERSONAL:** Born Jun 14, Campbell County, VA. **EDUCATION:** Miner Teachers College, graduate; District of Columbia Teachers Coll, MA; SUNY Plattsburgh, Catholic Univ, Graduate work. **CAREER:** District of Columbia Public Schools, teacher, counselor, supervising instructor and asst principal; District of Columbia City Council, member-at-large 1977-. **ORGANIZATIONS:** Chairperson Comm on Educ DC City Council 1981-82, 1983-84, 1985-86; voting rep apptd by Council of the District of Columbia Washington Metro Area Transit Authority Bd of Dirs; present and past mem Amer Personnel & Guidance Assoc, District of Columbia Educ Assoc, Amer Federation of Teachers, DC Counselor-sAssoc, DC Citizens for Better Public Educ, Washington Urban League, NAACP, Women Strike for Peace, The District of Columbia and Natl Women's Political Caucus, Nat Org for Women, Natl Cncl of Negro Women. **HONORS/ACHIEVEMENTS:** Authored research and professional studies and served as an educ consultant and lecturer.

MASON, HOWARD KEITH
Physician. **PERSONAL:** Born Mar 19, 1949, Harrisburg, IL; married Adrienne Marie Murfree. **EDUCATION:** Wayne State Univ, BS 1971; Univ of MI, MD 1974. **CAREER:** Pvt prac 1977-; USN Med Corps, gen med ofcr 1976-; USC Med Ctr, psychiat residency 1975-76; internship 1974-75. **ORGANIZATIONS:** Amer Psychiat Assc Conv 1975-77; Interstate Postgrad Med Assembly 1976 DC Med & Soc; Alliance for Psychiat Prog; Black Psychiat of CA. **MILITARY SERVICE:** USN lt 1976-. **BUSINESS ADDRESS:** 6601 14th St NW, Washington, DC 20012.

MASON, JESSE W.
Farm program consultant. **PERSONAL:** Born Oct 18, 1912, Elliot, AR; son of Solomon Mason and Lillie Bradley Mason; married Levada P Mason, Jun 1953; children: Jesse Jr, C Vernon, Michael, Darryl, Patricia. **EDUCATION:** Attended Arkansas Baptist College, Little Rock AR, 1930-32; Tuskegee Inst, Tuskegee AL, BSA, 1936. **CAREER:** Lincoln Jr High School, Fayetteville AR, vocation agriculture instructor, 1936-38; Immanuel High School, Almyra AR, principal, 1938-41; Farm Security Admin, Servier County AR, asst county supervisor, 1940-41; Crittenden County, Marion AR, extension agent, 1941-44; Farmers Home Admin, Crittenden County AR, asst county supervisor, 1947-53, admin aide and county supervisor-at-large, 1956-62; Farm Program Office, program officer; Cooperative Education Program at Philander Smith College, Little Rock AR, coordinator, 1973-75; National Green Thumb Program, Little Rock AR, consultant, district dir, 1975-. **ORGANIZATIONS:** Life mem, state treasurer, NAACP, Arkansas chapter; treasurer, Little Rock Arkansas Baptist College Alumni Assoc, 1929-; treasurer, Phi Beta Sigma, 1969-; pres, Tuskegee Alumni Assoc, Little Rock Chapter, 1979-89. **HONORS/ACHIEVEMENTS:** Outstanding Service Award, Crittenden County AR, 1958; Federal Employee of the Year award, 1966; A Friend of the Year Award, Shorter College, 1969; Meritorious Service Award, President Nixon, 1970; citation from US Dept of Agriculture, 1971; certificate of recognition, Tuskegee Inst, 1982; service award, Univ of Arkansas at Pine Bluff, 1989. **HOME ADDRESS:** 3015 S Battery, Little Rock, AR 72206.

MASON, KENNETH
College administrator. **PERSONAL:** Born May 24, 1949, Chicago, IL; children: Mayimuna, Chilembwe. **EDUCATION:** Augustana Coll, BA 1972; Western IL Univ, MS 1976; Kent State Univ, MA 1982; The Univ of TX at Austin, ABD 1986. **CAREER:** Davenport Comm Schools, teacher 1974-76; Chicago City Colls Dawson Skill Ctr, asst dir admissions 1978-80; Univ of IL at Chicago, asst dir admissions & records 1980-82; African History Roosevelt Univ, instructor 1980-81; St Philip's Coll, instructor 1985-; San Antonio Coll, instructor 1986-; Trinity Univ, assoc registrar 1982-. **ORGANIZATIONS:** Mem Organization of Amer Historians, Natl Assoc for the Study of Afro Amer Life & History, African Studies Assoc, Natl Assoc of College Deans, Registrars & Admissions Officers, Amer Assoc of Collegiate Registrars & Admissions Officers;American Historical Assoc; TX Assoc Black Personnel in higher education. **HONORS/ACHIEVEMENTS:** Phi Kappa Phi Honor Society Univ of TX at Austin 1986. **BUSINESS ADDRESS:** Associate Registrar, Trinity University, 715 Stadium Dr, San Antonio, TX 78284.

MASON, LUTHER ROSCOE
Elected official & business executive. **PERSONAL:** Born Feb 21, 1927, Georgetown, KY; married Anne Nutter; children: Gregory K, Kurt D. **EDUCATION:** Ed Davis High School, 1945. **CAREER:** Amer Red Cross, dir 1975-; KY School Bds, dir 1979-; Scott Bd of Educ, chmn 1983-84, mem 1976-. **ORGANIZATIONS:** Council mem Scott Cty Agr Extension Serv 1981-. **HONORS/ACHIEVEMENTS:** Treas Scott Cty NAACP 1984-85. **MILITARY SERVICE:** AUS corpl 1947-49. **HOME ADDRESS:** 1290 Delaplain Road, Georgetown, KY 40324.

MASON, MAJOR ALBERT, III
Research associate. **PERSONAL:** Born Jul 15, 1940, McKeesport, PA; married Ann Mathilde Floberg; children: Major Albert IV, Arianna Melany. **EDUCATION:** Univ of Pittsburgh, MEd 1976. **CAREER:** Comm Clge of Allegheny Co, research assc 1974-; NOW Enterprises Inc, exec dir 1968-73; Comm Clge of Allegheny Co, reseach planning consult 1974-75. **ORGANIZATIONS:** Bd mem Allegheny OIC 1972-76; bd mem United Mental Health Inc 1973-75; radio show host WEDO Radio 1973-75. **HONORS/ACHIEVEMENTS:** Outst Young Men of Amer 1971. **MILITARY SERVICE:** USN musician first class 1960-66. **BUSINESS ADDRESS:** Community Coll of Allegheny Co, 610 Smithfield St, Pittsburgh, PA 15222.

MASON, ORENTHIA DELOIS
Educator. **PERSONAL:** Born Jul 16, 1952, Tyler, TX. **EDUCATION:** TX Clge, BS 1973 magna cum laude; Stephen F Austin Univ, pursuing MEd. **CAREER:** Brownsboro Ind Sch Dist, tchr. **ORGANIZATIONS:** Pres Natl Christian Youth Fellowship CME Ch; mem Gen Bd Christian Educ CME Ch; mem Tyler Alumnae Chap Delta Sigma Theta Inc; supt mem Bd Christian Educ Miles Chapel CME Ch; mem TX State Tchrs Assc; Henderson Co Tchrs Assc; secr Henderson Co Unit TX State Tchrs Assc of Amer Mem NAACP; mem Trustee Bd Phillips Schl of Theol; Govt Bd Natl Coun of Ch of Christ; World Coun of Ch; Div of Educ & Ministry NCC of Amer. **HONORS/ACHIEVEMENTS:** Named Outst Young Woman of Amer 1974; listed Who's Who in the S & SW 1972. **BUSINESS ADDRESS:** PO Box 98, Chandler, TX 75758.

MASON, WILLIAM ALFRED
Physician. **PERSONAL:** Born Aug 25, 1898, Houma, LA; married Virgi Douglas; children: William, Charles. **EDUCATION:** OH State Univ, BS; Meharry Med Clge, 1929; Provident Hosp, intern 1930; Yale Med Clge, MPH 1945; Vanderbilt Univ, post grad; NIH; Harvard Med Sch; Univ PA; Univ GA; Emory Univ; Univ NC; Emory Univ School of Medicine. **CAREER:** Spelman Coll, consult family planning; Atlanta Univ Complex Family Planning Srv, cons; Human Sexualtiy Spelman Clge Atlanta, lectr; Atlanta Planned Parenthood Assc, med dir; GA Dept of Pub Hlth, physician 1942-74; VA Hosp Tuskeegee, resd; Pub Hlth Clinic, dir; US Pub Hlth Srv, AA Surgeon 1935; YMCA Baltimore, physical dir 1924; YMCA KS, 1920; YMCA Columbus, boys work dir 1919. **ORGANIZATIONS:** Mem bd Atlanta Urban League; dir past pres Atlanta Girls Club; assc prof Meharry Med Clge; past vis lectr Clark Clge; Atlanta Univ; Mercer Univ; Atlanta Comprehensive Hlth Ctr, admin dir 1967; fdr dir Nghbrhd Union Hlth Ctr 1943; mem Alpha Phi Alpha Frat; Chi Delta Mu Med Frat; 32nd degree Mason; Shriner Cert; Educator In Human Sexuality Amer Assc of Sex Edcr Cnslr & Therapists; mem Gov's Council on Family Planning; life mem GA Public Health Assn; health consult Atlanta Council Boy Scouts of Amer. **HONORS/ACHIEVEMENTS:** Silver Beaver Award BSA; Meritorious Srv Award GA Dept of Human Resources; Beavor Award WSB WS Radio-TV Sta publ "An Odyssey in Black & White" Vantage Press 1977; num publ in med & pub hlth journal; Recip Alan Guttmachet Medallion for Distg Srv in Contraceptive Prac Planned Parenthood Assc 1980; recip Aven Citizenship Awd Med Assn of Atlanta; listed in Marquis ho's Who in the South & Southwest; reg listing Who's Who in Amer 1978-79. **BUSINESS ADDRESS:** Consultant Family Planning, Spelmar College, Atlanta, GA 30303.

MASON, WILLIAM E.
City official. **PERSONAL:** Born Mar 12, 1934, Shuqualak, MS; married Catheryn; children: Terry, William, Jr. **EDUCATION:** TN State U, BS 1952; So IL U, MS;Univ of St Louis, PhD 1975. **CAREER:** Institutional Research & Assoc, pres; Dist 189, tchr, prin, personnel dir, dist supt; E St Louis, IL, former mayor, former precinct committeeman; State of IL, human rights splst. **ORGANIZATIONS:** Mem E St Louis C of C; first pres, exec bd Comprehensive Educ Com; mem original Model Cities Planning Com; mem, bd dir Madison, St Clair Urban League; mem Phi Delta Kappa; Alpha Phi Alpha; Friendshp Bapt Ch. **BUSINESS ADDRESS:** President, Institutional Research & Assoc, 1800 Tudor, East St Louis, IL 62207.

MASON, WILLIAM THOMAS, JR.
Attorney. **PERSONAL:** Born Jul 27, 1926, Norfolk, VA; son of William T Mason and Vivian C Mason. **EDUCATION:** Colby Coll, BA 1947; Howard Univ, LLB 1950. **CAREER:** William T Mason Jr Atty, private practice 1951-63; Dept of Justice ED of VA, asst US atty 1963-72; Mason & Robinson Attys, partner 1972-79; Robinson Eichler Zaleski & Mason, partner 1980-87; Robinson, Zaleski & Lindsey, counsel, 1987-. **ORGANIZATIONS:** Mem & vice chmn bd of dir Norfolk Comm Hospital 1975-; bd mem Planning Council Urban League 1976-; editor Newsletter Old Dominion Bar Assn 1980-; sec bd of dirs Norfolk State Univ Foundation 1980-; overseer Colby Coll 1982-; mem & sec Bd of Visitors Norfolk State Univ 1969-73; sec, vice pres, pres Old Dominion Bar Assn 1969-84; sec, Norfolk Community Hospital Assn, 1985-. **HONORS/ACHIEVEMENTS:** Editor Newsletter Old Dominion Bar Assn, 1980-; Award for Devoted Serv Old Dominion Bar Assn 1983. **BUSINESS ADDRESS:** Partner, Robinson, Zaleski & Lindsey, 256 W Freemason St, Norfolk, VA 23510.

MASS, EDNA ELAINE
Company executive. **PERSONAL:** Born Mar 17, 1954, Escatawpa, MS; children: Edward Juwan. **EDUCATION:** Tougaloo Coll, BS 1976, Jackson State Univ, MEd 1978. **CAREER:** AT&T Network Systems, supervisor software tools develop. **HOME ADDRESS:** 1251 Folkstone Ct, Wheaton, IL 60187. **BUSINESS ADDRESS:** Supervisor Software Tools Dev, AT&T Network Systems, 2600 Warrenville Rd, Lisle, IL 60532.

MASSAQUOI, HANS J.
Editor. **PERSONAL:** Born Jan 19, 1926, Hamburg, Federal Republic of Germany;divorced; children: Steve, Hans, Jr. **EDUCATION:** Univ of IL, BS 1957; Northwestern Univ Medill Sch of Journalism, grad studies 1958. **CAREER:** Ebony Mag, mng ed 1967-, asst Mng ed 1964-67, assc ed 1959-64; Jet Mag, assc ed 1958-59; Natl Assc of Educ Broadcasters, ed 1947; West Africa, travel 1948-50; Brit Occupation Forces in Germany, interpreter 1945-47. **HONORS/ACHIEVEMENTS:** Receip Outst Immigrant Award Travellers Aid Soc & Immigrant Serv League 1970. **MILITARY SERVICE:** AUS parachutist 1951-53. **BUSINESS ADDRESS:** 820 S Michigan Ave, Chicago, IL 60605.

MASSE', DONALD D.
Physician. **PERSONAL:** Born Dec 09, 1934, Lafayette, IN; son of Otto Masse' and Frances Maxine Johnson Masse'; married Mary Perkins; children: Stephanie, Mark. **EDUCATION:** Purdue Univ, BS 1956; Marquette Med Schl, MD 1964; Wayne State Schl Med Post Grad Trng, Ob Gyn 1969. **CAREER:** Catholic Soc Serv Wayne Co, mem brd of dir 1970-84; Kirwood Hosp, chmn dept OB/GYN, 1974-77; St Joseph's Mercy Hosp, chmn dept OB/GYN 1978-80; SW Detroit Hosp, chmn dept OB/GYN 1977-80; Wayne State Univ School of Medicine Dept of Obstetrics & Gynecology, instructor. **ORGANIZATIONS:** Fincl sec Detroit Medical Soc 1973-75; instr Wayne State Univ Schl of Med dept OB/GYN; diplomat Amer Bd of Ob/Gynecology 1971; mem Wayne Co Med Soc, Detroit Med Soc, Wolverine State Med Soc, MI State Med Soc, Amer Fertility Soc, Amer Assn of Gynecologic Laparoscopists. **MILITARY SERVICE:** AUS. **BUSINESS ADDRESS:** 3040 E Seven Mile Rd, Detroit, MI 48234.

MASSEY, CARRIE LEE
Business executive. **PERSONAL:** Born Apr 23, 1922, Newberry, SC. **EDUCATION:** Almanello Beauty Inst, grad diploma 1940; New York Univ 1941-43; Benedict Coll, 1943-44. **CAREER:** Massey's Beauty Shoppe, owner/oper 1950-; Tryon City Schools, sch bd mem. **ORGANIZATIONS:** Membership chairperson Polk Co NAACP 1960-; bd mem Roseland Comm Ctr 1961-; mem Tryon City Bd of Educ 1972-; bd mem Habitat for Humanity Inc 1982-; bd mem Polk Co Unit Amer Heart Assn 1978-; charter mem Polk Co Bus & Professional Women's Assn 1977; mem Polk Co Juvenile Task Force 1981-. **HONORS/ACHIEVEMENTS:** All State Sch Bd NC Sch Bd Assoc 1984. **HOME ADDRESS:** 200 Cleveland Rd, Tryon, NC 28782.

MASSEY, HAMILTON W.
Chief executive. **CAREER:** Tropical Ford, Inc, Orlando, FL, chief exec. **BUSINESS ADDRESS:** Tropical Ford Inc, 11105 S Orange Blossom Trail, Orlando, FL 32921. *

MASSEY, JACQUELENE SHARP
Human relations specialist. **PERSONAL:** Born Oct 08, 1947, Jackson, MS; married James Massey; children: Jermane Edward, Jamie Patrice. **EDUCATION:** Knoxville Coll TN, BA Sociology 1979; DC Teacher Coll, Washington, Cert, 1970; Univ Coll, Univ of MD Baltimore, MS Gen Mgmt. **CAREER:** Univ of MD-Baltimore, assoc dir, special prog, 1978-; Baltimore City Public Sch; Baltimore; 1977-78; Fed Educ Prog/Direct Search for Talent MD, admin prog coord 1973-77; Delta Sigma Theta Inc/Public Serv Sorority, Mem office, 1970-71; DC Public School, teacher; US Dept Housing & Urban Devel Washinton, DC, summer coordinator, 1970. **ORGANIZATIONS:** 2nd vice pres, Delta Sigma Theta Inc, Public Serv Sor, 1965-67; cons/decision making prog Coll Entrance Exam Bd, NY, 1976; vice pres, Girl Scouts of Central MD, 1977-; Speakers Bureau, United Fund of Central MD 1977-78; cons/cosmetic Business Fashion Two-Twenty Co 1978-; mem, chmn Hebbville Elementary School PTA, 1979-. **HONORS/ACHIEVEMENTS:** Ldrshp Award White House Natl Youth Conf on Natural Beauty & Conservation 1965; Mayoral Award/ldrshp Mayor City Council Baltimore 1978; Thanks Badge Mgmt Ldrshp Award Girl Scouts of Central MD 1979. **BUSINESS ADDRESS:** RCA/Woodstock Job Corps Center, P O Box 8, Woodstock, MD 21207.

MASSEY, JAMES EARL
Clergyman. **PERSONAL:** Born Jan 04, 1930, Ferndale, MI; married Gwendolyn Inez Kilpatrick. **EDUCATION:** Detroit Bible Coll, BRE, BTh 1961; Oberlin Grad School of Theol, AM 1964; Asbury Theol Seminary, DD 1972; Pacific School of Religion, addit study 1972; Univ of MI, Boston Coll Grad Sch. **CAREER:** Church of God of Detroit, assoc minister 1949-51, 1953-54; Metro Church of God, sr pastor 1954-76; Anderson Coll & School of Theol, campus minister, profof religious studies 1969-77; Christian Brotherhood, speaker 1977-82; Anderson School of Theol, prof of new testament 1981-84; Chapel & Univ Prof of Religion, dean 1984-. **ORGANIZATIONS:** Lecturer Gautschi Lectures Fuller Theol Sem 1975-1986; Freitas Lectures Asbury Theol Sem 1977, Rall Co-Lecturer Garrett-Evangelical Sem 1980, Mullins Lectures So Bapt Sem 1981, Swartley Lectures Eastern Baptist Sem 1982, Jameson Jones Lecturer Iliff School of Theol 1983, Rom Lectures Trinity Evangelical DivSchool 1984; northcutt lectures Southwestern Bapt Theol Sem 1986;l bd of dir Detroit Council of Churches; theol study commiss Detroit Council of Churches; corp mem Inter-Varsity Christian Fellowship; matl comm Black Churchmen; mem Wesleyan Theol Soc; ed bd Christian Scholars Review; bd of dir Warner Press Inc; vchmn Publ Bd of the Church of God; ed adv Tyndale House Publisher 1968-69; comm chmn Christian Unity; mem Natl Assoc of Coll & Univ Chaplains; bd of dir Natl Black Evangelical Assoc; life mem NAACP; mem Lausanne Continuation Comm 1974-; pres Anderson Civil Serv Merit Commiss 1975-81; ed bd Leadership Mag; bd of dir Natl Religious Broadcasteers; ed bd Preacking Mag 1987; Resource Scholar, Christianity Today Inst 1985. **HONORS/ACHIEVEMENTS:** Listed in Contemporary Authors vols 29-32, Who's Who in the Midwest 13th ed, Outstanding Educators of Amer 1972, Dict of Intl Biography 10th ed, Men of Achievement 1973, Who's Who in Religion 1976-77,78-79, The Writers Dir 3rd ed, Biographical Dictionary of Negro Ministers 3rd ed; Underwood Fellow Danforth Found 1972-73; Staley Disting Christian Scholar Staley Found 1977; Who's Who in the South and Southwest 1986-87. **MILITARY SERVICE:** AUS corpl 1951-53. **BUSINESS ADDRESS:** Dean of the Chapel, Professor, Tuskegee University, The Tuskegee Chapel, Tuskegee, AL 36088.

MASSEY, REGINALD HAROLD
Minister. **PERSONAL:** Born Jun 23, 1946, Rowan Co; married Arletta Bingham MD; children: Angela, Marc, Reginald, Jr. **EDUCATION:** Livingstone Coll, BS Sociology; Hood Theological Sem Livingstone Coll, MDiv; Rowan Tech Coll, Cert Crisis Counseling. **CAREER:** Town of East Spencer Police Dept, police officer 1971-73; Town of East Spencer, mayor 1973-76, 1977-81; Salisbury Rowan Community Serv Council Inc, asst planner 1976-78, asst dir 1978; Herndon Chapel AME Zion Church, pastor 1979-81; Ezekiel AME Zion Church, 1979-83; VA Med Center Salisbury, chaplain 1984-; Center Grove AME Zion Church, 1983-. **ORGANIZATIONS:** Mem E Spencer Planning Bd; Aux Police 1971-73; mem C of C; So Conf of Black Mayors; com chmn NC League of Municipalities Com; Boy Scout Troup 383;mem Am Legion Post 107; E Spencer Civic League; Salisbury-Rowan Civic League; Livingston Coll Alumni Assn; bd trustees So City AME Zion Ch; mem Nat League of Cities, Nat Conf Black Mayors; exec com Durham Coll; vice pres NC Conf of Black Mayors; intergovt relations comm NC League of Municipalities 1980; water quality policy adv comm Gov's Appointment 1st term 1980; mem Masonic Lodge Western Star #9. **MILITARY SERVICE:** AUS sgt e-5 1966-69; Cert of Accomplishment at General Supply Ft Bragg. **HOME ADDRESS:** 633 S Long St, East Spencer, NC 28039.

MASSEY, WALTER EUGENE
University official, physicist. **PERSONAL:** Born Apr 05, 1938, Hattiesburg, MS; son of Almar Massey and Essie Nelson Massey; married Shirley Anne Streeter, Oct 29, 1969; children: Keith, Eric. **EDUCATION:** Morehouse Coll, BS 1958; Washington U, MA, PhD 1966. **CAREER:** Argonne Natl Lab, staff physicist 1966-68, consultant 1968-75, dir 1979-84, vice pres 1984—; Univ of IL, assistant prof 1968-70; Brown Univ, associate prof 1970-75, prof, dean, 1975-79; Univ of Chicago, prof, 1979—, vice pres for research, 1983—. **ORGANIZATIONS:** Mem review committee Natl Science Foundation 1971; mem review committee Natl Academy of Science 1973; American Association of Physics Teachers; mem Natl Science Bd 1978-84; fellow, bd of dir, 1981-85, pres elect, 1987, pres, 1988, American Association for the Advancement of Science; American Nuclear Society; American Physical Society; NY Academy of Sciences; IL Governor's Commission on Science and Technology; IL Governor's Science Advisory Committee; Sigma Xi; bd of dirs Amoco, Argonne-Chicago Development Corp, Motorola, Chicago Tribune Co, Continental Materials Corp, First Natl Bank of Chicago; bd of fellows Brown Univ; bd of trustees, Rand Corp, Museum of Science & Industry, Chicago Orchestral Association. **HONORS/ACHIEVEMENTS:** Numerous science publications; NDEA fellowship, 1959-60; Natl Science Foundation fellowship, 1961; Distinguished Service Citation, American Association of Physics Teachers, 1975; recipient of 10 honorary Doctor of Science degrees. **BUSINESS ADDRESS:** Vice President for Research, Argonne National Laboratory, The University of Chicago, 5801 South Ellis Ave, Chicago, IL 60637.

MASSIE, SAMUEL PROCTOR
Educator. **PERSONAL:** Born Jul 03, 1919, N Little Rock, AR; married Gloria Thompkins; children: Herbert, James, Samuel III. **EDUCATION:** Dunbar Jr Coll, AA 1936; AMN Coll, BS 1938; Fisk U, MA 1940; IA State U, PhD 1946. **CAREER:** USN Acad, prof chem 1966-; NC Coll, pres 1963-66; NC Coll, chmn 1977-; Howard U, chmn prof 1961-63; Fisk U, chmn, prof 1953-60; Langston U, chmn prof 1947-53; Fisk U, instr 1946-47; AMN Coll, asso prof 1940-41; Eastman Kodak Co, rsrch chem 1946-47; OSRD, rsrch chem 1943-46. **ORGANIZATIONS:** Asso prgm dir NSF 1960-63; Am Chem Soc 1941-; bd trustee Coll of Wooster 1966; v chmn MD State Bd of Comm Colls 1968-79; chmn MD State Bd of Comm coll 1979-; bd of vistors Towson StateUniv 1970-; Lehman Adv Com 1968-; Sigma Xi; Phi Lamba Upsilon; Rho Chi; Am Men of Sci; Sigma Pi Phi; pres OK Acad Sci 1953; Sigma Xi Lectr Swarthmore 1956. **HONORS/ACHIEVEMENTS:** MCA award excellence in tchng 1961; merit award IA State Alumni 1964; hon LLDUniv AR 1970; Freedom Fund Award NAACP 1975; Outstanding Prof Award NOBCHCE 1980. **BUSINESS ADDRESS:** Chem Dept USN Acad, Annapolis, MD 21402.

MATABANE, SEBILETSO MOKONE
Educational administrator. **PERSONAL:** Born Oct 26, 1945, Johannesburg, Republic of South Africa;married William N Matabane. **EDUCATION:** Syracuse Univ, BA 1969, MS 1970; Univ of TX Austin, PhD 1986. **CAREER:** Cook Productions, asst to pres 1974-75; Austin Comm Coll, media coord 1975-76; Austin Comm Coll, acting campus admin 1984-, dir learning resources 1976-. **ORGANIZATIONS:** Admin asst Chamba Prod 1970-71; instr TV Grahm Jr Coll 1971-72; oper asst United Nations Devel Prog 1974; bd mem Austin Comm TV 1977-80; adv bd mem KLRU-TV Comm Adv Bd 1980-; commr Cable Commn City of Austin 1984-; pres, Zakhele found; l987-; bd mem, Texas Assn for Educ Technology, l987-; chair, Assess Comm, Cable Commn, Austin TX, l985-; mem, community advisory bd, KLRU-TV, 1984-. **HONORS/ACHIEVEMENTS:** Outstanding Young Women of Amer 1979; pres Zakhele Foundation l987-; bd mem Texas Association for Educational Technology l987-; chair Access Committee Cable Commission Austin TX l985-; mem Community Advisory bd KLRU-TV. **BUSINESS ADDRESS:** Media Coordinator, Austin Community College, PO Box 140707, Austin, TX 78714.

MATCHETT, JOHNSON, JR.
Manager-training. **PERSONAL:** Born Oct 17, 1942, Mobile, AL. **EDUCATION:** Alabama State Univ, BS 1963; Univ of Alabama, MA 1969; Univ of Southern MS, EdS 1975. **CAREER:** Anniston Public Schools, teacher 1963-64; Mobile Public Schools, teacher 1964-69; Miles Coll, dir of teacher educ 1969-73; Alabama State Univ, part-time instructor 1972-75; Univ of So Alabama, curriculum consultant 1974; BellSouth Services Inc, mgr/training 1974-. **ORGANIZATIONS:** Mem Amer Soc for Training and Develop 1975-, Phi Delta Kappa Hon Educ Frat 1975-, Natl Soc for Performance and Instruction 1982-, NAACP 1983-; mem exec bd AL State Univ General Alumni Assoc 1985-; mem Natl Black MBA Assoc 1986-, AL Initiative for Black Coll Recruitment and Retention Birmingham Chapt1987-, Holy Family HS Bd of Dirs 1987.

MATHABANE, MARK JOHANNES
Writer. **PERSONAL:** Born 1960, Alexandra Township, Republic of South Africa;son of Jackson Mathabane and Magdelene Mabaso Mathabane; married Gail Ernsberger, Aug 01, 1987; children: Bianca Ellen. **EDUCATION:** Limestone College, 1978; St Louis Univ, 1979; Quincy College, 1981; Dowling College, Oakdale NY, BA Economics, 1983; Columbia Univ, 1984. **CAREER:** Free-lance writer and lecturer, 1985—. **ORGANIZATIONS:** Authors Guild. **HONORS/ACHIEVEMENTS:** Christopher Award, 1986; author of Kaffir Boy: The True Story of a Black Youth's Coming of Age in Apartheid South Africa, 1986; finalist, Robert Kennedy Memorial Award. **BUSINESS ADDRESS:** c/o Kevin McShane, Fifi Oscard Agency, 19 W 44th St, New York, NY 10036.

MATHES, JAMES R.
Educator. **PERSONAL:** Born Feb 07, Philadelphia; married Ann Higgs; children: Sjonia, Ngina. **EDUCATION:** Shaw U, BA 1964; Rutgers U, completion credits for Masters Deg in Educ 1975; Tenton State Coll, grad work 1967-68. **CAREER:** RutgersUniv Camden, dir proj talent search 1973-; Camden City, tchr 1964-69; Rutgers U, coor of curriculum urban uni prog 1969-70; Bur of Comm Serv, deputy dir 1970-73; Rutgers U, hd coach bsbl team 1970-. **ORGANIZATIONS:** Trea BPUM Devel Corp 1972-; vice pres Camden City Bd of Educ 1973-; Alpha Phi Alpha; Beta Rho Chap 1960; bd of dir BPUM Day Care; chmn Educ Com 1969-72; bd dir Centerville Liberty Park Ftbl Assn 1970-; EOF Adv Bd Rutgers; v chmn EOF Adv Bd Camden Co Coll; adv bdUniv in Act Glassboro StateColl; Mayor's Open Space & Recrea Task Force; bd dir S Jersey Opport Indsl Ctr; Kappa Delta Phi Nat Hon Soc in Educ 1977; bd of dir Comm AdvocacyCoun of Camden Co. **HONORS/ACHIEVEMENTS:** Concerned Citizen Award Club Athens 1969; for outstndg work dedic to BPUM Day Care 1970; candid for tchr of year award Camden Jaycees 1968; Outstndg Young Men of Am 1973. **BUSINESS ADDRESS:** Bd of Education, Camden, NJ 08101.

MATHEWS, GEORGE
Chief executive. **CAREER:** WGPR, Inc, Detroit, MI, chief exec. **BUSINESS ADDRESS:** WGPR TV 62 and Radio, 3140 E Jefferson, Detroit, MI 48207. *

MATHEWS, KEITH E.
Attorney. **PERSONAL:** Born Mar 02, 1944, Steubenville, OH. **EDUCATION:** Morgan State U, BS 1966;Univ of Baltimore, JD 1972. **CAREER:** US Dept of Justice Antitrust Div, atty 1974-75; Congressman Parren Mitchell, legislative asst 1973-74; Legal Aid Br of Baltimore, atty 1972-73; Foster Mathews & Hill, atty 1975-82; States Atty Office Baltimore, asst states atty 1978-83; District Court of MD, judge 1983-. **ORGANIZATIONS:** Bd of govs Univ of Baltimore Alumni Assn 1973; vchmn Consumer Affairs Adb Bd for Howard Co 1978; mem Monumental Bar Assoc, Natl Bar Assoc. **HONORS/ACHIEVEMENTS:** Editorial Staff Law Review Univ of Baltimore 1972; Validictorian Police Acad Baltimore City 1968. **BUSINESS ADDRESS:** Judge, District Court of Maryland, 5800 Wabash Ave, Baltimore, MD 21215.

MATHEWS, LAWRENCE TALBERT
Financial administrator. **PERSONAL:** Born Oct 12, 1947, Michigan City, IN; married Beverly Ann Hoze; children: Gerald. **EDUCATION:** Univ of MI Flint, AB 1969; Univ of Detroit, MBA 1975. **CAREER:** Arthur Young & Co, sr audtr 1972-75; Comm Credit/Mc Cullagn Lsng, cntrlr/treas 1975-78; MI Penisula Airwys, vice pres fin 1978-80; Clipper Intl Manuf, vice pres fin 1980-82; Comprehensive Hlth Serv of Detroit, dir of fin oper. **ORGANIZATIONS:** Dir Natl Assn Blk Acctnts; mem MI Assn Hlth Mntnce Org Finance Comm; asst exec dir Detroit Area Agncy on Aging 1984. **HONORS/ACHIEVEMENTS:** Dstng-

shd Serv Natl Assn Blk Accts 1985; CPA State of MI 1975. **MILITARY SERVICE:** AUS 1st lt 3 yrs; Disngshd Mltry Grad/Off Cand Sch 1973.

MATHIS, DAVID
Government official. **PERSONAL:** Born Sep 16, 1947, Riverhead, NY; son of Freddie MacThompson; married Dorothy; children: Darren, David, Denise, Doreen. **EDUCATION:** Mohawk Valley Comm Coll, AAS 1970; Uitca Coll of Syracuse Univ, BS 1972. **CAREER:** Mohawk Valley Oppor Indus Ctr, dir of training 1972-73, exec dir 1973-74; Career Develop Ctr, dir of manpower serv 1974-79, dir of job develop 1979-80; Oneida Co Employment & Training, dep dir 1980-86, dir 1986-. **ORGANIZATIONS:** Bd of dirs Cosmopolitan Comm Ctr; bd of dirs pres Utica Head Start; bd of trustees Hope Chapel AME Zion Church; adv bd Oneida Co Youth Bureau; bd of trustees Mohawk Valley Comm Coll; Utica Coll Natl Alumni Council, mem; Assoc of Governing Bds of NY State Comm Colleges, exec comm; Mohawk Valley Frontiersmen, mem; Utica Coll Ed Bass Black Students Scholarship Fund, chmn; bd of dirs Ferre Institute 1988; bd of dirs Mohawk Valley Resource Center for Refugees 1986; bd of dirs Neighborhood Center of Utica 1988; Pres-bd of dirs Council of Churches of Mohawk Valley Area; bd of Trustees Munson-Williams-Proctor Institute 1988. **HONORS/ACHIEVEMENTS:** Outstanding Comm Serv Awd Mohawk Valley Frontiersman 1977; Man of the Yr Awd St Time 1978; 10th Yr Outstanding Grad Higher Educ Oppor Prog 1980; Outstanding Alumnus Mohawk Valley Comm Minority Union 1981; Citizen of the Yr Awd League of Women Voters Utica/Rome 1984; United Way of Greater Utica, Hero Awd; Utica Coll, Outstanding Alumnus; Len Wilbur Awd, Utica Kiwanis Club 1986; Outstanding Service Award Lambda Kappa MU 1987; Achievement Award, Oneida County NAACP 1987; Community Achievement Award, Aleppo # 140 1988; Outstanding Community Service Award Utica Salvation Army 1987. **BUSINESS ADDRESS:** Dir, Oneida Co Employment & Training, 800 Park Ave, Utica, NY 13501.

MATHIS, ELMERTHA BURTON
Physician. **PERSONAL:** Born Jul 12, 1948, Greenville, MS; married Paul Jr. **EDUCATION:** Howard U, BS; Meharry Med Coll, MD; Providence Hosp, resd. **CAREER:** Physician pvt prac. **ORGANIZATIONS:** Mem Wayne Co Med Soc; mem Detroit Bus Women Club; Barrister Wives. **HONORS/ACHIEVEMENTS:** Rsrch paper "The Effects of Oxytocin on Pre-elampsia and/or Essential Hypertension".

MATHIS, FRANK
Association executive. **PERSONAL:** Born Aug 04, 1937, Fort Valley, GA; son of Otis Mathis, Sr (deceased) and Laura B Lockhart Mathis Gibson. **EDUCATION:** Fort Valley State Coll, Fort Valley, GA, BS Zoology; Natl Exec Inst, Mendham, NS, professioanl scouter-BSA. **CAREER:** Boy Scouts of Am, dist scout exec 1954-72; Savannah Area Minority Contractors Assn Inc, dist dir 1972-. **ORGANIZATIONS:** Mem Natl Assn Minority Contractors; charter mem Natl Greene Sertoma Club; Alpha Phi Omega Frat; Natl Council Christian & Jews; owner, Mathis & Assoc-Advertising/Business Consultant, 1980-; consultant, Diocese of Savannah Social Apotlates, 1988-. **HONORS/ACHIEVEMENTS:** Boy of Yr Award 1955; Virgil Honor Order of the Arrow Natl Camping Soc 1967; Benedictine Medal 1971; St George Award Diocese of Savannah 1971; Leadership Award More Pure Heart of Mary's Parish 1972; Outstanding Citizen Award GA State Beauty Culture League 1974; DPC Service Award, Diocese of Savannah, 1981; Black Amer Hall of Fame, 1984; Masjid Jihad Award, 1985; Tought Love For Teenager, Salt Publication, 1985. **HOME ADDRESS:** 911 W 37th St, Savannah, GA 31401. **BUSINESS ADDRESS:** Office of Black Ministry, Diocese of Savannah, PO Box 1983, Savannah, GA 31402.

MATHIS, JOHNNY
Singer. **PERSONAL:** Born Sep 30, 1935, San Francisco, CA. **EDUCATION:** San Francisco St Coll, attended. **CAREER:** San Francisco Night Clubs, singer informal jam sesions; numerous recordings, film, stage &TV appearances; singing tours Europe, Australia, S Amer, Orient, Canada; Columbia Records, recording artist. **BUSINESS ADDRESS:** Rojon Productins, 3500 W Olive Ave #750, Burbank, CA 91505.

MATHIS, ROBERT LEE
Business executive. **PERSONAL:** Born Apr 21, 1934, Concord, NC; son of Minnie V Mathis; married Margaret Miller; children: Calven, Rodney, Jeffery, Kim West. **EDUCATION:** US Navy, Cooks & Bakers School 1956; Central Piedmont Comm Coll, AS Political Science 1976; NC State Univ, Personnel Mgmt Diploma 1978; St Louis Univ, Food Serv Diploma 1978. **CAREER:** Cabarras Memorial Hospital, cook spec diets 1958, cook & baker supvr 1965, asst food serv dir 1979. **ORGANIZATIONS:** Dir Cabarrus Cty Boys Club 1979-; mem Mt Zion Lodge 26 Concord NC 1980-, NC Chapter of Amer Soc Hospital; Food Serv 1980; advisory bd Salvation Army 1981-; leader Boy Scouts 1983; dir Cab County United Way 1983; mem bd of visitor Barber-Scotia Coll Concord NC 1984; delegate for the city NC Centralina Council of Government; elder First Christian Church; bd of dir Life Center and Logan Day Care. **HONORS/ACHIEVEMENTS:** Represented the largest ward in NC 1980; First Black elected Bd of Alderman Concord Bd of Alderman 1980-; Outstanding Citizen of the Year Kannpolis Daily Independence 1981; Co-Founder Fourth Word Devel Corp 1982; vice chmn Logan Optimist; Citizen of the Year by Phi Chi 1985. **MILITARY SERVICE:** USN third class commissaryman 5 1/2 yrs; Natl Defense, Korean Serv 1951-56. **BUSINESS ADDRESS:** Assistant Food Service Dir, Cabarrus Memorial Hospital, 920 Church St, Concord, NC 28025.

MATHIS, SALLYE BROOKS
Councilwoman. **PERSONAL:** Born in Jacksonville, FL; widowed. **EDUCATION:** Benedict Coll; Bethune Cookman, AA; Tuskegee Inst, BS; FL A&M U, M. **CAREER:** Dist 11 Jacksonville City Coun, city counwm; Duval Cty Sch, tchr; Matthew Gilbert Sch, dean of girls. **ORGANIZATIONS:** Mem city coun bd dir Leag of Women Voters; bd of dir City Mission Ashley St; bd of dir Health Maintenance & Operation (HMO); pres Minority Women's Coalition; mem Bethel Bapt Ch; Llongest tenure of 19 mem on council (13 yrs) elected 4 times two without opposition; com Citizens for Better Edn; bd dir Oppty Indsltn Ctr; bd dir YWCA; Delta Sigma Theta Sor; Alcoholic Advis Com; Chan 7 TV trustee; FL State NAACP bd; Meth Hosp Fnd; Prbtnrs Res Bd. **HONORS/ACHIEVEMENTS:** One of 1st 2 blk women elec cty coun; FL Publ Cmpy's Eve Aw 1973. **BUSINESS ADDRESS:** 10th Fl City Hall, Jacksonville, FL 32202.

MATHIS, SHARON BELL
Educator, author. **PERSONAL:** Born Feb 26, 1937, Atlantic City, NJ; daughter of John Willie Bell and Alice Mary Frazier Bell; married Leroy Franklin Mathis, Jul 11, 1957 (divorced 1979); children: Sherie, Stacy, Stephanie. **EDUCATION:** Morgan State Coll, BA, 1958; Catholic Univ of America, MLS, 1975. **CAREER:** Childrens Hosp of District of Columbia, Washington DC, interviewer 1958-59; Holy Redeemer Elem School, Washington DC, teacher 1959-65; Stuart Junior High School, Washington DC, special education teacher, 1965-75; Chas Hart Junior High School, 1972-; DC Black Writers Workshop, writer-in-charge of childrens lit div; Howard Univ, Washington DC, writer-in-residence, 1972-73; Benning Elem School, Washington DC, librarian 1975-76; Friendship Education Center, librarian 1976-. **ORGANIZATIONS:** Mem bd advisors, lawyers comm of District of Columbia Commn on the Arts, 1972; mem, Black Women's Community Development Foundation, 1973-. **HONORS/ACHIEVEMENTS:** Council on Interracial Books for Children Award, 1970, for Sidewalk Story; fellowship from Wesleyan Univ and Weekly Readers Book Club, Bread Loaf Writer's Conf, 1970; Child Study Assoc Awards, 1971, 1972; awards from New York Times and American Library Assn, 1972, for Teacup Full of Roses; Corretta Scott King Award and Boston Globe/Horn Book Honor Book, 1974, for The Hundred Penny Box; Arts and Humanities Award, Archdiocese of Washington Black Secretariat, 1978; fellowship, MacDowell Colony, 1978; nomination by Natl Conf Christians and Jews for Books for Brotherhood List. **BUSINESS ADDRESS:** Librarian, c/o Marilyn Marlow, Curtis Brown Ltd, 60 E 56th St, New York, NY 10022. *

MATHIS, THADDEUS P.
Educator. **PERSONAL:** Born Sep 08, 1942, Americus, GA; married Christine Harris (divorced); children: Latanya. **EDUCATION:** Bluefield State Coll, BS (Cum Laude) Secondary Ed 1965; Bryn Mawr Coll, MS Social Work 1968; Temple Univ, PhD Political Sci 1985. **CAREER:** Dept of Public Welfare, group leader 1965-66; Child Study Center of Philadelphia Temple Univ Hospital, social work intern 1966-68; Dept of Public Welfare, social worker 1968; Philadelphia Model Cities Program, planning coordinator 1968-70; Temple Univ, assoc prof of social admin 1970-. **ORGANIZATIONS:** Exec comm Philadelphia Congress of Racial Equality 1971-75; chairperson Philadelphia Black Political Convention 1971-80; presiding officer Natl Black Independent Political Party 1981-83; chairperson School of Soc Admin Grad Dept 1981-84; pres Philadelphia Alliance of Black Soc Workers; bd mem Housing Assocof Deleware Valley. **HONORS/ACHIEVEMENTS:** Shapp Found Scholar Shapp Foundation Philadelphia 1961-65; PEP Fellow State of PA Office of Children & Youth 1966-68; Fellow Urban Affairs Inst Amer Univ 1971; Outstanding Young Man 1973; Listed in Who's Who in the East 1981-82; Bernard C Watson Awd 1985. **HOME ADDRESS:** 163 W Wyneva St, Philadelphia, PA 19144. **BUSINESS ADDRESS:** Associate Professor Soc Admin, TempleUniv, RA 539 13th & Columbia Ave, Philadelphia, PA 19122.

MATHIS, VERDELL LEFTY
Athlete. **PERSONAL:** Born Nov 18, 1918, Crawfordville, AR; married Helen; children: Jean, Ann, Verdell Jr, Helen. **CAREER:** Memphis Red Sox, bsbl player 12 yrs; MX, winter bslb; PR. **HONORS/ACHIEVEMENTS:** S Am candidate Baseball Hall Fame; cert recog Blues Stad 1974; award for performance "Old Timers" of baseball.

MATHIS, WALTER LEE, SR.
County official. **PERSONAL:** Born Feb 02, 1940, Columbus, MI; married Patricia E Grier; children: Walter, Tracy, Daryl, Melissa. **EDUCATION:** Davenport Coll MI, ceret acctng. **CAREER:** Meijer Inc, shpng clerk mgr trainee; Mathis Tax Serv, owner; Party Store, owner; Co, comm. **ORGANIZATIONS:** Past mem Grand Rapids Hsng Bd of Appeals; past bd mem Freedom Homes Inc; mem NAACP; mem Kent-CAP Gob Bd. **HONORS/ACHIEVEMENTS:** Named VIP of Grand Rapids Press 1972. **MILITARY SERVICE:** AUS pfc 1959-62. **BUSINESS ADDRESS:** 1014 Franklin SE, Grand Rapids, MI 49507.

MATHIS, WILLIAM LAWRENCE
Law student. **PERSONAL:** Born Feb 27, 1964, Albany, GA; son of William L Reynolds and Eliza A Gorce. **EDUCATION:** Morehouse Coll, Atlanta GA, BA, 1985; Boston Coll Law School, Newton MA, JD, 1989. **CAREER:** US House of Representatives Select Comm on Narcotics Abuse & Control, Washington DC, staff asst, 1985-86; New York County District Attorney's Office, New York City NY, legal intern, 1987; Smith, Somerville & Case, Baltimore MD, summer assoc, 1988; The Honorable David Mitchell, Baltimore MD, judicial clerk, 1989-. **ORGANIZATIONS:** Mem, Morehouse Coll Alumni Assn, 1985-; natl chmn, Natl Black Law Students Assn, 1986-89; Northeast Regional dir, Natl Black Law Students Assn, 1987-88; bd mem, Natl Conference of Black Lawyers, 1988-, Natl Bar Assn, 1988-89; mem, consultant, Natl Assn of Public Interest Law, 1988-; bd mem, Natl Alliance Against Racism and Political Repression, 1988-; mem, Boston Coll Black Alumni Network, 1989-. **HOME ADDRESS:** 1405 Cromastre Beach Dr, Albany, GA 31705.

MATLOCK, KENT
Advertising manager, consultant. **PERSONAL:** Born in Chicago, IL. **EDUCATION:** Morehouse Coll, BA 1982. **CAREER:** Anheuser-Busch Inc, public relations rep 1979-80; Visual Persuasion Inc, accts exec 1980-81; Garrett/Lewis/Johnson, accts exec 1981-83; Georgia Pacific Corp, mgr adv & sales promo. **ORGANIZATIONS:** Mem NAACP 1977-78; co-chair publicity United Negro College Fund Inc 1984-85; mem Atlanta Adv Club 1984-85. **HONORS/ACHIEVEMENTS:** Lt Col Aide DeCamp Governors Staff 1982-85; Meritorious Serv Awd UNCF 1985. **HOME ADDRESS:** 1133 Scott Blvd, Decatur, GA 30030. **BUSINESS ADDRESS:** Manager of Adv & Sales Promo, Georgia-Pacific Corp, 133 Peachtree St NE, Atlanta, GA 30303.

MATNEY, WILLIAM C., JR.
Public affairs, communications consultant. **PERSONAL:** Born Sep 02, 1924, Bluefield, WV; son of William C Matney Sr and Jane A Matney; widowed; children: Alma, Angelique, William III. **EDUCATION:** Wayne State Univ, 1940-42; Univ of Michigan, BA 1946. **CAREER:** The Michigan Chronicle, reporter, sports editor, city editor, mng editor 1946-61; Detroit News, reporter, writer, 1962-63; WMAQ-NBC, TV and radio reporter 1963-65; NBC Network Television, correspondent 1966-72; ABC Network News, correspondent 1972-78; Who's Who Among Black Americans, founding editor 1974-88, consulting editor 1988-; US Bureau of Census, public affairs coord 1979-. **ORGANIZATIONS:** Mem, Big Ten Championship Track Team, 1943; pres, Cotillion Club, 1962-63; mem, NAACP; AFTRA; Alpha Phi Alpha; Natl Acad of Television Arts and Sciences. **HONORS/ACHIEVEMENTS:** 1st black exec sec, Michigan State Ath Assn, 1950-61; 1st black reporter, Detroit News, 1960-63; 1st black network news correspondent, NBC News, 1965-70; Natl Achievement Award, Lin-

coln Univ, 1966; Man of the Year, Intl Pioneers, 1966; Sigma Delta Chi Citation, 1967; Outstanding Achievement Citation (Emmy), Natl Acad of Television Arts and Sciences, 1967; 1st black correspondent permanently assigned to the White House, Washington NBC News, 1970-72; Natl Award, Southern Press Inst, 1976; Hon Dr Jour, Benedict Coll, 1973; Outstanding TV Correspondent, Women in Media, 1977; Outstanding Natl Corres Serv Award, Michigan Minority Business Enterprise Assn, 1977; Natl Advisory Comm, Crisis Magazine, NAACP, 1981-. **MILITARY SERVICE:** USAAF 1943-45. **BUSINESS ADDRESS:** US Bureau of the Census, Washington, DC 20233.

MATORY, DEBORAH LOVE
Clinical psychologist. **PERSONAL:** Born Apr 20, 1929, Norfolk, VA; daughter of Bishop David C Love and Nannie Reid Love; married William Earle Matory, Jul 26, 1949; children: William Earle Jr MD, Yvedt Love MD, James Lorand PhD. **EDUCATION:** Howard Univ, BS 1950, MS 1955. **CAREER:** DC Public School, clinical psychologist 1959-66; WA Tech Inst, assoc prof psych 1969-71; NMAF, rsch assoc, clin psych; Mod Cit Health Outreach Health Welfare Council, dir 1971; DHR DC, planning dir 1973-75; private practice, cons, clinical psych; DC Public Schools Handicap Svcs, coord. **ORGANIZATIONS:** Consultant, Albert Deutsch Rehab Ctr, Shaw Comp Health Ctr, Stanford Univ, Univ of Pacific, School of Educ; prog dir Phizer Pharm Co; plnd progs & conf Lederle Pharm Co, Natl Med Assoc, DC Men Health Assoc; mem US Civil Rights Comm; bd dir SAC; mem Inst of Mental Hygiene, Soc Hygiene Soc, Mental Health Assn, Epilepsy Foundation, Howard Univ Alumni, Amer Assn of Univ Women, Womens Auxiliary to the Med Chirurgical Soc; founder, pres Ward Four Dem Inc; bd mgr PTA Cong; ed chprsn Women's Natl Med Assn 1964-66; pres, Civic League of North Portal Estates; pres, Women's Auxiliary to Medico-Chirurgical Society, Inc. **HONORS/ACHIEVEMENTS:** Natl Hon Soc; Psi Chi Hon Soc; Fellowship to Grad School; Woman of the Year Awd Womens Aux to Med Chirurgical Soc 1967; Woman of the Year Afro-Amer Newspaper & Greyhound Bus Lines 1967; numerous citations, plaques for outstanding community involvement; NAACP Humanitarian Awd 1987. **HOME ADDRESS:** 1645 N Portal Dr NW, Washington, DC 20012.

MATORY, WILLIAM EARLE, JR.
Plastic surgeon. **PERSONAL:** Born Nov 20, 1950, Richmond, VA; son of William E Matory and Deborah Matory; married Yvonne Marie Johnson, Aug 01, 1989. **EDUCATION:** Yale, BS, 1972; Howard Univ, MD, 1976; Harvard Univ, Fellow, 1981. **CAREER:** Univ of Mass Medical Center, Worcester MA, Assoc Prof, Plastic Surgery, Anatomy, 1984-89. **HONORS/ACHIEVEMENTS:** Fellow, Amer Soc Plastic Reconstruction Surgeons, 1985; author of Rhinoplastics in The African American, 1985; Fellow, Amer Coll of Surgeons, 1987; One Clinic Award, 1988; author of Aging in the African American, 1989; author of Aesthetics in the African American, 1989. **BUSINESS ADDRESS:** Univ of Mass Medical Center, 55 Lake Avenue N, Worcester, MA 01605.

MATSON, OLLIE GENOA
Athlete. **PERSONAL:** Born May 01, 1930, Trinity, TX; married Mary Paige; children: Lesa, Lewis, Ollie III, Bruce, Barbara. **EDUCATION:** San Francisco City Coll, 1948;Univ of San Francisco, BS1952. **CAREER:** Prof scout 1966-68; Philadelphia Eagles, prof football player 1964-66; Detroit Lions, player 1962-63; LA Rams, player 1959-62; Chicago Cardinals, player 1952-59. **ORGANIZATIONS:** Pres Swinger Golf Club; mem Kappa Olympic Track Team 1952. **HONORS/ACHIEVEMENTS:** Prof Hall of Fame 1972; Coll Hall of Fame 1976. **MILITARY SERVICE:** AUS corpl 1953-54. **BUSINESS ADDRESS:** Los Angeles Sports Arena, 3911 Figueroa, Los Angeles, CA.

MATTHEW, CLIFTON, JR.
Educator. **PERSONAL:** Born Sep 25, 1943, Brooklyn, NY; married Claraleata Cutler; children: Darryl, Adrian. **EDUCATION:** NC A&T State Univ, BS 1966; Rutgers Univ, MEd 1973. **CAREER:** Baltimore Orioles, professional baseball player 1966-71; Camden Sch Sys, tchr 1966-71; Trenton State Coll, head baseball coach 1974; Upward Bound, dir; Educ Oppty Fund Trenton St Coll, asst dir 1971-74; Camden City Bd of Edn, supr recreation 1974-79; Pleasantville Pub Sch, dir comm educ 1979-83; Lower Camden Cnty Bd of Ed, asst principal 1983-. **ORGANIZATIONS:** Mem Kappa Alpha Psi; mem Natl Assoc of Secondary Sch Principals, NJ Principals and Supervisors Assoc. **BUSINESS ADDRESS:** Assistant Principal, Lower Camden Cnty Bd of Ed, 250 Coopers Folly Rd, Atco, NJ 08004.

MATTHEWS, ALBERT D.
Retired judge. **PERSONAL:** Born Feb 19, 1923, Oklahoma City, OK; son of Samuel Matthews and Della Matthews; married Mildred; children: Angela M. **EDUCATION:** Howard Univ School of Law, LLB 1954; Howard Univ, 1941-43, 1950-51. **CAREER:** State of CA, superior court judge, 1973-89 (retired); municipal court judge, 1968-73; Pro Tempr, superior court commr, 1962-68; Dept Employment, state referee hearing officer, 1960-62; LA County, deputy district attorney, 1958-60; private practice, 1955-58. **ORGANIZATIONS:** Mem LA Bar Assn; Langston Law Club, Natl Conf Trial Court Judges; Amer Bar Assn; mem, bd of dir, Henderson Community Center, S LA; bd mgrs, Amer Baptist Pac SW; chmn, MATE; deacon, church school admin, 2nd Baptist Church, LA; exec bd, Amer Baptist Churches, USA Valley Forge, PA; Sunday School Teacher, past 48 years, christian educator. **HONORS/ACHIEVEMENTS:** Graduated cum laude, Howard Univ, 1954. **MILITARY SERVICE:** AUS sgt 1943-45. **HOME ADDRESS:** PO Box 501, Claremont, CA 91711.

MATTHEWS, ALVIN LEON
Professional athlete. **PERSONAL:** Born Nov 07, 1947, Austin, TX; married Demille; children: Marcus, Kia Marie. **EDUCATION:** TX A&I U, BS 1970; B & A Sch Real Estate. **CAREER:** Green Bay Packers, professional football player; Seattle Seahawks;Univ of TX, asst coach 1977; Anderson-Wormley, real estate broker;Univ TX Austin First Black Coach Sch History, asst football coach 1972-74. **ORGANIZATIONS:** E Austin Optimist Club 1972; TX A&IUniv Alumni Assn; NAIA Distinguished Athletes Assn 1970-; Am Football Coaches Assn 1972-74; AP Little All Am 1969; Nat Student Register 1970; Kappa Alpha Psi Frat exec com Nat Football Leag Players Assn; Men of Achiev 4th Edit; Rishon Masonic Lodge # 1; All Decade Team Lone Star Conf. **HONORS/ACHIEVEMENTS:** Outstanding Young Men Am 1974; Outstanding Coll Athletes Am 1970; NAIA All Am 1969; All Lone Star Conf 1969. **MILITARY SERVICE:** Nat Guard spl 5 1970. **BUSINESS ADDRESS:** Anderson Wormley, 3724 Airport Blvd, Austin, TX 78722.

MATTHEWS, AQUILLA E.
Business executive. **PERSONAL:** Born in Danville, VA. **EDUCATION:** Columbia U, BS; Northwestern U, MS. **CAREER:** Guest Houses, owner 1985; VA State Coll, prof music edn; So U, prof music edn;; USO Hattiesburg MS Witchita Falls TX, dir; Mobile Serv AZ CA NE, dir; Atlantic City Parking Authority, sec 1985; US Pres Bd of Edn, 1st black women 1985. **HONORS/ACHIEVEMENTS:** Many Plaques & Awards For Disting Serv to Edn, Tchrs Assn, Youth Activites & Counseling; NAACP Citations.

MATTHEWS, BILLY
Professional athlete. **EDUCATION:** Attended Southern Univ. **CAREER:** UCLA, coach 1971-78; San Francisco 49'ers, running back coach 1979-82; Philadelphia Eagles, running back coach 1983-84; Indianapolis Colts, offensive coord.

MATTHEWS, CLAUDE LANKFORD, JR.
Television news producer. **PERSONAL:** Born Jun 18, 1941, High Point, NC; son of Claude Matthews and Georgianna Matthews; married Cynthia C Clark; children: Georgeanne N. **EDUCATION:** Howard Univ, BA 1963; Georgetown Univ Law Ctr, JD 1978. **CAREER:** WTOP-TV, reporter 1968-70, host of talk show "Harambee" 1970-74; NBC News, editor network radio 1976-77, editor network TV 1977-80, Washington producer weekend nightly news 1980-. **ORGANIZATIONS:** Mem Pennsylvania Bar Assn; mem American Bar Assn; mem District of Columbia Bar Association. **HONORS/ACHIEVEMENTS:** Host of Emmy Awd winning talk show "Harambee" on WTOP-TV Washington DC 1970-74. **HOME ADDRESS:** 2805 31st Pl NE, Washington, DC 20018. **BUSINESS ADDRESS:** Producer, NBC News, 4001 Nebraska Ave NW, Washington, DC 20016.

MATTHEWS, CYNTHIA CLARK
Attorney. **PERSONAL:** Born Aug 27, 1941, Nashville, TN; married Claude Lankford. **EDUCATION:** Wellesley Coll, Attended 1959-61; Howard U, BA 1965; George WashUniv Nat Law Center, JD 1973. **CAREER:** Ofc of Exec Dir Equial Employment Opportunity Commn, atty/adv 1985; Housing Com Council of DC, exec asst to council mem & atty 1976-79; Onyx Corp, vice pres for marketing & contract mgr 1975-76; US Comm on Civil Rights, equal opportunity specialist 1973-75; United Planning Orgn, pub information ofcr 1970-72; Hon John Conyers US Congress, legislative & press asst 1965-69. **ORGANIZATIONS:** Mem DC Bar 1975; mem Supreme Court Bar 1980; mem US Dist Ct for DC Bar 1980; mem Nat Assn of Black Women Atty/Am Bar Assn/Anacostia Mus Bd of Dir. **BUSINESS ADDRESS:** Equal Employment Opportunity C, 2401 E St NW, Washington, DC 20506.

MATTHEWS, DAVID
Clergyman. **PERSONAL:** Born Jan 29, 1920, Indianola, MS; son of Albert Matthews and Bertha Henderson Matthews; married Lillian Pearl Banks; children: Denise D. **EDUCATION:** Morehouse Coll, BA 1950; Natchez Coll, DD 1973; MI Coll, D of Humanities 1977. **CAREER:** Sunflower Cty & IN Public Schools, teacher 1950-83; Mt Heroden Baptist Church Vicksburg MS, pastor 1951-53; St Paul Baptist Church, pastor 1953-58; Baptist Church State Baptist Conv & Natl Convention USA Inc, pastor, pres & vice pres. **ORGANIZATIONS:** Appointed Southern Governor's Ecumenical Council of Infant Mortality 87. **HONORS/ACHIEVEMENTS:** Doctor of Divinity (Hon), Morris Booker Memorial College, 1988. **MILITARY SERVICE:** AUS pfc 1942-45; Good Conduct Medal, APTO Medal 1945. **HOME ADDRESS:** PO Box 627, Indianola, MS 38751.

MATTHEWS, DOLORES EVELYN
Educational administrator. **PERSONAL:** Born Jul 23, 1938, DuBois, PA; daughter of Evelyn Goodrich Matthews. **EDUCATION:** New York City Comm Coll of AA&S, Associate 1971. **CAREER:** Columbia Univ Coll of Physicians & Surgeons Dept of Psychiatry, program coordinator, postgraduate education; officer, Columbia Univ Dept of Psychiatry. **ORGANIZATIONS:** Past pres bd of trustees North Presbyterian Church; mem EDGES Group Inc; chorus mem Carnegie Hall's Oratorio Soc; founder/mem New York State Psychiatric Inst Women's Chorus; mem Continental Societies Inc; mem Harlem Hospital's Pastoral Care Comm; guest speaker Religious Coalition for Abortion Rights; mem Natl Assn of Negro Musicians; guest speaker Harlem Hospital's Comm Bd/Harlem Hospital's Medical Bd; natl parliamentarian Continental Societies Inc; Elder Commissioner Presbytery of New York City; chair, Education & Nurture Unit Presbytery of NY City. **HONORS/ACHIEVEMENTS:** Grant recipient Natl Endowment of the Arts 1977; Merit Awd Presbyterian Hosp Comm Adv Council 1978; President's Awd Continental Societies Inc 1982; Distinguished Music Alumna Awd DuBois Area HS 1985. **HOME ADDRESS:** 790 Riverside Drive, New York, NY 10032. **BUSINESS ADDRESS:** Program Coordinator Postgraduate Education, Department of Psychiatry, Columbia University, 72 W 168th St, New York, NY 10032.

MATTHEWS, DOROTHY
Advertising manager. **PERSONAL:** Born Jan 21, 1962, St Louis, MO. **EDUCATION:** Maryville Coll, BA 1983. **CAREER:** NY Ins, salesperson 1983; Channel 4 Newsroom, rsch person 1984; School Bd Dist 188, sec. **ORGANIZATIONS:** Mem Elks Purple Temple 126, Black Media Coalition St Louis, First Freewell Baptist Church, United Parcel Holiday Club. **HONORS/ACHIEVEMENTS:** Citizenship Lovejoy School 1979; Best Essay First Freewill Bapt Church 1979; Valedictorian Lovejoy HS 1979. **HOME ADDRESS:** 412 Jefferson St, Lovejoy, IL 62059.

MATTHEWS, GARY NATHANIEL
Professional athlete. **PERSONAL:** Born Jul 05, 1950, San Fernando, CA; children: Gary Jr, Delvon, Dustin, Dannon. **CAREER:** San Francisco Giants, outfielder 1972-76; Atlanta Braves, outfielder 1977-80; Philadelphia Phillies, outfielder 1981-83; Chicago Cubs, outfielder 1984-. **ORGANIZATIONS:** Active in Ronald McDonald House. **HONORS/ACHIEVEMENTS:** NL Rookie of the Yr BBWAA & Sporting News 1973; NL Player of the Month Sept 1981; NL All Star Team 1979. **BUSINESS ADDRESS:** Chicago Cubs, Wrigley Field, 1060 West Addison St, Chicago, IL 60613.

MATTHEWS, GREGORY J.
Business administrator. **PERSONAL:** Born Oct 25, 1947, Baltimore, MD; married Paula Allen. **EDUCATION:** Morgan State Univ, BA Sociology 1970; Coppin State Coll, MA Counseling 1973. **CAREER:** Adult Ed Economic Manpower Devl, instr 1970; Conciliation & Compliance-MD Comm on Human Rel, dir 1970-75; Intl Assn of Ofcl Human Rgts Agcies , EEO consultant 1975; Affirmative Action-Great Atlantic Pacific Tea Co, dir 1975-78; GJ Matthews & Assoc, mgng prtnr 1984-; Staffing and Equal Opp Prog, dir 1978-85; American

Express Travel Related Servics, Co, Inc, dir employee relations 1985-. **ORGANIZATIONS:** Chrmn Natl Urban Affrs Cncl 1983-; chrmn Fed of Corporate Profsnls 1983-; brd mem Assoc Black Charities; life mem NAACP; bd mem Natl Assoc Market Dev; mem Edges Group. **HONORS/ACHIEVEMENTS:** Key to the City Kansas City, MO 1984; Herbert H Weight Awd 1985; distinguished serv citation Natl Black MBA Assoc 1984. **BUSINESS ADDRESS:** Dir Employee Relations, American Express Travel, World Financial Center, New York, NY 10285.

MATTHEWS, HARRY BRADSHAW
Educational administrator. **PERSONAL:** Born Mar 01, 1952, Denmark, SC; son of James Edgar Matthews and Lucretia Killingsworth Parler Matthews; married Pamela Davis. **EDUCATION:** SUNY Coll at Oneonta, BA 1974; Carnegie Mellon Univ, 1979; Northern MI Univ, MA 1981. **CAREER:** NYS Minority Ways & Means Rsch Div, trainee, intern 1973-74; SUNY Coll Oneonta, asst dean in rsch 1974-78; Northern MI Univ, dir black student serv 1978-81; Hobart & William Smith Coll, asst to deans 1981-85; Gettysburg Coll, dean of intercultural advancement 1985-. **ORGANIZATIONS:** Mem MI Gov & Bd Educ Task Force 1980-82, Human Rights Commission Geneva NY 1983-85; consultant The Matthews Plan 1984-; fellow Coll of Preceptors UK 1985-, Royal Commonwealth Soc UK 1985-; mem July 3rd Comm Gettysburg Peace Celebration Commission 1987-; Pennsylvania Historical & Museum Commission's Black History Advisory Comm, 1989; chmn, Internship Program, Afro-Amer Historical & Genalogical Soc, 1989; dir & founder, Minority Youth Educ Inst, 1988-. **HONORS/ACHIEVEMENTS:** Presidential Classroom for Young Amers 1970; Amer Legion Leadership Award SUNY Oneonta 1974; Distinguished Visitor US 8th Air Force 1979; WEB DuBois Dist Lecturer Hobart & William Smith Coll 1986; Certificate of Merit, AAHGS, 1989; The Matthews Method in African Amer Genealogy, essay published by Univ of SC, 1989; founder & dir, Intercultural Resource Center, highlighting African Amer Genealogy Gettysburg Coll, PA, lst in the nation at a coll. **HOME ADDRESS:** 140 W Broadway, Gettysburg, PA 17325. **BUSINESS ADDRESS:** Dean of Intercultural Advance, Gettysburg College, Box 430, Gettysburg, PA 17325.

MATTHEWS, HEWITT W.
Educator, administrator. **PERSONAL:** Born Dec 01, 1944, Pensacola, FL; married Marlene Mouzon; children: Derrick, David. **EDUCATION:** Clark Coll, BS 1966; Mercer Univ School of Pharmacy, BS Pharmacy 1968; Univ WI Madison, MS 1971, PhD 1973. **CAREER:** Center for Disease Control, research chemist 1976, visiting scientist, summer 1987, 1988; TX Southern Univ, visiting assoc prof 1979; Mercer Univ School of Pharmacy, asst dean 1980-83; Mercer Univ Atlanta, prof & asst provost; Mercer Univ School of Pharmacy, prof, assoc dean 1985-. **ORGANIZATIONS:** Bd of dir, Metro Council on Alchol & Drugs, 1980-84, Atlanta Chapter Amer Red Cross, 1986-, Georgia Pharmaceutical Assn, 1988-; item writer, Natl Assn Bd of Pharmacy Licensure Examination, 1981-83; comm member, Amer Council on Pharm Educ, FDA Conf on Consumerism 1985; Continuing Educ, 1982-; editorial advisory bd, US Pharmacist Journal, 1982-83; ed comm, Paul D West Middle School, 1983-84. **HONORS/ACHIEVEMENTS:** Fellow, Amer Found for Pharmaceutical Educ, 1968; Natl Inst of Health, predoctoral fellow, 1970-76; prof of the year, Mercer Univ School of Pharm, 1980; Hood-Myers Alumni Chair, Mercer Univ School of Pharmacy, 1983-. **BUSINESS ADDRESS:** Professor & Assoc Dean, School of Pharmacy, Mercer Univ, 345 Boulevard NE, Atlanta, GA 30312.

MATTHEWS, JAMES VERNON, II
Roman catholic priest. **PERSONAL:** Born Oct 25, 1948, Berkeley, CA; son of James Vernon Matthews and Yvonne Feast Matthews. **EDUCATION:** St Patrick's Coll, Mountain View, CA, BA Humanities, 1970; St Patrick's Seminary, Menlo Park CA, MDiv, 1973; Jesuit School of Theology, Berkeley CA, DMin (candidate), 1977-79. **CAREER:** St Louis Bertrand Church, Oakland CA, assoc pastor, 1974-78; All Saints Church, Hayward CA, admin, 1978-80; St Cyril Church, Oakland CA, admin, 1980-83; Diocese of Oakland, Oakland CA, vicar of Black Catholics, 1983-87; St Cornelius Church, Richmond CA, admin, 1987-. **ORGANIZATIONS:** Knights of St Peter Claver Third and Fourth Degrees, 1971-; mem, past bd mem, Natl Black Catholic Clergy Caucus, 1973-; review bd, Alameda County Revenue Sharing, 1975-76; bd of dir, Campaign for Human Devel, 1979-84; commr, Oakland School District, Comm on Educ and Career Devel, 1982-83; Bay Area Black United Fund Religious Task Force, 1982-; bd of dir, Catholic Charities: Parish Outreach Program, 1983-87; advisory bd, Oakland Mayor's Task Force on Hunger, 1984-87, Oakland Mayor's Task Force on black/Jewish Relations, 1984-87; Diocesan coord, Natl Conference on Interracial Justice, 1984-. **HONORS/ACHIEVEMENTS:** Outstanding Black Sermons, Judson Press, Publishers, 1975; Rose Casanave Serv Award, Black Catholic Vicariate, Oakland CA, 1982; Martin Luther King Jr Award, United East Oakland Clergy, 1984; Marcus Foster Distinguished Alumni Award, Marcus Foster Educ Inst, 1984; Religion Award, Alameda/Contra Costa Chapter of Links Inc, 1985; Service Award, Xavier Univ Alumni Assn, 1985. **HOME ADDRESS:** 225-28th St, Richmond, CA 94804. **BUSINESS ADDRESS:** Administrator, St Cornelius Catholic Church, 225-28th St, Richmond, CA 94804.

MATTHEWS, JESSIE L.
Librarian. **PERSONAL:** Born Aug 18, 1935, Charleston, WV. **EDUCATION:** Kutztown State Coll, BS 1958;Univ IL, MS 1959; State Coll, Reference Libr Cheyney 1959-60; Morristown Coll, Libr 1960-62; RutgersUniv Law Sch Library 1962. **CAREER:** Mem Am Assn Law Libraries 1962-; chmn Directories Com 1972-74; editor co-author Indexer. **BUSINESS ADDRESS:** 5 Penn Sts, Camden, NJ 08102.

MATTHEWS, LAMOYNE MASON
Educator. **PERSONAL:** Born Aug 08, 1931, Emporia, VA; divorced; children: Derrick, Yvette, Kevin. **EDUCATION:** Morgan State Univ, AB 1951; Howard Univ, MSW 1961; Univ of MD, PhD 1976. **CAREER:** Baltimore City Dept of Soc Svcs, caseworker-dist suprv 1954-65; MD State Dept Soc Svcs, training spec 1965-68; Montebello Chronic Disease & Rehab Hosp,dir soc work 1968-69; Morgan State Univ, prof soc work, asst dean 1969-82; US Foreign Svc, citizens consular serv Monterey Mexico 1983-85, San Salvador1985-87; US Dept of State, chief post liaison serv 1987-. **ORGANIZATIONS:** Mem Acad of Cert Soc Workers 1961-, Delta Sigma Theta 1950-, Baltimore Urban League, NAACP. **HONORS/ACHIEVEMENTS:** Natl Teaching Fellow 1973-74; Univ of MD Grad School Fellowship 1973-75; Educ to Africa Study Grant 1974; 100 Outstanding Baltimore Women Delta Sigma Theta1974; Baltimore Cty Bd of Ed 1979-84; publ num works, presented num papers. **BUSINESS ADDRESS:** Chief Post Liaison Serv, US Department of State, Washington, DC.

MATTHEWS, LEONARD LOUIS
Educator/principal. **PERSONAL:** Born Dec 04, 1930, New Orleans, LA; married Dolores; children: Mallory Louis. **EDUCATION:** Southern Univ, BS/BA 1952-59; CA State Univ, Crdntl Psych 1964-65; Univ of CA Los Angeles, Crdntl Psych 1970-72, Pepperdine Univ Los Angeles, Crdntl Educ 1973-74; CA State Univ, MA Educ 1972-74. **CAREER:** St John School Dist, elem principal 1952-59; LA Unified School Dist, drama spec/master teacher 1959-70, counselor 1970-74; Inglewood Unified School Dist, secondary principal 1974-. **ORGANIZATIONS:** Organizer Citizens Against Prostitution 1982-84, Dr Martin L King Jr Memorial 1983-86, Citizens Against Crime & Drugs 1984-86; mem/officer Parents TeachersAssoc 1985-86, Young Men Christian Assoc 1985-86, Inglewood Mgmt Assoc 1986; mem CA Continuation Educ Assoc. **HONORS/ACHIEVEMENTS:** Awd of Recognition Project Investment 1978; Proclamation City of Inglewood 1980,82; Service Awd Assoc of CA Administrators 1982; Commendation City of Inglewood 1985. **MILITARY SERVICE:** AUS act/sgt 1976-78. **HOME ADDRESS:** 9626 5th Ave, Inglewood, CA 90305. **BUSINESS ADDRESS:** Principal, Inglewood Unified School Dist, 441 W Hillcrest Blvd, Inglewood, CA 90301.

MATTHEWS, MALLORY LOUIS
School administrator. **PERSONAL:** Born Mar 29, 1953, New Orleans, LA. **EDUCATION:** Univ of CA-Los Angeles, BA Psychology 1975; Pepperdine Univ, MA Educ Admin 1977. **CAREER:** Los Angeles Co, autism project counselor 1975; Averitt Youth Home/Prob Dept, counselor/teacher 1975; Junipero Serra HS, dir counseling/services 1976-79, admin/supervisor 1976-79; Archdiocese of LA, teacher social studies life science 1977-79; Inglewood Unified School Dist, dir actvts student council advisor 1979-81, school dist consultant 1980-82, adult educ coord 1980-, mem bd of dirs 1982-, asst principal 1981-. **ORGANIZATIONS:** Mem St Eugene's Church 1975-, CA Activities Dirs Assoc 1981-84, Assoc of CA Sch Admins CA Teachers Assoc 1981-, City of Inglewood Parks and Rec Commn1982-, YMCA 1984-, St mary's Acad Bd of Dirs 1984-, Inglewood Mgmt Assoc 1984-, Natl Assoc of Secondary Principals 1985-, Inglewood Democratic Assoc 1986-. **HONORS/ACHIEVEMENTS:** Commendations Hillcrest HS 1982-86, Morningside HS 1982-86, Morningside Dad's Club 1982-86, Inglewood Unified Sch Dist 1982-86, Mayor Edward Vincent Cityof Inglewood 1984-, Congressman Mel Levine 1984-86, Inglewood HS 1986, Senator Dianne Watson 28th Senatorial Dist 1986, Congressman Julian Dixon 1986; author "Self-Image in Black High School Students" 1975, "An Anthology of Political & Sociological Readings" 1977. **BUSINESS ADDRESS:** Assistant Principal, Inglewood Unified Sch Dist, 401 So Inglewood Ave, Inglewood, CA 90301.

MATTHEWS, MARY JOAN
Educator. **PERSONAL:** Born Dec 19, 1945, Boley, OK; married H Carl Matthews. **EDUCATION:** Langston Univ, BS Elem Ed 1967; CA State Coll Dominguez Hills, MA Learning Disabilities 1976; Univ of OK, Cert Psychometry 1980. **CAREER:** Paramount Unified School Dist, teacher 1st grade 1968-70; Sapulpa City School, teacher 5th grade 1971-74; Boley Public Schools, teacher LD 1976-79; OK StateDept of Ed, psychometrist 1979-. **ORGANIZATIONS:** Sec Greater Boley Area NAACP Branch 1981; mem OK Council for Vocational Ed 1982-; sec Boley Chamber of Commerce 1983-, Bd of Dir CREOKS Mental Health 1983-. **HOME ADDRESS:** PO Box 352, Boley, OK 74829.

MATTHEWS, MERRITT STEWART
Physician. **PERSONAL:** Born Jul 08, 1939, Atlantic City, NJ; son of George Matthews and Bessie Stewart Matthews; married Patricia Anne Delgado; children: Shari, Luis, Merritt Jr, Michael, Marguerite. **EDUCATION:** Howard Univ, BS Liberal Arts 1961, MD School of Medicine 1965. **CAREER:** St Joseph's Hospital, intern, 1965-66, resident, 1966-68, chief resident family practice, 1967-68; Otay Medical Clinic SD CA, medical dir, 1972-76; San Diego Acad of Family Physicians, pres, 1984-85; Family Practice Comm Paradise Valley Hospital, chairperson, 1983-86; Skilled Nursing Facility of San Diego Physicians & Surgeons Hospital, med dir, 1983-87; private practice, physician. **ORGANIZATIONS:** Physician, dir, San Diego County Jails, 1976-; bd of dir, San Diego Acad of Family Physicians, 1982-, Jackie Robinson YMCA San Diego, 1983-85, Logan Ave Community Clinic SD, 1985-87; co-dir, Wester Medical Group Lab, 1982-87; member, Task Force SD Police Dept, 1983; delegate 1987-, bd of dir 1988-, CA Acad of Family Physicians; alternate delegate, CA Medical Assn, 1987-. **HONORS/ACHIEVEMENTS:** Certified, Amer Bd of Family Physicians, 1970, re-certified 1976, 1982; fellow, Amer Acad of Family Physicians, 1974; published article "Cholelithiasis: A Differential Diagnosis in Abdominal Crisis of Sickle Cell Anemia," Journal of NMA, 1981; Special Achievement Award, Jackie Robinson YMCA, 1985. **MILITARY SERVICE:** USAF capt 1968-70. **BUSINESS ADDRESS:** 286 Euclid Ave #309, San Diego, CA 92114.

MATTHEWS, MIRIAM
Librarian, historian, consultant. **PERSONAL:** Born Aug 06, 1905, Pensacola, FL; daughter of Reuben H Matthews (deceased) and Fannie Elijah Matthews (deceased). **EDUCATION:** Univ of CA, AB 1926;Univ of CA, Cert of Librarianship 1927;Univ of Chicago, MA 1945. **CAREER:** Retired 1960; So Centrl Region Los Angeles Pub Lib, reg librarian, 1949-60; NY Pub Lib, exchange Libr 1940; Lib, br 1929-49; Los Angeles Pub Lib, libr 1927-29; LA Pub Lib, radio book reviewer 1927-35. **ORGANIZATIONS:** Life mem Am Lib Assn; counc 1947-51; mem Intellectual Freedom Com; CA Lib Assn; chmn Intellectual Freedom Com 1946-48; nominating com 1950; mem Youth Commn LA Co 1938-40; mem Adv Bd Nat Youth Adminstrn 1938-39; mem Mayor's Birthday Fiesta Com 1954-61; Mayor's Comm Adv Com 1961-65; pres vp Exposition Comm Coord Conc 1951-60; exec bd Nat Intercoll Christian Counc 1937-38; CA Cit Educ Adv Counc 1935-36; exec bd NAACP Legal Def Fund for So CA; lfe mem NAACP; bd of trustees, California Afro-Amer Museum Found, El Pueblo Park Assn, & Roy Wilkins Found, currently; advisory bd, Los Angeles City Historical Soc, currently. **HONORS/ACHIEVEMENTS:** LA Fellshp League 1935; LA Urban League 1948; LA Co Bd of Supr 1960; LA Sentinel 1960; Nat Cong of Parents & Tchrs 1960; Expo Com Coord Counc 1965; Nat Assn of Media Women 1975; Fedn of Black Hist & Arts 1974; Award of Merit, California Historical Soc, 1982; Woman of the Year Award, Women on Target, 1985; Distinguished Service Award, Black Caucus of the Amer Library Assn & California Librarians Black Caucus, 1987; Miriam Matthews Award inaugurated at California State Univ at Dominguez Hills, 1988; Elected Fellow, Historical Soc of Southern California, 1988; contrib to professional journals.

MATTHEWS, ROBERT L.
Educational administrator. **PERSONAL:** Born Jun 02, 1930, Tonganoxie, KS; son of Mark Hanna Matthews and Susie Jane Brown Matthews; married Ardelle Marie Dunlap, Aug 26,

1952; children: Mark Douglas, Brian Louis, Scott Wallace. **EDUCATION:** KS State Teachers (Emporia, KS), BS 1952; Columbia Univ, MA 1955; US Internatl Univ, PhD 1971; UCLA, Stanford, San Diego State Univ, Advanced Studies. **CAREER:** San Diego City Schl, tchr 1955-64, princpl 1965-72, dir of elem ed 1972-83, princpl 1983-84; Educ Cultural Complex, pres 1984-86; Continuing Education Centers San Diego Comm Coll Dist; pres 1986-. **ORGANIZATIONS:** Mem, Education Committee, San Diego Zoological Society 1973-; member and officer, San Diego Urban League, 1965-; NAACP; pres, Zeta Sigma Lambda Alpha Phi Alpha 1984-85; pres Elem Inst of Sci 1983-84; bd of dir Museum of Natl Hist 1984-. **HONORS/ACHIEVEMENTS:** Humanities Fellowship, Natl Endowment for Humanities 1976; fellowship Rockefeller Foundation 1971-72; NDEA fellowship US Govt 1965. **MILITARY SERVICE:** AUS cpl; Peace Medal, Marksmanship 1952-54. **HOME ADDRESS:** 4931 Dassco Court, San Diego, CA 92102. **BUSINESS ADDRESS:** President, Continuing Educ Centers, 5350 University Ave, San Diego, CA 92105.

MATTHEWS, VINCENT
Athlete. **PERSONAL:** Born Dec 16, 1947, Queens, NY. **EDUCATION:** Johnson C Smith Coll. **CAREER:** Olympic Track Runner. **ORGANIZATIONS:** Mem Olympic Teams 1968, 1972; Ran 440 yd in 444. **HONORS/ACHIEVEMENTS:** Won Silver Medal Pan-Am Games 1967; AAU 1968; ran on US 1600-m relay team which set world record; Founded Brooklyn Over the Hill Athletic Assn; won Gold Medal Munich Olympics 1972.

MATTHEWS, VIRGIL E.
Scientist, educator. **PERSONAL:** Born Oct 05, 1928, Lafayette, AL; son of Virgil W Matthews (deceased) and Iletta Roberta Ware Matthews (deceased); married Shirley E McFatridge, Jan 23, 1960 (divorced); children: Brian K, Michael A, Deborah M. **EDUCATION:** Univ of IL, BS 1951; Univ of Chicago, SM 1952, PhD 1955. **CAREER:** Univ of Chicago, teaching asst 1951-52; WV State Coll, instr part time chem 1955-60, prof part-time chem 1960-70; Union Carbide Corp, rsch chemist 1954-67, proj scientist 1967-75, develop scientist chem & plastics div 1975-86; WV State College, Dept of Chemistry, prof and chmn 1986-. **ORGANIZATIONS:** Councilman-at-Large Charleston 1967-83; mem Municipal Planning Commn Charleston 1971-83; chmn Planning Comm of City Council Charleston 1971-83; mem NAACP, vice pres Charleston Branch 1964-72; mem Charleston Bus & Professional Men's Club pres 1965-66; mem Amer Chem Soc; Fellow Amer Inst of Chemists; Fellow AAAS; mem Sigma Xi; Phi Lambda Upsilon; del Dem Natl Conv from WV 1968; Dem nominee for state senate 8th Dist of WV 1970; Amer Men of Sci; alternate delegate, Dem Natl Convention from West Virginia 1980; Democratic Nominee for City Treasurer of Charleston WV 1983. **HOME ADDRESS:** 835 Carroll Rd, Charleston, WV 25314. **BUSINESS ADDRESS:** Prof/Chmn Department of Chemistry, West Virginia State College, Institute, WV 25112.

MATTHEWS, WANDA DENISE
Elected official. **PERSONAL:** Born Nov 16, 1960, Washington, DC. **EDUCATION:** Univ of DC, Bus Admin 1978; Computer Learning Ctr, Computer Programmer/Operation 1981; Training & Oppty in Programming, Computer Programmer 1983. **CAREER:** Far Southeast Comm Org, housing counselor 1979-80; Information Sci Corp, data tech 1980-82; Wilson Hill Assoc, data tech 1982-83; Timesaver Inc, computer programmer 1983-. **ORGANIZATIONS:** Treas AL Ave Renaissance Task Force 1972-84; sec Far Southeast Comm Org 1980-; treas Advisory Neighborhood Comm 1982-84; ward volunteer Rainbow Coalition Presidential Election 1984; precinct coord Ward 8 City Council Election 1984. **HONORS/ACHIEVEMENTS:** Outstanding Young Woman of Amer 1983.

MATTHEWS, WESTINA LOMAX
Executive. **PERSONAL:** Born Nov 08, 1948, Chillicothe, OH; daughter of Rev Wesley Matthews and Ruth Matthews. **EDUCATION:** Univ of Dayton, BS 1970, MS 1974; Univ of Chicago, PhD 1980. **CAREER:** Mills Lawn Elem Sch, teacher 1970-76; The Chicago Comm Trust, sr staff assoc 1982-85; Merrill Lynch & Co, Inc, mgr corp contributions 1985-87, mgr corp contributions and comm affairs 1987-; Merrill Lynch & Co Foundation, Inc, secretary, 1985-. **ORGANIZATIONS:** Mem Mathematics Interpretation Team Natl Assessment of Educ Progress 1983; founder/chair Chicago Blacks in Philanthropy 1983-85; dir, Assn of Black Foundation Execs 1983-86; columnist "In Black and White" Dawn Magazine 1986; mem Governor's Adv Comm Black Affairs 1986-; dir NY Regional Assn of Grantmakers 1986-89; chair, Contributions Advisory Group 1989-; dir, Ms Foundation 1989. **HONORS/ACHIEVEMENTS:** Postdoctoral Fellow Northwestern Univ 1980-81, Univ of WI-Madison 1981-82; Kizzy Awd for Outstanding Women 1985; numerous articles published in educ journals on minorities participation in math and science; Black Achiever in Industry, YMCA of Greater New York Harlem Branch, 1989; Mary McLeod Bethune Recognition, Natl Council of Negro Women, 1989. **BUSINESS ADDRESS:** Vice President, Corporate Contributions & Community Affairs, Merrill Lynch & Co, Inc, World Financial Center, South Tower, New York, NY 10080-6106.

MAULDEN, JERRY L.
Utility company executive. **PERSONAL:** Born 1936, North Little Rock, AR. **EDUCATION:** Univ of AR, BS 1963. **CAREER:** Dyke & Assocs Inc, acct 1959-61; Madigan James & Co CPA's, sr auditor 1961-62; Dillard Dept Stores Inc, asst controller 1962-64; AR Power & Light Co, asst controller 1968-71, controller, asst sec, asst treas, spl asst to pres 1971-73, sec-treas 1973-75, vice pres fin svcs, sec-treas 1975-79, pres, ceo 1979-. **ORGANIZATIONS:** Dir AR Power & Light Co. **BUSINESS ADDRESS:** President, CEO, Arkansas Power & Light Co, PO Box 551, Little Rock, AR 72203.

MAULE, ALBERT R.
Business administrator. **PERSONAL:** Born Feb 18, Philadelphia, PA; son of Albert D Maule and Jessie R Maule; married Yvonne D; children: Albert C. **EDUCATION:** Hillyer Jr Coll, AS Accounting 1944; Wharton School of Finance Univ of PA, BSE Accounting 1947, MBA Personnel & Indus Mgmt 1949; Command & General Staff Coll (US Army), Diploma 1969; Industrial Coll of Armed Forces, Diplma 1976. **CAREER:** Amer Garages, Inc Parking Mgmt, mgr 1953-62; Hartford Housing Authority, project mgr 1962-67; Vietnam Bonus Div Off of State Treasurer, deputy dir 1967-70; Univ of CT Law School, asst to dean for fiscal affairs 1970-84; State of CT, Banking Commr, exec asst 1984-. **ORGANIZATIONS:** Exec bd Long Rivers Council Boy Scouts of Amer 1970-; pres Rocky Hill Civitan Club 1980-; club pres Res Officers Assoc Hfd Chapter 1967-1970; mem Natl Guard Assn 1975-; dist pres Omega Psi Phi Fraternity Inc 1974-74; commr Human Relations Comm Rocky Hill 1976-80. **HONORS/ACHIEVEMENTS:** Aide Camp Governor's Military Staff 1975-; Silver Beaver, Long Rivers Council, Boy Scouts of Amer 1987. **MILITARY SERVICE:** US Army 1949-53, US Army Reserve 1953-75, Connecticut Army Natl Guard 1975-82, brigade general. **HOME ADDRESS:** 7 Mark Lane, Rocky Hill, CT 06067. **BUSINESS ADDRESS:** Executive Asst To Banking Commissioner, State of CT Dept of Banking, 44 Capitol Ave, Hartford, CT 06106.

MAULTSBY, DOROTHY M.
Community organization director. **PERSONAL:** Born Feb 22, 1927, Wilmington, NC; divorced; children: James T Jr, Myra L, Wanda J (dec). **EDUCATION:** Wilberforce Univ, BS 1947; Dist of Col Tech & Coll UDC, 1971; US Civil Serv Mgmt Serv Ctr DC, 1976; US Dept Ag Grad School, 1972; George Washington Univ Grad School, 1973; Antioch School of Law, 1988. **CAREER:** US Navy Dept, phys sci tchr 1951-61; Dist of Columbia Pub Schl, pub schl tchr 1961-66; Dist of Columbia Gov, coord of volunteers 1966-67; Natl Conf of Chrstns & Jews Natl Capital Area, assoc dir 1968-1969; Un Plng Comm, spcl asst oper 1969; United Plng Org, exec rep for admin 1969-71; Dept Health, Ed & Welfare (US Govt), admnstrv ofcr 1971-76, sr mgmnt analyst 1976-78; Dist of Columbia Gov, comm org consult 1980-82; District of Columbia Superior Court, legal intern 1987; African Methodist Epicsopal Zion Church, dir of lay activities, reg I. **ORGANIZATIONS:** Mem Alpha Kappa Alpha Sor Xi Omega Chaptr 4 1982-; mem Mayors Comm on Budget & Res DC Govt 1983-; dir of lay activities Philadelphia & Balt Conf Am Zion Church 1981-; co-govnr Fed EMA Women Dept of HEW 1972-74; tchr Sligo Jr HS Montgomery Co, MD 1984. **HONORS/ACHIEVEMENTS:** Community Serv Ldrshp NAACP Dist of Columbia Chap 1971; Woman of the Year Grey Hound Bus Co & Afro Amer Newspaper 1976; ldrshp Lamond Riggs Citizens Assoc, Washington, DC 1976; Woman of the Year DC Women's Dem Club, Washington, DC 1976; Comm Serv Dist of Columbia Govt Washington DC 1982. **HOME ADDRESS:** 214 Oneida St NE, Washington, DC 20011.

MAULTSBY, PORTIA K.
Educator/university professor. **PERSONAL:** Born Jun 11, 1947, Orlando, FL; daughter of Clarence Maultsby and Valdee Maultsby. **EDUCATION:** Mt St Scholastica Coll, BM 1968; Univ of WI-Madison, MM 1969, PhD 1974. **CAREER:** Soc for Ethnomusicology, bd of dirs 1978-80, council chairperson 1982; The Children's Museum Indianapolis, consultant 1985-86; Smithsonian Inst, rschr & prog designer 1985-86; Natl Afro-Amer Museum & Cultural Ctr OH Historical Soc, consultant 1986-88; Indiana Univ Bloomington, assoc prof/chairperson. **ORGANIZATIONS:** Founder & dir of performing ensemble IN Univ Soul Revue 1971-81; guest editor Ethnomusicology XIX Special Issue on Black Music 1975; consult Young Black Programmers Coalition 1983-85; bd of dir Intl Assoc for the Study of Popular Music USA Chap 1987-; scholarly presentations given at various univs & professional conf throughout the country; keynote speaker for Florida Music Educators Assoc 1987; songwriter, arranger & producer for commercial recordings. **HONORS/ACHIEVEMENTS:** Rsch Fellowships Ford Foundation 1984; IN Comm for the Humanities 1984; Hon DM Benedictine Coll KS 1985; Smithsonian Inst Rsch FEllow 1985,86; published in Ethnomusicology, Journal of Popular Culture, Billboard, The Western Journal of Black Studies, The Black Perspective in Music, Jahrbuch Fur Liturgik und Hymnologie; Smithsonian Inst Publications; contrib articles to various books on Black Music & Culture; recipient of rsch fellowships from The Ford Found, IN Comm for the Humanities; hon doctor of music degree from Benedictine Coll 1985; Portia K Maultsby Day Proclaimed by Mayor of Orlando FL, 1975. **BUSINESS ADDRESS:** Assoc Professor/Chairperson, Indiana University-Bloomington, Dept of Afro-Amer Studies, Memorial Hall East, Bloomington, IN 47405.

MAULTSBY, SYLVESTER
Government official. **PERSONAL:** Born Oct 24, 1935, Whiteville, NC; son of Reather Maultsby; married Mildred Baldwin; children: Jerome, Hilda, Timothy. **EDUCATION:** Atlanta Coll, Mortuary Science 1959; Penn Univ, 1973; Hampton Inst (CT Sch Rel), Cert 1978; Liberty Univ, attended 1985; Liberty Bible Coll, Lynchburg, VA attending 1989-. **CAREER:** Edwards Co, expediter 1960-62; Norwalk Police Dept, patrolman 1962-68; Norwalk Area Ministry, youth dir 1968-70; New York Life Ins Co, underwriter 1970-75; General Motors Finance Div, 1973-75; CT State Police, chaplain 1985-; Prudential Life Ins Co of Amer, district agent 1975-. **ORGANIZATIONS:** Assoc minister Calvary Baptist Church, Norwalk, CT 1976-; vice president Greater Norwalk Black Democratic Club 1976-; city sheriff City of Norwalk 1977-80; councilman City of Norwalk 1981-; exec board NAACP; 32 degree Prince Hall Masonic Order; William Moore Lodge #1533 (Elks) IBPOEW; past patron Eastern Star PHA; founding bd of dir PIVOT (alcoholic and drug rehab center); founder/dir Norwalk Interdenom Youth Movement; First Black Democrat for State Senator from Fairfield County, CT 1980; Natl Black Caucus of Local Elected Officials 1976; Hampton Univ Minister Conf 1976; CT Baptist Missionary Conv; chmn Political Affairs Conn Missionary Baptist Convention 1987-; mem The Baptist Ministers Conference of Greater New York and Vicinity 1986-. **HONORS/ACHIEVEMENTS:** Distinguished Achievement Greater Norwalk Black Dem Club; Outstanding Citizen Norwalk Area Improvement League; US Jaycees Spoke Award Junior Chamber of Commerce; Service Award United Way; Holy Order of Past High Priesthood Award 1974; The Norwalk Youth Comm Concert Choir Man of the Yr Award 1983; CT Gen Assembly Official Citation for Presidential Campaign of Jesse Jackson 1984; Realities of Empowerment Awd CT State Fed of Black Dems 1985. **MILITARY SERVICE:** AUS paratrooper Cp Jumpmaster 1953-56; Sr Jumper; Good Conduct; Serv Medal; Leadership Medal Korean War. **BUSINESS ADDRESS:** Insurance Broker, Prudential Ins Co of America, PO Box 601, Norwalk, CT 06856.

MAUNEY, DONALD WALLACE, JR.
Business executive. **PERSONAL:** Born Oct 16, 1942, New Castle, PA; married Sharon Miller; children: Michael A, Dawnya M, Donovan T. **CAREER:** Diversified Payments & Loan Servicing Br, chief 1985; Tenant Ledger Br DC Dept of Housing & Comm, chief; Gen Accounting Br DC Land Agency, chief 1970-75; Robert Hall Store, asst mgr 1969-70; State Dept Fed Govt, budget analyst 1962-69. **ORGANIZATIONS:** Pres Tri-State Enterprises Inc 1974-; proprietor Tri-State Engraving Co 1969-70; state pres DC Jaycees 1975-76; 1st Blacknat; vP US Jaycees 1976-77; 1st black mem US Jaycees Exec Com; 1st black USA Elected Jaycess Intl World Vice Pres Johannesburg S Africa 1977; chmn of bd DC Council on Clothing for Kids Inc; exec com DC Vol Clearing House; bd dir DC Jaycee Youth Devel Trust; trustee Plymouth Congregational United Ch of Christ; treas Commerce Dept Toastmasters 1976-77. **HONORS/ACHIEVEMENTS:** Spl DC City Council Comm Award Resolution 1976; Jaycee of Year 1973; Hon Citizen Baton Rouge LA. **MILITARY SERVICE:** AUS 1965-67; AUS Reserves 1967-76; DC NG 1977. **BUSINESS ADDRESS:** 1325 G St NW, Rm 857 C, Washington, DC 20005.

MAXELL, CHARLES A.
Clergyman, business executive. **PERSONAL:** Born Sep 11, 1934, Sycamore, GA; married Bernese Shaw; children: Charles Jr, Carlynda Atha. **EDUCATION:** BS 1960; Johnson C Smith Theological Sem, MST 1963. **CAREER:** Coastal Area Planning & Devel Comm Burnswick GA, prog developer 1966; Liberty Co Community Serv Cntr OEO, dir 1966-71; Midway First Presb Ch & Midway Nursing Inn, minister & nursing home admin. **ORGANIZATIONS:** Pres FOCUS 1964-66; mem Ministerial Relations Com Presb of GA 1967-60; moderator Presbytery of GA United Presb Ch USA 1967; mem bd trustees Presbytery of GA 1973; chairperson Interpretation & Stewartship Com Presbytery of GA 1974; pres CAM Phar Inc 1977; Ministeria Comm Gen Assemply United Presbyterian Ch 1966. **HONORS/ACHIEVEMENTS:** Recipient leadership award 1954; Good Cit Awd 1954; Good Conduct Award 1956; Community Leaders & Noteworth Am Award 1973-74; also 1975-76. **MILITARY SERVICE:** AUS 1954-56. **BUSINESS ADDRESS:** PO Box 108, Midway, GA 31320.

MAXEY, CARL
Attorney. **PERSONAL:** Born Jun 23, 1924, Tacoma, WA; married Merrie Lou Douglas; children: William C, Bevan J. **EDUCATION:** Univ of OR, BS 1948; GonzagaUniv Spokane WA, LLB 1951. **CAREER:** Fredrickson Maxey Bell & Stiley PS, atty 1960; Domestic Rel GonzagaUniv Sch of Law, tchr 1972-76. **ORGANIZATIONS:** Bar adm Wash & US Dist Ct 1951; chmn Pres Appointment Wash St Adv Com to US Commn on Civil Rights 1963-78; Speedy Trial Act Planning Com US Dist Ct 1978; mem Spokane Co Bar Assn; past mem Judicial Selection Com; Judicial Liaison Com bar adm US Ct of Appeals; mem past chmn WA St Bar Assn;Criminal Law Sec Com; mem past sire archon Alpha Omicron Boul 1979; past pres NAACP Spokane WA Chpt.

MAXEY, JAMES, III
Psychological counselor. **PERSONAL:** Born Sep 30, 1943, Birmingham, AL; son of Mr. & Mrs. James Maxey, Jr; married Carolyn Wheeler; children: Katherine Arlene Wheeler Maxey. **EDUCATION:** Morehouse Coll, AB 1964; IN Univ, MS 1966; Temple Univ, Union Graduate School, PhD, 1983. **CAREER:** Dept of State, Harrisburg, PA, counseling psychologist; Dir Commn Charities, State of PA, special asst to sec 1980; OIC, asst dir 1979; MH/MR/PVT Youth Clinic/Prisons Bureau Vocational Rehabilitation, prof, consulting psychologist, 1973; Goodwill Industries, psychologist 1975; Adjunct prof, Antioch Univ, Lincoln Univ. **ORGANIZATIONS:** Mem, Natl Black Psychologist, mem, Alpha Phi Alpha Fraternity; Hon Mem, Phi Delta Kappa Fraternity, 1966; Amer Psychological Assn. **BUSINESS ADDRESS:** Executive Dir, State of Pennsylvania, Bureau on Charitable Org, 308 North Office Bldg, Harrisburg, PA 17120.

MAXEY, JO ANN (NEE STRICKLAND)
Senator. **PERSONAL:** Born in Chattanooga, TN; married Albert; children: Charlene, Michelle, Albert, Jr, Aaron. **EDUCATION:** Butler U; IN St U;Univ of NE. **CAREER:** NY Life Ins Co Lincoln NE, field underwriter; NE State Legis, senator. **ORGANIZATIONS:** Elected Lincoln Sch Bd; mem Lab Tech for Pediatricians Lincoln Found; Headstart Fed Prgm; WICS; Black Women's Caucus; League of Women Voters; City St Adv Commn; Lincoln Jaycees; Belmont Ctr; Multi-Cultural Com; Right to Read Com; Educ Commn of the States; Human Resources Com; steering com DisplacedHomemakers; NE Task Force on Abuse; bd of trustees Wesleyan U; life mem PTA; Child Guid PTA; Sigma Gamma Rho. **HONORS/ACHIEVEMENTS:** Mrs Jaycee Award; Mayor's Award partic on City Streets Adv Commn. **BUSINESS ADDRESS:** 1506 First Natl Bank, Lincoln, NE 68508.

MAXIE, PEGGY JOAN
State representative. **PERSONAL:** Born Aug 18, 1936, Amarillo. **EDUCATION:** Seattle U, BA 1970;Univ of WA, MSW 1972. **CAREER:** Peggy Maxie & Asso, pres 1978-. **ORGANIZATIONS:** Mem WA Ho of Rep 1971; mem Ho Rules Com 1977-; mem Ho Appropriations Com 1977-; mem Ho Ins Com 1977; Madrona Comm Counc; mem Capitol Hill Bus& Professional Women; Nat Assn of Social Workers; mem League of Women Voters; Alpha Kappa Alpha; NAACP. **HONORS/ACHIEVEMENTS:** Recipient Hon DDL St Martin's Coll 1975.

MAXWELL, BERTHA LYONS
Educator. **PERSONAL:** Born in Seneca, SC. **EDUCATION:** Johnson C Smith U, BA 1954; UNC Greensboro, MEd 1966; Union Grad Sch, PhD 1974; Cath U, Howard U,Univ of SC, further study. **CAREER:** Alexander St Sch, tchr 1954-60; corrective reading tchr 1960-67; Villa Heights Elem Sch, asst prin 1967; Morgan Elem Sch, prin 1967-68; Albemarle Rd Elem Sch, prin 1968-70;Univ of NC at Charlotte, asso prof edn, dir of black studies program 1970-. **ORGANIZATIONS:** Organized & coordinated Charlotte's first Volunteer Tchr Corps; provided first readiness program for 87 disadvantaged children at First Ward Sch 1964; consHead Start Winthrop Coll Rock Hill SC 1965; visiting com So Assn Accreditation of Gastonia City Sch System 1967; local consult ACE Workshop UNCC 1969; consult So Regional Educ Bd Regional Conf 1971; chmn, visiting com Harrisburg Sch; So Assn Accreditation of Cabarrus Co Sch 1972; chmn visiting com Greensboro City Sch 1973; mem NEA; Nat Assn of Elem Sch Prin; Afro-Am Study Assn; African Her*Itage Study Assn; mem Resolutions Com 1970; chmn Resolutions Com 1971; sec Charlotte-Mecklenburg Elem Pring Unit; mem Intl Reading Assn; mem bd dir 1969-72; Greater Charlotte Coun Intl Reading Assn; mem Intl Platform Assn; mem League of Women Votes; bd mem, chmn Charlotte-Mecklenburg Human Resources Com League of Women Voters; bd dir Johnston Memorial YMCA; mem Jack & Jill Inc; past pres Merry Makers Inc. **HONORS/ACHIEVEMENTS:** Outstanding Community Services Award Las Amagis Inc 1967; outstanding leadership Sigma Gamma Rho Sorority 1969; outstanding personalities of the s 1970; outstanding comm leader 1971; two thousand women of achievement Volume 3 1971; Who's Who Women of the World Volume 1 1972; outstanding educ of Am 1973; outstanding edcuator Las Amagis Inc 1973; Who's Who in the Black World 1974. **BUSINESS ADDRESS:** Univ North Carolina-Charlotte, Afro-Amer & African Studies, Charlotte, NC 28223.

MAXWELL, CEDRIC
Professional basketball player. **PERSONAL:** Born Nov 25, 1955, Kinston, NC. **EDUCATION:** Univ NC Charlotte, BA 1977. **CAREER:** Boston Celtics, professional basketball player (forward) 1977-. **ORGANIZATIONS:** Tournament backgammon player. **HONORS/ACHIEVEMENTS:** 1st round draft choice Boston Celtics 1977; led NBA in Field Goal Percentage (584) 1978-79; All-Time League Record in Field Goal Percentage (609) for a Forward 1979-80; Led Team in Most Field Goals Attempted & Made 1979. **BUSINESS ADDRESS:** Boston Celtics, Boston Garden at N Station, Boston, MA 02114.

MAXWELL, HAZEL DELORIS (NEE BRAMLETTE)
Retired secretary. **PERSONAL:** Born Oct 30, 1905, Chicago, IL; widowed; children: Anna Digg Taylor, Lowell D. **EDUCATION:** Howard Univ, BA 1935. **CAREER:** Milwaukee School of Engineering, part-time sec 1978-; DC Public Schools, jr high school teacher 1944-59. **ORGANIZATIONS:** Pres bd of trustees Milwaukee Pub Library 1965-79; pres bd dirs YWCA of Greater Milwaukee 1968-71; pres auxiliary Natl Med Assn 1973-74. **HONORS/ACHIEVEMENTS:** Headliner Award Milwaukee Press Club 1971; Pro Urbe Award Mt Mary Coll 1974; distinguished serv award Milwaukee Metro Civic Assn 1976; Hall of Fame YWCA of Greater Milwaukee 1979.

MAXWELL, MARCELLA J.
Educator & government official. **PERSONAL:** Born Nov 06, 1927, Asbury Park, NJ; daughter of William B Redwood and Ethel Click; married Edward C Maxwell, Apr 10, 1968 (deceased); children: Deborah Young. **EDUCATION:** Long Island Univ, Brooklyn NY, BS 1956, MS 1958; Fordham Univ, New York NY, EdD 1972. **CAREER:** New York City Comm on Status of Women, asst acad dean; Publ School Dist 20, elem sch teacher, teacher trainer 1958-63; Puerto Rico School Dist, exchange teacher 1963; Bank State Coll, curriculum coord; Medgar Evers Coll, City Univ, dean 1972-; NY City Commission on Human Rights, chairperson 1984-88; Board of Higher Education Medgar Evers College 1971-84. **ORGANIZATIONS:** Bd mem Women's Forum; vice pres Natl Council of Women 1989-; chairperson New York City Commn on the Status of Women 1978-84, 1988-. **HONORS/ACHIEVEMENTS:** Natl Achievement Awd Natl Assn of Negro Bus & Professional Women's Clubs; Exxon Scholarship Harvard Bus School; Keynote Speaker Older Women's League; NCCJ Human Rel Awd; Doctor of Law Pratt Instutute Brooklyn NY 1985; Doctor of Humane Letters Marymount Manhattan College 1984. **HOME ADDRESS:** 35 Prospect Park W, Brooklyn, NY 11215.

MAXWELL, ROGER ALLAN
Affirmative action officer, composer. **PERSONAL:** Born Jul 31, 1932, Marshalltown, IA; married Arenda; children: Jennifer, Courtney, David, Matthew. **EDUCATION:** Univ of N IA, BA 1954. **CAREER:** IA State Bd of Regents, affirmative action officer 1969-. **ORGANIZATIONS:** Nat pres Nat Assn of Affirmative Act Officers 1979-80. **HONORS/ACHIEVEMENTS:** Composer "Twelve Weeks to a Better Jazz Ensemble" pub CL Barnhouse Co 1978; composer "Fourteen Weeks to a Better Band" Books I & Ii pub CL Barnhouse Co1973-74; composer "Mass in Honor of the Uganda Martyrs" 1964. **MILITARY SERVICE:** AUS asst counductor AUS Band Pacific Honolulu HI 1956-58. **BUSINESS ADDRESS:** Lucas State Office Building, Des Moines, IA 50319.

MAXWELL, STEPHEN LLOYD
Judge. **PERSONAL:** Born Jan 12, 1921, St Paul, MN; married Betty Rodney. **EDUCATION:** Morehouse Coll, BA, BSL 1951; St Paul Coll of Law, JD 1953. **CAREER:** IRS, auditor 1945-48; St Paul Auditorium, accnt 1948-51; OPS, investigator 1951-53; Private practice, 1953-59; Ramsey Court, asst attny 1959-66; City of St Paul, corp counsel 1964-66; US Congressional Rep Candidate, 1966; Municipal Court, judge 1967-68; Dist Court State of MN, judge 1968-. **ORGANIZATIONS:** Mem Natl Bar Assoc, Judicial Council of Natl Bar Assoc, MN State Bar Assoc MN 1977, St Paul-Minneapolis Comm on Foreign Rel 1971, United Hosp Inc, Blue Cross & Blue Shield of MN. **MILITARY SERVICE:** USCG WWII; USNR capt retired.

MAXWELL-REID, DAPHNE ETTA
Business executive. **PERSONAL:** Born Jul 13, 1948, New York, NY; married Timothy L Reid; children: Christopher Tubbs; Tim Jr, Tori. **EDUCATION:** Northwestern Univ, BA 1970. **CAREER:** Screen Actors Guild, bd mem 1974-76; Screen Actors Guild, co-chmn, conservatory committee 1977; Daphne Maxwell Inc, pres. **ORGANIZATIONS:** Clothing designer and seamstress Daphne Designs; co-authored a limited ed cookbook In The Spirit of Food Tim & Daphne's Cookin' Book. **HONORS/ACHIEVEMENTS:** 1st Commercials 1967; 1st Black Homecoming Queen 1967; Cover Glamour Mag 1969; Selected by Ladies Home Jrnl as 1 of 14 Most Beautiful Women 1970; Currently re-occuring as Temple Hill on Simon & Simon. **BUSINESS ADDRESS:** President, Daphne Maxwell Inc, 1901 Ave of the Stars, #500, Los Angeles, CA 90067.

MAY, CHARLES W.
Songwriter, entertainer. **PERSONAL:** Born Jun 13, 1940, Macon, MS. **EDUCATION:** So IL U, BA 1962; So IL U, presently working on MA. **CAREER:** Ft Wayne IN, tchr pub sch; 1963; Los Angeles, tchr elementary sch including the mentally retarded 1966-70; club Harlem Atlanta City, performed 4 months 1970; Fairmont Hotel San Francisco, staed & vocally arranged Freda Payne's act 1970; Sands Hotel Las Vegas, played piano for Lola Falana's engaement 1 month; wrote title songs for movies, Wonder Women, Class of 74, Detroit 9000; numerous TV & radio appearances; produced wrote & sang several albums with Annette May Thomes & The 21st Century Ltd. **ORGANIZATIONS:** Formed group The 21st Centry Ltd; mem AFTRA. **HONORS/ACHIEVEMENTS:** Winner Quarter Finals of the Annual Song Writer Festival "If I Thought He Didn't Care". **BUSINESS ADDRESS:** PO Box 43402, Los Angeles, CA 90043.

MAY, CORNELIUS WALLACE
Director. **PERSONAL:** Born Oct 20, 1943, St Louis, MO; married Yvette Marion Myers. **EDUCATION:** Harvard Law School, JD 1969; Washington Univ St Louis, BA 1965. **CAREER:** The Rouse Co Columbia MD, sr attny 1970-79; Dept of Housing & Urban Devel Comm Plnng & Devel Wash DC, sr devel dir 1979-84; Festival Devel Corp, pres 1984-; The May Devel Co, pres 1984-. **ORGANIZATIONS:** Pres Columbia Interfaith Housing Corp 1979, Tenents Assoc of Boston Inc 1968-69; mem MD Bar Assoc, Amer Bar Assoc, Natl Bar Assoc, Sigma Pi Phi 1978-. **BUSINESS ADDRESS:** President, The May Development Co, 5615 Columbia Rd Apt 203, Columbia, MD 21044.

MAY, DICKEY R.
Corporate accounting administrator. **PERSONAL:** Born Dec 14, 1950, Dublin, GA; son of Clarence W May Sr and Zelma Smith May; married L Yvonne Fambrough, Jul 03; children: Andrea Lynette May, Ronald Maurice May. **EDUCATION:** Fort Valley State Coll,

Fort Valley GA, BBA, 1972. **CAREER:** Church's Fried Chicken, Atlanta GA, exec mgr candidate, 1972-73, mgr to area mgr, 1973-75, San Antonio TX, auditor, 1975-80, regional liason, 1980-84; Ron's Krispy Fried Chicken, Houston TX, regional controller, corporate controller, 1984-86; Church's Fried Chicken Inc, San Antonio TX, dir Corporate Planning, 1986-89, dir Operatoinal Acct, 1989-. **ORGANIZATIONS:** Mem, Inst of Internal Auditors, 1975-, Long Range Planning Comm, Northminister Presbyterian Church, 1988-. **BUSINESS ADDRESS:** Director of Operational Accounting, Church's Fried Chicken Inc, 355 Spencer Ln, San Antonio, TX 78250.

MAY, FLOYD O'LANDER
Government official. **PERSONAL:** Born Dec 02, 1946, Kansas City, MO; married Connie S Brown; children: Cheriss Dachelle, Floyd O'Lander Jr. **EDUCATION:** Kansas State College at Pittsburg, BS 1970, MS 1971. **CAREER:** Missouri Dept of Vocational Rehab, counselor 1971-75; Dept of HUD, investigator 1975-77, mgmt liaison officer 1977-85, dept dir/dir of comp 1985-. **ORGANIZATIONS:** Mem City of Lee's Summit Chamber of Commerce, Urban League of KC; president Channel 19 Public TV Comm Adv Bd, Heart of America Pop Warner Football Assoc. **HONORS/ACHIEVEMENTS:** Who's Who in MO Educ 1975; Outstanding Performance Awd US Dept of HUD 1977, 1985. **MILITARY SERVICE:** AUS capt 7 yrs; Outstanding Military Graduate. **HOME ADDRESS:** 5223 SW Raintree Pkwy, Lee's Summit, MO 64063.

MAY, JAMES F.
Educator, mayor. **PERSONAL:** Born Feb 10, 1938, Millry, AL; married Bessie Hill; children: Keita, Katrice. **EDUCATION:** Alabama A&M Univ, BS 1962; Tuskegee Inst, MEd 1968. **CAREER:** May's Plumbing & Elec Serv, owner; Uniontown AL, mayor pro tem; Perry County Bd of Educ, teacher; former city councilman. **ORGANIZATIONS:** Mem Uniontown Civic League; keeper of records Omega Chi Chap Omego Psi Phi; mem AVATA Perry Co Tchr Assn; AEA; NEA; Pride of AL Elks #1170. **HONORS/ACHIEVEMENTS:** First Black Councilman Award 1972. **MILITARY SERVICE:** AUS pfc 1956-58. **BUSINESS ADDRESS:** P O Box 24, Uniontown, AL 36786.

MAY, JAMES SHELBY
Educator, judge, trial attorney. **PERSONAL:** Born Jun 02, 1934, Louisville, KY; son of Shelby May and Arlee Taylor May; married Patricia Lynn Hunter; children: Angela Collen Weaver, James S May Jr, Sarita Maureen, Shara Lavorn Dickerson, Regina Grace. **EDUCATION:** Cornell Univ, BA Amer Studies 1971; Yale Univ Law School, Juris Doctor 1977, (distinction in all subjects); Natl Judicial Coll, trial judge course 1980; Georgetown Univ Law School, enrolled Master in Law Program. **CAREER:** USMC, infantryman 1953-60, officers candidate school 1960, officers basic course 1960-61, financial admin 1961-64, logistics officer 1964-69; US Naval Academy, history instructor 1972-74; Navy Marine Corps Court of Military Review, appellate judge; Marine Corps Base Camp Pendleton, staff judge advocate. **ORGANIZATIONS:** Mem Amer Trial Lawyers Assn; mem CA, FL, DC Bar Assns; mem Alumni Exec Comm Yale Law Sch 1982-85; mem Assn of Afro-Amer Life & History 1980-; mem Marine Corps Historical Foundation 1983-; mem Secondary Sch Comm Cornell Club of Washington 1983-; chmn Military Judges Comm Judiciary Sect Fed Bar Assn 1984-. **HONORS/ACHIEVEMENTS:** Woodrow Wilson Fellowship Finalist Cornell Univ 1971; White house Fellowship Finalist 1981; numerous published appellate court opinions in military law; first Black judge appointed to highest Navy Military Court (Ebony Jan 1983). **MILITARY SERVICE:** USMC col 1953-; Navy Commendation Medal; Meritorious Unit Commendation; Vietnamese Cross. **HOME ADDRESS:** 3305 S Stafford St, Arlington, VA 22206. **BUSINESS ADDRESS:** Administrator, Naval Council of Personnel Boards Petachment, Regional Physical Evaluation BD, Naval Medical Center, Bldg 1, Tower 9, Bethesda, MD 20814.

MAY, LEE ANDREW
Professional athlete. **PERSONAL:** Born Mar 23, 1943, Birmingham. **EDUCATION:** Miles Coll, student. **CAREER:** Player minor league teams 1961-65; Cincinnati Reds, 1st baseman, outfielder 1965-71; Houston Astros, 1st baseman 1972-74; Baltimore Orioles, 1974-. **ORGANIZATIONS:** Mem All-Star Teams 1969, 1971-72. **HONORS/ACHIEVEMENTS:** Named Nat League Rookie Player of Yr 1967; 1st baseman Sporting News & Nat League All-Star Team 1971; leader Nat League 1st baseman double plays 1970; tiedfollowing major league records, most home runs in 3 consec games 1969; most total bases (8) one inning & most home runs in one inning 1974; hit 3 home runs in one game 1973; led NL first basemen total chances & double plays 1972; led AL first basemen total chances & double plays 1975. **BUSINESS ADDRESS:** c/o Baltimore Orioles, Memorial Stadium, Baltimore, MD 21218.

MAY, SCOTT
Athlete. **PERSONAL:** Born Mar 19, 1954, Sandusky, OH. **EDUCATION:** IN U, BS 1976. **CAREER:** Chicago Bulls Corp Coll All Am, professional bskbl player 2 yrs. **ORGANIZATIONS:** Mem INUniv NCAA Champions. **HONORS/ACHIEVEMENTS:** Two-time Big-Ten Conf MVP/COLL Player of the Yr 1976; 1st round draft pick 1976; starting guard Gold Medal US Olympic Basketball Squad 1976; 1st Team All Rookie Squad 1977.

MAY, VERONICA STEWART
Educator. **PERSONAL:** Born Dec 05, 1920, Indianapolis; daughter of William Henry Stewart and Janie Morris-Lindsley-Stewart; married Jesse O; children: 1. **EDUCATION:** IN State Tchrs, BS 1950; Butler U, MS 1966; reading specialist Butler Univ, 1967. **CAREER:** Indianapolis Schs, tchr 1957; remedial tchr 1971-; hobby music and writing children's books. **ORGANIZATIONS:** Pres Indianapolis Educ Assn 1970-71; state dist vice pres 1971-73; NEA 1969-73; del conv1973; steering com Vocalist Midland House 3rd Church Christ Scientist; soloist first Ecumenical Conf Green Bay WI 1953 where Dr Martin Luther King asked to form So Leadership Conf Pubis in field. **HONORS/ACHIEVEMENTS:** First granddaughter of Phillip Van-Simpson Lindsley arranger of negro Spiritual found in the Natl Jubilee Melodies, more than one hundred thousand copies sold in 1921; first black pres of Indianapolis Education Organization of Teachers 1970-71.

MAYE, BEATRICE CARR JONES
Librarian. **PERSONAL:** Born Apr 23, Warren Cty, NC; daughter of James S Jones and Ellen Brown Jones; married John W Maye Sr (deceased); children: John Walter Jr, Mamie Ellene Maye-Bryan. **EDUCATION:** NC A&T State Univ, BS, English, French; NC Central Durham, BS, MS, Library Science; East Carolina Univ, postgraduate study. **CAREER:** WH Robinson School, librarian, 1947-68; EB Aycock Jr High School, media specialist, 1968-81; Greenville City Bd of Sheppard Memorial Public Library, 1972-74, dept of library science, library science consultant, 1972-; selected member of Elections Study Comm by mayor, 1981; Pitt/Greenville Media Soc, former pres, 1981-82; The Carolinian, columnist; Kinston-Greenville Dispatch and Bethel Herald, columnist, The "M" Voice; Pitt Community Coll, teacher, resource person on Black History Month. **HONORS/ACHIEVEMENTS:** Southeastern Black Librarian 1976; 25 Most Influential Black Women in Greenville/Pitt City 1983; Volunteer-of-the Year by the Greenville Pre-Release 1983; Citizen of the Year Award for Community Serv 1984; author, Personalities in Progress, Biographies of Black NC, Treasure Bits, An Anthology of Quotes 1984; editorials in We The People, The Daily Reflector, The News & Observer, The Wilson Library Bulletin, NC Libraries, Greenville Dispatch, The Carolinian & Bethel Herald; host, "Talk Show," WOOW Radio, WBZQ Radio, Sundays; Greenville Pre-Release & After-Care Center. **HOME ADDRESS:** 1225 Davenport St, Greenville, NC 27834.

MAYE, RICHARD
Clergyman. **PERSONAL:** Born Oct 26, 1933, Uniontown, AL; married Rose Owens; children: Darryl Kermit, Byron Keith. **EDUCATION:** Sangamon State U, BA/MA 1972;Univ of IA, PhD pending. **CAREER:** Pleasant Grove Baptist Church Springfield, IL, pastor 1970-; IL State Univ Normal, lecturer political science 1973-77; IL Dept of Corrections Springfield, admin asst 1970-72; Chicago Baptist Inst IL, faculty 1968-70; City of Springfield, commr civil serv 1979-72. **ORGANIZATIONS:** Mem Mayor's Complete Count Com Springfield 1980; bd of dir Morgan-Wash Sch for Girls 1977; mem Sch Integration Commn Springfield 1977-79; bd of dirLincoln Lib; grad dean fellow So ILUniv Carbondl 1975-76. **HONORS/ACHIEVEMENTS:** Citizen of the Year Award, NAACP Springfield 1976; Grad Fellow,Univ of IA 1977-80; Pub Serv Award, US Dist Ct Springfield, IL 1978; Who's Who in the Midwest. **MILITARY SERVICE:** AUS spec/3 1954-56. **BUSINESS ADDRESS:** 908 S 18th St, Springfield, IL 62707.

MAYES, CLINTON, JR.
Chief executive. **CAREER:** State Mutual Federal Savings and Loan Assoc, Jackson, MS, chief exec. **BUSINESS ADDRESS:** State Mutual Federal Savings and Loan Assn, PO Box 3199, Jackson, MS 39207. *

MAYES, DORIS MIRIAM
Concert artist, operatic performer, vocal technician. **PERSONAL:** Born Dec 10, 1928, Philadelphia, PA; daughter of James Mayes and Evelyn Bulter Mayes; married Jurgen Ploog, Jun 21, 1960; children: Flavia Miriam. **EDUCATION:** Philadelphia Conservatory of Music, Philadelphia PA, BM, teaching cert; attended Hochshule Fur Musik, Munich, Germany; attended Juilliard School of Music, New York NY. **CAREER:** Syracuse Univ, Syracuse NY, assoc prof, 1966-68; Oberlin College, Oberlin OH, asst prof, 1968-74; Western Reserve Univ, Hudson OH, voice technician, 1974-80; Univ of the Arts, Philadelphia, Pa, teacher in conservatory division, 1982-; Lincoln Univ, Lincoln PA, lecturer, voice technician, 1988-. **ORGANIZATIONS:** Scholarship chair, Pro Arts Soc, 1983-. **HONORS/ACHIEVEMENTS:** Key to city of Philadelphia PA, 1961; Presidential Commendation, Lincoln Univ, 1989; citation, Philadelphia City Council, 1989; Congressional citation, 1989; Philadelphia Orchestra Award; Bell Isle Award, Detroit Symphony; John Hay Whitney award; Fulbright fellowships; winner of Munich Intl Competition and Geneva Intl Competition; winner of Grande Prix at Toulouse Internationa Competition; debut at Carnegie Hall, New York, NY; performances with Philadelphia and Cleveland orchestras and Detroit, Wiesbaden, Paris, Delaware, and Akron symphonies; opera performances in Europe and the United States. **HOME ADDRESS:** 5415 Walnut St, Philadelphia, PA 19139. **BUSINESS ADDRESS:** Department of Music, Lincoln University, Lincoln University, PA 19352-0999.

MAYES, HELEN M.
Retired college official. **PERSONAL:** Born May 28, 1918, Waycross, GA; married Nathaniel H Mayes (deceased); children: Nathaniel H Mayes Jr. **EDUCATION:** Savannah State Coll, BS 1938; New York Univ, MA 1961. **CAREER:** Albany State Coll, GA, emeritus dir of admissions & records, ret 1976. **ORGANIZATIONS:** Exec sec Natl Assn of Coll Deans Registrars & Admissions Officers 1963-; first black pres GA Assn of Collegiate Registrars & Admissions Officers 1971-72; mem GA Teachers & Educ Assn; Natl Educ Assn; mem Alpha Kappa Alpha; mem Amer Assoc of Collegiate Registrars and Admissions Officers; mem selection comm Natl Merit Achievement Scholarship Program; mem United Way of Dougherty County Bd; bd of dirs Albany Symphony Assoc. **HONORS/ACHIEVEMENTS:** Who's Who in the South and Southwest; Who's Who in American Coll and Univ Admin; Who's Who of Amer Women; Honorary membership GA Assoc of Collegiate Registrars and Admissions Officers and Natl Assoc of Coll Deans, Registrars and Admission Officers; Top Leadership Awd Alpha Kappa Alpha Sor and Women of Distinction; Community Serv Awd Iota Phi Lambda Sor. **BUSINESS ADDRESS:** 917 Dorsett Ave, Albany, GA 31701.

MAYES, MCKINLEY
Government official. **PERSONAL:** Born Oct 07, 1930, Oxford, NC; son of Henry Mayes and Julia Mayes; married Mattie Louise Dupree, Aug 22, 1959; children: Byron Christopher Mayes. **EDUCATION:** North Carolina A&T State Univ, BS, 1953, MS, 1956; Rutgers Univ, PhD, 1959. **CAREER:** Southern Univ, Baton Rouge LA, prof, 1959-76; US Dept of Agriculture, Cooperative State Research Service, Washington DC, 1976-. **ORGANIZATIONS:** Mem, Amer Soc of Agronomy, 1959-, Sigma Xi, 1959-; global ministries, VA Conference, United Methodist Church, 1986-; vice chair, admin bd, Roberts United Methodist Church, 1987-; mem, USDA/1890 Task Force, 1988-. **MILITARY SERVICE:** AUS corporal, 1953-55. **BUSINESS ADDRESS:** Administrator, US Dept of Agriculture-Coop State Research Serv, Aerospace Bldg, Suite 329, 14th & Independence Ave, Washington, DC 20250-2200.

MAYES, NATHANIEL H., JR.
Consultant, educator. **PERSONAL:** Born Aug 22, 1941, Waycross, GA; married Constantina; children: Nathaniel III, Muriel, 009136. **EDUCATION:** Howard U, MS 1966, BS 1962. **CAREER:** Multi-cultural Progs, Gr Boston Area Pub Schs, Inst for Learning & TchgUniv MA, consult trainer 1971-; Soc Dynamics Inc Boston, prog mgr 1970-71; Organizational Dev Consltnt 1968-70; Clark Clg Atlanta, instr psychlgy 1966-68. **ORGANIZATIONS:** Co-founder mem Inter-Culture Inc Cambridge; mem SIETAR; Soc for Inter-Cultural Ed; Training & Rsrch. **HONORS/ACHIEVEMENTS:** Co-author booklet on Multi-Cultural

Tchr Training 1974; recip outst tchng cert Clark Clg 1965. **BUSINESS ADDRESS:** Inst for Learn & Teach Univ MA, Boston Harbor Campus, Dorchester, MA.

MAYES, RUEBEN
Professional athlete. **PERSONAL:** Born Jun 16, 1963, North Battleford, Saskatchewan, Canada. **EDUCATION:** Attended, Washington State Univ. **CAREER:** New Orleans Saints, running back. **HONORS/ACHIEVEMENTS:** All-America selection jr and sr year coll; appeared in Blue-Gray Classic and East-West Shrine games; holds every rushing record in WSU history incl career yds; gained over 1000 yds in each of last 2 seasons; mem Pro Bowl Team 1987. **BUSINESS ADDRESS:** New Orleans Saints, 1500 Poydras St, New Orleans, LA 70112.

MAYFIELD, CURTIS
Entertainer. **PERSONAL:** Born Jun 03, 1942, Chicago, IL; children: Tracy, Curtis, Todd, Sharon, Tymphani, Kirk. **CAREER:** Curtom Record & Pub Co, Chgo, singer, composer, recording artist, owner 1970-; The Impressions, lead singer 1958-70; The Alphatones & gospel groups & choirs. **HONORS/ACHIEVEMENTS:** Wrote & sang theme mus for 1972 film "Super Fly"; score for film "Sparkle" 1975; wrote score & appeared in "Short Eyes" 1977; compositions include "gypsy woman", "keep on pushing", "this is my country", "amen", "people get ready".

MAYFIELD, JOANN H.O.
City official. **PERSONAL:** Born Jul 01, 1932, Jackson Co; divorced; children: Joyce, Barbara, Theresa. **EDUCATION:** Louise Beauty Clg, Grad. **CAREER:** Cosmetology, active in. **ORGANIZATIONS:** Cnclwoman Cty of Commerce GA; unit pres Am Legion Aux 1963-64, dist pres Am Legion Aux 1965-66; chmn Cit Training Dist A B C 1966-67; unit Pres Am Legion Aux 1967-68; usher bd sec Am Legion Aux 1972; chmn Ed & Schlrshp 9th Dists; mem Celebrity Clb 1970; dist pres Am Legion Aux 1963-64. **BUSINESS ADDRESS:** 324 S Elm St, Commerce, GA 30529.

MAYFIELD, WILLIAM S.
Attorney, educator. **PERSONAL:** Born Mar 02, 1919, Gary, IN; son of William H Mayfield Sr and Elnora E Williams-Mayfield (deceased); married Octavia Smith (deceased); children: Pamela L, William E, Stephanie K. **EDUCATION:** Detroit Inst of Technology, AB 1946; Detroit Coll of Law, JD 1949. **CAREER:** Lewis Rowlette Brown Wanzo & Bell Detroit, atty pvt law pract 1949-51; US Office of Price Stabilization, atty 1951-53; Friend of the Court Detroit, referee1953-72; Southern Univ Sch of Law, prof of law. **ORGANIZATIONS:** Mem Natl Bar Assn; State Bar of MI; Amer Bar Assn; Wolverine Bar Assn; Louis A Martinet Legal Soc; World Assn of Law Prof of the World Peace through Law Ctr; Detroit Coll of Law Alumni Assn; The Retired Officers Assn; former vice pres Cotillion Club Detroit; mem Assn Henri Capitant; mem Delta Theta Phi Law Frat; past pres Krainz Woods Prop Owners Assn; former mem Regional Bd Boy Scouts of Amer; active in religious & civic affairs. **HONORS/ACHIEVEMENTS:** Outstanding Professor Awd of the Delta Theta Phi Law Frat 1982-83. **MILITARY SERVICE:** AUS lt col ret. **BUSINESS ADDRESS:** Professor of Law, SouthernUniv Sch of Law, Southern Branch Post Office, Baton Rouge, LA 70813.

MAYHAMS, NORRIDGE BRYANT
Business executive. **PERSONAL:** Born Aug 17, 1903, Georgetown, SC; divorced; children: Blondell Hensley, Julia Betty Coulthurst. **EDUCATION:** Christensen Sch of Music, attended 1939. **CAREER:** Mayhams Collegiate Records, pres/genl mgr. **ORGANIZATIONS:** Sor frat records ASCAP. **HONORS/ACHIEVEMENTS:** Music Song selected for inclusion by Musical Song Sound Review Ltd; composed & produced "We'll Build a Bungalow" composition featured in United Artist Motion Picture The Group during the war to sell war bonds and stamps Princeton Univ. **HOME ADDRESS:** PO Box 8027, Poughkeepsie, NY 12601.

MAYNARD, EDWARD SAMUEL
Educator. **PERSONAL:** Born Jul 16, 1930, Brooklyn, NY; son of Samuel Maynard and Robertine Maynard; married Ernestine Gaskin; children: Jeanne, Charles. **EDUCATION:** Brooklyn Coll, BA (Cum Laude) 1958; Columbia Univ, MA 1967; New York Univ, PhD 1972; Graduate Center City Univ of NY, PhD 1984. **CAREER:** NY City Bd of Educ, teacher 1958-67; Brooklyn Coll, lecturer 1967-69; Medgar Evers Coll, dir of public relations 1970-71; Hostos Comm Coll, professor 1971-. **ORGANIZATIONS:** Consulting psychologist Pastoral Counseling Ctr Flushing NY; lecturer various civic & professional organizations 1970-; mem NAACP 1980-, Amer Psychological Assoc1984-; mem bd dirs Hephzibah House 1983-; consultant Bedford-Stuyvesant Legal Serv 1985-; chmn bd of elders First Alliance Church 1985-. **HONORS/ACHIEVEMENTS:** Founders Day Award NY Univ 1972; mem NY Academy of Sciences 1983. **MILITARY SERVICE:** USMC corpl 2 yrs; Natl Defense Serv Medal 1951-53. **BUSINESS ADDRESS:** Professor of Humanities, Hostos Community College CUNY, 500 Grant Concourse, Bronx, NY 10451.

MAYNARD, ROBERT C.
Editor. **PERSONAL:** Born Jun 17, 1937, Brooklyn, NY; son of Samuel C. Maynard and Robertine Isola (Greaves) Maynard; married Nancy Hicks, Jan 01, 1975; children: Dori J, David H, Alex Caldwell. **EDUCATION:** Harvard Univ, Nieman Fellow, 1966. **CAREER:** York PA Gazette & Daily, reporter, 1961-67; Washington Post, reporter, 1968-,72, assoc editor, ombudsman, 1972-74, editorial writer, 1974-77; The Tribune, Oakland CA, editor/president, 1979-. **ORGANIZATIONS:** Former chmn, Inst for Journalism Educ, Univ of CA; bd trustees Rockefeller Found; bd of trustees Found for Amer Comm; mem, Council on Foreign Relations Inc; bd dirs, Bay Area Council; mem, Sigma Delta Chi Soc of Professional Journalists; bd dirs, Assoc Press; bd of dir, Pulitzer Prize. **BUSINESS ADDRESS:** Editor & President, The Tribune, PO Box 24304 409 13th St, Oakland, CA 94623.

MAYNARD, VALERIE J.
Artist. **PERSONAL:** Born Aug 22, 1937, Harlem, NY; daughter of William Austin Maynard, Sr and Willie-Fred Pratt Maynard. **EDUCATION:** Museum of Modern Art NY, Drawing & Painting 1954-55; Elaine Journet Art School New Rochelle NY, apprentice 1955-60; The New School NY, printmaking 1968-69; Goddard Coll Plainfield VT, MA 1977. **CAREER:** Studio Museum NY, instructor printmaking, artist-in-residence 1969-74; Langston Hughes Library NY, instructor sculpture 1971,72; Howard Univ Wash DC, instructor sculpture 1974-76; Jersey City State Coll NJ, instructor sculpture 1977-78; Baltimore School for the Arts, instructor sculpture 1980-81; Coll of the Virgin Islands St Thomas, instructor sculpture 1984-85; Northeastern Univ Boston MA, Goddard Coll Plainfield VT, Rutgers Univ NJ, Harlem State Office Bldg NY, Charlotte Amalie High School St Thomas, Coll of the Virgin Islands St Thomas, lecturer 1979-85; Orie's Potpourri St Thomas Cable TV, Newscenter 10 WBNB-TV St Thomas, AMVI WBNB-TV St Thomas, Sunday Morning CBS-TV NY, films & videos 1985-86. **ORGANIZATIONS:** Mem Natl Conf Artists; exhibitions ME St Exhibit 1967; IL St Exhibit 1970; Discovery '70, Links Cincinnati OH; Student Museum Harlem; Weusi Gallery; Amer Intnt Coll Springfield MA 1971; Howard Univ 1973; Amherst Univ 1974. **HONORS/ACHIEVEMENTS:** Travel Grant FESTAC Lagos Nigeria 1977; CEBA Design Award World Inst of Black Communication NY 1978; Citation of Merit Seward Park Alumni NY 1979; Living History Award NY Urban League Westchester 1980; Bedford-Stuyvesant Arts Award Brooklyn NY 1980; Finalist Natl Sculpture Competition Columbus OH 1980; Finalist Independence Monument Antigua West Indies 1981; one woman exhibitions, Reichhold Center for the Arts St Thomas US Virgin Island 1983, First PA Bank St Thomas US Virgin Islands 1984; two person exhibit, Works in Progress Valerie Maynard & Carol Byard Gallery 1199 1978; travelling exhibit, Impressions/Expressions, Black Amer Graphics Studio Museum NY 1979-84, Tradition & Conflict, Images of a Turbulent Decade 1963-73 Studio Museum NY 1985-87; Carribean Center NY, 1989; NY Community College, 1989; Womens Studio Workshops, residency, 1989. **BUSINESS ADDRESS:** 134-19 109th Ave, Richmond Hill, NY 11420.

MAYNOR, DOROTHY
Singer. **PERSONAL:** Born Sep 03, 1910, Norfolk, VA; married Rev Shelby Rooks. **EDUCATION:** Choir, Methodist Church, early musical educ; Hampton Inst, student home econ, studied music under J Nathanial Dett; Westminster Choir, Princeton NJ; Klamroth, NYC; Bennett Coll, MusD 1945; Howard Univ, 1960; Duquesne Univ, 1970; Oberlin Coll, LHD 1971. **CAREER:** Berkshire Music Festival, Tanglewood, auditioned by Koussevitzky 1939; NY Philharmonic & Boston, Philadelphia, Chicago, Cleveland, San Francisco, Los Angeles Symphony Orchestras; Harlem School of the Arts, NYC, founder 1965, retired exec dir. **ORGANIZATIONS:** Bd dirs Metropolitan Opera Assn; Westminster Choir College, Princeton, NJ. **HONORS/ACHIEVEMENTS:** Town Hall Endowment Series Award for outstanding performance at Town Hall, New York City 1939. **BUSINESS ADDRESS:** Harlem School of the Arts, 645 St Nicholas Ave, New York, NY 10030.

MAYNOR, KEVIN ELLIOTT
Opera singer. **PERSONAL:** Born Jul 24, 1954, Mt Vernon, NY. **EDUCATION:** Manhattan School of Music, Diploma 1972; Bradley Univ, BME 1976; Northwestern Univ, MM 1978; Moscow Conservatory, MMV 1980; IN Univ, DM 1987. **CAREER:** Chicago Lyric Opera, soloist 1978; Sante Fe Opera, soloist 1979; Bolshoi Opera, soloist 1980; VA Opera, soloist 1984; New York City Opera, soloist 1986; Alice Tully Hall, soloist 1985; Avery Fischer Hall, soloist 1985; Carnegie Hall, 1986; Nashville Opera, soloist 1986; Long Beach Opera, soloist 1986; Mobile Opera, soloist 1986; Orlando Opera, soloist 1986; Metropolitan Opera-Netherlands Dance Theatre, soloist 1986-87; Triangle Music Theatre Assn/Durham NC, soloist 1987; Opera Company of Boston, soloist 1988; Alice Tully Hall, New York NY, soloist 1988; Valparaiso Univ, soloist/recitalist 1988; Fort Worth Symphony, soloist 1988; Knoxville Symphony, soloist 1988; Music Under The Stars Festival, soloist 1988. **ORGANIZATIONS:** Mem NAACP 1983-85; soloist Carnegie Hall 1983-84, Acad of Music Philadelphia 1984, Wolf Trap Festival 1984; donor United Negro Coll Fund 1984; soloist TX Chamber Symphony 1985; New Orleans Symphony 1985; Long Island Philharmonic soloist 1985; Amer Symphony soloist 1985; Shreeveport Symphony 1986; Artpark Festival soloist 1986; Buffalo Philharmonic soloist 1986; Baltimore Choral Arts soloist 1986; New Haven Symphony soloist 1987; Spoletto USA soloist 1987; bd mem, Edler G Hawkins Foundation Inc 1989. **HONORS/ACHIEVEMENTS:** Fulbright Awd Fulbright-Hays Act of Constitution 1979; Sullivan Awd William M Sullivan Found 1983; Recitalist Awd Natl Endowment for the Arts 1984; Winner 1st Prize, Intl Singing Competition South Africa 1984; Natl Assn Teachers of Singing Award 1984; Richard Tucker Award 1985; George London Awd NIMT 1986; Tito Gobbi Awd 1986. **HOME ADDRESS:** 201 Egmont Ave, Mount Vernon, NY 10553.

MAYO, BARRY ALAN
Radio executive. **PERSONAL:** Born Jun 30, 1952, Bronx, NY; married Maisha Ware; children: Barry II, Alana Aisha. **EDUCATION:** Howard Univ, Major-radio 1974-76. **CAREER:** WRAP/Norfolk, prog dir 1978; WMAK/Nashville, prog dir 1978; WGCI-FM/Chicago, prog dir 1978-81; WJLB/Detroit, prog consultant 1981-84; WDMT/Cleveland, prog consultant 1984; WRKS-FM/New York, vice pres/gen mgr. **ORGANIZATIONS:** Bd of dirs, sec NY Market Broadcasters. **HONORS/ACHIEVEMENTS:** Black Achiever Awd NY Harlem YMCA 1983; Radio Awd Natl Black Media Coalition 1985. **BUSINESS ADDRESS:** Vice Pres/General Mgr, WRKS-FM, 1440 Broadway, New York, NY 10018.

MAYO, HARRY D., III
Business administrator. **PERSONAL:** Born Aug 28, 1939, Brooklyn, NY; son of Harry D Mayo Jr and Lillie Mae CLark Mayo; married Joan Etta Bradley. **EDUCATION:** Pace Univ, BBA Finance 1968, MBA Exec Mgmt 1978; Harvard Univ, Cert Exec Educ Prog Harvard Business School 1978; various other mgmt computer and communications courses, certificates. **CAREER:** Sperry P Hutchinson Co Inc, standards admin, Sr Systms Analyst, sr programmer, oper 1958-68; Facts, Inc (JP Morgan & Co), mgr financial serv 1968-69, dir mktg 1969-70; Borden's Inc, proj mgr 1970-73; Arthur Young & Co, mgr 1973-76; Intl Paper Co, mgr sys devel 1976-80; Merrill Lynch & Co Inc, dir MIS 1980-82; Peters, Mayo & Co, pres & chief oper officer 1983-85; SRI Intl, mgr info serv & systems div NY 1985-86; HD Mayo & Assoc, chmn/founder 1982-. **ORGANIZATIONS:** Mem seminar chrmn guest spkr Amer Mgmt Assc; prin mem Amer Natl Standards Inst 1967-70; mem Assc for Systems Mgmt; guest spkr Data Process MgmtAssc IBM Process Indstry Users Grp NY Univ; mem MENSA; asst vice pres Eastern Rgn, Chap pres, Pledge Line pres Alpha Phi Alpha Frat NC 1963-66; sec & mem Plng Bd of Township North Bergen 1979-87, vice chmn 1988-; pres & dir Parker Imperial Assc Inc 1975-; chmn & guest spkr Natl Inst for Management Rsch 1986-87. **HONORS/ACHIEVEMENTS:** Designated info systems expert Amer Natl Standards Inst 1967, Amer Mgmt Assc 1967; pres 1st vice pres treas dir Pace Univ Alumni Assc 1977-80; mem pres adv comm Pace Univ 1981-; chmn Stonehenge Tenants Comm 1969-72. **MILITARY SERVICE:** US Army Natl Guard pvt e2; Grad Trainee Ldrshp Schl 1962; Squad Ldr, Platoon Guide 1962. **HOME ADDRESS:** 7855 Boulevard East, North Bergen, NJ 07047. **BUSINESS ADDRESS:** Chairman, HD Mayo & Associates, 7855 Blvd East, North Bergen, NJ 07047.

MAYO, JAMES WELLINGTON
Educator, director. **PERSONAL:** Born Mar 02, 1930, Atlanta, GA; married Sandra Brat-

ton; children: Joanna, Janell, Jamila. **EDUCATION:** MIT, PhD 1964, MS 1961; Howard U, SM 1953; Morehouse, BS 1951. **CAREER:** Electtrochemical Energy Storage Dept of Energy, div dir 1979-; Dept of Energy, scntfc adv/asst sec energy 1978-79; Asst Dir Sci Ed, spl asst 1977-78; Sci Ed Rsrch Natl Sci Fnd, dep dir 1975-77; Natl Sci Found, sec hd 1973-75; NSF, %pgm dir 1971-73; Morehouse Clg, prof chmn 1964-72; MA Inst of Tech, tutor 1961-63; MIT, rsch asst 1957-63; Howard U, instr 1955-57; Natl Bur of Stndrds, physicist 1952-53; Howard U, Rsrch asst 1951-52. **ORGANIZATIONS:** Mem Natl Rsrch Cncl CHR 1975-; mem Sloan Found 1975; Mem BEEP Natl Urban League 1972-; pres Brown Station Sch PTA 1971; mem Natl Sci Found AdComm 1969-71; mem Ctr for Rsrch 1969-71; consult Atlanta Sci Cong 1969-71; commr Commn on Clg Physics 1968-71; mem Beta Kappa Chi; Sigma Pi Sigma; Sigma XI; Phi Beta Kappa; mem Am Phy Soc; Am Assc of Physics Tchrs; mem Am Assc for the Advcmt of Sci; mem GA Admy of Sci; mem Natl Inst of Sci. **BUSINESS ADDRESS:** Senior Technical Advisor, Sonicraft, Inc, 8859 S Greenwood Ave, Chicago, IL 60619.

MAYO, JULIA A. (JULIA MAYO JOHNSTON)
Behavioral scientist. **PERSONAL:** Born Aug 16, 1926, Philadelphia, PA; widowed; children: Wilvena. **EDUCATION:** Univ of PA, BA 1947; Bryn Mawr Clg, MS 1949;Univ of PA, DSW 1958. **CAREER:** St Vincents Hosp & Med Ctr NY, chief clncl stds & evaluation 1966-; NIMH St Elizabeth Hosp Wash DC, chief psychosocial stds 1960-66; Mental Hygiene-Clinic VA Hosp Wilmington, DE, asst chief 1953-60; Psychotherapy, indiv/group part time pvt prac 1966-; DHew Ofc of Ed, consult 1975-; South Beach Psycho Ctr NY, consult rsrch 1978-. **ORGANIZATIONS:** Mem ASA; APPA; AAP; AAMFT; NASW; AGPA. **HONORS/ACHIEVEMENTS:** Numerous scientific publ. **BUSINESS ADDRESS:** St Vincent's Hosp & Med Center, 203 West 12th St, New York, NY 10011.

MAYS, ALFRED THOMAS
Health care research & development executive. **PERSONAL:** Born Dec 29, 1947, East Meadow, NY; son of Benjamin L Mays and Marjorie (Stewart) Bamberg; married Deatrice Ward, Sep 07, 1969; children: Oneika, Ashley, Alexander. **EDUCATION:** Hampton Univ, Hampton VA, BA Chemistry, 1970. **CAREER:** Chicopee, Dayton NJ, project dir, mgr Scientific Serv, dir New Technology, dir Absorbent Technology, vice pres, dir, 1970-. **ORGANIZATIONS:** Mem, Amer Chemical Soc, 1973-89; advisor, bd of dir, Parents Anonymous, 1985-89; mem, Industrial Research Inst, 1987-89. **HONORS/ACHIEVEMENTS:** Philip B Hoffman Award for Scientific Achievement, 1976; Johnson Medal, 1984; Black Achievers Award, 1985; Honorary Chairperson, Big Brothers/Big Sisters, Middlesex County, 1988. **MILITARY SERVICE:** New Jersey Natl Guard, 1970-76. **HOME ADDRESS:** 33 Willis Dr, Ewing, NJ 08628.

MAYS, CARRIE J.
Funeral director. **PERSONAL:** Born Aug 30, 1928, Lincoln Cnty, GA; widowed; children: Willie H III. **CAREER:** WH Mays Mortuary, self-employed funeral dir. **ORGANIZATIONS:** Mem Augusta Plng & Zoning Comm; mem Augusta Waterworks Com; mem Recorders Ct & Stockade Com; chmn Cemetery Parks Trees Com; mem Augusta Recreation Comm; rep Ofc of Equal Opp Bd 1971; co-chmn Paine Clg Build It Back Dr 1972; mem GA Alcoholism Adv Com; mem Expansion Com Augusta YM-YWCA's; votingdel Natl YWCA Conv 1967; chmn of bd Phyllis Wheatly Br YWCA; bd of dir Green St YWCA; mem Augusta Lib Bd; mem Dem Party; sec State Dem Party; natl voting electorate State of GA; mem exec bd State Dem Party; mem Augusta OIC; mem Sickle Cell Anemia Bd Med Clg of GA; city adv bd Med Clg ofGA; mem Augusta Black Caucus/NAACP/SCLC/PAINE Clg Alumni Assc; Methodist Clb; Pinnacle Clb; GABEO. **HONORS/ACHIEVEMENTS:** Woman of yr Lincoln League 1971; Topsy Eubanks 1973; Augusta OIC Awrd 1973; comm serv awrd 1973; citizen awrd 1973; citizen of yr Augusta News Review 1973; outst serv 1970-74; mortician of yr GA State 1977; mortician of yr Eight Dist GFSPA 1977; comm serv awrd Civic Women's Clb 1979; GA State Comm Serv Awrd. **BUSINESS ADDRESS:** PO Box 754, Augusta, GA.

MAYS, DAVID
Athlete, dentist. **PERSONAL:** Born Jun 20, 1949, Pine Bluff, AR. **EDUCATION:** TX So U, BA 1971;Univ So CA, DDS 1976. **CAREER:** Los Angeles, dentist pvt prac 1978-; Comm Dentistry Dept & Pedodontic Dentistry DeptUniv of CA, clncl prof 1978-; Buffalo Bills, qtrbck/punter/place kicker 1979-; Celveland Browns, 1976-78; The Hawaiians, 1975; Houston Texans/Shreveport Streamer 1974. **ORGANIZATIONS:** Mem Western Dental Soc; Angel City Dental Soc; ADA; mem Alpha Phi Alpha Frat. **HONORS/ACHIEVEMENTS:** Named all-am TX SoUniv (Football) 1971; All-conf (SWAC) 4 Yrs. **BUSINESS ADDRESS:** 1414 Fairchild St, Baton Rouge, LA 70807.

MAYS, DEWEY ORVRIC, JR.
Physician. **PERSONAL:** Born Dec 24, 1929, Wichita Falls, TX; married Ruby; children: Dewey, Archie, Ealy, Jones, Ruby, Quintence. **EDUCATION:** Bishop Coll, BS 1949; Howard U, MD 1967. **CAREER:** Self Employed, physician; tchr hs sci 1959-62; instr aircraft mech 1956-57; prin coach hs 1952-56; Smithville TX, tchr, coach, sci 1949-52. **ORGANIZATIONS:** Mem AMaA; NMA. **BUSINESS ADDRESS:** 2114 Salem Ave, Dayton, OH 45406.

MAYS, EDWARD EVERETT
Educator. **PERSONAL:** Born Feb 21, 1930, Pine Bluff, AR; married Edythe Etherly; children: Pamela. **EDUCATION:** AR AM&N Clg, BS 1950;Univ AR, MD 1959; Infantry Sch, 1953; Brooke Army Med Ctr, intern 1960; Fitzsimons Army Med Ctr, resd 1960-63. **CAREER:** Meharry Med Clg, prof chmn dept of intrnl med; AUS, phys 1959-76;Univ HI, asst clincl prof of med 1968-70;Univ CA, 1970-75; AUS Hosp Ft Campbell,med consult 1977-; VA Hosp Tuskegee, consult 1977-. **ORGANIZATIONS:** Mem RF Boyd Med Soc 1976-; mem Nashville Soc of Internal Med 1978-; Am Soc of Internal Med 1977; mem Pulmonary Diseases Adv Com; NHLBI; NIH 1978-; Am Clg of Physicians 1977; TN Hypertension Adv Commn 1979; mem Aeromedical Biosci Panal Hq USAF 1979-; mem Am Clg of Chest Physicians 1970-; Gov 1972-75; consult Love Canal Project CDC Atlanta 1980; mem Am Thoracic Soc 1970-; AMA 1965-; NMA 1977-; Mil Thoracic Soc 1974-76; Assc of Prof of Med 1976-; mem Pgm Dir Internl Med 1977-; Omega Psi Phi Frat 1948; mem Alpha Kappa Mu Hon Soc 1948; Alpha Omega Alpha Hon Med Soc 1977. **HONORS/ACHIEVEMENTS:** Education achvmnt award SNMA Meharry 1977,Univ of AR 1978; publ 33 articles; one chpt; commendation medal AUS 1970; legion of merit AUS 1976; Infantry Hallof Fame 1977. **MILITARY SERVICE:** AUS lt 1951-53 col 1958-76. **BUSINESS ADDRESS:** Meharry Med Coll, 1005 18th Ave N, Nashville, TN 37208.

MAYS, JAMES A.
Physician, educator. **PERSONAL:** Born May 01, 1939, Pine Bluff, AR; children: James Arthur Jr, James Anthony, James Ornett, James Eddie. **EDUCATION:** Univ AR, BS, MD 1960;Univ CA Sch of Med, intern 1965; Wadsworth VA, Internal Medicine; UCLA Irvine, Cardiology. **CAREER:** Martin Luther King Hosp, cardiologist self chf comm ed; United High Blood Pressure Found, med dir 1974; LA & Chap Alumni Assc, pres 1972-73; AHA, gov cncl 1973; Merrill HS, stdnt cncl 1965; Stdnt Gov UAPB, vice pres 1960; owner of five medical clinics in Los Angeles County. **ORGANIZATIONS:** Mem State Cncl of Hypertension Cntrl CA 1975; publ edtrl LA Times 1974; chmn PUSH LA 1981; founder Adopt-a-Family; creator Black Super Heroes Radianand Radiance; chmn NY Public Serv Foundation; mem Philantropee Assoc; bd of dir Watt & Health Foundation; mem steering comm President Reagan's Comm onTax Reform. **HONORS/ACHIEVEMENTS:** News Maker Natl Assc of Media 1975; ANA Awd 1975; Citation CA State Senate 1976; WA Human Rels Com 1977; songs Baby Coy 1977, Resing Wright 1977, Disco Bill Happy Birthday 1977; Senator Natl Holder 50 Awrd; George Washington Medal Freedom Foundation Valley Forge; appeared on Donahue, Today Show; publ "Methods to Make Ethnic Foods Safer" 1976, "Monogram on High Blood Pressure" 1976, "Chameleon Released" 1977, "Circle of Five", "Blink of an Eye", "Doctor Dan-Man of Steel"; write-ups in Washington Post, Jet, Ebony, LA Times, LA Harold, Life, Look, Newsweek, CBS News, CNW News, ABC News, USA Today, AMA News, Christian Serv Monitor; spoke before comm of US Senate and House of Reps; cited in Who's Who in CA. **MILITARY SERVICE:** AUS capt 1966-68; Bronze Star, Combat Medic's Badge. **BUSINESS ADDRESS:** 9214 So Broadway, Los Angeles, CA 90003.

MAYS, NEBRASKA
Educator. **PERSONAL:** Born Sep 09, 1931, Laurel, MS; married Helen Moore; children: Curtis, Pamela, Mark Nebraska. **EDUCATION:** Alcorn A&M Clg Lorman, MS, BS 1953; SIU, MS 1958, PhD 1962. **CAREER:** Div Soc Sci, coordinator; Educ Dept, chmn; Fed Program Devel Fisk Univ, admin 1970-; Fisk Univ, asst to pres 1968-70; Educ Dir Inst Rsch TN State Univ, prof 1965-66; Prof Educ & Crdntr Rsrch in Educ, 1963-65; FL A&M Univ, assoc prof 1962-63; Ed SIU, lect 1959-62; Placement & Alum Relations Alcorn Coll, dir 1955-57; AUS Comnctns, 1953-55; US Office of Eucd, cons. **ORGANIZATIONS:** Mem State TN Comm on Comnty & Cont Ed; mem Pres Cab;Univ Exec Com; Exec Budget Com;Univ Ed Plcy;Univ Plng Comm;Univ Admsns Com;Univ Assmbly; Phi Delta Kappa;Univ Admn NEA; Assc Higher Ed Consult Natl Endowmt for Humanities; Natl Inst Hlth; mem Tax Modernization & Ref Comm TN; Urbn Afrs; Cnclon Faclts & Rsrcs. **HONORS/ACHIEVEMENTS:** Hon Magna Cum Laude; Alpha Kappa Mu Hon Soc; flwshp SIU ; lstd outst Edctrs of Am; Personalities of South; rcgntn & outst tchg SIU.

MAYS, SANDRA DENISE
Director. **PERSONAL:** Born Feb 18, 1953, Scotts AFB, IL; married Dr Dewey O Mays III; children: Clarissa Denise. **EDUCATION:** Howard U, BS 1975; Cntrl MI U, MA 1978. **CAREER:** Manpower Office, manpower specialist 1976-77, manpower coord 1977-78; Montgomery County Empl & Training Office, grants mgmt specialist 1978; Montgomery County Community Action Agency, publ info officer 1978-79; WONE/WTUE Radio, account exec, pub svc, pub relations dir; WSMV-TV, sales mktg rep 1985-. **ORGANIZATIONS:** Treas Delta Sigma Theta 1973-; exec bd dir Ben Franklin Club Inc 1978-79; bd dir Women Line 1978-80; mem Exec Women's Org 1978-; mem Intl Assn of Bus Communications 1978-; bd dir Amer Women in Radio & TV 1980-; assoc bd mem St Josephs Home for Children; adv bd mem Fam Serv Assn of the UnitedWay 1980; mem Jack & Jill of Amer, Dayton Jr League, Nashville Jr League; vice pres Amer Women in Radio & TV 1987-88. **HONORS/ACHIEVEMENTS:** Devel Leadership Awd Ben Franklin Club Dayton OH 1978-79; Cert of Achievement OH House of Reps 1979;Serv Awd for Meharry Pre-School. **BUSINESS ADDRESS:** Sales, Marketing Rep, WSMV-TV, PO Box 4, Nashville, TN.

MAYS, VERNON LEE
Engineer. **PERSONAL:** Born Mar 25, 1933, Cleveland, OH; divorced; children: Lynardo, Natalie. **EDUCATION:** OH State Natl School of Electronics, attending. **CAREER:** NASA 3 Mev Dynamitron, head of tech modifications, lead oper; NASA 300 Kev Neutron Gen, lead oper; NASA 60 Inch Rsch Cyclotron, lead oper; Lewis Rsch Ctr NASA, electron accelerator oper engr, retired 1982. **ORGANIZATIONS:** Mem NAACP 1965-, Steam Car Club of Amer 1965, Natl Tech Assoc 1979, NASA Equal Employment Comm, Past Exalted Rulers Council #15 Dist #1 IBPOEOW OH State Assoc, Past Grand Exalted Rulers Council Grand Lodge of IBPOEOW; leading knight & trustee King Tutt Lodge #389; mem Elks; no dist dir Beauty & Talent for OH Elks; col antler guard King Tutt Lodge #389; comdr King Tutt Lodge Color Guard; eastern div liaison officer Deputy Commander of Engineers of OH 1982-; exalted ruler King Tutt Lodge #389 1985. **HONORS/ACHIEVEMENTS:** 1st black apprentice NASA Lewis Rsch Ctr 1952; Master Jumpers Wings CIB; Six Incentive Awds; NASA Space Related Inventions; Outstanding Employee Awd; Student Motivation Prog. **MILITARY SERVICE:** Army Airborne sgt 1953-55.

MAYS, VICKIE M.
Professor. **PERSONAL:** Born Jan 30, 1952, Chicago, IL; daughter of Leonard Mays and Ruth Mays. **EDUCATION:** Loyola Univ of Chicago, Chicago IL, BA, 1972, MA, 1973; Univ of Massachusetts, Amherst MA, PhD, 1979. **CAREER:** Univ of California at Los Angeles, assoc prof, 1979-80. **ORGANIZATIONS:** Founder, Section on the Psychology of Black Women, Amer Psychological Assn, 1984-86; chair, Bd of Social and Ethical Responsibility, Amer Psychological Assn, 1989-; mem, Council of Representatives, Amer Psychological Assn, 1986-. **HONORS/ACHIEVEMENTS:** Outstanding Woman of the Year, 1984, 1986; Women and Psychotherapy Prize, Div on Women in Psychology, 1986; over 25 publications. **BUSINESS ADDRESS:** Assoc Prof, Univ of California at Los Angeles, 1283 Franz Hall, 405 Hilgard Ave, Los Angeles, CA 90024-1563.

MAYS, W. ROY, III
Attorney. **PERSONAL:** Born Jul 19, 1946, Atlanta, GA. **EDUCATION:** Fort Valley State Coll, BS 1967; Atlanta Univ, MA 1968; Temple Univ School of Law, JD 1972. **CAREER:** Commonwealth of Pennsylvania, deputy atty general 1972-75; City of Atlanta, asst city attorney 1976-. **ORGANIZATIONS:** Member Kappa Alpha Psi, Inc 1964-; board of trustees Shiloh Missionary Baptist Church 1975-; president Gate City Bar Assn 1983; board member Natl Bar Assn 1984; parliamentarian Natl Bar Assn 1984-85. **HONORS/**

ACHIEVEMENTS: Presidential Scholarship Atlanta Univ 1968; Distinguished Serv Award Fort Valley State College 1981. MILITARY SERVICE: AUS 2nd Lt served 2 years. HOME ADDRESS: 984 Cascade Ave SW, Atlanta, GA 30311. BUSINESS ADDRESS: Asst City Attorney, City of Atlanta, 1100 South Omni Intl, Atlanta, GA 30335.

MAYS, WILLIAM, JR.
Executive director. **PERSONAL:** Born Oct 12, 1929, Detroit, MI; married Marilouise; children: Elisabeth, Adrienne. **EDUCATION:** Eastern MI Univ, BA 1954; Univ of MI, MA 1958. **CAREER:** Ann Arbor Pub Schs, speech therapist 1958-66, elem prin 1966-72, asst supt 1972-74, dir elem educ 1974-75; MI Elem & Middle Sch Prin Assn, exec dir 1975-. **ORGANIZATIONS:** Bd trustees Washtenaw Comm Coll 1974; mem E MI Univ Alumni Assn; pres E MI Univ Track Alumni. **HONORS/ACHIEVEMENTS:** Churchmanship Awd 1st United Meth Ch 1969; article pub MI Assn of Sch Bds Journ 1976. **BUSINESS ADDRESS:** Executive Dir, MI Elem & Middle Sch Prin Assn, Rm 9 Manly Miles Bldg, 1405 S Harrison, East Lansing, MI 48823.

MAYS, WILLIAM O.
Physician, business executive. **PERSONAL:** Born Dec 21, 1934, Little Rock, AR; married Elaine Fisher; children: William, III. **EDUCATION:** Howard U, BS 1956;Univ of AR, MD 1960. **CAREER:** Wayne Co Gen Hosp, internshp 1960, residency 1965. **ORGANIZATIONS:** Pres & chmn of bd MI Hlth Maint Org Plans Inc; pres chmn of bd Detroit Medical Found; vice pres Harris Mays & Assc PC; mem NMA; AMA; Detroit Med Soc; Wayne Co Med Soc; MI State Med Soc; Wolverine Med Soc; mem bd dir & exec com & tres CHPC, SEM; mem bd dir Blue Shield of MI; pres DetroitMed Soc 1972-74. **MILITARY SERVICE:** AUS Med Corps 1962-63.

MAYS, WILLIE HOWARD, JR.
Professional athlete. **PERSONAL:** Born May 06, 1931, Westfield, AL; married Mae Louise Allen; children: Michael. **CAREER:** Birmingham Black Barons Baseball Team, mem 1948-50; NY now San Francisco Giants System, mem 1950; Trenton Team, mem 1950-51; Minneapolis Millers, mem 1951; Giants, mem capt 1951-72; NY Mets, mem 1972-73 retired from maj league baseball 1973; Bally Park Place Atlantic City, asst to pres; Ogden Corp & Gruntal & Co, public relations; SF Giants, asst to the pres; Say Hey Foundation, president (provides full scholarships for deserving students). **HONORS/ACHIEVEMENTS:** Voted Black Hall of Fame 1974; elected Baseball's Hall of Fame 1979; San Francisco Bay Area Hall of Fame 1980; George Mosone Meml Awd Big Bros 1980; A Phillip Randolph Awd 1980; played in 24 All Star Games; Rookie of Yr 1951; League's Stolen Bases Champion 1956-59; led Natl League in homeruns 1955, 1962, 1964-65; named Natl League's MVP 1954, 1965; named Player of Yr Sporting News 1954; Baseball Player of Decade 1970; named Male Athlete of Yr AD 1954; Hickock Belt 1954; 1st Commr's Awd 1970; author "Willie Mays, My Life In and Out of Baseball" 1966. **MILITARY SERVICE:** AUS 1952-54. **BUSINESS ADDRESS:** President, Say Hey, Inc, 51 Mt Vernon Ln, Atherton, CA 94026.

MAZIQUE, FRANCES MARGURITE (NEE BELAFONTE)
Educator. **PERSONAL:** Born Oct 12, Washington, DC; married Dr Edward C; children: Adrienne Biesemeier, Shari Harper. **EDUCATION:** Hampton Inst; NY U; BS, MA, PhD. **CAREER:** US Dept HEW, dir, acad prgms; psychologist; Early Childhood Educ Spec, TV-rADIO personality; HEW Fellows Prgm, dir; DC Commn on & Aging, chprsn; Child Devel Marriage & Family Life, cons; Child Serv Delta Sigma Theta, staff. **ORGANIZATIONS:** Bd mem DC Med Soc; Aux Nat Med Assn; Proidence Hosp Womens Bd; Hosp for Sick Children; DC Arthritis Found; Doll League Inc; NAACP; Urban League; Am Civil Liberties; Afro Arts; Performing Creative Arts Assn Internat. **HONORS/ACHIEVEMENTS:** Womens year award 1976; Who's Who In Colls U'S;Univ Women; Woman of Year; Commr DC. **BUSINESS ADDRESS:** 330 Independence Ave SW, Washington, DC 20201.

MBERE, AGGREY MXOLISI
Educator. **PERSONAL:** Born Jan 13, 1939, Johannesburg, Republic of South Africa;married Musa Violet Ngcobo; children: Jiyana Sobuya. **EDUCATION:** Occidental Coll, BA 1969; Cornell Univ, MA 1971; Harvard Univ, EdD 1979. **CAREER:** Accreditation Task Force on Faculty, chairperson 1984; Roxbury Comm Coll, dept chair 1979, pres of faculty 1981, prof of history. **ORGANIZATIONS:** Mem The Black Political Task Force 1984; mem Natl Council on Black Studies 1984; founding mem S African Council of Univ Profs 1985; faculty rep Bd of Trustees RCC 1985; Boston rep African Natl Congress 1985. **HONORS/ACHIEVEMENTS:** Post-doctoral Fellow Natl Inst of Educ 1981; NEH Summer Grant Natl Endowment for Humanities 1984. **HOME ADDRESS:** 68 Bird St #7, Boston, MA 02125-2351. **BUSINESS ADDRESS:** Prof of History, Roxbury Community College, 625 Huntington Ave, Boston, MA 02115.

MCADAMS, LINNIE M.
Claims representative. **PERSONAL:** Born Jan 28, 1938, Dallas, TX; married N Burkhardt; children: Novie Curtis, Karen Lynn. **EDUCATION:** TX Womans U, Attended 1963-64; Cooke Co Coll; Attended 1966. **CAREER:** Social Security Administrn, claims rep; Presby of Convenant, exec sec 1972; US Dept of Agriculture, adminstrn lk 1968-72; DOD Ofc of Civil Defense, clk stenographer 1965-68. **ORGANIZATIONS:** Mem planning & Zoning commn City of Denton 1976-; bd of dir United Way of Denton Co 1977-; bd of dir Denton Co Childrens' Protective Serv 1977-; chairperson Planning & Zonning Commn City of Denton 1979-80. **HONORS/ACHIEVEMENTS:** Outstanding young women in am 1972; cert outstanding performance social security adminstrn 1979; del White House Conf on Libraries Official TX Del 1979;cert of commendation TX His Commn 1980-. **BUSINESS ADDRESS:** Soc Sec Admin Box 2227, 300 N Carroll Blvd, Denton, TX 76201.

MCADAMS, ROBERT L.
Educator. **PERSONAL:** Born Aug 25, 1927, Durham, NC; widowed. **EDUCATION:** NC Central U, BSC 1949; MSC 1957. **CAREER:** Office Student Financial Aid NC Central U, asst instr sch bus & asst dir; NC Cen U, acting dean men; Tuskegee Inst, instr; Royal Music Co, bookeeper. **ORGANIZATIONS:** Mem NC Assn Student Financial Aid & Adminstrs; Southeastern & Nat Assns Financial Aid Adminstrs St Joseph's AME Ch; NC CentralUniv Nat Alumni Assn; Kappa Alphga Psi; One O'Clock Luncheon Club. **HONORS/ACHIEVEMENTS:** Meditorious achiev award NC CentralUniv Alumni Assn 1974; serv award Alfonso Elder Student Union 1969. **MILITARY SERVICE:** AUS corpl 1946-47. **BUSINESS ADDRESS:** 1800 Fayetteville St, Durham, NC 27707.

MCADOO, BOB
Professional athlete. **PERSONAL:** Born Sep 25, 1951, Greensboro, NC; married Charlina; children: Rita, Robert III, Ross. **EDUCATION:** NC Univ, 1972. **CAREER:** Buffalo Braves, player 1972-76; NY Knicks, player 1976-79; Boston, player 1979; Detroit Pistons, player 1980; Los Angeles Lakers, center, forward. **HONORS/ACHIEVEMENTS:** Rookie of the Year 1973; All Star Team 1974-77; leading scorer in the NBA (130); ranks 20th on NBA's all-time scoring list with 17,803 career points; led NBA in scoring for 3 consecutive years 1973-76 averaging more than 30 points per game each season; All-Rookie Team 1973; MVP & 2nd team All-League Honors 1974-75. **BUSINESS ADDRESS:** Los Angeles Lakers, PO Box 10, Inglewood, CA 90306.

MCADOO, HARRIETTE P.
Educational administrator. **PERSONAL:** Born Mar 15, 1940, Fort Valley, GA; married John McAdoo PhD; children: Michael, John, Julia, David. **EDUCATION:** MI State Univ, BA 1961, MA 1963; Univ of MI, PhD 1970; Harvard Univ, Post-doctoral 1974; Univ of MI, Post-doctoral 1982. **CAREER:** Milan/Ypsilanti HS, teacher 1964-67; Columbia Rsch System, rsch assoc 1976-77; School of Social Work Howard Univ, prof/assoc 1970-, acting dean 1984-85. **ORGANIZATIONS:** Bd of dirs Natl Coun on Family Relations 1979-82; publications com Soc for Res in Child Develop 1979-85; gov council Soc for Res in Child Develop 1979-85; bd of dirs Groves Conf on Mar & Fam 1983; dir of conf VIII,XI,XII Empirical Conf on Black Psych 1985,87,88; prog vice pres Natl Council on Family Rel 1985; mem at large AERA Spec Interest Group in Early Educ & Child Devel 1985-87. **HONORS/ACHIEVEMENTS:** Natl Adv Comm White House Conf on Families 1979-81; Outstanding Com Awd Howard Co Foundation for Black Educ 1980; Outstanding Soror Alpha Kappa Alpha Iota Lambda Omega Chap 1981; Marie Peters Awd Natl Coun on Family Relations 1984; Natl Acad of Science Comm on Status of Black Amers Demography & Health Panel. **HOME ADDRESS:** 3034 Chestnut St NW, Washington, DC 20015. **BUSINESS ADDRESS:** Professor, Howard University, School of Soc Work, 6th & Howard Place N W, Washington, DC 20059.

MCADOO, HENRY ALLEN
County official. **PERSONAL:** Born Feb 09, 1951, Murfreesboro, TN; son of John Allen McAdoo and Doris Ann Wade McAdoo; married Gayle Elizabeth Howse McAdoo, Dec 03; children: Carol, Allen Jr, Lauren. **EDUCATION:** Middle Tennessee State Univ, Murfreesboro TN, BS 1975; UTSI Tullahoma TN, graduate studies 1977; MTSU Murfreesboro TN, graduate studies 1979. **CAREER:** Sedrulp Technologies, application programmer 1972-82; NISSAN, sr analyst 1982-1986 sr systems analyst 1986-; Rutherford Co Comm, commissioner 18th Dist 1978-. **ORGANIZATIONS:** Chmn Law Enforcement Rutherford Co 1978-79; chmn Economic Committee Rutherford Co 1983-84; Mason Murfreesboro Lodge #12; Elks EA Davis Lodge #1138; Kappa Alpha Psi Fraternity, Murfreesbor Alumni Chapter; bd of Zoning Appeals; Rutherford County Board of Governors. **HONORS/ACHIEVEMENTS:** Nominated & appointed Rutherford Co Bd of Governors Mid-Cumberland 1978-79, Bd of Zoning Appeals 1979-. **HOME ADDRESS:** PO Box 3132, Murfreesboro, TN 37133-3132.

MCAFEE, CARRIE R.
Educator. **PERSONAL:** Born Dec 20, 1931, Galveston, TX; married Joshua McAfee. **EDUCATION:** Lincoln Univ, BA 1951; Columbia Univ, MA 1963; Univ of CA Berkeley, TSU. **CAREER:** NYC, tchr 1955-64, coun 1965-68, asst prin 1968-73, coun & coord 1969, 1972; Houston Ind Sch Dist, prin 1974-. **ORGANIZATIONS:** Mem TASSP, NASSP, ASCD, TSCD, HSCD; Natl Assn Women Exec; Natl Assn Sex Educ & Coun; TS&A Hon Prin Assn Bd Dirs; Amer Bridge Assn; mem YWCA; mem MacGregor Orioles Little League; state bd dirs American Lung Assn; bd dirs San Jacinto Lung Assn; Natl Coalition of 100 Black Women. **HONORS/ACHIEVEMENTS:** Lady of Yr 1951; Outstanding Master Bridge Player 1969; ABA Lady 1974; Outstanding Journ Tchr 1962; Achieve in Educ TSU 1974; Professional Awd Natl Assn of Bus & Professional Women 1975; Outstanding Women YWCA 1977; Newspaper Fund Fellow 1964; Big E Award, Boy Scouts of America 1989; Outstanding Women, Houston Woman Newspaper 1989. **BUSINESS ADDRESS:** Principal, Houston Ind Sch Dist, 13719 Whiteheather, Houston, TX 77045.

MCAFEE, CHARLES FRANCIS
Architect. **PERSONAL:** Born Dec 25, 1932, Los Angeles, CA; married Gloria Winston; children: Cheryl, Pamela, Charyl. **EDUCATION:** Univ NE 1958. **CAREER:** Charles F McAffee, architect. **ORGANIZATIONS:** Mem Am Inst Architects; KS Soc of Architects; cert Nat Cncl Archit Registration Bd; registered in KS, MO, GA; past pres Wichita Urban League; past vice pres Wichita C of C; past prs Phyllis Wheatley Children's Home Lectr Series. **HONORS/ACHIEVEMENTS:** FHA Hon Award 1964; KS AIA Award 1964,70-72,74-75; regional AIA award 1975. **MILITARY SERVICE:** AUS corpl 1953-55. **BUSINESS ADDRESS:** Architect, Charles F McAfee FA/A NOMA, 2600 N Grove, Wichita, KS 67219.

MCAFEE, LEO C., JR.
Educator. **PERSONAL:** Born Dec 15, 1945, Marshall, TX; married Sandra Wray; children: Leo III, La Ruth. **EDUCATION:** Prairie View A&M U, BS 1966;Univ of MI, MSE 1967;Univ of MI, PhD 1970. **CAREER:** Univ of MI, asso prof of elect & computer engr; Semiconductor Group Electronics Dept Gen Motors Research Labs MI, asso sr research engr 1973-74;Univ ofMI IBM Thomas J Watson Research Labs NY, summer & faculty 1971-78. **ORGANIZATIONS:** Mem tech staff summer Bell Telephone Labs NJ 1968; mem Inst of Elect & Electronics Engr Inc; mem Eta Kappa Nu; Tau Beta Pi; Sigma Xi; Phi Kappa Phi; Alpha Kappa Mu. **HONORS/ACHIEVEMENTS:** Listed in Who's Who Among Students in Am Coll & Univ 1965-66; outstanding engr student at Prairie View A&MUniv 1956-66; Nat Sci Found TraineeUniv of MI1966-68;Univ MI Predoctoral Fellowship 1969-70. **BUSINESS ADDRESS:** Elec Comp Engr, Dept Univ of MI, Ann Arbor, MI 48109.

MCAFEE, WALTER S.
Physicist. **PERSONAL:** Born Sep 02, 1914, Ore City, TX; married Viola Winston; children: Diane, Marsha. **EDUCATION:** Wiley Coll, BS (Magna Cum Lade) 1934; OH State Univ, MSc 1937; Cornell Univ, PhD 1949. **CAREER:** Columbus OH, teacher 1937-42; USAECOM, 1942-; Monmouth Coll, instr 1958-72; AUS Elect Command, sci adv 1971-78; AUS Elect R&D Command Ft Monmouth NJ, sci adv 1978-85 retired. **ORGANIZATIONS:** Mem bd 1970, v chmn 1974-75, chmn 1975- Trustees Brookdale Comm Coll; sr mem Amer Inst of Elect & Electron Engrs; mem APS, AAPT, Amer Astron Soc, AAAS, Eta

Kappa Nu, Sigma Pi Sigma; mem curriculum adv Council Electron Engrg Dept Monmouth Coll; bd trustees Brookdale Found Trust, Monmouth Cty Alcoholism Council, Monmouth Cty Mus; bd dir 1st Jersey Corp, 1st Jersey Natl Bank; Elected to bd of governors Jersey Shore Ctr 1983; bd of governors Jersey Shore Medical Ctr 1985-. **HONORS/ACHIEVEMENTS:** Rosenwald Fellow in Nuclear Physics Cornell Univ 1946; Cited for Contrib to Project Diana 1st Radar to the Moon 1946,71; Sec Army Fellowship Harvard Univ &Travel Abroad 1957-58; Sci Achievement Citation Delta Sigma Theta 1970; United Negro Bus & Professional Women 1971; NJ Council of Mayors 1971; Brotherhood Awd Natl Council of Christians & Jews 1976; Inducted into Wiley Coll Sci Hall of Fame 1982; Awd Mem on "the Honor Roll of Volunteers in Support of Higher Ed" Council for the Advancement of Ed 1983; Wiley Coll Alumni Hall of Fame 1985; Honorary DSc Degree Monmouth Coll 1985; The Stevens Honor Awd 1985. **BUSINESS ADDRESS:** Science Advisor, AMDEL-SA, Fort Monmouth, NJ 07703.

MCALISTER, JOE MICHAEL
Government official. **PERSONAL:** Born Nov 28, 1955, Durham, NC. **EDUCATION:** Fayetteville State Univ, BS 1978; Maxwell AFB Alabama, Squadron Officers School 1984. **CAREER:** US Air Force, 410 combat support squadron chief recreation serv 1978-80, 601 tactical control wing opers officer 1980-82, 93rd bomb wing opers officer 1982-85, 6170 combat support squadron chief morale welfare 1985-86, commander detachment 2 Okinawa Japan 1986-87. **MILITARY SERVICE:** USAF capt 9 yrs; Training Ribbon, Longevity Ribbon, Air Force Commendation Medal, Meritorious Serv Medal, Overseas Short Ribbon, Overseas Long Ribbon; inducted into Regular Air Force in 1986.

MCALLISTER, LEROY TIMOTHY, SR.
Elected government official. **PERSONAL:** Born Sep 01, 1918, Hamlet, NC; married Elizabeth Gwathmey; children: Leroy Jr, Ernest. **EDUCATION:** VA State Univ, BS 1947. **CAREER:** VA Hosp, supv corrective therapy 1948-75; King Williams Cty, chmn bd of supv. **ORGANIZATIONS:** Treasurer & bd mem Eastern VA Health Sys Agency 1976-; chmn NN-MP Agency on Aging 1976-84; bd of dir VA Statewide Health Coord Council 1976-; bd mem VA State Emerg Med Advisory Council 1980-; treas & bd dir VA Assoc of Counties 1981-; bd of dir Natl Assoc of Counties 1982-. **HONORS/ACHIEVEMENTS:** Omega Man of the Year Phi Phi Chap Omega Psi Phi Frat 1971; Serv Awd Paralized Vets of Amer 1975; Comm Serv Awd VA State Univ Alumni Assoc 1983; Serv Awd & Founder NNMP Area Agency on Aging 1984; Serv Awd Third Union Baptist Church 1984. **MILITARY SERVICE:** AUS sgt 3 1/2 yrs; Amer Defense & Good Conduct 1944.

MCALPIN, HARRY S.
Retired judge. **PERSONAL:** Born Jul 21, 1906, St Louis, MO; widowed; children: 4. **EDUCATION:** Univ of WI, Journalism attended 1926; Robert E Terrell Law Sch, attended 1931-33. **CAREER:** US Empl Serv, DC, supervising interviewer 1936-41; Dr McLeod Bethune Natl Youth Admin, admin asst 1941-42; 34th Judicial Dist KY, asst commonwealth atty 1941-43; Chicago Defender, Washington correspondent 1942-44; Natl Newspaper Publishers Assn, White House correspondent, Washington correspondent for 51 newspapers 1944-46; Navy war correspondent in the Pacific 1945-46; AUS, inf spcl officer of war inf Korea 1946-47; private practice attty, Louisville KY, 1949-68; KY Workmen's Compensation Bd, ref 1956-61; Mammoth Life & Accident Insurance Co, gen counsel, mem bd dirs 1959-68; Kentucky State Bd of Educ, mem 1966-68; GHA SSA LA CA, hearing examiner 1968-70; Soc Sec Admin Lansing, chief hearing examiner 1970-71; DALJ USDA, admin law judge 1971-72; US Dept of Agriculture, chief judge, Office of Admin Law Judges 1972-75; retired 1974. **ORGANIZATIONS:** Pres Louisville Br NAACP 1953; life mem NAACP 1955; legal counsel deseg of pub parks 1957, legal counsel placement of first black faculty mem on staff ofUniv of Louisville 1959 NAACP; mem Gov's Conf on Educ in KY; White House Conf to Fulfill these rights; bd dir Red Cross Hosp; bd dir Old KY Home Council Boy Scouts; bd dir Family Serv Orgn; bd dir Comm Action Commn; bd trustees Plymouth Cong Ch; chmn Stewardship Comm of United Meth Ch 1971; mem Admin Bd Holman United Meth Ch LA 1970; mem Admin Bd Good Shepherd United Meth Ch 1974-. **HONORS/ACHIEVEMENTS:** Capital Press Club's 1st Annual Awd Outstanding News Reporting 1943; first Black American accredited White House Corres 1944; first Black Amer accredited Navy War Corres 1945; first Black Amer hold Navy rank of Lt Comdr 1945; first Black Dir of Inf US Govt Agency 1947; first Black Amer Commissioned KY Col on staff of Gov of KY 1957; Outstanding Kentuckian Awd by Louisville Defender after apptmt to State Bd of Educ 1961; first Black Chief Adminis Law Judge US Govt when made Chief Judge at USDA 1972; Cert of Merit US Dept of Agriculture 1973; first Black Fed Judge hold adversary hearings in deep South without regard to racial identity of litigants 1971-74.

MCALPINE, ROBERT
Association executive. **PERSONAL:** Born Jul 13, 1937, New Haven, CT; married Carole J Robinson; children: Monique, Angie. **EDUCATION:** Southern CT State Coll, BS 1960, MS 1969; Yale Univ, Cert Urban Studies 1969; Occidental Coll, MA 1970. **CAREER:** Guilford Publ Schls, tchr 1960-67; New Haven Publ Schls, admin 1967-69; US Conf of Mayors, prog analyst 1970-74; Natl Urban League Inc, congressional liaison 1974-1989, director of policy and government relations 1989-. **ORGANIZATIONS:** NAACP; Washington Urban League. **HONORS/ACHIEVEMENTS:** Natl Urban Fellows 1969-70; New Haven Jaycees Key Man of the Year 1969-. **HOME ADDRESS:** 11700 Old Columbia Pike, Silver Spring, MD 20904. **BUSINESS ADDRESS:** Natl Urban League, Inc, 1111 14th Street, NW, Suite 600, Washington, DC 20005.

MCANULTY, BRENDA HART
Educator. **PERSONAL:** Born Jul 08, 1949, Williamstown, MA; daughter of Thomas Hart and Adalyne Monroe Hart; married William Eugene McAnulty, Jr; children: Patrick, Katheryn. **EDUCATION:** Boston Univ, BA 1970; Univ of Louisville, MEd 1972. **CAREER:** Community Action Comm, manpower coord 1973; Univ of Louisville Coop Educ Office, asst dir 1973-77; Univ of Louisville General Engrg, asst dir 1977-81, dir 1981-. **ORGANIZATIONS:** Bd dirs Planned Parenthood 1980-86, INCOME 1980-86, Family & Children's Agency 1980-86; bd dirs Univ of Louisville Sch of Educ 1983-86; bd directors Senior House 1986-. **HONORS/ACHIEVEMENTS:** Articles published in Journal of Non-White Concerns 1980, Measurement and Evaluation in Guidance 1981, Engrg Educ 1981, Applied Engrg Educ 1986. **BUSINESS ADDRESS:** Assoc Prof of Engrg Educ, University of Louisville, Speed Scientific School, Louisville, KY 40292.

MCARTHUR, BARBARA JEAN (NEE MARTIN)
Educator. **PERSONAL:** Born Jul 07, Dubuque, IA; daughter of James Lawrence Martin and Ada Boone Martin; divorced; children: Michele Jean, William Michael. **EDUCATION:** Provident Hospital & Training School, diploma in nursing; DePaul Univ, BSN, MS; Univ of Washington, MS, PhD 1976. **CAREER:** Knoxville Coll, nurse & asst prof Biology & Science Educ; Wayne State Univ, assoc prof, 1976-78; graduate program in institutional epidemiology, 1976-; assoc dept Immunology & Microbiology Med School, 1976-; adj prof Biology & Liberal Arts, 1980-88; prof of Nursing, 1978-. **ORGANIZATIONS:** Principal investigator Wayne State Univ 1976-83; consultant Plymouth Center for Human Devel 1978; bd mem WSU Phylon Soc 1979-; bd mem United Condo Owners of MI 1979-81; bd mem Planned Parenthood League Inc 1982-88; bd mem WSU Minority Biomedical Support Program 1979-81; consultant CURN Proj Self Catheterization in Rehabilitation Care 1979; dir MI Soc for Infection Control 1979-81; bd mem editorial advisory bd Infection Control 1979-; mem review bd Nursing Rsch 1979-; co-chair WSU Phylon Soc 1980-82; mem Oral Assessment Bd for Higher Educ; consultant MI Civil Serv Comm 1980; bd mem Total Health Care Inc 1981-84; bd mem First Certification Bd of Infection Control 1981-83; mem Amer Coll of Epidemiology 1982-; consultant Univ of AL Sch of Nursing Infection Control Program 1984-85; mem TaskForce Natl Council on Alcoholism & Chem Dependence, 1983-84; mem New Detroit Inc Health Comm, 1984-; mem Founder's Soc Detroit Inst of Arts, 1984-86; mem Womens' Economic Club, 1984-85; chair Public Relations Southfield Alumnae Chapter Delta Sigma Theta Inc, 1984-86; keynote speaker Southwest Hospital Nurses Day, 1985; WSU Graduate Council, 1985-; expert witness malpractice suites, 1984-; first assembly sec, governor, mem, bd of regents, mem, general comm, The Nightingale Soc, 1988-; mem, Coalition for Health Care, 1988-; mem, Friends of Southwest Hospital, 1988-. **HONORS/ACHIEVEMENTS:** A Wilberforce Williams Award Provident Hospital; Student Rsch Grant Sigma Theta Tau 1974; Nurse Traineeships from DePaul Univ & Univ of Washington 7 yrs; fellow Amer Acad of Nursing 1978; mem Sigma Theta Tau Nursing Honor Soc 1980; fellow NY Acad of Science 1980; numerous publications, chapters in books, journal articles, abstracts; Biography in Dr Elizabeth Carnegie's History of Black Nursing 1986; AIDS presentation at second intl conf and exhibition on infection control, England, 1988; first African Amer Faculty mem to win lawsuit against a predominantly white univ, 1987. **HOME ADDRESS:** 26500 Summerdale Dr, Southfield, MI 48034. **BUSINESS ADDRESS:** Professor of Nursing, Wayne StateUniv, 248 Cohn Hall, 5557 Cass Ave, Detroit, MI 48202.

MCBAY, HENRY CECIL
Educator. **PERSONAL:** Children: Michael, Ronald. **EDUCATION:** Wiley Clge, BS Chem 1934; Atlanta Univ, MS Chem 1936; Univ of Chicago, PhD Chem 1945. **CAREER:** Wiley Clge, assc prof of chem 1936-38; Morehouse Clge, prof of chem 1945-81; Atlanta Univ, prof of chem 1981-. **ORGANIZATIONS:** Tech expert UNESCO Mission To Liberia, West Africa 1951. **HONORS/ACHIEVEMENTS:** Outstanding Teaching Award Natl Assc for Black Chem & Chem Engrs 1976; Charles H Henry Award Georgia Sect of the Amer Chem Soc 1976; James Flack Norris Awrd Northeastern Sect of the Am Chem Soc 1978; Lamplighter Award Natl Beta Kappa Chi Soc 1983. **BUSINESS ADDRESS:** Professor of Chemistry, The Atlanta Univ, 223 Chestnut St, Atlanta, GA 30314.

MCBEE, VINCENT CLERMONT
Criminalist. **PERSONAL:** Born Nov 04, 1946, Greenville, SC; married Virginia Daniels; children: Vanessa Latasha, Victoria Simone. **EDUCATION:** Johnson C Smith Univ, BS 1971; FL Intl Univ, 1971; Univ of Miami, 1976. **CAREER:** Natl Brewing Co Southern Div, quality control chem dir 1971-75; Southland Corp Velda Farms, quality control supv 1975-76; Metro-Dade Police Dept, criminalist 1976-. **ORGANIZATIONS:** Mem Southern Assc of Forensic Sci, Prince Hall Masons, Omega Psi Phi Frat Inc Ordein Elder New Covenant Pres Church. **HOME ADDRESS:** 1841 NW 170th St, Opa-Locka, FL 33056.

MCBETH, VERONICA SIMMONS
Judge. **PERSONAL:** Born Feb 23, 1947, San Diego, CA; married James O McBeth; children: Ashley, Alison. **EDUCATION:** CA State Univ, BS 1972; Univ of CA, JD 1975. **CAREER:** Office of the Los Angeles City Attorney, trial deputy 1975-76, coordinator-domestic violence program 1976-78, special counsel to the city attorney 1978-79, supervising attorney 1979-81; Los Angeles Municipal Court, judge 1981-. **ORGANIZATIONS:** Pres Black Women Lawyers Assn of CA 1979-80; mem Natl Bar Assn 1975-; bd mem LA-NAACP 1979-80; mem Natl Assn of Women Judges 1981-; dir UCLA Law Sch Exec Comm 1981-; exec comm LA Muni Court 1982-, chair pers comm 1985, 1987; sec Judicial Division CA Assn of Black Lawyers 1984-85, vice pres 1986-; dir Harriet Buhai Center for Family Law; bd of dir judicial cncl Natl Bar Assn 1985-; bd of dir Coalition of 100 Black Women 1985-; lecturer Natl Judges Coll, PA Trial Judges Conf, ABA Appelate Judges Seminar. **HONORS/ACHIEVEMENTS:** UCLA Law Review 1973-74; Editor in Chief Black Law Journal 1974-75. **BUSINESS ADDRESS:** Judge, Los Angeles Municipal Court, 110 N Grand Ave, Los Angeles, CA 90012.

MCBRIDE, FRANCES (NEE EBERHART)
Educator. **PERSONAL:** Born Nov 04, Athens, GA; married Willie; children: Reginald. **EDUCATION:** Savannah St Coll, BS 1945; Atlanta U, MA 1953;Univ of GA, postgrad. **CAREER:** AIPS Rd Elem Sch Clarke Co, tchr 1954-; Polk Co, 1949-53; Lagrange GA, 1946-47; Jones Co, 1945-46; Savannah St Coll Alumni Assn, 1976-77; Atlanta UAlumni Assn;; 1976-77; Clarke Co Assn of Educs; GA Assn of Edn; Nat Educ of Educs. **ORGANIZATIONS:** Mem Resolution Comm NEA 1973-74; Ebenezer Bapt Ch; Am AssnUniv Women Athens Br; NAACP; Delta Sigma Theta Sor; mem Eval Team for So Assn of Schs Habersham Co Sch 1977; past pres Silhouette Club of Athens; chmn Kappa Alpha Psi Frat Clarke Co. **HONORS/ACHIEVEMENTS:** Tchr of Yr 1970; regnl Tchr of Yr GA St C of C 1970; st Tchr of Yr 1970; st Tchr of Yr Assn of Classroom Tchrs 1975-76; runner up Tchr Hall of Fame 1975-76; editor, publr 1st ch newpaper, The Messenger 1976; elected to GA Assn of Educs Exec Com 1977; cert Ebenezer Bapt 1977; century asso cert Savannah St & Coll 1972-73; apprec cert GAE 1976-77; 1st black female pres of local Clarke Co Assn of Educ 1971; 1st black female pres of GA Assn of Classroom Tchrs 1972-73; 1st black female dir 10th dist GAE 1974-78.

MCBRIDE, SHELIA ANN (NEE CORBETT)
Registered nurse. **PERSONAL:** Born Aug 27, 1947, Albany, GA; married Mathis; children: William Alexander Corbett, Erica Monique Corbett. **EDUCATION:** Albany State Coll, BS 1971. **CAREER:** ICU, Coatesville Vet Adminstrn Hosp, staff nurse 1976-77; ICU, Pheobe Putney Meml Hosp, charge nurse 1975-76; Albany Urban League Fam Planning Prgm, proj dir, nurse 1974-75; Orthopedics & Newborn Nursery, Pheobe Putney Meml Hosp, 1971-74. **HONORS/ACHIEVEMENTS:** Who's Who Among Black Am 1976.

MCBRIDE, ULLYSSES

Educator. **PERSONAL:** Born Nov 27, 1938, Atmore, AL; son of George McBride and Mamie McBride; married Mabel Copridge; children: Valeri. **EDUCATION:** Knoxville Coll, AB 1959; IN Univ, Masters Degree; Auburn Univ, Doctoral Degree 1974; Univ of NY Stony Brook, Coe Fellow; Troy State Univ, Post-Doctoral Studies. **CAREER:** Escambia Cty Training School Atmore AL, teacher, coach; No Norman HS Brewton AL, dir; James H Faulkner Coll, prof, secondary social sci. **ORGANIZATIONS:** Past pres Escambia Cty Teachers Assoc; pres Faulkner State Coll Ed Assoc; dist dir AL Council for Soc Studies; mem Polemarch So Province KAY, Kappa Delta Pi, Phi Delta Kappa, Alpha Kappa Mu; dir United Fund; bd mem AL Library; mem grand bd of dir Kappa Alpha Psi; mem pensions & security bd Escambia Cty; chmn bd of dir AL Dem Conf; reader Fed Grants Washington DC; dir self study Southern Assoc Coll & Schools Faulkner State Coll. **HONORS/ACHIEVEMENTS:** Achievement Awds; Teacher of the Year Faulkner State Coll 1974, 1975; 100 Most Influential Black Americans, Johnson Publishers 1989; International President, Kappa Alpha Psi Fraternity 1989. **HOME ADDRESS:** 173 Dr Martin Luther King Jr Ave, Atmore, AL 36502.

MCBRIER, VIVIAN FLAGG

Educator. **PERSONAL:** Born Apr 12, Lynchburg, VA; married Clyatt (deceased). **EDUCATION:** VA State Coll, BS Music, BS El Educ 1937; Columbia U, MA Music 1941; CathUniv of Am, PhD Musicology 1967. **CAREER:** DC Tchr Coll, prof, mnr Tchr 1944-72; Hampton Inst, tchr 1945-46; Pub Sch Lynchburg, VA, 1937-44; Cath Univ, lecturer 1971-72; Sch of Religion Howard U, lectr 1973-76. **ORGANIZATIONS:** Dir Coll Choir & num ch choirs in DC; lecturer Niagara Falls NY & Canada. **HONORS/ACHIEVEMENTS:** Publ "Finger Fun for Piano" 1949; Meyer Fellowship for Superior Serv in DC Sch 1963; book, "R Nathaniel Dett his life & works" 1974; num articles; Alpha Kappa Alpha Achvmnt Award.

MCBROOM, F. PEARL

Business executive. **PERSONAL:** Born in Louisville, MS; children: Lorelei, Pamela. **EDUCATION:** Univ of Chicago, BA 1946; Columbia Clge Physicians & Surgeons, BS 1949, MD 1953. **CAREER:** Bellevue Med Ctr NY, internship 1953-54; Columbia Univ Wing Goldwater Hosp NY, residency 1954-55; UCLA Los Angeles CA, residency 1955-57; USC Los Angeles CA, flwshp Cardiology 1957-58; NIH Grants, resrch fellow 1958-62; F Pearl McBroom MD Inc, spec intl med cardiology 1958-; Cardiovascular & Preventive Med, indpendent rsrch 1962-87; F Pearl McBroom MD Inc, dir. **ORGANIZATIONS:** Bd mem Frederick Douglas Child Dev Ctr 1958-62, EST Fnd 1972-82, Sidoha Yoga Fnd 1974-80; dir Found Blue Bindu Rsch Inst 1985-87; mem Assoc AUM Soc Univ So CA 1986-87. **HONORS/ACHIEVEMENTS:** Publ Who's Who CA, Am, World 1959-70, Who's Who World of Intellectuals 1980'S, Intl Bibliography 1970'S, Royal Blue Book England 1960'S; Who's Who World Women 1980; Fellow Assoc Clinical Investigators 1987; Medical Dir Pala Mesa Exec Spa 1987. **BUSINESS ADDRESS:** Dir, F Pearl McBroom MD Inc, 4560 Admiralty Way, Marina Del Rey, CA 90292.

MCCABE, EUGENE LOUIS

Hospital administrator. **PERSONAL:** Born May 18, 1937, New Haven, CT; son of Eugene Louis McCabe Sr and Edna Dawson McCabe; divorced; children: Kevin Louis. **EDUCATION:** Southern Connecticut State Univ, New Haven CT, BA, 1965. **CAREER:** Booz, Allen & Hamilton, New York NY, senior consultant, 1972-75; Governor's Commission for New York Fiscal Crisis, New York NY, staff director, 1976; Deleuw/Cathers & Assoc, New York NY, regional director, 1976-81; North General Hospital, New York NY, president, 1981-. **ORGANIZATIONS:** Trustee, Harlem Urban Development Corp, 1983-; trustee, Central Park Conservancy, 1985-; trustee, Stillman College, 1985-; trustee, New York Outward Bound, 1988-. **HONORS/ACHIEVEMENTS:** Vanguard award, Urban League Guild, 1983; Robert Wilson Kitchen award, American Cancer Soc, 1988; honorary doctorate, St Joseph's College, 1989. **MILITARY SERVICE:** US Marine Corps, corporal, 1954-58. **HOME ADDRESS:** 150 East 77th St, New York, NY 10021.

MCCABE, JEWELL JACKSON

Corporate director, civic leader. **PERSONAL:** Born Aug 02, 1945, Washington, DC; married Eugene L McCabe Jr. **EDUCATION:** Bard Coll, Liberal Arts 1963-66. **CAREER:** NY Urban Coalition, dir of pub affairs 1970-73; Special Serv for Children NYC, pub rel officer 1973-75; Women's Div Office of the Gov NY State, assoc dir, pub info 1975-77; WNET/Thirteen, dir gov comm affairs 1977-82; Natl Coalition of 100 Black Women, pres 1978-. **ORGANIZATIONS:** Bd dir Bus Mktg Corp, NY Urban League, New York City Planned Parenthood, Lenox Hill Hosp, Settlement Housing Fund Inc; mem Community Plng Bd 4; exec comm Assoc for a Better NY; bd dir Women's Forum; co-chair Women United for NY, Planned Parenthood of New York City Public Issues & Answers; mem Edges; bd dir Harlem Interfaith Counciling Svc, Comm Council of Gr NY; mem Policy Plng Comm NY Partnership David Rockefeller Chmn; mem Adv New York City Comm on Status of Women. **HONORS/ACHIEVEMENTS:** Publs "Women New York" 1975-77, "Give A Damn" 1970-73; Outstanding Young Woman of Amer 1977; E Region Urban League Guild Awd 1979; Seagrams Civic Awd 1980; Links Civic Awd 1980; Dep Grand Marshal The Annual Martin Luther King Jr Parade New York City 1980; Outstanding Comm Leadership Awd Malcolm/King Coll 1980. **BUSINESS ADDRESS:** President, Natl Coalition of 100, Black Women, 10 E 87th St, New York, NY 10128.

MCCAIN, CLAUDE, JR.

Business executive. **PERSONAL:** Born Jun 02, 1931, Dallas, TX; married Ramona C Franklin; children: Michael, Demetria. **EDUCATION:** WV State Coll, BS 1951; Cornell U, MPA 1969. **CAREER:** Garland Foods Inc, vice pres 1975-; Parkland Meml Hosp, asst adminstr, evening adminstr 1969-75; Pub Health Serv HEW Reg VI, fld invstgtr 1966-67; Samuel's & Co, asst plant mgr 1959-66; Met Bldg Maint Co, asst mgr 1957-59;Univ TX SW Med Sch, research tech 1954-57. **ORGANIZATIONS:** Exec bd mem Dallas C of C 1977-79; bd mem & 1st vice pres Dallas Urban League 1977-; exec bd mem United Way of Greater Dallas 1979-. **HONORS/ACHIEVEMENTS:** Trainee of the Month Award, AUS 1952; Trailblazer Award, Dallas Bus & Professional Women's Club 1973. **MILITARY SERVICE:** AUS pfc 1952-54. **BUSINESS ADDRESS:** Evening Administrator, Parkland Memorial Hospital, 5201 Harry Hines Blvd, Dallas, TX 75235.

MCCALL, AIDAN M.

University executive. **PERSONAL:** Born in Washington, DC. **EDUCATION:** St Johns Univ MN, BA 1950; St Johns Seminary MN, Ordination 1954; Univ of MI, AM Classics 1959; Univ of MN, NDEA Fellow 1967; Univ of WI Madison, Vilas Fellow 1976, AOF Fellow 1977-79; OH State Univ, NEH Fellow 1983. **CAREER:** St Johns Prep, instr of Latin 1950-54; St Augustines Clge Bahamas, instr of Latin 1954-57; St Johns Univ MN, instr of Latin/Greek 1957-58, 1959-64, dean of students 1968-71, vice pres student affairs 1971-74, Assc prof of classics 1980-. **ORGANIZATIONS:** Bd mem Central MN Council BSA 1969-74; staff mem Viking Council BSA 1963-73. **HONORS/ACHIEVEMENTS:** NEH Fellow OH State Univ 1983; AOF Fellow Univ of WI Madison 1977-79; Vilas Fellow Univ of WI Madison 1976; NDEA Fellow Univ of MN 1967. **BUSINESS ADDRESS:** Associate Prof of Classics, St JohnsUniv MN, MCL Dept St JohnsUniv, Collegeville, MN 56321.

MCCALL, BARBARA COLLINS

Educator. **PERSONAL:** Born Nov 17, 1942, Norfolk, VA; daughter of Joseph Collins, Sr and Gladys George Collins; children: Monsita McCall Allen, Monique Lavitia, Clifton III. **EDUCATION:** Norfolk State Univ, BS 1965, MA 1982. **CAREER:** Norfolk State Univ, confidential sec/pres 1966-75; instructor evening coll 1970; asst dir couns upward bound 1975-76, dir asst instr irc 1976-81, instructor English/language skills ctr 1981-. **ORGANIZATIONS:** Secty/treas Natl Sorority of Phi Delta Kappa Alpha Lambda Chap 1985-87; mem The Natl Council of Negro Women, The Natl Assoc of Negro Business & Professional Women's Club Norfolk; charter mem Metropolitan Club; mem Sigma Tau Delta Natl English Honor Society 1987-. **HOME ADDRESS:** 3032 Sunrise Ave, Chesapeake, VA 23324. **BUSINESS ADDRESS:** English Instructor, Norfolk State University, 2401 Corprew Ave, Norfolk, VA 23504.

MCCALL, CARL

Former state senator. **PERSONAL:** Married Cecelia; children: Marci. **EDUCATION:** Dartmouth Coll, Grad; Univ of Edinburgh, attended; Andover-Newton Theol Sem, attended. **CAREER:** UN under Pres Jimmy Carter, ambassador spec political affair; WNET-TV, sr vice pres 1981; New York State, candidate for lt gov 1982-; State of NY, senator 1974-9. **ORGANIZATIONS:** Founder, past pres Inner City Broadcasting Corp; past chmn, ed bd NY Amsterdam news; dep admin NY City Human Resources Admin; chmn NY City Council Against Poverty 1966-69; ordained minister United Church of Christ; preaching minister Met Comm Methodist Church in Harlem; trustee NY Med Coll; vchmn, bd Ctr for NY Affairs of the New School; dir Blue Hill Protestant Ctr 1961-63; consult urban renewal Action for Boston Comm Devel 1962-; dir church comm serv New York City Missionary soc 1964-; proj dir Taconic Found Inc, 1964-66; mem Gamma Delta Chi. **HONORS/ACHIEVEMENTS:** Hon Canon of Cathedral of St John the Divine. **BUSINESS ADDRESS:** 21702 Jamaica Ave, Jamaica, NY 11428.

MCCALL, EMMANUEL LEMUEL, SR.

Clergyman. **PERSONAL:** Born Feb 04, 1936, Sharon, PA; daughter of George McCall and Myra McCall; married Emma Marie Johnson; children: Emmanuel Jr, Evalya Lynette. **EDUCATION:** Univ of Louisville, BA 1958; So Bapt Theol Sem, BD 1962, MRE 1963, MDiv 1967; Emory Univ, DMinistry 1975. **CAREER:** Simmons Bible Coll Louisville, prof 1958-68; 28th St Bapt Church Louisville, pastor 1960-68; Cooperative Ministries w/Natl Bapt So Bapt Conv, assoc dir1968-74; So Bapt Theol Sem Louisville, adj prof 1970-; So Baptist Convention, dir dept of black church relations home missions bd 1974-88; Black Church Extension Division, Home Mission Board, SBC, director 1989. **ORGANIZATIONS:** Bd of dir Morehouse Sch of Religion 1972-85; mem Amer Soc of Missiology 1975-80; bd of trustees Interdenominational Theol Ctr 1978-. **HONORS/ACHIEVEMENTS:** Hon DD Simmons Bible Coll 1965; Ambassador of Goodwill City of Louisville 1967; Hon DD United Theol Sem 1977; Victor T Glass Awd Home Mission Bd So Bapt Conv 1979. **BUSINESS ADDRESS:** Dir, Division, Black Church Extension, Home Mission Board So Bapt Con, 1350 Spring St NW, Atlanta, GA 30367.

MCCALL, MARION G., JR.

Physician. **PERSONAL:** Born 1930, Birmingham. **EDUCATION:** Fisk U, BA; Univ of MI, MS, MD; Providence Hosp Detroit, intern, res int med; Kresge Eye Inst, WayneUniv Detroit, ophthal. **CAREER:** Pvt prac Detroit 1964-; MD MI & CA; cert Am Bd Ophthal 1968. **ORGANIZATIONS:** Mem NMA; AMA; Det, Wayne Co & MI Med Socs; Am Acad Ophthal; Gr Det Area Hosp Council; bd dirs Blue Cross Blue Shield, MI; adv com DeptSoc Serv Medicaid; chmn Com Socioeconomics, Wayne Co Med Soc.

MCCALL, REESE

Professional athlete. **PERSONAL:** Born Jun 16, 1956; married Ceola; children: Reese III, Shawna. **EDUCATION:** Auburn, attended. **CAREER:** Baltimore Colts, football player 1978-82; Tampa Bay, football player 1983; Detroit Lions, tight end 1983-. **HONORS/ACHIEVEMENTS:** Blocked a punt at Cincinnati 1983, the 1st punt blocked by the Lions since 1977.

MCCALLA, ERWIN STANLEY

Director. **PERSONAL:** Born Dec 10, 1928, New York, NY; married Ruth Elizabeth Thomas; children: Kim, Ruth, Christopher, Richard. **EDUCATION:** Elec Tech Acad of Aerontcs NY, AAS 1958; Engr Sci CW Post Coll Brookville NY, BS 1971. **CAREER:** Grumman Aerospace Corp, dir, engr test oprtns 1985; mgr affirm act progs 1976, grp head 1972, lab mgr 1970, proj test engr 1966, test engr 1958. **ORGANIZATIONS:** Mem AIAA 1975; mem Toastmasters Intrntl 1975; mem ITEA 1980; mem NY Pioneer Track Club 1947; mem 5th AF/FEC Champ Track Team 1950; mem Urban Leag of L I 1973. **HONORS/ACHIEVEMENTS:** Honoree Black Achievers in Ind YMCA of NY 1979; Occuptn Medal, 5 Bronze Stars AUS 1948-52. **MILITARY SERVICE:** AUS e6 1948-52. **BUSINESS ADDRESS:** Grumman Aerospace Corp, Mail StopC28/05, Bethpage, NY 11714.

MCCALLUM, LEO See SALAAM, ABDUL

MCCALLUM, WALTER EDWARD

Dentist. **PERSONAL:** Born Mar 13, 1936, Hendersonville, NC; son of Lucy Lillian Deborah Jones; married Dolores Johnson; children: Robin, Todd Jason. **EDUCATION:** Univ of Pittsburgh, BS 1959; Univ of Pittsburgh Sch of Dentistry, DDS 1962. **CAREER:** Lake Cty Comm Action Proj, treas of bd dir 1966-71; Lake Cty Jr College Med Dental Adv Comm,

mem charter comm 1973-; Lake County Urban League, pres bd dir 1971-73; VTU Dental 1314 Navy Reserves, commanding officer 1979-81; private practice; Naval Reserve Dental Unit 113, commanding officer 1986-88. **ORGANIZATIONS:** Mem adv comm Partnership for Health Clinic 1973-75; chapter mem Natl Naval Officers Assn 1971-; mem Amer Dental Assn 1962-, Lake Cty Health Dept Dental Adv Comm 1982-84, Senator's Adli Stevenson & Alan Dixon's Acad Selection Bds 1978-, North Suburban Branch of Chicago Dental Soc 1969-. **HONORS/ACHIEVEMENTS:** Plaque VTV Dental 1314 presented by Adm C Schreier for serv as Commanding Officer Navy 1981-83; citation presentd by Capt R D Porter of US Naval Acad for serv to Acad 1976; plaque Dental Adv Comm of Lake County Health Dept, Senators A Stevenson & A Dixon 1982-84; letter of appreciation for serv on Military Acad Selection Bd 1975-85; Plaque for Outstanding Naval Reserve Dental Unit in Redcom 13 1987. **MILITARY SERVICE:** USNR capt. retired 1988 after 30 years service, 27 years reserve and 3 years active duty. **HOME ADDRESS:** 594 Audubon Pl, Highland Park, IL 60035. **BUSINESS ADDRESS:** Private Practice, 1800 Grand Ave, Waukegan, IL 60085.

MCCAMPBELL, RAY IRVIN
Singer/songwriter. **PERSONAL:** Born Jun 22, 1959, Flint, MI; son of Ellsworth McCampbell and Victoria McCampbell. **EDUCATION:** Olivet Coll, Olivet MI, Music, 1979; Texas Southern Univ, Houston TX, Bachelor of Communications, 1982. **CAREER:** Self Employed, saxophonist, 1975-77, singer, 1977-82, singer/songwriter 1983-87; MCA Records, Los Angeles CA, singer/songwriter, 1987-; Lorimar Productions, Los Angeles CA, actor, 1988. **ORGANIZATIONS:** Mem, Kappa Alpha Psi Fraternity, 1980-; mem, Oak Cliff Bible Fellowship, 1983-. **HONORS/ACHIEVEMENTS:** Symphonic Award, Flint Northwestern High School, 1977; NBA Pre-Game Song, Dallas Mavericks, 1988; Appearance, Lorimar Productions, 1988; NBA Legend's Allstar Pre-Game Song, NBA, 1989; Soul Train Performance, 1988; McDonald's Commercial, 1989; Dallas City Proclamation, 1989; Houston City Proclamation, 1989; Arsenio Hall Show Performance, 1989; member of The MAC Band; debut album The MAC Band Featuring The McCampbell Brothers.

MCCANE, CHARLES ANTHONY
Retired educational administrator. **PERSONAL:** Born Oct 24, 1899, Jefferson, TX; married Margaret Maria Perea; children: Perea McCane Hopkins, Charlotte Antoinette. **EDUCATION:** Wiley Coll, AB 1922; Northwestern Univ, MS 1931; Catholic Univ, 1936-40. **CAREER:** Wiley Coll, prof of physics 1923-32; Bishop Coll, prof of physics 1931-32; Univ of DC, prof of physics 1932-66; Howard Univ, lecturer in math 1943-66; Cape Cod Comm Coll, lecturer in math 1968-72 retired. **ORGANIZATIONS:** Sec, vice chmn 12th St YMCA 1943-63; mem Central Atlanta YMCA Bd 1945-66; pres Brookland Civic Assoc 1950-52; bd mem USO DC 1950-60; mem exec comm Middle Atlantic YMCA 1950-66; mem Amer Assoc of Univ Prof. **HONORS/ACHIEVEMENTS:** Rosenwald Fellow Northwestern Univ 1928-29; listed in Amer Men of Sci; Man of the Year Wash DC 1963.

MCCANE, CHARLOTTE ANTOINETTE
Educator. **PERSONAL:** Born in Washington, DC; daughter of Charles A McCane and Margaret Perea McCane (deceased). **EDUCATION:** Albright Coll, BA Hist; Univ of Mysore India, Fullbright Grant 1964; Northwestern Univ, NDEA Grant 1968; Fairleigh-Dickinson Univ, MA Hist. **CAREER:** New London CT Bd of Ed, educator 1957; Red Bank NJ Bd of Ed, educator 1957-69; Ridgewood NJ Bd of Ed, educator 1969-. **ORGANIZATIONS:** Group leader World Youth Forum Tour of Europe 1965, Oper Crossroads Africa Liberia 1966; mem eval comm Middle State Assoc for Secondary School, Yorkers & Hempstead School; mem NASDTEC Eval Comm, Princeton Univ, Glassboro State; assoc inst, adv comm Racism & Social Justice Natl Council for Social Studies;sec, treas Multicultural Ed SIG; mem Life Assoc for Study of Afro-Amer Life & History; mem Amer Assoc of Univ Women, NAACP; life mem Natl Council ofNegro Women. **HONORS/ACHIEVEMENTS:** Article "Social Ed" Book Review Natl Council for Soc Studies 1980; publ article "Definition of Democracy" NY Herald Tribune 1964; extensive travel thru Africa, Asia, Europe, Latin Amer 1966-79. **BUSINESS ADDRESS:** Educator, Ridgewood High School, 627 E Ridgewood Ave, Ridgewood, NJ 07451.

MCCANNON, DINDGA FATIMA
Painter, printmaker, author, illustrator, fashion designer, quiltmaker, teacher, and muralist. **PERSONAL:** Born 1947, Harlem, NY; daughter of Ralph Miller and Lottie Porter; married Percival E McCannon, 1967; children: Afrodesia, Harmarkhis. **EDUCATION:** Attended Bob Blackburn Workshop, Nyumba Ya Sanaa Galleries, and under Charles Aston, Richard Mayhew, Al Hollingsworth, Abdullah Aziz. **ORGANIZATIONS:** Where We At, Black Women Artists. **HOME ADDRESS:** 800 Riverside Dr, New York, NY 10032. **BUSINESS ADDRESS:** 800 Riverside Dr, New York, NY 10032. *

MCCANTS, COOLIDGE N.
Attorney. **PERSONAL:** Born Nov 17, 1925, Mobile, AL; married Elaine J; children: Kevin, Gary, Lisa. **EDUCATION:** NY U, BS; Brklyn Law Sch, LLB. **CAREER:** Wshington Pvt Pract, atty 1960-; Legal Aid, Sup Ct Br, atty. **ORGANIZATIONS:** Mem Nat Am Washington & DC Bar Assns; Alpha Phi Alpha; Neighbors Inc. **MILITARY SERVICE:** USAF. **BUSINESS ADDRESS:** 7826 Eastern Ave, NW, Washington, DC 20012.

MCCANTS, JESSE LEE, SR.
Business executive. **PERSONAL:** Born Feb 13, 1936, Fairfax, AL; married Hettie Jane Lindsay; children: Sheree Yvonne, Jesse Jr, Jacinta Lariece, Jerel Lindsay, Janella Larose. **EDUCATION:** TN St U, M Deg Admin 1966; AL St U, BS 1958. **CAREER:** Allstate Loan & Inv Co, pres, fdr 1985; Peoples Bk of Chattanooga, chmn, organizer 1972-76; City Govt, admin 1969-72; Security Fed Svngs & Loan Assn, bd chmn, pres, fdr 1971-74; City of Chattanooga, tchr 1961-68. **ORGANIZATIONS:** Bd dir Chatta Chap of Nat Bus Leag; Am Diabetes Assn; Chatta Area Vo Tech Sch; Chatta E 5th St Day Care Ctr; bd chmn, dir Allstate Loan & Inv Co Inc; chmn, bd dir McCants Dev Co Inc; mem Kappa Alpha Psi Frat; active Corps of Execs; mem NAACP; mem Big Bros Assn; mem Better Bus Bur of Chatta. **HONORS/ACHIEVEMENTS:** Black Businessman of Yr Award 1975; Biography appears in Who's Who in Fin & Ind 1975; Disting Serv Award Jaycees 1972; Commd by Gov Winfield Dunn of TN rank of Col 1972. **MILITARY SERVICE:** AUS sp4 1959-61. **BUSINESS ADDRESS:** President, Allstate Investment Co, PO Box 16214, Chattanooga, TN 37416.

MCCANTS, ODELL
Medical doctor. **PERSONAL:** Born Sep 05, 1942, Winnsboro, SC; married Laura; children: Odell, Jr. **EDUCATION:** Howard Univ, BS 1965, MD 1970. **CAREER:** Howard Univ Hosp, resident 1975; Automobiles Intl, ceo 1984-; Greater SE Comm Hosp Washington, president/designate 1985-; Automobiles Intl, broker and founder 1984-; Odell McCants MD, PC, president 1975-. **ORGANIZATIONS:** Fellow Amer Coll of Obstetricians and Gynecologists 1977-, Intl Coll of Surgeons 1977-; mayor's task force Adolescent Health City of Alexandria VA 1986-; instructor Howard Univ Coll of Medicine; house specialist Alexandria Hosp, and Dept of Health Commonwealth of VA 1982-; former dir United Black Fund of WA; bd of dir Northern VA 1978-79; mem & bd of dir American Cancer Soc 1983-. **HONORS/ACHIEVEMENTS:** Daniel Hale Williams Awd Assoc of former Residents & Interns Freedmen's Hosp. **BUSINESS ADDRESS:** 1600-K Crystal Sq Arcad, Arlington, VA 22202.

MCCARRELL, CLARK GABRIEL, JR.
Engineering/construction official. **PERSONAL:** Born Apr 13, 1958, Chicago, IL; son of Mr Clark G McCarrell Sr and Mrs Melva Lee Washington McCarrell; married Ruby L Kirby, Aug 02, 1986. **EDUCATION:** Wright Coll, Chicago IL, AA Engineering, 1984; Washington Coll, Chicago IL, AAS Computer Science, 1986; Univ of Nevada, Las Vegas NV, BS Mechanical Engineering, 1989. **CAREER:** Donohue & Assoc, Milwaukee WI, engineering aide, 1978-80; Consulting Consortium, Chicago IL, engineering apprentice, 1980-82; Dunham & Assoc, Las Vegas NV, mechanical designer, 1986-87; Science Application Inter Corp, Santa Barbara CA, CAE designer, 1987-88; Clark County School District, Las Vegas NV, CAD designer, 1989-. **ORGANIZATIONS:** Mem, Amer Soc of Mechanical Engineering, 1977-, Amer Soc of Black Engineers, 1979-; asst to program coord, Ray Coll of Design, 1983-86; mem, Diaconate Bd, United Church of Christ, 1984-86, Natl Fire Protection Assn; procurement consultant, Nevada Economic Devel Co, 1986; mem, Amer Nuclear Soc, 1987-88, Amer Soc of Plumbing Engineering, 1987, Amer Soc of Professional Engineering; pres, (UNLV Chapter) Amer Soc of Heating, Ventilation & Air Conditioning Engineers, 1989. **HONORS/ACHIEVEMENTS:** Phi Theta Kappa Award, Phi Theta Kappa Honor Frat, 1984; Ashrae Scholarship, Amer Soc of HVAC, 1988; Engineer-In-Training (EIT) Candidate, State of Neveda, 1989. **HOME ADDRESS:** 1805 Green Acres Ave, Las Vegas, NV 89115.

MCCARTHY, FRED
Administration. **PERSONAL:** Born Jul 12, 1924, New York, NY; married Sybil Joshua; children: Louis. **EDUCATION:** Empire St Coll; Cornell U; St Francis Xavier 1971-. **CAREER:** Air Trans Local 504 AFL-CIO, 2nd vice pres 1985; Pan Am World Airways, mechanic 1975-. **ORGANIZATIONS:** Mem, past exec bd mem Cntrl Labor Cncl; Black Trade Ldrshp Com; adv cncl mem Affirm Act Com; Cncl for Airport Oppty Generic Training Prog; mem Urban Leag; NAACP; aav bd mem August Martin HS. **MILITARY SERVICE:** USN 1st class petty ofcr 1943-46. **BUSINESS ADDRESS:** 153-33 Rockaway Blvd, Jamaica, NY 11434.

MCCASKEY, DAPHNE THEOPHILIA (DAPHNE MCCASKY ROBINSON)
Physician. **PERSONAL:** Born Sep 26, 1912; married Dr Algernon Robinson; children: George A. **EDUCATION:** Washington Sq Coll NYU, AB 1936; Howard Med Sch HU, MD 1941; Am Acad of Family Practice, FAAFP 1976. **CAREER:** Pvt Practice, md 1985. **ORGANIZATIONS:** Mem Med Soc of Co of NY; mem AAFP; mem NMA. **HONORS/ACHIEVEMENTS:** Sojourner Truth Award, Nat Negro B & P Women's Clubs 1968.

MCCASKILL, EARLE
Associate judge. **PERSONAL:** Born Nov 20, 1937, Madison, IL; son of Wilson McCaskill and Rosie M King McCaskill; married Camille Williams; children: Ericka Denise. **EDUCATION:** Talladega Coll, BA 1959; Howard School of Law, LLB 1963. **CAREER:** St Clair Cty IL, asst publ defender 1970-71; Corp Counsel E St Louis, asst counsel 1971-73; Fire & Police Comm of E St Louis IL, attny 1973-79; private practice, attorney 1970-85; 20th Judicial Circuit of IL, associate judge 1985-. **ORGANIZATIONS:** Mem Alpha Phi Alpha 1956-; mem IL State Bar Assoc 1964-; asst dir Legal Aid Soc of St Clair County 1969-70; mem, bd of dir St Clair Cty Comm Mental Health Bd 1970-; attorney Civil Serv Comm E St Louis IL 1973-79; attny, bd of trustees State Comm Coll of E St Louis IL 1977-84; American Bar Association. **HONORS/ACHIEVEMENTS:** Community Leaders and Noteworthy Americans 1978. **MILITARY SERVICE:** AUS capt 1963-69. **HOME ADDRESS:** 601 Raintree Drive, Belleville, IL 62221.

MCCAULLEY, JAMES ALAN, III
Administrator. **PERSONAL:** Born May 22, 1948, Huntsville, AL; married Mary L Cassels; children: Chenessa Vay, James Alan IV. **EDUCATION:** Gen Motors Inst, Flint MI, BIE 1971; Michigan State Univ Lansing, MBA 1971; California Western Univ Santa Ana, PhD 1976. **CAREER:** Chenita Nursing Homes & Twin Oaks Living & Learning Ctr, adminstr 1985; Buick Motor Div Flint, personnel dir salaried employees 1971; Ashland Coll, prof 1985; North Central Tech Coll, prof 1985; McCaulley Dairy Inc, pres, owner; McCaulley Care Center, pres, owner; owner 4 other nursing homes. **ORGANIZATIONS:** Vice pres Ped Ctr 1985; qualified mental retardation professional OH Dept of Mental Health & Retardation 1985; bd mdm North Central Tech Coll 1985; bd mem Richland Ind 1985; mem Beta Gamma Sigma Man Hon Soc 1985; mem Tau Beta Pi Engr Hon Soc 1985; Licensed Social Worker. **BUSINESS ADDRESS:** President, Owner, McCaulley Care Center, 1670 Crider Rd, Mansfield, OH 44903.

MCCLAIN, ANDREW BRADLEY
Educator. **PERSONAL:** Born Nov 12, 1948, Akron, OH; son of Andrew H McClain and Margaret Greene McClain; married Patricia Ann Sampson; children: Sylvia, Andrew, Peter. **EDUCATION:** Univ of Akron, Akron, OH JD 1984-88; Kent State Univ Kent, OH, M Ed 1976-78; Univ of Akron Akron, OH, BA 1966-70. **CAREER:** Akron Bd of Educ, english teacher 1970-73; Western Reserve Acad, dir upward bound 1973-87; The Univ of Akron, dir upward bound 1987- Western Reserve Academy, Hudson, OH, dir Upward Bound 1973-87; Akron Public Schools, Akron, OH, teacher 1970-73. **ORGANIZATIONS:** Consultant A Better Chance 1975-86; dir School Scholarship Serv 1979-84; consultant Mid-South Assoc of Independent Schools 1981-83, Marquette Univ 1984; mem former dir and pres state chap MAEOPP; mem NAACP. **HONORS/ACHIEVEMENTS:** Fellowship Natl Assoc of Independent Schools 1982; Fellowship Inst for Educational Leadership 1982-. **BUSINESS ADDRESS:** Director, Pre College Programs, Gallucci Hall 111-7908, The University of Akron, Akron, OH 44320.

MCCLAIN, DOROTHY MAE (NEE HUNTER)
Government official. **PERSONAL:** Born Jun 17, 1931, Hartsville, SC; daughter of Chester Hunter and Eloise Eltridge Hunter; married Thurman McClain, Mar 31, 1950 (died 1987); children: Thurman Jr, Roxcella McClain Brown, Vaness McClain Smith. **EDUCATION:** Washington Tech Inst, Certificate 1972; Howard Univ, Univ Without Walls 1980; Morgan State Univ. **CAREER:** DC Govt, clerk-typist 1962-79; DC Govt Newspaper Recycling, program coord 1979-81; DC Govt Environmental Serv, office supvr 1975-79; DC Govt Dept Public Works Mayor's Beautification Comm, exec dir 1984. **ORGANIZATIONS:** Dir Ander-Mac Video Production 1983-84; bd dir Combine Communities in Action 1975-; councilwoman Town of Cheverly MD 1974-86; bd dir MD Municpal League 1977-78; pres Iota Phi Lambda Sor Epsilon Delta Chapter 1979-81. **HONORS/ACHIEVEMENTS:** Certificate of Appreciation Dept Environmental Serv Women's Prog 1984, Adams-Morgan Comm; Outstanding Job Performance Dept Environmental Serv 1974, 1975, 1979, 1980; plaque 25th Legislative Distinguished Alliance Club 1976, Sorority of Year Iota Phi Lambda Sorority 1984, Outstanding Community Serv Los Amigos Serv Club 1976. **BUSINESS ADDRESS:** Executive Dir, DC Govt Public Works Dept, 6523 Chillum Pl NW, Washington, DC 20012.

MCCLAIN, EARSALEAN J.
Educator. **PERSONAL:** Born Jul 28, 1910, Lexington, MS; children: 3 Children. **EDUCATION:** Jackson State Univ, BS; Eastern Michigan Univ, Graduate Work. **CAREER:** Holmes Co Tchng Unit, IPS tchr 1985; Holmes Co, IPS tchr 1975-; MAM Heroines of Jericho Local 7th Dist, jr atty; Holmes Co, notary pub 1975-; FDD Lexington MS, soc wkr. **ORGANIZATIONS:** Sec of Lexington Br NAACP; mem St Sci & Math Club; Lebanon MB Ch Chorus; pres Lebanon Pastors Aide Club; pres Women Fed Club; Lebanon MB ChGrp; grp capt, tchr Sun Sch; usher supervisor, Lebanon MB Church; pros, Lexington Branch, NAACP, 1982-. **HONORS/ACHIEVEMENTS:** Recip 30 yr Tchrs Award; life mem certificate, NAACP in 1985.

MCCLAIN, JAMES W.
Educator/administrator. **PERSONAL:** Born May 14, 1939, Southern Pines, NC; son of Wilton McClain and Mary McClain; married Mary E Rafferty; children: James W Jr, Ellen M, Elizabeth A, Kimberly A, Kara J, Matthew A. **EDUCATION:** Providence College, BA 1962. **CAREER:** McClain, McDaniel, Sullivan & Fowler Inc, pres 1968-77; Ford Motor Co, dealer develop 1977-80; Arthur D Little Co, sr consultant 1980-81; Boston Univ, dir of equal oppor 1982-. **ORGANIZATIONS:** Faculty mem Wheeler College Boston 1968-72, Newton College; mem Cardinal's Commn on Peace and Justice; chmn bd dirs Community Ctr School Newton MA 1985-86; bd mem Community Change Inc Boston 1985-86; regional dir Amer Assoc for Affirmative Action 1986-; bd mem Massachusetts chapter of Amer Society for Training and Development. **HONORS/ACHIEVEMENTS:** Stoughton MA Jaycee Man of the Year 1972. **HOME ADDRESS:** 32 Massapoag Ave, North Easton, MA 02356. **BUSINESS ADDRESS:** Dir of Equal Opportunity, Boston University, 25 Buick St, Boston, MA 02215.

MCCLAIN, JEROME G.
Business executive. **PERSONAL:** Born Jun 02, 1939, Cleveland, OH; married Jeanette. **EDUCATION:** Cntrl St U, BS; Am Inst of Bkng, Grad Cert. **CAREER:** Soc Nat Bk, working 1965-, mgmt trainee 1965, asst br mgr 1967, br mgr 1969, asst vp, br mgr 1972; vice pres community relations 1979, vice pres corporate community relations 1986. **ORGANIZATIONS:** Mem Urban Leag of Grtr Cleveland; bd mem United Way Srv; mem Consumer Pro Assn; mem Alpha Phi Alpha Frat Inc; bd mem The Karamu House; bd mem Cleveland Br NAACP; bd mem Eliza Bryant Ctr; mem Phi Alpha Theta Hon Hist Frat. **HONORS/ACHIEVEMENTS:** Bus Man of Yr Mt Pleasant Com Cncl 1974. **MILITARY SERVICE:** US Military comm 2 lt 1963; inactive 1st lt 1985. **BUSINESS ADDRESS:** VP Corporate Comm Relations, Society Natl Bank, 800 Superior, Cleveland, OH 44114.

MCCLAIN, MARLON L.
Musician. **PERSONAL:** Born Aug 08, 1955, Portland, OR; divorced; children: Devin Lamont. **CAREER:** Pleasure (Fantasy Record Artists), leader/guitarist 1974-; At Home Prodns, studio session guitarist 1974-78; 360 Music Inc, pres 1979-; guitarist; Solo LP Changes Fantasy Records 1980; productions incl Shock (Lets Get Crackin LP, Electrophonic Funk LP, Nite Life LP) 1980-83; Jeff Lorger Fusion, guitarist 1981-84;Kenny 6's (Kenny 6 and 6 Force LP, guitarist 1982-83; Nu Shooz Poolside LP Atlantic Records, co-producer 1986; Dazz Band Geffen Records, guitarist 1984-; MacMan Music Inc, pres 1980-. **ORGANIZATIONS:** Consult various musical artists; mem ASCAP 1974; mem BMA 1979. **HONORS/ACHIEVEMENTS:** Freedom Award NAACP 1978; Popular Music Award ASCAP 1978; producer Jeff Lorber Soft Space/Water Sign LP's 1978-79; producer Black Ivory LP 1978.

MCCLAIN, SHIRLA R.
Educator. **PERSONAL:** Born Feb 04, 1935, Akron, OH; daughter of Dumas Robinson and Marcella Macbeth Robinson; married Henry McClain, Apr 06, 1957; children: Kelli Shimabukuro, Scott McClain. **EDUCATION:** Univ of Akron, Akron OH, BS, 1956, MS, 1970, PhD, 1975. **CAREER:** Akron Public School, Akron OH, teacher and supervisor, 1956-76; Kent State University, Kent OH, prof of education, 1976-87; Walsh College, North Canton OH, prof of education, 1987-. **ORGANIZATIONS:** Mem, Assn of Teacher Educators Multicultural Education Special Interest Group, 1984-87, 1989; mem, Assn of Teacher Educators, 1984-87, 1989; mem, Univ of Akron Black Cultural Center advisory board, 1987; mem, Summit County Historical Society John Brown Inst Steering Committee, 1989-. **HONORS/ACHIEVEMENTS:** Author of numerous monographs, book chapters, and reviews; achievement award, Akron Urban League, 1975; distinguished black alumna award, Black Alumna Assoc of Univ of Akron, 1986; lifetime achievement award, Black United Students, Walsh College, 1988; distinguished educator award, Multicultural Education Special Interest Group of the Assn of Teacher Educators, 1989. **HOME ADDRESS:** 865 Packard Drive, Akron, OH 44320.

MCCLAIN, WILLIAM ANDREW
Attorney. **PERSONAL:** Born Jan 11, 1913, Sandford, NC; married Roberta White. **EDUCATION:** Wittenberg Univ, AB 1934; Univ of Michigan, JD 1937; Wilberforce Univ, LlD 1963; Univ of Cincinnati, LlD 1971; Wittenberg Univ, LHD 1972. **CAREER:** City of Cincinnati, asst city solicitor 1942-57; Berry & McClain, mem 1938-58; City of Cincinnati, deputy city solicitor 1957-63, city solicitor 1963-72, acting city mgr 1968, 1972; Keating, Muething & Klekamp, mem 1972-73; Cincinnati Branch Small Business Admin, general counsel 1973-75; Hamilton County Common Pleas Court, judge 1975-77; Hamilton County Municipal Court, judge 1977-1980; Manley, Jordan & Fischer, mem 1980-. **ORGANIZATIONS:** Mem bd of dir Cincinnati Chapter Red Cross 1975-; Natl Conf Christians & Jews Cincinnati 1975-; Cincinnati Bar Assn, Amer Bar Assn & Natl Bar Assn; Amer Judicature Soc; Amer Bar Fnd; Fed Bar Assn; World Peace Through Law; Prince Hall Mason 33 Degree; Alpha Phi Alpha. **MILITARY SERVICE:** Judge Advocate General USA 1st lt 1943-46; Army Commendation Award 1945. **BUSINESS ADDRESS:** Attorney, Manley, Jordan & Fischer, 4100 Carew Tower, Cincinnati, OH 45202.

MCCLAIN, WILLIAM L.
Automobile dealer. **PERSONAL:** Born Apr 25, 1958, Bronx, NY; son of Willie Lee McClain and Jacqueline Francis Jackson Winters; married Pamela Kay Johnson, May 18, 1985. **EDUCATION:** Oregon State Univ, Corvallis OR, BS Business Admin, 1981. **CAREER:** Zale Corp, Salem OR, mgr; Westside Timber Inc, vice pres, 1985-; Stayton Motors Inc, dealer, owner, 1985-; Jackies Ribs Inc, vice pres, 1985-; Reedsport Motors Inc, dealer, owner, 1988-.

MCCLAMMY, THAD C.
College president. **PERSONAL:** Born Oct 22, 1942, Evergreen, AL; son of T C McClammy and Ukla Maye McClammy; married Patricia Larkins McClammy, Jun 05, 1966; children: Christopher, Patrice. **EDUCATION:** Alabama State Univ, Montgomery AL, BA, 1966; Auburn Univ, Montgomery AL, MS, 1977; Selma Univ, Selma AL, Honorary LLD, 1984. **CAREER:** City of Montgomery, Montgomery AL, real estate officer/broker, 1967-68, developer, 1968-72; Lomax-Hannon Jr Coll, Greenville AL, devel officer, 1974; Trenholm State Technical Coll, Montgomery AL, instructor, 1974-77, coord Community Serv, 1977-81, pres, 1981-. **ORGANIZATIONS:** Mem, Omega Psi Phi Frat, 1963-, Phi Delta Kappa Professional Council; mem, President's Club, Natl Democratic Party, 1976-80; mem, bd of dir, Montgomery Area United Way, 1982; mem, Lion's Club, 1987-. **BUSINESS ADDRESS:** President, Trenholm State Technical College, 1225 Air Base Blvd, Montgomery, AL 36108.

MCCLANAHAN, BRENT ANTHONY
Athlete. **PERSONAL:** Born Sep 21, 1950, Bakersfield, CA; married Mae Lavonne Foster; children: Anthony Darnell. **EDUCATION:** Univ of MN, 1975; AZ St U, Agr Bus 1969-74. **CAREER:** MN Vikings, pro ftbl plyr 1973-; Viking Rep, pro bsktbl 1975; Transcntntl Oil Co, oilfld wrkr 1974; Windjammer Bar, 1973; St Dept, 1972; Asso Groc, dockman 1971; ASU, maint dept 1969-71. **ORGANIZATIONS:** Mem Kappa Alpha Psi 1975; dir Guide Right Prog; chmn Cancer Soc 1977. **HONORS/ACHIEVEMENTS:** Johnny Bench Superstar Tourn; Am Cancer Soc Ten Outstndng Yg Men of Am 1977; plyr Super Bowl 1974-75; plyr Fiesta Bowl 1971-72; plyr Peach Bowl 1970; 1st Team All WAC 1972; Ousts Fr ASU 1969; hon mem Prep All Am Sunkist 1968; Outst Back of the Yr S San Joaquin Valley 1968; SYL All Leag 1968; All CityBack of the Yr 1968; Athl of the Mo Jockey Club 1968; Most Val Plyr 1698; Most Outst Plyr 1967. **BUSINESS ADDRESS:** Minnesota Vikings, 7110 France Ave, Edina, MN 85423.

MCCLANE, KENNETH ANDERSON, JR.
Educator. **PERSONAL:** Born Feb 19, 1951, New York, NY; son of Dr Kenneth McClane and Genevieve McClane; married Dr Rochelle Evette Woods. **EDUCATION:** Cornell Univ, AB (with distinction) 1973, MA 1975, MFA 1976. **CAREER:** Colby College, instructor of English 1974-75; City Univ of New York, asst dir of SEEK 1977-78; Williams College, Luce visiting prof of English 1983-84; Cornell Univ, asst prof of English 1976-83, assoc prof of English 1983-89, prof of English, 1989-. **ORGANIZATIONS:** Dir, Creative Writing Program, Cornell Univ 1983-86; editor, Epoch Magazine, 1984-86; script consultant, "The Bluest Eye," 1984-; college scholar adv bd, Cornell Univ, 1984-; bd of dir, Human Affairs Training Program, 1986-; delegate, Modern Language Assn, 1989-. **HONORS/ACHIEVEMENTS:** Clark Distinguished Teaching Award, 1983; books of poetry include A Tree Beyond Telling, Poems, Selected and New, published 1983, and Take Five: Poems 1971-1986, published 1988; essays include "A Death in the Family" 1985 Antioch Review, "The School" 1985 Northwest Review, "Walls, A Journey to Auburn" 1987 Community Review; essay "Walls" selected for inclusion in Best American Essays of 1988, ed by Robert Atwan and Annie Dillard, Ticknor and Fields, 1989. **HOME ADDRESS:** 114 Glenside Rd, Ithaca, NY 14850. **BUSINESS ADDRESS:** Cornell University, Dept of English, Ithaca, NY 14853.

MCCLASKEY, WILLIAM H.
Attorney. **PERSONAL:** Born Jun 24, 1912, Louisville, KY; married Belma D Pleasant; children: William H. **EDUCATION:** Univ of Louisville (LMC), AB 1936; IN U, Bus Admin 1936-37; John Marshall Law Sch Chicago IL, JD 1950. **CAREER:** Priv Prac, atty 1985; Comm Serv Admin Chicago Reg Ofc, chief operatns div 1975-78; OEO/CSA Legal Serv Prog Chicago Reg, reg dir 1967-75; Ofc of Chief Cnsl IRS Philadelphia Reg Ofc, staff atty 1964-66; Purdue Univ Calumet Dev Found, atty 1960-62; Moore Ming & Leighton Chicago, atty 1950-59; Gary IN City Ct, spl judge 1963-64. **ORGANIZATIONS:** Dir Louiseville Urban Leag 1979-; life mem NAACP 1976; trustee Good Shepherd Cong Ch Chicago 1960-70; mem Kappa Alpha Psi Frat Louisville Alumni Chap 1978; %Dir Louisville Area Primary Care Consortium 1980-; KY Bar Assn Frankfort KY 1978; Louisville Bar Assn Louisville KY 1978; Plymouth Cong Ch Louisville KY 1980. **HONORS/ACHIEVEMENTS:** Recip Am & Victory Awards USN 1946; Order of John Marshall Hon, John Marshall Law Sch Chicago 1950. **MILITARY SERVICE:** USN av storekep 2c, 2 1/2 srvd.

MCCLEAN, VERNON E.
Educator. **PERSONAL:** Born Sep 17, 1941, St Thomas, Virgin Islands of the United States;married Freda McClean; children: 1 Child. **EDUCATION:** St Augustine's Coll, BA 1965; Atlanta U, MA 1967; Columbia U, EdD 1975; Johns Hopkins U, Further Study; Yale U. **CAREER:** Paine Coll, tchr 1966-67; William Paterson Coll NJ, asst prof 1969-. **ORGANIZATIONS:** Life mem S Hist Assn; mem Assn for the Study of Negro Life & Hist; Assn Soc & Behavioral Scintsts; former natl pres Sigma Rho Sigma Hon Soc; found BASE. **HONORS/ACHIEVEMENTS:** Pub UJAMAA, WPC Journal of Black Studies; estblshmnt of Vernon E McClean Award 1972; fellows Danforth Found 1971-72; inst in S & Black Hist 1967-69. **BUSINESS ADDRESS:** William Paterson Coll, 300 Pompton Rd, Wayne, NJ 07470.

MCCLEAVE, MANSEL PHILIP
Minister, educator. **PERSONAL:** Born Aug 07, 1926, Rock Hill, SC. **EDUCATION:** NC Agr & Tech Coll, BS 1950, MS 1959; NY School of Floral Design, Graduate 1953; NC St U;Univ of NC; Friendshp Coll Rock Hill SC, DD 1970. **CAREER:** First Bapt Ch Siler City NC, pastor 1957-70; Edwards Grove Church Liberty NC, pastor 1958-81. **ORGANIZATIONS:** Pres Deep River Bapt Training Union 1943-66; instr of horticulture NC Agr & Tech StUniv 1953-; pastor Edwards Grove Missionary Bapt Ch, Liberty NC 1958-; moderator Deep River Missionary Bapt Assn 1959-; mem Am AssnUniv Prof; mem gen bd Gen Bapt St Conv of NC; mem adv bd Hm Hlth Srvs, RandolphCo Hlth Dept; Intrntl Black Writers Conf, Greensboro Pulpit Forum; Liberty Ministerial Assn; Greensboro Ministers Flwshp; Am Horticultural Soc; org, found Liberty Imprvmnt Assn; committeeman BS of Am; mem Phi Beta Sigma Frat; Hayes-Taylor YMCA; Hampton Inst Alumni Assn. **HONORS/ACHIEVEMENTS:** Listed in Personalities of the S 1973; Honorary DD Frndshp Coll Rock Hill SC; listed in Dict of Intrntl Biography 1974; Gamma Sigma Delta Hon Soc of Agriculture; author of publs, Murmurs of the Heart A Collection of Poems Vantage press 1976, The Story of the Deep River Missionary Assoc of NC & It's Auxiliaries, Deep River Missionary Baptist Assoc Ushers' History & Resource Manual. **MILITARY SERVICE:** WW II staff sgt. **BUSINESS ADDRESS:** NC Agric & Tech St Univ, Greensboro, NC 27411.

MCCLEAVE, MILDRED ATWOOD
Retired educator. **PERSONAL:** Born Dec 19, 1919, Memphis, TN; daughter of Carl Poston (deceased) and Ellen Poston (deceased); married Ben F McCleaye, Jr; children: Benjamin F III, Robert A, William S, Bruce P. **EDUCATION:** LeMoyne Coll, BA 1941; Univ of Denver, MA 1971; postgraduate, Univ of Northern Colorado; postgraduate, Colorado University; Adams State. **CAREER:** Memphis Publ Schl, tchr 1941-52; Denver Publ Schl, tchr cnslr 1958-85; Hill Middle Schl, cnslr;retired. **ORGANIZATIONS:** Natl Educ Assn; CO Educ Assn; Denver Classroom Tchrs Assn; CO School Counselrs Assn; Amer Personnel & Guidance Assn; pres & charter mem Denver Chap Jack & Jill of Amer Inc 1954-; dist capt Denver Rep Party 1962-; alt delegate Natl Rep Conv 1972; secr CO Black Rep 1970-1980; Alpha Kappa Alpha Sor 1941-85; appeared in nationwide NBC-TV movie "The Case of the Long Lost Love," 1987, and in other Perry Mason films. **HONORS/ACHIEVEMENTS:** Distinguished Tchr Award Denver CO 1983; CO Tchr of the Year Special Recognition State of CO 1984; CO Educ Assn Human Rel Award State of CO 1984; Outstanding Serv in fld of Educ Epsilon Sigma Alpha Sor 1984; Award of Excellence Denver Chapter; by executive order of Richard D Lamm, Governor of Colorado, May 21, 1985 proclaimed Mildred McCleave Day. **HOME ADDRESS:** 2236 High St, Denver, CO 80205.

MCCLELLAN, EDWARD J.
Retired government official, transportation executive. **PERSONAL:** Born Dec 12, 1921, Chicago, IL; son of Jay McClellan and Clara Moses McClellan; married Emma G Johnson McClellan, May 28, 1943; children: Kenneth Wesley McClellan. **EDUCATION:** Governors State Univ, University City TN, BA, 1983. **CAREER:** City of Chicago Police Dept, patrolman, 1949-66; NAACP, Chicago IL, urban program dir, 1966-70; State of IL, Notary Public, 1970-; US Postal Service, Chicago IL, br mgr security, 1970-76, br mgr EEO, 1976-84; Willett Corporation, Chicago IL, pres Spears School Bus Div, 1984-86; EJ McClellan & Associates, pres, 1985-; Multi-Pure Corp, distributor, 1988-. **ORGANIZATIONS:** Mem, Salem Lutheran Church, 1953-; NAACP, Southside Chicago Branch, 1964-; mem, Museum of Science & Industry, 1983-; mem, Art Institute of Chicago, 1985-. **HONORS/ACHIEVEMENTS:** Service Award, Chicago Boys Club, 1969; Leadership Award, NAACP, 1970; Service Award, Illinios Law Enforcement Comm, 1971; Employee of the Year (nominee), US Postal Service, 1974; Distinguished Service Award, Willett Corp, 1987. **MILITARY SERVICE:** US Army Infantry, 1st lieutenant, 1942-48; received 4 campaign ribbons, combat infantryman badge.

MCCLELLAN, FRANK MADISON
Attorney, educator. **PERSONAL:** Born Feb 05, 1945, Marion, SC; married Linda J Hughey; children: Malik, Toussaint. **EDUCATION:** Rutgers U, AB 1967; Duquesne U, JD 1970; Yale U, LLM 1974. **CAREER:** Duquesne U, prof of law 1985, asso prof of law 1974-76, asst prof of law 1972-74; Wilmer Cutler & Pickering, asso atty 1971-72; Chief Judge William H Hastie, US Ct of Appeals, law clerk. **ORGANIZATIONS:** Mem PA Bar Assn; mem DC Bar Assn; bd dir House of the Crossroads; law rev ed United Way Rev Com. **HONORS/ACHIEVEMENTS:** Merit Award; Felix S Cohen Prize; publ Law Review Articles. **BUSINESS ADDRESS:** 600 Forbes Ave, Pittsburgh, PA 15219.

MCCLELLAND, ISAAC HOLLAND
Retired educator. **PERSONAL:** Born Oct 14, 1907, Oakland, CA; married Marion Alyce Bright. **EDUCATION:** Univ CA Berkeley, BA 1930, MA 1936; Univ of Southern CA, Sec & General Admin Credentials 1956. **CAREER:** Los Angeles Unified Schl Dist, sec tchr cnslr 1938-50, secr boys vice princ 1950-55; David Searil Jordan HS, sec princ 1955-65, sec Supt 1965-70, sec supt of instr dist 1970-72; Dollars for Scholars Inc, pres 1972-. **ORGANIZATIONS:** Consult Los Angeles Unified Schl Dist 1972-75; secr Pasadena Historical Soc Bd of Trustees 1981-; comm Sr Citizen Comm of Pasadena 1984-; past pres Pasadena Publ Libr Bd 1975-81; Metro Co-op Libr Syst Adv Bd 1976-82; Hillsides Home for Children Bd Trustees 1976-82; mem Pasadena Educ Fnd Bd Trustee 1981-; trustee Clge Entrance Examination Bd 1967-71; mem bd of dir Pasadena Child Health Fnd 1982-; pres Library Bd Pasadena City Lib 1976; consult LA United Sch Dist 1973-75; past pres Metropolitan Cooperative Library Serv 1976-; rep So CA UC Berkeley Found 1972-79; mem Univ CA Berkeley alumni Awds Comm 1982; mem Bd Dir Pasadena Child Health Found; mem bd dir Pasadena Educ Found 1982-; mem Pasadena Sr Citizen Commn 1984-; sec bd dir Pasadena Historical Soc; mem Commonwealth Clb 1956-; mem Phi Delta Kappa; mem & past pres Univ of So CA Alumni Assoc; past pres Educare. **HONORS/ACHIEVEMENTS:** Recg awards Los Angeles City Council, CA State Legislatures; srv awards Univ CA Berkeley Alumni Citation 1984, Fnd Fund Raising; Service 1984; Natl Honor Soc Univ CA; Beru English Club Outstanding Student; Arts & Humanities Honors Conf; Citations, LA City Council, CA State Legislators, USC Sch of Educ; 1st Black Boys vice prin, secondary prin, area supt, asst supt of instruction in CA; rep UC Berkley chancellor ar LaVerne Univ & Art Cnter Coll of Design, pres inaugurations. **MILITARY SERVICE:** USAAF sgt navigation instructor Tuskegee Army Airfield 1943-45; Ofc Candidate Bd Passed 1945. **HOME ADDRESS:** 540 Rosewood Ln, Pasadena, CA 91103.

MCCLELLAND, MARGUERITE MARIE
Educator. **PERSONAL:** Born Dec 06, 1919, St Louis, MO; daughter of Brooks Manuel Hubbard and Minnie Mae Marshall Hubbard; married John Clyde McClelland, Sep 02, 1972. **EDUCATION:** School of the Art Inst of Chicago, Chicago IL, BA, 1943; Wayne State Univ, Detroit MI, MA, 1949; postgraduate study at Temple Univ, Philadelphia PA, 1963, Univ of Michigan, Ann Arbor MI, 1975, and Wayne State Univ. **CAREER:** Chicago Public Schools, Chicago IL, art teacher, 1943-47; Detroit Public Schools, Detroit MI, student teacher and supervisor of Wayne State Univ teachers of art education, 1948-78, guidance counselor, 1963-78, guidance dept head, 1978-83. **ORGANIZATIONS:** Supreme basileus, Natl Sorority of Phi Delta Kappa, 1989-; mem, American Guidance Assn; mem, Natl Council of Negro Women; mem, Natl Assault on Literacy; life mem, NAACP; mem, Natl Assn of Univ Women; mem, Organization of School Administrators; mem, Michigan Personnel and Guidance Assn; mem, Michigan Assn for Career Education; mem, Detroit School Women's Assn; mem, United Methodist Women; mem, Top Ladies of Distinction. **HONORS/ACHIEVEMENTS:** Teachers Medal, Valley Forge Freedom Foundation; Teacher of the Year Award, Detroit Education Assn; Industrial Arts Award, Ford Motor Co; State of Mich, City of Detroit, and Detroit Board of Education resolutions; author of Art Education Guide, Grades 7-8-9 for Detroit Public Schools; author of The Language of Child Art; author of Education in Spain: A Comparative Report; author of A Handbook for Art Education Student Teachers. **HOME ADDRESS:** 19211 Pennington Dr, Detroit, MI 48221.

MCCLENDON, CAROL A.
Public official. **PERSONAL:** Born Aug 21, 1942, Cleveland; married William C; children: William Jr, Kelley. **EDUCATION:** So U. **CAREER:** Cuyahoga Co Auditors Ofc, dep admnstr; NE OH Area Wide Asso Agy, prgm mgr/compliance ofcr; City of Cleveland, councilman. **ORGANIZATIONS:** Exec com Cuyahoga Co Dem Party 1972; apptd to state com 1972; first black elected Dem Nat Committeewoman in history of state of OH; elected v-chmn Cuyahoga Dem Party 1975.

MCCLENDON, ERNESTINE
Career consultant, producer. **PERSONAL:** Born Aug 17, 1924, Norfolk, VA; married George Wiltshire; children: Phyllis. **EDUCATION:** Virginia State Coll. **CAREER:** Ernestine McClendon Enterprises NY & LA, former owner 1963; former artists' mgr; former actress appearing on TV & in live theater; Harlem Theatrical Workshop, former teacher, founder; drama coach, theatrical career consultant, writer, producer; MC Productions, pres. **ORGANIZATIONS:** Represents nearly 100 clients including actors in TV radio & theater & movies, dir, writers & variety acts 1960-80. **HONORS/ACHIEVEMENTS:** First in her field to be franchised by all unions as a theatrical agt & is largely responsible for getting blacks into TV commercials; recip Woman's Awd 1969; named one of Two Thousand Women of Achvmnt 1970; tribute to the black woman WISE 1979.

MCCLENDON, KELLEN
Lawyer. **PERSONAL:** Born May 07, 1944, New Castle, PA; son of Leroy McClendon and Sylest McClendon. **EDUCATION:** Westminster Coll, BA 1966; Duquesne Univ School of Law, 1974; Robert Morris Coll Legal Asst Program 198-89; Duquesne Univ School of Law; adjunct professor 1987-89; visiting professor 1989-; asst city solicitor, city of Pittsburgh 1982-89. **CAREER:** PA Dept of Justice, asst attny gen 1974-79; Consol Mgmt Enterprises Inc, pres 1977-; Private practice, attny 1979-; City of Pittsburgh, asst city solicitor 1982-89; Robert Morris Coll Legal Asst Prog, instructor 1985-89; Duquesne Univ School of Law, adjunct prof 1987-, visiting prof 1989-. **ORGANIZATIONS:** Mem Allegheny Cty Bar Assoc 1974-; minority bus enterprise review comm City of Pittsburgh 1982-. **MILITARY SERVICE:** USAF capt 1967-71; Bronze Star; Vietnam Serv Medal. **BUSINESS ADDRESS:** DuquesneUniversity, School of Law, 900 Locust Street, Pittsburgh, PA 15282.

MCCLENDON, MOSES C.
Materials engineer. **PERSONAL:** Born Dec 11, 1934, Graceville, FL; son of Harry McClendon and Virginia McClendon; married Grace Jones McClendon, Jun 24, 1962; children: Chantell M, Michelle R, Moses C II. **EDUCATION:** Edward Waters Coll, Jacksonville FL, AA, 1954; Morris Brown Coll, Atlanta GA, BA, 1957; North Carolina A&T State Univ, Greensboro NC, MS, 1967. **CAREER:** Washington Bd of Educ, Chipley FL, asst principal, math/science teacher, 1960-66; Bell Telephone Labs, Winston-Salem NC, assoc mem of tech staff, 1967-70; Western Electric, Greensboro NC, materials engineer, 1971-80; AT&T Technologies, Richmond VA, dept chief, Materials Engineering, 1980-88; AT&T Microelectronics, Richmond VA, sr materials engineer, 1988-. **ORGANIZATIONS:** Mem, The Soc of Plastic Engineers, 1975-87, The Amer Chemical Soc, 1980-86; instructor, Richmond Area Program for Minorities in Engineering, 1984-86; mem, YMCA, 1985-87, Amer Mgmt Assn, 1987-88, NAACP, 1987-, Black Exec Exchange Program, 1988. **HONORS/ACHIEVEMENTS:** Beta Kappa Chi, Natl Science Soc, 1956; Reaction of Selected Hydrazino Phosphonate, Phrosphorium Bromides and Phosphorane, 1967; Evaluation of One Component Silicone Encapsulant, 1967; Cost Reduction of Power Transformers by Plastics Encapsulants, 1968; Differential Scanning Calorimetric Evaluation of B-Staged Epoxy Resin, 1972; Sigma Man of the Year, Phi Beta Sigma Frat Inc, 1980; Morris Brown Coll Athletic Hall of Fame, Morris Brown Coll, 1988. **MILITARY SERVICE:** AUS, E4, 1957-60. **BUSINESS ADDRESS:** Senior Materials Engineer, AT&T Microelectronics, 4500 Laburnum Ave, Richmond, VA 23231.

MCCLENIC, DAVID A.
Attorney, business executive. **PERSONAL:** Born Mar 06, 1926, Akron, OH; married Zenobia; children: Lisa, Brian. **EDUCATION:** Akron U, BS 1951; Akron Law Sch, JD 1956; Life Underwrtrs Training Cncl; CLU. **CAREER:** Det Bank & Trust Co, asst vp, trust dept 1971-, Asst trust ofcr 1968-71, trust adminstr 1967-68, trust consult 1965-67; Metropolitan & Life Ins Co, ins consult 1961-65; Richard H Austin & Co, acct 1958; W Howard Fost Law Off, legal clk 1957-58; Peavy Rlty Co, salesman, gen mgr 1953-58; Goodyear aircraft Corp, assemblyman 1952-57; Notary Pub, 1985. **ORGANIZATIONS:** Mem MI & Detroit Bar Assns; Am Arbitration Assn; Wolverine Bar Assn; CLU. **MILITARY SERVICE:** AUS 1944-46.

MCCLENIC, PATRICIA DICKSON
Executive administrator. **PERSONAL:** Born Nov 13, 1947, Akron, OH; children: Richard L Jr; Dennis K, Nicole M. **EDUCATION:** Akron Univ, BA 1971-78. **CAREER:** WSLR Radio, dir of public affairs 1970-75; United Way of Summit Cty, dir of comm 1975-79; United Way of South Hampton, dir of comm 1979-83; Amer Cancer Society, state public information dir 1983-84; United Way of Amer, assoc dir 1984-. **ORGANIZATIONS:** Mem Public Relations Soc of America 1979-; mem Intl Assn of Bus Comm 1978-; mem Natl Press Club 1985.

HOME ADDRESS: 6050 Haverhill Ct, Springfield, VA 22152. **BUSINESS ADDRESS:** Associate Dir, United Way of America, 701 North Fairfax, Alexandria, VA 22314.

MCCLENNEY, EARL HAMPTON
Educational administrator. **PERSONAL:** Born Mar 04, 1907, Marion, AL; married Fannie M; children: Earl Jr, Clifton, Gail, Neil, Henry Clay IV. **EDUCATION:** A&T St U, BS 1930; Cornell U, MS 1938; PA St U, DD 1942; VA Theol Sem, LLD; St Paul's Coll, LLD. **CAREER:** Educ Admin, consult 1985; St Augustine's Coll, tchr 1938-47. **ORGANIZATIONS:** Pres Assn of Episc Coll 1970-83; coll pres Voorhees Coll St Paul's Coll 1947-49; mem St Bd Comm Coll VA 1985; mem VA Minority Commn 1985; chmn of bd Southside Sr Citizens Ctr Inc; vice pres PD XIII VA 1985; treasUniv of Black Episcopalian Inc.

MCCLINE, RICHARD L.
Executive. **PERSONAL:** Born Jul 13, 1944, Chicago, IL; children: Lamia, Al, Chari. **EDUCATION:** Univ of IL, BA 1966; Northwestern Univ Grad Sch of Business, MBA 1970. **CAREER:** Jewel Food Stores IL, general mgr grand bazaar 1970-77, buyer/merchandiser 1977-80; James H Lowry & Assocs, sr associate 1980-82; Golden State Business League, exec vice pres 1982-. **ORGANIZATIONS:** Corporate bd mem Assoc of Bay Area Govts 1983-87; mem East Bay Republican Cncl, Bay Area Purchasing Cncl, Minority Develop Ad-Hoc Comm for Bay Area 1983-87; mem adv cncl US Small Business Admin 1984-87; corporate bd mem Caelus Devices 1985-87; comm mem The Martin Luther King Jr Holiday Comm 1985-87; bd mem Upward Bound 1985-87; regional vice pres Natl Business League 1985-87; mem adv cncl Youth Entreprenuerial Ctr 1985-87; loan approval bd Oakland Revolving Loan Fund 1986-87; corporate bd mem United Engineering 1986-87. **BUSINESS ADDRESS:** Executive Vice President, Golden State Business League, 333 Hegenberger Rd Ste 315, Oakland, CA 94621.

MCCLINTON, CURTIS R., JR.
Investment banker. **PERSONAL:** Born in Muskogee, OK; married Devonne French MD; children: Tobi, Margot. **EDUCATION:** Cntrl MI U, MPA;Univ of KS, BS;Univ of NE, Sch of bkng;Univ of MO, Real Est Law; Am Inst of Bkng; Weaver Sch of Real Est Pract Franklin Fin Serv Inst; Real Est Bd Inst; Wharton Sch,Univ of PA. **CAREER:** Black Ec Union of Gr KC, pres, fdr, xec dir 1985; Midwest Prog Svc, lectr 1974-; Franklin Fin Svcs, reg securities broker, dealer 1974-; Tech Fab Inc, gen mgr, pres 1972-; Swope Pky Nat Bk, fdr, exec vice pres 1969; Douglass St Bk, comm loan ofcr, asst cashier 1965-67; KPRS, tv, radio brdcstr 1965-66; Interstate Securities, loan ofcr, collector 1964-65; Franklin Life Ins Co, ins salesman 1963-; Professional Ftbl Club 1962-70; Professional Concert Singer;U of KS, asst ftbl coach, recruiter 1962-63. **ORGANIZATIONS:** Mem Am Mgmt Assn; Black Ec Union of Gr KC; C of C fo Gr KC; Nat Assn of Mkt Devs; Nat Bkrs Assn; Nat Security Dealers Assn; past pres Comm Ec Dev Congress; Cnsl on Urban Ec Dev; Mid-Am Reg Cncl; Planned Ind Expansion Com of City of KC;Univ of MO Ext Prog Adv Cncl Flwshp of Christian Athlts; Kappa Alpha Psi Frat; NAACP; Urban Leag; YMCA; mem, bd of dir Who's Who of Outstndng Young Men of Am; St Mary's Hosp; United Negro Coll Fund; Selec Cnsl Sch of MedUniv of MO at KC. **HONORS/ACHIEVEMENTS:** All-Pro Fullback, KC Chiefs, World Champs 1970; All Am,Univ of KS; All Big 8 High Hurdle Champ 1960-61; recip C of C Ldr of Mon 1970; runner-up to MrKS Cit Annual C of C Hon 1970; Outst Cit Award, Presby Interracial Cncl; Outst Young Am 1971; Boss of Yr, KC Jr C of C 1975. **MILITARY SERVICE:** AUS. **BUSINESS ADDRESS:** 2502 Prospect, Kansas City, MO 64127.

MCCLOMB, GEORGE E.
Educator. **PERSONAL:** Born Apr 24, 1940, Long Island, NY; married Audrey Hamilton; children: George Jr. **EDUCATION:** Colgate U, BA 1962;Univ of Pittsburgh, MSW 1964, MA Polit Sci 1974, PhD Polit Sci 1984. **CAREER:** Univ of Pittsburgh, assoc prof 1973-, guest lectr 1970, adj asst prof 1969; hlth care consult 1971-72; Hlth Sys, asst dir 1971-73; Homewood Brushton Hlth Ctr, proj dir 1968-71, asst proj dir 1967-68. **ORGANIZATIONS:** Pres, bd dir Lemington Hm for Aged 1971-83; bd dir W PA Comprehensive Hlth Plng Agy; W PA Reg Med Prog; Visiting Nrs Assn; Pittsburgh Model Cities Hlth Task Force; Urban Leag Hlth Com; Comprehensive Care Task Force, Sickle Cell Anemia; commr Pub Pkng Auth City of Pittsburgh; commr Prog to Aid Citizen Enterprise; delegate White House Conf on Aging 1981; del Penna State Conf on Aging 1984. **HONORS/ACHIEVEMENTS:** Outstndng Vol Award, Allegheny Co United Way; Allegheny Co Med Soc Outstanding Citizens Awd 1981; Pittsburgh Fed Exec Bd 2nd Annual Black History Awd for Community Serv 1983. **MILITARY SERVICE:** USAF 1st lt 1964-67. **BUSINESS ADDRESS:** Assoc Prof, Chmn Admin, Univ of Pittsburgh, 2201 Cathedral of Learning, School of Social Work, Pittsburgh, PA 15260.

MCCLOUD, AARON C.
Educator. **PERSONAL:** Born Oct 28, 1933, Saginaw, MI; married Doris Jean Godbee; children: Sylvia Lynn, Monica Delis. **EDUCATION:** AA 1954; BA Pub Admin 1957; MA Guid & Cncl 1966-67; EdD Ldrshp in Curr 1973. **CAREER:** Eng & soc studies tchr 1960-68; cnslr 1968; evening adult ed 1967-69. **ORGANIZATIONS:** Pres MI Assn of Supv for Curr Dev 1969; mem Phi Delta Kappa 1972; pres, exec bd Hampton PTA 1971-72; exec bd Winterhalter PTA 1966-67; mem Concerned Cit for Action 1966-70; mem Messiah Bapt Ch; pres Mumford Constel Cit Grp 1968-71. **HONORS/ACHIEVEMENTS:** Recip Whitney Young, Outstndng Contri Black Culture 1971; WJR Radio, Outstndng Comm Contrib 1970. **MILITARY SERVICE:** US military 1958-59. **BUSINESS ADDRESS:** 2470 Collingwood, Detroit, MI 48206.

MCCLOUD, ANECE FAISON
Educational administrator. **PERSONAL:** Born May 29, 1937, Dudley, NC; daughter of Nancy Simmons Cole; married Verable L; children: Vernece Lynn, Carla D. **EDUCATION:** Bennett Coll, BS 1959; Univ of NE at Omaha, MA 1989. **CAREER:** Lincoln Jr High School, teacher 1959-60; Univ of NE Med Ctr, asst registrar 1972-76, dir of minority affairs 1976-85, asst instructor med jurisprudence & humanities 1980-85; Washington and Lee Univ, assoc dean of students 1985-. **ORGANIZATIONS:** Peer reviewer health career oppor prog grant 1982-84, consultant dean's forum on revitalizing health professional educ 1985; Div of Disadvantaged Assist Bureau of Health Prof HHS; consultant Life and Career Planning Workshop Urban League of NE 1985; mem bd dirs Rockbridge Comm Unit Amer Cancer Soc Virginia Div 1986; mem Natl Assoc for Women Deans Admins & Counselors, Amer Assoc for Counseling and Develop, Assoc for Multicultural Counseling and Develop, Natl Assoc for Foreign Student Advisors, The Assoc of Amer Medical Colls. **HONORS/ACHIEVEMENTS:** Certificate Black History Month Program Speaker Veterans Admin Medical Ctr Omaha 1984; Certificate Acknowledgement of Contribution to Educ Omaha Public Schools 1984; Plaque in Appreciation Minority Health Career Oppor 1984; Plaque in Appreciation Student Natl Medical Assoc UNMC Chap 1985. **BUSINESS ADDRESS:** Assoc Dean of Students, Washington & Lee University, Payne Hall 3, Lexington, VA 24450.

MCCLOUD, J. OSCAR
Clergyman. **PERSONAL:** Born Apr 10, 1936, Waynesboro, GA; married Robbie J Foster; children: Ann Michelle, Cassandra Anita, Tony Delancy. **EDUCATION:** Warren Wilson Coll Swannanoa NC, AA 1956; Berea Coll Berea KY, BA 1958; Union Theol Sem NY, MDiv 1961. **CAREER:** Davis St Untd Pres Ch, Raleigh NC, pastor 1961-64; Untd Pres Ch, Atlanta GA, fld rep, bd christian ed 1964-67; Div of Ch & Race Bd Nat Missns, asso 1968-69; Untd Pres Ch NY, Div of Ch & Race Bd of Nat Missns, asso chrmn for opertns 1969-71; Gen Sec Comm on Ecumcl Missn & Rel, asso 1971-72; The Program Agency United Presbyterian Church NY, gen dir 1972-86; The Fund for Theol Educ Princeton NJ, exec dir 1986-. **ORGANIZATIONS:** Gen dir Prog Agcy 1972-; mem bd dir Sthrn Chrstn Ldrshp Conf; GA Cncl of Chs; chmn Blk Pres Untd, Nat Conf of Blk; vchrprsn Div Overseas Ministries, Nat Cncl of Chs; mem Commn on World Mission & Evangelism, World Cncl of Chs; GZ Cncl on Hum Rel; mem NE Comnty OrgC Teaneck; Proj Eqlty Inc Nat; proj coord Am Forum for Intnl Stdy Tour to W Africa 1971; mem exec comm, central comm World Council of Churches; mem exec comm, governing bd Natl Council of Churches in the USA. **HONORS/ACHIEVEMENTS:** Hon Deg DD, Mary Holmes Coll, W Point MS 1974; Hon DHL, Whitworth Coll, Spokane WA; Black Congressional Caucus Comm Serv Awd 1978; 1st alumnus to receive Berea Coll Comm Serv Awd 1981. **BUSINESS ADDRESS:** Executive Dir, The Fund for Theological Educ, 421 Wall St, Princeton, NJ 08540.

MCCLOUD, RONNIE
Dentist. **PERSONAL:** Born Dec 29, 1947, Jacksonville, FL; son of Holley McCloud and Essie West McCloud. **EDUCATION:** Indiana Univ, BA 1970; NY Univ Coll of Dentistry, DDS 1974; Amer Dental Soc of Anesthesiology, FADSA 1976. **CAREER:** Dept of Anesthesiology, Maimonides Medical Ctr, fellow 1975-77; Dental Service, Maimonides Medical Ctr, attending staff 1980-86; private practice, dentist 1977-. **ORGANIZATIONS:** Amer Dental Assn; First District Dental Soc; Manhattan Dental Guild. **BUSINESS ADDRESS:** Dentist, 135 W 70th St, New York, NY 10023.

MCCLOUD, THOMAS HENRY
Business executive. **PERSONAL:** Born Jul 29, 1948, Jersey City, NJ; married Georgia. **EDUCATION:** Rutgers Univ, BA 1974, MPA 1977; Georgetown Univ Law Ctr, working on JD current. **CAREER:** Rutgers Univ, counselor, special programs 1974-76; City of Newark, deputy dir PSE 1977, acting dir 1977-78; Natl League of Cities Wash DC, dir, Employment & Training proj 1978-81, dir, Urban Noise Programs 1981-82; Wash Convention Ctr, dir, Human Resources & Bus Services 1982-86, asst general manager 1986-87; Natl League of Cities, dir membership service 1987-. **ORGANIZATIONS:** Chrmn EOF Comm Advisory Bd 1972; treas RutgersUniv Alumni Assoc, NCAS 1976; pres MPA Alumni Assoc 1976-77; trustee Leaguers Inc 1977-78; mem Amer Society for Pub Admin 1978-present. **HONORS/ACHIEVEMENTS:** Strauss Human Relations Schlrp 1972, Robert A Wynn Mem Awd 1974 Rutgers U; Pub Service Educ Fellow Dept of HEW Wash DC 1974; Outstanding Young Men of Amer Natl Jaycees 1978, 81 & 84; Manager of the Yr Wash Convention Ctr 1984. **MILITARY SERVICE:** USMC sergeant 1966-70. **HOME ADDRESS:** 4145 Alabama Ave SE, Washington, DC 20019. **BUSINESS ADDRESS:** Dir Membership Services, Natl League of Cities, 1301 Pennsylvania Ave, NW, Washington, DC 20001.

MCCLUNG, WILLIE DAVID
Clergyman. **PERSONAL:** Born Apr 03, 1939, Aliceville, AL; married Mary Jean Shamery; children: David, Rosemary, Bonita LaDawn, Rashawn. **EDUCATION:** Wayne Co Comm Coll, AA 1970; Wayne St U, BS 1971;Univ Detroit, MA 1972; Wayne St U, PhD 1975. **CAREER:** Detroit Council Bapt Pastors, sec 1966-67; Comm Human Rel Highland Park, 1969-73; New Grace &Univ Detroit, minister. **BUSINESS ADDRESS:** 25 Ford, Highland Park, MI 48203.

MCCLURE, EARIE
Educator. **PERSONAL:** Born in Atlanta. **EDUCATION:** Clark Coll, AB, Atlanta U; Wayne State U; Lund U;Univ London; Union of Soviet Socialist Republics Educ Seminar, post grad. **CAREER:** Atlanta Pub Schs & Special Edn, educator; Clark Coll Alumni Assn Atlanta Chpt, vp; Atlanta Pub Schs Silverbow & Clark Coll Alumni Atlanta, resourcespecialist for exceptional children. **ORGANIZATIONS:** Life mem NAACP; Nat Educ Assn; mem GA Assn of Retarded Children; Assn of Educators; chmn Pub Rel Assn of Classroom Tchrs; exec sec Nat Black Women's Polit Leadership Caucus Atlanta Chpt; chmn Program Com Atlanta Assn of Educators; comm organizer Citizens Rights; membership recruiter YWCA; precinct chmn Fulton Co Dem Party; mem GA Dem Party & Nat Dem Party; founder & assoc mem Museum of Confederacy; Am Forestry Assn; Museum of Nat Hist NY. **HONORS/ACHIEVEMENTS:** Plaque for outstanding serv in special educ parents; various awards from Clark Coll Alumni. **BUSINESS ADDRESS:** PO Box 92336, Atlanta, GA 30314.

MCCLURE, WESLEY C.
Educational administrator. **CAREER:** Virginia State University, Petersburg, VA, president. **BUSINESS ADDRESS:** Virginia State University, Petersburg, VA 23603. *

MCCLURKIN, JOHNSON THOMAS
Business executive. **PERSONAL:** Born Sep 25, 1929, Chester, SC; married Evelyn Rudd; children: Gary. **EDUCATION:** Morgan State U, BS 1958. **CAREER:** Nat Assn of Real Estate Brokers Inc, exec dir; Nat Corp for Housing, asst dir; Washington, DC, partner 1972-73; The Rouse Co, asst to dir of property mgmt 1970-72. **ORGANIZATIONS:** Bd dir Nat Assn Real Estate Brokers Inc; life mem NAACP; mem Ldrsp Conf on Civil Rights; Nat Bus League; mem St John Bapt Ch Columbia InterfaithCtr; Columbia Assn; Am Soc of Assn of Execs. **HONORS/ACHIEVEMENTS:** Pres's Award 1974, 77; lang & speech merit Award Morgan State Coll. **MILITARY SERVICE:** AUS 1951-53. **BUSINESS ADDRESS:** 1025 Vermont Ave NW, Washington, DC 20005.

MCCLUSKEY, JOHN A., JR.
Educator. **PERSONAL:** Born Oct 25, 1944, Middletown, OH; son of John A McCluskey and Helen Harris McCluskey; married Audrey T. **EDUCATION:** Harvard Univ, BA 1966; Stanford Univ, MA 1972. **CAREER:** Miles Coll Birmingham AL, teacher English; Valparaiso Univ IN, teacher humanities; Case Western Reserve Univ, assoc prof Afro-Amer Studies 1969-77; IN Univ, assoc prof Afro-Amer Studies 1977-83; adjunct prof English 1982-; prof Afro-Amer Studies 1983-; assoc dean Graduate School 1984-88; dir CIC Minorities Fellowships Program 1983-88. **HONORS/ACHIEVEMENTS:** Author "Look What They Done to My Song" 1974, "Mr America's Last Season Blues" 1983, "Blacks in History" 1975, "Stories from Black History, Nine Stories" 1975, "City of Refuge, Collected Stories of Rudolph Fisher" 1987; Best Amer Short Stories 1976; Yaddo Fellowship Yaddo Corporation 1984, 1986. **BUSINESS ADDRESS:** Professor, Indiana University, Dept of Afro-American Studies, Memorial Hall East M37, Bloomington, IN 47405.

MCCOLLOUGH, WALTER
Minister. **PERSONAL:** Born May 22, 1915, Great Falls, SC; son of Robert Bell and Janie Bell; married Clara Bell Price; children: Walter, Charles L, James E, Regina. **CAREER:** United House of Prayer Anacostia Mission, pastor 1941-56; United House of Prayer Natl Headquarters Washington DC, pastor and DC and MD state chmn 1956-60, bishop 1960-. **ORGANIZATIONS:** Grand inspector general 33 Degree United Supreme Council Southern Jurisdiction 1961-; exec dir McCollough Scholarship Coll Fund 1971-. **HONORS/ACHIEVEMENTS:** Presidential Citations Gerald Ford, Jimmy Carter 1976, 1980; Distinguished Comm Serv Awd Natl Urban Coalition 1985; Gold Medal Achievement Awd United Supreme Council 33 Degree AASR SJ 1986. **HOME ADDRESS:** 1665 North Portal Dr NW, Washington, DC 20012. **BUSINESS ADDRESS:** Bishop, United House of Prayer, 601 M St NW, Washington, DC 20001.

MCCOLLUM, ALICE ODESSA
Judge. **PERSONAL:** Born Feb 15, 1947, Oklahoma City, OK. **EDUCATION:** Univ of NC Greensboro, BA 1969; Univ of Cincinnati School of Law, JD 1972. **CAREER:** Reginald Heber Smith Community Lawyer fellow, 1972-74; Legal Aid Serv of Dayton, co-dir 1974-75; Wilberforce Univ, dir pre-law 1975-76; Univ of Dayton School of Law, asst prof, asst dir clinical legal 1976-79; Dayton Municipal Court, judge 1979-. **ORGANIZATIONS:** Bd member, United Theological Seminary, 1980-, United Way, 1980-, Dayton Contemporary Dance Co 1980-; member, OH Municipal Judges Assn, Amer Judges Assn, Natl Bar Assn, OH State Bar Assn, Amer Bar Assn, Dayton Bar Assn, Thurgood Marshall Law Soc; member, ethics comm, Dayton Bar Assoc 1978-. **HONORS/ACHIEVEMENTS:** Superior Judicial Serv Supreme Court of OH 1979-86; Outstanding Black Woman of 1979 Sinclair Community Coll Student Govt; Woman of the Year Iota Beta Lambda Sorority 1980; YWCA Salute to Career Women Special Achievement Award 1983; Woman of the Year, Unique Study Club 1985. **BUSINESS ADDRESS:** Judge, Dayton Municipal Court, 301 W Third St, Dayton, OH 45402.

MCCOLLUM, ANITA LAVERNE
Business executive. **PERSONAL:** Born Aug 20, 1960, Cleveland, OH. **EDUCATION:** Kentucky State University, BS 1983; Atlanta University, MBA 1985. **CAREER:** IBM, admin asst 1981; NASA Lewis Rsch Ctr, procurement coordin Summers 1981,82,83; IBM, sales asst 1984; Atlanta Exchange, asst to the exec vice pres 1984-;AT&T Communications, spvsr in Residence Marketing. **ORGANIZATIONS:** Undergraduate member of Natl Bd of Directors Alpha Kappa Alpha 1982-84; member Toastmaster's Intl 1983-85; student member Natl Black MBA Assn 1985; memberNAACP. **HONORS/ACHIEVEMENTS:** Outstanding Young Women of America 1982; Who's Who Among Students in Amer Colleges & Univ 1982; Soror of the Year Alpha Kappa Alpha 1982; Natl Dean's List KY State Univ 1981-83; Executive Management Scholarship AUGSBA 1983. **HOME ADDRESS:** 16512 Invermere Ave, Cleveland, OH 44128.

MCCOLLUM, CHARLES EDWARD
Educator. **PERSONAL:** Born Jan 24, 1942, Burlington, NC; married Joan C Torian; children: Marshane, Anthony, Charles Jr. **EDUCATION:** Durham Bus Coll, Diploma 1962; Shaw Univ, BA 1973; Shaw Divinity School, attended; VA Commonwealth Univ, attended; VA State Univ, attended. **ORGANIZATIONS:** Mem Natl Baptist Convention, Gen Baptist State Conv, Neuse River Assoc, Reedy Creek Assoc, Halifax & Adjacent Cty Ministrial Allience, Halifax Cty Bd of Ed, Participatory Council for Halifax Cty Tech Inst, Halifax Cty Branch of NAACP, Hampton Inst Ministers Conf, Rehab Ed Assoc; mem, chmn of caucus Halifax Cty Black Caucus; former dir Reedy Creek's Training Inst; pastor Pleasant Grove Baptist Church 1974-77, Oak Grove Baptist Church 1975-, Piney GroveBaptist Church 1977-, Hickory View Baptist Church 1981-. **HONORS/ACHIEVEMENTS:** Licensed to the Gospel Ministry 1973; Ordained to the Gospel Ministry 1973; VA Teachers Cert 1975. **BUSINESS ADDRESS:** Adult Basic Education Teacher, Auth of Richmond Rehab Schl, Deerfield Correctional Ctr, Capron, VA 23829.

MCCONNELL, DOROTHY HUGHES
Educator. **PERSONAL:** Born Apr 19, Cleveland, OH; daughter of Harry H Hughes and Genevieve Harris Hughes (deceased); divorced; children: Jan Yvette Evans. **EDUCATION:** Ohio State Univ, BS 1946; Western Reserve Univ, MA 1956; Loyola Univ, Admin Credential 1975. **CAREER:** Los Angeles Unified School Dist, training teacher 1960-79, school improvement coord 1979-80, integration coord 1980-81, lang arts spec 1982-. **ORGANIZATIONS:** State Comm of Credential State of CA Sacramento CA 1978-83; wrkshp org & ldr Parent Educ Workshops 1982-; mem Delta Sigma Theta Sor Century City Alumnus Chptr 1981-; treas Natl Assc of Media Women LA 1983-; mem NAACP Auxillary LA Branch 1984-; mem Natl Assoc Univ Women 1986. **HONORS/ACHIEVEMENTS:** Recg spec cert Outstanding Tchr Human Rel City of Los Angeles Human Rel Comm 1979; selected by USC & Dept Educ WashDC as Rsrch Participant in Egypt 1980; elected by LAUSD Tchrs as Mentor Tchr Evaluator in Mentor Tchrs Prog 1984-. **HOME ADDRESS:** 5547 Secrest Dr, Los Angeles, CA 90043.

MCCONNELL, ROLAND C.
Retired educator. **PERSONAL:** Born Mar 27, 1910, Amherst, Nova Scotia, Canada;son of Rev Thomas Benjamin McConnell and Helen Halfkenny McConnell; married Catherine Allen Taylor. **EDUCATION:** Howard Univ, AB 1931, MA 1933; NY Univ, PhD 1945. **CAREER:** Elizabeth City State Teachers College, Elizabeth City NC, hist dept instructor 1938-42; Natl Archives, Washington DC, archivist 1943-47; Morgan State Univ, prof 1948-78, hist dept chmn 1967-75, prof emeritus in history 1981-. **ORGANIZATIONS:** Chmn, Maryland Commn Afro-Amer History & Culture 1974-84; mem, Maryland Commn Afro-Amer History & Culture; Pub Comm Maryland Historical Soc 1981-; consultant, Maryland Branch Natl Hist Pub Exec Council for Study of Afro-Amer Life & Hist 1960-; Opera; Symphony; elder, Trinity Presbyterian Church. **HONORS/ACHIEVEMENTS:** Outstanding Serv Plaque, Phi Beta Sigma Frat, 1978; Maryland Commn Afro-Amer Hist & Culture; Patriotic Civilian Serv Dept of US Army, Morgan State Univ; Meritorious Plaque, State of Maryland & Morgan State Univ. **MILITARY SERVICE:** AUS quartermaster general pvt, ROTC 2nd lt Howard Univ 1931-37. **HOME ADDRESS:** 2406 College Ave, Baltimore, MD 21214.

MCCONNER, DOROTHY
Business executive. **PERSONAL:** Born May 15, 1929, Birmingham, AL; married Stanley J; children: Stanley Jr. **EDUCATION:** Hampton Inst; Cortez Peters Business Coll; Chic State Univ; Northwestern Univ. **CAREER:** Johnson Prod Co, exec vice pres 1983-, vice pres 1972-83, corp sec 1962-72; Johnson Prod Co, sec 1960-62; Fuller Prod Co, sec 1950-60. **ORGANIZATIONS:** Mem Am Soc of Cor Sec; bd of dir Chic Urban Leag; bd of dir Chic Econ Dev Corp; advis councChic State U; mem Operation PUSH; mem Nat Hook-up of Black Women; bd of dir Rehabiltn Inst of Chic; mem Black Women's Agenda; mem Chicago Comm Trust Asso; mem The Chicago Network; mem Chicago StateUniv Women's Club; bd of dirs Johnson Products Co Inc; mem Lakeside Comm Com; mem League of Black Women Inc; mem NWUniv Asso; mem The Ancillary Group Chicago StateUniv Found; mem Toastmasters Internat; mem Zonta Internat; chairwoman Chicago Urban League's Annual Golden Fellowship Dinners 1974-75. **HONORS/ACHIEVEMENTS:** Beautiful people award Chic Urban Leag; bus woman of yr Cosmpltn C of C; urban leagr of the yr Chic Urban Leag; salute to Women in Business Operation PUSH 1975f business woman of the yr Blackbook 1975; second runner-up woman of the yr Iota Phi Lambda Sor Inc 1977; great guys doing great things award Southtown YMCA 1979f Parkway Comm House Black Businesswomen 1979. **BUSINESS ADDRESS:** Executive Vice President, Johnson Products Co, Inc, 8522 S Lafayette Ave, Chicago, IL 60620.

MCCOO, MARILYN
Singer. **PERSONAL:** Born in Jersey City, NJ; married Billy Davis. **EDUCATION:** Univ of CA, BS. **CAREER:** The Hi-Fi's, singer; The Fifth Dimension formerly the Versatiles, orgl mem 1965-75; Art Linkletters Talent Scouts, singer; formed duo with husband; Solid Gold, co-host. **HONORS/ACHIEVEMENTS:** Jiss Bronze CA; Grammy Awd with Billy Davis for "You Don't Have to be a Star" 1977; 4 Grammy Awds for Up, Up & Awd; 2 Grammy Awds for Aquarius w/The 5th Dimensions; Grammy Awd "You Don't Have To Be A Star" duo w/husband; Awarded the Prestigious Grand Prize at Tokyo Music Fest.

MCCORMICK, LARRY WILLIAM
Journalist. **PERSONAL:** Born Feb 03, 1933, Kansas City, MO; married Anita Daniels; children: Alvin Bowens, Mitchell, Kitrina. **EDUCATION:** Lincoln Jr Coll Kansas City, MO, AA 1951;Univ of Kansas City UMKC; CA State Los Angeles, BA & MA (in progress). **CAREER:** KGFJ Radio Los Angeles, music prog host 1958-63; KFWB Radio Los Angeles, music prog host-columnist 1964-67; KGFJ Radio Los Angeles, music prog host, prog dir 1967-71; KABC Channel 7 Los Angeles, weathercaster 1971; KTLA Channel 5 Los Angeles,TV newscaster 1971-. **ORGANIZATIONS:** Mem Los Angeles NAACP 1960-; vp, bd of dirs Los Angeles Urban League; bd of dir Ebony Showcase Theatre 1978-; bd of dirs Challengers Boys Club; 100 Black Men of Los Angeles; Cal-State LA Support Group; Black Journalists Assoc of So CA; USC Ebonics Long-Range Dev Comm. **HONORS/ACHIEVEMENTS:** Outstanding Comm Serv Citation LA City LA Co Mayor Tom Bradley CA Senate CA Assembly 1976; Communicator of the Year Awd Nat Assn of Market Developers 1976; Nat Communication Award Nat Assn of Media Women 1977; LA Unified Sch Dist; So Christian Leadership Conf West; Women at Work; Los Angeles Lullaby Guild; Sons of Watts; Black Probation Officer's Assoc; Alpha Phi Alpha Frat; So CA Podiatry Assoc. **BUSINESS ADDRESS:** KTLA Channel 5, 5800 Sunset Blvd, Los Angeles, CA 90028.

MCCORMICK, MARGARET W.
Educator. **PERSONAL:** Born Aug 18, 1923, Baconton, GA; married James Mccormick; children: James Jr, Arvis, Kimberly. **EDUCATION:** BS MEd 1950; Columbia U, Post Grad Study 1954-56;Univ of GA, 1960, 63, 67, 70-71; W GA Coll, 1968; GA U, 1971-72. **CAREER:** Jackson Primary Sch, prin; Butts Co Bd Ed, 1969-75; Rome HS GA, instr coach 1954-58; Lang Arts Dept Henderson HS, instr chmn 1958-69. **ORGANIZATIONS:** Mem Bus & Prof Women's Clb 1964; trustee Hosp Authority Jackson, GA 1971; trustee United Appeal 1972; pres Jackson Theater Guild 1974-75; vice chmn Prof Practice Commn GA; NEA; BAE; NAESP; TEPS; PTD; coord Sun Sch Zion Bapt Ch; Choir Dir; asst sec Deaconess Bd; Youth Dir; music dir SS&BTU Cong; Tchr Ldrshp Tr Course; Adv Cncl; Day Care Ctr; Missionary Soc. **HONORS/ACHIEVEMENTS:** Tchr of yr 1961; prof achvmnt awrd 1973; working gal of the wk 1974; outstg prin of Fed Pilot Proj 1974-75; listed personalities of the south 1973. **BUSINESS ADDRESS:** 218 Woodland Way, Box 3908, Jackson, GA.

MCCOVEY, WILLIE LEE
Athlete. **PERSONAL:** Born Jan 10, 1938, Mobile, AL. **CAREER:** Sandersville, baseball player 1955; Danville, baseball player 1956; Dallas, baseball player 1957; Phoenix, baseball player 1958-59; San Francisco, baseball player 1959-73; San Diego/Oakland, baseball player 1973-76; San Francisco Giants, baseball player 1977-. **ORGANIZATIONS:** Chmn Willie McCovey March of Dimes Annual Charity Golf Tourn. **HONORS/ACHIEVEMENTS:** Natl League Rookie of the Yr 1959; led NL in home runs (36) & RBI 105 1968; NL in HR (45) & RBI (126) 1969; NL All Star Game 1963, 1966, 1968-71; leading left-handed home run hitter ever in NL; ranks 9th on baseball's all-time list of HR & 1st among active players; 18 grand slams 1st in NL & 2nd in history of major leagues; only player in baseball hist to hit 2 HR in same inning twice in career; NL Comeback Player of the Yr; Sporting News/UPI; NL MVP 1969; Hutch Award 1977; Willie McCovey Day Candlesticke Park 1977; inducted into Natl Baseball Hall of Fame 1986. **BUSINESS ADDRESS:** c/o Natl Baseball Hall of Fame, PO Box 590, Cooperstown, NY 13326.

MCCOY, CAROL TODMAN
Business executive. **PERSONAL:** Born Mar 25, 1947, New York, NY; married Shayim Ishmeal Todman; children: John McCoy, III, Leon McCoy, Shayim Todman, II, Alicia Todman. **EDUCATION:** Bronx Comm Fashion Institute of Technology. **CAREER:** Natl Recording/Video Center, post-production 1971-76; EUE/Columbia Pictures, post-production 1976-

80; VideoWorks, Inc, vice president operations. **ORGANIZATIONS:** Board of directors Videotape Producers Assn 1982-83; co-chairman Monitor Awards 1983; member Videotape Producers Assn 1984-85; SMPTE, mem, NY Bd of Dir 1987. **HOME ADDRESS:** 150 Archer St, Freeport, NY 11520. **BUSINESS ADDRESS:** Vice President Operations, VideoWorks, Inc, 24 West 40th St, New York, NY 10018.

MCCOY, FRANK MILTON
Pianist, educator, lecturer. **PERSONAL:** Born Sep 17, El Centro, CA. **EDUCATION:** Mus & Higher Edn, BA, MA, PhD 1980. **CAREER:** LA City Schs, edctr lectr; Europe, Mexico CAN 44 Other Countries (First Am To Present Concert on French & Protectorate Islands of St Pierre et Miquelon Ofcly Received by Gov Gen Clarence Campbell of Jamaica), concert piano tours. **ORGANIZATIONS:** Music drama critic El Centro CA 5 Yrs; concert piano tours in Europe Mexico CAN; 44 other countries; mem Nat Guild of Piano Tchrs; Intrnl Platform Assc; CA Music Tchrs Assc; Nat Negro Musicians Assc. **HONORS/ACHIEVEMENTS:** Black prof assc author Black Tomorrow - A Portrait of Afro-Am Culture, "We Too Are Americans" To Be Released 1981; contributor articles for professional journals;recip Leona M Hickman Awrd,Univ of WA Rotary Clb Schlrshp, San Fran State U; featured in Ebony Mag 1960; featured in Sepia Mag 1960 & 1965; 1st black adjudicator Nat Piano Playing Auditions Sponsers by Nat Guild of Piano Tchrs San Jose Co & San Bernadino CA; appeared on Canadian Broadcasting in TV Debut from Halifax Nova Scotia; recip awrd Natl Negro Clg Women; recip & awrd Our Author's Study Clb LA; fndr admnstr awrd Honoring His Mother Annie Lee McCoy Chopin Piano Meml; pub articles "A Corner of France at Your Doorstep" ; Travel & Arts Mag 1980.

MCCOY, FREDERICK DOUGLASS, JR.
Teacher, journalist, TV producer, director. **PERSONAL:** Born Aug 06, 1936, Jacksonville, FL; divorced; children: Michelle, Frederick III. **EDUCATION:** FL A&M U, Attended 1958-61; Bethune Cookman Clg, BS Prodcr Dir & Host 1966; Miami-Dade Community Coll, attended 1976; Nova Univ, Spec Educ 1987. **CAREER:** Dade Co Sch, tchr; Quardrophonic Soul & Productions & Host-Moderator of Nitelife TV Show, exec prdcr; Miami Times, reporter columist; N Dade Comm Sch, coord; various other tchng positions; Dade Co Sch Miami FL, tchr; "Moring Web" TV Show WKID TV Miami Ft Lauderdale, host producer & dir; "Our Magazine", columnist; Safety Patrols Rainbow Park Elem Sch Opa-locka FL, coord; Trojans Drill Team of Opa-locka FL, dir. **ORGANIZATIONS:** Mem FL Jaycees; BSA; Dade County Tchr Assc; Opa-locka North Dade Coalition; Dade Co News Media; News Media; Natl Comm Sch Ed Assc; NAACP & SCLC; Miami-Dade Black C of C; mem Natl Business League Inc, Amer Fed of Teachers, FL Educ Assoc. **HONORS/ACHIEVEMENTS:** Outs serv awrds for Comm Serv Daytona Beach & Orlando; cert of appreciation FL A&M Alumni Assc; outst serv awrd as Comm Sch Dir Opa-Locka & N Dade. **MILITARY SERVICE:** USAF airman first class 1954-58.

MCCOY, GEORGE H.
Administrator. **PERSONAL:** Born Dec 10, 1930, Philadelphia, PA; son of James Ross McCoy and Clara J Palmer; married Louise; children: Eva. **EDUCATION:** City Coll of NY, BA Biology 1970; Bernard Baruch NY, MBA Bus Health 1973. **CAREER:** Albert Einstein Hosp Bronx NY, asst admin 1973-75, sr asst admin 1975-77; Kings County Hosp Brooklyn NY, deputy dir 1977-78; West Co Med Ctr Valhalla NY, first deputy comm 1978-86; Erie County Medical Ctr Buffalo NY, chief exec officer 1986-. **ORGANIZATIONS:** Mem Amer Coll Hosp Admin 1972-; Amer Hosp Assn 1970-; adj Prof Marymount Coll Terrytown 1979-; mem bd dir West-Putnam March of Dimes 1984-; chmn bd dir Congregations Concerned with City Mt Vernon 1983-86; Greater Buffalo Chamber of Commerce, Buffalo Urban League; executive bd, United Way; Autistic Bd of Buffalo; Buffalo Eye Bank; executive comm, Natl Assn of Public Hospitals. **HONORS/ACHIEVEMENTS:** Comm srv Key Women of Amer Upper Westchester 1984; Professional of the Year, Buffalo Club, Natl Assn of Negro Business & Professional Women, 1988. **MILITARY SERVICE:** AUS capt 1951-59. **HOME ADDRESS:** 182 McNair Rd, Amherst, NY 14221. **BUSINESS ADDRESS:** Chief Executive Officer, Erie County Medical Ctr, 462 Grider St, Buffalo, NY 14215.

MCCOY, GLADYS
Government official. **PERSONAL:** Born Feb 28, 1928, Atlanta, GA; married William McCoy; children: Krista, William, Paul, Mary, Cecilia, Peter, Martha. **EDUCATION:** Talladega Coll, BA Sociology, 1949; Portland State Univ School of Social Work, MSW 1965-67; School of Work, Field Supvr, 1969-70. **CAREER:** Project Head Start Vancouver WA, dir of social serv 1967-70; Clark Coll, Pacific Univ, Portland Comm Coll, Intl Coll of Cayman Isle British WI, prof sociology & social work 1970-74; State of OR, ombudsman 1975-78; Multnomah County OR, commissioner 1979-84, chair/exec 1987-. **ORGANIZATIONS:** Planning/coordination specialist NW Regional Educ Lab 1978-79; supvr, field work students, Portland State Univ School of Social Work; bd mem Providence Medical Center Comm Bd Multnomah Co Ext Serv, KPBS Public Broadcasting, Sentinel Editorial Bd; trustee Amer Mothers Inc, Endowment Fund, Pres Assn of Oregon Counties. **HONORS/ACHIEVEMENTS:** Woman of Achievement Portland 1974; OR Mother of the Year 1980; Woman of Today Albina Womens League 1982, Abigal Scott Duniway Award, Women in Commun, 1984; OR Assembly of Black Affairs Political Devel Award, 1987; Community Serv Award, Natl Assn of Blacks in Criminal Justice Serv 1987. **BUSINESS ADDRESS:** Chair/Executive, Multnomah County, 1021 SW Fourth Ave #134, Portland, OR 97204.

MCCOY, JAMES F.
Retired librarian. **PERSONAL:** Born Aug 01, 1925, Clarkton, NC; son of Frank McCoy and Gertrude Smith McCoy. **EDUCATION:** Lincoln Univ, AB 1952; Rutgers Univ, MLS 1956; Univ of Denver, advanced cert 1973; Appalachian State Univ HEW Inst, attended. **CAREER:** NJ St Library, ref librarian 1956; Elizabeth Public Library, ref librarian 1956; Mercer Co Comm Coll, chmn library dept 1956-74; Hudson Valley Comm Coll, dir learn resources 1974-84 (retired). **ORGANIZATIONS:** Nom com ALA-ACRL 1971-72; Ad Hoc Comm on Interns 1972-77; AV Com 1975; edtrl bd CHOICE 1974; chmn schlrshp com 1966-67, vice pres 1969-70, pres coll & univ sect 1964-65; pres AAUP Mercer Co Coll; NJLA Exec Bd 1968-70; sec NJ Exec Bd 1970-72; pres Alumni Assn GSLS Rutgers 1958, 1975; NJ Jr Coll Assn 1960, 1965; adv comm Grad Sch Library Serv Rutgers 1958-59, 1975-76; Mayor's Adv Comm Trenton Model Cities 1968-73; adv comm Trenton Urban Renewal 1966-68; pres Trenton Nghbrhd Hlth Ctr 1971-72; Trenton Historical Soc 1965-74; chmn Adv Assoc GLIS Rutgers Univ 1979; pres Alumni Assn SLIM UnivDenver 1979; chmn Intellectual Freedom & Due Process NYLA 1979; sec Council of Head Librarians SUNY 1977; contrib Biblio of Negro in NJ 1967; Basic Books for Jr Coll Libraries 1963; Kappa Alphs Psi Frat; ALA; NJLA; NYLA; AAUP; NAACP; chair SUNY Cncl Head Librarians 1984; chair membership comm Amer Library Assn 1985; chair Comm & Jr Coll Lib Sect 1986. **HONORS/ACHIEVEMENTS:** Disting Serv NJLA Coll & Univ Sect Awd; Disting Alumni Awd Lincoln Univ; Cert of Achievement Trenton Model Cities; Founders Awd Black & Hispanic Faculty and Admins Assn 1984; Sire Archon Beta Psi Boule Sigma Pi Phi Frat 1984; 50th Anniversary Awd of Appreciation 1985; Appreciation Awd Beta Psi Boule, Sigma Beta Psi Fraternity 1986; Outstanding Contribution, Comm Org 1986. **MILITARY SERVICE:** AUS sgt 4th grade; 1944-46.

MCCOY, JESSIE HAYNES
Educational administrator. **PERSONAL:** Born Nov 17, 1955, Mound Bayou, MS; divorced; children: Raven, Tameka. **EDUCATION:** Coahoma Jr Coll, AA English 1975; Univ of S MS, BA Journalism 1976; MS State Univ, further study 1984; Bloomsburg Univ, further study 1985. **CAREER:** Hattiesburg Amer Newspaper, part-time reporter 1976; Delta Democrat-Times Newspaper, news reporter 1976-79; MS Valley State Univ, dir univ relations 1979-84; freelancer various print media; Bloomsburg Univ, univ relations dir 1984-86; J & R Enterprises, co-owner 1987-; Bloomsburg Univ, asst to city mgr, public info officer 1986-. **ORGANIZATIONS:** PTA pres Fulwiler & LS Roger Elem Schs 1978-1982; dist chairwoman MS Press Women 1981-83; pres College Public Relations Assn of MS 1982-83; public relations officer Amer Assn of Univ Women 1983; mem mgmt intern comm Bloomsburg Univ 1984-85; mem Columbia-Montour Tourist Promotion Agency 1984-85, Black Council on Higher Educ 1984-85; telecommun council, pres council Bloomsburg Univ; mayors task force War on Drugs; mayors bicentennial of the constitution comm, Jubilee Comm, C of C PR Comm, city hall grand opening comm, road bond referendum comm, mayors youth day comm; curricullum adv bd comm Tidewater Comm Coll; mem NAACP Chesapeake VA, Natl Forum for Black Public Admin, Intl City Mgrs Assoc, Public Relations Soc of Amer, Amer soc of Publ Admin, Amer Mktg Assoc, VA Municipal League, Conf of Minority Public Admin, PTA. **HONORS/ACHIEVEMENTS:** Journalism Scholarship Univ of S MS 1976; Ford Fellow in Journalism Ford Found Washington 1979; CASE Fellow Council for Advancement & Support of Educ 1981;Exec Council MS Valley State Univ 1982-84; Outstanding Young Woman of America 1983; only Black non-academic mgr Bloomsburg Univ 1984-86; Regional Finalist President's Commission on White House Fellows. **BUSINESS ADDRESS:** Assistant to City Manager, Bloomsburg Univeristy, City Hall, PO Box 15225, Chesapeake, VA 23320.

MCCOY, JOSEPH CLIFTON
Dentist, government administrator. **PERSONAL:** Born Jan 21, 1930, Chicago, IL; children: Joseph, Michael, Russell, Carla. **EDUCATION:** Morehouse Coll, BA 1956; Los Angeles Coll, 1957-58. **CAREER:** Allstate Ins Co, casualty claims suprv 1966-77; Intl House of Pancakes, owner 1970-73; Dunkin Donuts, owner 1973-79; MCCO Inc, owner 1980-81; Fulton County Voter Reg, chief registrar 1981-. **ORGANIZATIONS:** Pres Morehoue Torchbearers 1974-79; bd mem Atlanta Urban League 1976-82; pres GA Econ Council 1977-83; consult to African Nations for Votore Reg & Electoral Process 1984-85. **HONORS/ACHIEVEMENTS:** All Conf Quarter Back 19854-55; 1st balck to hold position of 2nd unit suprv in region Allstate Ins Co 1966-77; 1st known black to own & operate a businessin Royal Oak MI Intl House of Pancakes 1970-73; 1st known black to hold the position of chief registrar in the history of the 159 counties in GA 1981; AltantaUniv Sports Hall of Fame 1983; Outstanding Achievement in Voter Registration 1984. **MILITARY SERVICE:** AUS July 1951-July 1953 Hon Discharge. **BUSINESS ADDRESS:** Chief Registrar, Fulton County Government, 165 Central Ave #106, Atlanta, GA 30303.

MCCOY, LARRY ORLANDA
Business executive. **PERSONAL:** Born Sep 28, 1952, Beulah, MS. **EDUCATION:** Coahoma Jr College, AA Political Sci 1972-74; Alcorn State Univ, BA Political Sci 1974-76. **CAREER:** Sunflower Furniture Co, manager 1977-79; City Finance Co, manager/asst 1979-80; Capitol Furniture Co, manager 1980-81; Creditor Claims, manager 1981-83; McCoy & Associates, president 1983-. **ORGANIZATIONS:** Member Mississippi Offenders Effort 1979-85; member St Frances Credit Union 1983-85; vice president Small Businessmen's Association 1984-85.

MCCOY, LEAMON M.
Chief executive. **CAREER:** True Transport, Inc, Newark, NJ, chief executive, 1969-. **BUSINESS ADDRESS:** True Transport, Inc, 231 Johnson Rd, Newark, NJ 07108. *

MCCOY, MIKE C. (TAZ)
Professional athlete. **PERSONAL:** Born Aug 16, 1953, W Memphis, AR; married Margaret. **EDUCATION:** Univ of CO, Attended; W Los Angeles Jr Clg, Attended. **CAREER:** Green Bay Packers, professional football def back 1976-. **HONORS/ACHIEVEMENTS:** Co-player of the Yr 1976. **BUSINESS ADDRESS:** Green Bay Packer, 1265 Lombardi Ave, Green Bay, WI 54303.

MCCOY, WALTER D.
Public administrator. **PERSONAL:** Born Mar 17, 1930, Damascus, GA; married Toni Moynihan (divorced); children: Jonathan D, Wanda D Noble. **EDUCATION:** FL A&M Univ, BS 1951; Univ of TX El Paso, MS 1971; NM State Univ, ABD 1974; Univ of TX Arlington, PhD Admin 1980. **CAREER:** AUS, col 1950-70; Univ of TX El Paso, vice pres student affairs 1970-74; Univ of TX Arlington, dir of student serv 1974-76; Corpus Christi State Univ, assoc prof of mgmt 1975-85, dir public admin. **ORGANIZATIONS:** Mem Acad of Mgmt 1981-; chmn allocation comm United Way of Corpus Christi 181-83; pres bd Women's Shelter of Corpus Christi 1984-; mem Federal Mediator and Mediation Services 1989-. **HONORS/ACHIEVEMENTS:** Leadership Award United Way Coastal Bend 1970-80; Hon Soc Phi Kappa Phi 1974; Hon Soc Order of Omega 1974. **MILITARY SERVICE:** AUS col 20 1/2 yrs; Meritorious Serv Medal, Bronze Star w/Devices, Commendation Medal w/4 OLC; Pres Unit Citation, Republic of Korea. **BUSINESS ADDRESS:** Dir Public Administration, Corpus Christi StateUniv, Coll of Bus Admin, 6300 Ocean Dr, Corpus Christi, TX 78412.

MCCOY, WAYNE ANTHONY
Attorney. **PERSONAL:** Born Nov 05, 1941, Louisville, KY; married Sharron Lynne Gulliford; children: Jay Brandon Todd, Kamilah Nneka. **EDUCATION:** Univ of MI Law Schl, JD 1972; IN Univ, BS Bus Admin 1965. **CAREER:** General Dynamics Corp, graphic reprod 1962-63; RCA, distr & traffic 1963-65; Dow Chem Co, mrkt & sales mgr 1965-69; Schiff, Hardin & Waite, partner 1972-. **ORGANIZATIONS:** Dir Evanston Hosp Corp 1980-; visi-

tors comm Univ of MI Law Schl 1977-1979; mem Evanston IL Econ Dev Comm 1985-; general cnsl Jesse Owens Fnd 1983-; comm Evanston Human Rel Comm 1978-80; mem Evanston Comm on Schl Finance 1977-78; Evanston City Council Task Force on Police Serv 1973-1976; consult atty Evanston Fair Housing Review Bd 1972-73; trustee Evanston Environmental Assc 1977-79; mem Amer, Natl, IL, Cook Cty Chicago Lawyers Bar Assc; mem Kappa Alpha Psi 1960-; Oper PUSH; NAACP; Natl Assc Sec Prof. **HONORS/ACHIEVEMENTS:** Co-author "Advising Publicly-Held Corporation" Cont Legal Ed 1973, 1979, IL State Barn Assc Newsletter on Corp & Sec Law 1973, 1974. **BUSINESS ADDRESS:** Attorney, Schiff, Hardin & Waite, 7200 Sears Tower, Chicago, IL 60606.

MCCOY, WILLIAM
Government official. **PERSONAL:** Married Gladys; children: Krista, William, Paul, Mary, Cecila, Peter, Martha. **EDUCATION:** Univ Portland, BA Bus Admin & Political Sci; Univ of OR, grad studies in public admin; Univ of So CA, grad studies in gerontology. **CAREER:** State Representative 1972-74; State Senator 1975-. **ORGANIZATIONS:** Dir Foster Grandparent Pgm; state rep chmn Com on Aging; State House Rep. **HONORS/ACHIEVEMENTS:** Hon Doct ffrom Univ of Portland. **MILITARY SERVICE:** USN 1942-46. **BUSINESS ADDRESS:** Senator, State of Oregon, S-209 State Capitol Bldg, Salem, OR 97310.

MCCRACKEN, FRANK D.
Clergyman. **PERSONAL:** Born Jul 01, 1949, Reading, PA; married Charlene Flowers; children: Alicia, Frank, Stephanie. **EDUCATION:** PA State, 1967; Albright Coll, 1968; Kutztown State Univ, BA 1980; Lutheran Theological, attending. **CAREER:** Assoc Financial Svcs, mgr 1972-74; Police Athletic League, exec dir1977-; naternal Health Svcs, past pres, bd 1979-; NAACP Reading Branch, exec mem 1982-84; Berks County Resource Consortium, pres; St James Chapel COGIC, pastor. **ORGANIZATIONS:** Past mem Berks Cty Children & Youth Serv 1981-82; mem bd Prokids, Reading Ministerium; pres Berks Cty Training Inst, Berks Cty Resource Inc; mem, adv bd PA State Berks Campus; mem, bd of trustee Kutztown Univ. **HONORS/ACHIEVEMENTS:** Listed in Who's Who in Amer Univ & Coll 1978; Achievement IBPOEW Eastern Distr 1983. **MILITARY SERVICE:** AUS Intelligence E-5 3 yrs; Army Commendation w/OLC 1969; Presidential Unit Citation. **HOME ADDRESS:** 1716 N Third St, Reading, PA 19601. **BUSINESS ADDRESS:** Pastor, St James Chapel COGIC, 11 South 9th St, Reading, PA 19602.

MCCRARY-SIMMONS, SHIRLEY DENISE
Government attorney. **PERSONAL:** Born Nov 07, 1956, Boston, MA; daughter of Earlie McCrary and Eupha McCrary; married Nathaniel O Simmons. **EDUCATION:** Brown Univ, AB 1978; Boston Univ School of Law, JD 1982. **CAREER:** Georgia Legal Servs, law intern 1982; Internal Revenue Servs, tax rep/revenue officer 1983-84, attorney estate tax 1984-. **ORGANIZATIONS:** Pres Black Amer Law Student Assoc 1980-81; mem JD Curriculum Comm 1981-82; mem Natl Bar Assoc 1983; deputy registrar Fulton Co GA 1983; mem State Bar of GA 1983-; mem Gate City Bar Assoc 1985,87; union steward Natl Treasury Employees Union 1985-; legal advisor Africare Atlanta Inc 1985-. **HONORS/ACHIEVEMENTS:** First black female to be hired as an estate tax attorney in the Atlanta Dist; Superior Performance Award, IRS 1988. **BUSINESS ADDRESS:** Attorney Estate Tax, Internal Revenue Service, 401 West Peachtree Street, Room 738, Atlanta, GA 30308.

MCCRAVEN, CARL CLARKE
Business executive. **PERSONAL:** Born May 27, 1926, Des Moines, IA; son of Marcus H McCraven and Buena V; married Eva Louise Stewart; children: Carl Bruce. **EDUCATION:** Howard Univ, BS Elec Engr 1950; CA State Univ Northridge, MS Health Svr Admin 1976. **CAREER:** Natl Bureau of Standards Wash DC, radiation physicist 1950-55; Lockheed CA Co Burbank, CA, sr research engr 1955-63; Space Elec Power Engr Dept TRWSystems Inc, mem tech staff 1963-72; CA State Univ Northridge, asst prof 1974-76; Pacoima Mem Hosp Inc Lake Vw Terr CA, assc admin vice pres 1972-73; Hillview Mental Health Ctr Lake View Terr CA, founder, president 1973-. **ORGANIZATIONS:** Fellow Assc Mntl Hlth Admin 1984-; mem Amer Publ Hlth Assc 1976-; Am Mgmt Assc 1978-; Natl Assc Hlth Serv Exec 1976-; pres NAACP Soutern Area CA Conf 1967-71; natl bd dir NAACP 1970-76; vice pres Los Angeles Cty Contractors Assc 1983-; regent Casa Loma Clge Bd Dir 1970-85; bd dir San Fernando Valley Girl Scout Council 1980-82; past pres mem North San Fernando Valley Rotary 1981-85; mem Sigma Phi Xi Boule 1984-. **HONORS/ACHIEVEMENTS:** Recipient Citation CA Senate 1971, CA Assembly 1971, City of Los Angeles 1971, 1978; Cert of Appreciation Councilman Bob Ronka 1st Dist 1979. **MILITARY SERVICE:** AUS 1945-46. **HOME ADDRESS:** 17233 Chatsworth St, Granada Hills, CA 91344. **BUSINESS ADDRESS:** President and CEO, Hillview Mntl Hlth Ctr Inc, 11600 Eldridge Ave, Lake View Terrace, CA 91342.

MCCRAVEN, MARCUS R.
Business executive. **PERSONAL:** Born Dec 27, 1923, Des Moines, IA; married Marguerite Mills; children: Carol J, Stephen A, Paul A. **EDUCATION:** Howard Univ, BSEE; Univ of MD; Univ of CA. **CAREER:** Naval Research Lab, engr; Lawrence Radiation Lab, engr group leader nuclear test; Phelps Dodge Commun Co, chief engr; Bridgeport Elec Co, vice pres; United Illuminating Co, vice pres. **ORGANIZATIONS:** Dir First Constitution Bank Ct; pres Middletown Ave Assn Real Est; dir Metrodata Inc Okla City; bd trustees CT State Colleges; chrmn bd So Central CT Amer Red Cross; exec comm EPA Science Adv Bd; dir Quinnipiac Coll, The Graduates Club, Jr Achievement; chmn bd So Central Ct Health Planning; director Yale Univ Peabody Museum Assoc. **HONORS/ACHIEVEMENTS:** City Commissioner Menlo Park CA; Most Notable Citizen Award Hamden CT; pres North Haven CT Rotary; IRA Hiscock Award; mem Quinnipiack Club; New Haven Chamber of Commerce Award; Urban League; United Way; life mem NAACP. **MILITARY SERVICE:** AUS. **BUSINESS ADDRESS:** Vice President, United Illuminating Co, 80 Temple St, New Haven, CT 06510.

MCCRAY, BILLY QUINCY
Government official. **PERSONAL:** Born Oct 27, 1929, Geary, OK; son of John J. McCray and Ivory B. McCray; married Wyvette M Williams, Oct 12, 1952; children: Frankeleen Conley, Anthony, Melodie Miller, Kent. **EDUCATION:** Langston Univ Langston OK, 1945-47; CO Univ Boulder, 1949-50. **CAREER:** Boeing Co, Wichita, KS, industrial photographer, 1952-77; Govt of KS, Topeka, KS, state representative, 1967-72, state senator, 1973-84; KS Dept of Economic Development, Topeka, KS, dir, 1984-86; Sedgwick County Commissioner, 1987—. **ORGANIZATIONS:** Pres, Wichita Ach Club, 1953-55; me, Wichita Human Relations Committee, 1963-66; KS Drug Abuse Council, 1972-74; dir, Wichita A Phillip Randolph Inst, 1976-78; US Small Business Advisors Council, 1977-80. **HONORS/ACHIEVEMENTS:** Published Song of Autumn, 1948, and A Tree by the Highway, 1956; Outstanding Legislator, KS Association of Public Employees, 1977; plaque Outstanding Award, KS Credit Union League, 1975; Outstanding State Senator, KS Assc of Public Employees, 1983; Pres Award, Langston Univ Regl Alumni, 1982; Outstanding Service, Natl Advisory Council on Small Business, Pres Jimmy Carter. **MILITARY SERVICE:** USAF s/sgt 1947-51. **HOME ADDRESS:** 1532 N Ash, Wichita, KS 67214. **BUSINESS ADDRESS:** Commissioner, Sedgwick County, 525 N Main, Suite 320, Wichita, KS 67214.

MCCRAY, CHRISTOPHER COLUMBUS
Government official. **PERSONAL:** Born Sep 16, 1925, Waycros, GA; married Jewel Hollis; children: Cynthia, Linda Bacon, Christi. **CAREER:** SCL RR Co, equip operator 1943-; Waycross/Ware Co, co-chmn bi-racial comm 1966-71; Waycross GA, sch bd mem 1967-71; City of Waycross, mayor pro-tem. **ORGANIZATIONS:** Mem former pres NAACP 1955-; dir Waycross Jr Coll 1976-; dir SEGAPDC 1976-. **HONORS/ACHIEVEMENTS:** Who's Who Among Black Amers 1975; Miller Medal Awd of Civics Kiwanis Club Waycross 1976; Morris Jacobson Awd Hebrew Congregation 1976; Membership Awd NAACP1976. **MILITARY SERVICE:** USN petty officer 2/c 1943-46. **BUSINESS ADDRESS:** Mayor Pro Tem, City of Waycross, PO Drawer 198, City Hall, Waycross, GA 31501.

MCCRAY, JOE RICHARD
Business executive. **PERSONAL:** Born Nov 12, 1928, Bucksport, SC; married Gertrude E Bellamy; children: Sidney, Richard, Rhonda. **EDUCATION:** Univ MD, 1974. **CAREER:** Joe R McCray Enterprises Inc, pres. **ORGANIZATIONS:** Mem Washington Bd of Realtors DC; Prince George's Bd of Realtors MD; DC Chamber of Commerce; trustee Better Business Bureau; greater SE Comm Hosp; supt of Youth at E Washington Hts Baptist Church; Kiwanis Club; E Branch, DC Life Fellow, Kiwanis Intl. **HONORS/ACHIEVEMENTS:** Past pres awrd Disting Clb Kiwanis Intrnl 1973-74. **MILITARY SERVICE:** AUS lt col 1946-72. **BUSINESS ADDRESS:** 1315 Pennsylvania Ave SE, Washington, DC 20003.

MCCRAY, MACEO E.
Librarian. **PERSONAL:** Born Feb 10, 1935, Bucksport, SC. **EDUCATION:** Howard Univ Washington, BD 1962; SC State Coll, BS 1956; Univ of MD, MLS 1968. **CAREER:** Univ of PA, libry asst sch of social work 1964, Chas Van Pelt Libry lib asst 1964-65; Howard Univ, sch of rel libry 1959-62, fndrs library circ asst 1962-64, serials librian 1965-78, associate librarian 1978-. **ORGANIZATIONS:** Mem Med Lib Assn; Amer Libry Assn; HU Task Force on Libry Automation; HU Rep to Consortiums Union lst of Newspapers; faculty/staff Fellowship CommColl of Dentistry Howard Univ; Wash Urban League; Visiting Nurse Assn; Schl of Religion Alumni Assn; SC St Alum Assn of DC; Univ MD Alum Assn; Big Brothers of America; Omega Psi Phi; pres Mt Bethel Bapt Educational Congress 1983-. **HONORS/ACHIEVEMENTS:** Cert Washington Urban League 1964; Rosamond A Alston Chap Awd 1955; YMCA Ser Awd 1956; SC State Coll Sun Sch Awd 1956; PTA Key 1951; Cert the Fashion Grp of Washington DC 1966; Spl Librs Assn Flwshp Drexel; Rockefeller Theol Schlrshp Howard Univ; The WHC Brown Felwship; La Beza Ja Schlrshp; TheCraig Wall Felwshp; Citation Big Brothers 1972. **BUSINESS ADDRESS:** Associate Librarian, HowardUniv, Medical Dental Library, Washington, DC 20059.

MCCRAY, MELVIN
Maintenance director. **PERSONAL:** Born Aug 09, 1946, Ft Benning, GA; married Rosie M Thompson; children: Kimya Nicole, Keisha Michelle, Cora Danielle, Diedra Marie. **EDUCATION:** GA State Univ, BS 1972. **CAREER:** Atlanta City Aviation, admin asst II 1975-76, admin asst III 1976-77, project coord 1977-80, dir of maintenance 1980-. **ORGANIZATIONS:** Fin field City of Atlanta City Hall 1972-; collector dep marshal 1975; mem Amer Assoc of Airport Exec, Southeastern Airport Mgrs Assoc, Conference of Minority Public Admin, Natl Forum for Black Public Admin; mem bd of dir City of Atlanta Credit Union. **HONORS/ACHIEVEMENTS:** Cert of Appreciation ASPA 1982; Cert of Recognition GA Engrg Found 1982; Pres City of Atlanta Employees Club 1982; Cert of Merit City of Atlanta/Andrew Young 1983; Cert of Appreciation COMPA 1983 Christmas Fundraiser 1983. **BUSINESS ADDRESS:** Dir of Maintenance, Hartsfield Atl Int'l Airport, Commissioners Office, Atlanta, GA 30320.

MCCRAY, RODNEY CHARLES
Professional athlete. **PERSONAL:** Born Aug 29, 1961, Mt Vernon, NY. **EDUCATION:** Univ of Louisville, 1979-83. **CAREER:** Houston Rockets, forward 1984-. **HONORS/ACHIEVEMENTS:** Named to second All-Rookie team by NBA coaches; first All-Rookie team selected by Bsktbl Digest 1983-84. **BUSINESS ADDRESS:** Houston Rockets, The Summit, Ste 510, Houston, TX 77046.

MCCRAY, ROY HOWARD
Dentist. **PERSONAL:** Born Mar 14, 1946, Birmingham, AL; son of Maceo Cleggett and Annie Cleggett; children: Kenja, Kendyl, Kennethia. **EDUCATION:** AL A&M Univ, BS 1972; Meharry Medical Coll, DDS 1978. **CAREER:** Meharry Medical Coll, instructor operative dentistry 1978-81; AL Dental Soc, parliamentarian 1985-86; Private Practice, dentist. **ORGANIZATIONS:** Mem Huntsville Madison Co Dental Soc 1980-86; vice pres No AL Medical Assoc 1985-; mem NAFEO 1985. **HONORS/ACHIEVEMENTS:** CV Mosby III Awd Meharry Dental Sch 1977; Dr Martin Luther King Awd Meharry Dental Sch 1977; The Intl Coll of Dentists 1978; Amer Assoc of Endodontists and Orthodontists 1978. **MILITARY SERVICE:** AUS e-4/sp4 infantry 1967-69; Vietnam Overseas, Combat Infantryman, Unit Citation 1968. **BUSINESS ADDRESS:** President, McCray DDS PC, 2510 Pulaski Pk NW, Huntsville, AL 35810.

MCCRAY, THOMAS L.
Clergyman. **PERSONAL:** Born Jan 01, 1928, Valdosta, GA; married Elizabeth Wafier; children: Lois, Teresa, Thomas. **EDUCATION:** Wilberforce U, BA; Payne Theol Sem Wilberforce U, BD Candidate; Bucknell U, Extended Study; Cleveland State U, Western Reserve. **CAREER:** St Mathews AME Ch, pastor; Bethel AME Ch 1950-52; Milton PA, Circt pstr 1952-58; St James AME Ch Cleveland, assc pstr & dir chrstn ed 1958-67; MtMoriah AME Ch Maple Hghts, OH, pstr 1965-66; Avery AME Ch Clveland 1967-73; St James AME Ch Erie 1973; OH Civil Rights Commn, field Investigtr; Grtr Cleveland Interchr Cncl, dir.

ORGANIZATIONS: Past pres Cncl of Chs of Christ Grtr Clvlnd; past pres Grtr Clvlnd Mnstrl Assc; past pres Clvlnd Cncl of Chs Chld Dev Pgm; mem Div Chrstn EdnDept of Yth Mnstry; exec com Natl Cncl of Chs of Chrst; mem Div of Ch & Witness & of Prog & Plng Comm oH pstrs assc; OH Cncl of Chs; alt del Grtr Clvlnd Intrch Cncl; vice pres Clvlnd Advsry Bd; OH Ldrshp Conf; mem Gov Com; Migrant Affrs; Clvlnd Brnch; NAACP; E Urbn Bd; YMCA; bd of trust Forest City Hosp; mem Cnsmrs Lgue of OH; past vice pres Untd Area Ctzns Agcy; mem Training Com. **HONORS/ACHIEVEMENTS:** UACA Hon Degree DD Monrovia Clg Monrovia, W Africa 1972.

MCCRAY, WILLIAM JOEL
Retired educator. **PERSONAL:** Born Oct 03, Macon, GA. **EDUCATION:** Elem Edn, BS 1955. **CAREER:** Ach Jr HS, math sci instr; Elem Sch Tchr; Cincinnati Pub Sch, 6 lang arts soc stds. **ORGANIZATIONS:** Life mem NAACP 1986-; mem Taft Museum of Cinti Outreach Comm 1986-87; co-chmn Taft Museum 1986-87; mem Cinti Historical Soc Black History Archives AdvGroup; mem Resident Arts & Humanities Consortium 1986-87; mem Univ of Cincti Coll of Educ Alumni Adv Comm; chmn nom comm Cinti Chap The Friends of Amistad 1986-87; co-chmn 11th Anniv Luncheon Cinti Chap Friends of Amistad Inc. **HONORS/ACHIEVEMENTS:** President Awd for Outstanding Contrib to Ed Esquire Club Inc 1977; Cert of Appreciation of Devoted & Invaluable Serv South Avondale School 1983; Good Apple Awd for Dedicated Serv South Avondale School 1983-84; recipient of the President's Awd of Appreciation from the Cinti Chap Friends of Amistad; Cert of Appreciation from the Smithsonia Inst toward the Constr of the Center for Asians, Near East & Arican Cultures on the Natl Mall in Wash DC 1983; Cert of Apprec for Volunteer Serv to Parkam Public School 1986. **MILITARY SERVICE:** USAF corpl 1945-47.

MCCREARY, BILL
Reporter, co-anchorman. **PERSONAL:** Born Aug 18, 1933, Manhattan NYC, NY; married O'Kellon. **EDUCATION:** Cty Clg NYC; NYUniv Schl of Commnctns. **CAREER:** Radio Sta WWRL Woodside Queens, stf ancr eng 1960, co-prodcr 1961; Night Pgm, mgr 1962; Radio Sta WLIB, nwscstr 1963; News Dir 1965; Metro Media Brdcstg Inc,TV nwscstr 1967; WNEW & TV'S 10 O'Clock News, co-anchorman; 5 Min TV Newscast, anchorman; Black News, anchorman 1970, mng edtr & exec dir 1971; Gen Assgnmt Rptr; Fox Broadcasting Co, exec producer "McCreary Report", vice pres 1987-. **ORGANIZATIONS:** Mem Cambria Hghts Civ Assc Queens; vice pres Royal Crusdrs Bowling Clb. **HONORS/ACHIEVEMENTS:** Emmy Awd NY Chap Natl Acad TV Arts & Sci 1969-70; Citation of Merit 1971-72; Achievement Awd Bkly Chap Natl Assoc Negro Bus & Prof Wmns Clb Inc;Cambria Heights Serv Awrd 1975; Achievement Awd NAACP LI Chap 1975; Emmy Awd for co-anchoring 10 o'clock news 1980-81; Public Serv Awd FDA; Special Citation from the Commissioner; voted Most Watched and Belived Black Correspondent in Metro Area. **MILITARY SERVICE:** AUS corpl 1953-55. **BUSINESS ADDRESS:** Fox Broadcasting, 205 E 67th St, New York, NY 10021.

MCCREE, EDWARD L.
Clergyman. **PERSONAL:** Born Feb 24, 1942, Quitman, MS; married Mae Lois Heath; children: Anita, Edward, Michele. **EDUCATION:** Univ of Detroit, 1963; Detroit Bible Clg, 1961-62; Am Bapt Theo Sem, BA 1972. **CAREER:** Creeball Ice Cream Co, fndr 1961-62; Shell Oil Sta, Co-owner 1962; Cedar Grove Miss Bapt Ch Mt Juliet, TN, pastor 1968; Macedonia Bapt & Ch Pontiac, MI, pastor. **ORGANIZATIONS:** Mem Hoi Adelpos Frat; Ministerial Fellow; Gen Mtr Truck & Coach; Chapel Pontiac Gen Hosp; adv bd United Brotherhood; bd dirs Christians for Tomorrow;pres Boy of Hope Clb; Lecturer, cncl, advsr. **HONORS/ACHIEVEMENTS:** Recip Most Progressive Young Business Man of Royal Oak Twnshp 1962; most oust young man of Ferndale 1963; big brother awrd Royal Oak Twnshp 1963; activities awrd 1964. **BUSINESS ADDRESS:** 512 Pearsall Blvd, Pontiac, MI.

MCCREE, FLOYD J.
Register of deeds. **PERSONAL:** Born Mar 29, 1923, Webster Grove, MO; married Leeberta; children: Anita, Byron, Marsha, Melvyn. **EDUCATION:** Two Yrs Clg. **CAREER:** Genesee Co MI, reg of deeds 1971-, bd of sup 1956-68; Flint, city cncl 1958-70, mayor 1966-68. **ORGANIZATIONS:** Pres Model Cities Eco Dev Corp 1971-; pres Model City Dev Corp 1974-; bd of trus of NUL 1968-71; pres Local Urban League; Elks; Masons; PTA; NAACP; Human Rel Comm; bd of ed Adv Cncl. **HONORS/ACHIEVEMENTS:** Equal opp day awrd Urban League & NAACP; Fine Arts Thea Named After Him. **MILITARY SERVICE:** Stf sgt 1943-46. **BUSINESS ADDRESS:** 1101 Beach St, Flint, MI 48503.

MCCROOM, EDDIE WINTHER
Attorney. **PERSONAL:** Born Sep 11, 1932, Memphis, TN; married Shirley Kathery Lewis; children: Darren Winther, Audrey Jay, Sandra Marguerite. **EDUCATION:** Agr Mech & Normal Clge, BS 1955; Case Western Reserve Univ, LLB 1961. **CAREER:** OH Civil Rights Comm, fld rep 1961-63; US Dept of Justice, asst US atty 1964-69; State of OH Dept Adm Srv, state EEO coord 1972-74; Breckenridge & McCroom, priv prac law 1976-. **ORGANIZATIONS:** Exec vice pres Industrial Fed S & L Assc 1969-70; lecturer bus law Univ Cincinnati 1971-72; legal cnsl Jaycee 1970-; NAACP 1970-; IBPOE of W Elks 1980-. **MILITARY SERVICE:** USN seaman II 1955-57. **BUSINESS ADDRESS:** Attorney, Breckenridge & McCroom Law, 402 Legal Arts Centre, Youngstown, OH 44503.

MCCROREY, H. LAWRENCE
Educator. **PERSONAL:** Born Mar 13, 1927, Philadelphia, PA; son of Henry Lawrence McCrorey Jr and Marian Dawley McCrorey; married Constance Gilliam; children: Desiree, Lauren, Leslie, Larry. **EDUCATION:** Univ MI, BS 1949, MS 1950; Univ IL, MS 1958, PhD 1963. **CAREER:** Univ VT, dept of physiology & biophysics, asst, assoc, full prof 1966-, School of Alied Health Sciences, dean, 1981-; Acad Affairs Univ VT, assoc vice pres 1973-77; Physiology Univ IL, asst prof 1963-66; Sharp & Dohme Phila, rsrch assoc 1951-55; Howard Univ, vis prof; Tuskegee Inst; Goddard Clg; Univ CA; Charles Drew Med Sch; Coll of VI FL A&M; Dillard Univ; Statistics Walter Reed Army Inst of Rsrch, vis prof 1967-70; University of Colorado Medical College, visiting prof 1978-79. **ORGANIZATIONS:** Mem Gen Rsrch Support Pgm Adv Com NIH 1973-78 & 1980-84; bd trustee VT-NY Proj 1968-70; bd dir Am Civil Liberties Union 1971-75; Surgeon Gen's Ad Hoc Com on Health of Americans 1968-69; corporator Burlington Savings Bk 1976-; bd dir Burlington YMCA 1976-. **HONORS/ACHIEVEMENTS:** List of sci publ in Phsyiology; outst tchg awrds Coll of Nursing 1960,& 1964; Coll of Pharmacy 1965; Coll of Medicine, 1970, 1971, 1984; Univ of Vermont 1988. **MILITARY SERVICE:** AUS nco 1944-46. **BUSINESS ADDRESS:** Professor of Physiology & Biophysics and, Dean, School of Allied Health, Univ of Vermont, 301 Rowell Bldg, Burlington, VT 05405.

MCCUISTON, FREDERICK DOUGLASS, JR.
Engineering manager. **PERSONAL:** Born Nov 27, 1940, Wynne, AR; married Norma P; children: Frederick III, Marucs, Maria. **EDUCATION:** TN State Univ, BS 1961; Univ of Cincinnati, MS 1970, PhD 1976. **CAREER:** GM, asst staff engr. **ORGANIZATIONS:** Mem Amer Soc of Mechanical Engrs 1962-, Society of Automotive Engrs 1968-; mem NBCDI 1981-; pres Ann Arbor NAACP Branch 1982-. **HONORS/ACHIEVEMENTS:** Omega Psi Phi Comm Serv Awd 1984; Alpha Phi Alpha Man of the Year 1985; NAACP Leadership Awd 1986. **MILITARY SERVICE:** USAF capt 5 yrs. **HOME ADDRESS:** 3670 Larchmont Dr, Ann Arbor, MI 48105.

MCCUISTON, STONEWALL, JR.
Physician. **PERSONAL:** Born Feb 23, 1959, Chicago, IL. **EDUCATION:** Grinnell Coll, BA 1981; Meharry Medical Coll, MD 1985. **CAREER:** Cook County Hospital, resident physician. **ORGANIZATIONS:** Mem AMSA, SNMA 1981-85; rep Housestaff Assoc Cook County Hosp 1986; business liaison Black Physicians Assoc of Cook County Hosp 1986. **HONORS/ACHIEVEMENTS:** Research grant March of Dimes 1982,83; First place Research Day Medical Div Meharry Medical Coll 1983. **HOME ADDRESS:** 7810 South Ridgeland, Chicago, IL 60649. **BUSINESS ADDRESS:** Resident Physician, Cook County Hospital, 1825 W Harrison, Chicago, IL 60612.

MCCULLER, JAMES
Corporation executive. **PERSONAL:** Born Feb 27, 1940, El Dorado, AR; married Dorothy; children: James C, Daryl, Stacy D, Alecia M, Valerie D. **EDUCATION:** Central State Clg, BA 1962; NY U;; MA Pgm No Degree. **CAREER:** Action for a Better Comm Inc, exec dir 1967-; Neighborhood Youth Corps, dir 1965-67; NY State Employment Serv, emplymnt intrvwr 1965; Baden St Settlement, adult worker 1963-65. **ORGANIZATIONS:** Mem New Challenge Dev Corp; Anti-poverty Action Co Inc; Corp of Blacks in Pub Broadcasting; past chmn Rochester Hlth, Network; chmn Personnel Com; Natl Black Media Coalition; past 2nd vice pres Natl Exec Dir CAA Assc; 1st vice pres Home Ownership Promotion Corp; mem Greater Rochester Intergovernmental Panel; Genesee Reg Hlth Plng Cncl; Manpower Area Plng Cncl; Hsng Cncl of Monroe Co; Genesee Finger Lakes Reg Plng Bd; Am Civil Liberties Union; Cncl of Soc Agencies; mem Am Judicature Soc. **HONORS/ACHIEVEMENTS:** 1st prize Central State Clg Speech Champion 1962; Werner Hegeman Flwshp Awrd NYUniv 1962; recgnt & awrd Hospitality Clb 1975; comm serv awrd Madison Stdnt Cultural Assc 1974; Brockport StateUniv & Black StdntUniv 1974; Marcus Garvey Solidarity Com 1974-75. **BUSINESS ADDRESS:** 244 S Plymouth Ave, Rochester, NY 14608.

MCCULLERS, EUGENE
Business executive. **PERSONAL:** Born Jan 30, 1941, Garner, NC. **EDUCATION:** Shaw U, BA 1962;Univ of WI, Addistional Study 1963. **CAREER:** US Peace Corps, vol 1963-65; Capital Coca-Cola Btlg Co NC, sales Rep 1965-67; Coca-Cola Btlg Co TN, acct exec 1968-76; Cocoa-Cola USA Atlanta, GA,mkt mgr 1976-. **ORGANIZATIONS:** Bd dir Natl Assc of Mkt & Dev 1971-73; pres elect Natl Assc of Mkt Dev 1979; pres Cincinnati Chap of NAMD 1973-74; natl vice pres Natl Assc of Mkt Dev Kappa Alpha Psi Frat Chap Keeper of Records 1959; SNEA 1959-62; sunday sch supt Wake Bapt Grove Ch 1959-62; past pres Garner Consolidated Alumni Assc1961-63; YMCA 1968-; ShawUniv Alumni Assc 1963-; IBPOE of the World 1974-. **HONORS/ACHIEVEMENTS:** Outst young men of am 1971. **MILITARY SERVICE:** USAR.

MCCULLOUGH, FRANCES LOUISE (NEE FORD)
Personnel adminstrator. **PERSONAL:** Born Apr 05, 1941, Dermott, AR; married Leo McCullough; children: Nancy L. **EDUCATION:** Contra Costa Jr Coll, AA 1962; San Francisco State Univ, BA 1975, MA 1977. **CAREER:** Comm Vol, 1972-80; Employment Specialist, 1980-. **ORGANIZATIONS:** Chmn Comm Housing Resources Bd of Pacifica 1979-80; commr/pres San Mateo Co Human Relations Commn 1977-80; bd mem N San Mateo Co League of Women Voters 1974; chmn League of Women Voters Pacifica CA 1973; educ consult CA Educ Compliance Com 1977; desegregation consult Fellow-Coro Pub Affairs Found 1978; adv Skyline Comm Coll; mem African Hist Soc San Francisco 1976-80; prog dir Friends of Pacifica's Library 1979; mem Fair Hearing Com Pacifica's Childcare; Conferee Pacifica Rep Regional Bar Assn Conf 1975. **HONORS/ACHIEVEMENTS:** Fellowship Coro Pub Affairs Found San Francisco 1978; Manpower Fellowship San Francisco State Univ; producer/fndr First Black History Prog & Black Club inPacifica. **BUSINESS ADDRESS:** Employment Specialist, 444 El Camino, San Mateo, CA 94401.

MCCULLOUGH, FREDERICK DOUGLAS
Clergyman. **PERSONAL:** Born Mar 17, 1897, Magnolia, AR; married Octavia Anderson; children: Elsiree O Robinson (dec), Frederick M, Anna Z McKendall, Josephine R Murphy, Anderson, Henry G. **EDUCATION:** AR Baptist Coll, diploma 1922; Chicago Bapt Inst, diploma 1947, BTh 1955. **CAREER:** Shiloh Bapt Ch, deacon 1936-39, assoc minister 1938-45, sup of Sunday sch 1924-38; Candle Light Bapt Ch, pastor. **ORGANIZATIONS:** Vp New Era Dist Assn of Sun Sch Dept of Chicago & Vicinity; pers Chicago & Vicinity 1945; mem Sharvin Post # 397 Amer Legion. **HONORS/ACHIEVEMENTS:** Cert of Recognition for Serv Rendered to the Comm Bapt Ch Chicago Bapt Assn; Citation honoring Chicago Leaders. **MILITARY SERVICE:** AUS Private.

MCCULLOUGH, GERALDINE
Painter, sculptress. **PERSONAL:** Born Dec 01, 1922, Kingston, AR; married Lester; children: Lester Jr. **EDUCATION:** Art Inst of Chicago, BA 1948, MEd 1955. **CAREER:** Rosary Clg River Forest, IL, chmn prof of art dept; Wendell Phillips HS, former tchr; Century of Negro Progress Exposition Held in Chgo, sculpture work appeared 1963; Dr Martin Luther King, Jr W Side Dev Co, commd to do sculpture. **ORGANIZATIONS:** Mem IL Art Ed; Am Assc ofUniv prof; mem Alumni Assc; Art Inst of Chicago. **HONORS/ACHIEVEMENTS:** Amer Negro Heritage 1968; recipient John D Steindecker Schlrshp; the Meml Schlrshp; finger painting citation; Purchase Awrd 1959; first prize Annual Art Exhibit of Atlanta Univ 1961; sculpture entitled "Phoenix"; awrded George D Widener Meml Gold Medal; 159th Annual Exhibition of PA Acad of Fine Arts 1964. **BUSINESS ADDRESS:** 7900 W Division, River Forest, IL 60302.

MCCULLUM, DONALD PITTS
Judge. **PERSONAL:** Born Jan 28, 1928, Little Rock, AR; married Peggy T Cook; children: Donald A, Erica G, Peggy L. **EDUCATION:** Talladega Coll, AB 1948; Boston Univ Sch of Law, JD 1951; US Naval Sch Mil Justice, certified 1953. **CAREER:** Alameda Co Oakland CA, dep dist atty 1955-60; Law Offices Donald P McCullum, atty at law 1960-77; State of CA, state inheritance tax referee 1961-75; Berkeley CA, city atty 1972-76; Alameda Co CA, judge superior court 1977-. **ORGANIZATIONS:** Dir & pres Legal Arts World Oakland CA 1967-; dir Golden State Mutual Life Ins Co 1972-77; dir & pres Oakland's United Response 1979-; mem Amer Bar Assn, Natl Bar Assn, CA Assn Black Lawyers; pres/dir Oakland Br NAACP 1961-64 1967-70 1973-74; chmn W Coast Region NAACP 1966-70; commnr CA Constitution Revision commn 1970-72; dir Natl Urban Coalition Washington DC 1972-; chmn Adv Com Black Population 1980 Census 1976-80; life mem Natl Council Negro Women; life mem NAACP; mem MA Bar and CA Bar. **HONORS/ACHIEVEMENTS:** Outstanding Comm Serv CA Legislature City of Oakland Alameda Co 1977. **MILITARY SERVICE:** USN lt 1952-55; Korean (2 star) medal; Natl Defense Medal; UN Medal. **BUSINESS ADDRESS:** Judge, Superior Ct Alameda Co, Alameda Co Court House, Oakland, CA 94612.

MCCUMMINGS, LEVERNE
Educator. **PERSONAL:** Born Oct 28, 1932, Marion, SC; married Dr Betty L Hall; children: Gregory, Gary, Ahada. **EDUCATION:** St Augustine's, BA 1960; Univ of PA, MSW 1966; Ohio State Univ, PhD 1975. **CAREER:** Competency Certification Bd, Bd of Health & Human Svcs, Futures Think Tank, chmn 1981-82; Natl Conf of Grad Deans/Dirs & Off Soc Work Progs, pres 1982-85; Cheyney Univ of PA, pres. **HONORS/ACHIEVEMENTS:** Outstanding Educators Awd Univ of KY 1971; Recognition Awd NASW Sixth Biennial Prof Symposium 1980; Distinguished Alumni Awd Univ of PA 1980; Recognition Awd Council of Intl Prog 1981; Institute for Educational Management, Harvard University, 1989. **MILITARY SERVICE:** AUS 1955-57. **BUSINESS ADDRESS:** President, Cheyney University of PA, Cheyney, PA 19319.

MCCURDY, BRENDA WRIGHT
Microbiologist. **PERSONAL:** Born Jun 29, 1946, Richmond, VA; daughter of Rogers C Wright and Alcie Taylor Wright; married Howard Douglas McCurdy, PhD. **EDUCATION:** Virginia Union Univ, BS (Magna Cum Laude) 1968; Virginia Commonwealth Univ School of Medicine, MS 1970; Wayne State Univ School of Medicine, PhD 1980. **CAREER:** Henry Ford Hospital Detroit, microbiologist III 1970-72; Wayne State Univ, rsch asst 1972-75; Wayne State Univ, adj asst prof of immunology & microbiology 1980-; Veterans Admin Med Ctr, section chief of microbiology 1979-. **ORGANIZATIONS:** Mem Amer Soc for Microbiology 1970-; mem South Central Assoc for Clinical Microbiology 1978-; chairperson Medical Ctr Adv Comm for Equal Employment Oppor 1983-; pres Windsor Black Coalition (Canada) 1983-85; mem Delta Sigma Theta. **HONORS/ACHIEVEMENTS:** Graduate Professional Scholarship Wayne State Univ 1976-77; Natl Fellowship Awd 1977-78; Augusta T Calloway Fellowship Awd 1979. **BUSINESS ADDRESS:** Section Chief of Microbiology, Veterans Admin Medical Ctr, Southfield and Outer Dr, Allen Park, MI 48101.

MCCUTCHEON, LAWRENCE (CLUTCH)
Professional scout. **PERSONAL:** Born Jun 02, 1950, Plainview, TX. **CAREER:** Denver Broncos, running back 1980-; LA Rams, running back 1977-80. **ORGANIZATIONS:** Only Six Times In Ram Hist has a Ram Ball Carrier Gained More Than 1,000 Yds in a Season; McCutchoen has Done it the Top Three of Those Only Needs 1,132 to Catch Ram Record of 5,417. **HONORS/ACHIEVEMENTS:** NEA'S Third Down Awrd; 2nd Team ALL-NFC; UPI; Pro Bowl for 4th Staight Time; outst Ofnsv Back 1974; Daniel F Reeves Meml Awrd; MVP; All-Rookie Team UPI; All-Western Athletic Conf; CO State U; NFC All Star Team Sporting News 1974. **BUSINESS ADDRESS:** Los Angeles Rams, 2327 West Lincoln Ave, Anaheim, CA 92801.

MCDANIEL, ADAM THEODORE
Dentist. **PERSONAL:** Born Jun 08, 1925, Rock Hill, SC; married Lois Butler; children: Jenita, Frederic. **EDUCATION:** NC Central Univ, BS 1946; Howard Univ, DDS 1947-51; Jersey City Med Ctr, Internship 1951-52; Friendship Jr Clge. **CAREER:** Dentist; Rahway Geriatric Cntr, dental consultant. **ORGANIZATIONS:** Mem Rahway Rtry Club; pres Rahway Mun Council Caucus of Elected Black Officials 1960-72; mem Union Co & NJ Dental Soc; 100 Black Men of NJ; Omega Psi Phi Frat; NJ Chap Natl Guardsmen Inc; state rep Rahway Housing Auth 1959-70; mem Correctional Hlth Serv Invest Comm of NJ State Prisons; mem Lay Comm Publ Schl Systems; Urban League. **HONORS/ACHIEVEMENTS:** Beta Kappa Chi Hnr SJI Soc Honoree; Testimonial Dinner 1961, 1973. **MILITARY SERVICE:** USAF capt 1953-54. **HOME ADDRESS:** 97 E Milton Ave, Rahway, NJ 07065.

MCDANIEL, CHARLES WILLIAM
Government administrator. **PERSONAL:** Born Mar 17, 1927, Fairfield, AL; son of Charles Andrew McDaniel and Willie V Seldon McDaniel; married Rose L Bowen; children: Deborah Roberts, Charles F, Reginael. **EDUCATION:** Miles Coll, attended 1946; Civil Serv Comm, attended 1978; Coast Guard Acad, attended 1982; GA State Univ, attended 1981; US Army Logistics Mgmt Center, 1970-81; Exec Seminar Center, Kings Point NY, attended 1982; Exec Seminar, Denver CO, attended 1987. **CAREER:** US Army, Warren MI, system analyst 1967-70, budget analyst 1970-76; US Army, Washington DC, budget analyst 1976-80; US Army HQ FORSCOM, suprv budget analyst 1980-89; deputy dir Log Mgmt Div 1989, chief Mgmt Branch. **ORGANIZATIONS:** Pres Amer FED of Musicians #286 1965-73; church organist IN Baptist Church 1966-76; band leader Detroit MI 1968-76; mem NAACP 1970; bd mem Amer FED of Musician #15/286 1973-75; mem Amer Soc of Military Comptrollers 1981-; church organist Shiloh Baptist Church 1982-, treasurer 1987-; staff union negotiator US Army HQ FORSCOM Ft McPherson 1983. **HONORS/ACHIEVEMENTS:** Outstanding Award US Army 1973-75; Special Act US Army 1975; Letter from Pres Ford Cost Reduction US Army 1976; Outstanding Award US Army Pentagon 1980; Outstanding Award US Army Ft McPherson 1980; Outstanding Achievement US Army Ft McPherson 1983; Exceptional Performance, HQ FORSCOM, Ft McPherson GA 1986; Outstanding Chief Award Program & Budget Branch, HQ FORSCOM 1987. **MILITARY SERVICE:** USN stewards mate III 2 yrs. **HOME ADDRESS:** 5890 Riverdale Rd, Apt B 8, College Park, GA 30349. **BUSINESS ADDRESS:** Deputy Dir, Logistics Mgmt Div/Ch Mgmt Branch, US Army, HQ FORSCOM, Fort McPherson, GA 30330.

MCDANIEL, ELIAS BATES (BO DIDDLEY)
Musician. **PERSONAL:** Born Dec 30, 1928, McComb, MS. **CAREER:** Hits include Bo Diddley, I'm a Man, Diddley Daddy, Diddy Wah Diddy, Who Do You Love, Hey! Bo Diddley, Mona, Hush Your Mouth, Crackin' Up, Say Man, Road Runner,You Can't Judge a Book by the Cover.

MCDANIEL, ELIZABETH
Health service/educational administrator. **PERSONAL:** Born May 03, 1952, St Louis, MO; children: Paul. **EDUCATION:** Forest Park CC, BA Arts 1981. **CAREER:** Forest Park Admin Bldg, work study 1978; Forest Park Comm Coll, work study 1981, student asst 1982; Coalition for School Desegration, sec 1982; St Louis Comp N Health Center, secty/clerk 1982; Visiting Nurse Assn, billing clerk 1984; Wellston School Bd, vice pres; St Louis Univ Hosp, lead clerk 1986; St Louis Regional Physician's Billing, 1987. **HOME ADDRESS:** 6562 Jesse Jackson Ave, Hillside, MO 63121.

MCDANIEL, INEZ EUGENIA
Retired radiology student coordinator. **PERSONAL:** Born May 19, 1917, New York, NY; married Gordon L McDaniel; children: Eugenia L Brown, Sharon G Hollis, Rhonda L Tirfagnehu. **EDUCATION:** Hunter Coll, attended 1936-38; Manhattan Med Assts Sch, Certificate in X-ray technique 1948; Squibb Radioisotope Orientation Program 1971; Squibb Radioisotope Advanced Program, Certificate 1971. **CAREER:** St Agnes Hospital, staff tech, chief tech 1950-55; Phelps Memorial Hosp, staff tech 1955-57; Yonkers Professional Hosp, staff tech 1957; Doctors Duckworth, Huntington and Monteith, staff tech 1957-67; White Plains Hosp; sr technician 1967-72, student coord x-ray dept 1972-76 (retired). **ORGANIZATIONS:** Registry Amer Soc of X-ray Techs 1954; licensed NY State Dept of Health; charter mem, officer Westchester Soc of X-ray Techs; officer NY State Soc of X-ray Technologists 1975-76.

MCDANIEL, JAMES BERKLEY, JR.
Physician. **PERSONAL:** Born Aug 08, 1925, Pittsburgh, PA; widowed; children: James B III, Nancy Alben Lloyd. **EDUCATION:** HowardUniv Wash DC, BS 1950; Howard U, MD 1957. **CAREER:** Physician OB GYN, prv practice 1962; StateUniv of NY, asst clinical prof at Buffalo 1974. **HONORS/ACHIEVEMENTS:** First ach award Student Nat Med Assn & Buffalo 1972; ach award Buffalo Youth Bd. **MILITARY SERVICE:** USN musician 3/c 1944-46. **BUSINESS ADDRESS:** 50 High St, Buffalo, NY 14203.

MCDANIEL, MYRA ATWELL
Attorney. **PERSONAL:** Born Dec 13, 1932, Philadelphia, PA; daughter of Toronto C Atwell, Jr and Eva Yores Atwell; married Dr Reuben McDaniel Jr, Feb 02, 1955; children: Diane, Reuben III. **EDUCATION:** Univ of PA, English 1954; Univ of TX Law School, JD 1975. **CAREER:** Aviation Supply Office Philadelphia, mgmt analyst; Baldwin-Wallace Coll Berea OH, IN Univ Bloomington, admin asst jobs; Railrod Commiss of TX, asst spec counsel, asst atty gen in charge of taxation div; Gov Mark White, gen counsel; State of TX, sec of state 1984-87; Bickerstaff Heath & Smiley, atty 1987-. **ORGANIZATIONS:** Mem TX Bar Assoc, Amer Bar Assoc, Travis County Bar Assoc, Austin Black Laweyrs' Assoc, Travis County Women Lawyers' Assoc, Fellows of the TX Bar Found, Fellows of the Amer Bar Found; admitted to practice, State of TX, US Supreme Court, US Fifth Circuit Court of Appeals, US Dist Courts for the Eastern Western Southern & Northern Dist of TX; chmn atty sect Natl Assoc of Tax Admins 1980-81; mem Professional Efficiency & Econ Rsch 1978-84, Asset Mgmt Adv Comm State Treas 1984-86, Hobby-Lewis Joint Select Comm on Fiscal Policy 1984-86, Criminal Justice Policy Council State of TX 1984-86, Natl Assoc of Secretaries of State 1984-86; mem bd of dir Austin Consulting Group Inc 1983-86; mem bd trustees St Edward's Univ Austin 1986-88, TX Bar Found 1986-89, Episcopal Found of Houston TX 1986-90. **BUSINESS ADDRESS:** Attorney, Bickerstaff Heath & Smiley, 1800 San Jacinto Center, Austin, TX 78701.

MCDANIEL, PAUL ANDERSON
Clergyman. **PERSONAL:** Born Jul 05, 1930, Rock Hill, SC; married Edna Carolyn Phillips; children: Paul Jr, Pamela Anita, Patricia Ann, Peter Adam. **EDUCATION:** Morehouse Coll Atlanta, BA Hist Polit Sci 1951; Colgate Rochester Div Sch, MDiv 1955; Univ of Rochester, MA 1959. **CAREER:** Second Baptist Church Mumford, pastor 1952-56; Second Baptist Ch Rahway NJ, pastor 1956-66; Second Missionary Bapt Ch Chattanooga, pastor 1966-. **ORGANIZATIONS:** Former pres Clergy Assn of Greater Chattanooga; past pres TN Leadership Educ Congress; instr Natl Bapt Congress of Christian Educ; del TN Constitutional Conv 29th Dist Nashville 1977; chmn GA-TN Regional Health Commn 1978-80; chmn & past vice chmn Hamilton Co Commn Chattanooga 1979-. **HONORS/ACHIEVEMENTS:** DD Friendship Jr Coll Rock Hill SC 1975; various serv awds comm orgs. **BUSINESS ADDRESS:** Pastor, Second Missionary Baptist Ch, 2305 E Third St, Chattanooga, TN 37404.

MCDANIEL, REUBEN R.
Educator. **PERSONAL:** Born Jan 06, 1936, Petersburg, VA; son of Reuben R McDaniel and Nannie Finney McDaniel; married Myra Yores Atwell; children: Diane Castleberry, Reuben R III. **EDUCATION:** Drexel Univ, BMechEng 1964; Univ of Akron, MS Guidance Cnslng 1968; IN Univ, EdD Higher Educ 1971. **CAREER:** Baldwin-Wallace Clge, asst dean, asst prof educ, & dir div educ srv 1965-69; Indiana Univ, assoc instructor 1969-71; Florida State Univ, asst prof 1971-72; Univ of Texas at Austin, Jesse H Jones prof 1983-. **ORGANIZATIONS:** Acting deputy commnr Texas Dept of Human Resources 1979; consultant Seton Medical Center Austin 1980-; bd of trustees Seton Medical Ctr Austin 1985-; Priority Schools Comm, Austin Ind School District 1989-; Advisory Comm, Banaker Honors Coll, Prairie View A&M Univ 1987-. **HONORS/ACHIEVEMENTS:** J D Beasley Grad Teaching Awd UT Austin 1982; Jesse H Jones Professorship Grad Schl Business Univ TX at Austin 1983-; chmn Faculty Senate Univ of Texas at Austin 1985-87. **HOME ADDRESS:** 3910 Knollwood Dr, Austin, TX 78731. **BUSINESS ADDRESS:** Professor of Management, Univ of TX at Austin, Dept of Management CBA 4246, Austin, TX 78712.

MCDANIEL, WILLIAM T., JR.
Educator. **PERSONAL:** Born Sep 24, 1945, Memphis, TN; married Bernice Dowdy; children: William Theodore III. **EDUCATION:** Morehouse Coll, BA 1967;Univ IA, MA 1968, PhD 1974. **CAREER:** School of Music, OH State U, prof; NC A&T State U, prof, chmn dept of music; Morehouse Coll, dir of bands 1968-72, chmn dept of Music, dir of bands 1974-77;Univ IA, instr blk music 1973-74. **ORGANIZATIONS:** Mem Mus Edtrs Nat Conf; Am Musclgcl Soc; Coll Mus Soc; Coll Band Dir Nat Assn; Nat Assn Coll Wind & Percsn Instrs;

Nat Band Assn; mem Alpha Phi Alpha. **HONORS/ACHIEVEMENTS:** Advncd Study Felwshp for Black Ams, Ford Found 1972-73; IBM Fclty Flwshp, Untd Negro Coll Fund 1972-73; grant, Nat Endowmt for Arts 1972; Nat Flwshp, Ford Found 1973-74. **BUSINESS ADDRESS:** Professor, School of Music, Ohio State University, Room 313A, 1899 College Road, Columbus, OH 43210.

MCDANIELS, ALFRED F.
Head track and field coach, asst prof of physical education. **PERSONAL:** Born Sep 21, 1940, Muskogee, OK; son of Alvin McDaniels; married Cheryl McDaniels Kieser, Jun 11, 1971; children: Alfred Jr, Debbie. **EDUCATION:** Bakersfield Jr Coll, AA 1961; Univ of NV, Reno, B.S., 1965; Univ of NV, Las Vegas M.E.D., 1971; Univ of NV, BS 1965, MEduc, 1972. **CAREER:** PE Health Educ, tchr 1965-70; Varsity Football, asst varsity head jr varsity asst track coach, 1965-67; Merced HS, head track coach 1968-70; Univ of NV, asst football coach 1970-72, asst track coach 1971-74, asst prof phys educ head track coach. **ORGANIZATIONS:** Mem NEA, NSEA, NAHPER, AAHPER; United Tching Profsn; US Track & Field Coaches Assn; organized developed summer track & field prog for youths & adults 1971-75 (has more than 600 participants each summer). **HONORS/ACHIEVEMENTS:** Most Outstanding Sr Athlete Univ of NV Reno 1965; Most Outstanding in Track 1963; Most Outstanding in Football 1964; 1984 Women's PCAA Team Champion Track & Field; 1984-86, 1989 Women's PCAA Coach of the Yr Track & Field, 1984-86, 1989; big west coach of year, PCAA 1989; Outstanding Athlete, Bakersfield H.S., 1960, Bakersfield Coll, 1959, Univ of NV, 1965; publication in athletic journals, speaker at numerous clinics. **BUSINESS ADDRESS:** Head Track Coach, Univ of NV, 4505 Maryland Pkwy, Las Vegas, NV 89154.

MCDANIELS, JOHN EDWARD, SR.
Educational administrator. **PERSONAL:** Born Feb 23, 1921, Monmouth, IL; son of John Martin McDaniels and Helen Lucas McDaniels; married Margaret Currie; children: Charles Patterson, Erma Patterson, Sarah, Thomas, Capt Jeffrey, John E Jr. **EDUCATION:** Armed Forces Staff Coll, diploma 1968; Hampton Inst, BS History 1970; US Army Ware Coll, diploma 1974; Central MI Univ, MA Admin 1976. **CAREER:** US Army, col 36 yrs; Fayetteville Tech Inst, admin asst to pres, vice pres for personnel. **ORGANIZATIONS:** Post commander Ft Lesley J McNair 1972-76; vice pres Joe Barr United Serv Organ 1978-79; mem Omega Psi Phi Frat Inc Beta Chi Chap 1980; SERTOMA International 1989. **MILITARY SERVICE:** AUS col field artillery 36 yrs; Legion of Merit; Bronze Star; various combat and serv awds. **BUSINESS ADDRESS:** Vice President for Personnel, Fayetteville Technical Inst, PO Box 35236, Fayetteville, NC 28303.

MCDANIELS, ORRIN HUNTER
Business executive. **PERSONAL:** Born Feb 05, 1939, Washington, DC; married Rosemary Felitto; children: Nikki Allison, Sean Kedrick, Rikki Michele, Jeniffer Erin, Thomas Joseph. **EDUCATION:** Univ Chicago, BS 1960; UCLA, MBA Grad Sch 1963; USC, 1964. **CAREER:** WTOP Radio 15, vice pres gen mar post newsweek stas; WTOP Radio, gen sales mgr 1975-77; KYW Radio, sales mgr Philadelphia 1972-75; ALL News Spec NY Radio, adv rep 1970-72; KFWB Radio LA, acct exec 1967-70; 3M Co LA, mgr 1965-67; IBM LA, mgr 1962-65. **ORGANIZATIONS:** Bd dir Washington Ad Club; Washington Area Broadcasters Assn; Washington Media Research Council; consultant Lincoln Univ 1972-74; pres Quail Valley Home Owners Assn 1976-78; Washington Bd of Trade; bd dir Victoria Manor Home Owners Assn 1975-76; Kappa Alpha Psi. **HONORS/ACHIEVEMENTS:** Youth of Year Chicago Bd of Educ 1956; Youth of Year Chicago Metro YMCA 1957; Outstanding Serv Award Kappa Alpha Psi 1967. **BUSINESS ADDRESS:** 4001 Brandywine St, Washington, DC 20016.

MCDONALD, ALDEN J., JR.
Banking executive. **CAREER:** Liberty Bank and Trust Company, New Orleans, LA, president, 1972-. **BUSINESS ADDRESS:** Liberty Bank and Trust Company, 3939 Tulane Ave, New Orleans, LA 70119. *

MCDONALD, ANITA DUNLOP
Psychologist. **PERSONAL:** Born May 11, 1929, Morgantown, WV; married James J McDonald; children: Janice M Phillips. **EDUCATION:** WV State Coll, BA 1951; WV Univ, MSW 1953. **CAREER:** Syracuse Memorial Hosp, med soc worker 1954-56; Family Serv of Jamestown, social worker 1975-79; Chautauqua Co Mental Health-Jamestown, psychiatric socialworker 1980-. **ORGANIZATIONS:** Mem AAUW Jamestown Branch 1968-; sec bd of trustees Jamestown Comm Coll 1969-78; pres Bd of Dirs of YWCA 1973-75; chmn public affairs bd of dirs YWCA 1984-; Sunday sch tchr Emmanual Bapt Ch; financial sec & mem trustee bd Emmanuel Bapt Church. **HOME ADDRESS:** 40 W 22nd St, Jamestown, NY 14701. **BUSINESS ADDRESS:** Psychiatric Social Worker, Chautauqua Cnty Mntl Hlth, Jones Hill Professional Bldg, Jamestown, NY 14701.

MCDONALD, BERNARD
Foundation executive. **PERSONAL:** Born Feb 25, 1942, Brooklyn, NY; married Clara Marie Francis. **EDUCATION:** Hunter Coll, BA of Econ 1964; Brooklyn Coll, MA educ 1968. **CAREER:** Ford Found, program officer 1978; Bedford Stuyvesant Restor Corp, vice pres 1969-78; Manpwr Dev Train Prog, 1966-69; NY City Pub Sch Syst, 1964-66. **ORGANIZATIONS:** Pres Brooklyn Mang Club 1976-78; bd of dir ARC Geater NY Brooklyn Chap 1977; bd of dir Assn of Black Found Exec 1979; mem Comm Bd Three Brooklyn; bd of dir Magnolia Tree Earth Center Inc 1977; bd of dir Vanguard Urban Improvement Assn Inc 1977; mem Mayor's Adv Bd New York City Dept of Juvnl Justice 1979; dir Nat Cong for Comm Econ Dev 1976; Counc for Urban Econ Dev 1975-76. **BUSINESS ADDRESS:** 320 E 43rd St, New York, NY 10017.

MCDONALD, CHARLES J.
Physician, educator. **PERSONAL:** Born Dec 06, 1931, Tampa, FL; married Maureen McDonald; children: Marc, Norman, Eric. **EDUCATION:** NC A&T Univ, BS (Distinction) 1951; Univ of MI, MS 1952; Howard Univ, MD (Highest Distinction) 1960; Brown Univ, MS (Honorary) 1970. **CAREER:** Hosp of St Raphael New Haven, intern 1960-61, asst resident in med 1961-63; Yale Univ School of Med, asst resident 1963-65; US Public Health Serv, Special Rsch, Yale Univ School of Med, fellow & chief resident 1965-66; Yale Univ School of Med, Yale-New Haven Med Ctr, instr, assoc physician 1966-67, asst prof, asst attending physician 1967-68; Brown Univ Providence RI, asst prof 1968-69, assoc prof 1969-74; Roger-Williams Gen Hosp head dermatology, assoc chief of med 1968; Brown Univ, dermatology prog dir 1970, prof of med sci, head subsect dermatology 1974-. **ORGANIZATIONS:** Mem Amer Dermatology Assn, New England Dermatology Soc, Soc for Investigative Dermatology, Amer Fed for Clinical Rsch, Amer Acad of Dermatology, Natl Med Assn; chmn Sect of Dermatology 1973-75, AAAS, RI Dermatology Soc, Noah Worcester Dermatology Soc, Amer Soc for Clinical Oncology, Dermatology Found, Pan Amer Med Assn; mem Dermatology Coun, Assoc of Profs of Dermatology; consult Natl Inst of Arthritis Metabolism & Digestive Diseases; consult RI State Dept of Health; consult Providence Health Ctrs Inc; former chmn Health Task Force, RI Urban Coalition; former mem comm Governors Conf on Health Care Cost; mem bd dir, vice pres, pres elect RI Div Amer Cancer Soc; mem bd of trustees Citizens Bank Providence RI; mem bd dirs Natl Amer Cancer Soc; vice pres and pres New England Dermatology Soc 1983-85; mem bd dirs Amer Acad Dermatology 1986-. **HONORS/ACHIEVEMENTS:** Highest Academic Achievement Awd Coll of Medicine Howard; 1st Annual Distinguished Serv Award Hosp Assoc of RI; Distinguished Alumni Award Coll of Medicine Howard Univ 1983; author, co-author of approx 100 sci articles. **MILITARY SERVICE:** USAF mjr 4 yrs. **BUSINESS ADDRESS:** Department of Medicine, Roger Williams General Hospital/Brown University, 825 Chalkstone Ave, Providence, RI 02908.

MCDONALD, CURTIS W.
Educator. **PERSONAL:** Born Jan 29, 1934, Cedar Creek, TX. **EDUCATION:** Huston Tillotson Coll Austin, BS 1955; TX îSrthrn Univ, MS 1957; Univ TX, PhD 1962. **CAREER:** Alcorn A&M Coll Lorman MS, tchr 1961-63; AL State Univ Montgomery, 1963-68; Southern Univ Baton Rouge, 1968-73; TX Southern Univ Houston 1973-. **ORGANIZATIONS:** Mem Amer Chem Soc; Natl Inst Sci; Soc Applied Spectscpy; Soc Sigma Xi; LA Acad of Sci; Amer Inst Chemists. **HONORS/ACHIEVEMENTS:** Publications in Anal Chem 1964, 1967, 1969, 1973, 1974; Mikrochim 1970, 1972, 1974. **BUSINESS ADDRESS:** TX SouthernUniv, PO Box 35, Houston, TX 77004.

MCDONALD, EDMUND MORRIS
Dentist. **PERSONAL:** Born Sep 30, 1917, Sumter, SC; son of Samuel J McDonald and Adelaide Palmer McDonald; married Anna Louise Birnie; children: Edmund, Jr. **EDUCATION:** Benedict Coll, BS 1938; Colum Univ, MA 1941; Meharry Med Coll, DDS 1948. **CAREER:** Howard HS, teacher & coach 1938-39; Booker Washington HS, teacher & asst coach 1941-44; McDonald and McDonald, dentist 1984-, private practice since 1948. **ORGANIZATIONS:** Mem Pee Dee Dental Soc; mem SC Dent Assn; relief comm SC Dental Assn; mem Amer Dental Assn; Congaree Denta; Soc; Palmetto Med Dent & Pharmac Assn; pres Palmetto Med Dental & Pharmacy Assn 1971; mem Natl Dental Assn; House of Delegates Natl Dental Assn 1970-; mem Omega Psi Phi Frat; chmn life mem Comm NAACP; mem adv bd Pee Dee Boy Scouts; steward trustee Emmanuel United Methodist Church; captain Benedict Coll Football Team 1937. **HONORS/ACHIEVEMENTS:** 1st Benedict Coll football player to make Little All-Amer 1st team 1937; Dental Facility Honor Med Meharry Med Coll 1948; mem Omicron Kappa Upsilon Hon Fraternity; mem Kappa Sigma Pi Hon Fraternity; elected to Benedict Coll Athletic Hall of Fame 1982; elected to Sumter SC Athletic Hall of Fame 1984. **BUSINESS ADDRESS:** 7 W Liberty St, PO Box 368, Sumter, SC 29150.

MCDONALD, GABRIELLE K.
Judge. **PERSONAL:** Born Apr 12, 1942, St Paul, MN; married Mark T McDonald; children: Michael, Stacy. **EDUCATION:** Howard Univ, LLB 1966. **CAREER:** Legal Def Fund NYC, staff attny 1966-69; McDonald & McDonald Houston, partner 1969-79; TX So Univ Houston, asst prof 1970, adj prof 1975-77; Univ of TX Houston, lectr 1977-78; US Dist Court Houston, judge 1979-. **ORGANIZATIONS:** Bd dir Commun Serv Option Prog, Alley Theatre Houston, Natl Coalition of 100 Black Women, ARC; trustee Howard Univ 1983-; bd visitors Thurgood Marshall School of Law Houston; mem ABA, Natl Bar Assoc, Houston Bar Assoc, Houston Lawyers Assoc, Black Women Lawyers Assoc. **BUSINESS ADDRESS:** Judge, US District Court, 515 Rusk Ave, PO Box 61266, Houston, TX 77208.

MCDONALD, HERBERT G.
Architect. **PERSONAL:** Born Feb 11, 1929, Jamaica, NY; son of Herbert C McDonald and Priscilla A Young McDonald; married Debra H; children: Gail Louise, Cathy Allison. **EDUCATION:** Howard Univ, BArch 1953. **CAREER:** Gitlin & Cantor Architects, Wash DC, assoc 1959-60; Edwin Weihe, architect 1960-62; Herbert G McDonald & Assoc, architect 1962-65; McDonald & Williams AIA, architect, partner 1965-. **ORGANIZATIONS:** Dir, Lawrence Johnson Assoc, Wash DC; vice pres, dir, Barkingside Devel Inc, Bahamas; dir, sec, Davis Const Co; adv, Independence Federal Savings & Loan, Wash DC; mem, Amer Inst of Archit; mem, DC Council of Black Archit; mem, Aircraft Owners & Pilots Assn; mem, Omega Psi Phi Archit Clifton Terrace Apts, 1969; DC Correctional Detention Facility, 1974; archit NECIP 1977, Lincoln Westmoreland Apts 1972; mem, DC Legislative Comm on Housing; dir, Natl Housing Rehab Assoc; vice pres, dir, CEO, H Bear Enterprises Inc. **MILITARY SERVICE:** Corps of Engrs 1st lt 1954-56. **BUSINESS ADDRESS:** Architect, McDonald & Williams AIA, 7705 Georgia Ave, NW, Washington, DC 20012.

MCDONALD, JON FRANKLIN
Educator. **PERSONAL:** Born Jun 28, 1946, Jackson, MS; married Mary Ann Davies; children: Gabriel Charles, Beau Richards. **EDUCATION:** Kendall School of Design, Certificate 1969; San Francisco Art Inst, M Fine Arts 1972. **CAREER:** Spungbuggy Works, asst animator 1974-75; Everywomans Village, teacher 1977-79. **ORGANIZATIONS:** Visual arts advisor Frauenthal Center of Performing Arts/Muskegon MI 1986-89; comm mem Mayor's Advisory Comm on Art/Grand Rapids 1989-90; artist-in-residence Grand Haven Public Schools 1989-90. **HONORS/ACHIEVEMENTS:** Ellen Hart Bransten Scholarship San Francisco Art Inst 1970-72; Moscow/Manhatten Connection, 48 paintings will travel in USSR & USA 1989-91. **BUSINESS ADDRESS:** Assoc Prof Visual Communication, Kendall School of Design, 111 Division Ave N, Grand Rapids, MI 49503.

MCDONALD, MARK T.
Attorney. **PERSONAL:** Born Jun 20, 1935, Henderson, TX; married Babrielle Kirk; children: Mark T, Jr, Micheal K, Stacy Frances. **EDUCATION:** Prairie View A&M Coll, BA hon 1956; TX So U, LlB 1962. **CAREER:** McDonald & McDonald Atty at Law, atty 1962; Legal Serv Div OEO, consult 1965; TX So U, asst prof law 1964-70; Prarie View A&M Coll, asso prof Polit sci 1963-64. **ORGANIZATIONS:** Mem State Bar of TX; Am Bar Assn; Assn of Trial Lawyers of Am; NatL Bar Assn; Am Judicature Soc; Natl Assn of Criminal Def Attys; TX Trial Lawyers Assn; Houston Bar Assn; Houston Trial Lawyers Assn;

NAACP; Houston Bus & Professional Men's Club; ACLU of Houston; YMCA Century Club. **BUSINESS ADDRESS:** 1834 Southmore Blvd, Houston, TX 77004.

MCDONALD, R. TIMOTHY
Educational administrator. **PERSONAL:** Born Sep 29, 1940, Pittsburgh, PA; married Beverly Clark; children: Lawana, Monica, Lanita, Patrick. **EDUCATION:** Oakwood Coll, BS 1963; Atlanta Univ, MS 1968; Univ of Miami, EdD 1972. **CAREER:** AL A&M Univ, prof of educ 1972-78; Oakwood Coll, vice pres for develop 1975-78; Barber Scotia Coll, vice pres for academic affairs 1978-79; OH State Univ, develop officer 1979-83; Seventh-day Adventist Church, dir of educ 1983-. **ORGANIZATIONS:** Bd mem Columbus Mental Health Assn 1980-83; consultant Higher Educ Assns 1975-; proposal writer-reader Fed Govt 1975-; bdmem Columbia Union Coll 1983-. **HONORS/ACHIEVEMENTS:** Higher Educ Fellowship Fed Govt 1969-72; Title III Grant Fed Govt 1972-78; Spec Serv Awd OH State Univ 1981. **HOME ADDRESS:** 10516 E Wind Way, Columbia, MD 21044. **BUSINESS ADDRESS:** Dir of Education, Mid-Atlantic Region SDA Church, 5427 Twin Knolls Rd, Columbia, MD 21045.

MCDONALD, RICHARD E.
Attorney. **PERSONAL:** Born Jun 10, 1929, Pontiac, MI; married Edith W O'Neil; children: 7 Children. **EDUCATION:** Flint Jr Coll MI, AA 1955; Wayne State U, BS 1957; Wayne State U, MS 1957; UCLA Schl of Law, JD 1967. **CAREER:** Detroit City Schs, part & full-time tchr 1956-59; Compton Union HS 1959-65; Compton Coll, evening instructor 1961-65; Atty, 1968. **ORGANIZATIONS:** Mem Genesee Co Bar Assn; Nat Bar Asn; Am Bar Assn; Nat Judicature Soc; Am Trial Lawyers Assn; mem Pi Omega Pi Honor Soc; Nat Urban League; NAACP. **HONORS/ACHIEVEMENTS:** 15 publications in the law field; recip Hnrbl Mntn Flint Poetry Forum MI 1956; WayneUniv Alumni Scholarship 1955-57; Smead Manu Co Award, most outstndg Bsns Stdnt 1957; Detroit Bsns Tchrs Assn, most outstndg Stdnt 1957; Rsrc Sprkr CA Bsns Educ Assn Conf CA 1964-65; Arleo Corp, Main Speaker 1965; guest speaker, Unit Y Credit Union 1965; curriculum chmn Bsns Educ Compton Union HS Dist 1965-66. **MILITARY SERVICE:** USMC 1952-54; attended yeoman B sch US & naval training cntr 1952. **BUSINESS ADDRESS:** 2503 Detroit St, Flint, MI.

MCDONALD, TIMOTHY, III
Clergyman. **PERSONAL:** Born Jun 17, 1954, Brunswick, GA; married Shirley Ann Neal; children: Nikisha Lynette. **EDUCATION:** Berry Coll, BA 1975; EmoryUniv Candler Schl of Theology, MDiv 1978. **CAREER:** Ebenezer Bapt Ch, asst pastor 1978; Shiloh Bapt Ch Dalton GA, pastor 1976-78; EmoryUniv Candler Schlk of Theology, supr on faculty 1979; Interdenominational Theol Center, supr on faculty 1979. **ORGANIZATIONS:** Chmn State Wide Pub Assistance Coalition 1979; bd mem Atlanta Chap Nat Assn Of Black Social Workers 1979; sec of exec com Urban Training Orgn of Atlanta 1979. **HONORS/ACHIEVEMENTS:** Who's Who in Am Coll &Univ Berry & Emory 1975 & 78; fellow Fund for Theol Educ 1976-78; outstanding young men of Am OYMA Inc 1978; Cluade Thompson Award for Social Justice EmoryUniv 1978. **BUSINESS ADDRESS:** Dir Operation Breadbasket, SCLC, 334 Auburn Ave, Atlanta, GA 30312.

MCDONALD, WILLIAM EMORY
Engineer. **PERSONAL:** Born Mar 09, 1924, Detroit, MI; son of Emory S McDonald and Willie Mae Burrell McDonald; married widowed (deceased); children: Varnell, William, Jeannette. **EDUCATION:** Univ of Michigan, BS 1950. **CAREER:** Public Lighting Comm, jr engineer 1950-54; Detroit Arsenal, electronic scientist 1954-57; Farrara Inc, chief project engineer 1957-58; Chrysler Missile, design engineer 1958-59; Rockwell Intl, sr project engineer 1959-72; North Carolina Central Univ, physical plant dir 1972-. **ORGANIZATIONS:** Pres bd Urban Ministries 1970-71; Alpha Phi Alpha Fraternity; sec, treasurer, 1st black officer Southeastern Reg Assoc of Physical Plant Admin; treasurer Assn of Physical Admin (APPA) 1989-91; secretary/treasurer, South Eastern Reg APPA 1980-89; mem bd of Adjustment, City of Durham, NC 1981-; mem NC Synod, Evangelical Lutheran Church in Amer 1988-;. **HONORS/ACHIEVEMENTS:** Meritorious Serv Award SE Reg Assn of Physical Plant Admin 1987. **MILITARY SERVICE:** USAAF 1944-46. **BUSINESS ADDRESS:** Physical Plant Dir, North Carolina CentralUniv, Box 19735, Durham, NC 27707.

MCDONALD, WILLIE RUTH DAVIS
Educator. **PERSONAL:** Born Nov 04, 1931, San Antonio, TX; married Freeman; children: Ava Yvonne, Arva Yvotte. **EDUCATION:** Wiley Coll, BS 1952; TS U, MEd 1964. **CAREER:** Bonham Schl, elemen tchr 1954-77. **ORGANIZATIONS:** Dir SW Houston Tchrs Assn 1977-78; leg comm mem HTA; bd mem House of Bees Halfway House; vP Nat Council of Negro Women; mem Nat Conf of Christians & Jews; com mem Special Events for Senatorial Dist 7; asst coord Precinct Club 240; adv cncl bd mem Eliza D Johnson Home for the Aged; com mem Conf on Minority Concerns; com mem Human Relation for HISD; nom com Moderate Dem Orgn; group com Transportation for the Mayor of Housing & Citizens of Dist 19 1972-77; exec bd mem HTA 1976-78; polt educ comm Dist 4 TSTA 1976-78; Fac Rep HTA 1972-77. **BUSINESS ADDRESS:** 4815 Ligonberry, Houston, TX 77033.

MCDOWELL, BENJAMIN A.
Dentist. **PERSONAL:** Born Apr 12, 1939, Laurens, SC; married Bobbie Green; children: Robyn, Joy, Mark. **EDUCATION:** Morehouse Coll, BS 1960; Howard U, DDS 1965. **CAREER:** VA Hosp Tuskeegee, intern 1965-66; Pvt Practice, dentist. **ORGANIZATIONS:** Mem Nat Dental Assn; AL Dental Soc; Jefferson Co Dental Study Club; mem NAACP; Bessemer Cit Com; Assn Wmn's & Clubs Adv Bd; bd mem AG Gaston Boys Club of Am 1975-76. **BUSINESS ADDRESS:** 1931 Carolina Ave, Bessemer, AL 35020.

MCDOWELL, CLEVE
Attorney, judge. **PERSONAL:** Born Aug 06, 1941, Drew, MS; son of Mr & Mrs Fudge McDowell. **EDUCATION:** Jackson State Univ, 1963; Univ of Mississippi Law School, 1963; Texas Southern Univ Law School, JD. **CAREER:** Cook County Dept of Public Aid, staff consultant 1965-69; Coahoma Opportunity Inc, personnel dir 1969; Mississippi Head Start Training Coord Council, exec dir 1969-73; State of Mississippi, head start coord 1973-74; Mississippi Bar Legal Serv, assoc dir 1974-75; private practice, attny 1975-77; Clarksdale Office of Northern Mississippi Rural Legal Serv, managing atty 1977-79; Tunica County, judge; State Exec Field Dir of Mississippi NAACP 1985-87; Vice Mayor City of Drew MS 1986-. **ORGANIZATIONS:** Mem NAACP; former pres Delta Phi Chap Alpha Phi Alpha; mem Mississippi State Penitentiary Bd of Dir 1971-76. **HONORS/ACHIEVEMENTS:** Listed in Who's Who in Amer Colleges & Univ, Outstanding Young Men of Amer 1972. **BUSINESS ADDRESS:** Attorney-at-Law, Box 223, Drew, MS 38737.

MCDOWELL, EDWARD HOMER, JR.
Clergyman. **PERSONAL:** Born Jan 24, 1949, Greenville, SC; married Rhonda Jackson; children: Edward III, Timothy Isaiah, Erin Renee. **EDUCATION:** Claflin Coll, BA 1971; Gammon Theological Seminary, M Divinity 1974. **ORGANIZATIONS:** Mem Omega Psi Phi; church growth consult SC Conference 1980; bd mem Columbia Coll Advisory Council 1984, Adivosry Council Clinical Pastoral Educ 1985, Greater Columbia Literacy Council 1985. **HONORS/ACHIEVEMENTS:** Disting Serv Awd Interdenominational 1976; Outstanding Young Man Awd 1980; Disting Alumnus Awd Gammon Theol Seminary 1985. **BUSINESS ADDRESS:** Francis Burns Untd Meth Church, 5709 Ames Rd, Columbia, SC 29203.

MCDOWELL-HEAD, LELIA M.
Journalist. **PERSONAL:** Born Jun 07, 1953, San Francisco, CA; daughter of Steven Helmut Heims and Elenita McDowell; married Anthony Head, Dec 30, 1980; children: Layla. **EDUCATION:** New York Univ, New York NY, BFA, 1975. **CAREER:** Fenton Communications, Washington DC, senior account exec; WPIX TV, New York NY, reporter; WBLS-WLIB Radio, New York NY, reporter anchor; WHTM TV, Harrisburg PA, reporter; Natl Alliance of Third World Journalists, Washington DC, natl co-coordinator, 1989. **BUSINESS ADDRESS:** National Co-Coordinator, National Alliance of Third World Journalists, PO Box 43208, 1419 V St NW, Washington, DC 20010.

MCDUFFIE, HINFRED
Educational administrator. **PERSONAL:** Born Aug 08, 1949, Montgomery, AL; children: Paula, Barry, Toka. **EDUCATION:** Tuskegee Inst, BS 1971; Alabama State Univ, MS 1982, MS 1986. **CAREER:** Tuskegee Inst, assoc dir 1971-72, dir 1972-77; Alabama State Univ, dir of planning 1977-83, dir title III & planning 1983-. **ORGANIZATIONS:** Bd of dirs Montgomery Co Comm Action Agency; mem Election Law Commr State of Alabama, Kappa Alpha Psi Fraternity, Kappa Delta Phi Honor Soc in Educ, Soc for Coll & Univ Planning. **BUSINESS ADDRESS:** Dir, Alabama State University, 915 S Jackson St, Montgomery, AL 36195.

MCDUFFIE, JOSEPH DELEON, JR.
Certified public accountant. **PERSONAL:** Born Nov 09, 1950, St George, SC; son of Joseph McDuffie and Ernestine McDuffie. **EDUCATION:** SC State Coll, BSBA 1972; Columbia Univ, MBA 1974. **CAREER:** Touche Ross & Co, CPA 1974-77; CBS Inc, financial exec mergers & acquisitions 1977-79; SC State Coll, asst prof 1979-81; J deLeon McDuffie & Co, CPA 1979-; McDuffie Bros Inc, Registered Investment Advisors, 1989-. **ORGANIZATIONS:** Bd mem Eushua Arts Found 1983-; life mem Kappa Alpha Psi 1971-; mem Amer Inst of CPA's 1975-; sec asst, exec sec 1st Natl City Bank 1969; exec sec mgmt trne Amer Bank & Trust Co 1970-72; consulting Financial Pkg Corp 1973; IBM opr Ebasco Nuclear Engrg 1973; student advisor, consulting Lt Gov SC; mem SC State Student Leg; mayors comm Human Devel; bd dir SC State Coll Devel Fund; bd trustee SC State Coll; mem Kappa Alpha Psi; mem SC State Coll Alumni Assoc, SC State Coll Founders Club, SC State Coll Career Consultant, Columbia Univ Alumni Assoc of Business School, Columbia Univ Alumni Career Consult Assoc; vol Big Bros of NY Inc, Canaan Baptist Church; mem Amer Inst CPA, Natl Assoc Black Acct, Natl Soc Public Acct, NY State Soc CPA's; council Concerned Black Exec. **HONORS/ACHIEVEMENTS:** 100 Black Men of NY City IN; Provincial Achievement Awd Kappa Alpha Psi 1972.

MCEACHERN, KATHERINE VERDELL MCNEILL
Educator. **PERSONAL:** Born Oct 31, 1930, Rowland, NC; divorced. **EDUCATION:** St Teachers Coll, BS; IGY Conf Sci Found Grt, MS; Jersey City St; Temple Univ. **CAREER:** Pleasantville Bd of Educ, teacher; Proctorville, teacher athletic act 1950-56; R B Dean HS, adult sch tchr 1949-50; Pleasantville Educ Assn, sec 1957-58, pres 1973-74, vice pres 1974—75, pres 1975-77; Human Rights Atlantic Co Coun Educ Assn, chmn 1972-73; At Co Coun Educ Assn, parliamentarin 1974-; At Co Coun of Educ Assn, sec vice pres 1976-78; NJ Educ Assn, alt da 1975-77; NJ Educ Assn, da 1977-79; NEA Conv Hosp, chm 1973; Resol Comm, alt 1976-77; NEA Women's Caucus; NEA Blk Caucus. **ORGANIZATIONS:** Mem Oper PUSH; Nat Dem Club; Cancer Soc; pres Nat Sor Phi Delta Kappa Inc 1964-66 67-73; dir Eastern Reg 1971-75; natl dir Pub Rel 1975-79; staging dir Iota's Cotillion 12 Yrs; Atlantic Human Res Educ Coun 1963-67; pres Floral Soc of Sec Bapt Ch 6 Yrs; Choir Chaplan 4 Yrs; Hostess Club 1968-; prgm chrpsn Bible Sch Tchr 1959-67. **HONORS/ACHIEVEMENTS:** Tchr of the Mo Pleasantville Educ Assn 1968; Cert of Apprec Am Auto Assn 1964; Four Chaplains Legions of Hon Mem 1970; Cert of Apprec Alpha Mu Chap of Nat Sor of Phi Delta Kappa Inc 1972; Cert of Apprec Nat For Bldg Prog 1973; Nat Sor of Phi Delta Kappa Inc 1974; Outst Serv Rendered Iota Chpt. **BUSINESS ADDRESS:** 708 Maple Ct, Pleasantville, NJ 08232.

MCEACHERN, MACEO R.
Funeral director. **PERSONAL:** Born Nov 06, 1946, Pinehurst, NC; children: John. **EDUCATION:** NC Central U, BS 1968;Univ Cincinnati Sch Mortuary Sci, grad 1970. **CAREER:** McEachern Funeral Home, mortician, funeral dir 1971-; Campron Morrison Sch Hoffman, NC, tchr, coach 1971; Cincinnati Pub Schs, sub tchr 1970-71; YMCA Cincinnati, swimming instr 1969-71. **ORGANIZATIONS:** Mem Jaycees; bd dirs McLaurin Voc Training Cntr 1972-74; Richmond Co Sch Bd (1st black since Reconstruction); bd tr Richmond Meml Hosp 1975-; reg rep NC Med Emerg Serv Adv Commn 1974-; Richmond Co Indsl Devel Team 1975-; St Stephen's AME Zion Ch; Mason; Nat & State Sch Bd Assns 1972-; Nat & NC Embalmers & Fun Dirs Assn 1971-; Pi Sigma Eta; mem Appaloosa Horse Club 1975-; NC & Tarheel Appaloosa Assns 1975-. **HONORS/ACHIEVEMENTS:** NC Jaycee's Speak-Up Award 1971. **BUSINESS ADDRESS:** McEachern Funeral Home, 210 E Hamlet Ave, Hamlet, NC 28345.

MCEACHERN-ULMER, SYLVIA L.
Government official. **PERSONAL:** Born Mar 24, 1934, New York, NY; married Joseph Ulmer; children: Patricia McEachern, Brian McEachern. **EDUCATION:** Rutgers Extension School, certified as Registered Municipal Clerk, 1973-77. **CAREER:** Bd of Educ Passaic Co Voc & Tech Schl, commissioner 1980-, pres 1986-87. **ORGANIZATIONS:** Pres Passaic Co Municipal Clerk's Assc 1984; mem NJ State Muncipal Clerk's Assc 1972-; Intl

Municipal Clerk's Assc 1980-; Natl Black Caucus Schl Bd 1980-; vice pres NJ Cty Voc Schl Bd 1984-, pres 1986-87. **HONORS/ACHIEVEMENTS:** Honored Mother Women Active in Comm Affairs 1983; Salute to Blk Men & Women spec award Comm for Black History Month 1984; Christian Srv Award Calvary Baptist Church 1983, Canaan Baptist Church 1983; plaques from various comm grps; Testimonial Dinner 1975. **BUSINESS ADDRESS:** City Clerk, City of Paterson, City Hall, 155 Market St, Paterson, NJ 07505.

MCEACHIN, JAMES
Actor. **PERSONAL:** Born May 20, 1930, Rennert, NC; married Lois Davis; children: Alainia, Lyle. **CAREER:** Appeared in over 100 TV Prodns Including The FBI, Mannix, HI Five-O, Marcus Welby MD, That Certain Summer, actor 1965-; Tenafly Features McKnight ,PlayMisty For Me, Buck & The Preacher, Fuzz, Starred in; Universal Studios, actor writer dir 1969-. **HONORS/ACHIEVEMENTS:** Recipient Purple Heart. **MILITARY SERVICE:** AUS 1947-53. **BUSINESS ADDRESS:** PO Box 5166, Sherman Oaks, CA 91403.

MCELROY, ALFRED Z.
Business executive. **PERSONAL:** Born Mar 05, 1930, Sour Lake, TX; married Charlotte K; children: Alfred II, Austin, Arthur, Andrew, Anita, Adanna. **EDUCATION:** Wiley Coll Marshall TX, BS 1953; WA State Univ Pullman WA, MS 1956. **CAREER:** Lincoln HS Port Arthur TX, physical educ tchr 1956-62; Lincoln HS, head coach & athletic dir 1963-65; Nat Western Life Ins Co, presently div sales dir & salesman; Natl Western Life Ins Co, div sales dir 1965-; McElroy's Insurance Agency, owner, mgr. **ORGANIZATIONS:** Mem S Jeff Co Assn of Life Underwriters; president's club Natl Western Life Ins Co 1974; bd of trust, pres 1968-69,74-75,81-82, sec 198586, vice pres 1986-87 Port Arthur Independent School Dist; mem Natl Adv Council on Equality of Educ Oppty 1976-79; mem 1982-, sec 1984,85, pres 1986- Jefferson County Tax Appraisal Dist Bd; re-elected to PAISD Bd of Trust 1983,86. **HONORS/ACHIEVEMENTS:** Papal Award; 1970 Edition Outstanding Personalities of the S; Silver Beaver Award 1971; Contributing Editor Who's Who Among HS Students 1973-74; Five Year Quilifier Nat Sales Achievement Award; One Yr Qualifier TX Leaders Roundtable; Re-elected to PAISD Bd of Trustees 1980; Cited in 1975 by the Nat Educ Assnas the Recipient of the "Whitney M Young Jr Memorial Award" 1975; Recipient of a Special Human Relations Award TX State Teachers Assoc 1975. **MILITARY SERVICE:** AUS 1954-56. **BUSINESS ADDRESS:** Owner, Manager, McElroy's Insurance Agency, PO Box 1294, Port Arthur, TX 77640.

MCELROY, COLLEEN J.
Professor, writer. **PERSONAL:** Born Oct 30, 1935, St Louis, MO; daughter of Jesse D Johnson and Ruth C (Long) Johnson; divorced; children: Kevin D, Vanessa C. **EDUCATION:** Kansas State Univ, Manhattan KS, BS, 1958, MS, 1963; Univ of Washington, Seattle WA, PhD, 1973. **CAREER:** Rehabilitation Inst, Kansas City MO, chief, Speech & Hearing Serv, 1963-66; Western Washington Univ, Bellingham WA, asst prof, Speech, 1966-74; Univ of Washington, Seattle WA, supvr, EOP Composition, 1972-83, dir, Creative Writing, 1984-87, prof of English, 1983-. **ORGANIZATIONS:** Mem, Writers Guild of Amer East, 1978-, Dramatests Guild, 1986-, PEN Writers, 1989-. **HONORS/ACHIEVEMENTS:** Pushcart Prize, Best of Small Presses & Magazines, 1975; NEA Creative Writing, Natl Endowment for the Arts, 1978; Fiction 1st place, Callalvo Magazine, 1981; Poetry 1st place, Cincinnati Poetry R, 1983; Creative Writing Residency, MacDawell Colony, New Hampshire, 1984, 1986; Before Columbus Amer, Brock Award, 1985; Women of Achievement, Theta Sigma Phi, 1985; Creative Writing Residency Fugaslama, Fulbright Fellowship, 1988. **BUSINESS ADDRESS:** Professor of English, University of Washington, Dept of English GN-30, Padelford Hall, Seattle, WA 98109.

MCELROY, GEORGE A.
Journalist. **PERSONAL:** Born May 25, 1922, Houston, TX; married Lucinda Martin; children: Madeline Johnson, Toni, Linda, Kathleen, Sherri. **EDUCATION:** TX Southern Univ, BA 1956; USAF Systems Command, Honorary Doctorate 1966; Univ of MO-Columbia, MA 1970. **CAREER:** Houston Independent Sch Dist, journalism teacher 1957-69; Univ of Houston, asst prof of communications 1970-76; Houston Post, columnist 1971-78; TX Southern Univ, assoc prof of Journalism 1976-; Houston Informer, publisher/editor. **ORGANIZATIONS:** Chapter adviser Soc of Professional Journalists 1979-; publicist 9th and 10th Cavalry Assn; lay adviser TSU Catholic Newman Center; publicity chair United Negro College Fund/Houston; adviser Southwestern Journalism Congress. **HONORS/ACHIEVEMENTS:** Amigo de Guatemala Award govt of Guatemala 1977; Lynn C Eusan Serv Award Prof Amateur Boxing Assn 1979; Certificate of Recognition TSU Ex-Students Assn 1985; TSU Relays Service Award TX Southern Univ 1985. **MILITARY SERVICE:** USN steward 1st class 1940-46; USAF Information Specialist 1950-52. **BUSINESS ADDRESS:** Publisher/Editor, Houston Informer, PO Box 3086, Houston, TX 77001.

MCELVANE, PAMELA ANNE
Market manager/risk management. **PERSONAL:** Born Sep 04, 1958, Stockton, CA. **EDUCATION:** Univ CA Berkeley, BA 1981, MBA 1983. **CAREER:** US Dept of Labor, contract mgr 1980-82; Gelco-Cti Leasing Co, lease admin/sys supv 1982-84; Allstate Ins Co, market mgr 1984-. **ORGANIZATIONS:** Newsletter editor 1984-86, exec bd mem 1984-87, co-chair std affrs 1987, mgr editor 1987 SFMBA; coord Bay Blk Profls 1984-; bd mem, newsletter editor, vice pres UCB Alumni Assoc 1985-; recruiter Big Bros 1985-86; organizer March of Dimes 1986. **HONORS/ACHIEVEMENTS:** Coach of the Year Madeliene Sch 1984-86; Merit Awd Big Brothers 1984; Rosalie Stern Outstanding Comm Achiev UC Berkeley 1986; Who's Who Among Young Women of Amer 1986; Community Serv Awd March of Dimes 1986. **HOME ADDRESS:** 9004 Constitution Dr, Cincinnati, OH 45215.

MCEWING, MITCHELL DALTON
Educational administration. **PERSONAL:** Born May 16, 1935, Jacksonville, TX; married Verta Lee Ellis; children: Andre R, Veronica Lee. **EDUCATION:** Wiley Coll Marshall TX, BS 1958; TX Southern Univ, degree credits summers 1964; North TX State Univ, MEd 1973, degree credits 1974-75; TX State Bd of Examiners of Prof Counselors, Licensure Prof Counselor 1982. **CAREER:** Bethlehem United Com Ctr, athletic dir 1958-63; IM Terrell Jr-Sr HS, teacher/asst coach 1963-67, teacher/head coach 1968-69; Tarrant Cty Jr Coll, counselor/instructor 1971-75, dean of students devel svcs. **ORGANIZATIONS:** Soc worker Bethlehem United Com Ctr 1971; vice pres United Com Ctrs of Ft Worth 1971-73; bd mem Advisory Council in Counseling Student No TX State Univ 1981-82; mem Phi Delta Kappa; mem The Council of Black Amer Affairs; sec/treas E St Paul Bapt Church. **HONORS/ACHIEVEMENTS:** Dedicated Svs The Dukes 1975-76; Coach of the Year IM Terrell HS 1959-69; Serv Awd Phi Theta Kappa 1984. **MILITARY SERVICE:** AUS Spec 4 3 years; Berlin Serv Awd, Second Team Army Quarterback 1959; Hon discharge from the Army 1960. **HOME ADDRESS:** 3445 Denbury Dr, Fort Worth, TX 76133. **BUSINESS ADDRESS:** Dean, Student Devel Services, Tarrant County Junior College, South Campus, 5301 Campus Dr, Fort Worth, TX 76119.

MCFADDEN, ARTHUR B.
Minister. **PERSONAL:** Born Jan 05, 1940, Jacksonville, FL; married Marjesta Sanders; children: Anntoinette, Renee. **EDUCATION:** Stillman Coll, BA 1962; Johnson C Smith U, BD 1965; Eden Theological Seminary, STMD Min 1970, 1973; St Louis Univ, 1970-71; Southern IL Univ, 1984. **CAREER:** Calvary Presbyterian Church/Detroit, MI, asst minister 1965-66; Butler Memorial Church/Youngstown, OH, minister 1966-68; Third United Presbyterian Church/St Louis MO, minister 1968-. **ORGANIZATIONS:** Alumni bd dir, Stillman Coll 1973-79; adjunct prof, St Louis Univ 1974-82; bd const for blk clergy Eden Theological Seminary 1976-80; Omega Psi Phi Frat; bd dir KingFanow Mental Health Center 1985-; clergy support comm St Louis OIC; mem Men Organized Against Juvenile Crime. **HONORS/ACHIEVEMENTS:** Community Serv, St Louis Univ. **HOME ADDRESS:** 7112 Forest Hill Dr, St Louis, MO 63121. **BUSINESS ADDRESS:** Minister, 3rd United Presbyterian Ch, 2426 Union Blvd, St Louis, MO 63113.

MCFADDEN, CORA C.
Government admin. **PERSONAL:** Born Oct 03, 1945, Durham, NC; divorced; children: Lori Yvette, Larry Everette. **EDUCATION:** North. **CAREER:** Durham County Dept of Social Services, social worker 1969-76, foster care supervisor 1976-78; City of Durham, community services supervisor 1978-81, affirmative action dir 1981-. **ORGANIZATIONS:** One of the founders NC Association of Black Social Workers 1972; board member Volunteer Services Bureau 1980-83; board member YWCA 1983-84; state coordinatorAmerican Assn for Affirmative Action 1985; member Durham County Council for Women 1985; president Ebonettes Service Club, Inc 1985. **HONORS/ACHIEVEMENTS:** Founders Award North Carolina Association of Black Social Workers 1984. **BUSINESS ADDRESS:** Affirmative Action Dir, City of Durham, 101 City Hall Plz, Durham, NC 27701.

MCFADDEN, FREDERICK C., JR.
Physician. **PERSONAL:** Born Dec 04, 1927, New York, NY; married Jeannette Goddunn; children: Marianna Rox Buro, Lisa. **EDUCATION:** Howard U, MD 1952; NY U, BA 1948; Brandeis U, Post Doctoral Fellow 1961. **CAREER:** St Mary's Hosp, dir ambulatory care 1985; St Mary's Hosp, dir emergency dept; St Elizabeth, dir chest serv; Howard Med Sch Instr, instr bio. **ORGANIZATIONS:** Alcholism Studies; 1st AMA; Am Med Soc Alcholism; NY Cardiological Soc Bronze Star Korea; publ "Thoracic Aortograph"; Jour Am Heart 1957; "Temporal Lobectomy" 1963. **HONORS/ACHIEVEMENTS:** MED CORPS 1st lt 1952. **MILITARY SERVICE:** MED Corps 1st lt 1952. **BUSINESS ADDRESS:** 1298 St Marks Ave, Brooklyn, NY 11213.

MCFADDEN, GREGORY L.
Physician. **PERSONAL:** Born Jun 18, 1958, Tallahassee, FL; son of Robert L McFadden and Alma L Johnson McFadden; married Cynthia Williams, Dec 12, 1987; children: Desiree. **EDUCATION:** Florida A&M Univ, BS 1980; Howard Univ Coll of Medicine, MD 1984. **CAREER:** Orlando Regional Medical Center, resident physician 1984-87; Cigna Health Plan, staff physician, 1988-. **ORGANIZATIONS:** Mem Amer Coll of Physicians, Amer Medical Assoc, Alpha Phi Alpha Fraternity Inc; diplomate Natl Bd of Medical Examiners. **HONORS/ACHIEVEMENTS:** Natl Dean's List 1980; Physicians Recognition Award, Amer Medical Assn, 1987. **HOME ADDRESS:** 4308 Ellenville Pl, Valrico, FL 33594.

MCFADDEN, JAMES L.
Educator. **PERSONAL:** Born Nov 09, 1929, Darlington, SC; married Gertha Moore; children: Dionne Jametta. **EDUCATION:** Claflin Coll, AB 1954; NY U, MA; NY U, Further Study. **CAREER:** Morris Coll, Art instr 1954-56; Orangeburg City Sch Sharperson Jr HS, art tchr 1954-70; SC State Coll Orangeburg SC, prof of art 1970-; SC TextbookAdoption Com, selected to serve; Art & Music Texts, selected to serve 1969; Scholastic art awards in SC, regional adv comm 1969. **ORGANIZATIONS:** Treas SC Art Educ Assn 1971-Jan 1975; mem SC Educ Assn; Nat Educ Assn; Nat Art Educ Assn; mem Clafin & New YorkUniv Alumni Assn; Am Legion Post #210 1954; Edisto Masonic Lodge #39 AF&M 1966; Shriner Jeddah Temple No 160 1966; O-Burg IBOE of W Lodge #1627 Elks 1972; Orbg Alumni Chapter KAY; adv Alpha Lambda Chapter of KAY; Attend William Chapel AME Ch; mem NAACP; Honorable Mention & 3rd Place Sculpture Negro Nat Art Exhibition Atlanta 1950; grad Cum Laude Claflin Coll 1954; staff artist & asst mgr Post Theatre No 1 Ft & Benjamin Harrison IN 1951-53. **HONORS/ACHIEVEMENTS:** Southeastern Province Achievement Award Kappa Alpha Psi Frat 1950; Outst Ldrshp & Dedication Award Alpha Lambda Chap of Kappa Alpha Psi Frat 1976; 25 yr award SE Province of Kappa Alpha Psi Frat; Honored as Chartered Mem & Speaker 25th Anniv of Gamma Nu Chapter Kappa Alpha Psi Frat 1974. **MILITARY SERVICE:** AUS 1951-55. **BUSINESS ADDRESS:** PO Box 1962, SC State College, Orangeburg, SC 29115.

MCFADDEN, NATHANIEL JAMES
Elected official. **PERSONAL:** Born Aug 03, 1946, Philadelphia, PA; married Rachel Tift; children: Nathaniel Jr, Byron, Devon Dodson. **EDUCATION:** Morgan State Coll, AB 1968; Morgan State Univ, MS 1972. **CAREER:** Off-St Parking Commn Baltimore, 1983-; Jail Industries Adv Bd Baltimore City Jail, 1984-; Natl Youth Sports Prog Johns Hopkins Univ, adv comm 1984-; Sojourner-Douglass Coll, coord of comm affairs 1985-; Urban Serv Agency Baltimore, chmn 1985-; Morgan State Univ Dept of Educ, adv comm 1985-; City Council of Baltimore, councilmember. **ORGANIZATIONS:** Mem Assoc for the Study of Negro Life and History Baltimore City Chap 1980-82; mem Eastern Dist Police Community Relations Council Baltimore 1982-; mem adv bd Johns Hopkins Medical Plan 1985-; mem Optimist Club of East Baltimore 1985-. **HONORS/ACHIEVEMENTS:** Mem Kappa Alpha Psi Baltimore Alumni Chapt. **HOME ADDRESS:** 2702 Mura St, Baltimore, MD 21213. **BUSINESS ADDRESS:** Councilmember, City Council of Baltimore, 100 N Holliday Room 552, Baltimore, MD 21202.

MCFADDEN, SAMUEL WILTON
Physician. **PERSONAL:** Born Jun 17, 1935, Newark, NJ; married Nancy A Peters; children: Jonathan, Jesse. **EDUCATION:** NY University Coll, BA 1956;Univ Basel Switzer-

land, MD 1964. **CAREER:** BU Sch Med, pediatric radiologist/asst prof 1971-77; Child Abuse & Neglect Unit, chief 1973-75; Roxbury Comprehensive Comm Hlth Ctr, pediatrician 1973-77, chief radiology 1974-77; Eunice Kennedy Shriver Med Ctr, chief radiology 1974-83; Tobry Hosp, radiologist 1977-80, chief of radiology 1980-; Wareham Radiology Assoc, pres. **ORGANIZATIONS:** Pres New England Med Soc 1975-77; mem Bay State Peer Standards Rev Orgn 1976; treas New England Med Soc 1977-78; mem Am Coll of Radiology, Nat Med Assn; bd dir MA Radiol Soc; school comm ORR Regional HS 1981-; pres M & L Staff Toby General Hosp 1981-83; medical advisor Registry of Motor Vehicles 1983-; natl sec System Radiology Natl Medical Assoc 1987; medical advisor Marion UNA. **BUSINESS ADDRESS:** President, Wareham Radiology Assoc, 295 Delano Rd, Marion, MA 02738.

MCFADDIN, THERESA GARRISON
Teacher, counselor. **PERSONAL:** Born Jul 23, 1943, Philadelphia, PA; daughter of Alvin Prunty and Barbara Campbell Prunty; married Roslyn Ballard, Theresa McFaddin (deceased). **CAREER:** Motown Records, Los Angeles CA, writer, producer; Christian Broadcasting Network, Virginia Beach VA, writer, producer; Terri McFaddin & Friends, Pasadena CA, teacher, counselor. **HONORS/ACHIEVEMENTS:** Grammy Award, 1986; Citizen of the Year, Zeta Phi Beta Sorority, 1989. **BUSINESS ADDRESS:** Terri McFaddin & Friends, 1090 N Lake Ave, Suite A, Pasadena, CA 91104.

MCFALL, MARY (NEE SIMPSON)
Educational administrator. **PERSONAL:** Born Aug 30, 1938, San Angelo, TX; children: Jeannette, Owen III. **EDUCATION:** San Angelo Jr Coll, Honor Grad 1953-55;Univ of TX, BA Honor Grad 1957;Univ of TX, JD 1979; Cand. **CAREER:** Intercultural Devel So Meth U, dir 1971-; Tarrant Co YWCA, br exec 1969-71; Comm Action Agy, asst nghbrhd servs dir 1967-69; Soc Security Adm, serv rep 1965-66; Soc of Ethnic & Spec Studies, sec 1975-; TX Assn of Black Personnel in Higher Edn, co-founder 1st vice pres conf coord 1973-79; TX Assn ofBlack Personnel in Higher Edn, pres 1979. **ORGANIZATIONS:** Bd of dirs Family Guidance Assn 1979-; Coalition for Educ of Black Children; TX Assn of Coll;Univ Stu Personnel Adm Goals for Black Dallas Com 1976-77;vp Minority Cultural Arts Assn 1970-71; mem chmn Am Civil Liberties Union Ft Worth Chap 1968-70; mem Citizen's Plng Com Ft Worth 1971; co-fdr Students for Direct ActionUniv of TX; del Nat Students Assn 1961; Alpha Kappa Alpha Sor. **HONORS/ACHIEVEMENTS:** First Black Student Admitted to San Angelo Coll; 1st Black Student to Receive BA fromUniv of TX Austin; Listed Golden Profiles of Dallas Ft Worth 1980. **BUSINESS ADDRESS:** Box 355, SMU, Dallas, TX 75225.

MCFARLAND, ARTHUR C.
Attorney. **PERSONAL:** Born Feb 05, 1947, Charleston, SC; married E Elise Davis. **EDUCATION:** Univ Notre Dame, BA Govt 1970; Univ VA, JD 1973. **CAREER:** Private Practice, attorney 1974-; City of Charleston SC, assoc municipal judge 1976-78, chief municipal judge 1978-. **ORGANIZATIONS:** Mem Natl, Amer Bar Assns 1974-; mem Natl Conf of Black Lawyers 1974-; mem Amer Judges Assn, NBA Jud Council 1976-; bd dir Trident United Way 1977-; pres Robert Gould Shaw Boys Club 1978-; mem Chas SC NAACP Exec Com 1978-; pres Charleston Bus & Professional Assn 1983-85; mem Charleston Neighborhood Legal Assistance Prog Bd of Dir 1984-86; mem Charleston Waterfront Park Comm 1983-. **HONORS/ACHIEVEMENTS:** Earl Warren Fellow NAACP Legal Defense Fund 1973-74; Earl Warren Fellowship NAACP Legal Defense & Educ Fund 1973-77. **BUSINESS ADDRESS:** Chief Municipal Judge, City of Charleston, 205 King St, Ste 109, Charleston, SC 29401.

MCFARLAND, CLAUDETTE
Business executive, attorney, social worker. **PERSONAL:** Born Dec 08, 1935, St Louis, MO; married Vernon McFarland; children: Vernon Jr, Claudette II. **EDUCATION:** Roosevelt Univ, BA 1958; Univ NC, LLB; John Marshall Law School, LLM, JD; Univ of IL, MSW 1971, AM 1973, PhD. **CAREER:** Chicago Dwellings of Chicago Housing Auth, attny 1972; VAW Indust, corp lawyer, bus exec, exec vice pres 1975-; McFarland Enterprises, pres 1975-. **ORGANIZATIONS:** Mem Chgo, IL Assoc Commerce & Indust, C of C, Natl Assoc Univ Women, Amer Assoc of Univ Women; exec bd Girl Scouts of Amer; pres Chicago Section & Gr Chicago Sect of Natl Council of Negro Women Inc; pres emeritus Dr Claudette McFarland Ed Civic & Cultural Club of CNDA, No Dist Assoc of Women & Girls Clubs of Amer Inc, S Shore Natl Bank Bd; life mem NAACP; mem PUSH, Chicago Urban League; life mem Natl Council of Negro Women Inc; mem Wives Aux, Alpha Phi Alpha, YWCA; bd mem Provident Hosp Womens Aux, Chicago & IL Restaurant Assoc, Natl Bar Assoc, Jack & Jill; pres Chicago Chap Natl Council NegroWomen; life mem bd Alpha Kappa Alpha, Amer Bar Assoc, Natl Council Jewish Women; exec bd Chicago Links, Chicago Beautiful Comm trustee bd Du Sable Mus ofAfrican Amer History, League Women Voters, S Shore Comm; life mem Tau Gamma Delta; White House consult Women & Minority Affairs & Status of ERA invited by Pres Carter 1979; consult & partic White House Conf on Minority Human Experimentation 1975; ordained as interdenom minister Universal Life Church 1977. **HONORS/ACHIEVEMENTS:** Outstanding Achievement Awd Natl Council Negro Women 1972,73,75; Public Serv Awd WAIT Radio Natl Council Jewish Women; Nationally Outstanding Woman Awd Tau Gamma Delta 1975; Outstanding Comm Serv Awd Afro-Amer Patrolmen's League 1975; Outstanding Prof & Civic Awd Gamma Phi Delta 1975; Best Dressed Woman & Lane Bryant Fashion Awds 1975; Outstanding Women of the Year Girl Scouts of Chicago 1975; Guest at White House of Pres Ford 1975; Outstanding Humanitarian & CommServ Awd Intl Travelers Awd 1979. **BUSINESS ADDRESS:** President, McFarland Enterprises, 407 S Dearborn, Ste 950, Chicago, IL 60610.

MCFARLAND, OLLIE FRANKLIN
Educator. **PERSONAL:** Born Oct 25, 1918, Jacksonville, FL; married William A McFarland (dec) (deceased); children: William Michael. **EDUCATION:** Spelman Coll, BA 1940; Wayne State Univ, MM 1952; Columbia Univ, John Hay Fellow 1965-66. **CAREER:** Detroit Public Schools, music tchr Central High 1958-67, supvr music educ 1967-79, asst dir music educ 1979-81, dir music educ 1981-. **ORGANIZATIONS:** Life mem NAACP 1979-; singer Celeste Cole Opera Theatre; narrator Detroit Symphony Det Pub Schools Educ Concerts; concert/opera singer on radio/TV -St Joseph's Church; bd mem Detroit Comm Music Sch; bd mem Rackham Symphony Choir; mem Alpha Kappa Alpha Sor; mem Delta Kappa Gamma. **HONORS/ACHIEVEMENTS:** Honoree Natl Assn of Negro Musicians 1985; Educator's Achievement Award Booker T Washington Business Assn 1983; Achievement Award Omega Psi Phi Frat 1977;author music textbook, "Afro-America Sings" Det Pub Schools 1973, revised 1981. **BUSINESS ADDRESS:** Dir of Music Education, Detroit Public Schools, 5057 Woodward Ave, Room 850, Detroit, MI 48202.

MCFARLAND, ROBERT PHILLIPS
Business executive. **PERSONAL:** Born Apr 30, 1943, New Orleans, LA; married Vivian Johnson; children: Gaylynne, Brent, Aisha, Tanzia. **EDUCATION:** Xavier Univ of LA, BS 1965; Inst of Politics Loyola Univ of New Orleans, grad 1968. **CAREER:** New Orleans Educ Talent Search Prgm Inc, exec dir 1970-; Xavier U, dir consult 1968-70; A/Sci & Computer Programmer Chrysler Corp, math analyst 1965-68; US Geol Survey, civil engrng tech 1963-65; Mgmt Automated Info Sys Inc, sr consult sec 1974-; D White Realty, licensed real estate salesman 1973-; SWAssn of Student Assistance Prgrms, bd mem 1977; US China Peoples Friendship Assn, natl bd mem 1975-. **ORGANIZATIONS:** Chmn Carrollton Cntrl Inc 1968-; co-chrmn Comm Educ Coalition 1973-; mem State-Wide Vocat Adv Council LA Dept Of Corrections 1977; adv Council Nat Schlrshp Serv & Fund for Negrgo Students 1975; info ofcr Carver Booster Club. **HONORS/ACHIEVEMENTS:** Kiwanis Leadership Award 1975; contrib mem publ "Chou En-Lai & The Chinese Revolution" 1977; Comm Serv Award Joint Action & Comm Serv Inc 1975. **BUSINESS ADDRESS:** 3731 S Claiborne Ave, New Orleans, LA 70125.

MCFARLANE, FRANKLIN E.
Educator. **PERSONAL:** Born Apr 11, 1933, Jamaica; married Florence Maud Douglas; children: Valerie, Angela, Alychandra. **EDUCATION:** City Univ of NY, BS 1956; Columbia U, MS 1963; Claremont Grad Schl, M Bus Econ 1969. **CAREER:** Claremont Men's Coll Claremont CA, asst prof 1972-; Aerospace Corp El Segundo CA, consult 1972-; CA St PolytechUniv Pomona, asst prof 1970-72. **ORGANIZATIONS:** Pres MDR Corp 1968-69; pres Pac Mattrs Co LA 1965-68; Xerox Corp 1963-65; mem Amer Ec Assn Westrn Econ Assn; LA Cncl of Blk; Prof Eng's; mem NAACP. **HONORS/ACHIEVEMENTS:** Spl Act Commtn Dept of Army 1963. **BUSINESS ADDRESS:** 304 Bauer Ctr, Claremont Men's Coll, Claremont, CA 91711.

MCFARLIN, EMMA DANIELS
Government official. **PERSONAL:** Born Nov 14, 1921, Camden, AR. **EDUCATION:** Philander-Smith Coll Little Rock, BA 1950;Univ of WI Madison, MS 1961; US IntlUniv San Diego, PhD 1975. **CAREER:** US Dept HUD, regional adminstr 1977-;Univ of CA LA, asso prof 1975-77; Ofc of the Mayor LA, spl asst 1974-75; Menlo Parl CA, asst city mgr 1973-74; US Dept HEW, regional rep 1970-73; US Dept HUD, spl rep 1965-70; San Francisco Unified Sch Dist, tchr 1964-65; Low Rent Housing Proj Little RockRedevel & Housing Authority, mgr 1952-64. **ORGANIZATIONS:** Mem Omicron Nu Nat Honor Soc 1961; mem Nat Assn of Media Woman 1975; chmn Pub Utilities & Tran Commn LA 1976. **HONORS/ACHIEVEMENTS:** Cum laude Philander-Smith Coll 1949; recipient Emma McFarlin Day Award City of Menlo Park CAL 1974; newsmaker award Nat Assn of Media Women 1975; outstanding serv & achievement City Council LA 1975. **BUSINESS ADDRESS:** US Dept HUD, 450 Golden Gate Ave, San Francisco, CA 94102.

MCFARLIN, KERNAA D'OFFERT, JR.
Long range planner. **PERSONAL:** Born Oct 07, 1946, Jacksonville, FL; married Sandra Annette Williams; children: Kernaa D III, Brian Christopher, Patrick Allen. **EDUCATION:** Hampton Univ, BS 1968. **CAREER:** MA Mutual Life Ins Co, systems analyst 1969-71; IBM Corp, marketing rep 1971-77; Hartford Insurance Group, systems specialist 1978-79; Travelers Insurance Co, manager telecommunications 1979-. **ORGANIZATIONS:** Pres bd of dirs W W Johnson Life Ctr 1979-; vice pres Springfield Symphony Orchestra Assoc Marketing Comm 1983-; pres bd of dirs Longmeadow A Better Chance Inc 1985-. **HOME ADDRESS:** 124 Green Meadow Dr, Longmeadow, MA 01106. **BUSINESS ADDRESS:** Manager Telecommunications Div, Travelers Insurance Co, One Tower Square, Hartford, CT.

MCFERRIN, ROBERT
Educator. **PERSONAL:** Born Mar 19, 1921. **EDUCATION:** Chicago Musical Coll, BA. **CAREER:** Roosevelt Univ, visiting professor of voice 1976-. **HONORS/ACHIEVEMENTS:** First black to perform regularly with Metro Opera; performed in Canada, Latin Amer, Germany, Belgium, England, Italy, Greece, recorded album "Porgy & Bess Sound Track.".

MCFERRIN, SARA ELIZABETH COPPER
Musician, educator. **PERSONAL:** Born Sep 10, 1924, Washington, DC; daughter of Charles and Elizabeth; divorced; children: Robert, Brenda. **EDUCATION:** Howard Univ, attended 1942; Attended, Univ So CA LA; Attended, UCLA; Attended, California State University, Los Angeles. **CAREER:** CBS-TV, Christmas specials; solo recitalist & oratorio soloist throughout USA; symphony soloist; appeared in films Porgy & Bess, Elmer Gantry; appeared in Broadway prod "Lost in the Stars," "Troubled Island"; NY City Ctr Opera Chorus, soloist; Hollywood Greek Theatre Opera Chorus, soloist; CA State Univ, Long Beach/Nelson Sch of Fine Arts Canada, Pasadena City Coll, Cerritos Coll, tchr; Fullerton Coll Music Dept, chmn voice dept 1973-; University of Oklahoma, Norman, OK,visiting professor in voice 1966. **ORGANIZATIONS:** 2nd vice pres & prog chmn Natl Assn of Tchrs of Singing (NATS); exec bd treas Fullerton Coll Patrons of the Arts; mem Music Educators Natl Conf (MENC); mem Faculty Assn CA Com Coll (FACCC); faculty assn Fullerton Coll (FAFC); mem Music Assn CA Comm Coll (MACCC); Adjudicator Met Opera Western Region Audition in CA, AZ, NV 22 yrs; mem Adjudicating Panels Vocal comp in So CA, San Francisco Opera, South California Opera Guild. **BUSINESS ADDRESS:** Chmn Voice Dept, Fullerton Coll, Music Dept, 321 E Chapman Ave, Fullerton, CA 92634.

MCGATHON, CARRIE M.
Nurse. **PERSONAL:** Born Feb 03, 1936, Mendenhall, MS; married John A McGathon; children: Berlinda, Brenda, John Reginald. **EDUCATION:** Dillard Univ, BSN 1964; College of Holy Names, Advanced study 1970; Jackson State Univ, MEd 1978. **CAREER:** Naval Regional Medical Ctr Oakland CA, supervisor clinical Ob/Gyn 1975-80; Health Care Services Inc, director/administrator. **ORGANIZATIONS:** Mem Dillard Alumnus 1964-, NAACOG 1970-, Biblesway CIGOGC 1975-. **HONORS/ACHIEVEMENTS:** Merit Award Dept of United Navy 1975. **BUSINESS ADDRESS:** 2653 76th Ave, Oakland, CA 94605.

MCGAUGHY, WILL
Elected official. **PERSONAL:** Born Feb 23, 1933, Plantervills, MS; divorced; children: Felix Xavier. **EDUCATION:** Mildred Louis Bus Coll, 1954. **CAREER:** Citizen Participation, dir 1969-72, 1973-75; Will McGaughy Health Ctr, dir 1972-73; Health Educ & Wel-

fare, dir 1975-78; E St Louis Twp Citizen Prog, 1978-81; E St Louis Twp, asst to town super 1981-. **ORGANIZATIONS:** Adv to NAACP Youth Council 1966; pres Metro East Health Serv 1970-72; dir of Project Life 1970-73; precinct committeeman 1971-86; dir Dawson Manor Housing1954-; chmn E St Louis Transit Bd 1975-; vice pres City Central Democrate 1978-; cty bd mem Spec Asst to the Mayor of E St Louis 1978-; pres Southend Neighborhood Improvement Assn 1982-; mem Amer Red Cross. **HONORS/ACHIEVEMENTS:** Outstanding Leadership Awd E St Louis 1975; Politician of the Year 1976; Citizen Participation Workshop 1977; Resolution of Commendation from mayor of E St Louis 1980; Arson Awareness 1981; Project Hope 1982; Man of the Year E St Louis Monitor Newspaper 1982. **MILITARY SERVICE:** AUS corpl 3 yrs. **HOME ADDRESS:** 1402 So H, East St Louis, IL 62207.

MCGEE, ADOLPHUS STEWART
School administrator. **PERSONAL:** Born Jan 29, 1941, Dos Palos, CA. **EDUCATION:** Coalinga Coll, AA 1960; CA State U, BA 1963; CA State U, MA 1970; CA State U, MA Educ Adminstrn 1972. **CAREER:** Union High School Dist Sacramento, teacher math, head track coach football coach 1963-66; Luther Burbank High School Sacramento, teacher math science, track & football coach 1966-68; Sacramento City Unified School Dist, asst to supt 1968-70; inter-group relations adv 1969-70; Sacramento Sr High School, prin 1970-. **ORGANIZATIONS:** Mem Jount Legislative Com on Educ Goals & Evaluations Joint Task Force Goals & Evaluation For State of CA 1972-; pres Sacramento Sr High Sch Meml Scholarship Fund 1970-; Assn CA Sch Adminstrs; chmn Minority News Media Joint Task Force Urban Coalition 1969-71; mem YMCA; NAACP; Blue Key; Phi Delta Kappa; Omega Chi Delta. **BUSINESS ADDRESS:** 2315 34 St, Sacramento, CA 95817.

MCGEE, ARTHUR LEE
Business executive, designer. **PERSONAL:** Born Mar 25, 1933, Detroit, MI. **EDUCATION:** Wayne U, attended; Fashion Inst of Tech & Design, attended; Cybick Sch of Tailoring, attended. **CAREER:** Arthur McGee, pres designer 1958-; Ulla, design dir 1971-72; Sir for her, head designer 1969-71; Coll Town of Boston, head designer 1965-69. **ORGANIZATIONS:** Caswell Massey Men's Sprotswear 1959. **HONORS/ACHIEVEMENTS:** 1 of 2 Am Designers to Show in Intl Men's Show Europe 1965; contrib extrordinarie Oplehia Devore 1979; 1st Black Designer to work for a giant 7th Ave firm. **BUSINESS ADDRESS:** 80 E 11th St, New York, NY 10003.

MCGEE, BENJAMIN LELON
Company executive. **PERSONAL:** Born Feb 18, 1943, Booneville, MS; married Rose M Jackson; children: Ivy, Ben II, Brian, Holly. **EDUCATION:** AR AM&N Coll Pine Bluff AR, Agronomy Sci 1967; Memphis State U, 20 hrs 1975. **CAREER:** Liquor Center, owner 1977-; GMAC, credit rep 1976-77; Dept of Agr ASCS, compliance supr 1967-75. **ORGANIZATIONS:** Bd mem Marion Sch Dist 1975-; vice chmn bd of trustees AR StateUniv 1977-; state committeeman Dem Party 1979-; bd trustees AR StateUniv Jonesboro 1980; bd of trustees AME Ch. **BUSINESS ADDRESS:** The Liquor Center, 3109 E Broadway W, West Memphis, AR 72301.

MCGEE, EVA M.
Educator. **PERSONAL:** Born Jun 13, 1942, Nashvl, AR. **EDUCATION:** AM & N Coll, BS 1963;Univ AR Fayetteville, MEd 1971. **CAREER:** AM & N Coll Pine Bluff, AR, educ sec 1963-69;Univ AR, instr, dir of institutional advancement 1969-. **ORGANIZATIONS:** Pres AR Bus Ed Assn 1973-74, sec 1972-73; mem AR Coll Tchrs of Ec & Bus; Sthrn Bus Educ Assn; pres Nat Bus Educ Assn 1972-74, treas 1970-72, st coordntr 1974-; Pine Bluff Alum Chap Delta Sigma Theta; mem, bd dir Pine Bluff OIC 1973-74; Nat Cncl Negro Wmn; Jeff Cnty Advsry Com, Blk Adptn 1973-74. **HONORS/ACHIEVEMENTS:** Lstd Ldrs of Blk Amer 1973/74; named Outstndg Edtr of Amer 1974/75; Ldrshp Award, Pine Bluff Alum Chap Delta Sigma Theta 1973; Delta of the Yr 1974. **BUSINESS ADDRESS:** Dir of Institutional Adv, Univ of Arkansas, P O Box 4067, Pine Bluff, AR 71601.

MCGEE, HANSEL LESLIE
Attorney. **PERSONAL:** Born Jun 13, 1926, Miami, FL; married Mildred E Wareham; children: Elizabeth Florence, Leland Scott. **EDUCATION:** George Washington Law Sch, JD 1966; City Coll NY, BS 1952; Polytechnic Inst, MS 1960. **CAREER:** IBM, sr patent atty 1974-; IBM, pat atty 1966-74; Bronx Legal Svcs, chief atty proj dir 1972-74; IBM Rsrch, rstch staff mem 1960-63. **ORGANIZATIONS:** Pres bd dir SE Bronx Neighborhood Ctr; v chmn bd dir Bron Legal Svcs; mem Morris Educ Council; chmn Bronxwide Com for Voter registration; mem 100Black Men; consult Women of Am; mem Bronx NAACP; mem Harlem Lawyers Assn; mem Bronx OIC. **HONORS/ACHIEVEMENTS:** US Patents 3214460; 3342051; 3129104;3214282; sev outst serv awards. **MILITARY SERVICE:** USN 1943-45. **BUSINESS ADDRESS:** Acting Supreme Court Justice, New York Supreme Court, 851 Grand Concourse, Bronx, NY 10466.

MCGEE, HENRY W., JR.
Educator. **PERSONAL:** Born Dec 31, 1932, Chicago, IL; married Alice; children: Henry III, Kevin, Byron, Gregory, Erik. **EDUCATION:** NW Univ, BS 1954; DePaul Univ, JD 1957; Columbia Univ, LLM 1970. **CAREER:** Cook Co, asst state's atty 1958-61; Great Lakes Region USOEO, regional legal servs dir 1966-67; Univ of Chicago Ctr for Studies in Crim Justice Juv Delinq Rsch Proj, legal dir 1967-68; Wolfson Coll Oxford Univ England, visiting fellow 1973; Visiting Prof, Univ of Florence Italy Inst of Comparative Law 1976, Univ of Puerto Rico 1979, Univ of Madrid (complutense) 1982; Fed Univ Rio de Janeiro Brazil, grad planning prog 1987; UCLA, prof of law. **ORGANIZATIONS:** Mem Natl Bar Assn; mem Natl Conf of Black Lawyers; draftsman Natl Conf of Bar Examiners 1974-; consult City Poverty Com London England 1973; consult & lectr Urban Plng USIS Italy 1976; past editor in chief DePaul Law Review. **HONORS/ACHIEVEMENTS:** Blue Key Natl Honor Frat 1957; num publ. **BUSINESS ADDRESS:** Professor of Law, UCLA Sch of Law, 405 Hilgard Ave, Los Angeles, CA 90024.

MCGEE, JAMES H.
Mayor, attorney. **PERSONAL:** Born Nov 08, 1918, Berryburg, WV; married Elizabeth McCracken; children: Annette, Frances. **EDUCATION:** Wilberforce Univ, graduate 1941; OH State Univ Law School, JD, 1948. **CAREER:** Dayton, atty 1949-; City of Dayton, city commissioner 1967-70, mayor 1981-. **ORGANIZATIONS:** Mem bd dirs Town Affiliation Assn; Dayton Art Inst; mem OH Bar Assn; mem bd of dir Sister Cities Intl; mem adv bd, Natl League of Cities; memSupvr Counc on Crime & Deliquency; mem bd Melissa Bess Day Care Center mem Dayton Natl Amer Bar Assn; Juvenile Ct Adv Council. **HONORS/ACHIEVEMENTS:** Hon LLD Wilberforce & Central State Coll; Friend of the Boy Award, Dayton Westmont Optimist Intl. **MILITARY SERVICE:** AUS 1942-45. **BUSINESS ADDRESS:** Mayor, City of Dayton, 1526 W Third St, Dayton, OH 45407.

MCGEE, JAMES MADISON
Business executive. **PERSONAL:** Born Dec 22, 1940, Nashville, TN; married Mary Farncis Wilkins; children: Andrea, LaSandra, James Jr. **EDUCATION:** Fisk U, attended 1959-60; Mid-S Sch of Electronics Nashville, diploma 1968-70. **CAREER:** Ditrict Four Nat Alliance of Postal & Federal Emp, pres 1976-; US Postal Service, LSM instr trainer 1973-76; US Postal Service, LSM operator 1967; US Postal Service, clerk 1965. **ORGANIZATIONS:** Treasurer NAPFE Nashville Local #410 1968-72; pres NAPFE Nashville Local #410 1972-78; pres NAPFE Dist Four 1978; mem TN Voters Counc 1967-80; mem NAACP1968-80; mem Benevolent Protective Order of Elks TN 1970-80. **HONORS/ACHIEVEMENTS:** Mem HJ Johnson Honor Soc 1955-59; all conf basketball team High Sch 1959; all freshman basketball team FiskUniv 1959-60; recipient of good conduct medal USMC 1961-62; all marine basketball team USMC 1963-64. **MILITARY SERVICE:** USMC pfc 1961-65. **BUSINESS ADDRESS:** Ntl Alnc of Post & Fed Employ, 1644 11th St NW, Washington, DC 20001.

MCGEE, JOANN
Tutorial executive. **PERSONAL:** Born Jan 05, 1953, Buffalo, NY. **EDUCATION:** Elmira Coll Elmira NY, BA 1974, MS Ed 1975; SUNY at Binghamton, NY, 1974-77; New Life Bible School Cleveland, TN, Diploma, 1982; Southland Univ, Pasadena, CA, PhD, 1984. **CAREER:** George Washington Schl Elmira NY, smr tchr 1975; SUNY at Binghamton, NY, grad asst 1975-77; BCUL Teen Ctr Binghamton NY, asst ed coord 1978-80; SUNY at Binghamton, NY, instr 1980-81. **ORGANIZATIONS:** Supr volunteer tutors Elmira Corrtl Facility 1984-; trvlng artst/instr Arnot Art Museum Elmira NY 1982-; instr crafts Broome Cmnty Binghamton 1981-; instr Charles Harrison Mason Bible Schl Elmira 1982-83; mem Chemung Area Reading Cncl 1984-. **HONORS/ACHIEVEMENTS:** Grad asstshp SUNY at Binghamton NY 1975-77; Elmira coll schlrshp Elmira Coll NY 1970-73. **HOME ADDRESS:** 964 Farnham St, Elmira, NY 14901.

MCGEE, LAWRENCE VONETTA (VONETTA MCGEE)
Actress. **PERSONAL:** Born Jan 14, San Francisco, CA; daughter of Lawrence McGee and Alma Irene Scott McGee; married Carl Lumbly, May 29; children: Brandon Lumbly.

MCGEE, MIKE LAVELLE
Professional athlete. **PERSONAL:** Born Jul 29, 1959, Tyler, TX. **EDUCATION:** MI State Univ, 1981. **CAREER:** Los Angeles Lakers, guard. **HONORS/ACHIEVEMENTS:** Started 45 Games; est new NBA record for Fg pct by a guard (594); had a rookie-high 27 points vs San Diego to become the first non-starter in more than 4 years to lead the Lakers in scoring; had 4 of his 5 highest-scoring games his first 2 seasons vs the Clippers; shattered both Big Ten scoring records while at MI scoring 1,503 points in league games; holds the Wolverine mark for total Points; holds school career record for games started and field goals made and set asingle-season mark for field goals made; finished his college career as the 21st leading scorer in NCAA history. **BUSINESS ADDRESS:** Los Angeles Lakers, P O Box 10, Ste 510, Inglewood, CA 90306.

MCGEE, REBECCA E.
Business executive. **PERSONAL:** Born Aug 17, 1943, Toledo, OH; children: Kimberly Fawn, Stephanie Kara. **EDUCATION:** Univ Toledo, 1961-65; Univ of MI, BS 1968. **CAREER:** SETA, dir client services 1974-78; Central NY Reg Transp Authority, serv coord 1978-83; Consolidated Industries, placement counselor 1984-; WNDR Radio, talk show host/producer/news reporter 1978-. **ORGANIZATIONS:** Bd mem Syrcuse Urban League; mem Ch Women United; Jr League; Link Inc; Priority One; Black Political Caucus; mem Nat Council Negro Women; mem vol ctr bd mem Syracuse & Ondaga Co Econ Devel Com; past pres Urban League Guild; past chmn City Co Human Rights Comm; prod host "Black Comm" WNDR Radio;clmnst The Impartial Ctzn; mem Links. **HONORS/ACHIEVEMENTS:** Black Woman of Achievement Awd Delta Sigma Theta 1979; Directory of Distinguished Americans 1981; Who's Who Among the World's Women 1980; Who's Who Among the World's Intellectuals 1980; Comm Serv Awd for Publ Serv Celebrator's Club 1982; Impartial Citizen Comm Serv Awd 1984; Syracuse Police Dept Civilan Awd 1986; All Media Awd 1986. **BUSINESS ADDRESS:** Orange Comm WNDR-WNTO, PO Box 93-0, Syracuse, NY 13217-9300.

MCGEE, ROSE N.
Association coordinator. **PERSONAL:** Born Jan 23, 1921, Steubenville, OH; widowed; children: Robert, John, Thaddeus, Patricia Williams. **EDUCATION:** Steubenville Bus Coll, attended 1947;Univ of Steubenville, attended 1 yr. **CAREER:** OH Commn on Aging, area coordinator 1974-80; SSI OH Commn on Aging, dir 1970-74; Office City of Steubenville, clk treas 1968-70. **ORGANIZATIONS:** Area ldr Cancer Soc; area ldr ARC; area ldr Comm Chest Rec; steward Phillips Chapel CME; past pres life mem exec bd NAACP; vice pres League of Women Voters. **HONORS/ACHIEVEMENTS:** Recipient Awd of Commendation & Recognition, WSTV-TV Inc 1962; Outstanding Serv Awd OH Conf of NAACP 1968; Cert of Commendation, Nat Council of Negro Women Inc 1975; Cert of Appreciation for Falued Contribution, Bus & Professional Women, 1976; Comm Awd, City of Steubenville, 1976. **BUSINESS ADDRESS:** Area Coordinator, OH Dept of Aging, 50 W Broad St, 9th Floor, Columbus, OH 43266.

MCGEE, VONETTA See MCGEE, LAWRENCE VONETTA

MCGEE, WILLIE DEAN
Professional athlete. **PERSONAL:** Born Nov 02, 1958, San Francisco, CA. **EDUCATION:** Attended, Diablo Valley Jr Coll. **CAREER:** NY Yankees, outfielder; St Louis Cardinals, outfielder 1981-. **HONORS/ACHIEVEMENTS:** 17 consecutive steals; tied World Series record for outfielders with 24 putouts in the Series; set record for highest fielding average in 7 game series with most chances accepted; named to Howe News Bureau post-season All Star team 1981; Topps Chewing Gum All-Rookie team 1982; St Louis BBWAA Rookie of the Year; 3 Gold Glove Awds; Natl League MVP 1985; named to The Sporting News and

UPI NL All Star teams 1985; Sporting News NL Player of the Year 1985; winner of BBWAA Natl League MVP 1985; voted to first Silver Slugger Team 1985; Sports Illustrated and Natl League's Player of the Week June 3-9 1985; NL Player of the Month August 1985; mem All Star Teams 1983 and 1985. **BUSINESS ADDRESS:** St Louis Cardinals, 250 Stadium Plaza, St Louis, MO 63102.

MCGEHEE, MAURICE EDWARD
Retired educational administrator. **PERSONAL:** Born Aug 17, 1914, Chicago, IL; son of George E McGehee and Dorcas Lucille Appleby McGehee. **EDUCATION:** Chicago Teacher Coll, BA, 1941; DePaul Univ, MA, 1953; Univ of Southern CA, postgraduate, 1954-55; Los Angeles State Teachers Coll, 1954-63; Julliard School of Music, 1943; City Univ, EdD, 1981. **CAREER:** Wendell Phillips Evening High School, Chicago, asst principal counselor, 1950-54; Keith Elementary School, Chicago, asst principal, 1950-54; 96th St Sch Los Angeles, substitute vice principal, 1957-58, 1961-62; head thcr summer sessions 1961-62; Fremont Adult Sch Los Angeles, specialist 1966-67; Dorsey Adult School, head counselor 1957-67; Los Angeles Adult Sch, vice-principal, 1967-68; Watts Skill Center Los Angeles, manpower devel training acting principal, 1968-71; Principal, Manual Arts Community Adult School, 1972-74; Principal, Crenshaw-Dorsey Community Adult School, 1974-82 (retired). **ORGANIZATIONS:** Principal consultant curriculum div Career & Continuing Educ, Los Angeles Unified Sch District, 1972-73; mem, Commn on Evaluation of Language Arts Textbooks, Los Angeles 1957-; Adult Educ Guidance Counseling Commn, Los Angeles, 1964-; So Central Welfare Planning Comm, 1968-; mem Adult Educ Assn; Early Childhood Assn; Natl Assn Public School Adult Educ; NEA; Assn Classroom Teachers; CA Council Adult Educ Admin; CA Teachers Assn; CA Council Adult Educ; mem, Mayor's Comm Adv Com 1965-; Crenshaw Coordinating Council Los Angeles 1957-; 96th St PTA 1954-; exec dir Watts Summer Festival 1971; pres Negro History Assn 1961-; Nat CA Urban League; NAACP; Manpower Devel Assn Los Angeles Co Mus Assn; DePaul Univ Alumni Assn; Alpha Phi Alpha. **HONORS/ACHIEVEMENTS:** Named outstanding community citizen, Los Angeles City Council 1971; Community Man of the Year, Westminister Presbyterian Church, 1971; State of California Certificate of Commendation for Outstanding Service, 1971; Mayor's Certificate of Appreciation, 1976; Award for Community Service, Los Angeles Police Dept, 1978; Recipient of the Congressman's Medal of Merit, presented by Augustus F. Hawkins, 1974. **BUSINESS ADDRESS:** 430 N Grand Ave, Los Angeles, CA 90012.

MCGEHEE, NAN E.
University executive. **PERSONAL:** Born Mar 09, 1928, Chicago, IL; daughter of Winston T McGehee and Ethel Davis McGehee. **EDUCATION:** Univ of Chicago, BA 1947; Northwestern Univ, BSE 1958, MS 1959, PhD 1962; Harvard Univ, IEM Cert 1972. **CAREER:** Northwestern Univ Eve Div, instr 1960-61; Univ of IL Chicago Circle, instr 1961-62, asst prof 1962-66, assoc prof 1966-, dir univ honors progs 1967-70, dean of faculties 1970-72, assoc chancellor 1972-79 retired. **ORGANIZATIONS:** Sec, treas IL Psychol Assn 1968-70; consult US Civil Serv Comm, EEOC, FWP Reg & Training 1970-72; bd mem IL Reg Libr Council 1973; policy bd mem Natl Ctr for Study of Ed Policy Alternatives 1972; mem Sigma Xi, Alpha Kappa Alpha, Amer Psychol Assn, IL Psychol Assn, Midwest Psychol Assn, Amer Assn of Univ Profs, Alpha Lambda Delta, Phi Eta Sigma. **HONORS/ACHIEVEMENTS:** NIMH Fellow 1959; Univ of IL Rsch Fellow 1962; co-author several articles. **HOME ADDRESS:** Rt 5 Box 237, Vashon, WA 98070.

MCGHEE, GEORGIA MAE
Associate executive. **PERSONAL:** Born Dec 09, 1934, Joiner, AR; daughter of Webb Young and Marge Young; divorced; children: Curits L, Steven Alan, Garry Lynn, Cheryl Densie Johnson, Rita Lorain,Kenneth G. **EDUCATION:** Davenport Business Coll, 1958-59; Jr Coll, Data Processing, English 1973. **CAREER:** AFSCME AFL-CIO, vice pres council 07 1972-76, council vice pres 1977-79; pres local 261 1973-77, Coalition of Labor Union Women, convenor 1974, chap pres 1975; Coalition of Labor Union Women Natl Officers Council, 2nd vice pres 1977-80 & 1980-86; AFSCME AFL-CIO, intl vice pres 1977-80 & 1980-84 AFSCME Int vice pres two terms; MI Women's Commiss, commiss 1977-80 & 1980-84. **ORGANIZATIONS:** Pres Block Club 1969-70; intl vice pres AFSCME AFL-CIO 1977-80 & 1980-84; vice pres Coalition of Labor Union Women Natl Officers Council 1977-80 (coalition of Labor Union Women term from 1984-86; was re-elected (3rd term); MI Women's Commiss 1977; AFL-CIO Comm Serv Committee 1978-86; audit & review comm Kent Cty United Way Committee 1978-81; pres AFSCME AFL-CIO local 261; exec bd mem United Way Tent Co 1978-82. **HONORS/ACHIEVEMENTS:** Rosalyn Carter's Comm Plan Cert 1979; Kenneth W Robinson Comm Serv Kent Cty United Way 1982; Mary McLeod Bethune Awd Natl Council of Negro Women 1984; MI Women's Comm Disting Serv Awd MI Women's Commiss 1984; Martha Reynolds Labor Awd GR Giants Awd 1984. **HOME ADDRESS:** 612 Worden SE, Grand Rapids, MI 49507.

MCGHEE, JAMES LEON
Business executive. **PERSONAL:** Born Mar 03, 1948, Wayne, IN. **EDUCATION:** Univ of Puget Sound, BA 1974. **CAREER:** City Planning Commiss Tacoma WA, asst planner 1972-73; US Treasury Dept, asst bank examiner 1973-76; Housing & Devel Seattle, DC, dir 1977-78; Northwest Tech Inc, pres, chmn 1983-; Medsco Inc Med Supply Corp, pres, chmn 1983-. **ORGANIZATIONS:** Fin treas NW Black Elected Official Assoc 1973-85; founder United Trade Worker Assoc 1975; pres, chmn of bd WA State Bus League 1980-85; bd of dir NW Tech Inc 1981-85; plnng commiss City of Seattle 1981-85; asst reg vice pres Natl Bus League 1983-85; bd of dir Medsco Inc 1983-85; bd of dir UnitedNegro Coll Fund 1985. **HONORS/ACHIEVEMENTS:** Pres Alpha Phi Alpha/Sphinx OH State 1968; co-founder Seattle Central Comm Coll Found 1978; Honors for Serv EFP Rhomania 1979; Community Black Leader of 1980 NW Conf of Black Public Official 1980. **MILITARY SERVICE:** AUS sgt E-5 3 yrs; Hon Discharge; Viet Nam Medal; Serv Citation 1971. **BUSINESS ADDRESS:** President, Medsco Inc, 22030 W Valley Hwy, Kent, WA 98032.

MCGHEE, NANCY BULLOCK
Retired educator. **PERSONAL:** Born Mar 19, 1908, High Point, NC; daughter of Dr Oscar S Bullock and Mehala Bullock; married Samuel. **EDUCATION:** Shaw Univ, BA; Columbia Univ, MA; Univ of Chicago, PhD 1942; Univ of London; Cambridge Univ; Shaw Univ, HHD 1973. **CAREER:** Hampton Inst, dir, instructor in humanities 1964-69, chmn English dept 1967; Univ of Louisville, instructor; visiting prof of literature, Coll of William & Mary 1979; Hampton Inst, prof emeritus of English, commissioned by trustees to write history of Hampton Inst. **ORGANIZATIONS:** Exec comm member, Assn of Dept of English, 1972-75; sec bd dir, VA Found for Humanities & Public Policy, 1973-; pres, VA Humanities Conf, 1973-74; Grand Basileus Zeta Phi Beta Sorority Inc, 1948-54; bd chmn, Amer Council of Human Rights; vice pres, Natl Council of Negro Women 1954-56; comm member, Amer Assn of Univ Women, 1973-75. **HONORS/ACHIEVEMENTS:** Gen Educ Bd Scholarship Rockefeller Found; Julius Rosenwald Fund Scholarship; Distinguished Alumni Award Shaw Univ 1965; Avalon Found Chair in Humanities (first endowed chair at Hampton Inst). **BUSINESS ADDRESS:** Professor Emeritus, Hampton Univ, PO Box 6567, Hampton, VA 23668.

MCGHEE, PAMELA A.
Business executive. **PERSONAL:** Born May 22, 1946, Mount Vernon, KY. **EDUCATION:** PA State U, BS 1968; NYUniv Grad Sch of Bus Adminstrn, MBA 1977. **CAREER:** Mgmt Infor Systems Educ Programs RCA Corporate Staff Mgmt Info Systems, adminstr 1974-; Educ Coordinaro Lever Bros, sr systems analyst 1973-74; Chase Manhattan Bank, technical specialist 1971-73; 1st Nat Bank of Boston, sr analyst 1970-71; IBM Corp, jr programmer 1968-70. **ORGANIZATIONS:** Editor RCA Mgmt Info Systems Bulletin; pres Assn of Computer Educators; mem Am Soc for Training & Devel; mem New York City Chap of Assn for Computing Machinery; mem exec bd Video Users Edn; mem Metropolitan Museum of Art NYC; mem Museum of Modern Art NYC.

MCGHEE, REGINALD D.
Business executive. **PERSONAL:** Born Jan 20, 1927, Detroit, MI; married Christine; children: Reginald, Kathleen. **EDUCATION:** Detriot Inst of Technology, 1960. **CAREER:** Blue Cross-Blue Shield, spl rep 1964-. **ORGANIZATIONS:** V chmn first Dem Cong Dist Organization 1966-70; Precinct Delegate 1966-68; mem dist exec bd 1966-70; candidate Wayne Co Bd of Commissions 1968, lostby 7 votes; elected precinct delegate 1974; aptd to Zoning Bd of Appeals City of Detroit 1975; former pres Concerned Citizens for Action Inc; former pres Barton-MacFarlane Comm Coun; former speaker for New Detroit Inc; mem TV Study Com; mem UAW-CIO Local #1781, 1st vice pres; ruling elder Calvary Presbyterian Ch; former clerk of session Calvary Presbyterian Ch; former mem bd dir Metropolitan Detroit Coun of Ch; former chmn Pub Educ Com; chmn Com on Urban Crisis 1968. **HONORS/ACHIEVEMENTS:** First black hired as a spl rep for Blue Cross-Blue Shield; certificat of recognition City of Detroit 1974.

MCGHEE, SAMUEL T.
Educator, government official. **PERSONAL:** Born May 29, 1940, Jersey City, NJ; son of Samuel T McGhee Jr and Lucile Bitten McGhee; married Connie Bentley; children: Darren, Elissa, Samuel III, Jeffrey. **EDUCATION:** Jersey City State Coll, BA 1962; Seton Hall Univ, MA 1965, postgrad study. **CAREER:** Jersey City State Coll, asst dir admissions 1971-72, assoc dir admissions 1972-76, dir of admissions 1976-; Hillside, NJ Finance Commissioner 1987; HillsideTownship, Hillside NJ, mayor 1988; Hillside Township, Hillside NJ, police commissioner 1989. **ORGANIZATIONS:** Mem mayors adv council Hillside 1972-73; adv council, Bd of Educ 1973; chmn Shade Tree Commn Hillside NJ 1976-; mem Omega Psi Phi Fraternity 1988-; mem NatlConference of Black Mayors 1988-. **HONORS/ACHIEVEMENTS:** Black Merit Acad E St Louis 1973; Jersey City State Coll, Distinguished Alumni Award 1981. **BUSINESS ADDRESS:** Dir of Admissions, Jersey City State College, 2039 Kennedy Blvd, Jersey City, NJ 07305.

MCGHEE, WALTER BROWNIE
Musician, singer. **PERSONAL:** Born Nov 30, 1915, Knoxville, TN; children: Vedia Zella E,Vilhelmina,George,Valerie,Colin Che'. **EDUCATION:** Douglass High School 1936. **CAREER:** Cat On A Hot Tin Roof, actor 1955; Face In The Crowd, musician & actor 1955; Simply Heavenly, actor, musician, singer 1958; Buck & The Preacher, music. **ORGANIZATIONS:** Songwriter Publisher BMI 1950; song book Oak Publishing Co. **HONORS/ACHIEVEMENTS:** Local 802 Musician Union 1944; AFTRA. **HOME ADDRESS:** 688 43rd St, Oakland, CA 94609.

MCGILL, THOMAS L., JR.
Attorney. **PERSONAL:** Born Aug 13, 1946, Martinsburg, WV; son of Thomas L McGill, Sr and Dorthy Kathryn Baylor McGill; married Charisse R Lillie, Dec 04, 1982; children: Leslie Janelle, Thomas L III, Alison Charisse. **EDUCATION:** Lincoln Univ, BA 1968; Occidental Coll, MA 1972; Notre Dame Law School, JD 1975. **CAREER:** Olney HS, teacher 1968-71; Hon Kenneth Gibson Mayor, mayor's aide 1971-72; Hon Paul Dandridge Judge, law clerk 1975-82; PA Human Relations Commn, commissioner 1981-, chairperson 1986-; McGill & Seay, attorney 1975-. **ORGANIZATIONS:** Mem Philadelphia Bar Assn 1975-, Amer Bar Assn 1975-; mem Natl Bar Assn 1977-; Recording Sec Barristers Assn 1977-78; pres Barristers Assn 1980-81; mem of bd Veritas Inc 1980-83, Germantown Boys Club 1982-84; bd of dirs West Mount Airy Neighbors 1986-87. **HONORS/ACHIEVEMENTS:** All Conf Baseball Team Lincoln Univ 1967; Sr Class Awd for Creative Writing Lincoln Univ 1968; Natl Urban Fellow, Natl Conf of Mayors Yale Univ 1971-72. **HOME ADDRESS:** 6748 Emlen St, Philadelphia, PA 19119. **BUSINESS ADDRESS:** Attorney at Law, Robinson Building, Suite 1600, 42 South 15th St, Philadelphia, PA 19102.

MCGINNIS, GEORGE S.
Professional athlete. **PERSONAL:** Born Aug 10, 1950, Birmingham. **EDUCATION:** IN U, student 1969-71. **CAREER:** Philadelphia 76ers, 1975-; IN Pacers Indianapolis , forward professional basketball team 1971-75. **ORGANIZATIONS:** Mem Am Basketball Assn Players Assn. **HONORS/ACHIEVEMENTS:** Named to HS All Am Team 1968, 69; Coll All Am Basketball Team 1971; All Rookie Professional Team 1971-72; All Star Professional Team 1972, 73; NBA All Star Team 1976-77. **BUSINESS ADDRESS:** c/o NBA Players Association, 15 Columbus Circle, New York, NY 10023.

MCGINNIS, JAMES W.
Educator, attorney. **PERSONAL:** Born Jul 08, 1940, Fairfield, AL; son of Reatha Saunders Felton; married Debra Hughes, Mar 16, 1988; children: Ayana Marie. **EDUCATION:** Wayne State Univ, BS 1963; San Francisco State Univ, MA 1965; Yeshiva Univ, PhD 1976; Wayne State Univ Law School, JD 1977. **CAREER:** Coll Entrance Examination Bd, asst dir 1967-69; Univ of California Berkeley, instructor, 1970-72; Far West Lab for Educ Research, research assoc 1972-73; Oakland Univ, asst prof 1976-81; Private Practice, lawyer. **ORGANIZATIONS:** Pres Kappa Alpha Psi Frat Wayne State Univ 1961-62; mem Assn of Black Psychologist 1963-73; researcher Black Studies Inst Wayne State Univ 1975-76; office counsel Hall & Andary Law Firm 1982-84; chmn PAC-Natl Conf of Black Lawyers 1982-85. **HONORS/ACHIEVEMENTS:** Fellowship Project Beacon, Yeshiva Univ 1965-66; Ford

Found Fellowship Language Soc of Child, Univ of CA 1968. **BUSINESS ADDRESS:** Attorney, Bell & Gardner P C, 561 E Jefferson Ave, Detroit, MI 48226.

MCGINTY, DORIS EVANS
Educator, musician, author. **PERSONAL:** Born Aug 02, 1925, Washington, DC; daughter of Charles Evans and Vallean Richardson; married Milton Oliver McGinty, Sep 06, 1956; children: Derek Gordon, Dana Winston, Lisa Megan. **EDUCATION:** Howard Univ, BMus Educ 1945, BA 1946; Radcliffe Coll, MA 1947; Oxford Univ (LMH), DPhil 1954. **CAREER:** DC Public Library, music librarian 1943-45; Howard Univ, instructor, prof 1947-; TX Southern Univ, assoc prof musicology summer 1956; Howard Univ, chmn deptof music 1977-85, prof of music. **ORGANIZATIONS:** Contributing editor, The Black Perspective in Music, 1975-; Educ & Community Outreach Comm, Natl Symphony Orchestra 1978-81; bd trustees exec comm, WETA radio & TV 1979-85; bd trustees, Cathedral Choral Soc 1983-86; bd trustees & chair, Comm on Status of Minorities, Coll Music Soc 1982-85; consul, Afro-Amer Arts 1983-84; consul, L Bolliger Assoc Filming 1984-. **HONORS/ACHIEVEMENTS:** Gen Educ Bd Fellowship 1951-52; Fulbright Fellowship 1950-51, 1951-52; Caribbean-Amer Scholars Exchange Phelps-Stokes Fund 1974; Outstanding Teacher Awards 1973, 1976; Faculty Research Awards Howard Univ 1968-69, 1975-76; research grant Natl Endowment for the Humanities 1984, 1987. **BUSINESS ADDRESS:** Prof Dept of Music, HowardUniv, Washington, DC 20059.

MCGLOTHAN, ERNEST
Business executive. **PERSONAL:** Born Oct 25, 1937, Tuscaloosa, AL; married Willa Rean May; children: Wilma, Kecia, Corey. **EDUCATION:** Tuskegee Inst Sch of Arch, 1971; Tuskegee Inst Sch of Arch, BS 1971. **CAREER:** Mac-Pon Co Gen Contractors, pres owner; Gaillard Constrn Co Birmingham; A H Smith Constrn Co Birmingham. **ORGANIZATIONS:** Mem Alpha Phi Alpha Frat; Mayor's Adv Com; Nat Assn of Minority Contractors; Birmingham Zoning Bd of Adjustments; Omicron Lambda; bd dir BSA; chmn Cooper Green Golf Course Com. **HONORS/ACHIEVEMENTS:** Oustsnd bus men of yr Omega Psi Phi 1973; bus of the yr awd Dr Herman H Long 1977; licensed Minority Gen Contr AL. **MILITARY SERVICE:** AUS 1971-73.

MCGLOTHEN, GOREE
Councilman. **PERSONAL:** Born Aug 17, 1915, Huntsville, TX; married Allie Mae Hightower; children: Goree, Jr, Mattie Grant. **EDUCATION:** Indsl Educ Tuskegee Inst, BS 1937. **CAREER:** United Gas Corp, mstr gas meter repair 1941-45; State of TX, mstr electrical 1942-77, mstr plumber 1944-55; McGlothen Elect Co, owner; City of Huntsville, city councilman 1975-. **ORGANIZATIONS:** Sec Walker Co Negro C of C 1941-44; pres Coodgellows Club 1942-43; mem adult educ bd Huntsville HS 1975-76; chmn Janes Found 1976-77; deacon ss tchr fncl sec First Mission Bapt Ch; pres Cent Mission Bapt Assn of TX Brthd; mem NAACP Internt Bus Fellowship. **HONORS/ACHIEVEMENTS:** Golden Eagle Awd BSA 1967; 1st black to defeat a white polit opponent since Reconstruct Days Huntsville TX 1975; Ldr Celeb Bicent Year 1976; Plaque Trinity River Authority 1978; Black History Awd from Pres Jimmy Carter 1979; Hon Fine Lighter of the Year 1980; Outstanding Male Alpha Phi Alpha 1984; Plaque Huntsville Housing Authority 1985; Outstanding Achievement Awd Natl Council of Org 1986; vice pres Grand Persons Bd 1987.

MCGLOTHEN, LYNN EVEROTT (MAC)
Professional athlete. **PERSONAL:** Born Mar 27, 1950, Monroe, LA; children: Lynn Jr, Brandon. **EDUCATION:** Grambling State Univ, Attnd. **CAREER:** Chicago Cubs, pitcher 1978-; San Francisco Giants, pitcher 1977-78; St Louis Cardinals, pitcher 1973-76; Boston Red Sox, pitcher 1972-73. **BUSINESS ADDRESS:** Chicago Cubs, 1060 W Addison, Chicago, IL 60613.

MCGOODWIN, ROLAND C.
Dentist. **PERSONAL:** Born Jul 15, 1933, Evansville, IN; married Lillian Pollard; children: Nina Marie, Roland Jr. **EDUCATION:** Cntrl State Clge, BS 1955; Meharry Med Clge Sch Dentistry, DDS 1963; Hubbard Hosp, intern 1964; Albert Einstein Med Ctr, Resident 1965. **CAREER:** Cincinnati OH, pvt prac; Lincoln Hghts Health Ctr, staff; Bethesda Hospital. **ORGANIZATIONS:** Dentist crippled children; bd educ Amer Dental Assc; Natl Dental Assc; OH State Dental Assc; OH Valley Dental Soc; Cincinnati Dental Soc; Acad GenDentists Bd Mt Auburn Health Ctr; Walnut Hill Area Counc Adv; Health Manpower Linkage Sys; OH Dept Health. **MILITARY SERVICE:** AUS 1st lt 1956-59; LTC KC USAR 1978-. **BUSINESS ADDRESS:** 645 E Mc Millan St, Cincinnati, OH 45206.

MCGOWAN, THOMAS RANDOLPH
Director of religious ecumenism. **PERSONAL:** Born Apr 19, 1926, Baltimore, MD; son of Robert McGowan and Mary McGowan; married Roedean Olivia Oden; children: James, Karen White, Terry V Stevens, Kevin, Kurt. **EDUCATION:** Oakland City Coll, AA 1964; Attended, San Francisco State Coll 1964-66, Univ of CA at Berkeley 1966-67; Univ of MD, BS 1978. **CAREER:** San Francisco Procurement Agency, contract specialist 1963-68; US Army Harry Diamond Labs, branch chief 1972-79; US Army Yuma Proving Ground, dir proc directorate 1979-81; Roman Catholic Diocese of Oakland, dir for ecumenism 1983-. **ORGANIZATIONS:** Chmn of bd Columbia Found 1978-79; dir Youth for Serv 1985-. **MILITARY SERVICE:** AUS pfc 1944-46. **HOME ADDRESS:** 139 Pinto Dr, Vallejo, CA 94591. **BUSINESS ADDRESS:** Dir, Roman Catholic Diocese, 3014 Lake Shore Ave, Office of Ecumenical Affairs, Oakland, CA 94610.

MCGRADY, EDDIE JAMES
Supervisor. **PERSONAL:** Born Mar 06, 1928, Americus, GA; son of Will McGrady and Ola Scott McGrady; married Alice, Dec 26, 1952 (deceased); children: Broderick, Rodney, Valery McGrady Trice. **EDUCATION:** US Army Admin School Germany, Admin 1951; US Const NCO Acad, Sr NCO 1951. **CAREER:** US Army 555th Parachute Infantry, sgt 1946-66; Americus & Police Dept, one of first black patrolman 1966-71; Only Black Star Security Patrol, owner, mgr 1971; Campus Safety, lt, 1st black shift suprv 1973-, captain campus safety and asst dir, 1st black 1985. **ORGANIZATIONS:** Bd mem Americus City School Bd 1967-80, Natl Amer Council Amer Legion; chmn Seventh Dist Title 20 Council 1967-80; post commander CB Dowdell Amer Legion Post 558 1971-76; jr commander 3rd Dist Amer Legion Dept of GA 1976-80; adv Boy Scouts of Amer 1977; v chmn 3rd Dist of GA Assn of Black Elected Officials 1978; com mem GA Sch Bd Assn 1979; bd mem W Central GA Comm Act Councl 1979; commander The Amer Legion Third Dist Dept of GA 1979-80; Natl Membership Comm Amer Legion 1983; appt Patriotic Observance of Flag Etiquette Amer Legion State of GA 1984; chmn bd of directors of West Central GA Community Action Council, 1985-; served on Americus-Sumter County Bi-Centennial Commission, 1987-88. **HONORS/ACHIEVEMENTS:** Outstanding Dist Commander Natl Commander of Amer Legion for State of GA for Membership 1979-80; Mr legionnaire of the Year CB Dowdell Amer Legion 558 1976; Barnum Dosey-Comm Serv Awd Elks & Lodge 691 & BSAT 226 1977, Dedicated Serv Awd Student Union Bd GA SW Coll 1977-78; Cert Black Youth in Action 1979; Awd Support of Delta Sigma Theta GA SW Coll 1980, Support of Kappa Alpha Kappa 1980, Assn of Women Students 1980, Support of SABU 1980, 3rd Dit of Amer Legion Aux 1980, CB Dowdell Amer Legion Post 558 1980, CB Dowdell Amer Legion Ladies Aux 558 1980; Proclamation from Gov George Busbee State of GA 1981; Resolution from GA House of Reps 1981; Outstanding Dist Commander Natl Commander of Amer Legion for State of GA for Membership 1979-80; Lt Col Aide De Campfrom gov Joe Frank Harris State of GA 1984; Comm SV and Region VI of Noble 1987; Outstanding Leadership Award, West Central Georgia Community Action Council 1987; Community Service Award, United Holiness Church 1987; Life Achievement Award, Boy Scout Troup 226, 1988. **MILITARY SERVICE:** AUS 1st sgt E-8 20 yrs active 24 retired reserve; Sr Parachutist Army Commendation Ribbon 1946; Commendation Ribbon with Metal Pendant; 3 Awds by Sec of the Army 1957-66. **HOME ADDRESS:** PO Box 1305, 646 Rainbow Terr, Americus, GA 31709.

MCGRAW, TOM
Professional athlete. **PERSONAL:** Born Nov 21, 1940, Malvern, AR; children: Bryan, Marla. **CAREER:** White Soxs, first baseman 1963-70; Washington, 1971; Cleveland, 1972; CA, 1973; Cleveland Indians, player-coach 1975; Indians, miner league hitting instr 1976-79; Cleveland, firstbase coach 1980-82; San Francisco Giants, hitting instr 1983. **HONORS/ACHIEVEMENTS:** Am Assoc batting title 326 mark named circiuts All-Star tm 1962. **MILITARY SERVICE:** USNG. **BUSINESS ADDRESS:** San Francisco Giants, Candlestick Park, San Francisco, CA 94124.

MCGREGOR, EDNA M. (NEE MCGRUDER)
Educator. **PERSONAL:** Born in Toronto, Ontario, Canada;daughter of Walter Jay McGruder and Charlotte Maud Jackson McGruder; married Albert (dec) (deceased). **EDUCATION:** Howard Univ, BS 1945; Univ of Michigan, MA 1950; Michigan State Univ; Univ of Detroit. **CAREER:** Detroit Schools, health & physical educ teacher 1945-52, science teacher 1952-66; Butzel Jr High School, guidance counselor 1966-68; Osborn High School, guidance counselor 1982-85; retired 1985. **ORGANIZATIONS:** Exec comm counselors Detroit Fed of Teachers 1970-; mem House of Delegates, Detroit Assn of Black Organizations; delegate to the Michigan Senate 1980; mem metro Detroit Guidance Assn; Amer Assn of Univ Women; bd dir Detroit Assn of Univ of Michigan Women Alumnae; life mem NAACP; pres Detroit Urban League Guild; Alpha Kappa Alpha; Alpha Rho Omega; bd of mgmt YWCA; Howard Univ Alumni Club; recording sec Natl Howard Univ Alumni 1974-77; exec comm Natl Howard Univ Alumni Council; Women's Day chairperson Second Baptist Church 1984; project coordinator Health-O-Rama 1984; volunteer Southwest Detroit Hospital 1984; registration staff Metro Detroit Convention & Visitors Bureau 1985; Women's Comm NAACP 1985; pres Howard Univ Alumni Club of Detroit 1986-88; prog chmn Detroit Assn Univ of Michigaan Alumnae; travel agent, Ivery's Professional Travel Agency, 1985-; mem bd of dir, Univ of Michigan, 1989- . **HONORS/ACHIEVEMENTS:** Human Relations Award, Detroit Roundtable of Protestants, Catholics & Jews, 1955; Detroit Urban League, Guilder of the Year, 1972; Alumni Meritorious Award, Detroit Howard Univ Alumni, 1975; Who's Who of World's Women, 1976-77; Notable Americans 1976-77; Who's Who of Amer Women, 12th ed, 1980; Top Ladies of Distinction, 1984; Five-Year Pin for Volunteerism, Southwest Detroit Hospital, 1983. **HOME ADDRESS:** 17333 Muirland, Detroit, MI 48221.

MCGREGOR, ORAN B.
Retired business executive. **PERSONAL:** Born Oct 29, 1925, Marshall, TX; married Eulalia; children: Dietra Wade, Michelle. **EDUCATION:** Bishop Clge, BS 1949; TSU, addtl study 1950-51; Prairie View Clge 1951; LUTC Ins Course, grad; LIAMA Sch in Agency Mgmt, grad. **CAREER:** FW Urban League, bd dir 1958-61; Ft Worth Tarrant Co United Way, bd dir 1971-73; YMCA, bd dir 1962-72; Atlanta Life Ins Co Ofc 2, retired mgr 1972-82; First Fed Equities Mortgage Corp, vice pres 1967-68; Ft Worth Public School, substitute educ spec 1982-. **ORGANIZATIONS:** Trustee Mt Gilead Glen Garden Apts 1967-70; appointee/Elect Dallas-Ft Worth Airport Bd 1980-; mem Omega Phi Psi Frat 1951-; mem YMCA 1952; bd dir FWChap NAACP 1960. **HONORS/ACHIEVEMENTS:** Good Cit Award KNOK Radio 1967; mem Atlanta Life Ins Co Exclusive Pres Club 1953, 1957, 1959, 1961, 1963, 1965, 1969, 1970, 1976, 1977. **MILITARY SERVICE:** AUS 1944-46.

MCGRIER, JERRY, SR.
District attorney. **PERSONAL:** Born Apr 04, 1955, Dallas, TX; son of Joseph McGrier and Irve Leen Bass Looney; married Diane Jones, Aug 21, 1982; children: Jerry McGrier Jr. **EDUCATION:** The Coll of Wooster, Wooster OH, BA Political Science, 1977; SUNY, Buffalo NY, JD, 1980. **CAREER:** Neighborhood Legal Serv, Buffalo NY, staff attorney, 1980-82; Erie County District Attorney, Buffalo NY, asst dist attorney, 1982-. **ORGANIZATIONS:** Mem, Erie County Bar Assn, 1980-, Natl Dist Attorney's Assn, 1982-, Natl Bar Assn, 1984-, New York State Bar Assn, 1984-; chmn, Minority Bar Assn of Western New York, 1986-88; bd of dir, Grace Manor Nursing Home, 1987-. **HONORS/ACHIEVEMENTS:** Special Faculty Award, SUNY Buffalo Law School, 1989; Lawyer's Serv Award, Minority Bar Assn of Western New York, 1988. **BUSINESS ADDRESS:** Assistant District Attorney, Erie County District Attorney's Office, 25 Delaware Ave, Buffalo, NY 14204.

MCGRUDER, CHARLES E.
Physician, educator. **PERSONAL:** Born Jul 25, 1925, Alabama; married Curlie Haslip; children: Charles II, Jeffery. **EDUCATION:** AL A&M Clge; Xavier Univ; Meharry Med Clge, MD 1952. **CAREER:** Meharry Med Clge, assc prof; Flw Amer Clge Ob/Gyn, physician 1956-; Amer Bd Ob/Gyn, diplomate. **ORGANIZATIONS:** Scoutmaster Troop 279; mem exec com Middle TN Cncl BSA. **HONORS/ACHIEVEMENTS:** Recpt Woodbadge Beads in Scouting; Long Rifle; Silver Beaver. **BUSINESS ADDRESS:** 1005 18th Ave N, Nashville, TN 37208.

MCGUFFIN, DOROTHY BROWN
Counselor/educator. **PERSONAL:** Born Jul 27, 1944, Metropolis, IL; daughter of Lester Brown and Mary Brown; married Robert McGuffin; children: Denise, Toni Greathouse.

EDUCATION: Southern Illinois Univ, Carbondale IL, BS 1965, MS 1968; Drake Univ, MS 1985. **CAREER:** Lawrence Adult Ctr, adult educator 1977-81; Des Moines Area Community College, adult educator 1981-84; Young Women's Resource Ctr, community outreach counselor 1984-86; St Louis Community College at Forest Park, assessment specialist 1986-87. **ORGANIZATIONS:** Prog chair/sec/treas, Black Women's Coalition 1976-80; bd mem, Continuing Educ Comm, St Louis Assn for Counseling & Devel; licensed teacher and counselor in 4 states; mem, Amer Assn for Counseling & Develop; troop leader/consultant/bd rep, Girl Scouts Council. **HONORS/ACHIEVEMENTS:** Workshop presenter, Drake Univ Career Develop; Conference presenter, English as a Second Language, Kansas City MO; mem, Kappa Omicron Phi Honor Society. **HOME ADDRESS:** 1821 Lakemont Lane, St Louis, MO 63138. **BUSINESS ADDRESS:** Vocational Assessment Specialist, St Louis Community College, 5600 Oakland Ave, St Louis, MO 63110.

MCGUIRE, CHESTER C., JR.
Educator. **PERSONAL:** Born Oct 29, 1936, Gary, IN; married Julieivory; children: Michael, Angela, Gail. **EDUCATION:** Dartmouth Coll, AB 1958;Univ of Chgo, MBA 1964;Univ Qof Chicago Grad Sch of Bus, PhD 1974. **CAREER:** Inland Steel Co, financial analyst 1962-64; Real Estate Res Corp, economist 1965-68; Wington A Burnett Const Co, vice pres, gen mgr 1968-70; Dept of Cty & Regional Planning Univ of CA Berkeley, faculty mem 1970-. **ORGANIZATIONS:** Mem Am Inst of Planner; Am Econ Assn Mem Bd Dirs Acameda-contra Costa Co Transit Dist; vice chrprsn Berkely Master Plan Revision Com. **MILITARY SERVICE:** USN lt 1959-62. **BUSINESS ADDRESS:** Dept City & Regional Planning, U of CA, Berkeley, CA 94720.

MCGUIRE, CYRIL A.
Labor leader. **PERSONAL:** Born Apr 09, 1926, Lansing, MI; married Mary Jane Haithco; children: Cyril, Terence, Pamela. **EDUCATION:** Lansing Bus Univ, 1954-56; MI State Univ, 1957. **CAREER:** UAW Intl Union, educ rep; Gen Motors, employee 1947-. **ORGANIZATIONS:** Pres UAW Local 652; 1972-77, vice pres 1969-72, chmn shop com 1965-69, shop & committeeman 1959-69, dist committeeman 1956-59; dE UAW Intl Convs 1966, 68, 70, 72, 74, 77; com sec Intl Credentials 1974, com Chmn 1977; instr Labor Rel Studies Lansing Comm Clge 1976-77; vice pres Lansing Labor News Bd 1971-75, pres 1975-77; rec sec Capitol Area Comm Action Progs; mem Genesee Co Comm Action Progs Council; pres vice pres treas sec PTA; bd mem Gtr Lansing Urban League; Gtr Lansing Council Against Alcoholism; treas Dem Bus & Professional Org; Salvation Army; Boy Scouts of Amer; Big Bros Inc; Vol Action Ctr; Health Cntrl; Gtr Lansing Safety Council; Model Cities & Woldumar Nature Ctr; treas Dem 6th Cong Dist; precinct del Ingham Co Dem Exec Com; NAACP; Dem Party; Urban League; MI Labor History Soc; Labor Adv Com Lansing Comm Clge MI State Univ; laison consult Region 1-C Big Bros of Lansing. **HONORS/ACHIEVEMENTS:** Outst Serv award Lasing Model Cities; Man of Year Natl Assc of Negro Bus & Professional Women 1976-77. **MILITARY SERVICE:** AUS m sgt 1950-52. **BUSINESS ADDRESS:** 1940 W Atherton Rd, Flint, MI 48507.

MCGUIRE, JEAN MITCHELL
Business executive. **PERSONAL:** Born Apr 11, 1931, Canton, MA; married Clinton McGuire; children: Johanna, David, Clinton Jr. **EDUCATION:** Howard Univ, 1951; Boston State Coll, BS 1961; Tufts Univ, MEd 1963. **CAREER:** Boston Public Schools, pupil adjust counselor 1963-73; Simmons Coll, instr 1971-74; Boston School Comm, mem 1982-; Metro Council for Educ Opportunity, exec dir 1973-. **ORGANIZATIONS:** Mem, Boston Teachers Union 1962, Black Educ Alliance of MA, Negro Airmans Intl, Natl All Black School Educ; adv bd MA Womens Political Caucus; corporator Homes Savings Bank; mem bd MA Conf United Church of Christ; trustee Boston Children Museum; mem Negro Airmen's Intl New England Chpt; mem Delta Sigma Theta Sorority, Boston Alumnae Chapter; mem MA Black Political Task Force; life mem NAACP. **HONORS/ACHIEVEMENTS:** Alice K Pollitzer Awd, The Encampment for Citizenship 1978; Zeta Phi Beta Sor Awd 1980; Black Achievers Awd Boston 1982; Fred Douglass Public Serv YMCA 1982; Doctor of Humane Letters Salem State Coll 1983; WGBH Community Achvmnt Award; Bristol Co Juvenile Court Award; Big Brothers Assn Award; Founders Award Omega Psi Phi Fraternity Inc, Eta Phi Chapter; MA Teachers Assn Award; Pride Citation Simmons Coll. **BUSINESS ADDRESS:** Executive Dir, METCO, Inc, 55 Dimock St, Roxbury, MA 02119.

MCGUIRE, PAUL M., JR.
Business executive, clergyman. **PERSONAL:** Born Jul 15, 1935, Chicago; married Dorothy; children: Paul III, Andre, Tajuana, Gregory, Monee, Derrick. **EDUCATION:** BS phy educ 1957; US Army Guided Mis Sch, 1958;Univ Chicago, 1972. **CAREER:** Sea-Land Serv Inc, corp mgr equal oppor affairs; Second Bapt Ch Freehold, NY, pastor; Manpower Plan, mgr; Johnson & Johnson, employ; Minority Affairs,mgr 1969; spec proj mgr 1969; prod supvr 1968; RCA, prod supvr 1965-68; Fields Entpr, area mgr 1964-65; IL Nat Guard, fire con supr 1960-63. **ORGANIZATIONS:** Mem Chicago Assn of Commerce & Industry; mem Nat Assn of Market Dev; mem Chicago Urban Affairs Coun; Chicago Urban League; mem Alpha Phi Alpha Frat Inc; oper PUSH; Chicago bd edn; deacon trustee Mt Calvary Bapt Ch. **HONORS/ACHIEVEMENTS:** Placed in NC A&T StateUniv Hall of Fame; recip WGRT Great Guy Award 1973; WBEE Cit of Week Award May 1974. **MILITARY SERVICE:** AUS capt 1957-60. **BUSINESS ADDRESS:** PO Box 900, Edison, NJ.

MCGUIRE, ROSALIE J.
Educator. **PERSONAL:** Born Jan 27, Baltimore; married John McGuire; children: Elwyn Rawlings, Marsden Rawlings. **EDUCATION:** Coppin Tchrs Clge, grad; Morgan State Clge, BS; NY Univ, MA; Columbia Univ, post grad studies; Johns Hopkins Univ, post grad studies; Cath Univ, post grad studies. **CAREER:** Elementary classroom teacher, demonstration teacher, supvr teacher; prin; asst prin; elementary school prin. **ORGANIZATIONS:** Natl pres Natl Assc of Negro Bus & Professional Women's Clubs Inc 1971-75; 1st vice pres NANB&PW 1967-71; 1st vice pres MD League of Women's Clubs; Basileus Natl Sor of Phi Delta Kappa Gamma Chpt; pres Baltimore Club NANB&PW; sec bd trustees Provident Hosp; asst sec United Fund of Cntrl MD; mem at-large Natl Council of Women of US; historian For-Win-Ash-Garden Club; mem Steering Comm Pres Comm on Employment of Handicapped; mem bd dir Comm Cntr Union Bapt Ch, Adv Comm for Day Care Ctr, Sr Choir; Woman Power Negro Clge Women Cits Planning & Hsng Assc MD Council on Educ; NAACP; NEA; Elem Schl Prins Assc; Eastern Star; Queen of Sheba Chpt; Natl Council of Negro Women. **HONORS/ACHIEVEMENTS:** Recip Sojourner Truth Award Baltimore Club NANBPW; Professional Award Philadelphia Club NANBPW; Century Club Award YMCA; GSA Award; Appreciation Award Westchester ClubNANBPW; Comm Serv Award B&P League Ldrshp Westbury Club NANBPW; Extension Award Natl Assc of Negro Bus & Professional Women's Clubs Inc.

MCGUIRT, MILFORD W.
Certified public accountant. **PERSONAL:** Born Aug 15, 1956, Niles, MI; son of Milton McGuirt and Vhaness McGuirt; married Carolyn J Sconiers; children: Shavonne. **EDUCATION:** Western MI Univ, BBA (Cum Laude) 1978. **CAREER:** Coopers & Lybrand, audit mgr 1978-85; Peat Main Mitchell & Co, sr audit mgr 1985-. **ORGANIZATIONS:** Bd mem South Bend IN Chapter of Urban League 1981-82; mem Amer Inst of CPA's 1980, MI Assoc of CPA's 1980, GA Soc of CPA's 1986, Natl Assoc of Black Accountants 1986, Financial Mgr's Soc 1986; Atlanta Chamber of Commerce President's Comm 1986; mem Atlanta West End Rotary Club 1986. **HOME ADDRESS:** 1635 Links Overlook, Stone Mountain, GA 30088. **BUSINESS ADDRESS:** Senior Audit Manager, Peat Main Mitchell & Co, 245 Peachtree Ctr Ave NE, Atlanta, GA 30043.

MCHENRY, DONALD F.
Former ambassador, educator. **PERSONAL:** Born Oct 13, 1936, St Louis, MO; divorced; children: Michael Stephen, Christina Ann, Elizabeth Ann. **EDUCATION:** IL State Univ, BS 1957; So IL Univ, MS 1959; Georgetown U, post grad studies 1962. **CAREER:** Howard Univ Washington, english teacher 1959-62; Brookings Inst, guest scholar 1971-73; Council on Foreign Relations, intl affairs fellow 1971-73; School ofForeign Serv Georgetown Univ, professional lecturer 1971-72; American Univ Washington, professorial lecturer 1975; United Nations, former ambassador; Intl Relations Consultants Inc, pres; Georgetown Univ, rsch prof diplomacy & intl relations 1981-. **ORGANIZATIONS:** Dir Humanitarian Policy Studies Carnegie Endowment for Intl Peace Washington, DC 1973-77; US dep rep UN Security Council Dept of State 1977; US negotiator (Nambia) UN Western Five Contact Group; dir Intl Paper Co, Coca-Cola Co, SmithKline Beckman Corp, First Natl Boston Corp; bd govs Amer Stock Exchange; mem Cncl Foreign Relations, Amer Polit Sci Assoc; bd mem AT&T, Bank of Boston Corp. **HONORS/ACHIEVEMENTS:** Superior Serv Award, Dept of State 1966; author "Micronesia Trust Betrayed" 1975; mem editorial bd Foreign Policy mag; contrib articles to professional journals; Family of Man Awd NY Council Churches 1980.

MCHENRY, JAMES O'NEAL
Administrator. **PERSONAL:** Born Nov 11, 1940, Sterlington, LA; son of S O McHenry and Rebecca McHenry; married Esther C Johnson; children: Stephanie Diane, Ali Kenyatta. **EDUCATION:** Grambling State Univ, BS 1963; Wayne State Univ, MEd 1970, DEd 1979. **CAREER:** Monroe LA Bd of Educ, music tchr 1962-63; US Army Educ Center Europe, GED tchr 1965; Detroit, MI Bd Educ, res tchr 1966-67; Wayne Cty Recdrs Ct, prob officer 1967-73; Asst supvr Recorders Ct Probation Dept 1973-78; certified marriage counselor MI Dept Licensing & Reg 1975-; dir Recorders Ct Drug Prog 1978-80; dir Recorders Ct Pretrial Serv 1980-82; lecturer Oakland Univ 1984-. **ORGANIZATIONS:** Mem Omega Psi Phi Frat 1960-. **HONORS/ACHIEVEMENTS:** Second degree black Belt (Ea Dan) United Tae Kwon Do 1978; special awd NARCO 1983; leadership awd Recorders Ct Prob Dept 1983; pres awd Grambling State Univ 1983. **MILITARY SERVICE:** AUS e-4 3 yrs. **HOME ADDRESS:** 17191 Pennington Dr, Detroit, MI 48221. **BUSINESS ADDRESS:** Chief Officer, US Pretrial Serv Agency, US Courthouse, 231 W Lafayette St, Detroit, MI 48226.

MCHENRY, MARY WILLIAMSON
Educator. **PERSONAL:** Born Jan 23, 1933, Washington, DC; children: Michael S, Christina A, Elizabeth A. **EDUCATION:** Mt Holyoke Coll, AB 1950-54; Columbia Univ, MA 1955-60; George Washington Univ, 1962-65. **CAREER:** Howard Univ, instr in english 1960-62; George Washington Univ, asst prof of english 1964-69; DC Teachers Coll, guest lecturer in english 1967-68; Fed City Coll, asst prof of english 1969-74; Mt Holyoke Coll, assoc prof of english, assoc dean of studies 1974-. **ORGANIZATIONS:** Instr amer studies Peace Corps Training Prog 1962-63; adv bd Radcliffe Seminars Forum for Continuing Ed 1980; consult editor Univ MA Press 1978-79; mem Phi Beta Kappa MHC Chap 1954. **HONORS/ACHIEVEMENTS:** Fellowship John Jay Whitney Oppty 1954-55,57-58; Fellowship Danforth Found 1961-62; Natl Endowment for the Humanities 1972-73. **BUSINESS ADDRESS:** Associate Professor, Mt Holyoke Coll, South Hadley, MA 01075.

MCILWAIN, ALBERT HOOD
Executive director. **PERSONAL:** Born Apr 25, 1936, Lancaster Co, SC; married Nadine Williams; children: Jeaneen, Floyd. **EDUCATION:** Kent State U, 1959-60; Malone Coll, BS Elem Ed 1964. **CAREER:** Canton City Schls, elem instr 1964-70; Stark Metropl Hsg Auth, deputy dir 1970-82; Star Metropl Hsg Auth, exec dir 1982-. **ORGANIZATIONS:** Mem & sec Ohio Hsg Auth Conf 1983-84; exec brd mem Natl Asso of Hsg & Redevel Off 1984-85; mem Comm Hsg Res Brd; mem Public Hsg Auth DirAsso; brd of trte YMCA; chrmn Comm Bld Prog; brd of ttrte Stark County Lib; memshp chain Stark County NAACP. **HONORS/ACHIEVEMENTS:** Jenning schlr Martha Holden Jennings Found 1970; serv awd Buckeye Coun Boy Scouts of Am; treas Omega Psi Phi Frat. **HOME ADDRESS:** 2943 Coventry Blvd NE, Canton, OH 44705. **BUSINESS ADDRESS:** Executive Dir, Stark Metropolitan Hsng Auth, 1800 W Tuscarawas St, Canton, OH 44702.

MCILWAIN, NADINE WILLIAMS
Elected official, businesswoman. **PERSONAL:** Born Jul 29, 1943, Canton, OH; daughter of Willie J Williams and Mabel W Williams; married Albert H McIlwain; children: Jeaneen, Floyd. **EDUCATION:** Malone Coll, BA 1970; Univ of Akron, MA 1978. **CAREER:** Canton City Health Dept, lab asst 1962-65; OH Bell Telephone Co, opr & consult 1967-70; Canton City Schools, teacher 1970-; Nefertiti Nuptials, owner/operator 1984-; Canton City Council, ward councilperson 1984-86; Canton City Schools, curriculum specialist. **ORGANIZATIONS:** Pres Frontiers Intl Aux 1971; dir hs migrant program Canton City Schools 1975-82; pres Leila Green Educators Council 1978; sec Amer Business Womens Assoc 1980; state parliamentarian Natl Black Womens Leadership Caucus 1983-84; ward councilwoman Canton City Council 1984-; part-owner/operator Nefertiti Nuptuals 1984-. **HONORS/ACHIEVEMENTS:** Theses, Social & Structural Determinants of Methodone Clinic Attendance 1978; Woman of the Year Canton Negro Oldtimers Athletic Assoc 1979; Political Awd Black Women's Leadership Caucus 1981; Woman of the Year Greater Canton Amer Bus Women's Assoc 1982. **HOME ADDRESS:** 2943 Coventry Blvd NE, Canton, OH 44705.

MCINTOSH, ALICE T.
Management consultant. **PERSONAL:** Born Jan 10, 1933, Miami, FL; daughter of James S Jones and Thelma M Jones; married William R McIntosh, Sep 22, 1979; children: Otis Edwards, Yvonne Edwards, Jaynie Edwards, Zigmond Robinson. **EDUCATION:** Attended Savannah State College, Savannah GA, 1951; attended Indiana Business College, Muncie IN, 1953-56; attended Ball State Univ, Munice IN, 1980-81. **CAREER:** Action Inc, Muncie IN, manpower coordinator, 1968-70, executive dir, 1971-74, consultant, 1974-76; MSS Inc, Muncie IN, owner, consultant, 1976-83; Human Rights Comm, Muncie IN, executive dir, 1978-80; Muncie City Council, councilwoman, 1984-88; INC Inc, Muncie IN, Neighborhood Coordinator, 1986-. **ORGANIZATIONS:** Advisor, Black Achievers Inc, 1986-; mem, JTPA screening committee, 1987-. **HONORS/ACHIEVEMENTS:** Author of govt proposals and projects. **MILITARY SERVICE:** Women's Army Corps, private, 1951-52. **HOME ADDRESS:** 1412 East 8th St, Muncie, IN 47302. **BUSINESS ADDRESS:** 1121 East 7th St, Muncie, IN 47302.

MCINTOSH, JAMES E.
Dentist. **PERSONAL:** Born Jul 15, 1942, St Louis, MO. **EDUCATION:** Univ MO, BA 1965; Meharry Coll, DDS 1969; Sydenham Hosp, rotating internship 1970, periodentics residency 1971; Columbia U, MPH 1975. **CAREER:** Sydenham Hosp, dir 1975-; Tri-State Eval of Accident Ins, consult 1974-; Assn of NY Nghbrhd & Hlth Ctrs, consult 1974-; Columbia U, asst prof 1974-; Pvt Practice, 1971-; Dental Clinic Sydenham Hosp, adminstr 1971-; dental Hlth educ 1970; Cloverbottom Ment Hlth Inst, 1969; Nashville Hlth Dept, rsrch 1968-69;Univ MO, fellow 1963-65; Fed Food & Drug Div, insp 1965. **ORGANIZATIONS:** Pres of Medical bd & execl com mem Sydenham Hosp med bd 1976-; Sydenham Hosp med bd exec com 1976-; MO Dental Soc 1972-; 1st Dist Dental Soc 1970-; NY State Dental So 1970-; Am Pub Hlth Assn 1974-; Nat Dental Assn 1969-; Nat Student Dental Assn 1956-69; NAACP 1965-; Black Am Med & Dent Assn of Students 1969-; Ewell Neal Dental Soc 1965-69; Rose Hill Bapt Ch 1958-; rep Nat Conclave of Kappa Alpha Psi 1964; diplomate Nat Dental Bds 1969-; bd Eligible Am Acad of Pub Hlth & Preventive Dentistry 1974-. **HONORS/ACHIEVEMENTS:** Nat Hlth Professions Scholarship 1965-69; Omicron Sigma Nat Hon Ldrshp Frat 1976-; award for Table Clinic Presentation 1969; del Proctor & Gamble Rsrch-Symposium 1968; pres Student Faculty Rels Com Meharry Med Coll 1968-69; class pres Dental Sch 1967-69. **BUSINESS ADDRESS:** Dir of Dentistry, Harlem Hospital, City of NY Health & Hosp Corp, 506 Lenox Ave, New York, NY 10037.

MCINTOSH, RHODINA COVINGTON
Lawyer. **PERSONAL:** Born May 26, 1947, Chicago Heights, IL; daughter of William Covington and Cora Cain Covington; married Gerald Alfred McIntosh, Dec 14, 70; children: Gary Allen, Garvey Anthony, Ayana Kai. **EDUCATION:** MI State Univ, BA (Cum Laude) 1969; Univ Detroit, JD 1978. **CAREER:** MI State Univ Office of Equal Oppor, asst to dir 1969-70; Bell & Hudson PC Detroit, law clerk 1977-79; Covington McIntosh & Assocs Intl, pres Detroit MI, Washington DC, and Mbabane Swaziland 1980-83; Univ Swaziland and Botswana Kwaluseni Swaziland, lecturer 1981-83; US AID Office of Private and Voluntary Coop, chief information & tech assistance 1983-87, chief information & prog support 1987-88; Automation Research Systems, Limited, corporate counsel 1988-. **ORGANIZATIONS:** Founding bd mem Women's Justice Ctr Detroit 1975-77; coord Women's Leadership Conf Wayne State Univ Detroit 1979; bd mem/counselor Awareness Inc Detroit 1979-80; consultant Polit Educ Workshops Detroit, Flint, Lansing, Saginaw, Grand Rapids MI 1979-80; speaker Ohio Republican Co Leadership Conf 1980; founding bd mem Wayne Co Chap MI Republican Women's TAsk Force Detroit 1980; speaker Detroit Urban League 1980; main rapporteur 1st All Africa Law ConfUniv Swaziland and Botswana Kwaluseni Swaziland 1981; Detroit Urban League 1981; chairperson foreign relations subcom Natl Black Women's Polit Caucus Washington 1984; bd mem Amer Oppor Foundation Washington 1984-; charter mem Natl Assn of Female Executives 1983-; mem GOP Women's Network 1986-87; Phi Alpha Delta Law Fraternity, 1972-; Parent Teacher Association of Springbrook High School, 1986-; Naval Academy Athletic Assn, 1987-; Michigan State University Alumni Assn 1985-; St Teresa of Avila Roman Catholic Church, 1987-. **HONORS/ACHIEVEMENTS:** Scholar Martin Luther King Jr Ctr for Social Change Atlanta 1976; Awd Detroit Women's Justice Ctr 1978; Awd Goodwill Charity Club Chicago Heights IL 1978;Awd Outstanding Volunteer Service Reagan/Bush Campaign 1980; Awd Detroit Edison 1980; Awd Wayne County Chap Republican Women's Task Force 1980; New Republicans MI 1981; mem Delta Sigma Theta; The AID/PVO Partnership: Sharing Goals and Resources in the Work of Development 1984, 1987; Voluntary Foreign Aid Programs: Report on U.S. Private Voluntary Organizations Engaged in Relief and Development Registed by USAID 1983-86; The Individual Under African Law. **BUSINESS ADDRESS:** Corporate Counsel, Automation Research Systems, Limited, 4480 King Street, Suite 500, Alexandria, VA 22302.

MCINTOSH, SIMEON CHARLES
Educator. **PERSONAL:** Born Jul 14, 1944, Carriacou, Grenada. **EDUCATION:** York U, BA 1971; Howard U, JD 1974; Columbia U, LlM 1975. **CAREER:** Howard U, asst prof of law; Univ of OK, asst prof of law 1975-76. **ORGANIZATIONS:** Soc of Am Law Tchrs; Am Legal Studies Assn. **BUSINESS ADDRESS:** 2935 Upton St, Washington, DC 20008.

MCINTOSH, WALTER CORDELL
Educational administrator. **PERSONAL:** Born Jul 26, 1927, Lake Forest, IL; married Bernice Clay; children: Ann Elizabeth, David, Jeffrey. **EDUCATION:** Macalester Coll St Paul MN, BA Econ; Natl Coll of Ed Evanston IL, MA Ed; Columbia Univ NY, EdD. **CAREER:** Cuyahoga Welfare Dept, caseworker; Chicago Dept of Welfare, vocational counselor; LA Unified School Dist, teacher 1958-68; W Los Angeles Coll, instr english, spec reading 1972-73, coord basic skills 1973-76, dean evening div 1976-77; LA SW Coll, pres 1977-. **ORGANIZATIONS:** Mem Kappa Alpha Psi, Kappa Delta Pi, Phi Delta Kappa, NAACP, LA Urban League; bd of dir S Central LA Reg Ctr, LA Police Commiss Adv Comm. **HONORS/ACHIEVEMENTS:** Lifetime Awd Membership 10th Dist PTA LA 1968; Martin Luther King Fellow Columbia Univ NY 1968-71; Woodrow Wilson Fellow Columbia Univ NY; Social Sci Found Fellow Columbia Univ NY; Outstanding Teacher W LA Coll 1974. **MILITARY SERVICE:** AUS corpl 1946-48; Good Conduct Medal. **BUSINESS ADDRESS:** President, Los Angeles SW College, 1600 W Imperial Highway, Los Angeles, CA 90047.

MCINTOSH, WILLIAM E., JR.
Business executive. **PERSONAL:** Born Jun 13, 1945, Minneapolis, MN; married Helen B; children: Brian Justin, Blair Jason, Blake Jamone. **EDUCATION:** Metropolitan State Coll, AA 1970; MacAlester Coll, BA 1972; Univ of MN, 1973. **CAREER:** Chrysler Corp, staff exec to USAS vice pres 1982-83, USAS div 9 positions 1974-, mgr retail dealer devel prog 1983-. **ORGANIZATIONS:** Mem Urban League 1972-, Coll Alumni Bd 1972-, NAACP 1976-, Operation PUSH 1977-, Disabled Vets 1980-, Amer Prod & Inventory Control 1983-, Conf of Mayor's Auto Task Force 1985-; instructor Dale Carnegie Course 1983-84. **HONORS/ACHIEVEMENTS:** Dist Mgr of the Year Chrysler Corp 1976, 1977; Comm Excellence Awd Operation PUSH 1979; Black Achiever in Industry YMCA 1980. **MILITARY SERVICE:** USMC sgt E-5 1962-67; Good Conduct Medal, Expeditionary Medals, Cuba & Vietnam 1966.

MCINTYRE, DIANNE R.
Choreographer. **PERSONAL:** Born Jul 18, 1946, Cleveland. **EDUCATION:** OH State Univ, BFA dance. **CAREER:** Sounds Fin Motion dance co, choreog, Alvin Ailey's Co, chorog "Deep South Suite" & "Ancestral Voices"; Negro Ensemble Co, choreog "The Great Macdaddy" 1974 & 77; NBC-TV, choreog "Violence in Am" 1976; Off-Broadway, choreog "Bebop" 1979; Ozake Shange's Chorepoems, choreog "Boogie Woogie Landscapes" & "Spell #1" 1979; choreog "The Last Minstrel Show" 1980; Works by Cecil Taylor & Max Roach, collaborator; Sounds in Motion Dance Sch Harlem, NY founder; cntrl AL affiliate artists inc, performs, lec & tchs 1974-75; Harlem sch arts, fac mem 1971-73. **HONORS/ACHIEVEMENTS:** United Black Artists of Cornell Univ Audelco Award for choreography 1979. **BUSINESS ADDRESS:** c/o Sounds in Motion Dance, 290 Lenox Ave, New York, NY 10027.

MCINTYRE, JOHN HENRY, SR.
Clergyman. **PERSONAL:** Born Jun 03, 1925, Sylacauga, AL; married Estella Gaffney; children: Phyllis, John H. **EDUCATION:** Immunal Coll, BA BTh 1958; Calver Bible Coll, 1963; Union Bapt Sem, DD 1972. **CAREER:** Friendship Bapt Ch Talladesa Springs, AL, pastor; Shiloh Bapt Ch Pres Sylacauga Br & NAACP, pastor. **ORGANIZATIONS:** Bd mem Talladega Clay Randolph Comm Action Comm Inc; bd mem E AL Regional Planning & Devel Comm; exec bd Rushing Springs Assn chmn Sylacauga Blac Cemetery; mem Nat Bapt Conv Inc USA; mem AL Bapt Conv Inc Qmem NAACP Sylacauga IMP; sec treas Greater Sylacauga Minsterial Assn. **HONORS/ACHIEVEMENTS:** Man of Yr 1971; Minister of Yr 1975 Sylacauga Br NAACP & Shiloh Bapt Ch; treas Nat Singing Assn. **MILITARY SERVICE:** USAF s/sgt 1951-53. **BUSINESS ADDRESS:** P O Box 1164, Sylacauga, AL.

MCINTYRE, MILDRED J.
Clinical neuro-psychologist. **PERSONAL:** Born in Boston, MA. **EDUCATION:** Swarthmore Coll, BA 1965; Clark Univ, MA 1972, PhD 1975. **CAREER:** McLean Hosp, rsch asst 1966-68; Clark Univ, rschr 1968-72; Univ of MA, asst prof 1975-80, consulting psychologist 1977-. **ORGANIZATIONS:** Rsch assoc Childrens Hosp; mem Intl Neuropsych Soc. **HONORS/ACHIEVEMENTS:** Ford Foundation Fellow 1972-73; Natl Fellowships Fund Awd 1973-74.

MCIVER, JOHN DOUGLAS
Mayor. **PERSONAL:** Born Nov 07, 1941, Savannah, GA; son of James McIver and Hagar Norma McIver; married Gloria Grant; children: Andrea, Timothy, Anthony, Papneia, Cassandra. **EDUCATION:** Liberty Co HS, diploma 1959. **CAREER:** City of Riceboro, mayor; Interstate Paper Corp Riceboro, GA, papermaker 2nd asst 1968. **ORGANIZATIONS:** Mem Liberty Co Industrial Auth 1980; vice chmn Riceboro Comm Foundation 1982; chmn New Zion Baptist Church 1977-; pres Georgia Conference of Black Mayors 1989. **HONORS/ACHIEVEMENTS:** First Black Dorchester Credit Union 1978; comm leader Riceboro Comm Found 1983. **MILITARY SERVICE:** AUS spec 4th class 2 yrs. **HOME ADDRESS:** PO Box 246, Riceboro, GA 31323. **BUSINESS ADDRESS:** Mayor, City of Riceboro, PO Box 269, Riceboro, GA 31323.

MCIVER, MARGARET HILL
Educator. **PERSONAL:** Born Jun 03, 1925, High Point, NC; married Conerlious W; children: Conerlious W, Jr, Deborah Ann. **EDUCATION:** Bennett Coll Greensboro, NC, BA 1944; AtlantaUniv Sch of Social Work, MSW 1946; Harvard U, EdM 1967. **CAREER:** Douglass Middle Sch, guidance counselor 1969-; Douglass High Sch GA, tchr guidance counselor 1953-69; Morris Brown Coll, dean of women 1951-53; FL A&M U, counselor for women 1949-51: Clark Coll Atlanta, tchr counselor 1946-49; Proj Upward Bound Norman Park Coll GA, counselor 1968-70; GA Governor's Honors Program for Gifted Wesleyan Coll Macon, GA, guidance counselor 1972-74, 79. **ORGANIZATIONS:** Pres GA br Am Personnel & Guidance Assn 1968; pres GA Sch Counselors Assn 1973-74; dir district 2 GA Assn of Educators 1974-77. **HONORS/ACHIEVEMENTS:** Alpha Kapa Mu Honor Soc Bennett Coll Greensboro, NC 1943; Tchr of the Yr Thomasville, GA Tchrs Assn 1962; Counselor of the Yr District 2 GA Sch Counselors Assn 1972; Women of the Yr Thomasville, GA C of C 1975. **BUSINESS ADDRESS:** Douglass Middle School, Forrest St, Thomasville, GA 31792.

MCKANDERS, JULIUS A., II
Attorney, clergyman. **PERSONAL:** Born Jun 21, 1941, Jackson, MS; married Yvonne Mclittle. **EDUCATION:** Wayne St U, JD 1971; Henry Ford Comm Coll, 1962; Detroit Inst Tech, 1962; Eastern MI O, BS 1964;Univ MI Med Sch, 1966; Morehouse Scho of Religion, ITC 1976. **CAREER:** Metro Atlanta Rapid Transit & Auth, dir contracts & procur 1972-; Ebenezer Bapt Ch, asso minister; Council on Leg Ed Opp, deputy dir oper 1971-72; Detroit Bd Ed, mgr 1970-71; Price Waterhouse, sr mgmt 1969-70; IRS Detroit, sys analyst 1967-69; City of Detroit, sys analyst-programmer 1966-67; Univ MI Med Sch, research asst 1964-66; MI Bar, admitted 1972; GA Bar, 1974. **ORGANIZATIONS:** Mem Am Bar Assn; Detroit Bar Assn; Atlanta Bar Assn; Phi Alpha Delta; Purch Mgmt Assn #Of GA; Atlanta Jr C of C; bd dirs Martin L King Jr ChildDevelop Center; bd dirs NAACP Atlanta Br Program Comm Am Pub Transit Assn; adv council Martin L King, Jr Handicapped Child Project; bd mem Ebenezer Bapt Ch Charitable Found & life mem NAACP; ordained Bapt min. **BUSINESS ADDRESS:** 101 Professional Bldg, 2192 Campbellton Rd SW, Atlanta, GA 30311.

MCKAY, KAREN NIMMONS
Counselor. **PERSONAL:** Born Dec 21, 1947, Bronx. **EDUCATION:** BA sociology 1969. **CAREER:** State Univ of NY at Stony Brook, admissions counselor; Stony Brook Foundaton Inc, admin asst for operations Jan-Apr 1970. **ORGANIZATIONS:** Mem Nat Assn for Foreign Student Affairs 1974; StateUniv of NY Coll Admissions Personnel 1974-. **BUSINESS ADDRESS:** State Univ NY, Admiss Ofc Admins Bldg 125, Stony Brook, NY 11794.

MCKAYLE, DONALD COHEN
Choreographer, director, writer. **PERSONAL:** Born Jul 06, 1930, New York, NY; married Lea Vivante; children: Guy, Gabrielle, Liane. **EDUCATION:** Coll of the City of NY, 1947-49. **CAREER:** Choreog of films incl, "The Jazz Singer" 1980; "The Minstrel Man" 1975-76; "Bed Knobs & Broomsticks" 1970; choreog of Broadway plays incl, "Sophisticated Ladies" 1981; "The Last Minstrel Show" 1974, dir/choreog Raisin 1974; "Dr Jazz" 1975; "Golden Boy" 1964; dir/choreog TV incl, "The Annual Emmy Awds" 1979;"Free to Be You and Me" 1974; "The Hollywood Palace" (with Diana Ross) 1969; "The 49th Annual Acad Awards" 1977; "The Minstrel Man" 1976; "Good Times" 1974; "Komedy Tonite" 1977; "The Richard Pryor Special" 1977; "The 43rd Annual Acad Awards" 1973; choreog/creator of num otherTV shows, concerts and ballets; Regional Theatre, Denver Center Theatre, Mark Taper Forum, dir/choreog. **ORGANIZATIONS:** Bd dirs, Amer Dance Festival Durham NC, New Dance Group NYC; Clarke Cntr for Perform Arts NYC; Soc of Stage Dir & Choreog NYC; Modern Dance Found; The Dance Circle Boston, MA; Natl Cntr for Afro-Amer Artists Roxbury, MA; natl Endowment for the Arts Dance Panel; natl Arts Awards Dance Panel; mem of faculty, Julliard Sch of Music; Bennington Coll CA Inst of the Arts; Martha Graham Sch of Contemp Dance; Bard Coll; Connecticut Coll; Univ of OR; Inner City Cultural Center; Univ of WA; Portland State Univ; FL State Univ; Alvin Ailey Amer Dance Center; mem Soc of Stage Dir & Choreog; Assn of Amer Dance Companies; ASCAP; AEA; AGMA; AFTRA; AGVA; fellow Black Acad of Arts and Letters; fellow Dir Guild of Amer. **HONORS/ACHIEVEMENTS:** NAACP Image Award Writer/Concept & Best Stage Play "Sophisticated Ladies" 1981; Outer Circle Critics Award Choreography "Sophisticated Ladies" 1981; DramaLogue Critics Award Choreography "Evolution of the Blues" 1978; Capezio Award 1963; Emmy Nomination Choreography "The Minstrel Man" 1977; Antoinette Perry Nom-Direction "Raisin" 1974; Choreog "Raisin" 1974; Choreog "Dr Jazz" 1975; Choreog "Golden Boy" 1964; Choreog "Sophisticated Ladies" 1981; articles & publns, "The Dance Has Many Faces" Columbia Univ Press; "Modern Dance - 7 Points of View" Wesleyan Univ Press.

MCKEE, ADAM E., JR.
Veterinarian. **PERSONAL:** Born Apr 12, 1932, Fairfield, AL; married Barbara Nance; children: Adam III, Eric, Brett. **EDUCATION:** DillarUniv New Orleans, AB 1954; Tuskegee Inst, DVM 1958; Vet Path Armed Forces Inst Pathology, res 1963-66. **CAREER:** Naval Med Research Inst Nat Naval Med Cntr Bethesda, MD, chmn Qqqexptl path dept 1969-; Biol & Med Scis Div Naval Radiological Defense Lab San Francisco, chief vet & path 1967-69; Lackland AFB, TX, chief altitude chamber unit aerospace path 1966-67, sentry dog clinician 1960-63; Istanbul, Turkey, vet 1958-60. **ORGANIZATIONS:** Mem Am Vet Med Assn; Intl Acad Pathology; Washington So Scanning Electron Microscopy; Am Soc Microbiology; mem Post Doctoral Res Asso Prog Com; chmn Naval Med Res Inst Policy Adv Council scientific & managerial bd 1975-76; Am Assn Lab Animal Scis; Omega Psi Phi mem pres Tuskegee Vet Med Alumni Assn 1975-; mem USAF Distinguished Unit 1960-64. **HONORS/ACHIEVEMENTS:** Commendation medal USAF 1963; Special Merit Award Naval Med Research Inst 1976; keynote speaker 6th Annual Intl Scanning Electron Microscopy Symposium Chicago 1973; chrm Scanning Electron Cicroscopy Application in Med Microbiology 10th Annual Interna Scanning Electron Microsocpy Symposium Chicago 1977. **MILITARY SERVICE:** USAF 1975. **BUSINESS ADDRESS:** Naval Med Research Inst, Nat Naval Med Cntr, Bethesda, MD 20014.

MCKEE, CLARENCE VANZANT
Attorney. **PERSONAL:** Born Nov 16, 1942, Buffalo, NY. **EDUCATION:** Hobart Coll, BA 1965; HowardUniv Sch of Law, JD 1972. **CAREER:** Dept HEW, civil rights compliance ofcr 1966-67; Senator Jacob Javits, legal asst 1969-71; Sen Charles Macmathias, legal asst 1971-72; Office of Congressional Relations US Civil & Aeronautics Bd, acting dir 1972; Industry EEO Unit Office of Genl Cncl FCC, dep chief 1973-76; Fed Communications Commn, legal asst; Commissioner Ben Hooks FCC, legal asst 1976-77; WTVT Tampa, ceo/chairman. **ORGANIZATIONS:** Bd mem DC United Way; mem Am Bar Assn; Nat Conf of Black Lawyers; Fed Bar Assn; Unified Bar of DC; NY, PA, DC Bars; commentator FOX Broadcasting Co Washington. **HONORS/ACHIEVEMENTS:** Outstndg Young Men of Am Award 1970; Outstanding Alumni Public Serv Award 1969; outstanding Achievement in Intl Law Award 1972; Am Jurisprudence Award 1970-71; publ article Chineese Legal Sys 1972. **BUSINESS ADDRESS:** Pepper & Corazzini, 1776 K St, Suiet 200, Washington, DC 20006.

MCKEE, LONETTE
Actress. **PERSONAL:** Married Leo Compton. **CAREER:** Actress in one-woman off-Broadway Show "Lady Day at Emerson's Bar & Grill" about Billie Holiday; movies include Sparkle, 'Round Midnight, The Cotton Club, Brewster's Millions; appeared in Miami Vice episode; regional hit record Stop, Don't Worry About It. **HONORS/ACHIEVEMENTS:** Tony nomination for role as "Julie" in a pre-Broadway revival of Showboat 1983.

MCKEE, THEODORE A.
Judge. **PERSONAL:** Born in Rochester, NY; married Dr Ana Pujols. **EDUCATION:** State Univ of NY, BA 1965; Syracuse Univ Coll of Law, JD (magna cum laude) 1975. **CAREER:** Wolf Block Schorr & Solis-Cohen, assoc 1975-77; Eastern Dist of PA, asst US atty 1977-80; Law Dept City of Phila, deputy city solicitor 1980-83; Court of Common Pleas Commonwealth of PA, judge. **ORGANIZATIONS:** Bd of dirs Crises Intervention Network. **BUSINESS ADDRESS:** Judge Court Of Common Pleas, 1st Judicial Dist, 1516 One East Penn Square, Philadelphia, PA 19107.

MCKEEL, THOMAS BURL
Physician. **PERSONAL:** Born Jan 24, 1944, Pine Bluff, AR; married Rebecca Hill; children: Hilda Celeste, Trocelia Rana. **EDUCATION:** Fisk Univ, BA 1965; Univ of AR, MD 1969. **CAREER:** Private Practice, physician. **BUSINESS ADDRESS:** 6724 Troost, Ste 615, Kansas City, MO 64131.

MCKEEVER, VITO
Professional athlete. **PERSONAL:** Born Oct 08, 1961, Dunnellon, FL. **EDUCATION:** Univ of FL. **CAREER:** Oakland Invaders, corner back 1984-. **HONORS/ACHIEVEMENTS:** 4 yr letterman for Gators.

MCKELDIN, HARRY WHITE, JR.
Educator. **PERSONAL:** Born Mar 11, 1915, Athens, TN; married Lyda M Yette; children: Iris Yvonne Beard, Harriette E. **EDUCATION:** Knoxville Coll, BS 1947; Columbia U, MA 1955. **CAREER:** Univ of TN Chatt, dir, spl std prog 1985; Chattanooga Hamilton Co, exec dir comm act agency 1965-69; Chattanooga Pub Sch, prin 1964-69, asst prin 1960-64, tchr 1957-59; Camden AL, tchr, asst prin, coach 1947-57; Chattanooga Hum Serv Dept, interim dir; S Reg Ed Bd, consult Reg 4 Adv bd, Div of Std Spl Progs. **ORGANIZATIONS:** Pres St Assn of Std Spl Prog 1985; Planning Com SE Reg TN Conf on Soc Wlfr; St Dev Disabilities Bd; bd of asso Chatt St Tech Comm Coll;Chatt United Fund Allocation Com; dir Round TableUniv TN SE Clin Ed Ctr; NAACP; Nat Bus League; Alpha Phi Alpha Frat; Chatt Bd C fo C; bd Trustees Hosp Authority Co Manpwr Prog; Chatt Hamilton Co Team Evaluatn Ctr; past pres Delta Pi Field Ch, Phi Delta Kappa;Univ TN at Chatt Athltc Adv Com. **HONORS/ACHIEVEMENTS:** Serv Award Alpha Phi Alpha Frat 1975; Tchr of the Yr Wilcox Co 1956-57; Outstndng Serv Award Chatt Hum Serv Dept 1976; Key to the City Award City of Chatt 1969; Hon Memshp Award Kappa Delta Pi, Mu Alpha Chap 1976. **MILITARY SERVICE:** Aus staff sgt 1941-46. **BUSINESS ADDRESS:** 615 Mc Callie Ave, Chattanooga, TN 37401.

MCKELLAR, STEPHEN ALEXANDER
Elected city official. **PERSONAL:** Born Apr 26, 1956, Chester, PA; married Beverly Rice; children: Tamika, Jonee. **EDUCATION:** VA State Univ, 1974-76; St Joseph's Univ, BS 1980. **CAREER:** Dept of Sts & Public Improvements, 1st exec asst 1978-81; Co of Delaware, mun energy coord 1981-83; City of Chester, dir of parks pub prop & rec. **ORGANIZATIONS:** Mem St Michael Roman Catholic Church; mem NAACP; mem Franklin Lodge #58; F&AM chmn YMCA Bd of Mgrs; mem Republican Party of Chester PA 1974-; mem DelCo Republican Council 1984-; mem Alpha Phi Alpha; mem, Minaret Temple #174, AEAONMS 1987; mem, Charles E Gordon Consistory #65 Scottish Rite Freemasonry 1986. **HONORS/ACHIEVEMENTS:** Outstanding Comm Contribution Awd YIA 1974; Comm Involvement Awd Club Amoebia 1982; Humanitarian Awd Chester Black Expo 1984; Outstanding Young Men of Amer Awd 1984. **BUSINESS ADDRESS:** Councilman, 5th & Welsh Sts Municipal Bl, 838 W 6th St, Chester, PA 19013.

MCKELLER, THOMAS LEE
Educator. **PERSONAL:** Born Dec 31, 1940, Middletown, OH; children: Yolanda M, Monica L, Julia L. **EDUCATION:** Monmouth Coll, AA, Business Law 1962-64; Univ of Toledo, BA, Business & Educ, 1969-73; MI State Correctional Special School, Certificate, 1977; MI Constr Training Council, Certificate, 1979. **CAREER:** Berrien City State Correction Center Counselor, 1978-81; Benton Harbor Elementary School Advisory Comm, chmn, 1982-83; The Church of Our Lord & Savior, minister, 1982-; Benton Harbor Area Schools Bd of Educ, trustee, 1983-84; Educ instructor; Benton Harbor Schools, security 1984-. **ORGANIZATIONS:** Sgt major, OH Explorer Scouts Drill Council, 1964-65; coordinator, OH Model Cities Signing Comm 1965-67; corner back Cincinatti Bengals Professional Football Team 1966-67; pres Silver Tax & Bookkeeping Serv 1978-80; finance chmn supt Educ Task Force 1983; dir Brotherhood of Christian Ministers 1983; assoc dir BH Marriage Counselors Assn 1984; bd of dir Full Gospel Businessmans Assn 1984. **HONORS/ACHIEVEMENTS:** Published "I Am Gods Child" Oh Methodist Youth Dept 1960, "Black Is" US Black Legion of Scholars 1967; chmn OH Hi-Y Council 1971; Pres Chosen Few Literary Soc 1974. **MILITARY SERVICE:** USAF tech sgt E-6 6 yrs; Pres Citation, Special Merit Award, Special Serv Medal, 1960-66; USMC 2 yrs sgt Pres Citation 1958. **BUSINESS ADDRESS:** Security, Benton Harbor Area Schools, 880 Colfax, Benton Harbor, MI 49022.

MCKELPIN, JOSEPH P.
Educator. **PERSONAL:** Born May 06, 1914, Leflore Co, MS; married Peggy A Jones; children: Joseph P Jr, Emmett O. **EDUCATION:** SU, AB 1943;Univ WI, MS 1948, PhD 1952. **CAREER:** Fed City Coll, prof ed 1974-; Morris Brown Coll, dean 1973-74; S Assn Colls & Schs, dir resrch & eval 1967-73; SU, prof ed 1952-62. **ORGANIZATIONS:** Mem Phi Delta Kappa; Kappa Delta Pi; Kappa Phi Kappa; Omega Psi Phi. **MILITARY SERVICE:** AUS 2nd lt 1943-46. **BUSINESS ADDRESS:** 724 9 St NW, Washington, DC 20001.

MCKENZIE, EDNA B. (NEE CHAPPELL)
Historian. **PERSONAL:** Born Dec 29, 1923, Grindstone, PA; married Edmond (died 1986); children: Clyde Marc, Edmond Robert. **EDUCATION:** Univ of Pittsburgh, BSEd 1968, MA History 1970, PhD History 1973. **CAREER:** Community Coll of Allegheny County, assoc prof of History 1973-, chairperson black minority & ethnic studies 1973-; Seton Hill Coll Greensburg PA, assoc prof History 1970-72; Pittsburgh Bd of Educ Sec Schools, teacher 1968-70; The Pittsburgh Courier Hm Off, staff writer 1942-50. **ORGANIZATIONS:** Mem exec council Assn for the Study of Afro-Amer Life & History 1978-; bd of dirs PA Higher Educ Assistance Agency 1985; advisory council PA Historical & Mus Commn 1985; trustee Univ of Pittsburgh 1987-90; exec comm mem Pennsylvania Higher Educ Assistance Agency 1988-. **HONORS/ACHIEVEMENTS:** Outstanding Achievement Award, African Methodist Episcopal Church; Found Day Award Ministerial Alliance Pittsburgh 1975; pub "Freedom in the Midst of a Slave Soc" Univ Press Washington DC 1980. **BUSINESS ADDRESS:** 808 Ridge Ave, Pittsburgh, PA 15212.

MCKENZIE, ELI, JR.
Corporate director. **PERSONAL:** Born Dec 28, 1947, Byromville, GA; married Vera Lee Thomas; children: Jatun Kreatson, Eli III, Jennifer Ashley. **EDUCATION:** Ft Valley State Coll, BS 1969; Univ of IL, MS 1971, PhD 1975. **CAREER:** Univ of IL, rsch asst 1969-74; Ft Valley State Coll, rsch sci 1975; Prairie View A&M Univ, dept head soil sci 1976-78; M&M products Co, dir of R&D 1978-. **ORGANIZATIONS:** Mem Soc of Cosmetic Chemist 1978, Amer Soc for Quality Control 1979. **HONORS/ACHIEVEMENTS:** Rsch Grant Univ of IL 1969; "Effect of Pretreatment of Loss of Nitrogen" Soil Sci Soc Amer Proc 1976; "15-Labelled Fertilizer N from Waterlogged Soil During Incubation", "Phosphorus Fertility of Some Tropical Soils in Sierra Leone" Soil Sci Soc Amer Proc 1977. **BUSINESS ADDRESS:** Dir of Research & Devel, M & M Products Co, 29 Royal Dr, Forest Park, GA 30050.

MCKENZIE, FLORETTA D.
Educational administrator. **PERSONAL:** Born Aug 19, 1935, Lakeland, FL; children: Dana R, Kevin. **EDUCATION:** DC Teachers Coll, BS History 1956, Postgrad 1967-69; Howard Univ, MA 1957; George Washington Univ, Amer Univ, Catholic Univ of Amer, Union Grad School Baltimore, Postgrad; George Washington Univ, EdD 1984. **CAREER:** Balt & WA Schools, teacher 1957-67; DC Public Schools, asst supt charge secondary schools to dep supt educ prog & servs; 1969-74; Montgomery Cty Public Schools, area asst supt 1974-77, dep supt schools 1978-79; State of MD, asst dep supt schools 1977-78; US Dept of Educ,

1979-81; Office School Improvement, dep asst sec 1980-81; Ford Found, educ consult 1981; WA Office Coll Entrance Exam Bd, adv com 1970-; Educ Products Info Exchange, trustee 1970; DC Public Schools, supt 1981-. **ORGANIZATIONS:** Mem Amer Assoc School Admin, Urban League, Gamma Theta Upsilon, Phi Alpha Theta, Phi Delta Kappa; hon life mem MD PTA; bd of trustees George Washington Univ; bd of dirs Natl Geographic Soc, Potomac Electric Power Co, World Book, Acacia Life Insurance. **BUSINESS ADDRESS:** Superintendent, Washingtons Public Schools, 415 12th St NW, Rm 1209, Washington, DC 20004.

MCKENZIE, REGINALD
Professional athlete. **PERSONAL:** Born Jul 27, 1950, Detroit, MI; married Ethellean Hicks (divorced). **EDUCATION:** Univ of Michigan, BS, 1972. **CAREER:** Buffalo Bills, offensive guard, 11 yrs; Seattle Seahawks, offensive guard, 1983-84, asst dir of marketing and sales for Seattle Kingdome executive suites, spokesman for United Way, offensive line coach. **ORGANIZATIONS:** Comm Projects, Special Olympics, United Way, Boys Clubs of America; exec dir Reggie McKenzie Football Found Inc of Detroit; bd of dirs Central Area Youth Assoc Seattle; bd of dirs King County Boys and Girls Club. **HONORS/ACHIEVEMENTS:** Unsung Hero Awd Detroit Sports Media 1986; Sportsman of the Year Detroit March of Dimes 1986. **BUSINESS ADDRESS:** Seattle Seahawks, 1120 NE 53rd St, Kirkland, WA 98033. *

MCKENZIE, THERMAN, SR.
Business executive. **PERSONAL:** Born Jun 02, 1949, Byromville, GA; married Mollie Kaigler; children: Therman Jr, Carmisha Deniece, Christopher. **EDUCATION:** Ft Valley State Coll, BS 1970; Mercer Univ, RPh 1973. **CAREER:** Reeds Drug Chain, pharmacist 1971; Grady Mem Hosp, pharmacist 1971-73; Revco Drug Chain, pharmacist 1973-74; M&M Prod Co, exec vice-pres 1973-, chmn chief opers officer. **ORGANIZATIONS:** Mem Atlanta Bus League 1973-; mem, bd of dirs Amer Health & Beauty Aids Inst 1982-; vice-pres Intl Bus Fellows 1983-; trustee Mercer Univ 1983-; bdchmn Collections of Life & Heritage 1983-; treas Chamber of Commerce Atlanta 1984-; bd of trustees Leadership Atlanta 1984-; chmn CW Pettigrew Mem Endow Campaign; corp treas EAR Enterprises; apptd US Small Business Adv Comm, Morris Brown Coll Free Enterprise Inst; bd of dirs Citizen Trust Bank; mem natl bd Jr Entrepreneurial Traders Assoc; bd of dirs Citizen Banchares Corp; apptd to State Bd of Compensation and Postsecondary Vocational Educ Bdby Gov Joe Frank Harris; apptd to State Productivity Bd; bd of trustees Fort Valley State Coll; mem Natl Assoc for Equal Oppor in Higher Educ, Cncl of Natl Alumni Assocs. **HONORS/ACHIEVEMENTS:** Entrepreneur of the Year Stanford Univ Grad Sch of Bus 1980; People to Watch-Fortune Magazine 1984; Hon Doctorate of Laws Morris Brown Coll 1984; 100 TopAtlantans Under 40-Atlanta Magazine 1984. **BUSINESS ADDRESS:** Chmn and Chief Opers Officer, M&M Products Company, 3602 Brownsmill Rd, Atlanta, GA 30321.

MCKENZIE, WILFORD CLIFTON
Business executive. **PERSONAL:** Born Apr 01, 1913; married Mercia; children: Wilfred, Rona. **EDUCATION:** City Coll of NY, BA; Fisk U. **CAREER:** NY City Dept of Income Maint, admin mgr; HRA, emp 1985; Jamaica, civil srvnt 1933-45. **ORGANIZATIONS:** Mem 100 Black Men 1975; Managerial Empl Assn. **BUSINESS ADDRESS:** 250 Church St, New York, NY 10013.

MCKERSON, EFFIE M. (NEE STOKER)
Educator. **PERSONAL:** Born Mar 16, 1924, Henderson, TX; married Hayward Cornelious; children: Hayward Alton. **EDUCATION:** TX Coll, BA 1948;Univ WI, MS 1957; Boston U, Post Grad Study 1949; Sonoma St Coll, 1965; US Intrntl U, 1971-72; LaVern Coll Ctr, 1972; IGSE, 1973;Univ MN, 1973;Univ VA, 1974. **CAREER:** Longview TX, tchr 1948-59; Gary IN, 1959-68; Manilla Phillippine, 1968; Minn MN, 1968-69; Edina Pub Sch, 1969-. **ORGANIZATIONS:** Mem, pres Nat Adv Vo Rehab; Nat Cncl Soc Studies; Nat Ed Assn; Am Acad Pol & Soc Sci; Intl Assn Childhd Ed; Edina Historical Soc; rep Nat Cncl Soc Studies 1967, 1970; 1973-74; mem Nat Cncl Negro Women; vice chrwmn MN Rep; Minneapolis Girls Club Aux; past pres St Stephen Luth Ch Women. **HONORS/ACHIEVEMENTS:** Attend 1974 Presdntl Clsrm Wrkshp; cert Apprec from SecCasper Weinberger; del to US Dept St Foreign Policy Conf for Ed. **BUSINESS ADDRESS:** Creek Valley Sch, 6401 Gleason R, Edina, MN 55435.

MCKERSON, MAZOLA
Manager. **PERSONAL:** Born Jan 10, 1921, Bluff, OK; married Alfred; children: 4 children. **EDUCATION:** Grad HS; Many seminars 7 workshops related to restaurant bus. **CAREER:** Gourmet Rstrnt, mgr, owner 1962-. **ORGANIZATIONS:** Chrprsn Gov Commn St of Women; mem municipal bd St of OK; apptd commn on ed St of OK; chair Ardmore's 100th Birthday Centennial 1887-1987; adv bd Higher Educ Center. **HONORS/ACHIEVEMENTS:** 1st Lady Mayor Ardmore OK 1979-80; 1st Black Elected to City Commn Ardmore 1977-83; Lady of Yr Zeta Phi Beta Sor 1976-77; Hon for Srvng as Chrprsn C of C Bicentennial Com 1976; Woman of the Yr YMCA 1980; hon mem Sigma Gamma Rho 1986. **BUSINESS ADDRESS:** Manager, Owner, Gourmet Restaurant, 1606 McLish SW, Ardmore, OK 73401.

MCKINLEY, RAY E.
Agricultural consultant. **PERSONAL:** Born Jan 07, 1925, St James, Jamaica;married Icylin Woollery; children: Raymond, Ewan, Michelle Ann. **EDUCATION:** Jamaica School of Agr, Diploma 1948; Univ of Illinois, BS; Cornel Univ; Univ of Puerto Rico; Univ of West Indies. **CAREER:** Jamaican Ministry of Agr, agr consult 1973-; Agr Info Serv, dir 1964-73; Jamaica & Citrus Growers Ltd, sales mgr 1963; Daily Gleaner, feature writer 1949; Forestry Dept, rsch asst 1948; Farmlife Mag, ed, publisher; Cattle Farmer, 1974-. **ORGANIZATIONS:** Org, mktg officer, Jamaica Agr Soc 1950-62; mgr, dir, founder Farmlife Ltd. **HONORS/ACHIEVEMENTS:** Farming pub rel org, dealing in farm serv consult. **BUSINESS ADDRESS:** Ministry of Agriculture, Box 480, Kingston, Jamaica.

MCKINLEY, WILLIAM, JR.
Insurance executive. **PERSONAL:** Born May 05, 1924, Clarksdale, MS; married Doris Jean Stackhouse; children: Sandra, Cheryl, Kevin, Andrea Patrice Smith. **EDUCATION:** Waukegan Twp HS, grad 1947. **CAREER:** Naval Training Ctr Gr Lakes IL, mgr Hispanic employment 1978; Franklin Life Ins Co, life underwriter 1964-. **ORGANIZATIONS:** Bd mem Comm Action Project 1965-70; mem chair Waukegan Area Council of Churches 1970;

bd mem Elem Sch Dist # 64 1970-; 32 Mason North Shore Consistory # 91 1970-; chmn Adv Council Admin Comm 1984-85; pres IL Sch Bd Assn Lake Co Div 1984-85; mem NAACP Bi-Lingual Comm 1984-85. **HONORS/ACHIEVEMENTS:** Employee of the Yr EEO-Naval Training Ctr 1980. **HOME ADDRESS:** 2501 Argonne Dr, North Chicago, IL 60064.

MCKINNEY, ALMA SWILLEY
Educator. **PERSONAL:** Born Mar 04, 1930, Lamont, FL; children: Matthew M. **EDUCATION:** FL A&M Univ Tallahassee, BA 1951; FL State Univ, MS 1966; Univ of MN, attended. **CAREER:** Madison Cty School Bd Madison FL, teacher 1951-60; Greenville Training School Greenville FL, math instr 1960-63; Suwannee River Jr Coll Madison FL; head mathdept 1963-67; N FL Jr Coll, assoc prof of math 1967-73; Univ of MN, teaching asst 1973-76; N FL Jr Coll, coord learning lab 1976-80; State Dept of Ed Tallahassee, ons. **ORGANIZATIONS:** Chmn math dept N FL Jr Coll 1981-; chmn reg adv council Dept of Corrections 1977-79; corp dir ACTT Inc of Madison 1978-80; bd of dir Madison Cty Meml Hosp 198-84; pol action comm NAACP; mem Zeta Phi Beta Sor; mem voters League, RECS Serv Club, Recreation Assoc Senatorial Scholarship FL State Senate 1948-51. **HONORS/ACHIEVEMENTS:** Teacher of the Year Suwannee River Jr Coll 1964; Natl Sci Fellow NSF 1975-76; listed in Who's Who for Women in Ed 1978; Citizen of the Year Iota Alpha Zeta Chap Zeta Phi Beta 1979. **BUSINESS ADDRESS:** Consultant, State Dept of Educ, 530 Carlton Bldg, Tallahassee, FL 32301.

MCKINNEY, DAVID WALTER, III
Physician. **PERSONAL:** Born Dec 23, 1941, Detroit, MI; married Hattie Walls; children: Lisa, Tyra, Tiah, Sheba, David, Davyda. **EDUCATION:** Howard U, MD 1971. **CAREER:** Pvt Practice, med doctor 1971-. **ORGANIZATIONS:** Mem Chi Delta Mu (Frat of Doctors Dentists & Pharmacists); Med Assn; AMA; Detroit Med Soc; mem President's Club of Howard U. **BUSINESS ADDRESS:** 15901 Greenfield, Detroit, MI 48227.

MCKINNEY, E. DORIS
Educator. **PERSONAL:** Born Jul 26, 1921, Warrenton, GA; daughter of Aubrey Hill McKinney and Sallie Eva Dickson. **EDUCATION:** Sargent Coll, BS 1943; Boston Univ, MA 1945; Boston Univ, EdD 1958; Univ of Minnesota, MPH 1965; Indiana Univ, Michigan Univ, New York Univ, Univ of North Carolina, study. **CAREER:** Bennett Coll, Greensboro NC, 1943-45; Virginia State Coll, Petersburg VA, 1945-58; Boston Public Schools, substitute teacher, 1955-58; Richmond Public Schools, 1958-60; Bennett Coll, Greensboro NC, 1960-70; Univ of North Carolina, Greensboro NC, prof emeritus of Mtr Learning & Perf, 1970-86. **ORGANIZATIONS:** Mem Amer Psychological Assn; Amer Alliance of Health, Physical Educ and Recreation; Amer School Health Assn; Amer Coll of Sports Medicine; North Amer Soc of Psychology of Sport; Intl Soc of Sport Psychology; many other professional orgns; mem exec bd YMCA; community center, School of Psychology North Carolina Vocational Rehabilitation Panel Psychologists; tchr in Serv Workshops; volunteer, Community College of Guilford County, Shepherd Center, United Methodist Church of Greensboro NC. **HONORS/ACHIEVEMENTS:** Twinness Grad Hon Soc 1943; Pi Lamda Theta, 1958; So Fellowships Award 1957; US Public Health Study Grant 1964; Distinguished Alumni, Sargent Coll, 1969; Hon Award, North Carolina Assn for Health, Physical Educ and Recreation, 1974; Alumni Teaching Excellence Award, Univ of North Carolina-Greensboro, 1986. **BUSINESS ADDRESS:** Professor Emeritus, University of North Carolina-Greensboro, 901 Duke Street, Greensboro, NC 27406.

MCKINNEY, ELOISE VAUGHN (ELIOSE JOHNSON)
Educator. **PERSONAL:** Born in Greensboro, NC; children: Myron Herman Johnson Jr. **EDUCATION:** Spelman Coll, AB 1947; Boston Univ, Coll of Lib Arts, AM 1948; Johnson C Smith Univ, 1950; Univ of WI 1950-51; Univ of CO 1953; Univ of CA 1966,67,70; Univ of Pacific 1970; San Fran City Coll 1971; San Fran State Univ 1976; Stanford Univ, cert publishing course 1986. **CAREER:** Winston Salem St Coll, instr 1948-52; Carver Mun Jr Coll, instr 1951; Morehouse Coll, instr, asst prof 1953-61; NC Agr Tech St Univ, assoc prof 1961-65; SF Un School Dist, ed 1965, eng reader 1965-67; John Adams Adult School, eng lecturer 1966; San Fran Comm Coll, teacher 1966-71; Peralta Coll, instr, chrpsn 1971-73; No Peralta Comm Coll, instr engl 1973-75; Laney Coll, instr of engl 1975-. **ORGANIZATIONS:** Mem Amer Assoc of Univ Women, Coll Lang Assoc, Alpha Kappa Alpha, No CA Spelman Coll Club, NAACP, Class All of Western St, SF Afro-Amer Hist & Cult Soc Inc, Assoc for Study of Afro-Amer Life & History SF UN Assoc; co-chrpsn PTA Prog Comm 1968-69; life mem Coll Lang Assoc, Assoc for the Study of Afro-Amer Life & History; mem Friends of Ethnic Arts, Friends of Johnson C Smith Univ, McKinney-Ellis & Cannady Cousins Clans, Philological Assoc of the Pacific Coast; mem exec bd class of 1983 San Fran United Nations Assoc. **HONORS/ACHIEVEMENTS:** Junos "West"; Mothers Day Speaker Morehouse Coll 1959; Merrill Fac Fellowship Morehouse Coll 1959; NCTE Study Abroad Cert 1959; Hist PTA, Geo Washington Sr HS 1969-70; articles publ in JET Mag, Atlanta Daily World, Berkeley Post, San Francisco Sun Reporter, San Francisco Courier, CLA Jrnl, Black Art, IntlQuarterly, NAACP Crisis, Good News (Laney Coll Mag), other school pubs; African Heritage Course Univ of IFE 1970; Lge Fellowship Peralta Coll Dist 1972;Laney Coll Fac Sen Grants for studies in Greece, Crete, Egypt & Turkey, Laney Coll 1976; publ "The Jrnl of Negro History", "The Langston Hughes Review", "Black Women in Antiquity" Jrnl African Civilizations. **BUSINESS ADDRESS:** Instructor of English, Laney College, Dept of English, Oakland, CA 94607.

MCKINNEY, ERNEST LEE, SR. (MAC)
Educator. **PERSONAL:** Born Nov 26, 1923, Chesnee, SC; son of Jaffer McKinney and Corrie Dodd McKinney; married Marion L Birdwell; children: Ernest Jr, Kevin. **EDUCATION:** Tennessee State Univ, BS 1947; E Tennessee State Univ, MA 1964. **CAREER:** Swift Jr Coll, teacher 1947-49; Rogersville AL, teacher 1949-53; Booker T Washington, principal 1953-56; Langston HS, teacher 1956-65; Science Hill HS, teacher 1965-70; So Jr HS, guid 1970-76; Science Hill HS, asst principal 1976-85 (retired). **ORGANIZATIONS:** Alderman Town of Jonesborough 1968-73, 1976-84; mem/pres Jonesborough Kiwanis Club 1980; mem Omega Psi Phi Frat; mem First Tennessee Development Dist. **HONORS/ACHIEVEMENTS:** Listed in Personalities of the South 1969; Omega Man of the Year Iota Alpha Chap 1968,73,74,77,78,83.

MCKINNEY, GEORGE DALLAS, JR.
Clergyman. **PERSONAL:** Born Aug 09, 1932, Jonesboro, AR; married Jean Brown; children: George, Grant, Gregory, Gordon, Glenn. **EDUCATION:** AR State AM& N Coll

Pine Bluff, BA (magna cum laude) 1955; AR StateUniv Oberlin Coll, MA 1956;Univ of MI, Grad Studies 1957-58; CA Grad Sch of Theol, PhD 1974. **CAREER:** St Stephen's Ch of God in Christ, pastor 1962-; Private Practice, marriage family & child counselor 1971-; Comm Welfare Council, consult 1968-71; Econ Opportunity Com, asst dir 1965-71; San Diego Co Probation Dept, sr probation officer 1959-65; Family Ct Toledo, couns 1957-59; Toledo State Mental Hosp, prot chaplain 1956-57; Chargin Falls Park Comm Center, dir 1955-56. **ORGANIZATIONS:** Mem CA Probation Parole & Correctional Assn; founder & chmn of bd of dirs St Stephen's Group Home; mem Sandiego Co Council of Chs; bd of trustees Interdenominational Theol Center Atlanta; bd of dirs C H Mason Theol Sem Atlanta; bd of dirs Bob Harrison Ministries; bd of elders Morris Cerillo World Evangelism; mem Sigma Rho Sigma Social Sci Frat; mem San Diego Rotary Club (1st black); mem Alpha Kappa Mu Nat Hon Society; mem Operation Push; vol chaplain at summer camp BSA; mem San Diego Mental Health Assn; mem NAACP; mem YMCA; mem San Diego Urban League; bd of advs Black Communication Center SanDiego State U; mem CA Mental Health Assn. **HONORS/ACHIEVEMENTS:** Recipient JF Kennedy Award for servs to youth; outstanding pastor award San Diego StateUniv Black Students; award for servs to youth Black Bus & Professional Women of San Diego; listed "Who's Who in the West"; "Who's Who in Religion"; "Contemporary Authors"; social worker of the yr award San Diego Co 1963; one of the ten outstanding men in San Diego Jr C of C 1966; outstanding man ot the yr award Intenat Assn of Aerospace Workers Dist 50 1969; outstanding contributions to the San Diego Comm in Field of Religious Activities NAACP 1975; achievement award for Religion Educ & Dedicated Serv to Youth So CA Ch of God in Christ; pub "The Theol of the Jehovah's Witnesses" "I Will Build My Ch"; several other pubs; hon at Testimonial Dinner San Diego StateUniv by the New Friends of the Black Communications Center 1977; listed "Who's Who in Am Colls & U; listed "Today" one of twenty Authors Making Significant Contribution to Evangelical Christian Lit. **BUSINESS ADDRESS:** Bishop, St Stephen's Church, 5825 Imperial Ave, San Diego, CA 92114.

MCKINNEY, GREGORY L.
Paralegal, counselor. **PERSONAL:** Born Jan 11, 1953, Bowling Green, KY. **EDUCATION:** KS St Coll, 1971-72; Wstrn KY U, BA 1975; Wayne St U, 1978-79. **CAREER:** Cumberland Trace Legal Srvs, paralegal 1979-80; Std Aff Wstrn KY U, res hall cnsl, sr dir 1975-78. **ORGANIZATIONS:** Std mem Western KYUniv Bd of Regents 1974-75; rep St of KY Nat Oratorical Contest 1974; st trnr Substance Abuse "Couns from a Cultural Perspective"; strategus Bowling Green Alumni Kappa Alpha Psi 1978-80; pres NAACP 1979-81; v chmn Task Force Alcohol & Drug Abuse 1980. **HONORS/ACHIEVEMENTS:** Speech pub "Winning Oratories" 1974; Outstndng Yng Man in Am US Jaycees 1979; Outstndng Citizen Award Hum Rights Commn 1980; appointed dir Guide Rightfor S Cntrl Province, Alpha Psi S Cntrl Province 1980. **BUSINESS ADDRESS:** Cumberland Trace Legal Service, 1032 College PO Box 1776, Bowling Green, KY 42101.

MCKINNEY, JACOB K.
Publicist. **PERSONAL:** Born Jun 10, 1920, Columbus, OH; married Marjorie Weiss; children: Jacquelyn Kyle. **EDUCATION:** OH St U, 1 yr; LA City Coll, 1954-55. **CAREER:** Kyle Ldr mus variety act, 1940-50; UAW-CIO Local #927, pub dir 1950-53; LA Sentinel, adv mgr 1953-56; Bronze Am Mag, ed pub 1957-65; Columbia-Screen Gems, asst dir pub 1968-71; Am Intnl Pictures Inc, pub-comm rel dir 1972-80; Knott's Berry Farm, asst mgr pub rel; McKinney & Asso PR, pres. **ORGANIZATIONS:** Mem Nat Safety Coun 1950-52; mem bd dir Pub Guild Local 818; Elder Presb Ch 1963; bd dir Watts Comm Ctr 1969-70. **HONORS/ACHIEVEMENTS:** 1st black pub Nat TV network 1965-68; cited by LA Bd Ed for Summer Seminar UCLA 1973; Campaign Mgr for Pat Paulsen's pseudo Pres Campaign 1968. **MILITARY SERVICE:** USAAF pvt 1943-44. **BUSINESS ADDRESS:** Mc Kinney & Asso PR, 6515 Susnet Blvd, Los Angeles, CA.

MCKINNEY, JAMES RAY
Vocational counselor. **PERSONAL:** Born Apr 17, 1942, Arlington, KY; married Shirley J Bennett; children: James B, Zandra. **EDUCATION:** Lane Coll, AB 1967; MI St U, MA 1971; MSU, Ed Spec 1979. **CAREER:** Ins slsmn; nwspr ed; Boy's Dorm Lane Coll, undrtkr dir; TN Valley Auth, checker, pymstr; Comm Sch, dir Civic Rec Dept, plygrnd supr; Dept of Interior Rocky Mt Nat Pk CO, ranger; Calhoun Area Vo Ctr Battle Creek Pub Sch, spl needs cnslr 1985. **ORGANIZATIONS:** Mem Battle Creek Ed Assn 1970-72; st rep Nat Ed Assn 1971; bd dir Family & Children Srv 1973-80; chmn Pub Rel Com 1975; mem Urban League 1965-72; NAACP 1965-72; tchr Black History 1972; co-pres Ann J Kellog Elem PTA 1971-79; mem Alpha Phi Alpha 1961-64, vice pres 1963, dean of pledges 1962, hstrn 1964; founder of Battle Creek Track Club 1979. **HONORS/ACHIEVEMENTS:** Recip Ftbl Schlrshp 1960-64; pres Jr Class 1963; sports ed Yr Book Staff 1963-64; pres Pre Alumni Club 1963-64; Hon Guard, Reclamation Tour UT. **BUSINESS ADDRESS:** Special Needs Counselor, Battle Creek Publ School, 475 E Roosevelt Ave, Battle Creek, MI 49017.

MCKINNEY, JESSE DOYLE
Clergyman. **PERSONAL:** Born Oct 09, 1934, Jonesboro, AR; son of George D McKinney, Sr (deceased) and osie L McKinney (deceased); married Mary Francis Keys, Aug 05, 1978; children: Antionette, Patrick, Bruce, Gloria, Carla. **EDUCATION:** Univ of AR, BA 1957; San Diego State Univ, MSW 1972. **CAREER:** San Diego State Univ/Grossmont Comm Coll, teacher/lecturer 1972-74; Southeast Counseling and Consultant Svcs, counselor/director 1974-76; San Bernardino Co Mental Health Dept, mental health clinician II 1977-79; Pleasant Place Group Home, dir 1979-82; licensed clinical social worker; St Stephen's Church of God In Christ, pastor/social service dir. **ORGANIZATIONS:** Bd mem Home of Neighborly Serv 1985-; mem Natl Assoc of Social Workers; founder/pastor St Stephen's Church Samaritan Shelter; psychiatric social worker Dept of Mental Health San Bernardino Cty; mem San Diego County Health Adv Bd, CA Personnel and Guidance Assoc, Assoc of Black Social Workers; bd of dirs San Diego Operation PUSH; mem, advisory board, Graduate School of Social Work, 1989-. **HONORS/ACHIEVEMENTS:** Fellowship Grant Natl Inst of Mental Health. **HOME ADDRESS:** 1883 Myrtlewood St, Colton, CA 92324.

MCKINNEY, PAUL
State senator. **PERSONAL:** Born Apr 16, 1923, Albany, GA; widowed; children: Paula J, Diane B, Gwendolyn S, Elaine B, Vernill L. **EDUCATION:** Palmer Bus Coll; Allegheny St Coll. **CAREER:** State Dept of Transp, chief examiner Bur of Traffic Safety 1971-74; 60th Ward, dem exec com, dem state commiss; Commonwealth of PA, state senate 1974-84retired. **ORGANIZATIONS:** Mem Tuscan Morning Star & Masonic Lodge #48; OV Catto Elks Lodge; W Philadelphia Civic League; Cobbs Creek Civic Assn; Delancur Civic Assn; W Philadelphia Br 52nd St Busmns Assn; Hiram Chap #2 Royal Arch Masons; W Philadelphia YMCA; mem, bd trustee Cheyene St Coll; mem, bd trustee Lincoln U; chmn Sen Const Changes & Fed Rel Com; v-chmn Envirmntl Res Appropriations; Consumer Affairs; Labor & Ind; Mil Affairs & Aero; Pub Hlth & Wlfr; St Gov't. **HONORS/ACHIEVEMENTS:** 3rd Black in History of PA to Serve as St Sen. **MILITARY SERVICE:** US merch marines 1942-47.

MCKINNEY, RICHARD ISHMAEL
Educator. **PERSONAL:** Born Aug 20, 1906, Live Oak, FL; married Lena R Martin; children: George K, Phyllis McKinney Bynum. **EDUCATION:** Morehouse Coll, AB 1931; Andover Newton Theological Sch, BD 1934, STM 1937; Yale Univ, PhD 1942; Post-Doctoral Study, The Sorbonne, Univ of Chicago, Columbia Univ. **CAREER:** Medical Coll of GA, vstg prof 1972; Univ of PA, vstg prof 1973; Univ of Ife Nigeria, vstg prof 1974; Morgan State Univ, acting dean Coll of Arts & Scis 1977-78; Virginia Union Univ, acting vice pres for academic affairs 1978-79; Morgan Christian Ctr interim dir 1980-81; Coppin State Coll, disting prof 1984-. **ORGANIZATIONS:** Mem Soc for Values in Higher Educ 1938-; mem Amer Philosophical Assoc 1951-; mem Soc for Phenomenology and Existential Philosophy 1951-; natl pres Sigma Pi Phi Frat 1986-; life mem Natl Educ Assoc, NAACP. **HONORS/ACHIEVEMENTS:** Kent Fellow Soc for Values in Higher Educ 1938; Alpha Kappa Mu Honor Soc Pi Lambda Psi Chap 1955; DD St Paul's Coll 1978; Phi Beta Kappa Delta of GA 1981; 14 publications including "History of Black Baptists of Florida," Miami FL Memorial Coll Press 1987. **BUSINESS ADDRESS:** Disting Scholar in Philosophy, Coppin State College, 2500 W North Ave, Baltimore, MD 21216.

MCKINNEY, RUFUS WILLIAM
Business executive. **PERSONAL:** Born Aug 06, 1930, Jonesboro, AR; son of Rev G D McKinney, Sr. (deceased); married Glendonia Smith; children: Rufus Jr, Frederick Warren, Ann Marie, Paula Elaine. **EDUCATION:** UUniv AR, BS 1953; IN Univ School of Law, JD 1956. **CAREER:** US Dept Lbr, special asst solicitor 1956-69; Pacific Lgthg Corp, atty 1969-71, sr atty 1971-72; Southern CA Gas Co, asst vice pres 1972-75, vice pres for natl public affairs 1975-. **ORGANIZATIONS:** Vice pres Southern CA Gas Co 1975-; vice pres WA Chapter NAACP 1963-69; mem Nat'l Urban League; pres Gas Men's Rdtbl 1975; chmn Amer Assn of Blacks in Energy 1980-81; mem CA and IN Bar Assns, Kappa Alpha Psi, Sigma Pi Phi Frat. **BUSINESS ADDRESS:** Vice President, Southern CA Gas Co, 1150 Connecticut Ave NW #717, Washington, DC 20036.

MCKINNEY, SAMUEL BERRY
Clergyman. **PERSONAL:** Born Dec 28, 1926, Flint, MI; son of Wade Hampton McKinney and Ruth Berry McKinney; married Louise Jones; children: Lora Ellen, Rhoda Eileen. **EDUCATION:** Morehouse Coll, BA 1949; Colgate-Rochester Div Sch, MDiv 1952; Colgate-Rochester Div Sch, D of Ministry 1975. **CAREER:** Mt Zion Bapt Ch, pastor 1958-; Olney St Bapt Ch, pastor 1954-58; Antioch Bapt Ch, asst to pastor 1952-54; Aenon Bapt Ch, student asst 1950-52. **ORGANIZATIONS:** Life mem NAACP; mem Alpha Phi Alpha; Sigma Pi Phi Alpha Omicron Boule; Princehall Mason 33rd degree; mem Wash State Voc Educ Commn; past pres N Pacific Bapt State Conv; past pres Black Am Bapts; past pres Seattle Council of Chs; past bd exec com mem Am Bapt Bd of Natl Ministries; past bd exec com mem Amer Bapt Gen Bd ; fdr Seattle OIC; 2nd natl vice pres OIC of Amer; fdr past bd mem Liberty Bank of Seattle; mem bd trustee Wash Mutual Savings Bank;co-author Black Adminstrn in Black Perspective. **BUSINESS ADDRESS:** Mount Zion Baptist Church, 1634 19th Ave & E Madison Street, Seattle, WA 98122.

MCKINNEY, THEOPHILUS ELISHA, JR.
Executive. **PERSONAL:** Born Jan 20, 1933, Charlotte, NC; son of Theophilus Elisha McKinney and Martha Lloyd McKinney; married Sarah Louise Evans, Aug 17, 1957; children: Marie Alessandria, Margaret Celeste, Theophilus E III, Linda Maureen. **EDUCATION:** Bowdoin College, Brunswick, ME, BA 1954; Fletcher School of Law & Diplomacy, AM 1955, MA 1957, PhD 1963. **CAREER:** Danforth Fellow, Fletcher School of Law and Diplomacy, Tufts Univ, instructor, 1955-57; FL A&M Univ, associate prof, 1958-59; Southern Univ, prof, dept chmn, 1961-65; Sarah Lawrence College, faculty mem 1968-69; Educ & World Affairs, exec associate, 1965-69; Howard Univ, vice pres 1969-70; United Negro College Fund, exec, 1970-75; Forest Industries Inc, pres 1975-80, chairman, 1980—; Delaware State College, academic dean, prof, 1975-78; Research Industries Inc, consultant, guest lecturer, pres, chairman, 1966—. **ORGANIZATIONS:** Mem, NY State Civil Service Bd Examiners, 1974-78, Association American Colleges Commn on Liberal Learning, 1973-79; sr consult, Phelps-Stokes Fund Mgmt Development Survey, 1971-72; Natl Advisory Council on Comprehensive Minority Health Manpower; Natl Institute of Health Division of Research & Resources, 1972-75. **HONORS/ACHIEVEMENTS:** Recipient Nathan W Collier Award, FL Mem College, St Augustine, 1968; Fellow of numerous organizations. **MILITARY SERVICE:** AUSR lt 1954-55. **HOME ADDRESS:** 726 Forest St, Dover, DE 19901.

MCKINNEY, WADE H., III
Business administrator. **PERSONAL:** Born Sep 06, 1925, Flint, MI; married Sylvia Lawrence; children: Wade Hampton IV. **EDUCATION:** Western Reserve U, BA 1948. **CAREER:** Cleveland Press, copy editor/reporter 1949-53; Ft Wayne, indus relations sec 1953-56; Denver, indus relations sec 1956-59; Milwaukee, indus relations dir 1959-61; Chicago, youth guidance project dir 1961-63; Urban League, employment & guidance dir 1963-68, prog dir 1968-; Natl Skills Bank, midwest rep 1963-66; Econ Devel Corp, vice pres 1965-68; US Postal Serv Hdq Customer Serv, sr retail sales officer, program mgr. **MILITARY SERVICE:** USAAF 1943-46; USAFR 1946-67. **BUSINESS ADDRESS:** Program Manager, US Postal Serv Headquaters, 475 L Entant Plaza SW, Washington, DC 20260.

MCKINNON, DENNIS LEWIS
Professional athlete. **PERSONAL:** Born Aug 22, 1961, Quitman, GA. **EDUCATION:** Florida St, BA. **CAREER:** Chicago Bears, wide receiver 1983-85. **ORGANIZATIONS:** Honorary chmn, membership drive, Operation Push 1985-86; bd of educ spokesman, Volunteer Program 1986. **HONORS/ACHIEVEMENTS:** Established himself as the teams most consistent receiver; awarded game ball at Philadelphia 1983 after making 1 catch, 20 yards, TD, 5 punt returns for 48 yards; regarded by Mike Ditka as the best blocking wide receiver in pro football; scored since being with club; scored game winning touchdowns in back to back divisional championship games 1984-85; led team in scoring 1985; played in Superbowl XX. **BUSINESS ADDRESS:** Chicago Bears, Halas Hall, Lake Forest, IL 60045.

MCKINZIE-HARPER, BARBARA A.
Auditor/certified public accountant. **PERSONAL:** Born Jan 02, 1954, Ada, OK; daughter of Leonard McKinzie and Johnnie McKinzie. **EDUCATION:** East Central OK Univ, BS (Cum Laude) 1976. **CAREER:** Touche Ross & Co, supervisor & health care coord 1976-83; DeLoitte Haskins and Sells, mgr 1983-85; Alpha Kappa Alpha Sor Inc, exec dir 1985-87; Coopers & Lybrand, mgr 1987-. **ORGANIZATIONS:** Mem Amer Inst of Certified Public Accountants 1978; bd mem Natl Assoc of Black Accountants 1980; minority recruitment subcomm IL Soc of CPA's 1983; mem Amer Women's Soc of CPA's 1986. **HONORS/ACHIEVEMENTS:** Outstanding Alumnae of East Central OK Univ 1976; Valuable Contribution Awd Oklahoma City 1983; Outstanding Young Woman of Amer 1980, 1985. **HOME ADDRESS:** 1635 East Hyde Park Blvd, Chicago, IL 60615. **BUSINESS ADDRESS:** Coopers & Lybrand, 203 North LaSalle Street, Chicago, IL 60601.

MCKISSACK, LEATRICE B.
Company executive. **PERSONAL:** Born Jul 27, 1930, Keytesville, MO; married William DeBerry; children: Andrea McKissack Brown, Cheryl J, Deryl K. **EDUCATION:** Fisk Univ, BS 1951; TN State Univ, MS 1957. **CAREER:** Metropolitan Public Schools, teacher 1952-69; McKissack & McKissack, pres 1983-84; McKissack, McKissack & Thompson, ceo 1984-. **ORGANIZATIONS:** Mem Mental Health Bd Meharry Medical Coll 1977-78; treas Nashville Symphony Guild 1980-82. **BUSINESS ADDRESS:** Chief Executive Officer, McKissack McKissack & Thompson, 330 Charlotte Ave, Nashville, TN 37201.

MCKISSACK, WILLIAM DEBERRY
Architect. **PERSONAL:** Born Aug 29, 1925, Nashville, TN; married Leatrice Harriett Buchanan; children: Andrea Franklin, Cheryl Joan, Deryl Kaye. **EDUCATION:** Howard U, BArch 1951. **CAREER:** McKissack & McKissack Arch & Engrs Inc Nashivlle, 1951-; McKissack & McKissack Arch & Engrs Inc, pres 1968-; McKissack & McKissack Arch & Engrs chmn bd dir 1968-; TN StateUniv Nashville, instr gust lectr 1959-61. **ORGANIZATIONS:** Mem Nat Council of Registration Bds AIA; Nat Tech Assn; pres chmn bd dir Coll Hill Realty Co Nashville 1968-; mem Frontiers of Am; Sigma Pi Phi; Omega Si Phi. **MILITARY SERVICE:** USNR 1943-46. **BUSINESS ADDRESS:** Morris Meml Bldg, Nashville, TN 37201.

MCKISSICK, EVELYN WILLIAMS
Commissioner. **PERSONAL:** Born Aug 19, 1923, Asheville, NC; married Floyd Bixler; children: Joycelyn, Andree, Floyd Jr. **CAREER:** Soul City Sanitary Dist, comsnr chmn; Educ Enrichment Prog, dir 1970-72; Pre Sch Educ & Rec Bd , dir. **ORGANIZATIONS:** Mem Soul City Cultural Arts & Hist Soc 1975-; bd mem Soul City Pks & Rec Assn 1976-; bd mem Interfaith Comm of Soul City 1975-; mem Durham Comm on Negro Affairs; mem CORE; mem Durham Rec Dept; Union Bapt Ch Youth Prog; NAACP; vice chrm Warren Cnty Rep Party; mem Black Elected Officials. **BUSINESS ADDRESS:** PO Box 128, Soul City, NC 27553.

MCKISSICK, FLOYD B.
Business executive, attorney. **PERSONAL:** Born Mar 09, 1922, Asheville, NC; married Evelyn Williams; children: Joycelyn, Andree, Floyd, Jr, Charmaine. **EDUCATION:** Morehouse Coll, 1949; Univ of NC, 1951; NC Central Univ, AB 1951; LLD 1952. **CAREER:** The Soul City Co, pres 1974-80; Floyd B McKissick Enterprises Inc, pres 1968-74; McKissick & Burt Attys, sr partner 1960-66; McKissick & Bertry Attys 1957-66; State Univ of NY, Binghamton, visiting prof 1970; columnist Bny Amsterdam Newspaper 1965-71; Ordained Minister of the Gosepl 1979. **ORGANIZATIONS:** Admitted to NC Bar 1952; US Supreme Ct Bar 1955; Counsel Congress of Racial Equality NY 1960-68; natl chmn CORE 1963-66, natl dir 1966-68; Counsel Durham Bus Coll; rep March on Washington 1963; mem E End Betterment League 1963; DC Bar 1966; co-chmn Natl Conf on Black Lawyers 1969; chmn Natl Comm for Two-Party System; Natl & Southeastern Bar Assn; NC Central Univ Alumni Assn; Alpha Phi Alpha; US Comm on Civil Rights Advisory Committee; Assoc of Trial Lawyers; founder Natl Assoc of Black Manufacturers; Amer Bar Assn; co-founder NC Center for the study of Black History; life mem, NAACP. **HONORS/ACHIEVEMENTS:** Man of yr Award Durham Bu 1959-61; professional chain Housewives League of Am 1959-61; Ike Smalls Civil Rights Award NAACP 1962; conf award for Civil Right s AME Church 1964; NC Central Univ, Chapter Delta Theta Phi Law Fraternity named in hon F B KcKissick Senate; author "3/5 of a Man "; recipient, purple heart; 5 battle stars; Publications "Is Integration Necessary?", "A Black Manifesto, Constructive Militaney" 1966, "Genocide" 1967, "Three-Fifths of a Man" 1968,. **MILITARY SERVICE:** AUS t/sgt 1941-45. **BUSINESS ADDRESS:** 205 McClanahan St, Oxford, NC 27565.

MCKISSICK, MABEL F. RICE
Librarian. **PERSONAL:** Born Jun 12, 1921, Union, SC; married Wallace T McKissick; children: Wallace T Jr. **EDUCATION:** Knoxville Coll, AB 1943; SC State Coll, summer courses library science 1949-50; Tchrs Coll Columbia Univ, MA 1954; Sch of Library Serv Columbia Univ, MSLS 1966. **CAREER:** Sims HS, tchr/librarian 1943-48, librarian 1948-68; New London Jr HS, librarian/media specialist 1968-79; New London HS, librarian/media specialist 1979-. **ORGANIZATIONS:** Bd dir Public Library of New London 1979-81; adv task force ALA/SRRRT Coretta Scott King Awd 1969-; nom comm Natl Cncl of Negro Women 1979-, Amer Assoc of Univ Women 1978-; 2nd vice pres Delta Kappa Gamma Eta Chap 1969-; Delta Sigma Theta Sor 1943-; Educ Assns NEA, CEA, NLEA; Library Assns ALA, AASL,CEMA, NEEMA; founding mem CEMA 1976-; adv comm NLEA 1985-; mem CEA County Council Comm 1985-; mem CEMA Chair School Library Media Month 1985-86; nalt comm AASL Natl School Library Media Month 1986-88; mem New England Assoc of Schools & Coll Evaluation Com 1986-; dean's adv comm School of Library Sci & Instr Tech Southern CT State Univ 1986-88. **HONORS/ACHIEVEMENTS:** "Black Women of CT, Achievements Against the Odds" Exhibit Hartford CT Historical Soc 1984; Outstanding Woman of the Yr Awd CT Div Amer Assoc of Univ Women 1982; Rheta A Clark Awd CT Educ Media Assoc 1980; Outstanding Library Media Svcs; Coretta Scott King Awd ALA/SRRT Comm 1974; Dr Martin Luther King Jr Community Serv Awd 1981; New Haven Alumnae Chap Delta Sigma Theta Educ Devel Awd 1985; Citation Office of the Mayor City of New London for Outstanding Educ Achievements in Educ 1985; State of CT General Assembly Official Citation in Educ Achievements 1985; Community Serv Awd as an Educator Miracle Temple Church 1985; Cert of Apprec NEASC Commiss on Public Schools as a Vstg Comm Mem 1986. **HOME ADDRESS:** 201 Hempstead St, P O Box 1122, New London, CT 06320. **BUSINESS ADDRESS:** Librarian/Media Specialist, New London High School, 490 Jefferson Ave, New London, CT 06320.

MCKNIGHT, ALBERT J.
Financier, clergyman. **PERSONAL:** Born Aug 08, Brooklyn, NY. **EDUCATION:** St Mary's Sem, BA, BT; rcvd sem training under Holy Ghost Fathers in PA & CT. **CAREER:** So Cooperative Devel Fund Lafayette, LA, pres 1970-84; Southern Development Foundation 1972-. **ORGANIZATIONS:** Served on numerous LA econ devel task forces, So Consumers' Coop, Goals for LA Task Force, US Ofc of Econ Opty Task Force, People's Enterprise Inc 1970-; diocesan dir Credit Unions 1963; former assoc with Our Lady of Lourdes, Immaculate Heart of Mary & St Martin de Porres Chs in LA; helped organize over 10 credit unions in LA; bd mem of the Natl Consumer Coop Bank 1978-; chairperson of Consumer Coop Dev Corp; pastor of Holy Ghost Catholic Ch Opelousas, LA. **BUSINESS ADDRESS:** President, So Development Foundation, PO Box 3005, Lafayette, LA 70501.

MCKNIGHT, LANCESS
Physician. **PERSONAL:** Born Feb 05, 1901, Seminar, VA; married Thelma Watson; children: Lancess, Betty. **EDUCATION:** Howard U, MD 1930; Mercy Hosp, intern 1930-61; Hercy Hosp, chf resd 1931-32; Phips Inst, 1932-36; Harvard Med Sch, 1938-44; Beth Isreal Hosp, 1944-46. **CAREER:** Gen Prac, physician; DE Co, coroner's physician 1936-66; Mercy-Douglass Hosp, chf pathologist 1934-56; Mercy Hosp Sch for Nurses, thcr 1935-53; HowardU Med Sch, 1945-46. **ORGANIZATIONS:** Past mem Pathol Sect of Philadelphia Co Med Soc; flw Am Soc of Clinical Pathologist 1953; mem Bd of Hlth of Media PA; Freedom Fun Com NAACP of Media PA; Media Br NAACP. **BUSINESS ADDRESS:** 601 N Olive St, Media, PA 19063.

MCKNIGHT, LEE CASSELL
Business executive. **PERSONAL:** Born Apr 10, 1942, South Bend, IN; married Gloria A; children: Lajune Angela, Lisa Andrea, Lee Ann, Leslie Adrean. **EDUCATION:** TN State U, BS 1964; IN U, MS 1969. **CAREER:** Urban League of S Bend & St Joseph Co Inc, exec dir; Manpower, 1st state dir; Gov Office of Comm Affairs, 1970. **ORGANIZATIONS:** Dir Inner City Enterprises Corp; dir Lee Kemp Corp; mem Kappa Alpha Psi Frat.

MCKNIGHT, RONALD
Educator. **PERSONAL:** Born Feb 26, 1948, Baltimore, MD; married Margaret Ann Lennon. **EDUCATION:** Coppin State Coll, BS 1971; Cornell Univ, Fellowship Grant 1971-72; attended Univ of MD Med Sch 1973-74; attended Morgan State Univ Grad Sch 1974-76;Johns Hopkins Univ Sch of Med, summer fellow Lab Animal Med Program 1977; Tuskegee Inst, BS in Animal & Poultry Sci and DVM 1980, 1 year internshipin radiology 1980-81; Univ of MO Columbia Vet Med, 3 yrs residency in radiology 1981-84. **CAREER:** Argonne Natl Lab, student aid 1971; Coppin State Coll, instr physical sci 1972; Argonne Natl Lab, res asst Biological Med Sci Res Div 1974; CoppinState Coll, instr anatomy/physiology. **ORGANIZATIONS:** Student Natl Med Assn Inc 1973-74; mem the So Poverty Law Cntr Jan 1975; pres/vp Sci Soc 1968-71; jr counselor 1969-71; student mem Amer Chem Soc 1970-72; Cirrulus Scholarum Honor Soc 1971; student mem Amer Vet Med Assn 1976-80. **HONORS/ACHIEVEMENTS:** Afro-Amer Student of Yr 1965; Oratoratorical Awd 1968; Who's Who Among Students in Amer Univ & Coll 1969-70; Nominated for Woodrow Wilson Fellowship Award1971; Coppin State Coll Faculty Award 1971; Scholarship Johns Hopkins Univ Sch of Pub Health Developmental Sci 1973; Merck Scholarship 1974; Notable AmerAward 1976-77; Award Men of Achievement 1976; Dictionary of Intl Biography Award 1979; numerous Scouting Awards; The Directory of Distinguished Americans 1981edition for services to the community. **BUSINESS ADDRESS:** Assistant, Paine College, 1235 15th St, Augusta, GA 30910.

MCKOY, CLEMENCIO AGUSTINO
Editor. **PERSONAL:** Born Sep 09, 1928, Oriente, Cuba;married Jean Delores Lewis; children: Andre, Clemencio II, Gregorio. **EDUCATION:** Univ of London, BSc; London, FCI. **CAREER:** Minority News Digest Inc, editor-in-chief; PR Communications, pres 1975; Black Sports Inc, advertising dir 1972; Culinary Revs Inc, mgng editor 1968; Nat Publ House, exec vice pres dir 1961. **ORGANIZATIONS:** Mem Pub Relat Soc of Am; v chmn Black Athletes Hall of Fame 1975f dir Black Audio Network Inc; orgnzr coord Intl Inductions to Black Athletes Hall of Fame 1975; co-fdr 1st W Indian Standing Com African Afrs. **HONORS/ACHIEVEMENTS:** Co-publr The Jamaican Housewife, The Jamaican Builder, The Jamaican Nat Trade Rev; author This Man Smith. **BUSINESS ADDRESS:** Minority News Digest, 41 E 42nd St Ste #921, New York, NY 10017.

MCKOY, JOHN H.
Planning administrator. **PERSONAL:** Born Aug 25, 1944, Philadelphia. **EDUCATION:** Hamilton Coll, BA 1966;Univ of PA, MCP 1970. **CAREER:** Assn of Bay Area Governments, dir plnng progrmng; Match Inst Wash DC, consult 1971-73; Model Cities Agy, Springfield MA, dir plnnng 1970-71; Planning Dept Philadelphia, area planner 1969. **ORGANIZATIONS:** Mem Nat Assn Planners, Bay Area Chpt; plng com, Bay Area Urbn Leg 1975; chmn CA St Adv Com on Soc Profiles 1976; past mem Minority Affrs Com NAHRO 1973-74; corp mem Am Friends Serv Com 1971-73; Haverford Coll 1972; sch com Germantown Friends Sch, Phila, 1969; Comm Bd, Pickett Sch, Phila,1968-69; vol com Dvl prog W/Am Friends Serv Com Guatemala, 1966-68. **HONORS/ACHIEVEMENTS:** Author, "Recreation Preferences of Minority Groups in the East Bay", ABAG Berkeley 1973; "Distributive Effects of Transportation Decisios", Am Inst of Planners Conf on Transp, Berkeley, 1973. **BUSINESS ADDRESS:** Milton Company, Vienna, VA 22180.

MCLAREN, DOUGLAS EARL
Management consultant, attorney. **PERSONAL:** Born Nov 03, 1948, Wilmington, NC; son of Austen E McLaren and Huldah E McLaren; married Rosemarie P Pagon; children: Damion Earl, Kaili Elizabeth. **EDUCATION:** Univ of the West Indies, BSc Eng 1970; McGill Univ, MBA 1974; Harvard Law School, JD 1984. **CAREER:** Hue Lyew Chin, engr 1970-72; Peat Marwick Mitchell, management consultant 1974-76; Jamaica Natl Investment Co, project officer 1976-78; Exxon Intl Co, planning analyst 1979-84; ICF Inc, sr assoc 1984-. **ORGANIZATIONS:** Admitted to NY and DC Bars 1985; mem Amer Bar Assoc 1985, Natl Black MBA Assn 1986; mem Panel of Commercial Abritrators of the Amer Arbitration Assn. **HOME ADDRESS:** 515 Brummel Court NW, Washington, DC 20012.

MCLAUGHLIN, ANDREE NICOLA
Educator, poet. **PERSONAL:** Born Feb 12, 1948, White Plains, NY; daughter of Joseph Lee McLaughlin and Willie Mae Newman McLaughlin. **EDUCATION:** Cornell Univ, BS 1970; Univ of MA-Amherst, MEd 1971, EdD 1974. **CAREER:** Medgar Evers College/

CUNY, asst prof/project dir 1974-77, chairperson 1977-79, dean of administration 1979-82, planning coord of Women's Studies Rsch & Develop 1984-89; Hamilton Coll, Jane Watson Irwin Prof, Women's Studies, 1989-90. **ORGANIZATIONS:** Bd mem, "Where We At", Black Women Artists, 1979-87; mem Natl Women's Studies Assoc 1980-, Amer Assoc of Univ Profs 1982-; founding intl coord, Intl Resource Network of Women of African Descent, 1982-85, founding mem Sisterhood in Support of Sisters in South Africa 1984-86; adv bd mem Sisterhood of Black Single Mothers 1984-86; mem CUNY Acad for the Humanities & Sciences, 1986-; Intl Coordinator, Cross-Cultural Black Women's Studies Summer Inst, 1987; Chair, Editorial Bd, Network: A Pan African Women's Forum (journal), 1987-; mem, Policy & Publication Comm, The Feminist Press, CUNY, 1988-. **HONORS/ACHIEVEMENTS:** Natl Endowment for the Humanities, fellow, 1976, 1979, 1984; Honorary Visiting Scholar, Univ of London, 1986; 8 articles published; Amer Council on Educ; Fellow, in Acad Admin, 1980-81; NEH Fellow, Natl Endowment for the Humanities, 1989; Andrew W Mellon Fellow, CUNY Graduate School & Univ Center, 1987; Co-editor, Wild Women in the Whirlwind: Afra-American Culture & the Contemporary Literary Renaissance, Rutger's Univ Pres, 1989; Author, Double Dutch, poetry, 1989; article, "Black Women's Studies in America," 1989; article, "Urban Politics in the Higher Education of Black Women," 1988; article, "The International Nature of the Southern African Women's Struggles", 1988. **HOME ADDRESS:** PO Box 1964, White Plains, NY 10602. **BUSINESS ADDRESS:** Professor of Humanities, Medgar Evers College, CUNY, 1150 Carroll St, Brooklyn, NY 11225.

MCLAUGHLIN, BENJAMIN WAYNE
Corporate manager. **PERSONAL:** Born Feb 24, 1947, Danville, VA; son of Daniel McLaughlin and Lucy McLaughlin; married Gwen Stafford; children: LaShandra, Sonya. **EDUCATION:** Johnson C Smith Univ, Charlotte NC, graduated 1969. **CAREER:** Martin Marietta Energy Systems Inc/Union Carbide Corp, buyer 1969-70, maintenance engineering tech asst 1970-76, ORGDP affirmative action coord 1975-79, wage and salary associate 1979, ORGDP employment dept supervisor 1979-81, barrier mfg div supt 1981-82, maintenance engrg dept supt 1982-83, ORGDP wage and salary dept head 1983-84, energy systems dir of minority prog devel 1984-86, personnel mgr Portsmouth OH gaseous diffusion plant 1986-. **ORGANIZATIONS:** Owner, American Income Tax Serv, 1978-; Pike County OH Rotary Club. **HONORS/ACHIEVEMENTS:** Distinguished Serv Award, State of Tennessee, 1980; Martin Marietta Energy Systems Community Serv Award, 1985; Omega Man of the Year Award, Zeta Gamma Gamma Chap of the Omega Psi Phi Frat, 1985; Light From the Hill Award, Knoxville College, 1985; Jefferson Award for Community Service, 1986. **BUSINESS ADDRESS:** Personnel Manager, Martin Marietta Energy, PO Box 628, Piketon, OH 45661.

MCLAUGHLIN, CLARA J.
Television station executive. **PERSONAL:** Born in Brunswick, GA; married Richard A McLaughlin MD; children: Rinetta, Ricky. **EDUCATION:** Howard Univ, BA Journalism 1972; Prairie View A&M Univ, Grad Sch in Mgmt. **CAREER:** Journal of the Natl Medical Assoc, medical writer/editorial asst 1966; Amer Conservative Union, information specialist 1967-68; KUHT-Houston, talk show hostess 1976-78; KLMG-TV Inc (CBS) East Texas TV Network Inc, chmn/ceo 1983-. **ORGANIZATIONS:** Mem Houston Medical Forum; former mem bd of dirs Houston Area Urban League; campaign chairperson Wiley Coll Marshall TX; mem bd of dirs Africare; life mem Zeta Phi Beta Sor; mem Natl Assoc of Female Execs; mem panel of Amer Women and Top Ladies of Distinction. **HONORS/ACHIEVEMENTS:** The Essence Woman Awd Essence Magazine 1986; The Blackbook Awd Blackbook 1986; Who's Who of Amer Women 1987/88; author "The Black Parent's Handbook, A Guideto Healthy Pregnancy, Birth and Child Care," Harcourt Brace & Jovanovich New York. **BUSINESS ADDRESS:** Chairman and CEO, KLMG-TV, Inc (CBS), PO Box 5151, Longview, TX 75608.

MCLAUGHLIN, DAVID
Protozoologist, educator. **PERSONAL:** Born Nov 01, 1934, Sumter, SC; son of Arthur S McLaughlin and Iris Ladson McLaughlin; divorced. **EDUCATION:** Clark Coll, BS 1956; Howard Univ, MS 1962, PhD 1965. **CAREER:** Howard Univ, research asst USPHS grantee; NSF, teaching & rsch supr; summer research participant for HS students 1957-58, 1958-64; USPHS grantee, research assoc 1962-65; supr summer undergrad rsch participation 1965-66; IN Research Lab, prof zoology 1965-; NASA Wallops Sta Bio-Space Tech, post-doctoral studies 1965. **ORGANIZATIONS:** Gemini Summary Conf NASA Manned Space Craft Ctr Houston; participant 3rd Intl Congress on Protozoology Leningrad, USSR 1969; mem Soc Protozoologist; NY Acad Sci; Amer Inst Biol Sci; AAAS; Amer Micros Soc; Amer Soc Zoologists; mem NAACP. **HONORS/ACHIEVEMENTS:** Sigma Xi; Beta Chi Kappa; Omega Psi Phi; contrib articles to prof journals. **BUSINESS ADDRESS:** Prof of Zoology, Howard Univ, E E Just, G-37A, 415 College St, Washington, DC 20059.

MCLAUGHLIN, DOLPHY T.
Attorney. **PERSONAL:** Born Jul 10, 1922; married Nora Belle Facey; children: Norman Anthony. **EDUCATION:** Northwestern Univ, 1949-52; Loyola Univ Sch of Law, LLB 1955. **CAREER:** Brown, Brown, Greene & McLaughlin, attorney 1956-73; Victory Mutual Life Ins Co, asst gen counsel & mem bd dir 1962-67; Met San Dist of Greater Chicago, mem civil serv bd 1966-67, prin asst atty 1967-73; Govt of Jamaica, consul of Jamaica 1969-; Met San Dist of Greater Chicago, head asst attorney 1973-. **ORGANIZATIONS:** Pres Amer West Indian Assn 1962-67; mem Cook Co Bar Assn 1956-; mem Natl Bar Assn 1973-; mem Amer Bar Assn; Phi Alpha Delta Legal Frat 1956-. **HONORS/ACHIEVEMENTS:** Cert of Recognition Superior Pub Serv Award natl Civil Serv League 1971; Man of the Year Jamaican-Amer Caribbean Quarterly Mag 1982; Order of Distinction Govt of Jamaica 1983.

MCLAUGHLIN, EURPHAN
Government official. **PERSONAL:** Born Jun 02, 1936, Charlotte, NC. **EDUCATION:** Univ of MD Baltimore Coll of Commerce, 1958;Univ of Baltimore, AA 1963;Univ of Baltimore, LLB 1969;Univ of Baltimore, JD 1969;Univ of Baltimore, BS 1972;Univ of Baltimore, MBA (23 credits completed). **CAREER:** State of MD Dept of Personnel, asst sec for employee serv 1979-; MD Commn on Human Realtions, dep dir 1976-79; State of MD Dept of Health & Mental Hygiene, EEO supr 1975-76; MD Commn on Human Relations, intergroup relations rep 1973-75; Baltimore City Police Dept, intelligence div officer 1959-73. **ORGANIZATIONS:** Real estate asso & bd mem Century 21/Otis Warren & Co 1971-; mem NAACP; Nat Assn of Human Rights Workers; MD Assn of Equal Opportunity Personnel; Nat& MD Assn of Realestate Brokers; Baltimore Bd of Realtors. **HONORS/ACHIEVEMENTS:** Nine accommendations commendations City Police Dept 1959-73; award of merit MD Commn on Human Relations 1978; award of merit Staff of MD Commn on Human Relations 1978. **MILITARY SERVICE:** USAF a/2c 39 years. **BUSINESS ADDRESS:** MD Dept of Personnel, 301 W Preston St, Baltimore, MD 21201.

MCLAUGHLIN, GEORGE W.
Educator. **PERSONAL:** Born Feb 14, 1932, Petersburg, VA; married Sadie Thurston; children: Wesley, George Jr, Avis. **EDUCATION:** St Paul's Coll, BS Educ 1957; VA State Coll, 1958; Univ of VA, MEd, EdD 1970; Bank St Coll Univ of PA; Amer Bible Inst, DD 1974. **CAREER:** DE State Coll, dir of student teaching 1966-72, chmn educ 1972-75; St Paul's Coll, chmn educ & psych. **ORGANIZATIONS:** Assoc Blvd Cab Co 1962-; pastor Wayland Baptist Church 1974-; pres L&M Const Co 1976-; v chmn Alberta Child-Care Ctr 1978-; mem LA Cty Law Enforcement Comm 1980; vice pres Lawrenceville Optimist Intl 1982-84; pres Epsilon Omicron Lambda, Alpha Phi Alpha 1980-85. **HONORS/ACHIEVEMENTS:** Outstanding Citizen Awd LA Emancipation Org 1979; Faculty of the Year St Paul's Coll 1979; Alpha Man of the Year Alpha Phi Alpha Frat 1982; Disting Serv Awd Optimist Intl 1983. **MILITARY SERVICE:** AUS maj 1952-72. **HOME ADDRESS:** Rt 3 Box 1635, Trevilians, VA 23093. **BUSINESS ADDRESS:** Coordinator of Gifted Education, Mecklenburg County Public Schools, PO Box 190, Boydton, VA 23917.

MCLAUGHLIN, JACQUELYN SNOW
Dean of student development. **PERSONAL:** Born Aug 12, 1943, Camden, NJ; daughter of Mr & Mrs Arlington Reynolds Sr; married Herman McLaughlin; children: Jevon, Jacques. **EDUCATION:** Shaw Univ Raleigh NC, AB Sociology 1965;Univ of Bridgeport CT, couns cert 1965; Glassboro St Coll New Jersey, MA Couns 1972; Rutgers Univ New Jersey, DEd 1976. **CAREER:** Camden Co Coll, dean student devel 1975; Camden Co Coll, dir EOF program 1971-75; Camden Co Coll, counselor 1970-71; Washington Elementary School Camden NJ, teacher 1966-70; Div New Jersey Employment Serv, counselor 1965-66. **ORGANIZATIONS:** Team mem Middle St Accrdtn Assn 1980; pres NJ St Deans of Stud 1980-81; mem Nat Assn for Foreign Students; mem Assn of Coll Admnstrs; mem AlphaKappa Alpha Sor; mem Juvenile Resource Center 1986-89; Ad Hoc comm mem, Affirmative Action 1989. **HONORS/ACHIEVEMENTS:** Plaque of Outstanding Serv to Educ Oppor Fund Program, Camden Co Coll 1976; Certif Cited in Bicentennial Vol, Comm Leaders & Noteworthy Amer, 1976; chosen Outstndng Woman in Amer 1977; mem Delta Kappa Pi Honor Soc; Exec Leadership Inst, League for Innovations in the Community Coll; Leaders for the 80s Inst for Leadership Devel; Honorary Mem of Phi Theta Kappa Honor Fraternity; Outstanding Educator of the Year, Camden Church Organization, 1978. **BUSINESS ADDRESS:** Dean of Student Devel, Camden County College, PO Box 200 Wilson Hall East 105, Blackwood, NJ 08012.

MCLAUGHLIN, JOHN BELTON
Physician. **PERSONAL:** Born Jul 03, 1903, Birmingham, AL; son of Amasa A McLaughlin and Hattie B McLaughlin; married Mildred Woods; children: John Jr, William A, Harriet Stafford. **EDUCATION:** Talladega Coll, AB 1928; Fisk U, Advanced Study 1929; Meharry Med Coll, MD 1933. **CAREER:** Self-employed, retired physician; WW I promoting sale of US War Bonds, 4 minute speaker 1917-18; dr's aide influenza epidemic 1918; L Richard Meml Hosp, 2 yr intership 1933-35; med & surgery prac 1935; L Richard Meml Hosp, sec of med staff 1952-54; L Richardson Hosp Staff, pres 1962-63. **ORGANIZATIONS:** Mem Greensboro C of C 1965; Greensboro Men's Club 1942; sec pres 1950's; Hayes-Taylor YMCA 1948; Omega Psi Phi Frat 1926; mem Old N State Med Soc 1935-77; Natl Med Soc 1940-77; mem St James United Presbyterian Church of Greensboro; regular mem NAACP 1942-. **HONORS/ACHIEVEMENTS:** Cert of award & honor for 40 yrs devotion & serv to Omega Frat 1965; cert of award Free Med Care given to poor & indigent patients Natl Med Assn 1963; received the Meharry Medical Coll President's Awd for 50 years of Serv to Mankind 1933-83. **BUSINESS ADDRESS:** Physician, 1709 S Benbow Rd, Greensboro, NC 27406.

MCLAUGHLIN, JOSEPH C.
Business executive. **PERSONAL:** Born May 01, 1934, Washington, DC; married Katye Harris; children: Brian, Briget. **EDUCATION:** Amer Univ, 1966-70; Univ Detroit, 1975. **CAREER:** Black Nugget Restaurant, pres 1968-75; Creative Comm Develop Corp, pres 1972-75; Joe McLaughlin Olds, pres 1977-. **ORGANIZATIONS:** Mem/chmn Capital Headstart Inc; chmn Wash DC Econ Union Develop Corp; co-chmn Wash DC Urban League Mem Drive; chmn DC Chap Natl Black Rep Coun. **HONORS/ACHIEVEMENTS:** Apprec for Serv Rendered as Chmn Award Capital Headstart Inc 1974; Top Worker Fed Govt Award & Apprec Award Wash DC Urban League 1965. **BUSINESS ADDRESS:** President, Joe McLaughlin Olds, 7000 Wyndale St NW, Washington, DC 20015.

MCLAUGHLIN, LAVERNE LANEY
Educator. **PERSONAL:** Born Jul 29, 1952, Ft Valley, GA; daughter of John Laney and Gladys Laney; married Frederick; children: Frederick Laney. **EDUCATION:** Spelman Coll, BA (cum laude) 1974; Altanta U, MSLS (with honors) 1975. **CAREER:** Byron Elem Schl Bryon GA, tchr 1975-76; GA SW Coll Americus GA, asst prof/librarian 1976-. **ORGANIZATIONS:** Organist Allen Chapel AME Church 1977-81; pianist St John Baptist Church 1968-; bd of dir, Amer Cancer Soc; American Library Assn; Georgia Library Assn; Southeastern Library Assn. **HONORS/ACHIEVEMENTS:** Andrew Mellon Fellow Atlanta Univ 1974-75; cum laude Spelman Coll 1974; Beta Phi Mu Atlanta Univ 1975; Outstanding Young Women of Amer l983. **HOME ADDRESS:** 536 E Jefferson St, Americus, GA 31709. **BUSINESS ADDRESS:** Assistant Professor, GA Southwestern Coll, James Earl Carter Lib, Americus, GA 31709.

MCLAUGHLIN, MEGAN E.
Executive vice president. **PERSONAL:** Children: Afiya McLaughlin-White. **EDUCATION:** Howard Univ, BA 1966, MSW 1968; The Graduate Ctr CUNY, Doctoral work in Cultural Anthropology 1970-72; Columbia Univ Sch of Social Work, Certificate in Advanced Social Welfare 1976, DSW 1981. **CAREER:** Columbia Univ Sch of Social Work, lecturer 1975-78; The New York Community Trust, prog officer 1978-83, sr program officer 1983-86; Federation of Protestant Welfare Agencies Inc, exec vice pres 1986-. **ORGANIZATIONS:** Bd of dirs Assoc of Black Foundation Execs; adv council Columbia Univ Sch of Social Work; mem Caribbean Women's Health Assoc, Comm Council of GreaterNY, Dept of Social Serv Adv Comm; bd of dirs Edwin Gould Foundation for Children; mem Governor's Adv Comm on Black Affairs, Health System Agency, March of Dimes Steering Comm for Low Birth Weight Campaign, Neighborhood Family Serv Continuing Crisis Implementation, NY Alliance for the Public School, NY StateCommn on Child Care; mem President's Adv Comm

Hunter Coll Employee's Assistance Prog, Adv Comm Special Serv for Children, Task Force on Human Svcs. **HONORS/ACHIEVEMENTS:** 8 publications including "West Indian Immigrants, Their Social Network and Ethnic Identification" Distribution Columbia Univ 1981. **HOME ADDRESS:** 404 W 149th St, New York, NY 10031. **BUSINESS ADDRESS:** Executive Vice President, Fed of Protestant Welfare Agen, 281 Park Ave South, New York, NY 10010.

MCLAURIN, BENJAMIN PHILIP
Educational administration. **PERSONAL:** Born Apr 24, 1947, New York, NY. **EDUCATION:** Morehouse Coll, BA 1969; Rutgers State Univ, 1970. **ORGANIZATIONS:** Bd mem Southern Coll Placement Assoc 1977-78; vice pres GA Coll Placement Assoc 1978; bd mem GA Coll Placement Assoc 1984-85. **BUSINESS ADDRESS:** Dir Career Cnslng & Plcmnt, Morehouse College, PO Box 5, Atlanta, GA 30314.

MCLAURIN, DANIEL WASHINGTON
Business executive. **PERSONAL:** Born Nov 24, 1940, Philadelphia, PA; son of Abraham McLaurin and Dorothy E Foster McLaurin (deceased); married Delores E White, Sep 09, 1961; children: Craig Blair, Brian Keith. **EDUCATION:** LaSalle Coll, BS Marketing 1981. **CAREER:** Gulf Oil Corp, retail mktr 1970-73, EEO coord 1973-76, dir admin serv 1976-83; Chevron Gulf Oil Corp, dir security & safety 1983-85; Chevron Buildings Mgmt Co, supv bldgs mgmt 1985-. **ORGANIZATIONS:** Mem Amer Soc for Industrial Security; mem Society Real Prop Admin. **HONORS/ACHIEVEMENTS:** Chpl of Four Chplns 1973; Black Amer in Industry 1974. **HOME ADDRESS:** 15402 Evergreen Pl Dr, Houston, TX 77083. **BUSINESS ADDRESS:** Supervisor Bldgs Mgmt, Chevron Bldgs Mgmt Co, 11111 S Wilcrest, Houston, TX 77099.

MCLAURIN, FREDDIE LEWIS, JR.
Educator, mathematician. **PERSONAL:** Born Dec 06, 1943, Jackson, MS; son of Fred L McLaurin and Nora L Robinson McLaurin (deceased); married Dorothy Loretta Turner, Jul 10, 1965; children: Freddie Lewis III, Tanya Lynn. **EDUCATION:** CA State Univ, BA 1972, STC 1973; Webster Univ, MPA 1977; Univ of CO, MS 1978; Air Univ Air Command & Staff Coll Course, cert 1984-85. **CAREER:** USAF, electron syst spec 1964-73, auto flt cont syst tech 1973-74, electron syst ofcr 1974-75, logistics ofcr 1975-78; USAF Acad, asst prof dept math sci 1978-82; CA State Univ Fresno Dept Aerospace Studies, asst prof 1982-85; 2049 Comm Group, chf of operations 1985-88; Amer River College, mathematics instructor. **ORGANIZATIONS:** Commandant of Cadets Det 35 AF ROTC 1983-85; pres Black Faculty & Staff Assn 1983-84. **HONORS/ACHIEVEMENTS:** Distinguished Grad Sch Mil Sci 1974; Educ Achievement Award Tactical Air Command USAF 1976. **MILITARY SERVICE:** USAF Major 1964-88; USAF Meritorious Serv Medal 1982-85; 1st Oakleaf Cluster USAF Commendation Medal 1st Oak Leaf Cluster 1978-82; USAF Commend Medal 1975-77. **BUSINESS ADDRESS:** Mathematics Instructor, Dept Mathematics, American River College, Sacramento, CA 95841.

MCLAURIN, HOWARD WILSON
Director. **PERSONAL:** Born Dec 17, 1936, Jackson, MS; married Mary Lewis; children: Keith, Craig, Kirk. **EDUCATION:** Univ Chicago, MBA Prgm; Chicago Tchrs Coll; NY U, Cert IBM Data Processing for Govt Officials; Govt Data Sys Joint Ctr for Polit Studies; course in mgmt. **CAREER:** Ft Sam Houston BAMC, prgrm analyst; City Gary IN, dir data processing; Police System 1100 State Chicago, mgr; Ehlers Maremont Co, sr consult 1964-70.

MCLAURIN, JASPER ETIENNE
Physician. **PERSONAL:** Born Dec 12, 1927, Braxton, MS; married Doris Williams; children: Karen, Pamela, Toni. **EDUCATION:** Wayne State U, BA 1954; Meharry Med Coll, MD 1958; Harvard Med School, basic sci, neurology 1959-62; Univ MI, MS 1964; Mt Carmel Mercy Hosp, intern 1958-59; VA Hosp, resident 1959-62. **CAREER:** physician private practice, 1964-; Univ MI Med Center, assoc neurologist 1962-65;Univ MI Med Sch, instructor; chf neurology 1963-64; VA Hosp, asst chief neurology 1962; Wayne State Univ, asst prof present; Mt Carme Mercy Hosp, staff mem; Grace NW; Hutzel; Harper; MI Children's; SW Gen; Receiving Hospital of Detroit, Sameritan Med Center; Japser E McLaurin MD PC, pres. **ORGANIZATIONS:** Outer Drive mem Wayne Co Med Soc; MI State Med Soc; AMA; Detroit Med Soc; Nat Med Assn; MI Neurological Assn; Am Acad of Neurology; Amer Neurology Assn; flw Am Coll of Angiology Amer Geriatrics Soc; Am Heart Assn; bd dir Epileptic Ctr MI; World Med Relief 1970, 1972; consult MI State Dept Edn; Detroit Bd Educ; MI Cripple Children's Soc; MI Neuromuscular Inst; Soc Security Admin; mem, Pres Adv Com on Strokes & Heart Disease; Life mem NAACP; Urban League; Omega Psi Phi Frat; mem Nat Yacht Racing Union; bd dir Huron River Heights Property Owners Assn. **MILITARY SERVICE:** USN lt commander, 1946-50. **BUSINESS ADDRESS:** President, Japser E McLaurin MD PC, 6001 W Outer Dr, #137, Detroit, MI 48235.

MCLAWHORN, JAMES THOMAS, JR.
Association executive. **PERSONAL:** Born Apr 27, 1947, Greenville, NC; son of Mr & Mrs James T McLawhorn, Sr; married Barbara Campbell; children: Karla, James III, Mark. **EDUCATION:** NC A&T, BS Political Sci 1969; Univ of NC Chapel Hill, MS City & Reg Planning 1971; Univ of Miami, MBA 1977. **CAREER:** Model Cities, program planning coord 1971-74; City of Charlotte, program mgmt coord 1974-76; First Union Bank, loan devel analyst 1977-78; Democratic Natl Comm of Congressional Black Caucus, admin asst 1978-79; Columbia Urban League Inc, pres, CEO 1979-. **ORGANIZATIONS:** Mem City of Columbia Comm on Minority & Small Bus, Seven Thirty Breakfast Club, Governor's Volunteer Awds Selection Committee, Crime Stoppers, Indian Waters Boy Scouts of Amer Exec Council; sec Natl Urban League's Council of CEO's; chmn Governor's Primary Health Care Task Force for Richland Cty. **HONORS/ACHIEVEMENTS:** Ten for the Future Columbia Record; one of 60 civilian leaders in the nationinvited to participate in the Joint Civilian Orientation Conf Sec of Defense 1985; presenter, The South Carolina Great American Family Tour, Aspen Institute, 1988. **BUSINESS ADDRESS:** President & CEO, Columbia Urban League, Inc, Drawer J, Columbia, SC 29250.

MCLEAN, HELEN VIRGINIA
Educational administrator. **PERSONAL:** Born Jul 23, 1933, Southern Pines, NC. **EDUCATION:** NC Central U, BA 1954;Univ of PA, MA 1956;Univ of FL, EdD 1974. **CAREER:** St Petersburgh Junior Coll, dir div of communications 1975-; St Petersburg Junior Coll, chairperson directed studies dept 1964-75; Gibbs Junior Coll, chairperson communications dept 1958-64; Wilberforce U, asso prof languages 1956-58. **ORGANIZATIONS:** Am Assn ofUniv Women; Modern Languade Assn; Coll English Assn; FL English Assn; Council on Black Am Affairs So Region; various others YWCA; sec exec com Pinellas County Dist Mental Health Bd; mem NAACP; bd United Negro Coll Fund St Petersburg FL; mem The Greater St Petersburg Council on Human Rel;various others. **HONORS/ACHIEVEMENTS:** Tangley Oaks Educ fellowship 1972-73; EDDA-E grad fellowshipsUniv of FL 1972-74; Who's Who Win Am Edn; "Reading-A Total Faculty Commitment"; "Career Educ and Gen Edn"; "Every Tchr a Reading Tchr"; "Teaching Strategies for a Developmental Studies Curriculum"; various other publs. **BUSINESS ADDRESS:** Director, Communications, St Petersburg Junior College, 2465 Drew St, Clearwater, FL 34625.

MCLEAN, JOHN ALFRED, JR.
Scientist/educator. **PERSONAL:** Born Nov 08, 1926, Chapel Hill, TN; son of John Alfred McLean and Anna Belle Sheffield McLean; married Esther Ann Bush; children: Jeffery, David, Linda. **EDUCATION:** TN A&I State Univ, BS 1948; Univ of IL, MS 1956, PhD 1959. **CAREER:** State Bd for Pub Community & Jr Coll, chmn 1965-81; Univ of Detroit, prof of chem/chmn dept chem & chem engineering 1959-. **ORGANIZATIONS:** Bd of directors, American Heart Association 1988-. **HONORS/ACHIEVEMENTS:** Comm Service Awd Wayne County Comm Coll 1977; Amer Chemical Soc Certificate for Outstanding Leadership of Detroit Sect of ACS 1982; Annual Disting Serv Awd Detroit Sect of the ACS 1985; Univ of Detroit President's Awd for Excellence in Teaching and Research 1986; mem Phi Delta Kappa, Phi Lambda Upsilon, Sigma Xi. **MILITARY SERVICE:** AUS Sgt 1953-55. **BUSINESS ADDRESS:** Chmn Dept Chemistry, Univ of Detroit, 4001 W McNichols Rd, Detroit, MI 48221.

MCLEAN, JOHN LENWOOD
Saxophonist, composer, educator, historian. **PERSONAL:** Born May 17, 1931, NYC, NY; married Clarice Simmons; children: Rene, Vernon, Melonae. **EDUCATION:** Attended, A&T Coll. **CAREER:** The Living Theatre, actor musician 1959-63; played w/Thelonious Monk, Miles Davis, Bud Powell, Charlie Mingus and others; travelling extensively in Europe & Japan playing concerts & teaching; Univ of Buffalo, teacher w/Archie Shepp; NY State Correctional Dept, bandmaster; recorded on Prestige, Blue Note, United Artists, Steeplechase, RCA & Columbia labels; Joseph Papp's prod "Unfinished Women", composer 1977; Univ of Hartford Hartt Coll of Music, prof 1978; RCA Victor,recording contract 1979; Artists Collective Hartford, creative consultant; Hartt Coll Univ of Hartford, fndr & chmn african/amer music dept. **ORGANIZATIONS:** Honorary mem Omega Phi Epsilon Frat; panelist two Natl Endowment for the Arts Progs (expansion arts & jazz prog). **HONORS/ACHIEVEMENTS:** Mobilization for Youth New York City Outstanding Band Leader 1966-67; Downbeat TDWR Awd 1964; Humanities Awd Omega Phi Epsilon Delta Chap 1972; NAACP Awd for Artists Collective; State of CT Arts Awd 1983; Afro-Amer Museum Philadelphia PîA; Jazz Master Awd 1983; BMI Jazz Pioneer Awd 1984; Who's Who in Amer; New York Chap of Natl Black MBA Assoc Inc Gold Note Jazz Awd 1985; Upper Albany Ave Hartford CT Merchants Assoc Special Awd for Dedication to and Preservationof African American Culture and Service to the Comm; Univ of CA Berkeley Roots Awd 1986. **BUSINESS ADDRESS:** Professor, Hartt CollUniv of Hartford, 200 Bloomfield Ave, West Hartford, CT 06117.

MCLEAN, MABLE PARKER
Educator. **PERSONAL:** Born Mar 19, Cameron, NC; widowed; children: Randall P. **EDUCATION:** Barber Scotia Coll; Johnson C Smith U; Howard U; NW U; CathUniv of Am; Inst for Educ Mgmt HarvardUniv 1972; Johnson C Smith U, LHD 1976; Rust Coll, LHS 1976; Coll of Granada, LlD; JC Smith U, PedD. **CAREER:** Barber-Scotia Coll, prof of educ and psychology, coordinator of student teaching 1969-71, chairman dept of elementary educ 1970-71, dean of college 1971-74, apptd interim president 1974, apptd acting president of college 1974, apptd president of the college 1975-. **ORGANIZATIONS:** Mem Assn for Childhood Edn; Assn for Student Teaching; Nat & St NC Assn for Supr & Curriculum Devel; St Coun on Early Childhood Edn; Delta Kappa Gamma Soc of Women Edn; NC Adminstrv Women in Edn; Am Assn ofUniv Adminstr; Nat Coun of Adminstrv Women in Edn; mem exec com Metrolina Lung Assn; Dem Women's Org of Cabarrus Co; Alpha Kappa Alpha Sorority Inc; elder John Hall Presb Ch; elected bd of dir Children's Home Soc of NC; past pres United Presb Women's Org of John Hall United Presb Ch; pres Presidents Roundtable of UPC USA; bd dir NAFEO; mem United Bd for Coll Develop; mem United Way of Cabarrus Co; mem exec com NC Assn of Independent Colleges & U; mem exec com NC Assn of Colleges & U. **HONORS/ACHIEVEMENTS:** 5 Honorary Degrees; numerous awds and citations among which are Johnson C Smith Philadelphia Alumni Outstanding Achievement Awd 1977; Disting Alumna Awd 1977; Alumna of the Year Johnson C Smith Univ 1980; Dedicated Service Citation-Consortium on Rsch Training 1982; Disting Service Awd Grambling State Univ 1984; Presidential Scroll for devotion to higher educ by promoting achievement of excellence 1986. **BUSINESS ADDRESS:** President, Barber Scotia College, Concord, NC 28025.

MCLEAN, MARQUITA SHEILA MCLARTY
Consultant, management, personnel, environment. **PERSONAL:** Born Aug 05, 1933, Richmond, VA; daughter of William C McLarty and Daisey B McLarty; married Cecil P. **EDUCATION:** VA State Univ, BA 1953; OH State Univ, MA 1956; Univ of Cincinnati, postgrad 1957-69. **CAREER:** Delaware OH, teacher 1954-57; Robert A Taft HS Cincinnati, teacher 1957-62; Sawyer Jr HS Cincinnati, counselor 1962-65; Withrow HS Cincinnati, counselor 1965-67; Cincinnati Public Sch, assoc guidance serv div 1968-73; Ofc Univ Commitment to Human Resources Univ of Cincinnati, dir 1973-77; Univ Personnel Serv Univ of Cincinnati, assoc sr vice pres 1978-83; OH Environmental Protection Agency, deputy admin 1983-85; McLean Olohan & Associates, principal-in-charge. **ORGANIZATIONS:** Mem Alumni Advisory Council OH State Univ 1971-; past trustee Cincinnati Tech Coll; mem OH Educ Assn; mem Cincinnati Personnel & Guidance Assn; mem Amer School Counselor Assn; mem OH Sch Counselor Assn; mem Nat Assn of Sch Counselors; mem Delta Sigma Theta; mem OH State Alumni Club; mem and vice chairperson Ohio Water Advisory Council, Governor appointee 1985-89; mem Leadership Steering Comm Cincinnati 1986-87; mem Natl & Cincinnati Women Political Caucus; mem Citizens Scholarship Foundation of Amer Inc, Natl Bd of Governors; public manager, State and Local Govt Council 1988-92; mem, Cincinnati Environmental Advisory Council 1988-; charter member, Withrow Dollars for Scholars 1988. **BUSINESS ADDRESS:** Principal, McLean Olohan & Associates, 5324 Kenwood Road, Cincinnati, OH 45227.

MCLEAN, MARY CANNON
Retired special education administrator. **PERSONAL:** Born Sep 25, 1912, Cranford, NJ;

daughter of Rev Dr David W Cannon Sr (deceased) and Gertrude Moody Cannon (deceased); married Dr Eldon George McLean, Sep 03, 1942; children: Eldon James McLean. **EDUCATION:** Jersey City State Coll, Jersey City NJ, BS, 1935; Columbia Univ Teachers Coll, New York NY, MA, 1947, Professional Diploma, Supervisor of Work with the Mentally Retarded, 1948, Supervisor of Elementary Schools, 1949, PhD, Education, 1950. **CAREER:** Social Centers for Migratory Workers in Delaware and Maryland, Home Mission Council of Amer, New York City, organizer and director; Egg Harbor Township, Pleasantville NJ, primary grades teacher 1936-38; Springfield Public Schools, Springfield MA, teacher 1939, supervisor of special educ 1967-68, director of special educ 1968-79; Amer Intl Coll, Boston Coll, New York Univ, Queens Coll, Flushing LI, visiting professor and lecturer; Holyoke Public Schools, consultant 1980-85. **ORGANIZATIONS:** Bd dir, Massachusetts Blue Cross, 10 years; bd dir, Assn of Teachers of Children With Special Needs, Western Massachusetts; bd dir, Massachusetts Special Class Teachers Assn; bd dir, Springfield Day Nursery; bd dir, Hampden County Assn for Retarded Children; bd dir, Visiting Nurses Assn; bd dir, Springfield Hearing League Highland Branch YMCA; adv bd, United Cerebral Palsy of Western Massachusetts; bd of managers, Massachusetts Congress of Parents and Teachers; commr, Educational Development, Commonwealth of Massachusetts; chmn, Lyceum Comm, St John's Congregational Church UCC, 3 years; exec comm, Educ Comm, Citizen Action Commn, Springfield MA; exec comm; Springfield Branch NAACP; exec comm, New England Regional Conf, NAACP; steering comm, Region II, NAACP. **HONORS/ACHIEVEMENTS:** Distinguished Alumna, Jersey City State Coll, NJ, 1978; Hon Doctor of Humane Letters Degree, Westfield State Coll, Westfield MA, 1980; Hon Doctor of Laws Degree, Western New England Coll, 1981; Human and Civil Rights Award, Massachusetts Teachers Assn, Sturbridge MA, 1987; awarded commendations from the House of Rep, State Senate, Sec of State, Commonwealth Museum for contributions to the 350 years of African experience in Massachusetts, 1989; author of The History of St John's Congregational Church 1844-1962; author of "A Study of Occupational Opportunities for the Mentally Retarded in the City of Springfield, MA," School Dept, Springfield MA; contrib to Curriculum Guide for Auxiliary Classes in the Elementary Schools, Sprinfield Public Schools; author of "Easing the Load of the Limited," Amer Journal of Mental Deficiency. **HOME ADDRESS:** 909 Roosevelt Ave, Springfield, MA 01109.

MCLEAN, ZARAH GEAN
Physician. **PERSONAL:** Born Aug 28, 1942, Tallulah, LA; married Russell McLean; children: Paul, Crystal, Grant. **EDUCATION:** Fisk Univ, BA 1964; Howard Univ Coll of Medicine, MD 1968. **CAREER:** Medical Coll of WI, assoc prof of pediatrics 1972-86. **ORGANIZATIONS:** Bd dirs Emma Murry Child Care Ctr 1982-86; bd dirs WI Independent Physicians Group 1985-87. **BUSINESS ADDRESS:** Physician, Child Health Assoc, 2040 W Wisconsin Ave #580, Milwaukee, WI 53233.

MCLEMORE, LESLIE BURL
Educator. **PERSONAL:** Born Sep 17, 1940, Walls, MS; son of Burl McLemore and Christine Williams; divorced; children: Leslie Burl McLemore II. **EDUCATION:** Rust Coll, BA 1964; Atlanta Univ, MA 1965; Univ Of MA Amherst, PhD 1970. **CAREER:** Atlanta Univ, rsch asst 1960-65; So Univ, instr 1965-66; Univ MA Amherst, teaching asst 1966-69; Jackson State Univ, prof & ch 1971; Johns Hopkins Univ, post-doctoral fellow 1970-; Jackson State Univ, dean of grad sch & dir rsch admin & prof polit sci 1984-. **ORGANIZATIONS:** Pres Rust Coll Natl Alumni Assn; past vice pres So Poli Sci Assn; former pres Natl Conf of Black Polit Sci; mem Jackson League Task Force on Local Govt; mem exec comm Black Mississippians Council on Higher Educ; editorial bd Teaching Polit Sci summa cum laude Rust Coll 1964; chair liaison comm NCEA; chair Task Force on Minorities in Grad Ed. **HONORS/ACHIEVEMENTS:** Hon Woodrow Wilson Fellow Rust Coll; Pi Sigma Alpha Polit Sci; Outstanding Young Men of Amer 1967-75; Chancellor's Medal Univ of MA at Amherst 1986; appointed to the Comm on the Status of Black Americans, Natl Acad of Sci 1985-87; Rockefeller Foundation Research Fellowship 1982-83; Spotlight on Scholars Awd Jackson State Univ 1980-81. **HOME ADDRESS:** 746 Windward Rd, Jackson, MS 39206. **BUSINESS ADDRESS:** Dean, Grad Studies & Dir Rsch Adm, Jackson StateUniv, 1400 John Roy Lynch St, Jackson, MS 39217.

MCLEMORE, NELSON, JR.
City official. **PERSONAL:** Born Jan 29, 1934, Chicago, IL; married Ollie Stokes; children: Nelson III. **EDUCATION:** TN A&I State U, BS 1955; Governors StateUniv Park Forest S IL, MA 1978; Chicago Tchrs Coll & John Marshall Law Sch, addl study. **CAREER:** Dept of Public Works, dir of programming 1985-; Human Svcs, dep commr 1980, chief-of-staff; Human Svcs, dir of personnel & training 1979-80; Planning-Human Svcs, asst dir 1978-79; Chicago Dept of Human Resources, asst to Commr; coord of Comm Serv 1972-74; comm unit dir 1969-72; Chicago Commn on Youth Welfare, comm unit dir 1965-69; Chicago Pub Elem & Secondary Sch, tchr 1955-65. **ORGANIZATIONS:** Mem Nat Assn for Comm Develop; past pres & mem 2nd and Reg Dem Organization Boosters Club; Kappa Alpha Psi; Certified Social Worker. **MILITARY SERVICE:** AUS pfc 1956-58. **BUSINESS ADDRESS:** Dir of Programming, Dept of Public Works, 320 N Clark St, Chicago, IL 60610.

MCLENDON, JOHN B., JR.
Promotional representative. **PERSONAL:** Born Apr 05, 1915, Hiawatha, KS; married Joanna L Owens; children: Querida Banks, John III, Herbert Bryant, Nannette Adams. **EDUCATION:** U Univ KS, BS, Ed, 1936; Univ IA, MA, 1937. **CAREER:** Converse Rubber Co, natl & promotional rep present; Denver Rockets Am Basketball Assn, basketball coach 1969-70; Cleveland State Univ, 1966-69; KY State Coll, 1963-66; Cleveland Pipers, 1961-62; Cleveland Pipers Nat Indsl Bsktbl League, 1959-61; TN A&I State U, 1954-59; Hampton Inst, 1952-54; NC Coll, 1937-52; Lawrence Memorial HS, 1935-36; Health & Phys Educ, NC Coll, athletic dir, 1942-52; Athletics Hlth PE & Recreation TN State A&I U, co-ord 1962-63. **ORGANIZATIONS:** US Olympic Bsktball Com 1965-72; chmn Martin Luther King Chicago Boys Club; bd dir 1974-77; World BB Rules Com 1972-76; chmn Nat AAU Basketball 1967-68. **HONORS/ACHIEVEMENTS:** Coaching Award of Merit, NABC, 1970; 25-yr coaching award, Natl Assn Basketball Coaches of US, 1970; Natl Assn of Intercollegiate Athletes; Natl BB Championship, 1957-59; TN A&I State Univ; 1st team to win 3 Natl Championships consecutively; Natl AAU BB Championship, 1st Black Coach; Eastern ABA Championship, 1st black, 1962; Helms Athletic Hall of Fame, 1962; published, Fast Break Basketball, 1965; The Fast Break Game, 1974; Honorary DHL, North Carolina Central Univ, 1979, Jarvis Christian Coll, 1981; Breaking Through McLendon Katz, 1987; Alumni Award, Kansas Univ, highest honor given by Univ, 1979. **BUSINESS ADDRESS:** Promotions Consultant, Converse Inc, 15 Salt Creek Lane, Rm 301, Hinsdale, IL 60521.

MCLEOD, GEORGIANNA R.
Director, social worker. **PERSONAL:** Born Oct 06, 1937, NYC, NY. **EDUCATION:** NY Univ, BS 1959. **CAREER:** Morningside Comm Ctr Camp #41, group work/recreation 1952-; Rush Inst, recreation therapist 1957-58; Neighborhood House, 1959; New York City Dept Soc Serv Emer Asst Unit/Bronx, director/social wkr. **ORGANIZATIONS:** Mem APWA, NCSW, NABSW, Am Chama Soc, SSEU, Amer Soc of Professional Exec Women; officer Alpha Chap No 1 PH-OES 1982-; past pres Blk Hist Chap New York City DSS NAACP 1960-; Master Activist, Ch Sec Church of the Master 1984-. **HONORS/ACHIEVEMENTS:** Woman of the Yr Interboro Civic 5 1980; Comm Serv Awd DSS Branch NAACP 1983; Outstanding Serv Church of the Master 1983; Who's Who Among Professional and Executive Women Cert of Achievement 1987. **BUSINESS ADDRESS:** Director/Social Worker, New York City Dept of Serv Emer Asst, 434 E 147 St, Bronx, NY 10455.

MCLEOD, JAMES S.
Mortician. **PERSONAL:** Born Oct 14, 1939, Bennettsville, SC; married Shirley J Jeffries; children: Tracey, Maymia, Erica. **EDUCATION:** A&T State U, attended 1 yr; NC CentralUniv Durham NC, 2 yrs Eckels Coll Mortuary Science Philadelphia, grad. **CAREER:** Morris Funeral Home Bennettsville SC, mgr 1964-72, owner since 1972. **ORGANIZATIONS:** Mem 6 Dist Morticians Assn; SC State & Nat Morticians Assn; mem exec bd Pee Dee Regional Planning & Devel Coun Marlboro Co Betterment League; 6th Dist VEP bd dir Carolina Messenger Inc Mem Shiloh Bapt Ch trustee; Landmark Masonic Lodge #16; F&AM; CC Johnson Consistory #13-Cairo Temple #125 Shriners; Am Legion Post 213; Theta Phi Lambda Chap; dean of pledges Alpha Phi Alpha; NAACP. **HONORS/ACHIEVEMENTS:** Recipient certificate of merit United Supreme Coun 1970; distinguished serv award Alpha Phi Alpha 1971; certificate of achievement Omega Psi Phi Frat 1971; certificate of pub serv Mayor of Bennettsville SC; dean's award Eckels Coll of Mortuary Science; first black since Reconstruction to be appointed to a Boardin Marlboro Co Social Services 1968 & to be elected to Bennettsville City Coun 1971 presently serving 2 terms. **MILITARY SERVICE:** AUS signal corp 1962-64. **BUSINESS ADDRESS:** PO Box 551, Bennettsville, SC.

MCLEOD, MICHAEL PRESTON
Dentist. **PERSONAL:** Born Aug 16, 1954, Tulsa, OK; son of Wallace B McLeod, Jr and Jeanne McLeod; married Corlis Clay; children: Lauren Micah. **EDUCATION:** Howard Univ, BS (Cum Laude) 1976; Univ of OK, DDS 1980; Martin Luther King Genl Hosp, GPR 1981. **CAREER:** Private practice, dentist; Univ of Oakland College of Denistry, Oklahoma City OK, part-time faculty 1984-. **ORGANIZATIONS:** Mem Kappa Alpha Psi 1975-; mem Oklahoma City Med Dental-Phar 1982-; mem Citizen's Advisory Comm, Capital-Medical Center Improvement and Zoning Commn, 1984-. **HONORS/ACHIEVEMENTS:** Amer Acad of Periodontology Awd 1980; Amer Soc of Dentistry for Children Awd 1980; Div of Comm Dentistry Awd 1980; Univ of OK Assoc of Black Personnel Awd 1980. **BUSINESS ADDRESS:** Owner/Proprietor, M McLeod DDS Family Dentistry, 934 NE 8th, Oklahoma City, OK 73104.

MCLEON, NATHANIEL W.
Attorney. **PERSONAL:** Born Jul 13, 1944, Jersey City, NJ; married Lee; children: Jennifer. **EDUCATION:** Howard Univ, BA 1966; Howard Univ School of Law, 1970; NY Univ School of Law, LLM Taxation 1981. **CAREER:** Drew Hall Howard Univ Residence Hall Prog, grad asst 1967-70; Neighborhood Legal Serv, law intern 1969-70; Ernst & Ernst, staff atty 1970-71; Bank of Tokyo Trust Co NY, vice pres & dir of taxes 1979-84; Squibb Corp New York, tax atty. **ORGANIZATIONS:** Mem Natl Bar Assn; mem Omega Psi Phi Frat; Concerned Black Citizens Alliance; bd mem Jersey City Chap Operation PUSH. **HONORS/ACHIEVEMENTS:** Outstanding Intern Award, Ctr for Clinical Legal Studies, Howard Univ School of Law, 1969-70; Harlem YMCA Black Achiever, 1973; 100 Outstanding Young Men in Amer, 1973. **BUSINESS ADDRESS:** Attorney at Law, 521 Fifth Ave, Suite 1600, New York, NY 10175.

MCLIN, LENA JOHNSON
Educator, composer. **PERSONAL:** Born Sep 05, 1928, Atlanta, GA; married Nathaniel Mclin; children: Nathaniel G, Beverly. **EDUCATION:** Spelman Coll, AB 1951; Conservatory, MA 1954; RooseveltUniv Chicago State Coll. **CAREER:** Singer; composer of works too numerous to mention; clinician; Head of Music Dept Kenwood High Sch Chicago, tchr dir; leading small Opera Co "Mclin Ensemble", founder dir. **ORGANIZATIONS:** Mem Chicago Bd of Edn; TCI Educ Film Co Mem MENC; Nat Assn of Negro Musicians; NJE; Institute of Black Am Music. **HONORS/ACHIEVEMENTS:** Outstanding composer VA UnionUniv Award 1973; Tribune Newspaper article 1973; Best tchr of yr 1972-73; Critics Assn Outstanding Composer 1971; NANM Named Leading Black Choral Composer Sidney Alsop Critic 1970; outstanding musician NAACP; Gary Mayor Hatcher; hon degree HHD VA UnionUniv 1975.

MCLINN, HARRY MARVIN
Dental specialist. **PERSONAL:** Born in Huntsville, AL; married Angela; children: Teloca, Marvin, Jenol. **EDUCATION:** Columbia Univ, Cert of Proficiency; Amer Bd of Orthodontics, diplomate; Howard Univ, DDS 1947. **CAREER:** Private Practice, dentist 1947-51; Howard Dental Sch, chmn dept orthodontics & dental anatomy 1948-50; New York City Dept of Hlth, panel 1950-60; NYC, orthodontics 1951-71; NJ City Med Dental Coll, asst assoc prof 1973-75, assoc prof of orthodontics. **ORGANIZATIONS:** Mem ADA, NDA, NHDA, Columbia Univ Dental Alumni; NESO Amer Assn of Orthodontists; FICA Intl Coll of Dentists; mem Bd of Health; dir Englewood NJ Dental Prog for Sch Children; mem Longrange Hlth & Planning Com 1976-77; fellow Intl Coll of Dentists 1976; diplomate Amer Bd of Orthodontics 1958; mem Long Range Planning Comm of Englewood NJ Hosp serving 27 comms 1980. **HONORS/ACHIEVEMENTS:** 1st Louise Ball Teaching Fellow Howard Univ, Columbia Univ 1948; 1st Howard Univ Diplomate of Amer Bd of Orthodontics; Fellow Intl Dental Coll. **MILITARY SERVICE:** AUS Dental Corp WW II capt.

MCMATH, ALEXANDER S.
Educator. **PERSONAL:** Born Jun 14, 1945, Clinton, SC. **EDUCATION:** Morehouse Coll Atlanta GA, BA 1968; MA 1970;Univ CA Berkeley, MFA 1971. **CAREER:** Coll of Marin Kent Field, art prof present; Los Medonos Jr Coll Pittsburg CA; Hd Strt Prog Morehouse Coll Atlanta, counselor & consult 1964-67; Sanders Pub High Schl SC, tchr 1968-69; Spl Ser ProgUniv CA, cnsalr & tutor 1970-71; Art DeptUniv of CA Berkeley, instrctr 1972-74; Art DeptUniv SC Columbia,instrctr 1971-72. **ORGANIZATIONS:** Art exhibitions "A

Third World Painting & Sculpture exhibition" San Francisco Museum of Art San Francisco, CA June 8-July 28 1974; "Calligraphy Series Two" (One Man Show) Aha Gallery Chgo, IL Jan 23 1975; Lancers Galry NY 1963; Clark Coll Atlanta 1964; Spelman Coll Atlanta 1965;Univ CA Musm Berkly 1971; Morehouse Coll Atlanta 1967; Creative Cancer Art Galry Atlanta 1972, 1973; various group shows panlst particpnt USA 1971-1972 Art Conf Carnegie Inst Pittsburg 1971; Nat Conf of Artsts Conv; Chicago 1972 HowardUniv Washington 1973. **HONORS/ACHIEVEMENTS:** First place purchse award 21st Annual SC Gld Artsts Cntst 1971; eisner prize Art DeptUniv CA Brkly 1970-71; chsn for The Whitney Rebuttal Show Arts of Art Galry NY 1972; john hope prize Waddell Galry Atlanta 1969; one man show Clarence White Contemporary Art Gallery 1977; 1st place award Annual EmoryUniv RowArt Show GA 1968; 1st place annual exbhtn Waddell Glry Atlanta 1967; named in many art articles & periodicals.

MCMEANS, DONALD CURTIS
Business executive. **PERSONAL:** Born Oct 02, 1939, Westfield, AL; married Helen Carolyn; children: Michelle Denise, Monique Danielle, Malika Dionne. **EDUCATION:** Lincoln U, AB 1962;Univ of PA, MA 1964; Johns HopkinsUniv Sch for Advanced Intl Studies 1965. **CAREER:** Renaissance Broadcasting Corp, pres /gen mgr 1976-; NJ Pub Broadcasting Authority, dir of community serv 1971-76; NJ Dept of Community Affairs, asstdir model cities program 1968-71; W Main St Community Center Stamford CT, dir 1967-68; Community Renewal Team of Greater Hartford, program officer 1966-67; US Dept of Commerce, econ analyst 1965-66. **ORGANIZATIONS:** Bd of dir Nat Assn of Educ Broadcasters 1972-73; Am history adv bd Eastern Educ Network 1974; bd of Dir Wometco Home Theatre present; sec of bd Narcotic Addicts Rehab Center Orgn Atlantic City NJ 1975-77; mem Alpha Phi Alpha Frat/Price Hall Mason. **HONORS/ACHIEVEMENTS:** Foreign Affair Scholar Ford Found 1964-65; hall honor Chapel of Four Chaplins 1974; distinguished achievement Garden State Bar Assn 1979. **BUSINESS ADDRESS:** Route 130 & Levitt Pkwy, Willingboro, NJ 08046.

MCMICKENS, JACQUELINE MONTGOMERY
Government official. **PERSONAL:** Born Dec 10, 1935, Birmingham, AL; daughter of Zollie Coffer Montgomery and Flora B Walton Montgomery; married William McMickens; children: Lenell Myricks, Charles Maurice, Barry. **EDUCATION:** John Jay Coll of Criminal Justice, BA Criminal Justice 1972, MPA 1976; Brooklyn Law School, attending. **CAREER:** Kings Cty Hospital, CEO; Adolescent Ctr on Rikers Island, dep warden for security, dir training acad; New York City Dept of Corrections, commissioner; NY Housing Authority, vice chairwoman. **HONORS/ACHIEVEMENTS:** 1st woman to run security in a men's ward; 1st woman to head the dept acad; 1st woman to be named chief of King's Cty Hosp Prison Ward; 1st woman to be chief of oper; Hon DL St Joseph's Coll NY, Miles Coll Birmingham. **BUSINESS ADDRESS:** Vice Chairwoman, New York City Housing Authority, 250 Broadway, New York, NY 10007.

MCMILLAN, BENJAMIN EARL
Business executive. **PERSONAL:** Born Apr 29, 1936, Okmulgee, OK; divorced; children: Michael Alan. **EDUCATION:** Central State Univ Edmond OK, BS Math 1966; Pepperdine Univ Malibu, MBA 1973. **CAREER:** Fed Aviation Admin, prog 1963; Gen Dynamics Pomona Div, supr comp oper 1966, sr rsch engr 1969, group leader-computer hardware 1974, computer planning & acquisition spl 1974-76, tech purchasing spl 1976-81; United Technologies Comm Co, mgr mgmt info serv 1981-. **ORGANIZATIONS:** Instr Pepperdine Univ 1974; div mem Amer Mgmt Assn 1979; cons/speaker on computer related topics 1979-80; bd of dir Kiwanis Club of Pomona 1970-73; contrib ed Pomona Clairon-Comm Newspaper 1972-73. **HONORS/ACHIEVEMENTS:** Cert of Service Natl Assn of Bus Youth Motivational Task Force 1970; pub 4 part article "Facing up to Conversion" 1979. **MILITARY SERVICE:** AUS spec 3 1954-57; Good Conduct Medal Occupational Forces-Europe 1957. **BUSINESS ADDRESS:** Manager Mgmt Info Services, United Tech Comm Co, 12101 Woodcrest Exec Dr, St Louis, MO 63141.

MCMILLAN, ENOLIA PETTIGEN
Educator. **PERSONAL:** Born Oct 20, 1904, Willow Grove, PA; daughter of John Pettigen and Elizabeth Pettigen; married Betha D McMillan, Dec 26, 1936 (deceased); children: Betha D Jr. **EDUCATION:** Howard Univ Washington, DC, AB 1926; Columbia Univ New York, MA 1933. **CAREER:** Denton & Pomonkey MD, high school teacher 1926-28; Pomonkey High Schl, princ 1928-35; Jr High School Baltimore, teacher 1935-56; Clifton Pk JHS & Cherry Hill JHS, vprinc 1956-63; Dunbar Sr High Schl Baltimore, vice principal 1963-69; Baltimore City School System, apptd lifelong principal 1985-. **ORGANIZATIONS:** Secy MD Fed Clrd PTA's; pres D St Conf NAACP Brnchs 1938; reg vice pres Reg v Amer Teachers Assn 1939; pres Baltimore Brnch NAACP Trust Pub School Teachers' Assn 1948; bd mem & sec Bltmr Urban League; advisory com Dept of Juvnl Ser of MD; gov comm Strctr & Govrnce of Educ in MD; trust Calvary Baptist Church. **HONORS/ACHIEVEMENTS:** NAACP Merit Medal 1938; mem Afro Roll of Honor 1941; Cert of Merit Kappa Chap Iota Phi Lambda 1957; Merit Ser Award Nat Assn Negro Bus & Prof Wmn Clubs 1970; Fndrs' Day Award Tau Gamma Delta 1970; Dist Ctzn Award Dem Ladies Gld 1971; Douglass HS Hall of Fame 1972; Hon DHumane Letters Sojourner-Douglas Coll 1984; 1986 Brotherhood Citation of Natl Conf of Christians & Jews MD Region; one of Top 100 Black Business & Professional Women of 1986. **HOME ADDRESS:** 1015 Beaumont Ave, Baltimore, MD 21212.

MCMILLAN, HORACE JAMES
Physician. **PERSONAL:** Born Oct 30, 1919, Mineola, TX; children: Yvonne Camille, Michelle Louise. **EDUCATION:** Prairie View A&M Coll, BS 1942; St Louis Univ, Graduate Work 1945-46; Meharry Med Coll, MD 1950; UCLA, Certificate in Health Maintenance Org. **CAREER:** Family Medical Ctr in Santa Barbara, vice pres 1952-; Private Practice, physician 1952-, semi-retired 1978-. **ORGANIZATIONS:** Founder/bd of dir Goleta Valley Comm Hosp 1967-77; 1st chmn Mayor's Adv Comm on Human Relations 1968; forerunner of present Comm Relations Commn recommended the CRC; mem Comm Hlth Task Force 1973-81; pres, bd dir Comm Nghbrhd Ctr; staff mem St Francis Hosp, Santa Barbara Cottage Hosp, Goleta Valley Comm Hosp, Pine Crest Hosp; mem Santa Barbara Acad of Family Practice, Natl Academy of Family Practice; life mem NAACP. **HONORS/ACHIEVEMENTS:** Recognition Awd City of Santa Barbara as innovator of Franklin Neighborhood Serv Ctr on 10th Anniversary 1985; Recognition Awd Afro-Amer Comm Serv for the Martin Luther King Awd 1986. **MILITARY SERVICE:** USCG chief pharmacist mate 1942-46; 1st black pharmacist mate in history of USCG. **BUSINESS ADDRESS:** 2439 Vista Del Campo, Santa Barbara, CA 93101.

MCMILLAN, JAMES BATES
Dentist. **PERSONAL:** Born Jan 18, 1918, Aberdeen, MS; married Marie E; children: Jarmiell, James Bates III, Michelle Caliendo, John, Jacqueline (dec), Jeffrey. **EDUCATION:** Univ of Detroit 1937-39; Meharry Med Coll, DDS 1944. **CAREER:** Detroit, pvt practice dentistry 1946-55; Las Vegas, NV, pvt practice 1956-. **ORGANIZATIONS:** Condidate US Senat 1964; mem Acad Gen Practice; Acad Implant Dentures natl & am dental assn; mem las vegas golf bd 1965-; clark co NV central Dem Com 1960-; NV State Dom Com 1960; pres NAACP 1956-60; mem Intl Golf Assn; Alpha Phi Alpha; Roman Cath. **MILITARY SERVICE:** AUS maj dental corps 1955-57. **BUSINESS ADDRESS:** President, James B McMillan DDS, LTD, 2300 Rancho Rd, Ste 218, Las Vegas, NV 89102.

MCMILLAN, JAMES C.
Educator. **PERSONAL:** Born Dec 23, 1925, Sanford, NC; divorced; children: Eric Weslay, Frances Lynne. **EDUCATION:** Howard Univ, BA Art 1947; Skowhegan School Art ME, Fellowship 1947; Acad Julian(Paris France), Certificate 1951; Catholic Univ Amer, MFA 1952; Syracuse Univ NY, Fellowship (adv study) 1960-61. **CAREER:** US Naval Air Station, art instructor, illustrator 1945-46; Bennett Coll Greenboro NC, chmn art dept 1947-50, 1952-53, 1956-59; Guilford Coll (Summers), dir London/European arts seminar, 1968-72; Guilford Coll, prof of art, painter, sculptor. **ORGANIZATIONS:** Div cultural enrichment, EPDA Bennett Coll (summers) 1969-70; dir NY Art Sem Guilford Coll 1971-75; mem Coll Art Assn, 1984-85; mem DC Art Assn, 1985; mem Natl Conf Artists 1984-85. **HONORS/ACHIEVEMENTS:** Skowhegan art fellowship Howard Univ Washington, DC 1947; Danforth teacher fellowship (Bennett Coll) Syracuse Univ NY 1960-61; Fresco Mural Skowhegan School of Art ME 1947; MFA sculptor comm Catholic Univ (to LA Catholic Church) 1952; mural Providence Baptist Church Greensboro NC 1977. **MILITARY SERVICE:** USN aviation mach mate 2nd class 1944-46; Pacific Theatre of Oiper, WWII, 1946. **BUSINESS ADDRESS:** Professor of Art, Guilford Coll, 5800 W Friendly Ave, Greensboro, NC 27410.

MCMILLAN, JOHN-DOUGLAS JAMES
Clergyman, educator. **PERSONAL:** Born Feb 08, 1947, New York City, NY; son of James McMillan and Irene Wilson McMillan. **EDUCATION:** Community Coll Allegeny Co, AA (Eng) 1975; Univ Pittsburgh, BA (Lang Comm) 1977; Xavier Univ of New Orleans, Inst Black Catholic Studies, grad student theology. **CAREER:** Canevin High School, Pittsburgh, Pennsylvania, teacher, 1973-80; Assum Acad NY, tchr 1980-81; Bishop Grimmes HS NY, tchr 1981-. **ORGANIZATIONS:** Natl Black Catholic Clergy Caucus 1984-; bd mem, Office of Black Catholic Ministry for the Diocese of Syracuse. **MILITARY SERVICE:** AUS spclt 5th class 1966-68. **BUSINESS ADDRESS:** English Teacher, St Francis Friar, 812 N Salina, Syracuse, NY 13208.

MCMILLAN, JOSEPH H.
Association executive, university administrator. **PERSONAL:** Born Nov 17, 1929, Louisville, KY; children: Charles, Diane, Michael, Dwight, Joseph Jr. **EDUCATION:** Univ of Louisville, AB 1950;Univ of MI, MA 1959; MI State U, EdD 1967. **CAREER:** Dir Dept of Human Relations for Academic AffairsUniv of Louisville, asst vice pres 1977-; MI State U, 1972-77; State U, 1972-; Dir Equal Opp Progs MI StateU, 1969-72; Wstrn MI U, part-time instr fall 1969; Inner-City Schs Dir of Human Relations Dir Grand Rapids Head Start Prog Grand Rapis Bd of Edn, supr 1966-69; MI State U, extension lectr 1965-; Sheldon Elem Sch Grand Rapids, prin 1960-66; Elem Educ MI State U, asst instr 1963-64; Sheldon Elem Sch, tchr 1956-60; Webber Sch Baldwin, MI, tchr prin 1954-56; Idlewild, MI, tchr 1950-54. **ORGANIZATIONS:** Consult Project Follow Through in NY, Harlem, Louisville, E St Louis Pub Schs; consult Parent Child Cntr Louisville 1974-; instr PepperdineUniv 1974-77; cons-Roosevelt Comm Sch 1976-77; mem Adv Cncl to Bur of Pub Hlth 1977; instrUniv of No CO 1974; mem Conflict Mgmnt Workshops; Curriculum Workshops; consult SRA; Addison-Wesley Co; consult Behavioral Res Labs Proj Read; participated in deseg study Clairton PA 1968 Asso Educ Consult Inc; participated in SchoolReorgn Study Pontiac, MI 1969-70; participated in Elem Sch Decentralization Study at Detroit 1970-71 Title I Adv Bd Proposal 1970, 72, 73; testified as witness in Geo & Carolyn Higgins v Bd of Educ of City of Grand Rapids 1973; court appointed expert in Benton Harbor Schools Deseg Case 1978-; resourse personat Affirmative Action Workshop Urban Research Corp 1972; pres Louisville Urban League; co-chrmn Community Consortium on Black survival in Louisville; bd mem N St Baptist Ch; mem Louisville NAACP; mem Gr Lansing NAACP. **HONORS/ACHIEVEMENTS:** Recip Omicron Delta Kappa AwardUniv of Louisville 1950; outstanding man of Yr Grand Rapids Elks Club 1963. **BUSINESS ADDRESS:** 202 Adminstrn Bldg, Univ of Louisville, Louisville, KY 40292.

MCMILLAN, JOSEPH T., JR.
Educational administrator. **CAREER:** Huston-Tillotson College, Austin, TX, president. **BUSINESS ADDRESS:** Huston-Tillotson College, Austin, TX 78702. *

MCMILLAN, L. R.
Minister, educator. **PERSONAL:** Born Jul 19, Rosehill, MS; married Magnolia Kelly; children: Lee Roger Jr. **EDUCATION:** BS 1949; BD 1952; MA 1953. **CAREER:** United Meth Ch, minister present; HS MS, prin 1957-65. **ORGANIZATIONS:** Mem NAACP; Voters League 1948. **HONORS/ACHIEVEMENTS:** Recip Hon DD Campbell Coll 1953. **MILITARY SERVICE:** AUS 1942-45; chaplain 1953-56.

MCMILLAN, LEMMON COLUMBUS
Business executive. **PERSONAL:** Born Apr 17, 1917, Mineola, TX; married Vivian L Boyd; children: Drs Lemmon, Robert, Samuel. **EDUCATION:** Prairie View A&M Univ, BA 1939, MA 1951; Univ of TX, Doctoral Study 1952-54; Univ of VA, special prog 1963. **CAREER:** Dallas Public Library, librarian 1939-42; US Army Field Artillery, 1st lt 1942-46; Prairie View A&M Univ, asst registrar 1946-54, registrar 1954-63. **ORGANIZATIONS:** Exec dir Assoc of Huntsville AL Area Companies 1963-71; vice pres Natl Merit Scholarship Corp 1971-; vice pres Jr Engrg Tech Soc Bd 1973-; mem/supporter of NABSE, NAACP, Urban League, SCLC, NACME, NAFEOHE, UNCF, Exec Reserves, MPME, Alpha Phi Alpha Frat. **HONORS/ACHIEVEMENTS:** Plans for Progress Awd Natl Assn of Market Developers 1965; Outstanding Alumnus Awd Prairie View A&M Univ 1965; Outstanding Comm Serv Awd JF Drake State Tech Sch 1966; Disting Serv Awd Jaycees Huntsville 1971; Resolution of Commendation AL Legislature 1971. **MILITARY SERVICE:** AUS field artillery 1st lt 1942-46. **BUSINESS ADDRESS:** Vice President, Natl Merit Scholarship Corp, One American Plaza, Evanston, IL 60201.

MCMILLAN, MAE F.
Physician, educator. **PERSONAL:** Born May 12, 1936, Austin, TX. **EDUCATION:** Wiley Coll Marshall TX, BS BA (Summa Cum Laude) 1955; Meharry Med Coll, MD (Honors) 1959; Wayne Co Genl Hosp MI, Internship 1960; Baylor Univ Coll of Med Houston, affiliated hosp residency 1960-63 1963-65; Hampstead Child Therapy Course & Clinic London, Post-doctoral Fellowship 1965-67. **CAREER:** Baylor Coll of Med Depts Psych & Child Psych, asst prof 1966; Private Practice, part time child psychiatry specialty pre-schoolers 1966-; TX Rsch Inst of Mental Sci, asst dir div of child spych 1968-72, dir div of child psych 1972-74, dir early childhood therapy course & clinic 1974-; Univ of TX Med Sch at Houston, clinical assoc prof 1974-; Faculty for Advanced Studies Univ TX Sch of Biomedical Science, asst prof 1975; Univ of TX Health Sci Ctr at Houston, clinical assoc prof 1976; TX Woman's Univ Child Devel & Family Living, adjunct prof 1977-; Baylor Coll of Med Depts Psychiat & Child Psych, clinical assoc prof 1982-. **ORGANIZATIONS:** Bd mem CAN-DO-IT 1973-80; bd dirs Girls Clubs of Houston Sect 1983-; mem Natl Council of Negro Women, Delta Sigma Theta, Mental Health Assn; coord Child Care Cnclof Houston-Harris Co; United Methodist Women. **HONORS/ACHIEVEMENTS:** Criminal Justice Award, Delta Sigma Theta; One Amer Proj, 1973; Distinction of Merit; Natl Council of Negro Women, 1977; Woman of Distinction Award, YWCA Houston Sect, 1980; Fellow, Amer Psychiatric Assn, 1982; Notable Women of TX Award, Gov's Comm 1983. **BUSINESS ADDRESS:** Child Psychiatrist, 503 1/2 N Loop West, Houston, TX 77018.

MCMILLAN, RANDY L.
Professional football player. **PERSONAL:** Born Dec 17, 1958, Havre de Grace, MD. **EDUCATION:** Attended Hartford Community Coll, Univ of Pittsburgh. **CAREER:** Baltimore, 1981-84; Indianapolis Colts, fullback 1984-. **BUSINESS ADDRESS:** Fullback, Indianapolis Colts, PO Box 24100, Indianapolis, IN 46224.

MCMILLAN, ROBERT FRANK, JR.
Director of development. **PERSONAL:** Born Jul 08, 1946, Glassboro, NJ; married Constance Van Brunt; children: Ayisha-Nell, Marcia-Akillah. **EDUCATION:** Temple Univ, BS Civil Engrg 1972; Northwestern Univ, MBA Prog; State of IL, Real Estate Broker License 1985. **CAREER:** Turner Construction, field engr, supt 1972-76; Hudson Corp, proj mgr 1976-80; Urban Investment & Devel Co, devel mgr 1980-85; Joseph J Freed & AssocInc, dir of development 1985-. **ORGANIZATIONS:** Charter mem Rotary Intl 1984-; bd mem Oak Park Dist 1984-. **MILITARY SERVICE:** AUS 1st lt 3 yrs; Bronze Star; Meritorious Achievement Vietnam 1969. **BUSINESS ADDRESS:** Dir of Development, Joseph J Freed & Assoc Inc, 304 E Rand Rd, Arlington Heights, IL 60004.

MCMILLAN, WILLIAM ASBURY
Educator. **PERSONAL:** Born Feb 29, 1920, Winnabow, NC; married Mildred Geraldine Newlin; children: Pamela Jackson, Paula Jones, William Jr. **EDUCATION:** Johnson C Smith Univ, BA 1942; Univ MI, MA 1954, PhD 1954. **CAREER:** Gatesville NC, tchr 1942-44, 1946-47; Johnson C Smith Univ, asst dean of Instr 1947-48; Pomeroy PA, counselor 1948-49; Wiley Coll, dir 1949-58; Bethune-Cookman Coll, acad dean 1958-64, 1966-67; Rust Coll, pres 1967-. **ORGANIZATIONS:** Life mem NEA; ATA; Mid-S Med Assn; pres MS Assn of Pvt Coll 1977-78; Alpha Phi Omega; NAACP, Boy Scout Leader; chmn bd of educ N MS; Conf of United Meth Ch; Omega Psi Phi. **HONORS/ACHIEVEMENTS:** Hon LLD Cornell Coll, Johnson C Smith Univ, Bethune-Cookman Coll; Pres of Yr MS Tchrs Assn 1973-74. **MILITARY SERVICE:** USAAF 1945. **BUSINESS ADDRESS:** President, Rust College, Holly Springs, MS 38635.

MCMILLIAN, FRANK L.
Chemist, educator. **PERSONAL:** Born Jun 09, 1935, Mobile, AL; married Ruby A Curry; children: Franetta L, Kecia L. **EDUCATION:** Dillard Univ, BA 1954; Tuskegee Inst, MS 1956; Univ of KS, PhD 1965. **CAREER:** Ft Valley State Coll, instructor, Physical Sci 1956-58; NC Coll at Durham, instr chemistry 1959-60; Norfolk State Coll, asst prof Chemistry 1960-62; DillardUniv, visiting assoc prof Chemistry, 1969-70; EI du Pont de Nemours & Co, rsch chemist/sr technical specialist 1965-. **ORGANIZATIONS:** Mem Sigma Xi 1967-; mem Phi Lambda Upsilon Chem Soc 1964-; mem Omega Psi Phi Frat 1954-. **HONORS/ACHIEVEMENTS:** Natl Science Found Fellow 1963. **HOME ADDRESS:** 3117 Albemarle Rd, Wilmington, DE 19808.

MCMILLIAN, JIMMY, JR.
Manager. **PERSONAL:** Born Mar 22, 1953, Mt Pleasant, FL; married Marilyn Irene Wilson; children: Brian. **EDUCATION:** FL A&M Univ, BS 1974. **CAREER:** Deloitte Haskins & Sells, sr accountant 1974-77; Mariott Corp, corp auditor 1979; Watson Rice & Co, partner 1979-. **ORGANIZATIONS:** Bd mem Natl Assn of Black Accountants 1975-83; bd mem DC C of C 1981-85; bd mem Page One Communic 1984-; comm chr DC Inst of CPA's 1982-; lectrDC Inst of CPA's 1984-; lectr Howard Univ 1983-. **HONORS/ACHIEVEMENTS:** Founder's Award Miami Chap Natl Assn of Black Accountants 1985.

MCMILLIAN, JOSIE
Labor union executive. **PERSONAL:** Born Oct 21, 1940, Childersberg, AL; divorced; children: 1 son, 2 daughters. **EDUCATION:** Cornell Univ, Trade Union Study/George Meany Labor & Women Studies 1977. **CAREER:** NY Metro Area Postal Union, sector aide, chief steward, shop steward 1969, ex dir of clerk 1975, org'l vice pres 1976, exec vice pres 1979, pres. **ORGANIZATIONS:** Labor adv council NY Natl Urban League; mem Coalition of Labor Union Women; mem Natl Org of Women; mem New York City Black Trade Leadership Comm; adv bd mem Cornells Sch of Indus & Labor Relations; mem bd of dirs United Way of New York City; bd mem New York City & NJ combined Federal Campaign; life mem NAACP; clerk craft rep NYS Amer Postal Workers Union; adv mem New York City Central Labor Council; mem bd of dirs NYC Arthritis Foundation. **HONORS/ACHIEVEMENTS:** Hispanic Labor Comm Awd New York City Central Labor Council 1978; Outstanding Achievement Awd New York City Chap Coalition of Labor Union Women 1981; Mary McLeod Bethune Awd Natl Council of Negro Women 1981; Achievement Awd New York City Branch NAACP 1981; Distinguished Serv Awd New York City Central Labor Council 1981; Sojourner Truth Loyalty Awd NY Chap Blk Trade Unionist 1982; Hoey Ecumenical Awd NY Catholic Interracial Council 1982; Appted Admiral in the Great Navy of NE 1982; Awd of Appreciation NY Chap Arthritis Found 1983; Pacific Group Home Awd Little Flower Children's Serv 1983; Outstanding Labor Leader Awd Natl Assn of Negro Business & Prof Women's Clubs 1984; Citation of Appreciation Amer Legion Dan Tallon Post 678; Appreciation Awd Women for Racial & Econ Equality 1985; Citation of Appreciation Brooklyn Borough Pres H Golden 1984; Labor Leaders' Award New York City Arthritis Foundation, 1988; Women's Achievement Award, YWCA 1985; Leadership Award Borough of Manhattan Community College 1989. ppreciaiton Brooklyn Borough Pres H Golden 1984. **BUSINESS ADDRESS:** President, NY Metro Area Postal Union, 460 W 34th St, New York, NY 10001.

MCMILLIAN, THEODORE
Judge. **PERSONAL:** Born Jan 28, 1919, St Louis, MO; married Minnie E Foster. **EDUCATION:** Lincoln Univ, BS 1941; St Louis Univ Law School, LLB 1949. **CAREER:** St Louis Univ Law School, lecturer; Webster Coll, faculty mem; State of MO, circuit judge; City of St Louis, asst circuit attny 1953-56; MO Ct of Appeals, judge 1972-78; US Circuit Court of Appeals for 8th Cir, circuit judge 1978-. **ORGANIZATIONS:** Former mem bd of trustees Blue Cross 1974; former mem Danforth Found Adv Council 1975; mem Pres Council of St Louis Univ; former bd chmn Human Devel Corp 1964-77; former mem Natl Legal Aid Adv Bd; mem Alpha Sigma Nu, Phi Beta Kappa. **HONORS/ACHIEVEMENTS:** Alumni Merit Awd St Louis Univ; Awd of Honor Lawyers Assoc 1970; Man of the Year Awd 1970. **MILITARY SERVICE:** Signal Corps lt 1942-46. **BUSINESS ADDRESS:** Circuit Judge, US Circuit Court of Appeals for 8th Circuit, US Court & Customs Bldg, St Louis, MO 63101.

MCMORRIS, JACQUELINE WILLIAMS
Government employee. **PERSONAL:** Born Mar 18, 1936, Washington, DC; daughter of Mr and Mrs John D Williams; married James Oliver McMorris; children: Jameille Olivia, James Oliver Jr. **EDUCATION:** Temple Univ, AB 1958; Howard Univ Coll of Medicine, MD 1962. **CAREER:** Headstart Natl Office, pediatric consultant 1965; Public Health Dept Washington DC, medical officer 1965-69; DHS Commn of Public Health, developmental evaluation clinic dir 1969-87. **ORGANIZATIONS:** Church choir dir 1962-82; mem Howard Univ Med Alumni 1962-87; bd of dirs DC Special Olympics 1978-79; chairperson Mamie D Lee Neighborhood School Cncl 1982-86; Mayor's Devel Disabilities Council 1984-87, sec St Anthony's Grade Sch PTA 1984-86; Mayor's Comm Early Child Develop 1984-87, Medical Adv Rehab Serv 1985-87, Mayor's Comm on Handicapped 1985-87, Amer Medical Women's Assoc 1985-86; Howard Univ Transgenerational Project for Children with Learning Disabilities 1986-87. **HONORS/ACHIEVEMENTS:** Fellow Amer Acad of Pediatrics 1978. **HOME ADDRESS:** 4304 10th St NE, Washington, DC 20017. **BUSINESS ADDRESS:** Clinic Dir Eval Clinic, Commn of Public Health, 1900 Massachusetts Ave SE, Washington, DC 20003.

MCMORRIS, SAMUEL CARTER
Attorney. **PERSONAL:** Born Feb 24, 1920, Columbus, OH; divorced; children: Gina. **EDUCATION:** OH St U, JD 1951. **CAREER:** Priv pract atty. **ORGANIZATIONS:** Mem MENSA; CA Trial Lwyrs Assn. **MILITARY SERVICE:** AUS 1947-48. **BUSINESS ADDRESS:** Eastmont Mall Prof Bldg, Ste 3, Oakland, CA 94605.

MCMULLINS, TOMMY
Business executive. **PERSONAL:** Born Sep 15, 1942, Macon, GA; married Gwendolyn Williams; children: Tommy, Tyrone, Timothy. **EDUCATION:** Ft Vly State Coll, BS Social Sci 1964; Amer Inst Banking, Var Bank Courses 1969-75; Pepperdine Univ, 1972; Pacif Cst Banking School, Grad Cert 1980. **CAREER:** Ylwstn Natl Pk, seasonal pk rgr 1963-64; First Intst Bank, manager reg sales manager vice pres 1965-82; Crocker Natl Bank, vice pres 1982-85; Wells Fargo Bank 1985- . **ORGANIZATIONS:** Co-chrpsn Emerg Hispanic Mjty 1978-80; bd mem Pasadena NAACP 1979-82; bd mem Comm Bell Gdns Rotary 1981-85f bd mem Monrovia Kiwanis 1969-73; pres Pasadena Chptr Alpha Phi Alpha 1975. **HONORS/ACHIEVEMENTS:** Crusdr awd Am Cncr svcs1973-74. **MILITARY SERVICE:** USM corpl 2 yrs; Expert Riflmn 1967. **HOME ADDRESS:** 1245 Rubio Vista Rd, Altadena, CA 91001. **BUSINESS ADDRESS:** Vice President, Wells Fargo Bank, 900 N San Fernando Blvd, Burbank, CA 91504.

MCMURRY, KERMIT ROOSEVELT, JR.
Executive. **PERSONAL:** Born Jul 31, 1945, Kansas City, KS; married Thomasina Sandra; children: James Patrick, Chris, Nikii, Kermetria. **EDUCATION:** Univ CO, BS 1968, MS 1970;Univ NE, PhD 1975; Harvard U, Post-Dctrl Study 1979. **CAREER:** Dept Admin Serv Exec Brnh State Govt State of NE, asst to dir 1974-75; NE Coord Comm for Post Scndry Educ, exec dir 1975-77; Grambling State U, exec vice pres 1977-. **ORGANIZATIONS:** Asst dirLeisure ServUniv of NE 1970-74; vice chmn United Campus Mnstrs; mem Lincoln Total Com Action Prog. **HONORS/ACHIEVEMENTS:** Outstdng yng man NE Jaycees 1971; men Of achvmt 1975; pioneering coord Awrd NE Coord Commsn for Post Scndry Educ 1977.

MCMURRY, WALTER M., JR.
Business executive. **PERSONAL:** Born Mar 21, 1934, Canton, MS; married Reesa Anita Motley; children: Walter S, Stacie, James Randolph. **EDUCATION:** Univ of MI, BBA 1963. **CAREER:** Bank of the Commonwealth, loan officer 1965-68; Inner-City Bus Improvement Forum, exec dir 1967-71; COMAC Carribbean/West Indies, resident mgr 1969-70; Independence Capital Formation, pres 1973-; Inner City Bus Improvement Forum, pres 1971-. **ORGANIZATIONS:** Bd of gov Natl Assn of Small Bus Invest Co; chmn OMBE Reg 5 Adv Counc; chmn MI Dist 203 Adv Counc; mem bd dir MI Minority Tech Council; dirDetroit Housing Finance Corp; dir at large BSA Detroit Area Councl; founder Black United Fund. **HONORS/ACHIEVEMENTS:** Black Journal's 100 Most Influential Friends; guest lecturer Univ of MI. **BUSINESS ADDRESS:** President, Inner-City Bus & Improv Foru, 1505 Woodward Ave St #700, Detroit, MI 48226.

MCNAIR, BARBARA
Singer, actress. **PERSONAL:** Born Mar 04, 1939, Racine, WI; widowed. **EDUCATION:** Univ So CA. **CAREER:** Formerly night club singer; theatrical appearances include the body beautiful 1958; the merry world of natl king cole 1961; no strings 1962; films include spencers' mountain 1962; stiletto 1969; change of habit 1969; venus in furs 1970; they call me mister tibbs 1970; star & weekly TV show barbara Mcnair Show. **ORGANIZATIONS:** Mem Am Guild Variet Artists; Stage Artists Guild; AFTRA; Actors Equity Guild. **BUSINESS ADDRESS:** C/o Moss Agency Ltd, 113 N San Vicente Blvd, Beverly Hills, CA 90211.

MCNAIRY, FRANCINE G.
Educational Administrator. **PERSONAL:** Born Nov 13, 1946, Pittsburgh, PA. **EDUCATION:** Univ of Pittsburgh, BA, Sociology, 1968, MSW, 1970, PhD, Comm, 1978. **CAREER:** Allegheny Co Child Welfare Servs supvr & soc worker, 1970-72; Comm Action Regional training, tech asst specialist, 1972; Clarion Univ of PA, assoc prof/counselor 1973-82, coord of academic devel & retention 1983, dean of acad support serv & asst to the acad vice pres, 1983-88; West Chester Univ, Assoc Vice Pres for Acad Affairs, 1988-present. **ORGANIZATIONS:** Presenter Natl Conf on the Freshmen Yr Experience Univ of SC 1982-86; advisor Clarion Univ Black Student Union 1973-; vice chair Clarion Co Human Resources Develop Comm 1983-86; presenter, Intl Conf on the First Year Experience England, 1986, Creative Mgmt in Higher Educ, Boston 1986; consultant, Univ of NE, Briar Cliff Coll, Marshall Univ 1986; St Lawrence Coll 1984, Wesleyan Coll 1983; mem, PA Advisory Bd to ACT. **HONORS/ACHIEVEMENTS:** Publications "Clarion Univ Increases Black Student Retention"; co-authored "Taking the Library to Freshman Students via Freshman Seminar Concept" 1986, "The Minority Student on Campus" 1985. **BUSINESS ADDRESS:** Assoc Vice Pres for Acad Affairs, West Chester Univ, 151 E O Bull Center, West Chester, PA 19383.

MCNAIRY, SIDNEY A.
Educator. **PERSONAL:** Born Oct 16, 1937, Memphis; married Bobbie Nelson; children: Alicia, Sidney A III. **EDUCATION:** Lemoyne Coll Memphis, BS 1959; Purdue U, MS 1962; Purdue U, PhD 1965; ColumbisUniv New York 1968. **CAREER:** Biomedical Support Prog SoUniv Baton Rouge, dir 1972-; Health Research Cntr So U, dir 1971-. **ORGANIZATIONS:** Mem adv bd Sickle Cell Anemia Found New Orleans for planning a statewide Symposium on Sickel Cell Anemia; chmn steering com for developing a hypertension screening clinic Comprehensive Health Cntr & Social Serv of North Baton Rouge; consult Nat Institutes of Health-Biomedical Proposal Reviewer; consult Southeastern pilot study for feasibility of establishing Sickle Cell Screening Educ Counseling Cntrs across LA; mem Am Chemical Soc; consult Cntr for study of Alcoholism SouthernUniv 1974; chmn Sickle Cell Anemia Symposium Steering Com 1973; chmn Hypertension Symposium Steering Com 1974; chmn Health Career Symposium 1974; chmn Human Experimentation Com;Univ Building Com SoUniv 1973; consult pilot proj study on patent potential at predominantly black coll &Univ 1973; mem Research mgmt improvement proposal 1973; site visitation consult Nat Institutes of Health 1972; research biochemist Cntr for Disease Control 1972; consult So LA Sch Dist 1971; research chemist Chevron Research Co 1971. **HONORS/ACHIEVEMENTS:** Mem Alpha Phi Alpha, Beta Kappa Chi, Alpha Chi Sigma; Soc of Research Adminstrs; Am Assn for Advancement of Science; Coun on Research Policy & Grad Studies Nat Assn of StateUniv and Land Grant Colleges; del Am Found for Negro Affairs Conf Philadelphia 1974; Personalities of the S 1973; academic scholarship Lemoyne Coll Memphis 1955-59; Outstanding Young Men of Am 1965; grad research & tchr assistantship PurdueUniv 1959-65; Am Men of Science 1965; Nat Urban League Summer Fellow 1967, 69, 71, 72; Intensive Summer Study Prog ColumbiaUniv 1965. **BUSINESS ADDRESS:** Box 9921, SouthernUniv, Baton Rouge, LA 70813.

MCNARY, OSCAR LEE
Artist. **PERSONAL:** Born Mar 23, 1944, San Antonio, TX; married Maudene J; children: Omar. **EDUCATION:** Attended San Antonio Jr Coll 1964-65; attended TX So Univ 1967-68; attended So Meth Univ; attended Hunters Sch of Art 1973-74. **CAREER:** Visual artist. **ORGANIZATIONS:** Mem Dallas Mus of Fine Arts 1974-81; mem Natl Conf of Artists 1975-81; bd of adv/mem Phoenix Cultural Arts Cntr 1975-81; mem TX Arts Alliance; state & local mem TX Fine Arts Assn 1975-81; assoc mem Amer Watercolor Soc 1976-81; natl mem Artists Equity Assn 1977-81; elect mem the Intl Platform Assn 1978-81; 1st Black vice pres & 1st Black bd mem Artists Coalition of TX 1979; bd of trustees & 1st Black pres Richardson Civic Art Soc 1979-81; committeeman Cub Scouts of Amer Pack 584 1979-81; mem PTA Heights Elem Sch 1979-81. **HONORS/ACHIEVEMENTS:** Numerous Group exhibitions 1965-80; 1 Man Exhibit Promenade Natl Bank 1976; Man Exhibit Phoenix Cultural Arts Cntr 1979; 1 Man Exhibit Arthello's Gallery 1980. **BUSINESS ADDRESS:** Visual Artist, PO Box 832627, Richardson, TX 75083.

MCNATT, ISAAC G.
Judge. **PERSONAL:** Born Nov 19, 1916, Bladen County, NC; married Gladys C; children: Glenn, Robert. **EDUCATION:** Hampton Inst, BS 1937; St John's Law Sch, JD (magna cum laude) 1945. **CAREER:** Priv law pract 1947-; Municipal Teaneck Court, judge 1979-; Chic Title Ins Co NY, title examr 1945-46; HS NC, tchr 1938-42. **ORGANIZATIONS:** Pres Douglass-Carver Commun Devel 1967-77 & 80; NJ Bar Assn; Harlem Lawy Assn Bergen Co Bar; Garden State Bar; mem Teaneck Twnshp Counc 1966-74; depmay Teaneck 1970-74; chmn bd trustees Comm Ch; Nat Comm Agst Discrimnt in Housing 1959-65; chmn Teaneck Fair Housing Comm 1961-66; chmn Bergen CoMarch on Wash 1963; chmn Bergen Co Coordin Comm on Civ Rights 1963-66; chmn Polt Action Com Bergen Co NAACP 1963-67; chmn Teaneck Am Revoln Bicent Comm 1974-76; chmn Boy Sct Comm 1963-67; pres Garden State Bar Assn 1968-71, 73-74; prog chmn NAACP 1976-77 & 80; pres NY Hampton Alum Club 1953-56; pres Hamilton Grange Day Care Center 1954-57; chmn Bergen Blks for Action in Polit 1975-79. **HONORS/ACHIEVEMENTS:** Nat Bus & Pro Women's Aw 1974; Lay Leadershp Aw Commun Ch of NY 1963; commun serv aw Pieces of Africa 1974; citiz of yr aw Teaneck Political Assembly 1976. **MILITARY SERVICE:** USN seaman 1st cl 1942-43. **BUSINESS ADDRESS:** Judge, State of New Jersey, Compensation Court, 14 Commerce St, Newark, NJ 07102.

MCNEAL, DON
Professional athlete. **PERSONAL:** Born May 06, 1958, Atmore, AL; married Rhonda. **EDUCATION:** Alabama. **CAREER:** Miami Dolphins, cornerback 1980. **HONORS/ACHIEVEMENTS:** NFL all rookie, Tommy Fitzgerald mem awrd outstanding rookin 1980. **BUSINESS ADDRESS:** Miami Dolphins, 4770 Biscayne Blvd, Ste 1440, Miami, FL 33137.

MCNEAL, DOROTHY N. (NEE PAYNE)
Consultant, social worker. **PERSONAL:** Born May 03, 1922, NYC, NY. **EDUCATION:** Hunter Coll, BA 1943; Columbia Univ Teachers Coll, MA 1947; Hunter Coll Sch of Social Work, MSW 1960. **CAREER:** NY State Employment Service, interviewer/counselor 1943-49; New York City Police Dept, instr in grad prog of police science consul on comm relations & youth prog police woman training officer 1949-69; Genesee Co (Flint) Model Cities Prog, asst neighborhood dir 1970-71; Human Relations Comm Flint MI, exec dir 1971-77; State Univ, instr sch of criminal justice 1977-80; Comm Proj Unlimited, president/sr consul. **ORGANIZATIONS:** Proj dir Police/Comm Training Project Urban League of Flint 1981-84; state conf coord MI Chap Natl Assn of Black Social Workers; vice chairperson Flint Assn of Black Admins; chmn Prog Com & Del to Natl Assembly Flint Chap Natl Assn of Social Workers; mem Intl Assn of Official Human Rights Agencies; mem Academy of Police Science; Amer Soc for Pub Admin; Black Adminis Organ of Flint; pres Hunter Coll Sch of Social Work Alumni Assn 1969-70; pres Flint Club 1974-76; Natl Assn of Negro Bus & Professional Women's Clubs Inc 1974; Nat Third vice pres 1965-69; natl chmn Educ Asst Comm 1969-74; Flint YWCA; Flint Urban Coalition; Flint Soc of Afro-Amer Police; co-chmn Women's Inst; mem Natl Council of Women of USA; NAACP; Flint Urban League. **HONORS/ACHIEVEMENTS:** New York City Police Dept Thesis Aws & Hunter Coll George N Shuster Awd 1960; First female instructor in grad sch of police science Univ of the City of NY 1961; First Black and only female Dept Head City of Flint 1971; listed in Who's Who of Amer Women 1967; Social Worker of the Yr Flint Area Chap NASW 1976; organizer Black Comm Congress of Greater Flint 1977; Woman of the Yr 1984; Zeta Phi Sorority Social Worker of the Yr 1984; Michigan Assn of Black Social Workers.

MCNEAL, JOHN ALEX, JR.
Educational administrator. **PERSONAL:** Born Jun 18, 1932, Metter, GA; married Earlene Hazel; children: Lydia Tryphenia, Kezia Ruth. **EDUCATION:** Fort Valley State Coll, BS 1961; Grace Theol Sem, BRE 1964; GA State Univ, MEd 1975; Carver Bible Coll, doctor of divinity 1986. **CAREER:** Fundamentalist Baptist Assn, publicity chmn 1964, pres 1975-77, vice pres 1977-80; Atlanta Bible Baptist Church, pastor/founder; Carver Bible Inst & Coll, rev & dean of students 1964-; Baptist Mission of North America, ethnic rep 1985. **ORGANIZATIONS:** Mem Fellowship of Baptist for Home Missions. **HONORS/ACHIEVEMENTS:** Outstanding Educators of Amer 1972; Awd for Dedicated Serv Carver Alumni Assn 1972. **MILITARY SERVICE:** USAF airman 1st class 1952-56; Good Conduct Medal; Service Awd. **BUSINESS ADDRESS:** Rev & Dean of Students, Carver Bible Inst & Coll, 437 Nelson St SW, Atlanta, GA 30313.

MCNEAL, SYLVIA ANN
Manager. **PERSONAL:** Born Jan 29, 1947, Memphis, TN; married Lennie Jr; children: Andre Mario. **EDUCATION:** Am Inst of Banking 1966; LA City Coll 1966; El Camino Coll Torrance CA AA. **CAREER:** Allstate Savs & Loan Assn, affirmative lending mgr present; Mechanics Bank, dept couns 1975; USLIFE Savs & Loan Assn, sr dept loan counselor 1974; Union Fed Savs & Loan Assn, sr dept escrow sec 1972. **ORGANIZATIONS:** Mem LA Chap Assn of Professional Mortgage Women 1978; exec bd sec Inglewood Neighborhood Housing Serv 1979; mem St Mark United Meth Ch 1972; mem Crozier Jr High PTA 1979. **BUSINESS ADDRESS:** Allstate Savings & Loan Assn, 701 N Brand Blvd, Glendale, CA 91203.

MCNEELY, CAROL J.
Dentist, consultant. **PERSONAL:** Born Jul 17, 1954, Chicago, IL; daughter of Lewis W McNeely and Jessie O Woodfin McNeely; divorced; children: Matthews, Allan, Ivy. **EDUCATION:** Univ of IL College of Dentistry, DDS 1979. **CAREER:** Tyrone Holiday DDS, assoc dentist 1979-80; Provident Dental Assocs, owner 1984-; Dr Carol McNeely & Associates, owner 1979-; Soulful Expressions (A Practice Promotion Co), owner, 1987; Dental Network of America, Consultant, 1988-. **ORGANIZATIONS:** Speaker Amer Assoc of Women Dentists 1982; treas Lincoln Dental Soc Natl Dental Soc 1982-83; assoc bd mem Chicago Child Care Soc 1982-85, American Academy of Cosmetic Dentistry 1988; American Dental Association; National Dental Association; co-chairperson, Chicago Urban League Sholarship Committee, 1989. **HONORS/ACHIEVEMENTS:** Partners in the Comm Natl Bar Assoc Chicago Chap 1985. **BUSINESS ADDRESS:** Dentist, Dr Carol McNeely & Assocs, 7933 South King Dr, Chicago, IL 60619.

MCNEELY, MATTHEW
State representative. **PERSONAL:** Born May 10, 1920, Millen, GA; married Beatrice; children: Chris, Roy, Cloteele, Camille, Cynthia. **EDUCATION:** Lansing Comm Coll, Assoc degree. **CAREER:** Local 306 Dist, educ dir, 18 & 20 Wards, pres; MI State Bd of Escheats, cons; Houston House of Rep, elected 1964-80, assoc speaker pro tempore 1969, 1971, speaker pro tempore 1973-80; State of MI, state rep 16th dist. **ORGANIZATIONS:** Mem bd dir MI Partners of the Americas; mem exec com Natl Legislative Black Clearing House; adv bd Carmel Hall; chmn House Com in Insurance; mem Com on Educ State Affairs & Legislative Coun; past pres COIL Conf of Insurance Legislators; Pine Grove Bapt Ch; first past pres & fndr NCBSL; del Educ Comm of the States Advanced Leadership Prog; bd dirs MI Partners of the Americas. **HONORS/ACHIEVEMENTS:** 1978 Natl Conf of State Legislators MI Intl Cert of Leadership Awd; delegate to African-Amer Insts 9th Conf Khartoum Sudan; listed Who's Who in the Midwest. **BUSINESS ADDRESS:** State Representative 3rd Dist, MI House of Representatives, PO Box 30014, Lansing, MI 48909.

MCNEIL, ALVIN J.
Educator. **PERSONAL:** Born Apr 12, 1920, Hinds Co, MS; married Ella Edith Holmes; children: Charles, Needha, Adrian. **EDUCATION:** TN A&I State Coll, BA; Boston Univ, MA 1951; Univ Denver, EdD 1960; Univ of MO, post doctoral study. **CAREER:** Wynne, AR, asst prin/counselor 1947-49; MS Voc Coll, registrar/dean/dept head 1951-58; Grambling State Coll, prof/dept head 1958-68; Prairie View A&M, dean 1968-71; TX So Univ, prof/assoc dean/head dept of administration & higher educ. **ORGANIZATIONS:** City councilman Grambling 1965-68; past natl pres Phi Beta Sigma 1965-69; mem Lions Club; Prince Hall Masons; Shriner; Amer Legion; Kappa Delta Pi; Phi Delta Kappa; Alpha Kappa Delta; Sigma Delta Pi. **HONORS/ACHIEVEMENTS:** Crusade fellowship grant 1957-58; Citation for Meritorious Serv Town of Grambling; Distinguished Serv Chap Phi Beta Sigma; Distinguished Educator Award, MS; Christian Serv Award Wheeler Ave Baptist Ch; Appreciation Award Sch of Educ TX So Univ; Amer Assn for Higher Educ Black Caucus; Pioneering Efforts in Higher Educ Doctoral Students Appreciation Awd. **MILITARY SERVICE:** Military Serv WO-1 1942-45. **BUSINESS ADDRESS:** Prof/ Department Chairman, Texas SoUniv, Box 451, Houston, TX 77004.

MCNEIL, CLAUDIA MAE
Actress. **PERSONAL:** Born Aug 13, 1917, Baltimore. **CAREER:** NYC, debut as singer; NYC, Black Cat 1933; Jamaican Broadcasting Co, prog coord entainer 1951-52. **ORGANIZATIONS:** Mem Negro Actors Guild; vol worker, Harlem Hosp; St Vincent's Hosp. **HONORS/ACHIEVEMENTS:** Theatrical apperances in Raisin In The Sun 1959; Tiger, Tiger Burning Bright, 1962; TV apperances include, Simply Heavenly, 1952; Mem of the Wedding, 1958; The Nurses, 1963; motion picture apperances, The Last Angry Man, 1958; Black Girl, 1972; Nominee Tony Awd 1962; Emmy Awd 1963; recip Am Jewish Congress

1959. **BUSINESS ADDRESS:** c/o Actor's Fund of America, 175 West Hudson Ave, Englewood, NJ 07631.

MCNEIL, DEEDEE
Songwriter, singer, freelance journalist. **PERSONAL:** Born Sep 07, Detroit, MI; daughter of Frank Lawton and Mary Virginia Elkins; divorced; children: Maricea Lynn McNeil, Harry Lawrence McNeil III, William A Chappell, Jr. **EDUCATION:** Attended, Pasadena City Coll, Music, Journalism, one year. **CAREER:** Jobete Publishing Co, Motown Record Co, Detroit, contract songwriter 1968-71; Ala Record Co, Los Angeles, recording artist, 1971; The Watts Prophets, coll campus lecturer & traveling poet, 1971-77; A&M Record Co, Hollywood, first black publicist, 1972-73; United Artist Records, Hollywood, Natl Press & Media Coord, 1973-74; contributing writer, soul & jazz records, various newspapers & magazines in US & Canada, 1974-75; The Soul & Jazz Record Magazine, assoc editor, co-publisher, 1975-77; songwriter, singer, freelance journalist, publisher 1971-. **ORGANIZATIONS:** Asst, David Gest & Assoc PR Firm, Hollywood; coll speaker, seminars for promotional publications & publicity; co-establisher, Al-Bait Haram Publishing Co, CA, 1971; co-publisher, operator, House of Haram Publishing Found; co-producer, Ar-Tee/Double Dee Production Co; consultant & public relations specialist, KWANZA Org; established Eddie Beal Scholarship Fund for Creative Youth; bd of dir, The Jazz Heritage Found; program coord, free program for children, "Jazz & You" sponsored by Jazz Heritage Found. **HONORS/ ACHIEVEMENTS:** The Outreach Award, Pasadena, 1976; Shreveport Reg Bicentennial Comm Award, KWANZA Org, 1976; named Dir of Publicity, NATRA, 1976-77; founder, Fellow Fellowship of Intl Poets Assn, London; dean's honor list, Pasadena City Coll Music Dept; Certificate of Merit, Amer Song Festival, 1977; nominee, Best Spoken Word Image Award, NAACP, 1972; published numerous articles, Black Stars Magazine, Essence, Soul & Jazz Record Mag; published numerous poems; wrote numerous songs, Kiki Dee, Gladys Knight, Diana Ross, Nancy Wilson; performed various coll concerts with Watts Prophets; various TV appearances; featured vocalist, recordings & concerts.

MCNEIL, ERNEST DUKE
Attorney. **PERSONAL:** Born Oct 09, 1936, Memphis; married Sandra; children: 2 Children. **EDUCATION:** TN State Univ BS; Fisk U, BA 1957; Depaul U, JD 1965. **CAREER:** Mcneil Cheeks & Assoc, presently an atty. **ORGANIZATIONS:** Pres The woodlawn Organization; pres TWO Enterprises; pres woodlawn Redevel Assn; vice pres Cook County Bar Assn; Health Commr Cook Co Governing Comm; weekly columnist Chicago Defender Cook Co Dept of Pub Aid; interviewer & pub relations officer IL State Employment Serv; private investigator claimsadjuster Safeway Insurance Co; law clerk & defense atty Leo Gilfoy Attorneys; chmn Speaker Bureau Am Negro Emancipation Centennial Authority; adv youth div Chicago Urban League; co-founder & treas Organization of Black Am Culture; co-founder & treas Legal Found; mem Phi Alpha Delta; Kappa Alpha Psi; bd dirMandel Legal Aid Clinic; bd dir Mid S Health Planning Coun; bd dir Gateway House IL Drug Abuse Prog; mem Jackson Park-Woodlawn Businessmen's Assn; ch-chmn Civil Rights Com; chmn Woodlawn Comm Bd. **BUSINESS ADDRESS:** 1125 E 63 St, Chicago, IL.

MCNEIL, FRANK
City treasurer. **PERSONAL:** Born Jan 06, 1937, St Louis; married Annetta Cropp; children: Frank, Anita Louise, Patricia Ann, Betty Marie, Scott Kevin. **CAREER:** Wellston MO (1st Black Elected in MO), city treas; Block Mothers, dir 1973-. **ORGANIZATIONS:** Treas Wellston Youth League for Boys; FEPC Lincoln Eng Co Fair Employment Practices Com. **HONORS/ACHIEVEMENTS:** Recipient plaque Wellston Block Mothers 1973-74; mem Natl Roster of Black Elected Officials 1974. **MILITARY SERVICE:** AUS sp/4 hon discharge 1963. **BUSINESS ADDRESS:** 1804 Keinlin, St Louis, MO.

MCNEIL, FRANK WILLIAM
Lobbyist. **PERSONAL:** Born Dec 12, 1948, High Point, NC; son of Walter H McNeil and Madge Holmes McNeil; married Barbara Jean Curtain McNeil, Mar 17, 1977; children: Kwahme, Kofi. **EDUCATION:** NC Central Univ, Durham NC, BA, 1971; JD, 1974. **CAREER:** IL Law Enforcement Committee, Springfield Il, legislative spec, 1974-76; State Board of Ethnics, Springfield Il, admin asst, 1976-77; Secretary of State Corp Div, Springfield Il, corp spec, 1978-79, admin asst, 1979-81; Senate Democratic Staff Parleamentarian, Springfield IL, 1981-86; Chicago Urban League, govt rel coordinator, 1986-87; consultant/lobbyist, Springfield Il, 1987-. **ORGANIZATIONS:** Springfield Urban League Guild; Springfield Branch NAACP; Family Service Center Sangamon County Board of Directors; Boy's Club Board of Directors. **HONORS/ACHIEVEMENTS:** Political Action Award, NAACP, 1986; Omega Psi Phi Man of the Year, 1986, 87; Webster Plaque, NAACP, 1987; Plaintiff in successful voting rights suit, McNeil vs City of Springfield; Elected Alderman Ward 2 City of Springfield, 1987. **HOME ADDRESS:** 2010 Brown Street, Springfield, IL 62703. **BUSINESS ADDRESS:** Consultant/Lobbyist, Frank W McNeil & Associates, Inc, 1 West Old Capitol Plaza, Suite 501, Springfield, IL 62703.

MCNEIL, FREEMAN
Professional football player. **PERSONAL:** Born Apr 23, 1959, Jackson, MS. **EDUCATION:** Attended UCLA. **CAREER:** New York Jets, professional football player 1980-. **HONORS/ACHIEVEMENTS:** Voted Most Valuable Player New York Jets 1981-84; Holds New York Jets Rushing Record for Running Back 1984; Mackiey Award 1981; named AFC Offensive Player of the Month Sept 1986; All-NFL by AP, NEA, Football Digest; All-AFC by UPI; mem 1986 Pro Bowl team. **BUSINESS ADDRESS:** New York Jets, 598 Madison Ave, New York, NY 10022.

MCNEIL, OGRETTA V.
Educator. **PERSONAL:** Born Sep 02, 1932, Savannah, GA; married Kingsley R; children: John, Robert Vaughn. **EDUCATION:** Howard Univ, BS magna cum Laude 1954; Clark Univ, MA 1959; PhD (Danforth fellowship) 1967. **CAREER:** Worcester Youth Guidance Cntr, psychologist 1967-68; Worcester Pub Schs, clin psychologist 1968-70; Assumption Coll, asst prof 1968-71; Clark Univ, visit lectr 1972; Anna Maria Coll, consult clin psychologist 1968-78; Holy Cross Coll, assoc prof psychology 1971-. **ORGANIZATIONS:** Mem Amer Psychol Assn; New England Psychol Assn; steering com 1980-89; exec com Assn Soc & Behav Scis 1978-; AAUW corp laison; bd of trustees Univ of MA 1976-81; bd of trustees Consumers Savings Bank 1977-; bd of trustees LeMoyne Coll 1977-82; AAUP Phi Beta Kappa. **HONORS/ACHIEVEMENTS:** Sigma Xi; USPHS fellow 1956-58; VA Clin intern 1958-60; Danforth assoc 1971-77; NSF 1971. **BUSINESS ADDRESS:** Professor, Holy Cross Coll, College St, Worcester, MA 01610.

MCNEILL, JOHN L.
Business executive. **PERSONAL:** Married Carrie G. **EDUCATION:** Miles Coll AmUniv BA. **CAREER:** Interactions Inc, pres presently. **ORGANIZATIONS:** Mem Nat Bus League; Urban League C of C; adv com civ rights Sec Dept Agr Washington 1974. **HONORS/ACHIEVEMENTS:** Outstanding Young Man Am 1973; Race Relations/Equal Oppor Award Washington 1973. **MILITARY SERVICE:** AUS 1966-72. **BUSINESS ADDRESS:** Ste 43 Cross Country Office, PO Box 6508, Columbus, GA 31907.

MCNEILL-HUNTLEY, ESTHER MAE
Elected official, educator. **PERSONAL:** Born May 07, 1921, Fayetteville, NC; widowed; children: Micheline E, Karen D, Frances M. **EDUCATION:** NC A&T State Univ, BS Home Economics 1944; Bank St Coll NYC, teachers cert; NY Univ, Administration 1953; Fayetteville State Univ, Small Business Mgmt 1977. **CAREER:** NYC, postal clerk; day care teacher; Headstart teacher; Washington Ave Day Care Ctr, first dir; Rainbow Nursery Sch, proprietor/dir. **ORGANIZATIONS:** Former mem Girl Scout Leader NYc 1970-72; 3rd Dist Chairwoman Women in Municipal Govt 1982-85; found bd Bladen Tech Coll; mem NC Black Leadership Caucus; mem Natl Black Caucus of Local Elected Officials; vice pres NC Minority Public Officials; former mem Bladen Co Improvement Assn; charter & former mem Bladen Co Arts Council; mem Mt Zion AME Zion Church. **HONORS/ ACHIEVEMENTS:** County Chmn LINC Children's 100 1974; 1st Black elected to Elizabethtown's City Council 1979; represented City of Elizabethtown in the Natl League of Cities;1st woman to be elected to City Council; Lobbyist in Washington DC for Newtown Comm Block Grant awarded 1983; Outstanding Community Serv Zeta Phi Beta 1983;Cert of Appreciation Holshouser Jr; appointed by Gov James G Martin to serve on the Local Govt Advocacy Council 1985 (2 yr term). **HOME ADDRESS:** PO Box 1346, Elizabethtown, NC 28337.

MCNELTY, HARRY
Clergyman. **PERSONAL:** Born Jan 05, E, TX; married Edna Crossley; children: Michael. **EDUCATION:** Chicago Bapt Theo Sem. **CAREER:** First Bapt Ch of Melrose Park, IL 16 yrs first & only Black Ch in Melrose Park, pastor; Proviso-Lyons Council for Comm Action Inc, chmn bd dirs; Late Rev BSJ Ford, asst minister to 1958-59; Late Rev RA Hayden, ordained under Mar 24, 1957. **ORGANIZATIONS:** Pres Comm Orgn for Maywood; vice pres E Proviso Ministers Alliance; mem Black Men Moving Div SCLC Operation Breadbasket; bd dirs Maywood Br NAACP; tchr Ch Adminstrn Bapt Ministers' Conf of Chicago & vicinity; mem Adv Bd IL Citizens Conservation for Life Com Cook County Chpt; Am Soc Distinguished Citizens. **HONORS/ACHIEVEMENTS:** Honors SCLC Black Men Moving Div 1971; Foreign Mission Bd 1974. **BUSINESS ADDRESS:** First Bapt Ch, 2114 Main St, Melrose Park, IL 60160.

MCNORRIELL, MOZELL M.
Labor union executive. **PERSONAL:** Born Oct 20, 1922, Marshall, TX; divorced; children: Robert, Jr. **EDUCATION:** Wayne StateUniv Labor Sch 1971. **CAREER:** Am Fed State Co & Municipal Employees AFL-CIO, intl vice pres 1975-; Wayne Co Local 409 AFSCME AFL-CIO, pres 1967-; Metro Cist Council 23, sec 1969-. **ORGANIZATIONS:** Life mem NAACP; mem Elliottorian Bus Women's Club 1952-; Plymouth United Ch Christ; natl coordinating com mem Coalition of Labor Union Women; dir CivilRights Trade Union Leadership Council; mem Coalition Blak Trade Unionists; First Black woman MI Intl vice pres major union AFSCME AFL-CIO. **BUSINESS ADDRESS:** 24611 Greenfield, Southfield, MI.

MCPHAIL, IRVING P.
Educational administrator. **PERSONAL:** Born Mar 27, 1949, New York City, NY; married Carolyn Jean Carver; children: Kamilah Carole. **EDUCATION:** Cornell Univ, BS 1970; Harvard Univ, MAT 1971; Univ of PA, EdD 1976. **CAREER:** Morgan State Univ Baltimore, coord freshman reading prog 1971-73, assoc prof ed, chmn dept curr & instr 1977-80; The Johns Hopkins Univ Baltimroe, spec asst to pres & provost 1978-79; Univ of MD Coll Park, asst provost div of human & comm resrcs, assoc prof curriculum & instr; Baltimore City Public School, coo 1984-85; Kamilah Educ Enterprises Inc, pres, principal cons; DE State Coll, vp, dean of acad affairs, prof of educ 1985-. **ORGANIZATIONS:** Antioch Univ 1975-76,82-; co-found & pres Natl Assoc of Black Reading & Lang Ed; mem Natl Alliance of Black School Educators, Intl Reading Assoc, Amer Assoc for Higher Ed, Natl Council of Teachers of English, Phi Delta Kappa, Coll Reading Assoc; consult AID Prog Staff Devel School Dist of Philadelphia 1976; consult to off Right to Read Baltimore City Publ School 1977;author of over 25 articles chapters & menographs in professional lit; mem Alpha Phi Alpha, ZetaRho Lambda; vchmn DE Coalition for Literacy. **HONORS/ACHIEVEMENTS:** Amer Counc on Ed Fellow in Acad Admin 1978-79; Natl Fellowships Fund Doctoral Fellow Phi Delta Kappa Univ of PA; Certs for Outstanding Contribs & Svcs, Morgan State Univ 1973, MD Reading Inst 1977,81,85, Baltimore City Public Schools 1977,85, IRA 1978,81,82,85, Teacher Corps 1979, DC Public Schools 1983, Copping State Coll 1984, MD State Dept of Educ 1985, Concord Black Parents of Hartford Cty 1986; listed in Men of Achievement 1977; selected as Eminent Scholar Norfolk State Univ 1981, One of Amers Ten Outstanding Youn Men US Jaycees 1982. **BUSINESS ADDRESS:** VP, Dean Academic Affairs, Delaware State College, Grossely Hall, Dover, DE 19901.

MCPHAIL, WELDON
Administrator. **PERSONAL:** Born Jun 01, 1944, Washington, DC; married Ja-na Morrine Bordes; children: Ary, Ayanna. **EDUCATION:** Howard U, BA 1967; CatholicUniv Washington DC, MA 1969; CatholicUniv Washington DC, PhD 1975. **CAREER:** Gov Accounting Office, mgmt analyst 1980; Mgmt Innovations Systems Inc, pres 1979-80; PG Co Dept of Corrections, dir 1978-79; PG Co Dept of Corrections, deputy dir 1978; DC Gov, dir training &employee devel 1976-77; DC Gov, administrator 1972-76; Completed Am Mgmt Assn/ Adv Mgmt & Supervision 1976;US Government, exec leadership training 1977. **ORGANIZATIONS:** Mem Am Correctional Assn; mem Asm Soc for Training & Devel Fellowship Tchrs Corps 1967-69; mem Once-a-week Club Equitable Life Ins 1967. **BUSINESS ADDRESS:** President, Mgmt Innovations Systems Inc, PO Box 247, Lanham, MD 20706.

MCPHATTER, THOMAS H.
Association executive. **PERSONAL:** Born Oct 08, 1923, Lumberton, NC; married Genevieve R Bryant; children: Thomas, Doretha, Mary Elizabeth, Joseph, Neil. **EDUCATION:** Johnson C SmithUniv Charlotte, NC, BA 1948; Johnson C SmithUniv Charlotte, NC, MDiv 1951; Program in Human Behavior Urban Devel PhD. **CAREER:** Newport News Shipyard, ship rigger 1941-43; Clothing Store, clk & mgr 1946-51; St Paul Presb Ch KC, MO, pas-

tor 1951-58; navy chaplain 1958-69; LCDR Consult Religions & Race No CA 1969-70; Golden Hill Presb Ch, asso pastor 1970-71. **ORGANIZATIONS:** Pres Omega Housing & Devel Co; project dir MDTA; Dept Labor; deputyequal Employment Opportunity Officer Dept of Def 1974-75; commr United Presb Ch Gen Assembly 1968; comm Synod of MO 1953 & 1955; Moderator Presbytery of KC 1957-58; vice pres Council of Ch of Greater KC 1956-57; mem MO Synod Council 12th Dist ; rep Omega Psi Phi Frat; vice pres MO State Conf NAACP 1969-70; bd mem YMCA 1954-55; pres Eisenhowers Minority Adv Com 1954-58; Urban League Bd 1957-58; pres Any Boy Can 1968-69; SD Dist Chaplain & Post Chaplain Am Legion KC, MO 1955-58; Life mem Urban League Omega Psi Phi. **HONORS/ACHIEVEMENTS:** Key to City of San Diego 1963; listed in Who's What & Why in MO 1967-68; Intl Dictionary of Biography; Marquis Who's Who in the West; 12th Dist citizen of yr Omega Psi Phi Frat; honorary Life mem Council of CA PTA. **MILITARY SERVICE:** USMC sgt 1943-46; USN chaplain LCDR 1958-69. **BUSINESS ADDRESS:** 4297 Pacific Hwy, PO Box 80337, San Diego, CA 92138.

MCPHERSON, JAMES ALAN
Educator. **PERSONAL:** Born Sep 16, 1943, Savannah, GA; son of James A McPherson and Mable Smalls McPherson; divorced; children: Rachel Alice McPherson. **EDUCATION:** Morris Brown Coll, BA English/History 1965; Morgan State Coll, 1963-64; Harvard Law Sch, LLB 1968; Univ IA, MFA 1971. **CAREER:** Atlantic Monthly, contrib ed 1968-; Univs of CA VA IA, tchr 1969-85. **ORGANIZATIONS:** Judge lit panel Nat'l Endow for Arts 1977-79; judge Loft McKnight awd Mnpls 1981-82; judge CCLM General Elec Writing Aawds 1983-84; ACLU; NAACP; PEN. **HONORS/ACHIEVEMENTS:** Guggenheim Fellowship 1972-73; Pulitzer Prize 1978; MacArthur Prize Fellowship 1981. **BUSINESS ADDRESS:** Professor of English, U of Iowa, 430 English Philosophy Bldg, Iowa City, IA 52240.

MCPHERSON, WILLIAM H.
Technical editor. **PERSONAL:** Born May 18, 1927, Ft Worth; married Olivia T Denmon; children: Valencia D, Olivette R. **EDUCATION:** Morehouse Coll, BS 1948. **CAREER:** The Aerospace Corp El Segundo, CA, sr tech editor; N Am Rockwell Corp Autonetics Div, tech writer 1967-68; N Am Aviation Space & Info Systems Div,tech writer 1963-67. **BUSINESS ADDRESS:** 2350 E El Sequndo Blvd, El Segundo, CA 90245.

MCQUATER, PATRICIA A.
Attorney. **PERSONAL:** Born Sep 25, 1951, Washington, DC. **EDUCATION:** Boston Univ Coll of Busn Admin, BS 1973; Univ of San Diego Schl of Law, JD 1978. **CAREER:** San Diego City Cnsl, admin intern 1976-78; Cnty of San Diego, admin anlst 1979-82; Foodmkr Inc, corp cncl 1982-84; Solar Turbines Inc, corp cnsl 1984-. **ORGANIZATIONS:** Bd govs Earl B Gellium Bar Assn 1982-; mem Am Bar Assn, Natl Bar Assn 1981-; CA Assn Blk Lawyers; San Diego Cnty Bar Assn; Am Arbtrtn Assn; sec San Diego Urban League Bd Dir 1982-; EO-Chr Cnty San Diego Affirm Action Comm 1983-. **HONORS/ACHIEVEMENTS:** Law Merit awd USD 1978; Who's Who Amg Am CollUniv USD 1978. **BUSINESS ADDRESS:** Corporate Counsel, Solar Turbines Incorp, 2200 Pacific Hwy, P O Box 85376, San Diego, CA 92138.

MCQUAY, JAMES PHILLIP
Business executive. **PERSONAL:** Born Nov 15, 1924, Baltimore, MD; married Doris; children: James Jr, Kevin, Jamal. **EDUCATION:** NY Fashion Sch Design. **CAREER:** Retail & Wholesale, fur mfr; 12th Mt Vernon 100 Black Men Inc Conc Fur Flair, dist leader; Fur Wear Mt Vernon, businessmen. **HONORS/ACHIEVEMENTS:** Fur Design Award 1972, 75, 76; spl fur showing for congressional black caucus Wash 1977; 1st place award for design Century Fur Trade Show 1980. **MILITARY SERVICE:** AUS tech sgt. **BUSINESS ADDRESS:** President, James McQuay Furs, Inc, 247 West 30th St, New York, NY 10001.

MCQUEEN, BUTTERFLY See MCQUEEN, THELMA

MCQUEEN, THELMA (BUTTERFLY MCQUEEN)
Actress. **PERSONAL:** Born Jan 08, 1911, Tampa, FL. **EDUCATION:** New York City Coll, BA Spanish 1975. **CAREER:** Radio actress, The Goldbergs, Danny Kaye Show, Jack Benny Show, Beulah Show 1937; Broadway actress, Brown Sugar, Brother Rat, What A Life, Swingin A Dream, Bell Book & Candle, Harvey, You Can't Take It With You, Steal Away, One-Woman Show, 1937-77; movie actress, Gone With the Wind (Prissy), Duel in the Sun, Dood It, Mildred Pierce, Amazing Grace 1939-75; TV actress, Dinah Shore, Stan Shaw Show, Beaulah Show, appearances features & specials 1940-79; one woman show ch/sch/coll/clubs/restaurants; theatre teacher, Martin de Porres Community Serv Ctr Long Island, Mt Morris Marcus Garvey Rec Ctr NYC; wrote, produced and starred in bilingual playlet Tribute to Mary Bethune, Washington DC. **ORGANIZATIONS:** Mem Natl Council of Negro Women; also does volunteer work at a local elementary school. **HONORS/ACHIEVEMENTS:** Comm Serv Award; Black Filmmakers Award 1975; Rosemary Award; The Act One Play Tournament Washington, DC Dept of Recreation 1979.

MCRAE, CARMEN
Jazz singer. **PERSONAL:** Born Apr 08, 1922, New York, NY; divorced. **EDUCATION:** Private student in piano. **CAREER:** Benny Carter, pianist 1944; Count Basie, pianist 1944; Mercer Ellington Band, record debut 1946-47; made 1st records as solo singer during 1950's; appearances at, Ronnie Scott's in London, Lincoln Center, Carnegie Hall, Playboy Clubs, MGM Grand Las Vegas. **ORGANIZATIONS:** Appearances at, Monterey Jazz Festival, Newport Jazz Festival, Concord Jazz Festival, Concerts by the Sea Redondo Beach CA, 1980 Playboy Jazz Festival. **HONORS/ACHIEVEMENTS:** Recording "Two for the Road" with George Shearing for Concord Jazz Records; Recipient New Star Award Downbeat Critics Poll 1954. **BUSINESS ADDRESS:** c/o Abby Hoffer Enterprises, 223 1/2 E 48th St, New York, NY 10017.

MCRAE, HAROLD ABRAHAM (HAL)
Hitting instructor. **PERSONAL:** Born Jul 10, 1946, Avon Park, FL; married Johncyna Williams; children: Brian, Cullen, Leah, Deanna. **EDUCATION:** Attended FL A&M Univ. **CAREER:** Minor Leagues, baseball player 1965-68; Cincinnati Reds, baseball player 1968-72; Kansas City Royals, baseball player 1973-87, hitting instructor 1987-. **HONORS/ACHIEVEMENTS:** Played in World Series 1970 & 1972; played in League Championship Series 1970, 1972, 1976, 1977 & 1978; Royals Player of the Yr 1974; Third Highest Batting Avg 310 in Amer League; Highest batting avg of DH in Amer League; Played All-Star Games 1975-76; Tied major league record most long hits in a doubleheader (5doubles & 1 home run) 1974; Designated Hitter "Sporting News" All Star Team 1976-77; Led AL designated hitters in doubles (41), 1977; Led in doubles (39), 1978; Led AL designated hitters in runs (88) 1978.

MCRAE, HELENE WILLIAMS
Educator. **PERSONAL:** Born in New York, NY; married Lemuel C. **EDUCATION:** Trenton State Coll, BS 1945; Columbia Univ, MA 1948, Prof Diploma 1965; Lehigh Univ, EdD 1974. **CAREER:** Bates HS Annapolis, chmn math dept 1945-52; Teacher/reading coord/learning disability consult 1952-68; Trenton State Coll, prof/chairperson/grad supervisor dept of spl edn. **ORGANIZATIONS:** Past pres Trenton State Coll Chap of Amer Assn Univ Prof; past pres Lawrence Twp Educ Assn; mem Delta Kappa Gamma Intl Hon Soc; Kappa Delta Pi Hon Soc; Council for Except Children; Intl Reading Assn; mem Alpha Kappa Alpha Sor; Girlfriends Inc; Links Inc; field reader US Dept Educ, OSER. **HONORS/ACHIEVEMENTS:** Recip Comm Serv Award Trenton State Coll 1971; Recip Faculty Teaching Awd, Mary McLeod Bethune Plaque Trenton State Coll 1987; Recip Merit Awds TrentonState Coll 1980,85,86. **BUSINESS ADDRESS:** Prof/Grad Supervisor, Trenton State Coll, Dept of Special Education, Trenton, NJ 08625.

MCRAE, RONALD EDWARD
Salesman. **PERSONAL:** Born Feb 07, 1955, Dillon, SC; son of Betty M Dudley. **EDUCATION:** Macalester Coll, BA 1976; Northwestern Univ School of Management, MBA 1978; DePaul Univ School of Law, JD 1986. **CAREER:** The Toro Co, marketing intern 1976; Federal Savings & Loan Ins Corp, rsch asst 1977; Searle Pharmaceuticals Inc, asst product manager 1978-79, product manager 1979-84, key account hospital consultant 1984-88; Westwood Pharmaceuticals Inc, manager, new bus devel 1988-. **ORGANIZATIONS:** Mem Amer Management Assoc, Amer Bar Assn, Natl Black MBA Assoc, Midwest Pharmaceutical Advertising Club, Chicago Volunteer Legal Servs, Chicago Heart Assoc Church Based Hypertension Program; Licensing Exec Society. **HONORS/ACHIEVEMENTS:** Outstanding Young Men of Amer 1979. **BUSINESS ADDRESS:** Westwood Pharmaceuticals Inc., 100 Forest Avenue, Buffalo, NY 14213.

MCREYNOLDS, ELAINE A.
Business executive. **PERSONAL:** Born Feb 05, 1948, Louisville, KY; married George R McReynolds; children: Jennifer, Jason, Julie. **EDUCATION:** Attended Univ of Montepellier France 1965; attended Centre Coll of KY 1966-68; Univ of TN, BS 1975. **CAREER:** Natl Life and Accident Ins Co, computer programmer 1970-73, programmer analyst 1974-75, expense mgmt analyst 1975-76, adminstrv asst 1976-78, asst sec & mgr 1978-83, asst vice pres (Natl Life and Accident Ins changes to Amer General Life & Accident Ins) 1983-85; real estate 1985-87; commr Tennessee Dept Commerce & Insurance 1987-. **ORGANIZATIONS:** Dir Crisis Intervention Bd of Dirs 1977-78; trustee Univ of TN Bd of Trustees 1975-84; dir Cumberland Mus Bd of Dirs 1978-81; bd of dir Citizens Bank; bd of dir St Bernard Academy; bd of dir Harpeth Hall Middle School. **HONORS/ACHIEVEMENTS:** Who's Who Amer Coll & Univ 1975-76; Outstanding Young Women of Amer 1983-84; top ten outstanding grads Nashville Mag 1976; mem of 1st class Leadership Nashville 1976-; commencement speaker Univ of TN at Knoxville 1979; commencement speaker Univ of TN at Nashville 1979; reduced day care insurance rates in state. **BUSINESS ADDRESS:** Commissioner, TN Dept of Commerce & Insur, 500 James Robertson Parkway, Nashville, TN.

MCRIPLEY, G. WHITNEY
Government official. **PERSONAL:** Born Nov 29, 1957, Detroit, MI; married Sandie Cameron; children: Marlena L; Gil Whitney McRipley Jr. **EDUCATION:** Univ of Detroit, BA 1979; Univ of MI, MA 1983; Thomas M Cooley Law School, JD 1984. **CAREER:** Detroit Public Schools, teacher 1980-81; Waverly Public School, teacher 1981-83; City of Lansing, dir of div dept 1983-84; Charter Twp of Royal Oak, supervisor 1984-. **ORGANIZATIONS:** Mem Pi Sigma Alpha; Dem Party; pres Royal Oak Twp Bus Assoc, Royal Oak Twp Mainstream; sec MI Conf of Black Mayors. **BUSINESS ADDRESS:** Supervisor, Charter Twp of Royal Oak, 21075 Wyoming St, Ferndale, MI 48220.

MCROY, RUTH GAIL
Educator. **PERSONAL:** Born Oct 06, 1947, Vicksburg, MS; married Dwight D Brooks, Jul 16, 1988; children: Myra Louise, Melissa Lynn. **EDUCATION:** Univ of Kansas, BA w/honors 1968, MSW 1970; Univ of Texas, PhD 1981. **CAREER:** Family Consultation Serv, social worker 1970-71; KS Children's Serv League, adoption worker 1971-73; Univ of Kansas, asst prof 1973-77; Prairie View A&M Univ, asst prof 1977-78; Univ of Texas, asst prof 1981-86, assoc prof 1986-. **ORGANIZATIONS:** Bd pres Black Adoption Program & Services 1975-77; mem Council on Social Work Educ 1977-; mem Natl Assoc of Social Workers 1977-; bd pres Carver Museum 1983-86; mem Natl Assoc of Social Workers Steering Comm Austin 1986-; bd mem Carver Museum 1987-; mem Casey Family Advisory Comm 1989-; mem Adoptive Families of America Advisory Comm 1989-. **HONORS/ACHIEVEMENTS:** Danforth Fellow 1978; Black Analysis Fellow 1978; Phi Kappa Phi 1979; Outstanding Dissertation Award Univ of Texas 1981; author Transracial and Inracial Adoptees The Adolescent Years 1983; Lora Lee Pederson Teaching Excellence Award 1984; Ruby Lee Prester Fellow in Serv to Children and Families 1985; Phi Kappa Phi Scholar Awd 1985; Rishon Lodge Wilhemina Delco Award for Excellence in Educ 1987; books: Emotional Disturbance in Adopted Adolescents 1988; Openness in Adoption 1988; Social Work Practice with Black Families 1989. **BUSINESS ADDRESS:** Associate Professor, TheUniv of Texas at Austin, 2609Univ Ave, Austin, TX 78712.

MCSMITH, BLANCHE PRESTON
Researcher/writer. **PERSONAL:** Born May 05, 1920, Marshall, TX; divorced; children: Kymberly Blanche Walton. **EDUCATION:** Butler Jr Coll Tyler TX; Cert; Wiley Coll TX, BA Socio & Language; Univ of So CA, MSW; Wiley Coll, Hon Degree DL 1960. **CAREER:** Amer Red Cross, home serv consult 1944-49; AK, state legislator (first black) 1959-61; Mcsmith Enterprises TV Sales & Svcs, co-owner 1950-69; Anchorage Sch Dist, dir social serv Headstart prog 1968-70; Office of the Gov, state dir pub employ prog 1972-75; Self-Employed, rscher/writer. **ORGANIZATIONS:** Conducted weekly TV Show The NAACP Speaks; pres & organized Afro-Amer Hist Soc Inc 1975-; assoc ed Alaska Spotlight Newspaper. **HONORS/ACHIEVEMENTS:** Amer Cancer Soc Awd 1956; Human Rela Awd NAACP 1956; MCA-USO Leadership Awd 1959; Daus of Elks Achievement Awd Chicago 1960; Who's Who in Amer Women 1960; Hall of Fame Anchorage Daily News 1962; Sojourner Trath Club Awd LA 1965; Woman of the Yr No Lights Civic Club 1966; Comm Serv Awd

NAACP 1966 & 1974; Older Persons Action Grp Awd 1973; "Blanche McSmith Libr" renamed City Libr City of Whittier 1973; AK Black Caucus Awd 1978; Juneau Chamber of Commerce Awd 1978-83, each yr; Visitor Prog Volunteer; Honored by Taku Toastmasters Club 1984. **BUSINESS ADDRESS:** Researcher/Writer, PO Box 210-108, Auke Bay, AK 99821.

MCSTALLWORTH, PAUL
Educator. **PERSONAL:** Born Mar 04, 1910, Flatwoods, AL; married Charlotte Young; children: Ann M Wheeler, Carol M Higginbotham. **EDUCATION:** Geneva Coll Beaver Falls, BA 1936; Howard Univ, MA 1940; OH State Univ, PhD 1954. **CAREER:** St Augustine Coll Raleigh, instr 1940-43; Central State Univ Willerforce, asst prof 1947-49; Wright State Univ Dayton, prof & asst to pres 1969-76; Central State Univ, interim vice pres 1976-77; Wright State Univ, prof history, retired; Xenia Township, trustee 1980-88. **ORGANIZATIONS:** Consult North Central Accred Assoc 1972-73; prog chmn, life mem Optimist Intl Wilbergorce Xenia 1973; bd mem Greene Cty Health, Mental Guidance, Afro-Amer Museum Task Force 1978-, Dayton-Tri Cty Red Cross 1981-; mem Sigma Pi Phi Frat life mem Alpha Phi Alpha. **HONORS/ACHIEVEMENTS:** Minority Outstanding Awd OSU Grad School 1978; Man of the Year Xenia-Greene Cty Sertoma Club 1982. **MILITARY SERVICE:** AUS Infantry 1st lt 4 yrs. **HOME ADDRESS:** PO Box 238, Wilberforce, OH 45384.

MCSWAIN, BERAH D.
Executive. **PERSONAL:** Born Feb 06, 1935, Albany, NY; son of Berah McSwain and Willie McSwain; married Diane Bradd, Dec 25, 1966; children: Berah N McSwain. **EDUCATION:** Univ of Rochester, BS, 1956, MS, 1962; Univ of California, Berkeley, PhD, 1968. **CAREER:** Northrop Aircraft Inc, Anaheim CA, lab manager, 1956-58; US Naval Ordnance Laboratory, Corona CA, researcher and designer, 1958-61; Univ of Rochester, Rochester NY, researcher, 1961-62; Univ of California, Berkeley, Berkeley CA, researcher, 1962-76, dir of professional devel program, 1976-79; Dow Associates, vice pres and chief scientist, 1979-81; Lawrence Berkeley Laboratory, visiting research scientist, 1979-81; TEM Associates Inc, president, 1981-; consultant to govt and private organizations. **ORGANIZATIONS:** Mem, Amer Chemical Soc; mem, Optical Soc of Amer; mem, Amer Soc of Plant Physiologists; mem, Soc of Photographic Scientists and Engineers; lecturer, Amer Inst of Biological Sciences. **HONORS/ACHIEVEMENTS:** Author of book chapters, conference proceedings, and articles. **HOME ADDRESS:** 1220 Monterey Ave, Berkeley, CA 94707.

MCSWAIN, DAVID L.
Physician. **PERSONAL:** Born May 22, 1928, Detroit, MI; married Joyce Jondon; children: David III, Charles, Shary Anne, Horace Glenn. **EDUCATION:** Wayne State Univ, 1946-48; Lincoln Univ PA, 1948-50; Univ of Detroit, BS Chem 1953; Still Coll of Osteopathic Med, DO 1957. **CAREER:** Zieger Ost Hosp, chmn, staff 1968-69, pres 1969-70, bd of dir 1970-71; MI Coll Drug Abuse, dep dir, prof. **ORGANIZATIONS:** Pres Natl Alumni Assoc; mem Natl Alumni Assoc of Coms Des Moines; life mem NAACP, KAY Chap Alpha Beta, Phi Sigma Gamma; bd of dir Campfire Girls 1975-76; cubmaster BSA 1965-67; leader, adv Boy Scout. **BUSINESS ADDRESS:** Deputy Director, Professor, Michigan College, 6872 W Warren, Detroit, MI 48210.

MCSWEEN, CIRILO A.
Business executive. **PERSONAL:** Born Jul 08, 1929, Panama City, Panama;married Gwendolyn Amacker; children: Esperanza, Veronica, Cirilo Jr. **EDUCATION:** Univ of IL, BA 1954, MA. **CAREER:** McSween Ins Counselors & Brokers, 1957-; McDonalds, bus exec. **ORGANIZATIONS:** Mem, vchmn Independence Bank of Chgo; owner, oper Cirilo's Inc McDonald Franchise; vp, natl treas So Christian Leadership Conf; mem IL Adv Bd tothe Dept of Ins; mem IL State Prop Ins Study Comm; natl treas, bd mem PUSH; vice pres Chicago Econ Devel Corp; bd King Ctr for Nonviolent Soc Change in Atlanta; mem Univ of IL Athletic Bd; rep Panama in Olympic Games in Track & Field. **HONORS/ACHIEVEMENTS:** McDonalds Golden Arch Awd 1984; 1st Black Elected to State St Council 1984; 1st black in history to sell over $1,000,000 of life ins in 1 month; Life &Qualifying mem Million Dollar Round Table 1958-. **BUSINESS ADDRESS:** McDonalds, 230 S State St, Chicago, IL 60604.

MCTEER, GEORGE CALVIN
Dentist. **PERSONAL:** Born Mar 09, 1938, Barnwell, SC; son of Henry A McTeer and Janie Elizabeth Williams McTeer (deceased); married Norma Jean Eaddy, Aug 17, 1963; children: Sonja Nichelle, Arlene Veronica, George Calvin Jr. **EDUCATION:** South Carolina State Coll, BS 1960, MEd 1968; Medical Univ of SC Coll of Dental Medicine, DMD 1974. **CAREER:** Fairfield Co Schools, Math & Science teacher 1960-63; Charleston Co Schools, Math teacher and adult school teacher 1963-69; Franklin C Fetter Family Health Ctr Inc, chief of dental serv 1974-76; George C McTeer DMD, private practice 1976-. **ORGANIZATIONS:** Mem Alpha Phi Alpha Frat 1958-, Psi Omega Dental frat 1974-; chmn ad hoc comm on health Charleston Business and Professional Assoc 1981-; pres Charleston County Medical Assoc 1982-86; mem bd of dirs Sea Island Health Care Corp 1984-; mem of bd chmn Personnel Comm Cannon St YMCA 1986-87; mem Palmetto Medical Dental & Pharmaceutical Assoc, SC Dental Assoc, Coastal Dist Dental Soc, Amer Dental Assoc, Central Baptist Church, Charleston Dental Soc, The Acad of General Dentistry, NAACP, Jack and Jill of Amer Inc, Owl's Whist Club. **HONORS/ACHIEVEMENTS:** First black graduate Coll of Dental Medicine Medical Univ of SC 1974; Management Devel Award Franklin C Fetter Family Health Center 1976; Certificate of Achievement Alpha Phi Alpha Frat 1982; Appreciation for Outstanding Leadership Charleston County Med Assoc 1984; Volunteer Award Coming St YWCA 1985; Volunteer Award Stono Park Elementary School PTA 1986; Merit Award for Outstanding Support of the Student Natl Dental Assn 1987; Recognition of Service in Dentistry, Sigma Gamma Rho Sorority, 1987; Distinguished and Exemplary Service, Delta Sigma Theta Sorority, 1988. **HOME ADDRESS:** 2942 Ashley River Rd, Charleston, SC 29407. **BUSINESS ADDRESS:** 134-A Rutledge Ave, Charleston, SC 29403.

MCTHOMAS, DOROTHY B.
Retired government employee. **PERSONAL:** Widowed; children: 2 Children. **EDUCATION:** Bus Sch YWCA 1943; Madame CJ Walker Sch Beauty Cult 1940. **ORGANIZATIONS:** Treas Urban League Guild KC, MO; bd mem Urban League KC; mem Ward Chapel AME Ch; NAACP Mem Vol of Am KC, MO. **HONORS/ACHIEVEMENTS:** Achievement award & (courtesy) Nat Counc Urban League Guilds 1974.

MCWHORTER, GRACE AGEE
Agricultural scientist. **PERSONAL:** Born Jan 15, 1948, Mobile, AL; married George R McWhorter MD; children: Kenya, Lia. **EDUCATION:** Tuskegee Institute, BS (Honors) 1970, MS 1972; Univ of FL, PhD 1978. **CAREER:** Univ of FL, rsch assoc 1973-75; Univ of MO, vstg prof of biology 1976-77; Talladega Coll, asst prof of biology 1980; Jacksonville State Univ, asst prof of biology 1980-81; Univ of TX at San Antonio, lecturer-biology 1981-82; FL A&M Univ, assoc prof agriculture 1982-86; State Univ System of FL Bd of Regents, program review assoc 1986-. **ORGANIZATIONS:** Owner LaFontain Floral Design 1984-; vstg prof Farmers Home Admin USOA 1984-85; mem Delta Sigma Theta Sor, Jack & Jill Inc, Amer Assoc Higher Educ Black Caucus, United Faculty of FL Political Action Chmn; bd of volunteers Tallahassee Memorial Hospital; mem Toastmasters Intl, Tuskegee Alumni Club, Amer Assoc of Univ Women. **HONORS/ACHIEVEMENTS:** BOR Rsch Fellow 1977; several publications on small farm issues and concerns 1977. **HOME ADDRESS:** 2421 Tempest Dr, Birmingham, AL 35211. **BUSINESS ADDRESS:** Program Review Assoc, StateUniv System of FL, FL Board of Regents, 117 W Gaines St, Tallahassee, FL 32308.

MCWHORTER, MILLARD HENRY, III
Physician. **PERSONAL:** Born Nov 27, 1954, Hamilton, GA. **EDUCATION:** Morehouse Coll, BS 1976; Meharry Medical Coll, MD 1981. **CAREER:** Morehouse Family Practice Prog, residency training 1981-84; Natl Health Serv Corp, staff physician 1986-; Red Level Medical Clinic, medical director. **ORGANIZATIONS:** Mem Amer Acad of Family Physicians 1975-, NAACP 1984-, Amer Medical Assoc 1986-, Covington Cty Medical Assoc 1986-, Alabama Medical Assoc 1986-; mem Alpha Phi Alpha Fraternity Inc. **HONORS/ACHIEVEMENTS:** Beta Kappa Chi Natl Scientific Honor Soc 1975-. **HOME ADDRESS:** Shadowood Apts A-4, Andalusia, AL 36420. **BUSINESS ADDRESS:** Medical Dir, Red Level Medical Clinic, Rt 2 Box 210B, Red Level, AL 36474.

MCWILLIAMS, ALFRED E., JR.
Educator. **PERSONAL:** Born Feb 03, 1938, Wewoka, OK; son of Alfred E McWilliams, Sr and Elvira M Bowles McWilliams; married Wilmer Jean Bible; children: Kimberly Beatrice, (step-children) Esther Gabriel Moten,Cassandra Gabriel, Kenneth Gabriel, Fredericka Gabriel, Keith Gabriel. **EDUCATION:** CO State Coll, BA 1959, MA 1960; Univ No CO, PhD 1970. **CAREER:** Denver Public School CO, teacher, counselor & admin asst 1960-68; Proj Upward Bound Univ No CO, dir 1968-70; Univ No CO, asst dean-special educ & rehabilitation 1970-72; Fed of Rocky Mt States Inc, consultant & career educ content coord 1972-76; Univ No CO, dir personnel AA/EEO 1976-79, asst vice pres admin serv personnel 1979-82; Univ of CO, asst to vice pres for admin 1982-84; Atlanta Univ, vice pres for admin 1984-85; Atlanta Univ, dean, School of Educ, 1985-87; GA State Univ, professor, Educ Admin, 1987-. **ORGANIZATIONS:** Chmn/co-founder Black Educators United 1967-68; asst prof 1970-72, assoc prof educ 1976-82 Univ of No CO; bd mem CO Christian Home Denver 1977-; sec 1977-, chmn 1980-84 Aurora CO Career Serv Comm; bd mem Natl Brotherhood of Skiers 1978-79; mem 1978-, bd mem 1980-85 Amer Assn of Univ Admin; mem 1978-, Gov Lamm appointed chmn 1980-84 CO Merit System Council; council mem 1978-, chmn elect 1981-82 (EEO) Coll & Univ Personnel Assn; mem Am Soc for Personnel Admin 1979-; cons, trainer Natl Center for Leadership Development Atlanta Univ 1979-80; cons, trainer Leadership Develop Training Prog Howard Univ 1981-82; mem, Rotary Club of West End Atlanta, 1984-87, 1989-; mem & army committeeman, Greater Atlanta Chapter reserve Officers Assn of US, 1985-; mem & chairman of bd of dir, APPLE Corps, 1986-; mem, Professional Journal Committee, Assn of Teacher Educators, 1987-. **HONORS/ACHIEVEMENTS:** Appreciation Award Natl Brotherhood of Skiers 1979; Leadership Styles & Management Strategies, Management Education, series at Atlanta Univ, 1986; Review of KA Heller, et al Placing Children in Special Education: A Strategy for Equity, Natl Academy Press, 1987. **MILITARY SERVICE:** AUSR lt col 1961-68, 1977-; Army Reserve Component Medal, Army Achievement Medal, Army Commendation Medal, Meritorious Serv Medal. **HOME ADDRESS:** 1221 Ashley Lake Dr, Marietta, GA 30062. **BUSINESS ADDRESS:** Professor of Educational Administration, Georgia State University, University Plaza, Atlanta, GA 30303.

MCWILLIAMS, ALFRED EDEARD
Educator clergyman. **PERSONAL:** Born May 07, 1911, Guthrie, OK; married Elvira Minerva Bowles; children: Alfred E, Jr, Stanley Wilmax, Patricia Elaine Hunter. **EDUCATION:** Lane Coll Jackson TN, AB 1933; Yale Divinity Schl New Haven CT, BD 1936; Lane Coll Jackson TN, DD 1958; Univ of MS Oxford, MS, MEd 1967. **CAREER:** Christian Meth Epscpl Ch KS OK, pstr 1936-40; TX Coll Tyler TX, prof 1940-43; AUS, chpln 1943-46; USAF, lt col 1946-64; Anderson Chpl CME Chrh,pastor 1964-67; MS Indust Coll, coll dean 1967-70; Head Start Prog, dir 1967-79; MS Indstrl Coll, prof 1970-80; Evnglsm 4th Epis Dist CME Chrh, sec 1966-67; Acad Policy Comm (MI Coll), chmn fclty forum mem. **ORGANIZATIONS:** Sec Grtr Memphis Christian Meth Episcopal Chrh Memphis TN 1982-; pstr Armstead/ St Paul CME Chrhs 1979- Oxford MS; mem Alpha Phi Alpha Frat; Thirty Second Degree Mason. **HONORS/ACHIEVEMENTS:** 50th yr cert grad Lane Coll Jackson TN 1983; Memshp-at-large Gen Brd Christian Meth Episcopal Chrh 1982; delegate Gen Conf CME Chrh1952, 1978, 1982; ldr of E MS Delg 1982, Gen Conf. **MILITARY SERVICE:** USAF lt col; Bronze Star 1952; Meritorious Serv 1964; Retired 1964. **HOME ADDRESS:** 181 Golf Club Cir, Memphis, TN 38109.

MCWILLIAMS, JAMES D.
Attorney. **PERSONAL:** Born Dec 25, 1932, Fairfield, AL; married Anne; children: Laura, Susan. **EDUCATION:** h. **CAREER:** DC Govt Dept of Transp, asst dir 1979; Atty, pvt prac 1977-79; Opp Funding Corp, gen coun sec 1973-77; Coop Assistance Fund, asst sec; US Virgin Islands, asst att gen 1967-72; US Virgin Islands Port Authority, gen coun 1969-72; United Plng Organ, Wash DC CAP, asst gen coun 1966-67; US Dept of Interior, att adv 1962-66. **ORGANIZATIONS:** Mem Nat Bar Assn; Am Bar Assn; State Bar of WI 1962-; DC Bar Assn 1972. **HONORS/ACHIEVEMENTS:** Drafted legislation which establshd US Virgin Islands Port Authority. **MILITARY SERVICE:** AUS 1955-58. **BUSINESS ADDRESS:** 2021 K St NW, Washington, DC 20006.

MCWORTER, GERALD A.
Educator. **PERSONAL:** Born Nov 21, 1942, Chicago, IL; divorced; children: One. **EDUCATION:** Ottawa Univ, BA Soc & Philosophy, 1963; Univ of Chicago, MA, 1966, PhD, 1974. **CAREER:** Ottawa Univ Dept of Philosophy, teaching asst, 1962-63; Univ of Chicago Natl Opinion Research Center, research asst, asst study dir, 1963-67; Fisk Univ Center for Afro-Amer Studies, asst prof of sociology, 1967-68; Inst of the Black World, asst prof of sociology, 1967-68; Fisk Univ, asst prof, assoc prof of sociology & Afro-Amer studies, 1969-75,

dir, Afro-Amer Studies Program, 1969-75; Univ of Illinois at Chicago, assoc prof of Black studies, 1975-79; Univ of Illinois at Urbana-Champaign, assoc prof of sociology & Afro-Amer studies, 1979-87, dir Afro-Am Studies & Research Program, 1979-84; Twenty-First Century Books & Publications, sr editor, currently; State Univ of New York at Stony Brook, assoc prof of Africana studies, currently. **ORGANIZATIONS:** Founder & dir, Cooperative Research Network in Black Studies, 1984-; ed bd, Malcolm X Studies Newsletter, 1987-, Afro Scholar Newsletter, 1983-, Western Journal of Black Studies, 1983-, Black Scholar, 1969-; founder, chair, Org of Black Amer Culture, 1965-67. **BUSINESS ADDRESS:** Assoc Prof, Africana Studies Program, State Univ of New York at Stony Brook, Social & Behavioral Sciences Bldg, Stony Brook, NY 11794.

MCWRIGHT, CARTER C.
Elected official, business executive. **PERSONAL:** Born Feb 07, 1950; children: Carter, II. **EDUCATION:** Southern Univ, BA 1972. **CAREER:** Saginaw Black Business Assn, vice pres, 1982-84; Saginaw East Side Lions Club, vice pres, 1983-84; Saginaw City, councilman; Music Planet, owner. **ORGANIZATIONS:** Bd member, East Central Michigan Planners, 1984-87; member, NAACP, Tabernacle Baptist Church. **HONORS/ACHIEVEMENTS:** Businessman of the year, Saginaw Frontiers Club, 1983, Saginaw Black Business Assn, 1984; Lion of the year, Saginaw Eastside Lions, 1983. **BUSINESS ADDRESS:** Music Planet, 1722 E Genesee, Saginaw, MI 48601.

MCZIER, ARTHUR
Management consultant. **PERSONAL:** Born May 04, 1935, Atlanta; married Ruby Burrows; children: Sandra, Jennifer Rose. **EDUCATION:** Loyola U, BS 1959, study towards M 1960-61. **CAREER:** Resoursces Inc, mgmt consult 1974-; Gen Bahamian Co, bus exec 1973-74; US Small Bus Admin, asst adminstr for minority enterprise 1969-73; US Dept of Commerce Office of Foreighn Direct Investmts, 1968; Ford Motor Co, mktng analyst 1966-67; Seeburg Corp, intl sales & mktng rep 1962-66. **ORGANIZATIONS:** Adv Bd of Inst of Minority Bus Educ Howard U; Wash Bd of Couns Fed City Coll. **HONORS/ACHIEVEMENTS:** Who's Who in Am Adv Bd Robert Russo Moton Ldrshp Award, Natl Bus League 1971; hon dr laws degree Daniel Payne Coll 1971; gold medal disngshed serv USSmall Bus Admin 1969; award of merit Natl Econ Devel Admin 1971; spl achvmt award US Small Bus Admin 1969; recog award for outst contrib to minority econ dev Black Businessmen's Professional Assn 1971; recog award for outst serv to minority bus in TX & USA Pylon Salesmanshp Club 1971; hall of fame LoyolaU 1972; cert outst perform Small Bus Adm 1972; Who's Who in Govt 1972-73; city econ devel ctr award Miami 1972; pub serv award Houston Citizens C of C 1973; Arthur S Fleming award nominee Small Bus Adm 1972; key award Natl Assn Black Manufacturer's 1974. **BUSINESS ADDRESS:** President, Natl Business Services, 1420 N St NW, Washington, DC 20005.

MEACHAM, HENRY W.
Physician. **PERSONAL:** Born Apr 20, 1924, Jackson, TN; married Shirley; children: Paul, Henry, Brian. **EDUCATION:** Lane Coll, BS 1941; NYU, MS 1947; Howard Univ Med Sch, MD 1952. **CAREER:** Kings Co Hosp, hematology fellow 1955-56; Mt Sinai Hosp, attending physician internal med & hematology serv unit 1965-78; Carter Hlth Ctr, internist-hematologist 1968-80; Physician, prvt pract 1978-. **ORGANIZATIONS:** Mem NY Blood Soc 1970-80; bd mem Queens Urban League 1978-80; pres Empire State Med Assn NM Assn 1978-80; bd mem Am Cancer Soc Harlem Div 1980;pres Queens Clinical Soc Inc. **HONORS/ACHIEVEMENTS:** Past pres award Queens Clinical Soc Inc 1979. **MILITARY SERVICE:** USN pharmacist mate 2/c 1944-46. **BUSINESS ADDRESS:** 119-15 Sutphin Blvd, Jamaica, NY 11436.

MEACHAM, ROBERT ANDREW
Professional athlete. **PERSONAL:** Born Aug 25, 1960, Los Angeles, CA; married Gari Breeze. **EDUCATION:** San Diego State Univ. **CAREER:** NY Yankees, shortstop 1983-84. **HONORS/ACHIEVEMENTS:** All-Orange County and All-State in baseball; All-League in basketball and football; named All-American baseball; signed first pro contract by Marty Keough. **BUSINESS ADDRESS:** New York Yankees, Yankee Stadium, Bronx, NY 10451.

MEACHAM, ROBERT B.
Educator. **PERSONAL:** Born Mar 21, 1933, Tuscaloosa, AL; son of Armond Meacham and Manarah Meacham; married Grace A; children: Anthony, Alexander. **EDUCATION:** AB, EdM 1973; doctoral cand 1975. **CAREER:** Lecturer on Psychology; Univ of Cincinnati, counselor 1970-73; Univ of Cincinnati Coll of Applied Sci, asst dir 1973-74, dir student life & counseling 1974-, assoc vice provost minority programs & serv & intl serv; associate vice provost student services. **ORGANIZATIONS:** Mem Amer Personnel & Guidance Assn; mem Assn for Non-White concerns; mem Assn for Counselor Educ & Supervision United Black Faculty Assn, treas 1973; mem Paddock Hills Assembly Inc 1970-; mem Comm Devel Adv Cncl City of Cincinnati. **HONORS/ACHIEVEMENTS:** Affirmative action plan prepared for OH Coll of Applied Sci 1973; aided 200 Black students from 1971-80 in receiving industrial grant-in-aid scholarships. **MILITARY SERVICE:** USAF A/1C 1952-56. **HOME ADDRESS:** 1228 Westminster Dr, Cincinnati, OH 45229. **BUSINESS ADDRESS:** Assoc Vice Provost Student Services, Univ of Cincinnati, 350 T U C, Cincinnati, OH 45221.

MEADE, ALSTON B.
Research associate. **PERSONAL:** Born Jun 28, 1930; children: Alston B, Jr, Allison D, Jule Anne, Brandon D, Fred A. **EDUCATION:** Fisk Univ, BA 1956; Univ MN, MS 1959, PhD 1962. **CAREER:** EI du Pont de Nemours Co, rsrch biolgst 1964, sr rsrch biolgst 1971. **ORGANIZATIONS:** Mem Brd Ed W Cester Area Schl Dist 1970-80; v pres Brd Ed W Chester Area Schl Dist 1975-77; chrmn Joint Comm Spl Ed Chester Cnty PA 1974 80;mem Inter Unit Chester County PA 1974-80. **HOME ADDRESS:** 2014 Valley Dr, West Chester, PA 19382. **BUSINESS ADDRESS:** Research Associate, EI du Pont de Nemours & Co, Agr Chem Dept, Stine Haskell, Newark, DE 19711.

MEADE, MELVIN C.
Counselor. **PERSONAL:** Born Jan 16, 1929, Aliquippa, PA; married Beverly Ann Carter; children: Carroll Ann, Melvin Carter, Yolanda Alike, Natalie Marie. **EDUCATION:** W VA St Coll, BS 1953; Westminster Coll, MEd 1965; W MI U, 1967; Carlow Coll NSF, 1968-70; BostonUniv Pittsburgh Theol Sem, 1978, 1971. **CAREER:** Aliquippa Sch Dist, guidance couns; Aliquippa Sch Middle Sch, tchr 23 yrs. **ORGANIZATIONS:** Waterfront dir YMCA; dir Nghbrhd Yth Corp; dir Ch Bsktbll; dir YMCA Day Camp; mem Phi Delta Kappa; NEA; PA Educ Assn; Aliquippa Educ Assn; PA Sch Couns Assn; Midwstrn Couns Assn; Am Pers & Guid Assn; Assn for Non-White Concern; mem bd Christ United Beaver Co; Beaver Vly YMCA; Beaver Co Yth Serv Inc; Beaver Co Mental Hlth Red Cr; Alpha Phi Alpha; Phi Delta Kappa 1972; pastor Holy Institutional Bapt Ch; prgm coord Middle Sch 1974. **HONORS/ACHIEVEMENTS:** Man of yr Aliquippa Club 1971; Eagle Scout 1947. **MILITARY SERVICE:** AUS Corps eng PFC 1953-55. **BUSINESS ADDRESS:** Aliquippa Middle Sch, Aliquippa, PA 15001.

MEADE, WILLIAM F.
Educator. **PERSONAL:** Born Jan 04, 1925, Brooklyn, NY. **EDUCATION:** Brooklyn Coll, BA 1954, MA 1956; Teachers Coll, Columbia Univ, Diploma Special Educ 1960; Certified NLP practitioner level 1986, trainer 1987. **CAREER:** Dept of Physical Med & Rehabilitation Kingsbrook Jewish Med Center, chief speech therapist 1954-65; Long Island Univ Speech & Hearing Clinic, dir; Brooklyn Center, Long Island Univ, Assoc prof speech pathology & audiology. **ORGANIZATIONS:** Nursing home consultant speech problems of neurologically impaired adults geriatrics 1971-74; assoc mem Bedford Stuyvesant Jaycees 1974-75; treas of dirs Hosp Programs in Speech Pathology Audiology 1975-76; pres 1975-76; mem Am Speech & Hearing Assn; mem NY State Speech & Hearing Assn. **HONORS/ACHIEVEMENTS:** Recip Certificate of Appreciation for Civic Service Bedford Stuyvesant Jaycees 1975, Greenpark Care Center 1984. **MILITARY SERVICE:** USMC 1943-46. **BUSINESS ADDRESS:** Associate Professor, Long Island University, University Plaza, Brooklyn, NY 11201.

MEADE-TOLLIN, LINDA C.
Biochemist/university professor. **PERSONAL:** Born Aug 16, London, WV; daughter of Robert Meade and Virginia Meade; married Gordon Tollin; children: Amina Rebecca. **EDUCATION:** WV State Coll, BS cum laude 1964; Hunter Coll, MA 1969; City Univ of New York, PhD 1972. **CAREER:** Coll of Old Westbury, asst prof 1972-75; Rockefeller Univ, visiting asst prof, 1973-74; Univ of AZ, NIH postdoctoral fellow 1975-77, rsch assoc 1978-80; Univ of AZ, Coord Women in Science & Engrg 1980-82, University of Arizona, visiting asst prof 1982-85; Morehouse Schl of Medicine, Faculty Development Fellow, 1985-86; Univ of AZ, Sr Lecturer/NIH Minority Special Investigator, 1987, research asst prof 1989. **ORGANIZATIONS:** Natl Organization for the Professional Advancement of Black Chemists and Chemical Engineers, mem 1973-85,1987-, chair exec bd 1981; consultant Amer Med Women's Assn 1977-85; mem bd of dir Ododo Theatre Found 1977-85; mem Alpha Kappa Alpha Sorority 1962-; mem Jack and Jill Inc, 1987-. **HONORS/ACHIEVEMENTS:** Finalist Natl Merit Scholarship Corp 1960; contributor What People Eat Harvard Univ Press 1974; Rsch Fellow NIH at Univ of AZ College of Medicine 1975-77;indv preceptorship Amer Medical Women's Assoc 1979; Awd for Excellence in Medicine Scimitar Temple 108 1981; Scientist of the Year AZ Council of Black Engrs & Scientists 1983. **BUSINESS ADDRESS:** Research Assistant Professor, University of Arizona, Dept of Anatomy, Tucson, AZ 85724.

MEADOWS, CHERYL R.
City administrator. **PERSONAL:** Born Sep 07, 1948, Cincinnati, OH; married Geoffrey, 1982; children: Jerry C Wilkerson. **EDUCATION:** Tennessee State Univ, BA, 1970; Univ of Cincinnati, MS, 1975. **CAREER:** City of Cincinnati, planner, 1971-76, program mgr, 1976-82, asst to the city mgr, 1982-. **ORGANIZATIONS:** Mem, AS Conference of Mayor/City Human Serv, 1976-89, Women's City Club, 1982-88, Comprehensive Community Child Care, United Way Planning Bd, 1982-88, Free Store, 1984-86, Natl Forum for Black Public Admin, 1986-89, Amer Soc of Public Admin, 1989-, Hamilton County Clildren's Trust Fund, 1989-, Adolescent Pregnancy Task Force 1989-. **HONORS/ACHIEVEMENTS:** Aspo Ford Found Fellowship, 1975; Univ Scholarship, 1975; Oustanding Young Women of Amer, 1982; Community Chest's President Award, 1983; Community Action Comm Award, 1986; Community Serv Award, 1987.

MEADOWS, FERGUSON BOOKER, JR.
Educator. **PERSONAL:** Born Jan 23, 1942, Charleston, WV; son of Ferguson and Mary; married Hildred Jean Hutcherson; children: Leslie Michelle, Stephanie Dawn, Kimberlie Elizabeth. **EDUCATION:** West Virginia State College, BA Sociology 1962-67; West Virginia Univ, MA Counseling 1968-71; Virginia Polytechnic Institute & State Univ, EdD 1975. **CAREER:** West Virginia State College, dir of counseling 1968-71, dir guidance & placement 1971-72; Kanawha Co Bd of Education, dir project CARE 1972-73; VPI & State Univ, adjunct professor Summer 1975; Kent State Univ, assistant professor 1975-; Kent State Univ, Kent, OH asst dean Coll of Educ & Graduate School of Educ. **ORGANIZATIONS:** Bd of dir pres Portage County Housing Advocates 1981-82; member Amer Assn for Counseling & Devel 1971-; member Amer School Counselors Assn 1971-; member Assn for Non-White Concerns 1973-; member Assn of Counselor Educ & Supervision 1975-; bd of dir Portage County NAACP 1982-; bd of dir Portage County Headstart 1984-; bd of dir Portage County Comm Action Council 1984-; mem Amer Assn for Multicultural Counseling & Devel; pres Ohio Assn for Multicultural Counseling & Devel, 1988-89; Treasurer Ohio Assn for Counseling & Devel, 1988-90. **HONORS/ACHIEVEMENTS:** Kent State University Distinguished Advisor Award 1981; published book, Using Guidance Skills in the Classroom Eds Charles Thomas 1982; 15 articles and book chapters. **MILITARY SERVICE:** US Army Matl Guard, lieutenant colonel, 1960; Army Commendation Medal; Armed Forces Res Medal; Natl Defense Serv Medal; XO WV Military Acad; Army Achievement Medal. **HOME ADDRESS:** 1048 DeLeone Drive, Kent, OH 44240. **BUSINESS ADDRESS:** Asst Professor Coll of Educ, Kent StateUniv, 310 White Hall Kent State Unv, Kent, OH 44242.

MEADOWS, LUCILE SMALLWOOD
Educator. **PERSONAL:** Born May 23, 1918, Glen Ferris, WV; married Reginald Clinton; children: Benita Luanne. **EDUCATION:** WV State Coll, attended 1939. **CAREER:** Harlem Hgts Elem, princ 1957-67, teacher 1939-. **ORGANIZATIONS:** Pres Fayette Co Assn of Clsrm Tchrs 1975-78; sec Fayette Co Educ Assn 1975-77; NEA delg 1974-84; mem WVEA Human Rights Comm 1973-76; mem WVEA TaskForce on Reglztn 1976-77; mem WVEA Blk Caucus Strng Comm 1973-78; mem WVEA Polit Action Comm 1976-; chmn Fayette Co Blk Caucus 1974-85; WV State Adv Counc on Vocational Educ apptd by Gov Rockefeller 1977-86; chrpsn Tri Area Park Com; chrpsn Fayetteville Prop Owners Assn; spl adv com WV Tchrs Retirement Bd apptd by Gov Rockefeller; adv cncl WV Women's Commn; pub relat dir Upper Fayette Co Chap NAACP; past sec Fayette Co Chap WV State Alum Assn; registrar WV Bapt State Youth Camp 1961-71; delegate Dem Mid-term Natl Convention 1978;

delegate Dem NatlConv 1984; apptd to Gov Judiciary Adv Comm 1983 by Gov Rockefeller IV; assoc sec WV Dem Exec Comm; pres Fayette Co Dem Women's Club; mem bd dirs New River Family Health Ctr 1982-; mem Fayette Co Volunteer Steering Comm; adv council mem Eastern Highlands Area Agency on Aging. **HONORS/ACHIEVEMENTS:** Apptd WV for charter com 1976; Ten Persons of the Yr Fayette Co 1976; alt del 1976 Dem Conv; apptd Fayette Co Bicent Com 1976.

MEADOWS, RICHARD H.
Dentist. **PERSONAL:** Born Dec 07, 1928, Roanoke, VA; married Dorothy M Magee; children: William C. **EDUCATION:** VA Union U, BS 1951; HowardUniv Sch of Dentistry, DDS 1955; Freedman'‡ Hosp, intern 1956. **CAREER:** Dentist, pvt prac. **ORGANIZATIONS:** Pres PBR Dent Soc 1961-68; pres Old Dominion Dent Soc 1968-71; mem Nat Dent Soc; mem Intl Endodontic Soc; mem Aircraft Owners & Pilots Assn; mem Omega Psi Frat; NAACP. **HONORS/ACHIEVEMENTS:** Recip award in oral surg Beta Kappa Chi Nat Sci Soc HowardUniv 1955. **BUSINESS ADDRESS:** 215 W Clay St, Richmond, VA 23220.

MEANS, BERTHA E.
Educator. **PERSONAL:** Born May 01, 1920, Valley Mills, TX; married James H Means; children: Joan, Janet, James Jr, Patricia, Ronald. **EDUCATION:** Huston-Tillotson Coll, AB 1945; Univ of TX, MEd 1955; Univ of TX Austin, attended. **CAREER:** Prairie View A&M Univ, vstg instr 1959-68; Austin Independent School Dist Austin TX, dir head start 1969-70; Univ TX Austin, instr 1971-72; Austin Independent School Dist, instr coord secondary reading. **ORGANIZATIONS:** Mem Intl Reading Assoc; past pres Capitol Area Council; mem TX State Teachers Assoc; charter mem Ad Hoc Com for Enactment Human Relations Comm City ofAustin; bd mem YWCA; mem Epsilon Kappa Chap Delta Kappa Gamma Soc for Women Ed Area Ch, United Fund, Austin & Travis Cts 1965-67; 1st vice pres Austin NAACP 1970-74; chmn voter Reg & Ed, City Council appointee to Parks & Rec Adv Bd 1967-74; citizens comm for A More Beautiful Town Lake 1972-75; mem Local Citizens Adv Comm TX Constitutional Adv Comm 1973; past pres, org Austin Chap Jack & Jill of Amer Inc 1956-58; mem Alpha Kappa Alpha Sor, St James Episcopal Ch; pres Episcopal Women St James 1966-67. **HONORS/ACHIEVEMENTS:** Woman of the Year Awd Zeta Phi Beta Sor 1965; DeWitty Civil Rights Awd Austin Br NAACP 1966; selected 1 of Austins Outstanding Women of 1975; Austin Amer Statesman; NAACP Spec Awd for Serv to Parks & Rec Dept 1975; Comm Serv Awd Zeta Phi Beta 1976; Comm Leadership Cert Apprec Capital City Lions & Optimist Clubs 1972. **BUSINESS ADDRESS:** Instructional Coordinator, Austin Independent School Dist, 6100 N Guadalupe, Austin, TX 78752.

MEANS, CRAIG R.
Dental educator. **PERSONAL:** Born Aug 16, 1922, Shreveport, LA; children: Stephanie. **EDUCATION:** Southern U, BS 1950; Howard U, DDS 1954; OH State U, MSc 1963; Memorial Hosp Cancer, Certif 1964. **CAREER:** Coll of Dentistry Howard U, asst prof 1961-66, assoc prof 1966-70; Dept Rmvbl Prost, chmn 1968-70, prof 1970-; Coll of Dentistry Howard U, assoc dean 1970-81; Continuing Dental Ed, dir 1982-85, retired, professor. **ORGANIZATIONS:** Consult ADA Comm Dental Accreditation 1982-85; mem Amer Dental Assn; mem Natl Dental Assn; mem Amer Assn of Dental Schools. **HONORS/ACHIEVEMENTS:** Fellow Louise C Ball Fellowship Fund 1962-64; mem Omicron Kappa Upsilon Dental Honor Soc; fellow Amer Coll of Dentists 1971; alumni awd Howard Univ of Coll Dentistry 1984. **MILITARY SERVICE:** AUS 1st lt 1941-46.

MEANS, ELBERT LEE
Elected official. **PERSONAL:** Born Feb 03, 1945, Sandy Ridge, AL; married Harriet Ivory; children: Madelene, Jennifer, Kristen. **EDUCATION:** Selma Univ, 1964; AL State Univ 1964-66 & 1968-69. **CAREER:** Station Help Inc, supervisor 1969-73; General Motors, shipping clerk 1973-75; Brockway Glass, laborer 1975-79; Lowndes County, lst Black tax assessor 1979-. **ORGANIZATIONS:** State exec member Alabama Democratic Conf; county coordinator Lowndes Cty Democratic Party; member advisory board Lowndes Cty Community Org; vice-pres Selma Univ Alumni-Chapter; honorary lieutenant colonel aide-de-camp in the Alabama State Militia. **MILITARY SERVICE:** AUS E-5 sergant 1966-68; Bronze Star Vietnam Veteran. **HOME ADDRESS:** PO Box 69, Fort Deposit, AL 36032. **BUSINESS ADDRESS:** Tax Assessor, Lowndes Co, PO Box 186, Hayneville, AL 36040.

MEANS, FRED E.
Educational administrator. **PERSONAL:** Born in Pacolet, SC; son of Fred Means Sr and Lemor Tucker; married Helen Pryor; children: Chad, Marc, Vincent. **EDUCATION:** NY Univ, BS 1959; Trenton State Coll, MA 1963; Rutgers Univ, EdM 1973, EdD 1975. **CAREER:** NY City Schools, tchr 1959-60; Newark School System, tchr 1960-70; Rutgers Univ, lecturer & dir 1970-75; Jersey City State Coll, dir 1975-78, asst dean 1978-85, dean 1985-. **ORGANIZATIONS:** Mem Newark Bd of Educ 1973-76; trustee Action for Sickle Cell Anemia of Hudson City 1982-88; mem bd dirs Research for Better Schools 1983-; pres Org Newark Educators Newark 1967-70; trustee UCC Newark Anti Poverty Agency 1965-66; mem AACTE; mem AERA. **HONORS/ACHIEVEMENTS:** "Education: Key to America's Future," convocation address, Jersey City State Coll 1988; "Project PRIME (Program to Recruit Minority Educators)," paper presented at Norfolk State Univ 1988. **MILITARY SERVICE:** AUS Spec 3 1953-56. **BUSINESS ADDRESS:** Dean Professional Studies and Education, Jersey City State College, 2039 Kennedy Blvd, Jersey City, NJ 07305.

MEANS, KEVIN MICHAEL
Physician. **PERSONAL:** Born Jun 14, 1955, Brooklyn, NY; son of Phillip A Means Jr and Muriel C Means. **EDUCATION:** State Univ of NY at Binghamton, BS Biology 1978; Howard Univ Coll of Medicine, MD 1982. **CAREER:** Veterans Admin Medical Center, staff physician 1985-; UAMS Div of Rehab Medicine, asst prof 1985-; Univ Hospital of Arkansas, Staff physician, 1985-; a Veterans Admin Medical Center, Little Rock, AR asst chief Rehab Medical Serv 1988-; Veterans Admin Medical Center Little Rock, AR staff physician, Rehab Medical Serv 1985-88;. **ORGANIZATIONS:** Mem Urban League of Arkansas 1985-, Big Brother/Big Sister of Pulaski Co 1985-; fellow Amer Acad of Physical Medicine & Rehab 1986-; mem Assoc of Academic physiatrists 1986-, Amer Geriatric Soc and Amer Coll of Sports Medicine 1986-; mem ad hoc comm Geriatric Rehab Amer Acad of PM&R 1986-. **HONORS/ACHIEVEMENTS:** Outstanding Young Man of Amer 1986. **BUSINESS ADDRESS:** Assistant Chief, Rehabilitation Medicine Service, 117/NLR, Veterans Administrations Medical Center, 4300 W 7th Steet, Little Rock, AR 72205.

MEASE, QUENTIN R.
Association executive. **PERSONAL:** Born Oct 25, 1917, Buxton, IA; married Jewell Mary Mease; children: Barbara Ann (ranson). **EDUCATION:** Des Moines U, BS 1939; George Williams Coll, MS 1948. **CAREER:** Crocker Br YMCA, exec dir 1939-42; Metro YMCA Chgo, asst prgm sec 1946-49; Bagby Br YMCA Houston, exec dir 1950-55; So Central YMCA, exc dir 1955-75. **ORGANIZATIONS:** Chmn bd mgrs Harris Cnty Hosp Dist 1970-75; mem Rotary Club of Houston; bd mem TX Med Ctr; fdr pres Houston Area Urban League 1967-69; bd mem Alley Theater; Star of Hope Mission; exec sec Houston Bus & Professional Men's Club 1950-75. **HONORS/ACHIEVEMENTS:** Kappa Delta Pi Hon Soc 1948; diamond jubilee award George Williams Coll 1965; distngshd cit award Housont Citizens C of C 1955. **MILITARY SERVICE:** USAF capt 1942-46. **BUSINESS ADDRESS:** President, HELP, Inc, 5530 Van Fleet, Houston, TX 77033.

MEAUX, RONALD
Artist, educator. **PERSONAL:** Born Feb 15, 1942, Louisville. **EDUCATION:** Univ of KY, BA Art 1965. **CAREER:** Cleveland Public Schools, art instructor; Artist. **ORGANIZATIONS:** Mem Nat Conf of Artists; mem NAACP; mem Metro Opera Guild. **HONORS/ACHIEVEMENTS:** One man art show Karamu 1974; exhib work Clevelande Akron; recip Scholarshps Alpha Phi Alpha 1 yr; Mary E Johnston Art Sch 3 yrs. **BUSINESS ADDRESS:** Art Instructor, East Technical High School, 2439 E 55th St, Cleveland, OH 44105.

MEDEARIS, VICTOR L.
Clergyman, government employee. **PERSONAL:** Born Apr 03, 1921, Austin; married Gladys L Alexander; children: Victor L, Pamela Faye. **EDUCATION:** City Coll of San Fran, AA 1958; San Fran Bapt Bible Coll, Std Theol 1948-53; San Fran U, Std Soc Sci 1959-61. **CAREER:** Federal Employment, mechanic hlpr, warehse foreman, heavy duty drvr trainer, drvr examnr, mech inspec, equal employmt spec 1949-; Double Rock Bapt Ch San Fran, pastor. **ORGANIZATIONS:** Chmn San Fran Humn Rights Comm 1971-; sec bd instr Fellowshp Bible Inst; chmn Civic Com Bayview Bapt Min Fellowshp; past mod Bay Area Dist Assn;bd mem San Fran Chptr NAACP; bd mem Sickle Cell Anemia; West Bay Clergy Rep Northern CA Adv Bd of United Negro Coll Fund Bay Area Inter Alumni Com; ofcl Organist CA State Bapt Conven. **HONORS/ACHIEVEMENTS:** Recip highest award of merit City San Fran 1971; hon award Pelton Jr HS 1973; hon award Quartett Singers Assn of Am 1972. **BUSINESS ADDRESS:** 866 Malcolm Rd, Burlingame, CA 94010.

MEDFORD, ISABEL
Attorney. **PERSONAL:** Born Mar 15, Louisiana; children: Richard Kevin. **EDUCATION:** Univ of CA Berkley, BA Psych & Polit Sci 1972; Univ of CA Boalt Hall Sch of Law, JD 1975; Univ of CA, M Crim 1976. **CAREER:** Isabel Medford Law Firm, atty 1978-; Robert T Cresswell Inc, atty 1974-78; NAACP Legal Def Fund, law clerk 1974-75. **ORGANIZATIONS:** Bd dir A Safe Place 1979-; vice pres UC Black Alumni Assn 1979-; legal adv Oakland E Bay Chap Delta Sigma Theta 1979-; mem past chmn Memshp Com Niagra Movement Dem Club 1974-. **BUSINESS ADDRESS:** 645 Chetwood, Ste 302, Oakland, CA 94610.

MEEK, RUSSELL CHARLES
Educator, lecturer, consultant. **PERSONAL:** Born Sep 09, 1937, Springfield, IL; son of Albert Jackson Meek and Josephine Snowden Meek; divorced; children: 1 child. **EDUCATION:** Milliken Univ Natl Coll LaSalle U, student 1960; Hwa Rang Do Martial Arts Acad, 1970, Universal Life Ch, DD 1975; Natl Coll of Chiropractic Med, Doct Religious Humanities; Temple Univ. **CAREER:** Cook Co Dept of Corrections, 1966-; Search for Truth Inc, pres 1966-; Westside Art & Karate Center Inc, dir 1968-; Radio Sta WVON, prod host 1970-; Univ of IL, instr radio TV prod Psycholinguistics & Philology; CETA V "Devel Educ & Employ Prog," proj dir; Malcolm X Coll, instr 1970-72; Northeastern ILU, rehab educ specialist 1974-75; Natl Black Writer's Workshop, lecturer 1973-75; Study Commn for Residential Schs IL, hearing coord 1974; Investigative Jour & Historical Rsch, writer; Malcolm X Coll bd dir Parents Without Partners, comm adv commn. **ORGANIZATIONS:** Instr Martial Arts; pres Black Karate Fed; mem Black United Front, Black Enpowerment Comm; pres Search for Truth Inc; radio commentator, talk show host WBEE Radio; leader, Dr Russ Meek's Jazz AllSTARS; bd of dir African American Clergy for Action 1988-. **HONORS/ACHIEVEMENTS:** Poems for Peace, Justice and Freedom, 1966; songs "My Love," "You," and "Shadows of the Night," 1969; Blue Ribbon Panel Citizens for Police Reform, 1973-75; received ten humanitarian, community, integrity, merit & special awards, 1972-75; Westside Citizen of the Year, 1972-76; starred in two documentary films, "Crisis in the Cities" (Emmy Award winner) and "A Letter to Martin"; produced and directed TV and radio shows since 1966, first black to do so in country; editor, Search for Truth News; Comm Integrity Award, 1973; doctoral candidate, Univ of the Pacific; publicist, co-sponsor, African-Amer Culture Center Imo State; The Can Do It Awd, 1973; Champion of Imprisoned Award, 1974; The Get It Done Award, 1973; Special Commendation Award for Community Interest and Support, El Centro de La Causa 1975; Natl Community Leaders; Gentlemen of Distinction; Master of the Martial Arts; Outstanding Serv to the Martial Arts and Community; playwright, "The Message," 1976; co-author "Our Songs"; Image Makers Award, 1977. **BUSINESS ADDRESS:** Search for Truth, Inc, 10937 S Lowe Ave, Chicago, IL 60628.

MEEKS, CORDELL DAVID, JR.
Judge. **PERSONAL:** Born Dec 17, 1942, Kansas City, KS; son of Cordell D Meeks, Sr and Cellastine Brown; married Mary Ann Sutherland; children: Cordell, III. **EDUCATION:** Univ KS, BA Pol Sci 1964; Univ KS Law Schl, JD Law 1967; Univ PA Law Schl, Smith Fellowship 1968; Harvard Law Schl, Practicalities of Judging 1978; Natl Judicial Coll, Grad Gen Jrs 1981. **CAREER:** Wyandotte Cty Legal Aid Socty, staff counsel 1968-70; Meeks Sutherland McIntosh Law Firm, sr partner 1968-81; State of KS, special asst atty gen 1975; Kansas City KS, municipal judge 1976-81; 29th Judicial Dist of Kansas, dist court judge 1981-. **ORGANIZATIONS:** Amer Red Cross (MLK Chapter), pres 1971-73; Wyandotte Cty Legal Aid, pres 1971-73; Jr Achiev Greater Kansas City, vice pres 1975-76; KS Advisory Council Nat'l Leg Serv Bd, mem 1975; Mental Health Assoc Wyandotte Cty, pres 1980-82; KS Municipal Judges Assoc, pres 1980-81; Econ Oppor Fntd, pres 1981-84; Gov Comm on Crime Prev 1982-; Comm Professional Resp Natl Assoc of State Trial Judges 1984; Bd Govr KS Univ Law Schl, pres 1984-85; Natl Conf of Christians & Jews (Greater Kansas City region), exec comm 1984-; Substance Abuse Ctr of Eastern KS, pres 1985-87; KS Commission on Bicentennial of US Constitution, mem 1987-. **HONORS/ACHIEVEMENTS:** Omicron Delta Kappa 1964; Fellow Regn Heber Smith Comm Lawyer 1968; United Way, outstanding services awd 1979; Yates Branch, Men of Distinction Awd 1982; 100 Most Influential Black Men, Greater Kansas City, The KC GLOBE 1983-84. **MILITARY SERVICE:** AUS NG lt col 21 years; US Army, active duty 1968-70; Army Commendation Medal 1969; US Army

Command & General Staff Coll, graduate 1980; 35th Infantry Div KS Natl Guard, staff judge advocate 1983-. **HOME ADDRESS:** 7915 Walker, Kansas City, KS 66112. **BUSINESS ADDRESS:** District Court Judge, 29th Judicial Dist of KS, 710 N 7th St, Wyandotte County Courthouse, Kansas City, KS 66101.

MEEKS, LARRY GILLETTE
Director. **PERSONAL:** Born Apr 11, 1944, Bakersfield, CA; married Dinnie Jean Williams; children: Kimerley, Corey. **EDUCATION:** Bakersfield Jr Coll, AA 1963;Univ CA Davis, BS 1970; Golden Gate U, MPA 1973. **CAREER:** Lbr Aff Dept Tranp, chief 1972-74; Plng Cons't Dept Correct, chief 1974-77; Facil Develp Dept Hlth, chief 1977-82. **ORGANIZATIONS:** Prof Golden Gate U; mem Am Hlth Plnrs; advy brdUniv Of Southern Caine; chrmn trts Williams Meml Chrh God In Christ; life mem Nat'l Urban Leag; mem NAACP. **MILITARY SERVICE:** AUS 1st lt 1966-69; Army Cmndtn Combat Inftrymn Vietnam Serv Medals. **BUSINESS ADDRESS:** Dir, Office Statewide Hlth Plng, State of CA, 1600 9th St, Sacramento, CA 95814.

MEEKS, PERKER L., JR.
Judge. **PERSONAL:** Born Aug 06, 1943, Tallahassee, FL; married Patricia E Evans MD; children: Perker III, Alicia Nicole. **EDUCATION:** FL A&M Univ, BS 1965, JD 1968. **CAREER:** Gov State of FL, administrative aide 1968-69; San Francisco Sch Dist, teacher 1970-72; San Francisco Pub Defender's Office, trial lawyer 1972-80; San Francisco Municipal Ct, judge. **ORGANIZATIONS:** Sec/bd mem Charles Houston Bar Assn 1977-80; pres/bd mem OMI Com Assn 1970-80; bd mem San Francisco Chap NAACP 1978-79. **BUSINESS ADDRESS:** Judge, San Francisco Municipal Court, City Hall, San Francisco, CA 94102.

MEEKS, REGINALD KLINE
Elected official. **PERSONAL:** Born Mar 21, 1954, Louisville, KY; son of Florian Meeks and Eloise Meeks; divorced; children: Nilaja Nura-jehan. **EDUCATION:** Wabash College, BA History (minor Third World studies) 1976; Univ of Iowa Coll of Law, JD 1979; Univ of Louisville, Real Estate Law Course 1981. **CAREER:** Legal Aid Society, community development unit 1981-82; Christian & Bynum Attorneys, law clerk 1982-83; Bleidt, Barnett & Shanks Attorneys, law clerk 1983-88; City of Louisville, 11th ward alderman 1982-; Jefferson County Public Schools, Louisville KY, career developer 1988-. **ORGANIZATIONS:** Sec, board of directors Seven Counties Services 1983-88; board of directors Stage One - The Louisville Children's Theater 1983-87; Shawnee District chmn Old KY Home Council Boy Scouts 1984-87; NAACP; Natl League of Cities; KY Municipal League; mem Natl Bar Assn; Natl Black Caucus of Local Elected Officials 1982-; Chairman Museum Development Committee KY African American Museum 1987-; board of directors Farm & Wilderness Camps Plymouth VT 1987-; advisory council Salvation Army Boy's & Girl's Clubs 1987-. **HONORS/ACHIEVEMENTS:** Dean's List Wabash College; Black Achievers Award - YMCA 1983; One of Fifty Young Future Leaders - Ebony Magazine Sept 1983; Outstanding Young Men of America Award 1984. **HOME ADDRESS:** 2712 Virginia Ave, Louisville, KY 40211. **BUSINESS ADDRESS:** Alderman Ward 11, City of Louisville, 601 W Jefferson, Louisville, KY 40202.

MEHLINGER, KERMIT THORPE
Psychiatrist. **PERSONAL:** Born Jun 17, 1918, Washington, DC; married Lillian L Pettiford; children: Dianne, Bonnie, Renee, Jill. **EDUCATION:** Oberlin Coll OH, AB 1939; HowardUniv Med Sch, MD 1950; Yale U, Past Grad Training 195153; Cook Co Grad Sch Clinical Neurology, 1959. **CAREER:** Mental Hlth Ctr Chgo, sr psychiatrist 1954-59; Circuit Ct Chgo, sr pshychtrst 1960-69; Martin King Nghbrhd Hlth Ctr Chgo, proj dir 1969-71; Div of Pshyctry Cook Co Hosp, dir 1972-73; Rush Med Coll, prof 1976; Pvt Prac; Div of Behavior Sci & Psycholdynamic Med Jackson Park Hosp & Med Ctr Chgo, dir 1978-; Chicago Med Sch, asso prof clinical pshych 1969-; Columbia Coll, prof communication 1973-; Div Vocatnl Rehab, psych consult 1967-; West Side Orgn, psych consult 1973-; Friendship Med Clinic, psych consult 1974-. **ORGANIZATIONS:** Fdr chmn Image & Indentifctn 1961-; pres Coal Black Enterprise Inc 1971-; mem IL Dangerous Drug Adv Coun 1966-73; mem Am Med Assn Com on Alcoholism 1975-; mem Chicago Found for Med Care 1974-; mem IL State Med Soc Com on Drugs & Hazrds Substance 1973-; bd dir Gateway Houses Inc 1971-; past pres Cook Co Physician Assn 1968-69; pres S Side Br Chicago Med Soc 1970-; med adv com IL Criminologcl Soc; IL Psych Assn; Nat Rehab Assn; mem Am Veteran's Com; Kappa Alpha Psi. **HONORS/ACHIEVEMENTS:** Recip Fellow Inst of Med Chicago 1970; fellow Am Psych Assn 1973; distinctive award AMA 1969; diplomate Am Psych Assn 1961; author book "Coal Black &The Seven Dudes". **MILITARY SERVICE:** AUS capt med reserve ret 1941-46. **BUSINESS ADDRESS:** 7531 S Stoney Island Ave, Chicago, IL 60649.

MEHRETEAB, GHEBRE-SELASSIE
Foundation program officer. **PERSONAL:** Born Jun 29, 1949, Asmara, Ethiopia;married Sarah Brill Jones. **EDUCATION:** Haverford Coll, BA 1972. **CAREER:** Health & Welfare Council, staff assoc 1972-73; East Mt Airy Neighbors, dir 1974-76; YMCA of Germantown, assoc dir 1976-78; New World Foundation, assoc dir 1978-81; The Ford Foundation, program officer 1981-. **ORGANIZATIONS:** Dir Assoc of Black Foundation Execs Inc 1980-86, NY Regional Assoc of Grantmakers 1980-86; mem Columbia Univ Seminar on Philanthropy 1985-. **HONORS/ACHIEVEMENTS:** Citation Senate of Pennsylvania 1979; Key to the City Savannah GA 1987.

MEIER, AUGUST
Educator. **PERSONAL:** Born Apr 30, 1923, New York City, NY. **EDUCATION:** Oberlin Coll, AB 1945; Colubia, AM 1949, PhD 1957. **CAREER:** Tougaloo Coll, asst prof history 1945-49; Fisk U, rsrch asst to pres 1953, asst prof history 1953-56; Morgan State Coll, asst asso prof history 1957-64; Roosevelt U, prof history 1964-67; Kent Coll State U, prof history 1967-69;Univ Prof. **ORGANIZATIONS:** Sec Newark Br NAACP 1951-52, 56-57; chmn Balt Chap Ams for Dem Action 1960-61; mem Nat Bd Exec Com 1960-61; active Newark Chap CORE 1963-64; Balt Chap SNCC 1960-63; mem Am So Hist Assns; Assn Study Negro Life & History Orgn Am Historians; Am Studies Assn; Am Anthrop Assn; Unitarian; Gen Ed Atheneum Pubs for Negro in Am Life Series 1966-;Univ IL Press for Blacks in the New World Series 1972-. **HONORS/ACHIEVEMENTS:** Author- Negro Thought in Am 1880-1915, 1963; From Plantation to Ghetto 2nd Ed 1970 W/Elliott Rudwick; CORE a studey in the civil rights movement 1942-68, 1973; editor W/Francis Broderick Negro Protest Thought in the 20th Cent 1966; others; recip adv grad fellow Am Counc Learned Socs 1952; Guggenheim Fellow 1971-72. **BUSINESS ADDRESS:** 122 N Prospect St, Kent, OH 44240.

MELANCON, DONALD
Educator. **PERSONAL:** Born Nov 12, 1939, Franklin, LA; married Hortense Ferguson; children: Douglas Louis, Girard James. **EDUCATION:** So U, BS 1963;Univ IL, MEd 1971, PhD 1976. **CAREER:** Kankakee Sch Dist, elem sch prin 1973-, cent off adminstr 1971-72, sch psychol couns 1970; St Anne HS, tchr 1964-70; MO, tchr 1963; Nympum Mini-bike Prgm YMCA, consult 1972; Pembroke Consol Sch Dist, 1972; Opport Ind Ctr, 1972; Kankakee Boys Camp, 1972; Uof IL, lab trainer 1972; Ofc of Edn,1979; Union Grad Sch, 1979; St Ann Sch Bd of Educ 1976. **ORGANIZATIONS:** Bd of dir Kankakee Drug Abuse; Old Fair Pk Day Care; Kankakee Cult Prgm; YMCA Exten Dept; Cub Sct Mstr; Appt by Gov of IL Reg Manpwr Comm for CETA; mem NEA; IL Educ Assn; Humanist Assn; Sch Bd Assn of IL; Kankakee Co Adminstr Assn. **HONORS/ACHIEVEMENTS:** Sel Phi Delta Kappa-Hon Soc in Edn; Bicent Declar for Serv to Cub Sct 1976; Ebony Esteem Aw 1976; Men of prgss Outst Educator Award 1978; publ articles "As Stud See Things" IL Educ Assn Jour 1969; "Staff Dev on a Shoestring" IL Princ Journl 1973; "A System Apprch to Tension Monit & Tension Reduct in an Educ Setting" Journl of Rsrch in Educ 1973; "Model for Sch Commun Relat" Phi Delta Kappan 1974. **BUSINESS ADDRESS:** Principal, Kankakee School District, Warren Ave, Kankakee, IL 60901.

MELANCON, NORMAN
Educator. **PERSONAL:** Born Nov 06, 1939, Paincourtville, LA; married Joyce Carr; children: Norman Jr, Latisha, Marlon. **EDUCATION:** Dillard Univ, BA 1962; Nicholls State, MEd 1969; Loyola Univ, MSc 1972. **CAREER:** Assumption Parish, asst principal 1964-85; Ward 6, police juror 1976-85; Belrose Middle School, asst principal. **ORGANIZATIONS:** 4-H Club sponsor; Boy Scout coordinator. **BUSINESS ADDRESS:** Assistant Principal, Belle Rosese Middle School, PO Box 518, Belle Rose, LA 70390.

MELLETTE, DAVID C.
Business executive. **PERSONAL:** Born Dec 08, 1909, Sumter, SC; married Mary Way; children: Willie Wright, Gertrude M Ledbetter. **CAREER:** Comm Funeral Home, pres/owner 1950-. **ORGANIZATIONS:** Mem SC Mortician Assn; mem Dist 2 SC Mortician Assn; mem Natl Funeral Dir & Mortician Assn; masonic Corinthians Lodge #200; shriner YMCA of Sumter; mem Joint Stock of SC; mem Odd Fellows; chmn deacon bd Mt Zion Baptist Church; bd mem Sumter Sch Dist #17 1971-83. **HONORS/ACHIEVEMENTS:** Awd for Outstanding Service to Sumter Co Career Ctr; Awd for Dedicated Serv to Sumter Sch Dist #17. **HOME ADDRESS:** 9 West Williams St, Sumter, SC 29150. **BUSINESS ADDRESS:** Funeral Dir, Community Funeral Home, 353 Manning Ave, Sumter, SC 29150.

MELROSE, THOMAS S.
Electrical engineer/instructor. **PERSONAL:** Born Nov 23, 1922, Charleston, SC; son of Samuel Melrose and Lucy Melrose; married Shirley Chambers; children: Cassaundra T, Zhukov R, Thomas K. **EDUCATION:** Howard Univ School of Engineering, BSEE 1952. **CAREER:** Tennessee Valley Auth, elec design engr 1952-56; USAF Aeronautical Sys Div, lead proj engr instrument & visual flight simulators 1956-79; Sinclair Comm Coll, instructor engrg techn 1981-85 retired. **ORGANIZATIONS:** Assoc mem Inst of Elec & Electron Engrs; mem Tau Beta Pi Engrg Hon Soc; mem NAACP; bd mem & 1976 Layman of the Yr Dayton Fifth St YMCA; chmn Kettering Bd of Com Relations; past club pres & 1970 Copenhagen delegate Intl Assn of Y's Men; founder & past pres Carillon Civic Cncl; Scholarship Com chmn & chap ed Omega Psi Phi Frat; treas Sr Choir Bethel Baptist Ch; vice pres Howard Univ Alumni Club of Greater Dayton; trreasurer, Bethel Baptist Federal Credit Union. **HONORS/ACHIEVEMENTS:** Math Tutor with Distinguished Serv Award Dayton Public Schools VIPS Program 1980-84. **MILITARY SERVICE:** AUS WWII; Cited for Outstanding Performances with Simulators.

MELTON, FRANK E.
President/general manager. **EDUCATION:** Stephen F Austin State Univ TX, BS Educ. **CAREER:** TX Dept of Mental Health & Mental Retardation, 1969-74; Angelina Coll Lufkin TX, part-time teacher 1974-85; KTRE-TV Lufkin, weekend news anchor 1974; KLTV-TVTyler TX, exec vice pres and general mgr 1976-81; WLBT-TV Jackson MS, president/general manager 1984-. **ORGANIZATIONS:** Former pres broadcast div Buford TV Inc Tyler; apptd by Gov Mark White to TX Bd of Mental Health & Mental Retardation 1985.

MELTON, FRANK LEROY (GLOBE)
Clergyman, international representative. **PERSONAL:** Born May 26, 1921, Sumter, SC; married Gertrude Eleanor Van Dunk; children: Lawana Francine Mc Gee. **EDUCATION:** Rutgers; New York City Coll; PA State; 1950-70. **CAREER:** Interchem Corp Inmont Corp, union local reg sec 1956-73; New AME Zion & Wm Chapel AME Zion Ch, pastor's asst 1955-58; Mt Olive AME Zion Ch, pastor 1958-62; St Mark AME Zion Church, rev 1962-; Oil Chem & Atomic Workers Intl Union, intl rep 1973-80; Williams Chapel AME Zion Ch Passaic NJ, pastor 1980-. **ORGANIZATIONS:** Mem NAACP Paterson Br 1950-80; bd mem Paterson CETA & Paterson P/C 1979; mem Inter-faith Westwood NJ 1979; coord of Safety Paterson Rotary; mem Passaic& Vicinity Minster Fellowship; pres North Jersey Ministerial Alliance. **HONORS/ACHIEVEMENTS:** Plaque Labor Studies Seminar 1972; plaque 17 yrs of serv St Mark AME Zion Ch 1978; plaque OCAWIU Local 8-417. **MILITARY SERVICE:** USAF pfc 1945-47. **BUSINESS ADDRESS:** International Representative, Oil Chemical & Atomic Workers, 1155 W Chestnut St, Ste 1-A, Union, NJ 07083.

MELTON, HARRY S.
Judge. **PERSONAL:** Born Apr 18, 1915, Phila; married Dorothy; children: 2 Children. **EDUCATION:** Pioneer Bus Inst, 1950; Temple U, 1969. **CAREER:** Ins Broker, 10 Yrs; Commwlth PA, reg dir liquor audits 8 yr; Mun Ct Commwlth PA, ret judge. **ORGANIZATIONS:** Fin sec Ch of Redeemer 3 yrs; treas Ch of Redeemer 3 yrs; chmn bd trustees Ch of Redeemer. **MILITARY SERVICE:** Staff sgt 1943-45. **BUSINESS ADDRESS:** 1001 #1 E Penn Sq Bldg, Philadelphia, PA 19107.

MELVIN, HAROLD JAMES
Musician. **PERSONAL:** Born Jun 24, 1939, Philadelphia, PA; married Ovelia McDaniels; children: Trudy, Derrick, Garnell, Blondell, Harold, II. **CAREER:** Harold Melvin & The Blue Notes (Philadelphia Oldest Recording Grp), recording artist; Million Dollar Mangt Millioin Dollar Records, chenographer publ rec prod mngr & owner; ABC Record, recor prod. **ORGANIZATIONS:** Mem AFTRA. **HONORS/ACHIEVEMENTS:** 10 gold rec; Image award NAACP; spec achvmt 1973; Grammy Award; num hon citz awards; Citation "More

Than 20 Yrs of Musical Genius" Philadelphia Mayor; signed with Source Records "The Blue Album" 1979. **BUSINESS ADDRESS:** 1317 Filbert St, Philadelphia, PA 19107.

MENCER, ERNEST JAMES
General surgeon. **PERSONAL:** Born Apr 24, 1945, Baton Rouge, LA; son of George E Mencer, Jr and Mandra E Mencer; married Thomasine Haskins; children: Melanie Lynn, Marcus Kinnard. **EDUCATION:** Morehouse Coll, BS 1967; Meharry Medical Coll, MD 1972. **CAREER:** Our Lady of the Lake Regional Medical Ctr, chief of surgery 1983; Earl K Long Hosp LSU Medical Sch, asst prof of surgery 1984-; Baton Rouge General Medical Ctr, vice chief of surgery 1985-; Private Practice, general surgeon. **ORGANIZATIONS:** Diplomate Amer Bd of Surgery 1983; bd of dirs Baton Rouge Genl Medical Ctr 1984-; fellow Amer Coll of Surgeons 1985; bd of dirs East Baton Rouge Parish Amer Cancer Soc 1985-. **BUSINESS ADDRESS:** Physician, 5120 Dijon Dr Ste 100, Baton Rouge, LA 70808.

MENDENHALL, JOHN RUFUS
Athlete. **PERSONAL:** Born Dec 03, 1948, Cullen, LA. **EDUCATION:** Grambling Coll. **CAREER:** Green Bay Packers, professional football player 1980-; NY Giants, ftbll plyr 1972-80. **BUSINESS ADDRESS:** Green Bay Packers, 1265 Lombardi Ave, Green Bay, WI 54303.

MENDES, HELEN ALTHIA
Educator. **PERSONAL:** Born May 20, 1935, New York City, NY; daughter of Arthur Davenport and Louise Davenport; married Gregory R Love; children: Sheila, Leon. **EDUCATION:** Queens Coll, BA 1957; Columbia Univ, MSW 1964; UCLA, DSW 1975; Fuller Theological Seminary 1987-. **CAREER:** Big Brothers Res Treatment Center, acting dir 1967-69; Albert Einstein Coll Med, mental health consultant 1969; Hunter Coll School Soc Work, lecture 1970-72 ; UCLA, assoc 1972-75; Univ of Southern California, assoc prof 1975-86; Mendes Consultation Serv, founder, pres, 1976-. **ORGANIZATIONS:** Distrib Success Motivation Inst 1985-89; bd dir Jenesse Center Inc 1985-86; alternate Private Indus Cncl LA 1984-; chairperson Pastor Parish Rels Comm Wilshire Hm Church 1981-87; mem Natl Asso Black Soc Workrers; mem Black Womens Network; mem bd of dir House of Ruth 1985-; vice pres Professional Dev NASW CA 1986-88; 1st vice pres NASW, California 1988-. **HONORS/ACHIEVEMENTS:** Outstanding Educ Zeta Phi Beta Sor Altadena Pasadena Chap 1985; published book, The Africian Heritage Cookbook MacMillan Publishers Professional Journals 1971; publ articles on Single Parent Families, Religion/Therapy, Black Families 1976-; Outstanding Serv Award LA Comm Coll 1974; mem Acad Certified Soc Workers Natl Assn of Soc Workers; licensed clinical social worker, California; Bd Certified Diplomate. **HOME ADDRESS:** 5809 Vicstone Ct, Culver City, CA 90232. **BUSINESS ADDRESS:** President, Mendes Consultation Services, 3660 Wilshire Blvd, Suite 628, Los Angeles, CA 90010.

MENDEZ, HUGH B.
Educator, coach. **PERSONAL:** Born Dec 16, 1933, E Orange, NJ; married Dorothy L; children: Robert Hugh. **EDUCATION:** Springfield Coll, BS 1958; Whittier Coll, MEd 1975; Newark State Coll, Postgrad; Montclair State Coll; CA State Coll; UCLA. **CAREER:** Whittier Coll CA, instr afro-Am history & varsity bsbll coach; Long Beach, tchr bsbll coach 1968-70; Long Branch NJ, supvr elem phys educ 1960-66; Milwaukee Braves Bsbll Assn 1958-60. **ORGANIZATIONS:** Capt Springfield Coll Bsbll Team 1958. **HONORS/ACHIEVEMENTS:** Led NCAA in stolen bases; signed bonus contract with Milwaukee Braves 1958; 1st black coach maj sport Whittier Coll. **MILITARY SERVICE:** USN. **BUSINESS ADDRESS:** Whittier Coll, Whittier, CA 90608.

MENEWEATHER, EARL W.
Educator. **PERSONAL:** Born Sep 12, 1917, Marshall, TX; married Sarah E Thomas; children: Patricia, Earl, II, Leslie. **EDUCATION:** San Fran St, Adminstrv Degree 1967, MA 1965; Humboldt St U, BA 1941. **CAREER:** Univ Ombudsman Humboldt St U, spl asst to pres 1971-; Ravenswood HS E Palo Alto, prin 1968-71; Peralta Jr Coll Dist, asst dean of stdnt prsnl serv 1968; Madison Jr HS, prin 1967-68; Lowell Jr HS, dept chmn tchr 1955-57; McClymonds HS Oakland, tchr head coach 1957-66; Kaiser Shipyard, foreman 1944. **ORGANIZATIONS:** Dir & coord VIP's Oakland Raider Professional Ftbll Club 1960-; pofl ftbll plyr Oakland Giants & San Fran Bay Packers 1943-44; past mem Urban Rehab Proj Oakland CA; bd mem YMCA; Scattered Housing Com Oakland; City Info Counc for E Palo Alto; El Cerrito Rec Commn; St Dept of Educ Commn; CA Tchr Assn Plng Commn for Currclm Svc; mem Alpha Phi Alpha; CA Coll &Univ Prof Assn; CA Scndry Adminstrn Assn; United Prof Assn; Ombudsman Caucus of CA; Coll &Univ Prsnl Assn; mem Actin Com Humboldt St U; consult Minority Afrs Com Humboldt; chmn Afrmtv Action Com;Univ Prof Assn; consult Minority Recruit & Hiring Atomic Enrgy Comm Livermore & Berkeley 1967; chmn Mnrty Outrch Prgm; mgr dir Boys Clubs of Am Oakland 1945-55; del Luth Chs of Am 1967; dir Adminstrn Seirra Bckpck Prgm Luth Ch 1971; dir Summer Wrkshp Sequoia Union Sch Dist 1970; orgntr consult adv Blk Educ Corp Stanford 1970; mem Humboldt Co Hum Right Comm 1971; Ethinic Task Force Consult CA StUniv Humboldt. **HONORS/ACHIEVEMENTS:** 1st blk dept chmn phys educ No CA HS 1963; 1st Blk HS Prin Sequoia Union HS Dist 1968; 1st blk Adminstr CA StUniv 1971; 1st Athl Hall of Fame mem Humboldt StUniv 1955; author num publs on minority & educ subjects. **MILITARY SERVICE:** AUS 1st sgt 1942-45; Reserve 1945-50; Korean War 1950-51.

MERCER, ARTHUR, SR.
Retired chief master sergeant USAF. **PERSONAL:** Born Mar 31, 1921, Pachuta, MS; married Mildred Pugh; children: Arthur II, Lillian A, Lori A. **EDUCATION:** Attended, Laramie County Community Coll 2 yrs. **CAREER:** WY Private Industry Council, mem 1984-1989; US Army, 1942-47; USAF, 1947-74; Life/Hosp/Investment Ins, retired salesman 1974-85. **ORGANIZATIONS:** Pres Exchange Club of Cheyenne 1976-1977; mem bd of dir Laramie County United Way 1976-82; commander Amer Legion Carter Brown Post #83 1976,77; life mem NCOA 1977; life member Air Force Association 1978; life member Retired Enlisted Association 1985; member Air Force Sergeant Association 1985; member Cheyenne Rotary Club 1987; clerk Laramie County Sch Dist #1 Bd of Trustees 1978-85; re-elected to Laramie County School Dist #1 board of trustees for 4 yr term 1988- treasurer Laramie County School Dist #1 1988- mem Amer Legion Post #6 1979-; bd of dir, mem WY School Bd Assoc 1980-82; pres Rocky Mountain Dist Exchange Clubs 1981-82; 2nd vice pres WY School Bd Assoc 1983; 1st vice pres WY School Bd Assoc 1984; gov apptd mem WY Community Coll Commn 1984-89; pres WY School Bd Assoc 1985-8-87; mem Natl School Bds Assoc Resolutions & Policy Comm 1985; mem NSBA Delegate Assembly 1985,86. **MILITARY SERVICE:** USAF chief master sgt 31 yrs; UN Serv Medal; Korean Serv Medal w/1 Bronze Star; AFGCM w/2 OLC; AFGCM w/1 Bronze OLC; AFGCM w/1 Silver Cluster; AF Commendation Medal; AF Missileman Badge; APTO Medal; Army Good Conduct Medal; World War II Victory Medal; New Guinea Campaign Medal. **HOME ADDRESS:** 5131 Syracuse Rd, Cheyenne, WY 82009.

MERCER, WILLIAM A.
Business executive. **PERSONAL:** Born Feb 10, 1927, Metter, GA; married Elizabeth J Eggleston. **EDUCATION:** NY U, BS Journ 1955. **CAREER:** Mercermedia Inc Wash, pres; Black Viewpoint Publ, publshr; Minority Exec Matchmakers Inc, oper 1972-73; Newark Cable TV Inc, pres 1970-72; Broad NatBank Newark NJ, 1st black natl dir 1970-76; MEDIC Ent Inc, fdr dir 1968-72; 1 of 3 Div of Nat Urban Coalition Wash DC, dep dir communications 1968-70; Newark's ECO Devel Corp, chmn bd 1970-72. **ORGANIZATIONS:** Accredited mem Pub Relat Soc of Am 1960; MERCERMEDIA; mem PRSAs Couns Sec 1971-; adv bd mem Broad Nat Bank 1967-70; mem Nat Press Club 1974; Capitol Press Club 1969-; dir Travelers Aid Soc Nat Capital Area 1972-78; vice chmn Pub Relat United Way of Metro Wash 1973-74; commun & campaign coord Kenneth A Gibson Newark Mayoral Campaigns 1966 & 70, adv 1974; mem exec com Counc of Soc Agys of Essex & W Hudson Cos NJ 1968, 69; mem adv com Charles Engelhard Found 1967-71; mem Nat YMCAs Assn Press 1963-73; asst advertising mgr NJ Afro-Am Newspaper Newark 1956-57; asso pub relat dir Greater Newark United Way 1958-62; 1st black exec staffer United Way of Am NY 1963-64; com relations dir & coord of bus & industrial coord counc Greater Newark Area United Way 1964-68; full-time exec dir BICC 1966. **HONORS/ACHIEVEMENTS:** AUS sgt 1950-52. **BUSINESS ADDRESS:** PO Box 56311, Washington, DC 20011.

MERCHANT, JOHN F.
Attorney. **PERSONAL:** Born Feb 02, 1933, Greenwich, CT; son of Garrett M Merchant and Essie Nowlin Merchant; divorced; children: Susan Beth. **EDUCATION:** VA Union U, BA 1955; Univ of VA, LLB 1958. **CAREER:** CT, atty 1962-; ABCD Inc, dep dir 1965-67; State Dept Community Affairs, dep commr 1967-71; legislative lobbyist; Fairfield U, visiting lecturer 1970-75; Gen Elec Corp & Candeub Fleissig Assoc, consultant; Peoples Bank, dir, mem loan & Trust Committees 1969-. **ORGANIZATIONS:** Trustee of Peoples Bank & Univ of Bridgeport; partner Merchant & Rosenblum Attorneys At Law; mem Doric Lodge #4 F&AM; NAACP & other civic activities; pres Child Guidance Clinic; dir Regional Plan Assoc; pres Hartcom Inc; chmn Comm Council on Human Rights 1964-65; pres Brideport Area Mental Health Assn 1968; dir Bridgeport Hosp 1968-79; dir, Child Welfare League of America, chmn, Public Policy committee, 1986-. **HONORS/ACHIEVEMENTS:** 1st black grad, Univ VA law sch; Citizen of the Year, Omega Psi Phi 1983; Community Service Award, Sacred Heart Univ 1982. **MILITARY SERVICE:** USN lt comdr 1958-61. **HOME ADDRESS:** 480 Riders Ln, Fairfield, CT 06430. **BUSINESS ADDRESS:** Partner, Merchant & Rosenblum, 25 Bank St, P O Box 15430, Stamford, CT 06901-0430.

MERCY, LELAND, JR.
Educator. **PERSONAL:** Born Nov 01, 1942, Jacksonville, FL; married Dorothy McClellan; children: Michael, Leanne. **EDUCATION:** Univ of MD, Attnd 1964-65; Boise St U, BBA 1971. **CAREER:** Boise State U, dir of affirmative action/Exec asst to pres 1981; (Usaf, staff sgt 1961-69. **ORGANIZATIONS:** Pres ID Assn for Collegioat & Registars & Admissions Ofcrs; dir C of C of Boise; mem cmn Sped Student Srevs Com 1973-74; cmn Boise StUniv Affirmative Action Com 1974-75; cmn Boise StUniv Registration Task Force; mem Pacific Assn of Collegiate Registars & Admissions Ofcrs; v cmn Ada Cnty Planning Commn; Am Assn of Collegiate Registars & Admissions Ofcrs; v chmn & charter mem bd of dir Opptys Indsln Ctrs of Am of ID Fdr Salt & Pepper Soul radio prog KBBK; Webelo ldr BSA Boise; guest lectr Boise St U; guest spkr at num civic orgns. **HONORS/ACHIEVEMENTS:** Who's Who in Am Coll &Univ 1971; Outst Mktng Student Sales & Mktng Exec 1971; Speaking of People Ebony Mag 1974. **MILITARY SERVICE:** USAF staff sgt 1961-69. **BUSINESS ADDRESS:** Salt & Pepper Enterprise, 2710 W Sunrise Run Rd, Boise, ID 83705.

MEREDAY, RICHARD F.
Government employee. **PERSONAL:** Born Dec 18, 1929, Hempstead, NY; married Emma; children: Philip, Richard, Meta. **EDUCATION:** Hofstra U, BA 1951; licensed NY Ins Broker 1961; Brooklyn Law Sch, LLB 1958. **CAREER:** Ofc of Manpower Programs, coordinator of educ serv nassau co govt 1975-; Nassau Co Bur of Career Planning & Devel Dep of Gen Svcs, former dir 1971-75; Town of Hempstead Dept of Pub Works, adminstr 1965-70; probation officer supr 1964-65; Charles M Meredary Trucking Corp, vp; Tri-County Trucker Owners Assn, sec-scribe 1956-63; Nassau Co Met Regiona Council TV classes, speaker. **ORGANIZATIONS:** Rep exec Town Leader; former vp, Uptopia Comm Covoc Assn; past chmn Roosevelt United Fund; former institutional rep Nat Boy Scouts Counsils; past pres Lions Club; adv bd Salvation Army. **HONORS/ACHIEVEMENTS:** Recip good neighbor award Nassau Co Press Assn 1973; active participant Rep Leadership Conf 1975; plaque Unselfish Serv to Comm of Roosevelt 1969; recognition certificate Dist 20 K-2 Lions Intl 1973. **MILITARY SERVICE:** USN med corps 1951-53. **BUSINESS ADDRESS:** 33 Willis Ave, Mineola, NY 11501.

MEREDITH, JAMES HOWARD
Financial planner. **PERSONAL:** Born Jun 25, 1933, Kosciusko, MS; married Judy Alsobrooks; children: John Howard, Joseph Howard, James Henry, Kip Naylor, Jessica Howard. **EDUCATION:** Jackson State Univ, B 1962; Univ of MS, BA 1963; Ibadan Univ Nigeria, Certificate 1965; Columbia Univ Law Sch, JD 1968. **CAREER:** Meredith Enterprises, pres 1968-. **MILITARY SERVICE:** USAF s/sgt 1951-60. **BUSINESS ADDRESS:** President, Meredith Enterprises, PO Box 19385, Cincinnati, OH 45219.

MERENIVITCH, JARROW
Manager. **PERSONAL:** Born Jun 01, 1942, Alexandria, LA; married Hazel R Wilmer; children: Jarrow Jr, Marion, Jonathan. **EDUCATION:** Grambling State Univ, BA 1964; Inst for Applied Mgmt & Law, Certificate 1985. **CAREER:** Procter & Gamble Co, team mgr 1969-72, Albany GA plant personnel relations mgr 1972-75, Cincinnati corporate personnel develop consultant 1975-78, employee/employer relations mgr 1978-80, personnel mgr 1980-83, mgr industrial relations 1983-85, food mfg div human resources mgr 1985-. **ORGANIZATIONS:** Vice pres Grambling Univ Alumni 1986; mem Omega Psi Phi Frat; mem NAACP. **HONORS/ACHIEVEMENTS:** Outstanding Serv to Eta Omicron Chap Psi Phi Omega 1975; publication "Toward a Multicultural Organization," 1979; Citation Outstanding Contribution to Procter & Gamble Beverage Div 1984. **MILITARY SERVICE:** USAF

staff sgt 1964-68. **HOME ADDRESS:** 1817 Forester Dr, Cincinnati, OH 45240. **BUSINESS ADDRESS:** Human Resources Manager, Proctor & Gamble, Food Mfg Division, 5299 Spring Grove, Cincinnati, OH 45217.

MERIDETH, CHARLES WAYMOND
Educator. **PERSONAL:** Born Nov 02, 1940, Atlanta, GA; married Rebecca Little; children: Kelli, Cheryl. **EDUCATION:** Univ CA Berkeley, PhD 1965; Norehouse Coll, BS 1961;Univ IL, post doctoral 1956-66. **CAREER:** AtlantaUniv Cen, provost 1976-; AtlantaUniv Cen, dir of engineering 1969; Morehouse Coll, prof 1965. **ORGANIZATIONS:** Mem Phi Beta Kappa; Soc of the Sigma Xi; Beta Kappa Chi Sci Soc; Am Chem Soc; Am Physical Soc; Am Assn for the Advancement of Sci; NY Acad of Sci; bd of dir Blayton Bus Coll 1971. **HONORS/ACHIEVEMENTS:** Woodrow Wilson Nat Fello 1961; Charles E Merrill Early Admission Schlrshp Magna Cum Laude 1961; appointment Danforth Faculty Asso 167; Fresman Achievement Award in Chem 1957; one of 10 outstanding young people of atlanta TOYPA 1956. **BUSINESS ADDRESS:** Westview 360 Dr SW, Atlanta, GA 30310.

MERIWEATHER, JOE C.
Professional athlete. **PERSONAL:** Born Oct 26, 1953, Phenix City, AL; married Gail Ross. **EDUCATION:** Southern IL, BS Hlth Educ 1975. **CAREER:** Houston, 1975-76; Atlanta, 1976-77; NO, 1977-79; New York, 1979-80; Kansas City Kings, 1981-. **ORGANIZATIONS:** Bd Pro Bsktbl Flwshp Conf; works with youth groups Paseo Bapt Ch. **HONORS/ACHIEVEMENTS:** 16th in Nation in 1975 on all-time NCAA field goal accuracy charts; first round draft Houston 1975; 3rd in Nation as sr hitting 619 from the field; Southern IL Univ Bsktbl Hall of Fame.

MERIWEATHER, MELVIN, JR.
Elected official. **PERSONAL:** Born Oct 22, 1937, Hernando, MS; son of Melvin Meriweather and Virgie Meriweather; married Juliet Ilene Thomas; children: Kristel, Douglas, Dana. **EDUCATION:** Isaac E Elston, grad 12th 1957. **CAREER:** Eastport Improvement Assn, pres 1971-73; Michigan City PTA Council, pres 1974-75; Riley School PTA, pres 1968-79; N Central Comm Action Aency, pres 1979-84; Michigan City School Bd, pres; Michigan City Area School, bd pres 1987-88; sec 1988-89; Midwest Steel, Portage IN, crew coordinator 1989. **ORGANIZATIONS:** Treas and deacon New Hope Baptist Church 1963-85; parents adv bd Rogers HS 1978-79; hlth & safety chmn 1980-82, 2nd vice pres 1982-84 IN Congress of Parents & Teachers; mem Daniel C Slocum Mem Found 1982-85; vol fireman Fire Brigade Midwest Steel 1970-85; IN Dept of Education "Parent/Community Involvement" task force. **HONORS/ACHIEVEMENTS:** Mr Indiana IN AAU Amateur Bodybuilding 1966; Mr Most Muscular AAU Mid States Competition 1966; state life member IN Congress of PTA 1974; vice pres MI City Area School Bd 1982-86; School Board Pres 1986-87; IN Dept of Education certificate of merit. **HOME ADDRESS:** 616 Monroe St, Michigan City, IN 46360.

MERIWETHER, LOUISE
Author. **PERSONAL:** Born May 08, 1923, Haverstraw, NY. **EDUCATION:** NY Univ, BA; UCLA, MS. **CAREER:** Freelance writer; newspaper reporter LA Sentinel; Universal Studios, 1st black story analyst; Sarah Lawrence Coll, writing teacher. **ORGANIZATIONS:** Org Black Concern. **HONORS/ACHIEVEMENTS:** Author, Daddy Was A Number Runner 1970, The Freedom Ship of Robert Smalls 1971, The Heart Man, The Story of Daniel Hale Williams 1972, Don't Take the Bus on Monday, The Rosa Parks Story 1973, A Happening in Barbados, That Girl From Creektown 1972, The Tick End Is For Whipping 1968, James Baldwin, The Fiery Voice of the Negro Revolt 1963, No Race Pride 1964, The Negro Half a Man in a White World 1965, The New Face of Negro History 1965, The Black Family in Crisis, Teenage Pregnancy 1984. **BUSINESS ADDRESS:** Writing Teacher, C/O Janet Held, Faculty Secretary, Sarah Laurence College, Bronxville, NY 10708.

MERIWETHER, ROY DENNIS
Pianist/producer/arranger. **PERSONAL:** Born Feb 24, 1943, Dayton, OH; children: Tammi, Cyd. **CAREER:** Howard Roberts Chorale & Dayton Contempory Dance Co w/the Roy Meriwether Trio, composer arranger Black Snow 1976; Dayton Philharmonic Orchestra, guest artist 1980; Thomas A Edison State Coll, composer lyricist for college alma mater 1984; Gemini Records, producer arranger composer & recording artist 1985; Columbia-Capitol-Gambit-Stinger Recording Companies, pianist composer & recording artist 1960-. **ORGANIZATIONS:** Benefit performance of Black Snow for Wilburforce Univ & Central State Univ 1976; mem Amer Federation of Musicians Local 802 1960-; mem ASCAP 1960-. **HONORS/ACHIEVEMENTS:** Grant recipient Natl Endowment for the Arts 1974; proclamation to honor Black Snow Mayor City of Dayton OH 1976; Significant Achievement Awd Black Snow Powell & Assocs 1976; Outstanding Jazz Instrumentalist Manhattan Association of Cabarets 1987. **HOME ADDRESS:** 7 W 87th St, #4D, New York, NY 10024.

MERRICK-FAIRWEATHER, NORMA See SKLAREK, NORMA MERRICK

MERRITT, ANTHONY LEWIS
Automotive company executive. **PERSONAL:** Born Sep 15, 1940, New Haven, CT; married Ann Sarver; children: Eric, Heather. **EDUCATION:** Dodge City Jr Coll, AA 1958; Westminister Coll, BS 1964; Univ of UT, MBA 1966; Univ of Detroit, Post MBA 1968-70. **CAREER:** Pomona Unified School Dist, biology & business teacher 1966-67; Ford Motor Co, numerous mgmt assignments 1968-77, reg sales plnng & distribution 1977-78, gen field mgr 1978-81; Toyota Motor Sales USA, natl merchandising mgr 1981-. **HONORS/ACHIEVEMENTS:** Special recognition for group for exceeding assigned task United Way Coordinator Ford Motor Co 1972-73. **MILITARY SERVICE:** AUS pfc 1961-63. **HOME ADDRESS:** 24501 Mandeville Dr, Laguna Hills, CA 92653. **BUSINESS ADDRESS:** General Manager, Toyota Motor Distributors Inc, 2451 Bishop Drive, San Ramon, CA 94583.

MERRITT, BISHETTA DIONNE
Educator. **PERSONAL:** Born Dec 15, 1947, Greensboro, NC; married Owen Lee. **EDUCATION:** Fisk Univ, Nashville TN, BA 1970; Ohio State Univ Columbus, MA 1972; Ohio State Univ, Columbus OH, PhD 1974. **CAREER:** Shaw Univ, assoc prof 1980-; Univ of North Carolina, asst prof 1974-80; Ohio State Univ, grad assoc 1972-73. **ORGANIZATIONS:** Adv bd, WTVD-TV Channel 11, 1976; mem, Congressional Black Caucus Brain Trust on Communications, 1977; mem, Southern Coalition for Responsive Media 1978; mem, NAEB, 1980; mem, Delta Sigma Theta Sorority Inc, 1967; mem, The Links Inc, 1975; pres, Danville VA Chap, The Links Inc, 1977-79; mem, Southeastern Black Press Inst, 1978; mem, North Carolina Central Univ Mus Bd, 1979. **HONORS/ACHIEVEMENTS:** Graduate School Leadership Award, 1974; Motor Bd Honor Soc, 1975; published booklet, Stony the Way We Trod, 1976; received research grants from the Univ of North Carolina, 1976. **BUSINESS ADDRESS:** Shaw Univ, 118 E South St, Raleigh, NC 27602.

MERRITT, FRANK C.
Commissioner, educator. **PERSONAL:** Born Mar 31, 1906, Marianna, FL; widowed; children: Frank. **EDUCATION:** FL A&M Coll, BS 1930, MA 1958. **CAREER:** Gilmore Acad, tchr 1930-34; Greenville Training Sch, prin 1934-69; City of Madison, commnr. **ORGANIZATIONS:** Mem Mt Zion AME Ch; 3rd Jud Circuit Nom Commn FL Bar; bd dir Greater Madison Co C of C; mem Bd State Manpower Prog; Sr Citz Adv Comm; MadisonCo Voters Leg; Mens Civic & Soc Club; mem NAACP; Madison Cnty Rec Assn; pres Madison Cnty Chap FL A&m Alumni Assn; mem State & Cnty Retired Tchrs Assn. **HONORS/ACHIEVEMENTS:** Meritorious Serv FL Intersch Athletic Assn 1960; Outstanding Serv Edward Waters Coll 1962; Leadership State Dept of Educ 1963; Outstanding Serv Greenville Training Sch 1964; Man of the Yr Mt Zion AME Ch 1964; 35 Yr Serv Greenville Training Sch 1969; Appr Val Serv FL A&M Univ 1969; Cert of Merit FL Educ Assn 1969; Disting Serv FL St Dept of Educ 1969; Val Serv FL A&M Univ 1970; Cert 1974 Gubernat; elected Mayor City of Madison July 1978; 1st Black City Commr.

MERRITT, JOSEPH, JR.
Business executive. **PERSONAL:** Born May 24, 1934, Tunica, MS; divorced; children: Joseph, III. **CAREER:** Fillmore Taxi Svc, proprietor pres 1968-. **ORGANIZATIONS:** Black Men's Devel Found 1963; Buffalo Metro Bus Assn 1974; Buffalo C of C 1973; Better Bus Bur 1974; YMCA 1950; St John Bapt Ch 1961; NAACP 1963; Jefferson-Fillmore Revital Assn 1975; vice pres Dem Party 1976; apptd Civil Serv Commr Buffalo 1977; mem Local Devel Corp. **HONORS/ACHIEVEMENTS:** Black Achvmt Awd 1976. **BUSINESS ADDRESS:** Fillmore Taxi Service, 1000 E Ferry St, Buffalo, NY 14211.

MERRITT, LORENZO
Executive director. **PERSONAL:** Born Oct 25, 1931, New York, NY; divorced; children: Lori, Lisa, Kofi. **EDUCATION:** AdelphiUniv Garden City NY, BSW 1971; Adelphi U, MSE 1972; Adelphi U, DSE 1977. **CAREER:** Econ Opprtnty Commn, exec dir; Fam Serv Assn Hempstead NY, asst dir 1980. **ORGANIZATIONS:** Dir Comm Orgn Serv 1978; engr 15 yrs; founder Nas/Suf Chap ABSW 1972-76; mem LI Br Nat Blk Assembly 1972-; founder Afr Am Heritage Assn 1978-. **HONORS/ACHIEVEMENTS:** Social wrkr of the yr NASS/NASW 1972. **BUSINESS ADDRESS:** Economic Opportunity Commn, 106 Main St, Hempstead, NY 11590.

MERRITT, REUBEN ASA
Dentist, president retail trade. **PERSONAL:** Born Oct 06, 1928, Detroit, MI; married Esther Salome Green. **EDUCATION:** Western MI U, BS 1951;Univ Detroit, DDS 1958. **CAREER:** Detroit, dentist 1964-; Portsmouth, dentist 1961-64; Sci Tchr, 1951-54; William H Inc, pres 1974-. **ORGANIZATIONS:** Kappa Alpha Psi Frat 1950; mem Ch Choir 1950-; treas Sons of Abraham 1968-; pres Home Trste 1972-; pres Gen Ch Trste 1975-76; Sabbath Sch Supt 1974-; Prince Hall Mason 1970; pres Neophites 1971; Lodge Ahiff #21 32nd degree; Wolverine Consistory #6 1972. **HONORS/ACHIEVEMENTS:** Post grad fellow gen anestesia Wayne StUniv 1972. **BUSINESS ADDRESS:** 2923 E Seven Mile, Detroit, MI 48234.

MERRITT, THOMAS MACK
Insurance industry. **PERSONAL:** Born Jun 16, 1949, Homer, LA; son of Cordelus Merritt and Janelle Merritt; married Rosa M White; children: Kimberly R. **EDUCATION:** Grambling State Univ, BA 1971. **CAREER:** Liberty Mutual Ins, underwriter 1971-76, supervising underwriter 1976-78, asst mgr 1978-84, mgr large risks 1984-87, mgr reg risks 1987-; dist underwriting mgr 1988-. **ORGANIZATIONS:** Passed 9 of 10 exams leading to CPCU designation; founder 1st pres, Grambling State Univ Alumni Assoc of Metro Atlanta; mem Phi Beta Sigma. **HONORS/ACHIEVEMENTS:** Honoree Presidential Citation Natl Assoc for Equal Opportunity in Higher Ed 1983. **HOME ADDRESS:** 2924 Mesquite Dr, Carrollton, TX 75007. **BUSINESS ADDRESS:** Dist Underwriting Mgr, Liberty Mutual Insurance Co, Business Lines Underwriting, 2100 Walnut Hill Lane, Irving, TX 75038.

MERRITT, WILLETTE T.
Association executive. **PERSONAL:** Born in Reidsville, NC; married Dr Bishop (dec); children: Dr Bishetta D. **EDUCATION:** VA State Coll, BS 1935;Univ of NC, atnd; A&T State U;Univ of VA. **CAREER:** VA Polytechinic Inst & State U, extension agent home economist; Pittslvania Co VA VPI & SU Extension Div Blacksburg, extension agent; A&T State U, distsupvr 5 yrs; A&T U, subj matter specialist 2 yrs; Rockingham Co NC, extension agent 3 yrs; Reidsville NC, tchr pub sch 1935-37. **ORGANIZATIONS:** Mem Epsilon Sigma Phi Extension hon frat; Am AssnUniv Women; Am Home Economics Assn; pres Danville Chap Delta Sigma Theta Sor; organized Jack & Jill Inc; Danville Chap Links Inc; mem exec bd Mental Health Assn 1974-75; past mem exec bd Heart Assn 1973-74; past mem exec bd Cancer Assn 1973-74; past pres Wstrn Dist Home Economics Assn 1969; pres VA Home Economics Assn first black 1975; first vice pres Nat Assn of Extension 1974-75; deacon Holbrook St Presb Ch. **HONORS/ACHIEVEMENTS:** Recip Distin Serv Award 1968; Danville Woman of the Day 1975; first black first virginaina elected 1974-75 Nat ofcr of Nt Assn extension Home Economist. **BUSINESS ADDRESS:** PO Box 398, Chatham, VA 24531.

MERRITT-CUMMINGS, ANNETTE (ANNETTE MERRITT JONES)
Marketing, advertising, public relations executive. **PERSONAL:** Born May 14, 1946, Grady, AL; daughter of Henry W Merritt and Virgie Mathews Dowdell; married Iran Cummings, Aug 31, 1985; children: Michael O Jones, Angela J Jones. **EDUCATION:** Cleveland State Univ, BA, 1977; Cuyahoga Community Coll, AA, 1975. **CAREER:** EI DuPont de Numours, Wilmington DE; Occidental Petroleum, Madison Hts MI, sr sales rep, 1979-81; Publisher's Rep, Detroit MI, independent contractor, 1981-82; NW Ayer Inc, Detroit MI, sr acct exec, 1982-88; Natl Board for Prof Teaching, Detroit MI, dir of devel & marketing, 1988-. **ORGANIZATIONS:** Mem, Adcraft Club of Detroit, 1985-; mem, Literacy Volunteers of America, 1986-; Communications Committee Business/Education Alliance, Detroit Chamber of Commerce, 1987-; mem, Women's Economic Club of Detroit, 1987-; mem, Natl Society of Fund-Raising Executives, 1988-; mem, Detroit Rotary Club Intl, 1989-. **HON-**

ORS/ACHIEVEMENTS: Magna Cum Laude, Cleveland State Univ, 1977. **BUSINESS ADDRESS:** Director of Development & Marketing, Natl Board for Professional Teaching Standards, 333 W Fort St, Suite 2070, Detroit, MI 48226.

MERRIWEATHER, BARBARA CHRISTINE
Educator. **PERSONAL:** Born May 11, 1948, Philadelphia, PA; daughter of Robert C Merriweather and ElizabethLivingston Merriweather; divorced. **EDUCATION:** Cheyney State Univ, BS Ed 1969; Beaver Coll, 1986-; MA, Humanities, 1989. **CAREER:** Black Women's Ed Alliance, mem chair 1981-83, vice pres 1983, pres 1983-87; Philadelphia Fed of Black Bus & Professional Organizations, pres 1987-. **ORGANIZATIONS:** Bd dir Minority Assoc for Student Support 1981-;co-chair public rel Salem Baptist Church 100 Anniversary 1983-84; chair public rel Philadelphia Fed of Black Bus & Prof Org 1984-87; recruiter Amer Fed Teachers 1985; task force mem Youth Serv Coord Commiss 1986-; mem planning comm AFNA Educ & Rsch Fund 1987; pres Philadelphia Fed of Black Businesses & Prof Org. **HONORS/ACHIEVEMENTS:** Chapel of Four Chaplins 1970; Achievement Awd BWEA 1984, Women in Ed 1985; City Council Citation City of Philadelphia 1985; Outstanding Achievement BWEA 1986; House of Rep PA Citation for Outstanding Service 1987; Outstanding Serv Citation Commonwealth of PA House of Representatives 1987; PATHS Fellowship for Indep Study, Council for Basic Educ 1988. **BUSINESS ADDRESS:** President, Philadelphia Fed of Black Bus, 9200 New Bustleton Ave, 2112 Lloyd Bldg, Philadelphia, PA 19115.

MERRIWEATHER, MIKE
Professional athlete. **PERSONAL:** Born Nov 26, 1960, Albans, NY; married Djuna Mitchell. **EDUCATION:** Univ Pacific, History degree. **CAREER:** Pittsburgh Steelers, linebacker 1982-. **ORGANIZATIONS:** Mem Alpha Phi Alpha 1980-, Big Brothers Bowling for Kids 1986,87. **HONORS/ACHIEVEMENTS:** Twice named to All Pacific Coast team; NEA All-Amer team; played in East-West game; Olympia Gold Bowl; broke all-time Steeler sack record with 15 QB sacks ranking third in AFC and fifth in NFL 1983. **BUSINESS ADDRESS:** Pittsburgh Steelers, Three Rivers Stadium, 300 Stadium Circle, Pittsburgh, PA 15212.

MERRIWEATHER, ROBERT EUGENE
Business consultant. **PERSONAL:** Born Sep 01, 1948, Cincinnati, OH; son of Mr Andrew J Merriweather and Mrs Andrew J Merriweather; married Augustine Pryor, Sep 19, 1970; children: Tinia, Andre, Tarani. **EDUCATION:** Univ of Cincinnati, BA 1970. **CAREER:** Procter & Gamble Co, math consultant 1970-78, statistical analyst 1978-81, affirmative action mgr 1981-83, sr systems analyst 1983-. **ORGANIZATIONS:** Bd mem Mt Zion Federal Credit Union 1980-; trustee Mt Zion Baptist Church 1986-; Community Advisory Bd, University of Cincinnati 1988-. **HONORS/ACHIEVEMENTS:** Black Achiever YMCA 1983; Black Networking Awd Black Managers, Procter & Gamble 1986; Diversity Award, Procter & Gamble 1988. **HOME ADDRESS:** 9580 Heather Ct, Cincinnati, OH 45242.

MERRIWEATHER, THOMAS L.
Business executive. **PERSONAL:** Born Nov 15, 1932, Chicago, IL; son of Thomas L Merriweather and Mary Louise Merriweather; widowed; children: Anita Lynn Williams. **EDUCATION:** Chicago City Coll Am Cons, Music 1954; Roosevelt Univ/Loyola Univ, 1959-62; Chicago Conser Coll, BME, 1960; Columbia School of Broadcasting, 1971-72; United Inst Grad Coll of Performing Arts, DMA 1978. **CAREER:** Chicago Bd Educ, teacher, 1960-66; IL Dept of Labor, employment/training specialist, 1967-74; Chicago Urban League, trainee Adv (Counselor), 1974-76; The woodlawn Organ, vocational counselor, placement counselor/supvr, 1976-80; Creative Career Assn, exec dir, 1979-80; United Christian Fellowship, lay minister, entertainer, writer. **ORGANIZATIONS:** Dir/res artist Indigo Prod Merriweather Ent, 1956-; Chicago Fed of Musicians, 1966-; asst mgr, recruitng/govt program, Natl Alliance Business, 1968-71; chmn admin bd, St James United Methodist Church, 1968-72; mem, Am Guild Musical Artists, 1970-; res artist Lyric Opera Chicago, 1970, 1972-73, 1977, 1985; dir music, 1975-81; lcnd lay speaker 1975-86; church lay ldr, St James United Meth Church, 1979-86; pres/exec dir, Creative Music Studies Inc 1979-. **HONORS/ACHIEVEMENTS:** Commendation for Dedicated Serv, Natl Alliance Business, 1971-72; Certificate of Recognition, Natl Alliance Business, 1971; Serv Award, Musical Direction, St James United Methodist Church, 1981. **MILITARY SERVICE:** AUS pfc (e-3) 2; Natl Defense Serv Medal 1954-56. **HOME ADDRESS:** 5018 S Woodlawn Ave, Chicago, IL 60615. **BUSINESS ADDRESS:** Regional Vice President, Am Guild of Variety Artists, 184 5th Ave, New York, NY 10010.

MERTON, JOSEPH LEE
Association executive. **PERSONAL:** Born Oct 23, 1923, Chicago, IL; son of Joseph Merton and Harriet Brown Merton; married Valenia Olson; children: Joseph K, Geoffrey, David. **EDUCATION:** Chicago City Coll, Associate 1941-43/1946-47; Chicago Sch of Photography, Graduate 1948; Air Force Univ Ext, 1955-58; Chicago City Coll, 1961; Southern Methodist Univ, attended 1986. **CAREER:** Univ of Chicago Rsch Inst, chief photographer 1948-58; Chicago Area Council BSA, dir urban rels & field dir dist exec field scout exec 1958-68; Boy Scouts of Amer, faculty natl exec inst 1968-70, regional deputy reg 2 1970-71, scout exec Newark 1971-74, admin asst to chief scout exec 1974-77, natl dir boy scout div 1977-85, natl dir rsch & eval 1985-. **ORGANIZATIONS:** Club pres & lt gov IL Eastern Iowa Dist Kiwanis Intl 1962-68; adv Sigma Sigma Chap Alpha Phi Omega 1965-68; adv bd IL Youth Comm 1966-68; pres elect Chester Rotary Club NJ 1979; adjutant Military Order of the World Wars, Tuskegee Airman. **HONORS/ACHIEVEMENTS:** Faculty Prof Training Africa Region Accra Ghana World Scout Organ 1969; Disting Serv Awd Order of the Arrow BSA 1983. **MILITARY SERVICE:** AUS Aircorps fighter pilot 1st lt 1943-45; Disting Unit Citation; Air Medal w/Clusters; Seven Compaigns. **BUSINESS ADDRESS:** Director Research & Evaluation, Boy Scouts of America, 1325 Walnut Hill Lane, Irving, TX 75038-3096.

MESA, MAYRA L.
Dentist, educator. **PERSONAL:** Born Jul 20, 1949, Cuba. **EDUCATION:** Univ of Puerto Rico, BS 1968;Univ of Puerto Rico Dental Sch, DMD 1972; BostonUniv Sch of Grad Dentistry, MSc 1974. **CAREER:** CMDNJ NJ Dental Sch, assoc prof ora pathology 1977-, asst prof oral pathology 1974-77; Commonwealth Dental Soc, sec 1977-79. **ORGANIZATIONS:** Mem Commonwealth Dental Soc NDA 1975-; mem Am Bd of Oral Pathology 1978-; mem bd dirs Act for Boston Comm Devel 1973; supv Black Coalition Hlth Law Fair 1977-79; Table Clinics Nat Dental Assn 1977-79. **HONORS/ACHIEVEMENTS:** Hon mention Outstdg Young Women of Am 1978; various publ. **BUSINESS ADDRESS:** Assoc Prof of Oral Pathology, Univ of Medicine & Dentistry, Dental Schl C-854, 100 Bergen St, Newark, NJ 07103.

MESHACK, LULA M.
Retired vocational counselor. **PERSONAL:** Born in Dallas. **EDUCATION:** Univ of TX Ext Div, grad 1942; LA SW Coll Pasadena City Coll & UCAL Ext, certificate. **CAREER:** Fed Civil Serv Navy Dept Washington DC;; employed; LA County Assesor Prog Spec Neighborhood Adult Part Proj, rent con 1964-. **ORGANIZATIONS:** Charter mem, State Attorney General Advisory Bd; charter mem Dist Att Adv Bd; mem SC Vol Act Com; mem S Ctrl Reg Coun of Lung Assn; mem Martin Luther KingGuild; coord 25 Candy Stripers; mem Vol Act Com Natl Baptist Convention Women's Aux; past pres Russel Elementary Sch PTA 1955-56, 1956-57; past pres Fremont Coun PTA 1959-61; past bd mem LA 10th District PTA 1961-65; past pres Interdenominational Ministers' Wives of LA 1966-68; past pres Florence-Firestone Coord Coun 1971-74; mem Bapt Ministers' Wives; mem bd dirs LA Chptr & S Cntrl Dist Barc. **HONORS/ACHIEVEMENTS:** Recipient several Commendations from Co & city of LA for comm serv; vol serv award LA City Schools; Certificate of Merit, Baptist Ministers' Wives Unoin; LA Brotherhood Crusade; commr General Revenue Sharing LA Co; pastor worth matron Order of Eastern Star; past high preceptress New Beaulah Tab #2 of Tabor; Business & Professional Club Sojourner Truth Award; Lifetime CA Adult Sch Couns Cred.

MESHACK, SHERYL HODGES
Attorney. **PERSONAL:** Born Feb 25, 1944, Boston; daughter of Clyde H Hodges and Florence Norma Clifton; married John L Meshack; children: Norman, LaJohn, Derrick, Myles. **EDUCATION:** Howard Univ, BA 1965; USC Law School, JD 1972. **CAREER:** Atty. **ORGANIZATIONS:** CA State Bar; John M Langston Bar Assn; CA Women Lawyers Assn; Black Women Lawyers of So CA; bd of gov CA Assn of Black Lawyers 1979-81; CA Attorneys for Criminal Justice, 1972-76; Delta Sigma Theta Sorority; Pres, Assn of Black Attorneys, 1988-89. **BUSINESS ADDRESS:** Assistant City Attorney, Los Angeles City Attorneys Office, 200 N Main St, Suite 1800, Los Angeles, CA 90012.

MESIAH, RAYMOND N.
Technical manager. **PERSONAL:** Born Sep 01, 1932, Buffalo; children: 2 Children. **EDUCATION:** Canisius Coll, BS 1954; MS 1960. **CAREER:** Specialty Chem Group FMC Corp, various positions to dir of Commercial devel 1956-. **ORGANIZATIONS:** Mem Am Chem Soc; mem bd educ Franklentown 1969-75; press 1972-73; treas Frederick Douglass Liberation Library 1969-70; mem Franklin Twp Jaycees 1963-68; pres 1965; chmn Franklin Twp Civil Rights Commn 1967-68; treas Franklin Twp Pub Library 1967-69; mem Alpha Phi Alpha Frat. **HONORS/ACHIEVEMENTS:** 1 of 5 outstanding mem of yr NJ Jaycees 1967. **MILITARY SERVICE:** Corpl 1954-56f. **BUSINESS ADDRESS:** FMC Corp, 2000 Market St, Philadelphia, PA 19103.

MESSIAH, SONCERIA VON
Account executive. **PERSONAL:** Born Nov 24, 1953, Baytown, TX; married Jodie; children: Jodie, Brandon, Jiles. **EDUCATION:** Univ of Houston, BA Pol Sci 1974;Univ of Houston Sch of Real Estated cert 1978; RICE u publ prog, cert 1979. **CAREER:** Houston Defender Newspaper, assoc editor 1975-76; KYOK Radio, radio news reporter 1975-76; KHOU-TV Houston,TV co-host 1976-78; Houston Chronicle Newspaper, account exec 1976-80; KRIV-TV Houston,TV producer host 1978-86; KMJQ radio Houston, account exec 1980-81; Xerox Corp Houston, sales rep 1981-82; Houston Defender Newspaper, owner/publisher 1981-. **ORGANIZATIONS:** Mem Houston Citizen C of C 1978-; marketing consult S-Von Enterprises Inc 1978-; membership chmn Nat Assn of Market Developers 1980; mem Am Women in Radio & TV; mem NAACP; bd dirs Hester House Inc 1980; mem Natl Newspaper Publishers Assoc Adv Comm; mem Amer Newspaper Publishers Assoc; newsletter coord NNPA. **HONORS/ACHIEVEMENTS:** Presidential Award Houston Chapter NAMD 1979; pub chmn United Cerebral Palsy Telethon Telethon Houston 1980; Business Achievement Awd Houston Citizens C ofC 1986; (6) Merit Awds Natl Newspaper Publishers Assoc. **BUSINESS ADDRESS:** Publisher/Owner, Houston Defender Newspaper, P O Box 8005, Houston, TX 77288.

METCALF, ANDREW LEE, JR.
Government official. **PERSONAL:** Born Feb 21, 1944, Muskegon, MI; married Elizabeth Jane Lamb; children: Andrea, Andrew III. **EDUCATION:** Muskegon Comm Coll, AA 1971; Grand Valley State Coll, BS 1972. **CAREER:** US Dept of Justice, US marshall 1978-; McCroskey & Libner Law Firm, legal investigator 1971-78; Muskegon Heights Police Dept, patrolman juvenile officer 1967-71. **ORGANIZATIONS:** Asst regional dir Nat Assn of Legal Investigators 1976; mem W MI Law Enforcement Officer Assn 1978; charter mem Muskegon Hgts Lions Club 1975; treas Iota Phi Lambda Chap of Alpha Phi Alpha 1977-79; exec bd mem NAACP Grand Rapids MI Chap 1980. **HONORS/ACHIEVEMENTS:** Academic scholarship (375 gpa) Ford Found NY 1971. **MILITARY SERVICE:** USAF sgt 1962-66. **BUSINESS ADDRESS:** Dir of Enforcement, State of MI Dept of Licensing, Bureau of Commercial Services, 611 N Ottawa, Lansing, MI 48909.

METCALF, MICHAEL RICHARD
Physician. **PERSONAL:** Born Jan 04, 1956, Detroit, MI; son of Adele C Metcalf; married Ruth Chantell Holloman; children: Michael Jr, Leah, Jonathan, Christina. **EDUCATION:** Dartmouth Coll, BA 1978; Howard Univ Coll of Medicine, MD 1982. **CAREER:** DC General Hospital, internist 1982-83, resident 1983-85, chief resident 1984; CW Williams Health Center, internist 1985-; Charlotte Memorial Hosp, assoc div, active staff, dept of internal med 1987-. **ORGANIZATIONS:** Mem Charlotte Medical Soc 1986-; assoc mem Amer Coll of Physicians. **HONORS/ACHIEVEMENTS:** Diplomate Amer Bd of Internal Medicine 1985. **BUSINESS ADDRESS:** Assistant Health Services Director, CW Williams Health Center, 3333 Wilkinson Blvd, PO Box 668093, Charlotte, NC 28266.

METCALF, ZUBIE WEST, JR.
Educational administrator. **PERSONAL:** Born Jul 04, 1930, Ft Deposit, AL; son of Zubie W Metcalf Sr and Ella L Metcalf; married Maggie L Blake; children: DaVinci C, Caroletta A. **EDUCATION:** Univ of Dayton, BS 1957; Miami Univ, MAT 1961; State Univ of NY Buffalo, EdD 1972. **CAREER:** Ball State Univ, dir acad oppty prog 1971-73; Tuskegee Inst, asst vice pres for academic affairs/dean of grad prog 1973-76; East Carolina Univ Sch of Med, assoc dean, dir med center student oppty and minority affairs 1976-. **ORGANIZATIONS:** Dir Natl Sci Found Summer Inst FL A&M Univ 1966-69; coord Tchr Educ Prog State Univ

of NY Buffalo 1969-70; consult US Dept of Health & Human Serv Div of Disadvantaged Asst 1983-84; dir bd mem Pitt-Greenville C of C 1983-87; chairperson Southern Region Minority Affairs Sect of Assn of Amer Med 1984-; bd Planters Natl Bank 1986-; vice president, Natl Assn of Medical Minority Educators 1987-89. **HONORS/ACHIEVEMENTS:** Hon Soc in Ed Univ of Dayton OH 1957; Fellowship Natl Sci Found Washington DC 1960-61; Fellowship Ford Found NY 1970-71. **HOME ADDRESS:** 213 Churchill Dr, Greenville, NC 27834. **BUSINESS ADDRESS:** Assoc Dean and Director Minority Affairs, East Carolina University, School of Medicine, Greenville, NC 27834.

METOYER, CARL B.
Attorney. **PERSONAL:** Born Aug 08, 1925, Oakland; married Coline Apperson; children: Carl, Ronald, Monique. **EDUCATION:** Univ of CA, 3 yrs undergrad work econ; Hastings Coll, 1952. **CAREER:** Priv Prac Sole Practitioner, att 1968-; firm Metoyer & Sweeney, sen part 1959-68; Priv Prac Law Sole Practitioner, 1955-59; firm Fracois & Metoyer, partner 1953-55. **ORGANIZATIONS:** Vice-chmn exec com CA State Bar Conf of Del; mem State Bar of CA; mem Alameda Co Bar Assn; Lawyers Club of Alameda Co; Chalres Houston Law Club; mem Alameda Co Sup Cts Arbitration Panel; vice pres mem bd dirs CA Lawyers Serv; past vice pres Hastings Coll of Law Alumni Assn; past judge pro tem Oakland Mun Ct; past mem bd govs Alameda Co Comm Found; mem CA StateUniv Hayward Adv Bd; vice pres mem bd dirs Family Serv Bur Alameda Co; mem NAACP; mem UrbanLeague; mem Sigma Pi Phi Frat; past chmn Manpower Comm City of Oakland; Past mem Oakland Eco Dev Coun; past mem bd dirs Children's Home Soc of CA; past pres Sen Div Hayward Little League; past mem exec bd San Fran Coun Boy Scts Am. **HONORS/ACHIEVEMENTS:** Recip order of the coif Hastings Coll of Law 1952; mem thurston soc Hastings Coll of Law Hon Soc 1950-52; mem tower & flameUniv CA Berkeley Campus 1947-49. **MILITARY SERVICE:** USNR 1943-46. **BUSINESS ADDRESS:** 6014 Market St, Oakland, CA 94608.

METOYER, ROSIA G.
Librarian. **PERSONAL:** Born Mar 02, 1930, Boyce, LA; married Granvewl G; children: Renwick, Keith, Karlette, Toni Rosette. **EDUCATION:** Grambling Coll, BS Edu 1951; Webster Coll, MA; Nrthwstrn State U, stdy 1964; SthrnUniv Baton Rouge, stdy; TX Sthrn U; Nrthwstrn State U. **CAREER:** Acadian Elem Sch, libr; Lincoln Rd Elem Sch Rapides Parish Sch Bd, former school librarian; Rapides Parish Library, selections librarian. **ORGANIZATIONS:** Pres LA Classroom Teacher Assn LEA 1977-78; mem Exec Council of LA Assn of Educators 1978-80; mem United Teaching Professional LA Libr Assn, SW Libr Assn, Alexandria Zoning Bd of Adjustment & Appeals, Assn of Classroom Teachers, LA Libr Assn, YWCA, NAACP; negotiated the dedication of the Martin Luther King JrCenter; established the Black Awareness Resource Prog at Martin Luther King Jr Center; acquired $1200 from Jack & Jill Found to purchase resources for Center. **HONORS/ACHIEVEMENTS:** Recipient 1st James R Hovall Award; LA Assoc of Librarians Serv Awd; LA Beauticians Serv Awd; LA Assoc of Educators Outstanding Serv to Teachers Awd ZetaLambda Omega; Alpha Kappa Alpha Sor Community Serv Awd; SE Kiwanis Community Serv Awd. **BUSINESS ADDRESS:** Librarian, Rapides Parish Public Library, 411 Washington St, Alexandria, LA 71301.

METTLE-NUNOO, NII AHENE
Artist, designer, writer, educator. **PERSONAL:** Born Dec 03, 1945, Accra, Ghana;children: Naa Amanshia, Mokoledzen. **EDUCATION:** Inst of Languages Workers Coll, BA 1970; Printing Ind Evening Sch, production printing 1974-75; Fordham Univ, 1980-82. **CAREER:** Mettle-Nunoo Graphics, 1974-77; New Muse Community Museum NYC, asst cultural arts dir 1977; Jeffrey Norton Publ Inc, studio mgr 1983; N B Ward Assoc Inc, art dir; Integrated Communications Media, pres 1986-. **ORGANIZATIONS:** Mem Natl Conf of Artists 1972-; archivist/founder Ga-Dagme Oral Hist Rsch Inst 1979-; dep chmn Weusi Artists Inc New York City 1985; mem Printmaking Workshop New York City 1972-; mem Visual Artists & Galleries Assn Intl 1984-. **HONORS/ACHIEVEMENTS:** Represented in the permanent collections, Studio Museum in Harlem, Ghana Natl Museum, Ghana and Harlem Collection New York City 1975-; Letter of Apprec NYS Senate Spec Comm on the Culture Ind 1978; Graphic Art Award Amer Veterans Soc of Artists 32nd Annual New York City 1974; Cert of Recogn for Art Advancement Langston Hughes Libr & Cultural Cntr Corona, NY; Cert of Recogn Dept of Parks & Rec 4th Annual Banner Making Competition 1983; Carved Plaque Awd Black History Month Students of Sts Peter and Paul HS St Thomas US Virgin Islands 1987.

MEYERS, ISHMAEL ALEXANDER
Associate judge. **PERSONAL:** Born Feb 03, 1939, St Thomas, Virgin Islands of the United States;son of H Alexander Meyers and Elvira L Meyers nee Matthias; married Gwendolyn Lorraine Pate; children: Ishmael Jr, Micheline, Michael. **EDUCATION:** Morgan State Univ, BS with high honors 1962; Amer Univ, MBA 1964; George Washington Univ, JD with honors 1972. **CAREER:** Interstate Commerce Commn, acct/auditor 1963-64; VI Dept of Housing & Comm Renewal 1964-69; VI Dept of Law, asst atty gen 1973; US Dept of Justice, asst US atty 1973-78, US atty 1978-82; Territorial Court of the VI, assoc judge 1982-. **ORGANIZATIONS:** Mem Bar of the Supreme Court of the US 1980-; mem DC Bar Assn 1973-; mem VI Bar Assn 1973-; mem Amer Bar Assn 1973-; charter mem St Thomas Lions Club 1968-; v chmn Meml Moravian Sch Bd 1974; vice pres Theta Epsilon Lambda Chap Alpha Phi Alpha Frat Inc 1976. **HONORS/ACHIEVEMENTS:** Alpha Kappa Mu Natl Honor Soc Morgan State Univ 1960-62; John Hay Whitney Found Fellow 1962-64; US Atty Gen Special Achievement Award US Dept of Justice 1976; The Natl Alumni Assn of Morgan State Univ Special Achievement Award 1984. **BUSINESS ADDRESS:** Associate Judge, Territorial Ct of the VI, PO Box 70, St Thomas, Virgin Islands of the United States 00801.

MEYERS, MICHAEL
Association executive. **PERSONAL:** Born Feb 16, 1950, Manhattan, NY. **EDUCATION:** Antioch Coll, BA 1972; Rutgers Law School, JD 1975. **CAREER:** Marc Corp NYC, intern 1967,68, fellow 1968-75; Met Applied Rsch Ctr, asst to Dr Kenneth B Clark pres 1970-75; NAACP, asst exec dir 1975-84, dir res policy & planning 1977-84; RACE Inc NY, founder/dir/pres 1984-. **ORGANIZATIONS:** Mem spec comm HUD, Amer Bar Assoc 1974-75; bd dir Sponsors of Open Housing Investment Wash DC 1970-77; bd dir New Hope Housing Inc 1971-77; natl chmn comm of 25 SOHI 1972-74; exec comm SOHI 1970-77; bd dir Natl Child Labor Comm Inc 1976-82; bd dir NY Civil Liberties Union 1976-; exec comm Natl Coaltion Against the Death Penalty 1977-84, Amer Civil Liberties Union Equality Comm 1974-80, Acad Freedom Comm, Free Speech Assoc Comm; bd dir Amer Civil Liberties Union 1981-. **HONORS/ACHIEVEMENTS:** Staff Cit Comm Investigating Corpl Punishment in NYC's Publ School 1974; Law School Rep to Law Student Div Amer Bar Assoc 1972-75; publs in Integrated Ed Mag, Youth & Soc Jrnl, Civil Liberties, Wall St Jrnl, Change Mag, LA Times, Crisis, NY Times, Wash Post, Christ Sci Monitor, Newsday, Daily News, NY Post, Village Voice; Esquire Register 1986; Outstanding Young Men of Amer 1986. **BUSINESS ADDRESS:** Dir, RACE Inc, PO Box 1342, Riverdale, NY 10471.

MEYERS, ROSE M.
Research scientist. **PERSONAL:** Born Aug 18, 1945, Mt Pleasant, SC. **EDUCATION:** Bennett Coll Greensboro, BS Chem 1966; NY U, MS Biochem 1972, PhD Biochem 1976. **CAREER:** Philip Morris Rsrch Ctr, rsrch sci 1978-;Univ of Louisville Med Sch, postdoctoral fllwshp & rsrch tchng 1976-78; NYUniv Med Sch, rsrch tech II cancer rsrch 1972-76, rsrch tech I cancer rsrch 1968-72; YeshivaUniv NY, rsrch tech chem 1967-68; Howard HS Georgetown SC, math tchr 1966-67. **ORGANIZATIONS:** Mem Sister Cities Intl 1978-; mem Nat Assn Blk Chem 1978-; pres Bennett Coll Alumnae of Richmond 1980-82; mem Bus & Profes-sional Wmn's Club Mus of African Art. **HONORS/ACHIEVEMENTS:** Publ article "Studies on Nucleoside Deaminase" Jrnl Biol Chem 2485090 1973; publ "sialyltransferase in lympocytes" fdrtn prcdngs 351441 1976; Louisvillecitz awd Mayor Harvey Sloane Louisville 1976-77; publ "Immunosupprsn & Tobacco Smoke" Fdrtn Prcdngs 361230 1977.

MFUME, KWEISI
Congressman. **EDUCATION:** Morgan State Univ, Grad (Magna Cum Laude) 1976; Johns Hopkins Univ, M 1984. **CAREER:** US House of Representatives, congressman State of MD.

MICHAEL, CHARLENE BELTON
Assoiate director. **PERSONAL:** Born in Heath Springs, SC; married Joseph M, Sr; children: Joseph M Jr, Charles B. **EDUCATION:** Knoxville Coll, BA 1939; Teachers Coll, Columbia Univ, MaA 1955; Univ of TN, MS 1958; Univ of TN, PhD 1976. **CAREER:** Knoxville Cty Schls, tchr 1950-75; Knoxville Cty Schl & Univ TN, speech pathologist 1958-75; Knoxville/Knox Co Project Headstart, dpty dir 1965-66; Knoxville Coll-Upward Bound, assoc dir 1968-69 (Summer's); Educ & Training Adaption Serv Inc, ed dir 1971-75; MAAR-DAC/UNIV of TN, assoc dir 1974-;Univ Assoc,Johns Hopkins U, consultant 1979, 82-83; Mid Atlantic/Appalachian Race Desegregation Assistance Ctr, acting dir 1987. **ORGANIZATIONS:** Pres Phi Delta Kappa Univ of TN 1979-80; mem bd of trustees Knoxville Coll 1984; pres Knoxville Coll Natl Alumni Assoc Inc, pres Knoxville Educ Assoc, Delta Sigma Theta Sor Alumnae Chapt; bd of dirs Knoxville Women's Ctr, Matrix, Children's Ctr; mem Metropolitan Planning Commn. **HONORS/ACHIEVEMENTS:** Publications, "Why I Teach", "The Effect of Parental Invlmnt on the Lrng Process", "Advantages of Lang-Experience Approach in the Teaching of Reading" "Coping with Stresses in the Classroom", "Student Team Learning, An Educational Equity Tool", "Workshop Participants' Perception Rankings of Second Gen Schl Desegregation Issues"; Cert of Recgntn Knoxville Coll SE Regnl & Natl Alumni Assoc 1977; lic speech pathologist State of TN; Citizen of the Year Award/For Serv & Contrib to Humanity 1984; Selwyn Awd Knoxville Women's Ctr 1985; YWCA Awd Tribute to Outstanding Women 1986. **BUSINESS ADDRESS:** Acting Dir, Mid-Atlantic/Appalachian Race, 238 Claxton Addition, Knoxville, MS 37996.

MICHAEL, DALE R.
Attorney. **PERSONAL:** Born Oct 01, 1942, StThomas, VI; son of Cyril Michael and Elizabeth Michael; married Emilie Kheil. **EDUCATION:** Manhattan Coll, BChE 1962; Columbia Univ, MSChE 1967, LLB 1967, MBA 1968. **CAREER:** Robert S First, aup 1968-69; Coalition Venture Corp, exec dir 1969-72; NY Financial Serv, partner 1972-74; DPS Protective Systems, 1974-; JD Asset Protection Group, owner 1985-. **ORGANIZATIONS:** Mem NY Bar; mem California Bar; patron Metropolitan Opera 1982-. **BUSINESS ADDRESS:** Box 297, St Thomas, Virgin Islands of the United States 00801.

MICHAUX, ERIC COATES
Attorney. **PERSONAL:** Born Sep 23, 1941, Durham, NC; married Della Dafford. **EDUCATION:** Univ of NC, attended 1959; NC Central Univ Sch of Law, attended 1963-65; Boston U, BS Bus Adminstrn 1963; Duke Univ Sch of Law, B of Law 1966; Univ of Denver, attended 1968. **CAREER:** Eric C Michauz Law Firm, pres; 14th Solicitoral Dist, asst dist attorney 1973-75; Perason Malone Johnson & DeJormon, atty 1971-73; W G Pearson, atty 1967; Durham Coll Durham NC, tchr bus law 1965. **ORGANIZATIONS:** Vis prof N CA CentralUniv 1971-73; adj asst prof Dept of Health EducUniv of NC Chapel Hill 1972-73; %Congressional aide Congressman Nick Galifianakis 1971-72; pres Unoin Ins & Reality Co; vice pres Glenview Mem Park Washington Terr Apts Inc; bd of dir Harrison Constrn Realty Co; vchmn/bd of dir Cardinal Savs & Loan; mem Am Bar Assn; NAACP; So Christian Leadership Conf; mem Omega Psi Phi Frat; Phi Alpha Delta Legal Frat; Nat Soc of Perishing Rifles;Durham Com on the Affairs of Black People; mem United Citizens Against Drug Abusr; steward trustee treas St Joseph's African Meth Episcopal Ch; mem NC Bar Assn; bd of dirs Durham Chap of the Am Nat Red Cross. **HONORS/ACHIEVEMENTS:** Recipient of Nat Defencs Serv Medal; Vietnam Serv Medal; Vietnam Campaign Medal; Bronze Star USAF 1967-69. **MILITARY SERVICE:** USAF 1967-69. **BUSINESS ADDRESS:** PO Box 1152, Durham, NC 27702.

MICHAUX, HENRY G.
Educator. **PERSONAL:** Born Jan 19, 1934, Morganton, NC. **EDUCATION:** TX So Univ, BFA (Magna Cum Laude) 1959; PA State Univ, MEd 1960, DEd 1971, grad grant-in-aid 1959-60, grad asst 1966-67. **CAREER:** VA State Univ, tchr fine arts & art educ 1960-62; So Univ in New Orleans, 1962-67; Cntrl State Univ, 1967-68; TX So Univ, 1968-70; Coll of the VI, 1970; Appalachian State Univ, assoc prof art educ 1972-76; NC Central Univ, assoc prof art educ 1977-78; SC State Coll, assoc prof art educ 1978-. **ORGANIZATIONS:** Mem NC Coalition of Arts; mem Amer Craftsmen Council 1964-67; Amer Assn of Univ Profs 1962-71; natl Art Educ Assn 1974-87; Black Art Festivals; first pres Caldwell Arts Council Lenoir, NC 1976; designed and coord first indoor/outdoor regional (NC, SC, TN, VA) Sculptors Competition Lenoir NC 1986 through Lenoir Parks & Recreational Dept & the Caldwell Arts Cncl; developed Black Studies (African-Amer Studies for Caldwell Comm Coll Lenoir NC) Project proposal; ETV (WXEX-TV) participant VA State Coll. **HONORS/ACHIEVEMENTS:** Honorary mem Alpha Kappa Mu 1956-59; Jesse Jones Fine Arts Scholarship TX So Univ 1956-59; Selected Participant Japanese Seminar on Preserv of Cultural Continuity by SC Consortium for Intl Studies 1980; numerous exhibits; natl winner of competition for one-man shows; Madison Galleries, NY; work in Look Magazine;drawings owned by NC Arts Museum; "African American Artists, NC USA" NC Museum of Art 1980; interview and feature on "Carolina Camera" WBTV Charlotte 1981; apptd SC Acquisitions Comm

a part of the SC Museum Commn 1982-84; Natl Invitationals "Dimensions and Directions, Black Artists of the South" Jackson MS 1983. **BUSINESS ADDRESS:** Associate Professor, SC State College, Dept Art Education, Orangeburg, SC 29117.

MICHAUX, HENRY M., JR.
Government official. **PERSONAL:** Born Sep 04, 1930, Durham, NC; married Joyce; children: Jocelyn. **EDUCATION:** NC Central Univ, BS 1952; Rutgers Univ, 1954-55; NC Central Univ, BA, JD 1952, 1964. **CAREER:** Michaux & Michaux, sr partner; real estate broker 20 years; Durham Cnty, chf asst dist atty 1962-72; NC Gen Assembly & House Rep 1972-76; Middle Judicial Dist NC, US atty 1977-81; NC Gen Assembly 1985-. **ORGANIZATIONS:** Trustee NC Central Univ; mem exec com 14th Judicial Dist Bar; N State Bar; NC Bar Assn; George H White Bar Assn; Black Lawyers NC; Amer Bar Assn; Judicature Soc; Criminal Code Commn State NC 1973-77; Steering Com Caucus Black Dem; NC Commn Human Skills & Resources; NC Com Law Focused Edn; NC Central Alumni Assn; bd dir NC Central Univ Found Inc; Durham Bus & Professional Chain; Durham C of C; Durham Merchants Assn; NAACP. **HONORS/ACHIEVEMENTS:** Hon Dr Degree Durham Coll & NC Central Univ; Realist of Yr; Pub Affairs & Polit Achievement Award 1973-74 & 1976; Annual Award for Triad Sickle Cell Anemia Found 1973; Citiz Com Sickle Cell Syndrome Award 1976; Polit Achvmt Award NAACP 1975; Serv Award Phi Alpha Delta Law Frat; Achvmnt Award CA Real Estate Brokers 1974; Service Award 14th Judicial Dist Bar 1972; Triangle "J" Cncl Govt 1973; NC Bar Assn 1975; Pub Serv Award NC Chiropractic Assn 1977; NC Black Dem Leadership Caucus 1977. **MILITARY SERVICE:** AUS MC 1952-54.

MICHEAUX, LARRY LAVELLE
Professional athlete. **PERSONAL:** Born Mar 24, 1960, Houston, TX; married Annette; children: Keshia. **EDUCATION:** Univ of Houston, 1983. **CAREER:** Kansas City Kings, forward. **HONORS/ACHIEVEMENTS:** For 83-84 season tauted a rebound every 29 min played; in playoffs averaged 10 pts & 7 rebounds; in coll named Midwest Reg MV 1983; played in 11 NCAA town games & shot 50pct in all but 2; won honors ass Univ Houston's most improved player after soph & jr seasons.

MICHEL, HARRIET R.
Business executive. **PERSONAL:** Born Jul 05, 1942, Pittsburgh, PA; married Yves; children: Y Christopher, Gregory A. **EDUCATION:** Juniata Coll Huntingdon, BA. **CAREER:** Natl Scholarship Serv & Fund for Negro Students, dir spl projs 1965-70; NY Found, assoc 1970-71; City of NY Mayors Office, mayoral asst 1971-72; NY Found, exec dir; US Dept of Labor, dir office of youth employment 1977-79; Women Against Crime Found, pres 1980-83; New York Urban League, pres. **ORGANIZATIONS:** Pres Cano Taxi Corp; pres Y & H Enterprises; co-founder Assn of Black Found Execs; dir African Am inst; corp sec Private Indust Council; mayor's commission on Black New Yorkers; vchmn Mayor's Charter Revision Commiss; bd mem Jackie Robinson Found; adv bd WNET/13; rep Ditcheley Found Conf in London England; pres TransAfrica Forum. **HONORS/ACHIEVEMENTS:** Appointed to Mayor's Commission on Early Childhood Educ, State-City Commission on Integrity and the Gov's Liability Insurance Commission. **BUSINESS ADDRESS:** President, New York Urban League, 218 West 40th St, New York, NY 10018.

MICKENS, MAXINE
Business executive. **PERSONAL:** Born Dec 03, 1948, Clarksdale, MS; married Caesar Jr; children: Leonora. **EDUCATION:** Univ of MI, AB 1974; Comm Film Workshop of Chicago, cert 1976; ICBIF Sma Business mgmt Detroit, cert 1978. **CAREER:** Max Belle & Asso, vice pres 1977-; Simpson's Wholesale Detroit, adv mgr 1977; WJLB Radio Detroit, merchandising & promotion dir 1976-77; Detroid Bd of Edn, vocational & adult educ tchr 1974-80. **ORGANIZATIONS:** Mem WXYZ-TC Women's Adv Com Detroit MI 1974-76; mem Black Communicators Assn Detroit 1979-; mem Nat Assn of Media Women Detroit; communications chairperson Triedstone Bapt Church 1972-73; communications chairpersons Jeffersn Chalmers Com Assn 1974-75. **BUSINESS ADDRESS:** Max Belle & Associates, 1308 Broadway Ste 206, Detroit, MI 48226.

MICKENS, RONALD ELBERT
Educator, researcher. **PERSONAL:** Born Feb 07, 1943, Petersburg, VA; son of Joseph P Mickens and Daisey Brown Mickens; married Maria Kelker; children: Leah, James. **EDUCATION:** Fisk Univ, BA 1964; Vanderbilt Univ, PhD 1968. **CAREER:** MIT Center for Theoretical Physics, post doctoral researcher 1968-70; Fisk Univ Dept Physics, asst to prof 1970-81; MIT Dept Physics, visiting prof of physics 1973-74; Morehouse Coll/Atlanta Univ, visiting prof of physics 1979-80; Vanderbilt Univ Dept Physics, visiting scholar 1980-81; Joint Inst for Lab Astrophysics Boulder, CO, research fellow 1981-82; Atlanta Univ, chairperson 1984-86, Callaway prof 1985-. **ORGANIZATIONS:** Consult work for, natl Acad of Sciences, Los Alamos Sci Lab, Coll of Old Westburg etc; mem Amer Assn of Physics Tchrs, European Phys Soc, Amer Phys Soc, Amer Assn for Advancement of Sci, Sigma Xi, Beta Kappa Chi, Soc of Black Physicists, Amer Math Assn; mem London Mthematical Soc, Soc of Mathematical Biologists, Soc for Industrial and Applied Mathematics. **HONORS/ACHIEVEMENTS:** Phi Beta Kappa Fisk Univ Chap elect 1984; Woodrow Wilson Fellowship 1964-65; Danforth Fellowship 1965-68; Natl Sci Foundation Postdoctoral Fellowship 1968-70; Ford Foundation Postdoctoral Fellowship 1980-81; Joint Inst for Lab Astrophysics Fellowship 1981-82; research grants from, Army Ofc of Research, Dept Energy, NASA, Natl Sci Found, GTE Found; UNCF Distinguished Faculty Fellowship 1984-85; Callaway Professor 1985-; over 150 published papers, three books. **BUSINESS ADDRESS:** Professor, Atlanta University, Physics Dept, 223 James P Brawley Dr SW, Atlanta, GA 30314.

MICKEY, GORDON EUGENE
Educational administrator. **PERSONAL:** Born in Chillicothe, OH; married Dr Rosie Cheatham; children: Miguel Eugene,Madganna Mae. **EDUCATION:** Indiana Univ-Bloomington, BS 1962, MS 1966, EdD 1971; Cleveland State Univ, post doctoral work - psychology certification. **CAREER:** Indianapolis Public Schools, teacher/coach 1962-65; IN Univ Div of Univ Schools, instructor/coach 1966-69; New Castle Gunning Bedford Sch Dist, principal 1971-73; St Dept of Public Instruction (DE), state sup 1973-76; Mental Retardation Program-Lorain County OH, adm, consult 1976-77; Akron Public Schools-Akron OH, unit principal 1977-80; Stow City Schools-Stow OH, central office special educ supervisor 1981-. **ORGANIZATIONS:** Former Vice chmn trustee bd Second Baptist Church 1980-82; scholarship comm Beautillion Militaire 1980,81,83,85; founder/coord Minority Youth Recognition Programs 1982-84; vice pres Akron Frontiers Club 1982-84; chap consultant Jack and Jill of Amer Inc 1986; exec bd Neal-Marshall Alumni Club 1986; mem ASCD, NABSE, Phi Delta Kappa, Alpha Phi Alpha, Council for Exceptional Children. **HONORS/ACHIEVEMENTS:** Masters Fellowship Indiana Univ 1965-66, Doctoral Fellowship 1969-71; Presidential Natl Awd Frontiers Intl 1981; Certificate of Commendation Stow City Schools 1985; President's Awd Akron Frontiers Club 1986. **HOME ADDRESS:** 2415 Audubon Rd, Akron, OH 44320.

MICKEY, ROSIE CHEATHAM
Educational administrator. **PERSONAL:** Born Jun 13, Indianapolis, IN; married Dr Gordon Mickey; children: Miguel Eugene, Madganna Mae. **EDUCATION:** Indiana Univ Bloomington, BS 1970; The Univ of Akron, MS 1979, EdD 1983. **CAREER:** New Castle and Newark Sch Dists Delaware, business teacher 1971-76; Lorain City Schools OH, voc business teacher 1976-78; The Univ of Akron, grad asst 1978-80; Manfield City Schools OH, asst high school principal 1980-83; The Univ of Akron, asst dir fin aids 1984, asst dean & asst prof 1984-88; Indianapolis Public Schools, Indianapolis Indiana; consultant/admin. **ORGANIZATIONS:** Vice pres Akron Yokettes Club Aux of Frontiers 1983-84; mem exec bd Ecumenical Campus Ministry 1984-; general chairperson Beautillion Militaire J & J 1985; coord Individualized Study Program C&T 1985-; vice pres Pi Lambda Theta educ hon 1986-87; pres Jack and Jill of Amer Inc Akron Chap 1986-88; mem Phi Delta Kappa, NABSE, Natl Assoc Women Deans, Couns Admin; charter mem Neal-Marshall Alumni Club of Indiana Univ; mem Amer Assoc of Univ Women, United Way Allocations Panel Bd; urban consultation comm, steering comm United Methodist Churches; Indianapolis Black Expo Scholarship Committee. **HONORS/ACHIEVEMENTS:** Service Awd Vitiligo Symposiums Akron Frontiers Club 1983; Awd of Commendation House of Representatives of OH 1984; publication(s) from dissertation study 1983; papers presented Indianapolis, Atlanta, Chicago 1983, 1985, 1986; Community Service Award, Frontiers International Service Organization Sixth District; awards, Jack and Jill of America Inc.

MICKINS, ANDEL W.
Educator. **PERSONAL:** Born Oct 28, 1924, Central, SC; daughter of Ernest Watkins and Estelle Jamison Watkins; married Rev Isaac C Mickins, Jul 11, 1952; children: Isaac Clarence, II. **EDUCATION:** Tuskegee Inst, BS; Columbia Univ, MA; Iowa State Coll, std; Univ of Miami. **CAREER:** Sr HS, head home econ dept 1946-52; Holmes Elem School, teacher 1953-62; Curr Liberty City Elementary, asst principal 1962-67; Univ of Miami, summer supr tchr 1965;RR Moton Elem, principal 1967-72; Rainbow Park Elementary, principal 1972-81 (retired); Memorial Temple Baptist Church, dir early childhood educ center 1983-. **ORGANIZATIONS:** Pres Friendship Garden Club; vice pres Baptist Women's Coun; former supt Sunday School; mem Temple Baptist Church; adv Bus & profes Women's Club; pres Ministers Wivers Council of Greater Miami; spon Y-Teen; Comm Chr Boy Sct Troop 290; mem Alpha Kappa Alpha Sor; mem Phi Lambda Thet Honor Soc; mem Kappa Delta Pi Honor Soc; mem Amer Assoc of Univ Women; bd of dir Black Archives Foundation of Rsch of South FL; chmn exec bd Womens Aux Gen Baptist State Convention of FL; pres FL State Assoc of Ministers Wives. **HONORS/ACHIEVEMENTS:** Recip Sarah Blocker award FL Mem Col; plaque Rainbow Park Elementary School & Friendship Garden & Civic Club; plaque Alpha Kappa Alpha Sorority; Citation City of Miami; Natl Conf of Christians & Jews; listed in Who's Who Among Amer Women, Who's Who in Amer Educ, The Intl Who's Who of Intellectuals, The Intl Dictionary of Biographies, Notable Amers, Creative and Successful Personalities, Comm Leaders & Noteworthy Amers, Who's Who in the South and Southwest, Personalities of the South. **BUSINESS ADDRESS:** 15355 NW 19 Ave, Miami, FL 33054.

MICKLE, ANDREA DENISE
Educational administrator. **PERSONAL:** Born Jul 26, 1952, Kershaw, SC; daughter of John T Mickle and Mable Harris Mickle. **EDUCATION:** Hampton Univ, BA (Honor Graduate) 1974; Adelphi Univ, Certificate 1974; Howard Univ, MPA 1985. **CAREER:** Howard Univ, financial aid officer. **ORGANIZATIONS:** Conf participant, resource person Natl Assoc for Equal Oppor in Higher Educ 1975-; mem Amer Paralegal Assoc 1975-77; charter mem Lawyer's Assistants Inc 1975; pres Howard Univ Pi Alpha Alpha Honor Soc 1984-85; mem DE-DC-MD Assoc of Student Financial Aid Administrators; mem Amer Soc for Personnel Admin, Amer Soc for Public Admin, NAACP; speaker, coord of workshops for coll bound students sponsored by local organizations. **HONORS/ACHIEVEMENTS:** Outstanding Serv Awd Howard Univ Liberal Arts Student Council 1979, Howard Univ Upward Bound 1986; Certificate of Service Howard Univ Chap of ASPA 1982; Certificate of Appreciation Howard Univ Financial Aid Crisis Comm 1989; editorial reviewer for Black Excellence magazine 1989. **HOME ADDRESS:** 7543 Newberry Lane, Lanham, MD 20706. **BUSINESS ADDRESS:** Financial Aid Officer, Howard University, 2400-6th St NW, Washington, DC 20059.

MICKLE, ELVA L.
Business executive. **PERSONAL:** Born May 18, 1949, Oakland, CA; daughter of John C Mickle and Sadie Blanche Thomas Mickle. **EDUCATION:** Fisk Univ, BA (Magna Cum Laude) (Phi Beta Kappa) graduated first in class 1971; Harvard Univ, Grad Schl of Business MBA 1974. **CAREER:** Ford Div Ford Motor Co, statistician-mgmt trainee 1971-72, financial analyst 1974-75; Michigan-Wisc Pipe Line Co, Detroit MI, corp planning specialist/spvsr, financial modeling 1976-79; Michigan Bell Telephone Co, staff mngr Federal Issues & Analysis and Rates Proposals; University of TN at Chatanooga, Chatanooga TN, instructor in Business Policy/Strategic Management and Planning 1988-. **ORGANIZATIONS:** Mem Women's Economic Club, Detroit 1980-86; 2nd vice pres Natl Black MBA Assn Detroit chapter 1982, 1983; secretary 1982-84, mem Entrepreneur Conference Planning Comm 1983-85 Harvard Business Sch Alumni Assn of Detroit; moderator & speaker Strategies Annual Women's Career Conference 1983, 1984; mem Engineering Soc of Detroit 1983-85. **HONORS/ACHIEVEMENTS:** Outstanding Serv Award for leadership work on annual Banquet Committee Detroit chapter Natl Black MBA Assn 1981. **HOME ADDRESS:** 3131 Mountain Creek Rd, Apt 12B2, Chattanooga, TN 37415. **BUSINESS ADDRESS:** University of Tennessee at Chattanooga, 615 McCallie Avenue, Fletcher Hall, Room 412, Chattanooga, TN.

MICKS, DEITRA R. H.
Attorney. **PERSONAL:** Born May 26, 1945, Bronx, NY; divorced. **EDUCATION:** Howard U, BA 1967; Howard U, JD 1971. **CAREER:** Jacksonville, legal aid 1971-73; Pvt Prac, atty; Jackson & Micks; Univ N FL, tchr. **ORGANIZATIONS:** Bd dir Legal Aid 1974-; bd dir NAACP local Jackson chpt; student articles' Ed Howard Law Journal 1970-71. **BUSINESS ADDRESS:** 410 Broad St, Ste 208, Jacksonville, FL 32202.

MIDDLEBROOKS, FELICIA
Radio anchor, reporter. **PERSONAL:** Born May 29, 1957, Gary, IN; daughter of Raymond Middlebrooks Jr and Geraldine Rembert Middlebrooks. **EDUCATION:** Purdue Univ, Hammond IN, BA Mass Communications, 1982. **CAREER:** WBBA, W Lafayette IN, anchor, 1976-77; WGVE Radio for Handicapped, Gary IN, anchor, 1978-81; Jones & Laughlin Steel, E Chicago IN, laborer, 1978-82; WJOB Radio, Hammond IN, reporter, anchor, 1979-82; WLTH Radio, Gary IN, reporter, anchor, 1982-84; WBBM Radio, Gary In, morning drive anchor, reporter, 1984-. **ORGANIZATIONS:** Honorary chairperson, March of Dimes WalkAmerica, 1985-88; parliamentarian, CBS Inc, Minority Employees Assn, 1987-; mem, Chicago Assn of Black Journalists, 1987-; bd mem, Cris Radio (Chicagoland Reading Information Serv for the Handicapped), 1987-; mem, Sigma Delta Chi/ Professional Journalists, 1987-; bd mem, Little City Foundations's Project Vital, (Video Induced Training for Handicapped Youth), 1988-; bd of advisors, Med Care HMO/Educare Scholarship Found, 1988; mem, Women in Communications Inc, 1989. **HONORS/ACHIEVEMENTS:** Voice Behind State Farm Radio Spots Nationwide, 1986-; Benjamin Hooks Distinguished Achievement Recognition, NAACP, 1987; featured in Washington Journalism Review, 1987; Salute to Chicago's Up & Coming Black Business & Professional Women, Dollars & Sense Magazine, 1988; Tribute to Chicago Women, Midwest Women's Center, 1988; Skyaward of Merit, Women in Communications, 1989; Outstanding Excellence Award, Women in Communications, 1989; Outstanding Communicator, Women in Communications, 1989; Best Reporter Award, Illinois Assoiated Press, 1989. **BUSINESS ADDRESS:** Morning Drive Anchor, WBBM Newsradio 78, 630 N McClurg Ct, Chicago, IL 60611.

MIDDLETON, ERNEST J.
Educator. **PERSONAL:** Born Dec 25, 1937, Franklin, LA; married Rosa Metz; children: Lance, Owen. **EDUCATION:** Southern U, BA 1962;Univ of CO, EdS 1973;Univ of CO, EdD 1974. **CAREER:** Univ of KY, asso prof; Race & Sex Desegration Training Inst, dir 1974-; St Mary Par Publ Sch, prof 1962-63, 1965-70f St Mary Human Rel Cncl, vice pres 1966. **ORGANIZATIONS:** Pres St Mary Educ Assn 1967-70; chrm St Mary Comm Action Agency 1969; mem LA Educ Assn; SouthernUniv Mrch Band 1958-62; Kappa Alpha Psi Frat; NAACP; Phi Delta Kappa Frat; Nat Alliance of Black Sch Educ. **HONORS/ACHIEVEMENTS:** ASCD award Bowling GreenUniv 1968; EPDA fellowship SoutherUniv 1971; EPDA flwshpUniv of CO 1972; TDIS 1970-71; outstanding serv St Mary Par 1970-71; outstanding achvmnt LA Eudc Assn 1974. **MILITARY SERVICE:** AUS 1963-65.

MIDDLETON, MICHAEL A.
Government attorney. **PERSONAL:** Born Feb 24, 1947, Jackson, MS; married Julie Annette Nelson; children: Kimberly, Michael II, Marc. **EDUCATION:** Univ of MO, BA 1968; Univ of MO School of Law, JD 1971. **CAREER:** US Dept of Justice, trial attny 1971-75; Lawyers Comm for Civil Rights Under Law, dir govt employment proj 1975-76, dep chief counsel 1976-77; Dept of HEW Office of Civil Rights, dir div of policy devel 1977-79; Equal Employment Oppty Comm, assoc gen counsel, dir office of systemic progs 1979-80; Dept of Ed Office for Civil Rights, prin dep asst sec 1980-82; Equal Employment Oppty Comm, assoc gen counsel 1982-. **ORGANIZATIONS:** Mem DC Bar, Bar of State of MO, Bar of State of MS. **HONORS/ACHIEVEMENTS:** Special Achievement Awd Dept of Justice 1973-74. **BUSINESS ADDRESS:** Associate General Counsel, Equal Employment Oppty Comm, 2401 E St NW, Washington, DC 20506.

MIDDLETON, RICHARD TEMPLE, III
Educator. **PERSONAL:** Born Jan 17, 1942, Jackson, MS; married Brenda Marie Wolfe; children: Jeanna E, Richard T IV. **EDUCATION:** Lincoln Univ of MO, BS 1963, MEd 1965; Univ of Southern MO, EdD 1972. **CAREER:** Tougaloo Coll, instructor of educ 1967-70; Jackson State Univ, asst & assoc prof 1970-76, dir student teaching 1976-87. **ORGANIZATIONS:** Bd mem Ballet Mississippi 1983-85, Security Life Ins Co 1985; pres Beta Gamma Boule Sigma Pi Phi Frat 1985-87; bd mem Opera/South Co 1986-, Catholic Charities 1986-; vice pres Mississippi Religious Leadership Conference 1988-89; mem Natl Executive Council The Episcopal Church 1987-88. **HONORS/ACHIEVEMENTS:** Woodrow-Wilson King Fellowship Doctoral Study 1969; selected as mem of leadership, Jackson MS Chamber of Commerce 1987-88. **MILITARY SERVICE:** AUS 1st lt 2 yrs. **HOME ADDRESS:** 944 Royal Oak Dr, Jackson, MS 39209. **BUSINESS ADDRESS:** Dir of Student Teaching, Jackson State University, 1400 JR Lynch St, Jackson, MS 39217.

MIDDLETON, VERTELLE DELORES
Educational administrator. **PERSONAL:** Born Aug 10, 1942, Charleston, SC; daughter of Michael Graham and Nazarene Baldwin Graham; married James Middleton, Jr, Dec 21, 1963; children: Jamela V. **EDUCATION:** Johnson C Smith Univ, BS Psych/Soc 1964; NYU, Adult Educ Certificate 1975; Bank Coll, Adult Educ Certificate 1975; Temple Univ, Amin Training Certificate 1981; Webster Univ, Charleston SC, MA 1989. **CAREER:** Immacuale Consolidated High School, teacher 1964-67; Charleston County OIC Inc, exec dir 1968-82; Trident Teaching Coll Fair Break Center, center dir 1982-84; Trident Tech Coll Manpower Skill Center, dir; Beaufort Technical Coll, Walterboro SC, dir Career Success, 1987; Trident Technical Coll Berkeley Campus, Moncks Corner SC, dir JTPA 1987-. **ORGANIZATIONS:** Mem SC Higher Educ Assn 1983-; mem SC Chapter of SETA 1984-; mem SC Tech Educ Assn 1984-; Natl membership comm So Atlantic region; Alpha Kappa Alpha Sorority 1982-; sec Greater Bd Chapel AME Church 1980; sec Burke High School Advisory Bd 1983-; vice chmn Steward Bd Greater Bd Chapel 1980-; South Atlantic Region-Cluster Coordinator 1988-; chmn Burke High School Improvement Council 1988-; Trident Technical Coll Employee Assistance Program Advisory Council 1989. **HONORS/ACHIEVEMENTS:** Outstanding Community Serv, WPAL Radio Station 1984; Tribute to Women YWCA 1980; Alpha Kappa Alpha Sorority Outstanding Award S Atlantic Region 1986; Tribute to TWIN Woman-YWCA, Trident Technical Coll 1989. **HOME ADDRESS:** 1861 Taborwood Cir, Charleston, SC 29407. **BUSINESS ADDRESS:** Director, Trident Technical College, PO Box 482, Moncks Corner, SC 29461.

MIKELL, CHARLES D.
Association executive. **PERSONAL:** Married Jacqueline Henry; children: Michelene, Charles, II. **EDUCATION:** LincolnUniv PA, AB;Univ Pittsburgh, MPH. **CAREER:** Alcoholic Counseling & Recovery Prog CAP Inc, dir 1970-;Univ Pittsburgh, field supr grad students 1971-; Hill Rehab Center, dir 1968-70; Hill Rehab Center, asst dir 1967-68; Hill Emergency Lift Prog, supr 1966-67; Hill Dist Comm Action Program, asst coord 1965-66; neighborhood devel worker 1964065; Allegheny Co Health Dept, pub health san 1960-64; academic & prof consult 1968-69. **ORGANIZATIONS:** Scholarhsip Com United Mental Health Svc; Alcoholism Com United Mental Health Svc; former pres McKeesport Br NAACP 1964-74; bd dir treas Mon Yough Council Drug Abuse; former mem sec treas McKeesport Redevel Auth; Am Pub Health Assn; Program Aid Citizens Enterprise; New Image NAACP Health Com; exec com Mon-Yough Council Alcoholism; adv com McKeepsort Area Sch Dist; Am Legion Post 666; Booker T Wash Lodge 218 IBPOE of W. **MILITARY SERVICE:** USNR 1950-52; USMC 1952-55. **BUSINESS ADDRESS:** 107 6 St, Pittsburgh, PA 15222.

MILBOURNE, LARRY WILLIAM
Professional athlete. **PERSONAL:** Born Feb 14, 1951, Port Norris, NJ. **EDUCATION:** Cumberland Cnty Jr Coll; Glassboro St College. **CAREER:** Houston Astros, infielder 1971-76; Seattle Mariners, infielder 1977-80; Cleveland Indians, infielder 1982; minnesota Twins, infielder 1982; New York Yankees, infielder 1982-83; Philadelphia Phillies, infielder 1983; New York Yankees, infielder 1983; Seattle Mariners, infielder 1984-. **HONORS/ACHIEVEMENTS:** Grad from Milville High in 1969 where he earned All-State honors in Baseball for 2 yrs; signed by San Francisco's Class A affiliate at Decatur in 1971 & earned All-Star honors at second base; named to the TOPPS All-Rookie team.

MILBURN, CORINNE M.
Educator. **PERSONAL:** Born Sep 20, 1930, Alexandria, LA; married Dr Sidney E; children: Sidney E II, Deborah Anne. **EDUCATION:** Marian Coll Indpls, BS 1950; Univ of SD, MA 1970, EdD 1976. **CAREER:** IN Univ Med Cntr, lab tech (clin biochem) 1950-53; Carver Found-Tuskegee Inst, tissue culture tech 1954-57; Elk Point Pub Sch, hs sci teacher 1969-73, teacher corps team leader 1973-75; Univ of SD, asst prof/dir of outreach 1977-. **ORGANIZATIONS:** Grad intern sci consult AEA 12-Sioux City 1975-76; proj writer-HEW grant Univ of SD 1976-77; state pres Epsilon Sigma Alpha Int 1977-78; chap pres Phi Delta Kappa (USD chpt) 1979-80; state pres Assn of Tchr Educators 1979-80. **HONORS/ACHIEVEMENTS:** Pub in "Leaders of Amer Sec Educators" 1972; voc educ "A Challenging Alternative for the Gifted/Talented Student" 1976; voc educ "A New Dimension for the Gifted/Talented Student" 1976; "Education-A Lifelong Process" ESA Jour 1980. **BUSINESS ADDRESS:** Asst Prof/Dir of Outreach, Univ of SD, Vermillion, SD 57069.

MILES, CARLOTTA G.
Physician. **PERSONAL:** Born Sep 19, 1937, St Augustine, FL; married Theodore A; children: Wendell Gordon, Cecily Allison, Lydia Carlotta. **EDUCATION:** Wheaton Coll, AB 1959; HowardUniv Med Sch, MD 1964. **CAREER:** Pvt Practice, physician 1968-; Area B Children's Program, co-dir 1969-71. **ORGANIZATIONS:** Mem APA; Am Academy of Child Psychiatry; affiliate mem Am Psychoanalytic Inst; tching & supervising analyst Children's Hosp; asst prof psychiatry HowardUniv Coll of Med; faculty Washington Sch of Psychiatry; trustee Wheaton Coll; Black Student Fund of Washington The Potomac Sch; Woodley House. **HONORS/ACHIEVEMENTS:** Clerkship Prize for excellence in psychiatry HowardUniv Med Sch 1964. **BUSINESS ADDRESS:** 3000 Conn Ave NW, Washington, DC 20008.

MILES, DOROTHY MARIE
Military officer. **PERSONAL:** Born May 10, 1950, Gary, IN. **EDUCATION:** Oakland City Coll, BS 1973; Central MI Univ, MA 1981; Attending, Nova Univ. **CAREER:** Chicksands AFB England, position printer systems specialist 1975-77; Bolling AFB DC, equal oppor tech 1977-79; Barksdale AFB LA, shift commander security police 1980-82; Blytheville AFB AR, chief social actions 1982; Kunsan AFB Korea, chief social actions 1982-83; Military Personnel Ctr TX, chief equal oppor and treatment opers div 1983-85; Defense Equal Oppor Mgmt Inst FL, air force serv liaison officer 1985-. **ORGANIZATIONS:** Mem Tuskegee Airman Assoc 1984-, Natl Assoc for Female Execs 1984-; adjunct faculty mem Brevard Comm Coll 1985; Notable Amer Women 1987. **HONORS/ACHIEVEMENTS:** Outstanding Young Women of Amer 1980, 85; USAF Marksmanship Ribbon, Longevity Ribbon, Good Conduct w/one Oakleaf Cluster Ribbon, Overseas Long Tour Ribbon, Commendation Ribbon w/two Oakleaf clusters; also articles published. **MILITARY SERVICE:** USAF capt 13 yrs. **HOME ADDRESS:** 4850 Cobb Valley Dr, Kirby, TX 78219. **BUSINESS ADDRESS:** Air Force Serv Liaison Officer, Defense Equal Oppor Mgmt Inst, Patrick AFB, FL 32925.

MILES, E. W.
Educator. **PERSONAL:** Born May 04, 1934, Hearne, TX; married Frances Winfield; children: Tony W, Christopher W. **EDUCATION:** Prairie View Univ, BA 1955; IN Univ, AM 1960, PhD 1962. **CAREER:** Prairie View Univ, assoc prof 1962-65; Univ of NC, visiting faculty scholar 1965-66; IN Univ, visiting summer prof 1966; So Univ, 1967; Univ of TX, 1971; San Diego State Univ, prof polit sci 1966-. **ORGANIZATIONS:** Chmn of bd San Diego Urban League 1983-; mem bd dir Law in Amer Soc Found; chmn Com on Status of Blacks of the Amer Polit Sci Assn; past mem exec council Western Polit Sci Assn; mem adv panel CA Bd of Educ 1969-70; San Diego Blue Ribbon Com for Charter Review 1968; assoc edit West Pol Sci Quarterly; exec com CA State Assembly Fellowship Prog; mem State-Wide Anti-Discrim Com; mem Unit Prof of CA. **HONORS/ACHIEVEMENTS:** Recipient Distinguished Teaching Award San Diego State Univ 1968; co-author "Vital Issues of the Constitution" 1975; author of various scholarly articles. **MILITARY SERVICE:** AUS 1st Lt 1955-57. **BUSINESS ADDRESS:** Professor, San Diego StateUniv, Dept of Polit Science, San Diego, CA 92182.

MILES, EDWARD LANCELOT
Educator. **PERSONAL:** Born Dec 21, 1939; son of Cecil Miles and Louise (Dufont) Miles; married Wanda Elaine Merrick; children: Anthony Roger, Leila Yvonne. **EDUCATION:** Howard Univ, BA, w/honors, 1962; Univ of Denver Graduate School of Intl Studies, PhD, 1965. **CAREER:** Univ of Denver, instr 1965-66, asst prof, 1966-70; Univ of Denver Graduate School of Intl Studies, assoc prof 1970-74; Univ of WA, prof, Marine Studies & Public Affairs 1974-; dir, Inst for Marine Studies, 1982-. **ORGANIZATIONS:** mem, Ocean Policy Comm, Natl Rsch Council, 1970-74, chmn 1974-79; mem, bd of editors intl org, 1969-77; exec bd, Univ of Hawaii-Law of the Sea Inst, 1971-; assoc ed, "Ocean Devel & Intl Law Journal" 1973-; joint appointee Micronesian Maritime Auth Fed States Micr, 1977-83. **HONORS/ACHIEVEMENTS:** Honors in history Phi Beta Kappa 1962; Intl Affairs Fellow Cncl on Foreign Relations Inc 1972-73; James P Warburg Fellow Harvard Univ 1973-74. **BUSINESS ADDRESS:** Dir Inst for Marine Studies, U of WA, HF-05 3707 Brooklyn NE, Seattle, WA 98105.

MILES, FRANK J. W.
Business executive. **PERSONAL:** Born Dec 18, 1944, Orange, NJ; married Brenda. **EDUCATION:** Columbia U, MBA; Hampton U, BA. **CAREER:** State of NJ, major account relationships; Citibank NA Nat Black MBA Assn, vp; Urban Bankers Assn; NJ Real Estate Assn. **ORGANIZATIONS:** Vol Urban Consult Minority Bus; former Mayor's Appointee Exxex Co Econ Devel Corp Omego Psi Phi Frat. **MILITARY SERVICE:** AUS capt. **BUSINESS ADDRESS:** 100 Wood Ave, Iselin, NJ 08830.

MILES, FREDERICK AUGUSTUS
Psychiatrist. **PERSONAL:** Born May 25, 1928, Boston, MA; married Cora Edythe; children: Frederick, Felix, Andre. **EDUCATION:** VA St Coll, BS 1949; Columbia U, 1951; Army Lang Sch, 1952; Hunter Coll, 1955;Univ Basel Switzerland, 1958;Univ Freiburg, W Germany, MD 1964. **CAREER:** Brooklyn-Cumberland Med Cntr, internship & res pathology 1966-68; Brooklyn State Hosp, residency psychiatry 1969-72; Pvt Prac, psychiatrist; Brooklyn State Hosp, staff psychiatrist; Willia Hardgrow Mental Health Clinic, consult psychiatrist. **ORGANIZATIONS:** Mem AMA; APA; NY & Kings Co Med Soc; AAGP; ACEP; ACP; Provident Med Soc of Brooklyn; mem United Demo Club; Kappa Alpha Psi; bd trustees Redeemer Bapt Ch; AFAM. **MILITARY SERVICE:** AUS German interrogator 1952-55. **BUSINESS ADDRESS:** 808 New York Ave, Brooklyn, NY 11203.

MILES, KENNETH L.
Police captain. **PERSONAL:** Born Nov 29, 1937, Crewe, VA; married Carolyn D Garrett; children: Constance, Joan, Duane, Dana, David. **EDUCATION:** Long Island U, 1956; DE State Coll, 1957; Brandywine Coll. **CAREER:** City of Wilmington, police capt 1975-; Police Dept, lt 1973, sgt 1968, joined dept 1959. **ORGANIZATIONS:** Mem NOBLE; mem Boys Club of Am; bd of mgr Walnut St YMCA; bd dir Cen Br YMCA; mem NAACP. **HONORS/ACHIEVEMENTS:** Policeman of the Yr Award Martin Luther King Diner Com 1976. **BUSINESS ADDRESS:** 1000 King St, Wilmington, DE 19801.

MILES, LEO FIDELIS
Educator. **PERSONAL:** Born May 21, 1931, Washington, DC; married Recita Williams; children: Damita, Leolita, Recita, Leo. **EDUCATION:** VA State Coll, BS 1957, MS 1960. **CAREER:** NY Giants, professional football player 1953; Boys Jr Sr HS, tchr 1958; Bell Voc HS, tchr head football & track coach 1959-67; Alexandria VA, recreation supr 1960-65; Camp & Summer Enrichment Prog, asst dir of oper 1966-77; Lincoln Jr HS, asst prin 1967-70; Howard Univ, dir of athletics 1970-retirement. **ORGANIZATIONS:** Mem Kappa Alpha Psi; Professional Football Referees Assn; Nat Assn of Collegiate Dirs of Athletics; DC bd of Approved Basketball Officials; Eastern bd of Officials; VA State Alumni Assn; vice pres Brentwood Civic Assn; chmn "W" St Citizens Assn; Dept of HEW, spl consult 1968; natl football league official 1969; recording sec Lanham MD 1980. **HONORS/ACHIEVEMENTS:** Football Coach of the Year DC Public Schools 1964,65,66; mayor citizen advisor comm on resource & budget; CIAA Hall of Fame for Officials; USSA Bd of Visitors Emeritus; listed in Who's Who in Amer Colls & Univ; All-CIAA Football Player; Coll All Amer Football Player; officiated Superbowls VIII, X, XIX; recipient Citation as Natl Figure Awd Cath Youth Org; author "The Survival of the Black Athletic Conferences" Black Org Issues on Survival Techniques Yearwood, Lennox, Univ Press of Amer Inc Lanham MD 1980. **MILITARY SERVICE:** AUS capt 1954-55.

MILES, MARY ALICE
Elected official. **PERSONAL:** Born May 05, 1948, St Matthews, SC; children: Donald, Thaddeus, Handy Jr. **EDUCATION:** Orangeburg Tech Coll, AA 1968; SC State Coll, BS 1980; Univ of SC, MEd. **ORGANIZATIONS:** Vp Calhoun NAACP; adv Youth Council NAACP; bd mem Citizens Against Sexual Assault; mem Zeta Phi Beta, SC Personnel & Guidance Assoc, School Guidance Comm, Assoc for Counselor Ed, SC Mental Health Assoc, Eastern Star; pres Citizens in Action. **HONORS/ACHIEVEMENTS:** Concern Citizen Awd Zeta Phi Beta 1982; Presidential Scholar SC State Coll; Key SC Legislator Ebony Mag 1984; Woman of the Year Alpha Kappa Mu 1984. **HOME ADDRESS:** Rt 3 Box 1114, St Matthews, SC 29135.

MILES, NORMAN KENNETH
Clergyman, educator. **PERSONAL:** Born Dec 05, 1946, Toledo, OH; son of Mervin Miles and Sadie Miles; married Doris Calandra Goree; children: Erica Lynette, Norman Jr, Candace Renee, Kira Danette, Neal Mervyn. **EDUCATION:** Oakwood Coll, BA Theology 1964-68; Andrews Univ Seventh Day Adventist Theological Seminary, MDiv 1972-73; Univ of Michigan, MA 1974, PhD 1978. **CAREER:** Economic Opportunity Planning Assoc, work counselor 1968-69; South Central Conf & 7th Day Adventists, pastor 1969-72; Lake Regional Conf 7th Day Adventists, pastor 1974-77; 7th Day Adventists, prof 1977-; Andrews Univ, prof Urban Ministry; Univ of Michigan, Ann Arbor MI, adjunct prof of religion 1977-; Hyde Park Seventh-Day Adventist Church, Chicago IL, pastor 1989-. **ORGANIZATIONS:** Mp Ministerial Alliance, Hattiesburg MS, 1969-72; bd of dir Southern Mississippi Chapter Amer Red Cross; mem Natl Black Pastors Conf 1980-; dir Inst of Human Relations 7th Day Adventist Church 1983. **HONORS/ACHIEVEMENTS:** John Pierce Award, Historical Scholarship Univ of Michigan 1975. **BUSINESS ADDRESS:** Professor of Urban Ministry, Chairman, Dept of Christian Ministry, Andrews University, Berrien Springs, MI 49104.

MILES, RACHEL JEAN
Educator. **PERSONAL:** Born Sep 03, 1945, Memphis, TN; married Willie T; children: Lisa, Jason. **EDUCATION:** Lemoyne-Owen Coll, BS 1967; Memphis State U, EdM guidance & counseling 1970; Memphis StateUniv , post graduate 1971. **CAREER:** Shelby State Comm Coll, coor of counseling adv 1975-, prof coun 1972-75; Fairview Jr High Sch, coun engl tch 1971-72; Moorestown Township Coll Prep, guidance counselor 1971; Memphis State U, couns 1969-70; Memphis City Sch Sys, elem tchr 1967-68. **ORGANIZATIONS:** Pres bd of dirs Human Employment Resources Inc 1979-80; workshop presenter Am Personnel & Guidance Assn 1980; mem JUGS Charitable Orgn 1967-; mem Cherokee Com Civic Club 1969-; secr Westlawn-Galveston Block Club 1972-; bd of dirs Miss Black Memphis Pageant 1979-80. **HONORS/ACHIEVEMENTS:** Deans List Lemoyne-owen Coll 1967; Kappa Delta Pi H Onor Soc Memphis StateUniv 1970; Phi Delta Kappa Memphis StateUniv 1971; Colonel Aide De Camp Gov Ray Blanton 1977-78; appointed Limited Constitutional Convention of the State of TN Pres JD Lee & Delegates Micheal Hooks & Roscoe Dixon 1977-78; Honorary Staff Mem TN House of Repr 1977-78. **BUSINESS ADDRESS:** Shelby State Comm Coll, 737 Union Ave, Memphis, TN 38104.

MILES, VIC See LEVY, VICTOR MILES, JR.

MILES, WILLIE LEANNA
Association executive. **PERSONAL:** Born in Vienna, GA. **EDUCATION:** FL A&MUniv Tallahassee. **CAREER:** Asso for Prog & Dev of Assn for Study of Afro-Am Life & Hist, 1943-; Fed Gov Washington, DC, suprvr supply req officer 1942-57; ASALH Inc, admin asst 1957-72. **ORGANIZATIONS:** Visited most major cities in US promoting work of Assn for the study of Afro-Am Life & Hist. **HONORS/ACHIEVEMENTS:** Recep num awds for educ achive; Achieve Award Educ Assn 1968; Serv Award Assn for Study of Afro-Am Life & Hist 1971; Founder's Day Speaker Philadelphia Branch & Steadfast Devotion & outstanding service award Assn for the Study #Of Afro-Am Life & History Inc May 17, 1975. **BUSINESS ADDRESS:** Assn Study Afro Am Life & Hist, 1401 14 St NW, Washington, DC 20005.

MILEY, DEBRA CHARLET
Sales coordinator. **PERSONAL:** Born Dec 08, 1963, Atlanta, GA; daughter of Charles Miley Sr and Leila Mae Williams Miley; children: Brandy. **EDUCATION:** Georgia State Univ, Atlanta GA, BS Public & Urban Affairs, 1988. **CAREER:** Courtyard by Marriott, Atlanta GA, front desk supvr, 1986-89, sales coord, 1989-. **ORGANIZATIONS:** Mem, Natl Coalition of Black Meeting Planners, 1987-. **HOME ADDRESS:** 6900 Shenandoah Trl, Apt 315, Austell, GA 30001. **BUSINESS ADDRESS:** Sales Coordinator, Courtyard by Marriott, 380 Interstate N Pkwy, Suite 380, Atlanta, GA 30009.

MILLARD, THOMAS LEWIS
Educator. **PERSONAL:** Born Mar 08, 1927, Newark, NJ; son of James Millard and Elizabeth Millard; married P Anne Kelsic; children: Elizabeth Millard Reaves, Thomas Lewis Jr, James Edward. **EDUCATION:** Rutgers Univ, AB 1952; Columbia Univ, MS 1956; New York Univ, MA 1960; Columbia Univ, 3rd Year Certificate 1969; Fairleigh Dickerson Univ, EdD 1976. **CAREER:** New York Youth Serv Bureau, youth parole officer 1956-59; United Parent Assoc, New York City Bd of Educ, consultant in comm school rel 1959-60; Irvington House, social worker 1960-61; Public Schools, school soc worker Newark Brd of Ed 1961-65; Montclair State Coll, assoc prof of educ, social work and coord of school social work. **ORGANIZATIONS:** Bd of dirs Mental Health Assoc of Morris Cnty 1983-, The Mental Health Assoc in New Jersey; vice chmn bd of trustees New Jersey Neuro Psychiatric Inst 1977-79; bd of dir ALFRE Inc (Alcoholic Trmnt Fac) 1981-84; bd of dir New Jersey State Prison Complex 1979-81; fellow Amer Orthopsychiatric Assn 1982; pres, bd of educ Orange NJ 1968-71; delegate White House Conf on Children 1970. **HONORS/ACHIEVEMENTS:** Diplomate in Prfsnl Psychotherapy Int Assoc Prof Couns & Psychothaerapy 1983; licensed Marriage Counselor NJ 1983; Honored by NJ State Assembly in Resolution Citing Outstanding Teaching; appointed mem by Governor to New Jersey State Bd of Marriage Counselor Examiners. **MILITARY SERVICE:** AUS lt col USAR-RET ACTIVE & reserve; WW II Ribbon, Occupation Ribbon (Japan), Victory Medal 1946. **HOME ADDRESS:** 5 Overlook Ave, Randolph, NJ 07869. **BUSINESS ADDRESS:** Assoc Prof Educ & Soc Work, Montclair State College, Upper Montclair, NJ 07043.

MILLEDGE, LUETTA UPSHUR
Educational administrator. **PERSONAL:** Born in Savannah, GA; children: Dr Marshall L Upshur. **EDUCATION:** Ft Valley State Coll, BA English 1948; Atlanta Univ, MA English 1949; Univ Georgia, PhD English 1971. **CAREER:** Savannah State Coll, asst instructor 1949-, assoc prof, prof, chr div humn 1973-80, hd dept English 1972-80, hd dept humnl/fine arts 1980-84. **ORGANIZATIONS:** Brd mem GA Endowment for Humanities 1980-83; Elder Butler Presbytery Churh; mem Presid Comm Futr Savannah State Coll. **HONORS/ACHIEVEMENTS:** Regent's Scholarship 1944-48; Ford Found Fellowship 1969-71; George Washington Honor Medal; Freedoms Found Valley Forge Speech Vital Spchs 1973; Phi Kappa Phi, Phi BetaKappa (Univ of GA). **BUSINESS ADDRESS:** Head Dept of Humanities, Savannah State Coll, Savannah, GA 31404.

MILLENDER, DHARATHULA H.
City council member. **PERSONAL:** Born Feb 04, 1920, Terre Haute; daughter of Orestes Hood and Daisy Ernestine Eslick Hood; married Justyn L Millender, 1944 (deceased); children: Naomi Estelle, Justine Faye. **EDUCATION:** Indiana State Univ 1941, BS; Purdue Univ, MS 1958. **CAREER:** Dunbar-Pulaski School Gary, librn media specialist 1960-; Houston Jr High School Baltimore, librn 1953-60; Lincoln Jr High Montgomery Co, teacher 195-53; Serv Club # 2 Indianatown & Gap Mil Reser, army librn 1944; Netherlands Stds Unit Libr of Congress, ref asst 1943-44; Pmoney HS, librn teacher 1942-43; Bettis Jr Coll, librn 1941-42; Black Exper Film News Mag, ed 1973-82; Gary School System, Gary, IN, librarian/media specialist 1960-78; Gary School System, Gary,IN, reading lab coord 1979-82. **ORGANIZATIONS:** Chpsn Gary Hist & Cultural Soc 1977; Gary Precinct Committeewoman 1972-80; organist St Philip Luth Church; pres NIMM Educ Media Serv Inc; author 4 Books & num articles in journ & educ mags; libr Multi-Media Counsul Model Cities Dayton 1969-70; devel libr from storemroom using para-profes tchr help; libr Media Consul Model Cities Gary dev media cntr at Comm Research Cntr Gary; prog oord Cable TV Gary channel 3a 1973-; radio program Lift Every Voice & Sing sta WWCA, mat from Black Exper State dir Assn for Study of Afro-Am Life & Hist 1973; State Hist IN Black Pol Caucus 1973; hist Gary Chptr IN State Black Caucus 1973; former state chrmn Hist & Cul 1966-72; chrmn Gary NAACP Black Hist Com 1962-72; libr trustee Gary Pub Libr 1971-75; mem Amer Libr Assn; mem ALA Black Caucus; former mem NEA & IN Educ Assn; chmn & exec dir, Gary Historical & Cultural Society, Inc 1982-; historian, Natl Black Caucus - Natl League of Cities, 1984-; consultant, Follow Through Cultural Linquistic Approach 1989-. **HONORS/ACHIEVEMENTS:** Recip Commendable Book by an Indiana author Crispus Attucks Indiana Writers Conf 1966; outstanding serv Rendered to Comm Award Gary NAACP 1966; Media Women's Award, Natl Assn of Media Women 1974; Outstanding Women of Lake County, Indiana 1984; Brief Note on the Early Development of Lake County & Gary, Indiana, published by Gary Historical & Cultural Society, Inc 1988. **BUSINESS ADDRESS:** City Council Member, City of Gary, 401 Broadway, Gary, IN 46402.

MILLENDER, MALLORY KIMERLING
Editor, publisher & educator. **PERSONAL:** Born Jul 11, 1942, Birmingham, AL; married Jacqueline Stripling; children: Malbory, Jr, Marlon. **EDUCATION:** Paine Coll, BA (cum laude) English Lit, 1964; Univ Toulouse (French), 1966; KS State Teachers Coll, MS Foreign Lang, 1969; Columbia Univ, MS Journalism, 1977. **CAREER:** Paine Coll, asst prof 1967-; Augusta News Review, editor & publisher 1974-; Paine Coll, coord foreign lang 1977-, dean

admissions 1971-. **ORGANIZATIONS:** Tchr TW Josey High Schl 1964-67; mem Brd Trts of Paine Coll 1980-82; vice pres Brd Trts of Antioch Bpt Chrh 1971-; pres New Grow Inc 1971-. **HONORS/ACHIEVEMENTS:** Best column Natl Nwspr Publs Assoc Merit Awd 1983; flw Time Inc 1977; fclty flw United Negro Coll Fnd 1976-77; french govt tchg asst, Fulbright US and French Govt 1968-69. **BUSINESS ADDRESS:** Editor & Publisher, Paine Coll, 1235 15th St, Augusta, GA 30910.

MILLER, ANDREA LEWIS
Educator. **PERSONAL:** Born Sep 10, 1954, Memphis, TN; married Robert A Miller; children: Meredith Mechelle. **EDUCATION:** LeMoyne Owen Coll, BS 1976; Atlanta Univ, MS 1978, PhD 1980. **CAREER:** Univ of Cincinnati Coll of Med, postdoctoral fellow 1980-82; LeMoyne Owen Coll, prof of biol, assoc investigator 1982-83, pof biol, principal invest 1983-. **ORGANIZATIONS:** Mem Memphis Volunteer Placement Prog 1973, Alpha Kappa 1973, Amer Soc of Cell Biologist 1981; pres LeMoyne Owen Coll Faculty Org 1984-86; mem SoutheastElectron Microscopy Soc 1985, Electron Microscopy Soc of Amer 1985. **HONORS/ACHIEVEMENTS:** Predcotoral Fellowship Natl Inst of Health 1977-80; Rsch Awd Lederle Labs 1980; Rsch Grant Natl Inst of Health 1983-86; Premed Ed Grant United Negro Coll Fund 1984-; Doe Research Grant. **BUSINESS ADDRESS:** Assoc Professor of Biology, LeMoyne Owen College, 807 Walker Ave, Memphis, TN 38126.

MILLER, ANNA M.
Association executive. **PERSONAL:** Born May 15, 1923, New Orleans; married Martin W; children: Walter P, Loretta E, Fatima M. **EDUCATION:** XavierUniv New Orleans, BS (cum laude) 1943; Cath Sch Soc Serv Wash, DC, 1944; Howard U, 1945. **CAREER:** Chester Cit Info Cntr, chmn steering com 1969-; NAACP, chmn voter reg 1963-; League Women Voters, chmn 1964-70; Centennial Com IHMC, co-chairperson 1971-74; Human Concerns Com YWCA, chmn 1971-. **ORGANIZATIONS:** Mem Chester Rep Theatre 1969. **HONORS/ACHIEVEMENTS:** Comm Serv award 5th United Presb Ch 1967; Hum Serv award Chester Br NAACP 1973.

MILLER, ARTHUR J.
Management consultant. **PERSONAL:** Born Oct 07, 1934, New York, NY; son of Theodore R Miller and Rosalie White; married Mary Lee, Feb 19, 1966 (deceased). **CAREER:** Chase Manhatten Bank, dividend clerk 1952, supvr 1961, sys planning ofcr 1968, 2nd vice pres 1970, vice pres banking 1974-87; AJM Assoc, Inc, pres 1988; Business Systems Mgmt, Inc, principal, 1989. **ORGANIZATIONS:** Bd dir Reality House Inc; Advisory Bd, Urban's Bankers teller training, bd dir, Joan Miller's Dance player. **MILITARY SERVICE:** AUS Corpl 1955-58. **BUSINESS ADDRESS:** Business Systems Mgmt, Inc, 150 Broadway, Suite G12, New York, NY 10038.

MILLER, BENJAMIN T.
Educator. **PERSONAL:** Born Nov 23, 1934, Aliquippa, PA. **EDUCATION:** Univ Denver, BFA 1960; Carnegie-Mellon Univ, MFA 1967. **CAREER:** Dept of Art So IL U, chmn 1979-; Dept of Art & Art Educ IN Univ of PA, chmn 1972-79; CA State Coll, chmn 1970-72; Carlow Coll, instr 1968-69. **ORGANIZATIONS:** Bd dir Am Waterways Center for the Arts; IN Co Council for the Arts; Cambria Blair & IN Arts Consortium; exec bd PA Art Educ Assn Nat Assn of Art Adminstrs; Nat Art Educ Assn; PA Art Educ Assn; IN Co Council on the Arts. **HONORS/ACHIEVEMENTS:** Exhbn Am Waterways Consortium Show 1976; one man show Clarion State Coll 1977; 2nd World Black & African Festival of the Arts & Culture 1974. **MILITARY SERVICE:** AUS 1957-59. **BUSINESS ADDRESS:** Dept of Art, Southern IL Univ, Carbondale, IL 62901.

MILLER, BERNICE JOHNSON
Educational administration. **PERSONAL:** Born in Chicago, IL; married George Benjamin Miller; children: Benita, Michael. **EDUCATION:** Roosevelt Univ Chicago IL, BA; Chicago Teachers Coll, MA 1965; CAS Harvard Univ Grad School of Ed, 1968-69, EdD 1972; Harvard Univ Grad School of Ed, 1972. **CAREER:** Chicago Bd of Ed, teacher elem & hs 1950-66; The New School for Children Inc, headmistress 1966-68; Jackson Coll, assoc dean 1968-70; Radcliffe, instr1970-73; Harvard Grad School of Ed, assoc dir 1971-75; Boston Public Schools Lucy Stone School, principal 1977-78; Boston Public Schools, sr officer 1978-84; Harvard Grad School, dir high tech rsch proj 1983-84; City Coll of Chgo, pres. **ORGANIZATIONS:** Bd mem Children's World Day Care Ctr Boston 1972-84, Blue Cross/Blue Shield Boston, United Way; trustee Brigham's & Women's Hosp Med Found; mem 1968-84,pres 1983-85 United Commun Plng Corp; bd mem Chicago Metro History Fair Bd; mem Mayor's Commiss on Women. **HONORS/ACHIEVEMENTS:** Educator's Award Boston 350th Anniv of Boston MA 1980; Educator of the Year Urban Bankers Ed Awd Boston 1982; Woman of the Year Awd Assoc of Mannequins 1984; Woman in Ed Business & Professional Women Boston & Vicinity 1984; Freedom Awd Roosevelt Univ 1985; Disting Alumni of Chicago State Univ NABSE 1985; OutstandingAchievement Awd in Educ YWCA 1986; Minority Networking Org of Focus & Seana Mag Serv Awd 1986. **BUSINESS ADDRESS:** President, City Colleges of Chicago, 30 E Lake St, Chicago, IL 60601.

MILLER, CARROLL LEE
Educational administrator. **PERSONAL:** Born Aug 20, 1909, Washington. **EDUCATION:** Howard U, BA (magna cum laude) 1929, MA 1930; Columbia Tchrs Coll, EdD 1952. **CAREER:** Miles Coll, instr 1930-31; Howard U, mem faculty 1931-, prof educ 1957-, chmn dept 1961-68; Coll Liberal Arts, asso dean 1961-64; Grad Sch, dean 1966-74, prof higher educ 1974-, dir summer session 1964-70; DC Pub Schs Winings, instr social studies 1933-40; Commonwealth, VA, research asst 1938-39; Nat Conf Problems Rural Youth OK, mem adv com 1963; Commn Civil Rights, part conf 1962. **ORGANIZATIONS:** Mem exec council Episcopal Diocese WA 1964-68; mem Dept Coll Work 1957-67; mem standing com 1967-68; chmn Interracial Task Force 1969-70; mem Comm on Ministry 1970-72; rev bd 1973-74; Episcopal Council Overseas Students & Visitors 1960-63; mem Grad Record Exams bd 1965-70; exec com Council Grad Sch US 1968-71; exec com Grad Deans African-Am Inst; bd dirs DC TB & Assn 1953-59, 65; DC Epis Cntr for Children 1964-70; trustee Absolom Jones Theol Inst; mem Am Personnel & Guid Assn, del assembly 1963-65, 68-69; Nat Assn Student Personnel Adminstr Nat AssnUniv Research Adminstrs; Am Assn Coll Tchr Educ liaison rep DC 1963-65; Am Coll Personnel Assn; Nat Vocational Guid Assn; Student Personnel Personnel Assn Tchr Educ pres 1971-72; Nat Soc Study Edn; Assn Higher Edn; Soc Advancement Edn; Adult Educ Assn; AAAS; Assn for Gen & Liberal Edn; Nat Soc Coll Tchrs of Edn; Am Acad Polit & Social Scis; Phi Delta Kappa; Kappa Delta Pi Contrib ednl.

MILLER, CLEO CALVIN
Professional athlete. **PERSONAL:** Born Sep 05, 1952, Gould, AR; married Rosalyn; children: Latricia; Cleo III; Antoine. **EDUCATION:** AR Pine Bluff, Indus Educ. **CAREER:** Oakland Invaders, fullback 1984-. **HONORS/ACHIEVEMENTS:** Named honorable mention All-Am as a soph and All-NAIA as a soph & jr.

MILLER, DENNIS WELDON
Physician. **PERSONAL:** Born Mar 12, 1949, Roanoke, VA; married Carol Miller; children: Damon, Jared. **EDUCATION:** Fisk Univ, 1971; Meharry Med Coll, 1975; KC General Hosp & Medical Cntr, residency in OBGYN 1975-76; Truman Medical Center 1976-79. **CAREER:** Private practice, physician. **ORGANIZATIONS:** Mem Gynecological Soc, Southwest Clinical Soc, Natl Med Assn 1971-77; mem AMA 1971-77; mem NAACP; mem Kaw Valley Med Soc, Amer Assn of Gynecological Laparoscopists, Wyandotte Co Medical Soc, KS Medical Soc, KS Foundation for Medical Care; Gyn Laser Soc. **HONORS/ACHIEVEMENTS:** Omega Psi Phi Frat Outstanding Young Men of Amer 1976. **BUSINESS ADDRESS:** Dennis W Miller MD PA, 600 Nebraska Ste 102, Kansas City, KS 66101.

MILLER, DEXTER J., JR.
Business executive. **PERSONAL:** Born Dec 10, 1934, Kansas City, MO; married Martha L; children: Maelyn, Sherri, Candace, Dexter, Marcus. **EDUCATION:** Kansas City Univ, 1959-61; Rockhurst Coll, 1968-70; Natl Coll of Bus, BS Bus Admin 1975-76; completed both parts of LUTC Professional Sales Training Course 1959-61; completed 6 parts of CLU Prol Theoretical Ins Course 1969-72. **CAREER:** Atlanta Life Ins Co, life underwriter 1957-66, staff mgr, asst dist mgr 1966-68, dist mgr. **ORGANIZATIONS:** Mem MO Underwriters Assoc; mem exec com Underwriters Assoc of Gr KC; life mem NAACP; mem trustee bd Bethel AME Church; mem Laymans Org of AME Church, Millionaires Club, Natl Ins Assoc 1977-80; pres Ivanhoe Social Club 1978; pres Life Underwriters Hon Soc 1978; chmn bd of dir Blue Hills Comm Fed Credit Union 1978; mem Presidents Club Atlanta Life Ins 1978-80; appt chmn ins comm trustee bd Bethel AME Church 1980; mem exec comm Ivanhoe Soc 1980; elected fin sec Ivanhoe Club 1984. **HONORS/ACHIEVEMENTS:** Salesman of the Year 1958,59; Awd for Outstanding Sales Achievement Natl Negro Ins Week 1958-66; Outstanding Asst Mgr in Sales Natl Negro Ins Week 1967;Outstanding Mgrs Perf Natl Negro Ins Week 1968-74; Exceptional Performance & Leading all Others in the Field of Life Insurance-Sales & Serv for Mgrs Hornsby Trophy Natl Ins Assoc 1980,81,82. **BUSINESS ADDRESS:** District Manager, Atlanta Life Insurance Co, 4725 Pasen Blvd, Kansas City, MO 64110.

MILLER, DORIS JEAN
Educator. **PERSONAL:** Born Oct 13, 1933, River Rouge, MI; married Olie Miller; children: Carla A, Darryl S, Felicia C. **EDUCATION:** Wayne State Univ, BA 1957; MI State Univ, Cert 1963; Wayne State Univ, MA 1968. **CAREER:** River Rouge Public Schools, teacher 1959-73, principal 1973-74, teacher 1974-79; MI Fed of Teachers, field rep 1979-; Wayne County Community Coll, trustee. **ORGANIZATIONS:** Mem Alpha Kappa Alpha Sor 1952-; mem bd of dir Downriver Guidance Clinic 1970-; chmn Black Women's Task Force 1982-; mem Greater Metro Det Guidance Assoc 1982-; mem Women's Conf of Concerns 1982-; mem bd of dir Wayne County Private Indus Council 1983-; pres 1982-84, treas 1985 Wayne County Community Coll Found. **HONORS/ACHIEVEMENTS:** Scholarship Ford Motor Co Fund 1951-55; Community Activist/Educ NAACP 1973. **BUSINESS ADDRESS:** Trustee, Wayne County Community College, 801 W Fort, Detroit, MI 48226.

MILLER, DOROTHY RUTH
Educator. **PERSONAL:** Born Dec 09, 1915, Loreauville, LA; married Yeard; children: Floye, June Rose, Debra. **EDUCATION:** Huston Tillotson, BS 1938; Lamar Coll, ME; TX So U. **CAREER:** O J Thomas High School, tchr mus & eng 1938-40; Blessed Sacrament High School, tchr; Adams Elem Sch, tchr; Beaumont Indep Sch Dist, tchr. **ORGANIZATIONS:** Alpha Kappa Alpha Bus & Professional Women's Club; pres Musoleyet Soc Club; NEA; TSTA; TCTA; Direct # 5 OBC; bd trustees Carroll St Nursery Sch; Grand Ladies Aux; vice pres St TX-LA. **HONORS/ACHIEVEMENTS:** Tchr of yr United Appeal Rep 1965-67; mother of yr PTA Charlton Pollard HS 1965, 66; Most Outst Tchr of Yr 1973, 74; Silver Tray Awd; Orgnzr of HLHon Soc.

MILLER, E. ETHELBERT
Educational administrator. **PERSONAL:** Born Nov 20, 1950, New York, NY; son of Egberto Miller and Enid Miller; married Denise King; children: Jasmine Simone, Nyere-Gibran. **EDUCATION:** Howard Univ, BA Afro-Amer Studies 1972. **CAREER:** African-Amer Resource Ctr Howard Univ, dir 1974-. **ORGANIZATIONS:** Bd mem PEN American Center; adv bd The Washington School 1984-; council member DC Comm Humanities Council 1984-; be mem Pen/Faulkner Found, Blue Mountain Center. **HONORS/ACHIEVEMENTS:** Tony Taylor Awardd Cultural Alliance of Washington DC 1986; Mayor's Art Award for Literature 1982. **BUSINESS ADDRESS:** Dir, African-American Resource Center, Howard Univ, PO Box 746, Washington, DC 20059.

MILLER, EARL VONNIDORE
Physician. **PERSONAL:** Born May 09, 1923, Natchez, MS; married Rosalie; children: Miriam, Earl, Beryl, Kyle, Michael. **EDUCATION:** Dillard U, BA 1943; Atlanta U, postgrad 1944; Medharry Coll, MD 1947. **CAREER:** Pvt Prac, physician urology 1959-; VA, chf resd urology 1958-59;Univ of IA Hosp, 1st urology resd 1957-58; Hubbard Hosp, 2nd yr surg resd 1956-57; VA Hosp, 1st yr surg resd 1955-57; Columbus, GA, gen prac 1948-55; St Agnes Hosp, intern 1947-48;Univ WA, asso clinical prof urology 1972-; Harvorbiew Med Ctr, urologist-in-chief 1968-70; The Dr's Hosp, chf urology 1967-71, med staff 1974-75. **ORGANIZATIONS:** Mem Nat Med Assn; Kingco Med Soc; AMA; NW Urological Soc; Western Sect Am Urolog Assn; Am Urolog Assn; Intl Coll Surgeons Publ "Use of Intestines in Urolog Surgery" 1959; "Bladder Pouch for Tubeless Cystomstomy" Jour of Urology 1960; "Symtomatic Blindly Ending Bifid Ureter" Jour Urology 1964; "Use of DMSO in Peyronie's Disease" 1967; "Pseudocysts & of the Pancreas Presenting as Renal Mass Lsions" British Jour 1971; "Benign Testis Tumor", "Epidermoid Testicular Cyst" Nat Med Assn; "Epidermoid Cyst benign testicular tumor" intl sur; "simultaneous adrenal & multiple bilateral Renal Cysts" JourUrology. **BUSINESS ADDRESS:** 503 Med Dent Bldg, Seattle, WA 98101.

MILLER, EDITH
Judge. **PERSONAL:** Born in New York, NY; children: Janice, Brian. **EDUCATION:** Hunter Coll, BA; St John's Univ Sch of Law, JD, Hon LLD. **CAREER:** New York Univ

Sch of Law, adj assoc prof; Fordham Univ Grad Sch of Soc Svc, adj prof; New York City Family Court, admin judge; New York State Supreme Ct, supreme court justice. **ORGANIZATIONS:** Bd dirs Harlem Interfaith Counseling Servc; bd trustees Natl Council of Juvenile & Family Court Judges; mem Bar Assn of the City of New York; life mem Natl Bar Assn, League of Women Voters; commnr Officer of Black Ministry of New York Archdiocese; mem Women's City Club of the City of New York; mem Natl Council of Negro Women. **HONORS/ACHIEVEMENTS:** Mem Hall of Fame Hunter Coll; Hon DL degree St John's Univ; executive mem Assoc of the Bar of the City of New York. **BUSINESS ADDRESS:** Supreme Court Justice, NY State Supreme Court, 100 Centre St, New York, NY 10013.

MILLER, ERENEST EUGENE
Educator. **PERSONAL:** Born Jun 13, 1948, Farmville, VA; son of William C. Miller and Maria G. Miller; married Alice Robinson, Jun 08, 1985. **EDUCATION:** VA State Univ, BA 1970, EdM, 1978. **CAREER:** Gold Hill Elementary School, teacher 1970-71; Cumberland Co Schools, adult educ teacher 1973-; Longwood Coll Summer Inst for Talented & Gifted Students, facilitator 1979; Cumberland HS, educator 1971-. **ORGANIZATIONS:** Scout master Robert E Lee Scout Troop 6280 1971-74; dir proj VA Found for the Humanities & Public Policy 1979; pres Cumberland Co Branch NAACP 1976-80; bd mem VA State Conf NAACP 1978-; Sponsor SCA Cumberland HS; Dir, Summer Youth Employment and Training Program; Coach, Battle of the Brains, 1988; Coach, Social Studies AC Team, 1988; Vice pres, Virginia State NAACP, 1988; Vice Pres, Iota Tau Lambda Chapter, Alpha Phi Alpha, 1988; Mem, Sharon Baptist Church, Vice Pres, Inspirational Choir, Dir, Vocational Bible School. **HONORS/ACHIEVEMENTS:** Trophy & Plaque Luther P Jackson Faculty 1966; Engraved Plaque Robt E Lee Scout Troop 6280 1974; Certificate, VA State Conf, NAACP 1976; Plaque, Cumberland High School, 1987; Plaque, Central Piedmont Action Council, 1989. **HOME ADDRESS:** Route 4, Box 172, Farmville, VA 23901. **BUSINESS ADDRESS:** Social Studies Dept Chmn, Cumberland High School, PO Box 35, Cumberland, VA 23040.

MILLER, ETHEL JACKSON
Retired librarian. **PERSONAL:** Born Jul 20, 1916, Savannah, GA; divorced; children: Leroy Hebert, Jr. **EDUCATION:** A&T StateUniv Greensboro, NC, BS 1936; Hampton Inst Library Sch VA, BS in LS 1937; ColumbiaUniv Sch of Edn, 1951. **CAREER:** A&T State Univ Greensboro NC, asst librarian 1937-41; USMC Camp Lejeune NC, camp librarian 1942-45; VA Hosp Roanoke VA, hosp librarian 1945-50; Moultrie GAPubl School, hs librarian 1950-52; Tremont Branch NY Publica Library, first asst 1953-70; Lane Library Armstrong State Coll, coord of reader serv 1971-78, acting dir 1978-79, retired coord of reader serv 1979-81. **ORGANIZATIONS:** Bd of dir Greenbriar Children's Center 1975-; mem Alpha Kappa Alpha Soroity; mem Am Library Assn; mem GA Library Assn.

MILLER, EVANS ROYCE
Business executive, owner, mayor. **PERSONAL:** Born May 05, 1932, Bowling Green, KY; married Thelma J Waller; children: Steven Royce, Sheila Ann. **EDUCATION:** Eulien Barber Coll, 1950; Greer Tech Inst, 1968. **CAREER:** Markham Roller Rink Inc, pres owner 1974-; MARKHAM, IL City Council, alderman city council 1970-78; Exxon Oil Co Bedford Park, IL, union steward 1968-73; Markham Roller Rink Inc Markham, IL, pres bd of dirs 1974-. **ORGANIZATIONS:** Organizer & scoutmaster Cub & Boy Scouts of Am 1968-73; organizer & coach Little League, Babe Ruth Baseball 1968-75; bd of dirs S Suburban Br NAACP 1974-76; mem Operation PUSH 1976-. **HONORS/ACHIEVEMENTS:** Recip of Service Award USAAF 1951-55; Brotherhood Award Journal Newspaper Group 1972; Writer Recreation Columnist Standard Newspaper Oak Forest, IL 1973; Appreciation Award Greater St John Bapt Ch 1975; outstanding Serv Award Markham Jaycees 1976; Appreciation Award GSA 1980. **MILITARY SERVICE:** USAAF airman 1st/c 1951-55. **BUSINESS ADDRESS:** Markham Roller Rink Inc, 16630 S Dixie Hwy, Markham, IL 60426.

MILLER, EVELYN B.
Association executive, author. **PERSONAL:** Born in Atlanta, GA; daughter of Thomas F Bailey (deceased) and Willie Groves Bailey (deceased); married Charles R Miller, Aug 28, 1955 (deceased). **EDUCATION:** Southeastern U, BA; Spelman Coll, Hunter Coll, Columbia Univ, studies; New Sch for Social Research. **CAREER:** YMCA of Gr NY Harlem Br, senior dir of membership, adult prog and pub relations, retired. **ORGANIZATIONS:** Mem Assn Black Social Workers; life member NAACP; Metro Comm of 100 Inc; Assn Professional Dirs; 5th pres Knickerbocker Intl Business & Professional Women Inc; past mem Commn on Personnel & Security Matters YMCA; past reg co-commr on white racism YMCA; past chair Communications Cabinet YMCA Gtr NY; mem League of Women Voters; deacon 2nd Presb Ch; charter mem, Childsville Inc; trustee, Alexander Robertson Elem School, New York City. **HONORS/ACHIEVEMENTS:** Cert YMCA Sr Dir; 2nd place Woman of Yr Greyhound Bus Co 1967; Loyalty & Devotion Award Metro Comm of 100 Inc 1972; winner 3rd place poll taken by NY Daily Challenge newspaper "Ten Leading Harlemites" 1977; author "Footsteps on the Stair" under pen name "Leslie "Groves" 1977; Youth Serv Award, Harlem Branch YMCA, 1984. **HOME ADDRESS:** 415 Central Park W, New York, NY 10025.

MILLER, FREDERICK A.
Management consultant. **PERSONAL:** Born Nov 02, 1946, Philadelphia, PA; married Pauline Kamen Miller. **EDUCATION:** LincolnUniv PA, BA 1968. **CAREER:** CT Genl Life Ins Co, admin 1968-72, human devel consult 1972-76, asst dir training 1976-79; Kaleel Jamison Assoc Mgmt Consult Firm, partner vice pres 1979-85, pres 1985-. **ORGANIZATIONS:** Mem Kappa Alpha Psi Frat 1965-; pres Inst for Comm Orgnl & Personal Effectiveness 1972-78; bd of dir The Living Sch 1973-; mem Orgn Devel Network 1974-; mem Am Soc for Training & Devel 1974-; mem NTL Inst 1976-; mem Council of Concerned Black Execs Inc 1979-; bd of dir NTL Inst 1980-; bd of dirs Orgn Devel Network 1986-. **HONORS/ACHIEVEMENTS:** Recip John Mcgee Scholarship full 4 yr 1964; outstdng Young Men of Am 1977. **MILITARY SERVICE:** AUS sgt 1968-70. **BUSINESS ADDRESS:** President, Kaleel Jamison Associates, PO Box 6180, Albany, NY 12206.

MILLER, FREDERICK E.
Business executive. **PERSONAL:** Born Jan 28, 1931, Paulsboro, NJ; married Jean Reid; children: Frederick Jr, Darrel, Catheleen, Felecia. **EDUCATION:** Rutgers Univ, BA 1962; Temple Univ, EdM 1962, Grad Study, Mgmt & Fin 1975, MEd; Amer Grad Univ, MBA. **CAREER:** Miller Prods, bus entrepreneus 1955-62; Temple Univ, supvr instr in teacher training 1963-65; Philadelphia Publ Schools, teacher 1960-65; Temple Univ, supvr instr in teacher training 1963-65; Philadelphia OIC Inc, dep exec dir 1965-68, exec dir1968; OIC of Amer Inc, sr vp, exec dir 1968-73; Philadelphia Port Corp, finance dir. **ORGANIZATIONS:** Consult Govt Depts & Bus Orgs; mem Amer Mgmt Assoc New York City 1975-, Natl Indust Adv Council of OIC 1973-; chmn Independent Bus & Profession Com; adv HEW's Natl Inst of Health Prog for manpower placement & training of former drug addicts; consult to HUD & Gov's Priorities Comm; mem deacon Zion Bapt Church; mem Natl Assoc Community Devel, Wynnefield Civic Assoc, BSA, NAACP, Rutgers Univ Alumni Assoc, Temple Univ Alumni Assoc; mem bd of dir Philadelphia Port Corp. **HONORS/ACHIEVEMENTS:** Cited for Spec Recog as one of 1000 Successful Blacks Ebony Success Library 1973; 100 Top Black Bus Citation Black Enterprise 1973; Major Achievement RecogPhilly Talk 1973; HUD Merit Serv Awd 1973; OIC Reg Exec Dirs Awd 1973; Leadership Growth & Devel OIC Movement Awd 1973; Chapel of Four Chaplains Awd &Legion of Honor 1972; Cert of Apprec Conf Criminal Justice Univ of NE 1972; listed in Who's Who in Fin & Undist; publ "There is a Need for Militancy in Adult Basic Ed" Adult Leadership 1968; Spec Recog by Mayor & Pres of C of C; 10 Yrs Serv Awd Frontiers Intl. **BUSINESS ADDRESS:** Finance Dir, Philadelphia Port Corp, 1020 Public Ledger Bldg, 6th & Chestnut Sts, Philadelphia, PA 19106.

MILLER, GEORGE CARROLL, JR.
Management consultant. **PERSONAL:** Born Mar 03, 1949, Atlanta, GA; married Nawanna Lewis; children: George III, John Elliott, Mikah Alexis. **EDUCATION:** Amer Inst of Banking, 1971; GA State Univ, BBA 1971; GA State Univ, MBA 1974; Univ of OK, 1975; Amer Inst of Banking 1976. **CAREER:** Trust Co of GA, commercial officer 1971-76; US Treasury Dept, exec asst 1977-79; Cooper & Lybrand, dir state & local govt practice. **ORGANIZATIONS:** Fundraiser YMCA 1972-74, United Negro Coll Fund 1973-74, United Way 1973-74; v chmn, treas Atlanta Bus League 1974-75; bd dir Joint Action in Commun Serv 1982-; pres GA State Univ Natl Capital Alumni Club 1985-; bd dir DC Lung Assoc 1986-; mem Natl Asbestos Council. **HONORS/ACHIEVEMENTS:** WSB Beaver Awd 1968; Herbert Leman Educ Grant 1968-71; GA State Univ Alumni Appreciation Awd 1976; Outstanding Young Men of Amer 1977. **MILITARY SERVICE:** USA ROTC 2 yrs. **BUSINESS ADDRESS:** Dir, Coopers & Lybrand, 1800 M St NW, Washington, DC 20036.

MILLER, GEORGE N., JR.
Business executive. **PERSONAL:** Born Sep 12, 1951, Neptune, NJ. **EDUCATION:** Bowling Green State Univ, BS 1973; Miami Jacobs Bus Sch, attended 1974; Norfolk State Univ, grad study. **CAREER:** Gem City Savings & Loan, mgr trainee 1973-74; Comm Svgs & Loan, mgr trainee 1974-75, asst mgr 1975-76, exec vice pres 1976-77, pres 1977-83; First Development Enterprises Inc, pres ceo 1983-. **ORGANIZATIONS:** Bd dirs/sec Whittaker Meml Hosp 1978-80; bd of dir/sec Amer Svgs & Loan League 1979-80; adv com Fed Home Loan Mortgage Corp; FHLBB 1980; bd of dir Amer Cancer Soc 1977-; vice chmn Peninsula Area Adv Council to HSA 1979-; bd dirs Comm Fed Svgs & Loan Assn 1977-83; chmn NAACP 1977-; participant US Conference for Business Leaders of Foreign Affairs; life mem Omega Psi Phi Frat. **HONORS/ACHIEVEMENTS:** Alumni of the Yr Bowling Green State Univ 1982; Outstanding Contributions to the Comm & Business Alpha Phi Alpha Frat 1980; Scroll of Honor Omega Psi Phi Frat 1980; Outstanding Young Men in the Financial World in Amer American Svgs & Loan League 1978; Who's Who in Amer Univs & Colls 1973; Outstanding Citizenof the Yr Awd Zambda Lambda AOA Frat Inc 1977; Achievement Awd in Bus Office of Human Affairs 1978; Achievement Awd Under 30 Category Black Enterprise Mag NY 1980; Outstanding Schievement Bus & Commerce Heaven on Earth Restaurant Hampton VA 1980; Most Outstanding Man of the Yr Athenan Corp 1980. **BUSINESS ADDRESS:** President, First Develop Enterprises Inc, 1512 27th St, Newport News, VA 23607.

MILLER, HELEN S.
Nurse, educator. **PERSONAL:** Born Mar 29, 1917, Atlanta, GA; children: Ronald. **EDUCATION:** Univ Hosp Augusta, GA; Med Coll of VA, RN; Tuskeegee Inst Sch of Midwifery, BSNEd; Yale Univ Sch Nursing CNM, MSN; Sr Nurse Ofcr Resrv Corps Pub Health, MSN. **CAREER:** GA Dept Pub Health, staff nurse 1947-49; US Pub Health Serv, area suprv 1949-51; Army Nurse Corps, admin nurse 1951-53; City Philadelphia Dept Health, dist-suprv 1953-54; FL A&M Univ, pub health coord sch of nursing 1954-56; NC Cntrl Univ, chmn dept nursing 1956-77, assoc prof nursing research 1977-. **ORGANIZATIONS:** Sec Undergrad Cncl NC Cntrl Univ; mem Fac Exec Com NC Cntrl Univ; mem Long Range Planning Com NC Cntrl Univ; mem NC State Nurses Assn; mem Amer Nurses Assn; mem Com to Write Hist of Nursing in NC; NC State Nurses Assn; mem bd dir NC League for Nursing; mem Yale Univ Alumnae Assn; mem Amer Assn of Univ Women; mem Adv Com on Cont Educ Sch of Nursing Univ of NC at Chapel Hill; mem YWCA; former bd mem Local Chptr ARC; mem Exec Com NC Lung & Resp Assn; mem Health Careers Com NC Cntrs Univ Gubernatorial appt to NC Bd of Nursing 1966-70; natl pres Chi Eta Phi Sor Inc 1969-73. **HONORS/ACHIEVEMENTS:** Mary Mahoney Award Amer Nurses Assn 1968; bd mem 1st vice pres Natl League for Nursing 1971-75; Disting Alumni Award Yale Univ 1978; life mem Natl Councl Negro Women; life mem Chi Eta Phi Sor Inc; listed in, Minority Groups in Nrsg, Amer Nurses' Assn 1976, Personalities of the South, Historical Preservations of Amer 1975-76, World Who's Who of Women, Intl Biographical Ctr Cambridge, England, "Abstracts of Nursing Research in the South" Vol 1 1979; author "The History of Chi Eta Phi Sorority Inc 1968; publisher "The Assn for the Study of Afro-American Life & History Washington DC". **MILITARY SERVICE:** AUS Nurse Corps 1st Lt 1951-53. **BUSINESS ADDRESS:** Associate Professor, North CentralUniv, Dept Nursing, Box 19751, Durham, NC 27707.

MILLER, HENRY B., JR.
Clinic director. **PERSONAL:** Born Jun 03, 1940, San Diego; divorced; children: Holly, Amber. **EDUCATION:** Antioch Coll, MA Prgm. **CAREER:** YMCA Drug Proj, group facilitator 1969; Drug & Narcotic Educ Hlth Serv Div San Diego City Schs, speaker 1969-70; IL Drug Abuse Prgm, comm serv aide, trainee 1970; San Diego Narcotic Treatment Prgm Dept PsychiatUniv CA, clinic head 1970-72; Harbison Out-Patient Full-Serv Clinic, clinic dir 1972-. **ORGANIZATIONS:** Mem Nat Assn Concerned Drug Abuse Workers; CA Conf Methadone Prgms. **HONORS/ACHIEVEMENTS:** Biography Notable Am 1977; Biography Who's Who Amoung Black Am 1975-76; poems publs Arx Mag; selected poems "New Voices In Am Poetry" 1977. **BUSINESS ADDRESS:** Harbison Clinic, 5402 Division St, San Diego, CA 92114.

MILLER, HORATIO C.
Editor, publisher. **PERSONAL:** Born Jan 08, 1949, Birmingham, AL; married Judith Willoughby; children: Allison. **EDUCATION:** Univ of PA, BA 1970; Temple U, MusM 1973.

CAREER: Cheyney State Coll, instr 1973-74; Community Coll of Philadelphia, asst prof 1974-; My Point of View, editor, publisher. HONORS/ACHIEVEMENTS: Concert pianist gave performances throughout US, JFK Center for Performing Arts, Lincoln Center Library Auditorium New York City, Acad of Music Philadelphia, Inaugural Concert President Carter Washington, DC 1976; rated in the top 10 market timers in the gold market for 1988 by Timer Digest, a natl ratings publication. BUSINESS ADDRESS: My Point of View, PO Box 27712, Philadelphia, PA 19118.

MILLER, HOWARD M.
Judge. **PERSONAL:** Born Feb 17, 1929, Danville, IL; married Betty; children: Gregory, Victor. **EDUCATION:** IN U, BS 1951; Loyola Univ Sch Law, JD 1963. **CAREER:** Circuit Ct, judge; Gen Pract, atty 1963-74; Chicago Bd Elec Commr. **MILITARY SERVICE:** USN 1946-47. **BUSINESS ADDRESS:** Judge, Circuit Ct of Cook County, Daley Civic Ctr, Chicago, IL 60602.

MILLER, ISAAC H., JR.
Administrator. **PERSONAL:** Born Sep 26, 1920, Jacksonville, FL; married Effie; children: Isaac, III, Kevin, Eric, Keith, Kay. **EDUCATION:** Livingston Coll, BS 1938;Univ of WI, MS, PhD 1948 1951. **CAREER:** Meharry Med Coll Nashville, former prof biochemistry; Bennett Coll Greensboro NC, past pres (retired 1987). **ORGANIZATIONS:** Mem Am Chem Soc; Botanical Soc of Am; Am Assn for Advncmt of Sci; Assn of Southeastern Biologists; former vis sci Oak Ridge Inst of Nuclear Studies; panelist Nat Sci Found Prgm on Rsrch Participation for HS Tchr. **HONORS/ACHIEVEMENTS:** Recip Lederle Med Faculty Award Meharry Coll 3 Consecutive Yrs. **BUSINESS ADDRESS:** Past President, Bennett Coll, 900 E Washington, Greensboro, NC 27401.

MILLER, JACQUELINE ELIZABETH
Librarian. **PERSONAL:** Born Apr 15, 1935, New York, NY; daughter of Lynward Winslow and Sarah Winslow; children: Percy Scott. **EDUCATION:** Morgan State Coll, BA 1957; Pratt Inst, MLS 1960. **CAREER:** Brooklyn Public Library, young teen librarian trainee 1957-59, reading improvement instructor 1959-60, young teen specialist 1960-63, branch librarian 1963-64, dir young teen serv 1964-68; New Rochelle Public Library, head extension serv 1969-70; Yonkers Public Library, branch admin 1970-75, dir 1975-. **ORGANIZATIONS:** Member, Commr Commn on State-wide Library Devel 1980; exec bd member, Publ Library Dir Assn NY State 1984-; numerous other natl, state, county professional library org; mem, adv comm Work Opportunity Referrals for Kids (WORK); member, Rotaty of Yonkers. **HONORS/ACHIEVEMENTS:** Honored Citizen of Yonkers, Church of Our Saviour 1980; Annual Award West County Club Natl Assn Negro Business & Professional Women's Clubs 1981. **BUSINESS ADDRESS:** Dir, Yonkers Public Library, Seven Main St, Yonkers, NY 10701.

MILLER, JAKE C.
Educator. **PERSONAL:** Born Dec 28, 1929, Hobe Sound, FL; son of Jake Miller and Augustine White MIller; married Nellie Carrol; children: Charles, Wayne, Warren. **EDUCATION:** Bethune-Cookman Coll, BS 1951; Univ of IL, MA 1957; Univ of NC at Chapel Hill, PhD 1967. **CAREER:** Martin Co Sch Sys FL, instructor 1954-59; Bethune-Cookman Coll, asst prof 1959-64; Fisk U, assoc prof 1967-76; Bethune-Cookman Coll, prof 1976-. **ORGANIZATIONS:** Amer Political Sci Assn; Intl Studies Assn; Caribbean Studies Assn; TransAfrica. Natl Conference of Black Political Scientists; Alpha Phi Alpha Fraternity. **HONORS/ACHIEVEMENTS:** Fellowship Natl Endowment for the Humanities 1981-82; Prof of the Yr Finalist Cncl for Adv & Support of Educ 1984; book publ, Black Presence in Amer Foreign Affairs, Univ Press of Amer 1978; book publ, Plight of Haitian Refugees, Praeger 1984; Fellowship United Negro Coll Fund Distinguished Scholar 1986-87; Excellence in Research Award Bethune-Cookman College 1979, 1985, 1989; Ja Flo Davis Faculty member of the Year Bethune-Cookman College 1980, 1985, 1988; Distinguished Alumni Citation Natl Assn for Equal Opportunity in Higher Educ 1988; US Institute of Peace Fellowship 1989-90. **MILITARY SERVICE:** USMC cpl. **HOME ADDRESS:** 1103 Lakewood Park Dr, Daytona Beach, FL 32017. **BUSINESS ADDRESS:** Professor of Political Science, Bethune-Cookman Coll, Daytona Beach, FL 32015.

MILLER, JAMES, SR.
Insurance salesman. **PERSONAL:** Born Nov 03, 1944, Alexandria, VA; children: James II, Antoinette T. **EDUCATION:** Norfolk State Univ, BS 1968; Boston Univ, MEd 1975; Central MI Univ, MA 1980. **CAREER:** NY Life Insurance Co, sales manager 1982, field underwriter. **ORGANIZATIONS:** Life mem Kappa Alpha Psi 1968-; mem E Jerry Williams Lodge #141 FIAM 1986-. **HONORS/ACHIEVEMENTS:** All Awds from New York Life Ins Co mem Top Club, Million Dollar Round Table, Centurion, Rookie of the Year 1982, Retention Goal Leader 1982, 83, Life Leader 1985, Variable Life Leader 1985, Agent of the Month June, July, Sept 1985, Natl Sales Achievement Awd, Agent of the Year 1985. **HOME ADDRESS:** 5700 Norman Ct, Forestville, MD 20747. **BUSINESS ADDRESS:** Field Underwriter, New York Life Insurance Co, 8401 Corporate Dr #400, Landover, MD 20785.

MILLER, JAMES ARTHUR
Educator. **PERSONAL:** Born Aug 27, 1944, Providence, RI; son of John Miller and Elease Miller; married Edjohnetta Fowler; children: Ayisha, John. **EDUCATION:** Brown Univ Providence, RI, AB 1966; State Univ of NY Buffalo, PhD 1976. **CAREER:** Trinity Coll Hartford, CT, assoc prof English 1979-, asst prof 1972-78; City Univ of NY Medgar Evers Coll, asst prof humanities 1971-72; State Univ of NY, dir black studies 1969-71; CT Pub Radio, humanities consult 1979-80; WGBH Radio Found Boston, consult 1978-80; Lafayette Coll Easton PA, distinguished visiting prof 1982-83; Wesleyan Univ Middletown CT, visting assoc prof Afro-Amer studies 1985-86; Wesleyan Univ Middletown CT, visiting assoc prof English & Afro-Amer studies 1988-89. **ORGANIZATIONS:** Pres Blue Hills Civic Assoc Hartford 1976-78; bd of dir Big Bro of Greater Hartford 1978-80; pres, bd dir Artists Collective Inc Hartford 1984-86; Connecticut Humanities Council 1985-; trustee, Mark Twain Memorial, Hartford 1987-. **HONORS/ACHIEVEMENTS:** Outstanding Young Man of Am 1978; Fellowship, African Humanities Inst, Natl Endowment for the Humanities 1979. **BUSINESS ADDRESS:** Associate Professor, Trinity College, English Department, Hartford, CT 06106.

MILLER, JAMES S.
Library director. **PERSONAL:** Born Dec 23, 1924, Atlanta; married Nellie Jeter; children: Marilynn Maxine, James S. **EDUCATION:** Morehouse Coll Atlanta, AB 1950; Atlanta U, MS in LS 1951. **CAREER:** FL Mem Coll, head librn 1951-56; FL A&M U, asst prof libr sci 1956-60; AL A&M Coll, head librn 1960-62; Norfolk State Coll, libr dir 1962-;Univ of Chgo, libr workshops 1957, 58. **ORGANIZATIONS:** Mem Libr Adv Com State Coun Higher Educ VA; mem Act Com VA Libr Assn 1973; mem ALA; SELA; VA LA; vice pres FL State LA 1954-57. **MILITARY SERVICE:** USMC sgt. **BUSINESS ADDRESS:** Norfolk State Coll, 2401 Corprew Ave, Norfolk, VA 23504.

MILLER, JAMES S.
Educator. **PERSONAL:** Born Feb 20, 1923, Gastonia, NC; married Anne E Grier. **EDUCATION:** Howard U, BS 1949; A&T State U, MS 1956; NC Cntrl; Appalachian State U; UNC Extension Prog. **CAREER:** Arlington Elem Sch, principal 1970-; CF Gingles Elem Sch, prin 1952-70. **ORGANIZATIONS:** Mem Nat Educ Assn; NC Assn of Educators; Gaston Co Educ Assn Elder Loves Chapel Press Ch; mem Omega Psi Phi Frat; ofcr Local Chap treas past 19 yrs; treas Gaston Co Prin Assn; past mem bd dirs Excelsior Credit Union; Gastopn Boys Club; Gaston Co Red Cross; mem Gaston Co Bicentennial. **HONORS/ACHIEVEMENTS:** Recip Omega Man of Yr 1965; cert of Appreciation outstndg serv as prin cited Best Prin Schs PTA 1974; plaque serv rendered as pres of Gaston Co Tchrs Assn. **MILITARY SERVICE:** USMC 1st sgt 1943-46. **BUSINESS ADDRESS:** Arlington Elem Sch, 1621 N Webb St, Gastonia, NC 28052.

MILLER, JEAN CAROLYN WILDER
Program administrator. **PERSONAL:** Born Dec 17, 1932, Richmond, VA; daughter of Robert Judson Wilder Sr and Beulah Olive Richards Wilder; married Arnold Wilson, Aug 11, 1956; children: Maria Denise, Tara Anita, Anthony Wilson, Karlyn Jae. **EDUCATION:** VA State Univ, Petersburg, VA, BS Bus Educ 1956; Bradley Univ, Peoria, IL, MA Guidance Counseling 1974. **CAREER:** Manual HS, Peoria, IL, teacher, 1967-71; Richwoods HS, Peoria, IL, teachers, 1972-73; Bradley Univ, Peoria, IL, asst dean of women 1973-82, learning assistance program coordinator, 1982-84; Univ of IL, College of Medicine, Peoria, IL, conference coordinator, 1984-86; Ross Learning, Inc, Detroit, MI, counselor, 1986-87; UAW-Ford National Education Development and Training Center, Dearborn, MI, program assistant, 1987—. **ORGANIZATIONS:** Mem Am Personnel & Guidance Assn 1973-; mem Assn of Non-White Concerns 1973-; IL Guidance & Personnel Assn 1973-; mem IL Assn of Non-White Concerns 1973-; mem Jack & Jill of Am Inc Oakland County Chap 1985-; NAACP; Links, Inc; Delta Sigma Theta. **HONORS/ACHIEVEMENTS:** Engraved plaque George Washington Carver Comm Ctr 1980; cited for outstanding contribution to IL Guidance and Personnel Association. **BUSINESS ADDRESS:** UAW-Ford National Education Development and Training Center, 5101 Evergreen, Dearborn, MI 48121.

MILLER, JEANNE-MARIE A.
Educator, author. **PERSONAL:** Born Feb 18, 1937, Washington, DC; daughter of William Anderson (deceased) and Agnes Johns Anderson (deceased); married Dr Nathan J Miller. **EDUCATION:** Howard Univ, BA 1959, MA 1963, PhD 1976. **CAREER:** Howard Univ, instr English 1963-76, grad asst prof English 1977-79; Inst for the Arts & the Humanities Howard Univ, asst dir 1973-75, grad assoc prof of English 1979-, asst for academic planning office of the vice pres for academic affairs 1976-. **ORGANIZATIONS:** Ed Black Theatre Bulletin Amer Theatre Assoc 1977-86; mem exec council Black Theatre Prog Amer Theatre Assoc 1977-86; proposal reviewer Natl Endowment for the Humanities 1979-; adv bd WETA-TV Ed prog on Black Folklore 1976-77; mem Friends of JF Kennedy Ctr for Performing Arts, Amer Assoc of Univ Women, Amer Civil Liberites Union, Amer Film Inst; assoc mem Arena Stage, Washington Performing Arts Soc, Eugene O'Neill Memorial Theatre Ctr, Amer Soc of Business and Exec Women; assoc Art Inst of Chicago, Boston Museum of Fine Arts, Metropolitan Museum of Art, Corcoran Gallery of Art, Smithsonian Inst, Washington Performings Arts Soc, The Washington Opera Guild, World Affairs Council of Washington DC, Modern Language Assoc, Amer Studies Assoc, Coll Lang Assoc, Natl Council of Teachers of English, Amer Assoc for Higher Educ, Natl Assoc for Women Deans Administrators and Counselors, Natl Women's Studies Assoc. **HONORS/ACHIEVEMENTS:** Advanced Study Fellowship Ford Found 1970-72; Fellow So Fellowship Fund 1972-74; Grantee Amer Council of Learned Societies; 1978-79; Grantee Natl Endowment for the Humanities 1981-84; edited book From Realism to Ritual, Form & Style in Black Theatre 1983; publ over 50 articles in various jrnls & mags; Pi Lambda Theta Natl Honor and Professional Assn in Education 1987. **HOME ADDRESS:** 1100 6th St SW, Apt 515, Washington, DC 20024. **BUSINESS ADDRESS:** Assistant-Acad Planning, Prof, Howard University, 2400 6th St NW, Washington, DC 20059.

MILLER, JESSE P.
Mayor, business executive. **PERSONAL:** Born Nov 06, 1920, Longview, TX; married Easter V Anderson; children: Ronald, Dennis, Anthony. **EDUCATION:** OH St U. **CAREER:** City of Highland Park, mayor; Detroit Mason Cntr's Assn, cntrct compnc invstgtr; SA Healy Gargaro Co, foreman heavy constr 1952-58; Detroit Fattore Co, 1st blk supt heavy const 1959-61; Sinacola Const Co, supt 1962-64; Licensed Cntr in Heavy Const, 1965-68. **ORGANIZATIONS:** Mem AFL-CIO; 32 deg mason; NAACP; chmn Nghbrhd Adv Coun; former tr citz adv com; mem & former treas Wayne Co Nghbrhd Legal Svcs. **HONORS/ACHIEVEMENTS:** Commun awd of apprctn for dedctd & unslfsh serv 1972; councmn City of Highland Park 1978-. **BUSINESS ADDRESS:** 36 Louise, Highland Park, MI 48203.

MILLER, JOHN H.
Clergyman. **PERSONAL:** Born Dec 03, 1917, Ridgeway, SC; children: George F, John H Jr. **EDUCATION:** AB, BD 1941-45; Hartford Sem Found Religious Ed, further study 1954. **CAREER:** African Methodist Epis Zion Church, AME Zion Church, bishop 38 yrs. **ORGANIZATIONS:** Mem Alpha Phi Alpha 1941; past vice pres CT Council of Churchs 1955-60; mem Mayors Goodwill Comm Housing Comm Waterbury CT 1956; mem Winston-Salem NC GoodwillComm deseg all publ facilities 1963; mem Natl Council of Churchs 1966; charter mem Louisville Jeff Cty Crime Comm 1967-71; past pres Louisville AreaCouncil of Churchs 1969-71; sec treas Waterbury Ministers Assoc; mem exec bd NAACP, Urban League; dir Fed Fund for City of Winston-Salem; mem World Meth Council of Churchs; trustee Livingstone Coll Lomax-Hannon Coll. **HONORS/ACHIEVEMENTS:** KY Col Civic Title Outstanding Citizen of Commonwealth of KY 1966; Livingstone Coll Alumni Merit Serv Awd 1971; AR Traveller Civic Title given by Gov of AR1972; Greatest Hon Election to Episcopacy Mobile AL 1972; Citation City of Winston-Salem Outstanding Civic Contrib; Outstanding Contrib to Coll DD Livingstone Coll. **BUSINESS ADDRESS:** AME Zion Church, 8605 Caswell Ct, Raleigh, NC 27612.

MILLER, JOSEPH HERMAN
Insurance company executive. **PERSONAL:** Born Mar 05, 1930, Port Gibson, MS; married Cleo L Baines; children: Darryl, Stephen, Carrington, Vicki, Scott. **EDUCATION:** Talladega Coll, AB 1950; Howard Univ, JD 1957. **CAREER:** Miller Funeral Homes Inc, pres 1972-; Freedom Natl Ins Co, pres 1976-; Natl Ins Assoc, pres 1976-; Reliable Life Ins Co, pres. **ORGANIZATIONS:** Bd dir Monroe LA C of C 1976. **MILITARY SERVICE:** USA corpl 1951-53. **BUSINESS ADDRESS:** President, Reliable Life Insurance Co, PO Box 1157, Monroe, LA 71211.

MILLER, JUNIOR
Professional athlete. **PERSONAL:** Born Nov 26, 1957, Midland, TX; married Carol; children: Cara, Seth. **EDUCATION:** NE Univ, Phys Ed. **CAREER:** Falcons, football player 1984; New Orleans Saints, tight end 1984-. **HONORS/ACHIEVEMENTS:** All-Rookie, All-Pro Honors; selected to Pro Bowl 1981.

MILLER, KENNETH BERNARD (BEBE D'BANANA)
Radio executive. **PERSONAL:** Born Jan 18, 1951, Salisbury, NC; children: Keith Bernard. **EDUCATION:** FL Jr Coll, 1977-78; Chicago State Univ, 1983-84. **CAREER:** KNOK, on air personality 1975-76; WBOK, dir programming 1976-77; Rock 99/WCMB, sales exec 1977-78; WAPE, air personality 1978-79; WJPC/Johnson Publishing, dir programming 1979-83; Chicago State Univ, publicity affairs spec 1983-84; WLUM FM/All Pro Broadcasting, dir programming 1984-. **ORGANIZATIONS:** Mem Ancient Free and Accepted Masons 1977; mem NAACP 1984-85; mem Operation PUSH 1984-85. **HONORS/ACHIEVEMENTS:** Broadcaster of the Yr WI Music Indus/WAMI 1984-85; Youth Recogn Award Howalton Sch 1983-84; Platinum Album Capitol Records/Tina Turner 1984-85; Best Dressed Man 1983 Chicago's Fabulous Dressed Horseman 1983.

MILLER, LAMAR PERRY
Educator. **PERSONAL:** Born Sep 01, 1925, Ypsilanti, MI; married Deborah F Fox; children: LaMar Jr, Arianne E. **EDUCATION:** Univ MI, PhD 1968;Univ MI, EdS 1965;Univ MI, MA 1958; Eastern MI U, BA 1954. **CAREER:** NY U, sec ed & prof of metro studies present; Inst of Afro-Am Affairs, educ rsrch dir; Inst for Tchrs of Disad Youth, dir; Educ Ypsilani MI, asso prof; English Dept Willow Run, chmn; dir forensic activ. **ORGANIZATIONS:** Chief consult Nat Inst of Educ Dept of HEW; dir Tchrs Corps; ons Union Carbide Corp; NY Urban League; asso edit Am Educ Rsrch Jour AERA 1975-78; mem publ com Assn for Super & Curric Devel 1975-77; Nat Alliance of Black Sch Educ 1975-; edit bd NYUniv Quarterly 1972-75 ; sec Div G Am Educ Rsrch Assn 1972-74. **HONORS/ACHIEVEMENTS:** Publs "equality of educ opport a handbook for rsrch" 1974; "the testing of black students a symposium" 1974; "edn for an open soc" 1974. **MILITARY SERVICE:** AUS 1944-46. **BUSINESS ADDRESS:** New York University, Press Building, Room 72, 32 Washington Place, New York, NY 10003.

MILLER, LAUREL MILTON
Deputy chief of police, major. **PERSONAL:** Born Apr 29, 1935, Richmond, VA; married Betty Loggins; children: Yasmin, Nicole. **EDUCATION:** VA Union Univ, BS 1972; NWU, attended 1974; Univ of Louisville, grad study 1975; Nova Univ, MS 1980. **CAREER:** Richmond Bureau of Police, patrolman 1961-68, detective 1968-69, sgt 1969-73, lt personnel officer 1973-76, capt 1976-77, major 1978, deputy chief of police. **ORGANIZATIONS:** Mem Police Benevolence Assn; bd mem Natl Organ of Black Law Enforcement Execs; alumni So Police Inst. **HONORS/ACHIEVEMENTS:** First Black Traffic Sgt Richmond; First Black to Head Div in Bur of Police; First Black Capt of Bureau; First Black Major and Deputy Chief of Police; 36 Public Serv Commendations; Police Cit Certl 1963; Police Medal 1972; Merit Police Duty 1975. **MILITARY SERVICE:** USAF a/1c 1953-57. **BUSINESS ADDRESS:** Deputy Chief of Police, Richmond Bureau of Police, 501 N 9th St, Richmond, VA 23219.

MILLER, LAURENCE BRENT
Physician. **PERSONAL:** Born Sep 27, 1942, New York City, NY; married Marilyn S; children: Jennifer Kimberly, Katharine Emilie, Liza Alexandra. **EDUCATION:** City Coll of CityUniv NY, BS 1965; Meharry Med Coll, MD 1972. **CAREER:** Physician, pvt prac Parkway Day Sch Inc Inst for Learning, med dir 1979-; Work Adjstmt Ctr & Crossroads Prgm, med dir 1976-; Eagleville Hosp & Rehab Ctr, clinical dir 1976-79. **ORGANIZATIONS:** Mem Am Psychiatric Assn.

MILLER, LAWRENCE A.
Special projects coordinator, government official. **PERSONAL:** Born Aug 17, 1951, New York, NY; son of Lawrence A Miller and Adella B King; married Beverley McRae, Jun 17, 1981; children: Keisha Yvette, Dahra Ayanna. **EDUCATION:** York Coll, BA Publ Admin 1974; Brooklyn Coll, MPA 1989. **CAREER:** Dept of Juvenile Justice, juvenile counselor 1973-76; NY City Youth Bd, evaluation consult 1976-79; NYS Div for Youth, program mgmt spec, special projects coord. **ORGANIZATIONS:** Mem NAACP; bd mem Comm School Bd #28 1983-86, Comm Planning Bd #12 1983-, Rochdale Village Inc 1985-; vice pres Fred Wilson Regular Democratic Club 1987; chmn of the bd Youth Advocates through Educ & Sports 1987; producer and host of radio program WNYE Comm Trustees Report for the Borough of Manhattan; exec dir, Community Advocates for a Better Living Environment 1989. **HONORS/ACHIEVEMENTS:** Cert of Apprec NY City Office of Serv Coord 1975; Outstanding Young Men of Amer US Jaycees 1980; Outstanding Serv Awd NYS Div for Youth 1981; Comm Serv Awd Elmcor Youth & Adult Activites 1984; Certificate of Appreciation Bd of Educ New York City 1986; Chancellor's Awd for Outstanding Alumni 1986; Natl Assn of Negro Business and Professional Women's Club Comm Serv Awd 1987; Honor Service Award, Assn of Black Educators of NY 1988; Oustanding Community Service, York College 1986; Columnist, New York Voice Newspaper 1988; Producer/Host, Comm Affairs Talk Show, Radio 91.5 FM & Cable TV 1986, 1989. **HOME ADDRESS:** 170-12 130th Ave, Apt # 11 E, Jamaica, NY 11434. **BUSINESS ADDRESS:** Special Projects Coord, NYS Division for Youth, 163 W 125th St, Suite 1407, New York, NY 10027.

MILLER, LAWRENCE EDWARD
County official. **PERSONAL:** Born Aug 13, 1950, Columbia, SC; son of Ralph Carter and Mary E Miller. **EDUCATION:** Hard Barger Jr Coll, Raleigh NC, AAS, 1969; A&T State Univ, Greensboro NC, BA, 1974; Natl Theological Seminary, MA, PhD, 1983. **CAREER:** Wake-Raleigh Headstart, Raleigh NC, teacher, 1975-79, asst execeptional children coordinator, 1979, transportation coordinator, 1980; Housing Opportunity Unlimited, Laurel MD, dir of social services, 1980-83; PG County Housing, Landover MD, rental specialist, 1983; Arlington County Housing, Arlington VA, housing asst, 1983-. **ORGANIZATIONS:** Mem, NC State Elks Assn, 1972-; bd mem, PG County Headstart Policy Council, 1981-83; Eastern Region Security, Phi Beta Sigma Frat, 1987-; Executive Council, United Church of Christ, 1987-; Trustee, Alpha Sigma Chapter, Phi Beta Sigma Frat, 1988-; mem, Columbia Elks Lodge; mem, Alpha Sigma Frat, Phi Beta Sigma Frat; mem, Peoples Congregational UCC. **HONORS/ACHIEVEMENTS:** Brother Elk of the Year, Mississippi State Elks Assn, 1974; Director of the Year, Elks IBPOE of W, 1978; NC Longleaf, NC Governor, 1978; Doctor of Humane Letter, Natl Theological Seminary, 1982; Colonel Robert L Pollard Award, Alpha Sigma Chapter, 1989. **HOME ADDRESS:** 1318 Q Street, NW #3, Washington, DC 20009.

MILLER, LOREN, JR.
Judge. **PERSONAL:** Born Mar 07, 1937, Los Angeles, CA; married Gwen Allain; children: Pamela Allain, Michael, Stephanie Allain, Robin, Nina, Gregory Allain. **EDUCATION:** Univ of OR, BS 1960; Loyola Law School Los Angeles, JD 1962. **CAREER:** State of CA Dept of Justice, dep atty gen 1962-69; Western Ctr on Law & Poverty, dir of litigation 1969-70; Model Neighbor Legal Prog, dir 1972-73; Pacific Lighting Corp, asst gen counsel 1973-75; Los Angeles Municipal Court, judge 1975-77; Superior Court LA County, superior court judge. **BUSINESS ADDRESS:** Judge Superior Court, Superior Court LA County, 400 Civic Center Plz, Pomona, CA 91766.

MILLER, LORI E.
Senior account executive, writer. **PERSONAL:** Born Mar 02, 1959, Detroit, MI; daughter of Percy Miller and Mary Miller. **EDUCATION:** Univ of MI, BA 1981. **CAREER:** Carl Byoir & Assoc Public Relations, staff writer 1981-82; Metro Detroit Convention Bureau, communications asst 1982-83; Greater LA Visitors & Convention Bureau, public relations mgr; Ketchum/Bohle Public Relations, account exec 1985-86; Porter/Novelli, senior account exec 1986-. **ORGANIZATIONS:** Mem, Publicity Club of Los Angeles 1983-; public relations campaign dir Comm to Re-Elect George Vaughn to Detroit School Bd 1983; mem Public Relations Soc of Amer 1985; mem Amer Women in Radio and TV, Amer Film Inst, Public Relations Soc of Amer, Publicity Club of Los Angeles, Black Journalist Assoc Los Angeles Chapter. **HONORS/ACHIEVEMENTS:** LA Advertising Women's "Lulu Awards/Honorable Mention" for public relations. **BUSINESS ADDRESS:** Senior Account Executive, Porter/Novelli, 11755 Wilshire Blvd #1600, Los Angeles, CA 90025.

MILLER, LOUISE T.
Educator. **PERSONAL:** Born Mar 02, 1919. **EDUCATION:** Univ MI, BS 1949; Syracuse U, MS 1951; Yale U, MPH 1961;Univ RI, PhD 1970. **CAREER:** Spelman Coll, asso prof Biology 1973-;Univ RI, res asso in Animal Path 1963-72, res asst 1962-63; Syracuse U, tchng res asst 1951-60. **ORGANIZATIONS:** Mem Ad Hoc Com for Disad Students 1968-69; coun Special Prgm for Talent Dev 1970; instr Ed 900 Bio Workshop for Elem Sch Tchrs 1965-66, 68, 72; coll French Textbook by Jean S Hyland PhD. **HONORS/ACHIEVEMENTS:** Recip USPHS Trainee Grant Yale U, 1960-61. **BUSINESS ADDRESS:** 350 Spelman La SW, Atlanta, GA 30314.

MILLER, LUVENIA C.
Biological photographer. **PERSONAL:** Born Sep 14, 1909, Eden, NC. **EDUCATION:** Hampton Inst, BS 1934; NY Isnt of Photog, Cert 1939; Army Air Field Photo Lab, Cert 1945; Progressive Sch of Photog, Cert 1949. **CAREER:** Army Forces Inst of Pathology Med Illustration, chief of gross photography 1951-75; H Ec Gram Sch Greensboro NC, instr 1934-42. **ORGANIZATIONS:** Mem Biolog Photog Assn Inc 1961-74, dir 1973-76; bd mem Vol Serv DC Gen Hosp 1970-74; mem Methodist Women 1950-74; mem NAACP 1950-74; Hampton Inst Alumni Assn 1945-74. **HONORS/ACHIEVEMENTS:** Recip of 25 awards- Biolog Photog Assn Inc 1958-72; Am Mus of Nat Hist 1964; Defense Superior Perform 1965-72; Ladybird Johnson's Beautification Award "Lawn Ranger" Proj 1966; Chpn Beautification Com River Terr Wash DC 1967-70; Commend Vol Serv DC Gen Hosp 1972; 1st black woman in following- registered photog NC 1943; pub relations photog USAAF 1943-45; med photog Armed Forces Inst of Pathol Assn 1972; dir Biological Photog Assn Inc 1973-76.

MILLER, M. SAMMYE
Administrator. **PERSONAL:** Born Feb 23, 1947, Philadelphia, PA; son of Herman S Miller and Sammur Elizabeth Adams-Miller. **EDUCATION:** Delaware State Coll, BA 1968; Trinity Coll Washington, MAT 1970; The Catholic Univ of Amer, PhD 1977; Stanford Univ, Post Doc Fellow 1983. **CAREER:** Natl Endowment for the Humanities, humanist admin & policy analyst 1978-80; Assn for the Study of Afro-Amer Life & History Inc, exec dir 1983-84; Bowie State Univ, dept chmn/prof of hist. **ORGANIZATIONS:** Southern History Assn; Org of Amer Historian; The Amer Historical Assn; life mem Kappa Alpha Psi Fraternity Phi Alpha Theta Intl; Hon Soc in History. **HONORS/ACHIEVEMENTS:** HA NAFEO Research Achievemnt Award Natl Assn for Equal Opportuniy in Higher Educ 1984; felowships Knights of Columbus 1970; Penfield Fellow; Bd Trustees Scholar, Catholic Univ. **HOME ADDRESS:** 313 16th North East Street, Washington, DC 20002.

MILLER, MAPOSURE T.
Dentist. **PERSONAL:** Born Jul 17, 1934, Wadesboro, NC; married Bobbie J Grubbs; children: Teresa, Vickie, Gail. **EDUCATION:** Bluefield State Coll, BS 1956; WV Univ Sch Dent, DDS 1965. **CAREER:** Dr MT Miller Inc, pres. **ORGANIZATIONS:** Mem Natl Dent Assn; Amer Dent Assn; Buckeye State Dent Assn; OH State Dent Assn; Cleveland Dent Soc; Forest City Dent Study Club (pres-elect 1975-76); sec-treas Lee road Dent Cntrs Inc; bd tr Olivet Institutional Bapt Ch; chmn health & welfare E Cleveland Bus Men Assn; Urban League; NAACP. **HONORS/ACHIEVEMENTS:** Provincial Man of the Year Kappa Alpha Psi 1956; Beta Kappa Chi hon soc 1955-56. **MILITARY SERVICE:** AUS Sp4 1957-59; USN Lt 1965-68. **BUSINESS ADDRESS:** 13944 Euclid Ave, Cleveland, OH 44112.

MILLER, MARGARET ELIZABETH (NEE BATTLE)
Business executive. **PERSONAL:** Born Nov 19, 1934, Chapel Hill, NC; daughter of Ivy Battle and Johnnie M Battle; divorced; children: Lisa, Monica, William II. **EDUCATION:** NC Central U, AB 1955; Univ of NC, MSLS 1961; NC Central U, JD 1982. **CAREER:** Highland Jr & Sr HS, librarian 1955-59; Suwannee River Jr Coll, librarian 1959-66; Borgess Med Ctr, librarian 1968-79; Whitaker Sch, DHR administrator II 1981-89; MLM Svcs, pres. **ORGANIZATIONS:** Asst editor Commnty Courier Newspaper 1971-73; columnist Kalama-

zoo Gazette Newspaper 1973-75; commr Kalamazoo Co Bd of Commns 1975-78; chmn Orange Co Rainbow Coalition Educ Comm 1984-85; mem NAACP; mem Am Re-Educ Assn. **HONORS/ACHIEVEMENTS:** Fellow Newspaper Fund Fellowship 1965; fellow US HEW Fellowship 1967; recep of Mary M Bethune Award Delta Sigma Theta Sor 1978. **BUSINESS ADDRESS:** President, MLM Serv, 515 Hillsborough St, Chapel Hill, NC 27514.

MILLER, MARGARET GREER
Associate superintendent personnel. **PERSONAL:** Born Jan 25, 1934, Indianapolis, IN; married Charles E; children: Gregory Charles, Jennifer Charmaine. **EDUCATION:** Indiana State Univ, BS 1955; Indiana State Univ, MS 1965; Univ of Florida, Doctorate of Educ 1978. **CAREER:** Orange County Public Schools, speech clinician 1957-70; Univ of Central Florida, asst prof 1971-81; Orange County Public Schools, asst to supt for planning, research & testing 1981-83; Univ of Central Florida, assoc prof exceptional educ 1987-; Orange County Public Schools, assoc supt for personnel & office serv 1983-; Univ of Central Florida, dir of teacher educ center and extended studies 1989-. **ORGANIZATIONS:** Mem Alpha Kappa Alpha Sorority, Amer Speech & Hearing Assn, Amer Soc for Training & Devel, Florida Assn for School Admin, Council of Exceptional Children, Natl Sorority of Phi Delta Kappa; pres Valencia Comm Coll Fac Wives 1978-80; state treasurer CCBD-CNCL for Children with Behavioral Disorders 1975-81; mem ACLD-ASSOC for Children with Learing Disabilities, Mental Health Assn, ASCD Assn for Supervised Curriculum & Devel, Phi Delta Kappa, Inc, AERA Amer Educ Research Assn, AASPA Amer Assn of School Personnel Admin (Nom Comm), FASPA Florida Assn of School Personnel Admin (Comm Mem, Merit Pay, Records); comm sec Orange County Advisory Comm to Bd of Educ, bd of dir for Scholarship Fund, THEE Door 1979-81; bd of dir FLRS Brevard County; planning comm Teacher Corps Jones High School, Orange County School; Independent Research Project; Grant appl Summer Projec Emotnly Hn dcp Youth; chmn, bd of dir WA Shores Day Care Nursery 1978-; pres bd of dirs Greenhouse Family Counseling Center 1986-87, Human Serv Counsel 1987-88. **HONORS/ACHIEVEMENTS:** Dr Emory O Jackson Memorial Journalism Award South Atlantic Regional Conf of Alpha Kappa Alpha Sorority 1983; Pioneer Award Black Student Union Org at Univ of Central Florida First Minority Full Time Instructor UCF, and Outstanding Leadership 1985; State Health, Rehabilitation Serv Award for Outstanding Work in Child Abuse 1987; Certificate of Appreciation for Outstanding Work and Contributions to the Comm and State from Gov Robert Graham 1987. **BUSINESS ADDRESS:** Assoc Supt Personnel/Off SE, Orange County Public Schools, 434 N Tampa Ave, PO Box 25000, Orlando, FL 32816.

MILLER, MATTIE SHERRYL
Educator. **PERSONAL:** Born Jun 19, 1933, Adams, TN; married William E; children: Kori Edwin. **EDUCATION:** Tuskegee Inst AL, BS 1955; IN U, MS 1965, reading splst 1970;Univ of Evansville, adminstrn suprvsn 1975. **CAREER:** Evansville-Vanderburgh Sch Corp, guidance Couns 1975-, proj dir right to read 1972-75, reading clinician 1971-72, tchr 1959-71;Univ of Evansville, adjunctistr 1967-; IN U, practicum supv 1970-73; Vincennes U, field couns-upward bound 1975-77; Ball StateUniv Muncie IN, part-time instr. **ORGANIZATIONS:** Bd of dirs Channel 9 WNIN 1975-; sec bd of dirs Ldrshp Evansville 1976-; bd of dir IN State Tchrs Assn & Evansville Tchrs Assn. **HONORS/ACHIEVEMENTS:** Woman of yr in educ Evansville YWCA Ldrshp Award 1975; staff repr 8th dist Congressional Apptmnt 1975-78; black woman of yr in educ Evansville Comm Action Award 1978. **BUSINESS ADDRESS:** Evansville Vanderburgh School, 1 SE Ninth St, Evansville, IN 47708.

MILLER, MELVIN ALLEN
Public relations manager. **PERSONAL:** Born Nov 24, 1950, Hattiesburg, MS; married Alfredia Dampier. **EDUCATION:** UUniv of So Mississippi, BS 1972; Jackson State Univ, MS 1978. **CAREER:** Jackson Plant DeSoto Inc, communications asst 1975-76; Jackson State Univ, staff writer 1976-77, asst to dir of pub info 1977, acting dir of pub info 1977-78, dir of pub info 1978-86, dir of development 1987-. **ORGANIZATIONS:** Trustee, New Hope Baptist Church, Jackson, 1978-; 1st vice pres, Cystic Fibrosis Found, Mississippi Chap, 1980; unit commr, Boy Scouts of Amer, 1980; dean's list scholar, Univ of So Mississippi, 1970-72; Delta Omicron Hon Soc, Univ of So Mississippi, 1972; Phi Kappa Phi Natl Hon Soc, Jackson State Univ, 1978; pres, Coll Pub Relations Assn of Mississippi, 1979-80; bd mem, Jackson Chap of March of Dimes. **MILITARY SERVICE:** AUS 1st lt 1972-75. **BUSINESS ADDRESS:** Dir of Development, Jackson State University, 1400 Lynch St, Jackson, MS 39217.

MILLER, MELVIN B.
Publisher. **PERSONAL:** Born Jul 22, 1934, Boston, MA; divorced. **EDUCATION:** Harvard Coll, AB 1956; Columbia Law Sch, JD 1964. **CAREER:** US Justice Dept, asst US atty 1965-66; Unity Bank & Trust Co, conservator 1973-77; Bay State Banner, publ & editor 1965-; WNEV-TV, Inc, vice pres & genl counsel 1982-; Fitch Miller & Tourse, partner 1981-. **ORGANIZATIONS:** Trustee Boston Univ, Milton Academy, The Wang Center past trustee; New Eng Conserv of Music; James Jackson Putnam Children's Ctr, Family Serv Assn of Greater Boston, Family Couns & Guid Ctrs Inc; past dir Grtr Boston C of C; past dir MA Counc on Crime & Correc; past chmn Boston Comm Media Com; pastmem Visiting Comm; mem Overseers of Harvard Univ, MA Small Bus Adv Counc; NE Reg Area One Exec Com BSA; exec bd Minor Bus Oppor Com. **HONORS/ACHIEVEMENTS:** Boston Ten Outstanding Young Men Boston Jr C of C 1967; Annual Achiev Awd NAACP 1971; Awd of Excell Art Dir Club of Boston 1970; 1st prize Gen ExcellNew Eng Press Assn 1970; 2nd prize Make-up and Typography New Eng Press Assn 1970; 2nd prize Spec Sect Awd New Eng Press Assn 1971; hon ment Gen Excell New England Press Assn 1975; Honorary Doctor of Humane Letters Suffolk Univ 1984. **BUSINESS ADDRESS:** Publisher, Fitch Miller & Tourse, 189 State St, Boston, MA 02109.

MILLER, NATE CALVIN
Professional athlete. **PERSONAL:** Born Mar 21, 1958, Levenworth, KS. **EDUCATION:** Cameron Univ, Elem Educ Major. **CAREER:** Denver Gold, cornerback 1982-. **ORGANIZATIONS:** 2-yr mem Denver Gold Coed Charity Basketball Team. **HONORS/ACHIEVEMENTS:** Voted All-District; the District's Defensive MVP.

MILLER, OLIVER O.
Business executive. **PERSONAL:** Born Jul 23, 1944, Battle Creek, MI; son of Oliver and Edith; married Jeannette Claire Walker. **EDUCATION:** Dartmouth Coll, BA 1966; Stanford Univ, MBA 1968. **CAREER:** Business Week, Advertising Sales 1984-; McGraw-Hill Broadcasting Co, vice pres plng 1974-84, dir of acquisitions 1977-79; MECCO, vice pres 1975-77; Mc-kinsey & Co, mgmt consult 1973-75. **BUSINESS ADDRESS:** Business Week, 1221 ave of the Americas, New York, NY 10020.

MILLER, RAY, JR.
Government official. **PERSONAL:** Born Apr 06, 1949, Hampton, VA; married Marlene Rose Phillips; children: Inus Ray III. **EDUCATION:** OH State Univ, BA Pol Sci 1971, MA Public Admin 1974. **CAREER:** OH Legislative Serv Comm, rsch assoc; former State Rep Richard F Celeste, legislative asst; Rep CJ McLin Jr, admin asst; Correctional Inst Inspect Comm, exec dir; Amer Fed of State, Co & Municipal Employees, lobbyist; White House Staff of Pres Jimmy Carter, deputy spec asst; OH House of Reps, state representative 29th district. **ORGANIZATIONS:** Mem State Job Training Coordinating council; mem Private Indus Council of Franklin Co Adv Bd; mem Columbus Metro Comm Action Organ; mem Columbus Urban League; exec dir Employment & Educ Comm of Franklin; chmn Human Resources Subcommittee Finance; mem St Stephens Comm House; mem Coalition for Cost Effective Health Serv Planning; mem Review & Eval Group; mem Metro Human Serv Comm Cabinet of Execs. **HONORS/ACHIEVEMENTS:** Numerous civic, community and state awards. **BUSINESS ADDRESS:** Representative Dist 29, Ohio House of Representatives, Statehouse, Columbus, OH 43215.

MILLER, RICHARD CHARLES, JR.
Educator. **PERSONAL:** Born Jul 26, 1947, Ithaca, NY; son of Richard Miller and Marjorie Miller; married Doris Jean Boyd, Jul 14, 1973; children: Carin Lea Miller, Courtney Alison Miller. **EDUCATION:** Ithaca Coll, BS 1969, MS 1971; Springfield Coll, DPE 1976. **CAREER:** Tompkins Co Trust Co, bank teller 1965-70; San Francisco Giants Baseball Club, professional baseball player 1969-70; Ithaca Coll, grad asst 1970-71; Springfield Coll, research fellow 1972-74, instr 1974-75; Bowie State Univ, prof. **ORGANIZATIONS:** Mem Amer Coll of Sports Med; mem Amer Alliance for Health Physical Educ & Dance; chmn research sect MD Alliance for Health Physical Educ & Dance 1979-80; Natl Assn for Sport and Physical Educ. **HONORS/ACHIEVEMENTS:** All Amer Baseball Team Ithaca Coll 1969; Sports Hall of Fame Ithaca Coll 1979. **BUSINESS ADDRESS:** Professor, Bowie State University, Jericho Park Rd, Bowie, MD 20715.

MILLER, ROBERT HARRY
Mortician. **PERSONAL:** Born Jun 14, 1896, Leesburg, FL; married Ethel; children: 2 Dau. **EDUCATION:** State Coll Orangeburg; NW U; Worsham Mortuary Coll. **CAREER:** Miller Maj Funeral Home, pres. **ORGANIZATIONS:** Exec sec Nat Funeral Dir & Morticians Assn 32 Yrs; owner pub Funeral Dir & Embalmery; Nat Green Book; pres Marie's H&H Superior Beauty Prod; mem Kappa Alpha Psi Frat; Shriner Consistory; bd Manor Halfway House; past alderman Comillurman. **MILITARY SERVICE:** AUS sgt. **BUSINESS ADDRESS:** 73j W 79, Chicago, IL 60620.

MILLER, ROBERT LAVERNE
Professional athlete. **PERSONAL:** Born Jan 09, 1953, Houston, TX; married Lennie; children: Robert II, Samuel, Tiffanie. **EDUCATION:** Univ of KS Lawrence, B Bus Admin 1978. **CAREER:** James D Ryan Jr High, 1967; Jack Yates Sr High, 1968-70; MN Vikings, professional athlete 1975-80; CDC, admin 1981-. **ORGANIZATIONS:** Mem 9th St Missionary Baptist Church; deacon Church Org; asst tchr Sunday Sch; Campus Crusade for Christ; Fellowship of Christian Athletes; bd of reference Hospitality House. **HONORS/ACHIEVEMENTS:** MVP 1969-70; most determined and inspirational player 1973; Jayhawk 1974; has missed only one game in five years. **HOME ADDRESS:** RR 3, 285 Holyoake, Box 200A, Northville, MN 55057.

MILLER, RONALD BAXTER
Educator. **PERSONAL:** Born Oct 11, 1948, Rocky Mount, NC; son of Marcellus C Miller and Elsie Bryant Miller; married Jessica Garris; children: Akin Dasan. **EDUCATION:** NC Central Univ, BA (Magna Cum Laude) 1970; Brown Univ, AM 1972, PhD 1974; Yale Univ, Fellow. **CAREER:** Haverford Coll, asst prof English 1974-76; State Univ Coll of NY, lecturer 1974; Univ of TN, assoc prof/prof of English, dir of Black Literature Program, 1977-, prof 1982-. **ORGANIZATIONS:** Consultant, NEH sponsor, TV Series "The South" 1977-78; advisor and contributing editor "WATU, A Cornell Journ of black Writing" 1978-79, "Obsidian, Black Literature in Review" 1979-, "Callaloo" 1981-, "Black American Literature Forum" 1982-, "Middle Atlantic Writers Assn Review" 1982-,"Langston Hughes Review" 1982-; evaluator Div of Publ Programs Harlem Exec Comm Afro-Am Lit Discuss Group MLA 1980-83; chr/founder/1st chr Div on Black Amer Lit and Culture 1982-84; mem MLA delegate Assembly 1984-86; participant/consultant Black Writers South (GA Cncl for the Arts and Humanities) 1980-; vice pres Black History Month Lecture Series 1980; reader Univ of TN Press 1980-; chr Black Studies CLA 1982-; pres The Langston Hughes Soc 1984-88; Zora Neale Hurston Review 1986-; assoc ed Black Voices, An Interdisciplinary Journal, 1986. **HONORS/ACHIEVEMENTS:** Black Scholar Lectures Le Moyne Coll 1985, Univ of UT 1985; ACLS Conf Grant Black Amer Literature and Humanism Research 1978; NEH Summer Research 1975; Haverford Coll Rsch 1975; Natl Fellowships Fund Dissertation Grant 1973-74; Univ of TN Committee Awards for Excellence in Teaching of English 1978-79; United Negro Coll Fund, Distinguished Scholar, Xavier Univ, 1988; Honored teacher, Alpha Delta Pi, 1988; Natl Rsch Council, Ford Found, Univ of Tn, Sr Fellowship, 1986-87. **BUSINESS ADDRESS:** Professor of English, Univ of TN, Dept of English, Knoxville, TN 37996.

MILLER, ROSS M., JR.
Surgeon, city official. **PERSONAL:** Born Feb 19, 1928, Boston, MA; married Iris; children: 2 Children. **EDUCATION:** Howard U, BS 1947. **CAREER:** Jersey City Med Ctr, intrnshp 1951-52; VA Hosp Tuskegee AL, surg res 1952-54; VA Hosp Bronx, surg res 1956-58; EmoryUniv & Grady Mem Hosp Atlanta, surg res fellow 1958-59; US Pub Hlth Serv Clin Ctr, lt sr grade; Nat Cancer Inst Bethesda, 1954-56; Pvt Prac, 15 yrs; UCLA, asst prof of surg 7 yrs; City of Compton, former city councilman; UCLA & Harbor Gen Hosp, instr, asst prof 1966; UCLA, clinical prof of surgery; Charles R Drew MedicalSchools, clinical prof of surgery; Dominguez Vly Hosp, chief of staff. **ORGANIZATIONS:** Diplomate Am Bd of Surg 1961; surg chmn Nat Med Assn 1968; pres HowardUniv Alumni Assn of Southern CA 1961; vice pres Compton Council on Human Rel 1962; Compton Pks & Rec Comm 1963; bd dir Compton Chamber Comm 1964; pres Med, Dental, Pharm Assn of Southern CA 1965; pres elect Southern CA Chap Amer College of Surgeons; CA gov Amer Coll of Surgeons. **HONORS/ACHIEVEMENTS:** Fellow Am Coll of Surgs 1963; fellow Inter Coll of Surgs 1964; recip Man of Year Compton Bus & Prfl Assn 1968; listed in Who's Who in Am Politics 1969-

74 Ed; served US Pub Hlth Serv Nat Cancer Inst Lt Sr Grade. **BUSINESS ADDRESS:** Clinical Professor, 537 W Compton Blvd, Compton, CA 90220.

MILLER, RUSSELL L., JR.
Educator, physician, adminstrator. **PERSONAL:** Born Jun 30, 1939, Harvey, WV; son of Russel Miller and Corinne Miller; married Daryl Lawson; children: Steven, Laura. **EDUCATION:** Howard Univ Coll of Liberal Arts, BS 1961; Howard Univ Coll of Med, MD 1965. **CAREER:** Howard Univ, dean of coll of med 1979-88, vice pres for Health Affairs 1988-, prof of internal med & pharm, 1979-; Howard Univ Coll of Med, Assoc Prof, Internal Med & Pharm, dir, section of clinical pharm, 1974-79; visiting scientist, Natl Inst of Health, 1984-; Cardiovascular Rsch Inst, Univ of CA, Dept of Intl Med San Francisco Div of Clinical Pharm, rsch fellow, 1968-69 1971-73; Univ of MI Med Center, Ann Arbor MI, summer fellowships intern/Internal Med Rsch, 1965-68; Natl Inst of Health Bethesda MD, summer fellowships, 1961-63; Dept of Cellular Biology Div of Pharm & Immunopharmacology Roche Inst of Molecular Biology Nutley NJ, visiting scientist, 1973-74. **ORGANIZATIONS:** mem, AAAS; Am Fed for Clinical Rsch; Am Soc of Internal Med; Am Soc for Clinical Pharm & Therapeutics; Reticuloendotheolial Soc; DC Med Soc; DC Natl Med Assn; Med Chirurgical Soc; Mem, DC General Hospital Commn 1984-88, Mayor's Advisory Commn on Post-Secondary Education 1987-, Natl Advisory Council on Aging 1988-; bd of dir, Natl Resident Matching Program 1988; chmn, Council of Southern Deans, 1987-88. **HONORS/ACHIEVEMENTS:** Fellow, Am Coll of Physicians & Coll of Clinical Pharm; elected to Phi Beta Kappa, Howard Univ Chapter, 1961; elected to Alpha Omega Alpha Hon Med Soc, Howard Univ Chapter, 1964; Diplomate, Natl Bd of Med Examiners, 1966; Certified, Am er Bd of Internal Med, 1971; scholar in Clinical Pharm Burroughs Wellcome Fund, 1977-82; awarded grants, Dept of Health Educ & Welfare Rsch Grant 1977-80; Burroughs Wellcome Found, 1977-82; Bronze Star, AUS 1971; certificate of honor, Natl Medical Fellowships, 1988. **MILITARY SERVICE:** USAR, Major, 1969-71. **BUSINESS ADDRESS:** Howard Vice Pres for Health Affairs, 2041 Georgia Ave, NW, c/o Howard Univ Hospital, Washington, DC 20060.

MILLER, SAMUEL O.
Educator. **PERSONAL:** Born Jun 08, 1931, La Boca, Panama;son of Hubert Miller and Germaine Miller; divorced; children: Larisa, Mark. **EDUCATION:** Dakota Wesleyan Univ, BS (cum laude) 1957; Boston Univ School of Social Work, MSW (honors) 1961; Univ of Chicago Social Serv Admin, PhD 1970. **CAREER:** Family Serv Bureau Chicago, IL, social work 1959-62; Univ of Chicago Dept of Psy, instructor 1962-64; San Mateo County Mental Health Dept, sr social wkr 1964-67; Western MI Univ School of Soc Work, assoc prof 1970-73; Columbia Univ, prof of social work. **ORGANIZATIONS:** Consult Mental Health Organization Council on Soc Work Educ Sch; bd mem Manhattan Country School; NAACP; Natl Assn of Social Workers. **HONORS/ACHIEVEMENTS:** Natl Research Service Award, Natl Inst of Mental Health 1979; Fellowship Award, Whitney Young Found 1980; Career Tchr Natl Inst of Mental Health 1968-70; published various papers & chapters in social work books. **HOME ADDRESS:** 560 Riverside Dr 11c, New York, NY 10027. **BUSINESS ADDRESS:** Professor of Social Work, Columbia Univ, 622 W 113th St, New York, NY 10025.

MILLER, SHARON BERNARD
Banker. **PERSONAL:** Born Apr 19, 1943, Detroit, MI; son of John Bernard and Dorothea Bernard; children: Cylenthia, Sharon Gayle. **EDUCATION:** Univ of AR Sch of Law, BSL, JD 1969. **CAREER:** Self-employed, attorney 1970-74; Michigan Natl Bank, various mgmt positions, presently vice pres 1975-87. **ORGANIZATIONS:** Mem Kappa Beta Pi Legal Sor 1968-87, Women's Economic Club 1975-87; police commissioner Detroit Police Dept 1979-84; chairperson Children's Trust Fund 1982-, Detroit Urban League Bd 1984-89; pres, Neighborhood Services Organization Board 1987-; dir, National Committee, Prevention of Child Abuse Board 1984-. **HONORS/ACHIEVEMENTS:** Minority Achiever in Industry Awd YMCA 1980; Spirit of Detroit City Council of Detroit 1984; Humanitarian of the Yr Optimist Youth Foundation 1986; Outstanding Volunteer MI Natl Bank 1987; Kool Achiever Award Nominee, Brown & Williamson 1988; Michigan 150 First Lady Award, State of Michigan 1988. **BUSINESS ADDRESS:** Vice President, Michigan Natl Bank, PO Box 321006, Detroit, MI 48207.

MILLER, TELLY HUGH
Educator, clergyman. **PERSONAL:** Born Jun 18, 1939, Henderson, TX; married Glory D Bennett; children: Alanna Camille. **EDUCATION:** Wiley Coll, BA 1962; Interdenom Theol Cntr, MDiv 1965; Vanderbilt U, DMin 1973; Prairie View A&M Univ, EdM 1980. **CAREER:** St Paul Baptist Church St Albans WV, pastor 1965; WV State Coll, religious counselor 1967; Wiley Coll Marshall TX, coll minister 1968, financial aid dir 1970, assoc prof/chmn dept of religion 1973, vice pres for student affairs 1974, prof and chmn dept of religion and philosophy 1976-. **ORGANIZATIONS:** Relig consult Bapt WV St Coll Inst 1967; mem Am AssnUniv Profs; chmn Christmas Baskets for Needy St Albans 1967; bd dirs YMCA St Albans 1966-67; chmn mem drive NAACP 1967; mem exec com Kanawha Co chap 1967; v moder Mt Olivet Assn 1966-67; pres George Washington Carver Elem Sch PTA 1977; pres-Gamma Upsilon Lambda Chap Alpha Phi Alpha Frat Inc 1977; mem Alpha Phi Alpha Frat Inc, Alpha Phi Omega Natl Serv Frat Kappa Pi Chapt, AAUP, Morgan Lodge No 10 St Albans WV, NAACP; fellowship of Christian Athletes; bd of dirs Harrison County United Way Fund Dr 1983, bd of dirs Harrison County Red Cross. **HONORS/ACHIEVEMENTS:** East TX Educ Oppors Ctr Awd 1980; Kappa Alpha Psi Achievement Awd 1980; Omega Psi Phi Man of the Year Awd 1983; elected first Black Commissioner for Harrison County 1983; apptd by Gov of TX to East TX Regional Review Comm for the State's Comm Develop Block Grant Prog. **BUSINESS ADDRESS:** Chmn Dept of Religion/Philos, Wiley College, 711 Rosborough Springs Rd, Marshall, TX 75670.

MILLER, THELMA DELMOOR
Retired social worker. **PERSONAL:** Born Oct 22, 1921, New York, NY; married Tucson A Miller (deceased); children: Leslie Ann. **EDUCATION:** City Univ of NY (Queens Coll), MA 1975. **CAREER:** YMCA, 1942; Montclair, drama tchr 1945; New York City Play Sch Assn, 1948; Salvation Army Red Shield NYC, 1948-49; Harlem Br Boys Athl League, 1949-50; Queens Soc Preven Cruelty to Children Jamaica, NY, 1956-60; Drama Guild, adviser/cons 1957-60; Forest Neighborhood House Bronx, NY, rec group worker; Eastern Panhandle Mental Hlth Inc, counselor/therapist 1977-83, retired therapist 1983-; Medicaid Waiver Prog for Frail Elderly Special Federal Project Dept of Human Svcs, case mgr. **ORGANIZATIONS:** Council person Ranson City Council WV elected 1985; mem Migrant Adv Cncl 1980-; pres Jefferson Co Comm on Aging WV 1979-84; treas/bd mem Intercounty Health Inc 1979-85; former pres/bd mem Aging Nutrition Serv for Tri-County, WV 1978-; mem WV Human Resources Assn 1984-; mem St Philips Epis Ch 1979-;vestry mem/lay reader/chalice bearer; candidate for Mayor Renson WV 1987. **HONORS/ACHIEVEMENTS:** Senior Citizen of the Yr Ranson City Council WV 1984. **HOME ADDRESS:** PO Box 586, Ranson, WV 25438.

MILLER, THEODORE H.
Engineer. **PERSONAL:** Born Jan 27, 1905, Kansas City, KS; son of Harry W Miller and Otie B Miller; married Grace Eubank; children: Stanley E, Harry F. **EDUCATION:** Univ of NV, BS Elec Engrg 1930; Attended, KS State Coll. **CAREER:** Westinghouse Elec Co, comml refrig sales div 1935-42; USN Mare Island Naval Shipyard, supvr elec design 1941-46; VA Engrg Div, asst head 1946-51; US Govt GSA 9th Region, chief elec engr 1951-72; Self-Employed, consulting engr. **ORGANIZATIONS:** Licensed Professional Engr Elec State of CA; sr mem Inst of Elec & Electronic Engrs; instr part-time Radiological Defense Stanford Univ; pres Employees Assn 9th Region GSA 1962-66; Western Regional Dir Phi Beta Sigma Frat 1954-56; pres bd dirs Booker T Washington Comm Ctr San Francisco 1956-59; mem bd examiners US Civil Serv Commn 1949-52; Mason; Shriner. **HONORS/ACHIEVEMENTS:** Merit Serv Awd GSA 1964; High Quality Perf Awd GSA 1963; Commendable Serv Awd GSA 1964; Sustained Superior Perf Awd GSA 1968; Man of Month Awd GSA 1972.

MILLER, THOMASENE (NEE REPRESS)
Administrator. **PERSONAL:** Born Dec 06, 1942, Newcastle, PA; married David Lamar; children: David. **EDUCATION:** DePaul U. **CAREER:** City of Chicago, comm adminstr; Model Cities, asst comm adminstr 1970-76; Chicago Com on Urban Oppty, asst chief clk 1968-70, sec 1965-68. **ORGANIZATIONS:** Rua Consult Firm 1976-; Metro Home Hlth Adv Com 1976-; bd of mgrs Chicago Boys Club Martin Luther King Unit 1977; mem NAACP; mem Nat Assn for Comm Devel; mem Am Soc for Pub Adminstrn. **HONORS/ACHIEVEMENTS:** Recog of merit Chicago Com on Urban Oppty; Englewood Childrens Club Award 1970; recog of merit Chicago StateUniv 1970; recog of achvmt Model Cities/CCUO 1975. **BUSINESS ADDRESS:** 10 S Kedzie, Chicago, IL 60612.

MILLER, WARD BEECHER
Banking executive. **PERSONAL:** Born Jun 22, 1954, Kingstree, SC; son of Clifton Miller and Bertha McCray Miller; married Vicki Smith. **EDUCATION:** College of Charleston, BA 1976. **CAREER:** Wachovia Bank, personal banker 1977-79, branch mgr 1979-81, field analyst 1981-83, branch mgr 1983-85, exec banker 1985-. **ORGANIZATIONS:** Steward St James AME Church 1979-; bd mem Big Brothers/Big Sisters 1982-, March of Dimes 1983-, Lift Inc 1986-; financial partner Forsyth Investment Partners 1985-; at large mem Juvenile Justice Council 1986-. **HONORS/ACHIEVEMENTS:** Campaign Award for Fund Raising March of Dimes 1984-86. **HOME ADDRESS:** 2041 Claxton Dr, Winston-Salem, NC 27127. **BUSINESS ADDRESS:** Assistant Vice President, Wachovia Bank & Trust Co NA, 301 No Main St, Winston-Salem, NC 27150.

MILLER, WILBUR J.
Benefit authorizer, councilman. **PERSONAL:** Born Feb 16, 1928, Wilkes-barre, PA; married Gertha Wallace; children: Wilbur J. **EDUCATION:** BS 1975. **CAREER:** Roosevelt City, AL, city councilman; Soc Sec Admin SE Prgm Ctr Birmingham, benefit authorizer; AUS Ptr Pyramid Sporting Goods Co Inc Roosevelt City,1973-. **ORGANIZATIONS:** Pres Roosevelt Invest Corp; pres Citizens Econ & Ed Devel Corp; pres McDonald Chapel Sp Sch PTA; mem Civic League; Birmingham Grid Forecstrs. **HONORS/ACHIEVEMENTS:** Purple Heart; Bronze Star; Army Commendation; Outst Councilmn of Yr 1971. **MILITARY SERVICE:** AUS sgt 1945-66. **BUSINESS ADDRESS:** 301 Brighton Ave, Roosevelt City, AL 35020.

MILLER, WILLIAM NATHANIEL
Association executive. **PERSONAL:** Born Mar 15, 1947, Perry, GA; married Shirley Jones; children: Corbett Burgess, William Franklin. **EDUCATION:** Ft Valley State College, BA Economics 1969; American Inst of Banking, Advanced 1971. **CAREER:** Natl Bank of Georgia, banking officer 1972-77; US Small Business Admin, disaster loan specialist 1977-78; Atlanta Regional Minority Purchasing Council, executive dir 1978-. **ORGANIZATIONS:** Member Phi Beta Sigma Fraternity 1966-; life member Atlanta Chamber of Commerce 1976-; chairman of board John Harland Boys Club 1976; member Ft Valley State Coll Alumni Assn 1978-; member Atlanta & Natl Business League 1979-; member NAACP 1980-; chairman business com United Negro College Fund 1982; member Natl Assn of Exhibition Mgrs 1985; graduate Leadership Atlanta 1985. **HONORS/ACHIEVEMENTS:** Natl Top Achiever Atlanta Chamber of Commerce 1976; Business Dev Honors Collections of Life & Heritage 1984; Council of the Year Natl Minority Supplier DevCouncil 1984. **BUSINESS ADDRESS:** Executive Dir, Atlanta Reg Minority Purch Co, 235 International Blvd, Atlanta, GA 30303.

MILLER, WILLIAM O.
Association executive. **PERSONAL:** Born Apr 14, 1934, Philadelphia, PA; son of Joseph M Miller and Ethel Reed; divorced; children: William C. **EDUCATION:** Temple Univ, BS 1957; Antioch Univ, ME 1974. **CAREER:** Opportunity Indus Centrs Inc, instructor, 1965-73; Philadelphia Urban Coalition, instructor 1968-80; Fitzsimons Jr HS, dir publicity, 1968-70; Fellowship Commn Philadelphia, PA, dir educ, 1975-76; OIC/A Philadelphia, PA, asst dir funds devel, 1976-83, dir natl organization & special events, 1983-; Lincoln/Eagleville Program, l980-8l. **ORGANIZATIONS:** Mem bd dir Philadelphia Miniv; Temple Univ Downtown Club; Graduate Council of Antioch Univ; Philadelphia Tribune Charities; Voters Crusade; Delaward Valley Chapter of the natl Soc of Fund Raisers; bd dir Philadelphia Civic Ballet; Serv Acad Select Bd-Congr Gray; Prince Hall Masons King David #52 F and A of Penna PHA; Alpha Phi Alpha Fraternity; Deacon Board Zion Baptist Church; Comm Leaderships Seminar; mem Amer League of Lobbyist, Archival Comm OIC/Temple Univ. **HONORS/ACHIEVEMENTS:** Legion of Honor Award Chapel of Four Chaplins, 1967-75; Second Mile Award Prince Hall Masons PA, 1972; Distinguished Serv Award Philadelphia Chapter NAACP, 1965; published "Why Bus?" Urban Coalition Publication. **BUSINESS ADDRESS:** Dir, OIC/A, 100 W Coulter St, Philadelphia, PA 19144.

MILLER, WILLIE JAMES
Publisher. **PERSONAL:** Born Mar 24, 1902, Yazoo City, MS; married Lucille Stewart; children: Bobby, Dr Savannah Young. **CAREER:** MS Enterprise, owner pub 1933-; Voice of the S Newspaper, publ 1928-29. **HONORS/ACHIEVEMENTS:** Built & operated only pub entertainment arena for Blacks MidMS region 1940-50. **BUSINESS ADDRESS:** 604 N Farish, Jackson, MS.

MILLER, YVONNE BOND
Educator, senator. **PERSONAL:** Born Jul 05, 1934, Edenton, NC; daughter of John Thomas Bond Sr and Pency Cola Bond; married Wilbert Roy Miller (divorced). **EDUCATION:** VA St Coll, BS 1956; Columbia Univ Tchrs Coll, MA 1962; Univ of Pittsburgh, PhD 1973. **CAREER:** Virginia Senate, senator 5th senatorial district, 1988-; VA House of Delegates, delegate 89th dist, 1984-88; Norfolk State Univ, prof of educ, 1976-, head, Dept of Early Childhood/Elementary Educ, 1980-87, assoc prof, 1973-76, asst prof, 1968-72; Mid-S Tchr Corps Network, dir exec com 1976; Tchr Corps Corpsmen Train Inst, fac mem 1976; Old Dominion U, adj asso prof 1975-76; Mid-Atlantic Tchr Corps Network Bd of Dir, sec 1974-75, dir 1974-76; Norfolk Tchr Corps Proj, dir 1975; Norfolk/Chesapeake Tchr Corps Proj, dir 1974-75, asso dir 1973; Headstart, educ dir 1969; Norfolk City Sch, tchr asst 1966-68; Young Park Sch, headstrt tchr 1965-66, tchr 1956-66. **ORGANIZATIONS:** Life mem NEA; Am Assn of Elem Kinder Nurs Edn; Assn for Supv & Curr Devel; Nat Assn for Educ of Yng Child; Assn for Child Educ Internat; VA Assn of Early Child Edn; Tidewater Pre-Sch Assn; So Assn for Child Under 6; life mem Nat Alliance of Black Sch Edn; Am Assn ofUniv Prof; VA Educ Assn; CH Mason Meml Ch of God in Christ; editor Viewpoint Newsletter of VAECE 1979-80; am Assn ofUniv Women; Chrysler Mus at Norfolk; VA Mus; Beta Theta Zeta Chap Zeta Phi Beta; life mem Zeta Phi Beta Kappa Delta Phi 1962. **HONORS/ACHIEVEMENTS:** Outst Educ of Am 1975; acad excel award Zeta Phi Beta 1974; outst achvmt in educ Beta Theta Zeta 1974; trophy CH Mason Meml Ch of God in Christ 1974;cert Norfolk Counc of Intl Read Assn 1974; invit to memshp Prof of Curr; cert of serv Antoich Bapt Ch 1976. **BUSINESS ADDRESS:** Prof of Educ, Norfolk State Univ, Nursing Educ Bldg, Rm 125, 2401 Corprew Ave, Norfolk, VA 23504.

MILLER-JONES, DALTON
Educational administrator, psychologist. **PERSONAL:** Born Jul 06, 1940, St Louis, MO; married Cynthia L Miller; children: Dalton A Jones, Julie K Jones, M Luke Jones, Marcus N. **EDUCATION:** Rutgers Univ, BA & BS 1962; Tufts Univ, MS Experimental Psy 1965; Cornell Univ, PhD Psychology 1973. **CAREER:** Cornell Univ Africana Studies, lecturer & rsch assoc 1969-73; Univ of Mass/Amherst, asst prof 1973-82; Williams Coll, Henry Luce assoc prof 1982-84; City Univ of New York Grad School, assoc prof 1984-. **ORGANIZATIONS:** Adjunct prof & fellow Inst Comparative Human Cognition Rockefeller Univ, NY 1974-76; member Soc for Rsch in Child Dev 1978-; empirical rsch consultant in Black psychology for New York Board of Ed, Am Can Co & Black community organizations 1980; Jean Piaget Society 1981-; Amer Psych Assn 1982-; Amer Ed Rsch Assn 1981-. **HONORS/ACHIEVEMENTS:** NSF & Office Education Fellowships 1966-69; NSF 1972; Carnegie Corp New York Grant 1972-73; articles and book chapters on Black children's language & thought in J of Black Studies and Academic Press 1979-84. **BUSINESS ADDRESS:** Associate Professor Psychology, Developmental Psychology Prog, GSUC/CUNY, 33 W 42nd St, New York, NY 10036.

MILLER-REID, DORA ALMA
Retired educator. **PERSONAL:** Born Mar 24, Montgomery, AL; daughter of George Miller and Mary-Frances Ingersoll Miller; married Willie J Reid, Sep 28, 1949. **EDUCATION:** Florida A&M Univ, Tallahassee FL, BS, 1954; Wayne State Univ, Detroit MI, EdM, 1959. **CAREER:** Escambia County Bd of Public Instruction, Pensacola FL, teacher, 1955-71; Detroit Bd of Educ, Detroit MI, teacher, 1971-81. **ORGANIZATIONS:** The Detroit Fedn of Teachers, AFL-CIO, 1971-; Amer Fedn of Teachers, 1971-; bd of dir, mem, Co-Ette Club Inc, Detroit Chapter, 1971-; Wayne State Univ Alumni Assn, 1975-; Natl Retired Teachers Assn, 1981-; Retirement Coordinating Council, 1981-; mem, United Foundation's Heart of Gold Awards Council, 1982-, Metro Detroit Teen Conf Coalition, 1983-; Women's Comm, NAACP, 1983-. **HONORS/ACHIEVEMENTS:** Certificate of Merit, Detroit Bd of Educ, 1981; John F Kennedy Memorial Award, Co-Ette Club Inc, Detroit Chapter, 1987; Certificate of Appreciation, Detroit Bd of Educ, 1988; Governor's Volunteer Honor Roll, State of Michigan, Special Tribute, 1989; Certificate of Appreciation, Ronald McDonald House, 1989. **HOME ADDRESS:** 9000 E Jefferson, Apt 11-8, Detroit, MI 48214.

MILLETT, KNOLLY E.
Physician. **PERSONAL:** Born Aug 15, 1922; married Mavis DeBurg; children: Eileen, Mercedes, Denise, Maria, Jacques. **EDUCATION:** Long IslandUniv Brklyn, BS 1947; Univ of Paris Faculty of Med, MD 1959. **CAREER:** Brklyn Physicians, pvt prac. **ORGANIZATIONS:** Mem Nat Med Assn; AMA; Kings Col Med Soc; Provident Clinic Soc of Bklyn; Phi Beta Sigma; Gamma Rho Sigma; affil Brklyn-Cumberland Med Ctr Jewish Hosp of Bklyn; mem Urban League; NY Civil Liberties Union; Manhasset C of C; diplomate Am Bd of Family Prac; E. **BUSINESS ADDRESS:** 453 Franklin Ave, Brooklyn, NY 11238.

MILLETT, RICARDO A.
Social policy analyst, planner. **PERSONAL:** Born May 10, 1945, Panama City, Panama;son of William G Millett and Ometa Millett; married Jan Stepto; children: Sundiata Madoda, Miguel Stepto, Maya Alegre. **EDUCATION:** Brandeis Univ, BS Econ 1968; Florence Heller School Brandeis Univ, MA 1971, PhD 1973. **CAREER:** Atlanta Univ, assoc prof 1973-77; ABT Assoc, sr analyst, proj mgr 1977-80; Dept of Social Svc, dep asst comm mgr 1980-81; Boston Univ, dir, adjprof 1981-83; Roxbury Milti-Serv Ctr, exec dir 1983-85; Neighborhood Housing Development, asst dir 1985-. **ORGANIZATIONS:** Asst dir Boston Redevel Auth 1985-; bd mem, chmn Hillside Pre-Release Prog; mem, pres Black Political Task Force; mem Museum of Afro-Amer History African Meeting House Comm 1987; bd of overseers Florence Heller School, Brandeis Univ; bd of dirs Thomas Jefferson Forum; bd of dirs Social Policy Research Group. **HONORS/ACHIEVEMENTS:** "St Corner Alcoholics" Alton Childs Publ 1976; "Widespread Citizen Participation in Model Cities and the Demands of Ethnic Minorities for a Greater Decision Making Role in Amer Cities" 1977; "Simmering on the Calm presence and Profound Wisdom of Howard Thurman, 1981-82; "Racism and Racial Relations in Boston" 1982-83; Faces to Watch in 1986 Boston Mag 1986; "Urban Renewal and Residential Displacement in the South End" Boston Univ Afro-Amer Studies Dept 1987; "Enterprise Zones and Parcel to Parcel Linkage, The Boston Case" Univ of MA School of Public & Community Serv 1987; "New Players in Urban Development" Boston Redevelopment Authority 1989. **BUSINESS ADDRESS:** Senior Vice President for Planning, United Way of Mass Bay, Two Liberty SQ, Boston, MA 02109.

MILLICAN, ARTHENIA BATES
Retired educator, writer. **PERSONAL:** Born Jun 01, 1920, Sumter, SC; married Wilbert Millican (deceased); children: Wilbert James. **EDUCATION:** Morris Coll Sumter, SC, BA (Magna Cum Laude) 1941; Atlanta Univ, MA 1948; LA State Univ Baton Rouge, PhD 1972. **CAREER:** Westside HS Kershaw, SC, English teacher 1942-45; Butler HS Hartsville, SC, civics/English teacher 1945-46; Morris Coll, head English dept 1947-49; Mary Bethune HS Halifax, VA, English teacher 1949-55; MS Valley State Univ, English instructor 1955-56; Southern Univ, English instructor 1956-59, asst prof 1959-63, assoc prof 1963-72, prof English 1972-74; Norfolk State Univ, prof English 1974-77; Southern Univ Baton Rouge, LA, prof English & creative writing 1977-80; researcher, writer, freelance. **ORGANIZATIONS:** Mem Baton Rouge Alumnae Chap of Delta Sigma Theta; mem comm Arts and Letters Baton Rouge Sigma Alumnae Chapt; serve as poet prose reader and exhibitor ofcreative works for programs; mem Les Gayettes Civic and Social Club. **HONORS/ACHIEVEMENTS:** Natl Endowment for the Arts Award (1 out of 165 in the nation) 1976; prize short story "Where You Belong" publ in "Such Things From the Valley" 1977; cover story "Black World" July 1971; cover picture and interview "Nuance" with Adimu Owusu March 1982; contributing author, "James Baldwin, A Critical Evaluation"; "SturdyBlack Bridges, Visions of Black Women in Literature"; author of, "The Deity Nodded" 1973; "Seeds Beneath the Snow, Vignettes of the South" 1975; Prepared Black Culture Registry (Louisiana) a first 1985. **HOME ADDRESS:** PO Box 335, Baker, LA 70714.

MILLIGAN, HUGH D.
Manager. **PERSONAL:** Born Dec 08, 1931, Washington, DC; married Phyllis Louise Bivins; children: Sean Michael, Sharon Leslie. **EDUCATION:** FAA Acad, Cert 1958; FAA Mgmt Training Sch, Cert 1974, 76, 78. **CAREER:** FAA Tech Ctr, chief airport oper br 1978-, prgm mgr 1978, tch analyst 1976-78, prgm mgr 1974-76, air traffic cntrl splst 1960-74, 58-60. **ORGANIZATIONS:** Mem Orgn of Black Airline Pilots 1978; mem Am Inst of Aeronautics & Astronautics 1978-80; chap chmn Nat Tech Assn 1979-80. **HONORS/ACHIEVEMENTS:** Recip Korean Svc/United Nat Svc/Pres Unit Citation USAF 1952-53; quality perform award FAA 1966; publ article on Pilot Self-Briefing Tech Am Meteorological Assn 1976; cert of achvmt Orgn of Black Airline Pilots 1978; cert of apprctn Dept of Transp 1979. **MILITARY SERVICE:** USAF staff sgt served 4 yrs. **BUSINESS ADDRESS:** Mgr Air Traffic Control Facility, FAA, ACN-340, Atlantic City Airport, Atlantic City, NJ 08405.

MILLIGAN, UNAV OPAL WADE
Secretary. **PERSONAL:** Married Larry; children: Guren, Gary, Aaron, Mike, Gregory, Margarena, Ann. **EDUCATION:** Jr Coll & Bus Mgmt, 2 yrs. **CAREER:** First Integrated Beauty Salon Jasper TX, owner oper 1977-; Charmetts Beauty Salon, owner 1962-74; Gen & Masonry Contractors, sec. **ORGANIZATIONS:** Pres NAACP Alameda 1973-75. **HONORS/ACHIEVEMENTS:** Achvmt award fund raising NAACP 1973; recog award Alameda Unified Sch Dist 1976; apprectn award Alameda Br NAACP 1976; apprectn award Oakland Br NAACP1976; outst award Alameda Naval Airstation CA 1976. **BUSINESS ADDRESS:** Unav's Beauty Salon, R #2 Box 280, Jasper, TX 75951.

MILLIN, HENRY ALLAN
Elected government official. **PERSONAL:** Born Mar 17, St Thomas, VI; married Graciela Guzman; children: Leslie, Inez, Henry, Janet, Juliette. **EDUCATION:** Inter-Am U; OH State U. **CAREER:** Govt of the Vi, lt gov 1978-; 1st PA Bank of N Am, vp; VI Housing Authority, exec dir; Tax Assessor's Office, chief clk; Police & Prison Dept, chief clk. **ORGANIZATIONS:** Commr Pub Serv Commn; mem Rotary Club; sr warden All Saints Ch. **BUSINESS ADDRESS:** Govt of the VI, Box 450, St Thomas, Virgin Islands of the United States 00801.

MILLIONES, JAKE
Educational administrator. **PERSONAL:** Born Feb 24, 1940, Marietta, GA; married Barbara Sizemore; children: Beatena, Momar, Dubois, Marimba. **EDUCATION:** Lincoln Univ, 1958-61; Univ of Pittsburgh, BS Psych 1966; Langley Porter Neuropsychiatric Clinic 1971-72; Univ of Pittsburgh, PhD Clinical Psych 1973. **CAREER:** Univ of Pittsburgh, asst prof 1968-73, rsch asst 1977-80; Amer Civil Liberties Union, bd dir 1980-82; Spectrum Drug Treatment Prog, consultant 1980-; Western Psychiatric Inst & Clinic, asst prof, psychiatry & psychology. **ORGANIZATIONS:** Bd dir Program to Aid Citizens Entr 1969-80; consult Alpha House Therapeutic Comm for Treatment of Drug Addiction 1975-78; bd dir Allegheny Childrens YouthServ 1977-80, Pittsburgh Psychoanalytic Ctr 1977-80, Comm Action Pittsburgh 1978-81, Pittsburgh Bd of Public Ed 1978-. **HONORS/ACHIEVEMENTS:** Distinguished Serv Black Grad Students Org 1980; Community Serv Natl Assn of Black Accountants 1982. **MILITARY SERVICE:** AUS Reserves spec 4, 6 yrs. **BUSINESS ADDRESS:** Asst Prof, Psych & Psychol, Western PsychiatricInst, 3811 Ohara, Pittsburgh, PA 15260.

MILLIS, DAVID HOWARD
Physician. **PERSONAL:** Born Jun 26, 1958, Brooklyn, NY; son of Clovis B Millis and Ena G Whitaker Millis. **EDUCATION:** Yale Univ, BS Psychobiology 1979; Howard Univ, MD 1983; New School for Social Research, Certificate Microcomputer Systems 1986. **CAREER:** Univ of IL Chicago, resident general surgery 1983-84; SUNY Downstate Medical Center New York, resident psychiatry 1984-88; Stanford Univ Medical Center, postdoctoral fellow, currently. **ORGANIZATIONS:** Mem AMA, ACM, AAAI. **BUSINESS ADDRESS:** Postdoctoral Fellow, Stanford University Medical Center, Medical School Office Building, Room 215, Stanford, CA 94305.

MILLNER, DIANNE MAXINE
Attorney. **PERSONAL:** Born Mar 21, 1949, Columbus, OH; married Herb Anderson. **EDUCATION:** Pasadena City Coll, AA 1969;Univ of CA at Berkeley, AB 1972; Stanford U, JD 1975. **CAREER:** Hastings Coll of The Law, instructor 1977-78; Pillsbury Madison & Sutvo Law Firm, attorney 1975-80; Alexander, Millner & McGee, atty. **ORGANIZATIONS:** Dir Star Seven Broadcasting 1982-; pres & dir Black TV Workshop 1983-; dir Youth for Serv 1978-80; mem Commnty Redevel Agencys Assn 1983-; Nat Bar Assn; Black Woman Lawyers Assn; Charles Houston Bar Assn. **HONORS/ACHIEVEMENTS:** Pres Award

Womens Div Nat Bar Assn 1980; Phi Beta Kappa UC Berkeley 1975; Who's Who in Am Law; The World's Who's Who of Woman.

MILLS, BILLY G.
Judge. **PERSONAL:** Born Nov 19, 1929, Waco, TX; married Rubye; children: Karol, Karen, William Karl, John, James. **EDUCATION:** Compton Coll, AA High Hon 1949; UCLA, BA 1951; UCLA Law Sch, LLB 1954; UCLA, JD 1958. **CAREER:** LA Sup Ct, Fam Law Dept, suprvsg judge 1979-, judge Superior Court; Sup Ct, State of CA, judge 1974; LA City Counc, city councmn 1963-74; Atty, pvt prac 1957-74; LA Co, dep probation ofcr 1957-60. **ORGANIZATIONS:** Chmn LA Co Dem Cntrl Com; mem Dept of Justice Adv Com; exec bd LA Co Bar Assn; mem CA State Bar Assn; com on cts & the comm Am Bar Assn; mem Am Judicature Soc; mem num other legal & law enforcement orgn mem Trinity Bapt Ch; bd of trustees United Ch of Rel Sci; mem S Cntrl LA & Watts C of C; consult USC Sch of Pub Adminstrn; mem League of CA Cities; United Negro Coll Fund; Sickle Cell Found; CA Black Corr Coalition; CA Fedof Black Ldrshp; Crippled Child Soc; Kiwanis Club; mem num other orgns. **HONORS/ACHIEVEMENTS:** Outst grad Compton Comm Coll; outst achvmt S Cntrl Area Plng Counc United Way; IES Lamplighters Cert The Rdwy Ltg Forum; 2nd anniv comm serv award Met Gazette; cert of merit Un Supreme Counc Prince Hall Affil; outst cit of yr Jefferson Adult Sch; Hon D Humane Letters Un Ch of Rel Sci Schof Ministry; boss of yr Civic Ctr Women's Counc; num other certs plaques & awards. **MILITARY SERVICE:** AUS 1955-57. **BUSINESS ADDRESS:** Judge Superior Court, Los Angeles Superior Court, Family Law Dept, Los Angeles, CA 90012.

MILLS, DONALD
Entertainer. **PERSONAL:** Born 1915, Piqua, OH; children: John. **CAREER:** Sang during intermissions with Harold Greenamier's Band in Piqua, OH in 1923; Worked as "Four Boys and a Guitar" for WLW radio in Cincinnati in 1928; Performances on CBS radion in NY; US and European tours include Copenhagens Tivoli Gardens and New York's Rainbow Grill; presently touring as "John and Donald Mills of the Mills Brothers". **HONORS/ACHIEVEMENTS:** Between 1941 & 1946 recorded "Paper Doll" (more than 6 million copies sold), "I'll Be Around", "Till Then", "You Always Hurt the One You Love", "I'm Afraid to Love You", "Across the Alley from the Alamo"; to date The Mills Brothers have recorded over 1,264 songs. **BUSINESS ADDRESS:** c/o Henry Miller Associates, PO Box 195, Encino, CA 91426.

MILLS, ELIZABETH NATHANIEL
University administrator. **PERSONAL:** Born Jan 06, 1933, Charlotte, NC; married John Chambers; children: Joni, Candace, Reginald, Anthony. **EDUCATION:** Bennett Coll NC, BS 1954; Case-Western Reserve Cleveland, MSW 1968; Univ of Rochester, Rochester NY, doctorate in progress. **CAREER:** State Univ of NY, affirmative action adminstr; State Univ at Brockport, dir 1972-73; Coll Ctr State Univ, coordinator of counseling 1970-72; YWCA of Rochester and Monroe County, asso dir 1968-70; VA Hosp, group worker 1967-68; YWCA Charlotte Mecklenburg County, exec dir 1964-66. **ORGANIZATIONS:** Consult Project Upward Bound 1974-; consult State Educ Dept 1975-78; consult AtlantaUniv Nat Center Leadership Dev 1979-80; chairperson Affirmative Action Com Urban League of Rochester NY 1976-; chairperson Monroe County Youth Bd 1978-. **HONORS/ACHIEVEMENTS:** Dist serv award Urban League of Rochester 1978-79; dist serv award Project Upward Bound 1978-79; minority students StateUniv Coll at Brockport 1978. **BUSINESS ADDRESS:** 409 Admin Bldg, Brockport, NY 14420.

MILLS, GLADYS HUNTER
Coordinator, librarian. **PERSONAL:** Born Mar 13, 1923, Philadelphia, PA; daughter of Ephraim H Hunter and Charlotte Fisher Hunter; married E Thomas Mills; children: Alan Wayne. **EDUCATION:** Temple Univ, undergraduate study 1940-43; Cert Profes Sec, cert 1956. **CAREER:** CO Labor Coun AFL-CIO, sec 1954-57, 1964-67; Edu Comm of States, sec 1968; Res Cntr Edu Com of States, coor 1968-74; Libr Edu Comm of States, coord of & inf serv 1974-81; Storage Technology Corp, information specialist 1982-89. **ORGANIZATIONS:** Mem Spl Librs Assn; mem Am Libr Assn; mem Am Soc for Inf Sci; mem CO Comm on Civil Rights 1961-68; mem CO Coun on Instr 1964-68, Chrmn 1968; mem NAACP; mem Urban League; mem Peoples Presbyterian Church; mem National Black Presbyterian Caucus.

MILLS, GLENN B., JR.
Auditor. **PERSONAL:** Born Jul 05, 1948, Oakland, CA; married Ernestine Pratt; children: Tasha, Glenn III, Lennard. **EDUCATION:** Prairie View A&M Univ, Pol Sci 1969. **CAREER:** Transamerica Fin Corp, mgr 1970-75; State of TX Comptroller Office, auditor 1975-; Wilmer-Hutchins ISD, pres. **ORGANIZATIONS:** Deacon Concord Missionary Baptist Church 1976; pres Headstart (state & natl) 1976-82; deacon bd Concord Missionary Baptist Church 1976-; Master Mason Masonic Order 1977-; bd of trustees Wilmer Hutchins ISD 1980-; bd of dirs Headstart local-state-regional-natl. **BUSINESS ADDRESS:** President, Wilmer-Hutchins I S D, 3820 E Illinois Ave, Dallas, TX 75216.

MILLS, HERBERT
Retired entertainer. **PERSONAL:** Born 1913, Piqua, OH. **CAREER:** Sang during intermission with Harold Greenamier's Band in Piqua OH starting in 1923; Worked as "Four Boys and a Guitar" for WLW Radio in Cincinnati 1928; Performed on CBS radio in NY; US and European tours incl Copenhagens Tivoli Gardens and New York's Rainbow Grill. **HONORS/ACHIEVEMENTS:** Between 1941 and 1946 recorded "Paper Doll" (more than 6 million copies sold), "I'll Be Around", "Till Then", "You Always Hurt the One You Love", "I'm Afraid to Love You", "Across the Alley from the Alamo", "Bye Bye Blackbird", "Cab Driver"; to date The Mills Brothers have recorded over 1,264 songs. **BUSINESS ADDRESS:** c/o Henry Miller Associates, PO Box 195, Encino, CA 91426.

MILLS, HUGHIE E.
Association executive. **PERSONAL:** Born Mar 07, 1924, Fayette Co, WV; married Greta Tuck; children: Grace. **EDUCATION:** WV State Coll, BA 1949; NY U, MPA 1950; ColumbiaUniv Tchrs Coll, candidate for Ed D 1976. **CAREER:** ColumbiaUniv Sch of Bus, dir financial aid 1973-; asst dir admissions 1967-73; Council for Oppor in Grad Mgmt Edn, dir; John Hancock & Life Inst Co,agt 1960-67. **ORGANIZATIONS:** Mem Kappa Alpha Psi; NY State Financial Aid Adminstrs Assn; chmn Black Faculty & Adminstrs Columbia U; 100 Black Men; trustee Ch of The Good Shepherd; dir MBA Mgmt Cons; bd dir Faculty House Columbia U. **MILITARY SERVICE:** AUS 1943-46. **BUSINESS ADDRESS:** Dir of Alumni Affairs, Nassau Community College, 211 Nassau Hall, Garden City, NY 11530.

MILLS, JOEY RICHARD
Make-up artist. **PERSONAL:** Born Apr 02, 1950, Philadelphia, PA. **EDUCATION:** Temple U, BA 1970. **CAREER:** Vogue, make-up artist; Harper's Bazaar; Glamour; Red Book; Mccalls; Ladies Home Journal; Family Circle; Essence; Town & Country; The Next Man, created make-up for Cornelia Sharpe & Sean Connery; "Eyes of Laura Mars", appeared in role of make-up artist; has appeared on countlesTV and radio programs; Nancy Wilson & Melba Moore, num others, record album covers; Valerie Harper, regular Clients; Raquel Welch; Diana Ross; Naomi Sims; Beverly Johnson; Cissy Houston; MelbaMoore; Nancy Wilson; Jodie Foster; Jill Clayburgh; Brooke Shields; Twyla Thorpe; Margot Kidder; Mariel Hemingway; Olivia Newton-John; Lauren Hutton. **HONORS/ACHIEVEMENTS:** Guest appear WNBC Not For Women Only; For You Black Woman; appeared "Kenneth" Beauty Talk Show; appeared "AM New York"; appeared "PM New York"; appeared "The Morning Show" w/Regis Philbin; appeared "Today in New York"; appeared "The Barbara Walters Special" with Brooke Shields; 3 beauty books; cosmetic line 1978; designed make-up for Twyla Thorpe's first season on Broadway 1980; author "Joey Mills' Classic American Look".

MILLS, JOHN
Entertainer. **PERSONAL:** Born 1956. **CAREER:** Performances as "John and Donald Mills of the Mills Brothers" at Copa Room of the Sands Hotel in Las Vegas, Fiesta Dinner Theater in San Diego, Carleton in Minneapolis; European tour including performance in Copenhagen, West Germany, Sweden, England. **BUSINESS ADDRESS:** c/o Henry Miller Associates, PO Box 195, Encino, CA 91426.

MILLS, JOHN L.
Business executive. **CAREER:** DL&J Services, Chambersburg, PA, chief exec. **BUSINESS ADDRESS:** Chief Executive, DL&J Services Inc, PO Box 662, Chambersburg, PA 17201. *

MILLS, MARY ELIZABETH
Educator. **PERSONAL:** Born Jul 04, 1926, Franklin, TN; daughter of Daisy Johnson Knowles; married Latham L Mills, May 31, 1951; children: Latham L Mills, Joycelin M Blackman. **EDUCATION:** Tennessee State Univ, Nashville TN, BS, 1946, MS, 1965, certificate in adminand supervision; attended George Peabody College for Teachers at Vanderbuilt Univ. **CAREER:** Williamson County School System, Franklin TN, teacher, 1953-55; Franklin Special School District, Franklin TN, teacher, 1955-77, asst principal, 1977-80, principal, 1980-. **ORGANIZATIONS:** Pres, Franklin City Teachers Assn, 1977; board of trustees, William Medical Center, 1983-; chair, Community Child Care Center, 1983-; sec, Williamson County Tourism, 1983-; Natl Education Assn; Tennessee Education Assn; Assn of Elementary School Principals; Assn of Principals and Supervisors; Franklin Special School District Education Assn; Phi Delta Kappa. **HONORS/ACHIEVEMENTS:** Henry L. Hardison Humanitarian Award, Franklin Special School District Education Assn; Whitney M Young Jr Award, Boy Scouts of Amer; Helping Hand Award, Williamson County Chamber of Commerce; Black History Month Achievement Award; Outstanding Achievement in the Field of Education, Black Perspective Newspaper. **HOME ADDRESS:** 1776 West Main St, P O Box 486, Franklin, TN 37065.

MILLS, MARY LEE
Nurse consultant. **PERSONAL:** Born Aug 23, 1912, Wallace, NC; children: Lt Cmdr Robert S, David G. **EDUCATION:** Lincoln Sch of Nursing, dipl 1934; Med Coll of VA, cert in pub hlth nursing 1937; Lobenstine Sch of Midwifery, cert midwifery 1941; NYU, BS, MA 1946; George Washington Univ, cert 1973. **CAREER:** US Agency Intl Dev, detail 1946-66; Migrant Hlth Br, 1966-69; Howard Univ Div of Hlth Care Svc, 1969-71; The Nelsen Comm, sr hlth analyst 1971-72;Bur Comm Hlth Svc, consult 1973-. **ORGANIZATIONS:** Comm volunteer with Program on Aging in Pender Cnty; mem reg Adv Comm on Aging; chmn of fund raising Shiloh Columbia Volunteer Fire Dept; chmn Black History Cnty Comm; spec assignment on Natl Acad of Sci for Study of America's Role in Health and Sanitation in foreign aid; numerous speaking invitations toprofessional and comm groups. **HONORS/ACHIEVEMENTS:** NC State Volunteer Award James Rufus Herring Award; Lakes Chapel Bapt Ch Award; Shiloh Columbia Volunteer Fire Dept Disting Serv Award; Pleasant Hill BaptChurch Centennial Award; Included in, "Contemporary Minority Leaders in Nursing, Afro-Americans, Hispanics, Native Americans Perspectives" 1983; "Hope and Dignity - Older Black Women in the South" 1983.

MILLS, ROBERT
Business executive. **PERSONAL:** Born Aug 30, 1936, Chicago, IL; children: Vicky, Laura, Stacey. **EDUCATION:** Miami U; Fenn Coll. **CAREER:** Supreme Life Ins Co;; dist mgr 1974-; Columbus, dist mgr 1970-74; field supr 1969; staff mgr 1968; Mills Enter, owner oper 1962-68; Glidden Paint Co, supr exec ofc 1956-66. **ORGANIZATIONS:** Past treas Combin Mgrs Assn Life Ins Co; pres Athletic Club. **MILITARY SERVICE:** USNR 1954-62. **BUSINESS ADDRESS:** Supreme Life Insurance Co, 12025 Shaker Blvd, Ste 300, Cleveland, OH 44120.

MILLS, STEPHANIE
Singer. **PERSONAL:** Born Mar 22, 1957, Queens, NY. **EDUCATION:** Juilliard School Music. **CAREER:** 20th Century Fox Records, recording artist present. **ORGANIZATIONS:** Child star singing & act since 16 yrs old; at 16 starred in broadway mus "The Wiz"; many TV Appear; film "Piece of the Action" 1974. **HONORS/ACHIEVEMENTS:** Winner of 7 Tony Awds; 2 Gold Albums. **BUSINESS ADDRESS:** c/o Allen Mills, Starlight Music, 5807 Topanga Canyon Blvd D105, Woodland Hills, CA 91367.

MILNER, EDDIE JAMES, JR.
Professional athlete. **PERSONAL:** Born May 21, 1955, Columbus, OH; married Retha Sims. **EDUCATION:** Central State OH Univ; Muskingum Clge. **CAREER:** Cincinnati Reds, outfielder 1980-. **HONORS/ACHIEVEMENTS:** NL Player of the Week for the first week of season hitting 571 1984; named MVP of FL State League in 1978.

MILNER, MICHAEL EDWIN
Federal bank examiner. **PERSONAL:** Born Mar 16, 1952, Atlanta, GA; son of Edwin R

Milner and Ethel M Minor Milner; married Cathy Slack; children: Kimberly, Michaelyn. **EDUCATION:** Morehouse Coll, BA 1974. **CAREER:** General Finance Corp, mgr 1974-78; Federal Reserve Bank of Atlanta, federal bank examiner 1978-. **ORGANIZATIONS:** Consultant Atlanta Adopt-a-Student Prog 1986; mem Atlanta Urban Bakers Assoc 1987. **HONORS/ACHIEVEMENTS:** Competent Toastmaster Toastmaster Intl 1985. **HOME ADDRESS:** 4585 Spring Valley Pkwy, College Park, GA 30349.

MILNER, THIRMAN L.
Elected government official. **PERSONAL:** Born Oct 29, 1933, Hartford, CT; son of Marshall Henry Milner and Grace Milner Allen; divorced; children: Theresa, Gary, Thirman, Jr. **CAREER:** Allstate Ins Co, acct rep; Gen Electric Bus Div, acct rep; New York City Council Against Poverty CAA, exec asst; Comm Devel NYC, dep asst admin; Comm Renewal Team Conn Action Agency, pub relations dir; State of CT, rep; House of Reps, asst maj leader 1981-82; City of Hartford, mayor 1981-; First Natl Supermarkets, Inc, dir, govt affairs, 1987-. **ORGANIZATIONS:** Sub-comm chmn, Finance Revenue and Bonding legislative Comm, 1979-80; sub-comm chmn, Planning and Devel legislative Comm 1979-80; northeast region liaison, Minority Energy Technical Assistance Prog, 1979-81; bd dir, Hartford Branch NAACP, 1979-81; regional coordinator, Natl Caucus of Black State Legislators, 1979-81; Natl Conf of Black Mayors, first vice pres 1985-86, assoc mem 1987-; bd dir, Massachusetts Food Assoc, 1989-; bd mem Connecticut Food Assoc, 1989-; life mem, NAACP. **HONORS/ACHIEVEMENTS:** Comm Serv Awd Omega Phi Epsilon Frat 1980; Comm Serv Awd Guardians Afro-Amer Police 1980; Comm Serv Awd NAACP 1980; Comm Serv Awd Gr Hartford Black Soc Workers 1980; Jewish Tree of Life Award 1986; Univ of Hartford Chair-Establishing Thirman L Milner Scholar, 1987; dedication of Thirman L Milner Public Elementary School 1989; first African Amer mayor in New England popularly elected, 1981. **HOME ADDRESS:** 19 Colebrook St, Hartford, CT 06112.

MILTON, HENRY
Clergyman. **PERSONAL:** Born Apr 13, 1918, Arcadia, OK; married Corine; children: Leon, Antoinete. **CAREER:** Macedonia Baptist Church, pastor 1958-. **ORGANIZATIONS:** Mem Minst Cncl Bay Area Bapt Dist Assn; mem Peninsula Bapt Minst Union Bd; mem OICW; bd mem Nairabi Day Sch; clergy suprt OICW. **HONORS/ACHIEVEMENTS:** Certificate Comm Serv; Certificate Award Bay Area Baptist Dist Assn. **BUSINESS ADDRESS:** 1110 Berkeley, Menlo Park, CA 94025.

MILTON, HENRY BENFORD
Administrator/CEO. **PERSONAL:** Born Nov 28, 1961, River Rouge, MI. **EDUCATION:** Univ of MI Ann Arbor MI, BA Philosophy; Atlanta Univ, MBA Mktg;Univ of MI-Ann Arbor, AB 1984; Atlanta Univ, MBA 1986. **CAREER:** Milton Community Hosp, admin, chief exec officer;Milton Comm Hosp, administrator/ceo. **ORGANIZATIONS:** Mem Alpha Phi Alpha; mem, bd of trust Metro Detroit Area Hosp Serv Inc; ex officio mem, bd of trust Milton Comm Hosp;mem Alpha Phi Alpha Frat Inc 1981-. **HONORS/ACHIEVEMENTS:** Outstanding Youn Men of Amer. **BUSINESS ADDRESS:** Administrator/CEO, Milton Community Hospital, 234 SB Milton Dr, River Rouge, MI 48218.

MILTON, LEROY
Research analyst. **PERSONAL:** Born Apr 07, 1924, Los Angeles, CA; married Alma M Melonson; children: James E, Angela H. **EDUCATION:** Pepperdine U, BS 1949. **CAREER:** John Wesley Co Hosp, chf rsrch analyst 1970-; LA Co, admin deputy coroner 1969-70; exec asst bldg serv 1968-69; LA Co, head coll invest 1963-68; Secured Div LA Co, chief 1961-63; real est speculator 1950-70. **ORGANIZATIONS:** Pres Milton Enterprise 1960-; pres & dir Pub Ser Credit Union 1960-73; dir Eye Dog Found 1966-73; dir Beverly Hills Hollywood NAACP 1969-70; pres& mem Cosmos Club 1946-; Alpha Phi Alpha. **MILITARY SERVICE:** USN 1942-46. **BUSINESS ADDRESS:** Financial Consultant, Potomac View Properties, 4255 Cloverdale Ave, Los Angeles, CA 90008.

MILTON, OCTAVIA WASHINGTON
Educational administrator. **PERSONAL:** Born Apr 30, 1933, Greensboro, NC; divorced; children: James Jr, Lynne Michelle. **EDUCATION:** Hampton Inst, BS 1954; Atlanta U, MA 1968, EdS 1971, Edd 1986. **CAREER:** Greensboro NC City Schools, speech therapist 1954-62; Atlanta Public Schools, speech therapist 1962-73, coordinator speech/hearing impaired 1973-83, dir/program for exceptional children 1983-. **ORGANIZATIONS:** Outstanding Elementary Teachers of Amer 1973; mem Amer Speech-Language Hearing Assn; mem Council for Exceptional Children; mem Delta Sigma Theta Sorority. **HONORS/ACHIEVEMENTS:** Assist I & II Communication Skill Builders 1977, assist III 1981, assist combined 1983; grammarifics Imperial Intl Learning Corp 1980. **HOME ADDRESS:** PO Box 11246, Atlanta, GA 30310. **BUSINESS ADDRESS:** Dir, Atlanta Public Schools, 2930 Forrest Hill Dr SW, Atlanta, GA 30315.

MILTON, SAMUEL BYRON
Physician. **PERSONAL:** Born Mar 08, 1902, Washington, DC; married Isaure; children: Svane. **EDUCATION:** Northwestern U, MD 1927; Brown U, PhD 1924. **CAREER:** Sumby Hosp, physician, surgeon, founder. **ORGANIZATIONS:** Chmn bd tests Sumby Meml Hosp; bd educ City of River Rouge; hlth ofcr City of Ecorse; coroner Wayne Co; mem State & Nat Coroners Assn Life; mem NAACP; AMA; Detroit Med Soc; Wayne Co Med Soc; dir SA Sumby Meml Hosp; mem MI State Med Soc; med dir Wright Mutual Ins Co; mem Alpha Phi Alpha; Union Bapt Ch. **BUSINESS ADDRESS:** 240 Visger Rd, River Rouge, MI 48218.

MIMMS, MAXINE BUIE
Educational administrator. **PERSONAL:** Born Mar 04, 1929, Newport News, VA; married Jacques; children: Theodore, Tonie, Kenneth. **EDUCATION:** VA Union U, BA 1950; Union Graduate Sch, PhD 1977. **CAREER:** Evergreen State Coll, prof 1972-; Women's Bureau Dept of Labor 1969-72; Seattle Pub Schs administrator 1964-69; Kirkland Public Schs tchr 1961-64; Seattle Public Schs, tchr 1953-61. **ORGANIZATIONS:** Mem Nat Consultances in Edn; mem New Approaches to Higher Edn; mem NAACP; mem Urban League; mem NEA (WEA). **HONORS/ACHIEVEMENTS:** Women of the yr awards at several levels Seattle St Louis Tacoma. **BUSINESS ADDRESS:** Evergreen State Coll, Olympia, WA.

MIMS, GEORGE E.
Social service director. **PERSONAL:** Born May 14, 1932, Columbia, SC. **EDUCATION:** Howard Univ Washington DC, BA (Mag ı Cum Laude, Dist Military Grad) 1959; Amer Univ DC, MA 1960; Miami Univ OH, attended 1963-65; Univ of HI, attended 1965-68; Neotarian Coll of Philosophy, DD 1980. **CAREER:** USAF Race Relations Ed/Equal Opport, Drug/Alcohol Abuse, major 1951-55, 1959-76; Royal Thai Air Force Base Thailand, chief social actions 1973; USAF School of Social Actions San Antonio TX, chief of training 1973-76; Community Action Agency Ft Worth TX, exec dir 1976-78; Community Ed Extension Headstart, chief exec office 1979-81; Youngstown Area Urban League, pres and CEO. **ORGANIZATIONS:** Vp NAACP Honolulu HI 1965-68; instr Creighton Univ Omaha NE 1969-71, Eastern Washington State Coll Spokane WA 1971-72, Los Angeles City Coll Extension Thailand 1973; exec founder dir Black Unity Coord Council 1974-76; instr San Antonio Coll San Antonio TX 1976; pres Oper PUSH Columbia SC 1981; exec dir Black Leadership Summit Council 1982-85. **HONORS/ACHIEVEMENTS:** Disting Grad Squadron Officer School AL 1963; Military Man of the Year Owlers Mens Club Omaha NE 1969; Outstanding Achievement NAACP Honolulu HI 1968; Appreciation Awd Black Unity Coord Council San Antonio TX 1976; Youngstown/Warren Realtors Assoc, distinguished community serv awd 1986. **MILITARY SERVICE:** USAF maj 1951-55, 1959-76; Bronze Star, Commendation 1972-73. **BUSINESS ADDRESS:** President & CEO, Youngstown Area Urban League, 2516 Market St, Youngstown, OH 44507.

MIMS, GEORGE L.
Educational administrator. **PERSONAL:** Born Feb 27, 1934, Batesburg, SC; son of George W Mims and Mary Aletha Corley; married Clara Ann Twigg; children: Cheryl Ann, Carla Aletha. **EDUCATION:** FL A&M U, BS 1955; TC Columbia U, MA 1957, Prof Dip 1967; Rutgers U, EdD 1976. **CAREER:** Fisk U, head res counselor 1959-61; Volusia Co Comm Coll FL, dean of students 1961-63; Hunter Coll NY, asst placement dir 1963-67; Pace Univ NY, dir of special programs 1968-. **ORGANIZATIONS:** Mem editorial bd Journal, Educ & Psych Research 1983-86; mem adv comm Merck Sharp & Dohme 1983-; proposal reader US Ofc of Educ NY 1974-; pres AERA, Spec Int Group Black Educ 1982-86; chmn/designate AERA, Comm on Spec Int Groups 1984-87; res NY State Div of AACD 1982-83; pres Eta Theta Lambda Chap Alpha Phi Alpha 1980-87. **HONORS/ACHIEVEMENTS:** Minority Alumni Award Pace Univ NY, NY 1983; HEOP Award 1980; Leadership Award HEOP 1975; Cert of Merit Big Bro of NY 1969; Brothers Award, Eta Theta Lambda Chap 1987; Community Service Award Central Nassau Club 1989. **MILITARY SERVICE:** AUS sgt e5; Good Conduct 1957-59. **HOME ADDRESS:** 885 Seneca Rd, West Hempstead, NY 11552.

MIMS, MADELINE MANNING
Olympic runner. **PERSONAL:** Born Jan 11, 1948, Cleveland, OH. **CAREER:** 1968, 72, 76, 80 Olympic Teams, olympic runner mem. **HONORS/ACHIEVEMENTS:** Holds Am 800 m record at 1579; won gold medal & set olympic am records 1968; AAU champ indoor & outdoor; silver medal winner 1972 mile relay; gold medalistPan Am Games 1967; named outst athlete US Europe meet 1969; ran 2003 in us-USSR meet to win.

MIMS, MARJORIE JOYCE
Associate executive. **PERSONAL:** Born Sep 14, 1926, Chicago, IL; married Thomas S Mims; children: John, Raleigh. **EDUCATION:** Univ of IL, BS in LAS 1949, MS Admin 1974; Univ of Chicago, advanced study 1974-76; DePaul Univ, advanced study 1978-81. **CAREER:** Jack & Jil of Amer Chicago Chapt, pres 1974-78; The Moles, natl vice pres 1978-82; The Links Inc, central area dir 1983-. **ORGANIZATIONS:** Mem Amer & Guidance Assoc 1970-; bd mem Ada S McKinley Assoc 1972-82, Assoc for Family Living 1973-81; chmn Natl Nominating Comm of Jack & Jill of Amer 1978. **HONORS/ACHIEVEMENTS:** Woman of the Year Radio Station WAIT 1974; Anti-Basielus Theta Omega Chap Alpha Kappa Alpha Sor. **HOME ADDRESS:** 7016 S Constance Ave, Chicago, IL 60649.

MIMS, OSCAR LUGRIE
Public administrator. **PERSONAL:** Born Jun 07, 1934, Washington, DC; married Barbara C Crockett; children: Donna, Beverly Jackson, Oscar L Jr. **EDUCATION:** Univ of DC, BS 1959; Bank St Coll of Edn, Cert 1963; Howard U, MA 1964;Univ of MA, EdD 1971; Fed Exec Inst, Cert Pub Admin 1974. **CAREER:** DC Pub Sch, educator 1959-68; DC Tchrs Coll, asst acad dean 1967-68; US Dept of HUD, pub admin 1968-, dir affirmative action. **ORGANIZATIONS:** Life mem NEA 1959-; mem Am Soc of Pub Admin 1968-; bd of dir DC Branch NAACP 1972-76; bd of dir Wash Urban League 1972-76; natl dir C Rodger Wilson Leadershp Conf 1982-; Kappa Alpha Psi Frat. **HONORS/ACHIEVEMENTS:** Leadership Award Wash Urban League DC 1976; Nat Educ Fellow Bank St Coll of Educ 1963. **BUSINESS ADDRESS:** Director, Affirmative Action, US Dept of HUD, 451 7th St SW, Washington, DC 20410.

MIMS, ROBERT BRADFORD
Physician, educator, scientist. **PERSONAL:** Born Mar 24, 1934, Durant, MS; son of Dawson Mims and Laura Mims; married Eleanor Veronica Meeseburgh; children: Sharon Beverly, Valerie Tracy, Robin Eleanor, Bari Allen. **EDUCATION:** Shorter College, 1952-54; Philander Smith Coll, BS 1956; Univ AR School Med, MD 1960; USC School Med, Res 1961-64, Fellow 1964-66. **CAREER:** USC School of Medicine, acad prof1964-77; USN, LCDR 1966-68; John Wesley County Hospital, assoc med dir 1970-74; USC/LAC Med Center Home Health Servcs, dir 1974-78; Fndtn Med Center, pres/bd of dir 1978-82; USC School of Med, Associate Clinical Prof, 1978-86; Endocrine Metabolic Center of Santa Rosa, dir 1984-. **ORGANIZATIONS:** Mem Pasadena Unified School Dist; CA Med Assn; Endocriminology Soc; AAAS; Amer Federation Clinical Research; Amer Coll Phys; Amer Geriatric Assn; Natl Assn Home Health; vice pres bd dir Health Plan of Redwoods 1978-80; bd dir Sonora Co Diabetic Assn 1978-; bd dir Tri-Co Found for Med Care; dir Dept of Internal Med for Family Practice Santa Rosa Memorial Hospital 1979-; bd dir VNA Sonoma Co; CA Assn for Health Care at Home; Amer Diabetes Assn; CA Political Action Assn 1984; dir BSA 1979-81; bd of dir Visiting Nurses Assn 1978-83; pres N CA Amer Diabetic Assn 1985-86; Altadena Family Serv; Altadena Neighbors; Pasadena Intergration Plan; med admin advisor Southwest LA Community Med Corp; med lecturer at various public educ meeting 1977-; served on numerous community and hospital committees; Bd of dir & Executive Committee for CA Affiliate Amer Diabetes Assn, 1986-89; vice pres & bd of directors for the Laura & Dawson Mims Educ Foundation & The Mims Research Institute, 1985-. **HONORS/ACHIEVEMENTS:** Natl Honor Soc Philander Smith Coll 1952-56, Summa Cum Laude 1956; Honorary Life Membership CA & Natl Congress of PTA 1973; Natl Scientific Soc; numerous Collegiate Awards &

Honors; Award & Scholarship Pasadena Unified School Dist by CA Congress of Parents & Teachers Inc 1971; Award for dedicated serv to Med-Cor Affairs at USC School of Med 1972-74; numerours scientific presentations & publications, 1964-. **MILITARY SERVICE:** USN lt commander 1966-68. **BUSINESS ADDRESS:** Director, Endocrine Metabolic Center, 1109 Sonoma Ave, Santa Rosa, CA 95405.

MINCEY, W. JAMES
Association executive. **PERSONAL:** Born Feb 27, 1947, Statesboro, GA. **CAREER:** NC Mut Life Ins, empl. **ORGANIZATIONS:** Pres Bulloch Co Chapt; SCLC 1970-; co-chmn Mcgovern campaign Bulloch Co 1972-72; pub dir NAACP 1969-70; youth coun pres NAACP 1967-68; memJ Wesley Lodge #161; Mason; Ins Underwriters Assn Thomas Grove Bapt Ch. **HONORS/ACHIEVEMENTS:** Semi-finalist Ford Found Ldrshp Dev Prog.

MINER, WILLIAM GERARD
Architect. **PERSONAL:** Born May 12, 1950, Washington, DC; son of George Miner and Charlotte Miner. **EDUCATION:** Princeton U, AB 1972; MA Inst Tech, MArch 1974. **CAREER:** US Dept of State, Foreign Bldgs Operations, program mgr, 1985-; CRS Sirrine Intl Group, training & research coord, 1983-85; Amer Inst of Architects, dir of practice publications, 1978-83; Univ of Maryland School of Architecture, asst prof of architecture, 1977-81; Keyes Lethbridge & Condon, project architect, 1974-77; MIT Sch Archt & Urban Planning, tchr asst 1973-74; Keyes Lethbridge & Condon, intern archt 1973; MIT Sch Archt, rehab consult 1973; Keene Interior & Systems, designer draftsman 1972; Peoples' Workshop, co-fndr Designer 1972-72; Irving Wasserman Gulf Reston Inc, asst head planner 1971; PrincetonUniv Sch Arch & Planning, rsrch asst 1970-71; Princeton Alumni Cncl, trvlg rsrch 1970; Joseph Minor Nat Capital Housing Authority, asst sr archt 1970. **ORGANIZATIONS:** Mem Student Planning Team Metro Dist Commn 1972; instr Trenton Design Ctr 1970-71; stud rep bd dir AIA 1972. **HONORS/ACHIEVEMENTS:** Design competition finalist Nat Granite Quarry Assn 1974. **BUSINESS ADDRESS:** Program Mgr, US Dept of State, Foreign Buildings Operations, SA-6, Suite 1300, Washington, DC 20520.

MING, DONALD GEORGE K.
Bishop. **CAREER:** African Methodist Episcopal Church, president of council of bishops, presiding bishop of 8th Episopal district. **HOME ADDRESS:** 146-24 223rd, St Rosedale, NY 11413. **BUSINESS ADDRESS:** 28 Walmer Rd, Woodstock, Capetown 8001, Republic of South Africa. *

MINGO, FRANK L.
Business executive. **PERSONAL:** Born Dec 13, 1939, McComb, MS; married Sheila Breckenridge; children: Michael, Justin. **EDUCATION:** Univ of IL, BS 1961; NWU, MS 1970. **CAREER:** Mccann Erickson, vice pres mgmt supv; J Walter Thompson, sr acct exec; Field Enterprises NAACP, mgr; Mingo-Jones Advertising Inc, pres. **HONORS/ACHIEVEMENTS:** Outst acct serv HK Mccann awd 1974; Robert E Healy awd 1976; cit Nat Alliance of Bus 1970; cert Chic Pub Rel Club; coord Basis Advertising Course of 4a's 1st Lt 1962-63. **BUSINESS ADDRESS:** Chairman, Mingo-Jones Advertising Inc, 750 Third Ave34th Floor, New York, NY 10017.

MINGO, PAULINE HYLTON
Owner, manager. **PERSONAL:** Born Aug 08, 1945; daughter of Cecil and Martha; divorced; children: Martha Senetta, Elizabeth Joy, Nelson III. **EDUCATION:** Univ of Hartford, 1964-67. **CAREER:** State of CT, social worker 1964-67, private sec to chancellor of higher ed 1969-71; Natl Black Business & Professional Womens Org, chaplain 1971-74; Pan Am World Airways Eleuthera Bahamas, asst to base oper mgr 1972-74; Mingos World Travel Serv Hartford, owner, mgr 1974-. **ORGANIZATIONS:** Treas NW Family Day Care Ctr Hartford 1972-; vice pres Greater Hartford Bus Devel Corp Hartford 1975-78; member, Union Baptist Church, Hartford Conneticut. **HONORS/ACHIEVEMENTS:** Published pictoral article "The Watchman" Philadelphia Spring 1977; A Woman Worth Knowing Awd Ujima Inc 1978; appointed mem Gov's Vacation Council 1978-80; publ "Making It" Black Enterprise Mag 1980; featured CT Bus Times 1980; writer Bi-Weekly Travel Article No Agents Newspaper 1980. **BUSINESS ADDRESS:** Manager, Mingos World Travel Service, 279 Granby Street, Hartford, CT 06112.

MINION, MIA
Computer systems analyst. **PERSONAL:** Born Nov 05, 1960, Washington, DC; children: Daryn. **EDUCATION:** Coppin State Coll, BS 1985. **CAREER:** Coppin State Coll, clerk-typist 1981-85; Social Security Admin, computer systems analyst 1985-. **ORGANIZATIONS:** Vice pres Zeta Phi Beta Sor Inc 1984-85. **HONORS/ACHIEVEMENTS:** Mem Alpha Kappa Mu Natl Honor Soc 1983; Natl Deans List 1983,84,85; Outstanding Young Women of Amer 1983,84,85; John S Sheppard Scholarship Baltimore Mktg Assoc 1983. **HOME ADDRESS:** 5801 Bland Ave, Baltimore, MD 21215. **BUSINESS ADDRESS:** Computer Systems Analyst, Social Security Administration, 6401 Security Blvd, Baltimore, MD 21235.

MINOR, BILLY JOE
Educator. **PERSONAL:** Born Nov 10, 1938, Pine Bluff, AR; married Joanne Holbert; children: Billy. **EDUCATION:** CA State Coll at Hayward, BA 1968; CA State Coll at Hayward, MS 1969; IN U, PhD 1974. **CAREER:** Oakland U, asst prof 1974; Inner City Counselor Trg IN U, project dir 1971-74; San Francisco Sch, sch psychologist 1969-71. **ORGANIZATIONS:** Pres Behavioral Sci Consult & Inc 1974. **HONORS/ACHIEVEMENTS:** Guest editor "Counseling Practioner as Researcher & Consumer Research" Am Personnel & Guidance Assn to be publ Apr 1981. **BUSINESS ADDRESS:** Oakland Univ, Rochester, MI 48063.

MINOR, CLAUDIC DEE, JR.
Athlete. **PERSONAL:** Born Apr 21, 1951, Pomona, CA; married Vicki; children: Maisha, Keesha Sharinn. **EDUCATION:** Mt San Antonio Jr Coll; San Diego City Coll; San Diego State U. **CAREER:** Denver Broncos, offensive tackle 1974-; construction business. **ORGANIZATIONS:** Mem Fellowship of Christian Athletes. **HONORS/ACHIEVEMENTS:** Started every game at San Diego State; MV offensive lineman at San Diego State; MV & defensive lineman Mt San Antonio; played Coaches All Am game; started 88 consecutive games with broncos (team's 2nd longest consecutive streak); has not a game since joining Broncos. **BUSINESS ADDRESS:** Denver Broncos, 5700 Logan St, Denver, CO 80216.

MINOR, DAVID M.
Business executive-marketing. **PERSONAL:** Born May 25, 1947, St Louis, MO; married Janet Tillema; children: Aaron. **EDUCATION:** Ripon Coll, AB 1968; Northwestern U, MBA 1970. **CAREER:** General Mills Inc, prod mgr 1978-; US Dept of Commerce, sr policy analyst 1977-78; General Mills, product mgr 1976-77, asst prod mgr 1974-75; Proctor & Gamble, marketing asst 1970-73. **ORGANIZATIONS:** Dir CETA Adv Bd 1978-80; secy Pvt Industry Council (Minneapolis) 1979-80; mem Allocations Panel United Way 1977-78; mem Nat Assn of Market Devel . **HONORS/ACHIEVEMENTS:** Named White House fellow US Commn for White House Fellows 1977; named presidential interchange exec US Commn for Presidential Interchange Execs 1977. **BUSINESS ADDRESS:** General Mills Inc, 9200 Wayzata Blvd, Minneapolis, MN 55440.

MINOR, DEBORAH ANN
Educational administrator. **PERSONAL:** Born Aug 13, 1951, Long Branch, NJ; divorced. **EDUCATION:** Montclair State Coll, BA 1973, MA 1976; NYU, Doctoral candidate. **CAREER:** Neptune Sr HS, humanities instructor 1974-75; Webster Hall Res Hall Montclair State, dir 1975-76; Upward Bound, dir 1976-78; Stevens Tech Enrichment Pgm, dir 1978-83; Chicago Area Pre-Coll Engineering Pgm (CAPCEP), exec dir. **ORGANIZATIONS:** Bd mem/treas Assn for Equality & Excell in Edn; bd mem NJ Assn of Black Educators; bd mem Educ Oppor Fund Dir Assn; elected to steering comm formed NAMEPA, elected natl sec; mem Nat Assn of Pre-Coll Dir; mem Assn for Supr & Curr Devel (ASCD); mem The Coalition to Keep the School Open, Bd, Illinois Fair Schools Coalition, Blacks in Devel, Pres, The Right Source, an info network (education consulting firm), President-Partners for Profit (investment club), Youth on the move for Christ. **HONORS/ACHIEVEMENTS:** Named to Congressman Haye's Educ Leg Adv Cncl; published article, "Case for Retention Programs"; Served on educ comm Commission on The Status of Women IL; Published Article, "Overcoming Barriers"-Winning The Retention Battle (NSBE Jour nal Dec 85/Jan 86). **BUSINESS ADDRESS:** Executive Dir, CAPCEP, 300 W Adams Rm 614, Chicago, IL 60606.

MINOR, EMMA LUCILLE
Educator. **PERSONAL:** Born Mar 16, 1925, Pollard, AL; daughter of Berry Walton and Estella Dowell Walton; married James H Minor, May 24, 1946; children: Dale Michael Minor, Gail Minor Christopher, Valerie E Minor Alloy. **EDUCATION:** Kent State Univ, Kent OH, BS, 1971; Cleveland State Univ, Cleveland OH, MA Educ Admin, 1974; Bowling Green State Univ, Bowling Green OH, post graduate studies; Joh Carroll Univ, Univ Heights OH, post graduate studies. **CAREER:** Cleveland Public Schools, Cleveland OH, cadet teacher, 1968-72, consultant teacher, admin intern, asst principal, 1972-75, principal, 1975-85. **ORGANIZATIONS:** Natl Assn of Reading and Language Educ, 1975-85; mem, Phi Delta Kappa Educ Frat, 1976-89, Natl Alliance of Black School Educ, 1977-89; supreme basileus, natl officer, Natl Sorority of Phi Delta Kappa Inc, 1977-89; life mem, NAACP, 1977-89; local officer, Ohio Assn of School Admin, 1980-85; mem, Delta Sigma Theta Sorority, 1982-89; affiliate representative, Natl Urban League, 1985-89, Legal Council on Civil Rights, 1986-89, United Negro Coll Fund, 1986-89; affilliate pres, Natl Council of Negro Women, 1986-89; co-chairperson, Assault on Illiteracy, Professional Educ Comm, 1986-89. **HONORS/ACHIEVEMENTS:** Distinguished Serv Award, City of Cleveland, 1982; Teaching Reading for Competency, 1984; Distinguished Serv, Cleveland Public Schools, 1985; Organizational Growth and Change, 1986; Mission to Make a Difference, 1987; Distinguished Serv, Natl Sorority of Phi Delta Kappa Inc, 1987; 100 Most Influential Black Amer, Ebony Magazine, 1987, 1988, 1989. **HOME ADDRESS:** 1453 Blackmore Rd, Cleveland Heights, OH 44118.

MINOR, JESSICA
Psychotherapist, consultant. **PERSONAL:** Born in Chicago, IL. **EDUCATION:** Wittenberg Univ, BA, 1962; Univ of Chicago, MA, 1964; Univ of California, JD, 1988. **CAREER:** Mgmt consultant, corporate exec, & psychotherapist, 1970-. **ORGANIZATIONS:** Mem, Amer Bar Assn, Phi Alpha Delta Law Fraternity, Assn for Communications, Sports & Entertainment Law, United Nations Assn, Commonwealth Club of California, Amer Women for Intl Understanding, The Planning Forum, Intl Visitors Center; Founders Comm, United Nations World Centre in San Francisco; charter mem, San Francisco Symphony League. **HONORS/ACHIEVEMENTS:** Outstanding Young Woman in Amer, 1970; Semifinalist, White House Fellows Program, 1973-74; Outstanding Professional in Human Services, 1974; Honorary Consul, Republic of Liberia, 1979-84. **BUSINESS ADDRESS:** President, Minor & Co, PO Box 15505, San Francisco, CA 94115.

MINOR, JOHN A.
Chief executive. **CAREER:** Inner Harbor Ford, Inc, Baltimore, MD, chief executive, 1985-. **BUSINESS ADDRESS:** Inner Harbor Ford, Inc, 2900 S Hanover St, Baltimore, MD 21225. *

MINOR, JOHN S.
Construction executive. **PERSONAL:** Born Apr 02, 1948, Morristown, NJ; son of George Minor and Helen Nelson Minor; married Catherleen Webber, Jul 08, 1967; children: Jonn C, Keir S, Levar T, Maissha L. **EDUCATION:** New Jersey Inst of Technology, BSET 1981. **CAREER:** ET Killam Assoc, construction manager 1971-80; McKee Assoc, project manager 1980-81; JS Minor Corp, pres, CEO 1981-; Jacmin Inc, chmn of the bd 1982-89. **ORGANIZATIONS:** Esquire IBPOE-PON #93 1982-84; dir FSP Jaycees 1983,85; pres Sugar Bear Prod 1985-; coach YMCA Youth Basketball 1986-87.

MINOR, VICKI BEIZE
Administrative assistant. **PERSONAL:** Born Aug 16, 1938, Greenville, MS; married David E; children: Deborah Carol. **EDUCATION:** TX So U, BBA 1966. **CAREER:** Penn Mutual Life Ins Co Gordon Agency Houston, adminstrv asst 1979-; Riverside Gen Hosp, coordinator planning & devel 1971-79; TX So U, staff asst fordevel 1968-71; TX SoUniv of Bus, adminstrv asst 1966-68; Dow Chemical Co, information officer 1964-66. **ORGANIZATIONS:** Nat Assn of Market Developers, asst sec natl bd 1968-; Nat Assn of Devel, mem jour com co-chmn 1973-76; bd of dir Third Ward Reconstrn Finance Corp 1970-; mem 3rd Ward Planning Council; mem Windsor Village Civic Club. **HONORS/ACHIEVEMENTS:** Recipient Outstanding Award for Excellence in Achievement TX SoUniv 1972; pres's award NAMD 1975-79; Bettye Jane Everett award for Creative Involve-

ment NAMD 1976; outstanding comm serv award Black Communicators Assn 1976; incentive award NAMD 1978. **BUSINESS ADDRESS:** Penn Mutual Life Insurance Co, Gordon & Agency 2650 Fountain Vie, Houston, TX 77057.

MINOR, WILLIE
Educator. **PERSONAL:** Born Jan 31, 1951, Navasota, TX; son of Carl Minor Jr and Marjorie Williams. **EDUCATION:** Prairie View A&M Univ, BS 1973, MS 1974; Univ of Phoenix, MA 1980; AZ State Univ, EdD 1976. **CAREER:** Faculty Assn, sec 1984-85; Admin Mgmt Soc, pres 1984-85; Phoenix Coll, prof of business; Phoenix Coll Admin Intern 1989-. **ORGANIZATIONS:** Mem & sec Delta Mu Delta 1972; grad co-op NASA Space Ctr 1974; sponsor Afro Amer Club 1977; mem & sponsor Phi Beta Lambda 1972-; mem Business Comm Assn 1976-85; mem & officer Delta Pi Epsilon 1976-; pres Admin Mgmt Soc 1977-; mem Phi Delta Kappa 1980-; arbitrator Better Business Bureau 1984-. **HONORS/ACHIEVEMENTS:** Magna Cum Laude Prairie View A&M Univ 1973; Academic Recognition Prairie View Faculty 1976. **HOME ADDRESS:** 7333 West Roma, Phoenix, AZ 85033. **BUSINESS ADDRESS:** Professor of Business, Phoenix College, 1202 W Thomas Rd, Phoenix, AZ 85013.

MINTER, ELOISE DEVADA
Educational administrator. **PERSONAL:** Born Oct 24, 1928, Monroe Co, AL; children: Clifford B, Brenda Y. **EDUCATION:** Tuskegee Inst AL, BS 1949; Tuskegee Inst AL, MA 1961; Wayne State & Merril Palmer Inst Detroit, attended 1970 & 1974. **CAREER:** Pershing High Sch Detroit, asst prin 1979-; City of Detroit, real estate salesman & appraiser 1975-80; Telegram Newspaper, writer 1970-80; Longfellow MiddleSch Detroit, unit head 1978-79; Jefferson Middle Sch, dept head 1968-78; Southside Jr High Sch Mobile, asst prin 1965-68. **ORGANIZATIONS:** Pub speaker religious occasions civic groups & youth progs 1960-80; dir Bd of Christian Educ Dexter Ave Bapt Ch 1968-80; mem Nat Orgn of Sch Adminstrs Suprs 1968-80;; mem Sunday Sch & BTU Congress 1970-80; mem Alpha Kappa Alpha 1949; Mem NAACP 1965-80; mem PUSH 1965-80; Marie Clair Block Club 1970-80. **HONORS/ACHIEVEMENTS:** Pub audio presentation of Israel "In the footsteps of Jesus"; pub "A Drama for Your Ch 1980. **BUSINESS ADDRESS:** Pershing High Sch, Detroit Bd of Educ, Detroit, MI 48202.

MINTER, KENDALL ARTHUR
Attorney. **PERSONAL:** Born May 24, 1952, New York, NY; married Revola. **EDUCATION:** Cornell Univ, BA 1974, JD 1976. **CAREER:** Black Affairs Dept WVBR-FM, announcer, chmn 1970-71; WTKO, announcer, music dir, acct exec 1972-76; Cornell Univ, legal asst to vp, campus affairs 1975-76; Farichild Industries Inc, corp rep for broadcasting 1976-78; Burns Jackson Miller Summit & Jacoby NY, attny 1978-80; Private practice, attny. **ORGANIZATIONS:** Pres, chmn of bd Full Circle Enterprises Inc 1973-77; co-founder Black Entertainment Lawyers Assoc; bd dir 100 Black Men Inc; bd of dir Amer Youth Hostels Inc; dir HS Talent Search Intl Inc 1977-; media cons, lawyer, entertainment lawyer, adv counc Amer Youth Hostels Metro NY Council 1976-; fdg com Cornell Black Alumni Assoc 1977; mem Amer Bar Assoc, NY St Bar Asso, Fed Comm Bar Assoc, Comm Task Force Natl Conf of Black Lawyers, Natl Black Media Coalition. **BUSINESS ADDRESS:** Attorney, 221 West 57th St, New York, NY 10019.

MINTER, STEVEN ALAN
Administrator. **PERSONAL:** Born Oct 23, 1938, Akron, OH; son of Lawrence L Minter and Dorothy M Knox; married Dolores K; children: Michele, Caroline, Robyn. **EDUCATION:** Baldwin-Wallace Coll, BE 1960; Case Western Reserve Univ School of Applied Soc Servs, M Soc Adm 1963. **CAREER:** Cuyahoga Co Welfare Dept, dir 1969-70; Commonwealth of MA, commr of public welfare 1970-75; US Dept of Educ Washington DC, under sec 1980-81; The Cleveland Found, assoc dir & program officer 1975-80 & 1981-83, dir 1984-. **ORGANIZATIONS:** Dir OH Bell Tele Co 1984-; dir Goodyear Tire & Rubber Co 1985-; trustee Coll of Wooster 1978-; dir Society Natl Bank 1987-, Independent Sector 1987-, Amer Public Welfare Assoc 1987-; life mem NAACP; dir Society Corp 1987-; dir Consolidated Natural Gas 1989-. **HONORS/ACHIEVEMENTS:** Hon PhD Humane Letters Baldwin-Wallace Coll 1974; Disting Serv Awd The Sch of Applied Social Sci Case Western Reserve Univ 1979; Hon PhD Humane Letters Findlay Coll 1984; Social Worker of Yr OH Chap of Natl Assoc of Soc Workers 1984; Black Professional of Yr Black Professional Assoc Cleveland 1985; Hon PhD Humane Letters Oberlin Coll 1988; Hon PhD Humane Letters Kent State Univ 1988; Hon PhD Humane Letters Case Western Reserve Univ 1989. **BUSINESS ADDRESS:** Dir, The Cleveland Foundation, 1400 Hanna Bldg, Cleveland, OH 44115.

MINTER, THOMAS KENDALL
Educator. **PERSONAL:** Born Jun 28, 1924, Bronx, NY; married Rae Alexander; children: Thomas K Jr. **EDUCATION:** NY U, MA 1950; Union Theol Sem NY, SMM 1950; Harvard U, EdD 1971. **CAREER:** USOE, dep commr elem & secon edn; Wilmington Public Schs, supt 1975-77; Dist 7 Sch Dist of Phila, supt 1972-75; PA Advancement Sch, dir 1970-72;PA, adminstrv asst to supt 1968-70; Boston, adminstrv asst to dir of field serv 1967-68; Human Resources Adminstrn NY, consult 1967; Medford MA, arsrch asst 1967; Music Dept Benjamin Franklin HS, tchr acting chmn 1959-66; James Otis Jr HS, tchr 1955-59; MD State Tchrs Coll, inst 1949-53. **ORGANIZATIONS:** Coord Philadelphia Cluster Nat Ed D Prgm for Educ Leaders NOVAUniv 1973-76; coord Philadelphia Cluster Nat Ed D Prgm for Educ Leaders NOVAUniv 1973-76; consult Nat Alliance of Black Sch Educators; consult Nat EdD Prgm for Educ Leaders NOVA U; consult Rsrch for Better Schs PA; consult Supt of Schs Portland Learing Rsrch & Devel Ctr Rider Coll; Carter Mondale Transition Planning Group 1976; mem Assn for study of Afro-Am Life & History; memNAACP Fellow John HaySummer Inst in Humanities Williams Coll 1965; Phi Delta Kapp Hon Educ Frat 1966; Phi Mu Alpha Hon Music Educ 1949. **HONORS/ACHIEVEMENTS:** Publs Intermediate Sch 201 Manhattan ctr of controversy 1967; a study of NY city bd of ed demonstration projs IS 201 2 bridges ocean hill Brownsville 1967; The Role of Conflict in Devel Operation of 2 New York City Decentralized Sch Projs 1968; Covering the Desegreation Story current Experiences & Issues 1976; Sch Desegregation Making It Work. **BUSINESS ADDRESS:** Dean Div of Prof Studies, Lehman College, Bedford Pk Blvd West, Bronx, NY 10468.

MINTER, WILBERT DOUGLAS, SR.
Administrator. **PERSONAL:** Born Nov 17, 1946, Knoxville, TN; children: Wilbert Douglas, Jr. **EDUCATION:** Knoxville College, 1965-67; Univ of Tenn, 1970-. **CAREER:** Association of Records Managers & Administrators, pres (local chapter) 1974-; Administrative Management Society, pres (local chapter) 1982; Martin Marietta Corporation, suprv of engineering records. **ORGANIZATIONS:** Pres Oak Ridge Comm Relations Council 1972-73, Atomic City Sportsmen Club of Oak Ridge 1975; mem Human Resources Bd of Oak Ridge 1980-82, Oak Ridge School Bd 1983-, State Adv Comm US Civil Rights Cimmiss 1983-85, Dept of Energy Contractors & Micrographics Assoc 1985; natl conf speaker Assoc of Records Mgrss & Admin. **HONORS/ACHIEVEMENTS:** Distinguished service award Shriners of Knoxville 1973; outstanding chapter member Records Managers & Administrators 1975; outstanding certified records mamager1982. **BUSINESS ADDRESS:** Suprv of Engineering Records, Martin Marietta Corporation, P O Box Y, Oak Ridge, TN 37830.

MINTON, RUSSELL FARBEUX, SR.
Retired radiologist. **PERSONAL:** Born Sep 21, 1900, Philadelphia, PA; married Lucille Walton; children: Russell F Jr MD, Raymonde Mclure. **EDUCATION:** Penn State Univ, BS 1924; Howard Univ Medical Sch, MD 1929. **CAREER:** Tuskegee Inst, prof chemistry 1924-25; Sch Dist of Phila, school doctor 1939-40; Philadelphia Health Dept, radiologist 1940-62; Mercy Hospital Phila, superintendent 1949-55; Fed Civil Serv Commn, regional med dir 1965-75. **ORGANIZATIONS:** Former pres & historian Olde Philadelphia Club 1950-80. **HONORS/ACHIEVEMENTS:** Medical Alumni Assoc 50 Yrs Serv 1979; PA Historical Commn Awd Negro History 1981. **HOME ADDRESS:** 600 E Cathedral Rd #C 302, Philadelphia, PA 19128.

MINTZ, REGINOLD LEE
Real estate company executive. **PERSONAL:** Born Sep 27, Alexander, VA; son of John H Mintz and Dorothy Mintz; children: Reginold Lee Lewis. **EDUCATION:** Virginia State Univ, BS, 1983; IBM Programmers School, Dallas, TX, 1984; Century 21 Real Estate Mgmt Inst, 1988. **CAREER:** Natl Student Bus League, immed past natl pres 1981-83; MSP Landscaping Inc, vice pres 1983; IBM, program analy 1983-88; Investment Real Estate Annuity Corp, pres, 1988-; Century 21 Prestige Realty, realtor-assoc, currently. **ORGANIZATIONS:** Mem Natl Student Bus League Bus Advisory Comm; pres Minority Bus Assoc of VA 1984-85; mem Alpha Phi Omega Inc 1981-; bd mem, 1981-87, mem, currently, Natl Bus League; mem, Natl Assn of Real Estate Brokers, 1989-; mem, Natl Student Business League, 1981-; mem, Natl Assn of Realtors, currently. **HONORS/ACHIEVEMENTS:** Leadership Award, Natl Business League, 1982; Community Service Award, IBM; Outstanding Service Award, Minority Business Assn, 1987; author, "Buyer Beware," Real Estate Today, 1989. **HOME ADDRESS:** 1339 Irving St, NW, Suite 2, Washington, DC 20010. **BUSINESS ADDRESS:** Realtor-Assoc, Century 21 Prestige Realty, New Amsterdam Complex, 1375 Fairmont St, NW, Washington, DC 20009.

MINUS, HOMER WELLINGTON
Dentist. **PERSONAL:** Born Mar 21, 1931, Wyoming, DE; married Barbara; children: Carla M, Felicia Y. **EDUCATION:** Univ of Delaware, BS 1953; Temple Univ School of Dentistry, DDS 1959; Howard Univ School of Div, MDiv 1987. **CAREER:** Dentist; United Methodist Church, clergyman. **ORGANIZATIONS:** Vestryman Dioc Counc Conv DE Prot Episcopal Church; school bd mem Dover DE 1967-70; life mem NAACP; life mem Alpha Phi Alpha Fraternity Inc. **MILITARY SERVICE:** AUS s/sgt 1953-55. **BUSINESS ADDRESS:** Clergyman, United Methodist Church, 960 Forest St, Dover, DE 19901.

MINYARD, HANDSEL B.
Educator, real estate investments. **PERSONAL:** Born Mar 11, 1943, Phoenix, AZ; son of Richard Minyard (deceased) and Vivian Minyard; married Karen Flavell; children: Stacey B, H Blair. **EDUCATION:** Stanford U, AB 1964; Yale Law Sch, LlB 1967. **CAREER:** NLRB San Francisco, law clerk 1967-68; Fordham Univ NY, asst to exec 1968-69; Sullivan & Cromwell NY, assoc counsel 1969-72; Temple Univ School of Law Philadelphia, prof of law 1972-; City of Philadelphia, city solicitor. **ORGANIZATIONS:** Mem CA Bar Assn 1968; mem NY Bar Assn 1970; mem PA Bar Assn Philadelphia Bar Assn 1979; bd mem N PA Sch Dist Authority 1975-79; dir N PA Chap ARC 1975-79; bd mem Friends Hospital 1981-; bd of overseers Widener Law School 1986-; bd mem Franklin Institute 1988-. **BUSINESS ADDRESS:** Executive Vice President, Gravistone Realty Advisors Inc, B Mellon Bank Center, Suite 2360, Philadelphia, PA 19102.

MISSHORE, JOSEPH O., JR.
Insurance executive. **CAREER:** Gertrude Geddes-Willis Life Insurance Co, New Orleans, LA, chief executive. **BUSINESS ADDRESS:** Gertrude Geddes-Willis Life Insurance Co, 2120 Jackson Ave, New Orleans, LA 70113. *

MISTER, MELVIN ANTHONY
Business executive. **PERSONAL:** Born Jun 18, 1938, Memphis, TN; son of Mack A Mister, Sr. and Hattie A Cunningham; married Joan Devereux; children: 4 children. **EDUCATION:** Carnegie Inst of Tech, BS 1958; Princeton Univ, MA 1964. **CAREER:** US Conf of Mayors, assoc dir comm rel serv 1964-66; NW # 1 Urban Renewal Area DC, proj dir 1966-68; Ford Found NY, prgm ofcr 1968-69; DC Redevelop Land Agency, exec dir 1969-75; US Conf of Mayors, dir office of prog develop 1975-80, dep exec dir 1980-82; Citibank NA, vice pres 1982-84; Security Pacific Bank NA, vice pres 1984-86; Chase Manhattan Capital Mkts Corp, vice pres 1986-. **ORGANIZATIONS:** Asst exec dir US Conf of Mayors 1977-; dir Urban Econ Policy League of Cities Conf of Mayors 1975-77; act dep dir DC Dept of Housing & Comm Dev 1974-75; exec dir DC Redevelop Land Agency 1969-74; Natl Assn of Housing & Redevelop Officials; Natl Urban Coalition Housing; BSA; bd Potomac Inst; bd Interfaith Medical Ctr, Urban Land Inst; bd Hispanic Devel Proj; bd Seedco; Mortgage Bankers Assn. **MILITARY SERVICE:** AUS corp of engrs 1st lt 1958-62. **BUSINESS ADDRESS:** Vice President, Chase Securities, Inc, One Chase Plaza, 20th Fl, New York, NY 10081.

MITCHELL, ARTHUR
Executive director. **PERSONAL:** Born Mar 27, 1934, New York City, NY. **CAREER:** Premier Danseur New York City Ballet, prin 1952-69; Dance Theatre of Harlem Inc, exec dir/choreographer/founder. **ORGANIZATIONS:** Mem The Nat Conf on Soc Welfare 1973; US Dept of State Dance Adv Panel 1973; Nat Soc of Literature & The Arts 1975. **HONORS/ACHIEVEMENTS:** First black dancer to become a principal artist in the New York City Ballet; first male recip Dance Award HS of Performing Arts 1951; Cert of Recog The Harold Jackman Memorial Com 1969; spl tribute Arthur Mitchell & Dance Theatre of Harlem Northside Cntr for Child Develop Inc 1969; The Changers Award Mademoiselle Mag 1970; North Shore Comm Arts Cntr Award 1971; 20th annual Capezio Dance Award 1971; numerous other awards & tributes to Arthur Mitchell & The Dance Studio of Harlem.

MITCHELL, AUGUSTUS WILLIAM
Physician. **PERSONAL:** Born Apr 26, 1913, McKeesport, PA; married Dollie; children: Terrence, Wendell, Aiwur, Gail Jackson. **EDUCATION:** Lincoln U; Howard U, BS 1946; Homer G Phillips Hosp, Rotating Internship 1946-47;Univ MI, Post Grad Studies 1949. **CAREER:** Physician, self-employed; Fed Govt, mail clerk 1937-39; City of Ecorse, hlth offcr; City of River Beuge, hlth offcr 1960; Sumby Hosp, chief of staff; Outer Hosp, chief of staff. **ORGANIZATIONS:** Mem AMA; MI State SOE; Detroit Med Soc; Wayne Co Med Soc; Nat Med Soc; com chmn Accreditation of Hosp by Joint Com; nominating com, bd dir Wayne Co Gen Pract; bd dir Council of Med Staff Of Gen Prac; charter fellow Acad of Family Physicians; MI Assn of the Profession; Nat Med Vets Soc; mem bd dir Down River Guidance Clinic 1955; Omega Psi Phi Frat; Chi Delta Mu. **HONORS/ACHIEVEMENTS:** Recpt Award in Boxing Tennis; mem exec com Outer Hosp 1958; award in Med Nursing Com 1962. **MILITARY SERVICE:** USN lt commdr. **BUSINESS ADDRESS:** 12000 Visger, Detroit, MI 48217.

MITCHELL, B. DOYLE
Chief executive. **CAREER:** Industrial Bank of Washington, Washington, DC, chief exec. **BUSINESS ADDRESS:** Industrial Bank of Washington, 4812 Georgia Ave, NW, Washington, DC 20011. *

MITCHELL, BENNIE ROBERT, JR.
Clergyman. **PERSONAL:** Born Apr 24, 1948, Edgefield, SC; son of Mr. and Mrs. Bernie R. Mitchell; married Betty Tompkins, 1974; children: Benita Roshaunda, Bendette Renee, Bennie III. **EDUCATION:** Benedict Coll, BA 1970; Morehouse Sch of Religion, M of Div 1974. **CAREER:** Connors Temple Baptist Church, minister 1974-; Rock Hill Baptist Church, minister 1971-73; South Side Elementary, teacher 1970-71; NY City & Housing Authority, housing Officer, 1969; Mims Elementary, teacher 1969-70. **ORGANIZATIONS:** Mem, Exec Bd of General Missionary Baptist Convention of GA; Natl Baptist Convention; Natl Sunday School & Baptist Training Union; Savannah Baptist Ministerial Union; Political action Chmn of Interdenominatinal Ministerial Alliance; Spokesman of IMA Pilgrim Assn; Savannah Landmark Rehabilitation Project Inc; Savannah Emanicipation Assn; Chmn, MKL Jr Observance; bd mem, Savannah Chapter of PUSH; Life Mem, Omega Psi Phi Frat; Prince Hall Masonic Lodge; Volunteer Chaplain of Savannah Police Dept; bd of dirs, Natl Baptist Convention; bd of trustees, Morehouse school of religion; bd of trustees, Savannah Vocational & Technical School; Appointed to the MLK Jr State Holiday Commn. **HONORS/ACHIEVEMENTS:** Man of the Year, Savannah Tribune Newspaper; Ivan Allen Humantarian Award, Natl Chapter, Morris Brown Coll Alumni; May 2nd, Bernie R. Mitchell Jr, Day, Chatham County; Chaplain of the Day, Georgia State Senate; Preacher of the Year, Gospel Music Workshop of Savannah; Citizen of the Year, Omega Psi Phi Fraternity; Chaired the Jesse Jackson Campaign for Savannah, 1988; Person of the Week, WJCL-TV; guest Evangelist for the FL Baptist Convention & Outstanding Communty Service Award, Gamma Sigma Omega Chapter, AKA Sorority; Community Service Award, West Broad SDA Church. **BUSINESS ADDRESS:** Connors Temple Baptist Church, 509 W Gwinnette St, Savannah, GA 31401.

MITCHELL, BERT NORMAN
Business administrator. **PERSONAL:** Born Apr 12, 1938; married Carole Harleston; children: Tracey, Robbin, Ronald. **EDUCATION:** City Coll of NY, BBA 1963, MBA 1968; Harvard Grad Sch of Bus, 1985. **CAREER:** JK Lasser & Co CPA'S, sr auditor 1963-66; Interam Ins Co, controller 1966-67; Ford Found, asst controller 1967-69; Lucas Tucker & Co CPA'S, partner 1969-73; Assn of Black CPA Firms, dir/chmn 1970-; State Bd of Pub Acctncy, dir/chmn 1974-; AICPA, dir 1977-80; NYSSCPA, dir 1977-80, 1982-83; Mitchell/Titus & Co, managing partner. **ORGANIZATIONS:** Dir Greater NY Fund 1981-; treas 100 Black Men Inc 1976-; trustee Baruch Coll Fund 1969-; exec comm Assn for a Better NY 1980-; pres elect NY State Soc of CPA'S 1986-; pres NY State Soc of CPA's 1987. **HONORS/ACHIEVEMENTS:** Outstand Achievement Award Nat Assn of Black Accntnts 1977; Outstand Alumnus Award City Coll of NY 1982; CPA NY, NJ & DC; published over 50 articles in professional jour. **BUSINESS ADDRESS:** Managing Partner, Mitchell/Titus & Co, 2 Park Ave, New York, NY 10016.

MITCHELL, BILLY M.
Musician. **PERSONAL:** Born Nov 03, 1926, Kansas City, MO. **EDUCATION:** Cass Tech Detroit. **CAREER:** Billy Mitchell Inc; Lucky Thompson; Sonny Stitt; Julius Watkins; Mil Jackson; Nat Towles Orch Detroit, played 1948; Jimmie Lunceford; Milt Buckner; Gil Fuller; Woody Herman, 1949; Musician, self-employed; Dizzy Gillespie 1956, worked with 1956; Dizzy Gillespie, mes dir 1957; Count Basie 1957; Nasau County in School Jaza Ensemble, composer arranger, tchr, dir; Major Univ, tchr, lctr. **HONORS/ACHIEVEMENTS:** Played a big role in devel of Detroit Jazz Wave; toured Middle East for State Dept 1956; Renowned as modern tenor saxphnst; downbeat's New Star Awd for small combo 1962; recorded with Clarke-boland Orch in Europe on Atlantic Label; own LP's are on Smash Label; mus dir for Dizzy Gillespie, Della Reese, Sarah Vaughn, Stevie Wonder & Motown Recording Corp. **BUSINESS ADDRESS:** 407 Yale Ave, Rockville Centre, NY 11570.

MITCHELL, BUSH P.
Judge. **PERSONAL:** Born Nov 16, 1921, Lexington, KY; widowed; children: Phillip, Ronald, Michelle. **EDUCATION:** Franklin U, BA 1947; Capital U, LLB 1951; Capital U, JD 1966. **CAREER:** Dayton Munic Ct, judge; asst city pros; PvtPrac, 19 yrs. **ORGANIZATIONS:** Bd mem OH Indslztn Ctr; bd mem Comprehensive Offenders Prgm Eft. **HONORS/ACHIEVEMENTS:** NAACP Award of merit; Aff Contract of Am 1972; commend Congreg for recon 1972; law enforce award, Westmont Optimist 1973; commedn, Proj Cure Prgm 1973; commedn Dayton Pub Schl 1971-74; Sup Jud Serv Award Supreme Ct 1975. **MILITARY SERVICE:** AUS 1943-44. **BUSINESS ADDRESS:** Judge, 335 W 3rd St, Rm #306, Dayton, OH 45402.

MITCHELL, BYRON LYNWOOD
Orthodontist. **PERSONAL:** Born Mar 02, 1936, Miami, FL; divorced; children: Vanessa, Lynita, Patricia, Michael. **EDUCATION:** Savannah State Coll, BS 1959; Howard Univ, DDS 1966; Howard Univ, Orthod degree 1969. **CAREER:** General dentistry, private prac 1966-69; Family Health Ctr, chf family dentistry 1969-70, dentistry dir 1971-72; private practice, orthodontist 1970-. **ORGANIZATIONS:** Mem Alpha Phi Alpha Frat, Kiwanis Club, Elks, Dade Co Dent Soc, Dade Co Acad of Med, Grtr Miami Acad of Orthodon; mem Miami, E Coast, FL Dent Socs; mem So Soc of Orthodon; mem Amer Assn of Orthodon. **HONORS/ACHIEVEMENTS:** First black specialist in dentistry to practice in state of FL; first black orthodontist to practice in FL; 2nd black orthodontist to practist in entire South. **MILITARY SERVICE:** AUS 1959-61. **BUSINESS ADDRESS:** Orthodontist, 4885 NW 7th Avenue, Miami, FL 33127.

MITCHELL, CARLTON S.
Banker. **PERSONAL:** Born Sep 07, 1950, New York, NY; children: Howard Univ: BA 1972; Columbia Univ: MS 1984. **ORGANIZATIONS:** Mem Natl Assoc of Urban Bankers, Natl Bankers Assoc, Long Island Assoc. **BUSINESS ADDRESS:** Vice President, Marine Midland Bank, One Old Country Rd, Carle Place, NY 11514.

MITCHELL, CHARLES, JR.
Educational administrator. **PERSONAL:** Born Apr 21, 1938, Detroit. **EDUCATION:** Western MI U, BS 1959; Wayne State U, MEd 1965, EdS 1968; MA Inst Tech, MS 1970; Wayne State U, EdD 1972. **CAREER:** Fed & State Prog, div dir 1976-; Physical Edn, consult 1959-60; Detroit, tchr 1960-65; Highland Pk, coordinator 1965-67; Highland Pk, dir spl Proj 1967-69, asst supr personnel 1970-72; supt sch 1972-. **ORGANIZATIONS:** Mem Assn Sch CollUniv Staffing; Am Assn Sch Adminstrs; Am Assn Sch Personnel Adminstrs; Assn Supervision Curriculum Devel; Acad Mgmt; Booker T Wash Bus Assn; MI Assn Sch Adminstrs; MI Assn Sch Bds; MI Assn Supervision Curriculum Devel; Nat Community Sch Educ Assn; Nat Alliance Black School Adminstrs; Black Causes Assn Inc; NAACP; YMCA; Rotary Internat; Civic League; Human Relations Com; Civic & Industrial Com; Jaycees; mem Caucus Club; Alumni Assn; MI Inst Tech Western MIUniv Wayne State; Varsity Club Inc; adv Mothers Club. **HONORS/ACHIEVEMENTS:** Outstanding young man & yr 1968; sloan fellow MI Inst Tech 1969-70; Who's Who Midwest 1971; Danforth NAES fellow 1975; Ford Found fellow 1973; OutstandingEducators Am 1973; Comm Leaders Am 1973. **HOME ADDRESS:** 1130 3rd Ave, Apt 1703, Oakland, CA 94606. **BUSINESS ADDRESS:** Oakland Unified School Distric, 1025 2nd Ave, Oakland, CA 94606.

MITCHELL, CHARLES E.
Attorney. **PERSONAL:** Born Jul 07, 1925, Seymour, IN; married Julia Sarjeant; children: Charles L, Albert B. **EDUCATION:** Temple Univ Sch of Law, JD 1954; Brooklyn Law Sch; NY U, BA 1949; Morehouse Coll. **CAREER:** Philadelphia Schl Dist, tchr 1954-55; Fin Dept Phila, mgmt trainee 1955-56; Att Phila, legal asst 1956-60; Ofc of Dist Att Phila, legal asst 1956-60; NY US Soc Sec Admin, claim rep 1960-64; Labor Mgmt Rel Exam Nat Labor Rel Bd Phila, E I DuPont DeNemours & Co Inc, att labor mgmt. **ORGANIZATIONS:** Mem Am Bar Assn; mem Com on Prac & Proc under the Nat Labor Rel Act; Corp Banking & Bus Law; Legal Educ & Adm to Bar; Philadelphia & PA Bar Assn; pres Fed Bar Assn, DE Chptr; Am Jud Soc; Barristers Club of Phila; Lawyers Club of Phila; DE St Bar Assn; mem Com to Promote Equal Opp for Entry Legal Profes in DE; mem Philadelphia Inter-alumni Coun; United Negro Coll Fund; Indsl Rel Res Assn; Philadelphia Chptr; West MT Airy Neighbors Assn; subchrmn Zoning; Morehouse Coll Club of Phila; YMCA fund raiser; United Way of DE solicitor; mem Interested Negroes Inc; NACP; Rotary Club of Wilmington. **MILITARY SERVICE:** USN 1944-46. **BUSINESS ADDRESS:** Management Labor Counsel, E I DuPont DeNemours Co, Legal Department, 1007 Market St, Wilmington, DE 19898.

MITCHELL, CLYDE D.
Principal planner. **PERSONAL:** Born Aug 24, 1914, Greenville, SC; married Juanita; children: Clyde, Theo, Valerie, Carole. **EDUCATION:** Rutgers U; NY U; Syracuse U; Cornell U. **CAREER:** Newark Housing Authority, princ planner; Manpower Training Progs Newark NJ, dir; Frontiers Internat, intl pres; Essex County Youth & Econ Rehab CommnNJ, dir; Mayor of Newark, exec sec. **ORGANIZATIONS:** Pres Met Civic Club; exec bd NAACP; adv bd COED; bd dirs Newark Emergency Serv for Families; bd of trustees Boys Club of Newark. **HONORS/ACHIEVEMENTS:** Comm leadership award Nat Negro Coll Women; outstanding leadership award Frontiers Internat; Comm Serv Award NAFAD; distinguished serv award Met Civic Club; golden award Boys Club of Newark.

MITCHELL, CORINNE HOWARD
Retired educator. **PERSONAL:** Born Mar 10, 1914, Mecklenburg, VA; daughter of William E Howard and Elizabeth J Howard; married William E, Jan 06, 1938 (deceased); children: Lloyd, William, Charles. **EDUCATION:** St Paul's Coll, Asso 1935; VA State U, BS 1951; George Wash U, MA 1965. **CAREER:** Elem Sch, tchr 1935-82; Theta Sigma Upsilon Sor, founder 1979; Eta Phi Sigma Sor, natl pres 1981-; Smith Mason Art Gallery, tchr; retired art tchr; Mecklenburg Public Schools, teacher 1935-; Montgomery County, teacher 1965-81. **ORGANIZATIONS:** Mem of arts council DC Commn of Arts 1972; founder DC Art Assn Harlequin Ball 1971; chm Manor Pk Neighbors Inc 1960; founder Keep Washington Clean Soc 1960, pres 1975-85; mem Zeta Phi Beta Sor 1955; life mem Bethune; exec dir, Eta Phi Sigma Art Sorority 1981-89. **HONORS/ACHIEVEMENTS:** Outstanding Civic Work Neighbors Inc 1974-75; Appreciation Award Community Project Neighbors Inc 1974; CJ Black Emerg Fund Award 1976; Natl Conf of Artists Appreciation Awd 1979; Zeta Phi Beta Sor Awd 1981; Theta Sigma Upsilon Sor Awd 1982; Eta Phi Sigma Sor Awd 1986; Paul Jr HS Appreciation Awd; Harrison Elem Sch Awd 1986; Community Art Project Monetary Award; Founder, Eta Phi Sigma Art Sorority/Elizabeth Catlett Award of Excellence 1981; Leadership Appreciation, Theta Sigma Sorority; DC Commission on the Arts Neighborhood Councilwoman 1972; Founding Member, National Museum of Women in the Arts.

MITCHELL, DANIEL B.
Executive director. **PERSONAL:** Born Mar 19, 1941, Walterboro, SC; divorced; children: Jamal. **EDUCATION:** Clark Coll, BA 1962; SyracuseUniv Maxwell Sch, MA 1965; Course Wrk of PhD Completed. **CAREER:** Black Econ Resrch Ctr, exec dir 1977; City of Mound Bayou, conslt 1969; Nat Bus Planning Team Black Eco Union, chrm 1969; Tufts Delta Hlth Ctr, dir1967-69; Tufts Med Sch, instr; Emergy Land Fund, vice pres dir; pres Minority Constrn Supply Co Inc; Drune Communications Inc WENZ AM Richmand VA, chmn; Unified Limousine Service Inc NYC, chmn & pres; Twenty First Cent Fndt, sec dir; Delta Enterprises Inc, dir; Delta Fndt, dir; Delta Ministry, dir. **HONORS/ACHIEVEMENTS:** Fellow John Hay Whitney 1963; fellow Mellon 1969. **BUSINESS ADDRESS:** Vice President, C I I, 5430 Jimmy Carter Blvd, Ste 210, Norcross, GA 30093.

MITCHELL, DEBORAH KAREN
Marketing analyst. **PERSONAL:** Born Jul 28, 1962, New Haven, CT; daughter of Jerome Bosworth Mitchell and Elizabeth Foy Mitchell. **EDUCATION:** Drexel Univ, Philadelphia PA, BS Business Admin, 1985, MBA Marketing, 1987-. **CAREER:** Du Pont Co, Wilmington DE, assoc analyst, 1985-86, analyst, 1986-87, staff analyst, 1987-88; Sun Refining & Marketing; Philadelphia PA, marketing analyst, 1988-. **ORGANIZATIONS:** Advisor, Junior Achievement of Delaware, 1986-; pres, founder, Black Data Processing Assoc, Greater Wilmington Chapter, 1988-; vice-chair, Facilities Planning Comm, Brandywine Professional Assoc, 1988-; mem, Natl Black MBA's, 1988-; asst dir of Marketing, YMCA of Deleware, Black Achievers 1989-.

MITCHELL, DOLPHUS BURL
Optometrist. **PERSONAL:** Born Sep 09, 1922, Birmingham, AL; children: Dawn, Donald, Dori. **EDUCATION:** Alcorn A&M Coll, 1943; Northern IL Coll of Optometry, OD 1949; Union Bapt Sem Inc, Hon LLD 1952; Optometry Ext Pgm; Workshop So Coll of Optometry, 1973; Sch of Nut Sci, Diploma 1980; Chicago Med Coll Calcutta, India, MD Homeopathy 1981, PhD Homepathy 1986. **CAREER:** Birmingham, AL, private prac optometry 1949-73; Horner Rausch Optical of Huntsville, optician 1986; Huntsville, AL, private prac optometry 1973-; Royal Optical Madison Square Mall 1988. **ORGANIZATIONS:** Mem Better Vision Inst; Mason 1948; Shriners 1952; Boy Scout Comm 1952; part time asst prof opt Univ of AL Birmingham 1969-70; deacon mem sixth Ave Missionary Bapt Ch 1973-; mem NAACP; hon deputy sheriff Madison Co 1973; Amer Judicature Soc 1973-; assoc mem FOP Huntsville 1974; fellow Amer Biog Inst 1978; mem AL Assn of Optometry 1980-; mem Natl Optometric Assn 1980-; consult Amer Nutrition 1981; mem Chamber of Commerce Huntsville/Madison Ct 1984; life mem Natl Rifle Asson. **HONORS/ACHIEVEMENTS:** Cert of Merit Dic of Int Biog; Cert of Award BT Wash Bus Coll 1971; recip Wisdom Award of Hon 1973; listed Lib of Human Resources 1973; hon lt col AL State Militia 1977; Appreciation Award USN Recruiting Command Huntsville, AL 1981; Certificate of Merit Pearle Vision Center 1985. **MILITARY SERVICE:** AUS Inf pvt 1943-46; Good Conduct Medal; American Camp; USAF Civil Air Patrol, captain. **BUSINESS ADDRESS:** Madison Square Mall, Huntsville, AL 35806.

MITCHELL, DONALD
Actor. **PERSONAL:** Born Mar 17, 1943, Houston, TX; married Judy Pace; children: Dawn Marie, Shawn Michelle, Julia Anette. **EDUCATION:** Los Angeles City Coll, drama directing; Lee Strasberg Actors Studio; Los Angeles Reportory Co, Theatrical Mgmt; Beverly Hills Directors Lab, Directing; UCLAExt, Sculpture Ceramics; Tony Hill Ceramics, Ceramics Sculpture. **CAREER:** Don Mitchell Prodn, actor commr of Presidential Scholars; "Treemonisha" Los Angeles Opera Co, prod 1979; TV Series "Chips", actor 1979; "Police Story", actor 1978; "Perfume",co-dir movie 1977; Spl Proj for Theater, dir 1976; "Richard Pryor Live in Concert", pckgd movie 1976; "Medical Story", actor 1975; "The Blacks", prod & co-dir 1972; Mafundi Inst, tchr Acting 1971-72; The Watts Training Cntr, co-fndr 1967; "Ironside", actor 1966-75; Los Angeles, actor; New York, actor 1963-65. **ORGANIZATIONS:** Mc spl prog & or guest spkr, The US Jaycees; Nat Assn of Negro Bus & Professional Women; Boy Scouts; Am Cancer Soc; New Sch of Soc Res; Mot Pic Assn; Media Women; CA Spl Olympics; Charles Drew Med Soc; Am Black Vet Adminstrn; Am Polit Sci Assn; Handicapped Assn; Boys Club; UCLA Dept of Theater Arts; Black Filmmakers Hall of Fame; Nat Park Serv US Dept of Int; Nat Counc of Negro Women; Involvement for Young Achievers Inc; LAPD Drug Abuse Prog; Los Angeles Urgan League; Intl Year of the Child; Screen Actors Guild; El Monte City Counc; Ward Meth Episcopal Ch; L A Thespians; Inner City Cult Ctr; CA State Los Angeles; FL A&M U; Grambling U;Univ of Houston; Alcorn U; Howard U; New Fed Theater; Negro Emsemble Co; Mouehouse; Rockefeler Found; Un-Negrocoll Fund; Los Angeles Unified Sch Dist; NAACP; AFTRA; Actors Equity Assn; numerous others; campaigned Los Angeles Mayor, Tom Bradley; campaigned TXCongresswoman Barbara Jordan; campaigned State Sen Nate & Holden; campaigned Pres Jimmy Carter; Others.

MITCHELL, DOUGLAS
Electrical technician, mayor. **PERSONAL:** Born Apr 10, 1948, Leslie, GA; son of A J Mitchell and Lula Mae Jenkins Winbush; married Velma Jean Floyd, Jun 27, 1971; children: Rodney Purcell Mitchell. **CAREER:** Proctor and Gamble, Albany GA, line technician, 1975-82, team leader, 1982-84, electrical technician, 1984-; City of Smithville, Smithville GA, mayor, currently. **ORGANIZATIONS:** Past mem, Albany Area Primary Health Bd of Dir, 1985-86; mem, Lee County Chamber of Commerce Task Force, 1989, Highway 19 Improvement Task Force, 1989. **MILITARY SERVICE:** AUS, E-4, 1968-70. **BUSINESS ADDRESS:** Mayor, City of Smithville, PO Box 180 Main St, Smithville, GA 31787.

MITCHELL, DWAYNE OSCAR
Administrator. **PERSONAL:** Born Jul 13, 1959, Chicago, IL; son of Mr and Mrs Willie James Mitchell; married Debra Clifton, Aug 02, 1986; children: Daninelle Ashley Mitchell. **EDUCATION:** IL State Univ, BS 1982; Governor State Univ, MHA 1984. **CAREER:** Amer Cancer Society, asst youth coordinator 1982; Comm Mental Health, research assoc 1982-83; Cook County Hospital, lab admin 1984-85, Ob/Gyn admin 1985-. **ORGANIZATIONS:** Mem, Natl Assoc Health Care, 1982, treasurer, 1988; Alpha Phi Alpha Inc, 1985, Natl Black MBA Assoc, 1986; adjunct clinical prof, Governon State Univ, 1987; mem, Amer Public Health Assn, 1986. **HONORS/ACHIEVEMENTS:** Appreciation Award, Amer Cancer Society, Chicago, 1982. **HOME ADDRESS:** 15260 Waterman Dr, South Holland, IL 60473.

MITCHELL, EARL DOUGLASS, JR.
Educator. **PERSONAL:** Born May 16, 1938, New Orleans, LA; married Bernice Compton; children: Karen, Doug, Mike. **EDUCATION:** Xavier Univ of LA, BS 1960; MI State Univ, MS 1963, PhD 1966. **CAREER:** MI State Univ, research assoc 1966; OK State Univ, research assoc 1967-69, asst & assoc prof 1969-78, prof & asst dean 1978-82; NHLI of NIH, research chem 1978-79; OK State Univ, prof of biochemistry 1978-. **ORGANIZATIONS:** Mem US Commn on Civil Rights 1969-; chrmn SAC of OK 1980-86; chmn OK State Personnel Bd 1980-82; chmn OK Ethics & Merit Comm 1982-84; mem consult Biochem Study Sect Natl Inst of Health 1984-87; chmn Merit Protection Commn 1986-88; mem bd of trustees OK High School of Sciences & Math 1986-89. **HONORS/ACHIEVEMENTS:** NIH & NSF Research Grants 1969-75; 32 research journal publications & 35 research abstracts 1969-. **BUSINESS ADDRESS:** Professor of Biochemistry, OK State Univ, Dept of Biochemistry, Stillwater, OK 74078.

MITCHELL, EDWIN H., SR.
Educator. **PERSONAL:** Born Dec 21, 1921, Norfolk, VA; married Noella Pajaud; children: Tresa (Saxton), Kathryn, Cheryl (newsom), Edwin H. **EDUCATION:** Meharry Med Coll, MD 1948; certification in radiology & nuclear med 1960. **CAREER:** Harlem Hosp, internship 1948-49; Sydenham Hosp NY, admitting physician 1949; Sydenham Hosp, dir of clinics 1950-51; Camden SC, pvt practice 1952-56; Nat Cancer Inst Meharry Med Coll, trainee 1956-59; Columbia Presb Med Center, fellow 1959-60; Meharry Med Coll, asst prof 1960-62; Meharry Med Coll, asso prof 1962-72; Meharry Med Coll, prof of Radiology 1972-. **ORGANIZATIONS:** Mem Alpha Omega Alpha Honor Med Soc; Nashville Academy of Med; R F Boyd Med Soc; TN Med Assn; volunteer Med Assn; TN Radiol Soc; Nat Med Assn; Middle TN Radiol Soc; Am Coll of Radiology; pres of staff Meharry Med Coll 1974-75; chief dept radiology/Activing Chief Nuclear Medicine VA Hosp Murfreesboro TN; original bd mem & pres Davidson Co Ind Polit Council 1962-72; mem TN Voters Council 1962-; treas 1974; chmn Met Human Relations Commn 1967-70; chmn coordinating com Model Cities 1969-72; bd mem NAACP Nashville Br 1966-73; bd mem Easter Seals Soc; bd mem Urban Projects Inc 1968-72; mem Davidson Co Ind Polit Council; TN Voters Council; bd mem treas Voters Educ Project; mem Phi Beta Sigma Fraternity; Sigma Pi Phi Fraternity;Alpha Omega Alpha Med Honor Fraternity; Nat Assn of Human Rights Workers; Davidson Co Assn for Retarded Children. **HONORS/ACHIEVEMENTS:** Cit of yr Frontiersman 1967; Nat Assn of Intergroup Relations Officials 1968; Middle TN Council of BSA 1968; Nat Assn of Negro & Professional Women's ClubsNashville Br 1968; Dept of History & Polit Sci TN & StateUniv 1968; Agora Assembly 1969; Meharry Med Coll 1970; Met Human Relations Commn 1970; WelfareRights Orgn 1970; churchman of yr Religious Nashville Opportunities Industrialization Center 1970; citation Awards, POETS 1970; NAACP Youth Council1970; Model Cities Coordinating Com 1970; Phi Beta Sigma 1971; alumnus of yr Meharry Alumni 1971; pres award 25 yrs serv Meharry Med Coll 1973. **MILITARY SERVICE:** Sgt 1942-43; 1st Lt 1951-52. **BUSINESS ADDRESS:** Chief Radiology/Nuclear Med, A C York VAMC, Lebanon Road, Nashville, TN 37208.

MITCHELL, ELLA PEARSON
Theological educator, clergywoman. **PERSONAL:** Born Oct 18, 1917, Charleston, SC; daughter of Rev Dr Joseph R Pearson and Jessie Wright Pearson; married Dr Henry H Mitchell; children: Muriel, Elizabeth M Clement, Kenneth. **EDUCATION:** Talladega Coll AL, BA 1939; Union Theological Seminary & Columbia Univ, MA 1943; The School of Theology at Claremont, DMin 1974. **CAREER:** Berkeley Baptist Div School, instructor Christian educ 1951-59; Sunset Unified School Dist CA, kindergarten instructor 1961-66; Compton Coll CA, instr early child educ 1967-69; Amer Baptist Seminary of West & LaVernue Univ, adjunct prof 1974-82; Claremont Unified School Dist CA, kindergarten teacher 1973-80; Second Baptist Church Los Angeles, CA, minister of church educ 1980-82; School of Theology VA Union Univ, assoc prof Christian educ/dir Continuing Educ 1982-86; Spelman Coll, dean of sisters chapel; Interdenominational Theological Center, visiting professor of homiletics, 1988-. **ORGANIZATIONS:** Mem Claremont City Human Resources Comm 1975-79; mem Gov Bd Natl Council of Churches 1971-75; mem (pres 1969-73) Bd of Educ Ministries Amer Baptist Churches 1959-73; mem General Bd of Amer Baptist Churches 1984-. **HONORS/ACHIEVEMENTS:** Author/Editor "Those Preachin' Women 1985; Deputy Dir Martin Luther King Fellows Program 1972-75; Chaplain (life mem) Natl Delta Sigma Theta Sorority 1979; First Woman Dean of the Chapel Sisters Chapel Spelman Coll Atlanta; Talladega College, LHD, Granted 1989; Those Preaching Women, Vol 2, Judson Press, 1988. **HOME ADDRESS:** 46 McGill Place, NE, Atlanta, GA 30312.

MITCHELL, EMMITT W.
Chief executive. **CAREER:** Mitchell Lincoln Mercury, Kansas City, MO, chief executive, 1982-. **BUSINESS ADDRESS:** Mitchell Lincoln Mercury, 6300 E 87th St, Kansas City, MO 64138. *

MITCHELL, ERIC IGNATIUS
Physician. **PERSONAL:** Born Aug 01, 1948, Washington, DC; married Andrea. **EDUCATION:** St Joseph's Coll Phila, BS 1971;Univ of PA Philadelphia, MD 1974;Univ of PA Hosp, resident in orthopaedic surgery 1976-79; Philadelphia Gen Hosp, intern 1974-75. **CAREER:** ERJA Orthopaedics PC, physician; Team Physician, various sports teams Philadelphia 1973-79; Hosp of PA, instr of orthopaedics 1975-79;Univ of PA, instr 1975. **ORGANIZATIONS:** Mem Spl Biochem Prog TemplUniv 1970; sec treas Blockley Med Soc Philadelphia Gen Hosp 1974-75; mem Nat Assn of Interns & Residents 1974; mem PA Med Soc 1977; mem Sports Med Subcom Gov's Council on Physical Fitness & Sports PA 1979; sec Med Soc of E PA 1980; fndr & pres Black Awareness Soc St Joseph's Coll 1969-70; fndr crdntr tchr Wynnefield Summer Reading Prog 1970; bd of dirs Philadelphia Urban League; sec Student Nat Med Assn Region VIII1972-73; pres Student Nat Med AssnUniv PA Chap 1973-74; pres D & Hayes Agnew Surgical Society 1972-74; exec com Med Alumni Society 1972-74; mem Ten-man Com to Select Head Basketball Coach St Joseph's Coll 1974; bd dirs Germantown Boys' Club 1977-78; dir pr Germantown Boys' Club 1977-78. **HONORS/ACHIEVEMENTS:** Numerous Coll Basketball Awards 1968-71; Outstanding Coll Athlete of Am 1969; listed "Who's Who Among Students in AmUniv & Colls" 1970-71; researcher in Orthopaedic Surgery under Carl T Brighton MD Physical Structure of the Epiphyseal Growth Plate 1973; guest speaker on Orthopaedics, Numerous Coll; TV Progs; Med Assn Radio Progs 1974-80; fellowship in Orthopaedic ResearchUniv of PA 1975-76; researcher Electrically Induced & Osteogenesis Hosp ofUniv of PA 1975; researcher Pulse Current In Electrical Stimulation 1975; pub articles Parade & Ebony Mags 1975-76; hon mem Onyx Honor SocietyUniv of PA 1976; pub Treatment of Non-union with Constant Direct Current 1977; pub Radiographic Analysis of Non-unions with Treatment of Electricity 1978; pub A New Radiographic Grading Systemfor Blout's Disease The Epiphyseal Metaphyseal Angle; pub Treatment of Blount's Disease & Other Lower Limb Deformities with Osteoclasis & Osteotomy; listed Outstanding Young Men in Am 1978; recip The Stanley M K Chung Award for Orthopaedic Research 1979; fellowship Sports Med Prog of Dept of Orthopaedic Surgery Hosp ofUniv of PA 1979-80.

MITCHELL, GEORGE L.
Chief executive. **CAREER:** Dyersburg Ford, Inc, Dyersburg, TN, chief exec, 1985-. **BUSINESS ADDRESS:** Dyersburg Ford-Lincoln-Mercury, 920 Highway 51 By-Pass W, Dyersburg, TN 38024. *

MITCHELL, GROVER
Professional musician. **PERSONAL:** Born in Alabama. **CAREER:** Lionel Hampton, band mem; Duke Ellington, band mem; Count Basie and his Orchestra, 22 years as a featured

artist; Grover Mitchell Big Band, band leader. **HONORS/ACHIEVEMENTS:** Original compositions "The Devil's Waltz", "Frosty Blue", "Arica", "Hot Chocolate", "Blues Over Easy"; Recording "Live At The Red Parrot" (Hemisphere Records);Travels with Count Basie and his Orchestra to England, France, Switzerland, Germany, Sweden, Denmark and other countries.

MITCHELL, HENRY B.
Clergyman. **PERSONAL:** Born Nov 12, 1918, Ahoskie, NC; married Gertrude Phillips; children: Carolyn, H. **EDUCATION:** Hampton Inst, BS; Protestant Episcopal Theol Sem, 1957; YaleUniv Schl Alcohol Studies, 1960. **CAREER:** Danville Cure, priest 1957-58; Trinity Episcopal Ch, vicar 1958; VTS Alexandria VA, adj prof; Diocese of MI, asst to bishop 1977; Seabury Press & Bd 1978. **ORGANIZATIONS:** Bd of Bishop Whipple Schs 1979; bd trustees VA Theol Sem 1973; chmn Charlottesvl City Sch Bd 1972; mem Omega Psi Phi; exec bd NAACP 1970; bd sec Anglican Council No Am & Caribbean 1974. **HONORS/ACHIEVEMENTS:** Humanitarian award Secret 7 Soc,Univ of VA 1969; scroll honor VA State Assn Elks 1974. **BUSINESS ADDRESS:** 4800 Woodward, Detroit, MI 48201.

MITCHELL, HENRY HEYWOOD
Theological educator. **PERSONAL:** Born Sep 10, 1919, Columbus, OH; son of Orlando W and Bertha Estis; married Ella Muriel Pearson; children: Muriel, Elizabeth M Clement, Kenneth. **EDUCATION:** Lincoln Univ, AB (Cum Laude) 1941; Union Theol Sem NYC, MDiv 1944; CA State Univ, MA 1966; The School of Theol at Claremont, ThD 1973. **CAREER:** NC Central Univ, dean chapel instr 1944-45; Amer Bapt of Northern California, area staffer & editor 1945-59; Second Bapt Church Fresno, pastor 1959-60; Calvary Bapt Church Santa Monica, pastor 1966-69; Colgate Rochester/Bexley Hall/Crozer, black church studies 1969-74; Fuller Theol Sem Pasadena & Amer Bapt Sem of W Berkeley & LaVerne Coll, adj prof school of theology, Ecumenical Ctr for Black Church Studies of LA, prog dir 1974-82; CA State Univ Northridge, prof rel & pan-African studies 1981-82; VA Union Univ, dean school of theol 1982-86, prof history & homiletics 1986-; visiting prof of homiletics, Interdenominational Theological Center, Atlanta, 1988-; visiting prof of homiletics, United Theological Seminary, Dayton OH, 1989-. **ORGANIZATIONS:** Dir ML King Prog in Black Church Studies 1972-75; mem Soc for Study of Black Religion 1972-; pres North California Bapt Conv 1963; chmn bd 1964-65, pres Fresno Co Econ Oppor Commn 1966; mem Natl Comm of Black Churchmen 1968-; pres & chmn bd North California Bapt Conv 1963-64; pastor Calvary Bapt Church Santa Monica CA 1966-69, Second Baptist Church Fresno CA 1959-66; lit ed Martin Luther King Fellows Press 1975-; Lyman Beecher lecturer Divinity School of Yale Univ 1974. **HONORS/ACHIEVEMENTS:** Author Black Preaching 1970, Black Belief 1975, The Recovery of Preaching 1977, Soul Theology 1986 Harper & Row; numerous articles in books magazines & journals; Fellow Phelps-Stokes Fund E Africa 1973, 1974; Lyman Beecher Lecturer on Preaching Yale Divinity School 1974; Phi Kappa Epsilon Lincoln Univ Chap 1941; Phi Kappa Phi CA State Univ Fresno Chap 1966. **HOME ADDRESS:** 546 McGill Place, NE, Atlanta, GA 30312. **BUSINESS ADDRESS:** Prof History & Homiletics, Virginia Union University, 1601 W Leigh St, Richmond, VA 23220.

MITCHELL, HORACE
Educator. **PERSONAL:** Born Oct 04, 1944, Lambert, MS; married Barbara J; children: Angela, Kimberly. **EDUCATION:** Wash U, AB 1968; Wash U, MEd 1969; Wash U, PhD 1974. **CAREER:** Wash U, asst dean 1968-73; Educ Black Studies Wash U, asst prof 1973-76; Wash U, dir black studies 1976-. **ORGANIZATIONS:** Publ many art couns psycol; consult Midwest Cntr Equal Educ Opport 1974; mem APGA Com Standardized Testing Poten Disad; consult many sch dist; mem Kappa Delta Ph; Phi Delta Kappa; Phi Beta Sigma; Am Person & Guid Assn; Assn Black Psychol Assn; Non-White Concerns Person & Guid. **BUSINESS ADDRESS:** Univ of California - Irvine, 260 Administration Building, Irvine, CA 92717.

MITCHELL, HUEY P.
Attorney. **PERSONAL:** Born Dec 10, 1935, Bivins, TX; married Nelvia G; children: Huey, Jr, Janet H. **EDUCATION:** TX SoUniv Schl of Law, LLB 1960. **CAREER:** Law Firm of Mitchell & Bonner, atty; Reg Counsel US Dept HUD, asst 1967-73; City of Houston, asst city atty 1964-67; Office of Judge Advocate Gen; AUS FtHood, 1960-62; Pvt Prac Houston, 1962-64; Municipal Ct Ft Worth, sub judge 1973; TX Christian U, tchr Bus Law 1968-73. **ORGANIZATIONS:** Mem chmn of bd Tarrant Co Legal Aid Found 1972; mem & vice pres Ft Worth Chap Fed Bar Assn; mem Nat Bar Assn; Ft Worth Tarrant Co Sr Bar Assn; Hex Learning Cntr, prtnr; HPM Mgmt Devel & Co, owner & org; mem Nat Bd Dir Planned Parenthood Fedn of Am; Tarrant Co Hlth Plnng Cncl; orgnzng Com of Ft Worth Tarrant Comm Devel Fund. **HONORS/ACHIEVEMENTS:** First black asst city atty in history of Houston Apptd 1964; first black Municipal Judge in Ft Worth apptd 1973. **MILITARY SERVICE:** AUS splst e-5 62. **BUSINESS ADDRESS:** 700 Baker Bldg, Fort Worth, TX 76102.

MITCHELL, IVERSON O., III
Attorney. **PERSONAL:** Born Dec 20, 1943, Washington, DC. **EDUCATION:** Georgetown U, BSFS 1965; Wash Coll Law Am U, JD 1968. **CAREER:** Wilkes & Artis, atty 1976-; DC Corp Couns, 1971-76. **ORGANIZATIONS:** Mem DC Bar; Wash Bar Assn; Nat Bar Assn Gen Couns; bd dir Wash Bar Assn 1974-76, treas 1976-; mem DC Bd of Labor Relat 1977-. **HONORS/ACHIEVEMENTS:** Cert apprctn YMCA 1973. **MILITARY SERVICE:** AUS capt 1969-70. **BUSINESS ADDRESS:** Wilkes & Artis, 1666 N St NW, Washington, DC 20004.

MITCHELL, JACOB BILL
Company executive. **PERSONAL:** Born Jun 19, 1932, Boswell, OK; married Erma Jean Davis; children: Waymon, Victor, Erik, Mark, Kayla. **EDUCATION:** Armed Forces Inst, AE 1953; UCLA, BSEE 1958, MSEE 1963; CityUniv Los Angeles & Wichita State, PhD (Program) 1979. **CAREER:** Librascope Inc, sr engr analyst 1956-60; North Am Aviation, sys design engr 1960-62; Hughes Aircraft Co, sr electronic engr 1962-64; NASA, sr research engr 1964-68; Beech Aircraft, design engr 1968-73; Cessna Aircraft, design engr 1973-75; Jacob B Mitchell Asso, engineering consult 1975-79; NCR, sys engr 1979-81; Telemetry Sys Inc, pres. **ORGANIZATIONS:** Mem IEEE 1963. **MILITARY SERVICE:** AUS communications chief; Good Conduct Medal; European Occupation Medal 1951-54. **HOME ADDRESS:** 2210 E 13th St, Wichita, KS 67214. **BUSINESS ADDRESS:** President, Telemetry Sys Inc, 1601 E Harry, Wichita, KS 67211.

MITCHELL, JAMES H.
Business executive. **PERSONAL:** Born Sep 15, 1948, Danville, VA; married Linda T. **EDUCATION:** VA State Univ, BS 1972. **CAREER:** Mel Farr Ford, used car mgr; Park Motor Sales, asst used car mgr; Crest Lincoln-Mercury, asst used car mgr; Ford Motor Dealer Training Prog; Detroit Lions Inc, pro football 1970-78; Lynchburg Ford Inc, pres, gen mgr. **ORGANIZATIONS:** Dir Big Brothers & Big Sisters 1984-85. **BUSINESS ADDRESS:** President, General Manager, Lynchbury Ford, Inc, 2113 Lakeside Dr, Lynchburg, VA 24506.

MITCHELL, JAMES WINFIELD
Scientist. **PERSONAL:** Born Nov 16, 1943, Durham, NC; son of Eunice Hester Mitchell; married Alice J Kea; children: Veronica, Duane, Tonya. **EDUCATION:** State Univ of NC, BS Chem/Agr & Tech 1965; IA State Univ Ames, PhD Analytical Chem 1970. **CAREER:** Bell Laboratories, mem technical staff 1970-72, supvr 1972-75, head analyst chem research dept 1975-. **ORGANIZATIONS:** Adv bd Analytical Chem Amer Chem Soc 1977-80; adv bd Mikro Chim Acta 1978-82; mem Analytical Chem Div Program Comm; mem Fisher Award Comm 1980-83; mem Omega Psi Phi Frat 1963-; bd of dir Esseux Coounty Community Coll NJ 1972-74; bd dir Plainfield Science Center NJ 1972-. **HONORS/ACHIEVEMENTS:** Book, "Contamination Control in Trace Element Analysis" Wiley-Intersci Published 1975; Pharmacia Award in Analytical Chem Editorial Bd Atlanta 1978; 56 journal articles; 1 patent; Percey Julian Industrial Research Award 1980; IR100 Award 1982; Bell Labs Fellow 1985; Natl Academy of Engineering, 1989; Industrial Research Award, 1989. **BUSINESS ADDRESS:** Head Analytical Chem Research Dept, Bell Laboratories, MH 1D239, Murray Hill, NJ 07974.

MITCHELL, JOANN
University administrator. **PERSONAL:** Born Sep 02, 1956, Augusta, GA; daughter of Earl Mitchell and Alice King Mitchell. **EDUCATION:** Davidson Coll NC, AB 1978; Vanderbilt Univ Sch of Law, JD 1981. **CAREER:** Manson Jackson & Assocs, attorney/assoc 1981-86; TN Human Rights Comm, law clerk 1983-84; Vanderbilt Univ Opp Dev Ctr, asst dir 1983-86; Univ of PA, dir affirmative action 1986-. **ORGANIZATIONS:** Mem Amer Bar Assoc 1981-; treas bd of dirs Napier-Lobby Bar Assoc 1985, 1986; adv bd mem Vanderbilt Women's Ctr 1985, 1986; bd of dirs Assoc of Vanderbilt Black Alumni 1985, 1986; financial sec usher bd Mt. Oliver Miss Bapt Church 1985, 1986; deacon Mt Oliver Miss Baptist Church 1986-. **HONORS/ACHIEVEMENTS:** Outstanding Young Women of Amer 1983-; Affirmative Action Awd Vanderbilt Univ 1986. **BUSINESS ADDRESS:** Director, Affirmative Action, University of Pennsylvania, 1133 Blockley Hall, 418 Service Dr, Philadelphia, PA 19104-6021.

MITCHELL, JOANNE
Social worker. **PERSONAL:** Born May 30, 1938, Evansville, IN; married Robert Bright; children: Howard Polk, Karen Polk. **EDUCATION:** Roosevelt Univ Chicago, Sociology 1971; Univ of Chicago School of Social Serv Admin, AM SSA 1973. **CAREER:** IL Commn on Deliquency Prevention, exec dir; IL Law Enforcement Commn, assoc dir 1973-78; IL Dept of Corrections, community worker 1969-73; Brunswick Chicago Job Corps Center, admin asst 1966-69; IL Dept of Educ & Registration, social worker 1973; IL Dept of Financial Inst, asst director. **ORGANIZATIONS:** Acad of Certificate Social Workers; Natl Assn of Social Workers 1973; panelist Assembly of Behavioral & Social Science Natl Acad of Science 1979; mem League of Black Women 1976; mem NAACP; mem Natl Urban League. **HONORS/ACHIEVEMENTS:** Appointment Gov Advisory Council on Criminal Justice Legislation 1978; Outstanding Leadership & Dedicated Serv IL Health & Human Serv Assn 1978. **BUSINESS ADDRESS:** Assistant Dir, IL Dept of Financial Inst, 100 W Randolph, Ste 15-700, Chicago, IL 60601.

MITCHELL, JOSEPH CHRISTOPHER
Educational administrator. **PERSONAL:** Born Oct 08, 1922, Albany, GA; married Julia Louise Craig; children: Joseph Clovis PhD, Haazim Jawaad Abdullah, Michael Charles. **EDUCATION:** Fort Valley State Coll, BS Natl Sci-Math, 1939-43; Atlanta Coll of Mortuary Science Inc, diploma (summa cum laude), 1945-46; Atlanta Univ, MS (cum laude), 1947-48; Univ of Michigan, certificates, 1955-60; Princeton Univ, certificate, 1959; Duke Univ, certificate, 1961; Cornell Univ, PhD candidate, 1961-62, 1963, 1969-71; London School of Applied Rsch, ScD, 1972. **CAREER:** Albany & Mobile High School, head of science dept, head coach, 1943, 1946, 1948; Atlanta Coll of Mortuary Science, dir of labs, 1945-46; Fort Valley State Coll, asst prof of science, asst coach, 1949-52; Alabama State Coll Branch, asst prof of science, head of science dept, 1952-54; Albany State Coll, asst prof of biology, asst coach, 1954-63; Alabama State Univ, assoc prof of sci, head of science dept, 1963-65; Bishop State Jr Coll, interim pres, 1981, chmn of div of science & math, dir of mortuary science, 1965-. **ORGANIZATIONS:** Science consultant, Phelps Stokes Found, 1954-57; science consultant, Region 9, Georgia Teachers Assn, 1954-63; ESEA Title III proj consultant, US Office of Health, Educ & Welfare, 1964-67; dir, Natl Science Found, Minority Inst Science Improvement Prog, Bishop State, 1975-78; evaluator, Natl Science Teachers Assn, 1978; science consultant, visiting comm for Southern Assn of Schools, 1980, 1982, 1983; chmn of selection comm, Assoc Degree Nursing Prog, 1982-; rsch assoc, Dept of Medical Entomology Parasitology, Cornell Univ; bd mem, United Cerebral Palsy Mobile Inc; bd mem, Alabama Interdenominational Seminary Assoc; mem, NEA, AEA, AAAS, AAJC, NAACP, NABT; bd mem, Amer Cancer Soc. **HONORS/ACHIEVEMENTS:** Summer fellowships, Natl Science Found, Washington DC, summers 1959, 1961; fellowship, Natl Science Found, 1961-62; acad fellowship, Ford Found, New York, 1969-70; plaque Outstanding Interim Pres, Faculty and Students of Bishop State, 1981; published "The Effect of Inhibitors, Intermediates & Stimulants Upon the 02 Consumption in Ascaridia Lineata" Journal of Parasitology, Vol 35 Sect 6, 1949, "The Influence of Inhibitors on the Cytochrome System of Heterakis Gallinae," Transactions of Natl Inst of Science, Vol 45 No 1, 1952, "A Study of Endoparasites & Ectoparasites of the Cotton Rat, Sigmodon Hispidus," 1964-66, "A Cytogenetic Study of the Simuliidae of Tompkins County NY," 1969-71. **MILITARY SERVICE:** ERC of AUS 1942-43. **HOME ADDRESS:** 712 Bishop St, Mobile, AL 36617. **BUSINESS ADDRESS:** Chairman, Div Math & Science, SD Bishop State Jr College, 351 N Broad St, Mobile, AL 36690.

MITCHELL, JOSEPH RUDOLPH
Physician. **PERSONAL:** Born Aug 09, 1938, Chicago, IL; married Emi Yamashiro MD. **EDUCATION:** Morehouse Coll, BS 1959; Meharry Medical Coll, MD 1964. **CAREER:** Santa Clara Valley Medical Ctr, internship 1964-65; Kapiolani Hospital, residency 1968-71; Mama Yemo Hospital Zaire Kinshasa, chief of gyn pav 1972-74; Deltal Health Ctr Mound Bayou MS, med dir 1974-75; Gulfport MS, private practice 1975-. **ORGANIZATIONS:** Mem & vice chmn Mississippi Bd of Health 1980-86; bd of dirs Gulfport Area Chamber of

Commerce 1984-86; mem Governor's Infant Mortality Task Force 1985-;mem Amer Coll of Obstetricians & Gynecologists, Natl and Amer Medical Assocs, Coast Counties Medical Assoc, Natl Perinatal Assoc, MS Perinatal Assoc,Southern Perinatal Assoc, MS Medical & Surgical Assoc, MS State Medical Assoc. **HONORS/ACHIEVEMENTS:** Mem Alpha Omega Alpha Honor Medical Soc. **MILITARY SERVICE:** AUS Capt 1965-67. **BUSINESS ADDRESS:** Physician, Yamashiro & Mitchell PA, 1500 45th Ave Ste J, Gulfport, MS 39501.

MITCHELL, JUDSON, JR.
Internal auditor. **PERSONAL:** Born Oct 26, 1941, Jersey City, NJ; son of Judson Mitchell and Lucy Barnes Mitchell; married Patricia Roberts (deceased); children: Mark A, Judson, Steven C, Guy. **EDUCATION:** Rutgers Univ Coll, BS, Accounting, 1975; Rutgers GSBA, MBA 1979. **CAREER:** Public Service Electric & Gas Co, sr plant analyst 1980-81, assoc accountant 1981-82, internal auditor 1982-. **ORGANIZATIONS:** pres, Northern NJ Chapter, Natl Assn of Black Accountants, 1987-88; Mem, Natl Black MBA Assn; Amer Inst of CPA's, NJ Soc of CPA's; Inst of Internal Auditors, Minority Interchange; Natl Assn of Certified Fraud Examiners. **HONORS/ACHIEVEMENTS:** Certified Public Accountant NJ 1982; Certified Internal Auditor Inst of Internal Auditors 1986; Certified Fraud Examiners Award, IRS, 1989. **MILITARY SERVICE:** USMC lance corpl 4 yrs. **HOME ADDRESS:** 311 Randolph Ave, Jersey City, NJ 07304. **BUSINESS ADDRESS:** Sr Staff Auditor, Public Serv Electric & Gas Co, 80 Park Plaza, T22M, Newark, NJ 07101.

MITCHELL, JUDYLYNN
Educational administrator. **PERSONAL:** Born Aug 19, 1951, Salisbury, MD; married Fred; children: Cortni Lee-Lynn. **EDUCATION:** Bowie State Coll, BS 1969-72; Bowling Green State U, MEd 1973-74; Nova U, EdD (Expected) 1985. **CAREER:** Salisbury State Coll, academic cnslr 1974-79, project dir 1980-82, pgm splst 1982-83; Center for Human Svcs, educ spclst 1983-84, residential admin. **ORGANIZATIONS:** Mem Assn for the Study of Afro Life & Hist; bd of trustees Wicomico Co Lib; bd of dir Eastern Seals Soc; mem Wicomico Co Historical Soc. **HONORS/ACHIEVEMENTS:** Black Heritage Articles, "Salisbury Sunday & Daily Times" Salisbury, MD 1979; religious black hist play, "Yester-Days Women, Gone But Not Forgotten" 1983; Outstand Young Women of The Yr 1982-83. **HOME ADDRESS:** Rt 5 106 Southbury St, Salisbury, MD 21801. **BUSINESS ADDRESS:** Residential Administrator, Center for Human Serv, Univ of MD Eastern Shore, PO Box 1021, Princess Anne, MD 21853.

MITCHELL, JULIUS P.
Educational administrator. **PERSONAL:** Born Nov 05, 1941, Rome, GA; married Gwendolyn McLeod; children: Toni L, Shaune. **EDUCATION:** Clarkson Univ, Potsdam NY, Bachelor 1984; St Lawrence Univ, Canton NY, MED 1987. **CAREER:** US Army, special forces 1959-81; St Lawrence Univ, dir of HEOP/pres HEOP-PO; Clarkston Univ, Potsdam NY, dir of minority affairs, 1988-. **ORGANIZATIONS:** Pres Higher Educ Oppor Prog Prof Organ of NY State 1984. **MILITARY SERVICE:** AUS 1st sgt 22 yrs; Bronze Star; Meritorious Serv Awd. **HOME ADDRESS:** PO Box 146, Potsdam, NY 13676. **BUSINESS ADDRESS:** Dir of Miority Affairs, Clarkston Univ, Potsdam, NY 13676.

MITCHELL, KELLY KARNALE
Clergyman. **PERSONAL:** Born May 18, 1928, Newnan, GA; married Audrea Marie Martin; children: Kelyne Audrienne, Kelly Karnale Jr. **EDUCATION:** Nashville Christian Inst, 1948; Fisk U, BA 1952; AL Christian Coll, ThB 1968; Missionary of the New Truth Schl, DD 1971; AL Christian Sch of Religion, MRE 1978. **CAREER:** Southside Ch of Christ Montgomery AL, minister 1972; WRMA Radio Sta Montgomery, religious Supr 1963-67; Christian Echo LA, staff writer 1958-65; Holt St Ch of Christ Montgomery, minister 1955-72; Green St Ch of Christ Nashville, minsiter 1951-55; Greenlea Weekly Paper Nashville, editor 1951-55; Lawrenceburg Ch of Christ TN, minister 1946-51; Phi Beta Sigma Frat Inc, chaplain. **ORGANIZATIONS:** Pres Nat Christian Inst Alumni Assn; pres FiskUniv Debating Soc; pres Ecumenica Assn; chmn Car Pool Transp Montgomery Bus Boycott; chmn Montgomery Comm Action Bd. **HONORS/ACHIEVEMENTS:** Leadership award Danforth Found 1948; cert of Appreciation Montgomery Community Action Agency 1970; outstanding Ministry Plaque S Berkeley CA Ch of Christ 1970; cert of merit Montgomery Heritage Movement 1975; Nat Summer Youth Sports Prog Award AL StateUniv 1975; fndrs plaque AL Statewide Lectureship 1975; publ various religious books; spkr coll campuses, civic groups, frats. **BUSINESS ADDRESS:** 4214 Cleveland Ave, Montgomery, AL 36105.

MITCHELL, LEMONTE FELTON
Personnel director. **PERSONAL:** Born Feb 19, 1939, Wake Forest, NC; married Emma Jean Hartsfield; children: LaMarsha, Muriel, Andrea. **EDUCATION:** Johnson C Smith Univ, BA 1960. **CAREER:** NC Dept of Correction, personnel dir 1977; NC Dept of Admin, personnel analyst 1969-77; jr & sr high school teacher 1960-69. **ORGANIZATIONS:** Mem NC Chap IPMA; pres Wayne & Co Teachers Assn; Omega Psi Phi Frat; mem Young Democrats. **HONORS/ACHIEVEMENTS:** Outstanding Young Man of Amer 1971-72. **BUSINESS ADDRESS:** 840 W Morgan St, Raleigh, NC 27603.

MITCHELL, LEONA
Soprano. **PERSONAL:** Born Oct 13, 1949, Enid, OK. **EDUCATION:** OK City Univ, MBA 1971, DMus (Hon) 1979. **CAREER:** San Francisco Opera, soprano 1973,74,77; Edinburgh Scotland Festival 1977, Sacria Umbria Festival, Australia 1978, various maj symphonies in US, European debut, Barcelona Spain 1974, Met Opera 1974, soprano; appeared in films &TV shows. **ORGANIZATIONS:** Mem Amer Guild Musicians Assoc, Sigma Alpha Iota, Alpha Kappa Alpha, Church of God in Christ. **HONORS/ACHIEVEMENTS:** Named Ambassadress of Enid 1978; OK Hall of Fame 1983; performed for Pres Ford 1976, pres Carter 1978,79. **BUSINESS ADDRESS:** Columbia Artists, 165 W 57th St, New York, NY 10019.

MITCHELL, LEROY
Retired business executive. **PERSONAL:** Born Mar 25, 1921, Lima, OH; married Esther McClure; children: LeRoy III, Frederick Bruce, Steven Craig. **EDUCATION:** Univ of Cincinnati, BS 1945-49; IN U. **CAREER:** Inland Steel Co E Chicago, trainee 1951-52, div supr labor rel 1952-64, sr labor rel rep 1964-65; Inland Steel Co Chicago, asst supt labor rel 1965-69,supt labor rel 1969-79, supt indus relations planning 1979-80, retired. **ORGANIZATIONS:** Mem Calumet Ind Rel Group 1966-; mem E Chicago Lions Club 1973-80; chrmn

Blue Ribbon Comm to Settle Dispute Between Firefighters/City of Gary; pres Am Lung Assn of NW IN & IN 1977-80; pres E Chicago Lib Bd; mem Nat Bd of Dir Am Lung Assn 1978-; chmn Endowment Comm RT Andrews Schlrshp Commn 1982-; treas/sec Bd of Sch Trustees of Gary, IN 1965-67; mem bd of dir NW IN Urban League 1957-79; bd of trustees 1st Bapt Ch Gary 1957-78; mem Lake Cnty Liquor Bd 1965-66; vice pres bd of dir Fellowship Gdns Housing Gary, IN. **HONORS/ACHIEVEMENTS:** Hall of Fame Am Lung Assn of IN 1980; Black Achiever of Ind YMCA of Metro Chicago 1974; Accepting Commnty Resp Alpha Phi Alpha Frat 1966; Cert of Appreciation Nat Plans for Progress Youth Motivation Pgm 1968; Outstand Serv to Commnty Lake Cnty Womens Cncl 1977; Winner of the Murray A Auerbach Awd Amer Lung Assoc of IN 1985. **MILITARY SERVICE:** USN ph m. **HOME ADDRESS:** 2224 Van Ness Pl, Indianapolis, IN 46340-4702.

MITCHELL, LILYANN JACKSON
Public relations, promotion specialist,. **PERSONAL:** Born Jun 29, 1933, Greenville, MS; divorced; children: Craig, Claudia, Debra, Claude. **EDUCATION:** Stowe Jr Coll, AA 1950; MO U, 1951; MO U; Wash U; Dhaw Coll Detroit; Marygrove Coll Detroit. **CAREER:** Shaw Coll of Detroit, dir spec projects & promotion; Intl UAW Rep 1973-74; WTVS TV Detroit, dir pub rel 1972-73; Highland Pk, MI, deputy to the Mayor; Dir Pub Ser Careers 1971; UPI Internat, staff writers 1970-71; Intl Brotherhood of Teamsters, asst dir of pub rel; MO Joint Council of Teamsters Newspapers St Louis IBT 1965-70; Anheuser-beusch Inc St Louis, exec sec 1961-65; St Louis Job Corp Ctr for Women, instr; St Louis Argus Newspaper, bus& clerical subjects & Pub Rel staff Writer 1966-70; St Louis Am Newspaper 1968-70. **ORGANIZATIONS:** Mem Am Women in Radio TV; Pub Rel Soc of Am; Media Women Inc; Women in Comm; NAACP; SCLC; Urban League; Womens Conf of Concerns; Black in Comm; BlackComm Assn. **HONORS/ACHIEVEMENTS:** Outstanding Journalism & Unique Writing Style, Newspaper Pub Assn 1967; award of Black Entrepreneurs 1970; Dis Comm Serv Award 1969; award for Outstanding Serv to Youth St Louis City; award for Promoter of Muhammad Ali Shaw Coll benefit matches Olympia Stadium June 1975, Detroit; various other awards for comm serv. **BUSINESS ADDRESS:** 7351 Woodward Ave, Detroit, MI 48202.

MITCHELL, LOFTEN
Writer. **PERSONAL:** Born Apr 15, 1919, Columbus, NC; married Helen March, 1948. **EDUCATION:** City College, New York, NY, 1937-38; Talladega College, BA, 1943; Columbia University, MA, 1951; Union Theological Seminary; General Theological Seminary. **CAREER:** Worked as an actor in New York, NY; WNCY-Radio, New York, NY, writer of weekly program The Later Years, 1950-62; WWRL-Radio, New York, NY, writer of daily program Friendly Advisor, 1954; State University of New York, Binghamton, NY, department of theater and department of Afro-American studies, professor, 1971-85, professor emeritus, 1985—. **HONORS/ACHIEVEMENTS:** Black Drama: The Story of the American Negro in the Theatre, 1967; playwriting award, Research Foundation, State University of New York, 1974; Voices of the Black Theatre, 1975; Outstanding Theatrical Pioneer Award, Audience Development Committee, 1979; Bubbling Brown Sugar, 1984. **MILITARY SERVICE:** US Navy, served during WW II. **HOME ADDRESS:** 88-45 163rd St, Jamaica, NY 11432. *

MITCHELL, LOUISE
Educator. **PERSONAL:** Born in Beloit, AL. **EDUCATION:** AL State U, BS 1954; IN State U, MS 1964. **CAREER:** Dallas Co Bd of Edn, asst dir of guidance; Dallas Co Sch Sys, tchr; Dallas Co Sch Sys, counc. **ORGANIZATIONS:** Sec AL Future Parents & Tchrs 1959-63; sec Dallas Co Professional Educ Assn 1970-73; pres Dist VI, AL, Personnel & Guidance Assn 1973; coord Title IVB Proj; mem exec bd for United Appeal; mem AEA, NEA; sec Delta Sigma Theta Sor 1966-70; pres Delta Sigma Theta 1970; pres Entre Nous Club 1971-73; Trust Brown Chapel AME Ch. **HONORS/ACHIEVEMENTS:** Recip Tchr of Yr Dallas Co Tchr Assn 1960. **BUSINESS ADDRESS:** Rt 3 Box 361, Selma, AL 36701.

MITCHELL, MARIAN BARTLETT
Administrator. **PERSONAL:** Born Oct 27, 1941, Elizabeth City, NC; daughter of Mr & Mrs Paxton Bartlett; children: Lonzo Antonio Bartlett (son). **EDUCATION:** Elizabeth City State Univ, BS 1970; Norfolk State Univ, further study toward MA-Communications. **CAREER:** Elizabeth City State Univ, dir alumni relations. **ORGANIZATIONS:** Ex-officio mem bd of dirs General Alumni Assoc 1976-; former sec Council of Natl Alumni Assocs; mem CASE; mem Professional Business Women, Natl Assoc of Univ Women, General Alumni Assn; Delta Sigma Theta Sorority, North Carolina Alumni Dir. **HONORS/ACHIEVEMENTS:** Merit Awds from Tri-State Alumni Chapter 1986, Atlanta Alumni Chapter Alumni and Friends Coalition 1980, Class of 1946 1980; Woman of the Year Awd Natl Assoc of Univ Women 1981; Outstanding Service Awd General Alumni Assn 1971; Outstanding Service E A Johnson 1980. **BUSINESS ADDRESS:** Director-Alumni Relations, Elizabeth City StateUniv, Parkview Dr, Box 977, Elizabeth City, NC 27909.

MITCHELL, MARK RANDOLPH
Physician. **PERSONAL:** Born Jan 01, 1955, Washington, DC; children: Julien Randolph. **EDUCATION:** Univ of MD, (College Park) BS 1976, (Baltimore) RT 1977; Meharry Medical Coll, MD 1981. **CAREER:** Dept of Army Corps of Engrs, engineering intern 1972-76; Georgetown Univ Hosp & Affiliates, ob/gyn residency 1981-85; Natl Health Service Corps, physician 1985-; Biloxi Regional Medical Ctr, asst chief ob/gyn 1986-; coastal Family Health Ctr, dir ob/gyn 1985-. **ORGANIZATIONS:** Mem Amer & Natl Medical Assocs, Alpha Omega Alpha Natl Honor Med Soc, NAACP, Iota Phi Theta Frat Inc NY Chapt. **HONORS/ACHIEVEMENTS:** Natl Deans List 1981, CV Mosby Awd 1981, Hudson Meadows Awd 1981 all from Meharry Medical College. **BUSINESS ADDRESS:** Coastal Family Health Center, 300 E Division St, Gulfport, MS 39533.

MITCHELL, MARTHA MALLARD
Public relations executive. **PERSONAL:** Born Jun 11, 1940, Gary, IN; daughter of Louis B Mallard and Elizabeth Allen Mallard; divorced. **EDUCATION:** Michigan State Univ, East Lansing MI, BA, 1963, MA, 1968. **CAREER:** Univ of District of Columbia, Washington DC, dir continuing educ for women, 1970-74; Drug Abuse Council, dir info services, 1974-77; US Government Exec Office of Pres, special asst to pres, 1977-79, Dept of Commerce, assoc dir, 1979-81; Fleishman-Hillard Inc, St Louis MO, vice pres, 1985-87, sr vice pres, 1987-. **ORGANIZATIONS:** Pres, DC Women's Political Caucus; mem, Commission on Status of Women; mem, DC Democratic Central Committee; mem, KETC TV (public TV, St Louis) Board. **HONORS/ACHIEVEMENTS:** Public Service Award, Capital Press

Club, 1978; Distinguished Achievement Award, NAACP, Gary IN Branch, 1985; 100 Top Black Business & Professional Women, Dollar & Sense Magazine, 1988. **BUSINESS ADDRESS:** Senior Vice President, Fleishman-Hillard Inc, 200 N Broadway, Suite 1800, St Louis, MO 63102.

MITCHELL, MELVIN J.
Clergyman. **PERSONAL:** Born Feb 29, 1904, Girdon, AR; married Katherin Lambert; children: Melvin Thomas, Beverly Ann, William James, Mary Jane, Nathaniel. **EDUCATION:** Baltimore Coll of Bible, 1974. **CAREER:** Pilgrim Bapt Ch Columbus OH, pastor. **ORGANIZATIONS:** Founder Columbus Area Devel Action Training Sch 1967; fndr Boy's Own Youth Shelter Inc 1969; pres Model Neighborhd Assy; mem Mayor's Adv Bd; mem Columbus Bapt Ministerial Alliance; mem OH Minister's Conf; pres OH Bapt State Conv; pres Mt Calvary Bapt Assn; worshipful grand master St John's Masonic Lodge; bd mem Cath Social Svc; bd mem Neighborhood Comm Ctr; mem other civic orgns. **HONORS/ACHIEVEMENTS:** Recip Religious Achievement Award Gay St Bapt Ch 1972; Ather of the Week & One of Most Influential Black Men of Columbus WCOL 1973; One of Then Top Men of 1971 Citizen's Journal. **BUSINESS ADDRESS:** 26 N 21 St, Columbus, OH.

MITCHELL, MELVIN LESTER
Architect, educator. **PERSONAL:** Born Aug 11, 1939, New Orleans, LA; married Geraldine Vaughan, PhD; children: Marcus Quintana, Michelle Violet. **EDUCATION:** Howard U, B Arch 1967; Harvard Grad Sch of Design, M Arch. **CAREER:** Howard Univ, asst prof of arch 1970-75; Univ of District of Columbia, asst prof of arch 1986-; Melvin Mitchell Architects Washington DC, principal/sole owner 1979-. **ORGANIZATIONS:** Mem Am Inst of Architects; mem Nat Orgn of Minority Architects; mem Nat Tech Assn. **HONORS/ACHIEVEMENTS:** Awarded total expenses stipend to Harvard Grad School of Design 1968-70; author "The Case for Environmental Studies at Black U" AIP Journal 1968; author "Urban Homesteading" Washington Post 1974. **MILITARY SERVICE:** AUS spec 4 cl construction 1960-62, Thule Greenland & Fort Belvoir VA. **BUSINESS ADDRESS:** Owner, Melvin Mitchell Architects, 7300 Georgia Ave, Washington, DC 20012.

MITCHELL, MIKE CHARLES
Professional athlete. **PERSONAL:** Born Jan 01, 1956, Atlanta, GA; married Diane; children: Kiah; Michael Jr. **EDUCATION:** Auburn, studed Dstrbtv Educ 1978. **CAREER:** Cleveland Cavaliers, 1979-82; San Antonio Spurs, forward 1982-. **ORGANIZATIONS:** Originally drafted by Cleveland 15th 1978. **HONORS/ACHIEVEMENTS:** Had double pts in 74 of 79 games; had dougle pts-rebounds 16 times; career 47 pts 1984; his 6-14 on three's in 1983-84 were his career bests; twice was All-SEC selection. **BUSINESS ADDRESS:** San Antonio Spurs, HemisFair Arena, Ste 510, San Antonio, TX 78292.

MITCHELL, NELLI L.
Psychiatrist. **PERSONAL:** Born in Jersey City, NJ; daughter of Cullie Mitchell and Eloise Casey MItchell; children: Edward H Chappelle Jr DDS. **EDUCATION:** NYU, BA 1945; Columbia Univ, MA 1949; Howard Univ, MD 1950. **CAREER:** St Elizabeth's Hosp, staff psychiat 1956-57; Mental Hlth Cntr, med dir youth consultation serv 1963-65; Co of Monroe, 1966-; Hillside Children's Cntr, psychiat consult 1970-; Rochester Mental Hlth Cntr, training dir/child psychiat 1965-. **ORGANIZATIONS:** Fellow Amer Psychiatric Assn 1956; mem Natl Med Assn 1956; Amer Orthopsychiatric Assn 1960; Hudson City Med Assn 1960; Amer Acad of Child Psychiatry 1970; asst prof psychiat Rochester Sch of Med; bd mem Camp Fire Girls Inc 1967-73; YWCA 1974-75; Monroe Co Bd of Mental Hlth 1976-; mem NY State Bd Visitors Monroe Devel Ctr 1977-; Synod of the NE; UPC of the US 1975-; Diplomate Amer Bd of Psychiatry & Neurology, Psychiatry 1961; Amer Bd of Psychiatry & Neurology, Child Psychiatry. **HONORS/ACHIEVEMENTS:** Psi Chi Honor Society Psychology. **BUSINESS ADDRESS:** Supervising Psychiatrist, Rochester Mental Health Cntr, 1425 Portland Ave, Rochester, NY 14621.

MITCHELL, ORRIN DWIGHT
Orthodontist. **PERSONAL:** Born Oct 01, 1946, Jacksonville, FL; married Patricia Hill; children: Derrick, Kia. **EDUCATION:** Howard Univ, BS 1969, DDS 1973, Certificate of Orthodontics 1975. **CAREER:** Orrin D Mitchell DDS PA, orthodontist 1975-. **ORGANIZATIONS:** Mem, Amer Assn of Orthodontics, Amer Dental Assn, Natl Dental Assn, Acad of General Dentistry, Continental Orthodontic Study Club; Jacksonville Dental Soc, Northeast Dist Dental Assn, FL Medical, Dental & Pharmaceutical Assn, Southern Soc of Orthodontists, Jacksonville Medical Dental & Pharmaceutical Assn, Jacksonville Urban League; life mem Alpha Phi Alpha Frat; mem Chi Delta Mu Frat, Howard Univ Alumni Assoc, Sigma Pi Phi Frat; life mem NAACP; adv bd of dirs First Union Natl Bank of FL; mem FL Assoc of Orthodontists; trustee bd New Bethel AME Church; Fl Bd of Dentistry; Jacksonville Chamber of Commerce Bd of Governors, 1989; Stewart Bd of New Bethel AME Church; Secretary, Howard Univ Orthodontic Alumni Assn; Private Indus Council of Jacksonville; Pres, Northwest Council, Jacksonville Chamber of Commerce; Bd of Dir, Jacksonville Urban League, 1988-90; Bd of Dir, Midas Touch Day Care Center; Pres, Continental Orthodontic Study Club. **HONORS/ACHIEVEMENTS:** Diplomate Amer Bd of Orthodontics 1986; Alumni Achievement Awd Howard Univ Col of Dent 1986; Small Business Leader Jacksonville Chamber of Commerce Northwest Cncl 1986; Alpha Phi Alpha Frat Alumni Brother of the Year for the State of FL 1986, 1988. **BUSINESS ADDRESS:** 1190 W Edgewood Ave, Suite A, Jacksonville, FL 32208.

MITCHELL, OSSIE WARE
Educational administrator. **PERSONAL:** Born Oct 12, 1919, Uniontown, AL; widowed. **EDUCATION:** Tuskegee Inst AL, BS 1939; Daniel Payne Coll Birmingham AL, D of Humane Letters 1972; AL StateUniv Montgomery, MEd 1974. **CAREER:** Elberton Co Sch System, elem sch principal 1943; Palmer Meml Inst, instr 1945; Booker T Washington Bus Coll, asst dir 1947, asst dir. **ORGANIZATIONS:** Dir religious educ S Birmingham Huntsville Dist AME Church 1965-77; 1st Black Pres Dist V AL Sch Bds Assn 1977-78; 1st Black Woman Pres Birmingham Bd of Educ 1977-79; mem Steering Com Urban Sch Bd 1979-82; dir AL Sch Bds Assn 1980-82; mem exec bd Comm Affairs Comm Operation New Birmingham 1982-, Women's Network 1982-. **HONORS/ACHIEVEMENTS:** Woman of the year Zeta Phi Beta Sorority Inc 1973; community Serv Award Delta Sigma Theta Sorotity 1974; beautiful activist Birmingham Jaycees 1974; outstanding citizen award Lawson State Community Coll 1975; woman of distinction Iota Phi Lambda Sorority 1976; merit awd Booker T Washington Bus & Coll 1978; distinguished alumni merit award Tuskegee Inst 1978; woman of the year Birmingham Urban League 1979; cert of merit Jefferson Co Progressive Democratic Council 1979; Peggy Spain McDonald Award Birmingham Community Educ Council 1979; Life Membership Plaque NAACP 1981; Outstanding Serv Awd United Negro Coll Fund 1981; Black Heritage Awd 1983; Meritorious Serv Awd UNCF 1985; Certificate of Recog Metro Business and Professional Women's Club of Birmingham 1985; Friend of Educ Awd1985; Layman of Yr Awd 1984,85; Outstanding Contrib to Educ Birmingham Alumnae Chap Delta Sigma Theta Sor Inc 1986; Salute Silver Anniversary Celebration Alphi Xi Chap Gamma Phi Delta Sor Inc. **BUSINESS ADDRESS:** Assist Dir, Booker T Washington Bus Coll, 1527 5th Ave North, Birmingham, AL 35203.

MITCHELL, PARREN JAMES
Company executive. **PERSONAL:** Born Apr 29, 1922, Baltimore, MD; son of Clarence Mitchell, Sr and Elsie J Mitchell. **EDUCATION:** Morgan State Univ, Baltimore MD, BA, 1950; Univ of MD, College Park MD, MA, 1952; additional studies, Univ of Connecticut. **CAREER:** MD Commission of Human Relations, dir, 1961-65; Baltimore Anti Poverty Agency, dir, 1965-68; US House of Representatives, 1971-87; Minority Business Enterprise, chair of bd, 1980-. **HONORS/ACHIEVEMENTS:** Honorary Degrees: Lincoln Univ, Bowie State Coll, Univ of MD, Howard Univ, Coppin State, Morehouse Univ, VA Union Seminary, St Mary's Coll, Morgan State Univ; Natl and local consumer groups, civil rights groups, business and economic groups, fraternaties, sororities, religious groups, and educational organizations have presented more than 1200 awards to Mr Mitchell; He has recieved awards from such diverse groups as: The Natl Alliance of Black Educators, The Southern Christian Leadership Conference, the Greater New Haven Business and Professsional Assn, The Minority Contractors, The Alaska Black Caucus. **MILITARY SERVICE:** US Army, Infantry, Lieutenant, 1942-45; received Purple Heart. **BUSINESS ADDRESS:** Chairman, Minority Business Enterprise Legal Defense and Education Fund, 300 I Street, NE, Suite 200, Washington, DC 20002.

MITCHELL, ROBERT C.
Assistant general manager. **PERSONAL:** Born Jun 06, 1935, Hot Springs, AR; son of Albert Mitchell and Avis Mitchell; married Gwendolyn E Morrow; children: Terri Sue, Robert Jr. **EDUCATION:** Univ IL, BS 1958. **CAREER:** Pepsi Cola, marketing rep 1963-69; Bobby Mitchell Ins Agy, owner 1967-72; pro football scout 1969-72; Wash Redskins, dir of pro scouting 1972-78, exec asst to pres 1978-, asst gen mgr 1981-. **ORGANIZATIONS:** DC Boxing commn 1974-; adv com Howard Univ Cancer Rsch; bd mem Boy's Club of Metro Wash; chmn AAU Boxing; mem NAACP; Urban League; AFTRA; Huntsman Club Inc; Pigskin Club DC; YMCA; FCA; charter mem Heros Inc; past pres NAMD; past mem Jr Jaycees; Bd of Trade DC; Natl Football Found of DC; past bd mem Goodwill Inds; past secretary/vice president/president Washington Redskins Alumni Assn DC. **HONORS/ACHIEVEMENTS:** 1st Black to play for WA Redskins 1962; All Big-Ten 1955-57; hon mention All-Amer 1955-57; mem Big-Ten Track Championship 1958; 5 times All-Pro NFL; Most Valuable Player All-Star Coll Game 1958; Rookie of the Year 1958; AR Hall of Fame 1977; Inducted in NFL Pro Football Hall of Fame 1983; DC Stars Hall of Fame 1979; Washington Touchdown Hall of Fame 1983. **MILITARY SERVICE:** AUS 1958-59, 1962-62. **BUSINESS ADDRESS:** Assistant General Manager, Washington Redskins, 13832 Redskin Dr, Herndon, VA 22071.

MITCHELL, ROBERT L.
Educational administrator. **CAREER:** Edward Waters College, Jacksonville, FL, president. **BUSINESS ADDRESS:** Edward Waters College, Jacksonville, FL 32209. *

MITCHELL, ROBERT LEE, SR.
Metal chipman. **PERSONAL:** Born Nov 18, 1932, West Palm Beach, FL; son of Hezekiah Mitchell and Grace Mitchell; divorced; children: Verdette L, Marc A, Robert Jr. **CAREER:** Pratt & Whitney Aircraft, utility. **ORGANIZATIONS:** Founder Afro-Amer Civ Action Unit Inc 1960-69; mem bd of dir Palm Beach Co Comm Mental Health Center 1979-81; state chmn FL Minority Conf of Repub Clubs 1980-82; pres Frederick Douglass Repub Club 1979-81; mem Black Citizen's Coalition PB Co 1979-84; NAACP; past gen bd mem Urban League; Black Professional Caucus; bd mem Concerned Alliance Progressive Action Inc (CAPA); mem Palm Beach co Repub Exec Comm 1970-80; mem Policy Comm/Platform Com Rep Party of FL 1975-77; organz/chmn FL black Repub Councl 1975; del GOP Conv 1976; bd mem Tri-Cnty Chapter Natl Business League 1984-; Palm Beach Cnty Reagan-Bush Campaign - co-chmn Blacks for Reagan 1984. **HONORS/ACHIEVEMENTS:** Community Serv Award Tri-Cnty Natl Business League 1984; Accomp Pres Ford on historic riverboat trip down the MS river 1975; Man of the Year Professional Men's Bus League 1966; Official Particip FL Human Rel Conf 1977; Player KC Monarchs Baseball Team 1954-57; Man of the Year Omega Si Phi 1967; dep reg reg over 1000 persons.

MITCHELL, RODERICK BERNARD
Community development corporation executive. **PERSONAL:** Born Aug 14, 1955, Reidsville, NC; son of Hunter Lee Mitchell and Christine Odessa Dixon Mitchell; married Monica Boswell, Aug 12, 1979; children: Marcus Galen Mitchell, Akia Lee Mitchell. **EDUCATION:** UCLA, Los Angeles, CA, BA Economics, 1977; Columbia Univ, New York, NY, MBA, 1980. **CAREER:** Collins & Aikman Corp, Charlotte, NC, industrial eng, 1977-79; Celanese Corp, New York, NY, sr financial analyst, 1981-83; Bedford Stuyvesant Restoratoin, Brooklyn, NY, 1984-85, dir of operations, 1985-86, vice pres physical devel, 1987-88, pres, 1988-. **ORGANIZATIONS:** Treasurer, Men 'N' Ministries, 1986-; bd of dir, Brooklyn Academy of Cultural Affairs, 1988-; bd of dir, Brooklyn Chamber of Commerce, 1988-; bd of dir, Brooklyn Bureau of Community Serv, 1989; mem, 100 Black Men on Manhattan, 1989; Adult Sunday School Teacher, Bethel Gospel Assembly, 1989. **HONORS/ACHIEVEMENTS:** NOMMO Outstanding Graduate, UCLA, 1983; Outstandig Businessman Award, Central Baptist Church; 1988 Achievement Award, Brooklyn Urban League, 1988; RF Kennedy Minority Business Award; Brooklyn Chamber of Commerce, 1988; Merit Award, Natl Assn of Negro Business & Professional Women's Club, Inc, 1989. **BUSINESS ADDRESS:** Pres, Bedford Stuyvesant Restoration Corp, 1368 Fulton St, Brooklyn, NY 11216.

MITCHELL, ROSCOE E.
Business executive. **PERSONAL:** Born Aug 27, 1934, Chicago, IL; son of Roscoe E Mitchell and Mary G Taylor Mitchell; married Jacqueline L Abrams; children: Karen, Roslyn, Valerie, Robert. **EDUCATION:** Univ of IL Urbana, BS 1956; Univ of Chicago, MBA 1976. **CAREER:** Prudential Insurance Co of Amer, sr appraiser 1964-70; Talent Asst Program Business Consultants, exec dir 1970-73; Zenith Elec Corp, dir equal opportunity & admin serv

1981-88; Highland Community Bbank 1989. **ORGANIZATIONS:** Dir Chicago Community Ventures 1972-87; dir Chicago Regional Purchasing Council 1974-87; dir Cosmopolitan Chamber of Commerce 1976-; exec comm Chicago Council Boy Scouts of Amer 1977-, council commr 1983-85; bd of dir Chicago Alumni Kappa Alpha Psi 1983-; vice pres Chicago Council Boy Scouts of Amer 1986-. **HONORS/ACHIEVEMENTS:** Silver Beaver Boy Scouts of Amer 1985; Beautiful People Chicago Urban League 1981; Black Book Business Black Book Magazine 1979. **MILITARY SERVICE:** AUS captain 1956-66. **HOME ADDRESS:** 8620 S Dante, Chicago, IL 60619. **BUSINESS ADDRESS:** Vice President, Highland Community Bank, 1701 W 87th St, Chicago, IL 60620.

MITCHELL, SCOEY
Actor, comedian. **PERSONAL:** Born Mar 12, 1930, Newburgh, NY. **EDUCATION:** VA Union U, 1950. **CAREER:** Miami, comic 1955; "What's It All About World", stared 1967-68; "Barefot in the Park", 1970-71; "Police Story"; "Rhoda"; "Password". **ORGANIZATIONS:** Mem SAG; pres Scomi Prodns Hollywood CA 1970.

MITCHELL, STANLEY HENRYK
Attorney. **PERSONAL:** Born Sep 28, 1949, St Louis, MO; married Regina Braxton; children: Sherman. **EDUCATION:** Univ of MO St Louis, BS Spec Ed 1974; Washington Univ, MSW 1976; Temple Univ School of Law, JD 1979. **CAREER:** Solo Practicioner, attny 1980-; PA House of Reps, exec dir 1981-83; Elizabethtown Coll Soc Welfare, adj prof 1982-84; City of Harrisburg, solicitor 1984-; PA House of Reps, chief counsel. **ORGANIZATIONS:** Chmn Pro Bono Legal Redress City of Hbg NAACP 1981-; brother Omega Psi Phi Frat 1984-; adv bd Catholic Soc Svcs; mem PA Bar Assn; bd of dir Dauphin Cty Pretrial Svcs; committeeman 11th Ward City of Harrisburg. **HONORS/ACHIEVEMENTS:** Recipient Amer Jurisprudence Awd Conract Remedies 1976-77; Democratic Nominee City of Harrisburg City Council 1985. **BUSINESS ADDRESS:** Chief Counsel, PA House of Representatives, 512 E-2 Main Capital Bldg, Harrisburg, PA 17120.

MITCHELL, TEX DWAYNE
Supervisor. **PERSONAL:** Born Nov 19, 1949, Houston, TX; married Deborah Ann Earvin; children: Tonya DiBonne, Tess Dionne. **EDUCATION:** Lee Jr Coll, attended 1970; TX Southern Univ, BA 1977. **CAREER:** Courtesy Ford, parts delivery 1968-69; Petro-Tex Chem Corp, plant oper 1969; TX Petrochem, pumping suprv; Crosby ISD Trustee Bd, vp. **ORGANIZATIONS:** Pres Barrett-Crosby Civic League 1976-; mem Tenneco volunteers 1979-83. **HOME ADDRESS:** 407 Red Oak, Crosby, TX 77532. **BUSINESS ADDRESS:** Vice President, Crosby ISD Trustee Bd, 8600 Park Place Blvd, Houston, TX 77017.

MITCHELL, THEO W.
State senator/attorney. **PERSONAL:** Born Jul 02, 1938, Greenville, SC; married Greta JoAnne Knight; children: Emily Kaye, Tamara JoAnne, Megan Dawn. **EDUCATION:** Fisk Univ, AB 1960; Howard Univ Law Sch, JD 1969. **CAREER:** South Carolina General Assembly, state senator/attorney. **ORGANIZATIONS:** Pres Greenville Urban League Inc 1971-73. **HOME ADDRESS:** 522 Woodland Way, Greenville, SC 29607. **BUSINESS ADDRESS:** State Senator, South Carolina Genl Assembly, Nine Bradshaw St, Greenville, SC 29601.

MITCHELL, WILLIAM GRAYSON
Editor. **PERSONAL:** Born Mar 08, 1950, Mobile, AL; married Renee Grant. **EDUCATION:** Univ of IL, BS 1970. **CAREER:** Johnson Pub Co, assoc editor Ebony-jet magazines 1973; Washington Post, gen assignment reporter 1972-73; chicago Sun-times, 1970-72. **ORGANIZATIONS:** Nat Endowment for the Humanities Journalism Fellowship 1975-76. **BUSINESS ADDRESS:** 1750 Pennsylvania Ave NW, Washington, DC.

MITCHELL, WILLIAM P.
Retired association executive. **PERSONAL:** Born Jun 22, 1912, Pensacola, FL; widowed; children: Peggy M Peterman. **EDUCATION:** Attended Tuskegee Inst 1931-35; Univ GA & Auburn Univ, Certificates. **CAREER:** VA Hosp, phys therapist 1935-67; Tuskegee Housing Auth, exec dir 1967-75; John A Andrew Hosp Tuskegee Inst AL, credit/collection ofcr 1976-78. **ORGANIZATIONS:** Exec sec Tuskegee Civic Assn 1949-; past secy IBPOE of W Lodge #762; past pres AFGE Lodge #110 Tuskegee, AL; AL State NAACP; AL Assn Housing & Redev; Officials SERC-NAHRO; treas Tuskegee Branch NAACP. **HONORS/ACHIEVEMENTS:** Omega Phi Chap Omega Psi Phi Frat Man of Yr Award 1952-61; Recognition Award Tuskegee Civic Assn 1974 & 1981; Community Achievement Award Tuskegee Inst 1974. **BUSINESS ADDRESS:** 201 Azalea St, Tuskegee Institute, AL 36068.

MITCHELL-BATEMAN, MILDRED
Psychiatrist. **PERSONAL:** Born 1922, Cordele, GA. **EDUCATION:** Johnson C Smith U, BS 1941; Women's Med Coll of PA, MD 1946; NYC, intern; Menning Sch of Psychiatry, psychiatric residency cert 1957. **CAREER:** WV Dept of Mental Health, dir 1962; Philadelphia, pvt practice; Lakin State Hosp WV, phy Clinical dir & supt. **HONORS/ACHIEVEMENTS:** First woman to head such a dept in the US; The first black in WV history to direct an exec dept. **BUSINESS ADDRESS:** WV Dept of Mental Health, Charleston, WV 25305.

MITCHELL-KERNAN, CLAUDIA IRENE
Educator. **PERSONAL:** Born Aug 29, 1941, Gary, IN; married Keith Kernan; children: Claudia L, Ryan J. **EDUCATION:** Indiana Univ, BA Anthropology 1963, MA Anthropology 1964; Univ of California Berkeley, PhD Anthropology 1969. **CAREER:** Harvard Univ, asst prof of anthropology 1969-73; UCLA, asst prof of anthropology 1973-77, assoc prof of anthropology 1977-83, prof of anthropology 1983-, dir center for afro-american studies 1976-. **ORGANIZATIONS:** Researcher Natl Inst of Mental Health 1971-75; consultant Natl Urban League 1973; fellowship review comm Natl Sci Foundation 1974; bd of trustees Ctr for Applied Linguistics Washington DC 1979-81; bd mem Crystal Stairs Inc 1980-. **HONORS/ACHIEVEMENTS:** Fellow Natl Inst of Mental Health 1965-66; fellow Social Science Rsch Council 1966-68; fellow Ford Found 1968-69. **BUSINESS ADDRESS:** Dir Ctr for Afro-Amer Study, Univ of California-Los Angeles, Ctr For Afro-American Studies, 160 Haines Hall, Los Angeles, CA 91436.

MITCHEM, ARNOLD L.
Educator. **PERSONAL:** Born Sep 17, 1938, Chicago, IL; married Freda Kellams; children: Nichelle, Adrianne, Michael, Thea. **EDUCATION:** So CO State Coll, BS 1965; Haverford Coll, post bac study 1966;Univ of WI, grad Study 1968; Marquette U, doctoral study 1973. **CAREER:** History Dept Marquette U, instr 1968-71; Educ Opp Prog Marquette U, dir 1969; Mid-am Assn of Educ Opportunity Program Personnel, pres 1974-. **ORGANIZATIONS:** Mem Nat Bd Dir Inroads Inc; mem Exec Com Midwest Regional Assembly of Coll Entrance Examination Bd. **HONORS/ACHIEVEMENTS:** Recipient citation for outstanding serv to higher educ Region V Ofc of Educ 1974; spl Woodrow Wilson fellowship 1967-68, 1966-67; grant from So Educ Found 1966; honorary Woodrow Wilson fellowship 1965-66. **BUSINESS ADDRESS:** 1217 W Wisconsin Ave, Milwaukee, WI.

MITCHEM, JOHN CLIFFORD
Educational administrator. **PERSONAL:** Born in Terre Haute, IN; son of Clifford Mitchem and Clara Mitchem; married Anna Maria; children: Terence, Melanie. **EDUCATION:** Ball State Teachers Coll, Chem, Biol, BS Ed; State Univ of IA Iowa City, MA Phys Ed, PhD Phys Ed. **CAREER:** Northern IL Univ, spec asst to pres 1969-72; Baruch Coll, asst dean of faculty 1972-73, asst dean of acad affairs 1972-77; Bronx Comm Coll, prof, dean 1977-81; Univ of WI LaCrosse Coll of Health, PE & Rec, dean 1981-88. **ORGANIZATIONS:** Life mem Amer Alliance for Health, PE & Rec 1966-; ed Rsch Quarterly 1969-74; policy adv bd City Univ of NY Freshman Skills Assessment Prof 1977-; personnel & budget comm Dept of Compensatory Prog, Coll of Liberal Arts & Sci; univ council on instr, open admiss coord CUNY; middle state eval accred team; north central assoc accred team; southern dist accred team; life mem Phi Epsilon Kappa; mem Phi Delta Kappa, Amer Assoc of Univ Profs. **HONORS/ACHIEVEMENTS:** Numerous publ incl "Athletics:The Lab Setting for Character" 1967; "The Child that Bears Resentment" 1968; "Resolved that the Amer Acad of PE Support the Position that the Requirement of PE in Coll & Univ Should be Abolished" 1974; IL Assoc for Health, PE & Rec Quarter Century Club Awd 1972; Fellow Amer Acad of PE 1973. **BUSINESS ADDRESS:** Dean, Retired, Univ of Wisconsin-La Crosse, College of Health, Physical Educ,and Recreation, 1725 State, La Crosse, WI 54601.

MITCHEM-DAVIS, ANNE
Educator. **PERSONAL:** Born Dec 17, Boston, MA; daughter of Robert T Mitchem and Marian Frauklin Mitchem; divorced; children: Leah Anne Davis Hemphill. **EDUCATION:** Lincoln Univ, BS 1950; IN Univ School of Nursing, Diploma 1950-53; Simmons Coll, MS 1960; Boston Univ, CAGS 1966. **CAREER:** Visiting Nurse Assn of Boston, staff nurse 1954-59, asst supvr 1960-62; Hampton Inst, asst prof 1962-65; Boston Univ, Asst prof 1966-70; Mental Health/Retardation Center, public health nurse consultant 1970-71; Boston County Hospital, nursing dir out patient dept 1971-73; Howard Univ, asst dean Coll of Nursing 1973-75; College of Nursing Chicago State Univ, acting dean 1982-83, chairperson 1983-84, assoc prof 1980-. **ORGANIZATIONS:** Exec dir Alpha Kappa Alpha Sorority 1975-88; mem Amer Nurses Assn, Natl League for Nursing, Amer Public Health Assn, Alpha Kappa Alpha Sorority; North Atlantic Regional dir, 1970-74; Beta Kappa Chi; Sigma Theta Tau. **HONORS/ACHIEVEMENTS:** Special Serv Award, Alumni Assoc of IN Univ School of Nursing 1979; Advisor of the Year, 1983; Outstanding Faculty of the Year, 1984-85; Chicago State Univ. **BUSINESS ADDRESS:** Associate Professor, Coll of Nursing Chicago St Univ, 95th St at King Dr, Chicago, IL 60628.

MIXON, CLARENCE W.
Executive director. **PERSONAL:** Born Mar 07, 1934, Cleveland, OH; married Gayle; children: Rhonda Pheonix, Piper Gibson, William Gibson, Shelley Gibson, Donald, Heather, Lindsey. **EDUCATION:** Kent State U, BS 1961; Base Western Reserve U, MS 1968; MI State U, PhD 1974. **CAREER:** Cleveland Scholarship Programs Inc, exec dir; Mixon's Barber Shop, barber 1950-; Cuyahoga Comm Coll, dir comm serv 1968-69; Vista US, dir 1968; Cleveland Pub Sch, asst prin counselor tchr 1961-68; Singer Sewing Machine Co, salesman 1953-54; Roy & Eva Markus Found, educ consult 1969-80; Nat Episcopal Ch NYC, chmn black desk 1976-80; Garden Valley Neighborhood House Cleveland, bd pres 1977-78; OH Instructional Grants Program, adv bd 1978-80. **HONORS/ACHIEVEMENTS:** Kellogg fellow MI StateUniv 1970-71; educator of year Alpha Phi Alpha Frat 1975; elected dep Nat Conv Episcopal Ch 1976 & 1979; "Positive Cleveland" Emerson Press 1977. **MILITARY SERVICE:** AUS specialist 3rd 1954-56. **BUSINESS ADDRESS:** Cleveland Scholarship Programs, 1380 E & Sixth St, Cleveland, OH 44114.

MIXON, VERONICA
Editor. **PERSONAL:** Born Jul 11, 1948, Philadelphia, PA. **EDUCATION:** Long Island Univ, BA 1974. **CAREER:** Food Fair, bookkeeper 1966-68; Social Sec Admin, admin asst 1968-70; Doubleday & Co Inc, starlight romance editor 1974-. **ORGANIZATIONS:** Writer VM Media Service 1985; film reviewer Carib News 1983-. **HONORS/ACHIEVEMENTS:** Co-editor Freshstones, Women's Anthology 1979; author The World of Octavia Butler Essence Mag 1979; elected Who's Who of American Women 1985-86. **HOME ADDRESS:** PO Box 694, Grant Central Sta, New York, NY 10163. **BUSINESS ADDRESS:** Editor, Doubleday & Co Inc, 245 Park Ave, 42nd Floor, New York, NY 10167.

MIZZELL, WILLIAM CLARENCE
Data processing professional/mgr. **PERSONAL:** Born May 29, 1949, Ahoskie, NC; son of Eddie Lewis Mizzell, Sr and Myrtle Burke Mizzell; married Jomare Bowers, Dec 30, 1981; children: Jomare Elizabeth Bowers Mizzell. **EDUCATION:** Elizabeth City State Univ, Elizabeth City, NC, BS Mathematics, 1971. **CAREER:** Western Electric Co, Greensboro NC, spare parts analyst, 1971-73; Western Electric Co, Cincinnati OH, staff associate, 1973-74; Proctor & Gamble Co, Cincinnati OH, analyst/system analyst, 1974-77; Licoln National Corp, Fort Wayne IN, senior development analyst, 1977-80, senior programmer/analyst, 1980-82, project manager, 1982-83, senior project manager, 1983-87, lead project leader, 1987-. **ORGANIZATIONS:** Bd mem, Fort Wayne Branch, NAACP, 1980-; pres/host/founder, Minority Spectrum, Inc, 1982-; bd mem, WBNI Radio Community Advisory Bd, 1985-; mem, Fort Wayne Chapter Jack & Jill, Inc. 1985-; consultant, Business Assisted Summer Employment Program, 1986-; dir/bd mem, Al Stiles Talent Factory, 1987-; pres/found, Black Data Processing Assoc, Fort Wayne Chapter, 1987-. **HONORS/ACHIEVEMENTS:** Million Dollar Club, NAACP Natl Office, 1981-84; President's Award, NAACP, Fort Wayne Branch, 1981; Marjorie D Wickliffe, NAACP, Fort Wayne Branch, 1983; Community Serv, NAACP, Fort Wayne Branch, 1984; Minority in Media, Indiana/Purdue Fort Wayne Univ, 1989. **HOME ADDRESS:** 1509 Channel Ct, Fort Wayne, IN 46825-5934.

MOANEY, ERIC R.
Educator. **PERSONAL:** Born May 16, 1934, Easton, MD; children: Sara Elizabeth, Lucinda Jennifer. **EDUCATION:** RI Sch of Design, BFA 1956; Syracuse U, MFA 1965; San Diego State U, MS. **CAREER:** Dept of Art CA StateUniv San Diego, asst prof 1968-; Benton & Bowles Advertising Agy, asst art dir 1965-66; Syracuse & U, designer asst to dir of graphic arts 1963-65; freelance artist 1962-63; Darrel Prutzman Assoc,asst art dir 1957-62; Rustcraft Greeting Cards, designer 1956-57; Motown Record Corp, design consult 1968; NJ area library, 1966-70; Terry Phillips Enterprises, 1968-69; New Frontiers Corp, 1965; Four Guys Stores, 1969; Thomas Corp, 1970; Core Faculty ca Sch of Prof Psychology, series coordinator for the humanities 1973-76; San Diego Co Collegiate Council All Media. **ORGANIZATIONS:** Art Show 1975. **HONORS/ACHIEVEMENTS:** Recip certificate of merit, CA Governor's com 1971; commn sculpture bust of Beethoven to be completed for Beethoven Bi-centennial NJ 1970. **BUSINESS ADDRESS:** San Diego StateUniv, San Diego, CA 92115.

MOBLEY, CHARLES LAMAR
Educator. **PERSONAL:** Born Oct 09, 1932, Winter Garden, FL; son of Benjamin James Mobley and Mary Jayne Davis Mobley. **EDUCATION:** Morehouse Coll, 1953-55; Univ of Miami, BMus 1964, MMus 1971; FL Intl U, 1981-83; Barry U, 1984. **CAREER:** Mt Zion Baptist Church, organist/choir dir 1948-60; Beulah Baptist Church, organist/choir dir 1953-55; Fine Arts Conservatory, teacher 1963-64; Miami-Dade Community Coll, teacher 1971-79, dir choir 1971-80; Dade County Public Schools, teacher. **ORGANIZATIONS:** Mem MENC, FMEA, DMEA, UTD, FEA, AFT 1964-; pub rel chmn Dade Co Music Educ Assn 1974-75; treas DMEA 1983-; founder & dir Liberty City Elem String Ensemble 1976-; chmn Tract II Model City Prog 1974-75; bd of dir Greater Miami Youth Symphony 1982-. **HONORS/ACHIEVEMENTS:** Teacher of the Year, North Central Area, Dade Co FL 1977; recorded the liberty City Elementary String ensemble for the Dade County Florida Superintendent's Honors Music Festival 1983; Community Serv Award, Natl Assn of Negro Business and Professional Women's Clubs Inc, Miami Club 1985; Achievement Awd in Music Educ, Natl Sor of Phi Delta Kappa Inc, Gamma Omicron Chap 1987; Achievement Award Miami Alumni Chapter, Kappa Alpha Psi Fraternity 1989. **BUSINESS ADDRESS:** Teacher, Dade County Public Schools, 1855 NW 71st St, Miami, FL 33147.

MOBLEY, EMILY RUTH
Librarian. **PERSONAL:** Born Oct 01, 1942, Valdosta, GA; daughter of Emmett Mobley and Ruth Johnson Mobley. **EDUCATION:** Univ of MI, AB Ed 1964; Univ of MI, AM Library Sci 1967, additional coursework. **CAREER:** Chrysler Corp, engrg librarian 1965-69; Wayne State Univ, librarian 1969-75; Gen Motors Rsch Labs 1976-81; Univ of MI, adj lecturer 1974-75, 1983-85; GMI Engrg & Mgmt Inst, library dir 1982-86; Purdue University, assoc dir of lib 1986-. **ORGANIZATIONS:** Resolutions committee 1969-71; rsch comm 1977-80; comm on positive action 1972-74; Mi Chap Bulletin ed1972-73, ed comm 1974-76, prog comm 1976-80; pres elect 1979-80, pres 1980-81, career advisor 1980-83, program comm 1981-82, long range plnng comm chmn 1981-82; nominating comm chmn 1982-83; library mgmt div sec 1983-85; chap cabinet chmn elect 1984-85, chapter cabinet chairman 1985-86, president-elect 1986-87, pres 1987-88, past pres 1988-89, chmn, awards comm 1989-90, all with Spec Libraries Assn; bd of trustees Library of MI 1983-86; mem Alpha Kappa Alpha Sorority. **HONORS/ACHIEVEMENTS:** CIC Doctoral Fellow in Library Sci Committee on Inst Cooperation 1973-76; Various publ including "Special Libraries at Work" Shoe String Press 1984, "Library Operations within a Decentralized Corporate Organization" Issues & Involvement 1983; Distinguished Alumnus, Univ of Michigan School of Information and Library Studies, 1989. **HOME ADDRESS:** 1115 Trace Eleven, West Lafayette, IN 47906. **BUSINESS ADDRESS:** Assoc Dir of Libraries, Purdue University, Libraries, Stewart Center, West Lafayette, IN 47907.

MOBLEY, EUGENIA L.
Educator, dentist. **PERSONAL:** Born Dec 21, 1921, Birmingham, AL; married Charles W Mcginnis. **EDUCATION:** TN State U, BS 1943; Meharry Med Coll, DDS 1946;Univ Of MI, MPH 1948. **CAREER:** Sch of Dentistry Meharry Med Coll, interim dean 1976-; Dept of Prev Dent & Comm Health & Comm Health Sch of Dentistry Meharry Med Coll, assoc dean prof & chmn 1974-76; Div of Den Hygiene Meharry Med Coll, dir 1952-56; Meharry, pvt practice & part-time instr 1950-57; Jefferson Co Bd Health, staffdentist 1946-479. **ORGANIZATIONS:** Dental Health Res & Educ Adv Com; Nat Inst of Health PHS; mem TN State Dental Assn; Capital City Dental Soc,; Pan-TN State Dental Assn; Nat Dent TalAssn; Nashville Dental Soc; Council of Comm Agencies; Federation Intl Dentaire, mem various other prof orgns; mem Delta Sigma Theta; NAACP; Urban League; sec WA Bass Jr High PTA; St Vincent's Depaul Alter Soc & Ardent Gardners. **HONORS/ACHIEVEMENTS:** Recipient of several research grants Omicron Kappa, Upsilon Hon Dental Soc 1952; Kappa Sigma Pi Hon Dental Soc 1954; outstanding educ Of Am 1972. **BUSINESS ADDRESS:** 1005 18 Ave N, Nashville, TN 37208.

MOBLEY, JOAN THOMPSON
Physician. **PERSONAL:** Born Jun 02, 1944, New York, NY; married Stacey J; children: Michele T. **EDUCATION:** Fisk Univ, BA 1966; Howard Univ Coll of Med, MD 1970. **CAREER:** Thomas Jefferson Univ Hosp, resident 1971-75, staff pathologist 1975-77; Howard Univ Hosp, asst prof 1977-79; HHS Indian Health Svcs, dir of labs 1979-83; St Francis Hosp, dir of labs 1983-. **ORGANIZATIONS:** Vstg prof Howard Univ Coll of Medicine; spokesperson Coll of amer Pathologists; mem Medical Adv Comm Blood Bank of DE; dir Girls Clubs of DE, Opera House in Wilmington. **HONORS/ACHIEVEMENTS:** Fellow Coll of Amer Pathologists, Amer Soc of Clinical Pathologists. **BUSINESS ADDRESS:** Dir Dept of Pathology, St Francis Hospital, 7th & Clayton Sts, Wilmington, DE 19805.

MOBLEY, STACEY J.
Business administrator. **PERSONAL:** Born Nov 19, 1945, Chester, PA; married Dr Joan C Thompson; children: Michele. **EDUCATION:** Howard Univ Coll of Pharm, BPharm 1968; Howard Univ Sch of Law, JD 1971. **CAREER:** Del Co Legal Asst Assn, atty 1971-72; EI DuPont DeNemours & Co, atty 1972-76, Washington cnsl 1977-82, dir fed affairs 1983-86, vice pres federal affairs 1986-. **ORGANIZATIONS:** Mem of DC Bar 1977; mem Henry Clay Soc, Washington Rep Rsch Group; bd of dirs Arean Stage Washington DC, Delta Rsch & Educ Foundation; mem Wilmington Club DE. **HONORS/ACHIEVEMENTS:** Distinguished Alumni Awd Natl Assoc for Equal Oppor in Higher Educ 1987. **BUSINESS ADDRESS:** Vice Pres Federal Affairs, Dupont Co, 1701 Penn Ave NW, Washington, DC 20006.

MOBLEY, SYBIL (NEE COLLINS)
Educational administrator. **PERSONAL:** Born Oct 14, 1925, Shreveport, LA; married James Otis; children: James Jr, Janet Yolanda Sermon, Melvin. **EDUCATION:** Wharton SchUniv PA, MBA 1961;Univ IL, PhD 1964; State Of FL, CPA. **CAREER:** FL A&MUniv sch of business, prof acctg dean 1963-. **ORGANIZATIONS:** Mem Alpha Kappa Alpha; mem bd dir Amer Assembly of Collegiate Schools of Bus; bd of overseers of Wharton School, Univ of PA; bd dir Jr Achievement Inc, Intl Assoc of Black Bus Educators; consult panel Comptroller General of the US; mem bd dir Anheuser-Busch Co Inc, Champion Intl Corp, Hershey FoodsCorp, Premark Intl Inc, Sears Roebuck & Co. **HONORS/ACHIEVEMENTS:** Received three Hon doctorate degrees from Wharton School of Univ of PA, Babson Coll, Bishop Coll; presented Robert Russa Motel Leadership Awd Natl Bus League. **BUSINESS ADDRESS:** Dean, Schl of Busn & Industry, Florida A&M University, Tallahassee, FL 32307.

MOCH, LAWRENCE E.
Executive director. **PERSONAL:** Born Apr 28, 1929; married Gloria Domino; children: Jana, Larry. **EDUCATION:** Wiley Coll Marshall TX, BS 1954; Springfield Coll MA, further studies; Southern U. **CAREER:** Wiley Coll, vet affairs officer 1955-56; YMCA Baton Rouge, youth work sec 1956-61; YMCA Savannah, prog & camping dir 1961-63; YMCA Asheville, exec dir 1963-65; YMCA Baton Rouge, 1965-68; So Union SoUniv Baton Rouge, dir 1968-. **ORGANIZATIONS:** Past mem SoUniv Adminstrn Council Community Relations Com Spec Events Com;mem Student Personnel Serv Council; past proj dir City Ct Prob & Rehab Prog City Parish Council; mem Sheriff's Citizens Adv Com; LA Adv Council Vocational & Tech Edn; past mem Pontchartrain Levee Bd Commrs; treas Mayor Pres Council Youth Opportunity; sec S Baton Rouge Adv Com; Past Mem Cap Area United Givers Planning Council; mem Mayor Pres Jobs for Vet Task Force; Arts & Humanities Council; Mental Health Assn; spons Com Gov Prayer Breakfast; past pres Bethel Baton Rouge Fed Credit Union; sec Frontiers Intl; mem Citizens Com LA Crim Cts; div leader YMCA Membership Campaign; past ch City Ct Adv Com; past pres Legal Aid Soc; past vice pres Baton Rouge Council on Alcoholism & Drug Abuse; past mem City Parish Beautification Commn; past adv SoUniv Mem Assn Coll Unions; Am Assn Sch Administr; LA Sch Bd Assns; LA Educ Assn; mem YMCA; Istrouma Area Countil Boy Scouts Am; Vanguard Social Club; Pub Affairs Research Council. **HONORS/ACHIEVEMENTS:** Appreciation cert City Parish Council; So union staff humanitorious award; Bethel AME Ch plaque outstanding serv; City Ct Adv Com plaque; outstanding& meritorious serv award Baton Rouge City Ct & Probation & Rehab Plaque; St Francis Xavier Ath Club award; V Phalanx Frat outstanding serv award; outstanding serv student life trophy 1970; student govt appreciation trophy 1969-70; adv Plaque SoUniv Class 1972. **MILITARY SERVICE:** USAF, 1948-52. **BUSINESS ADDRESS:** Southern Union Southern Univ, Baton Rouge, LA 70813.

MODESTE, LEON EDGAR
Association executive. **PERSONAL:** Born Aug 19, 1926, Brooklyn, NY; son of Leon Modeste and Hattie Modeste; married Nettie C; children: Wendi, Leon III, Keith, Kharon, Joseph, Rhea. **EDUCATION:** LI Univ, BA 1950; Columbia Univ Sch of Soc Work, MSW 1953; Columbia Univ, attended Grad Sch of Business. **CAREER:** NY Univ, assoc prof; Univ So MS & Univ KY, guest lectr; State Univ of NY, assoc prof; Medgar Evers Coll, prof; Youth Consultation Serv Assoc, asst dir; Gen Conv Special Prog, dir; Manhood Found, exec dir; Brooklyn Br NY Urban League; dir; Syracuse Univ, adjunct prof; Urban League Onondaga Co Inc, president. **ORGANIZATIONS:** Exec dir Manhood Found; dir Urban Crisis Prog Natl Episcopal Ch; bd mem Unity Mutual Life Ins Co 1982; bd mem Syracuse Symphony Orchestra 1984; bd mem W New York City Public Broadcasting of CNY 1983; mem Syracuse Black Leadership Congress 1982; mem Assn of Black Social Workers; Natl Assn of Black Social Workers; Acad of Certified Social Workers; Certified Social Worker NY State; Phi Beta Sigma Frat. **HONORS/ACHIEVEMENTS:** Humanities Awd St Augustine Coll; Citizens Awd Farragut Houses; Exceptional Serv Manhood Found; Educ Awd Phi Beta Sigma Frat. **MILITARY SERVICE:** USN 1945-46. **HOME ADDRESS:** 2001 E Colvin St, Syracuse, NY 13210.

MOHAMED, GERALD R., JR.
Accountant. **PERSONAL:** Born Oct 03, 1948, New York, NY; son of Gerald R Mohamed and Helen Brown Mohamed; children: Gerald R III. **EDUCATION:** Duquesne Univ, BS 1970; Univ of Pittsburgh, MBA 1979. **CAREER:** Westinghouse Credit Corp, receivable accountant 1971-72, internal audit 1972-75, super genl ledger/accts payable 1975-77, mgr consumer receivables 1977-79, financial analyst/financial planning dept 1979-82, mgr general accounting 1982-84; Westinghouse Electric Corp, staff asst corp financial planning & procedures 1984-88, Westinghouse Broadcasting, mgr financial planning 1989-. **ORGANIZATIONS:** Mem Black MBA Assoc 1983-86; treas 1985-87, mem Omega Psi Phi Frat 1968-; mem Free Masonry PHA 1985-. **HOME ADDRESS:** 41 Sheppard Ave, Teaneck, NJ 07666-6119. **BUSINESS ADDRESS:** Westinghouse Broadcasting, 888 Seventh Ave, New York, NY 10106.

MOHR, DIANE LOUISE
Librarian. **PERSONAL:** Born Nov 24, 1951, Fairbanks, AK. **EDUCATION:** Alliance Francais Brussels Belgium, Deuxieme degree 1971; CA State Univ Long Beach, BA Black Studies 1977; Univ of So Ca Los Angeles, M Science in Library Sci 1978. **CAREER:** Getty Oil Co, indexer-reviewer 1978-79; Woodcrest Public Library, librarian in charge 1979-82; View Park Public Library, librarian in charge 1982-83; Compton Public Library, sr librarian in charge 1983-87. **ORGANIZATIONS:** Life mem Univ of So CA Alumni Assoc 1978-; mem Amer & CA Library Assocs 1980-; mem Vesta Bruner Scholarship Bd 1980-83; mem CA Black Librarians Caucus1981-, Alpha Kappa Alpha Sor Inc 1981-; mem SEIU Local 660 1983-87; mem The Links Inc 1985-. **HONORS/ACHIEVEMENTS:** President's Honor List Cal State Univ Long Beach CA 1975-77; mem Phi Kappa Phi Honor Soc CA State Univ Long Beach 1977-; Who's Who of Amer Women 1987-88. **BUSINESS ADDRESS:** Senior Librarian, Los Angeles Co Public Library, 240 W Compton Bl, Compton, CA 90220.

MOHR, PAUL B.
Educator. **PERSONAL:** Born Aug 19, 1931, Waco, TX; married Rebecca Dixon; children: Paul, Michelle. **EDUCATION:** FL A&M Univ, BS 1954; Univ NM, MS 1969; OK State Univ, EdD 1969. **CAREER:** St St Petersburg Jr Coll FL, instr 1954-55; FL A&M Univ Tallahassee, acad dean 1969; Norfolk State Univ VA, acad vp; Talladega Coll AL, pres 1984-. **ORGANIZATIONS:** Consult So Assn of Colls & Schools 1971-; evaluator of proposals Natl Inst Educ & Dept HEW 1975-; mem So Regional Educ Bd 1975-, FL Council on TeacherEduc 1976-. **HONORS/ACHIEVEMENTS:** Phi Delta Kappa Awd 1974; Recipient Liberty

Bell Awd FL A&M Univ Natl Alumni Assn 1976. **MILITARY SERVICE:** AUS 1955-57. **BUSINESS ADDRESS:** President, Talladega College, 627 West Battle St, Talladega, AL 35160.

MOLAND, WILLIE C.
Educational administrator. **PERSONAL:** Born Jan 19, 1931, Shamrock, OK; married Marianne; children: Charlotte, Debbie, Gary, Brent, Bryan. **EDUCATION:** Denver Art Acad Denver CO, certificate 1958. **CAREER:** Metropolitan State Coll, affirmative action staff officer 1971-; Denver Commn on Comm relations, consult 1970; Metropolitan State Coll, coordinator of resources & Support 1968-69; Martin Luther King Young Adults Center, dir 1955-68; Air Force Accounting & Financecenter, data devel technician. **ORGANIZATIONS:** Chrpsn Black Faculty Staff Caucus Metro State Coll; state dir of youth Prince Hall Grand Lodge CO; co-pres Phillips Elem PTSA; sec Syrian Temple #49 Chanters Group; pres Syrian Temple #49 Arabic Patrol; exec bd mem Greater Park Hill Community Inc; dir of youth programs Greater Park Hill Community Inc. **HONORS/ACHIEVEMENTS:** Citizens soldier of year 1959; man of year GPHC Tutorial Program 197 2; superior perf award USAF 1965; Golden Rule Award accounting & finance center. **MILITARY SERVICE:** USAF AUS 1951-54. **BUSINESS ADDRESS:** Metropolitan State Coll, 250 W 14 Ave Rm 208, Denver, CO 80204.

MOLETTE, BARBARA J.
Arts administrator. **PERSONAL:** Born Jan 03, 1940, Los Angeles, CA; daughter of Baxter R Roseburr and Nora L Johnson Roseburr; married Carlton W Molette, Jun 15, 1960; children: Carla E Molette, Andrea R Molette. **EDUCATION:** Florida A&M, Tallahasse FL, BA, 1966; Florida State Univ, Tallahassee FL, MFA, 1969; Univ of Missouri, Columbia MO, 1989-. **CAREER:** Spelman Coll, Atlanta GA, instructor, 1969-75; Texas Southern Univ, Houston TX, asst professor, 1975-85; Mayor's Advisory Committee on Arts & Culture, Baltimore MD, dir arts in educ programs, 1988-. **ORGANIZATIONS:** Mem, Dramatist Guild Of Amer, 1971-; President-Elect, Natl Assn For Africa-American Theatre, 1989-91; consultant for worshops in theatre and television. **HONORS/ACHIEVEMENTS:** Graduated with Highest Honors from Florida A&M, 1966; Graduate Fellowship, Florida State Univ, 1967-69; Graduate Fellowship, Univ of Missouri, 1986-87; author of Black Theatre, Wyndham Hall Publishers, 1986; Noahs Ark, published in Center Stage, 1981; Upstage/Downstage, column in Houston Informer, 1977-78; Rosalee Pritchett, performed at Negro Ensemble Company, 1971, Published in Black Writers of American. **HOME ADDRESS:** 255 West Lanvale, Baltimore, MD 21217.

MOLETTE, CARLTON W.
Educator, playwright, author. **PERSONAL:** Born Aug 23, 1939, Pine Bluff, AR; son of Carlton William Molette and Evelyn Richardson Molette; married Barbara Roseburr, Jun 15, 1960; children: Carla, Andrea. **EDUCATION:** Morehouse Coll, BA 1959; Univ of KC, graduate study 1959-60; Univ of IA, MA 1962; FL State Univ, PhD 1968. **CAREER:** Little Theatre Div of Humanites Tuskegee Inst, asst dir 1960-61; Des Moines Comm Playhouse, designer tech dir 1962-63; Howard Univ Dept of Drama, asst prof of tech production & design 1963-64; FL A&M Univ, asst prof & tech dir 1964-67, assoc prof 1967-69; Spelman Coll Div of Fine Arts, chmn 1969-75; School of Communications TX So Univ, dean 1975; Lincoln Univ, dean College of Arts & Sciences, 1985-87; Coppin State College, vice pres Academic Affairs, 1987-. **ORGANIZATIONS:** Mem The Dramatists Guild; Natl Assn of Dramatic & Speech Arts; past editor of "Encore"; US Inst for Theatre Tech; guest dir Univ of MI Feb-Mar 1974; mem bd dir Atlanta Arts Festival; vice pres Greater Atlantic Arts Council; chmn bd trustees Neighborhood Arts Center, Miller Theatre Advisory Council. **HONORS/ACHIEVEMENTS:** Graduate fellowship in theatre Univ of KC; Atlanta Univ Center Faculty Rsch Grant 1970-71; co-author Black Theatre, Premise & Presentation Wyndham Hall Press, 1986; Rosalee Pritchett (play) produced by Negro Ensemble Company, 1970. **MILITARY SERVICE:** AUS sp 5 1963. **BUSINESS ADDRESS:** Coppin State College, Dept of Academic Affairs, 2500 W North Ave, Baltimore, MD 21216-3698.

MOLETTE, WILLIE L.
Dentist. **PERSONAL:** Born Feb 15, 1919, Camden, AR; married Hattie J Center; children: Dr. **EDUCATION:** A M & N Coll, BS; Meharry Med Coll, DDS; Nat Dental & Chicago Dental Soc Mtgs, continuing educ dentistry. **CAREER:** Pine Bluff AR, dentist pvt prac 1947-;Univ of AR at Pine Bluff coll dentist, 1950-; hygiene a m & n coll, instr 1947-50. **ORGANIZATIONS:** Mem Nat Dental Assn 1949-; bd mem 1967-77; treas past pres AR Med Dental & Pharmaceutical Assn; mem SW Medical Dental & Pharmaceutical Assn; Am Dental Assn; Chicago Dental Soc; sec treas Delta Developers Inc; bd mem Union Enterprises Inc; bd mem Impex Corp; v chmn of bd Diversified Unlimited Corp; mem Educ Com Pine Bluff Hsng Authority 1968-; one of first four black men C of C; mem Pine Bluff Sch Bd 1968-69; first Black Mem; pres Nat Alumni AssnUniv Of AR at Pine Bluff 1970-74; treas of bd St John Apts; bd mem Cits Boys Club; past chmn Pine Bluff Boy Scout Div; mem Tau Phi Chap Omega Psi Phi Frat Inc; v chmn bd Pine Bluff & Opps Industrialization Cntr; mem trustee St John AME Ch; life mem NAACP; mem Adv Com City of Pine Bluff; commnr Pine Bluff Conv Ctr. **MILITARY SERVICE:** AUS capt. **BUSINESS ADDRESS:** 817 Cherry St, Pine Bluff, AR 71601.

MONAGAN, ALFRIETA PARKS
Educator. **PERSONAL:** Born Nov 27, 1945, Washington, DC; daughter of Frances T Parks. **EDUCATION:** George Washington Univ, AB 1969; Princeton, MA 1971, PhD 1981. **CAREER:** Hamilton Coll, visiting asst prof 1974-75; Univ Erlangen-Nuremberg, Fulbright Jr lecturer Amer Studies 1975-76; Univ of IA, asst prof Afro-Amer studies & anthropology 1976-. **ORGANIZATIONS:** Mem NAACP, Amer Anthropology Assn, Assn of Black Anthropologists, Popular Culture Assocs, Caribbean Studies Assn. **HONORS/ACHIEVEMENTS:** Fulbright Alumni Assn Gillen Scholarship 1968; Univ Fellowship Princeton 1969-70, 1973-74; Research Grant Princeton 1970; NSF Transportation 1972-73; Research Grant NSF 1972-73; Fellowship Soc Women Geographers; Research Grant Latin Amer Studies Princeton 1974; Lectrsp Fulbright-Hays Program 1975-76; Award from Natl Assoc for Foreign Student Affairs 1982, 1987; Old Gold Summer Faculty Research Fellowship 1985. **BUSINESS ADDRESS:** Adjunct Assistant Professor, University of Iowa, Dept of Anthropology, Iowa City, IA 52242.

MONAGAS, LIONEL JOHN
Communications executive. **PERSONAL:** Born Jul 08, 1921, Chicago, IL; married Natalie Hinderas; children: Michele. **EDUCATION:** Temple Univ, BA 1985. **CAREER:** Washington DC, postman 1947-52; WTOP-TV, asst dir 1952-54; Black Mrkt Cons, pub rel 1955-56; WHYY-TV, asst prog dir 1956-70; Natl Assn of Educ Broadcasters, dir office of minority affairs 1970-73; EEO Unit FCC, chief ind 1973-80; WRBV-TV, exec vice pres & station mgr 1980-82; Comcast Cable Comm Inc,dir franchise develop 1982-84; PYM Sight & Sound Inc, principal secty/treas 1984-85; Temple Univ, adjunct lecturer sch of comm & theatre radioTV film dept 1985-. **ORGANIZATIONS:** Founding mem Natl Black Media Prod Assoc 1968; founding mem Philadelphia Black Communicators 1968; chmn Luncheon Comm NCBL-TFC 1974-; mem Natl Assn of Educ Broadcasters; lectr Sch of Comm Howard Univ 1972-73; creator & exec producer Black Perspective on the News 1969. **MILITARY SERVICE:** AUS tech sgt 1940-42; AUS 1st lt 1942-46.

MONCRIEF, SIDNEY
Professional athlete. **PERSONAL:** Born Sep 21, 1957, Little Rock, AR; married Debra. **EDUCATION:** Univ of AR, BS Phys Ed. **CAREER:** Welch One on One Competition, spokesman; Milwaukee Buck, professional basketball guard. **ORGANIZATIONS:** Partner with AR Basketball Coach Eddie Sutton to do instr clinic for the Spec Olympics; bd of dirs Arkla Corp. **HONORS/ACHIEVEMENTS:** SW Conf Player of the Year; Broke the record of 504 FTM by Kareem Abdul-Jabbar in 1971-72 season; mem Sporting News All Amer Second Team 1979; All-Amer &SW Conf Player of the Year during sr season Univ of AR; NBA Defensive Player of the Year 1983,84; NBA All Defensive First Team 1983,84,85,86; mem 36th NBA All Star Team. **BUSINESS ADDRESS:** Milwaukee Bucks, 901 N 4th St, Milwaukee, WI 53203.

MONCURE, ALBERT F.
Business executive. **PERSONAL:** Born Apr 19, 1924, Lancaster, PA; married Dr Bennie Sue Morrison; children: Sheila Ann Belfon, Albert F Jr, Alexandria Marie. **EDUCATION:** Long Island Univ, BS Acctng 1950; NY Univ Grad Sch Business Adm, MBA 1956. **CAREER:** The Port of NY Authority, various positions through asst mgr operations 1951-67; New York City Dept Soc Svcs, dep comm 1967-70; The Port Authority of NYand NJ, asst personnel dir 1970, dep dir of gen serv 1970-71, dir gen serv 1971-84; Arlington Cnty VA Dept Human Services, admin serv div chief 1984-. **ORGANIZATIONS:** Chmn Child Health Assurance Prgm Subcomm for Citizen's Comm for Children 1973-80; conf chmn Inflation and Impact on Soc Serv at Ford Found 1974; vice pres Community Council of greater NY 1974-82; pres Purchasing Mgmt Assn of NY 1979-80; chmn Ethics Bd the Port Authority of NY and NJ 1980-83; chr Logistics Comm for the 1983 Conf of the Amer Soc for Publ Admin 1983; mem adv bd Sch of Busniess & Publ Admin Long Is Univ 1983; bd mem United Way of Tri-State. **HONORS/ACHIEVEMENTS:** Listed Who's Who Among Black Americans; Natl Urban League Black Exec Exch Prog Award 1979; One of 3 Disting Publ Leaders honored by People's Alliance 1983; Harlem YMCA Black Achievers Award 1973; Who's Who in the South and Southwest 1986. **MILITARY SERVICE:** AUS Master Sgt 1943-46 and 1950. **BUSINESS ADDRESS:** Admin Serv Div Chief, Arlington County, Dept of Human Services, 1800 N Edison St, Arlington, VA 22207.

MONK, ART
Professional athlete. **PERSONAL:** Born Dec 05, 1957; married Desiree; children: James Arthur Jr, Danielle. **EDUCATION:** Attended, Syracuse. **CAREER:** Washington Redskins, wide receiver 1980-. **ORGANIZATIONS:** Dir of Outside Sales for Record Den Inc; part owner Rick Walker's Scoreboard Restaurant Herndon VA; Broadcasts for WRC-TV. **HONORS/ACHIEVEMENTS:** Led Redskins in receptions 1980,82,84,85, and in yards 1980,81,84,85; all-Pro selections by AP, UPI, Pro Football Weekly, Pro Football Writers Assoc and The Sporting News; Player of the Year Washington Touchdown Club and Quarterback Club; named Offensive Player of the Game twice; voted Redskins 1984 MVP; mem NFL ProBowl teams 1986,87. **BUSINESS ADDRESS:** Washington Redskins, P O Box 17247, Dulles International Airport, Washington, DC 20041.

MONK, EDD DUDLEY
Business executive. **PERSONAL:** Born Apr 25, 1948, Magnolia, NC; married Marie Allen. **CAREER:** Edd D Monk Farms, farmer; Rose Hill Funeral Home Rose Hill, NC, pres 1948-. **ORGANIZATIONS:** Life chmn trust bd Missionary Bapt Training Inst 1973-80; pres /organizer Duplin Co Coastal Growers Coop 1968-78; pres/organizer Stanford Burial Soc Magnolia, NC 1932-64; bd dir FHA Kenansville 6 yrs; bd dir Neuse River Cncl of Govt 1968-79; bd trustees James Sprunt Tech Coll Kenansville 1971-80; v chmn Good Neighbor Cncl 5 yrs; bd of dir Duplin Co Farm Bur 10 yrs; chmn deacon bd Kenansville Bapt Ch 1953-76; pres Duplin Co PTA & EE Smith High PTA 1962-69; bd dir Duplin Co Planning Bd 1975-79; worshipful master Beulah Lodge #110 10 yrs. **HONORS/ACHIEVEMENTS:** Leadership Award Stanford Burial Soc 1962; Citizen of the Yr Duplin Co Adv Bd Ext 1966; Disting Serv Award E E Smith HS 1967; Disting Serv Award Kenansville Bapt Ch 1974; Disting Serv Cup Duplin Co Good Neighbor Cncl 1976; Citizen of the Year Duplin Co 4-H Club 1978; Disting Serv Award FHA 1978; Disting Serv Award Newuse Cncl of Govt 1979. **BUSINESS ADDRESS:** President, Rose Hill Funeral Home, PO Box 338, 302 W Church, Rose Hill, NC 28458.

MONROE, ANNIE LUCKY
Educator. **PERSONAL:** Born Dec 06, 1933, Milledgeville, GA; married Semon V Monroe; children: Angela V, Michael V. **EDUCATION:** Paine Coll, BA 1953; GA Coll, MEd 1977. **CAREER:** Boddie HS, tchr 1953-68; Baldwin HS, tchr 1968-76, asst prin 1976-77; GA Coll, instr of English 1977-80. **ORGANIZATIONS:** Mem GA Libr Assn 1976-80; mem GA Coll Alumni Assn 1977-80; mem GA Coll Women's Club 1978-79; trustee Mary Vinson Libr 1976-80; mem Trinity CME Ch; asst pianist Trinity CME Ch. **HONORS/ACHIEVEMENTS:** Teacher of the Year Boddie HS 1967; First Black Instr of English Baldwin HS 1968; First Black Woman chosen Bd of Trustees Mary Vinson Libr 1976; First Black Instr of English GA Coll 1977; Most Effective Teacher in Classroom Students of Baldwin HS 1977; First Black Woman Asst Principal Baldwin HS 1976-77. **BUSINESS ADDRESS:** Georgia College, Milledgeville, GA 31061.

MONROE, CHARLES EDWARD
Educational administrator. **PERSONAL:** Born Dec 09, 1950, Laurel Hill, NC; married Edwina Williams; children: Jarrod, Keisha. **EDUCATION:** Johnson C Smith Univ, BA (Summa Cum Laude) 1978; Univ of NC, MEd 1980; Univ of NC Greensboro, EdS 1989. **CAREER:** Greensboro City Schools, teacher 1980-84, asst principal 1984-86, principal 1986-. **ORGANIZATIONS:** Mem NC Assn of Educators 1981-, Natl Assn of Elementary School Principals 1986-, NC Assn of Administrators 1986-; teacher Cedar Grove Baptist Church

1985-; pres Alpha Kappa Mu Natl Honor Soc; vice pres Alpha Chi Natl Honor Soc; mem Pi Delta Tau Educ Honor Soc, Honors Program. **HONORS/ACHIEVEMENTS:** James B Duke Academic Scholarship; Babcock Academic Scholarship; George W Gore Grad Scholarship; Teacher of the Year Reidsville City Schools; Outstanding Young Educator in Reidsville City Schools Reidsville Jaycees. **MILITARY SERVICE:** AUS E-4 2 yrs; Purple Heart, Air Commendation Medal, Bronze Star, Soldier of the Month, Distinguished Graduate in Ranger School in Vietnam 1970-71. **HOME ADDRESS:** 2204 Cheltenham Blvd, Greensboro, NC 27407.

MONROE, EARL
Athlete. **PERSONAL:** Born Nov 21, 1944, Philadelphia, PA. **EDUCATION:** Winston Salem State, 1967. **CAREER:** Pretty Pearl Inc Entertainment Co, pres; NY Knicks, player. **ORGANIZATIONS:** Mem Groove Phi Groove Frat. **HONORS/ACHIEVEMENTS:** All star team 1969, 71, 75, 77; rookie of the year 1967-68. **BUSINESS ADDRESS:** NY Knicks, Madison Square Garden, 4 Pennsylvania Ave, New York, NY 10001.

MONROE, EARLY D., JR.
Engineer. **PERSONAL:** Born Mar 25, 1944, Shreveport, LA; divorced. **EDUCATION:** Southern Univ, BS 1966. **CAREER:** FCC Broadcasting Bur, radio &TV engr 1966-70; FCC Cable Bur, chief engr 1970-80; Howard Univ, adj prof 1973-78; EDM & Assoc Inc Wash DC, pres 1980-. **ORGANIZATIONS:** Bd mem Afro-Amer Datanamics 1973-, Farlington Meadows Cond Vlg 1974-75; former mem Civil Serv EEO Investigator 1975-; chmn Howard Univ Dept Applied Comm Curr Comm 1975-77; pres Rose Park/Georgetown Tennis Club 1983-; chmn bd, pres Natl Org Telecommun Engrs & Sci; mem IEEE; past vice pres Washington DC IEEE; mem NSPE; past mem Fed Cable TV Acv Comm, Soc of Cable TV Eng, Natl Conf of Black Lawyers Commun Comm; past exec dir AA Datanamics; consult African Bibliog Ctr-Telecomm; past bd mem Law & Consumer Affairs Div Natl Urban legue; life mem Omega Psi Phi Frat; mem Southern Univ Alumni. **HONORS/ACHIEVEMENTS:** Publ, "The Carriage of More than 12 Chnls" 1971, "Domestic Satellites" 1974, "The Electromagnetic Spectrum" 1974, "Broadcast Licensing" 1975, "Applied Commun-Baccalaureate & MD Proposals" 1976, "Studio & Central Room Equip" Hasting House 1977, numerous others.

MONROE, JAMES H.
Newspaper publisher. **PERSONAL:** Born Feb 23, 1946, Hartford, CT; son of James H Monroe and Rosalee Brown Monroe; married Sarah Jones Scott, Sep 30, 1979; children: Judy. **EDUCATION:** Parsons Coll, 1964-66; Central CT State Univ 1968-73. **CAREER:** Travelers Ins Co, acct 1968-69; enterpreneur 1969-; Conn Minority News, publisher; New England Minority News, Hartford, CT, 1969-. **ORGANIZATIONS:** Mem NAACP, 1970-, pres CT Business League, 1970-85; past pres, dir Greater Hartford Business Devel Center, 1973-; dir Hartford Econ Devel Comm, 1979-; mem SBA Task Force on Energy New England, 1979-81; dir CT Petroleum Council, 1981-; pres Greater Hartford Black Democratic Club, 1984-; dir Hartford Capital Corp. **MILITARY SERVICE:** AUS sgt E-5 2 yrs. **HOME ADDRESS:** P O Box 20080, Hartford, CT 06120.

MONROE, LILLIE MAE
Educational administrator. **PERSONAL:** Born Feb 15, 1948, Louisiana; married Egbert Thaddeus Lord; children: Alan Christopher Lord. **EDUCATION:** SU Baton Rouge LA, BS 1969; Freedmen's Hosp Washington DC, RD 1970; HowardUniv Washington DC, PhD, MS 1978, 1971. **CAREER:** CHANGE Inc, dir of nutrition prog 1970-72; Admin on Aging Dept Hlth Educ & Welfare, aging prog spec 1972-73; Med Assoc of NE Washington, private pract 1972-77; Comm Grp Health Found Inc, dir nutrition serv 1973-77; Univ of MD Eastern Shore, chmn, asst prof 1977-. **ORGANIZATIONS:** Mem Omicron Nu 1970; mem Soc Sigma Xi 1971; vol proj FIND 1971; judge/nutrition prog Phyllis Wheatley YMCA 1971; hmn diet therapy comm DC Dietetic Assoc 1973; mem Comm Nutrition Com DC Dietetic Assn 1971; mem Beta Kappa Chi 1972; mem pub rels com DC Dietetic Assn 1975; ed potomac post mag DC Dietitic Assn 1977. **HONORS/ACHIEVEMENTS:** Outstanding Young Dietitian of the Year 1973. **BUSINESS ADDRESS:** Chairperson Dept Human Ecology, Univ of Maryland, PO Box 1042, Princess Anne, MD 21853.

MONROE, ROBERT ALEX
Business executive. **PERSONAL:** Born in Sommerville, NJ. **EDUCATION:** Attended, Westchester Comm Coll, Hofstra Univ 1964. **CAREER:** Calvert Distillers, asst eastern div sales mgr, eastern div mgr; General Wine, mgr western upstate NY, NY mgr, natl brand mgr; asst metro NY sales mgr, eastern div sales rep; Calvert Distillers Co, vice pres/dir marketing; Summit Sales Co/Perennial Sales Co, pres. **ORGANIZATIONS:** Bd of dir, Joseph E Seagram & Sons Inc. **HONORS/ACHIEVEMENTS:** Outstanding Business & Professional Award, Blackbook Magazine, 1983; Man of the Year Award, Anti-Defamation League, 1985; first black to lead a major firm in the liquor industry; George M Estabrook Award, Hofstra Univ Alumni Assn, 1987. **MILITARY SERVICE:** USMC. **BUSINESS ADDRESS:** Vice Pres, Gen Mgr, House of Seagram, Southern Region, 5430 Bay Center Dr, Tampa, FL 33609.

MONTAGUE, LEE
Educational administrator, clergyman. **PERSONAL:** Born Jan 01, 1929, Philadelphia, PA; married Shirley Mae Demmons; children: Ricardo V, La Donna M, Michael A, Saunders L, Shirley M, Christina L, Deborah L, Denise A. **EDUCATION:** Coll of Marin, CA, 1965; Glendale Comm Coll, 1966-67; AZ Bible Coll, BA 1967-71. **CAREER:** USAF, sergeant 1947-67; Maricopa Med Ctr, med asst 1967-71; New Chance Inner City Ministries, dir 1972-84; Canaan Bible Inst, pres/dean 1983-. **ORGANIZATIONS:** Scoutmaster Boy Scouts of Amer 1966-69; chaplain Disabled Amer Vets 1971-74; brigade chmn Christian Serv Brigade 1973-75; pastor Luke AFB Gospel Chapel 1973-; administrator/director Inner City Children's Camps 1974-. **HONORS/ACHIEVEMENTS:** Recognition Black Chamber of Commerce; Meritorious Serv USAF 1966. **MILITARY SERVICE:** USAR t/sgt 20 years; AFOUA, AFGCM, GCM/5bl, NDSM/1bss, KSM, UNSM, AFLSA/4bolc 1947-67. **HOME ADDRESS:** 4935 West Berkely, Phoenix, AZ 85035. **BUSINESS ADDRESS:** President, Canaan Bible Institute, PO Box 1244, Phoenix, AZ 85001.

MONTAGUE, NELSON C.
Scientist. **PERSONAL:** Born Jul 12, 1929, Washington, DC; married Nancy L; children: Lennis Lee. **EDUCATION:** BS Elec Engr 1952. **CAREER:** Def Documentation Cntr, Def Logistics Agy, physical scientist, elec engr 1985 retired; Nat Bur of Standards, elec engr 1951-68. **ORGANIZATIONS:** Mem Inst of Elec & Electronics Engrs Inc 1951-; treas N VA Bapt Assn 1968-; mem exec bd NVB Assn; vice pres Commn on Hum Rights & Comm Rels, Vienna VA; Mayor's Adv Com 1966-70; coach Little Leag VA 1972-73; fin sec Northern VA Baptist Ministers & Laymen's Union 1985-. **HONORS/ACHIEVEMENTS:** Recip Grp Award Nat Bur of Standards 1964; Outstndng Perf Rating QSI Def Documentation Ctr 1974; finished 4 in 7 man race for 3 seats on Vienna Town Cncl 1968; Achievement Awd Arlington Branch 1986. **MILITARY SERVICE:** AUS pfc 1952-54.

MONTEIRO, MARILYN D.S.
University administrator. **PERSONAL:** Born Feb 22, 1941, Washington, DC; divorced; children: Chinyelu. **EDUCATION:** Univ of MA-Boston, BA 1970; Harvard Univ, EdM 1973, EdD 1982. **CAREER:** Delta Oppors Corp, teacher/teacher trainer 1970-71; YWCA Roxbury Branch, prog dir 1973-74; MA College of Art, dir affirmative action 1980-83; Univ of Northern IA, dir affirmative action progs 1983-. **ORGANIZATIONS:** Chair Cedar Falls Human Rights Commn; regional dir Amer Assoc for Affirmative Action; consultant Waterloo Dept of Correctional Svcs, Waterloo Civil SvcsCommn, Wendy's Restaurant Cedar Falls; bd mem YWCA Waterloo IA; mem NAACP, Phi Delta Kappa of Harvard and Univ of Northern IA, Amer Assoc on Higher Educ; mem Inter-Institutional Equal Employment Oppors Comm. **HONORS/ACHIEVEMENTS:** Listed Marquis Who's Who in the Midwest 1986; 2 publications; 8 articles published. **BUSINESS ADDRESS:** Affirmative Action Dir, University of Northern Iowa, 126 Gilcrist Hall, Cedar Falls, IA 50613.

MONTEITH, HENRY C.
Nuclear engineer. **PERSONAL:** Born May 10, 1937, Columbia, SC; married Joyce E; children: Biaia Monteith, Sheila Schoen, Perry Anglin. **EDUCATION:** Milwaukee Sch of Engrg, BS 1965; Univ of NM, MS 1970, PhD 1975. **CAREER:** RCA Indianapolis, elec engr 1965-67; Sandia Labs Albuquerque, math computer programmer, elec engr, tech staff mem 1967-80; Sandia Labs Albuquerque, nuclear engr 1976-. **ORGANIZATIONS:** Writer & lecturer on scientific/philosophical subjects; priv res Parapsychology; mem Amer Assn for Advancement of Sci, Soc of Physics Students, Intl Assoc of Math Physicists. **HONORS/ACHIEVEMENTS:** Sigma Pi Sigma Physics Honor Soc. **MILITARY SERVICE:** USN Electron Tech 2nd Class 1958-62. **BUSINESS ADDRESS:** Nuclear Engineer, Sandia Labs, Albuquerque, NM 87115.

MONTEVERDI, MARK VICTOR
Government official. **PERSONAL:** Born Jun 19, 1963, New York, NY; son of Marcella F Monteverdi-Monahan. **EDUCATION:** Hiram Coll, Hiram OH, BA, 1985. **CAREER:** Small Business Admin, New York NY, public affairs specialist, 1985-87; Black Enterprise Magazine/Earl G Graves, Ltd, New York NY, natl networking forum coordinator, 1987-88; Mayor's Office, New York Ny, mgr of public communications & outreach, 1988-. **ORGANIZATIONS:** Mem, Alpha Lamda Delta, 1981-; mem, Omicron Delta Kappa, 1983-; mem, Assn of Minority Enterprises of NY, 1985-; mem, Caribbean-Amer Chamber of Commerce, 1985-; mem, Natl Minority Business Council, 1985-; advisory bd mem, Self-Help Group, 1988-. **HONORS/ACHIEVEMENTS:** James A Garfield Memorial Award, Hiram Coll, 1981; Outstanding Political Science Major, Hiram Coll, 1985; Martin Luther King Jr Scholarship, Hiram Coll, 1985; received White House recognition for role as downstate coordinator for the 1985 White House Conference on Small Business, 1986; Outstanding Young Man in America, 1987. **HOME ADDRESS:** 210-16 Grand Central Parkway, Apt 1F, Hollis Hills, Queens, NY 11427.

MONTGOMERY, ALPHA LEVON, SR.
Attorney, judge. **PERSONAL:** Born Feb 01, 1919, Oklahoma; son of Emmett Montgomery and Melissa Montgomery; married Ann E; children: Alpha L Jr, Levonne, Adrien, Alain. **EDUCATION:** Fisk Univ, BA 1941; Howard Univ, 1943; Howard Univ, JD 1947. **CAREER:** Economist for fed govt, Washington, DC, 1945-47; Bussey, Montgomery & Smith 1948-49; Montgomery & Smith 1949-54; Montgomery & Rithcey San Diego, att 1964-79; Superior Court of San Diego, judge. **ORGANIZATIONS:** Mem Am Bar Assn; San Diego County Bar Assn; Am Arbitration Assn; bd architectural rev San Diego 1955-61; Legal Aid Soc 1958-59; psychology commn 1961-62; founder, San Diego Urban League 1963-79; NAACP; Forum Am Freedoms 1961- CA Adv Com US Commn Civil Rights 1962-66; vpv Citizens Interracial Com San Diego 1963-64; interview bd San Diego Civil Serv Commn 1963; Gov's Commn Rumford Act 1966; state bd educ Moral Guidelines Com 1970-72. **HONORS/ACHIEVEMENTS:** Fed ct serv certificate, San Diego Bar Assn 1959; certificate of appreciation San Diego 1963; superior accomplishment award, Federal Government, for work as an economist; participant in President Eisenhower's Conference for President's Commission on Equal Employment Opportunity, President Kennedy's Regional Conference of Community Leaders on Equal Employment Opportunity, and President Johnson's White Conference on Civil Rights; pub papers & booklets on economics and politics.

MONTGOMERY, BARBARA CURRY
Actress. **PERSONAL:** Born Jun 25, 1939, Orange, NJ; children: Byron. **EDUCATION:** Vinnette Carrol, dramatic study 1958-59; Margaret Murray Washington Schof Nursing Wash, DC, graduated 1966; Rodney K Douglas, classical study 1968; Prof Edward Boatner, mus study for voice 1977-79. **CAREER:** Old Reliable Theater Co NYC, actress 1968-69; Cafe LaMaMa Exptl Club NYC, actress 1970-73; Negro Ensemble Co NCY, actress 1975-80; Black Women In Theater Inc, founder (along with Mary Alice)/artistic dir; currently performing on Broadway in "The Tap Dance Kid"; recently completed filming "Evergreen" a three-part mini series for NBC. **ORGANIZATIONS:** Bd dir Roger Furman's New Heritage Rep Co Inc 1980; mem NAACP Creative Artists Br mem Jr League. **HONORS/ACHIEVEMENTS:** Obie Award Disting Performance in "My Sister My Sister" 1974; Award of Recognition AUDELCO 1974, 1976, 1979; Outstanding Contbd in the field of the Arts NJ Fedn of Colored Woman's Clubs Inc 1976.

MONTGOMERY, BRIAN WALTER
Education administrator. **PERSONAL:** Born Jun 29, 1957, Chicago, IL; married Teresa Viera. **EDUCATION:** St Mary's Coll, BA 1979. **CAREER:** De Paul Univ, asst dir annual giving 1979-84; North Central Coll, dir of annual funds 1984-. **ORGANIZATIONS:** Mem Phi Mu Alpha Sinfonia 1976-, Council for Advancement & Support of Ed 1979, Naperville Area Chamber of Commerce 1984, Naperville Chap American Cancer Soc, Naperville Jaycees. **BUSINESS ADDRESS:** Dir of Annual Funds, North Central College, 30 N Brainard, Naperville, IL 60566.

MONTGOMERY, CATHERINE LEWIS
Business executive. **PERSONAL:** Born in Washington, DC; divorced; children: Alpha LeVon, Jr. **EDUCATION:** Howard Univ, attended 1944-46; Univ CA ext 1948-49; Natl Inst Pub Affairs 1968. **CAREER:** USN elect Lab San Diego, admin asst to tech dir 1950-62; Republican State Central Comm, admin asst to field dir Jan 1966-June 1966; Economic Oppor Comm San Diego Cnty, pers dir admin serv 1966-69; State of CA Fair Empl Practice Commn, commissioner 1969-75; consult Urban Affairs 1972-; USN Dept, mgmtcons/equal opportunity spec 1978-. **ORGANIZATIONS:** San Diego Plang Commr 1966-73; Mental Hlth Serv Adv Bd 1968-72; President's Adv Cncl on Minority Bus Enterprise 1972-75; mem Western Gov Rsch Assn; Natl Assn of Planners; Amer Soc of Planning Officials; Commonwealth Club of CA; served on bds of Soroptimist Intl San Diego; pres Soroptimist Intl SanDiego 1979-80; Natl Girsl Clubs of Amer Inc; Urban League of San Diego Inc; Univ Hosp Adv Bd; mem NAACP; life mem Natl Cncl of Negro Women; League of Women Voters; San Diego Girls Club Inc; The Links, Inc. **HONORS/ACHIEVEMENTS:** Citizen of the Year Awd Omega Psi Phi 1977; Recognition Awd San Diego Br NAACP 1977; Cert of Apprec San Diego City Schools 1978; Natl Recognition Awd Lambda Kappa Mu 1978; Natl Trends & Serv Honoree The Links Inc 1978; Action Enterprises Devel Community Serv Awd 1979; Valuable Serv Awd Natl Fed Bus & Professional Women's Clubs 1980; Woman of Accomplishment Central City Assn & Soroptimist Intl of San Diego 1981; listed in many Who's Who books. **BUSINESS ADDRESS:** Management Consultant, USN Dept, PO Box 14041, San Diego, CA 921140041.

MONTGOMERY, DWIGHT RAY
Clergyman. **PERSONAL:** Born Apr 08, 1950, Memphis, TN. **EDUCATION:** Lane Coll, BA 1968-72. **CAREER:** New Zion Bapt Ch, minister 1985; Goodwill Ind, cnslr 1977; Memphis Reg Sickle Cell Cncl, dep dir 1973-76. **ORGANIZATIONS:** Kappa Alpha Psi Alumni Chap 1969; Masonic Lodge; 32 deg Scotish Rite; Elks; Shriners 1969-71; found, dir Coalition of Benevolent Yth 1974. **HONORS/ACHIEVEMENTS:** Memphis Hall of Fame, Alpha Kappa Alpha Sor 1973-75; outstndng Young Men of Am 1975; Outstndng Citizen of Memphis, Tri-St Def Nwspr 1976; 50 Future Black Ldrs, Ebony Mag Chicago 1978. **BUSINESS ADDRESS:** 1210 College St, Memphis, TN 38114.

MONTGOMERY, EARLINE (NEE SMITH)
Attorney. **PERSONAL:** Born Nov 15, 1944, Montgomery, AL; married Clarence; children: Rhonda Lynn, Clarence III. **EDUCATION:** AL St U, BA 1968; Emory U, JD 1971. **CAREER:** Pvt Prac, atty 1977-; Fulton Co Juvenile Ct 1973-77; Spaulding Montgomery & Asso, 1972. **ORGANIZATIONS:** Mem GA St Bar; Gates City Bar Assn; Nat Bar Assn; admitted to prac before all GA cts & US Dist Ct Pres, Neighbors Interested in Progress 1977; chmn Curriculum Com, Optimum Prog for Ed in DeKalb 1975; Gresham Pk Athl Assn 1974-77; S DeKalb Coalition 1977; DeKalp Bo PTA 1972-77. **BUSINESS ADDRESS:** 1485 Gordon St SW, Atlanta, GA 30310.

MONTGOMERY, EARLINE ROBERTSON
Corporate executive. **PERSONAL:** Born Aug 18, 1944, New Orleans, LA; daughter of Harold C Robertson and Ella Jones Robertson; married Murray Montgomery, Jr, Jun 03, 1983. **EDUCATION:** TX Southern Univ, Houston, TX, BS, 1977; Univ of Houston, Houston, TX, post graduate work, 1978. **CAREER:** City of Houston, Houston, TX, personnel mgr, 1974-88; Robertson & Assoc Inc, Houston, TX, owner & pres, 1988-; FamCorp USA Mktg, Houston, TX, vice pres, Human Resources, 1989. **ORGANIZATIONS:** Mem, Alpha Kappa Alpha Sorority, Inc, 1964-; mem, Amer Compensation Assn, 1978-; mem, Natl Forum for Black Public Admin, 1986-; commr, Mayor's Affirmative Action Advisory Commn, 1987-88; co-chmn of fund raising comm, Natl Urban League, 1988; chmn of membership comm, NFBPA, Houston Chapter, 1988; consultant, The Hackney Co, 1988; mem, Natl Urban League, 1988-; consultant, The Winning Edge, 1989; chmn of By-Laws Comm, NFBPA Houston Chapter, 1989; parlimentarian, NFBPA, Houston chapter, 1989. **HONORS/ACHIEVEMENTS:** Outstanding Young Woman of Amer Award, 1978; author, "Clerical Training Manual, 1980"; author "Job Performance Appraisal Manual," 1981; 1st Women of Achievement Award, 100 Top Women of Achievement, 1989. **BUSINESS ADDRESS:** Vice Pres, Human Resources, FamCorp-USA Mktg, Inc, 3100 Richmond Ave, Suite 213K, Houston, TX 77098.

MONTGOMERY, ETHEL CONSTANCE
Business executive. **PERSONAL:** Born Jul 10, 1931, Morristown, NJ; widowed; children: Byron, Lisa. **EDUCATION:** Fairleigh Dickinson U, Attend. **CAREER:** AT&T Bell Labs, supv 1985-, grp supr 1978, prsnl rep, affirm act coord 1975; Wstrn Elec Co, salaried prsnl rels, prsnl results invtgtr, tech clk, sec, steno sec 1968-75; Bell Tel Co, typist 1968; Silver Burdette, Morristown Ship, 1967; Warner Lambert Inc, coder 1965; Morristown Neighborhood House, prog dir, coord, vol, grp worker, sec 1951-64. **ORGANIZATIONS:** Ldr Girl Scout 1952; pres PTA 1957; Carettes Inc 1959; sec, treas, vp, corrs sec Carettes Inc 1959-76; mem, vp, pres Morristown Bd Ed 1966-70; corrs sec Morris Co Sch Bd Assn 1969; mem Morristown Civil Rights Commn 1969; Morristonw Comm Act Com 1969; Urban Leag & Family Srv 1970; Yth Empl Srv 1970; United Fund Adv Bd 1970; vice pres Morris Sch Dist Bd Ed 1972-74; mem St Bd Ed 1975; Juv Conf 1977; adv com Meml Hosp 1977; mem Gov Byrn's Govt Cost & Tax Policy Com 1977; mem 1982-, pres 1984,86,87 Morristown Council. **HONORS/ACHIEVEMENTS:** Morris Co Urban LeagAward 1953, 1963; Outstndng Women of NJ, Fairleigh DickinsonUniv 1964; Morris Co NAACP Award 1970; Lambda Kappa Mu Sor Award 1970; Trancendtial Meditaiton Award 1977; Nat Black Achiever 1979. **BUSINESS ADDRESS:** Supervisor, AT&T Bell Labortories, 1 Whippany Rd, Whippany, NJ 079810903.

MONTGOMERY, EVANGELINE JULIET
Business executive. **PERSONAL:** Born May 02, 1933, New York, NY. **EDUCATION:** Los Angeles City Coll, AA 1958; CA State Univ Los Angeles, attended 1958-62; Univ of CA Berkeley, attended 1968-70; CA Coll of Arts & Crafts, BFA 1969; Museum Studies and Workshops, 1970-83. **CAREER:** Freelance artist 1960-; EJ Assoc, art consultant to museums, comm organizations and colleges 1967-; Montgomery & Co, exhibits specialist/freelance art consultant 1969-73; AR Urban Systems Inc, vp/dir 1973-78; Amer Assn for State and Local Hist, workshop coordinator 1979; Arts America, program officer, 1983-. **ORGANIZATIONS:** Art commr San Francisco Art Commission 1976-79; natl coordinator of regions Natl Conf of Artists 1973-81; natl fine arts & culture dir Natl Assn Negro Business & Professional Women Clubs Inc 1976-78; pres Metal Arts Guild 1972-74; pres Art West Assn North Inc 1967-78; advisory bd Parting Ways Ethnohistory Museum 1977-; bd mem Museum Natl Center Afro-Amer Artists 1974-; mem Amer Museums Assn 1970-; mem Coalition 100 Black Women 1984-; mem of bd of dir, Dist of Columbia Arts Center, 1989-. **HONORS/ACHIEVEMENTS:** Natl Program Award NANB & P Women Clubs Inc 1977; Service Awards Natl Conf of Artists 1970, 1974, 1976; Museum Grant Natl Endowment for the Arts Smithsonian Prof Fellowship 1973; Grant 3rd World Fund 1974; Special Achievement Award, Arts America, 1989.

MONTGOMERY, FRED O.
Banking administrator. **PERSONAL:** Born Jan 23, 1922, Oak Ridge, LA; married Hazel White; children: Daryl Young, Cynthia. **EDUCATION:** Atlanta Coll, Mortuary Sci 1942. **CAREER:** Morehouse Funeral Home, mortician 1943-76; D&M Casket Co, owner, mgr 1959; Apex Vending Co, owner 1960-76; Ins Co, pres; Montgomery Funeral Home, owner; Security Natl Bank, dir. **ORGANIZATIONS:** Police juror Parish Governing Body 1974; pres Insurance Co 1976; dir Security Natl Bank 1985; treas, interim bd chmn 1987 Morehouse Concern Citizens Civil Club. **MILITARY SERVICE:** AUS 1st sgt 3 years; Battle Star & Good Conduct Medal 1940. **BUSINESS ADDRESS:** Dir, Security Natl Bank, 714 S Haggerty, Bastrop, LA 71220.

MONTGOMERY, GEORGE LOUIS, JR.
Realtor, banker. **PERSONAL:** Born Jul 13, 1934, St Louis, MO; children: Gay, Kelly. **EDUCATION:** St Louis U, BS 1956; Wash U, AD 1968. **CAREER:** St Louis Redeveal, real estate spec authority 1974; Kraft Foods Inc, salesman 1963-68; Conrad Liquor, salesman 1962-63; Universal Life Ins Co, salesman 1961-62. **ORGANIZATIONS:** Mem Indpd Fee Appraisers Assn 1974-; mem Realtist Assn of St Louis 1974-; vice-chmn Gateway Nat Bank of St Louis 1977; mem Wayman Temple AME Ch MemFrontiers Intl Inc 1974-; bd mem Annie Malone Children's Home 1976-; mem Pres Council of St LouisUniv 1973-; mem St Louis Jr C of C 1961-63; mem Nat Assn of Mrkt Dev 1961-63; past chmn Sel Ser Bd 1974. **HONORS/ACHIEVEMENTS:** Citizen of the Wk KATZ Radio 1961; Ebony Magz Most Eligible Bachelor 1964; Man of the Yr Frontiers Intl 1964. **MILITARY SERVICE:** USNR seaman 1956-58. **BUSINESS ADDRESS:** Vice Chairman, Gateway Natl Bank, 2838 N Union, St Louis, MO 63115.

MONTGOMERY, GREGORY B.
Attorney. **PERSONAL:** Born Mar 23, 1946, McKeesport, PA; married Patricia A Felton. **EDUCATION:** Rutgers Coll, AB 1968; Rutgers Law Sch Newark NJ, JD 1975. **CAREER:** Gregory B Montgomery PA, atty 1985; Forrestal Village Inc, corp sec 1978-79; S & E Const Corp, corp sec 1977-79; Fidelity First Corp, vice pres 1975-79. **ORGANIZATIONS:** Mem lwyr refferral & inform panel Nat Bar Assn; mem Am Bar Assn; mem Commercial Law Leag of Am; mem BA Law List; medm NJ Garden St & Camden Co Bar Assns; mem Nat Urban Leag. **HONORS/ACHIEVEMENTS:** USAF Commendtion Medal 1972. **MILITARY SERVICE:** USAF capt 1968-72. **BUSINESS ADDRESS:** 108 North Seventh St, Camden, NJ 08102.

MONTGOMERY, HARRY J.
Business executive. **PERSONAL:** Born Sep 25, 1939, Battle Creek; children: Victor, Meredith, Michelle. **EDUCATION:** Albion Coll, BA 1961. **CAREER:** Kellogg Co, sales rep 1961-65; MI Bell Telephone Co, div staff asst 1965-68; Estrn Airlines, mgr 1968-71; Gen Foods Corp Coor, Outrch Prog Tougaloo Coll, asso prsnl mgr 1985. **ORGANIZATIONS:** Adv bd Scormebe ProgUniv KS; del at large, bd dirs, conf rep Nat Urban Leag; mem Frontiers Intrntl; Jaycees; NAACP; mem Omicron Delta Kappa; Delta Sigma Rho. **MILITARY SERVICE:** MI Air Nat Guard. **BUSINESS ADDRESS:** 250 North St, White Plains, NY 10606.

MONTGOMERY, JAMES C.
Clergyman. **PERSONAL:** Born Feb 08, 1918, Lake, MS; married Mary I Roberts. **EDUCATION:** Rust Coll Holly Spg MS, 1952. **CAREER:** Mt Sinai Missionary Bapt Ch, pastor; Radio Shop, owner. **ORGANIZATIONS:** Mem NAACP. **HONORS/ACHIEVEMENTS:** Recip Award Comm Sch Improvement Prog 1961; Award of Apprec Metro Bapt Ch 1954; Award Dept of Christine Ed Nat Cncl Chs; Hon St of MI 68 Dist Ct Flint. **MILITARY SERVICE:** AUS pfc 1940. **BUSINESS ADDRESS:** Sinai Missionary Baptist Ch, 1215 Downey Avenue, Flint, MI 48505.

MONTGOMERY, JOE ELLIOTT
Public school teacher, mayor. **PERSONAL:** Born Jul 10, 1942, Hemingway, SC; son of Elliott Montgomery and Emma Jane Montgomery; married Phyoncia Montgomery, Apr 30, 1969; children: Charles Montgomery. **EDUCATION:** Allen Univ, Columbia, SC, BA, 1965, Univ of SC, graduate work. **CAREER:** City of New York, NY, counselor, 1965-66; Horry County Dept of Educ, teacher, 1966; Town of Atlantic Beach, Atlantic Beach, SC, mayor. **ORGANIZATIONS:** SC Educ Assn, Natl Educ Assn; Horry County Educ Assn. **HONORS/ACHIEVEMENTS:** Costa Carolina Coll, Certificate, 1979; Joint Center for Political Action, Certificate, 1979; Kappa Alpha Psi Fraternity, Certificate, 1982; Horry County Culture Assn, 1982; Natl Conf of Black, Certificate, 1984.

MONTGOMERY, KEESLER H.
Magistrate. **PERSONAL:** Born Oct 15, 1917, Carrollton, MS; son of Charlie Montgomery and Jennie Montgomery; married Josephine Chamberlain. **EDUCATION:** Prairie View State Univ, AB 1941; Suffolk Univ Law School, JD 1950; Boston Univ, MA 1960; Suffolk Univ, LLM 1961. **CAREER:** State of MA, asst atty gen 1953-60; US Circuit Ct of Appeals 1954; US Supreme Ct 1957; Roxbury Municipal Ct Comm of MA, magistrate. **ORGANIZATIONS:** Life mem & past Grand Exalted Ruler IBPOE; past Master JJ Smith Lodge of Prince Hall Masons 33rd degree; trustee Ebenezer Bapt Ch; trustee Andover Newton Theol Sch; life mem NAACP; bd mem Roxbury YMCA; Resthaven Nurs Home; United So Educ Settlements Greater Boston Fam Serv Assn; Visiting Nurse Assn. **HONORS/ACHIEVEMENTS:** Elks Alumni Award 1954 & 1957; Alumni Award Prairie View State Univ 1954; Disting Legal Serv Boston Policemen's Assn 1972; Paul Revere Bowl Past Masters Club, Prince Hall Masons. **MILITARY SERVICE:** USN Petty Officer 1943-45. **BUSINESS ADDRESS:** Magistrate, Roxbury Municipal Court, 101 Tremont St, Boston, MA 02108.

MONTGOMERY, MILDREN M.
Business executive. **PERSONAL:** Born Jan 27, 1929, Henderson, TX. **EDUCATION:** Prairie View A&M Coll, BS. **CAREER:** Dunbar HS Texarkana, tchr 1954-55; SW Med Sch

Dallas, resrch asso 1955-57; Samuels & Co Dallas, plant chemist, vice pres 1957-69; Garland Foods Inc, pres 1970-. **ORGANIZATIONS:** Mem Inst Food Tech; Am Inst Mgmt; Beta Kappa Chi; bd dirs Nat Assn Black Mfg Dallas C of C; dir Dallas Alliance Minority Enterprise; Alpha Phi Alpha Merit Schlrshp Com; adv dir Dallas Negro C of C; trustee St John Bapt Ch; mem NAACP; Boy Scouts of Am; YMCA; Gov Com to Rewrite Const; Nat Bus Leag; Urban Leag; Tri Racial Com. **HONORS/ACHIEVEMENTS:** Sam W Becker Award; Am Leg Award; AG Gaston Award 1971; Urban Leag Award 1971; Prairie View Alumni Award; Trail Blazers Award 1972; ICBO Award; Pan Helanic Award; Omega Award; Dallas County Comm Coll Award; Com 100 Award; Award Excel Off Minority Bus Enterprise; Alpha Merit Award. **MILITARY SERVICE:** 1 lt 1950-53. **BUSINESS ADDRESS:** 5003 S Lamar St, Dallas, TX 75215.

MONTGOMERY, OLIVER R.
Research assistant. **PERSONAL:** Born May 31, 1929, Youngstown, OH; married Thelma Howard; children: Darlene, Howard, Brenda, Oliver, Jr, Edwin. **EDUCATION:** BS 1956. **CAREER:** Untd Steelworkers of Am AFL-CIO, assoc res asst present. **ORGANIZATIONS:** Nat bd mem Sec Nat Afro-Am Labor Counc 1970-75; vice pres Untd Steelworkers Local 3657; natl bd & exec counc mem Coalition of Black Trade Unionists; bdmem Gr Pittsburgh ACLU 1972-75; chmn labor & ind com NAACP 1960-63; mem Kappa Alpha Phi Frat. **HONORS/ACHIEVEMENTS:** Recip A Philip Randolph Awd; awd cert of merit NAACP Urban League; Testimonial Dinner 1970; awds from Mayor, City Counc CAP ofcrs, OEO Progs. **MILITARY SERVICE:** AUS military sci instr. **BUSINESS ADDRESS:** Research Dept United Steelwork, Pittsburgh, PA 15222.

MONTGOMERY, OSCAR LEE
Educator. **PERSONAL:** Born Jul 19, 1949, Chapman, AL; married Alfredia Marshall; children: Paula Onese, Renita Falana. **EDUCATION:** Alabama A&M Univ, BS 1972; Purdue Univ, MS 1974, PhD 1976. **CAREER:** Union Hill PB Church, pastor 1977-; Alabama A&M Univ, asst prof 1976-81, assoc prof 1981, vice president. **ORGANIZATIONS:** Dir Alabama Ctr for Applications of Remote Sensing 1980-; pres GHIMF-Ministerial Fellowship 1980-; pres NAACP local chap 1982-84. **HOME ADDRESS:** 3800 Milbrae Dr, Huntsville, AL 35810.

MONTGOMERY, PAYNE
Educator, city official. **PERSONAL:** Born Nov 24, 1933, Bernice, LA; married Rosemary Prescott; children: Janice, Eric, Joyce. **EDUCATION:** Grambling Coll, BS 1956; Tuskegee Inst, MS 1969; NE LA U, 1969. **CAREER:** Morehouse Par Sch Bd, hum rel cnsl; City of Bastrop, city cnclmn; Morehouse HS, bsktbl coach 1959-69; Delta HS, soc stud tchr 1969-72. **ORGANIZATIONS:** Elec to City Cncl 1973; mem LA Ed Assn; Nat Ed Assn; Parish Rec Bd; C of C; Am Leg; bd dir Headstart; first pres Morehouse Comm Org; workedto increase black voter regist; evaluator Title VII Progs 1973-74. **HONORS/ACHIEVEMENTS:** Spl recog Coaching Record; Coach of Yr 1961. **MILITARY SERVICE:** AUS 1956-58. **BUSINESS ADDRESS:** Human Relations Office, Bastrop HS, Bastrop, LA.

MONTGOMERY, TRENT
University dean. **CAREER:** Southern University, School of Engineering, Baton Rouge, LA, dean. **BUSINESS ADDRESS:** Southern University, School of Engineering, PO Box 9969, Baton Rouge, LA 70813. *

MONTGOMERY, WILLIAM R.
Deputy secretary. **PERSONAL:** Born Dec 18, 1924, Uniontown; married Sarah Berger. **EDUCATION:** Wilberforce U, BA 1950; Grad Sch of Soc WrkUniv Pittsburgh, MSW 1955;Univ of Pittsburgh, Phd 1973. **CAREER:** Dept of Pub Welfare for Commonwealth of PA, program analyst 1985; PA Dept of Health, former dep sec for health sys devel; School of Health Professions Univ Pittsburgh, asst to vice chancelor 1970-75, asst prof, div of instructional serv 1972-78. **ORGANIZATIONS:** Exec dir Neighborhd Hlth Ctrs Assn 1968-70; dir Comm Orgn Planned Parenthood Ctr, Pittsburgh 1966-68; dir Neighborhood Prog Bus & Job Dev Corp Pittsburgh; DuquesneUniv Sch of Bus Asso in Continuing Ed, Pittsburgh 1964-66; consult PA Dept of Hlth 1960-64; dir Hlth Projs Urban Leag Pittsburgh; mem Am Pub Hlth Assn; Nat Assn of Black Soc Wrkrs; Nat Assn of Soc Wrkrs; Acad cert Soc Wrkrs; PA Pub Hlth Assn; Med Com on Hum Rights; Steering Com on Hlth Care in PA Black Caucus of Hlth Wrkrs of Am Pub Hlth Assn; chmn bd Homewood-Brushton Neighborhd Hlth Ctr; bd mem Pt Authority of Allegheny Co; bd trustees St Joh's Hosp; bd mem Wstrn PA Comp Hlth Planning Assn; Regional Cncl Am Arbritration Assn; mem various other civic orgns mem Zeta Sigma Pi Nat Hon Soc Sci Frat. **HONORS/ACHIEVEMENTS:** Recip Outstndng Cit Award Beltzhoover Neighborhd Cncl 1968; Outstndng Profls in Hum Svcs, Am Acad of Hum Serv 1974. **MILITARY SERVICE:** USN petty ofcr, 2nd class 1942-45. **BUSINESS ADDRESS:** PA Dept of Health, PO Box 90 Rm 807 Health & Welf, Harrisburg, PA 17120.

MONTGOMERY, WILLIE HENRY
Association executive. **PERSONAL:** Born Feb 20, 1939, Woodville, MS; married Thelma Johnson; children: Delores, Willie Jr, Monique. **EDUCATION:** YMCA Sch of Commerce, 1964; Loyola U, 1965; Nat AFL-CIO Hdqrtrs, internship 1973. **CAREER:** AFL-CIO, field rep 1985. **ORGANIZATIONS:** Past mem sec Young Dems of New Orleans; past chmn Labor Adv Com United Way of Gtr New Orleans; past exec bd mem LA Assn of Mntl Hlth; org LA APhilip Randolph Inst 1973; NAACP; Urban Leag of Gtr New Orleans; Met Area Com; LA Adv Cncl on Voc Tech Ed; LA Coop Org Com AFL-CIO. **HONORS/ACHIEVEMENTS:** Spl Serv Award Amalgamated Transit Union ALF-CIO; Testemonial Award LA A Philip Randolph Ins; Ldrshp Contrib Award New Orleans Chap A Philip Randolph Inst; Award United Way of Gtr New Orleans. **BUSINESS ADDRESS:** 1016 Carondelet Bldg, New Orleans, LA 70130.

MOO-YOUNG, LOUISE L.
Educator. **PERSONAL:** Born Dec 29, 1942, Lexington, MS; married Ervin; children: Troy, Tiffany, Tricia. **EDUCATION:** Nursing St Mary of Nazareth 1963; Roosevelt Univ, B Gen Studies 1974; Governors Univ BA; Roosevelt Univ, MPA 1975. **CAREER:** State Univ Instructor, Marion Adult Educ Center, com prof gov. **ORGANIZATIONS:** Pres Faulkner Sch Assn 1977-78; mem Bd Trustees Faulkner Sch 1977-78; beat rep 21st Dist Police; mem Gov Adv Cnc of Developmental Disabilites 1976-77; mem Comprehensive Sickle Cell Anemia Community Adv CncUniv of Chicago Neighborhood Health Cntr Adminstr Chicago Bd of Health Claude WB Holman Neighborhood Helath Cntr 1972-; pub health nurse supvr Chicago Bd of Health 1970-72; pub health field nurse Chicago Bd of Health 1964-70; staff nurse head nurse MI Ave Hosp Chicago 1963-64; part-time indu nurse Ryerson Stell; staff nurse Woodlawn Hosp; Past mem Am Nurses Assn; Economic & Gen Welfare Com; IL Nurses Assn; Pub Health Section IL Nurses Assn Sec 1975; ARC Nurse Active in Ch & Comm Affairs; chmn Health Task Force Chicago Urban League 1973-74; peer group educ com Loop Jr Coll; ex-oficio to Advisory Bd of Claude WB Holman Neighborhood Health Center; St Margaret Epis Church Vestery 1976-77; office mgr for Chicago Campaign Office 1975; mem Amer Soc of Pub Adminstrs; St Mary's Alumni; Roosevelt Univ Alumni. **HONORS/ACHIEVEMENTS:** Awarded by Jr Assn of Commerce Indus one of Chicago's Ten Outstanding Young Cits 1973-74; outstanding achvmt aw 4th Ward Dom Orgnz; recip cert The Emerging Women in Mgmt Workshop.

MOODIE, DAHLIA MARIA
Cable television communications executive. **PERSONAL:** Born Dec 19, 1959, San Francisco, CA; daughter of Alfred G Moodie and Nancy L Myers-Moodie. **EDUCATION:** Coll of the Holy Names, BA Organizational Soc, Bus & Indust, Indust Rec 1981; UC Berkeley, 1982-84, MSW 1984. **CAREER:** Inner City Youth Program, prog dir 1978-81; St Mary's Elderly Housing, retirement training asst 1980; Youth Employment Agency, work experience counselor, trainer 1980-83; Fairmont Hosp Psychiatric Day Treatment, treatment coord 1982-84; Holy Names High School, bus dept chair, school counselor 1984-85; City of Oakland, employee asst prog; Port of Oakland, employment resources devel coord 1985-. **ORGANIZATIONS:** Assoc mem Assn of Labor Mgmt Admin & Consult on Alcoholism 1985-; comm mem Women and Family Issues in the Work Place ALMACA 1985-; mem bd of advisors Turning Point Career Ctr 1986-; assoc mem Amer Soc for Training & Devel 1986-; employer adv bd mem Adelante/Asians for Job Oppty 1986-; classroom consultant Jr Achievement Project Business 1986; employer adv bd mem Local Employment Devel Dept 1987-; mem bd dir Youth Employment Corp 1987-; consultant, chair Job Preparation Sem. **HONORS/ACHIEVEMENTS:** Intl Dean's List 1980; Annual Scholarship Chi Kappa Rho 1980; Plaque Intl Youth in Achievement 1980; life mem Soc Sci Hon Soc Pi Gamma Mu 1981-; Scholarship CA Recreation Soc 1981; UC Berk Minority Fellowship Prog Grant 1982-84; Image Builder Awd Coll Bounders Comm 1986; publ Employment Resources Devel Prog Quarterly Newsletter for Port of Oakland tenants; media co-host Educ Highlights; Fellowship in Cable Television, Walter Kaitz Foundation 1989. **HOME ADDRESS:** 285 Van Bureau Ave #3, Oakland, CA 94610. **BUSINESS ADDRESS:** Cox Cable San Diego, 5159 Federal Blvd, San Diego, CA 92105.

MOODY, ANNE
Writer. **PERSONAL:** Born Sep 15, 1940, Wilkerson County, MS; daughter of Fred and Elmire Williams; married Austin Straus, Mar 09, 1967 (divorced); children: Sascha. **EDUCATION:** Natchez Junior College; Tougaloo College, BS, 1964. **CAREER:** Congress of Racial Equality, Washington, DC, organizer, 1961-63, fundaraiser, 1964; Cornell University, Ithaca, NY, civil rights project coordinator, 1964-65; writer. **ORGANIZATIONS:** International PEN. **HONORS/ACHIEVEMENTS:** Brotherhood Award, National Council of Christians and Jews, 1969; Best Book of the Year Award, National Library Association, 1969; Coming of Age in Mississippi, 1969; Silver Medal, Mademoiselle, 1970; Mr Death: Four Stories, 1975. **BUSINESS ADDRESS:** c/o Harper & Row, 10 East 53rd St, New York, NY 10022. *

MOODY, CHARLES DAVID, SR.
Educator, university administrator. **PERSONAL:** Born Aug 30, 1932, Baton Rouge, LA; son of James Nathaniel Moody and Rosetta Ella Hall Moody; married Christella Delois Parks; children: Charles David Jr, Corey Derrick, Cameron Dennis. **EDUCATION:** Central State Univ, BS Biology 1954; Chicago Tchrs Coll, MA Sci Ed 1961; Univ of Chicago, Cert Adv Study 1969; Northwestern Univ, PhD Ed Admin1971. **CAREER:** Mentally Handicapped Chicago Schs, tchr of educable 1959-62; Dist #143 1/2 Posen-Robbins IL, tchr of sci & soc studies 1962-64; Sch Dist #65 Evanston, asst principal 1964-68; Sch Dist #147, supt 1968-70; Urban Fellows TTT Prog North WU, instr 1979-70; Div of Educ Specialist Univ MI, chmn 1973-77;Proj for Fair Admn Student Disc Univ MI, dir 1975-80; Univ MI, prof educ SOE 1970-, dir prog for educ oppor 1970-87, dir ctr for sex equity in schs 1981-87, vice provost for minority affairs 1987-. **ORGANIZATIONS:** Fndr/ex bd NABSE 1970-; pres/fndr CD Moody & Assocs Inc 1981-; bd dirs Ann Arbor NAACP 1983-85. **HONORS/ACHIEVEMENTS:** Awd of Respect Washtenaw Comm Coll Ann Arbor MI 1984; Dr of Laws Degree Central State Univ 1981; Comm Leader Awd Ann Arbor Veterans Admn Med Ctr 1980; Professional of the Yr Awd Ann Arbor Chap of Natl Assn of Negro Businesses & Professional Women Inc 1979; Charter Inductee, Central State Univ, Wilberforce OH 1989. **MILITARY SERVICE:** AUS capt 1954-56. **BUSINESS ADDRESS:** Vice Provost for Minority Affairs, Office of Academic Affairs, The University of Michigan, 503 Thompson St, 3052 Fleming Admin Building, Ann Arbor, MI 48109-1340.

MOODY, ERIC ORLANDO
Attorney. **PERSONAL:** Born Jul 16, 1951, Petersburg, VA; married Sherrie Y Brown. **EDUCATION:** Lafayette Coll, AB Philosophy 1973; Univ of VA School of Law, JD 1976. **CAREER:** VA Beach Police Dept, uniformed police officer 1974; WINA/WOMC Radio, reporter & announcer 1974-75; Neighborhood Youth Corps, client counselor 1975-76; Norfolk State Coll, instr 1977-78;; Eric O Moody & Assoc PC, sr partner 1976-. **ORGANIZATIONS:** Mem Coll Bd of Trustees; mem VA State Bar, Portsmouth Bar Assoc, Old Dominion Bar Assoc, Amer Bar Assoc, Chesapeake Bar Assoc, Twin City Bar Assoc; bd of dir Chesapeake YMCA, NAACP, Chesapeake Men for Progress, Chesapeake Forward, Boy Souts of Amer; mem Fellowship United Church of Christ. **HONORS/ACHIEVEMENTS:** Dean's List; George F Baker Scholar; Debate Team; Substitute Judge City of Chesapeke; Indust Devel Authority. **BUSINESS ADDRESS:** Senior Partner, Eric O Moody & Assoc PC, 600 Crawford St Ste 202 A, Portsmouth, VA 23705.

MOODY, FREDREATHA E.
Business executive. **PERSONAL:** Born Dec 04, 1941, Washington, DC; divorced; children: Bruce L, Frieda D, Suzan C, Ron K. **EDUCATION:** Howard Univ, attended 1960-61; Montgomery Coll, attended 1971-72; Amer Univ, attended 1972-73. **CAREER:** Georgetown Univ, supr keypunch div 1964-70; Vitro Labs, data proc coord 1970-78; Tab Products, mkt & sales spec 1973-79; Market Concepts Inc, vice president 1980-83; Affairs by Freddi, president; Seagull Publishing & Rsch Co Inc, pres 1984; Emphasis Magazine, editor 1982-; Entrepreneuring Women Magazine, publisher & editor 1982-. **ORGANIZATIONS:** Chap sec Washington DC Chap Natl Assn of Market Developers Inc 1978-80; natl bd mem Natl

Assn of Market Developers Inc 1980-; com mem Mayor's Complete Count Com Wash DC 1979-; chairperson-pub relations Natl Council of Negro Women DC Chap 1980-; pres Forum for Women Bus Owners 1982-83; chair Task Force for Black Women Business Owners 1983; natl sec Natl Assn of Market Developers 1982-; pres Natl Assn of Market Developers DC 1984; in-house consul to dir of develop Congressinal Black Caucus Found. **HONORS/ ACHIEVEMENTS:** Data Entry Rookie of the Yr TAB Prods Rockville MD 1974; Outstanding Sales Performance TAB Prods Rockville MD 1975-77; 80/20 Club (top sales) TAB Prods Rockville MD 1978; Cert of Appreciation Census Adv Com Office of the Mayor Washington DC 1980.

MOODY, HAROLD L.
Educator. **PERSONAL:** Born Sep 06, 1932, Chicago, IL; married Shirley Mc Donald; children: Michele Marcia. **EDUCATION:** Chicago Teacher, BE 1954, ME 1961. **CAREER:** Williams Elem School, teacher 8 yrs; Ray Elem School, teacher 8 yrs; S Shore HS, audio visual con 1 yr; Deneen Elem School, principal 1970-. **ORGANIZATIONS:** Bd of dir Elementary Press Assoc, Phi Delta Kappa, Chicago Principal Assoc, Chicago Area Reading Assoc, Intl Reading Assoc, Block Club, Steering Comm Police Comm Workshops 3rd dist; mem bd of dir Salem House Luth Soc Serv Agency; mem First Unitarian Church. **HONORS/ ACHIEVEMENTS:** Best Teacher Awd Chicago Bd of Ed; Scholarship Harvard Univ 1963; Serv Awd Park Manor Neighbors Comm Org 1979. **MILITARY SERVICE:** USNG 2 yrs. **BUSINESS ADDRESS:** Principal, Deneen Elementary School, 7240 S Wabash, Chicago, IL 60619.

MOODY, LYNNE GATLIN
Actress. **CAREER:** Worked as stewardess; television and film actress. **HONORS/ ACHIEVEMENTS:** Regular appearances on That's My Mama, Soap, and E R; actress in Roots and Roots: The Next Generation; guest appearances on Murder, She Wrote, Amen, and Hill Street Blues; plays Patricia Williams on Knots Landing. **BUSINESS ADDRESS:** Lynne Moody, actress, Knots Landing, c/o CBS, 51 West 52nd St, New York, NY 10019. *

MOODY, WILLIAM DENNIS
Dentist. **PERSONAL:** Born Jun 06, 1948, White Plains, NY; daughter of R William Moody and Rebecca Moody. **EDUCATION:** North Central Coll, BA 1970; SUNY Buffalo, DDS 1974. **CAREER:** Private practice, dentist. **ORGANIZATIONS:** Program chmn Greater Metropolitan Dental Soc 1977-78; bd of dirs Greenburgh Neighborhood Health Center 1979-81, Greenburgh Comm Center 1982-83, Thomas H Slater Center 1984-87; mem White Plains Dental Forum, Scarsdale Dental Soc; bd of dir Union Child Day Care Center; mem Amer Dental Assn, Alpha Omega Frat, Natl Dental Assn, Greater Metro New York Dental Soc; pres, Greater Metropolitan Dental Society, 1987-89. **BUSINESS ADDRESS:** 48 Mamaroneck Ave, White Plains, NY 10601.

MOODY, YVONNE K.
Nurse. **PERSONAL:** Born Nov 27, 1936, Jacksonville, FL; divorced. **EDUCATION:** Grady Meml Sch Nursing, diploma 1957; Tuskegee Inst, BSN 1965; Nursing Adminstrn De paul U, MA. **CAREER:** Vet Adminstrn Cntrl Ofc, chief of nurs prog & leg affairs; VA Hosp Tuskegee, staff nurse; VA Resrch Hosp, staff nurse to asst chief nurse; VA Hosp Allen Park, presently chief nursing svc. **ORGANIZATIONS:** Mem Am Nurses Assn; Am Soc for Nursing Serv Adminstrs; Detroit Area Assn; Nursing Serv Adminstrn. **HONORS/ ACHIEVEMENTS:** Outstndg fed female empl Detroit Area 1975. **BUSINESS ADDRESS:** Veterans Administration, 810 Vermont Ave, Nursing Service 118H, Washington, DC 20420.

MOON, WALTER D.
Government official. **PERSONAL:** Born Aug 10, 1940, Marietta, GA; married Winford G Strong; children: Sonja, Sonita. **EDUCATION:** Kennesaw Jr Coll; Savannah State Coll; Inst Computer Tech 1967. **CAREER:** Mails US Postal Serv Marietta GA, foreman; part-time bldg contractor. **ORGANIZATIONS:** Treas Future Devel Assn Inc Pres Concerned Citizens of Marietta; mem NAACP; Mem Marietta Cobb Bridges Prog; v-chmn Marietta Bd Edn; only Black elected Marietta Civil Serv Commn; mem USN Manpower Speakers Team Freshman Scholastic Savannah State Coll USN 1960-64. **MILITARY SERVICE:** USNR chief petty ofcr 1966-. **BUSINESS ADDRESS:** 257 Lawrence St NE, Marietta, GA 30060.

MOON, WARREN
Professional football player. **PERSONAL:** Born Nov 18, 1956, Los Angeles, CA. **EDUCATION:** Univ of WA. **CAREER:** Houston Oilers, professional football player (quarterback) 1984-. **ORGANIZATIONS:** Began W Moon's Chocolate Chippery while in Edmonton - has since sold stores and formed new corp in Houston. **HONORS/ ACHIEVEMENTS:** Coll, mem of team winning Rose Bowl over MI in which was named MVP; career marks at WA 142 of 496 for 3,277 yds and 19 TDs with career long of 78 in 1975; profl, holds two Oilers' passing records after one season - most yds gained passing 3,338 breaking old mark of George Blanda and sharing with Blanda mark for most 300 plus yard games passing in a season; pass attempts and completions are third best in Oilers history; named All NFL Rookie Team by Pro Football Writers,UPI and Pro Football Weekly as well as Football Digest's Rookie All-Star Team; longest TD completion was 75 yarder to Tim Smith vs San Diego Chargers; third best interception percentage (31) in AFC behind Eason (19) and Marino (30). **BUSINESS ADDRESS:** Houston Oilers, BOx 1516, Houston, TX 77001.

MOONE, JAMES CLARK
Federal government administration. **PERSONAL:** Born Aug 11, 1940, Fountain Inn, SC; married Rev Ruby R; children: Malaika (Ruby), Afua (Jamesa). **EDUCATION:** SC State Coll, BS 1958; Morgan State Univ, MS 1967; Howard Univ, PhD 1976. **CAREER:** Pilgrim H&L Ins Co, asst mgr 1959-69; Washington DC Public Schools, principal 1969-72; Georgetown Univ, prof 1978-82, founding dir African Studies 1982-. **ORGANIZATIONS:** Exec bd NAACP 1950-87; mem-at-large PUSH 1969-87; mem Pythagoras Lodge #74 33 degree PHA 1969-87; bd dir Montgomery Co MD 1980-87; bd of appeals City of Rockville MD 1986-87; dir communications Alpha Phi Alpha 1987; vp, exec dir Intl United Black Fund Inc. **HONORS/ACHIEVEMENTS:** NSF Grants Univ of Akron 1965-70; Human Rights Awd City of Rockville 1979; author "The Physical Qualities of Life in Sub-Saharan Africa" Brunswick Publ Co 1985; Amer Leadership Awd City of Denver CO 1987. **HOME ADDRESS:** 1204 Potomac Valley Rd, Rockville, MD 20850.

MOONE, WANDA RENEE
Ombudsman. **PERSONAL:** Born Oct 12, 1956, Greensboro, NC; daughter of Connell Moone and Beulah Moone; children: Dedrick L. **EDUCATION:** NC A&T State Univ, BS (cum laude) 1982; Univ NC Chapel Hill, MSW 1983. **CAREER:** Bowman Group Sch of Medicine Amos Cotlage Rehab Hosp, social worker I 1983-85; St James Nursing Ctr Inc, dir social serv 1985-87; Rockingham Council on Aging, case manager 1987-89; Piedmont Triad Council of Governments, regional long term care ombudsman 1989-. **ORGANIZATIONS:** Mem NASW 1982-, Alpha Delta Mu 1982-; field instructor Bennett Coll 1985-86, NC A&T State Univ & UNC Greensboro 1986-; mem NC Assn of Black Social Workers 1987-, NAACP 1987-, NC Assn of Health Care Facilities 1987-88, Academy of Certified Social Workers, 1988, Alzheimer's Assn, 1989; advisory committee member United Services for Older Adults 1989-. **HONORS/ACHIEVEMENTS:** NC Dean's List 1979-80; Certificate Alpha Delta Mu Natl Social Work Hon Soc Rho Chap 1982-. **BUSINESS ADDRESS:** Regional Long Term Care Ombudsman, Piedmont Triad Council of Governments, Wilmington Bldg Suite 201, 2216 W Meadowview Road, Greensboro, NC 27407-3480.

MOORE, ACEL
Editorial board member. **PERSONAL:** Born Oct 05, 1940, Philadelphia, PA; divorced; children: Acel Jr. **EDUCATION:** Settlement Music Sch 1954-58; Charles Morris Price Sch 1966-64. **CAREER:** Philadelphia Inquirer, assoc editor 1981-, staff writer 1968-81, editorial clerk 1964; copy boy 1965. **ORGANIZATIONS:** Pres Philadelphia Assn of Black Journalists; founding mem Nat Assn of Black Journalists Sigma Delta Chi; mem Amer Soc of Newspaper Editors, Pulitzer Prize Juror. **HONORS/ACHIEVEMENTS:** Mng editors award PA Assn of Press 1975-76; PA Prison Soc award; humanitarian award House of Umoja; comm serv award Youth Devel Ctr; journalism award Philadelphia Party 1976; Philadelphia Bar Assn award; paul robeson award Afro-Am History Mus 1976; Nat Headliners award; natl clarion award Women in Communication; Nat Bus League of Philadelphia award; N Philadelphia Mothers Concern award; achievement award White Rock Bapt Ch; yvonne motley mccabe award Swarthmore Coll Annual UpwardBound 1977; nieman flwshp HarvardUniv 1979-80; scales of justice award Philadelphia Bar Assn 1970; Pulitzer Prize 1976; Robert F Kennedy Jour Awd 1976; Heywood Broun Awd 1976. **MILITARY SERVICE:** AUS 1959-62. **BUSINESS ADDRESS:** Associate Editor, Philadelphia Inquirer, 400 N Broad St, Philadelphia, PA 19101.

MOORE, ALBERT
Public relations consultant, educational administrator. **PERSONAL:** Born Feb 17, 1952, Johnsonville, SC; married Marie Durant; children: Porchia Atiya, Chelsey Maria. **EDUCATION:** Friendship Jr Coll, 1970-71; Benedict Coll, BA Pol Sci 1974; Univ of SC, Publ Admin 1979-80; SC Criminal Justice Acad, Cert Correction Officer 1981-. **CAREER:** Crayton Middle School, sub techer 1974-75; Square D Co, prod coord 1975-76; US Auto Assoc, vice pres mktg & publ relations 1976-77; Al's Drive In Restaurant, owner 1976-77; Benedict Coll, equip mgr 1977-79, tech asst, dean of acad affairs 1979-82; Natl Conf of Black Mayors Prog, asst dir 1979-82; Central Correctional Inst, correction officer II 1981-83; Benedict Coll, coord of spec svcs, publ relations 1982-84; St Augustines Coll, dir public relations1984-. **ORGANIZATIONS:** Attend confs & workshops in vairous cities Natl Conf of Black Mayors 1979,80,81,82; seminar Robert R Morton Mem Inst 1980; panalist Amer Census Bureau Workshop 1980; participant Assoc of Records Mgrs 1981; mem Benedict Coll Jr Alumni Club, Drexel Lake Residents Civic Org, NAACP, SCARMA, SC Correction Officers Assoc; charter mem Benedict Coll Tiger Club. **HONORS/ACHIEVEMENTS:** Alternate delegate Richland Cty Dem Convention 1984. **HOME ADDRESS:** 2020 Drexel Lake Dr, Columbia, SC 29223. **BUSINESS ADDRESS:** Dir of Publicity & Pub Rel, St Augustines College, 1315 Oakwood Ave, Raleigh, NC 27611.

MOORE, ALICE EVELYN
Educator. **PERSONAL:** Born Feb 16, 1933, Washington, NC. **EDUCATION:** Tuskegee Inst, Social Studies 1950-55; NM Highlands Univ, History/Ed 1961-62; Johns Hopkins Univ, Certificate Negro & Sou Hist 1969-70; North TX State Univ, Certificate Aging Specialist 1979,82. **CAREER:** Young Women's Christian Assoc, teen-age dir 1955-56; Emerson Settlement House, group work 1957-58; Friendship Jr Coll, instr social sci 1962-71; Elizabeth City State Univ, instr social sci 1971-73; Claflin Coll, asst prof social sci 1974-80; Allen Univ, assoc prof social sci 1981-, interim dir academic affairs 1985-86, coord gerontology prog 1981-. **ORGANIZATIONS:** Counselor Epworth Children's Home 1981; mem/secty Resource Mobilization Adv Council Dept Social Serv of Richland Co 1981-84; founder/secty/treas Orangeburg Branch Assoc for Study of Life & History. **HONORS/ACHIEVEMENTS:** Volunteer of the Year Epworth Children's Home 1986. **BUSINESS ADDRESS:** Coord Gerontology Prog/Soc Sci, Allen University, 1530 Harden St, Columbia, SC 29204.

MOORE, ALSTORK EDWARD
Airline executive. **PERSONAL:** Born May 12, 1940, Washington, DC; son of Charles E Moore; married Geraldine L Hagens; children: Anthony, Robert, Shannon, Samuel. **EDUCATION:** Montgomery Coll, Washington, DC, AA, 1967-71; Amer Univ, Washinton, DC, BS, 1971-73. **CAREER:** United Airlines, Philadelphia, PA, supvr passenger serv, 1977-78; New York, NY, operation mgr cargo, 1978-81, New York, NY, staff representative personnel, 1981-82, Lincoln, NE, mgr of station operations, 1982-85, Washington, DC, mgr cust serv, 1985-86, gen mgr, customer serv, 1986-. **ORGANIZATIONS:** Mem, United Methodist Men, 1982-. **HONORS/ACHIEVEMENTS:** Award of Merit, United Airlines, 1977, 1980. **MILITARY SERVICE:** US Air Force, sargeant, 1958-65; received Good Conduct, 1961, 1964, Outstanding Unit, 1964, Longevity, 1965. **BUSINESS ADDRESS:** Gen Mgr Customer Serv, United Airlines, Washington Natl Airport, Main Terminal Rm 9, Washington, DC 20001.

MOORE, ANNIE JEWELL
Couturiere/fashion designer. **PERSONAL:** Born Sep 20, 1919, Daytona Beach, FL; daughter of James Moore (deceased) and Ora Lee Moore (deceased). **EDUCATION:** Spelman Coll, AB 1943; Fashion Academy, Golden Pen Certificate 1951-52; Ecole Guerre-Lavigne, Paris France, Certificate 1954; Marygrove Coll, Certificate 1976. **CAREER:** Ann Moore Inc, couturiere 1952-70; Detroit Public Sch System, teacher 1972-82; Atlanta Public Sch System, teacher 1985-87; Rich's Academy, couturiere 1986-; Ann Moore Inc, Detroit Michigan, fashion designer/pres 1952-70. **ORGANIZATIONS:** Vice pres Detroit Chap of The

NAASC 1980-82; chairperson of awds comm of the Atlanta Chap of NAASC 1986-87; mem, Ad Hoc Committee for Clothing and Textile, S M Brownell, Superintendent of Detroit Public Schools. **HONORS/ACHIEVEMENTS:** Produced Cent Fash Focus Spelman's 100th Anniversary 1981; Michigan Women Civic Council Awd 1982; Certificate of Recognition, Detroit Chapter of the Natl Alumnae Assn of Spelman College. **HOME ADDRESS:** 988 Palmetto Ave SW, Atlanta, GA 30314.

MOORE, ANTHONY LOUIS
Business executive. **PERSONAL:** Born Jan 10, 1946, Chicago, IL; married Joyce M Watson; children: Jason A. **EDUCATION:** Southern Illinois Univ, BS 1971; DePaul Univ, Grad Study 1976; Univ of Illinois Chicago, Grad Study 1978. **CAREER:** Vince Cullers Advertising, media buyer 1971-73, media planner 1973-74; Proctor & Gardner Advertising, assoc media dir 1974-76, media dir 1976-78, vice pres advertising serv. **ORGANIZATIONS:** Bd mem Faulkner School 1984-; mem Amer Advertising Fed 1971-; mem Amer Mgmt Assn 1976-; mem Natl Assn Market Devel 1975-; advisory bd Chicago YMCA 1976-; Alpha Delta Sigma 1970-; mem Stepp School; mem Chicago Media Director's Council 1986. **HONORS/ACHIEVEMENTS:** Creative Advertising Certificate, Assn of Natl Advertisers; Black Media Merit, Black Media Inc; Employee of the Year, Proctor & Gardner; Achievement Award, YMCA. **MILITARY SERVICE:** USMC E-4 1967-69; USMC Combat Corres Assn 1968-. **BUSINESS ADDRESS:** Vice President, Proctor & Gardner Advert Inc, 111 E Wacker Dr, Chicago, IL 60601.

MOORE, ARCHIBALD LEE WRIGHT
Former light-heavyweight champion. **PERSONAL:** Born Dec 13, 1916, Benoit, MS; married Joan; children: Anthony, D'Angelo, Hardy, Joanie, Rena, Billy. **CAREER:** Former Light-heavyweight boxing champion for ten yrs; dr training Any Boy Can Clubs; Dept of Housing and Urban Development, special assistant to Samuel Pierce, LA, 1980-89. **ORGANIZATIONS:** Mem NAACP; Urban League; Optimists Club; founder, dir ABC (Any Boy Can) Club 1965-. **HONORS/ACHIEVEMENTS:** Winner of 194 out of 229 professional bouts; 2nd Greatest Light Heavyweight Champion Ring Mag; Light Heavyweight Champion 1952. **BUSINESS ADDRESS:** Boxing Instructor, 3517 E St, San Diego, CA 92102.

MOORE, ARCHIE BRADFORD, JR.
Educator. **PERSONAL:** Born Jan 08, 1933, Montgomery, AL; married Dorothy Ann Flowers; children: Angelo Juan, Kimberly D'Anna. **EDUCATION:** AL State univ, BS 1959, MEd 1961; KS State Univ, PhD 1974. **CAREER:** Russell Co Public School System, teacher 1959-61; Montgomery Co Public School Sys, teacher 1961-69; Clarke Coll, asst prof of soc sci 1970-75; AL State Univ, dir of TCCP 1975-77; AL State Univ, coord of continuing educ 1977-78, dean of evening & weekend coll & public serv 1978-83, assoc prof of educ & spec asst to dean of grad studies & cont educ 1983-. **ORGANIZATIONS:** Mem Natl Educ Assn; mem AL Assn of Social Science & History Teachers; mem Amer Fed of Musicians Affiliated with AFL-CIO; mem Phi Beta Sigma Frat; mem Phi Delta Kappa Prof Educ Frat; mem Assn for Continuing Higher Educ; mem Natl Comm Educ Assn; chmn Catholic Charity Drive; mem Holy Name Soc; mem AL Center for Higher Educ Comm Serv Comm; mem College of Educ Curriculum Comm AL State Univ; mem AL State Univ Council of Academic Deans; chmn Resurrection Catholic School System Bd of Educ. **HONORS/ACHIEVEMENTS:** Grant Natl Science Found 1965; Fellowship Natl Defense Educ Act 1967, 1968, 1969; Fellowship Educ Prof Develop Act 1972-74; State Awd AL Social Studies-Fair Teacher Recognition 1968. **MILITARY SERVICE:** USN petty officer 3rd class 1952-56. **HOME ADDRESS:** 2966 Vandy Dr, Montgomery, AL 36110. **BUSINESS ADDRESS:** Associate Professor Education, Alabama State University, 915 S Jackson St, Montgomery, AL 36195.

MOORE, ARNOLD D.
Hearings officer secretary of state. **PERSONAL:** Born Mar 31, 1916, Selmer, TN; married Emma; children: Joyce Parson, Barbara Rochelle. **EDUCATION:** Springfield Jr Coll. **CAREER:** St Paul AME Ch Springfield, asst pastor; Allen Chapel AME Ch Taylorville, IL, pastor; State Office, claims examiner 1947-49; Dept Pub Welfare, pubrel 1949-59; juv prob officer 1959; Sec of State Titles & Regist Vehicle Sect, adminstr/hearings officer. **ORGANIZATIONS:** Mem bd Salvation Arym; Comm Action; Mental Health; USO; ARC; Ministrial Alliance; AME Coalition; 1st pres local chap NAACP. **HONORS/ACHIEVEMENTS:** Outstanding Layman's Award 1965; Scouters Key. **MILITARY SERVICE:** AUS Capt; Commendation Medal. **BUSINESS ADDRESS:** Hearings Officer, Secretary of State, Centennial Bldg, Springfield, IL 62722.

MOORE, ARTHUR C.
Clergyman. **PERSONAL:** Born Jan 04, 1894, Philadelphia, PA; married Marguerite C Young. **EDUCATION:** Temple Univ Philadelphia Div Sch, MTh; Auburn Sem NY; Jewish Theol Sem. **CAREER:** St Cyprian's, 1924-45; St Simon's Ch New Rochelle, rector 1950-64; St Lukes Church, staff mem. **ORGANIZATIONS:** Mem Urban League; NAACP; founding mem Cncl Chs New Rochelle; pres Prot Min Assn; pres Minis Alliance; Alpha Phi Alpha; chmn Com Elderly NW Coalition Comprehensive Health Bd of Dir; NW Chap Philadelphia NAACP; NW Inter-Faith Movement. **HONORS/ACHIEVEMENTS:** Better Housing Award Philadelphia Afro-Amer 1944; Vol Serv Award NY State 1958; Award St Luke's Ch 1971; NW Chap NAACP Award 1972. **BUSINESS ADDRESS:** St Luke's Church, 5421 Germantown Avenue, Philadelphia, PA 19144.

MOORE, BOBBY See RASHAD, AHMAD

MOORE, BOOKER
Professional athlete. **PERSONAL:** Born Jun 23, 1959, Flint, MI; married Stephanie; children: Jashua. **EDUCATION:** PA State Univ, attended. **CAREER:** Buffalo Bills, fullback 1981-. **HONORS/ACHIEVEMENTS:** Twice caght a career high nine passes; scored his one professional touchdown in the Orange Bowl last year; played in 2 Fiesta Bowls along with a Liberty & Sugar Bowl.

MOORE, CARMAN LEROY
Composer, music critic, educator. **PERSONAL:** Born Oct 08, 1936, Lorain, OH; divorced; children: Martin, Justin. **EDUCATION:** OH State U, BMus 1958; Juilliard Sch of Music, MS 1966. **CAREER:** Manhattanville Coll, asst prof of music/composer; New School for Social Research, Queens Coll, NY; Univ Yale Graduate School of Music; The Village Voice, music critic 1965-, NY Times; contributed since 1969; The Saturday Review; rock lyricist. **HONORS/ACHIEVEMENTS:** Compositions include "African Tears"; "Drum Major"; "Wildires & Field Songs" (commissioned by NY Philharmonic Orch); "Gospel Fuse" (commissioned by San Francisco Symphony Orch); hit, A Concerto for Percussion and Orchestra "Wild Gardens of the Loup Garou" music theatre work "Paradist Lose-The Musical". **BUSINESS ADDRESS:** Composer/Conductor, The Carman Moore Ensemble, 148 Columbus Ave, New York, NY 10023.

MOORE, CAROL LOUISE (NEE WOOD)
Educator. **PERSONAL:** Born Sep 23, 1943, Columbus, OH; married Jesse T. **EDUCATION:** PA State U, PhD 1970; PA State U, MS 1969; OH State U, BS 1965. **CAREER:** Univ of Rochester NY, asst prof biology present; Dept of Radiation Biology & Biophysics School of Med & Dentistry Dept of Biology Univ of Rochester, assoc asst prof 1971-74; Div Human Genetics Dept of Anatomy School of Med & Dentistry Univ of Rochester, res asst 1970-71; The Highland School white Plains, science instr 1965-67. **ORGANIZATIONS:** Mem Genetics Soc of Am; Phi Epsilon Phi; Sigma Delta Epsilon. **HONORS/ACHIEVEMENTS:** Sicle Cell Anemia Vol in inner city comm &Univ of Rochester Liason; Cystic fibrosis fund raising vol; campus activities; Immaculate Conception Ch Recip Nat Sci Found Summer Fellowship 1965; Nat Defense Educ Act Fellow 1967-70; awards for genetics res to be conducted atUniv of Rochester Nat Sci Found Am Cancer Soc; Monroe Co Cancer & Leukemia Assn Inc. **BUSINESS ADDRESS:** Dept of Biology Univ of Rochester, Rochester, NY 14627.

MOORE, CHARLES D.
Business executive. **PERSONAL:** Born Jun 06, 1906, Seville, GA; married Julia Tilley. **EDUCATION:** Lane Coll TN; Malone Coll. **CAREER:** Plott Real Esate Agy; Fort Motor Co, asso 19 yrs. **ORGANIZATIONS:** Pres Canton NAACP 1952-56; pres CHIP Health Prog; 3rd vice pres Canton Urban League; co-dir FACE; trustee Bethel Christian Meth Episcopal Ch. **HONORS/ACHIEVEMENTS:** Honored by Mayor Stanley Cmich for founding CHIP Housing & Med Prog 1975; honored by Stark Co Club of Negro Bus & Professional Women 1968; honored for Outstanding Comm Serv Ford Motor Co 1975. **MILITARY SERVICE:** AUS sgt 1942-45. **BUSINESS ADDRESS:** 4646 W Tuscarawas, Canton, OH 44708.

MOORE, CHARLES W.
Educational administrator. **PERSONAL:** Born Nov 02, 1923, Macon, GA; married Mary Agnes DuBose; children: Tallulah Ragsdale. **EDUCATION:** Morris Brown Coll, AB 1950; NY U, MBA 1952; Univ of UT, MS 1975; Daniel Payne Coll, Dr of Humane Letters 1971; Morris Brown Coll, LLD 1980. **CAREER:** Morris Brown Coll, bus mgr 1951-66; US Dept of HEW, educ prog officer 1966-78; US Dept of HHS, financial mgr 1978-85; Morris Brown Coll, vice pres finance 1985. **ORGANIZATIONS:** Treas Am Assn of Coll & Univ Bus Off 1960-66; mem Assn of Govt Accountants 1983-; treas Atlanta Investment Assoc Inc 1956-; chmn bd of dir Butler St YMCA 1979-81; natl treas Phi Beta Sigma Frat Inc 1970-; pres Natl Alumni Assn Morris Brown Coll 1984-; mem bd of stewards Big Bethel AME Ch 1955. **HONORS/ACHIEVEMENTS:** Alumnus of the Yr Morris Brown Coll Natl Alumni Assn 1968 & 1975; Distinguished Serv Award Phi Beta Sigma Frat Inc 1978; Distinguished Serv Award Rust Coll 1971; Distinguished Leadership Award United Negro Coll Fund 1985; Special Achievement Award US Dept of Health & Human Serv 1984. **MILITARY SERVICE:** AUS staff sgt; Good Conduct Medal. **HOME ADDRESS:** 734 Flamingo Dr SW, Atlanta, GA 30311.

MOORE, CHARLIE W.
Retired supervisor civil engineer. **PERSONAL:** Born Feb 16, 1926, Chattanooga, TN; married Elva M Stanley; children: Charlie W Jr, Kelli Noelle. **EDUCATION:** Hampton Inst, BS 1950; Univ of AL, 1951; Villanova Univ, 1967-68. **CAREER:** USA Corps of Engr Anchorage AL Dist, struc engr 1951-52; AUS Corps of Engrs N Atlantic Div, constr mgmt engr 1952-55; USAF New Castle Co Airport, constr mgmt engr 1955-57; USAF Fifth AF Ashiya & Tokyo, Japan, gen engr 1957-58; Ankara Turkey USAFE HQ USLOG, maintenance engr 1958-61; AUS Corps of Engrs, civil engr 1962, Civil Defense Support Br, civil engr 1962-65, chief resident engr, support group 1975-79; Engrg Support Serv Corp, pres; FEMA NY, suprv civil engr; Fed Civil Serv RegIII, retired. **ORGANIZATIONS:** Mem Amer Soc of Civil Engrs, Soc of Amer Military Engrs, PA Soc of Professional Engrs, Camphor United Meth Church; mem Natl Defense Exec Reserve, Frontiers Intl. **HONORS/ACHIEVEMENTS:** Letter of Appreciation, Yahata Labor Mmgt Office (1st US civilian to receive a letter of apprec, Mssrs Schechet Kasparian Falcey support provied in connection with Mercer Cty Survey Briefing 1974, Mercer Cty CD Coord 1974; Outstanding Performance New England Div USC of E 1976; Outstanding Commendation DefenseCivil Preparation Agency 1978; Mr Lynch CommShelter Prog Jerry Vallery GSA Philadelphia Philadelphia Urban Coalition School Prog for Minority Contractors; Mr Duscha Qualified Instrs Briefing Conf New York City 1969. **MILITARY SERVICE:** USN 1944-46. **BUSINESS ADDRESS:** President, Engineering Support Serv Corp, 4950 Parkside Ave Ste 502, Philadelphia, PA 19131.

MOORE, CHRISTINE JAMES
Retired. **PERSONAL:** Born Sep 09, 1930, Windsor, NC; daughter of Henry James and Maude Boxley James; married Marcellus; children: Lisa M Barkley. **EDUCATION:** Morgan State Coll Baltimore, BA 1952; Columbia Univ New York, MA 1962; Johns Hopkins Univ Syracuse Univ. **CAREER:** Booker T Washington Jr HS, tchr 1952-59; counselor 1959-64; Balt Secondary Schs, specialist guidance 1965-69; Workshop Employment Opportunities for Disadvantaged Youth Johns Hopkins U, asst dir 1966; instr 1969-70; Dev Studies Community Coll Balt, dir 1969-74; Comm Coll Balt Harbor Campus, dean student services 1974-79; Comm Coll Balt, dean staff devel present; Comm Coll of Baltimore, retired exec asst to the pres 1979-83; House of Delegates of theMD Gen Assembly, reader. **ORGANIZATIONS:** Commn Higher Educ Middle States Assn Coll & Secondary Schs 1977-83; mem Am Personnel & Guidance Assn; Am Coll Personnel Assn; bd dir Mun Employees Credit Union of Baltimore 1975-83; bd dir Arena Players Comm Theater; bd of dir 4th Dist Dem Orgn 1980-82; Mayor's Steering Com Balt Best Promotional Camp 1976-87; NAACP; Nat Council Negro Women; Urban League Consult counseling & human relations; pub speaker; publs in periodicals; bd dir Baltimore MD Metro YWCA 1983-86; bd of examiners Speech Pathology 1983-85; commissioner Commission on Med Discipline for MD 1984-; bd of trust City Temple of Balto Baptist Church 1986-; mem Maryland State Bd of Physicians Quality Assurance 1988-90; mem Afro Amer empowerment Project 1987-. **HONORS/ACHIEVEMENTS:** Outstanding Educators of Am 1973; Who's Who Among Am Women 1972; Who's Who in

the E 1975; Outstanding Delta of Yr 1974; Arean Players Artistic Awd Community Theater Group 1979; One Hundred Outstanding Women in Baltimore Delta Sigma Theta Sor 1975.

MOORE, CLEOTHA FRANKLIN
Manager. **PERSONAL:** Born Sep 16, 1942, Canton, MS; married Norma Jo Ramsey; children: Faith Veleen, Sterling Kent. **EDUCATION:** IN Central Univ, BS 1960-64; Ball State Univ, Ed 1965-; IN Univ Purdue Univ Indpls, Bus Studies 1975-. **CAREER:** Wood HS Indianapolis Publ School Syst, teacher, coach 1964-69; IN Natl Bank, personnel admin 1969-74; RCA/Consumer Electronics, employee relations mgr 1974-. **ORGANIZATIONS:** Mem Natl Assoc Suggestion Syst 1976,79-80; vstg prof Black Exec Exchange Prog 1977-79; 1st vp, newsletter ed IN State Missionary Bapt Convention 1968-79; mem NAACP 1969-; asst scout master Boy Scouts of Amer 1970-73; adv Indianapolis Jr Achievement 1970-79; vol Head Start Prog 1974; bd of dir IN Central Univ Alumni Assoc 1977-79; big brother Big Brothers 1977-83; trustee, asst treas S Calvary Bapt Church 1977-; pres Audubon Terr Neighborhood Assoc 1978-; mem task force Mayors Ridesharing Work Rescheduling Task Force 1979; hs stg teacher Indianapolis Jr Achievement 1979-; bd mem Metro School Dist of Warren Twp (1st black to be elected to this post); instr Labor Relations IN Univ, Purude Univ Indpls. **HONORS/ACHIEVEMENTS:** Work Study Grant IN Central Coll 1960-64; IN State HS Wrestling Champion IN HS Athletic Assoc 1960; Coll Wrestling Championship Awds IN Little State Coll Conf 1962,64; Spoke Awd Indianapolis Jaycees 1971; Spark Publ Awd Indianapolis Jaycees 1972; Serv Awd Indianapolis Headstart Prog 1974. **BUSINESS ADDRESS:** Employee Relations Manager, RCA/Consumer Electronics, 600 N Sherman Dr, Indianapolis, IN 46201.

MOORE, COLIN A.
Attorney. **PERSONAL:** Born Apr 24, 1944, Manchester Village, Berbice, Guyana;son of Victor Emmanuel Moore and Olive Muriel Moore; married Ela Babb, May 18, 1985; children: Simone Moore. **EDUCATION:** Univ of the West Indies, Kingston Jamaica, BSc, 1963; Univ of London, London England, MA, 1968; doctoral study at Princeton Univ, Princeton NJ; Brooklyn Law School, Brooklyn NY, 1978. **CAREER:** Douglas College, Rutgers Univ, New Brunswick NJ, lecturer, 1971-75; Wachtell Lipton Rosen Katz, New York NY, paralegal, 1975-76; Attorney General, State of New York, New York NY, law clerk, 1976-78; Bronx County NY, New York NY, asst district attorney, 1978-79; self-employed attorney, Brooklyn NY, 1979-. **ORGANIZATIONS:** Legal Redress Committee, NAACP, Jamaica Chapter, chmn 1978-81, board mem 1979-82; St Albans Local Devel Corp, Queens NY, 1979-82; pres, Macon B Allen Bar Assn, 1980-83; pres, Carribean Action Lobby, 1981-82; board mem, Natl Bar Assn, 1981-83; mem, Natl Conference of Black Lawyers, 1982-84; board mem, Medgar Evers Center for Law & Social Justice, 1986-. **HONORS/ACHIEVEMENTS:** Amer Jurisprudence Award, Lawyers Coop Publishing House, 1976; Leadership Award, Sesame Flyers Intl, 1987; Achievement and Community Service Award, Medgar Evers College, 1987; Distinguished Service Award, Jamaica Natl Movement, 1988; Humanitarian Award, Vidcap Inc, 1989; author of The Simpson-Mazzoli Bill: Two Steps Forward, One Step Backward, 1984; author of The History of African Liberation Movements from Os Palmares to Montgomery, 1989; author of collection of articles, 1989. **BUSINESS ADDRESS:** Attorney-at-Law, 16 Court St, Suite 1212, Brooklyn, NY 11241.

MOORE, CORNELL LEVERETTE
Company executive, attorney. **PERSONAL:** Born Sep 18, 1939, Tignall, GA; son of Jesse L Moore and Luetta T Moore; married Wenda Lee Weeke's; children: Lynne M, Jonathon C, Meredith L. **EDUCATION:** VA Union Univ, AB 1961; Howard Univ Law School, JD, 1964. **CAREER:** US Treasurer, staff attorney, 1962-64; Crocker Bank, trust admin, 1964-66; Comptroller of Currency, US Treasurer, regional counsel, 1966-68; NW Natl Bank of Minneapolis, asst vice pres & legal officer, 1968-70; Shelter Mortgage Co Inc, exec vice pres & dir 1970-73; Shelard Natl Bank, dir 1973-78; Hennepin Co Bar Found, pres 1975-78; Golden Valley Bank, dir 1978-; Lease More Equipment Inc, pres & CEO. **ORGANIZATIONS:** Trustee Minneapolis Soc for Fine Arts; trustee Dunwoody Inst; dir Greater Minneapolis Housing Corp; trustee VA Union Univ. **BUSINESS ADDRESS:** Sr Vice Pres, General Counsel, Miller & Schroeder Financial Inc, 7900 Xerxes Ave S, Suite 2300, Minneapolis, MN 55431.

MOORE, DAVID BERNARD, II
Educator. **PERSONAL:** Born Jul 13, 1940, Uniontown, AL. **EDUCATION:** AL State Univ, BS 1960; Fordham Univ, Special 1962; Univ of AL, MA 1972. **CAREER:** Superior Graphics, dir 1973-79; RC Hatch HS, teacher 1981-. **ORGANIZATIONS:** Pres Uniontown Civic League 1970-; city councilman 1972-. **HOME ADDRESS:** PO Box 635, Uniontown, AL 36786.

MOORE, DONALD TORIAN
Physician. **PERSONAL:** Born May 04, 1933, Lagrange, GA; married Barbara Spcight; children: Karen, Donald Jr, Robin. **EDUCATION:** Morehouse Coll 1954; Meharry Med Coll 1958. **CAREER:** Physician self employed present; Detroit Receiving Hosp, intern 1958-59; Malden Hosp, resd physician; Ob-Gyn Hubbard Hosp; Duke Med Ctr Chf Ob-gyn Lincoln Hosp, fellow 1967-76; Duke Med Ctr, asst clinical prof; Am Bd of Ob-Gyn, diplomate; Am Coll Ob-Gyn fellow; Meharry Med Coll, asst prof. **ORGANIZATIONS:** Mem AMA, NMA; Bayard Carter Soc of Ob-Gyn; Old N State Med Soc; Am Coll of Ob-Gyn; Am Bd Ob-Gyn; Pan Am Med Assn; NC Med Soc Alpha Phi Alpha Frat; Am Assn of Gyn Laparoscopists. **HONORS/ACHIEVEMENTS:** Indsl Exhibit Com Publ "Abdominal Pregnancy" 1967; "Intussusception Complicating Pregnancy" 1967; "Endometriosis An Increasing Challange" 1970; "Hydrops Fetalis Asso with Idiopathic Arterial Calcification" 1972; "The Eyes of Gynecology" 1975. **MILITARY SERVICE:** USN 1959-61. **BUSINESS ADDRESS:** 601 Fayetteville Rd, Durham, NC 27701.

MOORE, DWAYNE HARRISON
Public housing. **PERSONAL:** Born Oct 27, 1958, Joliet, IL; son of William Moore and Patricia Moore; children: Latasha Ann Davis, Bryan Dwayne. **EDUCATION:** Joliet Jr Coll, AAS 1980; Northeastern Illinois Univ, BA (w/Honors) 1983; Univ of Chicago, Graduate Study 1984-85; Sangamon State Univ, MPA 1987. **CAREER:** Springfield Housing Authority, operations rsch & analysis. **ORGANIZATIONS:** Mem Amer Soc for Public Admin 1984-, Alpha Phi Alpha Frat Inc 1986-, Springfield Jaycees 1986-, Natl Black MBA Assoc 1987; Big Brothers KIDS & PALS Program 1988-89. **HONORS/ACHIEVEMENTS:** HUD Local Govt Internship Prog Scholarship 1984-86; Outstanding Achievement in Comm & Public Serv Minority Svcs/Black Student Caucus Sangamon State Univ 1985-86; interviewed on public service cable TV on subject of black history 1987; United States Achievement Academy Collegiate Academic All-Amer 1987; US Achievement Academy Natl Collegiate Student Govt Awd Winner 1987; Outstanding Young Men of Amer 1988. **HOME ADDRESS:** 308 Dickinson Road, Suite 11, Springfield, IL 62704.

MOORE, EARL B.
Clergyman. **PERSONAL:** Born Feb 02, 1930, Tulsa; married Cora Thornton; children: Julin, Jeanelle. **EDUCATION:** MDiv 1956; MST 1969; DMin 1976. **CAREER:** NY State Dept Correctional Svc, dir of ministerial serv 1973-; St Paul Bapt Ch, minister 1965-; New York City Dept of Corr, chpln 1963; Shilo Bapt Ch, pastor 1960-63; New York City Mission Soc, chaplain 1956-60. **ORGANIZATIONS:** Mem NY State Crime Control Com; State Select Com on Institutions; Attica Observance; founder Central Harlem Assn of Neighborhood Chs; adjunct prof Union Theol Sem Feild Services Program; mem NAACP, SCLC; Ford Fellowship; SCLC Ministerial Training Prog; Am Bapt Black Churchmen; pres Bapt Ministers Conf ofGreater NY & Vicinity. **HONORS/ACHIEVEMENTS:** History Makers Award; Ministerial Ser Award; Harlem Churchmen Award. **BUSINESS ADDRESS:** Dept of Correctional Serv, State Campus, Albany, NY 12226.

MOORE, EDWIN G.
Physician. **PERSONAL:** Born Oct 22, 1910, Carrollton, MO; married Trinidad Tabayoyong; children: Edwin, Mary. **EDUCATION:** Philander Smith Coll, BSE; Meharry Med Coll, MD. **CAREER:** Pvt Prac, Physician. **ORGANIZATIONS:** Mem Lk Co Med Soc; Am Acad of Family Physicians; IN St Med Soc; AMA; Nat Med Assn; life mem NAACP; life mem Kappa Alpha Psi Frat; Philippine Pro Assn; mem Nat Geog Soc 1972; mem Nat Police Res Ofcrs Assn; loyal mem St Mary Mercy Hosp Meth Hosp Staff. **HONORS/ACHIEVEMENTS:** Cert of Awd Countinuing Ed in Med. **MILITARY SERVICE:** AUS capt 1943-46.

MOORE, ELAINE
Insurance analyst. **PERSONAL:** Born Nov 18, 1947, Jersey City, NJ; daughter of Gerald Moore (deceased) and Lula Thompson Moore (deceased). **EDUCATION:** Rutgers Univ, BS Mgmt 1979. **CAREER:** Home Insurance Co, figure clerk 1966-72; Model Cities Employment, rsch clerk 1972-73; Hartford Ins Co, asst to underwriter 1973-80; Continential Ins Co,sr user analyst 1980-88. **ORGANIZATIONS:** Treas Concerned Comm Women of JC 1977-; bd of trustees YWCA 1981-87; voter serv dir Jersey City Area League of Women Voters 1983-88; mem officer NJ Chap Coaltion of 100 Black Women 1984-86; 2nd vice pres Hudson County Womens Political Caucus; 1st vice pres Metro Newark Chapter Natl Black Political Congress of Women; bd mem Hudson County Adoption Advisory Bd. **HONORS/ACHIEVEMENTS:** World's Who's Who of Women 1979; Outstanding Young Woman of Amer 1979; Who's Who of Amer Women 1979-; Outstanding Personalities of Amer 1982; Who's Who in the East 1984-; Who's Who in Finance & Industry 1984; Jersey Journal Woman of Achievement Jersey Journal News 1985; Comm Serv Awd Past Exalted Rulers Cncl No 17 1985; Black Woman of Achievement Comm Serv 1985; Martin Luther King Legislation & Women's Rights Martin Luther King Commn 1987. **HOME ADDRESS:** 42 Park St, Jersey City, NJ 07304.

MOORE, EMANUEL A.
Attorney. **PERSONAL:** Born Nov 22, 1941, Brooklyn, NY. **EDUCATION:** New York Univ, BS Willard J Martin Schlr, James Talcott Schlr 1963; NY Law Sch, JD Thurgood Marshall Schlr 1966. **CAREER:** Justice Dept Washington, atty civil rights div 1966-68; Queens Co NY, asst dist atty 1968; Ofc Gen Counsel AID Wash, legal adviser 1968-70; Eastern Dist NY, US atty 1970-72; US Atty Ofc Estrn Dist NY, chief consumer protect sec 1972-74; US Fed Energy Admin, dir compliance & enforcement 1974-77; private practice, attorney 1977-. **ORGANIZATIONS:** Mem NY Law Sch Alumni Assn; dir Natl Macon B Allen Black Bar Assn; Ed NY Law Forum 1965-66;Chinese American Lions Club, NY, Knighted Order of St Georgeand Constantine 1986. **HONORS/ACHIEVEMENTS:** Amer Jurisprudence Awd Academic Excellence in Law of Evidence 1965; Amer Jurisprudence Awd Academic Excellence in Law of NY Prac 1965; Vice Pres Awd Academic Excellence 1966; mem dir NY Law Sch Alumni Assn. **BUSINESS ADDRESS:** Attorney, Emanuel A Moore & Associates, 168 Canal St, New York, NY 10013.

MOORE, EMERSON J.
Clergyman. **PERSONAL:** Born May 16, 1938, New York City, NY. **EDUCATION:** Cathedral Coll NYC, attended; St Joseph's Sem NY, attended; NY Univ, Columbia Univ School of Social Work, attended. **CAREER:** Curubi, aux bishop; Diocese of NY, aux bishop 1982-. **HONORS/ACHIEVEMENTS:** Ordained priest Roman Cahtolic Church 1964. **BUSINESS ADDRESS:** 315 E 47th St, New York, NY 10017-2301.

MOORE, EVAN GREGORY
Psychiatrist. **PERSONAL:** Born Sep 05, 1923, Lima, OK; son of Eugene Ralph and Millicent Earl; married June Elizabeth Gibbs; children: Colleen Moore Jones, Evan Jr. **EDUCATION:** Meharry Medical Coll, MD 1948. **CAREER:** Harlem Hospital NY, intern 1948-49; Univ of IL, clinical asst prof psychiatry, 1958-70; Child Therapy Program, Inst Psychoanalysis Chicago, faculty 1968-85, faculty teacher training program, 1968-85; Erikson Inst Chicago, lecturer 1969-85; Cumberland Hall Nashville, attending staff 1985-88; Hubbard Hosp Nashville, attending staff 1986-88; Meharry Medical Coll, assoc prof, dept psychiatry and pediatrics 1985-88; clinical director, Children's Unit, HCA Montevista Hospital, 1989-. **ORGANIZATIONS:** Fellow, Amer Acad of Child Psychiatry; Life Fellow, Amer Psychiatric Assn; life fellow Amer Orthopsychiatric Assn; mem IL Council Child Psychiatry, Chicago Psychoanalytic Soc, Amer Medical Assn, Natl Medical Assn, IL State Psychiatric Soc, IL State Medical Soc, TN Psychiatric Assn; assoc examiner Amer Bd of Psychiatry and Neurology 1978-; impartial medical testimony panel IL Medical Soc/IL Bar Assn Chicago 1980-86; consultant Provident Hospital Chicago 1985; mem Academic Affairs Council, Honorary Degree Comm Meharry Medical Coll 1986-88. **HONORS/ACHIEVEMENTS:** Research, Longitudinal Study of Object Relations, Maternal Substance Abuse, Assault on Infant Morbidity and Mortality, Prenatal Head Start; numerous and varied informal presentations to staff students and public in a wide range of settings including radio and tv; Certified Amer Bd of Psychiatry and Neurology, General Psychiatry; Amer Bd of Psychiatry and Neurology, Child Psychiatry. **MILITARY SERVICE:** AUS Medical Corps capt 2 yrs. **BUSINESS ADDRESS:** 6000 West Rochelle Ave, Las Vegas, NV 89103.

MOORE, EVELYN K.
Agency executive. **PERSONAL:** Born Jul 29, 1937, Detroit, MI. **EDUCATION:** Eastern MI Univ, BS 1960; Univ of MI, MA 1960. **CAREER:** Natl Black Child Devel Inst Washington, DC, dir 1973-. **ORGANIZATIONS:** Mem bd dir Children's Lobby; mem N Amer Adoption Bd; adv com DC Citizens for Pub Edn; consult US Offc of Edn; mem Natl Assn for Educ of Young Children. **HONORS/ACHIEVEMENTS:** Chosen Outstanding Young Woman of State of MI 1970. **BUSINESS ADDRESS:** Dir, Nat Black Child Dev Inst, 1463 Rhode Island Ave NW, Washington, DC 20036.

MOORE, FRED HENDERSON (DANNY)
Attorney. **PERSONAL:** Born Jul 25, 1934, Charleston County, SC; married Louise Smalls; children: Fredena, Melissa, Fred, Louis, Rembert. **EDUCATION:** SC State Coll 1952-56; RooseveltUniv Chicago 1956; Allen U, BS 1956-57; Howard Episcopal, JD 1957-60; Teamers Sch of Religion, DD 1976; Stephens Christian Inst 1976; Reform Episcapal Seminary. **CAREER:** Atty self-employed 1977. **ORGANIZATIONS:** Corp cncl NAACP 1960; mem Black Rep Party; mem Silver Elephant Club; 1st Dist Coun SC Conf of NAACP; co-author "Angry Black South" 1960; asso pstr Payne RMUE Ch; asso cncl NC Mutual Ins Co; Mem Omega Psi Phy Frat. **HONORS/ACHIEVEMENTS:** Who's Who inam Coll 1956; youth award NAACP 1957; memorial award Charles Drew 1957; Youth March for Intergrated Schs 1958; stud body pres SC State Coll. **BUSINESS ADDRESS:** 39 Spring St, Charleston, SC 29403.

MOORE, GARY E.
Media specialist, educational administrator. **PERSONAL:** Born Dec 08, 1962, Rochester, NY; son of Frank Lewis Moore and Christine Enge Moore; married Marva Elaine Nabors-Moore, Jul 01, 1989. **EDUCATION:** Clarion Univ of PA, BS Accounting 1985, MS Communications 1988. **CAREER:** USAR, second lt, platoon leader, training & evaluation, equipment accountability 1984-; Clarion Univ, graduate asst; 1985-, admissions recruiter 1987-, project dir; Univ of PA, asst dir of admissiona; 332nd Eng Co (DT), Kittanning PA, company commander; GEM Presentation Graphics, pres/owner, presently/. **ORGANIZATIONS:** Graduate advisor Black Student Union 1985-87; chair, editor Amer Mktg Assn Newsletter 1986-87; chmn, editor Black Student Union Newsletter 1987; human relations subcomm Clarion Univ; mem Accounting Club, Amer Mktg Assn; Soc of Military Engineers 1987; Reserve Officers Assn 1989. **HONORS/ACHIEVEMENTS:** Black Student Union Acad Achievement Award; Graduate Assistantship Clarion Univ of PA 1985-87. **MILITARY SERVICE:** USA 2nd lt 4 yrs; Merit of Achievement 1986.

MOORE, GEORGE ANTHONY
Television producer. **PERSONAL:** Born Feb 08, 1914, Cleveland, OH. **EDUCATION:** OH St U, BA;Univ of IA, MA. **CAREER:** Gama Asso Inc, owns; US TV Station WEWS, first black prod & dir; Scripps-Howard Cleveland Press & Scripps-Howard's onlyTV station, formerly starting from news dir to present position; appeared as actor in over a dozen live stage & prod. **ORGANIZATIONS:** Mem Nat Acad of TV Arts & Sci; found dir Cath Theater of Cleveland OH StUniv Playmakers; mem Karamu House; Proj Equal; found pres Proj Peace Cath Commn on Comm Action. **HONORS/ACHIEVEMENTS:** The Dorothy Fuldheim prog which is his chief respons; Highlights of the News has been chosen as the outstndg Cleveland TV news show by many newspaper surv. **BUSINESS ADDRESS:** 1836 Euclid Ave, Cleveland, OH 44115.

MOORE, GEORGE THOMAS
Scientist. **PERSONAL:** Born Jun 02, 1945, Owensboro, KY; married Peggy Frances Jouett. **EDUCATION:** KY State U, BS chemistry/math 1967;Univ of Dayton, MS inorganic chem 1971; Env HealthUniv of Cincinnati Med Center, PhD 1978. **CAREER:** US DOE Pittsburgh Energy Tech Ctr, chief occupational health br 1979-; US DOE Pittsburgh Energy Tech Ctr, research indsl hygienist 1978-79; MonsantoResearch Corp Mound Lab, research chemist 1967-72. **ORGANIZATIONS:** Mem Am Chem Soc 1975-; mem Air Pollution Control Assn 1977-; mem Am Insl Hygiene Assn 1978-; Mem Unity Lodge # 115 Price Hall Affiliation 1963-; memOmega Psi Phi Frat 1964-; supt Ebenezer Bapt Ch Sunday Sch 1980-. **HONORS/ACHIEVEMENTS:** Who's Who Among Students in Am Coll andUniv 1967; hon french award Alpha Mu Gamma French Soc; Young Men of Am Outstanding Young Men of Am Inc 1980. **BUSINESS ADDRESS:** PO Box 10940, Pittsburgh, PA 15236.

MOORE, GERALD L.
Consultant. **PERSONAL:** Born Jul 31, 1933, New York, NY; children: Sharon-Frances, Meredith Adams. **EDUCATION:** City Coll of NY, BA Sociology (honors) 1974; Wharton School Univ of PA, Certificate Finance & Acctg 1978; Grad School & Univ Center City Univ of NY, PhD Sociology 1982. **CAREER:** Natl Urban League, proj dir 1965-67; Lance Moore Assoc, pres 1969-73; Consolidated Edison, sr training rep internal consultant 1973-77; Amer Express Co, mgr training 1977-79; NJ Inst of Tech, asst prof orgl behav 1979-82; consultant and educator 1982-. **ORGANIZATIONS:** Metro Council OD Network 1968-69; Amer Soc of Training & Develop 1974-77; Amer Soc Assn 1982-85; Assn of Black Sociologists 1982-85; recruited, selectedand made test-sophisticated the first Blacks and Hispanics to enter IBM, Pitney Bowes, Xerox and Bell Telephone in craft positions. **HONORS/ACHIEVEMENTS:** Book "The Politics of Management Consulting" 1984. **MILITARY SERVICE:** USAF Korean Vet. **HOME ADDRESS:** 19 Foxtail Ln, Monmouth Junction, NJ 08852.

MOORE, GWEN
Legislator. **PERSONAL:** Born Oct 28, Michigan; married Ronald Dobson; children: Ronald Dobson II. **EDUCATION:** CA State Univ LA, BA Tchng 1963; Univ S CA, MPA candidate. **CAREER:** LA County, deputy probation ofcr 1963-69; Gr LA Comm Action Agency, dir public affairs & dir of personnel 1969-76; Social Action Rsch Ctr LA, consul 1970-72; LA Comm Coll, mem bd trustees 1975; Compton Comm Coll, instr 1975; Inner City Information System LA, consul 1976-77; CA State Assembly,mem 1978-, chair assembly subcomm on cableTV 1982, chair assembly utilities & commerce comm 1983-. **ORGANIZATIONS:** Western regional chair Natl Black Caucus of State Legislators; reg v chair Natl Conf of Legislatures; mem CA Public Broadcasting Task Force; mem Commnon State Govt Orgn & Economy; platform comm of Dem Natl Comm; mem CA Elected Women's Assn for Educ & Rsch; mem Dem Women's Forum; mem LA Coalition of 100 Black Women; mem Natl Women's Political Caucus; mem YWCA, United Negro Coll Fund, CA Legislative Black Caucus; reg dir Women's Network of Natl Caucus o State Legislatures; sec Natl Org of Black Elected Legislative Women (Nobel/Women). **HONORS/ACHIEVEMENTS:** Natl Alliance of Supermarket Shoppers Golden Shopping Cart Awd for Legislator of the Yr 1983; Natl Caucus of Black State Legislators Awd 1984; CA State Package Store & Tavern Owner's Assn Awd 1984; Meritorious Awd for Outstanding Serv Women for Good Govt; Newsmaker of the Yr Awd Natl Assn of Media Women 1983. **BUSINESS ADDRESS:** Assemblywoman, CA Legislature, State Capitol Room 2117, Sacramento, CA 95814.

MOORE, HELEN BOULWARE
Educational & clinical psychologist. **PERSONAL:** Born Sep 01, 1936, Charlotte, NC; married Robert E; children: Michael, Robin. **EDUCATION:** Univ of PA, BA (cum laude) 1958; Univ of PA, MS 1961; Boston Coll, PhD 1977. **CAREER:** Boston Psychological Center for Women, staff psychotherapist present; Supportive Instrl Serv, dir; Dept of Psychology Simmons Coll, instr; Career Planning & Counseling Serv Simmons Coll, counselor, 1969-71; Tutorial Serv Newton METCO Prgm, coordinator, 1969; Dept of English & Reading, Philadelphia Public Schools, chmn 1965-67, reading teacher 1959-67, reading clinician, private practice 1959-66. **ORGANIZATIONS:** Mem, Am Psycological Assn; Natl Assn of Women Deans Administrs & Counselors; New England Assn of Acad Support Personnel; mem, Pi Lambda Theta Hon Soc, Alpha Kappa Alpha; NAACP; The Links Inc; Girl Friends Inc; Incorporator Greater Framingham Comm Church; Danforth Assn Visiting Com Afro-Am Artist in Residence Prog Northeastern U. **HONORS/ACHIEVEMENTS:** Who's Who Among Women; Simmons Coll Faculty Develop Fellowship 1975-76.

MOORE, HELEN D. S.
Educator. **PERSONAL:** Born Jan 21, 1932, Baldwyn, MS; married Elijah Moore; children: Michelle, Pamela, Elijah. **EDUCATION:** MS Industrial Coll, BA 1951; TN State Univ, MS 1957. **CAREER:** Jr, Sr, HS, teacher 4 yrs; Primary Grades, teacher 1953-56, 1960-75; Greenville Municipal School District, principal 1975-. **ORGANIZATIONS:** Mem Voter Reg; Political Camp; Ad Hoc Comm; lectr Wash County Political Action Comm; past pres YWCA 1950-51; past pres Greenville Teacher Assn; pres MS Assn of Educ 1978-79; youth advisor St Matthew AME Church 1977; advisor Teenette Art & Civic Club; mem Modern Art & Civic Club, NAACP, Natl Fed Colored Women's Club. **HONORS/ACHIEVEMENTS:** NSF Grant, Eastern MI Univ, 1963; Citizen Award, NAACP, 1975; Citizenship Award, WB Derrick Masonic Lodge, 1976; Educ Award Civil Liberties Elks 1976; Comm Seventh Day Adventist Church. **BUSINESS ADDRESS:** Principal, Greenville Municipal School District, Samson Rd, Greenville, MS 38701.

MOORE, HELEN J.
Educator. **PERSONAL:** Born May 11, 1904, St Louis. **EDUCATION:** Sumner Normal Certificate 1920-22; Stower Teachers Coll, AB, 1939; Lincoln Univ, AB, 1940; Univ IL, MA, 1943; Univ IL; Boston Univ, 1943. **CAREER:** St Louis Public Schools, retired teacher. **ORGANIZATIONS:** Mem del to conv MO State Tchrs Assn; PTA; Math Tchrs Greater St Louis; Math Tchrs MO; Nat Math Assn; city and natl mem officer LincolnUniv Alumnae Delta Sigma Theta Sor Inc; AssnUniv Women; NAACP; Urban League; Police Comm Relations; Aunts & Uncles; North Central Assn Report; United Negro Coll Fund; Union Sarah Comm Corp; Personnel adn Recruitment Com; Sr Citizens Com; Neighborhood Adv Bd; Health Educ Welfare Com Union Sarah Health Ctr; Youth Adv Com; Union Sarah Econ Dev Corp; YWCA; Top Ladies Distinction; Mayor's Adv Bd for Aged. **HONORS/ACHIEVEMENTS:** All Saint Episcopal Ch St Louis Argus Award 1969; NAACP Vol Award 1968; Tuberculosis Vol Award 1970; Lincoln Alumnae Award 1970; Delta Sigma Theta Award 1971; Omega Psi Phi Award 1969; nominee Retiring Tchr Award of MO 1974; ret mat tchr award Math Council Greater St Louis 1974; vol award Human Dev Corp 1973; Police Comm Relations 1966-73; Outstanding Secondary Tchr Math Award 1974; Alice Messerly Award 1974.

MOORE, HENRY J.
Appointed government official. **PERSONAL:** Born Jan 26, 1949, Philadelphia, PA; married Donna Morgan; children: Caprice. **EDUCATION:** NC A&T State Univ, BS English 1971; Univ of MD, MA Urban Mgmt 1976. **CAREER:** Bur of Govt Rsch/Univ of MD, public mgmt assoc 1974-76; Univ of MD, dir of student employment 1976-77; Seat Pleasant MD, city mgr 1977-79; Joint Ctr for Political Studies, dir of comm & eco dev 1979-81; City of Savannah, asst city mgr/public develop. **ORGANIZATIONS:** Mem Clean Comm Adv Council 1981-85; bd of dirs Neighborhood Housing Ser 1981-85; mem Amer Soc for Public Admin 1981-85; mem Leadership Savannah 1984-85; bd of dirs United Way 1984-85; mem Forum for Black Public Admin 1984-85. **HONORS/ACHIEVEMENTS:** Man of the Year Alpha Phi Alpha Beta Phi Lambda Chap 1983-84. **HOME ADDRESS:** 518 E Maupas Ave, Savannah, GA 31401.

MOORE, HILLIARD T., SR.
City official, educator. **PERSONAL:** Born Aug 18, 1925, Kingston, NC; married Gloria; children: Hilliard, Jr, Stephen, Donna. **EDUCATION:** Fayetteville State U, BS. **CAREER:** Camden Co, freeholder; Lawnside NJ, former mayor; Camden NJ, social studies tchr. **ORGANIZATIONS:** Dir Union Fed Savs & Loan Assn. **BUSINESS ADDRESS:** 203 Roberts Ave, Lawnside, NJ 08045.

MOORE, HIRAM BEENE
Physician. **PERSONAL:** Born Jan 01, 1914, South Pittsburg, TN; son of Levi Moore and Clara Beene Moore; married Stella M Epps, Dec 31, 1944; children: Clara Lynn Moore. **EDUCATION:** TN State U, BS 1938; Meharry Med Coll, MD 1944. **CAREER:** Physician, self-employed. **ORGANIZATIONS:** Med advsr Marion County Draft Bd 1952-; mem Marion County Bd of Health; chmn City Beer Commn; mem City Planning Commn 1956-66; commr Local Housing Authority 1956-66; mem Natl Med Assn; Amer Med Assn; mem Chattanooga Hamilton County Med Soc; life mem Omega Psi Phi Frat; trustee Lay Leader Randolph Univ Meth Ch; mem 32nd degree Mason; life mem NAACP; mem Shriner. **HONORS/ACHIEVEMENTS:** Family Doctor of the Year, Natl Med Assn 1964; Distinguished Alumni Natl Assn for Equal Opportunity in Higher Education 1989. **MILITARY SERVICE:** ASTP 2nd Lieutant 1943-1944. **BUSINESS ADDRESS:** 206 Elm Ave S, South Pittsburg, TN 37380.

MOORE, HOWARD, JR.
Attorney. **PERSONAL:** Born Feb 28, 1932, Atlanta, GA; married Jane Bond; children: Grace, Constance, Kojo. **EDUCATION:** Morehouse Coll, AB 1954; Boston Univ, LLB 1960. **CAREER:** Moore & Lawrence, attorney. **ORGANIZATIONS:** Admitted to prac-

tice MA 1961, GA 1962, CA 1973; admitted to practice before Supreme Ct of US all lower Fed Cts & US Tax Ct; mem Natl Conf of Black Lawyers; Charles Houston Law Club; Natl Lawyers Guild; Natl Emergency Civil Liberties Com; Amer Civil Liberties Union; Fedn of So Coop; former genl counsel Student Nonviolent Coord Comm. **HONORS/ACHIEVEMENTS:** Martin Luther King Jr Awd Howard Univ 1972; Disting Son of Morehouse Coll 1973; Centennial Awd Boston Univ 1973; Disting Serv Natl Coll of Advocacy Assn of Amer Trial Lawyers 1975. **MILITARY SERVICE:** AUS pfc 1954-56. **BUSINESS ADDRESS:** Attorney, Moore & Lawrence, 445 Bellevue Ave 3rd Fl, Oakland, CA 94610.

MOORE, JAMES L.
Clergyman. **PERSONAL:** Born in Atlanta, GA; married Gladys Stevens. **EDUCATION:** Bishop Coll, BA 1937; Pittsburgh Theol Sem, STB MDiv 1944;Univ Pittsburgh, MEd 1945;Univ of Pittsburgh Johns Hopkins U. **CAREER:** Sharon Bapt Ch pastor 1946-; KS & PA, pastored 1937-45; johns hopkins hosp, served on clergy staff. **ORGANIZATIONS:** Appointed mem Baltimore Comm on Human Relations by Mayor Harold Grady; appted Indorsing Agent & Dir of Chaplains Nat Bapt Conv USA Inc by Pres Dr JH Jackson; co-fdr & chmn bd of dir Opportunities Industralization Ctr of Baltimore; served as news reporter, auditor, vp, tchr at Bapt Ctr & AnnualInst Bapt Family in Baltimore; established & dir of Meml Scholarship Fund in mem of late dau Constance H. **HONORS/ACHIEVEMENTS:** Recipient Mayor's Citation for splendid quality of pub serv rendered City of Baltimore; Governor's Citation in apprec of outst serv to citizens of st St of MD. **BUSINESS ADDRESS:** 1373 N Stricker St, Baltimore, MD 21217R.

MOORE, JANE BOND
Attorney. **PERSONAL:** Born Sep 01, 1938, Nashville, TN; married Howard Moore; children: Grace, Constance, Kojo. **EDUCATION:** Spelman Coll Atlanta, AB 1959; Boalt HallUniv of CA, JS 1975. **CAREER:** Bank of CA, asst counsel 1977-; Open Road (a youth proj), admin 1976-77; Moore & Bell, asso atty 1975-76; So Christian Leadership Conf, research asst 1963-64; So Regional Council, research asst 1961-63. **ORGANIZATIONS:** Co-chairperson Consumer Interest Comm San Francisco Bar Assn 1979-80; mem Financial Inst Comm CA State Bar 1979-; mem Legal Affairs Com CA Bankers Assn 1979-; mem NAACP present; mem Am Bar Assn; mem Black Women Lawyers Assn present; mem Charles Houston Bar Assn present. **BUSINESS ADDRESS:** Bank of CA Legal Division, 400 California St, San Francisco, CA 94104.

MOORE, JEAN E. (NEE CAMPBELL)
Social worker, educator. **PERSONAL:** Born in New York City, NY; married Robert M Moore Jr; children: Robert III, Doreen. **EDUCATION:** Hunter Coll, BA 1947; Bryn Mawr Coll, MA 1949; Temple Univ, EdD 1978. **CAREER:** Childrens Serv PA, social worker 1949-52; Vet Admin PA, asst chief clinic social worker 1952-60; Redevel Auth City of PA, social work spec 1962-67; Model Cities US Dept Housing & Urban Devel, human resources adv 1967-69; Temple Univ, School of Soc Admin, assoc prof 1969-. **ORGANIZATIONS:** Mem Natl Assoc Social Workers, Acad Cert Soc Workers, Council Soc Work Ed, Natl Assoc Housing & Redevel Officials, Natl Conf Soc Welfare, Amer Publ Health Assoc, Black Caucus, Amer Personnel & Guidance Assoc, Natl Black Alliance on Grad Level Ed, PA Black Conf Higher Ed; chairperson PA State Bd Private Correspondence Schools; team chairperson, team mem Middle States Assoc of Coll & Schools; act 101 reviewer & eval Commonwealth of PA, mem Gov Task Force on Health Ed; mem Amer Assoc Univ Profs; past mem bd, trustees Metro YWCA Phila; bd of trustees Comm Coll of Phila; pres Spectrum Health Svcs; past bd dirs Comm Y Eastern DE Cty; mem Fair Housing Council DE Valley; elder Lansdowne Presbyterian Church; lecturer Delta Sigma Theta Sor Cons. **HONORS/ACHIEVEMENTS:** Award Medals for Writings; Outstanding Educator 1977; Educator Achievement Award 1979; Coll of Ed Alumni Award 1978; Phi Beta Kappa 1947; Award of Chapel of the Four Chaplains. **BUSINESS ADDRESS:** Associate Professor, Temple Univ, School of Social Admin, 406 Univ Serv Bldg, Philadelphia, PA 19122.

MOORE, JELLETHER MARIE
Computer systems manager. **PERSONAL:** Born Sep 04, 1949, Sacramento, CA; daughter of Oserine Moore and Artaive Daniels Moore; children: Cornealis N, Halima JJ. **EDUCATION:** Wagsburn Univ Topeka KS, BA 1973; Attended, California State Univ, Sacramento City Coll, Cosumnes River Coll, Univ of California at Davis. **CAREER:** State of California, computer software applications programmer/analyst 1976-84; Crystal Lightworks, owner 1986-; State of California, Dept of Conservation, Farmland Mapping and Monitoring Program, land & water use analyst/computer systems manager 1984-. **ORGANIZATIONS:** Mem California Assn of Professional Scientists 1984-, California Geographers Soc 1985-, Southwestern Anthropological Soc 1985-, Assn of Women Entrepreneurs, Chamber of Commerce of Sacramento CA, Better Business Bureau of Sacremento CA; reviewer Digital Cartographic Standards 1985-86;mem Multi-cultural Comm SUSD 1986-87; partner in Mooncraft/Minds Eye Images. **HONORS/ACHIEVEMENTS:** Superior Accomplishment Award for Excellence in Information Mgmt, State of California, Office of Information Technology 1988; Sustained Superior Accomplishment, State of California, Dept of Conservation 1988. **BUSINESS ADDRESS:** Computer Systems Manager, State of California, Farmland Mapping & Monitoring, 1516 9th St, Room 400, Sacramento, CA 95814.

MOORE, JERRY A., JR.
Clergyman, city official. **PERSONAL:** Born Jun 12, 1918, Minden, LA; married Ettyce Hill; children: Jerry III, Juran D. **EDUCATION:** Morehouse Coll, BA; Howard U, BD, MA. **CAREER:** USO New Orleans, asst dir 1943-; YMCA, boys work sec 1944; 19th St Bapt Ch, pastor. **ORGANIZATIONS:** Mem-at-large DC City Council; vice pres Bapt Conv Wash DC & Vincinity; vice pres Intl Soc Christian Endwavor; past pres Wash Metro Area Council Govts; chmn Transportation Com DC Counci; mem Northwest Boundary Civic Assn; Rock Creek Neighborhood League; NAACP; Pigskin Club; Rotary Club DC; Urban League; Capitol City Rep Club. **HONORS/ACHIEVEMENTS:** Washington Area Contractors Award 1971; NAACP Serv Award 1972; Capitol City Rep Club Lincoln Award 1974. **BUSINESS ADDRESS:** DC City Council Dist Bldg, 14 and E Sts NW, Washington, DC 20004.

MOORE, JOHN WESLEY, JR.
Business executive. **PERSONAL:** Born Mar 10, 1948, Martins Ferry, OH; married Brenda Scott; children: Kelly Shannon, Ryan Wesley. **EDUCATION:** W Liberty State Coll, BA 1970; WV Univ Morgantown, MA 1972. **CAREER:** Bridgeport HS, tchr 1970-71; W Liberty State Coll, dir counseling ctr & asst dir financial aids 1971-76; Wheeling Dollar Svgs & Trust Co, vice prespersonnel-human resources. **ORGANIZATIONS:** Mem bd trustees OH Valley Medical Ctr 1979; consult Ctr for Creative Comm 1974-75; consult No Panhandle Mental Health Ctr Wheeling 1977-79; bd of dir Big Bros/Big Sisters of Wheeling 1976-77; adv bd OH Co Bd of Vocational Educ 1977-; bd of dir Amer Inst of Banking Wheeling Chap 1979-; Ambassadors ClubWheeling Area C of C 1979-; adv com Upper OH Valley Employer Wheeling 1979-. **BUSINESS ADDRESS:** Vice Pres Personnel-Human Res, Wheeling Dollar Savings & Trst, Bank Plaza, Wheeling, WV 26003.

MOORE, JOHNNIE ADOLPH
Government administrator. **PERSONAL:** Born Sep 28, 1929, Cuero, TX; son of Nelson Moore and Eva Moore; married Tommye Dalphine Jordan; children: Carmalie Budgewater. **EDUCATION:** Tuskegee Inst AL, BS 1950; George Williams Coll, Grad Study. **CAREER:** Intl Personnel Mgt Assn Chgo, IL, editor 1963-66; US Dept of Labor Chgo, IL, pub aff ofcr 1966-67; US Civil Serv Commn Wash, DC, pub aff ofcr 1967-79; Bowie State Coll Bowie, MD, asst to pres 1980-82; US Office of Personnel Mgt Wash, DC, pub aff ofcr 1979-83; Am Nurses Assn, dir mrktng & pub aff div 1984-85; US Nuclear Regulatory Commission, public affairs officer 1985-. **ORGANIZATIONS:** Exec dir Nat Ins Assn 1961-62; info spclst Pres Comm on Gov't Contracts 1960-61; night editor Chicago Daily Defender 1959-61; bureau editor Norfolk Journal & Guide 1958-59; pres Capital Press Club Wash, DC 1972-74; visiting prof NUL Black Exec Exchange Pgm 1978-; mem Pub Rel Soc of Am 1977-; mem Kappa Alpha Psi Frat. **HONORS/ACHIEVEMENTS:** Spcl Citation US Civil Serv Commn 1978; Pearlie Cox Harrison Award Capital Press Club 1974; Image Maker Award Nat Assn of Media Women 1976; Citation Bowie State Coll 1982; citation US Nuclear Regulatroy Commission 1986. **MILITARY SERVICE:** USAF 1st lt 1953-55. **HOME ADDRESS:** 2212 Westview Ct, Silver Spring, MD 20910.

MOORE, JOHNNY CHARLES
Professional athlete. **PERSONAL:** Born Mar 03, 1958, Altoona, PA; married Natalie. **EDUCATION:** Texas, studied Phys Ed 1979. **CAREER:** San Antonio Spurs, guard 1980-. **ORGANIZATIONS:** Conducts youth camps. **HONORS/ACHIEVEMENTS:** 14th with a 396 rating in Shick Pivotal Player contest; led NBA with 96 assists in 1981-82; his career 29 pts were 2/25/83 vs Kansas City; twice was All-Southwest Conf at TX; as jr led team to NIT title & was teams MVP. **BUSINESS ADDRESS:** San Antonio Spurs, HemisFair Arena, Ste 510, San Antonio, TX 78292.

MOORE, JOSEPH L.
Administrator. **PERSONAL:** Born Nov 22, 1935, Ripley, TN. **EDUCATION:** St Louis Univ, BA 1959. **CAREER:** VA Med Ctr Lebanon PA, asst dir 1974-75; VA Med Ctr Louisville, asst dir 1975-76; VA Med Ctr Fresno, acting dir 1976; VA Med Ctr Cincinnati, asst dir 1976-79; VA Lakeside Med Ctr, dir 1979-. **ORGANIZATIONS:** Exec comm Chicago Fed Exec Bd 1979; bd of dir Mcgaw Med Center 1979; council of teaching hosp rep Assn of Am Med Coll 1979; comm Chicago Health Systems Agency 1979; chmn appropriateness rev com Chicago Health Systems Agency 1980. **HONORS/ACHIEVEMENTS:** Prestigious Presidential "Distinguished Executive" Rank Awd presented in a White House ceremony Dec 8, 1986. **BUSINESS ADDRESS:** 333 E Huron St, Chicago, IL 60611.

MOORE, JOSSIE A.
Educator. **PERSONAL:** Born Aug 20, 1947, Jackson, TN; married Jimmy L Moore; children: Juan, Jerry. **EDUCATION:** Lane College, BA 1971; Memphis State Univ, MEd 1975, EdD 1986. **CAREER:** Lane College, dir of audio visual 1970-74; Memphis State Univ/Memphis City Schools, teacher corps intern 1974-75; Lauderdale County Schools, resource teacher1975-76; Covington City Schools, spec ed teacher 1976-77; State Technical Institution, assoc prof reading. **ORGANIZATIONS:** Secretary PTA Lincoln School 1973-74; Sigma Gamma Rho; AUA; TEA, SCETC; NEA, 1977-83; secretary/adm vice pres Stimulus Toastmasters 1978-84; consultant Fed Corrections Inst 1978-79; representative Parent Advisory Comm 1979-82; consultant Expert Secretarial Serv 1981-84. **HONORS/ACHIEVEMENTS:** Honorable Mention Third World Writer's Contest 1979; Best Regional Bulletin Toastmasters Regional 1981-82; member Phi Delta Kappa 1982; publication co-author "Instructor Magazine" Feb 1984 issue. **BUSINESS ADDRESS:** Assoc Prof Reading, State Tech Inst at Memphis, 5983 Macon Cove, Memphis, TN 38134.

MOORE, KAREN E.
Attorney. **PERSONAL:** Born in Newark, NJ; children: Al-Shawki. **EDUCATION:** Essex Co Coll, AS 1976; Rutgers The State Univ of Newark, BA 1979; Montclair State Coll, MA 1981; Seton Hall Sch of Law, JD 1984. **CAREER:** Superior Court of NJ Appellate Div, law clerk 1982; State of NJ Bd of Public Utilities, legal asst 1983-84; Union Co Legal Svcs, staff atty 1984-85; Free-Lance Entertainment Atty, consultant/attorney 1985-; County of Essex NJ, asst county counsel. **ORGANIZATIONS:** Mem Natl Council of Black Lawyers 1985-; entertainment consultant Night Moves Inc 1986-; planning comm NY Chap Black Music Assoc 1986-; sales assoc Weichert Realtors. **HONORS/ACHIEVEMENTS:** Pi Gamma Mu Intl Social Science Honor Soc 1981; Comm Lawyer Fellowship Reginald Heber Smtih 1984-85, 1985-86.

MOORE, KERMIT
Cellist, conductor, composer, educator. **PERSONAL:** Born Mar 11, 1929, Akron, OH; married Dorothy Rudd. **EDUCATION:** Cleveland Inst Music 1951; NYUniv MA; Paris Conservatory 1956; Juilliard Sch Music. **CAREER:** Univ Hartford, formerly prof; numerous Concerts throughout US, Europe, Africa & Far East; toured NY Philharmonica to Argentina & Dominican Repub 1978; Nat Opera Ebony, permanent gst conductor; commd to compose serv works "Viola Sonata"; classical Radio WQXR, premiered 1979; Brooklyn Philharmonic at Lincoln Center NY, conductor 1984,85,86,87; Detroit Symphony Prog, conductor 1985; Berkeley CA Symphony, guest conductor 1986; commissioner by St Louis Arts Festival to compose work tor cello and piano, premiered work in Sheldon Hall 1986; Rud/Mor Publ Co, pres. **ORGANIZATIONS:** Founder proj dir Symphony of the New World 1964-; founder Soc Black Composers 1968. **HONORS/ACHIEVEMENTS:** Edgar Stillman Kelly Award State of Ohio; grant Knight Publs 1954; Lili Boulanger Award Paris 1953; found Riverside Symphony 1975; conducted concert UN Gen Assembly Hall 1976; composed "Many Thousand Gone"; special medal Queen Elizabeth of Belgium 1958.

MOORE, LARRY LOUIS
Educator. **PERSONAL:** Born Jul 21, 1954, Kings Mountain, NC. **EDUCATION:** Western Carolina Univ, BA 1978; Univ of NC-Charlotte, Graduate School 1980-. **CAREER:** Cleveland Tech Coll, instructor in black history and world civilization 1979-81; Southwest Junior High School, teacher chmn/foreign language dept. **ORGANIZATIONS:** Mem NEA/NCEA 1982-84; mem NC Teachers of Math 1983-84; chmn Student Activities Comm 1984-85; sec Parents and Teachers Org 1985-87; mem NAACP 1987. **HONORS/ACHIEVEMENTS:** Published articles on black topics in various newspapers. **BUSINESS ADDRESS:** Teacher/Chmn Foreign Lang Dept, Southwest Junior High School, #1 Roadrunner Dr, Gastonia, NC 28052.

MOORE, LENARD DUANE
Literary consultant. **PERSONAL:** Born Feb 13, 1958, Jacksonville, NC; married Marcille Lynn; children: Maiisha. **EDUCATION:** Attended, Coastal Carolina Comm Coll 1976-78, Univ of MD 1980-81, NC State Univ 1985. **CAREER:** Freelance Lecturer/Workshop Conductor, 1981-; The Black Writer Chicago, magazine consultant 1982-83; Pacific Quarterly Moana Hamilton New Zealand, acting advisor 1982-83; Intl Black Writers Conf Inc Chicago, regional dir 1982-83; Mira Mesa Branch Library San Diego CA, poet-in-residence 1983; NC Dept of Educ, div of admin serv clerk 1984-. **ORGANIZATIONS:** Mem Kuumba Festival Comm NAACP Onslow Co Branch 1982; bd of dirs Intl Black Writers Conf Inc 1982; mem Toastmasters Intl 1982-84; exec comm NC Haiku Soc 1983-; usher bd Marshall Chapel Missionary Bapt Church 1984-85; mem Poetry Soc of Amer, The Acad of Amer Poets, World Poetry Soc, NC Poetry Soc,Poets Study Club of Terra Haute, NC Writers Network, Intl Platform Assoc, The Poetry Council of NC Inc; The Haiku Soc of Amer; mem WV Poetry Soc; mem The Raleigh Writing Alliance. **HONORS/ACHIEVEMENTS:** Selected Best Poet of 1982 in Canada; Haiku Museum of Tokyo Awd Haiku Soc of Amer 1983; CTM Awd Toastmasters Intl 1983; Outstanding Young Man of Amer 1984; Dr Antonio J Waring Jr Memorial Prize The Poetry Soc of GA 1984; publishing grant NC Haiku Soc 1985; listed in Poets & Writers Inc; Gold Medal for Creative Writing Contest in West Germany; The Sallie Paschall Awd; numerous works published including "The Open Eye," NC Haiku Soc Press 1985; "North Carolina's 400 Years, Signs Along the Way," The Acorn Press; "The Haiku Anthology," Simon & Schuster. **MILITARY SERVICE:** AUS splst 4/E-4 3 yrs; Honorable Discharge, Good Conduct Medal. **BUSINESS ADDRESS:** Clerk, NC Department of Education, 116 West Edenton St, Raleigh, NC 27603.

MOORE, LENNY EDWARD
Promotions director. **PERSONAL:** Born Nov 25, 1933, Reading, PA; married Edith Randolph; children: Lenny, Leslie, Carol, Toni, Terri. **EDUCATION:** PA StUniv 1956; LA. **CAREER:** Juvenile Serv Admin State of MD, ad of spec projects; Baltimore Colts Ftbl Inc, promotions dir present; NW Ayer & Sons, field rep 1970-74; Baltimore Colts, professional ftbl 1956-67; WWIN Radio, sports dir 1962-64; pub relat for natl brewery 1958-63; WSID-RADIO, disc jockey sports dir 1956-58. **ORGANIZATIONS:** Chmn Heart Assn; helped start "Camp Concern" following 1968 riots upon death of King; CBS Pro-Football analyst 1968; asso Leukemia, Kidney Found, Multiple Schelorsis, Muscular Dystrophy, Spec Olympics 1975-; adv council Juvenile Justice 1985-. **HONORS/ACHIEVEMENTS:** Prof Ftbl Hall of Fame 1975; PA Hall of Fame 1976. **BUSINESS ADDRESS:** Ad of Special Projects, Juvenile Service Admin, 201 W Preston St, Baltimore, MD 21201.

MOORE, LEWIS CALVIN
Business executive. **PERSONAL:** Born Jun 22, 1935, Canton, MS; son of Sam A Moore and Louvenia McGee Moore; married Dolores Thurman, Sep 29, 1956; children: Kelly, Thurman, Andy. **EDUCATION:** Manual HS Indianapolis IN, 1954. **CAREER:** OCAW Local 7-706, pres 1970-75; OCAW Dist Council 7, pres 1970-75; OCAW Dist 4 Houston, intl rep 1975-77; OCAW Washington Office, citizenship-legislative dir 1977-79; Oil Chem & Atomic Workers Intl Union, vp. **ORGANIZATIONS:** Labor instr Univ of IN; charter mem, natl bd mem A Philip Randolph Inst; mem NAACP; mem of bd Big Brothers of Amer; leader Boy Scouts of Amer; mem TX Black Alcoholism Council; instr Health & Safety Seminars in Kenya 1984, 1988. **HONORS/ACHIEVEMENTS:** Recognition for serv in field of alcoholism & drug abuse. **BUSINESS ADDRESS:** Vice President, OCAW Intl Union, PO Box 2812, Denver, CO 80201.

MOORE, LOWES LAVELLE
Professional athlete. **PERSONAL:** Born May 05, 1957, Mt Vernon, NY. **EDUCATION:** WV Univ, 1980. **CAREER:** Kansas City Kings, guard. **HONORS/ACHIEVEMENTS:** 1983 named to CBA All-star first-team; 1981-82 averaged 175 ppg in reg season & 218 ppg in the playoffs; runner up to Brad Branson for CBA's Newcomber of the Year; voted WVU Most Valuable Player 1980.

MOORE, LUCILLE SANDERS
Educator. **PERSONAL:** Born Apr 06, 1920, Greenboro, NC; children: Rev. **CAREER:** I Dibner & Bro, commn bd educ district leader. **ORGANIZATIONS:** Past mem Town Com; vice pres Local 223 Intl Ladies Garment Workers Un Bd; mem Model Cities; OES; past matron Calisto Chap #4; spl dep Clock City Temple 895; exec bd mem Waterbury Br NAACP; mem Waterbury C of C; asst sec CT State Conf NAACP.

MOORE, M. ELIZABETH GIBBS
Retired librarian, library consultant. **PERSONAL:** Born in Boston, MA; daughter of Warmoth T Gibbs and Marece Jones Gibbs (deceased). **EDUCATION:** NC A&T State Univ, 1940; Univ of Chgo, BLS 1945; Univ of Chgo, Grad Study 1948-49. **CAREER:** NC A&T State Univ, instr 1940-43; NC A&T State Univ, asst librarian 1943-44; Fisk Univ, cataloger 1945-48, Library Sci, instr 1945-46; Detroit Publ Library, cataloger 1945-53; Detroit Publ Library, ref librarian 1953-54; cataloging supervisor 1955-67; Burroughs Corp, Detroit area librarian 1967-71; Corp Library Burroughs Corp, 1971-79; Library MI Bell, human resources supervisor 1979-82, library consultant 1982-. **ORGANIZATIONS:** Mem Women's Econ Club, Special Libraries Assn; life mem Amer Library Assn, YWCA, Womens Natl Book Assn; bd dir Delta Home for Girls 1974-76; mem Friends of Detroit Publ Library 1970-76, 1980-82, Your Heritage House 1969-82; bd dir Special libraries Assn 1981-84; mem Ctrl Adv Comm on Re-Accreditation of Wayne State Univ div of Libr Sci 1975-76; mem Adv Group for Selection of Head of Sci Libr Wayne State Univ 1976-77; life mem Delta Sigma Theta, NAACP; mem Guilford Cty Bd of Soc Serv 1984-87, 1988-90; bd dir Charlotte Hawkins Brown Historical Foundation 1985-; Women's Econ Club of Detroit 1967-82; bd dir Guilford Women's Network 1989-90; Library Serv & Construction Act Advisory Council to North Carolina State Library 1988-89. **HONORS/ACHIEVEMENTS:** Saslow Medal for Scholarship in Soc Sci; Awd for Meritorious Serv on Coll Newspaper; Alumni Awd for Outstanding Serv 1969; Outstanding Grad in Field of Soc Sci Alumni Awd 1973; Hall of Fame, Special Libraries Assn, 1986. **HOME ADDRESS:** 1000 Ross Ave, Greensboro, NC 27406.

MOORE, MARCELLUS HARRISON
Physician. **PERSONAL:** Born Apr 28, 1939, Griffin, GA; children: Marc, Michelle, Chris. **EDUCATION:** Morehouse Coll, BS 1959; Meharry Medical Coll, MD 1966. **CAREER:** Mercy Hosp, attending physician 1975-; Michael Reese Hosp, attending physician 1975-. **ORGANIZATIONS:** Mem Amer Medical Assn, Natl Medical Assn 1966-; mem Amer Acad of Ophthalmology 1975-. **HONORS/ACHIEVEMENTS:** Fellow Amer Acad of Ophthalmology 1979. **MILITARY SERVICE:** USAF capt 1964-67. **BUSINESS ADDRESS:** Attending Staff Physician, Michael Reese Hospital, 2600 S Michigan Ave, Chicago, IL 60616.

MOORE, MELANIE ANNE
Singer. **PERSONAL:** Born Feb 07, 1950, Dayton, OH. **EDUCATION:** Central State Univ Wilberforce OH, BS 1972. **CAREER:** Atlantic Records, singer; "The All Night Strut Boston Reperatory Theater, actress singer 1979; "The Autobiography of Lorraine Hansberry" Britanica Films Inc, actress 1976; Tymes RCA Records, singer 1975-78; Prudential Lines Inc, mgmt trainee 1976-77; JC Penney Co NY, asst buyer trainee 1972. **ORGANIZATIONS:** Mem AFTRA 1977; mem AGVA 1979; counselor adminstrv asst Veritas Therapeutic Drug Center 1976. **HONORS/ACHIEVEMENTS:** Miss homecoming Central State Univ 1972; biography Black Stars Mag Tymes 1977; biography Kleeer Black Stars Mag 1980; "Black Tress" Maginzine 1980. **BUSINESS ADDRESS:** Atlantic Records, 75 Rockefeller Plaza, New York, NY 10019.

MOORE, MELBA
Actress, singer. **PERSONAL:** Born Oct 29, 1945, New York, NY; married George Brewingston. **EDUCATION:** Montclair NJ State Tchrs Coll, BA. **CAREER:** Cotton Comes to Harlem 1970; made Broadway debut in Hair 1979; appeared in Broadway musical Inacent Black 1981; TV appearances incl Comedy is King, Ed Sullivan Show, Johnny Carson Show. **HONORS/ACHIEVEMENTS:** First Black to perform solo at Metro Opera House NY 1977; recip Tony Award for Best Supporting Actress in Musical Purlie. **BUSINESS ADDRESS:** c/o Capitol Records, 1750 N Vine St, Hollywood, CA 90028.

MOORE, MILTON DONALD, JR.
Dermatologist. **PERSONAL:** Born Aug 16, 1953, Aberdeen, MD; son of Dora Lee Moore; married Ramona Carter; children: Rahmon, Justin. **EDUCATION:** Xavier Coll of Pharmacy, RPh 1976; Meharry Medical Coll, MD 1980. **CAREER:** Hubbard Hospital, pharmacist 1976-80; Baylor Coll of Medicine, derm dept asst prof 1985-; private practice, physician 1985. **ORGANIZATIONS:** Bd mem Ensemble Theatre 1986. **HONORS/ACHIEVEMENTS:** Outstanding Young Men of Amer; American Academy of Dermatology. **BUSINESS ADDRESS:** Physician, 7553 South Freeway, Houston, TX 77021.

MOORE, N. WEBSTER
Retired educator. **PERSONAL:** Born Mar 05, 1913, Claremore, OK; married Fordine Stone. **EDUCATION:** KS State Coll of Pittsburgh, attended; Univ of KS, AB 1937, MA 1939; St Louis Univ, Washington Univ, Stowe Teachers, Harris Teachers Coll, Langston, attended. **CAREER:** Bristow OK Public Schools, teacher 1939-48; AR State AMN Coll, teacher 1947; Hadley Tech High School, teacher 1956-63; Vashon High School St Louis, teacher 1948-56, 1963-78; retired. **ORGANIZATIONS:** Pres, Natl Council for Social Studies, 1975-76; acting pres, St Louis Public Library, 1979-80; vice pres bd of dir, Arts & Educ Council, 1978-80; chmn bd, Page Park YMCA, 1972-74; bd of mgr, YMCA of Greater St Louis, 31 years; bd of dir, St Louis Prog Teachers Credit Union, Jr Kindergarten 1978-, KS Univ 1978-, Wells-Goodfellow 1978-79, Carver House, AARP, NRTA, Retired Teacher Assn of MO 1980, Retired St Louis School Employees Assn, Boy Scouts; dir, St Louis Public Library, 1972; committeeman, NAACP; grand historian, Kappa Alpha Psi, 1944-47; sr member, Monsanto YMCA; member, Natl Council for Social Studies, Greater St Louis Council for Social Studies, MO Council for Social Studies, St Louis White House Conf on Educ, Historical Assn of Greater St Louis, MO Historical Soc, State Historical Soc of MO, St Louis Teachers Assn, St Louis Teachers Union, United Churchmen, Metro Bd of YMCA, Urban League, Arts & Educ Council, US China Peoples Friendship Assn, Metro Dist & Branch YMCA Intl Program Comm, St Louis Westerners; former member, Natl Council of YMCA of the US; attended the World Council of YMCA in 1981. **HONORS/ACHIEVEMENTS:** Outstanding Serv Award, Kappa Alpha Psi, 1966; First N Webster Moore Humanitarian Award, Kappa Alpha Psi, 1971; Achievement Award, Mid-Western Provicne Kappa Alpha Psi, 1974; award from YMCA for 17 years serv to youth, 1965; author, several articles published in Bulletin of the MO Hist Soc.

MOORE, NAT
Professional athlete. **PERSONAL:** Born Sep 19, 1951, Tallahasse, FL; married Patricia; children: Trellanee, Natalie, Melanie. **EDUCATION:** Attended, Univ of FL. **CAREER:** Superstar Rollertheque, owner; Interno Lounge, owner; L & S Builders, partner, Miami Dolphins, wide receiver 1974-. **ORGANIZATIONS:** Bd mem Dade County United Way; bd mem Jackson Mem Children's Hosp; Boy Scouts of America. **HONORS/ACHIEVEMENTS:** All NFL Honors AP Pro-Football Writers 1977; All AFC Recognition; Tommy Fitzgerald Awd Outstanding Rookie in Training Camp 1974; Byron "Whizzer" White Humanitarian Awd NFL Players Assn 1986. **BUSINESS ADDRESS:** Miami Dolphins, 4770 Biscayne Blvd Ste 1440, Miami, FL 33137.

MOORE, NATHAN
Educator. **PERSONAL:** Born Jun 26, 1931, Mayaro, Trinidad and Tobago;son of William B Moore and Eugenie Samuel Moore; married Mary Lisbeth Simmons, Jul 02, 1967; children: Christine, Serena. **EDUCATION:** Caribbean Union Coll Trinidad, A 1958; Rockford Coll IL, BA 1963; CarletonUniv Ottawa, MA 1965;Univ of British Columbia, PhD 1972. **CAREER:** Barbados Secondary Sch, hs tchr 1958-61; Carleton U, sessional lecturer 1964-65, teaching fellow 1963-65; Barrier Sch Dist British Col, hs tchr 1966-67; Walla Walla Coll WA, coll tchr 1967-79; AL State U, u tchr 1979-, chmn dept of engl 1980-. **ORGANIZATIONS:** Mem Modern Lang Assn 1965-; mem Am Soc for 18th Century Studies 1971-; mem South Atlantic MLA 1980-. **HONORS/ACHIEVEMENTS:** Schlrshp Rockford Coll 1961; schl-

rshp Readers Digest 1962; Carleton Fellow CarletonUniv 1963-65. **BUSINESS ADDRESS:** Chairman, AL State University, S Jackson St, Montgomery, AL 36195.

MOORE, NOAH WATSON, JR.
Retired bishop. **PERSONAL:** Born Mar 28, 1902, Newark, NJ; son of Noah W Moore, Sr and Eliza A (Boyce) Moore; married Carolyn W Lee Moore (deceased); children: Carolyn Moore Weddington. **EDUCATION:** Morgan State Coll, AB 1926; LLD 1961; Drew Univ, BD 1931; Crozier Theol Sem, postgrad 1945-46; Grammon Theol Sch, DD 1951; So Meth Univ, 1968; NE, Wesleyan Univ, STD 1969. **CAREER:** Meth Ch ordained to ministry 1932; consecrated bishop 1960; NY State MD PA, pastor 1930-47; Eastern Dist MD, supt 1947-49; Tindley Temple Meth Ch Philadelphia, pastor 1949-60; New Orleans area, resident bishop 1960-64; SW area, bishop 1964-68; NE area, 1968-72. **ORGANIZATIONS:** Mem Meth Gen Overseas Relief 1952-60; del Gen Conf Meth Ch 1952, 56, 60; sec treas dir Philadelphia Housing Auth 1954-60; Gammon Theol Sem Houston-Tillotsen Coll Morriston Coll 1956-60; Hlth & Welfare Agency So Area Meth Ch Philadelphia 1957-59; pres Coll of Bishop Cntrl Juris 1956; mem Preaching Mission to AK 1956; study tour W Germany Berlin 1959; trustee Dillard Univ 1960-68; pres bd trustees Philander Smith Coll 1964-68; pres trustees Wiley Coll 1964-68; mem Gen Bd Educ pres United Meth Gen Bd Evangelism 1968-72; mem exec com World Meth Council; United Fund Philadelphia & vincinity; Bryan Meml Hosp; St Paul Sch Theol; Meth Kansas City MO; bd govs trustee NE Wesleyan Univ; bd dirs Urban League Philadelphia; NAACP; bd mgrs Christian St YMCA Philadelphia; mem Frontiers of Am; Natl Co uncil Chs; Omega Psi Phi; Mason; trustee Atlanta Comm Coll.

MOORE, OSCAR JAMES, JR.
Physician. **PERSONAL:** Born in Griffin, GA; children: Frederick, Elna. **EDUCATION:** Morehouse Coll, BS 1955; Atlanta U, 1955-56; Howard U, MD 1962; Howard U, intern 1963; HarvardUniv Thorndike Meml Lab Bostin City Hosp, resd 1963-Morehouse Coll Atlanta GA, BS 1955; Howard Univ Wash DC, MD 1962, internship 1963; Harvard Univ Boston MA, specialty residence 1967;66. **CAREER:** Self Employed, physician; Pritzker Med SchUniv Chgo, asso clinical instr 1972-; Rush Med Coll, asst prof med 1968-72; CT Gen Life Ins, asst med diHarvard Med School, instr 1965-66; Rush Med School, asst prof of med 1968-72; Med Univ of Chicago, asso clin prof 1972-79; UCLA Med School, asst cr 1967-68; Harvard Med Sch, instr 1965-66;lin prof 1979-87. **ORGANIZATIONS:** Dir med Mile Sq Hlth Ctr 1968-72; Mid-Southside Hlth Planning Orgn 1972-; sr atdng physician St Lukes Presb Med Ctr; Michael Reese Hosp & Med Cmem Omega Psi Phi, Beta Kappa Chi, Natl Urban League, NAACP;tr; IL Central Hosp; Woodlawn Hosp; bd dir New Eng Div Am Cancer Soc 1968-69; Chicago Urban League 1973; Abraham Lincoln Ctr 1973; Operation Breadbasket 1973; bd tst Grtr Bethesda Bapt Ch 1975; comm bd Olive Harvey Coll 1974. **HONORS/ACHIEVEMENTS:** Citz yr award Olive Harvey Coll 1976. **MILITARY SERVICE:** USN lt comdr 1966-68;USN lt cmdr 1966-68. **BUSINESS ADDRESS:** Clinical Professor, UCLA Medical School, 1828 S Western Ave, Los Angeles, CA 90008.

MOORE, OSCAR WILLIAM, JR.
Educator. **PERSONAL:** Born Mar 31, 1938, White Plains, NY; son of Oscar Sr and Helen; children: Derrick. **EDUCATION:** Southern IL Univ, BS 1969, MS 1970; graduate of Philadelphia Coll of The Bible; attending Trinity Coll of The Bible, Trinity Theological Seminary. **CAREER:** Southern Illinois Univ, asst dir 1969-71; Glassboro State Coll, asst prof, head track & field coach. **ORGANIZATIONS:** Sec/treas New Jersey Track Coaches Assoc 1975-; faculty sponsor Alpha Phi Alpha, Sigma Sor; dir Glassboro Summer Martin Luther King. **HONORS/ACHIEVEMENTS:** Teams have consistently placed in the top natl ranking including NCAA Div III Championships in 1980,81; recognized as one of the countries finest masters competitors; numerous speaking engagements in high schools; assists with Red Cross, Cancer Soc, YMCA fund raising campaigns. **MILITARY SERVICE:** USMC sgt 1956-60; Good Conduct Awd 1957. **HOME ADDRESS:** Park Crest Village 4A, Glassboro, NJ 08028. **BUSINESS ADDRESS:** Asstistant Professor, Glassboro State College, Health & Physical Ed Dept, Glassboro, NJ 08028.

MOORE, PARLETT LONGWORTH
Educational administrator. **PERSONAL:** Born Sep 17, 1907, Wetipquin, MD; married Thelma Crawford; children: Thelma Moore Smith, Parlett L Moore Jr, Daniel C Moore. **EDUCATION:** Howard Univ, AB 1930; Teachers Coll Columbia Univ, MA 1935; Univ of Chicago, 1946; Temple Univ, EdD 1952; Stanford Univ, 1955. **CAREER:** St Clair HS, principal 1930-38; Lincoln HS Rockville, MD, principal 1938-50; Morgan State Coll-Summer School, instr 1938-43; Carver HS Rockville, MD, principal 1950-56; Coppin State Coll Baltimore, MD, pres 1956-70; Middle States Acrdtg Assoc, evaluation comm 1950-70; MD Assoc for Higher Educ, pres 1968; Coppin State Coll, pres emeritus 1970-. **ORGANIZATIONS:** Bd of dir MD Region Natl Conf Christians & Jews 1956-63; bd of dir MD Assoc of mental health (15 yrs); bd of dir Baltimore Metro YMCA (8 yrs); prlmntrn Frontiers Internatl Baltimore Club 1957-85. **HONORS/ACHIEVEMENTS:** The Gnrl Alumni of Howard Univ Metitorious Award for Consipcuous Serv in the Field of Educ 1963. **HOME ADDRESS:** 7410 Rockridge Rd, Baltimore, MD 21208.

MOORE, RICHARD BAXTER
Attorney. **PERSONAL:** Born May 26, 1943, Erie, PA; son of Louis Tanner Moore and Jean Baxter Moore; married Brenda Robinson, Jun 25, 1989; children: Leonard, Richard Jr, Tiffiny. **EDUCATION:** Central State Coll, BS 1965; Howard Univ School of Law, JD 1969. **CAREER:** City of Phila, asst jury commissioner; Private Practice, attorney; Philadelphia, PA asst district atty 1971-77. **ORGANIZATIONS:** Mem Elks Chris J Perry Lodge 965, Phi Alpha Delta Law Frat, Omega Psi Phi Frat; bd of dirs NAACP; chmn Veterans Comm; vice chmn United Negro Coll Fund, City of Philadelphia; Juvenile Serv Sub Comm on Public Serv, vice chmn 1973-74; Compensation for Victims of Crimes Comm, sec 1974-75; Natl Bar Found, vice pres bd of dirs 1975-78; Philadelphia Bar Assn; Sigma Pi Phi Fraternity. **HONORS/ACHIEVEMENTS:** Service Awd Chapel of Four Chaplains; Outstanding Young Men of Amer 1977; Citation United Negro Coll Fund. **MILITARY SERVICE:** AUS capt 1969-71. **BUSINESS ADDRESS:** Attorney at Law, 406 South 16th St, Philadelphia, PA 19146.

MOORE, RICHARD EARLE
Educational administrator. **PERSONAL:** Born Apr 03, 1916, Marion, AL; married Rose Marie Greene; children: Richard E, Harriette M, Gwendelyn Tutt, Reginald E. **EDUCATION:** Talladega Coll, AB cum lauda 1939; Atlanta U, MS/MA 1961; Auburn Univ, EdS/EdD 1979. **CAREER:** Clayton Jr Coll, asst dean 1973-; JF Drake High Sch, high school prin 1949-71; Coffee Co Training School, high school prin 1945-49; Escombia Co Training School, high school science math teacher 1940-45. **ORGANIZATIONS:** Mem NAACP; Alpha Phi Alpha; NASSP; Phi Delta Kapa; Council on Black Am Affairs Commr; Fulton Co Voter Registration Bd 1977. **HONORS/ACHIEVEMENTS:** NDEA fellow Amherst Coll 1965; NDEA fellow Davidsons Coll 1966; CPSDI fellow Auburn Univ 1971-73; blacks in white coll Council on Black Amer Affairs 1976. **BUSINESS ADDRESS:** Assistant Dean, Clayton State College, Morrow, GA 30260.

MOORE, RICHARD V.
Educator. **PERSONAL:** Born Nov 20, 1906, Quincy, FL; married B J Jones. **EDUCATION:** Knoxville Coll, AB; Atlanta Univ, MA; NY Univ, post grad work. **CAREER:** Pinellas HS, instr coach 1932-34; Unoin Acad, prin 1934-37; Rosenwald HS, prin 1937-44; Booker T Washington HS, 1944-45; Negro Secondary Schools, state supr 1945-47; Bethune-cookman Coll, pres 1947-. **ORGANIZATIONS:** Mem Rotary Club Dayton Beach; conf lay leader FL Conf; mem Halifax Bd Commnrs; bd dirs Whinn-dixie Stores Inc; vice chmn FL Fed Savs & Loan Assn; mem Civic League; Daytona Beach Chamber of Commerce; NAACP; dir Central FL United Negro Coll Fund Inc; sec Independent Colleges & Univ of FL; Afro-Am Life Ins Co; Halifax Area Citizen's Scholarships Found; trustee So Coll & Gammon Theol Sem. **HONORS/ACHIEVEMENTS:** Lovejoy Award; St George Award; outstanding citizen of yr Daytona Beach; numerous hon degs honors. **BUSINESS ADDRESS:** 640 2 Ave Bethune, Cookman Coll, Daytona Beach, FL 32015.

MOORE, ROBERT F.
Educator. **PERSONAL:** Born Jan 30, 1944, Tuskegee Inst, AL. **EDUCATION:** Fisk Univ, BS 1965; IN Univ, MS 1966; IN Univ, EdD 1969. **CAREER:** Fisk Univ Nashville; assoc prof educ 1971-; Coppin State Coll, asst Prof 1968-70. **ORGANIZATIONS:** Mem bd dirs TN Assn Retarded Citizens; Davidson Co Assn Retarded Citizens; TN Foster Grandparents Assn; Grace Eaton Day Home; Personalities of S 1970; Phi Delta Kappa 1966. **BUSINESS ADDRESS:** Box 11, Dept Educ Fisk University, Nashville, TN 37203.

MOORE, ROSCOE MICHAEL, JR.
US health services veterinarian. **PERSONAL:** Born Dec 02, 1944, Richmond, VA; son of Roscoe Michaal Moore Sr and Robnette Johnson Moore; married Patricia Ann Haywood, Aug 02, 1969; children: Roscoe III, John H. **EDUCATION:** Tuskegee Univ, BS 1968, DVM 1969; Univ of Michigan, MPH 1970; Johns Hopkins Univ, MHS 1982, PhD 1985. **CAREER:** Natl Insts of Health, veterinarian 1970-71; Centers for Disease Control, epidemic intelligence serv officer 1971-73; Ctr for Veterinary Medicine, sr veterinarian 1973-74; Natl Inst Occup Safety & Health, sr epidemiologist 1974-81; Center for Devices and Rad Health, sr epidemiologist 1981-; US Public Health Servs, veterinary dir. **ORGANIZATIONS:** Mem Amer Veterinary Medical Assoc 1969-; mem bd of dirs FONZ 1979-; pres bd of dirs Friends of the Natl Zoo 1984-87; fellow Amer Coll of Epidemiology 1984-; adv comm Howard Univ Coll of Medicine 1985-; consultant, School of Veterinary Medicine, Tuskegee Univ 1988-; mem bd of governors, Univ of Michigan Public Health Alumni 1987-. **HONORS/ACHIEVEMENTS:** Commendation Medal US Public Health Serv 1976,83; USPHS Career Develop Awd to attend Johns Hopkins Univ 1977-79; Delta Omega Natl Honorary Public Health Society 1985. **HOME ADDRESS:** 14315 Arctic Ave, Rockville, MD 20853.

MOORE, SHELLEY LORRAINE
Writer, corporate communications consultant. **PERSONAL:** Born Mar 19, 1950, New York, NY; daughter of Dr Marcus W Moore and Sheppie Moore. **EDUCATION:** Syracuse Univ, BA 1971; Columbia Univ, MA, EdM 1973. **CAREER:** Natl Urban League, asst dir 1976-80; Natl Urban League, program coordinator 1980-83; Burson-Marsteller, Inc, acct exec 1983-85; Shelley Moore Communications, principal, 1985-; Mobil Corporation, staff assoc, 1988-. **ORGANIZATIONS:** Chairperson comm on minorities Public Relations Soc of Amer NY Chapter 1979-80 dir public relations Council of Concerned Black Exec 1981-82; mem NY Assn of Black Journalists; mem, Brooklyn Communications Arts Professionals. **HONORS/ACHIEVEMENTS:** Articles & photographs published in natl publications. **HOME ADDRESS:** 270 Jay St, Brooklyn, NY 11201.

MOORE, SUSIE M.
Government association executive. **PERSONAL:** Born Sep 03, 1918, Washington, DC. **EDUCATION:** Miners Tchr's Coll. **CAREER:** HEW Bur Comm Health Servs, training grant splst family planning; Fed Govt, employee 34 yrs; Vocational Rehab Serv, grants mgmt splst & adminstrv asst 22 yrs. **ORGANIZATIONS:** Mem dist pres Woman's Home For Miss Soc; AME Zion Ch 1961-; rec sec Nat Coun Negro Women 1971-73. **HONORS/ACHIEVEMENTS:** Superior serv award Vocational Rehab Ofc 1957. **BUSINESS ADDRESS:** 5600 Fishers Ln, Rockville, MD 20852.

MOORE, THOMAS H.
Postmaster. **PERSONAL:** Born Sep 04, 1927, Mount Bayou, MS. **EDUCATION:** BS Accounting Economics 1955; Tuskegee Inst NC Coll at Durham, atnd. **CAREER:** Mt Bayou, postmaster 1977-; Dist 3 Bolivar Co MS, justice of the peace; Mid-delta Educ Assn Greenville, adminstrv asst 1968-70; Mary Holmes Jr Coll West Point, chief finance ofcr 1966-68; Child Devel Group of MS, dir personnel 1965-66. **ORGANIZATIONS:** Mem Am Bar Assn 1974-; MS Justice Ct Ofcr Assn 1971-; exec dir Economic Devel Assn of Bolivar Co Inc 1969-; mem NAACP 1951-; Mound Bayou Recon League; Urban League; dem party Exec Com Bolivar Co; Mason; Elk. **HONORS/ACHIEVEMENTS:** Recip cert of proficiency Un Bus Assn; IBM cert Nat Ofc Mgmt Assn 1954; ldrshp cert AUS 1959; instr cert Nat Rifle Assn; first black to hold position of justice of the peace in history of bolivar co; first black to serve on MS justice ct ofcrs assn legislative com at state level; presided over congressional & depositions hearings on registration & voting in bolivar co Feb 1965. **MILITARY SERVICE:** AUS m/sgt 1945-61. **BUSINESS ADDRESS:** PO Box 238 Mound, Bayou, MS 38762.

MOORE, THOMAS L.
Business executive. **PERSONAL:** Born Jun 26, 1926, Burke Co, GA; married Alma Brown; children: Tommy, Yvonne, Dionne, Michael. **EDUCATION:** Swift Meml Coll; Knoxville Coll. **CAREER:** TAM Inc Constrn Co, pres; Tommy Moore Enter; Moore's Package Store. **ORGANIZATIONS:** Bd dir City & Co Bank of Knox Co; chtr commn Knox Co Bd of Commr; pres Knoxville Nat Bus League; Bus Devel Ctr C of C; bd dir Jr Achmvt; bd dir BSA; pres Cncl on Yth Oppt YMCA. **HONORS/ACHIEVEMENTS:** YMCA cert award Com-

monwealth of KY; KY Col Nat Soc of Vol of Am; TN Rep Capitol Club. **BUSINESS ADDRESS:** 1312 Mc Calla Ave, Knoxville, TN 37915.

MOORE, TIM CALVIN
Professional athlete. **PERSONAL:** Born Sep 27, 1960, New Orleans, LA; married Ramona. **EDUCATION:** Southern U. **CAREER:** Denver Gold, nose tackle; Oakland Invaders, nose tackle 1984-. **HONORS/ACHIEVEMENTS:** Named All-Southwest Athletic Conf as sr.

MOORE, TRUDY S.
Journalist. **PERSONAL:** Born Jan 06, 1957, Paterson, NJ; daughter of Queen E Moore. **EDUCATION:** Howard Univ, Washington, DC, BS, 1979; Northwestern Univ, Evanston, IL, MS, 1980. **CAREER:** Chicago Sun-Times, Chicago, IL, gen assignment reporter, 1980; Jet Magazine, Chicago, IL, asst editor, 1980-83, assoc editor, 1983-89, feature editor 1989; Ebony Man, Chicago, IL, contributing editor, 1988-. **ORGANIZATIONS:** Volunteer, Big Brothers/Big Sisters, Chicago, IL, 1982-85; mem, Chicago Urban League, 1986-; mem, NAACP, Women's Auxiliary, 1989; mem, bd of dir, NAACP, Ch icago, South Side Branch, 1989, mem, Chicago Assn of Black Journalists. **BUSINESS ADDRESS:** Feature Editor, Jet Magazine/ Johnson Publishing Co, 820 S Michigan Ave, Chicago, IL 60605.

MOORE, UNDINE SMITH
Educator, composer, lecturer. **PERSONAL:** Born Aug 25, 1907, Jarratt, VA; married Dr James Arthur. **EDUCATION:** Mus Sch Fisk U, AB 1st in class & honors 1926; Mus Tchr's Coll Columbia U, MA 1931; Howard Murphy, pvt study; Honoris Causa VA State Coll, MusD1972; Honoris Causa IN, U, MusD 1976. **CAREER:** VA State Coll Petersburg, ret prof mus 1927-72; Richmond Comm Sch for Gifted, scholar in residence 1978; VA State Coll, artist in residence 1976; VA Unoin U, adj prof 1972-77; Coll of St Benedict St Joseph MN, vis prof 1973-75; Carleton Coll Northfield MN, vis prof 1972; Goldsboro NC, mus supr pub 1926. **ORGANIZATIONS:** Co-founder Black Mus Center VA State Coll 1968; mus consult Arts Educ State of VA 1978; sr adv Afro-Am Arts Inst of IN U; mem John Work Meml Found;mem ASCAP; mem women's com Richmond Symphony Orchestra 1978; mem Mus Educators Nat Conf; mem Alpha Kappa Alpha; mem Gillfield Bapt Ch. **HONORS/ACHIEVEMENTS:** Recipient fine arts awards Fish U, Atlanta U, VA Unoin U, VA State So U, Norfolk State Coll, Nat Assn Negro Musicians, Huston-Tillotson, Morgan State U; cert of appreciation City of NY by Mayor John Lindsay; cert Mayor Arnold Petersburg VA; mus laureate VA 1977; lectr composer NY Philarmonic Celebration of Black Composers 1977; contributing author "The Black Composer Speaks" Scare Crow Press; pub "Reflections on Afro-Am Mus" Kent StateUniv Press; recipient first julliard scholarship in piano Fisk U; choral compositions pub Warner Bros; Augsburg Mus Home; documentary INUniv Black Artists Series.

MOORE, WALTER LOUIS
Government official. **PERSONAL:** Born Mar 14, 1946, Pontiac, MI; married Daisy Barber. **EDUCATION:** Attended Ferris State Coll 1966-68, Oakland Univ. **CAREER:** City of Pontiac MI, firefighter; County of Oakland MI, commissioner 1978; City of Pontiac MI, mayor. **ORGANIZATIONS:** Campaign mgr, Coalition for a Modern Charter, City of Pontiac; organized I-75 Mayor's Conference; mem, US Conference of Mayors; mem, Natl Conference of Black Mayors; dir, Pontiac Youth Assistance; charter mem, Pontiac Optimist Club; mason, Gibraltor Lodge #19 Prince Hall; bd mem, Offender Aid and Restoration. **HONORS/ACHIEVEMENTS:** America's Outstanding Young Men, Jaycees of Amer, 1984; Man and Boy Award, Boys and Girls Club of Pontiac, 1986; Community Serv Award, Oakland County NAACP; Community Serv Award, Natl Org of Negro Business and Professional Women's Clubs. **HOME ADDRESS:** 34 Ottawa Dr, Pontiac, MI 48053. **BUSINESS ADDRESS:** Mayor, City of Pontiac, 450 Wide Track Dr, Pontiac, MI 48058.

MOORE, WARFIELD, JR.
Judge. **PERSONAL:** Born Mar 05, 1934, Chicago, IL; son of Warfield Moore, Sr and Sally Moore; married Jeane Virginia; children: Warfield III, Sharon, Sally Anne, Janet. **EDUCATION:** Univ of MI, AB 1957; Wayne State Univ, LLB 1960. **CAREER:** Private Practice, attorney 1961-78; Recorders Court, judge 1978-. **HONORS/ACHIEVEMENTS:** Law Review, Wayne ST Univ; editor 1958-60. **BUSINESS ADDRESS:** Judge, Recorders Court, 1441 St Antoine #404, Detroit, MI 48226.

MOORE, WENDA WEEKES
Regent/researcher. **PERSONAL:** Born Dec 24, 1941, Boston, MA; daughter of Dr and Mrs Leroy R Weekes; married Cornell L Moore; children: Lynne, Jonathon, Meredith. **EDUCATION:** Howard Univ, BA 1963; USC, grad work 2 years. **CAREER:** Gov Wendell R Anderson, staff asst; Wash, DC Library, researcher. **ORGANIZATIONS:** Mem League of Women Voters 1964, 1974; dir YMCA; Women's Inst Social Change 1969-73; dir Children's Hosp 1974-83; appointed by Gov Anderson to bd of regents Univ of MN 1973; elected by MN Legislature to bd of regents 1975; elected v chairperson bd of regents 1975; chmn bd of regents 1977-83; mem Univ of MN Found; bd mem MN bd of Continuing Leg Edn; elected dir Gamble-Skogm Inc 1978-82; dir Greater Minneapolis Girl Scout Cncl 1979-81; leader First Educ Exchange Delegation Univ of MN to People's Republic of China 1979; Presidential appointee to Bd of Adv US Dept of Educ 1980; Adv Council 1980-83; Natl Commn on Foreign Lang 1980; mem Alpha Kappa Alpha; mem, pres 1987-89, Minneapolis/St Paul Chap of Links; Jacks and Jill; pres of the bd of dir, Chart/Wedco 1989- 90; mem, bd of dir Kellogg Foundation 1988-. **HONORS/ACHIEVEMENTS:** Outstanding Young Women Amer 1970; Torch & Shield Award 1982; Outstanding Woman in Education YWCA 1983; Outstanding Alumni Achievement Howard Univ 1989.

MOORE, WINSTON E.
Association executive. **PERSONAL:** Born in New Orleans; married Mabel Lee Woods. **EDUCATION:** WV State Coll, MA 1952;Univ LA, BA 1954. **CAREER:** Clinic IL Youth Commn Joliet, dir 1961-66; IL State Employment Serv Chicago, staff psychologist 1966-68; Cook Co Jail, supt cook 1968-70; Cook Co DeptCorrections, exec dir 1970-. **ORGANIZATIONS:** Mem Am Correctional Assn; Cook Co Criminal Justice Commn; IL Dept Corrections Adult Adv; bd mem Rotary 1. **MILITARY SERVICE:** AUS s/sgt 1945-49. **BUSINESS ADDRESS:** 2600 S California, Chicago, IL 60608.

MOORE-STOVALL, JOYCE
Medical doctor. **PERSONAL:** Born Nov 05, 1948, Washington, DC; daughter of Joseph Samuel Moore and Ida Barnes Moore; married Arthur J Stovall; children: Artis Jomar, Aaron Joseph. **EDUCATION:** Fisk Univ, BA 1970; Meharry Medical Coll, MD 1974. **CAREER:** Veteran's Administration, diagnostic radiologist. **HONORS/ACHIEVEMENTS:** "Parosteal Osteosarcoma" 1982, "Anorectal Abscesses" 1983 Journal of the Kansas Medical Soc; "Pneumatosis Coli" Journal of the Natl Medical Assoc 1983; "CT,Detecting Intraabdominal Abscesses" Journal of the NMA 1985; AMA Physician's Recognition Awds 1981,85; AIDS: The Role of Imaging Modalities and Infection Control Policies J.NMA 1988; Magnetic Resonance Imaging of an Adult with Dundy Walker Syndrome J.NMA 1988. **HOME ADDRESS:** 3707 Lakeview Dr, Leavenworth, KS 66048. **BUSINESS ADDRESS:** Diagnostic Radiologist, Veteran's Administration, 4th Trafficway, Leavenworth, KS 66048.

MOOREHEAD, BOBBIE WOOTEN
Educator. **PERSONAL:** Born May 26, 1937, Kelly, LA; daughter of Verdie C Wooten and Ora Lee Edwards Jones; married Erskine L Moorehead; children: Eric Lyn, Jennifer Lynne. **EDUCATION:** Atlanta Univ, attended 1958-59; TX Southern Univ, BS 1958, MEd 1977; Certification, Administration Supervision, 1977. **CAREER:** Goose Creek Consolidated School Dist, teacher 1959-62; Houston Independent School Dist, teacher 1963-. **ORGANIZATIONS:** Comm on administration YWCA 1977-84; regional dir Zeta Phi Beta Sorority 1978-80; 1978 Natl Convention Chmn Zeta Phi Beta Sorority; mem Commn on Accreditation for the Schools of TX 1978-83; natl first vice pres Zeta Phi Beta Sorority 1980-84; natl pres Top Ladies of Distinction Inc 1983-87; natl bd convention chmn Natl Council of Negro Women 1985, 1987, 1989; mem Speakers Bureau, Houston Planned Parenthood Federation, Houston Urban League Guild; Natl Executive Bd, Natl Council of Negro WOmen, Natl Chrmn Social and Legislative Action for Top Ladies of Distinction, Inc. **HONORS/ACHIEVEMENTS:** Service to the State Award Gov Dolph E Briscoe 1977; Hon Bd Mem TSU Maroon and Grey Ex-Students Assoc 1983, 1984; Woman of Achievement in Leadership Sigma Gamma Rho Sor 1986; Leadership Award Zeta Phi Beta Sorority 1986; Jack Yates High School Hall of Fame 1986; Distinguished Woman Award South Central Dist Women of Achievement Inc 1986; 1987 History Makers Award Educ Riverside Hospital. **HOME ADDRESS:** 3207 Parkwood Dr, Houston, TX 77021. **BUSINESS ADDRESS:** Teacher, HS of the Perf/Visual Arts, PO Box 600504, Houston, TX 77260.

MOOREHEAD, EMERY CALVIN
Professional athlete. **PERSONAL:** Born Mar 22, 1954, Evanston, IL. **EDUCATION:** Colorado, 1975-80. **CAREER:** Chicago Bears, tight end 1980-. **HONORS/ACHIEVEMENTS:** Finished 5th in receptions (29) and 2nd in reception yds (497); awarded to Bears via waivers 1984 from Broncos. **BUSINESS ADDRESS:** Chicago Bears, Halas Hall, P O Box 500 Sta M Montreal, Lake Forest, IL 60045.

MOOREHEAD, JUSTIN LESLIE
Banker. **PERSONAL:** Born Oct 31, 1947, St Thomas, VI. **EDUCATION:** Occidental Coll Los Angeles CA, BA History 1969; Woodrow Wilson School Princeton Univ, MPA Concentration, Econ Devel 1971; NY Univ Grad School of Bus Admin, Transp Econ 1974; Univ of MI Exec Acad, 1977; Bank of Amer, Municipal Credit & Money Mkt Instr 1978. **CAREER:** Government of Kenya, rural devel planner 1970; Government of the US Virgin Islands, economist office of the budget dir 1971-72; Virgin Island Dept of PublicWorks, admin 1972-73; Amerada Hess Corp, 1973-75; Virgin Island Office of the budget Dir, budget dir 1975-79; Lehman Brothers Kuhn Loeb Inc vice pres publ fin 1979-83; Dean Witter Reynolds Inc, managing dir public finance. **BUSINESS ADDRESS:** Managing Dir, Dean Witter Reynolds Inc, 2 World Trade Center, New York, NY 10048.

MOOREHEAD, THOMAS A.
Community service director. **PERSONAL:** Born Apr 21, 1944, Monroe, LA; married Deborah Williams. **EDUCATION:** Gramblin U, BA 1966;Univ of MI, MSW 1971; Chrysler Computer Mgmt Inst, attended 1970; United Auto Worker Leadership Training Inst, 1970. **CAREER:** Univ of MI, dir comm serv 1972-;Univ of MI, dir project comm 1971-72; Chrysler Corp Parts Div Detroit, sys analyst 1969-70; Mobil Oil Corp Detroit, marketing analyst 1966-67; Grambling U, IBM operator 1965-66. **ORGANIZATIONS:** Mem Assn of Black Social Workers; Assn of Vol Bur of Am; Assn of Voluntary Action Scholars; Nat Assn of Student Personnel Adminstr; mem Ann Arbor Bd of Better Chance Program;Univ of MI Rep Greater Ann Arbor C of C; mem Ann Arbor Bd of Ex-Offenders; mem Ann Arbor Young People Leather; Ann Arbor Sportsmen; adv com Recreation Intramurals & Club Sports; cit adv com of Camp Lauictoire. **MILITARY SERVICE:** AUS 1967-68. **BUSINESS ADDRESS:** Dealer/Development Program, General Motors Corp, West Grand Blvd, Detroit, MI 48202.

MOORHEAD, JOSEPH H.
Physician. **PERSONAL:** Born Mar 15, 1921, Frederiksted, St Croix, Virgin Islands of the United States;married Juanita; children: Joel, Karen, Frankie, James, Justina, Joseph, John. **EDUCATION:** Fisk U; Meharry Med Coll; Homer G Phillips Hosp; Hubbard Hosp; Pittsfield Gen; W MA. **CAREER:** Pvt Prac, gynecologist; Am Bd Ob-Gyn, diplomate. **ORGANIZATIONS:** Mem Atlanta Ob-Gyn Soc; Nat Med Assn; mem Kappa Alpha Psi Frat; FL Cattleman Ass; diplomate Nat Bd of Med Examrs; flw Am Coll Surgeons; Am Coll Ob-Gyn. **MILITARY SERVICE:** AUS capt 1952-55. **BUSINESS ADDRESS:** 75 Piedmont Ave NE, Atlanta, GA 30303.

MOORING, KITTYE D. (NEE SAMUELS)
Educator. **PERSONAL:** Born Mar 18, 1932, San Antonio; married Leon. **EDUCATION:** Prairie View A&M Univ, BA 1953, MS 1960; Univ Houston, EdD 1969. **CAREER:** Carver HS, dept head 1953-62; Prairie View A&M Univ, assoc prof 1962-68; Bus Educ & Off Administration TX Southern Univ, dept head 1970-. **ORGANIZATIONS:** Nat & TX Bus Assn; chmn TX Bus Tchr Educ Council 1973-75; TX Assn Coll Tchrs; Amer AssnUniv Prof; YWCA; Chadwick Manor Civic Club. **HONORS/ACHIEVEMENTS:** Many hon soc; State Service Youth Awd; Leaders Black Amer 1974; Who's Who Amer Coll &Univ 1954; Personalities South 1973, 74, 75. **BUSINESS ADDRESS:** Professor & Dept Head, Texas Southern University, 3100 Cleburne, Houston, TX 77004.

MOORMAN, CLINTON R. (BOB)
Athletic commissioner. **PERSONAL:** Born Mar 10, 1924, Cincinnati; married Tamiko Sanbe; children: Bobby, Kathy. **EDUCATION:** Univ MD, BS 1965. **CAREER:** Central Intercollegioate Athletic Ass, commnr; San Diego Chargers, talent scout 1969-; a combine

for the Packers, Cardinals, Browns, Flacons, Redskins,Giants, Patraiots, working for CEPO area scouts; Wiley Coll, head football coack 1966-68. **ORGANIZATIONS:** Mem Alpha Phi Alpha Res Officers Assn; fellowship Christian Ath 1969; Peninsula Sports Club 1973; Big Bros Inc 1973. **HONORS/ACHIEVEMENTS:** Bronze Star med & Purple Heart Korean conflict. **MILITARY SERVICE:** Corpl 1943-46; maj 1949-66. **BUSINESS ADDRESS:** Ste 322, 2013 Cunningham Dr, Hampton, VA 23666.

MOORMAN, HOLSEY ALEXANDER
Military officer. **PERSONAL:** Born May 18, 1938, Roanoke, VA; son of Holsey J. Moorman and Grace O. Moorman; married Carrie Boyd, Aug 03, 1963; children: Gary W. **EDUCATION:** Hampton Univ, attended 1956-58; Park Coll, BS 1986. **CAREER:** US Civil Service, training officer 1965-68, admin officer 1968-80, EEO officer 1980-86; Office of Dept Chief of Staff Personnel for the US Army, personnel policy intergrator. **ORGANIZATIONS:** Life mem, Natl Guard Assn of NJ 1964-, Natl Guard Assn of the US 1964-; mem, PHA, F&AM 1978-; EEO investigator Natl Guard Bureau 1982-86. **MILITARY SERVICE:** AUS lt col 1961-; Meritorious Serv Medal, Army Commendation Medal, Army Serv Ribbon, Armed Forces Reserve Achievement Medal, Armed Forces Reserve Medal, NJ Medal of Honor. **HOME ADDRESS:** 12501 Thunder Chase Dr, Reston, VA 22071.

MOOSE, GEORGE E.
Foreign service officer. **PERSONAL:** Born Jun 23, 1944, New York, NY; son of Robert Moose and Ellen Amanda Lane Jones Moose-McCloud; married Judith Roberta Kaufmann. **EDUCATION:** Grinnell Coll, BA 1966-; Syracuse Univ, postgraduate 1966-67. **CAREER:** Dept of State Washington DC, special asst to under sec for political affairs 1977-78, dep dir for Southern Africa 1978-79; Council For Relations NY, foreign affairs fellow 1979-80; US Mission to the UN NYL, dep political counselor 1980-83; Dept of State Washington DC, US ambassador to Benin 1983-86; deputy dir office of mgmt operations 1986-87, dir office of mgmt operations 1987-88; US ambassador to Senegal, 1988-. **ORGANIZATIONS:** Mem Amer Foreign Serv Assn 1967-; foreign affairs fellow Council on Foreign Relations NY 1979-80; mem Assoc of Black American Ambassadors 1985-, Policy Council Una Chapman Cox Foundation 1986-89. **HONORS/ACHIEVEMENTS:** Superior Honor Award Dept of State 1974; Meritorious Honor Award Dept of State 1975; Superior Honor Award Dept of State 1979; Senior Performance Pay 1985; Presidential Meritorious Serv Award, 1989. **BUSINESS ADDRESS:** US Ambassador to Senegal, American Embassy Dakar, Department of State, Washington, DC 20521-2130.

MOOTRY, CHARLES
Business executive. **PERSONAL:** Born Apr 05, 1948, Chicago, IL; married Estalla Eady; children: Charles IV, Anthony Kenneth. **EDUCATION:** Attended Boise State Coll. **CAREER:** Central City Mktg, account exec 1970-72; WVON Radio/Globe Broadcasting, account exec 1972, local sales mgr 1973, gen sales mgr 1975; Globe Broadcasting, vice pres GCI Sales 1975; Johnson Pub Co/WJPC Radio, vp/dir broadcast. **ORGANIZATIONS:** Black Advertising Club of Chicago 1975; bd of dir Wabash YMCA Chicago 1976; mem Chicago Urban League 1970; mem Operation PUSH 1972; Layman's group FellowshipBapt Ch 1975. **HONORS/ACHIEVEMENTS:** Black Achievers Award Met YMCA Chicago; Bus & Professional Award Dollars & Sense Mag. **MILITARY SERVICE:** USAF 1 year served. **BUSINESS ADDRESS:** VP/Dir Broadcast WJPC Radio, Johnson Pub Co, 820 S Michigan Ave, Chicago, IL 60605.

MORAGNE, LENORA
Publisher, editor. **PERSONAL:** Born in Evanston, IL; daughter of Joseph Moragne Sr and Linnie Lee Moragne; widowed. **EDUCATION:** IA State Univ, BS; Cornell Univ, MS, PhD 1969. **CAREER:** Comm Hosp Evanston IL, chief dietitian 1955-57; Cornell Univ, asst prof 1961-63; NC Coll, asst prof, foods & nutrition 1965-67; Gen Foods Corp, nutrition publicist 1968-71; Columbia Univ, lecturer nutrition prog 1971-72; Hunter Coll, prof foods & nutrition 1971-72; Food & Nutrition Serv USDA, head nutrition, ed & training 1972-77; Agr Nutrition & Forestry Comm US Senate, professional staff mem 1977-79, dep hhs nutrition policy coord 1979-84; Nutrition Legislation Svcs, founder, pres, 1985-present; Founding editor & publisher, Black Congressional Monitor, 1987-present. **ORGANIZATIONS:** mem, Amer Dietetic Assn, Soc Nutrition Ed, Amer Publ Health Assn, Cornell Club DC, Natl Council Women; mem Adv Council Major Univ, Cornell IA State, Univ of DE, Univ of MD; mem bd of dir Amer Dietetic Assoc 1981-84; mem APHA Prog Devel Bd 1984-87; nominee bd of trustees Cornell Univ 1984; pres Soc for Nutrition Educ 1987-88; mem adv council Meharry Med Coll Nutrition Center, 1986-present. **HONORS/ACHIEVEMENTS:** Co-author Jr HS nutrition text "Focus on Food"; authored baby record book for new parents "Our Baby's Early Years" author num food-nutrition related articles in professional publication; Elected to Cornell Univ Council, 1981; Distinguished Alumni Award, IA State, 1983; Certificate of Appreciation, USDA, 1973; Special Appreciation Award, Natl Assoc of Business & Professional Women, 1971; traveled W Africa, Central Amer, Europe; Nominee, Cornell Univ, Bd of Trustees, 1984; Inducted into Gamma Sigma Delta Honorary Agriculture Soc, 1987. **BUSINESS ADDRESS:** Founder Editor & Publisher, Black Congressional Monitor, PO Box 75035, Washington, DC 20013.

MORAGNE, RUDOLPH
Physican. **PERSONAL:** Born Feb 05, 1933, Evanston, IL; married Kathlyn Elaine; children: Donna, Diana, Lisa. **EDUCATION:** Univ IL, BS 1955; Meharry Med Coll, MD 1959; Cook Co Hosp, intern & resident 1961-65. **CAREER:** R Moragne, MD SC, physician. **ORGANIZATIONS:** Amer Coll Ob-gyn Surgeons; AMA; Nat'l Med Assn; IL & Chicago Med Soc; Cook Co Physicians AssnUniv Chicago Lying In Hosp staff; dir S Side Bank; memUrban League; Operation PUSH. **HONORS/ACHIEVEMENTS:** Beautiful people awd Chicago Urban League 1973; co-author Our Baby's Early Years 1974. **MILITARY SERVICE:** USAF capt 1961-63. **BUSINESS ADDRESS:** 8044 S Cottage Grove, Chicago, IL 60619.

MORAN, JOYCE E.
Attorney. **PERSONAL:** Born May 21, 1948, Chicago, IL; daughter of Theodore E Moran and Irma Rhyne Moran. **EDUCATION:** Smith Coll Northampton MA, AB 1969; Yale Law School New Haven, JD 1972; Univ of Chgo, MBA 1981. **CAREER:** Sidley & Austin Chgo, assoc attny 1972-78; Sears Roebuck & Co Chgo, attny 1978-. **ORGANIZATIONS:** Bd of dirs, vice pres, pres Legal Asst Found of Chicago 1974-88; chmn Lawyers Com Chicago Urban League 1980-82; mem, vice pres Chicago League of Smith Coll Clubs 1972-;ed review team leader mayor Washington Transition Comm Chicago 1983; mem Jr Governing Bd of Chicago Symphony Orchestra 1973-85; mem Chicago Symphony Chorus & Chorale Omega 1974-78; bd of dirs Alumnae Assoc of Smith Coll 1984-87; vice pres Smith Coll Class of 1969,74-79; vp, treas Yale Law School Assoc of IL 1975-78; coord Coppin AME Church Enrichment Prog 1981-84; bd dir Chicago Area Found for Legal Serv 1982-; bd dir, vice pres ACLU of IL 1983-; bd dir, v chair Chicago Found for Women 1985-; bd dir, treas Chicago School Fin Auth 1985-; mem Kennedy-King Community Chorus 1986-; mem Illinois Judicial Inquiry Bd 1987-; trustee, Smith Coll 1988-93; dir, ACLU 1987-89. **HONORS/ACHIEVEMENTS:** Dist Serv Awd Coppin AME Church Chicago 1972; Player of the Year Jr Master, Amer Bridge Assoc 1977; Beautiful People Awd Chicago Urban League 1979; YMCA of Metro Chicago Black & Hispanic Achievers of Indust Recog Awd 1981; Ten Outstanding Young Citizen Awd Chicago Jr Assoc of Commerce & Industry 1985. **BUSINESS ADDRESS:** Attorney, Sears Roebuck & Co, D/766 Sears Tower, Chicago, IL 60684.

MORAN, ROBERT E., SR.
Minister, retired educational edministrator. **PERSONAL:** Born Jul 24, 1921, Columbus, OH; son of Herbert Williams and Edna Carr; married Esther Quarles; children: Robert E Moran Jr. **EDUCATION:** Ohio State Univ, BS 1944; Ohio State Univ, MA 1947; Ohio State Univ, PhD 1968; Harvard Summer School, Certificate 1971. **CAREER:** Palmer Memrl Inst, teacher 1944-46; Xenia E High, teacher 1947; Allen Univ, teacher dir student teaching 1948-59; Southern Univ, prof dean 1959-87; Southern Univ, dean coll of arts & humanities, retired; minister 1989. **ORGANIZATIONS:** Historian Assn of Soc & Behavrl Science 1981; edtr br jrnl of Negro history Assoc for the Study of Negro Life & History 1982-; Omega Psi Phi Frat . **HONORS/ACHIEVEMENTS:** One Hundred Yrs of Child Welfare in LA 1980.

MORANCIE, HORACE L.
Appointed official, management consultant. **PERSONAL:** Born in San Fernando, Trinidad and Tobago. **EDUCATION:** Polytech Inst of Brooklyn BSc Civil Engrg 1958; Cornell Univ, MSc Civil Engrg 1960; Brooklyn Law School, Harvard Univ, John F Kennedy School of Govt, Cert 1982. **CAREER:** Office of the Mayor City of NY, asst admin 1968-74; Rockland Comm Action Council Inc, mgmt consult 1974-80, exec dir 1976-80; State of NY Div of Econ Opport, dir 1980-82; City of Harrisburg Dept of Community & Econ Devel, dir; Horace L Morancie & Assocs, devel housing & mgmt consultant. **ORGANIZATIONS:** Teaching fellow Cornell Univ 1958-60; rsch & civil engr Port Authority of NY & NJ 1960-68; bd chmn Urban Resources Inst, Addiction Rsch & Treatment Corp; v chmn Harrisburg Redevel Auth; bd mem Natl Comm Devel Assoc; chmn Harrisburg Property Reinvestment Bd. **HONORS/ACHIEVEMENTS:** Listed in Who's Who in Amer Univ & Coll 1958; Natl Reg of Prominent Amer & Intl Notables 1982; HUD Scholarship John F Kennedy School of Govt 1982. **BUSINESS ADDRESS:** Consultant, Horace L Morancie & Assocs, 469 Rockaway Parkway, Brooklyn, NY 11212.

MORCOM, CLAUDIA HOUSE
Judge. **PERSONAL:** Born Jun 07, Detroit, MI; daughter of Walter House and Glady Stuart. **EDUCATION:** Wayne State Univ, BA 1953; Wayne State Univ Law School, LLB-JD 1956. **CAREER:** City of Detroit Housing Commn, pub housing aid 1956-60; Law Firm of Goodman Crockett et al, atty/assoc mem 1960-66; natl Lawyers Guild So Legal Com, so regional dir 1964-65; City of Detroit, dir neighborhood legal serv 1966-68; State of MI Dept of Labor, admin law judge 1972-; Wayne Cnty Circuit Court, judge 1983-. **ORGANIZATIONS:** Instr Afro-Amer Studies Univ of MI 1971-73; instr Inst of Labor Industrial Relations 1972-73; bd of mgmt YMCA & YWCA 1971-; adv Wayne State Univ Council on World Affairs - Cntr for Peace & Conflict Studies 1974-; exec bd natl Alliance Against Racist & Polit Repression 1974-; mem State Bar of MI; mem and delegate to conf in Nicaragua 1981, Granada 1983, Argentina 1985 Assoc of Amer Jurists; participant Human Rights Workshop Natl Conf on the Nicaragua Constitution held in NY 1986; bd mem Merrill Palmer Inst; chmn adv bd Renaissance Dist Boy Scouts of Amer; mem Detroit Police Dept, Jr Cadet Adv Comm, Detroit Strategic Plan Comm; bd of dir Renaissance Club, Harmony Park Playhouse; vice pres Millender Fund. **HONORS/ACHIEVEMENTS:** Natl Shrine Scholarship Award Denver, CO 1953; Civil Rights Award Natl Negro Women 1965; Civil Rights Award Cook Cnty Bar Assn 1966; Human Rights Award Detroit Chap Amer Civil Liberties 1967; Human Rights Award Detroit Com on Human Rights 1969; MI State Legislative Cert of Merit 1977; Spirit of Detroit Award 1977; Cert of Recognition YWCA Met Detroit 1979; Damon J Keith Civic and Humanitarian Award 1984; Comm Leadership Awd Coalition of 100 Black Women; Women of Wayne Headliner Awd; Boy Scouts Appreciation Awd; John F Kennedy Awd of Co-Ettes Club; Heart of Gold Awd Boy Scouts of Amer; Natl Honor Soc Awd Cass Tech HS. **BUSINESS ADDRESS:** Circuit Court Judge, Wayne County, 1607 City County Bldg, Detroit, MI 48226.

MOREHEAD, FLORIDA MAE
Supervisor chemical industry. **PERSONAL:** Born Feb 22, 1948, Altheimer, AR; children: Sonya. **EDUCATION:** Univ of AR-Pine Bluff, BS (Magna Cum Laude) 1969; Univ of AR-Fayetteville, MS 1972. **CAREER:** The Dow Chemical Co, package purchasing, marketing sales, technical serv & development, manager. **ORGANIZATIONS:** Mem Alpha Kappa Alpha Sor 1968-; dir Christian Educ New Jerusalem Church 1980-; adv comm Natl Assoc Minority Engrg Prog Adm 1982; mem Natl Org ofBlk Chemists & Chem Engrs 1984-; industrial adv bd Natl Soc Blk Engrs 1985-; bd mem Woman to Woman Ministries Inc 1986-. **HONORS/ACHIEVEMENTS:** Special Service Awd New Jerusalem Church 1974, 86; Teacher of the Year New Jerusalem Church 1982; Special Recognition Univ of MI 1985; Outstanding Service Dow Chemical 1985.

MORELAND, LOIS BALDWIN
Educator. **PERSONAL:** Born in Washington, DC; daughter of Genis G Baldwin and Fannie Rives Baldwin; married Charlie J Moreland; children: Lisa Carol. **EDUCATION:** Sarah Lawrence Coll, BA; Howard Univ, MA; Amer Univ Washington, PhD. **CAREER:** Howard Univ, asst & instr soc sci 1956-57; NAACP, SE reg youth field sec 1957-58; US Senator R Vance Hartke, legis asst 1958-59; Spelman Coll instructor 1959-65, asst prof 1965-70, prof & chmn polit sci dept 1970-, acting Dean of Instruction 1970-72, chmn soc sci div 1980-. **ORGANIZATIONS:** Charter mem & first treas Natl Conf Black Polit Sci; consult So Assn Schs & Colls; mem Amer Assn Univ Women, NAACP, League Women Voters; former mem Fulton Co Bd Elections; Fulton Co Jury Commn; Gov's Council Human Rel; mem American Southern & GA Political Science Assoc, Assoc of Politics & the Life Sciences; Alpha Kappa Alpha; mem Professional Advisory Bd & bd of dir Epilepsy Foundation of America; former mem advisory council, Natl Inst of Nuerological, Communicable Disease and Stroke, Natl Institutes of Health. **HONORS/ACHIEVEMENTS:** Author, White Racism and the Law

1970; Amer Legion Award; Ford Foundation Fellow; The American Univ Govt Intern Fellow; Merit Achiev Amer Men of Sci; Outstanding Educator 1973; Amer Polit Sci So Conf Award; United Negro Coll Fund Fellow; Sarah Lawrence College Scholarship; honorary life mem, Natl Assoc of Business Women. **BUSINESS ADDRESS:** Chmn Soc & Political Sci Depts, Spelman College, PO Box 1006, Atlanta, GA 30314.

MORELAND, SALLIE V.
College president. **CAREER:** Clinton Junior College, Rock Hill SC, president. **BUSINESS ADDRESS:** Clinton Junior College, Rock Hill, SC 29732. *

MORGAN, ALICE JOHNSON PARHAM
Association executive. **PERSONAL:** Born Jul 17, 1943, Richmond, VA; daughter of Elmore W Johnson Jr and Fannie Mae Quarles Johnson; married Wilson M; children: Weldon Leo, Arvette Patrice. **EDUCATION:** VA Union Univ, BA 1965; VA Commonwealth Univ, MSW 1967; Univ of Southern CA (WA Public Affrs Cntr), MPA 1982. **CAREER:** Area D CMHC, supvr, soc worker 1981; St Elizabeth's Hosp, soc work prog 1981-82; Area D CMHC, soc worker 1982-83; Area D CMHC, dir special apt program, 1983-88; dir, Region IV Psychosocial Day Prog, 1988-. **ORGANIZATIONS:** program analyst, Public Health Serv, 1980-81; dir, comm placement office, Area D, CMHC 1980; ed & standards specialist, St Elizabeth's Hosp, 1979-80; dir, comm placement office, Area D, CMHC, 1972-79; chairperson (city of Alex, VA) Martin Luther King Planning Comm, 1973-; First Black Family City Council Candidate, Alex, VA, 1979; mem, First Black/First Female Planning Comm, 1971-79; bd of dir, Natl Conf of Christians and Jews, Alexandria Mental Health Assoc. **HONORS/ACHIEVEMENTS:** Dorothea Lynde Dix Award, St Elizabeth's Hosp, 1984; Human Rights Award, Alex Comm on Status of Women, 1984; Intergovtl Mgmt Appointee, Dept of Health & Human Serv 1980-81; Outstanding Comm Serv Award Alex Dept Pro Club, 1979; NAACP Community Serv Award, 1988; Community Serv Award, Alex Commn on Status of Women, 1986. **HOME ADDRESS:** 1513 Dogwood Dr, Alexandria, VA 22302. **BUSINESS ADDRESS:** Dir, Psychosocial Day Prog, Region IV, CMHC Allison Bldg, 2700 M L King Ave, SE, Washington, DC 20032.

MORGAN, BOOKER T.
Educator. **PERSONAL:** Born Sep 29, 1926, Boley, OK; married Ella L Parker; children: Travis W, Delois Jean. **EDUCATION:** Langston U, BS cum laude 1954; OK State Ud addl study 1964. **CAREER:** Langston Univ, dir graphic arts center 1970-; Langston Univ, asst dean mem 1961-70; Local 1140 Omaha, labor steward 1958-60; State Training School Boys Boley OK, farmsupt 1955-57. **ORGANIZATIONS:** Mem OK Educ Assn 1961-74; LangstonUniv Alumni Assn; deacon Mt Bethel Bapt Ch Rising Star Lodge #22; Jaycees; Langston Lions Club; polemarch Langston Alumni Chap of Kappa Alpha Psi. **HONORS/ACHIEVEMENTS:** Undergrad adv Alpha Pi Chap Kappa Alpha Psi 1961-; Kappa adv of Yr awd 1969; estab Booker T Morgan Achiev Awad most outstanding grad sr Alpha Pi Chap 1969. **MILITARY SERVICE:** AUS sgt 1949-52. **BUSINESS ADDRESS:** Development & Public Relations, Langston University, Langston, OK 73050.

MORGAN, CHARLOTTE THERESA
Educator. **PERSONAL:** Born Jun 28, 1938, Chicago, IL; daughter of Eleazar Morgan and Juanita Brewer Morgan; children: Theresa Isoke Morgan. **EDUCATION:** Univ of Chicago, BA 1960; Haile Selassie I Univ Addis Ababa, Certificate of Attendance 1965; Columbia Univ, Sch of Intl Affairs M Intl Affairs 1967, Teachers Coll MEd 1976, EdD 1979. **CAREER:** Chicago Bd of Educ, high school Social Studies teacher 1961-65; African-Amer Inst, teacher at Kurasini School 1967-70; Phelps-Stokes Fund, asst for african programs 1970-71; Lehman Coll CUNY, asst prof 1972-. **ORGANIZATIONS:** Mem adv comm adult learning Follett Publishing Co 1982-83; natl treasurer African Heritage Studies Assoc 1984-; alternate rep United Nations NGO Alpha Kappa Alpha Sor Inc 1985-86; mem Amer Assoc Adult/Cont Educ, Assoc Study of African-Amer Life and History, Natl Council for Black Studies, Alpha Kappa Alpha Sor. **HONORS/ACHIEVEMENTS:** Fulbright Award 1965; CUNY Faculty Fellowship Award 1978-79; Award Natl Fellowships Fund Emory Univ 1978-79; mem Kappa Delta Pi Honor Soc 1979; Research Grant Women's Research & Devel Fund CUNY 1986-87; published articles in Afro-Americans in NY Life and History, Grad Studies Journal (Univ DC). **HOME ADDRESS:** 800 Riverside Drive #3G, New York, NY 10037. **BUSINESS ADDRESS:** Asst Prof of Black Studies, Lehman Coll of CUNY, Bedford Park Blvd West, Bronx, NY 10468.

MORGAN, DOLORES PARKER
Performer. **PERSONAL:** Born in New Orleans, LA; daughter of Joseph Parker and Mabel Parker; married E Gates Morgan MD; children: Melodie Morgan-Minott MD. **EDUCATION:** Attended Chicago Musical Coll 1941; attended Wilson Coll. **CAREER:** Earl "Fatha" Hines, singer 1945-47; Duke Ellington, singer 1947-49; Solo Performer, singer 1949-56; Local Charity Events, singer 1960-; bd of dir Kent State Foundation 1987-90. **ORGANIZATIONS:** Bd mem, corres secy OH Ballet 1983-87; exec bd of trust Vstg Nurses Serv 1984-; devel council Akron Art Museum 1984-; exec bd Boy Scouts of Amer 1986-; bd mem Akron Symphony 1986-. **HONORS/ACHIEVEMENTS:** Hall of Fame Best Dressed Akron Beacon Jrnl 1971; Ebony Best Dressed List Ebony Mag 1972; Dolores Parker Morgan Endowed Scholarship in Music Kent State Univ1986; EL Novotny Award Kent State School of Art 1989. **HOME ADDRESS:** 3461 S Smith Road, Akron, OH 44313.

MORGAN, ELDRIDGE GATES
Corporate medical director. **PERSONAL:** Born Jan 09, 1925, Petersburg, VA; son of Waverly J Morgan and Emma Gates Morgan; married Dolores, Aug 30, 1956; children: Melodie Morgan-Minott. **EDUCATION:** VA State Coll, BS 1944; Meharry Medcl Coll, MD 1950; NY Univ Post Grad Surgery 1954; Harlem Hosp, NY City Res Surgery 1950-56. **CAREER:** St Thomas Hosp-Akron, staff surgeon 1956-78; Firestone Tire & Rubber Co, asst med dir 1978-82; Firestone Tire & Rubber Co, corp med dir 1982-. **ORGANIZATIONS:** Pres, Summitt County Med Soc 1970-72; treasurer, Summit County Med Soc 1968-84; lay advisory bd Akron Univ 1970-85; bd mem Independent Med Plan 1983-85; mem AMA, OSMA, NMA, Alpha Phi Alpha, AAOM, AOMA 1958-85; mem Wesley Temple AME Church 1956-present; bd mem, Med Serv Bureau 1986-present; treasurer, Independent Med Plan, 1986-present. **HONORS/ACHIEVEMENTS:** Fellow, Amer Coll of Surgery, Amer Coll of Med Hypnosis, 1958-present; bd certified Hypnosis Analysis, Hypno Therapy 1968-; 14 Articles Published, 1952-74; Fellow, Amer Coll of Occupational Med, 1984-present. **MILITARY SERVICE:** Med Admin Corp, 2nd lt, 1944-46. **HOME ADDRESS:** 3461 S Smith Rd, Akron, OH 44313. **BUSINESS ADDRESS:** Medical Dir, Firestone Tire & Rubber Co, 1200 Firestone Pkwy, Akron, OH 44317.

MORGAN, FLETCHER, JR.
Retired government administrator. **PERSONAL:** Born Oct 06, 1920, Bay City, TX; son of Fletcher Morgan and Ella Morgan; married Alice Mae Riggins; children: Nadine, Rita, Dennis L. **EDUCATION:** Prairie View A&M U, BS 1943, MS 1946; Lasalle Inst & Wharton Co Jr Coll, addl study re. **CAREER:** USDA Farmers Home Adm Bay City, TX, retired co supr 1970-86, asst co supr 1965-70; USDA FMHA Richmond TX Co, supr 1979-; Vets in Agri, instr & supr 1946-49. **ORGANIZATIONS:** Mem bd dir Ft Bend Co Taxpayers Assn; Centennial Council Prairie View A&M Univ 1968-69; Nu Phi; Omega Psi Phi; TX Soc Farm & Ranch Mgrs & Appraisers; NAACP; AME Ch; 32 deg Mason; Nat Assn Co Suprs USDA; Shriner; P V A&M Univ alumni assn; chmn Nat Housing Auth; mem Omega Psi Phi; bd of dir Coastal Plain SWCD, Pres Hilliard High Alumni Assn. **HONORS/ACHIEVEMENTS:** Alumni citation PV A&M 1969; dist Omega Man of Yr 1969; Omega Man of Yr Nu Phi Chap Houston 1973. **MILITARY SERVICE:** MIL serv 1943-45. **HOME ADDRESS:** PO Drawer 9, Thompsons, TX 77481.

MORGAN, GORDON D.
Educator. **PERSONAL:** Born Oct 31, 1931, Mayflower, AR; son of Roosevelt Morgan and Georgia Madlock Morgan; married Izola Preston Morgan, Jun 15, 1957; children: Marsha. **EDUCATION:** AR AM & N Coll, BA Soc Cum Laude 1953; Univ of AR, MA Soc 1956; WA State Univ, PhD Soc 1963. **CAREER:** Pine St School Conway, AR, teacher 1956-59; AR AM & N Coll Pine Bluff, instructor 1959-60; WA State Univ, TA/RA 1960-63; Teachers for East Africa Project, research asst 1963-65; Lincoln Univ, asst prof soc 1965-69; Univ of AR, assoc prof/prof 1973-. **ORGANIZATIONS:** Consultant So Regional Educ Bd, So-West MN State Coll, Philander Smith Coll, AR Program on Basic Adult Educ, AR Tech Assistance Program Quachita Baptist Coll, Natl Inst of Mental Health Washington, DC; fly-in prof St Ambrose Coll 1973, expert witness before Rockefeller Comm on Population and Future 1971, expert witness on fed judge panel on at-large voting in AR 1973, Washington Co Grand Jury 1974; mem, Rotary/Downtown, Fayelleville, AR, 1980-. **HONORS/ACHIEVEMENTS:** Guest on several programs dealing with topics as crime, human relations, Bakke, and foreign language study; Lecturer at more than 25 colleges and churches; Book reviewer; Numerous professional papers; Author of numerous books and manuscripts incl, "A Short Social History of the East Fayetteville Community" with Izola Preston Morgan 1978; "The Training of Black Sociologists, Tolbert H Kennedy and Washington State University" Teaching Sociology 1980; "African Vignettes, Notes of an American Negro Family in East Africa" New Scholars Press 1967; America Without Ethnicity Kennikat 1981; "The Little Book of Humanistic Poems" 1981; Law Enforcement Asst Admin Award SUNY 1975; Ford Found Postdoc Lincoln Univ 1969; Am Coll Testing Postdoc Lincoln Univ 1969; Russell Sage Postdoc Univ of AR 1972; Natl Endowment for Humanities Univ of WI 1980; Natl Endowment for Humanities Queens Coll SUNY 1983; The Ghetto Coll Student, ACT, Iowa City, IA 1970; Lawrence A Davis, AR Educator, Assoc Faculty Press, NY, 1985; Fellowship in Southern Studio, Mississippi, Oxford, MS, l987-88. **MILITARY SERVICE:** AUS 1953; Commission AUS Reserves 1959. **HOME ADDRESS:** 947 Oak Manor Dr, Fayetteville, AR 72701. **BUSINESS ADDRESS:** Professor,, Univ of Arkansas, Fayetteville, AR 72701.

MORGAN, HARRY
Educator. **PERSONAL:** Born Jun 06, 1926, Charlottesville, VA; son of John Morgan and Cheyney Lewis; children: Parris, Lawrence. **EDUCATION:** NY Univ, BS 1949; Univ of WI, MSW 1965; Univ of MA, Ed D 1970. **CAREER:** Bank St Coll, program coordinator 1966-69; Univ of NH, prof 1969-70; OH Univ, prof 1970-72; Syracuse Univ, prof 1972-84; W GA Coll, prof 1984-; WGA Coll, chmn early childhood educ. **ORGANIZATIONS:** Astr fdn Pre-Teen Resch Prjct 1960-64; US Govt dir Project Head Start North East Region 1964-66; mem AERA 1975-, NAEYC 1972-, AAUP 1980-; AACTE 1984; Phi Delta Kappa 1985. **HONORS/ACHIEVEMENTS:** Fellowship Ford Foundation 1967-69; consultant US Govt "Black Aged" 1970-74; book, The Learning Comm pub Charles Merrill, OH 1972; numerous articals for Learned Journals. **HOME ADDRESS:** 2284 Lakeview Parkway, Villa Rica, GA 30180. **BUSINESS ADDRESS:** Chairman, Early Childhood Ed, West GA College, Maple St, Carrollton, GA 30118.

MORGAN, HAYWOOD, SR.
Elected official, chemical plant technician. **PERSONAL:** Born Feb 06, 1936, Lakeland, LA; son of George Morgan Sr and Eloise Weber Morgan; married widowed (deceased); children: Althea, Haywood Jr, April. **EDUCATION:** Southern Univ, BS Educ 1968. **CAREER:** CIBA Geigy Corp, tech 1969-; West Baton Rouge Sch Bd, personnel & finance comm, trans & vocational skills comm, building equipt & maint comm 1972-84. **ORGANIZATIONS:** Mem Sunrise Baptist Church. **HONORS/ACHIEVEMENTS:** First Black elected official in West Baton Rouge Parish 1971; Comm Serv Scotts United M Church 1978. **HOME ADDRESS:** 1117 Maryland Avenue, Port Allen, LA 70767.

MORGAN, HAZEL C. BROWN
Educator. **PERSONAL:** Born Oct 25, 1930, Rocky Mount, NC; daughter of Rollon Brown and Beulah McGee Brown (deceased); married Charlie Morgan; children: Savoynne Fields. **EDUCATION:** A&T State Univ, BS Nursing 1960; East Carolina Univ, MS Rehab Counseling 1977, MS Nursing 1980. **CAREER:** Wilson Mem Hosp, charge nurse 1964-66; Northern Nash High School, health occupations teacher 1966-73; Nash General Hosp, team leader pt care 1971-; East Carolina Univ School of Nursing, asst prof of nursing 1973-; Veteran's Admin Hospital Richmiond VA & E Orange NJ, staff nurse 1960-62; Landis State Hospital Phildelphia PA, asst head nurse & instructor 1963. **ORGANIZATIONS:** Mem Amer Nurses Assoc, NC Assoc of Black Educators, NC Nurse's Assoc Dist 20, Carrie Broadfoot Org; mem ECU Org of Black Faculty & Staff; mem, Sigma Theta Tau 1988-; mem, The Assn of Black Nursing Faculty 1987-; health consultant, Wright Geriatric Day Care Center 1988-; supervisor & instructor, United Friendship Church Nurses Organization 1988-. **HONORS/ACHIEVEMENTS:** 10 yr Serv Awd East Carolina Univ School of Nursing 1983; Serv Awd for Achievement, Black Fac Mem with Greatest Numbers of Yrs Serv Omega Psi Phi Frat 1984; Soc & Civic Awd Chat-a-While Civic Orgn LA State Univ Eunice 1984; Devel Slide-Tape Program, Creativity in Documenting Nursing Interventions 1989. **HOME ADDRESS:** 913 Beal St, Rocky Mount, NC 27801.

MORGAN, JAMES
Manager. **PERSONAL:** Born Aug 23, 1914; married Justine. **EDUCATION:** Atlanta Life Ins, LTCU Course 1974. **CAREER:** Atlanta Life Ins Co, asst mgr; Atlanta Life Ins Co, supr, 1957; Atlanta Life Ins Co, staff mgr 1954; Atlanta Life Ins Co, deputy mgr 1947; Phillip66 Oil Refinery, general labor foreman 1945. **ORGANIZATIONS:** Pres BTU Mother Zion Bapt Ch 1956; pres Matagorda Council of Orgn 1958-80; chmn Deacon Bd Mother Zion Bapt Church 1967; pres Kiwanis Club Div 25 1979-80. **HONORS/ACHIEVEMENTS:** Recipient of good conduct medal & four battle stars AUS 1945; Thirty-third Degree the ancient & accepted scottish rite of free masons 1969; highest award of achievement Dale Carnegie Course 1974. **MILITARY SERVICE:** AUS pvt 1st/C 1942-45.

MORGAN, JANE HALE
Librarian, educator. **PERSONAL:** Born May 11, 1925, Dines, WY; daughter of Arthur Hale and Billie Wood; married Joseph C Morgan; children: Joseph Hale, Jane Frances, Ann Michele. **EDUCATION:** Howard Univ, BA 1947; Univ of Denver, MA 1954. **CAREER:** Detroit Pub Library, staff 1954-, exec asst dir 1973-75, dep dir 1975-78, dir 1978-87; Wayne State Univ, visiting prof 1989-90. **ORGANIZATIONS:** Mem Amer Libr Assn; mem MI Library Assn; exec bd Southeastern MI Reg Film Libr; LSCA adv council Lib of MI; mem Women's Natl Book Assn bd of trustees; New Detroit Inc; bd dir Rehab Inst; adv bd United Found; bd of dir YWCA; mem Assn of Municipal & Professional Women; mem Alpha Kappa Alpha; bd dir Univ Cultural Cntr Assn; mem Urban League; mem NAACP; bd of dir Women's Economic Club; bd dir United Community Svcs; brd dirs, Delta Dental Plan of MI; brd dirs, Metropolitan Affairs Corp; vice pres New Detroit, Inc; Michigan Council for the Humanities. **HONORS/ACHIEVEMENTS:** Recipient, "The Anthony Wayne Awd", Wayne ST Univ, Coll of Ed 1981; Detroit "Howardite of the Year", 1983; Summit Award, Greater Detroit Chamber of Commerce 1989.

MORGAN, JOHN PAUL
Dentist. **PERSONAL:** Born Oct 23, 1929, Kokomo, IN; married Pauline Marie Jones; children: Angela Marie. **EDUCATION:** IN Univ, pre-dental studies; Meharry Medical Coll, DDS 1960. **CAREER:** 6510 USAF Hospital Edwards AFB CA, officer-in-charge hospital dental 1960-64; 439th USAF Hospital Misawa AB Japan, oic security serv dental asst base dental surgery 1964-67; Lockbourne AFB OH, chief of prosthodontics 1967-71; 377th USAF Disp Tan Son Nhut AB Vietnam, chief of oral surgery 1971-72; USAF Hospital Kirtland AFB NM, asst base dental surgeon 1972-78; USAF Hospital Hahn AB Germany, base dental surgeon 1978-81; USAF Medical Center SGD Scott AFB IL, deputy dir of dental serv 1981-. **ORGANIZATIONS:** Mem Natl Dental Assoc, Acad of General Dentistry, Assoc of Military Surgeons, Prince Hall Lodge; life mem NAACP, Alpha Phi Alpha. **MILITARY SERVICE:** USAF col 26 yrs; Meritorious Serv Medal w/One Oak Leaf Cluster, Air Force Commendation Medal, Presidential Unit Citation AF Outstanding Unit Awd; Republic of Vietnam Gallantry Cross w/Palm; Republic of Vietnam Campaign Medal 1960-; The Legion of Merit, 1988. **HOME ADDRESS:** 4 Deer Run, O'Fallon, IL 62269-1209. **BUSINESS ADDRESS:** Deputy Dir of Dental Serv, USAF Medical Ctr, USAF Medical Ctr/SGD, Scott AFB, IL 62225.

MORGAN, JOSEPH C.
Deputy director. **PERSONAL:** Born Jan 10, 1921, Douglas, GA; married Jane Hale; children: Joseph, Jane, Michele. **CAREER:** Detroit Zool Park, dep dir 1974-; Pub Serv Employment Detroit, dir 1974. **ORGANIZATIONS:** Pres Frame Div of UAW 1955-67; appointed Intl Rep as Recruiter Couns 1967-74; pres Detroit Chap Nat Negro Labor Council 1957-59. **HONORS/ACHIEVEMENTS:** Recip of award for meritorious serv in field of soc econ leadership by UAW Assn 1974. **MILITARY SERVICE:** AUS corp of eng 1946. **BUSINESS ADDRESS:** 8450 W Ten Mile Rd, Royal Oak, MI 48068.

MORGAN, JOSEPH L.
Clergyman. **PERSONAL:** Born Aug 09, 1936, Pittsboro, NC; married Caroldine Leake; children: Sharon, Susan. **EDUCATION:** Johnson C SmithUniv Charlotte, NC, AB 1958; ShawUniv Raleigh, NC, MDiv 1961. **CAREER:** First Calvary Bapt Ch, pastor; Evening Curr Cntrl Carolina Tech Inst Sanford, NC, dir; Cntrl HS, tchr english 1968-74; First Bapt Dallas, NC Pleasant Grove Wendell, NC, New Light Hallsboro, NC, pastor. **ORGANIZATIONS:** Dir Gaston Boy's Club 1961-63; mem Sanford Redevel Comm 1968-; mem Lee Co Minister's Fellow 1964-74; mem ACT, NEA, NCEA; Gen Bapt State Conv; Lott Carey Foreign Miss Conv; Nat Bapt Conv USA mem NAACP, SCLC; inst rep BSA; mem Sanford Human Relations Coun & Coun on Aging. **BUSINESS ADDRESS:** Central Carolina Tech Inst, Kelly Dr, Sanford, NC.

MORGAN, JUANITA KENNEDY
Teacher. **PERSONAL:** Born Dec 16, 1911, Birmingham, AL; daughter of William Kennedy and Viola Skipper Kennedy; married William Morgan. **EDUCATION:** Attended Alabama State Teachers' College, Montgomery AL, 1930-35; Terrell Law School, Washington DC, LLB, 1949; DC Teachers' College, Washington DC, BS, 1962; attended Howard Univ, Washington DC; attended George Washington Univ, Washington DC. **CAREER:** Tennessee Coal & Iron Co, Birmingham AL, teacher, 1935-41; Dept of Treasury, Washington DC, examiner, 1941-60; DC Public School System, Washington DC, teacher, 1961-83; Ultra Realty Service, Washington DC, real estate broker, 1952-89. **ORGANIZATIONS:** Parlimentarian, Business and Professional Women's Club, 1965-70; mem, Common Cause, 1970-80; exec sec and dir, National Black Women's Political Leadership Caucus, 1981-89; mem board of dir, Kiwanianne Club, 1985-87; mem, Kiwanis Club, 1987-89; mem, NAACP; mem, Urban League. **HONORS/ACHIEVEMENTS:** Community Award, Urban League, 1965; Outstanding Grass Roots Community Leader Award, DC Civic Assn, 1968; Community Service Award, Southern Beauty Congress, 1977; Community Award, DC Citizens' Forum, 1983-87; Resolution, DC City Council, 1988; directly responsible for integrating cafeterias and restroom facilities in federal govt buildings during Roosevelt and Truman admins; author of A New Kind of Handbook in Retrospect: Informatives & Directives, Woodridge Civic Assn, 1967-68; lobbied for funding, conceived idea, and planned organizational structure of Federal City College (now Univ of the District of Columbia), 1966-68; delegate to numerous Methodist conferences. **HOME ADDRESS:** 630 11th Court West, Birmingham, AL 35204.

MORGAN, JUNE ELLOIE
Attorney. **PERSONAL:** Born Jun 14, 1949, New Orleans, LA; married Irvin. **EDUCATION:** Elmhurst Coll, BA 1971;Univ of Chicago Law Sch, JD 1974. **CAREER:** Morgan & Mcclarty, atty partner 1979-; BF Goodrich Co, atty 1978-79; Sears Roebuck & Co, atty 1976-78; Gen Motors Corp, atty 1974-76; Swift & Co, law clerk 1973; Urban League of Greater New Orleans, exec asst 1970-72; Fred Hampton Comm Coll of Law, instr 1976-77. **ORGANIZATIONS:** MI Bar Assn; Nat Conf of Black Lawyers; Am Bar Assn; Nat Bar Assn Instnl Lawyers Sect. **BUSINESS ADDRESS:** Morgan & McClarty, PC, 18353 West McNichols Road, Detroit, MI 48219.

MORGAN, KERMIT I.
Business executive. **PERSONAL:** Born Feb 22, 1942, Columbus, OH. **EDUCATION:** OH State U, BA 1964; Columbia U, MSW 1967. **CAREER:** LeMans Haberdashers Inc, pres. **ORGANIZATIONS:** Mem Omega Psi Phi 1961; social worker Harlem Hosp 1966-68; mem bd dir Menswear Retailer of Am; Nat Assn of Black Social Workers; Black Retail Action Group. **HONORS/ACHIEVEMENTS:** Bus & Achievement Award Oct 6, 1972. **BUSINESS ADDRESS:** President, LeMans New York, 2 Penn Plaza, New York, NY 10121.

MORGAN, LEON M.
Educator. **PERSONAL:** Born Nov 24, 1940, Camden, SC; married Shiryl Spells. **EDUCATION:** Benedict Coll, BA 1965; Univ SC, further study. **CAREER:** Burke HS Charleston, SC, teacher 1965-67; Carver Elem School Bethune, SC, 1967-70; Bethune HS, 1970-. **ORGANIZATIONS:** Mem Kershaw Co Tchrs' Coun; Dershaw Co Educ Assn; SC Educ Assn; Nat Educ Assn NAACP; Kershaw Co VEP; bd dir Kershaw Co Ment Hlth Assn 1973-75; co-chmn Camden-Kershaw Co Comm Rel Counc 1973-76; alt state exec committeeman of SC Dem Party 1972-76; SC Demo Black Caucus. **BUSINESS ADDRESS:** Bethune High School, Bethune, SC 29009.

MORGAN, MARY H. ETHEL
Retired educator. **PERSONAL:** Born Mar 11, 1912, Summerton, SC; married Dr C M; children: Carolyn M Morgan Brown;Williams. **EDUCATION:** SC State Coll, BA 1951; Ball State Univ IN, MA Ed 1975; Anderson Coll Theological Sem, MA Religion 1979. **CAREER:** Brd of Ed, tchr SC 1935-40; Nursery Schl, tchr FL 1941-44; IN Church Schl, tchr 1960-70; Comm Schls, tchr Anderson, IN 1970-82; Retired Tchr Minister; Substitute Tchr Anderson Community School; Minister Sherman St Church. **ORGANIZATIONS:** Mbrshp NAACP Local & Natl 1985; Ladies Republican Club Local & Natl 1985; State Tchrs Retirmnt Club IN 1985; Madison Cnty retired Teachers organization; Women United; Board of Directors CCCV. **HONORS/ACHIEVEMENTS:** Outstanding Tchr (Elem) of Amer 1974; Whos Who among Black Amer 1980-81; whos Who in Religion 1985; " Love Award" 1987; Women Ministers Organization Award for faithful service. **HOME ADDRESS:** 2011 Arrow Ave, PO Box 2041, Anderson, IN 46018. **BUSINESS ADDRESS:** Jackson St, Anderson, IN 46011.

MORGAN, MELI'SA (JOYCE)
Singer, songwriter, record producer. **PERSONAL:** Born 1964. **EDUCATION:** Attended Juilliard School, New York NY. **CAREER:** Former backup singer for Chaka Khan, Kahsif, Whitney Houston, and Melba Moore; singer, songwriter, and record producer. **HONORS/ACHIEVEMENTS:** Singer on two record albums, Do Me Baby, 1985, Good Love, 1987; three top five hit singles. **BUSINESS ADDRESS:** c/o Capitol Records, 1750 Vine St, Hollywood, CA 90028. *

MORGAN, MONICA ALISE
Public relations specialist, journalist. **PERSONAL:** Born May 27, 1963, Detroit, MI; daughter of Barbara Jean Pace. **EDUCATION:** Wayne State Univ, Detroit MI, BS, 1985. **CAREER:** Domino's Pizza, Ann Arbor MI, promotional coordinator; Detroit Public Schools, Detroit MI, public relations coordinator; WDIV-TV, Detroit MI, production assistant; Palmer Street Productions, Detroit MI, host and public relations dir; WQBH-radio, talk show host; Michigan Chronicle, Detroit MI, columnist and photojournalist, 1987-; US Dept of Census, Detroit MI, Community Awareness Specialist, 1988-. **ORGANIZATIONS:** Sec, Natl Assn of Black Journalists, 1981-; mem, Optimist Club, 1987-; board mem, Manhood Inc, 1988-; mem, Elliottorian Business Women Inc, 1988-. **HONORS/ACHIEVEMENTS:** Outstanding Young Woman of Amer, 1986, 1987; Civic and Community Award, Wall Street Inc, 1989; author of articles published in periodicals. **BUSINESS ADDRESS:** Columnist/Photojournalist, Michigan Chronicle, 479 Ledyard, Detroit, MI 48201.

MORGAN, RALEIGH, JR.
Educator. **PERSONAL:** Born Nov 12, 1916, Nashville, TN; son of Raleigh Morgan Sr and Adrien Beasley Morgan; married Virginia Moss; children: Carol M Russell, Jill M Bragdon. **EDUCATION:** Fisk Univ, AB 1938; Univ of MI, AM 1939; Univ of MI, PhD 1952. **CAREER:** Amerika Haus, Cologne, dir 1956-57; US Embassy, Bonn, dep chief, cultural op'ns 1957-59; Center for Applied Ling, assoc dir 1959-61; Howard U, prof of Romance linguistics 1961-65; Univ of MI, prof of Romance linguistics 1965-87, prof emeritus of Romance linguistics, 1987-. **ORGANIZATIONS:** Hd dept French NC Coll, Durham 1946-49; lectr linguistics in Several Countries; conslting linguist MLA Materials Devel 1962; dir summer lang instr HowardUniv 1962, 1963, 1965; ins mem USIA Eng Teaching Advisory Panel 1964-67; visiting prof lingustics Cornell Univ 1973; mem visiting Comm Germanic Harvard Overseers 1972-80; consultant Proj on French as a World Language 1978-80; chair Michigan Council for the Humanities 1974-77; Assembly of Behavioral & Soc Sci of Natl Rsch Council 1973-. **HONORS/ACHIEVEMENTS:** Regional French Of Cnty Beauce, Quebec (Mouton) 1975; alumnus mem Phi Beta Kappa Fisk Univ 1974; Fulbright Sr Rsch Scholar France 1974; author of Old French Jogleor and Kindred Terms 1954. **MILITARY SERVICE:** AUS 2nd lt 1942-46. **HOME ADDRESS:** 3157 Bluett Dr, Ann Arbor, MI 48105.

MORGAN, RANDALL COLLINS, SR.
Business executive. **PERSONAL:** Born Aug 31, 1917, Natchez, MS; married Joyce Tatum; children: Randall C Jr MD. **EDUCATION:** Rust Coll, AB 1938; Northwestern Univ, BS 1939; Northwestern Univ & IN Univ, grad studies;Loyola Univ; Grinnell Coll; Industrial Coll of the Armed Forces 1962-63. **CAREER:** Columbia & Gary, tchr; Vet Admin, voc counselor & supr 1946-51; Ironwood Drugs Inc, founder/pres 1950; Assoc Med Ctr, co-founder 1966; Eastside Med Ctr, pres/founder 1969-. **ORGANIZATIONS:** Alpha Phi Alpha 1947; Int'l Frontiers Serv Clb 1962-64 Pres; Nat'l Hlth Srvcs Exec 1972-76; Med Grp Mgmt Assn; Lay Leader Calumet dist United Meth Chrch 1976-82; Co-Chrmn NAACP, Life Membshp Comm; Spec Contrib Fund Brd Dir NAACP; Chtr Pres Gary East Chicago Serv Club; mem Ad Brd Bank of TN, adv comm In Univ; Brd DirMethodist Hosp; Brd of Trustees, Rust Coll, Grinnel Coll; Multi-racial Soc Comm trustee; Gary Chamber of Comm Trustee; NW Ctr for

Med Educn;mem & chrmn Lake CO Med Ctr Deve Agncy; Med Grp Mgmt Assn; Nat'l Assoc Hlth Srvcs; past mem & pres & 1st Black Gary Police Civil Serv Comm; past co-chrmn Negro Coll Fund; vice chrmn United Fund Grtr Gary Campaign; brd dir Gary Joint Hosp Fund; co fndr & busns mgr Assocs Med Ctr; Lake Cnty Comm Dev Comm; Lake Area United Way Camp vice Chrmn; NW Ind Compr Hlth Plng Cncl; Gary Cancer Crusade; Mayors Adv Comm; Better Buss Breau Nw Ind; Bank One Advis Brd. **HONORS/ACHIEVEMENTS:** Gary Est Chg Frontiers CLb Awd 1955; Chmb of Comm Certif of Apprectn 1961; Rust Coll Outstndg COntrib Awd 1966; NAACP Citation of Merit; Delaney United Meth Chrch Disting Serv 1967-68;Citizen Awd Chmb of Comm;1968;IU Gents Outstndg Citizen Awd 1967; United Fund Awd of Apprectn; 1968; Grinnell Coll Dr of Humane Ltrs 1971; NAACP Dist Ldrsp & Srvc Awd 1973; Greater Gary Arts Cncl Awd 1974; Gary Jaycees Outstndg Comm Awd 1976; Notable Americans 1st Ed 1976-77; Govrnrs Vol Actn Prgm Commendation 1977; Grinnell Coll Pres CLb 1978; Dist Ldrshp Awd NAACP 1983; Phi Beta Sigma Dist Citizen Awd 1984; The Cadre Awd of Recog 1984; Roy Wilkins Awd NAACP 1985; NAACP Nat'l Frdm Awd 1985; Rust Coll Trustee Emeritus Awd 1986; Great Garyite 4th Annual Awd 1986. **MILITARY SERVICE:** AUS maj93rd Infantry Div 1942-46. **BUSINESS ADDRESS:** Administrator, The Gary Professional Center, 3229 Broadway, Gary, IN 46409.

MORGAN, RICHARD H., JR.
Attorney. **PERSONAL:** Born Feb 12, 1944, Memphis; married Olga Jackson; children: Darrin Allan, Heather Nicole. **EDUCATION:** Western MI U, BA, MA;Univ of Detroit Law Sch, 1973. **CAREER:** Western MI U, counselor; Oakland Univ Project Pontiac, dir; Student Center, asst dir, asso dir; Dean of Students, asst; Comm Serv Program Urban Affairs Center, dir 6 yrs; Hatchett Mitchell Morgan & Hall, atty; Morgan & Williams, sr partner. **ORGANIZATIONS:** Pmem APGA & MPGA; MI State Bar; Oakland Co Bar; Wolverine Bar; Am Bar & Wayne Co Bar Kappa Alpha Psi Frat; Big Bro of Kalamazoo; Pontiac Area Urban Force on hs dropouts; treas vice pres Black Law Student AllianceUniv of Detroit Law Sch; bd mem Heritage Cultural Ctr. **BUSINESS ADDRESS:** Attorney at Law, Morgan & Williams, 47 North Saginaw, Pontiac, MI 48053.

MORGAN, ROBERT, JR.
Military officer. **PERSONAL:** Born May 17, 1954, Donaldsonville, LA; son of Robert Morgan Sr and Ruby Fields Morgan; children: Robyn Talana Morgan, Ryan Guanlao Morgan. **EDUCATION:** Southern Univ, BS 1972; Old Dominion Univ, grad work 1976; Natl Univ, MBA 1982; Armed Forces Staff Coll, Certificate 1986; Fort Gordon Signal School, Augusta GA Certificate 1987; Univ of Maryland, Foreign Language Studies, 1989. **CAREER:** USS America CV 66, Norfolk VA, deck/ASW officer, 1977-79; USS Cleveland LPD 7, San Diego CA, navigator/weapons officer, 1979-80; Surface Warfare Officer School, Coronado CA, instructor, 1981-83; USNS Ponchatoula FAO 108, Philippines Island, officer in charge, 1983-84; Naval Station Guam, Guam MI, operations officer, 1984-85; Central Texas College, Guam MI, instructor, 1984-85; HQ Central Command, Macdill AFB FL, comms staff officer, 1986-88; MSCO Korea, Pusan Korea, commanding officer, 1988-. **ORGANIZATIONS:** Life mem Alpha Phi Omega Frat 1973-, Omega Psi Phi Frat 1980-; mem Assoc of MBA Execs 1981, Accounting Soc 1982; St Joseph Masonic Lodge 1982; human resource mgmt instructor US Navy 1983; mgmt professor Central TX Coll 1985; master scuba diver Micronesian Diver Assoc 1985; Certified PADL and NAUL diver; mem Natl Naval Officers Assoc; mem NAACP; Armed Forces Communications and Electronics Association 1988-; American Chamber of Commerce in Korea 1988-. **HONORS/ACHIEVEMENTS:** Outstanding Black American Awd Comnav Marianas 1985; Outstanding Young Men of Amer 1986. **MILITARY SERVICE:** USN lt cmdr 1976-; Surface Warfare Officer, Humanitarian Service Medal, Navy Achievement Awd; Expert Rifle and Pistol Marksmanship 1976-; Joint Service Commendation Medal 1988; Commanding Officer 1988-89. **HOME ADDRESS:** MSCO, APO San Francisco, CA 96259-0264. **BUSINESS ADDRESS:** Commanding Officer, US Navy, MSCO Korea, APO San Francisco, CA 96259-0264.

MORGAN, ROBERT LEE
Architect, business executive. **PERSONAL:** Born Mar 06, 1934, Yazoo City, MS; married Janet Rogers; children: Allyson, Whitney, Peter. **EDUCATION:** LincolnUniv Jefferson City, MO; KS State U, BArch 1964. **CAREER:** Adkins-Jackels Asso Architects, exec vp, partner, stockholder, architect 1968-; Hammel, Green & Abrahamson, architect 1966-68; Cavin & Page Architects, architect 1964-66. **ORGANIZATIONS:** Mem Com on Architure for Artss & Recreation Am Inst of Architects 1974-77; MN Soc of Architects AIA; Nat Orgn of Minority Architects; Minneapolis Com on Urban Envir 1968-76; Minneapolis Schs Long-Range Facilities Planning Com; pres MN CDC 1971. **BUSINESS ADDRESS:** 1500 Pioneer Bldg, St Paul, MN 55101.

MORGAN, ROBERT W., II
Educator. **PERSONAL:** Born Sep 01, 1932, Poughkeepsie, NY; married Harriott V Lomax. **EDUCATION:** Durham, JD 1961. **CAREER:** Ability Devel Dept Kutztown State Coll, dir 1977; Prentice Hall, legal editor 1961-63; Flood & Purvin, defense counselor 1963-69; Univ Tech Corp, adminstr 1969-71; Morgan Assn & Urban Design Inc, adminstr 1970-74; Somerset Cnty Coll, adminstr 1970-72. **ORGANIZATIONS:** Mem Hlth Sys Coun 1977; mem State Coordin Coun on Health of PA 1977; mem State Allotment Com on Health of PA 1977; mem Black Conf on Higher Educ 1977; mem Nat Educ Assn 1977; mem Am Personal & Guidance Assn 1977; mem Natl Assn of Devel Studies 1977; chrprsn Ability Devel Dept at KSC 1977. **MILITARY SERVICE:** AUS pvt 1953-55. **BUSINESS ADDRESS:** Dept of Devel Studies Chair, Kutztown University, RM 152 Bukey Bldg, Kutztown, PA 19530.

MORGAN, ROSE
Business executive. **PERSONAL:** Born in Shelby, MS; divorced. **EDUCATION:** Morris Beauty Acad Chgo, attended. **CAREER:** Trim-Away Figure Contouring Ltd, franchiser; mail order bus natl & intl; Rose Morgan Enterprise, founder, pres. **ORGANIZATIONS:** Charter mem Cosmetic Career Women; mem NY State Beauty Culturists Assoc, Natl Assoc of Negro & Professional Women, Natl Assoc of Bank Women Inc; former mem Beauty Serv Minimum Wage & Hour Bd, NY State Labor Detp; incorporator Bethune Fed & Savings Loan Bank; dir Freedom Natl Bank of NY; dir Interracial Council for Bus Oppty; vice pres Natl Council of Negro Women; mem Assoc to Asst Negro Bus; life mem NAACP; Task Force Econ Adv Comm to Mayor of NYC; dir UptownC of C NYC, Mt Morris Park Hosp; pres Continental Soc of NY; bd of dir Kilamanjaro African Coffee; bd trustee Arthur C Logan Meml Hosp; bd of trustee Shaw Univ in Raleigh NC; mem Convent Ave Bapt Church; bd mem Assoc Black Charities; treas of Natl Coalition of 100 Black Women; mem New York City PartnershipInc. **HONORS/ACHIEVEMENTS:** Has been written about in numerous mag & appeared on localTV shows; listed in Who's Who in the East & the World, Who's Who in Commerce & Industry; Outstanding Achievement Awd NY State Beauty Culturists Assoc.

MORGAN, RUDOLPH COURTNEY
Health service administrator. **PERSONAL:** Born May 29, Buffalo, NY; son of Rudolph Morgan and Lillian Blue Donald; married Gwendolyn Young, Aug 12, 1973; children: Dawn J, Rudolph C, Jr. **EDUCATION:** Tuskegee Inst, Tuskegee, AL, BS Biology, 1973. **CAREER:** Univ Hosp, Cleveland, OH, dialysis technician, 1973-80; Organ Recovery Inc, Cleveland, OH, transplant coord, 1980-82, sr transplant coord, 1982-84; SC OPA, Charleston, SC, dir of procurement, 1984-85; Organ Procurement Agency of NY, Buffalo, NY, exec dir, 1985-; Buffalo, Eye Bank, Buffalo, NY, exec dir, 1987-. **ORGANIZATIONS:** Chmn mem, N Amer Transplant Coor Org, 1982-89; bd of dir (sec,) Assn of Independent Organ Procurement Agencies, 1986-87; bd of dir (treasurer) N Amer Transplant Coordinator Org, 1987-89; bd of dir, United Network for Organ Sharing (UMOS) 1987-89; mem comm, Professional Standard United Network for Organ Sharing Comm, 1987-. **BUSINESS ADDRESS:** Exec Dir, Organ Procurement Agency of Western New York, Inc, 1093 Delaware Ave, Buffalo, NY 14209.

MORGAN, SHARON ANTONIA
Business executive. **PERSONAL:** Born Jan 30, 1951, Chicago, IL; divorced; children: Vincent Scott. **EDUCATION:** Univ of IL Chicago Circle, 1968-69; Loop City Coll, 1970-71. **CAREER:** Provident Hospital, dir of comm serv 1974-79; Provident Comm Devel Corp, assoc dir 1978-79; James H Lowry & Assoc, assoc 1979-80; Morgan Comm Group Inc, pres 1980-83; Burrell Advertising Inc, vice pres public rel 1983-. **ORGANIZATIONS:** Mem Publicity Club of Chicago 1978-; mem Amer Mensa Ltd 1979-, Public Relations Soc of Amer 1981-; founder/pres Natl Black Public Relations Soc 1981-. **HONORS/ACHIEVEMENTS:** Listing Community Leaders & Noteworthy Amer, Outstanding Young Women of Amer, World Who's Who of Women; "My Daddy is a Cool Dude" book Dial Press 1979. **BUSINESS ADDRESS:** Vice Pres of Public Relations, Burrell Advertising Inc, 20 N Michigan Ave, Chicago, IL 60602.

MORGAN, STANLEY
Professional athlete. **PERSONAL:** Born Feb 17, 1955, Easley, SC; married Rholedia;; children: Sanitra Nikole, Monique. **EDUCATION:** TN State, BSE 1979. **CAREER:** Industrial Natl Bank; New England Patriots, wide receiver 1971-. **HONORS/ACHIEVEMENTS:** PFW All Rookie Team; Rookie of the Year by the Patriots' 1776 Fan Club; Patriots' all-time leading reception yardage leader 1983; mem NFL Pro Bowl team 1980,87. **BUSINESS ADDRESS:** New England Patriots, Schaefer Stadium, Rt 1, Foxboro, MA 02035.

MORGAN, WARREN W.
Educational administrator. **CAREER:** Paul Quinn College, Waco TX, president. **BUSINESS ADDRESS:** Paul Quinn College, Waco, TX 76704. *

MORGAN, WILLIE, JR.
Territory manager. **PERSONAL:** Born Sep 21, 1951, Birmingham, AL; children: Anita Louise. **EDUCATION:** Wilberforce Univ, BS Marketing (Cum Laude) 1974. **CAREER:** Union Carbide Corp, mgmt trainee 1974-75; Sandoz Pharmaceuticals, sales rep 1975-77; CR Bard Inc, Davol Div salles rep & mktg mgr 1977-83, Electro MedDiv mktg mgr & terr mgr 1983-. **ORGANIZATIONS:** Founding mem/pres SAIL organization professional sales 1974-; mgr Cernitin Amer Inc 1985-; assoc Pre-paid Legal Serv Inc 1985-; mem Wilberforce Univ Alumni. **HONORS/ACHIEVEMENTS:** Outstanding Sales Awd CR Bard Inc Davol Div 1978 & 1979; First Annual Bright Idea Awd C R Bard 1979. **HOME ADDRESS:** 17300 Columbia Dr, Castro Valley, CA 94546.

MORGAN-PRICE, VERONICA ELIZABETH
Judge, referee. **PERSONAL:** Born Nov 30, 1945, Chas, SC; daughter of Robert Morgan and Mary Cross Morgan; married Jerome Henry Price; children: Jerome Marcus. **EDUCATION:** TN State Univ, BS Eng 1966-69; Univ of Cincinnati Summer Law Scholarship, cert; TX So Univ, JD 1972; Univ of NV Natl Coll of Juvenile Judges, cert 1980. **CAREER:** Wade Rasmus & Washington, law clk & atty 1970-72; Baylor Coll of Med Alcoholism Prog, chief counselor coord 1972-75; Houston Comm Coll, law prof 1972-78; Harris Co Dist Atty Offices, asst dist atty 1975-80; TX Paralegal Sch, prof of law 1978-; Harris Co Juvenile Ct Office of Referee, judge. **ORGANIZATIONS:** Mem Houston Lawyers Assn 1973-; mem Natl Bar Assn 1975-; mem adv bd Safety Council of Gr Houston 1979-; former chairperson Med Legal Child Advocacy Comm 1980; mem adv bd Criminal & Juvenile Justice Educ Prog 1980; Ford Found Council on Legal Educ; bd of dir Assoc for Community TV Channel 8; mem Natl Council of Juvenile & Family Court Judges; mem Metro Court Judges; committee member, Learning Disabilities and Juvenile Delinquincy, National Council of Juvenile & Family Court Judges. **HONORS/ACHIEVEMENTS:** Law school Scholarship 1969-72; first black woman prosecutor TX Harris Co Dist Atty 1975-80; Serv Distinction Plaques Phi Alpha Delta/Thurgood Marshall Sch of Law/Houston Lawyers Assn/Natl Council of Negro Women/Harris Co Dist Atty; Black Women Lawyers Assn; Thurgood Marshall School of Law Alumni Assn; speaker, Hooding Ceremony, Thurgood Marshall School of Law 1984; speaker, Commencement Exercise, Tennessee State Univ 1985. **BUSINESS ADDRESS:** Judge, Harris Co Juvenile Court, Office of Referee, 3540 W Dallas, Houston, TX 77019.

MORGAN-SMITH, SYLVIA
Manager. **PERSONAL:** Born Dec 19, Alabama; married William Smith II; children: Shiva, Andre, Melody, Ramon Morgan. **EDUCATION:** Tchnl Comm Coll, Nursing 1956; Univ of CO-Denver, Jrnlsm Major 1970; Jones Real Estate Coll, Diploma 1976; Signal Broadcasting, Diploma 1971. **CAREER:** KBPI-FM Radio, radio producer & Announcer 1970-72; KWGN-TELEVISION 2, TV News Anchrwm 1972-77; Rockwell Int'l Rocky Flats, mgr pub afrs 1977-80; Nat'l Solar Energy Resch Inst, mgr comm relations 1980-. **ORGANIZATIONS:** Dir First Interstate Bank of Golden 1979-; rltr Champion Realty 1975-; TV announcer KOA-TV 1981-; dir Childrens Hosp 1981-; comsnr Denver Comm on Cmnty Rel 1973-; exec comm Jefferson Cnty Priv Indstry Cncl 1980-; pres Citizens Appreciate Police 1981-. **BUSINESS ADDRESS:** Manager of Community Relations, Natl Solar Rsrch Laboratory, 1617 Cole Blvd 17/3, Golden, CO 80401.

MORGAN-WASHINGTON, BARBARA
Dentist. **PERSONAL:** Born Nov 09, 1953, Richmond, VA; daughter of Calvin T Morgan

Sr and Florence Brown Morgan; married Fred S Washington Jr; children: Bria Renee, Fredrica Samone. **EDUCATION:** Virginia State Univ, BS 1976; Medical Coll of Virginia School of Dentistry, DDS 1980. **CAREER:** US Public Health Svcs, sr asst dental surgeon 1980-82; Private Practice, associate 1983-86; Beaufort/Jasper Comp Health Services, staff dentist 1982-. **ORGANIZATIONS:** Mem Acad of General Dentistry 1980-; treas Bd of Dirs St Mary Human Develop Ctr 1981-85; mem Tabernacle Baptist Church 1981-; mem Amer Dental Assoc 1982-, SC Dental Assoc 1982-; mem treas Beaufort Dental Soc 1982-88 mem NAAC 1986-. **HONORS/ACHIEVEMENTS:** Who's Who Among Students in Amer Univs & Colls 1975-76; Beta Kappa Chi Natl Scientific Honor Soc1975-; Outstanding Young Woman of Amer 1980,84. **HOME ADDRESS:** PO Box 325, Beaufort, SC 29901. **BUSINESS ADDRESS:** Dentist, Beaufort/Jasper Comp Hlth Serv, PO Box 357, Ridgeland, SC 29936.

MORGAN-WELCH, BEVERLY ANN
Business executive. **PERSONAL:** Born Sep 15, 1952, Norwich, CT; married Rev Mark RP Welch Jr; children: Michael, Dominique. **EDUCATION:** Smith Coll, BA 1970-74. **CAREER:** Creative Arts Com, admin asst 1975-76; Amherst Coll asst to the dean 1976-77; Amherst Coll, asst dean of admission 1977-78; CT Mutual Life, consult corp responsibility 1979-83; Avery Theater, gen mgr; Wadsworth Atheneum, corp & museum serv officer 1983-86; Wads Worth Atheneum, development offiver. **ORGANIZATIONS:** Chrpsn Urban Affairs Council 1981-82; sec CT Mutual Life Found 1981-83; charter bd mem CT Coalition of 100 Black Women 1982-; mem United Way Allocations Com Capitol Area 1982-86; bd of dir Newington Children's Hospital 1983-; bd dir, sec Jazz Inc 1983-86; bus assoc Gr Hartford C of C 1983-; bd dir Amer Red Cross Gr Hartford Chap 1985-86; pres Goodwin Tracr Conservancy 1986-; vice pres Horace Bushnell Management Resources, Inc 1985. **HONORS/ACHIEVEMENTS:** Recipient Gerald Penny Mem Awd 1979; producer co-founder PUSH Performing Ensemble 1980-82; recipient Big Brothers/Big Sisters Awd 1982; participant Leadership Greater Hartford Chair Poverty Task Force 1984; coord producer CPTV Video Ducumentary Paint by Mr Amos Ferguson 1985. **BUSINESS ADDRESS:** Development Officer, Wadsworth Atheneum, 600 Main St, Hartford, CT 06103.

MORIAL, ERNEST NATHAN
City official. **PERSONAL:** Born Oct 09, 1929, New Orleans, LA; son of Walter E Morial and Leonie Moore; children: Marc H, Julie C, Jacques E, Cheri M, Monique, Gayle. **EDUCATION:** Xavier Univ, BS 1951; LA State Univ Law School, JD 1954. **CAREER:** Keystone Life Ins Co, auditor 1951; Tureaud, Trudeau & Morial, partner 1954-60; Standard Life Ins Co of LA, gen counsel 1960-70; US Atty New Orleans, asst atty 1965-67; City of New Orleans, atty 1st black democrat elected to LA legislature 1967; Orleans Parish Juvenile Ct, judge 1970-72; LA Ct of Appeals, judge 1972-78; Tulane Univ Law School, prof of law; City of New Orleans, mayor. **ORGANIZATIONS:** Mem, officer NAACP; mem adv bd US Conf of Mayors; bd of dir Natl League of Cities AP Tureaud Medal; mem LA Conf of NAACP 1978; past gen pres Alpha Phi Alpha, Foreign Policy Conf WA, US Dept State; org, mem bd dir Liberty Bank & Trust Co; bd dir Gourmet Serv Inc, Loyola Univ; bd of govs Tulane Univ med Ctr; founding mem Lawyers Com Civil Rights Under Law; bd dir Total Comm Action; mem New Orleans Legal Aid Soc, LA Voter Ed Proj; adv bd Irish Channel Action Found; charter mem Commun Rel Council, Urban League; exec comm Mayors Criminal Justice Coord Council; mem US Superior Court, LA Superior Court, US Dist Court, US Court of Appeals, Amer Bar Assn, Fed Bar Assn, Louis Martinet Legal Soc, Amer Trial Lawyers Assn. **HONORS/ACHIEVEMENTS:** Outstanding Young Men of Amer 1965; One of Amers 100 Most Influential Blacks Ebony Mag 1971-80. **MILITARY SERVICE:** AUS Intell Corps. **BUSINESS ADDRESS:** Mayor, City of New Orleans, 1300 Perdido St, New Orleans, LA 70112.

MORIAL, SYBIL HAYDEL
Educational administrator. **PERSONAL:** Born Nov 26, 1932, New Orleans, LA; married Ernest Nathan Morial; children: Julie, Marc, Jacaues, Cheri, Monique. **EDUCATION:** Boston Univ, BS Ed 1952, MEd 1955. **CAREER:** Newton Public Schools, teacher 1952-55; Baltimore Public Schools, teacher 1955-56; New Orleans Public Schools, teacher 1959-71; Xavier Univ, dir spec serv 1977-85, assoc dean Drexel Center for Extended Learning 1985-. **ORGANIZATIONS:** Founder, pres, pres emeritus LA League of Good Govt 1963-; mem 1967-, pres1976-78 New Orleans Chap of Links Inc; mem United Fund of Greater New Orleans 1972-73; mem Audubon Park Commiss 1971-78; mem Children Arts Council of New Orleans 1974-77; co-chairperson LA Comm for the Humanities 1977-79; co-chair Mayor's Task Force on Arts Policy 1979; bd of dir WLAE-TV Adv Bd 1979-81, 1984-; Natl Conf on Children Having Children, Black Women Respond 1983; co-chair 1983 Year of the Healthy Birth; founder, pres, chmn I've Known Rivers Afro-Amer Pavilion LA World Exposition 1982-85; dir Liberty Bank & Trust Co 1979-; bd of trustees Amistad Rsch Ctr 1980-; trustee Natl Jewish Hosp Natl Asthma Ctr 1983-. **HONORS/ACHIEVEMENTS:** Natl Hon Soc in Ed Pi Lambda Theta; Torch of Liberty Awd Anti-Defamation League of B'nai B'rith 1978; Whitney M Young Brotherhood Awd Urban League of Greater New Orleans 1978; Zeta Phi Beta Finer Womenhood Awd 1978; Arts Council Medal LA Council for Music & the Performing Arts Co 1979; Weiss Awd Natl Conf of Christians & Jews 1979; Woman of the Year Links Inc 1981; Citizen of the Year Spectator News Jrnl 1984. **HOME ADDRESS:** 1101 Harrison Ave, New Orleans, LA 70122. **BUSINESS ADDRESS:** Associate Dean, Xavier University, 7325 Palmetto St, Drexel Cntr for Extended Learn, New Orleans, LA 70125.

MORISEY, PATRICIA GARLAND
Educational administrator. **PERSONAL:** Born Aug 01, 1921, New York, NY; daughter of Arthur L Williams and Dagmar McCabe Cheatum; widowed; children: Paul Garland, Jean Morisey, Alex Morisey, Muriel Spence. **EDUCATION:** Hunter Coll, BA 1941; Columbia Univ School of Social Work, MSS 1944, DSW 1970; Hunter Coll, New York, NY, BA, 1937-41; Columbia Univ, New York, NY, MIS, 1947-70. **CAREER:** Comm Serv Soc & NYANA, caseworker 1944-51; Louise Wise Adoption Servs, caseworker consultant 1951-59; Bureau of Child Welfare NY Dept Social Servs, proj dir, dir of training 1959-63; Youth & Corrections Comm Serv Soc, staff consultant 1963-64; Family & Child Welfare Fed of Protestant Welfare Agency, assoc prof 1968-69; Catholic Univ of Amer Washington DC, assoc prof 1968-69; Lincoln Center Fordham Univ Grad School of Social Science, asst dean, 1975-86; prof, Florida Univ Graduate School of Social Serv. **ORGANIZATIONS:** Mem Mayors Task Force on Child Abuse & Foster Care Mayor's Task Force on Task Force Youth & The Law, New York City Dept of Mental Health & Retardation, Council on Social Work Educ, Natl Assoc of Social Workers; vice pres Leake & Watts Childrens Svc; mem bd Citizens Comm for Children, Comm Council Rsch Utilization Unit; bd of dir Fed of Protestant Welfare Agencies; mem Subpanel on Spec Populations; pres Comm on mental Health 1977-78; Natl Council of Negro Women - NYC Comm; chmn, Greater NY Council Natl Council of Negro Women, 1984-. **HONORS/ACHIEVEMENTS:** Hall of Fame Hunter Coll 1975; Honoree Natl Assoc of Womens Business & Professional Club 1975. **HOME ADDRESS:** 186 Riverside Dr, New York, NY 10024.

MORNING, JOHN FREW, JR.
Art director. **PERSONAL:** Born Jan 08, 1932, Cleveland, OH; son of John Frew Morning, Sr and Juanita Kathryn Brannan Morning; divorced; children: Ann Juanita, John Floyd. **EDUCATION:** Wayne State Univ, 1950-51; Pratt Inst, BFA 1955. **CAREER:** McCann Erickson, Inc, art dir 1958-60; John Morning Design, Inc, owner 1960-. **ORGANIZATIONS:** Trustee Dime Savings Bank of NY, FSB 1979-; dir Henry St Stlmnt 1973, chmn 1979-86; trustee Pratt Inst 1973; dir Repertory Theatre Lincoln Cntr 1970-73, Council of Governing Brds 1984-. **HONORS/ACHIEVEMENTS:** Alumni medal Pratt Inst 1972; Pres Recognition Award/White House 1984. **MILITARY SERVICE:** AUS sp/3c 1956-58. **BUSINESS ADDRESS:** John Morning Design, Inc, 866 United Nations Plaza, New York, NY 10017.

MORRIS, ALFRED L.
Business executive. **PERSONAL:** Born May 15, 1933, Atlanta; married Dorothy L; children: Alfredalynn Y, Michael A, Marcellus A. **EDUCATION:** Morehouse Coll, AB 1957; Atlanta U, MA 1958; Atlanta U, MBA 1959; FL St U, PhD 1972. **CAREER:** Black Enter, dir of oper; Fidelity Bank Philadelphia, vice pres dir pub affairs 1974-; Am Inst Banking, instr 1972-; Sch Bus Adm Temple U, lectr 1972-;Fidelity Bank, asst training dir mktg plan 1971-72; Fidelity Bank, mktg consult 1969-70; FL A&M U, asst prof econ 1966-69. **ORGANIZATIONS:** Mem Am Econ Assn; So Econ Assn; Pi Gamma Mu; Omicron Delta Epsilon; Alpha Kappa Mu; Phi Beta Sigma; Frontiers Internat; Am Mktrs Assn; Am Inst Banking; PA Bankers Assn; bd dirs Jane Kent-St Nicholas Day Care Cntr; Brandywine Valley YMCA Camps; Carver Loan Co; Philadelphia Dance Co; Gr Philadelphia Commun Devel Corp; War Vets Fndtn; mem Philadelphia Urban Coalition Econ Devel Task Force; Minor Affairs Adv Counc; Philadelphia Coll Textiles & Sci; Untd Fund. **MILITARY SERVICE:** USMC sgt 1951-54; USMCR 1st lt 1954-65. **BUSINESS ADDRESS:** Black Enterprise, 130 Fifth Ave, New York, NY 10011.

MORRIS, ARCHIE, III
Educator, manager. **PERSONAL:** Born Mar 24, 1938, Washington, DC; married Irene Beatrice Poindexter; children: Giovanni, Ottiviani. **EDUCATION:** Howard Univ, BA 1968, MUS 1973; Nova Univ, DPA 1976. **CAREER:** US Dept of Commerce, dep asst dir admin 1972-73; US Dept of Commerce OMBE, R& D spec 1973-74; DC Govt, rent admin 1974-76; The MATCH Inst, proj dir, cons 1976-79; US Dept of Agr, chief facilities mgmt 1979-82; US Dept of Agri, chief mail & reproduction mgmt 1982-. **ORGANIZATIONS:** Mem bd of dirs HUD Fed Credit Union 1971-76; instr Washington Ctr for Learning Alternatives 1976; instr Howard Univ Dept of Publ Admin 1976-77; pres Natl Capital Area Chap Nova Univ Alumni 1980-81; mem Amer Soc for Publ Admin; mem Natl Urban League. **HONORS/ACHIEVEMENTS:** Honors & Plaque HUD Task Force Against Racism Washington 1972; Spec Achievement Awd OMBE Dept of Commerce Washington 1973; Outstanding Serv Awd HUD Fed Credit Union Washington 1976; Cert of Apprec Mayor Washington 1976. **MILITARY SERVICE:** USAF a/1c 1955-59. **BUSINESS ADDRESS:** US Dept of Agriculture, 12th & Independence Ave SW, Washington, DC 20250.

MORRIS, BERNARD ALEXANDER
Consultant, company executive. **PERSONAL:** Born Jun 25, 1937, New York, NY; married Margaret M Taylor; children: Myron, Michael, Loree Smith, Quincy. **EDUCATION:** Boston State Coll, BS 1975; Harvard Univ, EdM 1978. **CAREER:** MIT, academic admin 1971-77; New York City Bd of Educ, sr policy analyst 1979-80; Nolan Norton and Co, managing consultant 1980-85; Morris Associates, president/consultant 1985-87. **ORGANIZATIONS:** Mem Transafrica, Pi Sigma Alpha, Phi Delta Kappa. **MILITARY SERVICE:** USAF electronics/radar 4 yrs. **HOME ADDRESS:** 80 Irving St, Cambridge, MA 02138.

MORRIS, CALVIN S.
Educator. **PERSONAL:** Born Mar 16, 1941, Philadelphia, PA; children: Dorothy Rebecca, Rachel Elaine. **EDUCATION:** Friends Select Schl, Philadelphia, PA, Diploma 1959; Lincoln Univ, AB, Amer Hist 1963; Boston Univ, AM, Amer Hist 1964; Boston Univ Schl of Theology, STB 1967; Boston Univ, PhD, Amer Hist 1982. **CAREER:** SCLC Operation Breadbasket, assoc dir 1967-71; Simmons Coll, dir Afro-Amer Studies/Simmons Coll 1971-73; Urban Devel, Michigan State Univ, visitng lecturer 1973-76; Martin Luther King, Jr Ctr for Social Change, exec dir 1973-76; Howard Univ Divinity Schl, asst prof practical theology & dir min in church & soc 1976-82; Howard Univ Divinity Schl, assoc prof pastoral theology & dir Urban Ministries 1982-. **ORGANIZATIONS:** Mem Amer Historical Assn, Amer Soc of Church History, Assn for the Study of Negro Life & History, Assn for Theological Field Educ, Soc for the Study of Black Religion, Amer Civil Lib Union, Amer Friends Serv Comm Amnesty Intl, NAACP-Life Mem, Natl Urban League; mem Omega Psi Phi; Intl Peace Research Assn 1987-; bd mem, Arts in Action, 1988; bd mem, The Churches Conference on Shelter and Housing 1988. **HONORS/ACHIEVEMENTS:** Distinguished Alumni Award, Friends Select HS 1974; Jr Chamber of Comm Award One of Chicago's Ten Outstanding Young Men 1970; Crusade Schlr United Methodist Church 1963-66; Rockefeller Protestant Fellow 1964-65; Whitney Young Fellow 1971-72; Grad Fellowship for Black Amer, The Natl Fellowship Fund 1979-80; Black Doctoral Dis The Fund for Theological Ed 1979-80; Distinguished Alumni Award, Lincoln Univ, Pennsylvania, 1988. **BUSINESS ADDRESS:** Director of Urban Ministries, HowardUniversity School of Divinity, 1400 Shepherd Street NE, Washington, DC 20017.

MORRIS, CHARLES EDWARD, JR.
Educator/administrator. **PERSONAL:** Born Sep 30, 1931, Big Stone Gap, VA; son of Charles E Morris and Verta E Warner Morris; married Jeanne A Brown; children: David Charles, Lyn Elizabeth. **EDUCATION:** Johnson C Smith Univ, BS 1952; Univ of IL, MS 1959, PhD 1966. **CAREER:** William Penn High School, teacher 1954-58; Univ of IL-Urbana, teaching/rsch assoc 1959-66; IL State Univ, assoc prof math 1966-, sec of the univ 1973-80, vice pres for admin 1980-. **ORGANIZATIONS:** Bd dirs Presbyterian Foundation 1974-83, Presbyterian Economic Develop Corp 1975-85, Western Ave Comm Ctr 1978-86; chairperson IL Comm on Black Concerns in Higher Educ 1982-88, chmn emeritus 1988-; adv bd College Potential Program Council for the Advancement of Experiential Learning 1984-; chairperson IL Consortium for Educ Oppor Bd 1986-. **HONORS/ACHIEVEMENTS:**

Distinguished Alumnus Johnson C Smith Univ 1976; Citizen's Awd for Human Rel Town of Normal 1979; Distinguished Alum of the Year Citation Natl Assn for Equal Oppor in Higher Educ 1979; numerous speeches and articles on topics including mathematics educ, univ governance, blacks in higher educ. **BUSINESS ADDRESS:** VP for Administrative Serv, Illinois State University, Hovey Hall 301, Normal, IL 61761.

MORRIS, CLIFTON
Educator. **PERSONAL:** Born Jun 21, 1937, Fredericktown, PA. **EDUCATION:** Waynesburg Coll, BS (summa cum laude) 1959; WV Univ, MS 1961; OH State Univ, PhD 1968. **CAREER:** Whittier Coll, chmn biology dept 1979-; City of Hope Med Tech Training Program, lectr 1978; Whittier Coll, asso prof biology 1972; OH State Univ Lima, asst prof biology 1969; OH State Univ Columbus, teaching assn 1965-68; WV Univ, research fellow 1959-61; Natl Dental Aptitude Test Rev Course, consult & instr 1977-; Natl Med Coll Aptitude Test Rev Course, consult instr 1977-; Educ Testing Serv Advanced Placement, consult 1978. **ORGANIZATIONS:** Mem Xi Psi Epsilon Hon Scholastic Soc Waynesburg, PA 1959; treas Gamma Alpha Grad Sci Frat Columbus, OH 1963-65; appointed James Irvine Chair in Biological Sci Whittier Coll 1980. **HONORS/ACHIEVEMENTS:** Who's Who in Am Coll &Univ 1959; Rockefeller Found Grant WVUniv Physiology of Fung I 1959-61; NSF Cooperative Grad Fellowship OH StateUniv 1961; NSF summer fellowships OH StateUniv 1962-64; Muellhaupt Found fellowship OH StateUniv 1964; Distinguished Tchr Award OH State ULima 1971; Distinguished Tchr Award Whittier Coll 1977-78; joint authorship "Hormone-like substances which increase carotenogenesis in plus & minus sexes of Choanephora cucurbitarum" Mycologia 1967;highest honors WV U; highest honors OH State U. **BUSINESS ADDRESS:** 13406 Philadelphia St, Whittier, CA 90608.

MORRIS, DOLORES N.
Television executive. **PERSONAL:** Born Sep 11, 1948, Staten Island, NY; daughter of William A Morris, Jr and Norcie Allen Morris. **EDUCATION:** Hunter Coll, BA Physical Anthology 1970. **CAREER:** Port Richmond HS, teacher/advisor curriculum develop 1971-73, dir of curriculum develop; Presidio Hill School, teacher 1973-78; Children's TV Workshop, coord 1979-80; ABC Television, dir children's programs, 1980-87; vice pres Magical World of Disney. **ORGANIZATIONS:** Mem Women in Film NY, Hunter Coll Alumni Assoc, Amer Film Inst; comm organizer VISTA Clovis NM 1970-71. **HONORS/ACHIEVEMENTS:** Black Achievement Award Harlem YWCA 1985. **BUSINESS ADDRESS:** Vice President Magical World of Disney, Walt Disney Television, 500 S Buena Vista, TV 1 Room 8, Burbank, CA 91521.

MORRIS, DOLORES ORINSKIA
Clinical psychologist. **PERSONAL:** Born in New York, NY; daughter of Joseph Morris and Gertude Morris; divorced. **EDUCATION:** CUNY, MS 1960; Yeshiva Univ, PhD 1974; NY Univ, Certificate Psychoanalysis, Psychotherapy Post Doctoral Program. **CAREER:** Children's Center Dept Child Welfare, psychologist 1959-62; Urban League of Greater NY, staff psychologist 1962-65; Bureau of Child Guidance NYC, research psychologist 1965-74, supvr of school psychologists 1974-78; Urban Research Planning Conf Center, tech asst 1976; Bedford Stuyvesant St Acad, consultant 1977; Fordham Univ, asst prof 1978-87; New York City Public Schools Div of Special Educ Clinical Professional Devel, educ admin 1987-; supervisor of School Psychologists, Div of Special Educ. **ORGANIZATIONS:** Mem Amer Psychology Assn & E Psychology Assn; treasurer NY Assn Black Psychologist 1967-75; co-chair professional devel NY Assn Black Psychologists 1975-77; chair Schools Y Mental Health Amer Orthopsychology Assn 1978-81, 1986-87; Natl Assoc School Psychology; NY State Psychology Assoc pres Div of School Psychology 1985-86. **HONORS/ACHIEVEMENTS:** Yeshiva Fellowship NIMH 1970-72; fellowship Black Analysis Inc 1972-74. **BUSINESS ADDRESS:** Supervisor of School Psychologists, New York City Public Schools Spec Educ, 234 West 104th St, New York, NY 10025.

MORRIS, EFFIE LEE
Librarian, lecturer, consultant. **PERSONAL:** Born Apr 20, Richmond, VA; daughter of William H Morris and Erma Caskia Morris; married Leonard V Jones, Aug 25, 1971. **EDUCATION:** Univ of Chicago 1938-41; Case Western Res Univ, BA 1945, BLS 1946, MS in LS 1956. **CAREER:** Cleveland Publ Library, br children's librn 1946; Library of the Blind NY Publ Library, children's spec 1958-63; Univ of San Francisco, lecturer 1974-76; San Francisco Publ Library, coord children's serv 1963-78; free-lance lecturer/consultant; Mills College, lecturer 1979-. **ORGANIZATIONS:** Consult reading proj San Francisco Chap Natl Council Chris & Jews 1967-70; mem OH, NY & CA Library Associations, Black Caucus, American Library Association; council mem Newbery Caldecott Award Comm 1950-56, 1966-67, 1967-71, 1975-79, 1984-; mem Laura Ingalls Wilder Award Comm 1953-54, 1958-60; bd dir Natl Aid to Visually Handicapped; library adv bd New Book Knowledge; con children's serv Chicago Public Library Study 1968-69, Oakland Public Library Study 1974; adv comm Title II ESEA State of CA 1965-75; del White House Conf on Children 1970; bd dirs YWCA San Francisco 1968-73; dir children's serv div 1963-66, council 1967-71, 1975-79, 1984-88 ALA; pres, Public Library Association 1971-72; mem League Women Voters; mem 1958-, chap pres 1968-70 Women's Natl Book Assoc; mem Natl Council Teachers English; pres Natl Braille Club 1961-63; mem Amer Assoc Univ Women; mem CA Library Serv Bd 1982-84, vice pres 1984-; mem adv bd Center for the Book Library of Congress; chair, Coretta Scott King Book Award, 1984-88; Commonwealth of CA; mem Association of University Women, Mayor's Advisory Council on Child Care. **HONORS/ACHIEVEMENTS:** Author, Harcourt Brace Jovanovich 1977-80; Lola M Parker Award, Iota Phi Lambda Sor 1978; Apprec Award, Jewish Bur of Ed, San Francisco 1978; Distinguished Serv to Librarianship, Black Caucus of AL 1978; Distinguished Serv Award, CA Librarians Black Caucus 1978; Distinguished Alumni Award, School of Libr Serv, Case Western Reserve Univ 1979; Outstanding Negro Woman, Iota Phi Lambda Sor 1964; Black Women Organized for Action; EP Dutton-John Macrae Award, Advancement of Library Serv to Children & Young People 1958; Women's Natl Book Assoc Award 1984; San Francisco Public Library, Effie Lee Morris Historical and Research Collection of Children's Literature; Alpha Kappa Alpha Sor; life mem NAACP; June 12, 1984, named Effie Lee Morris Day by Mayor Diane Feinstein; keynote addresses and workshops for Assoc of Intl Schools in Africa, 1987. **HOME ADDRESS:** 66 Cleary Ct, #1009, San Francisco, CA 94109.

MORRIS, ELISE L.
Educator. **PERSONAL:** Born Oct 25, 1916, Deridder, LA; married John E; children: Monica Delphin, John T. **EDUCATION:** Xavier Univ, BA 1937; Prairie View A&M Univ, MEd 1965; TX So Univ, Univ of Houston, Southwestern Univ, post grad study; Univ of St Thomas, religious educ. **CAREER:** Archditoches Parish Training School, teacher 1973; Our Mother of Mercy School, 1942; Our Lady Star of the Sea Day School, dir 1956; Galena Park Ind School Dist, teacher 1962-. **ORGANIZATIONS:** Life mem Natl Educ Assn; honorary life mem, Natl PTA & TX PTA; golden life mem Delta Sigma Theta Sorority; life mem TX State Teacher Assn; mem Natl Assn of Univ Women; chmn founder Natl Assn of Univ Women Houston 1965; Harris Co Grand Jury Adv Com 1974-75; supreme lady Knights of Peter Claver 1970-75; steering com on black participation 41st Intl Eucharistic Congress 1975. **HONORS/ACHIEVEMENTS:** TSU listed Black Leader of Houston 1970, KOCH & TSU Newman; Dict of Intl Biog 1975; Silver Medal Award outstanding serv Knights of PC; outstanding citizenship & serv commendation Mayor of Houston; Woman Breaking New Ground Delta Sigma Theta 1974; outstanding Xavier Alumnae of Houston.

MORRIS, ELLA LUCILLE
Librarian. **PERSONAL:** Born Mar 13, 1923, Beachton, GA; daughter of Daniel Glenn, Jr and Maggie Thomas Glenn; married William Alexander (deceased); children: Daniel G. **EDUCATION:** Ft Valley State Coll, BS 1944; Atlanta Univ Sch of Libr Sci, BS LS 1949; FL A&M U, MEd 1959; FL State Univ Sch of LS, MSLS 1970. **CAREER:** Thomasville HS GA, head librarian 1969-; AL State Coll, acquisitions 1952; Douglass HS Thomasville, GA, librarian 1946-69; Boston HS Boston, GA, English instr 1944-45; Glenn-Mor Home Inc, sec 1970-; Southwestern State Hospital Thomasvill GA Library Consultant 1985-; Glenn-Mor Home Inc, pres 1986-; Southwestern State Hospital Thomasville GA, library consultant 1986-. **ORGANIZATIONS:** Pres Thomasville Assn of Educators 1975; mem GA Educ Assn State Legislative Com 1975-78; bd of dir E Side Sch Cultural Cntr 1979-; bd of dir Thomasville Diversion Cntr 1978-; mem NAACP, GEA, NEA, LWV; mem Thomas Co Jury Commn Hostess TV show "Input" WCTV 1974-; Alpha Kappa Alpha Thomasville, GA 1979; Thomas Coll, trustee 1984-; WAM Assoc Inc, bd of dir 1985-; pres Glenn-Mor Horne Inc 1986-; Historical Preservation Commission 1987-; mem Thomasville City Bd of Education 1987-; pres Natl Council Negro Women Thomasville Section 1987-. **HONORS/ACHIEVEMENTS:** Achievement Award in Communications Ft Valley Atlanta Alumni Assn 1976; Beta Phi Mu Intl Hon Soc in LS FL State Univ 1970. **BUSINESS ADDRESS:** President, Glenn-Mor Home, Inc, 308 W Calhoun, Thomasville, GA 31792.

MORRIS, ERNEST ROLAND
Educational administrator. **PERSONAL:** Born Dec 15, 1942, Memphis, TN; son of Benjamin C Morris and Ernestine Edwards Morris; married Freddie Linda Wilson; children: Ernest Jr, Daniel. **EDUCATION:** Rocky Mountain Coll, BS (Cum Laude) 1967; Eastern IL Univ, MS Educ (w/Distinction) 1968; Univ of IL Urbana Champaign, PhD 1976. **CAREER:** Minneapolis Pub Sch, history tchr 1968-69; Eastern IL Univ, admissions officer 1969-71; Univ of IL at Urbana-Champaign, asst dean, assoc dean 1971-78, exec asst to the chancellor 1978-80; Univ of WA Seattle, spec asst pres 1980-82, vice pres for student affairs 1982-. **ORGANIZATIONS:** Chmn educ div 1983, 1984, mem admissions and review comm 1984-85, vice chmn bd of dirs, Residential Care and Family Services Conference Panel 1985,1986,1987,1988; vice chmn planning and allocations comm 1986, chmn planning and distribution comm 1987,1988,1989 United Way Seattle/King Co; mem class of 1983-84, bd of dirs 1985-, sec exec comm 1987-, chmn selection comm 1987, Chamber of Commerce Leadership Tomorrow Prog; chmn Federal Emergency Mgmt Agency Local Bd Seattle/King Co 1984-86; founding trustee Seattle/King Co Emergency Shelter Foundation 1984-86. **HONORS/ACHIEVEMENTS:** Clark Meml Scholar 1966; Outstanding History Student Awd 1966; Alumni Distinguished Achievement Awd Rocky MT Coll 1982; mem Natl Assoc of Student Personnel Administrators, Natl Assoc of State Univ and Land Grant Colls; Outstanding Alumnus Award Leadership Tomorrow 1988. **BUSINESS ADDRESS:** Vice Pres for Student Affairs, University of Washington, PB-10, Seattle, WA 98195.

MORRIS, EUGENE
Journalist. **PERSONAL:** Born Feb 06, 1960, Cincinnati, OH. **EDUCATION:** Florida A&M Univ, bachelor's degree (magna cum laude) 1982. **CAREER:** St Louis Globe, summer intern 1981; The Virginian Pilot, education reporter 1982-84; St Petersburg Times, general assignment reporter 1984-85; Gainesville Sun, general assignment reporter 1985-. **ORGANIZATIONS:** Mem Natl Assoc of Black Journalists; lifetime mem Bethel AME Church. **HONORS/ACHIEVEMENTS:** Outstanding Young Men of Amer 1986. **BUSINESS ADDRESS:** General Assignment Reporter, Gainesville Sun, PO Drawer A, Gainesville, FL 32602.

MORRIS, FRANK LORENZO, SR.
Education executive. **PERSONAL:** Born Jul 21, 1939, Cairo, IL; son of Lorenzo Richard Morris, Jr and Frankie Mae Taylor (Honesty); married M Winston Baker, Jan 02, 59; children: Frank Jr, Scott, Rebecca, Kristina. **EDUCATION:** Colgate Univ, BA 1961; Syracuse Univ, MPA 1962; MIT, PhD, MS 1976. **CAREER:** US Dept Housing & Urban Devel, Seattle WA, urban renewal rep, 1962-66; US Agency for Intl Develop, reg coord 1966-72; Northwestern Univ, assoc prof 1972-77; US Community Serv Admin, chief of planning & policy 1978; USAID, deputy dir chief of operations 1979-83; Congressional Black Caucus Found, exec dir 1983-85; Colgate Univ, O'Connor prof 1986; Univ of MD School of Public Affairs, assoc dean 1986-88; Morgan State Univ, Baltimore MD, dean of graduate studies and research, 1988-. **ORGANIZATIONS:** Pres NAACP Tacoma 1963-66; vice pres NAACP Montgomery Cty 1977-79; trustee Lincoln Temple UCC 1984; moderator Potomac Assn, United Church of Christ 1987-; treas, bd of dir Global Tomorrow Coalition 1987-; mem Alpha Phi Alpha; bd of dir Center Immigration Studies, 1988-; bd of homeland ministries, United Church of Christ, 1988-. **HONORS/ACHIEVEMENTS:** NDEA Fellow MIT 1971; Dissertation Fellow Russel Sage Found 1972; selected as Father of the Year Chicago Defender 1975; Educ Policy Fellow Inst for Educ Leadership 1977; three awards NAACP Evanston Mont Cty MD; Superior Honor Awd Dept of State 1982. **MILITARY SERVICE:** US AID sr foreign service officer 18 yrs. **HOME ADDRESS:** 601 Bennington Ln, Silver Spring, MD 20910. **BUSINESS ADDRESS:** Dean of Graduate Studies & Research, Morgan State University, Baltimore, MD 21239.

MORRIS, GARRETT
Actor, comedian, musician. **PERSONAL:** Born Feb 01, 1937, New Orleans, LA. **EDUCATION:** Julliard Sch of Mus; Dillard Coll, BA; Manhattan Sch of Mus. **CAREER:** "Where's Poppa?", "The Anderson Tapes", "Cooley High"; film actor 1970-75; "Roll Out", Saturday Night Live";TV actor 1975-79; "The Great White Hope", "Show Boat", "Porgy & Bess", "Hallelujah Baby", "Ain't Supposed to Die a Natural Death"; theatre actor; Harry Belafonte Singers, former arranger; "If I Had a My Way", "Tell God All a My Troubles", composer. **ORGANIZATIONS:** Mem ASCAP 1963-; mem AFTRA. **HONORS/**

ACHIEVEMENTS: Tanglewood Conductors Award 1956; Omega Psi Phi Nat Singing Contest Winner. **BUSINESS ADDRESS:** NBC, Rockefeller Plaza, New York, NY 10020.

MORRIS, GREG
Actor. **PERSONAL:** Born Sep 27, 1933, Cleveland, OH; married Lee Keys; children: Iona, Philip, Linda. **EDUCATION:** OH State Univ, attended; Univ IA. **CAREER:** Actor, num plays, motion pict TV prog, series including "Mission Impossible" & " Vegas"; GLLIP prod co, owns. **ORGANIZATIONS:** Bd dirs Center Theatre Group of LA 1972; bd trustees Benedict Coll 1973. **HONORS/ACHIEVEMENTS:** Most Promising Newcomer to Fasion, TV & Costume Designers' Guild 1968-69; hon deg Miles Coll 1969; LA Father of Yr 1969; Emmy Nomin 1969, 1970, 1972; angel of yr Girls Friday of Show Bus 1971; TV father of yr Nat Father's Day Com 1971; image awd NAACP 1971; star of yr nomin Hollywood Women's Press Club 1971; VIVA cit 1971; ethics awd Sisterhood Temple Emanuel 1971; Unity Awd 1973. **MILITARY SERVICE:** AUS 1952-55; Honorable Discharge 1955, Good Conduct and Overseas Medals. **BUSINESS ADDRESS:** President, GLLIP, Prod, Inc, 9200 Sunset Blvd, Los Angeles, CA 90069.

MORRIS, HORACE W.
Executive director. **PERSONAL:** Born May 29, 1928, Elizabeth, NJ; divorced; children: Bradley, JoAnne, Horace, Jr, Bryan. **EDUCATION:** SyracuseUniv Sch of Edn, BA 1949; Rutgers The StUniv Grad Sch of Edn, MEduc 1962. **CAREER:** Burlington Public Schools, teacher, admin 1956-64; NY Urban League, exec dir 1964-72,75; Intl Center of the Meridan Found, lecture on "Civil Liberties & Race Relations in Amer" 1966-69; Dade County Community Relations Bd, dep dir 1970; Dade County Model Cities Prog, dir 1971; Garmco Inc, pres, ceo 1972-; Greater NY Fund/United Way, exec dir 1983. **ORGANIZATIONS:** Present mem Counc of Exec Dirs of Nat Urban League; Nat Conf of Soc Welf; Wash DC Br NAACP; Alumni Assn Syracuse U; Alpha Phi Alpha Frat; Frontiers Internatl; Chrtr mem Civitan Internatl Springfield OH Chpt; AME Zion Ch; mem, bd dir New York City Partnership. **HONORS/ACHIEVEMENTS:** Recip Pop Warner Serv to Youth Awd S Jersey area 1962; Outstanding Young Man of Yr Gr Burlington Area Jr C of C 1962; Father of Yr Burlington Jr HS PTA 1960; Four Yr Scholar SyracuseUniv 1945-49. **BUSINESS ADDRESS:** Executive Dir, Gr NY Fund/United Way, 99 Park Ave, New York, NY 10016.

MORRIS, JAMES F.
Executive director. **PERSONAL:** Born Nov 23, 1925, Washington, GA; married Charlene Ruffin; children: Sharon, James F. **EDUCATION:** Univ of MA Comm Action Agency Study, 1967-70; Skidmore Coll Bus Mgmt Study, 1975-77; Moody Sch of Commerce Bus Adminstrn. **CAREER:** Opporunities Industrialization Center, exec dir; Faf(Ir Bearing Co, work leader electric inspection gauges 1950-72; Burritt Mut Sav Bank, br adv 1976-80. **ORGANIZATIONS:** Pres local NAACP 1960-68; sec lodge 1437 IBPOE of W Elks 1965-70; chmn bd of Health Commr NB 1977-80. **HONORS/ACHIEVEMENTS:** Distinguished serv award New Britain NAACP 1967; devoted serv award May Mcloed Bethune Club 1970; Man of Yr Award Mt Pleasant Neighborhood Corp 1972; loyalsvc award A Philip Randolph Inst 1978. **MILITARY SERVICE:** USN bm/2c 3 yrs served. **BUSINESS ADDRESS:** Opportunities Industrializatio, 180 Clinton St, New Britain, CT 06053.

MORRIS, JOE
Professional athlete. **PERSONAL:** Born Sep 15, 1960, Fort Bragg, NC; married Linda; children: Samantha Ashley. **EDUCATION:** Syracuse Univ, BS 1982. **CAREER:** New York Giants, running back 1982-. **HONORS/ACHIEVEMENTS:** Played in Senior Bowl, East-West Shrine and Blue-Gray games; set all of the alltime rushing records at Syracuse; set 5 alltime Giant records rushed 1,336 yds,scored 21 touchdowns rushing, racked up seven 100 plus rushing games and scored three TD's in a game four times 1985; mem Pro Bowl Teams 1986,87; 1986 season rushed for 1516 yds, only Giant ever to have back to back 1,000 yd seasons; broke own record for yds rushing in a season. **BUSINESS ADDRESS:** New York Giants, Giants Stadium, East Rutherford, NJ 07073.

MORRIS, JOEL M.
Electrical/electronics engineer. **PERSONAL:** Born Aug 11, 1944, Washington, DC; married Beatrice Dianne Gilbert; children: Timothy Joel, Christopher Joel. **EDUCATION:** Howard U, BS 1966; Polytechnic Inst of Bklyn, MS 1970; Johns Hopkins U, PhD 1975. **CAREER:** Office of Naval Research Electronics & Solid State Sci Program, sci officer 1979; Naval Research Lab Communications Sci Div, research engr 1975; Bendix Corp, elec engr; Bell Telephone Labs, elec engr; Navy Oceanographic Office & Ibm, engr. **ORGANIZATIONS:** Mem IEE; mem Sigma Xi The Research Soc 1978; mem US Nat Comm The Intl Union of Radio Sci (URSI) 1978; mem Kappa Alpha Psi 1966; Tau Beta Pi 1965. **HONORS/ACHIEVEMENTS:** Recip NSF Traineeship Johns Hopkins U; Nat fellowships fund grant Johns Hopkins U; IEEE student award Howard U; awarded patent for work at Bell Labs.

MORRIS, KELSO B.
Educator. **PERSONAL:** Born in Beaumont, TX; married Marlene Isabella; children: Kenneth Bruce, Gregory Alfred, Karen Denise, Lisa Frances. **EDUCATION:** Wiley Coll, BS 1930; Cornell Univ, MS 1937, PhD 1940. **CAREER:** Wiley Coll, prof 1940-46; Howard Univ, prof 1946-77, dept head 1965-69; Atlanta Univ, visiting lecturer 1946, 1949, & 1951; NC Coll, 1957-59; Air Force Inst of TechWright Patterson AFB, prof sect head 1959-61; Amer Inst Chemists, fellow; TX Acad Sci; Washington Acad Sci; Amer Assn for Advancement of Sci; Wash Acad of Sci, sec 1977-78; Sci Achievement Awards Prgram Wash Acad of Sci, gen chmn 1974-78. **ORGANIZATIONS:** Mem Am Chem Soc; Nat Assn for Research in Sci Teaching; DC Inst Chemists pres 1974-75 Unitarian; mem Alpha Phi Alpha Frat; monographs in field; Sigma Xi. **HONORS/ACHIEVEMENTS:** Distinguished Teaching Award Washington Acad Scis 1968; Gen Educ Bd Fellow 1936-37; Cosmos Club of Washington 1969-; United Negro Coll Fund Dreyfus Found1974-80; listed in Who's Who in Am 40th edition; Am Men & Women of Sci Marquis Hon Scroll Award 1979.

MORRIS, LEIBERT WAYNE
Medical education administrator. **PERSONAL:** Born Nov 20, 1950, Cleveland, OH; married Cathy L. **EDUCATION:** OH Univ, BGS 1973, MEd 1980. **CAREER:** OH State Univ Office of Minority Affairs, coord of recruitment 1974-75; Oberlin Coll, asst dir admissions 1975-77; Coll of Osteopathic Med OH Univ, assoc dir admissions 1977-79, asst to regional dean 1979-85; OH State Univ Coll Med, associate to the dean 1985-. **ORGANIZATIONS:** Adv bd staff Buiders Home Health Care Agency 1983-; bd trustees Triedstone Missionary Baptist Church 1985-88; keeper of records & seal Omega Psi Phi Frat Inc 1984-85. **BUSINESS ADDRESS:** Associate to the Dean, Ohio State Univ, Coll of Med, 370 W 9th Ave, 270A Meling Hall, Columbus, OH 43210.

MORRIS, LEWIS R.
Educator. **PERSONAL:** Born Feb 17, 1926, Windsor, NC; son of Richard Morris and Brulena Morris; married Selena R Clark; children: Brenda J, Constance L, Lolita R, Richard J. **EDUCATION:** NC A&T Univ, BS 1947; Univ MI, MA 1950; Howard Univ, PhD 1970; Mount Hope Bible Coll, ThD 1978; Detroit Urban Bible College, DD. **CAREER:** TX Southern Univ, prof English chmn; Morris Coll Sumter, SC, dean dept chmn. **ORGANIZATIONS:** Mem CLA; CCCC; MLA; NCTE; YMCA; Magnolia Lodge #3; Douglass Burrell Consistory (32); Doric Temple; Alpha Kappa Mu; Lambda Iota Tau; chaplain Nu Phi, Omega Psi Phi; United Supreme Council 33 degree PHA. **MILITARY SERVICE:** Lt ww II. **BUSINESS ADDRESS:** Texas Southern University, 3300 Cleburne, Houston, TX 77004.

MORRIS, MAJOR
Educator. **PERSONAL:** Born May 12, 1921, Cincinnati, OH; son of Ellen Morris; married Anne-Grethe Jakobsen; children: Lia Jacqueline. **EDUCATION:** Boston Univ, attended 1949-51; Harvard Univ Graduate School of Educ, EdM 1976. **CAREER:** MIT, rsch technician 1953-66; Tufts Univ, program dir officer 1969-76; Southeastern MA Univ, affirmative action officer 1977-79; Portland State Univ, dir equity programs 1979-87. **ORGANIZATIONS:** Photographer/administrator Education Develop Ctr 1966-68; dir Deseg Training Inst Univ of Delaware 1976-77; state coord MA Region I AAAA 1977-79; vice chair Tri-County AA Assoc Portland 1981-83; state coord Oregon Region X AAAA 1983-; Willamette Valley Racial Minority Consortium (WVRMC); dir/photographer MaJac Assoc 1987-; bd mem Beaverton OR Arts Commission 1989-91. **HONORS/ACHIEVEMENTS:** Monographs EEO/AA In Postsecondary Institutions, Concepts in Multicultural and Intergroup Relations Ed, Click and Tell, Our Street; contributor Intergroup Relations Curriculum. **MILITARY SERVICE:** AUS staff sgt 1942-46; European Theatre; Po Valley; No Appenines; Good Conduct Medal; Victory Medal. **BUSINESS ADDRESS:** 13430 SW Weir Road, Beaverton, OR 97005.

MORRIS, MARGARET LINDSAY
Educator. **PERSONAL:** Born Dec 23, 1950, Princess Anne Co, VA; married Richard. **EDUCATION:** Norfolk State U, BA 1973; Iberian AmUniv Mexico City, 1975;Univ of IL Urbana-Champaign, MA 1974, PhD 1979; Univ of Madrid, summer 1982. **CAREER:** Lincoln U, asst prof of spanish 1980-; Central StateUniv Wilberforce OH, language lab dir 1980; Livingstone Coll Salisbury NC, asst prof 1981-85; Portsmouth City Schools, teacher 1986-. **ORGANIZATIONS:** Mem Am Assn of Tchr of Spanish & Portuguese 1976-80; mem Am Assn ofUniv Prof 1976-80; mem Coll Language Assn 1980; life mem Alpha Kappa Mu Honor Soc 1972-, life mem Sigma Delta Pi Spanish Hon Soc 1974-, life mem Alpha Gamma Mu Spanish Hon Soc 1972-, life mem Alpha Kappa Alpha Sor 1983-. **HONORS/ACHIEVEMENTS:** FellowshipUniv of IL 1973-74; Fellowship Grad CollUniv of IL 1975; 1st Black to Receive PhD in SpanishUniv of IL 1979; wrote proposal entitled "Personalizing Instruction in Modern Foreign Langugages" 1982-83,83-84. **BUSINESS ADDRESS:** Teacher, Portsmouth City School, 5601 High St, Portsmouth, VA 23703.

MORRIS, MARLENE C. (NEE COOK)
Staff chemist. **PERSONAL:** Born Dec 20, 1933, Washington, DC; daughter of Richard Cook and Ruby Cook; married Kelso B; children: Gregory A, Karen D, Lisa F. **EDUCATION:** Howard Univ, BS 1955; Polytechnic Ins of NY, postgraduate. **CAREER:** AUS, research assoc High Temp Research Project 1953-55; NBS JCPDS Associateship, research assoc 1955-, dir & research assoc 1975-; Intl Centre for Diffraction Data, research chemist 1986-. **ORGANIZATIONS:** Mem Amer Chemist Soc; Amer Crystallographic Soc; Amer Assn for Adv of Sci; Joint Comm on Powder Diff Stand; Intl Union of Crystallography; mem NBSSr Lunch Club; mem & fellow, Washington Acad of Sci Sigma Xi; Beta Kappa Chi Hon Sci Soc; mem Unitarian Church; mem, JCPDS-ICCD. **HONORS/ACHIEVEMENTS:** Published 50 articles in professional periodicals; author of 3 books.

MORRIS, MELLASENAH Y.
Educational administrator. **PERSONAL:** Born Aug 13, 1947, Norfolk, VA; married Thomas E Morris; children: Mellasenah Indira, Thomas Jared. **EDUCATION:** Peabody Conserv, BM 1968, MM 1971; Peabody Inst of JHU, DMA 1980, MS. **CAREER:** Howard Cty MD, elem school music teacher 1968-69; Peabody Prep Dept, priv & classroom instr 1969-85; Comm Coll of Baltimore, priv & classroom instr 1970-74; Peabody Conserv, instr & lectr 1973-84; Villa Julie Coll, music hist instr 1976-80; Peabody Conserv, acad counselor 1980-83, assist dean for acad affairs 1983-. **ORGANIZATIONS:** Mem "the friends" Douglas Meml Comm Church 1972-; Freelance Concert Pianist East Coast 1973; record sec Levindale - Sunset Comm Organiz 1974; mem Delta Sigma Theta 1978-; pres Baltimore Chap Delicados Inc 1980-84; mem Fine Arts Adv Comm Villa Julie Coll 1983; natl, vice pres Delicados Inc 1985-; mem Accredit Team Comm on Higher Educ 1985-; Balt Cntr Victims of Sexual Assault 1986; Sym Orch 1987. **HONORS/ACHIEVEMENTS:** Listed The World's Who's Who of Women 1982-83; recip Doctoral Fellowship Natl Fellowships Fund 1975; Grad Assistantship in Piano Peabody Conserv 1969-71; Pauline Favin Prize Peabody Conserv 1966; Alexander Sklarevski Prize Peabody Conserv 1965; Four-Year Scholarship Peabody Conserv 1964-68; First Prize Hermitage Foundation Competition 1963; First Prize Bland Meml Statewide Scholarship Competition 1961; Academic Conf presenter Univ of SC 1986. **BUSINESS ADDRESS:** Asst Dean of Academic Affairs, Peabody Inst of Johns Hopkins, 1 E Mt Vernon Place, Baltimore, MD 21202.

MORRIS, MELVIN
Attorney. **PERSONAL:** Born May 07, 1937, Chicago, IL. **EDUCATION:** Univ WI, BS 1959; John Marshall Law Sch, JD 1965. **CAREER:** Prv Prac, atty; Gary, IN, city atty. **BUSINESS ADDRESS:** 2216 Broadway St E, East Chicago, IN 46312.

MORRIS, MILTON CURTIS
Executive director arts organization. **PERSONAL:** Born Jul 07, 1936, Union Springs, AL; married Eleanor Christine Mayo; children: Stephanie, Ann, Milton. **EDUCATION:** Attended, OH Univ 1959; Case Western Reserve Univ, MSSA 1975. **CAREER:** City of Cleve-

land, dir NYC 1970-73; City of Cleveland Heights, asst dir of finance 1975-76; United Way Serv-Cleveland, dir agency mgmt 1976-83; Karamu HouseInc, exec dir 1983-. **ORGANIZATIONS:** Consultant State of MI Arts 1986; panelist State of OH Arts Counsel 1986; mem Vstg Comm Cleveland State Univ 1986, Univ Circle Bd of Trustees 1986, NatlAssoc of Social Workers 1986, Natl Assoc of Black Social Workers 1986. **HONORS/ACHIEVEMENTS:** Congressional Presentations 1971-73; Abrams Scholarship CWRU SASS 1973-75. **HOME ADDRESS:** 3048 Lincoln Blvd, Cleveland, OH 44118. **BUSINESS ADDRESS:** Executive Dir, Karamu House Inc, 2355 East 89th St, Cleveland, OH 44106.

MORRIS, SAMUEL SOLOMON
Clergyman. **PERSONAL:** Born Nov 01, 1916, Norfolk, VA; married Ermine Smith; children: Joyce Green, Ermine Laurel, Samuel III. **EDUCATION:** Wilberforce Univ, BS 1937; Yale Univ MDiv 1940; Payne Sem, DD 1964; Daniel Payne Coll, LLD 1963. **CAREER:** St Luke AME Ch & St John AME Ch, pastor 1940-41; Payne Sem & Wilberforce Univ, prof 1941-48; St Paul AME Ch, pastor 1943-46; Shorter Coll, pres 1946-48; Bethel AME Ch, assoc pastor 1948-49; 1st AME, pastor 1949-56; Coppin AME Ch & Builder Coppin Youth Ctr, pastor 1956-72; AME Ch, elected 89th bishop 1972; 12th Epis Dist AME Ch, presiding bishop 1972-76; 11th Epis Dist AME Ch, presiding bishop. **ORGANIZATIONS:** Bd chmn Edward Waters Coll; bd of dir Afro-Amer Life Ins Co; bd of trust Natl Urban League; sec bd of dir & developer Lake Grove Village Housing Complex 1969-72; chmn Gen Bd of Educ 1974-76; bd chmn Shorter Coll 1972-76; chmn Social Action Comm AME Ch 1972-74; pres Chicago Br NAACP 1960-62. **HONORS/ACHIEVEMENTS:** Silver Beaver Scout Awd Frontiers Intl; attnd World Council of Ch New Delhi India 1961 & toured 14 countries in Europe, Africa and the Holy Land, Near & Far East, Jamaica, W Indies 1965, Bahama Islands 1966; del World Counc of Ch Sweden 1968; World Council of Ch Nairobi Kenya E Africa 1974; publ "An African Methodist Priner, The Call to a Captive People". **BUSINESS ADDRESS:** Presiding Bishop, 11th Epis Dist AME Church, 101 E Union St, PO Box 2140, Jacksonville, FL 32203.

MORRIS, STANLEY E., JR.
Administrator. **PERSONAL:** Born Nov 15, 1944, Brooklyn, NY; married Sandra Brito. **EDUCATION:** Howard Univ, BA 1968. **CAREER:** State Univ of NY, asso dean 1970-, asst dir 1969-70; NY City Bd of Educ, teacher 1968-69. **ORGANIZATIONS:** Pres chmn of bd Elephant Ent Ltd 1975-; pres SE Morris Mgmt Assn 1976-; mem NY State Personnel & Guidance Assn; mem AfroAm Tchr Assn RepUniv Negro Coll Fund 1970; rep ASG; mem Dist of Columbia Sociological Soc. **HONORS/ACHIEVEMENTS:** Claude Mckay Award 1960; outst Young Men of Am 1976; publ "Beyong the Blue" 1961.

MORRIS, TOM
Professional athlete. **PERSONAL:** Born Apr 02, 1960, Anniston, AL; married Karen; children: Thomas Jr. **EDUCATION:** MI State Univ, Urban & Metro Degree. **CAREER:** Oakland Invaders, cornerback 1983-.

MORRIS, WAYNE LEE
Contractor/professional athlete. **PERSONAL:** Born May 13, 1954, Dallas, TX. **EDUCATION:** Southern Methodist Univ Dallas, BA 1976. **CAREER:** Wayne Morris Enterprises Inc, chmn of bd; St Louis Football Cardinals, runningback 1976-; Landmark Northwest Plaza Bank, loan officer 1978; Wayne Morris quarter Horse Ranch, owner 1979-. **ORGANIZATIONS:** Co-chmn YMCA. **HONORS/ACHIEVEMENTS:** Sustaining campaign 1976; Player of Yr Golden Knights 1975-76; Most Valuable Player Shringers Children's Hosp 1976; Most Improved Player St Louis Quarterback Club 1977. **BUSINESS ADDRESS:** Wayne Morris Enterprises Inc, 5715 Old Ox Rd, Dallas, TX 75241.

MORRIS, WILLIAM WESLEY
Clergyman. **PERSONAL:** Born Aug 07, 1937, Baltimore, MD; married Mary V Head; children: Loretta, Ava, Michael, William. **EDUCATION:** OH Wesleyan U, AB 1957; Garrett Evangelical Theol Sem, BD 1960; Scarritt Coll, MA 1969; Vanderbilt U, DMin 1973. **CAREER:** Conf council dir 1980; United Meth Conf, dist supt 1974-80; The Conf Council on Ministries Nashville, asso council dir 1971-74; John Wesley United Meth Ch, pastor 1967-71; Stanley Meth Ch, pastor 1962-67; Christ Meth Ch, pastor 1961-62; Union Ave Comm Meth Ch, pastor 1960-61; Bethany Meth Ch, student asst 1959-60. **ORGANIZATIONS:** Former mem Bethlehem Ctr Bd; TN-KY Annual Conf Merger Com; Minimum Salary Com TN-KY Annual Conf former youth dir TN-KY Annual Conf; chmn bd of ministry TN Annual Conf; chmn TN Conf Merger Com Inited Meth travel-study sem to Eastern & Central Europe, bd of Higher Educ & Ministry 1973. **HONORS/ACHIEVEMENTS:** Personalitites of the s 1976-77, 1978-79; Notable Ams 1977-78; Who's Who in Religion 1977-78; del SE Jurisdiction Conf 1972; del SE Jurisdiction Conf1976-80; del Gen Conf 1976-80.

MORRIS-HALE, WALTER
Educator. **PERSONAL:** Born Jan 30, 1933, Chicago, IL. **EDUCATION:** Univ of CA Berkeley, 1967; Univ of Stockholm Sweden, MA 1962; Univ of Geneva Switzerland, PhD 1969. **CAREER:** Smith Coll, asst prof 1969-75, assoc prof 1975-. **HONORS/ACHIEVEMENTS:** Publs "British Admin in Tanganyika from 1920-45, with Spec Reference to the Preparation of Africans for Admin Positions" 1969, "From Empire to Nation, the African Experience" in Aftermath of Empire Smith Coll Studies in History XIVII 1973. **BUSINESS ADDRESS:** Associate Professor, Smith College, Northampton, MA 01063.

MORRISEY, JIMMY
Association executive. **PERSONAL:** Born Mar 31, 1922, Raeford Hoke Co, NC; married Nina; children: Jo Belinda Morrisey, McPhatter Ben, John, Barbara. **EDUCATION:** New York City Trade Sch, cert mens tailoring 1951; Cardinal Health Agy, cert 1979. **CAREER:** Scurlock Comm Orgn Inc, pres 1972-; Hoke Co Voter Registration Edn, dir 1968-70. **ORGANIZATIONS:** Bd mem Cardinal Health Agency Inc 1975-; pres Hoke Co Branch NAACP 1968-; pres Scurlock Community Orgn Inc 1972-; v-chmn Hillcrest-scurlock Water System Inc 1972-. **HONORS/ACHIEVEMENTS:** Achievement Award Hoke Co Branch NAACP 1975; cert for Volunteer Serv State of NC 1976; contact person Hoke Co 7th Cong Black Caucus Leadership 1979-;first v-chmn Raeford Precinct No 3 1976-; recipient 3 European Battle Stars AUS 1943-44; cert AUS Artillery Gunner Sch 1943; Disabled Veteran. **MILITARY SERVICE:** AUS sgt 5 yrs served. **BUSINESS ADDRESS:** PO Box 501, Raeford, NC 28376.

MORRISON, CHARLES EDWARD
Director. **PERSONAL:** Born Jul 18, 1943, Longview, TX; married Geri Brooks; children: Constance, Rani, Kristi, Jennifer. **EDUCATION:** Bishop College, BS 1964; Wichita State Univ, Grad work. **CAREER:** General Motors, accountant 1965-70; Procter & Gamble, sales/mktg 1970-72; Schlitz Brewing Co, sales/mktg 1972-77, 1979-81; Burrell Advertising, advertising acct sup 1977-79; Coca-Cola USA, dir black consumer marketing 1981-. **ORGANIZATIONS:** Consultant WCLK Adv Bd 1985-86; vice pres Natl Assoc Mktg Developers 1985-86; consultant Southern Arts Federation 1985; trustee Bishop Coll 1985-86; bdmem South DeKalb YMCA 1986; life mem NAACP, Urban League; bd mem Atlanta Boys Club; mem Grambling State Univ Industry Cluster. **HONORS/ACHIEVEMENTS:** Top 10 Black Businessperson Dollar & Sense Magazine 1985; Beverage Exec of Year Cal-PAC Org 1986; several ad awards; CEBA's, CLIO's, Addy's. **BUSINESS ADDRESS:** Vice Pres Black/Hispanic Mktg, Coca-Cola USA, One Coca Cola Plaza, Atlanta, GA 30313.

MORRISON, CLARENCE CHRISTOPHER
Judge. **PERSONAL:** Born Feb 17, 1939, Charleston, SC; married Grace Fulton; children: Derricott M, Mark E. **EDUCATION:** Howard Univ Coll of Liberal Arts, BS Psych 1954; Howard Univ School of Law, LLB 1959. **CAREER:** Judge Carl B Shelly, law clerk 1960-61; State of PA Auditor Gen, legal asst 1961-62; Commonwealth of PA Dept of Revenue, asst attny gen 1962-65; DauphinCty Prosecutor's Office, asst dist attny 1965-69; PA State Ed Assoc, staff counsel 1969-76; Marrison & Atkins, law partner 1972-80; Court of Common Pleas, Dauphin Cty Court House, judge 1980-. **ORGANIZATIONS:** Bd of dir, pres Harrisburg Housing Authority; mem Mayor's Comm on Human Relations; vice pres Yoke Crest Inc; mem, vice chmn of bd of trustees, legal advisor, Sunday school teacher Tabernacle Baptist Church of Harrisburg PA; co-chmn South Central PA Chap of Heart Fund; legal advisor, chmn of bd of dir OpportIndust Ctrs Inc; pres Harrisburg Club of Frontiers Intl; mdm bd of dir Dauphin Cty NAACP; charter mem Optimist Club of Harrisburg; mem Omega Psi Phi-Frat. **HONORS/ACHIEVEMENTS:** Morrison Towers home for the elderly named after Clarence Morrison. **MILITARY SERVICE:** AUS commiss officer 1964-56. **BUSINESS ADDRESS:** Judge, Court of Common Pleas, Dauphin Cty Court House, Harrisburg, PA 17108.

MORRISON, CURTIS ANGUS
Attorney. **PERSONAL:** Born Jun 04, 1945, Pinehurst, NC; married Barbara. **EDUCATION:** Rutgers U, BA deans list 1971; RutgersUniv Sch of Law, jD 1974. **CAREER:** Prudential Ins Co of Am, asso counsel; St of NJ, deputy atty gen 1974-76. **ORGANIZATIONS:** Am Bar Assn; NJ Bar Assn; Garden St Bar Assn. **MILITARY SERVICE:** AUS sgt 1967-70. **BUSINESS ADDRESS:** 1111 Durham Ave, South Plainfield, NJ.

MORRISON, GWENDOLYN CHRISTINE CALDWELL
Educator. **PERSONAL:** Born Dec 11, 1949, Cunney, TX; daughter of John Caldwell (deceased) and Josephine Pierce Caldwell Ellis; married Ben; children: Paul, Brandon, Jonathan, Betsey. **EDUCATION:** Stephen F Austin State Univ Nacogdoches TX, BS home econ 1970; Stephen F Austin State Univ, MEd 1971; Cand TX Woman's Univ Denton, phD; Univ of North Texas, Denton, TX, Educational Leadership Post doctoral studies 1986-88; Texas Woman's Univ, Denton, TX, EdD Adult Educ 1986-88; Texas Womans Univ, Denton, TX, Doctor of Philosophy Awarded 1981. **CAREER:** Radio Shack, employee relations counselor 1977-81; Property Management Co, admin asst 1973-77; Palestine ISD TX, homemaking teacher 1971-73; Fort Worth ISD Fort Worth, TX, dir of Employee Staffing 1988-; E-Systems, Inc, Garland, TX, EEO specialist, 1987-88; dir of Personnel, City of Grand Prairie, TX 1982-84. **ORGANIZATIONS:** Trustee elected countywide Tarrant Co Jr Coll Dist 1976-; mem appointed by gov Coordinating Bd TX CollUniv System 1979-; bd of dirs St Citizens Center Inc 1976-; v gov S Central Dist Nat Assn Negro Bus Prof Women 1978-; bd of dirs Ft Worth Girls Club 1979-. **HONORS/ACHIEVEMENTS:** Outstanding Young Women of Amer Nominated for State 1976; Trailblazer of the Yr Award Ft Worth NB & PW Club 1976; "Characteristics of Black Executive Females" 1981. **BUSINESS ADDRESS:** Director of Employee Staffing, Fort Worth Independent School District, 3210 W Lancaster Avenue, Fort Worth, TX 76107.

MORRISON, HARRY L.
Educator. **PERSONAL:** Born Oct 07, 1932, Arlington, VA; married Harriett L; children: Vanessa L. **EDUCATION:** Catholic Univ of Amer, AB, 1955, PhD 1960. **CAREER:** Natl Inst of Health, rsch chemist 1955-56; Natl Bureau of Standards, post doctoral fellow 1960-61; Lawrence Radiation Lab, rsch physicist 1964-72; Univ of CA Lawrence Hall of Sci, assoc dir 1970-75; Coll of Letters & Sci Univ of CA, asst dean 1985-; Univ of CA Berkeley, prof of physics 1972-. **ORGANIZATIONS:** Governing council APS 1971-75; visiting prof Univ of CO 1972-73, Howard Univ 1973, MIT 1975-76; mem Amer Math Soc, Intl Assn Math Physics; fellow Amer Physical Soc 1971; co-founder MESA Out-Reach Prog 1970-. **HONORS/ACHIEVEMENTS:** Science Honor Soc Sigma Xi; edited book "Quantum Theory of Many Particle Systems". **MILITARY SERVICE:** USAF 1st lt 3 yrs; Commendation Medal 1963. **BUSINESS ADDRESS:** Professor, Physics, University of California, Department of Physics, Berkeley, CA 94720.

MORRISON, JAMES W., JR.
Consultant, lobbyist. **PERSONAL:** Born Jan 14, 1936, Bluefield, WV; son of James W Morrison Sr and Winnie E Morrison; divorced; children: Traquita Renee Morrison Reddix, James W III. **EDUCATION:** WV State Coll, BA 1957; Univ of Dayton, MPA 1970. **CAREER:** Dayton AF Depot Def Electronics Supply Ctr OH, inventory mgr 1959-63; AF Logistics Command Dayton OH, mgmt spec 1963-72; NASA Wash Dc, ex asst to dir mgmt sys 1972-74; Ex Ofc of Pres OMB Wash DC, s R mgmt assoc 1974-79; US Office of Personnel Mgmt Wash DC, asst dir econ and govt 1979, dir congressional rel 1979-81, assoc dir for compensation 1981-87; CNA Ins Co Rockville MD, sr mgr for prog support 1987-88; president, Morrison Associates, Washington, DC 1988-. **ORGANIZATIONS:** Visiting lecturer Publ Exec Proj State Univ NY Albany 1974-76; mem adv comm Dayton Bd of Educ 1971; mem Alpha Phi Alpha, Pi Delta Phi, Pi Alpha Alpha. **HONORS/ACHIEVEMENTS:** Except Serv Awd Exec Office of Pres OMB Wash DC 1977; Pres Cert Pres USA Wash DC 1979; Meritorious Serv Awd US Office of Personnel Mgmt Wash DC 1980; Pres Meritorious Exec Pres USA Wash DC 1983; Pres Distinguished Exec Pres USA Wash DC 1985. **MILITARY SERVICE:** AUS 1st lt 1957-59. **HOME ADDRESS:** 5225 Pooks Hill Rd, Apt 1710 North, Bethesda, MD 20814. **BUSINESS ADDRESS:** President, Morrison Associates, 815 Connecticut Ave NW, Suite 800, Washington, DC 20006.

MORRISON, JOHNNY EDWARD
Attorney. **PERSONAL:** Born Jun 24, 1952, Portsmouth, VA; son of Mary Bernard Morrison; married Cynthia L Payton, Aug 21, 1976; children: Melanie Yvette, Camille Yvonne. **EDUCATION:** Washington and Lee Univ, Grad 1974; Washington and Lee Univ School of Law, Grad 1977. **CAREER:** Legal Aid Soc Roanoke Valley, staff atty 1977-78; Norfolk Commonwealth's Atty's Office, prosecutor 1978-79; Portsmouth Commonwealth's Atty's Ofc, prosecutor1979-82; Overton, Sallee and Morrison, partner 1982; Portsmouth Commonwealth's Atty's Ofc, comm atty 1982-;. **ORGANIZATIONS:** Mem VA State Bar Assc, VA Assc of Commonwealth's Atty's, Kiwanis Intl; bd mem Tidewater Legal Aid Soc, United Way, Effingham St Branch YMCA; pres Tidewater Legal Aid Society; mem Tidewater Alumni bd of dirs for Washington & Lee; mem Virginia Black Caucus; mem Central Civic Forum; Old Dominion Bar Assn; Twin City Bar Assn; Natl Criminal Justice Assn; Natl Black Prosecutors Assn. **HONORS/ACHIEVEMENTS:** Young Man of the Year Eureka Club 1982; Reginald Heber Smith Flwshp Washington and Lee Schl of Law 1977; Man of the Year Disabled Amer Vets Portsmouth 1982; Outstanding Young Men of Amer Publ 1983; Man of Year, Eureka Club 1988; Martin Luther King, Jr Leadership Award, Old Dominion Univ, 1987. **BUSINESS ADDRESS:** Commonwealth's Attorney, Commonwealth's Attys Ofc, 601 Crawford St, Portsmouth, VA 23704.

MORRISON, JUAN LARUE, SR.
Educator. **PERSONAL:** Born Mar 22, 1943, Springfield, IL; married Clementine Lorraine; children: Juan L Jr, Daryl G, Cheryl L. **EDUCATION:** IL State Univ, BS Education 1969, PhD Higher Educ Admin 1980; IL State Univ, MA Ed Admin 1972; Sangamon State Univ, MA Human Dev/Counseling 1975. **CAREER:** Springfield School Dist #186, elemen teacher 1969-70, secondary teacher 1970-72; Prayer Wheel Church of God in Christ, copastor 1980-84; Emmanuel Temple Church of God in Christ, pastor 1984-; Lincoln Land Comm Coll, counselor and coordinator 1972-. **ORGANIZATIONS:** Test admin Amer College Test 1979-; test admin Amer Registry of Radiologic Technologists 1982-; test admin Natl Bd for Respiratory Care Mgmt Services Inc 1982-; publicity chmn Springfield Ministerial Alliance 1983-; test admin Educational Testing Serv 1984-; pres of music Dept for Central IL Jurisdictionof the Church of God in Christ 1984-. **HONORS/ACHIEVEMENTS:** Published article A Look at Community College Testing Programs; IL Guidance and Personnel Assn 1982. **HOME ADDRESS:** 49 W Hazel Dell, Springfield, IL 62707. **BUSINESS ADDRESS:** Counselor, Lincoln Land Comm College, Shepherd Rd, Springfield, IL 62708.

MORRISON, K. C. (MINION KENNETH CHAUNCEY)
Educator. **PERSONAL:** Born Sep 24, 1946, Edwards, MS; married Johnetta Bernadette Wade; children: Iyabo Abena. **EDUCATION:** Tougaloo Coll, BA 1968; Univ of WI Madison, MA 1969, cert in African Studies 1974, PhD 1977; Univ of Ghana, cert in African Studies 1972. **CAREER:** Tougaloo Coll, inst/asst prof 1969-71 1975-77; Hobart Coll, asst prof/coord 1977-78; Syracuse Univ, assoc prof 1978, chair afro-amer studies 1982-. **ORGANIZATIONS:** Mem African Studies Assn; mem Natl Conf Black Political Scientists; mem Amer Pol Sci Assn; consultant/fellow Ford Found Danforth Frost & Sullivan Huber Found 1968-84; bd of dirs NAACP; bd of dirs Intl Ctr of Syracuse; bd of dirs Partners of the Americas 1968-84; vice provost & professor of Political Science, Univ of Missouri, Columbia 1989-. **HONORS/ACHIEVEMENTS:** Listed in numerous biographies fellow/grants, Ford NSF NEH Huber 1969-82; books, "Housing Urban Poor in Africa" 1982, "Ethnicity and Political Integration" 1982; Black Political Mobilization 1987. **BUSINESS ADDRESS:** Vice Provost & Professor of Political Science, University of Missouri, Jesse Hall, Columbia, MO 65211.

MORRISON, KEITH ANTHONY
Educator/artist. **PERSONAL:** Born May 20, 1942, Linstead, Jamaica;son of Noel Morrison and Beatrice McPherson Morrison; married Alexandra, Apr 12, 1989. **EDUCATION:** School of Art Institute of Chicago, BFA 1963, MFA 1965. **CAREER:** Fisk Univ, asst prof of art 1967-68; DePaul Univ, chmn dept art 1969-71; Univ IL Chicago, assoc prof art 1971-79, assoc dean Coll of Art 1974-78; Univ of MD, chmn dept of art 1987-, prof of art 1979-. **ORGANIZATIONS:** Chmn of bd Washington Proj for the Arts 1984-85; adv bd New Art Examiner 1983-. **HONORS/ACHIEVEMENTS:** Award for Painting Natl Assn for Equal Oppty in Educ 1984; Bicentennial Award for Painting City of Chicago 1976; Intl Award for Painting OAU Monrovia, Liberia 1978; Danforth Foundation Teaching Assoc 1970-71. **HOME ADDRESS:** 3225 13th Street NW, Washington, DC 20017. **BUSINESS ADDRESS:** Professor of Art, University of Maryland, Art Department, College Park, MD 20742.

MORRISON, RICHARD DAVID
Educator. **PERSONAL:** Born Jan 18, 1910, Utica, MS; married Ethel. **EDUCATION:** Tuskegee Inst, BS 1931; Cornell U, MS 1941; State U, phD 1954. **CAREER:** AL A&M Univ in Normal, pres 1962-. **ORGANIZATIONS:** Former chmn Div of Agriculture; mem Joint Council on Food & Agr Sci; mem adv com of Marshall Space Flight Center AL A&MUniv 1937-62; affiliated withnumerous professional & civic groups. **BUSINESS ADDRESS:** AL A&M Univ, Normal, AL 35762.

MORRISON, RICK
Business executive. **PERSONAL:** Born Jul 15, 1957, New York, NY. **EDUCATION:** NY Univ School of Arts, BFA 1978. **CAREER:** CBS Inc, exec training intern 1977-78; The Creative Group Mgmt Corp, gen mgr 1979-80, intl activities mgr 1980-81; Amer Soc of Composers, dir talentacquisition 1981-. **ORGANIZATIONS:** Bd dir Black Music Assn 1982-; mem 100 Black Men 1984. **HONORS/ACHIEVEMENTS:** Gold Platinum Record Awds Capitol Records 1979, RCA Records 1980, CBS Records 1981. **BUSINESS ADDRESS:** Dir Talent Acquisition, ASCAP, One Lincoln Plaza, New York, NY 10023.

MORRISON, ROBERT B., JR.
Appointed government official. **PERSONAL:** Born Jul 09, 1954, Orlando, FL. **EDUCATION:** Loyola Univ, BA Pol Sci, Bus Admin 1975; Univ of FL, JD 1978. **CAREER:** Law Office of Warren H Dawson, attny 1978-79; Morrison Gilmore & Clark PA, partner 1986-; City of Tampa, exec asst to mayor. **ORGANIZATIONS:** Mem Amer Bar Assn, Natl Bar Assoc, FL Bar Assoc, FL Chap Natl Bar Assn 1979-; chmn Bi-Racial Adv Comm Hillsborough Cty School Bd 1978-81; chmn Mayor's Cable TV Advisory Comm 1979-83; pres St Peter Claver Parish Council 1979-83; mem Franklin St Mall Adv Comm 1979-, Tampa Org of Black Affairs 1979-; mediator Citizen Dispute Settlement Prog 1979-80; bd of dir Tampa Urban League 1980-, WEDU TV 1980-, March of Dimes of Hillsborough Cty 1980-; mem NAACP 1981; bd of dir Boy Scouts of Amer 1982-; mem State Job Training Coord Council 1983-, Rotary Club of Tampa 1983-; pres FL Chap Natl Bar Assoc 1986,87; mem Bi-Racial Commn 1987. **HONORS/ACHIEVEMENTS:** Who's Who in Amer Coll & Univ Awd Loyola Univ, Univ of FL 1975,78; Council of Ten Outstanding Law Student Group in Country 1976; Citizen of the Year Omega Psi Phi 1980; One of the Outstanding Young Men of Amer 1980,83; George Edgecomb Mem Awd for Outstanding Comm Serv at an Early Age Urban League 1981. **BUSINESS ADDRESS:** Executive Asst To Mayor, City of Tampa, 306 E Jackson St, Tampa, FL 33602.

MORRISON, RONALD E.
Television producer/writer. **PERSONAL:** Born Jun 26, 1949, Portland, OR. **EDUCATION:** Portland State U; Portland Comm Coll. **CAREER:** TV Prod, indpt 1973-; KCET-TV Hollywood, assoc prod 1973; KCET-TV "Doin It At The Stroefront, prodn asst, reporter 1972-73; Watts Writers Workshop LA, prod asst/video & instr 1972; KOAP-TV Portland OR "Feedback", floor dir, studio camerman 1971-72; KATU-TV "Third World", asst to producer 1971-72; Portland StateUniv TV Programming, producer, dir writer, production asst 1971-72; KION-TV, news film processor, news film careraman 1968-69. **HONORS/ACHIEVEMENTS:** Recipient Cert of Appreciation City of LA 1973. **BUSINESS ADDRESS:** 10100 Santa Monica Blvd, Ste 2500, Los Angeles, CA 90067.

MORRISON, SAMUEL F.
Association executive. **PERSONAL:** Born Dec 19, 1936, Flagstaff, AZ; son of Travis B Morrison and Ruth Morrison Genes; divorced. **EDUCATION:** Compton Jr Coll, Associates Degree 1956; CA State Univ, BA 1971; Univ of IL at Champaign, MSLS 1972. **CAREER:** Frostproof Living Learning Library, dir 1972-74; Broward County Library System, asst dir 1974-1987; Chicago Public Library, deputy libr commissioner & chief libr 1987-. **ORGANIZATIONS:** Pres FL Library Assn 1980-81; mem Amer Library Assn 1975-, Southeast Library Assn 1980-, FL Library Assn 1975-; bd dir Vinnette Carroll Repertory Theatre 1985, Oct Center; asst treasurer Broward Public Library Found 1984; parliamentarian and bd mem Area Agency on Aging of Broward County 1982-85; bd dir Urban League 1985; bd mem, La Rabida Children's Hospital of Chicago, 1988-89; bd mem, Children & Adolescents Forum of Chicago, 1988-89. **HONORS/ACHIEVEMENTS:** Deans's List CA State Univ 1971; English Honors Program CA State Univ 1971; Faculty Award Univ of IL Library School 1972; Employee of the Year Broward Co Library Advisory Bd 1977-78. **MILITARY SERVICE:** USAF a/1c 1955-59; Good Conduct Medal 1958; Air Force Longevity Award 1959. **BUSINESS ADDRESS:** Deputy Commissioner, Chicago Public Library, 1224 W Van Buren St, Rm 606, Chicago, IL 60607.

MORRISON, TONI
Senior editor, writer. **PERSONAL:** Born Feb 18, 1931, Lorain, OH; children: Harold Ford, Slade Kevin. **EDUCATION:** Howard Univ, BA 1953; Cornell Univ, MA 1955. **CAREER:** TX So Univ, Engl instructor 1955-57; Howard Univ, Engl instructor 1957-64; SUNY Purchase, assoc prof 1971-; Random House, senior editor/writer 1965-. **ORGANIZATIONS:** Visit lectr Bard Coll; visit lectr Yale Univ 1976-77; mem Author's Guild. **HONORS/ACHIEVEMENTS:** Author of, "Sula" 1973, "The Bluest Eye" 1979, "Song of Solomon" 1978, "Tar Baby" 1981; Periodical Publns, "What the Black Woman Thinks About Women's Lib" NewYork Times Mag 1971, "Cooking Out" New York Times Book Review 1973, "Behind the Making of the Black Book" Black World 1974, "Rediscovering Black History" New York Times Mag 1974, "Reading" Mademoiselle 1975; "Slow Walk of Trees (as Grandmother Would Say) Hopeless (as Grandfather Would Say)" New York Times Mag 1976. **BUSINESS ADDRESS:** Senior Editor/Writer, Random House, 201 E 50th St, New York, NY 10022.

MORRISON, TRUDI MICHELLE
Attorney, presidential aide. **PERSONAL:** Born Jul 25, 1950, Denver, CO; daughter of George Morrison and Marjorie Morrison; married Dale Saunders, 1981. **EDUCATION:** CO State Univ, BS 1971; The Natl Law Ctr, George Washington Univ, Georgetown Law Ctr, JD 1972-75; Univ of CO Denver, Doctorate of Publ Admin Candidate 1986. **CAREER:** States Atty Office Rockville MD, asst states atty 1975-76; Gorsuch Kirgis Campbell Walker & Grover, atty 1977; Denver Dist Attny Office, atty 1977-78; CO Div of Criminal Justice, criminal justice admin 1978-81; US Dept HUD, acting dep asst sec for policy & budget 1981-82; US Dept Health & Human Svcs, reg dep dir 1982-83; The White House, assoc dir office of publ liaison; US Senate, dep sgt at arms. **ORGANIZATIONS:** Exec sec of the student body CO State Univ 1969-71; bd of dir Natl Stroke Assoc 1983-87; mem Natl Council of Negro Women; founder CO Black Republican Council; mem Natl Urban League, NAACP. **HONORS/ACHIEVEMENTS:** 1st Black Homecoming Queen CO State Univ 1970-71; Outstanding Young Women of Amer 1978,79,82; Young Careerist for the Natl Org of Bus & Professional Women 1978;Highest Ranking Black Woman in the White House 1983-; 1984 Black Republican of the Year 1984; William E Morgan CSU Alumni Achievement Awd 1984; 1st woman & 1st Black dep sgt at arms for US Senate. **BUSINESS ADDRESS:** Deputy Sergeant at Arms, The Capitol of the US, United States Senate, United States Capitol, Washington, DC 20510. *

MORROW, CHARLES G., III
Customer service rep. **PERSONAL:** Born Jul 21, 1956, Chicago, IL. **EDUCATION:** Chicago Inst of Tech, 1974-76; attended Loop Coll Chicago. **CAREER:** School Dist, driver's ed instructor 1971-74; Metro Sanitary Dist, bookkeeper 1975-76; People Gas, customer serv rep 1977-. **ORGANIZATIONS:** Mem Boy Scouts of Amer, NAACP, Urban League. **BUSINESS ADDRESS:** Customer Service Rep, Peoples Gas, 122 So Michigan, Chicago, IL 60603.

MORROW, DION GRIFFITH
Judge. **PERSONAL:** Born Jul 09, 1932, Los Angeles, CA; married Glynis Ann Dejan; children: Jan Bell, Kim, Cydney, Lori, Carla Sando, Melvin Cavalier, Dion Jr. **EDUCATION:** Loyola Univ Law School, LLB 1957; Pepperdine Coll. **CAREER:** Los Angeles City Atty, asst city atty 1973-75; Los Angeles, atty at law 1957-73; Municipal Ct Compton CA, judge 1975-78; Superior Ct, judge. **ORGANIZATIONS:** Vice pres Gen Counsel dir Enterprise Savings and Loan 1962-72; pres John M Langston Bar Assc 1969-71; life mem NAACP; mem Natl Bar Assc 1969-. **BUSINESS ADDRESS:** Judge, Superior Court, 210 W Temple St, Los Angeles, CA 90012.

MORROW, E. FREDERIC
Bank executive. **PERSONAL:** Born Apr 20, 1909, Hackensack, NJ; son of John Eugene

Morrow and Mary Anne Hayes Morrow; married Catherine Louise Gordon, Sep 18, 1957. **EDUCATION:** Bowdoin Coll, AB 1930; Rutgers Univ Sch of Law, LLB, JD, 1948. **CAREER:** US Govt, Washington DC, business advisor to Dept of Commerce, 1953-55, admin officer, special proj group, The White House, 1955-61; African-Amer Inst, NYC, vice pres, 1961-64; Bank of Amer Intl, NYC, vice pres, 1964—. **ORGANIZATIONS:** Mem Presidential Elem Bd 1975-; mem Alpha Phi Alpha; former field sec NAACP; pub relations analyst CBS. **HONORS/ACHIEVEMENTS:** First black man to serve as White House aide when apptd admin asst by Eisenhower in 1955; Hon LLD, Bowdoin Coll, 1970; author, Black Man in the White House: A Diary of the Eisenhower Years, Coward, 1963, Way Down South Up North, United Church Pr, 1975, Forty Years a Guinea Pig: A Black Man's View From the Top, Pilgrim Press, 1980. **MILITARY SERVICE:** US Army, major, 1942-46. **HOME ADDRESS:** 1270 Fifth Ave, New York, NY 10029. **BUSINESS ADDRESS:** Bank of America, 41 Broad St, New York, NY 10004. *

MORROW, JESSE
Chief executive. **CAREER:** Leader Lincoln-Mercury-Merkur, Inc, St Louis, MO, chief executive, 1983-. **BUSINESS ADDRESS:** Leader Lincoln-Mercury-Merkur, Inc, 6160 S Lindbergh Blvd, St Louis, MO 63123. *

MORROW, JOHN HOWARD, JR.
Educator. **PERSONAL:** Born May 27, 1944, Trenton, NJ; son of Dr John H Morrow, Sr and Rowena Davis Morrow; married Diane Batts; children: Kieran, Evan. **EDUCATION:** Swarthmore Coll, BA (with Honors) 1966; Univ of PA Philadelphia, PhD History 1971. **CAREER:** Univ of TN Knoxville, asst prof to full prof & dept head 1971-; Natl Aerospace Museum Washington DC, Lindbergh prof of history 1989-; University of Georgia Athens, GA Franklin prof of history 1989-. **ORGANIZATIONS:** Mem Amer Historical Assn 1971-; consult Coll Bd & Ed Testing Serv 1980-84; mem AHA Comm on Committees 1982-85, AHA Prog Comm for 1984 Meeting 1983-84; mem educ adv bds Aerospace Historian 1984-; and Miliary Affairs 1987-; chairman History Advisory Committee to the Secretary of the Air Force 1988-. **HONORS/ACHIEVEMENTS:** Books Building German Airpower 1909-1914, 1976, German Airpower in World Ware I, 1982; Hon Soc Phi Kappa Phi 1980; Lindsay Young Professorship 1982-83; Outstanding Teacher UT Natl Alumni Assn 1983; UT Macebearer 1983-84; Univ Distinguished Serv Professorship 1985-. **HOME ADDRESS:** 130 Pine Tops Dr, Athens, GA 30606. **BUSINESS ADDRESS:** Franklin Professor of History, Univ of Georgia, Department of History, Athens, GA 30602.

MORROW, LAVEINE
Small business owner. **PERSONAL:** Born Mar 02, 1954, Kankakee, IL; daughter of George Morrow and Shirley Jackson Watson. **EDUCATION:** Illinois State Univ, Normal, IL, BS, 1976; Washington Univ, St Louis, MA Ed, 1978. **CAREER:** Urban League, St Louis, MO, specialist, 1978-79; Midtown Pre-Apprenticeship Center, St Louis, MO, dir, 1979-82; Coro Found, St Louis, MO, trainer, 1983-85; Emprise Designs Inc, St Louis, MO, founder/pres, 1985-. **ORGANIZATIONS:** First vice pres, Coalition of 100 Black Women Program, St Louis, MO, 1981-84; natl chmn, White House Conf on Small Business Minority Caucus, 1986-; comm chmn, Jr League of St Louis, 1986. **HONORS/ACHIEVEMENTS:** Appointed to the US Senate, Small Business Natl Advisory Council; featured and profiled as an Outstanding Business Woman in the September 1988 St Louis Business Journal. **BUSINESS ADDRESS:** President, Emprise Designs Inc, 5353 Union Blvd, St Louis, MO.

MORROW, NEBRASKA
Entrepreneur. **PERSONAL:** Born Jan 05, 1927, Eutaw, AL; widowed; children: Deborah, Valarie. **EDUCATION:** Attended, Alabama A&M Univ 1946-49, Univ of Omaha 1954-55. **CAREER:** Morrow Inc, president; M&G Enterprises, vice pres. **ORGANIZATIONS:** Elder Calvin Presbyterian Church 1957-87; mem American Legion Post #30 1970-87; bd of dirs Vstg Nurses Assoc 1975-87; chmn North Omaha Comm Develop 1981-83; vice pres Omaha Merchants Assoc 1981-87; mem Urban League. **MILITARY SERVICE:** AUS corpl 2 yrs. **BUSINESS ADDRESS:** Vice President, M&G Enterprises, 4002 Bedford Ave, Omaha, NE 68111.

MORROW, SAMUEL P., JR.
Attorney. **PERSONAL:** Born Jan 29, 1928, Jackson, TN; married Elizabeth B. **EDUCATION:** Lane Coll, BS 1948; Boston Univ, LLB 1958. **CAREER:** Carrier Corp, sr attorney. **ORGANIZATIONS:** Mem Amer, TN Bar Assns; Urban League; Lions Club Intl. **MILITARY SERVICE:** USAF major 5 yrs. **HOME ADDRESS:** 2264 Connell Terr, Baldwinsville, NY 13027. **BUSINESS ADDRESS:** Sr Attorney, Carrier Corporation, 6304 Carrier Parkway, DeWitt, NY 13201.

MORSE, JOSEPH ERVIN
Business executive. **PERSONAL:** Born Jul 31, 1940, Tuskegee, AL; married S Edwina; children: Ronald Elliot, Richard Eric. **EDUCATION:** Howard Univ DC, BArch 1964; Howard Univ, JD 1968; Howard Univ, MArch 1969. **CAREER:** JEMAR Assos, pres 1978-; So Consumers Conf, pres 1978-; Community Nutrition Inst, regl 1978-79; AL State & Community Serv Adminstrn, planning dir 1977-78; The Tuskegee Times & The Montgomery Times Wklys, founder & editor 1972-78; The Ford Found & PEDCO, consult 1972-76; Fedn of So Coops, consult 1976-; Nat Assn of Minority Consult & Urbanologists, dir & vP 1977. **ORGANIZATIONS:** Mem Shriners; 33 Masons; Wings USAF 1962-66; 1st Black Regional Comdr Arnold Air Soc. **HONORS/ACHIEVEMENTS:** Outstanding Pub Serv Award AL Press Assn 1974; pub 5 natl newsletters JEMAR Publs 1980. **MILITARY SERVICE:** USAF 2nd lt 1962-66. **BUSINESS ADDRESS:** P O Box 1059, Tuskegee Institute, AL 36088.

MORSE, MILDRED (NEE SHARPE)
Government official. **PERSONAL:** Born Oct 20, 1942, Dermott, AR; married Oliver; children: Stacey, Kasey. **EDUCATION:** Howard U, JD 1968;Univ of AR, BA 1964; Bowling Green State U. **CAREER:** Phase Ii White House Task Force on Civil Rights Presidents Reorganization Proj, deputy dir 1977-79; HUB, dir 1973-77 & 1979-80; HEW, staff asst to dir 1971-73; Civil Rights, spec 1968-71. **ORGANIZATIONS:** Nat Bar Assn; Nat Civil Rights Assn; steering com Dept of Justice Title VI Proj; mem Motgomery Co NAACP; sec Westover Elem Sch PTA 1977; Human Rights Com White Oak Jr HS 1976; mem Colesville Bapt Ch. **HONORS/ACHIEVEMENTS:** Spl Achvmt Award HUD 1975; cert of merit HUD 1977; scholarship Ford Found 1965-68; recongized among the World Whos Who of Women 1978-79; Recognized among the Young Women of Am 1978; Spec Achievement Award HUD 1980; Certificate of Service Award Fed Serv 1980; publ HUD Handbook on Title VI Cr Rts Act of 1964. **BUSINESS ADDRESS:** 7 H & D SW, Washington, DC.

MORSE, OLIVER
Educator. **PERSONAL:** Born May 17, 1922, New York, NY; married Mildred; children: Stacey, Kasey. **EDUCATION:** St Augustines Coll, BS 1947; Brooklyn Law Sch, LlB 1950; NY U, LLM 1951; Brooklyn Laws Sch, JSD 1952. **CAREER:** Howard Univ School of Law, acting dean, asso dean, prof 1960-; Hunter Coll, instr 1959; So Univ School of Law, prof 1956-59; Brooklyn Law School, prof 1968-69. **ORGANIZATIONS:** Vice-chmn HEW Reviewing Authority; Beta Lamba Sigma; Phi Alpha Delta; Omega Psi Phi; Am Assn of Law Schs; mem Nat Bar Assn; mem NY Bar Assn; 1st chmn of section on legal Educ of NBA 1971-72. **HONORS/ACHIEVEMENTS:** Most Outstdng Law Prof Howard Law Sch 1967, 70-72; written serveral publs including over 40 legal decisions of cases heard on appeal to HEW Reviewing Authority. **MILITARY SERVICE:** AUS sgt 1943-46.

MORSE, WARREN W.
Association executive. **PERSONAL:** Born Jul 25, 1912, Newport News, VA; married Maizelle; children: Madeline, Valerie, Warren Jr. **EDUCATION:** Wilberforce U, BS 1936. **CAREER:** Occupational Safety & Health Div W Conf of Teamsters, coord; Alameda Co, soc worker; Regnl Brewery, sales rep. **ORGANIZATIONS:** Mem Omega Psi Phi; bd dir Bay Area Urban League; bd dir Nat Housing Conf; Nat Adv Com on Agr Dept of Labor; No CA Med Pharm & Denatl Assn. **HONORS/ACHIEVEMENTS:** Recipient Cert of Apprec Kiwanis Club. **MILITARY SERVICE:** AUS lt col 1940-70. **BUSINESS ADDRESS:** 1870 Ogden Dr, Burlingame, CA 94010.

MORTEL, RODRIGUE
Physician, educator. **PERSONAL:** Born Dec 03, 1933, St Marc, Haiti;married Cecilia; children: Ronald, Michelle, Denise, Renee. **EDUCATION:** Lycee Stenio Vincent, BS 1954; Med Sch Port Au Prince Haiti, MD 1960. **CAREER:** General Practice, physician; PA State Univ, consultant; Lancaster General Hosp, prof; Penn State Univ, chmn, dept of Ob-gyn. **ORGANIZATIONS:** Mem AMA; PA Med Soc; James Ewing Soc; Soc of Synecologic & Oncologist; Amer Coll Ob-Gyn; Amer Coll Surgeons; Amer Radium Soc; NY Acad of Sci OB Soc of Phila. **HONORS/ACHIEVEMENTS:** USPHS Award 1968; Horatio Alger Awd 1985; Pennsylvania State Univ Faculty Scholar Awd for Outstanding Achievement in the Area of Life and Health Sciences 1986; Health Policy Fellow, Robert Wood Johnson Foundation 1988. **BUSINESS ADDRESS:** Chairman, Penn State University, Dept of Ob-Gyn, PO Box 850, Hershey, PA 17033.

MORTIMER, DELORES M.
Social science analyst. **EDUCATION:** HowardUniv Wash DC & Macalester Coll St Paul MN, BA 1971; M of Professional Studies CornellUniv Ithaca NY 1973. **CAREER:** Cornell Univ Ithaca, grad asst 1971-72; African Bibliog Ctr Washington, rsch coord-proj supr 1972-75, tech resource person/broadcaster 1973-; Free-lance Consultant, 1973-; Phelps-Stokes Fund Washington, adminis 1974-75; Smithsonian Inst Rsch Inst on Immigration & Ethnic Studies, social sci analyst 1975-79; US Commn Civil Rights, social sci analyst 1979-; US Information Agency, sr intl academic exchange specialist 1981-. **ORGANIZATIONS:** Mem Natl Assoc of Female Execs 1981-; vice pres Thursday Luncheon Group 1985-87; mem Intl Studies Assoc 1987. **HONORS/ACHIEVEMENTS:** Recipient Grant HowardUniv Wash DC Sponsors for Educ Opportunity Scholarship 1967; Scholarship Award Lambda Kappa Mu Black Professional Womens Sorority 1969; Scholarship Award Macalester Coll St Paul 1969; Scholarship Award Sponsors for Educ Opportunity 1970; Fellowship Award CornellUniv 1971; Elected Mem Cornell Univ Senate 1971, 72; Travel-study Grant CornellUniv 1972; Elected Mem Smithsonian Inst Womens Council 1976-79; pub various essays & book reviews in "A Current Bibliography on African Affairs," 1970-74; pub "Income & Employment Generation". **BUSINESS ADDRESS:** Sr Intl Acad Exch Specialist, U S Information Agency, 301 4th St SW, Washington, DC 20547.

MORTON, AZIE B.
Business executive. **PERSONAL:** Born Feb 01, 1936, Dale, TX; married James H; children: Virgie Clark, Stacey Dey. **EDUCATION:** Huston Tillotson Coll, BS 1956. **CAREER:** US, treasurer 1977-; Dem Nat Com, spl asst to chmn 1972-76; 1976 Dem Nat Conv, dep conv mgr 1975; 1974 Dem Conf, dep conv mgr 1974-75; Dem Nat Com Ofc of Minority Affairs, asst dir 1971-72; Model Cities Prog KS, dir of social serv 1969-71; US EEOC, officer & conciliator 1966-69; 1966 White House Conf on Civil Rights, spl asst to vice-chmn 1966; Com on Equal Opportunity in House David Lawrence pres, comm relations splst & adminstrv asst to chmn 1963-66; Pres Com on Equal Orrportunity in Housing, comm relations splst & adminstrv ass. **ORGANIZATIONS:** Mem Compliance Review Commn Dem Nat Com 1975; bd dir Urban League Wichita KS 1971; asso mem Smithsonian; mem Alpha Kappa Alpha Sorority. **HONORS/ACHIEVEMENTS:** Recipient Certificate of Achivent Brookings Inst 1970. **BUSINESS ADDRESS:** President, Stami Corporation, 317 N Broad St #412, Philadelphia, PA 19107.

MORTON, CHARLES E.
Clergyman, educator. **PERSONAL:** Born Jan 31, 1926, Bessemer, AL; married Jean; children: Joan, Carla. **EDUCATION:** Morehouse Coll, BA 1946; Unoin Theol Sem, BD 1949; Columbia U, PhD 1958. **CAREER:** Met Bpat Ch Detroit, pastor; OaklanUniv Rochester MI, adj prof philosophy; MI Bd of Edn, mem 1946-54; Div of Humanities & Philosophy Dillard U, former chmn; Albion Coll, asso prof of philosophy; Ebeneze Bapt Ch Poughkeepsie NY, minister. **ORGANIZATIONS:** Mem Gov Commn on Higher Edn; treas Urban Training Ctr for Christ Missions Chgo; bd dir First Indep Nat Bank of Detroit; MI Cancer Fund; Credit Couns Ctr; Detroit Indsl Mission; vchmn Inner City Bus Forum of Detroit; pres Met Housing Corp. **HONORS/ACHIEVEMENTS:** Author several art for religious jours. **BUSINESS ADDRESS:** 13110 14th St, Detroit, MI 48238.

MORTON, CYNTHIA NEVERDON
Educator. **PERSONAL:** Born Jan 23, 1944, Baltimore, MD; daughter of James Neverdon and Hattie Neverdon; married Lonnie George. **EDUCATION:** Morgan State Univ, BA 1965, MS 1967; Howard Univ, PhD 1974. **CAREER:** Baltimore Public School Syst, tchr of history 1965-68; Peale Museum, rschr/jr archivist 1965; Inst of Afro-Amer Studies, instructor curr develop 1968; MN Lutheran Synod Priority Prog, consultant 1969; Univ of MN, ad-

missions assoc 1968-69, coordinator special programs 1969-71; Coppin State Coll, asst dean of students 1971-72, assoc prof of history/chairperson dept of history, geography, international studies; prof of history/dept of history geography intl studies, prof. **ORGANIZATIONS:** Study grant to selected W African Nations 1974; participant Carribbean-Amer Scholars Exchange Program 1974; mem adv bd MD Commn of Afro-Amer Life 1977-; mem Assn of Black Female Historians 1979-; mem adv bd Multicultural Educ Coalition Com 1980-; mem Assoc for the Study of Afro-Amer Life & History; reader & panelist Natl Endowment for the Humanities Smithsonia Inst Fellow 1986. **HONORS/ACHIEVEMENTS:** Publ "The Impact of Christianity Upon Traditional Family Values" 1978; "The Black Woman's Struggle for Equality in the South" 1978; NEH Fellowship for CollegeTeachers 1981-82; publ "Self-Help Programs as Educative Activities of Black Women in the South 1895-1925, Focus on Four Key Areas" 1982; "Blacks in Baltimore 1950-1980, An Overview" with Bettye Gardner 1982; "Black Housing Patterns in Baltimore 1895-1925" publ MD Historian 1985; Annual Historical Review 1982-83, 1983-84; Ordnance Center & School Aberdeen Proving Ground 1986; mem consult ed bd Twentieth Century Black Amer Officials & Leaders publ Greenwood Press; recent publications book, "Afro-American Women of the South and the Advancement of the Rac 1895-1925" Univ of TN Press 1989; essay, "Through the Looking Glass: Reviewing Books about the African American Female Exerience" in Feminist Studies 1988. **BUSINESS ADDRESS:** Professor, Coppin State Coll, 2500 W North Ave, Baltimore, MD 21216.

MORTON, JAMES A.
Business executive. **PERSONAL:** Born Dec 20, 1929, Ontario, VA; married Juanita; children: James A, David L. **EDUCATION:** Am Acad of Mortuary Sci, 1950; Lincoln U, Howard U. **CAREER:** Morton & Dyett Funeral Homes Inc, first black owned funeral home in Baltimore, pres. **ORGANIZATIONS:** Past pres Funeral Dir & Morticians Assn of MD; past pres Opportunities Industrial Center; bd mem Nat Funeral Dir Mforticians Assn; chmn Tri-state Conv Comm; mem Adv com of Bus bd; bd mem Am Red Cross; committee man BSA; chmn House of Hope Financial Com; trustee Wayland Bapt Ch; adv bd Advance Fed Sav; bd mem YMCA; 3 times life mem NAACP; mem A Phillip Randolph Prince Hall Masons. **BUSINESS ADDRESS:** 1701 Laurens St, Baltimore, MD 21217.

MORTON, LEONA M.
Retired government employee. **PERSONAL:** Born Feb 25, 1912, Columbus, GA; married Bernard; children: Shirley M. **EDUCATION:** Spelman Coll; Fort Valley State Tchrs Coll. **CAREER:** Greensboro GA, elem tchr 1939-42; Sumter GA, 1936-39; Powder Springs, 1934-36; US Dept Commerce Patent Office Wash DC, clerk 1944-72; Shiloh Bapt ChDorcas Circle, leader 1952-; Circle Leaders Council, pres 1959-62. **ORGANIZATIONS:** Pres Hayesludlow Elem Sch PTA 1953-56; Den Mother of Cub Schouts 1954-57; numerous offices in Terrell Jr High & Dunbar Sr High PTA; rec sec Pub Interest Civic Assn 1958-61; membership ch 1974; sec Wash Spelman Club 1962-66, 1972-; pub relations Wash Sect Nat Council Negro Women 1972-75, sec 1968-72; mem Wash Urban League; vol worker Women in Community Serv for Womens Job Corps 1972-; vP St Citizens Club Shiloh Bapt Ch 1974-76; treas WA Sect NCNW 1975-76; mem Deaconess Bd Shiloh Bapt Ch; bd dir Hospitality House Inc 1975-79; sec to bd dir Women in Comm Serv Inc 1975; Task Force Rep for Nat Council of Negro Women with the Am Revolution Bicentennial Planning Com for Comm Resource Cntrs 1974. **HONORS/ACHIEVEMENTS:** Cert Award Pub Interest Civic Assn 1973; Plaque Nat Council Negro Women Wash sect 1972; Cert Award Dept Commerce 1972; Honor Award DC Federation Civic Assn 1973; hon WA Spelman Chap Alumnae Assn; cert award WA Intl Alumni Cncl of the United Negro Coll Fund; Cert of Merit Award US Labor Dept for work with women in Comm Serv Inc 1974; Cert Appreciation Vacation Bible Sch Shiloh Bapt Ch 1973, 1974; Cert Award Circle Leaders Council Shiloh BaptCh 1974; Appreciation Award Wash Section NCNW 1979.

MORTON, MARGARET E.
Senator, funeral director. **PERSONAL:** Born Jun 23, 1924, Pocahontas, VA; married James F Morton; children: James III, Robert Louis, Gerald Woods, Dawn Margaret. **EDUCATION:** Genoa HS Bluefield West Virginia, graduate 1941. **CAREER:** Funeral dir; Connecticut Gen Assembly; State of Connecticut, senator, asst majority leader, senate co-chmn exec & legislative nominations comm. **ORGANIZATIONS:** Mem, vice pres 1970, exec bd 1971-76 NAACP; bd dir Gr Bridgeport YWCA 1970-72; mem Gr Bridgeport C of C 1973-79; bd dirs Hall Neighborhood 1973-76, St Marks Day Care Ctr 1974-76; mem United Dem Club Bridgeport, State Fed Black Dem Clubs, Fed Dem Women, Org Women Legislators; Greater Bridgeport Chap Coalition of 100 Black Women, Fairfield Co CHUMS. **HONORS/ACHIEVEMENTS:** Sojourner Truth Awd Natl Council Negro Women 1973; Achievement Awd Barnum Festival 1973; Achievement Awd Bridgeport Chap Bus & Professional Women 1973; AMORE Ch Achievement Awd 1972. **BUSINESS ADDRESS:** Senator, State Legislature, State Capitol, Hartford, CT 06115.

MORTON, PATSY JENNINGS
Advertising executive. **PERSONAL:** Born Oct 02, 1951, Fauquier County, VA; daughter of Thomas Scott Jennings and Louise Dickson Jennings; married Allen James Morton, Jr, May 28, 1978; children: Valerie, Allen Christopher. **EDUCATION:** Jersey Academy, Jersery City, NJ 1965-69; Oberlin Coll, Oberlin, OH, BA, 1969-73; Columbia Univ, New York, NY, 1974-75. **CAREER:** Earl G Graves Publishing, New York, NY, mktg mgr, 1973-75; The New York Times Co, New York, NY, sales representative, 1975-81, assoc gen mgr, 1981-83; group mgr, 1983-87, advertising mgr, 1987-. **ORGANIZATIONS:** Mem, Business Comm, Admissions Comm, Obelin Coll, 1986; mem, proprietary assoc, 1986-; co-chmn-Transportation Comm, proprietary assoc, 1987; chmn-hospitality comm, proprietary assoc, 1988; mem task force, Five Star Newspaper Network, 1988-; bd dir, New York State Food Merchants, 1989-. **HONORS/ACHIEVEMENTS:** Rookie of the Year, Jersey Academy, 1965; Dean's Ust, Oberline Coll, 1970-73; Black Achievers Award, YMCA, 1989. **BUSINESS ADDRESS:** Advertising Mgr, The New York Times, 229 W 43 St, New York, NY 10036.

MORTON, WILLIAM STANLEY
Attorney. **PERSONAL:** Born Jul 18, 1947, White Plains, NY; married Mary. **EDUCATION:** Coll of Arts & Sci, BS 1969; Coll of Law OH State U, JD cum laude 1974. **CAREER:** Procter & Gamble Co, sr counsel 1974-. **ORGANIZATIONS:** Mem Black Lawyers Assn of Cincinnati; bd of dir Am Civil Liberties Union Central OH 1973; mem OH Bar 1974-; Nat & Urban League Black Exec Exchange, participation prof 1976-; mem Omega Psi Phi Frat; mem & bd of dir ProKids 1985-87. **MILITARY SERVICE:** AUS sp4 1970-72. **BUSINESS ADDRESS:** Senior Counsel, The Procter & Gamble Co, One Procter & Gamble Plaza, Cincinnati, OH 45202.

MORTON-FINNEY, JOHN
Attorney. **PERSONAL:** Born Jun 25, 1889, Uniontown, KY; married Pauline. **EDUCATION:** Lincoln Ints, PdB 1916, AB 1920; StateUniv IA, BA 1922; IN U, MA 1925, MA 1933; Lincoln U, LlB 1935; IN Law Sch, LlB 1944; IN U, LlB 1946; Butler U, AB 1965; IN U, Purdue U, certificate 1974. **CAREER:** MO, tchr, supr, administr, pub schs 1916-18 IN 1922-70; IN Pub Schs, state inspector 1935; Fisk U, tchr 1932; Lincoln Inst, 1919-22; atty pvt practice. **ORGANIZATIONS:** Mem IN State Pub Sch Survey Commn 1949; mem Am, Nat Bar Assns. **HONORS/ACHIEVEMENTS:** Distinguished Serv Award Indianapolis Educ Assn 1970; Recognition & Gratitude Award IN State Bd 1972. **MILITARY SERVICE:** AUS sgt 1911-14; USNA 1917-18.

MOSBY, CAROLYN BROWN
Administrator. **PERSONAL:** Born May 10, 1932, Nashville, TN; married John; children: William Edward Jordan III, Carolyn Elizabeth. **EDUCATION:** Univ of IL, attended; IN-Univ NW, attedned. **CAREER:** Carolyn Mosby Enterprises, pres; IN House of Rep, state rep;Univ of Chicago Grad Dept of Econ, administrative asst. **ORGANIZATIONS:** Chmn Gary Human & Relations Commn; membership chmn First Bapt Ch; vP Gary Bldg Authority; mem Nat Coun of Negro Women; mem Nat Hook-up of Black Women; life mem NAACP; charter pres Gary Dem Womens Club; charter pres Intl Toastmistress Club; editor League of Women Voters; resolutions chmn Nat Black Caucus of State Leg. **HONORS/ACHIEVEMENTS:** Outstanding Freshman Legislator IN Gen Assembly. **BUSINESS ADDRESS:** 328 Garfield St, Gary, IN 46404.

MOSBY, ESVAN SCOTT
Business executive. **PERSONAL:** Born Apr 21, 1910, Kansas City, MO; children: Esvan, Jr, Henry. **EDUCATION:** B Religious Sci 1959. **CAREER:** Varied show business career, 1935-40; Benson Men Shop Potentate of Shrines Al Ko Doch Temple, sales pub rel 1941. **HONORS/ACHIEVEMENTS:** Martin aw Youth Inc 1970; exemplary aw Lindsay-LA Cty Councmn 1970. **MILITARY SERVICE:** CA Nat Guard capt spl serv 1941. **BUSINESS ADDRESS:** 8667 S Broadway, Los Angeles, CA.

MOSBY, NATHANIEL
Service difficulty specialist. **PERSONAL:** Born Mar 24, 1929, Middletown, OH; married Gwendolyn Mizell; children: Natalyn, David, Warren, Howard, Phillip. **EDUCATION:** Morehouse Coll, AB 1951; Atlanta Univ, MBA grad School of Bus Admin 1961. **CAREER:** Lockhewed Aircraft Corp Marietta GA, 1955-58; SE Fidelity Fire Ins Co Atlanta, 1961-62; GSA, bldg mgmt prog (1 of 1st blacks hired) 1963, mgr fed ofc bldg 1964, area intergroup spec 1967, reg intergroup spec 1968-72; Fed Aviation Admin, personnel staffing spec 1972-77, serv difficulty spec. **ORGANIZATIONS:** Mem FL Coll Placement Assoc, so Coll Placement Assoc; charter mem Soc for Advancement of Mgmt Atlanta Univ Chapt; fed personnel council commiss Atlanta Reg Commn; commiss DeKalb Cty Comm Relations Commn; commiss, vchmn Commn; chmn DeKalb Cty Comm Rel Commn; bd dirs Grady Homes Boys Club; bd mgrs, past pres of bd SE Br YMCA, Alpha Phi Alpha, Mason; elder Oakhurst Presbyterian Church, Inst Rep of BSA; past chmn Atlanta Council for Publ Ed. **HONORS/ACHIEVEMENTS:** Outstanding Layman of the Year Atlanta YMCA 1973; listed in Who's Who in Religion 1974; Superior Achievement Awd for exemplary serv to FAA EEO 1983; Outstanding Fed Employee of the Year EEO 1984. **MILITARY SERVICE:** AUS ofcr 1951-53; Korean Conflict. **BUSINESS ADDRESS:** Service Difficulty Specialist, Fed Aviation Admin, PO Box 20636, Atlanta, GA 30320.

MOSEBY, LLOYD ANTHONY
Professional athlete. **PERSONAL:** Born Nov 05, 1959, Portland, AR; married Adrienne; children: Alicia Antoinette, Lloyd II. **CAREER:** Toronto Blue Jays, outfielder. **HONORS/ACHIEVEMENTS:** Named Pioneer League All-star 1978; named to FSL All-Star Team 1979; Topps Class A All-Star Team 1979; co-winner Labatt's Blue MVP 1983; named to AL All-Star Team The Sporting News & UPI 1983; Silver Slugging Team 1983; AL Player of the Week 1983; Labatt's Player of Month for July 1983; AL Player of Month for Aug 1983; LaBatt's "Blue" Player of the Month for Aug 1986; mem All Star Team 1986. **BUSINESS ADDRESS:** Toronto Blue Jays, Box 7777, Adelaide St PO, Toronto, Ontario, Canada M5C 2K7.

MOSEE, JEAN C.
Physician, educator, administrator. **PERSONAL:** Born Jun 06, 1927, Dallas, TX; married Dr Charles; children: Sheila Joan, Wren Camille, Meharry Med. **EDUCATION:** Hoawrd U, BS 1947; Middlebury Coll, MA 1951; Meharry Med Coll, MD (highest honors) 1960. **CAREER:** Dept of Human Resourc chf of clinic 1963-; DC gen hosp, pediatric resident 1961-63; instern 1960-61; fisk u, instr 1954-56; SC state Coll, asst prof of German 1951-54; VA Union U, instr of Gferman 1948-51. **ORGANIZATIONS:** Bd of dirs DC Mental Hlth Assn; mem Med-Chi Society Soc DC Wash Chap of Acad of Pediatrics; particip Career Confs at Pub & Parochial Sch; lectrChild Abuse; bd of tsts Nat Children's Intl Summer Villages; bd of mgrs Nat Meharry Alumni Assn; bd of tsts Friendship Settlemnt House. **HONORS/ACHIEVEMENTS:** Recip josiah macy rsrch flwshp Meharry Med Coll Pharm Dept; designated most outstndng stud in German Sch 1951; particip rsrch proj on Hypertension in Black Children; plaque fro otstndng alumna Meharry Med Coll. **BUSINESS ADDRESS:** Dept of Human Resources, Benning Rd & 46th St SE, Washington, DC 20019.

MOSEKA, AMINATA (ABBEY LINCOLN)
Actress, director. **PERSONAL:** Born in Chicago, IL. **CAREER:** The Girl Can't Help It, actress 1956; Nothing But a Man, lead role 1965; For Love of Ivy, title role 1968; A Pig in a Poke Prod Co, author, dir; African Amer Theatre CA State Univ, teacher. **ORGANIZATIONS:** Chairwoman, producers com Tribute to the Black Woman 1977. **HONORS/ACHIEVEMENTS:** Best Actess Nothing But a Man 1st World Fest of negro Arts 1966; Best Actess Nothing But a Man Fed of of Italian Film Makers 1964; Most Prom Screen Person For the Love of Ivy All Amer Press Assoc 1969; Black Filmmakers Hall of Fame 1975; worked with Coleman Hawkins, Sonny Rollins, Thelonious Monk, John Coltrane. **BUSINESS ADDRESS:** Teacher, California StateUniv, African Amer Theatre, Northridge, CA 91324.

MOSELEY, BARBARA M.
Computer specialist. **PERSONAL:** Born Feb 12, 1938, NYC; married Edward H. **EDUCATION:** BS Nathematics 1960. **CAREER:** Intl Telecommunication Satellite Orgn, senior computer system analyst; Computer Science, progmng with simulation team for commun net-

work models. **ORGANIZATIONS:** Mem ACM; sec IBM Share Inc Graphics Group; mem Urban League; NCNW; Delta Sigma Theta Inc. **BUSINESS ADDRESS:** 490 L Enfant Plaza SW, Washington, DC 20024.

MOSELEY, CALVIN EDWIN, JR.
Clergyman, educator. **PERSONAL:** Born Jan 07, 1906, Demopolis, AL; married Harriet F Slater; children: Harriet Ann, Barbara Jean. **EDUCATION:** Andrews Univ, BA, MA; Chicago Univ, Attended; Northwestern Univ, attended; Daniel Payne Coll, LLD. **CAREER:** Evanston & Springfield IL, pastoral minister 1929-31; St Louis KC, MO, pastor 1931-34; 7th Day Adventists Church Washington DC, gen field sec; ministerial workshops & field schools of evangelism 1951-71; Oakwood Coll, prof of religion 1934-51, chmn dept of religion 1943-51, teacher ministerial trainees 1934-51, 1972-74, part time teacher ministerial trainees 1974-87. **ORGANIZATIONS:** Columnist ed consult Message Mag. **HONORS/ACHIEVEMENTS:** Author "The Lords Day" 1949; "Information Please" 1973. **BUSINESS ADDRESS:** Teacher, Ministerial Trainees, Oakwood Coll, Huntsville, AL 35896.

MOSELEY, FRANCES KENNEY
Public relations manager. **PERSONAL:** Born Mar 20, 1949, Cleveland, OH; married Monroe Avant Moseley; children: Gavin. **EDUCATION:** Univ of Denver, BA Psych 1971. **CAREER:** State St Bank & Trust, security analyst 1974-77; Bank of Boston, trust officer 1977-79; WGBH-TV, dir of promo 1979-80; Boston Edison Co, sr publ info rep. **ORGANIZATIONS:** Mem & former officer Boston Branch NAACP 1976; mem Amer Assoc of Blacks in Energy 1980-; chmn of the bd Big Sister Assoc of Greater Boston 1984; pres of bd of Big Sisters Assn of Greater Boston 1982, bd mem since 1979. **HONORS/ACHIEVEMENTS:** Reddy Communications 1st Place Award for Boston Edison's 1983 Annual Report; Publicity Club of Boston Bellringer Award for Creativity 1982. **BUSINESS ADDRESS:** Senior Public Info Rep, Boston Edison Co, 800 Boylston St, Boston, MA 02199.

MOSELEY, JAMES ORVILLE B.
Educator. **PERSONAL:** Born Sep 21, 1909, Alcorn Coll, MS; married Vivian Leona Hyde. **EDUCATION:** Morehouse Coll, AB 1929; Univ of MI, M Mus 1947; Attended, NY Univ, Johns Hopkins Univ, Univ of Southern CA. **CAREER:** Natchez Coll, asst music dir 1929-32; Southern Univ, head music dept 1932-40; Tougaloo Coll, dir of music 1940-42; Morgan State Coll, acting head musicdept 1946-56; CA State Univ Long Beach, assoc prof 1975-77, music specialist 1956-73; LA Unified Sch Dist, resource music tchr 1973-75; Lincoln Music Studio, director/tchr. **ORGANIZATIONS:** Mem Amer Soc Composers Authors Publ; mem Elem Mus Tchrs Assn of LA; mem NEA, Natl Com of Music Educ Natl Conf; mem CA Textbook Adoptions Comm; dir Ebony Choraliers LA 1963; Comm Chamber Music Ensemble 1948; Organ dir HS & Coll State Rallies; Omega Psi Phi Frat; Phi Mu Alpha Sinfonia 1953; Music in Amer Educ 1955; dir of Amer Scholars 1957. **HONORS/ACHIEVEMENTS:** Listed in Who's Who in Amer Educ 1953-54; author composer numerous compos & arrangements in the larger forms; coll hymn "Dear Old Morehouse"; Piano Scholarship Intl Competition Chicago Mus Coll 1929; First prize winner Tuskegee Army Air Field Post Song 1943; Ford Found Fellowship 1952; listed Who Knows & What1949; Who's Who in Music 1951. **MILITARY SERVICE:** USAF res sr warrant officer, band leader 1942-46. **HOME ADDRESS:** 350 S Fuller Ave, Apt 4-H, Los Angeles, CA 90036.

MOSELEY-BRAUN, CAROL E.
Government official. **PERSONAL:** Born Aug 16, 1947, Chicago, IL; daughter of Joseph Moseley and Edna Moseley; divorced; children: Matthew Braun. **EDUCATION:** Univ of IL Chicago, Chicago, IL, BA 1969; Univ of Chicago, Chicago, IL, JD 1972. **CAREER:** Mayer Brown & Platt, law clerk 1970; Rose Hardies O'Keefe Babcock & Parsons, law clerk 1971; Davis Miner & Barnhill, assoc 1972; US Dept of Justice ND of IL, asst attny 1973-77; Jones, Ware & Grenard, oj counsel; 26th Leg Dist Chgo, state rep 1977-; Cook County, Chicago, IL, recorder of deeds/registrar of titles. **ORGANIZATIONS:** Mem Bar of the US Court of Appeals 7th Circuit, Bar of the US Dist Court Northern Dist of IL, Bar of the State of IL, IL State Bar Assoc, Natl Order of Women Legislators, Dem Policy Commiss of the Dem Natl Conv, Cook County Bar Assoc, Chicago Council of Lawyers, Amer Judicature Soc, Natl Conf of State Leg; comm on Courts & Justice; del Dem Natl Conv 1984; mem League of Black Women, Jane Addams Ctr for Social Policy & Rsch, Alpha Gamma Phi, Chicago Forum, DuSable Museum, Chicago Public Schools Alumni Assoc, IL women's Political Caucus, Coaltion to Save South Shore Country Club Park, Urban League, NAACP, South Shore Commiss. **HONORS/ACHIEVEMENTS:** Awardee Attny Gen's Commendation; Woman of the Year Awd Lu Palmer Found 1980; Best Legislator Awd Independent Voters of IL 1980; Recog & Appreciation Cert IL Sheriffs Assoc 1981; Award of Distinction Networking Together 1981; Outstanding Woman of Struggle Awd Chicago Alliance Against Racist & Political Repression 1981; Dist Serv Awd Concerned Black Execs of Social Serv Org 1983; Outstanding Legislator Awd IL Public Action Council 1983; Leadership Awd Assn of Human Serv Providers 1984; Legislative Leadership Awd Chicago Public Schools & Coaltion to Save Our Schools 1985; Beautiful People Awd Urban League 1985; Legislator of the Year Awd IL Nurses Assn 1986; Cert of Appreciation Chicago Bar Assn 1986; Serv Awd IL Pro-Choice Alliance 1986; Best Legislator Awd Independent Voters of IL Independent Precinct Org 1986; Friends of Educ Award, IL State Bd of Educ 1988; "Day Breaker" Award, Mayor Harold Washington 1988; Chicago Black United Communities "Secrets" Award, St Mark's United Methodist Ch, 1989; Karunya Educational Award for Legislative Excellence; certificate of appreciation, PTA. **BUSINESS ADDRESS:** Cook County Recorder of Deeds/Registrar of Titles, Cook County, 118 North Clark, #230, Chicago, IL 60602.

MOSES, ALICE J.
Educator. **PERSONAL:** Born Mar 25, 1929, Philadelphia, PA; married Paul B (deceased); children: Michael A. **EDUCATION:** Cheyney State Coll, BS 1951; Univ of PA, MS 1957. **CAREER:** Banks Ave School Asbury Park NJ, teacher; School Dist of Philadelphia, teacher 4-7, collaborator, social studies, sci workshop ldr in soc studies 1953-62; Fletcher Mem Art School, asst princ 1957-61; Univ of Chicago Lab Schools, teacher 1964-84; Nursery to HS, prin summer school 1970-84; Univ of Chicago Lab School, master teacher 1977-84; Natl Sci Found, prog dir. **ORGANIZATIONS:** Bd dirs Council for Elem Sci Intl 1969-72, Natl Sci Teachers Assoc Book Review Comm 1972-; bd dirs NSTA 1973-77; pres Council for Elem Sci Intl 1976-77; proposal evaluator NSF; consult Encyclopaedia Britannica Films; bd mem Renaissance Soc Univ of Chicago 1975-84, SE Chicago Commin 1976-84, Amer Assoc of Univ Women, Alpha Kappa Alpha; pres Natl Sci Teachers Assoc 1984-85. **HONORS/ACHIEVEMENTS:** Co-author, devel Elem Sci Ed Matls; co-auth DC Health & Co Sci Series Grades 106; hostess Read Me A Story publ affairs prog for children on NBC 1966-70; Fulbright Exchange Teacher Headington Oxford England; Selected to a Mem of Sci Del to look at sci ed in China; Cert for Outstanding Contribs Council Sci Intl; Named KY Col 1984; IL Sci Teachers Achievement Awd 1984. **BUSINESS ADDRESS:** Program Dierctor, Natinal Science Foundation, 1800 G St NW, Washington, DC 20550.

MOSES, ANDREW M.
Business executive. **PERSONAL:** Born Oct 25, 1926, Varnado, LA; married Velma Pittman; children: Walter, Coleman L, Eddie B. **EDUCATION:** Tri-state Coll of Industrial Arts, degree/mechanics 1950. **CAREER:** WBOX Radio, vice pres in charge of sales 1978-; WIK, sta mgr 1974-78; WIKC, announcer 1963-72; WBOX Radio, ANNOUNCER 1959-63; Keystone Ins Co, insur sales/sales mgr/dist mgr 1952-72; Bugalusa Voters League, organizer/1st pres 1964-65. **ORGANIZATIONS:** Bd of dirs United Fund; Camp Fire Coiuncil; vice pres Bogalusa Econ Devel Corp. **HONORS/ACHIEVEMENTS:** Opened Bogalusa's 1st drive in sandwich & malt shop The Dairy Palace 1964; 1st intergration of formally all shite eating establishments Bogalusa 1964; 1st bi-racial com Gogalusa 1964 very active in black civil rights bogalusa LA; 1st black admitted bogalusa c of c 1966; 1st black to serve A 3 year term-bogalusa C of C Bd of Dirs; 1st black to manage a radio sta in Bogalus 1965; 1st black radio announcer 1971. **MILITARY SERVICE:** AUS T-5 1945-47. **BUSINESS ADDRESS:** Old Varnado Hwy, Bogalusa, LA 70427.

MOSES, EDWIN
Athlete. **PERSONAL:** Born 1953, Dayton, OH; married Myrella;. **EDUCATION:** Morehouse Coll, Physics, Engrg. **CAREER:** Olympian hurdler. **HONORS/ACHIEVEMENTS:** Worlds Top Ranked Intermediate Hurdler 1976-; holds world record 400 meter hurdle (4702); 2 times Olympic Gold Medalist 1976,84; 1st US athlete to be voted del to Intl Amateur Athletic Fed; Sprotsman of the Year US Olympic Comm; 122 consecutive victories. **BUSINESS ADDRESS:** US Olympic Committee, 1750 E Boulder St, Colorado Springs, CO 80909.

MOSES, GILBERT
Film & theater director. **PERSONAL:** Born 2042, Cleveland, OH; son of Gilbert Moses and Bertha Moses; children: Tsia, China. **EDUCATION:** Oberlin Coll, Ba 1964; attended The Sorbonne, French Literature; attended NY Univ School of the Arts. **CAREER:** Director, Willie Dynamite, Ain't Suppose to Die a Natural Death, two segments of mini-series Roots, TV feature movie The Greatest Thing That Almost Happened, episodes of series Paper Chase and Call to Glory, HBO mini-series Maximum Security and the MOW, A Fight for Jenny, Buried Child, documentary The Facts of Life; developed and became one of the original creators of The Wiz; NY Univ School of the Arts, master teacher in acting 1971-72; Cornell Univ, visiting prof 1981; CA Inst of the Arts, visiting prof 1982; Carnegie-Mellon Univ, assoc prof of drama 1985. **ORGANIZATIONS:** Co-founder The Free Southern Theatre. **HONORS/ACHIEVEMENTS:** First Obie Awd as Best Dir for Slaveship, second Obie 1975 for The Taking of Miss Janie which also won New York Drama Critics Awd and the New York Critics Circle Awd for Best Amer Play; documentary The Facts of Life won awds at the New York and Chicago film festivals; Emmy nomination; Tony nomination. **BUSINESS ADDRESS:** Producer, Video Film Convergence Group, c/o Irv Schechter, 9300 Wilshire Blvd Ste 410, Beverly Hills, CA 90212.

MOSES, HAVEN CHRISTOPHER
Athlete. **PERSONAL:** Born Jul 27, 1946, Los Angeles, CA; married Joyce; children: Christopher, Bryan. **EDUCATION:** Harbor Jr Coll, LA; San Iego State Coll. **CAREER:** Samsonite Corp Denver, labor relations specialist; Denver Broncos, wide receiver 1972-; Buffalo, 1968-72. **HONORS/ACHIEVEMENTS:** Tactive in comm proj Played Pro Bowl 1973; two-year letterman & All-Amer at San Diego State; played E-W Shrine Game; MVP Sr Bowl; Coll & All-Stars; offensive end Coll All-Amer Sporting News 1967; AFC Championship Game 1977; NFL Championship Game 1977; 2nd leading active pass receiver AFC 1979; started 87 consecutive games with Broncos; never missed Bronco game. **BUSINESS ADDRESS:** Denver Broncos, 5700 Logan St, Denver, CO 80216.

MOSES, HENRY A.
Educator, educational administration. **PERSONAL:** Born Sep 08, 1939, Gaston County, NC; son of Roy and Mary. **EDUCATION:** Livingstone Coll, BS 1959; Purdue Univ, MS Biochemistry 1962, PhD Biochemistry 1964. **CAREER:** TN State Univ, vstg lecturer biochemistry 1966-70; Meharry Medical College, consultant clinical chemistry 1968-74, assoc prof of biochem and nutrition 1969-81, provost internal affairs 1976-83, dir of continuing educ 1981-, prof of biochem 1981-, asst vice pres for academic support 1983-, dir of continuing educ for area health educ ctrs 1984-. **ORGANIZATIONS:** Mem AAAS, ACS, Alpha Chi Sigma Frat for Chemists, Amer Assoc of Univ Profs, Beta Kappa Chi Scientific Honor Soc 1972-; chmn, mem Honors and Awds Comm The School of Medicine 1976-; mem Alpha Omega Alpha Honor Med Soc 1980; advisor The Meharrian Student Yearbook 1980-; chmn Academic Policy Comm The School of Medicine 1985-; mem Blakemore United Methodist Church and Bd of Trustees 1985-. **HONORS/ACHIEVEMENTS:** Service Awd Meharry Medical Coll 1971; Harold D West Awd Meharry Med Coll 1972; Kaiser-Permanente Awd for Excellence in Teaching Meharry Medical Coll 1976; Alpha Omega Alpha Honor Medical Soc 1981; Meritorious Service Awd Los Angeles Chap Meharry Medical Coll Natl Alumni Assoc 1985; Beta Kappa Chi Scientific Honor Soc Special Recognition Awd 1986; Presidential Citation as Outstanding Alumnus NAFEO 1986; also 29 publications. **BUSINESS ADDRESS:** Dir of Continuing Educ, Meharry Medical College, Nashville, TN 37208.

MOSES, JOHNNIE, JR.
Lab microbiologist. **PERSONAL:** Born May 24, 1939, Kinston, NC; married Mirian L Mosely; children: Nicholas G, Adrianne D. **EDUCATION:** Fordham Univ, BA 1978; New York Univ, MA 1982. **CAREER:** Mandl Medical Asst School, inst hematology 1982-84; Malcolm-King Harlem Coll, prof Afro-Amer history 1983-; Harlem Hospital Ctr, lab microbiologist 1962-. **ORGANIZATIONS:** Manhattan Christian Reformed Church 1963-, treas 1975-; mem Intl Soc for Clinical Lab Tech, NAACP; vice pres Lab Tech Council 1971-78; treas/exec bd Addicts Rehab Ctr 1975-; mem Fordham Univ Alumni Assoc 1978-; mem NY Univ Alumni Assoc 1982-. **HOME ADDRESS:** 990 Tinton Ave, Bronx, NY 10456. **BUSINESS ADDRESS:** Lab Microbiologist, Harlem Hospital, 506 Lenox Ave, New York, NY 10037.

MOSES, LOUISE J.
Librarian. **PERSONAL:** Born Jan 02, 1912, Anniston, AL. **EDUCATION:** Talladega Coll, AB 1933; AtlantaUniv Sch Library Svc, MSLS 1952-. **CAREER:** LA Co Pub Lib System Tchr Cobb Ave HS, adminstrn supr; Ft Mcclellan, hostess 1942-46; USAFE Ho's Zeppelhelm Roth Landsberg Air Force Bases, dir clubs; Morris Coll Sumter, lib; Albany State & Coll Albany, lib;Univ So CA LA, asst circulation lib; LA Co Lib System, lib in charge, three comm lib. **ORGANIZATIONS:** Author book of poetry "Shadow Castings" 1984; mem So CA Lib Black Caucas 1972-74; participant research study Talladega Coll Club LA; mem NAACP; asst Study Negro Life & History 1968-71; pres Brocknan Gallery Prodn LA; mem So Council Lit for children Jury Duty LA Co; mem 660 Union LA Co; speaker Claremont Reading Conf 1968; speaker Statler Hilton LA Co Bood Breakfact 1966; program coordntr Calif Lib Assn; reasearch com chrmn Lib Serv Juveniles in Instns So CA. **BUSINESS ADDRESS:** 150 E E1 Segundo Blvd, Los Angeles, CA 90061.

MOSES, MACDONALD
Educational administartor. **PERSONAL:** Born May 20, 1936, Bailey, NC; married Marie Biggs; children: Alvin, Jacqueline, Reginald, Kenneth. **EDUCATION:** Westchester Comm Coll; Alexander Hamilton Brooklyn Tech; IBM Education Center; American Management Assoc. **CAREER:** Church of Christ, Disciples of Christ, general bishop. **ORGANIZATIONS:** Manager MIS Botway Media Associates; pastor Mt Hebron Church of Christ. **HONORS/ACHIEVEMENTS:** Homoray Doctor of Divinity Goldsboro Disciple Institute 1978. **HOME ADDRESS:** 330 Warwick Ave, Mount Vernon, NY 10553.

MOSES, MILTON E.
Chief executive officer. **PERSONAL:** Born Aug 05, 1939, Chicago, IL; son of Jeffery Moses and Mary Moses; married Shirley C; children: Timothy E, Melody L. **EDUCATION:** DePaul Univ, 1965. **CAREER:** Supreme Life Insurance Co of Amer, agt 1963; The Robbins Ins Agency Inc, underwriter 1965; Community Insurance Ctr Inc, pres, CEO. **ORGANIZATIONS:** Mem Ind Insurance Agents of Amer 1980, Chicago Bd of Underwriters 1980, Insurance Inst of Amer 1980; pres Men for Provident Hosp 1971; chmn of bd Human Resources Devel Inst 1980; pres We Can Found Inc 1980. **HONORS/ACHIEVEMENTS:** Outstanding Support Awd Southtown YMCA 1974; Dedicated Serv Awd Third Ward Dem Party 1976; Black Businessman of the Year Blackbook Bus & Ref Guide 1980. **BUSINESS ADDRESS:** President, Community Ins Center Inc, 526 E 87th St, Chicago, IL 60619.

MOSES, WILSON JEREMIAH
Educator. **PERSONAL:** Born Mar 05, 1942, Detroit, MI; married Maureen Joan Connor; children: William Joseph, Jeremiah Showers. **EDUCATION:** Wayne State Univ, AB 1965, MA 1967; Brown Univ, PhD 1975. **CAREER:** Univ of IA, asst prof history 1971-76; Southern Methodist Univ, assoc prof history 1976-80; Free Univ of Berlin, sr fulbright lecturer 1983-84; Brown Univ, prof amer civilization. **HONORS/ACHIEVEMENTS:** Author The Golden Age of Black Nationalism 1978; author Black Messiahs and Uncle Toms 1982; author The Lost World of Alexander Crummell 1987. **BUSINESS ADDRESS:** Professor Amer Civilization, Brown University, Box 1892, Providence, RI 02912.

MOSLEY, CHARLES E.
Educator. **PERSONAL:** Born Feb 08, 1937, Neshoba County, MS; married Yvonne E Herring; children: Angela, Candace. **EDUCATION:** Univ of Chicago, PhD 1973; Northeastern IL U, MEd 1968; Roosevelt U, mA 1966; CA State U, BA 1961. **CAREER:** Governor's State U, Vice Pres 1977; Chicago State U, Chmn 1969-75; Thornton Comm Coll, dir 1968-69. **ORGANIZATIONS:** Pres & fndr African & Assn for Black Studies; pres Cncl on Academic & Comm SUS; mem bd of trustees Thornton Comm coll 1970-73; mem Continuing Educ Comm IL Bd of Higher Edn; mem Western Jour of Lack Studies; pres Black Jour. **HONORS/ACHIEVEMENTS:** Cited among 100 outstanding black am outstanding black am TV NY 1974; TV; outst young men of am 1972; edit Afro-am Jour; edit Nat Jour of Black Studies; Racial Crisis Review. **MILITARY SERVICE:** USAF sgt 1955-61. **BUSINESS ADDRESS:** Governor's State Univ, Park Forest, IL 60426.

MOSLEY, EDNA WILSON
Administrator. **PERSONAL:** Born May 31, 1925, Helena, AR; married John W; children: Edna L. **EDUCATION:** Univ of No CO, attended 1942-43; Adams State Coll, attended 1968-69; Met State Coll, BA 1969;Univ of CO, attended 1975-76. **CAREER:** Univ of Denver, affirmative action dir 1978-; CO State & Dept of Personnel, asst state affirmative action coordinator 1974-78; CO Civil Rights Commn, community relations coordinator 1970-74; Co Civil Rights Commn, civil rights specialist 1969-70; Women's Bank NA Denver, founder 1975. **ORGANIZATIONS:** Co-chmn Denver/Nairobi Sister-/City Com 1976-80; bd of dir Women's Bank NA Denver 1978-80; commr Nat Social Action Commn Delta Sigma Theta Sorority 1979-81; mem Higher Educ Affirmative Action Dir; mem Nat Assn of Affirmative Action Officers; mem CO Black Women for Polit Action; mem Delta Sigma Theta Denver Alumnae Chpt; mem Women's Forum of CO Inc Best Sustaining Pub Affairs Prog CO Broadcasting Assn 1972. **HONORS/ACHIEVEMENTS:** Lola M Parker Achievement Award Iota Phi Lambda Far Western Region 1977; Headliner Award Women in Communications Inc 1978; Appreciation Award Nat Assn of Black Accountants 1978; distinguished serv award Intl Student OrgnUniv of Denver 1979. **BUSINESS ADDRESS:** 2301 S Gaylord St, Denver, CO 80208.

MOSLEY, EDWARD R.
Physician. **PERSONAL:** Born in Chicago, IL; married Marian Kummerfeld; children: Cary, Laura, Kia, Rennie, Christopher, Caroline. **EDUCATION:** Meharry Med Coll, MD 1948. **CAREER:** Pvt Prac, Physician 1956-; Psychiatric Serv VA Hosp Tuskegee AL, med coord 1954-56; VA Hosp Tuskegee AL, residency 1949-52; Harlem Hosp, internship 1948-49; Reg Med Consult State Dept of Rehab. **ORGANIZATIONS:** Pres bd dir Westview Convalescent Hosp; John Hale Med Cntr; mem Nat Med Assn; AMA; Golden State Med Assn; CA Med Assn; Daniel Hale William Medical Forum; Fresno Co Med Soc; Am Soc of Internal Med; Fresno Co Soc of Internal Med; mem Alpha Phi Alpha; F & AM Prince Hall Shrine; 20th Century Elks; chmn Citizen's Resource Com State Cntr Comm Coll 1969; bd trustees State Cntr Comm Coll 1971-; pres 1975-; bd dir Sequoia Boy Scout Council; mem Co Parks & Recreation Comm 1958-68; Mayor's Biracial Com on Hum Rel 1966-68; bd dir Easter Seal Soc TB Assn. **HONORS/ACHIEVEMENTS:** AUS med corp capt 1952-54.

MOSLEY, ELWOOD A.
Training and development executive. **PERSONAL:** Born May 12, 1943, Philadelphia, PA; son of John Mosley and Ethel Glenn; married Eileen Carson, Jan 14, 1967; children: Danielle Mosley. **EDUCATION:** St Joseph's Univ, Philadelphia PA, Business Admin, 1972; Harvard Univ, Cambridge MA, MA, 1989. **CAREER:** Chase Mahatten Bank, New York NY, asst treasurer, 1972-76; CIGNA Insurance, Philadelphia PA, vice pres, 1976-82; USF&G Insurance, Baltimore MD, vice pres, 1982-85; Huggins Financial, Philadelphia PA, vice pres, 1985-87; US Postal Service, Washington DC, asst postmaster general, training & devel, 1987-. **MILITARY SERVICE:** US Marine Corp, corporal, 1964-70. **HOME ADDRESS:** 1684 Kingsbridge Court, Annapolis, MD 21401-6408. **BUSINESS ADDRESS:** Assistant Postmaster General, Training & Development Department, United States Postal Service, 475 L'Enfant Plaza, Room 9840, Washington, DC 20260-4300.

MOSLEY, GERALDINE B. (NEE BROWN)
Nursing educator. **PERSONAL:** Born Oct 22, 1920, Petersburg, VA; married Kelly; children: Lorraine Helms, Kevin. **EDUCATION:** Hunter Coll, NYC, BS 1945; Coll Columbia Univ NYC, MA teachers 1950; NYU, PhD 1970. **CAREER:** Div of Nursing Dominican Coll of Blauvelt, dir 1973-; Dept of Psychiatry Harlem Hospital Center, asso dir of nursing 1971-73; Mayor's Org Task For Comprehensive Health Planning, health planner 1970-71; Columbia Univ, asst prof dept of nursing 1968-71; Queens Coll NYC, lecturer, nursing 1956-58/1961-68; VA, instructor/supvr 1952-56; Dept of Health NYC, public health nurse 1947-52. **ORGANIZATIONS:** Bd of dirs, So NY League, Natl League for Nursing, 1974-76; sec, NY State Nurses Assn, Amer Nurses Assn; vice pres, Metro Regional Task Force for Nursing, 1975-; mem Assn of Univ Profs 1973-80. **HONORS/ACHIEVEMENTS:** Distinguished achievemtn in comprehensive health planning Chi Eta Phi 1971; Outstanding professional leadership award Dept of Psychiatry Harlem Hospital Center 1973; Distinguished serv to the Co of Rockland Co Leg & of Rockland Co 1976; professional Award Westchester County Club Natl Assn of Negro Business & Professional Women's Clubs Inc 1977. **BUSINESS ADDRESS:** Dir Division of Nursing, Dominican College of Baluvelt, 10 Western Hwy, Orangeburg, NY 10962.

MOSLEY, JOHN COLBERT
President/chairman of the board. **PERSONAL:** Born Jun 23, 1935, Rainelle, WV; married Rosalind Moore; children: Farah, Ferne. **EDUCATION:** WV State Coll, BS 1962;Univ of Pittsburgh, PhD 1976. **CAREER:** Holy Rosary School, prin 1968-70; Center for Educ Action, asso dir 1970-72; Mental Health Prg & Homewood-Brushton Nghbr Health Center Inc, coord 1973-75; Homewood-Brushton Nghbr Health Center Inc, developer special school for emotionally active children 1974; Port Authority Transit, consult 1975; Affirmative Action Prog Gen Foods Inc, co-designer 1976; Wm J Procter & Assn, consult 1976; Nigerian Teacher Devel Program Univ of Pitts, dir 1977, assoc prof counselor education 1978; Program Research and Development Inc, president/chairman of the board. **ORGANIZATIONS:** Mem bd of dir Shady Ln Sch 1970-72; bd of dir vice pres Pitts Free Clinic 1974; sec treas Prgm Rsch & Devel Inc 1977; asso Assn of Non-white Concerns;mem Intl Transaction Prgm Rsch & Devel Inc 1977; asso Assn of Non-white Concerns; mem Intl Transaction 1969. **HONORS/ACHIEVEMENTS:** Publ "An Educ Construct" 1969; co-author "Report of Drug Abuse Allegheny & County Citzs" 1970; publ "Problems of the Black Aged" 1977; Who's Who in Am Coll &Univ 1961-62; 1st black lay prin of a cath sch in USA 1968; citation of Merit Co of Allegheny 1971; alumnus of he yr W VA State Coll 1979; HonoreeUniv of Pitts Honors Covocation 1980. **MILITARY SERVICE:** USAF airman 1st class 1954-58. **BUSINESS ADDRESS:** President/Chmn of Bd, Program Rsch & Develop Inc, 6025 Broad St Mall, 2nd Fl, Pittsburgh, PA 15206.

MOSLEY, JOHN WILLIAM
Government administrator. **PERSONAL:** Born Jun 21, Denver, CO; married Edna W Wilson; children: Edna Lorette Futrell, John Gregory, Brian Wilson, William Eric. **EDUCATION:** CO State U, BS denver u, msw; tuskegee inst, attended; NC a & t u, attended. **CAREER:** Fed Regional Council Dept HEW Region Vii, spl asst prin regional ofcl for 1978-; Mtn Plains Fed Regional Council, staff dir 1978; James Farmer Dept HEW, spl asst asst sec 1970; NC A&T U, prof of air sci 1956. **ORGANIZATIONS:** Mem Acad of Cert Social Workers/Nat Assn of Social Workers 1980; bd mem Mile High United Way 1975-; chmn Aurora Human Relations Commn 1975; bd mem Denver People-to-people 1978-; bd mem YMCA; bd mem Goodwill Ind of Denver 1979-. **HONORS/ACHIEVEMENTS:** Award/command Pilot USAF; all conf football & wrestling CO StateUniv 1944; hon mention All Am Football; staff various White House Welfare Confs 1970-80; pub various articles "Educ today"/Wir-alle"; merit scholarship CO State U; Who's Who Among Students" CO & State U; "Who's Who in CO"; outstanding black in CO Histo Enver Pub Library. **MILITARY SERVICE:** USAF lt col 21 yrs. **BUSINESS ADDRESS:** Fed Bldg, 1961 Stout, Denver, CO 80294.

MOSLEY, LAWRENCE EDWARD, SR.
Clergyman. **PERSONAL:** Born Nov 07, 1953, Lynchburg, VA; son of Earl F Mosley Sr and Grace T Mosley; married Patricia Elaine Carr; children: Lawrence Jr, Tiffany. **EDUCATION:** Lynchburg Coll, BA 1976; VA Union Univ, MDiv 1980. **CAREER:** Second Baptist Church, asst to pastor 1979-80; Rising Mt Zion Bapt Ch, pastor 1980-85; Westbrook Hosp, intake counselor 1983-85; Lilydale Progressive MB Church, pastor 1985-. **ORGANIZATIONS:** Mem Chicago Chap VUU Alumni 1985-, Greater New Era Dist Assn Chicago 1985-, Baptist Genl State Convention of IL 1985-, Natl Baptist Convention USA Inc 1985-, Black on Black Love Inc 1986; bd mem 111th St YMCA Chicago 1986-. **HONORS/ACHIEVEMENTS:** Community of Scholars VA Union Univ 1972; Scholarship Awd Blue Key Honor Frat; Outstanding Young Men of Amer Jaycees 1982. **BUSINESS ADDRESS:** Pastor, Lilydale Progressive MB Church, 10706 S Michigan Ave, Chicago, IL 60628.

MOSLEY, MAURICE B.
Attorney. **PERSONAL:** Born Jun 04, 1946, Waterbury, CT. **EDUCATION:** SC St Coll, BS 1968; Cntrl CT St Coll, MS 1972;Univ of CT Sch of Law, JD 1975. **CAREER:** State of CT, Rep,Atty, pvt prac; CT, lgsltr 1976-; CT St Treas, exec asst 1975-77; Urban Leag, legis consult 1974; Tchr, 1968-72. **ORGANIZATIONS:** Adv bd Colonial Bank & Trust Co; chmn Legis Black Caucus; bd trustees Waterbury Hosp; exec bd NAACP 1974-77. **HONORS/ACHIEVEMENTS:** SC St Dist Bus Awd 1968. **BUSINESS ADDRESS:** Rep of 72nd Assembly Dist, State of Connecticut, Capitol Bldg, Hartford, CT 06702.

MOSLEY, MYRTIS H.
Educator. **PERSONAL:** Born Feb 06, 1939, Evergreen, AL; daughter of Arthur Hall and

Lula Hall; married Lavatus Powell; children: Kimberly, Robin, Judy, Lavatus III. **EDUCATION:** Univ of Cincinnati, AS 1968; Univ Cincinnati, BS 1969; Univ of Cincinnati, MA 1974, PhD 1978; Harvard Univ, certificate higher educ mgmt 1975; Saizburg Semianar in Amer Studies Saizburg Austria, certificate 1980. **CAREER:** Univ of Cincinnati, teacher asst 1969-71, asst to dean, lecturer 1971-73, assoc dean, adjunct, asst prof 1973-78; Edna McConnell Clark Found, program dir 1978-81; Miami Univ Oxford Campus, exec asst to the pres, adjunct asst prof of psychology; vice pres, Student Affairs 1989. **ORGANIZATIONS:** Mem Leadership Cincinnati Alumni Assoc, Goals & Long Range Plan Steering Comm Cincinnati Bd of Educ, Steering Comm The Roosevelt Centennial Youth Project Washington DC, Amer Council on Educ, OH Women's ID Project Planning Comm, Amer Assoc for Higher Educ, The Soc for Coll & Univ Planning, Natl Center for the Study of Collective Bargaining in Higher Educ & the Professions, Rsch Univ Network for Federal Legislative Liaisons; vice pres, bd mem Seven Hills Neighborhood Houses Inc Cincinnati; bd mem Community Chest Cincinnati, New Life Youth Serv; bd mem vice pres Natl Child Labor Comm NY; bd mem Jobs for Youth Inc Boston, Cincinnatians Active to Support Educ; chmn Natl Task Force on Educ & Employment Public Policy for Youth Southern Educ Found Atlanta; chmn Spring Forum Columbus 1984; preselect OH Conf for Coll & Univ Planning. **HONORS/ACHIEVEMENTS:** Univ of Cincinnati United Black Faculty Assoc Black Excellence Award 1973, 1978; Leadership Education & Serv Award 1976, 1978; New Hope Baptist Church Outstanding Black Amer Recognition Award 1983; Cincinnati Urban League Guild Leadership Award 1977; Natl Council of Urban League Guilds Leadership Award 1978; Salute to Outstanding Volunteer 1978; Community Serv Award 1978; Cincinnati Community Chest & Council Outstanding Leadership Award Allocations Div 1979; Natl Assn of Minority Women in Business 1980; Carver Community Center Leadership Award Peoria IL 1981; YWCA Career Woman of Achievement 1984; Leadership Cincinnati Graduate Class VIII 1984-85. **BUSINESS ADDRESS:** Vice Pres for Student Affairs, Miami University, 133 Warfield Hall, Oxford, OH 45056.

MOSLEY, TRACEY RAY
Education/assistant director admissions. **PERSONAL:** Born Nov 16, 1960, Kokomo, IN; married Jean Ann Prasher. **EDUCATION:** Univ of WI-Stevens Point, BS 1984. **CAREER:** Maryville Coll, asst dir of admissions/minority student advisor. **ORGANIZATIONS:** Mem Natl Assoc of Coll Admissions Counselors 1985-; marketing consultant Inst for Lifestyle Develop 1985-; advisor Maryville Coll Black Students Assoc 1985-; mem Knoxville Area Urban League Educ Task Force 1986-; mem The Coll Bd New York 1986-; mem human relations comm Southern Assoc of College Admissions Counselors 1986-; mem Natl Wellness Assoc Stevens Point WI. **HONORS/ACHIEVEMENTS:** Alexander Graham Bell Awd for Humanitarian Serv Bell Telephone 1976; Campus Leaders Awd Univ of WI-Stevens Point 1983; Chancellors Leadership Awd 1984. **HOME ADDRESS:** PO Box 2824, Maryville, TN 37801. **BUSINESS ADDRESS:** Asst Dir of Admissions, Maryville College, Offie of Admissions, Maryville, TN 37801.

MOSS, DANIEL CALVIN, JR.
Surgeon. **PERSONAL:** Born Dec 19, 1933, Miami, FL; married Alma Davis; children: Pamela, Sharon. **EDUCATION:** Claflin Coll, BS 1956; HowardUniv Coll Dentistry, dDS 1965;Univ PA, cert 1968. **CAREER:** Self, oral surgeon; HowardUniv Coll Dentistry, asst prof oral surg 1969-71; Dade Co Juv & Dom Rels Ct, asst probation ofcr 1959-61; Dade Co & Pub Sch, tchr 1959; Dade Co Pub Safety Dept, dep sheriff 1956; Cedar of Lebaon Hosp/Christian Hosp/Coral Reef Hosp/Variety Childrens Hosp/ Jackson Meml Hosp/Mt Sinai Hosp, attending staff; VA Hosp, consult oral surg. **ORGANIZATIONS:** Life mem Omega Psi Phi Frat; NAACP; mem Urban League; Claflin Coll Alumni Assn; HowardUniv Alumni Assn; bd dir FL Dental Serv Corp; bd tsts Ch of the Open Door; chmn UCC. **HONORS/ACHIEVEMENTS:** Num hon & awards. **MILITARY SERVICE:** AUS corpl 1956-58. **BUSINESS ADDRESS:** 7780 NW 7th Ave, Miami, FL 33150.

MOSS, ESTELLA MAE
Elected government official. **PERSONAL:** Born Sep 15, 1928, Upland, KY; married Charles E Moss Sr; children: Phyllis Johnson, Ardell, Sheila Spencer, Deborah L Ray, Charles E Jr, Angie V. **EDUCATION:** Central High, Business 1964; ISU of Evansville School of Public & Environ Affairs, 1975. **CAREER:** Superior Court, clerk probate 8 yrs; Pigeon Twp Assessor; chief deputy appointed 1974-76; Vanderburgh Cty, recorder 1976-84. **ORGANIZATIONS:** Vp Community Action Program 1969-77; bd of dir Carver Comm Day Care 1970-76; NAACP Coalition 100 Black Women Political Black Caucus 1978-85; bd of dir Liberty Baptist Housing Auth. **HONORS/ACHIEVEMENTS:** Community Leadership Awd YWCA 1976; Black Woman of the Year in Politics Black Women Task Force 1977; State of IN Black Expo 1978; Selected & Honored as one of 105 Outstanding Black Women of IN by Natl Council of Negro Women 1983. **HOME ADDRESS:** 804 Mulberry, Evansville, IN 47713.

MOSS, JAMES A.
Educator, psychoanalyst. **PERSONAL:** Born Mar 27, 1920, Newark, NJ; divorced; children: Jay Allen, Alison W. **EDUCATION:** Fordham Univ New Sch for Soc Research, BA 1948; Columbia Univ, MA 1949, PhD 1957; Adelphi Univ, MSW 1980, diploma in psychoanalysis 1987. **CAREER:** Univ of Puerto Rico, faculty 1949-50; Dillard Univ New Orleans, LA, instructor 1950-51; Orange Co Comm Coll Middletown, NY, instr 1952-56; Queen Coll City Univ of NY, instr 1956-57; Union Coll, Schenectady, NY, asst prof 1958-63; State Univ of NY at Buffalo, prof 1967-77; Private Practice, psychoanalyst; Adelphi Univ Garden City, NY, univ prof of soc sci 1977-. **ORGANIZATIONS:** Dir research Schenectady Welfare Cncl 1960; dir research So Reg Cncl Atlanta, GA 1961-62; supvr rsch officer Dept of State Wash, DC 1963; chief rschprog (INR/XR) Dept of State Wash, DC 1964; chief Academic Rel & spec asst for behav sci Dept of State Wash, DC 1965-67; assoc dean & act dean IntlStudies Univ of Buffalo 1968-71; vice pres Medgar Evers Coll (CUNY) 1971-72; dir African-American Studies Adelphi Univ 1977-80; consult Ford Foundation 1971, 1973; consult Vassar Coll NY 1968-69; consult Howard Univ Wash, DC 1974; bd of dirs Fifth Ave Psychiatric Ctr NY; co-dir Assoc for Interethnic Studies. **HONORS/ACHIEVEMENTS:** Fellow Woodrow Wilson Intl Center for Scholars 1972-73; mem rsch comm Coll Entrance Exam Bd NY 1968; Martin Luther King Award NY Soc of Clinical Psychologists 1981; author of, "The Black Man in America, Integration & Separation"; author of 40 articles on race and intl relations 1958-83. **MILITARY SERVICE:** AUS 1st Sgt served 3 1/2 yrs; Good Conduct Medal. **HOME ADDRESS:** 222 E 80 St, New York, NY 10021.

MOSS, JIMMY R.
City official. **PERSONAL:** Born Mar 13, 1941, Overton, TX; married Lauretta; children: Giselle, Derrick. **EDUCATION:** TX So U, BS 1963; OK U, MS 1974. **CAREER:** OK City Police Dept, crime analyst; OK City, urban planner 1974-77; Gen Foods, sales rep 1968-71; BSA, dist exec 1965-68. **ORGANIZATIONS:** Past vice pres treas Alpha Phi Alpha; past pres Frontiers Intl OK City & Chpt; scout mastger Troop 262. **HONORS/ACHIEVEMENTS:** Bruce Mcmillan Jr schlrsp; Housing & Urban Devel Flwsp.

MOSS, OTIS, JR.
Clergyman. **PERSONAL:** Born Feb 26, 1935, LaGrange, GA; married Edwina Hudson; children: Kevin, Daphne, Otis III. **EDUCATION:** Morehouse Coll, BA 1956, Morehouse School of Rel, BD 1959; Interdenominational Theol Ctr, spec studies 1960-61; Temple Bible Coll, DD, Morehouse Coll, DD 1977. **CAREER:** Raymond Walters Coll, instr; Old Mt Olive Bapt Church La Grange, pastor 1954-59; Prividence Bapt Church Atlanta, pastor 1956-61; Mt Zion Bapt Church, minister 1961-74; Olivet Inst Bapt Church Cleveland, pastor 1975-. **ORGANIZATIONS:** Mem bd dir Morehouse School of Religion & Morehouse Coll; bd of dir ML King Jr Ctr; bd of dir, vchmn Oper PUSH; mem Alpha Phi Alpha; past vice pres NAACP of Atlanta; past pres & founder Cinti Chap SCLC; bd of trustees Leadership Cleveland Civil Right Activist; mem of review comm Harvard Divinity School Harvard Univ 1975-82; mem bd of trustees Morehouse Coll 1979-; former columnist for Atlanta Inquirer Atlanta GA 1970-75; delivered speeches, sermons & addresses, Atlanta Univ, Colgate Rochester Divinity School, Coll of Mt St Joseph, Dillard Univ, Eden Theol Ctr, Howard Univ, Kalamazoo Coll, Miami Univ, Fisk Univ, Univ of Cincinnati, Vanderbilt Univ, Wilberforce Univ, Wright State Univ, Morehouse Coll; keynote speaker March on Cincinnati 1963. **HONORS/ACHIEVEMENTS:** Man of the Year in Religion Atlanta 1961; listed in Most Outstanding Men of Amer 1976; Consult with Pres Carter Camp David 1979; invited as part of clergy mission to Republic of China Taiwan 1984; consult with govt officials as part of clergy mission to Israel 1977-78; served as part of clergy mission to the Far East Hong Kong, Taiwan & Japan 1970; invited to act as delegate to World Bapt Conf in Beirut; visited W Africa 1963; Govs Awd in Civil Rights Gov Richard F Celeste; Black Professional of the Year Black Professional Assoc Cleveland OH 1983; Spec Awd in Leadership Central State Univ 1982; Human Rels Awd Bethune Cookman Coll 1976; Ranked as one of Clevelands 10 Most Influential Ministers Cleveland Press 1981; 1 of Amers 15 Greatest Black Preachers Ebony Mag 1984; twice honored by OH House of Reps Resolutions 1971,75; sermon "Going from Disgrace to Dignity" Best Black Sermons 1972; essays "Black Church Distinctives", "Black Church Revolution" The Black Christian Experience; listed in Ebony Success Library, Who's Who in Religion. **BUSINESS ADDRESS:** Pastor, Olivet Inst Bapt Church, 8712 Quincy Ave, Cleveland, OH 44106.

MOSS, ROBERT C., JR.
Educator, sports official, motivation consultant. **PERSONAL:** Born May 30, 1939, San Diego; son of Clinton and Lavern; married Edna Jean, Mar 17, 1962; children: Anita Louise, Parry Donald. **EDUCATION:** San Diego State U, BA 1961; US Intl Univ, teaching cred 1965; San Diego State U, MS 1975. **CAREER:** Phys Educ Dept Univ of CA San Diego, supervisor 1971-; professional baseball umpire 1969-71; San Diego HS, black studies tchr, black student motivation counselor 1969-71; Mission Bay HS, biology instr, football, baseball coach 1966-69; Lincoln HS, biology tchr 1965-66; founder/director of Moss-Cess Unlimited, a motivation consulting firm 1973-. **ORGANIZATIONS:** Kappa Alpha Psi Fraternity; Amer Alliance for Health, Physical Educ, Recreation & Dance; Amer Assn for Counseling & Devel; CA Assn for Health, Physical Educ, Recreation and Dance; CA Assn for Counseling & Devel; CA & Amer Assn for Multicultural Counseling & Devel; San Diego County officiating assn for football, basketball and baseball; Natl Assn of Sports Officials. **HONORS/ACHIEVEMENTS:** Ted Williams Award, 1960, leading hitter on San Diego State Univ baseball team; Byron Chase Memorial Award, 1960, most valuable lineman on SDSU football team; Most Outstanding SDSU Senior Athlete, 1961; Associated Students Man of the Month at SDSU, May, 1961; Blue Key Honorary Society, 1961; Ashanti Weusi Award for services in field of educ for the Southeast San Diego community; CAHPERD, San Diego Unit Meritorious Service Award, 1975; CAHPERD President's Citation, 1981; Oustanding Teacher Award, Univ of CA, San Diego African American graduates, 1985; CAHPERD Emmett Ashford Community Spirit Award, 1986; AACD President's Citation, 1986; CACD Black Caucus Service Award, 1986; CAHPERD Honor Award, 1987; Special Recognition Award, UC San Diego Intercollegiate Athletic Program; Special Recogni tion Award, United States International Univ basketball team, 1988; CACD Black Caucus Dedicated Service Award, 1989; CACD-CAMC President's Outstanding Professional Service Award, 1989. **MILITARY SERVICE:** Served USMC 1961-65. **BUSINESS ADDRESS:** Supervisor of Phys Education, University of CA, San Diego, PE Dept UCSD, C-017, La Jolla, CA 92093.

MOSS, SIMEON F.
Consultant, educator. **PERSONAL:** Born Apr 05, 1920, Princeton, NJ; son of Simeon C Moss and Mary Benning Moss; married Edith Ashby Moss, Apr 06, 1946; children: Simeon Jr, Deborah A. **EDUCATION:** Rutgers U, BS 1941; Princeton, MA 1949; Rutgers, EdD 1967. **CAREER:** Metro-ed Serv Inc, vice pres 1980-; Educ Dept Co of Essex, 1977-80; Essex Co Coll, exec vice pres 1969-77; Essex Co NJ Dept Educ, supt schools; Newark Schools, elem supt; NJ Dept of Labor and Industry, asst commr 1960-64; NJ Pub Schs, tchr adminstr 1954-60; NJ Manual Training Sch, field Rep 1949-53. **ORGANIZATIONS:** Trustee Essex Co Coll 1969-75; mem Essex Co Vocational Bd 1969-75; dir Essex Co Bd Educ Empl Pension Fund; dir City Natl Bank of Newark; mem adv comm teacher Educ Seton Hall Univ; chmn bd Inst Trustees NJ State Prison Complex 1972-73; membership chmn Orange Mtn Coun BSA 1973-74; sec-treas cham NJ Consultation Ethnic Factors in Educ; legislative chair ECREA. **HONORS/ACHIEVEMENTS:** Bancroft History Prize, Journal of Negro History 1949; White House Invitee Centennial of Emancipation Proclamation 1963; Distinguished Serv in Educ Award Alpha Phi Alpha 1965-69; Frontiers Community Serv Awd 1970; Loyal Son of Rutgers Awd 1987. **MILITARY SERVICE:** AUS 1st lt 1942-46; capt 1951-52; Njarng 1956-73; USAR; col retired. **HOME ADDRESS:** 440 Page Terr, South Orange, NJ 07079.

MOSS, THOMAS EDWARD, SR.
Deputy chief of police. **PERSONAL:** Born Nov 02, 1934, Detroit, MI; son of Thomas Whitting Moss (deceased) and Leola Lorraine Davis Moss (deceased); married Pearl Bonham, Nov 22, 1986; children: Thomas, Tonia Gadois, Monica, Marc. **EDUCATION:** Wayne State Univ, BA 1967; Univ of MI, MA 1975. **CAREER:** Wayne Co Youth Home, boys supr 1964-65; Detroit Public School, teacher 1966-70; Royal Oak Twp MI, police officer 1963-65; Oak Park MI, public safety officer 1965-74; Wayne Co Comm Coll, dir of law enforcement programs 1970-73; Detroit Police Dept, deputy chief of police 1974-. **ORGANIZATIONS:**

One of dir & coaches Detroit Jr Football League 1968-; pres Guardians of MI 1971-73; vice pres 1971; dir Three Day Conf on Black Problems in Law Enforcement 1972; 1st natl chmn Nat Black Police Assn 1973; mem MI Assn of Chiefs of Police; dirested security operations during Mayor Coleman Youngs First Campaign 1973; dir Detroit Police Dept Jr Police Cadet Program Involving Low Income Youth; aid Mrs Martin L King & Rev Martin L King Sr; mem Univ of MI Maize & Blue Club; mem Greater Alumni Assn of Univ MI; bd of dirs Detroit YMCA; bd mem Westside Cubs Athletic Assn; mem Am Psychological Assn. **HONORS/ACHIEVEMENTS:** Elected bd of govs Univ of MI Alumni Assoc 1986; developed Jr Police Cadet Prog; 1 of 18 for natl recognition by the Police Foundation Washington DC; Community service officer program, pre-police officer training program, high school, jr/sr's, 1988-. **MILITARY SERVICE:** AUS 1954-57. **HOME ADDRESS:** 3320 Spinnaker Lane, Detroit, MI 48207.

MOSS, WILMAR BURNETT, JR.
Educator. **PERSONAL:** Born Jul 13, 1928, Homer, LA; married Orean Sanders; children: Dwight, Victor, Gary, LaDonna. **EDUCATION:** AR Bapt Coll, attended 1949; So State Coll, attended 1955-57; AM&N Coll Pine Bluff, BS Bus Admin 1960; Univ of AR Fayetteville, MEd Educ Admin1970. **CAREER:** McNeil Cleaners, cleaner spotter presser; McNeil Lumber Co, tractor truck driver lumber grader; Partee Lumber Co, tractor driver; Navel Ordnance Plant Camden, light mach oper; Stuttgard, teacher 1960; E Side Lincoln Elem Schools Stuttgart, head teacher 1961-63; E Side Lincoln Holman, prin 1964-69; Holman Northside Elem Schools, prin 1969-72; Walker School Dist #33, supt of schools 1972-. **ORGANIZATIONS:** Mem AR Sch Admin Assn, AR Educ Assn, So AR Admins Assn, Columbia Co Educ Assn, Natl Educ Assn, Amer Legion former commander & vice dist commander; mem NAACP helped form Columbis Co Br; mem Natl Alliance of Black Sch Supts; mem Phi Delta Kappa; active Mason; mem Bethany Bapt Ch McNeil; Golden Diadem Lodge No 41; McNeil Jaycees; bd mem Pres Johnson's Concentrated Employ Prog 1971-72; active BSA; mem Stuttgart Civic League; organized WalkerAlumni Assn 1974. **HONORS/ACHIEVEMENTS:** Comm Serv Awd Stuttgart Civic League 1972; Outstanding Serv Awd Stuttgart Faculty Club 1970. **MILITARY SERVICE:** AUS 1951-53. **BUSINESS ADDRESS:** Supt of Schools, Walker Sch Dist #33, PO Box 1149, Magnolia, AR 71753.

MOSS, WINSTON
Writer. **PERSONAL:** Born in Selma, AL. **EDUCATION:** Bellarmine Coll KY, 1962-64; Western KY Univ, 1968. **CAREER:** The Flip Wilson Show, staff writer 1970; Laugh In, staff writer 1972; That's My Mama, story editor 1975-76; The Jackson-5 Show, staff writer 1977; Writers Guild of Amer/WST, freelance writer. **ORGANIZATIONS:** Staff writer The Clifton Davis Spec 1977, All in the Family 1977-79, Archie Bunkers Place 1979-80; vice chmn Black Writers Comm 1979-81; mem Hollywood Branch NAACP, Local Black Groups & Writers Groups. **HONORS/ACHIEVEMENTS:** 1st Black Story Editor for Network TV 1975; Golden Globe Awd for Writing on "All in the Family" 1977; Universal Studios TV Pilot Scheduled for ABC-TV Sep 1985; Stage Play "The Helping Hand" currently in production. **MILITARY SERVICE:** AUS spec 4 1965-67. **HOME ADDRESS:** 4714 Rodeo Ln #3, Los Angeles, CA 90016.

MOTEN, BIRDIA B. (NEE JENKINS)
Government consultant. **PERSONAL:** Born Apr 16, 1934, Kingsland, AR; divorced. **EDUCATION:** AM&N Coll, BS 1955;Univ AR, MEd 1956;Univ Chgo; No AZ U;Univ NV; Clark U; Columbia U; Yeshinv U. **CAREER:** Elem Secndry Tchr; EEO Nevada St Dept Educ Las Vegas, cons. **ORGANIZATIONS:** Mem League Women Voters; Am Civil Liberties Union natl council; NAACP; Am AssnUniv Women; Nat Western Reg Black Caucus Sch bd trustees; Nat Alliance Black Elected Officials; Nat Assn Sch Trustees; State Assn Sch Trustees; bd mem Clark Cnty Sch Dist; Task Force on Sch Desegregation; Adv Com toState Libr Bd; Operation Life Nat Welfare Rights Assn. **BUSINESS ADDRESS:** Dawson Bldg Ste 234, 4055 S Spencer, Las Vegas, NV 89109.

MOTEN, CHAUNCEY DONALD
Educator. **PERSONAL:** Born Jul 02, 1933, Kansas City, KS; married Barbara Jean; children: Allison, Dion. **EDUCATION:** TX Coll, BA 1955; Vandercook Coll, MA 1959;Univ of MO, MA 1969;Univ of MI, PhD 1972. **CAREER:** KS City Public School, teacher 1965-68; Univ of MO, dir 1968-70, 1971-73; Metro Comm Coll, exec & asst 1974-77; Metro Comm Coll Kansas City MO, exec dean ofc of human devel 1977-79; Penn Valley Comm Coll Kansas City MO, asst dean comm serv/instructional serv 1979-. **ORGANIZATIONS:** Review panalist HEW 1977; consult IO Assn for Equal Emplymnt Oppor/Affirmtn Action Prof 1977; consultUniv Resrch Corp 1978; consult Nat Counc for Staff Prog & Organztnl Devel 1978; consult Mid-am Regnl Counc 1978; consult OR StateUniv 1979; consult NW Coll Personnel Assn 1979; consult Am Assn for Affirmatv Action 1980; consult Thomas E Baker & Asso 1980; consult KCRCHE 1976; HEW 1976; Mott Found 1975; CBS 1974; Serengeti Res Inst 1972; KS & MO Bds of Educ pres MO Assn for Affirmatv Action 1980-81; exec bd mem Charlie Parker Mem Found 1978-80; mem MO Black Ldrshp Assn 1977-80; exec bd mem Kansas CitySpirit of Freedom Fountn Inc 1978-80; exec bd mem Yng Men's Christian Assn 1974-76; ofcr NatUniv Ext Assn 1975-77; mem Am Affr Act Assn 1975-77;comm MO Affm Act Assn 1976-80; exec bd mem MO Comm Educ Assn 1975-80; mem KCMO Serboma Club; NAACP; exec bd mem Black Archives of Mid-am 1974-80; bd mem AFRICARE KCMO 1975-80; mem Urban Leag; bd mem KS Assn for Blind 1977-80. **HONORS/ACHIEVEMENTS:** Mott Fellowship 1970-71; VFW VIP 1972; Man of the Yr 1972; Rockefeller Fellow 1973-74; Recog for Outstndg Srvc MO Assn for Affirmtv Actn 1977; Award of Apprec Am Assn for Affirmtv Actn 1978; Valuable Serv Award Spirit of Freedom Found 1978; Citation of Excellnc TX Coll 1980; Jefferson Award Am Inst for Public Serv 1980. **MILITARY SERVICE:** AUS bandsman 1955-57. **BUSINESS ADDRESS:** Dean, Penn Valley Comm College, 3201 Southwest Trafficway, Kansas City, MO 64111.

MOTHERSHED, SPAESIO W.
Librarian. **PERSONAL:** Born Jun 30, 1925, Bloomburg, TX; married Juliene Craven; children: Spaesio, Jr, Willa Renee. **EDUCATION:** Jarvis Christn Coll, BA 1952; Syracuse U, MS 1956; N TX State U, post-grad 1963. **CAREER:** TX So U, dir libraries 1966-; Jarvis Christn Coll, head librarian 1960-66; State Library MI, cataloger 1956-60; SyracuseUniv Library, grad asst 1954-56. **ORGANIZATIONS:** Mem TX & SW Library Assns; Houston Met Archives; mem COSATI Sub-com Negro Resrch Libraries 1970-73; editor News Notes 1968-72. **HONORS/ACHIEVEMENTS:** 2 gold stars USN 1945; Engl award; Journalism award; Who's Who Among Coll & Univ Students; Who's Who S & SW. **MILITARY SERVICE:** USN 1943-46. **BUSINESS ADDRESS:** 3201 Wheeler, Houston, TX 77004.

MOTLEY, CONSTANCE BAKER
Federal judge. **PERSONAL:** Born Sep 14, 1921, New Haven; daughter of Willoughby Baker and Rachel Baker; married Joel Wilson, Jr; children: Joel Wilson III. **EDUCATION:** NYU, AB 1943; Columbia Univ, LLB 1946. **CAREER:** NAACP Legal Def & Educ Fund NYC, staff mem and associate counsel 1945-65; NY State, senator 1964-65; Borough Manhatten, pres 1965-66; US Dist Court judge 1966-82, chief judge 1982-86, sr judge 1986-. **ORGANIZATIONS:** Mem NY State Adv Cncl Empl & Unempl Ins 1958-64; mem Assoc Bar City NY, Natl Bar Assoc. **HONORS/ACHIEVEMENTS:** Elizabeth Blackwell Award Hobart & William Smith Coll 1965; hon Dr Humane Letters Smith Coll 1965; hon LLD Western Coll for Women 1965, Morehouse Coll 1965, VA State Coll 1966, Howard Univ 1966, Morgan State Coll 1966, Brown Univ 1971, Fordham Univ 1970, Atlanta Univ 1973, Iowa Wesleyan Coll 1969, Univ of Hartford 1973, Alberta Magnus Coll 1976, John Jay Inst of Criminology New York City 1979, Spelman Coll GA 1979, Trinity Coll CT 1979, Univ of Puget Sound 1980, NY Law School 1982, Univ of Bridgeport Law School 1984; Hon LLB, New York Univer School of Law, New York, NY 1985; Hon LLB, Colgate Univ Hamilton, NY, 1987; Hon LlB, Yale Univ, New Haven, Ct 1987. **BUSINESS ADDRESS:** Chief Judge, US Courthouse, Foley Square, New York, NY 10007.

MOTLEY, JOHN H.
Business executive. **PERSONAL:** Born Sep 11, 1942, Chicago, IL; married Susan; children: Nicole Johnson, Michael Johnson. **EDUCATION:** S IL Univ, BS 1964; DePaul Univ, JD 1972; John Marshall Law Sch. **CAREER:** Central N/B, credit analyst 1969-73, atty law dept 1973-75, atty & loan officer 1975; Chemical Bank, vice pres & mgr legal dept 1975-79, vice pres disthead 1979-82, sr vice pres div head 1982-. **ORGANIZATIONS:** Mem Urban Bankers Coalition; mem Natl Assn of Urban Bankers; mem Amer Bar, NY Bar, IL Bar Assocations; bd mem & treas Tougaloo Coll; bd mem UnitedNeighborhood Ctrs 1984-. **HONORS/ACHIEVEMENTS:** Banker of Year Urban Bankers Coalition 1983; Outstanding Banker Awd Natl Assn of Urban Bankers 1983. **MILITARY SERVICE:** AUS 1st lt 3 yrs. **BUSINESS ADDRESS:** Senior Vice President, Chemical Bank, 633 Third Ave, New York, NY 10017.

MOTLEY, RONALD CLARK
Physician. **PERSONAL:** Born Jan 25, 1954, Dayton, OH; son of Claude L Dunson (stepfather) and Birdella M Rhodes Motley Dunson; married Charlyn Coleman, May 06, 1983; children: Melissa Charon. **EDUCATION:** Northwestern Univ, BA 1976; Howard Univ Coll of Medicine, MD 1983. **CAREER:** Northwestern Univ, lab tech 1972-74; Industrial Biotest Labs, toxicologist and group leader skin sensitization 1976-77; Avon Products Inc, process control chemist 1977-78; Southern Illinois Univ School of Medicine, vstg asst instructor 1978-79; Howard Univ Coll of Medicine, instructor and tutor 1980-81; Howard Univ Coll of Medicine Health Scis Acad, general coord 1981-83; Mayo Clinic, general surgery internship 1983-84, urology residency 1984-88. **ORGANIZATIONS:** Equal opportunity comm Mayo Clinci 1985-; assoc mem Minority Fellows Mayo Clinic 1985-; mem Natl Medical Assoc 1985-; educ comm Dept of Urology Mayo Clinic 1987-88; bd of dirs, Family Service Agency of San Bernardino, CA 1989-. **HONORS/ACHIEVEMENTS:** Who's Who Among Students in Amer Univs & Colls 1983; Lang Book Awd, Health Scis Acad Awd, Outstanding Geriatrics Awd, Excellence in Psychiatry Awd, CV Mosby Surgery Awd Howard Univ Coll of Medicine all rec'd in 1983; also numerous presentations and articles. **BUSINESS ADDRESS:** Urologist, San Bernardino Medical Group, Inc., 1700 North Waterman Avenue, San Bernardino, CA 92404.

MOTT, STOKES E., JR.
Attorney. **PERSONAL:** Born Mar 11, 1947, Tifton, GA; married Neilda E Jackman; children: Ako K, Khari S. **EDUCATION:** Long Island Univ, BS 1968; New York Univ, MS Urban Planning 1971; Seton Hall Law Sch, JD 1979. **CAREER:** Essex Co Comm Coll, instructor; Law Office of Stokes E Mott Jr, attorney. **ORGANIZATIONS:** Mem Alpha Phi Alpha, Pennsylvania Bar Assoc, Philadelphia Bar Assoc. **BUSINESS ADDRESS:** 12 So 12th St, Ste 1535, Philadelphia, PA 19107.

MOUTON, BARBARA ANNE
Mayor. **PERSONAL:** Born Jul 15, San Francisco, CA; children: Barbara, Michelle, David, Robin, Manon, Lauriene, Martin. **EDUCATION:** Univ of San Francisco, genl educ 1957-59; San Jose State, genl educ 1965-66; Foothill Coll, genl educ english 1968-69; Stanford Univ, english major 1969-71. **CAREER:** Nairobi Day & High Sch EPA, admin 1970-79; E Palo Alto Sr Ctr, dir 1979-82; CDI East Palo Alto, consultant 1982; Comm Develop Inst, prog dir 1983-. **ORGANIZATIONS:** Council mem East Palo Alto Mun Council 1976; intern Coro Fdn's Public Affairs Prog 1977; dir East Palo Alto Com Law Proj 1982; mayor City of East Palo Alto 1983; dir World Conf of Mayors 1984; 3rd vice pres Natl Conf of Black Mayors 1985. **HONORS/ACHIEVEMENTS:** Mem EPA Citizens Comm on Incorporation 1980; editorial bd East Palo Alto Progress 1983; author "Citizen Participation in Local Govt" 1984; bd mem Bay Area Black United Fund 1984. **HOME ADDRESS:** 2575 Emmett Way, East Palo Alto, CA 94303. **BUSINESS ADDRESS:** Program Dir, Comm Development Inst, 321 Bell St PO Box 50099, East Palo Alto, CA 94303.

MOUTON, CHARLES PETER
Physician. **PERSONAL:** Born Jan 09, 1960, New Orleans, LA. **EDUCATION:** Howard Univ, BSME 1981, MD 1986. **CAREER:** Natl Inst of Health, draftsman 1979; General Motors Corp, jr engr 1979-80; Martin Marietta Co, jr engr 1981; Howard Univ Hosp, house staff physician 1986-87. **ORGANIZATIONS:** Coord Grad Student Assembly 1983-85; mem Student Natl Medical Assoc 1981-86, Amer Medical Students Assoc 1983-86, Amer Medical Assoc 1986-; dean of pledges Alpha Phi Alpha Frat 1984-85. **HONORS/ACHIEVEMENTS:** General Motors Scholar Awd 1979-81; Certificate of Appreciation Howard Univ Student Council 1983; Outstanding Young Man of Amer 1983,86; Merit Awd Grad Student Assembly 1984. **HOME ADDRESS:** 313 Univ St NW, Washington, DC 20001.

MOUTOUSSAMY, JOHN W.
Architect. **PERSONAL:** Born Jan 05, 1922, Chicago, IL; married Elizabeth; children: John, Claude, Jeanne Marie Ashe. **EDUCATION:** IL Inst of Tech, BS 1948. **CAREER:** Dubin Dubin & Moutoussamy Archt Engr, partner; Chicago. **ORGANIZATIONS:** Fellow Am Inst of Archt; bd dir chicago Urban Leag; bd of tst LoyolaUniv of Chgo; Art Inst of Chgo; mem Appeal Bd of the Chicago Dept of Environ Control; vchmn Chicago Plan Commn; consult archt Chicago Metro Fair & Expo Authority. **HONORS/ACHIEVEMENTS:** Designed Johnson Pub Co bldg opened 1971.

MOWATT, OSWALD VICTOR

Surgeon. **PERSONAL:** Born Apr 05, Spanishtown, Jamaica;married Glenda; children: Cecilia, Oswald Jr, Cyril, Raoul, Enrico, Mario. **EDUCATION:** Roosevelt U, BS 1959; LoyolaUniv Med Sch, MD 1963. **CAREER:** Surgeon, self-emplyd; St Bernard Hosp, chmn Dept Surg 1976-, consult surg 1973-; Provident Hosp, sr atdng surg 1971-; Westside VA Hosp, 1969-76; instr surg 1969-76; Proficent Hosp, chf emer serv, dir med affairs 1972-74; St Bernard Hosp, atnd surg 1970-73; Westside VA, resd surg 1969-70;Univ IL, 1967-60, chf, resd surg; gen prac 1965-67; Michale Reese Hosp, resd surg 1964-65; Cook Co Hosp, intern 1963-64. **ORGANIZATIONS:** Mem AMA 1965-; IL State Med Soc 1965-; Chicago Med Soc 1965-; Nat Med Assn; Bylaws Com of Nat Med Assn 1975-; Judicial Cncl Nat Med Assn 1975-; nominating com Nat Med Assn 1977-; Hse of Del Nat Med Assn 1974-; Assn for Hosp Med Educ 1973-74; bd dir Martin Luther King Boys Club; chmn bd dir Martin L King Boys Club 1977; chmn Bylaws com Cook Co Physicians Assn 1974-76; pres Cook Co Physicians Assn 1977; diplomate Am Bd Surgery 1976;flw Am Coll Surgeons 1977. **BUSINESS ADDRESS:** 747 W 77th St, Chicago, IL 60620.

MOXLEY, FRANK O.

Business executive. **PERSONAL:** Born Jun 29, 1908, Bowling Green, KY; son of James Moxley and Hester Moxley; married Pearlee Goodbar, Sep 21; children: Donald, Shirley, Mary. **EDUCATION:** Wilberforce Univ, BS 1930; Western KY Univ, MA 1959; E Coast Univ, EdD 1973. **CAREER:** US Steel Gary works, 1940-42; Blue Label Foods, 1946-56; State St Sch, tchr coach 1931-55; High St Sch, coach 1956-65; Bowling Green High, counselor 1965-66; Western KY Univ, 1967-72; Bowling Green Schs, elem guidance 1967-72; Human Resource Consult Inc, pres. **ORGANIZATIONS:** Mem Amer Personnel & Guidance Assn; Proj Indy 1977; KY Personnel & Guidance Assn; 3rd Dist Personnel & Guidance Assn; Elem Sch Counselor Assn; Natl, KY, 3rd Dist, Educ Assns; Phi Delta Kappa; Kappa Alpha Psi; St Health Facilities Comm; Girls Club Bd; TB Bd; exec bd, sec Model City; Whitehouse Conf for Children & Yth; pilot Secondary Guidance Prog 1958-59; past chmn seven county OEO prog; rules comm KHHSAA; Natl Negro Basketbl Assn; chmn, Cumberland Trace Legal Service 1986-. **MILITARY SERVICE:** ROTC AUS Reserve 2nd lt. **HOME ADDRESS:** 303 Chestnut St, Bowling Green, KY 42101.

MOY, CELESTE MARIE

Business executive. **PERSONAL:** Born Jul 16, 1950, Detroit, MI; married L Edward Street. **EDUCATION:** MI State Univ, BA 1972; Univ of Detroit School of Law, JD 1976. **CAREER:** IRS, reviewer & processor estate & gift tax div 1973-76; Kirk Ellis & Moy, gen civil practice 1976-78; Celeste M Moy, gen bus practice 1978-80; Alexander Hamilton Life Ins Co of Amer, attny mktg dept 1980-81; Mutual of NY, attny 1981-83; Mahomes & Assoc, assoc attny gen bus practice 1983; Warner Amex Cable Commun of Dallas, vice pres legal affairs 1984-; Sphere Cable Comm, general counsel. **ORGANIZATIONS:** Mem State Bar of TX & MI, Natl Bar Assoc, Dallas Black Laywers Assoc, Intl Business Fellows, NAACP, Alpha Kappa Alpha Sor, Dallas Aboretum and Botanical Gardens. **BUSINESS ADDRESS:** General Counsel, Sphere Cable Comm Inc, 3131 Turtle Creek Blvd, Dallas, TX 75219.

MOYE, CARLA JOHNSON

Physician. **PERSONAL:** Born Jun 09, 1955, Independence, LA; married Allen Jerone Moye'; children: Andrea J. **EDUCATION:** Southern Univ, BS 1976, Grad Sch 1977-79; Meharry Medical Coll, MD 1984. **CAREER:** Meharry Medical Coll, physician 1984-. **ORGANIZATIONS:** Junior fellow Amer Coll of Ob/Gyn. **HOME ADDRESS:** 944 21st Ave North Apt 806, Nashville, TN 37208.

MOYLER, FREEMAN WILLIAM, JR.

Manager. **PERSONAL:** Born Dec 10, 1931, New York, NY; married Aline Veronica; children: Stephanie, Joy. **CAREER:** NY Times, assoc labor relations mgr 1971-75, dir genl serv 1979, bldg mgr 1975-79, asst dir genl serv 1979, mgr 1973-. **ORGANIZATIONS:** Mem NY Times Found Inc 1971; bd dir Capital Formation Inc 1977; mem bd dir Cncl of Concerned Black Exec 1968-75. **HONORS/ACHIEVEMENTS:** Achievement Awd Natl Youth Movement 1973; Hon MLK 1977. **MILITARY SERVICE:** USAF 1951-55. **BUSINESS ADDRESS:** Manager, New York Times, 229 W 43 St, New York, NY 10036.

MSHONAJI, BIBI See BELLINGER, MARY ANN

MTOTO, PEPO See PRIESTER, JULIAN ANTHONY

MUCKELROY, WILLIAM LAWRENCE

Attorney. **PERSONAL:** Born Dec 04, 1945, Los Angeles, CA; divorced; children: William II; Heather. **EDUCATION:** Univ Texas, BA 1967; Amer Univ, MS 1970, JD 1974. **CAREER:** Prothon Cyber Ltd, dir/pres; Riggs Liquor, dir/pres; Iram Amer Investments Ltd, dir/pres/chmn of bd; Amer Univ, teaching asst; Harry Diamond Labs WA, patent adv; RCA Corp, patent counsel; Muckelroy & Assoc, patent atty; US Patent Soc Inc, patent counsel. **ORGANIZATIONS:** Past pres Intl Soc for Hybrid Microelectronics Capital Chapt; pres elect dir Natl Patent Law Assn; mem NJ, Amer Bar Assns; trustee Montclair State Coll; dir Trenton Bus Asst Corp. **HONORS/ACHIEVEMENTS:** Teaching Fellowship Amer Univ; Teaching Fellowship Amer Univ; Honors Univ TX 1963-64; Alpha Phi Alpha Scholarship; NSSFNS Scholarship; Lawrence D Bell Scholarship. **BUSINESS ADDRESS:** Patent Counsel, US Patent Soc Inc, Ewing Professional Bldg, 1901 N Olden Ave, Ext, Trenton, NJ 08618.

MUDD, LOUIS L.

Marketing specialist. **PERSONAL:** Born Jul 29, 1943, Louisville, KY; married Marcella; children: Latonya, Darron, Bryan. **EDUCATION:** TN St U, BS. **CAREER:** KY Commerce Cabinet, sr bus devel off; Brown & Williamson Tobacco Corp Louisville KY, asst to prof planning mgr; Kool Cigarettes, former asst brand mgr. **BUSINESS ADDRESS:** 1600 W Hill St, Louisville, KY 40201.

MUHAMMAD, ASKIAA

Journalist. **PERSONAL:** Born Mar 28, 1945, Yazoo City, MS; married Marita Joy Rivero; children: Nadirah I, Raafi. **EDUCATION:** San Jose State Univ, 1966-70; Los Angeles City Coll, 1965; Los Angeles State Univ, 1963. **CAREER:** Newsweek Mag, corr 1968; Multi-

Cult Prog Foothill Coll, dir 1970-72; Muhammad Speaks News, edit-in-charge 1972-75; Chicago Daily Defender, WA corr 1977-78; Black Journalism Review, founder, Pacifica Radio Natl News Bureau, diplomatic corr 1978-79, reporter 1979-80; Natl Scene Mag, editor 1978-80; The WPFW Paper, editor. **ORGANIZATIONS:** Mem Natl Press Club, Sigma Delta Chi, Washington Press Club, Capital Press Club, Natl Assoc of Black Jrnl, Soc of Professional Jrnl. **HONORS/ACHIEVEMENTS:** Fred Douglass Awd Howard Univ School of Comm 1973; Annual Awd Fred Hampton Comm Serv Awd 1975; Outstanding Journalism Achievement Awd Natl Conf BlackLawyers 1977, Univ DC 1979. **MILITARY SERVICE:** USNR e-4 (ocs) 1963-69. **BUSINESS ADDRESS:** Editor, The WPFW Paper, 700 H St NW, Washington, DC 20001.

MUHAMMAD, MARITA See RIVERO, MARITA JOY

MUHAMMAD, SHIRLEY M.

President. **PERSONAL:** Born Apr 28, 1938, Chicago, IL; married Warith Deen Muhammad; children: Laila, Ngina, Warithdeen, Sadrud-Din. **EDUCATION:** Attended, Cortez Peters Business Coll 1957, Wilson Jr Coll 1958. **CAREER:** Clara Muhammad Memorial Fund, pres 1976-. **ORGANIZATIONS:** Pres CMMEF 1976-; bd of dirs Parkway Comm House 1982, Provident Hosp 1983. **HONORS/ACHIEVEMENTS:** Outstanding Woman of the Year Provident Women's Aux 1982-; Outstanding Business Woman Parkway Comm House 1982-83; Appreciation Awd Masjid Saahin Jr Youth 1984; Key to the City Newark NJ 1987. **HOME ADDRESS:** 8752 So Cornell, Chicago, IL 60617. **BUSINESS ADDRESS:** President, Clara Muhammad Memorial, Education Foundation Inc, 634 E 79th St, Chicago, IL 60619.

MUHAMMAD, WALLACE D. (WARITH DEEN MUHAMMAD)

Chief minister, Muslim leader. **PERSONAL:** Born Oct 30, 1933, Hamtramick, MI; married Shirley; children: Laila, N'Gina, Wallace II, Sadrud-Din. **EDUCATION:** Muhammad Univ of Islam, vocational training in welding. **CAREER:** Son of Elijah Muhammad; Philadelphia Temple, minister; Arabic & Islamic studies; leader of the American Muslim Mission (formerly World Community of Al-Islam in the West, formerly Nation of Islam and the Black Muslims). **ORGANIZATIONS:** Made pilgrimage to Mecca 3 times. **HONORS/ACHIEVEMENTS:** Recip four Freedom Awards; Pioneer Award from Black Press; Humanitarian Awards from many cities & groups. **BUSINESS ADDRESS:** Hon Elijah Muhammad Masjid #2, 7351 S Stony Island, Chicago, IL 60649. *

MUHAMMAD, WARITH DEEN See MUHAMMAD, WALLACE D.

MULDROW, CATHERINE (NEE JENKINS)

Educator, nurse. **PERSONAL:** Born Feb 03, 1931, Newark; married Howard B Muldrow; children: Michelle, Howard, Jr, Victoria. **EDUCATION:** Jersey City Med Cntr, diploma 1954; Nursing State Tchrs Clge NJ, BS 1954; Seton Hall Univ, MA 1966; Tchrs Clge Columbia Univ, currently doctoral student. **CAREER:** Essex Co Clge Newark, asst prof nursing; United Hospital of Newark, assoc nursing admin 1972-74; Rutgers State Univ Coll of Nursing, instr nursing 1966-68; Rutgers, asst prof nursing 1968-72; Newark Beth Israel Hospital, pediatric suprv 1961-65; School of Nursing St Mary's Hospital, educ dir 1960-61; Newark Beth Israel Hospital, instr nursing 1957-60; St Michaels Hospital, head nurse 1954-57. **ORGANIZATIONS:** Mem Cardiac Research Team St Michaels Hosp 1954-57; pres NJ State Student Nurses Assc 1952-54; adv 1954-56; bd dir Zonta Intl 1963-70; chmn MaternalChild Nursing Prac NJ State Nurses Assc 1972-75; NJ delegate Amer Nurses Assc Conv 1974; co-owner Children's World Nursery Sch 1964-65; vice pres Comm Council 1968-70; secr bd dir Area 9 United Comm Coup 1968-72; bd trustees Essex Unit NJ Assc for Retarded Children 1969-72; chmn Comm Health Adv Comm Newark Beth Israel Hosp 1968-73; mem Sigma Theta Tau Natl Hon Soc for Nurses 1971-; consult Textbook Pediatric Nursing for Prac Nurse Delmar Publ NY 1964. **HONORS/ACHIEVEMENTS:** Keynote Speaker VA State League for Nursing Conv; pubs, "Sibling Rivalry & Ordinal Position" Rutgers Univ Press 1968, "Now Its Students of Nursing Amer " Journal of Nursing 1969. **BUSINESS ADDRESS:** Essex Co Coll Allied Health Di, 375 Osborne Terr, Newark, NJ 07112.

MULLENS, DELBERT W.

Chief executive. **CAREER:** Flint Coatings, Inc, Flint, MI, chief executive, 1983-. **BUSINESS ADDRESS:** Flint Coatings Inc, 4221 James P Cole, Flint, MI 48505. *

MULLETT, DONALD L.

Educational administrator. **PERSONAL:** Born Apr 10, 1929, New York, NY; married Mildred James; children: Barbara L, Donna M, David R James, Lisa J James. **EDUCATION:** Lincoln Univ, AB 1951; New York Univ, MBA 1952; Univ of DE, PhD 1981. **CAREER:** United Mutual Life Insurance Co, vice pres & sec 1954-62; Equitable Life Assurance Soc, cost analyst 1962-63; Lincoln Univ, comptroller 1963-69, vice pres for finance 1969-85, interim pres 1985-. **ORGANIZATIONS:** Mem Omega Psi Phi Frat Inc 1948; mem & trustee Rotary Intl 1969-; mem New York Univ Club 1981-; dir Pan African Develop Corp DC 1981-; dir Urban Educ Foundation of Philadelphia 1983-; dir & treas Lincoln Univ Foundation 1986. **HONORS/ACHIEVEMENTS:** Achievement Awd Omega Psi Phi Frat 1969. **HOME ADDRESS:** 722 Laurel Grove Ln, Pearland, TX 77584.

MULLIGAN, CAROL HARRIS

Sales representative. **PERSONAL:** Born Jun 12, 1954, West Point, MS; married Michael R Mulligan. **EDUCATION:** Cornell Coll IA, BA 1976; Keller Graduate School of Business, MBA 1978. **CAREER:** Sales representative, ADT Security Systems, 1977-; vice pres, Mulligan Automotive Consulting Serv Co, 1989-. **ORGANIZATIONS:** Co-chmn, Natl Convention NBMBAA, 1981; member, Natl Black MBA Assn, 1981-87; treasurer, Young Exec in Politics, 1986-89; pres, MICAR, 1987; co-chmn, Young Exec in Politics Awards Banquet, 1989. **HONORS/ACHIEVEMENTS:** ADT Chicago Sales Representative of the Year, 1982, 1984, 1986; Outstanding Young Women in Amer, 1984; Young Exec of the Year, Young Executives in Politics, 1986. **HOME ADDRESS:** 1800 Sutton Lane, Schaumburg, IL 60194. **BUSINESS ADDRESS:** Sales Representative, ADT Security Systems, 455 W Lake St, Elmhurst, IL 60126.

MULLIGAN, MICHAEL R.
Management consultant, president. **PERSONAL:** Born May 12, 1950, Chicago, IL; married Carol Harris. **EDUCATION:** Indiana State Univ, BS 1973. **CAREER:** Ft Wayne Comm Schools, teacher 1973-75; McDonalds Corp, restaurant mgr 1975-78; Corporate Systems, mgr 1978; Chrysler Corp, manager 1978-89; Mulligan Automotive Consulting Service Co, president, 1989-. **ORGANIZATIONS:** Mem Omega Psi Phi Frat 1971-, Professional Serv Mgrs Guild 1982-; vice pres Mulligan Tours 1982-, MICAR 1987. **HOME ADDRESS:** 1800 Sutton Lane, Schaumburg, IL 60194. **BUSINESS ADDRESS:** Management Consultant/Pres, Mulligan Automotive Consulting Service Co, PO Box 681245, Schaumburg, IL 60168.

MUMFORD, THADDEUS QUENTIN, JR.
Writer, producer. **PERSONAL:** Born Feb 08, 1951, Washington, DC; son of Dr Thaddeus Q Mumford and Sylvia J Mumford. **EDUCATION:** Hampton Univ, 1968-69; Fordham Univ, 1969-71. **CAREER:** 20th Century Fox, Los Angeles CA, writer, producer, "MASH," 1979-83; Alien Productions, Los Angeles CA, writer, supervising producer, "ALF," 1986-87; Carsey-Werner, Studio City CA, writer, supervising producer, "A Different World," 1987-88, head writer, co-executive producer, 1988-. **ORGANIZATIONS:** Writers Guild of Amer, 1971-; American Society of Composers, Artists & Performers, 1973-; Humanitas Committee, 1984; mem, NAACP, 1984; mem, Save the Children, 1986-; mem, Friends of the Friendless, 1986-; mem, Los Angeles Partnership for the Homeless, 1986-. **HONORS/ACHIEVEMENTS:** Emmy Award, "The Electric Co," 1973; Writers Guild Award, "The Alan King Show," 1974, Writers Guild Award, "MASH," 1979.

MUMPHREY, JERRY WAYNE
Professional athlete. **PERSONAL:** Born Sep 09, 1952, Tyler, TX; married Gloria; children: Tamara, Jerron. **EDUCATION:** Chapel Hill HS Tyler, TX, grad. **CAREER:** St Louis Cardinals, outfielder 1971-80; San Diego Padres, outfielder 1981; New York Yankees, outfielder 1982-83; Houston Astros, outfielder 1983-. **HONORS/ACHIEVEMENTS:** All-Star Astros Representative; Recorded a high of 6 RBI tying the club record; had a string of 27 consecutive stolen bases without being caught in 1980; Career high of 52 steals - teamed in 1980 with Gene Richards and Ozzie Smith to form the first time in Natl League history three men on one team stealing 50 or morebases; Led the Amer Assn with 44 steals in 1975; Named to the Gulf Coast League all-star team in 1971. **BUSINESS ADDRESS:** Houston Astros, PO Box 288, Houston, TX 77001.

MUNCIE, CHUCK
Professional athlete. **PERSONAL:** Born Mar 17, 1953, Uniontown, PA; married Robyn. **EDUCATION:** CA, Deg Criminology. **CAREER:** New Orlean Saints, prof ftbl plyr. **ORGANIZATIONS:** Coached Ftbl Camps for Teenagers. **BUSINESS ADDRESS:** New Orleans Saints, 6928 Saints Drive, Metairie, LA 70003.

MUNDAY, CHERYL CASSELBERRY
Clinical psychologist. **PERSONAL:** Born Jan 20, 1950, Osaka, Japan;married Reuben Alexander Munday; children: Reuben Ahmed. **EDUCATION:** Cornell Univ, BA 1972; Univ of MI, MA 1978, PhD 1985. **CAREER:** Samaritan Hospital, staff psychologist 1982-83; Metro Youth Living Ctrs, consultant 1986-; Davis Counselling Ctr, private practice 1985-; Detroit Psychiatric Inst, psychologist/rsch coord 1983-. **ORGANIZATIONS:** Mem MI Soc for Psychoanalytic Psychology 1984-, Alliance for Mental Health Serv 1984-; mem Jack and Jill of Amer Inc, Cornell Univ Alumni Assoc, Africare/Detroit Chapt. **HONORS/ACHIEVEMENTS:** Research presentation Amer Psychological Assoc Annual Convention Washington DC 1986. **HOME ADDRESS:** 18994 Birchcrest, Detroit, MI 48221.

MUNDY, DAVID L., SR.
Business executive. **PERSONAL:** Born Feb 28, 1934, Lincoln Hts, OH; married Edythe. **EDUCATION:** Wayne U;Univ of MI Labor Sch; Muhammad'sUniv of Islam. **CAREER:** MI Casting Ctr UAW Ford Motor Co Local 600 UAW, pres; Local 600 Gen Counc, 11 yrs. **ORGANIZATIONS:** Mem Mayor's Labor Com Detroit; chmn Wolverine Wkrs Allnc; mem com TULC; chmn Foundry Wkrs for Action Prince Hall Masonic Affil; NAACP; Detroit Bus & Civ Leag; coach Westside Cubs Ftbll Team. **HONORS/ACHIEVEMENTS:** Recip commn ldrshp awd Ford Motor Co 1968, 72; num awards from Walter Reuther Educ Ctr, Trade Union Ldrshp Coun & Local 600 UAW 1964-. **MILITARY SERVICE:** USAF 1950.

MUNFORD, PAUL STANLEY
Clergyman. **PERSONAL:** Born May 11, 1949, Abington, PA. **EDUCATION:** Bucks County Comm College, AA 1970; Univ of Penna, BA 1972; Princeton Theological Seminary, Master of Divinity 1975. **CAREER:** Second Macedonia Baptist Church, preaching assist and church consultant 1972-74; Philadelphia Council of Boy Scouts, assoc dist executive 1976-78; Penna Baptist State Convention, state statistician 1982-84; Greater Zion Baptist Church, pastor 1979-. **ORGANIZATIONS:** Board member OIC 1979-82; member of the Community Advisory Board for Harrisburg Community Coll 1979-83; member Educational Committee Pa Christian ChurchesUnited 1979-85; educational secretary Harrisburg Interdenominational Ministers Conf 1980-85; consultant Central Baptist Assn 1980-85; member Social Action Committee Pa Baptist Convention 1980-85; religious advisor Harrisburg School Dist; bd mem Uptown Senior Citizens; conduct a religious radio program. **HONORS/ACHIEVEMENTS:** Book review published "Natl Baptist Voice" 1983; taught in the Natl Baptist Convention Congress 1983; Vice-President Pa Baptist State Convention 1984-; teaches, conducts seminars and preaches extensively throughout the country. **BUSINESS ADDRESS:** Pastor, Greater Zion Baptist Church, 4th & Reily Sts, Harrisburg, PA 17102.

MUNOZ, ANTHONY
Professional athlete. **PERSONAL:** Born Aug 19, 1958, Ontario, CA; married DeDe; children: Michael, Michelle. **EDUCATION:** Univ of Southern CA. **CAREER:** Cincinnati Bengals, tackle 1980-. **ORGANIZATIONS:** Crusade for Life & United Appeal. **HONORS/ACHIEVEMENTS:** Cincinnati Bengals Man of the Yr 1981; All-Pro offensive tackle 3 yrs; Pro Bowl 1982, 1983 & 1984; All-Pro; NFL Lineman of the Yr 1981. **BUSINESS ADDRESS:** Cincinnati Bengals, 200 Riverfront Stadium, Cincinnati, OH 45202.

MUNSON, EDDIE RAY
Certified public accountant. **PERSONAL:** Born Aug 04, 1950, Columbus, MS; son of Ray Munson and Rosetta Moore Munson; married Delores Butler, Jun 09, 1973; children: Eddie III, Derek. **EDUCATION:** Jackson State Univ, BS 1972. **CAREER:** Peat Marwick Main & Co, partner 1972-, audit partner 1983-. **ORGANIZATIONS:** Mem, MS Soc of CPAs, 1977-, American Institute of CPAs, 1980-, MI Assn of CPAs, 1980-; bd dir, Accounting Aid Soc, 1984-, Black Family Development Inc, 1984-, Boys and Girls Clubs, 1989-; bd dir, YMCA, Detroit, MI; bd dir, Urban League, Detroit, MI; mem, Natl Assn of Black Accountants. **BUSINESS ADDRESS:** Partner, Peat Marwick Main & Co, 3400-200 Renaissance Center, Ste 3400, Detroit, MI 48243.

MUNSON, ROBERT H.
Engineer. **PERSONAL:** Born Jan 15, 1931, Detroit, MI; married Shirley C Segars; children: Renee Angelique, Rochelle Alicia. **EDUCATION:** Detroit Inst of Tech, BS 1966; MI State Univ, MBA 1977. **CAREER:** Ford Scientific Lab, metallurgical engr, 1956; Ford Motor Co, materials design engr, section supvr front end section, bumper section, body engineering office, dept mgr elec components lighting dept body and elec engrg ofc, exec engr paint corrosion and matls engrg body and elec engrg ofc, exec engr lighting bumpers and grills, exec engr advanced and pre-prog engrg, exec engr instrument panels and elec systems, chief engr North Amer design, chief plastics engr plastics products div, dir of automotive safety ofc environmental and safety engrg staff. **ORGANIZATIONS:** Mem, Amer Soc of Body Eng; Amer Metals Soc; Ford Coll Recruiting Prog; Adv Bd Coll of Engr, Univ of Detroit; eng school sponsor, NC A&T State Univ; mem Engrg Soc of Detroit, Soc of Automotive Engrs. **HONORS/ACHIEVEMENTS:** Recipt Blue Ribbon Award Amer Soc of Metals 1963; co-author tech paper A Modified Carbide Extraction Replica Technique in Transactions Qrtly 1963; co-author tech paper Metallographis Examination of the Corrosion Mechanism of Plated Plastics 1969 SAE Intl Automotive Engr Congress & Exposition in Detroit. **BUSINESS ADDRESS:** Dir, Automotive Safety Office, Ford Motor Company, The American Road, Dearborn, MI 48121.

MURCHISON, E. P.
Clergyman. **PERSONAL:** Born Jun 18, 1907, Ft Worth, TX; married Imogene O Ford; children: Marcia Pierce, Elleen Yancy. **EDUCATION:** Paine Coll, 1925, DD (Hon) 1956; Clark Coll, AB 1930; Gammon Theol Sem, BD 1930; Boston Univ, AM 1932; Univ of Chgo, Postgrad 1932-33,38-44; Miles Coll, LLD (Hon) 1971; MS Indust Coll, DLitt 1950. **CAREER:** St John CME Church Atlanta, pastor 1926; CME Church Conyers GA, pastor 1927-28; Israel CME Church Jackson GA, pastor 1929; Elizabeth Chapel Dallas, pastor 1930; St Mark Church Springfield MA, pastor 1931-32; TX Coll Tyler, head dept religion & philosophy 1933-35; CME Church, gen dir leadership ed 1935-38; Jubilee Temple Chgo, pastor 1938-41; Chicago Dist CME Church, presiding elder 1941-46; Christian Index, editor 1946-58; CME Church, bishop 1958, presiding bishop over AL, FL 1958-70, OH & KY Conf 1970-78, MI MO IL & KS Confs 1978-, sr bishop, chief exec 1978-. **ORGANIZATIONS:** Patron bishop Womans Missionary Council; org CME Church Nigeria, Ghana, Africa 1959; founder CME Secondary School Accra Ghana; mem 1st Assembly World CouncilChurch Amsterdam Holland Nairobi; sec leadership ed div Fed Council Churches; charter mem, exec vice pres Natl Council Chs Amer; mem exec comm Consultation on Church Union, World Meth Council; mem Mayors Adv Comm Birmingham AL 1965; assoc Martin Luther King Jr Birmingham 1962-68; trustee, chmn bd Phillips School Theol; trustee Interdenom Theol Ctr Collins Chapel Hosp Memphis; mem KY Col; pres Natl Frat Council Chs Amer. **HONORS/ACHIEVEMENTS:** Author "Critical Analysis of the Elijah & Elisha Biblical Miracles" 1933, "A Critical Analysis of the Materialistic Concepts of Imortality" 1945, "Why I Believe in God" 1964.

MURPHY, ALVIN HUGH
Business executive. **PERSONAL:** Born Feb 22, 1930, Boston, MA; married Bobby Joan Tolbert; children: Marguerite Joan, Bernadette Joan, Annette Joan. **EDUCATION:** The Cath Univ of Amer, BME 1951; Univ Santa Clara, MBA 1964. **CAREER:** Lockheed Missiles & Space Co Inc, prog engr; DeAnza College, instr 1969-; Lockheed Aircraft, assc engr 1951-54; US Naval Surface Weapon Center White Oak Silver Spring MD, mech engr 1955-59. **ORGANIZATIONS:** Mem Amer Soc of Mech Engrs; secr Reliability Stress Analysis & Failure Prevention Comm; mem Amer Def Prepardness Assc; past chmn Reliability Tech Section; mem exec bd Quality & Reliability Div Amer Soc for Quality Control; fellow grade prog chmn Reliability Div; mem bd dir San Jose Symphony Assc; reg prof engr fellow election Amer Soc for Quality Controls. **BUSINESS ADDRESS:** PO Box 504, Sunnyvale, CA 94088.

MURPHY, ARTHUR G.
Attorney. **PERSONAL:** Born Jul 26, 1929, Baltimore; married Margaret Humphries; children: Terri Denise, Arthur Grant, Lynn Yvette. **EDUCATION:** Morgan State Clge, BA 1951; Univ MD Law Sch, LLB 1955. **CAREER:** Williams, Smith & Murphy, atty; Mem House of Delegates 41 Legislative Dist; Gov Mandel, spec asst 1969-73; US Atty, 1966-69; Dist MD, US atty 1962-66; Williams & Murphy, prac of Law 1958-62. **ORGANIZATIONS:** Mem bd dir Legal Aid Bureau; Travel Aid Soc; chmn Legal Srv to Indigent; mem MD State Bar Assc; Monumental City Bar Assc; Baltimore City Bar Assc; Jr Bar Assc; mem NAACP; Baltimore Urban League; YMCA; various assc & com. **HONORS/ACHIEVEMENTS:** Beta Sigma Tau Achievement Award. **BUSINESS ADDRESS:** Ste 310 Tower Bldg, Baltimore, MD 21202.

MURPHY, BEATRICE M. (BEATRICE MURPHY CAMPBELL)
Author, editor, journalist, poet, public speaker. **PERSONAL:** Born Jun 25, 1908, Monessen, PA; children: Alvin. **CAREER:** Secretary, 1932-41; columnist and book reviewer, 1933-41; stenographer, 1942; Office of Price Administration, Washington DC, correspondence reviewer; Venterans Administration, Washington DC, stenographer and purchase order writer, 1947-59; DC Statewide Health Coordinating Council, member, 1978-84; member of health care advisory committees on blindness and aging; public speaker, poet. **ORGANIZATIONS:** Exec dir, Beatrice M. Murphy Foundation at Martin Luther King Library, 1977-; mem, 1975-83, mem of advisory council, Retired Senior Volunteer Program, 1984-85. **HONORS/ACHIEVEMENTS:** Editor of Negro Voices: An Anthology of Contemporary Verse, 1938; author of Love Is a Terrible Thing, 1945; editor of Ebony Rhythm: An Anthology of Contemporary Negro Verse, 1948; coauthor of The Rocks Cry Out, 1976; founder of Negro Bibliographic and Research Center (now Minority Research Center), 1965; founder of Volunteer Counsel for the Blind, 1970; Meritorious Public Service Award, Mayor of Washington DC, 1981; Meritorious Service Award, State Health and DevelopmentAgency, 1984; Super Senior Award, Iona House Senior Service Center, 1986; certificate of appreciation, American Foundation for the Blind, 1988; nomination for DC Commission Women's Hall of Fame, 1989. **HOME ADDRESS:** 2737 Devonshire Place N W #222, Washington, DC 20008.

MURPHY, CHARLES A.
Physician/surgeon. **PERSONAL:** Born Dec 29, 1932, Detroit, MI; son of Charles L Murphy and Hazel C Robinson Murphy; married Sandra Marie Scott-Murphy; children: Charles A III. **EDUCATION:** Wayne State Univ, 1953; Coll of Osteopathic Med and Surgery, DO 1957; Flint Osteopathic Hospital, Internship 1958. **CAREER:** Martin Place Hospital chief of staff 1964-65; Art Center Hospital, chief of staff 1971-73; Wayne County Osteopathic Assn, past pres 1977-79; Detroit Police Dept, sr police surgeon 1977-79; CA Murphy DO PC, physician surgeon 1958-; Michigan Assn of Osteopathic Physicians and Surgeons, pres. **ORGANIZATIONS:** Bd mem Michigan Osteopathic Assn 1981-, Michigan Osteopathic Medical Center 1972-, Michigan Health Maintenance Org 1978-; clinical prof Michigan State Univ Coll Osteopathic Med 1973-; bd mem Michigan Peer Review Org 1985; House of Delgate Amer Osteopathic Assn 1975-, Michigan Osteopathic Assn 1970-; Osteopathic Rep Central Peer Review Comm Michigan Dept Health. **HONORS/ACHIEVEMENTS:** Cert Amer Osteopathic Bd of Gen Prac 1973; Fellow Award Amer Coll Gen Prac 1974; memb Psi Sigma Alpha (Schlst Hnry Frat) 1955. **BUSINESS ADDRESS:** President, CA Murphy DO Professional Corp, 12634 E Jefferson, Detroit, MI 48215.

MURPHY, CHARLES WILLIAM
Insurance company executive. **PERSONAL:** Born Dec 06, 1929, Kinston, NC; son of Edgar D Murphy, Sr and Blanche Burden Murphy; married Geneva McCoy, Aug 09, 1954; children: Charles, Jr, Donald Seth, Deanna Faye, Bryan Keith. **EDUCATION:** NC A&T State Univ, Greensboro, NC, BS, bio science/chemistry, 1954; attended Butler Univ, Indianapolis, IN, 1968-69. **CAREER:** City-County Govt, Indianapolis, IN, mgmt analyst, 1974-75; Indianapolis Life Insurance Co, Indianapolis, IN, vice pres office admin, 1975-. **ORGANIZATIONS:** Personnel dir, Indianapolis Chapter Admin Mgmt Soc, 1975-; subscribing life mem, Indianapolis Chapter NAACP, 1979-; basileus, Zeta Phi Chapter, Omega Psi Phi Fraternity, 1979-81; exec comm, Administrative Servs Comm Life Office Mgmt Assn (LOMA,) 1979-; Econ Devel Comm, Indianapolis Chapter Urban League, 1984-; bd of trustees, N United Methodist Church, 1985-; mem, Indiana Minority Supplier Devel Council, 1985-; volunteer action center, United Way Bd, 1988-; exec comm, Interfaith Housing Bd, 1988-. **HONORS/ACHIEVEMENTS:** Achievement in Military, NC A&T State Univ, 1974; Advancement of Minority Enterprises, Minority Supplier Devel Council, 1987, Achievement in Business, Center for Leadership Devel, 1988. **HOME ADDRESS:** 7016 Cricklewood Rd, Indianapolis, IN 46220.

MURPHY, CLYDE EVERETT
Attorney. **PERSONAL:** Born Jun 26, 1948, Topeka, KS; married G Monica Jacobs; children: Jamal Everett, Akua Edith. **EDUCATION:** Yale Coll New Haven, BA 1970; Columbia Univ Sch of Law NY, JD 1975. **CAREER:** Kings Co Addictive Disease Hosp, asst dir 1970-72; Vassar Coll, lectr 1981-84; NAACP Legal Defense & Educ Fund Inc, asst counsel 1975-. **HONORS/ACHIEVEMENTS:** Charles Evans Hughes Fellow Columbia Univ Sch of Law 1973-75. **BUSINESS ADDRESS:** Assistant Council, NAACP, Legal Defense & Education Fund, 99 Hudson St, Ste 1600, New York, NY 10013.

MURPHY, DELLA MARY
Law enforcement. **PERSONAL:** Born Nov 01, 1935, Mississippi; married Robert L Murphy; children: Peggy A Cruise. **EDUCATION:** Attended TN, MS, & IL Colleges. **CAREER:** Woolworth Five & Dime Store, cook 1956; St Clair Cty Vstg Nurse Inc, health aide 1964; East St Louis IL PD, juvenile spec 2 police matron. **ORGANIZATIONS:** Elected trustee East St Louis Twp Office 1981, 1985; charter mem East St Louis Volunteer's 1982; pres East St Louis Women's Club 1984; mem Intl Juvenile Officer Assoc, Knights of St Peter Claver St Moncia Court 260, St Joseph Roman Catholic Church. **HONORS/ACHIEVEMENTS:** Commun Serv Mental Health Assoc 1967, Natl Council of Negro Woman 1983, Elks Venus Temple # 1042 1983; Humanitarian City of E St Louis IL Mayor Carl Officer 1983; Outstanding Citizen Metro-East Ch Woman of Achievement 1985. **HOME ADDRESS:** 1383 North 39th St, East St Louis, IL 62204.

MURPHY, DONALD RICHARD
Attorney. **PERSONAL:** Born Aug 01, 1938, Johnstown, PA; married Carol Handy; children: Steven, Michael, Richard. **EDUCATION:** Wilberforce Univ, BA Econ 1960; NY Law Schl, JD 1969. **CAREER:** IBM Corp, acct supr 1963-66; Chem Bank of NY, oper mgr 1966-69; Soc Natl Bank, vice pres 1969-73; Sherwin Williams Co, staff atty asst dir of labor rel 1973-83; atty at law. **ORGANIZATIONS:** Mem EEO Sub Comm Amer Bar Assn 1974-; bd dir Health Hill Hosp 1970-78; bd trustees United Way Srvs 1980-; Cleveland Comm OH Fnd for Independent Coll 1970-; adv mem United Negro Coll Fund 1974-82; Cuyahoga City Bar Assn 1972-. **HONORS/ACHIEVEMENTS:** Distinguished Service Award, Outstanding Alumnus of Year Wilberforce Univ 1972; First Black recruited for IBM Mgmt and Training Course 1963. **MILITARY SERVICE:** AUS 1st lt 1959-62; Grad Army Adj General Schl 1960. **HOME ADDRESS:** 2987 Ludlow Rd, Shaker Heights, OH 44120. **BUSINESS ADDRESS:** Attorney, Forest City Enterprises, Inc, 10800 Brookpark Road, Cleveland, OH 44130-1199.

MURPHY, DWAYNE KEITH
Professional athlete. **PERSONAL:** Born Mar 18, 1955, Merced, CA; married Brenda Grimes; children: Dwayne, Scott, Christina. **CAREER:** Outfldr. **ORGANIZATIONS:** Bsbl bskbl ftbl at Antelope Vly H; selected All-League all 3 sports; shtstp bsbl; Little Leag, Pony Leag, Colt Leag/Am Leg bsbl Lancaster CA area; turned down AZ State ftbl schlshp sign with A'S. **HONORS/ACHIEVEMENTS:** AL behind Minnesota's Puckett; 5th straight Gold Glove for Fldg Excell; first Gold Glove awd Centrfld Ply; 2nd Gold Glove awd in 1981; named Sporting News All-Star tm led AL 15 game RBI'S; 3rd Gold Glover awd 1982; Won 4th Gold Glove. **BUSINESS ADDRESS:** Oakland A's, Oakland Alameda Cty Col, Oakland, CA 94621.

MURPHY, EDDIE
Comedian. **PERSONAL:** Born Apr 03, 1961, Brooklyn, NY. **CAREER:** Saturday Night Live NBC TV, actor, writer 1980; 48 Hours, co-star; Trading Places, star; Beverly Hills Cop and Beverly Hills Cop II, star; Eddie Murphy Raw,star; Coming to America, co-star; also recording artist. **HONORS/ACHIEVEMENTS:** Grammy Awd for Comeday Album of the Year "Delirious"; Recipient 1985 Dramatic Arts Award for achievements, talent and believability as a movie actor, and for starring role in "Beverly Hills Cop". **BUSINESS ADDRESS:** International Creative Mngmt, Hildy Gottlieb Agent, 8899 Beverly Blvd, Los Angeles, CA 90048.

MURPHY, FRANCES L., II (MRS. CHARLES J. CAMPBELL)
Educator, publisher. **PERSONAL:** Born Oct 08, Baltimore, MD; daughter of Carl J Murphy and Vashti Turley Murphy; children: Frances Murphy Draper, Dr James E Wood Jr, Susan M Wood Barnes, David Campbell. **EDUCATION:** Univ of WI Madison, BA 1944; Coppin State Coll, BS 1958; Johns Hopkins Univ, MEd 1963; Univ of Southampton England, Study Tour 1966. **CAREER:** Morgan State Coll, dir news bureau asst prof 1964-71; Afro Amer Newspapers, chmn bd, CEO 1971-74; Univ of MD Baltimore Cty, visiting prof 1974-75; State Univ Coll at Buffalo NY, lecturer to assc prof 1975-; Howard Univ, visiting prof 1984-85; Washington Afro-Amer Newspaper, publisher 1986-; Howard Univ, assoc prof 1985-. **ORGANIZATIONS:** Ex com mem bd dir Afro Amer Newspapers 1985-; advisory bd Howard Univ Partnership Inst 1985-, Crisis Magazine NAACP 1979-; mem exec comm Md Study Comm on Structure and Governance of Educ 1973-75; natl bd dir NAACP 1983-; bd trustees Spec Contribution Fund NAACP 1976-83, State Coll of MD 1973-75; mem MD Bicentennial Comm 1973-75; mem Capital Press Club, Sigma Delta Chi. **HONORS/ACHIEVEMENTS:** Ebony Mag 100 Most Influential Black Amer 1973-74; Fellowship Kiplinger Foundation 1980; SUC Buffalo Faculty Grant to write A Beginning Student's Guide to Word Star 1983. **HOME ADDRESS:** 5709 First Street NW, Washington, DC 20011. **BUSINESS ADDRESS:** Assoc Prof, HowardUniv Afro/Amer Nwspr, 2002 11th St NW, Washington, DC 20001.

MURPHY, GENE
Educator. **PERSONAL:** Born Mar 15, 1956, Mar, WV. **EDUCATION:** Marshall Univ, BA 1979; San Diego State Univ, WV Univ, grad work. **CAREER:** Educator, 7 years. **ORGANIZATIONS:** Mem Alpha Phi Alpha Frat 1978-; pres Black Pursuit Inc. **HONORS/ACHIEVEMENTS:** Co-author Black Pursuit Study Guide and co-creator Black Pursuit Computer and Board game 1985; appeared twice in USA Today 1986; creator of over twenty educational games and products 1986; recognized by ABC and NBC radio in NY as a Black History spokesperson 1986; motivational tape series called "The 10-2 System of Success; If It Is To Be It Is Up To Me" 1986; poet Amer Anthology; guest "700 Club" 1987. **BUSINESS ADDRESS:** PO Box 5524, Huntington, WV 25701.

MURPHY, GEORGE B., JR.
Educator, editor. **PERSONAL:** Born Oct 26, 1905, Baltimore; married Lillie; children: George B. **EDUCATION:** Dickinson Coll, BS 1927; Columbia U, grad work 1931. **CAREER:** Afro-american Newspapers, natl rep; Allen U, instructor 1927-30; Wash Afro Amer, managing editor 1931-38; NAACP, pub relations, dir 1938-41; Nat Negro Congress, adm, sec 1941-43. **ORGANIZATIONS:** Mem Nat Capital Press Club; IBPOE W 1926; Nat Council Am Soviet Friendship; mem Dusable Museum; New World Review Mag; Nat Conference Artists. **HONORS/ACHIEVEMENTS:** Author, Journey Soviet Union. **MILITARY SERVICE:** AUS sgt 1943-45. **BUSINESS ADDRESS:** Wash Afro Amer, 2002 11 St NW, Washington, DC 20001.

MURPHY, HARRIET LOUISE M.
Judge. **PERSONAL:** Born in Atlanta, GA; married Patrick H Murphy; children: Charles Wray. **EDUCATION:** Spelman Coll, AB 1949; Atlanta Univ, Masters 1952; Johns Hopkins School, school of advanced int studies 1954; Univ of TX Law School, JD 1969; Univ of Gratz, Austria 1971. **CAREER:** Fulton Co, GA, hs tchr 1949-54; Southern Univ, tchr 1954-56; Prairie View A&M Univ, teacher 1956-60; Womack Sr High, high school teacher 1960-66; Houston-Tillotson Coll, prof of govt 1967-78; City of Austin, assoc judge 1978-. **ORGANIZATIONS:** Mem Delta Sigma Theta Soror 1964-; bd mem Greater Austin Council on Alcoholism 1970-; bd mem Austin Area Urban League 1978-; mem Links Inc 1982-; bd mem Judicial Council NBA; bd mem TX Municipal Courts Found; mem Natl Bar Assn, TX Bar Assn; bd mem Austin Black Lawyers Assn; mem J Travis Co WomenLawyers Assn; mem Natl Cncl of Negro Women. **HONORS/ACHIEVEMENTS:** Appointed to two year term US State Dept Adv Council on African Affairs 1970; Outstanding Sorority Woman Delta Sigma Theta Sor 1974; first black woman to beappointed a permanent judge in TX 1974; first black woman democratic presidential elector for TX 1976; appointed Goodwill Ambassador State of TX 1976; most outstanding class member by class of Spelman Coll 1984. **BUSINESS ADDRESS:** Associate Judge, Austin Municipal Court, 700 East 7th St, Austin, TX 78701.

MURPHY, IRA H.
Attorney. **PERSONAL:** Born Sep 08, 1928, Memphis; married Rubye L Meekins. **EDUCATION:** TN State Univ, BS; City Clge of NY, atnd; NY Univ, grad sch bus; NY Univ Schl of Law, LLB, LLM. **CAREER:** Gen law prac 1956-; Riverside San & Hosp Nashville, acct; Geeter HS, commerce tchr. **ORGANIZATIONS:** State Rep 86, 87, 88, 89, 90, & 91st Gen Assem; chmn Labor Com House Rep 87th Gen Assem; chmn Jud Com House Rep 88, 89, 90 & 91st Gen Assem del Limited Constis Conv 1971; Mem Slpha Phi Alpha; Kappa Delta Pi; Elks; Masons; Shriners; past pres 26 Ward Civic Club; former legal adv Bluff City Coun Civic Clubs; legal adv IBPOE of W of TN. **MILITARY SERVICE:** AUS.

MURPHY, JEANNE CLAIRE
Volunteer. **PERSONAL:** Born Nov 07, 1929, Chicago, IL; married Col Donald G Murphy (deceased); children: Judith C. **EDUCATION:** Univ of Chicago, BA 1948; Eastern Michigan Univ, EdB 1949; Northwestern Univ, MA 1951. **ORGANIZATIONS:** Bd dir Fairfax Red Cross; cred chair GSCNC; mem AKA Sor 1949-, OWL 1984-; bd of dirs Vol Action Ctr Fx Cty VA; mem BWUFA, NAACP, Urban League; memWashington DC Metro Red Cross Consortium. **HONORS/ACHIEVEMENTS:** Thanks Badge/Adult Appreciation Pin GSUSA; Special Recognition Awd Red Cross; Volunteer Recognition Fairfax Cty VA; Gold Pin GS Assoc 54. **HOME ADDRESS:** 8902 Queen Elizabeth Blvd, Annandale, VA 22003.

MURPHY, JOHN H., III
Business executive. **PERSONAL:** Born Mar 02, 1916, Baltimore, MD; married Camay; children: Sharon, Daniel. **EDUCATION:** Temple U, BS 1937; Collumia U, Press Inst, 1952, 1971. **CAREER:** Washington Tribune, mgr 1937-61; Washington Afro-Amer, purchasing agent, asst bus mgr, bus mgr, chmn bd of dir 1974-. **ORGANIZATIONS:** Mem Churchman's Club; standing comm Diocese of MD; vestryman St James Episcopal Church; adv bd Morgan State Univ; mem School of Business, Morgan State Univ Cluster Prog, Sigma Pi Phi, Omega Psi Phi; bd mem Amalgamated Publs Inc, Natl Newspaper Publs Assoc, Council on Equal Bus Oppty, Natl Aquarium at Baltimore, Provident Hospital, Baltimore School for the Arts, Baltimore City Literacy Commiss. **HONORS/ACHIEVEMENTS:** City of Baltimore Citizen Awd 1977; Publisher of the Year Awd Univ of DC 1979; Father of the Year Awd Redeemer's Palace Baltimore MD 1980; Cert MD Comm on Sickle Cell Anemia 1980;

US Dept of Commerce Awd 1980; Appreciation Awd Race Relations Inst Fisk Univ 1981; Disting Citizens Public Serv Awd Coppin State Coll 1983; Hon degree Doctor of Humane Letters Towson State Univ 1984. **BUSINESS ADDRESS:** Chairman, Board of Dir, Afro-American Newspaper, 628 N Eutaw St, Baltimore, MD 21201.

MURPHY, JOHN MATTHEW, JR.
Dentist, president. **PERSONAL:** Born Mar 12, 1935, Charlotte, NC; divorced; children: John Matthew III, Brian Keith. **EDUCATION:** Morgan State Coll, BS 1959; MeHarry Med Coll School of Dentistry, DDS 1965; VA Hosp, Cert 1966. **CAREER:** Meharry Med Coll School of Dentistry, rsch assoc dept of orthodontics 1966; VA Center Dayton OH, staff dentist 1967-70; Charles Drew Health Ctr Dayton OH, clinical dir dentistry 1971-73; Metrolina Urban Health Initiative Charlotte NC, consult dentistry 1979; Private practice, gen dentist 1973-. **ORGANIZATIONS:** Pres elect Dayton Hosp Mgmt Assoc 1970-73; mem Charlotte C of C 1975-, Charlotte Bus League 1979-; treas Martin Luther King Mem Comm 1976-; council comm chmn Boy Scouts of Amer 1978; mem Sigma Pi Phi 1980. **HONORS/ACHIEVEMENTS:** Scroll of Honor Omega Psi Phi 1970; Cert of Appreciation Boy Scouts of Amer 1972; Fellow Royal Soc of Health 1974-; Fellow Acad of Gen Dentistry 1980. **MILITARY SERVICE:** AUS spec 4; 1959-61. **BUSINESS ADDRESS:** Dentist, 951 S Independence Blvd, Charlotte, NC 28202.

MURPHY, MARGARET HUMPHRIES
Administrator, government official. **PERSONAL:** Born in Baltimore, MD; married Arthur G Murphy (deceased); children: Terri, Grant, Lynn. **EDUCATION:** Coppin St Coll, BS 1952, ME; Morgan St Coll. **CAREER:** MD St, del 1978-; Baltimore City Public School, educ assn 1978-, teacher 1952-78. **ORGANIZATIONS:** Mem Pub Sch Tchrs Assn 1952-; mem MD St Tchrs Assn 1952-; mem Nat Ed Assn; mem NAACP; Lambda Kappa Mu; Red Cross; sec Leg Black Caucus; treasOrg of Wmn Lgsltrs; mem Delta Sigma Theta, Forest Park Neighborhood Assn; chmn Baltimore City Health Sub-Committee; bd mem Threshold Inc. **BUSINESS ADDRESS:** Delegate, Maryland General Assembly, 314 Lowe Bldg, Annapolis, MD 21401.

MURPHY, MICHAEL MCKAY
Business executive. **PERSONAL:** Born Aug 13, 1946, Fayetteville, NC; son of Charles L Murphy and Eleanor M Murphy; married Gwendolyn Ferguson; children: L Mark. **EDUCATION:** St Louis Univ, BS in Commerce 1964-68. **CAREER:** John Hancock Insurance Co, life underwriter 1968-71; Ford Motor Co, bus mgmt specialist 1971-75; Dunkin Donuts, purchasing mgr 1975-79; dir of quality control 1979-. **ORGANIZATIONS:** Canton, MA Board of Health, vice chmn 1986, chmn 1988-89; mem, Phi Beta Sigma Fraternity, Inc, Zeta Kappa Sigma Chapter, pres 1988-89; past pres, Blue Hill Civic Assn. **HOME ADDRESS:** 8 Flintlocke Ln, Canton, MA 02021. **BUSINESS ADDRESS:** Dir of Quality Control, Dunkin' Donuts of America, P O Box 317, Randolph, MA 02368.

MURPHY, RAYMOND M.
Government official. **PERSONAL:** Born Dec 13, 1927, St Louis, MO; married Lynette; children: Clinton, Krystal, Leslie, Raymond, Anita, James, Brandon, Alicia. **EDUCATION:** Attended, Detroit Inst of Tech, Wayne State Univ. **CAREER:** House of Representatives State of MI, representative elected Nov 2, 1982, re-elected for 3rd term 1986-. **ORGANIZATIONS:** Mem Natl Black Caucus of State Legislators; lifetime mem NAACP; imperial grand cncl Ancient Arabic Orders; Nobles of the Mystic Shrine; mem MI LegislativeBlack Caucus; exec bd mem Detroit Transit Alternative; mem Metro Elks Lodge; mem Eureka Temple No 1. **HONORS/ACHIEVEMENTS:** Legislator of the Year Minority Women Network 1987. **HOME ADDRESS:** 1724 West Grand Blvd, Detroit, MI 48210. **BUSINESS ADDRESS:** Representative, House of Representatives, 115-1/2 Capitol Bldg, Lansing, MI 48909.

MURPHY, RIC
Government official. **PERSONAL:** Born Jul 17, 1951, Boston, MA; son of Robert H Murphy and Joan Cornwall-Murphy. **EDUCATION:** Boston State Coll, BS 1973; Boston Univ Metro Coll, MBA 1976; Harvard Univ Kennedy School, Cert 1986. **CAREER:** City of Boston Public Schools, teacher 1973-76, team consult 1976-78, principal 1978-79, asst community supt 1979-82; Commonwealth of MA State Office of Affirmative Action, dir 1983-; Commonwealth of Massachusetts, Boston, MA, state purchasing Agent 1987-; Commonwealth of Massachusetts, Boston, MA, dir state office of affirmative action 1983-87. **ORGANIZATIONS:** Bd mem NAACP Boston Chap 1978-; vice pres Fort Hill Civic Assoc 1983-; mem Piggy Bank 1984-; mem adv bd Gannett Publ WLVI Channel 56 1985-; mem bd dir New England Hosp 1985-; chmn, principal Express Air Inc 1986-. **HONORS/ACHIEVEMENTS:** Outstanding Leadership Award MA House of Reps 1980; Outstanding Serv to Community Award NAACP 1980; Community Dist Adv Council Award 1981; Outstanding Community Service, Boston Chapter, National Conference of Christian and Jews 1987. **HOME ADDRESS:** 41 Highland Park Ave, Boston, MA 02120. **BUSINESS ADDRESS:** State Purchasing Agent, Commonwealth of Massachusetts, One Ashburton Place, Boston, MA 02120.

MURPHY, ROBERT L.
Educator. **PERSONAL:** Born Dec 23, 1935, Kinston, NC; married Gloria Walters. **EDUCATION:** NC Central Univ, 1962; NC Central Univ, addl study; E Carolina Univ, addl study. **CAREER:** Lenoir Co Bd of Educ, math lab coord; Phys Educ Coord; W Elm Jr HS Goldsboro, phys educ tchr & coach; Frederick Douglass HS Elm City. **ORGANIZATIONS:** Mem NEA; NC Assc of Educators; AHPER; NC Athletic Officials Assc; mem Amer Leg; NC Central Univ Alumni Assc; omega Psi Phi; Basilus Nu Alpha. **MILITARY SERVICE:** AUS 1954-57. **BUSINESS ADDRESS:** Savannah Middle School, Rt 2 Box 199, Grifton, NC 28530.

MURPHY, ROMALLUS O.
Attorney, educator. **PERSONAL:** Born Dec 18, 1928, Oakdale, LA; son of James Murphy and Mary Celeste Collins Murphy; married Gale L Bostic; children: Natalie, Kim, Romallus, Jr, Lisa, Verna, Christian. **EDUCATION:** Howard Univ, BA 1951; Univ NC, JD 1956. **CAREER:** Pvt law prac 1956-62; Erie Human Rel Commn, exec dir 1962-65; Mitchell & Murphy, 1965-70; Mayor's Comm Rel Committee, exec secr 1968; Shaw Univ, spec asst to pres 1968-70; Shaw Coll at Detroit, pres 1970-82; Gen Counsel NC State Conf of Branches NAACP; gen practice emphasis on civil rights; private practice, atty 1983-. **ORGANIZATIONS:** Mem Intermittent consult conciliator 1966-69; spec asst, vice pres Shaw Univ 1968-70; EEOC Wash DC 1968-; pres Shaw Coll Detroit 1970-; mem Amer Arbitration Assoc, Arbitrators & Community Dispute Settlement Panel, ACE, AAHE, NBL, NEA, Positive Futures Inc, Task Force Detroit Urban League Inc, NAACP; bd mem Metro Fund Inc; mem Central Governing Bd & Educ Com Model Neighborhood Agency; charter mem Regional Citizens Inc; mem Greensboro Task Force One; bd mem Good News Jail & Prison Ministry; trustee, sec trust bd Shiloh Baptist Church; pres Laymen's League Shiloh Baptist Church; mem Omega Psi Phi; bd mem Greensboro Br NAACP; mem Foreign Gravel for Intl Commun Agency & other govt agencies in South Africa, Zambia, Nigeria & Kenya; partic Smithsonian Inst Travel Seminar in India; mem NC Assn Amer Bar Assn, NC Black Lawyers Assn. **HONORS/ACHIEVEMENTS:** Omega Man of the Year 1968; Citation of Appreciation 1972; Detroit Howardite for Year Howard Univ Alumni 1974; Key to City Positive Futures Inc New Orleans 1974; Citizen of the Year Awd Omega Psi Phi 1977; Community Serv Awd Greensboro Br NAACP 1985; Tar Heel of the Week NC. **MILITARY SERVICE:** USAF 1st lt 1951-53. **BUSINESS ADDRESS:** Attorney, PO Box 20383, Greensboro, NC 27420.

MURPHY, WILLIAM EDWARD, JR.
Elected official. **PERSONAL:** Born Sep 04, 1941, Fayetteville, NC; married Marian Elizabeth Isler; children: Badru. **EDUCATION:** Morehouse Coll, BS 1963; Atlanta Univ, Grad Study Biology 1963-64 & 1965-66; Meharry Medical Coll, Medical Sch 1964-65. **CAREER:** Emory Univ, researcher (eye) 1966-68; Intl Business Machines, computer programmer/staff asst 1968-82, mgr admin serv 1982-. **ORGANIZATIONS:** Mem Alpha Phi Alpha Frat; mem Univ Club of White Plains; mem Ridgeview Congregational Church; mem White Plains Greenburgh NAACP; White Plains Bd of Educ mem 1979-84, vice pres 1982-83, pres 1983-84. **HONORS/ACHIEVEMENTS:** Special Awd St Paul's College Natl Alumni 1982-83; Appreciation Awd NY State Congress of Parents & Teachers 1984; Appreciation Awd Concerned Black Parents of White Plains 1984; Special Awd White Plains Bd of Educ 1984. **BUSINESS ADDRESS:** Manager of Administrative Serv, Intl Business Machines, 1000 Westchester Ave, White Plains, NY 10604.

MURRAIN, GODFREY H.
Attorney. **PERSONAL:** Born Mar 14, 1927, New York, NY; son of Walter Herbert Murrain and Ellouise Lorraine "Pearl" Jones; married Peggy Gray; children: Michelle. **EDUCATION:** Howard Univ, attended 1948-49; NY Univ, BS 1951; Brooklyn Law Sch, LLB, JD 1955. **CAREER:** Treasury Dept, IRS agent 1953-58; Godfrey H Murrain Esq, atty counsellor at law tax consult advising & counseling indivudal corp estates 1958-. **ORGANIZATIONS:** Mem Amer Arbitration Assn, NY Co Lawyers Assn, Metropolitan Black Bar Assn, Natl Bar Assn; mem Amer Civil Liberties Union; elder Hollis Presbyterian Church; Task Force for Justice Presbytery of the City of NY; adv bd Borough of Manhattan Comm Coll 1970; mem sec gen counsel One Hundred Black Men Inc; bd trustees Great Neck Library; bd mem NAACP of Great Neck Manhasset Port Washington Br; mem Departmental Disciplinary Comm First Judicial Dept Supreme Court of the State of NY. **MILITARY SERVICE:** AUS 1945-46. **BUSINESS ADDRESS:** Counselor at Law, Godfrey H Murrain, Esquire, 225 Broadway, New York, NY 10007.

MURRAIN, WILLIAM A.
Educator. **PERSONAL:** Born Jan 11, 1945, Panama, CZ. **EDUCATION:** BA 1968; MA 1972. **CAREER:** Western MI U, dir minority student servs; Western MI U, adminstr 1971-; Benton Harbor Pub Sch MI, adminstr 1968-71; Lake Michigan Jr Coll, instr 1971-72; Richard & Asso Consulting Firm, ptnr 1971-73. **ORGANIZATIONS:** Mem Nat Urban League; Model Cities & Citizens Adv Coun; Am Assn Univ Adminstrs; Nat Black Alliance Graduate Level Edn; Nat Assn Black Social Wrkrs; com Childrens TV; chmn Northside Assn Educ Advancet Scholarship Com; bd dirs Canamer Olympian Games. **HONORS/ACHIEVEMENTS:** Outstanding Young Man Am Award. **BUSINESS ADDRESS:** Adminstrn Bldg, Western MI Univ, Kalamazoo, MI.

MURRAY, ALBERT L.
Educator. **PERSONAL:** Born May 12, 1916, Nokomis, AL; son of Hugh Murray and Mattie Murray; married Mozelle Menefee; children: Michele. **EDUCATION:** Tuskegee Inst, BS 1939; NY Univ, MA 1948. **CAREER:** Tuskegee Inst, instr Engl 1940-43, 1946-51; Colgate Univ, O'Connor prof Engl 1970; Emory Univ, writer in res 1978; Colgate, prof humanities 1982; Barnard, adjunct prof writing 1981-83; Drew Univ, Woodrow Wilson Fellow 1983; author. **ORGANIZATIONS:** Alumni Merit Award Tuskegee 1972; Doctor of Letters Colgate 1975. **HONORS/ACHIEVEMENTS:** Books, "Omni Americans," "South to A Very Old Place," "The Hero and the Blues," "Train Whistle Guitar," "Stomping the Blues," Romare Bearden; The Visual Equivalent of the Blues; Lillian Smith Award for "Train Whistle Guitar," ASCAP Deems Taylor Award for "Stomping the Blues" 1977; "Good Morning Blues" The Autobiography of Count Basie as told by Albert Murray 1986. **MILITARY SERVICE:** USAF major. **HOME ADDRESS:** 45 W 132nd St, New York, NY 10037.

MURRAY, ANDREW EVANS
Educator. **PERSONAL:** Born Apr 02, N Arlington, NJ; married Phyllis. **EDUCATION:** Univ CO, AB 1939; Princeton Theol Sem, ThB 1942; ThD 1947. **CAREER:** Lincoln U, asso prof ch history 1949-51; Theol Sem, dean 1951-59; prof religion, chmn dept religion 1959-. **ORGANIZATIONS:** Mem Am Soc Ch History; Am Hist Assn; Presb Hist Soc trustee; Am Acad Religion. **HONORS/ACHIEVEMENTS:** Recip Lincback Award for distinguished teaching 1968; Makemie Award 1967; author Presbyns & the Negro-a History 1966; Skyline Synod 1971. **BUSINESS ADDRESS:** Lincoln University, PA 19352.

MURRAY, ANNA MARTIN
Educator. **PERSONAL:** Born Oct 31, Birmingham, AL; married Willie Alca Murray (deceased). **EDUCATION:** AL State Coll, BS 1952; Samford Univ, Cert Early Childhood Educ 1975; The CA Inst of Metaphysics, 1952; George Peabody Coll; A&M, post grad study towards Masters 1964. **CAREER:** St Clair Bd of Educ, teacher 1944-46; Birmingham City Bd of Educ, teacher 1947-72; Helping Hand Day Care, teacher 1976-77; Birmingham City Bd of Educ, substitute teacher 1977-87. **ORGANIZATIONS:** Vice pres Deaconess Bd Macedonia Baptist Church 1970-85; sec Alert Professional Club 1980-85; sec Tyree Chap 77 OES 1981-85; mem AL Retired Teachers Assoc Montgomery AL, Amer Assoc of Retired Persons Long Beach CA, Gamma Phi Delta Alpha Mu Chap 1968-, Natl Ed Assoc WA DC; mem Fraternal OES, Alert Twelve Profl, Alpha Mu Gamma Phi Delta Sor; mem Ultra Modern Club 1930-87. **HONORS/ACHIEVEMENTS:** New verses in American Poetry Vantage Press NY 1976; Inspiration from a Save in Action Vantage Press NY 1977; Dipl The Inst of Mentalphysics; Meritorious Serv Award Birmingham Educ Assn 1973; Outstanding Serv

Award by Supreme Chap of Zeta Phi Lambda Sor 1983; Meritorious Serv Award Field of Journalism 1980; AwardNatl Black Women's Polit Leadership Caucus 1978. **HOME ADDRESS:** 2112-18th St, Birmingham, AL 35218.

MURRAY, ARCHIBALD R.
Attorney. **PERSONAL:** Born Aug 25, 1933; married Kay C. **EDUCATION:** Howard U, BA 1954; Fordham U, LlB 1960. **CAREER:** NY County, asst DA 1960-62; Gov NY, asst counsel 1962-65; NYC, Priv law prac 1965-67; NY State Crime Control Council, counsel 1967-68; NY State Office of Crime Control Planning NYC, counsel 1968-71; NY State Div Criminal Justice NYC, adminstr 1971-72; NY State Div Criminal Justice Servs NYC, commr 1972-74; The Legal Aid Soc NYC, atty-in-chief, exec dir 1975-. **ORGANIZATIONS:** Mem NY State Interdept Commn Serv to Children & Youth 1974; consult NY Temporay State Commn on Preparation for Constitutional Conv Nyc 1966-67; mem NY State Council on Drug Addiction 1965-67; mem NY State Comm on Revision Penal Law & Criminal Code 1965-70; mem NY Govs Com on Consent to Abortn 1977; bd of dir New York City Health & Hosp Corp 1978-79; mem Am Mgmt Assn Crimes Agnst Bus Counc 1976-; mem Grievance Com 1975-78; mem NY State Am Bar Assns; bd dirs Harlem Lawyers Assn 1970-71; mem NY Co Lawyers Assn; mem Community Serv Soc 1969-72; vestryman St Philips Episcopal Ch 1970-; mem Standing Com Episcopal Diocese of NY 1971-75; trustee Venture Fund 1971-77; chancellor Episcopal Diocese of NY 1975-; trustee St Lukes Hosp Ctr 1971-78; membd of dir NY Urban Coaltn 1976-; mem bd dirs 100 Black Men 1972-. **HONORS/ACHIEVEMENTS:** Recipient William Nelson Cromwell Award 1977. **MILITARY SERVICE:** AUS 1954-56. **BUSINESS ADDRESS:** 15 Park Row, 22 Floor, New York, NY 10038.

MURRAY, DAVID KEITH
Musician, composer, arranger. **PERSONAL:** Born Feb 19, 1955, Berkeley, CA; married Ming; children: David-Mingus. **ORGANIZATIONS:** Founding mem World Saxophone Quartet 1977-; mem Amer Soc for Composers Authors & Publishers 1977, mem Soc of Authors Composers & Music Editors (France) 1978; leader David Murray Quartet 1978, David Murray Big Band 1978-, David Murrary Octet 1979-. **HONORS/ACHIEVEMENTS:** Proclamation David Murray Day Mayor of Berkeley CA 1981; Talent Deserving of Wider Recognition Down Beat Mag. **BUSINESS ADDRESS:** Kunle Mwanga, PO Box 3312, Jersey City, NJ 07303.

MURRAY, EDDIE CLARENCE
Professional athlete. **PERSONAL:** Born Feb 24, 1956, Los Angeles, CA. **EDUCATION:** Attended, CA State Univ. **CAREER:** Baltimore Orioles, infielder 1977-. **ORGANIZATIONS:** Involved in charitable activities with United Cerebral Palsy, Sickle Cell Anemia, Amer Red Cross, United Way, Johns Hopkins Children's Ctr, New Holiness Refuge Church and Park Heights Acad which dedicated a classroom in his honor; for past 7 seasons sponsored "Project 33". **HONORS/ACHIEVEMENTS:** BBWAA Rookie of the Year Awd 1977; won 3 Gold Glove Awds; Move Valuable Oriole 6 times; has more RBIs (733) than any other big leaguer in the 1980's; has ledthe club in home runs 7 times; has led club in average, home runs and rbi's in one season 4 times; named first baseman on The Sporting News Amer League All-Star fielding teams 1982-84; named first baseman on The Sporting News Amer League Silver Slugger teams 1983,84; mem All Star Team 1981,82,83,84,85. **BUSINESS ADDRESS:** Baltimore Orioles, Memorial Stadium, Baltimore, MD 21218.

MURRAY, EDNA MCCLAIN
Learning disabilities teacher. **PERSONAL:** Born Jan 02, 1918, Idabel, OK; daughter of Swingley Lee Moore and Ruberda Lenox Moore; married Mar 31, 1938 (widowed); children: Ruby J McClain Ford, Jacquelyn McClain Crawford. **EDUCATION:** Wilson Jr Coll, Chicago IL, AA; Roosevelt Univ, Chicago IL, BA; Chicago State Univ, MEd; Over 60 additional hours in Administration, Counseling & Human Relations. **CAREER:** Ru-Jac Charm Center & Beauty Shop, Chicago IL, owned/operated, 1948-59; Chicago Bd of educ, school teacher, 1959-, Learning Disabilities, resource teacher, 1974-, Teacher Corp unit leader, 1970-71; Chicago State Univ, guest lecturer. **ORGANIZATIONS:** Executive sec, Natl Sorority of Phi Delta Kappa, 1982-, Natl Supreme Grammateus of Sorority, 1979-83, Basileus, Local Chapter, 1968-72; Organized Chicag Chapter of Top Ladies of Distinction; Served as several Natl Officer in TLOD, as well as local pres; Mem of Chicago Psychological Club, NAACP, UNCF, NCNW, & Urban League; Mem, Board of Directors, Executive Council of The Natl Sorority of Phi Delta Kappa, Chicago African-American Teachers Assn, Phidelka Foundation, Michigan Avenue Block Club, Michigan Ave Condo Board; Served as voting Delegate of the Chicago Teachers Union over 20 yrs. **HONORS/ACHIEVEMENTS:** Woman of the Year, Chicago Daily Defender, 1966; Outstanding 100 Black Women , Copin Church, 1986; Woman of the Year, Top Ladies of Distinction, 1981; Inducted into Chicago Senior Citizens Hall of Fame, Mayor Washington, 1987; Special Honor and Recognition by members of my school, Womens History Month, 1988; Pioneer in the field of Modeling for Black Women as owner/operator of Ru-Jac Charm Center & Beauty Shop, 1948-59. **HOME ADDRESS:** 5417 S Michigan Ave, Chicago, IL 60615.

MURRAY, J. RALPH
Business executive. **PERSONAL:** Born Oct 04, 1931, Manatee, FL; married Alaine; children: James, Janmarie, Jodi. **EDUCATION:** BS 1960. **CAREER:** Am Cyanamid Co Research Labs, employed; Travelers Ins Co, 1967; life Iis agency. **ORGANIZATIONS:** Mem bd finance City Stamford dir Liberty Nat Bank 1970; mem SW CT Life Underwriters Assn; bd dirs St Lukes Infant Child Care; former ch bd trustees, 1st Congregational Ch. **HONORS/ACHIEVEMENTS:** Travelers Inner Circle Award 1970; Outstanding Political Serv Award Afro-am Club 1972; Civic Award Planning Bd City Stamford 1970. **MILITARY SERVICE:** AUS 1952-54. **BUSINESS ADDRESS:** 832 Bedford St, Stamford, CT 06901.

MURRAY, JAMES HAMILTON
Educator, dentist. **PERSONAL:** Born Nov 22, 1933, Washington, DC; married Joan; children: Christina, Michelle. **EDUCATION:** Howard U, BS 1956; Meharry Med Coll, DDS 1960; Jersey City Med Cntr , rotating dental internship 1960-61; Johns HopkinsUniv Sch of Health & Hygiene, mPH 1969. **CAREER:** VA Pub Health Dept, clinical dentist 1964-68; HowardUniv Coll of Dentistry Dept of Oprothodontics, asst prof 1964-68; HowardUniv Coll of Dentistry Dept of Community Dentistry, asst prof; Shaw Community Health Project Nat Med Found, dental dir 1969-70; Matthew Walker Heaith Cntr Meharry Med Coll, project dir; Dept of Family & Community Health, prof 1970-71; Dept Health Educ & Welfare Family Health Serv Rockville MD, health adminstrn 1972-; Dept of Human Resour Comm Hlth & Hosp Admintr Wash DC, 1977. **ORGANIZATIONS:** Mem Nat Dental Assn; Am Soc of Dentistry for Children; Am Acad of Gen Dentistry; Am Pub Health Assn; Am Dental Assn; Urban League; mem or membership com Health Adminstrn Sec Am Pub Health Assn 1974-75; mem Omicron Kappa Upsilon 1960. **HONORS/ACHIEVEMENTS:** Publisher of articles for dental journals; Am Soc of Dentistry for Children Award 1960; US Pub Health Traineeship Grant 1968-69; Dental Alumnus of the Yr Meharry Med Coll 1970-71; DC Dental Soc Award 1969; Nashville Dental Supply Co Award for Clinical Dentistry 1960. **MILITARY SERVICE:** USAF 1961-63. **BUSINESS ADDRESS:** Howard Univ Coll of Dentistry, Washington, DC.

MURRAY, JAMES P.
Editor. **PERSONAL:** Born Oct 16, 1946, Bronx, NY; son of Eddie Murray and Helena Murray; married Mary; children: Sean Edward, Sherron Anita, Angela Dawn. **EDUCATION:** Syracuse Univ, BA 1968. **CAREER:** White Plains Reporter Dispatch, copy editor 1968; ABC-TV News, news trainee 1968-71; Western Electric Co, pub relations asso 1971-72; freelance writer 1972-73; NY Amsterdam News, arts & entertainment editor 1973-75; Nat Broadcasting Co, press rep 1975-83; Black Creation Mag, editor in chief 1972-74; freelance-writer 1983-85; USA Network, mgr public relations 1985-. **ORGANIZATIONS:** 1st Black Member Fairview Engine Co #1 Greenburgh NY Volunteer Fire Company 1968; judge Newspaper Guild Page One Awd 1976-86; cont ed The Afro-Amer Almanac 1976,89; pres Fairview Engine Co #1 1980; judge Gabriel Awds 1986. **HONORS/ACHIEVEMENTS:** Man of the Year Fairview Engine Co #1 1971; 1st Black elected to NY Film Critics Circle 1972; author book "To Find An Image" 1974; Humanitarian Achievement Awd MLK Players 1975; ordained elder Christs Temple White Plaines NY 1978; Outstanding Youn Man of Amer 1980. **MILITARY SERVICE:** AUS 1st lt 1968-70. **BUSINESS ADDRESS:** Manager Public Relations, USA Network, 1230 AVe of Americas, New York, NY 10020.

MURRAY, JOHN W.
Broadcasting executive. **PERSONAL:** Born Jul 06, 1921, Washington, DC; children: John Jr. **EDUCATION:** Syracuse & Lincoln Univ, AB 1947; New York Univ, St Johns Univ Law School, Grad Studies. **CAREER:** NY Time, staff-writer, sch prom 1952-54; NY Mirror, circulation promo writer 1954-55; WNBC-TV & Radio, reporter, asst prod 1955; Tex McCrary Inc, acct exec 1955-57; Harold L Oram Inc, acct exec 1957-58; Natl TB Assoc, dir publ & promo 1959-63; WCBS-TV, publ rel cons, writer & prod 1963-65, mgr ofspecial proj 1965-66, dir publ info & advtsg 1966-67, dir comm rel 1967-68; NY Urban Coalition, vp, comm 1968-70; WOR-TV, dir publ affairs 1970-71, vice pres publ affairs 1971-73; RKO Gen TV Inc, vice pres publ affairs 1973-79, sr vice pres 1979-. **ORGANIZATIONS:** Mem Natl Acad of TV Arts & Sci, Intl Radio & TV; founder & dir Assoc of Black Broadcast Exec; past dir Community News Svc; consult CUNY; dir, past pres Urban League of Greater NY; mem exec adv comm Journalism Resources Inst Rutgers Univ. **HONORS/ACHIEVEMENTS:** Black Achievers Awd Harlem YMCA 1973; Citation of Merit NJ Conf of Mayors; Media Awd Natl Conf of Christians & Jews for Outstanding Editorials; Outstanding Comm Serv awd Massive Econ Neighborhood Devel Corp; Gold Key Awd Publ Rel News. **MILITARY SERVICE:** AUS sgt 1943-46. **BUSINESS ADDRESS:** Senior Vice President, RKO Gen TV Inc, 1440 Broadway, New York, NY 10018.

MURRAY, JUDSON T.
State official. **PERSONAL:** Born Dec 26, 1918, Shreveport, LA; married Julia B; children: Joyce A, Jacqueline T. **EDUCATION:** BA 1940. **CAREER:** Region Iv IL Dept of Pub Aid, asst regional dir 1975-; Bur of Resources of Pub Aid, asst chief 1975; Bur of Resources & Legal Serv Cook Co Pub Aid, caseworker, resources consult, tech adv, asst chief 1947-75. **ORGANIZATIONS:** Mem City Club of Chgo; NAACP; Chicago Urban League; Omega Psi Phi Frat; crerar mem Presb Ch; People United to Save Humanity PuSH. **MILITARY SERVICE:** AUS 1943-45. **BUSINESS ADDRESS:** 840 E 87th St, Chicago, IL 60619.

MURRAY, KAY L.
Government official. **PERSONAL:** Born Sep 08, 1938, Greenville, MS; daughter of Preston Mike Lance and Anne Dell Jackson Lance; married Otis Murray, Aug 01, 1981; children: Gary Michael. **EDUCATION:** Roosevelt Univ, Chicago IL, BA Public Admin, 1976; Northeastern Illinois, Chicago IL, Master Program candidate, 1989. **CAREER:** City Council, Chicago IL, sec to pres pro-tempore, 1960-74; City Dept of Public Works, Chicago IL, equal employment officer, 1974; Dept of Streets and Sanitation Commissioner's Office, Chicago IL, staff assistant commissioner, 1974-82; Bureau of Rodent Control, Chicago IL, asst commissioner, 1983-84; Dept of Streets and Sanitation Rodent Control, Chicago IL, deptuy commissioner, 1984-. **ORGANIZATIONS:** Mem, Natl Assn of Women Executives; mem, Hyde Park Community Organization; associate, Howard Univ School of Business, Management for Minority Women; mem, Amer Public Works Assn; community developer, John Marshall Law School; mem, NAACP, 1977; mem, 21st District Steering Committee, Chicago Police Dept, 1979; mem, Intl Toastmistress of Amer/Sirrah Branch, 1980; mem, Chicago Urban League, 1986; vice pres, Jackson Park Hospital, 1987-89; vice pres, Business and Professional Women, 1988-89. **HONORS/ACHIEVEMENTS:** Outstanding Community Efforts Award, 1986; Community Leaders and Noteworthy Americans, 1988.

MURRAY, MABEL LAKE
Educator. **PERSONAL:** Born Feb 24, 1935, Baltimoe, MD; daughter of Moses Oliver Lake and Iantha Alexander Lake; married Elmer R Murray, Dec 16, 1968; children: Mark Alfonso Butler, Sarita Murray. **EDUCATION:** Coppin State Teachers Coll, Baltimore MD, BS, 1956; Loyola Coll, Balitmore MD, MED, 1969; Virginia Polytechnic Institute, Blacksburg VA, Case, 1978-81, EdD, 1982. **CAREER:** Baltimore City Public Schools, teacher, 1956-68; Prince Georges County Public Schools, reading specialist, 1968-70; Project KAPS, Baltimore MD, reading coordinator, 1970-72; Univ of MD, reading coordinator, 1972-76; Johns Hopkins Univ, adjunct professor, 1972-76; Carroll County Public Schools, supervisor, 1976-87; Sojourner Douglass Coll, Baltimore MD, professor, 1987-. **ORGANIZATIONS:** Mem, Delta Sigma Theta Sorority, 1972-; first vice pres, Baltimore County Alumnae Chapter, Delta Sigma Theta; advisor, Lambda Kappa and Mu Psi Chapters, Delta Sigma Theta, 1972-89; consultant, Piney Woods School, 1984-89; commission chair-instruction, Natl Alliance of Black Shool Educators, 1987-89; executive board, Natl Alliance of Black School Educators, 1987-89; consultant, AIDS Project MSDE, 1988; consultant, Dunbar Middle School, 1989; consultant, Des Moines Iowa Schools, 1989. **HONORS/ACHIEVEMENTS:** Designed curriculum material for two school systems, 1968-72; Conducted numerous workshops, 1969-89; Guest speaker at variety of educ/human relations activities, 1969-89; Outstanding Educator, State of MD Intl Reading Assn, 1979; Guest Lecturer, Baltimore City Schools Special Educ, 1979; Developed reading program for state mental hospital, 1981; Mayor's Citation,

1982; Service Award, Baltimore City Chapter, Delta Sigma Theta, 1983; Mem of Congressman Louis Stokes Committee on Black Health Issues, 1989. **HOME ADDRESS:** 3 Kitridge Court, Randallstown, MD 21133.

MURRAY, NEVADA (NEE MACKEY)
Educator. **PERSONAL:** Born Sep 24, 1920, Austin, TX; married Marshall; children: Layle E, Marshall M. **EDUCATION:** Houston Tillotson Coll, BS 1942;Univ of PA, mS 1950. **CAREER:** Bucks Co Sch Dist, teacher 1969-; Commr Bucks Co, jury 1974-; Philadelphia, soc worker, teacher 1952-62; US Gov, chemist 1944-46; Austin Pub School Sys, teacher 1942-43. **ORGANIZATIONS:** Mem Dem Co Exec Com; NAACP; Zeta Phi Beta; Am Assn ofUniv Women; mem Leag of Women Voters; Racial Cristis Com Central Bucks Christian Council; co-organzr Martin Luther King Scholarship Fund. **HONORS/ACHIEVEMENTS:** NAACP Award 1975; first black person to receive nomination of major political party in hist of co; invited to Presidents Conference by President Carter on "Energy & Inflation" held at the White House March 20 1980. **BUSINESS ADDRESS:** Unami Jr HS, Chalfont, PA 18914.

MURRAY, R. A.
Advertising executive. **PERSONAL:** Born Sep 16, 1947, St Paul, MN; married Marcia Norman; children: Todd, Justin. **EDUCATION:** Univ of MN, BA 1974. **CAREER:** City of San Francisco, public rel coord 1968-69; New York City San Francisco, program dir 1970-71; Univ of MN, const compliance 1971-74; Fahden Advertising, vice pres 1974-76; RAM & Assoc Adv Agency, pres 1976-. **ORGANIZATIONS:** Chmn MN Motion Picture Bd 1984-87; v chmn MN Business League 1982-84; dir Minneapolis Red Cross 1978-80; bd dirs Media Adv Cncl 1984-85; mem Chamber of Commerce Minneapolis 1980-85.

MURRAY, ROBERT F.
Geneticist. **PERSONAL:** Born 1931. **EDUCATION:** Union College, Schenectady, NY, BS; University of Rochester School of Medicine, Rochester, NY, MD, 1958; Denver General Hospital, Denver, CO, intern. **CAREER:** Colorado General Hospital, resident; Carnegie-Mellon University, Department of Biological Sciences, Pittsburgh, PA, professor; National Institute of Health, DNA Advisory Committee, member, 1988-. **BUSINESS ADDRESS:** Carnegie-Mellon University, Department of Biological Science, 5000 Forbes Avenue, Pittsburgh, PA 15213. *

MURRAY, SYLVESTER
City official. **PERSONAL:** Born Aug 08, 1941, Miami, FL; children: Kimberly, Joshua. **EDUCATION:** Lincoln Univ PA, AB 1963; Univ of PA Phila, MGA 1967; Eastern MI Univ, MA 1976; Lincoln Univ PA, LlD 1984. **CAREER:** City of Inkster MI, city mgr 1970-73; City of Ann Arbor MI, city admin 1973-79; City of Cincinnati OH, city mgr 1979-. **ORGANIZATIONS:** Pres Intl City Mgmt Assc 1984; trustee general Amer Mgmt Assc 1984. **HONORS/ACHIEVEMENTS:** Publ Srv Award Amer Soc of Publ Admin 1984. **MILITARY SERVICE:** AUS sp5 1965-67.

MURRAY, THOMAS AZEL
Administrator. **PERSONAL:** Born Jan 15, 1929, Chicago, IL. **EDUCATION:** OH State Univ, BA 1974; Sangamon State Univ, MA 1976, MA 1977; Southern IL Univ, PLD 1982. **CAREER:** Univ of IL Chicago, proj coord 1959-72; IL Natl Guard, equal opport spec 1973-75; Fed Hwy Admin, civil rights ofc 1975-78; IL State Bd of Educ, affirmative action ofc 1978-84; Chicago Baptist Assc, dir Chicago Bapt assc 1971-72; IL Affirmative Action Ofc Assc, parliamentarian 1979-83; Sangamon StateUniv Alumni Assc, dir 1979-85; US Dept of HUD Region V, Dir Program Operations Div, Office of Fair Housing and Equal Opport. **ORGANIZATIONS:** Dir Springfield Sangamon Cty Youth Svs Bureau 1974-75; adv comm mem Land of Lincoln Legal Acct Fnd 1978-80; adv council mem Region IV Career Guid Ctr Springfield IL 1982-83. **HONORS/ACHIEVEMENTS:** Blk Aff Council Awd of Merit SIU, 1981; Phi Kappa Phi HE Honor Society SIU chapter. **MILITARY SERVICE:** USAF USAFR/USAR e8 sm8gt-msgt. **HOME ADDRESS:** 1715 N Major, Chicago, IL 60639. **BUSINESS ADDRESS:** Dep Dir of Fair Housing, US Dept of HUD Region V, 300 S Wacker Dr, Chicago, IL 60606.

MURRAY, THOMAS W., JR.
Clergyman. **PERSONAL:** Born Mar 11, 1935, Wilmington, NC; married Mable; children: Thomas R, Dean W, Darrell L. **EDUCATION:** BS, Ed 1968; ThM 1969; MEd 1973; DD 1973. **CAREER:** Shawtown HS, educator 1968-69; Community Coll, educator 1969-70; Bolivia HS, educator 1969-70; Philadelphia Sch Sys, educator 1970-74;Univ Bapt Ch, pastor. **ORGANIZATIONS:** Mem Black Economic Devel Self Help Prog Founder & Dir Operation Shout; Positive Self Image & Metaphysical Inst Cited Chapel 4 Chaplains 1974. **MILITARY SERVICE:** USAF E5 1955-64. **BUSINESS ADDRESS:** U Bapt Ch, 2041 E Chelten Ave, Philadelphia, PA 19138.

MURRAY, VIRGIE W.
Editor. **PERSONAL:** Born Sep 04, 1931, Birmingham, AL; daughter of Virgus Williams and Martha W Reese (deceased); divorced; children: Charles Murray. **EDUCATION:** Attended, Miles Coll, Booker T Washington Business Coll. **CAREER:** Dr John W Nixon, bookkeeper/recpt 1954-58; Thomas Floorwaxing Serv, bookkeeper 1954-64; Birmingham World, clerk/reporter 1958-64; First Baptist Church Graymont, sec 1960-64; religion editor, Los Angeles Sentinel 1964-. **ORGANIZATIONS:** Religion editor Los Angeles Sentinel 1964-; West Coast PR Dr Frederick Eikerenkoetter (Rev Ike) 1974-; pr & consul NBC, USA, INC, AMES & CME's Genl Confs; first black sec Religion Newswriters Assn 1971; bd mem Inst of Sacred Music 1979-; bd mem Ecumenical Black Campus Ministry UCLA 1982-; mem Trinity Baptist Ch, NAACP, Urban League, Angeles Mesa YWCA, Aux Cncl RSVP; former den mother Boy Scouts of Amer; former mem LA Chap Business & Professional Women's Club Inc; spec task force of United Nations Assn of USA's Ralph Bunche Awds; mem LA chapter Lane College & Mileans & Parker High School Alumni; serving on Awards Committee, Religious Heritage of Amer 1989-90. **HONORS/ACHIEVEMENTS:** Tribute Awd Good Shepherd Bapt Ch 1983; City County State Councilman Supervisors & Assemblymen 1983; Awd of Merit Crenshaw Christian Center 1980; Christian Example First Church of God 1982; 22 other awds; Woman of the Year, Women At Work, auxilary of Southwestern CC 1989; Southern Conf of CME Church, special award and honors 1988; Coverage of the 81st Annual Convocation of Church of God in Christ, Memphis, TN 1988; The AME Gen Conf in Ft Worth Texas 1988. **BUSINESS ADDRESS:** Religion Editor, Los Angeles Sentinel, 1112 E 43rd St, Los Angeles, CA 90011.

MURRAY, WINSTON LLOYD, JR.
Physician. **PERSONAL:** Born Sep 22, 1952, New Orleans, LA; married Teresa Ann Kearney; children: Winston III. **EDUCATION:** Tulane Univ, BS 1974; Howard Univ Coll of Medicine, MD 1978. **CAREER:** LA State Univ Medical Sch, asst prof of family medicine 1982-86; Private Practice, internal medicine 1986-. **ORGANIZATIONS:** Mem LA State Medical Soc 1982-, Natl medical Assoc 1985-. **BUSINESS ADDRESS:** 10555 Lake Forest Blvd 7A, New Orleans, LA 70127.

MURRELL, BARBARA CURRY
Educational administrator. **PERSONAL:** Born Jan 12, 1938, Starksville, MS; married Robert N Murrell. **EDUCATION:** TN State Univ, BS 1960, MS 1963; Univ of IL, Post Grad Cert 1970. **CAREER:** TN State Univ, dir student activities 1965-75, asst vice pres student affairs 1975-81, vice pres student affairs 1981-. **ORGANIZATIONS:** State coord Natl Assn for Student Personnel Admins 1973; Task Force of Human Resources Assn of College Unions Intl 1968-79; Harvard Univ Inst for EducMgrs Program 1984; consul Prof Development Workshop Assn of College Unions Intl; bd of dirs Bordeaux YMCA; Assn of College Unions Intl; Natl Entertainment and Campus Activities Assn; Beta Kappa Chi Natl Honor Soc; Delta Sigma Theta Sor Inc. **HONORS/ACHIEVEMENTS:** Omega Psi Phi Frat Sweetheart 1958-59; Miss TN State Univ 1960; Who's Who in American Universities and Colleges 1960; Outstanding Young Women of Amer 1973; Personalities of the South 1976; Kappa Alpha Psi Frat Perpetual Sweetheart 1960-. **BUSINESS ADDRESS:** VP for Student Affairs, Tennessee StateUniv, 3500 John A Merritt Blvd, Nashville, TN 37203.

MURRELL, CHARLAYNE E.
Director. **PERSONAL:** Born Jan 18, 1951, Denver, CO. **EDUCATION:** Wellesley Coll, BA 1973; Northeastern Univ, MEd 1974. **CAREER:** A Better Chance Inc, counselor 1971-73; MA Civil Service Comm, intern/consul 1972-74; Metro Cncl for Educ Oppor, group co-counselor 1974-75; Newton Public Schs, guidance counselor 1973-76; Cambridge Public Schs, coord of support serv 1976-77; WHDH, dir of comm affairs. **ORGANIZATIONS:** Mem Women in Comm; mem Natl Broadcast Assn for Comm Affairs; mem Boston Black Media Coalition; mem Boston Assn of Black Journalists; vice pres Natl Mental Health Assn 1983-; vice pres MA Assn for Mental Health 1981-; vice pres Patriots Trail Girl Scout Cncl 1983-; bd dirs Urban League of Eastern MA 1984-; bd dirs Comm Training & Resource Ctr 1982-; bd dir Boston Children's Serv Assn 1985-; Corp Sch Volunteers of Boston 1985-; develop comm Spaulding Rehab Hosp 1984-; adv United Way of Mass Bay 1983-; adv Boston Youth Theatre 1982-; adv Amer Cancer Soc of MA 1982-; adv Amer Lung Assn of MA 1980-; mem Wellesley Coll Alumnae Assn, Boston Alumnae Chap Delta Sigma Theta Sor, Sportsmens Tennis Club, Franklin Park Coalition. **HONORS/ACHIEVEMENTS:** Outstanding Young Women of Amer 1980-; Professional Develop Grant Natl Endowment for the Arts & Humanities 1980; Scholarship Outstanding Minority Grad Student MAPersonnel & Guidance Assn, Amer Personnel & Guidance Assn; numerous public serv & media citations. **HOME ADDRESS:** 1575 Tremont St #1107, Boston, MA 02120. **BUSINESS ADDRESS:** Dir of Community Affairs, WHDH Radio, 441 Stuart St, Boston, MA 02116.

MURRELL, PETER C.
Dentist. **PERSONAL:** Born May 14, 1920, Glasgow, KY; married Eva Ruth Greenlee; children: Peggy, Peter Jr, Linda, James. **EDUCATION:** KY State Coll, BS (Cum Laude) 1943; Marquette Univ, DDS 1947. **CAREER:** Howard Univ Coll Dentistry, instr 1947-48; Private practice, 1948-51,53-. **ORGANIZATIONS:** Mem Amer WI & Gr Milwaukee Dental Assoc; pres Gr Milwaukee Dental Assoc; mem Amer Soc Preventive Dentistry, Amer Acad Gen Practice; treas, bd mem Childrens Serv Soc 1962-77, Garfield Found; former mem Frontiers Intl; co-founder, 1st pres Milwaukee Chap Frontiers Intl; past pres Delta Chi Lambda; fellow Intl Coll of Dentists 1978, Academy of General Dentistry 1981; trustee, WI Dental Assoc 7th Dist 1983; WI State Medical Assistance Advisory Comm; exec comm WI Dental Assoc; mem, Pierre Fauchard Academy 1989; fellow, American College of Dentists 1989; advisory council, Marquette Univ School of Dentistry 1988. **HONORS/ACHIEVEMENTS:** Distinguished Serv Awd Opportunity Industrialization Ctr 1971; Service to Dentistry, Greater Milwaukee Dental Assn 1987. **MILITARY SERVICE:** AUS 1942-44; USAF Dental Corps capt 1951-53. **HOME ADDRESS:** 1302 W Capitol Dr, Milwaukee, WI 53206.

MURRELL, SYLVIA MARILYN
Mayor. **PERSONAL:** Born Sep 07, 1947, Arcadia, OK; daughter of Ebbie Parks, Jr and Inez Traylor Parks; divorced; children: Monica A, Alfred H, Cypreanna V. **EDUCATION:** Central State Univ, Edmond OK, 1964-66; Rose State Coll, Midwest City OK, 1981-82; Langston Univ, Oklahoma OK, 1986-87. **CAREER:** OK Business Devel Center, Oklahoma City OK, variety of positions, 1975-, executive dir, 1985-; Town of Arcadia, mayor, 1989. **ORGANIZATIONS:** Mem, OK City Chamber of Commerce, 1977-; sec & chairman Economic Devel Committee, Conference Black Mayors, 1986-; bd mem, Youth Services OK County, 1986-; bd mem, OK City Chp Assualt on Illiteracy, 1986-; steering committee, OK City Crime Prevention Task Force, 1988-; mem, Central OK economic Devel Task Force, 1988-; mem, Teamwork OK, 1988-; vice chair, OK Consortium for Minority Business Devel, 1988-89. **HONORS/ACHIEVEMENTS:** Creative Christian Award, Forrest Hill AME Church, 1987. **BUSINESS ADDRESS:** Mayor, Town of Arcadia, PO Box 189, Arcadia, OK 73007.

MUSE, WILLIAM BROWN, JR.
Banking official. **PERSONAL:** Born Jul 18, 1918, Danville, VA; son of William B Muse and Mayde S Muse; widowed; children: William K, Michael A, Eric V. **EDUCATION:** Hampton Inst, BS Bus 1940. **CAREER:** Wm B Muse Agency Real Estate Gen Ins & Property Mgmt, owner 1940-73; Imperial Savings & Loan Assn, pres managing officer 1973-. **ORGANIZATIONS:** Dir First State Bank 1950-; pres Martinsville Branch NAACP 1951-57; 1st vice pres NAREB 1954-59; pres VA Assoc of Real Estate Brokers 1963-; mem VA Adv Comm to US Civil Rights Commn 1968-80; trustee St Paul's Coll 1968-78 & 1981-; chmn Amer League Fin Inst 1983-84; dir Amer League of Fin; vice chmn bd NAREB; mem Federal Savings and Loan Adv Cncl 1985-86; mem bd of dir Martinsville County C of C 1986-; mem bd of governors VA League of Savings Institutions 1986-; mem exec comm Martinsville Democratic Party; treas Martinsville-Henry County Voters League. **MILITARY SERVICE:** Field Artillery chief warrant officer 1942-46; ETO. **HOME ADDRESS:** 611 First St, P O Box 391, Martinsville, VA 24112. **BUSINESS ADDRESS:** President, Managing Officer, Imperial Savings & Loan Assn, 211 Fayette St, P O Box 391, Martinsville, VA 24112.

MUSGROVE, MARGARET WYNKOOP
Teacher and author. **PERSONAL:** Born Nov 19, 1943, New Britain, CT; daughter of John T Wynkoop and Margaret Holden Wynkoop; married George Gilbert, Aug 28, 1971; children: Taura Johnene, George Derek. **EDUCATION:** Univ of Connecticut, BA, 1966; Central Connecticut State College, MS, 1970; Univ of Massachusetts, EdD, 1979. **CAREER:** High school English teacher in Hartford, Ct, 1967-69 and 1970; teacher at various community colleges; Community College of Baltimore, Baltimore, MD, English teacher, 1981-. **ORGANIZATIONS:** Society of Children's Book Writers, League of Women Voters. **HONORS/ACHIEVEMENTS:** Author of Ashanti to Zulu: African Traditions, Dial, 1976 (on Horn Book honor list and a Caldecott honor book). **HOME ADDRESS:** 6304 Wallis Ave, Baltimore, MD 21215. *

MUSKELLY, ANNA MARIE
Editor. **PERSONAL:** Born May 31, New York, NY; married Frederick Thomas Bryan, Dec 17, 1988. **EDUCATION:** Hunter Coll, BA 1969; Fashion Institute of Tech, AAS 1973. **CAREER:** House Beautiful Magazine, editorial 1969-71; Random House Inc, manuscript editor 1971-76, project editor 1976-86; Warren Gorham & Lamont Inc, senior editor 1986-; Warren, Gorham & Lamont Inc NYC Managing Editor 1988. **ORGANIZATIONS:** Vice pres students NY Women in Communications 1981-83; pres Black Women in Publishing Inc 1982-84; adv council mem Natl Council of Negro Women 1983-88; pres Women's Natl Book Assoc NY 1986-88; mem Natl Assoc of Female Execs; advisory council mem Women's Center 1988. **HONORS/ACHIEVEMENTS:** Role Model 1983-84 Coalition of One Hundred Black Women NY; WNBA Book Women Awd 1987; "Minority & Women Who Are First" Negro Business & Professional Women 1988; Founding Member Award Black Women in Publishing Inc 1989. **HOME ADDRESS:** 3555 Bruckner Blvd, Bronx, NY 10461. **BUSINESS ADDRESS:** Managing Editor, Warren, Gorham & Lamont Inc, One Penn Plaza, New York, NY 10119.

MUTALE, ELAINE BUTLER
Educator. **PERSONAL:** Born Aug 12, 1943, Templeton, PA; married Joseph Mutale; children: Amy Yvonne. **EDUCATION:** Univ of Pittsburgh, BS 1964, MLS 1966. **CAREER:** Slippery Rock State Coll, instr 1966-68; Union List Serials Pitts Reg Lib Center, editor spl proj 1968-70; Andrews Univ, instructor 1970-. **ORGANIZATIONS:** Mem Amer Assn Univ Prof; Berrien Co Co-operating Libraries Assn; ALA; Amer Assn Univ Women; Pathfinder Leader. **BUSINESS ADDRESS:** Instructor, AndrewsUniv, James White Library, Berrien Springs, MI 49104.

MUTCHERUON, JAMES ALBERTUS, JR.
Physician. **PERSONAL:** Born Mar 22, 1941, Tampa, FL; married Katherine; children: 's Hosp of DC, Kimberly. **EDUCATION:** FL U, A&M 1962; Am Intl Coll, BA 1966; HowardUniv Coll of Med, 1967-71. **CAREER:** Pediatric allergist self emp; HowardUniv Hosp, clinical instr 1975-; HowardUniv Hosp, pediatric allergy fellow 1973-75; Childrens Hosp of DC, pediatric resd 1971-73. **ORGANIZATIONS:** DC Med Soc; DC Allergy Soc; Am Acad of Allergy Pediatric Allergy Fellowship 1973-75. **BUSINESS ADDRESS:** 5223 Georgia Ave, Washington, DC 20011.

MUWAKKIL, SALIM (ALONZO JAMES CANNADY)
Writer. **PERSONAL:** Born Jan 20, 1947, New York City, NY; married Karimah; children: Salimah, Rasheeda. **EDUCATION:** Rutgers Univ; Newark Coll Arts & Science 1973. **CAREER:** Bilalian News, mng editor 1975-77; Muhammad Speaks, news editor 1974-75; Copy Editor 1974; AP, bur newsman 1972-74; Addiction Planning & Coordinator Agency of Newark, rsch specialist 1972; Livingston Nghbrhd Educ Ctr, co-founder educ 1971; Black Journalism Rev, consult editorial bd. **ORGANIZATIONS:** Pres Black Students Union 1970-72; consult Livingston Coll Nghbrhd Educ Ctr 1972-74; bd Gov S Shore Comm Ctr Several Publ; Spl Observer Orgn of African Unity 1975. **MILITARY SERVICE:** USAF 1964-69. **BUSINESS ADDRESS:** In These Times Magazine, 1300 W Belmont Ave, Chicago, IL 60649.

MUYUMBA, FRANCOIS N. (MUYUMBA WA NKONGOLA)
Educator. **PERSONAL:** Born Dec 29, 1939, Luputa Kasai-orien, Zaire;married Valentine Kanyinda; children: Walton MN, Muuka MK. **EDUCATION:** David & Elkins Coll Elkins WV, BA 1963-67; Portland State U, MS 1969-70; INUniv Boomington, MA & PhD 1977. **CAREER:** IN State Univ, asst prof 1977-; Univ Libre duCongo, asst prof/adminstrn asst 1968-69; Usaid-Kinshasa, asst training officer 1967-68; Youth Center (Carrefour deJeunes) Kinshasa Zaire, dir 1967. **ORGANIZATIONS:** Mem Tchrs of Engl as Second Lang 1973-80; mem Intl Peace Research Assn 1975-80; consult Inst for World Order's Sch Progs 1975-78; mem World Councilfor Curriculum & Instr 1974-80; mem Peache Educ Council 1978-80; mem Nat Council for Black Studies 1976-80. **HONORS/ACHIEVEMENTS:** Recipient Soccer Letters & Trophies Davis & Elkins Coll Elkins WV 1963-67; Listed Who's Who Among Students in Am Coll 1965-66; Travel Grant Intl PeaceResearch Assn 1975; Consult Grant Gilmore Sloane Presbyterian Center 1975. **BUSINESS ADDRESS:** IN State Univ, Terre Haute, IN 47809.

MWAMBA, ZUBERI I.
Educator. **PERSONAL:** Born Jan 03, 1937, Tanzania. **EDUCATION:** Univ WI, BS 1968;Univ Pitts, MA 1968; Howard U, PhD 1972. **CAREER:** Govt Tanzania, radio announcer, court clerk, interpreter, information asst 1957-62; Howard U, instr 1968-72; US State Dept 1969-70; African Studies TX So U, asst prof dir 1972-. **ORGANIZATIONS:** Mem Am Political Sci Assn 1971-; Nat Council Black Political Scientists 1971-; Educator to Africa Assn 1972-; pres Pan African Students Orgn 1965-67; Tanzania Students Union 1968-70 1971-72; exec com East African Students Orgn 1968-70; adv TX SoUniv Student Gov Assn 1974-75; faculty sponsor TSU YoungDemo 1974-75. **HONORS/ACHIEVEMENTS:** Fellows Fulbright 1965-68; WI Legislature 1965-67; HowardUniv Trust 1969-70. **BUSINESS ADDRESS:** Texas Southern Univ, 3201 Wheeler Ave, Houston, TX 77004.

MYATT, GORDON J.
Administrative law judge. **PERSONAL:** Born Jan 02, 1928, Brooklyn, NY; married Evelyne E Hutchings; children: Gordon, Jr, Kevin, Craig. **EDUCATION:** NY U, BS 1950; NYUniv Sch of Law, LLB 1956. **CAREER:** Pvt Practice, atty 1956-60; Nat Labor Relations Bd Chicago, trial atty 1960-62; Nat Larbor Relations Bd Chicago, supv atty 1962-64; First Black Bd, legal adv. **ORGANIZATIONS:** Mem Nat Labor Relations Bd Washington DC 1964-67; appt adminstrv Law Judge Nat Labor Relations Bd 1967 3rd Black in US to Hold Such Position; currently adminstrv Law Judge US Dept of Labor; chmn Conf of Adminstrv Law Judges of Am Bar Assn 1975-; mem Nat Bar Assn Pres; bd dir Bur of Rehab 1971-74; mem Alpha Phi Alpha 1945-; first black chmn of Conf of Adminstrv Law Judges of Am Bar Assn 1975. **BUSINESS ADDRESS:** Natl Labor Relations Board, Div of Judges, 901 Market St, Suite 300, San Francisco, CA 94103.

MYERS, BERNARD SAMUEL
Veterinarian. **PERSONAL:** Born Jun 02, 1949, Moultrie, GA. **EDUCATION:** Rollins Coll, BA 1970; Cornell U, DVM 1974. **CAREER:** Lynn Animal Hosp, vet 1985; Needham Animal Hosp, asso vet 1977-80; Stoneham Animal Hosp, asso vet 1975-77; Bruce Animal Hosp, asso vet 1974-75; Harvard Sch of Pub Health, res asst 1973. **ORGANIZATIONS:** Mem Am Vet Med Assn 1974-80; mem MA Vet Med Assn 1974-80; asst moderator Shiloh Bapt Ch 1980. **HONORS/ACHIEVEMENTS:** Academic Scholarship Rollins Coll 1966-70; Algernon Sidney Sullivan Award Rollins Coll 1969; Health Professions Scholarship CornellUniv 1970-74. **BUSINESS ADDRESS:** Lynn Animal Hospital, 110 Weber St, Orlando, FL.

MYERS, DEBRA J.
Physician. **PERSONAL:** Born Aug 03, 1952, Waynesville, NC; married Woodrow Myers, Jr; children: Kimberly L Myers, Zachary A Myers. **EDUCATION:** Stanford Univ, Stanford CA, BS, 1973; Harvard Univ, Boston MA, MD, 1977. **BUSINESS ADDRESS:** Medical Director Sleep Disorders Diagnostic Center, Methodist Hospital of Indiana, 1701 N Senate Blvd, Indianapolis, IN 46202.

MYERS, EARL T.
Engineer, manager. **PERSONAL:** Born Jul 26, 1930, Daytona Beach; married Clara Mills; children: Lesli, Linda. **EDUCATION:** Walden U, PhD 1973; Worcester Polytechnic Inst, MSME; Northeastern U, MS 1965; Claflin U, BS 1952. **CAREER:** Xerox Corp, prog mgr; Application Engineering Gen Elec Co, mgr 1973-77; Freedom Tool & Die Inc, gen mgr 1970-73; Raytheon Co, sr scientist 1966-67; AVCO Corp, sr consulting scientist 1956-66. **ORGANIZATIONS:** Mem Ordnance Soc 1958-60; Am Ins of Aeronautics & Astronautics; Am Astronautical Soc Pres Montachusett Br NAACP 1974-; mem Bd Corp Emerson Hosp 1974-; Minority Sci Study Consult 1970-. **HONORS/ACHIEVEMENTS:** Recip Outstanding Aurthors Award Raytheon Co 1967; Raytheon's Adv Study Fellowship 1967-70. **MILITARY SERVICE:** Served AUS pfc 1952-54. **BUSINESS ADDRESS:** 166 Boulder Dr, Fitchburg, MA 01420.

MYERS, EMMA MCGRAW
Association executive. **PERSONAL:** Born Nov 15, 1953, Hartsville, SC; married Kenneth E Myers. **EDUCATION:** FL State Univ, BA 1974, MSoc Wk 1975. **CAREER:** United Way of Amer, united way intern 1976-77, consul planning & allocations div 1979-80; United Way of Tarrant Co, mang vol training 1977-78, campaign divdir 1978-79; UWA, assoc dir natl ag relations 1980-83; United Way of the Midlands, dir planning & allocations div. **ORGANIZATIONS:** Parlimentarian Episcopal Church Women 1985; treas FSU Black Alumin Assn; bd mem Natl Assn of Black Social Workers 1985-; pres Dutch Fork Citivans 1985-; pres Alpha Kappa Alpha 1985-; corresp sec Columbia Chap NABSW. **HONORS/ACHIEVEMENTS:** Nominee Outstanding young Women of Amer 1983; NCNW Living the Legacy Awrd 1986; Civitan of the Year 1986. **BUSINESS ADDRESS:** Dir Planning & Allocations, United Way of the Midlands, PO Box 152, Columbia, SC 29202.

MYERS, ERNEST RAY
Educator, administrator, psychologist. **PERSONAL:** Born in Middletown, OH; son of David Myers and Alma Harper Myers; married Carole Ferguson. **EDUCATION:** Howard Univ, BA 1962, MSW 1964; Amer Univ, PhD candidate 1974; Union Grad Sch, PhD 1976. **CAREER:** VISTA, prog ofcr proj develop div 1964-66, sr eval officer 1964-66, proj devel officer 1966-67, program plans & policy develop ofcr 1967; Dept of Housing & Urban Develop, neighborhood serv prog ofcr & coord 1967-68; Natl Urban League, asst dir 1968; Westinghouse Learning Corp, mgr of prog develop 1968-69; Fed City Coll, dir coll comm evaluation office 1969-71; Bureau of Higher Educ US Office of Educ, dir servicemen's early educ counseling prog 1971; Federal City Coll, asst prof 1972-77; Univ of DC, assoc prof 1977-86, chmn dept of human resource dev 1986-. **ORGANIZATIONS:** Pres Myers Enterprises & Assocs 1982-; trustee Woodley House (Rehab) 1982-; mem Amer Psychological Assn 1975-84; chmn DC Govt Mental Health Admin Adv Bd 1984-86; chmn DC Mental Health Assn Professional Adv Comm 1984-86; chmn Howard Univ Alumni Sch of Social Work Fund Raising Comm 1984-86; mem Kiwanis Club GA Br1985-86; mem greivance comm Natl Assoc of Social Workers 1984-86; president, ERM Consulting Corp 1980-. **HONORS/ACHIEVEMENTS:** Outstanding Alumni Howard Univ Sch of Soc Wk 1982; Outstanding Serv Mental Health Assn (Natl) 1982; Outstanding Leadership Univ of DC Coll of Educ & Human Ecology 1981; Outstanding Scholar Assn of Black Psychologists 1981; numerous publs; Outstanding Leadership Awd Univ of DC 1985; Outstanding Scholarship Awd Univ of DC 1986; textbook, The Community Psychology Concept 1977; book, Race and Culture in the Mental Health Service Delivery SYstem 1981. **MILITARY SERVICE:** USAF s2 1956-60; 2 Good Conduct Medals. **BUSINESS ADDRESS:** Professor of Educ & Chmn, Univ of DC, Dept of Human Resource Develop, 2565 Georgia Ave, Washington, DC 20009.

MYERS, FRANCES ALTHEA
Physician. **PERSONAL:** Born Nov 12, 1957, Richmond, VA. **EDUCATION:** Howard Univ, Coll of Liberal Arts BS 1980, Coll of Medicine MD 1984. **CAREER:** Natl Inst of Mental Health, student researcher 1978-80; Howard Univ Hosp, postgraduate physician 1984-. **ORGANIZATIONS:** Chairperson Recreation Comm Women in Medicine Howard Univ Chap 1982-84; sec regional Student Natl Medical Asoc 1982-84; mem Amer Acad of Family Physicians 1982-, Amer Medical Assoc 1983-, Amer Medical Womens Assoc 1986-. **HONORS/ACHIEVEMENTS:** Mem Beta Kappa Chi Natl Scientific Honor Soc 1981; Chief Resident Family Practice Howard Univ Hospital 1986-87. **HOME ADDRESS:** 1353 Ingraham St, NW, Washington, DC 20011. **BUSINESS ADDRESS:** Postgraduate Physician, Howard University Hospital, 2041 Georgia Ave, NW, Washington, DC 20060.

MYERS, JACQUALINE DESMONA
Educator. **PERSONAL:** Born Jan 05, 1951, Charleston, SC; daughter of William Nicholas Myers (deceased) and Daisy Elouise Brown Myers (deceased). **EDUCATION:** Benedict College, Columbia, SC, BS 1971; Indiana Univ, Bloomington, MS 1972; Univ of Wisconsin,

Madison, PhD 1980. **CAREER:** Benedict College, work study secretary 1968-71; Medical Univ of SC, clinic accountant 1971; Indiana Univ, asst instructor 1971-72; Alabama State Univ, asst prof 1973-86, assoc prof 1986-. **ORGANIZATIONS:** Mem Natl Bus Ed Assoc 1971-, Amer Vocational Ed Assoc 1977-, Amer Ed Rsch Assoc 1980-, Natl Council of Negro Women 1983-, asst correspondence sec Delta Sigma Theta Montgomery Alumnae 1983-84, NAACP 1984-, AL Assoc of Teacher Ed, Delta Pi Epsilon, AL Council of Computer Ed, Phi Delta Kappa, AL Assoc of Univ Professors, Assoc of Suprv & Curriculum Devel, Southern Reg Assoc of Teacher Eds, AL Vocational Assoc, Southern Bus Ed Assoc, AAUP; correspondence sec Delta Sigma Theta 1986; Southern Business Education Assoc. **HONORS/ACHIEVEMENTS:** Cum Laude Benedict College 1971; Outstanding Young Women of Amer 1977, 1980, 1984; published article in SBEA Bulletin 1980. **HOME ADDRESS:** 1404 University Dr West, Montgomery, AL 36106.

MYERS, L. LEONARD
Business executive. **PERSONAL:** Born Jan 25, 1933, Aliquippa, PA; married R Elizabeth; children: Linda Ann; Larry Leonard. **EDUCATION:** Univ of Pittsburgh, BA; Life Underwriter Training Council LUTC; Chartered Life Underwriters, CLU; Amer Coll Amer Inst for Property & Liability Underwriter, CPCU. **CAREER:** First Summit Agency Inc, pres & ceo. **ORGANIZATIONS:** 1st black pres Long Island Chapter CPCU, Long Island Chap CLU, Hempstead Chamber of Commerce; past pres Natl Ins Ind Assoc, Lakeview Lions Club. **MILITARY SERVICE:** AUS spec 4 2 yrs. **HOME ADDRESS:** 19 Surrey Lane, Hempstead, NY 11550. **BUSINESS ADDRESS:** President, First Summit Agency, Inc, 126 North Franklin St, Hempstead, NY 11550.

MYERS, LENA WRIGHT
Educator. **PERSONAL:** Married Dr Julius Myers Jr (deceased); children: Stanley. **EDUCATION:** Tougaloo Coll, BA Sociology; MI State Univ, MA Sociology & Anthropology 1964, PhD Sociology & Social Psychology 1973. **CAREER:** Utica Jr Coll, instructor of soc & psych 1962-68; Washtenaw Comm Coll, asst prof of psychology 1968; Center for Urban Affairs MI State Univ, urban rsch 1970-73; Jackson State Univ, prof of sociology 1973-. **ORGANIZATIONS:** Mem of comm on status of women in sociology Amer Sociol Assoc 1974-77; rsch/consul TIDE 1975-78; pres Assn of Social/Behavioral Scientists Inc 1976-77; rsch/consul KOBA 1979-80; mem bd of dirs Soc for the Study of Social Problems 1980-83; rsch/consul Natl Sci Foundation 1983; pres Assn of Black Sociologists 1983-84. **HONORS/ACHIEVEMENTS:** Outstanding Young Women of America 1969; American Men & Women of Sci 13th Edition 1978; World's Who's Who of Women 6th Edition 1981; Who's Who in the South & Southwest 1982; State of MS House of Rep Concurrent Resolution No 70 Commendation 1981; Personalities of Amer 1981; Disting Amer Awd 1981. **HOME ADDRESS:** 2320 Queensroad Ave, Jackson, MS 39213.

MYERS, LEWIS HORACE
Business executive. **PERSONAL:** Born Apr 28, 1946, Carlisle, PA; married Cheryl; children: Donnell L, Marrielle, Lewis H III. **EDUCATION:** UNC, Cert Basic Ind Dev Course 1979; UNC, MBA 1974; Franklin & Marshall Coll, BA 1968; Govt Exec Inst, 1981. **CAREER:** Off of Spec Progs Franklin & Marshall Coll, assoc dir 1968-69; Upward Bound Prog Harvard Univ, exec dir 1969-71; Soul City Found Inc, assoc dir 1971-75; Soul City Co, vice pres 1976-79; NC Minority Bus Dev Agency, dir 1980-82; NC Dept of Commerce Small Bus Devel Div, asst sec 1982-. **ORGANIZATIONS:** Mem Assn of MBA Execs 1975, NC Ind Dev Assn 1979-, So Ind Dev Cncl 1979-; founder, mem NC Assoc of Minority Bus. **HONORS/ACHIEVEMENTS:** Series of 15 articles on Important Black People in Am Hist Lancaster Sun News 1968. **BUSINESS ADDRESS:** Assistant Secretary, Small Business Development Div, NC Dept of Commerce, 412 N Salisbury St, Raleigh, NC 27611.

MYERS, ROBERT L., JR.
Business executive. **BUSINESS ADDRESS:** Century Chevrolet, Inc, 6501 Market St, Upper Darby, PA 19082.

MYERS, SAMUEL L.
Educator. **PERSONAL:** Born Apr 18, 1919, Baltimore, MD; son of David Myers and Edith Myers; married Marion R Rieras; children: Yvette M May, Tama M Clark, Samuel L Jr. **EDUCATION:** Morgan State Coll, AB 1940; Boston Univ, MA 1942; Harvard Univ, MA 1948, PhD 1949; Morgan State Coll, LLD 1968; Univ of MD, LLD 1983. **CAREER:** Harvard Univ, rsch assoc 1949; Bureau Statistics US Dept of Labor, economist 1950; Morgan State Coll, prof, div chmn soc sci 1950-63; Inter-Amer Affairs US Dept State, adv 1963-67; Bowie State Coll, pres 1967-77, pres emeritus 1977-; Natl Assn for Equal Opportunity in Higher Educ (NAFEO), president, 1977-. **ORGANIZATIONS:** Mem MD Tax Study Comm 1958, Gov Comm on Prevailing Wage Law in MD 1962; vice chmn MD Comm for Humanities & Publ Policy; mem Alpha Kappa Mu, State Scholarship Bd 1968-77; vice chmn Gov Comm on Aide to Educ 1969-70; pres MD Assn Higher Educ 1971-72; chmn Comm Intl Prog, Amer Assn State Coll & Univ; rep Natl Adv Council for Intl Teacher Exchange; mem Steering Comm, Comm on Future Intl Studies; vice pres, bd of dir Natl Assn Equal Oppty in Higher Educ; mem Pres Comm on Foreign Lang & Intl Studies 1978-80; mem bd of dir Rassias Found 1980; mem Baltimore Urban League; rsch fellow Rosenwald Fellow Harvard Univ. **MILITARY SERVICE:** AUS capt 1942-46. **BUSINESS ADDRESS:** National Association for Equal Opportunity in Higher Education, 400 12th Street, NE, Washington, DC 20002.

MYERS, SAMUEL L., JR.
Economist. **PERSONAL:** Born Mar 09, 1949, Boston, MA; married Sharon E Smothers. **EDUCATION:** Morgan State Coll, BA 1971; MIT, PhD 1976. **CAREER:** Univ of Texas at Austin, asst prof of economics; Boston Coll, instr 1973; Bowie State Coll, Bowie MD, visiting instr 1972. **ORGANIZATIONS:** Mem, Amer Economics Assn; mem, Natl Economics Assn; mem, Amer Acad of Political & Social Science; mem, Amer Assn for the Advancement of Science; mem, Alpha Phi Alpha; co-coordinator, Black Grad Economics Assn 1973. **HONORS/ACHIEVEMENTS:** Alpha Kappa Mu Merit Award, 1970; Inst Fellow, MIT, 1971-73; Natl Fellowship Fund Fellow, 1973-75; Fulbright Lecturer in Economics, Cuttington Coll, Liberia, 1975-76. **BUSINESS ADDRESS:** Cuttington Coll & Div School, PO Box 277, Monrovia, Liberia.

MYERS, SERE SPAULDING
Dentist. **PERSONAL:** Born Feb 08, 1930, Oklahoma City, OK; married MaryJane Barbara Stewart; children: Dr Serese Si C'Annon, Dr Sere S Jr, Robin Lynn, Stewart, Sheryll. **EDUCATION:** Morehouse Clge, BS 1950; Univ of MO Kansas City, MS 1951; Howard Univ, DDS 1958; Queens Hosp, Cert in Oral Surgery 1959. **CAREER:** Forbes AFB, chief of oral surgery 1959-61; Priv Prac. **ORGANIZATIONS:** Pres Kansas City Howard Univ Alumni 1972-73, Natl Howard Univ Dental Assc 1983-85; Kansas City Dist Dental Soc; MO Dental Assc; Amer Dental Assc. **MILITARY SERVICE:** USAF capt 1959-61. **BUSINESS ADDRESS:** 5240 Prospect, Kansas City, MO 64130.

MYERS, WALTER DEAN
Writer. **PERSONAL:** Born Aug 12, 1937, Martinsburg, WV; son of George Ambrose and MAry Green Myers; children (previous marriage): Karen, Michael Dean; married Constance Brendel, Jun 19, 1973; children: Christopher. **EDUCATION:** State College of the City Univ of New York; Empire State College, BA. **CAREER:** New York State Dept of Labor, Brooklyn, employment supervisor, 1966-69; Bobbs-Merrill Co, Inc, New York City, senior trade book editor, 1970-77; writer, 1977-. **ORGANIZATIONS:** PEN, Harlem Writers Guild. **HONORS/ACHIEVEMENTS:** Author of Shadow of the Red Moon, Harper, 1987, Fallen Angels, Scholastic, 1988, Scorpions, Harper, 1988; author of It Ain't All For Nothin', Viking, 1978, The Young Landlords, Viking, 1979, Hoops, Delacorte, 1981, all of which were named by the Amer Library Assn "Best Books for Young Adults"; New Jersey State Council of the Arts fellowship, 1981, Natl Endowment of the Arts grant, 1982; author of Motown and Didi, 1984, whichwon the Coretta Scott King Award. **MILITARY SERVICE:** US Army, 1954-57. **HOME ADDRESS:** 2543 Kennedy Blvd, Jersey City, NJ 07304. *

MYERS, WOODROW AUGUSTUS, JR.
Physician. **PERSONAL:** Born Feb 14, 1954, Indianapolis, IN; son of Woodrow Myers and Charlotte Myers; married Dr Debra Jackson; children: Kimberly Leilani, Zachary Augustus. **EDUCATION:** Stanford Univ, BS 1973; Harvard Medical School, MD 1977; Stanford Univ Grad School of Business, MBA 1982. **CAREER:** US Senate Comm on Labor & Human Resources, physician health advisor 1984; Univ of CA, asst prof 1982-84; San Francisco General Hospital Med Center, quality assurance program chairman 1982-84, cost containment task force chairman, quality assurance/dept of med-computer system manager, dept of medicine/general internal medicine div-attending physician, medical/surgical intensive care unit-assoc director; Univ of CA Institute of Health Policy Studies, affiliated faculty mem; IN Univ Med Center, asst prof of medicine; Stanford Univ Med Center, physician specialist in surgery & attending physician; State of IN, state health commissioner. **ORGANIZATIONS:** Amer Coll of Physicians; Amer Medical Assn; Natl Medical Assn; Society for Critical Care Medicine; IN State Medical Assn; Marion County Medical Society; diplomat Amer Board of Internal Medicine 1980; advisor US Senate Comm on Labor and Human Resources 1984; mem bd of trustees of Stanford Univ 1987. **HONORS/ACHIEVEMENTS:** Book published, "Problems of Minorities at Majority Institutions, A Student's Perspective"; 15 articles published; medical licenses in states of Indiana, California, and DC; appointed by President Reagan to 13 member comm to find a strategy for battling AIDS 1987. **BUSINESS ADDRESS:** State Health Commissioner, Indiana State Board of Health, 1330 West Michigan, Indianapolis, IN 46206.

MYERS-MAY, YVETTE
Educator, business executive. **PERSONAL:** Born in New Orleans, LA. **EDUCATION:** Morgan State Univ, BS 1966; Columbia Univ, MA 1967; Harvard Univ, CAS 1970; Univ of MD, PhD 1982. **CAREER:** ABT Associates Cambridge, psychoeducator 1967; Head Start Program, ctr supervisor 1968, city-wide coord 1968-69; Towson State Univ, prog dir 1970-71, prof & researcher 1971-87; The Center for Human Devel Inc, pres 1976-. **ORGANIZATIONS:** Local regional and natl level task forces; adv bds and bd of directorships for institutions servicing children adults and families; mem Amer Psych Assoc, Amer Acad of Science, Alpha Kappa Alpha Sor. **HONORS/ACHIEVEMENTS:** Univ of MD Grad Sch Fellow 1978-82; Southern Fellowship Fund Doctoral Fellow 1979-80; Black Analysis Doctoral Dissertation Fellow 1980-82; Phi Delta Kappa; Pi Lambda Theta; Psi Chi.

MYLES, ERNESTINE (NEE JONES)
Educator. **PERSONAL:** Born Apr 19, 1921, Livingston, AL; son of Lilart Jeff Jones and Sophia Mae Abrams Jones; married Ernestine Jones (Long) Myles (divorced); children: Willie Long Jr. **EDUCATION:** Miles Coll, BA; Alabama State Univ, MEd; Univ Amherst; Auburn Univ; Troy State Univ; Sanford Univ; Alabama State Univ, AA, 1978; Howard Univ, Humanities, 1986. **CAREER:** Butler County Bd of Educ, teacher 1950-86; Dept Physical Educ, vice pres 1968-69. **ORGANIZATIONS:** Mem VISTA 1965; chmn Physical Educ Dept Dist Mtg Leader; consultant, dir Camp Bonnie Brae; Organized Classroom Teachers 1967; dir Dist VIII 1975; dir Dist VI 1972-77; League Advancement Educ 1967; chairperson Uni Serv District XIV 1976-77; mem AEA Bd 1977-80; mem Assn of Classroom Teachers; mem S Central Alabama Girl Scout Council USA; mem League for the Advancement of Educ, pres Alabama Assn of Classroom Teachers 1979-80; pres Butler County Educ Assn 1976; sec Butler County Civic League Alabama Democratic Conf 1972-; sec Secondary Congressional Dist Alabama Democratic Conf 1976-; sec Alabama Democratic Conf Bd 1973-77; sec S Regional Assn of Classroom Teachers1974-76; Girl Scout Troops 1971; S Central Alabama Girl Scout Council Inc Bd Mem 1977; Sunday School Teacher Friendship Baptist Church 1964-; dir BTU Friendship Baptist Church 1966-; US Award Sgt Shriver 1966; VISTA Pin Vice Pres; deputy registrar Butler County Alabama; Notary Public. Hubert Humphrey 1967. **HONORS/ACHIEVEMENTS:** Outstanding Educ Serv Plaque Alabama State Teachers Assn 1969; Con Serv Citation Natl Educ Assn 1971.

MYLES, HERBERT JOHN
City official, retired educational administrator. **PERSONAL:** Born Jul 31, 1923, Abbeville, LA; son of Alexander Myles (deceased) and Wilda A Myles. **EDUCATION:** USL-Lafayette, BA 1962; UNO-New Orleans, Med 1970; Nicholls St Univ, 30 plus 1971-72. **CAREER:** Vermilion Parish School System, teacher 1963-80; Herod Elem School, asst principal 1980-84; City of Abbeville, city councilman 1978-82, second term 1982-86; third term 1986-. **ORGANIZATIONS:** Member KPC Council #77 Knights Peter Claver 1965-85; member KPC Fourth Degree 3rd Assembly 1975-85. **MILITARY SERVICE:** USN aviation machinist 2nd class 6 yrs; American Campaign Medal-WW II Victory Medal 1943-49. **HOME ADDRESS:** 1009 Vernon Ave, Abbeville, LA 70510. **BUSINESS ADDRESS:** Councilmember, City of Abbeville, City Hall, 304 Charity St, Abbeville, LA 70510.

MYLES, STAN, JR.
Host, producer. **PERSONAL:** Born May 02, 1943, Los Angeles; divorced. **EDUCATION:** CA State U, BA 1966. **CAREER:** KABC-TV LA, host-producer; manpower develop specialist 1969-71; MI Mining Mfg Co, sales rep 1968-69; LA Hair Co, pub rel rep 1968-69; AL Locke HS LA, tchr 1968-June 1968. **ORGANIZATIONS:** Dir pub info Westminister Neighborhood Assn LA 1965-68; Nat Assn of Marketing Developers; Am Fed of TV & Radio Artists; Kappa Alpha Psi; YMCA; life-time mem NAACP; Urban League. **HONORS/ACHIEVEMENTS:** John Sweat Award CA Tchrs Assn; Urban Affairs Comm Rel Award LA City Schs; Man of Yr Award Bahai Faith. **BUSINESS ADDRESS:** PO Box 38796, Los Angeles, CA 90038.

MYLES, WILBERT
Business executive. **PERSONAL:** Born Aug 28, 1935, Winnsboro, LA; married Geraldine C Pinkney; children: Wilbert Anthony, Jr, Nicole Denise. **EDUCATION:** Am Inst of Banking, Atnd; Pace U. **CAREER:** Corp Trust Dept Nat Bank of North Am, asst vice pres 1973-; Asst Cashier 1968-73; Supvr 1964-68; Clerk Typist 1962-64; Mail Clerk Home Ins Co 1961-62; Baltman & Co, nyc porter 1961. **ORGANIZATIONS:** Mem Stock Transfer Assn 1968; Reorgn Group Securities Industries Assn 1975; bd of mgrs Harlem Br YMCA 1975; elected to the Nat Task Force Steering Comon YMCA in Black Comm 1975; mem BANWY's Black & Non-white YMCA's in Black Comm; mem Black Achiever's Com of Harlem YMCA of Gr NY 1974-. **HONORS/ACHIEVEMENTS:** Recip Plaque Harlem Br of YMCA of Gr NY 1974; A Salute to Black Achievers in Industry; Plaque Honor of Bank from Harlem Br of YMCA of Gr NY in Appreciation of Banks Support of 1975 Black Achievers Proj. **MILITARY SERVICE:** Served USAF a/2c 1956-61. **BUSINESS ADDRESS:** 44 Wall St, New York, NY 10005.

MYLES, WILLIAM
Associate athletic director. **PERSONAL:** Born Nov 21, 1936, Kansas City, MO; son of William Myles Sr and Vera L Phillips Myles; married Lorita Thompson, Jun 30, 1957; children: Debbie, Billy. **EDUCATION:** Drake Univ, Des Moines, IA, BS, 1962; Central MO State, MS, 1967. **CAREER:** Manual HS, Kansas City, MO, assistant football/basketball coach, 1962-63; Lincoln HS, Kansas City, MO, assistant football/basketball coach, head football coach, 1963-69; Southeast HS, Kansas City, MO, head football coach, 1969-72; Univ of NE, Lincoln, NE, assistant football coach, 1972-77; OH State Univ, Columbus, OH, assistant football coach, 1977-85, associate dir of athletics, 1985—. **ORGANIZATIONS:** Mem Christian Scientists Church, Fellowship of Christian Athletes, 1964—, american Football Coaches Association, 1972—, Natl Association of College Directors of Athletics, 1985—. **HONORS/ACHIEVEMENTS:** Kansas City Area Man of Year, Fellowship of Christian Athletes, 1970; Greater Kansas City Coach of Year, 1971; Double D Award, Drake Univ, 1981; Drake Natl Distinguished Alumni Award, Drake Univ, 1988. **BUSINESS ADDRESS:** Associate Director of Athletics, Ohio State University, 410 Woody Hayes Dr, St John Arena #227, Columbus, OH 43210.

MYRICK, CLARISSA
Associate producer. **PERSONAL:** Born May 24, 1954, Atlanta, GA. **EDUCATION:** Morris Brown Coll, BA 1976; OH St U, MA cand 1977. **CAREER:** WOSU-TV, asso prod "Inquiry" 1977; Lovely Atlanta Mag, contrib editor 1976; Atlanta Daily World Newspaper, gen assignment reporter 1975; Nat Endowment for the Arts Scriptwriters Contest, prod asst during taping of prize-winning teleplay "The Tie That Binds" 1974-75; WCLK-RADIO, newscaster, reporter 1974; Morris Brown Literay Mag, editor "Visions"; WXIA-TV, recited original poems; co-author "Hungry Souls". **ORGANIZATIONS:** 1st v chpsn Nat Coop Educ Assn 1975. **HONORS/ACHIEVEMENTS:** Dau of Am Revolution Medals 1967, 1972; Media Women Scholarship Awd Atlanta Chap 1974; 1st place Nat Endowment for the Arts Scriptwriters Prgm; Female Coop Educ Stud of Yr Awd Alpha Kappa Mu Honor Soc; Who's Who Among Black Am OH St MA Fellowship 1976; Who's Who Among Stud in AmUniv & Coll. **BUSINESS ADDRESS:** Curator, Collections of Life & Heritage, 135 Auburn Ave NE, Atlanta, GA 30308.

MYRICKS, NOEL
Educator, attorney. **PERSONAL:** Born Dec 22, 1935, Chicago, IL; married Sherralyn L Faine; children: Toussaint L. **EDUCATION:** San Francisco State Univ, BA 1965, MS 1967; Howard Univ, JD 1970; The American Univ, EdD 1974. **CAREER:** Howard Univ, prof 1967-69; Univ of Dist of Columbia, educ administrator 1969-74; Private Practice, attorney 1973-; (admitted to practice before US Supreme Court); Univ of Maryland, prof 1972-. **ORGANIZATIONS:** Certified agent NFL Players Assn 1984-; EEO investigator/cons The Match Assn 1984-; assoc editor Family Relations Journal 1978-. **HONORS/ACHIEVEMENTS:** Appointed by Pres Jimmy Carter Natl Adv Council on Extension and Cont Educ 1978-81; Outstanding & Dedicated Serv to Youth & Community Easton, PA NAACP1984; Outstanding Citizen of the Year Omega Psi Phi Frat Columbia, MD 1979; Alpha Man of the Year Alpha Phi Alpha Frat Columbia, MD 1979. **MILITARY SERVICE:** USN Musician 3rd Class served 4 yrs. **BUSINESS ADDRESS:** Assoc Professor/Attorney, University of Maryland, College of Human Ecology, College Park, MD 20742.

N

NABONNE, RONALD P.
Attorney. **PERSONAL:** Born May 11, 1947, New Orleans. **EDUCATION:** Loyola U, BA 1969. **CAREER:** Tulane Univ Sch of Law, pres scholarship, deans list; Douglas, Nabonne & Wilkerson, atty; Pub Interest Law Firm New Orleans LA, law clerk 1971-72; US Dept of Justice Civil Rights Div, law clerk 1970-71; Human Relations Com City of New Orleans, res analyst 1969-70. **ORGANIZATIONS:** Mem Am Bar Assn; Nat Bar Assn; LA State Bar Assn; Nat Conf of Black Lawyers; Lawyers Com for Civil Rights Under Law; mem Urban League; NAACP; State Bd of Dirs LA ACLU 1970-71; bd dirs Family Serv Soc 1974-75; instr Interracial Council for Bus Opp; campaign chmn LA State Sen Sidney Barthelemy 1974. **HONORS/ACHIEVEMENTS:** Recip Blue Key Hon Soc 1969; Who's Who in Am Colls &Univ 1969. **MILITARY SERVICE:** USAR 1st lt.

NABORS, CHARLES J., JR.
Educator. **PERSONAL:** Born Jan 11, 1934, Cleveland; married Joan Frances Washington; children: Brian Charles, Claire Kelley, Matthew James. **EDUCATION:** Wabash Coll, AB 1955;Univ of UT, PhD 1965. **CAREER:** Dept of Anatomy Univ of UT, instr 1965; Univ of UT, asst prof of attomy 1967; Dept of Anatomy Univ of UT, head of biochemistry group radiobiology div 1970-. **ORGANIZATIONS:** Mem Ednocrine Soc; mem Radiation Research Soc; mem NY Acad of Sci Trustee Alberta Henry Found; mem NAACP; mem US Commn on Civil Rights; delegate to Dem Nat Conv 1968; chmn UT Cit for McGovern 1972. **HONORS/ACHIEVEMENTS:** Recipient Markle Scholar in Academic Med 1969-74. **MILITARY SERVICE:** USAFR 1957-65.

NABORS, JESSE LEE, SR.
Educator. **PERSONAL:** Born May 17, 1940, Columbus, MS; married Rebecca Gibson; children: Sherri, Tejia, Jesse Jr, Marcellus III. **EDUCATION:** Tuskegee Inst, BS 1965; MEd 1968. **CAREER:** Stockton Unified Sch Dist, child welfare attendance 1971-; Tuskegee Inst, coord 1966; SUSD, tchr 1968; Tuskegee Inst, residence hall counselor 1967-68; City of Stockton, vice-mayor 1975. **ORGANIZATIONS:** Pres Stockton Br NAACP 1971-73; pres BTA 1972-73; polemarch Kappa Alpha Psi Frat; Stockton Alumni Chap 1975-77. **HONORS/ACHIEVEMENTS:** Outst serv NAACP 1973; outst serv BTA 1973; outst serv City of Stockton 1976. **BUSINESS ADDRESS:** 701 N Madison, Stockton, CA 95202.

NABRIT, HENRY CLARKE
Pastor. **PERSONAL:** Born Jul 11, 1915, Augusta, GA; married Vernice Smith; children: Henry, Jr, Barbara, Charles. **EDUCATION:** Morehouse Coll, BA 1937; Crozer Theol Sem, BD 1942; Colgate Rochester Bexley Hall Crozer, MDiv 1973; Memphis StateUniv Sch of Law, JD 1969; SimmonsU, DD 1958. **CAREER:** Third Bapt Ch Toledo, pastor 1968-; Nat Bapt Sunday Sch Pub Bd Nashville, ed quarterlies 1958-64; First Bapt Ch Memphis, pastor 1946-68; WV State Conf, dir 1945-46; Ebenezer Bapt Ch Beckly, pastor 1942-45; Am Bapt Theol Sem Nashville, prof 1938; MI, atty. **ORGANIZATIONS:** Mem Detroit Bar Assn; Monroe Bar Assn; MI State Bar Assn; Progressive Nat Pabt Conv; Am Bapt Chs in USA; NAACP; Omega Psi Phi; Mayor's Affirmative Action Com for City of Toledo; Lucas Co Mental Health Bd; Toledo-Lucas Co Legal Aid Bd; past pres Toledo Area Clergy Fellowship; atty Progressive Nat Bapt Conv; OH Migrant Com DD Inter-Faith Sem 1974. **HONORS/ACHIEVEMENTS:** Distinguished serv plaque NAACP Memphis Chap 1958. **BUSINESS ADDRESS:** Third Bapt Ch, 402 Pinewood Ave, Toledo, OH 43602.

NABRIT, JAMES M., III
Attorney. **PERSONAL:** Born Jun 11, 1932, Houston, TX; married Roberta Jacquelynn Harlan. **EDUCATION:** Bates Coll, AB 1952; Yale Law Sch, JD 1955. **CAREER:** NAACP Legal Def & Educ Fund Inc, atty 1959-. **ORGANIZATIONS:** Dir Lawyers Comm for Civil Rights. **MILITARY SERVICE:** AUS corpl 1956-58. **BUSINESS ADDRESS:** Associate Director/Counsel, NAACP Legal Defense/Educ Fund, 99 Hudson St 16th Flr, New York, NY 10013.

NABRIT, JAMES M., JR.
President emeritus. **PERSONAL:** Born Sep 04, 1900, Atlanta, GA; married Norma Walton (deceased); children: James M Nabrit, III. **EDUCATION:** Morehouse Coll, BA1923; Northwestern U, JD 1927. **CAREER:** Leland Coll, instr 1925-28; AR State Coll, dean 1928-30; Sch Law Howard U, faculty 1936-60; also active as attorney, 1936-60; Howard U, adminstrv assto pres 1938-39; Howard U, pres 1960-69 retired. **ORGANIZATIONS:** Apptd by Pres Johnson to US Dep Rep to Security Coun of UN 1965-67; mem numberous pub serv councils & coms; mem bd Nat Center for Educ in Politics; Washington Ctr for Met Studies; adv council Nat Fund for Med Edn; mem Commn on Professional & Grad Study Assn of Am Colls; mem NEA; Legal Adv Com Nat Soc for Med Research; mem Am Nat TX Bar Assns; Am Juridical Soc; Nat Lawyers Club; Nat Legal Com NAACP. **HONORS/ACHIEVEMENTS:** Numerous honorary degrees, other awards, & honors.

NABRIT, SAMUEL M.
Retired association executive. **PERSONAL:** Born Feb 21, 1905, Macon, GA; married Constance Crocker. **EDUCATION:** Morehouse Coll, BA 1925; Brown Univ, MS 1927, PhD 1932. **CAREER:** Morehouse Coll, prof of biology 1925-27; Atlanta Univ, instr chmn dept of biology dean of grad sch of arts & sci 1932-55; VI Educ Experimental Prog,prof of biology 1955; TX Southern Univ Houston, pres 1955-66; Atomic Energy Commn, appointed 1966-69; Southern & Natl Fellowships Fund, retired exec dir1967-. **ORGANIZATIONS:** Apptd to Natl Sci Bd 1956-61; bd dir Amer Council on Educ 1961; mgmt comm US So Africa Leader Exchange Prog; mem Natl Conf Christians & Jews Inc; chmn bd dirs Inst for Serv to Educ; chmn Natl Academy of Sci Panel on Hlth Svcs; served on several comms for depts of state & HEW; bd of dirof many colls & univs; pres Con Mortgage Co Atlanta; mem bd dir Afro-Am Life Ins Co Jacksonville; vice pres Standard Savings & Loan Houston; mem 1965 Houston Charter Review Commn; published several papers & articles; mem Amer Soc of Zoologists, Sigma Xi, Beta Kappa Chi, Pi Delta Phi, Omega Psi Phi, Sigma Pi Phi, Phi Beta Kappa. **HONORS/ACHIEVEMENTS:** Received many study & rsch grants; listed in Who's Who in America; World Biography and other reference works; received many honorary degrees.

NAGAN, WINSTON PERCIVAL
Educator. **PERSONAL:** Born Jun 23, 1941, Port Elizabeth, Republic of South Africa;married Judith Mattox; children: Jean, Catherine. **EDUCATION:** Univ of Ft Hare, BA 1964; Oxford U, BA1966; Oxford U, MA 1971; Kuke U, LLM, MCL 1970; Yale U, JSD 1977. **CAREER:** Univ of FL Coll of Law, prof 1975-; Monash Univ School of Law Australia, visiting prof 1979; Yale Coll, lectr 1974-75; CLEO Inst, asso prof; 1974; De PaulU Coll of Law, asso prof, asst prof 1972-75; Expedited Arbitration Proc, arbitrator 1972-74; Valparaiso Univ Sch of Law, asst prof 1971-72; VA Polytech Inst St U, asst prof 1968-71; AALS Law Tchrs Clinic, 1971; Duke Law Sch, rsch asst 1968; Ross Arnold atty-at-law, law clerk 1967. **ORGANIZATIONS:** Am Soc of Intl Law; African Stud Assn; Assn of Am Law Sch; Am Bar Assn; Ctr for Study of Dem Instn; Am Soc for Social Philosophy & Philosophy of Law; Arts & Civil SemUniv of FL; Am Civil SemUniv of FL; sec Intl Campaigtn vs Racism in Sports 1972-7(4; consult Am Bar Assn 1976; trust Intl Def Aid Fund 1971-74; Minority Com; Prom Tenure Com; Curr Com; Library Com; Fac Recruit Com; chmn Adm of Fgn Lawyers Com Univ Senate; edit Soviet Pub Intl Law 1970; exec com; Intl Def & Aid Fund for So Africa 1972-74; test UN 1968-73. **HONORS/ACHIEVEMENTS:** Faculty of Law prize Ft Hare 1963; Brasenose Oxford Overseas Scholar 1964-67; African-Am Inst Fellowship 1967-68;

James B Warburg Fellow 1974-75; num appear on radio & TV; num publ papers & speeches; Senior Fulbright Scholar MonashUniv Australia 1979.

NAILS, ODELL
Educator. **PERSONAL:** Born May 11, 1929; married Elizabeth K Thuston; children: Carla, Alicia, Odell III. **EDUCATION:** Univ of MI, post doctoral; MI State U; Wayne State U, EdD; Wayne State U, EdS; Wayne State U, EdM; Lincoln U, BS. **CAREER:** Pontiac School Dist MI, supt 1978; Pontiac School Dist MI, asst supt 1974-78; Pontiac School Dist, dir of secondary educ 1971-74; Jefferson Jr HS/Whitter Elem Pontiac, supv prin 1970-71; Jefferson Jr HS, prin 1969-70; Wayne Co Comm Coll Detroit, cons, instr 1969-; Detroit Pub Schools, staff coord 1968-69; Detroit Pub Schools, instr spec educ 1959-68; Ford Foundation (Greater Cities), instr 1961-68. **ORGANIZATIONS:** Mem Nat Alliance Black School Educ; Am Fed Tchrs; Detroit Fed of Tchrs; LincolnUniv Alumni Assn; Detroit Schoolmen's Club; Intl Platform Assn; Nat Assn of Mental Retardation; Poniac Urban League; many other prof affiliations; mem NAACP Detroit & Pontiac Chpts; Nat Council BSA; Res Officers Assn; Pontiac Council of PTA's; Area Wide Comm Council; Kappa Alpha Psi; Nat Exchange Club. **HONORS/ACHIEVEMENTS:** Listed in Community Leaders Of Am 1970; Dict of Intl Biog 1971-72.

NANCE, BOOKER JOE, SR.
Elected city official. **PERSONAL:** Born Apr 10, 1933, Crockett Cty, TN; married Everlena Lucas; children: Alice Eison, Booker J Jr, Mary, Phyllis, Gladys, Marvin. **CAREER:** Nance's Construction & Contracting, pres 1984-; Town of Gates, town board, alderman 1973-. **ORGANIZATIONS:** Chmn Parents Advisory Committee Halls Elementary. **MILITARY SERVICE:** AUS pfc 1953-55; Natl Defense Serv Medal. **HOME ADDRESS:** PO Box 97, Gates, TN 38037.

NANCE, HERBERT CHARLES, SR.
Guidance counselor/government. **PERSONAL:** Born Dec 30, 1946, Taylor, TX; son of Henry Nance, Jr and Alice Nance; married Linda Lee Brown; children: Charlinda Audlice, Herbert Jr. **EDUCATION:** Huston Tillotson Coll, BA 1969; Univ of TX at San Antonio, MA 1979. **CAREER:** Ross Jr High School, teacher/coach 1974-76; Kitty Hawk Jr High School, teacher/coach 1976-80; Vietnam Era Veterans Outreach Prog, counselor 1980-81; BASE Educ Serv Office, guidance counselor 1981-; Base Education Services SA-ALC/DPE Kelly AFB Texas Education Services Specialist 1987-. **ORGANIZATIONS:** Mem Amer Assoc Counseling 1981-; past pres Blacks in Govt 1984; trustee Lackland Indep Sch Dist Bd of Trustees 1986-; mem adv counsel Comm Coll of the Air Force 1986; asst keeper of records Omega Psi Phi Frat San Antonio Chap 1986; bd mem Bexar County Sickle Cell Anemia 1988-; Vice Basileus Psi Alpha Chapter Omega Psi Phi Fraternity Inc 1987-. **HONORS/ACHIEVEMENTS:** Outstanding Young Man in Amer 1979. **MILITARY SERVICE:** AUS sp-5 3 1/2 yrs; Army Commendation/Expert M-14. **HOME ADDRESS:** 2942 Lakeland Dr, San Antonio, TX 78222. **BUSINESS ADDRESS:** Education Services Specialist, BASE Education Services, SA-ALC/DPEPE, Kelly AFB, TX 78241-5000.

NANCE, JESSE J., JR.
Educational administrator. **PERSONAL:** Born Aug 02, 1939, Alamo, TN. **EDUCATION:** TN State Univ, Nashville, BS, 1961; Univ of WI Madison, MS 1971; Univ of TN, additional graduate studies. **CAREER:** TN High School, teacher 1961-67; Oak Ridge Assoc Univ, special training in atomic energy 1967, instructor nuclear science 1967-69; Atlantic Comm Coll, asst prof of biology 1971-76; Univ of TN Med Units Memphis, special training 1972; Jackson State Comm Coll, instructor, Biology 1976-78; Vol Comm Coll, assoc prof of biology 1978-. **ORGANIZATIONS:** Mem Phi Beta Sigma 1959; Intl Wildlife Fed 1972; church choir mem, dir male chorus, minister of educ, church school teacher. **HONORS/ACHIEVEMENTS:** Serv Key Award Baptist Student Union, 1961; Danforth Fellowship Award, Danforth Found, 1969; Acad Grant, NSF & Atomic Energy Commn 1972; Teacher of the Year, 1984-85; Martin Luther King Brotherhoold Award, 1988. **BUSINESS ADDRESS:** Associate Professor of Biology, Volunteer State Comm College, Nashville Pike, Gallatin, TN 37066.

NANCE, LARRY DONNELL
Professional athlete. **PERSONAL:** Born Feb 12, 1959, Anderson, SC; divorced. **EDUCATION:** Clemson Univ, 1981. **CAREER:** Phoenix Suns, forward 1981. **HONORS/ACHIEVEMENTS:** NBA slam dunk champ; named NBA Player of Week; honorable mention on 1980-81 Assoc Press All-Am team; NBA All-Star Player. **BUSINESS ADDRESS:** Forward, Phoenix Suns, P O Box 1369, Ste 510, Phoenix, AZ 85001.

NANCE, M. MACEO, JR.
Educational administrator. **PERSONAL:** Born Mar 28, 1925, Columbia, SC; married Julie E Washington; children: Maceo, Robert Milton. **EDUCATION:** SC State Coll, AB 1949; NY Univ, MA 1953; Morris Brown Coll, LLD 1968; Francis Marion Coll, LHD 1975; Clemson Univ, 1983; Citadel Mil Coll, 1983; Univ SC, LlD 1976. **CAREER:** SC State Coll Orangeburg, mil property custodian 1950-54, dir student union 1954-57, asst to bus mgr 1957-58, bus mgr 1958-67, vice pres bus fin 1967, acting pres 1967-68, pres 1968-1986; 1986 President Emeritus. **ORGANIZATIONS:** Dir Bankers Trust of SC; mem comm fed rel Amer Council Ed; mem Council of Pres of State Supported Insts Higher Ed SC; mem adv comm Natl Assoc Advancement of Public Negro Colls; chmn council pres Mid-Eastern Athletic Conf; mem SC State Council Boy Scouts Amer; bd dirs Coll Placement Svc, Blue Cross-Blue Shield SC; bd dir, mem exec comm United Way SC; mem Gov Comm on Police & Commun Relations; mem Natl Assoc State Univs, Land Grant Colls, NAACP; dir, treas Natl Assoc Equal Oppty in Higher Ed; mem NY Univ Alumni Assoc, Omega Psi Phi; past pres Sigma Pi Phi; mem Kiwanis, Masons. **HONORS/ACHIEVEMENTS:** Coveted Outstanding Civilian Serv Medal by the Dept of the Army; State of SC Order of the Palmetto; City of Orangeburg Citizen of the Year. **MILITARY SERVICE:** USN 1943-46. **BUSINESS ADDRESS:** President, South Carolina State College, Orangeburg, SC 29117.

NAPPER, BERENICE NORWOOD
Musician. **PERSONAL:** Born Dec 10, 1916, S Norwalk, CT; divorced; children: Patricia Knudsen, Alver Woodward Jr. **EDUCATION:** Howard Univ Washington DC, MusB 1935-40; Westport Famous Writer's School Westport CT, diploma 1950. **CAREER:** Concert artist 1940-; Am Cyanamid Co, librarian foreign div 1964; Napwood Asso, owner, dir 1953-; Natl NAACP NY, field sec, troubleshooter 1951; CT Labor Dept, unemployment comp supvr 1946-53; CT Welfare Dept, social worker 1945-. **ORGANIZATIONS:** Exec dir Urban League White Plains 1942-; Dist 12 RTM Greenwich CT Town Gov 1960-68; commr CT State Bd of Parole 1971-75; bd mem Sigma Gamma Rho Sorority 1940; bd mem State & Nat LWV/PPLI Social Serv 1940-; bd mem Norwalk Comm Coll 1973-. **HONORS/ACHIEVEMENTS:** 1st Negro woman cand Reb Nomination CT US Sen 1970; 1st Negro woman cand GOP Greenwich Nom 2nd Selectman 1979; 1st Negro vol nurse's aide Greenwich Chap ARC 1942-; Distinguished Alumni Award Howard Univ Alumni NY Chapter, 1970; Humanitarian Award Nigeria 1975; Outstanding Negro Woman CT Bicentennial Commn, 1976; Distinguished Black Women Greenwich YWCA 1977. **BUSINESS ADDRESS:** 62 N Sound Beach Ave, Riverside, CT 06878.

NAPPER, GEORGE, JR.
Adminstrator. **PERSONAL:** Born Jul 07, 1939, Berkeley, CA; married Imogene Delores Winston. **EDUCATION:** Univ of CA at Berkeley, BA 1963; Univ of CA at Berkeley, M Criminology 1968; Univ of CA at Berkeley, PhD Criminology 1970. **CAREER:** Atlanta Crime Analysis Team, exec dir; Atlanta Bureau of Police Serv, depty dir; Spelman Coll Atlanta, asso prof sociology; Psychiatry Dept Emory Univ Atlanta; Berkeley, asst to v chancellor for academic affairs 1968-69; consult state, fed, priv progs in areas of Urban Systems, jobs, econ opp, poverty, educ crime. **ORGANIZATIONS:** Mem GA State Crime Commn; Criminal Justice Coor*D Council Atlanta GA; Am Civic Lib Union Bd of Dirs; Cascade Youth Orgn Bd dirs. **HONORS/ACHIEVEMENTS:** Recip several local awards for serv to educ & comm activities; author Blacker Than Thou the struggel for campus unity 1973. **MILITARY SERVICE:** USMC pfc 1957-59. **BUSINESS ADDRESS:** 96 Mitchell St SW, Atlanta, GA 30303.

NAPPER, HYACINTHE T.
Retired government employee. **PERSONAL:** Born Feb 26, 1928, New York, NY; daughter of Charles Tatem and Georgiana Tatem; divorced; children: Cynthia, Guy, Geoffrey. **EDUCATION:** Fisk Univ, attended 1945-47; Howard Univ, AB 1951. **CAREER:** US Dept of Labor, sec Thomasina Norford Minority Groups consult 1951-53; Hon John Conyers Jr, admin asst retired 1988. **ORGANIZATIONS:** Mem Alpha Kappa Alpha Sor, Natl Urban League, NAACP, Amer Civil Liberties Union; interest in bringing greater polit awareness to Black comm improve voterturnout; mem US Figure Skating Assn, Ft Dupont Skating Club, Congressional Staff Club.

NAPPER, JAMES WILBUR
Educator. **PERSONAL:** Born Feb 25, 1917, Institute, WV; son of Walter J Napper and Zanphra D Robinson; married Cassie McKenzie, Dec 23, 1950; children: Gregory S, David M. **EDUCATION:** WV State Coll, BS 1937; WV Univ, MS 1949; Univ of CA Berkeley, Credential 1964. **CAREER:** Boyd School Charleston WV, teacher, coach 1950; Alameda Cty Oakland CA, dep probation officer 1954; DeAnza HS Richmond, teacher 1958; Richmond Unified School Dist, guidance consult 1965; Santa Rose Jr Coll, counselor 1969-82 retired. **ORGANIZATIONS:** Mem CA Teacher Assoc 1958-, NEA 1969, Phi Delta Kappa Ed Group 1976-; bd of dir NAACP 1969-74, Optimist Club of Santa Rosa 1974-76; ed adv Alpha Phi Alpha; council mem Sonoma County Area Agency on Aging 1988-; mem bd of dir Santa Rosa Suburban Kiwanis. **HONORS/ACHIEVEMENTS:** 2 Letters of Commendation Santa Rose City School 1969,70; Cert of Appreciation Dept of CA Youth Auth 1974. **MILITARY SERVICE:** AUS staff sgt 1944-46; ETO 5 Battle Stars. **HOME ADDRESS:** 3620 Williams Rd, Santa Rosa, CA 95404.

NASH, CURTIS
Attorney. **PERSONAL:** Born Jul 11, 1946, Tallulah, LA; married Betty Jean Gordon. **EDUCATION:** So Univ Baton Rouge LA, BA 1969; Univ of IL Coll of Law, JD 1972. **CAREER:** Tax Div Dept of Justice Washington DC, trial atty 1975-; Corp Tax Br IRS Nat Office, tax law spec 1972-75; Vermillion Co Legal Aid Soc Danville IL, law clk 1972; Firm of Kidd & McLeod Monroe LA, law clk 1971. **ORGANIZATIONS:** Vp Fairfax Co Wide Black Citizens Assn 1980; mem Pi Gamma Mu; mem Omega Psi Phi Frat. **HONORS/ACHIEVEMENTS:** Who's Who in Am Coll & U; recipient Equal Oppor FellowshipUniv of IL Coll of Law. **BUSINESS ADDRESS:** Department of Justice, Tax Division, 9th & Pennsylvania Ave, Washington, DC 20530.

NASH, DANIEL ALPHONZA, JR.
Physician. **PERSONAL:** Born Jul 15, 1942, Washington, DC; married Bettie Louise Taylor; children: Cheryl L, Daniel E. **EDUCATION:** Syracuse Univ, BS 1964; Howard Univ, MD 1968. **CAREER:** Georgetown Med Serv DC Gen Hosp, intership 1st yr resd 1968-70; Brooke Army Med Ctr, resd nephrology fellow 1970-73, asst chf 1973-76; Walter Reed Army Med Ctr, asst chf 1976-77, chf nephrology serv 1977-83; Private Practice Washington DC, physician 1983-. **ORGANIZATIONS:** Mem Amer Colls of Physicians 1974, fellow 1976; mem Natl Med Assn 1974; mem AMA 1975; mem Amer Soc of Nephrology 1975; mem Intl Soc of Nephrology 1975; med licensure Washington DC 1969; MD 1977; assoc prof med Howard Univ Col Med 1978; diplomat Amer Bd of Intl Med 1973; subspecialty Bd in Nephrology 1974. **HONORS/ACHIEVEMENTS:** 10 major medical publs; 12 publ abstracts; 4 sci presentations. **MILITARY SERVICE:** AUS col MC 1970-83; USAR 1983-. **BUSINESS ADDRESS:** 1328 Southern Ave S E, Ste 210, Washington, DC 20032.

NASH, EVA L.
Government association executive. **PERSONAL:** Born Jul 25, 1925, Atlantic City, NJ; widowed; children: Michele, Sharon. **EDUCATION:** Howard Univ, AB (magna cum laude) 1945; Univ of Chicago, Sch of Soc Serv Admin 1945-46; Univ of Pgh Sch of Soc Work, MSW (summa cum laude) 1959. **CAREER:** Hubbard Hosp, med soc worker 1947-49; Atlantic City NJ, sub tchr 1954-55; City of Pgh, market surveyor 1956-57; Travelers Aid, 1957; Freedman's Hosp, 1961-64; Child Guid Clinic, clinical soc worker 1964-67; DC Developmental Svc, chief soc worker 1967-69; DC Model Cities Prog, health planner 1969; HUD, comm serv officer 1969-72, asst to dir admin on aging 1972-. **ORGANIZATIONS:** Mem Natl Assn for Soc Workers 1947-; Academy of Certified Soc Workers 1962-; Amer Orthopsychiatric Assn 1965; Northwest Settlement House Aux 1972-, pres 1972-73; Budget Comm Washington Council of Planned Parenthood 1973-; Mental Health Sub-Comm Urban League 1963-64; Howard Univ & Interdisciplinary Faculty Seminar 1963-64; Bunker Hill Sch PTA 1959-64, chmn nominating comm 1960; chmn Sch Fair 1961; Western HS PTA 1965-66; DC Citizens for Better Pub Sch Educ 1966-, co-chmn spec serv comm 1968-70; Natl Comm for Support of Pub Sch 1968-; consult Group Counseling Prog Model Sch Div Sec Sch 1967-68; DC Public Sch Model Sch Div sum staff 1968; Educ Working Party of Mental Retardation

Planning Comm for DC 1968; workshop ldr Howard Univ Sch of Soc Work Sch Agency Inst 1967; NASW Regnl Conf Buffalo 1968; cnsltng seminar ldr Wash Sch of Psychiatry 1968-69; Comm Chest Area Capt Nashville 1951; World & Polit Disc Grp Pgh 1955-57, ldr 1956; bd dir DC Planned Parenthood 1968; Marriage Prep Inst Bd 1963-64; V St Proj Com 1963-64; NAACP; Nat Cncl Negro Women. **HONORS/ACHIEVEMENTS:** Urban League Vol Serv Awd 1967. **BUSINESS ADDRESS:** Dir Info & Referral, Administration on Aging/HHS, Chief Educ & Career Prep Br, 200 Independence Ave SW, Washington, DC 20201.

NASH, GEORGE T., III
Dentist. **PERSONAL:** Born Nov 06, 1935, Charlotte, NC; married Addie W Nash; children: Kimberly, Garrett. **EDUCATION:** NowardUniv Washington, BS 1957, DDS 1961. **CAREER:** Priv Prac, dr. **ORGANIZATIONS:** Sec Charlotte Med Soc 1965-66; mem Am Dental Assn 1975; Nat Dental Assn 1975; am Analgesin Soc 1975; Am Soc of Prosthodontia 1975; Am NC Dental Soc 1963-74; HowardUniv Alumni Assn. **HONORS/ACHIEVEMENTS:** Recip Turpin Memorial Award Nashville; spec consult to Picker X-Ray Corp. **MILITARY SERVICE:** AUS dentalcorps capt 1961-63. **BUSINESS ADDRESS:** 1063 S Cannon Blvd, Scottish Sq, Kannapolis, NC.

NASH, HELEN E.
Physician. **PERSONAL:** Born Aug 08, 1921, Atlanta, GA; daughter of Dr Homer E Nash, Sr and Marie Graves Nash; married James B Abernathy Sr (deceased). **EDUCATION:** Spelman Coll Atlanta, AB 1942; Meharry Med Coll Nashville, MD 1945. **CAREER:** WA Univ School of Med, clinical instr 1949-71; St Louis Childrens Hosp, vstg prof 1949; St Louis Maternity & McMillan Hosp, asst pediatrician 1949; Homer G Phillips Hosp, pediatric supr, assoc dir of pediatrics 1950-64; St Lukes Hosp St Louis, vstg prof 1962; Jewish Hosp of St Louis, vstg prof 1963; Washington Univ George Waring Brown Sch of Soc Work, lectuer 169-71; WA Univ School of Med, assoc prof clinical peds 1974, prof clinical peds 1984; St Louis Childrens Hosp, pres staff assoc 1977-79; Private Practice, physician 1949-. **ORGANIZATIONS:** Mem Amer Acad of Pediatrics 1953, Health & Welfare Council of Met St Louis, Comm of the State Welfare Dept of MO, St Louis Childrens Hosp Staff Soc, St Louis Med Soc; various committees St Louis Childrens Hosp 1948-79. **HONORS/ACHIEVEMENTS:** Honor mem St Louis Med Soc 1975. **BUSINESS ADDRESS:** 1441 N Grand, St Louis, MO 63106.

NASH, HENRY
Business executive. **PERSONAL:** Born Jun 07, 1932, Sparta, GA; children: Henry Gary, Gloria D. **EDUCATION:** Tuskegee Inst, 1 yr. **CAREER:** Subrena Artists Corp, pres 1979-; Happy Note Music Pub, pres 1979; Queen Booking Corp, vp, salesman, agt 1967-76. **ORGANIZATIONS:** Mem AGVA AF of M 1958; mem GMA 1979; col on staff of Gov Ednwin Edwards State of LA Exec Dept 1973. **HONORS/ACHIEVEMENTS:** Key to city of New Orleans Mayor Moon Landier 1973; Holy Name Soc Father Edward Donovan Green Haven Prison 1974-76; key to city of Indianapolis Mayor Richard G Luga 1975. **BUSINESS ADDRESS:** President, Subrene Artists Corp, 1650 Broadway #410, New York, NY 10019.

NASH, LEON ALBERT
Retired dentist. **PERSONAL:** Born Mar 19, 1912, Canton, MS; married Nora; children: Leon Jr, Anita. **EDUCATION:** Tongaloo Coll, 1934; Meharry Dental Sch, 1947. **CAREER:** Hathesbury MS, 1947-51; Detroit MI, retired dentist 1951-. **ORGANIZATIONS:** Omicron Kappa Epsilon Dental Soc; past pres Wolvermeed Dental Soc. **MILITARY SERVICE:** AUS 1941-44.

NASH, LEROY T.
Clergyman. **PERSONAL:** Born Sep 13, 1925, Holly Grove, AR; married Alberta Fitch; children: 4. **EDUCATION:** Moler Barber Coll St Louis , 1956; St Louis Sch Theology, 1960. **CAREER:** Christian Meth Episocpal Minister 1959-73; rebuilt Mitchell Tabernacle E St Louis 1972; organized Inc; Holsey Chapel First Independent Christian Meth Ch,St Joseph, Holsey Chapel is First Independent Christian Meth Ch Nation, pres; Holsey Chapel Ind Christian Meth Inc Barbering, minister 1956-74; electrical maint supr 1970-72; Weeden Constrn Co, supt 1973. **ORGANIZATIONS:** Master Barbers Assn St Louis 1968-73; Communications Division Master Barbers Assn 1972; Organized Inc AJEL Mt Vernon 1962-74; asst treas, incorporater of Met People Inc St Louis 1972-74; youth pres Dept Labor NAACP Mt Vernon 1962-64; youth organizer, chmn Budget Com NAACP Alton 1970-74; organized Alton Drugt Abuse Clinic 1972; servied Help Inc St Louis 1965-74; Meretorious Bus Achievement Help Inc 1965. **HONORS/ACHIEVEMENTS:** Certificated award Met People Inc 1973; key city St Joseph MO 1974. **MILITARY SERVICE:** AUS pfc 1943-46. **BUSINESS ADDRESS:** 1001 S 14 St, St Joseph, MO 64503.

NASH, THOMAS
Newspaperman. **PERSONAL:** Born Oct 05, 1919, Muskogee, OK; married Betty Jean (deceased); children: Charlotte Ann, Thomas Jr, Susan Carol, Stephen Charles. **EDUCATION:** Langston Univ, attended 1938-41, BA 1948. **CAREER:** The Post Newspaper Group, asst publisher. **ORGANIZATIONS:** Foreman pro-tem Monterey Co Grand Jury 1983-84; chmn of minority comm Monterey Co Affirmative Action Plan; state pres United Black Fund of CA. **HONORS/ACHIEVEMENTS:** Certificate of Appreciation Seaside Chamber of Commerce 1985, Monterey County Legal Aid Soc, Concerned Citizens of Monterey; Proclamation City of Seaside 1986. **MILITARY SERVICE:** AUS 1st sgt 1941-49; USAF 1st lt 1949-54. **BUSINESS ADDRESS:** Assistant Publisher, The Post Newspaper Group, 630 20th St, Oakland, CA 94612.

NATHAN, TONY CURTIS
Professional athlete. **PERSONAL:** Born Dec 14, 1956, Birmingham, AL; married Johnnie F Wilson; children: Nichole, Natalie. **EDUCATION:** Univ of AL Tuscaloosa. **CAREER:** Miami Dolphins, professional football running back 1979-. **HONORS/ACHIEVEMENTS:** Named All-NFL Kick Returner Assoc Press; All-AFC Punt Returner Sporting News; Played in Sr Bowl & Hula Bowl. **BUSINESS ADDRESS:** Miami Dolphins, 4770 Biscayne Blvd, Ste 1440, Miami, FL 33137.

NAYLOR, GLORIA
Writer. **PERSONAL:** Born Jan 25, 1950, New York, NY; daughter of Roosevelt Naylor and Alberta McAlpin Naylor. **EDUCATION:** Brooklyn Coll, BA English, 1981; Yale Univ, MA, Afro-Amer Studies, 1983. **CAREER:** George Washington Univ, Washington DC, visiting lecturer, 1983-84; New York Univ, New York NY, visiting professor, 1986; Princeton Univ, Princeton NJ, visiting lecturer, 1986; Boston Univ, Boston MA, visiting professor, 1987; Cornell Univ, Ithaca NY, senior fellow society for the humanities, 1988. **ORGANIZATIONS:** Executive bd mem Book of the Month Club 1989-. **HONORS/ACHIEVEMENTS:** Novel: The Women of Brewster Place 1982; American Book Award 1983; NEA Fellowship Natl Endowment for the Arts 1985; Novel: Linden Hills 1985; Guggenheim Fellowship 1988; Novel: Mama Day 1988. **BUSINESS ADDRESS:** Ticknor & Fields, 52 Vanderbilt Ave, New York, NY 10016.

NAYLOR, LAURETTA See THOMPSON, LAURETTA PETERSON

NAYMAN, ROBBIE L.
Psychologist. **PERSONAL:** Born Oct 07, 1937, Dallas, TX; married Dr Oguz B. **EDUCATION:** BS 1960; MS 1962; PhD 1973. **CAREER:** CO St U, sr cnslrUniv Cnslng Ctr, dirUniv Lrng Lab 1970-; WI St Dept of Hlth & Soc Svcs, affirm act coord 1969-70;Univ of WI, tchng asst 1964-69; StUniv Coll, asst dean of stds 1962-64; So IL U, cnslr 1960-62. **ORGANIZATIONS:** Mem Am Personnel & Guidance Assn; Am Psychol Assn; Pi Lambda Theta; mem Urban Leag NAACP. **HONORS/ACHIEVEMENTS:** Listed in Who's Who Among Am Coll Stds 1957; Outstndng Young Women of Am 1967. **BUSINESS ADDRESS:** Colorado State University, Univ Learning Lab, Aylesworth Hall NE Wing CO Sta, Fort Collins, CO 80523.

NDLOVU, CALLISTUS P.
Educator, government official. **PERSONAL:** Born Feb 09, 1936, Plumtree, Zimbabwe;married Angelina Wami; children: Siboniso, Mpumelelo, Nomalanga. **EDUCATION:** Univ of South Africa, BA 1965; New York Univ, MA 1968; SUNY, PhD 1973. **CAREER:** Hofstra Univ, Hempstead, Long Island, dir Africana Studies Inst, assoc prof history; Zimbabwe, minister of construction 1982-83, minister of mines 1983-85, minister of industry & technology. **ORGANIZATIONS:** Encyclopedia Africana; Comm of Concerned Afro-Amer Academics; mem, bd trustees, Ujamaa Acad for High School Dropouts, 1971-; asst ed, Pan-African Journal, 1971-73; mem, Friends of Museum of Natl History; chmn, Zimbabwe Comm, 1972; pres South African Rsch Assoc, 1974-; del, Geneva Conf on Rhodesia, 1976. **HONORS/ACHIEVEMENTS:** New York recipient, Outstanding Educators of Amer, 1972; Aggrey Fellow, Edward W Hazen Found. **BUSINESS ADDRESS:** Minister Industry/Technology, Country of Zimbabwe, PO Box 8434 Causeway, Harare, Zimbabwe.

NEAL, ALIMAM BUTLER
Physician, anesthesiologist, pain consultant. **PERSONAL:** Born Mar 29, 1947, Tuskegee, AL; son of Odis Neal and Gladys Neal; married Ruth Elizabeth Reid; children: Michael, Alimam Jr, Alaina, Angela. **EDUCATION:** Howard Univ, BS 1968; Howard Univ Coll of Medicine, MD 1973. **CAREER:** Walter Reed Army Medical Ctr, intern 1973-74, resident anesthesiology 1974-77; Eisenhower Army Medical Ctr, chief dept anesthesiology 1978-80; Medical Coll of Georgia, asst prof anesthesiology 1980-81; Univ Hosp Augusta GA, private anesthesiologist 1981-; Augusta Diagnostic Pain Center, pres; A B Neal and Assoc, pres; ABNA Realty, pres, CEO. **ORGANIZATIONS:** Mem Stoney Medical/Dental/Pharm Soc; life mem Alpha Phi Alpha; mem Natl Medical Assn, GA State Medical Assn, Amer Soc Anesthesiology, NAACP; trustee, Bethel AME Church. **HONORS/ACHIEVEMENTS:** Diplomate Amer Bd Anesthesiology 1979; Fellow Amer Coll Anesthesiology 1977; Spinal Cord Stimulation Workshop Phoenix, AZ, 1989. **MILITARY SERVICE:** AUS major 11 yrs; Army Commendation Awd 1978. **HOME ADDRESS:** 3415 Wheeler Rd, Augusta, GA 30909. **BUSINESS ADDRESS:** President, Augusta Diagnostic Pain Center, 1325 Troupe St, Augusta, GA 30904.

NEAL, BRENDA JEAN
Manager. **PERSONAL:** Born Jan 03, 1952, Greenville, SC; children: Damon Yusef. **EDUCATION:** New Mexico State Univ; Onondaga Community College, AA Social Work 1976; Le Moyne College, BA Sociology 1978. **CAREER:** Lincoln First Bank, teller 1974; Syracuse City School District, school social worker 1982-83; Xerox Corp, internal control mgr, customer service mgr 1983-. **HONORS/ACHIEVEMENTS:** Black Achievers Award 1490 Enterprise Buffalo 1983; Special Merit Award Xerox Corp 1984. **MILITARY SERVICE:** AUS Specialist 4; Outstanding Trainee Award (ranked 1st out of 34 men) 1971. **HOME ADDRESS:** 114 - Kay St, Buffalo, NY 14215. **BUSINESS ADDRESS:** Customer Service Manager, Xerox Corporation, 1 Marine Midland Center, Buffalo, NY 14203.

NEAL, EARL LANGDON
Attorney, chief executive officer. **PERSONAL:** Born Apr 16, 1928, Chicago, IL; son of Earl J Neal and Evelyn S Neal; married Isobel, Sep 24, 1955; children: Langdon D Neal. **EDUCATION:** Univ of IL, BA, 1949; Univ of MI, JD, 1952. **CAREER:** City of Chicago, Chicago, IL, attourney, Chicago Land Clearance Commission, 1955-61, assistant corporation counsel, 1961-68, special assistant corporation counsel, 1969—; Earl L Neal & Associates, proprietor, 1968—. **ORGANIZATIONS:** Trustee emeritus, Univ of IL; director, Chicago Title & Trust, Chicago Title Ins Co, Peoples Energy Corp, Lincoln Natl Corp, First Chicago Corp, First Natl Bank, Chicago Central Area Committee; life member, NAACP. **HONORS/ACHIEVEMENTS:** Outstanding Leader Award, Little Flowers, 1977; outstanding service award, Univ of IL Black Alumni, 1982; Man of the Year, Boys and Girls Clubs of Chicago, 1985; distinguished service award, Univ of IL Alumni Association, 1988. **MILITARY SERVICE:** US Army, cpl, 1953-54; served in Europe. **BUSINESS ADDRESS:** Earl L Neal & Associates, 111 W Washington St, Suite 1010, Chicago, IL 60602.

NEAL, EDDIE
Engineer. **PERSONAL:** Born Dec 18, 1943, Reidsville, NC; son of Charlie H Neal and Gertrude Farrish Neal; married Dianne Tyrance, Jun 28, 1986; children: Ayoka Z Neal, Damali C G Neal. **EDUCATION:** Howard Univ, BS, 1966; Catholic Univ, MA, 1971, PhD, 1986; Graduate Studies, Univ of MI; Univ Coll (London, UK) Webb Institute; Teesside Polytechnic Institute (UK). **CAREER:** US Dept of Transportation, research engineer, 1966-67; US Navy, research scientist, 1967-76; Chi Associates, vice pres, 1976-79; The Scientex Corporation, pres/CEO, 1979-. **ORGANIZATIONS:** Mem, Sigma Xi, 1973-; mem, Society of Naval Architects, 1975-; mem, Touchdown Club, 1985-; mem, NAACP, 1986-; mem, Kappa Alpha Psi, 1987-; mem, Honorary Committee, Charles R Drew World Medical Prize, 1989; dir, Assn of Small Research, Engineering and Technical Services Companies, 1989-. **HON-**

RS/ACHIEVEMENTS: Invited author, 8th and 10th International Symposia on Naval ydrodynamics, 1970, 1974; invited speaker, ASCE Conference, Highway Safety: At The ossroads, 1988. **BUSINESS ADDRESS:** President, The Scientex Corporation, 1750 w York Avenue, NW, Suite 200, Washington, DC 20006.

EAL, EDNA D.
lucational administrator. **PERSONAL:** Born Jan 19, 1943, Pine Bluff, AR; daughter of well L Devoe, Sr and Florell W Devoe; divorced; children: Yolande Aileen. **EDUCA-ON:** AM&N Coll, AB 1965; Univ of AR, MEd 1973; IN Univ, EdD 1978. **CAREER:** nployment Security Div, career counselor 1961-69; Univ of AR at Pine Bluff, asst dir counling ctr 1969-79; Youngstown State Univ, exec asst student svcs 1979-88; Sinclair Communi- College Dayton Ohio vice pres student serv 1988-. **ORGANIZATIONS:** 2nd Vice Pres oungstown YWCA Bd of Dirs 1983; mem Lake to River Girl Scout Council Bd 1982-; mem ahoning Co Transitional Homes Inc 1984-; mem Youngstown City Bd of Health 1986-88. **ONORS/ACHIEVEMENTS:** Nominee Who's Who Among Amer Women 1978; awd minee YWCA Tribute to Black Women 1983; Prof Woman Natl Assn of Negro Bus & Prof omen's Clubs 1983. **HOME ADDRESS:** 131 Folsom Drive, Dayton, OH 45405. **JSINESS ADDRESS:** Vice President for Student Services, Sinclair Community College, 4 West Third Street, Dayton, OH 45405.

EAL, GREEN BELTON
ysician. **PERSONAL:** Born Sep 04, 1946, Hopkins, SC; married Linda Mattison; chilen: Green II, Tiffany, Marcus. **EDUCATION:** Benedict Coll, BS 1966; Meharrymed oll, MD 1971; VanderviltUniv Med Sch, Flw 1973-75; GW Hubbard Hosp, Resid 1972-73. **AREER:** Self-empl, physician; Providence Hosp, med staff; Columbia; SC Richland Meml osp; Meharry Med Coll, asst prof med; GW Hubbard Hosp; dir cardiac catherization lab 75-76. **ORGANIZATIONS:** Mem NMA 1975; GA St Med Assn 1975; LA St Med Assn 75; consult Physician Tuskeegee Inst; Mem Nat Med Assn; AMA; bd mem Boy's Club of tr Columbia; Columbia Med Assn; mem Am Heart Assn; Congaree Med Dental & Pharm ssn. **HONORS/ACHIEVEMENTS:** Flwsp Grant in Cardiology NIH. **BUSINESS DDRESS:** Dir of Prof Medical Serv, South Carolina Dept of Correct, 4444 Broad River oad, Columbia, SC 29210.

EAL, HERMAN JOSEPH
ysician. **PERSONAL:** Born Dec 31, 1923, Alexandria, LA; son of Herman Joseph Neal d Catherine Johnson Neal; married Caridad Antigueno Neal, 1980; children: Ronald, Aninette, Renee, Eric John. **EDUCATION:** Wilson Jr Coll, AA 1943; Howard Univ 1943-; Northwestern Univ, pre-med 1945-48; Univ of IL Med School, 1952. **CAREER:** Cook ounty Hosp Chicago, phys (intern) 1952-53; Provident Hosp Chicago, physician 1953-67; ook County Hosp, phys/pediatrician 1955-57; Walther Meml Hosp, 1967-80; St Mary of azareth Hosp, physician 1976-80; physician. **HONORS/ACHIEVEMENTS:** "Paratyoid - Osteomyelitis in Sickle Cell Anemia" Cook Co Hosp Phys Bulletin 1957. **MILI-ARY SERVICE:** US Army Quartermaster, private first class, 1943-45; Overseas Serv Award 45; European Service Award, 1943-45. **BUSINESS ADDRESS:** Physician, 946 W 79th , Chicago, IL 60620.

EAL, HOMER ALFRED
ientist, educator. **PERSONAL:** Born Jun 13, 1942, Franklin, KY; married Donna Dans; children: Sharon; Homer Jr. **EDUCATION:** Indiana Univ, BS Physics 1961; Univ of ichigan, MS Physics 1963, PhD Physics 1966; Indiana Univ, DSc Hon Degree 1984. **CA-EER:** Indiana Univ, asst prof physics 1967-70, asso prof physics 1970-72, prof physics 1972-, dean research & grad dev 1977-81; Suny Stony Brook, provost 1981-86, prof of physics 86-. **ORGANIZATIONS:** Fellow Amer Physical Society 1972-; mem Natl Sci Bd 1980-; mem NY Seagrant Inst Bd of Directors 1982-86; fellow Amer Assoc for Adv of Sci 1983-; ustee Universities Research Assoc Bd of Trustees 1983-; mem SUNY Research Foundation d of Directors 1983-86; mem Scientist's Inst for Public Info Bd of Trustees 1985-87. **ONORS/ACHIEVEMENTS:** Fellow Natl Sci Found, Washington, DC 1966-67; fellow oan Found 1968; chrmn Argonne Zero Gradient Synchrotron Users Group 1970-72; trustee rgonne Univ Assoc 1971-74; mem Physics Advisory Panel Natl Sci Found 1976-79; mem igh Energy Physics Advisory Panel US Dept of Energy 1977-81; fellow JS Guggenheim ound 1980-81; chmn Natl Science Foundation Physics Adv Panel 1986. **BUSINESS AD-RESS:** Professor of Physics, StateUniv of NY, Department of Physics, Stony Brook, NY 794.

EAL, IRA TINSLEY
lucational administrator. **PERSONAL:** Born Nov 14, 1931, Memphis, TN; married Jaceline Elaine Wiley. **EDUCATION:** Evansville Coll IN, BA 1960; INUniv Bloomington, S 1964. **CAREER:** Evansville-Vanderburgh School Corp, dir of fed projs 1977-, supr 70-77; Comm Act Prog Evansville, exec dir 1966-70; Neighborhood Youth Corps, dir 1965-; Evansville-Vanderburgh School Corp, teacher 1960-65. **ORGANIZATIONS:** Pres ride Inc 1968-78; sec-treas New Hope Housing Inc 1979-80; ctr asso IL /IN Race Desegreation Assistance Ctr 1979-80; mem Kappa Alpha Psi Frat1966-80; bd mem Vanderburgh o Judiciary Nominating Com 1971-80; bd mem Inner City Cultural Ctr 1977-80. **HON-RS/ACHIEVEMENTS:** Nominated NEA's Carter G Woodson Award Local Black Tchrs 78; Black Comm Award Black Comm of Evansville 1978; plaque for Srv Rendered Head art of Evansville IN 1979. **MILITARY SERVICE:** AUS sfc 1947-56. **BUSINESS AD-RESS:** 1 SE Ninth St, Evansville, IN 47708.

EAL, JAMES S.
ssociation executive. **PERSONAL:** Born Sep 07, 1922, Washington, KY; married Manie; ildren: Patricia, Angela, John, Michael. **EDUCATION:** Xavier U, BS, BA; Xavier Eveing Coll; Chase Coll of Commerce; LaSalle Ext U. **CAREER:** Urban Leag of Cincinnati c, proj dir 1973-; Am Agr Chem Co, supr 1942-67. **ORGANIZATIONS:** Pres Chief Conact Neg Local Union of Intrntl Un Dist 50 United Mine Wrkrs 22 yrs; past pres Cincinnati hap Ohio Black Pol Assembly; past pres 13th Ward Avondale Dem Club; past mem Hamiln Co Dem Exec Com; precienct exec 8 yrs; past mem bd Seven Hills Neighborhood Houses c; past chmn Hlth & Safety Com Avondale Comm Cncl Inc; mem bd trustees, exec com egro Sightless Soc; labor rep Handicaps United for Betterment Inc; 3rd Deg KC; cand for H St Gen Assembly.

EAL, JOSEPH C., JR.
Investment, insurance agent. **PERSONAL:** Born Mar 23, 1941, Memphis, TN; son of Joseph C Neal, Sr and Hattie Counts Owens; children: Lisa M, Thomas Joseph. **EDUCATION:** Trade Tech Coll LA, AA 1960; CA State Coll LA, BA 1973. **CAREER:** Phoenix Mutual Life Ins Co & Phoenix Equity Planning Corp, agent/fin planner 1969-; Christian Method Episcopal Church, gen sec fin dept. **ORGANIZATIONS:** Mem NAACP 1965-; 32nd degree mason Prince Hall Grand Lodge 1966-; fin counselor Various businesses in CA 1969-; mem Los Angeles Life Underwriters Assoc 1969-; mem LA Kiwanis Club 1972-; licensed rep Natl Assoc of Securities Dealers 1974-; provisional mem Inst of Cert Fin Planners 1982-. **HONORS/ACHIEVEMENTS:** Outstanding Sales Phoenix Mutual Life Ins Co; Blue Vase Winner, presidents club mem; Honorary Dr of Laws Lane College 1989. **BUSINESS ADDRESS:** General Secretary Fin Dept, Christian Meth Episcopal Ch, PO Box 75085, Los Angeles, CA 90075.

NEAL, LYNWOOD
Systems manager. **PERSONAL:** Born Mar 29, 1932, Chattanooga, TN; married Billie Morrison; children: Lynwood, Jr, Wanda L. **EDUCATION:** So U, BS 1964; MI St U, MBA 1976. **CAREER:** Chrysler Corp, mgr sys 1974-, mgr indsl engr 1972-74, grp staff indsl engr 1967-69, indsl engr supr 1969-72. **ORGANIZATIONS:** Mem Nat Black MBA Assn; Nat Mgmt Assn; Chrysler Corp Mgmt Club; ordained deacon Presb Ch; mem SoUniv Alumnus Assn Detroit Chpt. **HONORS/ACHIEVEMENTS:** Candidate Chrysler Corp, MI St Advance Mgmt Prog Masters Deg. **MILITARY SERVICE:** Usaf s/sgt 1950-60. **BUSINESS ADDRESS:** Mound Road Engine Plant, PO Box 2919, Detroit, MI 48251.

NEAL, SYLVESTER (SAM)
Government official. **PERSONAL:** Born Sep 21, 1943, Austin, TX; son of Willis Neal and Ima L Jenkins Neal; married Doris Marie (Mims) Neal; children: Sylvia, Sylvester L, Keith, Todd, Angela Williams. **EDUCATION:** Univ of Alaska Fairbanks, Fairbanks AK, Justice, 1983. **CAREER:** City of Austin, Austin TX, firefighter, 1965-68; US Army, Fort Wainwright AK, firefighter, crew chief, 1968-70; State of Alaska, Dept of Transportation, Fairbanks AK, firefighter, security police, 1970-79, fire/security chief, 1979-83, Dept of Pulbic Safety, Anchorage AK, state fire marshal, 1983-. **ORGANIZATIONS:** Mem, bd (2 years), Alaska Fire Chiefs Assn, 1976-, Alaska Peace Officers Assn, 1979-; sec, Fairbanks Kiwanis Club, 1982-83; mem, Intl Fire Chiefs Assn, 1983-, Fire Marshals Assn of North Amer, 1984-; mem, consultant, Alaska Assn of Public Fire Educ, 1985-; pres, Anchorage Kiwanis Club, 1987-88; bd of dir, Community Action for Drug Free Youth, 1988-; lieutenant governor-elect, Kiwanis/Alaska-Yukon Div, 1989-90. **HONORS/ACHIEVEMENTS:** Student of the Year Justice Dept, Univ of Alaska Fairbanks, 1982; Kiwanian of the Year, Fairbanks Kiwanis Club, 1983; Magna Cum Laude Graduate, Univ of Alaska Fairbanks, 1983; Outstanding President, Kiwanis/Pacific Northwest Dist, 1989. **MILITARY SERVICE:** US Army, Sergeant E-5, 1968-70. **HOME ADDRESS:** 4812 Hunter Dr, Anchorage, AK 99502.

NEAL, WILLIAM J.
Educator. **PERSONAL:** Born Aug 22, 1913, Birmingham, AL; married Dorothy L Neal; children: William Jr, Barbara, Paul, Marguerite, Jolene, Louis. **EDUCATION:** Lane Coll, AB 1938; Wayne St U, M 1952;Univ of Chgo, Cert 1972. **CAREER:** School of Soc Work Valparaiso Univ, assoc prof 1968-; Fireman House Chicago exec dir 1958-68; Kenwood Ellis Comm Ctr, prog dir 1955-58; various positions in soc work since 1935. **ORGANIZATIONS:** Mem bd Grand Blvd Mntl Hlth Assn; Chicago Comm Fund Spkrs Bureau; past mem Bd Nat Presby Hlth & Wlfr Assn; mem Pub Rels Forum Chgo; mem bd Martin Luther King Urban Prog Ctr; Consult Nat Cncl on Aging Wash 1974-75; mem Am Assn Soc Wrkrs; mem ACSW; Kappa Alpha Psi; NAACP; Nat Fed of Settlements NY; exec comUniv Senate Coord of Spec Min Prog; mem Deans Club Valparaiso U; Century Club Ln Coll; faculty std advsr Dept of Soc Wrk; MIK Club; bd of dir Chase House Day Care Ctr;Univ Senate ValparaisoUniv 1969-79; mem Cncl on Soc Wrk Ed; Oper PUSH Chgo; USO; dir USO Club at Ft Leonard Wood; dir USO Club Ft Riley. **HONORS/ACHIEVEMENTS:** Recip Plaque for Woutstndng Comm & Civic Rels Ln Coll 1974; Outstndng Alumni Plaque Chicago Chap Ln Coll Alumni Assn 1980; listed Who's Who in Ed award Life Membership Kappa Alpha Psi Frat 1979; appoint rep ValparaisoUniv to IN St Inter Coll Cncl on Aging 1979. **BUSINESS ADDRESS:** Valparaiso University, Afro American Studies, Valparaiso, IN 46383.

NEALS, FELIX
Attorney. **PERSONAL:** Born Jan 05, 1929, Jacksonville, FL; married Betty Harris; children: Felice, Felix, Julien. **EDUCATION:** ID State Univ, BS; Washburn Univ, LLB, JD 1958. **CAREER:** Appellate Law NY, private practice 1960-64; ITT & RCA, mgmt positions 1965-69; Jazz Hall of Fame NYC, founder/partner; NY Dept of State, admin law judge; Private Practice, corporate law. **ORGANIZATIONS:** Mem dir Intl Bus Serv, Natl Minority Bus Council, Interracial Council for Bus Oppor; arbitrator Comm Dispute Serv Amer Arbitration Assn NY; assocAmer Assn of Minority Enterprises Small Bus Investment Co; founder "Psycho-Systematics" (course of mental control); authority and collector of matls on Black Magic; bd mem Kid Watch Inc (prevention of cruelty to children) 1986-; bd mem State Council of Societies for Prevention of Cruelty to Children Inc 1988-; bd mem NY Society for Prevention of Ageism and Cruelty to the Aged Inc 1989-. **HONORS/ACHIEVEMENTS:** US Natl Intercoll Oratorical Champion 1954-55; Who's Who in Amer Colls & Univs 1955; Who's Who in American Law 4th ed; Who's Who in the East 21st ed; Who's Who in the World 8th ed; Men of Achievement 5th ed 1986-87. **MILITARY SERVICE:** AUS corpl 1946-49. **BUSINESS ADDRESS:** Administrative Law Judge, NY State Department of State, 270 Broadway, New York, NY 10007.

NEALS, HUERTA C
Physician. **PERSONAL:** Born Oct 23, 1914, Fernandina, FL; son of Julious Neals and Hattie Neals; married Antoinette Johnson; children: Neal Byron, Huerta Johnson. **EDUCATION:** Edward Waters Jr College, 1932-34; Morehouse College, Atlanta GA, BS 1936; Howard Univ Medical School, Washington DC, MD 1942; Grad Fellow Cardiovascular Dis Harvard Univ Med Sch, 1957-58. **CAREER:** JC Med Center, intern 1942-43; Am Bd of Internal Med, diplomate 1962; Amer College of Physicians, fellow 1963-; JC Med Center, attend phys med 64-; Univ Med Dentistry of NJ, clinical assoc prof med 1967-; Med Center Jersey City, NJ, private phys attend phys med. **ORGANIZATIONS:** Life Mem NAACP 1962; pres Hudson County Heart Association, 1968-70; mem Hudson Health Sys 1983-; mem NJ Medical Soc Exec Council, 1984; past pres Alpha Phi Alpha Frat Beta; pres NJ Soc of Internal Med 1986-. **HONORS/ACHIEVEMENTS:** International attention & awards, The Pioneer in Motor Medical Outreach Care for the Disabled & Aged, 1970—; reognition of years of exemplary service NJ Soc Internal Med 1979; Whitney M Young Jr Award Urban League of Hudson County 1981; Medical Dental Staff Service Award 1981; Stanton HS Class

of 1932 for Dedicated Compassionate Humanitarian Service 1982; special recognition award Am Soc Internal Med 1983; tribute from Afro-American Historical & Cultural Soc, 1987; governor's award, 1988, for outstanding senior citizen of Hudson County. **MILITARY SERVICE:** AUS captain 1943-45; first black officer assigned to a General Hosp in Italy during WW II 1945. **BUSINESS ADDRESS:** Private Practice, Medical Cntr, 130 Atlantic St, Jersey City, NJ 07304.

NEAVON, JOSEPH ROY
Clergyman. **PERSONAL:** Born Dec 04, 1928, New York, NY. **EDUCATION:** Manhattan Coll NY, BA 1950; GregorianUniv Rome Italy, STD 1973. **CAREER:** Blessed Sacrament Fathers, rev, dr, prof 1985. **ORGANIZATIONS:** Parliamentarian Cath Theol Soc of Am 1970-; mem Black Cath Clergy Caucus 1978-; Faculty Flwshp John CarrollUniv Cleveland OH 1980-81. **BUSINESS ADDRESS:** 5384 Wilson Mills Rd, Highland Heights, OH 44143.

NEBLETT, RICHARD F.
Retired manager. **PERSONAL:** Born Mar 03, 1925, Cincinnati, OH; son of Nicholas Neblett and Haidee Neblett; married Barbara Kibble; children: Elizabeth. **EDUCATION:** Univ of Cincinnati, BS 1949, MS 1951, PhD 1953. **CAREER:** Exxon Corp, mgr 1973-86; Govt Rsch Lab, dir 1970; Agr Prod Lab, dir 1966; asst div dir 1965; Natl Action Council for Minorities in Engrg, pres 1986-89. **ORGANIZATIONS:** Mem Amer Chemical Soc; mem, pres Bd of Educ Plainfield 1963-74; trustee Union Coll; mem Council on Foundations 1981-87; Sci-Tech Center at Liberty State Park; Energy Conservation and Facilities Management Corp; Chemists' Club. **HONORS/ACHIEVEMENTS:** Phi Beta Kappa. **MILITARY SERVICE:** AUS 1st lt 1943-46.

NEDD, JOHNNIE COLEMON See COLEMON, JOHNNIE

NEELY, DAVID E.
Educational administration. **PERSONAL:** Born in Chicago, IL. **EDUCATION:** Fayetteville State Univ, BA Sociology 1975; Univ of ID, MA Sociology 1978; Univ of IA School of Law, JD 1981. **CAREER:** Univ of IA, univ omobudsman 1979-81; IL State Univ, assoc prof pol sci 1981-83, dir of affirm action 1981-83; Natl Bar Assoc, reg dir; John Marshall Law School, asst dean. **ORGANIZATIONS:** Legal counsel IL Affirm Action Officer Assoc, IL Human Relations Assoc, IL Comm on Black Concern in Higher Ed, Chicago Southside Branch NAACP. **HONORS/ACHIEVEMENTS:** Capital punishment discrimination An Indicator of Inst Western Jrnl of Black Studies 1979; innovative approach to recruiting minority employees in higher ed EEO Today 1982; Blacks in IL Higher Ed A Status Report Jrnl for the Soc of Soc & Ethnic Studies 1983; The Social Reality of Blacks Underrepresentation in Legal Ed Approach Toward Racial Parity 1985. **BUSINESS ADDRESS:** Assistant Dean, The John Marshall Law School, 315 S Plymouth Ct, Chicago, IL 60604.

NEELY, HENRY MASON
Attorney. **PERSONAL:** Born Jan 13, 1942, Washington, DC; married Elsie T; children: Allen, Frank. **EDUCATION:** Morgan St Coll, BA 1963; Howard Univ Sch of Law, LlB 1966. **CAREER:** DC, spl US dep marshal 1964; Met Police Dept DC, mem 1965; Armstrong Adult Ed Ctr, bus law & polit sci instr 1966-70; Clinton W Chapman Firm, asso atty 1967-71; pvt prac of law; Pub Serv Commn DC, v-chmn 1971-. **ORGANIZATIONS:** Mem Washington Bar Assn; mem Jud Br DC Bar Assn; Grt Lks Conf of Utility Commr; Nat Assn of Regulatory Untility Commr; mem Gamma Theta Upsilon Frat; Nat Soc of Pershing Rifles; Intrntl Moot Ct Team; Sigma Delta Tau Legal Frat; active in HowardUniv Child Dev Ctr; past mem Wash Bar Assn Leg Com; former vol, supr, atty HowardUniv Legal Interns; trustee DC Inst of Mntl Hygiene. **HONORS/ACHIEVEMENTS:** Recip Assn of AUS Medal 1962; Am Jurisprudence Prize, Joint Publ of Annotated Reports Sys, for Outstndng Academic Achiev in Commercial Law 1985. **MILITARY SERVICE:** AUS. **BUSINESS ADDRESS:** 1625 I St NW, Washington, DC 20006.

NEHEMIAH, RENALDO
Professional athlete. **PERSONAL:** Born Mar 24, 1959, Newark, NJ; married Patrice A Theard. **EDUCATION:** Univ of MD. **CAREER:** San Francisco 49ers, wide receiver 1982-. **ORGANIZATIONS:** Commentator for ABC-TV's Olympic track and field coverage this past summer. **HONORS/ACHIEVEMENTS:** Holds four wrld indoor hudles marks; broke the wrld record outdoors at the Bruce Jenner Classic; major wins include 1978 AAU, 1979 NCAA, AAU, Pan Am Games, World Cup; 1980 AAU/TAC, US Olympic Trials. **BUSINESS ADDRESS:** Chief Executive Officer, San Francisco 49ers, 711 Nevada St, Redwood City, CA 94061.

NEIL, CLEVELAND OSWALD
Company executive. **PERSONAL:** Born Oct 14, 1931. **EDUCATION:** Univ of CA, MBA Mgmt Theory & Policy 1962; Univ of CT, BS Indust Admin 1961. **CAREER:** ICBO, staff position 1970-73, exec dir 1973-78; BDCSC, pres & ceo 1978-. **ORGANIZATIONS:** Appt to Small Bus Adv Bd 1984; mem Trade & Commerce Comm 1984 Olympic Prog, Black Business's Assoc of Los Angeles, Office of Econ Devel Planning Comm, Los Angeles Spec Impact Area Overall Economic Devel Prog, State Comm on Intergroup Relations Ad Hoc Comm, Los Angeles Consular Corp-Hon Consul for Jamaica; bd of dir Los Angeles Training & Job Devel Prog, Kedren Mental Health & Chmn of Head Start Comm, Organization of Caribbean Amer People's Bd of Dir; task force LA Intl Airport Minority Concessions & Bus Opport, US House of Rep Small Bus & Minority Devel, Minority Enterprise, Minority Contractors. **HONORS/ACHIEVEMENTS:** Cert of Apprec Kedren Head Start & CA State Pre-School Ed 1975, S CA Small Bus & Econ Utilities Council, Councilman Robert Farrell 8th Council Dist, LA Area Chamber of Comm, LA Reg Purchasing Council, Lakewood Pan Amer Festival; Cert of Awd Project Dir; Cert of Membership the Black Businessmen's Assoc; Resolution of Commendation State Senator David Roberti Chmn Senate Select Comm on Small Bus Enterprises, Assemblyman Julia C Dixon 63rd Dist; Cert of Appointment State Senator David Roberti Chmn, Senate Select Committee on Small Bus Enterprises. **BUSINESS ADDRESS:** President, Business Dev Cntr of So CA, 3807 Wilshire Blvd #700, Los Angeles, CA 90010.

NEIZER, MEREDITH ANN
Transportation executive. **PERSONAL:** Born Jul 24, 1956, Chateauroux, France;daughter of Donald Frances Neizer and Roberta Marie Faulcon Neizer. **EDUCATION:** US Merchant Marine Acad, Kings Point NY, BS, 1978, USCG Third Mate License, 1978; Stanfo Graduate School of Business, Stanford CA, MBA, 1982. **CAREER:** Arco Marine, Lon Beach CA, third mate, 1978-80; Exxon Intl, Florham Park NJ, sr analyst, 1982-86; US Dep of Defense, Washington DC, special asst, 1986-87; New York/New Jersey Port Authority New York NY, mgr, 1987-. **ORGANIZATIONS:** Kings Point information representativ Kings Point Alumni Assn, 1979-89; minority representative, Stanford Graduate School Business Admissions, 1982-89;; corporate liason comm, New Jersey Black MBA Assn 198 89; consultant, Morris County Business Volunteers for the Arts, 1986; chair subcommitte #1; Defense Advisory Comm on Women in the Services, 1987-90; mem, Navy League, 198 89; young exec fellow, Fund For Corporate Initiatives, 1989. **HONORS ACHIEVEMENTS:** Partner, Creative Renovations Assoc, 1984-85; White House Fellow President's Commn on White House Fellowships, 1986, 1987; Leadership Award, New Jerse Black MBA Assn, 1986; Woman Pioneer, Kings Point Assn, 1988. **BUSINESS AD DRESS:** Assistant Manager, Port Department, The Port Authority of New York and Ne Jersey, One World Trade Center, Floor 64E, New York, NY 10048.

NELMS, OMMIE LEE
Association executive. **PERSONAL:** Born Jul 04, 1942, Houston, TX; married Donn Marie Ashley. **EDUCATION:** Dillard U;Univ of MO KC, BA 1965, Grad Study. **CA REER:** MO Dept of Ins, Wstrn Div, asst mgr 1975-; Allstate Ins Co, KC Reg Off, undrwrtn div mgr 1969-75; Jr HS, tchr. **ORGANIZATIONS:** Mem Nat Undrwrtrs Soc 1970-75;yt coord KC Br NAACP; dist lay ldr MO W Conf of United Meth Ch 1974; del S Cen Jurisdic tional Conf of UnitedMeth Ch 1972; lay ldr Centennial United Meth Ch KC 1967-75. **HONORS/ACHIEVEMENTS:** Recip Paragon Award for Undrwrtng Excell 1971; Arc Bow Award for Reg Achiev in Undrwrtng 1973. **BUSINESS ADDRESS:** MO State Offic Bldg, 615 E 13 St, Kansas City, MO 64106.

NELSON, A'LELIA (NEE RANSOM)
Business executive. **PERSONAL:** Born Aug 14, 1918, Indianapolis, IN; divorced; childrer Lynn, Jill, Stanley, Ralph. **EDUCATION:** Talladega Coll, AB 1938; Columbia Univ, M 1940. **CAREER:** Library of Congress, supr acquisitions dept 1942-47; Mme CJ Walker M Co, vice pres 1947-53, pres 1953-. **ORGANIZATIONS:** Mem NAACP, Delta Sigm Theta; bd dir N Side Ctr for Child Devel; bd dir ICBO New York City Chapt; bd dir Vande Zee Inst; bd dir Studio Mus.

NELSON, ARTIE CORTEZ
Physician. **PERSONAL:** Born Oct 06, 1955, Baltimore, MD; married Stacy Hayne Nelson MD. **EDUCATION:** Comm Coll of Baltimore, AA 1973-75; Towson State Univ BS 1975-79; Meharry Med Coll, MD 1979-84. **CAREER:** Sinai Hosp, pediatric res 1984-85 King Drew Hosp, pediatric res 1985-86; pvt practice 1986; pvt practice, creative psychiatr 1987; King/Drew Med Ctr,resident psychiatry. **ORGANIZATIONS:** Mem Amer Me Assoc 1979, Natl Med Student Assoc 1979, AMA 1980, Amer Psych Assoc 1986. **HON ORS/ACHIEVEMENTS:** Outstanding Young Amer 1983. **HOME ADDRESS:** 13705 Clarkdale Ave, Norwalk, CA 90650. **BUSINESS ADDRESS:** Resident Psychiatry, King Drew Medical Center, 12304 Santa Monica Blvd, Ste 300, Los Angeles, CA 90025.

NELSON, CHARLES J.
Educational administrator. **PERSONAL:** Born Mar 05, 1920, Battle Creek, MI; son c Schuyler A Nelson; married Maureen Tinsley. **EDUCATION:** Lincoln Univ, AB 1942; NY Univ, MPA 1948. **CAREER:** Rsch assoc state govt 1949-52, program asst MSA Manil 1942-53, public admin analyst FOA 1953-54, public admin specialist 1954-55, deputy specia asst for communications devel ICA 1955-57, chief commun devel advisor Tehran 1958, com mun devel adv dept of state 1960, chief Africa-Latin Amer branch 1960-61, detailed Africa branch 1961; Office Program Devel & Coord PC Washington, assoc dir 1961-63; Office Deve Resources AID, dir 1963-64; No African Affairs, dir 1964-66, dep dir Addis Ababa 1966-68 dir Dar es Salaam 1968-71; Botswana, Lesotho, Swaziland, Garborone, ambassador 1971 74,dir aid Nairobi; Howard Univ Sch Human Ecol, admin 1978-81, international consultan 1981-. **ORGANIZATIONS:** Chmn mayors Intl Adv Council; bd dir Girl Scouts US; Coun cil Nation's Capital; mem Georgetown Citizens Assoc, Voice of Informed Community Ex pression, Smithsonian Inst, Amer Political Sci Assoc, Soc Intl Devel Clubs, Intl Fed City WA Natl Bd of Dir Sister Cities Intl 1986-; co chair Africa Round Table SID; mem Beijing Friend ship Council, DC Dakar Friendship Council Bangkok; Council of the Overseas Developmen Council. **HONORS/ACHIEVEMENTS:** Council of Amer Ambassadors; Assoc of Black Amer Ambassadors; Lincoln Univ Hall of Fame. **MILITARY SERVICE:** AUS captai 1942-47. **HOME ADDRESS:** 1401 35th St NW, Washington, DC 20007.

NELSON, CLEOPATRA MCCLELLAN
Retired educator. **PERSONAL:** Born Sep 26, 1914, Norriston, PA; married Russell L Nelson. **EDUCATION:** Attended, Cheyney Training Sch for Teachers; Cheyney State Coll BS 1950; Temple Univ, Moore Inst, Dale Carnegie Inst, further study. **CAREER:** Kidd Culture, 1938-40; Norriston Youth Center, teacher counselor 1940; aircraft mech oper aircraf riveter 1st class, 1942-45; Frankfud Arsenal, clerk 1945-46;W Side Day Care Center, teache 1951-52; Bd of Educ Child Care Centres, teacher 1952-59; Blankenbury School Philadelphia teacher 1965-72; Wm Dick School, teacher 1960-83; Philadelphia Bd of Educ, teacher 1975-83 (retired). **ORGANIZATIONS:** V chair Lower Merion-Boro of Narberth Dem Comm; cmt wmn Montgomery Co Dem 1946-84, ward ldr 1970-81; past officer Zeta Phi Beta Sor Beta Delta Zeta Chap 1951-84; mem Main Line Mercy Douglass Hosp Club; sec Ardmore Comm Dev Corp; fund raising chmn ACDC; mem parlimentarian Main Line Charities; sec MainLine Br NAACP 1967-84; sec Mary E Gould Assembly #61 OGC; sec Labor & Indus Com NAACP; sec Golden Circle #61; vice pres Main Line Assn of Bus & Professional Womer 1978-80; appte Christian Ed Bd of Dirs Zion Bapt Ch Ardmore PA 1980; pres Dem Party Lower Merion & Narberth 1981-84, v chair 1984-85, cmtwmn 1984-86; mem Main Line Inc Dem; mem Bd Dirs Merion Dem Women; mem League of Women Voters; chmn Main Line Br NAACP Golden Anniv Marriott Hotel Philadelphia 1976-77-78-79-80; banquet chai Mary E Gould #61 OGC 1986. **HONORS/ACHIEVEMENTS:** Exhibition for Delta Sigma Theta Sor at Drexel Inst Philadelphia 1978, Haverford Coll, Martin Luther King Cele bration, Zion Bapt Church Ardmore PA; NAACP Most Outstanding Serv Awd Isabel Strick land Awd; Comm Serv Awd Calvary Baptist Ch Ardmore PA 1978; Dem Comm Lower Me rion Narberth Awd at Haverford Coll; exhibition of personal artifacts collection Merion Tribute House for Philadelphia Arts Soc 1980; Mary E Gould #61 Serv Awd 1983; Mary E Gould OGC Serv Awd 1986; Women's Literary Guild Golden Anniversary Chair 1987.

NELSON, DARRIN
Professional athlete. **PERSONAL:** Born Jan 02, 1959, Sacramento, CA; married Camilla; children: Jordan Darrin. **EDUCATION:** Stanford, BA. **CAREER:** MN Vikings, running back 1982-. **HONORS/ACHIEVEMENTS:** Miller NFL Man of Yr Awd in 1984; Led NFC kickoff returns; NCAA all time; all purpose yardge leader.

NELSON, DAVID E.
Coach, broadcaster, retired professional. **PERSONAL:** Born Jun 20, 1944, Fortsill, OK. **EDUCATION:** Compton Coll, 1963; CA State, 1965. **CAREER:** Chicago White Sox, coach; TX Christ U, Ft Worth, baseball coach 1979-; KBMA-TV Kansas City, MO, broadcaster 1977-79; KC Royals, professional baseball player 1976-77; TX Rangers, professional baseball player 1972-75; WA Senators, 1970-71; Cleveland Indians, 1968-69. **ORGANIZATIONS:** Athletes for Youth Found; Robintech Inc Big Brother of Am; co-chmn Am Cancer Soc 1971; head of baseball chapel for TX Rangers. **HONORS/ACHIEVEMENTS:** 1968 Rookie All-Star Team; mem Am League All-Star Team 1973; most valuable player, TX Rangers 1973. **MILITARY SERVICE:** AUS Reserve pfc 1965-71. **BUSINESS ADDRESS:** Chicago White Sox, 324 W 35th St, Chicago, IL 60616.

NELSON, DAVID S.
Judge. **PERSONAL:** Born Dec 02, 1933, Boston, MA. **EDUCATION:** Boston Coll, BS 1957, JD 1960. **CAREER:** Crane Inker & Oteri, assoc 1960-73; US Commissioner, 1968-69; State of Massachusetts, asst atty general 1971-73; Superior Court, Boston MA, justice 1973-79; US Dist Court Massachusetts, judge 1979-. **ORGANIZATIONS:** Fellow Amer Bar Found; mem Amer Law Inst. **HONORS/ACHIEVEMENTS:** Natl Award Christians & Jews, 1970; Thomas More Award, Boston College, 1973; Hon JD 1974-75. **BUSINESS ADDRESS:** United States District Court, Federal Court, 1525 Post Office & Courthouse, Boston, MA 02109.

NELSON, DOEG M.
Police official. **PERSONAL:** Born Sep 25, 1931, Daddridge, AR; married Rose Junior. **EDUCATION:** St Mary's Coll, BA 1977; AZ St U, 1953-54; Phoenix Coll, 1955-66. **CAREER:** Phoenix Police Dept, asst police chief 1973-; maj 1972-73; capt 1969-72; lt 1967-69; sgt 1960-67; patrolman 1954-60. **ORGANIZATIONS:** Vp, treas Progress Assn for C Dev Grand Master, Prince Hall Masons; Elks; Frat Order of Police; comm rel ofcr Nat Assn of Police; IACP; Nat Assn of Soc Serv Wrkrs. **HONORS/ACHIEVEMENTS:** Outst Serv Award Manpower Ctr 1969; Outst Cit Award Urban Leag 1971; Man of Yr Prince Hall Masonic Shriners 1970; Man of Yr Phoenix OIC 1972; Sup Serv Award Am Soc for Pub Adm 1973; Outst Serv Award LEAP 1974. **MILITARY SERVICE:** AUS corpl 3 yrs. **BUSINESS ADDRESS:** 620 W Washington, Phoenix, AZ 85003.

NELSON, EDWARD O.
Test engineer. **PERSONAL:** Born Feb 02, 1925, Johnsonville, TN; married Pauline; children: Stanley, Michael, Michelle, Cozetta, Richard, Viola. **EDUCATION:** St Louis U; Rankin Tech Inst. **CAREER:** Rockwell Insternat Envrnmntl Monitrng Serv Ctr, tech staff; US Envrnmntl Prtctn Agency St Louis, engr tech. **ORGANIZATIONS:** Mem Am Radio Relay Leag. **HONORS/ACHIEVEMENTS:** 1st blk admtd to Intl Brthrhd of Elec wkrs.

NELSON, EILEEN A.
Artist/designer. **PERSONAL:** Born in Chicago, IL; daughter of Summers Eileen Anderson and Frances Irons; married Alphonzo Nelson, Dec 07, 1975; children: Maisha Eileen Nelson. **EDUCATION:** Attended, IL Inst of Tech 1966-69, Art Institute of Chicago 1959-64, Los Angeles City Coll 1970-74, Indian Valley Coll 1975-79. **CAREER:** Permanent Dimensional Art Mural Chatworth CA 1975; Permanent Art Mural San Francisco CA 1978; Novato Library, solo showing 1984; Fairfax Library, solo showing 1984; The San Francisco African Amer Historical & Cultural Soc, solo showing 1985; Crown Zellerbach Gallery, solo showing 1985; Utilitarian Church Martin Luther King Jr Room, solo showing 1986; The San Francisco African Amer Historical and Cultural Soc, solo showing 1986; work appears on several album covers, films and TV graphic designs; Soft Sculpture, "Children of Planet Earth" "Impressions of Sao Paulo Brazil" 1986-87; Studio F, artist/designer. **HONORS/ACHIEVEMENTS:** Received awd for painting displayed at Henery Horner Boys Club of Chicago, IL; helped design the Afro-Amer Pavilion at the World's Fair in Spokane, WA; work included in an art showing at Los Angeles County Museum of Art; solo art show, San Francisco, 1989; solo art show, Chicago, IL 1989. **BUSINESS ADDRESS:** Designer, Artist, Studio F, 7 Regent Ct, Novato, CA 94947.

NELSON, GEORGE H.
Business executive. **PERSONAL:** Born Oct 03, 1924, Harris Co Houston, TX; married Annie Gooden. **EDUCATION:** So Bus Coll, Attend 1952;Univ of IA, 1969. **CAREER:** KYOK Radio Sta, comm rels dir. **ORGANIZATIONS:** Vp NASTRA; bd dir Operation PULL Houston; bd dir Christian Rescue Mission; publ bd of San Jacinto Lung Assn; mem Progressive & Amateur Boxing Assn; mem Houston Sprtwrtrs & Sprtscstrs Assn; MC at Many Black Ch in area; started KYOK Easter Sunrise Srvs; started Mtn of Food Camp at Christmas; dir Regigious Affairs KYOK. **HONORS/ACHIEVEMENTS:** Recip Sports Publ Merit Award Prairie View A&M Coll; Outstndng Achiev Award Charles Bush Enterprises 1974; cert of Appreciation TX SoUniv 1973; cert of Recognition Nat Cncl of Negro Women 1971; letter of Appreciation Proj PULL 1974. **MILITARY SERVICE:** AUS 1943-45. **BUSINESS ADDRESS:** Community Relations Dir, KYOK Radio, 3001 Labranch, Houston, TX 77004.

NELSON, GILBERT L.
Attorney. **PERSONAL:** Born Oct 05, 1942, Princeton, NJ; married J Mary Jacobs; children: Christine, Jessica. **EDUCATION:** Trinity College Ct, BA 1964; Georgetown Law School, JD 1967. **CAREER:** State of NJ, deputy public defender 1968-70; Middlesex Cty,NJ, assistant prosecuter 1970-72; New Brunswick, NJ, city atty 1975-86; Self Employed atty at law 1968-. **ORGANIZATIONS:** Dir Urban League of Greater NB 1968-70; dir Damon House 1975-81; mem Ntl Bar Assoc 1968-; mem New Jersey Bar Assoc 1968-. **HONORS/ACHIEVEMENTS:** Mayor New Brunswick, NJ 1978; Who's Who In Amer Law; archon Mu Boule-Sigma Pi Phi 1984-. **MILITARY SERVICE:** Army Reserve sgt 1968-74. **HOME ADDRESS:** 29 Goodale Cir, New Brunswick, NJ 08901. **BUSINESS ADDRESS:** Attorney, 148 Livingston Ave, New Brunswick, NJ 08903.

NELSON, H. VISCOUNT, JR.
Educator. **PERSONAL:** Born Jul 10, 1939, Oxford, PA; married Joan K Ricks; children: Christer V, Berk William. **EDUCATION:** West Chester State Coll, BS 1961; Univ of PA, MA 1962, PhD 1969. **CAREER:** The Center for Student Programing, Univ of CA, Los Angeles, dir Dartmouth Coll, assoc prof 1975-, asst prof 1972-75; UCLA, asst prof 1969-72; Univ of PA, teaching fellow, head teaching asst 1966-69; Abington High School, teacher, 1964-66; Oxford HS, public school teacher 1962-64. **ORGANIZATIONS:** Amer History Assn; Org of Amer Historians; former mem examining com Advance Placement in US History Educ Testing Serv; Danforth Assoc unofficial part-time track & field coach. **HONORS/ACHIEVEMENTS:** Author, "The Philadelphia NAACP race vs class consciousness during the thirties", journal of black studies 1975; "Black Philadelphia & the great depression" in press. **BUSINESS ADDRESS:** Center for Student Programming, University of California-LA, 405 Hilgard Ave, Los Angeles, CA 90024.

NELSON, HOWARD
Dentist. **PERSONAL:** Born Feb 10, 1923, Wash, DC; married Evelyn I Dunlap; children: Karen D. **EDUCATION:** Howard U, AB 1947, DDS 1954. **CAREER:** Self-empl, dentist;Univ of MO Sch of Dentistry, prof 1971-; Div of Preventive & Comm Dentistry, asst clinical prof; Model Cities Nghbrhd Hlth Ctr, 1971-72; Wayne Minor Hlth Ctr, ch bd dir 1968-72. **ORGANIZATIONS:** 1st Black mem Bd Govs MO Dental Assn 1975-78; pres Mdwstrn St Dental Soc 1964; pres Heart of Am Dental Soc 1964; Gr KS City Dental Soc; Dentist Invest Grp; chmn KC Chap CORE 1964-66; life mem NAACP. **HONORS/ACHIEVEMENTS:** Kappa Alpha Psi Hon Award Midtown Optimist Club of KC MO 1964; Srv Award Wayne Minor Hlth Ctr. **MILITARY SERVICE:** AUS 1st lt 1943-46; USAR 1946-52. **BUSINESS ADDRESS:** 2126 E 63rd St, Kansas City, MO 64130.

NELSON, IVORY VANCE
Educator. **PERSONAL:** Born Jun 11, 1934, Curtiss, LA; son of Elijah Nelson and Mattie Nelson; married Patricia; children: Karyn R, Cherlyn Y Kirk. **EDUCATION:** Grambling State Univ, BS Chemistry (Magna Cum Laude) 1959; Univ of KS, PhD Analytical Chem (Summa Cum Laude) 1963. **CAREER:** Grambling State Univ, chem tchr 1961; Amer Oil Co, research chem 1962; Southern Univ Baton Rouge LA, assc prof dept chem 1963-67; Universidad Autonomous de Guadalajara Fulbright Lectureship, visiting prof dept chem 1966; Loyola Univ, visiting prof 1967; Southern Univ Shreveport LA, chrmn div natural sci 1967-68; Prairie View A&M Univ, prof asst acad dean univ 1968-71; Union Carbide, sr research chem 1969; Prairie View A&M Univ, prof vice pres Research & Spec Prog 1971-82, acting pres 1982-83; TX A&M Univ Syst, exec asst to chancellor; Alamo Community College District San Antonio TX, chancellor 1986-. **ORGANIZATIONS:** Pres council 1984-, pub rel adv comm 1984-, chancellor's student adv bd 1984-, System Long-Range Plan Comm 1984-, System Research Council 1983-, TX A&M Univ System; reorg of TX A&M Univ System 1980, System-Wide Study of Marine & Marine-Related Sciences 1980, Energy & Minerals Adv Council 1977-81, Mining & Minerals Flwshp & Research Council 1980, Pres Council 1975-78 Prairie View A&M Univ; Amer Assn for Adv of Science 1963-; Amer Chem Soc 1963-; TX Acad Science 1968-; TX Coastal & Marine Council 1983-; Agr Research Inst 1980-83; Natl Assn of State Univ & Land Grant Colleges Exec Comm 1980-82; Exec Comm Council Research Policy & Grad Educ 1976-83; Natl Council Unic Research Admin 1983-86; NY Acad of Science 1976-83; Phi Delta Kappa Educ Prof Frat; S East Consortium for Intl Development Bd of Dir 1976-83; cnsl Oak Ridge Assn Univ; consult Natl Science Foundation; cnsl Natl Council for Accreditation of Teachers Educ; bd of dirs San Antonio Chamber of Commerce; bd of visitors Defense Equal Opportunity Management Institute; bd of dirs United Way San Antonio TX; bd of dirs United Way of San Antonio, Boy Scouts, Symphony of San Antonio, Southwest Research Institute, American Institute of Character Educ. **HONORS/ACHIEVEMENTS:** Omega Psi Phi Highest Freshman Schlst Award Grambling Univ 1956; TH Harris Schlrshp Grambling State Univ 1959; DuPont Tchng Flwshp Univ of KS 1962; Flwshp Natl Urban League 1969; Fulbright Lectureship; Phi Beta Kappa Hnry Soc; Phi Lambda Upsilon Hnry Chem Soc; Soc of Sigma Xi for Scientists; Beta Kappa Chi Sci Hnr Soc; Alpha Mu Gamma Foreign Lang Hnr Soc; Kappa Delta Pi Educ Hnr Soc; Sigma Pi Sigma Physics Hnr Soc; NAACP; Optimist Club of America Prairie View; Omega Psi Phi Frat. **MILITARY SERVICE:** USAF staff sgt 1951-55; Top Secret Cryptographic Clearance 1952-55. **BUSINESS ADDRESS:** Chancellor, Alamo Comm College District, 811 West Houston, PO Box 3800, San Antonio, TX 78284.

NELSON, JONATHAN P.
Business executive. **PERSONAL:** Born Jun 05, 1939, New York; married Dorothy Higgins. **EDUCATION:** St John's U, MBA 1974; Howard U, BS 1963. **CAREER:** Pfizer Inc, mgr oral prod pkg dept 1968-; EG&G Inc, electronics engr 1967-68; ACF Ind Inc, electronics design engr 1963-67; Nat Bur of Standards, std trainee 1961-63. **ORGANIZATIONS:** Mem Nat Black MBA Assn 1974-; Am Fin Assn 1973-; IEEE 1963-; Nat Mgmt Assn 1968-; mem exec bd Brooklyn BSA; mem Brooklyn Jaycees; mem bd dir MartinLuther King Male Glee Club; dir B-Q Enterprises Inc; Omega Psi Hi. **HONORS/ACHIEVEMENTS:** Recip Achiev Award Nat Assn of Negro Bus & Professional Women 1969; Black Achiever in Ind Harlem YMCA 1972, 1974. **BUSINESS ADDRESS:** Sr Packaging Engineer, Nabisco Brands, Inc, PO Box 1944, East Hanover, NJ 07936.

NELSON, NATHANIEL W.
Podiatrist. **PERSONAL:** Born Nov 28, 1921, Birmingham, AL; married Lee E; children: Altamease, Beth, Nolita, Stanley, Pierre, Milford. **EDUCATION:** WayneUniv of Detroit, attended; Inst of Tech, 3 yrs; doctor degree in podiatry. **CAREER:** Podiatrist to foot sergery Detroit; foot surgeon license in podiatric & medicine AL, MS, Tn; constructed a med bldg Detroit practice foot corrections & treatment; podiatrist admitted hosp surgical staff; Old Kirwood Hosp, chief of podiatry svc. **ORGANIZATIONS:** Mem MI Podiatry Assn; Am Podiatry Assn; Nat Podiatry Assn; OH Coll of Podiatric Med Alumni Assn; mem Bethal AME Ch BTA. **HONORS/ACHIEVEMENTS:** Political work on bill in Lansing MI that helped include podistrist work in the Blue Shield Act & the law that calls a podiatrist a physician & surgeon 1962; first black podiatrist to be aptd as examiner & consult in Detroit area of Aetna Life & Casalty Ins Co for foot & ankle disabilities Quarter Master Serv & Corp 1943-46. **BUSINESS ADDRESS:** 16451 Schoolcraft Rd, Detroit, MI 48227.

NELSON, NOVELLA C.
Actress, singer, director, producer. **PERSONAL:** Born Dec 17, 1939, Brooklyn, NY; children: Alesa Novella. **EDUCATION:** Brooklyn Coll. **CAREER:** J Papp, consult 5 yrs; NYSF, The Public Theatre, NEC, directed many plays incl Les Femme Noire, Sister Sonjii, Sweet Talk; "Purlie", "Caesar & Cleopatra", Passive Games", actress; Theatre, Division

Street, The Skin of Our Teeth, South Pacific, The Little Foxes, Trio, Purlie, Hello Dolly, House of Flowers, Ceaser & Cleopatra; TV, He's Hired She's Fired, Chiefs, The Doctor's Story, One Life to Live, You Are There, All My Children, As the World Turns, The Equalizer; Films, Orphans, The Cotton Club, The Flamingo Kid, An Unmarried Woman, The Seduction of Joe Tynan. **ORGANIZATIONS:** Mem ACT, Alliance Theatre, Seattle Rep; singer at many clubs, colleges, concerts; teacher "Creative Space" Argus School; mem Natl Council Negro Women, DeltaSigma Theta; mem bd DST Comm of Arts & Letters, Harlem Childrens Theatre, New Heritage Theatre; bd mem Studio WIS; dir The Public Theatre "Nigger Nightmare", "Sweet Talk", "Black Visions", "Les Femmes Noires"; Negro Ensemble Company "Perfection in Black", "Where We At", "Sister Sonj/II"; Manhattan Theatre Club revival of Nigger Nitemare; producer Sunday series at the Public Theatre, music at the Delacorte,TV The Public Theatre in the Park Cable TV. **HONORS/ACHIEVEMENTS:** Album "Novella Nelson". **BUSINESS ADDRESS:** c/o ICM, 40 West 57th St, New York, NY 10019.

NELSON, ORVILLE ALFONZO
Business executive. **PERSONAL:** Born Jul 11, 1925, Chicago, IL; divorced; children: Patricia, Pier, Janet, Orville, Michael. **EDUCATION:** Barber & Beauty Coll Crescent Sch Bty. **CAREER:** Kovado Inc, pres; Nelson Prod Inc; House of Nelson Bty Salon Consult Nelson's Rsrch & Devel Labs; Johnson Prod, asso prtnr. **ORGANIZATIONS:** Mem Faith Temple Ch of God; Free & Accepted Masons; 20th Ward Dem Hdqts Preceint Level Humanitarian. **HONORS/ACHIEVEMENTS:** Man of Yr Award; outsdng achvmt bty profession; concerned citz for fair & impartial justice. **MILITARY SERVICE:** AUS sgt 1942. **BUSINESS ADDRESS:** 8522 S Lafayette, Chicago, IL 60620.

NELSON, PATRICIA ANN
Agency executive. **PERSONAL:** Born Aug 20, 1955, Brooklyn, NY; daughter of Herbert Lee Nelson and Doretha Smith Nelson. **EDUCATION:** Long Island Univ Brooklyn Campus, AAS Bus Admin 1977, BS Mgmt 1978, MS Comm Health 1985. **CAREER:** Tri-State Health Svcs, office mgr 1978; Aspen Systems Corp, sr document analyst 1979; SUNY Health Science Center at Brooklyn, teaching hospital admin asst 1980; Kings Co Addictive Disease Hosp SUNY Health Science Center at Brooklyn, asst for univ financial analysis 1982-; Wyckoff Heights Hospital, asst dir admitting 1985-86; Long Island Univ Brooklyn Campus, learning specialist in writing; 1986-; Dime Savings Bank of NY, sales/management instructor, 1987-89; Girl Scout Council of NY, membership development director, 1989-. **ORGANIZATIONS:** Serv volunteer WNET Channel 13 1980-; program specialist Girl Scout Council of Greater NY 1980-; treasurer Long Island Univ Alumni Assn Brooklyn Campus 1983-85; pres bd of dirs Innervisions A Group of Young Performers Inc 1984-86; vice pres Long Island Univ Alumni Assn Brooklyn Campus 1985-86; bd mem Arnold & Marie Schwartz Coll of Pharmacy and Health Sciences Long Island Univ 1986-89; mem, American Society of Training & development, 1989-; mem, American Society of Notaries, 1989-. **HONORS/ACHIEVEMENTS:** Lifetime Membership Nursing Students Assoc of NY State 1977; cowriter refund grant Brooklyn Arts & Culture Assoc thru NEA NYSCA NYDA 1985; Outstanding Volunteer, Girl Scout Council of NY, 1989. **HOME ADDRESS:** 127 Chauncey St, Brooklyn, NY 11233. **BUSINESS ADDRESS:** Membership Development Director, Girl Scout Council of Greater New York, 76 Court Street, Rm 52, Brooklyn, NY 11201.

NELSON, PAUL DONALD
Business executive. **PERSONAL:** Born Mar 10, 1932, Pittsburgh, PA; married Joyce Ann Miller; children: Donna Jean Freeman, Donald, Paula. **EDUCATION:** Robert Morris Coll; Duuesne U. **CAREER:** Bus & Job Devel Corp, pres 1975-; vice pres corp devel treas 1972-75; OMBE asst to pres, ast treas, dep dir 1971-72; proj mgr, bus spec 1968-71; loan & officer 1967-68; bus counselor 1966-67; field coord 1965-66; Nelsons Auto Svc, managing partner 1965-; mgr 1960-65; asst mgr 1955-60; parking attendant 1950-55. **ORGANIZATIONS:** Chmn Homewood AME Zion Ch; Laymen's Council Allegheny Conf AME Zion Ch; mem Pitts Conv & Visitors Bur; Am Red Cross; Pittsburgh Afro-am Investment Devel; task force Homewood/Brushton Citizens Renewal Council; treas NAACP; US C of C; mem E Liberty C of C; Urban Youth Action Inc; bd dirSW PA Econ Devel Dist; parolees Sponsor; Nat Parking Assn; Boy Scouts of Am; econ devel com City of Pitts; econ devel com Allegheny Co; PA Minority Bus Devel Authority; Gtr Pitts C of C Minority Entrepreneurship; FEB/MBOC; solictor United Fund & Heart Fund of Allegheny Co; vice-chmn New WorldNat Bank; Rotary Club of Pitts; ilkinsburg Dem Party; mem Dem com. **BUSINESS ADDRESS:** 7800 Susquehanna St, Pittsburgh, PA 15208.

NELSON, PRINCE ROGERS (PRINCE)
Singer, composer, producer. **PERSONAL:** Born Jun 07, 1958, Minneapolis, MN. **CAREER:** Albums: "For You," 1978; "Prince," 1979; "Dirty Mind," 1980; "Controversy," 1981; "1999," 1982; "Around the World in a Day," 1985; "Parade," 1986; "Sign 'o the Times," 1987; "The Black Album," 1988; "Lovesexy," 1988. Motion picture soundtracks: "Purple Rain," 1984; "Under the Cherry Moon," 1986. **HONORS/ACHIEVEMENTS:** Academy Award Best Original Song Score "Purple Rain" 1984; 3 Amer Music Awds; 3 Grammy Awds. **BUSINESS ADDRESS:** c/o Tom Ross, Creative Artists Agency, 1888 Century Park East 14th Fl, Los Angeles, CA 90067.

NELSON, RICHARD Y., JR.
Executive director. **PERSONAL:** Born Aug 27, 1939, Atlantic City, NJ; married Nancy Allen; children: Michael, Michele, Cherie, Gregg, Nancy. **EDUCATION:** San Fran State Coll, BA 1961; TempleUniv Law Sch, JD 1969. **CAREER:** Nat Assn of Housing & Redevel Ofcls, dep exec dir 1970-; Philadelphia Regional Ofc Dept of Housing & Urban Devel, area coord 1965-70; Def Support Agency Phila, purchasing agt 1961-65; NJ Bar, admitted 1969. **ORGANIZATIONS:** Mem Am Soc of Assn Exec; mem Alpha Phi Alpha Frat; NAACP; officer Local PTA. **BUSINESS ADDRESS:** 2600 Virginia Ave NW, Washington, DC 20037.

NELSON, RICKY LEE
Professional athlete. **PERSONAL:** Born May 08, 1959, Elroy, AZ; married Deanna Nelson. **EDUCATION:** AZ St Univ, 1977-81. **CAREER:** Seattle Mariners, oufielder 1983-. **HONORS/ACHIEVEMENTS:** Attended AZ St univ winning All-Pac 10 honors while playing for the 1981 Coll World Series champions.

NELSON, ROBERT WALES, SR.
Physician. **PERSONAL:** Born Mar 26, 1925, Red Bank, NJ; married Pamela Diana Fields; children: Debra C, Renae V, Desiree M, Jason D, Roxanne W, Robert W. **EDUCATION:** Howard U, 1947-51; Howard Med Sch, 1952-56; USC Med Ctr, 1956-57. **CAREER:** Gardena Med Ctr, phys; W Adams Emergency Med & Grp, emergency physician 1967-80; LA Co, hlth dept 1965-66, bd educ 1959-60; Private Pract, 1957-65. **ORGANIZATIONS:** Am Coll of Emergency Physicians; mem Am Arabian Horse Assn 1974-77; Intl Arabian Horse Assn 1974-77; breeder of Arabian Horses 1974-; breeder of Black Angus 1975-. **MILITARY SERVICE:** USMCR corpl 1943-46. **BUSINESS ADDRESS:** 1849 Royal Oaks Dr, Bradbury, CA 91010.

NELSON, RONALD DUNCAN
Police chief. **PERSONAL:** Born Jun 17, 1931, Pasadena, CA; son of Harold O Nelson and Zenobia D Nelson; married Barbara Dorsey, Jul 03, 1954; children: Rhonda, Harold. **EDUCATION:** Drake Univ, Des Moines IA, BA, 1956; California State Coll, Los Angeles CA, attended, 1961-66; Pepperdine Univ, Malibu CA, MA, 1977. **CAREER:** Los Angeles Police Dept, Los Angeles CA, police lieutenant, 1956-77; Compton Police Dept, Compton CA, police commander, 1977-79; China Lake Police Dept, China Lake CA, police chief, 1979-80; City of Compton, Compton CA, city mgr, 1980-82; Berkeley Police Dept, Berkeley CA, police chief, 1982-. **ORGANIZATIONS:** Mem, Kappa Alpha Psi Frat, 1955-, Amer Legion, 1963-, Pasadena Planning Commn, 1976-79, Kiwanis Intl, 1978-88, Berkeley Boosters Assn, 1983-, Berkeley Breakfast Club, 1984-, Forum for Black Public Admin, 1987-; natl pres, Natl Org of Black Law Enforcement Exec, 1988-89; pres, Alameda County Chief of Police and Sheriffs Assn, 1989. **HONORS/ACHIEVEMENTS:** Community Serv Award, Natl Forum for Black Public Admin, 1988. **MILITARY SERVICE:** US Army, Sergeant, 1951-53; Good Conduct Award, 1953. **HOME ADDRESS:** 1460 Lincoln St, Berkeley, CA 94702.

NELSON, TERRY
Athlete. **PERSONAL:** Born May 20, 1951, Arkadelphia, AR; married Frances. **EDUCATION:** AR AM&N, BS 1973. **CAREER:** Los Angeles Rams, tight end 1973-. **HONORS/ACHIEVEMENTS:** Played all 14 games in 1976; Pittsburgh Courier All-am; NFC Championship Games 1974-76 & 1978-79; NFL Championship Game 1979. **BUSINESS ADDRESS:** Los Angeles Rams, 10271 W Pico, Los Angeles, CA 90064.

NELSON, WANDA JEAN
President. **PERSONAL:** Born Jul 05, 1938, Kingfisher, OK; married Earl Lee Nelson Sr; children: Marie, Stephen A, Earl Lee, Jr. **EDUCATION:** Madam CJ Walker's Beauty Coll, Graduated 1958; Natl Inst of Cosmetology Washington DC, B 1966, M 1968, D 1973; Penn Valley Comm Coll in Science, A 1973. **CAREER:** Le Cont'e Cosmetics, tech hairstylist & instructor; Air Cargo TWA, supervisor; USDA, keypunch & verifier; US Postal Svcs, guard 1979-80; Ms Marie Cosmetics,owner; Associated Hairdresser Cosmotologist of MO, pres. **ORGANIZATIONS:** Founder and 1st pres Young Progressors Beauty & Barbers; mem MO State Assoc of Cosmetology, Natl Beauty Culturist League Inc, Women's Political Caucus. **HONORS/ACHIEVEMENTS:** Certificates for Volunteer Serv in the Comm; Certificate from Jackson Conty State Sch for Retarded Children; elected Alpha Beta Sor Woman of the Year 1985;Top 100 Influential Black Amers in Greater Kansas City 1985; Theta Nu Sigma Natl Sor Woman of the Year 1986; Alpha Beta Local Chap Woman of the Year 1986. **HOME ADDRESS:** 9700 Buena Vista, Overland Park, KS 66207.

NELSON, WANDA LEE
Educational administrator. **PERSONAL:** Born Nov 16, 1952, Franklin, LA; daughter of James Green and Geraldine Minor Green (deceased); married Elridge Nelson; children: Michael, James. **EDUCATION:** Grambling State Univ, BA 1973; Ball State Univ, MA 1975; Natl Cert Counselor 1984; Louisiana State Univ, Ed S 1985; Northern Illinois Univ DeKalb Il Ed.D 1989. **CAREER:** Bicester Amer Elem School, England, learning specialist 1974-76; Summer Enrichment Program LSUE, music teacher 1984; LSUE, counselor; Northern Illinois Univ, counselor & minority programs coordinator, 1985-89. **ORGANIZATIONS:** Advisor Awareness of Culture, Ed & Soc Student Club 1978-85; Anti-Grammateus Epsilon Alpha Sigma chap - Sigma Gamma Rho Sorority, Inc 1979-80; consultant & presenter LA Health Occupations Students of Amer 1984; co-presenter LA Assn of Student Assist Programs Conf 1984; life member Grambling State Univ Alumni Assn; member Amer Assn for Counseling & Dev; Assn of Multicultural Counseling & Development; Amer college Personnel Assn. **HONORS/ACHIEVEMENTS:** Magna Cum Laude Grambling State Univ 1973; Outstanding Young Women of Amer 1979, 1986; President's Award Little Zion BC Matrons, Opelousas, LA 1985; Alpha Kappa Mu Honor Society, Grambling State Univ; Kappa Delta Pi Honor Society Norther Illinois Univ 1988. **BUSINESS ADDRESS:** Assistant Dean of Students for Retention Services, The University of Texas at Austin, Office of the Dean of Students, PO Box 7849, Austin, TX 78713-7849.

NELSON, WILLIAM EDWARD, JR.
Educator. **PERSONAL:** Born Mar 19, 1941, Memphis, TN; married Della Jackson; children: Nicholas. **EDUCATION:** AM & N College Pine Bluff, Ark, BA 1962; Atlanta, Univ, MA 1964; Univ of Ill, PhD 1971. **CAREER:** Southern Univ, instr 1963-65; Univ of Ill, research assoc 1966-69; OH State Univ, prof 1969-. **ORGANIZATIONS:** Regl dir Alpha Phi Alpha Frat 1976-82; proclamation Ohio Senate 1977; proclamation Columbus City Cncl 1977; pres Natl Conf of Black Pol Scientists 1978-79; pres Black Political Assembly 1979-81; chrmn Natl Cncl for Black Studies 1980-82. **HONORS/ACHIEVEMENTS:** Outstanding adminstr Black Stdnt Caucus 1976; mem exec bd African Heritage Studies Assn 1980-; NAACP; Urban League. **BUSINESS ADDRESS:** Prof Political Sci Chairman, Ohio StateUniv, 230 N Oval Mall, Columbus, OH 43210.

NELSON, WILLIAM W.
Business executive. **PERSONAL:** Born Mar 20, 1917, Bowling Green, KY; married Jewell; children: William Jr, Ronald J, Shirley Pickett. **EDUCATION:** Tuskegee Inst, attended; AL State Teachers Coll, attended; UCLA, attended. **CAREER:** Buick Dealer, salesman 1955; Chevrolet Dealer, salesman 1958; Bill Nelson Chevrolet Inc, owner, pres 1969-. **ORGANIZATIONS:** Past pres State of CA Publ Health Dept, Richmond Motor Car Dealers Assoc; past dir Chevrolet Oakland Zone Dealers Assoc; mem No CA Dealer Auto Assoc, Natl Auto Dealers Assoc; former mem Rotary Intl; former dir Chamber of Commerce Richmond; mem NAACP; past dir Richmond Boys Club. **HONORS/ACHIEVEMENTS:** Awd for Outstanding Business Achievement Omega Psi Phi 1954; Listed in Black Enterprise "The Top 100 Black Owned Firms". **BUSINESS ADDRESS:** President, Bill Nelson Chevrolet, 3233 Auto Plaza, Richmond, CA 94804.

NELSON-HOLGATE, GAIL EVANGELYN
Singer, actress, teacher. **PERSONAL:** Born Mar 29, 1944, Durham, NC; daughter of Reverend William Tycer Nelson (deceased) and Jane Avant Nelson; married Daniel A Holgate, Sep 27, 1987. **EDUCATION:** Oberlin Coll Oberlin OH, MMus 1965; New England Conserv of Music Boston MA, MMus 1967; Mozarteum Conserv Salzburg Austria 1963-64; Metropolitan Opera Studio, 1970-72; Amer Inst of Musical Studies Graz Austria 1972. **CAREER:** Private vocal teacher; adjunct prof of contemporary pop-vocal music, New York City College, 1986-89; Films, The Way We Live Now, I Never Sang for My Father, Cotton Comes to Harlem; Recordings, That Healin' Feelin' & Phase III from the US of Mind w/Horace Silver Blue Note Label, the original broadway cast album of Tap Dance Kid; many commercials & indust films & shows; numerous operas; orchs, The Maggio Musicale Orch Florence Italy, The Ball of the Silver Rose Deutsches Theatre 1984, Munich, Germ 1984, The Madame Mag Ball Baden Baden 1984, Detroit Symph Gala 1985, Buffalo Philharm, Philadelphia Pops, St Louis, Chicago Ravinia Fest, Wmsburg Fest; broadway theatre, Hello Dolly, Applause, On The Town, Music Music, Eubie; Minskoff Theatre; Tap Dance Kid; Bubbling Brown Sugar 1986; Lady Day at Emerson's Bar & Grill 1989 Vancouver Arts Club Theatre; Debut, London Philharmonic 1987; guest arti st Queen Elizabeth II Cruise Ship; Debut, New Jersey Symphony 1989. **ORGANIZATIONS:** Mem AEA 1968, AGMA 1967, AFTRA 1968, SAG 1968, BWIT 1984, Oberlin Alumnae, New England Conserv Alumnae, Amer Cancer Soc 1975-, Amer Lung & Respiratory Assoc 1970-; life mem Mu Phi Epsilon 1967-; mem Black Women in Theatre 1985-. **HONORS/ACHIEVEMENTS:** Carnegie Hall debut with Amer Symphony 1982; Lucretia Bori Awd NY Metro Opera Studio Performance Scholarship 1970-72; Humanitarian Plaque Oakwood Coll 1977; In Recog of Your Valuable Contrib to Human Life & Dignity and to Black Cultural Enrichment in Particular United Student Movement 1977. **BUSINESS ADDRESS:** Professional Singer, Ganel Productions, 401 West 44th St, New York, NY 10036.

NERO, DAVID M., JR.
Business executive. **PERSONAL:** Born Feb 18, 1924, Greenwood, MS; married Joyce Lee Conner; children: David III, Laurence, Darrell, Derek. **EDUCATION:** BA 1961; MA 1963; Postgrad Stud. **CAREER:** Nero & Asso Inc, pres; Nero Industries Inc, pres; Nero Construction & Devel Inc, pres; Oregon State U, asst prof; US Dept of Labor, expert consult 1970-71; The Albina Corp, vice pres 1968-69; Contracts & Procurement Admin Battelle Mem Inst, sr splst 1966-68; N Am Rockwell Corp, supr operations cntrl/sr engr planning analyst 1963-66; Litton Ind, supr operations cntrl 1961-63; Raymond Engring, chief prod cntrl 1961; Getz-Royman Inc, vp/gen mgr 1959-60; 3m Co, supr prod cntrl 1955-58. **ORGANIZATIONS:** Mem Am Prod & Inventory Cntrl Soc 1963; Nat Contract Mgmt Assn 1967; Portland C of C 1971; Nat Assn of Minority Consult & Urbanologists 1972; mem Career Oppor Pgm Adv Cncl 1974; Urban League 1950; NAACP 1950. **HONORS/ACHIEVEMENTS:** Bronze Star 1952; Soldiers Medal for Act of Heroism 1951; Small Businessman of Yr 1973; Selected Comm Ldrs & Noteworthy Am 1973-74; Who's Who in Finance & Ind 1974. **MILITARY SERVICE:** AUS capt 1943-55. **BUSINESS ADDRESS:** 208 SW Stark St, Portland, OR 97204.

NESBITT, PREXY-ROZELL WILLIAM
Government official. **PERSONAL:** Born Feb 23, 1944, Chicago, IL. **EDUCATION:** Antioch Coll, BA 1967; Columbia Univ, Certificate in African Studies 1968; Northwestern Univ, MA 1974. **CAREER:** World Council of Churches, dir 1979-83; District 65 United Auto Workers Union, administrator 1983-86; School of the Art Inst of Chicago, lecturer african literature 1983-; City of Chicago Mayor's Office, asst dir comm relations 1986-. **ORGANIZATIONS:** Mem NAACP 1970-, Assoc of Concerned African Scholars 1980-; bd of dirs CA Newsreel 1980-; consultant Amer Comm on Africa 1980-; bd of dirs TransAfrica 1981-, Crossroads Fund 1983-86. **HONORS/ACHIEVEMENTS:** Faculty Fellow Columbia Univ 1967; Steve Biko Awd Chicago TransAfrica 1987; 15 publications including "Beyond the Divestment Movement," The Black Scholar 1986; "Apartheid in Our Living Rooms, US Foreign Policy on South Africa," Midwest Research 1987. **BUSINESS ADDRESS:** Asst Dir Community Relations, City of Chicago, Mayor's Office-City Hall, 121 N LaSalle, Chicago, IL 60602.

NESBY, DONALD RAY, SR.
Law enforcement. **PERSONAL:** Born Feb 16, 1937, Austin, TX; married Ruby J Thomas; children: Donald R Jr, Alex L. **EDUCATION:** San Diego City Coll, 1964; Austin Comm Coll, 1975. **CAREER:** Travis Cty Sheriff Dept, deputy sheriff 1973-76; Constable Pct #1, constable 1976-. **ORGANIZATIONS:** Mem TX Peace Officer Assn 1978-; pres WH Passon Historical Soc 1983-85. **HONORS/ACHIEVEMENTS:** Outstanding Comm Serv Alpha Kappa Zeta Chap 1977; Outstanding Serv Awd St Mary's Comm 1978; Recog Awd MW Mt Carmel Grand Lodge 1982. **MILITARY SERVICE:** USN ao3 6 yrs. **BUSINESS ADDRESS:** Constable, Travis Co Pct #1, 3228 E Martin Luther Kind Bvd, Austin, TX 78721.

NETTERS, TYRONE HOMER
Legislative assistant. **PERSONAL:** Born Oct 11, 1954, Clarksdale, MS; married Beverly Bracy; children: Malik, Toure. **EDUCATION:** CA State Univ Sacramento, BS 1976. **CAREER:** Office of Majority Consultants, campaign specialist 1979-82; Assembly Ways & Means, consultant 1982-83; Office of Assemblywoman Moore, legislative assistant 1983-. **ORGANIZATIONS:** Bd of dirs Magalink Corp 1984-; mem A Philip Randolph Inst 1985-; founding mem Fannie Lou Hamer Demo Club 1985-. **HONORS/ACHIEVEMENTS:** SABC Comm Serv Awd 1980; Natl Black Child Development Merit Awd 1981. **HOME ADDRESS:** 8720 Cord Way, Sacramento, CA 95829. **BUSINESS ADDRESS:** Legislative Assistant, CA State Assembly, State Capitol Bldg Rm 2117, Sacramento, CA 95814.

NETTERVILLE, GEORGE LEON, JR.
Educational administrator. **PERSONAL:** Born Jul 16, 1907, Dutchtown, LA; married Rebecca Franklin. **EDUCATION:** So U, BS 1928; Columbia U, MA 1950; Wiley Coll, LittD 1968. **CAREER:** Natl Benefits Life Ins Co Baton Rouge, dist mgr 1928-32; LA Sausage Co, mgr 1934-38; So Univ Baton Rouge, former pres/acting pres/bus mgr 1938-80, dir of planning 1980-. **ORGANIZATIONS:** Mem Exec Cncl World Serv & Finance United Meth Ch 1964; mem Commn to Study Financing Meth Schs Theology 1964-68; Baton Rouge Civic Cntr Com 1970; LA Cncl Chs 1967; pres E Baton Rouge Parish Anti-Poverty Prog; Comm Assn Welfare Sch Chldrn; vice pres E Baton Rouge Parish Biracial Commn; LA Interch Cncl; sec Scotland Fire Prot Dist; mem/exec com LA Regl Med Planning Cncl; bd dirs Cerebral Palsy Ctr; Baranco-Clark YMCA; United Givers Fund Blundon Home; trustee Gammon Theol Sem; mem/past pres Am Assn Coll &Univ Bus Officers; past treas Nat Assn for Equal Opport in Higher Edn; Nat Alliance Bus Men; Phi Beta Sigma; Kappa Phi Kappa.

NETTLEFORD, REX MILTON
Educator. **PERSONAL:** Born Feb 03, 1933. **EDUCATION:** UCWI London, BA 1956; Oxon, BPhil 1959. **CAREER:** Jamaica, Trinidad & Tobago, resident tutor 1956-57, 1959-61, staff tutor in political educ 1961-63; Trade Union Ed Inst, dir of studies, 1963-; UWI Dept of Govt, tutor, lecturer, political thought; Extra-Mural Studies, deputy dir, 1969-71, dir 1971, prof 1975-. **ORGANIZATIONS:** Assoc fellow, Centre for African & African Amer Studies, Atlanta Univ; mem, Intl Soc for the History of Ideas, Acad Counselor Latin Amer Studies, Wilson Center, Washington DC; trustee, AFS Intl, New York; chmn, Commonwealth Arts Org, 1980; chmn, Inst of Jamaica, 1978-80; cultural advisor to Prime Minister of Jamaica, 1972-80; founder, artistic dir, Jamaica Natl Dance Theatre Co, 1962-; chmn, Tourism Product Devel Co, Jamaica, 1976-78; gov, Intl Devel Rsch Center, 1970-; mem, CIDEC, Org of Amer States; mem, Comm of Experts on Open Learning and Distance Educ, Commonwealth Secretariat, London UK 1986-87; mem, bd of dir, Natl Commercial Bank of Jamaica, 1987-; mem, bd of dir, Natl Comercial Bank (Jamaica,) 1987-; mem, bd of dir, Jamaica Mutual Life Assurance Soc, 1989-; Cultural Adviser Prime Minister of Jamaica, 1989-. **HONORS/ACHIEVEMENTS:** Order of Merit Award, Govt of Jamaica, 1975; Gold Musgrave Medal, Inst of Jamaica, 1981; author, editor, choreographer, principal dancer, Leader Cultural Missions to USA, Canada, Latin Amer, Australia, USSR; UCWI Exhibition Scholar, 1953: Issa Scholar, 1956; Rhodes Scholar 1957; ILO Fellow 1967; choreographer of over 50 major works for Natl Dance Theatre Co of Jamaica since 1962; author of many books and articles on Caribbean cultural devel; fellow, Jamaica Inst of Mgmt, 1988-89; pattern lecturer, Indiana Univ, 1989. **BUSINESS ADDRESS:** Professor, Extra-Mural Studies, Univ of the West Indies, Mona Campus, Kingston 7, Jamaica.

NETTLES, JOHN SPRATT
Clergyman, civil rights leader, social worker. **PERSONAL:** Born Jun 01, 1943, Darlington, SC; son of Townsend Nettles, Jr; married Gertrude Kidd, Oct 15, 1960; children: Madrica, John, Ralph. **EDUCATION:** Kittrell Coll, AA, 1963; Bluefield State Coll, BA, 1965; Morehouse School of Religion of ITC, Atlanta GA, hours towards MD, 1965-68. **CAREER:** Community Action Agency, Anniston AL, director, 1970; Mt Olive Baptist Church, Anniston Al, pastor 1968-. **ORGANIZATIONS:** Director, Producing Ambitious Youth, 1970-; state pres, Alabama Southern Cristian Leadership Conf, 1978-; Natl Board of Dir, SCLC, 1978-; founding dir, Educ Par Excellence, 1983-; chairman, Alabama New South Coalition 3rd district, 1985-; commissioner, Alabama Education Study Commission 1988-; founding chairman, Project DEED, 1988-. **HONORS/ACHIEVEMENTS:** Rosa Parks SCLC, National; Young Man of the Year, Anniston Community; MLK Humanitarion Award, SCLC; Frederick Douglass Christian Study Center of Alabama; Man of the Year; Education Award, AKA Sorority; The Ten Commandments for Becoming Productive Youth; The Beatitudes for Becoming Youth Employees; Crossing the Rubicon, Movement for A Just Society in South Africa; The Mirage of Racial Equity in Alabama (in process). **BUSINESS ADDRESS:** Reverend, Director of Education Par Excellence, Mt Olive Baptist Church Community Action Agency, 1300 Moore Avenue, Anniston, AL 36201.

NETTLES, WILLARD, JR.
City official, educator. **PERSONAL:** Born Jan 17, 1944, Hooks, TX; married Rosemary. **EDUCATION:** Lewis & Clark Coll, BA 1967. **CAREER:** Vancouver, WA, former city councilman; Portland School Dist, teacher; Crown Zellerbach Corp, prod planner 1967-70. **HONORS/ACHIEVEMENTS:** 1st Black & Youngest Cnclmn Vancouver, WA. **BUSINESS ADDRESS:** 210 E 13 St, Vancouver, WA.

NEUFVILLE, MORTIMER H.
Educational administrator. **PERSONAL:** Born Dec 10, 1939, Portland, Jamaica;married Masie Brown; children: Sonetta, Nadine, Tisha. **EDUCATION:** Jamaica School of Ag, Diploma 1961; Tuskegee Inst, BSc 1970; Univ of FL, MSc 1971, PhD 1974. **CAREER:** Univ of FL, grad asst 1971-74; Prairie View A&M, head dept of animal sci 1974-78; Lincoln Univ School of Appl Sci MO, assoc dean 1978-83; Univ of MD Eastern Shore, dean, agriculture and research dir 1983-. **ORGANIZATIONS:** Agr rsch asst Ministry of Agri-Jamaica 1961-68; mem Gamma Sigma Delta Hon Soc 1970, Gamma Sigma Delta Hon Soc 1970, Alpha Zeta Hon Soc 1971, Bd of Dir North Central R&D Ctr 1982-83; mem Sigma Pi Phi 1984, Natl Higher Ed Comm 1985; mem North East Regional Council 1986; Governor's Commn on Education in Agriculture 1987; mem International Science and Education Council 1987; Assn of Research Dir vice chariman. **HONORS/ACHIEVEMENTS:** Most Outstanding Jr Agr Tuskegee Inst 1969; Most Outstanding Grad Sr Tuskegee Inst 1970; Review of Animal Sci Rsch at 1890 Univ Devel of Rsch at Historically Black Land Grant Inst 1-75. **BUSINESS ADDRESS:** Dean, School of Agr Sciences, University of MD Eastern Shore, PO Box 1023, Princess Anne, MD 21853.

NEUSOM, THOMAS G.
Attorney. **PERSONAL:** Born Mar 07, 1922, Detroit; divorced. **EDUCATION:** Detroit Inst Tech, BA 1947; Detroit Coll Law, LLB, JD 1949. **CAREER:** Private Practice, law 24 yrs. **ORGANIZATIONS:** Pres NAACP 1954-56; NAACP Legal Com 1956-60; bd mem Welfare Planning Cncl 1960-70; treas Comm Rel Conf 1966-67; mem CA Hosp & Hlth Facilities Planning Com 1962-72; MC Mars Post Am Legion 1965; commander/mem LA Co Tax Assessment Appeals Bd 1962-69; bd mem Am Bar Assn 1960-; CA StateBar Assn 1949-; pres bd So CA Rapid Transit Dist 1973-, mem bd 1969-. **MILITARY SERVICE:** AUS lt 1943-46. **BUSINESS ADDRESS:** 1485 W Adams Blvd, Los Angeles, CA 90007.

NEVELS, ZEBEDEE JAMES
Physician. **PERSONAL:** Born Nov 13, 1926, Nowata, OK; married Virginia N Glass; children: Karen, James. **EDUCATION:** Univ of KS, BA 1950; KS State Coll, 1951; Howard U, MD 1958. **CAREER:** St Anthony Hosp Milwaukee, WI, chmn dept of surg 1975-; Interstate Blood Bank Inc, med dir 1967-; Private Pract Zebedee J Nevels MDSC, phys 1966-; Allis Chalmers Co W Allis, WI, staff/phys & consult 1966-74; USAF Wichita Falls, TX, civil tech train instr 1951. **ORGANIZATIONS:** Mem Nat Med Assn 1966; mem Am Med Assn 1966; mem Indsl Med Assn 1971; lifetime mem NAACP 1975. **HONORS/ACHIEVEMENTS:** Certification Am Bd of Surg 1969. **MILITARY SERVICE:** USNR lt 1955-72. **BUSINESS ADDRESS:** 2130 W Fond du lac Ave, Milwaukee, WI 53206.

NEVENS, JOHN CALVIN
Professional athlete. **PERSONAL:** Born May 09, 1963, Los Angeles, CA. **EDUCATION:** Cal-State Fullerton, Phys Educ Major. **CAREER:** Denver Gold, linebacker 1985-.

HONORS/ACHIEVEMENTS: Selected Special Teams Player of Year 1982; PCAA Co-Defensive Player of Year 1984.

NEWBERN, CAPTOLIA DENT
Educator, clergyman. **PERSONAL:** Born Sep 22, 1902, Dublin, GA; daughter of John W Dent and Arnetta E Rozier Dent; married Rev Samuel H Newbern, Dec 02, 1939 (deceased). **EDUCATION:** Paine Coll, Augusta, GA, Certificate Teacher Tgn 1921-23, BS Educ (cum laude), 1923-25, attended 1931-32; Hampton Inst, 1926; Northwestern Univ Graduate School, English, 1928; Case Western Reserve Univ, 1931-32; Talladega Coll, Talladega, AL, MusB, 1935-37, attended, 1937-38; School of Social Work, Columbia Univ, NYC, MSSW 1940-42; Teachers Coll, Columbia Univ, EdD 1954; United Theological Seminary, MDiv 1980; United Theological Seminary, D Min 1982. **CAREER:** Lane Coll, chmn, prof 1962-72; Lane Coll Vesper Choir, organizer, dir 1963-72; Upward Bound Program, Lane Coll, teacher, music instructor, 1966-67; Lane Coll Concert Choir, dir 1967-68; Undergrad Social Welfare Educ Program Lane Coll, instr, consultant, coordinator, 1969-72; US Dept of HEW Atlant, liaison consultant devel in black inst project 1971-72; Lane Coll Jackson TN, dir undergrad social welfare are 1972-75; Lane-Lambuth Social Welfare Consortium with Dir of Dept of Sociology & Family Devel Lambuth Coll, co-dir 1972-75; Lincoln Meml Univ Harrogate TN, prof social work 1975-80; NA Ministry of Ecumenical Education & Action, volunteer, 1982—. **ORGANIZATIONS:** Mem Am Assn of Univ Prof 1968-; mem Religious Educ Assn 1968; Nat Caucus on Black Aging & Black Aged 1972-77; Southern Poverty Law Center, 1973; Nat Council of Black Social Workers Inc 1974-76; life mem NAACP 1974; natl adv bd Am Security Council 1976-77; mem Am Biog Inst Research Assn 1979; mem N Am Acad of Ecumenists 1979; dir ecumenics CME Church Seventh Episcopal Dist 1980-83; mem Pan Methodist Fellowship com Philadelphia Area 1982; assoc minister Russell Tabernackle Church Philadelphia 1982-85; AARP, 1984; Nat Council of Senior Citizens, 1984; Intl Association of Women Ministers, 1985; mem dept sec Spiritual Life & Message 1985-87, 1989; mem Prison Fellowship Ministries, 1986; Habitat Partnership, 1986; Afro-American Historical and Cultural Museum; American Red Cross, 1989. **HONORS/ACHIEVEMENTS:** 1st Negro Woman Apptd by War Dept Employee Cnslr The Pentagon Bldg 1942; Book Cert/Cert of Appreciation Russell Tabernacle Christian Meth Episcopal Ch 1967; Lane Coll Plaque Lane Coll 1967-78; Citation Cert for Comm Serv The United Way of Jackson & Madison Co 1975; Ruth Pippert Core Meml Award United Theol Sem 1980; Pan Methodist Churches of Greater Philadelphia Bicentennial Awd for Outstanding Const to Spread of the Gospel through Methodism 1985; inducted in Two Thousand Notable Amers Hall of Fame 1985; World Biographical Hall of Fame Vol 1 Historical Preservation of Amer Inc 1985; selected chartered life mem World Inst of Achievement 1985; Russell Tabernacle CME Church Christian Woman of the Year Plaque Awd for many Years of serv to the Christian Methodist Episcopal Church 1986; many other plaques, awards, and recognitions of service.

NEWBERN, WALTER P.
Educator. **PERSONAL:** Born Feb 22, 1907, Medon, TN. **EDUCATION:** TN State U, BS 1934;Univ of Pittsburgh, EdM, MA 1946;Univ of HI, 1943; Carnegia Inst of Tech, 1937. **CAREER:** TN State Univ, asst teacher 1931-34; JL Cook HS TN, trade teacher & coach 1934-42, 1946-47; City School of Jackson, industrial coop coord 1947-72; TN State U, visiting teacher since retirement. **ORGANIZATIONS:** Pres NAACP Br; 32 degree Mason; Mystic Shriner; Knights of Pythian; TN Voters Cncl; life mem NEA; deacon/supt of sunday sch/choir mem Berean Bapt Ch; adv bd Salvation Army; bd dir C of C Mil Serv 1942-45.

NEWBERRY, CEDRIC CHARLES
Automobile aftermarket executive. **PERSONAL:** Born Aug 10, 1953, Perry, GA; son of Charlie C Newberry and Rubye L Allen-Newberry; married Lillie Ruth Brown; children: Carnice, Candice. **EDUCATION:** Fort Valley State Coll, BS 1975; Univ of WI-Madison, MS 1977; Southern IL Univ Edwardsville, MBA 1982. **CAREER:** Monsanto Co, sr rsch biologist 1977-83; Meineke Discount Mufflers/CC Newberry Automotive Corp, pres/general mgr 1983-. **ORGANIZATIONS:** Mem Amer Soc of Agronomy 1977-83; mem Comm to Support Black Business & Professionals 1983-; chmn educ comm Natl Black MBA Assoc 1986-87. **HONORS/ACHIEVEMENTS:** Honors Convocation Fort Valley State Coll; Fellow Shion Univ of WI 1975-77. **BUSINESS ADDRESS:** President/General Manager, CC Newberry Automotive Corp, 7760 Reading Rd, Cincinnati, OH 45237.

NEWBERRY, TRUDELL MCCLELLAND
Educator, government official. **PERSONAL:** Born Jan 30, 1939, Junction City, AR; daughter of Roosevelt McClelland; divorced; children: Fe Lesia Michelle, Thomas Walter III. **EDUCATION:** Univ of AR Pine Bluff, BA 1962; Roosevelt Univ Chicago, MA 1980; Governors State, Post-Grad Work 1982-84; Northern Illinois Univ post graduate work 1988-89. **CAREER:** Almyra Public School System, teacher 1962-65; Franklin-Wright Settlement, social worker 1965-69; North Chicago Grad School Syst, teacher 1970-; Foss Park Dist North Chicago, recreational suprv 1982-83; City Council North Chicago IL, alderwoman 5th ward 1983-87. **ORGANIZATIONS:** Mem Eureka Temple #1172 1972-, North Chicago Library Bd 1986-, UAPB Alumni Assoc 1982-, North Chicago HS PTO 1984-88, North Chicago Booster Club 1984-88; mem of North Chicago Teachers Assn 1982-87; building representative for NCTA 1985-87; mem of North Chicago Elementary Council of Federated Teachers 1987-; Council Representative to Lake County Federation of Teachers Executive Bd 1987-89; pres of North Chicago Elementary Council of Federated Teachers 1989-. **BUSINESS ADDRESS:** Alderwoman 5th Ward, City Council/North Chicago, 1850 Lewis Ave, North Chicago, IL 60064.

NEWBOLD, ROBERT THOMAS
Associate stated clerk/church exec. **PERSONAL:** Born Feb 26, 1920, Miami, FL; married Anne Worrell; children: Gregory. **EDUCATION:** FL Agriculatural & Mech Coll, AB 1942; Lincoln Theol Seminary, MDiv 1945; McCormick Theol Seminary, MA 1946; Mary Holmes Coll, DD 1976. **CAREER:** Second Presbyterian Church, pastor 1944-46; Radcliffe Pres Ch, pastor 1946-53; Grace Pres Church, pastor 1953-68; Dept of Ministerial Relations, assoc exec sec 1968-72; Council on Admin Svcs, assoc dir 1972-73; General Assembly, stated clerk 1975-. **ORGANIZATIONS:** Mem bd of trustees NY Theol Seminary 1978-86; mem bd of trustees McCormick Theol Sem 1978-83; chairperson bd of trustees NY Theol Seminary 1981-83; chairperson Black and Hispanic Fund NY Theol Seminary 1986-; mem Interdenominational Ministers Alliance; clergy vstg staff Baltimore City Hospitals; mem MD-DECouncil of Churches, Clergy Council Baltimore Urban League. **HONORS/ACHIEVEMENTS:** Richard Allen Awd Richard Allen Foundation 1964; Meritorious Alumni Awd FL A&M Univ. **BUSINESS ADDRESS:** Associate Stated Clerk, Presbyterian Church USA, 475 Riverside Dr Rm 1201, New York, NY 10115.

NEWBORN, ODIE VERNON, JR.
Physician. **PERSONAL:** Born Nov 05, 1947, Nashville, TN; married Sharlie. **EDUCATION:** TN St U, BS; Meharry Med Coll, MD; Flint MI, Intern, Resd. **ORGANIZATIONS:** Mem Am Acad Family Prac; GA St Med Soc; mem Colquitt Co Med Soc.

NEWELL, MATTHIAS GREGORY
Librarian. **PERSONAL:** Born Jun 26, 1927, Colon, Panama. **EDUCATION:** Univ of Dayton, BS 1951; Catholic Univ, MA 1960; Vatican Library School, diploma 1963; Vatican Archives School, diploma 1964; Catholic Univ, MSLS 1968; Simmons Coll, DA 1977; Latin Amer Tchng, fellow 1976. **CAREER:** Univ Centro-Americana, dir of library; Univ of Rhode Island, librarian 1973-; St Francis De Sales School, principal 1972-73; Eastern Michigan Univ, teacher 1971-72; Morgan State Univ, 1970-71; St Mary's Univ, librarian 1968-70; St Louis Milwaukee, teacher 1960-67; Rep of Peru, teacher 1951-58. **ORGANIZATIONS:** Mem, St Louis Province Soc of Mary, 1949-; mem, Black Caucus, Amer Library Assn; mem, Catholic Library Assn; mem, Common Cause; dir, Baltimore Black Catholic Lay Caucus, 1971; Patron de la Promocion Colegia San Antonio Callao, Peru, 1957; Latin Amer Teaching Fellowship, Tufts Univ, 1976-. **HONORS/ACHIEVEMENTS:** Published articles in Catholic Library World & Rila Bulletin. **BUSINESS ADDRESS:** Apartado 69, Managua, Nicaragua.

NEWELL, VIRGINIA K.
Educator. **PERSONAL:** Born Oct 07, Advance, NC; married George; children: Virginia, Glenda. **EDUCATION:** Talladega Coll, AB 1940; NY U, 1956;Univ Chicago, ASF fellow 1958-59;Univ of Sarasota, EdD 1976. **CAREER:** Winston-Salem State Univ, asso prof. **ORGANIZATIONS:** Pres NC Cncl Tchrs Math; life mem NEA; editor Newsletter Nat Assn Math; AMS; MAA; NCTM; life mem NAACP; State Comiener Nat Cncl Negro Women. **HONORS/ACHIEVEMENTS:** Zeta Phi Beta's Woman of Yr 1964; Outstand Tchr Award 1960. **BUSINESS ADDRESS:** Winston-Salem StateUniv, Winston-Salem, NC.

NEWELL, WILLIAM
Social worker. **PERSONAL:** Born Dec 28, 1938, Utica, MS; married Marie Bow; children: Raynard, Renee, Roseanne. **EDUCATION:** Riverside Comm Coll, AA 1970; Cal State Coll San Bernardino, BA 1972; Univ of CA Los Angeles, MSW 1974. **CAREER:** San Bernardino County Mental Health, psychotherapist. **ORGANIZATIONS:** Mem Soc for Clinical Social Work 1972-, North Amer Soc Adlerian Psy 1980-; past pres Inland Assoc Black Social Worker 1976-, Toastmasters #797 1980-; adv bd Hard to Place Black ADoption Children Insland Area Urban League 1981-83; founder/pres Family Adolescent Child and Elderly Serv 1984-; mem Omage Psi Phi Inc 1983-, Natl Assoc of Social Work 1985-. **BUSINESS ADDRESS:** Psychotherapist, San Bernardino Co Mental Hlth, 1777 W Baseline, San Bernardino, CA 92411.

NEWHOUSE, RICHARD H.
Legislator. **PERSONAL:** Born Jan 24, 1924, Louisville, KY; married Kathi; children: Suzanne, Richard, Holly. **EDUCATION:** Boston U, BS 1949, MS 1951;Univ of Chgo, JD 1961. **CAREER:** IL State Senate 24th Dist, senator. **ORGANIZATIONS:** Pres/founder Black Legislators Assn; dir Black Legislative Clearing House in Chgo; fellow Adlai Stevenson Inst; serves on Intergovtl Relations Commn; Cncl on the Diagnosis & Eval of Criminal Defendants; practicing atty. **HONORS/ACHIEVEMENTS:** Named Best Legislator by both Independent Voters of IL & Am Legion; Outstand Pub Servant Cook Co Bar Assn; Senator of the Yr Bapt Ministers Conf of Chgo. **BUSINESS ADDRESS:** Illinois State Senator, State of Illinois, 103B State Capitol Bldg, Springfield, IL 62706.

NEWHOUSE, ROBERT F.
Business executive. **PERSONAL:** Born Jan 09, 1950, Gregg County, TX; married Nancy; children: Roddrick, Dawnyel, Shauntel, Reginald. **EDUCATION:** Univ of Houston, MTH 1973; Univ of Dallas, MBA 1984. **CAREER:** Dallas Cowboys, player 1972-83; Tymeshare, computer oper; TX Bank & Trust, loan ofc; Trans Global Airlines, pres 1984; Dallas TX, real estate broker; Lone Star Delivery, pres; R Newhouse Enterprises Inc, pres. **ORGANIZATIONS:** YMCA; United Way; Boys Club. **HONORS/ACHIEVEMENTS:** Sport Hall of Fame Univ of Houston. **BUSINESS ADDRESS:** President, R Newhouse Enterprises Inc, 6847 Truxton, Dallas, TX 75231.

NEWKIRK, INEZ DORIS (NEE TUCKER)
Social worker. **PERSONAL:** Born Feb 27, 1921, Wilmington, NC; married William M; children: Kenneth, Barry, William P. **EDUCATION:** Talladega College, B in Sociology 1942; Atlanta Univ School of Social Work, Masters-Social Work 1944. **CAREER:** Hackensack Day Care Center, executive dir 1965-71; Home State Bank, bd 1st vp; Hackensack Day Care Center, bd pres 1983-; New York City Sch System, sch psychiatric social worker 1971-. **ORGANIZATIONS:** Mem bd Urban League-Bergen County 1981-. **HONORS/ACHIEVEMENTS:** Awards In Black; award from Home State Bank. **HOME ADDRESS:** 6112 Sleepy Hollow Lane, Wilmington, NC 28401.

NEWKIRK, QUEENIE HORTENSE
Educator. **PERSONAL:** Born in Tyler, TX; widowed. **EDUCATION:** TX Coll, BA; UC Berkeley, Post Grad. **CAREER:** Univ of CA Cooperative Exten, youth advisor; Contra Costa Co Vol Bur, project mgr/coord; Cleaning & Pressing Shop, owned/operated. **ORGANIZATIONS:** Life mem NAACP, 2nd term as pres Pitt Chpt/20 yrs mem exec bd; life mem Nat Cncl Negro Women, past 1st vice pres Contra Costa Sec; serving 3rd 1 yr term chmn Co Econ Oppor Cncl, 1st & only woman to serve; mem Bd Bay Area Social Planning; Contra Costa Easter Seal Soc; Alcohol Adv Cncl; Mt DiabloLeague Women Voters; Pittsburg & Key Women Dem Club; Dep Registar Voters; 1st Bapt Ch; finanical sec Missionary Soc; mem bd mgrs Woods Manor Housing Devel; matron Lilly Of Valley Chap UBF & SMT; mem CA St Bd of Easter Seal. **HONORS/ACHIEVEMENTS:** 1st Black Girl Scout Ldr in CC 1943-44; CC chmn of prop 14 no lead CC fight for TEPC legis in 50'S. **BUSINESS ADDRESS:** U of CA Extension, 960 East St, Pittsburg, CA 94565.

NEWKIRK, THOMAS H.
Director. **PERSONAL:** Born Nov 24, 1929, New York City, NY; divorced; children: Kori, Kisan, Kamila. **EDUCATION:** Univ of MA at Amherst, MEd 1974, EdD 1985. **CAREER:** Pres, consult Newkirk Assoc Tax & Bus 1958-; tax consult 1958-; ins broker 1959-63; Haryou-Act NYC, coord training testing youth div, dir mgmt training 6 yrs; SUNY Corland,

dir spec ed prog. **ORGANIZATIONS:** Founding mem Holcombe Rucker Scholarship Fund 1967; consult State Ed Dept 1967-72; consult State Ed Dept 1967-72; vice pres United Black Ed 1969; founding mem NYS Spec Prog Personnel Assoc 1973; chmn Spec Progs Inst on Teaching & Counseling 1979; mem Mayors Adv Comm at Cortland; swimming instr Cortland; lecturer Social Found Ed; past vice pres Spec Progs Pers Assoc State of NY. **HONORS/ACHIEVEMENTS:** Publ "Some Objective Considerations" 1974, "The New Disadvantaged" 1975, "Prob & Promises-Former Inmates on Coll Campuses" 1976, "History of Ed Oppty at Courtland Coll" 1968-73; Superlative Comm Serv Awd, Intl Key Women 1974; Awd for Excellence in Professional Serv State Univ Chancellor 1979. **MILITARY SERVICE:** NY Natl Guard 1946-48. **BUSINESS ADDRESS:** Dir Special Ed Program, StateUniv of NY, Cortland, NY 13045.

NEWLAND, ZACHARY JONAS
Podiatrist. **PERSONAL:** Born Dec 15, 1954, Ft Lee, VA; married Camillia Sutton; children: Yolanda. **EDUCATION:** SC State Coll, BS Chemistry 1975; Medical Univ of SC, BS Pharmacy 1978; PA College of Podiatric Medicine, DPM 1984. **CAREER:** Thrift Drugs, asst mgr pharmacist 1978-80; SC Army Natl Guard, medical platoon leader 1978-80; Laurel Pharmacy, pharmacist 1982-84; Lindell Hosp, resident poliatric surgery 1984-85; Lindell Hosp, chief resident podiatric surgery 1985-86; resident teaching staff & lecturer 1986-; Metro Community Health Ctr, dir of podiatric medicine & surgery 1986-. **ORGANIZATIONS:** Mem SC Pharmaceutical Assoc 1978-, Natl Health Serv Corps 1980-, Amer Podiatric Medical Assoc, Omega Psi Phi Frat. **HONORS/ACHIEVEMENTS:** Outstanding Young Men of Amer 1984; Who's Who of Amer Colls & Univs 1984; article published in Journal of Foot Surgery 1984. **MILITARY SERVICE:** AMSC Reserves capt 1978-. **BUSINESS ADDRESS:** Dir Dept of Podiatric Medicine, Metro Community Health Ctr, 2730 N Grand, St Louis, MO 63106.

NEWLIN, RUFUS K.
Educational administrator. **CAREER:** Morristown College, Morristown, TN, president. **BUSINESS ADDRESS:** Morristown College, Morristown, TN 37814. *

NEWMAN, COLLEEN A.
Business executive. **PERSONAL:** Born Feb 11, 1942, Georgetown, Guyana;married Alan. **EDUCATION:** Univ of the West Indies, BA 1964;Univ of London,. **CAREER:** UN, delegate/diplomat in Chile & Venezuela, Govnmnt of Guyana 1966-69; AT&T, editorial services supervisor 1969-72; Consolidated Edison, tech news mgr 1972-77, asst to vice pres 1977-79, asst vice pres 1979-80. **ORGANIZATIONS:** Lecturer Black Exec Exchange Prog 1977; lectutrer (in technical writing) Long IslandUniv 1977; chairman NY Power Pool/Pub Rels Com 1978-80; mem Edson Eng Soc 1980-81; mem Advisory Bd, Boys Choir of Harlem; mem Pub Rel Soc of Amer; mem Coalition of 100 Black Women; mem Amer Assn of Black in Energy; mem Advisory Comm of The Phelps-Stokes Ctr for Human Developmnt. **HONORS/ACHIEVEMENTS:** Black Achievers In Industry Award 1977; Women in Communications, Inc Clarion Award 1984; Hnry Member YWCA Academy of Women Achievers 1984. **BUSINESS ADDRESS:** Vice President, Consolidated Edison Co NY, 4 Irving Place, New York, NY 10003.

NEWMAN, DAVID, JR.
Musician. **PERSONAL:** Born Feb 24, 1932, Dallas, TX; married Esther Rae; children: Terry, Andr, Cadino, Benji. **EDUCATION:** Jarvis Christian Coll. **CAREER:** Newmanism, leader 1980; Muse Records, rec artist 1980; Fantasy Rec Co, rec artist 1978-80; Warner Bros, rec artist 1975-77; Atlantic Rec Inc, rec artist 1959-74; Herbie Mann & The Family of Mann, sideman 1970-71; Ray Charles Enterprises, sideman 1954-64. **HONORS/ACHIEVEMENTS:** Down Beat Nomination 1968-70; Outstand Musicianship TX Jazz 1970. **BUSINESS ADDRESS:** Head Publishing Co, 2623 Downing Ave, Dallas, TX 75216.

NEWMAN, DEBRA LYNN
Manuscript historian. **PERSONAL:** Born Aug 27, 1948, York, PA; daughter of Earl Newman and Eva Mitchell Newman Owens. **EDUCATION:** Howard Univ, Washington DC, BA 1970; Boston Univ, Boston MA, MA, 1971; Howard Univ, Washington DC, PhD 1984. **CAREER:** Natl Archives, Washington DC, archivist/black history specialist 1972-86. **ORGANIZATIONS:** Founding mem Afro-Amer Historial and Genealogical Society 1978-; publications dir, Assoc of Black Women Historians 1987-; chair, advisory board, Opportunities Industrialization Centers Archival Advisory Board; chair, advisory board, Mt Sinai Baptist Church Outreach Center. **HONORS/ACHIEVEMENTS:** Coker Prize, Society of Amer Archivists, 1985; Finding Aid Award, Mid-Atlantic Regional Archivists, 1985; Black History, A Guide to Civilian Records in the Natl Archives, 1984. **BUSINESS ADDRESS:** Specialist in Afro-Amer History and Culture, Manuscript Division, Library of Congress, Washington, DC 20540.

NEWMAN, ERNEST WILBUR
Minister. **PERSONAL:** Born Apr 09, 1928, Kingstree, SC; son of Meloncy Newman and Serena Hamilton Newman; married Thelma Heard, Aug 12, 1955; children: Kathy Newman McCoy, Ernest Wilbur, Jr.. **EDUCATION:** Claflin Coll, Orangeburg SC, AB, 1948; Gammon Theological Seminary, Atlanta GA, master's degree, 1956. **CAREER:** Minister, Summerville Charge, Summerville SC, 1950-52; Rockmill Charge, Anderson SC, 1952-53; Kelley Chapel, Miami FL, 1953; Talladega Charge, Talladega AL, 1954-55; St. Joseph Methodist Church, Jacksonville FL, 1955-57; Zion Methodist Church, Ocala FL, 1957-64; Ebenezer United Methodist Church, Jacksonville FL, 1964-72; Florida Conference, Melbourne Dist, dist superintendent, 1972-77; Plantation United Methodist Church, Plantation FL, 1977-82; Florida Conference, assoc coucil dir, 1982-83, dist superintendent, Deland Dist, 1983; elected bishop, 1984. **ORGANIZATIONS:** Mem, bd of dirs, Broward County Red Cross, Broward County Safety Council; mem, bd of trustees, Florida Conference; pres, Bishop's Cabinet, 1966-67; mem, Gen Commn on Religion and Race; pres, College of Bishops, southeastern jurisdiction, 1989. **HONORS/ACHIEVEMENTS:** Honorary doctorates from Bethune Cookman Coll, 1974, Lambuth Coll, 1987. **HOME ADDRESS:** 60 Revere Pk, Nashville, TN 37205. **BUSINESS ADDRESS:** United Methodist Church, 4731 Trousdale Dr Executive Pk, Nashville, TN 37205.

NEWMAN, GEOFFREY W.
Educator. **PERSONAL:** Born Aug 27, 1946, Oberlin, OH; son of Arthur Eugene Newman and Bertha Battle Newman. **EDUCATION:** Howard Univ, Washington DC, BFA, 1968;

Wayne State Univ, Detroit MI, MA, 1970; Howard Univ, Washington DC, PhD, 1978. **CAREER:** Actor, educator, consultant, theorist and director in theatre; Howard Univ, Washington DC, Owen Duston Distinguished Prof and drama dept chmn; Montclair State Coll, Upper Montclair NJ, dean of School of Fine and Performing Arts, 1988-. **ORGANIZATIONS:** Mem, grant screening panels, District of Columbia Commn on the Arts and Humanities, Pennsylvania State Council for the Arts, and Illinois State Arts Council; artistic dir and cofounder, Takoma Players, Takoma Theatre, Washington DC; artistic dir and cofounder, Ira Aldridge Theatre, Howard Univ, Washington DC; artistic dir, Park Place Productions, Washington DC; artistic dir, Young Audiences of District of Columbia. **HONORS/ACHIEVEMENTS:** Directed world premiere of Owen Dodson's Sound of Soul and European premiere of Robert Nemiroff's Raisin; received Amoco Award for Theatrical Excellence; honored by John F Kennedy Center for the Permorming Arts in conjunction with Amer Theatre Assn; received special commendations from Mayor Marion Barry Jr, Washington DC, Mayor Pat Screen, Baton Rouge LA, and Gov Harry Hughes, State of Maryland; published articles in professional journals; served as nominator for Washington DC Awards Society's Helen Hayes Awards. **BUSINESS ADDRESS:** Dean, School of Fine and Performing Arts, Montclair State College, Life Hall 130, Normal Ave, Upper Montclair, NJ 07043.

NEWMAN, KENNETH J.
Accountant/auditor. **PERSONAL:** Born Nov 07, 1944, Vallijo; married Barbara B; children: Kenneth J Jr, Eric J. **EDUCATION:** Gramblin Coll, BS 1967; Vet Adminstrn Data Processing Austin, TX, prgm instruction courses 1968; SACUBO & NACUBO, cont educ workshops 1969-; Univ NE atOmaha, course for bus mgrs 1977. **CAREER:** Grambling Coll, asst dir of computer ctr 1967; Veteran Admin Data Processing Ctr, acct trainee 1967-68, data processor 1968-69, asst auditor 1969-70; Grambling State Univ, bus mgr 1970-73; Mary Holmes Coll, bus mgr 1974-79; City of Monroe, prgms auditor 1979-81, dir of planning & urban develop. **ORGANIZATIONS:** Adv bd mem Special Serv Mary Holmes Coll; adv bd Gourmet Svcs; mem visiting com S Assn of Coll & Schs Atlanta 1976; mem Alpha Phi Alpha Frat 1979; mem bd of trustees Zion Travelor Bapt Church 1979-; bd mem Tri Dist Boys Club; mem United Way 1981-; PIC mem for JTPA 1984-90; mem Industrial Develop Bd 1986-92; mem Monroe Chamber of Commerce; pres Carroll HS PTA 1986. **HONORS/ACHIEVEMENTS:** Outstanding Young Man of Am 1978-79. **BUSINESS ADDRESS:** Dir of Planning & Urban Dev, City of Monroe, PO Box 7324, Monroe, LA 71201.

NEWMAN, KENYA MARIA
Entertainment company executive. **PERSONAL:** Born Nov 25, 1963, Flushing, NY; daughter of James Warren Newman and Gladys Maria Knight. **EDUCATION:** Univ of San Diego, BA, 1986. **CAREER:** Cedar Sinai Hospital, Los Angeles CA, lab research technician, 1982-84; Jeremiah's Steak House, Dallas TX, asst manager, head cashier, 1984-85; Marquee Entertainment, Los Angeles CA, asst executive vice pres, 1986-87; Shakeji Inc, Las Vegas NV, executive administrator, 1987-. **ORGANIZATIONS:** Sec/treas, Newman Management Inc, 1987-; corporate dir KNS Production Inc 1987-; corporate director Knight Hair Care Inc 1988-; sec treas Ms G Inc 1988-. **BUSINESS ADDRESS:** Executive Administrator, Shakeji Inc, 1589 Golden Arrow, Las Vegas, NV 89109.

NEWMAN, LEGRAND
Educator. **PERSONAL:** Born Jul 28, 1940, Danville, VA; son of James M Newman and Mildred Newman; children: Moya Marie. **EDUCATION:** Elizabeth City State Univ, BS (Cum Laude) 1967; Temple Univ, MEd (Distinguished) 1983. **CAREER:** DC Public School System, resource teacher 1967-70; Brookhave Natl Lab, personnel rep/educ coord 1970-73; Upsala Coll, dir sci program 1973-74; PA Coll of Podiatric Med, asst dean of students 1974-. **ORGANIZATIONS:** Consultant Natl Podiatry Medical Assoc 1974-; mem Amer Assoc of Higher Educ 1976-; natl sec Natl Assoc of Med Minority Educ 1983-85; mem Natl Assoc of Min Medical Educators 1976-. **HONORS/ACHIEVEMENTS:** Beta Beta Beta Biological Honor Soc 1964; Alpha Kappa Mu Honor Soc 1964; Dean's List 1965-67; Fellowship Elizabeth City State Univ 1966-67. **BUSINESS ADDRESS:** Asst Dean of Students, PA College of Podiatric Med, 8th at Race St, Philadelphia, PA 19107.

NEWMAN, MILLER MAURICE
Material stockclerk. **PERSONAL:** Born Oct 31, 1941, Terrell, TX; son of Miller Newman and Lillie Vee Coman Whestone; married Alice Faye Keith, Feb 10, 1963; children: Keith, Donald, Mark. **EDUCATION:** Eastern OK State Coll, 1968-71. **CAREER:** Hunt's Dept Store, Shipping & Recieving, 1960-66; Rockwell International, machine operator, 1966-83, stock clerk, 1983-. **ORGANIZATIONS:** Co-Owner, Teen's Vill USA, co-owner, B&B Skelly Station, 1968-76; mem, Keddo, 1972-; mem, Model Cities, 1971-76; pres, Pitts Co NAACP, 1972-; scoutmaster, Boyscouts of Amer, 1971-73; owner, Eastside Exxon, 1970-75; owner, Eastside Supperette, 1976-81; pres, UAW Local #1558, 1985-; chairman, McAlster Housing Auth, 1989. **HONORS/ACHIEVEMENTS:** Martin Luther King Jr, Pitts Co Holiday Commission, 1985, Natl Alliance Against Racism, 1984. **MILITARY SERVICE:** OK Natl Guard, Msg, ARCOM, Award for Valor, 1959-82; USAR, 1982-. **BUSINESS ADDRESS:** PO Box 13, McAlester, OK 74501.

NEWMAN, NATHANIEL
Investigator. **PERSONAL:** Born Aug 06, 1942, Altheimer, AR; son of Abraham Henry Newman and Marguerite Ruth Gordon Newman; married Constance Tate Newman, Jun 15, 1964; children: Mia Ruth Newman Williams, Angelique Marie. **EDUCATION:** Merritt, Coll, Oakland, CA, AA, 1971; San Jose State Univ, BS, 1974, MS, 1976; Spring Valley Bible Coll, Alameda, CA, BA, 1983; Fuller Theological Seminary, Pasadena, CA, certificate in religious studies, 1985. **CAREER:** City of Oakland, Oakland, CA, patrolman, 1968-74; Santa Clara County, San Jose, CA, inspector, 1974—; Antioch Baptist, San Jose, CA, assoc minister, 1981-86; Concord Missionary Baptist, San Francisco, CA, youth minister, 1986—. **ORGANIZATIONS:** Mem, chaplain, Alpha Phi Alpha, 1973—; sec, Alpha Phi Alpha Fraternity, Western Region, 1978-82; vice-pres, NAACP, San Jose Branch, 1980-84; pres, Black Peace Officers Assn, 1980-88; vice-chmn, mem, Minority Citizens Advisory Council, Metro Transportation Commission, 1980—; pres, District Attorney's Investigators Assn, 1982-84; pres/CEO, Frank Sypert Afro-Amer Community Service Agency, 1982-88; chaplain, Natl Black Police Assn, 1982—; chmn, Pack Committee, Boy Scouts of Amer, 1986—. **HONORS/ACHIEVEMENTS:** Doctor of Divinity, School of Gospel Ministry, 1982; Peace Officer of the Year, San Clara County Black Peace Officers, 1983, 1985, and 1988; community recognition, Omega Psi Phi, 1985; Community Service Award, San Jose Black Chamber of Commerce, 1986; Humanitarian Award, Ministers Alliance of San Jose, 1986; organized workshops and agencies for community blacks and students. **BUSINESS ADDRESS:** PO Box 2275, San Jose, CA 95119.

NEWMAN, PAUL DEAN
Automotive director of labor relations. **PERSONAL:** Born Dec 15, 1938, Zanesville, OH; married Norma Jean Guy; children: Vicki Newman Shields, Paula, Valerie, Paul II, Scott, Sharri. **EDUCATION:** Tri State Univ, BS 1966; Univ of VA Exec Devel Prog, Diploma 1985; Univ of MI Exec Devel Prog, Diploma 1986. **CAREER:** General Motors Corp, worked in several different positions with several different divisions and staffs presently dir of labor relations AC spark plug div 1964-. **ORGANIZATIONS:** Bd of dirs Mid-MI Chap Amer Soc for Training and Develop; treas mem of exec comm Urban League of Flint; vice pres mem of exec comm MI League forHuman Svcs; bldg and grounds comm Hurley Medical Ctr; bd of dirs Urban Coalition, Junior Achievement; treas, mem Flint Bd of Educ 12 yrs. **HONORS/ACHIEVEMENTS:** Disting Serv Awd Tri State Univ 1986. **HOME ADDRESS:** 3020 Westwood Pky, Flint, MI 48503. **BUSINESS ADDRESS:** Dir of Labor Relations, AC Spark Plug Div Genl Motors, 1300 No Dort Hwy, Flint, MI 48556.

NEWMAN, THEODORE ROOSEVELT, JR.
Judge. **PERSONAL:** Born Jul 05, 1934, Birmingham, AL; son of Theodore R Newman and Ruth Louise Newman. **EDUCATION:** Brown Univ, AB 1955; Harvard Law Sch, JD 1958. **CAREER:** DC Superior Court, assoc judge 1970-76; Brown Univ, trustee 1979-83; DC Court of Appeals, chief judge 1976-84, judge 1984-. **ORGANIZATIONS:** Pres Natl Ctr for State Courts 1981-82; fellow Amer Bar Foundation; mem Natl Bar Assn; past pres Judicial Council. **HONORS/ACHIEVEMENTS:** C Francis Stradford Awd 1984; Natl Bar Assoc; Brown Univ LLD 1980; William H Hastie Award Judicial Council Nalt Bar Assn 1988. **BUSINESS ADDRESS:** Judge, DC Ct of Appeals, 500 Indiana Ave NW, Washington, DC 20001.

NEWMAN, WILLIAM THOMAS, JR.
Attorney, elected official. **PERSONAL:** Born Sep 11, 1950, Richmond, VA; son of William T Newman and Geraldine Nunn Newman. **EDUCATION:** Ohio Univ, Athens OH, BA, 1972; Catholic Univ School of Law, Washington DC, JD, 1977. **CAREER:** US Dept of Commerce, Washington DC, attorney, 1977-80; Self-Employed, Arlington VA, attorney, 1980-; Arlington County, Arlington VA, mem Arlington County Bd, 1987-. **ORGANIZATIONS:** Mem, Virginia State Bar Assn, 1977-, District of Columbia Bar Assn, 1978-; bd of dir, Northern Virginia Black Attorney's Assn, 1984-88; chmn, Arlington County Fire Trial Bd, 1985-87; trustees council, Natl Capital Area YMCA, 1985-; bd of dir, Arlington County United Way, 1985-86; mem, Arlington Comm of PO, 1985-, Northern Virginia Urban League Advisory Comm, 1985-; vice pres, Old Dominion Bar Assn, 1986; mem, Virginia Medical Malpractice Review Panel, 1986-; commn in chancery, Arlington County Circuit Court, 1986-; vice chmn, Arlington Civic Coalition for Minority Affairs, 1986-88. **HONORS/ACHIEVEMENTS:** Corpus Juris Secundum, Catholic Univ School of Law, 1977; SAA, US Dept of Commerce, 1979; Community Serv, Alpha Phi Alpha, Theta Rho Lambda, 1987; Community Serv, Alpha Kappa Alpha, Zeta Chi Omega, 1988. **BUSINESS ADDRESS:** Member Arlington County Board, 1 Courthouse Plaza, 2100 Clarendon Blvd, Suite 300, Arlington, VA 22201.

NEWSOM, LIONEL H.
Educator. **PERSONAL:** Born Nov 11, 1919, Wichita Falls, TX; son of Lawson Newsom and Georgia Newsom; married Jane; children: Jacqueline Newsom-Peters. **EDUCATION:** Lincoln U, BA 1938;Univ MI, MA 1940; WA U, PhD 1956. **CAREER:** Central State U, pres 1972-; Johnson C Smith U, 1969-72; So Reg Educ Bd, asso proj dir 1966-68; Barber-Scotia C, pres 1964-66; Woodrow Wilson Schlrshp Prgm & Morehouse Coll, prof dir 1960-64; So U, head sociology 1956-60; St Louis Housing Auth, supr 1955-56; So U, prof sociology 1951-55; StoweTchr Coll, asso prof sociology 1949-51; So U, asso prof/social sci 1947-49; Lincoln U, instr 1946-47; Barber-Scotia Coll, disting UNCF scholar. **ORGANIZATIONS:** Life mem NAACP; Alpha Phi Alpha Frat; mem Nat Cncl Social Sci; So Social Assn; Assn Social Sci Tchrs; Alpha Kappa Delta Nat Hon Social Frat;Pi Gamma Mu Nat Soc Sci Hon Soc; Am Social Assn; WBT Black Adv Cncl; CIAA Pres Cncl; NC Ldrsp Inst Bd Tst; exec cabinet bd Nat Missions; Charlotte Rotary Club; HEXUS Com Bd Christian Edn; past mem Nat Com "S" of Univ Prof; adv cncl Danforth Found; Danforth Asso Pgm; SoUniv Chap AAUP; Self-Study Com So U; GA Cncl on Human Rel; Atlanta Summit Com; exec cncl Atlanta Negro Voters League; Wisteria Fairburn Comm Club; Charlotte/Radcliffe Presb Ch; Mechanics & Farmers Bank Commn on Liberal Learning Assn; NCNB bd of Dir. **HONORS/ACHIEVEMENTS:** LLD Davidson Coll 1972; Alumni Citation WA Univ 1973; LLD Bowling Green State Univ 1974; LHD Lincoln Univ 1975; LLD Wright State Univ 1975; Presidents Award for Excell Univ Cincinnati 1975; LLD Western MI Univ 1976; Alpha Phi Alphi Award of Merit 1979; Man of the Year Awd Natl Conf of Christian & Jews Dayton OH 1984; LHD Central State Univ 1984; Doctor of Humanities Wilberforce Univ 1984. **MILITARY SERVICE:** AUS 1st lt 1943-46; CMP. **BUSINESS ADDRESS:** Distinguished Scholar, Barber-Scotia College, Adm Bldg, Cozart Hall, Concord, NC 28025.

NEWSOME, BURNELL
Clergyman. **PERSONAL:** Born Apr 13, 1938, Wesson, MS; married Gloria J Wilson; children: Burrell Jr, Kenneth. **EDUCATION:** Marion Coll of Comm, Cert Business Admin 1962; Copiah Lincoln Jr Coll Wesson MS, Cert Carpentry 1977; MS Baptist Seminary Jackson MS, BTh. **CAREER:** Towne Shoes, store mgr, 1965; Commercial Credit Corp, dist rep, 1968; St Regis Paper Co, accountant 1973; BF Goodrich, budget control mgr; Mt Olive MB Church, pastor. **ORGANIZATIONS:** Trustee, Hazlehurst MS Separate School Dist 1982; advisory committee Southwest MS Elect Power Assoc 1983; bd mem MS Dept of Ed Comm on Accreditation 1984; chmn of steering committee "Copiah County Crusade for Christ" 1985; sec Copiah County Interdenominational Ministerial Alliance. **HONORS/ACHIEVEMENTS:** FHA Farm Family of the Year USDA Farmers Home Admin 1977. **BUSINESS ADDRESS:** Pastor, Mt Olive MB Church, Rt 4 Box 257, Wesson, MS 39191.

NEWSOME, CLARENCE GENO
Educator. **PERSONAL:** Born Mar 22, 1950, Ahoskie, NC; son of Clarence Shaw Newsome and Annie Butler Lewis Newsome; married Lynne DaNean Platt, Jul 29, 1972; children: Gina Lynn, Brittany Ann Byuarm. **EDUCATION:** Duke Univ, BA 1971; Duke Divinity School, M Div 1975; Duke U, PhD 1982. **CAREER:** Duke U, asst pro & dean of minority affairs 1973-74; Mt Level Baptist Church, Durham, NC Dem Nat'l Comm, asst staff dir demo charter comm 1974-75; Duke Divinity School, instructor 1978-82, asst prof 1982; Mt Level Baptist Church, Durham, NC Democratic Nat'l Comm 1974-75; Duke Univ, asst prof of Amer religious thought; Howard Univ DC Assistant Dean School of Divinity 1986-89, assoc dean, School of Divinity, 1989-. **ORGANIZATIONS:** Mem American Society of Church History 1980-; mem of finance comm Creative Ministries Assoc 1981; chrmn of the brd NC Gen Baptist Found, Inc 1982; mem of comm on educ Durham Comm on the Affairsof Black People 1983; co-chairman of comm on educ Durham Interdenominational Ministerial Alliance 1983-84; Planning Coordinator, Euro-American Theology Consultation Group, American Academy of Religion 1987-; pres Society for the Study of Black Religion 1989-. **HONORS/ACHIEVEMENTS:** 1st Black to receive Athletic Grant-in-Aid (Scholarship) Duke Univ 1968-72; 1st Black to be named to the All Atlantic Coast Conf Acad Team Duke Univ 1970-71; 1st Black stud Comm Speaker Walter Cronkite was the Keynote Duke Univ 1972; Rockfellow Doct Fellowship, Natl Fellowship, James B Duke Dissertation Fellowship, 1975-78; published number of articles and completed book length manuscript on Mary McLeod Bethund, A Religious Biography. **HOME ADDRESS:** 6761 Sewells Orchard Dr, Columbia, MD 21045. **BUSINESS ADDRESS:** Assoc Dean, The School of Divinity, Howard University, 1400 Shephard St, NE, Washington, DC 20017.

NEWSOME, COLA KING
Physician. **PERSONAL:** Born Sep 23, 1925, Ahoskie, NC; married Gerdine Hardin; children: Lars, Jon, Autumn, Ann, Peter. **EDUCATION:** WV State Coll, BS 1949; Meharry Med Coll, MS 1952; MD 1956. **CAREER:** Evansville, IN, Physician 1957-; St Mary's Hosp, staff mem; Deaconess Hosp; Hubbard Hosp, intern 1956-57. **ORGANIZATIONS:** Mem Evansville Rec Com 1970-; Evansville & Sch Bd 1964-; sec 1970-; IN Med Assn; AMA; Govtl Affairs Com 1969; Alpha; Dem; New Hope Bapt Ch; PlazaYacht Club Spl. **HONORS/ACHIEVEMENTS:** Recognition Black Expo 1977; listed Who's Who in Midwest W; personalities in the W Midwest; bd dir Child Guidance Ctr; Housing Com; SW IN Adult Ctr; Deaconess Med Records Utilization Com; dir Central Comm Clinic USMCR 1943-46. **BUSINESS ADDRESS:** 415 E Mulberry St, Evansville, IN 47713.

NEWSOME, EMANUEL T.
Educator. **PERSONAL:** Born Mar 21, 1942, Gary, IN; married Nellie Smith; children: Kim, Eric, Erika. **EDUCATION:** BS 1964; MA 1965; PhD counseling guidance & Psycho Service 1976. **CAREER:** Univ of Toledo 1976-; dir of student activities 1976-; IN State Univ, asst dean of student life for stud activities; dir coordinator state educ talent search search prog 1966-68; financial aid couns & field rep 1965-66; grad asst in physical educ 1964-65; head scout & asst basketball coach 1964-65. **ORGANIZATIONS:** Mem Midwest Stud Financial Aid Assn 1965-68; mem Nat Assn of Student Personnel Assn 1969-; mem bd dir Hyte Comm Center 1973-; mem bd dir Big Brother Orgn Kalamazoo MI 1965-66; basketball coach Terre Haute Boys Club 1973-; NAACP 1960-; Urban League 1967-; Gov Steering Com on Volunteerism 1975; adv bd Toledo March of Dimes; Western MIUniv Athletic Hall of & Fame 1974. **HONORS/ACHIEVEMENTS:** Outstanding Young Men of Am 1966; listed Who's Who Among Black Am 1974-75; All American in basketball 1964; 2nd leading scorer in nation major colleges 1964;All Mid-american Conf in basketball for 3 yrs 1961-64; participant Olympic Trials in basketball; IN All-star Basketball Team 1960. **BUSINESS ADDRESS:** Dean of Student Affairs, University of Toledo, 2801 W Bancroft St, University of Toledo, Toledo, OH 43606.

NEWSOME, MOSES, JR.
Education administrator. **PERSONAL:** Born Sep 06, 1944, Charleston, WV; son of Rev Moses Newsome and Ruth G Bass Newsome; married Barbara Newsome, Jun 08, 1968; children: Ayanna, Mariana. **EDUCATION:** Univ of Toledo, BA 1966; Univ of MI, MSW 1970; Univ of WI, PhD 1976. **CAREER:** Howard Univ Human Serv Eval Design Div, asst dir 1977-78; Howard Univ School of Social Work, asst dean 1979-80, assoc dean 1980-84; Norfolk State UnivSchool of Social Work, dean, prof 1984-. **ORGANIZATIONS:** Rsch consult Assoc consult Inc 1975-77; lecturer Upward Mobility Prog Univ of DC 1977-78; mem Natl Steering Comm Natl Assoc of Black Soc Workers 1979; elected mem Delegate Assembly Natl Assoc of Soc Workers 1983-84; mem Natl Steering Comm Group for the Advancement of Doctoral Ed 1983-85; chairman VA Social Work Educ Consortium; district chmn, Va. Chapter Natl Assn of Social Workers 1989-90; chmn, Norfolk City Council Task Force on Children in Need of Services 1988-89; vice chmn, Norfolk Area Health Study, Advisory Bd 1987-88; mem, Bd of Accreditation Council on Social Work Educ 1988-90; mem, State Bd Virginia Council on Social Welfare, 1989-91; mem, bd of dirs, Planning Council, Norfolk, VA, 1987-90. **HONORS/ACHIEVEMENTS:** Outstanding Young Man in Amer US Jaycees 1977; Outstanding Macro Faculty Mem Howard Univ School of Soc Work 1978; "Frequency and Distribution of Disabilities Among Blacks," in Equal to the Challenge, Bureau of Educ Research, Washington, DC 1986; "Job Satisfaction and Work Relationships of Social Service Workers," Dept of Human Resources, Norfolk, VA 1987. **MILITARY SERVICE:** USAF. **BUSINESS ADDRESS:** Dean, Professor, Norfolk StateUniv, School of Social Work, 2401 Corprew Ave, Norfolk, VA 23504.

NEWSOME, OZZIE
Professional athlete. **PERSONAL:** Born Mar 16, 1956, Muscle Shoals, AL; married Gloria Jenkins. **EDUCATION:** Alabama State, BS Recreation and Part Mgmt. **CAREER:** Cleveland Browns, tight end 1978-. **ORGANIZATIONS:** Active in Fellowship of Christian Athletes, Big Brothers, Athletes in Action; bd of dirs Police Athletic League. **HONORS/ACHIEVEMENTS:** Voted AL Amateur Athlete of Year by AL Sportswriters Assoc 1977; AFC Pro-Squad 1981; Teams Outstanding Player 1981; All Pro Pro-Football Writers Assn & Sporting News 1979; Browns All-Time Leading Receiver; MVP on Offense Cleveland TD Club (3 times); mem NFL Pro Bowl team 1981, 1985, 1986; ranked among NFL's top 10 in receptions; became 14th player in NFL history to grab 500 career passes; became the all-time leading TE in league history; leading receiver in AFC 1984. **BUSINESS ADDRESS:** Cleveland Browns, Cleveland Stadium, Cleveland, OH 44114.

NEWSOME, PAULA RENEE
Optometrist. **PERSONAL:** Born Jul 03, 1955, Wilmington, NC. **EDUCATION:** Univ of NC-Chapel Hill, BA 1977; Univ of AL-Birmingham Med Center, OD, 1981, MS, 1981. **CAREER:** The Eye Institute Philadelphia, residency 1982; Univ of MO-St Louis School of Optometry; asst prof 1982-84; VA Hospital St Louis, optometric consultant 1983-84; Private Practice, optometrist 1984-. **ORGANIZATIONS:** Mem, Delta Sigma Theta Sorority Inc 1974-, Amer Optometric Assn, 1981-; treasurer Region III Natl Optometric Assn, 1981-; mem NC State Optometric Soc 1982-;mem Mecklenburg Co Optometric Soc 1984-; mem Charlotte Medical Soc 1984-; state legislative affairs advisory comm Scope of Practice AOA 1984-; mem Young Professional Network Mecklenburg Co 1984-; free visual screening for area churches 1984-; speaker Role Model Series Charlotte-Mecklenburg School System 1985-; advisory bd Total Care Comprehensive Home Health Serv Charlotte 1985-; urban optometry Amer Optometric Assoc 1986-; mem of bd Charlotte Women Business Owners 1986-87; charter mem Doctors with a Heart 1986-; free visual screenings for Mecklenburg Co Parks and Recreation

1986; pres bd of dir Focus on Leadership 1986-, Mecklenburg Co, YWCA, 1988-present, Coalition for Literacy, 1988-present, Leadership Charlotte, 1986-present, Governor Morehead School for the Blind, 1988-present, Charlotte Civic Index, 1988-89. **HONORS/ACHIEVEMENTS:** Irv Borish Award for Outstanding Clinical Rsch 1981; The Las Amigas Outstanding Serv in Business Award 1985; 3 publications; numerous lectures. **BUSINESS ADDRESS:** Optometrist, 1812 Lyndhurst Ave, Charlotte, NC 28203.

NEWSOME, STEVEN CAMERON
Cultural administrator. **PERSONAL:** Born Sep 11, 1952, Norfolk, VA; divorced; children: Sanya. **EDUCATION:** Trinity Coll, BA 1974; Emory Univ, MLS 1975. **CAREER:** Northwestern Univ Library, afro-amer studies librarian 1975-78; Univ of IL Chicago Univ Library, asst ref librarian 1980-82, head of reference 1982-83; Vivian Harsh Collection of Afro-Amer Hist & Lit The Chicago Public Library, curator 1983-86; MD Commn on Afro-Amer History and Culture, exec dir 1986-. **ORGANIZATIONS:** Co-chair ACRL Black Studies Librarians Dis Group 1984-; mem Planning Committee Black Expressions/American Traditions 1985; coord Workshop The Black Woman Writer MI State Univ 1985; workshop leader Reference Resources in Afro-American Studies IL Library Assoc 1985. **HONORS/ACHIEVEMENTS:** Publication Literature of Illinois, The Afro-American Experience, IL Sec of State 1985. **BUSINESS ADDRESS:** Executive Dir, MD Commn on Afro-Amer History, 84 Franklin St, Annapolis, MD 21401.

NEWSON, ROOSEVELT, JR.
Concert pianist, educator. **PERSONAL:** Born Aug 30, 1946, Monroe, LA; son of Roosevelt Newson and Zipporah Newson; married Ethel Rae Whitaker; children: Erin, Meredith, Keirsten. **EDUCATION:** Southern Univ Baton Rouge, LA, BM 1968; Peabody Conserv of Music Baltimore, MD, MM 1971, DMA 1976; Juilliard Sch of Music NCY, professional studies 1982. **CAREER:** Appearances and performances with, York Symphony, Northeastern PA Philharmonic, Charlotte Symphony Orch, sev perf with Baltimore Symphony Orch; completed European tour incl perf in Salzburg, Vienna, Brussels, The Hague and a Wigmore Hall perf in London in 1978; numerous concerts on radio & TV; Western MI Univ,music faculty 1977-81; Wilkes Coll, chmn music dept/artist tchr. **ORGANIZATIONS:** Mgmt Affiliate Artists Inc 1970-78; mgmt Perrotta Mgmt New York City 1981-83; mem Leadership Wilkes-Barre 1985; minister of music Mt Zion Bapt Ch 1982-; mem Peabody Conservatory Alumni Council. **HONORS/ACHIEVEMENTS:** Ford Found Grant Peabody Conserv 1972-75; Ford Found Grant Juilliard 1982-83; Premier Performances at Kennedy Center Wash, DC 1980, Charlotte Symphony Orch 1983; Intl Who's Who in Music. **MILITARY SERVICE:** AUS Natl Guard Spec 4 1969-75. **HOME ADDRESS:** 160 Riverside Dr, Wilkes-Barre, PA 18766. **BUSINESS ADDRESS:** Assoc Dean, College of Arts and Sciences, Bloomsburg State Univ, Bloomsburg, PA 17815.

NEWTON, ANDREW E., JR.
Attorney, photographer. **PERSONAL:** Born Mar 09, 1943, Boston; married Joan Ambrose. **EDUCATION:** Dartmouth Coll, AB 1965; Columbia U, JD 1969. **CAREER:** Winston A Burnett Constr Co, asst gen counsel 1969-70; Amos Tuch Sch of Bus Adminstrn, Dartmouth Coll, 1970-71; Burnett Intl Dev Corp, gen counsel 1971-72; Honeywell Information Systems Inc, operations counsel 1972-74, staff counsel 1974-75, regnl counsel, Western Region 1975-77; Amdahl Corp, dir mkt oper cnsl 1977-; Digital Research Inc, gen counsel. **ORGANIZATIONS:** Mem Am, Boston, Fed, MA, Nat Bar Assns; mem NY & MA Bars; mem Peninsula Assn of Gen Counsel; Computer Lawyers Assn; Nat Contract Mgmt Assn. **BUSINESS ADDRESS:** Digital Research, Inc, 60 Garden Ct, PO Box DRI, Monterey, CA 93942.

NEWTON, DEMETRIUS C.
Attorney. **PERSONAL:** Born Mar 15, 1928, Fairfield, AL; married Beatryce Thomas; children: Deirdre Cheryl, Demetrius C, Jr. **EDUCATION:** Wilberforce U, BA 1949; Boston U, JD 1952. **CAREER:** Newton Coar Newton & Tucker, atty sr partner; City of Brightond city atty 1973-; city of brownsville, city judge 1975-. **ORGANIZATIONS:** Pres Tittisville & Powderly Br NAACP; forner natl pres WilberforceUniv Alumni Assn; former pres Fairfield Voters League UMDCA. **HONORS/ACHIEVEMENTS:** Man of Yr; Man of Yr So Beauty Congress; Man of Yr Phi Beta Sigma; counelor 82nd airborne div 1952-54. **BUSINESS ADDRESS:** Ste 1722-2121 Ave N, Birmingham, AL 35203.

NEWTON, ERNEST E., II
Elected official & business executive. **PERSONAL:** Born Feb 21, 1956, Fort Belvoir, VA; married Pamela A; children: Ernest E III, Chad J Newton. **EDUCATION:** Winston-Salem State Univ, BA 1978; Univ Bridgeport, grad prog 1980. **CAREER:** Bridgeport Bd of Educ, music teacher 1980-84; CT Natl Bank, personal banking rep 1984-; Peoples Bank, admin supv 1986-. **ORGANIZATIONS:** Former pres, former alderman, mem Bd of Aldermen 139th Dist; me Alpha Phi Alpha Frat; bdof mgrs YMCA; policy council Head Start; adv bd Greater Bridgeport Regional Narcotics Prog; comm Sikorsky Mem Airport; counsel of pres Red Cross; vice chmn 150th Anniversary of Bridgeport; pres of Bd of Alderman 139th Dist; mem Alpha Phi Alpha, James Wilkins Lodge #9 PHA afiliated FAMA. **HONORS/ACHIEVEMENTS:** Outstanding Merit Awd Natl Blk Teachers Assn 1974; Scholarship Awd Alpha Phi Alpha Grad Chap 1976; Outstanding Young Men of Amer Awd Natl Jaycees 1983; Comm Serv Awd Bus & Prof Women Youth Dept; Heritage Awd Alpha Kappa Alpha Sor 1983; City Govt Awd Omega Psi Phi Frat Inc 1983; Outstanding Achievement Awd Natl Assn of Negro Bus & Prof Women 1983.

NEWTON, JACQUELINE L. (NEE JEFFERSON)
Educator. **PERSONAL:** Born in Oklahoma City; divorced; children: Jeffrey, Richie. **EDUCATION:** SoUniv Lab Sch, Grad;Univ of OK, BBA, MEd 1974. **CAREER:** Univ Coll The Univ of OK, acad adv; OK Univ, finan aids couns; Apco Il Corp, various positions from clerk to accountant; OK City Law Firm, bookkeeper; OK Univ, Mobile Oil Co adminstrv Physical research coun, equal empl opp Com. **ORGANIZATIONS:** Chrd empl orgn reprsntng all non-tchng empl at univ 1972-73; active OKUniv Professional Empl Grp; pres OKUniv Assn of Blk Prsnl1975-76; NAACP Legal DefFund conjnctn with st deseg plans for hghr edn; supr training sem in Jan 1974; mem Alpha Kappa Alpha Sor; chmn Com of OK Blk Coaltn for Edn; intrst in hlpng yng blk ppl to rlz thr ptntl. **HONORS/ACHIEVEMENTS:** Voted outst achvmnt awd recip by fellow professional empl at OKUniv 1973. **BUSINESS ADDRESS:** 650 Parrington Oval, Norman, OK 73069.

NEWTON, JAMES DOUGLAS, JR.
Banker. **PERSONAL:** Born Jun 11, 1949, New Haven, CT; children: James D Newton III, Allen W Newton II. **EDUCATION:** Berkely Prep, 1969-70; S Central Comm College, LA 1971, AA 1973; New Hampshire Coll, BS Human Serv Admin 1979; Yale Univ, 1979-80; Attended, Public Health School. **CAREER:** AL Nellum & Assoc, comm liaison consultant 1968-69; Operation Breakthrough, placement interviewer 1969-79; Allied Radio Shack, asst mgr 1970-71; Bd of Educ, outreach worker 1971; Office of Comm Involvement, curriculum trainee 1971-73; Equal Employment Opportunity, officer 1973-76; Neighborhood Youth Corps Manpower Operation, field supervisor I; Kraft Dairy Group Inc, territory mgr 1976-78; Dept of Interior, asst dir work consultant 1978-79; Al Nellum & Assoc, dir of the New York City site 1979; City of New Haven, personnel & civil serv record system analyst 1979-82; CT Natl Bank, mgmt trainee. **ORGANIZATIONS:** Alderman Fifth Ward City of New Haven; mem Urban League, NAACP; bd of dirs YMCA; comm bd of dirs Yale Med Center; chmn bd dirs Hill NeighborhoodCorp; St Pauls Ch Planner for Organizational Activ; bd trustees Joy Temple Ch; mem Macedonia Ch of God and Christ; mem Intl Platform Assn; Joint Center for Polit Studies Washington, DC; chmn Black and Hispanic Caucus Bd of Aldermen City of New Haven CT. **HONORS/ACHIEVEMENTS:** Outstanding Young Man of America Jaycees; Outstanding Young Man of America awded by Genl Assembly & Gov Grasso. **HOME ADDRESS:** 547 Columbus Ave #1, New Haven, CT 06519. **BUSINESS ADDRESS:** Connecticut Natl Bank, 200 Orange St, New Haven, CT 06511.

NEWTON, JAMES E.
Professor, director higher education. **PERSONAL:** Born Jul 03, 1941, Bridgeton, NJ; son of Charles C Newton, Sr and Hilda H Newton; married LaWanda Williams Newton, Dec 1967; children: Regina, Walidah, KaWansi. **EDUCATION:** NC Central Univ, BA 1966; Univ of NC, MFA 1968; IL State Univ, PhD 1972. **CAREER:** Univ of NC, art instr 1967-68; W Chester State Coll PA, asst prof art 1968-69; IL State Univ Normal, asst prof art 1969-71; Western IL Univ Macomb, asst prof art 1971-72; Univ of DE Newark, asst prof ed 1972-73; Univ of DE Newark, prof, dir black amer studies 1973-. **ORGANIZATIONS:** Mem edit bd, Natl Art Ed Assoc; Editorial board Education 1974-; mem exec counselor Assoc Study Afro-Amer Life & History 1976-77; bd mem Western Journal of Black Studies 1983-; bd mem past chairman Walnut St YMCA Delaware 1983-; State Dir Assn for the Study of Afro-American Life & History 1988-. **HONORS/ACHIEVEMENTS:** Publ, College Student Jrnl, Jrnl of Negro Ed, Negro History Bulletin, Crisis, Education, Clearing House; books, A Curriculum Eval of Black Amer Studies in Relation to Student Knowledge of Afro-Amer History & Culture R&E Assoc Inc 1976, Roots of Black Amer; aduio-tapes Slave Artisans & Craftsmen, ContemporaryAfro-Amer Art Miami-Dade Comm Coll 1976; exhibitions, Natl Print & Drawing Show 11th Midwest Bienniel Exhib 1972; 1st prize Sculpture & Graphics 19th Annual Exhib of Afro-Amer Artists 1972; 23rd Annual Mid-States Art Exhibit 1972; Purchase Awd 13th Reg Art Exhibit Univ of DE 1974; DE Afro-Amer Art Exhib 1980; Exhibited Lincoln Univ, West Chester State Coll, FL A&M Univ, DE State Coll, Dover DE; Excellence in Teaching Award Univ of Delaware 1988; Eastern Region Citation Award Phi Delta Kappa National Sorority 1989. **MILITARY SERVICE:** US Army spec 4th class 1959-62. **BUSINESS ADDRESS:** Professor & Director, Black Amer Studies, Univ of Delaware, 417 Ewing Building, Newark, DE 19711.

NEWTON, MELVIN T.
Association executive. **PERSONAL:** Married Elizabeth Jackson; children: Latheria, Keith. **EDUCATION:** College, attended 1 yr. **CAREER:** Red Cap at PA Station in NYC, hotel worker; NAACP Mizpah Area Scholarship Fund, pres. **ORGANIZATIONS:** Adv comm Comm Svc; bd mem Atlantic Comm Coll, Mays Landing NJ; dir Summer Camp in Mizpuh Area; dir Meals on Wheels. **HONORS/ACHIEVEMENTS:** Chapel of Four Chaplains Awd 1969; Man of the Year Awd S Jersey 1971; NAACP Thalheimer Awd 1973; Freedom Equality & Justice Awd Mizpah Br NAACP 1971. **BUSINESS ADDRESS:** President, NAACP, Mizpah Area Scholarship Fund, P O Box 141, Mizpah, NJ 08342.

NEWTON, OLIVER A., JR.
Educator. **PERSONAL:** Born Jan 31, 1925, Long Branch, NJ; married Eleanor M Simmons; children: Martha Louise. **EDUCATION:** Howard Univ, BS 1949, MS 1950. **CAREER:** Inter-Amer Inst of Agr Sci Turrialba Costa Rica, rschr 1950-52; Univ of So CA, lab assoc 1952-56; Howard Univ, instr of botany 1956-58; William Paterson Coll of NJ, assoc prof 1958-. **ORGANIZATIONS:** Mem AAAS, AAUP, AIBS, Botanical Soc of Amer, Alpha Phi Alpha, Ridgewood Glen Rock Council Boy Scouts of Amer, Soc for Econ Botany, Glen Rock Adult SchoolCouncil, Glen Rock Civic Assoc; dir Glen Rock Human Relations Council, Cits Comm on Sch Plant & Classroom Eval; local asst bd Glen Rock 1966-74; Glen Rock Bd of Ed 1969-75; State Comm to Study Student Activism & Involvement in Ed Progs 1970. **HONORS/ACHIEVEMENTS:** Pan Amer Union Fellowship 1950-52; Natl Sci Found Coll Faculty Fellowship Rutgers Univ 1964. **MILITARY SERVICE:** USAF sgt 1943-46; USAFR maj retired. **BUSINESS ADDRESS:** Associate Professor, William Paterson College, 300 Pompton Rd, Wayne, NJ 07470.

NEWTON, ROBERT
Attorney. **PERSONAL:** Born Nov 13, 1944, Fairfield, AL; married Ruth Ann Boles; children: Robert Wade, Reginald Alan. **EDUCATION:** Lincoln Univ Jeff City MO, BS 1968; Howard Univ Sch of Law, JD 1971; Yale U; Harvard-Yale-Columbia, intensive summer studeis certificate summer 1966. **CAREER:** MO Comm on Human Rights, spec field rep 1968; Economic & Opportunity Wash, legal asst ofc 1969; US Atomic Energy Comm, staff atty 1971-74; Newton Coar Newton & Tucker Law Firm, atty. **ORGANIZATIONS:** Mem Am Bar Assn AL Bar Assn NAACP Legal Defense Fund Earl Warren Fellow; mem Jeff C Ity MO Com on Fiar Housing 1966-67; Omega Psi Phi Frat Inc;pres LincolnUniv Student Govt Assn 1966-67; Law Journal HowardUniv Law Sch 1969-70. **HONORS/ACHIEVEMENTS:** Who's Who in Am Coll &Univ 1966-67; LincolnUniv Man of Yr 1966-67; recipient Cobb-trustee Scholarship Howard Law 1969-70; 70-71; NAACP Earl Warren Legal Fellowship 1974-75. **MILITARY SERVICE:** AUSR 1st lt. **BUSINESS ADDRESS:** 2121 Bldg Ste 1722, 2121 Eighth Ave N, Birmingham, AL.

NEWTON, ROBIN CAPRICE
Physician. **PERSONAL:** Born Jan 31, 1957, Washington, DC. **EDUCATION:** Univ of WI-Milwaukee, BA 1979; Howard Univ Coll of Medicine, MD 1983. **CAREER:** DC General Hospital, chief resident internal medicine. **ORGANIZATIONS:** Mem Amer Medical Assoc 1980-, Amer Medical Women's Assoc, Alpha Omega Alpha Medical Honor Soc 1983-; mem DC Youth Chorale Alumni Chorus 1985-; assoc Amer Coll of Physicians 1985-; mem Medical Soc of the District of Columbia 1986-. **HONORS/ACHIEVEMENTS:** Raymond

P Jackson Awd for Tutorial Serv 1983; Emile C Nash Awd for Scholastic Achievement 1983; Citation of Scholastic Achievement Amer Medical Women's Assoc 1983; Outstanding Young Woman of Amer 1985; American Bd of Internal Medicine Certification 1986. **BUSINESS ADDRESS:** Chief Resident Internal Med, DC General Hospital, 19th & E Sts SE, Washington, DC 20003.

NEWTON, TOM CALVIN
Professional athlete. **PERSONAL:** Born Mar 08, 1954, Carmel, CA; married Donna. **EDUCATION:** California. **CAREER:** New York Jets, 1977-83; Oakland Invaders, fullback 1983-. **HONORS/ACHIEVEMENTS:** Holds club record by rushing for a touchdown in four consecutive games.

NEYLAND, LEEDELL WALLACE
College dean. **PERSONAL:** Born Aug 04, 1921, Gloster, MS; married Della Louise Adams; children: Beverly Ann, Keith Wallace, Katine Denise. **EDUCATION:** VA State Coll, AB 1949; NY U, MA 1950; PhD 1959. **CAREER:** Leland Coll Baker LA, prof social scis dean coll 1950-52; Grambling Coll, asso prof sociol scis 1952-58; Elizabeth City Coll, dean 1958-59; FL A&M U, prof hist dean humanities/soc sci 1959-; Black History & Edn, consult lectr. **ORGANIZATIONS:** Mem Phi Beta Sigma. **HONORS/ACHIEVEMENTS:** Author The History of FL A&M Univ 1963; Twelve Black Floridians 1970; contrib professional jours Am Assn State & Local History Grantee 1965; carnegie granted 1965. **MILITARY SERVICE:** USNR 1941-46. **BUSINESS ADDRESS:** Professor of History, Florida A&MUniv, Tallahassee, FL 32307.

NIBBS, ALPHONSE, SR.
Business executive, appointed official. **PERSONAL:** Born Nov 10, 1947, Charlotte Amalie, Virgin Islands of the United States;son of Ernest Albert Nibbs and Elenora Charles-Nibbs; married Paulette E Shelford Nibbs, Oct 30, 1967; children: Berecia Nibbs-Cartwright, Alphonse Jr, Antoninette Nibbs-Richardson,Annette, Anthony, Alyssa. **EDUCATION:** Coll of the VI 1980; Cert Labor Relations, Publ Admin, Personnel Mgmt 1980; Inst for Professional & Econ Devel 1981; Georgia Institute of Technology Atlanta GA Contract Administration, 1986. **CAREER:** Water & Power Authority, distribution engr 1967-76; Nibbs Brothers Inc, sec, treas 1974-; Dept of Housing, asst commiss 1977-84; Lt Governors Office, temp housing off hd-gar team, terr coord off 1979-86; VI Housing Authority, exec dir 1985-87; Legislature of VI 1988-89. **ORGANIZATIONS:** Mem Commiss on Aging 1977-87, Bd of Elections 1978-87, VI Soc on Public Admin 1980-87. **BUSINESS ADDRESS:** Secretary/Treasurer, Nibbs Bros Inc, PO Box 7245, 4A Estate Thomas, Charlotte Amalie, St Thomas, Virgin Islands of the United States 00801.

NICCO-ANNAN, LIONEL
Chief executive. **CAREER:** Clipper International Corp, Detroit, MI, chief executive, 1963-. **BUSINESS ADDRESS:** Clipper International Corp, 8651 E Seven Mile Rd, Detroit, MI 48234. *

NICHOLAS, DENISE
Performing arts. **PERSONAL:** Born in Detroit, MI. **EDUCATION:** Univ of MI, 1962-65; Univ of Southern CA, Professional Writer's Prog 1985. **CAREER:** Negro Ensemble Co, actress 1967-69; ABC, actress Room 222-series 1969-74; Masai Enterprises, Inc, producer 1976-. **ORGANIZATIONS:** Mem Neighbors of Watts, Inc 1976-; producer The Media Forum, Inc 1980-; bd of dir Communications Bridge Video School 1983-; mem & fund raiser Artists & Athletes Against Apartheid; mem Museum of African American Art LA; mem Museum of Afro-American History & Culture. **HONORS/ACHIEVEMENTS:** 2 LA Emmy Awards producer/actress Voices of our People in Celebration of Black Poetry 1981; 2 CEBA Awds Excellence for Advertising & Communications to BlackComm 1981, 1982; 3 Emmy nominations Room 222. **BUSINESS ADDRESS:** Masai Enterprises, Inc, 6922 Hollywood Blvd, Los Angeles, CA 90028.

NICHOLAS, FAYARD ANTONIO
Actor and entertainer. **PERSONAL:** Born Oct 20, 1914, Mobile, AL; son of Ulysses Nicholas and Viola Harden Nicholas; married Barbara January, Sep 17, 1967; children: Tony, Paul, Nina. **CAREER:** Dancer, with brother Harold, in group "Nicholas Brothers"; performer on radio shows and in vaudeville; actor, singer, dancer, or musician in films, including "The Big Broadcast," 1936, "Down Argentina Way," 1940, "Tin Pan Alley," 1940, "The Great American Broadcast," 1941, "Sun Valley Serenade," 1941, "Orchestra Wives," 1942, "Stormy Weather," 1943, "The Pirate," 1948, and "The Liberation of L. B. Jones," 1970; performer in Broadway shows, including "Ziefield Follies," 1936, "Babes in Arms," 1937, and "St Louis Woman," 1946; performer on television programs in Las Vegas, and on tour around US, Mexico, S Amer, Africa, and Europe ; teacher of private dance lessons; performer at numerous charitable events; choreographer for Broadway revue "Black and Blue," 1989. **HONORS/ACHIEVEMENTS:** Black American Life Achievement Award; gave Royal Command Performance for King of England at London Palladium, 1948; gave performances at the White House, Washington, D.C., 1942, 1955, and 1987; "Honorary Chmn for Month of May," Arthritic Foundation Telethon, 1986; Tony Award for best choreographer, 1989, for Broadway musical "Black and Blue.". **MILITARY SERVICE:** US Army, Special Service, 1943-44. **HOME ADDRESS:** 23388 Mulholland Dr, #58, Woodland Hills, Los Angeles, CA 91364.

NICHOLAS, GWENDOLYN SMITH
Licensing program analyst. **PERSONAL:** Born Jan 27, 1951, San Francisco, CA; married Alvin P Nicholas. **EDUCATION:** Univ of San Francisco, BA 1972; Atlanta Univ, MSW 1974. **CAREER:** Fireman's Fund Ins Co, business systems analyst 1976-77; W Oak Mental Health Dept, psychiatric social worker 1977-78; State of CA Dept of Mental Health, psychiatric social worker 1978-81, mental health prog specialist 1981-83, licensing program analyst II 1984-. **ORGANIZATIONS:** Area pub info officer, chap rec sec SF Chap of Links Inc 1975-; mem Bay Area Assoc of Black Social Workers 1977-; contributor United Negro Coll-Fund 1978-; contributor Bay Area Black United Fund 1980-; mem Soroptimist Intl Oak Founder Club 1986-; mem Alpha Kappa Alpha 1972; mem Black Advocates in State Serv, Bay Area Heath Consortium; mem Assoc of Black Career Developer. **HONORS/ACHIEVEMENTS:** Outsanding Young Women of Amer 1983. **HOME ADDRESS:** Box 8581, Oakland, CA 94662. **BUSINESS ADDRESS:** Licensing Program Analyst II, State of CA Dept of Soc Serv, Comm Care Licensing, 5850 Shellmound Ste 315, Emeryville, CA 94608.

NICHOLAS, MARY BURKE
Government official. **PERSONAL:** Born in Tuskegee, AL; children: Tracy Nicholas Bledsoe, Scott Cardozo. **EDUCATION:** Univ of WI Madison, BA High Hnrs 1948. **CAREER:** Housing Mayors Office NYC, exec asst 1960-66; US Dept of Housing & Urban Dev Reg II, congressional liaison 1966-70; Temporary Comm Local Govt NY State, deputy dir 1970-73; Public Affairs Cons1983-; Regional Econ Housing 1973-75; dir Women's Div Govt Office NY State 1975-82. **ORGANIZATIONS:** Fndr NY Coalition of 100 Black Women 1970-; mem Women's Forum of NY City 1974-; bd mem NY State Comm Aid Assc 1980-. **HONORS/ACHIEVEMENTS:** Pres Natl Assc of Commissions of Women 1980-82; mayoral appointee New York City Charter Revision Comm 1982-83; dir Fed Home Loan Bank Bd Reg II 1980-84; adv bd NY Univ Grad Schl of Public Admin. **BUSINESS ADDRESS:** Public Affairs Consultant, Self Employed, 201 E 21st St, New York, NY 10010.

NICHOLS, ALFRED GLEN
Commercial printing. **PERSONAL:** Born Mar 20, 1952, Jackson, MS; married Sylvia Lauree Robinson; children: Derek Allen, Shaunte Latrice. **EDUCATION:** Purdue Univ, BS 1975; Univ of Chicago, MBA 1985. **CAREER:** RR Donnelley & Sons Co, price admin estimator 1975-78, industrial engr 1978-80, project engr 1980-86, supervisor plng & facil engr 1986-. **ORGANIZATIONS:** Dir Hazel Crest Jaycees 1982-85. **HONORS/ACHIEVEMENTS:** Outstanding Young Men in Amer 1985; Black Achiever of Industry Chicago YMCA 1986. **HOME ADDRESS:** PO Box 315, 2918 Greenwood Rd, Hazel Crest, IL 60429. **BUSINESS ADDRESS:** Supervisor Plng/Facil Engr, RR Donnelley and Sons Co, 750 Warrenville Rd, Lisle, IL 60532.

NICHOLS, CHARLES HAROLD
Educator. **PERSONAL:** Born Jul 06, 1919, Brooklyn, NY; married Mildred Thompson; children: David G, Keith F, Brian A. **EDUCATION:** Brooklyn Coll, BA 1942; Brown Univ, PhD 1948. **CAREER:** Morgan State Coll, assoc prof, English, 1948-49; Hampton Inst, prof, English, 1949-59; Free Univ, prof, Amer Studies, 1959-69; Brown Univ, prof, English, 1969. **ORGANIZATIONS:** Mem Modern Lang Assn, Amer Studies Assn, Soc for Multi-Ethnic Lit of the US. **HONORS/ACHIEVEMENTS:** Author, "Many Thousand Gone", "The Ex-Slaves Account of their Bondage & Freedom" Brill, Leiden 1963, INUniv Press, 1969, "Black Men in Chains" 1971, Instr Manual for Cavalcade, Houghton, Mifflin, 1971, "African Nights, Black Erotic Folk Tales" 1971, "Arna Bontemps - Langston Hughes Letters 1925-67", Dodd Mead, 1980; sr fellow Natl Endowment for Humanities 1973-74; O'Connor Disting Vstg Prof Colgate Univ 1977. **BUSINESS ADDRESS:** Professor of English, Brown University, Box 1852, Providence, RI 02912.

NICHOLS, DIMAGGIO
Company executive. **PERSONAL:** Born May 08, 1951, Byhalia, MS; son of Emmitt Nichols, Jr and Lucille Bougard Nichols; married Lizzie Emma (Shelton) Nichols, Mar 16, 1974; children: Dimeka W, Dondra O. **EDUCATION:** Rust Coll, Holly Spring MS, BS 1973; General Motor Institution, Flint MI, Dealer Development 1983. **CAREER:** Buick Motor Division, Flint MI, dist sales manager 1974-1983; General Motor Institution, Flint MI, trainee 1983-84; Sentry Buick, Omaha NE, salesperson 1984-85; Noble Ford-Mercury, Indianola IA, pres 1985-, Earlham IA, pres 1987-; Alph Lincoln-Mercury Imports, Victoria TX, vice pres 1988-. **ORGANIZATIONS:** Mem, The Intl Lions Clubs 1987-; bd mem Chamber of Commerce Indianola IA 1987-; bd mem Black Ford Lincoln Mercury Assn 1988-. **HONORS/ACHIEVEMENTS:** Iowa Up and Comers Des Moines Register 1986; Quality Care Program Award for Excellence Ford Motor Company 1987; Top Return on Investment Ford Motor Company 1988. **BUSINESS ADDRESS:** President, Noble Ford-Mercury Inc, 947 Hwy 65-69 North, Box I, Indianola, IA 50125.

NICHOLS, EDWARD K., JR.
Clergyman, attorney. **PERSONAL:** Born Aug 10, 1918, Atlanta; married Ethel Williams; children: Charlotte A, Carolyn H, Eloise M, Lavra L. **EDUCATION:** Lincoln U, AB 1941; HowardUniv Law Sch, LLB 1950; PA Law Sch, grad study 1951; TempleUniv Sch of Theo, grad study 1957. **CAREER:** Atty 1951-; City of Philadelphia, asst dist atty 1952-53; Private Practice, 1954-58; ordained Minister Meth 1956; Norris Green Harris Higginbotham, assoc1958-63; Nichols & Nichols, partner; Greater St Matthew Independent Church, pastor. **ORGANIZATIONS:** Mem Fellowship Commn; life mem NAACP; 1st vice pres Black Clergy of Philadelphia. **BUSINESS ADDRESS:** Pastor, Grtr St Matthew Independent Ch, Race and Vogoes St, Philadelphia, PA 16139.

NICHOLS, EDWIN J.
Clinical/industrial psychologist. **PERSONAL:** Born Jun 23, 1931, Detroit, MI; married Sandra; children: Lisa, Edwin. **EDUCATION:** Assumption Coll CAN, attended 1952-55; Eberhardt Karls Universitat, Tubingen, Germany, 1955-57; Leopoline-franciscea Universitat, Innsbruck, Austria, on Fellow by Austrian Ministry of Edn, PhD 1961. **CAREER:** Natl Inst of Mental Health, Rockville, MD, chief Applied & Social Proj Review Branch; KS Neurological Inst Cleveland Job Corps Center for Women Meharry Med Coll & Fisk Univ, psychologist; Univ of Ibadan Nigeria, dir Childs Clinic 1974-77; Centre for Mgmt Devel Lagos Nigeria, mgmt consult 1974-77. **ORGANIZATIONS:** Veteran, Korean War. **BUSINESS ADDRESS:** 5600 Fishers Ln, Rockville, MD 20852.

NICHOLS, ELAINE
Archaeologist. **PERSONAL:** Born Oct 05, 1952, Charlotte, NC. **EDUCATION:** Univ of NC Charlotte, BA 1974; Case Western Reserve Univ, MSSA 1980; Univ of South Carolina, 1985-88. **CAREER:** Planned Parenthood Charlotte, crisis intervention counselor 1974-75; Big Brothers/Big Sisters, social caseworker 1975-78; City of Cleveland, neighborhood planner 1980-81, asst mgr of planners 1981-82; Univ North Carolina Charlotte, lecturer 1982-85; Univ of South Carolina, graduate student dept of anthropology, 1985-88; South Carolina State Museum, 1987-. **ORGANIZATIONS:** Charter mem Afro-Amer Serv Centtr 1974; mem Delta Sigma Theta Sor 1977-; lecturer Univ of NC Charlotte 1982-85; chairperson Afro-Amer Historical Soc Charlotte 1982-83; bd mem Metrolina Assoc for the Blind 1983-85; researcher Amer Heart Assoc Charlotte 1985. **HONORS/ACHIEVEMENTS:** "Pulse of Black Charlotte" Urban Inst Grant UNCC 1984; Research Assistantship Dept of Anthropology USC

1985-; Service Award Alpha Kappa Alpha Sor 1986; Sigma Xi Science Award 1987. **HOME ADDRESS:** 6400 Countryside Dr, #5, Charlotte, NC 28213.

NICHOLS, HENRY H.
Retired. **PERSONAL:** Born Jun 06, 1916, Philadelphia; widowed. **EDUCATION:** STB, BS 1941; Temple U, hon DD 1970; Lebanon Valley Coll, hon DD 1971. **CAREER:** Janes Mem United Meth Ch, minister 1947-. **ORGANIZATIONS:** Pres Philadelphia Fellowship Commn; coChmn Philadelphia Urban Coalition; trustee TempleUniv & Lebanon Valley Coll mem Eastern PA Conf of United Meth Ch;mem bd dir Nat Conf of Christians & Jews; bd dir Crime Commn of Philadelphia, Inc; mem exec com trustee, United Fund; mem Dept of Public Assistance; parole officer PA Bd of Parole; mem Lacour Special Evangelism Commn to Japan; visited Meth Mission Stations in Liberia, Ghana, Congo, Rodesia & South Africa; independently toured Kenya, Ethiopia, Egypt, Holy Land, India, Hong Kong & Japan 2959; Missioner to AK 1962; visited Union of S Africa under US-s Africa Cultural Leader Exchange Aprog 1965; mem Evangelistic Mission to Great Britian 1970; mem Evangelistic Mission to Lubumiashi, Congo 1971; affiliated with numerous civic & community organizations. **HONORS/ACHIEVEMENTS:** Recipient of many awds, including Interfaith-human Relations Awd, Nat Conf of Christians & Jews 1974; Citizenship Award, Black Political Forum 1972; Future Teachers of Am Awd 1969; various others.

NICHOLS, KAY BAILEY
Director of women's work. **PERSONAL:** Born Dec 15, 1908, Denton, MD; married D Ward; children: Wardean, Sioux. **EDUCATION:** Howard U, Attended 1928-31; Payne Coll, MA 1947. **CAREER:** Womens Work AME Ch SC, dir; Colonal Park Housing Comm Center, NYC, co-founder. **ORGANIZATIONS:** Life mem Fedn of Colored Womens Clubs 1961; New York City Ch W United 1954; Nat Negro Women 1970; mem exec bd Nat Negro Women 1970; sponsor of Forward 76; supv Womens Missionary AME Clh, AL 1940-48; supv Womens Missionary AME Ch NY Philadelphia, New England & Bermuda 1948-56; Baltimore & Washington 1954-56; mem Nat Bd Ch Women United 1950-64; dir Womens & Youth AME Ch AK & OK 1968-72; mem YWCA; NAACP; League of Women Voters; PUSH; listed in first edition of Whos Who of Am 1968; hon mem Nat Phi Delta Kappa Sor 1957; dir Family Life Dept, AME Lch 1950-58; mem Family Life Dept Nat Council of Ch 1951-58. **BUSINESS ADDRESS:** 70 Ashe St, Charleston, SC 29403.

NICHOLS, LEROY
Association executive. **PERSONAL:** Born Jan 24, 1924, E Chicago, IN; married Luella; children: Joanne, LeRoy, III, Gregory, Patty Sue, Cynthia, Kristopher, Michelle Denise. **EDUCATION:** Baker Bus U, 1946; Mott Comm Coll, 1948-50;Univ MI, 1967; GM Inst, cert Estate Selling Methods, Real Estate Selling Methods 1970-71;Univ MI,Univ MI, Flint, cert Mgmt Mgrs 1972. **CAREER:** Buick Motor Div, prodn worker 1942-44; Chev Motor Div, machine operator 1946; Genesee Co Comm Action Agy, organizer/EOO 1970; Genesee Co, bd supr 1964-68; Flint, MI, bd review 1968-69. **ORGANIZATIONS:** Flint Transp Authority 1969; Legal Aid Soc 1969; BSA bd dir 1970; mA Transp Authority chmn 1971; dist committeeman, Buick Motor 1944; chmn UAW, Civil Rights Comm 1955; chmn UAW Political Action Comm 1957; trustee Chev Local 659 1961; delegate UAW Conv CA 1966; delegate UAW Conv Detroit 1967; charter revision commr v chmn 1973; bd supr genesee co admin bldg, youth crime referral prog, bishop airport consol, new Mem McFarlen Park, Youth Summer Job Prog; Flint Youth Bureau; Urban League; Genesee Co Historical Soc; Comm Civic League; Bruin Club; YMCA Adv Comm; past Master John W StevensonLodge 56; F & AM Oman Temple No 72 Shriners, past potentate; NAACP; Mott Comm Coll Alumni; grand treas MWPH Grand Lodge MI; Imperial Auditor AEAONMS; Prince Hall Shriners; Mason 33 deg. **MILITARY SERVICE:** AUS 1943-44. **BUSINESS ADDRESS:** Executive Dir, Genesee County CAA, 601 S Saginaw St, Ste 301, Flint, MI 48505.

NICHOLS, NICHELLE
Actress, singer. **PERSONAL:** Married Foster Johnson. **CAREER:** Actress, singer, dancer; Women In Motion (consulting firm), president; NASA, public relations employee, minority recruitment officer. **ORGANIZATIONS:** Board mem, Natl Space Inst. **HONORS/ACHIEVEMENTS:** Played Lt Uhura on "Star Trek" television series and films. *

NICHOLS, NICK
Manager, manufacturing engineer. **PERSONAL:** Born Mar 26, 1944, Mobile, AL; son of Mr & Mrs C H Nichols. **EDUCATION:** Tuskegee Univ, BSEE 1967; Southern Methodist Univ, MBA 1975. **CAREER:** IBM Corp, systems engr 1966-67; Ford Motor Co, financial analyst 1976-79; Boise Cascade Corp, div staff engr mgr. **ORGANIZATIONS:** Life mem Kappa Alpha Psi Fraternity 1963-. **MILITARY SERVICE:** USAF major 1967-76; Air Medal (6), Air Force Commendation (2), Meritorious Service; Joint Service Commendation Medal; Vietnam Service Medal; Selective Service Meritorious Service Medal; USAFR Lieutenant Colonel, 1976-. **BUSINESS ADDRESS:** Division Staff Engineer, Boise Cascade Corporation, P O Box 50, Boise, ID 83728.

NICHOLS, OWEN D.
Educator. **PERSONAL:** Born Apr 08, 1929, Raleigh, NC; son of William Nichols and Pearl Nichols; married Delores Tucker; children: Bryan K, Diane Maria. **EDUCATION:** Shaw Univ, BS 1955; Howard Univ, MS 1958; HIghland Univ, EdD 1975. **CAREER:** SC State Coll, assoc prof 1958-59; US Naval Res Lab Washington DC, res chemist 1959-62; Dept Defense Alexandria VA, physical science analyst 1962-66; Air Pollution Tech Info Center, Natl Air Pollution Control Admin Washington DC, deputy dir 1966-68; Office of Tech Info & Publs Natl Air Polllution Control Admin Washington DC, dir 1968-69; Howard Univ Washington DC, exec asst to pres 1969-71; Howard Univ, vice pres admins & sec 1971-88. **ORGANIZATIONS:** Alpha Kappa Mu Soc; Beta Kappa Chi Science Soc; Amer Chem Soc; Air Pollution Control Assn; Soc of Sigma XI; Intl Platform Assn; Amer Mgmt Assn; Amer Assn High Educ; Amer Assn Univ Admin; Commn on Educ Statis & Admin Affairs, Amer Council on Educ MD Congress; PTA; Adv Con on Hospital Constructionn MD; town councilman, Seat Pleasant MD; Prince Georges County Housing Authority; legislative chmn, 2nd vice pres Prince Georges Co Council, PTA; Lay Speaker United Methodist Church. **HONORS/ACHIEVEMENTS:** Commin On Campus Ministry & Higher Educ; Baltimore Washington Conf United Methodist Church. **MILITARY SERVICE:** AUS Corps of Engrs 1st lt 1950-53. **BUSINESS ADDRESS:** 12713 Eldrid Pl, Silver Spring, MD 20904.

NICHOLS, PAUL
Clergyman. **PERSONAL:** Born Aug 12, 1939, Bowling Green, KY; son of George Nichols, Sr and Mary Nichols; married Brenda Coles Dabney; children: Colita, Kimberly, Camilla, Brandon. **EDUCATION:** VA Union Univ, BA & MDV 1961-64; Presbyterian School of Christian Educ, MA 1967; The Amer Univ, EdD 1976. **CAREER:** VA Union Univ 1968-69, campus pastor 1968-69; VA Union Univ School of Theology, interim dean 1974-75, dean 1976-82; Good Shepherd Baptist Church, pastor 1960-; Virginia Union Univ, assoc prof Christian educ, 1985-. **ORGANIZATIONS:** Lecturer Presbyterian School of Christian Educ 1972-74; vice-pres Natl Ministers Council/American Bapt 1982-85; chairman Richmond Redevel and Housing Authority 1983-85; vicepres VA Inst of Pastoral Care 1984-85; pres VA Interfaith Ctr for Public Policy 1985-87. **HONORS/ACHIEVEMENTS:** "Blacks and the Religious Education Movement," Changing Patterns in Religious Education, Abingdon Press, 1984; "The Pastor as Leader of Leaders" in Baptist Leader, Jan 1985; Brotherhood Citation, Natl Conf of Christian and Jews, 1988. **BUSINESS ADDRESS:** Pastor, Good Shepherd Baptist Church, 1200 N 28th St, Richmond, VA 23223.

NICHOLS, ROY CALVIN
Clergyman. **PERSONAL:** Born Mar 19, 1918, Hurlock, MD; son of Roy and Mamie; married Ruth Richardson, Jul 23, 1944; children: Melisande, Allegra, Nathan. **EDUCATION:** Lincoln U, BA 1941; Pacific Sch Religion, MDiv 1947, DD (hon) 1964;Univ Pacific, DD 1959; OH No U, D Pub Serv (hon) 1969; Allegheny Coll, DD (hon) 1969. **CAREER:** Bishop; S Berkeley Comm Ch, minister 1943-47; Meth Ch, ordained 1949; Downs Meml Meth Ch, Oakland, pastor 1949-64; Salem Meth Ch, NYC, 1964-68; United Methodist, emeritus bishop 1968-. **ORGANIZATIONS:** Pres Berkeley Bd Educ 1963-64; mem exec comm World Council of Churches 1968-75. **HOME ADDRESS:** 53 Ironwood, Oakland, CA 94605.

NICHOLS, SYLVIA A.
Public information specialist. **PERSONAL:** Born Nov 15, 1925, Washington, DC; married Herb Nichols; children: Cynthia, Louie, Albert Blalock-Bruce, Carl, Donna. **EDUCATION:** Univ of The DC, Washington, DD, MA. **CAREER:** Dept of Labor, Occupational Safety and Health Admin, public affairs specialist 1971-87. **ORGANIZATIONS:** Delegate Central Labor Council, DC 1972-85; founding member Washington Womens Forum 1977-; exec board Natl Assoc (BIG) DOL Chapter Blacks In Govt DC 1979-; pres Local #12, AFGE, Dept Labor 1982; dir Fed Credit Union, Dept Labor 1982-87; delegate Natl AFGE Convention 1984; delegate Natl AFGE Convention 1986; second vice pres #12 AFGE 1986-87; mem, Black Democratic Council Inc PG MD 1986-87. **HONORS/ACHIEVEMENTS:** Special serv Comm Award, The PG County Chapter of the Natl Hook Up of Black Women, Dept of Labor, 1982; Fed Serv Award for thirty years of honorable serv to the Dept of Labor. **BUSINESS ADDRESS:** Public Affairs Specialist, US Dept, Labor, 3rd & Constitution Ave,, Washington, DC 20210.

NICHOLS, WALTER L.
Automobile dealer. **CAREER:** Walt Nichols Chevrolet Inc, Lebanon, OH, chief executive, 1987-. **BUSINESS ADDRESS:** Walt Nichols Chevrolet Inc, 909 Columbus Ave, Lebanon, OH 45036. *

NICHOLS, WALTER LAPLORA
Educator. **PERSONAL:** Born Aug 31, 1938, Bolton, MS; married Louise Faye Harris; children: Anthony, Kala Faye. **EDUCATION:** MS Valley State Univ, BS 1964; Northern IL Univ, MS 1978; Independence Univ, DEd 1979. **CAREER:** Sheridan Ind for Boys, teacher 1965-67; Fairmont Jr HS, teacher/coach 1967-71; Argo Comm HS, teacher/coach 1971-. **ORGANIZATIONS:** Vp Dist 86 School Bd 1981-; mem Natl School Bd Assoc 1981-, IL School Bd Assoc 1981-; consult Joliet Job Corp 1982-83; bd mem PUSH 1983-; 1st lt marquette Joliet Consistory 1983; shriner 1984. **HONORS/ACHIEVEMENTS:** Article "You Either Move Up or Move Out" Chicago Tribune 1967, "Title Triumph by Charger Something Special, Walt" 1967, "Remember Walter Nichols Offensive Tackle" Joliet Herald newspaper 1964-67, "Stand by Valley State Alumni Urge Official" Clarion Ledger Paper 1983. **HOME ADDRESS:** 701 Spencer St, Joliet, IL 60433.

NICHOLS-ELLIOTT, RUTH L.
Business executive. **PERSONAL:** Born Apr 15, 1948, Los Angeles, CA; married Alexander William Elliott; children: Ernest Nichols. **EDUCATION:** Pasadena City Coll, Comm Coll Credential 1976; John Robert Powers Personal Devel Sch, attended 1978; UCLA Professional Training & Devel, Cert 1981; UCLA Personnel Mgmt, Cert 1981. **CAREER:** Los Angeles Co Dept Mental Health, exec sec 1966-72, jr administrator 1972-79; RL Nichols & Assoc, founder 1975; Pasadena City Coll, instr 1967-80; CA State Univ LA, instr 1978-80; CA State Univ Long Beach, instr 1978; Elliott-Elliott & Assoc, pres. **ORGANIZATIONS:** Assoc natl Secretarial Assn Intl 1980; chmp mem Amer Soc of Training & Devel 1978; natl mem Amer Soc of Training & Devel 1979; mem Business & Professional Women's Club Wilshire 1980.

NICHOLSON, ALFRED
Educator. **PERSONAL:** Born Jun 03, 1936, Edgefield, SC; children: Sharon Michell, Althea Gail. **EDUCATION:** Comm Coll of Philadelphia, AAS 1968; LaSalle Univ, BS 1974. **CAREER:** AAA Refinishing Company, tanner/inspector 1956-59; Strick Corp, elec wireman 1961-68, personnel asst 1968-69; Comm Coll of Philadelphia, personnel officer/aa dir 1974-. **ORGANIZATIONS:** Treas Coll & Univ Personnel Assoc 1972-74; bd of trustees United Way of Southeastern PA 1986-. **MILITARY SERVICE:** AUS corpl 2 yrs; Good Conduct Medal; Honorable Discharge. **BUSINESS ADDRESS:** Personnel Officer/AA Dir, Community College of Philadelphia, 1700 Spring Garden St, Philadelphia, PA 19130.

NICHOLSON, LAWRENCE E.
Educator. **PERSONAL:** Born Jul 10, 1915, St Louis. **EDUCATION:** LincolnUniv MO, BA 1938; Chicago U, MA 1942; Columbia U, MA, Doctorate. **CAREER:** Soc Caseworker, 1939-41; VA Couns Center, chief 1946-47; HS, teacher 1948-49; Harris Teachers Coll, prof Children Psych Dept 1950-. **ORGANIZATIONS:** Chmn Nat Schlrshp Comm Omega Psi Phi Frat 1950-60; Nat Bd ADA 1968-70; pres St Louis Dist MO St Tchrs Assn 1970-72; chmn bd Adult Wlfr SvcSt Louis 1968-; commnr chmn St Louis Hous Auth 1972-; bd St Louis Coun on Hum Relat 1972-F St Louis Sch Bd 1977; mem Bond Issue Supr Comm St Louis 1968-; bd St Louis Urban Leag 1972-; bd Chrctr Rsrch Assn 1965-69; bd NAACP 1963-65; bd Dept Chmn Relat Episcopal 1953-55; bd St Louis VocCouns Serv 1960-64; W End Comm Conf 1958-63; St Louis Opera Theatre 1963-65; Child Wlfr Comm MO Dept Wlfr 1968-70.

HONORS/ACHIEVEMENTS: Dist serv to comm medalUniv Chicago 1971; dist serv Nat Frat Omega Psi Phi 1972; man of yr awd St Louis ADA 1972; "Success Story" St Louis Globe DemNov 15, 1968; comm serv awd Sigma Gamma Rho 1972. **MILITARY SERVICE:** USN 1942-45. **BUSINESS ADDRESS:** 3026 Laclede, St Louis, MO 63103.

NICKERSON, WILLIE CURTIS
Religious administrator. **PERSONAL:** Born Apr 26, 1926, Macon Co, AL; married Sadie M Walker; children: Conway, Vernon, Christopher. **EDUCATION:** Tuskegee Inst, attended 1950; Columbia Coll, BA 1957. **CAREER:** Calvary Bapt Ch;; minister of Social Concerns 1974-; Calvary Bapt Comm Educ Prog, exec dir 1974; Calvary Bapt Ch Center, dir Vocational Exploration 1972; Quaker City IN, serv mgr 1964; Evans Fur Co;; mdse mgr L1954; Calvary Bapt Ch;; chmn deacon bd 1969; Calvary Bapt Ch, councilman 1970; Calvary Housing Corp, chmn 1973. **ORGANIZATIONS:** Am Mgmt Assn 1974; vice pres NW Clubster Am Bapt Ch of NJ 1974; mem Visions & Dreams Com Am Bapt Ch NJ 1979; Boys State Chmn, Am Legion Post #268 1970; mem Paterson Rotary Club #70 1975; mem NAACP 1979. **HONORS/ACHIEVEMENTS:** Nat Pub Speaking Awd NFA SoUniv Baton Rouge 1950; Korean Serv Awds AUS 1952; Roberta Johnson Guild, Calvary Bapt Ch 1971; Faithful Witness & Serv Calvary Bapt Ch 1979. **MILITARY SERVICE:** AUS corpl 1951-53. **BUSINESS ADDRESS:** 575 E 18th & St, Paterson, NJ 07501.

NICKS, WILLIAM JAMES, SR.
Retired football coach. **PERSONAL:** Born Aug 02, 1905, Griffin, GA; married Lillie Bell, Aug 20, 1931; children: William James Jr, Fredric Nicks. **EDUCATION:** Morris Brown Coll, AB 1928; Columbia Univ NY, MS 1941. **CAREER:** Morris Brown Coll, head football coach 1930-44; Prairie View A&M Coll, heal physical educ dept, athletic dir and head football coach 1945-66. **ORGANIZATIONS:** Regional dir Phi Beta Sigma Frat, Sigma Pi Phi Frat. **HONORS/ACHIEVEMENTS:** The Physical Educ Intramural Complex at Prairie View A&M Univ was named "The WJ 'Billy' Nicks Physical Education and Intramural Complex" in his honor; Hallof Fame inductee Natl Assoc of Intercollegiate Athletics 1964, Morris Brown Coll 1964, Extra Point Club ATlanta Univ Colls 1981; Coach of the Year 5 yrs. **HOME ADDRESS:** 3320 Rosedale, Houston, TX 77004.

NICKSON, SHEILA JOAN
Educational administrator. **PERSONAL:** Born May 20, 1936, Buffalo, NY; son of William Harris and Genevieve Martha Briggs Harris; children: Stephen Dwight, Roderick Matthew. **EDUCATION:** Attended, Buffalo State Coll 1953-54, 1966-70, Erie County Coll 1963-66. **CAREER:** SUNY, asst to chancellor coord of compus programs 1980-83; Buffalo State Coll, asst to chair dept of chemistry 1966-74, asst to pres dir of affirmativeaction 1974-. **ORGANIZATIONS:** Exec bd SUNY Black Faculty & Staff Assoc 1980-; educ adv comm Natl Urban League 1983-; bd dirs YWCA Buffalo 1983-; vice chair NY State Human Rights Adv Council 1984-; past pres Natl Org Amer Assoc of Affirmative Action; bd mem, past vice pres Girl Scouts of Amer; bd mem Sheehan Memorial Hospital 1988-; NAACP 1987-. **HONORS/ACHIEVEMENTS:** Citation for Serv to State Governor Carey NY State 1982; Citation of Appreciation Natl Alliance of Black Sch Educators 1984; Citation for Serv to Nation Commonwealth of VA 1986; Women Involved in Gloval Issues Alpha Kappa Alpha Awd 1987; Sojourner Truth Meritorious Service Award 1989; City of Buffalo Common Council Coalition 1988. **BUSINESS ADDRESS:** Asst to Pres/Dir Affirm Action, Buffalo State College, 1300 Elmwood Ave, Buffalo, NY 14222.

NIGHTINGALE, JESSE PHILLIP
Clergyman. **PERSONAL:** Born Jun 12, 1919, Nashville, TN; married Abigail C Clarke; children: Zelma Hockett, Rosalyn Bufford, Jesse Jr, Charles, Llewellyn. **EDUCATION:** Emannuel Bible Coll, BA, MDiv 1974-75; Bethel Seminary, dTh 1976; Vanderbilt Sch Div, postgrad;Univ of TN; TN St U. **CAREER:** Nat Bapt Pub Bd, chmn present; Evan Hill Bapt Ch, pastor. **ORGANIZATIONS:** Moderator Stones River Assn; NAACP; Ministers Conf; Interdenom Ministers Fellowship; Signet Lodge #10; Rosebud Chap #8; BO Lodge #29; TN St Conv Author, Confrontation with Reality, Nat Baptist Publ Bd 1977. **MILITARY SERVICE:** USN 2nd class petty ofcr 1943-45. **BUSINESS ADDRESS:** 7145 Centennial Blvd, Nashville, TN 37209.

NILES, ALBAN I.
Judge. **PERSONAL:** Born Jun 10, 1933, St Vincent, West Indies;children: Maria, Gloria, Angela. **EDUCATION:** UCLA, BS 1959, JD 1963. **CAREER:** Ernst & Ernst, auditor 1963-64; Private practice, attny 1964-82; Kedren Comm Health Ctr Inc, pres 1968-79; LA Cty Civil Serv Comm, commiss 1980; LA Municipal Court, judge 1982-. **ORGANIZATIONS:** Mem Natl Bar Assn, Langston Bar Assn; chmn of bd Bus Devel Ctr of S CA 1978-; mem NAACP, Urban League; Parliamentarian 100 Black Men Inc of Los Angeles; Commander Post 116 American Legion. **HONORS/ACHIEVEMENTS:** Selected as person of Caribbean birth to make signif contrib 1976; Carnegie Found Fellowship in Exec Leadership; UCLA Law Review; Passed the CPA examination 1960; appointed to the bench Feb 3, 1982. **MILITARY SERVICE:** USAF a/2c 1951-55. **BUSINESS ADDRESS:** Judge, Los Angeles Municipal Court, 110 N Grand Ave, Los Angeles, CA 90012.

NILES, LYNDREY ARNAUD
Educator. **PERSONAL:** Born May 09, 1936; married Patricia Aqui; children: Kathryn Arlene, Ian Arnaud. **EDUCATION:** Columbia Union Coll, BA 1963;Univ of MD, mA 1965; Temple U, phD 1973. **CAREER:** School of Communications Howard Univ, chmn Comm Arts & Sci Dept 1979-; Howard Univ, prof & asso dean 1975-79; Univ of MD, lectr 1971-75; Univ of DC, asst prof 1968-74, instr 1965-68; Columbia Union Coll, lectr 1964-65; Leadership Resources Inc, mgmt consult 1974-75. **ORGANIZATIONS:** Mem Speech Commn Assn/InternatrA Commn Assn/Am Soc for Training & Devel/NAACP; pres Met Wash Commn Assn 1974-75; pub article "Listening & Note TakingMethods" 1965; pub dissertation "The Defel of Speech Educ Problems at Predominately Black Colls 1973; "black rhetoric five yrs of growth, Encoder 1974; "Communication ind Dental Office", article in Encoder 1 979. **BUSINESS ADDRESS:** Howard University, School of Communications, 24 6th Street, NW, Washington, DC 20059.

NILON, CHARLES HAMPTON
Educator. **PERSONAL:** Born Jun 02, 1916, Maplesville, AL; son of Elbert Nilon and Vesta Brewer Nilon; married Nancy Mildred Harper, Aug 19, 1956; children: Charles H Jr. **EDUCATION:** TN State Coll, BS (Cum Laude) 1936; Univ of KS, MA 1946; Univ of WI, PhD 1951. **CAREER:** Washington School & Parker HS, English teacher 1936-43; Wayne State Univ, asst prof of English 1951-56; Univ of CO, prof of English 1956-85; Birmingham AL Public School, prof of English; Univ of CO prof of English Emeritus 1985-. **ORGANIZATIONS:** Mem Modern Language Assn 1952-, Boulder Housing Commission 1965-69; dir black studies Univ of CO 1969-73; chair, bd of dir HELP Inc 1969-73; chair, English dept Howard Univ 1974-76; language consultant School of Engrg 1976; mem Popular Culture Assn of Amer 1978-; treas Modern Humanities Rsch Assn; Coll Language Assn 1956-; MELUS 1978-. **HONORS/ACHIEVEMENTS:** Editor MHRA Annual Bibliography of Language & Literature 1958-66; Citadell Faulkner & the Negro 1965; Bibliography of Bibliographies in Amer Lit 1970; Danforth Found Fellow 1972; Thomas Jefferson Awd 1973; Stearns Award, Univ of Colorado, 1986; Award named in his honor, the Charles H and N Mildred Nilon Excellence in Minority Fiction Award, Univ of Colorado at Boulder, 1989; "The Science Fiction of Samuel R. Delany and the Limits of Technology" Black Amer Literature Forum 1984; "The Ending of Huckleberry Finn: Freeing the Free Negro" Mark Twain Journal 1984. **MILITARY SERVICE:** AUS corpl 1943-45. **HOME ADDRESS:** 702 Pine St, Boulder, CO 80302. **BUSINESS ADDRESS:** Professor of English Emeritus, Univ of Colorado-Boulder, Boulder, CO 80309.

NIMMONS, JULIUS
Educational administrator. **CAREER:** Jarvis Christian College, Hawkins, TX, president. **BUSINESS ADDRESS:** Jarvis Christian College, Hawkins, TN 75765. *

NIMS, THEODORE, JR.
Appliance distribution company executive. **PERSONAL:** Born Jun 06, 1942, Tallahassee, FL; son of Theodore Nims, Sr and Terri Courtney Nims (deceased); married Gloria Lee; children: Chandra, Marjorie. **EDUCATION:** Florida A&M Univ, BS 1964; various GE, AMA & Wharton management courses. **CAREER:** General Electric Co, various sales & mktg positions 1964-76, mgr compliance 1976-78, mgr retail parts 1978-79, zone mgr 1979-82, region manager 1982-86, mgr natl property mgmt sales 1986-89; pres Nims Distribution Inc Clearwater FL 1989-. **ORGANIZATIONS:** Roundtable mem Natl Minority Entre Devel Ment Ctr; co-founder/former chmn MN Black Networking Sys; mem Black Exec Exchange Program Natl Urgan League; mem Black MBA Assoc. **HONORS/ACHIEVEMENTS:** Many civic, community and company awards. **BUSINESS ADDRESS:** Pres Nims Distribution, Inc, 4480 107th Circle North, Clearwater, FL 34622.

NIPSON, HERBERT
Journalist. **PERSONAL:** Born Jul 26, 1916, Asheville, NC; married E Velin Campbell; children: Herbert, Maria. **EDUCATION:** Writers Workshop Univ of IA, MFA; Penn State, Journalism degree 1940. **CAREER:** Cedar Rapids Gazette, corres; Ebony Magazine, assoc editor 1949-51, co-managing editor 1951-64, managing editor 1964-67, exec editor. **ORGANIZATIONS:** Chmn bd dir South Side Comm Art Ctr; mem IL Arts Cncl, Joseph Jefferson Comm; bd of govs Urban Gateways. **HONORS/ACHIEVEMENTS:** IA Press Photographers Assoc Awds; Capital Press Clubs Awd as Outstanding Journalist 1965; Disting Alumnus of Penn State 1973; named to Phi Eta Sigma and Sigma Delta Chi Frats. **MILITARY SERVICE:** Armed Serv m/sgt 1941-45. **BUSINESS ADDRESS:** Johnson Publishing, 820 S Michigan Ave, Chicago, IL 60605.

NIVENS, BEATRYCE THOMASINIA
Author, lecturer. **PERSONAL:** Born Apr 01, 1948, New York, NY; daughter of Thomas J Nivens (deceased) and Surluta Bell Nivens. **EDUCATION:** Fisk Univ, Nashville TN, BA 1969; Univ of Ghana Legon, Ghana W Africa, Summer School Certificate, 1970; Hofstra Univ, Hempstead NY, MS in Ed, 1971. **CAREER:** Denison Univ, Granville OH, asst dean of women, 1969-71; Hosftra Univ, Hemptead NY, pre-law counselor, 1971-73; Queens Coll, Flushing NY, counselor 1974-79;District Council 37, New York NY, part-time counselor, 1979-87; columnist, Essence Magazine, 1977-; US Department of Health & Human Serv, Bronx NY, expert, 1980-; Career Marketing Int, New York NY, pres, lecturer, writer, 1985-; lecturer for colls, univs, corporations and civic women's and black groups, currently. **ORGANIZATIONS:** Delta Sigma Theta Sorority, 1987-. **HONORS/ACHIEVEMENTS:** Public Service Award US Dept of Labor 1982; author of The Black Woman's Career Guide 1982, 1987; Fellow, Virginia Center for the Creative Arts 1985; lecturer for Chevrolet's Natl Career Seminar to ten cities "Strategies for Success", 1985-86; Winthrop Rockefeller Distinguished Lecturer, Univ of AK, 1986; author of Careers for Women Without College Degrees, 1988; author of How to Change Careers (to be published in 1990). **BUSINESS ADDRESS:** Career Marketing International, 133 West 72nd Street, Suite 601, New York, NY 10023.

NIX, ROBERT N.C., JR.
Chief justice. **PERSONAL:** Born Jul 13, 1928, Philadelphia, PA; son of Robert N C Nix, Sr and Ethel Lanier Nix; married Dorothy Lewis (deceased); children: Robert Nelson Cornelius III, Michael, Anthony, Stephan. **EDUCATION:** Villanova Univ, AB 1952; Univ of PA, JD 1955; Temple Univ, postgrad bus admin & econs; Bar PA 1956. **CAREER:** State of PA, deputy atty general 1956-58; Nix Rhodes & Nix Phila, partner 1958-68; Common Pleas Court Philadelphia County, judge 1968-71; State of PA, justice supreme court 1972-. **ORGANIZATIONS:** Bd of dirs Germantown Boys Club 1968-; mem cncl pres assoc La Salle Coll 1971-; adv bd LaSalle Coll HS; bd consultors Villanova Univ Sch Law 1973-; mem Omega Psi Phi. **HONORS/ACHIEVEMENTS:** First PA Awd Guardian Civic League Achievement Awd;oree for achievements as Chief Justice of PA Supreme Ct, and for pioneering accomplishments as the highestranking Black official in history of PA. **MILITARY SERVICE:** AUS 1953-55. **BUSINESS ADDRESS:** Supreme Court of PA, Suite 3162 Federal Bld, 9th & Chestnut Street, Philadelphia, PA 19107.

NIX, ROSCOE RUSSA
Retired government employee, civil rights activist. **PERSONAL:** Born Jun 22, 1921, Greenville, AL; married Emma Coble; children: Veretta Tranice, Susan Lynette. **EDUCATION:** Howard Univ, AB; Amer Univ, Grad Work 195-52. **CAREER:** Labor Lodge #12 Civil Rights Comm US Dept of Labor, chmn 1964-66; US Dept of Labor Comm Rel Svc, field rep 1966-68; MD Comm Hum Rel, exec dir 1968-69; US Dept Justice Comm Rel Svc, chief state & local agencies sect 1969-73, chief tech support 1973-; 1980-86 Assoc DIrector, Office of Technical Assistance, Community Relations Service, US Dept of Justice. **ORGANIZATIONS:** Mem bd of trustees Stillman Coll, NAACP, Urban League 1964, Amer Civil Liberties Union 1969; mem Comm Church, Union Presbyterian Church; vice pres 1979, pres 1980, Montgomery Cty NAACP 1979-; mem Comm on Assembly Oper Presbyterian Church 1979-; exec bd Montgomery Cty Chap Natl Conf of Christians & Jews 1979; mem Alpha Phi Alpha,

United Way of Montgomery County; pres Montgomery County MD, NAACP 1980-; mem Montgomery County School Board 1974-78. **HONORS/ACHIEVEMENTS:** Publ, "When the Sword is Upon the Land", "What Color Are Good Neighbors?", If We Must Die", "The Ghost of Exec Order 10966", "Wanted Missionaries to the Suburbs", "God is White"; "Wanted, A Radical Black Church". **MILITARY SERVICE:** AUS T/4 1943-46. **HOME ADDRESS:** 11601 Le Baron Terr, Silver Spring, MD 20902.

NIX, THEOPHILUS RICHARD
Attorney. **PERSONAL:** Born Jul 21, 1925, Chicago, IL; married Dr Lulu Mae Hill; children: Theophilus R. **EDUCATION:** Lincoln U, PA, BA 1950; HowardUniv Law Sch Wash DC, LLD 1954. **CAREER:** Private Practice, atty 1954-; EEOC Phila, supr trial atty 1974-75; City of Wilmington, asst city solicitor 1955-56. **ORGANIZATIONS:** Mem DE Bar Assn 1956-; mem Bar St of MI 1957-; mem Nat Bar Assn 1970-; mem Bar MA 1975-; mem NAACP 1946-; legal coun DE Adolescent Prog Inc 1966-79; mem Correct Comm DE Bar Assn 1973-76; bd mem Martin Luther King Cntr Inc 1976-76; ETO/EUROPEAN Bandsmen/Drummajor, AUS 1943-46; Meretorfious Serv, DE PTA 1959; publ "How To Operate a School of Business" 1959; publ "St Tutorial & Job Training Program" 1962; publ "Statistical Analysis NCC Sup Court Drug Sentencing" 1972; Meretorious Commnty Serv DE Martin Luther Com 1978. **HONORS/ACHIEVEMENTS:** Dist Serv Awd DE Adolescent Prog Inc 1979. **MILITARY SERVICE:** AUS t/5 Bandsmen 1943-46. **BUSINESS ADDRESS:** 914 French St, Wilmington, DE 19801.

NIX, THEOPHILUS RICHARD, JR.
Construction/contract lawyer. **PERSONAL:** Born Oct 12, 1953, Washington, DC; son of Mr and Mrs Theophilus R Nix; married Myrtice Servance. **EDUCATION:** Cincinnati Coll of Mortuary Sci, 1975; Ithaca Coll, BFA 1979; Howard Univ Sch of Law, JD 1982. **CAREER:** Boston Housing Authority Construction attorney. **ORGANIZATIONS:** Mem Philadelphia Minority Contractors Assoc 1984-87, Philadelphia MBA Soc 1985-87, Philadelphia Barristers Assoc 1986-87; bd of dirs Bd of DE Contractors Assoc 1985-86. **HONORS/ACHIEVEMENTS:** Written up in alumni bulletin Ithaca Coll Alumni Dir 1986. **HOME ADDRESS:** PO Box 2298, Oak Bluffs, MA 02557.

NIXON, FELIX NATHANIEL
Clergyman. **PERSONAL:** Born May 27, 1918, York, AL; married Callie M. **EDUCATION:** Union Bapt Sem, bD, DD selma u, bth 1959; meridian bapt sem, 1955. **CAREER:** Abysinnia Bapt Ch, clergyman, present; Sumter Co Day Care Cntr, owner 1974-75; Nixon Ready to Wear Shop, owner 1974-75. **ORGANIZATIONS:** Mem Sumter Movedment for Human Rights 1960-67; Sumter Co Br NAACP 1964-75; dir Sumter Econ Devel Corp Inc 1970-75; Ensley Pratt City Br NAACP 1968-75; chmn Sumter Co Dem Conf 1967-75; chmn Sumter Co Bd Educ 1978-80. **HONORS/ACHIEVEMENTS:** Relcip The Most Dedicated Leader in West AL 1971. **BUSINESS ADDRESS:** 615 Broad St, York, AL.

NIXON, GEORGE W.
Airline pilot. **PERSONAL:** Born Mar 13, 1935, Pittsburgh, PA; son of James Nixon and Annie Nixon; married Heather Mary White; children: Lynnora, Rhonda, Nannette, George II, Vanessa. **EDUCATION:** Univ of Pittsburgh School of Engrg, 1953-54; USAF Aviation Cadet School, 1955-56; USAF Navigator Engrg School, 1956-57; USAF Aerial Bombardment School, 1958-59; USAF Pilot School, 1961-62. **CAREER:** USAF, mil combat Korea Loas & Vietnam, comdr Boeing 707, B-47 Bombardier, B-36 engr; United Airlines, pilot 1966-. **ORGANIZATIONS:** Mem United Airlines Pilot Speakers Panel, Arline Pilots Assoc, United Airlines Black Professional Org; Organization of Black Airline Pilots; Alpha Phi Alpha. **HONORS/ACHIEVEMENTS:** Won recognition & acclaim, filmed interview, Emmy Awd winning Realities in Black 1974; Nominee Cty Grand Jury. **MILITARY SERVICE:** USAF capt 1954-66; Natl Defense Serv Medal; AF Expeditionary Medal; AF Reserve Medal; AF Outstanding Unit Awd; Vietnam Serv Medal; AF Longevity Serv Awd.

NIXON, GLADYS (NEE ELLISON)
Retired educational administrator. **PERSONAL:** Born Jan 08, 1920, Palatka, FL; daughter of Rev Dr George F Ellison and Ethel Urline Ellison; married William B Nixon; children: William Jr, Ellen Finch, Camille Johnson. **EDUCATION:** Temple U, BS 1942, MEd 1952, EdD 1973. **CAREER:** EC Emlen Elem Sch, Sch Dist of Phila, prin 1970-80; Jacobs Shriners Hosp Classes, Torresdale Sch, spec educ prin 1964-70; Holy Family Coll, tchr 1964-65; John Hancock Elem Sch, prin 1962-64; James Rhoads, 1953-60; Martha Washington, tchr 1942-48. **ORGANIZATIONS:** Citywide Sch Math Com in Serv Intermediate Unit; Lu in Serv Tchr Educ Network; Philadelphia Assn of Sch Adminstrs; Nat Counc Tchrs of Math; Women in Edn; Nat Counc of Admin Women in Educ; DE Valley Reading Assn; AAUW; NAESP; CEC Chpsn Am Red Cross Youth Servs; bd of dir Germantown Br Settlement Music Sch; Student Welfare Counc; NW Br Am Red Cross; NW Br NAACP; elder Reeve Meml United Presb Ch; pres United Presb Women of Reeve 1973-74; Delta Sigma Theta Sor; Temple Univ Chap Phi Delta Kappa Educ Frat; moderator Presbyterian Women in Presbytery of Philadelphia 1989; chmn Committee on Representation 1988-. **HONORS/ACHIEVEMENTS:** Prin of Yr Awd Grtr NW Coord Counc 1975; 25 Yr Honoree Awd Women in Educ 1977; Chapel of 4 Chaplains Awd for Comm Serv; thesis, A Follow-up Study Pertaining to the Occupational Adjustment of Educable Mentally Retarded Pupils trained in Philadelphia Pub Schs 1973; author, History of Reeve Memorial Presbyterian Church 1920-82.

NIXON, GLENFORD DELACY
Physician. **PERSONAL:** Born Jul 11, 1956, POS, Trinidad and Tobago. **EDUCATION:** Brooklyn Coll, BSc Chem 1980; Howard Univ Coll of Medicine, MD 1985. **ORGANIZATIONS:** Mem GSA 1983-84, student council Howard Univ 1983-84; adm com Howard Univ 1984-85, Winthrop Univ Hosp House Staff 1986-; mem Natl & Amer Medical Assocs; assoc mem Amer Coll of Physicians. **HONORS/ACHIEVEMENTS:** Lloyd H Newman Awd for Service HUCM 1982; HUCM Student Council Recognition 1984; Dr John W Capps Memorial Scholarship 1984; Service Awd & Service CitationHUCM 1985. **HOME ADDRESS:** 270 First St, Mineola, NY 11501. **BUSINESS ADDRESS:** Resident Internal Medicine, 259 First St, Mineola, NY 11501.

NIXON, JAMES MELVIN
Association executive. **CAREER:** C of C, assoc exec professional dir. **ORGANIZATIONS:** Nat Cntr Youth Outreach Workers; mem Omega Psi Phi. **BUSINESS ADDRESS:** Effingham St Br YMCA, 1013 Effingham, Portsmouth, VA 23704.

NIXON, JOHN WILLIAM
Dentist. **PERSONAL:** Born Mar 02, 1922, Homeland, FL; married Ethyl Commons; children: John W, Jr, Karl H, Melba H. **EDUCATION:** Union Acad Bartow Fl, 1939; Bethune Cookman Coll, 1939-42; Fisk U, 1946-47; Meharry Med Coll, DDS 1951. **ORGANIZATIONS:** Vol ldr AL Negro Comm, secure, Imprv Cvl Rights; pres NAACP; aptdchmn SE Reg Conf NAACP Brs; Mayor's Comm Affairs Com; org Jefferson Co EmplrsCncl; aptd chmn Bi-Racial Jeff Co Manpower Coord Com; Helped inst Policy Comm Rltns Unit of Birmingham Police Dept; spearheaded negotiation prcdrs betweel Local Labor Ind & Nat Equal Empl Opp Commm ; spksmn Negro Comm & City Race Rltns; org, mem bd dirs Cits Fed Savings & Loan Assn; chmn Annual YMCA Mem Dr; chmn Birmingham Anti-TB Assn-Annual Christmas Seal Dr; bd dirs Oprtn New Birmingham; memUniv of AL Med Ctr Expansion Com; pres Birmingham Club Frntrs Intrntl; elected chmn Jefferson Co Biracial Manpower Coord Com; del Nat Cits Com for Comm Rltns; Comm Rltns Serv of US Dept of Just;aptd mem SE Regional Mnpwr Adv Com; aptd Birmingham Mnpwr Area Plng Cncl; apptd natl chmn, 21 mem Nat Pvt Rsrces Adv Com, US Ofc of Ec Opp. **HONORS/ACHIEVEMENTS:** Recip Outst Serv Awd Aeta Phi Lambda Sor; Dstngshd Serv Awd Iota Phi Lambda Sor; Man of Yr Awd Omega Psi Phi Frat, Alpha Phi Chpt; Outst Comm SvcAwd Miles Coll; Cit Merit Awd Phi Lambda Sor; Outst Comm Serv Awd The Birmingham Area Chap ARC; Outst Serv Awd Lawson St Jr Coll; Hon LLD, D Payne Coll; aptd Asso Clncl Instr UAB Sch of Dntstry 1974; aptd mem Adv Bd to Sch of Soc WrkUniv of AL 1973; aptd mem Birmingham Com on Frgn Rltns 1973-74. **MILITARY SERVICE:** AUS 1st sgt 1942-45. **BUSINESS ADDRESS:** 840 Miami Pl, Birmingham, AL 35214.

NIXON, NORM CHARLES
Professional athlete. **PERSONAL:** Born Oct 11, 1955, Macoun, GA; married Debbie Allen; children: Vivian. **EDUCATION:** Duguesne, 1977. **CAREER:** Los Angeles Clippers, guard 1983-. **HONORS/ACHIEVEMENTS:** 2nd best assist man in 6 seasons with Lakers; Laker's all time leader in steals; was named to the NBA All-Rookie Team in 1978. **BUSINESS ADDRESS:** Los Angeles Clippers, 3939 S Figueroa St, Ste 510, Los Angeles, CA 90037.

NJIIRI, RUTH STUTTS
Educational consultant. **PERSONAL:** Born Mar 16, 1929, Springfield, MA; divorced; children: Kari K, Bari. **EDUCATION:** BS (magna cum laude), 1971; MEd, 1972; EdD 1975. **CAREER:** Dr James H Robinson founder of Operation Crossroads Africa NY, admin asst 1952-57; Jomo Kenyatta Kenya, admin asst personal sec to pres 1961-68; Springfield Coll Continuing Educ, asst to dir 1969-72; Univ of MA Amherst, tchr assoc 1972-75; Intl Educ Programs Phelps-Stokes Fund, dir 1975-82; Presently, educational consultant. **ORGANIZATIONS:** Mem World Futures Soc, Comparative Educ Assn; founder Kenya Children's Library; mem several educ orgn in Kenya. **HONORS/ACHIEVEMENTS:** Who's Who in E Africa; Who's Who Among the World's Women.

NJOROGE, MBUGUA J.
Management consultant. **PERSONAL:** Born Jun 15, 1944, Banana Hill, Kenya;son of Wanjiku Njoroge and Wanjigi Njoroge; married Josephine; children: Wanjiku Felicia Mbugua, Njoroge Mbugua. **EDUCATION:** Baker Univ, Baldwin City KS, BA 1966; KS State Univ, Hayes KS, MS 1969; Univ of MO, Kansas City MO, masters of Public Admin 1972. **CAREER:** Edward D Jones & Company, stockbroker/investment banker; MCI Ltd/Mackenzie Consult Intl Ltd, managing dir 1978-; African Pavilion Ltd, Kansas City MO, pres 1973-78; Colum Union Natl Bank, Kansas City MO, marketing account exec 1969-70; Jones Store Co Kansas City, asst account dept 1969; KS State Univ, Hays KS, asst dept of Biology 1967-68; Woodlawn Jr High School Baltimore, science teacher 1966-67; Mackenzie Consultants Intl Ltd, intl Mgmt consultant 1970; Community Devel Corp, Kansas City MO, marketing analyst 1979. **ORGANIZATIONS:** Second vice pres Devel Corp 1977-80. **HONORS/ACHIEVEMENTS:** Honorary Youth of Honor, United Methodist Women, United Methodist Church, Everest KS 1963; Certificate of Leadership, Community Devel Corp, Kansas City MO 1977-78; Outstanding Leadership Award, Black Economic Union, Kansas City MO 1979. **BUSINESS ADDRESS:** 2450 Grand, PO Box 19842, Kansas City, MO 64141.

NKONGOLA, MUYUMBA WA See MUYUMBA, FRANCOIS N.

NKONYANSA, OSAFUHIN KWAKU See PRESTON, GEORGE NELSON

NNOLIM, CHARLES E.
Educator. **PERSONAL:** Born May 10, 1939, Umuchu-awka, Nigeria;married Virginia C; children: Emeka, Chinyere, Amaezeh, Azukah. **EDUCATION:** Catholic Univ of Amer, AB (cum laude), MA (sumna cum laude), PhD. **CAREER:** Univ of Port Harcourt, Nigeria, reader in Eng & literature studies, present; Babson Coll, Wellesley MA, asst prof 1970; Ferris State Coll, Big Rapids MI, asst prof 1969-70. **ORGANIZATIONS:** Mem, African Studies Assn; mem, Modern Lang Assn of Amer; mem, Natl Soc of Literature & the Arts. **HONORS/ACHIEVEMENTS:** Recipient, Doctoral Fellowship, Catholic Univ of Amer, 1968-72; author, Melville's Benito Cereno: A Study in Mng of Name-Symbolism, 1974; author, Pessimism in Conrad's Heart of Darkness, 1980; author, critical essays on African literature published in US and British journals. **BUSINESS ADDRESS:** Univ of Port Harcourt, Schl of the Humanities, Dept of Eng, Port Harcourt, Nigeria.

NOAH, LEROY EDWARD
Elected official. **PERSONAL:** Born Jul 25, 1934, Clarksdale, MS; married Grace Fulgham; children: Sharon Davis, Carolyn Mann, Brenda. **EDUCATION:** Forest Park Community College, AAS 1975. **ORGANIZATIONS:** Member/president School Board 1963-75. **HONORS/ACHIEVEMENTS:** Citizen of the Year Ward Chapel AME Church 1981. **MILITARY SERVICE:** USAF Sargeant; Korean Defense, Presidential Unit, Good Conduct, Korean Medal. **HOME ADDRESS:** 5900 Jefferson Ave, St Louis, MO 63140. **BUSINESS ADDRESS:** President Board of Aldermen, City of Kinloch, 5990 Monroe Ave, St Louis, MO 63140.

NOBLE, BEULAH CATHERINE (NEE LUMPKIN)
Food service executive. **PERSONAL:** Born Mar 23, 1924, Hartford, CT. **EDUCATION:** St Joseph Coll; BS 1947; Michigan State Univ, MS 1960; George Washington Univ, EdD 1976. **CAREER:** Tripler Army Med Ctr Honolulu, chief food serv div 1976-79; Walter Reed Army Med Ctr Wash DC, asst chief food serv div 1972-73, chief production & service

br 1971-72; US Army Hosp Camp Zama Japan, chief food serv ldiv 1968-71; Fitzsimons Gen Hosp Denver, chief diet therapy br 1964-68; 10th Evac Hosp Wurzburg, chief food serv div 1961-64; Frankfort Germany/Denver/Ft Carson CO, chief clinical diatetics br 1953-59; Percy Jones Army Hosp Battle Creek,staff dietitian 1951-53. **ORGANIZATIONS:** Mem Am Dietetic Assn 1948-; secr CO Springs Home Econ Assn 1958-59; ADA Repr, Am Hosp Assn 1972-73; vol worker St Benedict Cntr Hartford 1945-47;vol worker Hamblin Ave Comm Centger Battle Creek MI 1952-53; sponsor Big Sisters Orgn of Denver CO 1957. **HONORS/ACHIEVEMENTS:** Schlrshp St Joseph Coll 61944-46; selected to study for Masters Degree, Army Educ Prog 1959-60; Army Commendation Medal, Unit Citation 1968; Meritorious Serv Meda 1973; selected to study for Doct Degree under Army Educ Prog 1973-76; nominated Awd Outstndg Contribution of Minority Group Mem Field of Nutrition1975; Dist Alumni St Joseph Coll 1977; Legion of Merit 1979; US Army Med Dept Medallion 1979; nominated to be listed in Whos Who Among Black Am 1980-81; 1st Black Officer to recieve Regular Army Full Col Commn. **MILITARY SERVICE:** Army Med Specialist Corps.

NOBLE, GILBERT E.
Producer. **PERSONAL:** Born Feb 22, 1932; married Norma Jean; children: 5 children. **EDUCATION:** Humane Letters, D. **CAREER:** Seton Hall Univ NJ, artist-in-residence; WLIB Radio, producer, news correspondent; WABC-TV, producer, news correspondence. **ORGANIZATIONS:** Bd of dir Oper PUSH, Harlem's Confrontation. **HONORS/ACHIEVEMENTS:** Recipient Emmy 1969,76,77,78,79, & 2 in 1980; Harlem Prep Comm Serv Awd 1969,72; NY Urban League J Russwurm Awd 1969; 10 Emmy nominations; Cert of Merit NY Acad of TV Arts & Sci 1978; Frederick Douglass Awd NY Urban League 1979; 100 Black Men Humanitarian Awd 1980. **MILITARY SERVICE:** AUS corpl 1952-54. **BUSINESS ADDRESS:** Producer, News Correspondent, WABC-TV, 1330 Ave of Americas, New York, NY 10019.

NOBLE, JOHN CHARLES
Educational administrator. **PERSONAL:** Born Sep 21, 1941, Port Gibson, MS; married Colleen L; children: Michaelle, Leketha, Carlos, Tracy, Stephanie. **EDUCATION:** Claiborne Co Training Sch, 1959; Alcorn St U, bS 1962; TN A&I St U, MA 1971; Jackson St U. **CAREER:** Claiborne Co Schools, supt of educ, present; MS Chicago, teacher; Chicago, juvenile probation officer; Medgar Evers Comprehensive Health Center, dir research & evaluation; Opportunity Industrialization Center, instructor. **ORGANIZATIONS:** Omega Psi Phi; Am Assn of Sch Adminstgrs; fellow Inst of Politics; Rising Sun MB; chmn Bd trustees Hinds Jr Coll; bd trustee Utica Jr Coll; advanced ind instr Dr Thomas Gordons Parent Effectiveness Training & Tchr E Ffective Tng; Claiborn Co Chap NAACP; Port Gibson Masonic Lodge #21; bd dir MS Action for Progress; bd dir Urban League LEAP Prgm. **BUSINESS ADDRESS:** Superintendent, Claiborne County Public School, PO Box 337, Port Gibson, MS 39150.

NOBLE, JOHN PRITCHARD
Administrator. **PERSONAL:** Born May 31, 1931, W Palm Beach, FL; married Barbara Norwood; children: John Jr, Michael. **EDUCATION:** FL A&M Univ, BS 1959; Columbia Univ NYC, MA Hosp Admin 1963; Cornell Univ Ithaca, attended 1969. **CAREER:** Arabian Amer Oil Co Dhahran Saudi Arabia, hosp admin 1962-69; Winston-Salem NC Hosp Authority, pres/chief exec officer 1969-71; Forsyth Hosp Authority Winston-Salem, vice pres planning & devel 1971-73; Homer G Phillips Hosp St Louis, admin 1973-78; Acute Care Hosp City of St Louis, dir 1978-79; Dept of Health & Hosp City of St Louis, hosp commr; Lambert-St Louis Intl Airport, asst dir. **ORGANIZATIONS:** Mem Amer Coll of Hosp Admins 1965-; mem Amer Pub Health Assn 1976-; chmn Natl Assn of Health Serv Exec 1978-80; bd mem Family & Children Serv 1977-; bd mem King Fanon Mental Health 1978-; life mem Alpha Phi Alpha Frat; bd mem Tower Village Nursing Home 1978-. **HONORS/ACHIEVEMENTS:** Meritom Citation. **MILITARY SERVICE:** USAF A/2C 1951-53. **BUSINESS ADDRESS:** Assistant Dir, Lambert-St Louis Intl Airport, P O Box 10212, St Louis, MO 63145.

NOBLE, NORMA LYNETTE
Administrator. **PERSONAL:** Born Feb 10, 1944, Victoria, TX. **EDUCATION:** Northeastern St U, BS 1965, MED 1969;Univ of OK, MA 1974. **CAREER:** Mgmt Serv Dept City of Okla OK, admin coordinator 1980-; Human Resources Dept City of Okla City, asst dir 1974-80; Private, human relations cons1974;Univ of OK, research/teaching asst 1972-74; Muskogee OK Pub Sch tchr 1965-72; Evangelistic Bapt Ch Okla City, minister of music 1973-; Private, mgmt consult 1974-79; City of Okla City, technology agt 1980; Areawide Aging Agency Inc;; adv council 1978; Progressive Bapt Conv, coordinator of music 1978; Vocational & Tech Sch Dist, adv Bd 1979. **HONORS/ACHIEVEMENTS:** Outstanding Serv Awd YMCA 1970; Coordinator of Music Nat Bapt Reg Youth Conv 1974; Exec Com Okla City Literacy Council 1977; Dir Gospel Music Workshopof Am OK Chap 1978. **BUSINESS ADDRESS:** Assistant Dir, City of OK Human Resources Dpt, 609 West Sheridan, Oklahoma City, OK 73111.

NOBLES, PATRICA JOYCE
Attorney. **PERSONAL:** Born Jun 13, 1955, St Louis, MO; daughter of Ralph L Peters, Jr and Gwendolyn Bell Stovall; married Willie L Nobles, Jr, May 22, 1976. **EDUCATION:** Southwest Baptist Coll, BA, 1976; Univ of AK, JD, 1981. **CAREER:** US District Judge, law clerk, 1981-83; Southwestern Bell Telephone Co, attorney, 1983-. **ORGANIZATIONS:** Former mem of the executive bd, Urban League 1981-84; mem Amer Assoc of Trial Attorneys 1983-87; mem AK Bar Assn 1983-87; pres AK Assn of Women Lawyers 1985-86; mem of bd KLRE Public Radio Station 1986-87; mem NAACP 1989-. **HONORS/ACHIEVEMENTS:** Mem of UALR Law Review 1980-81; mem of 1988 Class of Leadership America. **BUSINESS ADDRESS:** Attorney, Southwestern Bell Telephone Co, 1010 Pine Street, Room 2114, St Louis, MO 63101.

NOEL, PATRICK ADOLPHUS
Physician. **PERSONAL:** Born Nov 09, 1940; married Evelyn Sebro; children: Carlita, Patrick Jr, John. **EDUCATION:** Howard U, BS 1960-64; Howard U, MD 1964-68; Johns Hopking U, flwsp 1972; Howard U, resd 1969-73. **CAREER:** Pvt Prac, physician 1973-; Bowie State Coll, coll physician 1973-; Ortho Surgery Howard U, instr 1973-; Univ MD Coll Pk, consult 1973-76; Bowie State Coll Ftbl Team, orth consult 1973-76; HowardUniv Hosp, atdng surg; Leland Hosp; SSE Comm Hosp; Laurel Hosp. **ORGANIZATIONS:** Treas Soc of Hlth Profls of PG Co 1977; Flw of Intl Coll Surgeons 1974; Meritorious Serv Bowie State Coll 1976; mem Am Bd Orthopedic Surgery1974; flw Am Acad Ortho Surgery 1976. **BUSINESS ADDRESS:** 8601 Palmer Hwy, Lanham, MD 20801.

NOGUERA, PEDRO ANTONIO
Educational administrator. **PERSONAL:** Born Aug 07, 1959, New York, NY; son of Felipe Noguera and Millicent Noguera; married Patricia Noguera, Jul 06, 1982; children: Joaquin, Amoya. **EDUCATION:** Brown Univ, Providence RI, BA & MA 1981 & 1983; UC Berkeley, Berkeley CA, PhD, 1989. **CAREER:** UC Berkeley, Course Instructor Dept, Ethnic Studies, 1983-84, Course Instructor, Dept of Sociology 1984-85; Goldberg & Assoc, Oakland CA, consultant, 1985; UC Berkeley, research specialist 1985-86; City of Berkeley, executive asst & mayor 1986, 1988; asst vice chancellor, Berkeley CA, 1988-. **ORGANIZATIONS:** Vice pres Berkeley Black Caucus 1985-; bd mem, Daily California Newpaper 1985-88; mem congressman Dellums Executive Committee, 1986-; pres Black Men United for Change, 1988-; bd mem Berkeley YMCA, 1988-. **HONORS/ACHIEVEMENTS:** Samuel Lampert Prize for International Understanding 1981; Rhodes Scholar Finalist, Rhode Island 1981; Adult Education and Political Socialization in Grenada, 1983; Making it in America, Kroeber Journal of Anthropology, 1984; Belize: A Nation at the Crossroads, published by Center for Latin American Studies 1984; Elected Chairman Graduate Assembly UC Berkeley 1984-85; Elected President Associated Student UC Berkeley 1985-86; Adult Illiteracy in Workplace, published by California Librian 1985; Fulbright Fellowship Recipient 1987-88; Presentation on Youth and Drugs at African American Summit, LA, 1989. **HOME ADDRESS:** 1536 62nd Street, Berkeley, CA 94703.

NOISETTE, RUFFIN N.
Association representative. **PERSONAL:** Born Mar 20, 1923, Summerville, SC; married Thelma Anderson; children: Shelley, Robin, Louis. **EDUCATION:** Howard U, AB 1946; Howard U, BD 1949; WilberforceUniv of OH, hon DD. **CAREER:** Fisk Univ Nashville, asst to dean of chapel 1949-50; Ebenezer African Meth Episcopal Ch Rahway NJ, pastor 1950-51; Bethel African Meth Episcopal Ch Wilmington DE, pastor 1951-65; Delaware OEO, dep dir 1965; EI Dupont De Nemours & Co, professional staffing consultant 1965-85; Emily P Bissell Hosp Wilmington DE, protestant chaplain 1986-. **ORGANIZATIONS:** Mem Eastern Coll Personnel Officers 1970-; mem DE Personnel & Guidance Assn 1968; mem bd dir YMCA Wilmington de; Boys Club of Wilmington; Opportunity Center Inc; Golden Beacon Coll; DE Council on Crime & Justice Inc; mem New Castle County Bd of Elections; mem bd of trustees DE State Coll Dover DE. **HONORS/ACHIEVEMENTS:** Citizenship Award Alpha Phi Alpha 1959; Meritorious Serv Award YMCA 1964; Recruiter of Year Award Lasalle Coll 1973; Black Heritage Disting Serv Awd 1981;Outstanding Services Awd Delaware State Coll Div of Student Affairs 1984.

NOLAN, ROBERT L.
Educator, music critic. **PERSONAL:** Born Jan 25, 1912, Cleveland. **EDUCATION:** Howard U, Mus B 1938; Juillard, M 1940. **CAREER:** Robert Nolan School Music, dean founder; MI Chronicle, music critic 1948-. **ORGANIZATIONS:** Fndr pres Pi Alpha Nu Stdnt Music Frat Howard U; mem Alpha Phi Alpha Frat; Music Critics Natl Assc; pianist accompanist arranger Eva Jessye Choir; fndr conductor Robert Nolan Choir Detroit; Detroit Musicians Assc natl assc negro musicians inc; music educators natl conf; NAACP; served as Piano Accoumpanist To Numerous Singing Stars, Many Outst Stdnts Dev ast Detroit & Serving in Distgshd Ldrshp Positions. **HONORS/ACHIEVEMENTS:** Recipient 1966 Annual Awrd Trophy; outst musician Music Critic Trophy 1969; 1966 honoree plaque Robert Nolan Choir; hon Detroit's Citizens of Interest Com1963; hon trophy Ebenezer AME Ch 1971; Current Topic Clbs man of yr 1954; hon cert Angelic Choir Peoples Bapt Ch; Annual Cilegna Awrd; achvmt awrd annual plaque Omega Psi Phi Frat 1976; awrd & plaque for outst musical contrib to Det Plymouth Chorale 1976. **BUSINESS ADDRESS:** C/O Michigan Chronicle, 479 Ledyard St, Detroit, MI 48201.

NOLES, EVA M.
Nurse, educator. **PERSONAL:** Born Apr 05, 1919, Cleveland, OH; daughter of Charles Bateman and Ola Bateman; married Douglas Noles; children: Tyrone M. **EDUCATION:** EJ Meyer Memorial Hosp Sch of Nursing, RN 1940; Nursing Univ of Buffalo, BS 1962; State Univ of NY at Buffalo, MEd 1967. **CAREER:** Roswell Pk Meml Inst, staff nurse & head nurse 1945-63, instr of nsg & asst dir of nsg 1963-68; State Univ of NY at Buffalo, clin assoc prof of nsg 1970-77; Roswell Pk Meml Inst, ret chief of nsg servs & training 1971-74; EJ Meyer Meml Hosp, coord fam planning nrs practitioner prog 1974-77; MedPersonnel Pool Inc, home care super/staff development 1977-84 (retired). **ORGANIZATIONS:** Mem NY State Nrs Assn, Amer Nrs Assn 1941-; mem (charter) External Deg in Nrsg NY State 1971-75; mem NY State Bd for Nrsg 1972-; comm adv councilState Univ of NY at Buffalo 1975-; chmn Nsg & Health Serv ARC Gtr Buffalo Chap 1978-; bd of govs Comm Mental Health Ctr Buffalo NY 1979-; bd of dirs ARC; bd of trustees Buffalo General Hosp; bd of dirs Boys & Girls Clubs of Buffalo and Erie Co 1985. **HONORS/ACHIEVEMENTS:** First black nurse educated in Buffalo NY EJ Meyer Meml Hosp 1936-40; Disting Service Awd for Outstanding Achievement in Public Health NY 1972; Disting Awd AAUW 1972; publ "Six Decades of Nursing 1914-1974"; Roswell Park Meml Inst 1975; Certificate of Merit ARC Greater Buffalo Chapt; Community Awds for Display "Buffalo Blocks-Talking Proud" 1986; published Buffalo's Blocks "Talking Proud" 1987; published Black History-A Different Approach.

NOR, GENGHIS
Musician, educator. **PERSONAL:** Born Jan 31, 1946, Brooklyn, NY; married Halemah; children: Selim Tahir, Amira Sakinah. **EDUCATION:** StateUniv of NY, BA 1971; Var Studies in Trumpet, Music Theory & Composition. **CAREER:** Genhis Nor & MAGIC, musician composer ldr; Bedford-Stuyvesant Restoration Corp, music consult Music coord; Restoration HERITAGE MUSIC ENSEMBLE, dir; Strong-Light Incorp, prdcr promoter; Simon F Rothschild, Jr HS, music cons; Media-Ecology Dept Jersey City State Clg, adjunct lectr. **ORGANIZATIONS:** Mem Trumpet; sec Frank Foster's Loud Minority; The Barron Band; Instr & Musical Arngr; Restoration HERITAGE MUSIC ENSEMBLE; Restoration SINGERS; instr Restoration Music Theory Wkshp; mem past v chmn pres & pres adv StateUniv Freedom Cncl; mem Consortium of Jazz Orgns; mem bd adv Afro-am Music Bicentennial Hall of Fame.

NORFLEET, FRED L., JR.
Manager. **PERSONAL:** Born Sep 07, 1950, Baltimore, MD; married Tina. **EDUCATION:** San Diego State Univ, BS Acctg 1973. **CAREER:** A&P Food Stores, journeyman clk 1967-70; IRS, revenue agent 1970-73; Phillips Ramsey Adv, media buyer 1973-74; KSEA-

FM, acct exec 1974-75; KFMB-TV, client serv rep 1975-78; McGraw Hill Broadcasting KGTV, dir community relations 1978-. **ORGANIZATIONS:** Mem Natl Acad of TV Arts & Sci San Diego Chapt; mem Kappa Alpha Psi Frat; bd of dirs Variety Club of San Diego, San Diego Urban League, ALBA '80 Society, Consumer Credit Counselors of San Diego; mem St Vincent De Paul Center for the Homeless. **HONORS/ACHIEVEMENTS:** Cert of Achievement A&P Food Stores 1968; Outstanding Young Men of Amer 1979; Outstanding Young Citizen of San Diego SD Jaycees 1978; San Diego Black Achievement Awd for Media 1980; CA State Assembly Resolution for "Exemplary record of dedicated contributions to the comm" 1981; City Council of San Diego Cert ofSpecial Recognition 1982; Elected to the Honor Roll for the Natl Conf of Christians & Jews 1983; Mexican & Amer Found "Amigo de Destincion" Awd 1984; Kappa Alpha Psi Frat Western Province Special Action Awd 1985; San Diego Women Inc Man of the Year Awd 1986. **BUSINESS ADDRESS:** Dir of Community Relation, McGraw Hill Broadcasting KGTV, Box 85347, San Diego, CA 92138.

NORFLEET, JANET
Postal government official. **PERSONAL:** Born Aug 14, 1933, Chicago, IL; married Junious Norfleet; children: Cedric Williams. **EDUCATION:** Olive Harvey Coll, AA 1977. **CAREER:** US Postal Service, supt of customer serv reps, public affairs officer, mgr of retail sales and svcs, mgr of delivery and collection, mgr North Suburban IL mgmt sect ctr, field div mgr/postmaster South Suburban IL div, field div gen mgr;postmaster Chicago IL div. **ORGANIZATIONS:** Mem bd of dir Carson Pirie Scott & Co 1988-. **HONORS/ACHIEVEMENTS:** First Woman Postmaster of the US Postal Serv Chicago Div; Partnership For Progress Awd Postmaster General TISCH 1986; Appointment Congressional Records by Congressman Savage 1987; Proclamation by Mayor Washington Janet Norfleet Day in Chicago 1987. **BUSINESS ADDRESS:** Field Div Gen Mgr, Postmstr, United States Post Office, 433 W Van Buren, Room 422, Chicago, IL 60607-9998.

NORFORD, GEORGE E.
Administrator. **PERSONAL:** Born Jan 18, 1918, NYC, NY; married Thomasina. **EDUCATION:** Columbia U; New Sch for Soc Rsrch. **CAREER:** Westinghouse Broadcasting Co NY, vice pres gen exec mem bd dir. **ORGANIZATIONS:** Former assc edtr Negro World Digest; mem Acad of TV Arts & Sci; bd mem Seven Civic Orgn; Began Writing for TV 1951; press writer for The Today Show. **HONORS/ACHIEVEMENTS:** Only Black Corr on Staff of Yank Mag During WW Ii; author Several Short Stories & Plays About Black Life; first black Producer of Network TV Pgms at NBC 1957; Has Had 6 Plays Produced in Off-Broadway Theaters.

NORMAN, ALEX JAMES
Educator. **PERSONAL:** Born Jul 02, 1931, Atlanta, GA; married Margaret Lawrence; children: Alex III, Keri Casady, Wendi Casady. **EDUCATION:** Morris Brown College, AB 1957; Atlanta Univ, MSW 1959; Univ Of CLA School of Social Welfare, DSW 1974. **CAREER:** USEEOc, investigations supervisor 1967-69; Univ of CLA Extention, dir urban affairs 1969-73; Univ of CLA, acting assoc prof 1975-79; Univ of CLA, assoc prof 1979-. **ORGANIZATIONS:** Charter member Academy of Certified Social Workers 1960-; founder/dir Jenesse Ctr Inc 1980-83; dir Crittenton Center, Inc 1983; dir Future Homemakers of Amer 1984; charter member Cert Consultants Intrnl 1984; mem Assn of Black Social Workers. **HONORS/ACHIEVEMENTS:** Who's Who in the West Marquis 1972; Who's Who in Amer Marquis 1977; Distinguished Educ Assn of Black Social Workers 1981. **MILITARY SERVICE:** USAF sgt 1949-52; Good Conduct, Presidential Unit Citation, Korean Medal, Dist Serv 1950-52. **BUSINESS ADDRESS:** Associate Professor, UCLA, 405 Hilgard Ave, Los Angeles, CA 90024.

NORMAN, BOBBY DON
Artist, technical writer, business administrator. **PERSONAL:** Born Jun 05, 1933, Dallas, TX; son of Ruben Norman and Bessie Norman; divorced; children: Parette Michelle Coleman. **EDUCATION:** San Francisco City Coll, 1950-51; USAF, Radio Electronics Tech 1951-55; SW Sch Bus Admin, Certificate 1956-59. **CAREER:** Mile High Club Restaurant & Cabins, gen mgr, 1955-57; D H Byrd Properties, property mgr, 1957-65; US Post Office, distribution clerk, 1957-67; Univ Chicago-Dallas, field evaluation researcher 1969-70; AAAW, Inc Cultural Gallery, dir 1972; SCLC Dallas, TX, co-founder ofc mgr, co-dir 1970-72; PPANET, Inc, comm liaison developer 1974-76; Davis Norman Zanders Inc, vice pres & gen mgr 1976-77; free-lance artist & inventor anti-collision car. **ORGANIZATIONS:** Pres, Forest Lakes Sportsmans Club; hunter safety instructor, NRA, 1963; pres & founder, Assn Advancing Artists & Writers 1969-74; commissioner Greater Dallas Community Relations Cmsn 1970-73; organizer & tech consult Greater DFW Coalition FFI 1971-74; alumnus Chi Rho Intrnl Business Frat; committeeman Block Partnership Comm of the Greater Dallas Council of Churches 1971-72; public speaking mem Intl Platform Assoc 1977-78. **HONORS/ACHIEVEMENTS:** Citizenship training SCLC 1969; service GDCRC 1973; fine arts Dallas Black Chamber of Commerce 1973; leadership service Assoc Advancing Artists & Writers 1973. **MILITARY SERVICE:** USAF corpl 1951-55; Korean Service Mdl, UN Service Mdl Good Conduct Mdl Nat Defense Mdl. **HOME ADDRESS:** 914 62nd St, Oakland, CA 94608. **BUSINESS ADDRESS:** Artist & Inventor, Free-Lance, 914 62nd St, Oakland, CA 94608.

NORMAN, CALVIN HAINES
Physician. **PERSONAL:** Born Sep 14, 1923, Jamaica, NY; married Ruth Elizabeth Gordon; children: Calvin H III, Robert Gregory, Wendy Beth. **EDUCATION:** NC Coll, BS 1952; Howard Univ, MD 1956; Columbia Univ, MPH 1961, FACR 1980. **CAREER:** Downstate Med Ctr, instr 1964; VA Hosp, attending radiologist 1964; Kate Bitting Reynolds Hosp, attending radiologist 1965-69; Bowman Grey Sch of Med, instr 1968; St Mary's Hosp, attending radiologist dir radiology 1969-84; Medical Comprehensive Health Prog, 1969; Downstate Medical Ctr, asst prof 1970-;MIH, attending radiologist 1984-. **ORGANIZATIONS:** Pres, vice pres, sec-treas, exec com mem Brooklyn Radiol Soc 1971-75; pres med bd St Mary's Hosp 1975-76; treas med bd Cath Med Ctr 1975; pres elect med bd St Mary's Hosp 1978; mem Kings Co, NY State Medical Soc; mem AMA. **HONORS/ACHIEVEMENTS:** Natl Medical Assn Fellow Columbia Univ 1960; Alpha Kappa Mu Natl Honor Soc 1952; Beta Kappa Chi Honor Sci Soc 1951; Amer Coll Student Ldrs 1952; Who's Who in Amer Colls & Univs 1952; articles published Nephrocalcinosis; Pycnodysostosis; Chronic Subdural Hematoma; Retroperitoneal Mesenteric Cyst; Multiple Ureteral Diverticula. **MILITARY SERVICE:** AUS sgt 1940-43; USAF, USAFR maj 1957-64. **BUSINESS ADDRESS:** Radiologist, MIH, 152 1189 Avenue, Jamaica, NY 11432.

NORMAN, CLIFFORD P.
Business executive. **PERSONAL:** Born Mar 22, 1943, Detroit, MI; son of Leavi Norman and Claudia C Norman; married Pauline C Johnson; children: Jays S, Rebecca L. **EDUCATION:** Wayne State Univ, BA 1974, MA 1980. **CAREER:** Fisher Body Div GM, engr test 1967-71, sr analyst qc 1971-72, sr srv & tool spec 1972-74, div process engr 1974-76; Ford Motor Co, div staff engr 1976-80; Glasurit Amer Inc, acct exec; BASF Corp Account Executive. **ORGANIZATIONS:** Mem ESD 1975-; mem Soc of Engr & Applied Sciences 1975-82; exec comm BB/BSA 1981-; mem Budget & Allocation Comm UCS Detroit 1981-84; chr Nominating comm BB/BS Detroit 1980-; u-f Speakers Bureau 1985-. **HONORS/ACHIEVEMENTS:** One In A Million WDME Radio Detroit 1976. **MILITARY SERVICE:** USAF a/2c. **BUSINESS ADDRESS:** BASF, PO Box 3065, 2855 Coolidge, Suite 300, Troy, MI 48007-3065.

NORMAN, GEORGE E.
Historian, business executive. **PERSONAL:** Born Dec 26, 1933, Detroit. **CAREER:** Black Odyssey History & Art Exhibit, creator nationally acclaimed. **ORGANIZATIONS:** Exhibited at Clgs, U, Conventions, Air Force Bases in Am & Panama. **HONORS/ACHIEVEMENTS:** Who's Who In Am 1970; Carter G Woodson Awrd 1969; prior foster awrd 1971. **BUSINESS ADDRESS:** Box 143, Detroit, MI 48232.

NORMAN, JAMES H.
Public administrator. **PERSONAL:** Born Aug 14, 1948, Augusta, GA; son of Silas Norman, Sr (deceased) and Janie M King Norman (deceased); children: James H Jr. **EDUCATION:** Mercer Univ Macon GA, AB Psych 1970; Western MI Univ Kalamazoo, MSW 1972. **CAREER:** Douglass Comm Assc Kalamazoo MI, coord job dev & placement 1972-74; Kalamazoo MI Publ Schls, parent consult 1974-75; Oakland Livingston Human Srvs, Pontiac MI div mgr comm dev 1975-78; MI Dept of Labor, dir bureau of comm srv 1978-87; MI Dept of Labor, deputy dir. **ORGANIZATIONS:** Chrmn & leg comm chr Natl Assc for State Comm Srv Prog 1981-82, 1985-87; exec secr MI Econ & Social Opp Commission 1983-87; mem NAACP; mem Lansing MI Assc of Black Soc Workers; mem Phi Mu Alpha Natl Music Frat; mem amer Soc for Public Admin 1984-; mem Assoc of State Govt Execs 1986-; mem Omega Psi Phi Frat Inc; life mem Western Michigan Univ Alumni Assoc; mem Friendship Baptist Church; mem Natl Council of State Building Code Officials 1988-; mem International Assn of Personnel in Employment Security 1988-; bd mem MI Assn of Black Organizations 1988-; mem Greater Lansing Urgan League 1989-. **HONORS/ACHIEVEMENTS:** Outstanding Young Man of Amer US Jaycees Publ 1978, 1979; Comm Srv Award Natl Alliance of Businessmen 1973, 1974; Full Univ Grad Flwshp Western MI Univ 1970-72; srv award Natl Assc for State Comm Srv Prog 1983; Wall of Distinction Western MI Univ 1980. **BUSINESS ADDRESS:** Deputy Dir, MI Dept of Labor, Box 30015, Lansing, MI 48909.

NORMAN, JESSYE
Singer. **PERSONAL:** Born Sep 15, 1945, Augusta, GA; daughter of Silas Norman Sr and Janie King Norman. **EDUCATION:** Howard Univ, BM (Cum Laude) 1967, D Music (hon) 1982; Peabody Conserv Music, 1967; Univ MI, MMus 1968. **CAREER:** Deutsch Opera Berlin, debut 1969; Deutsch Opera Italy 1970; appeared in, operas Die Walkure, Idomeneo, L'Africaine, Marriage of Figaro, Aida, Don Giovanni, Tannhauser, Gotterdammerung, Ariadne auf Naxos, Les Troyens, Dido and Aeneas, Oedipus Rex; La Scala Milan, Italy, debut 1972; Salzburg Festival 1977; Hollywood Bowl, US debut 1972; appeared with Tanglewood Festival MA, Edinburgh, Scotland Festival; Covent Garden, debut 1972; appeared in 1st Great Performers Recital Lincoln Center New York City 1973-; guest performances incl, Los Angeles Philharmonic Orch, Boston Symphony Orch, Amer Symphony Orch, Chicago Symphony Orch, San Fran Symphony Orch, Cleve Orch, Detroit Symphony, NY Philharmonic Orch. **ORGANIZATIONS:** Mem Gamma Sigma Sigma, Sigma Alpha Iota, Pi Kappa Lambda. **HONORS/ACHIEVEMENTS:** Appeared with, London Symphony Orch, London Philharm Orch, BBC Orch, Israel Philharm Orch, Orchestre de Paris, Natl Symphony Orch Australia; numerous recordings Columbia, EMI, Philips Records; recip 1st Prize Bavarian Radio Corp Intl Music Competitor; Grand Prix du Disque Deutsch Schallplatten; Preis Alumniat MI 1982; Outstanding Musician of the Yr Award Musical Am Grand Prix du Disque Academie Charles Cros 1983; Honorary Doctor of Humane Letters, Amer Univ of Paris, 1989; Honorary Doctor of Music, Cambridge Univ, 1989; Honorary Fellow, Newnham Coll, Cambridge, 1989; Honorary Fellow, Jesus Coll, Cambridge, 1989. **BUSINESS ADDRESS:** Soprano Concert & Opera Singer, Shaw Concerts Inc, 1900 Broadway, New York, NY 10023.

NORMAN, JOHN C.
Educator, physician. **PERSONAL:** Born May 11, 1930, Charleston, WV; married Doris S Sewell. **EDUCATION:** (magna cum laude) Harvard, BA 1950; Harvard Med Sch, MD 1954. **CAREER:** TX Heart Inst of St Luke's Episcopal & TX Children's Hospital Houston, TX, dir cardiovascular surg rsrch labs; Univ of TX Hlth Sci Ctr, prof of surgery. **ORGANIZATIONS:** Edtr CARDIOVASCULAR DISEASES Bulletin of TX Heart Inst; vis prof Biomedical Engr Seminar PgmUniv of Miami; dept of surg Harvard Med Sch; aoa vis prof DalhousieUniv Halifax Nova Scotia;Univ of Miamia Med Sch; Cntrl Adv Com Cncl on Cardiovascular Surg Am Heart Assc; Numerous Other Acad & Professional Apptmts; mem MA Med Soc; Phi Beta Kappa; NY Acad of Sci; Am Assc for Advcnmt of Sci; Am Clg of Surgeons; Soc ofUniv Surgeons; Soc of Thoracic Surgeons;Am Physiological Soc; Sigma XI RiceUniv Chap Thoracic & Cardiovascular NIH FellowUniv of Birmingham Eng 1962-63. **HONORS/ACHIEVEMENTS:** Listed Who's Who in Sci 1966; fellow am clg of cardiology 1965. **MILITARY SERVICE:** USN lt cmdr Inactive.

NORMAN, MAIDIE RUTH (NEE GAMBLE)
Actress, educator. **PERSONAL:** Born Oct 16, 1912, Villa Rica, GA; daughter of Louis Gamble and Lila Gamble; children: McHenry Norman III. **EDUCATION:** Bennett Coll, BA 1934; Columbia Univ, MA 1937; Actors Lab Hollywood, 1946-49. **CAREER:** Actress in radio, TV, motion pictures & stage since 1946; TX State Coll Tyler, TX, instr summers 1955-56; Stanford Univ Palo Alto, CA, artist in residence 1968-69; Univ CA at LA, lecturer, dir, acting tchr 1970-77; retired tchr. **ORGANIZATIONS:** Mem State Bd CA Educ Theater Assn 1969-; mem So CA Educ Theater Assn; co-founder/bd mem ANTA West retired 1967-; mem Actors Equity Assn; AFTRA; mem Screen Actors Guild; mem League of Allied Arts; life mem Actors Fund; pres bd of Stevens House Coop UCLA retired; bd mem LA Contemp Dance Theater; mem Coord Comm 1984 Olympics Arts Festival; mem CA Cncl for the Arts Theater Div. **HONORS/ACHIEVEMENTS:** Disting Serv CA Educ Theater Assn 1985; Black Filmmakers Hall of Fame Oakland, CA 1977; UCLA Chair of Honor upon retirement 1977; Black Student Faculty & Adm Award 1977; The Maidie Norman Award for Out-

standing Research by an undergrad in Black Theater is given annually at UCLA; LA Sentinel Woman of the Yr Award 1963; Negro Authors Study Club Civic Serv Award 1957; Bennett Coll Achievement Award 1953; Cabrillo Award Acting Achievement 1952. **HOME ADDRESS:** 3125 Creekside Dr, San Jose, CA 95132.

NORMAN, MOSES C.
Association executive. **CAREER:** Omega Psi Phi, Washington DC, grand basileus. **BUSINESS ADDRESS:** Omega Psi Phi, 2714 Georgia Ave NW, Washington, DC 20001. *

NORMAN, P. ROOSEVELT
Dentist. **PERSONAL:** Born Sep 08, 1933, Mound Bayou, MS; married DeLois Williams; children: Philippa J, David W. **EDUCATION:** Tougaloo Clg, BS 1955; Meharry Med Clg, DDS 1959. **CAREER:** Pvt Prac, dentist; Babe Ruth Leag Baseball Coach; Mound Bayou Comm Hosp, dental cons; Frances Nelson Hlth Ctr, adv cons; Union Med Cntr Dental Serv, formerly co-dir; Gen Dentistry Malcom Grow Reg Med Cntr USAF, ofcr in charge; Sheppard AFB TX, preventive dentistry ofcr; Misawa AFB Japan, air base oral surgeon; VA Hosp Tuskeegee, rotating dental internship. **ORGANIZATIONS:** Mem Natl Dental Assc; Am Dental Assc; Acad of Gen Diewntistry; Am Soc Of Preventive Dentistry; Am Endodontic Soc; Military Surgeons Assc; LicensedPrac in IL, TX, DC, MD, NH, PA, MS; mem Omega Psi Phi Frat; Champaign Co C of C; Neighborhood Commnr Boy Scouts of Am; Career Cnslg HS; bd dir Boys Clb of Am Champaign Co;Univ Dental Rsrch Team. **HONORS/ACHIEVEMENTS:** Recip music schlrshp; Athletic Schlrshp; mosby schlrshp awrd for Scholastic Excellance. **MILITARY SERVICE:** USAF; presently serving USAFR maj. **BUSINESS ADDRESS:** P O Box 2808 Station A, Champaign, IL 61820.

NORMAN, PATRICIA
Business executive. **PERSONAL:** Born Sep 03, 1947, New York, NY. **EDUCATION:** St John's Univ Jr College, AAS 1964-66; St John's Univ College of Business Admin, BS 1968-75. **CAREER:** North General Hospital, Asst Dir of Finance, Comptroller. **ORGANIZATIONS:** Advanced member Healthcare Financial Management Assoc. **BUSINESS ADDRESS:** Hospital Comptroller, North General Hospital, 1919 Madison Ave, New York, NY 10035.

NORMAN, ROY A.
Marketing manager. **PERSONAL:** Born Feb 08, 1941, Manhattan, NY; children: David Stokes, Sterling Bradley, Morgan Sage. **EDUCATION:** CityUniv of NY, 1959-61; Berklee Sch of Music, Cert Arranging/Composition 1964-65; LA City Clg, 1966-67. **CAREER:** Music Mktg Sys Co NY, pres 1979-; RCA Records NY, prdct mgr 1979; Polygram Distrib NY, mktg dev mgr 1978-79. **ORGANIZATIONS:** Pres Ronor Interntl Music Corp 1972-78; pres Great N Am Music Corp 1970-72; Ind Record Prod Arrngr 1970; Saxophonist Arrngr; "Chico" Hamilton Quartet 1965-66; Mktg Com Black Music Assc 1978-; mktg consult Unlimited Gold Records 1980; Advncd Comm Instr Grnd instr Priv Pilot 1978. **HONORS/ACHIEVEMENTS:** Hon disch good cond AUS 1963-65; schlrshp outst music performance Berklee Sch of Music Boston 1965. **MILITARY SERVICE:** AUS spec 4 1963-65. **BUSINESS ADDRESS:** 150 W 58th St, New York, NY 10019.

NORMAN, WILLIAM H.
Psychologist. **PERSONAL:** Born Dec 14, 1946, Sharon, PA; married Belinda Ann Johnson; children: Monica, Michael. **EDUCATION:** Youngstown State Univ, BA 1968; Howard Univ, MS 1971; Duke Univ Medical Center, psychology internship, 1974-75; Pennsylvania State Univ PhD 1975. **CAREER:** Butler Hospital, dir of psychological consultation program 1976-, dir of psychology 1982-, coord, eating disorders program, 1987-; Brown Univ Internship Consortium, coord adult clinical psychology track comm 1983-; Brown Univ Medical School, asst prof of psychiatry and human behavior, 1986-; HMO Rhode Island, evaluation specialist 1986-. **ORGANIZATIONS:** Mem, Amer Psychological Assn 1975-, Assn for the Advancement of Behavior Therapy 1975-, Soc for Psychotherapy Rsch 1986-. **HONORS/ACHIEVEMENTS:** Reviewer for several journals including Journal of Abnormal Psychology and Journal of Consulting and Clinical Psychology; Master of Arts ad eundem Brown Univ 1987; recipient of Natl Inst of Health grants, 1979, 1981, 1983. **BUSINESS ADDRESS:** Dir of Psychology, Butler Hospital, 345 Blackstone Blvd, Providence, RI 02906.

NORRELL-NANCE, ROSALIND ELIZABETH
Government official. **PERSONAL:** Born May 17, 1950, Atlantic City, NJ; daughter of Albert V Norrell, Jr and Vivian M Rhoades-Norrell; divorced; children: Kimberly. **EDUCATION:** Hampton Inst 1967-69; Atlantic Comm Coll, AS 1974-76; Glassboro State Coll, BA 1976-78. **CAREER:** Pleasantville Sch Dist, educator 1976-84; City of Atlantic City, mayorial aide. **ORGANIZATIONS:** Exec bd/youth advisor Atlantic City NAACP 1969-86; bd of dirs Atlantic Human Resources Inc 1981-89; mem natl Sor of Phi Delta Kappa Delta Lambda Chapt 1982-89; govtl affaris chairperson 101 Women Plus 1982-85; bd of dirs Minority Entrepeneur Develop Co 1984-85; bd of dirs United Way of S Jersey 1984-85 bd of dirs Black United Fund of NJ 1987; bd of dirs Atlantic City Costal Museum 1985-89; mem NJ State Business & Professional Women; bd dir Atlantic Human Resources; chairperson Atlantic Co Comprehensive Network Task Force on Homeless Svcs; Atlantic City Publ Rel Adv Bd; mem Natl Cncl of Colored Women's Clubs; bd dir Atlantic Community Concerts 1984-87; mem Ruth Newman Shaprio Cancer Fund; bd of dir Atlantic City Local Assistance; mem Healthy Mothers/Healthy Babies Coalition of Atlantic City, Hampton Alumni Assoc; mayor's youth adv bd, chair educ task force Congressional Black Caucus; mem NJ State Division of Youth & Family Services Advisory bd 1985-; bd of dir Coalition of 100 Black women 1987-; bd of dir Atlantic County Transportation Authority 1988-; Atlantic County Red Cross 1988-; founder Atlantic County Welfare Mothers Support Group 1988-; mem, Atlantic County Human Serv Advisory Bd. **HONORS/ACHIEVEMENTS:** Comm Serv Awd West Side Parent Adv Council 1976; Outstanding Leadership Black Atlantic City Magazine 1983; Outstanding Young Women in America 1984,85,86. **HOME ADDRESS:** 1105 Adriatic Ave, Atlantic City, NJ 08401. **BUSINESS ADDRESS:** Aide to Mayor/Dir Comm Relatio, City of Atlantic City, City Hall, 1301 Bacharach Blvd, Atlantic City, NJ 08401.

NORRELL-THOMAS, SONDRA
Administrator. **PERSONAL:** Born May 31, 1941, Richmond, VA; daughter of Edinboro A Norrell, Esq and Faith M Norrell; married Chauncey S Thomas, Jun 01, 1978. **EDUCATION:** Hampton Inst, BS 1961; Howard Univ, MS 1973. **CAREER:** Charlottesville Schools, teacher 1961-63; Richmond Public Schools, teacher 1963-64; Howard Univ, teacher 1964-77, assoc dir of athletics 1977-86, exec asst to vice pres for student affairs 1986-. **ORGANIZATIONS:** Mem Special Comm on Women's Interest NCAA 1983-85; council Natl Collegiate Athletic Assoc NCAA 1983-87; Division I Steering Comm (1st Black) NCAA 1983-87; special liasion Mid-Eastern Athletic Conference 1983-; pres Capital City Chapter, The Links Inc 1987-89; mem Alpha Kappa Alpha Sor, HUAA, NCNW, NAACP. **HONORS/ACHIEVEMENTS:** Resolution for Outstanding Contribution to Athletic and Community as a Woman in Male-Dominated field DC City Council 1983. **BUSINESS ADDRESS:** Exec Asst to Vice Pres Student Afrs, Howard University, 2400 6th St NW Room 201, Washington, DC 20059.

NORRIS, ARTHUR MAE
Educator. **PERSONAL:** Born Oct 07, 1911, Montgomery, AL; married Albert. **EDUCATION:** AL St U, BA, MEd; Gould Acad, Post Grad; Tuskegee Inst;Univ of AL. **CAREER:** Former Teacher, Principal Presently Retired. **ORGANIZATIONS:** Natl pres Sup Basileus; Natl Sor of Phi Delta Kappa Inc; 1st vice pres AL Fed of Womens Clbs; chmn Juvenile Prot Com; AL Cong of Parents & Tchrs; E Montgomery Dist Dir of Christ Ed; chmn Deserving Yth Com; Cleveland Ave YMCA; bd dir Com Action; mem Crim Just; bd Am Red Cross Bd; St Adv Com for Child & Yth; bd of dir Tumbling Waters Flay Mus; bd of dir Montgomery Area on Aging; bd of dir Black Caucus on Aging; Citizens Part Grp for Montgomery. **HONORS/ACHIEVEMENTS:** Achiev awrd Phi Delta Kappa Sor Inc; achvmt awd AL Assc of Womens Clbs; disting serv awrd Alpha Delta PDK; unit appeal awrd cent anniv awrd; AL St U;; cert of merit & apprec Emancip Proc Celebrat Com.

NORRIS, AUDIE
Professional athlete. **PERSONAL:** Born Dec 18, 1960, Jackson, MS. **EDUCATION:** Jackson State Univ, 1982. **CAREER:** Portland Trail Blazers, center 1982-. **ORGANIZATIONS:** Led Jackson State in rebounding all 4 seasons; Led Jackson State in scoring as a sophomore (181 points a game) & as a sr (167 average). **HONORS/ACHIEVEMENTS:** Led Jackson State in rebounding all 4 seasons; Led Jackson State in scoring as a sophomore (181 points a game) & as a sr (167 average). **BUSINESS ADDRESS:** Portland Trail Blazers, 700 NE Multnomah St, Portland, OR 97232.

NORRIS, CHARLES L., SR.
Clergyman. **PERSONAL:** Born Aug 14, 1926, Williston, SC; married Ruby Dent; children: Keith, Charles, Jr. **EDUCATION:** Queensboro Comm Clg; Bapt Ed Ctr of NYC. **CAREER:** Bethesda Missionary Bapt Ch, pastor ; Kitchen Modernization, prod mgr 1950-69. **ORGANIZATIONS:** Vp Queens Interfaith Clergy Cncl NYC; rec sec Bapt Minister Flwshp of Queens & Vicinity; past mem Comm Bd 14; mem NAACP. **BUSINESS ADDRESS:** 179 09 Jamacia Ave, Jamaica, NY 11432.

NORRIS, CURTIS H.
Retired business executive. **PERSONAL:** Born Dec 13, 1913, Knoxville, TN; married Minnie Calloway (deceased); children: Curtis Jr, Minette, Henri. **EDUCATION:** WV State Coll, BS 1937; Amer Coll of Life Underwriters, Chartered Life Underwriter Designation 1964. **CAREER:** NC Mutual Life Ins Co, various positions 1937-67, asst agency dir 1967-70, assoc agency dir 1970-76, vice pres admin 1976-80 (retired). **ORGANIZATIONS:** Mem Amer Soc of Chartered Life Underwriters; pres Frontiers Intl Indianapolis 1959-60; mem NAACP, YMCA; mem & clerk of vestry St Titus Episcopal Church; treas Mid Atlantic Sect of the Amer Bridge Assn; bd of dir Coordinating Council for Senior Citizens 1989-92. **BUSINESS ADDRESS:** Vice President, NC Mutural Life Ins Co, 411 W Chapel Hill St, Durham, NC 27701.

NORRIS, CYNTHIA CLARICE
Agency director. **PERSONAL:** Born Nov 16, 1956, Baltimore, MD; daughter of Robert John Norris, Sr and Clarice Gee Norris-Barnes; divorced. **EDUCATION:** Coll of Notre Dame, BA French Religious Studies, 1978; St Mary's Ecumenical Institute, MA Theology, 1986; Leadership Greater Chicago, Fellowship Program, 1989. **CAREER:** St Bernardine Church, dir of religious educ, 1978-85; Natl Office of Black Catholics, consultant, 1981-85; Silver Burdett Publishing Co, religion consultant, 1984-; Archdiocese of Chicago, executive dir, 1985-. **ORGANIZATIONS:** Mem, Regional Coordinator, 1984-; Natl Assn Black Admin, ex committee 1987-; mem League of Black Women 1986-; mem, Natl Assn Female Executives, 1986-. **HONORS/ACHIEVEMENTS:** Evangelization in the Black Community, profile; Unraveling the Evangelical Cord, filmstrip; Search for Black Catholic Identity: If Rivers Could Speak, filmstrip; Contributing Columnist, In A Word (monthly newsletter), The Chicago Catholic (weekly newspaper). **BUSINESS ADDRESS:** Executive Director, Office for Black Catholic Ministries, 155 East Superior Street, Chicago, IL 60611.

NORRIS, DONNA M.
Psychiatrist. **PERSONAL:** Born May 28, 1943, Columbus, OH; married Dr Lonnie H Norris; children: Marlaina, Michael. **EDUCATION:** Fisk Univ Nashville TN, BA 1964; OH State Univ Clge of Medicine, MD 1969; Mt Carmel Medical Ctr Columbus OH, internship 1970; Boston Univ Med Ctr, residency 1972; Childrens Hosp Judge Baker Guidance Ctr 1974. **CAREER:** MA Rehab Comm Roxbury & Quincy MA, psych consult 1974-79; Boston Juvenile Court Clinic, sr psych 1974-; Harvard Med Schl, instr psych 1974-; asst psych 1974-83; Charles River Hosp Wellesley MA, tchng fac 1981-; Family Srv Assc of Greater Boston, med dir 1981-; Children's Hosp Med Ctr & Judge Baker Guidance Ctr, assc in psych 1983-. **ORGANIZATIONS:** Minority rep to Assembly Amer Psych Assc 1981-85; mem Amer Acad of Child Psych 1974-; Amer Psych of Amer 1974-; Black Psych of Amer; mem Soroptomist Assc 1985-; mem Jack & Jill of Amer 1978-; staff consult Levison Inst 1981-; Amer Psych Assc 1973-; Falk Flwshp 1973-75; mem Exec Comm & Steering Comm to plan Conf on Psych Educ 1974-75; mem Task Force of Films 1975-77; edit bd Psych Educ, Prologue to the 1980'S 1976-; mem Committee on Women 1976-79; edit newsletter Comm on Women 1977-79; mem Spouses Sub-comm 1977-78; Minority Deputy Rep to Leg Assembly of Amer Psych Assc 1981-83; Minority Repto Leg Assembly of Amer Psych Assc 1983-; mem Task Force on Mbrshp Non-participation 1983-85; mem Comm of Black Psych Amer Psych Assc 1984-; Site Visitor Ach Awards Bd 1984; MA Psych Soc Boston 1973-; mem Ethics Comm 1978-; Amer Acad of Child Psych 1974-; Rep to MA Coalition of Mental Health 1984-86; Amer Orthopsychiatric Assc Inc 1983-. **HONORS/ACHIEVEMENTS:** Who's Who Among Women in Amer 1977-; Who's Who in Black Amer 1977-; Falk Fnd Amer Psych Assc 1973-75; Amer

Bds of Psych & Neurology 1978. **BUSINESS ADDRESS:** Medical Dir, Family Srv Assc Grtr Boston, 34 1/2 Beacon St, Boston, MA 02108.

NORRIS, ETHEL MAUREEN
Educator. **PERSONAL:** Born Mar 03, 1956, Petersburg, VA; daughter of Dr Granville M Norris and Marie Perry Norris. **EDUCATION:** East Carolina Univ, B Mus 1977; OH State Univ, MA 1978; summer study, Westminster Choir Coll 1985-86; Ohio State Univ, doctoral study in music history 1987-. **ORGANIZATIONS:** Instr Piano Lessons 1979-; mem Sigma Alpha Iota, Coll Music Soc, Amer Guild of Organists, Phi Kappa Phi. **HONORS/ACHIEVEMENTS:** Finalist Natl Achievement Scholarship Program for Outstanding Negro Students 1973; One-Year Minority Fellowship OH State Univ 1977-78; Graduate Teaching Assistantship OH State Univ 1987-88. **HOME ADDRESS:** 506 Byrne St, Petersburg, VA 23803.

NORRIS, EUGENE
Advertising executive. **PERSONAL:** Born Jul 25, 1939, Chicago, IL; son of J Eugene Morris and Willie Mae Mitchell Morris; married Beverly Coley-Morris, Sep 03, 1988. **EDUCATION:** Roosevelt Univ, Chicago Il, BSBA, 1969, MBA, 1971. **CAREER:** Foote, Cone & Belding, Chicago, IL, account exec, 1968-74; Burrell Advertising, Chicago, IL, sr vice pres, 1974-86; Morris & Co, Chicago, IL, pres, 1986-87; Morris/Randall Advertising, Chicago, IL, pres, 1987-88; E Morris, Ltd, Chicago , IL, pres, 1988-. **ORGANIZATIONS:** Instructor, Cosmo Chamber of Commerce, 1976-; vice pres, Youth Communication, 1985-; bd chmn, Chicago Urban League Public Relations Advisory Bd, 1986-; bd mem, Sickle Cell Planning Comm, 1988-; bd mem, Bethune Museum, 1989-. **HONORS/ACHIEVEMENTS:** Blackbook Business & Professional Award, Natl Publications, 1984; Citizen Professional Award, Citizen Newspapers, 1985. **MILITARY SERVICE:** US Army, E4, 1962-65. **BUSINESS ADDRESS:** Pres, E Morris, Ltd, 325 W Huron, Suite 512, Chicago, IL 60610.

NORRIS, FRED ARTHUR, JR.
Labor administrator. **PERSONAL:** Born Nov 25, 1945, Ecorse, MI; son of Fred Arthur Norris and Annie B Davis Norris; married Betty Sue Graves, Nov 26, 1982; children: Tracy M Graves, Shawna L Norris. **EDUCATION:** Attended, Wayne Cty Comm Coll, Wayne State Univ, IN Univ, Univ of WI, MI State Univ, George Meany School of Labor. **CAREER:** City of Ecorse, councilmember 1974-87; Local 616 Allied Ind Workers, pres 1977. **ORGANIZATIONS:** Mem United Black Trade Unionist 1976; SPIDER 1979; bd mem MI Downriver Comm Conv 1979-; bd mem Metro Detroit Chap A Philip Randolph Inst 1984, Allied Indust Workers Human Rights; pres Independence Alliance; mem Natl Black Elected Officials; sec, tres New Center Med CLinic; personal ministry dir Ecorse Seventh Day Adventist Church; Elder Ecorse Seventh Day Adventist Church 1989. **HONORS/ACHIEVEMENTS:** Community Serv Community Serv Awd Ecorse 1981, Wayne Cty 1982; Little League Awd Ecorse Little League 1982. **BUSINESS ADDRESS:** President, Allied Indust Workers #616, 191 LaBadie, Wyandotte, MI 48192.

NORRIS, JAMES ELLSWORTH CHILES
Plastic surgeon. **PERSONAL:** Born May 12, 1932, Kilmarnock, VA; son of Morgan E Norris, Sr and Theresita Norris; married Motoko Endo, Jun 21, 67; children: Ernest Takashi. **EDUCATION:** Hampton Inst VA, BS 1949-53; Case Western Reserve Cleveland OH, MD 1953-57; Grasslands Hosp, internship 1957-58; Queens Hosp Ctr Jamaica, gen surgery resd 1962-66; Univ of MI Med Ctr, plastic surgery resd 1972-74. **CAREER:** Kilmarnock VA & Melbourne Fl, gen practitioner 1958-62; VA Hosp Tuskegee Al, chief of surgical serv & dir surgical resd prog 1969-72; Burn Unit Div of Plastic Surgery Harlem Hosp Ctr NY, chief 1974-77; Hosp for Joint Diseases & Med Ctr NY, assoc attending plastic surgery 1975; Jamaica Hosp Jamaica NY, attending & chief plastic surgery 1975-88; Consultant in plastic surgery 1988-; Coll of Physicians & Surgeons Columbia Univ NY, asst prof 1976-87; Div of Plastic Surgery Harlem Hosp Ctr NY, attending 1977-87; St Lukes-Roosevelt Hosp Ctr Manhattan, asst attending plastic surgery 1981-; Private practice, physician. **ORGANIZATIONS:** Reed O Dingman Society 1974; Mem Amer Burn Assoc 1975, New York County Medical Society 1975, New York State Medical Socety 1975, Amer Soc of Plastic & Reconstr Surgeons 1975, New York Regional Socitey ASPRS 1976, Lipoplasty Society of North America 1987, Amer Cleft Palate Assn 1988, Amer Society for Laser & Medicine and Surgery Inc 1987, NorthEastern Society of Plastic Surgeons 1989. **HONORS/ACHIEVEMENTS:** Numerous med articles in various med jrnls 1954-73; licensed OH, FL, VA, NY, AL 1957-70; Cert Natl Bd of Med Examiners 1958; Cert Amer Bd of Surgery 1967; Cert Amer Bd of Plastic Surgery 1975; Vol Surgeon Albert Schweitzer Hosp Haiti 1965; Volunteer Surgeon Christian Mission Pignon Haiti 1986. **MILITARY SERVICE:** USNR comdr 1967-69. **BUSINESS ADDRESS:** Plastic Surgeon, 144 E 90th St, New York, NY 10128.

NORRIS, MICHAEL KELVIN
Professional athlete. **PERSONAL:** Born Mar 19, 1955, San Francisco, CA. **EDUCATION:** City Coll San Fran, 1yr. **CAREER:** Oakland A'S, pitcher 1975-83. **HONORS/ACHIEVEMENTS:** Runnerup AL-CY young vote; (AL pitchers awd Gold Glove for fielding; won second Gold Glove. **BUSINESS ADDRESS:** Oakland A's, Oakland Alameda Cty Col, Oakland, CA 94621.

NORRIS, WALTER, JR.
City official. **PERSONAL:** Born Jan 09, 1945, Jackson, MI; son of Walter Norris Sr and Willie Mae Glaspie-Neely; married Rosie Hill, Aug 07, 1963; children: Gloria J, Anthony W, Vernon D, Shannon D. **EDUCATION:** Spring Arbor Coll, Spring Arbor MI, BS 1970; Michigan State Univ, E Lansing MI, Graduate Study Educ Admin, 1979. **CAREER:** Jackson Community Coll, Jackson MI, financial aid dir 1968-70; Norris Real Estate, Jackson MI, owner & broker 1970-76; Jackson Public Schools, Jackson MI, dir minority affairs 1970-76; Jackson Housing Comm, Jackson MI, exec dir 1976-79; Lansing Housing Comm, Lansing MI, exec dir 1978-88; Housing Authority, Galveston TX, exec dir 1988-. **ORGANIZATIONS:** Natl Assn of Housing & Redevelopment Officials (NAHRO); Michigan Chapter of NAHRO; chmn, bd dir Legislative Comm; certification trainer HAHRO Public Housing Mgmt; Public Housing Authority Directors Assn; Texas Housing Assn; assoc mem Galveston Historical Found 1988-, Galveston Chapter NAACP 1988-; bd mem Galveston Boys' Club 1988-, Galveston Chamber of Commerce 1988-, Rotary Club of Galveston 1988-. **HONORS/ACHIEVEMENTS:** Men's Union Award, Most Outstanding Young Man of the Year, Jackson Community Coll 1965; Sophomore Class President, Jackson Junior Coll 1965; Outstanding Young Man of the Year, Jackson Jaycees 1968; Service Award, Outstanding Service & Contributions, HUD Program 1982; NAHRO Public Housing Mgmt Certification (PHM). **BUSINESS ADDRESS:** Executive Director, Galveston Housing Authority, 920-53rd St, Galveston, TX 77551.

NORTHCROSS, DAVID C.
Physician. **PERSONAL:** Born Jan 29, 1917, Montgomery, AL; children: David, Michael, Gale, Gloria, Derrick, Grace. **EDUCATION:** Univ Detroit; Meharry Med Coll, 1944; Univ of Pennsylvania, 1957. **CAREER:** Gen practice, physician; Mercy Gen Hospital, admin 1956-74. **ORGANIZATIONS:** Mem Detroit Medical Soc; Wayne County Medical Soc; Natl Medical Assn; Amer Medical Assn; Meharry Alumni Assn; Wolverine Medical Assnc; Michigan State Medical Assn; mem Booker T Washington Business Assn; Detroit C of C; UNA-USA; ACLU; Alpha Phi Alpha. **MILITARY SERVICE:** AUS MC capt 1953.

NORTHCROSS, DEBORAH AMETRA
Educational administrator. **PERSONAL:** Born Jun 27, 1951, Nashville, TN; daughter of Theron Northcross and Nell Northcross. **EDUCATION:** Mt Holyoke Coll, BA French 1969-73; Memphis State Univ, MEd Spec Educ 1973-75. **CAREER:** Shelby State Comm Coll, counselor 1973-76, dir/spec serv prog 1976-79, coord/fed affairs 1979-81, asst dir/stud develop 1981-83, dir/stud retention1982-83, grants officer 1983-84, dir of develop 1984-. **ORGANIZATIONS:** Field reader US Dept of Educ; pres TN Asso of Special Programs 1977-79; bd mem Southeastern Assn of Educ Oppor Program Personnel 1978-79; tutor Memphis Literacy Council 1983-87; chairperson Christian Educ Comm MS Blvd Christian Church 1984-; YWCA chair/nominating comm 1985, bd of dir 1986-, 2nd Vice Pres 1987; US Dept of Educ Special Programs Training Grant, evaluation consultant 1986-; Leadership Memphis, Vice Pres of alumni assoc 1987-88, bd mem 1987-89, vice chair bd of trustees 1989-; chair YWCA Financial Development committee 1988-. **HONORS/ACHIEVEMENTS:** Kate Gooch Leadership Award leadership Memphis 1989. **BUSINESS ADDRESS:** Dir of Development, Shelby State Community College, PO Box 40568, Memphis, TN 38174-0568.

NORTHCROSS, WILSON HILL, JR.
Attorney. **PERSONAL:** Born Dec 08, 1946, Detroit, MI; son of Wilson H Northcross, Sr and Gwendolyn Pinkney; married Winifred C Wheelock; children: Jill Inez, Christopher Wilson. **EDUCATION:** Wayne State Univ, BS 1969; Harvard Univ Law School, JSD 1972. **CAREER:** MI Supreme Court, assoc commissioner 1977-78; Private Law Practice, attorney 1981-83; Senior Citizens Law Program, dir 1983-87; Private Law Practice 1987-. **ORGANIZATIONS:** Attorney Miller, Canfield, Paddock & Stone 1973-75; attorney Private Law Practice 1975-77. **HONORS/ACHIEVEMENTS:** Publication "The Limits on Employment Testing", University of Detroit Journalof Urban Law, Vol 50, Issue 3 1973. **MILITARY SERVICE:** USAF 1st lt 1969-73. **HOME ADDRESS:** 801 Sunrise Ct, Ann Arbor, MI 48103.

NORTHERN, ROBERT A.
Educator, musician. **PERSONAL:** Born May 21, 1934, Kinston, NC. **EDUCATION:** Manhattan Sch of Music NYC, 1952-53; Vienna State Acad of Music Vienna Austria, 1957-58. **CAREER:** Brown Univ Afro Amer Studies Prg, lectr 1973-; Artist in Res Dartmouth Coll Music Dept, lectr 1970-73; Brass Instrmnts Pub School Syst NYC, Instr 1964-67; Metro Opera NYC, 1958-59; Symphony of the Air Orchester NYC, 1958-70; Broadway Theatre Orchestra NYC, 1969-71; Jazz Composer Orchestra NYC, 1969-71. **ORGANIZATIONS:** Performed as sideman & recorded with following artists, Thelonious Monk, Miles Davis, Gil Evans, Freddie Hubbard, Quincy Jones, Peggy Lee, Tony Bennett, Sun Ra, Ella Fitzgerald, Numerous Others; composer dir of following productions, Forces of Nature BrownUniv 1974, Symbols Dartmouth Clg 1972, Confrontaiton & Communication Dartmouth Clg 1971, Magical Mode Dartmouth Clg 1971, Ode to Creation Dartmouth Clg 1970, Ti-Jean Dartmouth Clg 1971, Child Woman BrownUniv 1973; chrtr mem Soc of Black Composers 1965; fndr Sound Awareness Ensemble 1968; fndr Radio Series Dimensions in Black Sounds WBAI-FM New York City 1970; fndr NY Wind Octet 1966; mus dir Black Fire Performing Arts Co Birmingtham; Producers First Album for Black Chorus of BrownUniv Sound Awareness Vol I 1973; Sound Awareness VolII Move Ever Onward III 1975; The New World Vol III 1980. **HONORS/ACHIEVEMENTS:** Owner publshr Umoja Music Publishing Co Founded 1973. **MILITARY SERVICE:** USAF a/1c 1953-57. **BUSINESS ADDRESS:** Afro Am Studies Brown Univ, Providence, RI 02912.

NORTHOVER, VERNON KEITH
Salesman. **PERSONAL:** Born Jan 03, 1934, New York, NY; married Lyn Brown; children: Vivia, Vernon, Paul, Fran, Orville. **EDUCATION:** London Sch of Econ, BS 1959. **CAREER:** GAF Corp, sales rep 1971-; British RR London, admstr 1960-71. **ORGANIZATIONS:** Bd of dir The Mus of Afro-Am Ethno History Inc 1977; pres Clb GAF Corp 1977. **BUSINESS ADDRESS:** 60 Curve St, Millis, MA 02360.

NORTON, AURELIA EVANGELINE
Clinical psychologist. **PERSONAL:** Born Feb 14, 1932, Dayton; divorced. **EDUCATION:** Wayne State, BA Distinction MA PhD 1961; Cntrl StateUniv of Dayton, Undergrad. **CAREER:** Wayne State, res psychologist; Childrens & Emergency Psychiat Clinic Detroit Gen Hosp, stf psychologist; Oak Pk Sch Sys, psychologist; Chrysler Corp, psychologist; Childrens Hosp Consulting Psychologist, res psychologist; Univ of Cincinnati Multi Ethnic Branch Psychological Svcs, assoc prof of psychology. **ORGANIZATIONS:** Numerous Orgns & Industries; Police Selec Cincinnati; mem Psychologist Examination Bd State of OH; term mem Amer Psychological Assc; Assc of Black Psychologists; NAACP; Mt Zion Baptist Church. **BUSINESS ADDRESS:** Assoc Prof of Psychology, Univ of Cincinnati, 221 Tangoman Univ Cntr, Cincinnati, OH.

NORTON, EDWARD WORTHINGTON
Government official. **PERSONAL:** Born Apr 10, 1938, New York, NY; married Eleanor K Holmes; children: Katherine Felicia, John Holmes. **EDUCATION:** Yale U, BA 1959; Columbia U, LlB 1966. **CAREER:** Dept of Housing & Urban Dev, dep gen cnsl; New York City Housing Authority, gen cnsl 1973-77; New York City Hlth Serv Admn, spl asst to admnstr 1970-73; NYUniv Law Sch;; adj asst proj 1971-73; Legal Serv Pgm NE Region OEO, dep dir 1968-70; Paul, Weiss, Rifkind, Wharton & Garrison, assc 1966-68; Lawyers Constitution Def Com 1966. **ORGANIZATIONS:** Tres Columbia Law Sch Alumni Assc 1970-74; bd dir 1969-; 100 Black Men Inc 1974-; Harlem Lawyers Assc 1976-; Equality Com Am Civil Liberties Union 1967-73; bd dir NY Civil Liberties Union 1971-74; vice pres Schlrshp Ed & Def Fund for Racial Equality 1972-; bd dir 1968-; bd dir Save The Children Fed 1975-.

MILITARY SERVICE: USN lt 1959-63. **BUSINESS ADDRESS:** 451 7th St SW Rm 10214, Washington, DC 20410.

NORTON, ELEANOR HOLMES
Educator. **PERSONAL:** Born Apr 08, 1938, Washington, DC; married Edward Norton; children: Katharine, John. **EDUCATION:** Antioch Coll, attended; Yale Univ, MA 1963; Yale Law School, JD 1964. **CAREER:** Georgetown Univ School of Law, prof. **ORGANIZATIONS:** Chmn US Equal Empl Oppty Comm 1977-83; mem NY Comm Human Rights 1970-76; asst legal dir Amer Civil Liberties Union. **BUSINESS ADDRESS:** Professor, GeorgetownUniv School of Law, 600 New Jersey Ave NW, Washington, DC 20001.

NORVEL, WILLIAM LEONARD
Clergyman. **PERSONAL:** Born Oct 01, 1935, Pascagoula, MS; son of William L Norvel, Sr and Velma H Norvel. **EDUCATION:** Epiphany Apostolic Coll, 1956; St Joseph's Seminary, BA 1959; St Michael's Coll, 1960-61; St Bonaventure Coll 1963; Marquette Univ, 1967. **CAREER:** Holy Family, asst pastor 1965; St Augustine HS, teacher 1965; Josephite Training Center, dir 1968; St Joseph's Seminary, staff asst 1970; St Benedict the Moor, pastor 1971; St Brigid, pastor 1979-83; consultant to Black Catholic Parishes in USA, 1983-; Josephite Soc, consultor-general 1983-; Most Pure Heart of Mary Church, pastor, 1987-. **ORGANIZATIONS:** Bd mem Lithurgical Conf 1978-82; bd mem SCLC/LA 1979/83; mem NAACP 1983-85; pres Black Catholic Clergy Caucus 1985-87; trustee bd Natl Black Catholic Congress 1987. **HONORS/ACHIEVEMENTS:** Comm Action Awd Secretariat for Black Catholics 1978; Ecumenical Fellowship Awd by Baptists, Muslims, AME, CME 1983; Church of God in Christ & Holiness Churches of LA Achievement Awd SCLC/LA 1983; Serv Awd Loyola Marymount Univ 1983. **BUSINESS ADDRESS:** Pastor, Most Pure Heart of Mary Church, 304 Sengstak St, P O Box 994, Mobile, AL 36601.

NORWOOD, BERNICE N.
Social worker. **PERSONAL:** Born Oct 02, 1917, Guilford County, NC; widowed. **EDUCATION:** Bennett Coll, BA 1938; Atlanta Univ School Soc Work, professional cert 1946. **CAREER:** Caldwell County NC Welfare Dept, case Worker 1945-50; Guilford Cnty NC Dept Soc Serv, case worker 1953-63, case work supr 1963-. **ORGANIZATIONS:** Mem, Natl Assn Social Workers; mem Acad Cert Soc Workers; mem NC Assn; Soc Workers; past program chmn pres Greensboro Branch Natl Council Negro Women; charter mem United Day Care Serv Bd, first sec exec com former chmn Admissions Metro Day Care Ctr; mem Greensboro, NC Mental Health Assn. **HONORS/ACHIEVEMENTS:** Directory of Professional Social Workers, 1972. **BUSINESS ADDRESS:** Guilford Co Dept of Social Serv, PO Box 3388, Greensboro, NC.

NORWOOD, CALVIN COOLIDGE
Association executive. **PERSONAL:** Born Apr 01, 1927, Tunica, MS; married Ida; children: Doris A, Deloris, Demetrice, Regina. **EDUCATION:** Coahoma Jr Clg, GED 1979. **CAREER:** Co Rd Dept in Co Turstee Bd Rosa Fort Sch, foreman; MS State Hwy Dept Tunica County, 1st black jury commiss supv. **ORGANIZATIONS:** Pres NAACP 1966-; mem EDA Bd; mem Co Dem Party; mem Legal Aide Bd Joint Communication Activity & Job Care; mem State Bd NAACP; mem VFW. **HONORS/ACHIEVEMENTS:** Job Core Cert Job Core 1979; Politician Action Awrd NAACP 1980; Ed Awrd NAACP 1980. **MILITARY SERVICE:** AUS std 3rd class 1944-46; served overseas Island of Guam 18 mo's.

NORWOOD, ELIZABETH LEE
Retired educator. **PERSONAL:** Born May 29, 1912, Shawneetown, IL; married James Robert Norwood; children: Robert Lee. **EDUCATION:** So IL Univ, BE 1955; Univ of IL, ME 1960. **CAREER:** Elem teacher 1937-51; pe consult 1952-60; Jr High School, pe instr 1960-65; elem teacher 1966-72 (retired). **ORGANIZATIONS:** Mem Phi Delta Kappa, IL Ed Assoc, NEA, NRTA, IL School Dist 118 Bd of Ed 1974-83, E Central IL Agency on Aging, IL Health Systems Agency, Comm Rsch & Serv Org Inc, Amer Assn of Univ Women, League of Women Voters, NAACP, Laura Lee Fellowship House, Neighborhood House; vice pres 1977-80, pres 1980-81, school bd IL Dist 118; state dir IL Assoc of School Bds. **HONORS/ACHIEVEMENTS:** Human Relations Awd joint awd with GC Lewis; UAW Social Justice Awd.

NORWOOD, JOHN F.
Retired clergyman, associate general secretary. **PERSONAL:** Born Nov 28, 1927, Darlington, SC; son of Rev J R Norwood and Benzina Norwood; married Zanthia; children: John F, Jr, Iris R, Lydia I. **EDUCATION:** BA 1951; BD 1957; MDiv 1969; Wiley Coll, DD 1976. **CAREER:** Council on Finance & Adminstrs United Meth Ch, assoc gen sec; Camden SC, prin elem sch; Health & Welfare United Meth Ch, asst gen sec; Gammon Theo Sem Atlanta, pres 1967-68; Huntsville, dist supt 1962-66. **ORGANIZATIONS:** Mem Nat Assn of Health & Welfare; Nat Alliance of Black Clergyman; delegate, jurisdoctoral conf mem Dist 65 Sch Bd Evanston IL 1972-75; re-elected 1975-; pres protem, bd dirs NAACP Evanston Br; Rotary Club Evanston; United Chris Ministry Bd. **HONORS/ACHIEVEMENTS:** Recip hon cit Huntsville 1968; key to city of Huntsville 1968; outstanding leadership citation Evanston NAACP 1974; key to city of Sparta TN 1974; NAACP Humanitarion award 1989. **MILITARY SERVICE:** AUS pvt 1945. **BUSINESS ADDRESS:** 1200 Davis St, Evanston, IL 60201.

NORWOOD, TOM
Educator. **PERSONAL:** Born Jul 19, 1943, Baton Rouge, LA; son of Edward A Norwood, Sr and Corinne Burrell Norwood; married Marjorie Marshall; children: Teri Lynn, Tony. **EDUCATION:** Southern Univ & A&M Clge, BS Art/English 1964, MEd Educ Admin 1969; Univ of NE Lincoln, PhD Ed Adm 1975. **CAREER:** Omaha Publ Schl, traveling art tchr 1964-65, jr high art tchr 1965-68, jr high cnsl 1968-70; Clge of Educ Univ of NE Omaha, asst dean 1970-83, assc prof 1983-88; asst dean and prof, Univ Wisconsin, River Falls. **ORGANIZATIONS:** Pres 1981-83, vice pres NE Council on Tchr Educ; wrkshp dir Joslyn Art Museum "Forever Free Exhibit" 1981; wrkshp dir Sioux Falls SD City Dept Heads, "Racism & Sexism" 1979; vice pres Greater Omaha Comm Action 1975; mem Appointed by US Dist Court Judge Albert Schatz 1976; mem Urban League of NE 1983-84; consultant to Omaha Public School re Implementing Discipline Based Art Educ Prog 1987-87. **HONORS/ACHIEVEMENTS:** Phi Delta Kappa Southern Univ & A&M Clge 1964; hnrbl mention Watercolor Council Bluffs IA Art Fair 1972; book "Contemporary Nebr Art & Artists" Univ of NE at Omaha 1978; article "Facilitating Multicultural Educ Via the Visual Arts" NE Humanist 1980; 1st pl award NE Art Educ Competition 1982; paintings selected natl & intl juried competitions, Natl Miniature Competition 1983, Natl Exhibition of Contemporary Realism 1983, Montana Intl Miniature Competition 1983, Intl Small Fine Art Exhibit 1984, Intl Miniature Competition 1984, Biennial Juried Competition (Natl) 1984, Tenth Intl Miniature Competition 1985; commissioned by St of NE to create poster design for first state observance of Martin Luther King, Jr holiday 1986; First Annual Natl NC Miniature Painting Show Cert of Merit 1985; Second Annual NC Natl Miniature Painting Show Second Place Watercolor 1986; participated in 17 exhibition 1985-1987. **BUSINESS ADDRESS:** Asst Dean, Coll of Educ, Univ of Wisconsin at River Falls, Hathorn Cottage, River Falls, WI 54022.

NORWOOD, WILLIAM R.
Pilot. **PERSONAL:** Born Feb 14, 1936, Centralia, IL; son of Sam Norwood and Allingal (Humble) Norwood; married Molly F Cross; children: William R, George A. **EDUCATION:** S IL U, BA 1959;Univ of Chicago, MBA 1974. **CAREER:** United Air Lines, captain 1983-, airline pilot 1st ofcr 1968-83; 2nd ofcr 1965-68. **ORGANIZATIONS:** Mem Air Line Pilots Assn; United Air Lines Speakers Panel; charter mem Orgn of Black Air Line Pilots; chmn Bd Trust S ILUniv at Carbondale Edwardsville1974-; bd of dir Suburban Chap So Christian Leadership Conf. **HONORS/ACHIEVEMENTS:** First black pilot with UAL; Chem News All Am Football at SIU 1958; 1st black quarterback SIU; commencement speaker Shawnee Comm Coll 1975; an exhibition in Smithsonian Inst "Black Wings". **MILITARY SERVICE:** AUS pilot B-52 capt 1959-65. **BUSINESS ADDRESS:** Captain, United Airlines, O Hare International Airport, PO Box 66140, Chicago, IL 60666.

NOTICE, GUY SYMOUR
Clergyman, educator. **PERSONAL:** Born Dec 06, 1929; son of Daniel E Notice and Eugena A Notice; married Azelma; children: Donald Hylton, Sandra. **EDUCATION:** Bethel Bible Coll, certificate 1954; Amer Divinity School, BTh 1972; Fordham Univ & Goddard Coll, BA 1974; Luther Rice Seminary, graduate studies. **CAREER:** Tutorial Coll, vice chmn, 1965-69; conv speaker, England, Canada, Dallas TX, Mexico, Eastern Caribbean, US Virgin Islands, 1968-81; Bethel Bible Coll, dir of educ 1973-77; Jamaica Theological Seminary, bd mem; New Testament Church of God, supt, 1982; justice of the peace, 1985. **ORGANIZATIONS:** Bd mem Jamaica Theological Seminary; chmn, Natl Chest Clinic, 1982; guest speaker, Conf Puerto Rico, 1985; chmn, Hope Inst; chmn of bd, Bethel Bible Coll. **HONORS/ACHIEVEMENTS:** Certificate of merit for books published (They Shall See Visions, If We Could Begin Again, Beyond the Veil), Opa Locka City, 1982; author of book, Prison Life: The Jamaican Experience, to be published 1989. **HOME ADDRESS:** 7068 Cardinalwood Ct, Orlando, FL 32818. **BUSINESS ADDRESS:** PO Box 680205, Orlando, FL 32818.

NUNERY, GLADYS CANNON
Educator. **PERSONAL:** Born Sep 07, 1904, Jersey City; divorced. **EDUCATION:** Jersey City State Tchrs Coll, BS1951; NY Univ, MA 1957. **CAREER:** Jersey City Public Schools, taught elem grades 1924-64; Bergen Study Center, dir 1964-69; Luth Parochial School, teacher 1969-71. **ORGANIZATIONS:** Volunteer ch & community work 1971-74; mem Nat Educ Assn; NJ Educ Assn; Nat Retired Tchrs Assn; NJ Retired Tchrs Assn; Hudson Co Retired Tchrs Assn; Local YWCA; mem Claremont-Lafayette Presbnyn Ch; supt Ch Sch 25 yrs 1930-55; ch treas 1962-75; life mem NAACP; serving 3rd term of 3 yrs Jersey City Bd Edn; rep out of town meetings; organized natl sorority Phi Delta Kappa 1923; held various natl & local offices; speaker woman's orgns & chs. **HONORS/ACHIEVEMENTS:** 1st woman elected trustee 1942; 1st woman elected an elder 1964; Outstanding Woman in City Jersey Journal 1965; Outstanding Soror Eastern Region 1966; Hon degree Dr of Humane Letters Jersey City State College 1986.

NUNERY, LEROY DAVID
Banker. **PERSONAL:** Born Dec 22, 1955, Jersey City, NJ; son of Leroy C Nunery and Thelma Jones Nunery; married Carolyn Thomas Nunery, Apr 24, 1982; children: Leroy David Nunery III. **EDUCATION:** Lafayette Coll, BA Honors, History 1977; Washington Univ, MBA Finance 1979. **CAREER:** Leroy Nunery & Sons Inc, vice pres, 1973-; Edward D Jones & Co, research analyst 1978-79; Northern Trust Co, comm banking officer 1979-83; First Natl Bank of Chicago, vice pres 1983-87; Swiss Bank Corp, vice pres, 1987-. **ORGANIZATIONS:** Natl pres, Natl Black MBA Assn Inc 1986-; dir Family Resource Coalition Inc 1988-; trustee, Lafayette Coll 1988-. **HONORS/ACHIEVEMENTS:** Black and Hispanic Achievers YMCA, 1983, 1986; Outstanding MBA of the Year Natl Black MBA Assn 1984; Amer Best & Brightest, Dollars & Sense Magazine 1987; Alumni Recognition Award, Washington Univ Business Minority Council 1987; frequent speaker to graduate, undergraduate, high school and elementary school student; quoted and profiled in several publications including New York Times, Black Enterprise, Ebony and Jet; profiled as a "Mover and Shaker" in Business Week, Oct 1987. **BUSINESS ADDRESS:** Swiss Bank Corp (NY Branch), 4 World Trade Center, PO Box 395, Church Street Station, New York, NY 10008.

NUNN, BOBBIE B.
Educator. **PERSONAL:** Born in Muskogee; married Josiah; children: Darla, Joe Darryl. **EDUCATION:** Portland State U, BS 1959;Univ of Portland, MEd 1970, Houston-Tillotson Coll; Prairie View Coll. **CAREER:** Paraprofl Devel System Portland Public School, dir; Career Oppor Program Portland Public School, dir; Environmental Educ Program Boise Elem School, dir 1968-70; Portland State Univ, demonstration teacher summer 1960-66; Portland Public School, teachers 1959-70. **ORGANIZATIONS:** Mem Am Assn of Sch Per*Sonnel Adminstr; Nat Council of Admin women in Edn; Cascade Adv Bd; Nat Alliance of Black Sch Educators; Child Devel Learning Cntr Bd; bd mem Model Cities Citizens Planning Bd; mem Metro Hum Rel Comm; chairperson Hum Rel Comm Oregon State Bd of Edn; NAACP; Alpha Kappa Alpha; Delta Kappa Gamma. **HONORS/ACHIEVEMENTS:** Albina Lions Club Award for comm ser 1974; award for comm serv in educ Nat Conf of Christians & Jews 1975. **BUSINESS ADDRESS:** 631 NE Clackamas St, Portland, OR 97208.

NUNN, JOHN, JR.
Company executive. **PERSONAL:** Born Sep 19, 1953, Berkeley, CA; son of John Nunn and Yvonne Hunter Nunn; married Valmere Fischer, Jul 03, 1977; children: Arianna M Nunn, Julian G Nunn. **EDUCATION:** St Mary's Coll, Moraga CA, BS Biology 1971-76; Univ of California at Berkeley 1975. **CAREER:** World Savings, Alamo CA, asst vice pres branch manager, 1976-78; American Savings, Oakland CA, asst vice pres branch manager, 1979-80, El Cerrito CA, vice pres regional manager, 1980-85, Stockton CA, senior vice pres

office chief admin officer, 1987-89, Stockton CA, senior vice pres dir Community Outreach 1989. **ORGANIZATIONS:** Mem Alumni Board, Bishop O'Dowd HS Prep, 1980-85; pres, 1985-87; mem Stockton Chamber of Commerce, 1987-; mem Stockton Black Chamber of Commerce, 1987-; memSacramento Chamber of Commerce, 1987-; mem California League of Savings Institutions, 1988-; mem Business School Adv Board, California State Univ, 1988-. **BUSINESS ADDRESS:** Sr Vice President, Director of Community Outreach, American Savings Bank, FA, 343 E Main, Stockton, CA 95201.

NUNN, ROBINSON S.
Judge. **PERSONAL:** Born Sep 29, 1944, Blytheville, AR; married Glanetta Miller. **EDUCATION:** MI State U, BA 1966; AmUniv Law Sch, JD 1969. **CAREER:** Admitted to Supreme Ct Bar 1976; US Tax Ct Wash DC, legal asst 1969; Little Rock AR, gen prac of law 1976. **ORGANIZATIONS:** Am Bar Assn; Nat Bar Assn; AR Bar Assn; NAACP; Kappa Alpha Psi Frat. **MILITARY SERVICE:** USMC captain 1976-. **BUSINESS ADDRESS:** Quarters 2947 D MCB, Quantico, VA 22134.

NUNN, WILLIAM GOLDWIN, JR.
Asst dir player personnel. **PERSONAL:** Born in Pittsburgh, PA; married Frances; children: Lynell Stanton, William III. **EDUCATION:** West Virginia State, graduate 1948. **CAREER:** Pittsburgh Courier, sports editor; Pittsburgh Steelers, training camp director/personnel scout 1968, asst dir of player personnel.

NUNNALLY, DAVID H., SR.
Educator. **PERSONAL:** Born Oct 16, 1929, Athens Clarke Co, GA; married Ileane I Nesbit. **EDUCATION:** Union Bapt Inst; Tuskegee Inst; Atlanta U;Univ of GA; Gov State U, mS; LoyalUniv of Chicago, PhD. **CAREER:** Kennedy-Ing Coll, counselor; teacher; Jr HS counselor; HS counselor; residential counselor; Sutdent Personnel Ser, dir; Comm Adult HS, asst dir; athletic coach; employment counselor; camp counselor. **ORGANIZATIONS:** Mem PTA; AFT; NEA; Phi Delta Kappa; VFW; APGA; IGPA; ICPA; GAE; past dir Dist IX Assn of Educators; past mem Assn of Educ Bd of Dir; Chicago Hghts Ldrshp Forum; founder Athens Chap Ita Iota Lambda; mem Lions Intl Club; Alpha Phi Alpha; Masonic Lodge; sponsor Comm Ser Club; troop scout master. **HONORS/ACHIEVEMENTS:** BSA Outstanding Male Tchr Am Tchr Assn 1964; Martin Luther King Hum Rel Award Eta Iota Lambda Chap 1970; Man of Yr Eta Iota Lambda Chap & GA Alpha Phi Alpha 1970; Who's Who Among Black Am Award 1974. **MILITARY SERVICE:** AUS sp 2 1951-53. **BUSINESS ADDRESS:** 7269 S Shore Dr, Chicago, IL.

NUNNERY, WILLIE JAMES
Deputy secretary for energy, attorney. **PERSONAL:** Born Jul 28, 1948, Chicago, IL. **EDUCATION:** Univ of KS Lawrence, KS, BS, CE 1971;Univ of WI Sch of Law, JD 1975. **CAREER:** State of WI, dep sec energy 1975-; Univ of WI Coll of Engrng, asst to dean 1972-75; Atlantic Richfield, legal intern 1972; Energy Research Ctr Univ of WI Coll of Engrng, asso dir; Atlantic Richfield, jr analytical engr, 1971. **ORGANIZATIONS:** Mem WI State Bar 1976-; Midwestern Gov Energy Task Force; scoutmaster, exec dir Four Lk Area Boy Scout Council WI; bd dir YMCA; mem Downtown KiwanisClub of Madison & Greenfield; mem Bapt Ch. **BUSINESS ADDRESS:** 101 S Webster St, Madison, WI 53702.

NURSE, ROBERT EARL
Business executive. **PERSONAL:** Born May 25, 1942, New York, NY; son of Earl Nurse and Miriam Nurse; married Ann Marie Jameson; children: Douglas Jamal, India Marie. **EDUCATION:** Univ VT, BA 1964; Fordham Univ, grad work. **CAREER:** Xerox Corp, sales rep, consultant, employee relations mgr, sales mgr, personnel operations mgr 1966-77; ITT, staffing mgr 1977-79; Citicorp, personnel mgr 1979-80; Pepsi-Cola, mgr of staffing 1980-81; Robert E Nurse Assoc Inc, pres 1981-88; J B Gilbert Assoc, vice pres, 1988-. **ORGANIZATIONS:** Mem CCBE; mem 100 Black Men; mem NAACP. **BUSINESS ADDRESS:** J B Gilbert Assoc, 420 Lexington Ave, New York, NY 10170.

NUTALL, JAMES EDWARD
Educational administration. **PERSONAL:** Born Aug 04, 1933, Oxford, NC; married Hazel Yville; children: Dexter Udell, Fawne J'nai. **EDUCATION:** VA Union Univ, BS 1956; George Washington Univ, MS. **CAREER:** DC Public School System, dep asst 1968-72; Howard Univ School of Bus & Public Admin, dir industry relations 1975-; Randall Hyland Pvt School, head master, pres. **ORGANIZATIONS:** Pres Wilson of Grandville; vice pres Anocostia Professional & Merchants; mem Council to Devel Natl Agenda for Black Progress, Mayors Overall Econ Devel Corp, Mayors Riverfest Comm. **HONORS/ACHIEVEMENTS:** Commun Health Fellow East of the River Health Network; Consult to US Office of Ed; Expert on Title VII. **HOME ADDRESS:** 1312 You St SE, Washington, DC 20020. **BUSINESS ADDRESS:** President, Randall Hyland Pvt School, 2910 Pennsylvania Ave SE, Washington, DC 20020.

NUTT, AMBROSE BENJAMIN
Engineering consultant. **PERSONAL:** Born Mar 16, 1920, Milwaukee, WI; son of Ambrose Nutt and Willette Nutt; married Viola Elaine Henderson; children: Jacqueline Nutt Teepen, Sandra. **EDUCATION:** Univ of MI, BSc 1940; OH State Univ, MSc 1950; Air Force Command & Staff Coll, Graduate 1955; Industrial Coll of the Armed Forces, Graduate 1960. **CAREER:** Air Force Aircraft Lab, project engr 1941-43, 1946-56; Air Force Flight Dynamics Lab, chief mech & sp proj branches 1956-64, chief plans office 1964-69, chief tech operations office 1969-73, chief mgmt opns ofc 1973-76, dir vehicle equip div 1976-81; Wilberforce Univ, dir engrg & computer science 1981-88. **ORGANIZATIONS:** Pres bd of trustees SCOPE (5 county anti-poverty program) 1967-79; pres Yellow Springs (OH) School Bd 1968-74; mem bd of trustees Dayton (OH) Honor Seminars 1974-. **HONORS/ACHIEVEMENTS:** Assoc Fellow AIAA 1964; Literary Awd Armed Forces Mgmt Assoc 1971; Meritorious Civilian Serv Medal USAF 1977; Exceptional Civilian Serv Medal USAF 1981. **MILITARY SERVICE:** USAF maj 1944-46 reserves 1950-60. **HOME ADDRESS:** 8379 Adams Rd, Dayton, OH 45424.

NUTT, MAURICE JOSEPH
Roman Catholic priest. **PERSONAL:** Born Dec 20, 1962, St Louis, MO; son of Haller Levi Nutt and Beatrice Lucille Duvall Nutt. **EDUCATION:** Holy Redeemer Coll, BA Philosophy, 1985; Catholic Theological Union, Master of Divinity, 1989; Xavier Univ of LA, Master of Theology, 1989. **CAREER:** St Alphonsus Rock Church, St Louis Mo, associate pastor, 1989-. **ORGANIZATIONS:** Pres, Natl Black Catholic Seminarians Assn 1986-87; mem bd of dir, Natl Black Catholic Clergy Caucus 1986-87; pres Pan African Studdents Assn of Catholic Theological Union, 1988-89. **HONORS/ACHIEVEMENTS:** Man of the Year Award, St Joseph Preparatory Coll, 1980; preacher of the 1st Chicago Archdiocesan Black Catholic Youth Revival 1986; publication: Black Vocations: The Responsibility and Challenge 1987; keynote speaker Chicago Archdiocesan Youth Congress 1988; The Fr Clarence Williams Award, Natl Black Catholic Seminarians Assn 1988; organizer and speaker of the Redemptorist Conference on Black Ministry, 1989. **HOME ADDRESS:** St Alphonsus Rock Church, 1118 N Grand Blvd, St Louis, MO 63106.

NWANNA, GLADSON I. N.
Educator. **PERSONAL:** Born May 12, 1954, Mbonge, Cameroon. **EDUCATION:** Essex Cty Coll, AS acct 1977, AA 1978; Rutgers State Univ, BA acct 1979; St Johns Univ, MBA fin 1980; Fordham Univ, PhD econ 1984; Amer Inst of Banking, banking for prof cert 1985. **CAREER:** NJ Blood Center, distrib clerk 1978-79; St Benedict HS, math teacher 1979-80; Essex Cty Coll, adj prof of math & bus 1981-84; Kean Coll of NJ, asstprof fin & econ 1983-85; Rutgers State Univ, adj prof of math 1984; Morgan State Univ, asst prof fin, econ & acct 1985-. **ORGANIZATIONS:** Mem Rutgers State Univ Intl Student Org 1978-79, Amer Econ Assoc 1983-, Eastern Fin Assoc 1985-, World Acad of Devel & Coop 1986-; chief cons, founder African Rsch & Consult Serv 1985-; pres CAMA Trans Inc 1986-; mem NAACP 1986-, Natl Urban League 1986-, World Acad of Devel & Coop 1986-, Soc for Intl Devel 1986-. **HONORS/ACHIEVEMENTS:** Student of the Month Essex Cty Coll 1978; Who's Who in Amer Jr Coll Essex Cty Coll 1978; Alpha Epsilon Beta Essex Cty Coll 1979; Omicron Delta Epsilon1980; Beta Gamma Sigma St Johns Univ 1981; author; publ several articles in prof jrnls. **BUSINESS ADDRESS:** Professor Fin, Econ & Acctg, Morgan State University, Box 476, Baltimore, MD 21239.

NYAHUMA, TAHIYA R. M. W.
Economic development specialist, consultant. **PERSONAL:** Born Aug 09, 1951, Philadelphia, PA; married Mujahid BW; children: Jawanza, Naledi. **EDUCATION:** Windham Coll, BA 1973; State Univ of NY, MA 1977, PhD 1987. **CAREER:** Richmond Coll London, lecturer pol sci 1980-81; Lewisham Way Comm Ctr, lecturer african studies 1979-81; Amer Friends Ser Com, asst coor african pro1983-85; Opportunities Ind Cen Intl, consultant 1985-86; Aprotech Intl, founder/director. **ORGANIZATIONS:** Mem African Heritage Studies Assoc 1984-85, Concerned Black Women Philadelphia 1985-86, World Affairs Council Philadelphia 1986-87; vice chairperson Natl Pol Cong of Black Women 1985-, Amer Women's Heritage Soc 1986-. **HONORS/ACHIEVEMENTS:** Fellowship NY State Grad 1977; Harambe Grad Awd SUNY 1977. **HOME ADDRESS:** 1509 W Lehigh Ave, Philadelphia, PA 19132. **BUSINESS ADDRESS:** Founder/Dir, Aprotech International, PO Box 50077, Philadelphia, PA 19132.

O

OAKLEY, CHARLES
Professional basketball player. **PERSONAL:** Born Dec 18, 1963, Cleveland, OH. **EDUCATION:** Attended, VA Union Univ. **CAREER:** Chicago Bulls, professional basketball player 1985-. **HONORS/ACHIEVEMENTS:** Led NCAA Division II in rebounding 1985; named to NBA All-Rookie Team 1986. **BUSINESS ADDRESS:** Chicago Bulls, 980 N Michigan Ave, Chicago, IL 60611.

OATES, CALEB E.
Clergyman. **PERSONAL:** Born Apr 05, 1917, Shelby, NC; married Authella Walker; children: Bernard D, David C. **EDUCATION:** Union Sem, attended; Jewish Theol Sem, attended. **CAREER:** Baptist Church, ordained minister 1947; Bethany Baptist Church, pastor 1947-. **ORGANIZATIONS:** Mem Local, State, Fed Bapt Church Orgs, pres, chmn Howell-Farmingdale Juvenile Bd 1965-; pres Howell-Farmingdale Council Chs 1968-72; mem bd of dirHowell Rotary Club 1973-. **HONORS/ACHIEVEMENTS:** Pastor of the Year in NJ 1953; Cert of Merit Comm Act Jewish War Vets 1961; Listed in Who's Who in the East, Marquis Who's Who. **MILITARY SERVICE:** AUS, ETO, chaplain 1943-45; Bronze Star; 5 Battle Stars. **BUSINESS ADDRESS:** Pastor, Bethany Baptist Church, RFD 1 W Farms Rd, Farmingdale, NJ 07727.

OATES, WANDA ANITA
Teacher, coach. **PERSONAL:** Born Sep 11, 1942, Washington, DC; daughter of Robert L. Oates, Sr. and Ruth Richards Oates. **EDUCATION:** Howard Univ, Washington DC, BS, 1965; George Washington Univ, Washington DC, MA, 1967. **CAREER:** F. W. Ballou High School, Washington DC, athletic coach, c. 1967—, athletic director, 1980—. **HONORS/ACHIEVEMENTS:** Twice named coach of the year by Eastern Bd of Athletic Officials; natl honorary basketball official rating, Washington DC Bd of Women Officials; outstanding achievement award, Howard Univ Alumni Club; named by Washingtonian Magazine one of Washington's 100 most powerful women. **HOME ADDRESS:** 5700 Fourth St NW, Washington, DC 20011.

O'BANNON, ALVIN JAMAL
Educational administrator. **PERSONAL:** Born Aug 25, 1953. **EDUCATION:** Attended, SUNY at Geneseo, 1971-73; SUNY at Albany, BA 1975, MA 1977; Adult Educ Certificate; Life Skills Certificate. **CAREER:** Trinity Institution Inc, business mgr 1977-79; Capital District Educ Oppor Ctr, admin asst 1979-82; Hudson Valley Comm Coll, dir of educ opp progs1982-. **ORGANIZATIONS:** Bd mem Renn Co Alch Ctr 1984-; adv council Glenmont Job Corps Ctr 1984-; comm mem Educ Comm/RCAC 1984-; mem Northern Region Black & Hispanic Political Caucus; alumni advisor to Black Student Alliance at SUNY Albany, Hudson Valley Comm Coll. **HONORS/ACHIEVEMENTS:** Cert of Appreciation Benjamin Ward Commissioner of Corrections 1980.

OBAYUWANA, ALPHONSUS OSAROBO
Physician. **PERSONAL:** Born Jul 26, 1948, Benin City, Nigeria;son of William Obayuwana and Irene Osemwegie Obayuwana; married Ann Louise Carter, Jun 11, 1977; children: Alphonsus, Anson. **EDUCATION:** High Point Coll, BS (Summa Cum Laude) 1973; How-

ard Univ, MS 1977; Howard Univ Coll of Medicine, MD 1981. **CAREER:** South Baltimore General Hospital, intern 1981-82, resident 1982-85; The Johns Hopkins Univ Sch of Medicine, instructor 1985-86; Group Health Assoc, obstetrician/gynecologist 1986-. **ORGANIZATIONS:** Principal investigator Institute of Hope 1982-; mem Amer Medical Assoc, Amer Coll of Obstetrics and Gynecology, Natl Medical Assoc, Amer Soc of Psychosomatic Obstetrics and Gynecology; Consultant The Female Care Center Silver Spring MD 1985-. **HONORS/ACHIEVEMENTS:** Co-author "The Hope Index Scale," 1982; Natl Resident Research Paper Awd; "Psychosocial Distress and Pregnancy Outcome" 1984; Who's Who in Biobehavioral Sciences 1983. **HOME ADDRESS:** 613 Manorbrook Dr, Silver Spring, MD 20904. **BUSINESS ADDRESS:** Staff Physician, Group Health Association, 8401 Colesville Rd, Silver Spring, MD 20910.

OBI, JAMES E.
Manager. **PERSONAL:** Born Sep 02, 1942, Lagos, Nigeria;married Olubosede Cecilia; children: Funke, Femi, Siji, Uche. **EDUCATION:** St Peter's Coll Oxford England, BA 1963; Amer Coll of Life Underwriters, CLU 1973. **CAREER:** Equit Life Assurance Soc of the US, agent 1967-68, dist mgr 1968-72, agency mgr 1972-. **ORGANIZATIONS:** Bd mem Nigerian-Amer Friendship Soc 1979. **BUSINESS ADDRESS:** Manager, Equitable Life Assurance Soc, One Penn Plaza Ste 4315, New York, NY 10119.

OBINNA, ELEAZU S.
Educator. **PERSONAL:** Born Jun 04, 1934, Ogbeke-Obibi, Imo, Nigeria;married Carol Jean Miles; children: Iheanyi, Obageri, Marvin. **EDUCATION:** BA 1969; Inst of Bookkeepers London , FCBI 1972; Loyola Univ of Los Angeles, MEd 1973; Univ of CA UCLA, EdD 1978; Univ of Hull England, post doc. **CAREER:** Redman Western Corp, acct controller 1968-69; Sec Pacific Bank, fin planning spec 1970-71; Pan African, prof bus econ educ 1971; CA State Univ Northridge, studies dept. **ORGANIZATIONS:** Vp Natl Alliance of Bus for youth motivation Wash DC 1984-; chrmn Pan African Studies Dept 1971-75; prof Bus Econ Educ Pan African Studies Dept 1971-; dir of fac & students affairs Pan African SD 1984-86; life mem NAACP 1972; bd dir NAACP San Fernando Valley 1973-74; pres United Crusade Fnd 1982-. **HONORS/ACHIEVEMENTS:** Phelp Stokes Flw 1966-69; Phi Delta Kappa Prof Org 1977-; Black Educ Commissioner LAUSD 1972-82; Black Urban & Ethnic Dir 1972-; African Studies Assc 1971-. **BUSINESS ADDRESS:** Prof of Business Econ Educ, CA StateUniv Northridge, 18111 Nordhoff St, 18111 Nordhoff St, Northridge, CA 91330.

O'BRYAN, JAMES ALVANLEY, JR.
Senator. **PERSONAL:** Born Jun 07, 1956, St Thomas, VI. **EDUCATION:** Boston Univ Sch of Public Communication, BS 1978. **CAREER:** Luis Millin Campaign Comm, campaign mgr 1978; Lt Gov of the Virgin Islands, special aide 1979-83; Legislature of the VI, senator 1985-87; Just A Thought Amusement, pres 1981-84. **BUSINESS ADDRESS:** Consultant, Just A Thought Amusement Inc, 392 Annas Retreat, St Thomas, Virgin Islands of the United States 00801.

O'BRYANT, JOHN D.
Association executive. **PERSONAL:** Born Jul 15, 1931, Boston, MA; married Cicily; children: John, James, Richard, Paul, Bruce. **EDUCATION:** Boston Univ, BS 1952, MEd 1956; State Coll at Boston, attended. **CAREER:** Boston Publ Schools, teacher, guidance counselor 1954-69; Tufts Univ Inst for Teachers of Disadvantaged Youth, assoc dir 1964-65; Urban Ed Prog Simmons Coll Grad School of Ed, instr 1967-72; Upward Bound Prog Northeastern Univ, dir of counseling & guidance 1966-74; Harvard Univ School of Publ Health, lecturer 1971-72; Simmons Coll Grad School of Soc Work, lecturer 1974; Boston School Comm, vp; NE Univ of Boston, vp. **ORGANIZATIONS:** Co-chmn Ed Counseling Comm Boston NAACP 1964-; pres Bridge Fund Inc 1970-; chmn Scholarship Fund for Black Studied, United Church of Christ 1970-; formerpres Black Black Educators Alliance of MA 1971-; pres Governor's Adv Bd Roxbury Comm Coll 1972-; mem bd of trustees Boston Hosp for Women 1973-; past treas MA Publ Health Assoc, Amer Publ Health Assoc,; chmn Council of Urban Bds of Ed, Natl School Bds Assoc 1983-85. **HONORS/ACHIEVEMENTS:** Awd of Merit for Disting Publ Serv Youth Activities Comm Office of Mayor Boston 1966; Citation of Merit Boston Br NAACP 1966; Cert of Merit Graham Jr Coll 1968; Champion of Black Youth Awd 1970; Citizen of the Year Black Big Brothers Alliance Boston 1974. **MILITARY SERVICE:** AUS corpl 1952-54. **BUSINESS ADDRESS:** Vice President Student Affairs, NEUniv of Boston, 360 Huntington Ave, Boston, MA 02115.

O'BRYANT, TILMON BUNCHE
Administrator. **PERSONAL:** Born Aug 14, 1920, Edgefield, SC; son of Lawrence O'Bryant and Annie O'Bryant; married Deidre. **EDUCATION:** Amer Univ, 1967-70; FBI Natl Acad, graduate; Fed City Coll, MEd 1971. **CAREER:** Gen Acct Office, clerk 1954-57; Washington Technical Inst, teacher Police Admin, conducted promotional examination preparatory classes 1958-63, constructed entire promotional examination for Metropolitan Police Dept 1967; Metro Police Dept, plainclothes officer 1952-57, patrolman 1952-57, detective lieutenant 1960-62; detective captain 1966-68, uniformed captain 1968, inspector 1968-69. dept chief of police in command of patrol div 1969, dept chief of police for personnel & training 1970-73, asst chief of police field operations 1973-74, asst chief of police 1974-. **ORGANIZATIONS:** Chmn Friends for Help for Retarded Children 1962; US Senate Advisory Panel on Armed Violence in Urban Areas 1969; bd of dirs Police & Community Relations Commn, Natl Conf of Christians & Jews 1970; mem Pigskin & Kiwanis Clubs 1971-; supvr, civic training, dir, bd of dirs Minority Recruiting in Law Enforcement 1974; pres bd of dirs 12th St YMCA; speaker Univ Pennsylvania, Mansfield Coll, Univ Wisconsin, Amer Univ, George Washington Univ, Univ of Miami; civic, business & serv orgs & chs on Modern Concept of Law Enforcement in Urban Soc. **HONORS/ACHIEVEMENTS:** Police Dept Honorary Mention Award 1950; Protective Community Award by Washington Bd of Trade 1966; Washington DC Commr Oral Commendation for Outstanding Police Work 1968; Metropolitan Womens' Democratic Club Man of the Year Award 1971; over 100 letters of commendation from White House, business, religious & civic leaders. **MILITARY SERVICE:** AUS 1943-45.

O'CONNOR, RODNEY EARL
General dentist. **PERSONAL:** Born Jun 25, 1950, Sharon, PA; son of Dr. Lauriston E. O'Connor and Helena B. McBride O'Connor; divorced; children: Elena Moi O'Connor. **EDUCATION:** Kentucky State Univ, Frankfort, KY, 1968-71; Univ of Kentucky, Lexington, KY, College of Dentistry, DMD, 1975; Eastman Dental Center, Rochester, NY, 1975-76; Rochester Institute of Technology, 1983—. **CAREER:** Rushville Clinic, dental consult 1976; Rochester Health Network, dental consult 1978-87; LE O'Connor AAS PC, vice pres. **ORGANIZATIONS:** Treas, Operation Big Vote, 1983; member, Acad of General Dentistry 1984-, Amer Dental Assoc, Natl Dental Assoc, Northeast Regional Dental Board. **HONORS/ACHIEVEMENTS:** Strong Hospital Dental Research fellowship, 1972; abstract/patent search, "Method of Ultrasonic Pyrogenic Root Canal Therapy," 1976. **HOME ADDRESS:** 311 Aberdeen St, Rochester, NY 14619. **BUSINESS ADDRESS:** Vice President, LE O'Connor DDS PC, 503 Arnett Blvd, Rochester, NY 14619.

O'CONNOR, THOMAS F., JR.
City councilman. **PERSONAL:** Born Mar 16, 1947, New Bedford, MA. **EDUCATION:** Roger Williams Coll Bristol, RI, AA, BA 1975. **CAREER:** Ward II Providence, city councilman, sch committeeman 1973-79. **ORGANIZATIONS:** Mem ILA Local 1329; bd dir Afro Arts Cntr; bd dir S Providence Tutorial. **HONORS/ACHIEVEMENTS:** Recip 2 Purple Hearts, Vietnam; Biography, Leaders of Black Am, Harco Press 1973; Biography, Who's Who in Am 1973. **MILITARY SERVICE:** USMC 1966-70.

O'DANIEL, THERMAN BENJAMIN
Educator. **PERSONAL:** Born Jul 09, 1908, Wilson, NC; son of John Wesley O'Daniel and Ernestine Williams O'Daniel; married Lillian Gertrude Davis, Jun 04, 1935. **EDUCATION:** Lincoln Univ, BA 1930; Univ of PA, MA 1932; Univ of Ottawa, PhD 1956. **CAREER:** Allen Univ, Columbia SC, instr, 1933-34, asst prof, 1934-35, assoc prof, 1935-36, prof of Eng, head of Div of Lang and Lit, 1936-37, dean of Liberal Arts Coll, 1937-40, acting pres, 1939; Fort Valley St Coll, GA, assoc prof, 1940-43, prof of Eng, 1944-45, acting admin dean, registrar, 1945-46, head of Eng dept, 1946-52, registrar, dir of summer sch, 1952-55; Dillard Univ, New Orleans LA, assoc prof of Eng, 1955-56; Morgan State Univ, Baltimore MD, asst prof, 1956-63, assoc prof, 1963-67, prof of Eng, 1967-78. **ORGANIZATIONS:** Life mem Coll Lang Assn; NAACP; NEA; Modern Lang Assn; mem NCTE; Melville Soc; Assn for the Study of Afro-Am Life & Hist; Soc for the Study of Southern Lit, MD Council of Tchrs. **HONORS/ACHIEVEMENTS:** Gen Educ Fellowship, Univ of Chicago; Ford Foundn fellowship; Alice E. Johnson Memorial Fund Awd, Black Acad of Arts & Letters, 1972; author of intro, The Blacker the Berry, by Wallace Thurman, Collier, 1970; editor of Langston Hughes, Black Genius: A Critical Evaluation, Morrow, 1971; author of James Baldwin: A Critical Evaluation, Howard Univ Pr, 1977; co-fndr, ed, College Language Assn Journal. **BUSINESS ADDRESS:** PO Box 480, Jefferson City, MO 65102. *

ODEN, GLORIA C.
Educator, poet. **PERSONAL:** Born Oct 30, 1923, Yonkers, NY; married John Price Bell. **EDUCATION:** Howard Univ, BA 1944, JD 1948; NY Univ, grad study. **CAREER:** Amer Inst of Physics, editor 1961-66; Inst of Electric & Electronic Engrs, sr editor 1966-67; Appleton-Century-Crofts, supr 1967-68; Holt Rinehart & Winston, proj dir for language arts books 1968-71; Univ of MD Baltimore, assoc prof, prof of english. **ORGANIZATIONS:** Mem PEN, The Poetry Soc of Amer 1977; contrib to numerous poetry & literature anthologies; author of various articles published in magazines books; has given poetry readings at my colls & univs since 1966. **HONORS/ACHIEVEMENTS:** Creative Writing Fellowships John Hay Whitney Found 1955-57; Fellowship to Yaddo Saratoga Springs NY 1956; Breadloaf Writers Scholarship Middlebury College 1960; interviewed for Black Oral History Prog Fisk Univ Library 1973; listed in Dictionary of American Poets 1973; Living Black American Authors 1973; Intl Who's Who in Poetry 1974; Black Writers Past & Present 1975; The World Who's Who of Women 3rd ed. **BUSINESS ADDRESS:** Professor of English, Univ of MD Baltimore County, University of Maryland, Catonsville, MD 21228.

ODEN, WALTER EUGENE
Educator. **PERSONAL:** Born Feb 26, 1935, Stuart, FL; married Edith; children: Walter II, Darin. **EDUCATION:** Bethune-Cookman Coll, BS 1956; FL Atlantic Univ, MEd 1966; FL Atlantic, EdD 1975. **CAREER:** Brownsville Jr HS, principal 1955-68; Radio Station WSTU, ancr, dj; Univ of Miami, teacher 1956-63, dir 1963-66, principal 1966-67, consult 1967, guidance consult 1968-69, asst principal 1969; FL Atlantic Univ, asst prof 1971; FL Atlantic Univ, adj prof 1971-76; Jan Mann Oppty School North, principal 1982-. **ORGANIZATIONS:** Mem Phi Delta Kappa, 2nd Baptist Church, Omega Psi Phi, Bethune-Cookman Coll Alumni Assoc, Dade Cty Secondary School Principal Assoc. **HONORS/ACHIEVEMENTS:** Natl Assoc Secondary School Principal Plaque; Disting Serv Recruiting Students Bethune-Cookman Coll 1968; Outstanding Leadership CEEB Club Martin Co 1969;Listed in Personalities of the South; Outstanding Serv Plaque 1973; Dep Prin Amer School; Outstanding Serv Young Mens Prog Org 1975. **BUSINESS ADDRESS:** Principal, Jan Mann Oppty School North, 4899 NW 24th Ave, Miami, FL 33142.

ODOM, CAROLYN
Communications director. **PERSONAL:** Born Aug 31, 1944, Augusta, GA; daughter of P C Odom and Marjorie Odom. **EDUCATION:** Spelman Coll, BA (Hon roll) 1966; Amer Univ, MA Comm 1970. **CAREER:** Coll of Medicine & Dentistry of New Jersey, materials developer 1970; Minority Economic Devel Corp, admin asst, Educ 1971; New York City Addiction Serv Agency, deputy dir, public relations, community info 1972-76; Natl Health Council, asst dir, communications coordinator 1976-77; Earl G Graves Ltd, dir, public affairs 1977-83; Corporate Communications, vice pres 1983-, sr vice pres 1987-. **ORGANIZATIONS:** Bd of dirs Natl Black Child Devel Inst; advisory council Natl Advisory Council on Minorities in Higher Educ, Univ of Oklahoma; co-chair Corporate Women's Roundtable, Spelman Coll; The EDGES Group; Women in Communications. **HONORS/ACHIEVEMENTS:** Natl French Hon Soc Pi Delta Phi 1963; YWCA Acad of Women Achievers 1984; publications: "Talking with the Inner City" Public Relations Journal 1969, "The Enigma of Drug Abuse" Journal of Practical Nursing 1974. **BUSINESS ADDRESS:** Senior Vice President, Earl G Graves, Ltd, 130 Fifth Ave, New York, NY 10011.

ODOM, CLIFF LOUIS
Professional football player. **PERSONAL:** Born Sep 15, 1958, Beaumont, TX. **EDUCATION:** Attended Univ of TX at Arlington. **CAREER:** Cleveland, 1980-81; Oakland Raiders, 1982; Los Angeles Raiders, 1982; Baltimore Colts, 1982-84; Indianapolis, linebacker 1984-. **BUSINESS ADDRESS:** Linebacker, Indianapolis Colts, PO Box 24100, Indianapolis, IN 46224.

ODOM, STONEWALL, II
Public policy organization executive. **PERSONAL:** Born Nov 01, 1940, Petersburg, VA;

son of Stonewall Faison and Flossie Odom; married Marlena (Hines) Odom, Feb 29, 1989; children: Terrance, Jacqueline, Nicole, Stonewall III, Marlena, Marcus, Malcolm. **EDUCATION:** Attended John Jay Coll of Criminal Law. **CAREER:** Metropolitan Life, sales representative; City of New York, New York NY, police officer, 1965-73; Yonkers CORE, Yonkers NY, chmn, currently. **ORGANIZATIONS:** Mem, Sammuel H Dow Amer Legion Post #1017; master mason, James H Farrell Lodge; mem, Vietnam Veterans of Amer; coordinating mem, The Yonkers Crack Task Force; founder, chmn, Tower Soc Citizens for Responsible Govt, 1985-89. **HONORS/ACHIEVEMENTS:** Two Meritorious Awards, New York Police Dept, 1969-72; Chairman of Veterans Comm for the Yonkers Branch of the NAACP, 1986; Ethiopian Orthodox Church Public Award, 1988; ran for The New York State Assembly on the Conservative Line and Right to Life (received 7,000) votes), 1988. **MILITARY SERVICE:** US Army, Sp4, Airborn, 1961-64. **HOME ADDRESS:** 79 Oak St, Yonkers, NY 10701. **BUSINESS ADDRESS:** Chairman, Yonkers CORE, PO Box 467, Yonkers, NY 10703-0467.

ODOM, VERNON LANE, JR.
TV correspondent, broadcast journalist. **PERSONAL:** Born Sep 16, 1948, Atlanta, GA. **EDUCATION:** Columbia Univ NYC, Broadcast Journalism Course 1970; Morehouse Coll Atlanta, BA 1970. **CAREER:** WSB Radio Atlanta, radio, newsman 1970; WXIA-TV Atlanta,TV newsman, anchorman 1970-76; WPVI-TV Channel 6 Philadelphia, 1976-. **ORGANIZATIONS:** Chmn bd of dir Philadelphia Assoc of Black Journalists 1976-; mem Natl Assoc of Black Journalists 1976-. **HONORS/ACHIEVEMENTS:** Media Man of the Year Award, Atlanta Assoc of Media Women 1972; Comm Serv Awd Philadelphia UNCF Alumni Assoc 1979; Comm Serv Awd Philadelphia Assoc of Black Accountants 1980. **BUSINESS ADDRESS:** WPVI-TV Channel 6, 4100 City Line Ave, Philadelphia, PA 19131.

ODOMS, WILLIE O.
Data processing consultant. **PERSONAL:** Born Mar 03, 1950, Eatonton, GA; son of Willie Cleve Odoms and Helen Reid Odoms; married Paulette Copel, Jul 25, 1987; children: Antoinette, Cristy Helena, A'seem Evans. **EDUCATION:** Clayton State Coll, Morrow GA, AA, 1974; Dekalb Community Coll, Clarkston GA, AS, 1981; Brenau Professional Coll, Gainesville GA, BS, 1989. **CAREER:** State of Georgia, Atlanta GA, planner, 1981-84; Information Systems of Amer, Atlanta GA, product specialist, 1984-86; Equifax Inc, Atlanta GA, sr planner, 1986-89; Odoms Contracting Serv Inc, Ellenwood GA, consultant, 1989-. **ORGANIZATIONS:** Pres, Black Data Processing Assoc Inc, Atlanta Chapter, 1988-. **HONORS/ACHIEVEMENTS:** DOAs Commissioner's Award, State of Georgia, 1983. **MILITARY SERVICE:** US Army, sergeant first class, 1968-71; Vietnam Campaign Medal, 1971; Arcom, 1970-71. **HOME ADDRESS:** 3693 Windmill Rd, Ellenwood, GA 30049.

O'DONNELL, LORENA MAE
Educational administration, clergyman. **PERSONAL:** Born May 01, 1929, Cincinnati, OH; children: Alena. **EDUCATION:** Univ of Cincinnati, BS Ed 1951; Miami Univ, ME 1960; Yale Univ, Post Grad 1972; Nova Univ, EdD 1976. **CAREER:** Cincinnati Publ Schools, teacher 1951-61, personnel assoc 1961-65, suprv 1965-69; North Avondale School, principal 1969-72; Cincinnati Public Schools, dir of staff devel 1972-81; Hillcrest School, chaplain 1982-; Cincinnati Bd of Ed, past pres, member. **ORGANIZATIONS:** Ed consult 1960-; dir Hamilton Cty State Bank 1976-; 1st black female mem Cincinnati Bd of Ed 1980-; dir Franchise Devel Inc 1980-; partner Loram Entr 1981-83; dir Red Cross Adv Bd 1981-; mem Juvenile Court Review Bd 1981-86. **HONORS/ACHIEVEMENTS:** God in the Inner City Juv Regilious Book 1970; God is Soul Juv Religious Book 1971; Kellogg Found Grant Yale Univ 1972; Grand Deputy Dist 6 State of OH, OES Amaranth Grand Chap 1985; One of Ten 1986 Enquirer's Women of the Year. **BUSINESS ADDRESS:** Member, Cincinnati Board of Education, 230 E 9th St, Cincinnati, OH 45202.

O'FERRALL, ANNE F.
Educator. **PERSONAL:** Born Jun 28, 1906, Marshall, TX; daughter of Mack Flowers (deceased) and Ardella Dawson Flowers (deceased); married Ernest B O'Ferrall, Sep 03, 1938. **EDUCATION:** Bishop Coll, BS; Univ of So CA, BS Ed, MS Math 1962, MS Ed 1963; FL A&M Univ, USC Educ of Mentally Retarded. **CAREER:** LA Unified Sch District, math teacher, teacher of trainable mentally retarded; Dade Co Miami, FL, math & sci tchr; English Enterprises, bookkeeper/accountant, 1944-; LA City School System, teacher, 1958-81. **ORGANIZATIONS:** Natl Council of Negro Women; past sec & vice pres United Nation Assn, LA; mem LA World Affairs Council; NAACP Legal Defense & Educ Fund; mem Freedom from Hunger Com; mem Comm Relations Conf of So CA; sec CA State Council UN Assn; mem, Phi Delta Gamma, Omicron Chap Univ So CA; UNA, Pasadena, 1st vice pres; bd mem, Community Relations Conf, Southern California. **HONORS/ACHIEVEMENTS:** Cit of outstdng serv LA Co Conf on Comm Relations 1954; Outstanding Women of Yr in Intl Relations, LA Sentinel 1958; Certificate of Merit, Zeta Phi Beta 1956; UNICEF chmn/del to Biennial Conv UNA-USA 1977; Cert of Merit, appreciation, outstanding serv & devotion to volunteer duty, Vet Admin 1951, 1953, 1955, 1958.

OFFICER, CARL EDWARD
City official. **PERSONAL:** Born Apr 03, 1952, St Louis, MO. **EDUCATION:** Western Coll of Miami Univ Oxford OH, BA Pol Sci, Philosophy 1974; So IL Univ Carbondale, Mortuary Sci 1975. **CAREER:** St Clair Cty IL, dep coroner 1975-77; State of IL, dept dir driver serv 1977-79; Officer Funeral Home E St Lois IL, vice pres 1970-; City of E St Louis IL,mayor 1979-. **ORGANIZATIONS:** Chmn subcom on intergov affairs US Conf of Mayors; founder chmn Metro- E Conf of Black Mayors; mem Sigma Phi Sigma; life mem Kappa Alpha Psi, E St Louis Jaycees, NAACP. **HONORS/ACHIEVEMENTS:** Listed in Outstanding Young man of Amer 1979, Who's Who Among Black Amer 1979; Cert of Commendation Top Ladies of Distinction 1980; Humanitarian Awd Campbell Chapel AME Church 1980. **MILITARY SERVICE:** IL NG 2nd lt 2 yrs. **BUSINESS ADDRESS:** Mayor, City of East St Louis, 7 Collinsville Ave, East St Louis, IL 62201.

OFFUTT, NARDA JULIE
Attorney. **PERSONAL:** Born Jul 03, 1948, Normal, IL; married Gerald M Offutt. **EDUCATION:** Grinnell Coll Grinnell, IA, BA Biol 1969; Sch for Intl Training Brattleboro, VT, earned 6 credits in spoken Japanese 1970; IL State Univ Normal, IL, course of study microbiology 1970; Georgetown Univ Law Center, JD 1975. **CAREER:** US Info Agency Exhibit in the Soviet Union, Russian speaking guide 1972; Sen Adlai E Stevenson III Wash, DC, legislative aide 1973-74; US Dept Justice Appellate Sect Tax Div Wash, DC, law clerk 1974-75; The Northern Trust Co Chicago, IL, staff attorney 1976; Robert Levin Chicago, IL, attorney 1976; US Attorney's Office Chicago, IL, asst US attorney 1977-80; Private Practice, attorney 1980-83; Hill, Hubbard, Cole & Couch Chicago, IL, attorney 1983-84; attorney. **ORGANIZATIONS:** Mem Dist of Columbia Bar Assn 1975; mem Supreme Court of IL Bar 1976-; mem US Court of Appeals for the Seventh Circuit Bar 1977-; poll watcher Project LEAP Chicago, IL 1982-83; tutor "Get in the Know" Comm Tutorial Prog Evanston, IL 1980-81; mem US Dist Court for the Northern Dist of IL 1977-. **HONORS/ACHIEVEMENTS:** Cast Wennetka Comm Theater "Brigadoon" 1978; 1st violinist Pit Orchestra Chicagoland Theatrical Troupe Productions 1981-82; 1st violinist Skokie Vallye Symphony Orch 1981-86; 1st violinist "Do It-Yourself Messiah" Orchestra Marg Hillis Conductor Orch Hall Chicago IL 1983-84; violinist Univ of Chicago Symphony Orch Barbara Schubert Conductor 1987-.

O'FLYNN-THOMAS, PATRICIA
Business executive. **PERSONAL:** Born Jul 28, 1939, E St Louis, IL; daughter of James E O'Flynn and Margarette O'Flynn; divorced; children: Terence, Todd. **EDUCATION:** Southern IL Univ, BS 1963; Univ of WI Milwaukee, MA 1973; St Martins Acad, Hon Doct 1983. **CAREER:** Natl Newspaper Publishers Assn, pres 1987-, 2nd vice pres secy 1983-86; Milwaukee Minority C of C, dir 1986; Milwaukee NAACP; dir 1983; Milwaukee Community Journal Inc, newspaper publisher. **ORGANIZATIONS:** Founder Eta Phi Beta Milwaukee Chap 1976; founder Milwaukee Comm Pride Expo 1976; mayoral appt Lakefront Design Comm 1979; founder Milwaukee Chap Squaws1980; gov appt Comm of Small Business 1980; dir Milwaukee Chap of PUSH 1980; del White House Comm 1980. **HONORS/ACHIEVEMENTS:** Publisher of the Year NNPA 1986. **BUSINESS ADDRESS:** Publisher, Milwaukee Community Journal, 3612 N Martin L King Dr, Milwaukee, WI 53212.

OGLESBY, JAMES ROBERT
Higher education administrator. **PERSONAL:** Born May 30, 1941; married Barbara; children: James R Jr, Regina, David. **EDUCATION:** SC State Coll, BS 1966; Univ of Missouri-Columbia, MEd 1969, PhD 1972. **CAREER:** Jefferson Jr High School, classroom teacher; Univ of Missouri-Columbia, graduate research asst 1969-70, graduate teaching asst 1970-71, coord of space & facilitiesand asst prof of educ 1972-74, asst prof of educ and asst provost for admin 1974-80, asst prof of educ and dir facilities utilization 1980-. **ORGANIZATIONS:** Guest lecturer for educ courses Univ of MO-Columbia 1972-; bd dirs Columbia Day Care Corp 1973-; mem Bd of Educ Columbia MO 1974-; mem MO State Teacher's Assoc 1974-; mem Natl Sch Bd Assoc 1976-, MO School Bd Assoc 1977- (holding various positions and serving on numerous bds in both assocs); sec Bd of Trustees Columbia Coll 1978-; mem Ambassador Club 1982-; comm develop consultant on Educ and Politics for Minneapolis MN; consultant Task Force on Governance-Natl Sci Foundation; consultant site visitor Secondary Sch Recognition Program US Dept of Educ. **HONORS/ACHIEVEMENTS:** Published material includes "Education for the "Twenty First Century," Natl Science Foundation Comm on Public Educ 1983; grant received, Boone Country CommServ Council to partially fund a building addition for Columbia Day Care Corp, City of Columbia to fund a summer youth employment prog titled CARE. **MILITARY SERVICE:** AUS 2nd lt 2 yrs. **HOME ADDRESS:** 1441 N Countryshire Dr, Columbia, MO 65202. **BUSINESS ADDRESS:** Dir Facilities Utilization, University of Missouri, 310 Jesse Hall, Columbia, MO 65211.

OGLIVIE, BENJAMIN A.
Professional athlete. **PERSONAL:** Born Feb 11, 1949, Colon, Panama;married Tami; children: Trianni, Benjamin. **EDUCATION:** Bronx Community Coll; NortheasternUniv Boston; Wayne StateUniv Detroit. **CAREER:** Boston Red Sox, outfielder 1971-73; Detroit Tigers, outfielder 1974-77; Milwaukee Brewers, outfielder 1978-. **HONORS/ACHIEVEMENTS:** Harvey Kuenn Award 1978; tied for the Home Run Title 1980; named to several post-season All-Star Teams 1980; Silver Slugger Team The Sporting News 1980; namedto the All-Star Team 1980, 1982-83; ranks in every Brewer category on the All-Time Top Ten Hitting List 1983. **BUSINESS ADDRESS:** Outfielder, Milwaukee Brewers, Milwaukee County Stadium, Milwaukee, WI 53214.

OH, HARRY K.
Business executive. **PERSONAL:** Born Oct 03, 1935, Korea; married Soon Jean; children: Richard, Philip. **EDUCATION:** Univ PA, BS 1958; George Washington Univ, MEE 1961. **CAREER:** Harry K Oh & Assocs, pres; OH & Chen Assoc, pres. **ORGANIZATIONS:** Mem Natl Soc of Professional Engrs 1965; mem MD Soc of Professional Engrs 1965. **HONORS/ACHIEVEMENTS:** Natl Medal Korea 1975. **BUSINESS ADDRESS:** President, Harry K Oh & Assocs, 11900 Parklawn Dr, Rockville, MD 20852.

O'HARA, LEON P.
Clergyman, oral surgeon. **PERSONAL:** Born May 13, 1920, Atlanta; married Geraldine Gore; children: Scarlett, Leon, Michael, Jeri, Mark, Miriam. **EDUCATION:** Talladega Coll, AL, BA, BS 1942; Meharry Med Col, DDS 1945; Washington U, first Negro, post-grad Sch 1952; Providential Theol Sem, DD. **CAREER:** Oral surgeon, St Louis 1945-; Holy Metro Bapt Ch, fdr, pastor 1955-; City of St Louis, pub health oral surg. **ORGANIZATIONS:** Vp, pres Mound City Dental Soc 1952-56; pres Midwestern States Dental Soc; staff mem St Mary's Hosp, Peoples Hosp, Faith Hosp, Christian Hosp; mem, commr St Louis Mayor's Council on Human Relations; chmn Way Out Drug Abuse Prgm; parole adv Penal Adoption Prgm; bd dirs Urban League, St Louis; bishop Indep Peng Assemblies Chs; Omega Psi Phi; West Urban Renewal Dirs 1968-70; life mem NAACP; former mem CORE; former mem Ecumenical Coun of Chs. **HONORS/ACHIEVEMENTS:** Pub Serv Award, 25 yrs svc, Pres Johnson; 8-state shotgun skeet shooting champ 1966; ETO Tennis Champ 1947; Ft Monmouth Tennis Champ (singles & doubles) 1945; Who's Who in Midwest. **MILITARY SERVICE:** AUS maj Dental Corps 1943-48. **BUSINESS ADDRESS:** Mound City Med Center, 2715 Union Blvd, St Louis, MO 63113.

O'KAIN, MARIE JEANETTE
Educator. **PERSONAL:** Born in Magnolia, AR; married Roosevelt O'Kain; children: Gregory L. **EDUCATION:** Univ of AR Pine Bluff, BS (cum laude) 1953-59; Univ of MO St Louis, MEd 1968-71, Specialist 1981-82; St Louis Univ, Advanced Graduate Study toward Doctorate. **CAREER:** St Louis Co Elem Public School, teacher 1960-75, principal 1975-81; MINACI Inc/Job Corps, consultant 1982; St Louis Co Public School, unified studies lecturing and curriculum develop 1982-. **ORGANIZATIONS:** Mem Assn of Elem Sch Principals 1975-84; Alternate Prof Liability Review Bd 1978-80; alderwoman 3rd wd city of Pine Lawn MO 1979-; mem Welfare Bd 1979-; mem Parks & Recreation Comm 1979-; mem Streets &

Lights Comm 1979-; mem Re-districting Comm 1979-; mem Norhill Neighborhood Adv Council 1979-; dir Budget & Finance 1979-; dir Public Relations 1979-; mem Conf of Educ; mem St Louis Univ Metro Coll Scholarship Selection Comm; mem St Louis Univ Metro College Upward Bound Adv Bd 1983-; mem Performance Based Teacher Eval Task Force, Human Rel Comm & Spec Activities; public speaker, pianist Church; pres Margaretta Block Unit #1. **HONORS/ACHIEVEMENTS:** Certificate three consecutive yrs Natl Guild of Piano Teachers 1967-69; Disting Serv Awd Teachers Assn St Louis 1970; Key Principal Awd Elem Principals Assn 1975-81; cert of appreciation 1st Congressional District 1980; meritorious cert Chap 9 OES Eastern Star 1980. **HOME ADDRESS:** 6032 Margaretta, Pine Lawn, MO 63120. **BUSINESS ADDRESS:** Administrator, Parkway Public Schools, 6250 Forest Ave, Pine Lawn, MO 63120.

O'KAIN, ROOSEVELT
City official. **PERSONAL:** Born Aug 21, 1933, Clarendon, AR; married Marie J Haymon; children: Gregory Lynn. **EDUCATION:** Forest Park Comm Coll, A 1973; Harris Teachers Coll, BS Educ 1978. **CAREER:** US Post Office, carrier 1965; City of Pine Lawn, alderman 1973-79; Pine Lawn MO, mayor. **ORGANIZATIONS:** Mem Bd of Jail Visitors St Louis Co 1977; mem Cit Adv Bd Job Corp Ctr 1978; mem bd of dir Normandy Council 1980. **HONORS/ACHIEVEMENTS:** Awd of Appreciation St Louis Job Corps Ctr 1980. **MILITARY SERVICE:** AUS pfc 1953-55; Good Conduct Medal & Natl Def Ribbon. **BUSINESS ADDRESS:** Mayor, City of Pine Lawn, 6250 Forest Ave, Pine Lawn, MO 63121.

OKHAMAFE, E. IMAFEDIA
Educator. **PERSONAL:** Son of Obokhe Okhamafe and Olayemi Okhamafe. **EDUCATION:** Purdue Univ, PhD, Philosophy, English, 1984. **CAREER:** Univ of NE at Omaha, prof of Humanities 1985-. **ORGANIZATIONS:** GRE/LSAT consultant; humanities consultant; area chair Popular Culture Assoc. **HONORS/ACHIEVEMENTS:** Purdue Univ David Ross Fellow 1983; Natl Endowment for the Humanities Summer Fellow 1985; Humanities Grant from Andrew W Mellon Foundation 1985; Natl Endowment for the Humanities summer grant 1987 for workshop on humanities for non-traditional students; articles have appeared in periodicals such as Black Scholar, Journal of the British Soc for Phenomenology, UMOJA, Intl Journal of Social Educ, Auslegung, Rsch in African Literatures, Soundings, Philosophy Today, Africa Today and The Omaha Star; presented papers at such institutions as Univ of TX at Austin, Ohio Univ, Miami (of Ohio) Univ, and MI State Univ. **BUSINESS ADDRESS:** Prof of Humanities, Univ of NE-Omaha, Annex 39, Omaha, NE 68182-0208.

OKORE, CYNTHIA ANN
Social worker. **PERSONAL:** Born Nov 15, 1945, Philadelphia, PA; daughter of William Reed (deceased) and Jessie M Reed; married Caleb J Okore; children: Elizabeth A. **EDUCATION:** Cheyney Univ, BA 1974; Rutgers Univ, M of Social Work 1981. **CAREER:** JFK Mental Health/Mental Retardation, social worker 1981-84; Veterans Administration, social worker 1984-. **ORGANIZATIONS:** Therapist private practice; mem Philadelphia Chap of Social Workers 1979-, Natl Assoc of Social Workers 1979-; Notary Public; Natl Assn of Black Alcoholism Counselors 1989-90. **HONORS/ACHIEVEMENTS:** Public Service Awd Knights of Columbus St Benedict the Moor Council 1986. **HOME ADDRESS:** 5543 Windsor Ave, Philadelphia, PA 19143. **BUSINESS ADDRESS:** Social Worker/Family Therapist, Veterans Admin Medical Center, 39th & Woodland Ave, Philadelphia, PA 19104.

OKUNOR, SHIAME
Educator. **PERSONAL:** Born Jun 03, 1937, Accra, Ghana;son of Benjamin Okunor and Dorothea Okunor; children: Dorothy Ometse. **EDUCATION:** New York Univ, Certificate 1968; Grahm Jr College, AAS 1971; The Univ of NM, BA Speech Communications 1973, MPA 1975, PhD 1981. **CAREER:** The University of NM, afro-amer studies 1981-82, dir academic affairs afro-amer studies 1982-, acting dean univ coll 1985-86, dean general coll 1986-, asst prof educ found, dean and dir, Acting Assoc Dean Graduate Studies 1988-89. **ORGANIZATIONS:** Mem exec bd NAACP 1975-86; mem Affirmative Action Comm; bd of dirs, presNM Sickle Cell 1981-85. **HONORS/ACHIEVEMENTS:** Outstanding Sr Awd 1971; Outstanding Intl Awd 1971; listed in Who's Who in Amer Univs & Colls 1975-76; Pres Recognition Awd Univ of NM 1981, 82, 83, 84, 85; AP Appreciation Awd Albuquerque Public Schools 1981; Comm Serv Awd NAACP 1982; WM Civitan Merit Awd 1984; Black Communication Serv Awd 1984; Presidency Awd Schomburg Ctr New York City 1985,86; NM Sec of State Cert of Apprec 1985; NM Assoc of Bilingual Teachers Awd 1986; US Military Airlift Command Cert of Recognition 1987; Cert of Apprec US Corps of Engrs 1987. **BUSINESS ADDRESS:** Acting Assoc Dean of Graduate Studies &, Dir, Afro-Amer Studies, Albuquerque, NM 87131.

OKWUMABUA, BENJAMIN NKEM
Business executive. **PERSONAL:** Born Jun 20, 1939, Issele-Uku, Nigeria;married Constance Lee; children: Benjamin Nkem Jr, Obiamaka P, Richard Ikeduba, Daniel Ikeduba. **EDUCATION:** Central State Univ Wilberforce, OH, BS 1967; MI State Univ, E Lansing, MI, MBA & MLIR 1969-71; MI State Univ, E Lansing, MI, PhD 1974. **CAREER:** MI State Univ, asst prof 1969-71; Saginaw Valley St Coll, chairman prof 1971-75; Gen Motors Corp Oldsmobile Div, area sales mgr 1975-78; AFRO-LECON, Inc Watson Ind Div; pres & CEO 1978-. **ORGANIZATIONS:** Member Academy of Management, 1974; President Greater Jamestown Area Minorita Leadership Assoc, 1983; member NY StateGovernors Advisory cncl on Minority Business, 1983; member WNY Regional Econ Deve Cncl 1984. **HONORS/ACHIEVEMENTS:** Beta Gamma Signa MI State Univ 1971; Sigma Iota Epsilon MI State Univ E Lansing 1974; Black Achievers in Industry 1983. **BUSINESS ADDRESS:** President/Chief Exec Officer, AFRO-LECON, Inc Watson Ind, 335 Harrison St Box 1028, Jamestown, NY 14702.

OLAJUWON, AKEEM CHARLES
Professional athlete. **PERSONAL:** Born Jan 21, 1963, Lagos, Nigeria. **EDUCATION:** Univ Houston, 1981-84. **CAREER:** Houston Rockets, center 1984-. **ORGANIZATIONS:** Played on the Nigerian Natl team in the All-African games as a 17-year old. **HONORS/ACHIEVEMENTS:** Voted Top Player of the 1983 Final Four; mem 2nd Team All-NBA; mem 36th & 37th NBA All Star Teams. **BUSINESS ADDRESS:** Houston Rockets, The Summit, Ste 510, Houston, TX 77046.

OLAWUMI, BERTHA ANN
Employment counselor. **PERSONAL:** Born Dec 19, 1945, Chicago, IL; married Aina M; children: Tracy, Tanya. **EDUCATION:** Thronton Comm Coll, AAS 1979; John Marshall Law School, Cert 1980; Governors State Univ, BA Human Justice 1981-. **CAREER:** Tinley Park Mental Health Ctr, mental health tech 1979; Robbins Juvenile Advocacy, juvenile advocate 1979-83; John Howard Assoc Prison Watch Group, intern student 1984; Minority Econ Resources Corp, employment spec/instr. **ORGANIZATIONS:** Mem chairperson Thornton Comm Coll Mental Health Club 1978-79; mem bd of dir Worth Twp Youth Serv 1981; mem 1981-83, pres 1982 Amer Criminal Justice Assoc; mem Blue Island Recreation Commiss 1982-84; bd mem School Dist 143 1/2. **HONORS/ACHIEVEMENTS:** Student Found Scholarship Awd Thornton Comm Coll 1979; Cert Cook Cty Sheriffs Youth Serv 1980; Cert Citizens Info Serv 1980; Cert Morraine Valley Comm Coll 1980; Cert St Xavier Coll 1981. **HOME ADDRESS:** 3032 West 140 St, Blue Island, IL 60406.

OLDHAM, ALGIE SIDNEY, JR.
Educator. **PERSONAL:** Born May 18, 1927, Dyersburg, TN; married Sarah Mae Graham; children: Roslynn Denise, Bryan Sidney. **EDUCATION:** TN State Univ Nashville, BA 1949; Univ of Notre Dame, MA 1954. **CAREER:** South Bend Comm School, elem principal 1966-75, asst high school principal 1975-83, principal 1975-; Riley High School, principal 1983-. **ORGANIZATIONS:** Mem Phi Delta Kappa Educ Frat, Natl Assoc of Secondary School and IN Principal's Assoc; adv bd Vocational/Special Educ Handicapped for South Bend Comm Schools; life mem NAACP; bd mem South Bend Police Merit Bd; life mem Kappa Alpha Psi Frat; Most Worshipful Grand Master Prince Hall Grand Lodge Jurisdiction of Indiana 1981-83; Deputy Orient of Indiana, Ancient Accepted Scottish Rite Prince hall Grand Lodge IN 1986. **HONORS/ACHIEVEMENTS:** Invited to the White House during President Carter's administration for conference on Energy 1980; Sovereign Grand Inspector General Ancient Accepted Scottish Rite Prince Hall Northern Jurisdiction 1980; first Black High School Principal South Bend IN 1983; elevated to 33 degree United Supreme Council AASR, PHA, NJ. **MILITARY SERVICE:** AUS supply sgt 1950-52. **HOME ADDRESS:** 1758 N Elmer St, South Bend, IN 46628. **BUSINESS ADDRESS:** Principal, James Whitcomb Riley H S, 405 E Ewing St, South Bend, IN 46613.

OLDHAM, JAWANN CHARLES
Professional athlete. **PERSONAL:** Born Jul 04, 1957, Seattle, WA. **EDUCATION:** Seattle Univ. **CAREER:** Denver Nuggets, center 1980-81; Houston Rockets, center 1981-82; Chicago Bulls, center 1982-. **HONORS/ACHIEVEMENTS:** One of three Bulls to shoot 500 or better from the field. **BUSINESS ADDRESS:** Chicago Bulls, 333 N Michigan Ave, Ste 510, Chicago, IL 60601.

OLIVER, AL
Professional athlete. **PERSONAL:** Born Oct 14, 1946, Portsmouth, OH; married Donna; children: Felisa, Aaron. **EDUCATION:** Kent State Univ, attended. **CAREER:** Los Angeles Dodgers, pitcher 1984; Philadelphia Phillies, 1984; Montreal Expos, 1982-83; Houston Astros, 1978-81; Pittsburgh Pirates, 1968-77. **ORGANIZATIONS:** Hit 300 for ninth consective season and 11th overall; collected the 2,500th hit of his career 1983; played 2,00th major league game 1983. **HONORS/ACHIEVEMENTS:** Natl League batting title with Expos 1982; tied Dale Murphy for NL RBI crown; First player in history to have 200 hits & 100 RBI in same season in both leagues (1980, TX, 1982, Montreal); Amer League record with 21 total bases in doubleheader 1980; Silver Bat offensive excellence at his position (OF) 1981, (DH) 1982); Seven career grand slams; named to The Sporting News NL All-Star team in 1975 & 1982.

OLIVER, DAILY E.
Educator. **PERSONAL:** Born Aug 05, 1942, Ft Devons, MA; married Mary E McConaughy; children: Brennen, Mona. **EDUCATION:** Univ of Utah, BS 1965; Univ of Utah, MEd 1973; Univ of Utah, PhD 1978. **CAREER:** Utah Board of Pardons, member 1979-83; Weber State College, dir Ethnic Stuies 1985. **ORGANIZATIONS:** Member Prof Ski Instructor of Amer 1964-. **MILITARY SERVICE:** UT Natl Guard staff sgt 1959-69. **HOME ADDRESS:** 735 E 800 S, Salt Lake City, UT 84102. **BUSINESS ADDRESS:** Dir Ethnic Studies, Weber State College, 3750 Harrison Blvd, Ogden, UT 84408.

OLIVER, FRANK LOUIS
State official. **PERSONAL:** Born Apr 15, 1922, Philadelphia, PA; married Wilma Wooden; children: Donna, Frank Jr, Shawn. **CAREER:** 29th Ward Dem Exec Comm, ward leader; Bd Educ, supr 15 yrs; state rep. **BUSINESS ADDRESS:** State Representative, 1205 N 29th St, Philadelphia, PA 19121.

OLIVER, JAMES L.
Automobile dealer. **PERSONAL:** Born Oct 02, 1934, Little Rock, AR; son of Willie Oliver and Jessie M McKinley; married Doreatha, Jun 1952; children: Cornell, Patricia, Cheryl, Barbra. **CAREER:** Faust Polishing, Chicago IL, foreman, 1952-65; United Saving Life Insurance, regional mgr, 1970-75; Self-Employed in Ice Cream Business, 1975-80; Bonnie Brook Ford, mgr, 1982-84; Willow Brook Ford, mgr, 1984-85; University Ford, owner, CEO, 1985-. **BUSINESS ADDRESS:** University Ford, 3403 N University St, Peoria, IL 61604.

OLIVER, JESSE DEAN
Elected official. **PERSONAL:** Born Nov 10, 1944, Gladewater, TX; married Gwendolyn Lee. **EDUCATION:** Dallas Baptist Univ, B Career Arts Mgmt 1976; Univ of TX Sch of Law, JD 1981. **CAREER:** Sanger Harris Dept Stores, asst dept mgr 1971-72, dept mgr 1972-73; Intl Bus Machines Corp, admin spec 1973-78; Univ of TX Sch of Law, student asst to assoc dean Byron Fullerton 1979-80; Mahomes Biscoe & Haywood, assoc atty 1981-83; Attorney at Law, practicing attorney 1983-; TX House of Reps, mem of 68th & 69th TX Legislature 1983-. **ORGANIZATIONS:** Adv comm mem Licensed Voc Nurses Assn; participant Information Seminar for Amer Opinion Leaders Hamburg & Berlin Germany 1983; participant Natl Forum onExcellence in Educ 1983; planning comm mem Secretarial Initiative on Teenage Alcohol Abuse Youth Treatment Regional Conf 1983; exec comm Mayor's Task Force on Housing & Economic Development in S Dallas 1983-84; participant 19th Annual Women's Symposium The Politics of Power & conscience 1984; mem Natl Ctr for Health Serv Rsch User Liaison Prog 1984; speaker TX Public Health Assn Conf 1984; speaker Natl Conf of State Legislators Conf on Indigent Health Care 1984; speaker TX Public Health Assn Conf. **HONORS/ACHIEVEMENTS:** "The Jesse Dean Oliver-Student Bar Assn Student Loan Fund" Honored by the Univ of TX; Perigrinus Awd for Outstanding Leadership TX Sch Student Bar Assn Bd of Govs; Student Bar Assn Bd of Govs Awd TX Sch of Law; Consul Awd

for Outstanding Serv to TX Sch of Law; Gene Woodfin Awd Univ of TX Sch of Law; J L Ward Disting Alumnus Awd Dallas Baptist Coll 1984; Certificates of Appreciation, East Garland Neighborhood Serv Ctr 1974 & 1975; Dallas Plans for Progress Youth Motivation Comm 1976 & 1977; Outstanding Young Men of Amer Awd 1981; Natl Fed of the Blind Progressive Chap 1983; TX State Council Natl Organ of Women 1983; Good St Baptist Church 1983; Harry Stone Middle Sch 1984; South Oak Cliff HS 1984; Dallas Independent Sch Dist Bus & Mgmt Ctr 1983, 1984. **BUSINESS ADDRESS:** Representative, TX House of Representatives, P O Box 2910, Austin, TX 78769.

OLIVER, JOHN J., JR.
Attorney. **PERSONAL:** Born Jul 20, 1945, Baltimore, MD. **EDUCATION:** Fisk U, BA 1969; ColumbiaUniv Sch of Law, JD 1972. **CAREER:** GE Information Serv Co, couns asst sec 1980-; Assigned Components GE Co Headquarter, couns 1978-80; Davis Polk & Wardwell, corp atty 1972-78. **ORGANIZATIONS:** Bd dir 1972-; chmn bd of trust Afro-Am Newspapers; mem Kappa Alpha Psi; asso mem Musm of Natl Hist; Columbia Law Sch Alum Assn. **HONORS/ACHIEVEMENTS:** Listed Who's Who Among Am Coll &Univ 1969-70. **BUSINESS ADDRESS:** Gen Electric Information Serv, 401 N Washington St, Rockville, MD 20850.

OLIVER, KENNETH NATHANIEL
Business executive. **PERSONAL:** Born Mar 06, 1945, Montgomery, AL; married Thelma G Hawkins; children: Tracey, Karen, Kellie. **EDUCATION:** Univ of Baltimore, BS 1973; Morgan State Univ, MBA 1980. **CAREER:** Equitable Bank NA, sr banking officer 1973-83; Coppin State Coll, asst prof; Devel Credit Fund Inc, vp. **ORGANIZATIONS:** Treas Baltimore Mktg Assoc; mem Baltimore Cty Private Ind Council, St of MD Advisory Bd, Walter P Carter Ctr. **MILITARY SERVICE:** AUS E-5 4 yrs. **HOME ADDRESS:** 8818 Greens Ln, Randallstown, MD 21133. **BUSINESS ADDRESS:** Vice President, Development Credit Fund Inc, 1925 Eutaw Pl, Baltimore, MD 21217.

OLIVER, MELVIN L.
Educator. **PERSONAL:** Born Aug 17, 1950, Pittsburgh, PA; son of Rev Loman Oliver and Ruby Oliver. **EDUCATION:** William Penn Coll, BA 1968-72; Washington Univ, MA 1972-74, Ph D 1975-77; Univ of MI, postdoctoral 1979. **CAREER:** Univ of MO, visiting asst prof 1977-78; UCLA, asst prof 1978-85, assoc prof 1985-. **ORGANIZATIONS:** UCLA Center for Afro-American Studies, faculty assoc 1978-; Resource Allocation Committee, mem 1981-86, chair 1986-. **HONORS/ACHIEVEMENTS:** Nat'l Fellowship Fund, dissertation fellow 1975-77; Ford Foundation, post doctoral fellowship 1982-83; Rockefeller Foundation, research fellow 1984-85; Natl Science Foundation Research, Initiation Planning Grant, 1988; Social Science Research Council Grant on the Black Underclass, 1989. **BUSINESS ADDRESS:** Assoc Professor of Sociology, UCLA, Dept of Sociology, Los Angeles, CA 90024.

OLIVER, WILLIAM HENRY
Labor business executive. **PERSONAL:** Born Jan 13, 1915, Chattanooga, TN; married Alice Suvilla Smith. **EDUCATION:** TN A&I State Coll, extension course sociology 1936. **CAREER:** Chattanooga World Newspaper, asst editor 1934; Ford Motor Co Dearborn, Ford 8-tenor 1937-39; UAW Local 400 Ford Motor Co Highland Park MI, rec sec 1942-44; UAW Natl Ford Dept Detroit, intl rep 1944-46; UAW Fair Practices & Anti-Discrimination Dept, dir 1946-80. **ORGANIZATIONS:** Natl coord Natl Com for Fair Play in Bowling 1946-50; bd mem Leadership Conf on Civil Rights 1950-80; bd mem Natl Housing Conf 1960-80; trustee Natl Urban League 1952-55; vice pres Natl NAACP 1967-80; pres NAACP Natl Housing Corp 1972-; pres NAACP Nevada Housing Develop Corp. **HONORS/ACHIEVEMENTS:** Hon Dr of Humanities Wilberforce Univ 1955; Urban League Awd Detroit Banch.

OLLEE, MILDRED W.
Educational administrator. **PERSONAL:** Born Jun 24, 1936, Alexandria, LA; married Henry P Ollee Jr; children: David Michael, Darrell Jacques. **EDUCATION:** Xavier Univ of LA, BA 1956; Univ of SW LA, Grad Courses 1960; Walla Walla Coll, Masters 1967; Univ of WA, Grad Work 1977-78. **CAREER:** Various cities in LA & WA schools, hs teacher 1956-62; George Washington Carver HS LA, soc sci lead teacher 1960-61; WA Assoc of Retarded Children WallaWalla Lillie Rice Activ Ctr for Youths & Adults, dir 1964-66; Walla Walla Cty Sup Ct, marriage counselor, therapist 1967; Walla Walla Comm Coll, instrfaculty 1968-70; Birdseye Frozen Foods Div of Gen Foods Walla Walla WA, consult 1968; Seattle Central Comm Coll dist VI, counselor faculty 1970-73, dir spec serv to disadv students 1973-; AIDP SSDE FIPSE Dept of HEW Office of Ed, consult 1977-80; Comm Coll Dist VI, assoc dean of students 1976-. **ORGANIZATIONS:** Bd mem Amer Red Cross Walla Walla 1962-64, Puget Sound Black Ed Assoc Seattle 1970-72; chmn pres search comm Seattle Central Comm Coll 1979; pres elect NASP, NW Assoc of Spec Prog Reg X 1979-81; mem Delta Sigma Theta, Citizens Transit Adv Comm, METRO Council 1979-80; area rep Fed Way Comm Council 1979-80. **HONORS/ACHIEVEMENTS:** Most Outstanding Young Coll Woman Awd, Xavier Univ 1956; Workshop Leader Compensatory Ed for the New Learner Univ of WA 1975; Co-author SSDS-TRIO Project Dir Manual Dept of HEW Office of Ed 1978; Presented paper "3 R's for Black Students, Recruitment Requirements & Retention" 4th Annual Conf of Council on Black Affairs. **BUSINESS ADDRESS:** Associate Dean of Students, Seattle Central Comm Coll, 1701 Broadway, Seattle, WA 98122.

OLLISON, IDA BELL
Retired educator. **PERSONAL:** Born Dec 30, 1926, Bayboro, NC; married Joseph Ollison; children: Joseph. **EDUCATION:** Elizabeth City State Univ, BS 1948; Temple Univ, grad studies 1951; Frankenton Ctr, certificate religious studies 1953; Bricks, certificate religious studies 1953; NC Central Univ, reading spec 1960; Wingate Coll, certificate religious studies 1964; Peace Coll, science workshop 1973. **CAREER:** Williamsburg Co Public Schs, teacher 1948-49; Pamlico Co Sch System, teacher 1949-79; NC Council of Churches, teacher (migrant children) 1960; Pamlico Tech Coll ABE, instructor 1965; Headstart, 1967-68-69. **ORGANIZATIONS:** Mem Sr Choir 1950-; dir/teacher Vacation Bible Sch 1964-84; finan sec Greenhill MB Church 1968-; mem Pamlico Co Bd of Health 1973-82; worthy matron Order of Eastern Star 1975-; pres New Bern Eastern Missionary Baptist Women's Auxiliary 1978; mem Pamlico Co Bd of Educ 1980-84; mem bd of trustees Pamlico Tech Coll 1981-; chairperson Bayboro Precinct of Democratic Party 1982-; mem Neuse River Council on Aging 1984-; mem bd of dirs Carteret Comm Action 1984-; volunteer Meals on Wheels 1986-; notary public; volunteer Caller for Pamlico Co Christian Aid Serv 1986-; commissioner, mayor pro-tem Bayboro Town. **HONORS/ACHIEVEMENTS:** Awd Amer Red Cross 1972; awd Amer Cancer Soc 1978-80; awd Bayboro Headstart Ctr 1981; Voter's League Awd Local Voters League 1981; Ambassador Extraordinary Order of Long Leaf Pine JB Hunt's Office 1981; Retired Teachers Awd Pamlico Cty Bd of Educ 1982; awd Mental Health Assn 1982-84. **HOME ADDRESS:** PO Box 216, Bayboro, NC 28515.

OLOGBONI, TEJUMOLA F. (ROCKIE TAYLOR)
Writer, editor. **PERSONAL:** Born May 02, 1945, Salina, KS; children: Charles, Olatoyin. **EDUCATION:** Univ of WI, BS 19668. **CAREER:** Mojo, owner; Unique Intl Magz for Men, editor 1975-; Olatunji, musician 1976-; WI Arts Cncl, poet 1973-76;Univ of WI, instr 1969-74; Domican Coll, lect 1971; Marquette U, lect 1969-70; Inner City Arts Cncl, dir of art 1969; Youth Opp Proj Comm Relation Bd, art dir 1968. **ORGANIZATIONS:** Mem Gov Comm for Children & Youth 1963; Alpha Phi Alpha Frat Black Petic Messg; bd mem WI Humanities Comm; mem Milwaukee Pub Museum Northside Writers Workshop De Gallery Art Gallery Inmate Outreach Conslr; lect Wales Sch for Boys 1972-73. **HONORS/ACHIEVEMENTS:** Hall of Fame W Div HS 1970; flwhp Fed Forg Lang 1968; Water Buffalo, WI State Fair Art Exhibit 1966. **BUSINESS ADDRESS:** MOJO, PO Box 16706, Milwaukee, WI 53216.

OLUGEBEFOLA, ADEMOLA
Artist. **PERSONAL:** Born in Virgin Islands. **CAREER:** Artist lectr works include vibrant cover designs & illustrations for leading authors pub by Doubleday, Broadside, William Morrow, Harper & Row, Am Museum ofNatrl History; has been in numerous major exhibitions over 15 yr period; had over 20 one man exhibitions; work is in collections throughout US, S Am, Africa, Caribbean. **ORGANIZATIONS:** Mem bd dirs Harlem Cultural Council; Inter-Am Artists Inc; Createadrama Cultrual Cntr; Benin Enterprises; chmn Educ Dept of Weusi Acad of Arts & Studies; natl vice pres NCA; served as consult to Mtro Museum of Art. **HONORS/ACHIEVEMENTS:** Won critical acclaim for innovative set designs for Lew Lafayette Theatre, NY Shakespeare Fest, Nat Black Theatre; working on several books including a biography. **BUSINESS ADDRESS:** Vice President, Gumbs & Thomas Publishers, Inc, 2067 Broadway, New York, NY 10023.

OMOLADE, BARBARA
Educator. **PERSONAL:** Born Oct 29, 1942, Brooklyn, NY; children: Kipchamba, Ngina, Eskimo, Krishna. **EDUCATION:** Queens Coll, BA 1964; Goddard Coll, MA 1980. **CAREER:** Ctr for the Elimination of Violence in the Family, co-dir 1977-78; Women's Action Alliance, 1979-81; Empire State Coll Ctr for Labor Studies, instructor 1980-81; WBAI Radio, producer/commentator 1981-83; CCNY-CWE, higher educ officer/adjunct faculty 1981-; freelance writer 1979-. **ORGANIZATIONS:** Bd mem Sisterhood of Black Single Mothers 1983-, Wellspring Foundation; co-founder CUNY Friends of Women Studies 1984-. **HONORS/ACHIEVEMENTS:** Unit Awds in Media Lincoln Univ of MO 1981; Malcolm X Awd The East 1982; Susan B Anthony Awd New York City Natl Org of Women 1987.

O'NEAL, CONNIE MURRY
Government official. **PERSONAL:** Born Oct 09, 1951, Detroit, MI; married Booker L. **EDUCATION:** MI State U, BS 1973, MA 1976. **CAREER:** MI Dept of Transportation, Bur of Urban & Mass Pub Trans, adminstr govtl relations & consumer affairs; Gov Milliken's Ofc, policy/legisltv liaison to MI Hs of Reps 1979; MI Hs of Reps, legisltv analyst rep caucus of MI 1977-79; Gov Milliken, dir vol for gubernatorial candidacy 1978; Greater Lansing Urban League, dir of comm devel 1976-77; Cath Orgn, community orgr 1973-74. **ORGANIZATIONS:** Pres Ctr of Urban Affairs MI StateUniv 1976-77; bd of trustees Fam & Child Serv 1976-; del at lg Nat Women Polit Caucus 1979-; bd mem Am Soc for Pub Adminstrn 1980; mem Urban League Guild 1978-; life mem NAACP 1978-; co-chmn MI ERAmerica 1979; v-chmn Ingham Co Rep Party 1979. **BUSINESS ADDRESS:** State Capitol, Lansing, MI 48909.

O'NEAL, EDDIE S.
Clergyman. **PERSONAL:** Born Mar 28, 1935, Meridian, MS; married Onita; children: Vallerie, Eddie III, Nancy, Michael. **EDUCATION:** Tougaloo So Christian Coll, AB 1963; Andover Newton Theol Sch, BD 1967, STM cum laude 1969, DMin 1972. **CAREER:** Peoples Bapt Church, assoc minister; Clinton Ave Bapt, co-pastor; Myrtle Bapt, pastor; St Mark Congrtnl, assoc pastor; Mt Olive Bapt Ch, pastor; PineGrv Bapt Ch, pastor; Andover Newton Theol Sch, prof;, reverend, doctor. **ORGANIZATIONS:** Chmn Black Studies Comm of the Boston Theol Inst 1970-76; ministries to Blks in Higher Edn; Interfaith Coun on Ministry & Aging; Rockefeller Protestant Flwshp Prgm; trustee Andover Newton Theol Sch; auditor /parl United Bapt Conv of MA & RI; mem Nat Com of Blk Chmen; mem Soc for the Study of BlkRelgn; mem City Missionary Soc of Boston; mem Am Bapt Conv; mem NAACP; mem Omega Psi Phi Frat; consult Women's Serv Club. **HONORS/ACHIEVEMENTS:** Rockefeller Protestant Fellowship 1962-66; Woodrow Wilson Flwshp 1963; Who's Who in AmUniv & Coll 1963; Key to the City of Newton, MA 1969; Outst Young Menof Am 1970; articles Christian Century 1971; Andover Newton Quar 1970. **BUSINESS ADDRESS:** Reverend, Doctor, Andover Newton Theol School, 210 Herrick Rd, Newton, MA 02159.

O'NEAL, FREDERICK DOUGLAS
Actor, director, lecturer, retired trade union executive. **PERSONAL:** Born Aug 27, 1905, Brooksville, MS; son of Ransome James O'Neal and Ninnie Bell Thompson; married Charlotte Talbot Hainey, Apr 19, 1942. **EDUCATION:** New Theatre Schl NY; Amer Theatre Wing NY; Brooksville Elementry School Brooksvill Miss; High School St Louis Public School. **CAREER:** Actor dir lecturer theatre motion pictures radioTV since 1927; Southern IL Univ, visiting prof 1962; Clark Clge, visiting prof 1963; Actors' Equity Assc, pres 1964-73. **ORGANIZATIONS:** Intl pres Assc Actors & Artistes of Amer 1970-89; pres emeritus Actors' Equity Assc 1973; vice pres AFL/CIO 1969-; chmn AFL/CIO Civil Rights Comm 1970-; pres 1979-81, pres emeritus 1981 Catholic Interracial Council; chrmn Harlem Cultural Council Adv Bd vice pres Catholic Actors' Guild; adv consult Fnd for Extension & Dev of Amer Prof Theatre; vice pres A Philip Randolph Inst; pres emeritus Schomburg Corp 1978; secr treas African-Amer Labor Ctr 1974-; co-chrmn Natl Urban League Labor Adv Council; co-chrmn NAACP Ad Hoc Labor Comm; bd mem & secy AmerTheatre Wing; bd mem Sickle Cell Anemia Fnd of Greater NY; bd mem & secy Muscular Dystrophy Assc Inc; bd mem Inst for Adv Studies in Theatre Arts; bd mem AFL/CIO Labor Studies Ctr bd mem Natl Comm on US/China Rel; bd mem League for Industrial Democracy; bd mem Actors' Fund of Amer; mem Adv Bd Amer Vets Comm; bd mem UN Dev Corp; bd mem Asian/Amer Labor Inst. **HONORS/ACHIEVEMENTS:** Derwent Award 1944-45; New England Theatre Conf; OH Comm Theatre Assc; Distg Srv Award New York City Cntrl Labor Council

1967; DFA Columbia Clge Chicago IL 1966; Loeb Student Ctr Citation NY Univ 1967; hnry mem Kappa Delta Pi; City of St Louis 1968; Natl Urban League Equal Opport Day Award 1965; Hoey Award 1964; David W Petegorsky Award for Civic Ach 1964; Ira Aldridge Award 1963; George W Norris Civil Rights Award 1970; Canada Lee Fnd Award; Frederick DouglassAward 1971; Yiddish Theatrical Alliance 1971; League for Industrial Democracy 1973; 75th Aniv Trustee Award 1974; Humanitarian Award 1974; Black Filmmakers Hall of Fame 1975; Brooklyn Chptr Links Inc 1970, 1975; Edward Waters Clge & Alumni Assc 1975; Dr of Humanities Lincoln Univ 1976; Cynthia Sicle Cell AnemiaFund of Greater Boston 1976; DFA Clge of Wooster 1976; Women's Council of Brooklyn 1970, 1977; Audelco Fndrs Award 1976; Schomburg Corp Citation 1980; Distg Trade Unionists Award Natl Urban Coalition 1980; George M Cohan Award 1980; Distg Srv Plaque Natl Urban League Labor Affairs Prog; Hnry Doctor of Humanities Degree Tougaloo Clge 1982; Hnry Doctor of Human Letters St Johns Univ 1981; Distg Ach Award Comm Black Involvement Drama. **MILITARY SERVICE:** Armed Forces 93rd inf div 1942-43. **HOME ADDRESS:** 41 Convent Ave, Apt 2F, New York, NY 10027.

O'NEAL, FREDRICK WILLIAM, JR.
Government official, principal systems engineer. **PERSONAL:** Born Dec 08, 1948, Chicago, IL; son of Fredrick W O'Neal and Essie M Reed O'Neal. **EDUCATION:** Roosevelt Univ, Chicago IL, BS, 1985; Keller Graduate School of Management, Chicago IL, MBA, 1987. **CAREER:** Commonwealth Edison Co, Chicago IL, efficiency technician, 1966-71; Western Union Telegraph Co, Chicago IL, computer technician, 1972-88; City of Chicago, Chicago IL, principal systems engr, dept of general services, 1988—. **ORGANIZATIONS:** Telecommunications Professionals. **BUSINESS ADDRESS:** City of Chicago, Department of General Services, 320 North Clark St, Room 519, Chicago, IL 60610.

O'NEAL, JOHN M.
Director, playwright, poet. **PERSONAL:** Born Sep 25, 1940, Mound City, IL; married Marilyn Norton; children: Wendi Autumn, William Edward Burkhardt. **EDUCATION:** Southern IL Univ, BA 1962. **CAREER:** Free So Theater, producing dir; Commn for Racial Justice, UCE, field program dir; Haryou Act, field sec, SNCC trainer. **ORGANIZATIONS:** Dir Comm Action Cntr; mem Alpha Phi Alpha.

O'NEAL, MALINDA KING
Printing company executive. **PERSONAL:** Born Jan 01, 1929, Cartersville, GA; daughter of Mr & Mrs Dan King; married Sheppard Dickerson, Sr; children: Sheppard, II, Sherod Lynn. **EDUCATION:** Morris Brown Coll, BA cum Laude 1965; Atlanta Univ, MA 1970; Alumni Admn Am Alumni Counc Wash, DC, Cert; Skillings Bus Coll Kilmarnock, Scotland, Professional Cert. **CAREER:** Radio Station WERD, record librarian/disc jockey/continuity writer 1949-50; Mammy's Shanty Restaurant Atlanta, sec bookeeper (only Black in mgmt with firm for 11 years prior to integration 1951-53; Natl Congress of Colored Parents & Teachers Atlanta, ofc dir; Emory Univ Center for Res in Soc Change, field supr for spl projects; Morris Brown Coll, former dir alumni affairs/gov rel/ dir of admissions, dean of students; Owner/President MKO Graphics and Printers Atlanta GA 1987-. **ORGANIZATIONS:** Editor "The Alumni Mag" Morris Brown Coll 8 years; editor "The Ebenezer Newsletter"; writings, "How to Rear a Blind Child" 1959; mem United Negro Coll Fund; NAACP; YWCA; Kappa Omega of Alpha Kappa Alpha Sor; vol for Atlanta Counc of Intl Visitors; mem of trustee bd Ebenezer Baptist Church; mem Better Business Bureau 1988; mem Atlanta Business League 1988. **HONORS/ACHIEVEMENTS:** Recipient Morris Brown Coll Natl Alumni Assn WA Fountain & JH Lewis Status Achievement Award 1975; Hon by Morris Brown Coll Natl Alumni Assn for Outstanding Dedicated Serv as Dir of Alumni Affiars 1974; cited by many student organs on Morris Brown Campus for outstanding svcs; Hon by Natl Congress of Colored Parents & Teachers on 2 occasions for outstanding & dedicated svcs; cited on 2 occasions for outstanding serv as Adv to the Undergrad Chap of Alpha Kappa Alpha Sor on Morris Brown Campus. **BUSINESS ADDRESS:** Owner, President, MKO Graphics & Printers, 853 M L King, Jr Drive, NW, Atlanta, GA 30314.

O'NEAL, REGINA (NEE SOLOMON)
Retired writer, educator. **PERSONAL:** Born Mar 27, Detroit, MI; widowed; children: Phillip, Keith. **EDUCATION:** Wayne State Univ, BA, MA 1965. **CAREER:** Edward MacDowell Sch Milwaukee, workshop dir; Detroit Public School, reading coordinator; Jam Handy Org, writer; Detroit Public School, teacher; Wayne State Univ, writer/producer. **ORGANIZATIONS:** Minority program Natl Assn of Educ Broadcasters Convention; Comm Conf Univ of MI; Cable RV Sem AL A&M Univ; mem Natl Assn of Educ Broadcasters; mem Amer Wmn in Radio & TV; trustee Professional & Admins Assn; UAW; mem NAACP; mem Alpha Kappa Alpha Sor; Black Causes; Intl Afro-Amer Museum; editorial advisory bd Public Telecomm Review; mem NAEB; advisory comm Impact of Mass Media on Urban Life; comm arts advisory panel MI Council for the Arts 1980-; appointed Citizens Advisory Comm Water Pollution Control 1982; coordinator Telecomm Career Recruitment for Group W Cable 1983-84. **HONORS/ACHIEVEMENTS:** Nominee Comm Serv Award of Women's Advisory Club 1981; author "And Then The Harvest"; 3 TV plays Broadside/Crummell Press; coproducer/dir African Fables Wil-Cas Records; guest Profiles in Black Issues & Answers 1975; exec prod writer Inner City Freeway TV Series 1972-80; guest speaker Comm Sem Univ of Windsor; guest speaker IL Broadcasters Sem So IL Univ; guest speaker Susan B Anthony Celebration; Emmy Award, Detroit Chapter Natl Acad of TV Arts & Sciences 1979; NAEB Leadership in Minority Telecomm Award 1979.

ONLI, TURTEL
Artist, art therapist, publisher. **PERSONAL:** Born Jan 25, 1952, Chicago, IL. **EDUCATION:** Olive-Harvey College, AA 1972; L'Academie De Port-Royal, 1977; School of the Art Institute of Chicago, BFA 1978; Art Institute of Chicago Master in Art and Art Therapy 1989. **CAREER:** Columbia Coll Chicago, instructor 1978-81; Dysfunctioning Child Center, art therapist 1978-82; Black on Black Love Fine Arts Center, acting dir 1984-85; Ada S McKinley Developmental Sch, art therapist; Onli-Wear Studio, master artist 1978-85, director/producer. **ORGANIZATIONS:** Founder BAG (BLACK Arts Guild) 1971-76; usa rep FESTAC (Second World Festival of African Art and Culture 1976; inventor of rhythmistic style of art. **HONORS/ACHIEVEMENTS:** Certificate of award Natl Conference of Artists 1972 & 1974; founder of Rhythmistic School of Art 1976; premiere prix aux foyer internatl D'Accueil De Paris 1978; Award Of Excellence Artist Guild of Chicago 1979; Publisher of NOG Protector of the Pyramides and Future Funk News, the only black-owned & published comic characters. **BUSINESS ADDRESS:** Director, Producer, Onli-Wear, 5121 S Ellis, Chicago, IL 60615.

ONYEJEKWE, CHIKE ONYEKACHI
Physician. **PERSONAL:** Born Jun 08, 1960, Okigwe; son of Engr E Onyejekwe. **EDUCATION:** Western KY Univ, BS Biology, BS Chemistry 1981; Howard Univ, MD 1986. **CAREER:** DC General Hospital, physician house staff. **ORGANIZATIONS:** Sec Intl Red Cross 1976-78; sec Revolutionary Youth Congress 1976-80; pres Freedom These 1978-82; mem Intl Forum WKU 1978-81; capt WKU Soccer Club 1980-81. **HONORS/ACHIEVEMENTS:** Alpha Epsilon Delta Premed Honor Society; Chief Resident, Howard Medical Service, DC General Hospital. **BUSINESS ADDRESS:** House Staff, DC General Hospital, 19th & Mass Ave SE, Washington, DC 20003.

ORGAN, CLAUDE H., JR.
General surgeon. **PERSONAL:** Born Oct 16, 1928, Marshall, TX; married Elizabeth; children: Claude III, Brian, Paul, Gregory, David, Sandra, Rita. **EDUCATION:** Xavier Univ New Orleans, BS 1944-48; Creighton Univ School of Med, MD 1948-52, surg residency 1952-57, MS surg 1957. **CAREER:** Creighton Univ School of Med, instr of surg 1960-63, asst prof of surg 1963-66, assoc prof of surg 1966-71, prof & chmn of surg 1971-82; Univ of OK Health Sci Ctr, prof of surg 1982-. **ORGANIZATIONS:** Dir Father Flanagan's Boys Town 1969-83, Northwestern Bell Telephone Co 1975-83, St Paul Co 1976-; chmn, bd trust Xavier Univ 1976-78; dir Alpha OmegaAlpha 1979-87; pres Southwestern Surg Congress 1984; chmn Amer Bd of Surg 1984-86; mem Residency Review Comm 1986-. **HONORS/ACHIEVEMENTS:** Sinkler Awd 1970; Hon Deg Univ of NE at Omaha 1976; Hon Fellowship Royal Coll of Surgeons of South Africa 1986; Disting Serv Awd Minority Med Educ ofAmer 1986; editor A Century of Black Surgeons, The USA Experience 1987; Hon Deg Xavier Univ 1987. **MILITARY SERVICE:** USN, lt cdr, mc USNR 1957-59. **BUSINESS ADDRESS:** Professor of Surgery, OklahomaUniv Health Sci Ctr, Dept of Surgery PO Box 26307, 920 Stanton L Young Blvd, Oklahoma City, OK 73126.

ORR, CLYDE HUGH
Director. **PERSONAL:** Born Mar 25, 1931, Whitewright, TX; son of Hugh Orr and Melissa Orr; married Maizie Helen Stell; children: 3 children. **EDUCATION:** General Staff Coll, Grad Army Command 1965; Prairie View A&M Coll, BA Political Sci 1953; Maters in Public Admin Univ of Oklahoma 1974. **CAREER:** US Army Ford Ord, CA, mgr 1968-70; US Army, mil advisor/ethiopian div 1970-72; Lincoln Univ, administrator ROTC 1973-75; Metropolitan St Louis Sewer District, dir human resources 1976-. **ORGANIZATIONS:** Prepared Affirmative Action Plan for St Louis Red Cross 1985; chmn YMCA Bd of Mgrs; mem of corp YMCA Bd; mem Amer Cancer soc Bd of City North Unit; chmn Personnel Comm Edgewood Childrens Home. **HONORS/ACHIEVEMENTS:** Lay Participant Awd St Louis School System; Boy Scouts of Amer Awd St Louis Chap 1984; Chairman of YMCA Bd Awd Monsanto 1985; Lay Participant Awd American Cancer Soc 1985. **MILITARY SERVICE:** US Army lt col 22 yrs; Legion of Merit; Bronze Star and Air Medal 1975. **BUSINESS ADDRESS:** Dir of Human Resourcs, Metropolitan Sewer District, 2000 Hampton Ave, St Louis, MO 63139.

ORR, DOROTHY
Insurance company executive. **EDUCATION:** Atlanta Univ, M; Columbia Univ, Accelerated Grad study. **CAREER:** Fordham Univ School of Social Work, assoc prof (first female); Equitable Life Assurance Soc, vice pres (first black woman officer of a major insurance co); Orr DaCosta Balthazar & Orr, pres/sr partner. **ORGANIZATIONS:** Former commr NY State Commn on Human Rights.

ORR, EARL LAWTON
Physician. **PERSONAL:** Born Jul 12, 1934, Savannah, GA; son of Alphonso Orr, Sr and Genava Marki Orr; widowed; children: Rhonda, Vanessa, Andrea, Sasha, Earl III. **EDUCATION:** NC A&T Univ, BS 1955; Adelphi Coll, MS 1956; Meharry Med Coll, MD 1960; Lakeland Hospital San Antonio TX, internship 1961; Huron Rd Hosp Cleveland OH, residency 1965. **CAREER:** Martin L King Health Ctr, chrmn 1967-74; Chicago Bd of Health, consultant 1969-; Louise Burg, consultant 1969-; Tabernacle Hosp, chmn 1973-77. **ORGANIZATIONS:** Diplomat Am Bd of Ob/Gyn 1968; mem Amer Med Assc; mem Natl Med Assc; flw Amer Coll of Ob/Gyn; fellow, Amer Coll of Surgeons; fellow Intl Coll of Surgeons; mem Fertility Soc. **HONORS/ACHIEVEMENTS:** Josiah Macy Fellowship Macy NY 1960; Biochem Fellowship Meharry Med Coll 1960; mem NAACP; mem Operation PUSH; mem Urban League. **BUSINESS ADDRESS:** 3233 Martin L King Dr, Chicago, IL 60616.

ORR, LOUIS M.
Professional athlete. **PERSONAL:** Married Amerine Lowry. **EDUCATION:** Syracuse Univ. **CAREER:** New York Nicks, basketball player. **HONORS/ACHIEVEMENTS:** Named First Team All-East by the Baketball Writers and Basketball Weekly. **BUSINESS ADDRESS:** New York Nicks, Madison Sq Garden, 4 Pennsylvania Plaza, New York, NY 10001.

ORR, RAY
Mailing service executive. **PERSONAL:** Born Feb 13, 1953, Marks, MS; married Patrice Ann Clayton; children: Jacqueline Denise, Ray Jr, Reuben Patrick. **EDUCATION:** Memphis State Univ, B Bus Admin 1978. **CAREER:** US Post Office Memphis, clerk/loader/sorter 1975-77; Methodist Hosp, distribution agent 1977-78; Federal Express Corp, cargo handler, sales trainee, sales rep sr sales rep 1978-82; Big "D" Mailing Service Inc, pres/ceo 1983-. **ORGANIZATIONS:** Chmn of bd Big "D" Mailing Serv Inc; bd mem Word of Grace Church, American for a Better America. **HONORS/ACHIEVEMENTS:** Outstanding Sales Performance Federal Express Corp 1980; Letters of Praise from Vice Pres of Sales, Sr Vice Pres of Marketing, District Dir, Dist Sales Mgr Federal Express Corp 1980; Businessman of the Day KKDA Radio Dallas 1985; Entrepreneur of the Week Dallas Morning News 1986; Quest for Success Awd Dallas Black Chamber 1987. **BUSINESS ADDRESS:** President & CEO, Big "D" Mailing Services, Inc, PO Box 10841, Dallas, TX 75207.

ORTIQUE, REVIUS OLIVER, JR.
Judge. **PERSONAL:** Born Jun 14, 1924, New Orleans, LA; son of Revius O Ortique (deceased) and Lillie Long (deceased); married Miriam Marie Victorianne; children: Rhesa Marie McDonald. **EDUCATION:** Dillard Univ, AB 1947; IN Univ, MA 1949; So Univ, JD 1956; Campbell Coll, LLD; Ithaca Coll, LHD; Univ of Indiana, LLD. **CAREER:** Full-time practicing attorney New Orleans, LA, 1956-; Civil Dist Court, judge 1979-. **ORGANIZATIONS:** US Dist Ct Eastern Dist LA; US 5th Circuit Ct Appeals; US Supreme Ct; former pres Natl Legal Aid & Defender Assn; mem Amer Lung Assn; Natl bd dir; Antioch Coll Law

bd dir; Natl Bar Assn exec bd; exec bd Natl Bar Found; bd Natl Sr Citizens Law Center, LA; exec com Amer Bar Assn; Amer Bar Assn Comm Legal Aid & Indigent Defenders; Amer Bar Assn House of Dels; LA State Bar Assn House of Dels; sr vice pres Metro Area Comm MAC Affiliate Urban Coalition; bd trustees Dillard Univ; exec com Criminal Just Coord Com; former bd mem LEAA; bd mgmt Flint Goodridge Hosp; bd City Trusts City of New Orleans; exec com Indus Devel New Orleans Metro Area; adv bd League Women Voters Greater New Orleans; bd New Orleans Legal Assist Corp; bd dir United Fed Savings & Loan Assn; bd dir Comm Relations Cncl; men's adv bd YWCA; LA State Bar Assn; Ad Hoc Com Devel Central Business Dist New Orleans; general counsel eight dist AME Ch LA/MS; former mem Pres's Commn on Campus Unrest/Scranton Commn; past pres Amer Lung Assn LA; chart mem World Peace Through Law. **HONORS/ACHIEVEMENTS:** Alpha Kappa Delta Honor Soc; Blue Key Honor Soc; Arthur von Briesen Medal of Distinguished Serv to Disadvantaged Americans 1971; Brotherhood Award Natl Conf of Christians and Jews 1976; Outstanding Person in LA (one of ten persons cited by the Institute of Human Understanding) 1976; many other citations, awards and plaques. **MILITARY SERVICE:** AUS 1st Lt. **BUSINESS ADDRESS:** Judge, Civil District Court, 421 Loyola Ave, New Orleans, LA 70112.

ORTIZ, DELIA
School board official. **PERSONAL:** Born Nov 25, 1924; married Steve Oritz; children: Rosie, Vickie, Steven Jr, Clara, Sandra, Beinaldo. **EDUCATION:** Columbia, 2 yrs. **CAREER:** PS 43-PS125, pres; Fama Film Prod, pres; Knickerbocker Hosp Ambulatory Care, pres; Drug Referral, pres; Community School Bd, pres 1973-75, sec 1982-. **HONORS/ACHIEVEMENTS:** Tenant of the year Grant Housing Project 1966; Community Awd Salinas Socia Club 1970; School Service Awd President's council District 5 1972. **BUSINESS ADDRESS:** Secretary School Board, Community Sch Dist 5, 433 W 123rd St, New York, NY 10027.

OSAKWE, CHRISTOPHER
Educator. **PERSONAL:** Born May 08, 1942, Lagos, Nigeria;married Maria Elena Amador; children: Rebecca Eugenia. **EDUCATION:** Moscow State Univ School of Law, LL B (First Class Hons) 1966, LL M 1967, Ph D (Law) 1970; Univ of IL College of Law, JSD 1974. **CAREER:** Univ of Notre Dame Law School, prof of law 1971-72; Tulane Univ School of Law, prof of law 1972-81; Univ of MI Sch of Law, vis prof of law 1981; Univ of PA sch of law, vis prof of law 1978; St Anthony's Coll, Oxford Univ, visiting fellow 1978; Washington & Lee Univ Sch of Law, visiting professor of law 1986; Tulane Univ School of Law, prof of comparative law 1981-. **ORGANIZATIONS:** Carnegie doctoral fellow Hague Academy of Int'l Law 1969; member Am Law Inst (since 1982), ABA (since 1970), Am Soc Int'l L 1970; research Fellow Russian Research Cntr, Harvard Univ 1972; dir Eason-Weinmann Cntr for Comparative Law 1978-86; dir bd of dir Am Assoc for the Comparative Study of Law 1978;visiting fellow Cntr for Russian and East Europ Studies Univ of MI 1981; scholar Sr US-Soviet Exchange Moscow State Univ Law Sch 1982; dir, bd of review and dvlpt, American Soc of Int'l Law 1982-87. **HONORS/ACHIEVEMENTS:** Author The Participation of the Soviet Union in Universal International Organizations 1972; co-author Comparative Legal Traditions in a Nutshell 1982; co-author Comparative Legal Traditions-Text, Materials, Cases 1985. **BUSINESS ADDRESS:** Prof Comparative Law & Dir, Tulane Univ Sch of Law, TulaneUniv Sch Of Law, New Orleans, LA 70118.

OSBORNE, ALFRED E., JR.
Educator, educational administrator. **PERSONAL:** Born Dec 07, 1944; son of Alfred Osborne and Ditta Osborne. **EDUCATION:** Stanford Univ, BS Elec Engr 1968, MA Economics 1971, MBA Finance 1971, PhD Business-Economics 1974. **CAREER:** Western Development Labs, elec engr 1968; UCLA Grad School of Mgmt, asst prof 1972-78, assoc prof 1979-; Sec & Exchange Commn, economic fellow 1977-80; UCLA Grad Sch of Mgmt, asst dean & dir MBA prog 1979-83; Associate Dean 1984-87; Dir Entrepreneurial Studies Center 1987-. **ORGANIZATIONS:** Dir, The Times Mirror Co, 1980-; past pres, Natl Economic Assn, 1980-81; dir & chair, Municipal Financial Advisory Comm City of Los Angeles, 1981-; mem, Bd of Economics, Black Enterprise Magazine, 1982-85; dir, Nordstrom Inc; dir Industrial Bank, 1983-; dir, Natl Conf of Christians & Jews, 1985-. **HONORS/ACHIEVEMENTS:** Outstanding Faculty Award, UCLA Grad School of Mgmt, 1975-76; fellow, Brookings Inst Economic Policy, 1977-78; author of several scholarly articles in economics and finance. **BUSINESS ADDRESS:** Associate Dean, UCLA Grad School of Mgmnt, 405 Hilgard Ave, Los Angeles, CA 90024.

OSBORNE, ERNEST L.
Government official. **PERSONAL:** Born Nov 15, 1932, New York, NY; married Elizabeth; children: Mrs. **EDUCATION:** Long Islan Du, 1953. **CAREER:** Travelers Corp, dir of natl & comm affairs; Dept of Hlth & Human Svcs, dep under sec for intergovtl affairs; Dept of Hlth Educ & Welfare Wash, DC, commnr APS/OHDS 1978-80, dir OSCA/OHDS 1977-80; Sachem Fund New Haven, CT, exec dir 1972-77; Yale Counc on Com Affs Yale U, exec dir 1968-71. **ORGANIZATIONS:** Bd mem Coop Assis Fund Wash 1972-75 & 80; bd mem HowardUniv Press Wash, DC 1979-80; bd mem Counc on Found Wash, DC 1980-81; mem NAACP 1963-. **HONORS/ACHIEVEMENTS:** Dist Serv Awd Dept of Hlth Educ & Welfare Wash, DC 1980. **BUSINESS ADDRESS:** Travelers Corporation, 1 Tower Square, Hartford, CT 06115.

OSBORNE, ESTELLE MASSEY
Nursing director. **PERSONAL:** Born May 03, 1901, Palestine, TX. **EDUCATION:** Tchrs Coll, Columbia U, BS 1930, MA 1931. **CAREER:** KC Gen, Harlem, Lincoln, Freedmens Nursing Schs, tchr; Julius Rosenwald Fund, social explr 1934-36; Nat Nrsg Counc for War Svc, consult 1943-48; Sch of Educ NY U, fac mem 1946-52; Nat League for Nrsg, asso gen dir 1946-57. **ORGANIZATIONS:** 1st vice pres Nat Council Negro Women 1952; chmn Nat Health Project, Alpha Kappa Alpha Sor; 1st Negro nurse on bd dirs Am Nurses Assn 1948; Am del, Intl Council of Nurses Assembly, Stockholm 1949.

OSBORNE, GWENDOLYN EUNICE
Journalist. **PERSONAL:** Born May 19, 1949, Detroit, MI; daughter of George William Osborne and Ida Jackson Osborne; married Harry K Rye, Feb 12, 1977; children: Kenneth A Rye. **EDUCATION:** Detroit Conservatory of Music, AA 1966; MI State U, BA 1971; Medill School of Journalism NW U, MSJ 1976; Roosevelt Univ, paralegal cert 1986. **CAREER:** The Crisis/NAACP, contributing editor 1973-78; Players Magazine, book editor 1974-78; Unique Magazine, arts book & entertainment writer 1976-78; Scott-Foresman& Co, asst editor permissions asst 1978-79; Pioneer Press Newspapers, Inc, lively arts editor 1978-80; Rand McNally, production editor 1979; News Election Service, Chicago regnl personnel mgr 1980; Amer Bar Assoc, publishing specialist 1980-82; Southeastern MI Transp Authority, publications specialist 1982-84; Debbie's Sch of Beauty Culture/Debbie Howell Cosmetics, spec asst to the pres 1985; 21st Century Woman, assoc editor 1986; ABA Commission on Opportunities for Minorities in the Profession, Chicago, IL, communications consultant, 1988-89; American Civil Liberties Union, Chicago, IL, public information director, 1989—. **ORGANIZATIONS:** National board of directors, Michigan State University Black Alumni Association; Second Baptist Church; Delta Sigma Theta; Interdisciplinary Arts Panel, Evanston Arts Council; Chicago Urban League; associate member, American Bar Association; Chicago Society of Association Executives; Chicago Association of Black Journalists; Black Public Relations Society; Chicago Press Club; National Association of Black Journalists; Society of Professional Journalists; Women in Communications, Inc; National Conference of Artists. **HONORS/ACHIEVEMENTS:** Nominated for Governor's Award for Arts, IL Arts Council, 1979-81; fellow, National Endowment for the Humanities summer seminar for journalists at UC Berkeley, 1979; fellow, National Endowment for the Arts Office for Partnership, Washington, DC, 1980; certificate of merit, Family Law Section, American Bar Association, 1981-82; proclamation from Office of the Mayor, City of Detroit, 1983; certificate of appreciation, Office of the Governor, State of IL, 1983. **HOME ADDRESS:** 413 Liberty St, Waukegan, IL 60085. **BUSINESS ADDRESS:** Director of Public Information, American Civil Liberties Union of Illinois, 20 East Jackson Blvd, Suite 1600, Chicago, IL 60604.

OSBORNE, HUGH STANCILL
Business executive. **PERSONAL:** Born Jul 18, 1918, Birmingham, AL; married Ruby Jewel Williams; children: Sidney, Cheryl. **EDUCATION:** Loyola U, MA 1977; Loyola U, grad study 1947-48; KY St U, BA 1939. **CAREER:** Chgo, 1st dep commr; Chgo, acting commr 1975-77; Chgo, dep commr 1969-75; Chgo, dep dir 1969-75; Chicago Housing & Authority, dep dir 1946-65. **ORGANIZATIONS:** Commr Chicago Co Cook Criminal Justice Commn; mem Nat Council on Crime & Devinquency; Comm Devel & Housing Coord com Chgo; Chicago Manpower Planning Council; Muni Fin Off Assn; Am Soc for Pub Adminstrn; mem citz com Juvenile Ct of Cook Co; Nat Assn for Comm Devel; com for Full Employment; ChgoAssn for Collaborative Effort; Kappa Alpha Psi; Conf on Minority Pub Adminstrs; com for Full Employment Chicago Assn of Commercy & Industry. **HONORS/ACHIEVEMENTS:** Brotherhood awd Chicago Conf of Brotherhood 1976; cert of appre Abraham Lincoln Ctr 1976. **MILITARY SERVICE:** AUS 1st sgt 1941-45. **BUSINESS ADDRESS:** 640 N LaSalle St, Chicago, IL 60610.

OSBORNE, JEFFREY LINTON
Singer. **PERSONAL:** Born Mar 09, 1948, Providence, RI; married Sheri; children: Tiffany, Dawn, Jeanine. **CAREER:** LTD, producer, singer 10 yrs. **HONORS/ACHIEVEMENTS:** Recorded num albums incl, The Last Time I Made Love, Stay With Me Tonight, Don't You Get So Mad, On The Wings of Love; Recoreded 10 albums. **BUSINESS ADDRESS:** Recording Artist, Almo-Irving Publishing Co, 1358 N LaBrea, Hollywood, CA 90028.

OSBORNE, JIM
Professional athlete. **PERSONAL:** Born Sep 07, 1949, Sylvania, GA; married Emma. **EDUCATION:** So IL U, BA Accntg. **CAREER:** Chicago Bears, professional football def tackle 1973-. **HONORS/ACHIEVEMENTS:** Brian Piccolo Award 1972; NAIA All-Am. **BUSINESS ADDRESS:** Chicago Bears, PO Box 204, Lake Forest, IL 60045.

OSBORNE, OLIVER HILTON
Educator. **PERSONAL:** Born Feb 17, 1931, Brooklyn, NY; children: Martin, Mary, Michael, Michelle, Mathew. **EDUCATION:** Hunter Coll NY, BS Nursing 1958; NY Univ, MA Psychiatric/Mental Health Nursing 1960; MI State Univ, PhD 1968. **CAREER:** Wayne State Univ, assoc prof nursing/adj prof anthropology 1960; McGill Univ Montreal, mental health consult 1969; Univ of WA Dept of Psychosocial Nursing, assoc prof & chmn 1969-74; Univ of Botswana So Africa, assoc rsch fellow 1976-78; Univ of WA Dept Anthropology, adj prof 1979-; Univ of WA Dept of Psychosocial Nursing, prof 1974-. **ORGANIZATIONS:** Mem Amer Anthropological Assn, Amer Nurses' Assn, Soc for Applied Anthropology, Soc for Med Anthropology (sec/treas 1970-73), Council on Nursing and Anthropology; numerous consultations including, East Model Cities Health Task Force Seattle, WA 1971; Rockefeller Foundation Univ del Valle Cali, Columbia 1973; Mental Health Clinic Group Hlth Coop Seattle, WA 1974; ANA Fellowship Pgm for Doctoral Training of Racial/Ethnic Minorities in Clin Mental Hlth Serv 1977-82; mem Interdiv Cncl on Certification Amer Nurses Assn 1976-80; Natl Adv Comm Center for Health Care and Research Sch of Nursing Univ of TX at Austin 1979-80; Psychiatric Nursing Educ Review Comm NIMH 1980-83; Natl Comm on Devel of Minority Curric in Psychiatric and Mental Health Disciplines Howard Univ NIMH 1980-; lay mem Judicial Screening Comm Seattle-King County Bar Assn; 1982-. **HONORS/ACHIEVEMENTS:** Visit Prof Sch of Nursing Yale Univ 1979; Visit Prof Afro-Amer Studies Dept School of Nursing Univ of WI Milwaukee, WI 1979; Disting Lectr Sch of Nursing East Carolina Univ 1979; Listed in"Black Nursing Pioneers, Leaders and Organizers" The Assn for the Study of Afro-Amer Life and History 1979; numerouspapers including, "Violence and the Human Condition, A mental Health Perspective" Univ of WI Milwaukee, WI 1979; "Psychosocial Nursing Research, The State of the Art" presented at the Conference "Perspectives in Psychiatric Care" 1980 Phila, PA; Research Approaches to the Social Ecology of Health School of Nursing Columbia Univ New York, NY 1982; 37 publications including, "Violence and the Human Condition, A Mental Health Perspective" Occasioning Factors of Urban Violence Occasional Paper African-Amer Studies Center Madison, WI; "Point Prevalence Study of Alchoholism and Mental Illness Among Downtown Migrants" (with Whitley, Marilyn P and Godfrey, M) accepted for publication in "Social Science and Medicine, An Intl Journal" in 1985. **BUSINESS ADDRESS:** Professor, Univ of WA Dept Psychosoc Nurs, School of Nursing SC-76, Seattle, WA 98195.

OSBORNE, WILLIAM REGINALD, JR.
Medical director. **PERSONAL:** Born May 10, 1957, Worcester, MA; son of William Reginald Osborne, Sr and Dolores Everett Osborne; married Cheryl Lowery, Jun 1980; children: Justin, Blake. **EDUCATION:** Morehouse Coll, BS (Cum Laude) 1979; Howard Univ Coll of Medicine, MD 1983; Emory Univ Sch of Medicine, Dept of Internal Medicine. **CAREER:** Morehouse Coll, asst instructor of anatomy & physiology 1979-80, summer careers prog instructor of physics 1980; Morehouse Coll of Medicine Dept of Internal Medicine, clinical instructor 1986-; Health South, internist 1986-89; Health South, medical director 1989-. **ORGANIZATIONS:** Mem Omega Psi Phi Frat 1976-; mem Southern Christian Leadership

Conf 1978-; mem Amer Coll of Physicians 1986; mem Natl Medical Assn; mem Georgia State Medical Assn 1989-. **HONORS/ACHIEVEMENTS:** Scholastic Awd Omega Psi Phi Frat 1978,79; mem Atlanta Univ Center Biology Honor Soc; Fraternity 7th District Scholar Awd Omega Psi Phi Frat 1978; Beta Kappa Chi Scientific Honor Soc; Board Certified in Internal Medicine. **BUSINESS ADDRESS:** Medical Director, Health South, 1039 Ridge Ave, Atlanta, GA 30315.

OSBY, SIMEON B., JR.
Journalist. **PERSONAL:** Born May 15, 1909, Springfield, IL; married Annabel Marie Anderson. **EDUCATION:** Univ of IL, 1929-32. **CAREER:** Fed Transient Bur, caseworker 1934-36; Natl Youth Admin, field rep 1936-43; Capitol City News, publ weekly paper 1947-51; Chicago Daily Defender, legislative corr 1953-86; Capitol City News Serv, editor & publisher 1980-. **ORGANIZATIONS:** Organizer IL State NAACP; sec IL State NAACP 1933-36; past pres Springfield NAACP 1939-43; mem Omega Psi Phi Frat 1940-; mem IL Legislative Corr Assn 1953-; Comdr Col Otis B Duncan Post 809 Amer Legion 1962-63; exec dir IL Legislative Com Minority Group Employment 1969-73; Soc Prof Journalist Sigma Delta Chi 1972-; bd trustees Lincoln Library Springfield 1980-. **HONORS/ACHIEVEMENTS:** Appointed to Press Comm of IL State Senate 1975. **MILITARY SERVICE:** AUS 1st lt 1943-46; AUSR 1947-52. **BUSINESS ADDRESS:** Editor & Publisher, Capitol City News Service, Press Rm Mezzanine Floor, State Capitol, Springfield, IL 62706.

OSENI, HAKEEM O.
Engineer. **PERSONAL:** Born May 26, 1938, Lagos, Nigeria;married Naomi; children: Iyabo, Tunde. **EDUCATION:** BS 1965; MS 1969; PhD 1974. **CAREER:** Exxon Production Research Co, sr research engr 1974-; SUNY Buffalo, Cooperate Coll Ctr, lectr 1972-74; EI DuPont, Yerkes Research Lab, research engr 1969-70; Shell-BP, Nigeria, jr pet engr. **ORGANIZATIONS:** Mem AIChE; SPE; pres African Students Union of Buffalo 1972-73. **BUSINESS ADDRESS:** Box 2189, Houston, TX 77001.

OSIBIN, WILLARD S.
Physician. **PERSONAL:** Born Feb 02, 1925, Oakland, CA; married Shirley M Wilson; children: Willard S. **EDUCATION:** Univ of CA Berkeley, 1946-49; Meharry Med Coll Nashville, TN, MD 1953. **CAREER:** Physician & surg, pvt prac 1656-80. **ORGANIZATIONS:** Mem CA Med Assn Com on Collective Bargaining 1980; mem CA Med Assn Com on Evolving Trends in Soc Affecting Life 1978-80; v-chmn CA Med Com on Emergency Med Care 1978-80; alternate del CA Med Assn, AMA 1976-80; hs of del CA Med Assn 1973-80; past diplomate/mem Am Bd Family Practice 1971-; trustee San Luis Obispo/Santo Barbara Med Care Found 1973-80; exec com sec & fdg dir Area XVI PSRO 1974-80; mem CA State MQRC # 8 Bd of Med Quality Assurance 1975-80; med ofcr Composite Squadron # 103 Civil Air Patrol; past pres & current dir San Luis Obispo CA Fair Bd; past pres San Luis Obispo Co Civil Serv Commn 1970-78; past cmdr W States Assn of Sheriffs Aero Squadron; past pres Atascadero Lions Club; past pres San Luis Obispo Co Alcoholic Adv Com 1975. **HONORS/ACHIEVEMENTS:** M Airman Award & others, AUS 1943-45; Bronze & Silver Medallions, Am Heart Assn 1973 & 1977; Lion of the Yr, Lions Intl 1975; Citizen of the Month, Atascadero Businessmen's Assn 1976; Citizen of the Yr, Atascadero C of C 1977; Who's Who in the West; Dir of Med Specialists Marquis Who's Who 1978. **MILITARY SERVICE:** AUS corpl 1943-45; AF Aux 1979. **BUSINESS ADDRESS:** 1400 Las Tablas Rd, Templeton, CA 93465.

OTEY, FLEM B., III
Business executive. **PERSONAL:** Born Jul 11, 1935, Nashville, TN; married Yoshiko; children: Francoise, Flem, IV, Mimi. **EDUCATION:** TN A&I State U, BS 1957;Univ TN, cert in real est; TN State U, serv sch mgmt, adminstrv inst, owners sm bus;Univ TN, Vanderbilt Sch of Div, MBA grad prgm 1975-; Indsl Coll Armed Forces, Nat Sec Seminar, Middle TN State U, 1974. **CAREER:** Otey's Northtown Big Star Supermarket Nashville, TN, prop (a fam enterprise since 1904, listed in Black Enterprise Mag). **ORGANIZATIONS:** Mem adv bd OIC; Banks Com, Minority Bus Dev; Alcoholic Rehab Prgm; Phi Beta Lambda; fdr & chmn bd Middle TN Bus Assn; life mem & past bd mem NAACP; mem Frontiers Internat; partic integration, mem first bd mgrs Nashville YMCA; first black mem Nashville Area C of C; bd dirs TN Voters Council; Davidson Co Indep Pol Council; former deacon & treas, asst minister Pleasant Green Bapt Ch. **HONORS/ACHIEVEMENTS:** Bigger & Better Bus Award, Phi Beta Sigma 1971; Bus & Achvmt Awards, Interdenom Ministers Fellowship, Nashville 1969; Businessman of Yr Award, Middle TNBus Assn 1969; est Washington-Carver Scholastic Achvmt Award, Pearl High Sch 1969; North High Sch 1970; Cert Excellence in Comm Svc, Sterling Brewers Inc 1971. **MILITARY SERVICE:** USAF res maj; base supply mgmt & proced ofcr, Little Rock AFB. **BUSINESS ADDRESS:** 2230 Morena St, Nashville, TN 37208.

OTIENO-AYIM, LARBAN ALLAN
Dentist. **PERSONAL:** Born Sep 15, 1940; son of Janathan Ayim and Dorcas Ayim; married Agness Auko; children: Peter, Paul, James, Anna. **EDUCATION:** Univ of WI, 1969; Meharry Med Coll Nashville, TN, DDS 1973; Univ of MN Sch of Public Health, MPH 1975. **CAREER:** Dentist, private practice 1977-; State of MN Dept of Public Welfare, staff dentist 1975-77; Pilot City Health Ctr Minneapolis, clinical dentist 1974-75. **ORGANIZATIONS:** Mem Am Dental Assn; mem Minneapolis Dist Dental Soc; mem MN Dental Assn; mem Am Public Health Assn; mem MN Public Health Assn; mem Masons. **BUSINESS ADDRESS:** 2126 West Broadway, Minneapolis, MN 55411.

OTIS, AMOS JOSEPH
Professional baseball player. **PERSONAL:** Born Apr 26, 1947, Mobile, AL. **EDUCATION:** NY Mets Nat League Baseball Team, outfielder, third baseman 1967-69; KC Royals Am League Baseball Team, outfielder 1969-. **HONORS/ACHIEVEMENTS:** Sporting News Am League All-Star Team 1973; Sporting News Am League All-Star Fielding Teams 1971, 72 & 74; mem Am League All-Star Team 1970-71, 1973-76; tied major league records for fewest times caught stealing one season, 50 or more stolen bases (8) 1971; set league records for highest stolen base percentage life-time 300 or more attempts (799) 1975; most stolen bases 2 consec games (7) 1975; led Am League in stolen bases (52) 1971; played in 3 Championship Series 1976-78; tied series record most stolen bases one series (4) & total series (6) 1978. **BUSINESS ADDRESS:** c/o San Diego Padres, 9449 Friars Rd, San Diego, CA 92108.

OTTLEY, AUSTIN H.
Association executive. **PERSONAL:** Born Jun 17, 1918, NYC; married Willie Lee; children: Federic Wayne, Dennis. **EDUCATION:** Empire State Coll, BS. **CAREER:** Mayors Com Exploitation Workers NY, sr rep 1965-67; IBEW Local 3, shop steward 1959-65; New York City Central Labor Council ALF-CIO, asso dir. **ORGANIZATIONS:** Mem Local 3 IBEW; F Div Adv Bd, Local 3 IBEW 1954-; Lewis Howard Latimer Progressor Assn 1958-; Independent United Order of Scottish Mechanics 1936-; Chap 80 St Geo Assn 1972; mem Labor Com Jamaica NAACP 1962-66; Negro Am Labor Council 1962. **MILITARY SERVICE:** USAF sgt 1942-46; USAFR s/sgt 1948-52, active duty 1951-52. **BUSINESS ADDRESS:** 386 Park Ave S, New York, NY 10016.

OTTLEY, NEVILLE
Physician, surgeon. **PERSONAL:** Born Dec 18, 1926; married Esther; children: Russell Mark, Melanie Dawn. **EDUCATION:** Andrew U, BA 1953; HowardUniv Coll of Med, MD 1957; DC Gen Hosp, intern 1957-58; HowardUniv Freedmen's Hosp, resident, gen sergery 1958-62. **CAREER:** St Elizabeth's Hosp, chf dept of surgery 1965-, med ofcr & gen surgeon 1962-65. **ORGANIZATIONS:** Diplomate Am Bd of Surgery 1963; fellow Am Coll of Surgeons; fellow Intl Coll of Surgeons; fellow Am Geriatrics Soc; diplomate mem Pan Am Med Assn; mem DC Med Soc; St Elizabeth's Med Soc; mem Credentials Com, Res Review Bd, Environ & Infection Control Com, St Elizabeth's Hosp. **HONORS/ACHIEVEMENTS:** Monographs the effect of adrenalectomy on electrolye balance in rats; carcinoma of the esophagus treated with right & left colon transplant. **BUSINESS ADDRESS:** 2642 12 St NE, Washington, DC 20018.

OTUDEKO, ADEBISI OLUSOGA
Educator. **PERSONAL:** Born Jun 10, 1935, Ibadan, Nigeria;married Bernice Green; children: Oluwole, Folashade. **EDUCATION:** Eastern Nazarene Coll, BA 1953; Boston U, MA 1955; Stanford U, MA 1974, PhD 1977. **CAREER:** Washburn Univ of Topeka, chmn of Soc anthropology; Franklin & Mashall Coll, asst prof; Nigerian Fed Gov, asst sec 1959-60; Bennett Coll, instr 1960-62; Hampton Inst Inst of African Life & Hist, dir prof 1966. **ORGANIZATIONS:** Mem African Studies Assn Am Asso ofUniv Prof Negeian Soc & Anthropological Asso Flwshp,Univ Negro Coll Faculty 1964-65. **HONORS/ACHIEVEMENTS:** Rsrch flw NISER 1975-76; flwsp Danforth Found 1971-76; flwshp Nat Sci Found 1975-76. **BUSINESS ADDRESS:** WashburnUniv of Topeka, 1700 College St, Topeka, KS 66621.

OUBRE, HAYWARD LOUIS
Artist. **PERSONAL:** Born Sep 17, New Orleans, LA; son of Hayward Oubre and Amene Oubre; widowed; children: Amelie Geneva. **EDUCATION:** Dillard U, BA 1939;Univ of IA, MFA 1948. **CAREER:** FL A&M College, assoc prof of art 1949-50; AL State College, prof of art chrmn 1950-65; Winston-Salem State U, prof of art chrmn 1965-81, curator selma burke art gallery 1984-89. **ORGANIZATIONS:** Researcher in color. **HONORS/ACHIEVEMENTS:** 1st prize oils Ia State Fair, Ia 1947; 8 prizes Atlanta U, Atlanta, GA 1947-68; 3rd prize sculpture Emancipation Proclamation Centennial 1963; author of directors in modern art Art Review Magazine Natl Art Exhibit New Orleans 1966; corrected color triangle Devised by Johann Wolfgang Vongoethe 1976. **MILITARY SERVICE:** Engr m sgt 1942-43; PTO good conduct medal 1942-43. **HOME ADDRESS:** 2422 Pickford Ct, Winston-Salem, NC 27101.

OUBRE, LINDA SEIFFERT
Financial manager. **PERSONAL:** Born Dec 26, 1958, Los Angeles, CA; married Nathaniel L Oubre Jr. **EDUCATION:** Univ of CA Los Angeles, BA (Cum Laude) 1980; Harvard Business Sch, MBA 1984. **CAREER:** Security Pacific Natl Bank, mgmt assoc 1980-82; Syndicated Communications Capital, financial analyst 1983; Harvard Business School, asst dir MBA admissions 1984-85; Times Mirror Co, sr financial analyst 1985-. **ORGANIZATIONS:** Publisher UCLA Daily Bruin 1978-79; alumni rep Harvard Business Sch Exec Cncl 1984-85; student relations officer Harvard Business Sch Black Alumni Assoc 1985-87; mem Natl Black MBA Assoc 1985-, Inst of Certified Mgmt Accounts 1986-; newsletter editor Harvard Business Sch Black Alumni Assoc 1987-. **HONORS/ACHIEVEMENTS:** Chancellor's Banner Mar UCLA 1980; Council for Oppor in Grad Mgmt Educ Fellow Harvard Univ 1982-84. **BUSINESS ADDRESS:** Senior Financial Analyst, Times Mirror Company, Corporate Finance, Times Mirror Square, Los Angeles, CA 90053.

OUSLEY, HAROLD LOMAX
Performer, composer. **PERSONAL:** Born Jan 23, 1929, Chicago; son of Nellie Ousley Farabee; married Alice Inman; children: Sheronda. **EDUCATION:** Dusable HS, 1943-48. **CAREER:** Jamaica Art Center, music dir 1982-85; Queens Council on The Arts, jazz music coord 1982-85; Jazz Interactions, music coord 1980-85. **ORGANIZATIONS:** Therapeutic music coord Key Sch York Manor Branchdekey Women of Amer 1970-85. **HONORS/ACHIEVEMENTS:** Comm serv Key Women of America 1981; jazz achievement Jazz at Home Club 1972; Jazz Pioneer Award Broadcast Music Inc 1984. **BUSINESS ADDRESS:** Music Coord & Dir, Jamaica Art Center, GPO Box 1119, New York, NY 10116.

OUTLAW, LUCIUS T., JR.
Educator. **PERSONAL:** Born Dec 28, 1944, Starkville, MS; married Freida Hopkins. **EDUCATION:** Fisk U, BA (magna cum laude) 1967; Boston Coll, PhD 1972. **CAREER:** Moton Ctr for Indep Studies 1976; Morgan State U, asso prof 1977-; Fusk U, assoc prof relig & philosoph studies dir gen honors prog 1970-76; BlackStudies Boston Coll, interim dir 1970. **ORGANIZATIONS:** Mem Nat Collegiate Honors Counc; mem Am Philosoph Assn; Phi Beta Kappa.

OUTLAW, PATRICIA ANNE
Educator, psychologist. **EDUCATION:** Mt Providence Jr College, AA 1966; Townson State U, BA 1968, MA 1971;Univ of MD College Park; Ph D 1977; St Mary's Seminary & U, MA Th 1984. **CAREER:** Balto City Sch, school pscyologist 1970-71; Townson State U, dir of study skills center 1971-77, assoc Deans of students 1977-79; Cheltenham Ctr, psychologist 1979-83. **ORGANIZATIONS:** Social worker Balto Dept of Social Services 1968-69; job counselor Dept of Defense 1969-70; assoc minister St John AME Church, Balto MD 1984-85; assoc prof of mental health Morgan StateUniv 1984-85. **HONORS/ACHIEVEMENTS:** Outstanding Young Women of America 1977. **HOME ADDRESS:** 3605 Old York Rd, Baltimore, MD 21218.

OUTLAW, WARREN GREGORY
Counselor. **PERSONAL:** Born Mar 25, 1951, South Bend, IN; married Iris L Hardiman; children: Lauren, Gregory. **EDUCATION:** Lincoln Univ, BS 1974; IN Univ-South Bend, MS Educ 1980. **CAREER:** South Bend School Corp, substitute teacher 1974-75; YMCA Comm Service Branch, asst dir 1975-80; Educ Talent Search, assoc dir 1980-83, dir 1983-. **ORGANIZATIONS:** Chmn scholarship comm NAACP 1984-; chmn financial dev comm IN Mid-Amer Assoc Educ Oppor Prog Pers 1985-; chmn Black Comm Sch Comm 1986-. **HONORS/ACHIEVEMENTS:** Service Citation YMCA 1980; IN Black Achievers IN Black Expo 1984; Youth Leadership & Service John Adams High School 1985. **HOME ADDRESS:** 2902 Bonds Ave, South Bend, IN 46628. **BUSINESS ADDRESS:** Director, Educ Talent Search, Univ of Notre Dame, PO Box 458, Notre Dame, IN 46556.

OUTTERBRIDGE, JOHN WILFRED
Artist. **PERSONAL:** Born Mar 12, 1933, Greenville, NC; married Beverly Marie McKissick; children: Tami Lyn. **EDUCATION:** A&T Univ, 1952-53; Amer Acad of Art, 1957-59, 1960-61; State of CA Teaching Credential, 1970. **CAREER:** Traid Corp, artist/designer 1964-68; CA State Univ, lecturer african amer art history 1970-73; Communicative Arts Acad, artistic dir 1969-75; Pasadena ArtMuseum, art instructor & installation 1968-72; Watts Towers Arts Center, dir. **ORGANIZATIONS:** Group study aesthetic eye proj 1974, panelist expansion arts 1977-79, task force crafts div 1981 Natl Endowment of the Arts; panelist instr & train CA Arts Council 1978-80; bd of dir Watts Towers Comm Trust; adv bd Friends of the Jr Arts Ctr, The J Paul Getty Trust; Fullbright Fellowship to New Zealand 1986. **HONORS/ACHIEVEMENTS:** Citizen of the Week, KNX Newsradio 1977; Bicentennial Salute Los Angeles Human Relations Commission, 1980; Cultural Awareness Los Angeles Unified School Dist 1981; Certificate of Commendation, Los Angeles 15th Dist 1982; Certificate of Appreciation, City of Los Angeles 1983. **MILITARY SERVICE:** AUS corpl 1953-56. **BUSINESS ADDRESS:** Dir, Watts Towers Art Ctr, Cultural Affairs Dept, 1727 E 107th St, Los Angeles, CA 90002.

OVERALL, MANARD
Marketing, engineering program manager. **PERSONAL:** Born Sep 20, 1939, St Louis, MO; married Arclethia Ann Abbott (divorced). **EDUCATION:** Hampton Inst Hampton, VA, BS 1973; Fairleight DickinsonUniv NJ, MBA 1977. **CAREER:** Aerospace Geoup Tracor Inc, mrktng mgr 1979-82; TX Inst Inc, computer sys mrkt engr mgr 1978-79; TX Inst Inc, prodr eng mgr 1977-78; St Edward's U, instr 1978; Austin Comm Coll, instr 1978-; Mgmt Objectives Co Bus Consultant, managing dir/owner; Modular Power Systems Director Mktg and programs 1981-1986; Eldec Corporation Engineering Manager 1986-. **ORGANIZATIONS:** Coach youth sports teams 1960-80; vice pres Pond Springs Sch PTA 1977-78; CO rep TX Alliance for Minority Engrs 1977-78; President Puget Sound Black Proffessional Engineers 1988-; Advisory bd Seattle WA, MESA. **HONORS/ACHIEVEMENTS:** Legion of merit (Plus 12) USCG 1957-77; scholastic honors Hampton Inst Engineering 1973. **MILITARY SERVICE:** US Coast Guard CPO 1957-67; US Army chief warrant ofcr 1967-77. **HOME ADDRESS:** PO Box 126, Lynwood, WA 98046.

OVERBEA, LUIX VIRGIL
Staff writer. **PERSONAL:** Born Feb 15, 1923, Chicago, IL; married Elexie Culp. **EDUCATION:** NWU, PhB 1948; MS 1951. **CAREER:** Assoc Negro Press, chf copy desk 1948-54; OK Eagle Tulsa, cty editor 1954-55; The Winston-Salem Journal, staff writer 1955-68; The St Louis Sentinel, mng edtr 1968-70; the St Louis Globe-Dem, asst mkup editor staff & reporter 1970-71; The Christian Sci Monitor, staff writer 1971-; Winston-Salem State Coll, tchr 1965-68. **ORGANIZATIONS:** Mem Sigma Delta Cig; mng edtr The Black Ch Mag 1974; commentary Black News TV Show 1973-; mem NAACP; Kappa Alpha Psi; Prnts Counc; Metco; 2nd Ch of Christ. **HONORS/ACHIEVEMENTS:** Sci NNPA Aws St Louis Sentinel. **MILITARY SERVICE:** AUS ASTP corpl 1943-46. **BUSINESS ADDRESS:** 1 Norway St, Boston, MA 02115.

OVERBY, ERNESTINE BENITA (MOTHER HEN)
Retired nurse. **PERSONAL:** Born Jul 25, 1915, Evansville, IN. **EDUCATION:** Homer G Phillips Hosp, RN 1938. **CAREER:** HG Phillips Hosp, staff nurse 1939-41, head nurse 1942-43; Public Health City of St Louis, staff nurse 1943-66, supervisor 1966-80. **ORGANIZATIONS:** Mem Amer Nurses Assn & 3rd Dist MO Nurses 1943-80; bd mem Planned Parenthood 1969-71; charter mem & sec Black Nurses Assn Greter St Louis Inc 1974-80; mem Natl Black Nurses Inc 1974-80; chmn Allied Health Comm for United Negro Coll Fund 1977-80; bd of dir 3rd Dist MO Nurses Assn 1976-80; human rights chmn 3rd Dist MO Nurses Assn 1976-80. **HONORS/ACHIEVEMENTS:** Plaque for Comm Serv Yeatmen Dist Corp St Louis 1973; Plaque for Outstanding Service Black Nurse's Assn Greater St Louis Inc 1977; Pendant for 40 yrs with the City of St Louis 1979.

OVERSTREET, HARRY L.
Architect. **PERSONAL:** Born Jun 20, 1935, Conehatta, MS; son of Joe Overstreet and Cleo Huddleston-Overstreet; divorced; children: Anthony, Harry II. **EDUCATION:** Attended CCAC, Oakland CA. **CAREER:** Gerson/ Overstreet, San Francisco CA, vice pres, partner, 1968-85, pres, 1985-. **ORGANIZATIONS:** Past pres, mem, Berkeley Planning Comm, 1967-73; bd mem, Hunter Point Boys Club 1975-; co-founder, Amer Inst of Architects; pres, Natl Org of Minority Architects, 1988. **HONORS/ACHIEVEMENTS:** Award of Merit, Palace of Fine Art's, 1975; Serv for Engineering Career Day, U C Davis, 1979; Career Workshop, City of Berkeley, 1979. **MILITARY SERVICE:** US Army, 1960. **BUSINESS ADDRESS:** President, Gerson/Overstreet, 57 Post St, Suite 804, San Francisco, CA 94104.

OVERTON, BETTY JEAN
Educational administrator. **PERSONAL:** Born Oct 10, 1949, Jacksonville, FL; daughter of Henry Crawford and Miriam Crawford; divorced; children: Joseph A, Jermaine L. **EDUCATION:** TN State Univ, BS 1970, MA 1973; George Peabody of Vanderbilt Univ, PhD 1980. **CAREER:** Metropolitan Nashville School Bd, teacher 1970-72; TN State Univ, teacher, program dir 1972-76; Univ of TN at Nashville, instructor 1973-78; Nashville State Tech Inst, asst prof 1976-78; Fisk Univ, asst prof, asst dean 1978-83; Univ of Arkansas, assoc dean, dean 1983-. **ORGANIZATIONS:** Race Relations Information Center, reporter 1970-71; Nashville Panel of American Women, bd mem 1973-83; Natl Council of Teachers of English 1979-; ACE, admin fellow 1980; Arkansas Women's History Inst, bd mem 1983-; Teak Reportory Theatre, bd mem 1983-; Women of Color United Against Domestic Violence, bd mem, founding mem 1985; Scarritt Coll, consultant; YMCA, counsultant. **HONORS/ACHIEVEMENTS:** Alpha Kappa Alpha, Outstanding Leadership Award 1981; articles published in: Southern Quarterly 1985; The Race Relations Reporter 1971; Tennessee Developmental Studies Notes 1977; Calloloo Magazine 1981; W K Kellogg Natl Leadership Development Fellowship, W K Kellogg Foundation 1988-91; Award for Meritorious Achievement, Office of Research and Sponsored Programs, Univ of Arkansas at Little Rock 1989. **HOME ADDRESS:** 521 Springwood Drive, Little Rock, AR 72211. **BUSINESS ADDRESS:** Dean of Graduate School, Univ of Arkansas-Little Rock, 2801 University Ave, Little Rock, AR 72204.

OVERTON, VOLMA ROBERT
Association executive. **PERSONAL:** Born Sep 26, 1924, Travis Co, TX; married Warneta. **EDUCATION:** Huston-Tillotson Coll, BS 1950. **ORGANIZATIONS:** Pres Austin Br NAACP since 1962; 1st vice pres TX State Conf NAACP 1970-72; started Credit Union 1969; sec, streas Austin NAACP; Fed Credit Union scoutmaster 1954-65; pres PTA. **HONORS/ACHIEVEMENTS:** Arthur Dewitty Award 1967; Scoutmaster Award 1960; Zeta Phi Beta Civic Award 1970; Sakarroh Temple #1 Award Outstanding Comm Serv 1973. **MILITARY SERVICE:** USMC 1943-46; USAR ltc 1947-. **BUSINESS ADDRESS:** 1704 E 12 St, Austin, TX.

OWENS, ANDI
Educator. **PERSONAL:** Born Jul 21, 1934, Minneapolis, MN. **EDUCATION:** Columbia Univ, BA 1962; NY School for Social Work, graduate work 1963. **CAREER:** Genesis II Museum of Intl Black Culture, dir 1980-; Brooklyn Museum, museum prep 6 curatorial depts work proj 1978-80; Afro-Amer Cultural Found Westchester Co, coordinator, 1976-77; Black History Museum of Nassau Co, museum curator 1974-75; The Met Museum of Art, Rockefeller fellow 1973-74; Genesis II Gallery of African Art, co-fdr 1972; Indus Home for the Blind, asst dir recreation 1965-72; Church of St Edward the Martyr, dir recreation 1962-65. **ORGANIZATIONS:** Fdr experimental drama group The Queens Revels ColumbiaUniv 1958-62; orkshopws Documentation & Exhbn for Mus Educators 1974; Fedn of Prot Welfare Agys "Creative Comm Involvement" 1974; Met Mus of Art "Art Discovery Workshop for Comm Grps" 1974; Met Mus rep designer for YM-YWHA 1974; chmn Visual Arts Discipline for Mid-West Regn; 2nd World Festival of Black & African Arts & Culture 1975; panelist Blacks & Mus; Am Assn of Mus 1974; bd advr Bronx Comm Bd 7 Cultural Arts Ctr 1974; NY State chmn of exhbns Nat Conf of Artists 1974; part NY State Cncl on the Arts 1975; Smithsonian Inst Mus Prgm 1975; panel chmn Mus & Visual Art Instns for Rgnl Nat Conf of Artists 1976. **HONORS/ACHIEVEMENTS:** Grant recipient NY State Cncl on Arts for Genesis II Traveling Exhbn Prgm 1973. **MILITARY SERVICE:** USAF sgt 1953-57. **BUSINESS ADDRESS:** 509 Cathedral Pkwy, New York, NY 10025.

OWENS, ANGLE B., JR.
Superintendent. **PERSONAL:** Born Sep 17, 1922, Wilmington, NC; married Mattie L Bagby. **EDUCATION:** Hampton Inst, BS; VA Polytechnic Inst; State U;Univ of NE at Omaha; GA Tech;Univ of Cincinatti; Lasalle U. **CAREER:** AUS, horticulturist 1951-52; Hampton Inst, asst grounds supt 1952-55; Hampton Inst, grounds supt 1955-59; Hampton Inst, asst supt maint 1959-66; Building & Grounds Hampton Inst, supt 1966-. **ORGANIZATIONS:** Mem Peninsula C of C 1965-71; mem Assn Physical Plant Adminstr %For Coll & Univ; Nat Safety Council Coll Div; Hampton Inst Alumni Assn; consult various Penninsular Garden Clubs; Pioneer Lodge #315 Free & Accepted Masons PM; Hampton Inst Commn 1970-71; past v chmn Hampton Dem Com 1959-60; mem Am Numismatic Assn; Nat Negro Commerative Soc; NAACP; Wythe Southampton Action Com; consult Moton Found; consult FL Meml Coll; served on Review Com Handbook for Physical Plant Operations for Small Coll; served on Transportation Policy Review Com Hampto Pub Sch. **MILITARY SERVICE:** AUS 1944-46; USAR 2nd lt 1946-53. **BUSINESS ADDRESS:** Hampton Inst, Hampton, VA.

OWENS, BRIGMAN
Personal services. **PERSONAL:** Born Feb 16, 1943, Linden, TX; married Patricia Ann; children: Robin, Tracey Lynn. **EDUCATION:** Univ of Cincinnati, BA 1965; Potomac Sch of Law, JD 1980. **CAREER:** Dallas Cowboys, prof athlete 1965-66; Washington Redskins, prof athlete 1966-78; NFL Players Assn, asst exec dir 1978-84; Brig Owens & Assocs, pres. **ORGANIZATIONS:** Exec bd Boy Scouts of Amer 1974; vice pres Mondale's Task Force on Youth Employment 1978; mem Comm on Caribbean for Governor of FL 1978; bd of dirs USATelecomm Inc 1985; bd of dirs Natl Bank of Commerce 1985; bd of dirs Big Bros of America 1985; vice pres Leukemia Soc 1985. **HONORS/ACHIEVEMENTS:** All American Univ of Cincinnati 1965; author "Over the Hill to the Superbowl" 1971; Distinguished Alumni Fullerton Jr Coll 1974; Washingtonian of the Year Washington magazine 1978; Washingtonian of the Year Maryland Jaycees 1978; Hall of Stars Washington Redskins; Hall of Fame Univ of Cint; Hall of Fame Orange Co CA. **MILITARY SERVICE:** ANG 1965-70. **BUSINESS ADDRESS:** President, 600 New Hampshire Ave NW, #800, Washington, DC 20037.

OWENS, C. BURGESS
Professional athlete. **PERSONAL:** Born Aug 02, 1951, Columbus, OH. **EDUCATION:** Univ of Miami, BS 1974. **CAREER:** NY Jets, professional football player def back 1973-79; Oaklanders Raiders, 1980. **ORGANIZATIONS:** HS Am Legion Boys St 1968; pres com Student ActUniv of Miami 1972-73. **HONORS/ACHIEVEMENTS:** Iron arrow hon socUniv of Miami 1972; Asso Press All So Team 1972; Sports-News All Am; Time Mag All Am; NEW All Am Team; most valuable player ldrshp Ernie David Awd 1973; most valuable def player Jimmie Peane Meml Awd 1973; Shrines All Am Game 1973; Coll Stars vs Miami Dolphins 1973; selected to Hall of Fame Outstnd Coll Athl of Am 1973; #1 draft choice on NY Jets; Un Press Intl first team All Rookie Pro Team 1973; rookie of yr NY Jets. **BUSINESS ADDRESS:** c/o Dee Rauch, NFL Players Association, 1300 Connecticut NW Ste 407, Washington, DC 20036.

OWENS, CHARLENE B.
Business executive. **PERSONAL:** Born Sep 24, 1926, Jeff Davis Co, MS; divorced; children: Jerry, Johnnie R, Judy. **EDUCATION:** Alcorn A&M U. **CAREER:** Charlene's Enterprises Hattiesburg MS, pres; Kiddy Haven Kindergarten, tchr, owner; The Style Shop, owner; Golden Gate Funeral Home; Jerry's Modern Day Apts; Jerry B Ownens Bus & Prof Plaza; Charlene's Realty Co; Shopper's World Plaza. **ORGANIZATIONS:** Mem Nat Assn Negro Bus & Prof Women's Club; pres Nat Morticians & Funeral Dirs Assn; mem Gov's Adv Bd; Mayor's Planning Council; C of C; bd trustees Hattiesburg Pub Lib; mem Am Leg Aux; NAACP; City Fed Women. **HONORS/ACHIEVEMENTS:** BSA Award Excellence Pres

US; Peraonalities of S Alpha Kappa Alpha; honor award C of C; Gov's Commn Who's Who in Black Am 1970. **BUSINESS ADDRESS:** 208 Rosa Ave, Hattiesburg, MS 39401.

OWENS, CHARLES CLINTON
Dentist. **PERSONAL:** Born Sep 03, 1942, Smithville, TX; married Dianne Burdel Banks; children: Euau Cha, Chelsi Dion. **EDUCATION:** Prairie View A&M Univ, BS 1965; Howard Univ Sch of Dentistry, DDS 1970. **CAREER:** Model Cities Lawton, dentist 1971-72; OK State Health Dept, dentist 1972-79; dentist. **ORGANIZATIONS:** Consult OK State Health Dept 1972-79; 2nd vice pres PIC Invest Corp 1978-; treas Northside C of C 1979; treas PIC Invest Corp; mem OK Health Planning Com 1973. **HONORS/ACHIEVEMENTS:** Outstanding Young Man of the Year lawton Jaycees 1972; Appreciation Award Great Plains Vo Tech 1979; Appreciation Award Eisenhower Sr High Sch 1979. **BUSINESS ADDRESS:** 1316 Ferris, Lawton, OK 73501.

OWENS, CHARLES EDWARD
Educator. **PERSONAL:** Born Mar 07, 1938, Bogue Chitto, MS; married Otis Beatrice Holloway; children: Chris Edward, Charles Douglas, Bryant Holloway. **EDUCATION:** WV State Coll, BA 1961; WV U, MA 1965;Univ of NM, EdD 1971. **CAREER:** Psychology Dept Univ of AL, assoc prof 1973-; VA Commonwealth Univ Richmond, counselor 1971-73; Univ of WI Madison, counselor 1969-71; Albuquerque Job Corps Center for Women NM, counselor 1967-68; Charleston Job Corps Center for Women WV, coordinator of testing & referals 1966-67; Wheeling WV, teacher 1965-66. **ORGANIZATIONS:** Mem Am Psychol Assn; mem Nat Assn of Black Psychol; mem Nat Assn of Blacks in Crimnl Just; mem NAACP; mem Tuscaloosa Mental Health Assn; Plemarch Kappa Alpha Psi WV State Coll 1960-61; Phi Delta Kappa WVUniv 1965. **HONORS/ACHIEVEMENTS:** Who's Who in Am Coll &Univ 1961; US Office of Educ FellowshipUniv of NM 1968-69; book publ "Blacks & Criminal Justice" 1977; book publ "Mental Health & Black Offenders" 1980. **MILITARY SERVICE:** AUS 1st lt 1961-64. **BUSINESS ADDRESS:** Box 2968, Tuscaloosa, AL 35486.

OWENS, CURTIS
Business executive. **PERSONAL:** Born Oct 18, 1938, Philadelphia, PA; children: Curtis Derek. **EDUCATION:** Central State Univ Wilberforce, OH, BS 1962; Temple Univ, MPA 1970; California Coast Univ Santa Ana, CA, working towards PhD. **CAREER:** Mercy Douglass Hosp PA, asst adminstr; Gen' Elect PA, operations & rsch analyst; Philco Ford Corp, sr instr; Neighborhood Health Svc, cntr adminstr;Temple Univ Comprehensive Health Svcs, prog adminstr, director. **ORGANIZATIONS:** Mem Polit Sci Soc; mem Natl Health Consumer's Orgn; past pres Natl Assn of Neighborhood Health Centers Inc; mem Health Task Force Philadelphia Urban League; bd dirs Regional Comprehensive Health Planning Cncl. **HONORS/ACHIEVEMENTS:** Recip Congressman's medal of Merit 1975; Key to City of San Francisco 1975. **MILITARY SERVICE:** AUS 1st Lt Med Serv Corp. **BUSINESS ADDRESS:** President, One Buttonwood Square, Philadelphia, PA.

OWENS, DANIEL WALTER
Educator. **PERSONAL:** Born Jul 14, 1948, Malden, MA. **EDUCATION:** Univ of MA at Boston, BA eng 1971; Yale Sch of Drama; Harvard Grad Sch of Edn, EdM 1974. **CAREER:** Frederick Douglass Creative Arts Center, dir of tngt 1978-; Coll of New Rochelle, instr; Coll of Human Serv, consult humanities 1976-78; Univ of MA Boston Theatre Dept, instr 1974-76; Natl Playwights Conf Eugene O-Neill, visiting playwright 1972-75. **HONORS/ACHIEVEMENTS:** Grants to playwrights Rockefeller Found9 1978.

OWENS, DAVID K.
Engineer. **PERSONAL:** Born Jun 14, 1948, Philadelphia; married Karen P. **EDUCATION:** BS elec engr 1969; Howard U, MSEE 1977; Geo Wash U, MSEA 1977. **CAREER:** Securities & Exchange Commn, chief engr; Fed Power Commn, 1970-74; Gen Elec Co, 1969-70; Philadelphia Elec Co, 1968. **ORGANIZATIONS:** Mem Inst of Elec & Electronics Engrs; Kappa Alpha Psi Frat; Am Fed of Govt Employees; mem Nativity BVM Ch; campaign com DC Council aspirant Durwood Taylor 1974; shop steward of AFGE 1974. **HONORS/ACHIEVEMENTS:** Recip Superior Perf Award 1972; Utstanding Award 1974; Kappa Alpha Psi Frat Schroller of Yr Award 1969. **BUSINESS ADDRESS:** 1100 L St NW, Washington, DC 20549.

OWENS, DEBBIE A.
Journalist. **PERSONAL:** Born Jan 23, 1956, Brooklyn, NY. **EDUCATION:** Brooklyn Coll CUNY, BA (Cum Laude) 1977; Univ of IL Urbana-Champaign, MS 1982. **CAREER:** Chicago Tribune Newspaper, reporter 1976; NY Amsterdam Newspaper, reporter 1977; New York City Bd of Educ, hs English teacher 1978-79; JC Penney Co NY, catalog copywriter 1979-81; WPGU-FM "Black Notes", public affairs reporter 1981-82; WCIA-TV, news reporter/minority affairs prog prod 1982-85; Edward Waters Coll, radioTV broadcast instr 1982-85; Edward Waters Coll, radio/tv broadcast instr 1985-. **ORGANIZATIONS:** Mem Mayor's Vol Action Ctr of NY 1980; mem NY Vol Urban Consulting Group 1980; mem Radio-TV News Dir Assn 1982-; writer for grad newsletter Univ of IL 1981-82; mem IL News Broadcasters Assoc 1983-85. **HONORS/ACHIEVEMENTS:** Scholars Program Brooklyn Coll of CUNY 1975-77; Scholarship/Intern Newspaper Fund Prog 1976; Book Reviewer Freedomways Magazine NY 1980; Scholarship Scripps-Howard Found 1981; Grad Fellowship Univ of IL at Urbana-Champaign 1981-82. **BUSINESS ADDRESS:** Radio/TV Broadcast Instructor, Edward Waters College, 1658 Kings Rd, Jacksonville, FL 32209.

OWENS, EDWARD
Attorney. **PERSONAL:** Born Aug 18, 1957, Lexington, KY. **EDUCATION:** Univ of KY, BBA 1979, JD 1982. **CAREER:** Ed Owens III Attorney at Law, attorney 1982-84; Commonwealth of KY, asst commonwealth atty 1984-. **ORGANIZATIONS:** Legal counsel Lex NAACP 1982-84; sec Lexington Transit Auth 1984-; bd of dir Lexington Optimist Club 1984-; bd of dir Main St Manor Inc 1984-; bd dir pilot prog "One Single-Parent Housing Facility 1985-.

OWENS, EDWARD OLIVER
Business executive. **PERSONAL:** Born Jan 29, 1948, Cambridge, MA; married Maureen Baker; children: Sarhu R, Edward Oliver Jr. **EDUCATION:** NE U, BS crim just 1972. **CAREER:** Henry F Owens Inc, vice pres 1980; New Eng Minority Purch Counc, chmn adv com 1979-80. **ORGANIZATIONS:** Bd of dir MA Movers Asso Boston MA 1957-80; bd of dir Cambridge C of C 1977-80; mem Governors Task Force of Minority Businessmen 1980; mem NAACP; Black Enterprise On the Move for More 1979; Boston Magz Business You Can Trust 1979. **HONORS/ACHIEVEMENTS:** Very Important Producer Award Henry F Owens Inc Raytheon Co 1980. **BUSINESS ADDRESS:** 130 Fawcett St, Cambridge, MA 02138.

OWENS, GEORGE A.
Administrator, educator. **PERSONAL:** Born Feb 09, 1919, Hinds Co, MS; son of Charlie Owens and Robbie Henry Owens; married Ruth B Douglas, Apr 22, 1944; children: Paul Douglas Owens, Gail Patrice Owens Baity. **EDUCATION:** Jackson State Coll MS; Tougaloo Coll, AB 1941; Columbia U, MBA 1950. **CAREER:** Security Life Ins Co, clk 1946; Jersey City, bookkeeper hardware store 1947-48; Talladega Coll, bus mgr chief financial officer 1949-55; Vis Commit forContin Educ Exten Programs Harvard Univ, pres 1965; Tougaloo Coll, chief financial officer 1955-64, acting pres 1964, pres 1965-84; LeMoyne Owen Coll,interim pres 1986-87. **ORGANIZATIONS:** Mem Alpha Phi Alpha Frat Incor; bd mem United Bd for Coll Devel; pension bd United Ch of Christ; United Negro Coll Fund; life mem NAACP; Nat UrbanLeague; Phi Delta Kappa Frat; Boy Scouts of Amer; Bd of Dir Amistad Research Center 1978-; Sigma Pi Phi Fraternity. **HONORS/ACHIEVEMENTS:** Recipient honorary LLD degrees from Bethany Coll 1967, Huston-Tillotson Coll 1967, BrownUniv 1967; LHD WilberforceUniv 1970; 1st black pres of Tougaloo Coll; Hon LLD Tougaloo Coll 1984; president emeritus Tougaloo Coll; President Emeritlis Tougaloo College 1986; Silver Beaver Award Boy Scouts of America 1988. **MILITARY SERVICE:** AUS Corps of Engrs Captain 1941-46 Honorable Discharge. **HOME ADDRESS:** 815 Winthrop Circle, Jackson, MS 39206.

OWENS, HUGO ARMSTRONG
Rector, dentist. **PERSONAL:** Born Jan 21, 1916, Chesapeake, VA; son of James E. Owens and Grace Melvin Owens; married Helen West Owens, Sep 02, 1941; children: Paula Parker, Patrice, Hugo A Jr. **EDUCATION:** Virginia State University, BS, 1939; Howard University, DDS, 1947. **CAREER:** Crisfield, MD, high school teacher, 1939-42; Portsmouth, VA, high school teacher, 1942; Dr Hugo A Owens Ltd, dentist, 1947—; City of Chesapeake, vice mayor, 1970-80; Virginia State University, rector, 1982—. **ORGANIZATIONS:** Founder, president, Epsilon Nu Lambda AQA, 1952; founder, president, John L McGriff Dental Society, 1955; president, Old Dominion Dental Society, 1958-59; founder, treasurer, American Society for Preventive Dentistry, 1970; director, Eastern Region United VA Bank, 1975-; speaker of house of delegates, 1981-83, president, 1988, National Dental Association; director, Network Synergy Inc. **HONORS/ACHIEVEMENTS:** Associate editor, Trident News, Virginia Tidewater Dental Association, 1972—; First Citizens Award, Alpha Phi Alpha, 1973; poems published in The Chesapeake Collection, 1977; citation as Citizen of Decade, Norfolk newspapers, 1980; first citizen, City of Chesapeake, 1988; LLD, Virginia State University, 1988; Howard University distinguished alumni award, 1988; cited as one of 100 most influential African Americans, Ebony magazine, 1988. **MILITARY SERVICE:** US Army, cpl, 1943-44; received Good Conduct Medal, Honorable Discharge, 1944. **HOME ADDRESS:** 4405 Airline Blvd, Chesapeake, VA 23321.

OWENS, ISAIAH H.
Educator, business executive. **PERSONAL:** Born Jan 08, 1920, Columbus, GA; married Nell Craig; children: Whitlynn, Isaiah, Jr, Bert, Barrington. **EDUCATION:** Univ of IL, BFA 1948; IN U, BS 1959. **CAREER:** Roosevelt HS Gary, teacher; Owens & Craig's Inc, pres; Standard Oil, industiral distributor 1950-58; Owen's Gift & Toy Shoppe, owner 1949-65; Chicago Rockets, pro football 1948. **ORGANIZATIONS:** Vp Midtown Pusinessmen Assn 1970-73; mem Residence Com Model Cities; chmn Economic Task Force; mem Gary Alumni Chap Kappa Alpha Psi; NAACP; Roosevelt HS Alumni Assn. **HONORS/ACHIEVEMENTS:** Big Ten Football 1941, 1945, 1947; All American 1947; Most Valuable to Team 1947; All Big Ten 1947; All Midwest 1947. **MILITARY SERVICE:** AUS sgt 1941-45. **BUSINESS ADDRESS:** 1638 Broadway, Gary, IN.

OWENS, JAMES ALVIN, JR.
Business executive. **PERSONAL:** Born Feb 24, 1948, Boston, MA; married Grace E Tinch; children: Kiesha Diane, Renee Nicole. **EDUCATION:** Amos Tuck Sch of Bus Adminstrn, MBA 1975; Lincoln U, BA 1969. **CAREER:** Am Cyanamid Internat, sr market analyst; Ortho Pharmacy Corp, asst marketing research mgr 1977-78; Ocean Co Coll, adf faculty mem 1977-; Unity Bank &Trust Co, mgmt trainee 1969-71; Pfizer Internat, asst to vice pres 1977; Pfizer Internat, prod mgr 1975-77; Sudler & Hennessey Inc, advertising 1974; UpJohn Pharm Co, sales rep 1971-73. **ORGANIZATIONS:** Mem Nat Black MBA Assn; Am Mktg Assn; Omega Psi Phi Frat Gogme Fellow 1973-75; Richard M Wheeler mem. **HONORS/ACHIEVEMENTS:** Lincoln Lion Editorial Key; Achvmt Award Omega Psi Phi Frat; #1 gen terr salesman in New Eng 1972. **MILITARY SERVICE:** USNG sp 5 1975.

OWENS, JAMES E.
President. **PERSONAL:** Born Sep 07, 1937, Stonewall, MS; married Evelyn Robinson; children: James, III. **CAREER:** Chicago Metro Mutual Ins Co, mgr 1959-71; Supreme Life Ins Co, sr vice pres 1971-82, mem bd of dir 1976-82; American Investors Life Ins Co, regional dir1983-; Owens Enterprises, president 1983-. **ORGANIZATIONS:** Bd of dir Chicago Ins Assn; asst dean Cosmopolitan CC Free Sch of Bus; sect Natl Ins Assn; instr Chicago Ins Assn; mem Southend Jaycees; mem NAACP; Boy Scouts of Amer; Amer Assn of Comm & Indus; Chicago Ins Assn 1975-76; mem Natl Assn of Life Underwriters. **HONORS/ACHIEVEMENTS:** Chicago Merit Chicago Assn of Life Underwriters 1968-69; Outstanding Man of the Year Chicago Southend Jaycees 1973; Golden Scepter Award 1974. **MILITARY SERVICE:** AUS E4 1960-62. **BUSINESS ADDRESS:** President, Owens Enterprises, 523 E 67th St, Chicago, IL 60637.

OWENS, JAY R.
Dentist. **PERSONAL:** Born Feb 17, 1944, Pine Bluff, AR; married Staggie Darnelle Gordon; children: Kevin, Jay II, Latitia. **EDUCATION:** Howard Univ, BS 1967; Meharry Medical Coll, DDS 1971. **CAREER:** Private Practice, dentist. **ORGANIZATIONS:** Pres AR Medical Dental Pharmaceutical Assoc 1982-83; vice speaker of house Natl Dental Assoc 1984-85; bd of dirs Urban League of AR 1984. **MILITARY SERVICE:** AUS capt 2 yrs. **BUSINESS ADDRESS:** Ste 714 University Tower Bl, Little Rock, AR 72204.

OWENS, JEFFERSON P.
Educator. **PERSONAL:** Born Jul 10, 1917, Wharton, TX; son of Isaac Owens and Manola

Struber Owens; married Addye B Leroy; children: Sharynn. **EDUCATION:** Prairie View State Coll, Prof, Shoemaking Certificate, 1933-35; Boy Scout Exec School 89th, Exec Certificate 1943; Knoxville Coll; BA 1961; Univ of TN, MS, Educ 1977; Intl Univ Found of Europe, PhD 1985. **CAREER:** Knoxville Coll, coordinator of Alumni Affairs 1962-70; Knoxville Recreation Dept, recreation supvr 1957-62; Knoxville City Schools, classroom teacher 1971-84; TN Dept of Educ, teacher evaluator 1984-; Vine Middle School Knoxville, language arts teacher, 1985-87. **ORGANIZATIONS:** Field scout exec, Boys Scouts of Amer 1943-53; charter pres Y's Men's Club (YMCA) 1960; bd of mgmnt YMCA 1964-70; sec-treasurer educ Carpetbag Theatre 1970-80; minister of christian Ed Mount Zion Baptist Church 1980-; life mem, Alpha Phi Alpha Fraternity; Vice Moderator of Educ, Knoxville Dist Baptist Assn, 1987-88; Deputy Governor, Amer Biographical Inst, Rsch Assn, 1989. **HONORS/ACHIEVEMENTS:** Knoxville Sponsored Negro Man of the Year 1945; Religious Service Award NCCJ 1974; Outstanding Homeroom Teacher Park Jr HS 1980; Golden Apple Award by Knoxville News-Sentinel 1985. **HOME ADDRESS:** 310 Ben Hur Ave Se, Knoxville, TN 37915. **BUSINESS ADDRESS:** Language Arts Teacher, Vine Middle School, 1401 Vine Ave SE, Knoxville, TN 37915.

OWENS, JERRY SUE
Educational administrator. **PERSONAL:** Born Jan 16, 1947, Kentucky; married Ronald L Owens. **EDUCATION:** Murray St Univ, BA 1969, MA 1970; Univ of TX, PhD 1983. **CAREER:** Earlington Elem Sch, 6th grade educator 1970; Murray High School, Jr/Sr english 1970-71; Triton Coll, instructor 1971-77, asst/ assoc/ & dean of arts & sciences 1978-85; Lakewood Comm Coll, president 1985-. **ORGANIZATIONS:** Mem Natl Cncl of Teachers of English, Amer Assoc of Comm & Jr Colls, Amer Assoc of Higher Educ, Women in Higher Educ; vice pres bd YWCA St Paul MN; bd mem United Way St Paul; mem Urban League, NAACP. **BUSINESS ADDRESS:** President, Lakewood Community College, 3401 Century Ave, White Bear Lake, MN 55110.

OWENS, JIMMY
Musician, trumpeter, composer, educator,. **PERSONAL:** Born Dec 09, 1943, New York, NY; married Lola M Brown; children: Milan, Ayan. **EDUCATION:** Univ of MA, MEd 1976. **CAREER:** The Collctv Blk Artsts Inc, co-fndr 1969-; Atlantic Records, recs "You Had Better Listen" 1967; Polydor Records, "No Escapin' It" 1970; A&M Records, "Jimmy Owens" 1976; "Headin' Home" 1978; performed at the concerts & workshops USA & Eur 1973-80; Teaching Positions, Queens Borough Comm Coll 1985-86, SUNY-Old Westbury 1981-86; Jazzmobile Jazz Workshop, dir; Jay-Oh Music Co, composer/musician/educator. **ORGANIZATIONS:** Bd dir NY Jazz Reptry Co; mem Jazzmobile Workshop Staff; bd of dirs Am Arts Alliance; mem Amer Fed Mscns, Brdcst Music Inc, Recg Mscn Assn; Newport Jazz Fest Adv Bd Awards Dowbeat Critic's Poll; mem bands led by Lionel Hampton, Slide Hampton, Hank Crawford, Herbie Mann, Charles Minque, Duke Ellington, Count Bassie, Thad Jones, Mel Lewis, Billy Taylor, NY Jazz Sextet; concerts in Europe Senegal Morocco Tunisia Algeria Egypt Pakistan South America with band "Jimmy Owens Plus"; mem Natl Assoc of Jazz Educators 1974-, Universal Jazz Coalition 1977-, United Univ Profs 1981-; faculty Queensborough Comm Coll 1984-85; mem Natl• Jazz Serv Org 1985,. **HONORS/ACHIEVEMENTS:** Pres Citation for Excellence in Advancement of the Contributions of Black AmS ot Music in Am 1978; major articles written on Jimmy Owens NY Times, Downbeat Mag, Jazz Mag, Arts Midwest Jazz Letter, Jazz Journal; cited in Black Enterprise Magazine "New Leaders for the 80's"; Intl Success Awd Marabu Club (Italy); Borough President of Manhattan Awd for Excellence in the Arts 1986. **BUSINESS ADDRESS:** Composer, Jay-Oh Music Co, 236 Park Avenue South, New York, NY 10003.

OWENS, JOAN MURRELL
Educator, invertebrate paleontologist. **PERSONAL:** Born Jun 30, 1933, Miami, FL; daughter of William H Murrell and Leola Peterson Murrell; married Frank A Owens; children: Adrienne Johnson, Angela. **EDUCATION:** Fisk Univ, BA (Magna Cum Laude) 1954; Univ of MI, MA (Pi Lambda Theta) 1956; George Washington Univ, BS 1973, M Phil 1976, PhD 1984. **CAREER:** Children's Psych Hosp Univ of MI, reading therapist 1955-57; Howard Univ Dept of Eng, reading specialist 1957-64; Inst for Services to Educ DC & MA, curriculum Spec 1964-71; Smithsonian Inst DC, museum technician 1972-73; Howard Univ Washington, DC, 1976-, assoc prof of Geology. **ORGANIZATIONS:** Speaker 4th Intl Symposium Fossil Cnidaria 1983; mem, Minority Affairs Committee, Natl Assn of Geology Teacher, 1988-90. **HONORS/ACHIEVEMENTS:** College Reading Skills (Co-author), Alfred J Knopf 1966; Ford Fellowship Nat'l Fellowships Fund, Atlanta 1973-76; "Microstructural Changes in the Micrabaciidae and their Taxonomic & Ecologic Implications," Palaeontographica Americana, 1984; 1st Black American Woman Geologist with PhD in the field; mem Delta Sigma Theta; "Evolutionary Trends in the Micrabaciidae, An Argument in Favor of Pre-Adaptation," 1984 Geologos Vol II No 1; "Rhombopsammia: A New Genus of the Family Micrabaciidae," 1986 Proceedings of the Biological Soc of Washington Vol 99 No 2; "On the Elevation of the Stephanophyllia Subgenus Letepsammia to Generic Rank," Proceedings of the Biological Soc of Washington Vol 99 No 3; Scientist, Black Achievers in Science, Exhibit Museum of Science & Indus, 1988. **HOME ADDRESS:** 1824 Upshur St NE, Washington, DC 20018. **BUSINESS ADDRESS:** Assoc Prof of Geology, Dept of Geology, Howard Univ, Washington, DC 20059.

OWENS, JUDITH MYOLI
Educator. **PERSONAL:** Born Jun 18, 1940, Carlisle, PA; daughter of B Myoli Owens and Estella Pickens Owens. **EDUCATION:** Shippensburg Univ, BS Educ 1962; Monmouth Clge, MS Educ 1975. **CAREER:** NJ Educ Assc, pres 1975-77; Asbury Park Bd Educ, elem tchr, math resource room tchr, chrprsn spec educ, affirmative action ofcr, supr, vice principal; Asbury Park Bd Educ Bradley School Asbury Park NJ principal 1987-. **ORGANIZATIONS:** Natl Educ Assoc; NJ Ed Assoc; American Assoc of School Admin; Mammouth County Elementary Middle School Administrators Assoc; NJ Principals and Supervisors Assoc; Order of Kentucky Colonels; Delta Kappa Gamma; Central Jersey Club NANB PWC Inc; Asbury Park Assoc of School Administrator. **HONORS/ACHIEVEMENTS:** Natl Ach Award Natl Assc of Negro Bus & Prof Women's Clubs; Mini-grant Prog NJ State Dept of Educ; Educ Ach Award Central Jersey Club NANBPW Inc; Educ Ach Award Asbury Park Study NJ Org of Tchrs; Educ Ach Award Psi Upsilon Chptr Omega Psi Phi Frat; Educ Ach Award Monmouth Cty Bus & Prof Women's Council; Woman of Year 1976 Camden Area Club NANBPW Inc; Gold Award The United Way; Womon of the Year, Educ; Monmouth Cnty Advisory Committee on The Status of Women 1986. **HOME ADDRESS:** 64 Kathy Ct, Brick, NJ 08724. **BUSINESS ADDRESS:** Asbury Park Board of Educ, Asbury Park, NJ 07712.

OWENS, LILLIE ANNE
Business executive. **PERSONAL:** Born Oct 14, 1935, Kansas City, KS; married Chester C Jr; children: Cynthia Marie, Karen Lenora, Carla Anne. **EDUCATION:** Univ KS, 1953-54. **CAREER:** Am Woodmen's Life, pres, ceo 1969-; Cursader Life Ins Co, 1958-69. **ORGANIZATIONS:** Mem NE Bus Assn; mem Kansas City KS Womens C of C; exec bd NAACP; mem 1st AME Chand Steward Bd; bd of dirs Ave Area Merchants; advisory bd Black Adoption Program and Services. **HONORS/ACHIEVEMENTS:** 2nd place Black Bus Women of Spl Year KC Chap SCLC 1975; appeared in issue of Ebony Mag 1977; Top Execs in Biggest Black Bus; Essence Women Essence Magazine 1985; KC Star Corporate Business News 1985; Black Chamber of Commerce Black Business Women of Year 1986; Gentlemen of Distinction Black Business Women 1986. **BUSINESS ADDRESS:** President/CEO, American Woodmen's Life Ins, PO Box 507, Denver, CO 80201.

OWENS, MAJOR R.
US representative. **PERSONAL:** Born Jun 28, 1936, Memphis, TN; son of Ezekiel Owens and Edna Davis Owens; children: Christopher, Geoffrey, Millard. **EDUCATION:** Morehouse Coll, BA 1956; Atlanta Univ, MLS 1957. **CAREER:** Brooklyn Public Library, comm coord 1964-66; Brownsville Comm Council, exec dir 1966-68; NYC, commr 1968-73; Columbia Univ, instr 1973-; Communovation Assoc, pres cons; State of New York, senator 1974-82; NY State Senate Albany NY Senator 1975-82; US rep 12th dist 1983-; NY City Deputy Administrator Community Development Agency. **ORGANIZATIONS:** Commn on XVI Intl Conf Hague Netherlands 1972; mem 100 Black Men; mem NY State Black & Puerto Rican Caucus; mem Beta Phi Mu; mem Central Brooklyn Mobilization for Polit Action; NY chmn Brooklyn Congress Racial Equality; Lifetime member NAACP. **HONORS/ACHIEVEMENTS:** Awds in Black Found for Rsch & Educ in Sickle Cell Disease 1973; Honoree Awd Fed of Negro Civil Serv Orgn 1973; Achievement Awd Widow Sons' Lodge #11 Prince Hall Masons 1973; Major R Owens Day Sept 10, 1971 Pres of Borough of Brooklyn; pub author and lecturer on library sci; keynote speaker White House Conf on Libraries 1979; Honorary Doctorate of Law Degree Atlanta Univ 1986; Appointed Chairman House Subcommittee on Select Education 1987-. **BUSINESS ADDRESS:** US Representative 12th Dist, State of New York, 114 Cannon House Ofc Bldg, Washington, DC 20515.

OWENS, NATHANIEL DAVIS
Judge. **PERSONAL:** Born Feb 17, 1948, Hartsville, TN; married Barbara Catlin; children: Marsha. **EDUCATION:** Univ of South Sewanee TN, BA (with Honors) 1970; Emory Univ Law School, JD 1973; Northwestern Univ School of Law, Grad Prosecutors Course 1976; Univ of NV at Reno, Grad Natl Judicial Coll 1979. **CAREER:** Atlanta GA, rsch 1971-72; USMC Asst Defense Counsel, spec prog 1972; Atlanta Legal Aid Soc 1972; Thelma Wyatt Atty, 1972-73; Kennedy Bussey Sampson Attnys 1973-74; Huie Brown & Ide Attnys, 1974-US Army AGO Basic Course AGOBC, 1974, Ft McClellan 1974-76; Jacksonville State Univ, adj prof 1975-; 7th Judicial Circuit, asst dist attny 1976-79; Distric Court of Cleburne & Calhoun Counties, dist court judge 1979-. **ORGANIZATIONS:** Mem Mt Olive Baptist Church 1975-; 32nd Degree Master Mason 1976-; Royal Arch Mason Chap 47; Hartsville Commandry No 5 TN 1976-; 1st vice pres Assoc of US Army 1978-; former mem bd of dir Anniston Area Chamber of Commerce 1978-79; pres Club of AL State Demo Party 1978-; Omega Psi Phi Theta Tau Chap 1978-; chmnState & Local Govt Comm Chamber of Comm 1978-80; co-chmn Citizens Org for Better Ed 1979-82; Beta Kappa Boule Sigma Pi Phi 1981-. **HONORS/ACHIEVEMENTS:** Omega Man of the Year Awd Theta Tau Chap 1979; Outstanding Serv Awd Alpha Kappa Alpha Sor 1980; Case Club Awd Appellate Arguments; Case Club Judge; Moot Court Competition Awd Emory Univ School of Law. **MILITARY SERVICE:** AG/FA/CML capt 1974-; commander 496 chem detachment. **HOME ADDRESS:** 5529 Ashwood Dr, Anniston, AL 36206.

OWENS, O'DELL M.
Endocrinologist. **EDUCATION:** Yale University, New Haven CT, received medical degree, 1980, completed residency. **CAREER:** University of Cincinnatti Medical Center, Cincinnatti, former director of reproductive endocrinology and infertility division; Christ Hospital, Cincinnatti OH, currently director of reproductive endocrinology and infertility; also currently vice-chairman, Cincinnatti Board of Health. **HONORS/ACHIEVEMENTS:** Irving Friendman Award, Yale University, for most outstanding resident; fellowship in reproductive endocrinology and infertility from Harvard University Medical School; named one of Cincinnatti's 200 greatest achievers during city's bicentennial, 1988. **BUSINESS ADDRESS:** Director, Reproductive Endocrinology and Infertility, Christ Hospital, 2139 Auburn Ave, Cincinnati, OH 45219. *

OWENS, ROBERT LEE
Business owner. **PERSONAL:** Born Aug 27, 1932, Calipatria, CA; children: Reolar Thomas, Hazel, Norma, Laura, Raymond, Rachael, Robert Jr, Michael, Monique. **EDUCATION:** Bakers Field Coll, AA 1953; Pepperdine Coll, 1963; UCLA, 1965. **CAREER:** North Amer Aviation, design engr 1955-65; Aerospace Corp, rsch asst 1965-72; Owens Const Co, owner 1979-; West Fresno School Dist, pres bd of trustees. **MILITARY SERVICE:** AUS corpl 2 yrs. **HOME ADDRESS:** 844 W Hardy, Fresno, CA 93706.

OWENS, ROBERT LEON, III
Educator. **PERSONAL:** Born Nov 03, 1925, Arcadia, FL; married Nancy Gray; children: Raymond, Ronald, Nancy. **EDUCATION:** Tuskegee Inst, BS summa cum laude, class valedictorian 1949; StateUniv of IA, MA 1950; StateUniv of IA, PhD 1953; N Park Coll, LHD 1968; New York U, 1954; Columbia U, 1957; Inst for the Study of Acad Leadership, 1961; Harvard U, 1965; PA State U, 1967;Univ of MI, 1970. **CAREER:** Coll of Liberal Arts Howard U, dean 1971-;Univ of TN, v prof educ psychol 1969-71; Knoxville Coll, pres, prof of psychol 1966-71; Coll of Arts & Sci, dean; SoUniv Baton Rouge, prof of psychol & educ 1962-66; SoUniv Baton Rouge, dean grad sch, prof of psychol & educ 1958-62; So U, prof psychol & educ 1957; So U, asso prof psychol 1956; So U, asst prof psychol 1953-55; StateUniv of IA, instr psychol of reading 1953. **ORGANIZATIONS:** Mem exec com Land Grant Assn of Deans of Grad Schs 1959-71; mem Exec Com of Deans of Arts & Sci Land Grant Univs 1963-65; symposium participant Am Psychol Assn 1959, 1962, 1964; panelist Assn for Higher Educ 1959, 1963, 1972; mem exec com Am Soc for Curriculum Devel 1970; duscussant Am Conf ofAcad Deans 1973; group leader Am Conf of Acad Deans 1977; chmn, nominating com Am Conf of Acad Deans 1976; mem, bd of dir Am Conf of Acad Deans1977-80; Mem Exec Com of the Cncl on Religion & Higher Educ Research Assbn 1974-77; symposium leader Annual Conf of Inst for Intl Educ 1971-76; lectr convocation & commencement addresses at various instutions of higher educ 1975-; life mem Phi Delta Kappa. **BUSINESS ADDRESS:** HowardUniv, Coll of Liberal Arts, Washington, DC 20059.

OWENS, RONALD
Attorney. **PERSONAL:** Born Feb 04, 1930, Newark; married Louise Redding; children: Randall, Pamela. **EDUCATION:** Seton Hall Law, LLB 1959. **CAREER:** Asso Newk Muni, Judge Charles A Stanziale Jr ofcs in Newark, atty; NJ, acting governor 1976; Pro-Tempore, assembly speaker; Dist 29 Essex Co, assemblyman 1965-; NJ Gen Assembly, asst dem ldr 1972-73; City of Newark, asst corp counsel 1968-70; served in following, Assembly Educ Com; Assembley Tax PolicyStudy Commn; Assembly Welfare Commn; Assembly Criminal Law Revision Study Commn; Assembly Sex Educ Commn; Assembly Ins Revision Commn; Assembly Child Abuse Study Commn; Assembly Permanent Commn on Sch Aid; Assembly Bateman Commn; NJ Hist Commn. **ORGANIZATIONS:** Mem Nat Bar Assn; Am Bar Assn; NJ Bar Assn; Essex Co Bar Assn; Commerical Law League Of Am; trustee Anna Whittington Scholarship Fund; trustee NewarkPub Library; commr Newark Wathershed Commn; BSA; Robt Treat Council; Weequahic Comm Council; YMCA Newar Br; NAACP. **MILITARY SERVICE:** US Signal Corp 1953-55. **BUSINESS ADDRESS:** 50 Park Pl, Newark, NJ 07102.

OWENS, RONALD C.
Attorney. **PERSONAL:** Born May 01, 1936, Conway, AR; married Lois Adamson; children: Ronald, Alan, Veronica. **EDUCATION:** Morehouse Coll, 1952-54; Univ of AR at Pine Bluff, BS 1957; Univ of Baltimore Law Sch, JD 1973. **CAREER:** Baltimore City, former asst states atty; asst city solicitor; att pvt prac; Johns Hopkins U, pre-law advisor 1975-; Johns Hopkins U, former asst dir of admissions 1969-73; Ft Howard Am Bar Assn, corrective therapist. **ORGANIZATIONS:** Monumental City Bar Assn; Phi Beta Gamma Legal Frat; steward Douglas Memorial Ch. **HONORS/ACHIEVEMENTS:** Recip Ford Found Scholarship Morehouse Coll; Law Review ofUniv of Baltimore Sch of Law 1972-73; Outstandin Advocate for 1972-73;Univ of Balt Sch of Law. **MILITARY SERVICE:** AUS. **BUSINESS ADDRESS:** 3705 Dorchester Rd, Baltimore, MD 21215.

OWENS, THOMAS C.
Educational administrator. **PERSONAL:** Born May 11, 1922, Dillion Cty, SC; married Dorothy Stevens; children: Jacquelyn Hillman, Thomas C III, Brenda Hamlett, Linda Cooper, Darwin. **EDUCATION:** SC State Coll, BS 1948; SC State Coll, MA 1957; Atlantic Univ, Fellowship to study the middle school concept 1969. **CAREER:** Amer Legion Post 222, 1st post commander 1950-70; Kappa Alpha Psi, historian 1975-80; Charleston/Columbia Dist, district lay leader 1978-81; NC & SC Conf ofthe Methodist CME Churches, vice pres 1981-84; Riverside School, principal. **ORGANIZATIONS:** Advisor to registrant Bd of Registration 1972-; 1st black elected City Council 1977; mem NAACP, SCEA, SC Assn of School Admin. **HONORS/ACHIEVEMENTS:** Achievement Award Outstanding Serv to School & Community 1980, SC Admin Leadership Acad 1982; Outstanding & Dedicated Service Awd, Child Devel Class 1985; Loyal and Dedicated Service 12 year Award, Town Council 1985; Award in Appreciation for Developing "Little Minds of the Future" 1986. **MILITARY SERVICE:** AUS sgt 3 years; Purple Heart, Five Battle Stars, Good Conduct Medal, Medal of Honor 1944. **BUSINESS ADDRESS:** Principal, Riverside School, Bauknight Ferry Rd, Saluda, SC 29138.

OWENS, TREKA ELAINE
Certified public accountant. **PERSONAL:** Born Dec 06, 1953, Chicago, IL; married Johnny C Owens; children: Kellie. **EDUCATION:** DePaul Univ, BSC Acctg 1975. **CAREER:** Arthur Young & Co, auditor 1975-77; Avon Products, staff accountant 1977-78; Borg-Warner Corp, corporate acct 1978-80; Johnson Publishing Co, chief accountant 1980-86, vice pres finance 1986-. **ORGANIZATIONS:** Mem Amer Inst of CPA's 1982-, IL Soc of CPA's 1982-; treas bd of dirs Literacy Volunteers of Chicago 1985-; mem bd of dirs Chicago Equity Fund Inc 1986-. **HONORS/ACHIEVEMENTS:** Outstanding Young Women in Amer 1981. **BUSINESS ADDRESS:** Vice President Finance, Johnson Publishing Co, 820 So Michigan Ave, Chicago, IL 60605.

OWENS, VICTOR ALLEN
Telecommunications executive. **PERSONAL:** Born Sep 30, 1945, Bronx, NY; married Ruth Morrison; children: Malcolm. **EDUCATION:** Wilberforce Univ, BA 1967; Univ of Dayton, MA 1971. **CAREER:** Ohio Bell Telephone, mgr 1967-71; YWCA, business mgr 1971-76; Colonial Penn Group, mgr 1976-79; The Equitable, vice-pres 1979-. **ORGANIZATIONS:** Chmn Minority Interchange; assoc mem Big Brothers; mem Intl Communications Assoc. **HOME ADDRESS:** 169 Rutland Rd, Brooklyn, NY 11225. **BUSINESS ADDRESS:** Vice President, The Equitable, 787 7th Ave, New York, NY 10019.

OWENS, WALLACE, JR.
Educator. **PERSONAL:** Born in Muskogee, OK. **EDUCATION:** Langston Univ, BA Art Educ 1959; Central State Univ Edmond, OK, MTA 1965; Instituto Allende-Mexico, MFA Painting 1966; Univ Rome, Italy, Fulbright Scholor 1970; N TX State Univ, Doctoral Studies 1970-71. **CAREER:** Sterling HS Greenville SC, art instructor, 1969-71; Lockheed Missile Co Sunnyvale, CA, electronics tech 1971-74; Langston Univ, prof art 1966-80; Central State Univ, prof art 1980-. **ORGANIZATIONS:** Member Lions Intl 1976; Natl Conference of Artists. **HONORS/ACHIEVEMENTS:** Educators to Africans, African Amer Inst Study Tour W Africa 1973; painting owned by State Arts Collection OK. **MILITARY SERVICE:** AUS cpl. **HOME ADDRESS:** Rt 6, Box 782, Guthrie, OK 73044. **BUSINESS ADDRESS:** Asst Professor of Art, Central StateUniv, Edmond, OK 73034.

OWENS, WILLIAM
Government official. **PERSONAL:** Born Jul 06, 1937, Demopolis, AL; married Cora; children: Curtis, Laurel, William Jr, Adam. **EDUCATION:** Harvard U, MEd 1971; Boston U, 1970;Univ MA, doc cand. **CAREER:** MA, state senator 1975-; MA, state rep 1973-75; Proj JesiUniv MA, local proj dir 1971-72; State Dept Edn, dir career oppt prgm 1970; Urban League Grtr Boston, proj coord 1968-70; Sunrise Dry Cleaners, owner, mgr 1960-68. **ORGANIZATIONS:** Mem MA Leg Black Caucus; MA Black Polit Assembly; Nat Black Polit Assembly; Cncl state Govts; Ad Hoc Com on Prison Reform; Dept Corrections Adv Task Force on Voc Edn; bd dir Roxbury Defenders; Resthaven Corp; Boston Black Repertory Co; Roxbury Multi-Serv Ctr; Pre-Release Prgm; S End Nghbrhd Action Prgm; mem Harvard Club of Boston; Carribean Am Carnival Day Assn; New Hope Bapt Ch. **HONORS/ACHIEVEMENTS:** Man of Yr Award; Black Big Bros Award of Excellence; Houston Urban League Plaque; Ft Devens Black Hist Mth Plaque. **BUSINESS ADDRESS:** State House Rm #405, Boston, MA 02133.

OWENS-HICKS, SHIRLEY
State official. **PERSONAL:** Born Apr 22, 1942, Demopolis, AL; daughter of Reverand Johnathan Owens and Mary Owens; children: Dawn Deirdre, Stephanie Alicia. **EDUCATION:** Chandler School for Women, Certificate 1961; Boston Univ School of Educ, 1969-71; Harvard Univ Graduate School of Educ, EdM 1972. **CAREER:** Massachusetts Senate, chief aide to senator 1975-80; Urban League of Eastern Mass, Inc, deputy dir 1980-81, president/exec dir 1981-83; Boston School Committee, vice president 1984-88; Univ of Massachusetts at Boston, advocacy counselor 1984-86; Commonwealth of Massachusetts, state rep 1987-. **ORGANIZATIONS:** Mem Delta Sigma Theta Sorority, St Paul AME Church, Harvard Univ Alumni Assn, Urban League, NAACP, Massachusetts Black Legislative Caucus, Joint (House & Senate) Comm on Educ, Human Serv and Elderly Affairs; co-founder Mothers Against Drugs. **HONORS/ACHIEVEMENTS:** Certificate of Appreciation Simmons College 1978; Achievement Plaque Urban League Guild of Eastern Massachusetts 1983; Woman of the Year Zeta Phi Beta Sorority 1984; Certificate of Appreciation Boston Students Advisory Council 1985, 1987; Promoting Excellence in Educ Freedom House Inst on Schools and Educ 1986; Educ Award Black Educators Alliance of MA 1986; Bi-Lingual Master Parents Advisory Council Award 1986; Woman of the Year Univ of MA at Boston Black Students Org 1987. **HOME ADDRESS:** 115 Hazelton St, Mattapan, MA 02126. **BUSINESS ADDRESS:** State Representative, Commonwealth of Massachusetts, State House Room 473-G, Boston, MA 02133.

OWENS-SMITH, JOYCE LATRELL
Association executive, administrator. **PERSONAL:** Born Jul 21, 1949, Leland, MS; divorced; children: Kevin, Kelli. **EDUCATION:** Seattle Pacific Univ, BA Sociology 1973-77; Univ of Washington Seattle, MSW 1977-79. **CAREER:** Highest High Inc, prog coord 1973-76; New Careers Inc OJSD, career counselor 1976-; Seattle Counseling Svc, exec dir 1976-78; CA State Office of Econ Devel, field rep 1978-79; Human Resources Bureau Train & Employ, planner III 1979-80; Urban League of Portland, comm svcdir 1981-83, vice pres prog 1983-84; Orange Cty Urban League, pres. **ORGANIZATIONS:** Suprv bd mem WA State Fed Feminist Credit Union 1977; newsletter ed grant writing Assoc of WA Comm Youth Serv 1977; grant writer/resource devel Sacramento Women's Ctr 1978-79; past pres, vice pres Multnomah Cty Comm Health Council 1980-84; chap sponsor Parent's Anonymous 1982; mem Delta Sigma Theta 1983-. **HONORS/ACHIEVEMENTS:** Acad Scholarship WA State Black Soc Workers 1977; nominee CA State Assembly Fellowship 1979; Cert Labor Market Info & CETA Planning US Dept of Labor Training 1980; Cert Contemporary Issues for the Black Family Howard Univ School of Continuing Ed Washington DC 1981. **BUSINESS ADDRESS:** President, Orange County Urban League, 106 W 4th St, #302, Santa Ana, CA 92701.

OXENDINE, JOHN EDWARD
Financial administrator. **PERSONAL:** Born Jan 20, 1943, New York, NY. **EDUCATION:** Hunter Coll CityUniv of NY, AB 1965; HarvardUniv Grad Sch of Bus, MBA 1971. **CAREER:** FAD FSLIC Fed Home Loan Bank Bd, acting chief 1979-; First Nat Bank of Chicago Mexico, asst rep 1977-79; First Nat Bank of Chicago, asst mgr 1974-77; Korn & Ferry Internat, sr asso consulting 1973-74; Fry Consultants, mgmt consultant 1971-73; Bedford Stuyvestant Restoration Corp, mgmt adv 1968-70; Bd of Educ NY City, tchr 1965-68;Univ of Redlands Redlands CA, lectured 1974. **ORGANIZATIONS:** Bd of trustees mem Nat Urban League 1972-78. **HONORS/ACHIEVEMENTS:** Award of Excellence in Russian Language & Studies USMCR 1968; "Importance of Profit Motivation & Mgmt Assistance in Develop Programs" DukeUniv Lawy Review 1970; JH Whitney Grad Fellowship Grant JH Whitney Found 1970. **MILITARY SERVICE:** USMCR staff sgt 1967-73.

OXLEY, LEO LIONEL
Psychiatrist. **PERSONAL:** Born Jul 09, 1934, Raleigh, NC; children: Keith Charles, Claire Elaine. **EDUCATION:** St Augustine CollRaleigh NC, BS 1955; Meharry Med Coll, MD 1959. **CAREER:** William Beaumont General Hosp, internship; Walter Reed General Hosp, chief resident 1960-63; Brooklyn-Staten Island Mental Health Serv of Hlth Insurance Plan of Greater NY, dir 1971-73; Natchaug Hospital, staff psychiatrist 1973-74; Newington Veterans Admin Hosp, chief psychiatry serv 1974-78; GA Mental HealthInst, supt 1978-80; The Institute of Living, sr staff psychiatrist 1980-82; VA Medical Ctr Chillicothe OH, chief psychiatry serv 1982-83; VA Medical Ctr Leavenworth KS, chief psychiatry serv 1983-84; Brecksville VA Med Ctr Natl Ctr for Stress Recovery, assoc clinical dir 1984-85; VA Med Ctr, chief mental hygiene clinic 1985-86; VA Med Ctr Cleveland, staff psychiatrist. **ORGANIZATIONS:** Life mem Alpha Phi Alpha Frat; mem Amer Medical Assoc, Amer Psychiatric Assoc, World Federation for Mental Health, Medical Soc State of NY, State of CTMedical Soc; licensed to practice medicine in NY, MO, CT, GA. **HONORS/ACHIEVEMENTS:** Mem Alpha Omega Alpha Honor Medical Soc; publication "Issues and Attitudes Concerning Combat Experienced Black Vietnam Veterans," Journal Natl Medical Assoc Vol 79 No 1 1987 pp 25-32. **MILITARY SERVICE:** AUS col 1958-67; USAR 1977-. **HOME ADDRESS:** 2837 Lee Rd, Shaker Heights, OH 44106.

OXLEY, LUCY ORINTHA
Physician. **PERSONAL:** Born Aug 19, 1912, Harrisburg, PA; widowed. **EDUCATION:** Univ Cincinnati, BS 1935; DNB 1938; Am Acad Family Physicians, flw 1974. **CAREER:** Family physician self; Southwestern OH Coc of Family Physicians Institutum Divi Thomae, pres elect 1945-52; Wilberforce U, 1937-39; Bennett Coll for Women, stud hlth physician 1936-37; Bethesda Hosp, staff; Freedmen's Hosp, intern 1935-36. **ORGANIZATIONS:** Mem Cincinnati Acad Med; Am Acad Family Physicians; Am Med Women's Assn; Med Women's Intrnat Assn; Southwestern OH Assn Family Physicians; Adv Cncl of Catherine Booth Home of Salvation Army; pres Woodward HS Alumnal Assn 1975-77; tst Woodward HS 1973; pres SW OH Society of Family Physicians 1979-81. **HONORS/ACHIEVEMENTS:** Spl achvmt award AMA 1967-; US rep Intl Med Women Con 1968, 1970, 1974, 1976; appointed OH State Med Bd by Gov Rhodes for 7 yr term 1980-87. **BUSINESS ADDRESS:** Physician, 1621 Dexter Ave, Cincinnati, OH 45206.

OYALOWO, TUNDE O.
Senior corporate consultant. **PERSONAL:** Born Oct 16, 1953, Lagos, Nigeria;married Marie Bongjoh; children: Akin. **EDUCATION:** State Univ of NY Brockport, BS 1979; Atlanta Univ, MBA 1980. **CAREER:** APC Skills Co FL, project mgr 1981-86; APC Mgmt Serv Brussels, project mgr 1983-84; Mellon Bank Corp NA, sr corporate consultant. **ORGANIZATIONS:** Mem Amer Mgmt Assoc 1980-84, Amer Soc for Quality Control, Natl Assoc of Black MBA's, 100 Black Men of Western PA, Toastmaster Intl; volunteer United Way; dir Kolet Construction. **HONORS/ACHIEVEMENTS:** Beta Gamma Sigma Atlan-

ta Univ 1980. **HOME ADDRESS:** 168 Thunderwood Dr, Bethel Park, PA 15102. **BUSINESS ADDRESS:** Sr Corporate Consultant, Mellon Bank Corporation NA, One Mellon Bank Ctr, Pittsburgh, PA 15258.

OYESHIKU, PATRICIA DELORES WORTHY
Educator. **PERSONAL:** Born Nov 03, 1944, Miami, FL; daughter of Inez Brantley; married Anthony A Oyeshiksu, May 25, 1968; children: Kama Charmange Titilola, Chaundrissa Morenike. **EDUCATION:** Knoxville Coll, Knoxville TN, BS English, 1964; San Diego State Univ, San Diego CA, MA Curriculum, 1971; US Intl, San Diego CA, PhD Educational Leadership, 1980. **CAREER:** Peace Corps, Brazil, volunteer, 1964-66; Peace Corps, San Francisco CA, recruiter, 1966-67; Peace Corps, Boston MA, deputy dir recruiter, 1967-68; San Diego City Schools, San Diego CA, teacher, 1970-. **ORGANIZATIONS:** Volunteer, Homeless Shelter, San Diego CA. **HONORS/ACHIEVEMENTS:** Outstanding Peace Corps Volunteer, presented by Hubert Humphrey, 1966; California Teacher of the Year, 1980-81; Natl Teacher of the Year Finalist, 1980-81; Press Club Award, San Diego CA; Outstanding Alumni in Education, San Diego State Univ; doctoral dissertation "The Effect of the Race of the Teacher on the Student.". **HOME ADDRESS:** 7985 Hillandale Dr, San Diego, CA 92120.

OYEWOLE, SAUNDRA HERNDON
Educator. **PERSONAL:** Born Apr 26, 1943, Washington, DC; daughter of Laurence Homer Herndon and Helen Kirkland Herndon; married Godwin G Oyewole, Mar 21, 1970; children: Ayodeji Babatunde, Monisola Aramide, Kolade Olufayo. **EDUCATION:** Howard Univ, BS (Magna Cum Laude, Phi Beta Kappa, Beta Kappa Chi) 1965; Univ of Chicago, MS 1967; Univ of MA Amherst, PhD 1973. **CAREER:** Hampshire Coll, asst prof of Microbiology 1973-79, assoc prof of Microbiology 1979-81; Trinity Coll, assoc prof of Biology/Electron Microscopist 1981-87; prof of Biology, 1988-. **ORGANIZATIONS:** Mem Amer Soc for Microbiology; mem Comm on the Status of Minority Microbiologists of the Amer Soc for Microbiology 1984-; exec comm Northeast Assoc of Advisors for the Health Profs 1984-87; coord Health Professions Adv Comm Trinity Coll; coord Pre-Nursing Prog Trinity Coll; mem, advisory council of North East Assn of Advisors for the Health. Professions, 1987-. **HONORS/ACHIEVEMENTS:** Danforth Associate 1979; pres Epsilon Chap of Phi Beta Kappa 1983-85. **BUSINESS ADDRESS:** Associate Professor Biology, Trinity College, 125 Michigan Ave NE, Washington, DC 20017.

OZIM, FRANCIS TAIINO
General surgeon. **PERSONAL:** Born Oct 01, 1946, Lagos, Nigeria;married Margaret Fay Taylor; children: Brion Olufemi, Frances Adetola, Melissa Funmilayo. **EDUCATION:** St Finbarr's Coll Lagos Nigeria, WASC 1965; St Gregory's Coll Lagos Nigeria, HSC 1967; Howard Univ Medical Sch, MD 1976. **CAREER:** Georgetown Univ Med Ctr, intern 1976-77; Howard Univ Hosp, resident surgery 1977-81; District of Columbia General Hosp, attending in surgery 1981-82; Charlotte Memorial Hosp & Medical Ctr, active staff 1982-86; Norfolk Comm Hosp, active staff 1987-; Sufnor Surgical Group, general surgeon. **ORGANIZATIONS:** Active staff Louise Obici Memorial Hosp Suffolk 1987-, Maryview Hosp Portsmouth 1987-, Norfolk Comm Hosp 1987-, Norfolk General Hosp 1987. **HONORS/ACHIEVEMENTS:** Fellow Southeastern Surgical Congress 1982-, Amer Coll of Surgeons 1986-. **BUSINESS ADDRESS:** General Surgeon, Sufnor Surgical Group, 549 E Brambleton Ave, Norfolk, VA 23510.

P

PACE, KAY ROBERTINE
Educator. **PERSONAL:** Born in Mobile, AL. **EDUCATION:** Xavier Univ LA, BA 1968; Southern IL Univ Carbondale, MM 1970; Peabody Conservatory of Johns Hopkins Univ Baltimore, DMA 1984. **CAREER:** Southern IL Univ, instr music & coord of accompanying 1970-73; AL State Univ, asst prof of piano. **ORGANIZATIONS:** Coord Univ Piano Guild 1975-; mem Delta Omicron Music Frat for Women 1976-; coord of keyboard AL State Univ 1979-; pres & founder Soc of Friends of Music Montgomery 1979; mem AL Theory Teachers Assoc 1981-; chairperson Dean Selection Comm Music ASU 1982-83; mem Delta Sigma Theta Sor 1983. **HONORS/ACHIEVEMENTS:** Elected mem Phi Kappa Phi Natl Honor Soc 1969, Pi Kappa Lambda Music Honor Soc 1970; Solo piano concerts throughout US 1970-; 1st Place Winner IL State Music Teachers Young Artist Comp 1972, St Louis Artist Presentation Comp 1973; Spec Study Grant Van Cliburn Intl Piano Comp 1977; Otto Ortmann Theory Awd Peabody Conserv of Music 1978; Fellowship Ford Foundation for Doctoral Study 1978-81; SE Reg Winner Natl Black Music Comp 1979; A Portrait of Kay Pace AL Public TV 30 min spec 1979. **HOME ADDRESS:** 3252 Virginia Loop Court, Montgomery, AL 36116. **BUSINESS ADDRESS:** Asst Prof of Piano, Alabama State University, 915 S Jackson St, Montgomery, AL 36195.

PACKER, LAWRENCE FRANK
Dentist. **PERSONAL:** Married Erma Hill. **EDUCATION:** Tougaloo Coll; Megarry Med Coll, DDS 1927. **CAREER:** Rollins United Meth Ch, lay pastor; Beasley United Meth Ch; Meharry, 50 yrs dental serv 1927-77. **ORGANIZATIONS:** Mem OBE; IBPOE. **BUSINESS ADDRESS:** 634 E Harrison, Ruleville, MS 38771.

PADDIO-JOHNSON, EUNICE ALICE
Education administrator. **PERSONAL:** Born Jun 25, 1928, Crowley, LA; daughter of Henry Paddio and Cecile A Chesle; married John David Johnson, Sr; children: Deidre Reed Dyson, Clarence III, Henry P, Bertrand J, Cecile A Reed. **EDUCATION:** Leland Coll Baker, LA Grmblg State Univ Grambling LA, BS 1949; UCLA, MA 1960; LA State Univ Baton Rouge, 1966, 1975; Univ MN St Paul, 1975; State Univ NY Albany, 1980; Cornell Univ, Ithaca, MS, 1987. **CAREER:** St Helena Parish Shls (LA), tchr/cous, 1949-72; St Helena Smr Hd Start (LA), asso dir 1965-69; St Helena Assis Resou Est (LA), pres/dir 1972-73; Cornell Univ (NY), admin 1973-85; St Helena Head Start, dir 1986-; Paddio-Johnson Enterprises Inc, pres. **ORGANIZATIONS:** Mem Am AssocUniv Wmn 1980-; edt jour exec comm hee mem LA Ed Assoc 1964-69; schl brd mem St Helena Parish Schl (LA) 1972-73; Ithaca City Schl NY 1975-82; pres Paddio Ent (Hmn Relat Consu & Comp Portr 1980-; brd dir Fmly & Childs Serv, Plnd Parenthd of Tompkins Co, Ithaca Nbhd Hsg SvcsP-R Found Atlanta Child 1975-; pres Martin Luther King Jr Schlshp Fund Inc 1982-86. **HONORS/ACHIEVEMENTS:** Grd assoc Matron for LA Esther Grand Chptr OES 1963-74; outstdng cit City of New Orleans 1973; blk & gold awd Grambling StateUniv 1973; Creat Career Exp Prog 1975; author Gene Wng Behvr Skills 1976-77; hnr Eunice Paddio-Johnson Foundt Inc 1972-. **HOME ADDRESS:** PO Box 245, Greensburg, LA 70441.

PADGETT, JAMES A.
Educator, artist. **PERSONAL:** Born Nov 24, 1948, Washington, DC; son of James Padgett and Pauline C Flournoy; married Joan M Jemison; children: Anthony A. **EDUCATION:** Corcoran Sch of Art, WW; Howard U, BFA 1972; HowardUniv Grad Sch, MFA 1974. **CAREER:** WilberforceUniv Dept of Art, instr. **ORGANIZATIONS:** Mem HowardUniv Mural Proj Com 1968-; mem DC Comm on the Arts Mural Proj Comm 1968-72; murals erected & various sites Howard U, Anacostia Museum, Smithsonian Inst, Sch of Soc Work, Howard U; traveling mural touring 30 states; Shaw Com Comp Health Cntr Nat Med Assn Found HowardUniv Hosp Coll of Med; co-dir Martin Luther King Jr Arts Festival; man gallery exhibitions. **HONORS/ACHIEVEMENTS:** Selected to participate in touring art exhib "Paintings from Am U"; recip Cert of AppreciationUniv Neighborhood Coun 1964; Cert of Accom Summer EnrichProg Art Dir 1965; Wash Rel Arts Exhib Am Savings & Loan Assn DC; first prize Collage & Painting 1966; Cert of Commen Upward Bound Coll Prog HowardU 1966; Corcoran Schlship Award W W Corcoran Sch of Art 1967; Cert of Art DC Rec Dept Art & Splst Instr 1967-68; scnd prize The Town Square Art Show Inc Collage & Painting 1969; thrd prize Outdoor Art Exhib Painting 1969; thrd prize Artists Unlmtd Painting 1969; first & scnd prize Artists Unlmtd Painting 1970; Monitor Asst Grant HowardUniv Coll of Fine Arts 1970; first prize Hon Mention Ch of the Brethren Arts Exhib Painting 1971; scnd prize SkowheganSch of Painting & Sculp Painting 1971; Schlrshp Award HowardUniv Coll of Fine Arts 1968-72; Schlrshp Award HowardUniv Grad Sch of Fine Arts 1972-73; Schlrshp Award Skowhegan Sch of Painting & Sculp summer 1971; Afro-Am Artist a bio-bibliog directory; Images of Change-1 Art Society in Transition; Chrmn 4th International Conference on Art, in honor of her majesty Queen Elizabeth II, 1977; K Miller Galleries LTD, the Old Bank Gallery, 1979; Galerie Des Deux Mondes Gallery of Art, 1980. **BUSINESS ADDRESS:** Wilberforce Univ, Wilberforce, OH.

PADULO, LOUIS
Education administrator. **PERSONAL:** Born Dec 14, 1936, Athens, AL; married Katharine Seamans; children: Robert, Joseph. **EDUCATION:** Fairleigh Dickinson Univ, BS 1959; Stanford Univ, MS 1962; GA Inst Tech, PhD 1966. **CAREER:** RCA, systems analyst 1959-60; San Jose State Coll, asst prof 1962-63; GA State Coll, asst prof 1966-67; GA Tech Eng Experiment Station, consult 1966-69; Morehouse Coll, assoc prof chmn of math dept 1967-69; Stanford Univ, assoc prof 1969-75; Columbia Univ, 1969; Harvard Univ, visiting prof 1970; Stanford, 1971-72 1973; Atlanta Univ Center & GA Tech, founder & dir dual degree prog; Boston Univ, dean coll of engrg prof of math & engrg 1975-. **ORGANIZATIONS:** Chmn planning commn Expanding Minority Oppors Engrg 1973-; mem Natl Acad Engrg Com Minorities Engrg. **HONORS/ACHIEVEMENTS:** Awd for Excellence in Sci & Engrg Educ Natl Consortium for Black Professional Devel 1977; W Elec Fund Awd 1973; Walter J Gores Awd Stanford Univ 1971; Vincent Bendix Awd 1984; Reginald H Jones Awd of NACME 1983. **BUSINESS ADDRESS:** Dean/Prof of Math & Engrg, BostonUniv, Coll Engrg, 110 Cummington St, Boston, MA 02215.

PAGE, ALAN CEDRIC
Professional athlete, attorney. **PERSONAL:** Born Aug 07, 1945, Canton, OH; son of Howard Felix Page and Georgianna Umbles; married Diane Sims; children: Nina, Georgianna, Justin, Khamsin. **EDUCATION:** Univ of Notre Dame, BA 1967; Univ of MN Law Sch, JD 1978. **CAREER:** Minnesota Vikings, professional football player 1967-78; Chicago Bears, professional football player 1978-81; Lindquist & Vennum (Law Firm), associate 1979-84; State of MN, spec asst atty gen 1985-87, asst atty general 1987-. **ORGANIZATIONS:** Amer Lung Assn Run for Your Life 1978; exec com Artists & Athletes Against Apartheid 1984; Mixed Blook Theatre Adv Bd 1984; Fedn for Progress ad hoc comm to keep S Africa out of Olympics 1984; search com Univ of MN football coach 1983; adv bd League of Women Voters 1984; comm mem Honeywell Literacy TaskForce 1948; hon co-chair Child Care Works 1984; concert sponsor Natl multiple Sclerosis Soc 1985; player rep Natl Football League Player's Assn 1970-74 and 1976-77; mem NFLPA's exec com 1972-75; weekly commentary for Morning Edition on Natl Pub Radio 1982; Color commentary work for TBS Sports - Coll Football Game of the Week 1982; speaker to young teens with emphasis in minority areas on the importance education; MN State Bar Assn; Natl Bar Assn; Amer Bar Assn; Hennepin Cnty Bar Assn; bd mem Chicago Assn Retarded Citizens; Chicago MS Read-A-Thon 1979; former chmn Amer Cancer Soc State of MN; chmn United Negro Coll Fund 1972; chmn MN Cncl on Physical Fitness 1972; Minneapolis Urban League, bd mem 1987-; bd of regents, Univ of Minnesota 1987-. **HONORS/ACHIEVEMENTS:** First defensive player in hist of NFL to rec Most Valuable Player Award 1971; Amer's Ten Outstanding Young Men US Jaycees 1981; NFL's Marathon Man First NFL player to complete a full 262 mile marathon; inducted into NFL Hall of Fame, 1988; completed Edmund Fitzgerald Ultra-Marathon (62 miles) 1987; established Page Education Foundation to assist minority youth in post secondary education 1988. **BUSINESS ADDRESS:** Assistant Atty General, State of Minnesota, 520 Lafayette, St Paul, MN 55155.

PAGE, CEDRIC DANIEL
Educator. **PERSONAL:** Born Sep 08, 1945, Syracuse, NY. **EDUCATION:** Syracuse U, AB 1967; Rutgers U, MA 1969; Rutgers U, PhD 1977. **CAREER:** Univ of CO, asst prof 1977; USAF Acad, asst prof 1969-73; Univ of CO, inst 1970-73; Natl Endowment for the Humanities CO Dept of Hwys Planners Etc of Denver, consultant 1980-; Natl Science Found, reviewer 1976-80; Natl Conf on the Black Family, cord 1976; Urban Studies Prog Univ of CO, dir 1977-; Partners Inc, bd of dir 1976; Park East Center for Community Mental Health, bd of dir. **ORGANIZATIONS:** Mem Comm on Geography & Afro Am 1972-75, 1979-80; Fellowship Black Am in Higher Educ 1974-75. **MILITARY SERVICE:** USAF cpt 1973. **BUSINESS ADDRESS:** 1100 14th St, Denver, CO 80202.

PAGE, GREGORY OLIVER
Dentist. **PERSONAL:** Born Feb 26, 1950, Philadelphia, PA; children: Dylan Mikkel. **EDUCATION:** Howard Univ, BS 1972; Univ of Pennsylvania, DMD 1976. **CAREER:** North Central Bronx Hosp, attending dentist,1978-80; Health Insurance Prog of New York, Bronx, dir of dentistry, 1978-82; private practice, dentist, 1982-; Hostos Community Coll, CCNY, asst adjunct prof, 1978-87. **ORGANIZATIONS:** Mem, Howard Univ Alumni Club of New York City, 1976-; mem, Acad of Gen Dentistry, 1976-; mem, Amer Dental Assn, 1976-; mem, Amer Dentists for Foreign Serv, 1983-; mem, St Phillip's Church of New York

City, 1986-; mem, 100 Black Men of New York City, 1987-. **HONORS/ACHIEVEMENTS:** Fellowship in Restorative Dentistry, Albert Einstein Coll of Medicine, 1976; author of "Some Wisdom About Teeth," Ebony magazine, 1987. **BUSINESS ADDRESS:** Asst Adjunct Professor/Dentist, Hostos Community College, 10 W 135th St, #1-E, New York, NY 10037.

PAGE, MARGUERITE A.
Educator. **PERSONAL:** Born in Savannah, GA; married Charles D (deceased); children: Carrie, Gregory Allen, Charles, Jr, Linda. **EDUCATION:** Howard U, BS 1944; NY Inst of Dietetics, 1945; NY U, MS 1951. **CAREER:** St Francis Hosp Trenton NJ, dietitian 1946-47; NYC, nursery sch tchr 1947-49; helped organize Guidance Guild Nursery 1949; Guidance Guild Nursery, tchr, dietitian 1949-51; Paterson Pub Sch, tchr 1951-54; Newark NJ, tchr of trainable mentally retarded 1954-; Headstart, tchr summer 1966; Passaic Summer Headstart, asst dir 1967; Passaic Summer Headstart, dir 1968-69. **ORGANIZATIONS:** Former mem Fair Housing Commn; mem Passaic Human Relations Commn; mem NAACP; sec Passaic Rub Orgn; v chmn Passaic Rep Orgn; League of Women Voters; Cit Action Com; Black Women's Council; bd dir Guidance Guild Nursery Sch; mem Alpha Kappa Alpha Sor; mem Roger Williams Bapt Ch; supt of Sunday Sch; mem Passaic Bd of Educ 1971-77; Passaic; Commissioner NJ Advisory Commission Status of Women 1985-. **HONORS/ACHIEVEMENTS:** Bd of trustees St Mary's Hosp Passaic 1st bld so honored; received GOP nom for Passaic Co freeholder 1st black woman to receive legis nom for either party in Passaic Co; testimonial dinner Black Women's Council 1975; 1st black woman elected official in Passaic; Comm Involmt Award Nat Counc of Negro Women 1975; outstanding community service Pi Xi Omega Chapter Alpha Kappa Alpha Sorority 1989. **BUSINESS ADDRESS:** 2 Cedar St, Newark, NJ 07055.

PAGE, ROSEMARY SAXTON
Attorney. **PERSONAL:** Born Jan 29, 1927, New York, NY; divorced; children: Marjorie, Christopher. **EDUCATION:** Fisk Univ, BS 1948; Howard Univ Sch of Law, 1959. **CAREER:** Legal Aid Soc of NYC, assoc coun 1967-70; Nassau Co Law Svcs, atty 1970-72; Fordham Univ Sch of Law, adjunct prof 1983-; Amer Arbitration Assn, assoc gen counsel; Touro Law Sch, adjunct 1986. **ORGANIZATIONS:** Editor Digest of Ct Decisions 1973-76; Arbitration Com Bar Assn of New York City 1974-77; Labor & Employment Com Bar Assn of New York City 1981-85; Natl Bar Assn 1977-; NBABd of Govs & chmn NBA Arbitration Sect 1981-; NY State Bar 1961-; USDC, SDNY 1969; USDC, EDNY 1969; USDC, NDNY 1984; US Ct of Appeals 1969; US SupremeCt 1973; bd of dir Huntington Youth Bd 1972-77, vice chmn of bd 1976-77; published numerous articles. **BUSINESS ADDRESS:** Associate General Counsel, American Arbitration Assn, 140 W 51st St, New York, NY 10020.

PAGE, WILLIE F.
Educator. **PERSONAL:** Born Jan 02, 1929, Dothan, AL; married Gracie Tucker. **EDUCATION:** Wayne State U, BSME 1961; Adelphi U, MBA 1970; NY U, PhD 1975. **CAREER:** Brooklyn Coll CUNY, asso prof 1979-; Dept of Africana Studies Brooklyn Coll, chmn, asso prof 1974-79; Nassau-Suffolk CHES, exec dir 1972-74; Glen Cove Coop Coll Center SUNY, dir, lectr 1971-72; Grumman Aerospace, asst to dir prodn 1967-70; The Boeing Co, engr 1961-63; New York City Head Start Regional Training Office, consult 1975-79; Natl Endowment for the Humanities, consult 1977-78; NY State Educ Dept, consult 1977-79. **ORGANIZATIONS:** Mem African Heritage Studies Assn 1974-80; mem Am Educ Research Assn 1974-80; bd mem Weeksville Soc Brooklyn 1979-80. **HONORS/ACHIEVEMENTS:** EPDA Fellowship USOE NYU 1973; Dissertation Year Fellowship Nat Fellowships Fund Atlanta 1975; Henry Meissner Research Award Phi Delta Kappa NYU 1975; NEH Fellowship Seminar on Slavery HarvardUniv 1978. **MILITARY SERVICE:** AUS 1st lt 1950-53. **BUSINESS ADDRESS:** Brooklyn, NY 11210.

PAIGE, ALVIN
Education administrator, artist. **PERSONAL:** Born Jul 13, 1934, LaGrange, GA; son of Edward Paige and Dora Jane McGee Paign; married Susan Lee, Feb 29, 1988; children: Monica L, Paige,Gaila R Paige, Alvin Jr, Shaneane Paige Foster. **EDUCATION:** American International College, BA Political Sci 1980; Antioc Coll, MA Administ 1981; advanced graduate studies, Harvard Univ. **CAREER:** The Beeches Resort Rome, NY, art dir 1965-67; Display workshop Hartford, CT, chief designer 1967-68, dir of art 1968-69; Paige Innovations Enterprise, managing dir 1970-75; American Intl Coll, resident artist/designer & dir of cultural and perf arts center 1978-. **ORGANIZATIONS:** Bd dirs Natl Collegiate Conf Assn 1979; chmn Symphony Hall Promotion Comm; mem Inst of Urban Design Architectural League of NY; mem Natl Sculptors Soc; mem British Sculptors Soc; mem Free Painters and Sculptors of London, England; bd of directors Berkshire Ballet 1987-89; bd of directors Springfield Mayors Office of Cultural Affairs 1988-89; bd of directors Springfield Neighborhood Housing Services 1988-89; cooperator: Stage West Theatre Company 1988-89. **HONORS/ACHIEVEMENTS:** "The Gift" public art Springfield, MA 1978 largest indoor public art installation 20,000 sq ft Springfield, MA 1980; Produced sculpture "Dignity" for year ofHandicapped at United Nations NY, NY 1981; Largest outdoor conceptual art installation 6 ton limestone "Stage of Dionysus" 1984 Springfield, MA; Rome, NY largest statue of Christ in US 1959; 1960-61 two 55 foot conceptual kinetic art install Rome, NY; Natl One man sculptors exhibit tour 1984-85; Acad Polit Sci Achvmnt American Intl College 1980; US Steel Cost Incentive Award 1982; Alvin Paige Day LaGrange, GA 1983; Council for Advance Support to Education "ExceptAchvmnt" Award 1982; Outstanding Amer Spirits of Honor Medal 1957; Governor TX Citizenship Award 1958; 3 Intl Art Exhibits People's Republic of China 1989; Invitational Intl E xhibit Royal Hibernian Academy Dublin Ireland 1988. **MILITARY SERVICE:** USAF 8 years; Maj; Non-Commissioned Officers Award (4-times). **HOME ADDRESS:** 3 East St, North Grafton, MA 01536. **BUSINESS ADDRESS:** Resident Artist/Designer, American International College, 1000 State St, Springfield, MA 01109.

PAIGE, EMMETT, JR.
Military officer. **PERSONAL:** Born Feb 20, 1931, Jacksonville, FL; son of Emmet Paige and Elizabeth Core Paige; married Gloria Mc Clary, Mar 01, 1953; children: Michael, Sandra, Anthony. **EDUCATION:** Univ of MD, BA 1972; Penn State, MA 1974; Army War Coll, 1974. **CAREER:** 361st Signal Brigade US Army Vietnam, comdr 1969; 11th Signal Brigade US Army Ft Huachuca, AZ, comdr 1975; US Army Comm Elec Engr & Install Agy, comdr1976-79; US Army Comm & Syst Agy, comdr 1976-79; US Army Inform Sys Command, commanding gen; US Army Communicat Rsrch & Devel Command, comdr 1979-; advanced through grades to Lieutenant General on July 1, 1984. **ORGANIZATIONS:** Bd of dir Armed Forces Comm Elect Assn 1980 mem Am Leg Post 224 1976-; mem Amer Radio Relay League. **HONORS/ACHIEVEMENTS:** Legion of Merit with three oak leaf clusters 3 times AUS; only blck signal corps ofcr ever promoted to Grade of Gen AUS 1976; Major Gen AUS 1979; Army Commendation Medal; Bronze Star; Meritorious Service Medal. **MILITARY SERVICE:** US Army, gen, 33 yrs. **BUSINESS ADDRESS:** Commander, US Army Information Systems, Systems Command, Fort Huachuca, AZ 85613. *

PAIGE, RODERICK
Educator. **PERSONAL:** Born Jun 17, 1935, Brookhaven, MS; divorced; children: Rod Paige Jr. **EDUCATION:** Jackson State Univ, BS 1955; Indiana Univ, MS 1964, DPEd 1969. **CAREER:** Utica Jr Coll, head football coach 1957-67; Jackson State Univ, head football coach 1962-69; TX Southern Univ, asst/head football coach, asst prof, dean, athletic dir 1971-. **ORGANIZATIONS:** Pres Hirma Clarke Civic Club; sec Houston Job Training Partnership Council; adv bd mem Professional United Leadership League; mem of dirs Tri-Civic Assoc; former commnr Natl Commn for Employment Policy; coord Harris Co Explorer Olympics for the Boy Scouts of Amer. **HONORS/ACHIEVEMENTS:** Brentwood Dolphins Comm Serv Awd; Natl Assoc of Health PE and Recreation; "An Employment Policy for America's Future" Natl Commn for Employment Policy; "Grading in Physical Education" MS Teachers Journal. **MILITARY SERVICE:** USN hospital corpsman 2 yrs. **BUSINESS ADDRESS:** Dean College of Education, Texas Southern University, 3100 Cleburne St, Houston, TX 77004.

PAINTER, NELL IRVIN
Professor. **PERSONAL:** Born Aug 02, 1942, Houston, TX; daughter of Frank Edward Irvin and Dona Donato McGruder Irvin; married Glenn R Shafer, Oct 14, 1989. **EDUCATION:** Univ of CA Berkeley, BA 1964; Univ of CA Los Angeles, MA 1967; Harvard Univ, PhD 1974. **CAREER:** Harvard Univ, teaching fellow 1969-70, 1972-74; Univ of PA, asst prof 1974-77, assoc prof 1977-80; Univ of NC Chapel Hill, prof of history 1980-88; Princeton Univ, Professor of History, 1988-. **ORGANIZATIONS:** Natl dir Assoc Black Women Historians 1982-84; amer studies comm Amer Council of Learned Societies 1982-; exec bd Organization of Amer Historians 1984-87; beveridge prize comm Amer Historical Assoc 1985-87; mem NOW, The Nation Assocs; mem Harvard and Radcliffe Alumni/ae Against Apartheid. **HONORS/ACHIEVEMENTS:** Fellow Natl Humanities Ctr NC 1978-79; Fellow John Simon Guggenheim Foundation 1982-83; Candace Awd Natl Coalition of 100 Black Women 1986; 30 publications; 18 reviews and review essays; fellow, Center for Advanced Study in the Behavioral Science, 1988-89; 1989 Alumnus of the Year, Black Alumni Club, Univ of California, Berkeley, 1989. **BUSINESS ADDRESS:** Professor of History, Princeton University, History Dept, 129 Dickinson Hall, Princeton, NJ 08544-1017.

PAJAUD, WILLIAM E.
Business executive. **PERSONAL:** Born Aug 03, 1925, New Orleans, LA; married Donlaply. **EDUCATION:** Xavier U, BAFA 1946; Chouinard Art Inst. **CAREER:** Golden St Mutual Life Ins Co, pub rels. **ORGANIZATIONS:** Mem Life Ins Advertisers Assn; Pub Rels Soc Am; Graphic Designers Assn; Nat Watercolor Soc; pres Art Ed Found. **BUSINESS ADDRESS:** 1999 W Adams Blvd, Los Angeles, CA 90018.

PALMER, BERTHINA E.
Administrative assistant. **PERSONAL:** Born Nov 07, 1927, Cleveland, OH. **EDUCATION:** LLD (cum laude) 1954; BS 1951. **CAREER:** Cleveland AFL-CIO Fed of Labor, Worked since HS grad; admin asst 1985. **ORGANIZATIONS:** Sec, treas A Philip Randolph Inst Cleveland Chpt; mem Black Women's Lwyrs of Cleveland; mem Alpha Kappa Alpha Sor; v-pres Cleveland Bd of Ed; exec sec Black Labor Ldrshp Caucus; mem NAACP **BUSINESS ADDRESS:** 3250 Euclid Ave, Cleveland, OH 44115.

PALMER, DARLENE TOLBERT
Government broadcasting administrator. **PERSONAL:** Born Jul 04, 1946, Chicago, IL; married Mickey A; children: Terri, Jonathan, Tobi. **EDUCATION:** StUniv of NY Albany, BA 1973, MA 1974; Harvard Grad Sch of Bus Admin, Cert of Broadcasting Mgmt 1978-79. **CAREER:** Minority Telecomm Dev Nat Telecomm & Info Admin, prog mgr 1979-; Nat Assn of Brdcstrs Wash DC, asst dir brdcst mgmt 1977-79; Litt Enterprises Wash DC div pres 1975-77; WTEN-TV Albany, prod 1973-75; Palmer Media Asso Schenectady, prtnr 1970-75. **ORGANIZATIONS:** Media rels dir Nat Hookup of Black Women 1976-78; rec sec Am Women in Radio & TV 1980; chmn Affirm Act Am Women in Radio & TV 1980; co-chmn MinorityOwnrshp Cong Black Caucus Communications Brain Trust DC 1977-78; mem Com on Media & Natural Disaster Nat Acad Sci DC 1979; bd dirs Am Nat Metric Cncl Wash DC 1979. **HONORS/ACHIEVEMENTS:** Prod "Black English" WTEN-TV Albany; Nat Med Assn. **BUSINESS ADDRESS:** Nat Telecommunications & Info, Washington, DC 20230.

PALMER, DENNIS
Retired educator. **PERSONAL:** Born Jan 23, 1914, Steubenville, OH; son of Dennis Palmer and Ruth Merriman Palmer; married Soundra Lee Palmer, Feb 29, 1974; children: Denise Evans Dickerson, Jeffrey, Mark. **EDUCATION:** WV St Coll; Coll of Steubenville. **CAREER:** Post Office, employee 1937-67; Washington Hdqs, reg post office 1968-71; Coll Steubenville, dir finan aid 1971-85. **ORGANIZATIONS:** Mem Nat Assn Student Finan Aid Asminstrsn; Midwest & OH Adminstrs Assn; jury commr Equal Opport Com Fed; exec bd mem Rotary Club; bd advs Coll Steubenville;life mem NAACP; trust Quinn AME Ch; past grand lctr Prince Hall Grand Lodge of OH; past jury commn Equal Employment Oppr Commn; fed exec bd bdof adv Coll of Steubenville; past vice pres Dollars ofr Scholars; past pres Jefferson Co OEO; Prince Hall Mason. **HONORS/ACHIEVEMENTS:** Outstnd citz Elks Club; outstnd citz OH 1974; Educators of Am 1975; 1st black elected Sch Bd Steubenville; sur Steubenville PO; host of weekly TV talk show The Problem Is. **HOME ADDRESS:** 802 Lawson Ave, Steubenville, OH 43952.

PALMER, DOREEN P.
Physician. **PERSONAL:** Born Jun 01, 1949, Kingston, Jamaica;daughter of Granville Palmer and Icilola Dunbar. **EDUCATION:** Herbert H Lehman Coll, Bronx NY, BA, 1972; Downstate Medical School, Brooklyn NY, MD, 1976; Johns Hopkins Univ, Baltimore City Hospital, fellow gastroenterologist, 1981. **CAREER:** New York Medical Coll, Valhalla NY, asst prof, 1981-86; Metropolitan Hospital, New York City, asst chief GI, 1981-88, chief GI, 1983-86; Lenox Hill Hospital, New York City, adjunct physician, 1986-; Cabrini Hospital, New York City, atteding physician, 1986-; Doctors Hospital, New York City, attending physician, 1986-. **BUSINESS ADDRESS:** Physician, 185 E 85th St, New York, NY 10028.

PALMER, DOUGLAS HAROLD
Elected official. **PERSONAL:** Born Oct 19, 1951, Trenton, NJ. **EDUCATION:** Hampton Inst, BS 1973. **CAREER:** Trenton Bd of Educ, sr accountant 1976-78, coord of comm educ 1981-82, asst sec of purchasing 1982-; Mercer County Legislator, freeholder. **ORGANIZATIONS:** Pres mgr West End Little League; treas Trenton Branch of the NAACP; bd of dirs Amer Red Cross; mem Forum Project, Boy Scouts, WE Inc, Carver Center, Urban League Guild of Metro Trenton, Project Help; pres Freeholder Bd; served on Memorial Comm, Comm on the Status of Women, TRADE Adv Bd, Disabled Adv Bd, Mercer Co Bd of Social Svcs, Cultural & Heritage Comm. **HONORS/ACHIEVEMENTS:** Comm Serv Awds Fai-Ho-Cha Club, Twig Mothers, Hub City Distributors, Voice Publications, NJ Assn of Black Social Workers; Outstanding Young Man of Amer 1975; Outstanding Chmn DE Valley United Way 1977; Man of the Year Omega Psi Phi Frat 1984; Community Serv Awd Lifeline Energy Shelter. **BUSINESS ADDRESS:** Mercer Co, 640 S Broad St, Trenton, NJ 08608.

PALMER, EDWARD
Physician. **PERSONAL:** Born Jul 25, 1937, New York, NY; son of Edward Palmer, Sr. and Thelma Palmer; married Maria PaLmer; children: Neeco. **EDUCATION:** Adelphi Univ, attended 1960; Meharry Med Coll, attended 1964; Kings Co Hosp Cen, attended 1964-65. **CAREER:** Elmhurst Hosp Cen, staff attending; Mt Sinai Sch of Med, lectr; Hosp of the Albert Einstein Coll of Med, staff attending; Montefiore Hosp & Med Ctr, staff attending; Albert Einstein Coll of Med, assoc clinical prof; Bronx Mun Hosp Cen, dir eye clinics. **ORGANIZATIONS:** Mem Cen NY State Ophthalmogic Soc; Amer Acad of Ophthalmology & Otolaryngology; fellow Amer Coll of Surgeons; NY Clinical Soc; Intl Eye Found The Soc of Surgeons; Amer Assn of Ophthalmology; rsch to prevent blindness; diplomate Amer Bd of Ophthalmology. **HONORS/ACHIEVEMENTS:** Founding editor Journal of Cataract; numerous publs; listed as one of best black physicians in America: "Black Enterprise" mag 1988. **MILITARY SERVICE:** USN lt 1965-67. **BUSINESS ADDRESS:** Dir Eye Clinics, Bronx Mun Hosp Cen, 100 Casals Pl, Bronx, NY 10475.

PALMER, EDWARD
Educator. **PERSONAL:** Born Jul 26, 1928, Williamsburg, VA; divorced; children: Karen, Brian. **EDUCATION:** VA Coll, 1946-48, 1954-56; AB 1962; City Coll, CityUniv of NY; Columbia U, MS 1967; EdD Cand 1975. **CAREER:** Coll Ent Exam Bd, asso dir 1973-; US Dept, ofcr; CEEB, asst dir 1970-73; CUNY, asst ofcr; New York City Bd of Ed, tchr, vo nsl 1960-68; Yth House for Boys, cnsl, supr 1959-60; VA St Coll Variety Show WXEX-TV, IC 1954-55. **ORGANIZATIONS:** Distrib UNRA & Brethern Serv Ctr 1946; ldr Operation Crossroads Africa; consult EPDA Summer Inst New York City Comm Coll; cons, com mem UFT Coll Schlrshp Fund; mem bd of dir Urban Leag for Bergen Co 1979-; NY St Regents Adv Bd on Tchr ed, Cert & Prac 1966-69; NAACP Labor & Ind Com 1960-61; New York City Bd of Ed tchr consult 1964-68; curr dev com New York City Bd of Ed 1966; APGA; NYSPGA; NAFSA; NY Assn of Std Fin Aid Admin; bd of dir Harlem Coll Asst Proj; LOGOS Drug Rehab Ctr; New York City Coll Bound Prog; Operations Crossroads Africa Screen & Sel Com 1969-76; pres Nu Psi Chpt, Omega Psi Phi 1955-56; pres Radio-TV Grp 1954-55; vice pres VA St Vet Assn. **HONORS/ACHIEVEMENTS:** Outst Achiev Award VA St Plyrs Guild 1954-55; 1st Prize Frgn Lang Declamation VA St 1956; compiled resource book Serv for Disadvtg Stds 1970; num publ. **MILITARY SERVICE:** AUS 1950-53. **BUSINESS ADDRESS:** 170/ Market St, Ste 1418, Philadelphia, PA 19103.

PALMER, ELLIOTT B., SR.
Associate executive secretary retired. **PERSONAL:** Born Mar 07, 1933, Durham, NC; married Marjorie Taylor; children: Elliot, Douglas, Ruth, Tonya. **EDUCATION:** NCCU, AB 1855, MA 1961; Duke U, post Grad. **CAREER:** Little River HS Durham Co, tchr 1956-60; Lakeview Elem Sch Durham Co, prin 1960-64; NC Tchrs Assn Raleigh, exec sec 1964-71; NC Assn of Educators, asso exec sec 1970-. **ORGANIZATIONS:** Mem Nat Ed Assn; chmn Nat Cncl Off of St Tchrs Assn 1969-71; mem Pi Gamma Mu Nat Soc Sci Org; Pres Std Gov 1954; found Diversified Invest Spec Org 1960; mem NAACP; Hunter Lodge FM & AM; Mayor's Comm on Plan & Dev Raleigh 1974; pres Comm on Urban Redev of Durham 1958; gov comm Study of NC Pub Schls 1972; natl pres Offical Black Caucus of Nat Ed Assn 1985; 1st Black chrprsn Nat Comm of Ed for Hum Rights; exec dir Hammocks Beach Corp; co-chmn NEA Joint Comm Publ & Textbook Comm 1972-73; Boy Scouts Raleigh 1974; initiated Leg Def & Prot of Educrs by Prof Assn in NC 1965. **HONORS/ACHIEVEMENTS:** Rec H Cncl & Trenholm Award NEA for Outstndg Alumni Award Hillside HS Durham 1974; inv to White House Conf on Ed 1964; cited by two Govs for Outstdg Cont to Fld of Ed 1972-73; Who's Who Am Coll & U's. **BUSINESS ADDRESS:** NCAssociation of Educators, 119 Sunnybrook Rd, Raleigh, NC 27610.

PALMER, JAMES E.
Educator, minister. **PERSONAL:** Born Jul 06, 1938, Butler, AL; children: two. **EDUCATION:** Selma U, BTh; StateUniv Montgomery, AL, BS; Appalachian State Boone, NC, addl study; NC State U; Birmingham Bapt Coll, DD. **CAREER:** Univ Park Bapt Church Charlotte, past 3 yrs; Iredell Co Public Schools Statesville, NC, teacher 5 yrs; Jones Chapel Bapt Church Mooresville, NC, past 5 yrs; Catawba Coll & Catawba Co Public School, teacher & counselor, 7 yrs. **ORGANIZATIONS:** Moderator Mt Catawba Assn which incl 39 Chs with app 5000 membrs 3 yrs; mem Jaycees; mem Mayor's Counc; ex bd mem Gen State Bd Conv NC Inc; mem Nat Educ Assn; BSA; ex bd mem YMCA; mem Black Pol Caucus; mem NAACP. **HONORS/ACHIEVEMENTS:** NDEA Grant for stud in Asia; Sst Tchrs grant for stud in Communism; Who's Who among Bapt Minis. **BUSINESS ADDRESS:** Pastor, University Park Baptist Church, PO Box 16128, Charlotte, NC 28216.

PALMER, JAMES L. D.
Physician. **PERSONAL:** Born Oct 10, 1928, Sumter, SC; son of Edmund Palmer and Ellie Dibble Palmer; married Rose Martin; children: James Jr. **EDUCATION:** Fisk Univ 1949; Meharry Med Coll 1954. **CAREER:** Atlanta Life Ins Co, sr vice pres & med dir 1968-; Private Practice, physician internal med 1961-. **ORGANIZATIONS:** Bd dir Atlanta Life; trustee AF & NB Herndon Found; trustee Clark-Atlanta Univ and Gammon theological Seminary; past pres Atlanta Med Assn; mem GA State Med Assn; Natl Med Assn; Med Assn of Atlanta; Med Assn of GA; Amer Med Assn; mem Med Assn of Med Directors; life mem NAACP; mem Omega Psi Phi Frat; Kappa Boule of Sigma Pi Phi Frat; Warren United Meth Church Lay Leader; Atl Guardsmen. **MILITARY SERVICE:** USAF Ret Maj. **BUSINESS ADDRESS:** Senior Vice President, Atlanta Life Insurance, 970 M L King Drive, Ste 305, Atlanta, GA 30314.

PALMER, JOE
Therapist. **PERSONAL:** Born Oct 04, 1951, Charleston, SC; married Katie E Givens; children: Shannon Denise. **EDUCATION:** Livingstone Coll, BS 1974; USC affiliation w/ VAMC, cert in therapy 1975; Univ of AK, 29 hrs MS Spec Ed 1978; US Sports Acad, MSS 1985. **CAREER:** Charleston Rec Ctr, center super 1974; Statesville Public Sch System, teacher 1975; US Army, recreation specialist 1976-79; Municipality Parks & Rec of Anchorage, super 1979-80; Rehab Medicine Serv Vets Admin Med Ctr, corrective therapist 1980-83; US Sports Acad, sports trainer Mobile AL 1983; VAMC, corrective therapist. **ORGANIZATIONS:** Instructor Red Cross Life Saver; instructor First Aid; instructor Tae Kwon Do & Kuk Sool Won; olympic counselor Bartlett HS Anchorage 1976-80; phys fitness & aerobic instructor Vet Admin Hosp 1980; 1978-82 certificates and letters obtained Special Olympics, Dept of the Army, Heart Assn, Vets Admin, Cardio-Pulmonary Resuscitation. **MILITARY SERVICE:** AUS spec 4 3 yrs; Good Conduct Medal. **HOME ADDRESS:** PO Box 27055, Raleigh, NC 27610-7055. **BUSINESS ADDRESS:** Corrective Therapist, VAMC Tuskegee, Tuskegee, AL 36083.

PALMER, JOHN A.
Educator. **PERSONAL:** Born Aug 21, 1944, Mathiston, MS. **EDUCATION:** Rust Coll, BA 1967; Atlanta U, MA 1968;Univ of IA, Attend;Univ of I, MS 1972; Marquette U, phD Candidate. **CAREER:** Dept of Afro-Amer Studies Univ of WI, chmn 1975-, instr 1974-; Crime Prevention Dept Atlanta Police Dept, comm rels spec 1968; Milwaukee Children's Hosp Child Dev Center, consult 1975; St Francis Children's Activity & Achiev Center Milwaukee, consult 1974; Curative Workshop & Rehab Center, consult 1973. **HONORS/ACHIEVEMENTS:** Selected Outstndng Young Men of Am Volume XXI 1972. **BUSINESS ADDRESS:** Dept of Afro Am Studies Univ of W, 8708 Sandburg Hall, Milwaukee, WI.

PALMER, NOEL
Educational administrator. **PERSONAL:** Born Nov 14, 1926, Jamaica, WI; married Daisy Mae; children: Janet, John, Jules. **EDUCATION:** Union Theological Coll, 1951-54; William Penn Coll, BA 1956; Columbia Univ Teachers College, BSc 1977, MA 1959. **CAREER:** SUNY Farmingdale, assist to president 1968-70, vice pres Urban Center 1970-73, vice pres Educational Opportunity Center 1973-80, vice pres student affairs 1980-. **ORGANIZATIONS:** Superintendent Swift Purscell Boys Home 1964-66; dir on-the-job training Five Towns Community House 1966-68; part-time teacher Lawrence Public School 1967-69; president Advisory Council-BOCES 1978-82; president Half Hollow Hills Rotary 1980-81; vice chairman WLIW Educational TV 1982-84; Religious Society of Friends (Quakers). **HONORS/ACHIEVEMENTS:** Appeared "Outstanding Educators in America" 1972-74; member Friends World Committee for Consulation; President Central Westbury Civic Assn; Education Committee Westbury Branch NAACP. **HOME ADDRESS:** 609 Oxford St, Westbury, NY 11590. **BUSINESS ADDRESS:** Vice President Student Affairs, StateUniv of NY-Farmingdale, Administration Bldg, Melville Rd, Farmingdale, NY 11735.

PALMER, RONALD DEWAYNE
Appointed government official. **PERSONAL:** Born May 22, 1932, Uniontown, PA; married Princess Tengku Dato Intan; children: Derek, Alyson. **EDUCATION:** Howard Univ, BA (Magna Cum Laude) 1954; Inst de'Etudes Politiques Univ of Bordeaux France, 1954-55; School of Advanced Intl Studies Johns Hopkins Univ, MA 1957. **CAREER:** Togo, ambassador 1976-78; The Foreign Svc, dep dir gen 1979-81; Malaysia, ambassador 1981-83; Dept of State, foreign service officer on detail to CSIS/Georgetown 1957-. **ORGANIZATIONS:** Mem Kappa Alpha Psi 1952-, Amer Foreign Serv Assn 1957-, Council on Foreign Relations 1979-; Included in Who's Who in Amer, Who's Who in the World. **HONORS/ACHIEVEMENTS:** Knight commander Order of Mono, Republic of Togo 1978; commander Setia Mahkota Johor, Malaysia 1984. **BUSINESS ADDRESS:** Senior Foreign Affairs Fellow, GeorgetownUniv, Ctr Strat & Intl Studies, 1800 K St NW, Washington, DC 20006.

PALMER-HILDRETH, BARBARA JEAN
Educator. **PERSONAL:** Born Jan 10, 1941, Jackson, MS; daughter of John Palmer and Thelma Palmer; married Truman A Hildreth, Aug 15, 1970. **EDUCATION:** Jackson State Univ, BS 1964; Natl Coll of Educ, MS 1986. **CAREER:** Canton Public Schools, teacher 1964-67; Rockford Bd of Educ, teacher 1967-, head-teacher 1984-. **ORGANIZATIONS:** 2nd vice pres/life mem Natl Council of Negro Women 1984; mem Legislative Comm IEA 1986-87; Big Sisters Inc, 1975-89. **HONORS/ACHIEVEMENTS:** Mary McLeod Bethune Serv Awd Natl Council of Negro Women 1976; service award Rockford Memorial Hospital 1989. **HOME ADDRESS:** 2228 Pierce Ave, Rockford, IL 61103.

PALMORE, LYNNE A. JANIFER
Advertising, public relations executive. **PERSONAL:** Born Oct 03, 1952, Newark, NJ; married Roderick Palmore; children: Jordan, Adam. **EDUCATION:** Yale Univ, BA 1974. **CAREER:** J Walter Thompson, media trainee 1975-76, media planner 1976-78; Creamer Inc, media super 1978-80; Needham Harper Worldwide Inc, vice pres assoc media dir. **ORGANIZATIONS:** Mem Northshore Chapter Jack & Jill. **BUSINESS ADDRESS:** Vice Pres & Assoc Media Dir, DDB Needham Worldwide, 303 E Wacker Drive, Chicago, IL 60601.

PANDYA, HARISH C. (H. CHRISTIAN POST)
Business executive. **PERSONAL:** Born Oct 22, 1945, Zanzibar, United Republic of Tanzania. **EDUCATION:** Univ IN, MA 1971; NE MO St U, BS 1968;Univ Cambridge, 1966;Univ London, 1964. **CAREER:** Essence Mag, mid-west dir of Advertising 1977-; Tuesday Publs, dir of mrktng 1971-76; Johnson Pub Co, mrktng-editorial rsrchr 1970-71; Westinghouse Corp, 1969-70; Clopton HS, cnslr, tchr 1969. **ORGANIZATIONS:** MO Hist Soc; Wrtrs & Edtrs Guild; Nat Assn of Mrkt Dvlprs; Chicago Advertising Club; Chicago Press Club; Am Mrktng Assn; bd mem Pullen Sch for Execeptional Children 1973; bd dir Coalition of Concerned Women in War on Crime 1977; Pro & Con Screening Bd 1975. **HONORS/ACHIEVEMENTS:** 10 Outst Young Citizens Jr C &Of C 1976; Spl Achiev US Citizen 1976. **BUSINESS ADDRESS:** Essence, C/O 919 N Michigan Ave Ste #1, Chicago, IL 60611.

PANNELL, PATRICK WELDON
Artist. **PERSONAL:** Born Apr 13, 1936, New York City, NY; son of Patrick S. Pannell and Gwendolyn Pannell; children: Duffman Pannell. **EDUCATION:** Morgan State Coll, BA; CollUniv & New Sch Social Rsch, attended. **CAREER:** Public & Private Art Projects, dir 1962-64; Profiles in Cultural Revolution, 1964-66; S Bronx Comm Arts Prog, dir 1967-69;

Marcus Garvey Ctr, dir; New Experience Gallery, co-owner, co-founder; Rhino Arts Inc, head of co 1980-; NY City, dir special progs. **ORGANIZATIONS:** Artist Professional Rec Union; Artists Coalition; charter mem The Committee of Concerned Artist and Profls; co-founder of Panox Inc Silk Art Co; Panox Inc produces fine art and wearable art. **HONORS/ACHIEVEMENTS:** Special Awd for Work with Youth in New York City Wham-O Mfg Co 1978. **MILITARY SERVICE:** AUS Engrs 1957-59. **BUSINESS ADDRESS:** Dir of Special Programs, NY City, 830 5th Ave, New York, NY 10021.

PANNELL, WILLIAM E.
Director/associate professor. **PERSONAL:** Born Jun 24, 1929; married Hazel Lee Scott; children: 2 sons. **EDUCATION:** Wayne State Univ, BA Black History; Univ of So CA, MA Social Ethics; Malone Coll, Hon Doctorate. **CAREER:** Brethren Assemblies, asst pastor, youth dir; Christian Assemblies, pastor; School of Theol Fuller Theol Sem, dir black ministries, assoc prof evangelism. **ORGANIZATIONS:** Vp Tom Skinner Assoc; Staley Found lecturer George Fox Coll Newburg OR; speaker at many confs incl consult on the Gospel & Culture Lausanne Comm 1978, USConsultation on Simple Lifestyle Ventnor NJ 1979; spkr Church and Peacemaking in a Nuclear Age Conf Pasadena CA 1983; bd mem, chmn Youth for Christ USA 1980; pres Acad for Evangelism 1983-84. **HONORS/ACHIEVEMENTS:** Author "My Friend My Enemy" 1968; DDiv Malone Coll 1975; mem Delta Epsilon Chi Honor Soc of the Accrediting Assoc of Bible Colls; numerous articles in Eternity, The Other Side, Sojourners, The Amer Scientific Affiliation, The Herald, The Gospel Herald, Theology, News & Notes, Christianity Today, Leadership Magazine, etc. **BUSINESS ADDRESS:** Dir Black Min/Assoc Prof Evang, Fuller Theological Seminary, 135 N Oakland Ave, Pasadena, CA 91101.

PANTON, YVONNE B. F.
Physician. **PERSONAL:** Born Nov 03, 1946, Portsmouth, OH; married Adrian K; children: Nadra Layla. **EDUCATION:** OH St U, BS 1967, MD 1971. **CAREER:** UCLA, summer flwshp comm psychiatry 1969; Mt Carmel Hosp Columbus, intrnshp 1971-72; LA USC Med Ctr, res psychiatry; MLK & Charles R Drew Postgrad Sch, res psychiatry; Child Fellow I MLK UCLA, res psychiatry; MLK LA, co-chief res psychiatry 1985. **ORGANIZATIONS:** S CA Psychiat Soc 1974-; chap mems in Training Com; Black Psychiatrists Am 1974-; Sol W Ginsberg Fellow of Grp for Advancement Psychiatry 1974-76; Alpha Kappa Alpha Sor, Theta Chap 1966-; Prisoners Support Grp 1975; chrprsn Legal Com MLK Housestaff Assn Morrors Nat Hon Fr Women. **HONORS/ACHIEVEMENTS:** Publ Individual Perceptual Variability Predictor of Hallucinogenic Drug Induced Behavior, Archives Gen Psychiatry 1973. **BUSINESS ADDRESS:** NeuropsychiatricInstitute, 760 Westwood Plaza, Los Angeles, CA 90024.

PARHAM, BRENDA JOYCE
Nursing administration. **PERSONAL:** Born Jun 03, 1944, Ft Lauderdale, FL; daughter of Mr & Mrs Clarence Ray Sr; divorced; children: Grant III, Valorie, Stephanie, Deidra. **EDUCATION:** FL A&M Univ, BS 1966; Memphis State Univ, MEd 1972; Univ of TN Ctr for the Health Sci, MSN 1981. **CAREER:** Holy Cross Hosp, staff nurse 1966-67; Plantation Gen Hosp, staff nurse 1967; US Air Force, staff nurse 1967-68; Methodist Hosp, charge nurse 1966-69, instr 1969-71; Shelby State Comm Coll, dept head of nursing. **ORGANIZATIONS:** Liaison nurse & suprv Baptist Mem Hosp 1971-72; asst Prof Memphis State Univ 1972-80; staff nurse, suprv, asst dir Reg Med Ctr 1973-81; staff devel coord Methodist Hosp 1982; assoc prof, instr Shelby State Comm Coll 1982-83; dept head, nursing Shelby State Comm Coll 1984-; mem TN Nurses Assoc 1984-, Natl League for Nurses 1985. **HONORS/ACHIEVEMENTS:** Licensed Evangelist Missionary Church of God in Christ 1983; Advisory Bd Mem Amer Home Health Agency 1984. **MILITARY SERVICE:** USAF 1st lt 1 1/2 yrs. **BUSINESS ADDRESS:** Department Head of Nursing, Shelby State Community College, 737 Union Ave, Memphis, TN 38174.

PARHAM, MARJORIE B.
Publisher, editor. **PERSONAL:** Born in Batavia, OH; married Hartwell; children: William M Spillers Jr. **EDUCATION:** Wilberforce Univ; Univ of Cincinnati; Chase School of Business. **CAREER:** Cincinnati Herald, vice pres, advertising mgr 1963-. **ORGANIZATIONS:** Bd mem Comm Chest & Council United Appeal; Hamilton County YMCA; Natl Newspaper Publishers Assn; trustee Univ of Cincinnati; former bd mem Cincinnati OIC; Hamilton County Amer Red Cross; Greater Cincinnati Urban League; former chmn of bd Cincinnati Tech Coll; Women in Communications Inc; Iota Phi Lambda Business Women's Sor; St Andrew's Episcopal Church. **HONORS/ACHIEVEMENTS:** Iota Phi Lambda Business Woman of the Year 1970; Outstanding Woman in Communications 1973; named 1 of 12 most influential to the Queen City 1974; Outstanding Citizen Award, Omega Psi Phi 1975; Community Serv Media Award, Natl Conf of Christians & Jews 1977; Hon DTL, Cincinnati Tech Coll 1977.

PARHAM, SAMUEL LEVENUS
Educator. **PERSONAL:** Born Oct 03, 1905, Henderson, NC; married Erma Price; children: Marcia, Morma Lowe. **EDUCATION:** Shaw U, AB 1929; Columbia U, MA 1932. **CAREER:** Retired 1985; cosmetic mfr, exporter 1943-71; Lincoln Acad, prin 1934-43; Tillotson Coll, prof hist, acting dean 1933-34; Jr Coll Palmer Meml Inst, teacher, acting dean 1930-33; Afro-Amer Hist, lectr. **ORGANIZATIONS:** Former mem, bd of trustees Westchester Comm Coll; v-pres Urban Leag of W; former chrm Hum Rels Com, Bd of Ed; former pres NAACP Greenburgh & White Plains; mem Steering Com Urban Renewal of White Plains; mem, resolution com NY St Sch Bd Assn; mem Bd of Ed White Plains; pres White Plains Housing Auth. **HONORS/ACHIEVEMENTS:** Recip Annual Brotherhood Award Interchurch Cncl of White Plains 1964.

PARHAM, THOMAS DAVID, JR.
Clergyman. **PERSONAL:** Born Mar 21, 1920, Newport News, VA; son of T D Parham Sr and Edith Seabrook Parham; married Marion Cordice, Jun 01, 1951; children: Edith Evangeline Greene, Mae Marian, Thomas David III. **EDUCATION:** NC Central Univ, BA (Magna Cum Laude) 1941; Pittsburgh Theol Seminary, STB, STM (Summa Cum Laude) 1944; Amer Univ Washington, MA 1972, PhD 1973. **CAREER:** Butler Memorial Presby Church, pastor 1941-50; US Navy, chaplain 1944-82; Duke Univ Medical Ctr, chaplain 1982-84; Duke Divinity Sch, asst for black church affairs 1984-86; NC Central Univ, campus minister 1985-86; Messiah Presby Church, senior minister. **ORGANIZATIONS:** Life mem Kappa Alpha Psi; mem NAACP; life mem Military Chaplains Assoc; executive committee, Chaplaincy, Full Gospel Churches 1985-88; corporate, Presbyterian Ministers Fund. **HONORS/ACHIEVEMENTS:** Alumnus of the Year Pittsburgh Seminary 1983; Doctor of Divinity, Ursinus College, 1970. **MILITARY SERVICE:** USN Chaplain 37 yrs; Meritorious Serv Medal 1972, Legion of Merit 1982. **BUSINESS ADDRESS:** Senior Minister, Messiah Presbyterian Church, 1485 Johnston's Road, Norfolk, VA 23513.

PARIS, CALVIN RUDOLPH
Business executive. **PERSONAL:** Born Sep 05, 1932, New Haven, CT; son of Samuel and Nellie; married Gaudiosa; children: Calvin Jr, Priscilla, Theodore, April. **EDUCATION:** Howard U, BS 1956. **CAREER:** Fld Enterprises Educ Corp, asst vp, gen mgr sales 1958-81 (retired); Paris Health Systems Mgmt Inc dba Nutri/Systems Weight Loss Centers, pres & treas; Baskin Robbins 31 Flavors Chicago IL, franchiser. **ORGANIZATIONS:** Life mem NAACP. **HONORS/ACHIEVEMENTS:** Superior Srv Key; 15 yr mbrshp 100 Order Club; winner (2) Top Mgmt Award; Flying Circus 1969, 1973; runner-up 1974; pres & major stockholder in largest black owned chain of weight loss centers in world.

PARISH, ROBERT
Professional athlete. **PERSONAL:** Born Aug 30, 1953, Shreveport, LA; married Nancy; children: Justin. **EDUCATION:** Attended, Centenary Coll. **CAREER:** Golden State Warriors, center 1976-80; Boston Celtics, center 1980-. **HONORS/ACHIEVEMENTS:** Named to The Sporting News All-Amer First Team 1976; Gold Medalist World University Games 1975; named to the All-NBA Second team 1982; scored the 10,000th point of career on 2/26/84 in Phoenix; represented Boston in the All-Star Game 6 seasons. **BUSINESS ADDRESS:** Boston Celtics, Boston Garden, Boston, MA 02114.

PARKER, ARNITA WALDEN
Educator. **PERSONAL:** Born Sep 27, 1905, Chicago, IL; married Cleveland Parker. **EDUCATION:** Univ of Chicago, PhB 1934, MBA 1944; Univ of Hawaii, grad study 1958 1959; Univ of IL, attended 1961. **CAREER:** Farren Elem Sch, teacher 1928-38; DuSable HS, teacher 1938-68, chmn bus educ dept 1964-68. **ORGANIZATIONS:** Sec reader Eighth Ch of Christ Scientist Chicago 1954-57; bd mem/treas Howalton Day School in Chicago 1965-68; rec sec Chicago Tchrs Union 1966-68; memfirst Neg Com for First Coll Barg contract between Chicago Bd of Ed & Chicago Tchrs Union 1967; mem bd dir Stevens House integra dorm for women enr at UCLA 1974; Epistoleus Natl Sor of Phi Delta Kappa Inc Beta Theta Chap 1975-77; mem Natl Sor Phi Delta Kappa Beta Theta Chapt;bd mem sec/treas Las Angelenas Mayor's Volun Corps to City Gobt Los Angeles 1976-77. **HONORS/ACHIEVEMENTS:** Cert of Appreciation serv rendered in observ of IL Sesquic Gov Samuel H Shapiro 1968; Awd of Merit serv to City of LA Mayor Tom Bradley 1974.

PARKER, AVERETTE MHOON
Physician. **PERSONAL:** Born Jan 27, 1939, Memphis, TN; divorced; children: Rosalind. **EDUCATION:** Hillsdale Coll, BS 1960; Howard U, MD 1964. **CAREER:** Children & Family Mntl Hlth & Mntl Retardation Unit of N Cntrl Philadelphia Comm Mntl Hlth & Mntl Retardation Ctr, dir 1974-; Corinthian Guidance Ctr forSrvs to Children, aso dir 1973-74; Woodburn Ctr for Comm Mntl Hlth, dir 1973; N Cnty Ctr Fairfax Falls Ch Mntl Hlth Ctr, dir 1972-73; Com Mntl Hlth Ctr, dir adult outpatient dept 1970-71; Area B to DC Pub Sch, consult 1969-70; Hillcrest Children's Ctr to DC Headstart Prog, consult 1968; WNVT TV Natl Instrnl TV, consult 1973-74. **ORGANIZATIONS:** Gen mem Am Psychiatric Assn 1969-; mem PA Psychiatric Soc 1974-; professional adv com Soc Ctr 1973-75; adv cncl N VA Hot Line 1973; appearance in WKBSTV DE Vly Today Mntl Hlth Srvcs 1975; SPVI TV Woman's Perspective & Perspective on Yth "The Black Family" 1975; "Hostility in the Black Male" 1976; "Aggression in Children & Adolescents" 1976; "Crisis Intervention-effects on Women & their Family" 1976; panel mem Blk Hlth Consumer Conf N Cntrl Philadelphia Comm Mntl Hlth & Mntl Retardation Ctr 1975; panel mem PA Assn of Mntl Hlth Providers-Annual Meeting 1975; panel mem Orthopsychiatry Annual Meeting Primary Prevention & Early Intervention Progs 1976; panel mem, lectr "Hostility in the Blk Male-Fact or Fiction" N Cntrl Philadelphia Comm Mntl Hlth & Mntl Retardation Ctr 1976; lects Blk Family & Roles Swarthmore Coll Upward Bound Parents 1976; selected for externship Obstet & Gynecol 1963. **HONORS/ACHIEVEMENTS:** Rec Neuro-Psychiatry Dept Award for Achiev 1964. **BUSINESS ADDRESS:** Adult & Child Psychiatry, 3645 Veazey St, NW, Washington, DC 20008.

PARKER, BARRINGTON D.
Judge. **PERSONAL:** Born Nov 17, 1915, Rosslyn, VA; children: Jason Holloman, Barrington D Jr. **EDUCATION:** Univ of PA, AB 1936, MA 1938; Univ of Chicago, JD 1947. **CAREER:** Private Practice, attorney 1947-68; Dist Court of DC, judge 1970-. **ORGANIZATIONS:** Mem DC Human Rel Cncl 1963-66; mem ABA, Natl Bar Assn, Bar Assn of DC; adjunct prof Wash Coll of Law Amer Univ 1972-77; mem DC Comm on Judicial Disabilities & Tenure 1981-; mem local chap ACLU; co-chmn United Negro Coll Fund. **HONORS/ACHIEVEMENTS:** Recip Univ of Chicago Professional Achievement Award 1982. **BUSINESS ADDRESS:** Judge, Dist Court of DC, US Court House, 3rd & Constitution Ave NW, Washington, DC 20001.

PARKER, BERNARD F., JR.
Administrator. **PERSONAL:** Born Dec 16, 1949, Detroit, MI; married Sandra Bomar; children: Bernard III, Bukika, Bunia, Damon Bomar, Deric Bomar. **EDUCATION:** Univ of Michigan, BA 1973. **CAREER:** Operation Get Down, exec dir 1973-. **ORGANIZATIONS:** Vice pres Universal Variable Staffing 1979; bd mem Southeast Michigan Food Coalition 1979; vice pres Midwest Group Mgmt 1980; bd mem Governors Task Force Infant Mortality 1985, Michigan Bell Citizen Adv Group 1986; comm mem Detroit Strategic Planning Commn 1987; pres CAD Cable 1987-. **HONORS/ACHIEVEMENTS:** Natl Community Serv Awd United Community Serv 1979; Detroit City Council Community Awd 1984; Michelob Comm Serv Awd 1985. **BUSINESS ADDRESS:** Executive Dir, Operation Get Down, 9980 Gratiot, Detroit, MI 48213.

PARKER, CHARLES MCCRAE
Biological science technician. **PERSONAL:** Born Aug 13, 1930, Farmville, NC. **EDUCATION:** NC A&T State Univ, BS 1951, BS 1958; Natl Inst of Health. **CAREER:** Natl Inst Health, messinger-clerk 1961-65; USDA, biol sci tech 1965-67, biol sci tech path 1967-80, sr biol sci tech 1980-87. **ORGANIZATIONS:** Mem Phi Beta Sigma. **HONORS/ACHIEVEMENTS:** Quality Increase APHIS USDA 1975; Letter of Achievement FSIS USDA 1983; Special Achievement FSIS USDA 1985. **MILITARY SERVICE:** AUS sp3

1954-57; Honor Graduate NCO School 1956. **BUSINESS ADDRESS:** Sr Biological Science Tech, USDA Government, ARC East Bldg 318C, Beltsville, MD 20705.

PARKER, CHARLES THOMAS
Law enforcement. **PERSONAL:** Born Oct 26, 1918, Cleveland, TN; married Zilla Mae Goldston; children: Garland E. **EDUCATION:** College Hill School. **CAREER:** Charleston Police Dept, patrolman 1954, sgt of police 1956, asst chief 1974, chief of police 1979. **ORGANIZATIONS:** Mem Blue Lodge 1960, Shriner's Org 1974; adv capacity North East Advisory Bd 1981. **HONORS/ACHIEVEMENTS:** Awd for Outstanding Serv to Comm Amer Legion 1970; Future Farmer of Amer Charleston FFA Chap 1978; Ordained Elder Green's Chapel Cumberland Presbyterian Church 1979; 2nd Chief of Police City of Charleston TN 1979; Citizen of the Year Hiwassee Mental Health Ctr 1981; 1st Black Chief of Police for State of TN. **MILITARY SERVICE:** AUS corpl 1942-46; Battle Star Awd, Good Conduct Medal 1942-46. **HOME ADDRESS:** PO Box 154, Bates St, Charleston, TN 37310.

PARKER, CLAUDE A.
Quality control manager. **PERSONAL:** Born Oct 24, 1938, Branchville, VA; son of Claude A Parker Sr and Alma Virginia Wyche; married Constance Yvonne; children: Ryan. **EDUCATION:** Comm Coll of Baltimore, AA 1960; Morgan State Univ, BS 1964. **CAREER:** Joseph E Seagram & Sons Inc, chemist 1965-66, supr quality control 1966, distiller 1967-70, quality control mgr 1970-. **ORGANIZATIONS:** Mem Amer Mgmt Assn 1971, Applied Mgmt Sci Inc 1972, Wine Adv Bd of CA 1972; mem Meritocrats Inc, YMCA. **HONORS/ACHIEVEMENTS:** Listed in Who's Who 1975 Ebony Success Library, Who's Who in America 1977-78, Personalities of the South. **BUSINESS ADDRESS:** Quality Control Manager, Joseph E Seagram & Sons Inc, PO Box 357, Baltimore, MD 21203.

PARKER, D. LAVERNE
Entrepreneur/software develop comp exec. **PERSONAL:** Born Jan 14, 1949, New York, NY; daughter of Tommie B Parker (deceased) and Emma Smith Parker. **EDUCATION:** Bernard M Baruch Coll CUNY, BA 1974; Fordham Univ, MSW 1978. **CAREER:** Harlem Dowling Children's Svcs, caseworker 1974-77; Greater NY Fund/Tri-State United Way, tech asst 1977-78; Abraham & Straus Dept Stores, coord of public affairs 1978-79, asst mgr/computer opers 1979-81, internal consultant/special projects mgrs 1981-82, data processing financial controller 1982-85; Software Integration Serv Inc, vice pres finance/product rsch 1985-. **ORGANIZATIONS:** Mem Randolph Evans Scholarship Awds Dinner Comm 1979-; bd mem Software Integration 1985-; mem Mgmt Assistance Comm Greater NY Fund/United Way 1985-87; pres Brooklyn Mgmt Club 1986-87; mem NY Coalition 100 Black Women 1986-; school volunteer NY City School Volunteer Prog 1986-; mem Natl Assoc of Social Workers, Natl Assoc of Black Social Workers. **HONORS/ACHIEVEMENTS:** Disting Service Awd Salvation Army Brownsville Corps 1979; Outstanding Young Women of Amer 1983. **BUSINESS ADDRESS:** Vice President, Software Integration Serv Inc, 60 East 42nd Street, Suite 2238, New York, NY 10165.

PARKER, DARWIN CAREY
Electronic engineer. **PERSONAL:** Born Feb 22, 1956, Detroit, MI; son of Arthur Parker and Melvina Theresa Parker; children: Kenyota, Aisha, Omega, Alpha. **EDUCATION:** OH Institute of Tech, EET 1976; Highland Park Comm Coll, AAEE 1980; Siena Hieghts Coll, BAS 1982; Wayne State Univ MI Graduate Student 1987-. **CAREER:** Lanier Business Products, customer serv eng 1976-78; WGPR Radio & TV, radio engr 1977-79; Howe-Richardson Scale Co, electronic field engr 1978-81; ShiningStar Intl, owner/producer 1980-83; FAC Enterprises, vice pres sales & public relations 1981-82; Omega Star, owner/engineer 1983-; Detroit Engrg SSI, cons/prog coord, elect engr, author 1985-; Wayne State Univ MI Lab, Research Technician 1987-. **ORGANIZATIONS:** Dir Young Democrats 13th District 1980-; mem NAACP 1981-; mem Operation PUSH 1982,83; sr mem Soc of Mfg Engrs 1986-; mem Soc Auto Eng 1986-; Steward UAW Local 2071 1988-. **HONORS/ACHIEVEMENTS:** First completely full service black owned ad agency in Detroit Shining Star Intl 1980-83; Outstanding Community Leader Budd Local 306 1984; publication "Electronic Troubleshooting, Art & Science," DEI 1986; publ "A Day In The Life of The Civil Rights Movement, The Story of Dr William V Banks" 1987; Distinguished Service UAW Local 2071 1988. **MILITARY SERVICE:** ARNG pfc 1984-85. **BUSINESS ADDRESS:** Electronic Engineer, Author, Detroit Engineering/SSI, 4420 Townsend, Detroit, MI 48214.

PARKER, DAVID GENE
Professional athlete. **PERSONAL:** Born Jun 09, 1951, Jackson, MS; married Kellye Crockett; children: Danielle, David II, Dorian. **CAREER:** Pittsburgh Pirates, outfielder 1973-83; Cincinnati Reds, outfielder 1984-. **HONORS/ACHIEVEMENTS:** Named to the NL All-Star team five years in succession 1977-81 and 1986; three-time Gold Glove Awd 1977-79; played in three Championship Series; NL MVP in1978; All-Star game MVP in 1979; Red's MVP 3 yrs 1984,85,86; led the NL in total bases, finished second in homers and RBIs and was in the top ten in hits; voted by managers and coaches to the Silver Slugger team; NL Player of the Week May 1885, Sept 1986; picked by The Sporting News for its post-season All Star team; first player ever to homer into the second deck in right field at Dodger Stadium. **BUSINESS ADDRESS:** Cincinnati Reds, 100 Riverfront Stadium, Cincinnati, OH 45202.
*

PARKER, DAVID RUSSELL
Attorney. **PERSONAL:** Born Jun 06, 1950, Buffalo, NY. **EDUCATION:** Syracuse Univ, BA Econ (Cum Laude) 1974; Univ of MI Law School, JD 1977; Univ of WI Grad School of Bus 1975. **CAREER:** Civil Aeronautics Bd, attny, advisor 1978-83; Office of Inspector Gen US Dept of Health & Human Svcs, attny 1983-; ANCIB, commissioner. **ORGANIZATIONS:** Mem PA & DC Bar 1978; mem Howard Univ Comm Relations Comm 1981-; pres LeDioit Park Civic Assn 1982-; chmn Adv Neighborhood Commiss 1985-. **BUSINESS ADDRESS:** Commissioner, ANCIB, 519 Florida Ave NW, Washington, DC 20001.

PARKER, DORIS S.
Educator. **PERSONAL:** Born Aug 23, 1931, Marvel, AR; daughter of Percy L Watson and Earlie Mae Sims; divorced; children: Karen Parker Stewart, Terri L. **EDUCATION:** IN Central Coll, BA 1959; Pomona Coll, Certificate of Completion Peter Drucker Seminar 1981; Natl Bd YWCA Trainer 1983; Sales & Marketing The Winning Edge 1987; Advanced Facilitator Training Institute of Cultural Affairs 1986; Devel & Funding Lilly Endowment 1978-79. **CAREER:** Finance Center US Army, military pay clerk 1952-66; Veterans Admin Regional Office, adjudicator veteran claims examiner 1966-73; IN Vocational Tech Coll, asst dir student serv 1973-75, regional relations coordinator 1975-82; Young Women's Christian Assn, exec dir 1982-85; Independent Consultant 1985; Alpha Kappa Alpha Educational Advancement Foundation, Chicago IL, exec sec 1987-. **ORGANIZATIONS:** Mem Fund for Hoosier Excellence 1983-; mem State Advisory Council on Vocational Educ 1976-83; vice chmn Greater Indianapolis Progress Comm 1982-87; mem Natl Comm Campaign for Human Development USCC 1975-78; past pres Hoosier Capital Girl Scout Council 1979-82; past pres Indianapolis Urban League 1976-78; St Mary of the Woods Coll Trustee 1985; US Judicial Nominating Comm 1978-80; Past Pres Comm Action Against Poverty 1970-73; Marion County Welfare Bd 1974-86; US Selective Service Review Bd; Alpha Kappa Alpha; Women's Leadership Bd Comm Hospital 1985-87; Archidiocesean Black Catholics Concerned. **HONORS/ACHIEVEMENTS:** Woman of the Year B'nai B'rith Indianapolis 1968; Brotherhood Award IN Chapter Natl Conf Christians & Jews 1975; Human Relations Award Indianapolis Educ Assn 1976; Those Special People Women in Communications 1979; Badge Hoosier Capital Girls Scouts 1982; Sagamore of the Wabash-Governor of Indiana 1986; Achievement Plus Public Service center for leadership Development 1985. **BUSINESS ADDRESS:** Consultant, Doris Parker, 1330 W Michigan St, Indianapolis, IN 46206.

PARKER, EDWARD EVERETT
Educator, sculpture. **PERSONAL:** Born Feb 07, 1941, Pittsburgh, PA. **EDUCATION:** Central State Univ, BS; Kent State Univ, MA Ed; Toledo Art Museum, Additonal Studies; Family Art Course; Toledo Univ; Cleveland Art Museum; IL StUniv Normal, Wrkng Toward Doctorate Degree. **CAREER:** Cuyahoga Comm Coll Parma OH, teacher, sculpture & ceramics 1985; Jr & Sr HS Toledo & Cleveland & Case Western Reserve Univ, teacher adult & retarded art; Cleve Bd of Ed, head art dept 1969; Original Ceramics E Cleve, asst dir 1969. **ORGANIZATIONS:** One man sculpture exhibs 1st Bk & Trust Cleve 1974; Kent StUniv 1974; Karamu House Cleve 1972; Bowling Green StUniv 1972; Wright StUniv 1972; Cuyahoga Comm Coll Cleve Mus of Art; Toledo Art Club; Avant Grade 1970-71; Cleve Tchr Credit Un; Nat Org of Black Artists 1972-74; Ashland Coll 1970; Faculty ArtShow Kent OH; All OH Art Exh; Cleve Invitational Lk Erie Coll. **HONORS/ACHIEVEMENTS:** Recognition by Black World; spl mention in Cleve Jrnl.

PARKER, FRED LEE CECIL
Educator, clergyman. **PERSONAL:** Born Jun 16, 1923, Calvert, TX; married Elsie Evans; children: Patricia Ann. **EDUCATION:** Southwestern Baptist Theological Seminary, Ft Worth, Diploma 1956; Bishop Coll Dallas, BA 1968; E TX State Univ Commerce, MEd 1975; S Bible Sem Burnwsick GA, ThD 1978. **CAREER:** Geochem Surveys, lab tech 1944-70; Dallas Independent Sch Dist, tchr 1969-84; Goodwill Baptist Ch, Assoc minister, 1977; D Edwin Johnson Baptist Inst, seminary & ext teacher 1979-, administrative dean 1984-. **ORGANIZATIONS:** Mem GT Dallas Math Tchrs TSTA NEA 1970-; mem Classroom Tchrs of Dallas 1970-; local & state chaplain Phi Beta Sigma Frat Inc 1970; Elem Math Tchrs Dev, US Off of Ed Bishop Coll Dallas 1971; Nat Sci Found, Math Bishop Coll Dallas 1972-73; Professional Growth in Ed Dallas Independent Sch Dist 1973-74; regvp, natl dean Universal Bible Inst Inc 1978-79; reg dir, dean S Bible Sem Inc 1978-79; fld rep, cnslr World-Wide Bible Inst Inc 1979-. **HONORS/ACHIEVEMENTS:** Panalist Radio Sta KNOK Dallas-Ft Worth 1954-71; hon DD Universal Bible Inst Inc Brunswick GA 1977; cert Pastoral Cnsl Birmingham AL 1977. **BUSINESS ADDRESS:** Administrative Dean, D Edwin Johnson Baptist Inst, 2212 Robert B Cullum Blvd, Dallas, TX 75210.

PARKER, GEORGE ANTHONY
Equipment leasing company executive. **PERSONAL:** Born Jan 29, 1952, Norfolk, VA; son of Milton A Parker and Lillian B Carr; married Michele Annette Fleuranges; children: Jenifer Ann. **EDUCATION:** Wake Forest Univ, BS 1974; Univ of NC Chapel Hill, MBA 1976. **CAREER:** Continental IL Natl Bank, banking assoc 1976-78, banking officer 1979-80, 2nd vice pres 1980-82; DPF Computer Leasing Corp, vice pres & treas 1982-84; Atlantic Computer Funding Corp, chmn of bd & pres 1984-; CT Bancorp Inc, dir 1986-; The Norwalk Bank, dir 1986-; Leasing Tech Intl Inc, dir/vice pres/chief financial officer 1984-. **ORGANIZATIONS:** Bd of dirs Consortium for Grad Studies in Mgmt 1975-76; vice pres Urban Bankers Forum Chicago 1981-82; mem Glenwood Lake Comm Assoc 1983-, Natl Black MBA Assoc 1986-, YMCA 1986; dir CT Bancorp Inc 1986-, The Norwalk Bank 1986-; mem Wake Forest Univ Alumni Letterman Club 1986-. **HONORS/ACHIEVEMENTS:** Western Electric Scholarship Awd 1971,72,73; Consortium for Grad Studies in Mgmt Fellowship Awd 1974-76; Who's Who in Finance & Industry 1987. **BUSINESS ADDRESS:** Dir/VP/Chief Financial Ofcr, Leasing Tech Intl Inc, 24 Old King's Hwy South, Darien, CT 06820.

PARKER, H. WALLACE
Attorney. **PERSONAL:** Born Dec 08, 1941, North Carolina; married Patricia W; children: Meriel S Parker. **EDUCATION:** Winston-Salem State Univ BS, 1967; NCC Univ JD, 1970. **CAREER:** Reg Herb Smith Lwyr Fellow Prog, 1970-72; Legal Dept, City of Pontiac, Deputy City Atty 1971-75; Pres, Law Office of H Wallace Parker, 1975-; pres/owner, Check Mate Transportation System 1974-; v pres/atty, V-Tech Corp 1976-. **ORGANIZATIONS:** Mem Am St Nat, Oakland Co Wolverine Bar Assns; chief legal counselor, NAACP 1984-; atty/bd of dirs, OAR Program 1987-. **HONORS/ACHIEVEMENTS:** First black deputy city atty, City of Pontiac,1971; Norcroff Award, NAACP 1986; Outstanding Service Award, 0AR 1987; modified jury selection system and statue for state of MI, 1987; judgement to remove discrimination, Pontiac Police Dept. 1988. **MILITARY SERVICE:** USMC, Sgt 1960-63; Outstanding Soldier Award, 1962. **BUSINESS ADDRESS:** Attorney, Law Offices of H Wallace Parker PC, 1275 S Woodward Ave #200, Bloomfield Hills, MI 48013.

PARKER, HENRY ELLSWORTH
Elected official. **PERSONAL:** Born Feb 14, 1928, Baltimore, MD; married Janette; children: Curtis, Janet. **EDUCATION:** Hampton Inst, BS 1956; Southern CT State Univ, MS 1965; Sacred Heart Univ, JD (Hon) 1983. **CAREER:** State of CT Hartford, treasurer 1976-. **ORGANIZATIONS:** Pres Natl Assoc of State Treasurers 1985; pres Kappa Alpha Psi Found; mem Fed Natl Mortgages Assoc Advisory Comm; Past Grant Exalted Ruler of the Elks; 33 Degree Mason; trustee Instnl Responsibility Rsch Corp; bd dirs Inst Living. **HONORS/ACHIEVEMENTS:** Prince Hall Masons Bicentennial Awd 1975; Civil Rights Awd CT NAACP 1976; One of Ebony Mag 100 most influential Black Amers 1978-; Lovejoy Awd Elks 1984. **MILITARY SERVICE:** AUS 1951-53. **BUSINESS ADDRESS:** Treasurer, State of Connecticut, 20 Trinity St, Hartford, CT 06115.

PARKER, HENRY H.
Educator. **PERSONAL:** Born Sep 11, 1933, Memphis, TN. **EDUCATION:** St Thomas Coll, BA 1956; Univ of MN, MA 1959; Univ of IL, PhD 1975. **CAREER:** Univ of MN, asst prof 1961-65; Univ of N Iowa, asst prof 1965-68, Univ of IL, asst prof 1968-71; Univ of N Iowa, asst prof 1971-84, full prof 1984-. **ORGANIZATIONS:** Pres the Off-CampusUniv consulting firm; founder & principal Waterloo-Pre-Sch Acad; pres The Parker Reading Co; pub The Parker Reader Elem Sch Newspaper;producer & star the Hank Parker Show Ch 7; co-dir with Marilyn Crist of CP Collegians Gifted Children's Prog. **HONORS/ACHIEVEMENTS:** NDEA Lecturer in Rhetoric 1965; Danforth Assoc Danforth Found; Iowa's Most Outstanding Prof Awd 1972; Geo Wash Carver Disting Lecturer Awd 1975. **BUSINESS ADDRESS:** Professor, Univ of N Iowa, Cedar Falls, IA 50613.

PARKER, HERBERT GERALD
Administrator. **PERSONAL:** Born May 13, 1929, Fayetteville, AR; son of Otis J Parker and Anna B Parker; married Florida Fisher; children: Christie Lynne. **EDUCATION:** Univ of NE, BS 1962; NC A&T State Univ, MS 1972; FL State Univ, PhD 1982. **CAREER:** Rep of China Taipei Taiwan, adv ministry of natl defense 1962-65; NC A&T State Univ, prof of mil sci 1965-68; AUS Spec Forces The Delta of Vietnam, commander 1968-69; US Army Civil Affairs Sch Fort Bragg, dir 1969-73; FL A&M Univ, prof of mil sci 1973-77; State of FL Bureau of Crimes Compensation 1979-87; chief internal auditor Florida Dept of Education. **ORGANIZATIONS:** Bd dir Civil Affairs Assn 1970-73; mem Natl Assn of Soc Scientist 1973-; bd of dir Three C's Corp 1974-79; bd of dirs Tallahassee Urban League 1981-; Board Chrmn 1986-88; Tallahassee Area C of C 1974-82; Bd of Dirs Oppor, Indus Ctrs 1975-78; bd dirs, United Way of Leon Co 1978-82; pres Natl assn of Crime Victim Compensation Bd 1984-87; bd dirs FL Victim & Witness Network 1984; mem Tallahassee NAACP. **HONORS/ACHIEVEMENTS:** Disting Serv Awd Boy Scouts of Amer 1968; Disting Serv Awd Civil Affairs Assn 1974; Outstanding Serv Awd Coll of Humanities & Soc Sciences FL A&M Univ 1977; Phi Kappa Phi Hon Soc 1979; Youngest Black Promoted to Col AUS 1969; Distinguished Service Awd, Natl Assn Crime Victim Compensation Brds, 1986; FL Network of Victim Witness Services; James Fogarty Distingushed Service Award 1988. **MILITARY SERVICE:** AUS col 1947-77; 2 Legion of Merit; Silver Star; 3 Bronze Stars; Purple Heart; meritorious Serv Awd 12 other awds Airborne Ranger & Spec Forces Qualified; Joint Service commendation medal; 3 air medals; 2 army commendation medals; United Nations Ribbon; Korean Campaign Awd; Vietnamese Cross of Gallantry with Palm; reserve forces award with 10 year device, good conduct medal. **BUSINESS ADDRESS:** Chief Internal Auditor, Florida Department of Education, 111 W Saint Augustine Street, Tallahassee, FL 32399.

PARKER, JACQUELYN HEATH
National president. **PERSONAL:** Born Dec 29, Memphis, TN; daughter of Mr & Mrs Fred Heath; married William A Parker; children: Kimberly, Shane. **EDUCATION:** Southern IL Univ, BS 1963, MS 1967; post graduates: Univ of Illinois. **CAREER:** Community High School Dist 218, reading specialist/adm 1970-; Top Ladies of Distinction Inc, natl pres 1987-. **ORGANIZATIONS:** Program coord Teaching Homebound Students 1980-; scholarship chmn Build Inc 1983-; sponsor NIYA Club for Girls 1985-; pres Theta Rho Omega Chap of Alpha Kappa Alpha Sor 1987-89; Jack & Jill, Inc; Links, Inc. **HONORS/ACHIEVEMENTS:** Soror of the Year Theta Rho Omega Chap of Alpha Kappa Alpha Sor; Lady of the Year Top Ladies of Distinction Chicago 1985; Top 40 Finest Women of Community Women Together of South Suburban Chicago 1988; Nominee-Top Women of Chicago Midwest Center of Chicago 1989; Orchid Award Top Ladies of Distinction, Inc. 1989. **HOME ADDRESS:** 254 E Denell Dr, Crete, IL 60417.

PARKER, JAMES E.
Biomedical products executive. **CAREER:** V-Tech Inc, Pomona CA, chief executive. **BUSINESS ADDRESS:** V-Tech Inc, 270 E Bonita Ave, Pomona, CA 91767. *

PARKER, JAMES L.
Retired contract administrator. **PERSONAL:** Born Oct 29, 1923, Salina, KS; son of John H Parker and Classie Meadows Parker; widowed; children: Cheri D, Jami L, Beryl J, Kathleen L, Rosalind A, Donna J, Janice E, Gloria J. **EDUCATION:** KS Wesleyan U, BS 1950; Brown Mackie Sch of Bus, Attend. **CAREER:** Carver Rec Ctr Salina KS, asst rec dir 1947-50; E Side Rec Ctr Freeport IL, exec dir 1951-67; Sundstrand Oper Advanced Tech Div Pub Acctng & Income Tax Srv, contract adminstr 1950-. **ORGANIZATIONS:** Mem Gov Commn on Minority Entrepreneurship; Gov Commn on Emancipation Centennial; Freeport Hum Rels Commn; IL Law Enforcement Commn; Freeport Adult Ed Cncl Freeport Nrthwstrn IL Comm Act Prog Bd; Intrntl Toastmasters Club Ed Commn; adv bd Freeport Jr Coll; ML King Jr Comm Ctr Bd N IL Constr Affirm Act Prog. **HONORS/ACHIEVEMENTS:** Recip Yth Award Freeport C of C 1956. **MILITARY SERVICE:** US Army, Sgt maj 1943-45. **HOME ADDRESS:** 632 E Iroquois St, Freeport, IL 61032.

PARKER, JAMES THOMAS
Businessman. **PERSONAL:** Born Apr 03, 1934, Macon, GA; married Easther; children: Pamela, Sheri, James Jr, Diane, David, Maisha, Anwar, Christian. **EDUCATION:** OH St U. **CAREER:** Baltimore Colts, professional ftbl plyr 1957-68; Jim Parker Publs, owner 1985-. **ORGANIZATIONS:** Bd of gov Goodwill Ind; Woodlawn Football Prog 1969; Forest Pk Little Leag 1971. **HONORS/ACHIEVEMENTS:** Pro-ftbl Hall of Fame; Nat Ftbl Hall of Fame; GA & Toledo Hall of Fame; All Am OH St 1955-56; Outland Trophy 1956; All Pro 8 Consec Seasons 1958-65; College Hall of Fame; Baltimore Hall of Fame; Ohio State Hall of Fame. **BUSINESS ADDRESS:** 333 Garrison Blvd, Baltimore, MD 21215.

PARKER, JEAN L. (NEE LANE)
Educator. **PERSONAL:** Born Feb 22, 1923, Cincinnati, OH; widowed; children: Anthony. **EDUCATION:** H&PE Wilberforce U, BS 1942; Wayne U, MA 1949; Columbia U; MI St. **CAREER:** Detroit Bd of Ed, conselor, consult 1962-72; H&PE Ft Vly St Coll, dept head 1942-43; City Detroit Highland Pk, rec lead 1944-48; H&PE Detorit Bd Ed, special educ teacher 1944-70; Joy Cleaning & Pressing Srv, co-owner 1965-76; Detroit Bd of Ed, pres, voc special 1970-76; Parke Lanie Jewelry, distrib 1970-75; Parker's Party & Bridal Consult Service, founder, owner 1954-. **ORGANIZATIONS:** Dir N Reg Eta Phi Beta Sor 1975-; past grand dir, Ed 1962-66; past grand Jour 1968-70; past Nat Pres Cntrl StUniv Nat Alumni Assn 1967-69; past bd dir Lucy Thurman YWCA; past bd mem Detroit Fed Tchrs Local #231; past mem, bd Delta Hm for Girls; past mem, bd dir Wayne StUniv Alumni Assn; Coll Ed Cur; pres Shay Ladies Aux; mem NAACP; NCNW; Narcerima Wives. **HONORS/ACHIEVEMENTS:** Town Sq Coop Schlrshp COUniv Detroit Roundtable Ch 1951; 25 yr Award for Srv Am Fed Tchrs 1973; Recog Award Detroit City Cncl 1977; Spl Award USO; YWCA; Grt Cities; Detroit Fed Tchr; Delta Sigma Theta; Detroit Bd of Ed. **BUSINESS ADDRESS:** PO Box 32159, Detroit, MI 48232.

PARKER, JEFF, SR.
Physician. **PERSONAL:** Born Aug 19, 1927, Big Cane, LA; son of Edmond Parker and Stella Parker; married Patricia O; children: Jeff Jr, Jacqueline, James, Janice. **EDUCATION:** Howard Univ, BS 1962, MD 1966; Union Meml Hosp Baltimore, MD, rotating internship 1966-67; Sinai Hosp of Baltimore, MD, asst resid internal med 1967-69; Univ of MD Hosp, fellowship in cardiology 1969-70. **CAREER:** Private Practice, internist/cardiology. **ORGANIZATIONS:** Mem Black Cardiologists Assn 1974-; active staff Maryland General Hosp, Union Memorial Hosp; pres Medical Foundation Baltimore Inc; pres Reliable Medical rental and Serv Inc. **HONORS/ACHIEVEMENTS:** Phi Beta Kappa Howard Univ 1962; Presidential Medallion/Recognition of Medical Arts by Church of God in Christ Bishop JO Patterson 1984; Alan Locke Meml Plaque Howard Univ 1958; Dean's Honor Roll Under-Grad Howard Univ 1962; Natl Honor Soc Psychol Psi Chi Howard Univ 1962; Magna Cum Laude Coll Liberal Arts Howard Univ; Honors Coll of Med Ped & Psych Howard Univ 1966; author: A christian Guide to the War on Drugs; A Christian Child's Guide to the War on Drugs. **MILITARY SERVICE:** AUS Sgt 1st Class 1947-58; Good Conduct Medal. **HOME ADDRESS:** 1012 Argonne Dr, Baltimore, MD 21218. **BUSINESS ADDRESS:** Internist, 2300 Garrison Blvd, Baltimore, MD 21216.

PARKER, JERRY P.
Attorney. **PERSONAL:** Born Mar 01, 1943, West Blocton, AL; married Patricia Wall; children: Jerry, Jennifer. **EDUCATION:** Bowling Green St U, BS, BA 1965; Cleveland Marshall Sch of Law, JD 1970. **CAREER:** Sears Roebuck & Co, tax atty 1973-; Ernst & Ernst Cleveland, tax supr 1968-73; E OH Gas Co, syst analyst 1965-68. **ORGANIZATIONS:** Am Bar Assn; Nat Bar Assn; Cook Co Bar Assn; Chicago Bar Assn; iL bar assn; mem iL & oH st bar bd of trust consult prot assn; bd of trust, exec com Child Srv; bd of trust Friendly Inn Settle House. **BUSINESS ADDRESS:** Tax Dept #568, Sears Roebuck & Co Sears Tower, Chicago, IL 60684.

PARKER, JOSEPH CAIAPHAS, JR.
Trial attorney. **PERSONAL:** Born Sep 25, 1952, Anniston, AL; son of Rev Dr Joseph C Parker Sr (deceased) and Addie Ruth Fox Parker; married J LaVerne Morris, Aug 14, 1976; children: Jessica, Jennifer. **EDUCATION:** Morehouse Coll, BA 1974; Univ of Georgia, M Public Admin 1976; Univ of TX at Austin, JD 1982. **CAREER:** City of Dallas, admin asst mgmt serv 1976-77, admin asst office of the city mgr 1977-79, mgr summer youth employment program 1979; Travis Co Attorney Office, trial attorney 1983-84, chief trial div 1985-86; David Chapel Missionary Baptist Church, assoc pastor 1984-; Long, Burner, Parks & Sealy PC, attorney 1986-. **ORGANIZATIONS:** Mem Natl Conf of Minority Public Administrators 1974-80; mem Amer Soc for Public Admin; bd dirs Morehouse Coll Natl Alumni Assoc; bd dirs Austin Child Guidance and Evaluation Ctr; mem Conference of Christians and Jews; mem Black Austin Democrats; mem Urban League, NAACP, Austin Jaycees; mem Travis County Public Defender Task Force; mem State Bar of TX, TX and Austin Young Lawyers Assns, Natl Bar Assns; mem Austin Black Lawyers Assn and Federal Bar Assn; mem Association of Trial Lawyers of America. **HONORS/ACHIEVEMENTS:** Man of the Year Spelman College Student Govt Assoc 1973-74; Univ of GA Fellowship 1974-76; Pi Sigma Alpha Honor Soc 1976; Dallas Jaycees Rookie of the Yr 1978-79, Presidential Awd 1978-79; Outstanding Achievement Awd Natl Conf of Minority Public Administrators 1979; Gene Woodfin Awd Univ of TX 1982; Leadership Austin 1984-85; Distinguished Morehouse Coll Alumni Citation of the Year 1986; Baptist General Convention of TX Theological Scholarship 1986-87; Benjamin E Mays Fellowship in Ministry, Fund for Theological Studies; publication "Prosecuting the DWI", True Bill Vol 6 No 4 TX Prosecutor Council. **BUSINESS ADDRESS:** Trial Attorney, Long, Burner, Parks and Sealy, PC, PO Box 2212, Austin, TX 78768.

PARKER, JOYCE LINDA
Educator, educational administrator. **PERSONAL:** Born Aug 16, 1944, New Orleans, LA; children: Cynthia Lorraine. **EDUCATION:** Santa Ana Coll, AA psychology 1977; Chapman Coll, BA Social Work/Personnel 1979; Univ of LaVerne, MS Business Mgmt 1986. **CAREER:** Univ of CA-Irvine, admin asst, 1970-78; North Orange County Comm Coll, business instructor 1981-85 (part time); AME Johnson Chapel, assoc minister 1984-; Rockwell Intl, coord educ prog 1978-84, EEO Rep, 1984-. **ORGANIZATIONS:** Mem Natl Womens Assoc of Orange County 1978-; speaker Youth Motivation Task Force of Orange Co 1979-; mem Santa Ana Comm Coll APL Adv Bd 1981-83; sec bd dirs Youth Motivation Task Force 1985-; mem Governor's Comm for Employment of the Handicapped 1985-. **HONORS/ACHIEVEMENTS:** Personnel Administration Fellowship, Chapman Coll, 1979; Special Recognition Award, Orange Coast Comm Coll, 1982-83; Outstanding Achievement Award, EEO, 1983; Gold & Bronze Key Award O C Youth Motivation Task Force 1985-86. **HOME ADDRESS:** 1303 N Kraemer Blvd, Placentia, CA 92670. **BUSINESS ADDRESS:** EEO Representative, Rockwell International, 3370 Miraloma Ave, Anaheim, CA 92670.

PARKER, KAI J.
Appointed official, business executive. **PERSONAL:** Born Aug 06, 1939, Abilene, TX; married James Parker; children: Darren, Darnel. **EDUCATION:** Compton Coll, AA Social Welfare 1965; Loyola Marymount Univ, grad studies in Psychology & Guidance Counseling 1979, the Human Construction of Sexuality 1980, Alcohol & Drug Studies 1982; Univ of Redlands, BA Management 1981. **CAREER:** Amer Telegraph & Tele, customer serv rep 1966-68; LA Co Dept of Social Svcs, eligibilty worker 1968-70; LA Co Dept of Public Social Svcs, eligibility super 1970-79; Aide Sanitary & Supply Co, mgmt consultant 1979-80; LA Co Assessment Appeals Bd, comm 1980-82; Group W Cable, public affairs & govtl relations coord 1982-. **ORGANIZATIONS:** 20 memberships including NAACP; Asian-Pacific legal Defense & Educ bd of dir;United Negro Coll Fund; Gardena Local Manpower Adv Bd; Gardena Interagency Health Comm; Gardena Martin Luther King Cultural Comm; Asian Amer Drug Abuse Prog; CA Afro-Amer Museum Art Council; Museum of African Amer Art; vice pres S Bay Coalition on Alcoholism; adv bd LA Co Child Health Disease Prevention. **HONORS/ACHIEVEMENTS:** Outstanding Leadership Award City of Gardena; Recognition Awd Gardena Elks Leadership; Outstanding Serv Award AFL-CIO; Community Involvement Award Soroptimist Intl; Comm Involvement Award, Gardena Soroptimist; Comm Serv Awd CA Black Comm on Alcoholism; Commendations, LA Co; Outstanding Serv Bd of

Supvr, Dept of Public Soc Serv, 1982. **BUSINESS ADDRESS:** Public Affairs & Govt Relations, Group W Cable, 1730 Gardena Blvd, Gardena, CA 90249.

PARKER, KEITH DWIGHT
Educator. **PERSONAL:** Born Oct 15, 1954, Philadelphia, MS; married Emery W Woodruff; children: Narroyl. **EDUCATION:** Delta State Univ,BA 1978; Miss State Univ, MA 1981, PhD 1986. **CAREER:** Delta State Univ, assistant to the dean 1979-82; Mississippi State Univ, resident asst 1982-85, teaching assistant 1982-86; Auburn Univ, asst prof 1986-89; Univ of Nebraska-Lincoln 1989-. **HONORS/ACHIEVEMENTS:** Pres Graduate Black Student Org 1983; advisor Black Student Org 1982; Minority Fellowship Mississippi State 1982; Outstanding Young Men of America 1980; Alpha Kappa Delta MS State 1983, Outstanding Student 1986; Outstanding Minority Faculty, Auburn Univ, 1989. **BUSINESS ADDRESS:** Dept of Sociology, University of Nebraska-Lincoln, 711 Oldfather Hall, Lincoln, NE 68588-0324.

PARKER, KELLIS E.
Educator, attorney. **PERSONAL:** Born Jan 13, 1942, Kinston, NC; children: Kellis, Kimberly, Emily. **EDUCATION:** Univ NC, BA 1960; Howard Univ Sch of Law, JD cum laude 1968. **CAREER:** Columbia U, prof of law 1975-; Columbia U, asso prof of law 1972-75; Univ CA, acting prof of law 1969-72; Judge Spottswood W Robinson III, law clk 1968-69. **ORGANIZATIONS:** Consult NAACP Legal Def Fund; New World Found; chprsn Comm Action Legal Serv 1977-79; mem Nat Conf on Black Lawyers; chrpsn Minority Groups Com; Assn of Am Law Schs 1976-77; mem Nat Com on Legal & Ethical Implications of Sickle Cell Anemia; bd mem Comm Action for Legal Svcs. **HONORS/ACHIEVEMENTS:** Publ "Modern Judicial Remedies" Little Brown & Co 1975; editor in chf Howard Law Jour 1967-68. **BUSINESS ADDRESS:** Columbia University, School of Law, 435 W 116th St, New York, NY 10027.

PARKER, LEE
Business consultant. **PERSONAL:** Born May 31, 1949; children: 2 children. **EDUCATION:** LeMoyne Owen College, BS, BBA (Magna Cum Laude) 1979. **CAREER:** US Treasury, assoc natl bank examiner 1979-83; Natl Bank of Commerce Memphis, vice pres 1983-84; Gospel TV Network Inc, business consultant 1984-. **ORGANIZATIONS:** Co-chmn Memphis Housing Comm; registered with Securities and Exchange Commission; elected to LeMoyne Owen Coll Religious Life Comm; apptd naval advisor NAUSUPPACT forces. **HONORS/ACHIEVEMENTS:** Natl Science Award, Eastman Kodak Co; Distinguished Alumnus, Natl Assn for Equal Opportunity in Higher Educ; UNCF Awd. **MILITARY SERVICE:** USN petty officer 1966-76; Naval Commendation Medal.

PARKER, LUTRELLE FLEMING
Government official. **PERSONAL:** Born Mar 10, 1924, Newport News, VA; married Lillian M Cobb; children: Lutrelle F Jr, Wendell E, Raymond D. **EDUCATION:** Cornell Univ US Naval Reserve Midshipmen's Sch, commissioned ensign 1945; Howard Univ, BS Civil Engineering 1947; Georgetown Univ Law Sch, JD 1952. **CAREER:** US Patent & Trademark Office, assoc solicitor 1964-70, examiner-in-chief 1970-75, deputy commr 1975-80, mem bd of patent appeals & interferences 1980-. **ORGANIZATIONS:** Mem & chmn Arlington Co Planning Commn 1969-70; mem Bd of Visitors George Mason Univ 1972-80; mem vice chmn VA State Council of Higher Educ Bd/Arlington Hosp 1970-80; chmn of the bd Hosp Council Natl Capital Area 1980-; pres Nauck Citizens Assn 1970-78; bd mem Blue Cross 1975-; Sire Archon Sigma Phi Beta Nu Chap 1984-. **HONORS/ACHIEVEMENTS:** Silver Medal Dept of Commerce 1969; Outstanding Alumni Awd Howard Univ. **MILITARY SERVICE:** USN/USNR capt 36 yrs. **HOME ADDRESS:** 2016 S Fillmore St, Arlington, VA 22204.

PARKER, MARYLAND MIKE
Journalist. **PERSONAL:** Born Feb 05, 1926, Oklahoma City, OK; married John Harrison Parker (deceased); children: Norma Jean Brown, Janice Kay Shelby, Joyce Lynn, John H Jr, Cherie D Hite, Patrick Scott, Charles Roger, John H III. **EDUCATION:** Univ of AR Pine Bluff, 1970-71; Marymount Coll Salina KS, 1974-77. **CAREER:** MD House of Beauty Salina KS, beautician 1964-69; NAACP Salina, youth adviser 1970-72; BACOS Newsletter, newspaper reporter 1971-77; KINA BACOS Report, radio announcer 1973-84; Kansas State Globe, reporter & photographer. **ORGANIZATIONS:** Mem YWCA 1958-, Saline Cty Democratic Women 1960-, VFW Aus 1971-, Amer Leg Aux 1973-, Natl Fed of Press Women 1973-, KS Press Women 1973-; bd of dir Salina Chilc Care Assoc 1973; part time volunteer Salvation Army 1979-; mem Intl Platform Assoc 1983-; bd of dir Gospel Mission 1984. **HONORS/ACHIEVEMENTS:** Lifetime member NAACP 1980; Good Citizenship Award from VFW 1432 Salina KS 1982; Award of Merit, Salina Human Relations, 1986. **HOME ADDRESS:** PO Box 2412, Salina, KS 67402.

PARKER, MATTHEW
Educational administrator. **PERSONAL:** Born Nov 14, 1945, Cincinnati, OH; son of Matt Parker; married Karon Lanier Parker, Aug 08, 1981; children: Matthew Lloyd Parker, Jr. **EDUCATION:** Grand Rapids School of Bible & Music, diploma Bible 1970; Wheaton Coll, BA Sociology 1976; Univ of Detroit, MA Educ Admin 1981; Westminister Theological Seminary, D of Ministry Applicant 1987. **CAREER:** Campus Crusade for Christ, black campus staff 1971-72; Wheaton Coll, minority student adv 1973-77; Great Commiss Comm Ch, founder, pastor 1978-83; Detroit Afro-Amer Mission Inc, consultant 1979-80; J Allen Caldwell Schs, admin 1981-83; William Tyndale Coll, faculty mem 1982-87, assoc vice pres urban academic affairs; Institute for Black Family Development, pres. **ORGANIZATIONS:** Mem, Natl Religious Broadcasters; mem, Christian Management Assn. **HONORS/ACHIEVEMENTS:** MVP Grand Rapids School of Bible & Music Basketball team 1969; MVP MI Christian coll Conf 1969; Achievement Awd Minority Student Organ at Wheaton Coll 1974; publ, "God Sent Him" 1984, "Black Church Development" 1985; Mission Leadership; Destiny Movement Inc, 1987; Leadership Development Natl Black Evangelical Assn, 1988; The Black American Family: A Christian Legacy (film).

PARKER, PAUL E.
Engineering educator. **PERSONAL:** Born Oct 23, 1935, Jenkins Bridge, VA; married Ann Withers. **EDUCATION:** NCA&T State Univ, BS ME 1961; State Univ of NY Buffalo, MS ME 1969. **CAREER:** Bell Aerosystems, stress analyst 1961-67; NCA&T State Univ, asst prof mech engrg 1967-73, asst to dean engrg 1971-73; Univ of IL, asst dean engrg. **ORGANIZATIONS:** Engrg coop dir NCA&T State Univ 1970-73; pres Natl Assn of Minority Engrg Prog Adminstrs 1985; consul Battelle Lab 1984; bd dirs Urban League of Champaign Co 1983-; bd of trustees Mt Olive Bapt Ch 1980-; chmn adv comm Unit 4 Schools 1975-78; bd dir GEM 1986-. **HONORS/ACHIEVEMENTS:** Pi Tau Sigma Hon Soc; Tau Beta Pi Hon Soc. **MILITARY SERVICE:** AUS sp3 instr engrs sch 1955-57. **BUSINESS ADDRESS:** Asst Dean Engineering, Univeristy of Illinois, 1308 W Green St #207, Urbana, IL 61801.

PARKER, RAY, JR.
Singer, song writer, producer. **PERSONAL:** Born 1954, Detroit, MI. **CAREER:** Herbie Hancock "Keep on Doin It", Chaka Kahn & Rufus "You got The Love", Stevie Wonder, Barry White, Temptations, Gladys Knight & The Pips, Spinners, writer. **HONORS/ACHIEVEMENTS:** 5 gold albums; grammy nom "Keep on Doin' It"; Academy Award Nomination Best Orig Song from "Ghost Busters" 1984.

PARKER, STEPHEN A.
Psychologist, educator. **PERSONAL:** Born in Chicago, IL; married Diana Louise; children: Stephen A II, Daniel Edmond. **EDUCATION:** IL Teacher Coll S, BS 1965; Chicago State Coll, MS 1970; Northwestern Univ Evanston IL, PhD 1974. **CAREER:** Chicago State Univ, instr of psychology 1970-74, asst dir 1970-74, assoc asst instr of psychology 1978-84, prof of psychology 1983-85, dir of financial aid, actg dean of admissions & records 1983-86, full professor of psychology 1983-. **ORGANIZATIONS:** Mem/affiliate Henry Horner Chicago Boys Club 1957-; tchr Chicago Bd of Educ 1965-70; recreational instr Chicago Bd of Educ 1966-70; mem Amer Psychological Assn 1974-; mem Phi Delta Kappa 1975-; affiliate Ctr for Creative Mgmt, Natl Rsch Cncl, Ford Foundation; panel mem Doctoral Fellowships 1987. **HONORS/ACHIEVEMENTS:** General Robert E Woods Scholarship Chicago Boys Club 1962; Special Teaching Recognition Award, Chicago State Univ 1977; Chicago Urban League Achievement Award 1976; Black Students Psychological Assn 1975; Natl Assn of Bahamian Cosmetologists 1979; Appreciation Award Business Educ Student Assn CSU 1982; Distinguished Alumni Award Crane HS Hall of Fame 1985; Special Guest Speaker Award 1986; Distinguished Serv Award Henry Horner Boys & Girls Club 1987. **BUSINESS ADDRESS:** Professor of Psychology, Chicago State Univ, 9500 King Dr, Chicago, IL 60628.

PARKER, THOMAS E., JR.
Clergyman. **PERSONAL:** Born Jul 14, 1916, Floyd, VA; son of Thomas E. Parker, Sr. and Cleopatria Brammer Parker; married Bessie Locke; children: Gwendolyn E, Thomas E III, Louis W. **EDUCATION:** VA Theol Sem & Coll Lynchburg, BA & BD 1951; VA Theol Sem & Coll, DD 1964, D Human Letters 1964; Am Bapt Theol Sem Nashville TN. **CAREER:** Zion Bapt Ch Ambler PA, ret pastor 1961-80; Montgomery County OIC, found & ret exec dir; Castle View Bapt Ch Calloway VA, pastor 1937-47; Shiloh Bapt Ch Salem VA, 1945-52; 1st Bapt Ch Oxford NC, 1952-61; pres Virginia Seminary & College Lynchburg, VA 1982-87 (retired). **ORGANIZATIONS:** Pres VA Sem & Coll Alumni Assn 1962-66; pres Ambler Ministerium 1965-67; pres Rose Valley Cemetery Assn 1971-79; bd mem Lott Carey Bapt Foreign Mission Exec Bd; trustee VA Sem & Coll; moderator Suburban Bapt Ch Assn; mem Progressive Nat Bapt Conv; Am Bapt Conv; PA Bapt Philadelphia Bapt Assn; Big Bros Assn; mem Prince Hall Free & Accepted Masons; Phi Beta Sigma; Kiwanis Club; mem VA Bapt State Convention, Natl Bapt Convention of Amer. **HONORS/ACHIEVEMENTS:** Distinguished serv awd Gr Ambler Jaycees 1968; community serv awd Montgomery Co Business Community 1971; distinguished achievement awd Borough of Ambler for 40 yrs of continuous pastorate 1977; rec Humanitarian Awd on Retire as Exec Dir Montgomery Co OIC; honored for 50 years in ministry 1935-86.

PARKER, THOMAS EDWIN, III
Public & government affairs advisor. **PERSONAL:** Born Dec 11, 1944. **EDUCATION:** Princeton U, MPA 1971; Howard U, BA 1967; Woodrow Wilson Sch of Pub & Intrntl Affairs. **CAREER:** Standard Oil Co, prog coord, pub & govt aff 1985; Am Soc for Pub Admin Wash, dir of progs 1974-76; City Cncl of DC, legis asst 1971-74; Wash Concentrated Empl Prog, prog coord 1967-69. **ORGANIZATIONS:** Admin prog dev consult Ghana W Africa; OIC Rsrch Asso NJ St Landlord; Tenant Relationship Study Commn Pub Defenders Off NJ Am Soc for Pub Admin; Intrntl City Mgmt Assn; Urban Leag; NAACP. **HONORS/ACHIEVEMENTS:** Woodrow Wilson Flwshp; Pub Affairs Intrnshp; Outstdng Young Men of Am 1972. **BUSINESS ADDRESS:** Amoco Oil Co, 6 Executive Park Dr NE, Atlanta, GA 30329.

PARKER, WALTER GEE
Physician. **PERSONAL:** Born Feb 11, 1933, Branchville, VA; son of Roosevelt Parker and Theresa Parker; married Henri Mae Smith; children: Jennifer L, Walter G Jr, Brian K. **EDUCATION:** Hampton Inst, BS 1955; Meharry Medical Coll, MD 1962; University of MI, MPH 1967. **CAREER:** Univ of MI Sch of Public Health, rsch assoc 1967-69; Wayne County Health Dept, public health phys 1969-75; Southwest Detroit Hospital, vice pres of medical affairs 1975-86; State of MI Dept of Corr, medical dir 1986-. **ORGANIZATIONS:** Mem Amer Public Health Assoc 1967-, Amer Acad of Pediatrics 1973-, Detroit Medical Soc 1975-, Wayne Co Medical Soc 1975-. **HONORS/ACHIEVEMENTS:** Mem Delta Omega Public Health Honorary Society 1967-; Bd Certified Amer Bd of Pediatrics 1971; article "Michigan Rheumatic Fever Study," in Michigan Med 1969. **MILITARY SERVICE:** AUS sp-3 1956-58; Good Conduct Medal. **HOME ADDRESS:** 3626 Deerfield Pl, Ann Arbor, MI 48103. **BUSINESS ADDRESS:** Medical Dir, W Wayne Correctional Facility, 48401 Five Mile Rd, Plymouth, MI 48170.

PARKER, WILLIAM C., JR.
Real estate developer. **PERSONAL:** Born Apr 16, 1939, Mt Gilead, NC; son of Mr and Mrs William C Parker, Sr; married Markethia Baldwin; children: Kamala, Keisha D. **EDUCATION:** North Carolina A&T State Univ, BS 1961, BS 1965; Univ NC-Chapel Hill, ME 1967; Indiana Univ, Doctorate 1971. **CAREER:** Shepargib Foods Inc Burger King Franchise in Greensboro & Winston-Salem, founder/pres/ceo 1976-84; Wilpar Develop Corp, founder/pres/ceo 1977-; Wilpar Construction Co, founder/pres/ceo 1977; Parker Brothers Restaurant, founder/pres/ceo 1980; Wilpar Corp, founder/pres/ceo 1983; Southeastern Develop Group, founder 1985; Joint Ctr for Economic Develop, founder 1985; Piedmont Develop Corp, founder/pres/deo 1974-. **ORGANIZATIONS:** Mem Omega Psi Phi Frat 1963-, Phylaxis Soc 1975-, Natl Restaurant Assoc 1976-; life mem Univ of NC at Chapel Hill Alumni Assoc 1977-; mem Natl Bd of Realtors 1979-; mem adv bd Carolina Peacemaker Newspaper

1980-; mem Greensboro Bd of Realtors 1979-; deputy grand master Prince Hall Grand Lodge of NC and its Jurisdictions 1980-; sec A&T Univ Foundation Inc 1982-; bd of dirs Foundation of Greater Greensboro 1983-; mem The Greensboro Conversation Club 1985-, Greensboro Men's Club 1985-; past chmn NC A&T State Univ Bd of Trustees 1985-; mem Beta Epsilon Boule Sigma Pi Phi Frat 1986-, Greensboro Natl Bank Adv Bd 1986-; vice pres NC Black Leadership Caucus 1986; mem bd of trustees, chmn long range plng comm Shiloh Bapt Church 1986; life mem NAACP; mem Greensboro Merchants Assoc. **HONORS/ACHIEVEMENTS:** James T Isler Comm Serv Awd Family Children Serv of Greater Greensboro 1982; presented the "Order of the Long Leaf Pine" by Gov James B Hunt 1985; Econom-ic Develop Awd NAACP 1985; Outstanding Alumnus Awd Natl Assoc on Higher Educ 1985; Levi Coffin Awd for Leadership and Human Serv Greensboro Area Chamberof Commerce 1986. **MILITARY SERVICE:** AUS 2 yrs. **BUSINESS ADDRESS:** Chief Executive Officer, Piedmont Development Corp, 1604 East Market St, Greensboro, NC 27401.

PARKER, WILLIAM HAYES, JR.
Director/producer. **PERSONAL:** Born May 02, 1947, Mt Vernon, NY; married Yvonne Kelly; children: Eric Hayes, Steven Lee, Stella Cailan. **EDUCATION:** Univ of Cincinnati, 1965-66; Macomb Co Coll, 1967-69; Los Angeles City Coll, 1973-75. **CAREER:** EUE Screen Gems, prod mgr 1977-78; New Genesis Prods, producer 1978-79; BAV Inc, producer/LD 1980-82; BPP, director/producer 1982-. **MILITARY SERVICE:** USAF sgt 1966-70. **BUSINESS ADDRESS:** Director-Producer, B Parker Prods/ Renge Films, 8400 DeLongpre Ave, Los Angeles, CA 90069.

PARKS, ARNOLD GRANT
Educator. **PERSONAL:** Born Nov 19, 1939, St Louis, MO; married Lennette Bogee; children: LaShawn Michelle, Anna Louise, Alicia Victoria. **EDUCATION:** Harris Teachers Coll, AA 1959; Washington Univ, BS 1962; St Louis Univ, MA 1964, PhD 1970. **CAREER:** St Louis Univ, instructor 1964-66; Delta Educ Corp, deputy dir 1966-69; Malone & Hyde Inc, training dir 1969-71; Memphis State Univ, assoc prof 1971-76; Lincoln Univ, prof of sociology, acting coord Coll of Arts & Scis. **ORGANIZATIONS:** Mem Mid-Amer Congress on Aging; mem Assn of Black Sociologists; mem Midwest Sociological Soc mem Sigma Phi Omega Natl Gerontology Hon Soc; mem MO Acad of Sci mem Assn for Gerontology & Human Develop in the Historically Black College & Univ; pres-elect Lincoln Univ Found; life mem Alpha Phi Alpha; mem NAACP; chmn Jefferson City Police Personnel Review Bd; vice pres Wesley Found at Lincoln Univ Campus Ministry; mem bd of dirs The Ethnic Minority Local Church Task Force; received federal & state grants including the following, MO Gerontology Inst 1977-82; grant MO Comm on the Humanities; grant MO Gerontology Inst; grant MO Div of Aging; grant MO Div of Aging; grant Admin on Aging; pres MO State Sociological Assn 1985-86; chmn Gerontology Sect MO Acad of Science 1985. **HONORS/ACHIEVEMENTS:** Faculty Fellowship Natl Science Found 1976-77 1977-78 1978-79; Fellowship from Natl Ctr on the Black Aged 1978 1980; Fellowship from Joint Ctrs on Aging Studies; Fellowship from Ethel Percy Andrus Gerontology Ctr; mentioned in Leaders in Educ 5th edition; mentioned in Personalities of the South; mentioned in Dictionary of Intl Biography vol 13 1976-77; book publication "Urban Education, An Annotated Bibliography" Century 21 Publishing Co 1981; have published numerous articles in journals. **BUSINESS ADDRESS:** Prof of Sociology, Lincoln University, 820 Chestnut St, Jefferson City, MO 65101.

PARKS, BERNARD
Attorney. **PERSONAL:** Born Jun 10, 1944, Atlanta; married Joyce Williams; children: Bernard Jr. **EDUCATION:** Morehouse Coll, BA 1966; Emory Univ Sch of Law, JD 1969. **CAREER:** Patterson Parks Jackson & Howell, ptr 1973-; Jackson Patterson Parks & Franklin, ptr 1970-73; Jackson & Handler, Asso 1970; Jud Elbert Parr Tuttle United Cir Ct of Appeals, law clk 1969-70; Atla Leg Aid Soc Inc, law asst 1968-69; Sen Horace Ward Atla, leg intern 1968; Aldmn Q V Williamson Atla City, gov intern 1967 Cts admitted to prac Fulton Co GA Sup Ct, GA Ct of Appeals, GA Sup Ct, US Dis Ct, US Ct of Appeals, US Sup Ct. **ORGANIZATIONS:** Co-chmn Men Hlth Com Yng Law Sect; Am Bar Assn; Atla Bar Assn; bd of dir Atla Coun Yng Law; co-chmn Ment Hlth Com GA Bar Assn; vice pres GA Leg Serv Prog Inc; Gate Cty Bar Assn; Nat Bar Assn; Law Com Civ Rights under Law; Chmn bd of dir Opp Ind Cent of Atla; bd dir Opp Ind Cent of Am ; chmn bd of mgrs E Cent Br Butler St YMCA; bd dir Butler St YMCA Assn; Gov Ment Hlth Com Task Force; Met Atla Coun on Crime & Juv Del; chmn Pri Alloc Com Uni Way Allo Com for Comm Sec; Local Govt Task Force Com Atla C of C; Atla Crim Just Coord Com; bd of dir Big Bros Assn; Atla Bus League; Atla Urban League; NAACP; Am Civ Lib Un; SE Region Bd YMCA; Atla Coal on Curr Comm Aff; Omega Psi Phi Frat; Phi Alpha Delta Frat; Y'S Men Int. **HONORS/ACHIEVEMENTS:** Omega Chap Outstndg Young Man of Year in Prof; Mr Psi 1967f Omega Psi Phi Frat Psi Chap Morehouse Coll; WSB Nesmaker Award 1972; five Outstndg Young Men In 1974. **BUSINESS ADDRESS:** 101 Marietta Towers, Atlanta, GA 30303.

PARKS, GEORGE B.
Educator, consultant. **PERSONAL:** Born Feb 18, 1925, Lebanon, KY; son of George W. Parks and Eleanor Parks; children: Paula Lynn, William Earle. **EDUCATION:** Howard Univ Sch of Law, LLB 1948; George Washington Univ Sch of Law, LLM 1951. **CAREER:** Coleman Parks & Washington law firm, atty 1948-60; professional consul to title companies 1963-73; LA City Councilman David Cunningham, spl asst 1973-74; Glendale Univ Sch of Law, asst dean/prof of law 1979-80; Summa Corp, consult 1979-84; land use and polit procedure, consul 1984-. **ORGANIZATIONS:** Mem KY Bar Assn; mem DC Bar Assn; mem Amer Bar Assn; educ consul to consol Realty Bd; CA Real Estate Advancement Adv Comm; life mem SW Music Symphony Assn; consol Realty Bd; Mid-City C of C; Luth Housing Corp; LA Co Dist Atty Adv Comm; Amer Bar Assn; mem Soc of Amer Law Tchrs; founding dir CA Timeshare Owners Found; consul Timeshare Mgmt Corp; owner/pres Parks Course in Continuing Real Estate Educ 1979-. **HONORS/ACHIEVEMENTS:** Spl Serv Awd Law Enforcement Council Wash 1959; Man of Yr Natl council Bus & Professional Women 1968; Spl Citizens Testimonial Awd LA 1969; Human Rel AwdLA 1970; Man of Yr Crenshaw C of C 1972; LA City Council Awd 1969; Who's Who in the West 1972-73; Disting Alumni Awd from Howard Univ Alumni Club ofSouthern CA 1982; Natl Soc of Real Estate Appraisers Educ Awd 1981; Lutheran Housing Corp Awd for Outstanding Leadership 1980; CA State Assoc of Real Estate Brokers Awd 1980; numerous city/county/state awards and citations. **BUSINESS ADDRESS:** Consultant, 1122 S LaCrenega Blvd, #104, Los Angeles, CA 90035.

PARKS, GILBERT R.
Psychiatrist. **PERSONAL:** Born May 14, 1944, Arcadia, OK; married Jenice L; children: Garmez, Melanese, Ronee. **EDUCATION:** Cntrl St, BS 1967; Thomas Jefferson Med Coll, MD 1973. **CAREER:** Topeka St Hosp, psychiatrist; Menninger Found, Topeka, present; Priv Prac, part-time; HEW, 3 yr res Psychiatry complete 1976. **ORGANIZATIONS:** Chmn bd Student Nat Med Assn 1972-73; dir Health Career Progs Philadelphia 1970-72; OK St Dept of Pub Hlth, Environ Hlth Div of Water Quality Control 1967-69; psychiatry asst Hosp ofUniv of oK 1965-67; rancher 1960-69; adminstrv consult adv Student Nat Med Assn; mem KS Dist Br of Am Psychiatric Assn; consult Ofc of Hlth Resources Opp, Hlth Resources Adminstrn Dept of HEW; sec Nat Assn of Post Grad Physicians; bd dirs Boys Club Topeka. **HONORS/ACHIEVEMENTS:** Recip Outstanding Ldrshp Awd Stdnt Nat Med Assn; Outstanding Stdnt Awd Med Com Concerned with Civil Rights 1970; Solomon Fuller Fellowship 1975. **BUSINESS ADDRESS:** 629 Quincy, #205, Topeka, KS.

PARKS, GORDON A.
Author, photographer, composer. **PERSONAL:** Born Nov 30, 1912, Fort Scott, KS; married Genevieve Young; children: Gordon Jr (dec), David, Toni, Leslie. **EDUCATION:** The MD Inst, Hon Degree 1968; Fairfield Univ, Hon Degree 1969; Boston Univ, Hon Degree 1969; KS State Univ, Hon Degree 1970; St Olaf Coll, Hon Degree 1973; Colby Coll, Hon Degree 1974; Macalester Coll, Hon Degree 1974; Lincoln Univ, Hon Degree 1975. **CAREER:** Farm Security Admin, correspondent 1942; OWI, correspondent 1943-45; Standard Oil of NJ, correspondent 1945-49; Life, photo-journalist 1949-70; Essence, ed dir 1970-73; Paramount Pictures, film dir. **ORGANIZATIONS:** Mem, natl bd dir Guild of Amer; past dir ASMP, Authors Guild; mem NAACP, Urban League, Newspaper Guild, Assoc Composer & Dir, Kappa Alpha Mu. **HONORS/ACHIEVEMENTS:** Awd Natl Council Christians & Jews 1964; author, The Learning Tree 1966, Born Black 1971, Whispers of Intimate Things 1971, In Love 1971; author num articles, composer of popular songs & sonatas, Symphonic Set, A Piece for Piano & Wind Instruments, The Learning Tree Symphony; produced, directed, wrote script & music for The Learning Three Warner Bros 1968; directed Shaft MGM 1971, Shaft's Big Score MGM 1972, The Super Cops MGM 1973, Leadbelly Paramount 1976; author "Moments Without Proper Names" 1975; President's Fellow Awd RI Sch Design 1984; named Kansan of Year Native Sons and Daughters Kan 1986. **BUSINESS ADDRESS:** Film Dir, Paramount Pictures, 860 United Nations Plaza, New York, NY 10017.

PARKS, JAMES CLINTON, JR.
Marketing manager. **PERSONAL:** Born May 12, 1944, Kannapolis, NC; married Corine Musgrave; children: Crystal Westray, James III, Shawnda M. **EDUCATION:** Livingstone Coll, BS 1965. **CAREER:** EI Du Pont, employment supv 1965-77; US Army, 1st lt 1967-69; Miller Brewing Co, mgr spec mktg prog 1977-. **ORGANIZATIONS:** Mem Phi Beta Sigma 1963-; bd of dir Milwaukee Min Chamber of Comm 1983-86, Waukesha County WI NAACP 1984-86; mem Frontiers Intl 1987-; bd mem Fayetteville State Univ Foundation; bd mem Cal-Pac Corp Advisory Bd. **HONORS/ACHIEVEMENTS:** Order of Long Leaf Pine St of NC 1984; Distinguished Alumnus, Livingstone Coll 1989. **MILITARY SERVICE:** AUS 1st lt 1966-69. **BUSINESS ADDRESS:** Manager-Spec Mkt Programs, Miller Brewing Co, 3939 W Highland, Milwaukee, WI 53201.

PARKS, JAMES DALLAS
Educator. **PERSONAL:** Born Aug 25, 1906, St Louis, MO; married Florence Wright; children: James Peter. **EDUCATION:** Bradley U, BS 1927; StUniv of IA;; MS 1943; Academyy Italia Delle Artiedellavorse Parma Italy, Dliploma of Academician of Italy 1980. **CAREER:** Lincoln U, emeritus prof of art 1976-, head art dept 1927-76; Sphinx Mag Alpha Phi Alpha, art ed 1956-50. **ORGANIZATIONS:** Past pres Natl Conf of Artists 1961-62; past pres MO Coll Art Conf 1955-56; past commr MO Negro Inter-sch Ath Assn 1943-54; "Juan Paraja the Man in 5 1/2 Million Dollar Painting", St Louis Post-dispatch 1970; Co-author Comprehensive Exam for Undergrad; Majors in Asrt History, Educ Testing Serv Princeton NJ 1970. **HONORS/ACHIEVEMENTS:** Spl Honored Alumnus, BradleyUniv 1973; "Robert Scott Duncanson-19th Cent Black Painter", Assn for study of Negro Life & History 1980.

PARKS, JAMES EDWARD
Attorney. **PERSONAL:** Born Mar 22, 1946, Pine Bluff, AR; married Gwendolyn Jean Fane; children: James Jr, Latina, Lisa. **EDUCATION:** CA St Univ at Fresno, BS 1972; Harvard Law Sch, JSD 1975. **CAREER:** Dawson & Ninnis Fresno CA; atty 1977-; San Fernando Val Neighborhood Legan Serv Van Nuys CA, atty 1975-77. **ORGANIZATIONS:** Mem Fresno Co Bar Assn present; mem CA St Bar & Assn, present; mem Assn of Defense Counsel, present; bd of dirs Fresno Co Legal Servs Legan Advis, Black Polit Council of Fresno 1980. **BUSINESS ADDRESS:** Dawson & Ninnis, 2409 Merced St, Fresno, CA 93721.

PARKS, LYMAN S.
City official, clergyman. **PERSONAL:** Born Mar 12, 1917, Princeton, IN; married Cleo; children: Linda, Larry, Leo, Lana, Londa, Lyman Jr, Lawana. **EDUCATION:** IN St Tchrs Coll, 1936-37; Wilberforce U, BA 1944; Payne Theol Sem, 1944; Allen U, hon DD 1951. **CAREER:** Bethel AME Ch Marion, pastor 1944-47, Richmond 1947-52; Ann Arbor 1952-64; River Rogue 1964-66; AME First Comm Ch Grand Rapids, pastor; served as sec Grand Rapids Council Chs 1966-. **ORGANIZATIONS:** Officer chmn Manpower Area Planning Council bd dir; MI Conf Mayors; bd dir TB Emphysema Soc; Nat Council Alcholism, MI Div; MI Municipal League; mem US Conf Mayors; Nat League Cities; Lastin Am Council; Hlth Serv Task Force; Dist Ct Probation Steering Com; Kent Co Regional Planning Com; Assn Grand Rapids Area Govts; Grand Rapids Conv Bur; United Fund & Comm Svcs; elected Mayor 1973; acting Mayor 1971; elected pres City Commn 1971; elected Third Ward Commr NAACP; Urban League; Downtown Kiwanis; Prin Ce Hall F & AM; Alpha Phi & Alpha Frat, life mem; Interdenominational Ministerial All; Grand Rapids Ministerial Assn. **HONORS/ACHIEVEMENTS:** Founders Day Awd, Outstanding Leadership Comm 1969; Liberty Bell Awd sponsored by Bar Assn 1972; Floyd Skinner Awd sponsored NAACP; Chicago's AME Nminiksterial Assn, Serv Awd 1974; Grand Rapids Lions Club Cert Appreciation 1974; Charter, Boss of Yr Awd, Bus Womens Assn LaGrande-vitesse Chap 1974.

PARKS, PAUL
Corporate executive. **PERSONAL:** Born May 07, 1923, Indianapolis, IN; married Virginia Loftman; children: Paul, Pamela, Stacey. **EDUCATION:** Purdue Univ, BS 1949; MA Inst of Tech, postgrad 1958. **CAREER:** Commonwealth of MA, sec Educ Affairs 1975-; Boston Model City Admin, admin 1968-75; Architecture & Engineering Firm, Boston, partner 1957-67; Pratt & Whitney Aircraft, nuclear engr 1953-57; Chance Vought Aircraft; missile designer 1952-53; Fahy Spofford & Thorndike, Boston; Stone & Webster Engring, designer 1951; IN St Hwy Commn Indianapolis, 1949-51; Mayors Com for Admin of Justice, consult gen ac-

counting office. **ORGANIZATIONS:** Mem Atty Gen Adv Com on Civil Rights 1961-71; mem Hlth Task Force, Boston Fed Exec Bd; adv Boston Mothers for Adequate Welfare 1966-68; speech therapist, Vets Lang Clinic 1964-66; mem MA Ad Council on Educ 1968-71; MA Commn on Children & Youth 1962-67; chmn MA Adv Com to US Civil Rights Commn 1961-73; chmn Urban Affairs com, MA Fedn of Fair Housing & Equal Rights 1961-67; mem Comm Educ & Council 1961-73; pres com for Comm Educ Devel Inc 1968-74; adult leader Youth Prgms Roxbury UMCA; trustee Peter Bent Brigham Hosp; bd dir MA Planned Parenthood Assn; MA Mental Hlth Assn; MA Soc for Prevention of Blindness; Boston Coll, Upward Bound Prog; registered professional engr; Am Soc of Civil Engrs; Nat Soc of Professional Engrs; Nat Acad of Pub Adminstrn; NAACP; Nat Bd of the Ams for Dem Action 1971-74; St Bd of the Am for Dem Action 1970-74; Steering Com, Educ Commn of the States Books; "Racism", "Elitism", "Professionalism Barriers to Comm Mental Hlth" 1976. **MILITARY SERVICE:** AUS 1st sgt 1942-46. **BUSINESS ADDRESS:** 1 Ashburton Pl, Boston, MA 02108.

PARKS, ROSA
Civil rights leader. **PERSONAL:** Born Feb 04, 1913, Tuskegee, AL. **EDUCATION:** Alabama State Coll, attended. **ORGANIZATIONS:** Former clerk, insurance saleswoman, tailor's asst; former youth advisor, Montgomery N NAACP; active with SCLC, Detroit & Women's Public Affairs Comm; refused to give up her bus seat to white passenger & triggered bus boycott which resulted in outlawing of segregation on city buses in Montgomery 1955; known as the Mother of the Modern Civil Rights Movement. **HONORS/ACHIEVEMENTS:** SCLC sponsors an annual Rosa Parks Freedom Awd; honored by Women's Missionary Soc, AME Church at Quadrennial Conventions, Los Angeles 1971; recipient honorary degree Shaw Coll Detroit. **BUSINESS ADDRESS:** 305 Fed Bldg, 231 W Lafayette, Detroit, MI 48226.

PARKS, SHERMAN A.
Judge. **PERSONAL:** Born May 15, 1924, Topeka, KS; married Alberta Lewis; children: Sherman Jr. **EDUCATION:** Washburn U, Bba 1949; Washburn Univ Sch of Law, Llb 1955, JD 1970. **CAREER:** KS Ct of Appeals, judge 1977-; Sec of St, dep asst 1971-76; Atty Gen KS, asst 1968-71; KS Alcoholic Beverage Control, atty 1966-68; Co Atty, 1st asst 1961-66; Pvt Law Prac, 1955-61; KS Supreme Ct; US Dist Ct for KS; 10th Judicial Circuit; US Supreme Ct; Washburn Univ Sch of Law, lectr 1969. **ORGANIZATIONS:** Mem Omega Psi Phi Frat; Chmn pro tem Steward Bd of St John AME Ch 1972-76; chmn bd of regents WashburnUniv 1968-76; mem Selective Serv Bd #71 1967-76; bd dir Topeka UMCA 1966-76; bd trustee Topeka YMCA 1976; bd of gov Washburn Law Sch Assn 1964-72; pres Topeka Council of PTA 1962 st francis hosp adv bd 1962-65; first black to serve on appellate-level ct kS; first black to serve on washburn u bd of regents; first black to serve on the Selective Serv Bd, KS. **MILITARY SERVICE:** USN yhoeman 1st class 1943-46. **BUSINESS ADDRESS:** Judge, Court of Appeals State House, Topeka, KS 66612.

PARKS, THELMA REECE
Educator. **PERSONAL:** Born Apr 04, 1923, Muskogee, OK; divorced. **EDUCATION:** Langston U, BS 1945;Univ of OK, M 1955; Central St U, professional Cert 1963; Central State Univ, additional study 1980-81. **CAREER:** Oklahoma City Housing Authority, commr 1977-84; US Grant High School; counselor/dept head 1973; Douglass High School, counselor 1970-71, English teacher/dept head 1961-70; Dunbar & Truman Elem Schools, teacher 1951-61. **ORGANIZATIONS:** Past pres OK City Guidance Assn 1976-77; life mem NEA; mem OEA COA; mem McFarland Br YWCA 1973-; first black female trustee Faith Meml Bapt Ch 1975;adv mem Capitol Improvement Plan Oklahoma City 1975-; mem Adv Com Black Family; mem NE YMCA; mem Alpha Kappa Alpha Sor; mem NAACP; mem Urban League; mem Urban League Guild; Womens Day Speaker, Wildwood Christian Ch 1978; first Black Female Mem Kappa Delta Pi Gamma ChapUniv of OK 1955; chmn Blue RibbonComm Fund Raising 1982-86; mem bd dir YWCA 1983-86; sec OK City Langston Alumni 1986-88; panelist OK State Dept of Ed Conf on Educ 1987; bd mem elect Langsotn Univ Alumni Assoc 1987-90; task force comm OEA improving schools in OK 1987-; mem Natl Sor of Phi Delta Kappa. **HONORS/ACHIEVEMENTS:** Recipient Outstanding Serv Awd Nu Vista Club 1972; Guest Feature Writer Black Educ Black Dispatch Pub Co 1976; Couns of Yr, Okla City Pub Sch OK CityGuidance Assn 1977; Employee of Month Okla City Pub Schs, Assn of All Sch Personnel 1978; Received Awd 20 Year Reunion from Class 1965 1985; Received Awd 20 Year Reunion from Class 1966 1986. **BUSINESS ADDRESS:** Counselor, Oklahoma City Bd of Education, 900 North Klein St, Oklahoma City, OK 73119.

PARKS-DUNCANSON, LOUISE
Entertainer. **PERSONAL:** Born Mar 19, 1929, Raleigh, NC; married David. **EDUCATION:** Emerson Coll, BA 1951. **CAREER:** Lu Parks Jazz & Soul Dance Ensemble, dir/leader 1951; prog initiated by Gov Rockefeller & Bd of Educ, dance drama specialist, taught in underprivileged area of NYC; performer in several Broadway plays; appeared w/ensemble on all major TV networks throughout country; concert tour of US colleges & universities.

PARMS, EDWIN L.
Attorney. **PERSONAL:** Born Jun 18, 1937; married Margaret; children: Stephanie, Deborah. **EDUCATION:** Univ of Akron, BA 1960, JD 1965. **CAREER:** Parms, Purnell & Gilbert, atty 1965-; Akron Pub Schs, tchr 1960-65; St Univ of Akron, co-counsel. **ORGANIZATIONS:** Mem Local, State & Am Bar Assn; mem Black & Barristers Club; legal counsel Akron NAACP, past br pres; Salvation Army Bd; United Way Bd; Visiting Nurses Bd; Local Urban League Bd; Fair Housing Bd; Co Legal Aid Bd; co-author Akron Plan, plan to get more blacks in Akron construction industry; mem Akron Rewdevel Bd; mem Eta Tau Lambda Chpt, Alpha Phi Alpha Frat; chmn spl library proj working to improve reading abilities minority youth; mem States Citizens Task Force on Higher Edn; pres Akron Frontiers Inc; Wesley Temple AME Zion Ch; sec of Akron Bar Assoc. **HONORS/ACHIEVEMENTS:** First black chosen Young Man of Yr, Akron Jr C of C. **MILITARY SERVICE:** AUS 1st lt.

PARNELL, ARNOLD W.
Business executive. **PERSONAL:** Born Jan 21, 1936, Philadelphia, PA; son of Jesie Parnell and Eva Parnell; married Thelma; children: Steven, Paula, Michael. **EDUCATION:** Villanova Univ, BSCE 1957; USC, MSCE 1962; USC & UCLA, postgraduate.. **CAREER:** Nellson Candies, original owner & founder 1962-68; N Amer Aviation, sr research engineer 1957-62; P&L Mgmt Systems, corporate dir 1972-; TRW Systems Group, div staff mgr 1962-82, dir indus research center 1982-86; ELI Mgmt Corp, general mgr 1986-. **ORGANIZATIONS:** Professional license Mechanical Engineering; mem Small Business Devel Advisory Bd; Amer Inst of Aeronautics & Astronautics 1967-; assoc fellow AIAA 1970. **BUSINESS ADDRESS:** General Manager, ELI Management Corporation, 15201 So Broadway, Gardena, CA 90248.

PARNELL, JOHN VAZE, III
Business executive. **PERSONAL:** Born Oct 04, 1944, Boston, MA; married Patricia Meehan; children: Elizabeth, Monica, Andrea. **EDUCATION:** Univ MA, BS 1966. **CAREER:** General Foods Corp, sr food tech 1966-72; Latouraine Bickford's, new prod devel mgr 1972; Miralin Co, prod devel mgr 1972-74; General Foods Corp, lab mgr, sr lab mgr. **ORGANIZATIONS:** Pres AEPI Frat 1965, vice pres Class 66; mem Inst of Food Technologist; pres Univ MA Alumni Assn 1975-77, vice pres 1973-75; bd of dir Univ MA Alumni Assn 1970-; Univ MA Found Inc 1977-; mem Sportsmens Club of Greater Boston. **HONORS/ACHIEVEMENTS:** Listed in Who's Who in Amer Colls & Univs 1966; Outstanding Sr Awd 1966; Distinguished Serv to Univ Awd Univ MA 1977; Black Achievers in Industry AwdYMCA of Greater NY Harlem Br 1979. **BUSINESS ADDRESS:** Senior Lab Manager, General Foods Corp, 555 S Broadway, Tarrytown, NY 10591.

PARNELL, WILLIAM CORNELLUS, JR.
Accountant. **PERSONAL:** Born Feb 10, 1940, Burton, SC; married Carolyn E Howard; children: Wanda, Debra, Monique. **EDUCATION:** Univ Detroit, MBA 1974; Howard U, BA 1962; Mil Comptrollership; honor cert 1969; walsh coll bus, efta, m. **CAREER:** Independent Fin Serv Inc, pres, chief fin dir; Vickers Inc, bus analyst 1974-86; Ford Mtr Co Birmingham MI, financial analyst 1968-74; Citizens Crusade Against Poverty, Washington, comptroller 1966-68; Defense Contract Audit Agy, Alexandria VA, auditor 1965-66; Practicing Accountant & Tax Practitioner; US Treasury Card Holder. **ORGANIZATIONS:** MI Ind Accounts Assn; Nat Assn Accountants; Inst Mgmt Accountants; Nat Black MBA Assn; Assn of MBA Exec; Nat Assn of Black Accountants; Nat Soc Enrolled Fed Tax Accountants; treas, vice pres Howard U; Alumni Club Detroit; Omega Psi Phi Frat; Luth Intl Mens League; panelist Detroit Ind Adv Group; life mem NAACP 1980. **MILITARY SERVICE:** AUS 1st lt 1962-64; USAR capt 1964-75; Mil Hon Ribbon 1961; Army QM Theater Operations Ft Lee VA 1967; Letter of Commendation Command Post Exercise. **BUSINESS ADDRESS:** President, Chief Fin Dir, Independent Financial Serv Inc, 19750 James Couzens Dr, Detroit, MI 48235.

PARRIS, GUICHARD
Business executive. **PERSONAL:** Born Mar 03, 1903; son of Esau Parris and Laure Parris; married Willie Ferron; children: Mary, Frederick, Louise. **EDUCATION:** Amherst Coll, AB (with honors) 1927; Columbia Univ, MA 1932. **CAREER:** Livingstone Coll, Atlanta Univ, Lincoln University MO, instructor 1930-36; Negro Affairs Natl Youth Adminstration Region I, dir 1939-42; Natl Urban League, dir public relations 1944-68; Underwood Jordan Assocs, consul urban affairs 1968-78. **ORGANIZATIONS:** Pres Catholic Interracial Council 1956-61; trustee Hospital for Special Surgery NYC 1968-; chmn Parish Council Corpus Christi Ch 1966-68; pres Schomburg Corp, NY Public Library 1984-86; Trustee Catholic Big Brothers of New York 1962-. **HONORS/ACHIEVEMENTS:** Phi Beta Kappa Amherst Coll 1927; Rosenwald Fellow Julius Rosenwald Fund 1938; "Blacks in the City" co-author G Parris & Lester Brooks 1971; Silver Anvil Awd Public Relations Soc of America 1965; Man of the Yr NY Chap PRSA 1968; Doctor of Humane Letters, Jersey City State College 1988. **HOME ADDRESS:** 501 W 123rd St, New York, NY 10027.

PARRISH, CHARLES HENRY
Educator. **PERSONAL:** Born Jan 12, 1899, Louisville, KY; married Frances Murrell; children: Ursula. **EDUCATION:** Howard, AB 1920; Columbia, MA 1921; Chicago, PhD 1944. **CAREER:** Univ Louisville, prof dept sociology, present, head, dept sociology 1959-64; Belknap Campus, 1951-69; Louisville Mun Coll, 1931-51; Simmons Univ, 1921-30. **ORGANIZATIONS:** Mem Urban League; CLSEA Com; consult So Student YMCA; US Nat Student Assn; mem Lincoln Key; chmn Comm Action Com. **HONORS/ACHIEVEMENTS:** Recpt Ottenheimer Awd for Comm Serv; mem Const Revision Com; publ "desegregation in pub edn-a critical summary", jour negro edn; "Desegregated Higher Educ in KY"; "Principles of Police Work With Minority Groups" 1950. **BUSINESS ADDRESS:** University of Louisville, Dept Sociology, Louisville, KY 40208.

PARRISH, CLARENCE R.
Circuit court judge. **PERSONAL:** Born Oct 22, 1921, Louisburg, NC; married Mildred; children: Sheila, Sharon. **EDUCATION:** St Johns Univ, LLB; Univ WI, LLM. **CAREER:** Private Practice, Milwaukee attorney; Circuit Court Milwaukee, judge. **ORGANIZATIONS:** Mem Am WI & Milwaukee Bar Assns, Natl Bar Assn; mem bd State Bar Commrs; appeal counsel Local Draft Bd #44; past pres Milwaukee NAACP; past pres Chaplaincy Ct Serv; mem adv bd trustees Gr Milwaukee YWCA; lectured 3 yrs Milwaukee Area Teach Coll evening sch part time lecturer 2 yrs on law politics& religion; mem Amer Bd Arbitration; writer short stories & essays; Univ WI Law Sch Charter mem Omega Frat Milwaukee; Ct Commr for Milwaukee Courts; magistrate Milwaukee Co; trustee & deacon Calvary Baptist Ch; author novel; contrib literary pubs. **HONORS/ACHIEVEMENTS:** Honors & awds, from Omega Phi Psi, YMCA; former gen counsel Central City Dev Corp. **MILITARY SERVICE:** Veterab WW II overseas. **BUSINESS ADDRESS:** Judge, Circuit Court, 901 N 9th St, Milwaukee, WI 53233.

PARRISH, JAMES W.
Clergyman. **PERSONAL:** Born Mar 28, 1908, Louisa Co, VA; married Henrietta V Thomas. **EDUCATION:** Gordon Coll Theol & Missions, Boston, ThB 1932; Univ Pittsburgh, edM 1940; VA Theol Sem Lynchburg, DD 1946; Western Theol Sem, Pittsburgh; Lutheran Sem, Columbus OH. **CAREER:** Shiloh Bapt Ch Columbus OH, pastor 1944-; Ebenezer Bapt Ch Providence RI, 1928-33; Bethesda Bapt Ch Port Chester NY, 1933-38; Metro Bapt Ch Pittsburgh, 1938-44; WBNS, radio preacher 1944. **ORGANIZATIONS:** Pres OH Bapt Gen Assn 1968-71; organized OH St Youty Rally; conducted revivals & preaching missions since 12 yrs of age; known as "The Boy Preacher"; guest speaker at colls, univs, seminaries and before Nat Bapt Conv, USA, Inc; Nat Bapt cong; Pastors Cong; Pastors Sect NCC; New Eng Bapt Conv;Conv Pacific NW; mem Urban League; NAACP; Mayors Adv Bd; Com for Better Columbus; spec com Bd Educ Columbus Pub Schs; trustee No Bapt Sem, Chgo; lecturer Black Ch Studies, Lutheran Theol Sem; spec lecturer Methodist Theol Sem, Delaward OH; mem Phi Beta Sigma. **HONORS/ACHIEVEMENTS:** Recd more than 30 awds Ch Orgns;

Civic Grps; Educ Groups; Chosen Alumnus of Yr,Univ Pittsburgh Alumni Assn 1974. **BUSINESS ADDRESS:** 720 Mt Vernon Ave, Columbus, OH 43203.

PARRISH, JOHN HENRY
Clergyman. **PERSONAL:** Born Dec 14, 1924, Clarkdale, AR; married Marie Jones; children: John Jr, Roland. **EDUCATION:** Manassas High School, diploma 1942. **CAREER:** Hammond Branch NAACP, pres 1959/1972; 3rd Dist Hammond, councilman 1972-; First Tabernacle Baptist Church, pastor 1977-. **MILITARY SERVICE:** USN seaman 1st class 3 yrs. **HOME ADDRESS:** 1108 Cleveland St, Hammond, IN 46320. **BUSINESS ADDRESS:** Pastor, First Tabernacle Baptist Church, 643 W 41st St, Gary, IN 46408.

PARRISH, LEMAR
Professional athlete. **PERSONAL:** Born Dec 13, 1947, Riviera Beach, FL; married Donna Brogden; children: Tracy, Lemar. **EDUCATION:** Lincoln U, 1971. **CAREER:** Washington Redskins, prof football player 1978-; Cincinnati Bengals, cornerback & punt kick-off splst 1970-78; Matrix Enterprises, vp. **ORGANIZATIONS:** Mem Urban League W Palm Beach; mem Nat Football Players Assn & All-pro 1971-72, 74; Leading Punt Returner AFC 1974; Leading Kick-off - Return AFC 1971; All Star Game 1970, 71, 74-76. **HONORS/ACHIEVEMENTS:** MVP many team records; led NFC 9 pass interceptions 1979; played in 7 Pro Bowls; All Pro AFC 1971-77; Outstanding Rookie 1970.

PARRISH, MARY
Writer, actress. **PERSONAL:** Born May 20, 1942, Mississippi; married Cedar Walton; children: V-Etta V, Naisha O. **EDUCATION:** Chicago U, St JohnsUniv Coll of Gen Studies; NY Sch of Announcing & Speech. **CAREER:** Haans Woltgers Theatrical Agy, NY, TV Commercials, professional modeling, actress 1963-; NY Rep St Com Urban Affairs Div, asst dir, present; free lance writer, present; Former research asso for Gov Rockefeller; Carl Vergari, vote coord; Black Rep Youth Crusade, prin speaker; Elizabeth Holtzman, coord; Shirley Chisholms Pres Campaign, fundraiser. **ORGANIZATIONS:** Comm devel co-founder Black Womens Polit Caucus; mem Coalition of Black Rep; Women in City Govt United; Black Womens Polit Caucus; Ripon Soc; ManhattanWomens Polit Caucus; Nat Black Rep Council. **HONORS/ACHIEVEMENTS:** Comm Serv Awd E Flatbush Civic Assn; noted in Congressional Records, Oct 11, 72; co-found NY St Cncl of Black Rep; presently writing 1st play for theatre.

PARRISH, RUFUS H.
Physician. **PERSONAL:** Born in Donora, PA; son of Rufus Parrish and Mary E Wright Parrish; married Alma Marion, Nov 24, 1957. **EDUCATION:** St Augustine's Coll, BS (magna cum laude) 1938; Meharry Med Coll, MD (honors) 1944. **CAREER:** Wayne Co Genl Hosp, staff psychiatrist 1964-68, asst dir psych serv 1969-73; Wayne Co Mentl Health Clinic, dir 1973-76; Kirwood Mental Health Ctr; consultant; Highland Park Mental Health Ctr, consultant; Wayne State Univ Coll of Medicine, instructor 1969-; Walter P Reuther Psychiatric Hosp Westland MI, dir of psychiatric serv 1979-. **ORGANIZATIONS:** Courtesy staff Psychiatric Div Harper-Grace Hosp 1977-; Met Regional Psychiatric Hosp Westland MI dir after-care 1977-; dir of admissions 1978; dir psychiatric serv Walter P Reuther Psychiatric Hosp Westland 1979-; mem NAACP, Mason (Prince Hall Affil) 32nd degree shriner; Detroit Chap of Natl Guardsmen Inc; mem Kappa Alpha Psi, St Matthew-St Joseph Episcopal Church; diplomate of Amer Bd Psychia and Neurology 1967; diplomate Amer Bd of Quality Assurance and Utilization Review Physicians 1985.

PARRON, DELORES L.
Government offical senior executive service. **PERSONAL:** Born Jan 14, 1944, Red Bank, NJ; daughter of James Parron and Ruth Parron. **EDUCATION:** Georgian Court Coll, BA 1966; Cath Univ Amer, MSW 1968, PhD 1977. **CAREER:** Dept Human Resources, soc worker 1968-69; Childrens Hosp Natl Med Ctr, psychiat soc worker 1969-71; Coll Med Howard Univ, asst prof 1971-78; Fed City Coll, lecturer 1973-75; Pres's Comm on Mental Health White House, soc sci analy 1977-78; Inst Med Acad Scis, prin staff ofcr 1978-83; Natl Inst of Mental Health, assoc dir. **ORGANIZATIONS:** Bd mem Assoc Catholic Charities; bd dir Bur of Rehab 1977; bd mem Pacifica WPFW-FM 1976-78, Area A Comm Mental Health Ctr 1977-79; mem Acad of Certified Soc Workers 1975-, Natl Assoc of Soc Workers; bd dir Phyllis Wheatley YWCA 1974. **HONORS/ACHIEVEMENTS:** Kappa Gamma Phi Acheivement Awd Georgian Ct Coll 1966; Fellowship Grad Study Cath Univ of Amer; mem Sigma Phi Sigma Natl Hon Soc 1964; parron Soc &psychol Dimensions of Behavior; A Reader for Student Physicians 1974; parron Mental Health Serv in Gen Health Care 1980, Health & Behavior 1982. **BUSINESS ADDRESS:** Associate Dir, Natl Inst of Mental Health, 5600 Fishers Lane, Rockville, MD 20857.

PARSON, HOUSTON
Business executive. **PERSONAL:** Born May 10, 1925, Florence County, SC; married Viola Hilton; children: Houston Jr, Lillie, Estelle, James, Hermon. **EDUCATION:** Intl Found of Employee Benefit Plans, sC Cert. **CAREER:** Intl Longshoremens Local #1751, pres 1970-; Charter Bus Co, sch bus optr; Parsons Grocery, optr; Lt Cross, personal aide; Intl Longshoremens Assn, aus Negotiator. **ORGANIZATIONS:** Odd Fellows Lodge, United Supreme; Counc of Shriners; Georgetown Co Dem Party; SC Progressive Dem; NAACP; SC Sch Bd Assn; mem bd of trustees Georgetown Co; co-chmn trust fund ILA Welfare Dept; apptd bd gov SC Ports Auth Adv Bd; trustee 1st Calvary Bapt Ch; 320 Mason Consistory #189. **HONORS/ACHIEVEMENTS:** Spec Awd Andrews Civic Assn; Disting Serv Awd, Citizens Com; Apprec Cert Congressman Edwin Young 1973; started 1st sch bus serv for blacks in Georgetown Co 1942; 1st black elected ofcl Georgetown Co 1968. **BUSINESS ADDRESS:** Vicechmn Cty Bd of Education, Georgetown County Schools, 624 Front St, Georgetown, SC 29440.

PARSON, WILLIE L.
Educator. **PERSONAL:** Born Apr 25, 1942, Newellton, LA; married Sylvia Sanders. **EDUCATION:** So Univ Baton Rouge, BS Biol 1963; Washington State Univ, MS Microbiology 1967, PhD Microbiology 1971. **CAREER:** SoUniv Baton Rouge, instructor biology dept 1963-65; WA State Univ, teaching asst 1965-67, rsch asst 1965-67; The Evergreen State Coll, mem of the faculty 1971-74, sr acad dean 1974-78, mem of the faculty-microbiology 1978-. **ORGANIZATIONS:** Panelist for grants review Natl Sci Found 1977-80; mem Amer Soc for Microbiology; mem Amer Assn for the Advancement of Scis; mem Phi Delta Kappa Educ Soc; mem Alpha Phi Alpha Frat. **HONORS/ACHIEVEMENTS:** Outstanding Young Man of Amer-Outstanding Young Men of Amer Inc 1977. **BUSINESS ADDRESS:** Faculty-Microbiology, The Evergreen State Coll, Lab II 2249, Olympia, WA 98505.

PARSONS, JAMES B.
Judge. **PERSONAL:** Born Aug 13, 1911, Kansas City, MO; son of James B and Maggie; married Amy Margaret Maxwell; children: Hans-Dieter. **EDUCATION:** James Milliken Univ, 1934; Conservatory of Music;Univ of WI Grad Schl, Pol Sci;Univ of Chgo, Masters Deg;Univ of Chicago Law Schl, Dr of Law 1949. **CAREER:** Lincoln Univ, field agent, asst to dean of men & instructor in political science & music, 1934-38, acting head music dept, 1938-40; Public Schls of Greensboro, supvr of instrumental music, 1940-42; Gassaway, Crosson, Turner & Parsons, private practice, 1949-51; City of Chgo, asst corp cnsl 1949-51; Off of US Atty Chgo, asst US Atty 1951-60; Superior Ct of Cook Cty, judge 1960-61; US Dist Court, judge, chief of ct, chief judge emeritus, sr judge, 1961-. **ORGANIZATIONS:** Mem Natl Advsry Cncl Boy Scouts of Amer 1985-; mem Exec Brd Citizenshp Cncl of Metro Chicago 1975-; mem Advsry Brd of IL Masonic Hosp 1975-; fndr Honry Chrmn Chicago Conf on Religion & Race; mem IL Comm on Ed for Law & Justice of the State Brd of Ed; mem Brd of Dir Harvard-St Schl; IL Acad of Criminology, The Bar Assoc of Seventh Fedl Cir, The Fedl Bar Assoc, The Natl Bar Assoc, The Amer Bar Assoc, The Cook Cnty Bar Assoc, The Amer Judicature Soc, The Berrien Cnty Bar Assoc (State of MI), The Law Club of Chgo, comm Probation & Sentencing Seminars, Chicago Comm on Police & Comm Rel; cncl Criminal Law Sec of the Amer Bar Assoc; Natl Lawyers Club of Washington, DC, Navy League Club, Standard Club, Royal Coteria of Snakes,; mem Church of the Good Shepherd in Chgo; hon pres Men's Club. **HONORS/ACHIEVEMENTS:** Honorary degrees, Lincoln Univ, Millikin Univ, DePaul Univ Law School; Designated Judge B Parsons' Day in his honor Feb 26, 1967; dedicated Elem Schl Decatur, IL; mem Court's Exec Comm; 1st Race US Dist Court Judge; Citation of Recognition for Outstanding Service as Chief Judge of the District Court, Chicago Bar Assn, 1981; Outstanding Service Award, Chicago State Univ, 1984. **MILITARY SERVICE:** US Navy, volunteered V-8 active service program, 1942, continental duty, 1942-43, pacific duty, 1944-45. **BUSINESS ADDRESS:** Sr Judge & Chief Judge Emeritus, US Dist Court of N Dist IL, 219 S Dearborn St, Chicago, IL 60604.

PARSONS, PHILIP I
Food & beverage manufacturing executive. **PERSONAL:** Born Nov 18, 1941, Cherry Hill, NJ; son of Nathaniel I Banks Parsons and Kathyrn M Brooks Beverly Parsons; children: Andrea LaVerne. **EDUCATION:** Gettysburg Coll, BA 1964; Harvard Business School, MBA 1972; IL Inst of Tech, MPA 1988. **CAREER:** Scott Paper Co, sales mgr 1964-70; Quaker Oats Co, market mgmt 1973-78; AT&T, staff mgr 1979-82; Perfect Pinch Inc, Soft Sheen Products, general mgr 1982-. **ORGANIZATIONS:** Bd mem Hyde Park Neighborhood Club 1978; pres 3100 S King Dr Condo Assn 1984-87; trustee Gettysburg Coll 1986-91; mem East Bank Club 1987. **HONORS/ACHIEVEMENTS:** Trainee of the Cycle Fort Dix NJ 1964; Outstanding Salesman Scott Paper Co 1968; Regional Representative Tau Kappa Epsilon 1975; Article on Minority Business Grocery Marketing 1986; Calvary Youth Council Award, Calvary Baptist Church, 1982. **MILITARY SERVICE:** USA lt. **BUSINESS ADDRESS:** General Manager, Perfect Pinch, Inc, 1024 E 87th St, Chicago, IL 60616.

PARTEE, CECIL A.
Attorney, city official. **PERSONAL:** Born Apr 10, 1921, Blytheville, AR; children: Paris, Cecile. **EDUCATION:** TN St, BA 1944; Northwestern Univ Law Sch, JD 1946. **CAREER:** City of Chgo, treas present; Pvt Atty, 1946; Cook Co, asst states atty 1948-56; State Legislator, 1957-77; Dept of Human Serv City of Chgo, commr 1977. **ORGANIZATIONS:** Mem Dem Nat Com 1972; mem numerous bar assn; mem Park Manor Cong Ch; mem numerous civic & serv orgn. **HONORS/ACHIEVEMENTS:** Most Outstanding Frshmn Senator 1967; Most Effective Senator 1971; Northwestern Outstanding Alumnus Awd 1972; hon doc Kennedy-king Coll 1973. **BUSINESS ADDRESS:** Chicago City Hall, 12u N La Salle, Chicago, IL 60602.

PASCHAL, ELOISE RICHARDSON
Educator. **PERSONAL:** Born Feb 07, 1936, Hartsville, SC; married Willie Lee Paschal; children: William. **EDUCATION:** Benedict Coll, AB 1954-58; Atlanta Univ, MSLS 1967. **CAREER:** Tooms Cty GA Public Schools, teacher 1958060; Americus Public Schools, teacher 1960-65, career media spec 1965-. **ORGANIZATIONS:** Mem Sumter Cty Mental Health Assoc 1971-, Flint River Girl Scout Council 1982-; chmn sumter Cty Mental Health Mental Retardation Bd of Dir 1982-84; memAmer Library Assoc, Amer Assoc of School Librarians, Natl Ed Assoc, GA Assoc of Educ, GA Library Assoc, Third Dist Dept; pres GA Library Media. **HONORS/ACHIEVEMENTS:** Woman of the Year Boy Scout Units #226 1980; Disting Serv Awd Sumter Cty Mental Health Assoc 1982. **HOME ADDRESS:** 310 Vista Drive, Americus, GA 31709. **BUSINESS ADDRESS:** Career Media Specialist, Staley Middle School, 915 North Lee St, Americus, GA 31709.

PASCHAL, WILLIE L.
Educational administration. **PERSONAL:** Born May 09, 1926, Americus Sumter, GA; married Eloise Richardson; children: William Stanley. **EDUCATION:** Morehouse Coll, BA Bus Admin 1949; Atlanta Univ, MA Educ & Admin 1957; GA State Univ Atlanta GA, EdS EAS 1978. **CAREER:** Webster Cty Bd of Educ Preston GA, principal/teacher 1949-52; Twiggs Cty Bd of Educ, teacher 1952-53; Sumter Cty Bd of Educ, principal/teacher 1953-72; Amer Bd of Public Ed, principal 1972-; Eastview Elementary School, principal. **ORGANIZATIONS:** Life mem Alpha Phi Alpha Frat Inc 1949-; asst sec Amer/Sumter Cty Payroll Dev Auth 1980-; sr vice comm Amer Legion Dept of GA 1984-85; mem NAESP,GAESP 3rd Dist 1984-85, Phi Delta Kappa 1984-85, GAEL 1984-85; mem team chmn Chamber of Comm 1985. **HONORS/ACHIEVEMENTS:** Distinguished Citizen Mental Health Assoc of Sumter Cty 1982; Disting Serv Mental Health Assoc of Sumter Cty 1982. **MILITARY SERVICE:** AUS corpl 1 yr 4 mo's. **HOME ADDRESS:** 310 Vista Dr, Americus, GA 31709.

PASSMORE, JUANITA (NEE CARTER)
Business executive. **PERSONAL:** Born Mar 04, 1926, Chicago, IL; married Maymon Passmore. **EDUCATION:** Long Beach City Coll; Columbia Coll. **CAREER:** Johnson Prod Co, dir spl promotion; Totaly Beauty Y Ou, TV Prgm, host 2 yrs. **ORGANIZATIONS:** Fndr 69 Choppi Block Club; chmn Nat Media Women; parliamentarian Chicago Chap Womens Bd Operation PUSH; chmn Fashion Therapy Mental & Hlth; mem OperationSnowball. **HONORS/ACHIEVEMENTS:** Media Woman of Yr Awd Chicago Chap 1974; Outstng

Woman of Yr, Chicago S End Jaycees Women Assn 1977; Comm Wrkr Debutante Master AME Ch 1977.

PASSMORE, WILLIAM A.
Job developer. **PERSONAL:** Born Apr 04, 1929, E Chicago, IN. **EDUCATION:** Calumet Coll, BS; Wayne St U; E Chicago Bus Coll IN U. **CAREER:** Red Top Cab Co, dispatcher 1951-63; Vetold Photo, ofc mgr 1950-51; INUniv Spl Services, adminstrv asst 1970-73; Chicago Daily Defender, columnist 1954; Neighborhood Youth Corps, work coord 1965-73; E Chicago Fed Prog, manpower splst 1973; Com on Emp of Handicapped, pres 1969, gov 1970. **ORGANIZATIONS:** Mem Nat Rehab Assn 1970; vice pres E Chicago Lib Trustees; mem Am Lib Trustees Assn; del White House Conf on Handicapped Indvls 1977; adv council IN St;Civil Rights Commn 1 975; adv bd mem E Clhgo Salvation Army 1976; Urban League for Veterans 1976; adv bd St Catherines Hosp for Accessibility 1977; bd dir E Chicago Exchange Club; Com on New Central HS; bd dir Consumer Credit Cnslng Serv of NW IN; mem Mid Am Educ Oppty Personnel Prgm; Whos Who in Black Am 1975-76; Nat Parpalegic Found 1972; past pres E Chicago Exchange Club; bd dir Camp Fire Girls; bd dir Tri-city Mental Hlth; past bd dir Nat Easter Seal Soc; past pres E Chicago Jaycees; past sec Anselm Forum; bd dir Referral Emerg Serv NW IN; past bd dir Twin City Comm Serv; past asst supt St Mark AME Ch; mem Pirate Trade Winds; co-chmn Wheel Chair Bsktbl & JCI Intl Senate 5817; exec bd Trade Winds Rehbabv Ctr; gov St Youth Counc; gov St Commn on Handicapped. **HONORS/ACHIEVEMENTS:** Recipient EC Cit of Month, Book of Golden Deeds E Chicago Exchange; Outstndng New Jaycees; Evelyn Davis Eastern Star Awd for Achvmnt; Hoosier Handicapped Awd for 1968; Handicapped Am 1969 Duble Amputee; hon mem cert for IN St Prison; St Catherine Visitor of Yr Awd; IN Mason Outstndng Man of Yr Awd; E Chicago Mason Otstndng Achvmnt Awd; St Mark AME Zion Ch Handicapped Awd 1968; Rotary Club Good Cit Awd 1971. **BUSINESS ADDRESS:** 3522 1/2 Main St, East Chicago, IN 46312.

PASTEUR, ALFRED BERNARD
Educator. **PERSONAL:** Born Apr 14, 1947, Ocalo, FL. **EDUCATION:** FL A&M Univ, AB; IN Univ, MS; Northwestern Univ, PhD. **CAREER:** Temple Univ, asst prof; Chicago Bd of Educ, counselor admins; Hunter Coll, prof. **ORGANIZATIONS:** Mem Dayton OH Model Cities, Morgan State Coll, Bethune Cookman Coll, MN State Dept of Educ, Kennedy Found, Atlanta Univ, Chicago Career Oppor Prog, Southern Univ, Savannah State Coll, OIC Phila, Princeton Univ, Univ of Delaware, Univ of TX Austin, Virgin Islands Univ; mem Amer Personnel & Guidance Assn, Amer Psychol Assn, Assn of Black Psychol, Phi Delta Kappa, Assn for Non-White Concerns in Personnel & Guidance; devel stages of Black Self-Discovery Journal of Negro Educ 1972; soul music technique for therapeutic intervention Journal of Non-White Concerns 1972; Therapeutic Dimensions of the Black Aesthetic Journal of Non-White Concerns 1976; publication "Roots of Soul, A Psychology of Black Expressiveness" Doubleday Press 1982; "Black Academic & Cultural Excellence" Alliance for Black Sch Educators 1984; rsch travel to Nigeria, W Africa, Senegal, Ghana, Haiti, Trinidad, Barbados, Brazil, Jamaica, Virgin Islands. **BUSINESS ADDRESS:** Hunter College, 695 Park Ave, New York, NY 10021.

PATE, JOHN W., SR. (JOHNNY)
Retired film, TV composer, arranger, conductor. **PERSONAL:** Born Dec 05, 1923, Chicago Heights, IL; son of Charles Pate, Sr. and Nora R Pate; married Carolyn; children: John Jr, Yvonne, Donald, Brett. **EDUCATION:** Midwestern Conservtory of Music Chicago 1950; UCLA Elec Music, Script Writ, Act-Dir workshop. **CAREER:** Career began as bass player Chicago 1946-; formed the Johnny Pate Trio 1957-62 (Chicago); composing & arrang career comm, also record producing; arrang & prod for many musical stars; involved in motion picture & TV scoring; was Midwest Dir of A&R for ABC Records (Chicago) 1963-65; was East Coast Dir of A&R (Artists & Repetoire) for MGM-Verve Records (New York) 1966-68; produced and/or arranged albums for The Bee Gees, Peabo Bryson, Natalie Cole, Gladys Knight & The Pips, BB King, Stan Getz, Ruth Brown, Curtis Mayfield, the late Minnie Riperton, Ahmad Jamal, Donny Hathaway and Jimmy Smith. **ORGANIZATIONS:** Pres of Yvonne Publ & Nod-Jon Mus pub cons. **HONORS/ACHIEVEMENTS:** First Black to become pres of Local NARAS Rec Acad Chicago Chapter; mem of BMI 25yrs; Composer of Musical Scores for following films: Shaft in Africa 1973, Satan's Triangle 1975, Bucktown 1975, Dr Black & Mr. Hyde 1976, Sudden Death 1976, Every Girl Must Have One 1978; Musical Director for the following TV productions: Lou Rawls Special 1979, Future Stars 1979, Richard Pryor Specials 1977. **MILITARY SERVICE:** AUS dir of dance and jazz band 218th AGF Band Ft Benning GA, Marseille France, Salzburg Austria.

PATERSON, BASIL ALEXANDER
Attorney. **PERSONAL:** Born Apr 27, 1926, New York, NY; son of Leonard Paterson and Eva Paterson; married Portia Hairston; children: David, Daniel. **EDUCATION:** St John's Coll, BS 1948; St John's Univ, JD 1951. **CAREER:** Paterson Michael Jones & Cherot Esqs, partner 1956-77; Inst for Mediation & Conflict Resolution, pres & chief exec officer 1972-77; City of NY, dep mayor for labor relations 1978; State of NY, sec of state 1979-82; Meyer, Suozzi, English & Klein, PC, partner. **ORGANIZATIONS:** Mem NY State Senate 1965-70; mem NY State Temp Commn for Revision of New York City Charter; v chmn Dem Nat Com 1972-78; Judicial Screening Comm for Second Dept chair 1985-; NYS Judicial Nominations Commission mem 1986-. **HONORS/ACHIEVEMENTS:** Eagleton Inst of Politics Award Excellence in Politics 1967; Black Expo Award f1973; Interracial Justice Cath Interracial Counc 1978; Humanitarian Award Coalition of Black Trade Unionists 1980; St John's Univ Medal of Excellence; City Univ of NY Kibbee Awd for Outstanding Public Serv & Achievement, 1987; PSC Friend of CUNY Award, 1989. **HOME ADDRESS:** 40 W 135th St, New York, NY 10037.

PATES, HAROLD
Educational administrator. **CAREER:** Kennedy-King College, Chicago IL, president. **BUSINESS ADDRESS:** Kennedy-King College, Chicago, IL 60621. *

PATIN, JOSEPH PATRICK
Physician. **PERSONAL:** Born Jan 10, 1937, Baton Rouge, LA; married Rose; children: Joseph, Karla. **EDUCATION:** Univ MI, BS Meharry Med Coll, MD 1964. **CAREER:** Pvt Prac, physician; 85th Evac Hosp, chf surgery 1970-71; Raymond W Bliss Army Hosp, 1969; St Elizabeth Hosp, res 1964-69; LA St U, asso prof. **ORGANIZATIONS:** Mem Baton Rouge Parish Bd Hlth; Kappa Alpha Psi; Cancer So of Grtr Baton Rouge; Operation Upgrade Baton Rouge;; Baton Rouge Med Soc; flw Am Coll L Surgeons; So Med Assn; Nat Med Assn Diplomate Bd Surgeons 1970. **HONORS/ACHIEVEMENTS:** Bronze Star; Dist Med. **MILITARY SERVICE:** AUS maj. **BUSINESS ADDRESS:** 4731 North Blvd, Baton Rouge, LA 70806.

PATNETT, JOHN HENRY
Business executive. **PERSONAL:** Born Nov 21, 1948, New Orleans, LA; son of Melvin Patnett and Mary Patnett; married Lynn J Patnett. **EDUCATION:** Southern Univ of New Orleans, BA 1971; Southern Univ Baton Rouge LA, Cert Furn Upholstery 1980. **CAREER:** LA Bk Republican Council, dir of publ relations 1983-85; Mel & Son Upholstery Inc, pres. **ORGANIZATIONS:** Bd mem US Selective Service 1980. **HONORS/ACHIEVEMENTS:** Certificate of Merit Outstanding Comm Serv 1974; apptd to Orleans Parish Republican Exec Comm 1985. **BUSINESS ADDRESS:** President, Mel & Son Upholstery Inc, 2001 Touro, New Orleans, LA 70116.

PATRICK, CHARLES NAMON, JR.
Company owner. **PERSONAL:** Born Feb 05, 1949, Birmingham, AL; son of Charles Patrick and Rutha Mae Robbins Patrick; married Gwendolyn Stephanie Batiste Patrick, Apr 13, 1975; children: Gentry Namon Patrick, Jessica Sherrie Patrick, Charles Stephan Patrick III, Hope Naomi Patrick, John Paul Patrick. **EDUCATION:** Coll of Data Processing, Los Angeles CA; Life Underwriters Training Council, certificate of completion, 1979. **CAREER:** VIP Manufacturing, North Hollywood CA, sales dist, 1970-76; Prudential Insurance Co, Los Angeles CA, sales agent/manager, 1976-82; Pioneer Capital & Associates, Dallas TX, western reg vice pres, 1982-83, owner, 1982-84; Patrick, Patrick & Associates, Lawndale CA, pres, 1984; Austin Diversified Products, Ingelwood CA, corp sales mgr, 1985-88; PPA Industries, Compton CA, owner, 1988-. **ORGANIZATIONS:** Admin/asst, The Way Church at Ingelwood, 1981, block club president, Action Block Club, 1982-85; mem, Greater LA Visitors & Convention Bureau, 1984, program coordinator, Black Amer Response to the African Community (BARAC), 1987-88; counselor, Fellowship West Youth Ministries, 1987-88. **HONORS/ACHIEVEMENTS:** Business Man of the Year, ACC News, 1985. **BUSINESS ADDRESS:** Owner, PPA Industries/Pioneer Patrick & Associates Industries, PO Box 5365, Compton, CA 90224-5365.

PATRICK, JAMES L.
Business executive. **PERSONAL:** Born Nov 11, 1919, Prairie View, TX; married Gladys A Holloway; children: Charles, James, Harold, Wayne, Sheldon. **EDUCATION:** TX Coll, AB 1941; LoyolaUniv Chgo, MSA 1949. **CAREER:** N Central Region, Cook Co, IL Dept of Pub Aid, dir 1949-. **ORGANIZATIONS:** Vp chmn budget United Comm Serv of Evanston; registered social worker; mem Am Mgmt Assn; mem NAACP; mem Urban League; mem Alpha Phi Alpha Frat; mem Teelan Coll of LoyolaUniv Alumni Assn; mem APWA; mem IWA Sr warden, ch sec, St Andrews Episicopal Ch; sec Mens Club, St Andrews Episicopal Ch; mem Phi Delta Psi Hon Soc; Supply Officer 1941-46. **HONORS/ACHIEVEMENTS:** Made Deans List. **BUSINESS ADDRESS:** 624 S Michigan, Chicago, IL.

PATRICK, JENNIE R.
Engineer. **PERSONAL:** Born Jan 01, 1949, Gadsden, AL; daughter of James Patrick and Elizabeth Patrick. **EDUCATION:** Tuskegee Inst, 1967-70; Univ of CA Berkeley, BS 1973; MIT, PhD 1979; Tuskegee Inst, Hon PhD 1984. **CAREER:** Dow Chem Co, asst engr 1972; Stauffer Chem Co, asst engr 1973; MIT, rsch assoc 1973-79; Chevron Rsch, engr 1974; Arthur D Little Inc, engr 1975;Gen Elect Co, rsch engr 1979-83; Phillip Morris Inc, sr engr 1983-; Rohm and Haas Co, rsch section mgr. **ORGANIZATIONS:** Mem Sigma Xi, AIChE, NOBCChE. **HONORS/ACHIEVEMENTS:** 1st black woman in US to earn doctorate in chem engrg 1979; NOBCChE Outstanding Women in Science & Engrg Awd 1980; a subject in Exceptional Black Scientists Poster Prog CIBA-GEIGY 1983. **HOME ADDRESS:** PO Box 1088, Bristol, PA 19007.

PATRICK, JULIUS, JR.
Educational administrator, mayor. **PERSONAL:** Born May 16, 1938, Natchitoches, LA; married Beatrice M Jackson; children: Ronald, Karen, DiAnthia, Riqui. **EDUCATION:** Dillard Univ, BA 1966; Tuskegee Inst, MS Ed 1970. **CAREER:** Rapide Parish School Bd, teacher 1966-69, vice prin 1972-75, Town of Boyce LA, mayor; Rapides Parish School Bd, principal 1975-. **ORGANIZATIONS:** Pres Boyce Civic Improvement League Inc; v chmn Police Jury's Rehab Com 1977-80; mem Parish's Housing Auth Bd 1978; chmn Natl Conf of Black Mayors;pres boyce Civic Improvement League Inc; mem Rapides Parish Housing Auth, Rapides Area Planning Commission, Trade Mission to People's Republic of China, UMTA Rural Transportation Mission to Peurto Rico; pres Rapides Assoc of Principals and Asst Principals. **HONORS/ACHIEVEMENTS:** Hon Ambassador of Goodwill Exec Branch State of LA 1980. **MILITARY SERVICE:** AUS sp/4 1961-64. **BUSINESS ADDRESS:** Principal, Rapides Parish Sch Bd, PO Box 1052, Alexandria, LA 71301.

PATRICK, LAWRENCE CLARENCE, JR.
Lawyer. **PERSONAL:** Born Feb 08, 1945, Detroit, MI; son of Bishop Lawrence C Patrick and Ada D Patrick; married Rayona R Fuller, Jun 23, 1973; children: Lawrence C Patrick III, Joseph E Patrick, Ayana B Patrick, Goldie EPatrick. **EDUCATION:** Wayne State Univ, Detroit MI, BA, 1972, JD, 1975. **CAREER:** Honigman Miller Schwartz & Cohn, Detroit MI, assoc, 1975-77; Patrick, Reid & Lewis, Detroit MI, partner, 1977-. **ORGANIZATIONS:** Mem, bd of dir, Wolverine Bar Assn, 1978-81; corp dir and bd chmn, Black United Fund, 1978-88; mem, Michgan Transportation Commn, 1979-84, vice chmn, 1981-84; chmn of bd, Black United Fund, 1985-88; chmn of bd, Wayne County Social Services Bd, 1986-88. **HONORS/ACHIEVEMENTS:** Michigan Senate Resolution, Michigan Senate, 1981; Trio, Wayne State Univ, 1988; Founder's Award, Student Motivational Program, 1989, Outstanding Service, Church of God in Christ, 1989. **BUSINESS ADDRESS:** Pres, Detroit Bd of Educ, 5057 Woodward Ave, Rm 274, Detroit, MI 48202.

PATRICK, LINNIE
Professional athlete. **PERSONAL:** Born Aug 12, 1961, Monroeville, AL. **EDUCATION:** Alabama. **CAREER:** Oakland Invaders, halfback 1984-. **HONORS/ACHIEVEMENTS:** Ended career With 265 carries for 1,063 yards (40 Avg) and 16 touchdowns).

PATRICK, ODESSA R.
Educator. **PERSONAL:** Born Oct 22, 1933, Mt Gilead, NC; married Joe L; children: Krystal, Joseph, Jasmine. **EDUCATION:** NC A&T St U, BS 1956;Univ of NC, MA 1969. **CAREER:** Univ of NC Greensboro, instr Biology Dept 1969-, lab techn 1958-69. **ORGANIZATIONS:** Mem Am Assn ofUniv Women; Girl Scout Ldr; Delta Sigma Theta; Scientific paper published in Journal of Elisha Mitchell Scientific Soc 1969. **BUSINESS ADDRESS:** Biology Dept, U of NC, Greensboro, NC.

PATRICK, OPAL LEE YOUNG
Educator. **PERSONAL:** Born Jul 16, 1929, Tatums, OK; married Charles; children: Jacqueline R. **EDUCATION:** Langston Univ, BA 1951; Univ of NM, MA 1963; Univ of UT, PhD 1974. **CAREER:** Public School OK, teacher 1951-56; Bur Ind Affairs, inst counselor 1956-63; Univ of MD Educ Centers Deptnd School, 1963-66; USAFE W Germany, instr lecturer teacher; Clearfield Job Corp, inst counselor adminstr 1966-70; Univ of UT, inst of educ 1971-74, asst prof of educ 1974-77; political activities, guest lecturer & coordinator 1979-. **ORGANIZATIONS:** Presenter various conf; participant presenter Natl Organ; guest lectr coord of various projects & research activities; mem State Mental Health Assn; 1973-; UT Acad of Sci 1974-; natl Coll of Soc Studies 1976-; Assn of Teach Educ 1974-; Natl Cncl Tchrs of Eng 1973-; vice pres Natl Cncl Tchrs of Eng 1973; Assn of Sch & Currs Develop 1975-; pres Davis Co NAACP 1978. **HONORS/ACHIEVEMENTS:** Doctoral dissertation "An Effective Teacher Profile" 1976; article "A Receipe for Effective Teaching" 1977; speech "The Culturally Unique" 1973; speech "MentalHealth & the Cultural Differ" 1975; speech "Blacks in Edn" 1976.

PATRICK, WILLIAM T., JR.
Business executive. **PERSONAL:** Born Mar 28, 1920, Washington, DC; married Betty; children: Michelle. **EDUCATION:** Howard U, AB 1942;Univ of MI, LLB 1946;Univ of Detroit, LHD 1972. **CAREER:** Am Telephone & Telgraph Co NYC, dir comm rel; MI Bell Telephone Co, former dir of environ affairs;Univ of MI, former vis lectr polit Sci 1965-67;Univ of Detroit, consult lectr 1960-71. **ORGANIZATIONS:** Bd mem Cntr for Governmental Studies Wash DC. **HONORS/ACHIEVEMENTS:** Recip HowardUniv Outsndg Alumni Awd 1964;Univ of MI Regents Awd 1965; Beta Gamma Sigma Hon Schol Soc Awd hon mem 1967; Wayne Co Comm Coll Outstnd Serv Awd 1971.

PATTEN, EDWARD ROY (COUSIN EDS)
Entertainer. **PERSONAL:** Born Aug 22, 1939, Atlanta, GA; married Renee Brown; children: Stephanie, Steve, Sonya, Edward II, Elliott. **CAREER:** Gladys Knight & the Pips, entertainer 1956-; Lagoons, sing group 1955; Cashmere, sing group 1954; Overalls, performer 1952; travelled through GA doing plays & dances 1950; Barber Shop Quartet, 1949. **ORGANIZATIONS:** Exec pres, Patten & Guest Production Co Inc; NAACP. **HONORS/ACHIEVEMENTS:** Recognition Mayors M Jackson & Coleman Young helping in their campaign; grammy award best R&B Group 1969, 1971, 1972; Am Music Award 1973; grammies, Record World, Cash Box, Billboard, Rolling Stone, Bobby Pop's Pop, Soul Magazine Awards; rock music award Radio CLIO 1975; Entertainer of the Year, 1974. **BUSINESS ADDRESS:** 1414 Ave of the Americas, New York, NY 10019.

PATTEN, W. GEORGE
Educator. **PERSONAL:** Born Jun 29, 1931, Alexandria, Jamaica;married Zenobia Oliver; children: Wessel Jr, Kimberly. **EDUCATION:** Mico Training Coll, diploma 1955; London U, cert 1958;Univ NC, BS 1960;Univ WI, MS 1967, PhD 1968. **ORGANIZATIONS:** Mem Nat Soc for the Study of Edn; Adult Educ Assn USA; Phi Delta Kappa Madison Br; Alpha Phi Alpha Frat Chi Lambda Chpt; WI Counc of Educ Opp Progsmem Milwaukee Mid-Town Kiwanis; Milwaukee Cricket Club, vice pres 1975. **HONORS/ACHIEVEMENTS:** Hon adv & Man of Yr Awd Student GovtUniv WI 1972-73; Outstdg Educator 1973; Who's Who in Am Higher Edn; Who's Who in Midwest; Who's Who in WI. **MILITARY SERVICE:** Univ of WI Whitewater, assoc dean of continuing educ & outreach; Madison Area Techers Coll, coor teacher 1966-68; Oppor Industrlztn Center & Greater Milwaukee, exec dir 1968-70; Univ WI, asst dean 1970-71; Univ WI, prof dir tutorial & supportive serv prog for minor & educationally disadv students 1971-. **BUSINESS ADDRESS:** Univ of WI-Whitewater, Roseman Building, Whitewater, WI 53190.

PATTERSON, ALONZO B.
Clergyman. **PERSONAL:** Born Nov 05, 1937, New Orleans, LA; married Shirley May Smith; children: Edna, Mitchell, Norris, Janet, Kim. **EDUCATION:** Am Bible Inst, ThD 1977;Univ AK, BA 1974; AA 1974;Univ AK, AA 1973. **CAREER:** Shilo Misionary Bapt Ch, pastor; Anchorage Sch Dist, person spl 1976; Shilo Bapt Ch, religious adminstr 1970-75; MHE, supr 1966-70; AUS, food serv supr 1956-66. **ORGANIZATIONS:** NAACP; Comm Action; Human Rel Commn; Anchorage OIC; Ministerial Alliance; Civilian & Mil Cncl; Anchorage Comm Hlthl Ctr; Minority Culture Assn; vice pres March of Dimes. **MILITARY SERVICE:** AUS 1956-66. **BUSINESS ADDRESS:** 855 E 20th, PO Box 3156 ECB, Anchorage, AK 99501.

PATTERSON, BARBARA ANN
Association executive. **PERSONAL:** Born in Pennsylvania; married Billy W Patterson; children: Gwendolyn, Kimberly, Damali. **EDUCATION:** Trinity Coll, BA Ed 1984; Trinity College DC Graduate Study. **CAREER:** Independent & Public Schools, teacher 1962-80; Family & Child Svcs, pre-school & home day care 1975-80; Black Student Fund, executive dir; Howard Univ Continuing Education Dept DC Trainer/Family to Family program 1988-89. **ORGANIZATIONS:** Bd mem Hisher Achievement Prog 1983,84,85; devel DC Youth Orchestra 1985; adv bd DC Youth Orchestra & Project Match; Tutor non-reading adults 1988-89. **HONORS/ACHIEVEMENTS:** Washington Woman of the Year WA Women Mag; Friend of the School Awd 1984 Gonzaga Coll HS; Chapter Contributor "Promoting Independent School Enrollment", Visible now Blacks in Private School by Slaughter & Johnson 1989; researcher & resource for a History Deferred, A Guide for Teachers. **BUSINESS ADDRESS:** Executive Dir, Black Student Fund, 3636 16th St NW, Suite AG15, Washington, DC 20010.

PATTERSON, CECIL BOOKER, JR.
Superior court judge. **PERSONAL:** Born May 15, 1941, Newport News, VA; son of Cecil B. Patterson, Sr. and Marie E. Patterson; married Wilma M Hall; children: Angela D, Cecil M. **EDUCATION:** Hampton Inst VA, BA 1963; AZ State Univ, JD 1971. **CAREER:** Maricopa Cnty Legal Aid Soc, staff atty 1971-72; Bursh & Patterson, private law practice 1972-73; Phoenix Urban League, house counsel 1973-75; Maricopa Cnty Publ Defend Office, trial atty 1975-80; Maricopa Cnty Superior Ct, judge. **ORGANIZATIONS:** Mem rep Amer Bar Assn House of Del 1978-80; mem bd governors AZ State Bar 1977-79; pres AZ Black Lawyers Assn 1979-80; mem Natl Conf of Christians & Jews 1981-; mem Tempe, AZ United Way bd 1984-; mem bd Maricopa Cnty Red Cross 1978; mem AZ Academy 1975 & 1978. **HONORS/ACHIEVEMENTS:** Law Fellowship Reginald Heber Smith Program 1971; Law Scholarship Scholarship Educ & Defense Fund 1970; Grant Martin L King Jr Woodrow Wilson Found 1969. **MILITARY SERVICE:** USAF Captain 1963-68; Outstanding Weapons Controller Officer 27th Air Div Luke AFB 1968; Good Conduct Ribbon; Marksmanship Ribbon 1967. **BUSINESS ADDRESS:** Judge Maricopa Cnty Supr Ct, State Judiciary, Juvenile Court Complex, Phoenix, AZ 85003.

PATTERSON, CECIL LLOYD
Educational administrator. **PERSONAL:** Born Jun 10, 1917, Edna, TX; married Vivian Rogers. **EDUCATION:** Samuel Houston Coll, BA Eng 1941; Univ of PA, MA English 1947, PhD English 1961. **CAREER:** Ft Valley State Coll GA, instructor 1947-48; NC Central Univ, instructor-prof 1950-68, dean-undergrad sch 1968-78, chancellor for acad affairs 1978-. **ORGANIZATIONS:** Mem So Conf of Deans & Acad Vice Pres 1970-; chmn NC Com on Coll Transfer Students 1974-78; chaplain Gen Bd of Examining Chaplains of the Epis Church 1976-. **MILITARY SERVICE:** AUS engrs col 1941-74; Southwest Pacific Theater; Misc Battle Stars; Campaign Medals. **BUSINESS ADDRESS:** Chancellor for Acad Affairs, NC CentralUniv, 1801 Fayetteville St, Durham, NC 27707.

PATTERSON, CHARLES JERRY
Business executive. **PERSONAL:** Born Jan 08, 1925, Ft Wayne, IN; married Dorothy Smith; children: Mark Watson, Tracy Jacqueline. **EDUCATION:** Antioch Coll, BA 1951; Case Western Res U, Ma 1956;Univ CA, post grad 1958063. **CAREER:** World Airways Inc, dir; Wold Am Investment Co, dir; World Airways Inc, sr vice pres asst to pres of bd; US Dept of Commerce Econ Devel Adminstrn, spec asst to dir 1966-68; Peace Corps, asso dir for prgm devel & operations 1965-66; Inst of Current World Affaris New York City & Africa, fellow 1961-64. **ORGANIZATIONS:** Dir Herrick Hlth Care Found; trst Antioch Coll; dir KQED TV Inc9; dir San Francisco Found; manower adv bd City of Oakland; dir African Student Aid Fund; dir New Oakland Com; past dir SF Unitarian Ch; Intl Hse Barkeley; United Bar Area Crusade; Unitarian Universalist Serv Com; Friends of LangleyPorter Neuropsychiat Inst; Yth for Understanding; Art Commn Berkeley; life mem NAACP; mem Coun of Fgn Rels; mem ACLU. **BUSINESS ADDRESS:** Oakland Intl Airport, Oakland, CA 94614.

PATTERSON, CLARENCE J.
Business executive. **PERSONAL:** Born Feb 23, 1925, Bogalusa, LA; children: Clarence, Robert. **EDUCATION:** SF State U, BA 1949;Univ of CA, MA 1951. **CAREER:** CJ Patterson Co, pres; Oakland CA, real dev ins broker 19 yrs; Focus Cable TV Oakland, org chmn of bd of dir. **ORGANIZATIONS:** Mem bd of dir Oakland RE Bd; pres chmn bd of dir Golden St Bus Leag Oakland; mem exec com natl bd of dir Nat Bus Leag; vice pres Reg 11 Nat Bus Leag; pres Nat Mortgage Co; chmn of bd Cty Cen Econ Dev Corp; mem Civic & Leg Com of Oakland RE Bd; mem US dept of Comm Nat Min PurcCoun; mem bd of dir Peralta Coll Dist Found; mem bd of dir Northwestern Title Co Inc; mem bd fo dir New Oakland Com; mem bd of dir Manpower Area Plan Coun; mem Bd of dir East Bay Bus & Prof Org; mem bd of dir Plan & Red Com & Educ Com Oakland C of C; chmn bd of dir Asso Real Prop Brok Inc; consult Dept Parks & Rec CA on Lnad Acq; also form mem of many org bd o Fdir NAACP; ex bd NAACP Oakland Br; mem SF Bay Area Coun Boy Scouts; co-found chmn E Oakland Ad-Hoc Com for Hsg & Econ Dev; mem bd of dir Uplift Corp Oakland; mem Cooper AME Zion Ch; mem of trst bd; also mem of many polit org. **HONORS/ACHIEVEMENTS:** Horace Sudduth Aws Nat Bus Leag 1974; mer awd City of Oakland 1972; CA awd Nat Asso RE Bd 1970; cong awd for cont toward econo dev City of Oakland 1966. **BUSINESS ADDRESS:** Golden State Business League, 333 Hegenberger Rd Ste 203, Oakland, CA 94621.

PATTERSON, CLINTON DAVID
Clergyman, staff manager. **PERSONAL:** Born Nov 11, 1936, Uniontown, AL; son of David Patterson and Mattie Mason Patterson; married Lillie Young, Dec 24, 1961; children: Michael, Florencia, Donnetta, Clintonia, Edshena, Bernita. **EDUCATION:** Birmingham Bapt Coll, 1963; Liamia, 1969; Elba Sys, 1970; Liamia, 1973. **CAREER:** Beulah Bapt Ch, pastor; Booker T Washington Inc Co, mgr; New Morning Star Bapt Ch, pastor 1965-72; Demopolis Fed Credit Union, vp; Fed Credit Union, loan off teller; Asst Trea Manager, BBM Federal Credit U. **ORGANIZATIONS:** Pres Demopolis Ministeral Fellow; bd dirs Together Inc Demopolis AL; bd dirs BBM Fed Fredit Unoin; Prof Bus Men's Assn 1964-75; mem bd dirs BBM Brimingham AL; mem Demopolis Fed Credit Union; mem AL Cntrl Credit Union; mem AL Bapt State Conv & Congress; Nat Bapt Sunday Sch & Training Union Congress; Nat Bapt Conv Inc; Birmingham Bapt Min Conf; Jeff Co Dist Assn; NW Dist Conv; lectr Jeff Co Dist Sun Sch & BTU Congress; hon mem AL Sheriff Assn 1974; AL Motorist Assn 1974; pres S Pratt City Civic Leag 1967; mem AL Fed Civic Leag; mem trst bd Peace Bapt Ch 1957; Geometry Lodge 410; NAACP; AL Chris Movement for Human Rights; mem Tuxedo Height Civic Leag. **HONORS/ACHIEVEMENTS:** Cit Fed Savings & Loan Assn; recip C J McNear Awd 1963; com serv awd Pratt City 1971; com serv awd Demopolis AL 1972; NIA Awd for Outsnd Salesmanhip 1974. **BUSINESS ADDRESS:** 1022 Second Ave N, Bessemer, AL 35020.

PATTERSON, CURTIS RAY
Educator. **PERSONAL:** Born Nov 11, 1944, Shreveport, LA; married Gloria M Morris; children: Curtis R. **EDUCATION:** Grambling State U, BS educ 1967; GA State U, MVA 1975. **CAREER:** Atlanta Coll of Art Atlanta GA, art instr 1976-; Atlanta Pub School, art instr chpsn 1970-76; Caddo Parish School Bd Shreveport LA, art instr 1968-70; Muscogee Co School Columbus GA, art instr 1967-68; Gov Hon Prog, instr 1973; Atlanta Life Ins Co, adv com art 1979-80; Piedmont Arts Festival, juror 1980. **ORGANIZATIONS:** Mem Black Artist of Atlanta 1974-80; mem 13 Minus One Sculpture Group 1975-80; adv bd mem Atlanta Bur of Cutlural Affairs 1975-80; sculpture commn Met Atlanta Rapid Transity Authority 1978. **HONORS/ACHIEVEMENTS:** Rep in Visueal Arts Festival of Arts & Cultur Lagos Nigeria 1977; "Sculpture in the Park" Commn Atlanta Bur of Cultural Affairs 1977; bronze jubilee awd visual arts WETV Network Channel 30 1979; Atlant Ainternat Airport Sculpture Commn Atlanta Bur of Cultural Affaris 1980. **BUSINESS ADDRESS:** Atlanta Coll of Art, 1280 Peachtree St NE, Atlanta, GA.

PATTERSON, DAVID LEON
Educator. **PERSONAL:** Born Oct 10, 1949, Des Moines, IA. **EDUCATION:** Univ of IA, BA 1971;Univ of IA Coll of Bus Adm, cert in supv & mgmt 1973;Univ of No IA, MA 1975. **CAREER:** Coll Coll of Denver, dir educ oppty ctr 1976-; Grad EOP, dir 1974-76; EOP Research & Devel, asst dir 1973-74; Ednlo Talletn Search, dir 1971-73. **ORGANIZATIONS:** Educ adminstrv cons; natl steering com Nat Black Alliance for Grad Level Edn; Co Assn of Finan Aid Adminstrs. **HONORS/ACHIEVEMENTS:** Produced educ films.

PATTERSON, DESSIE LEE
City official. **PERSONAL:** Born Jul 06, 1919, Grand Cane, LA; daughter of Clinton Jackson, Sr. and CarLee Guice Jackson; widowed; children: Willie Leroy, Betty Marie P Smith, Corrie Jean P Reed. **EDUCATION:** Attained 9th grade. **CAREER:** Mansfield Desoto LA NAACP, secretary since 1971; City of So Mansfield, mayor 1971-. **ORGANIZATIONS:** Anti Proverty Prog Natchitoches Area Action Assn 1979; mem Desoto Parish Chamber of Commerce 1979-; library bd of controls; mem policy council Head Start. **HONORS/ACHIEVEMENTS:** First Black female Mayor of the State of LA; first Black female Mayor in the US. **BUSINESS ADDRESS:** Mayor, City of So Mansfield, PO Box 995, Town Hall, Mansfield, LA 71052.

PATTERSON, ELIZABETH ANN
Radiologist. **PERSONAL:** Born Feb 02, 1936, Wilkes-Barre, PA; daughter of Benjamin A Patterson and Edythe Enty Patterson; divorced; children: Tonya L Henry. **EDUCATION:** Univ of MI, BS 1957; Howard Univ Coll of Medicine, MD 1961. **CAREER:** Mercy Hospital, radiology 1972-80; Univ of Pgh/Magee Women's Hosp, asst prof of radiology 1981-85; Central Medical Ctr & Hosp, diagnostic radiologist 1985-88; assistant professor of radiology, Hospital of Univ of Pennsylvania, 1988-. **ORGANIZATIONS:** Pres Pittsburgh Roentger Soc 1982-83; pres Gateway Medical Soc 1983-88; councilor Amer Coll of Radiology 1985-; secty/program chair Radiology Section of Natl Medical Assoc 1985-87, vice chariman 1987-; bd of dirs Amer Cancer Soc Pittsburgh 1986-88; mem Amer Assoc of Women in Radiology, Alpha Kappa Alpha. **HOME ADDRESS:** 232 Berwin Rd, Radnor, PA 19087.

PATTERSON, ELIZABETH HAYES
Attorney. **PERSONAL:** Born Jun 25, 1945, Boston, MA; daughter of Lucille Hayes Young; married Jerome Alexander; children: Sala Elise, Malcolm Atiim. **EDUCATION:** SorbonneUniv of Paris, diploma with honors 1966; Emmanuel Coll, AB with distinction in french 1967; Stanford U, 1967-68; Columbus Sch of Law CathUniv of Am, JD 1973. **CAREER:** Georgetown Ul Law Cntr, asso prof 1980-; DC Pub Sev Commn, chmn 1978-80; DC Pub Serv Commn, commr 1977-80 Columbus Sch of Law Cath U, adj prof1976; Hogan & Hartson Law Firm, asso 1974-77; Hon Ruggero Aldisert US Ct of Appeals, law clk 1973-74; Treasurer, District of Columbia Bar 1987-88. **ORGANIZATIONS:** Trst Family & Child Sev Wash DC 1977-; mem ACLU Litigation Screening Com 1977-80; mem DC Bar Div I Steering Com 1980-82, DC Bar Screening Comm 1985-86; mem bd editors Washington Lawyer 1986-; mem Sec of State's Adv Comm on Private Intl Law; study group on the Law Applicable to the Intl Sale of Goods1983-85; mem adv comm Procedures Judicial Council of the DC Circuit 1981-84. **HONORS/ACHIEVEMENTS:** Woodrow Wilson Fellow Woodrow Wilson Soc 1967; A Salute to Black Women in Gov Iota Phi Lambda Sor Gamma Cht 1978; "UCC 2-612(3): Breach of an Installment Contract and a Hobson's Choice for the Aggrieved Party," 48 Ohio State Law Journal 227, 1987; "UN Convention on Contracts for the Intl Sale of Goods: Unification and the Tension Between Compromise and Domination," 22 Stanford Journal of Intl Law 263, 1986. **BUSINESS ADDRESS:** Assoc Professor of Law, GeorgetownUniv Law Center, 600 New Jersey Ave NW, Washington, DC 20001.

PATTERSON, EVELYNNE (NEE ROBERTS)
Educational administrator. **PERSONAL:** Born Feb 28, 1930, Meadville, PA; married Herman; children: Alice, Patricia. **EDUCATION:** NY U, BS 1962; NY U, post grad. **CAREER:** NY Univ, exec asst to pres dir office for affirmative action dir office for comm rel asso prof 1975-; asst dep chancellor dir asso prof 1972-75; NY Univ, dir asso 1968-72. **ORGANIZATIONS:** Mem adv bvd HarvardUniv 1974-77; mem Comm Bd #2 Borough of Manhattan 1977-; bd of dir WA Sq Assn 1977-. **BUSINESS ADDRESS:** 70 Washington Sq s, New York, NY 10012.

PATTERSON, FLOYD
Retired boxer. **PERSONAL:** Married Janet; children: Janene, Jennifer, Tracy. **CAREER:** Professional Heavyweight Boxer, 1952-72; Huguenot Boxing Club New Paltz NY, owner. **ORGANIZATIONS:** Mem New York State Athletic Commn; presently working on behalf of a variety of charitable orgs including New York City's Inner-City Scholarship Fund. **HONORS/ACHIEVEMENTS:** Middleweight Gold Medal winner 1952 Olympic Games in Helsinki; World Heavyweight Champion 1956-59, 1960-62; first man to win the heavyweight title twice and youngest man to ever capture the heavyweight crown.

PATTERSON, GERALD WILLIAM
Logistics manager. **PERSONAL:** Born May 09, 1953, Cleveland, OH; son of William Robert Patterson and Willa Mae Harris Patterson; divorced; children: Monique Camille Patterson. **EDUCATION:** Michigan State Univ, East Lansing, MI, BA, 1975; Wayne State Univ, DLetroit MI, specialist, 1977; Central Michigan Univ, Mt Pleasant MI, MA, 1978; Univ of Wisconsin, Madison WI, transportation certificate, 1987. **CAREER:** Ford Motor Co, Dearborn MI, sr transportation agent, 1978-80; Amway Corp, Grand Rapids MI, traffic coordinator, 1980-82, traffic supvr, 1982-83; Kellogg Co, Battle Creek MI, truck pricing mgr, 1984-87, mgr logistics services, Lancaster/San Leandro, 1988, currently mgr outside warehouses & dist centers. **ORGANIZATIONS:** Mem, Phi Beta Sigma, 1975-; mem, Delta Nu Alpha, 1982-89; mem, Southwest Michigan Traffic Club, 1984-; mem, Battle Creek Area Urban League, 1985-; advisor, Jr Achievement, 1986-88; mem, 60NR Committee, 1987-88; mem, NAACP, 1988-; advisor, Upward Bound, 1989-; mem, Council of Logistics Mgmt, 1989. **HONORS/ACHIEVEMENTS:** Transportation Negotiation Strategies, 1987; Service Award, Governor of Tennessee, 1989. **HOME ADDRESS:** 203 Eaton St, Battle Creek, MI 49017.

PATTERSON, JACQUELINE J.
Administrator. **PERSONAL:** Born Jul 01, 1928, Ft Wayne, IN. **EDUCATION:** Howard Univ, BS 1950; Univ of MI, MSW 1967. **CAREER:** Ft Wayne Urban League Inc, assoc dir health family & ind serv 1967-70, dep dir 1970-71; Child Care Comm Educ Prog St Louis, coord 1971-73; Health &Social Welfare St Louis, asst dir 1973-74; Social Welfare Natl Urban League, asst regional dir 1975-79; Field Operations, asst vice pres 1979; Natl Urban League Eastern Regional Office, dir 1979-. **ORGANIZATIONS:** Interim exec dir Urban League of Ft Wayne 1967-68; interim exec dir Marion IN Urban League 1978; interim exec dir Urban League of Ft Wayne Inc 1978-79; interim exec dir Urban League of Madison Co Inc 1972; consult St Louis Child Care Assn 1972-74; mem adv com IL Commn on Aging. **HONORS/ACHIEVEMENTS:** Natl Urban League Fellow 1965-67; Sojourner Truth Awd Natl Assn of Negro Bus & Professional Women 1978. **BUSINESS ADDRESS:** Dir, Nat Urban League East Reg, 500 E 62nd St, New York, NY 10021.

PATTERSON, JAMES
Business executive. **PERSONAL:** Born May 10, 1935, Augusta, GA; married Phyllis Black; children: Katy, Jacqueline, Jennifer. **EDUCATION:** State Clge, MD 1957. **CAREER:** Mutual of NY, field underwriter 1966-; Supreme Life Phila, debit & staff mgr 1960-66 business unlimited inc, pres 1975-. **ORGANIZATIONS:** Mem Million Dollar Round Table; Mutual of New York Hall of Fame; mutual of NY Pres's Council; Natl Assc of Life Underwriters; past mem Philadelphia Jaycees; mem Philadelphia chap Natl Bus League, vice pres 1972. **HONORS/ACHIEVEMENTS:** Rec'd Mutual of New York's highest hnr Hall of Fame 1974; agcy Man of yr 1967. **MILITARY SERVICE:** Mil srv 1958-60. **BUSINESS ADDRESS:** 146 Montgomery Ave, Bala-Cynwyd, PA 19004.

PATTERSON, JAMES OGLETHORPE
Clergyman. **PERSONAL:** Born Jul 21, 1912, Derma, MS; married Deborah Mason; children: James Jr, Janet Davis. **EDUCATION:** Howe School of Religion, ThM; Pillar of Fire Sem, DCL 1969; Trinity Hall Coll, PhD 1970. **CAREER:** Charles Harrison Mason Found, gen sec; Church of God in Christ Book Store, gen sec; Church of God in Christ Hosp Fund, gen sec; CH Mason System of Bible Inc, gen sec; Charles Harrison Mason Theol Sem, gen sec; Church of God in Christ, gen sec; Pentecostal Temple, pastor; Churches Publ House, mgr; Highland Park of God in Christ, sec, exec com; Church of God in Christ Inc, presiding bishop. **ORGANIZATIONS:** Bd dir YMCA, Memphis Landmark Comm, Mayors Task Force, Big Bros, NAACP, Collins Chapel Hosp, Shelby Cty Sheriffs Assoc, Tri-State Bank, TN Burial Assoc; founder Mason Found. **HONORS/ACHIEVEMENTS:** Recipient numerous awards, honors & citations. **BUSINESS ADDRESS:** Church of God in Christ Inc, 272 Main St, Memphis, TN 38103.

PATTERSON, JOAN DELORES
Education specialist. **PERSONAL:** Born Mar 17, 1944, Columbia, SC; daughter of David Creech; divorced; children: Torrey. **EDUCATION:** City Colleges of Chicago, AA 1976; Chicago State Univ, BA 1979; Univ of North FL, MEd 1982. **CAREER:** Univ S Navy, dir of personal serv 1982-83, educ tech 1983-84, personnel clerk 1984; Univ S Air Force, guidance counselor 1984-. **ORGANIZATIONS:** Mem Amer Soc for Training and Devel 1982-85; chief counselor Equal Employment Opportunity 1984-85; mgr Federal Women's Program 1984; mem Amer Assn for Counseling & Devel 1985-; mem Military Educators & Counselors Assn 1985-; mem Assn for Multicultural Counseling & Devel 1985-; bd of dir, Military Educators Counseling Assn, 1989-. **HONORS/ACHIEVEMENTS:** Outstanding Performance Award, Univ S Navy 1983; Letters of Commendation (5), Univ S Air Force 1986. **MILITARY SERVICE:** US Army Reserves, staff sgt 1977-85. **BUSINESS ADDRESS:** Education Services Office, US Air Force, 6550 ABG/DPE, Patrick AFB, FL 32925-6505.

PATTERSON, JOHN T., JR.
Business executive. **PERSONAL:** Born Apr 04, 1928, New York City, NY; married Jamelle G; children: Ramona Jamelle, Jodie Miishee. **EDUCATION:** Lincoln Univ PA, AB 1950; Brooklyn Law Sch, LLB 1954, JD 1967. **CAREER:** Bache & Co, Investment Broker 1961-65; Interracial Council for Business Opportunity, natl exec dir 1965-68; self-employed econ devel consultant 1968-72; South Bronx Overall Econ DC (SOBRO), pres 1972-; owner Patterson & Co. NYC 1957-1961. **ORGANIZATIONS:** Exec com Assn for Better NY 1980-; trustee Herbert H Lehman Coll Foundation 1983-; mem Bronx C of C. **HONORS/ACHIEVEMENTS:** The Frederick Douglass Award New York Urban League 1986. **BUSINESS ADDRESS:** President, SOBRO, 370 E 149 St, Bronx, NY 10455.

PATTERSON, KAY
State representative. **PERSONAL:** Born Jan 11, 1931, Darlington County, SC; married Jean James; children: Eric Horace, Pamela Maria. **EDUCATION:** Allen Univ, AB 1956; SC State Coll, MEd 1971. **CAREER:** WA Perry Middle School, teacher 1956-70; Benedict Coll, teacher 1966; SC Educ Assn, uniserv rep 1970-; SC House of Representatives, rep 1975-85; elected SC Senate 1985. **ORGANIZATIONS:** Life mem Natl Educ Assn; life mem NAACP; commnr Educ Comm of the States 1978-84; mem Southern Regional Educ Bd 1985-; Univ of SC Trustee, former mem 1985. **MILITARY SERVICE:** USMC buck sgt 1951-53. **BUSINESS ADDRESS:** Senator, SC Senate, PO Box 142, Columbia, SC 29202.

PATTERSON, LAWRENCE PATRICK
Editor. **PERSONAL:** Born Aug 12, 1932, Jamaica, NY; married Ruthetta; children: Karen, Lawrence, Kathy. **EDUCATION:** NY Univ, BS 1957. **CAREER:** Black Enterprise Mag, founding editor & editor-at-large; editorial & mag cons; NY Univ & Howard Univ, instr of journalism. **ORGANIZATIONS:** Pub rel consult Assc of Mag Editors; Amer Soc of Bus Editors; Alpha Phi Alpha; NY Univ Alumni Assc; NAACP; NY Univ Alumni Assc; Natl Black United Fund. **HONORS/ACHIEVEMENTS:** Silurian Award; Paul Tobenkin Award. **MILITARY SERVICE:** Military srv sgt 1950-52. **BUSINESS ADDRESS:** 295 Madison Ave, New York, NY 10017.

PATTERSON, LLOYD
Police executive, law enforcement consultant. **PERSONAL:** Born Feb 02, 1931, Cleveland, OH; son of Ambrose and Willa; married Lena Burgan. **EDUCATION:** Cuyahoga Comm Coll, attended 1965-66; FBI Natl Acad, grad 1975; Natl Training Ctr of Polygraph Science NYC, graduate; Attended, Dignitary Protection School, US Treasury Dept, OPOTA Hypnosis School. **CAREER:** Cleveland PD, police officer ptlmn thru lieut 1957-82, deputy chief of police 1982-83; CWRU Law Medicine Ctr, staff instructor 1978-83; L & L Patterson Consultants Las Vegas, exec dir. **ORGANIZATIONS:** Past potentate El Hasa Temple #28 Shriners 1961-; mem 32nd Degree Bezaleel Consistory AASR 1961-; mem Eureka Lodge #52 Prince Hall Masons 1961-; disting fellow Acad of Certified Polygraphists 1976; pres Black Shield Police Assoc 1980-; trustee Cleveland Police Hist Soc 1982-; co-owner Bar 2 L Ranch 1983-; parlimentarian Las Vegas Appaloosa Club 1985; imperial dir NAACP; charter mem Natl Org of Black Law Enforcement Execs, NBPA, FOP, Intl Assoc of Chiefs of Police, Black

Shield Police Assoc, NV Black Police Officers Assoc, FBINAA. **HONORS/ACHIEVEMENTS:** Appeared in Disney Movie "You Ruined My Life" 1987 and HBO Special "VIVA-SHAF" 1987; movie: Crime Story, 1988; movie: Midnight Run, 1988; Author: Chicken Every Sunday (cookbook), Pet Peeves Etc (humor), 1989. **MILITARY SERVICE:** AUS sgt 1952-53; Korean Svc; Good Conduct Medal 1952-53. **BUSINESS ADDRESS:** Executive Dir, L & L Patterson Consultants, 5654 Smithsonian Way, Las Vegas, NV 89130.

PATTERSON, LYDIA R.
Bank officer. **PERSONAL:** Born Sep 03, 1936, Carrabelle, FL; married Berman W Patterson; children: Derek, Kelley, Corley. **EDUCATION:** Hunter Coll, BA 1958. **CAREER:** US Energy Dept, industrial rel specialist 1966-68; NY State Div Human Rights, regional dir/mgr 1962-66, 1969-76; Extend Consultant Serv, pres/CEO 1985-; Bankers Trust Co, vice pres 1976-87; Merrill Lynch & Co, vice pres, mgr corp EEO serv dept 1987-. **ORGANIZATIONS:** Govt affairs commn Fin Women Assn/Natl Assn Blk Women 1978-; prof devel comm Urban Bankers Coalition 1978-; mem Amer Soc Personnel Admin 1979-, Employment Managers Assoc 1979-, NY & Natl Urban League 1979-; exec bd NY Women Employment Ctr 1985-; exec bd, mem EDGES 1985-. **HONORS/ACHIEVEMENTS:** Seminar speaker Columbia Univ, Wharton Sch, Harvard Univ, Duke Univ, Cornell Sch of Industry Relations 1976-; Women in Industry Natl Council of Negro Women 1978; article Columbia Univ Sch of Industrial Social Welfare Journal 1981; Women Who Make A Difference, Minorities and Women in Business Magazine 1989; Corporate/Community Partnership Award, Greater New York Chapter Links 1989; Economic Justice Award, Judicial Council, Natl Bar Assn. **HOME ADDRESS:** 183 Rhododendron Dr, Westbury, NY 11590. **BUSINESS ADDRESS:** Vice President, Manager, Merrill Lynch & Co, World Financial Center, South Tower, New York, NY 10080-6111.

PATTERSON, MICHAEL DUANE
Attorney, managing partner. **PERSONAL:** Born Jul 27, 1949, Detroit, MI; son of Harry B Patterson Dr and Myra Howard Patterson; children: Lisa Marie. **EDUCATION:** Ferris State Coll, Big Rapids MI, attended, 1967-68; Western Michigan Univ, Kalamazoo MI, BS, 1970; The Natl Law Center, George Washington Univ, Washington DC, JD, 1974. **CAREER:** Mayor Robert B Blackwell, Highland Park MI, special asst to mayor, 1971; US Senator Birch Bayh, Washington DC, legal intern, 1971-72; US Senator Philip A Hart, Washington DC, staff asst, 1972-74; Herman J Anderson PC, Detroit MI, law clerk, 1974; Wayne County Community Coll, Detroit MI, instructor, 1974-81; Community Youth Serv Program, Detroit MI, legal coord, 1975; Stone, Richardson, Grier & Allen PC, Detroit MI, assoc, 1975-80, partner, 1978-80. **ORGANIZATIONS:** Mem, Wolverine Bar Assn, Natl Bar Assn, NAACP, Amer Bar Assn, New York State Bar Assn, Joint Center for Political Studies, 1971-72; chmn of bd of trustees, Renaissance Baptist Church of Detroit, 1984-86, 1987-89. **HONORS/ACHIEVEMENTS:** Spirit of Detroit Award, Mayor's Certificate of Merit Award. **BUSINESS ADDRESS:** Patterson, Phifer & Phillips, PC, 1274 Library St, L B King Bldg, Suite 500, Detroit, MI 48226.

PATTERSON, ORLANDO HORACE
Educator. **PERSONAL:** Born Jun 05, 1940; married Nerys; children: Rhiannon, Barbara. **EDUCATION:** Univ West Indies, BS 1962; London Sch Econs, PhD 1965; Harvard Univ, AM hon 1971. **CAREER:** Harvard Univ, prof vis lectr 1970-71; Allston Burr Sr, tutor 1971-73; Univ West Indies, lectr 1967-70; London Schl Econs, asst lectr 1965-67. **ORGANIZATIONS:** Mem Tech Adv Com to Prime Minister & Govt of Jamaica 1972-; Jamaica Govt Exhbn; mem Amer Social Assc. **HONORS/ACHIEVEMENTS:** Author, "The Sociology of Slavery" 1967, "The Children of Sisyphys" 1964, "An Absence of Ruins" 1967, "Die the Long Day" 1972. **BUSINESS ADDRESS:** 520 James Hall, Harvard Univ, Cambridge, MA 02138.

PATTERSON, PAUL
Supervisor, director. **PERSONAL:** Born Aug 06, 1926, Aurora, IL; married Shirley Glenn; children: Charles, Carrie. **EDUCATION:** Univ IL, 1950. **CAREER:** Chicago Bears, dir player rels; Anheuser-Busch Inc, sales supr; Chicago Bears, traveling sec 1973, scout dir of player rel 1967; Anheuser-Busch, sales rep 1965; owned & oper food & liquor store 1965; Capitol Dairy 1950. **ORGANIZATIONS:** Bd dir IL Athl Assc at Univ IL 1974; State of IL Athl Bd 1974; bd chmn Athletic Bd of State of IL 1975; Rose Bowl 1947; Jr Mens Hon Soc SACHEH; Mawanda Sr Men Hon Soc; Kappa Alpha Psi. **MILITARY SERVICE:** USN 1945-46. **BUSINESS ADDRESS:** Anheuser Busch, 4841 S California, Chicago, IL 60632.

PATTERSON, PAUL A.
Business executive. **PERSONAL:** Born Mar 05, 1929, Richmond, IN; divorced; children: 3 Children. **EDUCATION:** Earlham Coll, BS 1951; IN Mortuary Coll, 1964. **CAREER:** Patterson's Funeral Home, mortician & prop; Wayne Co, coroner 1984-88. **ORGANIZATIONS:** Mem Lions Club; pres Townsend Comm Ctr; pres Wayne co Fed Welfare Adv Bd; bd Amer Red Cross; bd Boys Club; bd Jr Achievement; vice pres IN Voc Tech Coll; bd Salvation Army; Richmond Funeral Dirs Assn; IFDA & NFDA; Buckeye State Funeral Dir Assoc of OH; past pres Richmond Comm Sch Bd 1966-77;Mayor's Select Group 1972-73; past exalted ruler IBPOEW #479; 32 deg Malta-Consistory #34 shriner; Quinn Lodge #28 F&AM; Tyre Temple #129 Trustee Bethel AME Church.

PATTERSON, POLA NOAH
Librarian. **PERSONAL:** Born Aug 07, 1935, Jennings, LA. **EDUCATION:** Univ of IL, BA French 1970, MS Libr Sci 1971. **CAREER:** Calcasieu Parish Sch Bd LA, sub elem tchr 1956; Univ of IL Library, afro-amer biblio librn 1971-78; CA State Univ Libr San Bernardino, head automation serv 1979-. **ORGANIZATIONS:** Mem Amer Libr Assn; Black Caucus of Amer Libr Assn; mem CA Libr Assn Sucl Chapt; Amer Fed of Tchrs; life mem Zeta Phi Beta Sor Inc; mem CA Black Faculty & Staff Assn; mem Urban League. **HONORS/ACHIEVEMENTS:** Cert Internship in Black Studies Librnshp Fisk Univ 1972; Hon Soc Chi Gamma Iota, Pi Delta Phi, Beta Phi Mu. **MILITARY SERVICE:** USAF capt 1958-69; USAFR retired major. **BUSINESS ADDRESS:** Head Automation Services, CA StateUniv Library, 5500 StUniv Pkwy, San Bernardino, CA 92407.

PATTERSON, RAYMOND R.
Educator. **PERSONAL:** Born Dec 14, 1929, NYC, NY; son of John Patterson and Mildred Clemens; married Boydie Alice Cooke; children: Ama. **EDUCATION:** Lincoln Univ, AB 1951; NY Univ, MA 1956. **CAREER:** Youth House for Boys NY, children's super 1956-58; Benedict Coll, instructor 1958-59; New York City Public Schs, teacher 1959-68; City Coll CUNY, assoc prof. **ORGANIZATIONS:** Dir author Black Poets Reading, Inc; dir City College Langston Hughes Festival; mem Poetry Society of Amer; trustee Walt Whitman Birthplace Assoc; bd of dirs, PEN - Center. **HONORS/ACHIEVEMENTS:** Borestone Mountain Poetry Awds 1950; Natl Endowment for the Arts Awd 1970; Creative Artists Pub Serv Fellowship 1977; City Coll Langston Hughes Awd 1986; honorary mem Golden Key National Honor Society - The City College, 1989; book of poems - Elemental Blues, 1983; opera libretto - David Walker, 1989. **MILITARY SERVICE:** AUS corpl 1951-53. **BUSINESS ADDRESS:** Associate Professor, City Coll CUNY, English Dept, 138 St at Convent Ave, New York, NY 10031.

PATTERSON, RONALD E.
Bank executive. **CAREER:** Commonwealth National Bank, Mobile AL, chief executive. **BUSINESS ADDRESS:** Commonwealth National Bank, 2214 St Stephens Rd, Mobile, AL 36617. *

PATTERSON, THEODORE CARTER CHAVIS
Physician. **PERSONAL:** Born Aug 14, 1932, Sparrows Point, MD; married Sylvia Louise Tureaud; children: Gina Louise, Tina Marie, Chavis Alan. **EDUCATION:** Morgan State Coll, BS 1954; Howard Univ Grad Sch, attended 1957; Univ of MD Sch of Medicine, MD 1962. **CAREER:** Franklin Square Hosp, S Baltimore Genl Hosp, staff; Meridian Home Health Care Agency, Baltimore Co Bd of Med Examiners for Retired Police & Firemen, med dir; Meridian Nursing Ctr Heritage, med dir; staff Church Hosp; Private Practice, physician. **ORGANIZATIONS:** Mem Southern Medical Assn; past pres Baltimore Co Med Assn; mem Amer Acad of Family Practice; mem MD Acad of Family Practice; past pres Dundalk Famrs Improvement Assn 1983-85; elected sec bd of dirs Patapsco Savings & Loan Assn; adv bds Dundalk Comm Coll, Essex Comm Coll; life mem NAACP; recertified Amer Bd of Family Prod; diplomate Amer Acad of Family Physician; bd of dir Med Alumni Assn Univ of MD; chmn Minority Scholarship & LeadershipGuild Univ of MD. **HONORS/ACHIEVEMENTS:** Comm Serv Awd Medical & Chirurgical Faculty of MD 1973; Disting Serv Awd Dundalk Jaycees 1969; Community Serv Awd Baltimore Tuskegee Alumni Assoc. **MILITARY SERVICE:** Infantry 1st lt 1954-56. **HOME ADDRESS:** 1940 Robinwood Rd, Dundalk, MD 21222. **BUSINESS ADDRESS:** Physician, 3427 Dundalk Ave, Dundalk, MD 21222.

PATTERSON, WILLIAM BENJAMIN
Retired recreation administrator. **PERSONAL:** Born May 19, 1931, Little Rock, AR; son of William B Patterson Sr and Perrish Childress Patterson; married Euradell Logan; children: William, David. **EDUCATION:** California State Univ San Francisco, BS Recreation 1956, MS Recreation Admin 1963. **CAREER:** City of Oakland Office of Parks & Recreation, recreation dir 1952-56, head recreation dir 1956-62, district supervisor 1962-74, admin supervisor 1964-74, visitor services mgr, recreation serv mgr 1987-89; City of Oakland, Office of Mayor Lionel J Wilson, special consultant 1989; Growth Opportunities Inc, pres/CEO 1988-. **ORGANIZATIONS:** Foreman Alameda County Grand Jury 1982-83; mem Oakland Baseball Athletics Advisory Bd 1982-; mem Natl Life Mem Comm NAACP 1982-87; treasurer, bd of dirs Joe Morgan Youth Foundation 1983-; vice pres/dir Mitre Business Org Inc 1983-88, pres/CEO 1988-; past pres 1984, chairperson of bd New Oakland Comm Inc 1985-; pres bd chair Greater Acorn Community Improvement Assn Inc 1985-87; mem California Parks and Recreation Soc East Bay Recreation Exec Assn, Amer Assn of Zoological Parks and Aquariums; life mem Kappa Alpha Psi Frat 1982-; mem Sigma Pi Phi Frat 1984-. **HONORS/ACHIEVEMENTS:** Outstanding Contributions Award, California Youth Authority 1977; Outstanding Serv Award, Alameda County Bd of Supervisors 1977; Comm Testimonial, McClymonds Alumni Assn 1982; Commendation for Community Serv, Oakland City Council 1983. **MILITARY SERVICE:** AUS pfc EII 1951. **BUSINESS ADDRESS:** Retired Municipal Administrator/ Community Consultant, Mayor Lionel J Wilson-City of Oakland, One City Hall Plaza, City Hall, Oakland, CA 94612.

PATTERSON, WILLIS CHARLES
Educator, performer. **PERSONAL:** Born Nov 27, 1930, Ann Arbor, MI; married Frankie Bouyer; children: Sharon, Kevin, Shelia. **EDUCATION:** Univ of MI, MusB, M Mus. **CAREER:** VA State Coll, assoc prof 1962-68; Univ of MI, prof 1977; Univ of MI School of Music, assoc dean 1979; Major Orchestra, Our Own Thing Inc, performer; Univ of MI School of Music, assoc dean/prof of voice. **ORGANIZATIONS:** Mem Natl Opera Assn; Natl Assn Teachers Singing Alpha Phi Alpha Frat; NAACP; Natl Assn of Negro Musicians; Natl Black Music Caucus. **HONORS/ACHIEVEMENTS:** Compiled "Anthology of Art Songs by Black Amer Composers" Edward B Marks Music Corp 1977; Recorded with RCA Victor, Philips Records, TV NBC, BBC. **MILITARY SERVICE:** USAF staff sgt 1949-52. **BUSINESS ADDRESS:** Assoc Dean/Prof of Voice, Univ of MI, 225 Earl V Moore Bldg, School of Music, Ann Arbor, MI 48109.

PATTILLO, ROLAND A.
Physician, educator. **PERSONAL:** Born Jun 12, 1933, DeQuincy, LA; married Marv; children: Catherine, Michael, Patrick, Sheri, Mary. **EDUCATION:** Xavier Univ, BS 1955; St Louis Univ, MD; Johns Hopkins Univ, postdoc flwsp 1965-67. **CAREER:** Med Coll WI, prof; WHO, consult 1977, prof dir cancer research & research sci; Med Coll WI, physician 1968-; Harvard Univ, resd 1960-64; Marquette Univ. **ORGANIZATIONS:** Bd dir Amer Cancer Soc; mem Milwaukee Div Sci Jour Reviewer; Jour of Natl Cancer Inst Sci; Cancer Rsrch; Amer Jour OB/GYN; OB/GYN Jour NIH flwsp 1965-67. **HONORS/ACHIEVEMENTS:** Rsrch award Amer Clge OB/GYN 1963; Found Thesis Award Amer Assc OB/GYN 1975; author publ. **BUSINESS ADDRESS:** 8700 W Wisconsin Ave, Milwaukee, WI 53226.

PATTMAN, VIRGIL THOMAS, SR.
Electronic engineer. **PERSONAL:** Born Nov 29, 1940, Detroit, MI; children: Virgil Thomas Jr, Randall H, Tiffaney Lynn. **EDUCATION:** Lawrence Inst of Tech, BS 1969; Detroit Inst of Tech, BS 1981; Central MI Univ, MA 1983. **CAREER:** General Electric Co, electronic tech 1964-67; GM Corp Proving Ground, elec engr 1967-78; GM Corp Tech Ctr Mfg Div, safety engr 1978-82; GM Corp Tech Ctr Adv Eng Staff, sr safety engr 1983-. **ORGANIZATIONS:** Bd of trustees 1968-84, church treas & finance sec asst 1972-84, audio engr 1984-, church school tchr 1985-, bd of christian educ 1986- Peace Bapt Church Detroit; mem Amer Soc of Safety Engrs 1980-. **HONORS/ACHIEVEMENTS:** Appeared in Ebony Magazine Who's Who 1982; First black senior safety engr at the GM Tech Ctr responsible

for staff of 1500 persons. **MILITARY SERVICE:** AUS Reserves sgt 1963-69; instructor of chemical biological & radiological warfare. **HOME ADDRESS:** 15015 Glastonbury St, Detroit, MI 48223. **BUSINESS ADDRESS:** Senior Safety Engineer, GM Tech Center, Advanced Engrg Staff, 30300 Mound Rd, Warren, MI 48090.

PATTON, CAROLYN VANNETTE
Manager. **EDUCATION:** Hampton Inst, BA 1970; Univ of Puget Sound, MEd 1974. **CAREER:** Aerojet Genl Corp, personnel tech 1972-73; Univ of Puget Sound, adm asst to pres 1974-77; Weyerhaeuser Co, proj mgr 1977-78, mgr 1978-83; Office of Minority & Women's Bus Enterprises, dir. **ORGANIZATIONS:** Mem bd of trustees Univ of Puget Sound 1984; mem Women Executives in State Govt 1983-85; mem Amer Assn of Women Deans & Adminstrs 1974-78; mem Puget Sound Hosp Commn Adv Comm 1977-83; mem Northwest Conf of Black Officials 1978-80; mem adv comm Washington State Vocational Education Sex Equality Commn; 1978-83; mem Bellevue Comm Coll Business Scholarship Adv Bd 1978-82; mem Pacific NW Personnel Mgmt Assn Inc 1978-84; mem Weyerhaeuser Found Review-Comm 1979-83; mem Tacoma Urban League 1975-85; chmn mem Tacoma Pierce Co March of Dimes 1975-83; exec bd bd of trustees mem Tacoma Urban League 1975-83; chair Washington State Women's Council 1976-77; Commr Washington State Lottery 1982-83; mem NAACP 1973-84; mem Tacoma Human Relations Commn Tribunal 1976-78; mem Washington Women's Polit Council 1978-80; mem Alpha Kappa Alpha Sor 1985. **HONORS/ACHIEVEMENTS:** Academic Scholarship Hampton Inst 1966; HEW Grad Fellowship Univ of Puget Sound 1973-74; Who's Who in the West 17th Ed 1979; Outstanding Young Women of Amer 1980. **BUSINESS ADDRESS:** Dir, Off of Min & Women's Bus Ent, 406 S Water; MS: FK-ll, Olympia, WA 98504.

PATTON, CURTIS L.
Scientist, educator. **PERSONAL:** Born Jun 13, 1935, Birmingham, AL; married Barbara Beth Battle; children: Lynne Martine. **EDUCATION:** Fisk Univ, BA 1956; MI State Univ, MS 1961, PhD 1966; Rockefeller Univ, Postdoct 1967-70. **CAREER:** MI State Univ, instructor 1963-67; Rockefeller Univ, guest investigator & fellow 1967-70; Yale Univ, asst prof of microbiology 1970-76, co-dir grad studies in microbiology 1972-75; Intl Lab of Rsch on Animal Disease Nainobi Kenya, visiting scientist; Yale Univ, assoc prof epidemiology & public health 1976-; Yale Univ School of Med, asst 1970-74, asst with tenure 1974-78, prof 1985-. **ORGANIZATIONS:** Review comm Natl Inst of Gen Med Scis Study Sect 1978-82; consult Natl Rsch Council 1979-80; consult AUS Med Rsch & Devel Command 1979-84; exec com Soc of Protozoologists; mem Amer Soc of Parasitologists; mem Amer Assn for Advancement of Sci; mem Royal Soc of Tropical Med & Hygiene; mem Amer Soc of Tropical Med & Hygiene; mem Sigma Xi, Alpha Phi Alpha; bd dirs Clifford Beers Clinic; consult Natl Inst of Health, Walter Reed Army Inst of Rsch. **HONORS/ACHIEVEMENTS:** USPHS Doctoral Fellowship 1967-70; USPHS Rsch Grant 1972-; USPHS Career Devel Awd 1972-77; USAID Rsch Grant 1976-77; USPHS Training Grant 1977-; USPHS Rsch Grant 1978-; World Health Organ Rsch Grant 1983-; Natl Inst of Health rsch grant. **MILITARY SERVICE:** AUS spec 6th class 1956-59. **BUSINESS ADDRESS:** Professor, YaleUniv, School of Medicine, New Haven, CT 06510.

PATTON, GERALD WILSON
Educator, educational administrator. **PERSONAL:** Born Nov 13, 1947, Chattanooga, TN; married Linda S Williams; children: Germond Che'. **EDUCATION:** Kentucky State Univ, BA 1969; Western Illinois Univ, MA 1973; Univ of Iowa, PhD 1978. **CAREER:** North Carolina State Univ, asst prof history 1978; Washington Univ, asst dean of graduate school of arts & science 1978-81. **ORGANIZATIONS:** Coordinator "St Louis A Policy Framework for Racial Justice, an Agenda for the 80's" sponsored by the Danforth Found 1984-85; chmn Educ Comm 100 Black Men of St Louis 1983-; chmn MO Comm of Black Studies 1984-. **HONORS/ACHIEVEMENTS:** "War and Race, Black Officer in the Amer Military" 1981; Congressional Black Caucus Found Scholars lecturer 1984. **BUSINESS ADDRESS:** Assistant Director, North Central Association of Colleges & Schools, 159 N Dearborn, Chicago, IL 60601.

PATTON, JOYCE BRADFORD
Educator. **PERSONAL:** Born May 31, 1947, Shreveport, LA; married Jerry A Patton (deceased); children: Blythe. **EDUCATION:** Grambling State Univ, BA 1969; SUNY Teacher Coll at Buffalo, MS 1972; LA State Univ at Shreveport, attended 1983. **CAREER:** Caddo Parish Schools, teacher of earth science. **ORGANIZATIONS:** Mem Prog Scholarship Comm Alpha Kappa Alpha Inc 1966-; mem Natl Educ Assn 1972-, YWCA 1983-, Natl Science Teachers Assn 1984-; local school chmn Substance Abuse Prevention Educ 1984-; local board 1st vice pres Parent Teacher Student Assn 1984-85; mem Natl Earth Sci Teachers Assn 1986-; youth Sunday school supt Mt Canaan Baptist Church 1986-; member Phi Delta Kappa 1987-89. **HONORS/ACHIEVEMENTS:** Presidential Awds for Excellence in Science & Math Teaching LA State winner 1986, natl winner 1986; Teacher Enhancement Program Evaluator Natl Science Foundation 1987; Educator of Distinction Louisiana PTA 1987; Middle School Teacher of the Year Caddo Parish School Bd 1988; Selected for the National Science Foundation Sposored "Operation Physics," 1988; Teacher Enhancement Program Evaluator, National Science Foundation 1988-89. **HOME ADDRESS:** 6306 Kenwood Lane, Shreveport, LA 71119. **BUSINESS ADDRESS:** Teacher of Earth Science, Caddo Parish Schools, 7635 Cornelious Dr, Shreveport, LA 71106.

PATTON, LEROY
Business executive. **PERSONAL:** Born Apr 14, 1944, Alabama; married Jessie Maple; children: Mark A, Edward L, Audrey Maple. **EDUCATION:** IN Central Coll; IN Univ, 1967; CA Film Inst for Filmmakers, 1971. **CAREER:** LJ Film Prod, pres/dir of photography; "Ft Apache, The Bronx" Time Life Prod Inc, cameraman; "Fame" MGM Prod Inc, stand-by dir of photography 1979; "Will" LJ Film Prod Inc, dir of photography 1978; "Black Econ Power - Realty or Fantasy", dir of photography. **ORGANIZATIONS:** Pres Concerned Black Filmmakers of NYC; mem 100 Black Men Inc mem found for independent video & film; mem cameraman union iatse local 644. **HONORS/ACHIEVEMENTS:** Publ "How to Become a Union Camerawoman Film-Videotape" 1977; 1st & 2nd prize NY Black Film Festival 1977; Freedoms Found Award WCBS-TV spec "My Seeds Are Gone" 1979. **BUSINESS ADDRESS:** President, Concerned Black Filmmakers, 1270 Fifth Ave, Ste 10 C, New York, NY 10029.

PATTON, ROBERT
Educator. **PERSONAL:** Born Jun 29, 1947, Clarksdale, MS; married Dorothy J Johnson; children: Kamela. **EDUCATION:** Jackson State Univ, atnd 1968; Delta State Univ, mA 1976. **CAREER:** Bolivar Co School Dist 3, teacher; Bolivar Co, city alderman. **ORGANIZATIONS:** Mem Jackson State Alumni Assc; mem St Andrews Bapt Ch; vice pres PTA Broad St Sch. **HONORS/ACHIEVEMENTS:** Recip Outst Comm Ldr 1974-75.

PATTON, ROSEZELIA L.
Sales representative. **PERSONAL:** Born Sep 25, 1934, Cincinnati, OH; daughter of Robert L Leahr and Rosezelia Bradshaw Leahr (deceased); widowed; children: Councill M Harris III, Rebecca Leah Harris. **EDUCATION:** Miami Univ 1975-1984; Western College 1970-72. **CAREER:** DuBois Bookstore Oxford OH, trade buyer 1962-69; The Western Coll Oxford OH, registrar 1969-74; Miami Univ Sch of Ed & Allied Prof, prog consul 1974-82; Miami Univ Roudebush Hall Oxford, asst to dir aff act 1982-84; Sears Roebuck & Co, sales rep 1987-. **ORGANIZATIONS:** Housemother Alpha Phi Alpha Miami Univ 1959-62; bd dirs Butler Co Mental Health/Retardation 1966-69; volunteer Planned Parenthood 1965-70; treas Church Women United Oxford 1962-63; vice pres treas Oxford Bus & Professional Women 1973-74 1974-75; Minister of Music Bethel AME Oxford 1962-72 1977-; chair of budget & financial estimates Conf Branch of the Women's Missionary Soc 1978-86; pres Women's Missionary Soc 1977-84; bd of dir Oxford Crisis and Referral Center 1984-. **HOME ADDRESS:** 520 S Main St, Oxford, OH 45056.

PATTON, WILLIAM C.
Retired educator. **PERSONAL:** Born Jul 12, 1912; married Marguerite B Patton; children: William Jr, Celestra R Teele, Jacqueline, Jarvis E. **EDUCATION:** Attended jr college 1936; attended AL State Coll. **CAREER:** York Jr High School, York, AL, prin 1930-36; Greenville City School, prin 1936-45; Amer Woodmen, dist mgr 1945; NAACP AL, state pres 1947-55; NAACP Voter Edn, natl dir 1956-78. **ORGANIZATIONS:** Pres Comm Action Agency JCCED 1966; pres Bham Emancipation Assn 1969; mem 16 other bds/commns/com. **HONORS/ACHIEVEMENTS:** Omega Man of the Year Bham, AL; Man of the Year 16th St Bapt Ch Bham, AL; Citizen of the Year Tushegee Inst 1975; Citizen of the Year Miles Coll Bham, AL 1980.

PAUL, ALVIN, III
Educator, administrator. **PERSONAL:** Born Feb 17, 1941, New Roads, LA; son of Alvin Paul and Pearl Paul; married Vera; children: 3 Sons. **EDUCATION:** Southern Univ, Baton Rouge LA, BS 1961; Northeastern Illinois Univ, MEd 1970; Nova Univ Ft Lauderdale, EdD. **CAREER:** Pointe Coupee Parish Schools, New Roads LA, History, Math & Science teacher 1961-62; Gary Public Schools, Math teacher 1962-71, team leader & asst principal 1967-69; Prairie State Coll, Math & Educ teacher 1971-; Marcy Newberry Center Chicago, acting exec dir & dir 1971; Our Lady of Solace Catholic School Chicago, principal 1974-75; Triton Coll, River Grove IL, Math teacher 1979-; Prairie State Coll, dir, teacher aide, Educ and Math teacher 1971-. **ORGANIZATIONS:** Mem St Dorothy Parish Council 1976-; pres St Dorothy School Bd 1976-79; mem Personalized Learning Program Advisory Bd Prairie State Coll 1976-; mem Human Serv Advisory Bd Prairie State Coll 1977-; mem Archdiocese of Chicago Bd of Educ 1979-84; chmn Human Serv Dept Prairie State Coll 1980-83; mem metric adv bd Prairie State Coll 1980-82; Keeper of Records 1982; Kappa Alpha Psi Chapter Guide Right Comm 1982, 1985, 1987; chmn Academic Program Review Comm PSC 1983-85; vice polemarch Kappa Alpha Psi Frat 1985-87; mem Knights of Peter Claver Council #158 deputy grand knight 1987-89; chmn Academic Program Review Comm Prairie State Coll; former chmn Financial Comm St Dorothy School Bd; mem Coll Teacher Union; mem Curriculum Comm & Faculty Senate (PSC); chmn Teacher Aide Advisory Bd Prairie State Coll; former business mgr Our Lady of Peace Ho me Sch Assn; former mem, Our Lady of Peace Parish Council; pole march, Kappa Alpha Psi Frat, 1987-88; bd mem, Chicago Heights CEDA, 1983-. **HONORS/ACHIEVEMENTS:** Research Study Founds & Procedures for Math Assts & Teacher Aides in Elementary School 1976; Research Study A Study of Academic Performance of Students Taught by Traditional Classroom Methods as Compared to Programmed Learning 1977; Research Study The Effects of Test Scores & Prerequisite Requirements on Students' Success in Tech Math 1977; Research Study An Evaluation of the Governance Structure of Human Serv Dept Prairie State Coll 1977; Research Study A Comparison of Effects of Competency Based Instruction on Achievement Attitudes & Persistency of Non-Traditional Students at Prairie State Coll 1978; Dissertation Perceived Satisfaction of Traditional Students with Traditional Coll Programs Prairie State Coll 1979.

PAUL, BEATRICE (NEE LITTLE)
Business executive. **PERSONAL:** Born Mar 13, 1943, Portsmouth, VA; divorced; children: Kellene, Keith Jr, Kerrith. **EDUCATION:** Empire State Clge, BA 1973. **CAREER:** 19th Ward Youth Proj, dir; SUC Brockport, adj prof; Early Childhood Devel Ctr, exec dir; Early Childhood Learning Ctr Rochester Assc for Educ of Young Child, dir 1973-75. **ORGANIZATIONS:** Chmn Staff Devel & Training Task Force 1973-75; Rochester Chap Natl Assc of Black Social Workers; bd dir Western NY Child Care Council 1974-75; Natl Caucus of Black Sch Bd mems; Rochester Sub-region N Eastern Black Polit Caucus; Black Ldrshp studies grp; adv bd Comm Educ Ctr 1971-72; FIGHT Inc vice pres bd of educ 1977-78; pres Rochester Bd of Educ 1978-79. **HONORS/ACHIEVEMENTS:** Comm Involvement Award Comm Schl Council 1976; Oustst Comm Serv Award Nghbrhd St Acad; Comm Serv Award Wilson Jr High 1975-76; Comm Srv Award CommSch Council 1977; Comm Srv Award Title I 1978; Outst Citizen Award Genesee Settlement House 1978; Political Srv Award Eureka Lodge 1979; Political Srv Award Electric City Lodge 1979; Comm Srv Award Marcus Garvey Meml 1979; Appreciation Award Franklin High 1979; Spec Recog Class of '79 Franklin 1979; Meritorious Srv Award Title I 1979; Outst Citizen Award Comm Sch Council 1980. **BUSINESS ADDRESS:** 447 Genesee St, Rochester, NY 14611.

PAUL, JOHN F.
Business executive. **PERSONAL:** Born Sep 13, 1934, Miami, FL; married Betty; children: Dana, Derek, Darryl, Darin. **EDUCATION:** BA 1964; MPA 1970; Cert Mgmt Devel Inst, 1970; Cert Inst for Ct Mgmt, 1971; Cert Inst of Labor & Industrial Rel 1972; Cert Natl Inst of Corrections, 1973-74. **CAREER:** CEA Dept of Human Resources Devel Los Angeles CA, mgr 1969-71; State Serv Ctr Los Angeles, asst mgr 1968-69, supr cnslr 1967-68; CA Youth & Corrections Agy, parole ofcr 1964-67; CA Youth & Corrections Agency Norwalk CA, sr grp supr 1960-64; Circuit Ct Probation Dept, dir. **ORGANIZATIONS:** Consult US Dept of Justice Comm Rel Ofc 1974; consult Univ of So CA Cntr for Adm of Justice 1974; mem Amer Soc for Pub Admin; mem Natl Council onCrime & Delinquency; mem MI Correctional Assc; mem Acad of Ct Admin; mem NAACP; Trade Unionist Ldrshp Conf; MI Black

Caucus. **HONORS/ACHIEVEMENTS:** Recip Flwshp Univ of Denver Inst of Ct Mgmt; China Serv Award. **MILITARY SERVICE:** USN petty ofcr 3rd class 1952-56; Good Conduct Award. **BUSINESS ADDRESS:** 3600 Cadillac Tower, Detroit, MI 48226.

PAUL, VERA MAXINE
Educator. **PERSONAL:** Born Dec 14, 1940, Mansfield, LA; daughter of Clifton Hall and Virginia Elzania Smith Hall; married Dr Alvin James Paul III, Jun 14, 1964; children: Alvin Jerome, Calvin James, Douglas Fairbanks. **EDUCATION:** Southern Univ, Baton Rouge LA, BS, 1962; Chicago State Univ, Chicago IL, 1968-69; Roosevelt Univ, Chicago IL, MA, 1975. **CAREER:** Union Street High School, Shreveport LA, teacher, 1962-64; Chicago Bd of Educ, Chicago IL, teacher, asst principal, 1964-67, 1968-; South Bend Community School System, South Bend IN, 1967-68. **ORGANIZATIONS:** Mem, Chicago Teacher Union, 1964-; mem, Natl Assn for the Advancement of Colored People, 1965-; mem, Illinois Teacher Union, 1968-; mem, Natl Mathematics Assn, 1969-88; mem, Illinois Mathematics Assn, 1975-88; mem, Operation Push, 1975-88; mem, Amer Federation of Teachers, 1978-; mem, Urban League, 1980-88; mem, Chicago Area Alliance of Black School Educators, 1982-87; life mem and Great Lakes regional dir, Zeta Phi Beta Sorority, Inc, 1986-89. **HONORS/ACHIEVEMENTS:** Distinguished Volunteer Leadership, March of Dimes, 1982; Mayoral Tribute from City of Pontiac MI, 1987; Zeta of Year, Zeta Phi Beta Sorority, Inc, 1988; Distinguished Service Award, City Council of Detroit, 1988; Award Excellence in Education, New School Administrator, 1988. **HOME ADDRESS:** 8505 S Phillips Ave, Chicago, IL 60617.

PAULK, BERNICE HERRING
Foreman. **PERSONAL:** Born Jul 13, 1926, Gainesville, FL; divorced; children: Rosa Okpara, Marva Swint, Ira, Atheas, Loretta, Earthera. **CAREER:** USMC Logistic Support Base Atlantic Warehouse, foreman. **ORGANIZATIONS:** GARC sec of bd 1971-72, regional vice pres 1973, bd liaison to youth 1973-77, chairperson 1976; reg coord Citizen Hearing on Key Legis for Mentally Retarded Offender Act 1974-75; chairperson Annual Registration Comm 1975; sec United Way; vol Probation-Juvenile Delinquests; comm on Minority Affairs, Environmental Influences; mem SE Reg Task Force on Minority Involvement, Wage & Survey Fed Women's Program; council comm EEO; pres GA ARC; mem Hines Mem CME Church. **HONORS/ACHIEVEMENTS:** Most Outstanding Vol for Mentally Retarded in GA GARC 1975; Plaque Atlanta GARC 1975; Outstanding Advisor Awd Youth GARC 1976; 1st Black to be elected to Natl Bd of Dirs Natl Assn for Retarded Citizens 1977; 1st Black elected to Natl Exer Comm Assn for Retarded Citizens 1978 (re-elected 1979); Most Outstanding Albany Mem ARC 1977-78; presented resolution for contributions to State of GA & its people GA House of Reps 1980.

PAWLEY, THOMAS D., III
Retired professor. **PERSONAL:** Born Aug 05, 1917, Jackson, MS; son of Thomas D Pawley and Ethel John Woolfolk; married Ethel Louise Mc Peters; children: Thomas IV, Lawrence. **EDUCATION:** VA State Coll, AB (with distinction) 1937; Univ of IA, AM 1939, PhD 1949. **CAREER:** Prairie View A&M State Coll, instr 1939-40; Lincoln Univ of MO, div chmn 1967-77, dean of arts & scis 1977-83, instr/asst prof/assoc prof/prof 1940-, writer in residence, head dept of communications 1983-85, curators disting prof of speech and theatre, head dept of communications 1985-88. **ORGANIZATIONS:** Visit prof at, Univ of CA Santa Barbara 1968; Northern IL Univ 1971; Univ of IA 1976; Univ of MO 1980, 1988; pres Natl Assn of Dramat and Speech Arts 1953-55; adv com Am Educ Theatre Assn 1953-55; comm on Theatre Educ Am Theatre Assn 1977-79; pres Speech & Theatre Assn of MO 1977-78; Theatre Adv Comm of the MO Arts Cncl 1979-87; Exec Com Black Theatre Prgm Am theatre Assn 1980-; delegate to the Episcopal Diocesan Conv St Louis 1963; treas Jefferson Reg Libr Bd 1974; pres J C Library board 1970-72; v chmn Mayor's Comm on Resid Standards; mem organiz comm Jefferson City Cncl on Race and Religion; delegate Governor's Conf on Libr Services 1978; bd of dirs Mid Amer Arts Alliance 1980-, MO Arts Council 1981-87; mem Natl Endowment for the Arts Theatre Panel 1986,87,88; pres National Conferenc e on African American Theatre 1987-90. **HONORS/ACHIEVEMENTS:** Dir of Amer Scholars; Contemporary Authors 1971; Living Black Authors 1973; Who's Who in Amer; Personalities in the South 1974; Who's Who in the World 4th ed; Shields-Howard Creative Writing Award VA State Coll 1934; Natl Theatre Conf Fellowship 1947-48; Winner of 1st Prize Jamestown, VA Corp Playwriting Contest 1954 for play "Messiah"; Elected to Outstanding Educators of Amer 1970; Outstanding Teacher Award Speech and Theatre Assn of MO 1977; Elected to Coll of Fellows Amer Theatre Assn 1978; Author of numerous books/articles/plays incl, "The Black Teacher and the Dramatic Arts" with Wm Reardon Negro Univ Press 1970; "The Black Theatre Audience" Players Mag Aug-Sep 1971; "FFV" Full-length drama 1963 First production by Stagecrafters Lincoln Univ 1963; "The Tumult and the Shouting" Drama in Two Acts 1969 First production by Inst in Dramatic Arts Lincoln Univ 1969 Publ in Hatch and Shine 1974; Natl Assoc of Dramaticand Speech Arts Outstanding Serv Awd 1984; Natl Conf on African Amer Theatre Mister Brown Awd 1986; Distinguished Alumnus NAFEO Virginia State Univ 1988. **HOME ADDRESS:** 1014 Lafayette, Jefferson City, MO 65101. **BUSINESS ADDRESS:** Professor Emeritus, Lincoln University Box 212, Jefferson City, MO 65101.

PAXTON, GERTRUDE GARNES
Dentist. **PERSONAL:** Born Oct 09, 1931, Raleigh, NC; married Lawrence Paxton; children: Lynn, Lori, Lawrence Jr. **EDUCATION:** Univ CA, 1966; DDS 1956; Howard Univ Clge Dentistry, flw; Howard Univ, BS 1956. **CAREER:** Dentist pvt prac; Pub Hlth, 1966-71, 1956-58; Howard Univ Clge Dentistry, instr 1956-58. **ORGANIZATIONS:** Mem Dental Adv Bd S Cntrl Multi-Srv & Child Devel Ctr; Alain Lock HS 1976-; Adv Cncl Reachout Com Cncl; Performing Arts Music Ctr; mem Omicron Kappa Upsilon Natl Dental Hon Soc; Beta Kappa Chi Sci Hon Soc; Links Inc; Angel City Chpt; Jack & Jill of Amer; pres Circle-Lets 1973-75; Med Dental & Pharm Aux 1968-70; Alva C Garrott Dental Aux 1966-68; mem Natl Dental Assc; Amer Dental Assc. **HONORS/ACHIEVEMENTS:** Listed Who's Who of Amer Women; Outst Black Women in Dentistry Alpha Kappa Alpha Heritage Series; cited Natl Arthritis Found; bd dir YWCA LA. **BUSINESS ADDRESS:** 3310 W Slauson Ave, Los Angeles, CA 90043.

PAXTON, PHYLLIS ANN
Health services administrator. **PERSONAL:** Born May 05, 1942, Birmingham, AL; daughter of Dan Roland Perry and Neida Mae Perry; married Herbert W Laffoon, Apr 02, 1979; children: Terella. **EDUCATION:** Emory Univ, MN in Maternal & Child Health Educ 1970; The Atlanta Ctr of Med Clge of GA, BS nursing 1968. **CAREER:** Univ of AL Birmingham, asst prof nursing; UCLA Extension-Continuing Educ in Health Sci Div of Nursing, proj dir Family Planning Nurse Practitioner Prog 1957-77; LA Regional Family Planning Cncl, training assc 1973-75; UCLA, asst prof of nursing 1970-73; L A Regional Family Planning Council, principal assoc 1978-85; JWCH Institute Inc, manager 1985-89, exec dir 1989-. **ORGANIZATIONS:** Mem Cncl of Black Nurses Inc; mem Natl Black Nurses Assc 1974-; consult Western Interstate Commn on Higher Educ Proj, Models Intro Cultural Diversity in Nursing Curricula 1974-; consult list Amer Pub Health Assc 1974-76; CA Nurses Assc Minority Grp Task Force 1971-73; field rep Proj Breakthrough recruitment of Blacks, Amer Indians, Chicanos, Puerta Ricans & Males into Nursing Schl leading to RN licensure 1972-73; devel 1st Summer Pre-entry Retention Prog for Ethnic Students of Color at UCLA Sch of Nursing 1972; sec Redeemer Alternative School Board 1988-;mem bd of dirs, California Reproductive Health Assoc, 1989-. **HONORS/ACHIEVEMENTS:** Outst Nurse Award Nursing Fund Inc of LA 1973; Natl Med Assc Fnd Award Commitment to action in increasing number of minorities in Health Careers 1972; publ "Providing Safe Nursing Care to Ethnic People of Color" 1976; "Continuing Educ Needs of Nurses Serving Minorities & The Poor" Jour of Continuing Educ in Nursing 1974; National Association of County Organizations Award 1987; developed a comprehensive perinatal services program which served as a model for the Lost Angeles County Dept of Health Services programs in 1985. **BUSINESS ADDRESS:** Executive Director, JWCH Institute Inc, 1910 Sunset Blvd Suite 650, Los Angeles, CA 90026.

PAYDEN, HENRY J., SR.
Clergyman. **PERSONAL:** Born Apr 03, 1923, Columbus; married Phyllis M Smith; children: Garnet, William B, Linda, Henry J. **EDUCATION:** Capital Univ; Cleveland Bible Clge Westminster; Western Res Univ; Cert in Clin Psychology & Pastoral Counseling 1971. **CAREER:** Holy Trinity Bapt Ch, fndr & pastor 1961-; St Paul Bapt Ch New Castle PA, former pastor; Macedonia Bapt Ch Toledo; Gr Abyssinia Bapt Ch Cleveland. **ORGANIZATIONS:** Featured soloist with "Wings Over Jordan"; Cleveland Women's Sym Orch; Chpln of Amvets; Mem Mt Pleasant Comm Ctr; mem Pub Bd & Tchr Prog Natl Bapt Conv Inc. **HONORS/ACHIEVEMENTS:** Hnrd as Pastor of Year 1956; awarded automobile as Soloist in Burts Hour Cleveland 1947. **MILITARY SERVICE:** US 9 Cav sgt. **BUSINESS ADDRESS:** Pastor, Holy Trinity Baptist Church, 3808 14 E 131 St, Cleveland, OH 44120.

PAYNE, BEVERLY
Anchorperson. **PERSONAL:** Born in San Francisco, CA; children: 3 Children. **EDUCATION:** Univ San Francisco. **CAREER:** TV 2 News, anchorperson present; Focus, co-host 1973; Tokyo-Eleven PM, co-hostess; Japanese TV, taught eng. **ORGANIZATIONS:** Bd dir Detroit Hearing & Speech Ctr; Keep Detroit Beautiful Inc; Worked on Jerry Lewis MD Telethon; NAACP Telethon; The Childrens Leukemia Found; Am Diabetes Assn. **HONORS/ACHIEVEMENTS:** Only black woman in country who holds position of lead anchorperson for Prime Time Newscast; City of Detroit Majors awd of mer for Media Present 1974; The Dist Serv Awd 1975; the NOW Media Woman of Yr Awd 1975; The Women Lawyers Assn Awd for Women in the Media 1976; The Met Arts Complex Media Awd 1976; The MI Chronicale Citizen of Yr Awd 1977; Detroit Chap of Am Women in Radio & TV 1977; awd for Outst Women in Broadcasting 1977. **BUSINESS ADDRESS:** #2 Storer Pl, Southfield, MI 48075.

PAYNE, BROWN H.
Attorney. **PERSONAL:** Born Jan 27, 1915, Buffalo Gap, VA; married Ruth E Boyd; children: Brown W, Cynthia B, John H, Wilbert A. **EDUCATION:** Hampton Inst, 1934-35; Fisk Univ, 1937-38; Bluefield State, BA 1945; Howard Univ, LlB 1948; Geo Wash Univ, LlM 1951. **CAREER:** Priv prac 1951-61; Nat Labor Rels Bd 1961; State Tax Dept WV, atty 1961-63; Florida A&M Coll of Law, asst prof 1962-65; NC Coll Durham, asso prof of law 1965-70; priv prac 1970-; Beckley Coll Introd to Crim Just, instr 1976-77; VA Loan Closer; WV Workmen's Comp, invest. **ORGANIZATIONS:** Mem Nat Bar Assn; WV Bar Assn; Raleigh Co Bar Assn; Kappa Alpha Psi Frat; pres Raliegh Co Civil Serv Commn; Masons Elec Alt Del Rep Nat Conv1944; Adv of NCC Law Jour Vol 1969; mem Elector Coll 1972 pres elec. **MILITARY SERVICE:** AUS warrant off. **BUSINESS ADDRESS:** 338 S Fayette St, Beckley, WV 25801.

PAYNE, ETHEL LOIS
Columnist, commentator. **PERSONAL:** Born Aug 14, 1911, Chicago, IL; daughter of William Payne (deceased) and Bessie Austin Payne (deceased). **EDUCATION:** Chicago Training School (now Garrett Inst), Evanston IL; Medill School of Journalism, Evanston IL. **CAREER:** Chicago Defender, Chicago IL, feature writer, 1951-53, Washington DC, Washington correspondent, 1953-73, Chicago IL, assoc editor, 1973-78; Ford Foundation, George Washington Univ, fellowship in educ journalism, 1978; CBS Opinion Program, "Specrum," 1972-78; Jackson State Univ, Jackson MS, writer-in-residence, 1981; WBBM-CBS, "Matters of Opinion" Chicago, 1978-82; Fisk Univ, Nashville TN, "Ethel L Payne," professorship in journalism, 1982-83; columnist, free lance writer, 1982-. **ORGANIZATIONS:** Honorary mem, Delta Sigma Theta Sorority, 1973; bd mem, Africare, Washington DC, 1983-. **HONORS/ACHIEVEMENTS:** First Prize, Illinois Prees Assn (series on adoptions), 1952; Third Annual World Understanding Award, Chicago Council on Foreign Relations, 1956; Outstanding Reporting, Windy City Press Club 1957; Capial Press Club Award for Vietnam Report Washington DC, 1967; author of: A Profile on Black Colleges, "Roots, Rewards, Renewal," published under the auspices of Delta Sigma Theta Sorority and George Johnson, Chicago, 1980; report on women refugees in Somalia, Sudan, Zambia and Zimbabwe, sponsored by Africare and the Bd of Global Ministries, United Methodist Church, 1982; Candace Award, Coalition of 100 Women, 1988; elected to Washington DC Women's Hall of Fame, 1988, Black Press Hall of Fame, 1988. **HOME ADDRESS:** 6101-16th St NW, Washington, DC 20011.

PAYNE, FREDA
Singer, nightclub performer. **PERSONAL:** Born 1944, Detroit, MI; married Gregory Abbott; children: Gregory Jr. **CAREER:** Invictus Record Co, artist. **ORGANIZATIONS:** Appeared in Hallelujah Baby; on tour with Quincy Jones, Duke Ellington Orchs; worked with Billy Eckstine/Bob Crosby; num nightclubs TV shows.

PAYNE, JAMES FLOYD
Higher education administrator. **PERSONAL:** Born Jul 19, 1943, Boonville, IN; married Madelyn Brown; children: Detra, Niambi. **EDUCATION:** Los Angeles City Coll, AA 1968; CA State Univ-Los Angeles, BA 1970; Harvard Univ, MEd 1971; Univ of CA-Irvine, PhD 1975. **CAREER:** California State Univ-Los Angeles, coordinator of advanced educ and occupational services 1968-70; Harvard Univ and Educational Development Center, rsch assoc 1970-71; California State-Univ Los Angeles, asst prof 1971-82; Oregon State System of

Higher Educ, asst in academic and student affairs 1984-86, asst vice chancellor for curricular affairs 1986-. **ORGANIZATIONS:** Mem, Natl Council for Black Studies, 1976-84; bd dirs, California Black Faculty & Staff Assn, 1979-81. **HONORS/ACHIEVEMENTS:** Regents Fellowship, Univ of California-Irvine, 1974. **MILITARY SERVICE:** USMC cpl-E4, 1961-65. **BUSINESS ADDRESS:** Assistant Vice Chancellor, Oregon State Sys of Higher Ed, PO Box 3175, Eugene, OR 97403.

PAYNE, JERRY OSCAR
School administrator. **PERSONAL:** Born Jul 31, 1955, Madera, CA; son of Oscar Payne, Jr and Sallie Ophilia Smiley-Payne; married Monette Balkzagar, Oct 30, 1982; children: Deidre Avery, Jonathan. **EDUCATION:** San Jose State Univ, San Jose CA, BA, 1975; Arizona State Univ, Tempe AZ, MA, 1978; Lewis and Clark Coll, Portland OR, education administration certification, 1984. **CAREER:** El Dorado High School, Las Vegas NV, special education instructor, 1978-80; Clark County Classroom Teachers Assn, Las Vegas, negotiations chairman, 1978-80; Grant High School, Portland OR, special education instructor, 1980-83; Benson Polytecyhnic High School, Portland, integration counselor, 1983-84, admin asst to principal, 1984-87; Lincoln Summer High School, Portland, principal, summers, 1985-87; Martin Luther King, Jr, Junior High School, Sacramento CA, principal, 1987-. **ORGANIZATIONS:** Association for California Administrators; Association for Supervision and Curriculum Development; American Association of School Administrators; member of Commision of Local School Administrators, chairman of Affiliate Council, National Alliance of Black School Educators; American Vocational Association; National Council of Local Administrators of Vocational, Technical and Practical Arts Education. **BUSINESS ADDRESS:** Principal, Martin Luther King Jr Junior High School, 3051 Fairfield St, Sacramento, CA 95838.

PAYNE, JESSE JAMES
Association executive, clergyman. **PERSONAL:** Born Apr 26, 1947, Fayette, AL; son of R P Payne and Lydia R Payne; married Regina Ann Payne, Apr 13, 1989; children: Robert, Yolanda, Jesse III, Jarred. **EDUCATION:** Univ of Nebraska, Lincoln NE, BS, 1973, MS, 1977, attended, 1981-84. **CAREER:** Lincoln Public Schools, Lincoln Ne, teacher, 1973-75; Lincoln Action Program, Lincoln NE, exec dir, 1975-78; Nebraska Dept of Educ, Lincoln NE, program dir, 1980-81; Kansas State Univ, Manhattan KS, assoc prof, 1981; Lincoln OIC, Lincoln NE, exec dir, 1982-84; Newman Methodist Church, Lincoln NE, pastor, 1982-84; Urban League of Broward County, Ft Lauderdale FL, pres/CEO, 1986-. **ORGANIZATIONS:** Mem, Couuncil of Chief Exec, Natl Urban League, Council of Exec, United Way of Broward County, Vision "94" Comm, City of Ft Lauderdale, BETA Indus Council, City of Ft Lauderdale, Health Access Comm, Broward County Bd Comm, NAACP, 1980-, Natl Urban League, 1986-, Leadership Broward Alumni Assn, 1987-. **HONORS/ACHIEVEMENTS:** Graduated with Honors, Univ of Nebraska-Lincoln, 1973. **BUSINESS ADDRESS:** President and Chief Executive Oficer, Urban League of Broward County, 11 NW 36th Ave, Fort Lauderdale, FL 33311.

PAYNE, JUNE EVELYN
Psychologist. **PERSONAL:** Born Jun 11, 1948, Charlottesville, VA; daughter of Walter A. Payne and Theola Reaves Payne; married Charles R Payne EdD; children: Lauren R, Gregory A. **EDUCATION:** VA State Univ, BA 1970; Ball State Univ, MA 1974, PhD 1980. **CAREER:** Charlottesville Dept of Public Welfare, social worker 1970-72; The Cambridge House Inc, counselor 1974-75, dir of treatment 1976-78; Comprehensive Mental Health Serv of East Central IN, psych 1980-83; Ball State Univ Counseling and Psychological Serv Ctr, counseling psychologist 1983-. **ORGANIZATIONS:** Pres, mem, sec 1984-85 IN Assoc of Black Psych; mem bd of dir Wapahani Girl Scout Council; mem NAACP, Riley-Jones Womens Organization, Delta Sigma Theta Sor. **HOME ADDRESS:** 2905 W Woodbridge, Muncie, IN 47304. **BUSINESS ADDRESS:** Counseling Psychologist, Ball StateUniv, Counseling & Psychological Serv, Muncie, IN 47306.

PAYNE, LESLIE
Journalist. **PERSONAL:** Born Jul 12, 1941, Tuscaloosa, AL; married Violet S Cameron; children: Tamara Olympia, Jamal Kenyatta, Haile Kipchoge. **EDUCATION:** Univ of Connecticut, BA Eng 1964. **CAREER:** "Newsday," natl correspondent/columnist 1980-, investigative reporter 1972-80, minor affairs specialist, 1973-78, editor, writer 1971, asst editor 1970, Babylon Town Beat reporter 1969. **ORGANIZATIONS:** Mem Natl Assn of Black Journalists 1978; mem NY Assn of Black Journalists, 1977-80. **HONORS/ACHIEVEMENTS:** Bronze Star, 2 commednation medals, AUS 1968; published "The Heroin Trail" & "Life & Death of the Symbionese Liberation Army"; received Pulitzer Prize Headliner Awd 1974; Sigma Delta Chi Awd 1974; Tobenkin Awd Columbia Univ 1978; Man of the Year Award, Natl Assn Black Business & Professional Women 1978; Frederick Douglass Prize, Natl Assn of Black Journalists 1978; Journalism Prize, 100 Black Men; 2 Unity Awards Lincoln Univ; Pulitzer Prize for Foreign Reporting 1978. **MILITARY SERVICE:** AUS capt 6 yrs. **BUSINESS ADDRESS:** Asst Managing Editor, Newsday, 235 Pinelawn Rd, Melville, NY 11747.

PAYNE, MARGARET RALSTON
Educator. **PERSONAL:** Born Jan 31, 1946, Louisville, KY; daughter of Henry Morris Ralston and Rena Owens Ralston; married James Edward Payne, Dec 11, 1976; children: Maya Renee. **EDUCATION:** Kalamazoo Coll, BA 1968; Fourah Bay Coll Univ of Sierra Leone, attended 1966-67; Kent State Univ, MA 1972, PhD in progress. **CAREER:** Kent State Univ, asst prof psychology 1972-78, adjunct asst prof psychology 1978-, asst dean prof for developmental services 1973-89, special asst to vice provost for student affairs, 1989-. **ORGANIZATIONS:** Mem OH & Natl Assn for Women Deans Administrs & Counselors 1979-; mem OH Planning Comm ACE Natl Identification Prog for Advancement of Women in Higher Educ Adminstrn 1983-; pres Kent Area Chap The Links Inc 1984-88; bd mem Western Reserve Girl Scout Council; bd mem Portage Co Comm Action Council 1979-85; dist advisor Natl Alpha Lambda Delta 1985-87; mem National Council Alpha Lambda Delta 1985-88; mem Natl Advisory Committee, SAGE: a scholarly journal on black women 1985-; bd mem Akron Urban League 1988-. **HONORS/ACHIEVEMENTS:** Fellow Natl Educ Policy Fellowship Prog 1979-80; Grants OH Rehabilitation Serv Commn 1974, 1975, Lilly Endowment (for NAWDAC) 1982, Fed Dept Health Educ & Welfare Dept of Educ 1974, 1978-; Service Certificate, Assn on Handicapped Student Service Programs in Post Secondary Education 1987; national finalist, White House Fellowship Program 1979; Leadership Award, Kent State University Upward Bound 1989. **HOME ADDRESS:** 797 Cliffside Drive, Akron, OH 44313. **BUSINESS ADDRESS:** Special Asst to Vice Provost for Student Affairs, Kent State Univeristy, 225 Student Services Center, Kent, OH 44242.

PAYNE, MITCHELL HOWARD
Government official. **PERSONAL:** Born Feb 02, 1950, Shelbyville, KY; son of Llewellyn Payne and Hattie Cohrell; married Dr Karen W Bearden, Jul 11, 1987; children: Janell Mitchet. **EDUCATION:** Western Kentucky Univ, Bowling Green KY, BA, 1972, MPA, 1973; Univ of Louisville, Louisville KY, JD, 1978. **CAREER:** Univ of Louisville, Louisville KY, dir minority affairs; Commonwealth of Kentucky, Frankfort KY, exec asst to sec of finance comm for admin. **ORGANIZATIONS:** Mem, Natl Bar Assn, Amer Soc for Public Admin, Natl Assn of State Dir of Admin & Gen Serv, 1987-, Kappa Alpha Psi Frat; bd mem, Prichard Comm on Academic Excellence, 1987-, Kentucky State Child Abuse & Sexual Exploitation; advisory council, Kentucky State Univ School of Public Affairs, 1987-; mem, Natl Forum for Black Public Admin, 1988-; steering comm, YMCA Black Achievers Program, 1989-; mem, Sigma Pi Phi Frat, 1989-. **HONORS/ACHIEVEMENTS:** Kappa Alpha Psi Frat Alumni Achievement Award, 9185; Dr Martin Luther King Appreciation Award, Western Kentucky Univ, 1986; Alpha Kappa Alpha Sorority (granter org)- "Men Who Cook," 1988; Volunteer of the Year, Louisville YMCA Black Achievers, 1989; Shelbyville KY Black Achiever of the Year Award, NAACP, 1989. **BUSINESS ADDRESS:** Commissioner, Commonwealth of Kentucky, Dept for Administration Finance and Administration Cabinet, #238 Annex Bldg, Frankfort, KY 40601.

PAYNE, OSBORNE ALLEN
Business executive. **PERSONAL:** Born May 26, 1925, Bedford, VA; married Famebridge Cunningham; children: Andrea Kyles, Famebridge S, Sarita S. **EDUCATION:** VA Union Univ, BS 1950, VA State Univ MS 1955; Univ of VA, 1961; Univ of MD, 1974. **CAREER:** Richmond, VA, tchr 1950-57, principal 1957-62; Cuttington Coll Liberia, W Africa, act dean of instr 1963-65; TAP Roanoke, VA, field dir 1965-66, educ dir 1966-68; NEA Search, dir 1968-70; NEA Special Svcs, field coord 1970-73; Natl Educ Assn, consumer adv 1974-75; Baltimore-Specialty Tours, pres; Broadway-Payne Inc, pres. **ORGANIZATIONS:** Pres Baltimore City McDonald's; mem McDonald's Balt Market Coop; bd mem Natl Black McDonald's Operators Assn 1978-82; bd of dir VA Union Univ 1980; bd of assoc St Paul's Coll 1983; mem Pres's Roundtable; mem Greate Balt Comm 1984-; bd of dir The Fund for Educ Excellence 1984; United Way 1984;bd of governors Natl Aquarium 1985; mem United Way 1985; Arena Players 1985; bd of dir Baltimore Museum of Art 1986; bd of dir Natl Conference of Christians & Jews 1986. **HONORS/ACHIEVEMENTS:** Golden Arch Elite McDonald's 1976-77; Governor's Citation for Outstanding Serv MD 1982; Presidential Citation Natl Assn for Equal Oppty in Higher Educ 1983;Senator's Citation for Many Years of Dedicated Serv to the Community 1984; Presidents Citation, Baltimore City Cncl 1985; Citations MD Senate, Governors MD, Citizens by Mayor WD Schaefer, MD Black Caucus 1985; Honorary Degree Dr of Intl Law, 1985; Citations Md House of Delegates, 41st Dist Baltimore, Congressional Merit, US Senate, 1985; Businessman of the Year Intl Assn of Negro & Professional Women; "An Evening With" honoree Project Survival 1985; Ronald McDonald Awd for community involvement 1985; small business awd by Mayor of Baltimore 1985; Baltimore Mktg Assoc Man of the Year 1985. **MILITARY SERVICE:** USN 3rd Class Petty Officer 1943-46. **BUSINESS ADDRESS:** President, Broadway-Payne, Inc, 11 West North Ave, Baltimore, MD 21201.

PAYNE, SAMUEL, SR.
Government official. **PERSONAL:** Born Jun 16, 1919, Zion, IL; son of Samuel Lincoln Payne and Dora Smith; married Pearl V Darnell; children: Richard, Robert, Irene, Samuel Jr. **EDUCATION:** Lake Forest Coll, attnd. **CAREER:** Mem of bd Lke Co Dist #3 1972-; US Steel Wire Co 37 yrs. **ORGANIZATIONS:** Mem Zion Boy Scouts 1949-55; mem Zion Pub Library Bd 1958-62; Spl Zion Police 1958-68; mem Zion Christian Bus Men Com; mem bd of adv Zion Bento Hosp; found mem Mt Zion Missionary Bapt Ch. **HONORS/ACHIEVEMENTS:** 1st Black elem sch bd mem 1970; 1st Black mem bd Lake Co Bd 1972. Special Citizen Award, City of Zion, 1975; Special Citizen Award Mt Lebannon Lodge #715 1985; instrumental in making the first Lake County documentary for the preservation of Lake County's Natural Resources, 1988.

PAYNE, VERNON
Athletic coach. **PERSONAL:** Born Apr 20, 1945, Michigan City, IN; married Dorphine; children: Linda, David, Arthur. **EDUCATION:** Indiana State Univ, BS Educ 1968. **CAREER:** NBC TV, Color Commentator 1970-71; Indiana Univ, Graduate Asst Basketball Coach 1970-71; ABC TV, Commentator 1971-72; Indiana Univ, Assoc Instructor 1971-72; Univ of Denver, Asst Basketball Coach 1972-73; Michigan State Univ, Asst Basketball Coach 1974-77; Wayne State Univ, Head Bsktbl Coach 1977-81, Dir Intercollegiate Athletics/Hd Bsktbl Coach 1981; Western Mich Univ, Head Bsktbl Coach 1982- . **ORGANIZATIONS:** Wayne State Univ, Presidents Select Blue Ribbon Task force on Athletics;Univ Task force on Women's Rights; Edison Comm Corp Detroit, Chairman Personnel; Greater Lansing Urban League Speakers Bureau; LaPorte Cnty Shelterd Work Shop, Brd of Directors; Michigan City Youth Coord Council, Brd & Vice Chairman; Greater MichYMCA Bldg Fund, Group Leader; Michigan City Planned Parenthood Assoc, Brd of Directors; Lakeland Improv Assoc Counsultant. **HONORS/ACHIEVEMENTS:** Indiana Daily Student, Selected as one of twenty outstanding men of sr class 1968; LG Balfour Award for honor and distinction in Indiana Univ athletics 1966-67 and 1967-68; Indiana Univ Bsktbl, Captain & MVP 1967-68; Omega Psi Phi, Secretary. **HOME ADDRESS:** 131 E Candlewyck Dr, Apt 115, Kalamazoo, MI 49001. **BUSINESS ADDRESS:** Head Basketball Coach, Western Michigan University, Kalamazoo, MI 490083899.

PAYNE, WILFORD ALEXANDER
Chief executive officer. **PERSONAL:** Born Jan 04, 1945, Youngstown, OH. **EDUCATION:** Blufton Coll Blufton OH, attnd 1963-65; Youngstown StateUniv OH, bA Soc 1973; OH State U, MHA 1975. **CAREER:** Primary Care Hlth Serv Inc Alma Illery Med Ctr Pittsburgh, proj dir 1977-; Monongahela Valley Assn of Hlth Cntrs Inc Fairmont WV, admin asst 1976-77; Monongahela Valley Assn of Hlth Cntrs Inc, hlth main coord 1976-77; OH StateUniv Hosp Columbus, admin asst 1975; St Joseph's Riverside Hosp Warren OH, admin resident 1974. **ORGANIZATIONS:** Bd of dir Eastern Allegheny Co Hlth Corp 1977-; bd of dir Family Plng Counc of Southwestern PA 1977-; instr Tri Reg Cluster Training Cntr NY 1979-; mem Nat Assn of Comm Hlth Cntrs Inc 1977-; com mem Untd Way Review Com of Plng & Allocations Com present. **HONORS/ACHIEVEMENTS:** Awd Who's Who in AmUniv & Coll 1973; scholar Hlth & Welfare Assn 1973-75. **MILITARY SERVICE:** USAF sgt 1966-70. **BUSINESS ADDRESS:** Primary Care & Health Services, 7227 Hamilton Ave, Pittsburgh, PA 15208.

PAYTON, ALBERT LEVERN
Scientist. **PERSONAL:** Born Feb 08, 1944, Hattiesburg, MS; married Maggie Belle Smith;

children: Al Michaelis, Andriae Monique. **EDUCATION:** Alcorn StateUniv Lorman MS, BS 1965; SoUniv Baton Rouge LA, MS 1969;Univ of So MS, PhD 1976. **CAREER:** MS Valley State Univ, asso prof of chem 1974-; Univ of So MS, teaching & research asst chem 1971-74; Dillard Univ New Orleans, instr chem math 1969-71; So Univ Baton Rouge, teaching asst chem 1967-69; Hattiesburg Public School MS, high school teacher chem phys 1965-67; NSF High School Teachers Training Prog Alcorn State Univ, chem lab instr 1965; MS Test Fac, materl analy 1966. **ORGANIZATIONS:** Mem & undergrad adv Beta Kappa Chi Scientific Soc 1979; Am Men & Women of Sci Jacques Cattell Press Tempe AZ 1979. **HONORS/ACHIEVEMENTS:** Outstndg Young Men of Am 1979; resrch article lithium-Amine reduction journal of org chem acs 1979; resrch grant acetylenic acid syntheses Nat Sci Found 1978-81. **BUSINESS ADDRESS:** Hwy 82 W, Itta Bena, MS 38941.

PAYTON, BENJAMIN FRANKLIN
Educator. **PERSONAL:** Born Dec 27, 1932, Orangeburg, SC; son of Sarah M Payton; married Thelma Plane; children: Mark Steven, Deborah Elizabeth. **EDUCATION:** SC State Coll, BA (honors) 1955; Harvard Univ, BD 1958; Columbia Univ, MA 1960; Yale Univ, PhD 1963. **CAREER:** Howard Univ, asst prof 1963-65; Office of Church & Race The Protestant Council of NY, dir 1965-66; Commn on Religion & Race Dept Natl Cncl of Churches in USA, exec dir of social justice 1966-72; Benedict Coll, pres 1967-72; The Ford Found, prog officer 1972-81; Tuskegee Univ, pres 1981-. **ORGANIZATIONS:** Dir Am South Bancorporation; dir Natl Assn for Equal Oppor in Higher Educ; mem AL Industl Relations Cncl; dir Phelps-Stokes Fund; dir Nat'l Assoc ofIndependent Coll and Univ; dir Southern Reg Council; mem Bd of Visitors of the Wm Jewett Tucker Found; mem Business-Higher Education Forum; mem CorpVisiting Comm for the Dept of Humanities-MIT; mem Amer Soc of Scholars; mem Exec Bd of the Nat'l Consortium for Educ Access; mem Leadership Alabama; dir, ITT Corp, 1987-; dir, Challenger Center for Space Science Educ, 1988-. **HONORS/ACHIEVEMENTS:** Phi Beta Kappa Delta of Morehouse Atlanta; Alpha Kappa Mu Honor Soc SC State Coll; Hon Degrees, Eastern MI, Morris Brown, Benedict, Morgan State; FellowshipDanforth Graduate Fellowship 1955-63; Napoleon Hill Foundation Gold Medal Award 1987; Benjamin E Mays Award, South Carolina State College 1988; Team Leader, Presidential Task Force on Agricultural Development in Zaire, 1984; Educational Advisor to VP George Bush, Seven Nation Tour of Africa, 1982. **HOME ADDRESS:** 399 Montgomery Rd, Tuskegee, AL 36083. **BUSINESS ADDRESS:** President, Tuskegee University, Kresge Center, Tuskegee, AL 36088.

PAYTON, CAROLYN ROBERTSON
Educator. **PERSONAL:** Born May 13, 1925, Norfolk, VA; daughter of LeRoy Robertson and Bertha Robertson; married Raymond Rudolph (divorced). **EDUCATION:** Bennett Coll, BS 1945; Univ WI Madison, MS 1948; Columbia Univ Tchrs Coll, EdD 1962; Lake Erie Coll for Women, LLD 1978. **CAREER:** Howard Univ, asst psych prof 1959-64; US Peace Corps, chief field selection ofcr 1964-66; Peace Corps Eastern Caribbean, dep dir to dir 1966-71 Howard Univ Counseling Svcs, dir 1970-78; US Peace Corps, dir 1978-79; Howard Univ Counseling Svcs, dean 1980-. **ORGANIZATIONS:** Dir Ctr for Multicultural Awareness 1979; sec DC Psychologist's Examiners Bd 1980-83; mem DC Commn on Homelessness 1984-87; chair & mem Comm on Scientific & Professional Ethnics & Conduct APA 1972-77. **HONORS/ACHIEVEMENTS:** Apptd by Pres of USA to Bd of Dirs of the Inter-American Found 1978-82; Disting Professional Contributions to Public Serv Awd APA 1982; publ "Who Must Do the Hard Things?" Amer Psychologist 39 391-397 1984. **BUSINESS ADDRESS:** Dean, Counseling & Career Dev, HowardUniv, 6th & Bryant St NW, Washington, DC 20059.

PAYTON, JEFF
Attorney. **PERSONAL:** Born Sep 11, 1946, Canton, MS; married Carol E Rooks. **EDUCATION:** Ashland Coll, BS 1969; John Carroll U, attnd; John Marshall Coll of Law-Cleveland State U, JD 1975. **CAREER:** Richland Co Legal Serv, dir 1977-; Cleveland Legal Aid Soc, atty staff 1975-77; US Dept of Just, legal intern 1972-73; Cleveland HS OH, biology instr 1969-71. **ORGANIZATIONS:** Mem OH State Bar Assn; mem Richland Co Bar Assn; bd of trustees Ashland Alumni Assn; bd of trustees Planned Parenthood Assn 1979-; bd of trustees Heritage Trls Girl Scouts Counc 1979-; bd of trustees Richland Co Juvenile Just Commn 1980; mem exec com Mansfield Chap NAACP; chmn NAACP Legal Redress Commn. **BUSINESS ADDRESS:** Richland Co Legal Servs, 35 N Park St, Mansfield, OH 44902.

PAYTON, NOLAN H.
Attorney. **PERSONAL:** Born Dec 23, 1919; children: 1 Child. **EDUCATION:** AZ St, BA; USC, MA 1940; Am Clg Life Undrwrtrs, CLU 1954, LlB 1962. **CAREER:** Golden St Mut Life Ins, agnt 1938-42, mgmt 1942-49; Priv Prac, atty 1969-. **ORGANIZATIONS:** Mem Twn Ha; Am Bar Assc; Bvrly Hills Bar Assc; Langston Law Assc; LA Cnty Bar Assc; Lwyrs Clb of LA; SW Bar Assc; Am Arbrtn Assc; Sigma Lambda Sigma; Alpha Phi Alphi; mem Alpha Mu Gamma. **BUSINESS ADDRESS:** Payton Law Center, 1728 W King Blvd, Los Angeles, CA 90062.

PAYTON, VICTOR EMMANUEL
Physician. **PERSONAL:** Born Jun 03, 1948, Savannah, GA; married Gwendolyn Middleton Payton; children: Khary, Kurlen, Kurtis, Kalere. **EDUCATION:** Mercer Univ Macon, GA, BS Chem 1971; Med Clg of GA Augusta, MD 1975. **CAREER:** Noble Army Hosp Ft McClellan, AL, pediatrician 1978-; Tripler Army Med Ctr Honolulu, residency (pediatrics) 1977-78; Med Clg of GA Augusta, residency (pediatrics) 1976-77, intrnshp (pediatrics) 1975-76; Dept of Human Resources, Georgia Retardation Center, Athens, GA, medical director 1981-. **ORGANIZATIONS:** Flw Natl Bd of Ed Examiners; candidate mem Am Acad of Pediatrics; pres, Advisory Committee, Head Start 1987-. **MILITARY SERVICE:** AUS capt 1978-81; Army Commendation Medal, 1980. **BUSINESS ADDRESS:** Dr Victor E Payton, MD, PC, 1270 Prince Ave, Suite 302, Athens, GA 30606.

PAYTON, WALTER JERRY (SWEETNESS)
Professional athlete. **PERSONAL:** Born Jul 25, 1954, Columbia, MS; married Connie; children: Jarrett, Brittney. **EDUCATION:** Jackson State U, BA Communications. **CAREER:** Walter Payton Enterprises Investments, owner 1979; Chicago Bears, running back 1975-. **ORGANIZATIONS:** Hon chmn IL Mental Health Assoc 1978-80; aids with the Boy Scouts, March of Dimes, Piccolo Rsch Fund, United Way, Peace Corps; hon chmn Heart Assoc Jump Rope for Heart 1983; hon chmn Ben Wilson Memorial Dinner 1985. **HONORS/ACHIEVEMENTS:** Youngest player to be voted NFL MVP 1977; NFC Player of the Year Sporting News 1976-77; NFC Player of Yr UPI 1977; NFC All-Star Team 1976-78; NFL MVP 1978; 6th All Time NFL Rushing Yards 8,178 1980; selected All-Pro by TSN, PFW, Football Digest, AP, NEA, UPI, PFWA; broke club record for career receptions; broke Brown's record for most 100 yard games in career (58), now has 63 in 10 yrs; owns league single game rushing record of 275 yds; owns 23 Bear records, 7 NFL records (rushing, combined yards, most 100 yard games, single game, rushing attempts) & shares another 8 1,000 yard seasons w/Harris; has back-to-back 2,000 yards combined during 1983-84 seasons; Chicago Red Cloud Athlete of the Year; UPI Athlete of the Year; NEA Thorpe Trophy, Mutual Radio, AP, FB Digest, Sport Mag NFL Player of the Year, AP NFL most valuable offensive player; unanimous choice to NFC Pro Bowl squad; Pro FB Weekly Offensive Player of the Year; Seagram's "Oscar" Awd for football; WI Pro Football Lombardi Dedication Awd 1983; Black Athlete of the Yr voted on by black media members nationwide 1984; biography "Sweetness" published 1978 by Contemporary Books; player NFL Pro Bowl teams 1986, 1987. **BUSINESS ADDRESS:** Chicago Bears, 55 E Jackson St, Ste 1200, Chicago, IL 60604.

PAYTON, WILLIS CONWELL
Attorney. **PERSONAL:** Born Feb 09, 1923, Grifton, NC; son of Sidney Payton and Lillian Payton; married Mary E; children: Paula. **EDUCATION:** NC Cntrl Univ, 3 yrs; Terrell Law Sch, LLB 1950. **CAREER:** Cortez Peters Bus Coll, prof 1950-52; Pvt Practice, atty 1952-; Payton & Vance, attorney. **ORGANIZATIONS:** Mem Natl Bar Assn; Washington Bar Assn DC Bar Assn; VA Bar Assn; Old Dominion Bar Assn 1952; mem Sigma Delta Tau Legal 1947-;Univ S Supreme Ct Bar &Virgina Bar. **HONORS/ACHIEVEMENTS:** Juvenile ct award 1960. **BUSINESS ADDRESS:** Attorney, Payton & Vance, 733 15th St, N W, Washington, DC 20005.

PEACE, EULA H.
Educator. **PERSONAL:** Born Jul 22, 1920, Norfolk, VA; children: Wesley H III. **EDUCATION:** VA Union U, VA St Coll & NJ St Tchr Coll, grad. **CAREER:** City of Playground, teacher; World Book, mgr. **ORGANIZATIONS:** Norfolk Chap Assn of Coll Women; pres former bd mem League Women Voters & Demo Women's Club; pres Norfolk Club Assn of Negro Bus & Prof Women ; mem Phi Delta Kappa; city-wide Girls' Week 1948-68; bd mem Hunterville Heighborhood Cntr 1974; adv bd mem Area III Model City Prog 1974; Demo Committeewoman 1968-77; City Dem Com 1972-74; build rep Educ Assn of Norfolk 1973-80; del VA Educ Assn 1974-80; mem VA Educ Assn Women in Educ 1977-78; del Nat Educ Assn 1978-80; sec/treas Dist 19 Yr of the Child 1978-80; part Gov Conf on Edn; bd mem Educ Assn of Norfolk; chrprsn Women in Edn-Educ Assnof Norfolk; mem Legisltr & Polit Action Commn/Women Abuse Com/Mental Retard Assn/Children in Need Com/ Les Gemmes Civic & Soc Club. **HONORS/ACHIEVEMENTS:** Who's Who in Am Women 1974-75; Dictionary 1971; Commun Ldrshp 1960; city coord for Gov's campaign.

PEACE, G. EARL, JR.
Educator, scientist. **PERSONAL:** Born Feb 04, 1945, Norfolk, VA; son of George E Peace and Margaret Douthit Peace; married Renee Marlene Filas; children: Trevor Daniel, Nicole K. **EDUCATION:** Lafayette Coll, BS Chem 1966; Univ of IL at Urbana-Champaign, MS Chem 1968, PhD Analyt Chem 1971. **CAREER:** Lafayette Coll, asst prof of chem 1971-78, assoc prof of chem 1978-79; CO State Univ, vstg assoc prof chem 1985-86; Coll of the Holy Cross, assoc prof of chem 1979-. **ORGANIZATIONS:** Mem of exec com NE Assn of Advisors to the Health Prof 1974-79; mem Citizen Adv Council to the PA Dept of Environ Resources 1976-79; mem American Chemical Society 1967-; mem American Assoc for the Advancement of Science 1979-; mem Shrewsbury (MA) Conservation Commission 1989-. **HONORS/ACHIEVEMENTS:** Rsch Grants Natl Sci Found 1972, 1974; Student Govt Superior Teaching Awd Lafayette Coll Student Govt 1974; Citizens Adv Council PA Dept of Env Res(named by Gov Milton Shapp) 1976-79; AAAS/EPA Environmental Sci & Engrg Fellow 1981; Summer Faculty Rsch Fellowship; Amer Cyanamid Corp CEEOP Rsch Grant1986-87. **MILITARY SERVICE:** USAAF/SCEEE 1980. **BUSINESS ADDRESS:** Associate Professor, College of the Holy Cross, 218D Oberlin Hall Dept of Chem, Worcester, MA 01610.

PEAGLER, FREDERICK DOUGLASS
Educator. **PERSONAL:** Born Mar 23, 1922, New Milford, CT; married Dr Joyce Reese; children: Douglass Frederick Jr. **EDUCATION:** Wilberforce Univ, 1940-43; Howard Univ, DDS 1948; Univ of MN, MSD 1965. **CAREER:** Private Practice, 1953-59; Howard Univ, prof 1960-73; Univ of MN, visiting prof 1973-74; Job Corps, consul lab dept; Natl Cancer Inst, consul; St Elizabeth Hosp, consul; Howard Univ, dent educ prof 1974-. **ORGANIZATIONS:** Mem pres Amer Assn for Cancer Educ; fellow Amer Acad of Oral Pathology, ADA, Amer Cancer Soc, Amer Coll of Dentists, Amer Acad of Oral Pathology; mem Sigma Xi, Omicron Kappa Upsilon. **HONORS/ACHIEVEMENTS:** Harold Krogh Awd Amer Cancer Soc. **MILITARY SERVICE:** USAF capt 1949-53. **BUSINESS ADDRESS:** Dental Education Professor, HowardUniv, 600 W St NW, Washington, DC 20059.

PEAGLER, OWEN F.
Educator. **PERSONAL:** Born Nov 28, 1935, New Milford, CT; son of Robert J. Peagler and Myrtle Gary Peagler; married Teresa Balough; children: Catherine Ann, Robert G, Kirin E. **EDUCATION:** Western CT State Univ, BS 1956; New York Univ, MA 1958, Prof diploma 1962. **CAREER:** NY State Office of Economics, deputy director; New York City Metro Area Opportunity 1966-69; Pace Univ, dean school of continuing educ 1969-78; Dept of Comm Affairs Delaware, sec 1982-83; Eastern CT State Univ, dean school of continuing educ. **ORGANIZATIONS:** Pres 70001 Development Found 1975-; bd dirs 70001 Training & Employment Inst 1975-; chmn President's Adv Council on Disadvantaged Children 1973-80; vice chairman, bd of dir of the 70001 Training and Employment Institute 1988-. **HONORS/ACHIEVEMENTS:** Young Man of the Yr NY State Jr Chamber of Commerce 1964; Distinguished Serv Awd White Plains NY JCC 1964; Science Fellowship Weslyan Univ 1956; outstanding educator CT Natl Guard 1988. **BUSINESS ADDRESS:** Eastern Connecticut State University, Dean, School of Continuing Education, State of Connecticut, Willimantic, CT 06226.

PEAKE, EDWARD JAMES, JR.
International director. **PERSONAL:** Born Jan 19, 1933, Akron, OH; son of Edward J Peake, Sr. and Minnie L Peake; married Louise; children: Teresa E, Linda K, Kenneth T. **EDUCATION:** Akron Univ, Fin 1965-69. **CAREER:** Goodyear Tire & Rubber Co, rubber

worker-tirebuilder 1950-; US Dept of Labor, team mgr 1967-68; United Rubbers Workers Intl, field rep, spec rep 1969-75,dir fair practices dept 1975-78, dir pension & ins dept 1978-80; United Rubber Workers Intl, pres 1980, dir fair practices 1983. **ORGANIZATIONS:** Bd mem Natl Urban League Akron, AIA Homes Inc; life mem Alpha Phi Alpha Frat Eta Tau Chap Akron; mem Natl Labor Comm NAACP, Natl Oper Comm, A Philip Randolph Inst; urw rep Leadership Conf on Civil Rights; bd mem Akron Comm Serv Ctr & Urban League; natl bd A Philip Randolph; state and local bd of APRI. **MILITARY SERVICE:** AUS pfc 1954-56. **BUSINESS ADDRESS:** Dir Fair Practices, United Rubber Workers Intl, 87 S High St, Akron, OH 44308.

PEARCE, RICHARD ALLEN
Business executive. **PERSONAL:** Born Oct 04, 1951, New York, NY; married Lois A Mayo; children: Alysia Daphine, Ryki Desiree. **EDUCATION:** Hampton Inst, BS 1973;Univ Bridgeport, MBA; Williams Sch of Banking. **CAREER:** State Natl Bank, admn ofcr; Union Trust Co, tres; Carteret Savings & Loan Assc asst mgr; carver fed savings & loan assc, admn asst. **ORGANIZATIONS:** Bd dir Hampton Alumni Fed Credit Union 1973-74; Alpha Phi Alpha; Dean of Mens Stf Concert Clg Chapel Choirs; Karate Clb; 1969 Track Team; Bus Clb; MensAssc; Hampton Inst Concert Master; Hampton Concert Choir 1972; Dean of Pledges Gamma Iota Chap Alpha Phi Alpha 1973. **BUSINESS ADDRESS:** Colonial Bancorp Inc, 81 W Main St, Waterbury, CT 06702.

PEARSON, CLIFTON
Educator. **PERSONAL:** Born Jun 24, 1948, Birmingham, AL; married Clementene Hodge; children: Monica Denise, Clifton Anderson. **EDUCATION:** AL A&MUniv Normal AL, BS in Art 1970; IL State U, MS 1971, EdD in Art 1974. **CAREER:** AL A&M Univ, chmn/assc prof 1974-; Art Dept AL A&M Univ, acting chmn 1973-74; IL State Univ, grad teaching asst 1971-73. **ORGANIZATIONS:** Consultant, Art More Than 10 Coll & Univ 1973-; creator & host Educ TV Series "For Art's Sake" 1976; mem Natl Art Educ Assn 1973; mem Natl Conf of Artist 1975; bd mem, Huntsville Museum of Art 1978-. **HONORS/ACHIEVEMENTS:** Ford fellowship, Ford Found NY; southern fellowship, Southern Fellowship Fund; Acad fellowship, IL State Univ; acad scholarship, AL A&M Univ. **BUSINESS ADDRESS:** AL A&M University, Normal, AL 35762.

PEARSON, DREW
Athlete. **PERSONAL:** Born Jan 12, 1951, S River, NJ; married Marsha Kaye Haynes; children: Tori, Britni. **EDUCATION:** Tulsa U, Grad 1973. **CAREER:** Dallas Cowboys, wide receiver 1973-; CBS Sports, color commentator; Smokey's Express Barbecue Rest, partner; Drew Pearson Enterprises, president/owner. **ORGANIZATIONS:** Past chmn March of Dimes Crusade; natl spokesman Distilled Spirits Cncl; serves Pres's Com for Advancement of Underpriviledged Youth; NFL Champ Game 1973, 75; Pro Bowl 1974, 76 , 77; All Pro 1974-77; Offensive Co-capt 1977-78; Passes Caught 188 for 3,103 Yds 18 Td's; 165 Yds Avg Per Catch in 56 Games.

PEARSON, HERMAN B.
City contract coordinator. **PERSONAL:** Born Mar 02, 1947, Omaha; divorced; children: Nicole, Carmen, Selina, Quatica. **EDUCATION:** Univ of NE, BS 1972. **CAREER:** Minister 1973-; Mayor's Ofc City of Omaha, contract coord. **ORGANIZATIONS:** Evaluator Mental Retardation Pgm; Comm Ldr Among Young Adults; Professional Ftbl Plyr Washington Redskins 1972; professional dj co-founder First Black Owned Radio Station Omaha Area 1969; asst pastor Tabernacle Bapt Ch Council Bluff, IA; Recreational Activities Ldr; mem NATRA. **BUSINESS ADDRESS:** 723 N 18 St, Omaha, NE 68111.

PEARSON, JAMES A.
Judge. **PERSONAL:** Born Apr 25, 1925, Cincinnati, OH; married Julia Carter; children: 4 children. **EDUCATION:** OH State Univ, BS 1951, LLB 1953, JD 1969. **CAREER:** Private practice, 1953-55; Franklin Cty Probate Court, chief dep 1955-61, asst pros 1961-69, judge 1969-. **ORGANIZATIONS:** Mem OH & Columbus Bar Assoc, OH Mun Judges Assoc, Amer Judicature Soc, Robert B Elliott Law Club; bd trustees Maryhaven Inc; bd govs Columbus Bar Assoc; mem Columbus Area Leadership Lab; mem bd trustees Cath Social Svcs, J Ashburn Jr Youth Ctr, Franklin Cty Com Criminal Justice. **MILITARY SERVICE:** USN 1943-46. **BUSINESS ADDRESS:** Judge, Franklin Cty Municipal Court, 375 S High St, 14th Floor Courtroom 14D, Columbus, OH 43215.

PEARSON, JESSE S.
Controller. **PERSONAL:** Born Apr 24, 1923, Gasden, AL; married Mary Lee; children: Milbrun, Eric Hart, Peter Hart, Kelli Hart. **EDUCATION:** Wayne State Univ, BS Bus Admin 1969. **CAREER:** Highland Park Genl Hosp, deputy dir 1971; Bon Secours Hosp, asst controller 1967-71, controller 1971-. **ORGANIZATIONS:** Dir Homemaker's Agency MI 1982-83; dir Agape House Hartford Ch 1985; natl bd mem Health Care Financial Mgmt Assn 1978-80; pres Eastern MI Chap HFMA 1976-77. **HONORS/ACHIEVEMENTS:** William G Follmer Awd HFMA Eastern MI 1974; Robert Reeves Awd HFMA Eastern MI 1978; Frederick C Muncie Awd HFFMA Eastern MI 1981; Ernest C Laetz Awd HFMA 5 MI Chapts 1978. **MILITARY SERVICE:** AUS sgt, 2 yrs; South Pacific Combat Ribbon. **HOME ADDRESS:** 20467 Basil, Detroit, MI 48235. **BUSINESS ADDRESS:** Controller, Bon Secours Hosp, 468 Cadieux, Grosse Pointe, MI 48230.

PEARSON, MARILYN RUTH
Financial consultant. **PERSONAL:** Born Nov 12, 1955, Saginaw, MI; daughter of Hollis Townsend and Bernice Richard Townsend; married Tommie L Pearson, Sr, Aug 09, 1975; children: Tamara Bernice, Tommie L Jr. **EDUCATION:** Saginaw Valley State Univ, University Center MI, BA, 1978. **CAREER:** Ford Motor Credit Co, Saginaw MI, credit investigator, 1977-80; Merrill Lynch, Saginaw MI, financial consultant, 1980-84, New York NY, sr training consultant, 1984-87, Princeton NJ, AVP mgr sel & devel, 1987-. **ORGANIZATIONS:** First vice pres, Zeta Phi Beta Sorority Epsilon XI Zeta, 1980-; Executive Club Merrill Lynch, 1981-82; mem, President's Club, Merrill Lynch, 1983; Natl Assn Securities Professionals, 1987-; bd mem, Jr Achievement of Mercer County, 1987-; bd mem, Literacy Volunteers of Amer State NJ, 1988-; bd mem, YWCA, Trenton, 1989-; mem, NAACP; mem, Shiloh Baptist Church. **HONORS/ACHIEVEMENTS:** Achievement Award Natl Assn of Negro Business & Prof Women, 1982; designed, developed and implemented Auditors Training Program, 1984; creative director for Black FC ads; nominated for 1988 CEBA Award; Zeta of the Year Epsilon Xi Zeta Zeta Phi Beta Sorority, 1988; Faith, Hope & Charity Award, FAI HO CHA, Trenton NJ, 1988; featured in Merrill Lynch ad in Black Enterprise, Essence, Ebony, 1988-89; Intl Business & Professional Women Dolars & Sense, 1989; Black Achievers in the Industry Award, Harlem Branch YMCA, 1989; special tributes from State of Michigan and Mercer County NJ. **BUSINESS ADDRESS:** AVP Financial Consultant Training, Merrill Lynch, PO Box 9032, Princeton, NJ 08543-9032.

PEARSON, MICHAEL NOVEL
Senior loan review officer. **PERSONAL:** Born Feb 12, 1956, Memphis, TN. **EDUCATION:** Fisk Univ, BS 1978; Pepperdine Univ, MBA 1980; Coll for Financial Planning, CFP 1984. **CAREER:** Ford Motor Credit Co, cust acct rep 1978-79; M-Bank Houston NA, energy loan officer 1981-83; Pearson Assoc, financial planner 1982-; First City Bank Corp, sr loan review officer 1984-. **ORGANIZATIONS:** Series 7 Registered Rep Lowry Financial Serv Corp 1986; Life Health Disability Ins license State of TX 1986; Registered Investment Adviser US Securities & Exchange Commn 1986; treas Natl Black MBA Assoc Houston Chap 1987; mem Alpha Phi Alpha Frat; mem Inst of Certified Financial Planners, Intl Assoc ofFinancial Planners, Urban Bankers Assoc; adjunct instr Amer Inst of Banking Houston Chapt. **HONORS/ACHIEVEMENTS:** Young Achiever Awd Riverside General Hosp 1986; Human Enrichment Awd Human Enrichment of Life Progs Inc 1987. **HOME ADDRESS:** 2011 Spenwick, Houston, TX 77055.

PEARSON, PRESTON JAMES
Company executive, former professional athlete. **PERSONAL:** Born Jan 17, 1945, Freeport, IL; married Linda; children: Gregory, Matthew. **EDUCATION:** Univ IL. **CAREER:** Dallas Cowboys, running back 1975-; Pitts Stealers, 1970-75; Baltimore Colts, 1967-70; Preston Pearson Inc, owner; Time Inc & Am Tel Communication, mktg exec. **ORGANIZATIONS:** Fndr tres Consult Mgmt Enterpises; Played Super Bowl 1968; NFL Champ Game 1968 1974-75; Led NFL in Kickoff Returns Ave 351 Yds; Kickoff Returns for Td's 2;No Kickoff Returns 31 1969; Set Clb Receiving Record for a Running Back 46 Catches 1977. **HONORS/ACHIEVEMENTS:** Broke His Own Record 47 Catches 1978; Only Player to Appear in Super Bowl with 3 Different Teams. **BUSINESS ADDRESS:** President, KeJay Enterprises, Inc, 9304 Forest Lane, #119, Dallas, TX 75243.

PEARSON, STANLEY E.
Physician. **PERSONAL:** Born Oct 21, 1949, Quitman, GA; son of Rev Oliver Pearson, Jr. and Mattie A. Bowles. **EDUCATION:** Univ of FL Gainesville, attended 1967-71; Meharry Medical Coll, MD 1975. **CAREER:** Providence Hospital, residency 1975-78; Fitzsimons Army Medical Ctr, fellowship 1978-80; Landstahl Army Regional Medical Ctr West Germany, chief cardiology serv 1981-83; United States Army Europe 7th Medical Command, cardiology consultant 1982-83; Madigan Army Medical Ctr, staff cardiologist 1983-84; CIGNA Health Plan of Arizona; dir cardiac rehab 1984-, chief of staff 1986-88; chmn, department of internal medicine 1988-. **ORGANIZATIONS:** Mem Alpha Omega Alpha Honor Med Soc; fellow Amer College of Cardiology; mem Colorado Medical Soc, Tau Epsilon Phi Frat; chairman, Department of Internal Medicine Dec. 1988-. **HONORS/ACHIEVEMENTS:** Diplomate Amer Bd of Internal Medicine 1978, Amer Bd of Internal Medicine Cardiovascular Disease 1981. **MILITARY SERVICE:** US Army, lieutenant colonel, 6 years; Army Commendation Medal 1st Oak Leaf Cluster. **BUSINESS ADDRESS:** Chairman, Department of Internal Medicine, CIGNA Health Plan of Arizona, Phoenix Div, McDowell Health Care Facility, 755 E McDowell Rd, Phoenix, AZ 85006.

PEASE, DENISE LOUISE
Financial institution regulator. **PERSONAL:** Born Mar 15, 1953, Bronx, NY; daughter of William Henry Pease, Jr and Louise Marion Caswell Pease. **EDUCATION:** Columbia Univ, New York NY, BA, 1980; Columbia Univ Graduate School of Business, Special Certificate, 1982; Bernard Barauch Graduate School of Public Administration, 1982-83. **CAREER:** Elmcor Youth & Adult Activities, dir of community services, 1980-82; Essex County, Newark NJ, special asst to county exec, 1982-83; New York State Department of Banks, urban analyst III, 1983-86, exec asst to supt 1986-87; deputy supt, 1987-. **ORGANIZATIONS:** Bd mem, Handier, 1974-; mem, Governor's Economic Devel Sub-Cabinet, 1985-; bd mem, Cornell Univ Cooperative Extention Advisory Comm, 1986-; bd mem, Elcor Youth & Adult Activities, 1986-87; mem, Coalition of 100 Black Women, 1988-; life mem, Natl Council of Negro Women, 1988-; representative, Governor's, Housing Policy Cabinet, 1989; mem, Financial Women's Assn, 1989. **HONORS/ACHIEVEMENTS:** Outstanding Young Women of America, 1979-81; Professional Achievement Award, Natl Assn of Negro Business and Professional Women, 1980; Charles H Revson Fellow on the Future of New York, Columbia Univ, 1981; Natl Urban Fellow, Natl Urban Fellows Org, 1982; Citation of Merit, New York State Assembly, 1989. **BUSINESS ADDRESS:** Deputy Supt, New York State Dept of Banking, 2 Rector St, 18th Floor, New York, NY 10006.

PEAVY, JOHN W., JR.
Judge. **PERSONAL:** Born Apr 28, 1943, Houston, TX; married Diane Massey; children: 4 Children. **EDUCATION:** Howard Univ, AB 1964; Howard Univ School of Law, Postgraduate 1964-67. **CAREER:** Natl Aero & Space Council, The White House, Washington DC, acct, 1961-64, admin asst 1964-67; Berry Lott Peavy & Williams, practice law 1967-72; Harris Cty Comm Action Assoc, assoc field coordinator, 1967-68; County Judge Bill Elliott, exec asst 1968-70; Home Pilot Program, Amer Bar Assn, Houston Bar Assn funded by Ford Found HUD Houston, assoc counsel for projects 1970-71; Harris County Court Precinct 7, judge-justice of the peace position 2 1973-77; 246th Dist Judicial Dist Ct Harris County Houston, judge. **ORGANIZATIONS:** Chmn WL Davis Div Sam Houston Boy Scouts 1976; mem Alpha Phi Alpha, Urban League, Harris Cty Council of Orgs; life mem NAACP; mem nom comm Houston Bus & Professional Men's Club, YMCA Century Club; former dem precinct chmn Precinct 292 Houston TX; mem adv bd KYOK Radio Sta; legal adv Riverside Lion's Club;mem bd of dir Mercy Hosp; mem steering comm A Phillip Randolph Inst; mem bd of dir Houston Citizens Chamber of Commerce, Project Pull, Eliza JohnsonCtr for the Aged, So Ctr Br YMCA, United Negro Coll Fund, Julia C Hester House, St Elizabeth Hosp, Houston Council of Human Rel, Volunteers of Amer;appt mem Housing Asst Tech Adv Group 1974; hon co-chmn Citizens for Better Transit 1978; mem Downtown Rotary Club of Houston, Urban Policy Task Force for the City of Houston 1978; mem Pol Action Comm Houston Lawyers Assoc; mem bd of dir Natl Bar Found, Houston Bar Assoc, Natl Bar Assoc, Amer Bar Assoc, State Bar of TX, Jr Bar Assoc of Houston, St Jr Bar Small Claims Court Handbook Comm 1977, State Bar TX Ct Reorg Comm, Judicial Council. **HONORS/ACHIEVEMENTS:** Outstanding Military Student Chicago Tribune Award; Contributor, Most to the Comm YMCA; Acad Scholarship to Howard Univ School of Law; Eagle Scout & mem Order of the Arrow of Boy Scouts of Amer 1960; Distinguished Achievers Award

YMCA 1973, 1977; YMCA Award for Outstanding Serv to the Community 1974, Certificate of Citation by the State of TX House of Reps 1975; Natl Judicial Intl Achievement Award; Houston Lawyers Assn Achievement Award, 1980; Outstanding Young Business & Professional Man, Houston Young Adult Club, 1979; Appreciation Award, Exploring Div, Sam Houston Area BSA, 1979. **BUSINESS ADDRESS:** Judge, State District Court, 246th Dist, 1115 Congress, Houston, TX 77002.

PEAY, FRANCIS
Football coach. **PERSONAL:** Born in Pittsburgh, PA; married Patricia; children: Aryca, Aisha. **CAREER:** Professional football player with New York Giants, Green Bay Packers, Kansas City Chiefs; Univ Sr HS in St Louis, defensive coord; Notre Dame, jr varsity and offensive line coach; Univ of CA, outside linebacker coach; Northwestern Univ, defensive coordinator, head coach. **BUSINESS ADDRESS:** Head Coach, Northwestern University, 633 Clark St, Evanston, IL 60201.

PEAY, ISAAC CHARLES, SR.
Clergyman. **PERSONAL:** Born Jun 03, 1910, Stone Co, MS; married Velma L Bluitt; children: Minnie Lee Purnell, Isaac Charles Jr, Mary Nell, Robert James, Sylvia Hennings, James Hennings. **EDUCATION:** MS Bapt Sem, BTh 1948, MCT 1949, ThM 1951, ThD 1953; Jackson Clg, BS 1953; MS Bapt Sem, DD 1960; MO Bapt Clg, LlD 1979. **CAREER:** Galilee Bapt Ch St Louis, MO, pastor 1954-80; MO Bapt Clg St Louis, tchr 1975-80; MO Bapt Messenger, edtr 1968-74; Mt Zion Bapt Ch Hattiesburg, MS, pastor 1950; Friendship Bapt Ch Laurel, MS, pastor 1943. **ORGANIZATIONS:** Dir fndr Beautification Youth Corps Inc 1968; vice moderator Berean Dist Assc 1973; vice pres Missionary Bapt State Convention of MO 1979; vice pres Conf on Religion & Race 1966; pres Bapt Ministers Union 1967, 77; mem Mayor's Commn on Human Relations 1968. **HONORS/ACHIEVEMENTS:** "Stewardship Made simple" Copyrighted 1969; minister of yr awrd St Louis Argus Nwspr 1972; 50 yr pastorate & awrd MO Bapt State Conv of MO 1979; 20 yr awrd St Louis Bapt Missionary Flwshp 1979. **BUSINESS ADDRESS:** Galilee Baptist Church, 4300 Delmar Blvd, St Louis, MO 63108.

PEAY, SAMUEL
Judge. **PERSONAL:** Born Jun 02, 1939, Ridgeway, SC; son of English Peay and Geneva Peay; married Lillian Bernice Chavis; children: Clifton Delmineo, Ira Aloysius. **EDUCATION:** Basic Law Enforcement Training, certificate; Univ of Nevada Nat'l Judicial Acad 1985, 1986. **CAREER:** Richland Co Sheriff's Dept Cola SC, dep sheriff 1964, 1st Black sgt in law enforcement 1969, juvenile/arson/criminal invest 1971-78; Magistrate's Court, judge. **ORGANIZATIONS:** Mem Nat Sheriff's Assn, SC Law Enforcement Assn, SC Magistrate's Assn, life mem; Richland Cnty Magisterial Assoc, pres 1986-88; Nat'l Judges Assoc, vice chairman, bd of deacons, & chairman; Zion Canaan Baptist Church, Columbia SC, family activities comm. **HONORS/ACHIEVEMENTS:** Nat'l Council of Negro Women, honored as outstanding South Crolinan 1980; featured in article-"Judges Plus" Feb 1985 issue of The Carolina Reporter 1985; honored by Capital City Lodge #47 Columbia SC 1985; Optimist Club of Columbia, "Respect for Law" awd 1986; Dept of Military Sci Army ROTC, Benedict Coll Serv awd 1986. **BUSINESS ADDRESS:** Magistrate's Court, 4919 Rhett St, Columbia, SC 29203.

PECK, DOUGLAS ROBERT
Program coordinator. **PERSONAL:** Born Nov 16, 1960, Cleveland, OH. **EDUCATION:** Univ of Cincinnati, BS Urban Planning & Design 1984; Natl Academy of Voluntarism, Certificate 1985. **CAREER:** City of Cleveland, intern Dept of Comm Dev 1982; intern Office of the City Manager 1983-84; intern City Planning Commission 1984; Community Chest & Council,planner/project coordinator. **ORGANIZATIONS:** Member Alpha Phi Alpha Frat, Inc 1980-; member Ohio Citizens Council 1984-85; coordinator Greater Cincinnati Emergency Services 1984-85; alternate Citizens Committee on Youth 1984-85; member Conference of Minority Public Admin 1984-85; member Natl Forum of Black Public Admin 1984-85; member Amer Planning Assoc 1985. **BUSINESS ADDRESS:** Planner/Project Coordinator, Community Chest & Council, 2400 Reading Road, Cincinnati, OH 45202.

PECK, GREGORY LESTER
Director. **PERSONAL:** Born Mar 31, 1952, Bronx, NY; married Judith Crayton. **EDUCATION:** OH Wesleyan U, BA 1970-74; Bowling Green State, MA 1975-76. **CAREER:** Columbia Promotion CBS Records, natl dir; CBS Recrods, reg promotion mgr 1979; CBS Records Chgo, local promotion mgr 1977-79; Atlantic Records Cleveland,local promotion mgr 1976-77. **ORGANIZATIONS:** Elem tchr NY Bd of Ed 1974-75; 3rd Class FCC Broadcast License/Common Br Tchng License NY; MVP Football Dewitt Clinton HS Bronx 1970. **BUSINESS ADDRESS:** CBS Records, 51 W 52nd St, New York, NY 10019.

PEDEN, S. T., JR.
Company representative. **PERSONAL:** Born Aug 19, 1944, Greenville, SC; married Carolyn Brown; children: Seldon Tremayne. **EDUCATION:** SC State Clg, BS 1966. **CAREER:** Gen Elec Co, rep pers relations 1968-; EI DuPont Co, accnt 1966. **ORGANIZATIONS:** Mem Am Soc for Pers Admn; Greenville Area Pers Assc; chmn Black Cncl for Progress; vice pres Greenville Br of NAACP; pres bd dir Phillis Wheatley Ctr; mem bd dirs Op PUSH Greenville; mem bd dir SC Cncl on Human Rights. **HONORS/ACHIEVEMENTS:** Recip outst young men of am awrd 1972; comm ldrs & noteworthy am awrd 1974. **MILITARY SERVICE:** AUS spec 4th cls e-4 1966-68. **BUSINESS ADDRESS:** PO Box 648, Greenville, SC 29602.

PEEBLES, ALLIE MUSE
Educator. **PERSONAL:** Born Apr 12, 1926, Danville, VA; daughter of William Brown Muse and Maude Smith Muse; married Millard R. Peebles, Sr., Aug 16, 1947 (deceased); children: Martha Elaine Peebles Brown, Brenda LaVerne, Millard R., Jr.. **EDUCATION:** Hampton Univ, Hampton VA, BS, 1943-47; St. Augustine's Coll, Raleigh NC, certificate renewal; attended North Carolina Central Univ, Durham NC, 1965-69; North Carolina State Univ, Raleigh NC, certificate renewal. **CAREER:** Prince Edward County School System, Farmville VA, English teacher, 1947-48; Raleigh-Wake County School System, Raleigh NC, English teacher, 1963-78; M. R. Peebles and Son Masonry Contractors, Raleigh, owner and pres, 1978-82; Telamon Corp, Smithfield NC, job counselor, 1983-86; The Carolinian (newspaper), Raleigh, columnist, 1984-; St. Augustine's Coll, Raleigh, English instructor, 1987-. **ORGANIZATIONS:** Mem, Martin St Baptist Church Choir, 1955-; pres 1962-64, 1984-86, vice pres, 1979-84, Raleigh Hampton Univ Alumn Assn; treas, Jack and Jill of America, 1966-68; mem 1969-, sec, 1972-74, chmn of publicity and public relations 1985-89, Delta Sigma Theta-Raleigh Alumnae Chapter; chmn of nat recruitment 1978-82, 2nd vice pres of NC region 1983-89, Nat Hampton Alumni Assn; life mem and chmn, Raleigh-Apex NAACP, 1978-; mem, Wake County Private Industry Council, 1980-82; mem, Raleigh Civil Service Commision, 1980-82; board mem, YWCA of Wake County, 1980-86; consultant, Women in Communication workshop, 1987; mem, Delta's Nat Comm on Neritage and Archives; solicitor for several fundraising drives; volunteer for voter registration and political candidates. **HONORS/ACHIEVEMENTS:** NC Hamptonian of the Year Award, Hampton Univ, 1974; mem, Million Dollar Club, NAACP, 1981-89; recognition of service from nat office of NAACP; writes column, "Raleigh's Social Scene," for local black paper; editor-in-chief, "Tar-Heel AHamptonian," NC newsletter of Nat Hampton Alumni Assn. **BUSINESS ADDRESS:** Instructor, St. Augustine's College, 1315 Oakwood Ave, Raleigh, NC 27610.

PEEBLES-MEYERS, HELEN MARJORIE
Physician. **PERSONAL:** Born Oct 06, 1915, New York, NY; daughter of James Peebles and Elizabeth Peebles; married Frederic Rickstord Meyers, Dec 27, 1939 (deceased); children: Joy V Lilly. **EDUCATION:** Hunter Coll, BA 1937; Columbia Univ, MA 1938; Howard Univ Med Sch, 1938-40; Wayne State Univ Sch of Med, MD 1943. **CAREER:** Detroit Gen Hosp, intern 1943, asst resident, resident 1944-47; private practice 1947-77; Hutzel Hosp, sr attending physician; Evang Deaconess Hosp courtesy staff; Alexander Blain Hosp, cons; Wayne State Univ, clinical assoc prof; Ford Motor Co World Headquarters, chief physician retired 1985. **ORGANIZATIONS:** Bd mem MI Heart Assn 1966-71; treas Detroit Adventure 1969-71; past bd of govs Wayne State Univ Med Sch Alumni Assn 1970-72; mem Nat Med Assn; del to MI State Med Soc from Wayne Co Med Soc; AMA; Wayne Co Med Assn; Am Diabetes Assn on Com on Prgm & Planning; MI Diabetes Assn; Fdrs Soc of Detroit Inst of Arts; Oakland Univ Arts Soc; Detroit Symphony Orch; bd dir Amer Diabetes Assn; United Found; Detroit Urban League; Nghbrhd Serv Organizations; Arts Commn Detroit Inst of Arts; exec bd Mt Carmel Hosp Med Alumni Assn; United Com on Negro History. **HONORS/ACHIEVEMENTS:** Hall of Fame Hunter Coll 1977; YWCA Metro Detroit 1978; Alpha Kappa Alpha Patron of the Arts Awd 1982; Mercy Medallion Mercy Coll of Detroit 1983; DowntownYWCA 1984; Focus and Impact Awd Black Awareness Month Comm Oakland Univ 1984; Summit Awd Greater Detroit C of C 1984; Detroit Urban Center Awd 1985; President's Cabinet Awd Univ of Detroit 1985; Heritage Awd in Med Little Rock Baptish Church 1985; Union of Black Episcopalians 1985; Disting Warrior Awd Detroit Urban League 1986; MI Women's Hall of Fame 1986; Spirit of Detroit Awd 1986; One of Amer Top 100 Citizens Newsweek Mag 1986. **HOME ADDRESS:** 1321 Nicolet, Detroit, MI 48207.

PEEBLES-WILKINS, WILMA CECELIA
Educator. **PERSONAL:** Born Apr 21, 1945, Raleigh, NC; married James Alexander Wilkins; children: Keith, Kenneth. **EDUCATION:** NC State Univ, BA, 1967; Case Western Reserve Univ, MSSA, 1971; Univ of NC at Chapel Hill, PhD 1984. **CAREER:** Cuyahoga Co Div of Child Welfare, social worker 1967-72; Mental Develop Ctr, dir of intake 1972-76; Eastern KY Univ, asst prof 1976-77; NC Memorial Hosp, chief pediatric social worker 1977-78; NC State Univ, assoc prof of social work 1978-. **ORGANIZATIONS:** Mem Natl Assoc of Black Social Workers 1976-; consultant Wake Co Council on Aging 1979, Raleigh Housing Authority 1979; vice chairperson NC Certification Bd for Social Work 1984-; competence certification bd Natl Assoc of Social Workers 1984-; commn on minority group concerns Council on Social Work Education 1985-87. **HONORS/ACHIEVEMENTS:** Irene Sogg Gross Serv Awd 1971; Swedish Intl Fellowship for Youth Leaders/Social Workers 1980; articles in Encyclopedia of Social Work, Black Caucus Journal, Children and Youth Services Review, Journal of Education for Social Work. **HOME ADDRESS:** 2620 Cottage Circle, Raleigh, NC 27612. **BUSINESS ADDRESS:** Assoc Prof of Social Work, North Carolina StateUniv, Box 8107, Raleigh, NC 27695.

PEEK, BOOKER C.
Educator. **PERSONAL:** Born May 22, 1940, Jacksonville, FL; married Annette Jones; children: Cheryl, Joseph, Angela. **EDUCATION:** FL A&M U, BA; Oberlin Coll, MAT;Univ FL, further study; Case Wessstern Reserve. **CAREER:** Hampton Jr Coll, teacher; Matthew W Gilbert HS; Ribault Sr High; Albany State Coll; Oberlin Coll, asst prof. **ORGANIZATIONS:** Mem Am AssnUniv & Professions; NAACP; former mem Intl Longshoremen Assn; mem Oberlin Comm Welfare Council; pres Toward Am Togerthernes Comm Orgn 1968; FL Star Tchr 1968; So Fellow 1969-70. **HONORS/ACHIEVEMENTS:** Scholarship Jacksonville Univ 1969. **BUSINESS ADDRESS:** Associate Professor, Oberlin College, Department of Black Studies, Oberlin, OH 44074.

PEEK, MARVIN E.
Educator. **PERSONAL:** Born Aug 21, 1940, Cleveland, OH; married Venice Lee Long; children: Marvin Eugene Jr, Monica Elizabeth, Marcy Evette. **EDUCATION:** Allen Univ, BA History 1964-65; IN Univ, MA History 1965-67; Univ of TN, PhD History 1971. **CAREER:** US Park Service, park ranger 1963-65; Lane Coll, chair social scis div 1970-71; Univ of TN Afro-Amer Studies, dir 1971-86, asst to the provost 1987-. **ORGANIZATIONS:** Sec Natl Cncl for Black Studies 1984-86; pres elect Assn of Social & Behavorial Scientists 1986; consul Memphis State Univ Wm Patterson Coll Comm for the Humanities; reader Natl Endowment for the Humanities; LSU Press; Univ TN Press. **HONORS/ACHIEVEMENTS:** Alpha Phi Alpha Scholarship; Ford Found Educ Study Grant; Faculty Develop Grant. **BUSINESS ADDRESS:** Asst to the Provost, Univ of TN, 812 Volunteer Blvd, Knoxville, TN 37916.

PEELE, JOHN E., JR.
Patent attorney. **PERSONAL:** Born May 19, 1934, Durham, NC; married Lucia F; children: John III, Steven, Beverly. **EDUCATION:** NC Central U, BS 1955; GeorgetownUniv Law Cntr, JD 1962. **CAREER:** Northrop Corp Hawthorne CA, pat couns 1980-; Vivitar Corp Santa Monica CA, pat couns 1977-79; Bell & Howell Co Chicago, pat atty 1963-77; US Patent & Trademark Off DC, pat & exam 1955-63. **ORGANIZATIONS:** Mem Omega Psi Phi; mem Photograph Soc of Am; mem Am Bar Assn; mem Nat Bar Assn; mem Nat Patent Law Assn. **BUSINESS ADDRESS:** Northrop Corp, 3901 W Broadway, Hawthorne, CA 90250.

PEELER, DIANE FAUSTINA
Instructor/orthopedically handicapped. **PERSONAL:** Born Mar 14, 1959, Greeneville, TN. **EDUCATION:** Univ of TN Knoxville, BS 1982; Attended, Southern Univ of New Or-

leans, Xavier Univ. **CAREER:** Orleans Parish Comm Schools, modern dance teacher 1983-85; Office of Employment & Develop, summer youth counselor 1986; Orleans Parish School Bd, instructor 1982-. **ORGANIZATIONS:** Vice pres Delta Sigma Theta Sor Inc 1980-81; physical therapy volunteer Meadowcreast Hosp 1985-86. **BUSINESS ADDRESS:** Instructor, Orleans Parish School Bd, 3411 Broadway, New Orleans, LA 70125.

PEEPLES, AUDREY RONE
Social service administrator. **PERSONAL:** Born May 22, 1939, Chicago, IL; daughter of John Drayton Rone and Thelma Shepherd Rone; married Anthony Peeples; children: Jennifer Lynn, Michael Anthony. **EDUCATION:** Univ of IL, BA; Northwestern Univ, MBA. **CAREER:** Continental Bank, trust admin 1961-72; Girls Scouts of USA, asst reg dir 1972-76; GS of Chicago, assoc exec dir 1976-83, exec dir 1983-87; exec dir YWCA of Metropolitan Chicago 1987-. **ORGANIZATIONS:** Natl bd GS of USA 1971-73; mem & sec Jack & Jill of Chicago 1973-; mem Jr Govt Bd Chicago Symphony Orchestra 1976-83; mem of bd Women in Charge 1983-, Black Exec Dir Coalition 1984-; mem Chicago Network 1988-; mem Economic Club of Chicago 1988; mem bd United Way of Chicago, 1988-. **BUSINESS ADDRESS:** YWCA of Metropolitan Chicago, 180 N Wabash, Chicago, IL 60601.

PEEPLES, DARRYL
Designer. **PERSONAL:** Born Mar 20, 1943, Detroit, MI. **EDUCATION:** Steelcase Mfg Co, 1974; Soc of Arts & Crafts, MA 1970; Tapahagen Sch of Design, cert 1967; NY Phoenix Sch of Design, MA 1967; Pratt Inst, BA 1965; Sch of Interior Design, AA 1963. **CAREER:** Inter Internat, design admin; James Hill & Co, contract specif int design sales rep; Larwin Homes Ctr, int design 1973; Sofas Inc, sr design 1969; House of Living Rooms, design consult 1968; Decors Unlimited, inter Design 1967; United Nations NYC, master design 1965; Professional Rendering Serv, design consult 1977; Environ Design of San Francisco, design adv 1977. **ORGANIZATIONS:** Mem Victorian All; Native Sons of San Francisco; 3rd World Tours House Beautiful 1969; house Restor & Remldg Show 1977; Presidio Mall 1977; Interior InterShowrooms 1977. **BUSINESS ADDRESS:** 1451 McAllister St, San Francisco, CA 94115.

PEER, WILBUR TYRONE
Educator. **PERSONAL:** Born Apr 28, 1951, Lee County, AR; married Patricia Nelson; children: Andre B, Yolanda, Wilbur T II. **EDUCATION:** AM&N College, BA History & Govt 1973. **CAREER:** Phillips College, vet counselor 1974-76; Lee County Coop clinic, project mgr 1976-81; Phillips County Comm Coll, voc counselor 1982-. **ORGANIZATIONS:** Owner/oper Wilbur Peer Farm 1977-; justice of the peace Lee County quorum Court 1980-; owner/broker Wilbur T Peer Realty Co 1982-; exec dir Delta Improvement 1982-; PIC mem East AR Private Industry Council 1983-. **HONORS/ACHIEVEMENTS:** Mem Phi Beta Sigma 1972l. **MILITARY SERVICE:** USAR 1lt transportation 8 yrs. **HOME ADDRESS:** P O Box 34, La Grange, AR 72352. **BUSINESS ADDRESS:** Justice of the Peace, 33 N Poplar St, Marianna, AR 72360.

PEERY, BENJAMIN FRANKLIN, JR.
Astronomer. **PERSONAL:** Born Mar 04, 1922, St Joseph, MO; married Darnelle; children: Yvany. **EDUCATION:** Univ of Minnesota, bachelor's degree in physics 1949; Fisk Univ, MA 1955; Univ of Michigan, PhD 1962. **CAREER:** Howard Univ, prof 1977-; Indiana Univ, prof 1959-76; Univ of Michigan, instr 1958; Agricultural & Techical Coll of North Carolina, instr 1951-53; California Inst of Tech, visiting assoc 1969-70; Harvard Univ, visiting assoc prof 1971; Kitt Peak Natl Observer, visiting research astronomist 1975-76. **ORGANIZATIONS:** Mem US Natl Comm Intl Astron Union 1972-77; mem Amer Astron Soc; chmn Comm on Manpower & Employment 1977; mem Astron Adv Panel Natl Sci Found 1974-78; consultant NSF NASA Ind Syst of Sci Instr Florida State Univ; writ Elem Sch Sci Prgm 1961-66; participant Visiting Prof AAS 1964-; trustee Adler Planetarium; mem Astron Soc of The Pac; fellow Amer Assn for the Adv of Sci Rec; NSF Res. **HONORS/ACHIEVEMENTS:** Grants; published numerous articles in Astrophysical Journal of the Astron Soc and in Japan Astron & Astrophysics Journal. **MILITARY SERVICE:** AUS 1942-45. **BUSINESS ADDRESS:** Dept of Physics & Astron, Howard Univ, Washington, DC 20059.

PEETE, CALVIN
Professional golfer. **PERSONAL:** Born Jul 18, 1943, Detroit, MI; son of Dennis Peete and Irenia Bridgeford Peete; married Christine Sears, Oct 24, 1974; children: Charlotte, Calvin, Rickie, Dennis, Kalvanetta. **CAREER:** Worked as farm laborer in FL, 1957-60; itinerant peddler, 1961-71; professional golfer, 1971—; real estate investor. **ORGANIZATIONS:** Professional Golfers Association. **HONORS/ACHIEVEMENTS:** Eleven PGA victories, including Greater Milwaukee Open, 1979, Anheuser-Busch Classic, 1982, Phoenix Open, 1985; member, US Ryder Cup team; honorary degree, Wayne State University, 1983; Ben Hogan Award, 1983; Jackie Robinson Award, 1983; two-time winner of Vardon Award for lowest stroke average on PGA Tour; winner of awards for driving accuracy and hitting most greens in regulation number of strokes; over $1 million in career earnings. **HOME ADDRESS:** Route 21, Box 81, Tarpon Way N, Fort Myers, FL 33903. **BUSINESS ADDRESS:** Calvin Peete Enterprises, 2050 Collier Ave, Fort Myers, FL 33901. *

PEGUES, ROBERT L., JR.
Educational administrator. **PERSONAL:** Born Mar 06, 1936, Youngstown, OH; children: Tamara Pegues Brooks, Robert L III. **EDUCATION:** Youngstown State Univ, BS 1958; Westminster Coll PA, MS 1963; Kent State Univ OH, Doctoral Prog. **CAREER:** Youngstown City Schools, teacher/admin 1959-72; Educ Research Council of Amer Cleveland, OH, dir urban education 1969-70; Youngstown City Schools, superintendent 1972-78; Youngstown State Univ, dir/instr 1978-79; Warren City School Dist, supt of schools. **ORGANIZATIONS:** Bd of trustees St Elizabeth's Med Cntr Youngstown, OH; bd dir Warren Redevel & Planning Corp Warren, OH; bd dir Warren-Trumbull Urban League. **HONORS/ACHIEVEMENTS:** Humanitarian Award Trumbull Co Br NAACP 1984; Outstanding Educator Warren-Trumbull Urban League 1981; Finis E Engleman Scholarship Amer Assn of Sch Admin 1981; Bowman Fellowship Kent State Univ 1979. **MILITARY SERVICE:** AUS Capt (active & reserves) 1954-68. **BUSINESS ADDRESS:** Superintendent of Schools, Warren City School District, 261 Monroe NW, Warren, OH 44483.

PEGUES, WENNETTE WEST
City administrator. **PERSONAL:** Born Nov 25, 1936, Pittsburgh, PA; married Julius Pegues; children: Mary Pamela, Michael David, Angela Suzette. **EDUCATION:** Carlow Coll Pittsburgh, BSN 1958;Univ of Tulsa, CCS 1974;Univ of Tulsa, EdD 1978. **CAREER:** Langston Univ Urban Center, assoc acad dean 1979-80; Univ of Tulsa, asst dean 1978-79; asst dean 1976-78; Univ of Tulsa, grad Research fellow 1975-76; Univ of Tulsa, grad asst 1974-75; RN adminstr teacher & staff position 1958-74. **ORGANIZATIONS:** Mem AAUW; mem Am Personnel & Guid Assn; mem Nat Conf on Acad Advising; mem Pub Welfare Assn Sch Bd; mem Osage Co Dept Dist #55 Acad Cent Sch 1979-80; commr OK State Dept of Human Serv 1979; mem Delta Sigm Theta 1980; sch bd pres Osage Co Dept Dist #55 Acad Cent Sch 1980-81; mem bd of dir Tulsa Sr Citizens Inc 1980. **HONORS/ACHIEVEMENTS:** Educ Honor Soc Kappa Delta Outstndg Wom in the comm N Tulsa B & P Wom; Disting Alumni Serv awd in the Educ Calow Coll 1979; whoS Who Am Wom; listed Worlds Who's Who of Women; listed person of The S. **MILITARY SERVICE:** ANC 2 lt 1956-59. **BUSINESS ADDRESS:** Div Mgr - Human Development, City of Tulsa, 200 Civic Center, Tulsa, OK 74103.

PEGUESE, CHARLES R.
Librarian. **PERSONAL:** Born Aug 03, 1938, Philadelphia, PA. **EDUCATION:** LaSalle Coll Phila, BS 1960; Drexel Univ Phila, MLS 1962-65. **CAREER:** NE Area Young Adult Free Library of Phila, coord 1960-69; Action Library Learning Ctr Philadelphia Sch Dist, dir 1970-74; State Library of PA, coord networking & academic libraries 1974-. **ORGANIZATIONS:** Mem Omega Psi Phi Frat 1957-; pres bd of dirs N City Cong of Philadelphia 1966-74; comm mem PA Library Assn 1970-; comm chmn Amer Library Assn 1971; adv bd Philadelphia United Way 1972-74; mem & chair Harrisburg Historical Architectural Review Bd 1980-; mem Historic Harrisburg Assn 1980-; articles PA Library Assn Bull Library Jour. **MILITARY SERVICE:** AUS E-5 1961-66. **BUSINESS ADDRESS:** Coord Networking & Acad Lib, State Library of PA, Harrisburg, PA 17105.

PEIRSON, GWYNNE WALKER
Educator. **PERSONAL:** Born Nov 16, 1921, Oakland, CA; married Margaret Ballard; children: Kerry, Scot. **EDUCATION:** Univ of CA Berkeley, BA 1969, M Criminology 1971, D Criminology. **CAREER:** Howard Univ, asso prof soc dept 1979-; US Justice Dept Law Enforce Assist Admin Natl Minority & Adv Counc, sr research 1977-79; UMSL, lectr training dir 1970-72; Oakland CA, police officer 1947-70. **ORGANIZATIONS:** Mem res com Nat Orgn of Black Law Enforce Offic (NOBLE) 1976-; air medal (6) dist flying cross USAF 1944; pub pub Pol Oper (book) Nelson Hall Chgo1976; "The Role of the Police in Reducing Crime" Black Crime A Police View 1977, "Instit Racism & Crime Stat" Black Perspect on Crime & The Crim Justic System 1978. **MILITARY SERVICE:** USAF capt 1943-45. **BUSINESS ADDRESS:** PO Box 987, Admin Bldg, Washington, DC 20059.

PELOTE, DOROTHY B.
Elected official. **PERSONAL:** Born Dec 30, 1929, Lancaster, SC; daughter of Abraham Barnes and Ethel Green; married Maceo R Pelote (deceased); children: Deborah Pelote Allen, Miriam Pelote Heyward. **EDUCATION:** Allen Univ, BS 1953. **CAREER:** Chatham Co Bd of Educ, teacher 1956-85; Chatham Co GA, co commissioner. **ORGANIZATIONS:** Mem Legislative Study Comm for Memorial Med Ctr; pres Carver Height Organ; mem Adv Comm on Local Govt; mem Water & Sewer Auth of Chatham Co; mem Chatham Assn of Educ; mem Phi Delta Kappa Educ Frat 1978; pres Savannah Fed of Teachers 1982-83; mem Coastal Comm Food Bank; mem bd dir YMCA; bd mem United Way; mem Business and Professional Women's Club. **HONORS/ACHIEVEMENTS:** Carver Heights Comm Serv Awd 1981-82; Rep Roy Allen Awd for Excellence 1982; Zeta Phi Beta nomination for Minority Women of the Yr 1984; Dorothy Pelote Day City of Savannah & Chatham Co 1985; First Female elected Co Commission Chmn Pro Tem; mem State Bd of Postsecondary Vocational Educ by appointment of theGov of GA; Mem of the Chatham Co Employees Retirement Bd; Mem of Coastal Area Planning & Devel Commn for Seminar Agendas; electec vice pres of the Black Caucus of the Assoc of County Commissioners of GA; Testimonial Banquet by Constituents of Eighth Commission District.

PELTIER, ARMA MARTIN
Physician. **PERSONAL:** Born Apr 22, 1938, New York, NY; married Maria Virginia Gonzalez; children: Coulissa, Michelle. **EDUCATION:** Fordham U, BS 1965; Long Island U; Meharry Med Coll, MD 1973. **CAREER:** Hunter Found, intrnst 1977-; Prospect Hosp, phys 1976-77; Harlem Hosp Ctr, intrn, res 1973-76; Exlay, chemist 1965-69; Brooklyn Coll of Pharm, chem instr 1962-65; Good Samaritan, atdng phys; St Joseph; Cntrl Bapt Hosp. **ORGANIZATIONS:** Mem Nat Assn of Intrns & Rsdnts; asso Am Coll of Phys. **BUSINESS ADDRESS:** 212 N Upper, Lexington, KY 40507.

PEMBERTON, DAVID M.
Business executive. **PERSONAL:** Born Apr 24, 1926, Chicago; married Masseline; children: Diana, Debra, Denise, Kim. **CAREER:** Midwest Nat Life Ins Co, reg mgr 1965-. **ORGANIZATIONS:** Mem Life Underwriters Assn Miami; elder Bethany SDA Ch; NAACP; treas Locka Br; chmn Commun Act Nghbrhd Counc. **HONORS/ACHIEVEMENTS:** Civic awd 1969; natl qual Awd; natl & sales achvemnt awd 1974; 51st All-Star Honor Roll 1973. **BUSINESS ADDRESS:** 3900 NW 79 Ave, Miami, FL.

PEMBERTON, PRISCILLA ELIZABETH
Educator. **PERSONAL:** Born Jan 04, 1919, New York; married William. **EDUCATION:** Brooklyn Coll, BA 1952; Bank St Coll Edn, MS 1960. **CAREER:** Non-Matric Stud Bank St Coll Educ NYC, dir 1966-; NY City Pre-schs, tchr 1944-48; Intl Nurs Sch & Kinder NY, dir 1949-65; mis cler pos 1937-43; Ministry Educ British Guyana, educ consult 1962-63; One Summer's Tchr Training Barbados 1969; Pub & Ind Schs Various States, consult 1967-. **ORGANIZATIONS:** Mem Early Childhood Educ Council New York City 1961-; mem bd trustees New Lincoln Sch New York City 1971-74; mem bd trustees Clinton Pre-sch Head Start 1972-; mem Allen AME Ch Jamaica 1935-; membership NAACP 1939-50; Bus & Professional Women's Clubs 1959-64. **HONORS/ACHIEVEMENTS:** Achievement Educ Awarded by Bus & Professional Women's Clubs 1963. **BUSINESS ADDRESS:** 610 W 112 St, New York, NY 10025.

PENA, ANTONIO FRANCESCO
Professional athlete. **PERSONAL:** Born Jun 04, 1957, Monte Cristi, Dominican Republic;married Amaris; children: Tony Jr, Jennifer Amaris. **CAREER:** Pittsburgh Pirates, catcher 1980-. **HONORS/ACHIEVEMENTS:** Led all league catchers in double plays 1979; Gold Glove Awd winner 3 times; led NL catchers in putouts, assists, total chances, &

double plays; set a record, 12 stolen bases for Pirate catchers; Pirate rep on the NL All-Star team 1984; selected starting catcher on The Sporting News 1983 post-season NL All-Star team, led all NL catchers in putouts, & total chances 1983; mem NL All-Star team, NL Player of the Week for 7/4 1982; Was TOPPS Rookie All-Star catcher & mem Eastern League All-Star team; fourth major league catcher in 40 years to reach the 100 mark in assists 1985; named to Sporting News first Latin Amer All-Star Team; mem major league all-star team that toured Japan; MVP of the US squad by the Japanese mgr and coaches; Most Popular Pirate in poll of fans 1986; mem All Star Team 1982,84,85,86. **BUSINESS ADDRESS:** Pittsburgh Pirates, Three Rivers Stadium, Pittsburgh, PA 15212.

PENA, ROBERT BUBBA
Professional athlete/actor. **PERSONAL:** Born Aug 08, 1949, Wareham, MA. **EDUCATION:** Dean Jr Coll, AA, Univ of MA, BA candidate. **CAREER:** Actor, Love of Life, Dogs of War, Ft Apache, The Four Seasons; Cleveland Browns, professional football player 1971-74 traded to Kansas City Chiefs & waived then signed w/Atlanta Falcons; business ventures, Domingo's Chowder House Restaurant, W Falmoreth Fish Market, Health Club Enterprises; TV pilot, , "Street" a Lorimar Production; principal roles in various commercials; Robert Pena & Assocs, pres (real estate develop). **ORGANIZATIONS:** Founder & co-chairman of "Roche Pires Scholarship Fund"; mem Cape Verdean Club of Falmouth MA; mem Lambda Chi Alpha Frat; volunteer work Northampton Jail inMA; worked with Black students at Barnstable HS MA Jr Coll. **HONORS/ACHIEVEMENTS:** All-Amer 2 yrs; All-East 2 times; All New England 2 times; MVP 3 yrs in coll; Special Athletic Awd for Jr Coll; played in Coll All-Star Game in Lubbock TX1971; Awd from Falmouth MA Local Real Estate Beautification Comm for restoring a piece of historically zoned real estate. **BUSINESS ADDRESS:** President, Robert Pena and Assocs, 621 Main St, East Falmouth, MA 02536.

PENCEAL, BERNADETTE WHITLEY
Educator. **PERSONAL:** Born Dec 16, 1944, Lenoir, NC; daughter of Walter Andrew Whitley and Thelma Simmons Whitley; married Sam Penceal, Apr 29, 1967. **EDUCATION:** Syracuse Univ, Syracuse NY, BS, 1966; The City Coll, New York NY, MA, 1973, Letter of Completion, 1974; Fordham Univ, New York NY, PhD, 1989. **CAREER:** Fashion Inst of Technology, New York NY, instructor of English, 1973-74; Green Haven Maximum Security Prison, Stormville NY, instructor of English, 1974-76; Malcolm-King Coll, New York NY, instructor of English, 1974-78; Hunter Coll, New York NY, instructor of reading, 1974-79; Coll of New Rochelle, New Rochelle NY, instructor of English, 1977-89; New York Univ, New York NY, mentor of English, 1980-. **ORGANIZATIONS:** Mem, Assn of Black Faculty & Admin, New York Univ, 1981-, Phi Delta Kappa, 1981-; pres, Assn of Black Women in Higher Educ Inc, 1985-87, J & B Whitley's Inc, 1985-; bd mem, Urban Women's Shelter, 1985-87; mem, New York Urban League, 1987-, Amer Assn of Univ Women, 1989-. **HONORS/ACHIEVEMENTS:** "Bernadette Penceal Day," Office of the President of the Borough of Manhattan, City of New York, 1987; "Non-Intellective Factors as Predictions of Academic Performance of Non-Traditional Adult College Freshmen," 1989. **BUSINESS ADDRESS:** English Mentor, New York University, 239 Green St, 8th Floor, New York, NY 10039.

PENDER, MELVIN
Business executive. **PERSONAL:** Born Oct 31, 1937, Atlanta, GA; married Christina Marittza Diaz. **EDUCATION:** Adelphi U, BA 1976. **CAREER:** Mel Pender's Athletic Attic, bus owner 1976-; Mitre Sports, marketing coord 1985; USMA W Point, head track 1975-76; asst track coach 1970-75; Ann Mel Pender Track & Field Devel Camp, dir 1975; ITA Intl Track Assistance, professional track runner 1972-75. **ORGANIZATIONS:** Mem CRC 1977; laison for Lynwood Park Comm Group 1977; mem Extra Point Club; Atlanta Track Club; Track & Field 1964-65, 1968, 1972; intl champion Trinidad Eng Germay France Greece Austria Chile; Olympic Games 1968; Gold Medal 4x100 Meter Relay World Rec 1972, 1973, 1970; 1st black Hall of Fame 1976. **MILITARY SERVICE:** Military Serv capt 1955-76.

PENDERGRASS, EMMA H.
Attorney. **PERSONAL:** Born Jun 01, Orangeburg, SC; married Bailey Jr; children: Bailey III, Gary W. **EDUCATION:** Howard U, BS 1949; Westfield State Coll, MEd 1964; Armstrong Law Sch, JD 1976; CA Western U, phD 1976. **CAREER:** Law Office of Emma H Pendergrass, atty of law 1976-; Hayward Unified Sch Dist, career educ counselor 1971-76; Hayward Unified Sch Dist, sci tchr 1967-71; Chicopee High Sch, sci tchr 1960-67; US Govt, chemist 1955-56. **ORGANIZATIONS:** Bd of dirs Charles Houston Bar; bd of dirs YMCA Oakland 1979-; mem Nat Bar Assn; mem Delta Sigma Theta Sorority Inc 1946-; mem Alameda Co Bar Assn 1977-80; Pro Bono Serv Judicare Program Charles Houston Bar Assn 1977-80. **BUSINESS ADDRESS:** One Kaiser Plaza, Ste 1135, Oakland, CA 94612.

PENDERGRASS, MARGARET E.
Librarian. **PERSONAL:** Born Aug 09, 1912, Springfield, IL. **EDUCATION:** Hampton Inst, BS 1934; Extra Mural Courses in Lib Sci 1967-68; LaSalle U, certificate in computer programming 1972. **CAREER:** Phyllis Wheatley Br, br libr 1934-41; War Dept Ft Custer, army libr 1941-43; Camp Ellis 1943-45; Camp Miles Standish 1945-46; Camp Joyce Kilmer 1946-49; IL State Libr, cataloger 1950-57; head juvenile unit 1957-70; Head Children's Book Reviewing Ctr, asst ref libr 1970-73; Order Libr, Juvenile cataloger 1973-79; Ault Books & Spcl Proj "Fed Doc Switching Proj", catalouger 1979-; IL State Library, librarian. **ORGANIZATIONS:** Mem Am Libr Assn 1942-44, 1950-; past pres & sec Springfield Lib Club 1953-; mem Springfield Chap NAACP 1954-; v chmn Children's Sect IL Libr Assn 1956-57; chmn Edit Com James Weldon Johnson Study Guild 1962-; chmn of Children's Sect 1957-58; mem Belleville Springfield Chap Cath Lib Assn; asst sec Order of Golden Circle 1973-; Zion Bapt Ch; pres Missionary Soc; bd mem World Federalists 1980-. **HONORS/ACHIEVEMENTS:** Citizens Award NAACP 1974; Citation Award Am Bicentennial Research Inst 1974; Certificate of Appreciation Historical Project "Black Women in the Middle West"1985. **BUSINESS ADDRESS:** Librarian, IL State Library, Centennial Bldg, Springfield, IL 62756.

PENDERGRASS, THEODORE D.
Business executive, single artist. **PERSONAL:** Born Mar 26, 1950, Philadelphia, PA; married Karin Still; children: Teddy Jr, Tisha, LaDonna, Tamon. **CAREER:** Teddy Bear Prodns Inc T-Bear Music, chmn of bd, pres 1985; Harold Melvin & Blue Notes, Teddy Pendergrass To Be True & Wake Up Everybody; Platinum Albums, "Teddy Pendergrass", "Teddy", "Life is a Song Worth Singing", "Teddy Live Coast to Coast"; Hit records incl, "The Love I Lost", "Wake Up Everybody", "If You Don't Know Me By Now", "Close The Door", "Choose Me and Hold Me". **BUSINESS ADDRESS:** President, Chmn of Bd, Teddy Bear Enterprises, 35 Rockhill Rd, Bala-Cynwyd, PA 19004.

PENDLETON, TERRY LEE
Professional athlete. **PERSONAL:** Born Jul 16, 1960, Los Angeles, CA. **CAREER:** St Louis Cardinals 3rd baseman 1982-. **ORGANIZATIONS:** 5th player to Steal 20 Bases 1984; selected Texas League All-Star Team 1983. **BUSINESS ADDRESS:** St Louis Cardinals, 250 Stadium Plaza, St Louis, MO 63102.

PENELTON, BARBARA SPENCER
Educator. **PERSONAL:** Born Apr 08, 1937, Chicago, IL; married Richard; children: Kim, Lisa. **EDUCATION:** Univ of IL, BS Elem Educ 1958;Univ of IL, MS Guidance/Counseling 1961;Univ of IN, edD Higher Educ 1977. **CAREER:** Bradley Univ Peoria IL, dir student teaching 1978-, asso prof of educ 1969-; Tri-County Urban League Peoria, dir of educ programs 1966-69; McCosh Elementary School Chicago, teacher 1958-66; Ten-year Review Team IL State Board of Educ, evaluation team Consult 1979; IL Council of Right to Read, adv/cons 1980; Rockefeller-Kellogg Found Leadership Training Project, consult 1980. **ORGANIZATIONS:** Bd of trustees Nat Urban League 1980; bd of trustees Proctor Hosp Peoria 1980; pres bd of dirs Tri County Urban League 1980. **HONORS/ACHIEVEMENTS:** Outstanding Educator Young Women's Christian Assn 1973; Outstanding Grad Adv Central Region Alpha Kappa Alpha Sorority 1975. **BUSINESS ADDRESS:** Bradley University, 1501 W Bradley Ave, Peoria, IL 61604.

PENN, CHARLES E.
Association executive. **PERSONAL:** Born Oct 10, 1928, Pittsburgh; married Mavis V; children: Robert E, Ronald L. **EDUCATION:** Bluefield State Coll WV 1951; Univ MI, BS 1957. **CAREER:** Todd-Phillips Children's Home Detroit, exec dir 1965-; MI Dept Soc Servs, child welfare wrkr 1956-59; Wayne Co Juv Ct, prob officer & counselor 1959-65. **ORGANIZATIONS:** Founder & dir Boy's Club of Inkster MI 1957-; pres MI Assn Children's Agencies 1974; bd dirs MI Council on Crime & Delinquency 1973-; bd dirs Boys Work Council 1962-64; pres People's Action Com of Inkster & Dearborn Hts MI 1971-; community resources coord Inkster Br NAACP 1973-; exec bd mem 2nd Dist Rep Nat Assn of Homes for Boys, First Black to Hold Membership & Office in Hist of Orgn; v-chmn Soc Dev Com City of Inkster 1974; 50 Anniv Medallion Services to Humanity 1970; Jaycees (Name Enshrined at Nat Jaycee Hq Tulsa, OK); Sigma Rho Sigma Honoary Soc of the Soc Scis; Alpha Phi Alpha. **HONORS/ACHIEVEMENTS:** Lafayette Allen Sr Dist Serv Award 1971; Dist Serv To Youth Wayne Co Sheriffs Assn 1972; Cert Merit Plymouth United Ch Christ 1972. **MILITARY SERVICE:** USAF 1951-55. **BUSINESS ADDRESS:** 1561 Webb Ave, Detroit, MI 48206.

PENN, JOHN GARRETT
Judge. **PERSONAL:** Born Mar 19, 1932, Pittsfield, MA; son of John Penn and Eugenia (Heyliger) Penn; married Ann Elizabeth Rollison; children: John II, Karen, David. **EDUCATION:** Univ of MA, BA 1954; Boston Univ School of Law, LLB 1957; Princeton Univ, attended; Woodrow Wilson School of Intl & Public Affairs; Natl Coll of St Judicial. **CAREER:** AUS, judge, advocate general corps 1958-61, trial attorney 1961-65, rev 1965-68, asst chief 1968-70; US Dept of Justice, general litigation section 1961-70; Court of General Sessions, judge 1970-71; Superior Court of DC, assoc judge 1970-79; US District Court for Washington DC, district judge 1979-. **ORGANIZATIONS:** DC Bar Assn, MA Bar Assn, Amer Judicial Assn, Boston Univ School of Law Alumni Assoc; fellow Princeton Univ 1967-68; honorary bd mem District of Columbia Dept of Recreation Day Care Program; boule Sigma Pi Phi. **HONORS/ACHIEVEMENTS:** Natl Inst of Public Affairs Fellow, Princeton Univ 1967-68; Outstanding Jurist, District of Columbia Bar Assn; Fort Lewis Certificate of Achievement, US Army 1960. **MILITARY SERVICE:** US Army, Judge Advocate Judges Corp, 1st lieutenant 1957-61. **BUSINESS ADDRESS:** United States District Judge, United States District Court of the District of Columbia, Third and Constitution Ave, NW, Suite 6600, Washington, DC 20001.

PENN, LUTHER
Association executive. **PERSONAL:** Born Oct 08, 1924, Barnsville, GA; married Maggie Scott; children: Cydni Charise. **EDUCATION:** Pol Sci, BA 1970; Correctional Admin, MA 1974; Wolverine Trade Sch 1946. **CAREER:** Comprehensive Offender Manpower Prog MI Dept of Corrections, asst dir; Dep Dir Corrections Dept Detroit, mayoral appointee 1975-; Criminal Jus StudiesU of Detroit, instr 1974; Employee & Indsl Rel Hygrades Corp, mgr 1971; Model Neighborhood Detroit, mgr 1969; Ford Mtr Co, supr 1964; bus consul, prog writer, invest proposal writer; Prinson Constr & Prog to Smith Henchman Grylls Architects, cons. **ORGANIZATIONS:** Pres Bramblewood Country Club Inc; mem Cotillion Club Unity Lodge; AMFM Prince Hall; Peoples Com Ch; chrtr mem Trade Union Leadership Coun; Mayors ComManpower Area Planning; Block Clubs; bd mem Self Help Prog; Indsl Rel Assn Special Asst to Gov John B Swainson 1962; consult Mayors Manpower Ofc on Ex-Offenders; mem Planning Com Model Neighborhood Prog; campaign mgr Various Candidates Local & State Ofcs. **HONORS/ACHIEVEMENTS:** Listed Intl Men of Achvmt Vol IV 1977; Notable Am 1976-77. **MILITARY SERVICE:** AUS ssgt 1943-46. **BUSINESS ADDRESS:** Box 174, Plymouth, MI.

PENN, NOLAN E.
Educator. **PERSONAL:** Born Dec 01, 1928, Shreveport, LA; married Barbara Pigford; children: Joyce, Carol. **EDUCATION:** CA State Univ, AB 1949; Univ of So CA, MS 1952; Metro State Hosp, psych intern 1955; Univ of Denver, PhD 1958; Univ of WI School of Med, Postdoctoral fellow 1959-61; Harvard Med School, Cert in Comm Mental Health 1969. **CAREER:** Larue Carter mem Hosp Indianpolis, staff psychologist 1958-59; Mendota State Hosp, staff psychologist 1961-63; Univ of WI Madison, asst prof to prof 1963-70; Univ of CA San Diego School of Med, prof of psychiatry 1970-, reg dir area health ed ctr office of the dean 1982-88; Associate Chancellor, Univ of Cal-San Diego, 1988-. **ORGANIZATIONS:** Pres WI State Psychological Assoc 1967-68; mem WI Leg Comm to recodify the Mental Health & Mental Retardation Codes 1967-70; founder & chmn Afro-Amer Studies Dept Univ of WI Madison 1969-70, Urban & Rural Studies Univ of CA San Diego 1970-73; dir Comm & Forensic Psych Trg UCSD 1974-; mem Amer Psych Assoc, Inter-Amer Soc of Psych, Sigma Xi; ed bd Jrnl of Consulting & Clinical Psych, Amer Jrnl of Publ Health perceptual and motor skills, psychological reports. **MILITARY SERVICE:** AUS corpl 1952-54. **BUSINESS**

ADDRESS: Assoc Chancellor, UCSD School of Med, Office of the Dean, Office of the Dean, La Jolla, CA 92093.

PENN, ROBERT CLARENCE
Public policy administrator. **PERSONAL:** Born Mar 06, 1943, Buffalo, NY; son of William C Penn and Jeanette Robinson Penn; married Barbara Bowman; children: Robert C Jr. **EDUCATION:** Morgan State Univ, BS 1965; Howard Univ 1967; MIT 1976. **CAREER:** US Dept of Justice, asst 1967; Manhattan, spec asst borough pres 1967-68; Sen Robert Kennedy campaign staff, mem 1968; Model Cities Agy, dir 1971-73; City of Buffalo, commr of parks 1973-75, commr human resources 1975-78; Manpower Demonstration Rsch Corp, senior vice pres 1978-85; New York Works Inc, pres 1985-86; Universal Management Consulting Grp, pres 1986-; vice pres, African American Men of Westchester Inc, 1987-; Sec/Treas MDC Inc, 1989-. **ORGANIZATIONS:** V chmn United Way of Buffalo & Erie Co; Natl League of Cities/US Conf of Mayors Vet Educ Trng; prog chmn NY State NAACP Legisl Comm; vice pres CatholicDiocese Timon Towers Hous Corp; dir Natl Child Labor Comm; NY Statewide Adv Council on Youth; Alpha Phi Alpha; Bd of dir Natl Child Labor Comm; mem MDC Inc; bd of dir and exec comm New York City Vietnam Veterans Memorial Commn; vice pres, African Amer Men of Westchester Inc, 1987-; sec/treasurer, MDC Inc, 1989-. **HONORS/ACHIEVEMENTS:** Ford Found Scholarship. **MILITARY SERVICE:** AUS 1968-71; numerous military awards. **BUSINESS ADDRESS:** President, Universal Mgmt Consulting Grp, One Don Lane, White Plains, NY 10607.

PENN, SHELTON C.
Judge, attorney. **PERSONAL:** Born Dec 09, 1925, Winston Salem, NC; married Sadie W. **EDUCATION:** Morehouse Coll, BA 1948; Univ of Mich Law School, JD 1951. **CAREER:** Attorney pvt practice 1951-75; chief asst pros attorney 1963-66; asst pros attorney Calhoun County, MI 1957-66; practicing attorney & civil rights hearing referee 1973-75; appointed judge Tenth Dist Ct Calhoun County 1975-. **ORGANIZATIONS:** Member Calhoun Co Bar Assn; MI Bar Assn; Amer Bar Assn; Natl Bar Assn; Natl Conf of Black Lawyers; past bd of dir Cripple Childrens' Soc; YMCA, Urban League, ARC; Humane Soc; Battle Creek Human Rel Comm; past pres Battle Creek NAACP; Legal Aid Soc; bd of dir South Central MI Planning Cnc ofMI Crime Comm; bd of dir Big Brothers & Big Sisters of S Central MI. **MILITARY SERVICE:** AUS WWII. **BUSINESS ADDRESS:** Judge, Hall of Justice, Battle Creek, MI 49017.

PENN-ATKINS, BARBARA A.
Business executive. **PERSONAL:** Born Nov 11, 1935, Gary, VA; married Will E Atkins; children: Lawrence Nichols, Cheryl Nichols Smith, Brian L Nichols. **EDUCATION:** MI State Univ 1954-55; Wayne State Univ 1962-64; Oakland Comm Coll, 1979; Wayne Co Comm Coll, 1977-79. **CAREER:** Univ of Detroit, adm asst; Wayne Co Comm Coll, accts rec super 1968-72; BPA Enterprises, Inc, vice pres 1972-; Pica Systems Inc, pres 1980-. **ORGANIZATIONS:** Past pres Amer Business Women's Assn/MCCC 1981; gen co-chair/MI United Negro College Fund 1983,84,85; mem allocations/review United Foundations 1983,84,85; 2nd vice pres/bd of dirs Minority Tech Council MI 1985; bd dir Detroit C of C. **HONORS/ACHIEVEMENTS:** Woman of the Year Motor City Charter Chap of Amer Bus Women's Assn 1979; Spirit of Detroit Detroit Convention Bureau 1980; Founders Awd United Negro Coll Fund 1984; Minority Business Awd MI Dept of Commerce 1984; Who's Who in the Midwest 1982-83; Who's Who of American Women 1981-82; Pioneering Business Award Natl Assn of Women Business Owners MI Chapter 1985. **BUSINESS ADDRESS:** President, Pica Systems, Inc, 19980 James Couzens Hwy, Detroit, MI 48235.

PENNICK, AURIE ALMA
Attorney. **PERSONAL:** Born Dec 22, 1947, Chicago, IL; children: Faith, Keidra. **EDUCATION:** Univ of IL, BA 1971, MA 1981; John Marshall Law Sch, JD 1986. **CAREER:** Coalition of Concerned Women Inc, exec dir 1976-78; Chicago Abused Women Coalition, exec dir 1978-81; Citizens Alert, exec dir 1981-82; Chicago Comm Trust Fellowship, staff assoc 1982-84; John D & Catherine T MacArthur Foundation, asst dir spec grant; Chicago Transit Authority Chief Adminstrative Atty. **ORGANIZATIONS:** Part time trainer Vista/Action Region V 1980-81; part time faculty Roosevelt Univ 1986-; mem Chicago Police Bd, Chicago Women in Philanthropy, Chicago Blacks in Philanthropy, Phi Alpha Delta Legal Frat; mem Cook County Bar Assoc 1988-; mem American Bar Assoc 1988-. **HONORS/ACHIEVEMENTS:** Ten Outstanding Young Citizens Chicago Jr Assoc of Commerce & Industry 1984; Kizzy Image & Achievement Awd 1985. **BUSINESS ADDRESS:** Chief Administrative Atty, Chicago Transit Authority, Merchandise Mart Suite 429A, Chicago, IL 60654.

PENNIMAN, RICHARD (LITTLE RICHARD)
Performer. **PERSONAL:** Born Dec 25, 1935, Macon, GA. **EDUCATION:** Oakwood Coll. **HONORS/ACHIEVEMENTS:** Records include Big Hits, Very Best, Together, Roots, Cast a Long Shadow, Greatest Hits & others; TV Merv Griffin, Tonight Show, Midnight Spl, Rock 'n' Roll Revival 1975; Night Dreams 1975; Dinah 1976; Tomorrow 1976; appeared Radio City Music Hall 1975; became church soloist at age 14; singer & dancer in Medicine Show age 15; won Talent contest in Atlanta 1952; became rhythm & blues recording star; featured in "Down & Out in Beverly Hills" film 1986. **BUSINESS ADDRESS:** c/o Warner Bros Records, Burbank, CA.

PENNINGTON, JESSE C.
Attorney. **PERSONAL:** Born Jul 01, 1938, Percy, MS; married Roberta; children: Bradford, Johnny. **EDUCATION:** Howard Univ, BA 1964, JD 1969; Wright Jr Coll, AA 1969; Central YMCA Real Estate Inst, certificates; Natl Coll Criminal Lawyers & Public Defenders, 1974; Regional Heber Smith Fellow, 1969-71. **CAREER:** US Postal Serv, clerk 1957-60; Seyfarth, Shaw, Fairweather & Geraldson Law Firm, office boy 1957-60; Travis Realty Co, real estate broker 1960-61; Sen Paul H Douglas, legislative asst 1964-67; Natl Labor Relations Bd, legal asst 1967-68; Fed Home Loan Bank Bd, 1968-69; Mary Holmes Coll, instr 1970-71; Northern Mississippi Rural Legal Serv, managing staff atty 1969-72; Pennington Walker & Turner, sr partner 1973-; Micronesian Legal Serv Corp, directing atty. **ORGANIZATIONS:** Mem, Mississippi Bar Assn, Iowa Bar Assn, Natl Bar Assn; Natl Conf Black Lawyers; pres, Mississippi Assn Attys Inc, 1974-; Natl Defense Lawyers Assn; bd dirs, Northern Mississippi Rural Legal Serv, 1973-; Black Appalachian Commn; Clay County Community Devel Prog Inc; mem, Trust Terr of the Pacific Bar, 1976-.

PENNINGTON, LEENETTE MORSE
Educator. **PERSONAL:** Born May 10, 1936, Webster, FL; married Bernard; children: Bernadette, Brigette. **EDUCATION:** Morgan State Coll, BS 1956; Univ of Miami, EdM 1970; Univ of FL 1974-76. **CAREER:** Elem Basic Skills Project Dade Co Public Schools Miami, project mgr 1973-; Dade Co, admin asst 1970-72; Inst Dade Co Div of Staff Dev, coord 1971; curriculum writer 1969-70; educator 1963-69; FL State Welfare, caseworker 1958-63. **ORGANIZATIONS:** Mem Adv Coun of Elem Educ FL Intl U; mem Assn of Supervision & Curriculum Dev; mem Intl Reading Assn; past pres Nat Coun of Negro Women; Sigma Gamma Rho; consult Desegration CtrUniv of Miami; mem Dade Co Comm on Status of Women; African Meth Epis Ch. **HONORS/ACHIEVEMENTS:** Recipient Outstanding Educ Achievement Award Sigma Gamma Rho 1972; Outstanding Religious Serv AME Ch 1970; Cited by Bishop Hatcher as Outstanding Young AME Churchwoman 11 Epis Dist. **BUSINESS ADDRESS:** 7100 NW 17 Ave, Miami, FL 33147.

PENNY, ROBERT
Physician. **PERSONAL:** Born Jun 06, 1935, Cincinnati, OH; son of Ralph Penny and Marie Penny; married Joselyn E; children: Angeline E Penny. **EDUCATION:** Univ of Cincinnati, BS 1959; OH State Univ, MD 1963. **CAREER:** Children's Hosp Columbus, internship pediatrics 1963-64; Children's Hosp Cincinnati, residency pediatrics 1964-66; Loma Linda Univ, instructor pediatrics 1967-68; Johns Hopkins Hosp Baltimore, fellow ped endocrinology 1968-71; Univ of So CA, asst prof ped 1971-75, assoc prof ped 1975-81, prof of pediatrics 1981-; Univ of So CA Med Cntr, dir, div of pediatric endocrinology. **ORGANIZATIONS:** Mem The Endocrine Soc; mem The Lawson Wilkins Ped Endocrine Soc; mem Soc for Pediatric Rsch; mem Amer Pediatric Soc; editorial board of AJDC 1988; associate mem The American Board of Pediatrics 1989-. **HONORS/ACHIEVEMENTS:** 47 articles in peer review journals; 8 chapters; 45 abstracts; chairperson Endocrinology Sect Western Soc for Ped Rsch 1983; question writer 1986 PediatricEndocrinology Examination; Rho Chi Soc Beta Nu Chap Cincinnati 1959; reviewer, J Endo & Metabolism, AJDC, and pediatric research. **MILITARY SERVICE:** USAF Med Corps capt 1966-68. **BUSINESS ADDRESS:** Professor of Pediatrics, Univ of So CA, 1129 North State St, Room 4E8, Los Angeles, CA 90033.

PENNY, ROBERT L.
University educator. **PERSONAL:** Born Aug 06, 1940, Opelika, AL; married Betty Jean Johnson; children: John, Robert Jr, Kadumu Jua. **EDUCATION:** Central Dist Catholic High School, 1958. **CAREER:** US Post Office, clerk 1965-67; Opportunities Indust Ctr, counselor 1967-69; Univ of Pittsburgh/Black Studies Dept, teacher 1969-, chairperson 1978-84, assoc prof. **ORGANIZATIONS:** Coord/co-founder Kuntu Writers Workshop 1976-; playright-in-residence Pittsburgh Public Theatre 1976-77; sec Pittsburgh Front for Black Unity 1980. **HONORS/ACHIEVEMENTS:** Black Tones of Truth (poetry collection) Oduduwa Prod 1970; "Little Willie Armstrong Jones" (play) Kuntu Repertory Theatre 1974; Bus & Professional Awd The Natl Assoc of Negro Business & Professional Women's Club Inc 1979; "Who Loves the Dancer" (play) The New Fed Theatre 1982. **HOME ADDRESS:** 1845 Bedford Ave, Pittsburgh, PA 15219. **BUSINESS ADDRESS:** Associate Professor, University of Pittsburgh, 230 S Bouquet St 3T01 FQ, Pittsburgh, PA 15260.

PENNYWELL, PHILLIP, JR.
Educational administrator & psychologist. **PERSONAL:** Born Aug 01, 1941, Shreveport, LA; married Janet E M; children: Phyllis, Twanda, Pamela, Phillip, Wayne. **EDUCATION:** Southern Univ, BS 1972, MEd 1974; N TX State Univ, PhD 1980. **CAREER:** Caddo Parish Sch Bd, teacher 1972-74; Parish Govt, police juror 1984-85; Southern Univ, chmn div social sci/educ. **ORGANIZATIONS:** Mem Phi Delta Kappa 1976; mem Kappa Alpha Psi Frat 1983; bd of dirs Shreveport Leadership sponsored through the Shreveport Chamber of Commerce; chmn bd of dirs Socialization Serv Inc funded through the State of Louisiana (Gerontology). **HOME ADDRESS:** 7412 McArthur Dr, Shreveport, LA 71106. **BUSINESS ADDRESS:** Chmn Div of Social Sci/Educ, SouthernUniv, 3050 Dr ML King Jr Dr, Shreveport, LA 71107.

PENTECOSTE, JOSEPH C.
Educator, psychologist. **PERSONAL:** Born Jul 30, 1918, Selma, AL; children: Joseph, Maria, Tai. **EDUCATION:** Roosevelt Univ, BA 1954; Northeastern IL Univ, MA; Purdue Univ, PhD. **CAREER:** United Farm Equipment Workers, P&E dir, 1941-52; Hall & Brock Accts, 1952-63; Better Boys Found, rsch dir 1965-70; Northeastern IL Univ, grad faculty 1969-72; IN Univ Northwest, chmn Afro-Amer studies 1972-81, minority studies 1981-. **ORGANIZATIONS:** Am Psychol Assn; Assn Black Psychologists; Am Educ Rsrch Assn; Kappa Alpha Psi Frat; editorial bd of Coll Student Jr. **HONORS/ACHIEVEMENTS:** 20 articles published in scholarly publs Psi Chi Phi Delta Kappa "Systems of Poverty" 1977, "Rats, Roaches & Extension Cords" 1977. **BUSINESS ADDRESS:** Associate Professor, IN Univ, Northwest, 3400 Broadway, Gary, IN 46408.

PEOPLES, EARL F., SR.
Community relations director, educator, account executive. **PERSONAL:** Born Oct 12, 1930, Bastrop, LA; son of Fate Peoples and Fannie Williams Peoples; married Lillie Jefferson (divorced); children: Earl F Jr, Vincent Edward. **EDUCATION:** Southern University, Baton Rouge, LA, attended 1948-50; Grambling University, Grambling, LA, BS, 1954; Cleveland State University, Cleveland, OH, grad work, 1967. **CAREER:** Galion Elem Sch, Galion, LA, teacher 1954-55; Our Lady of Christian HS, Bastrop, LA, teacher 1954-55; OH Bur Unemployment, stenographer 1958-61; Sun Finance & Loan Co, supr multilith dept 1961-69; Cleveland Urban League, employer relations rep 1969-72; Action Against Addiction Job Devel Comm, dir 1972-73; Cleveland Vocational Educ Proj, supr 1973-76; Fed Govt Emp Opportunity Commn, Detroit, investigator 1976; OH Commn on Aging, asst coord 1976-77; County Employment & Training, account exec 1977-85; NCMD, Inc, Cleveland, OH, community relations dir, 1989—. **ORGANIZATIONS:** Exec bd mem 21st Cong Dist Caucus 1972-; chmn memb com 21st Cong Dist Caucus 1972-; chmn Sr Citizen Com 21st Cong Dist Caucus; 2nd vice pres Cleveland Heights Lions Club 1980; memb chmn Cleveland Hts Lions Club 1980; bd of dir The Triangle Indsl & Econ Soc Inc of Shaker Heights Comm Ch 1980; chmn Econ Com; vice pres membshp serv Econ Com; Bd of Dir Job Serv Empl Comm for Richard Celeste; Fndr 5% Cash Refund Pilot Prgm for Senior Citizens 1987; Fndr Mr Sirloin Prgm. **HONORS/ACHIEVEMENTS:** Recipient, 21st Caucus Achievement Award, 21st Congressional Dist Caucus, 1979, 21st Caucus Small Businessmen/women Award, 1989, Businessmen/women Economics Development Award, 1989; established Willie Jackson Transportation Program for East Surburban Montessori school; established National Coalition Business Enterprise, 1988; Cleveland Black Beautiful Award, Explorer 12 Club, United

Labor Agncy; Intl Platform Speaker Ladder Awd, 1986; Appointment to Advsory Bd, Job Serv Empl Comm, by John R Tasin, Chpsn for Governor Richard Celeste. **HOME ADDRESS:** 10201 Gibson Ave, Cleveland, OH 44105.

PEOPLES, ERSKINE L.
Salesman. **PERSONAL:** Born Oct 16, 1931, Gadsden, AL; married Dorothy Thompson; children: E Ladell Jr, Tamatha M. **EDUCATION:** Mus Educ TN A&I State U, bS 1953; TN A&I State U, Addl Studies; Chattanooga Assn of Life Underwriters. **CAREER:** Mutual Benefit Life Ins Co, salesman 1966-; BT Washington HS Chattanooga, band dir 12 yrs; Security Fed Savings & Loan Assn Chattanooga, vice pres & dir 1971-. **ORGANIZATIONS:** Chmn Hamilton Co Sch Bd Chattanooga 1973-75; mem bd Greater Chattanooga C of C; Goodwill Industries Inc; Meth Neighbrohood Ctrs; deacon Mt Calvery Bapt Ch; mem Alpha Phi Alpha; Chattanooga Underwriters; pres Club Mutual Benefit Life; Man of Yr Psi Lambda 1968. **MILITARY SERVICE:** AUS spl/4 1956-58. **BUSINESS ADDRESS:** The Mutual Benefit Life Ins Co, Ste 500 Pioneer Bldg, Chattanooga, TN 37402.

PEOPLES, FLORENCE W.
Hospital supervisor. **PERSONAL:** Born Jul 21, 1940, Charleston, SC; married Earl Calvin Peoples; children: Patricia Peoples Lowe, Jonelle Elaine Washington, Deborah Simmons Jones, Sheyla Simmons, Pamela, Calvin. **EDUCATION:** Roper Hosp School of Practical Nursing, Diploma 1963; Northeastern Univ, BSN 1977. **CAREER:** New England Reg Black Nurses, bd dir 1982-85; H McCall Nurses Unit/Grant AME Church, pres 1986-87; Amer Cancer Soc William Price Unit, bd of dir, co-chairperson 1987; MA Mental Health Ctr, hospital supv. **ORGANIZATIONS:** Mem Natl Black Nurses 1978-, New England Regional Black Nurses 1978-, Amer Nurses Assoc 1978-, MA Nurses Assoc 1978-, NAACP 1982-, Eastern MA Urban League1983-. **HONORS/ACHIEVEMENTS:** Public Serv Awd NERBNA Inc 1982; 5 Yrs Membership Natl Black Nurses 1986; Committee of the Year NERBNA Inc 1987. **HOME ADDRESS:** 70 Nelson St, Boston, MA 02124. **BUSINESS ADDRESS:** Hospital Supervisor, Massachusettes Mental Health, 74 Fenwood Rd, Boston, MA 02115.

PEOPLES, GREGORY ALLAN
Educational administrator. **PERSONAL:** Born May 17, 1951, Ravenna, OH; married Alice Leigh; children: Allaina Terice, Ashleigh Gail. **EDUCATION:** Allegheny Coll, BA 1973; Kent State Univ, MEd 1977. **CAREER:** Allegheny Coll, asst dir of admissions 1973-75; Kent State Univ, resident hall dir 1975-77; Center-Eastern MI Univ, coord of campus info 1978-80; Eastern MI Univ, asst dir of admiss 1980-82, assoc dir of admiss 1982-83; GMI Engrg & Mgmt Inst, admiss, corp spec 1983-84, dir of admiss. **ORGANIZATIONS:** Mem Delta Tau Delta 1973-; treas Black Faculty & Staff Assn 1978-82; mem Delta Sigma Pi 1980; mem bd of dir Natl Orientation Dir Assn 1981-; advisor Delta Sigma Pi 19081-83, Delta Tau Delta 1984-. **HONORS/ACHIEVEMENTS:** Outstanding Young Men of Amer 1984. **HOME ADDRESS:** 8961 Oxford Court, Ypsilanti, MI 48197.

PEOPLES, HARRISON PROMIS, JR.
Organizational development executive. **PERSONAL:** Born Mar 23, 1940, Anawalt, WV; son of Harrison P Peoples; children: Jacqueline Phaedra, Nikki-Nicole. **EDUCATION:** Chapman Coll, Orange CA, BA, 1976; Pepperdine Univ, Malibu CA, MS, 1986. **CAREER:** Motorola, Cupertino CA, manager, 1980-85; Transition Strategies, Los Altos CA, vice pres, 1985-88; Natl Traffic Safety Institute, San Jose CA, instructor, 1988-89; US Census Bureau, San Jose CA, mgr, 1989-. **ORGANIZATIONS:** Mem, Penninsula Assoc Black Personnel Admin, 1981-88; recorder, Human Resources Planning Soc, 1983; mem, Org Devel Network, 1984-86; NAACP, pres, state, 1987-89, vice pres, 1989. **HONORS/ACHIEVEMENTS:** Recognition, Salinas NAACP, 1983; Service Award, Palo Alto NAACP, 1988; DEA Appreciation, Drug Enforcement Admin, 1988; Omega Man of the Year, Omega Psi Phi. **MILITARY SERVICE:** US Army, major, 1959-80. **HOME ADDRESS:** 1065 Rankin Dr, Milpitas, CA 95035.

PEOPLES, JOHN ARTHUR, JR.
University president. **PERSONAL:** Born Aug 26, 1926, Starkville, MS; son of John A Peoples Sr (deceased) and Maggie Rose Peoples; married Mary E Galloway; children: Dr Kathleen, Mark. **EDUCATION:** Jackson State Univ, BS 1950; Univ of Chicago, MA 1951, PhD 1961. **CAREER:** Gary IN Pub Sch System, principal 1951-64; Jackson State Univ, asst to pres 1964-65; State Univ of NY at Binghamton, asst to pres 1965-66; Jackson State Univ, vice pres 1966-67, pres 1967-84. **ORGANIZATIONS:** Bd of trustees Amer Coll Test Corp 1973-79; bd of control Southern Regional Educ Bd 1974-86; consul Kellogg Foundation 1981-84; consul Killy EndowmentFd 1976-77; mem Noon Optimist Club Jackson 1981-; life mem NAACP; bd of dirs MS Ballet Intl Inc 1980-. **HONORS/ACHIEVEMENTS:** Fellow Amer Council on Education 1965-66; Education Specialist US State Dept 1977; Man of Yr Alpha Chi Chap 1962. **MILITARY SERVICE:** USMC sgt 1944-47. **BUSINESS ADDRESS:** Trstes Disting Professor, Universities Center, 3825 Ridgewood Road, Jackson, MS 39212.

PEOPLES, JOYCE P.
Educator. **PERSONAL:** Born Aug 27, 1937, Huntsville, AL; divorced; children: Alycia Peoples-Behling. **EDUCATION:** AL A&M Univ, BS (Cum Laude) 1957, MS 1965; The Amer Univ, PhD (with Distinction) 1977. **CAREER:** AL A&M Univ, asst prof 1967-76; Voorhees Coll, dir interdisciplinary studies 1976-77; Univ of MD-ES, asst vice chancellor 1977-78; Inst for Serv to Educ, special asst to pres 1978-83; Southern Univ, vice chancellor academic affairs 1983-. **ORGANIZATIONS:** Regional dir Black Women Academicians 1982-83; consultant Amer Council on Educ 1982-86; parliamentarian NAUW 1985-87; pres Top Ladies of Distinction Inc 1985-87; bd mem Natl Assoc of Univ Women 1986-87. **HONORS/ACHIEVEMENTS:** Listed in Intl Dictionary of Biography London, England 1973; Natl Citation for Assault on Illiteracy AOIP 1985-86; selected Woman of the Year Natl Assoc ofUniv Women 1986-87; Natl Top Lady of the Year TLOD Inc 1986-87; listed in Who's Who of Amer Women 1986-87. **BUSINESS ADDRESS:** V Chancellor, Academic Affairs, Southern University, 3050 ML King Jr Dr, Shreveport, LA 71107.

PEOPLES, SESSER R.
Educator. **PERSONAL:** Born Dec 07, 1934, Newark; married Irma; children: 4 Children. **EDUCATION:** Jersey City State Coll, BA 1963; Kean Coll, MA. **CAREER:** Mentally Retarded Plainfield Public School, teacher; Urban Processes Coordinated, coor 1971-; Black Studies Jersey City State Coll, dir 1969-73; Jersey City State Coll, affirmative action officer 1973-. **ORGANIZATIONS:** Mem Phi Delta Kappa 1972-; Nat Assn Black & Urban Ethnic Dirs 1971-72; African-Am Studies Assn 1970-73; African Heritage Studies Assn; Urban Processes Coordinated Consulting Firm 1971-; Third World Enterprises 1968-; mem bd dirs Leaguers Inc. **MILITARY SERVICE:** AUS 1957-59. **BUSINESS ADDRESS:** Jersey City State Coll, Jersey City, NJ 07305.

PEOPLES, VEO, JR.
Attorney. **PERSONAL:** Born Sep 13, 1947, St Louis, MO; married Linda Sing; children: Nicole, Nissa. **EDUCATION:** Univ of MO Rolla, BS Chem Engr 1970; St Louis Univ School of Law, JD 1975. **CAREER:** Ralston Purina Co, patent agent 1973-75; Ralston Purina Co, patent attny 1975-78; Monsanto's Patent Dept, patent trainee; Monsanto Co's Cntrl Engrg Dept, process design engr; Monsanto Co, engrg intern; Anheuser-Busch, assoc gen council 1978-84; private practice, patent attorney. **ORGANIZATIONS:** Mem Ralston Purina Corp Devel Bd 1977; spec task force MO Bar Assoc 1976-77; entertainment chmn Mound City Bar Assoc 1976-77; sec exec comm bd of dir Legal Serv of Eastern MO Inc; dist commiss Western Dist of St Louis for Boy Scouts of Amer; bd of dir W Co Amer Cancer Soc; dist exec Mark Twain BSA 1976-; mem Optimist Club of St Louis; circuite comm 22nd Judicial Bar 1984-87; chmn patent section BAMSL; pres, founder CADRE 19 Inc. **HONORS/ACHIEVEMENTS:** Achievement Awd Urban League 1975; Rosalie Tilles Scholarship 1966-70; Univ of MO Curators Scholarship 1966; Student Chap Awd of Excellence AIChE 1970; Univ Scholar Awd Univ of MO 1976; Undergrad Rsch Fellowship 1970.

PEOPLES, WOODROW (WOODY)
Professional athlete. **PERSONAL:** Born Aug 16, 1943, Birmingham, AL. **EDUCATION:** Grambling Coll, BSBA 1965. **CAREER:** San Francisco 49ers, professional football 1968-75, 1977; Philadelphia Eagles 1978-; Pro Bowl 1973 & 1974; NFC Championship Game 1970-71. **MILITARY SERVICE:** AUS 1966-68.

PERARA, MITCHELL MEBANE
Physician. **PERSONAL:** Born Feb 11, 1924, Tulsa, OK; married Jean Wolfe; children: Susan, Mark, Georgianna. **EDUCATION:** VA Union Univ, BS 1944; Howard Univ, MD 1948. **CAREER:** Amer Coll of Surgeons, diplomate 1955-85; Private Practice, physician 1955-85. **HONORS/ACHIEVEMENTS:** Fellow Amer Cancer Society 1955. **BUSINESS ADDRESS:** 1828 S Western Ave, Los Angeles, CA 90006.

PERDUE, FRANKLIN ROOSEVELT
Psychologist, author. **PERSONAL:** Born Jan 30, 1944, Birmingham, AL; married Carolyn Jean Walton; children: Stephannie Denise, Francis Renee. **EDUCATION:** Miles Coll, BS 1974; AL State Univ, MEd 1979; Century Univ, PhD 1984; UCLA Marriage Family Child Counsel Sem, Post Doct 1984; LA Hypnotism Training Inst, post doct hypnotist; Coastview Memorial Hosp-Long Beach CA, marriage family child counsel alcohol & drug abuse internship 1985-86; Kaizer Permanente Hosp, hospice intern. **CAREER:** Los Angeles Comm Coll, college instructor 1980; US Naval Sea Cadet Corp, commanding officer 1980-; Vantage Pres, author 1980-; Lincensed hypnotist 1985; LA & State of CA chapters, psychologist, MFCC, internist 1984-87. **ORGANIZATIONS:** Mem Phi Beta Sigma Frat 1970-73; cadet USAF Res Officer Training Samford Univ 1970-74; teacher, educator Birmingham Bd of Ed 1973-80; mem Retired Military Officers Assoc 1981-; postal carrier/clerk Los Angeles Postal Serv 1963-67, 1980-; Los Angeles Chapter, internist-marriage, family, child counseling 1984-; CA marriage, family, child counseling chapter, mem 1987. **HONORS/ACHIEVEMENTS:** Authored reports on The Privite Life of Petty Officer FDR Perdue, Segregation & Integration 1983. **MILITARY SERVICE:** USNR lt 26 years. **HOME ADDRESS:** 575 West Cocoa St, Compton, CA 90220. **BUSINESS ADDRESS:** Commanding Officer, US Navy Sea Cadet Corp, 1700 Stadium Way, Los Angeles, CA 90052.

PERDUE, JOHN F.
Retired education executive. **PERSONAL:** Born Dec 14, Ypsilanti, MI; son of John Wesley Perdue and Maggie B Saxon Perdue; married Trunetta V Perdue, Dec 29, 1954. **EDUCATION:** Toledo U, BED;Univ MI, MA; OaklandUniv MI St U, atnd. **CAREER:** Union Mutual Hlth Life & Acc Ins Co Phila, salesman agncy dir 1934-42; Toledo Urban League, indus rel sec 1946-50; MI Sch Dist, tchr 1950-56; Bagley & Whittier Ele Schs Jefferson Jr HS Pontiac MI, prin 1956-66; Sch Com Rel of Pontiac Sch Dist, dir 1966-; Wayne StUniv Desegregation Inst, on staff summer 1966; Sch Com & Rel Pontiac Sch Dist, dir; Emergency Sch Aid Act, dir. **ORGANIZATIONS:** Mem DESP reg, state & nat; ASCD; MASSP; NSPRA; PTA Coun of Pontiac; Pi Gamma Mu; Nat Soc Sci Hon Soc; past vice pres AFT Ferndale MI Chptr; life mem Alpha Phi Alpha Frat; mem Hum Rel Com of St Dept of Educ of MI; mem Assn for Study of Afro-Am Life & Hist; mem Nat Assn of Sch Pub Rel Assn; mem Nat Alliance of Black Sch Edu; organ W Philadelphia Youth Civic League 1936; worked with Armstrong 1975. **HONORS/ACHIEVEMENTS:** Outstndg achiev awd Nat Allian of Blk Sch Edtrs 1975; spec tribute St of MI Legisl 1976, 77; Res of Commend from City Commis of City of Pontiac 1976; Assn of Phila; mem bd dirs Pontiac Urban League past sec vp; past mem Detroit Presb Comm on Religion & Race; testified for NAACP in Desegregation Case Davis vs Sch Dist of City of Pontiac 1970; rec Dabney Awd outstndg civic contri for yr 1937; Prin of Yr 1961; Arthur Croft Pub Co Annual Pontiac Urban League Awd 1961; citznshp awd St Stephens Ch 1962; awd of merit Jefferson Jr HS PTA & Whittier Elem Sch PTA 1966; Lakeside Tenants OrganAwd 1970; Oakland Co Br of NAACP 1971; Cert of Mer; 761st Tank Batalion Allied Vets Assn 1974; cit of yr MI Chronicle Newspaper 1968; listed Outstndg Blacks in Pontiac MI 1975. **MILITARY SERVICE:** 1st sgt 1942-46. **HOME ADDRESS:** 2327 Horseshoe Bend Rd, Marietta, GA 30064.

PERDUE, JULIA M. WARD
Educator. **PERSONAL:** Born Oct 06, 1938, Cincinnati, OH; divorced; children: Audrey Lynn, Andre Maurice. **EDUCATION:** Univ of Cinicnnati, BS 1963;Univ of Cincinnati, postgrad; Xavier U; IN U. **CAREER:** City of Cincinnati Bd of Edn, title i tchr 1963-; Real Estate, saleslady 1961. **ORGANIZATIONS:** Mem Assn for Educ of Children; mem Upper Grade Study Coun; mem Cincinnati Fed Tchrs; mem OH Am Fed of Tchrs; mem NAREBS past pres 1975-77, past vice pres 1974; Pub Rec Commn Cincinnati 1973-; pres 7th Ward Dem Club Cincinnati; vice pres exec com Hamilton Co Dem Party; mem OH Dem Party Exec Com; bd dir Charter Com of Grtr Cincinnati; com of mgnt YMCA; mem Whithrow HS & Rothenberg Elem Sch PTA'S; mem NAACP; past mem Riverfront Adv Coun Cincinnati; pub adv Delta Sigma Theta Sor; mem Pan City Garden Club; mem Zion Bapt Ch; asst fin sec Inspir Chorus; sec Credit Com Fed Credit Union; trustee Adolphus Ward Jr Meml Schlrshp

Fund; past mem St Social Serv Adv Coun; past bd of dir Cath Big Bros; past bd of dir Hamilton Co Black Caucus; past bd of dir Madonna Comm Ctr Best Am Block Club Lieblos W Germay 1960. **HONORS/ACHIEVEMENTS:** Outst Serv Award Hamilton Co Blk Caucus 1972; Disting Serv Award Delta Sigma Theta Sor 1974; Consecrated Serv Award Zion Cincinnati Fed Credit Union 1975;Disting Serv Award St John's AME Zion Ch 1975; Who's Who Among Black Am 1975; 20th Century Patroit Award Grtr Cincinnati Bicent Commn 1976; Outst Serv Award YMCA 1976; Music Maker Award Zion Bapt Ch 1977; 10 Outst Black Women in Cincinnati.

PERDUE, ROBERT EUGENE
Educator. **PERSONAL:** Born Sep 17, 1940, Barnesville, GA. **EDUCATION:** Morehosue Coll, BA 1961; Atlanta U, MA 1963;Univ GA, PhD 1971. **CAREER:** Fayetteville State Univ, instr 1963-66; Ft Valley State Coll, asst prof 1968-70; Spelman Coll, asso prof acting chmn 1972-. **ORGANIZATIONS:** Mem Org of Am Histrns; Am Hist Assn; Nat Assn for Stdy of Afro-Am Life Hist; GA Assn of Histrns; mem YMCA; Barnesvl Civ Lgue; Morehouse Coll Atlanta Alum Club 1972-74; Awards Flwshp Fund; Ford Found Grant. **BUSINESS ADDRESS:** Box 21 Dept of Hist, Spelman Coll, Atlanta, GA.

PEREIRA, SARAH MARTIN
Educator. **PERSONAL:** Born Dec 12, 1909, Cleveland, OH; daughter of Alexander H Martin and Mary B Martin; widowed; children: Carlos Martin. **EDUCATION:** OH State Univ, AB (with honors & distinction in French) 1931; Western Reserve Univ Cleveland, MS French 1935; OSU, PhD Romance Langs 1942. **CAREER:** Shaw Univ Raleigh, instr spanish/french 1931-41; Miner Teachers Coll, instr spanish/french 1941-46; Howard Univ Grad Sch, part-time assoc prof french 1942-46; Cleveland Coll, part-time lectr in spanish 1946-50; Fenn Coll, part time lectr in spanish 1946-52; WV State Coll Inst WV, prof & chair of dept1952-58; DC Tchrs Coll Washington, prof & chair dept of for langs 1971-76; Univ of Dist Col, acting academic dean Harvard Campus 1976-78, prof of spanish & portuguese 1978-70; Johnson C Smith Univ, visiting prof of spanish. **ORGANIZATIONS:** Mem Natl Spiritual Assembly Baha'i Faith 1961-73; mem Continental Bd of Counsellors Americas Baha'i World Faith 1973-85; mem Spiritual Assembly of Baha's of Charlotte, NC 1986-. **HONORS/ACHIEVEMENTS:** Phi Beta Kappa OH State Univ Epsilon Chap 1931; Kappa Delta Pi DCTC Washington DC 1965; appeared on first edition Who'sn Who Among Amer Women; Delta Sigma Pi (Spanish Honors); Phi Delta Kappa (French Honor Soc); Phi Lambda Beta (Portugese Honor Soc); honored in formal ceremony as Disting Alumna OH State Univ Cols O 1972 first Black so honored at OSU. **HOME ADDRESS:** 5801 J Sharon Rd, Charlotte, NC 28210.

PEREZ, BOBBIE M. ANTHONY
Educator. **PERSONAL:** Born Nov 15, 1923, Macon, GA; daughter of Solomon Cotton, Sr (deceased) and Maude Alice Lockett Cotton (deceased); married Andrew S Perez; children: Freida M Chapman. **EDUCATION:** DePaul U, BS 1953, MS 1954; Univ of IL at Urbana, MS 1959; Univ of Chgo, PhD 1967; DePaul U, MA 1975. **CAREER:** Chicago Pub Schs, math tchr 1954-68; Univ of Chgo, math consult 1965; Chicago St U, psych tchr 1968-; Worthington Hurst, psych Head Start 1971-72; Howard U, Inst for Urban Afrs rsrch cood 1977; Chicago St U, acting Ccrd for Black Studies 1981; Chicago St U, prof of psych 1977. **ORGANIZATIONS:** Local rep, Midwestern Psych Assoc 1979-; Am Ed Rsrch Asso 1980-; Vice Pres for comm affairs Chatham Bus Assoc 1981; chp bus rltns Chatham Avalon Pk Comm 1982-; chp pub ed Am Cancer Soc 1982-87; local rep Chicago Psych Assoc 1984-; secy Chatham Bus Assn 1986-87; chp pub inform Amer Cancer Soc 1987-; public information chairperson Chatham-Avalon Unit of American Cancer Society 1987-; conference presenter International Assn for Applied Psychology 1988; conference presenter International Assn for Cross-Cultural Psychology 1988; chp Communications Ingleside Whitfield Parish 1989. **HONORS/ACHIEVEMENTS:** Outstndng comm serv Chicago Area Asso of Black Pshcys 1983; outstndng comm serv Chatham Bus Asso 1984; appreciation serv Yng Adults of Ingleside Whitfield Parish 1984; cert for serv & support Chatham Bus Asso 1984; many plaques & certificates for services to students and for Black studies teaching & curriculum development; distunguished bd mem Chatham Business Assn 1988; visited all 7 continents in 10 1/2 months to study cultural factors through ethnography; developed Chatham Business Assn Directories 1987 & 1988; 10 yrs distinguished serv as bd mem Chatham Business Assn 1988. **BUSINESS ADDRESS:** Professor of Psychology, Chicago StUniv, 9500 S King Dr, Chicago, IL 60628.

PERINE, JAMES L.
Educator. **PERSONAL:** Born Jun 23, 1943, St Louis; married B Rosalie Hicks; children: Lori, Keith, Kelly. **EDUCATION:** NE MO State U, BA 1964;Univ MD, MA 1967; PA State U, PhD 1979. **CAREER:** Washington, research psychol 1964-68; Univ MD, oeo grad & teaching asst 1965-67; Coll Human Devel PA State Univ, presently asst to dean. **ORGANIZATIONS:** Mem Phi Delta Kappa; Nat Educ Hon Frat; Am Vocational Assn; Am Personnel & Guidance Assn; Am Psychological Assn; St Paul's United Meth Ch State College; NAACP; adv bd Lewisburg Prison; bd dirs State Coll Comm Theatre; Comm Vol to Mountainview Unit Centre Comm Hosp. **HONORS/ACHIEVEMENTS:** Blue Key; State Coll Kiwanis Club; Spl Citation Optimists Club 1970. **BUSINESS ADDRESS:** PO Box 654, Centreville, MD 21617.

PERINE, MARTHA LEVINGSTON
Business executive. **PERSONAL:** Born Jun 27, 1948, Mobile, AL; married David Andrew; children: David Jr, Alissa, Alison. **EDUCATION:** Bus Adminstr Clark Coll Atlanta GA, BA 1965-69; WashingtonUniv St Louis, MA Econ 1969-71. **CAREER:** Fed Reserve Bank of St Louis, asst vice pres 1971-. **ORGANIZATIONS:** Mem Nat Assn of Bank Women 1985; mem Am Inst of Banking 1985; financial sec Gamma Omega Chap Alpha Kappa Alpha Sor Inc 1985; fin sec Holy Metro Missionary Bapt Ch 1985. **HONORS/ACHIEVEMENTS:** Outstanding Yng Woman in Am Outstanding Yng Am's 1970; Achievement Nominee St Louis Jaycee Wives 1978; Outstanding Young Women in Am, Outstanding Yng Am's 1979. **BUSINESS ADDRESS:** Federal Reserve Bank of St Lou, 411 Locust St, St Louis, MO 63102.

PERKINS, CHARLES WINDELL
Business executive. **PERSONAL:** Born Mar 12, 1946, New Orleans, LA; children: Evany Joy. **EDUCATION:** Univ of CA Berkeley, BA 1968; Southwestern Grad Sch of Banking SMU Dallas, grad degree banking 1978. **CAREER:** Security Pac Nat Bank, vp; San Leandro, vice pres & mgr 1978. **ORGANIZATIONS:** Asst vice pres San Mateo & SF; mgr Foster City 1974; asst mgr Hayward Fremont; asst cashier SF; supr SF & Berkeley; mgmt trainee Security Pacific Bank 1968; bd mem Hunters Point Boys' Club of SF 1972; treas Foster City C of C 1974; co-founder Black Officers Group Sec Pac Bank 1980; memUniv of CA Alumni Assn. **HONORS/ACHIEVEMENTS:** All-conf basketballUniv CA Berkeley 1967; $1,000,000 trust award Security Pacific Bank 1979. **BUSINESS ADDRESS:** Vice President and Manager, Security Pacific Nat'l Bank, 4929 Wilshire Blvd, Los Angeles, CA 90010.

PERKINS, EDWARD JOSEPH
Ambassador. **PERSONAL:** Born Jun 08, 1928, Sterlington, LA; son of Edward Joseph Perkins Sr and Tiny Estella Noble Holmes; married Lucy Chen-mei Liu, Sep 09, 1962; children: Katherine Karla Shih-Tzu, Sarah Elizabeth Shih-Yin. **EDUCATION:** Univ of MD, BA 1968; Univ of Southern CA, MPA 1972, PhD 1978. **CAREER:** AIDS Far East Bureau Washington, asst general serv officer; US Operations Mission to Thailand Bangkok, asst genl serv officer 1967-69, mgmt analyst 1969-70, deputy asst dir for mgmt 1970-72; Office of the Dir General of the Foreign Serv Washington, staff assistant 1972, personnel officer; Bureau of Near Eastern & South Asian Affairs, admin officer 1974-75; Office of Mgmt & Opers, mgmt analysis officer 1975-78; Accra, counselor for polit affairs 1978-81; Monrovia, deputy chief of mission 1981-83; Bureau Of African Affairs Office of West African Affairs, dir 1983-85; Dept of State, ambassador to Liberia 1985-86, ambassador to South Africa 1986-89, dir general The Foreign Service 1989-. **ORGANIZATIONS:** Mem Amer Foreign Serv Assoc 1966-, Amer Soc for Public Admin 1967-, Kappa Alpha Psi, Phi Kappa Phi Honor Soc. **HONORS/ACHIEVEMENTS:** Hon Soc of Phi Kappa Phi Univ of So CA 1972; Certificate of Army Dept of the Army 1966; AID's Meritorious Honor Award; State's Superior Honor Award; Kappa Alpha Psi Fraternity Eastern Region Award for Achievement in Foreign Affairs 1985; author rsch document "The Priorities Policy Group, A Case Study of the Institutionalization of a Policy Linkage and Resource Allocation Mechanism in the Department of State"; Honorary Doctor of Laws, Lewis and Clark Coll, Portland OR 1988; Presidential Honor Award, The President of the US 1989. **MILITARY SERVICE:** USMC sgt 1954-58. **BUSINESS ADDRESS:** Director General of the Foreign Service, Department of State, 2301 "C" St, NW, Washington, DC 20520.

PERKINS, EUGENE
Social worker, educator. **PERSONAL:** Born Sep 13, 1932, Chicago, IL; married Janis; children: Julia, Russell. **EDUCATION:** George Williams Coll, BS 1961; MS 1963. **CAREER:** Fiaman House, group worker 1963-66; Henry Horner Boys Club, prog dir 1966-68; Better Boys Found, exec dir; Malcolm X Coll, instr 1969-72; Chicago St Coll, instr 1974-. **ORGANIZATIONS:** Mem Nat Assn of Black Soc Workers. **HONORS/ACHIEVEMENTS:** Recip Malcom X Black Manhood Awd black express newspaper awd. **MILITARY SERVICE:** USAF. **BUSINESS ADDRESS:** 1512 S Polaski, Chicago, IL.

PERKINS, FRANCES J.
Educator. **PERSONAL:** Born Dec 14, 1919, Boston, MA; married W Wentworth; children: Joseph W. **EDUCATION:** Boston State, BSE 1941; Tufts Univ, EdM 1957; Boston Univ, EdM counseling 1981. **CAREER:** Tufts Univ, summer faculty Eliot-Pearson Dept of Child Study 1960-65, lecturer 1965-66; Garland Jr College, instructor summer inst 1965-66; Head Start Training Prog Wheelock Coll sum, dir 1966-67; Peace Corps, project dir Tunisia Training Prog Wheelock Coll 1966-67; EPDA Inst Garland Jr Coll, asst dir 1969; Wheelock Coll, instr psychology 1970-73, assoc prof psychology retired 1985; Center for Individual & Family Serv Family Mediation Prog, social worker. **ORGANIZATIONS:** Dir Lemberg Lab Sch Brandeis Univ 1961-73; dir Suburban Parent Coop Presch Belmont 1953-61; dir Inner City Comm Preschool Boston 1946-53; consult Jackson-Mann Early Childhood Program Horace-Mann Sch for the Deaf 1974-75; Head Start Programs Eastern Reg 1967-73; Action for Boston Comm Devel 1965; mem NatlAssn for Educ of Young Children; Amer Assn of Univ Women; past pres bd dir Freedom House Inc; mem Parents & Children's Serv; MA Com for Children & Youth; Professional Adv Com Ft Hill Mental Health Assn; life mem Delta Sigma Theta; bd mem Urban League of Eastern MA; bd mem NAUSET Workshop, Center for Individual & Family Svcs.

PERKINS, GLADYS PATRICIA
Retired engineering specialist. **PERSONAL:** Born Oct 30, 1921, Crenshaw, MS; daughter of Douglas Franklin and Zula Crenshaw Franklin. **EDUCATION:** LeMoyne Coll, BS Math 1943; Univ of MI, Math; Hughes Aircraft, ATEP; UCLA Ext. **CAREER:** Amer Missionary Assoc Athens AL, teacher 1943-44; Natl Advisory Comm for Aeronautics, 1944-49; Natl Bureau of Standards, mathematician 1950-53; Aberdeen Bombing Mission, mathematician 1953-55; Lockheed Missle Systems, assoc engr math analyst 1955-57; Hughes Aircraft Co, staff engr 1957-80; Rockwell Intl, engrg specialist 1980-87 (retired). **ORGANIZATIONS:** Mem Alpha Kappa Alpha Sor 1941-, LeMoyne-Owen Coll Alumni Assoc 1943-, Assoc of Computing Machinery 1964-, Soc of Women Engrs 1981-, NAFEO 1983. **HONORS/ACHIEVEMENTS:** Lunar Trajectory Program (surveyor), Three Dimensional Boost-Coast Trajectory, High Speed Trajectory Simulator Hughes Aircraft Co; Program to Determine a Satellite Ground Trace Hughes Aircraft 1978; Alumnus of the Year Awd LeMoyne Owen Coll 1982; Golden Parade Galery of Outstanding Alumni LeMoyne-Owen Coll 1982; Natl Assoc for Equal Oppor in Higher Educ NAFEO 1983; "Users Guide to Ascent, Insertion, Orbit, Deorbit Program" Space Shuttle Rockwell Intl 1987.

PERKINS, HUEL D.
Educator. **PERSONAL:** Born Dec 27, 1924, Baton Rouge; married Thelma O Smith; children: Huel Alfred. **EDUCATION:** So U, BS highest honors 1947; Northwestern U, MusM 1951, PhD 1958. **CAREER:** So U, dean coll of arts & humanities 1968-78; Nat Educ for Humanities, dep dir educ prog 1978-79; Acad Affairs LA St U, asst vice chancellor 1979-; So U, asso prof music 1951-60; Lincoln U, instr music 1948-50. **ORGANIZATIONS:** Mem visiting fac prog HarvardUniv 1968; part Caribbean-Am Scholars Exchange Prog 1974; part So Assembly 1973; visiting prof LA StateUniv 1972, 74; mem Mayor's Commn of Youth Activities 1969; Nat Bd of Consult Nat Endowment for the Humanities; bd of dir LA Arts & Sci Ctr; mem Alpha Phi Alpha; Pi Kappa Lambda; Phi Mu Alpha; Pi Gamma Mu; Alpha Kappa Mu; Sigma Pi Phi; ASCAP; mem bd dirs Blundon Orpahnage 1970-71; bd dirs Baton Rouge Symphony Orchestra 1971-;pres bd dir Capital Area United Way 1986; bd mem Baton Rouge Opera, New Orleans Museum of Art, Salvation Army; mem Rotary Club of Baton Rouge, Baton Rouge C of C, Omicron Delta Kappa Leadership. **HONORS/ACHIEVEMENTS:** Recip Outstdg Prof Student Govt Assn 1970, 74; Danforth Tchr Grant 1957-58; flwshp Nat Endowment for Humanities 1972; chmn Dean's Sec of Conf of LAColl &Univ 1974; recip Brotherhood Awd Natl Conf of Christians & Jews 1987. **MILITARY**

SERVICE: USN musician 1st class 1943-46. **BUSINESS ADDRESS:** Asstistant Vice Chancellor, Louisiana StateUniv, Officeof Academic Affairs, Baton Rouge, LA 70803.

PERKINS, JOHN M.
Business executive. **PERSONAL:** Born in New Hebron, MS; married Vera Mae; children: Spencer, Phillip, Joan, Derek, Debbie, DeWayne, Priscilla, Betty. **CAREER:** Voice of Calvary Ministries, pres; num lecuring posts travelled over US as Ford Found 1972-73; through Israel to study cooperatives 1968; through Caribbean to study econs of disad 1966; through Germany on NEA 1972; through Germany to speak to servicemen 1976; to Gr Britain 1977; Fed of S Cooper, co-fdr; S Cooper Devel Fund, co-fdr; Voice of Calvare Ministries; Voice of Calvary Cooper Hlth Clinic; People Devel Inc; several other coopers; Gen Session spkerUrbana 1976; MS Billy Graham Crusade, steering com 1975; Tom Skinner MS Mgmt Sem, sponsor 1975. **ORGANIZATIONS:** Pres Voice of Calvary Ministries; bd mem Bread for the World; Nat Black Evangelical Assn; Convenant Coll; S Devel Found; Koinonio Partners. **HONORS/ACHIEVEMENTS:** Author, Let Justice Roll Down; A Quiet Revolution; contrib editor Sojourners mag The Other Side mag, Radix mag; Decision mag; several other periodicals. **MILITARY SERVICE:** AUS 1951-53. **BUSINESS ADDRESS:** 1655 St Charles St, Jackson, MS 39209.

PERKINS, LEONARD L.
Educator. **PERSONAL:** Born Apr 04, 1933, Nashville, TN; married Patricia; children: Lynn, Lowery, Conrad. **EDUCATION:** BA; MS; MA. **CAREER:** Horace Mann Educators, dist asso mgr; Plus Ltd Mgmt Cons, exec dir; Purude U, dean of stud, stud affairs ofcr; Upward Bound, couns dir; tchr Spanish, French, English. **ORGANIZATIONS:** Founder PurudeUniv Black Student Union; charter mem IN Assn Afro-Am Studies; consult Educ Asso Office of Edn; educ consult splst Encyclopedia Britannica; mem counc of elders African Asso for Black Studies; NAACP; chmn Harvey Commn on Hum Rel; part IL Black Caucus. **MILITARY SERVICE:** AUS corpl 1953-55.

PERKINS, LEWIS BRYANT, JR.
Director. **PERSONAL:** Born in Newark, NJ; son of Lewis Perkins and Madelaine Perkins. **EDUCATION:** Benedict Coll, BS 1952; Rutgers Univ, Mgmt courses 1964; The Professional Sch of Business, Real Estate Mgmt 1971. **CAREER:** P Ballantine and Sons Brewers, trade relations mgt 1956-66; New York Titans-Jets, defensive end 1960-63; City of Newark NJ, deputy mayor 1966-70; Central Cadillac Inc, sales mgr 1970-80; The Equitable Life Assurance Soc of US, National director of recruitment and advancement 1980-87; advertising and sales director, Smith Motors Cadillac 1987-. **ORGANIZATIONS:** Mem Natl Football League Alumni; mem Natl Progressive AThletes Comm; dir Professional Athletes Unlimited; tri-state chrmn (New York, New Jersey, Conn), Natl Football League Retired Players Assoc; excutive bd mem, Nat Football League Players Assn 1985. **HONORS/ACHIEVEMENTS:** Disting Alumni of Yr Natl Assoc for Equal Oppor in Higher Educ 1983; Man of the Yr State of OK 1984; article published "When It's Over," Sports Financial Network 1984; Man of the Year, NJ Jaycees, 1969; Honorary Doctorate of Humane Letters, World Music Assn, Rutgers Univ, 1978. **HOME ADDRESS:** 648 Haxtun Ave, Orange, NJ 07050.

PERKINS, LINDA MARIE
Educator. **PERSONAL:** Born Nov 22, 1950, Mobile, AL; married Vincent Lee Wimbush. **EDUCATION:** Kentucky State University, BS 1971; Univ of Illinois, C-U, MS 1973; PhD 1978. **CAREER:** Univ of Ill-Champaign Urbana, Asst Dir of Minority Affrs 1973-75; William Paterson Coll Dir of Affirmative Action 1978-79; Radcliffe College The Mary Bunting Institute, Research Fellow, Asst Dir 1979-83; The Claremont Coll, asst vice pres 1983-86; Center for Afro-Amer Studies UCLA, visiting scholar 1986-. **ORGANIZATIONS:** Big Sisters of Boton, 1981-83; Pomona Valley YWCA Board Member 1984-; Los Angeles United Way, Allocation Team 1984-86. **HONORS/ACHIEVEMENTS:** Research Grant, Natl Inst of Educ 1979-81; Natl Endowment for the Humanities 1984; Spencer Foundation 1986-. **HOME ADDRESS:** 738 Santa Barbara Dr, Claremont, CA 91711. **BUSINESS ADDRESS:** Visiting Scholar, UCLA, Campbell Hall, 738 Santa Barbara Drive, Los Angeles, CA 90024.

PERKINS, LUCY ANN
Social worker. **PERSONAL:** Born in Louisville, KY. **EDUCATION:** Univ of Louisville, BA 1944; Atlanta U, MSW 1946; Werstern Reserve U, postgrad 1951; Coll of William & Mary, 1957. **CAREER:** Cuyahoga Co Child Welfare Bd Cleveland, sr caseworker 1947-52; Family Serv Soc Hartford, CT, sr worker in charge dist ofc 1952-56; Family Serv & Travelers Aid Inc Utica, NY, casework supr 1957-63; Wiltwyck Sch for Boys NYC, casework supr 1963-65; N Central Regional Comm Mental Hlth, former chf psychiat soc work. **ORGANIZATIONS:** Bd dir Soundview Comm Mental Hlth Cntr Bronx, NY; consult lectr supr project demonstrator Marcy State Hosp NY 1958-63; mem Nat Assn Soc Work; Am Orthopsychiat Assn; Soc Work Vocat Bur; Conf Soc Welfare; mem Zeta Phi Beta.

PERKINS, MYLA LEVY
Educator. **PERSONAL:** Born Feb 25, 1939, Pueblo, CO; married Edgar L Perkins; children: Julie, Steven, Todd, Susan. **EDUCATION:** Wayne State Univ, BS 1960. **CAREER:** Detroit Public Schools, teacher, 1960-66; Sugar N Spice Nursery School, co-owner, 1966-; Pyramid Elementary School, co-owner 1976-. **ORGANIZATIONS:** Mem Alpha Kappa Alpha Sor 1957-; mem Tots & Teens of Amer 1967-. **BUSINESS ADDRESS:** Pyramid Elem/Sugar N Spice Nur, 17151 Wyoming Ave, Detroit, MI 48221.

PERKINS, ROBERT E. L.
Oral/maxillofacial surgeon. **PERSONAL:** Born May 17, 1925, Carthage, TX. **EDUCATION:** Wiley Coll, BS 1945; Howard Univ, DDS 1948; Tufts Univ, MSD 1956. **ORGANIZATIONS:** Mem Amer Dental Assoc 1949-87, Natl Dental Assoc 1963-87; pres and founder DSACE 1964-87; courtesy staff Children's Hosp of MI 1960-87, Metro Hosp of Detroit 1965-87; mem MI and Amer Assoc of Oral and Maxillofacial Surgeons 1970-87; bd of dir and Treas Your Heritage House 1977-87; bd of dirs Detroit Symphony Orchestra 1980-87; jr staff mem Hutzel Hosp Detroit 1983-87; life mem NAACP, Natl Urban League, United Negro Coll Fund. **HONORS/ACHIEVEMENTS:** Key to the City of Detroit; Patron of the Arts Awd Detroit Musicians Assoc, The Alpha Kappa Alpha Sor; Alumni Awds Coll of Dentistry; Howard Univ Alumni Awd 1983. **MILITARY SERVICE:** USAF major 1949-54. **BUSINESS ADDRESS:** Oral Maxillofacial Surgeon, 2673 W Grand Blvd, Detroit, MI 48208.

PERKINS, SAM CHARLES
Professional athlete. **PERSONAL:** Born Jun 14, 1961, New York, NY. **EDUCATION:** North Carolina, BA 1984. **CAREER:** Dallas Mavericks, forward/center 1984-. **HONORS/ACHIEVEMENTS:** Currently 1st season NBA experience; drafted by Dallas 1st round 1984 (4th overall); pick acquired from Cleveland on 9/16/80 in exchange for Mike Bratz; Olympic champnshp followed titles in the 1983 Pan Am Games, the 1982 NCAA tournmnt & high school all-star tournmnt in 1980. **BUSINESS ADDRESS:** Dallas Maverick, Reunion Arena, Ste 510, Dallas, TX 75207.

PERKINS, THOMAS P.
Church executive. **PERSONAL:** Born Jan 12, 1940, Jersey City, NY; children: Thomas Jr, Susan, Stephen. **EDUCATION:** Univ IA, BA 1965; Seton Hall U, JD 1968. **CAREER:** Pvt Prac, atty 1970-; former state assemblyman; Judiciary Law & Pub Safety Com, atty pvt prac chmn house; State NJ Affirmative Action Com. **ORGANIZATIONS:** Bd tst Jersey & State Coll. **HONORS/ACHIEVEMENTS:** Human Rights Awd State NJ. **BUSINESS ADDRESS:** 7887 Walmsley Ave, New Orleans, LA 70125.

PERKINS, WILLIAM O., JR.
Government official. **PERSONAL:** Born Jun 05, 1926, Gregory, NC; married Arthur; children: 4 Children. **EDUCATION:** Elizabeth City State U, BS 1949; Atlanta U, addtl study;Univ of GA. **CAREER:** Atlanta Pub Schs, tchr 1957-76; Turner Co Schs, tchr 1952-53; Morgan Co Schs, tchr 1949-51, 53-56. **ORGANIZATIONS:** Mem bd of dir Atlanta Asn of Educ 1973-75; GA Assn of Educ 1976-77; mem bd of dirs GA Assn of Classroom Tchrs; mem NEA 1957-77; mem Metro Atlanta Counc Intl Reading Assn mem bd of dir Metro Atlanta Girls Club 1972-75; YWCA 1957-77; NAACP; sec Atlanta Dist Bapt Missionary Soc 1976-77; Beulah Bapt Ch; Gate City Tchrs Assn 1957-70; mem Alpha Kappa Mu Nat Hon Soc Article Four Tchrs Sound Off About Class Size Today's Educ 1976. **HONORS/ACHIEVEMENTS:** Nom Bronzew Woman 1976; Atlanta Classroom Tchr of Yr 1976-77; GA Tchr Classroom of Yr 1976-77. **BUSINESS ADDRESS:** Attorney at Law, 921 Bergen Ave, Jersey City, NJ 07306.

PERPENER, WINIFRED UVEDA
Educational administration. **PERSONAL:** Born May 01, 1929, Fort Worth, TX. **EDUCATION:** Jarvis Christian Coll, BA 1953; East TX State Univ, Masters work 1969. **CAREER:** Nursery School Ft Worth, teacher 1951-52; Fisk Univ, residence hall dir 1952-58; Jarvis Coll, dean of women 1958-79, dean of students 1979-. **ORGANIZATIONS:** Zeta Phi Beta Sorority. **HONORS/ACHIEVEMENTS:** Concert Singer Opera, Sacred Music, World & Intl Conventions, Schools, Churches 1952-; Appeared in Canada Europe US & VI 1952-; Personalities of the South; Govt Commiss on Status of Women, Govt Commiss Tech Vocation 1960-80. **BUSINESS ADDRESS:** Dean of Student Affairs, Jarvis Christian College, Drawer G, Hawkins, TX 75765.

PERRIMON, VIVIAN SPENCE
Educator. **PERSONAL:** Born Jan 14, 1937, Petersburg, VA; married Clarie; children: Petronia, Geraldine. **EDUCATION:** VA State Coll, AB 1958, MS 1960; FL State U, PhD 1972; INUniv Med Cntr, diploma 1972. **CAREER:** Crownsville Hosp, psychologist intern 1959; Central State Hosp, staff psychol 1960; FAMU, asst prof psychol 1961-68; IU Med Cntr, psychol intern 1971; FAMU, prof psychol 1969-72, chmn dept of psychol 1972-; Mental Hlth Svcs, clinical psychol Apalachee Comm 1972-. **ORGANIZATIONS:** Assn Black Psychol; Psi Chi; Southeastern Pyschol Assn; FL Psychol Assn; Asn Soc & Behaviorial Scientists; Phi Delta Kappa; Pi Gamma Mu; Leon Co Mental Hlth Assn Omega Psi Phi Frat. **HONORS/ACHIEVEMENTS:** Who's Who Am Men & Women Sci Cargegie Fellow 1968; NSF Summer Fellow 1964; FL A&MUniv Tchr of Yr 1961-62; FAMU Psychol Tchr of Yr 1974, 75.

PERRIN, DAVID THOMAS PERRY
Pastor. **PERSONAL:** Born May 16, 1951, Cleveland, OH; married Elizabeth Ann Jackson; children: Caleb Karamo, Quianne Shapearl, MiLeah Niambi. **EDUCATION:** Hamilton Coll, 1969-71; Carnegie Mellon Univ, BFA 1975; Gordon-Conwell Theological Seminary, MTS 1978; Howard Univ, PhD Program 1983-. **CAREER:** Corning Comm Coll, instr 1981-83; Friendship Baptist Church, pastor 1981-83; Elmira Correctional Inst, vstg lecturer 1982-83; TDX Systems Inc, sales analyst 1984-85; Parkway Baptist Church, pastor. **ORGANIZATIONS:** Campus ministry dir Howard Univ 1978-80; ed consult Perrin & Perrin 1978-; computer coord The Alliance of Interdenominational Ministers 1983; mem Natl Speakers Assoc 1983, Amer Soc for Training & Dev 1983; vstg lecturer Elmira Correctional Inst 1983. **HONORS/ACHIEVEMENTS:** Article "Making Senses of the Sixties" in Hawken Review 1983; Hosted TV Spec Dr ML King Birthday Elmira NY 1983; Hosted Mayoral Political Forum, 1983; Alliance of Ministers 183. **HOME ADDRESS:** 11317 Kettering Pl, Upper Marlboro, MD 20772. **BUSINESS ADDRESS:** 6arkway Baptist Church, 6809 District Heights, District Heights, MD 20747.

PERRY, ALEXIS E.
Corporate executive. **PERSONAL:** Born Feb 09, 1944, New York, NY; daughter of Elex W. Perry and Eliza McBurnett Perry; children: Ronald Earl Arlington Kirby. **EDUCATION:** Nancy Taylor Secretarial School, NY, degree, 1965; attended Borough of Manhattan Community Coll, 1972-78, received associates degree; attended Queens Coll, Flushing NY, 1982-83. **CAREER:** Norton Simon Inc, New York NY, legal sec, 1973-76, equal employment coord, 1976-78, equal employment analyst, 1978-81, worked in charitable contributions, 1978-81, mgr of corp progams, 1981-84; RKO General, New York NY, corp mgr of equal employment opportunity, 1984-87, corp dir of affirmative action and equal employment opportunity, 1987-. **ORGANIZATIONS:** Mem 1983-, sec 1988-, Natl Urban Affairs Council; mem of advisory comm 1985-87, Comm Associates Devel Corp; mem 1985-, Coalition of 100 Black Women (NY); mem 1987-, Harlem YMCA Black Achiever Comm; mem 1988-, EDGES Group Inc. **HONORS/ACHIEVEMENTS:** Black Achiever in Industry, Harlem YMCA, 1980. **BUSINESS ADDRESS:** Corporate Director—Affirmative Action and Equal Employment Opportunity, RKO General Inc, 1440 Broadway, 20th Floor, New York, NY 10018.

PERRY, AUBREY M.
Psychologist, educator. **PERSONAL:** Born Jan 14, 1937, Petersburg, VA; married Clarie; children: Vanessa, Aubrey Jr, Kenneth. **EDUCATION:** VA State Coll, AB 1958, MS 1960; IN Univ Med Ctr, Diploma 1972; FL State Univ, PhD 1972. **CAREER:** Crownsville Hosp,

psychologist intern 1959; Central State Hosp, staff psychologist 1960; FAMU, asst prof psychology 1961-68; IU Med Center, psychologistintern 1971; Apalachee Comm Mental Health Svcs, clinical psychologist 1972-; FL A&M Univ, assoc prof psychology 1969-, dean Coll of Arts & Sci 1972-. **ORGANIZATIONS:** Mem Assn Black Psychologists, Psi Chi, Southeastern Psychol Assn, FL Psychol Assn, Assn Social & Behavioral Scientists, Phi Delta Kappa, Pi Gamma Mu, Leon Co Mental Health Assn, Omega Psi Phi. **HONORS/ACHIEVEMENTS:** FL A&M Univ Teacher of the Year 1961-62; NSF Summer Fellow 1964; listed in Who's Who Amoung Men & Women of Science; Carnegie Fellow 1968; FAMU Psychology Teacher of the Year 1974,74. **BUSINESS ADDRESS:** Dean, Coll of Arts & Sciences, Florida A&M University, 208 Tucks Halls, Tallahassee, FL 32307.

PERRY, BENJAMIN
Fire chief. **PERSONAL:** Born Feb 12, 1939, Gary, IN; son of Bennie Perry and Mary Ellen Childress (deceased); married Kathryn A Gillespie, Nov 17, 1978; children: Sharlan Renee',Lonydea Marie, Gina Dyan. **EDUCATION:** Indiana Univ, 1957-58; Ocean Side Carlsbad CA, 1958-59; Marine Inst, 1959-60/. **CAREER:** Inland Steel Co, E Chicago IN, headleader, 1961-65; Gary Fire Dept, Gary IN, firefighter, 1965-68, lieutenant, 1968-71, captain, 1971-78, battalion chief, 18-80, asst chief, 1980-86. **ORGANIZATIONS:** Mem, Intl Assn of Firefighters, 1965-, Intl Fire Chiefs, 1978-, Indiana Fire Chief's Assn, 1978-, Marine Corp Assn, 1980-, Natl Fire Protection Assn, 1981-;mem, advisory bd, Ivy Technical Coll, 1988-. **HONORS/ACHIEVEMENTS:** Developed Large Diameter Hose Conception, Gary IN, Tactics Manual for Gary IN Fire Dept; Developed the Drivers Training Program for Gary Fire Dept. **MILITARY SERVICE:** US Marine Corps, Sergeant E-5, Good Conduct, Indo-China Medal, 1961; Expert, rifle, piston, machine gun, automatic rifle, 1958-61. **BUSINESS ADDRESS:** Fire Chief, City of Gary Fire Dept, 200 E Fifth Ave, Gary, IN 46402.

PERRY, BENJAMIN L., JR.
Education administrator, consultant. **PERSONAL:** Born Feb 27, 1918, Eatonville, FL; married Helen N Harrison; children: Kimberly. **EDUCATION:** FL A&M Coll, BS 1940; IA State Coll, MS 1942; Cornell U, PhD 1954; Claremont Coll CA, adv study 1955. **CAREER:** MGT Inc, consult 1980-; Kellogg Found, consult 1980-; FL A&M U, pres 1968-80, dean admn 1968; Intl Educ Assn Workshop, 1970; US Dept Treas Wash, consult 1970; Higher Educ Columbia Sch Bus NY, mgmt planning instr 1971; So Assn Land-Grant Coll & U, pres 1972-73; FL Assn Colls & U, pres 1972-73. **ORGANIZATIONS:** Pres Tallahassee Urban Leage 1972; Phi Delta Kappa; C of C; Fronties Intl Club BSA; Pythian Knights of City State & Tallahasse, FL; Tiger Bay Club;Alpha Kappa Mu; adv com Ofc of Adv Pub Negro Colls 1972. **HONORS/ACHIEVEMENTS:** Recip Danforth Flwshp Grant for Travel & Study Abroan on Promotion for Human Understanding 1972-73; Phi Delta Kappa Man of Yr 1970; Reg of Prom Am & Notables 1973-75; Outstdg Civilian Serv Medal Dept of Army 1973; Disgshd Leader of Educ Awd Lily White Assoc 1969; Awd of Excellence Tallahassee Urban League1973. **MILITARY SERVICE:** US armed forces 1942-46.

PERRY, BRENDA L.
Educator. **PERSONAL:** Born Nov 08, 1948, New Bedford, MA; daughter of Frank Andrade and Mary Mendes; married Clyde L Perry; children: Lisa Marie, Scott Anthony. **EDUCATION:** Middlesex Comm Coll, AS 1975; Goddard Coll, MA 1977; Stonehill Coll, BA 1981. **CAREER:** Roxbury Multi Svcs, asst dir of female residential serv 1976-78; Commonwealth of MA Dept of Youth Svcs, dir of female serv 1978-81; Commonwealth of MA Dept of Social Svcs, program evaluator & monitor 1981-83; Rollins Coll, asst dir of admissions 1983-. **ORGANIZATIONS:** Mem Theosophical Soc; natl mem The Smithsonian Assocs; voting mem Natl Assoc of College Admissions 1983-; voting mem Southern Assoc of College Admissions 1983-; mem Natl Assoc of Foreign Student Serv 1984-; mem bd dirs Seminole Co Mental Health Serv 1985-; mem Natl Assoc of Black School Educators 1986; mem Natl Arbor Day Foundation 1988-90; mem Natl Wildlife Assn 1989-. **HONORS/ACHIEVEMENTS:** Certificate of Appreciation Seminole Co Bd of Mental Health; Certificate in Drug Abuse Counseling Simmons Sch of Social Work 1975; poetry publication, American Poetry Anthology 1988. **BUSINESS ADDRESS:** Asst Dir of Admissions, Rollins College, P O Box 2720 Admissions, Winter Park, FL 32789.

PERRY, CARRIE SAXON
State representative. **EDUCATION:** Attended, Howard Univ. **CAREER:** Amistad House Inc, exec dir; Community Renewal Team of Greater Hartford Inc, administrator; Ambulatory Health Care Planning Inc of Hartford, administrator; Hartford Comm Trainers, administrator; CT Welfare Dept, administrator; CT General Assembly, state rep. **ORGANIZATIONS:** Life mem NAACP; pres Hartford Chap of 100 Black Women; exec bd mem Greater Hartford Black Democrats; exec bd mem Organized North Easterners; delegateFederation of Democrat Clubs; mem CT Caucus of Black Women for Political Action; mem Hartford Federation of Democratic Women; nominating chmn Permanent Commn on the Status of Hartford Women; corporator Oak Hill Sch for the Blind, Hartford Public Library, CT Black and Hispanic Urban Inst Inc; regional dir NatlOrg of Black Elected Women Legislators, Nat Black Caucus of State Legislators; pres Order of Women Legislators; chairperson NBCSL 1987 Conference; apptd Natl Conf of State Legislatures. **HONORS/ACHIEVEMENTS:** WKND's & CT Mutual's Leader of the Month Awd; Black People's Union, Univ of Hartford Outstanding Comm Serv Awd; Greater Hartford YWCA's Woman of the Year Awd; The World's Who's Who of Women; Certificate of Merit for Disting Achievement; Ancient and Accepted Scottish Rite of Freemasonry Certificate of Merit; CT Minority Business Assoc Salute. **BUSINESS ADDRESS:** Mayor, PO Box 3989, Old State House Station, Hartford, CT 06103.

PERRY, EUGENE CALVIN, JR.
Sports management company executive. **PERSONAL:** Born Feb 08, 1953, Charlottesville, VA; son of Eugene C Perry, Sr and Elizabeth Blair Perry; married Shelia Herndon, Sep 01, 1978; children: Shannon Janine Xavier Perry, Eugene Calvin Perry III. **EDUCATION:** Washington & Lee Univ, BA History 1975, JD 1978. **CAREER:** Justice Dept FBI, special agent 1978-86; Wilkinson & Perry Ltd, pres 1986-; Perry Group Intl Inc, pres 1987-. **ORGANIZATIONS:** Mem Phi Alpha Delta Legal Fraternity 1977-; parliamentarian Jr Chamber of Commerce 1979-; mem Amer Mgmt Assoc 1983-, Washington & Lee Alumni Council 1985-, Washington & Lee Univ Alumni Bd of Dirs 1987-; mem Speical Olympics, Philadelphia Adopt-A-School Program, Omega Psi Phi Inc 1988-. **HONORS/ACHIEVEMENTS:** Honor Award, Norfolk Jaycees 1980; co-producer of album "Ringing in the New Year," Philadelphia Mummers String Bands 1987. **HOME ADDRESS:** 6 Hamlet Court, Somerset, NJ 08873.

PERRY, FELTON
Actor, playwright. **PERSONAL:** Born Oct 11, Evanston, IL. **EDUCATION:** Wilson Junior College, Chicago IL; Roosevelt University, Chicago IL, BA; University of Chicago, graduate study. **CAREER:** Actor in "Hooperman" television series; actor in films "Walking Tall," "Magnum Force," "Towering Inferno," "Down and Out in Beverly Hills," "Robocop," and "Weeds"; television appearances in "Hill Street Blues," "LA Law," and "Cagney & Lacey"; actor in television films and in plays; director, YAY production company; playwright. **ORGANIZATIONS:** Amer Federation of Television and Radio Actors; Screen Actors Guild. **HONORS/ACHIEVEMENTS:** Author of plays "Or," "by the bi and bye," and "Sleep No More". **MILITARY SERVICE:** US Marine Corps, sgt, 4 years. **BUSINESS ADDRESS:** c/o Lori De Waal, Executive Vice President, Public Relations, The Garrett Co, 6922 Hollywood Blvd, Los Angeles, CA 90028. *

PERRY, FRANK ANTHONY
Educator, physician. **PERSONAL:** Born Dec 16, 1921, Lake Charles, LA; married Helena; children: Clara, Frank Jr, Robert, David. **EDUCATION:** Attended Xavier Univ; Meharry Med Coll, MD. **CAREER:** Sloan Kettering Inst, 1955-56; Naval Med Rsch Inst, 1956-57; Meharry Med Coll, assoc prof 1956-58, dir learning resources ctr 1968-75, prof of surgery 1968-; vice chmn dept of surgery 1983-. **ORGANIZATIONS:** Bd of dir Amer Cancer Soc, Children's Music, United Cerebral Palsy; life mem NAACP; mem Davidson Co Ind Council; mem Alpha Phi Alpha Frat, Sigma Pi Phi Frat, Amer CollSurgeons, Soc of Head & Neck Surgeons, Soc of Surgical Oncologists. **MILITARY SERVICE:** USN lt comdr 1956. **BUSINESS ADDRESS:** Vice Chairman Dept of Surgery, Meharry Med Coll, 1005 18th Ave N, Nashville, TN 37208.

PERRY, FRANKLIN D.
Automobile dealer. **CAREER:** Perry Lincoln-Mercury Inc, Montgomery AL, chief executive; Youngblood-Perry Lincoln-Mercury, Montgomery AL, chief executive. **BUSINESS ADDRESS:** Perry Lincoln-Mercury, 1040 Eastern Bypass, Montgomery, AL 36117. *

PERRY, HAROLD
Physician. **PERSONAL:** Born Jun 26, 1924, Hamtramck, MI; married Agnes; children: Harold, Karen, Michael. **EDUCATION:** Wayne State Univ, 1941-43; Cornell Univ, 1944; Howard Univ Coll of Medicine, MD 1948; Freedmen's Hospital, intern 1948-49, resident 1949-52; Memorial Hospital for Cancer & Allied Diseases 1952, 1955; Diploma Amer Bd Radiology 1955; licensure, OH 1957, DC 1960, MI 1970; Kress Fellow in Radiation Therapy at Memorial Hospital and Dept of Biophysics, Sloan-Kettering Inst, New York 1956-57. **CAREER:** Daniel Drake Memorial Hospital, asst attending rad 1957-60; Univ of Cincinnati Coll of Medicine, 1957-66; Cincinnati General Hospital, attending rad therapy 1957-66, assoc dir rad 1957-66; VA Center, attending rad 1961-66, consultant 1965-66; Sinai Hospital, sr assoc attending physician 1966-73; Abraham & Anna Srere Radiation Therapy Center, dir radiation therapy 1966-; Detroit General Hospital, sr assoc 1968-; VA Hospital, consultant radiotherapist 1972-; Sinai Hospital of Detroit, attending physician 1973-; Detroit-Macomb Hospital Assn, consultant 1976; Wayne State Univ School of Medicine, clinical prof dept of radiation oncology 1982; Sinai Hospital of Detroit, chmn dept of radiation therapy 1982-, physician 1973-. **ORGANIZATIONS:** Bd dir MI Cancer Found 1968; Hospital Advisory Council SE MI Reg Med Program 1969-; mem MI State Medical Soc Com on Cancer 1971; Wayne County Med Soc Resolutions Com 1974; MI Cancer Found 1974; MI Cancer Coord Com 1974; alt del MI State Med Soc 1974-75, del 1975-76; pres elect MI Radiol Soc 1976-77; chmn Radiation Therapy Advisory Panel Comp Health Plan Council of SE MI 1978-; speaker, Univ WI 1978, Nuclear Med Liege Belgium 1979, 7th Intnl Conf Tokyo/Kawasaki Japan 1980; Radiology Section Natl Med Assn 84th Annual Convention & Science Assembly 1979; pres elect MI Soc of Therapy Radiology 1981-82; del Wayne County to MI State Med 1982-83; pres NSTR; chmn of bd NSTR 1983-84; reg rep council for Affiliated Radiation Oncology Soc; al Bio-Medical Computwn E Allen Jr lectr; org & prog comm 8th ICCRToronto, Ontario Canada 1984; mem exec com MI Cancer Found 197AAs, NY A-; AMA; MI State Med Soc; Wayne County Med Soc; vice pres of alumni assoc dept of radiation oncology Mem Sloan Kettering Canter Center 1986-87; vice chairman, bd of trustees, MI Cancer Found 1985-87; mem Exec Comm of the Council of Affiliate Reg Radiation Oncology Soc 1986; MI Rad Soc alt counselor to Amer Coll of Rad 1986-87. **HONORS/ACHIEVEMENTS:** Licensure DC 1960, OH 1957, MI 1966; mem Kappa Pi Hon Med Soc; Hon mention A Cressy Morrison Award 1963; Amer Men of Sci 1967; Alumni Hall of Hon Hamtramck HS 1970; Fellowship Amer Coll of Radiology 1976; numerous rsch projects presentations bibliographies; listed in Amer Men & Women of Sci 1975, 1976, 1979. **MILITARY SERVICE:** USAF capt 1953-55; AUS pfc 1942-46. **BUSINESS ADDRESS:** Chairman, Dept of Radiation Therapy, Sinai Hospital of Detroit, 6767 W Outer Dr, Detroit, MI 48235.

PERRY, HAROLD ROBERT
Clergyman. **PERSONAL:** Born Oct 09, 1916, Lake Charles, LA. **EDUCATION:** St Augustine Sem; St Mary's Sem. **CAREER:** Ordained priest Roman Catholic Ch 1944; apptd provincial of so province of Soc of the Divine Word 1964;-65; New Orleans Archdiocese, aux bishop. **ORGANIZATIONS:** Mem Bd of Admin for the US Cath Conf of Bishops; Comm Rel Cncl of New Orleans; Natl Assembly for Social Policy & Devel of NY. **HONORS/ACHIEVEMENTS:** Citation for Outstanding Work on Gov's Commn on Law Enforcement & Admins of Criminal Justice for LA 1970; Consecrated Bishop by Archbishop Egidio Vagnozzi 1966; 1st Amer Black raised to Fullness of Priesthood 1965; aptd Vicar Gen of Archdiocese of New Orleans 1965; 1st Black Provincial Superior of St Augustine Province for the Fathers of the Soc of the Divine Word 1964; 1st Black Clergyman to act as guest chaplain, give invocation for opening of US Congress 1963; 1st Black priest to serve a full term as rector of St Augustine Sem 1985. **BUSINESS ADDRESS:** Archdiocese of New Orleans, 7887 Walmsley Ave, New Orleans, LA 70125.

PERRY, JEAN B.
Educator. **PERSONAL:** Born Aug 31, 1946, New York City. **EDUCATION:** Fashion Inst of Tech, AA 1968; NY Univ, BS 1970; NY city Tech Coll, AA 1980; Teacher Coll Columbia Univ, MA 1986. **CAREER:** NY Daily News "Good Living" section, feature writer; NY Daily News, reporter 1970; Black Enterprise Mag, wrote "Black Bus in Profile" column on free lance basis 1973-74; Daily News Conf for HS Editors, speaker 1974 & 75; Essence Mag, health & fitness editor 1982-84; Ethical Culture School, asst teacher 1985-87; Los Angeles Unified School Dist, teacher 1987-. **ORGANIZATIONS:** Mem Kappa Tau Alpha 1970-, Kappa Delta Pi 1986-. **HONORS/ACHIEVEMENTS:** Recip Martin Luther King Alumni Assn Awd for Print Journalism NYUniv 1978; Media Awd for an Invest Feature Story for NY Daily News on Childhood Obesity NY Heart Assn 1979; Conceived and edited story on

hypertention for Essence which received a William Harvey Awd from the Squibb Corp and the Amer Med Writers Assoc 1984; Conceived and edited story on Diabetes for Essence which received the Media Awd from the Amer Diabetes Assoc 1984. **BUSINESS ADDRESS:** Educator, Los Angeles Unified School, 315 Holmby Ave, Los Angeles, CA 90024.

PERRY, JERALD ISAAC, SR.
Clergyman & consultant. **PERSONAL:** Born Jun 03, 1950, Edenton, NC; son of John Isaac Perry and Evelyn Jones Perry; children: Jerald I Jr, Davin E, Felicia Shantique Mayo. **EDUCATION:** Automation Machine Training Center, diploma 1968; Elizabeth City State Univ, BA matriculating; Shaw Divinity School, MA matriculating; Aviation Storekeeper "A" School Meridian MS. **CAREER:** Edenton Housing Auth, be member 1979-86; Amer Heart Fund Assoc, bd member 1980-86; bd member Edenton Chowan Bd of Education 1982-86; Elizabeth City State Univ, computer oper, programmer. **ORGANIZATIONS:** Bd mem Church of God in Christ Trustee Bd; mem NC Corsortium Comm 1972; gospel disc jockey/ acct mgr WZBO-AM 1975-; mem NC State School Bd Assn 1982-;mem Natl School Bd Assn 1982-; mem NC Humanities Comm 1982-; bd mem State Employees Assoc of NC 1985; mem Black State Ministers Coalition; bd mem EdontonChowan Civic League; disc jockey/acct mgr WBXB-Love 100 FM Station; Sunday school supt Eastern NC Greater NC Diocese of Church of God in Christ Inc; mem Meridian Lodge #18; JW Hood Consistory #155 United Supremem Council; 33 degree AASR of Freemasonry Prince Hall Affiliation. **HONORS/ACHIEVEMENTS:** Outstanding Young Man of America 1979;1983; Kappa Delta Phi Honor Soc Eliz City State Univ 1982-83; Letter of Accomodation Commanding General for ExpeditingH1 Priority Documents; Letter of Accomodation for Serving as Wing NCO of Barracks when received Barracks of Quarter Selection; Bluejacket of the Month and Bluejacket of the Quarter MCAS Cherry Point, NC. **MILITARY SERVICE:** USN. **HOME ADDRESS:** PO Box 1211, Edenton, NC 27932. **BUSINESS ADDRESS:** Computer Operator/Programmer, Elizabeth City State Univ, Information Systems Div, Elizabeth City, NC 27909.

PERRY, JOHN B.
Transportation services manager. **PERSONAL:** Born Jan 14, 1945, Americus, GA; married Yvonne P Halback; children: Monique, Keith. **EDUCATION:** Stony Brook Univ Stony Brook, NY, 1973-74; Miami Dade Community Coll Miami, FL, 1978-79. **CAREER:** Eastern Airlines, senior instructor Miami, FL 1977-80; operating manager Atlanta, GA 1980-83; manager sales & services Daytona Beach, FL 1983-85; manager ramp services Atlanta, GA 1985-86; Newark Intl Airport NJ, dir sales & serv 1986-. **ORGANIZATIONS:** Member Black Caucus of Eastern Airlines 1977-; member Amer Soc of Travel Agents 1983; co-chairman United Negro College Fund Drive Volusia County 1984-85; chairman business ed & youth comm Rotary Intl 1984-85; board of directors Richard V Moore Comm Center Daytona Beach, FL 1984-85. **HONORS/ACHIEVEMENTS:** Salute to Leadership Award United Negro College Fund Daytona Beach, FL 1984; Carter G Woodson Award Westside Business & Prof Assn Daytona Beach, FL 1984. **HOME ADDRESS:** 151 Country Club Dr #8, Union, NJ 07083. **BUSINESS ADDRESS:** Dir Sales & Service, Eastern Airlines, Newark International Airport, Newark, NJ 07114.

PERRY, JUNE CARTER
Foreign service officer. **PERSONAL:** Born Nov 13, 1943, Texarkana, TX; daughter of Bishop W Carter and Louise Pendleton Carter; married Frederick M; children: Chad Douglass, Andre Frederick. **EDUCATION:** Mundelein Coll Fine Arts Scholarship Mundelein Coll Scholarship, BA cum laude 1965; Univ of Chicago Woodrow Wilson Fellow, MA 1967; Hamline Coll, St Paul MN Faculty Fellowship at Middle East Inst, Certificate 1968. **CAREER:** US Community Serv Admin, special asst for public affairs 1977-79; Amer Embassy Lusaka, 1983-85; dir of publlic affairs ACTION 1979-83; Amer Embassy Harare, 1986-87; Dept of State, political officer, desk officer Botswana 1987-89; special asst, Secretary of State, 1989-. **ORGANIZATIONS:** Dir of public affairs WGMS-AM/FM 1974-77; producer/ commentator WGTS-FM & WTOP-AM 1973-74; coll instructor/ high school teacher NC A&T Univ, Univ of of Maryland, Marianas High School Micronesia 1967-70; mem Amer Assn of Univ Women 1973-76; mem AFTRA 1974-78; vice pres Women's Inst/Amer Univ 1975-; mem of bd Greater Washington Boys & Girls Club 1975-79; mem Finance Comm Natl Capital YMCA 1975-79; vice pres Friends for the Advancement of African Civilization 1979. **HONORS/ACHIEVEMENTS:** Blacks in Indus Award, Harlem Y & Time Magazine 1975; Sup Achiever Award, RKO General Broadcasting 1976; Human Rights Award, UN Natl Captial Chapter 1977; Cited in Women's Book of World Records & Achievements, Doubleday/Anchor Press 1979; Distinguished Alumna Award, Mundelein Coll 1980; Special Achievement Award, Action Agency 1980; "Ancient African Heroines", article, Washington Post, 1983; Outstanding Performance Award, Action Agency 1982; State Dept Meritorious Serv 1985, 1987. **BUSINESS ADDRESS:** Office of the Deputy Secretary of State, Dept of State, Washington, DC 20520.

PERRY, JUNE MARTIN
Executive director. **PERSONAL:** Born Jun 10, 1947, Columbia, SC; daughter of Mark Anthony Martin and Junie Alberta Martin; divorced; children: Kevin Martin Perry, Krystle Martin Perry. **EDUCATION:** North Carloina Central Univ, Durham NC, BS Psychology, 1965; Univ of Wisconsin, Milwaukee WI, MSSW Social Welfare, 1969. **CAREER:** Milwaukee Co DSS, Milwaukee WI, social worker, 1971-73, purchase of service coord, 1973-75; New Concept Self Devel Center, Milwaukee WI, co-founder exec dir, 1975-. **ORGANIZATIONS:** Mem, Delt Sigma Theta Sorority, 1969; mem, NASW, 1971; mem, Natl Black Child Devel Inst, 1986; mem, bd of dir, Girl Scouts of Amer, 1986-88; mem, bd of dir, Wisconsin Council on Human Concerns, 1986; mem, bd of dir, Wisconsin Advocacy Coalition, 1987; mem, bd of dir, Milwaukee Mgmt Support Org, 1987; mem, Natl Forum for Black Public Admin, 1988. **HONORS/ACHIEVEMENTS:** Sojourner Truth Award, Eta Phi Beta, 1986; Trailblazer of the Year, Black Women's Network, 1986; Toast & Boast Award, Natl Women's Political Caucus, 1986; author of "Parents As Teachers of Human Sexuality," 1986; Top Ladies of Distinction Comm Service Award, 1987; Social Worker of the Year, Health Service Professionals of Wisconsin, 1988. **BUSINESS ADDRESS:** Exec Dir, New Concept Self Devel Center, Inc, 636 W Kneeland St, Milwaukee, (414)271-7496, 53212.

PERRY, LARRY STEVEN
Physician. **PERSONAL:** Born May 22, 1948, Baltimore, MD; married Inez Braye; children: Lisa L, Leah N, Linda M. **EDUCATION:** Mrgn St U, bS Biol 1970; Mhry Med Coll, MD 1975; Med Coll of WI, Res Intrnl Med 1978. **CAREER:** Mlwk Co Med Hosp, crdlgst 1979-; Prvdnt Hosp Bltmr, intnsv care staff 1978-79. **ORGANIZATIONS:** Mem Am Coll of Physcns 1979-80; mem Am Hrt Assn 1979-80; mem Hyprtnsn Scrng Com 1979-80; dir Ch Nurse Scrng Prog; dir of crnry risk fctr clnc affirm actn com Med Coll of WI. **HONORS/ACHIEVEMENTS:** Crdlgy fellow Med Coll of WI 1979-81; publ Echo Dgnss of Left Atrl Thrmbs AHA/CABG for Ptnts with Hypthyrdsm & Angn AHA/2 Dmnsnl Echo in Myxm's of the Hrt Abstrct ACC 1980.

PERRY, LEE CHARLES, JR.
Regional product coordinator. **PERSONAL:** Born Feb 22, 1955, St Louis, MO; married Rena Armstrong; children: Raimon, Jonathan. **EDUCATION:** Forest Park Comm Coll, AS Elec Engrg Tech 1974; Comm Coll of the Air Force, Electronics Honor Grad 1975; Eastern KY Univ, BS 1980; Industrial Tech, grad with recognition. **CAREER:** IBM St Louis, customer engr 1980-83, program support rep 1983-85; IBM Regional Office Kansas City, sr nsd specialist 1985-. **ORGANIZATIONS:** Minister United Pentecostal Church 1984-. **MILITARY SERVICE:** USAF e-5 staff sgt equipt chief 4 yrs; Good Conduct Medal, Certificate of Recognition for Outstanding Performance as Peer Instructor USAF. **BUSINESS ADDRESS:** Sr NSD Specialist, IBM Corporation, 9401 Indian Creek Pkwy, Ste 700, Overland Park, KS 66210.

PERRY, LEONARD DOUGLAS, II
Educator. **PERSONAL:** Born Mar 14, 1952, Philadelphia, PA. **EDUCATION:** Temple Univ, BS, MEd; Purdue Univ, EdS. **CAREER:** Temple Univ, resident coord 1976-77, assoc to dean of students 1977-80; Purdue Univ, asst dean of students 1980-85; FL State Univ, assoc dean of student develop 1985-. **ORGANIZATIONS:** Consultant peer counseling training Indiana Teen Inst 1984-86; Midwest Regional Coord Ethnic Minority Network NASPA 1984; coord Conf Volunteer Serv Natl Assoc of Student Personnel Admin 1984-86; consultant needs assessment Hollins Coll 1985; consultant peer counseling training Univ of South Carolina 1986; chair educ comm NAACP Lafayette IN; mem Natl Assoc of Student Personnel Administrators, Assoc for Educ Comms and Tech, Amer Soc for Training and Develop, Natl Soc for Performance and Instruction; consultant Min Stdnt Prog Dev St Josephs Col 1981, Staff Dev Big Bend Cmty Coord Child Care Agcy 1986, Organizational Structure & Dev Hanna Area Cmty Ctr 1984, SADD 1984 & 85, peer ministry training IN Stdnt Mnstry Retreat 1983, minority stdnt prog dev West GAColl 1986, needs assessmentUniv of NC 1986; mem Crisis Cntr 1985, planning comm 1st NASPA 4 East Reg Conf 1985, 1984 Ntl Conf; creator/producer "Soul Plus Mag; instructor Peer Cnslg Trng, Minority Ldrshp Dev, Experiential App to Ldrshp Dev, Coll Tchg Wkshop, Career Dev. **HONORS/ACHIEVEMENTS:** Martin Luther King Awd FL State Univ/BSU 1986. **HOME ADDRESS:** 2161 Victory Garden Dr, Tallahassee, FL 32301. **BUSINESS ADDRESS:** Associate Dean, Florida State Univeristy, 324 Bryan Hall, Tallahassee, FL 32306.

PERRY, LOWELL W.
Business executive. **PERSONAL:** Born Dec 05, 1931, Ypsilanti, MI; son of Lawrence C Perry and Lillian Bass Perry; married Maxine Lewis; children: Lowell Jr, Scott, Merrideth. **EDUCATION:** UUniv MI, BA 1953; Detroit Coll of Law, JD 1960. **CAREER:** Pittsburgh Steelers Football Club NFL, player 1956, asst coach 1957, scout 1958-60; Frank A Picard, law clrk 1960-61; Chev Motr Div GM Detrt, personnlrep 1961-62; Nat Lbr Rel Bd 7th Reg Dtrt, atty 1962-63; Chrysler Corp, dir of personnel 1963-79; LIP Inc, pres 1979-83; Michigan Bell Telephone Co, dir of government affairs 1983-; chrmn US Equal Opportunity Commission (EEOC) 1975-76. **ORGANIZATIONS:** Mem MI St Bar Assn; Dir Sky-pac Entrprs Inc mem bd dir NFL Charities NY; bd dir Untd Found Met Dist; bd dir Boys Clubs Met Dist; bd GovUniv MI Club of Detroit; bd dir Black child and Family Inst Lansing; bd of dirs, Detroit College of Law; bd of dirs, Starr Commonwealth Schools. **HONORS/ACHIEVEMENTS:** Nat Hnr Soc Ypsilanit High Sch; Sr HopnUniv MI; All-Amer Ftbl HonUniv MI; NCAA Silver Anniversary Athlete Scholar Awd 1978; Honorary Doctorates of Laws, Ferris State Univ, 1976, Wilberforce Univ, 1976. **MILITARY SERVICE:** USAF 1st ltn. **BUSINESS ADDRESS:** Dir of Government Affairs, Michigan Bell Telephone Co, 444 Michigan Avenue Rm 818, Detroit, MI 48226.

PERRY, LOWELL W., JR.
Business executive. **PERSONAL:** Born May 10, 1956, Ypsilanti, MI; son of Lowell Perry and Maxine Perry; married Kathleen Tucker, Mar 21, 1987; children: Lowell W, Tucker Nichol. **EDUCATION:** Yale Univ, BA Admin Sciences 1978; graduate work marketing, Seattle Univ 1987. **CAREER:** Nutone Div Scovill, sales rep 1978-81; Seattle Seahawks, dir sales & mktg 1981-88; Access Plus Communications Sr. Sales Executive. **ORGANIZATIONS:** Bd mem Kirkland C of C 1984-; bd Kidsplace-Action Agenda Taskforce 1985; corresp sec Zeta Pi Lambda Chap of Alpha Phi Alpha 1983-84; 1st vice pres Zeta Pi Lambda of Alpha Phi Alpha 1984-; bd East Madison YMCA 1985-; pub rel comm Eastside Mental Health Cntr 1983-84; bd Cooperative Charities; bd Washington Generals. **HONORS/ACHIEVEMENTS:** Rookie of the Year Nutone Div Scovill 1978-79; Chairman Sustaining Membership Drive East Madison YMCA 1984-85; Project Developer & Coord of "Blow the Whistle on Drugs" a statewide family substance abuse prog; Outstanding Young Men of America 1987; speaker of the house Seattle Marketing Executives. **HOME ADDRESS:** 17909 NE 129th, Redmond, WA 98052. **BUSINESS ADDRESS:** Access Plus Communications, 325-118th Ave SE Suite 300, Bellevue, WA 98005.

PERRY, MARGARET
Library director. **PERSONAL:** Born Nov 15, 1933, Cincinnati, OH; daughter of Rufus Patterson and Elizabeth (Anthony) Perry. **EDUCATION:** Western MI Univ, AB 1954; Cath Univ of Amer, MSLS 1959; Universite de Paris, Certificat d'Etudes Sum 1956; NY City Coll, attended 1957-58. **CAREER:** New York Publ Library, young adult/reference librarian 1954-55, 1957-58; US Army Europe, post librarian 1959-67; US Military Acad West Point, circulation librarian 1967-70; Univ Rochester, head educ library 1970-75, assoc prof 1975-82, joint appt asst prof English dept 1973-75, head reader serv div acting dir of libraries; asst dir of libraries for reader serv 1975-82; Valparaiso Univ, dir of libraries 1982-. **ORGANIZATIONS:** Mem Amer Civil Liberties Union; life mem Amer Library Assn; assoc editor Univ Rochester Library Bulletin 1970-73; chair education comm, 19th Ward Community Assoc Rochester 1972-73; mem, 2nd vice pres Urban League of Rochester 1978-80; pres Northern IN Area Libraries 1986-88; mem Delta Kappa Gamma 1984-. **HONORS/ACHIEVEMENTS:** Scholarship to Seminar Amer Writing and Publishing, Schloss Leopoldskron Salzburg, Austria, 1956; honorable mention 1965, first prize 1966, Armed Forces Writers League Short Story Contest; second prize, Frances Steloff Armed Forces League Short Story Contest, 1968; bibliog Directory of Librarians in the US and Canada; author of A Bio-Bibliography of Countee P Cullen, Greenwood Press 1971, Silence to the Drums: A Survey of the Literature of the Harlem Renaissance, Greenwood Press 1976, The Harlem Renaissance: An Annotated Bibliography and Commentary, Garland 1982, The Short Fiction of Ru-

dolph Fisher, Greenwood Press 1987, and numerous articles. **BUSINESS ADDRESS:** Dir of Libraries, ValparaisoUniv, Moellering Library, Valparaiso, IN 46383.

PERRY, PATSY BREWINGTON
University professor. **PERSONAL:** Born Jul 17, 1933, Greensboro, NC; daughter of James C Brewington and Rosa Kirby Brewington; married Wade Wayne Perry, Dec 23, 1955; children: Wade Wayne Perry, Jr. **EDUCATION:** North Carolina Coll, Durham, NC, BA (magna cum laude), 1950-54; North Carolina Coll, Durham, NC, MA, 1954-55; Univ of North Carolina, Chapel Hill, NC, PhD, 1968-72. **CAREER:** Georgetown High School, Jackson, NC, teacher, 1955-56; North Carolina Central Univ, Durham, NC, reserve book librarian, 1956-58, instructor, 1959-63, assoc prof, 1972-74, prof, 1974-79, prof and English dept chmn, 1979-; Duke Univ, Durham, NC, visiting prof, 1975. **ORGANIZATIONS:** Mem, YWCA, 1976-; mem The Links Inc, 1976-; life mem, Coll Language Assn; mem, senator 1986-, Philological Assn of the Carolinas; mem, South Atlantic Modern Language Assn; mem, Assn of Departments of English; mem, The Langston Hughes Soc; reader, College Board English Composition Test (ETS), 1985-. **HONORS/ACHIEVEMENTS:** Alpha Kappa Mu Honorary Soc, 1953; Danforth Scholarship Grant, Summer, 1967; Career Teaching Fellowship, Univ of North Carolina, 1968-69; Faculty Fellow, North Carolina Central Univ, 1968-71; nominee, ACE Fellow Program in Academic Admin, Amer Council on Educ, 1977; Ford Foundation Writing Fellow, Recognition for Excellence in Teaching Writing, 1989; author of "The Literary Content of Frederick Douglass' Paper Through 1860," CLA Journal 1973, "One Day When I Was Lost: Baldwin's Unfulfilled Obligation," chapter in James Baldwin: A Critical Evaluation, edited by Therman B O'Daniel, Howard Univ Press 1977, and biographical sketches in Southern Writers-Biographical Dictionary, Louisiana State Univ Press 1979, and The Dictionary of Literary Biography, Gale Research 1986. **BUSINESS ADDRESS:** Prof and Chmn, Dept of English, North Carolina Central Univ, Communications Bldg, Rm 307, Durham, NC 27707.

PERRY, RICHARD
Novelist, educator. **PERSONAL:** Born Jan 13, 1944, New York, NY; son of Henry Perry and Bessie Draines Perry; married Jeanne Gallo, Sep 14, 1968; children: Malcolm David, Alison Wright. **EDUCATION:** City College of the City University of New York, BA, 1970; Columbia University, MFA, 1972. **CAREER:** Pratt Institute, Brooklyn NY, associate professor of English, 1972—. **ORGANIZATIONS:** PEN, Teachers and Writers Collaborative, National Writers Union, National Council of Teachers of English. **HONORS/ACHIEVEMENTS:** New Jersey State Council on the Arts Award, 1980; New Jersey Writers Conference citation, 1985; author of Changes, Bobbs-Merrill, 1974; author of Montgomery's Children, Harcourt, 1984. **MILITARY SERVICE:** US Army, 1968-70. **BUSINESS ADDRESS:** Department of English, Pratt Institute, 215 Ryerson St., Brooklyn, NY 11205.
*

PERRY, ROBERT CEPHAS
Government official. **PERSONAL:** Born Mar 01, 1946, Durham, NC; married Blossom N Sanborn; children: Jessica Lahela, Benjamin Lono. **EDUCATION:** Wittenberg Univ, BA Political Sci. **CAREER:** Dept of State, foreign serv officer Vietnam 1969-70, foreign serv officer Santiago Chile 1971-72, foreign serv officer Asmara Ethiopia 1973-75; foreign serv officer 1975-77; foreign serv officer Mexico City Mexico 1977-80; foreign serv officer 1980-84. **HONORS/ACHIEVEMENTS:** Meritorious Honor Awd Dept of State 1975.

PERRY, ROBERT LEE
Educational administrator. **PERSONAL:** Born Dec 06, 1932, Toledo, OH; son of Rudolph R Perry and Katherine Bogan Perry (deceased); married Dorothy Larouth Smith; children: Baye' Kito, Kai Marlene, Ravi Kumar. **EDUCATION:** Bowling Green St Univ, BA Sociology 1959, MA Sociology 1965; Wayne St Univ, PhD Sociology 1978. **CAREER:** Lucas Cnty Juv Ct Toledo, OH, probation counselor 1960-64, juvenile ct referee 1964-67; Detroit Inst Techn, asst prof 1967-70; Department of Ethnic Studies, Bowling Green State Univ chmn, 1970-; Licensed Practicing Counselor, 1988. **ORGANIZATIONS:** Consult Natl Inst of Law Enf and Crimin Just 1978-82; consult Div Soc Law and Econ Scis Natl Sci Found 1980; consult Children's Def Fund Task Force on Adoption Assist 1980; chair Status of Women & Minorities Comm N Cent Sociol Soc 1983-85; bd mem Citizens Review Bd Lucas Cnty Juv Ct Toledo, OH 1979-85; bd mem Inst for Child Advocacy Cleveland, OH 1981-85. **HONORS/ACHIEVEMENTS:** Sigma Delta Pi natl Spanish Hon Soc 1958; Alpha Kappa Delta Natl Soc Honor Soc 1976; $37,00000 Grant Dept HEW 1979; Post Doct Fellowship Amer SociolSoc Inst for Soc Research UCLA 1980. **MILITARY SERVICE:** USAF A/IC Air Man First Class 1953-57. **BUSINESS ADDRESS:** Chair/Dept Ethnic Studies, Bowling Green State University, Ethnic Studies Prog, Bowling Green, OH 43403.

PERRY, ROD
Athlete. **PERSONAL:** Born Sep 11, 1953, Fresno, CA. **EDUCATION:** Fresno City Coll; CO State. **CAREER:** Los Angeles Rams, defensive back 1975-. **HONORS/ACHIEVEMENTS:** Lead Rams to the League ldrsp in interceptions with 32; NFC All-Star Sporting News 1978; NFC Championship Games 1975-76 & 78-79; NFL Championship Game 1979; Pro Bowl 1978. **BUSINESS ADDRESS:** Los Angeles Rams, 10271 W Pico, Los Angeles, CA.

PERRY, THELMA DAVIS
Retired executive editor. **PERSONAL:** Born in Wagner, OK; widowed; children: 3. **EDUCATION:** Howard U, AB, JD, MA. **CAREER:** Fisk Univ TN, rsch staff mem 1940-42; Langston Univ OK, chmn soc sci dept 1948-57; Johnson C Smith Univ NC, fac mem 1957-68; Geo Washington Univ DC, assoc prof lect 1971-72; Assn for Study of Negro Life & Hist, retired exec ed, guest editor Negro Hist Bulletin. **ORGANIZATIONS:** Mem Nat Lawyers Club; mem Acad of Pol Sci. **HONORS/ACHIEVEMENTS:** Author Hist of Amer Tchrs Assn pub by Nat Educ Assn 1975; held 2 Rosenwald fellowships 1943-45; held gchng asst & fellow Howard Univ 1935-36; valedictorian of law class 1931; numerous publications, Soc Forces, Journal of Soc Psych, Journal of Negro Educ, Journal Hist, Negro Hist Bulletin, articles, poems, book review, etc; co-author, The Washington DC Chapter of The Links, Inc.

PERRY, WAYNE D.
Research economist. **PERSONAL:** Born Oct 14, 1944, Denton, TX; married Linda Jackson; children: LaNitha, Chelese, Wayne. **EDUCATION:** Tuskegee Inst, BS 1967; B NM, MS 1969; Carnegie Mellon U, PhD 1975. **CAREER:** Ford Motor Co, co-op student mfg eng 1964-67; Tuskegee Inst, resrch & tchng asst 1963-67; Sandia Lab, mech engr dir adv computer aided design proj1967-71; Manpower Studies Proj Carnegie Mellon U, instr mgr rsrch coor 1971-75; Housing Studies Defense Manpwr & Energy Pol Studies The RAND Corp, econ pol proj dir 1975-. **ORGANIZATIONS:** Mem Am Statis Assn; The Inst of Mgmt Sci; Econometric Soc N Am; Am Soc Mech Engr; pub many rsrch papers mem Omega Psi Phi; NAACP; co-fndr Concerned Black Employees Sandia Lab; Black Coalition Albuquerque & Pitts; LA Yth Motivat Task Force; dir LA Carnegie-MellonUniv Alum Assn; dir Ladera Heights Civic Assn. **HONORS/ACHIEVEMENTS:** Rsrch grnts from US Dept of Labor; Dept of Energy; Dept of Defense; HUD; HEW; Sandia Lab & Serv Awd Nuclear Weapons Devel Atomic Energy Comm 1969; edit reviewer "Policy Analysis"Univ of CA Berkeley 1978-; Resrch Paper Winner Am Soc Mech Engr 1967; Adad Schlshp Tuskegee Inst 1962-67; grad flwhp Carnegie-MellonUniv 1971-75. **BUSINESS ADDRESS:** 1700 Main St, Santa Monica, CA 90406.

PERRY, WILLIAM ANTHONY
Professional football player. **PERSONAL:** Born Dec 16, 1962, Aiken, SC. **EDUCATION:** Attended Clemson Univ. **CAREER:** Orlando, 1985; Chicago Bears, defensive tackle 1985-. **HONORS/ACHIEVEMENTS:** Played in NFC Championship Game following 1985 season; played in NFL Championship Game following 1985 season. **BUSINESS ADDRESS:** Defensive Tackle, Chicago Bears, Halas Hall, 250 N Washington Rd, Lake Forest, IL 60045.

PERRY, WILLIAM E.
Educator. **PERSONAL:** Born Nov 20, 1932, New York. **EDUCATION:** VA Union U, BA 1955;Univ of Buffalo, MSW 1957; ColumbiaUniv Assoc, doctoral study. **CAREER:** Temple Univ, prof chmn graduate dept school of soc admin; Harlem Hosp Patient Care Prog Eval Unit Columiba Univ School of Public Health, research assoc exec dir 1967-69; consultant variety of public & private agency in human serv field. **ORGANIZATIONS:** Mem Nat Assn of Black Soc Workers; chmn Black Faculty & Staff TempleUniv 1970-72. **BUSINESS ADDRESS:** Temple Univ Sch of Soc, Adminstrn Ritter Annex, Philadelphia, PA 19122.

PERRY, YVONNE SCRUGGS
Urban planner, educator. **PERSONAL:** Born Jun 24, 1933, Niagara Falls, NY; children: Cathryn, Rebecca. **EDUCATION:** NC Central U, BA 1955; FreeUniv of Berlin German Huchschulefiir Politik, cert 1956;Univ MN, MAPA 1958;Univ of PA, PhD. **CAREER:** Howard Univ, prof of city planning; Comm Planning & Devel Dept of HUD, dep asst sec 1977-79; Dept of City & Regional Planning Howard Univ, asso prof chpn 1974-77; Univ PA, faculty administration 1970-74; HUD, fed Liaison off 1967-70; Ford Found Philadelphia Council for Comm Advancement, assoc dir, dir of planning 1964-67; Philadelphia, comm renewal spec 1961-64; Research & Planning Wharton Center, dir 1959-61. **ORGANIZATIONS:** Mem Am Inst of Planners; vice pres Assn Collegiate Schs of Plng; vice pres PA Housing Fin Corp 1974; commr Mobile Homes Commn; lectr US Info Serv in Ethiopia, Kenya, S Africa, Nigeria, Ghana; bd mem World Affairs Counc 1970-73; Phiula Council for Comm Advancement 1970-74; Nat Workshop YMCA 1971-74; Crime Prevention Assn 1964-69; Gov's Commn IPPA 1971-72. **HONORS/ACHIEVEMENTS:** Fulbrigh fellow 1955-56; SAIS schlshp Johns Hopkins 1956-57; Elks Schlshp 1951-55; grad students council awd Grad Educators 1975. **BUSINESS ADDRESS:** Rm 7100 HUD Bldg, 7th & D Sts SW, Washington, DC 20410.

PERRYMAN, LAVONIA LAUREN
Journalist. **PERSONAL:** Born in Detroit, MI. **EDUCAȚION:** Wayne State U, BA 1971; Ferris Coll, 1969; Howard U, MA 1978. **CAREER:** Soc Rsrch Applic Corp, comm dir; owner opr 1st girls bskbl clinic; Pizazzz Corp, pres; Afbony Modeling & Talent Agy, professional model instr; Teai & Record, pub rel dir; WCAR Radio, reprt 1973-76; WTVS-56, black journal reprt. **ORGANIZATIONS:** Vp Nat Assn of Media Women; mem NAACP; Negro Counc of Women; Black Commctrs; All Star Bsktbl Player; Congressman John Conyers Women Orgn; Stud Non-violents Orgn. **HONORS/ACHIEVEMENTS:** Athletic awd Ferris State Coll 1969; Ms Soul of MI & Ms Autorama 1972; speech awd VFW 1973-74; Ms Black MI; Ms Black Detroit; Ms Elks; Ms Swimsuit; Ms Congeniality; Ms Misty of MI 1974-75; Media Woman of the Yr; Spirit of Det Awd City of Detroit; Citz Awd Booker T Wash Bus Assn; Most Unique Dresser Detroit News 1976-77; Citz Awd Detroit City Counc; Detroiter's Awd Detroit Experience; Disco Martin Citz Awd. **BUSINESS ADDRESS:** 800 18th St NW, 3rd Floor, Washington, DC 20006.

PERSAUD, INDER
Business executive. **PERSONAL:** Born Oct 23, 1926, Georgetown, Guyana;married Nalini Singh; children: 4 Children. **EDUCATION:** London Engl, prof degree in hosp admin Inst Hosp Admin 1956. **CAREER:** Berbice Group Guyana, hosp admin 1958-60; Georgetown Hosp, 1960-67; Morrisania Hosp Bronx, acting admin 1967-68; Cumberland Hosp Brooklyn, asso exec dir 1968-73, exec dir 1973-. **ORGANIZATIONS:** Mem Hlth Com Nat Urban League; New York City chap Nat Assn Hlth Serv Exec pres 1972; founder mem Consumers Accreditation Counc; fdr vch Ft Greene Coop. **BUSINESS ADDRESS:** 39 Auburn Pl, Brooklyn, NY.

PERSON, DAWN RENEE
Educational administrator. **PERSONAL:** Born Dec 10, 1956, Sewickley, PA; daughter of Conrad Person Sr and Fannie Mae Person (deceased); married Harold Eugene Hampton; children: Bryson Thomas Person-Hampton. **EDUCATION:** Slippery Rock Univ, BS Educ 1977, M Educ 1979; Teachers College Columbia Univ (ABD) 1986-. **CAREER:** Slippery Rock Univ, human relations counselor 1978-79, minority affairs coord 1979-80, advisor to black & intl students 1980-81; CO State Univ, dir black students 1981-85; Lafayette Coll, asst dean academic serv 1985-. **ORGANIZATIONS:** Workshop facilitator Male/Female Relation 1978-; mem ACPA, AACD 1981-; mem NAACP Easton PA Chap 1985-87; mem Black Conference-Higher Educ PA 1986-87; NASPA; Leadership Lehigh V.lley 1989-90. **HONORS/ACHIEVEMENTS:** Outstanding Young Professional Women of Amer 1984,85,86; Outstanding Women of Amer 1986; NASPA graduate case study competition winner 1988. **BUSINESS ADDRESS:** Assistant Dean Academic Serv, Lafayette College, 219 Markle Hall, Easton, PA 18042.

PERSON, EARLE G.
Dental surgeon. **PERSONAL:** Born Apr 28, 1928, Mt Vernon, IL; married Estelle Mccraty. **EDUCATION:** Univ IL, BS 1950; CreightonUniv Omaha, DDS 1958. **CAREER:** Pvt Pract dentistry 1958-; Creighton U, faculty 1960-62. **ORGANIZATIONS:** Mem IL Soc Microbiologists; Amer & NE Dent Assc; surg staff Archbishop Bergan Mercy Hosp & Doctor's Hosp Omaha; state chmn NDA Council Dental Care Prog 1974-; pres NE Soc Clin Hypnosis 1973; mem Creighton Univ Adv Council 1972-; bd dir KOWH AM/FM Radio; Acad Gen Dentistry 1972-; pres bd dir Comprehensive Health Assc Omaha 1973-; pres Urban League 1965-68; assemblyman Natl Black Pol Assembly 1972-; del Natl Black Conv Gary 1972; Little Rock1974; natl Dem Conv 1972; mem Alpha Sigma Nu, Omicron Kappa Upsilon. **HONORS/ACHIEVEMENTS:** Owler's Award dist srv dent & civic affairs 1968; Who's Who Amer Politics 1973-74; Who's Who Midwest 1974; Noteworthy Amers & Commun Ldrs 1974; Intl Biogs 1975; Intl Platform Assc 1974-75. **MILITARY SERVICE:** AUS 2nd lt 1950-52, 1st lt 1952-53. **BUSINESS ADDRESS:** 3707 N 24 St, Omaha, NE 68110.

PERSON, LESLIE ROBIN
Deputy ATC operations officer. **PERSONAL:** Born Nov 14, 1962, St Louis, MO; married Kyro Jonathan Carter. **EDUCATION:** Attended, Nichols State Univ 1979-80, Kent State Univ 1980-81; Univ of Cincinnati, BA 1982. **CAREER:** US Air Force, 2012 communications squadron atc officer trainee 1984-85, 1903 communications squadron deputy atc ops officer 1985-86, 2146 communications group deputy atc ops officer 1986-. **ORGANIZATIONS:** Mem 2012 CS Unit Adv Council 1984-85; assoc mem Pima Country Special Olympics Group 1985; sec Davis-Monthan Company Grade Officer GP 1985-86; founding mem Davis-Monthan Special Olympics GP 1985-86; mem Santas in Blue 1985-86; base chairperson Combined Federal Campaign 1985. **MILITARY SERVICE:** USAF 1st lt 3 1/2 yrs; Air Force Commendation Medal 1985-86. **HOME ADDRESS:** 11991 Hitchcock Dr, Cincinnati, OH 45240. **BUSINESS ADDRESS:** Deputy ATC Operations Ofcr, United States Air Force, 2146 CG, PSC Box 2431, APO San Francisco, CA 96366.

PERSON, WAVERLY J.
Geophysicist. **PERSONAL:** Born May 01, 1926, Blackridge, VA; son of Santee Person and Bessie Butts Person; married Sarah Walker Person, Nov 06, 1954. **EDUCATION:** St Paul's Coll, Lawrenceville VA, BS, 1949; American Univ, Washington DC, attended, 1959-60; George Washington Univ, Washington DC, attended, 1960-63. **CAREER:** Dept of Commerce, NOAA, Boulder CO, geophysicist, 1958-73; US Geological Survey, Denver & Golden CO, geophysicist, 1973-. **ORGANIZATIONS:** Seismological Soc of Amer, 1965-, treasurer, Eastern Section, 1968-; past pres, Flatirons Kiwanis, 1972-; Amer Geophysical Union, 1975-; bd of dir, Boulder County Crimestoppers, 1986-. **HONORS/ACHIEVEMENTS:** Honorary Doctorate, St Paul's Coll, 1988; Outstanding Govt Communicator, Natl Assn of Govt Communicators, 1988; Distinguished Alumni: Citation of the Year Award, Natl Assn for Equal Opportunity in Higher Educ, 1989; Meritorious Serv Award, USGS, 1989; many publications on earthquakes in scientific journals and contribution to a number of text books in the Earth Sciences. **MILITARY SERVICE:** US Army, 1st Sergeant, 1944-46, 1951-52; Good Conduct Medals, Asian Pacific Medal. **HOME ADDRESS:** 5489 Seneca Place, Boulder, CO 80303.

PERSON, WILLIAM ALFRED
Educator. **PERSONAL:** Born Aug 29, 1945, Henderson, NC; married Juanita Dunn; children: William Alfred II; Wilton Antoine. **EDUCATION:** Johnson C Smith Univ, BA 1963-67; University of Georgia, MEd 1972-73, EdD 1973-77. **CAREER:** Wilkes Cty Board of Education, teacher 1967-72; Univ of Georgia, Grad Asst/Admin Asst 1973-77; Mississippi State Univ, asst prof 1977-80, assoc prof 1980-. **ORGANIZATIONS:** Treasurer Phi Delta Kappa 1982-83; vice pres Phi Beta Sigma 1982-83; pres Phi Beta Sigma 1983-; bd of directors Starkville Kiwanis Breakfast Club 1984-. **HONORS/ACHIEVEMENTS:** Two academic scholarships 1963-65, Who's Who Among Students 1966-67 Johnson C Smith University; Sigma Man of the Year Phi Beta Sigma 1979; Outstanding Young Men of America 20th ed 1982. **HOME ADDRESS:** PO Box 424, Starkville, MS 39759. **BUSINESS ADDRESS:** Associate Professor, Mississippi State University, P O Box 5365, Mississippi State, MS 39762.

PERSONS, W. RAY
Attorney, partner. **PERSONAL:** Born Jul 22, 1953, Talbottan, GA; son of William Persons and Frances Crowell Persons; married Wendy-Joy Mottley Persons, Sep 24, 1977; children: Conrad Ashley, April Maureen. **EDUCATION:** OH State Univ, 1971-72; Armstrong State Coll, BS 1975; OH State Univ, JD 1978. **CAREER:** Armstrong State Coll, coll prof 1979-80; Natl Labor Rel Bd, attny 1980-82; Wells Braun Persons Law Firm, partner/owner 1982-; Cong Lindsay Thomas, legislative counsel; Arrington & Hollowell, P.C., attorney 1986-. **ORGANIZATIONS:** Mem State Bar of GA 1979-; treas Riceboro Comm Improvement Found 1982-83; gen counsel Congressional Black Assoc 1984-85; mem Fed Bar Assoc 1984-85, Leadership GA Foundation 1985-; Legal Advisor to Brook Glen Neighborhood Assn 1986-; Ohio State Univ Alumni Assn 1981-. **HONORS/ACHIEVEMENTS:** Regents Scholar Armstrong State Coll 1973-75; Silver "A" Awd Armstrong State Coll 1975; Co-author OH Civil Rules Supplement 1978. **HOME ADDRESS:** 3883 Holy Cross Dr, Decatur, GA 30034. **BUSINESS ADDRESS:** Attorney & Partner, Arrington & Hollowell, PC, 2200 First Atlanta Tower, 2 Peachtree St, NE, Atlanta, GA 30383.

PETERMAN, LEOTIS
Educational administration. **PERSONAL:** Born Sep 19, 1934, Abbeville, AL; married Lucy Bell; children: Karen Yvette, Sharron Yvonne. **EDUCATION:** AL State Univ, BS 1955; IN Univ, MS 1959; Univ of AL, Doctorate in Ed 1982. **CAREER:** Lemoyne-Owen Coll, registrar, bus mgr 1955-62; AL State Univ, asst to pres, bus mgr 1962-67, vice pres for admin 1967-75, budget dir, controller 1975-84, vice pres for bus & finance 1984-85; Fisk Univ, chief financial officer 1986-. **ORGANIZATIONS:** Pres Pan-Hellenic Council 1977-85; state dir Alpha Phi Alpha 1979-85; mem Phi Delta Kappa, Delta Pi Epsilon, Kappa Delta Pi, Montgomery United Way, YMCA, The Comm Council; past pres Alpha Phi Alpha; trustee bd mem & deacon First Baptist Church; mem Assoc of Supervision & Curriculum Develop, Natl Assoc of Coll & Univ Business Officers, First Baptist Capitol Hill Church. **HONORS/ACHIEVEMENTS:** Listed in Who's Who in Ed 1960; Dir of the Year Alpha Phi Alpha 1980; Listed in Outstanding Young Men of Amer 1982. **BUSINESS ADDRESS:** Chief Financial Officer, Fisk University, 1000 17th Avenue North, Nashville, TN 37208.

PETERMAN, PEGGY M.
Newspaper columnist. **PERSONAL:** Born Oct 06, 1936, Bessemer, AL; daughter of William P Mitchell and Annie M Townsend Mitchell; divorced; children: Frank W, John M. **EDUCATION:** Howard Univ Sch of Lib Arts, BA 1958; Howard Univ of Law, LLD 1961. **CAREER:** St Petersburg Times, columnist news features dept 1986-, women's dept 1968-70, news reptr 1965-67; White, Peterman & Sanderlin, legal secr 1963. **ORGANIZATIONS:** Mem FL Press Club; Delta Sigma Theta Sor Inc; Delta Sigma Theta Sor St Petersburg Chpt; mem National Coalition of 100 Black Women 1988-; mem National Association of Black Journalists 1980-. **HONORS/ACHIEVEMENTS:** Comm Serv Award African People's Socialist Party; Meritorious Achievement Award 1988, Florida A & M Univ; Gwen Cherry Freedom Fighters Award, Heritage Foundation 1988; Woman of Achievement Award, St. Petersburg Links; fellow Multicultural Management Program, Univ of Missouri 1988; Speakers Bureau, Florida Endowment for the Humanities 1987-88. **HOME ADDRESS:** 1015 28 Ave S, St Petersburg, FL 33705.

PETERS, AULANA LOUISE
Appointed government official. **PERSONAL:** Born Nov 30, 1941, Shreveport, LA; married Bruce Franklin Peters. **EDUCATION:** Notre Dame School for Girls, diploma 1959; College of New Rochelle, BA Philosophy 1963; Univ of S CA, JD 1973. **CAREER:** Publimondial Spa, secty/English corres 1963; Fibramianto Spa, secty/English corres 1963-64; Turkish Delegation to Org for Economic Coop and Develop, English corres 1965; Cabinet Braconnier AAA Translation Agency, translator/interpreter 1966; Organ for Economic Coop and Develop Scientific Rsch Div, admin asst 1966-67; Gibson Dunn & Crutcher, attorney 1973-84; US Securities and Exchange Comm, comm 1984-. **ORGANIZATIONS:** Former mem Los Angeles Co Bar Assn, State of CA Bar Assn, Hughes Langston Bar Assn, Women Lawyers of Los Angeles Bar Assn; mem Black Women Lawyers Assn, Amer Bar Assoc; mem Univ of S CA Law Sch Law Alumni Assoc; mem Women's Forum Washington, Council on Foreign Relations Inc NY; panelist Los Angeles Co Bar Assoc Law & Motion Bd 1980; panelist Los Angeles Co Bar Assoc sponsored prog entitled "Bridging the Gap" 1980; lecturer Rutter Group Prog entitled "Successful Discovery in the Los Angeles Superior Court" 1981; panelist Assoc of Bus Trial Lawyers Seminar on Unfair Competition Los Angeles 1982. **HONORS/ACHIEVEMENTS:** Co-chairperson Exec Bd of the Univ of S CA Hale Moot Court Honors Program Los Angeles; finalist runner-up Univ of S CA Hale Moot Court Honors Prog Los Angeles; Natl Assoc of Bank Women Inc Washington Achiever Awd 1986. **BUSINESS ADDRESS:** Commissioner, Securities & Exchange Commsn, 450 5th St NW, Washington, DC 20549.

PETERS, BROCK G.
Actor, singer, producer. **PERSONAL:** Born Jul 02, 1927, New York City, NY; married Di Di Daniels; children: Lise. **EDUCATION:** Univ of Chgo, 1944-46; City Coll NY, 1946-47; student of acting with various individuals. **CAREER:** Porgy & Bess 1943, South Pacific 1943, Anna Lucasta 1944-45, My Darlin' Aida 1952, Great White Hope 1970, Lost in the Stars 1974, theatrical appearances; num stock engagements; DePaur Inf Chorus, bass soloist 1947-50; films incl, Carmen Jones 1954, Porgy & Bess 1959, To Kill a Mockingibrd 1962, The L-Shaped Room 1963, The Pawnbroker 1968, The Incident 1969, Slaughter II 1976, Lost in the Stars 1975, Soylent Green 1977; actor Five on the Black Hand Side 1973, This Far by Faith 1975, co-producer; actor Roots II Next Gen, Huckleberry Finn 1981, Star Trek IV; numTV guest appearances; PBS Network "Voices of Our People" actor & supervising producer. **ORGANIZATIONS:** Mem Actors Equity Assoc, AFTRA, Screen Actors Guild, Amer Guild Variety Artists; founder and chmn Dance Theatre of Harlem, Free So Theatre, Third World Cinema, Media Forum; former chmn CA State Arts Comm; bd of trustees Dance Gallery of LA; founder/chmn Maga Link Inc and Communications Bridge Inst; commnr CA State Film Commn. **HONORS/ACHIEVEMENTS:** All Amer Press Assoc Awd; Box Office Blue Ribbon Awd; Allen & AME Awd; Amer Soc African Culture Emancipation Awd 1962; Man of the Year Douglas Jr HS1964; Golden Globe Awd 1970; Drama Desk Awd 1972; Outer Circle Critics Awd 1972; Tony Nomination 1973; Best Actor Mar del Plata Film Fest 1974; Neil Smith Awd S Afr Film Fest 1974; Hon Docts Sienna Hgts Fine Arts Coll Univ of MI, Otter Beia Coll 1975,78; Inducted Black Filmmakers Hall of Fame 1976; Life Achievement Awd Natl Film Soc 1977; Image Awd NAACP 1979,82,87; Emmy Awd 1982. **BUSINESS ADDRESS:** Delbro Enter Inc c/o Morse, 15900 Ventura Blvd, Encino, CA 91436.

PETERS, CHARLES L., JR.
Real estate developer, business executive. **PERSONAL:** Born Sep 20, 1935, New Orleans; married Doris Jackson; children: Leslie Jean, Cheryl Lynne. **EDUCATION:** So Univ, BS (cum laude) 1955; USC, MS 1959, grad study. **CAREER:** Natl Housing Consult Inc, pres ch bd 1973-. **ORGANIZATIONS:** Admin consult for bus serv LA Unified Sch Dist; mem Omega Psi Phi; LA Urban League; YMCA; Natl Assn of Housing & Redev Officials, Omega Life Membership Foundation. **HONORS/ACHIEVEMENTS:** Natl Assn of Homebuilders Man of Yr Omega Psi Phi 1964, 1974, 1983; Outstanding Educator LA City Cncl 1970; listed Who's Who Among Students in Amer Colls & Univs 1953. **MILITARY SERVICE:** AUS capt 1955-67. **BUSINESS ADDRESS:** President, Natl Housing Consult Inc, 4640 Lankershim Blvd, Ste 202, North Hollywood, CA 91602.

PETERS, ERSKINE ALVIN
Educator. **PERSONAL:** Born Mar 16, 1948, Augusta, GA; son of George Raymond Peters Sr and Marie Johnson Peters. **EDUCATION:** Yale Univ, summer study 1968; Paine Coll, BA English 1969; Oberlin Coll, Post-baccalaureate study 1969-70; Princeton Univ, PhD English 1976; Sorbonne Paris, summer study 1984. **CAREER:** Morristown Coll, tutor 1970-72; Univ of CA Berkeley, assoc prof of Afro-Amer Literature. **ORGANIZATIONS:** Advisor Oakland Scholar Achiever Program 1980-82; discussion leader SATE Program at San Quentin Prison 1980-83. **HONORS/ACHIEVEMENTS:** First Recipient of Frank J Henry Award, Univ of GA 1968; Rockefeller Fellowship in Afro-Amer Studies 1972-76; Books, William Faulkner, The Yoknapatawpha Worldand Black Being 1983, African Openings to the Tree of Life 1983, Fundamentals of Essay Writing 1983. **BUSINESS ADDRESS:** Professor of English, Univ of Notre Dame, Notre Dame, IN 46556.

PETERS, FENTON
Educational administrator. **PERSONAL:** Born Jul 10, 1935, Starkville, MS; son of Pellum Peters and Cora Peters; married Maggie Teresa Malone; children: Avis Campbell Wilcox, Pellum, Alton. **EDUCATION:** Rust Coll, AB 1958; MS State Univ, MEd 1969, Ed D 1983. **CAREER:** Henderson HS, principal 1968-70; Henderson Jr HS, principal 1970-76; Starkville HS, principal 1976-81; Starkville Public Schools, chap 1 coord 1981-84, admin asst to supt; Superintendent, Holly Springs Public Schools 1986-. **ORGANIZATIONS:** Presenter Stu-

dent Teaching MS St Univ 1978; presenter Continuing Educ MS St Univ 1979; bd of dirs Starkville Chamber of Comm 1983-84; bd of trustees Oktibbeha Co Hosp 1984-; bd of dirs Holly Springs Chamber of Commerce 1988-89. **HONORS/ACHIEVEMENTS:** Natl Science Found science fellowship 1962, 1962-63, 1967; state choir dir Church of Christ 1983; Public Serv Awd United Way 1985; Presidential Citation, Natl Assn for Equal Opportunity in Educ, 1987. **HOME ADDRESS:** 375 North West Streeet, Holly Springs, MS 38635.

PETERS, JAMES SEDALIA, II
Educator & psychologist. **PERSONAL:** Born in Ashdown, AR; married Marie Ferguson (deceased); children: James S III, Donna Marie, Kimberly C Bourne-Vanneck. **EDUCATION:** Southern Univ Baton Rouge, BS; Hartford Seminary Found, MA; IL Inst of Tech, MS; Purdue Univ, PhD. **CAREER:** US Naval Training Ctr Great Lakes IL, tchr psychologist 1942-45; Veterans Adminstration, clinical & counseling psychologist 1946-55; Springfield Coll, dir asst prof of psychology 1955-56; Div of Vocational Rehab CT, administrator 1956-81; Univ of Hartford, adjunct prof; Private Practice, psychologist. **ORGANIZATIONS:** Dir New England Bank & Trust Co 1968-; dir Amer Automobile Assn 1970-; mem Alpha Phi Alpha Frat, Society for Sigma Xi, Sigma Pi Phi Frat, Episcopal Church. **HONORS/ACHIEVEMENTS:** TH Harris Fellowship Southern Univ; Genl Educ Atlanta Univ; Veterans Admin Fellow Purdue Univ; Dept of Health Educ & Welfare Harvard Univ. **MILITARY SERVICE:** USN specialist tchr 1st class 1942-45. **HOME ADDRESS:** PO Box 431, Storrs, CT 06268.

PETERS, KENNETH DARRYL, SR.
Government official. **PERSONAL:** Born Jan 27, 1949, Englewood, NJ; son of John C Peters, Jr and Lena Jones Peters; married Katie Coleman, Nov 27, 1976; children: Kenneth Jr, Kevin. **EDUCATION:** Fisk Univ, BA 1967-71; Univ of KS, MSW 1971-73; Univ of CA, Cert 1973; Acad of Health Sci Ft Sam Houston, Cert 1981. **CAREER:** Catholic Social Svc, school consult 1973-78; State of CA Stockton, psychiatric soc worker 1978-80; State of CA Sacramento, soc serv consult 1980-84, program analyst 1984, soc serv admin. **ORGANIZATIONS:** Bd of dir Fisk Student Enterprises 1968; vice pres NAACP-Collegiate Chapter Nashville 1968-69; minority recruitment comm Univ of KS 1971-72; mem San Joaquin Mental Health Advisory Bd 1978-; bd of dir Maternal & Child Health Disability Prevention Bd 1979-; sec Alpha Phi Alpha Frat Inc 1980; mem Natl Conf on Social Welfare 1982-, CA Respiratory Examining Bd 1983-. **HONORS/ACHIEVEMENTS:** Dean's List Univ of KS 1972-73; Acad Honors Spanish Fisk Univ 1968; Eligible Bachelor Ebony Mag 1975; Biography in Outstanding Young Men of Amer Inc 1983; Commendation CA Assemblyman Pat Johnston 1983, CA Senator John Garamendi 1983. **MILITARY SERVICE:** AUS Res maj 1979-; Appt Asst Detach Cmdr 1982; Commend for Combat Environ Transition Training 1983; Appt Annual Training Module Officer in Charge 1985, participated in Team Spirit '86 in Republic of Korea. **HOME ADDRESS:** 2663 Fallenleaf Dr, Stockton, CA 95209. **BUSINESS ADDRESS:** District Contracts Officer, California Department of Transportation, 1976 E Charter Way, Stockton, CA 95205.

PETERS, MICHAEL
Dancer, choreographer. **CAREER:** Videos Beat It, Thriller, Running With The Night, Hello Uptown Girl, Love is a Battlefield, choreographer; broadway musical Dream Girls, choreographer; Pieces of Ice, Donna Summers 1st concert tour of US, German prod of Jesus Christ Superstar, The Awakening, Quartet, choreographer; Purlie, Raisen, The Wiz, dancer. **HONORS/ACHIEVEMENTS:** Tony Awd Broadway Musical Dream Girls 1981; Image Awd NAACP 1983; Amer Music Awd for Best Video Choreography.

PETERS, ROSCOE H., JR.
President. **PERSONAL:** Born Mar 03, 1945, Charleston, WV; married Brenda Marie Adams; children: Kenneth, Roscoe, Jeaninne. **EDUCATION:** General Motors Inst, attended 1973. **CAREER:** IBM Corp, customer engr 1969-72; Chevrolet Motor Div, zone serv mgr 1972-82; RH Peters Chevrolet, pres 1982-. **ORGANIZATIONS:** Owner Peters Fuel 1976-; president Peters Realty 1980-; dir of engrg Peters Broadcasting 1984-. **MILITARY SERVICE:** USAF staff sgt 4 yrs active, 3 yrs reserves; Airman Medal for Valor. **BUSINESS ADDRESS:** President, RH Peters Chevrolet, Inc, 102 Orchard Park Rd, Hurricane, WV 25526.

PETERS, SAMUEL A.
Attorney. **PERSONAL:** Born Oct 25, 1934, New York, NY; son of Clyde Peters and Amy Matterson; married Ruby M Mitchell; children: Robert, Samuel Jr, Bernard. **EDUCATION:** New York Univ, BA 1955; Fordham Univ Sch of Law, LLB 1961. **CAREER:** Federal Communications Comm, law clerk 1961; Lawyer's Comm for Civil Rights Under Law, staff atty 1968-69; US Dept of Justice, trial atty 1961-68; Legal ir Atlantic Richfield Co, employee relations counsel 1970-80, sr counsel public affairs; Rio Hondo Coll, instructor; Self-Employed, attorney. **ORGANIZATIONS:** Mem Langston Bar Assn; mem American Bar Assn; mem Fordham Law Review Alumni Assn; pres A Creative Network; mem CA Museum of Afro-Amer History & Culture; mem NAACP LA Chapt; mem bd of dirs Weingart Ctr Assoc; mem Central City East (Los Angeles) Task Force. **MILITARY SERVICE:** AUS sp-2 3 yrs. **HOME ADDRESS:** 11471 Kensington Rd, Los Alamitos, CA 90720. **BUSINESS ADDRESS:** Attorney, 11471 Kensington Rd, Los Alamitos, CA 90720.

PETERS, SHEILA RENEE
Psychologist. **PERSONAL:** Born Jun 27, 1959, Columbus, MS. **EDUCATION:** Univ of NC at Chapel Hill, BA (w/Honors in Psychology) 1981; Vanderbilt Univ, MS 1985. **CAREER:** Luton Community Mental Health Ctr, dept of psychology/human develop doctoral candidate in clinical psychology prog, clinical therapist. **ORGANIZATIONS:** Pres Org of Black Grad & Professional Students 1982-85; steering comm 1983 Eco-Psychology Conf 1982-83; dir of youth ministries Key-Stewart UM Church 1983-87; treas Assoc of Black Psychologists 1984-85; mem Div of Psychology of Women 1984-87, Div of Comm Psychology 1984-87, Southeastern Psychological Assoc 1986-87, Nashville Alum Chap of Delta Sigma Theta 1986-87. **HONORS/ACHIEVEMENTS:** Outstanding Young Woman of Amer 1981; Peabody Minority Fellowship vAnderbilt 1981-84; Crusade Scholarship Bd of Global Ministries 1982-85; NIMH Traineeship 1984-85. **HOME ADDRESS:** 4224 Kings Ct, Nashville, TN 37218.

PETERS, WILLIAM ALFRED
Manager. **PERSONAL:** Born Mar 01, 1940, Atlantic City, NJ. **EDUCATION:** Temple Univ, BS 1963; Pace Univ, MBA 1978. **CAREER:** Fortune Circulation Time Inc, natl sales dir 1979-; Fortune Mag Time Inc, asst circulation dir 1978-79; Time Inc, dir of edn; Emerson Hall Pub, vpof mrkt 1970-72; Harper & Row Pub, editor 1968-70, mrkt & rep 1976-80. **HONORS/ACHIEVEMENTS:** Recipt Black Achgievers in Industry Award Harlem Br YMCA 1978. **BUSINESS ADDRESS:** Time Inc, 1271 Sixth Ave, New York, NY 10020.

PETERSEN, ALLAN ERNEST
Manager. **PERSONAL:** Born Dec 13, 1918, New York, NY; married Florence Ridley; children: Robert. **EDUCATION:** W Hervey Bus Coll, AD 1952; City Coll of NY, 1954. **CAREER:** Ny State Unemployment Div, supv 1946-52; Our World Mag, bus mgr 1952-54; Distilled Brands, sales rep, salesman supv, sales mgr 1954-78; Peerless Importers, general sales mgr 1987. **ORGANIZATIONS:** Mem NAACP; Urban Leg; Bottle & Cork Sales Club; Nat Negro Golf Assn. **HONORS/ACHIEVEMENTS:** AUS 1st lt 1941-45. **BUSINESS ADDRESS:** General Sales Manager, Peerless Importers, Inc, 16 Bridgewater St, Brooklyn, NY 11222.

PETERSEN, ARTHUR EVERETT, JR.
Business development consultant. **PERSONAL:** Born Feb 05, 1949, Baltimore, MD; son of Arthur Peterson and Marguerite Peterson. **EDUCATION:** Comm Coll of Baltimore, AA 1971; Morgan State Univ, BA 1973; Atlanta Univ, MBA 1975. **CAREER:** Transportation Inst NC A&T State Univ, rsch assoc 1975-77; Exec Office of Transportation & Construction, sr planner 1977-79; Simpson & Curtin, Inc, consultant 1979-80; Lawrence Johnson & Assoc, rsch assoc 1980-82; Ctr for Transportation Studies, Morgan State Univ, project dir 1982-83; Public Tech projectmgr 1983-88; Baltimore Minority Business Develop Ctr, procurement specialist 1986-86; Associated Enterprises, Inc Consultant 1988-89; Boone, Young & Assoc Inc Consultant 1989-. **ORGANIZATIONS:** Mem Conf of Minority Transp Officials Transp Rsch Board, Natl Forum for Black Public Admin, Baltimore Marketing Assoc; mem Toastmasters Inc. **HOME ADDRESS:** 1823 W North Ave, Baltimore, MD 21217. **BUSINESS ADDRESS:** Director, Management Services, Balto-Minority Business Development Center, 2901 David Park Dr Ste 201, Baltimore, MD 21217.

PETERSEN, EILEEN RAMONA
Judge. **PERSONAL:** Born Apr 18, C'sted, St Croix, VI. **EDUCATION:** Hampton Inst, BS 1959, MA 1959; Howard Univ, JD 1966; Geo Wash Univ, Advanced Studies MA 1970. **CAREER:** Territorial Court of the VI, judge. **ORGANIZATIONS:** Mem VI, Natl, Wash DC, Amer Bar Assocs 1967-72; Natl Assoc of Women Judges, mem; Amer Judges Assoc, mem; World Assoc of Judges of the World Through Peace Law Ctr, mem; League of Womens Voters & Bus and Professional Women's Club, mem; VI Cncl of Boy Scouts of Amer, cncl mem; VI Girl Scouts ofAmer, board mem 1982-85. **HONORS/ACHIEVEMENTS:** William Hastie Awd Natl Bar Assoc 1982; Women of the Yr Business & Professional Women's Club 1976; Outstanding Woman of the Yr Howard Univ 1970; Alpha Kappa Alpha Sorority, Inc 1970. **BUSINESS ADDRESS:** Judge, Territorial Court of the VI, RFD 2 Box 9000, Kingshill, St Croix, Virgin Islands of the United States 00850.

PETERSON, ALAN HERBERT
Association executive philanthropist. **PERSONAL:** Born Jul 09, 1948, East Orange, NJ; son of William Willis Peterson (deceased) and Evelyn Lucretia Hughes Peterson; married Michelle Monica Morrison Peterson, Sep 27, 1986. **EDUCATION:** Central TX Coll, Criminal Invest Cert 1970; LaSalle Law School, Cert 1971; Essex Co Police Acad, 1971-72; Bergen Co Police Acad, Cert 1978; Law Enforcement Officers Training Sch, Cert 1979; Doctor of Divinity 1985. **CAREER:** Rutgers Univ Police Dept, police officer 1971-72; East Orange NJ Aux Police, patrolman 1972-; Essex Cty Sheriff's Dept NJ, spec deputy 1972-75; Modern Carpet Serv NJ, vice pres 1972-75; Conrail Police Dept, police officer/investigator 1975-85; Survival Assoc, pres, ceo 1975-; Masters of Philanthropy, ceo 1982-; Suicide Prevention Group PA, exec dir, suicidologist 1985-; ordained minister 1985-; Natl Police Officers' Assoc of Amer, NJ state pres 1985-; Nat'l Exec Dir, USCCCN National Clearing House on Satanic Crime in America 1988-; Publisher, The American Focus Publishing Co, 1986-; Law Enforcement Special Agent - Law Enforcement Division, New Jersey Society for the Prevention of Cruelty to Animals 1988-. **ORGANIZATIONS:** Commis E Orange NJ Welfare Dept 1975-; mem Frat Order of Police NJ 1976-; mem NY Transit Police Hnr Lgn NY 1976-, NJ Police Hnr Lgn NJ 1976-, Natl Blk Police Assoc NJ 1976-, NJ Narcotic Enf Officers Assn NJ 1976-; 1st black So NJ Police Invest for Conrail Police Cmtr Div 1978; mem Amer Criminal Justice Assn 1979-, Police Benev Assoc NJ #304 1982-, Natl Disabled Law Officers Assn NJ 1983-; 1st black bd mem, vp, chmn of the bd Make A Wish FoundNJ 1983-86; mem Candlelighters Fnd DC 1984-; prtcpnt/spnsr Phone Pal/Pen Pal Prog The Ctr for Attitudinal Healing of CA-NJ 1984-; 1st blk sec 1984, 1st blk pres1985 NJ Law Enf Lions Club; mem Burntout Policemen & Friend Assn NJ 1985; media prod asst US Vet Admin NJ 1985; corp dir Ctr for Blind MI 1985; mem Amer Legion Montclair, NJ 1985; mem Gavaliers Toastmasters 1985-; suicide presenter NJ Educ Assn 1985-; charter mem Amer Assoc of Suicidology 1987; co-chrmn Citizens' Sickle Cell Commission 1989-; Chaplain, Minority Involvement Committee of New Jersey 1988-. **HONORS/ACHIEVEMENTS:** Police Commendation Newark NJ Police Dept 1971; Senate Resolution NJ Senate 1977; Police Commendation Conrail Police Dept NJ 1978; 1st black Heroism Commendation Recipient from Conrail Police Dept for heroic actions during Jan 7, 1983 Texaco Oil Co explosion 1984; Recip of Citation for Bravery Natl Police Ofcrs Assn of Amer Louisville, KY 1985; Recip of Veterans Admin Leadership Award 1985; Recip of Veterans Admin Voluntary Serv Award 1985; Jerseyan of the Weekby the Newark, NJ Star Ledger as result of receipt of Citation for Bravery; Natl Fundraising Chmn Center for the Blind Lansing, MI; nom Amer Focus on Millionaires in Amer 1987, 1989; Cert of Appreciation Southern NJ Region of Hadassah; Outstanding Community Service Award, International Yo uth Organization 1988; Author: The American Focus on Satanic Crime - Volume 1, 1988; Author: Satanic Crime and the SPCA, 1988; first black national exec bd of dir mem: The National Police Officers' Assoc of America, 1987. **MILITARY SERVICE:** AUS spec agent ci 1967-70; Vietnam 1968-69; Vietnam Cmpgn Mdl & Serv Mdl; AUS Crim Invest Div Awd, RVN Div Awds, Good Conduct Mdl; Hon Dschg Cert. **HOME ADDRESS:** PO Box 403, Chatham Road, Short Hills, NJ 07078. **BUSINESS ADDRESS:** National Executive Director, United States Citizens' Commission on Crime and Narcotics, P O Box 1092 - National Headquarters, South Orange, NJ 07079.

PETERSON, ALPHONSE
Dentist, dental educator. **PERSONAL:** Born Sep 09, 1926, St Louis; married Jessie Clark; children: Alphonse Jr, Alan, Alex. **EDUCATION:** Howard Univ, Washington DC, BS

1948; Meharry Med Coll, School of Dentistry, Nashville TN, DDS 1954; Royal Soc of Health, England, DDS 1954; postgraduate study, Northwestern Univ Dental School 1961, State Univ of Iowa 1963, St Louis Univ 1965, Washington Univ School of Dentistry 1969, Univ of Nebraska Medical Center 1971, Harvard Univ 1971, Armed Forces Inst of Pathology 1972. **CAREER:** Gen practice dentist, 1957-; Washington Univ School of Dental Medicine, St Louis MO, assoc prof of oral diagnosis and radiology, 1972-89; Homer G Phillips Hospital and Ambulatory Center, St Louis MO, asst chief, dept of oral surgery, and dir of cardiopulmonary resuscitation educ, 1973-85; Meharry Medical College School of Dentistry, Nashville TN, 1981-. **ORGANIZATIONS:** Sec-treas, Guam Dental Soc, 1956-57; pres, Amer Acad Dental Electrosurgery, 1977; mem, pres 1983, Downtown St Louis Lions Club; mem, Kappa Alpha Psi Frat; mem, Pleasant Green Missionary Baptist Church; mem, Chi Delta Mu Medical-Dental Fraternity; mem, 33rd Degree Prince Hall Free Masons; mem Medinah Temple #39 AEAONMS; bd dir, Ferrier Harris Home for the Aged; bd dir St Louis Branch of the Opportunities Industrialization Center. **HONORS/ACHIEVEMENTS:** Selected to represent the US at the Third Kenyan-Amer Dental Seminar, Nairobi, Kenya, 1973; elected Fellow, Royal Soc of Health, England, 1972; published "Diagnostic Electrosurgery, To Rule In or Out Malignacy of Oral Tissues," Quintessence Intl-Dental Digest, 1977, and "The Use of Electrosurgery in Reconstructive and Cosmetic Maxillofacial Surgery," Dental Clinics of North Amer, 1982; mem Kappa Sigma Pi Scholastic Hon Frat; mem Gamma Chap, Omicron Kappa Upsilon Natl Dental Hon Soc; lectr "The Use of Electrosurgery in Reconstructive Surgery of the Tongue, Lip, Ear and Nose," 66th Annual World Dental Congress of Federation Dentaire Internationale, Madrid Spain, 1978. **MILITARY SERVICE:** USAF, oral surgery resident, capt 1955-57, chief of oral surgery, major, 1970-72. **BUSINESS ADDRESS:** 3737 N Kingshighway Blvd, St Louis, MO 63115.

PETERSON, BENJAMIN See ALLEN, ROBERT L.

PETERSON, CARL M.
Surgeon, business executive. **PERSONAL:** Born Jun 05, 1914, Opelika, AL; son of William L Peterson Sr and Carrie Belle Prince Peterson; married Hulda Hayward; children: Carl M, Louis H. **EDUCATION:** Morehouse Coll, AB 1937; Meharry Med Coll, MD 1941; KC Gen Hosp, resident 1946-49. **CAREER:** The Doctors Clinic KC MO, founding partnr, Surgeon. **ORGANIZATIONS:** Diplomate Am Bd Surgery 1953; fellow Am Coll of Surgeons 1956; fellow Intl Coll of Surgeons 1956; fellow SW Surgical Congr 1968; pres Jackson CoMed Soc 1972; pres KC Surgical Soc 1973-74; pres Truman Med Ctr West Med Dentl Stf 1975; bd Trustees KC Blue Shld 1975; life NAACP 1963; curator LincolnUniv 1960-66; commr Urban Renewal Bd of KC 1967-72; Urban Leg Bd KC 1960; chmn Citizens Assn 1968; elder United Presby Ch USA. **MILITARY SERVICE:** AUS maj med corps 1942-46. **BUSINESS ADDRESS:** The Doctors Clinic, 2701 E 31st St, Kansas City, MO 64128.

PETERSON, CLARENCE JOSEPHUS
Labor rep. **PERSONAL:** Born Sep 18, 1932, Stubenville, OH; married Diane Gladys Johnson; children: Robin Whitaker, Dana W Scott, Phillip P Scott, Marla J Peterson. **EDUCATION:** Findlay HS, grad 1951. **CAREER:** City of Jamestown, council at large 1971-75; Cty of Chautauqua 1976-79; Jamestown Com Coll, bd of trustees 1981-; IAMAW Dist 65, bus rep. **ORGANIZATIONS:** Mem United Way Planning Council Chautaugua Cty 1982-, Full Gospel Bus Men's Org 1983-. **HOME ADDRESS:** 33 W 18th St, Jamestown, NY 14701.

PETERSON, EUGENE K.
Pharmacist. **PERSONAL:** Born Jul 15, 1920, LeRoy, NY; married Julia Wright; children: Eugene C, Keith F. **EDUCATION:** BPharm. **CAREER:** Gen Hosp #2 KC MO, chief phar & instr 1954-61. **ORGANIZATIONS:** Del 1964, conv chmn 1970 MO Phar Assn Conv; mem Min Schlrshp Com Univ MO Schl of Phar 1970; pres Phar Assn Grtr KC 1971; pres 1973 Grtr KCChap ACA; pres KC Chap Amer Phar Assn; councilman MO Phar Assn; mem Amer Phar Assn, Amer Soc Hosp Phar, Natl Phar Assn, Amer Coll ofApoth, Natl Assn Retl Druggists; mem Exec Comm & Adv to Youth Council, NAACP; co-fndr vice chmn bd dir chmn pol & actn com Community Comm for Social Action; vice pres Frontiers Intl Inc; vice pres chmn of bd Beau Brummel Soc & Civic Club; pres Beta Lambda chap Alpha Phi Alpha; vestryman St Augustine's Epis Church. **HONORS/ACHIEVEMENTS:** Cert of Awd for Prof Leadership Jack & Jill Chap 1964; Alpha Man of Midwestern Reg 1965; Alpha Phi Alpha Honors Hosp Fellow 1965 Amer Coll of Apoth Full Fellowship 1969; Honorary Alum 1974 Univ MO Sch Phar. **MILITARY SERVICE:** USAAC flight eng 1944-46.

PETERSON, GERARD M.
Business executive. **PERSONAL:** Born Sep 10, 1932, Hartford, CT; son of Rufus Peterson and Edythe Peterson; divorced; children: Brian, Bradford. **EDUCATION:** Univ CT, BA 1957; Cert Data Processing 1965. **CAREER:** Aetna Life & Casualty, adm roles 1957-69, dir mktg 1974-83; OUR Corp, pres 1969-72; Natl Alliance Businessmen, exec vice pres 1969-70; Hubbard & Co, dir 1970; Stanford U, asst dean grad sch bus 1970-73; Star Lite Industries, dir 1970-71; Hartford Civic Center, ceo, exec dir 1983-. **ORGANIZATIONS:** Mem Alpha Phi Alpha, NAACP, Urban League, Intl Assoc of Auditorium Mgrs; vchmn Greater Hartford Red Cross; dir, trustee Hartford Club, Hartford Hospital, St Francis Hospital, Mount Sinai Hospital, St Joseph Coll. **HONORS/ACHIEVEMENTS:** Arena and Mgr of the Year Performance Mag Readers Poll 1986. **MILITARY SERVICE:** AUS corpl 1953-55. **BUSINESS ADDRESS:** Executive Dir, Hartford Civic Center, One Civic Center Plaza, Hartford, CT 06105.

PETERSON, HARRY W.
Business executive. **PERSONAL:** Born May 13, 1923, Chanute, KS; son of Harry Peterson and Bertha Peterson; married Kathryn Elizabeth Boggs (divorced); children: Donna (Waller), Jerry Ronnell. **CAREER:** Lincoln Police Dept, 1956-66; King's Food Host USA Inc, 1966; dir, Motor Vehicles, NE, 1979-83. **ORGANIZATIONS:** Mem bd dir Lincoln General Hospital; chmn Human Rights Comm Lincoln 1962; Advisory Comm Head Start 1967; St Selection Comm Natl ROTC Scholrships 1970; dir Nebraska Red Cross bd; mem City Council 1969-73; v chmn 1971-73; mem Volunteers in Probation; NE Citizens Advisory Alcoholism Chcl; pres mem bd trustees NE Human Resources 1973; mem Chamber of Commerce; mason; Kiwanis; squires; Methodist Church. **HONORS/ACHIEVEMENTS:** Outstanding Public Serv Award 1970, Kiwanis Club; Good Govt Award 1972, Lincoln JC'S. **MILITARY SERVICE:** AUS 1943-46. **BUSINESS ADDRESS:** 8601 NE Highway #6, Lincoln, NE 68524.

PETERSON, LLOYD, JR.
Educator. **PERSONAL:** Born Jul 20, 1958, San Antonio, TX. **EDUCATION:** CO State Univ, BA English 1980, M Higher Educ 1982. **CAREER:** CO State Univ, admissions counselor 1982-83; CO College, asst dir/admissions 1983-. **ORGANIZATIONS:** Bd dirs Jolly Jills Civic and Social Club 1983-; 1st vice pres El Paso County Black Caucus 1984-86; bd dirs Urban League of Colorado Springs 1984-. **HONORS/ACHIEVEMENTS:** Mem Outstanding Young Men of America 1983; guest instructor College Board Summer Admission Inst 1986. **BUSINESS ADDRESS:** Assistant Director/Admissions, Colorado College, Admissions Office, Colorado Springs, CO 80903.

PETERSON, MARCELLA TANDY
Educator. **PERSONAL:** Born in Detroit, MI; married Harvey Hughes Peterson. **EDUCATION:** Wayne St Univ, BS 1949, DEd 1973; Univ of MI, MA 1955; Univ of Chicago; MI State Univ; Merrill-Palmer; Univ of Detroit; Trinity Coll; George Washington Univ, Paralegal certificate 1983. **CAREER:** Detroit Bd of Educ, reg asst supt; Detroit Public School, teacher; Miller Jr HS, counselor; Condon Jr HS, asst principal; Noble Jr HS, principal; Delta Sigma Theta Sorority Inc, exec dir. **ORGANIZATIONS:** Mem, Detroit Home Econ Assn 1949-57; et Guidance Assn 1957-61, Detroit Counselors' Assn 1957-61; chmn bd Delta Home for Girls 1957-58; mem Detroit Asst Principals' Assn 1961-63; Negotiating Team Org of School Admin & Supvr 1969, 1971, 1973; Detroit Women Admins; Phi Upsilon Omicron Fraternity, 1949-57; Delta Kappa Gamme Soc; Beta Sigma Phi Fellow; MI Assn for Supvr & Curriculum Devel; Amer Assn of Univ Women; Natl Council of Admin; Women in Educ; pres Detroit Principals' Assn 1965-66; Defense Advisory Comm on Women in the Serv 1967-70; sec Org of School Admins & Supvrs 1972-75; chmn Residence Com YMCA Bd of Mgmt Downtown Branch 1972-73; mem bd of dirs St Mary Cou 1985-86; mem bd of governors Women's Natl Democratic Comm 1987-; mem Washington Comm A Better Chance; mem, Governing Bd Womens' Natl Democratic Club, 1987-89. **HOME ADDRESS:** 101 Executive Center Dr, #3-612, West Palm Beach, FL 33401. **BUSINESS ADDRESS:** Partner, DMP Associates Inc, 2295 General Motors Blvd E, Suite 3, 4, Detroit, MI 48202.

PETERSON, MAUREEN LAURETT
Education administrator. **EDUCATION:** Trenton St Coll, BA 1976, MEd 1978; Univ of PA, PhD in progress. **CAREER:** Trenton St Coll, graduate assist 1977-78; GA Southern Coll, hall dir 1978-80; Univ of PA, assist dir 1980-. **ORGANIZATIONS:** Delta Sigma Theta, mem 1974; Univ of PA Education Alumni Assoc, board of directors 1984; Big Brothers / Big Sisters of PA, volunteer 1985; PA Literacy Project, tutor 1985; Region 11 NASPA, chair ethnic minority task force 1986; Assoc of Black Admin; Assoc of Women Faculty and Admin atUniv of PA; Mid Atlantic Coll and Univ Housing Officers.

PETERSON, MAURICE
Writer. **PERSONAL:** Born Feb 19, 1952, Harlem, NY. **EDUCATION:** Columbia U, BA 1973. **CAREER:** 20th Cent Fox, unit publicist 1973; The NY Met Rev Mag, edtr, film dept 1972-72; Manhattan Cable TV "New York Now", host & producer 1974-75; Afro-am Total Theater, "Manhattan Muses" 1975-76; Essence Mag, contrbtg Edtr 1970-79; NY Telephone's Daily Entrtnmnt Srv, prod, writr, dir "Theater Phone" 1979-80. **HONORS/ACHIEVEMENTS:** Mus Comedy, "The Soul Truth"; mus comedy (book music lyrics) "Hot Dishes", 1978; screenplay, "Growing Pairs" 1980; Seymour Brick Awd, ColumbiaUniv 1973; awd NY Met Mus of Art 1968. **BUSINESS ADDRESS:** C/o Wm Morris Agency, 1350 Ave of the Americas, New York, NY 10019.

PETERSON, MICHELLE MONICA
State association executive director. **PERSONAL:** Born Oct 21, 1959, Newark, NJ; daughter of Alvin Morrison and Christine (Hall) Morrison; married Dr Alan H Peterson, Sep 27, 1986. **EDUCATION:** Ward Baking Company, Newark NJ, CRT operator, 1977-80; First Natl State Bank, Newark NJ, direct deposit admin, 1980-81; Schering-Plough Corp, Kenilworth NJ, lead terminal operator, 1981-. **ORGANIZATIONS:** Supporter, Make-A-Wish Found of New Jersey, 1983-; consultant, Natl Police Reserve Officers Assn (New Jersey State), 1987-; bd mem, Heath Center Black History Comm, 1987-; exec dir, New Jersey State Chapter, Natl Police Officers Assn of Amer, 1987-; mem, Pride In Excellence, 1988-, United States Citizens' Commn on Crime & Narcotics, 1988-; bd mem, Masters of Philanthropy, 1988-. **HOME ADDRESS:** PO Box 350, East Orange, NJ 07019. **BUSINESS ADDRESS:** Lead Terminal Operations-Computerized Hi-Rise Div, Schering-Plough Corporation, Galloping Hill Rd, K-2-1, Kenilworth, NJ 07033.

PETERSON, OSCAR EMMANUEL
Professional jazz pianist, singer. **PERSONAL:** Born Aug 15, 1925, Montreal, Quebec, Canada;son of Daniel Peterson and Olivia John. **CAREER:** Pianist; singer. **HONORS/ACHIEVEMENTS:** Performed on radio show with Johny Holmes Orch, Can 1944-49; Jazz at the Philharmonic, Carnegie Hall, 1949; toured US & Europe freq 1950; ldr Trio with Roy Brown, Irving Ashby, latr Barney-Kessel, Herb Ellis, Ed Thigpen, Sam Jones, Louie Hayes & others; concert & apprncs with Ella Fitzgerald, Eng , Scotland, 1955; apprd Stratford Shakespeare Fest, ON Newport Jazz Festvl; faclty Schl Jazz, Lenox MA; rcrdngs Billie Holiday, Fred Astaire, Benny Carter, Count Basie, Roy Eldridge, Lester Young, others; compsr svrl muscl wrks; wrts bckgrnd music for films, TV & Stage; performs reglrly Can, USA, Europe, Eng, Japan, freq S Am, New Zealand, Australia, Mexico, Spain, Carribean & Russia; made apprnces St Dept; gstd White House former Pres Johnson; recip Awd Piano, Down Beat Mag 1950-54, 60-63, 65; Toronto Civic Medal 1971; hon LLD, Carlton Univ 1973; hon LLD Queen's Univ 1976; Order of Can 1973; Diplome D'Honneur, Ottawa 1975; recip 12 Play Boy Awds, 12 Down Beat Awrds; Grammy Awd 1974, 75, 77; silvr mdl NY Intrnat Film Festvl; slvr plaque Chicago Intl Film Fstvl; Edison Awd; Adhvmt Awd Toronto 1966; Awd of Apprctn Montreal 1969. **BUSINESS ADDRESS:** c/o 2421 Hammond Rd, Mississauga, Ontario, Canada L5K 1T3.

PETERSON, SUSHILA JANE-CLINTON
Dentist. **PERSONAL:** Born Jun 04, 1952, New Delhi, India;daughter of Audrey Clinton Peterson. **EDUCATION:** Howard Univ, BS 1974; Howard Univ Dental School, DDS 1979. **CAREER:** Private Practice, Dentist 1984-. **ORGANIZATIONS:** Mem Amer Dental Assoc 1980-, Alpha Kappa Alpha Sor 1982-, Amer Assoc of Univ Women 1982-, District of Columbia Dental Soc 1984-, MD State Dental Assoc 1984-, Howard Univ Dental Alumni Assoc 1984-; US Chamber of Commerce 1987-88. **MILITARY SERVICE:** AUS capt 4 yrs active 2 yrs reserves, Servicemen's Merit Awd 1983. **HOME ADDRESS:** 3816 8th St NW, Washington, DC 20011.

PETERSON, WILLIAM E.
Judge. **PERSONAL:** Born Apr 30, 1913, Oxford, MS; widowed. **EDUCATION:** Alabama State Univ, BS 1935; The John Marshall Law School, LLB 1950; The John Marshall Law School, JD 1970. **CAREER:** High school teacher 1935-43; lawyer, private practice 1951-72; Circuit Court Cook County, assoc judge 1972-76, circuit judge 1976-. **ORGANIZATIONS:** Pres, Cook County & Bar Assn, 1966-68; pres, Natl Bar Assn, 1969-70; mem bd of mgrs, Chicago Bar Assn, 1969-71; mem bd of gov, Am :r Acad of Matrim Lawyers, 1968-72; mem, Natl Conf of Lawyers & Soc Workers, 1969-70; mem, Assn of Family Conciliation Cts Inc, 1970; mem, Alpha Phi Alpha Frat; mem, NAACP; mem, Urban League; past chmn, Bd of Trust; mem, Cong Ch of Park Manor; mem bd of trustees, John Marshall Law School. **HONORS/ACHIEVEMENTS:** Cook County Bar Assn Awd; Natl Bar Assn; Chicago Bar Assn Awd; Alabama State Univ Awd. **MILITARY SERVICE:** USNA sgt 1943-46. **BUSINESS ADDRESS:** Judge, Circuit Court of Cook County, 2600 Daley Center, Chicago, IL 60602.

PETERSON, WILLIAM T.
Educational administrator. **PERSONAL:** Born Jun 15, 1930, Tuskegee, AL; married Amelia Wyckoff; children: Patrice Annell. **EDUCATION:** Tuskegee Inst, BS 1956, MEd 1957. **CAREER:** Macon County Sch System, principal 1969-73 1979-85; City of Tuskegee, judge 1973-78; 5th Judicial Circuit of AL, magistrate 1975-79; City of Tuskegee, councilman 1967-72 1980-. **ORGANIZATIONS:** Mem Selective Serv System Dist IV 1983-; mem Macon Co Sesqui Centennial Comm 1983; historian City of Tuskegee AL 1980-. **HONORS/ACHIEVEMENTS:** Nominee US Dist Judge 1981; Dictionary of Intl Biographies 1972; Personalities of the So 1974. **MILITARY SERVICE:** AUS pfc (RA) 2nd lt (rsigned) 6 yrs; apptmt to USMA; Disting Military Student 1948. **BUSINESS ADDRESS:** Councilman, City of Tuskegee, Municipal Complex, 101 Fonville St, Tuskegee, AL 36083.

PETERSON, WILLIE DIAMOND
Clergyman. **PERSONAL:** Born Oct 13, 1911, Trumble, TX; married Lydia D Smith; children: 8 Children. **EDUCATION:** Trinity Hall Coll & Seminary, DD 1975. **CAREER:** Calvary Dist, supt; Plaino TX, pastor 1937; White Rose Ch, Stockton CA, fndr 1945; Wayside Ch Weed CA, 1949; Gospel Ctr Ch, San Diego, Pstr. **ORGANIZATIONS:** Pres Interdenmntl Min All; orgnzr Evangelist Bd of N CA St. **HONORS/ACHIEVEMENTS:** Awd NAACP; received Proclmtn naming Rev W D Peterson Park 1974. **BUSINESS ADDRESS:** PO Box 13131, San Diego, CA 92113.

PETETT, FREDDYE
Public official. **PERSONAL:** Born Dec 27, 1943, Monroe, LA; daughter of Barbara Mansfield; divorced; children: Andre. **EDUCATION:** Portland State Univ, BS 1969-73; Portland Comm Coll, AS 1968-69; Southern Univ, 1961-62; Portland State Univ. **CAREER:** Portland Urban League, exec dir 1979; mayor's Office City Portland, asst to mayor 1976-79; Crime & Prevention Bureau, dir 1974-76; Office of Emergency Servcs, coordinator 1973-74; Nero & Assoc, project dir 1971-73; Portland Model Cities, syst coordinator 1970-71; Portland Comm Coll, programmer analyst 1969-70; State of OR, Public Welfare Admin, 1987-. **ORGANIZATIONS:** Chmn outreach com OR Women's Conf 1977; bd of dirs Center for Urban Educ; bd dirs Conf of Minority Public Admin; mem Portland Chamber of Commerce Urban Affairs Com; mem desegregation task force Portland City Club; bd dirs, Housing Authority Portland; Portland City Club; sec Delta Sigma Theta 1976-77; bd dirs YWCA; mem regional selection panel White House Fellowships; mem, World Affairs Council; bd mem, Federal Home Loan Bank of Seattle. **HONORS/ACHIEVEMENTS:** Published, Towards A Self-Evaluative Public Program Mgmt 1972; WK Kellogg Natl Fellowship, Kellogg Found, 1983; Woman of Excellence, Delta Sigma Theta Sorority, 1985. **HOME ADDRESS:** 1108 Cayuse Cir, SE, Salem, OR 97306. **BUSINESS ADDRESS:** State Capital, Salem, OR 97310.

PETIONI, MURIEL M.
Physician, educator. **PERSONAL:** Born Jan 01, 1914; children: Charles M Woolfolk. **EDUCATION:** New York U, 1930-32; Howard U, BS 1934, MD 1937; Harlem Hosp Internship, 1937-39. **CAREER:** New York City Dept Hlth, sch phys 1950-80; prvt practice 1950-; NY Hlth & Hosp Corp Harlem Hosp, med stf 1960-80; New York City Dept Hlth, spvr/sch phys 1980-84; Harlem Hosp Dept Peds, spvsing phys & cnsltnt 1982-; Dept of Peds Columbia U, asst clncl prof 1982-. **ORGANIZATIONS:** Natl Med Assc; Empire State Med Assc; tres Manhattan Cntr Med Assc; flw Am Acad Fmly Phys; HowardUniv Med Alumni Assc; founder pres Susan SmithMcKinney Steward Med Assc 1974-84; fndr 1st chrprsn Med Women of NMA 1977-83; tres Doctors Cncl of City of NY 1980-84; mem Doctors Cncl City NY 1950-80; pres Trinidade & Tobago Gyap Orgn; mem Delta Sigma Theta Soc; mem Coalition of 100 Black Women; mem New York City Dept Hlth Child Hlth Forum; mem NAACP; mem NY Urban League. **HONORS/ACHIEVEMENTS:** Woman of yr Morrisania Youth & Comm Serv Ctr Inc 1969; awrds in black Found Rsrch & Ed Sickle Cell Disease 1973; first harlem humanitarian awrd NY Cncl Smlr Chrchs 1975; Martin Luther King, Jr Democrates Salute 1975; harlem brnch ymca world serv awrd Harlem YMCA 1978; women of yr Everybody's Mag 1979; practitioner of yr Natl Med Assc 1979; ed dept awrd City Tabernacle SDA Chrch 1979; dstngshd serv awrd Lehman HS Bio-Med Inst 1981; profsnl ed awrd Harlem Unit/Am Cancer Soc 1982; black achvmnt awrd Comm Church NY 1983; cert aprctn Pioneer in Treatment of Drug Abuse Edward I Koch Mayor of City of NY 1983; spec rcgntn Muriel Petioni MD Fndr of NMA Women in Medicine Task Force on Conserns of Women Phys; harlem wk 83 hlth serv awrd Harlem Week Inc 1983; harlem hosp meritorious serv awrd Harlem Hospt Ctr & NY Hlth & Hosp Corp 1983; Whitney M Young Jr Comm Rltns Awrd Annual BlckAm Heroes & Heroines Day 1984; distngshd serv awrd Doctors Cncl 1984; city of ny Proclamation Ofc of City Clrk David N Dinkins City of NY 1984; outstndg serv to chldrn harlem awrd Med Stf & Med Bd Harlem Hosp 1984. **BUSINESS ADDRESS:** 114 West 131st, New York, NY 10027.

PETRIE, HARRY R.
Business executive. **PERSONAL:** Born Sep 13, 1926, New York, NY; married Marie-Therese; children: Jean Pierre. **EDUCATION:** Bennett Clge Jamaica W Indies, 1946. **CAREER:** Corporate Personnel Serv Revlon Inc, dir. **ORGANIZATIONS:** N Jersey Compensation Assc. **HONORS/ACHIEVEMENTS:** 100 Black Men; Award of Merit Black Media Inc; cert of appreciation Natl Urban League; Hispanic Charities Assc. **MILITARY SERVICE:** AUS sgt maj 1946-68. **BUSINESS ADDRESS:** 767 5th Ave, New York, NY 10022.

PETROSS. PRECIOUS DORIS
Association executive. **PERSONAL:** Born in Chicago, IL; divorced; children: Charles H, Janice E Muhammad, Michael A. **EDUCATION:** Univ of MI, BA 1967; Eastern MI Univ, MA 1974; Detroit College of Law, JD 1982. **CAREER:** City of Flint, personnel tech 1967-69, sr personnel tech 1969-72; Hurley Medical Ctr, asst pers dir 1972-74, personnel dir 1974-80, asst dir 1980-85; UAS-GM Lega Services, staff attorney 1985-. **ORGANIZATIONS:** Various clerical pos City of Flint 1958-67; instructor Mott Adult Educ Prog 1967-70; past pres Zeta Phi Beta 1961-; past pres Flint Club Natl Assn of Negro Bus & Professional Women 1961-; Natl Bd Dir Girl Scouts USA 1984-; bd dir YWCA of Greater Flint 1983-; mem Amer Bar Assn State Bar of MI 1983-. **HONORS/ACHIEVEMENTS:** Woman of the Yr Zeta Phi Beta 1978; Congressional Cert of Amer US House of Rep 1978; Who's Who in the Mid-West 1982; Resolution of Achievement City of Flint 1983; Outstanding Citizen Natl Sor of Phi Delta Kappa Flint 1984. **HOME ADDRESS:** 6013 Detroit St, Flint, MI 48505. **BUSINESS ADDRESS:** Staff Attorney, UAW-GM Legal Service, 1501 Genesee Towers, Flint, MI 48502.

PETRY, ANN (NEE LANE)
Author. **PERSONAL:** Born Oct 12, 1908, Old Saybrook, GA; daughter of Peter C Lane and Bertha James Lane; married George D Petry; children: Elisabeth, Petry Milbert. **EDUCATION:** CT Coll of Phar, PhG 1931. **CAREER:** Self-employed, author;Univ of HI, prof of eng 1974-75. **ORGANIZATIONS:** Mem Am PEN; mem Auth Guild; mem Authors Leag. **HONORS/ACHIEVEMENTS:** Books pub "The St" 1946; "Cntry Place" 1947; "The Narrows" 1953; "Miss Muriel & Other Stories" 1971; "The Drugstore Cat" 1949; "Harriet Tubmam Cond on the Underground RR" 1955; "Tituba of Salem Vill" 1964; "Leg of the Sts" 1970; short stor pub in New Yorker & Red Bk; wilmer hougthon miffin lit fellow award 1945; Doctor of Letters - Sulfolk Univ 1983; Doctor of Letters - Univ of CT 1988; Doctor of Humane Letters Mount Holyoke 1989. **BUSINESS ADDRESS:** c/o Russell & Volkening, 50 W 29th St, New York, NY 10001.

PETTAWAY, CHARLES, JR.
Pianist, educator. **PERSONAL:** Born Jun 07, 1949, Philadelphia, PA; son of Charles Henry Pettaway and Lorraine Thornton Pettaway; married Terri Lynne Jenkins, Oct 05, 1985; children: Sean, Ashley. **EDUCATION:** Philadelphia Mus Acad, BM 1971; Temple Univ, MM 1976; Fontainbleau Acad France, 1973; Ravel Acad France, Cert 1974. **CAREER:** Performed throughout the US and some European countries making European debut in 1974; important musical performances incl, Tour of Switzerland summer 1981;Great Hall of Moscow Conserv Russia; Carnegie Hall NY; Acad of Music Phila; Philharmonic Hall NY; Yacht Club of Chicago; Boston Univ; Music Hall at Ciboure; Palais de Fontainebleau France; Center Coll KY; Windsor Sch NC; Tanglewood Music Fest Recanti Auditorium Tel Aviv, Isreal; Kennedy Center Wash, DC; Orchestra Hall Chicago; Settlement Sch of Music, concert pianist/tchr; Lincoln Univ Lincoln PA Lecturer of Music 1988-. **ORGANIZATIONS:** Performing artist-piano, arranger, choir director. **HONORS/ACHIEVEMENTS:** International Piano Competition - France, 1st prize winner 1974; article publ in Society Newsletter (musical publ) "The American Audience" 1984; 1st commercial recording released "Charles Pettaway Performs Music by Russian Composers" 1985. **HOME ADDRESS:** 1267 Cox Rd, Rydal, PA 19046.

PETTERWAY, JACKIE WILLIS (JACKIE O OF HOUSTON)
Fashion designer. **PERSONAL:** Born in Galveston, TX; married Arthur L Petterway; children: Chiquita. **EDUCATION:** Prairie View A&M Univ, BS Clothing and Textiles 1970; Magnolia Business Ctr Inc, Small Business Certificate of Merit 1972; Natl Sch of Dress Design, attended 1973; Univ of Houston, M Retailing 1979. **CAREER:** Jackie O Designs Inc Houston, designer/proprietor 1970-80, designer/chairperson of the bd 1980-. **ORGANIZATIONS:** Developed produced and directed several spectacular fashion shows for charitable orgs; presented Jackie O's 1982 holiday collections during 2nd annual fashionextravaganza benefitting the Sickle Cell Anemia Foundation 1982; presented 3rd annual fashion extravaganza benefitting The Greater Houston Civic Ballet Co 1983. **HONORS/ACHIEVEMENTS:** Ebony FAshion Fair featured Jackie O designs in their Yearly Fashion Extravaganza (internationally) 1982-83, 1983-84, 1984-85, 1985-86; YWCA Woman of the Yr Awd 1983; Designer of the Yr Awd and Key to the City from Cincinnati OH 1986; Beefeater Fashion and Jazz Competition grand Awd 1986; Natl Awd Natl Best Dressed Awd and Civic Org Inc of Chicago. **BUSINESS ADDRESS:** Chairperson of the Bd, Jackie O Designs Inc, 718 E 29th St, Ste B, Houston, TX 77009.

PETTIFORD, QUENTIN H.
City official. **PERSONAL:** Born Dec 06, 1929, Marion, IN; married Betty I. **EDUCATION:** IN Univ Kokomo, ABA Banking 1978. **CAREER:** Marion Police Dept, asst chief police 1975-75; Amer Bank & Trust, asst vice pres 1975-; Grant County, councilman. **ORGANIZATIONS:** Pres bd dir Marion Urban League 1980-81, 1984-; bd dir Grant Cty Economic Growth Council 1981-, Grant Cty Convention Bureau 1982-; mem Grant Cty Tax Council 1983-84; Grant Blackford Opportunities Ind 1984-. **HONORS/ACHIEVEMENTS:** Serv Awd Marion Pal Club 1972; Serv Awd United Way 1979-84. **HOME ADDRESS:** 1819 S Selby, Marion, IN 46953.

PETTIFORD, STEVEN DOUGLAS
Plant manager. **PERSONAL:** Born Aug 24, 1948, Dayton, OH; son of Edwin E Pettiford and Martha E Streaty Pettiford; married Donna F McKeever Pettiford, Aug 17, 1970; children: Yvonne Michelle, Yvette Rene. **EDUCATION:** General Motors Inst, Flint MI, bachelor mechanical engineering, 1972; Massachusetts Inst of Technology, Cambridge MA, masters mgmt, 1978. **CAREER:** General Motors, Dayton OH, production engineer, 1972-75, asst supt prod engineering, 1975-76, asst supt mfg, 1976-77, plant mgr mfg, 1977-82; Warren MI, dir ind engineering, 1982-85, Lansing MI, mgr product assurance, 1985-87, Kalamazoo MI, plant mgr, 1987-. **ORGANIZATIONS:** Mem, GMI Alumni Assn, 1972-; mem, Tau Beta Pi Inc, 1972-; mem, Engineering Soc of Detroit, 1985-; mem, Engineering Bd of Visitors, Western Michigan Univ, 1987-; trustee, Nazareth Coll, 1987-; bd mem, Forum, 1987-; mem, NAACP, 1988-; bd mem, CEO of Kalamazoo, 1989-; mem, exec bd, Chamber of Commerce, 1989; sec exec bd, United Way, Kalamazoo, 1989-. **HONORS/ACHIEVEMENTS:** Honoree, Tau Beta Pi, 1972; instructor and developer of pre-apprentice training course, 1973-77; Alumnus for a Day, GMI-EMI, 1986; America's Best and Brightest, Dollars and Sense, 1988. **BUSINESS ADDRESS:** Plant Mgr, General Motors Corp, 5200 E Cork St, Kalamazoo, MI 49001.

PETTIGREW, GRADY L., JR.
Judge. **PERSONAL:** Born Jun 21, 1943, Forrest City, AR; married Carolyn Landers; chil-

dren: Dawn Karima, Grady Landers. **EDUCATION:** OH State Univ, BA 1965; Howard Univ School of Law Wash DC, 1968-69; OH State Univ, JD 1971. **CAREER:** Columbus State Hosp, activities therapist 1965; Huntington Natl Bank Columbus, mgr trainee 1968; Legal Aid Agency DC, investigator law clerk 1969; Vorys Sater Seymour & Pease, assoc atty 1971-77; US Bankruptcy Court, judge 1977-86; Arter & Hadden, partner. **ORGANIZATIONS:** Mem Columbus & OH State Bar Assoc, ABA; corr sec Robert B Elliott Law Club 1977-, Natl Conf of Bankruptcy Judges Adj Prof of Law Capital Univ 1979, OH State Univ 1980; bd of trustees chmn Comm Devel Com Ctrl Comm House 1972-75; bd of trustees Ecco Manor 1973, United Way of Franklin Cty 1974-75; solicitor Village of Urbancrest OH 1975-76. **HONORS/ACHIEVEMENTS:** Natl Moot Ct Championship Young Lawyers Comm NY Bar Assoc 1971; Outstanding Young Men of Amer Chicago 1972. **MILITARY SERVICE:** AUS 1st lt 2 yrs. **BUSINESS ADDRESS:** Partner, Arter & Hadden, 180 E Broad St 44th Fl, Columbus, OH 43215.

PETTIS, GARY GEORGE
Professional athlete. **PERSONAL:** Born Apr 03, 1958, Oakland, CA. **CAREER:** CA Angels, outfielder 1982-84. **BUSINESS ADDRESS:** California Angels, PO Box 2000, Anaheim, CA 92803.

PETTIS, JOYCE OWENS
Educator. **PERSONAL:** Born Mar 14, 1946, Columbia, NC; daughter of Howard Owens and Victoria Hill Owens; married Bobby Pettis; children: Darryl. **EDUCATION:** Winston Salem State Univ, BA 1968; East Carolina Univ, MA 1974; Univ of NC-Chapel Hill, PhD 1983. **CAREER:** NC Public Schools, teacher 1968-71; Pitt Tech Inst, teacher 1972-74; East Carolina Univ, asst professor of Eng 1974-; NC State Univ, asst prof of english 1985-. **ORGANIZATIONS:** Alpha Kappa Alpha; Popular Culture Assn; College Language Assn; teacher North Carolina History Summer Inst 1984; teacher Summer Institutes Incorp the New Scholarship on Women 1984; criticism editor Obsidian II, Black Literature in Review. **HONORS/ACHIEVEMENTS:** Minority Presence Fellowship Univ of NC - CH 1978-80; UNC Board of Gov Doctoral Award Univ of NC - CH 1981; Danforth Associate 1981; Natl Humanities Faculty Mem 1984. **HOME ADDRESS:** 1108 Cedarhurst Dr, Raleigh, NC 27609. **BUSINESS ADDRESS:** Professor of English, North Carolina StateUniv, Box 8105, Raleigh, NC 27695.

PETTIT, ALVIN DWIGHT
Attorney. **PERSONAL:** Born Sep 29, 1945, Rutherdfordton, NC; married Bobbie N Moore; children: Alvin Dwight Jr, Nahisha Tamara. **EDUCATION:** Howard Univ, BA 1967, JD 1970. **CAREER:** Mitchel & Pettit, law part 1973-; Baltimore, asst pub def 1974; Fed City Clge, part-time prof 1972; Wash DC Area Dist Ofc, dist couns 1972-73; Small Bus Admin, gen couns & staff trial atty 1970-72. **ORGANIZATIONS:** Pres Monum City Bar Assc; mem NBA; ABA; NAACP; mem bd trustee Prov Hosp; mem sub-comm on Min Affairs John Hopkins Univ; mem bd dir Champ Assc; hon Fund Raising chmn Balt YMCA; state Co-chmn Jimmy Carter for pres; dele at large 1976 Dem Natl Conv; floor whip The Carter Forces at Conv. **MILITARY SERVICE:** USAF 1st lt. **BUSINESS ADDRESS:** 222 St Paul Pl, Baltimore, MD 21202.

PETTRESS, ANDREW WILLIAM
Printing company director. **PERSONAL:** Born Jul 11, 1937, Steubenville, OH; son of Andrew Pettress and Bessie Louise Pettress; divorced; children: Andrews W Pettress IV, Andrew W Pettress Jr. **EDUCATION:** Xavier Univ, Cincinnati OH, BA, 1966; Univ of Cincinnati, Cincinnati OH, Master/Labor Relations, 1977. **CAREER:** City of Pontiac, Pontiac MI, exec asst to mayor, 1982-86; Dan T Murphy for Governor, State of Michigan, deputy finance dir, 1986; Amer Speedy Printing, Bloomfield Hills MI, dir/special market devel, 1986-; Metro Substance Abatement Center, Detroit MI, self-employed; affiliated with Amer Football League, San Diego CA; Pettress & Associates, Detroit MI, self-employed. **ORGANIZATIONS:** Mem, Amer Society for Training and Devel; mem, Intl Assoc for Inter-Group Relations officials; mem, Intl Personnel Mgmt Assn; mem, Amer Mgmt Assn; president (3 terms) Alpha Phi Alpha Fraternity (Oakland County Graduate Chapter); mem, Natl Black Republican Council, MI; mem, Kiwanis Club Intl, Detroit MI; bd mem, Pontiac Creative Art Center of Pontiac, MI; mem, Michigan Comm for Honest Elections; mem, President's Commission, Oakland Univ, Rochester MI; vice-chmn, Minority Enterprise Comm, Intl Franchise Assn Conf of Black Mayor's Economic Devel Task Force. **HONORS/ACHIEVEMENTS:** Money Mgmt of Methadone Clinics (State of Michigan), 1979; George E Baker Foundation fellow at Harvard Univ, 1980; Amer Speedy Printing Co (Midwest Devel Dir Mgr of the Year for Outstanding Sales Performance, 1987, Team Player of the Month, 1988; Broadcaster of the year, WCIN, Cincinnati OH. **MILITARY SERVICE:** US Marine Corps, staff sgt, 1958-60, Sec to Admiral of the Fleet. **BUSINESS ADDRESS:** Dir of Special Market Devel, Amer Speedy Printing Centers, 2555 S Telegraph Rd, Bloomfield Hills, MI 48013.

PETTUS-BELLAMY, BRENDA KAREN
Pediatrician. **PERSONAL:** Born May 07, 1957, Washington, DC; married K Daniel Bellamy; children: Daniel K Jr. **EDUCATION:** GA Southern Coll, BS Biology 1979; Howard Univ, MD 1983. **CAREER:** Howard Univ Hosp, intern/resident 1983-86; West Baltimore Health Ctr, pediatrician 1986-. **HONORS/ACHIEVEMENTS:** Ruth E Moore Serv Awd Howard Univ 1982. **HOME ADDRESS:** 340 Taylor St NE, Washington, DC 20017. **BUSINESS ADDRESS:** Pediatrician, West Baltimore Health Ctr, 1850 W Baltimore St, Baltimore, MD 21223.

PETTWAY, JO CELESTE
Government official. **PERSONAL:** Born Mar 18, 1952, Consul, AL; daughter of Joseph Pettway and Menda Gamble Pettway; divorced. **EDUCATION:** Auburn Univ, BA 1973; The Univ of AL, BSW 1976, MSW 1978, JD 1982. **CAREER:** Children's Aid Soc, social worker 1975-77; Jefferson Co Dept of Pensions and Security, social worker 1977; Miles Coll, instructor of social work 1978-79; Legal Serv Corp of AL, summer clerk 1980; England and Bivens PC, assoc 1982-84; Jo Celeste Pettway Attorney at Law, solo practitioner 1984; Wilcox County, district judge 1984-. **ORGANIZATIONS:** Mem Natl Bar Assn, Amer Bar Assn, Natl Assn of Women Judges, Natl Assn of Juvenile and Family Court Judges, AL Lawyers Assn; parlimentarian Zeta Eta Omega Chap of Alpha Kappa Alpha Sor Inc; bd of dirs Health Improvement Project; Natl Council of Negro Women; 2nd Anti Basileau - Zeta Eta Omega Chapter of Alpha Kappa Alpha Sor Inc. **HONORS/ACHIEVEMENTS:** Outstanding Young Women of Amer 1983; Outstanding Achievement Awd BLSA Univ of AL; Humanitarian Award Concordia College 1988; Outstanding Alumni Black Law Students Assn of Univ of Alabama 1987. **HOME ADDRESS:** PO Box 86, Alberta, AL 36720. **BUSINESS ADDRESS:** District Judge, Wilcox Co, PO Box 549, Camden, AL 36726.

PETTY, BOB
Reporter, anchorman. **PERSONAL:** Born Nov 26, 1940, Memphis; married Cora; children: Bobby, Cory. **EDUCATION:** AZ State U, BS 1969. **CAREER:** KAET TV Tempe AZ, 1968; KPHO TV News, 1969; KOOL TV News 1969-70; WLS TV News 1970-; with the exception of KAET TV all experience is in news as film cameraman, soundman, lightingman, asst editor, writer, producer & reporter-anchorman reporter, producer; "Your Comment", community affairs program dirested at black community. **ORGANIZATIONS:** Mem fun raising com Hyde Park YMCA; mem Provident St Mel Cath HS only black cath HS on Chicago's Westside. **HONORS/ACHIEVEMENTS:** One of several black broadcasters honores by Club Date Magazine of Chicago 1974. **BUSINESS ADDRESS:** c/o WLS-TV, 190 N State St, Chicago, IL 60601.

PETTY, BRUCE ANTHONY
Company executive. **PERSONAL:** Born Nov 15, 1938, East St Louis, IL; son of Bruce Petty and Helen Petty; married Madeline C; children: Tanya, Avril Petty Weathers, Anthony. **EDUCATION:** Southern IL Univ, BA 1960; Howard Univ, MPA 1973. **CAREER:** AL Nellum & Assoc, exec vice pres 1973-77; Univ Rsch Corp, vice pres 1978-80; AL Nellum & Assoc, exec vice pres 1981-83; Pettsons Inc, pres 1984-. **ORGANIZATIONS:** Former assoc dir Natl Civil Service League. **BUSINESS ADDRESS:** President, Pettsons Inc, 2804 M Luther King Jr Ave SE, Washington, DC 20032.

PETTY, RACHEL MONTEITH
Educator/psychologist. **PERSONAL:** Born Jun 21, 1943, Columbia, SC; daughter of Frank H Monteith, Sr (deceased) and Susie E Monteith; married LaSalle Petty, Jr, Sep 03, 1966; children: Adrienne, Erin. **EDUCATION:** Univ of Maryland, PhD, 1980; Howard Univ, MS 1968, BS 1964. **CAREER:** Howard Univ, lecturer 1968-71; Prince Geo Pub Sch, sch psych 1968-72; DC Pub Sch, sch psych 1967-68; Univ of the Dpstrict of Columbia, chairperson, and asst prof of psych, assoc prof of Psychology 1971-. **ORGANIZATIONS:** Assc Black Psychologists; Amer Assc Advancement Sci; MD Assc Sch Psychologists; research on Black Child; consultant DC Dept Human Services 1987-88; consulting psych St Ann's Infant Home Hyattsville, MD 1974-; bd mem Lutheran Social Services of the Natl Capital Area 1989-. **HOME ADDRESS:** 2124 Sudbury Pl, NW, Washington, DC 20012. **BUSINESS ADDRESS:** Chairperson, Dept of Psychology, Univ of the District of Columbia, 4200 Connecticut Ave NW, Washington, DC 20008.

PETTY, REGINALD E.
Executive director, educational publisher. **PERSONAL:** Born Oct 07, 1935, St Louis, MO; son of Bruce Petty and Helen Smith Petty; married Lucy Klaus; children: Joel, Amina. **EDUCATION:** Southern IL Univ, BS 1956; MS Educ 1966. **CAREER:** Educ Resources Intl Inc, pres, 1986-; Your World Intl Newspaper for Students, publisher; Peace Corps, Kenya 1979-82, Swaziland, dir 1977-79; Natl Advisory Council Vocational Educ, deputy dir 1974-, dir rsch, 1971-74; General Learning Corp, assoc dir, Educ, 1970-71; Peace Corps W Africa Upper Volta, dir, 1969-70, deputy dir 1967-69; St Clair County IL Community Action Program, community relations consultant, 1966-67; Training Corp Amer, asst dir 1965-66; Breckenridge Job Corps Ctr, 1964-65; S IL, graduate rsch asst, 1962-64; IL State Dept Welfare, Child Welfare Div, 1961-62. **ORGANIZATIONS:** Amer Vocational Assn; Natl Sociological Soc Mid-Western Sociological Soc; Natl Educ Assc; Natl Alliance Black School Educators; Natl Assn of Black Adult Educators; Educ consultant, Gary IN, Newark NJ, E St Louis IL; Africare on West African Famine Relief Program, 1973; Corp Public Broadcasting, 1973-74; mem NEA, Kappa Alpha Psi, Urban League, NAACP, Natl Alliance of Black School Educators; TransAfrica; African Natl Congress. **HONORS/ACHIEVEMENTS:** Published "Minorities & Career Education," 1973; chmn, 1st minority conf career educ, 1973; Outstanding Dir, Peace Corps, 1979, 1980, 1982. **BUSINESS ADDRESS:** President, Educational Resources Intl Inc, 7219 Blair Rd, NW, Washington, DC 20012.

PEYTON, HENRY E.
Automobile dealer. **CAREER:** Peyton Olds-Cadillac-GMC, Inc, Alton IL, chief executive. **BUSINESS ADDRESS:** Peyton Oldsmobile-Cadillac-GMC, Inc, 3550 Homer Adams Pkwy, Alton, IL 62002. *

PEYTON, JASPER E.
Assistant educational director. **PERSONAL:** Born Dec 30, 1926, Richmond; widowed; children: Rose La Verne Abernathy. **EDUCATION:** Univ Philippines, attended 1946; City Coll NY, 1952. **CAREER:** Local 66 Intl Ladies Garment Workers, trade unionists, shop steward 1952-64; Civil Rights Comm Dir Educ, exec bd mem dir 1965-69, asst dir educ. **ORGANIZATIONS:** Mem Council Chs Brooklyn Div 1971-; Assc minister Bethany Bapt Ch; bd dir CLICK-cOMMERCE Labor Industry Corp of Kings for Brooklyn Navy Yard; bd memFulton Art Fair. **HONORS/ACHIEVEMENTS:** Award Pub Rel Dir Bethany Bapt Ch. **MILITARY SERVICE:** AUS sgt. **BUSINESS ADDRESS:** 1710 Broadway, New York, NY 10019.

PHEARS, WILLIAM D.
Association executive. **PERSONAL:** Born Sep 03, 1917, Arkansas; children: William D, Jr, Jo Alison. **EDUCATION:** Long Island Univ, BS, MS 1967. **CAREER:** Brevard Engr Co Cape Canaveral FL, consult 1975; Water Hempstead NY, commr 1972-, dep commr pub wks 1966-72; real est broker; clge instr. **ORGANIZATIONS:** Trustee Uniondale Pub Lib 1963-64. **HONORS/ACHIEVEMENTS:** APWA Top Ten Engr Award 1969. **MILITARY SERVICE:** USAF lt col 1941-64. **BUSINESS ADDRESS:** 1995 Prospect Ave E, Meadow, NY 11554.

PHELPS, C. KERMIT
Clinical psychologist. **PERSONAL:** Born Dec 04, 1908, Newton, KS; son of James Clifford Phelps and Eva Bradshaw Phelps; married Lucille Mallory, Sep 11, 1936; children: Patricia Ann Phelps Evans, Sr Constance Kay Phelps. **EDUCATION:** Univ of KS, Lawrence KS, AB, 1933, MA, 1949, Ph.D, 1953. **CAREER:** Veteran's Admin, Topeka KS, psychologist, 1949-52, Kansas City KS, psychologist, 1952-55, chief psych service, 1955-75, assoc chief of staff-educ, 1975-78; Avila Coll, evening div, Kansas City MO, prof psych, 1955-72; Kansas

City MO, private practice, 1955-81; KU Medical Center, Kansas City, KS, assoc prof psych,1961-69; Univ of Kansas, Lawrence KS, asst prof psych, 1962-64; Shepherds Center, Kansas City MO, dir life enrichment, 1974-80. **ORGANIZATIONS:** Mem, Bd of Regents Rockhurst Coll, 1962-; co-chmn, Natl Conf of Christians & Jews, 1965-67; chmn, Jackson County Civil Rights Comm, 1967-72, mem, Rotary Club 13 Kansas City, 1972-73; mem, Red Cross Bd of Dir, 1977-79; mem bd, 1981, chmn natl bd, 1986, AARP. **HONORS/ACHIEVEMENTS:** Civil Servant of the Year, VA, 1964; Man of the Year, Ivanhoe Club, 1966; Knight of Holy Sepulchre, Pope Paul VI, Rome, 1966; Getting Ready for Retirement, Intl Gerontolological Congress, paper presented in Vienna, 1966; Aging in Youth Oriented World, Spain, 1970; Life Enrichment, Hew, 1975; Honorary PhD, St Mary's Coll, 1976; Counseling the Elderly, MO Counsel of Churches, 1980. **HOME ADDRESS:** 3437 Quincy St, Kansas City, MO 64128.

PHELPS, CONSTANCE KAY
Educational administrator. **PERSONAL:** Born Sep 16, 1940, Topeka, KS; daughter of C Kermit Phelps and Lucille Mallory Phelps. **EDUCATION:** St Marys Coll, BA 1962; Wash Univ St Louis, AM 1970, PhD 1977. **CAREER:** St Mary Clge, assc prof of soc 1970-; Denver Parochial Sch System, tchr 1962-68; Harvard MIT, research asst 1970; Comm Crisis Intervention Ctr, research asst 1974-75; HEW, grant reviewer 1979; St Mary Coll, dean of students 1986-. **ORGANIZATIONS:** Mem, Sisters of Charity of Leavenworth, 1959-; Mem Amer Soc Assc 1969-; proj mgr Long Range Planning proj St Mary 1977-78; on campus coord small clge consortium Wash DC 1977-80; consult Natl Consult Network 1977-; asst w/ docuemnts Ghana Mission to UN 1981; coord Social Justice Network Sisters of Charity ofLeavenworth 1985; bd dir Leavenworth City-County Alcohol & Drug Abuse Council 1985; Civilian Based Defense, 1986; bd of dirs, St Vincent Clinic, 1988-; Catholic Social Services, 1988-; consultant/evaluator, N Central Assn of Colleges & Schools, 1988-; mem, Natl Assn of Student Personnel Admin. **HONORS/ACHIEVEMENTS:** Natl Delta Epsilon Sigma Acad Honor Soc, 1970-; fellowship, Hamline Univ, 1973; fellowship, Washington Univ, 1973-75; Fulbright Hays Fellowship, Ghana, W Africa, 1975-76; assoc mem, Danforth Assn, 1980. **BUSINESS ADDRESS:** Dean of Students, St Mary College, 4100 S 4th St TFWY, Leavenworth, KS 66048.

PHELPS, DONALD GAYTON
Educational administrator. **PERSONAL:** Born Jul 22, 1929, Seattle, WA; son of Donald G Phelps and Louise E Gayton Adams; married Pamela, Jul 04, 1981; children: Richard W, Michael K, Dawn S. **EDUCATION:** Cornish School of Allied Arts, Seattle WA, Music Major 1948-51; Seattle Uni v, Bachelor of Educ 1959, Master of Educ 1963; Univ of Washington, Doctor of Educ 1983; Harvard Graduate School of Educ, Inst for the Mgmt of Lifelong Educ, 1987. **CAREER:** Bellevue Community Coll, Bellevue WA, exec asst to the pres and dir of personnel 1969-72; Natl Inst on Alcohol Abuse and Alcoholism, dir 1972-76; Lake Washington School Dist, interim supt 1976-77; King County WA, dir of exec admin 1977-80; Seattle Central Community Coll, Seattle WA, pres 1980-84; Seattle Community Coll Dist VI, Seattle WA, chancellor 1984-88; Los Angeles Community Colleges, Los Angeles CA, chancellor 1988-. **ORGANIZATIONS:** Natl Council on Black American Affairs, AACJA; bd of dirs Amer Council on Educ; Amer Council on Educ, Commission on Minorities in Higher Educ; bd of advisors, Inst for the Mgmt of Lifelong Educ, Harvard Univ; Sigma Pi Phi Fraternity, Phi Delta Kappa; bd of trustees, Seattle Univ; life mem NAACP; mem Seattle Urban League, Los Angeles Chamber of Commerce Educ Committee. **HONORS/ACHIEVEMENTS:** Author of Measuring the Human Factor of Classroom Teaching 1978, The Progress of Developmental Students at Seattle Central Community Coll 1981-83; dissertation presented to the School of Educ, Univ of Washington 1983; author of articles "What Can Be Done to Enhance the Status of the Associate Degree?" AACJC Journal 1985, "A Nation Comfortable With Its Prejudices," article taken from speech delivered to the Girl Scout Leaders of Amer 1987, "The Legacy of Martin Luther King Jr and Its Continuing Effect on Today's Society" 1987; nominee for Seattle Post Intelligencer Jefferson Award 1987; Natl Business League President's Washington State Award 1987; selected in The Univ of Washington's first group of Alumni Legends 1987; President's Award, Natl Business League, Washington State Affiliate 1988; Amicus Collegii, Faculty Senate, Los Angeles Harbor Coll 1989; Frederick Douglass Award, Black Faculty Staff Assn, Los Angeles Harbor Coll 1989. **MILITARY SERVICE:** US Army 1951-53, Honorable Discharge.

PHELPS-PATTERSON, LUCY
Educator. **PERSONAL:** Born Jun 21, 1931, Dallas, TX; daughter of John C Phelps Jr and Florence Harllee Phelps; married Albert S Patterson; children: Albert H. **EDUCATION:** Howard Univ, BA 1950; Univ Denver, MSW 1963. **CAREER:** Educ Transformation Inc, pres/CEO, currently; Bishop Clge, Ethel Carter Branham prof & dir soc work prog 1978-88; N TX State Univ, asst prof 1974-78; Dallas Co Child Care Coun, exec dir 1971-74; Grtr Dallas, plng dir Comm Coun 1971-72; Inter-Agency Proj, dir 1968-71; Dallas Co Dept Pub Welfare, casework supr 1963-68. **ORGANIZATIONS:** Chrtr mem N TX Assc Black Social Workers; Natl Assc Social Workers; Acad Cert Social Workers; publs in field; city councilwoman Dallas 1973; pres TX Mun League Region 13 1974-; chrwmn Human Devel Com Dallas; mem Mun Ct Com & Inter-govtmntl Affairs Com; mem Natl League of Cities Comm Devel Policy Com 1973-76; mem Human Resources Com Policy Com 1976; mem Coun on Social Work Educ; ldrshp com E Oak Cliff Sch Dist Cert of Recog House of Reps State of TX 1973, 75; pres NASC elected, 1989. **HONORS/ACHIEVEMENTS:** Woman of Year Zeta Phi Beta Soc 1975; Social Worker of Year; NASW Dallas 1975; Civil Rights Worker of Year; Phi Delta Kappa 1975; Gold Plate Award Alpha KappaAlpha Sor; Outst Educ of Amer NTSU 1975; Com of 100 Award Outst Contrib in Politics 1975; Achvmt Award Henry W Longfellow Sch 1976; Citizens Award TSABCL 1976; Mother of Year John Neely Bryan Elem Sch 1976; awarded Endowed Chair in Social Work Bishop Clge; Fair Housing Award 1979; City of Dallas 1980; Ldrshp Dallas Cert of Award 1979-80; Recognition of Dedicated Service to Citizens of Dallas County, Appraisal Review Board 1988. **HOME ADDRESS:** 2779 Almeda Dr, Dallas, TX 75216. **BUSINESS ADDRESS:** President/CEO, ETI (Educational Transformation, Inc), 1901 Industrial Blvd, Colleyville, TX 76034.

PHILANDER, S. GEORGE H.
Scientist. **PERSONAL:** Born Jul 25, 1942; son of Peter J. Philander and Alice E. Philander; married Hilda Storari; children: Rodrigo. **EDUCATION:** Univ Cape Town, BS 1963; Harvard Univ, PhD 1970. **CAREER:** MA Inst Tech, rsch assoc 1970-71; NOAA/Dept of Commerce, sr rsch oceanographer 1978; Princeton Univ, rsch assoc 1971-78. **ORGANIZATIONS:** Consultant World Metrology Organization 1973-; numerous articles in oceanographic rsch journal; contributor "The Sea" 1977; mem, Natl Academy of Sciences Gate Comm, 1977-79; chmn, EPOCS Steering Comm, 1978-85; mem, SEQUAL Steering Comm, 1981-87; chmn, CCCO Atlantic Panel, 1981-; mem, Mass Inst of Tech Visiting Comm; mem, Natl Acad of Sciences TOGA Panel, 1985-; mem, Dynamics of Atmospheres and Oceans; mem, Geofisica Intl; mem Oceanographie Tropicale; lecturer with rank of professor in geological and geophysical sciences, Princeton Univ, 1980-. **HONORS/ACHIEVEMENTS:** NOAA Environmental Rsch Labs, 1979; Distinguished Authorship Award, 1979; NOAA Environmental Rsch Labs, 1983; Distinguished Authorship Award, 1983; Awarded Sverdrup Gold Medal by Amer Meteorological Soc, 1985; Dept of Commerce Gold Medal, 1985; Elected Fellow of the Amer Meterological Soc, 1985; Book published El Nino, La Nina & The Southern Oscillations, acad press, 1989. **BUSINESS ADDRESS:** Research Associate, PrincetonUniv, Geophys Fluid Dyn Lab, Princeton, NJ 08544.

PHILLIP, MICHAEL JOHN
Educator. **PERSONAL:** Born May 27, 1929, Port-of-Spain, Trinidad and Tobago;married Germaine Victor; children: Roger, Brian. **EDUCATION:** Univ of Toronto, BSc 1960, MSc 1962; MI State Univ, PhD 1964. **CAREER:** John Carroll Univ Cleveland, assoc prof biology 1969-72; Univ of Detroit, prof microbiology 1977-, dir genetics 1982-. **ORGANIZATIONS:** Mem bd trustees St Mary's Hosp 1983-; vice chmn bd of dirs Alexandrine House Detroit 1979-. **HONORS/ACHIEVEMENTS:** Distinguished Faculty Awd Univ of Detroit Black Alumni 1983; Outstanding Foreign Student MI State Univ 1963. **BUSINESS ADDRESS:** Dir of Genetics, Univ of Detroit, 2985 E Jefferson Ave, Detroit, MI 48207.

PHILLIP, WHITE, III
Educator. **PERSONAL:** Born Jun 23, 1956, Beckley, WV; son of Phillip White Jr. **EDUCATION:** Beckley Coll, AA 1974-76; WV State Coll, BSEd 1976-78; WVCOGS, MA 1980-83; ME 1980-83; Scholastic All-American, 1981. **CAREER:** Job Corps, coll prep inst 1979-82; Raleigh Co Public Sch, spec ed teacher 1983-86; Educational Handbook/Curriculum Guide, staff writer/proofreader/editor 1986-, consulting editor 1986; DC Public Sch, ed specailist 1986. **ORGANIZATIONS:** Mem Alpha Phi Omega 1977, Kappa Delta Pi 1977-80; WV-W Germany Friendship Force Exchange, ambassador 1979; WV Rehab Center Vol Serv, vol 1979-81; Lambda Iota Tau, pres 1980-81; Assoc of Supervision & Curriculum Dev, mem 1980-82; Nat'l Ed Assoc, mem 1983-86; youth committee NAACP 1985-86; mem Phi Delta Kappa, Howard Univ 1988; mem National Council of Teachers of English 1980; mem Concerned Black Men, Inc 1989; mem Kiwanis 1977; mem Black Caucus - Council of Exceptional Children 1986. **HONORS/ACHIEVEMENTS:** Reg Intergovernmental Council, researcher/writer 1978-79; Higher Ed Inst, guest lectuer; Liberty High School, teacher of the year 1985-86; guest lecturer, Higher Education Institution 1982. **HOME ADDRESS:** 201 Eye Street SW, #412, Washington, DC 20024.

PHILLIPS, ACEN L.
Clergyman, business executive. **PERSONAL:** Born May 10, 1935, Hillhouse, MS; married E La Quilla Gaiter; children: Acen Jr, Gregory, Delford, Vicky Lynn, Aaron La Bracc, Carole Knight. **EDUCATION:** Denver Univ, BA, MA; Conservative Baptist Theol Seminary, BD; Iliff Sch of Theology, MRC; Amer Baptist Theology Seminary, DD. **CAREER:** Denver Public Schs, educator; Ace Enterprises, pres; Mt Gilead Bapt Ch, minister. **ORGANIZATIONS:** Pres WSBC; state vice pres NBC USA Inc; pres East Denver Ministers Alliance; organizer of Denver OIC; organizer/founder first chmn of bd & pres Productions Inc; organizer/founder pres & bd chmn Ace Enterprises Inc; pres Natl Amer Church Union Inc; chmn Intl Interdenominational Ministers Alliance; bd chmn DTP Ministers Inc. **HONORS/ACHIEVEMENTS:** Brought opening prayer for US Congress 1976; listed in Congressional Record; Man of the Yr. **BUSINESS ADDRESS:** Minister, Mt Gilead Bapt Church, 195 S Monaco, Denver, CO 80224.

PHILLIPS, BARBARA (NEE KINARD)
Educator. **PERSONAL:** Born Sep 05, 1936, Winston-Salem, NC; married Garret Elroy Phillips Jr; children: Eleanor. **EDUCATION:** WSSU, BS 1957; IN Univ, MS 1958; UNC, EdS 1975, EdD 1979. **CAREER:** Winston-Salem Forsyth Co School, principal; teacher; guidance counselor; librarian; psychometrist. **ORGANIZATIONS:** Dir Continuing Educ; coord Model Cities Natl Pres Alpha Kappa Alpha; trustee Winston-Salem State Univ 1974-79; former bd mem YWCA; former bd mem GSA;former bd mem Robert Vaughn Agcy; bd dir Big Bros-Big Sisters; trustee 1st Bapt ch. **HONORS/ACHIEVEMENTS:** Jessie Smith Noyes Flwshp to grad student 1957; Ldrshp Award NC/VA Alpha Kappa Alpha Sor 1977. **BUSINESS ADDRESS:** Lowrance Int School, 2900 Ave, Winston-Salem, NC 27105.

PHILLIPS, BASIL OLIPHANT
Administrator. **PERSONAL:** Born Feb 19, 1930, Kansas City, MO. **EDUCATION:** Roosevelt Univ & Inst of Design at IL Inst of Tech, atnd. **CAREER:** Johnson Pub Co Inc, photo editor; JPC Book Div, dir spec mrkts & promo & former sales mgr 1950-; Abraham Lincoln Bookstore, former employee. **BUSINESS ADDRESS:** 820 S Michigan Ave, Chicago, IL 60605.

PHILLIPS, BERTHA (NEE PARKER)
Coordinator. **PERSONAL:** Born Sep 11, 1940, Tillman, SC; married Vincent Phillips; children: Vincent Parker, Kia Rosetta. **EDUCATION:** Benedict Clge, AB; Atlantic Univ, MSLS; GA State Univ, MEd. **CAREER:** Children's Cottage Inc Atlanta GA, prog coord 1979-; Atl Pub Libr, zone coord 1976-79; Child Srv, coord 1969-75; NY Pub Lib, child libr 1965-69;Robert Smalls HS, libr 1962-64. **ORGANIZATIONS:** Chmn Eval of Child Mag; mem Amer Libr Assc; mem Natl Assoc of Young Child; educ Lucky Book Club; mem Beta Phi Mu Intl Lib Sci Hon Soc. **HONORS/ACHIEVEMENTS:** Recorded 2 vols of African Folk Tales for Children; mem CMS Records Co label; recd the EP Dalton-John Macrae Award to Clge folktales in the S 1969. **BUSINESS ADDRESS:** Children's Cottage Inc, 575 Woodlawn Ave NW, Atlanta, GA 30318.

PHILLIPS, BERTRAND D.
Painter, photographer. **PERSONAL:** Born Nov 19, 1938, Chicago, IL. **EDUCATION:** Art Inst of Chicago, BFA 1961; NWU, MFA 1972. **CAREER:** Northwestern Univ, asst prof; Elmhurst Coll, instructor, 1970-72. **ORGANIZATIONS:** Bd mem Chicago Alliance for the Performing Arts, 1975; bd mem, Chicago Public Art Workshop 1975-. **HONORS/ACHIEVEMENTS:** G D Brown Foreign Traveling Fellowship, 1961; Ponte dell'Arte Award School of Art Inst of Chicago Srcs 1961; Blk Artst of the New Generation, Elton Fax 1977; Afro-Amer Slide Depositry Catalog 1970-75; Afro-Am Artist; A Biobibliography Dir Boston

Public Library, 1973. **MILITARY SERVICE:** AUS pfc 1962-64. **BUSINESS ADDRESS:** Art Dept, Northwestern Univ, Evanston, IL 60201.

PHILLIPS, COLETTE ALICE-MAUDE
Public relations, communications executive. **PERSONAL:** Born Sep 20, 1954, St John's, Antigua-Barbuda;daughter of Douglas Phillips and Ionie Phillips. **EDUCATION:** Emerson Coll, BS Speech Communications 1976, M Business & Org Communications 1979. **CAREER:** Press sec to prime minister of Antigua, 1976-78; Patriots' Trial Coun, public relations dir 1980-84; Cablevision of Boston, public relations dir 1984-85; Royal Sonesta Hotel, public relations dir 1985-86; APR Company, pres. **ORGANIZATIONS:** Mem bd of dirs Urban League Eastern MA 1980-85; bd mem Women in Communication Boston Chap 1984-86; vice pres Financial Develop MA Assoc of Mental Health 1984-87; vice pres Horizons for Youth 1986-87; bd mem Boston AIDS Action Comm 1986-; mem Amer Cancer Soc Public Information Comm, Public Relations Soc of Amer, Develop Comm of Spaulding Rehab Hosp; bd mem Museum of Fine Arts Council 1988-; bd mem Freedom House 1989-92; trustee Friends of Boston Ballet. **HONORS/ACHIEVEMENTS:** United Way Communications Awd 1981; Certificate of Appreciation Boston Univ PRSA Student Chap 1982; Outstanding Alumni Awd Emerson Coll 1983; 100 Most Influential Blacks in Boston 1986; named one of the 100 most powerful people in Boston by Boston Herald; named one of 100 most interesting women in Boston by Boston Woman Magazine, 1989; named "face to watch in 1988," Boston Magazine. **BUSINESS ADDRESS:** President, APR Company, 41 Colborne Road, Ste B2, Brighton, MA 02135.

PHILLIPS, CONSTANCE ANN
Sales manager. **PERSONAL:** Born Jun 19, 1941, Hamilton, OH; married Lloyd Garrison Phillips Jr; children: Allan Lloyd, Garrison Loren. **EDUCATION:** Miami Univ of OH, BA 1964; St Elizabeth Hosp Sch of Med, ASCP Registered Med Tech 1962. **CAREER:** St Elizabeth Hosp Dayton, medical tech 1962-64; Miami Valley Hosp Dayton, medical tech chemistry 1964-66; Univ of MN Hosp, medical tech supv pulmonaryfunction lab 1966-69; Mary Kay Cosmetics, beauty consultant 1974-, sales dir 1976-. **ORGANIZATIONS:** Mem Alpha Kappa Alpha Sor; sec Gem City Medical Dental & Pharm Aux 1982-83; mem Natl Assoc for Female Execs 1982-, Black Career Women 1983-84; editor, newsletter Jack & Jill of Amer 1983-85; pres Twentig Inc 1985-; mem hospitality comm Dayton Philharmonic Womens Assoc; mem Montgomery County Medical Assoc Aux. **HONORS/ACHIEVEMENTS:** Miss Go Give Awd Mary Kay Cosmetics Inc 1980; Jill Business Woman of Year Jack & Jill of Amer 1983; 6 Pink Cars Mary Kay Cosmetics 1986. **BUSINESS ADDRESS:** Senior Sales Dir, Mary Kay Cosmetics Inc, 9572 Bridlewood Trail, Spring Valley, OH 45370.

PHILLIPS, DANIEL P.
Business executive. **PERSONAL:** Born Feb 20, 1917, Sharon, PA; married Dorothy Weston; children: Dana Jean Johnson, Robin Dale. **EDUCATION:** Lincoln U, BA 1939. **CAREER:** Chem Proc Fed Tool & Plstcs Co, plnt mgr div of ethyl corp; Cyrus Realtors Inc, realtor. **ORGANIZATIONS:** Pres Evnstn Pk & Rec Bd 1953-73; vice pres Evnstn YMCA Bd 1959-76; mem 1964-, pres Evnstn HS Bd of Educ 1969-73, 1987,88; mem dir Evanston Rotary Club 1969-; mem bd of dirs IL Assoc of School Bds 1983-; pres Evanston Rotary Club 1989-1990. **HONORS/ACHIEVEMENTS:** Recip Outstanding Sch Bd Mem St of IL 1974; Disting Comm Contrib NAACP 1974; St Awd Otstndng Rehab Empl 1973. **BUSINESS ADDRESS:** Sales Associate, Cyrus Realtors, Inc, 2929 Central St, Evanston, IL 60201.

PHILLIPS, DILCIA R.
Bilingual educator. **PERSONAL:** Born Nov 30, 1949, Colon, Panama;children: Melbourne Alexander Hewitt Jr. **EDUCATION:** Kingsborough Comm Coll, AA 1977; Brooklyn Coll, BA Educ 1979, MS Educ 1982; Brooklyn Coll, advanced degree Guidance/Couns 1982. **CAREER:** Maternal Infant Care Family Planning Project, counselor 1978-81; Women's Medical Serv at Kingsbrook Hosp, counselor 1981-83; Women Medical Serv at Kingsbrook Hosp, dir of public relations and agency afrs 1983; New York City Bd of Educ, bilingual teacher 1983-. **ORGANIZATIONS:** Dept coord STEP Prog/Columbia Univ 1986-; chairperson Comprehensive School Improvement Prog 1986-. **HONORS/ACHIEVEMENTS:** Outstanding Serv to the Grad Students of Brooklyn Coll 1982. **HOME ADDRESS:** 244-30 137 Road, Rosedale, NY 11422. **BUSINESS ADDRESS:** Teacher Elem Bilingual Educ, New York City Public School, 51 Christopher St, Brooklyn, NY 11212.

PHILLIPS, EARL W.
Educator. **PERSONAL:** Born Sep 20, 1917, Teague, TX; married Dorothy S Reid; children: Eart, Jr, Betty, Carol. **EDUCATION:** Huston Tillotson, BA 1940; Boston Univ, MBA 1947; NC Central Univ, JD 1953; Univ NC, MA 1960; Univ CO, PhD 1965. **CAREER:** Met State Coll, prof; CO Dept Educ, cons; US Dept State & US Dept Commerce, economist; Univ CO, asst prof; NC Central Univ, asst prof. **ORGANIZATIONS:** Mem Presbyterian Mens Assn; elder Peoples Presbyterian Church; mem W Reg Sic Assn; Amer Economic Assn; Indus Relations Rsch Assn; Natl Business Law Assn; Soc Intl Devel; mem bd dir Home Neighborly Serv; trustee Wasatch Acad & Westminster Coll; chmn Personnel Com Gen Council; mem Urban League CO. **HONORS/ACHIEVEMENTS:** Fellowship Univ Oslo Norway 1956; Certificate of Merit CO Dept Educ 1970; Human Relations Awd CO Educ Assn 1975. **MILITARY SERVICE:** USN 1942-45. **HOME ADDRESS:** 3085 Fairfax, Denver, CO 80207.

PHILLIPS, EARMIA JEAN
Executive director. **PERSONAL:** Born Apr 21, 1941, Edwards, MS. **EDUCATION:** Bus Edn, 2yrs; Utica Coll, Cosmet 1yr. **CAREER:** Delta Rsrcs Com, exec dir1976-; Delta Ministry, rep 1968; Nat Cncl Chs USA MS, adminstr asst fnncs 1967-71; Intrcntntl Msns Jcksn TN PrdUniv Lfytt, rep. **ORGANIZATIONS:** Chmn Frdmn Dem Prty Hinds Co Edwrds Br; bd mem Wash Co NAACP; bd mem Wash Issqn Comm Actn Prog; bd mem Sr Ctzn Cmpn Prog Adv Com; mem of Peoples Educ Prog Area Cncl Prnts to Save the Chldrn of Peoples Educ Prog; mem St Mark MB Ch; bd mem Plnd Prnthd Jcksn Ch Wmn Untd; NAACP-Wash Co Chpt; bd mem Wash Co Un for Prog Frdm Vlg Inc; adv com No MS Rural Lgl Serv Inc. **BUSINESS ADDRESS:** PO Box 584, Greenville, MS 38701.

PHILLIPS, EDWARD MARTIN
Chemical engineer. **PERSONAL:** Born Dec 23, 1935, Philadelphia, PA; son of Edward M Phillips and Sylvia D Phillips; married Audrey Henrietta Longley. **EDUCATION:** Lafayette Coll, BS ChE 1958; Northwestern Univ, MS ChE 1959; Univ of Pittsburgh, PhD ChE 1969. **CAREER:** Arco Rsch & Engrg, engr 1959-64; Exxon Engrg Co, project engr 1968-72; Tufts Univ, assoc prof 1972-74; Air Products & Chemicals Inc, engrg assoc, 1974-86; Rutgers Univ, professor, 1987-. **ORGANIZATIONS:** Mem Amer Inst of Chemical Engrg 1958-; mem Amer Chem Soc 1969-; dir Lehigh Valley Child Care 1977-. **HONORS/ACHIEVEMENTS:** NASA Predoctoral Fellow Univ of Pittsburgh 1964-68; Fellow of Amer Institute of Chemical Engineers. **BUSINESS ADDRESS:** Professor & Associate Director, Center for Packaging Science & Engineering, Rutgers Univ, Bldg 3529, Bush Campus, Piscataway, NJ 08855.

PHILLIPS, ERIC MCLAREN, JR.
Supervisor. **PERSONAL:** Born Oct 19, 1952, Georgetown, Guyana;married Angela; children: Takeisha Sherrill. **EDUCATION:** McMaster Univ, BS Engrg 1976; New York Univ, MBA 1983; Stevens Inst of Tech & Bell Laboratories, Certificate in Telecommunication Engrg 1985. **CAREER:** Apollo Technologies, test engr 1977-78, project engr 1978-79, sr project engr 1979-80, r&d product development leader 1980-82; AT&T Communications, staff mgr local area networks 1983-84, 1984-85, staff mgr network planning 1985-86; AT&T Bell Laboratories, supervisor mem tech staff 1986-. **ORGANIZATIONS:** Pres Phillips Smith & Assocs Inc 1982; exec dir The Caribbean Theatre of the Performing Arts New York City 1983; program dir 1986, pres 1985 NYU Black Alumni Assoc. **HONORS/ACHIEVEMENTS:** Top Engineer 6 consecutive Quarters Apollo Technologies Inc 1979,80; R&D Scientific Achievement of the Year Awd Apollo Technologies Inc 1981; Merit Awd Grad Sch of Business Admin New York Univ 1983; AT&T Management Succession Roster 1983-86. **BUSINESS ADDRESS:** Supervisor/Mem Tech Staff, Bell Laboratories, Crawford Corners Rd, Holmdel, NJ 07783.

PHILLIPS, EUGENIE ELVIRA
Physician. **PERSONAL:** Born Jan 04, 1918, New York, NY; widowed; children: Eugenie, Randolph. **EDUCATION:** Hnter Coll, BA 1940; Meharry Med Coll, MD 1944. **CAREER:** Harlem Hosp, intern 1944-45; Provident Hosp, ob/gyn 1945-47; Maternity Hosp, ob/gyn 1945-47; Mrgrt Hague, ob/gyn res 1945-47; Coppin State Teachers Coll,assoc sch phy 1959-74; Morgan State Univ, medical dir health svcs; Private Practice, ob/gyn physician 1947-. **ORGANIZATIONS:** Mem Nat Med Assn; Mnmntl Med Soc; MD St Med Soc; Bltmr City Med Soc; Med & Chrrgcl Fac of MD; Ob-Gyn Soc of MD; Am Med Wmns Assn; So Med Soc; Am Frtlty Soc; Am Soc for Clpscpy & Clpmcrscpy; NAACP. **BUSINESS ADDRESS:** 1612 Edmondson Ave, Baltimore, MD 21223.

PHILLIPS, F. ALLISON
Clergyman. **PERSONAL:** Born Jan 05, 1937, Brooklyn, NY; married Velma Carr; children: Denise Mitchell, Alyson. **EDUCATION:** Virginia Union Univ, BA 1958; Colgate Rochester Divinity School, BD 1967; New York Theological Seminary, STM 1975, DMin 1981. **CAREER:** YMCA, assoc dir 1958-64; Garrison Blvd Comm Ctr, dir 1967-71; North Congregational Church, pastor 1971-82; Mt Zion Congregational Church, pastor 1982-. **ORGANIZATIONS:** Mem Alpha Phi Alpha 1955-; bd mem Amer Red Cross 1983-87; pres Inner City Renewal Soc 1984-; moderator African Amer Family Congress 1986-; bd mem Greater Cleveland Roundtable 1986-, Leadership Cleveland 1986-. **HONORS/ACHIEVEMENTS:** Service Awds YMCA 1966, Council of Churches 1971, UCC Clergy Black Caucus 1981; Leadership Awd ISTEM 1982. **BUSINESS ADDRESS:** Pastor, Mt Zion Congregational Church, 10723 Magnolia Dr, Cleveland, OH 44106.

PHILLIPS, FITZGERALD
Attorney. **PERSONAL:** Born Nov 29, 1893; married Kathleen; children: Joyce Phillips Austin, Mildred E. **EDUCATION:** City Coll NY; Frdhm Law Sch, LLB 1925. **CAREER:** New York City Dept Corr, dep commr 1946-50; New York City Parole Commn, 1950-67; Priv Prac, atty. **ORGANIZATIONS:** Mem NY St Bar 1927-; Prince Hall Masons; Epsilon & Sigma Frat; Grand St Boys Assn; NY Co Lwyrs Assn; Harlem Lwyrs; Harlem YMCA; NAACP; Frdhm Law Sch Almn City Coll Almn Assns; 369th Vet Assn; Am Legion; New York City Corr Post; frmr mem Rotary Club Upper Mnhttn. **HONORS/ACHIEVEMENTS:** Num hon awds. **MILITARY SERVICE:** AUS Ww I vet 1918-1919. **BUSINESS ADDRESS:** 271 W 125 St, Ste 410, New York, NY 10027.

PHILLIPS, FRANK E.
Government official, attorney. **PERSONAL:** Born Mar 03, 1930, Pittsburgh, PA; married Mary E; children: Nancy, Judith. **EDUCATION:** Shaw Univ, AB 1952; Howard Univ, LLB 1955. **CAREER:** IRS, Washington DC, rev officer 1955-62; IRS LA CA, off chief counsel tax atty 1962-66, sr tax atty 1966-69, staff asst to regional counsel. **ORGANIZATIONS:** Natl Bar Assn; Fed Bar Assn; VA St Bar; bd dir Crenshaw YMCA; mem Chrstn Dcsn Dept Episcopal Church. **HONORS/ACHIEVEMENTS:** Many hon & frat. **BUSINESS ADDRESS:** Assistant District Counsel, Internal Revenue Service, 300 N Los Angeles, Rm 3018, Los Angeles, CA 90053.

PHILLIPS, FREDERICK BRIAN
Psychologist. **PERSONAL:** Born Sep 02, 1946, Philadelphia, PA; married Vicki Altemus, May 25, 1986; children: Jamali, Jasmine. **EDUCATION:** Penn State Univ, BA 1968; Univ of PA, MSW 1970; The Fielding Inst, PsyD 1978. **CAREER:** Dist of Columbia Govt, psychologist 1978-81; Institute for Life Enrichment, assoc dir 1981-83; Progressive Life Inst, director/pres. **ORGANIZATIONS:** Mem Assoc of Black Psychologists 1978-85; mem Kappa Alpha Psi 1965-85. **MILITARY SERVICE:** AUS capt 3 yrs. **BUSINESS ADDRESS:** Director/President, Progressive Life Center, 1123 11th St, NW, Washington, DC 20001.

PHILLIPS, GLENN OWEN
Educator. **PERSONAL:** Born Sep 26, 1946, Bridgetown, Barbados;son of E Owen Phillips and Dorothy E Phillips; married Ingrid Denise Tom, Aug 27, 1972; children: Mariette. **EDUCATION:** Atlantic Union College, BA 1967; Andrews Univ, MA 1969; Howard Univ, PhD 1976. **CAREER:** Caribbean Union Coll, lecturer 1969-71, Howard Univ, asst prof history 1981-82, Morgan State Univ, asst prof history 1978-, asst dir Univ Honors Program 1981-82, research assoc 1982-, acting dir of Institute for Urban Research 1986-89. asst prof 1989-. **ORGANIZATIONS:** Liason Officer NAFEO, DC 1985; E. Comm. Council of Caribbean Organizations, DC 1985-; School Bd Mem G. E. Peters Elementary School 1987-. **HONORS/ACHIEVEMENTS:** HBCU Faculty Fellshp United Negro Coll Fund/US Dept of Lab 1980; Morgan State Univ Honorary Member (Promethean Kappa Tau) 1982; Cited Nat'l Dir Latin

Americans; Assoc Editor Afro- Hispanic Rev, Jrnl of Negro Hist, co-editor Dic of Negro American Biography Bks 1984; Book "The Caribbean Basin Initiative" co-editor 1987; Article for Maryland Historical Society 1988. **BUSINESS ADDRESS:** Department of History, Morgan StateUniv, Cold Spring Ln & Hillen Rd, Baltimore, MD 21239.

PHILLIPS, HELEN M.
Educator. **PERSONAL:** Born May 29, 1926, Norfolk, VA; daughter of Thomas Battle and Rosa Battle; married Orman Decoursey Phillips, May 26, 1951; children: Marcia Anita Baynes, Brian O D. **EDUCATION:** VA State Univ, Petersburg VA, BS 1954; Suffolk Univ, Boston MA, MEd 1983; studied at Univ of MD, Fairleigh Dickinson Univ, Salem State Coll, Catholic Univ of Amer & Boston Univ. **CAREER:** Carnegie Inst, dir of prog for medical sec & assistants; Staff Norfolk State Coll 1951, East Boston HS, Boston Sch of Business, Brighton HS, Carnegie Inst; Malden Public Sch System, Malden MA, teacher of typewriting, word processing, and money and banking. **ORGANIZATIONS:** Mem Natl Business Educ Assn, Natl Educ Assn, MA Teachers Assn; mem NAACP, Malden Teachers Assn, Eastern Business Teachers Assn, The Resolutions Comm of the MA Teachers Assn 3 yrs; mem, assoc vice pres, VA State Coll Alumni Assn; bd dir & charter mem, Cynthia Sickle Cell Anemia Fund; mem Concord Baptist Church, Boston MA; former project dir of Women in Community Serv Boston; organizer & founder of Black Student Union at MHS; mem Alpha Kappa Alpha Sor; former columnist for the Boston Graphic and the Boston Sun newspapers; served on Ad Hoc Comm responsible for incorporating black studies into the Malden School System; natl bd dir, representing the 17th dist, VA State Univ Alumni Assn, 1982-85, 1986-87; mem of task force comm, Restructuring Malden High School, 1988-89. **HONORS/ACHIEVEMENTS:** Listing 1972 edition of Comm Leaders of America; selected to serve on Evaluation Team New England Assn for Accreditation of Coll & Secondary Schs 1972; selected by MA Teachers Assn to represent MA in Cadre Training Session Univ of NH 1973; selected to attend MIP Conf Cheyney State Coll MA Teachers Assn; responsible for starting MIP Conf in MA; First Place Dist Representative Awd, VA State Univ Alumni Assn, 1986; one of five educators in Malden School System selected as a mem of Needs Assessment Comm for Students at Risk-Dropouts, Updating Junior High Schools in Malden to Middle Schools, 1987. **BUSINESS ADDRESS:** Teacher, Malden High School, Boyle Bldg B-321, 77 Salem St, Malden, MA 02148.

PHILLIPS, JAMES LAWRENCE
Physician, educational administration. **PERSONAL:** Born Mar 01, 1932, Sharon, PA; son of Daniel S Phillips and Roxie B Phillips; married Barbara A Eiserman; children: James Jr, Jeffrey, Steven. **EDUCATION:** Washington & Jefferson Coll, BA 1954; Case Western Reserve Univ School of Medicine, MD 1958; Harvard Univ, advanced mgmt program 1979. **CAREER:** Kaiser Found Hospital Parma 1970-; Case Western Reserve Univ School of Medicine, asst clinical prof in pediatrics 1972-87; Cleveland Cavaliers Basketball Team, asst team physician 1973-79; West OH Permanente Med Group Inc, physician-in-chief 1968-86; Rocky River Med Off, physician in charge 1986-87; Case Western Reserve Univ School of Med, assoc dean for student affairs. **ORGANIZATIONS:** Mem Acad of Medicine of Cleveland; mem OH State Med Assn; mem N OH Pediatric Soc; pres Case Western Reserve Univ School of Med Alumni Assn 1980-81; bd trustees Washington & Jefferson Coll 1982-; mem Case Western Reserve Univ School of Med Comm on Students 1982-87; bd trustees Mt Pleasant Church of God 1976-82; chmn United Way Serv New Programs Comm 1985; pres Northern OH Pediatric Soc 1988-89; bd of trustees, Washington & Jefferson College, 1988-94; pres, Northern Ohio Pediatric Society, 1988-89; mem, Cleveland Medical Association, 1988-. **HONORS/ACHIEVEMENTS:** Bd Certified Amer Bd of Pediatrics 1963; Birch Scholarship Award Washington & Jefferson Coll 1954; Jessie Smith Noyes Found Med School Scholarship 1954-55; Leadership Cleveland, 1989-90. **MILITARY SERVICE:** USNR lt comdr 2 yrs; Commendation from Commanding Officer. **BUSINESS ADDRESS:** Assoc Dean of Student Affairs, Case Western ReserveUniv, 12301 Snow Road, School of Medicine, Cleveland, OH 44106.

PHILLIPS, JOHN M.
Business executive. **PERSONAL:** Born Mar 10, 1920, Hampton, VA; married Effie Banks; children: John Mallory, Jr. **EDUCATION:** Hampton Inst, BS 1943. **CAREER:** Phllps Sea Co Inc, dir; Amory Sea Co, plnt supr 1943-63; Hampton City Cncl, elctd 1974-78. **ORGANIZATIONS:** Mem VA Sea Cncl; VA Pckrs Assn; C of C 1st Bapt Ch; Omega Psi Phi Frat; Hampton Almn Assn; Elks; Exclsr & Ldg No 4; Dochiki Club; mem HamptonCity Cncl; Zeta Omicron Chptr. **HONORS/ACHIEVEMENTS:** Ctzn of the Yr 1974.

PHILLIPS, JUNE M. J.
Educator, writer. **PERSONAL:** Born May 31, 1941, Ashdown, AR; married AW Phillips; children: Roderick, Calandra Camille. **EDUCATION:** Philander Smith Coll, BA English (Magna Cum Laude) 1963; LA State Univ, MA English 1971; Northwestern State Univ, doctoral candidate; Bakers Prof Real Estate Coll, license 1977. **CAREER:** Port Arthur TX Schools, teacher 1963-65; Caddo Parish Schools Shreveport, teacher 1965-68; Board of LA Colls & Univs, trustee 1983-; consultant on educ for minorities; orator and poet; Southern Univ Shreveport, asst prof english 1968-. **ORGANIZATIONS:** Sales assoc Century 21 1977-79; sales assoc Lester Realty 1979-83; sales assoc Ferdinand Realty 1984-; consul Lynell's Cosmetics 1984-; bd mem United Way of NW LA 1979-; secty-treas Caddo Parish Charter Study Com 1981-82; delegate Democratic Natl Conv 1984; NAUW; OEO #175; Shreveport Chap of Links; Zeta Phi Beta Sor; pres elect LA Philosophy of Educ Soc; vice pres CODAC; mem bd of trustees La Colleges and Universities gubernatorial apptmt; chairs academicaffairs comm for 9 LA colls; First black woman to serve on state bd. **HONORS/ACHIEVEMENTS:** Woman of the Yr Zeta Phi Beta Sor Inc 1975; Woman of Amer Outstanding Young Woman of Amer 1977; mem Caddo Parish Sch Bd 1976-77; Fellowship NDEA, TX So & So Univ; editor/critic Holbrook Press NY & Roxbury Press CA; selected by City of Shreveport as "Woman Who Has Made a Difference". **HOME ADDRESS:** 1820 Jones Mabry Rd, Shreveport, LA 71107. **BUSINESS ADDRESS:** Asst Prof of English, SouthernUniv, 3050 ML King Drive, Shreveport, LA 71107.

PHILLIPS, LEO A.
Scientist. **PERSONAL:** Born Feb 21, 1931, Nashville, AR; married Hattie M; children: Philip, Phyllis, Pebbles, Phil. **EDUCATION:** Univ of So CA, BS 1954; AZ St U, MS 1963;Univ of KS, PhD 1967; Am Acad of Microbiol. **CAREER:** Nat Cancer Inst, sci, sr staff fellow 1971-73, staff fellow 1969-71, past proj ofcr 1972-73; Pub Hlth & Rsrch Inst of NYC, rsch fellow 1967-69. **ORGANIZATIONS:** Ext Revw Com HowrdUniv Cancer Rsrch Ctr; mem Am Soc for Mcrbiol; mem Sigma Xi; Bphyscl Soc; Am Assn for Cancer Rsch; Intl Assn for Comp Rsrch on Luek & Rltd Disea;Am Soc for Biol Chem Spkr Cold Spr Hrbr Sympsm 1969; spkr ICN-UCLA Sympsm 1973; spkr Grdn Rsrch Conf 1973. **MILITARY SERVICE:** AUS 1955-57. **BUSINESS ADDRESS:** Bldg 41 Ste 300, 9000 Rockville Pike, Bethesda, MD 20205.

PHILLIPS, LEROY DANIEL
Consultant. **PERSONAL:** Born Jul 10, 1935, Texarkana, TX; son of L D Phillips and Jessie Mae Phillips; married Mary A; children: Kevin V. **EDUCATION:** Los Angeles City Coll, AA 1967; California State Univ Los Angeles, BA 1972; Century Univ Los Angeles, MBA 1979. **CAREER:** Los Angeles County, various positions including pharmacy storekeeper, pharmaceuticals supply mgmt for med center, div chief supply & transportation mechanical dept, building crafts mgr 1956-85; Business Mgmt Consulting, commodities broker 1986-. **ORGANIZATIONS:** Apptd Interview Bds Dept of Personnel LA County 1977-83, 1979-81; chmn Coastal Mental Health Governing Bd 1980-83; president Diane Watson Semi-Professional Sports Assoc 1986-; volunteer role player LA County Sheriff Dept 1986-; trustee Intergroup Trust 1987-; lifetime mem LA County Employees Assoc. **HONORS/ACHIEVEMENTS:** Special Citation Serv Employees Intl Union 1985; United Way Award 1985; Leadership Award Brotherhood Crusade 1986; Leadership Award United Negro College Fund 1986. **HOME ADDRESS:** 914 Oakmere Dr, Harbor City, CA 90710.

PHILLIPS, LLOYD GARRISON, JR.
Surgeon. **PERSONAL:** Born May 23, 1941, Dayton, OH; married Connie Cunningham; children: Allan, Garrison. **EDUCATION:** Miami Univ Oxford OH, BA 1962; Meharry Medical Coll, MD 1966; Univ of Minnesota, PhD 1973. **CAREER:** Univ of Minnesota, grad stud anat 1966-73, resident genl surgery 1966-74; OH State Univ, resident thoracic & Cardiovascular surg 1974-76; Dayton VA Medical Ctr, chief thoracic & cardiovascular surgery 1978-. **ORGANIZATIONS:** Medical advisor Concerned Citizens for Cancer 1982-; mem bd dirs Otterbein Home Lebanon OH 1983-; founding mem Amer Assoc of Clinical Anatomists 1983-; mem Alpha Phi Alpha, Alpha Omega Alpha. **HONORS/ACHIEVEMENTS:** Published papers, monographs, book chapter. **HOME ADDRESS:** 9572 Bridlewood Tr, Spring Valley, OH 45370. **BUSINESS ADDRESS:** Chief Thoracic/Cardiovasc Surg, VA Medical Center, 4100 W Third St, Dayton, OH 45428.

PHILLIPS, MEL
Defensive backfield coach. **PERSONAL:** Born Jan 06, 1942; married Patricia; children: Paulette, Yvette. **EDUCATION:** Attended, North Carolina A&T. **CAREER:** San Francisco 49ers', player 1966-77; Detroit Lions, defensive backfield coach 1980-84; Miami Dolphins, defensive backfield coach. **HONORS/ACHIEVEMENTS:** Twice won 49ers' Len Eshmont Awd symbolic of team's MVP.

PHILLIPS, RALPH LEONARD
Investment analyst. **PERSONAL:** Born May 11, 1925, Sacramento, CA. **EDUCATION:** Univ of CA Berkeley, AB (Cum Laude) 1949, MA; Institute of African Studies Northwestern Univ, Special Studies. **CAREER:** Bureau of Intl Relations Univ of CA, rsch assoc 1950; Univ of CA, teaching fellow political science 1952-55; USIA, information officer/cultural attache 1956-68, special asst to the dir Near East & Southeast Asia Washington Headquarters 1963-64; Mobil Oil Community & Public Affairs Tripoli Libya, 1969-71; International Gov Rels New York, sr planning analyst 1971-. **ORGANIZATIONS:** Dir of Planning Educ Task Force Council of Econ Develop New York City as Mobil rep 1971-72; bd of dirs DPF Inc (NYSE) 1972-74; mem Mayor's Adv Council on Housing Princeton 1973-75; bd of dir Council on Intl Programs 1975; mem Campanille Soc Univ of CA 1976-; mem Zoning Bd for Variance Princeton 1977-79; vice pres Princeton Republican Assoc 1978-80; mem Princeton Regional Planning Bd 1981-; mem bd of trustees St Paul's Coll Lawrence VA 1983-; mem Prince Hall F&A Masons Aaron #9 Princeton NJ; 32nd Degree Ophir Consistory, Trenton NJ; Shriner Prince Hall Masons Kufu, Princeton NJ; American Legion Post #218 Princeton NJ. **HONORS/ACHIEVEMENTS:** Hon Students Soc Univ of CA Merit Awd Dept of St 1956; Merit Awd Dept of St 1967; Pi Sigma Alpha Natl Polit Sci Hon Soc; Delta Sigma Rho Natl Forensic Hon Soc. **MILITARY SERVICE:** AUS T/4 Med & Phil Islands; AUS Ready Reserve Presidio of San Francisco Military Intelligence 1957-61. **BUSINESS ADDRESS:** Senior Planning Analyst, Mobil Oil Corp, 3225 Gallows Rd, Fairfax, VA 22037-0001.

PHILLIPS, ROD
Athlete. **PERSONAL:** Born Dec 23, 1952, Meridian, MS; married Brenda; children: Erin. **EDUCATION:** Cincinnati U; Jcksn St, BA. **CAREER:** LA Rams, running back 1975-78; St Louis Crdnls, athlete 1978-. **HONORS/ACHIEVEMENTS:** Ram's 3rd Ldng Rshr Carrying 34 Times for 206 yds 1976; NFC Champ Game 1975-78. **BUSINESS ADDRESS:** Los Angeles Rams, 10271 W Pico, Los Angeles, CA.

PHILLIPS, ROMEO ELDRIDGE
College professor. **PERSONAL:** Born Mar 11, 1928, Chicago, IL; married Deloris R Jordan; children: Pamela Marlene, Arthur JH. **EDUCATION:** Chicago Conservatory Coll, MusB 1949; Chicago Musical Coll, MusM 1951; Eastern MI Univ, MA 1963; Wayne State Univ, PhD 1966. **CAREER:** Chicago IL Public Schools, teacher 1949-55; Detroit MI Public Schools, teacher 1955-57; Inskster MI Public Schools, teacher 1957-66; Kalamazoo Coll, chmn dept of educ 1974-86, tenured prof of educ/music 1968-. **ORGANIZATIONS:** Mem Amer Assoc of Coll for Teacher Educ, Music Educators Natl Conf, MI Sch Vocal Assoc, Assoc for Supervison & Curriculum Develop, MI Assoc for Supervision & Curriculum Develop, MI Assoc for Improvement of Sch Legislation, Natl Alliance of Black School Educators, Natl Assoc of Negro Musicians, Phi Delta Kappa, Kappa Alpha Psi; conductor AfraAmerican Chorale. **HONORS/ACHIEVEMENTS:** Invited by the govt of the Republic of Nigeria West Africa to be a guest to the World Festival of Black and African Art 1977; Omega Psi Phi Leadership Awd 1982; Committee of Scholars for the Accreditation of MI Colls 1982-84; Kalamazoo NAACP Appreciation Awd 1982; Fulbright Scholar to Liberia West Africa 1984-85; 13 journal publications; 1 magazine article; 1 book review; chapters contributed to or credit given in 6 books. **MILITARY SERVICE:** AUS sgt 1951-53. **HOME ADDRESS:** 6841 Welbury, Portage, MI 49081. **BUSINESS ADDRESS:** Prof of Educ/Music, Kalamazoo College, 1200 Academy, Kalamazoo, MI 49007.

PHILLIPS, ROSEMARYE L.
Retired educator. **PERSONAL:** Born Jun 21, 1926, McNary, AZ; daughter of William LeForbes and Octavia McNealy Howard; married David Phillips, Nov 1949 (divorced); children:

Pamela Phillips, Margaret McCalla, Darryl A Phillips. **EDUCATION:** Arizona State Univ, Tempe AZ, AB, 1947; Univ of Southern California, Los Angeles CA, MS, 1956, MEd, 1958; Brigham Young Univ, Provo, UT, Ed, 1974. **CAREER:** Phoenix Dist #1, Phoenix AZ, teacher, 1947-50; Los Angeles City Schools, Los Angeles CA, teacher K-6, reading and math coordinator, supervising training teacher for USC, UCLA, Mt St Marys Coll, Los Angeles CA, asst principal, 1952-86; prof educ, Mt St Mary's Coll, Pepperdine Univ, California State Univ, Los Angeles, Dominguez Hill. **ORGANIZATIONS:** Mem and recording sec, Natl Alliance of Black School Educators (NABSE); mem, Health and Educ Groups, Congressional Black Caucus; past pres, Delta Sigma Theta, Beta Theta Chapter; 1945-46; past pres, Council of Black Admin, Los Angeles, , 1981-82; mem and sec, UNCF advisory bd, Los Angeles CA; trustee, First AME Church, Los Angeles CA; telephone coordinator, floor mgr, Lou Rawls Parade of Stars production, Los Angeles CA, 1982-. **HONORS/ACHIEVEMENTS:** Scholarship, Delta Sigma Theta to Arizona State Univ, 1943-47; scholarship, Minister of Educ, Korea, 1983.

PHILLIPS, ROY G.
Educational administrator. **PERSONAL:** Born Nov 26, 1934, Minden, LA; married Vira L Goosby; children: Roy Jr, Kevin, Crystal, Kelley. **EDUCATION:** E MI U, BA 1957; Wayne St U, 1964;Univ of MI, PhD 1971. **CAREER:** Met Tech Com Coll, vice pres campus dir 1977-; Seattle Central Com Coll, campus pres 1975-76; Wayne Co Com Coll, vice pres for admin 1972-75; Detroit Public School, science teacher affirm action officer second prin 1958-65. **ORGANIZATIONS:** Consult Knox Found Hrtfrd 1974; dir Wash Enviro Trd Assn1975-77; dir Priv Sctr Inc 1976-77; vchmn Omaha Priv Ind Cncl 1978-; bd mem Omaha CETAPlng Cncl 1978-; exec bd Omaha NAACP 1979-. **HONORS/ACHIEVEMENTS:** Mott Flw in Urban Educ Ldrshp Mott FndUniv of MI 1968-69; acad schol Mskgn Rotary Club; acad schol Mskgn Wmns Club St of MI 1953-57; natl sci summer flw Nat Sci Fnd/ Wayne St/W MI U/Cornell/INUniv 1959-63; master plan devel of 5 com oll campuses Wayne Co Com Coll 1973-74. **BUSINESS ADDRESS:** PO Box 3777, Omaha, NE 68103.

PHILLIPS, VEL R.
Judge. **PERSONAL:** Born Feb 18, 1924, Milwaukee, WI; married Dale; children: Dale, Michael. **EDUCATION:** Howard U, BS 1946; WI Law Sch, LLB 1951;Univ of NV, Grad Smr Coll for Jvnl Ct Jdgs 1971. **CAREER:** WI, sec of state 1978-; Mlwk Co Br 13 of Chldrn's Ct, judge 1972-74; Phillips & Phillips, atty;Univ of WI Dept of Afro-Am Stds, vis lectr. **ORGANIZATIONS:** Mem Am Assn of Univ Wmn; Wmn's Intl Leag for Peace & Frdm; bd mem NAACP; Day Care & Child Devel Cncl JFK Sch; adv bd Dept of Lcl Afrs; mem Delta Sigma Theta; co-chmn Nat Dem Conv Com on Rules & Ordr of Bus 1960. **HONORS/ACHIEVEMENTS:** Recip Mlwk Star Awd For Serv 1967; nmd wmn of the yr Mlwk Mrqt-tUniv Chp Theta Sigma Phi Sor 1968; one of doers of the decade Theta Sigma Phi Sor; frmrly 1st blk elctd to Mlwk Common Cncl 1956; 1st blk prsn in the US ever elctd to serve on Nat Com of either of the major prts 6 yrs. **BUSINESS ADDRESS:** State Capitol, 13 W Capitol, West Madison, WI 53702.

PHILLIPS, W. THOMAS
Business executive. **PERSONAL:** Born Aug 02, 1943, Charleston, MS; married Carline Bradford; children: Craig, Lee, Ernest. **EDUCATION:** Univ Northern IA, Bus Admin 1966; Northeastern Univ Boston MA, Mgmt Devel 1978. **CAREER:** General Foods, sales rep dist mgr 1966-72; Quaker, sales planning zone mgr 1973-77, mgr sales devel 1978-79, mgr dir corp prog 1980-84, vice pres corp prog. **ORGANIZATIONS:** Mem Loaned Exec Assoc United Way of Chicago 1979-; bd mem Chicago Hearing Soc 1979-82, Donors Forum of Chicago, Natl Charities Info Bureau 1984-; mem Assn of Black Foundation Executives. **HONORS/ACHIEVEMENTS:** 1st Black Vice Pres & Corp Officer elected by Quaker. **HOME ADDRESS:** 2415 N Douglas Ave, Arlington Heights, IL 60004. **BUSINESS ADDRESS:** Vice President Corp Programs, The Quaker Oats Company, Merchandise Mart Plz, Chicago, IL 60654.

PHILLIPS, WILBURN R.
Bank executive. **CAREER:** Home Federal Savings Bank, Detroit MI, chief executive. **BUSINESS ADDRESS:** Home Federal Savings Bank, 9108 Woodward Ave, Detroit, MI 48202. *

PHILYAW, CHARLES
Athlete. **PERSONAL:** Born Feb 25, 1954, Shreveport, LA. **EDUCATION:** TX So U. **CAREER:** Oakland Raiders, def tackle 1976-. **HONORS/ACHIEVEMENTS:** AFC & NFL Championship Games 1976. **BUSINESS ADDRESS:** Oakland Raiders, 7811 Oakport St, Oakland, CA 94621.

PICKARD, WILLIAM FRANK
Business executive. **PERSONAL:** Born Jan 28, 1942, La Grangee, GA. **EDUCATION:** Flint Mott Coll, AA 1962; W MI Univ, BS 1964; Univ of MI, MSW 1965; OH State Univ, PhD 1971. **CAREER:** Cleveland Urban League, dir educ 1965-67; NAACP, exec dir 1967-69; Wayne State Univ, prof 1971-74; McDonalds Res, owner 1971-. **ORGANIZATIONS:** Chmn Detroit Urban League 1981-82; vice chmn MI Republican Party 1977-83; dir First Indepen Natl Bank 1981-; dir Detroit Chamber of Comm 1983-; chmn African Develop Found 1984-; vice chmn Grand Valley State Coll Bd 1985. **HONORS/ACHIEVEMENTS:** Mental health NIMH Fellowship 1964; Haynes Fellowship Natl Urban League 1965. **HOME ADDRESS:** 335 Pine Ridge Dr, Bloomfield Hills, MI 48013. **BUSINESS ADDRESS:** McDonald's Restaurant, 2990 W Grand Blvd #M-15, Detroit, MI 48202.

PICKENS, WILLIAM, III
Business entrepreneur. **PERSONAL:** Born Sep 27, 1936, New York, NY; married Audrey Patricia Brannen; children: Pamela Alison, William IV, John Montier. **EDUCATION:** Univ of VT, BA 1958. **CAREER:** B Pickens Asso Inc, fdr pres; P Morris USA, dir prsnnl admin 1976-79; Marine Mdlnd Bank, vice pres 1972-76; Booz Allen & Hmltn Inc, mgmt consult 1968-72;Wstrn Elctrc Co, prsnnl 1962-68; Cncl of Cncrnd Blk Execs Inc, co-fdr 1968. **ORGANIZATIONS:** Mem Blk Exec Exch Prgm Nat Urban Leag 1972; mem US Vice Pres Task Frc on Yth Mtvtn 1965; mem Assn for a Better NY 1974; mem natl bd dir exec com-NAACP 1975; mem Fed City Club 1972; co-chmn Boys Hrbr Inc 1968; mem bd dir Untd Nghbrhd Hss NY 1977; chmn bd dir Std Mus of Harlem 1975; treas New York City Dem Com Inc 1976; bd of dirs exec com Nat Com on Am Fgn Plcy 1978; mem Sigma Pi Phi; Tau Epsilon Phi; mem Pres's Assos DukeUniv 1979. **HONORS/ACHIEVEMENTS:** Coauthor Blks in Mgmt, MBA Mag 1969; author The Interview The Blks Vwpnt Bus Hrzn 1970; cntrbtng edtr Cncl of Cncrnd Blk Execs Newsltr 1975-. **MILITARY SERVICE:** USAF 1st lt 1958-61. **BUSINESS ADDRESS:** 200 Park Ave, New York, NY 10017.

PICKENS, WILLIAM GARFIELD
Educator. **PERSONAL:** Born Dec 27, 1927, Atlanta, GA; son of William Pickens; married Ernestine Williams, Sep 30, 1977; children: Leslie, Reese, Todd, Marc. **EDUCATION:** Morehouse Coll, Atlanta GA, BA, 1948; Atlanta Univ, Atlanta GA, MA, 1950; Univ of Hartford, Hartford CT, 1953-54, 1964-65; Trinity Coll, Hartford CT, 1954-59; Univ of Connecticut, Storrs CT, Ph.D., 1969. **CAREER:** Hillside High School, Durham NC, teacher, 1950; Chandler Evans, W Hartford CT, clerk, 1952-54; Hartford Bd of Educ, Hartford CT, teacher and dept head, 1954-70; US Post Office, Hartford CT, clerk, 1954-56; Morehouse Coll, Atlanta GA, dept chmn/prof, 1970-. **ORGANIZATIONS:** Mem, Coll Language Assn, 1970-; mem, Natl Council of Teachers of English, 1971-; mem, Conf of Coll Composition and Communication, 1972-; mem, Amer Dialect Soc, 1975-; mem, Friendship Baptist Church, 1977-; mem, Peyton Woods Chalet Community Org, 1978-. **HONORS/ACHIEVEMENTS:** Magna cum laude, Morehouse Coll, 1948; service plaque, Realty Bd of Greater Hartford, 1964; Trends in Southern Sociolinquistics, 1975; Phi Beta Kappa, Delta of Georgia, 1984; Social Dialectology in Chesnutt's, House behind Cedars, 1987. **MILITARY SERVICE:** US Army, SFC, 1950-52. **HOME ADDRESS:** 2617 Peyton Woods Trail, Atlanta, GA 30311. **BUSINESS ADDRESS:** Prof, Morehouse Coll, 830 Westview Dr, Brawley Hall, Atlanta, GA 30311.

PICKERING, ROBERT PERRY
Government administrator. **PERSONAL:** Born Oct 23, 1950, Charleston, SC; married Deborah DeLaine; children: Robert, Richard, Russell, Randall. **EDUCATION:** Voorhees Coll, BS 1972. **CAREER:** Chas Co Health Dept, environ tech 1976; SC Swine Flu Prog Cola, state coord 1979; DHEC SC State, epidemiologic Asst 1978-80; Health Dept Chas CoSC, prog dir 1980-81; Congressman TH Harnett, spec asst. **ORGANIZATIONS:** Treas Mitchell Elem Sch PTA 1978-85; pres St Patrick Parish Council 1979-82; chmn Mitchell Elem Sch Adv Council 1979-83; bd mem Charleston OIC 1980-83; bd mem Morris Coll Indus Bd 1983-86; adv SC Natl Black Republican Council 1984-. **HONORS/ACHIEVEMENTS:** Comm Serv Omega Psi Phi Frat Mu Alpha Chas SC 1978; OYMOA US Jaycees 1981 & 1982. **HOME ADDRESS:** 179 Line St, Charleston, SC 29403. **BUSINESS ADDRESS:** Special Assistant, Congressman TH Hartnett, Rm 640 334 Meeting St, Charleston, SC 29403.

PICKETT, ALVIN L.
Business executive. **PERSONAL:** Born May 22, 1930, Mt Morris, MI; married Patricia L Lett; children: Rocky, George, Tricia. **CAREER:** MI Dept of Lbr, chf dept dir; MI St Empl Assn, lgsltv agnt-adm asst 1965-72; MI St Senate, chf snt dcmnts rm 1957-65; Boys Training Sch, super 1955-57. **ORGANIZATIONS:** Mem Intl Assn of Govt Lbr Ofcls IAGLO; Am Soc for Training & Devel ASTD; Intl Assn of Indus Accid Bds & Commns IAIABC; pres Lnsng Urban Leag 1971-73; pres Lnsng Old Nwsbys 1970-71; bd of dir Mid-MI Chap Am Red Cr 1968-73; bd of dir Lnsng NAACP 1960-62; Cub Mstr 1960-64; Sct Mstr 1964-66; Cptl Ldg No 8 Pnnslr Cnsstry No 44; Shrine Tmpl No 167 Prince Hall Affil; Dlgt Nat Rep Cov 1972; Rep St Cntrl 1971-; DAV Am Leg. **MILITARY SERVICE:** USMC sgt 1950-53. **BUSINESS ADDRESS:** 7150 Harris Dr, State Secondary Complex, Lansing, MI 48909.

PICKETT, DOVIE T.
District chairperson. **PERSONAL:** Born Nov 22, 1921, Hinze, MS; widowed; children: Fosterson Eddie Lee Brown. **EDUCATION:** Lewis Bus Coll, 1952; Int Data Proc Inst, 1956;Univ of MI Cntr for Adlt Std, 1969; Wayne Co Comm Coll. **CAREER:** 13th Cong Dist Repub Com, pct del/chrprsn 1954-, 13th dist coord, elected 13th dist repub com chrprsn 1969-, exec sec 1963-66; MI Chmn Com & MI State Repub Com, v chrprsn; Eisenhower/ Nixon for Pres & VP, dist cam chrprsn 1954; 13th Cong Dist Hdqtrs, apptd exec sec 1962-67; 13th DistRep Women Club, pres 1963-67; Rep Women's Fed of MI, elected sec; 13th Dist Cam for Pres Nixon & Sen Robert P Griffin, coord 1972. **ORGANIZATIONS:** Mem Elec Coll MI 1972; co-chrprsn MI Nat Black Com for Re-elect of Pres Nixon 1972; del Repub Nat Conv 1972; 1st vice-chrprsn Nat Black Repub Coun MI Chpt; mem Black Coun for Rep Pol Inc; mem Intl Platform Assn; bd of dir United Rep of MI; mem Wayne Co Rep Educ Coun; mem Rep Women's Fed of MI; bd mem Wayne Co Juvenile Fac Network; mem Friends of Equal Justice Com; Cit Governing Bd Model Neighborhood Agency; chrprsn Economic Devel Loan Group; mem Economic Devel Com; Trans & Comm Com 1971-73; life mem NAACP; mem Order of Estrn Star; mem Star of Bethlehem Chap III; mem People's Comm Ch; mem Sigma Gamma Rho; vol GM Red Cross Open Heart Surgery Prog; adv bd The Optometric Inst & Clinic of Detroit Inc; mem Citizen's Adv Counc Wayne Co Comm Coll; pres stdnt govt Wayne Co Comm Coll; chrprsn Balch-Thomas Comm Counc 1976-78; Nat Black Women's Caucus. **HONORS/ACHIEVEMENTS:** Recip Cert of Accomplishment Div of Bus AdminUniv of MI 1971; Serv Award Black Nat Voters Div for Re-Elect of the Pres & Vice Pres 1972 & 1976; Cert as Mem of Elec Coll 1972 Election; delegate to Repub Nat Conv 1972 & 1976; Citation Pres Richard Nixon 1972; Citation Sen Robert P Griffin 1972; Listed in Who's Who in Am Politics 1973-76; Elected to Serve on Com on Orgn Repub Nat Conv 1976; Spl Tribute MI Repub House of Rep 1977; Outstand Serv Award MI Repub Party 1977; Cert of Apprec Wayne Co Repub Educ Counc 1977; Cert of Recog Detroit Pub Sch Reg I 1977; Outstand Serv Award Gov Wm G Milliken1977; Who's Who Among Stdnts in Am Jr Coll 1980. **BUSINESS ADDRESS:** c/o Office of Student Act, Wayne Co Community Coll 4612 W, Detroit, MI 48201.

PICKETT, HENRY B., JR.
Clergyman, educator. **PERSONAL:** Born Mar 21, 1938, Morehead City, NC; married Mary Louise Hoffler; children: Marquis DeLafayette, Sherry Louise. **EDUCATION:** Elizabeth City State Univ, BS 1961; NC Central Univ, MA 1973; Shaw Divinity Sch, Shaw Divinity Sch, Master of Divinity 1977. **CAREER:** Raleigh City, elem tchr 1963-72; St Augustine's Coll, counselor foreign student adv 1972-73; Fuguay Varina, counselor 1973-76; Oberlin Bapt Ch, pastor 1977-80; Wendell First Baptist Ch, pastor 1983-; East Millbrook Middle Sch, counselor 1976-. **ORGANIZATIONS:** Bapt minister Wake Co Bd Edn; Amer Personnel & Guidance Assn; Amer Sch Counselor Assn; NEA; NCPGA; NC Assn Educators; Phi Delta Kappa; NAACP; Kingwood Forest Comm Assn Inc; pres Black Dem Caucus; Wake Co chmn 1974; Omega Psi Phi Frat Inc. **HONORS/ACHIEVEMENTS:** Outstanding Young Man Amer 1973; Man of Yr Oberlin Bapt Ch 1968; Personalities of S 1974; Phi Delta Kappa 1975; Omega Achieve Award; Citizen of Yr 1974;Iota Iota Chpt; Boy Scout Dist Award Merit 1971. **MILITARY SERVICE:** AUS E-4 1961-63. **BUSINESS ADDRESS:** Counselor, East Millbrook Middle Sch, 3801 Spring Forest Rd, Raleigh, NC 27604.

PICKETT, ROBERT E.
Educator. **PERSONAL:** Born Sep 08, 1936, Brookhaven, MS; married Dorothy Owens; children: Deborah Denise, Ritchie Elyot. **EDUCATION:** Alcorn State U, BS 1957; MS Jackson State U, 1969; MS State U; Atlanta U; Jackson State U. **CAREER:** Vicksburg Jr High School, prin; Vicksburg High School, admin prin 1973-77; Randolph High School Passchristian, MS, teacher/coach 1957-59; Weathers High School Rolling Park, MS, teacher 1959-60; Temple High School Vicksburg, MS, teacher/coach/adm asst 1960-64; McIntyre Elem Jr High School Vicksburg, MS, prin 1964-66; Jefferson Jr High School Vicksburg, MS, prin 1966-73. **ORGANIZATIONS:** Mem Vicksburg Tchr Assn; 8th Dist Tchrs Assn; MS Tchrs Assn; Nat Ed Assn; MS Secondary Prin Assn; Nat Assn of Secondary Sch Admin; Am Assnof Sch Admin; Phi Delta Kappa Intl; mem/2 yr vice-chmn Elks Fidelity Lodge #507; 3 Rivers Dist Boy Scouts of Am 1971-72; ETA TAU Chap Omega Psi Phi Frat Basileus 1969-71; pres Warren Co United Fund 1973; bd mem mgmt/5 yrs as chmn Jackson St YMCA 1966-70; mem Vicksburg Park Comm 1970-80; pres Port City Kiwanis Club 1975-76; mem bd dirs Warren Co Red Cross; bd dirs Communications Improvement Inc WLBT-TV 3. **HONORS/ACHIEVEMENTS:** Listed in, 1970 Edition "Outstand Personalities of the South", "Outstand Leaders Am Secondary Ed" 1971, "Two Thousand Men of Achievement" London, Eng 1972, "Outstand Educators of Am" 1975; Received YMCA Serv Award 1969; UGF Serv Award 1973. **BUSINESS ADDRESS:** Principal, Vicksburg High School, 1630 Baldwyn Ferry Road, Vicksburg, MS 39180.

PICOTT, J. RUPERT
Association executive. **PERSONAL:** Born Aug 25, 1916, Suffolk, VA; married Altia Hodges; children: John Rupert. **EDUCATION:** VA Union U, BS 1938; PhD 1950; Temple U, MEd 1940; VA State Coll, LLD 1960; VA Sem & Coll, DHL 1972. **CAREER:** Assn for Study of Afro-Am Life & Hist, exec dir 1972; NEA, asst dir/mem 1967; VA Tchr Assn, exec sec 1944-66; White House Conf on Children, del 1955, 1960, 1965. **ORGANIZATIONS:** White House Conf on Youth 1970; pres VA Statewide Indep Voters League 1965-70; chmn bd of mgmt Leigh St YMCA 1965-67; state treas Richmond Br VA Cncl on Human Rel; bd dir Richmond Urban League 1960-66; mem Richmond Friends Assn for Chldrn 1958-67; vice pres NEA 1955-56; pres Am Tchr Assn 1963-64; chmn Nat Cncl State Tchr Assn 1956-63; editor Negro Hist Bulletin 1972; mem Alpha Phi Alpha; Alpha Bta Boule; Sigma Pi Phi. **BUSINESS ADDRESS:** 1401 14 St NW, Washington, DC 20005.

PICOU, THOMAS MAURICE
Journalist. **PERSONAL:** Born Oct 25, 1937, Los Angeles, CA; divorced; children: Tracey. **EDUCATION:** Los Angeles City Coll, AA 1957; UCLA; Roosevelt U, BA 1959. **CAREER:** Sengstacke Newspapers, vice pres 1978; Chicago Daily Defender, former mng editor 1970. **ORGANIZATIONS:** Bd dir Robert S Abbott Publ Co; Tri-State Defender Publ Co; FL Courier Publ Co; Gateway Nat Bank Frank L Beam Adv; chmn Robert-Bruce Co; bd of trustees Chicago StateUniv Found; FL IntUniv Found; pres Pullen Sch for Exceptl Chldrn; bd dir Coalition for United Comm Action.

PIERCE, CHESTER MIDDLEBROOK
Educator. **PERSONAL:** Born Mar 04, 1927, Glen Cove, NY; son of Samuel Pierce and Hettie Pierce; married Jocelyn Patricia Blanchet, Jun 15, 1949; children: Diane Blanchet Williams; Deirdre Anona. **EDUCATION:** Harvard Coll, AB 1948; Harvard Med Sch, MD 1952; Westfield State, ScD 1977 (Hon); Tufts Univ, ScD 1984 (Hon). **CAREER:** Univ of Cincinnati, instructor 1957-60; Univ of OK, asst prof, prof 1960-69; Harvard Univ, prof 1969-. **ORGANIZATIONS:** Pres Amer Bd of Psychiatry & Neurology 1978; pres Amer Orthopsychiatric Assn 1983; founding natl chmn Black Psychiatrists of Amer 1969; advisor Children's TV Workshop (Sesame Street) 1969-; sr consul Peace Corps 1965-69; natl consul to the surgeon genl USAF 1976-82. **HONORS/ACHIEVEMENTS:** Pierce Peak (in Antartica for biomedical rsch) 1968; Special Recog Awd Natl Med Assn 1974; Honorary Fellow Royal Australian & New Zealand Coll of Psychiatrists 1978; mem Inst of Medicine at the Natl Acad of Sciences; Solomon Carter Fuller Awd, American Psychiatric Assn 1986; Chester M Pierce Annual Research Seminar Natl Medical Assn 1988-. **MILITARY SERVICE:** USNR comdr. **HOME ADDRESS:** 17 Prince St, Jamaica Plain, MA 02130. **BUSINESS ADDRESS:** Prof of Educ Psych Pub Hlth, HarvardUniv, Nichols House Applan Way, Cambridge, MA 02138.

PIERCE, CYNTHIA STRAKER
Educator. **PERSONAL:** Born Jul 20, Brooklyn, NY; daughter of Milton Straker and Enid Bayley Straker; married Lawrence W Sr. **EDUCATION:** Hunter Coll, AB 1950; Brooklyn Law Sch, LLB 1953, LLM 1956. **CAREER:** Private Practice, atty 1954-56; Howard Univ, faculty 1956-62; FAA, atty, advisor 1962-69; US Dept of Transp, atty ofc of sec 1969-82; St John's Schoolof Law, assoc prof 1983-. **ORGANIZATIONS:** NY, WA & DC Bar Assn; US Supreme Ct Nat Bar Assn; Fed Bar Assn; NAACP; Nat Urban League. **HONORS/ACHIEVEMENTS:** Fed Women's Award Dept of Transp 1979; books, "DC Lawyer's Handbook"; Hunter Coll Hall of Fame 1983. **BUSINESS ADDRESS:** Assoc Professor, St JohnsUniv School of Law, Grand Central & Utopia Pkwy, Jamaica, NY 11439.

PIERCE, DELILAH W.
Artist, retired art educator. **PERSONAL:** Born Mar 03, 1904, Washington, DC; daughter of George Frank Williams and Sara F Jackson Williams; married Joseph L Pierce, Dec 12, 1936. **EDUCATION:** Miner Normal, Washington DC, Teacher Cert Domestic Art 1923, Teacher Cert Art & Art Ed 1925; Howard Univ, Washington DC, BS Art & Art Educ 1931; TC Columbia Univ, New York City, MA Art Educ 1939; Univ of Pennsylvania, Chicago Univ, New York Univ, postgraduate studies in art educ. **CAREER:** District of Columbia Public Schools, jr and sr high school art teacher, 1925-52; exhibiting artist, locally, nationally and internationally, 1948-; District of Columbia Teachers College, teacher of art & art educ, 1952-71; Howard Univ, Washington DC, visiting prof of art and teacher educ, 1968-69. **ORGANIZATIONS:** Natl basileus, Natl Sorority of Phi Delta Kappa Inc, 1934-38; exhibiting/associate artist & cofounder, District of Columbia Teachers College, Margaret Dickey Gallery, 1956-70; exhibiting/associate artist, Artists' Mart Gallery, Georgetown, DC, 1960-74; treasurer, Soc of Washington Artists, 1966-84; natl treasurer, Natl Conference of Artists, 1973-81; cofounder & exhibiting artist, Canal House Gallery, Co-Op, Georgetown, DC, 1978-82; treasurer, Washington Water Color Assn, 1978-83. **HONORS/ACHIEVEMENTS:** Author of "Can Art Serve as a Balance Wheel in Educ?" Eastern Arts Journal, 1949, and "The Significance of Art Exper in Educ of Negro," Negro History Journal, 1952; Agnes Meyer Fellowship Award 1962; exhibitor, US Art in Embassies Prog, 1973-83; traveling show, "Forever Free, Art by Afro-Amer Women," 1982; received achievement awards from Natl Sorority of Phi Delta Kappa Inc, Natl Conf of Artists, Amer Assn of Univ Women, US Equal Employment Opportunity Commn, Univ of the District of Columbia, Washington Bar Assn, Gallarie Triangle, Smith-Mason Gallery, and Evans-Tibbs Gallery; Apr 2 1980 designated as Delilah W Pierce Day by DC mayor; participant in NMAA-Smithsonian "Continuing Traditions, A Festival of Afro-American Arts Conversations With Artists," 1985; participant in "Focus International, American Women in Art" in Nairobi, Kenya, 1985; Distinguished Black Women Award, BISA, 1988; Alumni Award, Howard Univ Art Dept, 1989.

PIERCE, EARL S.
Clergyman. **PERSONAL:** Born Nov 29, 1942, Bridgeton, NJ; married Joyce; children: Amy. **EDUCATION:** Glassboro State Coll, AB 1965; Philadelphia Div Sch, MDiv 1970. **CAREER:** Dicoese of NJ, episcopal priest; A & A Frat Rho Chap Phila, chaplain; Migrant Laborers in NJ, chaplain 1966-74; St Cyprians Glassboro, NJ, seminarin in charge 1969-70. **ORGANIZATIONS:** Mem Inter & Borough Ministerium; pres Lawnside Bd of Educ 1974-; chaplaing US Army Nat Guard of NJ; Black Elected Ofcls of NJ; trustee Lawnside Five Co; Lawnside Dem Club. **HONORS/ACHIEVEMENTS:** Recip Chapel of Four Chaplains Award.

PIERCE, FREDERICK WATSON
Physician. **PERSONAL:** Born Sep 05, 1903, Covington, VA; married Marylynn Guthrie. **EDUCATION:** VA Union U, BS 1938; Meharry Med Coll, 1933. **CAREER:** Private Pract; Med Arts Hosp, resd 1975-77; Madison Ave Hosp, chf resd 1968-75; Westchester Acad of Med, flw 1965. **ORGANIZATIONS:** Mem Royal Soc Hlth 1970-77; life mem Kent Rod & Gun Club 1972-77; mem Westchester Stickmen Golf Club 1971-77; Alpha Phi Alpha Frat 1926; fellow Westchester Acad of Med.

PIERCE, GREGORY W.
Physician. **PERSONAL:** Born Sep 25, 1957, Vallejo, CA; son of Raymond O Pierce, Jr and Geraldine B Pierce. **EDUCATION:** Wabash Coll, BA 1979; Meharry Medical Coll, MD 1983. **CAREER:** Univ of TN Jackson-Madison Co General Hospital, intern & resident 1983-86; Family Health Assocs, staff physician 1986-. **ORGANIZATIONS:** Chmn Journal Comm Malcolm X Inst of Black Studies Wabash Coll; jr class pres, sr class pres Meharry Medical Coll; term trustee Meharry Medical Coll Bd of Trustees; certified instructor Advanced Cardiac Life Support; mem Amer and TN Medical Assocs; mem Amer and TN Acad of Family Physicians; mem Southern Medical Assoc, Natl Medical Assoc. **HONORS/ACHIEVEMENTS:** Honor Scholarship & Dean's List Wabash Coll; Alvin P Hall Scholarship; Mosby Scholarship Book Award; Upjohn Award for Excellence in Clinical and Academic Obstetrics and Gynecology; Pre-Alumni Assoc Annual Senior Recognition Award; Alpha Omega Alpha Honor Medical Soc; Board Certified Amer Bd of Family Practice 1986-93. **BUSINESS ADDRESS:** Staff Physician, Family Health Associates, 1121 Greenland Dr, Murfreesboro, TN 37130.

PIERCE, JOSEPH LEROY
Insurance broker. **PERSONAL:** Born Jun 28, 1905, Wilson, NC; son of Nazareth Pierce and Ella Armstrong Pierce; married Delilah Williams, Dec 12, 1936. **EDUCATION:** Univ of PA, business & finance grad 1930; Amer Inst for Property & Liability Underwriters, CPCU 1959. **CAREER:** Natl Benefit Life Ins Co, GA state mgr 1931-35; special agent NC Mutual Life Ins Co, 1935-43; John R Pinkett Inc, ins broker & consultant, vice pres & mgr ins dept 1943-89 (retired) Mutual Benefit Life Insurance Co, 1943- broker 1943-. **ORGANIZATIONS:** Chmn St Mary's PECH WA Diocese Mission Dev Fund 1969; vestry & mem Parish Coun; life mem NAACP; mem Friends of Mus of African Art, Friends of KennetyCtr, Smithsonian Assn, YMCA Bachelor-Benedict Club Inc. **HONORS/ACHIEVEMENTS:** 1st Black to receive the CPCU designation from the Amer Inst for Property & Liability Underwriters and elec to the CPCU Soc, 1959.

PIERCE, LAWRENCE WARREN
Judge. **PERSONAL:** Born Dec 31, 1924, Philadelphia, PA; son of Harold E Pierce and Leora Bellinger Pierce; married Wilma Taylor, Sep 1948 (died 1978); children: Warren Wood, Michael Lawrence, Mark Taylor; married Cynthia Straker, Jul 08, 1979; children: Warren Wood, Michael Lawrence, Mark Taylor. **EDUCATION:** St Joseph Univ, BS 1948; Fordham Univ, JD 1951; St Joseph Univ, DHL 1967; Fairfield Univ, LLD 1972; Fordham Univ, LLD 1982. **CAREER:** Gen law practice New York City 1951-61; Kings Co NY, asst dist atty 1954-61; NYC, dep police comm 1961-63; NYS Div Youth Albany, dir 1963-66; NYS Narc Addiction Cont Comm, chmn 1966-70; SUNYA Grad Sch Crim Justice, vis prof 1970-71; S Dist NY, US dist judge 1971-81; US Foreign Intelligence Surveillance Ct, judge 1979-81; US Court of Appeals, judge 1981-. **ORGANIZATIONS:** Former pres Cath Inter Council 1957-63; trustee Fordham Univ; mem NBA, ABA Comm Jud Admin; vice pres bd of dir, Lincoln Hall for Boys; bd mgrs, Havens Relief Fund Soc; bd of trustees Practising Law Inst; mem Amer Law Inst; mem of delegations to Africa, Sweden, England, Japan, Vietnam, Korea, West Germany, and People's Republic of China to discuss legal, judicial and correctional systems; formerly bd of dir CARE USA. **HONORS/ACHIEVEMENTS:** Fordham Univ Sch of Law BALSA's Ruth Whitehead Whaley Awd for Distinguished Legal Achievement; NBA's Judge Jane Bolin Awd; Doctor of Laws Degree, Hamilton College 1987. **MILITARY SERVICE:** AUS 1943-46 MTO. **BUSINESS ADDRESS:** Judge, US Court of Appeals, US Courthouse, Foley Sq, New York, NY 10007.

PIERCE, PONCHITTA A.
Magazine writer, television host. **PERSONAL:** Born Aug 05, 1942, Chicago, IL; daughter of Alfred Pierce and Nora Pierce. **EDUCATION:** Univ of Southern CA, BA 1964; Cambridge Univ, attended summer 1962. **CAREER:** Ebony Magazine, asst editor 1964-65, assoc editor 1965-67; Johnson Publishing Co, NY editorial bureau chief 1967-68; CBS News, special correspondent 1968-71; McCall's Magazine, contributing editor 1973-76; Reader's Digest, staff writer 1975-77, roving editor 1977-80; WNBC-TV, magazine writer/TV host. **ORGANIZATIONS:** Mem Theta Sigma Phi NY Chapter, Amer Fedn of TV & Radio Artists, Amer Women in Radio & TV, Natl Acad of TV Arts & Sciences, NY Chapter dir African Student Aid Fund; mem Women's Forum, mem Manhattan advisory comm NY Urban League. **HONORS/ACHIEVEMENTS:** Penney-Mo Magazine Award 1967; Headliner Award Natl Theta Sigma Phi 1970. **BUSINESS ADDRESS:** WNBC-TV, 30 Rockefeller Cntr, #315 W, New York, NY 10020.

PIERCE, RAYMOND O., JR.
Educator, physician. **PERSONAL:** Born May 17, 1931, Monroe, LA; married Geraldine Brundidge; children: Raymond III, Gregory, Leannette, Geralyn, Lori. **EDUCATION:** Fisk Univ Nashville, TN, BA 1951; Meharry Med Clg Nashville, TN, MD 1955; VA Hosp Des Moines, IA Univ of IA, Residency 1963. **CAREER:** 3151 N IL Indpls, IN, prvt prctc 1963-69; INUniv Med Ctr, asst prof 1970-76, assc prof 1976-80, prof of ortho 1981-. **ORGANIZATIONS:** Courtesy stf Methodist Hosp 1969-; hon stf Winona Hosp 1969-; cnsltng stf US Army Hosp Ft Benjamin Harrison 1976-79; bd dir Martin Ctr 1970-; bd dir St Elizabeth's Home 1980-83; bd dir Flanner House 1980-; pres Aesculapian Med Soc 1972-75; Am Acad Ortho Surg; Am Assc Advncmnt Sci; Am Assc Surg Trauma; exmnr cert Am Bd Ortho Surg 1976-84; credentials com Am Clg Surgeons 1983-84; Am Fracture Assc; Am Soc Sports Medince; chrtr memAm Trauma Soc; chrmn bd Group Practice Inc 1973-79; sec pres Hoosier State Med Assc 1968-75; pres sec/Tres IN Bone & Joint Clb 1980-; chrmn cont med ed com IN Ortho Soc 1970-80; Intrl Clg Surgeons; bd trustee MDDS 1968-74; house delegates co-chrmn ortho sect exec com ortho sec Natl Med Assc 1963-76; Pan-Pacific Surg Soc; Sigma XI-Rsrch Soc. **HONORS/ACHIEVEMENTS:** One of 50 black distngshd blck ldrs Honoree FAC Clb Indianpolis, IN 1973; summer furness awrd Outstndg Comm Serv 1977; phys rcgntn awrd AMA 1977-83; Phys Rcgntn awrd NMA 1981-83; third place scntfc award "Treatment of Osteonecrosisof the Hip" IN State Med Assc Meeting 1980; first place scntfc awrd "The Assessment of Bone Healing in Bone Impedance" IN State Med Assc Meeting 1982; third pl scntfc awrd "The Effect of Alcohol on the Skeletal Systm" IN State Med Assc Meeting 1984; govnr awrd Cncl of the Sagamore of Wabash 1984; pblctns incldng Alcohol, Underlying Cause of Many Skeletal Lesions Ortho News Vol 6 2 Mar/Apr 1984 P3, The Effect of Alcohol on Skeletal Systm Ortho Review Vol XIV 1 Jan 1985 P45-49, Treatment of Subtroc hanteric Fractures with a Flexible Intramedullary Rod Ortho Transctns Vol 8 3 Fall 1984 P441, The Effect of Alcohol on Skeletal Systm IN State Med Assc Scntfc Awrd Third Pl Indpls, IN Oct 1984, Immediate Intrnl Fixation of Gunshot Fracturs Am Acad Ortho Surgeons Las Vegas, NV Jan 1985. **MILITARY SERVICE:** USAF capt 1976-79. **BUSINESS ADDRESS:** Professor of Orthopaedic Surg, INUniv Medical Center, 960 Locke St, Indianapolis, IN 46202.

PIERCE, REUBEN G.
Educator. **PERSONAL:** Born Nov 30, 1926, Omaha, NE; married Leslie Ann Hazur; children: 5 Children. **EDUCATION:** Univ Omaha, BA 1949;Univ Omaha, MS 1952; Columbia U, Grad Work 1957-60;Univ MA, EdD 1974. **CAREER:** Johnson C Smith Univ, instr 1953-54; VA State, 1954-60; VA State Coll, asst prof 1960-61; asso prof 1961-65; Bennett Coll, asso prof 1965-67; Dept Science DC Schools, asst dir 1967-69; Dept Science DC Public Schools, supr dir 1969-74; Washington DC HS, prin; Natl Science Found Coop Coll School Science Program Amer Univ Cath Univ, asso dir 1968-70; Fed Funded Projects DC, dir 1971-73. **ORGANIZATIONS:** Chmn Assn Central Office of School Ofcrs 1969-; Nat Sci Tchrs Assn; chmn NSTA Black Caucus 1971-72. **HONORS/ACHIEVEMENTS:** Ford Found Fellow 1972-73; Phi Delta Kappa Hon Frat; Kappa Delta Pi Hon Soc; Beta Kappa Chi Hon Soc; Sigma Pi Sigma Hon Soc. **MILITARY SERVICE:** USAAF sgt 1945-46. **BUSINESS ADDRESS:** Ballou Sr HS, 4 & Trenton Sts, Washington, DC 20032.

PIERCE, RICKY CHARLES
Professional athlete. **PERSONAL:** Born Aug 19, 1959, Dallas, TX. **EDUCATION:** Rice Univ Houston, TX, 1979-83. **CAREER:** Milwaukee Bucks, guard 1983-. **HONORS/ACHIEVEMENTS:** Appeared in 69 games on the year, 35 of which came in starting role; scored a career high 30 points & 12 rebounds in starting debut agnst San Antonio Nov 25th. **BUSINESS ADDRESS:** Milwaukee Bucks, 901 Fourth St, Ste 510, Milwaukee, WI 53203.

PIERCE, RUDOLPH F.
Judge. **PERSONAL:** Born Aug 12, 1942, Boston, MA; married Carneice T; children: Kristen, Khari. **EDUCATION:** Hampton Inst, BA 1967; Harvard Law Sch, JD 1970. **CAREER:** Superior Ct of MA, judge; Magistrate US Dist Ct, Judge; Keating Perretta & Pierce, Ptnr 1975-76; Crane Inker & Oteri, ptnr 1974-75; Crane Inker & Oteri, asso 1972-74; Roxbury Multi-svc Ctr, dir legal serv 1971-72; Mayor's Safe St Act Com, legal adminstr 1970-72; Atty David S Nelson, asso; Harbridge House Inc, 1970; Boston Legal Asstnc Proj, legal intern 1968-69. **MILITARY SERVICE:** AUS sp-4 1960-63. **BUSINESS ADDRESS:** Superior Court, New Courthouse Pemberton Sq, Boston, MA 02108.

PIERCE, SAMUEL R., JR.
Attorney, government official. **PERSONAL:** Born Sep 08, 1922, Glen Cove, NY; son of Samuel R and Hettie E; married Barbara Wright; children: Victoria Pierce Ransmeier. **EDUCATION:** Cornell Univ, AB (Hon) 1947, JD 1949; NY Univ, LLM Taxation 1952; NY Univ, LLD 1972; Hon Degrees incl, LLD, LHD, DCL, D. Litt. **CAREER:** New York City, asst dist atty 1949=52; S Dist NY; asst U.S. attny 1952-54; Undersecretary of Labor, asst 1954-56; US House of Rep, Subcom Antitrust of Jud Comm, counsel 1956-57; private practice, attny 1957-59, 1961-70, 1973-81; NY Court Gen Sess, judge 1959-60; Battle Fowler Stokes & Kheel, partner 1961-70; US Treas, gen couns 1970-73; Battle Fowler Jaffin Pierce Kheel partner l973-81; Sec, Housing & Urban Devel, 1981-l989. **ORGANIZATIONS:** Dir Prudential Ins Co of Amer 1964-70, 1973-81, US Industries 1964-70, 1973-79, Intl Paper Co 1973-81, 1989-, Gen Elect Co 1974-81, Intl Basic Econ Corp 1973-80; adj prof NY Univ School of Law 1957-70; trustee Mt Holyoke Coll 1964-80, Hampton Inst 1964-, Inst Intl Ed 1967-, Cornell Univ 1973; mem bd Overseers Visiting Comm for Psych & Soc Rel Harvard Univ 1969-74; mem, natl exec bd Boy Scouts of Amer 1969-; mem Alpha Phi Alpha, Alpha Phi Omega, Ford Found Fellow Yale Law School 1957-58; chmn impartial disciplinary rev bd New York City Transit System 1968-81; mem natl adv com Comptroller of Currency 1975-80; mem Natl Wiretapping Comm 1973-76; dir NY Worlds Fair Corp 1964-65; gov Amer Stock Exchange 1977-80; contrib articles to professional journals, l976-81; mem panel arbitrators Amer Arbitration Assn; Fed Mediation & Conciliation Serv, 1957-. **HONORS/ACHIEVEMENTS:** Alexander Hamilton Awd US Treas Dept 1973; New York City Jr C of C Ann Distinguished Serv Awd 1958; Fellow Amer Coll Trial Lawyers; Martin Luther King, Jr. Center Salute to Greatness Award l989; Reagan Revolution Medal of Honor l989; The Presidential Citizens Medal l989. **BUSINESS ADDRESS:** Secretary, Housing & Urban Development, 451 7th St SW, Washington, DC 20410.

PIERCE, WALTER J.
Educator. **PERSONAL:** Born Jan 16, 1941, Minden, LA; married Iopha Douglas; children: Gay, Gwenevera, Iopha Anita. **EDUCATION:** BS 1964; gad study. **CAREER:** Kiwanis Club, counselor 1968-70; Atascadero State Hosp, recreation therapist 1964-69; Tulare View, dir rehabilitation 1969-70; Northside Hosp, dir activities 1970-71; CA State U, affirmative action coordinator 1972-74; coordinator, faculty advising 1974-. **ORGANIZATIONS:** Mem Kiwanis Club 1968-70; NAACP; Black Educator Fresno; Fresno Housing Affirmative Com; Bapt Sun Sch Supt; Plan Variation; chmn Man Power & Econ Area 6. **HONORS/ACHIEVEMENTS:** Outstanding young men am 1970. **BUSINESS ADDRESS:** Counselor, California StateUniv Fresno, Advisor Center, Fresno, CA 93740.

PIERCE, WILLIAM DALLAS
Psychologist. **PERSONAL:** Born Nov 16, 1940, Sunbury, NC. **EDUCATION:** Univ of Pitts, BS 1962; OH State U, MA 1965; OH State U, PhD 1967. **CAREER:** Priv Prac San Francisco CA, clinical psychologist 1969-; Dept of PsychologyUniv of CA at Berkeley, lectr 1970-; Dept of Mentl Hlth Commn of MA, regional serv admin 1979-80; Westside Coimm Mental Hlth Cntr San Francisco, exec dir 1973-77; Westside Comm Mental Health Cntr, dir of clinical serv 1971-73. **ORGANIZATIONS:** Founding mem Assn of Black Psychologists 1968; chmn com on mental hlth Assn of Black Psychologists 1971-73; pres Bay Area Assn of Black Psychologists 1978-79. **HONORS/ACHIEVEMENTS:** Apprec aw Assn of Black Psychologists 1970; Blacks in the West Hall of Fame San Francisco Africam Hist Cultural Soc 1976; annual aw for ldrshp & serv Assn of Black Psychologisgts 1980. **BUSINESS ADDRESS:** 361 Upper Terr, San Francisco, CA 94117.

PIERRE, DALLAS
Dentist. **PERSONAL:** Born Jun 09, 1933, Charenton, LA; married Carol Ann Yates; children: James Darian. **EDUCATION:** Prairie View A&M Coll, BS 1955; TX So Univ, MS 1963; Univ of TX Dental Br, DDS 1968; Trinity Univ, adv study. **CAREER:** Private Practice, dentist. **ORGANIZATIONS:** Mem E TX Area BSA; mem Natl Platform Assn, Phi Beta Sigma, Univ of TX Alumni Assn, Citizens C of C Angelina Co; pres Area Adv Council of Manpower Educ & Training of E TX; mem Pub Rel Organ for Comm Laity Improvement; deacon finance com chmn Baptist Ch; mem Piney Woods Kiwanis Club; pres Gulf State Dental Assoc; sec East TX Med Dent Phar Assoc; life mem NAACP; mem E TX Minority Bus Devel Found Inc 1974-. **HONORS/ACHIEVEMENTS:** Who's Who of Black Men & Women in TX; Comm Leaders & Noteworthy Amers; Who's Who in the S & SW. **MILITARY SERVICE:** USAF airman 1st class 1956-60. **BUSINESS ADDRESS:** PO Box 1236, 809 Kurth Dr, Lufkin, TX 75901.

PIERRE, GERALD P.
Physician. **PERSONAL:** Born Oct 14, 1951, Cayes, Haiti;divorced; children: Jeanette C. **EDUCATION:** Bard Coll, AB 1975; Meharry Medical Coll, MD 1980. **CAREER:** Physician in Practice, ob/gyn 1980-. **ORGANIZATIONS:** Mem Amer Coll of Obstetrics & Gynecology 1980, Hartford Co & CT State Medical Assocs 1984; diplomate Amer Bd of Ob/Gyn 1986. **HONORS/ACHIEVEMENTS:** Teacher of the Year Ob/Gyn Dept Mt Sinai Hosp 1985; Plaque Hartford Police Dept 1986. **HOME ADDRESS:** PO Box 94, Bloomfield, CT 06002. **BUSINESS ADDRESS:** Obstetrician/Gynecologist, One Regency Dr, Bloomfield, CT 06002.

PIERRE, PERCY ANTHONY
Educational administrator. **PERSONAL:** Born Jan 03, 1939, Donaldville, LA; married Olga A Markham; children: Kristin Clare, Allison Celeste. **EDUCATION:** Univ Notre Dame, BS Elec Engrg 1961, MS 1963, DEng (hon) 1977; Johns Hopkins Univ, PhD Elec Engrg 1967; Univ of MI, postgrad 1968; Rensselaer Polytechnic Inst, hon doc degree 1985. **CAREER:** So Univ, asst prof elec engrg 1963; Johns Hopkins Univ, instr elec engrg 1963-64; Morgan State Coll, instr physics 1964-66; Univ MI, intr info &control engrg 1967-68; UCLA, instr systems engrg 1968-69; RAND Corp, rsch engr in communications 1968-71; Office of Pres, White House fellow spl asst 1969-70; Howard Univ, dean sch engrg 1971-77; Alfred P Floan Found, prog officer for engrg educ 1973-75; US Dept of Army, asst sec for rsch Devel& acquisition 1977-81; engrg mgmt consul 1981-83; Prairie View A&M Univ, pres 1983-. **ORGANIZATIONS:** Dir engrg coll council Amer Soc for Engrg Educ 1973-75; mem sci adv group Def Communications Agency 1974-75; mem adv panel Office Exptl Rsch & Devel Incentives NSF 1973-74; mem Comm Scholars to Rev Grad Progs IL Bd Higher Educ1974; mem panel on role US engrg sch in fgn tech assistance 1972; co-chmn symposium on minorities in engrg 1973; mem rev panel for Inst for Applied Tech Nat Bur Standards 1973-77; chmn com on minorities Natl Acad Engrg 1976-77; consult to dir ERDA 1976-77; mem adv bd Sch Engrg Johns Hopkins Univ 1981-; consult Office Sec Def 1981-. **HONORS/ACHIEVEMENTS:** Contrib articles on communications theory to professional publs Trustee Univ Notre Dame 1974-77 1981; Trustee Mem Exec Comm Natl Fund for Minority Engrg Students 1976-77; recipient Disting Civilian Serv Awd Dept Army 1981; Awd of Merit from Sen Proxmire 1979; mem IEEE (sr mem Edison Awd Comm 1978-80); Sigma Xi; Tau Beta Pi. **BUSINESS ADDRESS:** President, Prairie View A&M Univ, PO Box 2152, Prairie View, TX 77446.

PIERRE-LOUIS, CONSTANT
Physician. **PERSONAL:** Born Feb 11, 1939; married Jeany; children: Marilyn, Pascale, Carolyn. **EDUCATION:** State Univ Port-au-Prince Med Sch, MD 1963. **CAREER:** Columbis Univ, 1971-75; Downstate Univ, clinic asst prof of urology 1975-; Adelphi Med ARt Assn, fndg mem partner 1975-; staff mem Brookdale Hosp, St John's Epis Hosp, Unity Hosp; Private Practice, urologist 1971-. **ORGANIZATIONS:** Mem Amer Bd Urology; fellow Amer Coll Surgery; mem NY State Med Soc, Natl Med Assn; bd mem pres Assn of Haitian Drs Abroad 1975-76; publications "Lymphoma of the Urethra Masquerading as a Caruncle" 1972; "Morphologic Appearance of Leydig Cells in Patients with Prostatic Cancer & Benign Prostatic Hypertrophy" NY Acad Med Urol Resd; "Delayed Subcapsular Renal Hematoma" Urology 1977. **HONORS/ACHIEVEMENTS:** Essay Contest 3rd prize 1969. **BUSINESS ADDRESS:** Urologist, 60 Plaza St, Brooklyn, NY 11238.

PILKINGTON, EDWARD ARTHUR
Attorney. **PERSONAL:** Born Mar 13, 1945, Radford, VA. **EDUCATION:** Wesleyan U, BA 1966; Yale Law Sch, JD 1971; Yale Graduate Sch, MA 1971. **CAREER:** Coca-Cola Co, atty; Legal Aid Soc Roanoke, atty 1971-72; Legal Aid Soc Louisville KY, atty 1972-73; Legal Aid Soc Louisville, staff atty 1973-74. **HONORS/ACHIEVEMENTS:** Yadoo Medal 1962; Davenport Flwshp 1965.

PILLOW, VANITA J.
Sales representative. **PERSONAL:** Born Dec 16, 1949, Nashville. **EDUCATION:** BS 1971; MS 1985. **CAREER:** Fayette Co Bd Edn, secondary instr & Beta Honor Soc sponsor

1973; Experimental Theatre sponsor; Electric Dance Workshop Sponser 1972; des Moines Main PO Supply & Procurement Asst; TN State U, part time istrn 1971; speech dramatics arts grad asst; S Central Bell Bus Office, sales rep teller. **ORGANIZATIONS:** Mem NAACP; Minority Consumer Communications Theatre Nashville 1974; mem USO Tour Germany, Holland, Belgium 1970; mem Women's Bowling League 1971; Theta Alpha Phi 1969;Univ Couns; pres TN State Plyrs Guild. **HONORS/ACHIEVEMENTS:** Miss TN State Plyrs Guild; Who's Who Among Am Coll Students; best female actress 1971; Children's Theatre Chicago Grad top 10 percent class.

PILOT, ANN HOBSON
Musician. **PERSONAL:** Born Nov 06, 1943, Philadelphia, PA; daughter of Harrison Hobson and Grace Stevens Hobson Smith; married R Prentice; children: Lynn, Prentice. **EDUCATION:** Cleveland Inst, BM 1966. **CAREER:** Pittsburgh Symphony Orchestra, 2nd harpist 1965-66; Washington Natl Symphony, principal harpist 1966-69; Ambler Music Festival, faculty 1968-69; Boston Symphony Orchestra, asst principal harpist, principal harpist 1980-. **ORGANIZATIONS:** Participant Marlboro Music Festival; faculty New England Conservatory of Music, Berkshire Music Center; soloist Boston Symphony Orchestra; founder mem New England Harp Trio 1971-; mem Contemporary Music Ensemble, College performances in Europe, Japan, China and Haiti; bd of dir, Holy Trinity School of Haiti. **HONORS/ACHIEVEMENTS:** Honored by the Professional Arts Soc of Philadelphia 1987; Honorary Doctorate of Fine Arts, Bridgewater State College, 1988. **BUSINESS ADDRESS:** Principal Harpist, Boston Symphony Orchestra, Symphony Hall, Boston, MA 02115.

PINADO, ALAN E.
Business executive. **PERSONAL:** Born Dec 15, 1931, New York, NY; married Patricia LaCour; children: Alan E Jr, Jeanne M, Anthony M, Steven L. **EDUCATION:** Fordham Univ of Coll of Bus Admin, BS Mktg 1953; Univ of Notre Dame, MBA 1958. **CAREER:** Wm R Morris Agency South Bend IN, real estate sales, devel 1960-61; Allied Fed Savings & Loan Jamaica NY, exec vp, mortgage loan officer 1961-67; IBM Corp NY, mktg rep 1967-68; NY LIfe Ins Co NY, vice pres re fin 1968-84, vp, mgmt coord/trng 1984-85; Real Estate Inst of Atlanta Univ/Morehouse Coll, dir 1986-. **ORGANIZATIONS:** Dir Oppty Funding Corp 1979-, Urban Home Ownership Corp 1980-, NY Life Pac 1983-85; Wilton CT United Way 1983-85; dir emeritus Minority Interchange Inc 1975-; United Mutual Insurance Co 1985-87. **HONORS/ACHIEVEMENTS:** Dr of Literary Letters Mary Holmes Coll 1976; Horace Sudduth Awd Natl Bus League 1978; James J & Jane Hoey Awd Catholic Interracial Council of NY 1972. **MILITARY SERVICE:** AUS 1st lt 1953-55; Commendation Medal 1954. **BUSINESS ADDRESS:** Dir, Real Est Inst of AtlantaUniv, Morehouse Coll Economics Dept, 830 West View Dr, Atlanta, GA 30314.

PINCHAM, ROBERT EUGENE, SR.
Judge. **PERSONAL:** Born Jun 28, 1925, Chicago, IL; married Alzata Cudalia Henry; children: 3 children. **EDUCATION:** Tennessee State Univ, BS 1947; Northwestern Univ School of Law, Juris Dr Deg 1951; admitted to the bar of Illinois, 1951. **CAREER:** Circuit Ct of Cook Co, judge 1976-; Attorneys T Lee Boyd Jr & Isaiah S Gant, assoc 1974-76; Atty Charles B Evins, assoc 1955-76; Atty Joseph E Clayton Jr, assoc 1951-55; criminal trial lawyer appellate litigation; Notre Dame Univ School of Law, lecturer/instructor; Northwestern Univ School of Law; Univ of Illinois School of Law; Univ of Houston Bates Coll of Law, lecturer/instructor; Natl College of Criminal Defense Lawyers & Public Defenders; Univ of Colorado-Boulder College of Law; Natl Inst of Trial Advocacy, Univ of Nevada. **ORGANIZATIONS:** Mem Chicago Bar; Cook County Bar; Illinois Bar; Natl Bar; Amer Bar Assn; The Chicago Council of Lawyers; life mem NAACP; mem Amer Civil Liberties Union; Kappa Alpha Psi Frat; the Amer Judicature Soc; mem, former trustee Faith United Methodist Church. **HONORS/ACHIEVEMENTS:** Award of merit, the Northwestern Univ Alumni Assn, 1975; certificate of appreciation, Chicago Bar Assn, 1974; Richard E Westbrook Award for Outstanding Contrib to the Legal Profession, Cook County Bar Assn; certificate of serv, the Lawyers Constitutional Def Comm of the Amer Civil Liberties Union, 1965. **BUSINESS ADDRESS:** Illinois Appellate Court—First District, Richard Daley Center, 28th Fl, 50 W Washington St, Chicago, IL 60602.

PINCKNEY, ANDREW MORGAN, JR.
Administrator. **PERSONAL:** Born Jul 02, 1933, Georgetown, SC; married Brenda Cox; children: Meika, Margo. **EDUCATION:** Morris Brown Coll Atlanta, BS 1960; Lasalle Coll Phila, Bus Adminstrn 1967-68;Univ of PA Phila, Wharton Mgmt 1974-76. **CAREER:** Merck Sharp & Dohme West Point PA, adminstsr 1973-; Merck Sharp & Dohme, rsrch Biol 1963-73; Skin & Cancer Hosp Phila, rsrch asso 1962-63; Frnaklin Inst Lab Phila, rsrch chemist 1961-62. **ORGANIZATIONS:** Mem Am Mgmt Assn 1975-; mem BlackUniv Liasion Com Merck & Co 1977-; mem of steering com United Way Campaign Merck Sharp & Co 1976-79; pres Philadelphia Alumni Chap of Morris Brown 1970-; pres Club Noble Gents 1971-; finan sec Black Polit Forum 1975. **HONORS/ACHIEVEMENTS:** Medal of Merits; good conduct; marksman USAF 1951-55; taste & odors Jour of Water Pollu Franklin Inst Philadelphia 1961; Morris Brown Coll Athletic Hall of Fame TAY Club Atlanta 1975; Purple & Black Serv Award Morris Brown Coll Nat Alumni Atlanta 1979; racquetball trophy North Penn Racquetball Club N Wales PA 1980. **MILITARY SERVICE:** USAF a/1c 1951-55. **BUSINESS ADDRESS:** Sumneytown Pike, West Point, PA 19486.

PINCKNEY, JAMES
Elected official. **PERSONAL:** Born Jun 24, 1942, Fairfax, SC; married Gladys M Simmons; children: Janet, Jerome, Zachary, Lorraine. **EDUCATION:** Allen Univ, BS Phys Ed 1964. **CAREER:** Lower Saunnal Council of Govts, bd mem 1984-; Allendale Co, co councilman 1985-. **ORGANIZATIONS:** Bd mem Allendale-Fairfax HS Advisory Council 1982-84. **BUSINESS ADDRESS:** Councilmember, Allendale County, PO Box 677, Allendale, SC 29810.

PINCKNEY, LEWIS, JR.
Business executive. **PERSONAL:** Born Dec 25, 1932, Columbia, SC; married Johnnye Caver; children: Lewis III, Johnette V. **EDUCATION:** DePaul U, 1975; Benedict Coll, 1952-53; Cook Co Grad Sch of Med, ARRT 1956-57. **CAREER:** Cook County Hosp, staff tech 1957-64, qual control supv 1964-68, chief x-ray tech educ dir 1968-69, admin asst to chmn 1969-73, admin; St Bernard Hosp, dir radiological svcs. **ORGANIZATIONS:** John Jones Lodge # 7 F&AM IL 1963-; IL State Soc of Radiologic Tech 1971-74; Lions Assn 1971-73; Amer Soc of Radiologic Tech 1973; Amer Hosp Radiology Admin 1973-76; WA Park YMCA 1974; conf ledr Inst for Graphic Communication 1974; Oakdale Covenant Church; Local Bd # 84 Selective Service; adj faculty mem Chicago Edm School; adv comm mem Malcolm X Coll; evaluating quality control Cook Co Grad School of Med 1977; treas Kenwood Oakland Health Ctr; chmn Affirmative Action Comm Adv Bd City of Chicago Fire Dept. **MILITARY SERVICE:** AUS sgt 1953-56. **BUSINESS ADDRESS:** Dir, St Bernard Hospital, 64th & Dan Ryan Expressway, Chicago, IL 60612.

PINCKNEY, STANLEY
Artist, educator. **PERSONAL:** Born Sep 30, 1940, Boston, MA. **EDUCATION:** Famous Artist School, Westport CT, commercial art, 1960; Music School Fine Arts Boston MA, Diploma 1967; Music School Fine Arts Boston MA, Certificate, Graduate Program, 1969. **CAREER:** Music School Fine Arts, teacher, 1972-; Coll Art, guest-artist 1979; Boston Univ Program In-Artisanry, guest-artist 1967. **ORGANIZATIONS:** Mem, African-Amer Artists-in-Residency Northeastern Univ Boston MA 1978. **HONORS/ACHIEVEMENTS:** Blanche E Colman Fellowship Blanche E Colman Found Boston 1978; Ford Found Grant Music School, Fine Arts Boston 1978; Albert H Whitin Fellowship Music School, Fine Arts, Boston 1978. **BUSINESS ADDRESS:** c/o Music School of Fine Arts, 230 Fenway, Boston, MA 02115.

PINCKNEY, THEODORE R.
Physician. **PERSONAL:** Born Sep 10, 1901, Albany, NY; married Hermena M Clay; children: Theodore C. **EDUCATION:** Bates Coll, BS 1923; Med CollUniv IN, MD 1929. **CAREER:** Gen Hosp Kansas Cty, intern residency 1929-32; Priv Prac, 1932-; Morehouse Coll, faculty 1923-25f HowardUniv Coll Med, 1932-69; Dept Motor Vehicles DC, med ofcr 1969-. **ORGANIZATIONS:** Mem Am Nat Interstate Postgrad Med Assns; Med Soc of DC; Med Chirurg Soc; Am Rheumatism Soc; bd dirs Arthritis & Rheumatism Assn of Metro Washington; vol worker Am Cancer Soc 1948-. **MILITARY SERVICE:** USAF Med Corps maj 1942-46. **BUSINESS ADDRESS:** Municipal Center, Washington, DC 20001.

PINDELL, HOWARDENA D.
Painter, curator, educator. **PERSONAL:** Born Apr 14, 1943, Philadelphia, PA; daughter of Howard Douglas Pindell and Mildred Lewis. **EDUCATION:** Yale U, MFA 1967; Boston U, BFA 1965. **CAREER:** Pratt Inst, guest lecturer 1972; Hunter Coll, 1972; Morivian Coll, 1973; Queens Coll, 1973; Sch Visual Arts, 1973,75; Montclair State Coll, 1974; Brooklyn Mus, 1976; SUNY at Stony Brook, prof. **ORGANIZATIONS:** Mem Intl Art Critics Assoc, Intl House of Japan. **HONORS/ACHIEVEMENTS:** Afro-Amer Artists 1973; Who's Who of Amer Women 1975-76; Who's Who in Amer Art 1980; Dictionary of Intl Biography 1980; Natl Endowment for the Arts Grant1983-84; Boston Univ 1983 Alumni Awd for Disting Serv to the Profession; Ariana Foundation Grant 1984-85; Guggenehim Fellowship 1987-88; US/Japan FriendshipCommn Creative Arts to Fellowship. **BUSINESS ADDRESS:** Professor, SUNY at Stony Brook, Art Department, Stony Brook, NY 11794.

PINDER, FRANK E.
Foreign service officer. **PERSONAL:** Born Feb 24, 1911, Key West, FL; children: Terrecita E, Frank E III, Dorothea I. **EDUCATION:** FL A&M Coll, BS 1933; Cornell Univ, Dept State Fellow 1951-52; Monrovia Coll Liberia, LLD 1955; Campbell Coll, LHD 1956; Morris Brown Coll, attended 1973. **CAREER:** Alachua Co, co agr asst 1933-41; US Dept of Agr Wash, asst coop specialist 1941, agriculturist 1942, agr econ 1943; US Econ Mission Dept State Liberia, head agriculturist 1944-48; TCA Liberia, agr adv 1949-51; FOA & successor agency, chief agricul 1952-57; ICA Ghana, food & agr officer 1958-64; UN Econ Comm for Africa, cons; US Aid Mission to Ghana, dep dir 1964, dir 1964-68; UN Econ Comm for Africa, spl adviser to exec sec 1968-. **ORGANIZATIONS:** Mem Amer Acad Pol & Social Scis, Amer Pub Health Assn, Assn for Advancement of Agr Scis in Africa, Amer Fgn Serv Assn; life mem Soc for IntlDevel; mem Alpha Phi Alpha, Urban League, NAACP; Protestant Episcopal Mason. **HONORS/ACHIEVEMENTS:** Meritorious Serv Awd Dept of State 1951; ICA 1955; Citation Govt Liberia 1957; Govt Chana 1961; Disting Serv Awd AID 1967; The Mary McCleod Bethune Medallion 1973; appointed Pres Comm on Liberia-US Relations 1980.

PINDER, NELSON W.
Clergyman. **PERSONAL:** Born Jul 27, 1932, Miami; son of George Pinder and Coleen Saunders Pinder; married Marian Grant; children: Gail, Squire. **EDUCATION:** Bethune-Cookman Coll, BA 1956; Nashotah House Sem, BD 1959; Inst IN U, Adult Educ 1959; Urban Training Cntr, 1964; FL A&M, MEd 1974; Bethune-Cookman Coll Daytona Beach FL, DD (honoris causa) 1979. **CAREER:** St John the Bapt Epis Ch Orlando, priest 1974-; Diocese of Cntrl FL, staff mem 1971-; Awareness Cntr Orlando, dir 1969-71f St John the Bapt Epis Ch, vicar 1959-69. **ORGANIZATIONS:** Chmn Recruitment & Equal Employ Oppor Com Province VI Epis Ch 1972-; mem bd dir Union of Black Episcopalians 1973-74; mem Joint Commn on Ch in Small Comm 1970-; assoc trst Bethune-Cookman Coll; mem bd of trsts Bethune-Cookman Coll; mem Orlando C of C; Dept of Urban Affairs; mem Phi Delta Kappa; Walt Disney World Awards Com 1973; past Pres Delta Ix Lambda; mem Natl Commn on Social & Specialized Ministry 1989-; trustee Univ of the South, Sewanee, TN 1983-. **HONORS/ACHIEVEMENTS:** Knights of Columbus Citznshp Award 1974; US Congress Chaplains' Award 1973; 1st Annual Disney World Comm Serv Award 1972f black comm Award 1972; United Negro Coll Fund Award 1971f Alpha Kappa Alpha Comm Award 1972; Bethune-Cookman medallion 1975. **MILITARY SERVICE:** AUS 1953-55. **BUSINESS ADDRESS:** St John the Baptist, 1000 Bethune Drive, Episcopal Church, Orlando, FL 32805-3480.

PINDERHUGHES, CHARLES ALFRED
Psychiatrist. **PERSONAL:** Born Jan 28, 1919, Baltimore, MD; married Elaine Brazier; children: Charles Jr, Robert, Ellen, Richard, Howard. **EDUCATION:** Dartmouth, AB 1940; Howard Univ Sch Med, MD 1943; Boston Psychoanalytic Soc & Inst 1955. **CAREER:** Boston VA Hosp, chief psychiatry 1960-65; E N Rogers Memorial Veterans Hosp, asst chief psychiatry serv for clinical training 1975-; Boston Univ Sch of Med, psychiatrist psychoanalyst 1950-72, prof 1971-. **ORGANIZATIONS:** Mem Surgeon Gen Sci Adv Com on TV & Soc Behavior 1970-74; chmn Task Force on Aggression & Violence 1972-75; mem Amer Psychiat Assn, bd trustees 1974-77; numerous articles. **MILITARY SERVICE:** AUS med corps capt 1944-46. **BUSINESS ADDRESS:** Prof Psychiatry, BostonUniv Sch of Medicine, 200 Springs Rd, Bedford, MA 01730.

PINDLE-CONAWAY, MARY WARD
City official. **PERSONAL:** Born Jan 26, 1943, Wilson, NC; married Frank M Conaway;

children: Frank M Jr, Belinda, Monica. **EDUCATION:** NC Central Univ, BA 1964, 1970; Julliard School of Music, Performers Cert 1971-72; Coppin State Coll, MEd 1975; Univ of MD College Park, Spec Advanced Stud Clinical Psy 1978. **CAREER:** Yonkers Bd of Ed, music teacher 1970-71; Martin Luther King Jr Parent & Child Ctr, coord 1971-72; Baltimore City Schools, music teacher 1972-74, spec teacher 1974-81; Baltimore City, registrar of wills. **ORGANIZATIONS:** Mem NAACP; Ashburton Neighborhood Assoc, NC Central Univ Alumni Assoc, Gillis Mem Comm Church; pres & founder Woman Inc, The United Order of Tents-Annie's Endeavors; vip panelist Cerebral Palsy Telethon; bd mem at-large Natl Political Congr for Black Women; exec mem MD Assn of Register of Wills; exec treas Polytechnic Inst; policitcl action comm chrperson to Natl Conv of United Order of Tent. **HONORS/ACHIEVEMENTS:** Woman of the Month Ebeneezer Baptist Church Wilson NC; Afro-Amer Cert of Apprec for Outstanding Serv to the Student Population of Baltimore City; Baltimore City Mayor's Citation of Merit & Appreciation; Baltimore City Council Special Achievement Awd; Amer Business Women's Assoc Inner Harbor Chapt; Citation of Appreciation, Speaker of the Year 1983 Awd of Merit; Awd for Demonstrating Outstanding Courage HUB Inc; Honoree Natl United Affiliated Beverage Assoc Convention Baltimore City; Delegate Democratic Natl Convention 1984. **HOME ADDRESS:** 3210 Liberty Hts Ave, Baltimore, MD 21215. **BUSINESS ADDRESS:** Register of Wills, Baltimore City, 111 N Calvert St #344, Baltimore, MD 21202.

PINKARD, BEDFORD L.
Recreation supervisor. **PERSONAL:** Born Oct 09, 1931, Jacksonville, TX; divorced; children: Derek Louis. **EDUCATION:** Attended LA State Coll 1956-58, California Polytechnic Coll 1950-51; Ventural Coll, AA 1953; Cal State Univ Northridge, BS 1973. **CAREER:** City of Oxnard Comm Youth Project, dir 1979-80; City of Oxnard, recreation supervisor 1959-. **ORGANIZATIONS:** Mem Oxnard Noontimers Lions Club 1964-; pres Bd of Educ Oxnard Union High School Dist (served 4 terms as pres of bd) 1972-. **HONORS/ACHIEVEMENTS:** PTA Hon Serv Awd; Esquire Social Club Citizen of the Yr Awd; Resolution of the Oxnard City Council for Dedicated Svcs; Eighteen Years Perfect Attendance Oxnard Noontimers Lions Club. **MILITARY SERVICE:** AUS pfc 2 yrs. **HOME ADDRESS:** 1246 So M St, Oxnard, CA 93033.

PINKARD, DELORIS ELAINE
Personnel director, educational administrator. **PERSONAL:** Born Oct 22, 1944, Kansas City, KS; daughter of Andrew D Jackson and Ella Mae Williams Jackson; married William G Pinkard II, Dec 30, 1985; children: Karisse W Grigsby, Robert C Edwards. **EDUCATION:** Emporia State Univ, Emporia KS, BS Elementary Educ, 1966; Univ of Kansas, Lawrence KS, MS Educ Psychology & Research, 1980; Emporia State Univ, Emporia KS, MS Educ Admin, 1984. **CAREER:** Washington Dist Schools, Kansas City KS, teacher, 1966-69; Kansas City KS Catholic Diocese, Kansas City KS, teacher, 1970-72; Kansas City KS Public Schools, Kansas City KS, teacher, 1972-82, admin intern, 1982-83, principal, 1983-86, personnel dir, 1986-. **ORGANIZATIONS:** Past bd mem, Yates Branch YWCA, 1969; bd of dir, Wyandotte County Mental Health Commn, 1971; mem, Missouri Valley School Personnel Admin Assn, 1986-, Assn for School, Coll & Univ Staffing, 1986-, Amer Assn of School Personnel Admin, 1986-, Kansas City KS Women's Chamber of Commerce, 1987-; sec, Kansas-Natl Alliance of Black Schoool Educ, 1988-; bd of dir, Martin Luther King Urban Center, 1988-; interim sec, NAACP, 1989; Kansas City KS coord, United Negro Coll Fund Drive, 1989. **HONORS/ACHIEVEMENTS:** Cum Laude, Emporia State Univ, 1966; Kappa Delta Pi, Honors Soc in Educ, 1966; research thesis, Teacher Attitudes as Related to the Differences in Achievements of Reflective and Impulsive Children, 1980; Phi Delta Kappa, Emporia State Univ, 1982; conf presenter, Networking for Women in Educ Admin, 1984; Admin-in-Residence, Emporia State Univ, 1985; induction speaker, Lyons County Phi Delta Kapa, Fighting Teacher Burnout, 1985; Woman of Distinction for Community Serv, Friends of Yates, 1986; keynote speaker, Delta Sigma Theta Founders Recognition, Equity With Excellence, 1986; conf presenter, Kansas Black Legislative Conf, The Direction of Educ for Minority Students and Legislative Alternatives, 1987. **BUSINESS ADDRESS:** Director of Elementary Personnel, Kansas City, Kansas Public Schools, USD #500, 625 Minnesota Ave, School Administration Building, Kansas City, KS 66101.

PINKARD, NORMAN THOMAS
Government official. **PERSONAL:** Born Feb 26, 1941, Orange, NJ; married Betty Holmes; children: Anthony, Gail, Cathy, Lisa. **EDUCATION:** Syracuse U, BA 1968; Syracuse U, MA 1969. **CAREER:** Indus & Corp Devel NYS Dept of Commerce, dep commr; NYS Div for Youth, exec dep dir 1975-77; Human Rights Commn Syracuse & Onondaga Co, exec dir 1970-75; State Assemblyman Mortimer Gallivan, legis aide 1967-69; Syracuse U, urban econ devel spec 1968-70. **ORGANIZATIONS:** Host Straight to the Sourc Pub Affairs Prgm 1973-75; host PULSE Pub Serv Prgm 1976-; NY State Bd of Regents; rep NY State Adv Coun for Voc Edn; appointed by Gov Ofc to Bny State Aprenticeship & Training Coun; 1st vice chmn NY State Black Polit Caucus. **HONORS/ACHIEVEMENTS:** HUD Flwshp 1967-68; outstndg comm serv Award Careerco. **MILITARY SERVICE:** AUS s/sgt 1959-67. **BUSINESS ADDRESS:** 99 Washington Ave, Albany, NY 12245.

PINKELTON, NORMA HARRIS
Educator. **PERSONAL:** Born Oct 15, 1927, Philadelphia, PA. **EDUCATION:** Lincoln Sch of Nursing NY, nursing dip reg nurs 1950; Univ of Cincinnati, BSN 1963, MSN 1963, EdD 1976. **CAREER:** Jewish Hosp, psych unit gen staff spec duty 1962-65; Prep Employment Prog for Spec Youth, couns 1965-67; Univ of Cincinnati Coll of Nursing & Health,assoc prof psych nursing 1967-70; Univ of Cincinnati Inst for Rsch & Higher Ed, psychology of interracial relationships group leader 1971-73; Univ of Cincinnati & Coll of Nursing & Hlth, asst prof 1973-74; Cincinnati Health Dept, asst health comm, prof serv div 1980-81; Hampton Univ School of Nursingprof nursing, dir gerontological nursing pract proj. **ORGANIZATIONS:** Mem Natl League for Nurses, Amer Nurses Assoc, United Black Fac Assoc Univ of Cincinnati, Council for Exept Children, Black Nurses Assoc; pres bd dir Winton Hills Med & Health Ctr 1979-81, Black Child Devel Inst; bd mem Cincinnati Ctr for Devel Disability; mem Mental Health & Mental Retard Children's Svcs; mental health adv Cathcment Area 3; mem Women's City Club Cincinnati; ind gr & family coun Independent Pract 1975-81,85; dir min nursing recruit Univ of Cincinnati 1978-80; dir ger nursing pract prog Hampton Univ 1982-; facilitator Inst Rsch & Higher Ed Black-White Rel 1970-73; lay readerChrist Ed comm, choir St Cyprinas Epis Church, St Andrews Eipscopal Church; health serv comm Alpha Kappa Alpha 1977-81. **HONORS/ACHIEVEMENTS:** Nom Dictionary of Intl Biography 1973-75, World's Who's Who of Women; NDEA Fellow Univ of Cincinnati 1970-73; Sigma Theta Tau Natl Nursing Hon Soc 1973-; listed in Who's Who in the Midwest 1979-80, Who's Who in Amer 1979-80, Intl Who's Who 1978,80; "Mental Health" Osborne Carter Pinkelton & Richards 1976-80, "People of Color" 1983, "Devel of African Amer Cur Content in Psych Mental Health Nursing" 1982. **BUSINESS ADDRESS:** Professor, Dir, HamptonUniv, School of Nursing, Hampton, VA 23668.

PINKETT, HAROLD THOMAS
Consultant. **PERSONAL:** Born Apr 07, 1914, Salisbury, MD; son of Rev Wilson Pinkett and Catherine Richardson Pinkett; married Lucille Cannady, Apr 24, 1943. **EDUCATION:** Morgan Coll, AB; Univ of PA, AM; Columbia Univ, Grad Study; Amer Univ, PhD. **CAREER:** Natl Archives, suprv archivist 1959-79; Livingstone Coll, prof of history; Howard Univ, adjunct prof of history and archival admin 1970-76; American Univ, 1976-77; Natl Archives, staff archivist 1942-59; Private practice, archival & historial consult 1980-. **ORGANIZATIONS:** Editor Soc of Amer Archivist 1968-71; mem bd of dirs US Capitol Historical Soc 1972-; mem adv bd District of Columbia Historical Records 1978-; archival consult Howard Univ 1980, Natl Bus League 1982-84, United Negro Coll Fund 1983-84; mgmt cons, archival consult Cheyney Univ 1984-85; mem Links Inc 1986,NAACP 1986-87; mem Amer Historical Assoc, Soc of Amer Archivists, Org of Amer Historians, Assoc for Study of Afro-Amer Life and History, Agricultural History Soc pres 1982-83, Forest History Soc pres 1976-78, Southern Historical Assoc, Omega Psi Phi Frat; Sigma Pi Phi Fraternity. **HONORS/ACHIEVEMENTS:** Fellow Soc of Amer Archivists 1962-; Fellowship Grant Council on Library Resources 1972-73; Book Awd Agricultural History Soc; Carroll Lecturer in History Mary Baldwin Coll 1986; author of many historical and archival publications, including Gifford Pinchot (1970) and Research in the Administration of Public Policy (1975). **MILITARY SERVICE:** AUS t/sgt 1943-46; European & Asiatic-Pacific Serv Awds. **HOME ADDRESS:** 5741 27th St NW, Washington, DC 20015.

PINKNEY, ALPHONSO
College professor. **PERSONAL:** Born Dec 15, 1930, Tampa, FL; divorced. **EDUCATION:** Cornell Univ, PhD 1961. **CAREER:** Univ of Chicago, prof of sociology 1969-71; Howard Univ, prof of sociology 1972-73; Univ of CA-Berkeley, prof of criminology 1973-75; Hunter Coll CUNY, prof of sociology 1961-69, 1975-. **ORGANIZATIONS:** Mem Amer & Eastern Sociological Soc 1960-; mem Intl Sociological Assoc 1970-; mem or contributor to all major civil rights and civil liberties orgs. **HONORS/ACHIEVEMENTS:** Ford Foundation Fellowship; Publications 6 books incl "The Myth of Black Progress," 1984. **BUSINESS ADDRESS:** Professor of Sociology, Hunter College CUNY, 695 Park Ave, New York, NY 10021.

PINKNEY, ARNOLD R.
Educator. **PERSONAL:** Born Jan 06, 1931, Youngstown, OH; married Betty; children: Traci. **EDUCATION:** Albion Coll MI, BA. **CAREER:** Cleveland Bd of Edn, pres; Pinkney-Perry Ins Agency Cleveland, bd Chmn. **ORGANIZATIONS:** Mem OH Nat Life Underwriters Assn; exec com Grtr Cleveland Growth Assn; Cleveland Bus League; orgn dir The First Nat Bank Assn; mem vice pres & pres Cleveland Bd of Educ 1967-; bd of tst Albion Coll; pres bd of tst Central State U; chmn Devel & Goals Com; Com on Black Phys; bd of tst Cncl on Human Rel; Phyllis Wheatley Found; mem Urban League of Grtr Cleveland; bd mem Metro Hlth Planning Corp; past treas Black Econ Union; bd of tst The Citz League; life mem NAACP; candidate Mayor of Cleveland 1971, 75; dir Nat Deputy Campaign Senator Humphrey's 1972; exec com v chmn Cuyahoga Co Dem Party 1973; chmn Dem Party's Vice-pres Selection Com 1973; co-chmn Dem Nat Cpgn Com 1974; bd of elections Cuyahoga Co 1974; steering com Nat Caucus of Black Dem 1974; del Dem & Mini-conv Kansas Cty 1974; Dem Nat Conv 1976; adv Local State & Nat Dem Officials 1976; state chmn OH State Voter Registrtn Drive 1976; headed crive Get Out The Vote 1976; mem Olivet Int Bapt Ch. **HONORS/ACHIEVEMENTS:** Listed Who's Who in Am Coll & U; 1000 Successful Black in Ebony Mag; apt Exec Order of the OH Commodore; num lctr. **MILITARY SERVICE:** AUS 1952-54. **BUSINESS ADDRESS:** 2131 Fairhill Rd, Cleveland, OH 44106.

PINKNEY, DOVE SAVAGE
Medical technologist. **PERSONAL:** Born May 18, 1932, Macon, GA; daughter of Edward W Savage and Mildred Goodwin Savage; divorced; children: Rhonda Michelle Pinkney Washington, Roderick S. **EDUCATION:** Talladega Coll, 1954; Inst of Pathology Case-Western Reserve Univ, Cleveland OH, Certificate Medical Techn 1955. **CAREER:** Univ Hospital Cleveland, technician and supervisor 1955-59; Children's Hospital Los Angeles, technician in charge of out-patient clinic lab 1960-73, hematology lab supervisor 1973-. **ORGANIZATIONS:** Chairperson Children's Hospital Los Angeles Employee Recognition Comm 1973-; campaign chairperson Children's Hospital Los Angeles United Way Campaign 1975; treasurer 1978-80, mem 1981-, chair 1988-89, Bd of Mgrs Crenshaw 28th St YMCA; pres CA Assn for Medical Technology pres 1982-83; mem New Frontier Democratic Club trustee and exec bd mem 1982-; CA Soc for Medical Technology dir 1981-83, 1983-85; coord CSMT Student Bowl 1983; delegate to 15 state conventions; delegate to eight natl conventions; chairperson ASMT Minority Concerns Forum By-Laws Com, 1979-86; natl pres Talladega College Alumni 1984-87; advisory bd mem and fund raiser 1982-84 United Negro College Fund 1984-; life mem Natl Council of Negro Women; life mem Delta Sigma Theta Sorority; mem Urban League, NOW, PUSH, NAACP; mem Comm Relations Council of Southern CA; mem Black Women's Forum, Museum of Afro-Amer History and Culture, Trinity Baptist Church; Delta Sigma Theta Head Start Bd, 1970-76; Delta Sigma Theta Life Devel (seniors citizens program) Bd of Dir, 1984-89. **HONORS/ACHIEVEMENTS:** Awards received from Delta Sigma Theta Los Angeles Chapter, Talladega Coll Local Alumni Assoc, Talladega Coll Natl Alumni Assoc, Crenshaw YMCA, UNCF, Amer Soc of Medical Technology, Children's Hospital Los Angeles Employees, Federal Credit Union; co-author of two professional (scientific) papers. **HOME ADDRESS:** 5601 Coliseum St, Los Angeles, CA 90016. **BUSINESS ADDRESS:** Hematology Laboratory Supervisor, Children's Hospital Los Angeles, 4650 Sunset Blvd, Los Angeles, CA 90027.

PINKNEY, JERRY
Illustrator. **PERSONAL:** Born Dec 22, 1939, Philadelphia, PA; son of James H Pinkney and Willa Mae Landers Pinkney; married Gloria Jean Maultsby Pinkney; children: Troy Bernardette Pinkney Johnson, Jerry Brian Pinkney, Scott Cannon Pinkney, Myles Carter Pinkney. **EDUCATION:** Univ of the Arts, Philadelphia PA, 1957-59. **CAREER:** Rustcraft Publishing Co, Dedham MA, designer, 1960-62; Barker-Black Studio, Boston MA, designer-illustrator, 1962-64; Kaleidoscope Studio, Boston MA, designer-illustrator, 1964-66; Jerry Pinkney Studio, Boston MA, designer-illustrator, 1966-70; Rhode Island School of Design, visiting critic, 1969-70; Jerry Pinkney Inc, Croton-on-Hudson NY, pres, 1970-; Pratt Inst, Brooklyn NY, assoc prof, 1986-87; Univ of Delaware, distinguished visiting prof, 1986-88,

assoc prof of art, 1988-; US Military Academy, West Point NY, lecturer. **ORGANIZATIONS:** Mem, Society of Illustrators; mem, US Postal Service Citizens Stamp Advisory Comm, 1982; mem, Artist Team NASA, Space Shuttle Columbia, 1982; mem, US Postal Service Quality Assurance Comm, 1986-; mem, bd of scholars, Children's Art Carnival, New York NY, 1988-. **HONORS/ACHIEVEMENTS:** Annual Show, NY Soc of Illustrators, 1965-83, 1986-88; Christian Science Monitor, Boston MA, 1969; Idea Magazine #123, 1974; Communication Arts Magazine May/June, 1975; One of Fifty Best Books, Amer Inst of Graphic Arts, 1978, 1979; Graphic World, London, England, 1979; Christopher Award, The Christophers, 1986; Coretta Scott King Award, Amer Library Assn, 1986, 1987, 1989; Retrospective, Philadelphia, Boston MA, Newark DE, Ithica NY, 1987-88; How Magazine, July/August, 1987; Caldecott Honor Book, Amer Library Assn, 1989; CEBA Award, World Inst of Black Communications, Inc, 1989; Amer Visions Magazine, 1989; designer of eleven commerative postage stamps, US Postal Service. **BUSINESS ADDRESS:** Pres, Jerry Pinkney Inc, 41 Furnace Dock Rd, Croton-on-Hudson, NY 10520.

PINKNEY, JOHN EDWARD
Division manager. **PERSONAL:** Born May 06, 1948, Landover, MD; married Gloristine Wilkins; children: Nikole, John, April. **EDUCATION:** Prince George Comm Coll, AA 1973; Bowie State Coll, BS 1976. **CAREER:** Dept of Agriculture, computer operations 1970-71; Shadyside Barber & Beauty Salon, hair stylist/co-owner 1971-; Philip Morris USA, sales rep 1977-79, military mgr 1979-80, division mgr. **ORGANIZATIONS:** Natl Business League of Southern MD pres 1981-83, bd dirs 1984-; youth task force participant Natl Alliance of Business 1981-83. **HONORS/ACHIEVEMENTS:** Community Serv Award, Dist of Columbia; Presidential Citation Natl Assoc for Equal Opportunity in Higher Educ. **MILITARY SERVICE:** AUS E-5 3 yrs; Bronze Star; Vietnam Serv Medal; Vietnam Campaign Medal; Natl Defense Serv Medal. **HOME ADDRESS:** 6110 Joyce Dr, Camp Springs, MD 20748. **BUSINESS ADDRESS:** Division Manager, Philip Morris USA, 6101 Executive Blvd, Ste 270, Rockville, MD 20852.

PINKNEY, WILLIAM D.
Business executive. **PERSONAL:** Born Sep 15, 1935, Chicago, IL; married Ina Brody; children: Angela Walton. **EDUCATION:** NY City Comm Coll, AAS 1964; Adelphi Univ, BA 1973. **CAREER:** Astarte, natl sales mgr 1971-72; Cleopatra Creations, vice pres 1972-73; Revlon, mktg mgr 1973-77; Johnson Products Co, dir of mktg 1977-80; Dept of Human Serv City of Chicago, dir of family serv 1980-84; Combined Construction Co, vice pres; The Dessert Kitchen Ltd, dir. **ORGANIZATIONS:** Mem Natl Assoc Broadcast Engrg & Tech 1970-, Lake Michigan Yacht Racing Assoc 1974-; rear commadore Belmont Yacht Club; life mem Lake Michigan Singlehanded Soc. **HONORS/ACHIEVEMENTS:** Guest Lecturer Worton School of Business Univ of PA 1978; Contrib Writer Great Lakes Boating Mag 1982,83. **MILITARY SERVICE:** USN hm2 1953-60; 2 Good Conduct Medals 1953-57. **HOME ADDRESS:** 3532 N Pinegrove, Chicago, IL 60657. **BUSINESS ADDRESS:** Dir, The Dessert Kitchen Ltd, 721 Wrightwood, Chicago, IL 60614.

PINKSTON, MOSES SAMUEL
Clergyman. **PERSONAL:** Born Jan 14, 1923, Camden, NJ; married Esther Miller; children: M Samuel Jr, Steven A. **EDUCATION:** VA Union Univ Richmond, VA; Howard Univ Washington DC; Gordon Coll Boston MA, BA 1949; Temple Univ Sch of Theology, MDiv 1952; Rutgers Univ School of Social Work New Brunswick NJ, MSW 1969; CA Grad School of Theology, PhD 1977. **CAREER:** Pastor Mt Olivet Bapt Ch Newport RI 1953-57; pastor Mt Pisgah Bapt Temple Asbury Park NJ 1957-65; pastor Faith Bapt Tabernacle Asbury Park NJ 1965-69;organized & Dir of Shore Comm Child Care Center & Nursery Sch Asbury Park NJ 1966-69; social worker Monmouth Co Welfare Dept 1966-69; dir Public Ministries & East Bay Area Minister Am Bapt Churches of West Oakland, CA 1970-75; pastor Antioch Bapt Ch San Jose CA 1974-. **ORGANIZATIONS:** Past pres Ministerial Alliance San Jose & Vic 1978-80; prof - lecturer San Jose StUniv San Jose CA 1977-83; former mem commr Santa Clara Co Comm of Human Relations 1975-77; mem San Jose Downtown Redvlpmnt Comm under Mayor Janet Gray Hayes 1981-82; mem Mayors Comm on Minority Affairs for San Jose CA 1984-; hold Permanent Life Time St of CA Tchng Crdntls in Cnslng Psych, Pub Serv, Rel & Soc Studies, Soc Welfare & Hist; NAACP; Free & Accepted Masons, R C Marshall Lodge #15-San Jose; Natl Assn of Soc Welfare; Natl Assn of Social Workers (Golden Gate Chapter); Acad of Certificate, Social Workers (ACSW). **HONORS/ACHIEVEMENTS:** Travelled extensively in Europe, Middle East & Holy Land directed Organized tour groups to Hawaiian Islands, Caribbean Islands & Greek Islands. **MILITARY SERVICE:** AUS 1943-46; honorable discharge. **BUSINESS ADDRESS:** Senior Pastor-Administrator, Antioch Baptist Church, 268 E Julian St, San Jose, CA 95112.

PINN, SAMEUL J., JR.
Educator. **PERSONAL:** Born May 25, 1935, Brooklyn, NY; married Cynthia; children: Samuel III, Gregory, Charles. **EDUCATION:** Morgan State U, BA 1959; Rutgers U, MSW 1970. **CAREER:** Ramapo Coll, asso prof; SJP Cons, pres 1968-; Wiltywck Sch, dir 1971-72; Mayors Action Task Force, dir 1968-71; thcr 1957-68. **ORGANIZATIONS:** Consult Nassau & Co Equal Oppty Commin 1976; mem Coll for Human Serv 1973-75; Nat Conf on Penal Reform 1975-76; pres Bedford Study Inst of Afro- am Studies & Cont Edn; chmn & fdr Ft Greene Sr Citzn Ctr; chmn Brooklyn Core; sr citzn colmnst NY Amsterdam News; mem Human Resource Dist #11; mem Omega Ps Phi Frat; mem Assn of Blk Soc Wrkrs; chmn Comm Sch Bd Dist 196. **HONORS/ACHIEVEMENTS:** Comm serv Awrd John Jay Coll; Civic Ldrshp Brooklyn Civic Assn; Comm Educ JHS 117; Yth Ldrshp Recreation Tchr Assn; author "Comm Organizinga for Small Groups 1970. **MILITARY SERVICE:** Military Serv first lt 1959.

PINSON, THOMAS J.
Educator, surgeon. **PERSONAL:** Born Aug 01, 1927, Vicksburg, MS; married Margo Dean; children: Tracey. **EDUCATION:** Wilberforce Univ, BS 1948; Univ MI Coll Dent, MS 1957; Howard Univ Coll Dentistry, DDS 1953. **CAREER:** Freedman's Hosp Howard Univ Coll Dentistry, asst prof 1957-59, assoc prof 1959-60, prof & head dept oral surg 1960-65, dir clinics 1966-68, assoc dean hosp affairs & dir oral surg 1968-. **ORGANIZATIONS:** Mem Natl, Amer Dental Assns; Robert T Freeman & DC Dent Socs; Amer Bd Oral Surg; Amer Cancer Soc; Intl Assn Dental Rsch; Amer Soc Oral Surg; mem NAACP, Urban League; Alumni Club Univ MI & Wilberforce Univ. **HONORS/ACHIEVEMENTS:** Alumni Awd for Outstanding Contribution to Dental Educ and Admin 1973; Amer Cancer Soc In Grateful Acknowledgement of Outstanding Serv to the Cause of Cancer Control 1973; The Amer Cancer Society's Harold W Krogh Awd for Outstanding Work in the Control of Oral Cancer 1979; Faculty Recognition Awd for High Quality Instruction Scholarly Endeavors and Serv as Hallmarks of Excellence in Dental Educ 1986. **BUSINESS ADDRESS:** Associate Dean Hospital Affair, HowardUniv Hospital, 2041 Georgia Ave NW, Washington, DC 20060.

PINSON, VADA EDWARD, JR.
Athlete. **PERSONAL:** Born Aug 11, 1938, Memphis, TN. **CAREER:** Seattle Mariners, coach; Cincinatti Reds, played 11 yrs; St Louis Cardinals, played 1 yr; Cleveland Indians, played 2 yrs Kansas City Royals, played 2 yrs. **HONORS/ACHIEVEMENTS:** Lifetime bat avg 288; rbi 1148; hr 252; one of 12 plyrs to have 200 or more hits in rookie yr; led Nat league in at bats & doubles 1959; led Nat League in hits 1961 & 1967;; selected to 4 All-Star Teams; twice led Nat League outfldrs in Fldng 1965-69; ranks among all-time Top Reds in Career Marks in 10 Categories; inducted Cincinnati Hall of Fame 1977. **BUSINESS ADDRESS:** Seattle Mariners, PO Box 4100, Seattle, WA 98104.

PINSON, VALERIE F.
Legislative representative. **PERSONAL:** Born Apr 30, 1930, Newburgh, NY; divorced; children: Tracey. **EDUCATION:** Howard U, 1948-50; Bus Sch, 1950-51. **CAREER:** Sen Thomas J Dodd, asst 1960-64; White House Hon Hobart Taylor, exec asst 1965-66; Ofc Econ Opp, 1966-71; Comm Action Spec 1971-72; Congresswmn Yvonne B Burke Dem CA, admin asst; The White House, spec asst; Nat Assn of Counties, leg repr. **ORGANIZATIONS:** Bd mem Wash Urban League; bd Family & Child Serv; Com Minority Fellow Prgm Am Univ. **BUSINESS ADDRESS:** The White House, 1600 Pennsylvania Ave NW, Washington, DC 20500.

PIPER, CAROL VARDIMAN
Educator. **PERSONAL:** Born Jun 18, 1942, Detroit, MI; divorced; children: James Jr. **EDUCATION:** Harris Tchr Coll, BS 1966;Univ IL, 1967; Wayne State U, MEd 1970; Wayne State U, EdD 1975. **CAREER:** Detroit Pub Sch, reading spec coord 1971-; Wayne StateUniv ITE Prgm, co-dir, instr, comm rep 1974-75;Univ Detroit, guidance cnslr 1970; Detroit & Pub Sch, tchr 1968-71; St Louis Pub Sch, 1966-68. **ORGANIZATIONS:** Mem Nat Alliance of Black Sch Edcrs 1977; Intl Reading Assn 1973-74; MI Assn Middle Sch Edctrs 1973-; exec bd Metro Detroit Reading Cncl 1971-; Wayne Educ Options 1974-; consult Ctr for Professional Growth & Devel Wayne StateUniv 1976-; mem Cncl Negro Women 1969-70; NAACP 1968-; Women's Art & Econ Guild; 1st Independence Nat Bank of Detroit 1972-73; Friends of Belle Isle 1975-; Nat Negro Coll Found; St Paul AME Zion Ch 1942-; judge Detroit Edison Co Comm Beatuification Proj 1974.

PIPER, ELWOOD A.
Educator. **PERSONAL:** Born Apr 13, 1934, Bastrop, TX; married Ora Lean Williams; children: Malcom, Karen, Adrian, Kenneth. **EDUCATION:** Wiley Coll, BA 1956; TX So U, MA 1965. **CAREER:** Houston Indep Schl Dist, prin 1977; tchr; King St Bank, asst prin dir. **ORGANIZATIONS:** Mem Pleasantville Civ Club; mem bd of dir Riverside Meth Ch; mem Rotary of Houston; Phi Delta Kappa; Natl Assoc of Sec Prin; Boy Scouts of Amer; Big Broth of Amer; TXJ Prin Assn. **HONORS/ACHIEVEMENTS:** Man of the yr Civ Club 1965; serv awrd in Ngro Hist 1968; cit of the wk KNUZ-rADIO 1973; silver beaver awrd Boy Scouts of Amer 1976. **BUSINESS ADDRESS:** 1101 Taft, Houston, TX 77019.

PIPER, PAUL J.
Physician. **PERSONAL:** Born Jun 19, 1935, Detroit; married Mary K Harris; children: Paul, Michael. **EDUCATION:** Univ MI, BS 1962; MS 1967; Wayne State U, MD 1973. **CAREER:** MI Dept of Corrections, physician; Pvt Pract, Phys; HS, Tchr; coach track & cross country. **ORGANIZATIONS:** Mem Detroit Med Soc, Sigma Phi Pi; Detroit Surg Soc; Nat Med Assn. **MILITARY SERVICE:** USAF 1955-58.

PIPER, W. ARCHIBALD
Physician. **PERSONAL:** Born Apr 13, 1935. **EDUCATION:** Mt Allison U, BSc 1961; Dalhousie U, MD 1966; McGillUniv Can, MSc 1969; FRCS 1972; FACS 1976. **CAREER:** W Archibald Piper PC, plastic surgeon; MI St U, asst prof surgery. **ORGANIZATIONS:** AMA; MI St Med Soc; Am Coll of Surgeons; Am Soc of Plastic Recons Surgeons; Flint Acad of Surgeons; MI Acad of Plastics Surgeons; Rotary Club; pvtpilot; mem Intl Coll of Surgeons. **HONORS/ACHIEVEMENTS:** Bd cert Am Bd of Plastic Surgery; MSc thesis "The Fibrolast in Wound Healing". **BUSINESS ADDRESS:** Plastic Surgeon, 2313 Stone Bridge Drive, Flint, MI 48504.

PIPES, WILLIAM H.
Educator. **PERSONAL:** Married Anna Russell; children: Harriet Mc Adoo, Willetta, William III. **EDUCATION:** Tuskegge Inst, BS 1935; Atlanta U, MA 1937;Univ of MI, PhD 1943. **CAREER:** Ft Valley State Coll, Instr 1937, 1938-43; W KY State Coll, instr 1937-38; Langston Univ, prof 1943; English & Speech So Univ, prof & dept chmn 1943-45; Alcorn State Univ, pres & prof 1945-49; Philander Smith Coll, dean & prof 1949-56; Wayne State Univ, vis prof 1956-57; MI State Univ, prof 1957-77; MI State Univ, prof emeritus 1977-. **HONORS/ACHIEVEMENTS:** Author 3 books & serveral articles; Gen Educ Bd Schlrshp; Fulbright Grant to teach in Japan. **BUSINESS ADDRESS:** Michigan State University, East Lansing, MI.

PIRES, LAURA J.
Foundation officer. **PERSONAL:** Born in Wareham, MA; daughter of John M Pires and Adeline Pires; divorced. **EDUCATION:** Smith Coll, BA Eng 1961; Columbia Univ School of Social Work, MSW 1963, MA, M Phil, Anthro 1981. **CAREER:** Harlem Youth Opp Prog Action Inst, program analyst 1963-64; Harlem Youth Prog Emp Prog, dir 1964-65; Harlem Youth Opp Prog Com, dir 1965-66; Coll for Human Serv, v pres 1966-74, const 1974-82; New York City Welfare Mgmt Sys, dir of trng, 1982-88; program officer, Edwin Gould Foundation for Children 1988-. **ORGANIZATIONS:** Assoc of Black Social Workers 1969-73; scholarship comm Cape Verdeau Amer Scholarship Comm 1975-80 natl pres Friends of Ernebtina/Norrissey 1976-87; Amer Anthr Assoc 1977-; bd mem, bd of dir Smith Alumnae Assoc 1980-83; bd mem, bd of counselors Com on AFro-Amer Studies Smith Coll 1984-. **HONORS/ACHIEVEMENTS:** Human Serv Awd Coll for Human Serv 1973; Travel & Study Awd Ford Found 1975; DOL Doctoral Rsch Awd NYS/DOL 1980; Humanitarian Awd Cape Verdeans United CT 1982; Achievement Awd Verdean Vets 1982. **HOME ADDRESS:** 245 E 40th St, New York, NY 10016. **BUSINESS ADDRESS:** Program Officer, Edwin Gould Foundation for Children, 126 East 31st Street, New York, NY 10016.

PITCHER, FREDERICK M. A.
Airline captain, pilot. **PERSONAL:** Born Mar 09, 1932, Washington, DC; son of Sylvia Saunders Hardy; divorced; children: Frederick II, Riccardo, Tia Pitcher Clarke, Mikela, Ericka, Elliott. **EDUCATION:** DeVry Tech Inst, Diploma 1953; Northrop Univ, Cert, License A&P 1965; Fowler Aeronautical, Diploma 1966; LA Trade Tech Coll , AS Dean's List 1969; UCLA, Teaching Credential 1977; Natl Radio Inst, Diploma 1977; KIIS Radio Broadcasting, Diploma 1979. **CAREER:** US Naval Model Basin, engrg aide 1955; Burroughs Corp Computers, electronic tech 1955-59, electronics engr 1959-64; Tech Enterprises, owner, oper 1961-; Electronic Memories Inc, quality control 1964; Rose Aviation, flight instr 1975-85; Western Airlines, airline pilot, 1966-87; Delta Airlines, airline pilot, 1987-. **ORGANIZATIONS:** Mem/restorer, March Air Force Base Museum, California, 1988-89; founder, Soc for Preservation of Antique Technical Equipment, 1989; industry resource person, Los Angeles School Distict, 1986-; mem/builder, Experimental Aircraft Assn, 1965-; pilot/instructor, Civil Air Patrol, 1948-; Pres Mktg Intl Ltd 1983-; exec vice pres Worldwide Tax & Bus Consult Inc 1984-85; ceo Tech Enterprises 1966-; chief fin officer the DW Ford Corp Inc 1982-85; dir DW Ford Seminar Assoc 1983-85; mem LA Urban Bankers Assoc 1984-85; cert flight instr Worldwide 1961-85; station engr KFAR-TV 1962-63; west reg vice pres Org of Black Airline Pilots 1984-86; dir mem Northrop Univ Alumni 1979-; reading tutor CA Literacy Prog 1984-87; comm rel officer AirlinePilots Assoc 1983-85; guest lecturer LA School Dist 1968-85; mem Educare USC Alumni 1977. **HONORS/ACHIEVEMENTS:** Certificate of Recognition, State Senator Bill Greene, California, 1989; Professional Recog Edges Group Inc of Fortune 500 1984; Commendation CA State Senator Green Comm Asst 1980; Disting Alumni Northrop Univ 1976; Good Samaritan Awd Church of Jesus Christ of Latter Day Saints 1976; Community Serv LA School Dist 1971; Scholarship Sci Bosch & Lomb 1950; People & Choices Harcourt BraceJovonovich Publ Co 1971. **MILITARY SERVICE:** USNR-R atr-2 10 yrs. **HOME ADDRESS:** PO Box 73CN, Broadway-Manchester Station, Los Angeles, CA 90003.

PITCHFORD, GERARD SPENCER
Business executive. **PERSONAL:** Born Dec 08, 1953, Jersey City, NJ; son of Gordon Pitchford and Gloria Oliver Pitchford; married Janet F Hardy, Nov 25, 1987; children: Uonisha, Paris. **EDUCATION:** Rutgers Univ, 1970. **CAREER:** Dynamic Service Unlimited, sales mgr 1976; Time to Order Corp, pres 1984-86;Communications Equipt Repair, pres 1977-. **ORGANIZATIONS:** Bd mem treasuer Chicago Regional Purchasing Council 1980-; bd mem Chicago State Univ Found 1982-; bd mem Private Industry Council 1984-; bd mem Push International Trade Bureau; commissioner City of Chicago Dept of Human Rights; chairman Chicago Reg Purchasing Council Comm on Certification; Deacon, Chicago United 1987. **HONORS/ACHIEVEMENTS:** Vendor of the month, state of Illinois 1986. **BUSINESS ADDRESS:** President, Communication Equipt Repair, 738 S Wabash, Chicago, IL 60605.

PITTMAN, AUDREY BULLOCK
Educator. **PERSONAL:** Born Dec 16, 1916, Philadelphia, PA; married James Pittman, Jan 17, 1942 (died 1989); children: Joyce. **EDUCATION:** Morgan State Univ, BA 1948; Univ of Pennsylvania, MSW; Waldon Univ, PhD 1984. **CAREER:** Philadelphia Dept Welfare, supervisor 1951-57; Pennsylvania State Dept Welfare, day care dir 1964-69; Children's Aid Soc, adoption super & consultant 1957-64; Temple Univ, assoc prof 1969-84, prof emeritus. **ORGANIZATIONS:** Founding mem Philadelphia Assoc Black Social Workers 1969-; dir Christian Educ AME Church 1971-; trustee Cheyney Univ 1977-89; adv bd Philadelphia Dept Welfare 1981-; bd mem Black Family Serv 1984-; bd mem Women's Christian Alliance 1986-. **HONORS/ACHIEVEMENTS:** Linback Awd Excellence in Teaching Temple Univ 1981; Service Awd Natl Alliance Black Social Workers 1984; Alumni of Year Awd William Penn High School 1985. **BUSINESS ADDRESS:** Professor Emeritus, Temple University, Ritter Hall Annex, 13th & Columbia Ave, Philadelphia, PA 19107.

PITTMAN, CHARLES MATTHEW
Professional athlete. **PERSONAL:** Born Mar 23, 1958, Rocky Mount, NC; married Verma; children: Kale Edward. **EDUCATION:** Maryland, 1982; Merced Jr Coll. **CAREER:** Phoenix Suns, forward 1982-. **HONORS/ACHIEVEMENTS:** Competitive Spirit & Most Unselfish Contribution Awrd. **BUSINESS ADDRESS:** Phoenix Suns, P O Box 1369, Ste 510, Phoenix, AZ 85001.

PITTMAN, DARRYL E.
Government official. **PERSONAL:** Born Jul 11, 1948, Pittsburgh, PA; son of J Ronald Pittman and Eunice W Pittman; married Deborah Durham, Aug 08, 1980; children: Darryl M, Sholah, Jordan, Cassi, Nolan. **EDUCATION:** Columbia Coll, New York NY, AB, 1970; Columbia Univ School of Law, New York NY, JD, 1973. **CAREER:** Hardiman, Alexander, Pittman & Howland, Cleveland OH, partner; Hahn Loeser, Freedheim, Dean & Wellman, Cleveland, OH, assoc; City of East Cleveland OH, mayor. **ORGANIZATIONS:** Pres, Software Specialist; mem, Norman Minor Bar Assn; former pres, Ohio Chapter of Black Mayors; mem, 21st District Congressional Caucus, bd mem, Cleveland Branch NAACP. **HOME ADDRESS:** 16119 Oakhill Rd, East Cleveland, OH 44112.

PITTMAN, INEVA (NEE MAY)
Educator. **PERSONAL:** Born Jul 06, 1934, Jayess Lawrence Co, MS; married Joe; children: Albert Jefferson. **EDUCATION:** BS 1956; MS 1973; AA 1974. **CAREER:** Local NAACP; 1st vice pres 1965; Natl Council Negro Women, pres 1974; Bus & Professional Women's Club, 2nd vice pres; CSA, bd mem poverty program; Jackson School System, first grade teacher. **ORGANIZATIONS:** Stonewall Missionary Bapt Ch; 1st vpres N Jackson Comm Boy's Club; chmn trst bd NCNW; pres Missionary Soc; supt Adult Dept Sunday Sch; adult sponsor Youth Ministry Team; bd mem Jackson Tchrs Assn; NAACP; vol voter registrtn & edn; asst tchr Jackson Missionary Bapt Dist Assn; life mem JacksonStateUniv Nat Alumni Assn; MS Tchrs Assn; Nat Counc Negro Women; Bus & Professional Women's Club; subscribing life mem Nat Educ Assn. **HONORS/ACHIEVEMENTS:** Tchr of yr 1959; pres of yr Jackson Dist missionary 1970; NAACP Fight for Freedom Cert of Merit 1973. **BUSINESS ADDRESS:** 1716 Isable St, Jackson, MS 39204.

PITTMAN, JAMES RONALD
Corporation executive. **PERSONAL:** Born Nov 11, 1925, Richmond; married Eunice Walker; children: Darryl, Ronald F, Toni L, Joni R. **EDUCATION:** VA Union U; WV State Coll;Univ of Pitts, BA;Univ O Fpitts, Grad Studies; Grad Sch of Urban StudiesUniv of Akron. **CAREER:** J Ronald Pittman & Assos, pres; Cty of Youngstown, urban consult comm devel dir 1978-80; Youngstown Area Devel Corp & Plaza View Inc, exec dir 1970-78; Youngstown Fair Employment Prac, exec sect 1964-70; Pitts Urban League, dir hsng 1963-64; Human Relations Commn PA, rep 1961-63; PA Dept Pub Welfare, 1954-62. **ORGANIZATIONS:** Mem Omega Ps Phi Frat; Assn Housing Redevel Officials; C of C; instr Police Comm Rel 1969; columnist Mahoning Vly Challenger Catholic Exponent; presbd dir of Catholic Charities; mem of bd Catholic Serv League; mem of bd NAACP; mem of bd Human Rel Commn; mem of bd Budget Com; Mayor's Tech Adv Com; Society Blind. **HONORS/ACHIEVEMENTS:** Comm serv awrd OH, Beauticians 1966; BD Mason comm serv awrd 1969; B'Nai B'Rith man of yr awrd 1969; Omega Psi Phi outstndg comm serv Awrd 1974. **MILITARY SERVICE:** AUS 1943-46. **BUSINESS ADDRESS:** 1555 Belmont Ave, Youngstown, OH 44504.

PITTMAN, MARVIN B.
Dentist. **PERSONAL:** Born May 31, 1931, Blakely, GA; married Amanda B Nelson; children: Marvin B Jr. **EDUCATION:** Savannah State Coll, BS (Hon) 1953; Univ of MI, MS 1957; Howard Univ, DDS (Hon) 1966. **CAREER:** VA Center Los Angeles, rsch biochemist 1957-62; AUS, dental officer 1966-70; Private practice Los Angeles, dentist 1970-. **ORGANIZATIONS:** mem, Amer Dental Assn, CA Dental Assn, Angel City Cental Soc, Century Club Univ SC, Holman Meth Church, Urban League, NAACP, Alpha Phi Alpha, YMCA, Reserve Officers Assn; bd of dirs, pres, JW Ross Med Ctr Los Angeles; bd of dir Omicron Kappa Upsilon, Beta Kappa Chi. **MILITARY SERVICE:** AUS non-commiss officer 1953-56, naval res officer ensign 1964-66, capt 1966-70, lt col Army Res 1971-84; Bronze Star, Army Commendation, Good Conduct. **BUSINESS ADDRESS:** JW Ross Medical Center, 1828 S Western Ave #18, Los Angeles, CA 90006.

PITTMAN, SAMPLE NOEL
Educator. **PERSONAL:** Born Apr 22, 1927, Texas; married Vivian Jo Byars; children: Sample Jr, Ava, Nicholas. **EDUCATION:** NYU, PhD, 1974; TX Southern Univ, MA 1952; Samuel Houston Coll, BA 1949. **CAREER:** Borough of Manhattan Comm Coll City Univ of NY, dean of admin 1970-, asso dean of students 1971; Corp Consortium-Harlem Inst for Teachers NYC, dir teacher 1970; Poverty Program, Training Resources for Youth Educ Dept, dir 1969; Inst of Strategic Study United Presbyterian Church, New York City rsch assoc 1967; New York City Housing & Redevel Bd Hudson Consev Project, asst dir 1966; Dillard Univ, dean of students 1964; Chicago Comm Coll, instructor 1962; Chicago Commn on Race Relations; asst dir; Mayors Com on New Residents, 1959; IL Youth Commn, juvenile parole officer 1957; St Charles St Training School. **ORGANIZATIONS:** Mem bd dir, Chicago Halfway House 1962; consulting lecturer, Natl Conf of Chrstns & Jews Chicago 1962; Chicago City Comm Coll Faculty Rep United Natl Inst 1962; vice pres Parents Teachers Students Assn 1962; vice pres Greenview Comm Council, Chicago 1962; Chicago City Comm Coll Faculty Rep Intercollegiate Counc 1961; panelist, DePaul Univ & Natl Conf of Christians & Jews, Chicago 1962; treasurer, Comm Bd #9 Manhattan NY. **HONORS/ACHIEVEMENTS:** Diploma de hon Borough of Manhattan Comm Coll 1975; Outstanding Educ of Amer Award 1975; adminstr of yr award Borough of Manhattan Comm Coll 1974; founders day award NYU, 1974; Phi Delta Kappa mem 1966; Alpha Phi Alpha mem 1948; Bertha Lockett achievement award Brownwood TX 1975. **MILITARY SERVICE:** AUS. **BUSINESS ADDRESS:** Borough Manhattan Comm Coll, 199 Chambers St, New York, NY 10031.

PITTS, BRENDA S.
Executive director-personnel. **PERSONAL:** Born Aug 29, 1950, Madison, IN; daughter of Kenneth W Hunter and Theola Brewer Hunter; married Joseph David; children: Nichole, Christopher. **EDUCATION:** IN Univ, BS Educ 1972. **CAREER:** Knox Co News, writer 1972-73; Cummins Engine Co Inc, communication spec 1974, couns 1975, personnel admin 1975-78, mgr EEO 1978-82, mgr personnel 1982-83; director, personnel 1983-88; executive director of personnel 1988-. **ORGANIZATIONS:** Mem Alpha Kappa Alpha Sorority 1970-72; scholarship chmn Laws Found 1975-79; commr Columbus Human Rights Commn 1978-79; mem First Call for Help bd, recording secretary, Columbus East Band Boosters. **HONORS/ACHIEVEMENTS:** Freshman Hon Soc IN Univ 1968-69; Dean's List IN Univ 1968-72; Outstanding Young Women of Amer 1978. **BUSINESS ADDRESS:** Executive Director, Engine Business Personnel, Cummins Engine Co, mail code 60630PO Box 3005, Columbus, IN 47202.

PITTS, DONALD FRANKLIN
Judge. **PERSONAL:** Born Aug 30, 1933, Pontiac, MI; married Patricia Florence Washington; children: Gregory Leroy, Gail Lynn, Kimberly Marie Thomas, Mark Robert Brown, Donald F Jr, Maureen Alyce. **EDUCATION:** East Los Angeles Coll, AA 1952; CA State Univ, BA 1954; Southwestern Univ, JD 1962. **CAREER:** LA CA, probation officer 1955-63, attny at law 1963-71; CA State Univ Long Beach, assoc prof 1972-75; Superior Court, referee 1969-71, commissioner 1971-84, judge 1984- (Court of Appeals State of CA 2nd District, justice pro tem Dec 1985 & Jan 1986). **ORGANIZATIONS:** Mem State Bar of CA, Natl Bar Assoc, John M Langston Bar Assoc, LA Cty Bar Assoc, Long Beach Bar Assoc, YMCA, NAACP; bd dir Comm Devel Inc of Long Beach. **BUSINESS ADDRESS:** Judge, Superior Court, 200 W Compton Bld, Compton, CA 90220.

PITTS, DOROTHY L. (NEE WALLER)
Retired social worker. **PERSONAL:** Born Jun 29, 1913, Memphis, TN; married Walter L Pitts; children: Edolia Goudeau. **EDUCATION:** LeMoyne Coll, AB 1935; Howard Univ, MA 1940; Univ of CA, Cert Soc Welfare 1957. **CAREER:** DeFremery Rec Ctr, rsd dir 1947-48, head dir 1948-56; Summer Workshop in Ed for Human Rel, staff teacher 1952; Oakland Rec Dept, suprv 1956-62, trngcons 1962-63, suprv of rec 1964; Richmond comm Devel Demo Proj, suprv new careers 1965-66; Advance Negro Council for Comm Improvement, exec dir 1966; Social Plng Dept Berkeley, neighborhood cons, soc plng analyst 1966-73; Div on Aging City of Berkeley CA, chief 1973-78, dir 1978-retirement. **ORGANIZATIONS:** Mem Western Gerontological Soc, CA Spec on Aging, Natl Council of Sr Cit Inc, CA Assoc for Health & Welfare, Natl Council on Aging, Howard Univ Alumni Assoc, NAACP El Cerrito Br, Natl Council of Negro Women Inc; charter mem, natl bd dir The Older Women's League 1980-; org sponsor & 1st pres RainbowSign; past pres Natl Assoc of Negro Bus & Professional Womens Clubs Corp Inc 1969-73; pres Progressive Black BPW Inc 1974-, Sojourner Truth Housing Inc 1974-; co-org Black Women Org for Political Action 1972; adv bd Univ of CA, chrpsn of bd dir YWCA 1974-; 1st vice pres Berkeley Bar Area Alumnae Chap Delta Sigma Theta; mem task force Constitution & By-Laws Comm; convenor NCNW CA State Mechanism 1983-84; vice pres Older Women's League 1986. **HONORS/ACHIEVEMENTS:** Woman of the Yer Zeta Phi Beta 1954; Citizenship Awd Alpha Phi Alpha 1955; Outstanding Contrib to Youth Awd Sunset Dist Comm Council 1962; author of article Rec Mag Sep 1966; CA Park & Rec Assoc Awd for Exceptional Achievement in

Field of Parks & Rec 1963; Delta Women of Achievement Delta Sigma Theta 1965;listed in Who's Who of Amer Women 1966-67, Who's Who in the West, Who's Who in CA 1966; Cal-Pal Awd for Outstanding Serv to Community 1974; Woman of the YearSun Reporter Merit Awd 1973; Disting Alumna Awd Bay Area Howard Univ Alumni Assoc 1975; WAVE Awd Women of Achievement Vision & Excellence Alumnae Resources 1984; Awd for Outstanding Community Serv Natl Inst for Minority Women of Color 1984; Community Service Awd Alameda Contra Costa Links Inc 1985; Ella Hill Hutch Awd Black Women Organized for Political Action 1986.

PITTS, GREGORY PHILIP
Artist, clerk. **PERSONAL:** Born Nov 24, 1949, Los Angeles, CA; married Diane Germaine Easley; children: Aisha Makini. **EDUCATION:** LA Valley Coll, AA 1967-70; CA State Univ at Long Beach, BA 1971-74; Otis Art Inst Parsons School of Design, MFA 1980. **CAREER:** So CA Rapid Transit Dist, info clk; Travel & Art Mag, contbng ed 1977-; Pearl C Wood Gallery, dir 1975-. **ORGANIZATIONS:** Mem Art Educ Consult Serv 1975-; Studio Mus in Harlem; Friends of Claude Booker; mem Nat Conf of Artists; yth adv Triangular Ch of Rel Sci. **HONORS/ACHIEVEMENTS:** Watts Fest Art Exhibit 1972; TV Prgm Storefront KCET 1973; Comm Afrs Prgm KCOP 1974; Livin' KTTV 1974; fdr Witness Inc Orgn of Black Art Crit Histrns 1979; publ newsletter "Witness" Witness Inc. **BUSINESS ADDRESS:** 1938 S Western Ave, Los Angeles, CA 90018.

PITTS, JAMES DONALD, JR.
Natural gas utility company executive. **PERSONAL:** Born Aug 07, 1938, Chicago, IL; son of James Donald Pitts, Sr and Jewell Johnson Richmond-Anderson. **EDUCATION:** Illinois Inst of Technology, Chicago IL, BS, 1968; Univ of Chicago, Chicago IL, MBA. **CAREER:** The Peoples Gas Light & Coke Co, Chicago IL, 1956-. **ORGANIZATIONS:** Mem, Amer Gas Assn; mem, Amer Assn of Blacks in Energy; mem, Chicago Urban League; mem, Executive Program Club-Graduate School of Business, Univ of Chicago; co-chmn and dir, Centers for New Horizons; sec, Mental health Assn of Greater Chicago, commr and treasurer, Guardianship and Advocacy Comm; dir, Greater State St Council. **MILITARY SERVICE:** US Army, SP4 E4, 1962-64, Army Commendation Award, 1964. **BUSINESS ADDRESS:** Vice Pres, The Peoples Gas Light & Coke Co, 122 S Michigan Ave, Chicago, IL 60603.

PITTS, JOHN MARTIN
Business executive. **PERSONAL:** Born Feb 28, 1945, Birmingham, AL; divorced; children: Gioia. **EDUCATION:** Arizona St U, BS 1971, MPA 1977. **CAREER:** Vly Nat Bank of AZ, asst vice pres 1976-, comm loan ofcr 1969-80; Denver Broncos, professional ftbll plyr 1973-76; Buffalo Bills, professional plyr 1967-73. **ORGANIZATIONS:** Players rep NFL Players Assn 1967-73; Pop Warner coach Pop Warner Assn bd Tempe AZ 1976; mem Kappa Alpha Psi-Alumni Chap 1978-; mem AZ StUniv Bd of Alumni 1979-; mem Boys Club Bd of Dir Phx 1979. **HONORS/ACHIEVEMENTS:** Most valuable plyr for Buffalo Bills 1970; black man of yr Black Caucus Assn Tempe AZ 1970. **BUSINESS ADDRESS:** Vice President, 1st Interstate Bank of Arizona, 100 W Washington, PO Box 53456, Phoenix, AZ 85072.

PITTS, LORENZO, JR.
Senior sales representative. **PERSONAL:** Born May 19, 1946, Boston, MA; widowed; children: Derek, Jared. **EDUCATION:** Northeastern Univ, BSEE 1977, MBA Mktg 1983. **CAREER:** Procter & Gamble, project engr 1977-81; Texas Instruments, mfg supervisor 1981-82; L Pitts Inc, manager 1982-83; Corning Glass Works, sr sales rep 1983-87. **ORGANIZATIONS:** Exec comm Elmira/Corning Branch NAACP 1985-87; advisor Junior Achievement 1986; mem NBMBAA 1986-87; consultant Master Industries 1987. **HONORS/ACHIEVEMENTS:** Million Dollar Club NAACP 1985-86. **MILITARY SERVICE:** USN FTMI E6 1966-71; Vietnam Service 1968. **BUSINESS ADDRESS:** Sr Sales Representative, Corning Glass Works, Advanced Products Dept, Corning, NY 14831.

PITTS, M. HENRY
Educator. **PERSONAL:** Born Dec 19, 1916, Montgomery, AL; married Helen Lowery; children: Delia Carol, Steven Carlton. **EDUCATION:** Univ IL, AB 1936;Univ Chgo, AM 1938, PhD 1951. **CAREER:** Roy Littlejohn Asso, sr asso; Comm Clincl Psych Prgm Howard U, dir 1973-77; Garfield Park Comm Mntl Hlth Ctr, dir 1969-73;Univ IL, asso prof 1961-69, asst prof 1956-58; Psych Inst of Municpal Ct, asst dir 1951-56. **ORGANIZATIONS:** Sec Div of Clncl Psych IL Psych Assn 1969; consult Worthington Hurst Assn 1962-73; bd mem Nat Serv & Schlshp Fund for Negro Stdnts 1969-77; mem AmPsych Assn 1951-; mem exec com Nat Assn of Black Psych 1976-77. **HONORS/ACHIEVEMENTS:** Involved in rsrch, Antecedents & Dynamics of Black Self Concept; diploma Am Bd of Professional Psych Clncl Psych 1956; publ Racism in Comm Psych 1977. **MILITARY SERVICE:** AUS warrant ofcr jg 1943-47. **BUSINESS ADDRESS:** 1328 New York Ave NW, Washington, DC 20050.

PITTS, RONALD JAMES, SR.
Attorney. **PERSONAL:** Born Nov 02, 1942, Wheeling, WV; married Nellie M Price; children: Ronnelle, Rhonda; Ronald J II. **EDUCATION:** BS 1966; LLB 1969; JD 1970. **CAREER:** Atty, pvt prac; IRS Estate & Gift Tax Reg Analyst Cincinnati, est tax grp mgr; IRS, Atty; Greensboro Dist Greensboro NC, quality & productivity coord. **ORGANIZATIONS:** Vp NAACP Huntington WV; Huntington URA Commr; Legal Counc Bluefield St Alumni; sec NAACP 1973-74; chmn C-H Hum Rights Counc 1970-73; mem WV Black Caucus; supvs C/UNIDN chmn; pres Chap 64 Nat Treas Empl Union; mem Mtn St Bar Assn, sec 1972-73, histrn; mem WV St Bar Assn; Am Bar Assn 1969;mem Pres Cncl of Wheeling Coll; EEO Consult RJP Consult Fdr Fed Bsktbll Leag 1970; cmmr 1970-75; bd mem Tri-St Tax Inst 1975; mem St Legist Interim Com; quality instr Regional 1987; natl exec bd AIM-IRS 1986-87. **HONORS/ACHIEVEMENTS:** Disting Performer 1986,87.

PITTS, VERA L.
Educator. **PERSONAL:** Born Jan 23, 1931, Wichita, KS; daughter of Wade Johnson and Maggie Johnson; widowed. **EDUCATION:** Mills Coll, AA 1950; NC Berkeley, BA 1953; Sacramento State Univ, MA 1962; MI State Univ, PhD 1969. **CAREER:** Stockton Unified School Dist, teacher, counselor, admin 1954-65; City Coll NY, asst prof 1967-69; Palmer Handwriting Co, consult 1975-; CA State Univ Hayward, prof, dept chair ed admin 1969-86; program mgr, Dept of Educ, 1986-87; assoc supt, Oakland Unified School District 1987-88. **ORGANIZATIONS:** Mem bd dir League of Women Voters 1975-; mem Western Assoc Accrediting Teams 1975-; pres San Mateo Br Amer Assoc Univ Women 1976-77; vice pres CA State Div Amer Assoc Univ Women 1978-82; mem Foster City Ed Facilities Comm 1983; counselor Univ of CA Alumni Assoc 1979-83; Natl Urban League EdAdv Comm 1979-; dir-at-large Natl Council Admin Women in Ed 1982-; Phi Delta Kappa 1982-85; Pacific School of Religion Bd of Trustees, 1989-; Rotary Intl, 1988-. **HONORS/ACHIEVEMENTS:** Outstanding Young Women of Amer Bay Area 1965-76; Mott Fellowship Natl Awd MI 1965-67; Danforth Assoc Found 1974-; Vstg Professorships Univ Houston UnivMI, Pepperdine Univ 1974-; Rockefeller Postdoctoral Fellowship 1978-80; Natl Faculty Exchange to US Dept of Ed 1986-87. **HOME ADDRESS:** 600 Sandy Hook Ct, Foster City, CA 94404. **BUSINESS ADDRESS:** Professor, Dept Chair, California StateUniv, 25800 Carlos Bee Blvd, Hayward, CA 94542.

PITTS, WILLIAM HENRY
Dentist. **PERSONAL:** Born Sep 19, 1914, New Haven, CT; son of William Henry Pitts and Lillian Seabrooks Pitts; married Eleanor Mable Eaton; children: William H III, James J, Clarence E. **EDUCATION:** Lincoln Univ, AB 1937; Meharry Medical Coll Sch of Dentistry, DDS 1942; NYU, post grad 1946; New Orgn Sch for Grad Dentist, attended 1946; State of CT, post grad work 1965. **CAREER:** Yale New Haven Hosp, staff 1955; PA Dental Soc of Anesthesiology, post grad course pain control & patient mgmt; State of CT Correction Dept, dentist 1982; private practice, dentist. **ORGANIZATIONS:** Mem Amer Dental Assoc 1942-, New Haven Dental Assoc 1947-, CT State Dental Assoc 1947-; mem Intl Acad of Anesthesiology 1951, Natl Dental Assoc 1955-; PGER of IBPO Elks of the World; Prince Hall Mason 32nd degree. **HONORS/ACHIEVEMENTS:** 1st Black Sch Dentist New Haven 1952-57; Certificate of Qualifications Natl Bd of Dental Examiners; Fellow Royal Soc of Health. **MILITARY SERVICE:** AUS Dental Corps capt 1942-46. **BUSINESS ADDRESS:** Dentist, Dr William H Pitts, 206 Dixwell Ave, New Haven, CT 06511.

PLATT, RICHARD A.
Construction executive. **CAREER:** Platt Construction Inc, Franklin WI, chief executive. **BUSINESS ADDRESS:** Platt Construction Inc, 3321 W Rawson Ave, Franklin, WI 53132. *

PLAYER, WILLA B.
Educational consultant, retired educational administrator. **PERSONAL:** Born Aug 09, 1909, Jackson, MS; daughter of C C Player and Beatrice D Player. **EDUCATION:** OH Wesleyan Univ, BA; Oberlin Coll, MA; Univ Grenoble France, Cert d'Etudes; Univ of Chicago & Univ of WI, grad student; Columbia Univ, DEduc 1948; OH Wesleyan Univ, LD 1953; Lycoming Coll, LD 1962; Morehouse Coll, LD 1963; Albion Coll, LD 1963; Keuka Coll, DH Litt 1967; Univ NC Greensboro,HD Litt 1969; Prairie View A&M Coll, DPS 1971; Bennett Coll, HD Litt 1976. **CAREER:** Bennett Coll, French & Latin instr, dir admissions, coord of instr, vp, pres 1955-66; Bureau of Postsecondary Educ Wash, DC, dir div institut devel 1966-77; consultant in higher edn. **ORGANIZATIONS:** Mem bd trustees Charles Stewart Mott Found; mem adv comm on Black Higher Educ Mott Found; mem bd dir United Negro Coll Fund NYC; mem Univ Senate United Meth Ch Nashville, TN 1976-84; mem Comm on Funding Black Colls Nashville, TN 1976-84; mem Ford Found Study of Black Coll CAEL Baltimore, MD; mem steering comm ISATIM ACE/UNCF/Kellogg Found Study; mem First United Meth ChAkron, OH. **HONORS/ACHIEVEMENTS:** Superior Serv Award & Disting Serv Award Dept HEW 1970 & 1972; Disting Achievement Citation OH Wesleyan Univ 1980; Gen Educ Bd Fellowships 1945 & 1947; Frank Ross Chambers Fellow Columbia Univ 1948; Ford Fellow on study tour of 12 colleges and universities in US; study made possible by grant from Fund for Educational Advancement; Presidential Ldrshp Grant to Japan Carnegie Corp of NY; travel to England, France, Italy, Switzerland, East and West Africa, Japan, Israel and Egypt. **HOME ADDRESS:** 684 Schocalog Road, Akron, OH 44320.

PLEAS, JOHN ROLAND
Psychologist. **PERSONAL:** Born Nov 11, 1938, East St Louis, IL; children: Chandra. **EDUCATION:** McKendree Coll, BA 1960;Univ of IL Urbana, MEd 1967; VanderbiltUniv Nashville TN, PhD 1980. **CAREER:** VanderbiltUniv Weight Mgmt Prgm, adminstrv dir & co-dir 1976-; St Leonard House, dir com devel 1967-71;Univ of Chicago Billings Hosp, rsrch tech 1963-67; Competence Inc, pres 1975-. **ORGANIZATIONS:** Inactive mem WA Graham Lodge #9 1976-79; inactive mem Cumberland Vly Consistory 1978-79. **HONORS/ACHIEVEMENTS:** Good conduct medal AUS; danforth fllwshp VanderbiltUniv 1971-73; couns fllwshp Inter Univ Couns Ctr 1976. **MILITARY SERVICE:** AUS spec 5th class 1960-63. **BUSINESS ADDRESS:** VanderbiltUniv, 134 Wesley Hall, Nashville, TN 37240.

PLEASANT, ALBERT E., III
Administrator. **PERSONAL:** Born May 22, 1944, Cincinnati, OH; divorced; children: Albert E IV. **EDUCATION:** Univ of Cincinnati, BS 1973. **CAREER:** Children's Hospital Medical Ctr Div of Neonatology, business mgr 1974-; Univ of Cincinnati, dean's office fiscal asst 1969-74, dept peds bus affairs asst 1974-79, sr business admin 1979-. **ORGANIZATIONS:** Mem Natl Council of Univ Rsch Adminis 1974-; mem Soc of Rsch Administrators 1974-; lay delegate 51st Reg Conv of the Lutheran Church Missouri Synod 1975; mem Assoc of Amer Medical Colls Group on Business Affairs 1982-; assoc mem Natl Health Lawyers Assoc 1984-; Business Mgmt Consultant NICHHD, PHS, DHHS 1985-; mem OH Dist Bd for Parish Serv 1985-87. **HONORS/ACHIEVEMENTS:** Elected mem Republican Central Comm Hamilton Co Cincinnati OH 1982-86. **MILITARY SERVICE:** AUS specialist 5th class 1967-69; Vietnam Serv Medal; Good Conduct Medal; Army Commendation Medal.

PLEASANT, MAE BARBEE BOONE
Retired educational administrator. **PERSONAL:** Born Jul 08, 1919, Kentucky; daughter of Zelma C Burks and Minnie Burks; married Noel J; children: Eugene Jr. **EDUCATION:** Tennessee State Univ, BS 1941; Hampton Inst, MA 1962; George Washington Univ. **CAREER:** Hampton Inst, admin asst to pres, sec of corp 1973-, faculty mem 1968-71, admin asst to pres 1957-63, business mgr 1946-53; African Amer Affairs, assoc dir 1971-73; OEO, educ specialist 1966-68; Univ MD, dean of women 1963-66; Clark Coll, past sec pres 1953-57; Virginia State, past sec supt 1944. **ORGANIZATIONS:** Mem Alpha Kappa Mu; Girl Scout Leader; area chmn UNCF; chmn Human Relations Comm, League of Women Voters; pres Peninsula Pan Hellenic Council; state chmn Assn for Study of Negro Life & History 1973-75; bd dir YWCA 1953-57; vice-chmn Professional Sec 1955-57; mem Vestry & Register, St Cyprean's Episcopal Church 1974, 1984, 1989; basileus, Alpha Kappa Alpha, Gamma Upsilon Omega 1977-79; Quarter Century Club of Hampton Univ; bd of dir, Children's Home Society,

Richmond VA; former vice chairman, King Street Community Center. **HONORS/ACHIEVEMENTS:** Citation HEW 1967; citation TN St Univ 1962; woman of yr Hampton Inst 1957, 1963; editor, History of Mid-Atlantic Region of Alpha Kappa Alhpa Sorority, 1981. **BUSINESS ADDRESS:** Hampton Inst, Hampton, VA 23668.

PLEASANTS, CHARLES WRENN
Educational administrator. **PERSONAL:** Born Feb 28, 1937, Newport News, VA; married Anna Hines Pleasants; children: Charles W Jr, Michael L, Linda Y. **EDUCATION:** Norfolk State Univ, BA 1961, MA 1973; The Coll of William and Mary, advanced study. **CAREER:** Carver HS, instr 1962-69; VA Sch for Deaf & Blind, dir student serv 1969-73; Norfolk State Univ, dir intensive recruitment 1978-81, alumni dir 1973-81, asst dir admissions 1981-84, assoc dir admissions 1984-. **ORGANIZATIONS:** Past dist treas Cncl for Advancement & Support of Educ 1981-83; mem Natl Educ Assn; mem Natl Assn of Coll Admiss Couns; mem VA Assn of Coll Admiss Officers; pres Natl Alumni Assn Norfolk State Univ 1973; mem Omega Psi Phi Frat; mem Norfolk State Athletic Found. **HONORS/ACHIEVEMENTS:** Listed in Personalities of the South 1972, Outstanding Young Men of America 1972; Case III Southeastern Dist Chair Citation Southeastern Dist 1981; Outstanding Leadership and Serv Award Norfolk State Univ Natl Alumni Assn 1981; Cert of Merit Inter-Collegiate Press 1983. **HOME ADDRESS:** 4528 Boxford Rd, Virginia Beach, VA 23456.

PLEDGER, VERLINE S.
Educator. **PERSONAL:** Born May 11, 1927, Macon, GA; married Charles L Pledger; children: Charles III, Bever Lyne. **EDUCATION:** Morris Brown Coll, BS with Hon 1957. **CAREER:** Atlanta Bd Educ, teacher execp children (EMR) 1957-; Atlanta Girls Club, teacher 1946-48; Pilgrim Health & Life Ins Co, bookkeeper 1950-51. **ORGANIZATIONS:** Mem exec bd NAACP chmn voter reg Atlanta Br; mem AAE; NEA; CEC; past pres Atlanta Chap Las Amigas 1969-71; mem Wheat St Bapt Ch; secy Deacon's Wives' Cir; treas Adamsville Garden Club 1972-74; parliamentarian Atlanta Chap The Cont Socs Inc 1972-; vice pres Loyal Friends Birthday Club 1972-; mem AltantaChldrns Theatre Guild 1969-; mem 5 yr breast cancer screening proj. **HONORS/ACHIEVEMENTS:** Award of merit Gov of GA for Civic Work 1971; most dist exhib award Conclave Las Amigas 1970; merit outst work CF Harper 1965; yrly cert Voter Reg Fulton Co 1968-; asst chmn Procedure Book CF Harper 5 yrs, Blue Ribbon ea yr; chmn cultural prgm chmn Girl Scout Prgm. **BUSINESS ADDRESS:** 200 Casanova SE, Atlanta, GA 30315.

PLINTON, JAMES O., JR.
Airline executive. **PERSONAL:** Born Jul 22, 1914, Westfield, NJ; son of James O Plinton, Sr and Mary Williams Plinton; married Kathryn Hancock, May 14, 1952; children: James Norman, Kathryn Ann Breen. **EDUCATION:** Lincoln Univ, PA, BS, 1935; Univ of Newark, Newark NJ, received commercial pilots certificate and flight instructors rating, 1942. **CAREER:** Haitian-American Drycleaners and Laundry Inc, president, 1947-57; Quisqueya Airways Ltd, Port-au-Prince, Haiti, co-owner and chief pilot, 1947-49; Trans World Airlines (TWA), New York NY, exec asst to sr dir of mktg, 1957-71; Eastern Airlines Inc, Miami FL, corp vice pres, 1971-79; Metropolitan Fellowship of Churches, Miami, exec dir, 1980-; Tacolcy Economic Development Corp, Miami, chmn of bd, 1983-. **ORGANIZATIONS:** Charter member, Negro Airmen Intl, 1958-; dir, Caribbean Tourism Assn, 1972-79; pres, vice chmn of bd, comm chmn, YMCA of the United States, 1973-81; mem of bd dir, South Florida Jail Ministry, 1975-; trustee, Embry-Riddle Aeronautical Univ, 1976-; sec to bd of dir, P L Dodge Found, 1977-; trustee, South Florida Center for Theological Studies, 1985-; mem of advisory comm, Urban Coalition of Miami, 1985-; mem of bd of dir, Miami Museum of Science and Space Transit, 1988-. **HONORS/ACHIEVEMENTS:** First African-Amer to complete the Army Air Corps' Central Instructors School, 1944; first African-Amer to co-organize and operate a passenger/cargo airline outside the USA, Quisqueya Ltd, Port-au-Prince, Haiti, 1948; first African-Amer corp exec for major US airline, 1957; received doctor of laws degree, Fisk Univ; doctorate in aeronautical science, Embry Riddle Aeronautical Univ; National Order of Honour and National Order of Labor from three different presidents of Haiti; distinguished serv award, Lincoln Univ; Outstanding Man of the Year Award in intl mktg, Long Island Univ; award for outstanding achievement in aviation, Negro Airmen Intl; President Kenneth David Kaunda Award for Humanism; CHIEF Award, Assn of Pres of Ind Coll and Univ of Florida, 1980; first of 15 Americans and first African-Amer to be elected to YMCA of the USA Natl Treasure body (Hall of Fame) out of 11 million members; numerous other honors. **MILITARY SERVICE:** US Army Air Corps, flight officer, 1944-46; Army Air Corps flight instructor at Central Instructors School, Tuskegee Institute, Tuskegee AL, 1944. **BUSINESS ADDRESS:** Chairman of the Board, Tacolcy Economic Development Corporation, 645 NW 62nd St, Miami, FL 33150.

PLUMMER, MATTHEW W., SR.
Attorney. **PERSONAL:** Born Apr 14, 1920, Bexar Co, TX; married Christine J; children: 4 Children. **EDUCATION:** Tuskegee Isnt, Trade Diploma 1939, BA 1947; TX So Univ, LLB 1951. **CAREER:** Atty, pvt prac. **ORGANIZATIONS:** Pres Tuskegee Civic Club 1945-46; 2nd pres of TCV; chmn TX Del to Nat Black Polit Conv; pres Harris Counc of Orgns 1962; fdr past pres Bronze Eagles Flying Club; past pres Houston Lawyers Assn; District Judge 133rd Court of Harris County. **HONORS/ACHIEVEMENTS:** Org 1st Flying Club Tuskegee forerunner of Aviation Airbase & Schs; org Tuskegee Br NAACP 1947; 1st class at TSU Law Sch; 1st Invstgtr Harris Co Dist Attys Ofc; org TX Counc of Voters; outst stdnt interested in Govt Affairs 1947. **MILITARY SERVICE:** AUS flight instr 1941-45; USAAF Res WW II. **BUSINESS ADDRESS:** Attorney at Law, Jefferson, Mims, Plummer, Rice, 2100 Travis St, Houston, TX 77002.

PLUMMER, MICHAEL JUSTIN
Nonprofit corporation developer, fiscal manager. **PERSONAL:** Born Apr 15, 1947, Cambridge, MA; son of Justin Plummer and Kathleen Plummer. **EDUCATION:** Trinity Coll, BA Religion 1970; Harvard Univ Grad Sch of Educ, MEd 1972; Brandeis Univ Florence Heller Sch, MMHS 1986; Boston College, Ph.d candidate, sociology. **CAREER:** Integrated Systems Information Serv Co, founder/principal 1986-; Independent Assoc of Minorities in Mgmt Inc, founder/pres 1987-; MA State Dept of Public Health, Family Health Serv Div, policy analyst; Aid to Incarcerated Mothers, Business Manager 1988-. **ORGANIZATIONS:** Chmn Proposal Review Comm 1983; bd mem Cambridge/Somerville MA Council for Children 1983-; co-founder/pres Independent Assoc of Minorities in Mgmt 1987-. **HONORS/ACHIEVEMENTS:** Lifetime certification from Commonwealth of MA as Teacher of Secondary Sch Social Studies; Certificate of Accomplishment MA Governor Dukakis 1986. **HOME ADDRESS:** 154 Fayerweather St, Cambridge, MA 02138.

PLUMMER, MILTON
Bank executive. **CAREER:** City National Bank of New Jersey, Newark NJ, chief executive. **BUSINESS ADDRESS:** City National Bank of New Jersey, 900 Brood, Newark, NJ 07102. *

PLUMMER, ORA B.
Educator. **PERSONAL:** Born May 25, 1940, Mexia, TX; daughter of Macie I Echols; children: Kimberly, Kevin, Cheryl. **EDUCATION:** Univ NM Coll Nursing, BS 1961; UCLA, MS 1966; Faculty Practitioner Nursing Course, 1973; Univ of Co, postgraduate; Training Coordinator Conf, 1988, 1989; Variety of continuing educ courses, 1973-89. **CAREER:** Staff Nurse, 1961-62, 1962-64, 1967-68; Staff Nurse & Relief Super, 1962-64; USPHS, nurse traineeship 1964-66; NM Coll Nursing Albuquerque, instructor 1968-69; Univ of CO School of Nursing, sr instructor 1971-74; Univ of CO School of Nursing, asst prof 1974-76; West Interstate Comm for Higher Educ, staff assoc III 1976-78; Garden Manor, dir of nursing service 1978-79; CO Dept of Health, nursing consultant 1979-; long term care process trainer 1986-; Educ Coordinator, Colorado Dept of Health, 1987-. **ORGANIZATIONS:** Mem, Amer & CO Nurses' Assn; Alpha Tau Delta; Phi Delta Kappa; CO Black Nurses Council; master ceremonies recruitment day; Black Educ Day Boulder 1971; NavyOrientation trip for educators & admins 1971; Air Force Orientation Trip 1971; faculty devel comm School of Nursing 1974-; mem Interdisciplinary AMSA Proj 1975-76; rsch The Effects of Nursing Reassurance on Patients Vocal Stress Levels 1976; coordinator Comm for Bacc Program postgraduate drug therapy for elderly; Minority Affairs Comm 1971-74; WICHE Project Faculty Devel to Meet Minority Group Needs 1971-73; coordinator & implementation pre-nursing program Univ of CO School of Nursing 1972; mem, Natl Black Nurses Assn 1976-; advisory bd of sickle Cell Anemia 1976-; advisory commttee mem State Institutional Child Abuse & Neglect 1983-89. **HONORS/ACHIEVEMENTS:** Feature story NM Alumnus Mag 1974; scholarships NM Med Soc Women's Aux 1960; co-author "A Demonstration Model for Patient Educ", "A Final Report" WICHE 1978; Keynote Speaker ID Nurses Assn Conv "Patient Educ-The Politics & The Nurse" 1979; Amer Business Women's Assn 1958-60; Confederated Art Club 1958-59; Authored, Long Term Care, Implications of Medical Practice, 1988; Final Report, Improvement of Rehabilitative Nursing Service to the Elderly in Long Term Care Facilities in Colorado, co-author, 1989.

PLUMPP, STERLING DOMINIC
Professor. **PERSONAL:** Born Jan 30, 1940, Clinton, MS; son of Cyrus H Plumpp and Mary Emmanuel; divorced; children: Harriet Nzinga. **EDUCATION:** Attended St Benedict's Coll, Atchison KS, 1960-62; Roosevelt Univ, Chicago IL, BA, 1966-68, further study, 1969-71. **CAREER:** US Postal Service, Chicago IL, distribution clerk, 1962-69; North Park Coll, Chicago, counselor, 1969-71; University of Illinois at Chicago, professor, 1971-89. **ORGANIZATIONS:** Mem 1980-89, Black Amer Literature Forum. **HONORS/ACHIEVEMENTS:** Illinois Arts Council Literary Awards, 1975, 1980, 1986; Carl Sandburg Literary Award for Poetry, 1983. **MILITARY SERVICE:** US Army, spec 4, 1964-65. **BUSINESS ADDRESS:** Associate Professor, Black Studies Program, University of Illinois at Chicago, Box 4348, Chicago, IL 60680.

POE, BOOKER
Physician. **PERSONAL:** Born Jul 09, 1936, Eustis, FL; son of Rev William Poe (deceased) and Janie Jackson Poe (deceased); married Gloria Reeves, Aug 15, 1959; children: Janita L, Brian D. **EDUCATION:** TN State U, (With Hnrs) BS 1953; McHarry Medl Coll, MD 1963. **CAREER:** Private Prctc, pediatrician. **ORGANIZATIONS:** Chrmn medl legs GA State Medl Assoc 1976; breakfast prog chmn Atlanta Medl Assoc 1970-76; chmn awds GA State Medl Assoc 1977; comm advisor MinDent/Physns GA 1980; pblc rels Atlanta Medl Assoc 1980-; chmn bd dir GA Medical Assoc 1973-; bd dir prec Morehouse Sch Med 1980-; ex brd Atlanta Branch NAACP 1982-; assoc clin prof of Peds GAUniv 1974-; leglt GA Am Acad Peds 1982-; mem of Chmn's Council Scholarship Fund, Morehouse School of Medicine 1987-; bd of dir/treasurer, Health 1st (HMO) 1979-89. **HONORS/ACHIEVEMENTS:** Young Physician of the Year Atlanta Med Assn 1974; listed in Who's Who in Atlanta 1978; listed in Personalities of the South 1979-80; listed in Directory of Disting Amers 1980; Physician of the Year Atlanta Med Assn 1980; Doctor of the Year GA House Rep 1980; Pres Awd GA Medl Assoc 1982; publ, "EPSDT and the Black Medical Community in Georgia" Natl Med Assoc Jrnl 1979, "Why Attend a Legislative Breakfast?" The Microscope Newsletter 1980; President's Awd GA State Med Assoc 1982,86; 25 years of Service Award, Atlanta Medical Assn 1989; President's Award, 25 years of service McHarry Medical Coll 1989. **MILITARY SERVICE:** USAF capt 1965-69. **HOME ADDRESS:** 3518 Lynfield Dr, Atlanta, GA 30311. **BUSINESS ADDRESS:** Pediatric Physician, Private Practice, 2600 Martin Luther King Jr Dr, Atlanta, GA 30311.

POELLNITZ, FRED DOUGLAS
Educational administrator. **PERSONAL:** Born Aug 03, 1944, Philadelphia, PA; married Stephanie Snead MD; children: Andrew, Michelle. **EDUCATION:** Univ of Pittsburgh, BSEE 1966; NY Univ, MSEE 1970; Harvard Univ, MBA 1972. **CAREER:** Bendix Corp, project engr 1967-70; Touche Ross & Co, consult 1972-76; Sorbus Inc, dir of acctg 1976-80; Smith Kline Beckman, asstmgr 1980-81; Meharry Medical Coll, vp. **ORGANIZATIONS:** Mem Alpha Phi Alpha Frat 1963-; bd of dir Electronic Typesetting Corp 1972-76; mem Natl Assoc of Accountants 1974-; mem Financial Exec Inst 1983-; bd of advisors TN State Univ Business School 1983-. **HONORS/ACHIEVEMENTS:** Cogme Fellow Harvard Univ 1970-72. **BUSINESS ADDRESS:** Vice Pres for Finance & Business, Meharry Medical College, 1005 D B Todd Blvd, Nashville, TN 37208.

POGUE, D. ERIC
Business executive. **PERSONAL:** Born Feb 12, 1949, Southampton, NY; married J Marie; children: Eric Spencer. **EDUCATION:** Heidelberg Coll, BS Psych 1970; Bowling Green State Univ, MA Personnel 1971. **CAREER:** Case Western Reserve Univ, asst dir acad support, 1971-72; Cleveland State Univ, staff devel trainer, 1972-76; Diamond Shamrock Corp, mgr human resources, 1976-82; Cuyahoga Comm Coll, adj prof 1978-79; Reichhold Chem Inc, White Plains NY, senior vice pres human resources, 1989; Philip Morris Co Inc, New York NY, vice pres personnel, 1989-. **ORGANIZATIONS:** Mem Amer Soc of Personnel Admin 1980-, Westchester Personnel Mgmt Assoc 1982-, Westchester/Ct Personnel Round Table 1983-; coord-annual dr United Way of Greater Cleveland 1982. **HONORS/ACHIEVEMENTS:** Outstanding Young Men of Amer Montgomery AL 1982. **BUSINESS ADDRESS:** Vice President of Personnel, Philip Morris Co Inc, 120 Park Ave, New York, NY 10017. *

POGUE, FRANK G.
Educator. **PERSONAL:** Born Nov 03, 1939, Mobile, AL; married Dorothy Dexter; children: Constance L. **EDUCATION:** Bishop Jr Coll, SD 1960; AL St U, BA 1961; Atlanta U, MA 1962;Univ of Pitsburgh, PhD 1971. **CAREER:** Dept African & Afro-Am Studies, StUniv NY at Albany, prof chmn vice pres for student affairs 1974-; Philander Smith Coll Little Rock, dean stdnts & chmn dept soc 1962-66; Chatham Coll Pittsburgh, asst prof soc & coord Afro-Am stud prgm 1969-71; Meharry Med Coll Nashville, sr rsrch asso 1971-73; DeptSoc SUNY-A, adjunct prof 1974-; SUNY Poverty Rsrch & Training Prgm, coord 1974-. **ORGANIZATIONS:** Mem Am Soc Assn; NE Soc Assn; Am Pub Hlth Assn; Assn Black Soc; Nat Assn Black Soc Wrkrs; Alpha Phi Alpha; life mem Alpha Phi Omega; NAACP; Urban Leag; Alpha Kappa Delta Soc Assn. **HONORS/ACHIEVEMENTS:** Alpha Kappa Mu Hon Soc Most Outst Yng Men of Am 1968-69; Who's Who in Coll Educ 1965-66; Intl Biog of Contmpry Achvmnt 1969-70; Men of Sci 1974-75; Man of Yr 1971, 72, 73; listed Notable Am 1976-77. **BUSINESS ADDRESS:** Vice Pres for Student Affairs, State University of New York, at Albany, 1400 Washington Ave, Albany, NY 12222.

POGUE, LESTER CLARENCE
Private consultant in education. **PERSONAL:** Born Apr 04, 1943, Marysville, CA; children: Paul, Karl, Alonzo, Lester Jr, Exavier. **CAREER:** Bridge the Gap EOPS Newsletter, dir & ed 1976-; EOPS Yuba Comm Coll, co-dir 1969-76; Yuba Co Probtn Dept, grp supr 1969-71; Sacramento City Coll, consult 1971-75. **ORGANIZATIONS:** Sec Parliamentarian treas vice pres CA Comm Coll Extended Oppor Prgm Assn 1971-; past mem Exofficio CA Comm Coll EOPS Adv Com 1975-76; mem Task Force1976-; pres Eval Training Inst 1976; consult mem reg coord CA Prsnl Guid Assn; Black Caucus 1972-; pnlst CA Comm Colls Chief Stdnt Prsnl Serv Assn1976; chmn spkr Martin Luther King Jr Day Com 1976; mem consult Western Reg Counc on Black Am Afrs 1973-; chmn Yuba Co Minrty Recruitmnt Adv Com 1975-; consult Tahoe Nat Forest Minority Awareness Prgm 1975; reader CA St Schlrshp & Loan Commn 1975-; moderator EDPA Wrkshp on Career Educ 1975; mem NoCA Rural Legal Asst Adv Bd 1974-75; spkr Career Plng & Job Oppor Wrkshp Chaffey Coll 1975; mem Proj Alph Adv Com 1975-; mem CA Comm Coll Career Educ Task Force 1974-75; mem CA Comm Coll Ad Hoc Com to State EOPS Adv Bd 1974-75; consult Task Force on Tutorial & Peer Couns Serv 1974; pres CCCEOPSA; mem Sacramento Area Plng Commn Com on Transp 1975-77; presenter CCCEOPSA Annual Conf 1977-80. **HONORS/ACHIEVEMENTS:** Apprctn plaque Yuba Coll Mecha 1976; outst serv CCCEOPSA 1975-76; cert of rec CCCEOPSA Stdnt Segment 1976; outst yng men Nat Jr C of C 1977; pres Plaque & Past Pres Plaque CCCEOPSA 1977-78; outst serv award CCCEOPSA 1978. **MILITARY SERVICE:** USAF sgt 1961-69. **BUSINESS ADDRESS:** Bridge the Gap c/o Chancellor', 1238 S Ave, Sacramento, CA 95814.

POGUE, RICHARD JAMES
Civil service. **PERSONAL:** Born May 25, 1943, Cortelyou, AL; married Birdie Raine; children: Tiffany Denise, Karen Lanise. **EDUCATION:** Alabama Univ, BS (High Honors) 1971; Pepperdine Univ, attended 1977. **CAREER:** Robins Air Force Base, personnel mgmt specialist 1971-73; Air Force Reserves, personnel mgmt specialist 1973-75; Keesler Air Force Base, chief employment & staffing 1975-76; Randolph Air Force Base, personnel mgmt specialist 1976-79; Headquarters USAF Pentagon Washington DC, deputy eeo 1979-80; Robins AFB GA, equaloppor/affirmative action officer 1980-86, chief employee devel & training section 1986-. **ORGANIZATIONS:** Mem NAACP 1980-; pres K&R Shoes Inc 1983-85; pres Intl Personnel Mgmt Assoc 1984-85; mem Better Mgmt Assoc 1985-; bd of career advisors Atlanta Univ 1986; historian Alpha Phi Alpha Frat Inc 1986-87; bd dirs Middle Georgia Educ Talent Search 1986-; bd dirs Air Force Assoc 1986-. **HONORS/ACHIEVEMENTS:** Outstanding Young Men of Amer Awd 1971; Key to the City of New Orleans 1975; Affirmative Action of the Year Robins AFB 1981. **MILITARY SERVICE:** USN third class petty officer 1963-67; Natl Defense. **HOME ADDRESS:** 139 Stewart Dr, Warner Robins AFB, GA 31093. **BUSINESS ADDRESS:** Chief, Employee Dev & Training, Robins Air Force Base GA, 2853 ABG/DPCT, Civilian Personnel, Warner Robins AFB, GA 31098.

POINDEXTER, GAMMIEL GRAY
Attorney. **PERSONAL:** Born Sep 22, 1944, Baton Rouge, LA; married Geral G; children: John LR, Christopher R. **EDUCATION:** Univ of IN, AB Government 1965; LA State Univ, JD 1969. **CAREER:** Office of Solicitor US Dept of Labor, staff attorney 1968-70; Richmond Legal Aid Soc, dept dir 1971-73; Poindexter & Poindexter, partner 1973-; Surry Co VA, commonwealth's atty 1976-. **ORGANIZATIONS:** Past pres Old Dominion Bar Assn 1980-82; mem Bd of Visitors Old Dominion Univ 1982-; chmn Surry Co Democratic Party 1983-; bd of dirs VA Assn of Black Elected Officers. **BUSINESS ADDRESS:** Commonwealth Attorney, Surry Co, PO Box 766, Surry, VA 23883.

POINDEXTER, HILDRUS A.
Educator. **PERSONAL:** Born May 10, 1901, Memphis; married Ruth V Grier; children: Patchechole Barbara. **EDUCATION:** Lincoln U, AB cum laude 1924; Dartmouth Harvard, MD 1929; ColumbiaUnivUniv of PR, AM 1930; PhD 1932; MSPH 1937; Lincoln U, Hon DSc 1946; Dartmouth, 1956; Howard U, 1961. **CAREER:** HowardUniv Coll of Med, prof comm hlth; US Pub Hlth Svc, sr surg med dir 1947-65; Howard U, prof microbio comm hlth 1931-43; US Foreign AidMission in Liberia, French Endochina, Surinam, Iraq, Jamaica, Sierra Leone, Nigeria, chief, hlth & sanitation div. **ORGANIZATIONS:** Mem bd trustees Lincoln U;Univ of NSUKKA of Nigeria; med dir US Pub Hlth Svc; dir Nat Finan & Invest Corp of DC; chmn Int Hlth Section of APHA. **HONORS/ACHIEVEMENTS:** Recip Bronze Star; 2 Commndtn Medals; 4 Battle Stars; Knight Commdr of Liberia; listed in Who's Who in Am; Nat Civil Serv Leag Award; Browning Apha Award; AID PHS Dist Serv Award. **MILITARY SERVICE:** AUS lt col 1943-47. **BUSINESS ADDRESS:** Howard Univ Coll of Medicine, 520 W St NW, Washington, DC 20059.

POINDEXTER, MALCOLM P.
Newscaster, commentator. **PERSONAL:** Born Apr 03, 1925, Philadelphia, PA; son of Malcolm Poindexter and Alda Poindexter; married Lottie; children: David, Lynne E Poindexter-Garrett, Malcolm III. **EDUCATION:** Several private and military schools, 1943-47; Temple Univ, 1953. **CAREER:** The Philadelphia Tribune, reporter/columnist/business mgr/controller 1949-60; The Evening Bulletin, reporter 1960-65; KYW-TV, editorial spokesman/reporter/producer/program host 1965-. **ORGANIZATIONS:** Manager/consultant Opera North, Inc 1977-; honorary bd chmn Norris Square Neighborhood Project 1984-; Phila Press Assn Bd; advisory council, Scleroderma Assn of Delaware Valley. **HONORS/ACHIEVEMENTS:** Received more than 200 awards for professional and civic achievement. **MILITARY SERVICE:** AUS T-Sgt served 4 years. **BUSINESS ADDRESS:** Editorial Spokesman, KYW-TV, Independence Mall East, Philadelphia, PA 19106.

POINDEXTER, ROBERT L.
Educator. **PERSONAL:** Born Mar 12, 1912, Philadelphia, PA; married Josephine. **EDUCATION:** Temple U, BSE 1942, ME 1944, PdM 1972. **CAREER:** Educator, Elem Prin; Jr HS Prin; Dist Supr; Dep Supr; Exec Dep Supr. **ORGANIZATIONS:** Vp Philadelphia Tchrs Credit Union; mem Philadelphia Bicentennial Comm; YMCA; Exec Bd; BSA; March of Dimes; McKee Schlrshp Com; bd trustees Messiah Coll.

POINDEXTER, ZEB F.
Dentist. **PERSONAL:** Born Apr 05, 1929, Fort Worth; married Ruby Revis; children: Zeb, Merlene (Gilbert), Patricia. **EDUCATION:** Wiley Coll, BS 1945; TX So U, MS 1952;Univ of TX Dental Br, DS 1956. **CAREER:** Gulf St Dental Assn, pres 1966-67; Nat Dental Assn, local conv chmn 1968; Univ of TX, asso prof of Comm dentistry 1973, dentist, Dental Br. **ORGANIZATIONS:** Mem NAACP; bd mem Negro Coll; treas Charles A George Dental Soc; bd mem Baker-Jones Invest Co; Houston Dist Dental Soc; Nat Dental Assn; mem Alpha Phi Alpha Frat 1947; YMCA Century Club 12 yrs; Eldorado Soc Club; Gulf St Dental Assn; Am Dental Assn; trustee NDA 1973; del Nda 1971 & 73; del TX Dental Assn 1968. **HONORS/ACHIEVEMENTS:** YMCA Century Man 10 yrs 1972; elected to OKUniv Hon Soc Zeb F Poindexter Chap Stdnt Nat Dental Assn 1980; 1st black to finishUniv of TX as Dentist 1956. **MILITARY SERVICE:** USAF capt. **BUSINESS ADDRESS:** 7703 Cullen Blvd, Houston, TX 77051.

POINSETT, ALEXANDER C.
Journalist. **PERSONAL:** Born Jan 27, 1926, Chicago, IL; son of Alexander A Poinsett (deceased) and Ardele Leola Prindle Poinsett; married Norma Ruth Miller, Aug 24; children: Pierrette M, Alexis Pierre. **EDUCATION:** Univ IL, BS (Journlism) 1952, MA (Phlsphy) 1953; Univ Chicago, completed all work execpt Thesis for MA in Lbry Sci 1956. **CAREER:** Johnson Publ Co, contributing editor 1959-, sr staff edt 1956-82; Grumman Corp, mgr edtl serv 1982-83; Johnson Prod Co, mgr corp commu 1983-85; The Ford Found, cons. **ORGANIZATIONS:** Const US Off Ed; spch wrtr Mayor Richard G Hatcher (Gary IN) 1969-75; guest lectr More Then 50 US Coll/U 1969-81; past pres, Chicago Prairie Tennis Club. **HONORS/ACHIEVEMENTS:** Atr Blk Power Gary Style 1970; PUSH awd Optn PUSH 1977; outstdng person awdUniv IL Blk Alumni Assn 1980; CEBA awd CEBA 1982; J C Penney Award, Univ of Missouri 1967; Author of "Black Power Gary Style", 1970. **MILITARY SERVICE:** US Navy, yeoman 3rd class 1944-1947. **HOME ADDRESS:** 8532 S Wabash Ave, Chicago, IL 60619.

POINTER, NOEL
Violinist. **PERSONAL:** Born 1956; children: Richard. **CAREER:** Concert Violinist; Sym of New World; Carnegie Recital Hall for Newport Jazz Fest; Chicago Chamber Orch; Detroit Sym; many others. **BUSINESS ADDRESS:** c/o William Morris Agency, 1350 Avenue of the Americas, New York, NY 10019.

POINTER, RICHARD H.
Scientist/educator. **PERSONAL:** Born Jun 04, 1944, Covington, GA; son of H B Pointer and Sarah Eunice Weaver Pointer; married Rosie Lee Davis, Apr 30, 1966; children: Richard Hamilton Jr., Rawlinson Lee, Robert Lewis. **EDUCATION:** Morehouse Atlanta Ga, BS 1968; Brown U, ScM 1973; Brown Univ Providence RI, PhD 1975. **CAREER:** Research assoc Vanderbilt Univ 1975-77; research biochemist Massachusetts General Hosp 1977-78; Harvard Univ Instructor 1977-80; assistant professor Howard Univ 1980-87; assoc professor Howard Univ 1987-. **ORGANIZATIONS:** Mem Sigma Xi 1973; Am Assn Advancement Sci 1972-; rec sec exec bd PACE 1973-74; research papers pub biochem & pharmacol jrnls; American Physiological Society 1975-; American Diabetes Assn 1979-; Adult Leader Boy Scouts of America 1979-; science fair judge Southern MD School Area 1988-; bd of dir P.G. County Chapter American Diabetes Assn 1988-89; vice pres P.G. County Chapter American Diabetes Assn 1989-90. **HONORS/ACHIEVEMENTS:** Publications in Biochemical Journals 1973-; research grants from NSF and NIH 1976-; research fellow Howard Hughes Medical Institute 1978-80; Commissioners Award Boy Scouts of America 1988. **BUSINESS ADDRESS:** Assistant Professor of Biochemistry, Howard University College of Medicine, 520 W St, NW, Pre-Clinical Bldg, Washington, DC 20059.

POITIER, SIDNEY
Actor, director, producer. **PERSONAL:** Born Feb 20, 1927, Miami, FL; married Joanna Shimkus; children: Beverly, Pamela, Sherri, Gina, Anika, Sydney. **CAREER:** Acted & starred in over 38 motion pictures; made film debut in "No Way Out" 1950; other include "Cry the Beloved Country" 1952, "Go Man Go" 1954; "Blackboard Jungle" 1956; "Edge of the City" 1957; "Something of Value" 1957; "Porgy & Bess" 1959; directed and starred in "Buck & the Preacher", "A Warm December", "Uptown Saturday Night", "Let's Do it Again", "A Piece of the Action" 1977; starred in Broadway production of "Raisin in the Sun" 1959; directed Richard Pryor & Gene Wilder in "Stir Crazy" 1980; directed Gene Wilder & Gilda Radner in "Hanky Panky" 1982; directed youth musical "Fast Forward" 1985; acted in "Little Nikita" 1987;"In the Hall of the Mountain King" 1987; "Hard Knox" 1987. **HONORS/ACHIEVEMENTS:** First black actor nominated for Academy Award for "The Defiant Ones"; first Black actor to record footprints in concrete of Grauman's Chinese Theater 1967; first black actor to win an Oscar "Lilies of the Field" 1963; autobiography published "This Life" by Alfred Knopf Pubs 1980. **MILITARY SERVICE:** AUS WWII. **BUSINESS ADDRESS:** c/o Verdon Productions Ltd, 9350 Wilshire Blvd, Beverly Hills, CA 90212.

POLITE, CARLENE HATCHER
Dancer. **PERSONAL:** Born Aug 28, 1932, Detroit, MI. **EDUCATION:** Sarah Lawrence Coll NY, attended; Martha Graham School of Contemporary Dance, attended. **CAREER:** Concert Dance Theatre of NYC, dancer 1955-59; Vanguard Playhouse, dancer 1960-62; The King & I, The Boy Friend, Dark of the Moon, dancer 1963; Wayne State Univ, visiting instructor; SUNY Buffalo, assoc prof, English. **ORGANIZATIONS:** Guest instr Detroit YWCA 1960-62; org No Negro Leadership Conf; mem Detroit Council for Human Rights. **HONORS/ACHIEVEMENTS:** Author The Flagellants, Sister X & The Victims of Foul Play 1975. **BUSINESS ADDRESS:** Farrar, Straus & Giroux, Publicity Department, 19 Union Square West, New York, NY 10003.

POLITE, CRAIG K.
Educator, psychologist. **PERSONAL:** Born Aug 29, 1947, New York, NY; married Cheryl Yvonne Bradford; children: Kimberly L, Craig K II, Adam. **EDUCATION:** Univ of Toledo, BA 1969; Michigan State Univ, MA 1971, PhD 1972; NY Univ, Certificate, psychoanalysis 1983. **CAREER:** Michigan State Univ, research asst center urban affairs 1970-72; Economic Opportunity Planning Assn of Greater Toledo, employee 1968-69; industrial & clinical psychologist; State Univ of NY at Stony Brook, asst prof 1972-76; Private Practice, clinical psychologist 1976-; Midtown Psychological Serv Inc, president. **ORGANIZATIONS:** Teaching fellow Michigan State Univ 1971-72; consultant School Dental Med SUNY Stonybrook 1974-; Metro Comm Mental Health Center NY 1974-; New York City Head Start 1973; mem Amer Psychology Assn; Assn of Black Psychologists; Omega Psi Phi. **HONORS/ACHIEVEMENTS:** Dean's List Univ Toledo 1968. **MILITARY SERVICE:** AUS capt 1969-77. **BUSINESS ADDRESS:** President, Midtown Psychol Serv Inc, 340 East 52nd St Ste 4C, New York, NY 10022.

POLITE, MARIE ANN
Educator. **PERSONAL:** Born Jan 26, 1954, Savannah, GA; daughter of Lucius Levett, Sr and Leola Denegal Levett; married Alan Polite, Sep 01, 1972; children: Sharmona, Nakisha. **EDUCATION:** Armstrong State Coll, BS (Cum Laude) 1976; GA Southern Coll, MEd 1980, MPA 1987; Georgia Southern Coll Statesboro GA EdS 1989. **CAREER:** MAP to Success, consultant 1985-; Georgia Employers Assoc, consultant 1986; Savannah-Chatham Bd of Educ, learning disabilities specialist 1976-; Savannah-Chatham Bd of Educ, Bartlett Middle School, Assistant Principal 1988-. **ORGANIZATIONS:** Bd of dirs Savannah Police Athletic League 1975-; mem Phi Delta Kappa, Chapter 1219 1982-; state vice pres GA Federation of Teachers 1983-87; Deputy Vote Registrar 1984-85; bd of dirs GA HEAT Prog 1984-85; pres MAP to Success Consulting Agency 1985-; dist vice dir 1986-87; mem Zonta Club of Savannah 1986-; dist dir 1987-88 GA Fed of Business & Professional Women; bd of commissioners Savannah Housing Auth 1987-92; mem, Education's Leadership Georgia, 1988-89; Site Visitor, US Dept of Educ Secondary School's Recognition Program, 1989. **HONORS/ACHIEVEMENTS:** Outstanding Young Women of Amer 1980; Outstanding Serv Savannah Police Dept 1982; Outstanding Serv Port City BPW Inc 1984,86; GA Regents Scholarship GA Southern Coll 1985-86; Georgia Regent's Scholarship, GA Southern Coll, 1989; Pi Alpha ALpha Honor Society, GA Southern Coll, 1989; participant/selected to Harvard Univ Graduate School's Principalship Seminar, 1989. **HOME ADDRESS:** 10446 Gray Fox Way, Savannah, GA 31406. **BUSINESS ADDRESS:** Assistant Principal, Savannah-Chatham Bd of Educ, 207 W Montgomery Crossroad Bartlett Middle School, Savannah, GA 31406.

POLITE, THERON JEROME
Elected official, private investigator. **PERSONAL:** Born Feb 24, 1930, Tampa, FL; divorced; children: Jimmy Lee, Celinda Joyce West, Kenneth Jerome. **EDUCATION:** Monterey Peninsula Coll, AS 1972; Golden Gate Univ, BA 1976, MPA 1978; CA Comm Coll, Police Sci 1979, Public Serv & Admin 1983. **CAREER:** Jerome Consistory #328 Ancient & Accepted Scottish Rite of Free Masonary, founder & 1st commanding-in-chief 1975-; Jeremiah Chap #19 Royal Arch Mason, founder & 1st excellent high priest 1976-; Attica Guild #7 Heroines of Templars Crusade, founder & 1st past royal adv 1976-; Attica #16 Pacific Prince Hall Grand Commandery Knights Templar, founder & 1st past grand eminent comm 1977-; Polites Investigation Agency, owner, pres, mgr 1981-; City of Seaside, councilman. **ORGANIZATIONS:** Mayor pro tem City of Seaside 1982; Retired Men's Social Club 1970-; life mem Golden Heritage Mem NAACP 1976-, Amer Legion #591 1977-; pres Comm Devel Corp 1980-; mem Chamber of Commerce Seaside 1981-; bd mem Monterey Reg Water Pollution Control Agency 1982-, Canyon Del Rey Water Shad 1984-; vice chairperson Econ Devel Task Force City of Seaside 1984-, Redevel Agency of the City of Seaside 1984-; life mem Non-Commissioned Officers Assoc of USA 1984-. **HONORS/ACHIEVEMENTS:** 1st Black Bailiff Deputy Sheriff Monterey Cty Sheriff's Dept 1971-83; Disting Noble Awd for Outstanding Contrib to the Spirit & Reclaiming Mem for the Temple & the Imperial Council AEAONMS 1975-78; Citizen of the Year Omega Psi Phi 1978-82; Mr NAACP for the Monterey-Seaside Branch NAACP 1981; Listed in Who's Who in CA 1985-86. **MILITARY SERVICE:** AUS 1st sgt E-8 24 yrs; Bronze Star Medal w/1 OLC, Commendation Medal w/1 OLC, Natl Defense Serv Medal w/1 OLC, Amer Defense Medal, UN Serv Medal. **BUSINESS ADDRESS:** Councilman, City of Seaside, 1630 Marietta St, Seaside, CA 93955.

POLK, CHARLES CARRINGTON
Retired physician. **PERSONAL:** Born Apr 12, 1892, Barrington, NJ; married Olive (deceased); children: Carolyn, Gene-Ann, Barbara, Josephine. **EDUCATION:** Howard Univ, AB 1917, MD 1921; Rutgers Univ, attended; Seton Hall Univ, attended; Univ of PA, attended. **CAREER:** Retired physician. **ORGANIZATIONS:** Established Roselle-Linden Negro Health Comm 1934, Baby Keep Well Clinic 1934, Social Disease Clinic 1939; past pres, sec NJ Med Soc; mem AMA, Natl Med Soc, Howard Alumni House; org BSA Troup 1933, Urban League Eastern Union Co, Roselle NAACP, Alpha Phi Alpha, Chi Delta Mu, Sigma Pi Phi, Howard Univ Alumni Assn, Comm Chest of Eastern Union Co. **HONORS/ACHIEVEMENTS:** Citation, Rahway Hospital Devel Bd 1954; General Practitioner of the Year NJ Med Soc 1959; Good Citizen Award NJ Herald News 1959; Citizen Award B'Nai B'rith of Linden 1968; 50 Yr Awards NJ Med Soc; Howard Univ Med Alumni 1971; Outstanding Serv Award Roselle Bd Health 1971; Roselle NAACP Citizen of the Year 1986. **MILITARY SERVICE:** AUS 1917-18.

POLK, DON
Director. **PERSONAL:** Born Feb 05, 1955, Los Angeles, CA; married Pamela Lopes; children: Tiffany Marie, Brandon Elliot. **EDUCATION:** Boston Univ, BS, BA 1973-77. **CAREER:** Ipswich River Watershed Assoc, asst editor 1976; Sierra Club, asst editor 1977; Roxbury MA Headstart, teacher 1977-78; Bruce Walker Campaign, mgr 1979; Emmanuel Romar Companies, dir of sales. **ORGANIZATIONS:** Consultant Canadian Club, Fashion Across Amer; comm serv AYC.

POLK, EUGENE STEVEN, SR.
Professional/personnel administrator. **PERSONAL:** Born Oct 24, 1939, Detroit, MI; son of Wardell and Josephine; married Barbara Jean Edwards; children: Camille, Kent, Eugene Jr, Chris. **EDUCATION:** Shaw Coll at Detroit, BA 1971. **CAREER:** Ford Motor Co, employment coord 1966-69; Pontiac General Hosp, asst dir personnel 1970-74; Comprehensive Hlth Serv of Detroit, personnel dir 1975-79; Kelly Services Inc, mgr headquarters personnel 1980-87; Mazda Manufacturing, Proffessional, Personnel Administrator 1987-. **ORGANIZATIONS:** Bd mem Metro Detroit Youth Foundation 1983-87; polemarch Detroit Alumni Chap Kappa Alpha Psi Frat 1984-88; bd mem Northside Family YMCA 1985-88; pres Industrial Relations Assoc of Detroit 1985-86; chmn bd of dir South Oakland Family YMCA 1986-87; bd mem Don Bosco Hall 1986-89; mem NAACP, Detroit Urban League. **HONORS/ACHIEVEMENTS:** Minority Achiever Kelly Serv Inc Metro Detroit YMCA 1987. **BUSINESS ADDRESS:** Professional, Personnel Administrator, Mazda Manufacturing, MMUC - ADM 106, 1 Mazda Drive, Flat Rock, MI 48134.

POLK, GENE-ANN (GENE-ANN P. HORNE)
Physician. **PERSONAL:** Born Oct 03, 1926, Roselle, NJ; daughter of Charles C Polk, MD and Olive Bond Polk; married Edwin C Horne, DDS, Aug 23, 1952; children: Carol Anne Horne Penn, Edwin Christian Horne. **EDUCATION:** Oberlin Coll, BA 1948; Wmn's Medl Coll PA, MD 1952; Columbia U, MPH 1968. **CAREER:** Englewood NJ, prv prac 1959-68; Harlem Hosp Ctr/Columbia U, chief pedt clinic 1968-75, dir Peds (Acting) 1975-77; Columbia Univ/Harlem Hosp Center, dir of Ambulator Care Services 1977-1988; Columbia Univ/Harlem Hosp Center Dept of Pediatrics Attending Phsician 1988-. **ORGANIZATIONS:** Fellow American Bd of Medical Examiners 1952; Fellow American Academy of Pediatrics 1958; Schl phys City Englewood, NJ 1960-67; Basileus Alpha Kappa Alpha Iota Episilon Omega 1971-73; bd mem Grtr Harlem Nrsng Hme Chap 1982-84; area rep United Negro Coll Fund. **BUSINESS ADDRESS:** Dir of Ambulatory Care, Columbia U/Harlem Hosp Ctr, 506 Lenox Ave, New York, NY 10037.

POLK, GEORGE DOUGLAS
Business executive. **PERSONAL:** Born Oct 06, 1919, St Louis, MO; married Mary Attyberry; children: Mary Olivia MD. **EDUCATION:** LincolnUniv Of MO, BA Mod Lang 1940; St LouisUniv Inst Tech, BSEE 1949;; St LouisUniv Grad Schl, MS in Eng Res 1960. **CAREER:** UniDynamics St Louis, sr elec engr 1953-, mgr prod supt. **ORGANIZATIONS:** Brd mem Ctl Inst Deaf St Louis MO 1984-; past polemarch St Louis Alumni Kappa Alpha Psi 1958-60; past kpr recds and exchequer mdl western prov KappaAlpha Psi 1955-67. **MILITARY SERVICE:** USN radarman 2/c 1943-45. **HOME ADDRESS:** 5160 Norwood Ct, St Louis, MO 63115. **BUSINESS ADDRESS:** Manager of Product Support, UniDynamics St Louis, 472 Paul Ave, 472 Paul Ave, Ferguson, MO 63135.

POLK, LORNA MARIE
Educational administrator. **PERSONAL:** Born Aug 03, 1948, St Louis, MO; daughter of Ora Polk and Louise Polk. **EDUCATION:** Fisk Univ Nashville TN BA Psychology 1968; George Washington Univ DC MAE Human Resource Developement 1973; Catholic Univ of Amer EdD Educational Admin 1982. **CAREER:** US Dept of Educ, ed prog spec, Ed Personnel Development 1968-69; Career Opp Program 1969-73; Postsecondary Ed 1973-75; Migrant Education 1975-83; White House Initiative on Historically Black Coll & Univ, educational administrator 1983-. **ORGANIZATIONS:** Mem American Assoc of Public Admin; mem American Soc of Prof and Exec Women; mem Phi Delta Kappa; mem Council of 100; mem Natl Alliance of Black Sch Administrators; mem Blacks in Govt; mem Ed Joint Dissemination Review Panel, Educ, 1981-88; vice pres for Personnel & Director of Friends of Flair, Flair Promotions Inc 1986-87; vice pres Southwest DC Neighborhood Assembly 1986-87; vice pres River Park Members Council 1986-87. **HONORS/ACHIEVEMENTS:** Outstanding Young Women of Amer 1981; published "The Effects of Migrant Educ Centers in the State of FL" 1981; article presented in the Natl Society of Black Engineers Journal March Commemorative Issues 1986-87; Council of 100 Outstanding Leadership Award 1989. **HOME ADDRESS:** 1306 4th St, SW, Washington, DC 20024.

POLK, RICHARD A.
Association executive. **PERSONAL:** Born Jun 04, 1936, Moss Point, MS; married Mary Dennis; children: Clay, Phyllis, Beverly, Richard. **EDUCATION:** Alcorn StUniv Lorman MS, BS 1957; TN A&IUniv Nashville, MS 1965. **CAREER:** Fed Equal Empl Opport Comm, invstgtn supr; Newton & Carthage MS, tchr, ath coach 1957-66; STAR Inc, 1966-70; Mound Bayou Comm Hosp, dir 1970; Hosp & Hlth Ctr, dir 1972. **ORGANIZATIONS:** Mem NAACP; Jackson Urban Leag 1968-70; STAR Inc 1971-; Delta Ministry 1975-; S Legal Rights Corp 1975-; Leake Co Voters Leag 1975-; Delta Found Greenville MS 1975-; MS Cncl Hum Rels 1970; MS ACLU 1974; MS Cath Found 1975; pres Parish Cnsl St Anne Cath Ch Carthage MS; MS Cath Blue Ribbon Com to make Cath Ch more relevant to needs of Blacks & other minorities. **HONORS/ACHIEVEMENTS:** Applicant for opertnl rights for a Jackson MS TV sta OEO Award 1969; MS Inst of Politics Fellow 1971; Personalities of S 1974. **BUSINESS ADDRESS:** 203 W Capitol St, 203 Bldg, Jackson, MS 39201.

POLK, ROBERT L.
Clergyman, educational administrator. **PERSONAL:** Born May 08, 1928, Chicago, IL; son of Tillman Polk and Lillie Bell Polk; divorced; children: George R. **EDUCATION:** Doane Coll, BA 1952; Hartford Theol Sem, MDiv 1955; Doane Coll, Hon Dr of Div 1971; Huston-Tillotson, Hon Dr of Div 1984. **CAREER:** 1st Congregational Church Berthold ND, pastor 1955-57; YMCA Minot ND, youth prog coord 1957-60; Riverside Church, minister to youth 1960-66; Dillard Univ New Orleans, dean of chapel & dean of students 1966-68; Riverside Church, minister of urban affairs 1969-76; Edwin Gould Serv for Children, exec dir 1976-80; Council of Churches City of NY, exec dir, 1980-88; City Coll of New York, City Univ of New York, acting vice pres External Relations & Community Affairs, 1988-. **ORGANIZATIONS:** Chmn CUNY Constr Fund; Mayor's Comm of Religious Leaders, Assoc Black Charities, Hole-in-the-Wall-Gang Camp Inc; New York City Bd of Educ, Capital Task Force on Construction & Renovation of Public Schools; New York State Dept of Educ Interfaith Educ Advisory Council to the Commr of Educ; Governor's Comm on Scholastic Achievement; Health Watch Advisory Bd. **HONORS/ACHIEVEMENTS:** Distinguished Service Award, Black Christian Caucus Riverside Church 1983; Sam Levinson Memorial Award, Jewish Community Relations Council, New York City 1984. **BUSINESS ADDRESS:** Acting Vice Pres, External Relations and Community Affairs, City Coll of New York, 138th St & Convent Ave, A-2050, New York, NY 10031.

POLK, RON LAMONT
Entrepreneur. **PERSONAL:** Born Feb 05, 1955, Los Angeles, CA; married Portia M; children: Ron L II. **EDUCATION:** Attended, Cal-State San Bernardino 1972-74; UCLA, BS 1976. **CAREER:** Mayor Holcom, advisor 1973-74; Various Non-Profit Orgs, speaker. **BUSINESS ADDRESS:** General Partner, 110 E 9th St, Ste B522, Los Angeles, CA 90079.

POLK, WILLIAM C.
Educator. **PERSONAL:** Born Aug 02, 1935, Philadelphia; married Aundria Willis; children: Catherine Collette, William David. **EDUCATION:** Westchester St Coll, BS 1958; Columbia U, MA 1961; PA St U, DEd 1970. **CAREER:** Neshaminy Sch Dist, tchr 1958-68; PA St U, grad asst 1968-70; asso prof; Elippery Rock St Coll, prof ed 1970-. **ORGANIZATIONS:** Mem Nat Cncl for Soc Studies; coms for Tchr Certifications, & Rural Ed; sec Mdwstrn PA Cncl for Soc Studies 1973-; guest lectr Intrntl Studies Inst, Westminster Coll 1974-75; consult Commodore Perry Schs 1976; mem Nat Geographic Soc; mem Alpha Tau Chpt; Phi Delta Kappa 1968-; Rho Chap Alpha PhiAlpha; bd dirs EL Cunningham Comm Ctr 1963-70; faculty sponsor Black Action Soc, Slippery Rock St Coll 1972, 1975-77. **HONORS/ACHIEVEMENTS:** Nat Sci Found Grant 1966; Outstndng Eductgor 1972. **BUSINESS ADDRESS:** Educ Bldg, Slippery Rock State Coll, Slippery Rock, PA 16057.

POLLARD, ALTON BROOKS, III
Educator. **PERSONAL:** Born May 05, 1956, St Paul, MN; son of Alton B. Pollard, Jr and Lena L Pollard; married Jessica Bryant; children: Alton Brooks IV, Asha Elise. **EDUCATION:** Fisk Univ, BA 1978; Harvard Univ Divinity School, MDiv 1981; Duke Univ, PhD 1987. **CAREER:** John St Baptist Church, pastor 1979-82; Clark Univ, dir 1981-82; New Red Mountain Baptist Church, pastor 1984-86; St Olaf Coll, asst prof 1987-88; Wake Forest Univ, asst prof 1988-. **ORGANIZATIONS:** Mem Soc for the Scientific Study of Religion 1984-, Assoc for the Sociology of Religion 1985-; mem (clergy) Amer Baptist Convention; mem NAACP, The Visions Foundation, Amer Acad of Religion 1987; Religious Research Assn 1988-. **HONORS/ACHIEVEMENTS:** Thomas J Watson Fellowship Fisk Univ 1978; Fund for Theological Educ Fellowships Princeton NJ 1978-81, 1983-86; Andrew Mellon Fellowship Duke Univ 1986-87;article "Religion, Rock, & Eroticism," The Journal of Black Sacred Music 1987; "The Last Soul Singer in Amer," The Journal of Black Sacred Music 1989; review of "The Color of God" and "Black Theology in Dialogue," Perspectives in Religious Studies 1989. **HOME ADDRESS:** 2026 Storm Canyon Rd, Winston-Salem, NC 27106. **BUSINESS ADDRESS:** Assistant Professor of Religion, Wake Forest Univ, Dept of Religion, Box 7212, Winston-Salem, NC 27109.

POLLARD, DIANE S.
Educator. **PERSONAL:** Born Oct 31, 1944, Richmond, VA; daughter of Elric Stewart and Clara Stewart; married Scott; children: Amina, Almasi. **EDUCATION:** Wellesley Coll, BA 1966; Univ of Chicago, MA 1967, PhD 1972. **CAREER:** Roosevelt Univ, instructor 1969-72; Univ of WI, asst prof 1972-76, assoc prof 1976-, assoc prof of educ psychology & dir ctr for study of minorities& disadvantaged 1979-85. **ORGANIZATIONS:** Mem Amer Educ Rsch Assn 1972-; mem Assn of Black Psychologists 1973-; mem Eta Phi Beta Inc 1978-; articles "Patterns of Coping in Black School Children"; "Motivational Factors Underlying Achievement" several others; mem Soc for the Psychological Study of Social Issues; mem Alpha Kappa Alpha, Inc. **HONORS/ACHIEVEMENTS:** Author of: "A Profile of Black Professional Women in Educ, Psychology and Sociology"; "Perceptions of Black Parents Regarding the Socialization of their Children". **BUSINESS ADDRESS:** Associate Prod of Educ Psych, Univ of Wisconsin-Milwaukee, Milwaukee, WI 53201.

POLLARD, EMILY FRANCES
Physician. **PERSONAL:** Born Oct 19, Milwaukee, WI. **EDUCATION:** Smith Coll, attended 1975-77; Univ of WI Madison, BS 1980; Meharry Medical Coll, MD 1984. **CAREER:** Georgetown Univ Hosp, general surgery resident. **ORGANIZATIONS:** Mem Alpha Kappa Alpha sor 1978-. **HONORS/ACHIEVEMENTS:** Alpha Omega Alpha Medical Honor Soc 1983. **HOME ADDRESS:** 1520 Massachusetts Ave SE, Washington, DC 20003. **BUSINESS ADDRESS:** General Surgery Resident, GeorgetownUniv Hospital, 3800 Reservoir Rd, Washington, DC 20007.

POLLARD, FREEMAN WALLACE
Educational administrator. **PERSONAL:** Born Aug 08, 1922, Mobile, AL; married Helen Louise. **EDUCATION:** Univ of South Alabama, AB 1973; Indiana Univ, MA 1978, PhD 1981. **CAREER:** Mobile Cty Voter Educ Proj, dir 1962-69; St Ambrose Coll, prof of political sci 1978-, dir public admin. **ORGANIZATIONS:** Dir of black student union Promotion & Amplification of (Negro) Black Culture 1980-; chmn, consultant, Davenport Civil Rights Comm 1981-84; co-organized & dir Freedom Road Found St Ambrose Coll 1983-84; commissioner Scott Cty Alcohol & Drug Abuse Rehab Bd 1984-; mem of bd of dir Scott Cty Comm Univ 1984-. **HONORS/ACHIEVEMENTS:** Black Scholar & Fellow Amer Assoc Pol Sci 1973; Outstanding Accomplishment in Pol Sci & Philosophy & Cert for 37 GPA in a double major Univ of South AL 1973. **MILITARY SERVICE:** USMC Sgt 1943-46, 1950-52; Pres Citation 1945. **HOME ADDRESS:** 4023 N Lillie Ave, Davenport, IA 52806. **BUSINESS ADDRESS:** Dir Public Admin Prog, St Ambrose College, 518 W Locust St, Davenport, IA 52803.

POLLARD, MURIEL RANSOM
Engineer. **PERSONAL:** Born Nov 05, 1953, Isola, MS; daughter of Mr & Mrs Arthur Ransom; divorced; children: Kendra, Eyphra, Elverna. **EDUCATION:** Meharry Medical Coll, attended biomedical science summer program 1972-74; Dillard Univ New Orleans, BA Chem 1975. **CAREER:** South Central Bell Telephone Co, engr supervisor 1977-; Sunflower-Humphries Co Project Headstart Policy Council, chairperson. **ORGANIZATIONS:** Mem Delta Sigma Theta Sorority 1973-, Telephone Pioneers of Amer 1981-; consultant religious speech writing & delivery 1984-; pres Inverness Elementary School PTA; mem admin comm MS Political Action Comm for South Central Bell 1986-; rep MS Headstart Parents Assn. **HONORS/ACHIEVEMENTS:** President's Award, Mississippi Head Start Parents Assn, 1989; Recognition of Service, Mississippi Delta Community College, 1989. **HOME ADDRESS:** PO Box 1484, Indianola, MS 38751. **BUSINESS ADDRESS:** South Central Bell, 600 West Park Ave Policy Cncl, Greenwood, MS 38930.

POLLARD, PERCY EDWARD, SR.
Senior manager. **PERSONAL:** Born Jun 03, 1943, King & Queen, VA; son of George T Pollard and Hattie Bell Taylor; married Annie Randolph, May 22, 1965; children: Tracie Anita, Percy Jr. **EDUCATION:** VA State Univ, BS 1966; Emory Univ, Certificate Mgmt Dev Program 1985. **CAREER:** IBM Corporation, jr instructor 1966, sr educ specialist 1969, equal oppor admin 1970, mgr of equal oppor 1972, mgr equal oppor & comm progs Gaithersburg 1973, district personnel programs mgr Office Products Div 1976, regional personnel mgr Washington/Baltimore Metro area 1977, personnel planning mgr Office Products Div Franklin Lakes, NJ 1979, corporate mgr equal oppor prog 1981, admin asst to the vice pres of personnel 1982, personnel mgr Rsch Div Yorktown, NY 1984, mgr staff services White Plains, NY 1986-; Special Asst for Employee Charitable Contributions 1988, IBM Corporate Headquarters Personnel Manager 1989-. **ORGANIZATIONS:** Contributing editor Alpha Phi Alpha Sphinx Magazine; mem Bergen Co Urban League; trustee Franklin Lakes United Methodist Church; mem President's Exec Exchange Assoc; steering comm Organizational Resource Counselors; mem VA State Univ Alumni Assoc No NJ Chapt; mem Kappa Theta Lambda Chap Alpha Phi Alpha Frat; founder/chmn VA State Univ Special Action Team. **HONORS/ACHIEVEMENTS:** Certificate of Merit, Broome Co NY NAACP 1972; Family and Children's Soc Special Recognition Certificate 1973; Kiwanis Club President's Awd 1975; Alpha Phi Alpha Outstanding Tenure Awd 1976, Sustained Serv Awd 1977, President's Impact Awd 1978; Outstanding Young Men of America 1975, 78, 79; Notable Amers 1977;IBM Office Products Div People Management Awd 1979; Presidential Exec Exchange 1980-81; Sr Management Citation Dept of Health and Human Serv 1981; Outstanding Natl Achievement Awd 1981; Alpha Phi Alpha Iota Theta Lambda Chap Awd 1983; SES Candidates Certificates of Recognition Dept of Health & Human Serv 1983; Alpha Phi Alpha New York/New Jersey Archives Awd 1983; NAFEO Presidential Citation Awd 1986; Most Outstanding Classmember Central High Sch Class of 1961, 1986; Division Exellence Award IBM 1988; Lead IBM's Charitable Contribution Program for 1988, $31.8M raised; Alumnus of the Year, Virginai State Univ, 1989. **HOME ADDRESS:** 8 Monroe Dr, Mahwah, NJ 07430. **BUSINESS ADDRESS:** Corporate Personnel Manager, IBM, Old Orchard Road, Armonk, NY 10504.

POLLARD, RAYMOND J.
Retired general vice president. **PERSONAL:** Born Mar 31, 1932, Lamar, SC; married Eloise Wilson. **EDUCATION:** FSU, EdB 1953;Univ of PA, M Edquivalent 1957; Antioch Coll, MS 1977. **CAREER:** Internal Revenue, mail clerk 1953-54; AUS, communication coding clerk 1954-56; Kenderton Sch, spl educ tchr 1957-58; McIntyre Sch, tchr 1958-61; CPA, caseworker male clerk 1961-62; LP Hill Sch, 1962-64; Levering Sch, 1966-67; LPHill Sch, 1967-71; Turner Middle Sch, phys educ tchr 1971-73; PA Fedn of Tchrs, staff rep 1973, general vice president retired. **ORGANIZATIONS:** Finan sec mem usher bd chsch schlshp com co-dir rec Met Bapt Ch; past pres bus mgr chmn hospitality com Fayetteville StateUniv Alumni; mem exec bd co-chmn Progressive Philadelphia Fedn of Tchrs; bldg rep LP Hill Sch & JP Turnr Sch; mem NAACP; PUSH; CORE; SCLC; APHI; treas BSA; vice pres Negro Trade Unoin Ldrshp Coun 1971; 1st v,chmn A Phillip Randolph Inst 1972. **MILITARY SERVICE:** AUS 1954-56.

POLLARD, WILLIAM E.
Director. **PERSONAL:** Born Sep 14, 1915, Pensacola, FL; married Josephine Mays; children: Constance Lagness, Barbara Ann LaCarra. **EDUCATION:** UCLA; LA City Coll. **CAREER:** Dining Car Employees #582, sec treas 1941-45; Dining Car Employees #456 & #582, gen chmn 1945-; LA Co Fedn Labor, vice pres 1959-64; AFL-CIO Dept Civil Rights, staff rep 1964-74; Dept Civil Rights AFL-CIO, dir 1974-86; NAACP, deputy exec dir 1986-. **ORGANIZATIONS:** Pres Joint Counc Dining Car Employees 1954-68; former orgn LA Joint Exec Bd Hotal & Restaurant Employees & Bartenders Intl Union; mem natl exec bd NAACP; natl exec bd Ldrshp Conf on Civil Rights; natl labor adv com Nt Urban Leag; natl exec bd A Philip Randolph Inst; Mason. **HONORS/ACHIEVEMENTS:** Serv Awds Natl Urban League, NAACP, Metrop Red Yth Adv Coun,, Metrop Police Dept, Cath Labor Inst 1974; Public Serv Awd Dept of Justice 1978; Scroll of Merit Natl Medical Assoc 1983. **BUSINESS ADDRESS:** Deputy Executive Dir, NAACP, 4805 Mt Hope Dr, Baltimore, MD 21215.

POLLARD, WILLIAM LAWRENCE
Educator. **PERSONAL:** Born Nov 27, 1944, Raleigh, NC; married Merriette Maude Chance; children: William Lawrence, Frederick Touissaint. **EDUCATION:** Shaw Univ, AB 1967; Univ of NC Chapel Hill, MSW 1969; Univ of Chicago, PhD 1976. **CAREER:** Livingstone Coll, instr 1969-71, asst prof & dir social welfare prog 1973-76; Univ of Pittsburgh, asso prof & chairperson of comm orgn skill set school of social work 1976-82; Grambline State Univ, assoc prof & dir of undergrad social work 1984-. **ORGANIZATIONS:** House of dels Council on Social Work Educ 1974-77, 1979-82; bd of dir Friendship House Salisbury NC 1974-76; sec bd of dir Dial Help Salisbury 1974-76; bd of dir YMCA Salisbury 1975-76; bd of dirs Council on Social Work Educ; adv comm Citizen Educ Action Group for Criminal Justice. **HONORS/ACHIEVEMENTS:** Fellowship Grant Met Applied Rsch Corp 1974; A Study of Black Self Help R&E Rsch Assocs 1978; "The Black Child" in proceedings of New Concepts in Human Serv for the Developing Child 1978. **BUSINESS ADDRESS:** Associate Professor & Dir, Grambling State University, School of Social Work, Grambling, LA 71245.

POLLEY, WILLIAM EMORY
Physician. **PERSONAL:** Born Feb 16, 1921, Huntington, WV; married Revella Justice; children: William, Aaron, Sharon Nott, John, Brenda, Susan, Leslie, Douglass. **EDUCATION:** WV State Coll, BS 1943; OJ Coll of podiatry 1953. **CAREER:** Podiatrists 22 yrs. **ORGANIZATIONS:** Treas WV State Alumni Assn 11 yrs; chaplain 9 yrs; 33rd degree Mason; mem Forest City Hosp; Royal Craft & Grand Lodge; sec 20 yrs; past pres Credit Union; Holy Trinity Bapt Ch9; pres of trst bd Mt Olive Bapt Ch 1962-69; life mem Alpha Phi Alpha Frat; NAACP; Phyliss Wheatley Assn; Northeastern OH Podiatry Assn 22 yrs; Am Podiatry Assn 22 yrs; PTA 10 yrs; Boy Scouts; Cub Scouts Com 1957-67. **HONORS/ACHIEVEMENTS:** Awd plaque from WV Alumni Assn for 21 yrs of serv 1975. **MILITARY SERVICE:** AUS sgt 1943-46. **BUSINESS ADDRESS:** 14011 Kinsman Rd, Cleveland, OH 44120.

POMARE, ELEO
Artistic director. **PERSONAL:** Born Oct 20, 1937, Columbia, SC. **EDUCATION:** Studied with Louis Horst, Curtis James, Kurt Joos & Jose Limon. **CAREER:** Organized many dance groups all over coutry including expanding the Am dance Co; choreographed for theater andTV in the US & Europe. **ORGANIZATIONS:** John Hay Whitney Fellowship Europe 1962-64; Guggenheim Fellowship grant 1973. **HONORS/ACHIEVEMENTS:** John Hay Whitney Fellowship Europe 1962-64; Guggenheim Fellowship grant 1973. **BUSINESS ADDRESS:** 325 W 16 St, New York, NY 10011.

POMPEY, CHARLES SPENCER
Retired educator. **PERSONAL:** Born Jul 31, 1915, MacClenny, FL; married Hattie Ruth Keys; children: Cheryl Zaneta. **EDUCATION:** FL Meml Coll, AA 1935; Bethune Ckmn

Coll, AA 1936; Johnson C Smith U, AB 1939;Univ MN, MA 1947. **CAREER:** Pinemount Elem School, prin 1936-37; Washington Jr/Boynton Elem, prin 1939-45; Carver High School, teacher coach 1946-64; Carver H/Seacrest H, asst prin 1964-69; Jr H Atlantic H Carver Middle School, prin 1969-80; Delray Beach Planning/Zoning/Cty Land Use Adv Com, 1968-82; retired educator/writer. **ORGANIZATIONS:** Author "A sch& its cmnty-prtnr's in Soc Engrng" 1956; Negro Jrnl Of Higher Ed "An Analysis of The Wash-DuBois Contrvrsy" The Bulletin, Mn Cncl forSocial Studies 1957; "More Rivers to Cross" Copyright 1984; co-fndr & 1st pres Palm Bch Co Tchrs Assn 1941; chmn FL State Tchrs Assn Pgm Action Com 1966-67; chmn mem Budget Comm Exec Com-FL Ed Assn 1968-71; pres Phi Delta Kappa Ed Frat. **HONORS/ACHIEVEMENTS:** 1st annl hmn relt awd FL Tchg Prof 1977; coach yr EE FL Athl Conf 1949,50,54, 1961-64; 1st Marthin Lugher King ctzn awd Palm Beach Cty 1977f "Pompey Pk/Rec Ctr" Cty Delray Beach 1976; "Black FL hall fame"Univ FL 1984. **HOME ADDRESS:** P O Box 1533, Delray Beach, FL 33447. **BUSINESS ADDRESS:** PO Box 1533, Delray Beach, FL 33447.

POMPEY, MAURICE
Judge. **PERSONAL:** Born May 14, 1923, S Bend, IN; married Josephine; children: Maurice Jr, Tina Marie. **EDUCATION:** Howard U; Roosevelt Coll; DePaul Univ Law Sch Chicago, JD 1951. **CAREER:** Circuit Ct of Cook Co IL, judge; former asst corp counsel magistrate circuit ct 1964-70; circuit judge 1970-. **ORGANIZATIONS:** Mem Cook Co IL & Am Bar Assn; mem Orginial Forty Club; mem 4mth Bombardment Group. **MILITARY SERVICE:** WW-II.

PONDER, EUNICE WILSON
Educator. **PERSONAL:** Born Sep 04, 1929, Oklahoma; daughter of Austin Wilson and Kate Wilson; married Dr Henry; children: Cheryl, Anna. **EDUCATION:** Langston U, BS 1951; OK State U, MS 1958;Univ of SC, EdD 1977. **CAREER:** Planning Research & Mgmt Benedict Coll, institutional researcher 1977-; Benedict Coll, tchr 1977-; Millie Lewis Agency Columbia SC, model; OK, tchr pub schs 1951-58. **ORGANIZATIONS:** Mem Nat Delta Pi Epsilon Bus Frat 1958-; mem Nat Asso of Institutional Researchers 1977; vol worker Rd Cross; Scouting; PTA several state 1959-75; mem NCATE Self-Study Team HEW 1978-80; reader tite IV HEW 1979-80; life mem Delta Sigma Theta Sor; mem Jack & Jill of Am Inc; mem Links Inc. **HONORS/ACHIEVEMENTS:** Dissertation "A Study of Selected Characteristics Affecting the Survival Rate of Black & White Student at theUniv of SC" 1977.

PONDER, HENRY
Educator. **PERSONAL:** Born Mar 28, 1928, Wewoka, OK; married Eunice Wilson; children: Cheryl, Anna. **EDUCATION:** Langston Univ, BS 1951; OK State Univ, MS 1958; OH State Univ, PhD 1963. **CAREER:** OK State Univ, rsch asst 1961-63; VA State Coll, asst prof 1958-61; OH State Univ, rsch asst 1961-63; VA State Coll, chmn dept agri/business 1963-64; Fort Valley State Coll, chmn dept business & econs 1964-66; Irving Trust Co, econ consult 1968; AL A&M Univ, dean 1966-69, vice pres academic affairs 1969-73; Benedict Coll, pres 1973-84; Fisk Univ, pres 1984-. **ORGANIZATIONS:** Mem Amer Econ Assoc; mem Amer Farm Econ Assoc; Mason 32nd Deg C of C; mem Alpha Phi Alpha. **HONORS/ACHIEVEMENTS:** Comm Leader Amer 1972; Personalities of S 1973; Who's Who in S & SW, in Finance, in Industry; Men of Achievement 1980; Internat'l Who's Who of Intellectuals 1981; OK State Univ, distinguished alumnus award 1986; 100 Most Effective College Presidents in US 1986. **MILITARY SERVICE:** AUS chief computer fdc sgt 1953-55. **BUSINESS ADDRESS:** President, Fisk University, Office of Pres, Nashville, TN 37203.

POOL, MARQUITA JONES
Journalist. **PERSONAL:** Born Feb 19, 1945, Aurora, IL; daughter of Maris E Jones and Jeanne Boger Jones; married Knut Eckert, May 21, 1988. **EDUCATION:** Boston Univ, BS 1966; Columbia Univ, MS 1969. **CAREER:** WABC-TV New York, producer 1970-74; WNET/13 Public TV, producer 1974-75; CBS News, assoc prod 1975-84, producer 1984-. **ORGANIZATIONS:** Bd of dirs Nzingha Soc Inc 1976-, pres 1976-85; mem NY Assoc Black Journalists 1985-, Womens Media Group 1986-. **HONORS/ACHIEVEMENTS:** Emmy Awd Producer "The Bombing of Beirut" 1983; Emmy Awd Producer "The Black Family - A Dream Deferred" 1983; Dollars and Sense Magazine Awd 100 Top Professional Black Women 1986; Natl Monitor Award 1988. **BUSINESS ADDRESS:** News Producer, CBS News, 524 W 57th St, New York, NY 10019.

POOLE, CECIL F.
Judge. **PERSONAL:** Born 1914, Birmingham, AL; son of William T Poole and Eva L Poole; married Charlotte Crump, Apr 03, 1942; children: Gayle, Patricia. **EDUCATION:** Univ of MI, LLB; Harvard Univ, LLM 1939. **CAREER:** Practiced law in San Francisco; former asst dist atty for San Francisco; Gov Brown of CA, clemency sec 1959-61; N Dist of CA, US atty 1961-70; Univ of CA at Berkeley, regents prof of law 1970; Jacobs Sills & Coblents, counsel 1970-76; N Dist of CA, appointed US Dist Judge 1976; US Circuit Ct, circuit judge 9th circuit 1979-. **ORGANIZATIONS:** Mem Adv Comm to Natl Comm for Reform of Federal Criminal Laws 1968-70; trustee Natl Urban League 1969-75; chmn Section of Individual Rights Amer Bar Assn 1971-72; mem House of Delegates ABA 1972-74; dir Levi Strauss & Co 1972-76; dir NAACP Legal Defense & Educ Fund 1973-76; mem ABA, San Francisco Bar Assn; Black Women Lawyers Assn; CA Assn of Black Lawyers; mem, United Way Agency Relations Council; chair, United Way Regional Admissions Committee; Amer Bar Assn; Langston Bar Assn; Los Angeles County Bar Assn; Los Angeles County Bar Assn Committee on the Status of Minorities in the Profession; Altrusa Club of Pasedena, CA, mem, Bd of Dir; Delta Sigma Theta Sorority; Licnoln Ave Baptist Church, Pasadena CA. **MILITARY SERVICE:** USAF, Lt 1942-45. **BUSINESS ADDRESS:** Judge, US Court of Appeals, PO Box 547, San Francisco, CA 94101.

POOLE, DILLARD M.
Educator. **PERSONAL:** Born Sep 15, 1939, Birmingham, AL. **EDUCATION:** BA 1971; MA 1977. **CAREER:** State OH, clerk; Warner & Swasey Machine Tool Co, tool supply worker; Cleveland State Univ, asst to dean for student life 1971-72; Afro-Amer Cultural Center Cleveland State Univ, dir. **ORGANIZATIONS:** Nat Conf Artists 1973-74; trst Parkwood CME Ch 1974-. **HONORS/ACHIEVEMENTS:** Mem dean's list Cleveland StateUniv 1970. **MILITARY SERVICE:** USAF airman 2nd class 1959-63. **BUSINESS ADDRESS:** 2121 Euclid Ave, Cleveland, OH 44115.

POOLE, JAMES F.
Investment counselor. **PERSONAL:** Born Apr 12, 1936, Laurens, SC; married Martha; children: Stephanie, Heather. **EDUCATION:** Benedict Coll, 1959;Univ of PA,Univ of CO & CO Coll, grad work. **CAREER:** Central HS Pueblo, tchr math 1962-67; Amer Capital Financial Serv Inc, investment couns div mgr 1967-. **ORGANIZATIONS:** Mem Est Planning Coun of Colorado Springs; Sale & Mrkt Exec Club; mem Alpha Phi Alpha Frat; Pueblo Country Club; apptd CO Centennial-Bicentennial Commn 1975; bd trst Benedict Coll Columbia SC; mem Millionaires Club of Amer Capital Financial Serv Inc. **MILITARY SERVICE:** AUS e-5 1959-62. **BUSINESS ADDRESS:** Certified Financial Planner, Ste 414, United Bank Bldg, Pueblo, CO 81003.

POOLE, MARION L.
Reading instructor. **PERSONAL:** Born May 25, 1921, Sumter, SC; son of Edward Poole and Rena Poole; married Dr Rachel Johnson; children: M Brevard El, Andrea, Adriene. **EDUCATION:** BS 1959; MEd 1964; EdD 1972. **CAREER:** Pennsylvania Welfare Dept, sr visitor; Pittsburgh Public Schools, teacher, admin; Univ of Pittsburgh, consultant & faculty 1968-84 retired; teacher corps dir 1969-72; Univ Pittsburgh & General Assembly Center School Desegregation & Conflict, principal research asst lecturer staff specialist; Comm Coll, Alleghany County, part-time instructor, 1984-. **ORGANIZATIONS:** Natl Training Labs 1970; current ed Center Communicator 1973-; Phi Delta Kappa Doctoral Assn Educ 1973-; AERA; pres current bd dirs Promethenas Inc 1972-74; vice pres Emanons; mem NAACP. **HONORS/ACHIEVEMENTS:** Astp Howard Univ; 92nd INF Div Hq 1944-45; co-author, Comprehensive Affirmative Action for Equal Educational Opportunity in the Racially isolated school district, 1981; Bronze Medallion, Outstanding Service to Students in DE, 1984; Merit Plaque, Service to Students. **HOME ADDRESS:** 137 Kilmer St, Pittsburgh, PA 15221.

POOLE, RACHEL IRENE
Retired educational administrator. **PERSONAL:** Born Dec 02, 1924, Uniontown, PA; married Dr Marion L Poole; children: Andrea Lynell, Adriene Charisse Sharif. **EDUCATION:** Univ of Pittsburgh PA, BS nursing 1947;Univ of Pittsburgh, ML nursing educ 1952;Univ Pittsburgh, PhD 1977. **CAREER:** Allegheny Campus Community Coll of Allegheny Co Pittsburgh PA, retired asst dean of life sci and dir of nursing prog 1979-84; Community Coll of Allegheny Co, adminstrv intern/Adminstrv asst to pres 1977-79; Inst for Higher Educ Sch of EducUniv of Pittsburgh, lectr/adminstrv asst 1974-77; Western Psychiatric Inst and Clinics, dir of Nursing; Dept of Psychiatric Mental Hlth Nursing Sch of NursingUniv of Pittsburgh, asso prof and asso chmn 1967-72; Deptof Psychiatric Mental Hlth Nursing Sch of NursingUniv of Pittsburgh, asso prof 1972-73;hlth integrator 1972; Homewood-Brushton Branch Allegheny Comm Coll, part-time advisor, counselor 1984-. **ORGANIZATIONS:** Mem Am Nurses Assn 1958-73,79-84; Nat Leag for Nursing 1963-73,79-84; mem Group for the Advncement of Soc Psychoanalysis 1968-70; com Recruitment of Minorities Into Nursing Commonwealth of PA Dept of Hlth 1972-73; mem Am Assn of Higher Educ 1975-76; planner coor first aid classes for Black yth in Homewood Brushton and Hill Dist 1968-69; bd of dirs Ille Elegba 1968-74; orgn & treas Black Women's Forum 1969-71. **HONORS/ACHIEVEMENTS:** Interviewee "Racism" WIIC's TV Prog Face to Face 1968; natl hon soc in nursing Elected to Sigma Theta Tau 1953; elected PA Nurses Assn "Brain Trust" 1965-67; Who's Who of Am Women 1979; author of many writings; "Proposal for a Plan of Action" Com on Recruitment of Minorities Into Nursing Dept of Hlth Commonwealth of PA 1973; Panelist Nursing Programs WTAE's TV Prog Pgh Today 1982; Panelist Minorities and Nursing WQED's TV Prog Black Horizons 1981; Black Achiever of Year, NIP Magazine 1986; Special Recognition Award, Community Coll of Alleg County 1986; frequent speaker to many groups such as Bus/Prof Women, sec, nurses, ex-convicts, fed women employees, & women in military on the subject of "Assertiveness" 1979-88. **BUSINESS ADDRESS:** Advisor, Counselor, Comm Coll of Allegheny Cty, 701 N Homewood Ave, Pittsburgh, PA 15221.

POOLE, THOMAS H., SR.
Educator. **PERSONAL:** Married Rena; children: Rene', Hank Jr. **EDUCATION:** FL A&M U, BS;Univ CA, MS. **CAREER:** Mt Dora Middle School, teacher coach 1964-; Drew HS, athletic dir head football coach 1955-64; Eustic Voc HS, athletic dir head football coach, basketball coach 1950-53; Poole's Radio & TV Reparis Serv, owner & operator. **ORGANIZATIONS:** Mem United Tchg Prof Human Resl Com Lake Co Nego Team; life mem NAACP; pres Tri-City Br NAACP; Lake Co Voters Leag; SW Eustis Improvement Assn Inc; past pres Lake Co Econ Oppt; chmn tsts St James AME Ch; steward St James AME Ch; appt by Gov Human Rel Commn for State of FL 1977. **HONORS/ACHIEVEMENTS:** Distgd serv awd 1972; black awareness awd Outsdng Serv 1973; grtr serv to humanity Gethsemane Bapt Ch 1969; one of ten most influential men in lake Co Lake-Sumter Comm Coll 1969. **MILITARY SERVICE:** AUS 1953-55. **BUSINESS ADDRESS:** 1033 Smith St, PO Box 1334, Eustis, FL 32726.

POOLE-HEARD, BLANCHE DENISE
Information administrator. **PERSONAL:** Born Aug 09, 1951, Washington, DC; married Emanuel F Heard Jr; children: Latricia Poole, Michael Poole, Mannikka Heard. **EDUCATION:** Attended, Montgomery Co Jr Coll 1969, University Coll 1976; TN State Univ, 1972. **CAREER:** American Security Bank, supervisor 1974-75, sr edp auditor 1976-83; Savings Bank of Baltimore, sr edp auditor 1984-85; United States Fidelity & Guaranty, information interity admin 1985-. **ORGANIZATIONS:** Membership chair EDP Auditors Assoc 1980-81; intl sec EDPP Conference 1982; mem Data Processing Mgmt Assoc 1986, Insurance Data Mgmt Assoc 1986, United Black Fund of Greater Baltimore 1986-7. **BUSINESS ADDRESS:** US Fidelity & Guaranty Co, PO Box 1138 Div A, Baltimore, MD 21203.

POPE, ADDISON W.
Psychiatrist. **PERSONAL:** Born May 16, 1926, Baltimore; married Pauline Humphries; children: Jerilyn. **EDUCATION:** Howard U, BS 1948; Meharry Med Coll, MD 1957;Univ MD, psychiat res 1960; Rutgers U, 1963; Howard U, neurololgy. **CAREER:** Out Patient Clinic Crownsville State Hosp, dir 1962-65; Soc Sec Adminstrn, consult 1964-68; Baltimore City, reg mental hlht dir 1967-73; Drug Abuse Adminstrn, commr 1969-70; Nat Inst Mental Hlth, career tchrs prog 1973-; Correctional Sys State MD, consult 1969-73; W Elec Corp 1971-; Johns Hopkins Hosp, instr 1967-; Sinai Hosp, attending phys psychiat 1968-; Univ MD, instr 1968-; Provident Hosp, chief psychiat 1967-73. **ORGANIZATIONS:** Mem Jail Bd Baltimore City; chmn exam study grp Baltimore City Fire Dept 1972-73. **HONORS/ACHIEVEMENTS:** Awd signt contrib field mental hlth Comm Hlth Coun MD 1974. **MILITARY SERVICE:** AUS 1944-46; AUSR 1948-53. **BUSINESS ADDRESS:** 2403 Garrison Blvd, Baltimore, MD 21216.

POPE, HENRY
Psychiatrist. **PERSONAL:** Born May 01, 1922, Athens, GA; children: 4 Children. **EDUCATION:** Howard U, BS 1949; Meharry Med Coll, MD 1958. **CAREER:** Provident Hosp, intern 1958; St Elizabeth's Hosp, 1960; St Elizabeths Hosp, staff physician 1960-65; Self-employed, 1960-; Crownsville Hosp Cntr, res psychiat staff psychiat 1970-. **ORGANIZATIONS:** Mem Nat Med Assn 1960-; DC Med Soc 1970. **MILITARY SERVICE:** Sgt 1943-45. **BUSINESS ADDRESS:** 5502 Colorado Ave NW, Washington, DC 20011.

POPE, ISAAC S.
Physician. **PERSONAL:** Born Mar 06, 1939, S Pittsburgh, TN; married Joan Darby; children: David, Stephen, Theresa. **EDUCATION:** Gonaaga Univ, Spokane WA, BS 1965; Univ WA Seattle, MPA 1970; Univ WA Seattle, MD 1974. **CAREER:** Peace Corps in Sierra Leone, volunteer 1965-67; Peace Corps Training Program Gambia dir 1969; model cities program Seattle, asst dir employee economic devel 1969-70; US Army Ft Leonard Wood MO, staff pediatrician, 1977-79; Private Practice, pediatrician, 1979-. **ORGANIZATIONS:** Regional dir Studies Natl Med Assn 1972-73; mem WA State Med Assn Lewis Co Med Socty; mem Amer Acad Pediatricians, WA State Soc of Pediatrics; 1985 pres Kiwan's mem 1979-; bd mem Lewis County Work Opportunity, 1981-86; bd mem St Helen Hospital Chehalis WA 1982-; bd mem Lewis County Special Olympic 1983-86; bd mem Stmary's Center 1985-86; pres The Center Found 1986-. **HONORS/ACHIEVEMENTS:** Conc patient care Ft Leonard Wood Army Hospital 1978; Army Commendation Medal, AVS, 1979. **MILITARY SERVICE:** USAF airman 1/c 1956-59; USA major 1974-79. **BUSINESS ADDRESS:** Pediatrician, 370 S Market Blvd, Chehalis, WA 98532.

POPE, JAMES M.
Government official. **PERSONAL:** Born Apr 17, 1927, Sharon, PA; married Cora Silver; children: Anthony V, Michael R. **EDUCATION:** OH Wesleyan U, BA 1950; Boston U, MA 1951; Harvard U, 1955. **CAREER:** Bureau of African Aff State Dept, deputy publ aff dir 1972-76, publ aff adviser 1976-77; US Arms Contl/Disarm Agen, deputy publ aff adviser 1977-82; Washington Foreign Press Ctr, dir. **ORGANIZATIONS:** Pi Delta Epsilon 1950; Omicron Delta Kappa 1950; vice pres Cpt Press Club 1971. **HONORS/ACHIEVEMENTS:** Meritorious hnr awd US Infor Agency 1964; meritorious hnr awd Dept of State 1974; meritorious hnr awd Arms Ctrl/Disarm Agency 1980. **MILITARY SERVICE:** AUS corpl 1945-46. **HOME ADDRESS:** 1402 Sheridan St NW, Washington, DC 20011. **BUSINESS ADDRESS:** Dir, Washington Foreign Press Ctr, Ste 898, Natl Press Bldg, Washington, DC 20045.

POPE, JOSEPH N.
Automobile dealer. **CAREER:** Pope Chevrolet, Inc, Modesto CA, chief executive. **BUSINESS ADDRESS:** Pope Chevrolet Inc, 1234 McHenry Ave, Modesto, CA 95350. *

POPE, MARY MAUDE
Clergyman. **PERSONAL:** Born Jan 27, 1916, Wake Co, NC; widowed. **EDUCATION:** Amer Sch of Chicago;Univ NC; NC St U. **CAREER:** Mt Sinai Saints of God Holy Chs & Mt Sinai Chs Worldwide, bishop. **ORGANIZATIONS:** Past fndr Mt Sinai Chs 1946. **HONORS/ACHIEVEMENTS:** Plaques Who's Who in NC 1973. **BUSINESS ADDRESS:** Mt Sinai Ch, 301 S Swain St PO Box J27411, Raleigh, NC 27611.

POPE, MIRIAN ARTIS
Business executive. **PERSONAL:** Born Nov 03, 1952, Franklin, VA; married Johnnie Lee Pope, Jr; children: Ebonee Johndrea, Courtney LaVerne. **EDUCATION:** Norfolk State University, BS 1975; Old Dominion University, graduate school. **CAREER:** United Virginia Bank, branch manager 1975-81; Community Federal S/L Assn, managing officer 1981-. **ORGANIZATIONS:** Adv bd of banking & fin comm Norfolk State Univ 1977-81; mem Natl Assn of Bank Women, Inc 1977-81; dir Norfolk C of C 1980; dir Amer Red Cross Tidewater Chap 1979-81; dir United Way 1981-82; mem, sec Order of Eastern Star of VA, PHA 1979-; adv to Jr Achievement of Tidewater 1976. **HONORS/ACHIEVEMENTS:** Scholarship Norfolk State University 1971; appreciation Junior Achievement of Tidewater 1976; appreciation Norfolk Chamber of Commerce 1980; appreciation American Red Cross 1981. **HOME ADDRESS:** 387 Brock Circle, Norfolk, VA 23502. **BUSINESS ADDRESS:** Chief Executive Officer, Community Fed S & L Assn, 1512 27th St, Newport News, VA 23607.

POPE, RUBEN EDWARD, III
Personnel administrator. **PERSONAL:** Born Jun 28, 1948, Cleveland, OH; married Cheryl Ann Jones; children: Walter, Yolanda, Yvonne. **EDUCATION:** Kenyon Coll, BA 1970; Boston Coll Law Sch, JD 1973. **CAREER:** Wyman-Gordon Co, dev benefits mgr 1975-; Arthur Andersen & Co, auditor 1973-75. **ORGANIZATIONS:** Mem OH Bar 1978; mem Am Bar Assn 1978; bd of dir Untied Way of Central MA 1979-; treas Yth Guid Assn Inc 1979-; bd of dir Prospect Hse Inc 1980; finan sec Quinsigamond Lodge #173 IBPOE OFW Elks; sec Belmont St AME Zion Ch. **BUSINESS ADDRESS:** 244 Worcester St N, Grafton, MA 01536.

PORTEE, FRANK, III
Pastor. **PERSONAL:** Born Jun 16, 1955, York, SC; son of Frank Portee Jr (deceased) and Alvon Pendergrass Portee; married Yvonne Fersner, Sep 10, 1983; children: Alyssa Shanee. **EDUCATION:** Carson-Newman Coll, BA 1977; Interdenominational Theological Seminary, MDiv 1980. **CAREER:** New Light UM Church, pastor 1980-83; United Methodist Church SC, coord of youth ministry 1980-83; Coll of Charleston, campus minister 1983-; Old Bethel UM Church, pastor 1983-. **ORGANIZATIONS:** pres Greater Charleston Community Development, Inc 1988-; chrmn Avery Research Bd. 1988-; Vice pres Natl Kidney Foundation 1984-; bd mem Action Council Comm Mental Health 1984-; columnist Charleston Chronicle 1985-; bd mem Comm Relations Council 1985-, Florence Crittenton Homes 1986; consultant General Bd of Global Ministries 1987; chrmn First Congressional District Rainbow Coalition, 1988. **HONORS/ACHIEVEMENTS:** Rsch Fellow Emory Sch of Theology 1982-83; Disting Serv Prince Hall Lodge #46 F&AM 1986; Disting Serv Chas Air Force Base 1987; Social Action, Phi Beta Sigma 1989; Delegate - Democratic National Convention 1988. **HOME ADDRESS:** 513 Huger St, Charleston, SC 29403. **BUSINESS ADDRESS:** Senior Minister, Old Bethel United Meth Church, 222 Calhoun St, Charleston, SC 29401.

PORTER, ALBERT S.
Judge. **PERSONAL:** Born Dec 15, 1930, Laurel, MS; married Mildred; children: Alvita, Darryl, Richard, Kimberly. **EDUCATION:** Univ of IL, BS 1955; John Marshall Law Sch, LLB JD 1962; also studied at Wilson Jr Coll, Roosevelt Univ, IL Inst of Tech; Northwestern Law Sch, criminal law certificate. **CAREER:** US Post Office, clerk 1952-53; Argonne Natl Lab, chemist 1955-57; serv station prop 1958-59; teacher 1957-62; State Atty Office, trial atty 1962-66; Chicago Dept of Investiga, dep commr 1966-70; Circuit Ct, judge Cook Co 1970-. **ORGANIZATIONS:** Mem Chicago, IL, Cook Co, Natl Bar Assns; mem Natl Honor Soc. **HONORS/ACHIEVEMENTS:** Amer Legion Awd for Scholarship. **BUSINESS ADDRESS:** Judge, Cook Co Circuit Court, Chicago Civic Center, Chicago, IL 60602.

PORTER, ARTHUR L.
Business executive. **PERSONAL:** Born Jun 25, 1940, Los Angeles, CA; married Miriam J; children: Karen, Shawn. **EDUCATION:** Los Angeles City Coll, AA 1966; CA State Univ LA, BA, MA 1969, 1972. **CAREER:** LA Unified Sch Dist, teacher 1963-69, financial coord 1963-69; Bache & Co, stock broker 1969-73; Amer Savings & Loan, vice pres 1973-. **ORGANIZATIONS:** Mem real estate adv comm LA Trade Tech Coll 1974-; chmn of bd pres Home Loan Counseling Ctr 1979; mem Urban Affairs Com CA Savs & Loan League; mem adv bd Home Ownership Workshop City of Compton. **MILITARY SERVICE:** USNR sn 6 yrs. **BUSINESS ADDRESS:** Vice President, Amer Savings & Loan, 2701 Wilshire Blvd, Santa Monica, CA 90403.

PORTER, BLANCHE TROULLIER
Educator. **PERSONAL:** Born Nov 22, 1933, New Orleans; divorced; children: Louis Porter, II. **EDUCATION:** Dillard U, BA 1955;Univ of So CA; Xavier U; So U. **CAREER:** Elementary school teacher, 15 years prior to becoming resource teacher. **ORGANIZATIONS:** Mem United Tchr of New Orleans; Nat Educ Assn; Am Fedn of Tchr; LA Educ Assn; Parent Tchr Assn Andrew Jackson Ele Sch; McDonogh #35 High; mem Nat PTA Grammeteus Alpha Kappa Sor 1954; Grace United Meth Ch Adm Bd; sec United Meth Women; sec Coun on Ministries mem Parents Aux Club BSA Troop 155. **HONORS/ACHIEVEMENTS:** Granted key to city of Louisville KY 1968. **BUSINESS ADDRESS:** 703 Carondelet St, New Orleans, LA.

PORTER, CAROL DENISE
Graphic designer. **PERSONAL:** Born Mar 04, 1948, Washington, DC; daughter of Wiley W Porter and Alma D Porter. **EDUCATION:** Howard Univ, attended 1966-67; Independent Study Tour European Capitals, 1970; Moore College of Art, BFA 1971; Sterling Institute, attended 1975; Hartford Graduate Ctr, attended 1976; Poynter Inst of Media Studies, attended 1986. **CAREER:** WJLA-TV7 Washington, graphic artist 1971-73; WBBM-TV2 Chicago, graphic artist 1973-75; WFSB-TV3 Hartford, art dir 1975-77; WDVM-TV9, asst art dir/graphic designer 1977-79; Needham Harper and Steers Advertising Falls Church, art dir/graphic designer 1979-80; Ketchum Advertising, art dir 1984-85; WashingtonPost, graphic designer 1980-84, 1985-. **ORGANIZATIONS:** Mem Alpha Kappa Alpha Sor; sec Natl Academy of TV Arts & Sciences; mem Capital Press Club; volunteer Family Place; freelance design/art director; mem Speakers Bureau Washington Post; mem Broadcast Designers Assoc; mem Soc of Newspaper Design; 2nd vice pres, Capital Press Club 1987-89; moderator/participant, Howard Univ Comm Conference: workshop on careers in newspaper communication 1988. **HONORS/ACHIEVEMENTS:** Washington Art Directors Club Awds of Merit 1973, 79, 81, 83 (two); Emmy Awd Outstanding Individual Achievement in Scenic Design 1972; Awds of Excellence Chicago '75 Communications Collaborative Show for TV Spots 1975; bd of govs Washington Chap Natl Acad of TV Arts and Scis 1979; Awd of Merit Soc of Newspaper Design 1986; award of excellence "page design", Print Magazine 1988; award of excellence "portfolio of 6 page designs", Society of Newspaper Design 1989; award of excellence "page design" Washington Art Directors Club 1989. **HOME ADDRESS:** 2242 Washington Ave, Silver Spring, MD 20910.

PORTER, CHARLES WILLIAM
Editor, publisher. **PERSONAL:** Born Oct 06, 1939, Mobile, AL; son of Mr & Mrs Puillie Porter (deceased) and Mrs Puillie Porter (deceased); married Joyce A Wallace; children: Nikki, Terri, Michael, Stanley. **EDUCATION:** Bishop State Jr Coll, AS 1960; AL State Univ, BS 1962; Univ of AL, MA 1970; Chicago City Coll, 1973. **CAREER:** Public school teacher 1962-68; news reporter, dir of public relations, 1970-71; Northwestern Univ, publishing editor 1971-74; Mobile Beacon, editor 1974-76; Bishop State Jr Coll, dir of public relations 1982-86; Inner City News, owner 1976-, editor & publisher 1976-; Bishop State Jr Coll, instructor of Journalism 1982-87; Inner City Public Relations, relations consultant 1986-; Inner City Printers, owner 1977-. **ORGANIZATIONS:** Founder & pres Media Coalition 1976-; chmn of bd OIC Mobile Area 1980-81; mem Sigma Delta Chi; Natl Assn of Black Journalist; Amer Coll Public Relations Assn, Educ Writers Assn; Natl Council of Coll Public Advisors; NAACP; Sickle Cell Rsch Found, Omega Psi Phi Fraternity Inc; Operation PUSH; Concerned Citizens for Police Reform, Chicago, Southern Christian Leadership Conf: YWCA (honorary); YMCA; Urban League; former mem MCEA; mem NEA; AEA. **HONORS/ACHIEVEMENTS:** Natl, regional & local honors for establishing the Southern AL Task Force on Illiteracy; Numerous honors for community serv. **BUSINESS ADDRESS:** Editor & Public Dir of Public Relations, Inner City News, 551 Summerville St, PO Box 1545, Mobile, AL 36633-1545.

PORTER, CLARENCE A.
Educator. **PERSONAL:** Born Mar 19, 1939, McAlester, OK; children: Richard, Cory. **EDUCATION:** Portland State Univ, BS 1962; OR State Univ, MS 1964, PhD 1966. **CAREER:** OR State Univ, grad asst 1961-64, asst vet med 1964-66; Portland State Univ, asst prof 1966-70, exec asst to pres & assoc prof 1970-72; Univ of NH, asst v provost acad affairs 1972-76; State Univ of MN, assoc v chancellor acad affairs 1976-78; Phyllis Wheatley Comm Cntr, exec dir 1979-83; Cheyney Univ of PA, vice pres for acad affairs 1983-84; Montgomery Coll Tacoma Park, MD, instructional dean 1985-. **ORGANIZATIONS:** Mem Sigma Xi; Amer Assn for Advancement of Sci; Amer Assn Parasitology; Helminthological Soc of Wash; Amer Assn Higher Edn. **HONORS/ACHIEVEMENTS:** AIBS Summer Fellow LA State Univ 1968. **BUSINESS ADDRESS:** Instructional Dean, Montgomery College, Takoma Park Campus, Takoma Park, MD 20912.

PORTER, CURTISS E.
Educator. **PERSONAL:** Born Dec 29, 1939, Braddock, PA; divorced; children: Dennis, Janice, Natiata, Tajudeen, Lelle, Omar, Jolan. **EDUCATION:** Univ Pgh, BA;Univ Pgh,

PhD cand. **CAREER:** Univ Pittsburgh, chmn dept of black comm educ research & devel; DBCERD/PITT, asso dir 1969-72; DBCERD-PITT, dir program devel 1972-74. **ORGANIZATIONS:** Chmn Reg 3 Nat Counc of Black Studies; consult Def Race Rels Inst; spl guest 6th Pan African Congress; mem Commn on Educ & Rsrch African Heritage Studies Assn; exec bd Nat Coun of Black Studies; mem Assn for the Study of Afro-Am Life & Hist; part Kuntu Writers Workshop; fdr Black Horizons Theatre; fdr Black Action Soc; mem Adv EST; mem EST Hunger Proj Com. **MILITARY SERVICE:** USAF a/1c 1958-63. **BUSINESS ADDRESS:** 3804 Forbes Ave, Pittsburgh, PA 15260.

PORTER, DOROTHY B.
Library administrator. **PERSONAL:** Born May 25, 1905, Warrenton, VA; married Charles H Wesley; children: Constance Vzelac. **EDUCATION:** Howard U, BA 1928; Columbia U, BS 1931; Columbia U, MS 1932; Preservation & Adminstrn of Archives Am U, cert 1937; HowardUniv & Am U, grad courses. **CAREER:** Morrland-Spingarn Collection of HowardUniv Lib Washington, retired libr. **ORGANIZATIONS:** Mem Phi Beta Kappa. **HONORS/ACHIEVEMENTS:** Aurthor numerous articles on black hist for book & various publ; recip hon LLDUniv of Susquehanna 1971; distngd serv awd students of Howard's Coll of Liberal Arts 1971.

PORTER, E. MELVIN
Attorney, legislator. **PERSONAL:** Born May 22, 1930, Okmulgee, OK; married Leona; children: 6 Children. **EDUCATION:** TN State U, BS 1956; Vanderbilt Univ Sch of Law, LLB 1959. **CAREER:** OK, senator 1964-; Black Voices Mag, co-owner publ. **ORGANIZATIONS:** Chmn Social Welfare Com; vchmn Rules Com; mem Judiciary Com; OK Co Bar Assn; OK Bar Assn; Am Bar Assn; Am Judicature Soc; life mem NAACP; pres OK City Chap 1961-64; 32 degree Mason. **HONORS/ACHIEVEMENTS:** Recip hon LLD Shorter Coll AR; drafter Anti-discrimination Act which is now law in OK; bill requiring a hist of black am be included in various textbooksthroughout OK; authored bill requiring the state to test for sickle cell anemia & sickle cell trait; first black to serve in State Senate of OK. **BUSINESS ADDRESS:** 2116 NE 23 St, Oklahoma City, OK 73111.

PORTER, ELLIS N.
Clergyman. **PERSONAL:** Born Apr 26, 1931, Sumter, SC. **EDUCATION:** St Coll Orangeburg, BS; Epis Div Scl Educ at Hofstra Coll, MDw. **CAREER:** Church of Redeemed, St Stehen's Ch, St Titus' Ch, Urban Crisis Prog, vicar assoc vicar; Howard U, epis chaplain 1972-. **ORGANIZATIONS:** Bd mem Union Black & Epis; Angus Dun Fellowship Comm; Citz Comm on Adoption 1965-66; exec bd Citz antiPoverty Comm 1956-66; exec bd Better Hlth Found 1968-72; Black Sol Comm 1968-72; Smithsonian Inst Copr 1952-55. **BUSINESS ADDRESS:** PO Box 6, Howard Univ, Washington, DC 20051.

PORTER, EVERETTE M.
Judge. **PERSONAL:** Born Nov 10, 1910, Franklin, LA; married Ida Bell; children: 4. **EDUCATION:** SW U, JS 1940; Chapman Coll, BA 1951; LA & USC Sch Law, grad work 1959-61. **CAREER:** CA Adult Auth Congress Corrections & Bd Corrections, 1955-59; LA Police, commr 1961-63; Juvenile Ct Superior Ct, referee 1962-64; LA Suerior Ct, judge pro tem 1964-65; Commr Superior Ct State CA, elect appt 1965; Municipal Ct LA Judicial Dist, appt 1972. **ORGANIZATIONS:** Past couns CA State Bapt Conv; past pres CA State Bapt Laymens Orgn; mem LA Co Bar Asn; Themis Soc; Judicatur Soc; NAACP; YMCA; Conf CA Judges; 2 elected exec com LA Municipal Ct. **HONORS/ACHIEVEMENTS:** Layman yr Nat Bapt Conv 1956; Geo Wash Carver Awd outstnd cit 1964; many art speeches &TV appearances Family Law Juvenile Law & Criteria Parole Slection 1957; combat inf badge; bronze star. **MILITARY SERVICE:** Inf capt 1942-46. **BUSINESS ADDRESS:** Criminal Courts Bldg, 210 W Temple St, Los Angeles, CA 90012.

PORTER, GLORIA JEAN
Business administrator. **PERSONAL:** Born Apr 15, 1951, Baltimore, MD. **EDUCATION:** Adelphi Univ, BSW (Summa Cum Laude) 1973; Univ of Illinois, MSW (Summa Cum Laude) 1974. **CAREER:** Univ of Mass Mental Health Service, therapist 1975-78; Univ of Southern Cal Counseling Serv, psychotherapist, asst dir, dir 1978-84; Univ of Southern Cal; Dataproducts Corp, employee assist mgr 1984-. **ORGANIZATIONS:** Mem bd of dir, Ebonics, Alcohol Info Ctr San Fernando Valley Council on Alcoholism, NAACP, Black Women's Forum, Black Women's Network, Black Agenda, Women in Mgmt, Amer Personnel & Guidance Assoc, NASW Reg of Clinical Soc Workers, Natl Assoc of Soc Workers, Assoc of Black Soc Workers; Natl Health Attitudes Research Project; Amer Personnel and Guidance Assn; NASW Register of Clinical Social Workers. **BUSINESS ADDRESS:** Employee Assistance Manager, Data Products Corp, 6200 Canoga Ave, Woodland Hills, CA 91365.

PORTER, GRADY J.
County employee. **PERSONAL:** Born Sep 01, 1918, Carrollton, GA; son of James Porter and Amanda Porter; married Marcella M Larriere; children: Liliane, J Anthony, Sylviane, Patricia. **CAREER:** Dem Ward Chairman, 4 yrs; State Convention, delegate 10 yrs; Oldsmobile Gen Motors Corp, retired employee; Ingham Co, commr 1967-; Law & Cts Comm, chmn pro-tem; Ingham County, bd of commr chairperson. **ORGANIZATIONS:** Chmn Fair Prac Anti-Discrim Com Local 652 UAW 17 yrs; Unit chmn Local 652 UAW 1952-54; transportation officer US Zone Germany UNRRA & ORT 1945-48; mem MI Assn Co; NACO; Capitol Lodge AF & AM Prince Hall; life mem NAACP; attended & participated in all the NAACP Natl Conv for the last 17 yrs; mem Union Baptist Ch; Boy Scouts; Urban League; mem Lansing Human Relations Comm 1952-53; spl comm on Sch Needs & Sights 1953; NABCO; chairperson Laymen League Union Baptist Church; mall advisory bd Mayor committee. **HONORS/ACHIEVEMENTS:** Nominated Outstanding Man of Yr 1966; 1st Black elected official in history of Ingham Co; Fredrick Douglass Awd 1986; special recognition to Black History Ingham County housing; outstanding community serv awd NAACP; Ingham County Democratic Party, 20 year elected county commr 1988; Ingham County Bd Commrs Service Award 1988. **MILITARY SERVICE:** AUS 1941-45. **HOME ADDRESS:** 745 W Lenawee, Lansing, MI 48915.

PORTER, JAMES H.
Educator. **PERSONAL:** Born Nov 11, 1933, Portchester, NY; divorced; children: Michael Brandon, Adrienne Michelle, Lynn Sharon. **EDUCATION:** Renselaer Polytechnic Inst, BChE 1955; MIT, ScD 1963. **CAREER:** MIT, assoc prof, chem engineering; Energy Resources Inc, consultant 1974-; MA Inst Tech, visiting assoc prof 1971-72; Abcor, mgr computer application design 1967-72; Cornell Univ, visiting lecturer 1970; Chevron, sr research engineer 1963-67. **ORGANIZATIONS:** Visiting staff mem Elect Systems Lab 1966-67; engr Exxn 1955-58; mem Am Inst Chem Engrs; United Comm Devel; MIT Alumnit Adv Coun; vchmn SocProfessional Advancement Black Chemists & Chem Engrs; consult NIH; Num Publs Patent on Gas Well Sulfur Removal by Diffusion through Polymeric Membranes 1970. **HONORS/ACHIEVEMENTS:** Jesse smith noyes found fellowship 1953,54; Chevron Research Fellowship 1962; outstanding professor award MIT 1974,75. **BUSINESS ADDRESS:** c/o AICE, 345 E 47th St, Attn:Member Records, New York, NY 10017.

PORTER, JOHN HENRY
Educator in chiropractics. **PERSONAL:** Born Nov 13, 1950, Spartanburg, SC; married Errie Marie Bobo; children: Michael, Princess. **EDUCATION:** Claflin Coll; Spartanburgh Tech; Sherman Coll of Chiropractics, DD 1974. **CAREER:** Sherman Chiropractic Coll, dc 1979-; Sherman Coll of Chiropratics, admission comm 1979; Sherman Coll of Chiropractics, instr 1979. **ORGANIZATIONS:** Mem Int Chiroptractic Assn 1979; mem Sigma Chi Sigma Frat 1975-80; mem Holdens Chapel. **HONORS/ACHIEVEMENTS:** Recip merit unit comm USS Springfield clg-7 1971; natl def serv medal USS Springfield clg-7 1971; achvmnt awd Sherman Coll 1975; radiographic awd Sherman Coll 1977. **MILITARY SERVICE:** USN e-3 2 yrs. **BUSINESS ADDRESS:** Sherman Chiropractic Coll, 2020 Springfield Rd, Spartanburg, SC 29301.

PORTER, JOHN RICHARD
Clergyman. **PERSONAL:** Born Apr 02, 1932, Mineral Springs, AR; married June Carol McIntosh; children: John Thomas, Joseph Dubois, Julia Magdalene, Jessica Retha, Jorja Angela, Jerrianne Carol. **EDUCATION:** IO Wesleyan Coll, BA 1959; Garrett Evan Theol Sem, MDiv 1962; Union Grad Sch, PhD 1975. **CAREER:** Christ United Meth Ch, pastor 1962-71 & 1979-; Urban Young Life, vice pres 1974-79; Chicago Cntr Black Religious Studies, dir 1971-74; Sch of Human Dignity, dir1967-70. **ORGANIZATIONS:** Chmn Repression Com Chicago Black United Comm 1980; adj prof Agarrett Theol Sem Chicago Religious Inst 1980; chmn Chicago United Meth Fellowship 1980; pres Englewood United Meth Cluster 1980; mem Intl Black Writers 1980; pres Student Assn Garrett Theol Sem 1961. **HONORS/ACHIEVEMENTS:** Pub book "Dating Habits of Young Black Ams" 1979; pub articles best b Lack sermons Vol II Judson Press 1979; pub articles Metro Ministgry David C Cook Pub 1979. **MILITARY SERVICE:** AUS sgt 1954-57. **BUSINESS ADDRESS:** Christ United Meth Church, 6401 S Sangamon St, Chicago, IL 60621.

PORTER, JOHN T.
Business executive. **PERSONAL:** Born Feb 21, 1941, Brady, TX; children: John Jr, Christian. **EDUCATION:** IL Coll, BA 1968; Sangamon State U, MA 1971. **CAREER:** IL Bell Telph Co, various 1968-79, dist mgr training 1979-80, dist mgr AA/EEO 1980-. **ORGANIZATIONS:** Exec brd mem Govr's Coucl on Devep Disb 1984-; brd mem IL State Assoc Retd Citiz 1984-; pres Hope Schl 1975-81; mem Disbl Am Vet's 1963-. **MILITARY SERVICE:** AUS e-5 3 yrs, 7 mos. **HOME ADDRESS:** 190 S Wood Dale Rd, Unit 905, Wood Dale, IL 60191. **BUSINESS ADDRESS:** District Manager AA/EEO, IL Bell Tele Co, 212 W Washington, HQ 2g, Chicago, IL 60606.

PORTER, JOHN W.
Superintendent of school/chief executive officer. **PERSONAL:** Born Aug 13, 1931, Ft Wayne, IN; son of James Porter and Ola Mae Porter; married Lois Helen French; children: Stephen James, Donna Agnes. **EDUCATION:** Albion Coll, Albion MI, BA, 1953; Michigan State Univ, East Lansing MI, MA, 1957, PhD, 1962. **CAREER:** Lansing Public Schools, Lansing MI, counselor 1953-58; Michigan Dept Public Instruction, consultant, 1958-61; Michigan Dept HE Asst Auth, dir, 1961-66; Michigan Dept of HE, assoc supt, 1966-69, state supt, 1969-79; Eastern Michigan Univ, Ypsilanti MI, pres, 1979-89; Detroit Publ Schools, gen supt 1989—; Urban Educ Alliance, Inc, chief exec officer 1989—. **ORGANIZATIONS:** Chmn Natl Sel Comm for Outstanding HS Seniors sponsored by NASSP/Cent III 1981; chmn AASCU Task Force on Excellence in Educ 1983; mem MI Cncl for the Humanities 1984; chmn Coll Ent Exam Bd NY 1984; apptd by Sec of HEW Jos Califano to the Natl Adv Cncl on Soc Svcs; chmn Amer Assoc of State Colls & Univs Task Force on Excellence in Educ 1984-86; mem MI Council for the Humanities; mem holiday commn MI Martin Luther King 1986; mem Natl Commn for Coop Educ 1986, Governor's Blue Ribbon Commn on Welfare Reform 1986-87; vice chmn Natl Commn on the Future of State Colls & Univs 1986. **HONORS/ACHIEVEMENTS:** Marcus Foster Disting Educator Award Natl Alliance of Black Sch Educators' Conv 1979; Cert of Recog Alpha Kappa Alpha Sorority Eastern MI Univ 1979; State Admin Bd Ten-Year Serv Resolu State Cap Lansing, MI 1979; Educator of the Decade Award MI Assn of State and Fed Program Spec 1979; MI Pub Sch Cert of Award Pontiac Pub Sch 1979; Res of Serv as Supt of Pub Instr Metro Detroit Alliance of Black Sch Educators 1979; Anthony Wayne Award Coll of Educ Wayne State Univ 1979; Disting Alumni Award MI State Univ 1979; Recong Award for Contrib to Educ Wayne Cnty Comm Coll 1979; Momemento for Serv as Supt ofPub Inst Coll of Educ Alumni Assn Wayne St Univ 1979; Cert of Commendation Educ Serv Award MI Cong of Parents Teachers and Students 1979; President's Award as Disting Educator Natl Alliance of Black Sch Educators 1977; Who's Who in Black America; Who's Who in America; numerous publications incl, "The Counselor as Educationalist" The Personnel and Guidance Journ 1982; "Why Minimum Competency Now?" JC Penney Forum 1980; "Education, The Challenging Frontier" Colorado Journ of Educ Research 1976; "Better Education Through Accountability, Research, Program Budgeting" Michigan Challenge 1973. **BUSINESS ADDRESS:** Chief Executive Officer, Urban Education Alliance, 2835 Carpenter Rd, Ann Arbor, MI 48108. *

PORTER, JOSEPH E., III
Attorney. **PERSONAL:** Born Feb 15, 1946, Kansas City, KS. **EDUCATION:** CA St Univ LA; Univ So CA Sch of Law. **CAREER:** Kaplan Livingston Goodwin Berkowitz & Selvin, clerk; Motown Record Corp, atty; Motown Prods Inc, asst vp; Amer Int Pictures, leg counsel; Ziskin Kahan & Porter, atty. **ORGANIZATIONS:** Co-fndr Black Amer Law Stus Assn; mem Beverly Hills Bar Assn; mem exec bd Langston Bar Assn; mem US Crt App for Ninth Cir; mem US Supreme Ct; US Dist Ct of Appeals for DC; US Tax Ct; founder Enter Law Sectn for the CA Assn of Black Lawyers; Black Enter Lawyers Assn Beverly Hills Brch-NAACP; mem Kappa Alpha Psi; mem Cpyrght Assn; mem bd dirUniv So CA Law Cntr. **HONORS/ACHIEVEMENTS:** Hon resltn CA Legisltr.

PORTER, KARL HAMPTON
Musician, conductor, educator. **PERSONAL:** Born Apr 25, 1939, Pittsburgh, PA; son of

Naomi Givens. **EDUCATION:** Carnegie-Mellon; Peabody Conservatory; Juilliard Sch of Music; Domaine Sch of Conductors; Fordham Univ. **CAREER:** Baltimore Symphony, conductor 1971-72; Massapequa Symphony, conductor 1975-78; Park West Symphony, conductor; Harlem Philharmonic, conductor; NYCTC/CUNY, instructor; Josephine Baker - Musical Director/Cond, 1974. **ORGANIZATIONS:** Pres Finale Productions 1978-87; Sickle Cell 1970-; Arts & Letters 1974-; Dance Theatre of Harlem 1971-78. **HONORS/ACHIEVEMENTS:** Listed Who's Who in America; Natl Endowment Grant. **HOME ADDRESS:** 425 Central Park West, New York, NY 10025. **BUSINESS ADDRESS:** PO Box 445, New York, NY 10025.

PORTER, KEVIN
Athlete. **PERSONAL:** Born Apr 17, 1950, Chicago, IL; married Cleota; children: Kevin, Kandace, Kelly. **CAREER:** Detroit Pistons bsktbl player 1975-79; Wash Bullets, bsktbl player 1974-75; Baltimore, bsktbl player 1972-74. **HONORS/ACHIEVEMENTS:** Led NBA in assists three times; holds leag record for assists in ne Game (29) 1978; holds NBA assist record 1099 in a season 1978-79; Bullets assist record 650 in one seasn & 80 average 1974-75; holds Bullets career record 59 average during playoffs. **BUSINESS ADDRESS:** Washington Bullets, 1 Harry S Truman Dr, Landover, MD 20786.

PORTER, LIONEL
Business executive. **PERSONAL:** Born Jan 26, 1943, Canton, MS. **EDUCATION:** IN State Univ, BA 1966; Univ of CT, MA, ABD 1975, JD 1985. **CAREER:** Arsenal Tech HS, english teacher 1966-68; Aetna Life & Casualty, mgmt trainee 1968-69; Hartford Public HS; english teacher 1969-70; Univ of Hartford, instr/am lit 1975-78;Univ Conn Health Ctr, title XX cons, training dir 1978-. **ORGANIZATIONS:** Vp Blue Hills Civic Assoc 1978-80; participant Leadership Greater Hartford 1980-81; bd mem Community Council of Capitol Reg 1981-82, Amer Heart Assoc 1984-. **HONORS/ACHIEVEMENTS:** Outstanding Young Men in Amer Awd; EPDA Fellowship Univ of CT 1970-75.

PORTER, MICHAEL LEROY
Deputy director general. **PERSONAL:** Born Nov 23, 1947, Newport News, VA; son of Leroy Porter and Doretha Bradley Porter. **EDUCATION:** VA State Univ Petersburg, BA Sociology (Hon) 1969; Atlanta Univ, MA Hist 1972; Leonardo DaVinci Acad, Rome, Italy, MCP Contem 1983-84; Emory Univ, PhD Hist/Amer Studies 1974; Thomas Nelson Community Coll, Hampton VA, Cert Crim Justice 1981; US Armed Forces Staff Coll, Norfolk VA, US Pres Appt, 1987. **CAREER:** WA State Univ, asst prof of history, black studies prog 1974-75; Dept History Molegan Comm Coll, lectr 1975-76; Newport News VA, asst editorial coord, editor comp, target proj prog 1977; Hampton Univ, asst prof history 1977-80; NC Mutual Ins Co, life ins underwriter 1980-81; Mullins Prot Serv VA Bch, private instr 1981-83; Amer Biographical Inst Raleigh, media freelancer 1984-85, publications dir/deputy governor 1985-; Old Dominion Univ, Norfolk VA, consultant 1985; Intl Biographical Ctr, Cambridge England, deputy dir gen 1986-. **ORGANIZATIONS:** Life patron World Inst of Achievement 1985; curator "Michael L Porter Historical & Literary Collection"; mem World Literary Acad 1984-; mem World Biographical Hall of Fame 1985; mem City of Hampton Stand-By Selective Serv Bd 1986-; mem Intl Advisory Council, 1989-; mem Republican Inner Circle, 1988-; chairperson US Selective Service Training Conference, 1987; mem US Presidential Transition Comm, 1989-. **HONORS/ACHIEVEMENTS:** World Medal of Achievement 1983; Commemorative Medal of Honor 1984; US Presidential Medal of Merit 1985; US Presidential Commn 1986; Grand Ambassador of Achievement Amer Biographical Inst 1986; VSU Alumni Memorial Gold Medallion 1987; Intl Hall of Leaders, Amer Biographical Inst, 1988; participant (exhibit), DuSable Museum of Black History, 1988; honoree, Intl Exhibit, Singapore, Malaysia, 1988; Outstanding Man of the World, Ormiston Place, Tasmania, Australia, 1989. **MILITARY SERVICE:** AUS pfc, 1969-71; Natl Defns Medal, 1971; Certificate of Appreciation, AUS, 1971; Certificate of Appreciation, US Armed Forces, 1971; Vietnam Vets Natl Medal, 1986. **HOME ADDRESS:** 3 Adrian Cir, Hampton, VA 23669-3814.

PORTER, OTHA L.
Educator. **PERSONAL:** Born Apr 02, 1928, Indianapolis, IN; son of Theodore Porter and Addie J Porter; married Ruth; children: Theodore C, Otha Jr, Lola Geneva. **EDUCATION:** IN Univ, BS 1949, MS 1950, EdD 1970. **CAREER:** Langston HS, teacher 1950-51; Ft Valley State Coll, teacher 1951; Carver Elem School, instr 1954-57; Pulaski Jr HS, asst princ 1957-58; Drew Elem School, prin 1958-66; Horace Mann HS, asst prin 1966-67; Edison HS, prin 1967-68; Pulaski Jr HS, 1968-69; IN Univ, admin asst 1969-70; Gary Publ Schools, suprv 1970-71; Schools City of Gary, dist supt 1971-72; E Orange NJ Publ Schools, supt 1972-82; Plainfield NJ HS, suprv of science 1982-84, vice principal 1984-88; Hubbard Middle School, principal, 1988-. **ORGANIZATIONS:** Mem various offices, commiss Northwest Div IN State Teachers Assoc; mem Northwest IN Assoc Elem School Princ, Assoc Gary Elem Princ, IN State Teachers Assoc, NJ Ed Consortium, Title I State Adv Council, E Orange Publ Library Bd Trustees, NJ Schoolmasters Club, Phi Delta Kappa, Kappa Kappa Psi, NEA, Assoc of Childhood Ed, Intl Reading Assoc; life mem IN Univ Alumni Assoc; bd treas Gary Legal Aid Soc; bd sec St Timothy Comm Ch; mem Alpha Phi Alpha Soc Frat; mem NAACP; bd pres Gary Sanitary Dist; elder Elmwood Presbyterian Church East Orange NJ 1988. **MILITARY SERVICE:** Instructor SE Signal Sch Camp Gordon GA 1951-53. **HOME ADDRESS:** 110 Woodland Ave, East Orange, NJ 07017.

PORTER, PATRICK A.
Safety engineer. **PERSONAL:** Born Sep 10, 1944, Maryville, TN. **EDUCATION:** TN State U, BS 1966. **CAREER:** Union Carbide Nuclear Div, radiographer 1967-72; lab supr 1972; eng 1974. **ORGANIZATIONS:** Mem Am Soc of Safety Engrs; Am Soc Nondestrctv Testing Inc; mem NAACP; Jaycees; TN Council Human Relatns; hon mem Sheriffs Assn. **HONORS/ACHIEVEMENTS:** Who's Who Politics S & SW. **BUSINESS ADDRESS:** Union Carbide Co, Y12 Plant, Oak Ridge, TN 37830.

PORTER, RICHARD SYLVESTER
Business executive. **PERSONAL:** Born Jun 09, 1923, Gloster, MS; married Annie Mae Matthews; children: Shirley Ann, Erick Lynn, Justin Paul. **EDUCATION:** US Army, SS 1943; Leland Baptist Coll, BA, BTh 1952-53; Amer Baptist Coll & Seminary Citation 1977; Harper Baptist Seminary, DD 1977. **CAREER:** NAACP, pres meridian chap 1963-71; Meridian Ed Found Inc, pres 1964-69; Weem's Mental Health Ctr, therapeutist 1967-70; Lauderdale Cty reg 10 Mental Bd, commissioner 1970-73; Harper Baptist Seminary, pres. **ORGANIZATIONS:** Pastor Owens Chapel Baptist Church Columbia MS 1953-59, 1973-; pres EMS Baptist State Convention Inc 1969-; mem of bd Natl Baptist Convention USA Inc1969-; advisor Marion Cty Civic Club 1980-; chmn of bd of dir Owens Gymnasium Found 1981-; lecturer MS Seminary Ctr Columbia MS 1984-; advisor to governor Prison Reform 1985. **HONORS/ACHIEVEMENTS:** Human Devel Columbia Devel Prog Inc 1981; Commun Serv Governor's Office 1983. **MILITARY SERVICE:** AUS sgt 1942-46; 4 Bronze Stars 1943. **BUSINESS ADDRESS:** President, Harper Baptist Seminary, 1310 Marion Ave, Columbia, MS 39429.

PORTER, SCOTT E.
Dentist. **PERSONAL:** Born Nov 15, 1924, Humboldt, TN. **EDUCATION:** Univ of Toledo Coll of Arts & Sci, BS 1949; OH State U, BS Scndry Educ 1952; OH StateUniv Coll of Dentistry, DDS 1957. **CAREER:** Dentist, pvt prac; Toledo Health Dept, asst to dir of Dental Serv 1960-66. **ORGANIZATIONS:** Mem Bd Mgrs YMCA 1958-; life mem NAACP; mem Am & OH Dental Assn; Toledo Dental Soc; OH StateUniv Alumnae Assn;Univ of Toledo Alumnae Assn; life mem Kappa Alpha Psi Frat; Rep Party; Mason; Shriner; mem Worldwide Sportsmen's Club. **HONORS/ACHIEVEMENTS:** Recip Spl Award for Support of YMCA Serv 1974, 75, 76, 77; listed Marquis Who's Who in Am Reg Listing 38th Edit 1974-75; listed Marquis Who's Who in the Midwest 14th Edit 1974-75. **HOME ADDRESS:** 1023 Lincoln Ave, Toledo, OH 43607.

PORTER, YVONNE
Representative. **PERSONAL:** Born Nov 01, 1942, Gary, IN. **EDUCATION:** IN U, 1960-62; Chicago Sch of Dental Nursing, 1962-63; Roosevelt U, 1971-75. **CAREER:** United Steelworkers of Am, leg & polit action rep; USWA Job Related Female Problems, consult 1977; Inland Steel Co, 1966-75; Lake Co Bd of Registration 1965. **ORGANIZATIONS:** Gary Commn on & Statues Of Women 1974; Del Dem Nat Conv 1974; Gary League of Women Voters; Nat Black Polit Caucus 1972; =IN Black Caucus 1972; del USWA Intl Convs 1970,72,74; NOW; CLU Feted at testimonial dinner given by Black Steelworkers of Dist 31 1976. **HONORS/ACHIEVEMENTS:** Award for comm involvement NAACP 1976; award in black comm, award for 1976; nominated for 1977 award by Intl Women's Yr Conf 1977.

PORTIS, KATTIE HARMON (JESSIE KATE HARMON)
Organization executive. **PERSONAL:** Born Oct 28, 1942, Kinterbish, AL; married Jesse; children: Dawn, Luther, Torris. **EDUCATION:** Franconia Coll, BA 1976; Antioch Coll, MA, Human Service Mgmt. **CAREER:** Women Inc Dorchester MA, founder/exec dir; Concilio Drug Program, counselor 1974; Stamford Outreach Proj Turnabout, 1973; 1st Residental Drug-Free Program for Women & Children Who are Abusing Alcohol or Drugs, founder, 1973; Community Coordinator/founder, Boston Women and Aids Risk Network, 1987-present. **ORGANIZATIONS:** Consultant, Women & Health 1975; Northeastern Univ 1974; Research & Demonstratn Project, 1975; Treatmnt conf for Women 1976; mem 3rd World Womens Caucus 1974; mem Policy Advisory Bd; chmn BostonUniv Screening Bd; mem Mayor Coordinating Council on Drug Abuse; MA Comm Children & Youth Advisory Bd. **HONORS/ACHIEVEMENTS:** Certificate Yale Univ 1973; Testimony US House of Reps Select Comm on Narcotics Abuse & Control Task Force on Women & Drug Abuse 1980; presentation "Lack of Serv for Women" Sec of State Patricia Harris 1980; Hero Award, Boston Parents Paper; Abigal Adams Award; Metro Boston Alive Leadership Award; Dept of Public Health Leadership Award; Office for Children, Outstanding Service for Children. **BUSINESS ADDRESS:** 244 Townsend St, Dorchester, MA 02124.

PORTLOCK, CARVER A.
Business executive. **PERSONAL:** Born Jun 08, 1934, Muskogee, OK. **EDUCATION:** Bethune Ckmn Coll, BA Religion/Philosophy 1955; Syracuse U, Grad Study 1956-57. **CAREER:** Bethune Cookman Coll, asst instr speech & drama 1955-56; Dade Cty Jvnl Ct/Miami, cnslr of dlnqnt boys 1959-61; CME Church Paine Coll, admin asst/bdlay actvts 1961-62; Natl Alumni Assoc/Bethune Ckmn Coll, exec sec 1962-66; SmithKline Corp, cmnty rels coord 1966-68, mgr cmnty rels. **ORGANIZATIONS:** Pres Natl Alumni Assoc/Bethune Cookman Coll 1982-84; mem bd of dirs Big Brother/Big Sister Assoc 1981-. **HONORS/ACHIEVEMENTS:** United Negro Coll Fund Achvmnt Awrd 1984; Cmnty Serv Awd Berean Inst 1983; Professional Serv Awd Crisis Intrvntn Network 1981; Hon LLD Bethune-Cookman Coll 1986. **MILITARY SERVICE:** AUS Korea 1957-59. **BUSINESS ADDRESS:** Manager of Community Relations, Smithkline Beckman Corp, 1500 Spring Garden St, Philadelphia, PA 19101.

POSEY, BRUCE KEITH
Regulatory counsel. **PERSONAL:** Born Mar 22, 1952, Baton Rouge, LA. **EDUCATION:** Univ of OR, BS 1970-74;Univ of MI, JD 1974-77. **CAREER:** US West Communications; Pacific Northwest Bell; Stoel Rives Boley Fraser & Wyse, attorney 1977-; Urban League of Portland, dir 1979-; Martin Luther King Jr Scholarship Fund of OR, pres 1979-. **ORGANIZATIONS:** Mem ACLU 1978-; sec OR State Bar Affirmative Action Steering Com 1979-; mem Assn of OR Black Lawyers 1979-. **BUSINESS ADDRESS:** US West Communications, 1801 California St #5100, Denver, CO 80202.

POSEY, EDWARD W.
Psychiatrist. **PERSONAL:** Born May 29, 1927, Youngstown, OH; married Fanny Berryman; children: Bruce, Ada, Michael. **EDUCATION:** Ohio Univ, 1944-48; MeHarry Medical Coll, MD 1952; Univ of Minnesota, Psychiatry 1965. **CAREER:** Minneapolis VA Medical Center, dir day hospital 1965-71, chief psychiatry serv 1971-79, chief outpatient psychiatry 1979-; Univ of Minnesota, psychiatrist, asst prof 1965-. **ORGANIZATIONS:** Const Pilot City Health Center 1969-; chmn minority studies program comm Univ of Minnesota Medical School 1971-; Sigma Pi Phi; Natl Medical Assn. **HONORS/ACHIEVEMENTS:** Fellow Amer Psychiatric Assn 1972; diploma Amer Bd of Psychiatry/Neurology 1968; examiner Amer Bd of Psychiatry/Neurology. **MILITARY SERVICE:** USNR lieutenant 1953-55. **HOME ADDRESS:** 2808 W Highland Dr, Burnsville, MN 55337. **BUSINESS ADDRESS:** Chief Outpatient Psychiatry, MN VA Medical Ctr, Minneapolis VA Medical Ctr, Minneapolis, MN 55417.

POSEY, RONALD ANTHONY
Architect. **PERSONAL:** Born Feb 19, 1953, San Diego, CA. **EDUCATION:** Southern Univ, BA (Magna Cum Laude) 1976; Univ of CA-Berkeley, MA (w/Highest Honors) 1978. **CAREER:** Pacific Gas & Elec, summer inst 1974; Perkins & James, internship 1975-76; Burns

& McDonnell, project architect 1978-83, project mgr 1983-87. **ORGANIZATIONS:** Career awareness Urban League 1979-82; educ comm Amer Inst of Arch 1980; program comm of architects 1982; pres Southern Univ Alumni Assoc KCMO 1982-87; bd of dirs Clymer Comm Ctr 1983-87; mem Urban League 1986, Legislative Action 1987; cultural arts presentor KCMO; bd of dirs Euphrates Art Gallery; mem Alpha Kappa Mu Natl Honor Soc. **HONORS/ACHIEVEMENTS:** Amer Inst of Architects Medal of Excellence 1976; cultural and artistic production presentations Gentlemen of Distinction 1981-87; Black Achiever in Business& Industry Southern Christian Leadership Conf 1982; Centurion Leadership Develop Kansas City Chamber of Commerce 1983; Urban Design Publication Baton Rouge LA; Man of the Yr Gentlemen of Distinction Civic Inc Kansas City 1986. **HOME ADDRESS:** 1505-50 Citadel Dr, Kansas City, MO 64110. **BUSINESS ADDRESS:** Architectural Project Manager, Burns & McDonnell, 4800 East 63rd St, Kansas City, MO 64141.

POST, H. CHRISTIAN See PANDYA, HARISH C.

POSTEN, WILLIAM S.
Judge. **PERSONAL:** Born Mar 10, 1931, E Moline, IL; son of Vernie Teague and Aquilla Teague; married Pauline Ann; children: Karen, Scott, David, Elaine, Melissa. **EDUCATION:** Minneapolis Coll Law, BSL 1953; Wm Mitchell Coll Law, JD 1959. **CAREER:** US Govt SS Admin, 1960-61, asst cty attny 1961-73; Hennepin Cty, mun ct judge 1973-76; Minneapolis Dist Court, judge 1976-. **ORGANIZATIONS:** Past mem, adv bd Turning Point; adv bd Genesis II; adv bd Salvation Army; mrm Amer, MN & Hennepin Cty Bar Assoc, Amer Assoc Black Lawyers, NAACP, Amer Leg; former Comm Health & Welfare Cty; mem Met Minneapolis March of Dimes. **MILITARY SERVICE:** Mil Serv 1953-55. **BUSINESS ADDRESS:** Judge, District Court of Minneapolis, Hennepin Co Gvt Cntr, 18 Fl Courts Tower, Minneapolis, MN 55487.

POSTON, CARL C., JR.
Attorney. **PERSONAL:** Born Oct 13, 1921, Memphis; married Thelma Kirkland; children: Carl, Keith, Kevin, Craig. **EDUCATION:** LeMoyne Coll, BA 1942; Univ Training Ctr Florence Italy, 1945; Wayne St U, Law Degree 1950. **CAREER:** Attorney, self-emplyd; Saginaw City Cncl, 1970-73; Mayor Pro Tem, 1971-73; Asst Co Prosecutor, 1966-68; Human Relatns, 1961-68; Civil Rights Referee, 1967-70. **ORGANIZATIONS:** Mem Fraternities; Press Club; MI St Bar Grievnc Referee 1972; St Bar Econ Com 1969; Workmens Compenstn Sec 1960; Negligence Sec 1960-; St Bar Legisltv Com 1972-73; mem & past pres Saginaw Co Youth Protectn Cncl 1962-; vice pres Big Brothers 1966-67; treas & mem OIC Metropolitan Saginaw 1968-; mem Alpha Phi Alpha Frat; city rep Saginaw Co Bd of Supervis 1960-66, 68-70; past pres Frontiers 1963. **HONORS/ACHIEVEMENTS:** Outstndg Servc as mem chrmn NAACP; award C of C civic respnsblty; Frontiersman of Yr 1968. **MILITARY SERVICE:** AUS sgt tech 1943-46. **BUSINESS ADDRESS:** 1515 E Genesee St, Saginaw, MI 48601.

POSTON, ERSA HINES
Retired business executive. **PERSONAL:** Born May 03, 1921, Paducah, KY; widowed. **EDUCATION:** KY State Coll, AB 1942; Atlanta U, MSW 1946; Union Coll, honorary LLD 1971. **CAREER:** NY State Civil Serv Comm, pres 1967-75, commr 1975-; NY State Offc Econ Opportnty, dir 1965-67; NY Exec Chamber, confidntl asst Gov Nelson A Rockefeller 1964-65; NY State Div Youth, youth work prog coord 1962-64; NY State Youth Commsn, area dir 1957-62; NY City Youth Bd, asst dir 1955-57; NYCity Welfare & Hlth Cncl, field sec 1953-55; Clinton Comm Ctr, dir 1950-53, asst dir 1949-50, young adult prog dir 1948-49; W Side Branch Yng Women's Christn Assoc, teenage prog dir 1947-48; Hartford TB & Hlth Assoc, comm org sec 1946-47. **ORGANIZATIONS:** Vp United Fund of Albany Area Inc; mem Intl Personnel Mgmt Assoc; mem Nat Assoc Social Wrkrs; mem Nat Conf Social Welfare; mem Nat Academy PubAdm; mem NAACP; mem Academy Certfd Social Wrkrs; mem Am Soc Pub Adm; mem NY State Welfare Conf Inc; various other mem; hon mem Nu Chap Lambda Kappa Mu; Delta Kappa Gamma; 369 Vet Assoc; chmn, pres Adv Cncl Intergovtl Personnel Policy 1971-74; vice pres Nat Urban Leag 1972-74. **HONORS/ACHIEVEMENTS:** Nat'l Assoc Negro Bus & Prof Women's Club Achvmnt Award 1965, Nat'l Achvmnt 1967; Woman of Yr Awards twice in 1967; Jamaica Club Nat'l Assoc Negro Bus & Prof Womens Clubs Trail Blazer 1967; NY Careerists Soc Inc Good Govt Award 1967; Bus & Prof Women's Club NY Woman of Yr 1970; AtlantaUniv Distngshd Alumna 1971; Caucus Black Legisltrs State of NY Distngshd Serv 1971; mem US Delgtn to UN Gen Assemb 1976; NY StateUniv Pres Distngshd Serv Citation 1973; numerous other achievmnts.

POTTER, JUDITH DIGGS
Educator. **PERSONAL:** Born Jul 23, 1941, Norwood, MA; divorced; children: Wende Beth, Kimberly Ann. **EDUCATION:** Lesley Coll, BS Educ 1964; Wheelock Coll, MS Educ 1977. **CAREER:** Boston Public Schools, teacher 1964-65; Medway Public Schools, teacher 1965-66; Brookline Headstart, teacher 1968; Boston Public Schools, teacher 1968-. **ORGANIZATIONS:** Delegate MA Federation of Teachers, Amer Federation of Teachers 1977-85; delegate Boston Labor Council, Building Rep-Boston T Union 1977-87; founder secty/treas Black Caucus Boston Teachers Union #66 1978-83; coord Try Arts & Chap 188 Boston Public Sch 1978-86; grad advisor Delta Sigma Theta Inc Boston Alumnae 1980-81; co-author Boston Public School Kindergarten Exam 1981; panelist Natl Endowment for the Arts 1984. **HONORS/ACHIEVEMENTS:** Teacher of the Year Boston Public Schools 1983; featured in Christian Science Monitor and Albuquerque Journal 1986. **HOME ADDRESS:** One Brook St, Brookline, MA 02146.

POTTINGER, ALBERT A.
Attorney. **PERSONAL:** Born Apr 24, 1928, Topeka, KS; married Delores Johnson. **EDUCATION:** Washburn Munic U, BBA 1951; Cleveland St Law Sch, LLB 1959. **CAREER:** Atty, self; City Cleveland, cnclmn 1968-69, relocator, property mgr 1968-69, 1st asst prosecutor 1964-65. **ORGANIZATIONS:** Bd tsts Children Serv; Cath Big Bros; Cath Charities; Harvard-Lee Comm Serv. **BUSINESS ADDRESS:** 33 Pub Sq, Cleveland, OH 44113.

POTTS, HAROLD E.
Educator. **PERSONAL:** Born Jun 26, 1921, Youngstown, OH; married Audrey; children: Stephen, Stephanie, Christopher. **EDUCATION:** Springfield Coll, Doctoral Study 1962, MS 1961; NY U, MA 1954, Certf 1951; Springfield Coll, BS 1950. **CAREER:** Quinnipiac Coll, prof, dir physical Therapy 1969-; Springfield Coll, bd of Trustee; Quinnipiac Coll, bd of trustee; US Dept Health Educ & Welfare, prog specialist 1966-69; Gaylord Hosp, admin asst 1962-66; Springfield Coll, research asst 1961-62; Neuromuscular Diagnostic Serv Hospital Center, W Orange NJ, chief physical therapist, research asst, conselor, asst 1960-61; St CT Veterans Hospital Rocky Hill, research asst, supr, clincal instr 1958-60; Kessler Inst Rehabilitaion Physically Handicapped, W Orange NJ, dir physical therapy 1956-58, asst dir physical therapy, supr clinical exprnc for student therapists 1955-56. **ORGANIZATIONS:** Numrs publs speakg experne 1951-75; bd of dir New Haven Easter Seal Goodwl Ind Rehab Ctr; Am Phys Therapy Assn; CT Chap APTA bd dir; Nat Rehab Assn; Nat Athltc Trnrs Assn; Am Coll Sports Medicine; Intl Soc Electromyogrphc Kinesiology; NE Phys Therapy Eductrs; Rotary Club Wallingford CT bd dirs, schlrchp awards com, vocatnl serv com; Comm Devel Action Prog N Branford Hlth Com; N Branford Schlrshp Assn Inc bd dir; New Haven Schlrshp Assn; Greater New Haven Area Rehab Cncl; Wallingford YMCA bd dirs Bldg Com; Springfield Coll Alumni Assn; Springfield Coll Corp Academic Affrs Com; Zoning Bd Appeals N Branford. **HONORS/ACHIEVEMENTS:** Nat Found Phys Therapy Schlrshp 1950; Offc Vocatnl Rehab Traineeship 1957; Am Phys Therapy Assn Traineeship 1961; Rotarian of Yr 1973. **MILITARY SERVICE:** USCG signal man 2nd class. **BUSINESS ADDRESS:** Co-Chm of Physical Therapy, Quinnipiac College, Mt Carmel Ave, Hamden, CT 06518.

POTTS, SAMMIE
College administrator. **CAREER:** Mary Holmes College, West Point MS, president. **BUSINESS ADDRESS:** Mary Holmes College, West Point, MS 39773. *

POUNDER, C. C. H.
Actress. **PERSONAL:** Born Dec 25, 1952, Georgetown. **EDUCATION:** Ithaca Coll, BFA 1975. **HONORS/ACHIEVEMENTS:** Nominated for NAACP Image Awd for Best Actress in TV Drama 1986.

POUNDS, AUGUSTINE WRIGHT
Educator, educational administrator. **PERSONAL:** Born Jul 20, 1936, Wadley, AL; daughter of Cortelyou Busbee (deceased) and Flossie Wilkes Busbee (deceased); married Russell G Pounds, Jul 04, 1981; children: Karen V Williams, Georgina Young. **EDUCATION:** Pontiac Business Inst, attended 1958-60; Oakland Comm Coll, attended 1965; Oakland Univ, BA 1973, MA 1975; IA State Univ, PhD 1980. **CAREER:** Oakland Univ, consultant black cultural ctr 1966-68, admin asst to vice pres for urban affairs 1968-71, asst dir of commuter serv 1971-73; Oakland Univ, asst dir student ctr 1973-75; Univ of Zambia, vstg prof 1984; IA State Univ, asst dir minority student affairs 1975-76, asst dean of student life 1976-80, assoc dean of student life 1980-84, dean of students 1984; Murray State Univ, vice pres of student devel, currently. **ORGANIZATIONS:** Mem White House Conf on Families Des Moines IA 1980; consultant evaluator North Central Assoc of Colls and Schools 1987; mem Ames Human Relations Commn; bd mem United Way of Ames, Amer Coll Personnel Assoc; mem Oakland Univ; adv bd Fine Arts Inst for Region V US Office of Educ; staff adv Assoc of Black Students; mem City Human Relat Commn; bd mem Family Serv of Oakland Co; first vice pres Oakland Co NAACP; bd mem New Horizons of Oakland Co; mem Amer Cncl on Educ, Natl Identification Prog, IA Student Personnel Assoc, Natl Assoc of Student Personnel Administrators; admin bd All Univ Comm Cncl; birthday celebration comm Martin Luther King Jr; mem Natl Assoc of Women Deans Adminis and Counselors; vice pres of assn relations, NAWDAC, 1989-90; exec comm, ACPA/CMA, 1988-; bd mem, Iowa Student Personnel Journal, 1987-. **HONORS/ACHIEVEMENTS:** Citizen of Yr Oakland Co Ministerial Assn 1970; Cert of Appreciation Cit Finance Study Com City of Pontiac Sch Dist 1968; Serv Awd OU Credit Union Adv Council 1973; Matilda Wilson Awd 1974; Outstanding Contribution to Quality of Life of all Students Oakland Univ 1977; Woman of the Year Story Co Women's Polit Caucus 1983; Martin Luther King Service Award, MLK Inc, State of Iowa; author of 2 publications on black students. **BUSINESS ADDRESS:** Vice Pres of Student Devel, Murray State Univ, Curris Center, Murray, KY 42071.

POUNDS, ELAINE
Media executive. **PERSONAL:** Born Dec 31, 1946, Detroit, MI; daughter of George Pounds and Ethel Loyd Pounds; divorced; children: Adrian Molett, Allen Parks. **EDUCATION:** Attended Los Angeles Southwest Coll, 1971; California State Univ, Los Angeles, BA, 1978; attended Los Angeles City Coll and Santa Monica City Coll, 1979-80. **CAREER:** Former production asst, KNBC-TV; former producer, KACE-Radio; former programming asst, Theta Cable Television; former promotions coord and traffic mgr, Group W Cable/Westinghouse Broadcasting Co; former asst traffic mgr, KTTV/Metromedia Television; KCET-TV, Los Angeles CA, currently works as corp mktg asst; Los Angeles Black Media Coalition (LABMC), current dir. **ORGANIZATIONS:** Natl Assn of Media Women, Alliance of Black Entertainment Technicians, Women in Show Business, NAACP, REEL Black Women, Southern Christian Leadership Conf. **BUSINESS ADDRESS:** Director, Los Angeles Black Media Coalition, P O Box 48899, Los Angeles, CA 90027.

POUNDS, KENNETH RAY
Business executive. **PERSONAL:** Born Jan 02, 1942, Herminie, PA; married Patricia Dore; children: Kenneth Troy. **EDUCATION:** Univ of Wash, BA 1971, MA/Urban Planning 1975. **CAREER:** PACE Property Mgmt Co Inc, pres 1980-; city of Seattle, asst supt of bldg 1979-80; Security Pacific Inc, vice pres 1976-78; Fed Energy Adminstrn, spl asst 1974-76; Dept of HUD, housing mgmt offcr 1971-74; city of Seattle-Dept of Comm Devel, loan offcr 1970-71. **ORGANIZATIONS:** Vp Central Area Fed Credit Union 1975-76; treas NW Conf of Black Pub Officials 1979; first vice pres Nat Bus League-Seattle chap 1979; mem Seattle KingCo Bd of Realtors 1978-80; mem Hercules Lodge No 17 1979; mem Central Area Kiwanis 1980. **HONORS/ACHIEVEMENTS:** Employee of yr Fed Reg Adminstrn Region X 1974; Potential Black Ldr NW Conf of Black Pub Officials 1979. **MILITARY SERVICE:** AUS e-5 1967-69. **BUSINESS ADDRESS:** 1801 E Yesler Way, Seattle, WA 98122.

POUNDS, MOSES B.
Educator. **PERSONAL:** Born Feb 18, 1947, Baltimore, MD; son of Moses B Pounds, Sr and Katherine McCutcheon Pounds; married Ann P McCauley, Dec 27, 1981; children: M Andrew M Pounds. **EDUCATION:** Univ of CA Santa Cruz, AB Anthrop 1974; Univ of CA Berkeley, MA Anthrop 1975; Univ of CA Berkeley and San Francisco, PhD Med Anthrop 1982. **CAREER:** The Johns Hopkins Univ Sch of Hygiene and Publ Health, asst prof dept behavioral scis & health educ 1982-88; Univ of Maryland at Baltimore, asst to the pres, project director and principal investigator, Mid-Atlantic AIDS Regional Educ and Training Center,1988-91. **ORGANIZATIONS:** Mem Amer Anthropological Assn, Assn for Asian Studies, Society for Med Anthrop, Kroeber Anthropological Soc. **HONORS/**

ACHIEVEMENTS: Biolog Sci Rsch Grant NIH The Johns Hopkins Univ 1982-84, 1984-85; Fellow Grad Minority Fellowship Univ of CA Berkeley 1979-81; Trainee Natl Inst of Gen Medical Serv NIH Grant 1977-79; Fellow Natl Sci Found Pre-doctoral Fellowship 1974-77; recip natl Fellowship Fund Fellowship (declined) 1974; Amer Found for AIDS Rsch Grant 1987-88; Natl Cancer Inst Grant 1988; Health Resources and Services Admin Grant 1988-91. **MILITARY SERVICE:** AUS Admin Asst Sgt E-6; hon discharged after 4 yrs (1966-70). **BUSINESS ADDRESS:** Asst to the Pres, Proj Dir and Principal Investigator, Mid-Atlantic AIDS Regional Educ and Training Center, 520 W Lombard, Office of the Pres, Univ of Maryland at Baltimore, Baltimore, MD 21201.

POURCIAU, KERRY L.
Business executive. **PERSONAL:** Born Sep 04, 1951, Baton Rouge. **EDUCATION:** LA State U, 1973. **CAREER:** Bauerlein Inc New Orleans, acct exec; Sen Russell B Long, spl asst;Sst. **ORGANIZATIONS:** Wash chap LSU Alumni Assn; vice pres SoUniv Sigma Delta Chi; Theta Alpha Phi; mem Pendulum Club Capit Hill; Capit Hill Dem; Smith Asso 1974-. **HONORS/ACHIEVEMENTS:** Who's Who Am Coll & U; first blck stud bdy pres LA StateUniv 1972-73.

POUSSAINT, ALVIN FRANCIS
Educator. **PERSONAL:** Born May 15, 1934, East Harlem, NY; married Ann Ashmore; children: Alan. **EDUCATION:** Columbia Coll, BA 1956; Cornell Univ Medical Coll, MD 1960; Univ CA Los Angeles, MS 1964. **CAREER:** STufts Univ Medical School, sr clinical instructor 1965-66; Med Com Human Rights, so field dir 1965-66; Tufts Univ Medical School, asst prof 1967-69; Columbia Pt Health Center, dir psychiatry 1968-69; MA Mental Health School, assoc psychiatrist 1969-; Harvard Medical School, assoc dean students 1969-; Judge Baker Guidance Center, senior assoc psychiatrist 1978-; Harvard Medical School, assoc prof Psychiatry. **ORGANIZATIONS:** Mem bd trustees Wesleyan Coll 1968-69; mem bd trustees Natl Afro Amer Artists 1968; chmn bd Solomon Fuller Inst 1975-81; mem bd dirs Operation PUSH 1971-; fellow Amer Spychiat Assn 1972-; mem Natl Medical Assn 1968-; natl treasurer Med Com Human Rights 1968-69; fellow, Amer Assn for the Advancement of Science, 1981-; affiliate mem, Amer Academy of Child Psychiatry, 1985-; chairman, Select Committee on the Educ of Black Youth, 1985-; fellow, Amer Orthopsychiatric Assn, 1987-. **HONORS/ACHIEVEMENTS:** Honorary degrees, Dr Humanities Wilberforce Univ 1972; Human Letter Govs State Univ 1982; Amer Black Achievement Award in Business and the Professions, 1986; John Jay Award for Distinguished Professional Achievement, 1987; Medgar Evers Medal of Honor, Johnson Publishing Co, 1988. **BUSINESS ADDRESS:** Assoc Professor of Psychiatry, Harvard Med Sch, 295 Longwood Ave, Boston, MA 02115.

POUSSAINT, ANN ASHMORE
Psychologist. **PERSONAL:** Born Jun 23, 1942, Atlanta, GA; married Alvin F Poussaint; children: Alan Machel. **EDUCATION:** Spelman Coll Atlanta, BA 1963; Simmons Coll Sch of Social Work, MS 1965; Univ of CA Berkeley, MA 1976, PhD 1979. **CAREER:** San Mateo Co CA Child Guidance Clinic, psychiatric social worker 1965-68; Roxbury Multi-Serv Center, social work supr 1968-69; PHP NY Hosp, patient coord 1969-70; Pacific Psychotherapy Assn, consult clinician 1970-73; Pacific Training Assn State Univ of CA at San Francisco, consult 1970-73; Private Practice, clinical psychologist 1974-81; Min Training Prog for Psychol BU & City Hosp, supr 1978-; Urban Psychological Associates, founder & dir 1981-. **ORGANIZATIONS:** Consult Howard Univ Press 1980; mem pub rel com Amer Psychol Assn; mem Assn of Black Psychologists; mem Links Inc. **HONORS/ACHIEVEMENTS:** Lectr & Contributor of articles in field to mags; Outstanding Young Women of Amer Spelman Coll 1969; Fellowship US Pub Health Scholar 1971-73; Cert of Appreciation Precedent Setting in Jury Selection Assn of Black Psychologists 1974; Who's Who of Amer Women 1981. **BUSINESS ADDRESS:** Dir, Urban Pschological Associates, 51 Brattle St, Ste 67, Cambridge, MA 02138.

POUSSAINT, RENEE FRANCINE
Journalist. **PERSONAL:** Born Aug 12, 1944, New York, NY; married Henry J Richardson. **EDUCATION:** Sorbonne Paris France/Yale Law Sch, attended 1965-67; Sarah Lawrence Coll Bronxville NY, BA 1966; UCLA, MA 1971; IN U, PhD studies 1972; Columbia USch of Jornalism, attended 1973. **CAREER:** WJLA-TV, anchor/reporter 1978-; CBS Network News Chicago Wash DC, reporter 1977-79; WBBM-TV Chicago, reporter/anchor/show host 1973-77; INUniv Bloomington, lectr/doctoral candidate 1972-73; African Arts Mag Los Angeles, editor 1969-73. **ORGANIZATIONS:** Program dir AIESEC New York 1967-69; dancer Jean Leon Destine Haitian Daznce 1967; translator UC Press 1970; peaker various pvt & govt orgn 1977-; mem Sigma Delta Chi; lifetime mem NAACP; mem Women in Communications Awards TV Reporting Nat Assn of Media Women 1975; Illinois Mental Health Assn 1975; Young Achiever YMCA Chicago 1976; Am Firefighters Assn 1977; Am AssnUniv Women 1979. **HONORS/ACHIEVEMENTS:** Outstanding serv US Dept of Labor Ed Women 1979; emmy Nat Acad of TV Arts & Scis 1980; religiton in Media 1980. **BUSINESS ADDRESS:** News Anchor, WJLA-TV, 4461 Connecticut Ave NW, Washington, DC 20008.

POWE, JOSEPH S.
Engineer. **PERSONAL:** Born Jul 26, 1946, Bremerton, WA. **EDUCATION:** Univ of WA, BS 1968; MS Physics 1971; MS Aero & Astro Engineering 1972. **CAREER:** Hughes Aircraft Co, senior scientist. **ORGANIZATIONS:** Mem Mensa. **BUSINESS ADDRESS:** Senior Scientist, Hughes Aircraft Co, 1950 E Imperial Hwy, BS41/MSA315, El Segundo, CA 90245.

POWELL, ADAM CLAYTON, III
Broadcasting. **PERSONAL:** Born Jul 17, 1946, New York, NY; son of Adam Clayton Powell Jr and Hazel Dorothy Scott (Powell). **BUSINESS ADDRESS:** Vice President, News, National Public Radio, 2025 M Street, NW, Washington, DC 20036.

POWELL, ADDIE SCOTT
Community organization founder and volunteer coordinator. **PERSONAL:** Born Nov 14, 1922, Augusta, GA; daughter of Matthew Marion Scott and Tillie Lyons Scott; divorced; children: Frances Powell Harris. **EDUCATION:** Paine Coll, AB 1943;Univ of IA, MA; Atlanta U, MA 1949. **CAREER:** Brooklyn Public Library, dist supv of adult svcs, 1970-74 (retired); Branch Lib Augusta GA, 1961-62; librarian various posts 1949-74; freelance writer resrchr & lecturer. **ORGANIZATIONS:** Mem Am Lib Assn; mem Round Table Coll Res Libraries; mem So Cncl on Human Relatns 1960-62; YMCA; Sickle Cell Anemia Assn; TV appearance "Voices of Bklyn" (intercultrl series Brooklyn Coll); Leadership Augusta 1986; bd of directors Fund for Southern Communities 1984-87; bd of directors Georgia Housing Coalition 1983-. **HONORS/ACHIEVEMENTS:** Carnegie Fellow 1951-52; author various works, tech publicatns; listed Who's Who in Lib Serv 1955; Community Service, Seventh Day Adventist Church 1982; Citizen of the Year, Augusta Unit, Natl Assn Social Workers 1983; Citizen's Participlation Study of Black Residents of Bethlehem 1980-81; Economic Devel Study: Marketable Skills Among Low Income Residents of Bethlehem; Land Use Study of Low Income Community of Bethlehem 1985-86. **BUSINESS ADDRESS:** Coordinator, Bethlehem Area Community Assn, Inc (BACA, Inc), 1634 Milledgeville Rd, Augusta, GA 30901.

POWELL, ALFRED
Attorney & educational administrator. **PERSONAL:** Born in Montgomery, AL; married Sherri V Thompson. **EDUCATION:** AL State Univ, BS 1965; Auburn Univ, PhD 1970; Washington Univ, JD 1981. **CAREER:** Calgon Corp, sr chemist 1970-72; AL State Univ, chem prof 1972-75, head chem dept 1975-76; KY State Univ, head chem dept 1976-78; Hon Charles Price Judge, law clerk & atty 1980-81; St Augustine Coll, chmn sci div 1983-84; GA Southwestern Coll, asst to pres 1984-. **ORGANIZATIONS:** Mem Amer Chem Soc; mem Amer Bar Assn; mem Bar US Dist Court. **HONORS/ACHIEVEMENTS:** Rsch Fellow Auburn Univ; President's Awd AL State Univ; mem Phi Lambda Upsilon Hon Chem Soc 1969-; mem Bar State of AL 1981-.

POWELL, ARCHIE JAMES
Educator. **PERSONAL:** Born Jun 01, 1950, Lakeland, FL; children: Kevin J. **EDUCATION:** Univ of Nantes, France, certificate 1971; Morehouse Coll, BA 1972; Brown Univ, MA 1974, PhD 1984. **CAREER:** RI Dept of Educ, planning specialist 1978-81; Brown Univ, minority affairs office 1981-85; Albany Medical Coll, asst professor 1985-, asst dean for minority affairs 1985-. **ORGANIZATIONS:** New England Assoc of Black Educators, mem; Organization of Amer Historians, mem; American Historical Society, mem; Assoc for the Study of Afro-American Life and History, mem; Rhode Island Black Heritage Society, mem; Natl Assoc of Medical Minority Educators, Inc, mem, northeast regional coord, 1987 conference co-chair; Albany Symphony Orchestra, bd of directors 1986-; Albany Boys Club, bd of directors 1986-; Black Dimensions in Art, Inc, bd of directors 1986-; Israel African Methodist Episcopal Church, trustee 1986-. **HONORS/ACHIEVEMENTS:** Morehouse Coll, merrill overseas travel-study grant 1970-71; The Ford Foundation, doctoral fellowship 1972-75; Phi Beta Sigma, distinguished service as as reg dir 1985; Mt Hope Day Care Center, Inc, distinguished service as board pres 1985; Outstanding Young Men of America 1986. **HOME ADDRESS:** 285 Hudson Ave, Albany, NY 12210. **BUSINESS ADDRESS:** Asst Dean for Minority Affair, Albany Medical College, 47 New Scotland Ave, Albany, NY 12208.

POWELL, ASTON WESLEY
Educator. **PERSONAL:** Born May 21, 1909, Santa Cruz, St Elizabeth, Jamaica;married Cynthia Marguerite; children: Leighton, Marilyn Yvonne Robinson, Douglas. **EDUCATION:** Columbia Univ, BSc 1945, MA 1946; Univ of the West Indies, Hon LLD 1983. **CAREER:** Blackman (daily newspaper), reporter 1929; Excelsior School, founder/headmaster 1931; Excelsior Educ Centre, founder/dir 1971, consultant/fund-raiser 1981-; North St Excelsior, dir. **ORGANIZATIONS:** Chmn, Amer Univ Grad Assn, 1954-57; pres, YMCA, 1972-77; pres, Jamaica Tchrs Assn, 1964-66; chmn, JTA Prof and Dev Comm, 1970-83; mem, Inst Bd of Tchr Educ (Univ of West Indies), 1970-76; dir, Kingston Rotary Club, 1972-83; mem, Jamaica Club, 1973-75; mem, Ministry of Educ Working Party on Post-Secondary Educ, 1973-74; mem, Coun Coll of Arts Science and Tech (CAST), 1975-79; mem, Jamaica Natl Reserve Coun, 1976-77; mem, Jamaica Honour Awards Comm, 1976-83; mem, Western New York/Jamaica Partners and mem of its Personal Comm, 1978-83; bd mem, Inst of Jamaica, 1980-83; mem, Jamaica/New York Concerned Citizens Christian Educ, 1981-83; mem, The Victoria League for Commonwealth Friendship, 1982-85. **HONORS/ACHIEVEMENTS:** Order of the British Empire; Outstanding Contrib to Jamaica in the Field of Educ, Jamaica Progressive League of New York Inc, 1970; Norman Manley Awd of Excellence, 1971; Catholic Tchrs Assn Jamaica, Special Awd, 1972; Dictionary of Intl Biography Certificate of Merit Distinguished Serv, 1973; Order of Jamaica, 1976; Jamaica Teachers' Assn Natl Roll of Honour, 1977; pres emeritus, YMCA, 1979; Outstanding & Unequalled Contrib to the Prov & Advancement of Educ for all Jamaicans, Rotary Club of Kingston, 1979; Recognition of Excellent & Dedicated Serv in Field of Educ, Jaycees of Jamaica, 1980; Daily Gleaner Certificate of Merit, 1980; Long Service Awd, Excelsior Old Students' Assn, 1981; Jamaica Distinguished Methodist Church Recog Outstanding Serv Field of Educ 1981; Plaque Contribution to the Devel of Higher Educ for the Blind in Jamaica, 1982; pres emeritus, Jamaica Tchrs Assn, 1983; chmn, Leila Tomlinson Wareika Basic Sch Bd, 1983; LLD Hon Dr of Laws, Univ of the West Indies, 1983; Outstanding Service to Independent Schools in Jamaica, 1983; Jamaica Geog Soc, Pioneer Geographer of Jamaica Awd, 1985; Nova Univ Citation of Merit, 1986. **HOME ADDRESS:** Doumarleigh Skyline Jacks Hill, PO Box 209, Kingston, Jamaica. **BUSINESS ADDRESS:** Dir, North St Excelsior, 16 North St, Kingston, Jamaica.

POWELL, BERNICE FLETCHER
Public relations manager. **PERSONAL:** Born Mar 09, 1949, Washington, DC; married Robert CS. **EDUCATION:** Wilson Coll, BA 1971; ColumbiaUniv Grad Sch of Journalism, MS 1975. **CAREER:** Women's Div Gov Offc NY, spl asst for pub info 1979-; Equitable Life Assur Soc, asso mgr pub relatns 1977-79; Nat Urban Leag, communctns spec1975-77; Renewal Mag, asst managing editor 1974-75; Nat Cncl of Ch, Africa dept asst 1972-74; Wash DC Sch System, tchr 1971-72. **ORGANIZATIONS:** Bd mem Manhattan Br NY Urban Leag 1978-; chrprsn Riverside Ch Video Project 1979-; vice pres Coalition of 100 Black Women 1980-81. **BUSINESS ADDRESS:** 1350 Ave of the Americas, New York, NY 10019.

POWELL, C. CLAYTON
Vision specialist. **PERSONAL:** Born Apr 11, 1927, Dothan, AL; son of Willie Powell and Evelyn Powell; married Romae Turner, Mar 11, 1954; children: C Clayton, Jr, Rometta E. **EDUCATION:** Morehouse Coll, AB; IL Coll of Optometry, BSc; Coll Optometry, OD; Univ of MI, graduate study MPH Program; Atlanta Univ, MEd; Illinois Coll of Optometry, DOS 1987. **CAREER:** Metro-Atlanta Child Devel Center & Health & Vision Clinic, devel vision specialist/exec dir; Atlanta Southside Comprehensive Health Center, exec dir 1973-76, chief of Optometry Dept 1968-73; AL, jr high school teacher/asst prin; PA Coll of Optometry, adjunct prof. **ORGANIZATIONS:** Mem Natl Eye Inst; adv com State Univ; Natl Assn

Neighborhood Health Centers; Amer Public Health Assn; legis com NANHC; mem 5th Dist, GA, Amer, Natl Optometric Assns; mem GA Vision Serv Inc; organizer, chmn Metro-Atlanta OEP Study Group; Ad Hoc Com Group Practice by pres Amer Optometric Assn; mem, offcr, coms, numerous other orgs; mem Beta Kappa Chi Natl Science Hon Soc/Tomb & Key Natl Hon Optom Soc/Beta Sigma Kappa Intl Hon Optom Soc/Mu Sigma Pi Professional Fraternity. **HONORS/ACHIEVEMENTS:** Recipient Outstanding Man of the Year Clark Coll, Morehouse Coll, Morris Brown Coll; Atlanta Graduate Chapter Omega Psi Phi; Outstanding Achievement Award Fulton Co Rep Club, Atlanta Postal Acad, Pine Acres Town & Country Club; Optometrist of the Year, Natl Optometry Assn 1984; Honorary Degree, Doctor of Ocular Science, Illinois Coll 1987. **HOME ADDRESS:** 403 Fielding Ln SW, Atlanta, GA 30315. **BUSINESS ADDRESS:** The Health and Vision Clinic, 2039 Stewart Ave, SW, Suite A, Atlanta, GA 30314.

POWELL, CHARLES L., JR.
Educator. **PERSONAL:** Born Jun 19, 1931, Laramie, WY. **EDUCATION:** Tuskegee Inst, BS 1952;Univ WV, BA 1953;Univ WY, MA 1955; The Am U, professional diplomas in commun & educ 1958. **CAREER:** ESL Prgms Hope Coll, prof fgn student adv dir 1971-; Hope Coll, 1971-; Fulbright, tchr prof spec in US Govt Tchr Training Prgms in SE Asia 1957-71; Am U, professional lectr 1956-58; Morgantown WV, tchr 1952-54. **ORGANIZATIONS:** Sec vice pres pres MI Assn TESOL; consult Micronesian Bilingual tchr training prgms; consult Vietnamese refugee educ prgms for MI; consult ESL instr Adult Educ Continuing Educ Prgms Am Assn ofUniv Profs; NEA; Soc for Intl Devel; Am Studies Assn; Nat Council of Tchrs of Eng; Overseas Educ Assn; Coop Coll Registry; Intl House of Japan; Ctr for Applied Linguistics; TESOL tchrs of Eng to Spkrs of Other Lang Vietnamese-Am Assn; Inst of Chinese Culture; Nat Assn of Fgn Student Affairs; Linguistic Soc of Am Adv Bd of Holland Lit Counc; adv area counc for Vietnamese Edn; Resrc Prsn for MI Counc for Humanities; pres MI Tchrs of Eng to spkrs of other lang; Alpha Psi Omega; Theta Alphu Mu; Phi Alpha Theta; Phi Delta Kappa; Alpha Kappa Delta; Phi Mu Slpha Sinfonia; Alpha Phi Omega; Pi Kappa Delta; Alpha Phi Alph; Sigma Nu. **HONORS/ACHIEVEMENTS:** Scholar Paul A Ewert 1949-52; grad study grants 1953-54; William R Coe grad fellow 1954-55; Outst Educator of Am Awd 1974. **BUSINESS ADDRESS:** Hope Coll, Holland, MI 49423.

POWELL, CHARLES P.
Retired physician. **PERSONAL:** Born Sep 20, 1923; married Margaret (deceased); children: Patricia, Leslie, Sylvia. **EDUCATION:** Howard Univ, 1941-44; MD 1948; Harlem Hosp, intern 1948-49; New Britain Gen Hosp, resident 1953-54; post-grad Yale, Harvard, Boston Univ, Tufts, Oak Ridge Inst Nuclear Med, Princeton. **CAREER:** Univ CT Med Ctr & Western Res, post-grad rsch fellow 1949-51; VA Hosp, 1954-59; VA Ctr, sr physician 1959-65; Prudential Ins Co, asst med dir 1965-75; Samuel Shattuck Hosp, consul 1966-67; clincial asst OH State Sch Med 1961-65, Tufts Sch Med, clinical asst 1967-70; Dreyfus Consumer Life Ins Co, med dir 1984-85; Hartford Ins Grp, med dir 1975-85; Internal Med Consultant 1986. **ORGANIZATIONS:** Certified Amer Bd Intl Med; past mem Soc Nuclear Med; past mem Exec Council Assn of Life Ins Med Dirs of Amer; Fellow Amer Coll Physicians; past bd mem Roxbury MA Fed of Neighborhood Ctr; Vis Nurses Assn of Boston; stadium phys in charge New England Patriots 1971, 1974. **MILITARY SERVICE:** USAF mc capt 1951-53. **HOME ADDRESS:** 8 Boulder Circle, Glastonbury, CT 06033.

POWELL, CLARENCE DEAN, JR.
Business executive. **PERSONAL:** Born Aug 26, 1939, Kansas City, MO; children: Pamela Diane. **EDUCATION:** Attended Univ of Kansas City, 1957-60. **CAREER:** US Army Aviation, chief warrant officer 1962-66; Darben Clifton & Gordon Construction Co, proj engr 1968-69; Hadden Investment & Devel Co, proj engr &cons 1971-72; Afro Air Inc, pres & ceo 1974-77; Organ of Black Airline Pilots, eastern region vice pres 1979-; Prof Photographer; TWA Inc, first officer. **ORGANIZATIONS:** Mem Negro Airmen Intl 1967-; mem NAACP 1967-; consult Natl Urban League 1967-77. **HONORS/ACHIEVEMENTS:** Honor grad AUS Basic Training & Warrant Officer Training 1962-63; Awd of Excellence TWA Airlines 1979. **MILITARY SERVICE:** AUS; Vietnamese Cross of Gallantry; Gold Leaf Air Medal w/4 Silver Leaf Clusters & v for Valor; Commendation Medal w/V for Valor. **BUSINESS ADDRESS:** First Officer, TWA Inc, JFK Intl Airport, Jamaica, NY 11430.

POWELL, CLILAN BETHANY
Physician. **PERSONAL:** Born Aug 08, 1894, Suffolk, VA; married Lena Dukes. **EDUCATION:** VA St Coll, 1913; HowardUniv Schl of Med, 1920; Bellevue, internship. **CAREER:** Brown Bomber Baking Co, estbld; Victory Mut Life Ins Co, pres 1936-45; priv med prac/retired/roentgenologist 1922; Amsterdam News, purchased largest black newsppr. **ORGANIZATIONS:** Life mem NAACP; dir NAACP; legal Def & Educ Fund; dir NY St Fair 1960. **HONORS/ACHIEVEMENTS:** 1st blk Roentgenologist in NY; 1st blk Ath Comm in Boxing Hist; One of Found first FEPC law in nation; Estbld Unity Funeral Homes 1954; lrgst Black FH in country; recvd Haitian Govt's highest Award Honneur de merite order of Chevalier; Dist Ach HowardUniv 1968; 50 Yrs in Med Serv HowardUniv Med Alumni Assoc 1970; recvd numerous awards & plaques for servc to com & nation. **BUSINESS ADDRESS:** 401 W 153rd St, New York, NY 10031.

POWELL, COLIN L.
Soldier, administrator. **PERSONAL:** Born Apr 05, 1937, New York, NY; married Alma Vivian Johnson; children: Michael, Linda, Anne Marie. **EDUCATION:** City Coll of NY, BS 1958; George Washington Univ, MBA 1971; Nat War Coll, attended 1976. **CAREER:** AUS, career army infantry officer 1958-, brig comdr 101st airborne div 1976-77, asst div comdr 4th inf div Ft Carson, CO 1981-82, mil asst Dep Sec of Def 1982-86; The White House, dep asst to the pres for Natl Security Affairs (first black); Dept of Defense, military asst to Secretary of Defense. **HONORS/ACHIEVEMENTS:** White House Fellow. **MILITARY SERVICE:** Purple Heart 1963, Bronze Star 1963, Legion of Merit awds 1969 & 71, Dist ServMedal, AUS lt. **BUSINESS ADDRESS:** Military Asst to Sec of Def, Department of Defense, The Pentagon, Room 3E 880, Washington, DC 20301.

POWELL, DAVID L.
Dental specialists. **PERSONAL:** Born Apr 09, 1938, Tuskegee, AL; son of David Powell and Emma Powell; married Carol June Gandy; children: Paul, Mark, Melanie, Peter. **EDUCATION:** St Michael's Coll, AB 1959; Howard Univ Coll of Dentistry, DDS 1963; OH State Univ, MS 1971. **CAREER:** USAF, lt col 1963-75; prv practice, dental specialist endodontics 1975-. **ORGANIZATIONS:** Assoc bd mem Dayton Art Inst 1979-84; pres OH Assoc of Endodentist 1982-83; bd trust Miami Valley School 1982-; mem Centerville Optomist 1984-; bd dir Superior Dental Care 1986; pres Dayton Dental Soc 1987-88. **HONORS/ACHIEVEMENTS:** Diplomate Amer Bd of Endodentics. **MILITARY SERVICE:** USAF lt col 12 yrs. **BUSINESS ADDRESS:** Dentist, 529 E Stroop Rd, Dayton, OH 45429.

POWELL, DUDLEY VINCENT
Business executive, pharmacist, physician. **PERSONAL:** Born Jul 23, 1917; married Beryl Mae Prettigar Henry; children: Dudley Vincent Jr, Hubert Barrington, Tyrone Anthony. **EDUCATION:** SyracuseUniv Hosp, internship; Met Hosp Cleveland, residency Ob-Gyn 3 yrs;Univ of Rochester Sch of Medicine & Dentistry NY, MD 1950. **CAREER:** Western Reserve U, instr ob-gyn 1 yr; Ft Carson CO, chief ob-gyn 2 yrs; Dallas, pvt prac ob-gyn 1958-; Ob-Gyn Hlth Sci Cntr Univ of TX, clinical prof; St Paul Presb Med Arts Hosp. **ORGANIZATIONS:** Dir Planned Parenthd of NE TX 1960-76; mem Nat Planned Parenthd Bd 1968-72; life mem NAACP. **HONORS/ACHIEVEMENTS:** Margaret Sanger Award; Man of the Yr Omega Psi Phi; Merit Award AUS Reserve; Legion of Merit AUS Reserve. **MILITARY SERVICE:** AUS Reserve col 1958-77. **BUSINESS ADDRESS:** St Paul Professional Bldg, 1906 Peabody Ave, Dallas, TX 75215.

POWELL, GAYLE LETT
Business executive. **PERSONAL:** Born Dec 18, 1943, Manhattan, NY; daughter of Robert A Lett and Claire Lett. **EDUCATION:** Central Univ, BSE 1966. **CAREER:** Newark Bd of Educ, teacher 1966-72; She Creations Ins, corp pres 1969-83; The Fur Vault, fur sales 1981-82; G Letts Shop, corp pres 1982-; Antonovich Furs Inc, fur sales 1982-84; Fur You Inc Outside Fur Sales, corp off 1984-; The Fur Mart Inc, retail furs & service corp pres 1984-. **ORGANIZATIONS:** Mem Alpha Kappa Alpha Sorority, Master Furriers Guild, Amer Bridge Assoc. **BUSINESS ADDRESS:** President, Fur Mart Inc, 1220 Rt 46, Parsippany, NJ 07054.

POWELL, GEORGETTE SEABROOKE
Artist, art therapist. **PERSONAL:** Born Aug 02, 1916, Charleston, SC; married Dr George W (deceased); children: George W III, Phyllis A Manson, Richard V. **EDUCATION:** Harlem Art Workshop NYC; Cooper Union Art School NYC; Fordham Univ NYC; Turtle Bay Music Sch NYC; Dept Agr Grad School Washington, DC; DC Teachers Coll; WA School Psychiatry, Howard Univ, BFA; grad Metro Mental Health Skills Center. **CAREER:** Numerous exhibits and collections including, Carnegie Inst; Natl Exhibit Hall Gallery; Harmon Found; Waltha Daniels Libr; "Forever Free" a traveling art exhibit of Amer Black Women Artists; Charleston Black Arts Festival; Ormond Beach Art League; Palm Coast, FL Art Festival; 18th Art Festival of Capital City Artists; Numerous art positions including, DC Gen Hosp, art therapist 1963-66; Art in Action, inceptor/cons 1967-68; Comm Art Happening Annual Art Show, inceptor/dir 1967-; George Wash Univ Grad Sch Art & Sci, art therapy program 1972-; Flagler County Bunnell FL, minority arts coord 1982-; Tomorrow's World Art Center, dir/fdr 1975-. **ORGANIZATIONS:** Amer Art Therapy Assn; Amer Art League; DC Art Assn; bd mem Howard Theatre Found; mem Natl Conf of Artists; consult bd Createadrama Educ Centre of IN; Women in the Arts WI/NYC/Wash,DC; mem DC Mental Health Assn; DC Commn on the Arts & Humanities; Natl Endowment of the Arts; des cover & illustrator, Black Arts Calendar Josephite Pastoral Center, 1976-80; designed brochure cover Sidwell Friends Summ Program; booklet of drawings of Black Artists Natl Afro-Amer Hist Kit 1977; exhibited "Forever Free" Black Women's Natl Traveling Art Show; exhibits Intl NCA Natl Conf of Artists Dakar Senegal 1984; guest Comm Folk Art Gallery 1986; panelist WPA & the Harlem Artists Guild New York. **HONORS/ACHIEVEMENTS:** 1st Prize Cooper Union Art Sch, Dillard Univ, Amer Art League 1967; Outstanding Perf Awd DC Publ Hlth Art Therapy Acute Psychiatry 1964; Quality Perf Awd DC Dept Rec 1974; Natl Achvmnt Awd Natl Conf of Artists 1975; Natl Exhbn of Minority Artists of Amer 1976; DC Art Assn Awd 1977; Festac Ptcpt Awd 1977; select particip 2nd World Black & African Fest of Arts & Culture Lagos, Nigeria 1977; Listed in, Ebony, Jet Mag, WA Artists Dir 1972, Artists USA1973, WA Post, Evening Star News, Afro-Am Newspapers, Intl Artist Dir 1974-75; Panelist Amer Art Therapy Conv 1972, 1974; Merit Award Howard Univ Comm Action Prog DC 1978; Comm Serv Award Neighborhood Plng Cncl 1979; Jos Parks Spl Award Natl Conf of Artists 1979; Juris Art Citation Plaque WA Bar Assn 1980; Humanities Awd Black History Month Peoples Congregational Church 1985; Outstanding Comm Serv in the Arts Awd St Patrick's Episcopal Church Sr Ctr 1986and Honoree Salute to Georgette Seabrooke Powell 1986; Comm Serv Plaque DC Art Assoc; Art Serv Plaque NCA Conf Los Angeles CA 1987. **BUSINESS ADDRESS:** Dir, Tomorrow's World Art Cntr Inc, 616 "E" St NW, Washington, DC 20004.

POWELL, GLORIA J.
Physician. **PERSONAL:** Born Aug 11, 1936, Boston, MA. **EDUCATION:** Holyoke Coll, BA 1958; Meharry Med Coll, MD 1962. **CAREER:** Parent-Child Learning Found LA, dir 1971-; Meharry Coll Nashville, adj prof div behavioral sci, grad studies, rsch 1971-; CA Coll Med Univ of CA Irvine, asst clinical prof dept psych, div child psych 1972-; UCLA Ctr Health Sci, assoc prof dept psych 1974-; neuropsychiatric Inst LA, asst dir child outpatient dept 1974-76, dir child outpatient dept 1976-84. **ORGANIZATIONS:** Hon lecturer psychiatry Tanzania Uganda; lecturer, writer, rschr & psych consult to comm agencies dir Parent-Child Learning Found; mem bd dir Child Care& Devel Svc; mem APA, Soc Rsch Child Devel, Amer Acad Child Psych, So CA Psych Assoc, Delta Sigma Theta; med dir Child Sexual Abuse Prog Neuropsych Inst UCLA; sr ed The PsychoSocial Devel of Minority Group Children 1984. **HONORS/ACHIEVEMENTS:** Author Black Mondays Children; Awd for Outstanding Youn Women 1967; listed in Outstanding Young Women of Amer 1968; Mary P Dole Med Fellowship Mt Holyoke Coll 1969; UCLA Women Faculty Awd 1970. **BUSINESS ADDRESS:** Dir Child Outpatient Dept, Neuropsychiatric Inst, 760 Westwood Plaza, Los Angeles, CA 90024.

POWELL, GRADY WILSON
Clergyman. **PERSONAL:** Born Aug 06, 1932, Brunswick Co, VA; married Dr Bertie J; children: Sandra Z, Dorthula H, Grady W, Jr, Herbert C, Eric C. **EDUCATION:** St Paul's Coll, BS 1954; VA Union Univ Sch of Theol, MDiv 1959; St Paul's Coll, DD (hon) 1976. **CAREER:** Amity Bapt Church S Hill VA, pastor 1953-58; Greensville Co Pub Schools Emporia VA, teacher 1954-56; Quioccasin Bapt Church Richmond, pastor 1958-61; Richmond Pub Schools, teacher 1959-60; Gillfield Bapt Church, pastor 1961-. **ORGANIZATIONS:** Treas/bd member Children's Home of VA Bapt Inc 1959-70; sec/governing bd VA Council of Churches 1960-66; Petersburg Biracial Comm City of Petersburg VA 1961-62; bd member/sec, State Bd of Corrections of VA 1974-78; governing bd Natl Council of Church of Christ 1979-. **HONORS/ACHIEVEMENTS:** Distinguished Serv NAACP 1961; Man of the

Year Omega Psi Phi Frat Petersburg 1963; Honorary Degree St Paul's Coll 1976; Presidential Citation Nat Assn Equal Opportunity in Higher Educ 1979. **BUSINESS ADDRESS:** Perry & Farmer Sts, Petersburg, VA 23803.

POWELL, J. OTIS
Producer & poet. **PERSONAL:** Born Nov 25, 1955, Huntsville, AL; married Elizabeth Craig-Powell. **EDUCATION:** AL A&M Univ, BA 1977; SECA and BBC "Producing Drama for Television" Seminar 1985. **CAREER:** AL A&M Telecommunication, actor/talk show 1975-77; Charlie Parker Found, actor/poet 1978; Huntsville City Schools, teacher 1979; VISTA, comm organizer 1980-81; Pensacola Jr College WSRE-TV,TV producer/poet 1981-. **ORGANIZATIONS:** Trainer Action Office for Vista in FL 1980-81; acting coach WSRE TV 1981-; actor/playwright's repertory Festival Univ of West FL 1985; serveral Poetry Recital's 1985-; grant recipient INPUT 1986. **HONORS/ACHIEVEMENTS:** First graduate in Telecommunications AL A&M 1977; published Huntsville Mirror 1979; profiled Corsair & Pensacola News Journal 1984, 1985; published Poetry magazine Bolder CO 1985; published Corsair 1985; also published in the Pensacola Voice 1985; silver awd Pensacole Press Club for Video Photography 1985, gold awd Best Art Entertainment Series 1986; pictured on the cover of Preview 1985. **BUSINESS ADDRESS:** TV Producer, WSRE-TV Pensacola Jr College, 1000 College Blvd, Pensacola, FL 32504.

POWELL, JOHN LEWIS
Clergyman. **PERSONAL:** Born Nov 02, 1902, McKeesport, PA; married Ruth Marie Davidson. **EDUCATION:** Johnson C Smith U, AB 1931, BD 1934, DD 1956;Univ of Pittsburgh, MEd 1947. **CAREER:** ABT Sem, dean of stds; Progressive Bapt Ch Nashville TN, pastor 1951-74; Freindship Bapt Ch Charlotte NC, pastor 1932-47; Unity HS Statesville NC, tchr 1944-47; Faith United Bapt Ch Nashville, paston 1974-. **ORGANIZATIONS:** Recrology Com NACDRAO; mem Nashville IMA; Alpha Phi Alpha Frat; Prince Hall Order of Free & Accepted Masons; mem So Coll Personnel Assn; treas Comm Ec Dev Corp. **HONORS/ACHIEVEMENTS:** Hon DD Deg Alma Mater Johnson C Smith U, Charlotte NC 1956. **BUSINESS ADDRESS:** 1800 Whites Creek Pike, Nashville, TN 37207.

POWELL, JOSEPH HANSFORD
Director. **PERSONAL:** Born Mar 22, 1946, Macon, GA. **EDUCATION:** Morris Brown Coll Atlanta, BS 1968; CornellUniv Sch of Hotel Admin Ithaca NY, 1967. **CAREER:** St Christophers Hosp for Children, dir of food srv 1985; Grad Hosp ofUniv of PA, dir of food srv 1976; Bell of PA, dir of food srv 1975; Soc Security Admin Woodlawn MD, dir of food srv 1974; Sinai Hosp of Baltimore Inc, dir of food srv 1973; Mercy-Douglas Hosp Philadelphia PA, dir of food srv 1970. **ORGANIZATIONS:** Bd mem Food Srv Craft Adv Com for Chester-Upland Sch Dist Chester PA 1977-80; mem Omega Psi Phi Frat Inc 1965; mass care spec SE PA Chap ARC 1974-80; alumni chap treas Philadelphia Alumni of Morris Brown Coll 1975-80. **HONORS/ACHIEVEMENTS:** Most outstndng grad std of Food Prod Mgmt, Morris Brown Coll Atlanta GA 1968; recip Statler Found Grant, Further Studies at CornellUniv Sch of Hotel Admin 1969; listed amoung Outstndng Young Men in America 1971; named Food Srv Dir of Yr, Hosp Food Mgmt Div 1972.

POWELL, JOSEPH T.
Clergyman. **PERSONAL:** Born Nov 11, 1923, Baltimore; married Alice Pettiford; children: Cynthia R, Jo Anne M. **EDUCATION:** Oakwood Coll Huntsville AL, BA 1946; AndrewsUniv Berring Spgs MI, MA 1951. **CAREER:** AUS Ft Ord CA, chaplain 1960-; Academy Ch, pastor 1948-52; AUS chpln 1952-57; Immanuel Temple Seventh Day Adv Ch Durham NC, chpln 1957-60. **ORGANIZATIONS:** Mem NAACP Durham Interden Minis Assn 1957-60; Durham Com Negro Affairs 1957-60. **HONORS/ACHIEVEMENTS:** Merit serv awd Durham Com Negro Affairs 1960; achievement awd Oakwood Coll 1974; Col AUS Res; numerous medals & commendatiosn Korea, Viet Nam, Armed Forces. **BUSINESS ADDRESS:** Oakwood College, Office of the Chaplain, Huntsville, AL 35896.

POWELL, JUAN HERSCHEL
Civil engineer. **PERSONAL:** Born Aug 11, 1960, Roanoke, VA; son of John Henry Powell and Shirley Oliver Powell. **EDUCATION:** Howard Univ, BSCE 1978-82; Univ of MD, MBA 1985-88. **CAREER:** The CECO Corp, construct engr 1983-85; The George Hyman Construction Co, project engr 1985-. **ORGANIZATIONS:** Mem Amer Soc of Civil Engrs 1979-, Alpha Phi Alpha Frat Inc 1980-, Tau Beta Pi Natl Engrg Honor Soc 1982-, Natl Black MBA Assoc 1986-; Chrmn of Fundraising Howard Univ Engineering Alumni Assoc 1988-89; pres, George Hyman Chapter, Toastmasters Inc, 1988; DC Contractors Assn, 1989. **HONORS/ACHIEVEMENTS:** Who's Who in Amer Colls & Univs 1982; Leadership Awd ASCE Howard Univ 1982; Certificate of Appreciation Alpha Phi Alpha Beta Chap 1983; Outstanding Young Men of Amer 1985. **HOME ADDRESS:** 2124 Flagler Place NW, Washington, DC 20001.

POWELL, KENNETH ALASANDRO
Vice president/manager. **PERSONAL:** Born Nov 26, 1945, Mobile, AL; son of William O Powell Sr and Myrtle E Powell (deceased). **EDUCATION:** Howard Univ, BS Mathematics 1967; Harvard Business School, MBA Finance 1974. **CAREER:** McKinsey & Co, associate mgmt consulting 1974-77; Chase Manhattan Bank, 2nd vice pres vice pres strategic mgmt 1977-83; Marine Midland Bank, vice pres and manager 1983-. **ORGANIZATIONS:** Pres 1989 Harvard Business School Assoc (all alumni); pres 1983-86 Harvard Business School Club of NY; mem Harvard Club West Point Soc; bd mem Foundation for Dance Promotion 1987; bd mem Metropolitan Assistance Corp 1989-; mem American Society for Training and Development (ASTD), 1988-. **HONORS/ACHIEVEMENTS:** COGME Fellowship (Honorarium) Cncl of Grad Mgmt Educ Boston 1972-74; Martin Luther King Fellowship Woodrow Wilson Foundation 1972-74; Howard Univ Disting Alumnus Natl Assoc for Educ Oppor 1984. **MILITARY SERVICE:** AUS and Reserves major 5 yrs active, 8 yrs reserves; Bronze Star; Vietnam Cross of Gallantry 1969. **HOME ADDRESS:** 245 E 87th St, Apt 11E, New York, NY 10128. **BUSINESS ADDRESS:** Vice President and Manager, Marine Midland Bank, 140 Broadway, 9th floor, New York, NY 10015.

POWELL, LEOLA P.
Educator. **PERSONAL:** Born Oct 09, 1932, Dawson, GA; married Benjamin; children: Gwendolyn, Benita, Benjamin Jr. **EDUCATION:** Edward Waters Coll, BS 1962; FL A&M U, MA 1966. **CAREER:** School Psychology Services, Duval County School Bd, acting supr, psychologist 1967-74; School Psychology Services, Duval County, coordinator; teacher 1963-67; bookkeeper 1960-63; sec 1955-60. **ORGANIZATIONS:** Phi Delta Kappa 1975; mem St Pius Cath Ch; am Black FL NE FL Psychologist Assn; FL & Duval Co Prsnl Guidance Assn; treas Wmn's Political Caucus;Black Coalition; Charmettes Inc; mem Delta Kappa Gamma Soc Intrntl; mem St Bernadette Guild; mem Minority Womens Coalition. **HONORS/ACHIEVEMENTS:** Am Heritage Tchng Accomps 1966; Academic Hons 1962. **BUSINESS ADDRESS:** Counselor, Duval County School Board, 1701 Prudential Drive, Jacksonville, FL 32202.

POWELL, MARVIN
Professional athlete. **PERSONAL:** Born Aug 30, 1955, Ft Bragg, NC; married Kristen; children: Amerique, Beronique. **EDUCATION:** Southern CA Univ, BA. **CAREER:** NY Jets, tight end 1977-. **ORGANIZATIONS:** Vice pres NFL Players Assn; player rep NY Jets. **HONORS/ACHIEVEMENTS:** Selected to Pro Bowl 5 times; Forrest Gregg Offensive Lineman of the Yr Awd 1982; MVP 1979; honored by Women's Natl Republican Club NY; named to NFL All-Rookie Team UPI 1977; played in 3 Rose Bowls and 1 Liberty Bowl. **BUSINESS ADDRESS:** New York Jets, 1000 Fulton Ave, Hempstead, NY 11550.

POWELL, PHILIP MELANCTHON, JR.
Educator. **PERSONAL:** Born Jan 30, 1941, Greenwood, MS; son of Philip Melancthon Powell, Sr and Mamie Lee McCain Powell; married Sharon; children: David, Aaron, Robert. **EDUCATION:** Roosevelt Univ, BA 1964; Univ of Chgo, MA 1970, PhD 1971. **CAREER:** St Xavier Coll, instr 1971; Univ of Chicago Vocational Counseling Inst, instr 1971; Yale Univ, asst prof psych 1971-76; Univ of TX, assoc prof ed psych 1984-. **ORGANIZATIONS:** Dir Philosophy-Psychology Track is Psychology Yale Coll 1974-76; consult ed MENSA Rsch Jrnl 1975-85; contrib ed Roeper Review 1980-85; mem Natl Assoc of Gifted Children; mem The Natl Assoc of Black Psychologists; mem Amer Psychological Assoc, AERA Study Group 1974-75; mem adv bd Umoja Family 1975-; caseworker Cook Cty Dept of Publ Aid 1964; rsch asst Woodlawn Mental Health Ctr Chicago 1965-67; co-investigator Yale Criterion Study 1971; com mem Equal Rights Yale Psychology Dept 1971-76; former policy com mem Yale Dept of Afro-Amer Studies; speaker Columbia Univ 1974, Mensa Natl Conv 1974, Conf on Empirical Rsch in Black Psychology 1974-; chmn Devel Soc Personality Area of Dept Ed Psych Univ TX Austin 1984-85. **HONORS/ACHIEVEMENTS:** Listed in Amer Men & Women of Sci 1974, Notalbe Amer 1976-77, Who's Who in the East 1977; postdoctoral fellow Ford Found/NRC 1980-81. **BUSINESS ADDRESS:** Associate Professor, Univ of Texas, Martin Luther King & Speedway, Ed Bldg 506F, Austin, TX 78712.

POWELL, ROBERT E.
Association executive. **PERSONAL:** Born Jan 31, 1919, Kansas City, KS; son of Manuel Powell and Helen Powell; married Della Mae Weaver; children: Peggy Delores. **EDUCATION:** Harvard Univ Bus Sch, 1960. **CAREER:** Laborers LU 1290, asst bus mgr 1956-59; Laborers' Intl Union of N Amer, 1st vice pres 1961; Mrs JW Jones Meml Chapel Inc; bd of dir pres, Douglass Bank (kck) bd of dir. **ORGANIZATIONS:** Helped set up first Labor Educ Cntr Columbus, OH; Civil Rights Act through Country; Urban League; SCLC; A Philip Randolph Ins Natl Consumers League; execbd mem Indust Union Dept AFL-CIO. **HONORS/ACHIEVEMENTS:** Disting Serv Award natl Urban League; Labor Affairs Prog in Recognition of 7 Years of Support & Devotion. **MILITARY SERVICE:** USN Fireman 1st Class 1944-46. **BUSINESS ADDRESS:** President, Mrs JW Jones Meml Chapel, 703 North 10th St, Kansas City, KS 66102.

POWELL, ROBERT MEAKER
Clergyman. **PERSONAL:** Born Apr 23, 1930, Cumberland, MD. **EDUCATION:** Morgan St U, AB 1954; VA Theol Sem, MDiv 1957; NY Sch of Soc Wrk, 1958-61. **CAREER:** St Philip's Epis Ch, vicar 1971-; Chapel of the Holy Trinity, vicar 1964-67; St James' Ch, asso rector 1963-64; Lafayette Sq Comm Ctr, exec dir 1958-63; diocesan, missionary 1957-63. **ORGANIZATIONS:** Sec Stndng Com 1969-; pres Stndng Com 1976-77; mem Ecclesiastical Ct 1965-69; mem Yth Commn 1963-70; dir Summer Yth Conf 1959-71; mem Christian Soc Relat Commn of the Diocese; supr Mid-Atlantic Parish Training Inst 1966-69; epis chaplain Morgan StUniv 1962-71; instr Lay Sch of Theol; vice pres MD Clericus 1965; num Ad Hoc Com of thebishop; supr Deacon Training Prog 1969; nom Suffragan Bishop of Diocese of MD 1972; Ch Mission of Help; Florence Crittenton Svcs; Citizens Plng & Housing Assn; Citizens Sch Adv Bd; Urban Leag Bd; MD St Interracial Commn 1963-67; MD Cncl of Chs; Harlem Pk Urban Renewal Bd; ABCD Adoption Agy; consult Clifton T Perkins St Hosp, Criminally Insane; Girl Scouts of Ctrl MD; Camp Fire Girls of MD; Literacy Cncl of MD; trustee Balt Comm Chest; Prisons Aid Soc; Balt-Cntrl MD Leag for Crippled Children & Adults; Planned Prnthd Assn of AA Co; Anne Arundel Co EOC Bd; chaplainClifton T Perkins St Hosp; consult Anne Arundel Co Bd of Ed; num other orgs. **HONORS/ACHIEVEMENTS:** Awards Balt Urban Leag; Anne Arundel Co Comm Svcs; Balt-Cntrl MD Leag for Crippled Children & Adults; NAACP; nom Outstndng Men of Yr, MD Jaycees; Afro-Am Hon Roll Plaque, Afro-Am Nwspr 1961, 1967; nom Caroline Brady Humanitarian Award, Anne Arundel Cncl of Comm Svcs; num comm & orgs awards. **BUSINESS ADDRESS:** St Phillip's Episcopal Ch, Bestgate & Severn Grove Rds, Annapolis, MD 21401.

POWELL, THOMAS FRANCIS A.
Physician. **PERSONAL:** Born Feb 13, 1925, Philadelphia, PA; married Mary Elizabeth Holloway; children: Thomas Jr, Allyson, Linda, Tracy [illegible]rl Patrick. **EDUCATION:** Univ PA, 1952; Philadelphia Coll Osteo Med, 1956. **CAREER:** Met Hosp, chf of staff, co-chmn gen surg; Philadelphia Coll Osteo Med Des Moines [illegible]l, asst prof surg; Philadelphia Coll Podiatric Med, adj faculty; Am Coll, osteo Surgs. **ORGANIZATIONS:** AOA; POMA; Am Assn ofUniv Profs Inner City Cncl; SE PA Heart Assn; past bd Houston Comm Ctr, Med Com Concerned Civil Rights; AFNA. **HONORS/ACHIEVEMENTS:** Publ several med articles on Surg. **MILITARY SERVICE:** USAF 1943-46. **BUSINESS ADDRESS:** 5725 Lansdowne, Philadelphia, PA 19131.

POWELL, WAYNE HUGH
Financial administrator. **PERSONAL:** Born Jul 29, 1946, Petersburg, VA; son of Willie Powell and Lena Powell; married Leslie J; children: Farrah, Brandi, Kristin. **EDUCATION:** Lincoln Univ, BS Bus Admin 1970; Rockhurst Coll, MBA Fin 1979. **CAREER:** General Mills, reg office mgr 1975-79, reg credit mgr 1980-81, mgr gp fin analysis 1981-82, mgr of admin 1982-85. **HOME ADDRESS:** 1403 Torrington Ct, San Jose, CA 95120. **BUSINESS ADDRESS:** Manager of Administration, General Mills Inc, 1701 Technology Drive, San Jose, CA 95110.

POWELL, WILLIAM
Dentist. **PERSONAL:** Born Mar 06, 1935, Greenville, MS; married Carolyn M. **EDUCATION:** XavierUniv New Orleans, 1957; Mehary Med Coll Sch of Dent, 1963. **CAREER:** DDS Inc Bakersfield CA, pvt prac dent 1965-. **ORGANIZATIONS:** Mem Am Dent Assn; CA Dent Assn; Kern Co Dent Soc; Am Endodontic Soc; Aca Gen Dent; Pierre Favehard Acad; Assn Military Surg; Nat Dent Assn; pres Kern Co Dent Soc 1974; sec 1972; treas 1971; Kappa Alpha Psi Frat; NAACP. **MILITARY SERVICE:** USAF capt 1963-65.

POWELL, WILLIAM J.
Clergyman. **PERSONAL:** Born Nov 02, 1908, Crenshaw County, AL; married Bessie Ford Powell. **EDUCATION:** Livingston Coll Salisbury NC, AB 1947, Doc Div Deg 1980; Hood Theol Sem Salisbury, MDiv 1950. **CAREER:** YMCA Birmingham, sec 1927-43; William's Chpl AME Zion Ch, pstr 1974-78; Oak St AME Zion Ch, 1978-; Birmingham & Montgomery AL, pastor; Cherryville Charlotte & E Spencer NC, pastor; Ridgewood & Asbury Pk NJ, pastor. **ORGANIZATIONS:** Mem Bd of dirl Montgomery Multi-Co Chpt, AL Caucus on Black Aging; del Wrld Meth Conf London 1966; del Denver 1971; bd dir YMCA Ridgewood NJ; memBd Mgnt Ridgewood Comm Chest; pres Wmancptn Procl Com Montgomery AL; sec, 1st vice pres Montgomery Impvmnt Assn; mem exec com Fair Hsng Com Ridgewood; mem Vlg Com on Yth; Kiwanis Club Ridgewoos & Asbury Pk; Mayor's Adv Com Asbury Pk; pres Shore Area Cncl Chs; led the Cong of St Stephen AME ZionCh, Asbury Pk NJ, in bldng a 90-unit, $1,501,000 hsng proj as means of identifying the ch with a real comm need; led same cong in estb a credit union. **HONORS/ACHIEVEMENTS:** Spl cit 1956 Nat Bible Guild Inc Montgomery; Minister of Yr Award Asbury Pk Yth Cdts 1973; Award AME Zion Mnstrs All of NJ 1974. **BUSINESS ADDRESS:** 2816 Tremont St, Montgomery, AL 36110.

POWELL, WILLIAM O., JR.
Dentist. **PERSONAL:** Born Sep 19, 1934, Andalusia, AL; married Anna D Thompson; children: Rosalyn F, Michelle R. **EDUCATION:** Talladega Coll, AB 1955; Howard Univ Coll of Dentistry, DDS 1967. **CAREER:** Ft Detrick Dept of Defense, histopath tech 1958-61; Mt Sinai Hosp, internship 1968; Walter Reed Army Medical Ctr, rsch biologist 1961-63; Howard Univ Coll of Dentistry, asst prof 1968-69, dir dental therapist training 1969-75; Private Practice, dentist 1969-. **ORGANIZATIONS:** Mem, Omega Psi Frat, Amer Dental Assn, Natl Dental Assn, MD State Dental Assn, So MD Dental Soc, Robt T Freeman Dental Soc, Kiwanis Intl, Montgomery Co MD Drug Abuse Adv Council, NNGA. **HONORS/ACHIEVEMENTS:** Published paper on "Comparison of Dental Therapists Trainee and Dental Students" Journal of Dental Education. **HOME ADDRESS:** 14801 Waterway Dr, Rockville, MD 20853. **BUSINESS ADDRESS:** 809 Viers Mill Rd, Ste 213, Rockville, MD 20851.

POWELL, YVONNE MACON (YVONNE MACON COOK)
Corrections administrator. **PERSONAL:** Born Dec 08, 1936, Harlem, NY; daughter of James Macon and Eugenia Wright Jackson; married Alfred J Powell, Jr, Sep 02, 1962; children: Richard L Cook III, Stacy D Powell, Alfred Edward Powell, Natasha N Powell, Ronald L Gardner, Towano Y Pittman, Terrence L Gardner, Sharon M Gardner. **EDUCATION:** Tennessee State Univ, Nashville TN, 1955-57; Mercy Coll, Dobbs Ferry NY, BS criminal justice, 1980; Natl Academy of Corrections, Denver CO, 3 certificates, 1981, 1982; Long Island Univ, Dobbs Ferry NY, 1981. **CAREER:** Dept Public Safety, White Plains NY, parking enforcement, 1962-65; Westchester County Sheriff's Dept, White Plains NY, deputy sheriff, 1967-; West County Dept of Correction, Valhalla NY, correction officer, 1969-71, sergeant, 1971-82, captain, 1982-84, asst warden, 1984-88; assoc warden, 1988-. **ORGANIZATIONS:** Mem, NAACP; mem, Urban League of Westchester; mem, Daughter of Elks-Rosebud Temple; mem, Alpha Kappa Alpha; mem, Alpha Psi Epsilon. **HONORS/ACHIEVEMENTS:** Commissioner's Award, Westchester County Dept of Correction, 1981, 1983; Community Service, Central 7, Greenburgh NY, 1982; Mem of the Year, Northeast Region Natl Black Police Assn, 1983; Guardian of the Year, Westchester Rockland Guardians Assn, 1984; Contribution to Law Enforcement, Tri-County Federation of Police, 1984; Community Service, Westchester Co-op, 1985; Coach of the Year, Kenisco Little League, 1986; Achievement Award, Natl Negro Business and Professional Women, 1989.

POWER, ROBERT CORNELIUS
Attorney. **PERSONAL:** Born Apr 03, 1922, Plumerville, AR; married Elizabeth McCord; children: Wanda, Karen, Stephen. **EDUCATION:** Morehouse Coll, 1941-43; Univ Florence (Armed Forces Inst), 1945; John Marshall Law Schl, JD 1949. **CAREER:** Chicago Gazette, clmnst 1967-73; State IL, asst atty gen 1969-83; Progg Natl Bapt Convt, atty 1976-78; Private Prac, atty 1980-82. **ORGANIZATIONS:** Mem Natl Bar Assoc 1951-; mem Cook Cty Bar Assoc 1951-; mem Chicago Bar Assoc 1983-. **HONORS/ACHIEVEMENTS:** LLD McKinley Theolog Semin 1980. **MILITARY SERVICE:** AUS sgt 2 yrs 1943-45. **BUSINESS ADDRESS:** Attorney, Private Practice, 7 W Madison, Chicago, IL 60602.

POWERS, GEORGIA M.
Elected government official. **PERSONAL:** Born Oct 29, Springfield, KY; married James L; children: William F Davis, Cheryl Campbell, Deborah Rattle, J Cartlon. **EDUCATION:** Lou Munic Coll, 1940-43. **CAREER:** KY State Senate, senator. **ORGANIZATIONS:** Chmn Senate Lbr & Indstry Com; mem Jeff Co Dem Exec Comm 1964-66; mem Lbr & Indstry Comm; Cities Comm; YWCA; NAACP; Urban League; frmr Bd of ovrsrsUniv of Louisville; 1st wmn & 1st blck elected to KY Sen; mem bd of dir Fund for Women, Inc. **HONORS/ACHIEVEMENTS:** Kennedy King awd Young Dem KY 1968; Ky Cong of Barb & Beau Ach Awd 1968; AKA Recg Awd 1970; Zeta Phi Beta; Sor outsdng serv awd 1971; Merit awd Zion Bapt Ch 1969. **HOME ADDRESS:** 733 Cecil Ave, Louisville, KY 40211.

POWERS, MAMON, SR.
Construction executive. **CAREER:** Powers & Sons Construction Co Inc, Gary IN, chief executive. **BUSINESS ADDRESS:** Powers & Sons Construction Co Inc, 2636 West 15th Ave, Gary, IN 46404. *

POWERS, MAMON M., JR.
Business executive. **PERSONAL:** Born Mar 10, 1948, Gary, IN; son of Mamon Powers and Leolean Powers; married Cynthia R Berry, Jul 23, 1972; children: Kelly, Mamon. **EDUCATION:** Purdue Univ, BS Civ Eng 1970. **CAREER:** Powers & Sons Const Co, sec treas 1971-; reg professional engr; Am Oil Co Whiting IN, design engr 1970-71; Powers & Sons Const Co, Pres 1988-. **ORGANIZATIONS:** Treas Gary Econ Devel Corp; former pres Calumet Chap IN Soc of Professional Engrs; bd of dirs Constr Advance Found; mem Asso Gen Contrs; chrm Const Advancement Foundation 1983-85; pres Calumet Builders Assoc 1985-87. **HONORS/ACHIEVEMENTS:** 59th largest black owned business (industrial & service) 1988. **BUSINESS ADDRESS:** President, Powers & Sons Construction Co Inc, 2636 W 15th Ave, Gary, IN 46404.

POWERS, RUNAS, JR.
Physician. **PERSONAL:** Born Dec 11, 1932, Jackson's Gap, AL; married Mary Alice; children: Tiffany, Trina, Runas III. **EDUCATION:** TN State, BS 1961; Meharry Med Coll, MD 1966. **CAREER:** Private Practice, physician. **ORGANIZATIONS:** Mem Arthritis Foundation, Amer Rheumatism Assoc, Natl Med Assoc, Amer Fed Clinical Rsch. **MILITARY SERVICE:** USN Reserve lt cmdr 1967-69. **BUSINESS ADDRESS:** 101 Madison St, Alexander City, AL 35010.

POWERS, WINSTON DONALD
Lieutenant general. **PERSONAL:** Born Dec 19, 1930, Manhattan, NY; married Jeanette Wyche; children: Diane E Nock, David. **EDUCATION:** McKendree Coll, BA 1961; George Washington U; Industl Coll Armed Forces, Grad 1974. **CAREER:** HQ US Air Force Washington DC, dir c3 1978, d/dir c3 1975-78, chief c3 plns 1974-75; 2146 Comm Grp Osan AB Korea, commander 1974; HQ US Air Force Washington DC, spec asst c3 div 1973-74; J-6 OJCS Washington DC, staff Off 1971-73; 360th Tac Elec Warfare Sq Vietman, navgt 1970-71; Comm Sys Div Langley AFB, VA, chief 1967-70; Defen Jcomm Agcy RAF Croughton UK, comm engr 1964-67; Air Force Command Post Washington DC, emer actions ofcr 1961-63; Scott AFB IL, comm ofcr 1959-61; Det 2 6123 Air Ctrl & Wang Sq, Korea, commd 1957-58. **ORGANIZATIONS:** Intl vice pres Armed Force C-E Assoc. **HONORS/ACHIEVEMENTS:** EM Zuckert Awd for mgmt USAF 1982. **MILITARY SERVICE:** USAF lt gen 35 yrs Dstnghd Serv Med; Legion of Merit; Meritorious Serv Med; Air Med; AF Commendation Med; Mstr Nvgtrs Wings; Space Badge 1950-.

PRATER, OSCAR L.
Educational administrator. **PERSONAL:** Married Jacqueline P; children: Lamar, Marcus. **EDUCATION:** Talladega College, BA 1961; Hampton University, MA 1967; The College of William and Mary, MS 1968, EdD 1977. **CAREER:** Middlesex Co Public Schools, mathematics teacher 1961-62; Wmsbg-James City Public Schools, mathematics teacher 1962-72; Rappahanock Community College, chairman, division of mathematics 1972-79; Hampton University, vice-president for administrative services, 1979-. **ORGANIZATIONS:** Member Human Services Board, Hampton Roads Cultural Action Committee, trustee, chairman First Baptist Church 1980-84; institutional representative American Council Teacher Education 1980-; management consultant HU Administrative Leadership Team 1982-83-84; member Board of Visitors/VA State Univ 1982-; management associates 1983-. **HONORS/ACHIEVEMENTS:** Citizen of the Year Chamber of Commerce 1970; publication Faculty Perceptions of Selected Student Characteristics 1978; Outstanding Man of the Year Omega Psi Phi Fraternity 1982. **BUSINESS ADDRESS:** Vice Pres Administrative Serv, HamptonUniv, Hampton, VA 23668.

PRATHER, GUY TYRONE
Professional athlete. **PERSONAL:** Born Mar 28, 1958, Olney, MD. **EDUCATION:** Grambling Univ, BS. **CAREER:** Green Bay Packers, linebacker 1981-. **HONORS/ACHIEVEMENTS:** Packer Special Teams Player of the Year as a rookie in 1981,82; 2 time All Southwest Athletic Conf selection. **BUSINESS ADDRESS:** Green Bay Packers, 1265 Lombardi Ave, Green Bay, WI 54307.

PRATHER, JEFFREY LYNN
Administrator. **PERSONAL:** Born May 14, 1941, New York, NY; son of James and Mary. **EDUCATION:** Howard Univ Washington DC, 1959-60; Queens Coll CUNY Flushing NY, BA 1965; CA State Univ Northridge CA, MS Equiv 1967; Rochdale Coll Toronto Canada, PhD (Hon) 1971. **CAREER:** Operation Head Start Brooklyn NY, consult psychologist 1967-71; MDTP Bd of Ed of City of NY, asst in guidance 1968-72, counseling suprv 1969-72, admin asst adult training ctr 1969-72; Sacramento City Coll, instr 1978; Malcoln-King Harlem Coll Ext NYC, instr, interim chmn psych 1979-80; Dept of State USA, escort/interpreter 1979-; Sacramento CA, consult juristic psych 1982-; Pratherian Enterprises, director, 1972-. **ORGANIZATIONS:** Action Co-op Volunteer, Attica Correctional Facility, Literacy Vol of Amer 1975-76; corr proj dir NY, CA Literacy Vol of Amer 1976-77; consult CA State Dept of Ed Migrant Ed 1977-79; mem Intl Assoc of GP Psychotherapy, Intl Council of Psych, Assoc of Black Psych. **HONORS/ACHIEVEMENTS:** Author, "A Mere Reflection, The Psychodynamics of Black & Hispanic Psychology," Dorrance & Co, 1977; author, "400 Days at Attica," Dorrance & Co, 1983. **BUSINESS ADDRESS:** Director, Pratherian Enterprises, 1201 P St Suite 4, Sacramento, CA 95814-5827.

PRATT, ALEXANDER THOMAS
Educational administrator. **PERSONAL:** Born Sep 18, 1938, StMartinville, LA; married Mable Agnes Lee; children: Thomas, Thaddeus. **EDUCATION:** Prairie View A&M, BA 1961, MA 1963. **CAREER:** Prairie View A&M, asst circulation librarian 1962-63; La Marque Ind School, teacher & head of history dept 1963-70; Coll of the Mainland, instructor 1970-76, chairman Social Science Dept 1976-. **ORGANIZATIONS:** Member adv Com Webb Soc 1974; mayor pro tem City of La Marque 1974-; Galveston Co Hist Commn 1975-; Galveston Co Mayors Assn 1979-80; TX State Comm onUrban Needs 1980-; member Phi Alpha Theta. **HONORS/ACHIEVEMENTS:** HK "Griz" Eckert Award Coll of the Mainland 1975; Jaycee of the Year The La Marque Jaycee 1975-76; Disting Serv Award La Marque Jaycee 1978; Outstanding Comm Serv Delta Sigma Theta 1980. **BUSINESS ADDRESS:** College of the Mainland, 8001 Palmer Hwy, Texas City, TX 77591.

PRATT, J. C.
Educator, author, clergyman. **PERSONAL:** Born Nov 15, 1927, Selina, TX; son of Jack and Annie; children: Cardelia Marie, John Curtis. **EDUCATION:** Langston U, BS 1961. **CAREER:** Kiamichi Area VO-TECH Sch E Star Bapt Ch Mcalester OK, educ bapt min civ ldr 1974-; US Civil Svc, 1947-52, 1962-72; BTU & Bible Inst Centralwayland Bapt Dist, 1962-65; Bethlehem Bapt Ch, past 1959-66; E Star Bapt Ch, assoc min 1967. **ORGANIZATIONS:** Not pub OK 1962-64; chmn Soc Ser Task Force for Mod Cit 1970-73; chmn bd dir Eastsde Comm Ctr 1972-; chmn Voc Serv Prog 1974-; mem Pitts CoYth Shelt Bd 1971-; assn exec NAACP OK 1965-67; assn exec Pitts Co CORE 1967-; most worship mstr Prince Hall

Mason Ldge Eufaula OK 1962-; OK Dept of Agric for the state of OK 1976; comm Amer Leg Post 293 1959-. **HONORS/ACHIEVEMENTS:** Nat def arm forces med 1954; cert for dist serv in hum rhts 1969; pub "The blck Ldrs in Indus" The Blck Voices 1973; list Men of Achieve Intnl Biograph Cambrid Eng 1977-79. **MILITARY SERVICE:** AUS E-5 1952-57. **BUSINESS ADDRESS:** Rt 2 Box 104, Eufaula, OK 74432.

PRATT, LOUIS HILL
Educational administrator. **PERSONAL:** Born Aug 11, 1937, Savannah, GA; married Darnell Myrtice Dixon; children: Karen Lynnette, Kenneth Dwayne. **EDUCATION:** Savannah State Coll, BS (cum Laude) 1958; Columbia Univ Teacher Coll, MA 1967; FL State Univ Tallahassee, PhD 1974. **CAREER:** Public School State of GA, teacher 1958-62, 1964-69; US Army Air Def Command, operations asst 1962-64; FL A&M Univ Language Dept, instr 1969-74; FL A&M Univ Freshman Comp Dept of Language & Lit, asst prof & dir 1974-75; FL A&M Univ Div of Languages & Lit, prof of English div 1975-. **ORGANIZATIONS:** Life mem Coll Language Assn; mem Editorial Bd Middle Atlantic Writers Assn; life mem Alpha Phi Alpha Frat Inc; charter mem Seven Hills Toastmasters Club. **HONORS/ACHIEVEMENTS:** Recipient NDEA Fellowship FL State Univ 1972-74; J Russell Reaver Award FL State Univ (best creative scholarship in Amer Lit in dissertation) 1974-75; Natl Endowment for the Humanities Stipend to attend Afro-Amer Culture Inst Univ of IA 1977; Man of the Year Award Alpha Phi Alpha Frat Inc 1979. **BUSINESS ADDRESS:** Professor of English, FL A&M University, Room 415 Tucker Hall, Tallahassee, FL 32307.

PRATT, MABLE
Elected official, educator. **PERSONAL:** Born May 27, 1943, Houston, TX; married Alexander Pratt; children: Thomas, Thaddeus. **EDUCATION:** Prairie View A&M, BS Home Econ Ed 1967; Univ of Houston, MS Ed Mgmt 1978, starting in doctoral program summer 1985. **CAREER:** Queen of Peace School Lamarque, second teacher 1969-70; Sacred Heart School Galveston, third grade teacher 1970-71; Rosenberg Elem Galveston, fifth grad teacher 1971-77; Rosenberg Elem Galveston, title I reading/math teacher 1977-82; Alamo Elem Galveston, fifth grade teacher 1982-; LaMarque School Dist, bd mem. **ORGANIZATIONS:** Mem Assoc of Childhood Ed, TX Classroom Assoc, TX professional Ed, Alpha Kappa Alpha Sor, Amer Business Women's Assoc, Amer School Bd Assoc, Gulf Coast Area Assoc of School Bds, Lamarque Gifted and Talented, School Home Adv Panel of Ed, Amer Bus Women Assoc, Alpha Kappa Alpha Sor of LaMarque; dir LaMarque Youth Aid Proj, United Way of the Mainland; LaMarque School Bd; Queen of Peace Instr of Interior Decorating COM; LaMarque Parent Teachers Assoc; Helped toorganize Non-Graded Reading Program in GISD; served on Teacher Adv Council, Policy Revision Comm, Pres & several other offices of ACE, state vice pres of Assoc of Childhood Ed; hospitality chmn at Rosenberg; served as Admin Designee for ARD Meetings; attended many seminars on HB 246, HB 72, Chap 75. **HONORS/ACHIEVEMENTS:** Jaycee-ette of the Year 1974,75; TX Hon Life Mem Jayceeettes 1978; TX Hon Life Mem PTA 1980; Serv Above Self-Rotary Intl Awd 1978; Outstanding Young Woman of Amer 1979. **HOME ADDRESS:** 2616 Lake Park Dr, LaMarque, TX 77568.

PRATT, MELVIN LEMAR
City manager. **PERSONAL:** Born Mar 16, 1946, Jackson, MS; married Mary Frances Buchanan; children: Kim Evette, Yuvette Patriece, Eric Marlowe, Justin Lavelle, Aaron Antion. **EDUCATION:** John Marshall HS, diploma 1961-64. **CAREER:** Maywood Concerned Citizens Org, second in command 1976-85; Village Bd, 3rd dist trustee. **ORGANIZATIONS:** Mem NBC-LEO 1983-; parent helper Boy Scouts of Amer 1978-80; usher St James Catholic Church 1977-84. **HONORS/ACHIEVEMENTS:** Image Awd Fred Hampton Scholarship Awd 1982. **HOME ADDRESS:** 214 So 7th Ave, Maywood, IL 60153. **BUSINESS ADDRESS:** Trustee Dist 3, Village Board, 115 So 5th Ave, Maywood, IL 60153.

PRATT, RUTH JONES (RUTH J. KING)
Educator. **PERSONAL:** Born Aug 02, 1923, Baltimore, MD; married James; children: Karl. **EDUCATION:** Coppin State Tchrs Coll, BS 1943; Howard U, MA 1948; Johns Hopkins U, attnd;Univ of MD; Towson State U; Morgan State U. **CAREER:** Baltimore City Public Schools, sr educ officer to supt of public instr present; elem prin 1968-75; asst prin elem school 1963-68; curriculum specialist elem school 1961-63; sr teacher master teacher 1959-61; supr teacher 1952-55; demo teacher 1945-49; teacher 1943; Morgan State Univ, asst prof reading devel & educ psychology 1969-73; Reading Workshops, consultant 1968-71; Human Relations Inst Towson State Univ, consultant 1968-70; Youth Summer Human Relations Workshop Natl Conf of Christians & Jews 1969-70; cosmetics consultant wig stylist 1968-77. **ORGANIZATIONS:** Chmn Miss Untd Negro Coll Fund Contest 1972-76; vice pres Provident Hosp Aux 1974-75; exec com dir search for talent 1969-76; chmn Untd Fund CICHA Campaign Baltimore City Pub Schs 1975-77; allocation panel Untd Fund 1976-77; bd dir Untd Way 1976-79; chmn Baltimore Employ Adv Com 1976-77; pres Professional Untd in Serv to Cherry Hill Comm 1970-75; long range plng com Girl Scouts of Central MD 1976-79; bd dir YWCA Central MD 1977; com for Preserv of OrchardSt Ch 1977; pres Baltimore Alumnae Chap Delta Sigma Theta Sor 1974-76; Mayor's Bicent Ball Com 1976; Afro Am Expo Steering Com 1976-77; mem Sharon Bapt Ch; organ dir Sunday Sch Choir; chrpsn annl mus Schlrshp Benefit; chmn 85th Anniv of Sharon 1970; Comm Leaders of Am 1971. **HONORS/ACHIEVEMENTS:** Serv plaque Untd Negro Coll Fund 1974; serv cert SE Br Kiwanis Club 1975; cert awds plaque Delta Sigma Theta Sor; sincere ded serv plaque PUSH 1975; outstnd woman panelist St John's Bapt Ch 1977; comm serv awd Untd Fund-CICHA Campaign 1975-76. **BUSINESS ADDRESS:** Principal, Baltimore City Public Schools, 5025 Dickey Hill Rd, Baltimore, MD 21207.

PRATTIS, LAWRENCE
Judge. **PERSONAL:** Born Jun 16, 1926, Philadelphia, PA; married Marie; children: Susan, David. **EDUCATION:** Howard Univ, AB 1946; Temple Univ School of Law, JD 1951. **CAREER:** Maple Corp, sec 1967-69; HAAS Comm Fund, sec 1969-72; Eastern Dist of PA, asst city solicitor; private practice 1953-73; Court of Common Pleas, judge 1973-. **ORGANIZATIONS:** Mem Distrib Com Philadelphia Found 1971-73; Lectr in Law Law Sch Villanova Univ 1976-80; mem Exec Com PA Conf of State Trial Judges. **MILITARY SERVICE:** USMC 1951-53. **BUSINESS ADDRESS:** City Hall, 1400 Market St, Philadelphia, PA 19107.

PREISKEL, BARBARA SCOTT (NEE SCOTT)
Attorney. **PERSONAL:** Born Jul 06, 1924, Washington, DC; married Robert H Preiskel; children: John S, Richard A. **EDUCATION:** Wellesley Coll, BA 1945; Yale Univ, LLB 1947. **CAREER:** Hon Charles E Wyzanski Boston, law clerk 1948-49; Dwight Royall Harris Koegel & Caskey, assoc free lance 1950-59; Motion Picture Assn of Amer, dep atty/vp 1959-77, sr vice pres & general counsel 1977-83; attorney. **ORGANIZATIONS:** Dir Jewel Co 1973-84; dir Amstar Corp 1974-84; dir Textron Inc 1975-; dir Levi Strauss & Co 1980-; dir RH Macy Corp 1981-86; dir Gen Elect Co 1982-; dir Mass Mut Life Ins Co 1983-; dir Washington Post Co 1985-; mem Pres Comm on Obscenity and Pornography 1968-70; mem New York City Bd of Ethics 1976-; mem Distrib Com New York Com Trust 1978-; successor trustee Yale Corp 1978-; trustee Ford Found 1982-; dir Med Educ of South African Blacks 1985-; mem Amer Women's Econ Devel Co 1982-. **HONORS/ACHIEVEMENTS:** Meritorious Award Natl Assn of Theatre Owners 1970-72; Theatre Owners of New England Award 1971; Wellesley Coll Alumni Achievement Award 1975; Catalyst Award for Women of Outstanding Achievement 1979; YWCA Elizabeth Morrow Achievement Awd 1986. **BUSINESS ADDRESS:** Attorney, 36 W 44th St, New York, NY 10036.

PREJEAN, CHERYL RENEE
Business executive. **PERSONAL:** Born Jul 30, 1947, Houston, TX; married Robert Bruce Greaux. **EDUCATION:** Univ of TX, MA 1973; TX Southern Univ, BA (Magna Cum Laude) 1967. **CAREER:** NASA Johnson Spacecraft Ctr, procurement spec 1968-71; Dept of Labor, supr compliance officer 1973-80; MA Inst of Tech, consult 1979; Allied Corp, corporate manager - EEC Programs. **ORGANIZATIONS:** Mem Delta Sigma Theta Sorority 1965-, Counterparts of NY 1980-, Natl Urban Affairs Council 1980-; chmn, fund raising NJ Inst of Tech 1981-; bd mem Morris Cty Urban League 1983-; committee Pre-Coll Ctr Bd. **HONORS/ACHIEVEMENTS:** Ford Found Scholarship TX Southern Univ. **BUSINESS ADDRESS:** Corp Manager, EEO Programs, Allied Corporation, Columbia Rd & Park Ave, Morristown, NJ 07960.

PREJEAN, RUBY D.
Educator. **PERSONAL:** Born Feb 20, 1925, Terrell, TX; married Wilbur. **EDUCATION:** BS 1958; Southwestern Christian Coll, teaching fellow. **CAREER:** Quinlan Schools, teacher 1942; NV Public Schools, 1948; Southwestern Christian Coll Terrell, 1958; Hardin-Jefferson Ind School Dist Sourlake, presently. **ORGANIZATIONS:** Hardin-Jefferson Educ Assn; TX State Tchrs Assn; Hardin Jefferson Classroom Tchrs Assn; TX State Classroom Tchrs Assn; Nat Educ Assn YMCA; pres Zeta Phi Beta Sor Inc Pub Relations 1966-68; spl liason com Welfare Dept Beaumont 1975. **HONORS/ACHIEVEMENTS:** Classroom tchr awd outstndg serv Hardin-Jefferson 1969-70; Outstndg Tchrs Am Elem 1972. **BUSINESS ADDRESS:** PO Box 398, China, TX.

PRELOW, ARLEIGH
Graphic designer. **PERSONAL:** Born Feb 01, 1953, Los Angeles, CA; daughter of Clifford Nathaniel Prelow and Leona Kern Prelow; divorced; children: Alison Guillory, Kara Guillory. **EDUCATION:** Univ of California, Berkeley, BA, 1974; attended Laney Coll, Oakland CA, 1984-86; attending Univ of California, Los Angeles, 1986-. **CAREER:** KQIV-Radio, Portland OR, program producer, host, writer, and spot announcer, 1975; KPIX-TV, San Francisco CA, segment producer and writer, researcher, production asst, sec, 1975-77; WTBS-TV, Atlanta GA, producer, writer, researcher, on-air dir, 1977-78; WSB-TV, Atlanta, segment writer and researcher, 1977; WETA-TV, Washington DC, associate producer, 1978-80; Scott Hall Productions, San Anselmo CA, administrator, 1980-81; Moti-Vision, Richmond CA, exec dir and producer, 1981-84; Arleigh Prelow Design, Los Angeles, owner and graphic designer, 1984-. **ORGANIZATIONS:** Sec and mem, Natl Assn of Negro Business and Professional Women's Clubs, 1986-89; mem, Worship '89 Conference Planning Comm, Synod of Southern California and Hawaii Presbyterian Church USA, 1988-89; treas and mem, Presbyterian Women, Redeemer Presbyterian Church, Los Angeles, 1988-. **HONORS/ACHIEVEMENTS:** Feature editor and writer, Black Thoughts Newspaper, Berkeley CA, 1973-74; writer, Portland Observer, Portland OR, 1975; writer, Soul Newsmagazine, 1978; Emmy Award for producer of cultural affairs prog, Acad of Television Arts and Sciences, Atlanta, 1978; third place in publication design Californiar, Cappy Awards, California Public Information Officers Assn, 1988; gold winner in magazine design intl, Mercury Awards, 1988; grand prize, best publication US and Canada, City Hall Digest Awards, 1988; featured in newspaper articles. **BUSINESS ADDRESS:** Owner, Arleigh Prelow Design, 727 W 7th St, Suite 1258, Los Angeles, CA 90017-3707.

PRESLEY, CALVIN ALONZO
Educator. **PERSONAL:** Born Jun 11, 1914, Statesboro, GA; married Viola Brown. **EDUCATION:** Savannah State Coll, BS 1940; Tuskegee Inst, MAgrEd;Univ WI, addl study;Univ of GA; Auburn U; GA So. **CAREER:** Randolph Co Comprehensive HS, teacher vocational agriculture; Randolph Co Sys, teacher vocational agriculture 1942-75; Jeffersonville GA, teacher 1940-42. **ORGANIZATIONS:** Mem Duroc Breeding Assn; Farm Bureau; Randolph Co Assn Educators; GA Assn of Educators; GA Voc Agr Assn; NEA; Am Voc Asso; master mason S T Thomas #70 Cuthbert GA; Eta Omicron. **HONORS/ACHIEVEMENTS:** Serv awd GA Voc Educ Agr 10 yr cert 1950, 20 yr cert 1960, 30 yr plaque 1970; letter of rec from Pres F D Roosevelt.

PRESLEY, OSCAR GLEN
Veterinarian. **PERSONAL:** Born Dec 19, 1942, Kosciusko, MS; married Ethel Rita Scott; children: Wanda, Glen Jr, Corey. **EDUCATION:** Rust Coll, BS 1966; TX Southern Univ, MS 1971; Tuskegee Inst, DVM 1974. **CAREER:** Meridian Public School, teacher 1967-69, dir independent study 1968-69; Tuskegee Sch of Vet Med Freshman Class, president 1969-70; Lexington Animal Clinic, pres. **ORGANIZATIONS:** Bd mem Jackson Chap Natl Bus League 1977-; bd mem K & S Chemical 1979-; bd mem New Hope Church 1980-84; vice pres MS Vet Med Assn 1983; natl chmn Fund Raising Rust Coll 1983; Phi Beta Sigma 1985; pres Lexington & hanging Moss Clinics. **HONORS/ACHIEVEMENTS:** Outstanding Young Man of Amer 1972; Outstanding Service Awd Jackson State Univ Minority Student 1985, 86. **MILITARY SERVICE:** AUS capt 2 yrs. **HOME ADDRESS:** 571 Woodson Dr, Jackson, MS 39206. **BUSINESS ADDRESS:** President, Lexington Animal Clinic, 1250 Forest Ave, Jackson, MS 39206.

PRESS, HARRY CODY, JR.
Educator. **PERSONAL:** Born Aug 22, 1931, Chesapeake, VA; married Francella Jane Teele; children: H Cody III, Lillian Jan. **EDUCATION:** VA Union U, BS 1952; Medl Coll VA, MD 1957; Am Brd Radlgy, Diplomate 1965; Am Coll Radlgy, Flw 1980. **CAREER:** Howard U, chmn dept radlgy 1966-79, prof radlgy 1978-. **ORGANIZATIONS:** Advy brd Washington Inst Techlgy 1970-78; const radlgy Commty Grp Found 1969-; commt grants

James Picker Found 1972-74; brd dir Silver Spring Boys Club 1971-74; sr warden Trinity Epis Chrh 1972-74; tm phys Bethesa Chevy Chase Ftbl Tm 1984. **HONORS/ACHIEVEMENTS:** Spel serv awd HowardUniv Const 1975; medl tm Urban Leag Trk Run 1981-82; ingested foreign bds Am Jourl Roentlgy 1976; evalu renal outline plus 50 publ Radiology 1980. **MILITARY SERVICE:** USN lt med Ofc 2 yrs. **HOME ADDRESS:** 6745 Newbold Dr, Bethesda, MD 20817. **BUSINESS ADDRESS:** Professor of Radiology, Howard Univ, 2041 Georgia Ave NW, Washington, DC 20060.

PRESSEY, JUNIUS BATTEN, JR.
Business executive. **PERSONAL:** Born Apr 06, 1947, Hampton, VA; married Elaine F Jenkins. **EDUCATION:** Central StateUniv Bus Adminstrn, 1971-72; IN Univ, BS 1975; Attending, Coll for Financial Planning. **CAREER:** Magnavox Corp, account intern 1972-73; City Util of Ft Wayne IN, acct trainee 1974; Natl Life & Acc Ins Co, life ins agent 1975-76; Metropolitan Life Ins Co, sales rep 1976-79; Lincoln Natl Sales Corp, tax deferred prog mgr 1979-; Lincoln Natl Life Employee Benefits Div, pensions mktg 1984-86; The Pressey Financial Planning Group Inc, pres/chairman. **ORGANIZATIONS:** Mem Ft Wayne Nat Life Underwriters Assn 1976-; bus consult Proj Bus of Jr Achievement 1978; bd mem Ft Wayne Opport Indsl Cntr Inc 1975-; bd mem Ft Wayne Sickle Cell Found 1978-; pres Ft Wayne NAACP 1978-; chmn econ task force Ft Wayne Future Inc C of C 1978-79; chmn Ft Wayne Affirmative Action Adv Cncl 1980-86; mem Comm Harvest Food Bank 1983-87; chmn Ft Wayne NBE/WBE Cncl 1984-86; mem Ft Wayne Anti-Apartheid Action Comm 1985; pres Ft Wayne/Allen Cty Martin Luther King Jr Memorial Inc 1985-87; bd mem Ft Wayne Business Cncl 1986; mem Intl Financial Planners Assoc 1986. **HONORS/ACHIEVEMENTS:** Who's Who Among Students in Am Coll IN Univ 1974-75; Metropolitan's Ldrs Club Met Life Ins Co 1976; Natl Sales Achievement Awd Natl Life UnderwritersAssoc 1977-79; IN Life Ins Ldrs Club Nat Life Underwriters Assn 1977; Pres Con Awd Met Life Ins Co 1978; Agent of the Yr Awd Gen Agent & Mgmt Assn 1978; The Cosmopolitan Outstanding Leadership Awd 1981; FWES Black Heritage Achievement Awd 1982; The Frederick Douglass Awd 1982; IN Grand Lodge Prince Hall Freedom Awd 1983; The NAACP Marjorie D Wickliffe Awd 1983. **MILITARY SERVICE:** USAF a/1c 1966-70; Natl Defense Awd. **BUSINESS ADDRESS:** President/Chairman, The Pressey Financial Plng Grp, PO Box 11763, Fort Wayne, IN 46860.

PRESSEY, PAUL MATTHEW
Professional athlete. **PERSONAL:** Born Dec 24, 1958, Richmond, VA; married Elizabeth; children: Ashley. **EDUCATION:** Univ of Tulsa, BS 1982. **CAREER:** Milwaukee Bucks, guard 1982-. **HONORS/ACHIEVEMENTS:** Emerged as Plyr of the Future according to NBA Today colmnst and CBS-TV play-by-play commentator Dick Stockton; led Bucks in scoring twice on the season hitfor double figures 32 times (twice over 20 points). **BUSINESS ADDRESS:** Milwaukee Bucks, 1001 N St, Milwaukee, WI 53203.

PRESSLEY, STEPHEN, JR.
Administrator social work. **PERSONAL:** Born Feb 01, 1947, Canton, OH; children: Lance E, Akima M, Stephen III. **EDUCATION:** Kent State Univ, AS 1975, BA 1977. **CAREER:** Stark Co CAP, dir of manpower 1971-73; Canton Urban League, dir of employment 1973-78; Lorain Co Urban League, exec dir 1978-80; Pittsburgh Urban League,dir of employment 1980-83; Urban League of Muskegon, exec dir 1983-. **ORGANIZATIONS:** Mem Alpha Phi Alpha; pres Civil Serv Commn Muskegon. **HOME ADDRESS:** 1274 5th St, Muskegon, MI 49440. **BUSINESS ADDRESS:** President/CEO, Urban League of Muskegon, 469 W Webster, Muskegon, MI 49440.

PRESTAGE, JEWEL LIMAR
Educator, educational administrator. **PERSONAL:** Born Aug 12, 1931, Hutton, LA; daughter of Brudis L Limar and Sallie Bell Johnson Limar; married Dr James J Prestage; children: Terri, J Grady, Eric, Karen, Jay. **EDUCATION:** Southern Univ & A&M Coll, BA 1951; Univ of Iowa, MA 1952, PhD 1954. **CAREER:** Prairie View A&M Coll, assoc prof Political Science 1954-56; Southern Univ, assoc prof Political Science 1956-62, prof Political Science 1965-, chairperson dept of Political Science 1965-83, dean school of Public Policy & Urban Affairs 1983-. **ORGANIZATIONS:** Pres SW Soc Science Assoc Scintists 1973-74; pres Natl Conf Black Politics 1976-77; pres Southern Political Science Assoc 1975-76; vice pres Amer Political Science Assn 1974-75; mem bd Voter Educ Project, Atlanta GA 1978-; state chmn mem Louisiana State Advisory Committee US Commission on Civil Rights 1974-81; mem bd Louisiana Common Cause 1983-; mem of bd Louisiana Capital Area Chapter Amer Red Cross 1985-; mem Alpha Kappa Alpha Sor Inc, Jack & Jill of Amer Inc. **HONORS/ACHIEVEMENTS:** Citizen of the Year, Alpha Kappa Alpha Sorority S Central 1971; Honor, Women's Pavillion 1984; World's Fair 1984; postdoctoral research Fellow Ford Found 1969-70; Honored Contributer Prof Amer Political Science Assoc 1984; co-author A Port Marginality The Political Behavior Of Amer Women 1977; Distinguished Alumni Award, Natl Assoc for Equal Opportunity in Higher Educ 1981; Baton Rouge Women of Achievement Award 1983; Distinguished Alumni Achievement Award Univ of Iowa 1986; Hancher-Finkbine Medallion, Univ of Iowa, 1989; Fannie Lou Hamer Award, Natl Conf of Black Political Scientists, 1989. **HOME ADDRESS:** 2145 77th Ave, Baton Rouge, LA 70807. **BUSINESS ADDRESS:** Dean, Southern Univ, Box 9222, Southern Branch P O, Baton Rouge, LA 70813.

PRESTON, BILLY See PRESTON, WILLIAM EVERETT

PRESTON, CAREY MADDOX
Educational administrator. **PERSONAL:** Born Apr 28, 1915, Columbia, MS; widowed. **EDUCATION:** Tougaloo Coll, BA 1937; Atlanta Univ, MSW 1939. **CAREER:** Chicago Bd of Educ, vice pres 1969-; Alpha Kappa Alpha Sor Chicago, exec sec retired 1974. **ORGANIZATIONS:** Pres Chicago Urban League 1970-; Natl Urban League; bd mem Hyde Park Fed Savs & Loan Assn; mem women's bd Univ of Chicago. **BUSINESS ADDRESS:** 5211 S Greenwood Ave, Chicago, IL 60615.

PRESTON, EDWARD LEE
Musician. **PERSONAL:** Born May 09, 1925, Dallas, TX; son of Swanee Preston, Sr and Beulah Mae Williams; divorced. **EDUCATION:** UCLA, 1945-47; Wiley Coll, 1941-42. **CAREER:** Count Basie Orchestra, trumpet player 1963; Charles Mingus Sextex, trmpt plyr 1963-66; NY Committee Young Audiences, bnd ldr musician 1975-; Jazzmobile Inc, lectr instr 1974-87; Jazzmobile Inc 1974-. **ORGANIZATIONS:** Trump plyr Duke Ellington Orchest 1963 1971-72, Archie Shepp Band 1979, Hamptons Band 1955-56; mem Mscn Local 802 1962-; mason Thomas Waller Masonic Lodge 1947; mem Musicians Local 47 1945-; made rcrdngs with all bands except "All Am Brass Band". **HONORS/ACHIEVEMENTS:** Russian Tour Duke Ellington Orch 1971; Japan tour Chas Mingus Combo 1970; Afrn tour All Am Brass Bnd 1964; Israel & European Tour Lionel Hampton Bnd 1955. **BUSINESS ADDRESS:** Jazzmobile Inc, 154 W 127th St, New York, NY 10027.

PRESTON, EUGENE ANTHONY
Business executive, city official. **PERSONAL:** Born Jan 10, 1952, Zanesville, OH; married Karen Y Booker. **EDUCATION:** Central State Univ Wilberforce OH, 1969-71; Franklin Univ Columbus OH, BS Bus Mgmt; Eastern Union Bible Coll Columus OH, attended. **CAREER:** Perry Cty Drug Abuse Council, pres 1973-; Rendville, mayor 1975-80; Rendville Housing Auth, vice pres 1976-; Perry Cty Plng Comm, exec dir 1976-; Arvin Systems Inc, former asst serv mgr; Amer Electric Power, bus exec. **ORGANIZATIONS:** Mem Rendville Village Cncl 1973-75; Lancaster-Fairfield Co NAACP 1972-; mem & deacon First Bapt Ch; 2nd vice pres OH Bapt Gen Conf Laymens Aux; vice pres Bapt Training Union; mem Lampado of Omega Psi Phi Frat; vice pres Providence Baptist Assoc, BTU; treas Providence Baptist Assoc Laymen's Aux; N Amer Baptist Men's Fellowship; spec projects comm Natl Baptist Convention USA Laymens Aux; committeeman Dem Central 1971-79; political action comm OH State Conf of Br NAACP; mem Golden Rule Lodge #30 PHF & AM; exec dir Perry Cty Plng Commiss 1976-78. **HONORS/ACHIEVEMENTS:** Listed in Natl Jaycee's Outstanding Young Men of Amer 1983.

PRESTON, GEORGE NELSON (OSAFUHIN KWAKU NKONYANSA)
Educator. **PERSONAL:** Born Dec 14, 1938, New York City, NY; married Adele Regina; children: Matthew, Afua-Magdalena, John. **EDUCATION:** City Coll of NY, BA 1962; Columbia, Univ, MA 1967; Columbia Univ, PhD 1973. **CAREER:** Dept of Art City Coll City Univ NY, assoc prof, Art & Art Hist 1980-, asst prof art & Art History, 1973-80; Dept of Art, Livingston Coll Rutgers Univ, asst prof, Art & Art Hist 1970-73. **ORGANIZATIONS:** Special consult NY State Commn on the Arts 1967-68; spl consult New World Cultures Brooklyn Museum, 1968; assoc, Columbia Univ Seminar on Primitive & Precolumbia Art 1973-80; bd of dir Bd of Adult Educ Museum of African Art Washington, DC 1972-80; mem Roger Morris-Jumel Hist Soc 1973-80; bd of dir Cinque Gallery New York City 1977-79. **HONORS/ACHIEVEMENTS:** Foreign area fellow Joint Com of the Amer Council of Learned Soc & the Soc Science Rsch Council 1968-70, 1972; numerous publications. **BUSINESS ADDRESS:** 133 St at Covent Ave, New York, NY 10031.

PRESTON, JOSEPH, JR.
Elected official. **PERSONAL:** Born May 28, 1947, Pittsburgh, PA; married Odelpa Smith; children: Joseph III, Diana. **EDUCATION:** Wilberforce Univ, attended; Univ of Pittsburgh, BA, 1979. **CAREER:** PA House of Reps, rep. **ORGANIZATIONS:** Bd mem, Homewood Revit Devel Corp, Allegheny Academy, Pittsburgh Water & Sewer Authority. **BUSINESS ADDRESS:** Representative Dist 24, PA House of Representatives, PO Box 153 Main Capitol, Harrisburg, PA 17120.

PRESTON, LEONARD
Automobile dealer. **PERSONAL:** Born Sep 08, 1948, LaGrange, TX; son of Verge Preston and Lula Gates Preston; married Cleo Jacko, Sep 26, 1970; children: LaTrondria, Byron, Germain. **EDUCATION:** Prairie View A&M Univ, Prairie View, TX, Industrial Ed, 1971. **CAREER:** Ford Motor Co, Memphis, TN, field zone sur mgr, 1971-78, Lansing, MI, owner relations mgr, 1979-85; All American Ford-Lincoln Mercury, Covington TN, owner. **ORGANIZATIONS:** Mem, Covington Rotary Club, 1985; mem, Chamber of Commerce, 1985; coach, Dixie Youth Baseball, 1987, sponsor, 1988.

PRESTON, RICHARD CLARK
Clergyman. **PERSONAL:** Born Aug 19, 1933, Paraloma, AR; married Hazel I Witherspoon; children: Belinda F, Ulysses V, Felecia M, Antonio L. **EDUCATION:** Philander Smith Coll Little Rock, attnd; Gammon Sem Conf Course of Study Atlanta; Henderson StateUniv Arkedelphia AR. **CAREER:** St Mark Untd Meth Ch Wichita KS, pastorate 1973-; Mallalieu Untd Meth Ft Smith AR, pastorate 1969; Mt Carmel Untd Meth Lockesburg AR, pastorate 1963; First Untd Meth Sweet Home AR, pastorate 1961; Mt Zion Untd Meth Cntr Ridge AR, pastorate 1952. **ORGANIZATIONS:** Pres NAACP Ft Smith AR 1971-73; pres NE Ministerial League Wichita 1975-77; rep KS W Conf Counc on Ministries 1973-80; bd mem Area Agency on Aging 1974-75; bd mem Interfaith Ministries Bd Wichita 1979-80; First Fire Dept Ecumenical Grp Sweet Home AR 1961; Mallalieu Comm Devel Ctr/ Richard Preston Ctr for Human Devel Ft Smith AR 1971. **HONORS/ACHIEVEMENTS:** Cert of awd ded NAACP KS State Conf Topeka 1972; bldg New Ch Wichita 1980. **MILITARY SERVICE:** AUS pfc 1955-61. **BUSINESS ADDRESS:** 1914 E 11th St, Wichita, KS 67214.

PRESTON, SWANEE H. T., JR.
Physician. **PERSONAL:** Born Mar 10, 1924, Dallas, TX; son of Swanee Preston and Beulah Preston; married Hazel Elizabeth Bjorge; children: Dorrlyn Jean, Tyrone Hudson, Wayne Raynard. **EDUCATION:** Great Lakes Coll Clvlnd OH, MM 1948, DM 1952; Am TUniv Arcade MO, ND 1953; Wiley Coll Marshall TX, BS 1943;Univ Cincinnati CT, Counseling 1981 . **CAREER:** Hair Weev Inc, admin 1957-72; City Cleveland, EMT para medic 1973-79; Operation Newstart, soc wrkr 1976-80; Salvation Army (Adult Rehab Ctr), supr stores 1980-83; Dept Inmate Svcs, actng unit dir soc serv 1982-; Private Practice, 1952-. **ORGANIZATIONS:** Past vice pres NY Naturapathic Soc; founder Phys Medl Soc; Am Techlgy Assn; 1st aid emer care inst Am Red Cross; CPR instr trnr Am Heart Assn bd dir YMCA. **HONORS/ACHIEVEMENTS:** ausn Man yr Hair Inc 1964; Busn Man Day Radio Sta WDOK; mem Myr Cncl City Cleve Carl Stokes Mayor; LA soc intl Who's Who (work in Liberia, Africa 1969). **MILITARY SERVICE:** USCG lt 1/c 3 yrs 5 Battle Stars & Medals & Theater Ribbons 1943-46. **HOME ADDRESS:** 6270 Dawson Blvd, Mentor, OH 44060. **BUSINESS ADDRESS:** Acting Dir of Soc Serv, Dept of Inmate Serv, 9002 Empire Ave, Cleveland, OH 44108.

PRESTON, WILLIAM EVERETT (BILLY PRESTON)
Recording artist. **PERSONAL:** Born Sep 02, 1946, Houston, TX. **EDUCATION:** Dorsey HS Los Angeles CA, grad; began career when he was 3 yrs old at keyboard; toured with Beatles & Rolling Stones 1960's. **CAREER:** Active in St Elmo's Village a ctr for children; NightlifeTV show, musical dir. **ORGANIZATIONS:** Gold single Will it go Round in Cir-

cles 1972, Space Race 1973, Nothing from Nothing 1974; BMI cit of achvmt You Are So Beautiful 1975-76; apprd in St Louis Blues; movie with Nat King Cole; played with James Cleveland, Ray Charles, The Beatles, The Rolling Stones; recrded album in hon of St elmo's Village, Billy Preston, The Kids & Me; teamed with Syreeta "It's My Pleasure" 1975, for movie soundtrack "Fast Break", "Syreeta"; 1 of 1st to fuse gospel W/pop/R&R/R&B.

PRESTWIDGE, BARBARA ELIZABETH
Bank official. **PERSONAL:** Born Dec 05, 1945, Baltimore, MD; divorced; children: Monique Jackson, Melanie Jackson. **EDUCATION:** Howard Univ, BA Lib Arts 1967; Southern CT State Univ, MS Ed 1972; CT Sch of Broadcasting, graduate 1979. **CAREER:** Essex Co Coll, adjunct instructor 1972-77; Kean Coll, adjunct instructor 1974-77; Farleigh Dickinson Univ, adjunct instructor 1975-77; Sacred Heart Univ, adjunct instructor 1980; South End Comm Day Care Ctr, exec dir 1972-74; Messiah Luthern Day Care Ctr, dir 1976-77; Child Care Gtr Bpt, exec dir 1977-78; Peoples Bank Bridgeport, mgmt trainee admin super 1978-80, asst branch mgr 1982-84, asst branch mgr Wilton Office 1980-82; branch mgr 1984, asst treasurer 1984-. **ORGANIZATIONS:** Grp leader Explorers 1977-78; vol Women Helping Women Program YWCA 1979-80; bd mem Big Brothers/Big Sisters of Fairfield Co 1981-82; bd mem & housatonicGirl Scout Council treas 1981-83; Action for Bridgeport Comm Dev Inc vice chmn 1982, chmn 1982-; loaned exec United Way of Fairfield Co 1983; allocation comm United Way of Fairfield Co 1980-; mem & editorial staff Women In Mgmt 1982-; choir mem St Mark's Episcopal Church 1983-; youth group adv St Mark's Episcopal Church 1983-; mem Finance Comm YWCA 1984-; mem Natl Assn Bank Women 1984-; mem Coalition of 100 Black Women 1984-; vestry mem St Mark's Episcopal Church 1985-; mem Black Women of Corporate Amer 1985-; moderator "Today's Woman" radio talk show WICC Radio Bridgeport 1979; mem bd of dirs Conn Friends of Ernestina Morrissey Ocean Classroom 1985-. **HONORS/ACHIEVEMENTS:** Glamour Magazine 10 Best Dressed Coll Girls Contest 1 of 25 Natl runners up 1965; Alpha Phi Alpha Sweetheart 1965; Who's Who Among Howard Women 1967; Pi Sigma Alpha Pol Sci Honor Soc 1967; Outstanding Young Women of Amer 1981 & 1982; Chairman's Awd People's Bank 1984. **HOME ADDRESS:** 715 Frenchtown Rd, Bridgeport, CT 06606. **BUSINESS ADDRESS:** Asst Treasurer, Peoples Bank-Bridgeport, PO Box P, Monroe, CT 06468.

PRETTYMAN, QUANDRA
Educator. **PERSONAL:** Born Jan 19, 1933, Baltimore, MD. **EDUCATION:** Antioch Coll, BA 1954; Univ of MI, graduate study 1955-57. **CAREER:** Barnard Coll, assoc in English, foreign student advisor; Coll of Ins, instr 1962-67; New School for Social Research, lectr 1959-62; Scholastic Book Serv NY, editor The Open Boat & other short stories by Stephen Crane 1968. **HONORS/ACHIEVEMENTS:** "Out Of Our Lifes a selection of contemporary black fiction Howard Univ Press 1975; poems in many anthologies Most Notable Arnold Adoff, The Poetry of Black Amer, Black World Barnard Publ. **BUSINESS ADDRESS:** Associate in English, Barnard College, 3009 Broadway, New York, NY 10027.

PREWITT, AL BERT
Educator, elected official. **PERSONAL:** Born Feb 17, 1907, Tuscaloosa, AL; married Audrey Monroe; children: Jean, AB, Jr, Juan, Maryann Davis, Gloria P Cooke, Jessee D. **EDUCATION:** Langston University, BSA 1935. **CAREER:** Langston Univ, instructor 1934-47; Langston High School, teacher 1947-57; Boley High School, teacher 1958-65; City of Langston, chairman-trustee board. **BUSINESS ADDRESS:** Chairman, Board of Trustees, City of Langston, PO Box 116, Langston, OK 73050.

PREWITT, LENA VONCILLE BURRELL
Educator. **PERSONAL:** Born Feb 17, 1932, Wilcox, AL; married Moses K Prewitt; children: Kenneth Burrell. **EDUCATION:** Stillman Coll, BS in Business Educ, 1954; Indiana Univ, MA in Business Educ, 1955, EdD in Business Educ, 1961, postdoctoral study, 1965; postdoctoral study in France, Czechoslovakia, and Germany, 1968-69; postdoctoral study, Texas Southern Univ 1969, Univ of California at Los Angeles 1978, Georgia Tech Univ 1980, Harvard Univ 1987, Univ of South Carolina 1987, Univ of Bocconi, Milan Italy, 1988. **CAREER:** Pacific Telephone & Telegraph, Los Angeles CA, special mgmt consultant 1968; Marshall Space Flight Ctr, Huntsville AL, employee devel officer 1964; Stillman Coll, asst prof, assoc prof, prof 1955-67; Texas Southern Univ, assoc prof, dept chmn 1967-69; Florence State Univ, assoc prof 1969-70; Univ of Alabama, assoc prof 1970-74, prof 1974-. **ORGANIZATIONS:** Special rsch consultant, TTT Proj, Texas Southern Univ, 1969; mem, Acad of Mgmt; mem, European Found for Mgmt Devel, 1968-; mem, Southern Mgmt Assn; mem, Amer Assn for Univ Women; mem, Natl Business Educ Assn; mem Delta Pi Epsilon; mem gen exec bd, Presbyterian Church US, 1973-; vice pres, FOCUS on Sr Citizens; bd dir, Tuscaloosa Opportunity Prog, 1970-74; bd dir, Tuscaloosa Planning Comm, 1974-75; mem, Century Club YMCA; mem, United Fund Steering Comm, 1974; chair, US Selective Service Appeals Bd, 1980-; bd dir, AMI-West Alabama Hospital, 1986-. **HONORS/ACHIEVEMENTS:** SUrban League Fellowship 1966; Ford Found Fellow 1965; Presbyterian Church US Fellow 1958-60; Maritime Admin Fellowship 1965; published numerous articles incl "The Role of Human Resources Mgmt in Econ Devel" 1982, "Selling Cable TV as Career Opportunity for Coll Students" 1979, "Black Capitalism: A Way or a Myth?" Journal of Small Business, 1973, "Facing the Realities of Executive Burnout and the Need to Manage Stress," Intl Mgmt Devel, 1982; participated in numerous lectures including Human Resources Mgmt & Motivation 1982, Preventing Discrimination Complaints, a Guide for Line Managers 1980, The Black Experience in Higher Educ; numerous seminars & workshops; TV appearances in "Work and the Modern Family," program taped for NBC-TV for the Natl Endowment for the Humanities. **BUSINESS ADDRESS:** Prof of Human Resources Mgmt, Univ of Alabama, PO Box 5237, University, AL 35486.

PREZEAU, LOUIS E.
President, CEO. **PERSONAL:** Born Mar 04, 1943, Port-au-Prince, Haiti;son of Emile Prezeau and Yua Roy; married Ramona A Prezeau, Apr 04, 1964; children: Jasmine, Louis Jr, Rodney. **EDUCATION:** Bernard M Baruch, New York NY, BBA, 1970. **CAREER:** Freedom Natl Bank of New York, New York NY, chief operating officer, 1975-88, acting pres, 1987-88; City Natl Bank of New Jersey, Newark NJ, pres/CEO, 1989-. **ORGANIZATIONS:** New York State Soc of Certified Public Accountants, 1973-; treasurer, trustee, Community Serv Soc, 1985-; trustee, New York Uran League, 1988-, investment comm, Natl Council of Churches, 1988-. **BUSINESS ADDRESS:** President & Chief Executive Officer, City National Bank of New Jersey, 900 Broad St, Newark, NJ 07102.

PREZEAU, MARYSE
Educational administrator. **PERSONAL:** Born Feb 20, 1942, Port-au-Prince, Haiti. **EDUCATION:** Hunter Coll, BA (Cum Laude) 1970, MA 1971; CUNY, PhD 1976. **CAREER:** Hunter Coll, adj lecturer 1970-76; York Coll, adj asst prof 1973-77; Barnard Coll, lecturer 1977-78; NY Inst of Tech, asst provost. **ORGANIZATIONS:** Bd mem Nassau Cty Med Ctr 1978-; mem & NYIT Corp rep Amer Assoc of Univ Women 1982-. **BUSINESS ADDRESS:** Assistant Provost, NY Inst of Technology, NYIT Central Islip Campus, Central Islip, NY 11722.

PRICE, A. YVONNE CONN
Business executive. **PERSONAL:** Born Feb 09, 1930, Toledo, OH; children: Allyson. **EDUCATION:** Central State Coll. **CAREER:** DC Public Schools, government emp; NAACP, legal assist; Leadership Conf on Civil Rights, exec asst; United Black Fund, natl coord; NAACP, dir combined federal campaign; Yvonne Price & Assocs, pres. **ORGANIZATIONS:** Nat Women's Com for Civil Rights; Nat Urban League; Consult Fed Exec Inst; OIC's of Am; steering com Nat Policy on Career Educ for Blacks; Black Educ Policy Conf; co-chmn Adv Cncl of Nat Orgn Corp for Pub Brdcstg; mem Task Force on Minorities & Women CPB; White House Conf Civil Rights; White House Conf on Aging; Nat Black Women's Polit Caucas chmn; Nat Cncl Negro Women; Govtl Affairs Nat Assn Negro Bus & Professional Women's Clubs; past chmn Govt Affairs Nat Assn Mkt Devel; bd mem & sec Women's Campaign Fund; mem Ad Hoc Com on Women's Appts in Carter Admin; chairperson DC Apprent Council; mem Capital Press Club; bd dir Private Indust Council. **HONORS/ACHIEVEMENTS:** Salute to Yvonne Price Sept 1984; 100 Black Women of DC; Special Award Salute to Black Women by Black Men SCLC; listed Who's Who in Amer Women; Woman of the Year Afro Amer Newspaper; Pres Award Nat Assn of Kkt Devel; Serv Award WA Urban League; Past Pres Award Urbanite Guild; Outstanding Serv Award DeVore School of Charm; Mayors Meritorious Public Serv Awd; Govt of the Dist of Columbia Cert of Commendation NANBPWC Inc.

PRICE, ALBERT H.
Business executive. **PERSONAL:** Born Jun 21, 1922, Somerville, MA; married A Terry; children: Glenn, Kendal, Byron. **EDUCATION:** Howard U, BA 1942; cum laude, Grad Sch of Bus Adminstrn NY U, MBA (cum laude); Grad Sch Pub Adminstrn NY U, MPA 1955. **CAREER:** Ronson Corp, vice pres & asst treas 1968-81; controller 1965; chief accountant 1954; jr accountant 1948. **ORGANIZATIONS:** Dir First Nat Bank of Princeton 1972-76; dir UJB 1976-87; dir Princeton YMCA 1967-74; trustee Middlesex Co Coll Scholar Fund 1971; dir Interracial Counc for Bus Oppor of NJ 1968-; mem Nat Alliance of Bus 1972; srvd on various sch study com 1970-72; Dir Easter Seal Soc of NJ 1986-; trustee, Medical Center at Princeton. **MILITARY SERVICE:** AUS infantry capt 1942-46.

PRICE, ALFRED DOUGLAS
Educator. **PERSONAL:** Born Jul 06, 1947, Buffalo, NY; son of Alfred D Price and Virginia M Allen; divorced; children: A Douglas, V. **EDUCATION:** Princeton Univ, M Arch & Urban Plan'g 1975; Princeton Univ, AB-SOCIOLOGY 1969. **CAREER:** Harvard Univ, co-dir AAEO 1969-71; Schl of Arch-nJ Inst of Tech, asst dean 1975-77; Sch of Architecture-SUNYAB, assoc dean 1977-84. **ORGANIZATIONS:** Mem US Assn for Club of Rome 1980-; mem & chair of selection Bflo City Arts Comm 1980-; chrm architectural comm Episcopal Diocese of Western NY 1980-;brd of dir Buffalo Convtn Cntr 1981-84; chrmn City of Buffalo Urban Design Task Group 1980-; brd of dir Seventy-Eight Restoration Corp 1979-. **HONORS/ACHIEVEMENTS:** Grants Exceeding 1/4 Million Dollars Harvard 1969-71; Butler Travelling Flwshp Princeton Univ 1973; Jury Member, 1975 Honor Awards, Amer Inst of Architects1975. **HOME ADDRESS:** 77 Huntington Ave, Buffalo, NY 14214. **BUSINESS ADDRESS:** Assoc Professor of Planning, Sch of Architecture, StateUniv of NY at Buffalo, Buffalo, NY 14214.

PRICE, CHARLES
Judge. **PERSONAL:** Born May 09, 1940, Montgomery, AL; married Bernice B; children: Susan Y, Charles II. **EDUCATION:** VA Union Univ, BS 1969; Natl Law Ctr; George Washington Univ, JD (Honors) 1972. **CAREER:** US Dept of Justice Washington DC, intern 1972-73; State of AL, asst atty gen 1973-75; Escambia Cty AL, acting dist atty 1974; Montgomery Cty AL, depdist atty 1975-78; Private practice, law 1978-83; State of AL, circuit judge. **ORGANIZATIONS:** Mem Natl Bar Assoc; reg dir Headstart; asst municipal judge Montgomery 1978-83; pres Montgomery Cty Trial Lawyers Assoc 1982-83; circuit judge Montgomery Cty AL 1983-. **MILITARY SERVICE:** USAR Judge Advocate Corps maj. **HOME ADDRESS:** 134 N Haardt Dr, Montgomery, AL 36105. **BUSINESS ADDRESS:** Judge Circuit Court, State of Alabama, 251 S Lawrence St, Montgomery, AL 36104.

PRICE, CHARLES EUGENE
Attorney. **PERSONAL:** Born in Apalachicola, FL; married Mrs Lennie B; children: Charles E Jr (deceased). **EDUCATION:** Johnson C Smith U, BA 1946; Howard U, AM 1949; Johns Hopkins U, further study 1951-52; Boston U, further study 1956; Johnson Marshall Law Sch jd 1967; Harvard Law Sch, cs 1980. **CAREER:** NC Mutual Life Ins, ins mgr 1949-50; Butcen Coll, dean of coll 1950-53; FL Mem Coll, dean of coll 1953-55; NAACP (assgnd to GA), field dir 1955-57; Livingstone Coll, asst prof 1957-59; Morris Brown Coll, assoc prof/atty. **ORGANIZATIONS:** Bd dir Hemphill Food Serv 1982-; cnsltnt Thomas & Russell 1979-; atty at law State Bar of GA Fed Bars 1968-; bd dir Dekalb, GA EOA 1965-70; pres Dekalb, GA NAACP Chptr 1962-70; adv bd Sm Bsns Adm GA 1968-82. **HONORS/ACHIEVEMENTS:** Ldrshp Awrd GA NAACP 1965-66; schlrshp Alpha Kappa Mu 1954; artcls pub Atlanta Daily Wrld & Pittsbrgh Courier 1955-57; Tchr of Yr Morris Brown Coll 1972, 1980-81. **HOME ADDRESS:** 1480 Austin Rd SW, Atlanta, GA 30331. **BUSINESS ADDRESS:** Associate Prof/Attorney, Morris Brown Coll, 643 MLK Dr NW, Atlanta, GA 30314.

PRICE, DAVID B., JR.
Chemical company executive. **PERSONAL:** Born Nov 09, 1945, St Louis, MO; son of David B Price and Ethel Armstrong Price; married Joyce A Jacobs, Dec 03, 1966; children: Danyale A Price, Jason J Price. **EDUCATION:** Univ of Missouri, Rolla MO, BS, 1968; Harvard Business School, Boston MA, MBA, 1974-76. **CAREER:** Laclede Gas Co, St Louis MO, project engineer, 1968-72; Monsanto Co, St Louis MO, sr engineer, 1972-74, various managerial jobs, 1976-81, mgr, commercial devel, 1981-83, dir, investor relations, 1983-86, dir, commercial devel, 1986-87; vice pres & gen mgr, 1987-. **ORGANIZATIONS:** Mem, Harvard Business Club of St Louis, 1976-; commr, Missouri Housing Devel Commn; 1986-; bd mem, Synthetic Organic Chemical Assn, Inc. 1987-; bd mem, Young Men's Christian Assn

of St Louis, 1988-; mem, Society of Chemical Industry, 1988-. **MILITARY SERVICE:** US Army, staff sergeant, 1969-71. **BUSINESS ADDRESS:** Vice Pres & Gen Mgr, Specialties Div, Monsanto Chemical Co, 800 N Linbergh Blvd, G5NG, St Louis, MO 63167.

PRICE, DAVID LEE
Educator. **PERSONAL:** Born Jan 11, 1934, Greenville, NC; married Eva Elizabeth Walker; children: David L. **EDUCATION:** A&T State U, BS 1959;Univ of VA, MEd 1971;Univ of MD, MEd plus 30 1973. **CAREER:** Fairfax Co VA Public Schools, adminstrative aide 1978-; Fairfax Co VA Public Schools, reading specialist 1968-78; Newport News Public Schools, reading specialist 1966-68; Newport News VA Public Schools, teacher 1961-66. **ORGANIZATIONS:** Spl police ofcr Hampton VA Police Dept 1961-68; ldr-supr Fairfax Co VA Rec Dept 1968-; lib asst Fairfax Co Pub Lib VA 1968-72; mem Fairfax Educ Assn; VA Educ Assn; Fairfax Co Reading Assn; various others; mem Mt Vernon Civic Assn 1975-; coach-mgr Mt Vernon Youth Ath Assn 1975-; mem Woodley Hills Sch PTA 1975-; mem H&T StateUniv Alumni Chpt;Univ of VA Alumni Chpt; Big Brothers of Am; Toastmasters Intl 1971-; num others. **HONORS/ACHIEVEMENTS:** Outstndg tchr of the month John Marshall Elem Sch 1965; Epsilon Delta Chi Soc 1965; Kappa Delta Pi Hon SocUniv of MD Chap 1973; Outstndng Educ of Am 1974; Personalities of the S 1974; listed Who's Who in N Am 1976; listed Who's Who in the S & SW 1978; listed Personalities of Am & Notable Am 1979; num other awds & hons; Nat Def Serv Medal AUS. **MILITARY SERVICE:** AUS corpl 1953-55. **BUSINESS ADDRESS:** Fairfax Co VA Pub Sch, 10700 Page Ave, Fairfax, VA 20230.

PRICE, ELIZABETH LOUISE
Association executive. **PERSONAL:** Born Jan 07, 1934, Worcester, MA; married Elwood B; children: Dante, Stacey. **EDUCATION:** ClarkUniv u of RI. **CAREER:** Prospect House Inc, exec dir 1971-; Worcester Sch Com, 1973-; Lyman Sch for Boys, 1968-69; Severeux Sch for Emotionally Dist, 1969-70; Worcester Detention Cntr, 1968. **ORGANIZATIONS:** Exec bd MA Min Counc on Alcoholism 1973; mem State Library Com 1973; dir Nat Black Caucus Sch Bd; dir bd Campaign for Human Devel 1974; NAACP 1973; mem Affirmative Act Com Worcester State Coll. **HONORS/ACHIEVEMENTS:** Rec Laurel Clayton Civic Awd 1962; Geo Washington Carver Crum & Bugle Corp 1970; Nat Miss Black Fox 1973. **BUSINESS ADDRESS:** 67 1/2 Laurel St, Worcester, MA 01605.

PRICE, FAYE HUGHES
Mental health administrator. **PERSONAL:** Born in Indianapolis, IN; married Frank Price Jr; children: Faye Michele. **EDUCATION:** WV State Coll, AB (honors scholarship) 1943; IN Univ Sch of Social Work, scholarship 1943-44; Jane Addams Sch of Social Work Univ IL, MSW 1951; Univof Chicago, summer institutes 1960-65; IL MH Inst Abra Lincoln Sch of Med; Fam Inst of Chicago; Inst of Psych Northwestern Meml Hosp; Northwestern Medical Sch. **CAREER:** Flanner House, supv youth activities 1945-47; Parkway Comm House, prog dir 1947-56; Parway Comm House, dir 1957-58; Bureau Mental Health Chicago Dept of-Health, dir social work 1958-61; Chicago Dept Health, asst dir bureau of mental health. **ORGANIZATIONS:** Consul various health welfare & youth agencies; field instr Univ IL-Univ Chicago-Atlanta Univ-George Williams Univ; lecturer Chicago State Univ-Univ ILother professional workshops seminars and confs; mem Art Inst Chicago; mem Chicago Lyric Opera; mem Chicago Urban League; mem Southside Comm Art Ctr mem Chicago YWCA; mem Parnell Ave Block Club; mem DuSable Mus; mem Psychotherapy Assn; mem Amer Public Health Assn; mem IL Public Health Assn; mem Alpha Gamma Phi; mem Alpha Kappa Alpha; mem NAACP; mem natl Council Negro Women; life mem WV State Coll; life mem Univ of IL; Jack and Jill Assn; The Chums Inc; Chicago Chap The Links Inc; Natl parliamentarian Natl Assn of Parliamentarians; Zonta Intl; Les Cameos Social Club; Assn of Retarded Citizens of IL; Natl Assn of Soc Wkrs; Acad of Cert Soc Wkrs; Certified Soc Wkrs of IL; Assn of Clin Soc Wkrs; Natl Conf Soc Wel; Natl Assn Black Soc Wkrs; IL Grp Psych Assn. **HONORS/ACHIEVEMENTS:** Listed in Who's Who of Amer Women; Who's Who in the Midwest; Who's Who in America; Who's Who in the World; Mother of the Yr Award Chi State Univ; Natl Outstanding Serv Award Links Inc; Outstanding Serv Award Links So Suburban Chpt. **HOME ADDRESS:** 9815 S Parnell Ave, Chicago, IL 60628. **BUSINESS ADDRESS:** Assistant Dir, Chicago Dept of Health, Richard J Daley Center LL139, Bureau of Mental Health, Chicago, IL 60602.

PRICE, GEORGE BAKER
Retired brigadier general, business executive. **PERSONAL:** Born Aug 28, 1929, Laurel, MS; son of Mr James A Price and Mrs James A Price; married Georgianna Hunter; children: Katherine, James, William, Robert. **EDUCATION:** SC State Coll, BS 1947-51; US Army Command & Genl Staff Coll, certificate 1964-65; US Army War College, certificate 1970-71; Shippensburg State Coll, MS 1970-71. **CAREER:** US Army, platoon leader headquarters 1951, platoon leader L Company 1952, company commander specialist training regiment 1953-57, opers officer 1957-61, personnel mgr 1961-62, adv 1st vietnamese infantry div 1964-65, dept of army staff 1965-68, battalion commander 1968-70, brigade commander 1971-73, chief of staff 1973-74, asst div commander 1974-76, chief of staff 1976-78; Techdyn Systems Corp, dir govt operations 1978-81; Unified Industries, special asst to pres 1981-82; Southern Brand Snack Inc, exec vice pres 1978-81; Price Enterprises, personal mgr Leontyne Price. **ORGANIZATIONS:** Mem Kappa Alpha Psi Frat; mem Military & Veterans Adv Comm Natl Urban League; mem Vietnam Veterans Memorial Fund 1980-85; bd of visitors US Military Academy, West Point; bd of Advisors Womans Vietnam Veterans Memorial. **HONORS/ACHIEVEMENTS:** Distinguished Patriot Awd Natl Womens Republican Club; Distinguished Serv Awd SC State Coll 1975; distinguished Vietnam Veteran National Association Paramedics 1989-. **MILITARY SERVICE:** AUS brigadier gen 1951-78; Legion of Merit; Bronze Star; Meritorious Serv Medal; Commendation Medal; Air Medal; Purple Heart; Combat Infantryman Badge, airborne, ranger. **BUSINESS ADDRESS:** Personal Manager, Price Enterprises, 1133 Broadway, New York, NY 10010.

PRICE, GILBERT
Performer. **PERSONAL:** Born Sep 10, 1942, Brooklyn, NY; son of Leon Price and Carmen Christian Price. **CAREER:** Featured singer on Ed Sullivan, Merv Griffin, David Frost, Red Skelton, Harry Belafonte Singers, Leonard de Paur Chorus; Langston Hughes' Jericho Jim Crow 1963; host of Canadian TV Series, One More Time, Kicks & Co, Fly Blackbird 1972; Jacques Brel is Alive & Well, Chita Rivera 1972; Gentlemen of Verona Australia 1973; Leonard Bernstein Mark Taper Forum 1974; Mahogonny Yale Repertory Theatre 1974; The Night That Made America Famous Harry Chapin 1975; 1600 Pennsylvania Avenue Leonard Bernstein & Alan Jay Lerner 1975-76; The King in Spite of Himself NY Opera 1977; Timbuktu 1977; freelance performer. **ORGANIZATIONS:** Mem Equity; mem St Cecilia's Roman Catholic Church. **HONORS/ACHIEVEMENTS:** Nominated for Antoinette Perry Awds Lost in the Stars, The Night that Made America Famous. **BUSINESS ADDRESS:** c/o Warren Allen Smith, 130 W 42nd St Variety #551, New York, NY 10036.

PRICE, HUGH BERNARD
Attorney. **PERSONAL:** Born Nov 22, 1941, Washington, DC; married Marilyn Lloyd; children: Traer, Janeen, Lauren. **EDUCATION:** Yale Law Sch, LLB 1966; Amherst Coll, BA 1963. **CAREER:** City of New Haven Human Resources, adminstrn; Cogen Holt & Asso, partner; The Black Coalition of New Haven, exec dir; Urban Renewal Agency New Haven Redevel Agy, asst couns; New Haven Legal Asst Assn, neighbrhd atty. **ORGANIZATIONS:** Mem bd dir Cntr for Comm Change Washington DC; mem bd dir exec com real estate com New Haven Water Co; past mem Distrib Com New Haven Found; past mem bd dir past vice pres for planning United Way of Grtr New Haven; mem Nat Bus Leag; mem NAACP; mem Alpha Phi Alpha Frat; mem Proj Planning Com Grtr New Haven Black Soc Civic Orgn Higher Educ Fund; past mem bd dir New Haven Legal Asst Assn Daytop Inc; Polly T McCabe Cntr; Grtr New Haven UMCA;Lewis Latimer Found. **HONORS/ACHIEVEMENTS:** Co-authored several art. **BUSINESS ADDRESS:** 16u Church St, New Haven, CT 06510.

PRICE, JAMES ROGERS
Personnel administrator. **PERSONAL:** Born Sep 19, 1942, Atlanta, GA; married Jean Wade; children: Roderick. **EDUCATION:** Morris Brown Coll Atlanta, BS 1964. **CAREER:** Dobbs House Inc, reg personnel mgr 1972-76; EEO Affairs Dobbs-Live Savers Inc, mgr 1976-78; Metro Atlanta Rapid Transit Auth, dir of personnel 1978-81;M&M Products Co, employment serv mgr 1981-. **ORGANIZATIONS:** Bd mem TAY Morris Brown Coll 1983; mem Amer Soc of Personnel Admin, Morris Brown Coll Natl Alumni Assoc; mem Alpha Phi Alpha 1977; chmn Indust Adv Council Atlanta Job Corps Ctr 1983-; mem Adv Comm on Vocational Ed; past mem Leadership Fort Worth; deacon Union Bapt Church, Soloist Union Bapt Church Choirs. **HONORS/ACHIEVEMENTS:** Outstanding Young Men in Amer 1967; Outstanding Alumnus Morris Brown Coll 1975; Employee of the Month Lockheed- GA Co 1969; listed in Who's Who Among Black Amer 1981. **BUSINESS ADDRESS:** Employment Services Manager, M&M Products Co, PO Box16549, Atlanta, GA 30321.

PRICE, JOHN ELWOOD
Musician. **PERSONAL:** Born Jun 21, 1935, Tulsa, OK; son of Carter E and Irma V. **EDUCATION:** Lincoln Univ, BMus 1957; Univ of Tulsa, MM 1963; attended Washington Univ 1967-68. **CAREER:** Karam Theatre Cleveland, staff composer/pianist/vocal c 1957-59; FL Meml Coll Miami, chmn Music/Fine Arts, composer-in-residence 1967-74; Tuskegee Univ, composition/history 1980; Portia, Washington-Pittman Fellow 1981-82; Eastern IL Univ, mem music dept 1970-71, 1974-80; Tuskegee Univ, mem music dept 1982-. **ORGANIZATIONS:** Five hundred ninety-two compositions 1943-; life mem Alpha Phi Alpha 1954-; life mem Phi Mu Alpha Sinfonia 1954-; mem ASCAP 1970-; mem Assn for the Study of Afro-Amer Life & History 1970; mem Amer Music Soc 1970-; mem Natl Black Music Caucus; mem The Soc for Ethnomusicology 1974; mem The Mediaeval Acad of Amer 1975; Spirituals for the Young Pianist Book I Belwin Mills NY 1979; pub Invention I for Piano 1952; pub Blues & Dance I Clarinet & Piano 1955; pub Scherzo I Clarinet & Orch 1952 & 1955; Two Typed Lines 1959; The Lamp FMC 1969; The Lamp FL Memorial Coll; pub Prayer, Martin Luther King Baritone Solo SSAATTBB a cappella 1971; pub Barely Time to Study Jesus 3rd Version Solo Gospel Choir 7 speakers percussion ensemble 1977; pub A Ptah Hymn Unaccompanied Cello 1978; pub Menes, The Uniter Unaccompanied C Bass 1979; mem Natl Assoc Composers USA 1982; Slave Ship Press Tuskegee Inst AL 1983. **HONORS/ACHIEVEMENTS:** The Black Musician As Artist & Entrepeneur Awd Phelps-Stokes Fund Scholarship Exchange 1974-; Disting Faculty Awd Eastern IL Univ Charleston 1979-80; 2nd Disting Faculty Awd Black Student Union E IL Univ 1980; Tischler Alice "Fifteen Black American Composers," 1981; listed Roach, Hildred Black American Music Vol II 1985; Fellowship Grant AL Arts Council 1986; Rural Arts Coord State of AL apptd 1986; featured Alabama Adver Dowrnal Feb 1987; "Composers of the Americas" Pan Amer Un Vol 19 1977 Washington DC; "The Sphinx" mag of Alpha Phi Alpha Frat 1976; photographic posters of the Tuskegee City Dance Theatre in eight rest areas for the State of AL; honored as one of the musical "gems" of Oklahoma Musical History during American music week 1988. **MILITARY SERVICE:** AUS sp4 1959-61. **BUSINESS ADDRESS:** Professor, TuskegeeUniv, The Chapel, Tuskegee, AL 36088.

PRICE, JOSEPH L.
Clergyman. **PERSONAL:** Born Dec 25, 1931, Gary, IN; married Edria Faye; children: 6. **EDUCATION:** East Los Angeles Jr Coll; Moody Bible Inst; Chicago Bapt Bile Inst; Indiana Christian Theol Sem, 1969. **CAREER:** St Jude Deliverance Ctrs of Amer, pastor Evangelist minister organ & fndr 1971-; Church of God in Christ, bishop dist supr & pastor 1963-71; photo, welder, owner, furniture & appliance store; real estate & ins broker. **HONORS/ACHIEVEMENTS:** Award for community serv & leadership Mayor Richard Lugar; hon DDiv Natl Inst of Relig Sci & Arts. **MILITARY SERVICE:** AUS airborne spl/4c 1951-56. **BUSINESS ADDRESS:** 975 N Delaware, Indianapolis, IN.

PRICE, JUDITH
Business executive. **PERSONAL:** Born Feb 10, 1937, New York City, NY; children: Toni, Marc. **EDUCATION:** City Coll of NY, attnd; Bernard Baruch Sch of Bus Adminstrn. **CAREER:** James B Beam Import Corp subsidiary of James B Beam Distilling Co NY, vice pres dir 1972-; James B Beam Import Corp, former adminstrv dir & asst sec. **ORGANIZATIONS:** Mem Traffic Assn of the Liquor Industry. **BUSINESS ADDRESS:** 5800 Arlington Ave, Riverdale, NY 10471.

PRICE, LEONTYNE
Opera diva, recording artist, concert and recital artist, humanitarian. **PERSONAL:** Born Feb 10, 1927, Laurel, MS; daughter of Mr and Mrs James A Price; divorced. **EDUCATION:** Central State Coll, BA Doct Music 1949; Julliard School of Music NYC, 1949-52; Florence Page Kimball, private study. **CAREER:** Actress, Porgy & Bess, Europe, 1952-54; recitalist, soloist with symphonies in US, Canada, Australia, Europe, 1954; performed in Tosca, NBC Opera Theater, 1954; appeared in concert, India, 1956-64; soloist, Hollywood Bowl, 1955-59, 1966; Berlin Festival, 1960; San Francisco Opera, 1957-59, 1960-61, 1963, 1965, 1967, 1968, 1971; Vienna Staatsopera, 1958-59, 1960-61; RCA, recording artist 1958-; opened new Metropolitan Opera House Lincoln Center in 1968; 6 performances at the White

House; performed Live from Lincoln Center; performed at 2 presidential inaugrations and for the Pope. **ORGANIZATIONS:** Hon bd mem, Campfire Girls; co-chairperson, Rust College Upward Thrust Campaign; trustee, Intl House; hon vice chmn, US Comm UNESCO; mem AFTRA, Amer Guild Mus Artists, Actors Equity Assn, Sigma Alpha Iota, Delta Sigma Theta, Natl Inst of Music Theater, NAACP, Whitney Young Foundation, New York Univ Bd of Trustees. **HONORS/ACHIEVEMENTS:** 20 Grammy Awds; Spirit of Achievement Awd, Albert Einstein College Med, 1962; Silver Medal of San Francisco Oper Italy's Order of Merit; Presidential Medal of Freedom, 1964; Spingarn Medal, NAACP, 1965; Schwann Catalog Awd, 1968; Natl Medal of Arts, 1985; Handel Medallion New York City; Associated Black Charities Grammy Lifetime Achievement Award; 26 honorary doctorates. **BUSINESS ADDRESS:** c/o Columbia Artists Mgmt Inc, 165 W 57th St, New York, NY 10019.

PRICE, MICHAEL D.
Radio broadcaster. **PERSONAL:** Born Nov 07, 1957, Cincinnati, OH; married Paula A Hall. **EDUCATION:** OH Univ, BS Communications 1980. **CAREER:** Armour-Dial Co, sales rep 1981-83; WKQX/NBC Radio, acct exec 1983-86; WBBM/CBS Radio, sr acct exec 1986-. **ORGANIZATIONS:** Mem CBS Black Employees Assoc Chicago, Field Museum of Natl History Chicago, Art Institute of Chicago.

PRICE, MICHAEL J.
Association executive. **PERSONAL:** Born Nov 28, 1950, Yazoo City, MS. **EDUCATION:** Dillard U, BA 1971; Purdue U, MA 1973; Columbia Coll Chicago, addl studies. **CAREER:** Alpha Phi Alpha Frat Inc, asst execsec; The SPHINX, editor-in-chief 1974-. **ORGANIZATIONS:** Mem Am Philos Assn 1971-73; Soc of Phenomenology & Existential Philosophy 1971-73; mem & Chicago Inter-alumni Coun; DillardUniv Alumni; Alpha Chi Nat Honor Soc; staff asso Safer Found; charter mem DillardUniv Chpt. **HONORS/ACHIEVEMENTS:** Listed in Notable Am of 1976-77; Comm Ldrs & Noteworthy Am 1977; Who's Who in AmUniv & Coll 1969-70; Chicago Negro Almanac 1975; nom Outst Young Men of Am 1977; black dotoral flwshp PurdueUniv 1971. **BUSINESS ADDRESS:** c/o Alpha Phi Alpha, 4432 S Martin Luther King Dr, Chicago, IL 60653.

PRICE, RAMON B.
Educator. **PERSONAL:** Born 1933, Chicago, IL. **EDUCATION:** Art Inst of Chicago, BFAE 1958. **CAREER:** Du Sable High School, teacher 1959-72; South Side Community Art Center, dir 1960-68; George Williams College, dept chmn 1969-73; Indiana Univ, presently assoc instructor. **ORGANIZATIONS:** Liason vol Blacks in Chicago auspicies; mem Natl Conf of Christians and Jews 1960-73; visual art consultant and instructor Urban Gateways 1971-74; visual art dir Amer Friends Serv Comm 1963-66; youth dir Natl Conf of Artists 1972-74; bd dirs South Side Community Art Ctr; advisor Du Sable Museum of African-Amer Art and Hist. **HONORS/ACHIEVEMENTS:** Numerous awards, prizes, comm in sculpture & painting. **MILITARY SERVICE:** USMC 1952-54. **BUSINESS ADDRESS:** Afro-Amer Studies, IndianaUniv, Bloomington, IN.

PRICE, RUBY JEWELL TIMMS
Educator, chairperson. **PERSONAL:** Married Ralph Sr; children: Jessie Tave (dec), Marqueax, Ralph Jr, DeAne, Deon, DeVon. **EDUCATION:** Butler Coll, cert; Philander Smith Coll, BS & BA; Weber Coll Ogden Utah, certs & deg kindergarten & early childhood edn; Butler Coll Tyler TX, bookkeeping & bus edn; Wiley Coll Marshall TX; Utah StateUniv Logan, grad schs psychol & couns;Univ of UT SLC; Brigham YoungUniv Provo UT. **CAREER:** W Pt Elem School, vice prin 1938-39; Gregg Co Independent School Dist, dir of preschool & kind 1939-40; Pleasant Hills Jr HS, dept head 1940-43, dept head 1947-48; Ogden Arsenal, supvr mail & records 1948-49; Hill AFB, data trans 1949-50; Intermountain Indian School, teacher 1950-56; Gregg County School Dist, teacher summer 1952; Intermt Ind School, acting dept head 1952; Vae View Elem School, retired teacher 1963-75; Davis County Republican Party, chairperson. **ORGANIZATIONS:** Mem Natl & State Comm for the Handicapped; state delegate White House Conv 1976-; mem Gov Black Adv Coun; mem St Professional Cert & Recert Com Dir Yth Beaut Layton City; mem chmn Comm Ch Layton UT 1979-81; mem UT Civil Rights Adv Comm 1979-; mem UT State Coalition of Sr Citizens 1979-81; natl advbd Amer Sec Counc 1979-81; vice chmn Davis Co Rep Party 1979-81; mem Davis Co NAACP Layton 1980; mem Utah Civil Rights Comm; mem KSL-TV Adv Bd Bonneville Corp Utah; charter mem President's Task Force; mem Davis County Task Force for Substance Dependency. **HONORS/ACHIEVEMENTS:** Who's Who in Am Politics 6th edit 1977-78; Outstanding Layton Citizen Awd 1977; UT Mother of the Year 1977; 1st black PTA pres; 1st Woman Hon Sheriff Davis Cty; hon appt Natl Bd of Adv Amer Biograph Inst; The Intl Who's Who of Intellectuals; The World Who's Who of Women; one of 350 delegates in the world selected by Dr Kay of Cambridge England to attend the 7th IBC Intl Congress on Arts and Communications in Amsterdam Holland; Governor's Black Scholars Disting Comm Awd.

PRICE, SUZANNE D.
Educator. **PERSONAL:** Born Aug 19, 1921, Baltimore, MD; daughter of J Steward Davis and Blanche Moore Davis Lindsay; married Charles K Price, Nov 07, 1953. **EDUCATION:** Howard Univ, BA, MA. **CAREER:** Retired, Div of Prog Devel Bureau of Elementary & Secondary Educ US Dept of Educ, dir 1973-81; USOE, chief analyst res & mat staff 1968-73; Div of Equal Educ Opportunity USOE, educ program specialist 1965-68; HEW, asst rev office 1964-65; Coll of Liberal Arts Howard Univ, instructor 1960-64; US Dept of State, intell rsch specialist 1961. **ORGANIZATIONS:** Mem Phi Alpha Theta Natl Hist Hon Soc; mem Kappa Delta Pi Natl Educ Hon Soc; mem Amer Hist Assn; mem Asm Assn of Univ Women; mem Delta Sigma Theta Inc; mem The Links Inc Columbia MD Chapter; mem Natl Council of Negro Women Howard Co MD Chapter. **HONORS/ACHIEVEMENTS:** Cash Award for Super Performance US Office of Educ 1968; Letter of Commendation US Commr of Educ Harold Howe 1968; Group Award F Div of Equal Educ Opportunity 1970; Cash Award for Super Performance US Office of Educ 1973; Super Serv Award US Office of Educ 1974.

PRICE, WALLACE WALTER
Business executive. **PERSONAL:** Born Mar 10, 1921, East St Louis, IL; son of Samuel P Price and Pennie Johnson Price; married Adrienne Walton, Jun 05, 1982; children: Sandra D, Wallace W II, Catherine A Counts. **EDUCATION:** So IL Univ Carbondale, BE 1942; E Univ Sch of Commerce & Law Baltimore MD, attnd 1947-48; Univ of MD Aberdeen Coll Pk MD, attnd 1948-49; master of science, VA State Coll Petersburg, 1952-53; Univ of PA Grad Sch, post grad work 1958-61; Seton Hall Univ Sch of Law Newark NJ, attnd 1977-79; tchng permits IL/NJ/VA. **CAREER:** VA State Coll, commandant of cadets 1951-53; MS&T VA State Coll, assoc prof 1951-53; OLIN Corp Stamford CT, mgr proc finance chem gr 1964-72; SeatrainShipbuilding Corp Brooklyn, asst vice pres 1972; Pan Am World Airways NY, corp dir 1972-75; Becton Dickinson Co Rutherford NJ, corp mgr affirm prog 1976-77; United Cerebral Palsy Assoc of NJ, exec dir 1978-82; Consultants Admin Mgmt, consultant. **ORGANIZATIONS:** Bd of dir Comm Chest Englewood NJ 1968-87; treas & finan sec Nat Assn of Mrkt Devel NY 1966-70; asso dir Herbert Lehman Educ Fund NY 1971-72; pres Bus & Professional Men's Opportn Inc NY 1970-73; spl consult Gov of VI Plan Gr 1974; bd of dir Citibank Cap Corp NY 1973-74; affirm act counc NJ Sports & Expo Auth 1973-75; affirm act counc Teaneck Bd of Educ NJ 1975-76; treas former pres & co-found The Edges Gr Inc NY-NJ-CT 1979-; cnclmn Teaneck Township, NJ 1977-78; former pres & treas Alpha Phi Alpha Frat IL & Germany; mem Fair Hous Counc of Bergen Co Hackensack; mem bd of dir Untd Way of Bergen Co NJ 1972-85; pres emeritus Urban League of Bergen Co NJ. **HONORS/ACHIEVEMENTS:** Collegiate Professional Tchng Permit Commonwealth of VA 1953; Annl Awd of Mer E Reg Alpha Phi Alpha Frat Inc 1960; Life mem European Cong of Am Parents &Tchrs Germany 1963; One of the Ten Great Men of Bergen Co NJ 1970; Who's Who in Fin & Ind; Who's Who in the E; Master Mason Prince Hall F&A Masons DE 1970; Urban League of Bergen Co Outstndg Achiev Awd Englewood NJ 1972; AUS awd for Outstndg Support of Northeastern Reg Comman 1975; v chmn Black Am Law Students Assn Seton Hall Law Sch 1978-79. **MILITARY SERVICE:** AUS lt col USA 1943-64. **BUSINESS ADDRESS:** Consultant, Consultants Admin Management, 585 W Englewood Ave, Teaneck, NJ 07666.

PRICE, WILLIAM S., III
Judge. **PERSONAL:** Born Sep 30, 1923, Hennessey, OK; married Dilys A. **EDUCATION:** Washburn U, AB JD 1950. **CAREER:** Genesee County, atty asst pros 1951-72; asst pros 1956-59; 68th Dist Ct Flint MI, presently presiding judge. **ORGANIZATIONS:** Pres Genesee County Bar Assn 1970-71; Genesee County Legal Aid 1956-57; pres Flint Civil Serv Commn 1969-72; mem & jud counc Nat Bar Assn. **HONORS/ACHIEVEMENTS:** Achieve awd No Province Kappa Alpha Psi. **MILITARY SERVICE:** Capt A&M Soc Corps ETO 1944-45; ETO 1942-46. **BUSINESS ADDRESS:** 120 E 5 St, Flint, MI 48502.

PRICE-CURTIS, WILLIAM
Educator. **PERSONAL:** Born Nov 10, 1944, OklahomaCity, OK; son of Jonathan Curtis and Algie Price Curtis. **EDUCATION:** OK State U, BA 1966, MS 1970; OK U, PhD 1976. **CAREER:** Hoffmann Laroche Inc, mktg spl 1971; Oscar Rose Coll, prof 1972-79; Youth Career Devel Nat Urban League, natl dir 1979-86; Okla City Public Schools, Equity Officer, 1987-. **ORGANIZATIONS:** Mem OK Psycholosical Assn, Am Assn for Cnslng & Dev, Am & Personnel & Guidance Assn, Am Psychological Assn, Councial Black Am Affairs, OK City Urban League Dept Health Ed & Welfare, Rehabilitation Couselor Fellowship 1969, Alpha Phi Alpha; bd dir US Youth Council 1983-86; gov bd Intl Youth Year Commission 1983-85; bd of directors, Urban League of Okla City 1989-. **HONORS/ACHIEVEMENTS:** Publs "Black Amer Progress in the Attainment of Educational Equity" Educ Leadership 1981, "An Examination of the Variables Related to Minority Youth Employment" Jrnl of Employment Counseling 1982. **HOME ADDRESS:** 4404 Thompson Ave, Oklahoma City, OK 73105.

PRIDE, ARMISTEAD SCOTT
Retired educator. **PERSONAL:** Born May 27, 1906, Washington, DC; son of Armistead Pride and Belle Scott Pride; married Marie Schoffen Pride, Jun 16, 1951. **EDUCATION:** Univ of MI, AB 1927; Univ of Chicago, AM 1932; Northwestern Univ, MSJ 1942, PhD 1950, LHD (Hon) 1976. **CAREER:** TN State Univ, English instr 1928-30; Bishop & Wiley Coll, instr 1932-33; Bishop Coll, instr 1933-34; MA Geodetic Survey Boston, editor dept forms & reprod 1935-37; Lincoln Univ, asst prof English 1937-41, asst prof journalism 1942-43, acting dir, asst prof 1944-45, dir 1945-47; School of Journalism, dean & prof 1947-57; Cairo Univ, Amer Univ of Cairo, Univ of Rome, visiting Smith-Mundt prof 1956-57; School of Journalism, chmn journalism 1957-76; Chungang Univ Seoul, visiting Fulbright lecturer 1963-64; Temple Univ, visiting prof communications 1969-70. **ORGANIZATIONS:** Mem adv bd MO State Library; rsch & travel Amer Council Learned Soc 1946-47; mem Comm on Negro Studies ACLS 1948-50; vice pres 1956, pres 1958 Amer Soc Journalism School Admin; vice pres Assoc Coll & Univ Concert Mgrs 1967; mem Assoc for Educ in Journalism, Amer Assoc Univ Prof. **HONORS/ACHIEVEMENTS:** Contributed articles to scholarly and professional journals. **MILITARY SERVICE:** AUS pvt 1944.

PRIDE, CHARLEY
Entertainer. **PERSONAL:** Born Mar 18, 1939, Sledge, MS; married Rozene; children: Kraig, Dion, Angela. **CAREER:** Detroit, Birmingham Black Barons, Memphis Red Sox, baseball player; Los Angeles Angeles, professional baseball player; Anaconda Mining; Decca Productions Inc, recording artist. **HONORS/ACHIEVEMENTS:** Sold more than 20 million albums & five million singles; twelve of his 40 LP's have gone gold in the US Market; 31 gold & four platinum LP's; awarded the firstGolden Opal Awd in Australia for album sales in excess of one and a half million; listed in Book of Lists as one of the top fifteen all-time world-wide recordsellers; won three Grammy Awds-Best Country Vocal Performance Male "Charley Pride Sings Heart Songs" 1972, Best Gospel Performance "Let Me Live" 1971, Best Sacred Performance "Did You Think to Pray" 1971; won Entertainer of the Year Awd 1971; Best Male Vocalists Awd CMA; Amer Music Awd Favorite Male Vocalist in Country Music 1976. **MILITARY SERVICE:** AUS 1956-58. **BUSINESS ADDRESS:** Recording Artist, Decca Productions Inc, PO Box 670507, Dallas, TX 75367.

PRIDE, HEMPHILL P., II
Attorney. **PERSONAL:** Born May 19, 1936, Columbia, SC; divorced; children: Hemphill III. **EDUCATION:** SC State Coll; Johnson C Smith U; FL A&M U. **CAREER:** Self Emp, atty; NAACP, cola br 1964-; SC Housing Auth, vchmn 1972-77; Nat Bar Assn, adv bd 1972-76; Gov's Bi-Centennial Com, 1976; SC Taxpayers Assn, atty 1973; Cty of Columbia, asst pros 1973; 1st black to construc 55 unit high-rise 236 housing proj 1970; Jenkins Perry & Pride, prtnr 1965. **ORGANIZATIONS:** Mem SC Bar 1963; Nat Bar Assn 1964; admitted to practice US Supreme Ct 1968; State Dem Com of 100 1970; gen counsel allenUniv 1977; legal counsel NAACP1977. **BUSINESS ADDRESS:** Attorney at Law, 1401 Gregg St, Columbia, SC 29201.

PRIDE, J. THOMAS
Business executive. **PERSONAL:** Born Jan 18, 1940, Highland Park, MI; married Vernester Green; children: Leslie, Thomas, Alesia. **EDUCATION:** Highland Park Jr Coll, 1958-59, 1962; Wayne State U, 1962-64. **CAREER:** Ross Roy Inc, vice pres adv 1972-; J Walter Thompson Co Detroit, media buyer 1964-69; Campbell Ewald Co, acct exec 1969-72; Amer Assn Advertising Agys, tchr. **ORGANIZATIONS:** Adcraft Club of Detroit Nat Assn of Market Devel; Black Applied Res Cent; Detroit Boat Club; spkr Black Applied Res Cntr 1972; mem Blacks Against Racism 1969; trustee Kirkwood Gen Hosp Club. **BUSINESS ADDRESS:** Health Alliance Plan, 2850 W Grand Blvd, Detroit, MI 48202.

PRIDE, JOHN L.
Association executive. **PERSONAL:** Born Nov 04, 1940, Youngstown, OH; married Sallie Curtis; children: Jacqueline, Curtis. **EDUCATION:** Capital Univ Columbus, BA 1963; Howard Univ, grad work in Psy. **CAREER:** US Office of Educ, chief SE oper Bran 1970-72, deputy asst dir for oper 1972-74; US Dept HEW, spec asst to dep asst sec for human dev 1974-. **ORGANIZATIONS:** Consult to White House Conf on Food Health & Nutrition 1969; US Senate Select Comm on Human Needs 1968; Natl Adv Com on Civil Disorders 1968; mem Adv Comm on Special Educ Montgomery Co MD Pub Schls; mem Adv Comm on Family Life & Human Dev Mont Co MD Pub Schls; pres Mont Co Assn for Language Handicapped Children; mem Big Brothers of the Natl Capital Area. **HONORS/ACHIEVEMENTS:** 4 yr coll Athletic Scholarship; MVP Coll Track Team 1963; 5 ltrs basketball & track in coll. **BUSINESS ADDRESS:** Spec Asst to Dep Asst, U S Department HEW, 330 Independence Ave SW, Ste 5717, Washington, DC 20202.

PRIDE, MARCUS O., SR.
Educational administrator. **PERSONAL:** Born Feb 15, 1962, Los Angeles, CA; married Charlotte Faye Rose; children: Marcus Orlando, II. **EDUCATION:** Dillard University, BS Biology 1981-84; Pasadena College of Chiropractic, Dr of Chiropractic 1985. **ORGANIZATIONS:** Member Social & Recreational Committee Dillard Univ 1982; member Roentgenological and Technology Society; keeper of records Kappa Alpha Psi; treasurer & public relations officer Student American Chiropractic Assn; assoc student body vice pres Pasadena Coll of Chiropractic 1985. **HONORS/ACHIEVEMENTS:** Academic Scholarship Dillard Univ 1982, United Negro College Fund 1982, Harvey Lillard Chiropractic Soc 1984; The Natl Deans List 1985. **HOME ADDRESS:** 720 N Marengo #6, Pasadena, CA 91103.

PRIDE, WALTER LAVON
Attorney. **PERSONAL:** Born Apr 04, 1922, Birmingham, AL; son of George T Pride and Althea Pride; divorced; children: Karen, Pamela. **EDUCATION:** Roosevelt Univ, BS; John Marshall Law Sch, JD; Univ of Michigan, Roosevelt Univ, grad study. **CAREER:** Chicago Assn of Defense Lawyers, former pres 1967-69; Pride Leaner Stewart & Elston Chicago, attorney-at-law. **ORGANIZATIONS:** Mem Chicago Bar Assn, IL State Bar Assn; attended Legal Seminars Northwestern Univ, Univs of MI IL WI; mem Alpha Phi Alpha; Il State Bar Assn; mem bd of dir Stuart Townhomes Corp; mem Chicago Conf on Brotherhood; Norman LaHarry Golf Classic; mem Cook Co Bar Assn; mem Natl Bar Assn; mem Natl Assn Defense Lawyers; life mem NAACP. **HONORS/ACHIEVEMENTS:** Listed in Who's Who in Amer Law. **MILITARY SERVICE:** AUS s/sgt WW II. **BUSINESS ADDRESS:** Attorney, Pride Leaner Stewart & Elston, 180 N La Salle St, Chicago, IL 60602.

PRIESTER, JULIAN ANTHONY (PEPO MTOTO)
Jazz artist, composer. **PERSONAL:** Born Jun 29, 1935, Chicago, IL; son of Lucius Harper Priester and Colelia Smith-Priester; married Jaymi Goodenough; children: Julia Antoinette, Claudette Ann Campbell, Adebayo Goodenough, Foster Lucian. **EDUCATION:** Sherwood School of Music, Chicgo IL, attended. **CAREER:** ECM Riverside Records, trombonist/bandleader 1954-80; Max Roach Quintette, trombonist/soloist 1959-61, 1964-65; Art Blakey's Jazz Messingers, trombonist/soloist 1968; Duke Ellington Orchestra, lead trombonist 1970; Herbie Hancock Sextette, trombonist/soloist 1971-73; Cornish College of the Arts, jazz program administrator/faculty 1979-87. **ORGANIZATIONS:** Adj to the faculty Lone Mountain Coll 1976-77; program dir/faculty Cazadero Music Camp 1978-80; sec Music Adv Council 1979-80; faculty Naropa Inst 1981-83; faculty Center for the Arts 1984-87; bd of dirs Pacific Jazz Inst 1987; commr Seattle Arts Commn 1988-90. **HONORS/ACHIEVEMENTS:** Commemorative Plaque Msingi Workshop 1972; Grant NEA 1975; Best Horn Player Award Bay Area Music Magazine 1978; Commemorative Plaque San Francisco Jazz Comm 1979; King County Arts Commn Grant 1987. **MILITARY SERVICE:** AUS corpl 1955-63. **BUSINESS ADDRESS:** Jazz Program Administrator, Cornish College of the Arts, 710 E Roy St, Seattle, WA 98102.

PRIMAS, BARBARA JEAN
Executive director. **PERSONAL:** Born May 03, 1949, Jacksonville, FL; divorced; children: Aprelle. **EDUCATION:** Edward Waters Coll, BA 1971. **CAREER:** PA State Dept of Justice, personnel assoc 1972-74; Mathematica Inc, personnel mgr 1974-84; Princeton Tehological Seminary, dir of personnel 1984-. **ORGANIZATIONS:** Mem Delaware Valley Personnel Assoc 1983-; mem Amer Mgmt Assoc 1984-; mem Churchwide Compensation Council of Presbyterian Church 1984-; mem College & Univ Personnel Assoc 1984-; treasurer Princeton Personnel Assoc 1985-; mem Amer Compensation Assoc 1986-. **HOME ADDRESS:** 131 Bluebird Dr, Hillsborough, NJ 08876. **BUSINESS ADDRESS:** Dir of Personnel, Princeton Theological Seminary, CN 821, Mercer St, Princeton, NJ 08542.

PRIMM, BENY JENE
Physician, business executive. **PERSONAL:** Born May 21, 1928, Williamson, WV; married Annie Delphine Evans (deceased); children: Annelle Benne, Martine Armande, Jeanine Bari. **EDUCATION:** WV State Coll, BS 1950; Univ of Geneva Switzerland, MS 1959. **CAREER:** MJ Lewis Coll of Podiatry NYC, co-med dir 1969-72; Hunter Coll NY, adj asst prof 1971-72; Eckerd Coll Div Behavioral Sci FL, visiting prof 1977; Dept of Anesthesiology Harlem Hosp, attending phys 1977-; Urban Resource Institute, pres 1983; Addiction Rsch & Treatment Corp, exec dir. **ORGANIZATIONS:** Mem Special White House Briefing Team 1972; consult Spl Act Office Drug Abuse Prevention at White House 1972-73; chmn Drug Abuse Com Empire State Med Assn1976-; mem Natl Med Assn 1964-; bd dirs Com on Problems of Drug Dependence 1977-; mem Drug Abuse Adv Com Food & Drug Admin 1978-; fellow Amer Collof Anesthesiology; US Delegate UNESCO Conf Youth & Drug Use in Indsl Countries France. **HONORS/ACHIEVEMENTS:** Cert of Appreciation Exec Off Pres Spl Action Off Drug Abuse Prev; listed Who's Who in America. **MILITARY SERVICE:** AUS 1st lt 1950-53. **BUSINESS ADDRESS:** Executive Dir, Addiction Rsch & Trtment Corp, 22 Chapel St, Brooklyn, NY 11201.

PRIMO, QUINTIN E., JR.
Clergyman. **PERSONAL:** Born Jul 01, 1913, Liberty Co, GA; married Winifred; children: Cynthia, Quintin III, Susan. **EDUCATION:** Lincoln U, BA 1934; Lincoln U, STB 1937; VA Theological Sem, MDiv 1941, DD 1973; Seabury-Western Sem, DD 1972; General Theol Sem, STD 1973. **CAREER:** Ch in FL, NC, NY, DE, former pastor; Woodward Convoction of the MI Epis Diocese; St Matthew's & St Joseph's Ch Detroit, former rector; Epis Diocese of Chgo, suffragan bishop 1972-retirement; interim bishop of DE, 1985-86. **ORGANIZATIONS:** Life trustee Rush-Presbyterian-St Luke's Med Center Chicago; trust Penninsula United Methodist Home Inc Wilmington, Kalmar Nyckel Found Wilmington. **HONORS/ACHIEVEMENTS:** Fifth black ever elected as a bishop of the ch; recip DD honor degrees from Gen Theol Sem of NY & VA Theol Sem; hon DD Seabury-Western Sem Evaston, IL; LHD honor degree St Augustine's Coll Raleigh.

PRIMOUS, EMMA M.
Educator. **PERSONAL:** Born Oct 05, 1942, Olive Branch, MS; married Commodore Cantrell; children: Commodore, Christopher. **EDUCATION:** Memphis State U, BS 1964; Memphis State U, EdM 1971. **CAREER:** Memphis Public Schools, teacher 11 years; MSU Reading Workshop Elem School Teachers, cons; WKNO-TV County Schools Program, panel mem; Open-Space Schools Benoit, cons; MSU TN State Univ LeMoyne-Owen Coll, supr teacher & student teachers; Program on Problem-solving Skills Memphis County Bd Educ, staff teacher. **ORGANIZATIONS:** Mem Ant Educ Assn; TN Educ Assn; Memphis Educ Assn; mem past vpres Rubaiyats Inc; mem Les Casuale Bridge Club; Cherokee Civic Club; NAACP; Delta Sigma Theta Sor; Kappa Delta Pi. **HONORS/ACHIEVEMENTS:** Listed outsdng yng women of Am 1976; named outsdng Yng Eductr of Yr Parkway Village Jaycees 1974.

PRIMUS, PEARL
Dancer. **PERSONAL:** Born Nov 29, 1919. **CAREER:** Cafe Soc, solo dancer 1943; New York City Chicago Trenton Newark, various solo concerts 1944-45; appeared at Belasco Theatre Broadway 1944; Roxy Theatre 1944; made cross country tours 1946-48; appeared in revival of Show Boat 1946; Chicago Opera Emperor Jones 1946; starr Caribbean Carnival 1947; open ed sch of dance New York City 1947. **ORGANIZATIONS:** Mem Am Negro Theatre; New Dance Group; Am Guild Mus Artists Inc; Actors Equity; Am Guild Variety Artists. **HONORS/ACHIEVEMENTS:** Contributed article The African Dance; NY Univ Ernest O Melby Award for Distinguished Serv in Human Relations. **BUSINESS ADDRESS:** c/o Dances Mag, 503 West 33rd St, New York, NY 10101.

PRINCE See NELSON, PRINCE ROGERS

PRINCE, A. CHERYL
Educator. **PERSONAL:** Born Sep 04, 1945, Louisville, KY; married Ernest S; children: Lisa, Michelle. **EDUCATION:** Univ of Akron, BEd 1968; Westminster Coll, Grad Study; AmUniv Cairo Egypt, Sum Study. **CAREER:** Westminster Coll New Wilmington PA, asst dir of admissions; Upward Bound Baldwin-Wallace Coll Berea OH, teacher 1970; Canton Public School, teacher 1968-69. **ORGANIZATIONS:** Mem Kappa Delta Pi; adv Black Stud Union Westminster Coll; mem bd mem White Plains Counc of Comm Serv; mem Mayor's Youth Bd White Plains NY; UrbanLeague Guild; League of Women Voters; treas Interfaith Counc Counc of Jewish Women; Coll Club of Sharon; Altruist Guild; Phi Alpha Theta. **HONORS/ACHIEVEMENTS:** Sociology honorary Akron U; Laurels Jr Women's honorary; outsndg Yng Women of Am 1975.

PRINCE, ANDREW LEE
Athlete, educator. **PERSONAL:** Born Dec 14, 1952, Victoria, TX. **EDUCATION:** Abilene Christian Univ, BSEd 1975, MEd 1980. **CAREER:** Barcelona, Spain, pro basketball 1975; Graz, Austria, pro basketball 1979; Gottingen, Germany, pro basketball 1981; Abilene Christian Univ, asst coach 1983-. **HONORS/ACHIEVEMENTS:** Who's Who Am Abilene Christian Univ 1975. **BUSINESS ADDRESS:** Assistant Basketball Coach, Abilene ChristianUniv, PO Box 8131, Abilene, TX 79699.

PRINCE, CHERYL PATRICE
Marketing manager. **PERSONAL:** Born Mar 29, 1956, Atlanta, GA. **EDUCATION:** GA State Univ, AS 1977, BBA 1979; Atlanta Univ, MBA Finance 1982. **CAREER:** Six Flags Over Georgia, lead food serv supervisor 1977-78; Honeywell Inc, customer opers rep 1978-79, serv sales rep 1979-82, market sales mgr customer training serv 1983-84, market sales mgr serviceline products 1984-. **ORGANIZATIONS:** Musician, community involvement; volunteer Big Brothers/Big Sister; mentor Career Beginnings Prog. **HONORS/ACHIEVEMENTS:** Sales Rep of the Quarter 1980,81; Outstanding Woman of the Year 1981; Top Hat Club Awd Honeywell Inc 1981; Honeywell Focus Awd for Scholastic Achievement 1983; Young Personalities of Amer 1984; YWCA Leadership Awd Recipient 1986. **BUSINESS ADDRESS:** Marketing Sales Manager, Honeywell, Inc, Plaza West MN 27-4156, Minneapolis, MN 55408.

PRINCE, EDGAR OLIVER
Elected official. **PERSONAL:** Born Sep 13, 1947, Brooklyn, NY. **EDUCATION:** CUNY at NYCCC, AA Liberal Arts 1968; SUNY at Stony Brook, BA Sociology 1971, MA Sociology 1974; CW Post Center of LIU, MPA Public Admin 1980; NY Univ, PhD candidate in Publ Admin 1981-. **CAREER:** Mission of Immaculate Virgin 1968, St Agatha's Home for Children 1969, St Vincent Hall Inc 1970-71, sr residential child care counselor; Suffolk Co SummerIntern Prog Youth Bd, rsch analyst 1972; SUNY at Stony Brook, dept of sociology grad teaching assistantship 1971-73; CW Post Ctr of LIU Dept of Criminal Justice, adjunct asst prof 1974-79; Suffolk Co Criminal Just Coord Cncl, co exec offices sr rsch analyst 1974-75; Suffolk Co Dept Health Svcs, sr rsch analyst 1975-. **ORGANIZATIONS:** Mem Amer Public Health Assn 1975-; mem Amer Soc for Public Admin 1976-; mem Intl Soc for System Sci in Health Care 1980-; mem Natl Forum for BlackPublic Admins 1983-; official sponsor GOP Victory Fund 1984-; charter mem Statue of Liberty Ellis Island Found Inc 1984-; mem Congressional Black Caucus Health Brain Trust chaired by Louis Stokes 1984-; charter mem and trustee Republican Presidential Task Force 1984-. **HONORS/ACHIEVEMENTS:** Grad Teaching Assistantship SUNY at Stony Brook Dept of Sociology 1971-73; Honorarium Co-

lumbia Univ 1976; Pi Alpha Alpha CW Post Ctr Chap NASPAA 1981; Outstanding Young Men of Amer Outstanding Americans Found 1982; Presidential Medal of Merit Pres Reagan 1985; Presidential Honor Roll Pres Reagan 1985; Cert of Merit, Presidential Commn Republican Presidential Task Force 1986; several publications & presentations including "Welfare Status, Illness and SubjectiveHealth Definition," Amer Journal of Public Health 1978 presented at 103rd annual meeting of the Amer Public Health Assoc Chicago 1975, "Productivity Monitoring & Improvement, Managing Primary Care Svcs" System Science in Health Care 1984 presented at the Third Intl Conf on System Sci in Health Care Germany 1984; "Needs Assessment Through Analysis of Social Indicators" Systems Sci in Health and Social Serv for the Elderly and the Disabled presented at the First IntlConf on Systems Sci in Health and Social Serv for the Elderly and Disabled Canada 1983; Cert of Recognition Natl Republican Congressional Comm signed by Congressmen Guy Vander Jagt 1985. **MILITARY SERVICE:** Commissioned 2nd lt US Army Reserves Medical Serv Corp 1981-. **HOME ADDRESS:** 22 E 29th St Apt 214, New York, NY 10016.

PRINCE, ERNEST S.
Association executive. **PERSONAL:** Born Nov 07, 1942, Alliance, OH; married A Cheryl; children: Lisa, Michelle. **EDUCATION:** Baldwin-Wallace Coll, Liberal Arts Dgree 1965. **CAREER:** Westchester Co Urban League, pres 1974-; Shenango Valley PA Urban League, exec dir 1968-74; Comm Servs Canton OH Urban League, dir 1967-68; Stark Co OEO Canton OH, asso dir 1965-67. **ORGANIZATIONS:** Mem Sigma Pi Phi Frat 1978. **BUSINESS ADDRESS:** Westchester Co Urban League, 61 Mitchell Pl, White Plains, NY 10601.

PRINCE, JOAN MARIE
Hematologist. **PERSONAL:** Born Jan 14, 1954, Milwaukee, WI. **EDUCATION:** Univ of WI-Milwaukee, BA 1977, BS 1981. **CAREER:** St Luke's Hosp, lab tech 1977-78; St Joseph's Hosp, hematologist 1981-. **ORGANIZATIONS:** Assoc mem Amer Soc of Clinical Pathologists 1981-; mem Delta Sigma Theta Sor 1981-; sec Black Women's Network 1981-; mem Cancer & The Black Amer Comm 1982-; task force mem Black Women's Health Project 1983-; speakers bureau Ronald McDonald House 1984-86; bd of dirs Amer Cancer Soc 1985-; assoc mem Amer Soc of Medical Technologists; bd of dir UW Milwaukee Alumni Assoc 1985-86; mem Citizens Review Bd 1987; mem Future Milwaukee 1988-. **HONORS/ACHIEVEMENTS:** Published article "Black Women & Health," 1984; 1989 Black Role Model Milwaukee Public Library 1989; 12 articles in "The Business Journal" magazine, topic: Instilling Entreprenurial Spirit In Youth" 1989. **HOME ADDRESS:** 8712 W Spokane, Milwaukee, WI 53224. **BUSINESS ADDRESS:** Staff Medical Technologist, 11020 W Plank Court, Suite 100, Wauwatosa, WI 53226.

PRINCE, RICHARD EVERETT
Journalist. **PERSONAL:** Born Jul 26, 1947, New York, NY; son of Jonathan Prince and Audrey White Prince. **EDUCATION:** New York Univ, BS 1968. **CAREER:** Newark Star Ledger, reporter 1967-68; Washington Post, reporter 1968-77; Democrat and Chronicle, asst metro editor 1979-81, asst news editor 1981-85, editorial writer/columnist 1985-87; Democrat and Chronicle/Times-Union, editorial writer/columnist 1987-; Gannett News Service, columnist 1988-. **ORGANIZATIONS:** Mem Natl Assoc of Black Journalists 1984-; pres Rochester Assoc of Black Communicators 1986-87; bd mem Writers & Books 1988-; mem National Society of Newspaper Columnists 1989-. **HONORS/ACHIEVEMENTS:** 2nd place writing competition, National Society of Newspaper Columnists 1989; 3rd place writing competition, commentary, National Assn of Black Journalists 1987, 1988. **MILITARY SERVICE:** USAF Reserve sft 1968-73. **HOME ADDRESS:** 140 Troup St, Rochester, NY 14608. **BUSINESS ADDRESS:** Editorial Writer/Columnist, Gannett Rochester Newspapers, 55 Exchange Blvd, Rochester, NY 14614.

PRIOLEAU, PETER SYLVESTER
Banker/loan officer. **PERSONAL:** Born Dec 10, 1949, Hopkins, SC; son of Jessie Prioleau and Ruth Byrd Prioleau; married Brenda Mickens, Nov 24, 1984. **EDUCATION:** Midland Technical Coll, AA Retail Mgmt 1974; Benedict Coll, BS Business 1975. **CAREER:** Davison-Macy's Dept Store, assoc mgr 1972-75; NCNB of South Carolina, vice pres 1975-. **ORGANIZATIONS:** Mem SC Bankers Assoc 1975-, Greater Columbia Chamber of Commerce 1975-, Columbia Urban League 1975-, NAACP 1978-, SC Assoc of Minorities & Public Administrator Inc 1979-. **HONORS/ACHIEVEMENTS:** Awd of Appreciation United Negro Coll Fund 1983-85; Appreciation Awd United Way of the Midlands SC 1983; Natl Assoc for Equal Oppor in Higher Educ 1986. **MILITARY SERVICE:** AUS specialist (E-5) 2 yrs; S.C. Air Natl Guard; US Air Forces Reserves TSGT 1975-. **HOME ADDRESS:** P O Box 1823, Columbia, SC 29202. **BUSINESS ADDRESS:** Vice President, NCNB of South Carolina, P O Box 448, Columbia, SC 29202.

PRIOLEAU, SARA NELLIENE
Director of dental services. **PERSONAL:** Born Apr 10, 1940, Hopkins, SC; daughter of Willie Ore Prioleau and Wilhelmina Prioleau; married William R Montgomery; children: Kara I, William P. **EDUCATION:** SC State Coll, BS 1960, MS 1965;Univ of PA, DMD 1970. **CAREER:** Comph Grp Hlth Svcs, pbl hlth dent 1971-72; Hamilton Hlth Ctr, dir dental serv 1972-; Commu Dental Assco PC, pres 1976-. **ORGANIZATIONS:** Nat'l Dntl Assoc 1970-; Am Dental Assoc 1970-; Hbg Dental Assoc 1972-; pres (1979-81) Links Inc Hbg Chap 1976-; vice chmn hlth Socoptomist Int'lHbg 1982-84; mem Exec Women Intl Hbg Chap 1984-; vchmn The Status of Women Soroptomist Intl North Atlantic Reg 1986-; vice pres Soroptomist Intl Hbg 1986-; bd dir Mental Health Assoc Tri County Inc 1986-88; pres Soroptomist International of Harrisburg 1987-89; regional chrmn for Health - Soroptomist International of North Atlantic Region 1988-. **HONORS/ACHIEVEMENTS:** Wkg wmn of the yr Hlth Serv Pomecoys 1982; wmn of the yr Blck Wmn's Caucus; Cumberland Co Mental Retardation Award 1987. **BUSINESS ADDRESS:** Dir of Dental Services, Hamilton Hlth Ctr, 2451 N 3rd St, Harrisburg, PA 17110.

PRITCHARD, DARON
Elected official. **PERSONAL:** Born Aug 26, 1954, Vicksburg, MS; married Juanita Hill; children: LaTonzia, LaToya, LaKeita, Daron Jamaal. **EDUCATION:** Utica Jr Coll, attended; Alcorn State Univ Lormaums, BA 1977. **CAREER:** Eastern Foods Inc, branch mgr; Town of Edwards, mayor. **ORGANIZATIONS:** Deacon Friendship MB Church. **HOME ADDRESS:** Rt 2 Box 11-C, Edwards, MS 39066. **BUSINESS ADDRESS:** Mayor, Town of Edwards, PO Box 215, Edwards, MS 39066.

PRITCHARD, MARION K. SMITH
Attorney. **PERSONAL:** Born in Valdosta, GA; children: Jonathan, Abena, DuBois, and Harriet King. **EDUCATION:** Spelman Coll, BA 1953; Univ of PA, Cert Phys Therapy 1953; Mercer Univ, JD 1976. **CAREER:** King & King Inc, real estate & ins broker 1962-69, pres 1969-79; Young & Smith, 1977-79; City of Albany Recorders/Court, Alternate Judge, 1978-79; City of Atlanta Law Dept, attorney 1979-. **ORGANIZATIONS:** Dir Dougherty County Resorces Assn 1961-65, Southwest GA Assn for Convalescent & Aging Persons 1966-, Albany Urban League 1967-72; bd mem, sec New Communities Inc 1969-73; bd mem Southwest GA Land Devel Co Inc 1971-79; mem New Era Enterprises 1983-; part LdrshpGA 1978. **HONORS/ACHIEVEMENTS:** Natl Found Grant NY 1953; Family of the Year Awd Albany Urban League 1969. **BUSINESS ADDRESS:** Associate City Attorney, City of Atlanta, 1100 S Tower, One Cnn Center, Atlanta, GA 30303.

PRITCHARD, ROBERT STARLING, JR.
Concert pianist; composer; educator; foundation executive; publisher. **PERSONAL:** Born Jun 13, 1929, Winston-Salem, NC; son of R. Starling Pritchard, Sr. and Lucille Pickard Pritchard; children: Tyrone Shardel Pritchard (adopted). **EDUCATION:** Syracuse Univ, Syracuse NY, BS, 1948, MM, 1950; private piano study with Edwin Fischer, Arturo Benedetti Michelangeli, Carl Friedberg, Hans Neumann, and Robert Goldsand, 1948-59. **CAREER:** Touring concert pianist, 1951-; Conservatoire Nationale D'Haiti, Port-au-Prince, Haiti, artist in residence, 1958; Univ of Liberia, Monrovia, artist in residence, 1959; New School for Social Research, New York NY, faculty member, 1962; Panamerican/Panafrican Assn, Baldwinsville NY, co-founder and chairman, 1968-; Kahre-Richardes Family Found, Baldwinsville, cofounder and chairman, 1972-; Impartial Citizen Newspaper, Syracuse NY, publisher, 1980-; Lincoln University, Lincoln University PA, artist in residence, 1988-. **HONORS/ACHIEVEMENTS:** Doctorate honoris causa, Nat Univ of Haiti, 1968; citation, Org of Amer States, 1969; founder and organizer, Louis Moreau Gottschalk Intl Pianists and Composers Competition, Dillard Univ, 1970; artistic dir, Gala Concert on Peace and Reconsiliation DAR Constitution Hall, Washington DC, 1970; artistic dir, United Nations General Assembly Concert Gala for US Bicentennial and 13th Anniv of Org of African Unity, 1976; artistic dir, Martin Luther King Concerts, Riverside Church and Cathedral of St. John the Divine, 1978; Black History Month Founder's Citation, Governor of New York, 1987; Bayard Rustin Human Rights Award, A. Philip Randolph Inst, 1988; President's Centennial Medal, Lincoln Univ, 1988; artistic dir, Black History Month Concert Gala, Lincoln Univ, 1989. **BUSINESS ADDRESS:** Chairman, Two Foundations at "Applecrest", Panamerican/Panafrica Association Inc, P O Box 143, Baldwinsville, NY 13027.

PROBASCO, JEANETTA
Counselor, educator. **PERSONAL:** Born Aug 30, Needville, TX; married James A; children: Wardell. **EDUCATION:** Prairie View A&M U, BS 1941; MEduc 1950;Univ of TX, completed couns certif work 1965. **CAREER:** Kilfore Jr HS, counselor; CB Dansby HS, counselor teacher math 1953-59; Fredonia School, teacher homemaking 1953-59; Fredonia School, teacher homemaking math 1942-53. **ORGANIZATIONS:** Asst chmn Texarkana Dist of New Homemakers of Am 1958-59; served on stud activities Com Kilgore Jr HS; served as sec PTA; elected chmn TEPS 1974-75;bd mem Kilgore Br TSTA; bd mem Kilgore Br TX State Tchrs Assn 1973-74; mem NEA; Piney Woods Pers & Guid Assn; TX Am Pers & Guid Assn; CntrlSteering Com Kilgore Indpt Sch Dist 1972-73; organized co-sponsored a chap of Future Tchrs of Am Dansby HS 1969; organ currently Spons FTA Kilgore Jr HS; mem co & dist adult 4-H ldrs Assn; organized 3 new 4-H Clubs active particip in num 4-H Functions; clk Fedonia Bapt Ch Kilgore; mem Heroniesof Jerioch; Am Assn ofUniv Women; Gregg Co Home Economics Assn; Marquis Library Soc. **HONORS/ACHIEVEMENTS:** Recip State 4-H Alumni Award 1967; State 4-H Adult Ldrs Award 1969; WD McQueen 4-H Award 1971; Nat 4-H Alumni Recog Award 1975; selected outstndng FTA sponsor Dist VIII TSTA 1974.

PROCOPE, ERNESTA G.
Business executive. **PERSONAL:** Married John L. **CAREER:** EG Bowman Co Inc, pres 1953-. **ORGANIZATIONS:** Bd dir Avon Prod Inc, Urban Natl Corp, Chubb Corp, Columbia Gas System Inc; bd trustees Cornell U, Adelphi U, NY Zoological Soc, NAACP, Grtr NY Ins Brokers Assoc, Siloam Ch Achievement Bus Bethel Temp & Ch; Comm Serv F & M Schaefer Brewing Co, Black Achievers, YMCA. **HONORS/ACHIEVEMENTS:** Sojourner Truth Awd Negro Bus & Prof Wmn's Club Inc; Woman Yr Tuesday Mag 1972; Bus Achievement Awd Interracial Council Bus Oppor 1973; Jet Mag Cover 1st wmn cover black ent 1974; Brotherhood Awd Concord Bapt C 1974; 36 Women of Power Cosmopolitan Mag Apr 1975; one of nominees for Woman of Yr in Bus Ladies Home Journal Feb 1975; Hon mem Alpha Kappa Alpha Sor 1976; Bus Awd Natl Business League; Catalyst Awd Women Dir on Bds 1977. **BUSINESS ADDRESS:** President, EG Bowman Co, Inc, 97 Wall St, New York, NY 10005.

PROCOPE, JOHN LEVY
Insurance company executive. **PERSONAL:** Born Jun 19, 1925, New York, NY; married Ernesta G Procope, Jul 03, 1954. **EDUCATION:** Morgan State Coll, BS 1949; New York Univ Grad School of Business, 1955. **CAREER:** Tuesday Publ Inc, vice pres 1965-66; Slant Fin corp, dir mktg 1969-70; NY Amsterdam News, vp, gen mgr 1966, 1970, pres & publisher; NY Amsterdam News, editor & publshr 1974-; EG Bowman Co Inc, chmn; Batton, Durstein & Osborn, Marketing Specialist; Advertising Representative, Associated Publishers, Inc; Advertising Prepresentative, the Afro-American Newspapers. **ORGANIZATIONS:** Dir Apple Savings Bank, Shopwll Inc, YMCA, 100 Black men Inc, Siloam Presbyterian Church; chmn Task Force on Minority Bus Devel for White House Conf on Small Bus; pres, bd mem Natl Assoc of Newspaper Publs 1980-84; trustee Springfield Coll; mem United Way of Tri-State; bd dir New York City Indust & Commercial Incentive Bd; gov's appointee States Council on Intl bus; trustee Grad School of Bus NY Univ; bd mem Howard Univ; pres, Harlem Business Alliance, 1986-. **HONORS/ACHIEVEMENTS:** Hon commiss, "Civic Affairs & Public Events", "Cultural Affairs" NYC; Doctor of Humanities, Universal Orthodox College-Nigeria. **MILITARY SERVICE:** Vetern USA Corp of Engineers, private. **BUSINESS ADDRESS:** Chairman of the Board, EG Bowman Co Inc, 97 Wall St, New York, NY 10005.

PROCTER, HARVEY THORNTON, JR.
Executive. **PERSONAL:** Born Dec 29, 1945, Monongahela, PA; son of Harvey T Procter Sr and Charlene McPherson Procter; children: Karyn Michele. **EDUCATION:** Southern IL Univ, BA 1967; Roosevelt Univ, MA 1970; Wayne State Univ, JD 1976. **CAREER:** Chicago Comm on Youth Welfare, asst zone dir 1966, dir special events 1967; Ford Motor Company, various human res 1968-. **ORGANIZATIONS:** Mem Amer, MI State, Detroit Bar

Assocs, Assoc of Trial Lawyers of Amer; mem Amer Mgmt Assoc, Midwest Co-op Educ Assoc, Employer Management Assoc; life mem Alpha Phi Alpha Inc, NAACP; parish council team St Thomas the Apostle Church; assy & comm chmn Midwest Coll Placement Assoc 1983-; pres bd of dirs Earhart Village Homes; pres, exec bd, Midwest College Placement Assoc 1988-90; mem Business Advisory Council Univ of MI Comprehensive Studies Program 1989-; mem Business Advisory Council Atlanta University Center 1988-89; mem Business Advisory Council GMI Mgt Instit 1989-90. **HONORS/ACHIEVEMENTS:** Univ of IL Law Fellowship; IL General Assembly Scholarship; Vice President's Award - youth motivation, vice pres of US 1970. **BUSINESS ADDRESS:** Associate Director, Ford Motor Co, UAW - Ford National Education, Development, and Training, PO Box 6002, 5101 Evergreen Rd Rm 421, Dearborn, MI 48121.

PROCTOR, BARBARA GARDNER
Business executive. **PERSONAL:** Born Nov 30, Black Mountain, NC; divorced; children: Morgan. **EDUCATION:** Talledega Coll, BA Psych Sociol, BA Engl Ed. **CAREER:** Downbeat mag, contrib ed; Vee Jay Records Intl, intl dir 1961-64; Post-Keyes-Gardner Advt, 1965-68; Gene Taylor Assoc, 1968-69; North Advertising Agency, copy suprv 1969-70; Proctor & Gardner Advertising Inc, pres. **ORGANIZATIONS:** Mem contg ed Down Beat Mag 1958-; mem Chicago Econ Devel Corp, Chicago Media Women, Natl Radio Arts & Sci, Chicago Advertising Club, Chicago Womens Advertising Club, Female Exec Assoc; mem bd dir Better Bus Bur, Cosmopolitan C of C; chmn WTTW TV Auction; mem Chicago Econ Devel Corp, Chicago Urban League, NAACP, Smithsonian Inst, Chicago Symphony; bd dir Seaway Natl Bank, Mt Sinai Hosp, IL State C of C, Council of Univ of IL. **HONORS/ACHIEVEMENTS:** Listed in Who's Who in Amer Women, Blue Book of London; 20 Industry Awds incl Clio-Amer TV Commercial Festival; 2 CFAC Awds; Fredrick Douglas HumanitarianAwd 1975; Amer TV Commercial Awds, 1st Pl TV, 1st Pl Print 1972; Blackbook Businesswoman of the Year; Chicago Advertising Woman of the Year 1974-75; listed in World's Who's Who of Women 1973; Small Bus of Year 1978; Headline Awd 1978; Charles A Stevens Intl Org of Women Exec Achievers Awd 1978. **BUSINESS ADDRESS:** President, Proctor & Gardner Advertising Inc, 111 E Wacker Dr Ste 931, Chicago, IL 60601.

PROCTOR, EARL D.
Business executive. **PERSONAL:** Born May 20, 1941, Philadelphia, PA; son of Earl M Proctor and Louise Culbreath Proctor; married Jean E Matlock, Sep 27, 1978; children: Denise, Eric, Monica. **EDUCATION:** Temple Univ, BS 1963; Temple Univ, Grad 1965; NY Univ, Grad Courses 1966-69; Harvard Business Schl, MBA 1975. **CAREER:** Cummins Engine Co, mktg dir; Rockwell Internatl, mktg dir 1977-79; Ferguson/Bryan Assoc, partner 1979-80; DOT/MBRC, exec dir 1980-81, commission on the Bicentennial of the United States Constitution dep dir mktg. **ORGANIZATIONS:** mem Amer Acad of Poltcl & Soc Sci; mem PA Soc World Affairs Cncl; life mem NAACP; PA Society, Natl Urban League-Beep Visiting Professor. **HONORS/ACHIEVEMENTS:** Who's Who in Amer; Honarary Citizen New Orleans; US Small Business Natl Award of Excellence 1983. **HOME ADDRESS:** 2332 McGregor Ct, Vienna, VA 22180.

PROCTOR, LEONARD D.
Auditor. **PERSONAL:** Born Jun 09, 1919, Jackson, MS; married Dell; children: One Child. **EDUCATION:** Tougaloo Coll, BA 1941; Wayne State U, MEd 1961. **CAREER:** Detroit Pub Sch, tchr 1946-66; 1st black cty assessor 1966; Woayne Co Bd of Auditors, 1972-; 1st black chmn 1971-72. **ORGANIZATIONS:** Mem Municipal Finance Ofcrs Asso; Nat'l Assoc Counties; exec bd SE MI Counc Govts; mem Exec counc Trade Union Ldrshp Counc; trea Detroit Chap Coal of Black Trade Unionists; bd trsts Wayne Co Gen Hosp; Detroit Econ Club; past pres Detroit Counc Polit Ed; past pres Cotillion Club; life mem NAACP & various Frats. **HONORS/ACHIEVEMENTS:** Man of yr Cotillion Club 1959; citation aw Nat'l Med Assoc for work on hosp-med probs 1960; cited for ldrshp in prep of hosp discrimination ordinances adopted Cotillion Club 1964; cert of apprec for contrib in Negro Hist 1968. **MILITARY SERVICE:** USAC 1942. **BUSINESS ADDRESS:** 1236 City County Bldg, Detroit, MI 48226.

PROCTOR, SAMUEL DEWITT
Clergyman, educator. **PERSONAL:** Born Jul 13, 1921, Norfolk, VA; married Bessie Louise Tate; children: Herbert, Timothy, Samuel, Steven. **EDUCATION:** VA Union Univ, AB 1942; Univ of PA, grad student 1944-45; Crozer Theol Sem, BD 1945; Yale Div Sch, student 1945-46; Boston Univ, ThD 1950. **CAREER:** Baptist Church, ordained to ministry 1943; Pond St Ch Providence, pastor 1945-59; VA Union Univ, prof religion & ethics 1949-50, dean sch of religion 1949-50, vice pres 1953-55, pres 1955-60; Agr & Tech Coll NC, pres 1960-64; Peace Corps, assoc dir 1963-64; Natl Council Chs, asso gen sec 1964-65; Office Econ Oppor, dir NE region spl asst to natl dir 1965-66; Inst for Serv to Educ, pres 1966-68; Univ WI Madison, univ dean spl projects 1968-69; Rutgers Univ, prof educ grad sch 1969-84; Abyssinian Bapt Ch, minister 1972-. **ORGANIZATIONS:** Adjunct prof Union Theol Seminary New York City, Princeton Theol Seminary NJ; trustee Middlebury Coll; trustee Overseas Devel Cncl; trustee Christian Childrens Fund; United Negro Coll Fund; Crozer-Colgate Theol Sem; mem Kappa Alpha Psi, Sigma Pi Phi; life mem NAACP. **HONORS/ACHIEVEMENTS:** Disting Serv Awd State Univ of NY at Plattsburgh 1966; Outstanding Alumnus Awd Boston Univ 1964; Hon Degrees, Bethune-Cookman Coll, Dillard Univ, UnivRI, Bloomfield Coll, Howard Univ, Bryant Coll, Bucknell Univ, Davidson Coll, Morehouse Coll, Ottawa Univ, Rider Coll, Stillman Coll, Atlanta Univ, Wilberforce Univ, VA Union Univ, Univ of MD, Coe Coll, St Peter's Coll, Fisk Univ, NC A&T State Univ, Central MI Univ, Southeastern Mass Univ, VA StateUniv, NC State Univ, Monmouth Coll, Boston Univ, Fairleigh-Dickenson Univ.

PROCTOR, TIMOTHY DEWITT
Attorney. **PERSONAL:** Born Dec 15, 1949, Fredericksburg, VA; son of S D and B T Proctor; married Karen L McNulty, Dec 1977; children: T David, Kathryn Amanda. **EDUCATION:** Yale Univ, 1967-68; Univ of WI, 1968-71; Univ of Chicago, MBA, JD 1975. **CAREER:** Union Carbide Corp, attorney 1975-80; Merck & Co Inc, sr attorney 1980-83, secretary new products comm 1984-85, assoc counsel-international 1985-88; Merck Sharp & Dohme Division, 1988-. **ORGANIZATIONS:** Mem Abyssinian Baptist Church, Yale Spizzwinks Singing Club 1968, Amer Bar Assn 1975, NY Bar 1976, US Supreme Court Bar 1979, NJ Bar 1980; board of dir Edwin Gould Serv for Children 1978-80; mem PA Bar 1981, Natl Bar Assn 1984-, Natl Black MBA Assn 1984-, Kappa Alpha Psi 1969, Amer Mensa Ltd 1982, Sigma Pi Phi (Mu Boule) 1985; merit selection panel Fed Magistrate US Dist Court (NJ), 1985; Dept of Health & Human Services Advisory Comm on Childhood Vaccines, 1989-91. **HONORS/ACHIEVEMENTS:** Black Achievers in Industry Awd YMCA Harlem Branch 1979 & 1983. **HOME ADDRESS:** 52 Clarke Ct, Princeton, NJ 08540.

PROCTOR, WILLIAM H.
Educator. **PERSONAL:** Born Jan 15, 1945, Baltimore, MD. **EDUCATION:** PA St U, BS 1967; NC CentUniv Law Sch, JD 1970;Univ PA, MBA 1973. **CAREER:** Fed Trade Comm, examiner mgmt mktg 1970-71; Pagan & Morgan, consultant 1973; Morgan St Univ, asst prof business & management. **ORGANIZATIONS:** Mem US Supreme Ct 1976; mem Kappa Alpha Psi Frat 1963; ptnr Harris & Proctor 1973-; pres CBH Invstmt Corp 1966-; mem Phi Alpha Delta Law Frat 1971;US Supreme Ct 1976; Phi Alpha Delta; Kappa Alpha Psi; Am Bar Assn; mem Rapid Transit Coal Balt 1973-; Proctor Enterprises 1974-; mem PA Bar Assn; mem York Co Bar; mem US Dist Crt. **HONORS/ACHIEVEMENTS:** Who's Who in Am 1973; 500 Black Ldrs 1973; Who's Who in East 1973. **MILITARY SERVICE:** US Army Res capt. **BUSINESS ADDRESS:** Morgan StateUniv, Baltimore, MD 21239.

PROPES, VICTOR LEE
Government official, instructor. **PERSONAL:** Born Dec 22, 1938, Fort Worth, TX; son of Arthur L Propes and Verlene V Propes; married Beverly P Galloway, May 28, 1966; children: Pashell, Tarik Yusef, Hakin Malik. **EDUCATION:** CA State Univ-Los Angeles, BA Bus Ed 1970; Univ of MN, MA Bus Ed 1981. **CAREER:** Minneapolis Dept of Civil Rights, exec dir 1974-76, 1978-80; Comm Dvlpmnt Agncy of LA, equal emplymnt ofcr 1976-78; Propes & Assoc, consltnt 1980 -83; State of MN Council on Black Minnesota, exec dir 1983-; Metropolitan Univ, history instructor 1989-. **ORGANIZATIONS:** Pres NAACP-ST Paul, MN Branch 1985-87; fndr MN State Affirmative Action Assoc 1974-84; corp fndr Neighborhood Housing Servcs N Minneapolis 1981-85; exec producer Focus-On; exec producer The Grand Lizard and the Kute Little Koulored Kids; mem National Forum of Black Public Administrators 1987-; mem MN adult literacy campaign 1987-; bd mem U of MN Black Learning Resource Center 1988-. **HONORS/ACHIEVEMENTS:** Fdn flw Woodrow Wilson 1972-74. **MILITARY SERVICE:** AUS cpl. **HOME ADDRESS:** 1141 Thomas Ave N, Minneapolis, MN 55411. **BUSINESS ADDRESS:** Executive Dir, Council on Black Minnesota, State of Minnesota, 2223 University Ave #426, St Paul, MN 55114.

PROPHET, RICHARD L., JR.
Automobile dealer. **CAREER:** Gulf Freeway Dodge, Inc, Houston TX, chief executive. **BUSINESS ADDRESS:** Gulf Freeway Dodge Inc, 7250 Gulf Freeway, Houston, TX 77017.
*

PROPHETE, BEAUMANOIR
Physician. **PERSONAL:** Born Sep 06, 1920, Cap Haitien, Haiti;married Anne-Marie Charles; children: Maud, Yve Robert, Mary Kathleen, Jo Anne, Myrtha, John Pierre. **EDUCATION:** Faculte de Medecin D'Haiti Port-Au-prince Haiti, Grad 1948; Freedman Hosp HowardUniv Wash DC, Fellwoship In Urology; Homer G Phillips Hos Wash U, Residency 1949-50; Am Bd of Urology, Cert 1954. **CAREER:** Pvt Prac, phys 1954-; Dept of Urology Homer G Phillips Hosp, supr; Dept of Urology St Louis Univ Med Sch, asst. **ORGANIZATIONS:** Pres Mound Cty Med Forum 1970-72; exec sec Homer G Phillips Hosp Interns Alumni 1973-; treas W End Comm Conf 1970-71; chmn Bd of Educ St Rose of Lima Sch 1973-75. **HONORS/ACHIEVEMENTS:** Recip Fulbright Grant Fellowship in Urology HowardUniv Wash DC. **BUSINESS ADDRESS:** 3737 N Kingshighway, St Louis, MO 63112.

PROTHRO, JOHNNIE WATTS
Educator. **PERSONAL:** Born Feb 26, 1922, Atlanta, GA; son of John Devine Hines and Theresa Louise Young; married Charles E Prothro Jr; children: 1. **EDUCATION:** Spelman Coll, BS 1941; Columbia Univ, MS 1946; Univ of Chicago, PhD 1952. **CAREER:** Tuskegee Inst, asst prof 1952-63; Univ of CT, assoc prof 1963-68; Emory Univ, prof 1975-79; GA State Univ, prof 1979-. **ORGANIZATIONS:** Bd mem Intl Food & Agr Devel 1978-81; mem Geo Washington Carver Rsch Fdn 1979-85; mem Intl Union of Nutritional Scientists 1982-85. **HONORS/ACHIEVEMENTS:** Borden Award Amer Home Ec Assoc 1950-51; Special Fellow Natl Inst of Health 1958-59; OEEC Fellow Natl Sci Fdn 1961; Fellow March of Dimes 1984. **BUSINESS ADDRESS:** Professor, Georgia State University, PO Box 873, Atlanta, GA 30303.

PROTHRO, LOUISE ROBINSON (NEE GRAY)
Association executive. **PERSONAL:** Born Feb 10, 1920, Macon, GA; divorced; children: Joanne. **EDUCATION:** Columbia U, MA 1951; Framingham MA, BS 1941. **CAREER:** VI Port Auth, pub rel 1974-; VI Govt, sec pub rel 1971; Farley Manning Assn Inc, acct exec 1968; Pet Inc, pub rel mgr 1963; Pet Milk Co, publicty pub rel 1952; Home Economics FL A&M U, instr 1948; NJ Urban League, comm orgn sec 1943-44; MA Reformator Wmn, asst dietitian 1941. **ORGANIZATIONS:** Food edit Essence Mag; contr edit Pet Mag; Lectr Educ Civi Coll Frat Groups; promotor Fultz Quads; mem Planning Counc Youth Motiv; Nat Alliance Bus; Nat Assn Market Devel; Home Economists Bus; Am Home Economics Assn; Am Wmn Radio & TV; Wmn Advertising; Publicity Club NY; St Louis Adv Club; St Thomas Pub Info Assn; Delta Sigma Theta Sor. **HONORS/ACHIEVEMENTS:** First eetye Jane Everett Awa NAMD; 1st Rosa L Gragg Awa PR Serv; wmn yr Framingham Coll. **BUSINESS ADDRESS:** VI Port Authority, St Thomas, Virgin Islands of the United States 00801.

PROVOST, MARSHA PARKS
Educational administrator. **PERSONAL:** Born Feb 06, 1947, Lynchburg, VA; married George H Provost; children: Geoffrey. **EDUCATION:** Hampton Inst, BA 1969; Univ of TN Chattanooga, MEd 1976; Univ of TN Knoxville, working toward EdD 1982-; Univ of MI, C3 Experience, counselors computers & creative change 1984; Univ of TN, Inst of Leadership Effectiveness 1983-84. **CAREER:** Guilford Co Dept of Social Svcs, counselor-intern 1968; City of Hampton, juvenile probation officer 1969-71; Guilford Co Dept of Social Svcs, social worker II 1971-75; Counseling & Career Planning Ctr UTC, counselor 1977-81, asst dir 1981-. **ORGANIZATIONS:** Mem Amer Assn for Counseling & Develop 1975-; mem Amer Coll Personnel Assoc 1977-; mem Chattanooga Area Psychological Assn 1977-; mem vice pres Women in Higher Educ in TN 1981-82; pres mem Chattanooga Alumnae Chap Delta Sigma Theta Inc 1977-; mem New Dimensions Club of Toastmistress Inc 1982-; Chattanooga Bus & Prof Women's Club 1982-83; mem Chattanooga Chap Amer Soc for Training & Develop 1982-84. **HONORS/ACHIEVEMENTS:** Outstanding Young Woman of Amer-Outstanding Young Women of Amer Inc 1981; Woman of the Yr Chattanooga Bus &

Prof Women's Clubs 1981-82; Natl Certified Counselor Natl Bd of Certified Counselors 1984; mem Leadership Chattanooga 1984-85. **HOME ADDRESS:** 2441 Leann Circle, Chattanooga, TN 37406. **BUSINESS ADDRESS:** Asst Dir Cnslng/Career Ctr, Univ of TN at Chattanooga, 231 University Ctr, Chattanooga, TN 37403.

PRUDHOMME, NELLIE ROSE
Educator. **PERSONAL:** Born Aug 28, 1948, Lafayette, LA; daughter of Richard August and Mary August; married Hilton James Prudhomme; children: Eunisha, Shannon. **EDUCATION:** Univ of Southwestern LA, BS Nursing 1970; Tulane Univ School of Public Health, M Publ Health 1974; Univ of Southern MS, 9 cr hrs 1974-77; Univ of Southwestern LA, 15 cr hrs 1981-84. **CAREER:** Lafayette Charity Hosp, staff nurse 1970; Vermilion Parish School Bd, health nurse 1971-72; Touro Infirmary City Health Dept, staff nurse 1972-73; Univ of Southern MS Nursing School, asst prof 1973-78; Family Health Found, staff nurse summer 1973; Univ of Southwestern LA Nursing School, instr 1978-81; Univ Medical Ctr, staff nurse II 1981-82; TH Harris Vo-Tech School, instr 1983-84; Univ Med Center at Lafayette, rn iv nurse consult 1986-; LA State Univ, asstprof. **ORGANIZATIONS:** Mem Sigma Theta Tau 1978-, USL Nursing Hon Soc 1981-; vice pres for mem Reserve Officers Assoc 1983-85; mem at large Amer Publ Health Assoc, Amer Nurses Assoc, natl League for Nursing, Assoc for Military Surgeons of the US; mem Zeta Phi Beta Sorority Inc 1988; bd mem March of Dimes Birth Defects Foundation 1989-; mem Mayor's Human Services Commission 1989-. **HONORS/ACHIEVEMENTS:** Aaron Fellowship Tulane Univ School of Publ Health 1972-73; USPHS Traineeship Univ School of Publ Health 1972-73. **MILITARY SERVICE:** US Army Reserve,lieutenant colonel, 11 years; 4 yrs Achievement 1983. **HOME ADDRESS:** 157 S Richter Dr, Lafayette, LA 70501. **BUSINESS ADDRESS:** Assistant Professor, Univ of Southwestern Louisiana, PO Box 40294, Lafayette, LA 70502.

PRUITT, ANNE SMITH
Educational administrator. **PERSONAL:** Born in Bainbridge, GA; daughter of Loring Smith and Anne Ward Smith; widowed; children: Dianne Newbold, Pamela Green, Sharon, Ralph Jr, Leslie. **EDUCATION:** Howard Univ, BS cum laude 1949; Teachers Coll Columbia Univ, MA 1950, EdD 1964. **CAREER:** Howard Univ, counselor 1950-52; Hutto HS, dir of guidance 1952-55; Albany State Coll, dean of students 1955-59; Fisk Univ, dean of students 1959-61; Case Western Reserve Univ, prof of educ 1963-79; OH State Univ, assoc dean grad school 1979-84, assoc provost 1984-86, dir Center for Teaching Excellence 1986-, prof of Educ Policy and Leadership 1986-. **ORGANIZATIONS:** Mem Alpha Kappa Alpha Sor; mem Links Inc; consultant Women's Job Corps creation Pres Lyndon Johnson's War on Poverty 1964; mem bd of trustees Cleveland Urban League 1965-71; consultant Southern Regional Educ Bd 1968-81; mem Bd of Trustees Central State Univ 1973-82; moderator Mt Zion Congregational Church 1975-78; pres-(1st Black) Amer Coll Personnel Assn 1976-77; Research Task Force Southern Educ Found 1978-87; mem Adv Comm US Coast Guard Acad 1980-83; Amer Assn for Counseling and Devel; sec, Journal bd mem, pres-elect, pres 1976-77, Amer Coll Personnel Assn; Amer Educ Research Assn; Amer Assn for Higher Educ; Amer Assn of Univ Professors; mem Mayor's Task Force on Private Sector Initiatives 1986-88, bd of trustees, Case Western Reserve Univ 1987-. **HONORS/ACHIEVEMENTS:** Outstanding Alumnus Howard Univ 1975; Amer Council on Educ Fellow 1977-78; honorary degree DHum Central State Univ 1982; Named one of America's Top 100 Black Business & Professional Women, Dollars & Sense Magazine 1986; Ohio State Univ Distinguished Affirmative Action Award 1988; Amer Coll Personnel Assn Senior Scholar Award 1989; Phi Beta Delta Honor Soc for Intl Scholars 1989. **BUSINESS ADDRESS:** Dir, Center for Teaching Excellence, OH State University, 124 W 17th Ave Rm 1 Lord Hall, Columbus, OH 43210.

PRUITT, CLARENCE O.
Dentist. **PERSONAL:** Born Jan 17, 1927, Hot Springs, AR; married Joy E Brock; children: Clarence Michael, Paul W, Andre Brett. **EDUCATION:** Wilberforce State, BS 1948;Univ of OR Dental Sch, DMD 1954. **CAREER:** OR State Bd of Higher Edn, dent asso prof; Vets Hosp Portland, former cons; Free Peoples Dental Clinic, dir 1971; Restorative & Dentistry, lectr; Pacific NW Ceramic Study Club, pat master clinician; part-time tchr; part time priv prac; Univ of OR Dental Sch, acting dept chmn crown & bridge 1956-57. **ORGANIZATIONS:** Mem Multnomah Co Dental Soc; Am Soc of Dentistry for Children; Fedn Dentaire Internat; OR State Dental Soc; Am Dental Soc; devel Fed Low Income Hsng of Portland; Portland NAACP; former mem Boy Scouts Exec Bd Prtland Area Council. **MILITARY SERVICE:** USAF capt 1954-56.

PRUITT, FRED RODERIC
Physician. **PERSONAL:** Born Dec 17, 1938, Birmingham, AL; married Joan Simmons; children: Christopher, Lisa. **EDUCATION:** TN State U, BS 1961; Howard U, MS 1963; Meharry Med Coll, MD 1967. **CAREER:** Phys splst internal med 1973-; St Elizabeth Hosp, resd 1971-73; St Elizabeth Hosp, intern 1967-68. **ORGANIZATIONS:** Med dir Mahoning Co Drug Prgm Inc; mem Lions Internat; pres Boardman Lions Club; mem Nat Med Assn; Boh State Med Assn; Alpha Phi Alpha Frat; Mahoning Co Med Soc. **MILITARY SERVICE:** USAF mc maj 1968-71. **BUSINESS ADDRESS:** 407 Belmont Ave, Youngstown, OH 44502.

PRUITT, GEORGE ALBERT
Educator. **PERSONAL:** Born Jul 09, 1946, Canton, MS; married Delores Walker; children: Shayla Nicole. **EDUCATION:** IL State Univ, BS 1968, MS 1970; The Union Grad School, PhD 1974. **CAREER:** IL State Univ, asst to vice pres for acad affairs 1968-70; Towson State Univ, dean of students 1970-72; Morgan State Univ, vp/exec asst to pres 1972-75; TN State Univ, vice pres 1975-81; Council for the Advancement of Experiential Learning, exec vice pres 1981-82; Thomas A Edison State Coll, pres 1982-. **ORGANIZATIONS:** Reg corrd AAHE/Mid-Atlantic Reg 1973-75; bd trustees CAEL 1983-; mem Middle State Assn 1980-; accredit evaluator So Assn of Colleges & Schools 1973-75; comm on Urban Affairs AASCU 1982-; bd trustees Greater Balt Med Ctr 1973-75; mem Educ Comm Natl Conf Christians & Jews 1973-75; bd trustees Nashville Urban League 1976-81; mem Nashville C of C 1976-81; chmn Committee on Alternatives and Innovation in Higher Education, AASCU 1985-87; mem Labor/Higher Education Council, ACE 1982-; mem, Commission on Higher Education and the Adult Learner, ACE 1982-. **HONORS/ACHIEVEMENTS:** Governor's Citation for Outstanding Serv Gov Alexander St of TN 1981; Outstanding Serv to Educ Award TN State Univ 1981; Honorary Mem House of Representatives TN Gen Assembly 1981; Honorary Mem of Congress US House of Representatives 1981; Recip of Resolution of Commend Bd of Trustees Morgan St Univ 1975; named one of the most effective college presidents in the United States by EXXon Education Foundation Study 1986; Outstanding Alumni Achievement Award, Illinois State Univ 1984; Achievement in Education Award, Natl Assn of Negro Business and Professional Clubs Inc, New Jersey 1987. **BUSINESS ADDRESS:** President, Thomas A Edison State College, 101 W State St CN 545, Trenton, NJ 08625.

PRUITT, GREGORY DONALD
Professional athlete. **PERSONAL:** Born Aug 18, 1951, Houston, TX. **EDUCATION:** Working on BS Pub Rel; degree in journalism Oklahoma. **CAREER:** Cleveland Browns, offensive running back. **ORGANIZATIONS:** Work along with bus advisors; unlimited sports in Houston. **HONORS/ACHIEVEMENTS:** Two yr consensus All Am 1972-73; 2nd to Heishman Trophy 1973, 3rd 1972; All Professional 1973-74, 1976; Offensive Player of the Yr Cleveland Browns 1974; 2 times at OK Bluebonnett Bowl & Hula Bowl 1972-73; led Browns Rushing 1974-79; Pro Bowl 1973-77; Brown's Offensive Player of the Yr 1977. **BUSINESS ADDRESS:** Cleveland Browns Tower B, Cleveland Stadium, Cleveland, OH 44114.

PRUITT, LARRY
Professional athlete. **PERSONAL:** Born Nov 27, 1956, Chicago, IL. **EDUCATION:** Central State OH. **CAREER:** Tampa Bay Buccaneers, professional ftbl plyr. **BUSINESS ADDRESS:** Tampa Bay Buccaneers, 1 Buccaneer Pl, Tampa, FL 33607.

PRUITT, MIKE
Professional athlete. **PERSONAL:** Born Apr 03, 1954, Chicago, IL; married Karen Boulware; children: Aaron Michael. **EDUCATION:** Purdue Univ, BA Bus Admin. **CAREER:** Pruitt & Grace Develop Corp, pres; Cleveland Browns, fullback 1976-. **HONORS/ACHIEVEMENTS:** 22nd NFL Player to crack 6000 yrd barrier; Cleveland's Player of the Yr Awd Akron Booster Club 1981; Best Offensive Player TD Club Cleveland 1980; Miller Man of the Yr 1980. **BUSINESS ADDRESS:** Cleveland Browns, Cleveland Stadium Tower B, Cleveland, OH 44114.

PRUNTY, HOWARD EDWARD
Social worker. **PERSONAL:** Born in Maybeury, WV; son of Leon C Prunty and Ruth Eleanor Carter. **EDUCATION:** Bluefield State Coll, Bluefield WV, BS, 1953; Univ of West Virginia, Morgantown WV, MSW, 1955; Univ of Pittsburgh, Pittsburgh PA, MPHA, 1976. **CAREER:** Univ of Pittsburgh MH/MRC, Pittsburg PA, director, 1974-76; Project Hope MH/MRC, Detroit MI, dir, 1976-78; Center for Advocacy, Family Service of Greater Boston, Boston MA, dir, currently. **ORGANIZATIONS:** Chmn, Natl Black Admin in Child Welfare, 1969-; chmn, Brookline Human Relations Commn, 1988-. **MILITARY SERVICE:** US Army, Cpl, 1950-52. **BUSINESS ADDRESS:** Dir, Center for Advocacy, Family Service of Greater Boston, 34 1/2 Beacon St, Boston, MA 02108.

PRYCE, EDWARD L.
Landscape architect. **PERSONAL:** Born May 26, 1914, Lake Charles, LA; married Woodia Smith; children: Marilyn Alim, Joellen G Elbashir. **EDUCATION:** Tuskegee Inst, BS Agric 1937; OH State Univ, BLA 1948;Univ CA at Berkeley, mS in LA 19553; Tuskegee Inst, Alumni Merit Award 1977; OH S tate Univ, Dist Alumnus Award 1980. **CAREER:** Ornamental Horticulture, Tuskegee Inst, head dept 1948-55, supt of bldgs grds 1955-69; Dept of Architecture, prfsr 1969-77; Private Practice La ndscape Architect 1948-. **ORGANIZATIONS:** Chmn AL State Brd of Examiners of Landscape Architects 1981-83; mem Tuskegee City Plng Comm 1970-76; mem Tuskegee Model Cities Comm 1968-72; mem ALState Outdoor Rec Plng Bd 1978-. **HONORS/ACHIEVEMENTS:** Fellow Am Soc of Landscape Archts 1979; fellow Phelps-Stoke African Fac Exch Prog 1976. **BUSINESS ADDRESS:** Edward L Pryce Landscape Arch, P O Box 246, Tuskegee Institute, AL 36088.

PRYDE, ARTHUR EDWARD
Mechanical designer. **PERSONAL:** Born Jul 08, 1946, Providence, RI; married Lydia. **EDUCATION:** RI School of Design, BA 1968-72. **CAREER:** AVID Corp E Prov RI, designer 1971-74; General Motors Corp, designer 1974-85. **ORGANIZATIONS:** Owner LPA Design 1983-85; design consult to Different Drummer; crew tech C Little Racing 1983-85; racing 2 liter Can-Am Championship Car 1984. **HOME ADDRESS:** 17249 Melrose, Southfield, MI 48075. **BUSINESS ADDRESS:** Assistant Chief Designer, General Motors Corp, G M Technical Center, 3100 Mound Rd, Warren, MI 48090.

PRYOR, AARON (RICHARD PRYOR)
Comedian, actor, writer, producer. **PERSONAL:** Born Dec 01, 1940, Peoria, IL; children: Renee, Richard Jr, Elizabeth Ann, Rain. **CAREER:** Bustin Loose, The Wiz, The Toy, Richard Pryor, Live on the Sunset Strip, Some Kind of Hero, Superman III, actor; Lady Sings the Blues, actor 1972; Silver Streak, actor 1976; Stir Crazy, actor 1980; Sanford & Son, Flip Wilson Show, writer; Indigo Prod, owner; comedian, actor, writer, producer; Jo Jo Dancer, producer, director; Critical Conditions, actor. **ORGANIZATIONS:** Supporter to charities & human rights orgs. **HONORS/ACHIEVEMENTS:** 4 Emmys for comedy albums; 5 grammys for screen plays; 4 cert gold albums; 1 cert platinum. **MILITARY SERVICE:** AUS Airbone Div 2 yrs. **BUSINESS ADDRESS:** Actor, C/o Mr Buddy LaRosa, LaRosas, Inc, 5870 Belmont Ave, Cincinnati, OH 45222.

PRYOR, CALVIN CAFFEY
Attorney. **PERSONAL:** Born Oct 16, 1928, Montgomery, AL; married Mable M; children: Linda Pryor Elmore, Debra E. **EDUCATION:** AL State Univ, BS 1950; Howard Univ, LLB 1957. **CAREER:** Sote Prac, atty 1958-70; US Dept Justice, atty 1971-. **HONORS/ACHIEVEMENTS:** Spec Ach Award Dept of Justice 1975; Spec Alumni Award AL State Univ. **BUSINESS ADDRESS:** Assistant US Attorney, US Dept Justice, PO Box 197, Montgomery, AL 36101.

PRYOR, CHESTER CORNELIUS, II
Ophthalmologist. **PERSONAL:** Born Jan 02, 1930, Cincinnati, OH; married Audrey; children: Marcus. **EDUCATION:** Cntrl State Univ, BS 1951; Howard Univ Coll of Medicine, MD 1955. **CAREER:** Boston City Hospital, resident 1957-58; MA Eye & Ear Infir, heed fellow 1959; Univ of Cincinnati Coll of Med, asst prof; Deaconess & Christ Good Samaritan Hosp, assoc; Jewish Bethesda & Children's Clermont Co Hosp, staff; Private Practice, ophthal 1961-. **ORGANIZATIONS:** Pres Cinn Ophthal Soc 1976; treas Cinn Acad of Med 1969; chmn sec opthal Natl Med Assn 1970-71; dir Unity State Bank 1970-76; mem bd of dir Cinn

Assn for the Blind 1968-; mem Counc on Aging 1962-68; life mem Alpha Phi Alpha Frat; treas Delta Gamma Lambda Chap 1963-77; charter mem Delta Xi; life mem NAACP; mem Argus Club; mem True Am Ldg #2; mem FA&M 1962; mem Worshipful Master 1972; mem Noble of Sinai Temple #59; mem King Solomon Consis #20 1962; comdr in chief King Solomon Consis #20 1972-73; mem GIG 1975; Beta Kappa Chi 1950; Alpha Kappa Mu 1950; mem Amer Chem Soc 1951; fellow Amer Coll of Surgeons 1971-; diplomat Amer Bd of Ophthal 1960; Eye & Ear Infir. **MILITARY SERVICE:** AUS capt 1959-61. **BUSINESS ADDRESS:** 2828 Highland Ave, Cincinnati, OH 45219.

PRYOR, JAMES D.
Government employee. **PERSONAL:** Born May 03, 1914, Cedartown, GA; married Ersena J Harris; children: Ruby, Gregory. **EDUCATION:** Postal Serv Inst Wash DC; OK Postal Training Ops. **CAREER:** Mail Processing US Postal Svc, dir; Mamouth Ins, ins salesman. **ORGANIZATIONS:** Bd dirs Am Woodmen Ins; scnd vice pres IN PTA; pres NW IN Postal Supvrs; sec Postal Clerks & Union; parliamentarian Tolleston Comm Club; prog chmn Gary Rotary; treas St Augustine Epis Ch. **HONORS/ACHIEVEMENTS:** Recip Silver Beavr BSA. **BUSINESS ADDRESS:** 1499 Martin Luther Dr, Gary, IN 46401.

PRYOR, JULIUS, JR.
Physician. **PERSONAL:** Born Jul 19, 1924, Montgomery, AL; married Joan Scales; children: Julius III, Pamela, Jonathan. **EDUCATION:** Lincoln Univ, AB 1947; Meharry Dental Sch, DDS 1952; Meharry Med Coll, MD 1957. **CAREER:** John A Andrew Hosp, surgeon 1968-; St Margaret's Hosp, 1968-; Firview Med Ctr, 1964-; VA Hosp, consult surg 1968-; Meharry Med Coll, surg instr 1963-64; Hubbard Hosp, attending surgeon, 1963-64. **ORGANIZATIONS:** Mem Montgomery Area Chamber of Commerce; bd mem YMCA; Omega Psi Frat Inc; Am Coll of Surgeons; diplomate Natl Bd Dentistry; Am Bd Surgery; bd trustees, Old Ship AME Zion Church. **HONORS/ACHIEVEMENTS:** Omega man of yr Sigma Phi Cpt 1973; bd. **MILITARY SERVICE:** USN phm 3/c. **BUSINESS ADDRESS:** Pryor-Winston Ctr, 1156 Oak St, Montgomery, AL 36108.

PRYOR, LILLIAN W.
Educator. **PERSONAL:** Born Dec 13, 1917, New Orleans, LA; divorced; children: Mignon M Schooler. **EDUCATION:** Univ of CA Berkeley, BA 1942; Roosevelt U, MA 1966; LoyolaUniv Sch of Soc Work. **CAREER:** Chicago Bd of Educ, teacher physically handicapped children 1963-; elem teacher 1948-53; Cook Co Hospital, medical social worker 1948-53; Dept Public Asst, social worker 1943-48. **ORGANIZATIONS:** IL State co-chmn educ NAACP; women's bd Am Cancer Soc; mem Mus of Contemporary Art; Art Inst; bd mem Chicago S Side NAACP; bd mem Counc for ExcepChildren; bd mem S Side Comm Art Cntr; mem Women's Benefit Board Operation PUSH; Bravo Chap Lyric Opera; com mem Harris "Y"; life mem NAACP; mem Urban League Women's Counc Proj 75. **HONORS/ACHIEVEMENTS:** Serv aw Women's Aux NAACP; top tagger NAACP. **BUSINESS ADDRESS:** Bd of Educ, 228 N La Salle St, Chicago, IL 60601.

PRYOR, RICHARD **See PRYOR, AARON**

PUCKETT, KIRBY
Professional athlete. **PERSONAL:** Born Mar 14, 1961, Chicago, IL; married Tonya Hudson. **EDUCATION:** Attended, Bradley Univ Peoria IL, Triton Jr Coll River Grove IL. **CAREER:** Minnesota Twins, player 1982-. **HONORS/ACHIEVEMENTS:** Region IV Jr Coll Player of the Year 1982; Topps Player of Month for Aug 1982 Appalachian League; 1982 Player of the Year in Appalachian League by Baseball Amer; 1983 CA League All-Star Player of the Year; voted by league mgrs as Best Batting Prospect and Rookie of the Year 1983; named to Topps 1984 Major League All Rookie Team; Amer League Player of Week April 21-27 1986; Amer League Player of the Month for April 1986; named to Assoc Press Major League All-Star Team 1986; named centerfielder on The Sporting News and Baseball Amer American League All Star squads 1986; voted to Amer League Silver Slugger Team 1986; Gold Glove Awd 1986; named by Twin Cities Chap of Baseball Writers Assoc of Amer as Twins MVP 1986; Chicago Pitch & Hit Club as Chicago Area Major League Player ofYear 1986. **BUSINESS ADDRESS:** Minnesota Twins, 501 Chicago Ave South, Minneapolis, MN 55415.

PUCKREIN, GARY ALEXANDER
Publisher. **PERSONAL:** Born Aug 18, 1949, New York, NY; married Joanne Harris; children: 1. **EDUCATION:** CA State Univ, BA 1971; Brown Univ, MA 1974, PhD 1978. **CAREER:** Rutgers Univ, asst prof 1978-82, assoc prof 1982-; The Visions Foundation, exec dir; American Visions Magazine, publisher. **ORGANIZATIONS:** Mem Assoc of American Historians; mem Assoc of Caribbean Historians. **HONORS/ACHIEVEMENTS:** Free to Die (monograph) RI, Black Heritage Soc 1978; Fellow Vstg Scholar Smithsonian Inst 1982-84; Little England NY Univ Press 1984. **BUSINESS ADDRESS:** American Visions Magazine, Natl Museum of Amer Hist, Smithsonian Inst, Room A1040, Washington, DC 20560.

PUGH, CLEMENTINE A.
Educator. **PERSONAL:** Born in Raleigh, NC; daughter of Otho High and Alberta Harris High; married George Douglas Pugh; children: Douglas, Janet. **EDUCATION:** Shaw Univ, BA 1945; Columbia Univ, MSW 1948; Univ of MA Amherst, EdD 1982. **CAREER:** Hunter Coll, soc worker, rsch assoc educ clinic; Comm Serv Soc Family, psych soc; Herbert H Lehman Coll, prof of educ 1970-. **ORGANIZATIONS:** Fellow Amer Orthopsychiatric Assc 1975-, prog fac 1980-; mem Natl Assc of Black Social Wrkrs 1980-; bd dir Homes for the Homeless; mem Assoc of Black Women in Higher Educ, Natl Women's Studies Assoc; lifetime mem NAACP. **HONORS/ACHIEVEMENTS:** Book Publ "Those Children" Wadsworth Publ 1970; Article "Multi-Ethnic Collaboration to Combat Racism" Journal of Applied Behaviorial Sci 1977; numerous articles & publ 1980-85; book chapter: collaboration through validation of difference: an interracial model for change 1988. **BUSINESS ADDRESS:** Prof Dept of Education, Herbert H Lehman Coll, New York, NY 10468.

PUGH, G. DOUGLAS
Administrator. **PERSONAL:** Born Dec 14, 1923, New York, NY; married Clementine A; children: Douglas E, Janet A. **EDUCATION:** Columbia Univ, BS 1951, MBA 1957. **CAREER:** Urban League of Greater NY, ind rel dir 1955-60; Trafalgar Hosp, personnel dir 1960-62; Fed Mediation & Conciliation Svc, commiss 1962-67; Haryou-Act Inc, assoc exec dir Ford Found, prog adv on urban affairs 1966-69; Dormitory Auth NY, dir labor rel & urban affairs 1970-75; Unemployment Inst Appeal Bd, commiss, mem of bd 1976-87, chmn, 1987—. **ORGANIZATIONS:** AFSCME AFL-CIO officer, 1958—. **HONORS/ACHIEVEMENTS:** Publ "Black Economic Development" 1969. **BUSINESS ADDRESS:** Chairman, Unemployment Ins Appeal Bd, 2 World Trade Cntr, New York, NY 10047.

PUGH, MARLANA PATRICE
Educator. **PERSONAL:** Born Dec 26, 1952, Cleveland, OH. **EDUCATION:** John Carroll Univ, BA (Cum Laude) 1970-74; Cleveland State Univ, attended 1976-78; Purdue Univ, attending 1982-. **CAREER:** Cleveland State Univ Libraries, film library asst/film library head 1975-79; East Cleveland City Schools, speech/drama teacher 1979-80; Purdue Univ, teaching ast 1982-84; Cleveland Public Schools, english/reading teacher 1980-82, 1984-. **ORGANIZATIONS:** Mem Northeast OH Jazz Soc 1978-, Natl Council of Teachers of English 1980-; volunteer United Negro College Fund 1980-; mem Rhetoric Soc of Amer 1983-; charter mem Southeast Toastmasters 1986-; mem Metro Cleveland Alliance of Black School Educ 1986-; admin vice pres Southeast Toastmasters 1986-87; pres SoutheastToastmasters 1987-. **HONORS/ACHIEVEMENTS:** Alpha Sigma Nu Honor Soc 1973-; Writing Project participant Martha Holden Jennings Found, 1981-82; Graduate Assistantship Purdue Univ 1982-84.

PUGH, ROBERT WILLIAM, SR.
Business executive. **PERSONAL:** Born May 10, 1926, New York, NY; son of William R Pugh and Vennett I Pugh; married Barbara Johnson; children: Robert Jr, Lori. **EDUCATION:** Newark Sch of Fine Indsl Art, 1946-49; Mus of Moder Art, 1946; NY U, 1947-48. **CAREER:** Wynson Inc, designer 1945-46; Desagnet Hsng Corp, 1946; Nowland & Schladermundt, designer 1949-51; Assn Granite Craftsman's Guild Inc, pres 1975; Keystone Monument Co Inc, founder/pres. **ORGANIZATIONS:** Mem Indusl Designer's Inst; Design Guild of NJ bd of mgrs Harlem YMCA; bd of trsts Youth Consult Serv; pres Asso Granite Craftmen's Guild Inc 1976-77& 1979-80; bd mem NY State Monument Bldrs Assn Inc; mem Monument Bldrs of N Amer; bd dirs New York State Monument Builders Assn Inc; mem Frank Silvera Workshop. **HONORS/ACHIEVEMENTS:** Disting Serv Awd Assn Granite Craftsman's Guild 1976; designed and erected a public monument to Dr Martin Luther King in Harlem 1976; Man of the Yr HarlemYMCA 1977; First place awd design contest Monument Builders of North Amer 1977; only Black owner of monument co NY; spkr Tri-State Funeral Dirs Conv Granit NY 1979; guest AUS War Coll Nat Security Seminar 1979; Unity Award Assoc Granite Craftsman's Guild & Met Meml Indust Inc 1979; first Black man to serve as pres of Assoc Granite Craftsman Guild of NY (served 5 terms); Archie L Green Awd for Excellence 1982 and 83; donated and designed memorial dedicated to the slain children of Atlanta; Excellent Achievement Award, Nancy R Cherry Association 1989. **MILITARY SERVICE:** AUS pvt 1944-45. **BUSINESS ADDRESS:** President, Keystone Monument Co, Inc, 37 Conway St, Brooklyn, NY 11207.

PUGH, RODERICK W.
Clinical psychologist, educator. **PERSONAL:** Born Jun 01, 1919, Richmond, KY; son of George W Pugh and Lena B White Pugh; divorced. **EDUCATION:** Fisk Univ Nashville TN, BA 1940; OH State Univ, MA 1941; Univ of Chgo, PhD Clinical Psych 1949. **CAREER:** Hines VA Hosp Chgo, staff psych 1950-54, asst chief clin psych for psychotherapy 1954-58, chief clin psych sect 1958-60, suprv psych & coord psych internship training 1960-66; Private practice, clin psych 1958-; Loyola Univ of Chgo, assoc prof psych 1966-73, prof of psych 1973-. **ORGANIZATIONS:** Mem Ctr Inner City Studies NE State Univ Chicago 1966-67, IL Div Voc Rehab 1965-, Chicago VA Reg Psych Training Prog 1966-, Amer Psych Assoc & Natl Inst Mental Health Vis Psych Prog 1968-, Juv Problems Rsch Review Com, Natl Inst Mental Health 1970-74; invited lectr Clinical Psych Univ of Ibadan Nigeria 1979; consult adv editor "Contemporary Psychology" 1975-79; mem Natl Inst of Mental Health Ctr for Minority Group Mental Health Prog 1975-77; professional adv com Div of Mental Health City of Chicago 1979-; mem natl adv panel Civilian Health & Med Prog of the Uniformed Serv Amer Psych Assoc 1980-83 civilian adv comm US Army Command and Genl Staff Coll 1981-83; fellow Amer Psych Assoc, Soc for Psych Study of Soc Issues; mem Assoc of Black Psych; IL Psych Assoc; Midwestern Psych Assoc; IL Group Psych Assoc; Amer Assoc Univ Profs; Alpha Phi Alpha; vstg scholar psych Fisk Univ 1966; mem 1968-78, sec 1970-77 Fisk Univ Bd Trustees; mem Psi Chi Psych, Sigma Xi Sci Univ of Chicago 1948; diplomate clin psych Amer Bd Prof Psych 1975. **HONORS/ACHIEVEMENTS:** Listed in Amer Men & Women of Science, Who's Who in Amer; author, "Psychology & The Black Experience" 1972, "Psychological Aspects of the Black Revolution"; Disting Serv Awd Amer Bd of Professional Psychology 1986; Illinois Psychological Assn, Distinguished Psychologist Award (top annual IL State Award) 1988; Assn Black Psychologists, Chicago Chapter, Award for Distinguished Service to Black Community 1984 & 1988; Natl Assn Black Psychologists Guiding Light Award for Pioneering Service 1979. **MILITARY SERVICE:** AUS 2nd lt 1943-46; Battlefield Commn as 2nd lt Patton's 3rd UA Army Alsfeld Germany 1945. **BUSINESS ADDRESS:** Clinical Psychologist, 30 N Michigan Ave, Suite 1515, Chicago, IL 60602.

PUGH, THOMAS JEFFERSON
Educator. **PERSONAL:** Born Oct 25, 1917, Lewiston, NC; married Lillian Ruth; children: John. **EDUCATION:** Clark Coll, AB 1940; Gammon Theo Sem, MDiv 1942; Atlanta U, MA 1947; Boston U, PhD 1955. **CAREER:** Theol Center, vice pres acad servs interdenominat 1979-, exec vice pres 1980; Acad Affairs, acting vice pres 1978-79; Theol Center, prof interdenom 1958-78; Albany State Coll, chap 1948-58; Bryant Theo Sem, tchr 1944-47; Bethesda Bapt Ch, pastor 1943-46; Tri-Comm Consol HS, prin 1942-44; Jas Andrews Farm, dir religion educ to migrants 1942. **ORGANIZATIONS:** Contrib YMCA; life mem Alpha Phi Alpha Frat; ldr Career Devel Inst for AF; indiv grp marriage therapy to alcoholic patients GA Clinic; Psychol Eval ofCand for Ministry; Marriage & Family Enrich Workshops; mem Friendship Bapt Ch, Amer Psych Assn, GA Psych Assn, Soc for Sci Study of Rel; supr AAMFt; AAUP; GA AMFt; Atlanta MHA; bd of dirs GA Assn for Past Care; bd trust ITC; faculty rep; pastoral therapist GA Clinic for Alcoholics elected mem Intl Soc of Theta Phi. **HONORS/ACHIEVEMENTS:** NIMH Fellow; grant Lilly Endowment Couns Educ Prgm; cit Judge Baker's Ct; ldr 2 CDI Missions to Air Force Chaplains etc overseas 1973; Fellow The Case-Study Inst 1975; Fellow Ecumenical Cultural Inst 1975; num publ in professional & ch journals; Fellow in Gerontology GSU 1986-87. **BUSINESS ADDRESS:** Professor, Interdenominational Theol Ctr, Psy of Relig & Pastoral Care, 671 Beckwith St SW, Atlanta, GA 30314.

PULLEN-BROWN, STEPHANIE
Educator. **PERSONAL:** Born Dec 11, 1949, Baltimore, MD; married Gerald O Brown; children: Margot. **EDUCATION:** MD Inst of Art, BFA 1970; Coppin State Coll, MEd 1973; Loyola Coll, MEd 1979. **CAREER:** Balta City Public Schools, teacher 1970-74, admin specialist 1974-80; Univ of MD, coop extn serv city dir 1980-86, asst to vice president/dean 1986-. **ORGANIZATIONS:** Commissioner Baltimore City Commn for Women 1984-86; mem Johnson Foundation Bd Baltimore Museum of Art 1985-; mem Bd YMCA 1985-. **HONORS/ACHIEVEMENTS:** Search for Professional Excellence Natl Assoc of County Agricultural Agents 1983; Woman Manager of the Year, Conf of Women in MD State Serv 1984. **BUSINESS ADDRESS:** Asst to Vice Pres/Dean, University of MD, Symons Hall, College Park, MD 20742.

PULLEY, CLYDE WILSON
Educator. **PERSONAL:** Born Sep 21, 1934, Durham, NC; children: Mary A, Jessie F. **EDUCATION:** Culver-Stockton Clge Canton MO, BS 1973; Xavier Univ Cincinnati OH, MS 1978. **CAREER:** USAF, police admin 1952-74; OH Dept Rehabilitation & Corrections, correction admin 1974-77; NC Dept of Corrections, corrrection dir 1977-79; Wilson Co Tech Inst NC, prof correction social services 1979-81; Metro State Coll, prof criminal justice & crime 1981-. **ORGANIZATIONS:** Consult Amer Corr Assc 1979-; spec correspondent Afro-Amer Newspapers Balto MD 1979-81; mem bd dir Comitis Crisis Cntr Aurora CO 1983-84, CO Prison Assc Denver CO 1984-, Williams St Ctr Denver CO. **HONORS/ACHIEVEMENTS:** Mem Natl Assc of Blacks in Criminal Justice 1982-, Amer Correctional Assc 1977-; recipient Outstanding Educ Award Goldsboro NC 1980-; candidate Lt Gov NC Demo Primary 1980. **MILITARY SERVICE:** AUS & USAF mstr sgt e7 1952-74; AFCM NDSM KSM VSM GCM UNSM 1952-74. **BUSINESS ADDRESS:** Professor of Criminal Justice, Metro State Clge, 1006 11th St, Denver, CO 80204.

PULLEY, REGINALD
Government official. **PERSONAL:** Born 1926, Bronx, NY. **EDUCATION:** Lincoln U, AB 1950. **CAREER:** Correctional Training Facility Soledad, CA, supt 1980; San Quentin Prison, dep warden 1977-80; CTF Soledad, dept supt 1975-76; CA Adult Auth, hearing ofcr 1973-75; CTF Soledad, prog adminstr 1971-73; CA Dept Corr CCCC LA, parole agent Iii 1969-71; CA Dept Corr LA Modesta, parole agent III; LA Co Santa Monica, dep probation ofcr. **BUSINESS ADDRESS:** Correctional Training Facility, PO Box 686, Soledad, CA 93960.

PULLIAM, BETTY E.
Business executive. **PERSONAL:** Born Jun 04, 1941, Woodruff, SC; daughter of Shewerl Douglas Ferguson and Gertrude Greene Ferguson; married Herman; children: Trudy, Vanessa, Herman Jr. **EDUCATION:** Wayne State U. **CAREER:** St Mark's Comm Ch, sec 1958-64; Mayor's Youth Employment Prog Comm for Human Resources Devel, 1965-69; Robert Johnson Asso Training Inst, office mgmnt 1971-73; Payne-Pulliam Sch of Trade & Commerce, pres dir 1973-. **ORGANIZATIONS:** 1st female pres of Booker T Washington Business Assoc; mem of the Detroit Stategic Planning Cncls (Jobs & Economic Devel Task Force); Designated Educ Planning Entity for Job Training Partnership Act, bd mem; Mich Dept of Educ Adult Exte Learning Adv Bd mem; Commerce High School Alumni bd mem; Mich Org of Private Schools mem; Greater New Mt Moriah Bapt Church choir mem; Women's Economic Club. **HONORS/ACHIEVEMENTS:** Business Woman of the Month; Pinch Cert of Ach 1978; Spirit of Detroit Awd 1983; Golden Heritage Awd for Educ Exc 1984; Detroit City Cncl Cmty Awd 1983; Black History Month Recog Awd 1985; Wayne Cnty Exec Office Ach Awd 1986; Proclamation from the Mayor Detroit 1983; Cert of Appr for Natl Business Week 1985; Cert of Recog City of Highland Park 1987; Cert of Rec from the Mayor 1987; Outstanding Ach for Historical Accomplishment 1987; Community Service Award, Councilwoman Barbara R Collins 1988; appointment to Michigan Liquor Control Commission, by Governor James Blanchard, 1989. **HOME ADDRESS:** 18945 Woodingham, Detroit, MI 48221. **BUSINESS ADDRESS:** President, Payne-Pulliam Sch of Trade/Com, 2345 Cass Ave, Detroit, MI 48201.

PURCE, THOMAS LES
Chief operating engineer. **PERSONAL:** Born Nov 13, 1946, Pocatello, ID. **EDUCATION:** BA Psychology 1969; MEd 1970; EdD 1975. **CAREER:** Washington State Univ, counsel psychologist 1970-72; ID State Univ, dir coop educ 1974-75, asst prof of counselor ed 1975-77; Pocatello, ID, mayor 1976-77; State of ID Dept of Adminstrn, adminstr div of gen serv 1977-79, dir 1979-81; State of ID Dept of Health & Welfare, dir 1981-83; POWER Engineers Inc, chief operating engineer 1983-. **ORGANIZATIONS:** Mem Assn Univ Prof; Assn of Counselor Educ & Supr; Assn of ID Cities; Assn of Black Psychologists; v chmn City Council; mem ID Water & Sewage Cert Bd; NAACP; Urban League Task Force; SE ID Cncl of Govt; ID Housing Agency; Kappa Alpha Psi; City Councilman. **HONORS/ACHIEVEMENTS:** Outstanding Young Men of Amer; mem State Exec Com Dem Party. **BUSINESS ADDRESS:** Chief Operating Engineer, Power Engineers Inc, 724 O'Farrell Ave, Olympia, WA 98501.

PUREIFORY, DAVE
Professional athlete. **PERSONAL:** Born Jul 12, 1949, Pensacola, FL. **EDUCATION:** E MI Univ, MA 1972. **CAREER:** Green Bay Packers, football player; Detroit Lions, football player; Birmingham Stallions, defensive end. **HONORS/ACHIEVEMENTS:** Tremendous pass rusher; 3 time All-Mid Amer Conf; twice name All-Amer.

PURNELL, ALTON
Musician. **PERSONAL:** Born Apr 16, 1911, New Orleans, LA. **CAREER:** Crescent Jazz Prod (LA "Legends of Jazz), musician (jazz singer & pianist); various US college tours; European tour with New Orleans ALL Stars 1964; 1st solo European tour 1962-63; Australian tour 1965; solo artist tours in Japan & Australia 1976, Canada 1977; many solo tours of Europe completed by demand. **ORGANIZATIONS:** Pres S Cal Hot Jazz Soc 1970-72; mem ASCAP (composer); mem AFM LA; mem Com "Louis Armstrong Statue Fund" 1970; mem Com to Commemorate Louis Armstrong (Shrine Aud "Hello Louis") featured in "Family Album" Al Rose. **HONORS/ACHIEVEMENTS:** "Who's Who of Jazz" John Chilton London; "Pictorial History of Jazz". **BUSINESS ADDRESS:** Crescent Jazz Productions, PO Box 60244, Los Angeles, CA 90054.

PURNELL, CAROLYN J.
Attorney. **PERSONAL:** Born Aug 16, 1939, Memphis, TN; divorced; children: Monica, Mardine. **EDUCATION:** Univ of WA, BA 1961; Univ of WA School of Law, JD 1971. **CAREER:** Pros Attny Office, sr legal intern 1971, civil dep 1972-74; City of Seattle, legal couns to mayor; Weyerhaeuser Co Fed Way Wash, corp attny, dir of corp matls; Washington Round Table, exec. **ORGANIZATIONS:** Vp Housing Corp Devel of Washington; panelist Human Rights Comm Tribunal; past exec bd sec March of Dimes; bd of trustees Epiphany School; mem Phi Alpha Delta Legal Frat; sec Delta Sigma Theta Sor; former mem Providence Hosp Found; mem WA State Bd of Bar Examiners, City of Seattle Bd of Adjustments, Scholastic Honor Soc; mem Pacific Med Ctr Bd, Mayors Centennial Parks Commiss, Mayors Zoo Commiss. **HONORS/ACHIEVEMENTS:** Outstanding Young Women Dir for US 1976; 1 of 100 Lawyers in US to attend Amer Assembly on Law; Selected 1st Class of Leadership for Tomorrow Seattle C of C.

PURNELL, LEE J.
Engineer. **PERSONAL:** Born Oct 11, 1896, Washington, DC; married Olga Smith; children: Joyce Lee, Lee J Jr, Katherine M. **EDUCATION:** Univ of CA, AB 1919; MA Inst of Tech, BS 1921;Univ of CA, MS 1929. **CAREER:** Lee J Purnell Consult Engrs, consult engr 1942-; Bonneville Pw Admin Portland, assoc sys engr 1939-51; Pca Gas & Elec Co San Francisco, engr dept 1925-30; Howard U, asso prof, chmn, elec engr dept 1942-72. **ORGANIZATIONS:** Mem v chmn sec chmn DC Bd of Registration for Professional Engrs 1950-61; mem Commrs Planning Adv Counc 1962-65; life mem Nat Soc of Professional Engrs; mem Nat Tech Assn; Tau Beta Pi. **MILITARY SERVICE:** AUS 2nd lt 1918.

PURVIS, ARCHIE C., JR.
Business executive. **PERSONAL:** Born May 24, 1939, New York, NY; son of Archibald Purvis, Sr. and Millicent Purvis; married Candace H Caldwell; children: Victoria, Christian. **EDUCATION:** Univ of Munich, 1960; City Coll of NY Sch of Business, BS 1969; Stanford Executive Program l989. **CAREER:** Gen Foods Corp, account manager 1963-66; Polaroid Corp, natl sales mgr 1966-74; Lear Purvis Walker & Co, exec vice pres 1974-75; MCA Inc Univ Studios, dir indsl mktg 1975-79; Amer Broadcasting Co, vp, general mgr video sales div; ABC Distribution Co, sr vice pres. **ORGANIZATIONS:** Mem Amer Mktg Assn; mem Amer Mgmt Assn, mem Sales Exec of NY; dir San Fernand Fair Housing, 1979; dir Intl Children's Sch; dir Corporation for Public Broadcasting 1987; Academy of Motion Picture Arts & Sciences, Hollywood Radio & TV Society. **MILITARY SERVICE:** AUS Sp-5; Advanced Commendation Award. **BUSINESS ADDRESS:** Senior Vice President, American Broadcasting Co, 2040 Ave of the Stars, Los Angeles, CA 90067.

PURYEAR, ALVIN N.
Educator. **PERSONAL:** Born Apr 06, 1937, Fayetteville, NC; married Catherine; children: 3 Children. **EDUCATION:** Yale Univ, BA 1960; Columbia Univ, MBA 1962, PhD 1966. **CAREER:** Mobile Oil Corp, employee relations advisor 1965-66, financial analyst 1966-67; Allied Chem Corp, computer systems specialist 1967-68; Rutgers Univ, assoc prof 1968-70; Baruch Coll, dean 1972-75, prof of mgmt 1980-84; The Ford Foundation, vice pres organiz & mgmt 1980-82; City of NY, first deputy comptroller 1983-84. **BUSINESS ADDRESS:** Professor, Baruch Coll CityUniv of NY, 17 Lexington, New York, NY 10010.

PURYEAR, BOYD ALFRED
Administrator. **PERSONAL:** Born Mar 18, 1945, Cleveland, OH; married Joann Minter; children: Aki, Maia, Asinna. **EDUCATION:** Williams Coll, BA 1967; Princeton Theol Sem, BD (incomplete) 1969;Univ of Pittsburgh, PhD educ admin 1972; Carnegie-MellonUniv Coll, cert mgmt prog1979. **CAREER:** Comm Coll of Allegheny Co, asst mgr of employ serv 1979-, asst to pres 1973-79; Univ of Pittsburgh, instructor graduate school of public & internal affairs 1969-72; Univ & City Ministries Pittsburgh, PA, asso minister 1970-71; Congress of Racial Equality Cleveland, economical devel coordinator 1967-68; United Ministeries in Higher Educ PA Commn, prog strategy com 1973-77. **ORGANIZATIONS:** Chmn Archives Inst of Creative Arts 1977-78; vP human resources Bowman Puryear Lioon Asso 1980-; co-chmn Vibrations Ii Prisioners' Justice Com 1971-78; bd mem Ch & Soc Inst 1972-76; bd mem Prog to Aid Citizens Enter 1976-; bd mem Family & Children's Serv 1977-79. **HONORS/ACHIEVEMENTS:** Herbert H Lehman Scholshp Williams Coll 1964-67; bd of Christian Educ Fellowship Princton Theol Sem 1968-69; Provost Devel FellowshipUniv of Pitts 1972-73; Outstdg Educator of Am, Outstdg Am Wash, DC 1975; Outstdg Young Men of Am, Outstdg Am Wash, DC 1977. **BUSINESS ADDRESS:** Personnel Administrator, Comm Coll of Allegheny Cnty, 800 Allegheny Ave, Pittsburgh, PA 15233.

PUTNAM, GLENDORA M.
Attorney. **PERSONAL:** Born Jul 25, 1923, Lugoff, SC; daughter of Simon P McIlwain and Katherine Steward McIlwain. **EDUCATION:** Barber Scotia Jr Clge, Cert 1943; Bennett Clge, AB 1945; Boston Univ, JD 1948. **CAREER:** Dept of HUD, deputy asst secr 1975-77; MA Office of Atty Gen, asst atty gen 1963-69; MA Comm Against Discrimination, chair 1969-75; MA Housing Finance Agcy, equal opport ofcr. **ORGANIZATIONS:** Mem MA Bar 1949-, Federal Bar 1st Dist 1956-, US Supreme Court Bar 1964-, MA Bar Assc 1971-; bd trustee Boston Conservatory of Music 1972-; bd trustees Barber Scotia Clge 1980-; pres YWCA of the USA 1985; bd NAACP Legal Educational Defense Fund; Boston Bar Assoc; Boston Lawyers Committee for Civil Rights Under Law; life mem Exec Committee BU Law School Alumni Assn. **HONORS/ACHIEVEMENTS:** Women of the Year Greater Boston Bus & Prof Club 1969; Humanitarian Award Boston Branch NAACP 1973; Academy of Distinguished Bostonians, Greater Boston Chamber of Commerce 1988; Doctor of Laws (hon), Southeastern Mass Univ 1986; Woman of Achievement, Boston Big Sisters 1985; Silver Shingle for Distinguished Public Service, Boston Univ Law School 1988. **HOME ADDRESS:** 790 Boylston St, Boston, MA 02199. **BUSINESS ADDRESS:** Equal Opportunity Officer, MA Housing Finance Agcy, 50 Milk St, 3rd floor, Boston, MA 02109.

PUTNAM, ROSALIND (NEE LAWSON)
Educator. **PERSONAL:** Born Aug 02, 1906, Hartford, CT; children: Hubert P Jr. **EDUCATION:** Fisk Univ NY Univ, BS 1943; NY Univ, MA 1959. **CAREER:** Home Relief Bureau, case worker 1933-34; YMCA Harlem Branch, prog & camp dir 1934-47; Meth Church Rural Extension Svc, dir 1940-41; N End Comm Center, dir 1950-54; Univ Hartford, adjunct faculty mem 1952; Comm Orgn, dir 1954-59; Univ Hartford, asst prof 1959; Chung Chi Coll, prof group work; Lei Cheug Uk Settlement House Hong Kong, prog dir 1966-68; Univ of Hartford, assoc prof 1977, prof emeritus. **ORGANIZATIONS:** Chmn Summer Prog Coord Com Hong Kong; mem Div of Children & Youth Hong Kong Cncl of Soc Svcs; mem Youth

Workshop Com Hong Kong; mem Bd of Family Welfare Soc Hong Kong; working with Wm Copford of the Student Christian Ctr in developing a Golden Age Seminar Wkshp Family Planning Hong Kong; mem lectr Hong Kong Social Welfare Dept Training Unit; chmn Summer Prog Week-end Conf on Leadership Training for Social Agency Suprs Hong Kong; chmn Div of Children & YouthHong Kong Cncl of Social Svcs; chmn Regional Youth Conf Prog Com Hong Kong; mem Regional Youth Conf Planning Com Hong Kong; mem Women's League Univ ofHartford; memUniv of Hartford Women's Assn; mem bd of dir Capitol Region YWCA 1974-75; mem World Mutual Serv Comm; mem Hartford alumna Chap Delta Sigma Theta Sor; arbitrator Am Arbit Assn Better Business Bureau Grtr Hartford; mem Natl Conf Christian & Jews; mem Dept of Aged State of CT. **HONORS/ACHIEVEMENTS:** Awd Honor Arabic Temple #40 AEAO Nobles of Mystic Shrine Prince Hall Affiliation 1962; Cert of Recog Natl Conf of Christians & Jews 1962; 10 yrs of devoted serv Leadership Devel Commn Univ of Hartford 1965; testimonial dinner Awd of Love & Serv Hong Kong 1968; Cert of Appreciation Kiwanis Club of Hartford 1969; WDRC First Lady of the Day 1970; Serv Awd 15 yrs of valued service Univ of Hartford 1970; Blk Peoples Union Awd 1974; Citation Civic Committment & Public Dedication Ct of Common Cncl City of Hartford 1974; Who's Who of Amer Women Vol II; Hon Deg Dr of Humane Letters Univ of Hartford 1976; Who's Who ofAmer Women Marquis Vol II 1961-62; publ "An Experimental Project in the Application of Group Work Principles in Large Group Settings" Hong Kong Jour of Social Wk 1967; "Children & Youth Activities During Summer Months" Chinese Quarterly 1967; Disting Serv Awd Hartford Alumnae Chap Delta Sigma Theta Sor 1981;Citation by CT Historical Soc "Black Women Against the Odds" honoring 81 Black Women of CT 1984; Official Citation Genl Assembly State of CT. **BUSINESS ADDRESS:** Professor Emeritus, Univ of Hartford, 200 Bloomfield Ave West, Hartford, CT 06117.

PYKE, WILLIE ORANDA
Educator. **PERSONAL:** Born May 06, 1930, Plymouth, NC. **EDUCATION:** NC A&T State Univ Greensboro, BS 1953; ColumbiaUniv NY, MA 1965f No IL U, EdD 1972. **CAREER:** Dept of Bus Educ & Adminstrv Services So IL Univ, prof and chairperson 1972-; Hampton Inst VA, assoc prof of business 1971-72; Langston Univ OK, asst of business 1967-69; Albany State & Coll GA, asst prof of business 1965-67; Teachers Coll Columbia Univ NY, TC fund officer 1963-65; St Augustine's Coll Raleigh NC, execsec 1960-63. **ORGANIZATIONS:** Mem lgislative com IL Bus Educ Assn 1979-80; mem bd of dir SW IL Intern'l Word Processing Assn 1979-80; mem State of IL Adv Com for Bus Mkt & Mgmt Occupations; sec bd of dir E St Louis Met Ministry 1978-81; mem Commn of Ministry So IL. **HONORS/ACHIEVEMENTS:** Award for Doctoral study Ford Found 1969-71; oman of achievement award Edwardsville Bus & Professional Women's Club; author of several articles in Nat Professional MagS and Yearbooks; numerous service awards Bus Orgns. **BUSINESS ADDRESS:** Southern Illinois University, PO Box 106, Edwardsville, IL 62026.

PYLES, J. A.
Educational administrator. **PERSONAL:** Born Feb 23, 1949, Sanford, FL. **EDUCATION:** Bethune-Cookman Coll, BA 1971; Roosevelt Univ MA 1975. **CAREER:** United Negro Coll Fund, asst area dir; Alpha Kappa Alpha Sorority Inc, program specialist; Social Security Admin St Petersburg, 1970; Bethune Cookman Coll, vice pres for development. **ORGANIZATIONS:** Mem commn on Religion & Race United Methodist Church Washington, DC; mem Chicago Soc of Fund-Raising Execs; Natl Soc of Fund-Raising Execs; Bethune-Cookman Coll Alumni Assn; Roosevelt Univ Alumni Assn. **HONORS/ACHIEVEMENTS:** Recipient United Negro Coll Fund Alumni Achievement Award 1980. **BUSINESS ADDRESS:** Vice President for Development, Bethune-Cookman College, 640 Second Ave, Daytona Beach, FL 32015.

PYLES, JOHN E.
Attorney, judge. **PERSONAL:** Born Jan 11, 1927, Memphis, TN; married Deborah; children: 8 children. **EDUCATION:** BCL 1951; JD 1968. **CAREER:** Office of John E Pyles, attorney 1968-; municipal judge 1979-81. **ORGANIZATIONS:** Mem Wichita Bar Assn; Sedgwick County Bar Assn; Wichita Bd of Realtors 1960-; Multilist Serv of Wichita 1967-; MS Trial Lawyer Assn 1967-. **MILITARY SERVICE:** USAF Signal Corp Sgt 1945-47. **BUSINESS ADDRESS:** Judge, 2703 E 13, Wichita, KS 67214.

Q

QAMAR, NADI ABU
Freelance performer. **PERSONAL:** Born Jul 06, 1917, Cincinnati, OH; son of William Givens and Alberta Bennett Givens; married Rose Ann Dolski; children: Fabian Billie. **EDUCATION:** Attended Intl Univ Foundation Independence MO. **CAREER:** Jazz Pianist, Composer and Arranger, 1934-65; Inaugural History of Jazz series 1965; composer, musician, 1965-77; Bedford Study Youth in Action, oratorio composer/mus dir; Countee Cullen, concerts 1965-68; New Lafayette Theatre, artist in residence 1970-72; Nina Simone World Tours 1972-74; "Wy Mbony Sita", ballet at 20 Spruce St New York City 1973; Museum of Natural History NY, perf series 1976; Bennington Coll, prof of voice, piano and orchestra 1978-85; lecturer, leader of workshops at various universities and study centers, 1980-89; Nuru Taa Arts, afromusicologist, director. **ORGANIZATIONS:** Broadcast Music, 1958—; American Federation of Musicians; Mechanical and Copyright Protective Society of London; Percussive Arts Society, 1989. **HONORS/ACHIEVEMENTS:** Drummer & singer with Zulu Singers & Dancers at World's Fair African Pavillion, Flushing Meadows, NY, 1965; composer/scorer/director, premiere performance of Likembican Panorama, 1969; asst mus dir of "Black Picture Show" at Jos Papp Shakespeare Festival 1974; Likembi/mbira Performance Workshop Series Dir Museum of Natural History Dr Barbara Jackson Coord 1976; Certificate of Recognition for Exemplary Representation of African Amer Artistic and Cultural Expression at FESTAC 1977; records Nuru Taa African Idiom, The Mama Likembi Instruction Manual CRB 14, The Likembi Songbook Manual of Annotated Songs & Recorded Compositions CRB 15 Folkway Records; citation for concerts at FESTAC 1977; performed at Detroit Inst of Art Inaugural Nok Igbo Sculpture Show 1980; Folkways recording artist; debut records of strings & keys duo w/Charles Mingus, original composition, 1989. **BUSINESS ADDRESS:** Director, Nuru Taa Arts/Publishers, Route 1, Box 274, Kewaunee, WI 54216.

QUANDER, ROHULAMIN
Attorney. **PERSONAL:** Born Dec 04, 1943, Washington, DC; son of James W Quander and Joheora Quander; married Carmen Torruella; children: Iliana Amparo, Rohulamin Darius, Fatima de los Santos. **EDUCATION:** Howard Univ, BA 1966, JD 1969. **CAREER:** Neighborhood Legal Serv, 1969-71; Geo Wash Univ, 1970-72; Intl Investors, Inc, market cons, attorney, state dir 1973-; private practice 1975-; Office of Adjudication DC Govt 1986-; geneological hist and researcher for private groups; attorney examiner under consulting contract to various DC Govt agencies. **ORGANIZATIONS:** Mem Superior Ct of DC 1975; US dist Ct of DC 1976; mem Amer Bar Assn; Natl Bar Assn; DC Bar Assn; Bar of Supreme Ct of PA; US Dist Ct for Eastern PA; Ct of Appeals DC; Phi Alpha Delta Law Frat 1967; Phi Alpha Theta His Soc; founder Howard Univ Chap of Black Amer Law Students Assn 1968; mem Omega Psi Phi Frat 1964-; pres Student Bar Assn 1968-69, vice pres 1967-68; mem bd of dir The Wash DC Parent & Child Center 1977-81; chief archivist Quander Family History 1977-; reg chmn Howard Univ Alumni 1979-87; chmn Educ Inst Licensure Commn of DC 1979-; bd dir Wash Urban League 1969-70; pres Howard Univ Alumni Club for Wash DC 1970-71; guest lecturer on the geneology hist & contributions of the Quander Family (America's oldest documntd black fam); wrote "The History of the Quander Family" 1984; mem MLK Holiday Commission for DC 1987-89; pres Quanders United, Inc 1983-; mem of, Columbia Hist Soc, Int'lPlatform Speakers Assoc 1985-, Republican Party of DC; bd of dir Pigskin Club 1986-; have published numerous articles for Howard Univ alumni newspaper. **HONORS/ACHIEVEMENTS:** Listed Who's Who Among Students in Amer Univs & Colls 1965; Man of Yr Award Omega Psi Phi Frat 1965 & 1968; Spl Award Howard Univ Outstdg Serv to Law Sch, the Community and the Univ 1969; Dean's List Howard Univ 1964, 65 & 68; Travel Fellowship to 13 foreign countries 1964. **BUSINESS ADDRESS:** Attorney, 1703 Lawrence St NE, Washington, DC 20018.

QUANSAH-DANKWA, JULIANA ABA
Dentist. **PERSONAL:** Born Aug 11, 1955, Apam, Ghana;daughter of S T Quansah and Elizabeth Quansah; married Joseph Ofori-Dankwa. **EDUCATION:** Univ of Michigan Dental School, Zoology 1974-76, DDS 1980. **CAREER:** Lawrence D Crawford DDS PC, assoc dentist 1980-83; Comm Action Comm, dental dir 1981-85; Riverfront Dental Ctr, dentist 1982-83; Private Practice, dentist 1984-. **ORGANIZATIONS:** Mem, NAACP 1984; chmn, Intl Trends & Serv Tri City Links Inc 1984-; mem, African of Greater Flint Inc 1984-; mem, Saginaw Chamber of Commerce 1985; bd mem, Headstart Saginaw 1985-. **HONORS/ACHIEVEMENTS:** Commendation Award, Ross Medical Educ Center, 1986; Appreciation Award, Averill Career Opportunities, 1986.

QUARLES, BENJAMIN A.
Educator. **PERSONAL:** Born Jan 23, 1904, Boston, MA; son of Arthur Quarles and Margaret Quarles; married Ruth Brett; children: Roberta Knowles, Pamela Pourzal. **EDUCATION:** ShawUniv Raleigh, NC, BA 1931;Univ of WI, MA 1933, Doc of Philosophy in Hist 1940. **CAREER:** Shaw U, inst in hist 1935-39; DillardUniv New Orleans, LA, asso & prof of hist/dean of instrctn 1939-53; Morgan StateUniv Baltimore, MD, emeritus prof of hist. **ORGANIZATIONS:** Editorial bd Frederick Douglass Papers Project Yale U; natl cncl Frederick Douglass Museum of African Art Smithsonian Inst; advisory bd Am Hist & Life Am Bibliographical Ctr; com of advisors Nat Humanities Ctr; bd of editors MD Hist Mag; hon chmrn MD State Commn on Afro-Am Hist & Culture; hon fellow Ctr for African & African-Am Stud Atlanta; exec cncl Assn for Study of Afro-Am Life & Hist 1948-84; hon consult US Hist Lib of Congress 1970-71; fellowship select com 1976-77; Am Cncl of Learned Soc 1977-78; The Dept of the Army Hist Advis Com 1977-80; has 17 Hon Doctorates from Coll & U. **HONORS/ACHIEVEMENTS:** Books published, "Frederick Douglass" 1948; "The Negro in the Civil War" 1953; "The Negro in the Am Revolution" 1960; "Lincoln & the Negro" 1962; "The Negro in the Making of Am" 1964; "Black Abolitionists" 1969; "Allies for Freedom, Blacks & John Brown" 1974; "The Black Am" a documentary 1976; "Narrative of Life ofFrederick Douglass" 1962; "Frederick Douglass" in "Great Lives Observed Series" 1968; "Blacks on John Brown" 1972; Has published 23 articles, 70 shorter pieces, 11 chap in books; 26 articles biographical sketches in encyclopedias, 5 doc sources edited, 12 introd to reprints of books, 4 forewords to orig books, 2 forewords to fed govt publ, 1 foreword to microfilm collection, 107 book reviews. **HOME ADDRESS:** 10450 Lottsford Road, #2115, Mitcheville, MD 20716.

QUARLES, GEORGE R.
Educational administrator. **PERSONAL:** Born Jul 14, Morgantown, WV; son of George and Mable; married Barbara; children: Diane, Karen, Niama. **EDUCATION:** Hampton Inst, BS 1951; NY U, MA 1956. **CAREER:** Ctr for Career & Occup Edn, chief admin; NYC, bd of edn; CityUniv of NY, dir regional oppor cntr; Sam Harris Asso Ltd Washington, DC, exec vp;NJ State Educ Dept, dir voc educ dept; Newark Skills Cntr, dir; New Rochelle HS New Rochelle, NY, tchr; US Dept of Educ, Washington DC, Office of Vocational and Adult ED, 1980-81; Sewanhaka Central High School District, Floral Park, NY, dir of occupational educ, 1985-. **ORGANIZATIONS:** Mem Am Vocational Assn; former mem NY State Adv Counc for Vocat Edn; adjunct staff New Sch for Soc Research; consult Vocat Educ mem Omega Psi Phi Frat; mem tech review panel Nat Inst of Edn's Study of Vocat Edn; former mem Nat Faculty for the Nat Center for Research in Vocat Educ OH State U; consultant, US Aid African Bureau, 1983-84; consultant, Academy for Educational Devel, 1984-. **HONORS/ACHIEVEMENTS:** Recip Winged Trophy Newark Anti-Poverty Agy; Omega Man of Yr Omicron Iota Chpt; num radio & TV appearances articles for various newspapers on vocat edn; Bronz Star for Valor; Purple Heart with Oak Leaf Cluster; major paper on "Equity in Vocational Edn" Nat Cntr for Research in Vocat Edn; num articles & studies Vocat Educ & Youth Employ; Education Secretary's Special Achievement Pin. **MILITARY SERVICE:** 1st lt field artillery. **BUSINESS ADDRESS:** Director of Occupational Education, Sewanhaka Central High School District, 500 Tulip Avenue, Floral Park, NY 11001.

QUARLES, JOSEPH JAMES
Physician. **PERSONAL:** Born Aug 10, 1911, Norfolk, VA; divorced. **EDUCATION:** WV State College, BA 1934; Meharry Med Coll, DR of MED 1941. **CAREER:** Retired Physician. **ORGANIZATIONS:** Retired dir Berkley Citizens Mutual Savings and Loan 1951; pres chrmn of board, CEO 1974; v chrmn Community Facilities Comm City of Norfolk, VA 1975. **MILITARY SERVICE:** USMC cap.

QUARLES, NORMA R.
Reporter. **PERSONAL:** Born Nov 11, 1936, New York; divorced; children: Lawrence, Susan. **EDUCATION:** Hunter Coll; City Coll of NY. **CAREER:** NBC NY, TV news report 1970-; WKYC Cleveland, news report & anchorwoman 1967-70; NBC News Training

Prog, 1966-67; Pub Serv Dir WSDM FM Chicago, news report 1965-66; Katherine King Assoc Chicago, real estate broker 1957-65. **ORGANIZATIONS:** Mem Nat Academy of TV Arts & Sci; Sigma Delta Chi; mem bd of Gov Nat Academy of TV Arts & Sci. **HONORS/ACHIEVEMENTS:** Awd for TV journalism Sigma Delta Chi 1974; Front Page Awd for TV journalism Newswomen's Club 1973.

QUARLES, RUTH BRETT
Retired educator. **PERSONAL:** Born Nov 23, 1914, Murfreesboro, NC; daughter of Arthur Brett and Julia Pierce Brett; married Benjamin Quarles; children: Roberta Knowles, Pamela. **EDUCATION:** Shaw Univ Raleigh, NC, AB 1935; Hartford Seminary Foundation, MA 1936; Teachers College, Columbia Univ, EdD 1945. **CAREER:** Spelman College, Atlanta, assistant to dean 1936-38; Dillard Univ, New Orleans, dean of women 1938-42; Bennett Coll Greensboro, dean of students 1942-44; Tuskegee Inst, assoc personnel dir 1945-49; Univ of Munich Student Ctr Munich, Germany, asisstant in student ctr 1949-51; Fisk Univ, dean of students, 1951-53; Morgan State Univ, dir of counseling ctr 1956-80. **ORGANIZATIONS:** Pres Assoc of Deans of Women and Advisers to Girls 1944-46; fellow Natl Cncl Religion in Higher Education 1944-; consultant Amer Cncl Ed 1953-57; member Comm on Ed of Women Amer Cncl on Ed 1953-57; member Brd of Dir of YWCA on US 1956-60; mem Bd of Trustees of Morgan Christian Ctr 1960-; life member of NAACP; mem MD Intl Women's Year Coord Comm 1977; mem Exec Bd of Dir and Dir of Coll Sect of Natl Assoc for Women Deans, Cnslrs and Admin 1977-80; published article Journal of the NAWDAC 1984-86 on "Our Living History, Reminiscences of Black Participation in NAWDAC"; prgm participant in annual conf of NAWDAC 1984, 1986. **HONORS/ACHIEVEMENTS:** Member Kappa Delta Pi Honor Soc 1944-; member Pi Lambda Theta Honor Soc 1944-; citee Outstanding Achvmnt NAWDAC 1980; symposium set up by NAWDAC in her honor on Counseling for Minorities 1982; Promethean honor soc at Morgan St named for one of founders and advisor for 23 yrs, Grant-Brett Kappa Tau honor soc. **HOME ADDRESS:** 10450 Lottsford Road, # 2115, Mitchellville, MD 20716.

QUARRELLES, JAMES IVAN
Charitable director. **PERSONAL:** Born Apr 02, 1926, Morgantown, WV; married Gladys; children: Tracy Marie, Jamie C. **EDUCATION:** Hilltop Radio & Electronic Inst, 1947. **CAREER:** Martha Table non-profit corp, chmn 1984-; NAC of NDC # 1 UPO, pres 1982-. **ORGANIZATIONS:** Mem Mayor's Task Force on Ambulatory Health Care for the Metro Area 1975; mem Childrens Hosp Comprehensive Health Care Prog 1978; mem Childrens Hosp Natl Health Ctr task force comm 1978; mem Childrens Hosp Natl Health Ctr Spec Comm 1978; mem Notre Dame Acad PTA Assn 1980; mem 3rd Dist Adv Council 1980. **HONORS/ACHIEVEMENTS:** Certificate of Appreciation US Dept of Commerce 1970; Certificate of Appreciation United Planning Organ 1984. **MILITARY SERVICE:** USN petty officer 2nd class 3 yrs; Amer Theater Ribbon. **HOME ADDRESS:** 2101 New Hampshire Ave NW, Washington, DC 20009. **BUSINESS ADDRESS:** President, NAC of NDC # 1 UPO, 1336 8th St NW, Washington, DC 20001.

QUAYNOR, THOMAS ADDO
Educator. **PERSONAL:** Born May 22, 1935, Accra, Ghana. **EDUCATION:** Philander Smith Coll, BA 1961; So IL U, MA 1962; SIU, PhD 1965. **CAREER:** MS Valley State Univ, prof, chmn soc sci div 1964-70; Morgan State Univ, assoc prof 1970-. **ORGANIZATIONS:** Scoutmaster Boy Scouts of Am; author A Documented History of Black Consciousness NY Vantage Press 1986. **HONORS/ACHIEVEMENTS:** Outstdg Young Men of Am Alpha Kappa Mu Nat Hon Soc 1971; Outstdg Educators of Am Phi Kappa Phi Nat Hon Soc 1972; Personalities of the South Pi Sigma Alpha Nat Polit Sci Hon Soc 1970. **BUSINESS ADDRESS:** Associate Professor, Morgan State Univ, Baltimore, MD 21239.

QUEEN, ROBERT CALVIN
Editor. **PERSONAL:** Born Jun 10, 1912, Newark, NJ; divorced; children: Delores H Fields, Roberta L Burroughs, Robert C Jr. **CAREER:** NJ Guardian, reporter 1938-40; NJ Herald News, reporter city editor 1941-49; Philadelphia Independent, managing editor 1950-57; Philadelphia Edition Pittsburgh Courier, managing editor 1957-63; Philadelphia Afro-Amer, managing editor 1963-67; NJ Afro-Amer, editor 1968-. **ORGANIZATIONS:** Mem Philadelphia Citizens Comm City Planning 1954-67; mem Sigma Delta Chi Journalistic Soc 1964; pr comm Philadelphia Child Devel Prog; panelist "Ben Hur" Centennial Crawfordsville IN 1980. **HONORS/ACHIEVEMENTS:** Disting Serv Free & Accepted Mason 1961; Philadelphia Cotillion Soc Plaque 1964; Journalism Awd Temple Univ School of Journalism 1968; WEB Dubois Awd Newark Branch NAACP 1982; Awd NJ Assoc of Black Journalists 1984; Assoc in Arts Liberta Arts Humanitis Honoris Causa Essex Co Coll Newark NJ 1986. **BUSINESS ADDRESS:** Editor, New Jersey Afro-American, 439 Central Ave, East Orange, NJ 07018.

QUICK, CHARLES E.
Clergyman. **PERSONAL:** Born Oct 29, 1933, Raeford, NC; married Ruby Lee Williams; children: Charliss Quinae. **EDUCATION:** Clinton Jr Coll, 1958; Livingstone Coll, BA 1960; UCLA, further studies 1974; Temple U, 1976; Rutgers U; Hood Theo Sem, MDiv 1963;Univ of MD;Univ of NC; VA Chpln Sch, 1971. **CAREER:** VA Hosp, v chmn hire the handicap com, chpln; Coatesville, PA VA Med Center, chpln 1975-; Clinton Jr Coll Rock Hill, SC, tchr 1964-71; Western NC Conf Charlotte, NC, pastor 1960-71; AME Zion Ch Pee Dee Conf SC, pastor 1958-60; NC, TN, VA AME Zion Ch, Christ educ dir 1969-71. **ORGANIZATIONS:** Mem bd dirs NC Coun of Chs 1968-71; mem NAACP Charlotte Augusta 1951-; SC Educ Assn 1964-71; mem Legion 505 Augusta 1971-; mem bd dirs Prog Assn for Econ Devel 1968-71; mem Elks 1966; chmn Chpln Serv VA Hosp Augusta 1974; mem Charlotte-mecklenburg Sch Bd Com 1965-69; Com of Equal Empl OppVA Hosp 1972-; Vietnam ERA Com VA Hosp 1971-; originator & coor Annual Dr Martin L King Jr Meml Day Celebration at Coatesville VA Med Cntr; mem Black History Com Coatesville VA Med Cntr; instr Assaultive Behavior & Suicide Prevention Class Coatesville VA Med Cntr; chmn 50th Anniversary Com Coatesville VA Med Cntr. **HONORS/ACHIEVEMENTS:** Recip Oratorical first place winner Clintor Jr Coll Rock Hill, SC 1958; Hon DD Teamers Sch of Religion Charlotte 1968; Humanitarian Awd Charlotte 1971; Outstdg Serv Awd AME Zion Ch Communion 1971; comm awd Coatesville 1976; Augusta, GA 1974; recip Good Citizenship Awd. **BUSINESS ADDRESS:** VA Hosp, Augusta, GA 30904.

QUICK, MIKE
Professional athlete. **PERSONAL:** Born May 14, 1959, Hamlet, NC; son of James Quick and Mary Quick. **EDUCATION:** Attended, NC State. **CAREER:** Philadelphia Eagles, wide receiver 1982-. **ORGANIZATIONS:** Active in community affairs especially Big Brothers/Big Sisters; madeTV announcements for KYW-TV's Project Homeless Fund, WCAU-TV's School Vote Program, the Franklin Inst, 7-Eleven/Coca Cola Freedom Run for Sickle Cell; co-owner All Pro Fitness and Racquet Club in Maple Shade NJ. **HONORS/ACHIEVEMENTS:** Played in the Blue-Gray Game and Olympia Gold Bowl; became first Eagle in history to surpass 1,000 yards receiving in 3 straight seasons; first team all-pro selections by AP, Newspaper Enterprises Assoc, College and Pro Football Newsweekly, The Sporting News, Sports Illustrated and NFL Films 1985; named first team All-NFC by UPI; led NFC with 11 TD receptions 1985; honored in 1985 with a special night "The Pride of Hamlet-The Fantastic Four"; mem Pro Bowl teams 1986,87. **BUSINESS ADDRESS:** Philadelphia Eagles, Veterans Stadium, Broad St & Pattison Ave, Philadelphia, PA 19148.

QUICK, R. EDWARD
Travel agent. **PERSONAL:** Born Jan 22, 1927, Youngstown, OH; married Constance D; children: Cheryl Quick Pope, Renee C. **EDUCATION:** OH State Univ, 1944-45, 1947-49; Howard Univ, LLB 1952. **CAREER:** Rural Electrification Adm US Dept of Agriculture, special asst to administrator 1968-69; Federal Hwy Admin US Dept of Transportation, chief contract compliance Div 1969-76, acting deputy dir 1976-77, dir office of civil rights 1977-86; pres El Dorado Travel Service, Washington, DC, 1982-. **ORGANIZATIONS:** Mem Natl Assn of Human Rights Workers 1970-; bd of dirs El Dorado Travel Service 1982-; mem MD Assoc of Affirmative Action Officers 1984-; mem NAACP, Urban League. **HONORS/ACHIEVEMENTS:** Administrator's Special Achievement Awd Federal Hwy Admin 1977; Sr Executive Service Bonus Awd Federal Hwy Admin 1980; Vice President Washington Sub Chapter Amer Society of Travel Agents. **MILITARY SERVICE:** USAF sgt 18 months. **BUSINESS ADDRESS:** President, El Dorado Travel Service, 1444 Eye St NW, Washington, DC 20005.

QUIGLESS, MILTON DOUGLAS, JR.
General surgeon. **PERSONAL:** Born Oct 15, 1945, Durham, NC; son of Milton Douglas Quigless, Sr and Helen Gordon Quigless; married Anita Regina LeVeaux; children: Leslie, Matthew, Christine, Ashley, Maryanna. **EDUCATION:** Morehouse College, BS 1970; Meharry Medical Coll, MD 1971. **CAREER:** Meharry Medical Coll, instructor in surgery 1976-77; UNC Chapel Hill, clinical assoc prof of surgery 1986-; Wake County Med Ctr, president/medical staff. **ORGANIZATIONS:** St Augustine College Bd 1985-88. **HONORS/ACHIEVEMENTS:** Doctor of the Year Old North State Medical Soc 1984. **HOME ADDRESS:** 3320 Marie Dr, Raleigh, NC 27604. **BUSINESS ADDRESS:** President/Medical Staff, Wake County Medical Center, 100 Sunnybrook Rd, PO Box 14445, Raleigh, NC 27620.

QUINCY, RONALD LEE
Government official. **PERSONAL:** Born Sep 08, 1950, Detroit, MI. **EDUCATION:** Univ of Detroit, BA, MA; Michigan State Univ, PhD; John F Kennedy Sch of Govt Harvard Univ, completed Senior Managers in Govt Program. **CAREER:** State of MI Contractual Program for Minority and Woman-Owned Businesses, chief administrator; Michigan Equal Employment Opp Council, exec dir; Office of Human Resource Policy and Spec Projects, director; former Governor William G Milliken, spec asst; US State Dept, foreign affairs advisor; US Dept Housing andUrban Develop, special asst to the secty; Michigan Dept of Civil Rights, director. **ORGANIZATIONS:** Bd mem MI State Univ Natl Criminal Justice Alumni Assn; past co-chair of the Governor's 1980 US Census Special Population Comm; mem State Criminal Justice Comm. **HONORS/ACHIEVEMENTS:** Who's Who in the Midwest 1983-; White House Fellowship 1985-86; Outstanding Young American Awd 1986; Who's Who in the World 1988. **BUSINESS ADDRESS:** Dir, Michigan Dept of Civil Rights, 309 N Washington Square, Room #103, Lansing, MI 48913.

QUINN, ALFRED THOMAS
Educational administrator. **PERSONAL:** Born Sep 21, 1922, Omaha, NE; married Sylvia Price. **EDUCATION:** Univ of CA Los Angeles, BA 1950, MEd 1956, EdD 1964. **CAREER:** USAF, 1942-45; Vet Admin, emp relation off 1946-48; Santa Monica Sch Dist, teacher 1951-63; Santa Monica Coll, prof 1963-73. **ORGANIZATIONS:** Mem Phi Delta Kappa Ed UCLA 1955; mem Santa Monica Parks Recreation Comm 1958-63; mem Santa Monica Charter Review Comm 1962; mem Santa Monica Housing Comm 1980-84; bd of dirs Natl Conf of Christians & Jews; mem NAACP; mem Rotary Intl. **HONORS/ACHIEVEMENTS:** Outstanding teacher awd Santa Monica Sch Dist 1956; awd League United Latin Amer Citizens 1970; NCCJ Brotherhood awd 1973; publications "Schools in Racial Transition" 1964, "Schools in the Later 20th Century" 1980. **MILITARY SERVICE:** USAF psnl sgt/major 3 yrs. **BUSINESS ADDRESS:** Dean of Student Services, Santa Monica College, 1900 Pico Blvd, Santa Monica, CA 90405.

QUINN, DIANE C.
Manager. **PERSONAL:** Born May 09, 1942, Chicago, IL; children: Caren Clift. **CAREER:** Illinois Bell Telephone Co, sales mgr 1974-79; C&P Telephone Co, industry mgr 1978-79; AT&T, market mgr 1979-83, mgr mgmt employment 1983-84, mgr univrelations 1984-87. **ORGANIZATIONS:** AT&T rep Natl Urban League 1972-; lecturer Natl Alliance of Business 1972-74; consultant Wilberforce Univ 1979; consultant R Burton & Co Inc 1986; lecturer College Bd Conference on Industrial Partnerships 1986. **HONORS/ACHIEVEMENTS:** Black Achiever YMCA 1973, 74; AT&T Loaned Executive Univ of MD 1987. **HOME ADDRESS:** 1708 15th St NW, Washington, DC 20009. **BUSINESS ADDRESS:** Executive Vice President, Giga Tek International Inc, 4501 E Forbes Blvd, Lanham, MD 20706.

QUINN, LONGWORTH D., JR.
Judge. **PERSONAL:** Born Oct 05, 1943, Chicago, IL; son of Lungworth M Quinn and Dorothy Dodd Quinn. **EDUCATION:** Alma Coll, BA Biol 1963; Wayne State Univ Law School, JD 1973. **CAREER:** Detroit Pub Schools, tchr 1966-67; City of Detroit Commn on Comm Relations, 1967-74; US Congr Asst, 1974-78; Private Practice, attorney 1974-79; Atty Gen, spec asst 1974-79; City of Detroit Law Dept, Atty 1979-82; 36th Dist Ct, magistrate 1982-83, judge, 1983-. **ORGANIZATIONS:** Mem MI Bar Assoc 1974, Wolverine Bar Assoc 1974; mem Detroit Bar Assn; former mem New Detroit Bd of Dir; former mem Detroit Bd of Edn; former mem Region 1 Detroit Bd of Edn; former mem Detroit Human Rights Commn; Alpha Phi Alpha Frat. **HONORS/ACHIEVEMENTS:** Many Comm Serv and Professional Awards. **HOME ADDRESS:** 2033 Atkinson, Detroit, MI 48206. **BUSINESS ADDRESS:** District Court Judge, 36th Judicial Dist, 1441 St Antoine, Detroit, MI 48226.

QUINTON, BARBARA A.
Educator. **PERSONAL:** Born Jul 01, 1941, Sharptown, MD; children: Keith F Nichols, Kyle B Nichols. **EDUCATION:** Morgan State Univ, BS 1963; Meharry Medical Coll, MD 1967. **CAREER:** Hubbard Hosp, intern 1967-68; St Louis Children's Hosp, resident 1968-69, fellow 1969-71; Howard Univ, fellow 1971-74, asst prof 1974-76, assoc prof 1976-. **ORGANIZATIONS:** Church rep NAACP 1985-. **HONORS/ACHIEVEMENTS:** Outstanding Teacher Howard Univ 1975,78; Honorary Mem Intern/Resident Assoc Howard Univ 1983. **BUSINESS ADDRESS:** Assoc Professor of Pediatrics, Howard University, 2041 Georgia Ave NW, Washington, DC 20059.

QUINTYNE, IRWIN SINCLAIR
Director. **PERSONAL:** Born Jul 25, 1926, NYC; married Delores; children: 8 Children. **EDUCATION:** Stony BrookUniv NY,. **CAREER:** Women's wear cutter, patternmaker, marker, prod mgr 1949-69; Suffolk County Econ Oppor Counc, vocational couns 1969-70; Wyandanch Coll Cntr, part-time faculty 1971-72; Stony Brook Coll, dir field serv EEO 1970-; Congress of Racial Equality Suffolk Cnty, dir 1966-; Suffolk Cnty Core, co-founder 1964, dir1967-; Nassau/Suffolk Minority Coalition, chmn 1971; Alba-Neck Halfway H3use Drug Prog, bd chmn 1970-. **ORGANIZATIONS:** Bd mem Alliance of Minority Group 1970-; co-founder bd mem Black Students Assistance Fund Stony BrookUniv 1972-; mem Central LI Br NAACP; 100 Black Men Nassau/Suffolk Counties 1975. **HONORS/ACHIEVEMENTS:** Num honors, awds, spl achvmnts. **MILITARY SERVICE:** USN 1944-46. **BUSINESS ADDRESS:** State Univ NY, Stony Brook, NY.

QUIVERS, ERIC STANLEY
Physician. **PERSONAL:** Born Oct 27, 1955, Winston-Salem, NC; married Mara Williams; children: Micah Stanley. **EDUCATION:** Morehouse Coll, BS (Magna Cum Laude) 1979; Howard Univ Coll of Medicine, MD 1983. **CAREER:** Howard Univ Hosp Dist of Columbia, pediatric resident 1983-86; Park West Medical Center, staff pediatrician, 1986-. **ORGANIZATIONS:** Mem Natl Medical Assoc 1983-; junior fellow Amer Acad of Pediatrics 1986-; provisional medical staff Sinai Hospital 1986-. **HONORS/ACHIEVEMENTS:** Phi Beta Kappa 1977; Beta Kappa Chi 1977; Certificate of Appreciation Howard Univ Coll of Med SGA 1983; Roland B Scott Departmental Awd in Pediatrics 1983; publication "Hepatic Cyst Associated with Ventricular Peritoneal Shunt in a Child with Brain Tumor," w/SR Rana, TB Haddy Child's Nervous System 1985. **HOME ADDRESS:** 7567 Alaska Ave NW, Washington, DC 20012. **BUSINESS ADDRESS:** Staff Pediatrician, Park West Medical Center, 3319 W Belvedere Ave, Baltimore, MD 21215.

QUIVERS, WILLIAM WYATT, SR.
Physician. **PERSONAL:** Born Sep 14, 1919, Phoebus, VA; son of Robert McK and Irma M Quivers; married Evelyn C Seace; children: William Jr, Eric, Celia. **EDUCATION:** Hampton Inst, BS 1942; Atlanta Univ, 1946-47; Meharry Medical Coll, MD 1953; Pediatric Cardiology Fellowship USPH grant at Univ Los Angeles 1962-63, 1964-65. **CAREER:** KB Reynolds Meml Hosp, internship and pediatric residency 1953-55; Meharry Medical Coll Hubbard Hosp, pediatric resident 1959-63; Meharry Medical Coll, assoc prof pediatrics 1965-68, med dir child & youth project 1967-68; Reynolds Memorial Hosp, dir of pediatrics 1968-72; Bowman-Gray Sch of med, assoc prof of ped 1968-72; Provident Hosp Inc, dir of ped 1972-85; Univ of MD Sch of Med, assoc prof of ped 1972-85; Liberty Medical Ctr, actg chief of pediatrics 1986-. **ORGANIZATIONS:** Fellow Amer Academy of Pediatrics, Natl Medical Assoc; diplomate Amer Bd of Pediatrics, Royal Soc of Health, Amer Heart Assoc, People to People Intl, Chinese Amer Scientific Soc, East Coast Ch Tuskegee Airmen; bd of dirs Homewood School and Baer School; mem Assoc of Black Cardiologists; mem Central MD Heart Assoc. **HONORS/ACHIEVEMENTS:** Certificate of Appreciation Essex Comm Coll and Baer Sch; Orchids from Emma's. **MILITARY SERVICE:** USAF 1st lt 1942-46. **HOME ADDRESS:** 6110 Benhurst Rd, Baltimore, MD 21209.

R

RAAB, MADELINE MURPHY
Business executive. **PERSONAL:** Born Jan 27, 1945, Wilmington, DE; married Dr Maurice F Rabb Jr; children: Maurice F III, Christopher. **EDUCATION:** Univ of MD, 1961-63; MD Inst Coll of Art, BFA 1966; IL Inst of Tech, MS 1975. **CAREER:** Tuesday Publ, asst dir of art & prod 1966-68; Myra Everett Design, vice pres bus mgr 1977-78; Corp Concierge, acct exec 1978-79; Rabb Studio & Gallery, artist 1978-83; Chicago Office of Fine Arts, exec dir 1983-. **ORGANIZATIONS:** Bd mem The Hyde Park Arts Ctr 1981-83, Univ of Chicago Women's Bd 1980-85, Afro-Amer Newspaper Co Baltimore MD 1981-84; adv Folk Art Exhibition Field Museum of Natl History 1984; treas US Urban Arts Fed 1984-86; adv Black Creativity Celebration Museum of Science & Industry 1985-86, Arts Culture & Entertainment Comm 1992 Chicago World's Fair 1985; bd mem Channel 20 WYCC-TV 1985-86, IL Arts Alliance 1986-88; co-chair Special Interest Areas Natl Assembly of Local Arts Agencies 1986-88; panelist Natl Assembly of Local Arts Agencies Convention Wash DC 1986; moderator IL Arts Alliance Annual Conf 1986; panelist Local Arts Agencies IL Arts Council; panelist Natl Assembly of Local Arts Agencies Annual Conv Portladn OR 1987; panelist Local Programs Natl Endowment for the Arts 1987-88. **HONORS/ACHIEVEMENTS:** Paintings drawings & prints "The Chicago Exchange Group" Chicago State Univ Gallery 1981, "Emma Amos & Madeline Rabb" Jazzonia Gallery Detroit MI 1983, "A Portfolio of Prints by Madeline Murphy Rabb" Fells Point Gallery Baltimore MD 1987; publ, "Removing Cultural Viaducts, Initiative for Traditionally Underserved Audiences" Connections Quarterly 1986, "Chicago, An Artistic Renaissance Under Way" Amer Visions Afro-Amer Art 1986; permanent collections, Standard Oil Co Chicago IL, Johnson Publish Co Chicago IL, IL Inst of Tech, Inst of Design Chicago IL, The Chicago Community Health Ctr Chicago IL, The Evans-Tibbs CollectionWash DC. **BUSINESS ADDRESS:** Executive Dir, Chicago Office of Fine Arts, 78 E Washington, 2nd Floor, Chicago, IL 60602.

RABB, MAURICE F.
Ophthalmologist. **EDUCATION:** Studied premedicine at Indiana University, Bloomington IN; University of Louisville, Louisville KY, received bachelor's degree, received medical degree, 1958; postgraduate study at Kings County Hospital, Brooklyn NY, and Eye and Ear Infirmary, University of Illinois. **CAREER:** Operated private medical practice, Chicago IL, beginning 1965; staff member, Illinois Central Hospital, beginning 1965; medical director, Illinois Eye Bank, beginning 1969; Mercy Hospital, Chicago, currently chief of ophthalmology; also professor of ophthalmology, University of Illinois. **ORGANIZATIONS:** President beginning 1975, Chicago Ophthalmological Society. **HONORS/ACHIEVEMENTS:** Honorary degree, University of Louisville, 1983; author of five books. **BUSINESS ADDRESS:** 680 N Lake Shore Dr, Chicago, IL 60611. *

RABY, CLYDE T.
Government official. **PERSONAL:** Born Sep 14, 1934, Baton Rouge, LA; married Elaine Miller; children: Dwight Tillman, Iris R Locure, Wayne A, Eric C, Trudi E. **EDUCATION:** Southern Univ, BS 1960; Tuskegee Inst, DVM 1964. **CAREER:** Southern Univ, asst prof 1964-70; Plant Road & Port Allen Animal Hosps, owner 1970-; LA Dept of Agriculture, asst commissioner 1980-. **ORGANIZATIONS:** Mem AVMA 1963-; mem Beta Beta Beta Siol Soc 1970-; chmn LA Veterinary Med Assoc 1982; bd of dirs Reddy Cultural Ctr 1985. **HONORS/ACHIEVEMENTS:** Veterinarian of the Year LA Vet Med Assoc 1982; Bigger and Better Business Awd Phi Beta Sigma Frat 1986; article published Journal of Dairy Science, Journal of Animal Science, Amer Journal of Vet Research. **MILITARY SERVICE:** USAF airman 2st class 1954-57. **HOME ADDRESS:** 2737 Brandywine Dr, Baton Rouge, LA 70808. **BUSINESS ADDRESS:** Assistant Commissioner, LA Dept of Agricultura, PO Box 1951, Baton Rouge, LA 70821.

RACKLEY, LURMA M.
Reporter. **PERSONAL:** Born Apr 24, 1949, Orangeburg, SC; children: Rumal. **EDUCATION:** Clark Coll, BA honors; ColumbiaUniv Sch of Journalism, spec masters deg 1970. **CAREER:** Wash Star News, reporter 1970; THE PLACE WRC-TV Wash DC, script writer 1972-; free-lance writer; O'Field Dukes Assoc, writer, editer Office of Planning; District of Columbia Gov, deptuy press sec to mayor; Office of Communications Wash DC Govt, dep dir. **ORGANIZATIONS:** Mem Communications Assoc; mem Alpha Kappa Alpha; mem DC Clark Coll Club; mem Capital Press Club. **HONORS/ACHIEVEMENTS:** Listed in Outstanding Young Woman of Amer 1974; Commitment to Excellent Awd Dep Mayor for Economic Devel 1985.

RADCLIFFE, AUBREY
Educator. **PERSONAL:** Born Aug 27, 1941, NY, NY; married Katherine; children: Rick, Deborah. **EDUCATION:** Mich State Univ, BA 1968, MA 1972, PhD 1975. **CAREER:** White Plaines Public School, counselor 1962-63; Lansing Public School, counselor 1966-74; Univ of MI, prof 1974-75. **ORGANIZATIONS:** Mem assn of Governing Bds; Assn of Admin & Higher Ed; Amer Guidance & Personnel Assn; program dir Am Legion Boys' State; Lansing Jaycees; Phi Delta Kappa; Greater Lansing Urban League; former young rep natl committman, MI 1966; former state dir & adv MI Teenage Rep 1967; former ad hoc rep chmn Human Relations 1968; mem MI Veteran Trust Fund 1980; mem E Lansing Lions' Club 1980; v comdr E Lansing Amer Legion Post 205 1980; bd of trustees MI State Univ 1980; rep candidate US Congress 1980. **HONORS/ACHIEVEMENTS:** Outstanding Teacher of the Year Award 1965; MI Republican's Youth Award 1966; Outstanding Young Man in Amer 1973. **BUSINESS ADDRESS:** PO Box 806, East Lansing, MI 48823.

RADDEN, THELMA GIBSON
Nurse, association executive. **PERSONAL:** Born Feb 18, 1913, Oakland, CA; widowed. **EDUCATION:** BA nursing educ 1952; Wayne State Coll of Nursing, 1952; HS & KC Gen Hosp Sch of Nursing, 1933; UC Hosp, post grad 1934. **CAREER:** Sacramento Area Long Term Care Ombudsmen Inc Advocacy Orgn, coor; Continuing Patient Care Met Hosp Detroit, coor; Norfolk Com Hosp, adminstr 1936-40; Trinity Hosp Detroit, supr & dir of nurses 1940; Homer G Phillips Hosp St Louis, surgical supr instr surical nursing; Grace Hosp Detroit, surgical wards 1942; Detroit Chap ARC, asst dir nursing serv 1955-; Detroit Dist MI State Nurses Assn, past prog chmn. **ORGANIZATIONS:** Detroit League for Nursing; mem Gerontological Sect Detroit Dist MI State Nurses Assn past pres Urban League Guild; pres Detroit Br AAUW; mem Detroit Chap KC Hosp Alumni Assn; mem Delta Sigma Theta; Chi Eta Phi; Detroit Intl Inst; vice pres Citizens for Better Care; past Matron Dorician Chap # 32 OES-PHA & Daus of Isis Marracci Ct; mem E Bay CA Negro Hist Soc. **BUSINESS ADDRESS:** Met Hosp, 1800 Tuxedo St, Detroit, MI.

RAGLAND, MICHAEL STEVEN
Physician obstetrics/gynecology. **PERSONAL:** Born Aug 23, 1958, Brooklyn, NY; son of Fountain W Ragland and Violet B Ragland; married Laurena Mooré, Aug 10, 1985. **EDUCATION:** Fisk Univ, BS 1980; Meharry Medical Coll, MD 1984. **CAREER:** Physician obstetrics/gynecology. **ORGANIZATIONS:** Mem Student Natl Medical Assoc 1980-84, Amer Medical Assoc 1980-; junior fellow Amer Coll of Obstetrics/Gynecology 1986-; Bay Area Medical Society 1988. **HONORS/ACHIEVEMENTS:** Beta Kappa Chi Natl Scientific Honor Society; Alpha Omega Alpha Honor Medical Soc. **HOME ADDRESS:** 6600 Cedarwood Ct, Mobile, AL 36616.

RAGLAND, SHERMAN LEON, II
Real estate developer. **PERSONAL:** Born Jul 04, 1962, Stuttgart, Federal Republic of Germany;son of Lt Col Sherman L Ragland and G Anita Atkinson Ragland; married Chevelle Loreen Calloway, Jun 15, 1986. **EDUCATION:** Towson State Univ, Towson MD, BS Mass Communications, 1984; The Wharton School of the Univ of Pennsylvania, MBA Finance/Real Estate. **CAREER:** Xerox Realty Corp, Stamford CT, financial analyst, 1986-87, Leesburg VA, assoc devel dir, 1987-88; The Oliver Carr Co, Washington DC, devel mgr, 1988-. **ORGANIZATIONS:** Pres, Natl Assn of Black Real Estate Professionals, 1988-; bd of dir, Christmas in April USA, 1988-, Christmas in April Alexandria, 1988-; bd of advisors (alumni), Wharton Real Estate Center, 1988-; bd of dir, Towson State Univ Alumni Assn, 1989; commr, Alexandria Human Rights Commn, 1989, Alexandria Equal Opportunities Commn, 1989; pres, The Wharton Alumni Club of Washington, 1989-. **HONORS/ACHIEVEMENTS:** Johnson & Johnson Leadership Award, Johnson & Johnson, 1984; Wharton Public Policy Fellow, The Wharton School, 1985; Black Alumni of the Year, Towson State Univ, 1989; author of 2 publications, Motivation, 1985, and Lease vs Purchase of Real Estate, 1989. **BUSINESS ADDRESS:** Development Manager, The Oliver Carr Company, 1700 Pennsylvania Ave NW, Washington, DC 20006.

RAGLAND, WYLHEME HAROLD
Clergyman. **PERSONAL:** Born Dec 19, 1946, Anniston, AL; son of Howard Ragland and Viola Pearson Ragland; married Donna Theresa Barker; children: Seth H III. **EDUCATION:** Jacksonville State Univ, BA 1972, attended grad school 1972-73; Emory Univ, MDiv

(Cum Laude) 1975; Vanderbilt Univ, DMin 1978. **CAREER:** Center Grove United Methodist Church, pastor 1975-77; King's Memorial United Methodist Church, sr pastor 1977-; North AL Regional Hospital, dir of religious service and coordinator-The Employee Assistance Program 1984-. **ORGANIZATIONS:** Charter mem The Employee Assistance Soc of North Amer 1985; mem Phi Alpha Theta, Pi Gamma Mu, Sigma Tau Delta, The North AL Study Club, The Morgan County Historical Soc, The Mental Health Assn of Morgan Co; chairperson The Rights Protection Advocacy Committee 1987-89; mem The Needs Assessment Committee, The Decatur City Bd of Educ, The Advisory Committee The Albany Clinic 1989. **HONORS/ACHIEVEMENTS:** Outstanding Young Men of Amer 1984; "Pierce Pettis, Guitar Man" Speaking Out newspaper Decatur AL 1984. **MILITARY SERVICE:** USNR communication yeoman 3rd class 3 yrs; Highest Honor and 1st in Class CYN School. **HOME ADDRESS:** 511 Walnut St NE, Decatur, AL 35601. **BUSINESS ADDRESS:** Dir of Religious Studies, North AL Regional Hospital, PO Box 2221, Decatur, AL 35602.

RAGSDALE, CHARLES LEA CHESTER
Manager. **PERSONAL:** Born Aug 07, 1929, Coweta, OK; married Joyce E Phillips; children: Theresa (Chappelle), Sylvia, Angela, Tammy, Tamara. **EDUCATION:** Langston U, BS; OK St U, grad studies. **CAREER:** Wagoner Sch, tchr July 1949, Sept 1950, 1951-55; Beggs Sch, tchr 1955-56; Mcdonnell Douglas Tulsa, OK, sr employ repr 1956-, pres (currently $5 million in asset); Tulsa Urban Leag Found, pres; Mcdonnell Douglas Tulsa Man Club, past 1st vP; Ex Comm So Cal Pro Eng Assn, past chmn; Tulsa Urban League, past pres & vp. **ORGANIZATIONS:** Mem Tulsa Pub Sch Bd of Edn; past chmn CPAC; mem Tulsa Co Sch & Tulsa Met CC Speaker's Bureau; Tulsa Econ Oppor Task Force Bd Dir; Mcdonnel Douglas Coor Youth Motivation Prog mem Christ Emple Christian Meth Epis Ch; past supt ch Sch; chmn steward bd. **HONORS/ACHIEVEMENTS:** Plaque from Mcdonnell Douglas for Contr of Comm Rel. **BUSINESS ADDRESS:** Mc Donnell Douglas Tulsa, 2000 N Memorial Dr, Tulsa, OK 74115.

RAGSDALE, LINCOLN JOHNSON
Business executive. **PERSONAL:** Born Jul 27, 1926, Muskogee, OK; married Eleanor Dickey; children: Elizabeth, Gwendolyn Madrid, Lincoln J III, Emily. **EDUCATION:** Tuskegee Inst, Instrument and Commercial Flying diploma; Lamson Business Coll Phoenix, Acctg and Mgmt diploma/certificate; CA Coll of Mortuary Science, diploma (Magna Cum Laude); Phoenix Coll, AA (w/Distinction); AZ State Univ, BS (w/Distinction). **CAREER:** Home Realty and Insurance Agency; partner; Natl Conf of Christians and Jews, mem bd of dirs 1957-; Natl Business League Washington DC, bd of dirs; The AZ Club, bd of dirs; Rust Coll, bd of trustees; Sun State Savings and Loan Assoc, bd of dirs; Universal Memorial Ctr, Universal Sunset Chapel, chmn of bd of dirs; Intl Investment Co, owner/pres/chmn of the bd of dirs; Valley Life & Casualty Ins, pres/chmn bd of dirs. **ORGANIZATIONS:** Founder Intl Investment Co, Intl Construction Co, Valley Life and Casualty Insurance Group; cofounder Vesco Land Co, Home Security Finance Corp; licensed funeral dir and embalmer for State of AZ; licensed embalmer for State of OK; licensed real estate broker for the State of AZ; licensed general insurance agent for the State of AZ; licensed building contractor for the State of AZ; past sec & mem of the bd of dirs Southwest Savings & Loan Assoc; mem Natl Urban League Bd of Trustees 1977-82; mem Memorial Hosp Foundation Bd of Trustees 1978-85; mem Iota Sigma Alpha Honor Soc, Omega Psi Phi Frat; mem American Legion Post #41, 33rd Degree Mason Masonic Lodge, Shriners; grand boule Sigma Pi Phi Frat. **MILITARY SERVICE:** AUS Air Corps 2nd Lt, fighter pilot 1944-46; Honorable Discharge. **BUSINESS ADDRESS:** Chairman of the Board, Valley Life & Casualty Ins, 1100 E Jefferson, Phoenix, AZ 85034.

RAGSDALE, PAUL B.
Government official. **PERSONAL:** Born Jan 14, 1945, Jacksonville, TX. **EDUCATION:** Univ TX, BA. **CAREER:** State rep 1972-; chf planner Dallas 1968-72. **ORGANIZATIONS:** Bd mem Black C of C; numerous others. **HONORS/ACHIEVEMENTS:** Numerous awards. **BUSINESS ADDRESS:** 1209 E Red Bird Ln, Dallas, TX 75241.

RAHMAN, MAHDI ABDUL See HAZZARD, WALT

RAIFORD, ROGER LEE
Orthopedic surgeon. **PERSONAL:** Born Nov 01, 1942, Greensboro, NC; married Pamela Gladden; children: Gregory, Brian. **EDUCATION:** Howard Univ, BS 1964; Howard Medical School, MD 1968. **CAREER:** Howard Univ, asst prof orthopedic surgery. **ORGANIZATIONS:** Mem Amer Bd of Orthopedic Surgery, Amer Acad of Orthopedic Surgery, DC Medical Soc. **BUSINESS ADDRESS:** Asst Prof Orthopedic Surgery, Howard University, 8601 Martin Luther King Hwy, Lanham, MD 20706.

RAINBOW-EARHART, KATHRYN ADELINE
Retired psychiatrist. **PERSONAL:** Born Mar 21, 1921, Wheeling, WV; daughter of John Henry and Addaline Holly Rainbow; married William; children: Frederic Jr, Holly. **EDUCATION:** Ft Valley State Coll, BS 1942; Meharry Med Coll, MD 1948; Menninger Sch of Psychiatry, 1965. **CAREER:** Rocky Mount, private pediatric practice 1952-54; Lakin State Hosp, staff physician 1954-59, clinical dir 1959-60, supt 1960-62; Topeka State Hosp, staff psychiatrist 1965-79; Shawnee Comm Mental Health Center Inc, staff psychiatrist 1979-81; Kansas Reception and Diagnostic Center, staff psychiatrist 1981-83. **ORGANIZATIONS:** Mem Shawnee County Med Soc; past pres WV Med Soc; KS Med Soc; Amer Med Assn; Med Women's Assn; Am Psychiatric Assn; Black Psychiatrists of Amer; Natl Med Assn; Courtest Staff of Stormont-Vail & St Francis Hosps; mem Alpha Kappa Alpha Sor; past pres Topeka Chap Links, Inc; past pres Quota Intl of Topeka; Life mem NAACP; St John AME Church; bd of dir The Villages; Natl Med Fellowships, Inc Pediatric Fellowship 1950-52; NIMH Fellowship 1962-65; board of directors Topeka Assn for Retarded Citizens 1972-78, 1983; Honorary Member of Delta Kappa Gamma Society International. **HONORS/ACHIEVEMENTS:** 25 year service Humanity Plaque Meharry Med Coll. **HOME ADDRESS:** 2916 Kentucky Ave, Topeka, KS 66605.

RAINE, CHARLES HERBERT, III
Physician. **PERSONAL:** Born Oct 31, 1937, Selma, AL; married Martha A Lewis; children: Charles IV, Christopher, Shani. **EDUCATION:** Attended, Miles Memorial Coll 1953-55, TN A&I State Univ 1955-57; Meharry Medical Coll, MD 1961. **CAREER:** GW Hubbard Hosp, internship 1961-62, resident 1962-65; Smith Clinic Glasgow MT, physician/partner 1970-72; Kurten Medical Group Racine, physician/partner 1972-. **ORGANIZATIONS:** Human subjects rsch committeeman Univ of WI Parkside 1983-; assoc clinical prof of allied health Univ of WI Parkside 1984-; medical dir Area 19 Wisconsin Div Amer Cancer Soc 1985-; editorial bd mem State Medical Soc of WI Medical Journal 1985; chmn dept of medicine St Mary's Medical Ctr 1986-87. **HONORS/ACHIEVEMENTS:** Published contemporary health journal (a health newsletter) 1983-86. **MILITARY SERVICE:** USAF lt col 1965-70. **BUSINESS ADDRESS:** Kurten Medical Group, 2405 Northwestern Ave, Racine, WI 53404.

RAINES, COLDEN DOUGLAS
Dentist. **PERSONAL:** Born Oct 17, 1915, Apex, NC; married Frances Johnson; children: Tajuana Raines Turner, Colden Jr, Romley H. **EDUCATION:** Shaw Univ, BS 1940; Howard Univ, DDS 1946. **CAREER:** Mary C Leonie Guggenheim Dental Clinic, intern 1948. **ORGANIZATIONS:** Mem Bergen Co Dental Soc; Amer Dental Assn; Natl Dental Assn; Essex Co Dental Soc; Commonwelath Dental Assn; past pres Dental Sect Acad of Med; Acad of Gen Dentristry; Soc of Oral Physiology & Occlusion; trustee Acad of Med of NJ; pres Howard Univ Dental Alumni 1977; past pres Bergen Passaic Howard Univ Alumni Club; Alpha Phi Alpha Frat; Chi Delta Mu Frat; fellow Acad of Med NJ. **HONORS/ACHIEVEMENTS:** Alumni Award Howard Univ Coll of Dentistry 1975; Fellow Acad of Gen Dentistry 1979; Fellow Amer Coll of Dentists 1979; Fellow Amer Soc for Advancement of Anesthesia in Dentistry 1982; Howard Univ Alumni Achievement Awd 1984. **MILITARY SERVICE:** AUS Maj 1957. **BUSINESS ADDRESS:** 603 Clinton Ave, Newark, NJ 07108.

RAINES, TIM
Professional athlete. **PERSONAL:** Born Sep 16, 1959, Sanford, FL; married Virginia. **EDUCATION:** Seminole HS Sanford, FL. **CAREER:** Montreal Expos, outfielder 1980-. **ORGANIZATIONS:** Works with youngsters at baseball camps during off-season. **HONORS/ACHIEVEMENTS:** Led the Natl League in stolen bases with 75; led the league in steals each of his first four seasons; all-time leader in stolen base percentage; first winner of the Player's Performance Trophy donated by Imperial Tobacco to the player with the highest Total Average on the team; 10th in NL MVP vote; NL Player-of-the-Week for period ending Aug 19th; Expos' Player-of-the-Month for August; voted Rookie-Player-of-the-Year in 1981 by Sporting News; runner up to Fernando Valenzuela in Rookie-of-the-Year voting; Expos' April Player-of-the-Month in 1981; named co-Expos' Player-of-the-Year with Andre Dawson in 1983; The Sporting News Gold Shoe Awd 1984; named outfielder on The Sporting News Natl League All-Star Team 1983,86; named outfielder on The Sporting News Natl League Silver Slugger team 1986; mem All Star Team 1981-86. **BUSINESS ADDRESS:** Montreal Expos, P O Box 500, Station M, Montreal, Quebec, Canada H1V 3P2.

RAINES, WALTER THE BARON (SIR WALTER)
Choreographer. **PERSONAL:** Born Aug 16, 1940, Braddock, PA. **EDUCATION:** Carnegie-Mellon Univ, 1958-59; School of Amer Ballet, 1959-63. **CAREER:** Alvin Ailey American Dance Center, scholarship director, choreographer; Dance Theatre of Harlem, res choreographer/faculty; The Ice Break Royal Opera London, choreographed & staged; Peter & The Wolf, Haiku, After Corinth, Dance Theatre of Harlem, choreographed; TN Williams, Lady of the Larkspur Lorion, Birmingham, dirested; Syrinx, Chamber Ballet & Summerset, Panamanian Ballet, choreographed; New York City Ballet Munich Opera Ballet, guest artist; Arthur Mithcells Ballets, created leading male roles. **ORGANIZATIONS:** Mem Stuttgart Ballet 1963-67; choreographed opera Carmen, Regansburg Opera; in fashion field staged the Von Furstenberg Collection; designed costumes for Ballet, Ipera, Drama & Burlesque; served as dancing palnelist NY State council on the Arts For Am Jewish Congress created Choreo styles with Harriett Pitt; artist in residence for Co of City of NY; taught & lectured for 1st congress of Black & Dance in Am; lectured at State U; discussed music of Sir Michael Tippett & genius of Arthur Mitchell, BBC London; student of Japanese Philosophy; 1st black to choreograph for Royal Opera 1977; ballet "After Corinth" included in Balanchine's Complete Stories of the Great Ballets. **HONORS/ACHIEVEMENTS:** 1st black to teach classic ballet for AL Dance Conf 1976; 1st black to becom permanent mem of Suttgart Ballet 1963-67. **BUSINESS ADDRESS:** Alvin Ailey American Dance Cnt, 1515 Broadway-Arcade Level, New York, NY 10036.

RAINES, WILLIAM C.
Attorney. **PERSONAL:** Born Nov 15, 1909, Apex, NC; married Katherine Hobson; children: William C Jr, Earle. **EDUCATION:** Shaw U, AB 1939; Fordham Law Sch, JD 1946; NY U, LlM 1947; Shaw U, hon LlD; Southeastern U. **CAREER:** Shaw Coll, pres 1965; Prv Prac, atty; Carver Fed Savs Bank, bd dirs 1947-65; Shaw U, trustee bd 1965-; Shaw Coll, 1965-; instrum in establ black banks throughout US 1950-. **ORGANIZATIONS:** Mem Elks Lodge; 33 deg Mason; life mem NAACP; mem Alpha Phi Alpha Frat chmn bd dirs Assn of Trade & Commerce 1947-50; vP & bd mem Bergen Co UrbanLeague 1956-58; pres ShawUniv Alumni Assn NY Chap 1949-52; pres Gen Alumni Assn of ShawUniv 1952-54. **HONORS/ACHIEVEMENTS:** Unofficial mayor Citizens of Harlem; leading citizen of Harlem Mil. **MILITARY SERVICE:** Serv pilot WW II.

RAINEY, BESSYE COLEMAN
Educator. **PERSONAL:** Born Jul 15, 1929, Boydton, VA; daughter of John W Coleman and Rosa Jones Coleman; married Bob; children: Martin, Karl. **EDUCATION:** Saint Paul's Coll, BS 1962; Union Coll, MS 1965; Univ of VA, EdD 1977. **CAREER:** East End High School, Sci & Math teacher 1961-69; Saint Paul's Coll, dean of women 1969-74, acting chmn dept Sci & Math 1977-79, dir acad comp & inst rsch 1984-87, prof of education 1987-. **ORGANIZATIONS:** Adjunct prof Univ of VA 1982; consultant Brunswick Co Public Sch 1984-85, Chase City Elementary School 1986; mem Phi Delta Kappa. **HONORS/ACHIEVEMENTS:** Membership Awd Lychnos Soc of Univ of VA 1976; Natl Science Found Fellowship. **BUSINESS ADDRESS:** St Paul's College, Professor of Education, 406 Windsor Ave, Lawrenceville, VA 23868.

RAINEY, SYLVIA VALENTINE
Marketing communications consultant. **PERSONAL:** Born in Chicago, IL; children: Meredith Terzol. **EDUCATION:** Univ of IL Champ Urbana, BA 1967;Univ of IL Circle Campus, MBA Uncompleted. **CAREER:** Compton Adv Agy, cpywtr 1973-75; Am Hosp Sply Corp, mgr of mktg comm 1975; Nalco Chl Co, dir of mktg comm 1978-84. **ORGANIZATIONS:** Consult AT & T Infor Syst 1984-; consult William A Robinson Mktg 1984-; consult Paul Simon for Str Agency Camp 1984; Alpha Kappa Alpha Sorority; pres of brd SJnrl Truth Child Care Ctr; Am Mktg Assoc. **HONORS/ACHIEVEMENTS:** Advertising

Awds; Outstndg Young Wmn of Am 1979; Who's Who in Black Am 1983. **BUSINESS ADDRESS:** Marketing Communications Consult, Sylvia V Rainey Consult Firm, 323 S Franklin Bldg, Ste R-202, Chicago, IL 60606.

RAINS, HORACE
Physician. **PERSONAL:** Born Jan 13, 1912, Atlanta, GA; married Frances Mary Mchie; children: Anthony, Kimberly. **EDUCATION:** Wilberforce U, BS 1937; OH State U, MA 1938; Meharry Med Coll, MD 1953. **CAREER:** LA Co Gen Hosp, intern 1953-54; Atlanta Life Ins Co, ins salesman 1938-40; Lincoln U, instr hlth & phys educ 1940; Wilberforce, OH, recreation dir natl youth admin 1941; Wilberforce U, asst prof, mil sci & tactics 1941-44; Long Beach, CA, prac of med 1954-. **ORGANIZATIONS:** Mem staff St Mary's Long Beach Hosp 1954-, bd dir 1971-; Long Beach Meml Hosp Med Cntr 1954-; Comm Hosp 1954-; Long Beach Hosp 1964; chmn Med Educ Sub-com CA Rsrch Med Educ Fund 1970-71; chmn Long Beach Human Relations Commn 1972-; mem Am Acad Gen Prac; Am Geriatrics Soc; TB & Respiratory Disease Assn CA bd dir 1966-, pres Long Beach chap 1964-65; chmn United Civil Rights Com 1963-65; bd dir Family Serv Long Beach 1966-; Fair Housing Found 1965-; WilberforceUniv Aluni Assn & pres So CA chap 1969-. **HONORS/ACHIEVEMENTS:** Recip Man of Yr Awd Bernard & Milton Sahl Post Am Legion 1965. **MILITARY SERVICE:** AUS 1944-45. **BUSINESS ADDRESS:** 1533 Alamitos Ave, Long Beach, CA 90813.

RAINSFORD, GRETA M.
Pediatrician. **PERSONAL:** Born Dec 28, 1936, New York, NY; daughter of Maurice and Gertrude; married Samuel K Anderson; children: 5. **EDUCATION:** AB 1958; MD 1962; Internship 1962-63; Pediatric Res 1963-65; Dipl Bd of Ped 1967. **CAREER:** Mercy Hosp, Assoc Attending Pediatrician 1965-; NCMC, Asst Attending Pediatrician 1965-; Sickle Cell Clinic, dir 1971-85; Planned Parenthood Council, med adv board 1971-; Roosevelt School Dist, school physician 1975-; Hempstead Sch Dist, school pediatrician 1975-77; Old Westbury Campus State Univ of NY, clinic phys 1976-; Private Practice, physician/pediatrician 1965-. **ORGANIZATIONS:** Comm for Handicapped Child 1971-73; Com for Comm Health & Ed 1971-; Nassau Pediatrician Soc Me Sch Bd Trustees since 1969 & pres 1971-74; bd dir Natl Conf of Christians & Jews 1975-78; bd dir Roosevelt Ment Health Ctr 1976-; NC Coalition for Fam Planning 1977-78; bd of trustees Hofstra Univ 1978-; chmn Comprehensive Planning Comm Nassau Co Youth Bd 1978-83; chmn steering comm Long Island Gate 1978-79; pres bd of dirs Long Island Gate 1979-81; SUNY Stony Brook Council 1981-; mem Nassau Co Med Soc; NY Med Soc. **HONORS/ACHIEVEMENTS:** Placque for Service to Sickle Cell Anemia 1972; Placque for Service to Youth & Mankind 1974; Commendation for Service to Youth Hempstead C of C 1974; Disting Serv Award HCTA 1974; Comm Serv Award Natl Assn of NBPWC Inc 1974; Comm Serv Award Black Hist Museum 1977; Med Serv Award LI Sickle Cell Proj 1977. **BUSINESS ADDRESS:** 312 Greenwich St, Hempstead, NY 11550.

RAKESTRAW, KYLE DAMON
Purchasing agent/manufacturing. **PERSONAL:** Born Apr 09, 1961, Dayton, OH; son of Delores Rakestraw. **EDUCATION:** Univ of Cincinnati, BSIM 1984; Xavier Univ Cincinnati, MBA 1988. **CAREER:** General Motors Corp, professional practice 1982-84, purchasing agent 1984-. **ORGANIZATIONS:** Mem Natl Black MBA Assoc 1987. **HONORS/ACHIEVEMENTS:** Voorheis Coll Scholarship Univ of Cincinnati 1979; Dorothy Gradison Memorial Scholarship Univ of Cincinnati 1983. **HOME ADDRESS:** 128 Shenandoah Trail, West Carrollton, OH 45449. **BUSINESS ADDRESS:** Purchasing Agent, Delco Moraine Div General Motors, 1420 Wisconsin Blvd, Dayton, OH 45401.

RALSTON, EDWARD J.
Director. **PERSONAL:** Born Jun 04, 1938, St Louis, MO. **EDUCATION:** Univ of Mo, BA 1973. **CAREER:** Malcolm Bliss Hosp St Louis Hosp, co-dir of drug prog 1974-, drug couns 1972-74; Archway House, dir legal dept 1971-72. **ORGANIZATIONS:** Mem Drug Abuse Dist Agencies; mem Drug & Sub Counc; mem Drug Abuse Coord Counc; mem Phi Thetta Kappa Forest Pk Comm Coll; consult Parole & Probation Bd on Drug Abuse Detection & Prevention.

RALSTON, ELRETA MELTON ALEXANDER
Judge. **PERSONAL:** Born Mar 21, 1919, Smithfield, NC; married John D (deceased); children: 1 Son. **EDUCATION:** A&T State U, BS 1937; Columbia Univ Sch of Law, JD 1945. **CAREER:** State of NC, judge, dist ct, gen ct of justice; Alexander Ralston, Pell & Speckhari, attorney. **ORGANIZATIONS:** Mem Am Bar Assn; former mem Am Judicature Soc Am Trial Lawyers Assn Nat Assn Conferee Eisenhower & Kennedy EEOC; mem Atty Gen Robt Morgan's Ad Hoc Com on Revision of Criminal Law of NC 1969; former mem Bd Gov's Sch; bd of mgmt Hayes-Taylor YMCA; adv bd Henry Wiseman Kendall Cntr; bd for Disadvntaged Students UNC-G; bd of Un Comm Serv of Greensboro; lectr to civic, religious, endl, bus, professional govt, frat, youth, sr cits orgns, groups & convens; appntd mem 1976 Atlatna Regional Panel pres Commn on White Hse Fellwhps 1975; hon mem Future Homemakers of Am 1958. **HONORS/ACHIEVEMENTS:** 1st Black woman elec judge in US & 2nd Blck elec in US 1968; only Rep elec; re-elec for 4-yr term 1972; ldg Tckt with more than 50,000 votes in Guilford Co; re-elec without oppos 1974; candidate without oppos 1980; widely acclaimed for rehab, innovative, meaningful Judicial Progs for youths & other offenders; recip recog plaque for Initiative Ldrship Wake Co Chap A&T Alumni Assn 1958; hon recog & penned 1971 Triad Counc GSA in hon of late father& mother who est 1st Negro GS Troup in Greensboro 1936; Centruy Club Awd serv to youth Hayes Taylor Br YMCA 1968; Dolly Madison Awd Contrib of woman Power to comm Greensboro C of C 1969; cit Law-Dedication schshp Bus & Professional Mens Club of High Point 1969; hon mem Delta Kappa Gamma Intl Soc of WomenEducators 1970; sel as most admired blck cit of Greens inducted as hon mem Guys & Dolls Inc Nat Family Orgn; Cherokee Counc BSA Cit Awd 1970; featured by Donald Dale Jackson in book Judges; featrd in many natl period & Newpprs such as Nat Observer Columbia Observer, Miami Herald, Ebony, including Wake Forest Jurist. **BUSINESS ADDRESS:** Attorney, Alexander Ralston, Pell &, 220 Commerce Pl, Greensboro, NC 27401.

RAMBO, BETTYE R.
Educator. **PERSONAL:** Born Sep 02, 1936, Jasper, CO; married Leon Taylor, Jan 01, 1980; children: Valencia A, Sherryle B. **EDUCATION:** Stillman Coll, BA 1959; IN Univ, MA 1968; Postgrad study at Univs of IL, Laverne Coll, Moray House Coll Edinburgh Scotland 1974; Illinois State Univ, attending. **CAREER:** Educator various positions since 1959; Bd of Educ Springfield, educator 1968-. **ORGANIZATIONS:** Mem Jasper Co Tchrs Assoc 1959-68; life mem Natl Educ Assoc 1959-74; mem MS Teachers Assoc 1959-68, IL Educ Assoc 1968-74; human relations coord REgion #32; mem Hum Rel Comm for IL Educ Assoc 1974 & 75; local minority caucus; mem Zion Missionary Baptist Church; bd dir Stillman Coll Alumni Assoc; participant NDEA Inst for Culturally Disadvantaged Youth; delegate to NEA Conventions; mem NAACP, The Smithsonian Assoc, NRTA; sec PDK 1985-87; education chair ABWA 1986; worthy matron Order of Eastern Star (Estella Chapter) 1989; life mem Springfield Civic Garden Club 1988. **HONORS/ACHIEVEMENTS:** Airline Passengers Assoc; Teacher of Excellence, Iota Phi Lambda Sorority 1986; Education Award, NAACP (Springfield Branch) 1983; NCATE Evaluation Team Member 1982-87; Spotlight Feature, Springfield Public Schools 1986; Women's Day Speaker 1981, 1983, 1988. **HOME ADDRESS:** 2025 Gregory Ct, Springfield, IL 62703.

RAMIREZ, GILBERT
Judge. **PERSONAL:** Born Jun 24, 1921, Puerto Rico; son of Virgilio and Paulita; married Maria. **EDUCATION:** Univ of PR, BA edn; NYU Grad Sch; Columbia Univ Tchrs Coll; Brooklyn Law Sch, JD 1956. **CAREER:** New York State Supreme Court, justice 1976-; Family Ct of State of NY, judge 1968-75; NY State Constitutional Conv, del 1967; NY State Assembly, assemblyman 1966; General Prac of Law, atty 1957-68. **ORGANIZATIONS:** Vice chmn of bd Bedford-Stuyvesant Lawyes Assn; mem Natl Bar Assn; dir Brooklyn Law Sch Alumni Assn; mem Bedford-Stuyvesant Beautification Assn; mem Natl Fedn of Blind; dir Guiding Eyes for Blind. **BUSINESS ADDRESS:** New York State Supreme Court, 360 Adams St, Brooklyn, NY 11201.

RAMOS, GENE MAURICE
Interior designer. **PERSONAL:** Born Aug 10, 1932, Cincinnati, OH; married Jackie; children: Gene, Gia. **CAREER:** Gene M Ramos & Assoc, interior designer owner. **ORGANIZATIONS:** Bd mem Gal Golden Oaks 1970; treas Watts Summer Festival 1969; sec LA Urban League 1970; corporate bd LA United Crusade; mem Amer Soc Interior Deisgners; mem NAACP. **BUSINESS ADDRESS:** 2903 W Vernon Ave, Los Angeles, CA.

RAMSEUR, ANDRE WILLIAM
Poet, employment specialist. **PERSONAL:** Born Jan 15, 1949, Manhattan, NY; son of Otho William Ramseur, Jr and Crola William; children: Creola, Otho William. **EDUCATION:** St Augustines Coll Raleigh, BA Eng 1971; Miami Univ Oxford OH, MA Eng 1972; George Washington Univ DC, further study 1980. **CAREER:** Miami Univ Oxford OH, grad asst 1971-72; St Augustines Coll, instr of eng 1972-74; Equitable Life Assurance Soc of US, agency sec Wash DC, asst suprv New Bus Indianapolis, admin trainee Washington DC 1974-77; Eton Towers Tenants Assoc, legal coord 1975; Pres Comm on White House Fellowships, staff asst 1977-79; Office of Personnel Mgmt Washing DC, ed specialist 1979-86; Defense Communications Agency, employee devel specialist 1986-. **ORGANIZATIONS:** Founder Organizing Consultantship to Aid Individual in Job Counseling & Asst; co-founder Station to Station Performance Poets & Writers Collective 1980; asst to program dir, Natl Society for Performance & Instruction 1988-89; mem of Federal Educations and Training Assoc 1988-. **HONORS/ACHIEVEMENTS:** Outstanding Young Man Dees & Fuller Org 1975; finalist Clover Intl Poetry Contest Wash DC 1975; Notable Amer Awd Notable Historian Soc Raleigh 1976-77; Spec Achievement Awd Pres Comm on White House Fellowship 1979; poetry publ "You Never Tried" Clover Publ 1976, "After the Fact" Young Publ 1978, "Greenhouse Poetry" Collection of Love Poems Triton Press 1977-78, "Greenhouse Poetry" Vol 2 1979-80; author dramatic play "Father My Father" 1979; author musical drama "My Fathers House" 1980; annual 1 man poetry performance 1982-; group performances with Station to Station 1980-85; special achievement OPM Director's Award 1984; author of dramatic play "Spotlights in Black History" 1985; special act or service Defense Comm Agency 1986; poetry collection in progress "It's About Time" 1989. **HOME ADDRESS:** 4900 Beauregard St #103, Alexandria, VA 22312.

RAMSEUR, DONALD E.
Retired judge. **PERSONAL:** Born Dec 17, 1919, Cleveland County, NC; married Prince Alma Whitworth; children: 3 children. **EDUCATION:** Johnson C Smith Univ, BS 1941; NC Coll Sch of Law, LLB 1954. **CAREER:** 27th Judicial Dist, dist judge (retired 1985). **ORGANIZATIONS:** Past pres, founder, Gaston Boys' Club; bd of trustees Gaston Mem Hosp; former memb Gastonia City Bd of Ed; mem Mayor's Comm on Human Relations; past pres, mem, Gaston County Bar Assn; mem NC Bar Assn; NC Black Lawyers' Assn; NC conf Dist Ct Judges; bd of trustees St Paul Baptist Church. **HONORS/ACHIEVEMENTS:** Man & Boy Award Boys' Clubs of Amer 1968; Omega Man of the Year; Citizen of the Year. **MILITARY SERVICE:** AUS T/Sgt.

RAMSEUR, ISABELLE R.
Councilwoman. **PERSONAL:** Born Feb 21, 1906, North Carolina; married Charles; children: Harold D, Albertine. **CAREER:** Philadelphia Gen Hosp, nursing vol work; Mercy Douglas Hosp; Nursery Sch Fernwood, tchrs asst; Boro Darby, councilwoman. **ORGANIZATIONS:** Mem Needlework Guild Am 1933; Ladies Aux to WMCA Phila; Blessed Virgin Mary Ch; mem NAACP; past matron Order E Star; chrtrd mem Rose of Sharon Chap #80. **HONORS/ACHIEVEMENTS:** 1st prize ARC Talent Rally Rose of Sharon.

RAMSEY, CHARLES EDWARD, JR.
Mayor. **PERSONAL:** Born Dec 22, 1956, Moorseville, NC; married Nora Elizabeth Hosch; children: Erraull LaRonne. **EDUCATION:** Clark Coll & GA Tech, 1975-77; E Carolina Univ, BFA Int Arch 1980. **CAREER:** E Carolina Univ Student Chap of the Amer Soc of Int Design, pres 1978-79; Town of E Spencer, alderman 1983-84; K-Town Furniture, interior designer 1984; NC Conf on Black Mayors, 2nd vice pres 1984-; Town of East spencer, mayor 1984-. **ORGANIZATIONS:** Mun rep NC League of Municipalities 1983-; state rep World Conf of Black Mayors 1984; mun rep Rowan Co Economic & Indus Develop 1984-. **HONORS/ACHIEVEMENTS:** Disting Serv to Humanity GAP Prods Inc 1984; Youngest Black Mayor in State of NC World Conf of Black Mayors Tuskegee 1984; Pres's Achievement Awd for Distinguished Serv to Humanity Gen Baptist State Convention of NC 1985. **HOME ADDRESS:** PO Box 324, East Spencer, NC 28039. **BUSINESS ADDRESS:** Mayor, Town of East Spencer, PO Box 338, East Spencer, NC 28039.

RAMSEY, HENRY, JR.
Judge. **PERSONAL:** Born Jan 12, 1934, Florence, SC; married Eleanor Anne; children: Charles, Githaiga, Robert, Ismail, Yetunde, Abeni. **EDUCATION:** Univ of California, Riverside CA, AB 1960; Univ of California, School of Law, Berkeley CA, LLB 1963. **CAREER:** Contra Costa County, CA, dep dist atty 1964-65; Ramsey & Rosenthal, Richmond CA, partner 1965-71; Univ of California Sch of Law, Berkeley CA, prof of law 1971-80; Univ of Texas, Austin TX, visiting prof of law 1971-77; Univ of Colorado, Boulder CO, visiting prof of law 1977-78; Univ of New Mexico School of Law, Special Scholarship Prog for Amer Indians, Albuquerque NM, visiting prof of law 1980; ,State of California, County Co of Alameda, superior ct judge 1980-. **ORGANIZATIONS:** Past mem Curriculum Devel & Supplemental Materials Comm of State of CA; mem CA Bar Assn, 1964-80; mem CA Judges Assn; past mem Human Rel Comm City of Richmond; past mem bd dir Redevelopment Agency; United Bay Area Crusade; bd dir Amer Civil Liberties Union of Northern CA; past mem Berkeley City Council; past mem exec comm Assn of Amer Law Sch; past mem Council on Legal Educ Oppor; mem 1987-, pres Council on Legal Educ Oppor; mem Council of the Sect on Legal Educ and Admission to the Bar of the Amer Bar Assn, 1982-; mem Amer Law Inst; past mem Accreditation Comm of the Sect of Legal Educ & Admissions to the Bar Amer Bar Assn; mem Commn on Trial Court Performance Standards, Natl Center for State Courts, 1987-; mem Blue Ribbon Commn on Inmate Population Mgmt, 1987-; mem Judicial Council of California, 1988-; chairperson, Judicial Council Advisory Comm on Change of Venue, Judicial Council of California, 1988-; Natl Commn on Trial Court Performance Standards; life mem NAACP; life mem Amer Civil Liberties Union; mem Amnesty Intl. **HONORS/ACHIEVEMENTS:** Author, "Affirmative Action at Amer Bar Assn Approved Law School: 1979-1980," Journal of Legal Educ, 1980; author, "California Continuing Education of the Bar," chapter in California Criminal Law Procedure and Practice, 1986; Fellow, Amer Bar Foundation; mem Amer Law Inst; Distinguished Alumnus Award, Univ of California (Riverside) Alumni Assn, 1987. **MILITARY SERVICE:** USAF 1951-55. **BUSINESS ADDRESS:** Superior Court Judge, Alameda County Superior Court, 1225 Fallon St, Oakland, CA 94612.

RAMSEY, JEROME CAPISTRANO
Attorney. **PERSONAL:** Born Mar 28, 1953, San Bernardino, CA. **EDUCATION:** Univ of CA, BA honors 1975, JD 1978. **CAREER:** Holland and Hart, attorney 1978-80; US Dept of Justice, asst US attorney 1980-82; Mile Hi Cablevision, vp/genl counsel 1982-. **ORGANIZATIONS:** Genl partner Assoc Capital Enterprises 1979-; mem Amer Bar Assn 1978-; mem CO & Denver Bar Assn 1978-; mem Sam Carey & Natl Bar Assn 1978-; gen counsel/sec Mile Hi Small Bus Investment Co 1984-. **HONORS/ACHIEVEMENTS:** Distinguished Service US Dept of Justice 1982; Executive Excel the Minority Prof Directory 1984. **BUSINESS ADDRESS:** Associate Counsel, American TV & Communications, 160 Inverness Dr West, Englewood, CO 80112.

RAMSEY, OTTO BRYANT
Educator. **PERSONAL:** Born Feb 07, 1909, Sparta, TN. **EDUCATION:** Howard U, AB 1931; Columbia, MA 1940; Deams Scholar Tchrs Coll, spring 1945; NatUniv Mexico, postgrad summer 1948; Spanish Cultural InstUniv Madird, exchange scholar 1951-52; Universidad Interamericana Saltillo Mexico, PhD in Spanish 1966. **CAREER:** Xavier Univ New Orleans, instr dir remedial reading clinic 1945-47; TX So Univ Houston, asst prof spanish 1948-51; asso prof spanish 1952-70; prof 1973-; head dept foreign languages & lits 1970-73. **ORGANIZATIONS:** Bd dirs La Universidad Interamericana de Saltillo Coahuila Mexico 1969-; instr Hispanic Culture Houston 1970-72; mem Am AssnUniv Profs; Am Assn Tchrs Spanish & Portuguese; La Sociedad Nacional Hispanica; mem Sigma Delta Pi. **HONORS/ACHIEVEMENTS:** Author "the development of reading rate & comprehension in spanish a simplified spanish guide" revised ed pts 1, 2, 3 1972.

RAMSEY, WALTER S.
Business executive. **PERSONAL:** Married Grace E Walker; children: Dr Walter S Jr. **EDUCATION:** Coll of City of NY, BS. **CAREER:** Sylvania Electric, proj engr 1946-53; Raytheon Mfg Co, proj engr 1945-46; Standard Eletronics, physicist 1943-45; US Signal Corps, physicist 1942-43; Ramsey Electronics, owner mgr consult 1953-. **ORGANIZATIONS:** Mem adv com August Martin HS Jamaica NY; mem bd Queens Child Guidance; bd chmn NAACP Jamaica; Montauk Day Care Cntr; educ chmn Queensboro Fed of Parents Clubs; pres Jamaica Br NAACP. **BUSINESS ADDRESS:** 114-74 176 St, St Albans, NY 11434.

RAND, A. BARRY
Corporate vice president. **PERSONAL:** Born 1945, Washington, DC; son of Addison Penrod Rand and Helen Matthews Rand; divorced. **EDUCATION:** Rutgers University, Camden, NJ; American University, Washington, DC, BS; Stanford University, Stanford, CA, MBA, MS. **CAREER:** Xerox Corp, Rochester, NY, sales representative, 1968-70, regional sales representative, 1970-80, corporate director of marketing, 1980-84, vice president of eastern operations, 1984-86; Xerox Corp, Stamford, CT, corporate vice president, 1986-, president of US Marketing Group, 1986-. **BUSINESS ADDRESS:** Xerox Corp, 800 Long Bridge Road, Box 1600, Stamford, CT 06902. *

RANDALL, ANN KNIGHT
Educator, librarian. **PERSONAL:** Born in NYC; married Julius T; children: Christine Renee. **EDUCATION:** Barnard Coll, BA 1963; NY U, post grad study 1967; Columbia U, DLS 1977. **CAREER:** US Social Security Admin NYC, claims adjuster 1963-64; AUS Bamberg Germany, lib asst 1964-65; Brooklyn public library, library adult trainee 1965-67; City Univ of NY Queens Coll, instr 1967-69; Brookyn Coll, adjunct lectr 1976-; Columbia Univ, Pratt Inst, Queens Coll, Rutgers Univ, teacher part-time 1970-73; Univ S Educ Resources Info Center ERIC, indexer 1967-68; Urban Center Columbia Univ, library consultant 1970-; Urban Resources Sys Univ of MI, 1973; RR Booker, public consultant 1973. **ORGANIZATIONS:** Mem YWCA Brooklyn; Acad of Pol Sci; Am Lib Assn 1966-; Assn for Study of African Am Life & History 1968-; exec bd Spl Lib Assn NY Group 1969-71;pres NU chap ColumbiaUniv Beta Phi Mu 1971-72. **HONORS/ACHIEVEMENTS:** Publ review & art in jour and book chpt; recip NDEA Fellowship Awd for doctoral studies; Who's Who of Am Women 1975-76 ed.

RANDALL, CLAIRE
Former church executive. **PERSONAL:** Born Oct 15, 1919, Dallas, TX. **EDUCATION:** Schrener Coll, AA 1948; Scarritt Coll, BA 1950; Berkeley Sem, Yale Univ, DD (hon) 1974; Austin Coll, LLD (hon) 1982; Notre Dame Univ, LLD 1984. **CAREER:** World Missions Presbyterian Church US Nashville, assoc missionary educ bd 1949-57; Gen Council Atlanta, dir art 1957-61; Christian World Mission, dir; Church Women Univ NYC, prog dir 1962-73; Natl Council Church of Christ in USA NYC, gen sec 1974-84. **HONORS/ACHIEVEMENTS:** Recipient Woman of the Year in Religion Awd Heritage Soc 1977; Empire State Woman of the Year in Religion Awd State of NY 1984; Medal Order of St Vladimir Russian Orthodox Church 1984. **BUSINESS ADDRESS:** Past General Secretary, Natl Council of Churches, 155 West 68th St, New York, NY 10023.

RANDALL, DUDLEY FELKER
Librarian, publisher, poet. **PERSONAL:** Born Jan 14, 1914, Washington, DC; son of Arthur George Clyde Randall and Ada Viola Bradley Randall; married Ruby Hands, May 27, 1935; children: Phyllis Ada; married Mildred Pinckney, Dec 20, 1942; married Vivian Spencer, May 04, 1957. **EDUCATION:** Wayne Univ, Detroit MI, BA, 1949; Univ of Michigan, Ann Arbor, MALS, 1951; Univ of Ghana, 1970. **CAREER:** Lincoln Univ, Jefferson City MO, librarian, 1951-54; Morgan St Coll, Baltimore MD, assoc librarian, 1954-56; Wayne Co Federated Library Sys, Wayne MI, branch librarian, 1956-63, head of ref, 1963-69; Univ of Detroit, MI, ref librarian & poet-in-res, 1969-75. Visiting lecr, Univ of MI, 1969; fndr, gen editor, Broadside Pr, 1965-77; fndr, Broadside Poets Theatre, Broadside Poetry Wkshp, 1980; consultant, 1977—. **ORGANIZATIONS:** Mem, New Detroit Inc com on arts, 1970—; MI Coun Arts Adv Panel on Lit, 1970—; Detroit Coun Arts, 1975-76; mem, Intl Afro-Amer Museum, NAACP, Amer Libr Assoc, MI Libr Assoc, MI Poetry Soc, Detroit Soc for Advncmt of Culture & Educ. **HONORS/ACHIEVEMENTS:** Tompkins Awd, Wayne St Univ, 1962, 1966; Kuumba Libn Awd, 1973; Arts Awd in Lit, MI Found for Arts, 1975; Creative Artist Awd in Lit, MI coun for Arts, 1981; NEA fellowshps, 1981, 1986; appt 1st Poet Laureate of Detroit by Mayor Coleman A. Young, 1981. Author num poems; author of books A Capsule Course in Black Poetry Writing (with others), Broadside Pr, 1975, Broadside Memories: Poets I Have Known, Broadside Pr, 1975, A Litany of Friends: New & Selected Poems, Lotus Press, 1981, Homage To Hoyt Fuller, Broadside Pr, 1984; ed, contr to anthologies. **MILITARY SERVICE:** US Army, signal corps, 1942-46. **HOME ADDRESS:** 12651 Old Mill Pl, Detroit, MI 48238. *

RANDALL, PHILLIP MELVIN
Business executive. **PERSONAL:** Born Dec 15, 1946, Youngstown, OH; married Maureen Elaine Williams; children: Evelyn Tracy. **EDUCATION:** Youngstown State Univ, BS 1968; Univ of MI, MA 1974; Univ of Akron, PhD 1986; Inst of Geromtology Univ of MI, Specialist in Aging Certification 1974. **CAREER:** OH Bell Tele Co Cleveland OH, mgr 1969-80; The Hay Group Philadelphia PA, dir 1980-81; Amer Intl Inc Chicago IL, corp dir human resources 1981-83; Rockefeller Group New York NY, corp dir 1983-. **ORGANIZATIONS:** Consult Multiple Organizations 1975-; prog coord Univ of Akron 1975-80; mem Life Long Learing Coord Comm 1975-80; mem & chmn Comm on Aging 1978-80; memNatl Nomination Comm Amer Soc of Training & Devel 1982; mem Statewide Comm of Minority Participation 1984; adjunct faculty The New School for Soc RschRsch 1985; instr Univ of Akron. **HONORS/ACHIEVEMENTS:** Outstanding Graduate Phi Kappa Phi Honor Soc 1974; Distinguished Services Mayor's Awd City of Akron 1980; Fellow Univ of Akron Inst Life Span Devel 1979-.

RANDALL, QUEEN F.
Educational administrator. **PERSONAL:** Born Jan 28, 1935, Pine Bluff, AR; children: Barbara J. **EDUCATION:** Lincoln Univ, BS Ed 1956; Indiana Univ, AM 1961; Nova Univ, EdD 1975. **CAREER:** Lincoln Univ, math instructor 1956-58; American River Coll, math instructor 1962-70, math & engineering dept chair 1970-72, assoc dean of instr 1972-76; Pioneer Comm Coll, dean, instructional systems & student development 1976-78, president 1978-80; Metropolitan Comm Coll, asst to chancellor 1980-81; El Centro Coll, president 1981-84; American River Coll, president 1984-. **ORGANIZATIONS:** Pres Delta Kappa Gamma; mem Alpha Kappa Alpha 1953-; pres Soroptimist Club Kansas City MO 1981; bd of dirs Industrial Develop Corp 1982-85; adv bd Treescape Dallas, Contact Dallas; bd of dirs American River Hosp, Crocker Art Museum. **HONORS/ACHIEVEMENTS:** Fellow John Hay Whitney Foundation 1961; Fellow Delta Kappa Gamma 1974; Trailblazer So Dallas Business & Professional Club 1982; Outstanding Educator YWCA 1985; Outstanding Alumni Nova Univ 1985; Women of Distinction Award Soroptimist Intl of Sacramento North 1986; Dollars and Sense Magazine's Second Annual Salute to America's Top 100 Business and Professional Women 1986. **BUSINESS ADDRESS:** President, American River College, 4700 College Oak Dr, Sacramento, CA 95841.

RANDLE, BERDINE CARONELL
Business executive. **PERSONAL:** Born Mar 18, 1929, Lufkin, TX; married Lucious; children: Lydia. **EDUCATION:** Prairie View A&M U, BA 1949; Prairie Vew A&M U, Ms 1955;Univ of Houston, post grad. **CAREER:** Miss Lucy's Acad & Early Chldhd Educ Cntr, exec dir 1969-; Friendship Rlty Co, owner 1970-; HI SD Houston, 1957-72; Marlin ISD, phys educ tchr1951-57; tchr elem sch 1951-55; phys educ tchr 1946, 48, 49, 51; YMCA Waco, dance instr. **ORGANIZATIONS:** Adv bd consult Clanthe Hse of Bees Halfway Hse 1973-77; vice pres North Forest Sh Bd 1974-76; vice pres Fontaine Scenic Woods Civic Club 1976-; golden life mem Delta Sigma Theta Sor 1972; life mem YWCA 1975; Nat State & Houston Area Assn for the Educ of Young Children 1976-; ACEI 1974-77; SACUS 1973-; NAESP 1973-; AAHPER 1955-; mem chrpsn NFTFO 1976-; AUCW 1974-77; HALBPWC 1973-; NALBPWC 1973-; mem chrpsn F SWCC 1976; Alpha Tau chptr Theta Nu Sigma Nat Sor. **HONORS/ACHIEVEMENTS:** Comm serv awd 1974; natl coun of negro women's awd 1973; outstdng comm serv awd 1973; TX Assn of Sch Bd Awd 1975; Kashmere Gdns HS Comm Srev Awd 1975; Fontaine Scenic Woods Civic Club's Civic Minded Awd 1973, 74; Pres Coun on Phys Fitness Awd 1966; Bd of Educ North Forest Sch Dist Awd 1976;Miss Lucy's Acad Outstdng Serv & PTO Awd 1977; ded serv awd Houston Ind SchDist 1977; Gulf Coast Comm Serv Awd 1977; ded serv awd Calanthe Hse of Bees 1977; cert of merit serv Mayor of Houston Gov of TX Hse Spkr Bill Clayton 1977; achiev awd for excell in educ & comm serv Houston Leag of Bus & Prof Women's Club. **BUSINESS ADDRESS:** 10620 Homestead Rd, Houston, TX 77016.

RANDLE, CARVER A.
Attorney. **PERSONAL:** Born Jan 12, 1942, Indianola, MS; married Rosie Knox; children: Regina, Carver Jr, Rosalyn. **EDUCATION:** MS Valley State U, BS 1965; Univ MS, JD 1973. **CAREER:** Pattonlane HS, tchr coach 1965-67; Washington Co Schs, tchr 1967-68; Quitman Co, spl proj dir 1968-69; N MS Rural Legal Svcs, staff atty 1973-. **ORGANIZATIONS:** Mem Nat Conf Black Lawyers; MS Nat Bar Assn; cand Mayor City Indianola 1968;

cand state rep MS 1971; mem bd dirs Indianola Fed Credit Unoin 1969-; ACSC 1967-70; pres Sunflower Co MS Br NAACP 1967-; mem MS Coun on Human Rel 197-. **HONORS/ACHIEVEMENTS:** Coach of yr N Central Athletic Conf 1965-66; awd for outstdng achvmnts & ldgrshp Indianola 1973. **BUSINESS ADDRESS:** PO Box 546, Indianola, MS 38751.

RANDLE, LUCIOUS A.
Educator. **PERSONAL:** Born Aug 15, 1927, Mcgregor, TX; married Berdine C Reese; children: Lydia Louise. **EDUCATION:** BS 1949; MEd 1953;Univ of TX, post grad work. **CAREER:** Robert E Lee Sr HS Houston Indendent School Dist, vice prin 1970-; Attucks Jr HS, teacher part-time prin 1962-70; Worthing HS, science teacher 1958-62; Charlie Brown HS, 1957-58; OJ Thomas HS 1949-57; Friednship Realty Co, owner-broker 1970-; Homestead Rd School of Dance, owner 1971-; Miss Lucy's Acad & Early Childhood Educ Center, owner-dir 1969-; Homefinders Real Estate Inc, co broker 1965-70. **ORGANIZATIONS:** Mem NEA; TSTA Houston Prin Assn; Nat Assn Real Est Brokers; Houston Realtors Assn; TX Realtors Assn; N Forst Task Force Orgn; Fontaine-Scenic Woods Civic Club; Masonic Lodge; Lions' Club. **HONORS/ACHIEVEMENTS:** Tchr of Yr 1954-55; Real est Salesman of Yr 1964-65; comm serv awd Nat Coun of Negro Women 1974; hon mem FFA awd 1973. **MILITARY SERVICE:** AUS signal corps med br oc classification 1951-53. **BUSINESS ADDRESS:** 10620 Homestead Rd, Houston, TX 77016.

RANDOLF, ALMA LOUISE
Elected official. **PERSONAL:** Born Jan 13, 1957, Beaver Dam, KY. **EDUCATION:** Davies Cty Voc School, 1975; Owensboro Business Coll, 1976. **CAREER:** Nestaway Div of Axio Inc, admin asst 1976-; Task Force on Drunk Drivers, vice pres 1983; United Way Allocation Comm, bd mem 1984; HUD Grant & City of Beaver Dam, liaison Officer 1980-; City of Beaver Dam, council mem. **ORGANIZATIONS:** Chairperson City Parks, Leg Comm, Apply for State & Fed Grants 1980-. **HONORS/ACHIEVEMENTS:** Listed Who's Who High School Students 1975; 1st Woman elected to Beaver Dam Council 1980; 1st Black to hold political office in county 1980; Named Kentucky Colonel 1982.

RANDOLPH, BERNARD CLYDE
Physician. **PERSONAL:** Born May 22, 1922, New York, NY; son of William F Randolph and Jessie K Briggs Randolph; married Bille Jean Coleman; children: Dana Grace, Bernard C Jr MD, Paul Allen. **EDUCATION:** City Coll of New York, BS 1943; Howard Univ Coll of Med, MD 1947. **CAREER:** Mound City Medl Forum, pres 1963-65; MO Pan-Medical Assoc, pres 1966-67; Talent Rec Council of Natl Med Assoc, chmn 1972-81. **ORGANIZATIONS:** Founder and pres St Louis County Env Health and Safety 1975-; past pres Gamma Chapter Chi Deltu Mu Frat; mem Phi Beta Signa Frat; life mem and golden heritage mem NAACP; chmn Hlth & Hosp Com of St Louis Chapter; mem NAACP Health Comm; chmn Hlth Comm of 5th Senatorial Dist Corporate and Professional Round Table. **HONORS/ACHIEVEMENTS:** Mem Mission to W Africa Natl Med Assoc Mem 1961; mem NMA delegate Conference on Hosp Discrimination Pres John F Kennedy 1963; Practitioner of the Year, National Medical Assn 1988; Community Service Award, Legal Services of Eastern Missouri 1989. **MILITARY SERVICE:** USAF capt 1952-54. **BUSINESS ADDRESS:** 3737 N Kinshighway, St Louis, MO 63115.

RANDOLPH, BERNARD P.
Air force commander. **PERSONAL:** Born Jul 10, 1933, New Orleans, LA; son of Philip Randolph and Claudia Randolph; married Lucille Robinson; children: Michelle, Julie, Michael, John, Liane, Mark. **EDUCATION:** Xavier Univ LA, BS Chem (cum laude) 1954; Air Force Inst Tech, BS (magna cum laude) 1964; Univ of N Dakota, MS Electrical Engineering 1965; Auburn Univ, MS Business Admin 1969. **CAREER:** 834th Air Div Tan Son Nhut Air Base Vietnam, airlift ops officer Chu Lai, airlift coord 1969-70; Hdqrs Air Force Systems Command Andres AFB MD, chief command plans br office dep, chief staff ops 1970-72, exec officer to dep chief staff ops 1972-73; Space & Missile Systems Orgn Los Angeles Air Force Sta, dir space systems plnng 1974-75; Air Force Satellite Commun System Space & Missile Systems Orgn, system program dir 1975-78, prog dir space defense systems 1978-80; Warner Robins Air Logistics Ctr Robins AFB CO, vice comdr; 1980-81; US Air Force, Washington DC, dir, space systems/CCC, 1981-84; Air Force Systems Command Adrews AFB, vice comdr 1984-85; USAF Washington, chief staff for R&D & acquisition hdqrs 1985-87; Air Force Systems Command, Andrews AFB, dir, 1987-. **HONORS/ACHIEVEMENTS:** Disting Grad Air War Coll 1974; second Black named a Four-Star General in Air Force; third Black Four-Star General to be named in US. **MILITARY SERVICE:** US Air Force, general, 1964-; Decorated Disting Serv Medal, Legion of Merit w/oak leaf cluster, Bronze Star Medal, Meritorious Serv Medal, Presidential Unit Citation. **BUSINESS ADDRESS:** Dir, Air Force Systems Command, Andrews Air Force Base, Washington, DC 20334.

RANDOLPH, DAVID E.
Business executive. **PERSONAL:** Born Feb 07, 1936, Tampa; married Mary El Hagwood; children: David II, Katrena, Dwayne. **EDUCATION:** FL A&MUniv Tallahassee, BS 1957. **CAREER:** Family-Owner Bus, bus ptnr mgr. **ORGANIZATIONS:** Mem Grtr Delray Beach C of C; Nat Bus Leag; Kiwanis; Kappa Alpha Psi; Delray Beach Civic Assn; pres Delray Beach Sickle Cell Fund 1973; mem Migrants& Labor Policy Bd; pres Delray Beach Young Men's Investment Club. **HONORS/ACHIEVEMENTS:** Mayor 1966-69; bronze star Viet Nam 1967-68. **MILITARY SERVICE:** AUS trans corps 2nd lt 1958. **BUSINESS ADDRESS:** 945 W Atlantic Ave, Delray Beach, FL 33444.

RANDOLPH, ELIZABETH
Educator. **PERSONAL:** Born Mar 18, 1917, Farmville, NC; daughter of John Schmoke and Pearl Schmoke; married John D Randolph (deceased). **EDUCATION:** Shaw Univ, AB 1936; Univ of MI, MA 1945; Univ of NC, Certificate School Admin 1964; Shaw Univ, Hon DHL 1979. **CAREER:** NC Public School, teacher 1936-58; Charlotte Mecklenburg School, principal 1958-67; ESEA Title I, dir 1967-73; Charlotte Mecklenburg Bd of Educ, admin asst 1973-76, asst supt 1976-77, assoc supt 1977-82 (retired). **ORGANIZATIONS:** Mem bd of mgrs Charlotte Mem Mecklanburg Hospital 1971-; mem Charlotte Mecklenburg Human Relations Comm 1972-75; supreme parliamentarian Alpha Kappa Alpha Sorority Inc 1974-78; pres ASCD 1977; bd of dirs Mecklenburg Boy Scout Council 1978-; mem Charter Review Comm 1979-80; mem Phi Delta Kappa Educ Fraternity; bd oftrustees Shaw Univ; bd of trustees NC A&T State Univ; bd of trustees Public Library of Charlotte and Mecklenburg Co; cochmn Friends of Johnson C Smith Univ; bd of commissioners Charlotte-Mecklenburg Hospital Authority; mem bd of trustees Davidson Coll 1987-, Queen's Coll 1988-. **HONORS/ACHIEVEMENTS:** Citation Local Press Civic Educ Org 1958-77; Citation Alpha Kappa Alpha Sor 1977; Citation ASCD 1977; Citation Public Library of Charlotte and Mecklenburg County; Citation Mecklenburg County Commissioners; Citation Charlotte-Mecklenburg Bd of Educ; Citation Mecklenburg General Baptist Convention.

RANDOLPH, JAMES B.
Educator. **PERSONAL:** Born Jul 23, 1923, Richland, LA; married Gloria D Jackson; children: Gina Lynne, Cecily Karen, James Bolton. **EDUCATION:** FL A&M U, BA 1950; Western Reserve U, MA 1951; KARAMU Theatre, spec stud;Univ of Miami Barry Coll , addl Stud. **CAREER:** Westveiw Jr HS, prin 1973-; Carol City Jr HS, asst prin admin 1970-73; Educ Testing Serv, writer 1969-71; Units on Negro History & Culture Dade County School, 1969; Dade County School, teacher drama 1958-69; Prairie View A&M Coll, asst prof of speech 1956-58; Comm Youth Center Springfield, dir 1954-56; FL A&M Univ instructor asst prof of drama 1951-54. **ORGANIZATIONS:** Mem Phi Delta Kappa; Nat Educ Assn; 1st vice pres FL Interscholastic Speech & Drama Assn; bd of dir Sec Sch Theatre Conf; pres Dade Co Speech Tchr Assn; mem FL Assn Sec Sch Prin; Nat Assn Sec Sch Prin; chmn; Ch Coun Ch of the Open Door; chmn Scholarship Com Miami Edison PTSA; Omega Psi Phi; exec bd Sigma Alpha Chap Miami. **HONORS/ACHIEVEMENTS:** Distngd ser to N Dade HS honor soc 1962-63; outs serv Dramatic Arts Deerfield Bch Elem Sch 1963; awd of exec ser to N Dade HS Faculty & Students 1958-66; cover DRAMATICS Mag 1962. **MILITARY SERVICE:** AUS. **BUSINESS ADDRESS:** Westview Jr HS, 1901 NW 127 St, Miami, FL 33167.

RANDOLPH, LOUIS T.
Business executive. **PERSONAL:** Born May 05, 1928, Washington, NC; married Betty Jean Barr; children: Naomi Ann. **EDUCATION:** NC Central U, BS 1951. **CAREER:** Randolph Funeral Home, owner funeral serv dir; Wash NC, mayor pro-tem; VA Washongton, educator 1951-52. **ORGANIZATIONS:** Chmn bd of trst Beaufort Co Tech Inst; mem Human Rel Coun; bd dir Nat Funeral Dir & Morticians Assn Inc; Odd Fellow Lodge; IBPOE of W; Masonic Lodge; NC Assn of Educators; NEA; Elite Club; life mem Kappa Alpha Psi; sec bd of govUniv of NC; mem United Supreme Cncl Ancient & Accepted Scottish Rite of Freemasonry So Jurisdiction Prince Hall Aff 32nd degree; life mem NAACP; bd dir Grtr Washington C of C. **HONORS/ACHIEVEMENTS:** Oustndg ldrshp awd Funeral Dir & Morticians Assoc of NC Inc 1971, 1972; man of yr E Dist Funeral Dir & Morticians Assn 1971-72; Nat Mortician of Yr 1975-76; distngd serv awd Princee Hall Free & Accepted Masons of NC; man of yr Kappa Alpha Psi Frat 1976; outsdng citz of Beauford Co & Wash NC 1976; distgsd serv awd Funeral Dir & Morticians Assn 1977. **BUSINESS ADDRESS:** 208 W 4 St, Washington, NC 27889.

RANDOLPH, NANCY ELIZABETH
Educational administrator. **PERSONAL:** Born in Boston, MA. **EDUCATION:** Boston Univ, BS; Smith Coll School for Social Work, MSS; Univ of AL, PhD. **CAREER:** Econ Oppty Council for Five Towns Woodmere NY, dir 1963-65; Comm Serv soc, dir 1969-72; Smith Coll School for Social Work, teacher 1969-72,77-; Hunter Coll NY, adj prof 1971-72; Univ of AL School for Social Work, assoc dean & assoc prof 1972-77; Harvard Univ, spec asst to pres; Council on Social Work Educ, dir. **ORGANIZATIONS:** Bd of counselors Smith Coll School for Social Work 1978-; pres Natl Smith Alumni Assoc 1979-; house of dels Council on Soc Work Ed Prog; chmn Black Faculty & Admins Org Harvard Univ 1978-80; mem Omicron Delta Kappa; adv Delta Sigma Theta Natl Serv Sor 1980; bd dirs Natl Assoc of Social Workers MA Chapt; mem Links Inc Middlesex Cty Chapt; bd mem Elma Lewis School of Fine Arts; trustee Intl Defense Fund of S Africa. **HONORS/ACHIEVEMENTS:** Outstanding Woman Awd IWY 1976; listed in Outstanding Educator 11th Ed, Who's Who Amoung Women 11th Ed.

RANDOLPH, ROBERT LEE
Educator/economist. **PERSONAL:** Born Jan 02, 1926, East St Louis, IL; children: Heather. **EDUCATION:** DePauw Univ, AB 1948; Univ IL Urbana, MS 1954, PhD 1958; Case Western Reserve Univ 1960, Univ of MI 1962, Postdoctoral study. **CAREER:** Springfield Coll MA, from instructor to assoc prof 1958-65, chmn dept 1960-63, dir evening and summer schs 1960-64; Job Corps, deputy assoc dir 1965-67; Equal Employment Oppor Commn Washington, dep exec dir 1967-68; Chicago State Univ, exec vice pres 1969-73; Westfield Coll MA, pres 1973-79; MA State Coll System, vice chancellor 1979-81; Alabama State Univ, pres 1981-83; Univ Montevallo AL, prof economics 1983-. **ORGANIZATIONS:** Vice pres Springfield Urban League 1962-66; pres Randolph Assocs Birmingham AL, Boston 1983-; consultant to industry; mem Amer Assoc State Colls & Univs, Amer Assoc Polit and Social Scis, Amer Economic Assoc, Phi Delta Kappa, Alpha Phi Omega, Kappa Alpha Psi. **HONORS/ACHIEVEMENTS:** Danforth Foundation Awd 1943; State of IL Scholar 1952-56; Bailey Fellow 1957-58; Carnegie Fellow 1962; Vice President's Awd Excellence Pub Serv US Govt 1967; Outstanding Alumni Awd Lincoln HS East St Louis 1973.

RANDOLPH, WILLIE LARRY
Professional athlete. **PERSONAL:** Born Jul 06, 1954, Holly Hill, SC; married Gretchen Foster; children: Daniesha, Chantre, Andre, Ciara. **CAREER:** Pittsburgh, 1975; NY Yankees, 2nd baseman 1976-84; Los Angeles Dodgers, 1989-. **HONORS/ACHIEVEMENTS:** On 4 All-Star teams in 9 full seasons; leading Intl League in hitting when called up in 1975 to Pirates; named James P Dawson Award Winner as top rookie in 1976 Yankee camp; rookie on All-Star ballot; named to Topps All-Rookie team in 1976; 1977 named to AP, UPI and TSN All-Star t eams; named to UPI & TSN All-Star teams and won TSN Silver Bat Award for AL 2nd baseman; solo HR in Game 3 of 1981 ALCS was game winner To AL pennant; tied major league record for most assists by 2nd basemane in extra-inning game since 1900 with 13, August 25, 1976; establishe d AL record for most chances accepted by 2nd baseman in extra-inning game with 20, August 1976; led AL 2nd basemen in putouts 355, assist s 478, and doubleplays 128, 1979. **BUSINESS ADDRESS:** Los Angeles Dodgers, Dodger Stadium, 1000 Elysian Park Ave, Los Angeles, CA 90012. *

RANGE, M. ATHALIE
State official. **PERSONAL:** Born Nov 07, 1918, Key West, FL; widowed; children: 4 Children. **CAREER:** FL Dept of Comm Affairs, sec retired; Miami City Comm, mem 1966; Miami City Commn, vice-mayor 1 yr; Martin Luther King Blvd Corp, pres. **ORGANIZATIONS:** Licensec embalmer & funeral dir; mem Dade Co's Model Cities Governing Bd; mem Dem & Women's Club; Links of Am Inc. **HONORS/ACHIEVEMENTS:** Recip Cath Diocese of Miami Awd for Mer Svc; sojourner truth awd of Bus & Professional Negro Women's Club; Nat Assn of Christ & Jews Awd.

RANGEL, CHARLES B.
Congressman. **PERSONAL:** Born Jun 11, 1930, New York City, NY; married Alma Carter Rangel; children: Steven, Alicia. **EDUCATION:** NY Univ, BS Bus Admin 1957; St Johns Univ, JD 1960; Wagner Coll, LLD 1982; Atlanta Univ, LLD 1983; St John's Univ, LLD 1983. **CAREER:** Weaver Evans Wingate & Wright, attny 1960; US Attny So Dist of NY, asst attny 1961; NY State Assembly, mem 1967-70; US House of Rep, congressman 1970-. **ORGANIZATIONS:** Mem House Judiciary Comm 1973-74; chmn Congressional Black Caucus 1974-75; mem House Comm on Ways and Means 1975-; mem House Select Comm on Narcotics Abuse & Control 1976-82; chmn House Select Comm on Narcotics Abuse & Control 1983-. **MILITARY SERVICE:** AUS 1948-52; Bronze Star, Purple Heart, US Korean Presidential Citations. **BUSINESS ADDRESS:** Representative, US House of Representatives, 2330 Rayburn Office Building, Washington, DC 20515.

RANKIN, CHARLES I.
Association executive. **PERSONAL:** Born Dec 06, 1937, Winfield, KS; married Sandra Brown; children: 1 Son. **EDUCATION:** Cowley County Jr Coll, AA 1957; Wichita U, BA 1964; Wichita St U, MEd 1968; KS St U, PhD 1973. **CAREER:** Wichita, tchr, asst prin 1964-68; Cooperative Urban Tchr Edn, dir 1968-71; Preparation Retraining Inst & Devl Educ KS St U, dir 1971-73; Midwest Ctr Equal Educ Opportunity,Univ MO Consult Srv; dir; numerous instns, pub schls systems; Wichita Cncl Alcoholism Inc, professional confs, bd dirs. **ORGANIZATIONS:** Mem Urban Leg; NAACP; bd dirs, UMCA; mem Phi Delta Kappa; Assn for Suprervision & Curriculum Dev Citation, Tchrs KS 1968. **HONORS/ACHIEVEMENTS:** Nominated for Outstanding Young Man of Am, St KS 1975.

RANKIN, EDGAR E.
Educator. **PERSONAL:** Born Apr 25, 1914, Holly Springs, MS; married Robbie Lee; children: Edward, Michael, Janet. **EDUCATION:** MI Indsl Coll, AB 1936; Springfield Coll, MS 1953; Univ IL & KS State U, postgrad. **CAREER:** MS Indsl Coll, retired pres 1975-78; HS teacher & coach 1936-40. **ORGANIZATIONS:** Mem NAACP; Phi Delta Kappa; C of C; Am Assn Coll Pres; Am Assn Colls & Univs; Am Assn Pvt Colls; BSA; Omega Psi Phi; Mayor's Com; Mason; lay leader N MS Conf CME Ch; sr pres CME Colls. **HONORS/ACHIEVEMENTS:** Anderson Chapel Ch L M McCoy awd Educ & Comm Betterment 1967; Serv to Humanity awd 1972; Educ & Soc Devel awd 1974.

RANKIN, EDWARD ANTHONY
Surgeon. **PERSONAL:** Born Jul 06, 1940, Holly Springs, MS; son of Edgar E Rankin Jr and Robbie Lee Rankin; married Dr Frances Espy; children: Tony Jr, Marc. **EDUCATION:** Lincoln Univ (MO), BS 1961; Mehary Med Coll (TN), MD 1965. **CAREER:** Howard Univ School of Med, asst prof 1973-78, assoc prof 1978-; Georgetown Univ School of Med, assoc prof 1982-. **ORGANIZATIONS:** Pres Washington Ortho Soc 1982; sec tres Washington Soc for Surgery Hand 1983-; delegate bd coun Am Acad Ortho Surgery 1982-; comm mem Regl Advisors Am Acad Ortho Surgery 1984-; comm mem Regl Advisors Am Coll Surgeons 1980-; oral examiner Am Bd Ortho Surgery 1980-84; editorial Bd, Sports Medicine Today; Chief Orthopedics, Providence Hosp; pres, Metro Washington Society for Surgery of the Hand 1989; vice pres, Metro Washington Chapter, American College of Surgery 1989; program chmn, Liberia Project, Ortho Overseas 1989; American Ortho Assn 1988; Washington Academy of Surgery 1989. **HONORS/ACHIEVEMENTS:** Bronze Star USNA (Vietnam) 1971; army comm medical USNA 1973; public works 2 Chptr. **MILITARY SERVICE:** USNA MC major 1965-73. **BUSINESS ADDRESS:** 1160 Varnum St NE, Suite 312, Washington, DC 20017.

RANN, EMERY LOUVELLE
Retired physician. **PERSONAL:** Born Mar 09, 1914, Keyestone, WV; son of Emery Rann Sr and Vicie Froe; married Flossie Aurelia Fox; children: Judith Rann Thompson, Emery L Rann III, J D, Lara Diane; Jonathan Cheshire, Flossie Aurelia. **EDUCATION:** JC Smith U, BS (cum laude) 1934; Univ MI, MS 1936; Meharry Med Coll, MD 1948; Johnson C Smith U, ScD (Hon) 1981. **CAREER:** Old N State Med Soc, pres 1959; Mecklenburg Co Med Soc, v pres 1958; NC Acad Fmly Pract, dist dir 1981; Imhotep Conf (For Hosp Integ), chrmn 1961-63. **ORGANIZATIONS:** Pres Natl Med Assn 1973-74; fellow Amer Acad Family Practice 1975; mem past chmn bd of trustees, Johnson C Smith Univ 1966-; boule sire archon Sigma Pi Phi Fraternity 1968; Alpha Phi Alpha (Life Mem) 1931-. **HONORS/ACHIEVEMENTS:** Award of Merit, Johnson C Smith Univ 1954, 1968; Doctor of the Year Old N State 1961; Charlotte Med Soc 1972; ZOB mert ZOB Sor 1981; mer scs awd Family Practice Div NMA 1984. **MILITARY SERVICE:** USNA capt 1955-57. **HOME ADDRESS:** 4301 Hamilton Cir, Charlotte, NC 28216.

RANSBURG, FRANK S.
Educator. **PERSONAL:** Born Jan 29, 1943, Keatchie, LA; married Ivory Bowie; children: Ursula. **EDUCATION:** So U, BA 1965; LA State U, MA 1970. **CAREER:** Southern Univ, counselor 1965-69, asst dean men 1969, instructor 1969-71; Jr Div LA State Univ, counselor 1969-73; HS Rel LA State Univ, named asst dir 1975; Southern Univ, dean of students act 1969-. **ORGANIZATIONS:** Adminstr asst Lt Gov's Office summers 1973, 1974; mem LA Commn on Campaign Prac 1974; mem Am Polit Sci Assn; So Polit Sci Assn; AAUP; NAACP; Am Personnel & Guid Assn; Nat Assn Personell Workers. **HONORS/ACHIEVEMENTS:** Faculty awd SoUniv 1970; hon mem LA State Senate 1974.

RANSOM, BURNELLA JACKSON
Business executive. **PERSONAL:** Born Nov 16, 1940, Louisburg, NC; daughter of Burnal James Hayes and Elizabeth Day; divorced; children: Elizabeth Jackson, Brooke Jackson, Maynard Jackson III,Rae Yvonne Ransom. **EDUCATION:** NC Coll, BS 1961; NC Cent U, MS 1969. **CAREER:** Bennett Coll, inst 1962-63; EOA Inc, dir planning 1965-70; BJT Inc Self-employed, pres 1979-83; GA State Univ, inst 1981-; First Class Inc, pres, CEO 1975-. **ORGANIZATIONS:** Mem Public Relations Soc Arenek; mem Natl Assn of Media Women; mem Natl Org of Women; various posts held, Delta Sigma Theta Sorority 1951-85; various posts held, Jack & Jill of Amer 1978-85; bd mem NWGA Girl Scouts 1978; bd mem Atlanta Symp 1975. **HONORS/ACHIEVEMENTS:** Special Award, Bronze Jubilee 1984; mem The Links, Inc. **BUSINESS ADDRESS:** President, Atlanta Artists Mgmt Inc, 1422 W Peachtree St NW, 816, Atlanta, GA 30309.

RANSOM, GARY ELLIOTT
Judge. **PERSONAL:** Born Dec 23, 1941, New Brunswick, NJ; married Gloria P. **EDUCATION:** Rutgers Univ BA Econ 1965; Univ of the Pacific-McGeorge School of Law, JD 1974. **CAREER:** Sacramento Cty Publ Defenders Office, asst publ defender 1974-81; Court of Appeals-Third Appellate Dist, justice pro tem 1983; NJ Div on Civil Rights, field rep 1965-66; Sacramento Municipal Cty Dist, judge 1981-88; California Superior Court, judge 1988-. **ORGANIZATIONS:** Bd of dir Planned Parenthood Assn of Sacramento 1978-81; pres Wiley Manuel Bar Assn 1981; bd of dir Family Serv Agency of Greater Sacramento 1981-; mem CA Judges Assn 1981-; mem Sigma Pi Phi, Gamma Epsilon Boule, Prince Hall F&AM 33rd Deg; life mem Kappa Alpha Psi; bd dir Easter Seals Soc of Gr Sacramento 1978-; life mem No CA Peace Officers Assn; vice pres CA Assoc of Black lawyers 1981; mem Intl Platform Assn; pres, bd of dirs Greater Sacramento Easter Seals Society 1988-. **HONORS/ACHIEVEMENTS:** Phi Nu Pi Awd from Kappa Alpha Psi Frat 1981; Sacramento Wardens & Masters Achievement Awd 1982; Earnest E Robinson Jr Awd Black Law Students Assoc of Univ of the Pacific 1982; Justice Pro Tem Court of Appeals Third Appellate Dist 1983; Bernard S Jefferson Jurist Award, California Assn of Black Lawyers 1989. **MILITARY SERVICE:** USAF capt 1966-71. **HOME ADDRESS:** 1406 Commons Dr, Sacramento, CA 95825. **BUSINESS ADDRESS:** State of California, County Courthouse, 720 9th St, Sacramento, CA 95814.

RANSOM, NORMAN
Clergyman. **PERSONAL:** Born Aug 23, 1923, St Stephen, SC; married Martha Cole; children: Helen, Alice, Norman Jr, Melvin. **EDUCATION:** SC State Coll, BS 1948, PE 1951, Masters 1951; AL A&M Coll, Chem 1955; MI Tech Univ, PhD & BS physics 1966; Duke Univ, DD 1970. **CAREER:** Orangeburg SC, athlete 1946-51; Cainhoy HS, teacher/coach 1949-54, admin 1957-69; Alston HS, teacher/coach 1969-79; St Stephen SC, councilmember 1974-85;Cainhoy HS, admin 1979-84; United Methodist Church, minister 1960-85. **ORGANIZATIONS:** Commissioned notary public SC 1950-85; athletic dir SC League 1953-77; mgr McGowan Corp 1967-71; sec Snack Land Corp 1973-74; ordained minister SC Conf 1974-85; sec United Supreme Council 1975-84; dir St Stephen Play Gound 1975-80. **HONORS/ACHIEVEMENTS:** Most Valuable SC State Coll 1946-48; Pass Tryouts Pittsburg Pirates, St Louise Cardinals 1946; All Ammer SC State Coll 1947-48; Athletic Awd & AchievementSC League 1976; many trophies and plaques in high school and college. **MILITARY SERVICE:** USN warren officer 3 yrs 8 mos; Pass Examination Officers Training 1944. **HOME ADDRESS:** PO Box 295, St Stephen, SC 29479.

RANSOM, PRESTON L.
Educator, educational administrator. **PERSONAL:** Born Jan 02, 1936, Peoria, IL; married Mildred D Murphy; children: Patricia Lynn, Michael Murphy. **EDUCATION:** Univ of IL at Urbana-Champaign, BS 1962, MS 1965, PhD 1969. **CAREER:** Raytheon Co Bedford MA, electrical engr 1962-63; Univ of IL, grad rsch asst 1963-67, instr 1967-70, asst prof electrical engr dept 1970-72, assoc prof electrical engr 1972-88, prof elec engr, 1988-; asst dean and dir cont engineered educ, 1988-. **ORGANIZATIONS:** Sr mem Inst of Elec & Electronic Engrs 1970-; mem Amer Soc of Engrg Educ 1972-; mem Optical Soc of Amer 1972-. **HONORS/ACHIEVEMENTS:** Paul V Golvin Teaching Fellow Univ of IL 1967-68; Hon Rsch Fellow Univ Coll London 1976. **BUSINESS ADDRESS:** Asst Dean and Dir,, Univ of Ill at U-C,, 422 Engineering Hall, 1308 W Green St, Urbana, IL 61801.

RANSOM, VICTOR L.
Engineer. **PERSONAL:** Born Mar 22, 1924, New York, NY; married Dorothy Wilkie; children: Victor Jr, Pamela. **EDUCATION:** MA Inst of Technology, BS 1948; Case Inst of Tech, MS 1952. **CAREER:** Bell Telephone Labs Inc, head syst engr dept 1953-; NJ Coll of Engring, instr 1956-65; Nat Adv Com of Aearonautics, elec engr 1948-52. **ORGANIZATIONS:** Chmn NJ Coast & Section IEEE; past pres bd Red Bank Comm Cntr; mem New Shrewsbury Planning Bd. **MILITARY SERVICE:** USAAF 2nd lt 1943-46. **BUSINESS ADDRESS:** Bell Labs, Holmdel, NJ 07733.

RANSOM, WILLARD BLYSTONE
Attorney. **PERSONAL:** Born May 17, 1916, Indianapolis, IN; married Gladys L Miller; children: Philip F, Judith Ellen, Andrew L. **EDUCATION:** Talladega Coll, AB (Summa Cum Laude) 1936; Harvard Law School, LLB 1939. **CAREER:** Lawfirm Bamberger & Feibleman, assoc, 1971-; Madamme CJ Walker Mfg Co, general mgr 1954-71; IN, deputy attorney general, 1940-41. **ORGANIZATIONS:** dir, Merchants & Natl Bank & Trust Co 1969-; bd trustees, YMCA 1965-77; trst Sarah Walker Est 1954-; past state pres NAACP; former pres Legal Serv Org of Indianapolis; former dir Indianapolis Chamber of Commerce; chmn, State Legal Redress NAACP; mem bd, Madame Walker Urban Life Center. **HONORS/ACHIEVEMENTS:** Distinguished alumni award Talladega Coll 1964; Traylor Award, promoting legal serv for poor 1975; 1 of 250 black citizens of IN for outstanding serv & leadership, Indianapolis Black Bicentennial Comm, 1976. **MILITARY SERVICE:** Military serv capt 194-46.

RAO, KODURU V. S.
College administrator. **PERSONAL:** Born Mar 01, 1940, Vigayawada, IN; married Beverlye Taylor; children: Kishore, Kristina. **EDUCATION:** Andhra Univ India, BA 1959, MA 1962, LLB 1965; Atlanta Univ, MBA 1967. **CAREER:** FL Memorial Coll, vice pres for business & fiscal affairs. **ORGANIZATIONS:** Mem Natl Assoc of Coll and Univ Business Officers 1975-; consultant Robert R Moton Memorial Inst 1975-86; consultant Business Mgmt 1975-; mem Alpha Phi Alpha Frat 1977-; consultant ISATIM Amer Council on Educ 1983-; mem Natl Assoc of Black Accountants 1985-; mem Small Colls and Minority Institutions Comm 1986-. **HONORS/ACHIEVEMENTS:** Grantsmanship US Education Dept 1977. **HOME ADDRESS:** 20049 NW 65 Ct, Miami, FL 33015.

RAPHAEL, BERNARD JOSEPH
Educational administrator. **PERSONAL:** Born May 04, 1935, Rock Castle, VA; married Lynne Keyes. **EDUCATION:** Xavier Univ of LA, BA 1959; St Thomas Coll, MA 1968; Univ of No CO, EdD 1976. **CAREER:** MN Public Schools, teacher/writer coord 1966-67; Hopkins Public Schools, teacher 1967-68; Normandale Comm Coll, chmn div eng 1968-71, dir coop ed 1971-75, assoc dean/instruction 1975-. **ORGANIZATIONS:** Consult Twin Cities OIC 1966-72; mem Affairs Natl Coun Teachers of English 1971-73, Commiss of Curriculum & Intercultural; pres MN Council Teacher of English1973-74; consult US Dept of Ed 1973-; pres Phi Delta Kappa 1975-76. **HONORS/ACHIEVEMENTS:** Excellence in English Xavier Univ New Orleans 1959; Bush Summer Fellow Bush Found St Paul 1975; Harvard Univ Mgmt Lifelong Ed 1984; Publication "Cooperative Education in Higher Ed Univ of No CO; Fulbright Fellow to West Germany, administrator's prgm spring 1986. **BUSINESS ADDRESS:** Associate Dean of Instruction, Normandale Community College, 9700 France Ave S, Bloomington, MN 55431.

RAPHAEL, PAUL W.
Clergyman. **PERSONAL:** Born Sep 29, 1894, Plaquemines Parish, LA; married Dora Smith; children: Ernest, Marion, John. **EDUCATION:** Union Bapt Sem, BTh 1941; Union Bapt Sem, MTh 1942; Union Bapt Sem, honorary DD 1947. **CAREER:** 2nd Bapt Ch, pastor 1933; Union Bapt Sem, sec 1935-58; Union Bapt Ch, trst of gov bd 1935-; pres trst bd 1960-; Union Bapt Sem, tchr theol classes 1947-49. **ORGANIZATIONS:** Mem trst bd Leland Coll 1950-; pres 1st Dist Missionary Bapt Assn 1950-; vice pres LA Missionary Bapt State Conv 1951-; mem Nat Bapt Conv USA Inc; mem NAACP. **HONORS/ACHIEVEMENTS:** Cert of merit New Orleans 1971; honorary dep Criminal Sheriff of Orleans Parish 1973; honorary mem of New Orleans Police Dept 1960; honorary State Senator1974. **MILITARY SERVICE:** AUS 1917-18. **BUSINESS ADDRESS:** 4218 Laurel St, New Orleans, LA 70115.

RASBERRY, ROBERT EUGENE
Clergyman, educatar. **PERSONAL:** Born in Philadelphia, PA; married Gloria E Hooper; children: Roslyn, Robert, John, Denise. **EDUCATION:** Morgan State Coll, AB 1955; Howard U, sch of soc work 1956; NY U, MA 1958; Andover-Newton Theol Sch, BD 1966. **CAREER:** Bethany Baptist Church Syracuse NY, pastor; Mt Calvary Baptist Church Springfield MA, pastor 1965-73; Episcopal Church of Atonement Westerfield MA, asst to rector 1970-72; Messiah Bapt, pastor 1962-65; Friendship Bapt, pastor 1959-62; First Bapt, pastor 1957-59; Springfield Tech Comm Coll, asst prof 1969-73; Bureau of Child Welfare NYC, social investigator 1956-57; Big Bros of Baltimore, social case worker 1954-56. **ORGANIZATIONS:** Exec com Am Assn ofUniv Prof; Urban Leag; Human Righst Commn; Protestant Comm Ministries; bd dir SyracuseUniv Hill Corp Syracuse Chap OIC's of Am; coun of rep NY State Counc of Chs; past exec com TABCOM; assn moderatr Pioneer Valley Am Bapt Chs of MA. **HONORS/ACHIEVEMENTS:** Host producer WSYR Words & Music for a Sunday Morning Syracuse; ten most watchable men Post-Standard Newspaper Syracuse 1977; Nat Forsensic Coun; natl hon soc Philosophy. **BUSINESS ADDRESS:** 601 Irving Ave, Syracuse, NY 13210.

RASHAD, AHMAD (BOBBY MOORE)
Athlete. **PERSONAL:** Born Nov 19, 1949, Portland, OR; married Phylicia; children: Keva, Maiysha, Ahmad Jr, Condola Phylea. **EDUCATION:** Univ OR, degree in edn. **CAREER:** MN Vikings, wide receiver 1976-; Seattle, 1976; Buffalo, 1974-75; St Louis, 1972-74; KMSP-TV Minneapolis, host monday night football preview show; WCCO-TV Minneapolis, sports reporter; NBC Sports, host. **HONORS/ACHIEVEMENTS:** Played NFL Champ Game 1976; set NFL record for longest non-scoring play from scrimmage when he caught a 98 yd pass from Jim Hart 1972; caught more passes (250) as wide receiver in four years with Vikings than any other wide receiver in NFL during that time; All Am Running Back; All Conf 3 Times; Pro Bowl 1979. **BUSINESS ADDRESS:** NBC, 30 Rockefeller Plaza, New York, NY 10020.

RASHAD, PHYLICIA AYERS-ALLEN
Performing artist. **PERSONAL:** Born Jun 19, 1948, Houston, TX; daughter of Andrew A Allen and Vivian Ayers; married William Lancelot Bowles, Jr (divorced 1975); children: William Lancelot III; married Victor Willis, 1978 (divorced 1980); married Ahmad Rashad, Dec 1985; children: Condola Phylea, 3 stepchildren. **EDUCATION:** Howard Univ, Washington DC, BFA, 1970. **CAREER:** Off-Broadway and Broadway actress, 1970s, including "Into the Woods," "Dreamgirls," "The Whiz," and "Ain't Supposed to Die a Natural Death"; played Courtney Wright on television soap "One Life to Live," and Claire Huxtable on "The Cosby Show," 1984-; actress in television films "False Witness," 1989, and "Polly," 1989. **HONORS/ACHIEVEMENTS:** 2 Emmy nominations for "The Cosby Show"; 2 People's Choice Awards for most popular actress on network television; NAACP Image Award as the best actress in a comedy series for 3 consecutive seasons; Ace Award nomination for best supporting actress in television film "Uncle Tom's Cabin.". **BUSINESS ADDRESS:** c/o "The Cosby Show ", Kaufman Astoria Studios, 34-12 36th St, Astoria, NY 11106. *

RASHEED, HOWARD S.
Financial executive. **PERSONAL:** Born Feb 03, 1953, Chicago, IL; son of Howard L. Lee, Sr. and Kathlene P. Lee; married Barbara; children: Candace, Derick, Hassan, Mikal. **EDUCATION:** Univ of West FL, BS Marketing 1978, MBA Finance 1979. **CAREER:** FSC Business Development, financial analyst 1973-74; AMM Journal, purchasing mgr 1974-75; Southern Bell, account exec 1978-83; Ver Val Enterprises, dir of finance 1983-87. **ORGANIZATIONS:** Dir Pensacola Private Industry Council 1982-85; mem Assoc of MBA Execs 1983-87; commissioner Pensacola-Escambia Develop Commn 1984; dir Ft Walton Beach Comm of 100 1986-; mem Natl Black MBA Assoc 1987. **HOME ADDRESS:** 16 Neptune Dr, Mary Esther, FL 32569.

RASHFORD, JOHN HARVEY
Educator/anthropologist. **PERSONAL:** Born May 10, 1947, Port Antonio, Jamaica;son of Hector G. Rashford and Winifred Jacobs Rashford; married Grace Maynard. **EDUCATION:** Friends World Coll, BA 1969; CUNY Grad Center, MA, PhD 1982. **CAREER:** Crossroads Africa, group leader 1971; Rutgers Univ, visiting lecturer 1980-82; Coll of Charleston, asst prof anthropology. **ORGANIZATIONS:** Mem Soc for Econ Botany 1979-, SC Acad of Science 1982-; clerk Charleston Friends Meeting 1984-. **BUSINESS ADDRESS:** Asst Prof of Anthropology, Coll of Charleston, Dept of Sociology/Anthropolgy, Charleston, SC 29401.

RASHIED, A. JOHN
Educational administrator, training officer. **PERSONAL:** Born Oct 05, 1941, Bridgeport, CT; married Marcella A Grace; children: John Jr, Kamilah Ayisha, Khadijah Anne. **EDUCATION:** San Jose City Coll, attended 1960-62; Roosevelt Univ, BS 1973, MA 1974. **CAREER:** IBM Corp, sr staff admin 1964-74; St Acad, dir 1974-79; Atlanta Bd of Educ, counselor 1979-80; Fulton Co Govt, training officer 1980-. **ORGANIZATIONS:** Adjunct prof DeKalb Comm Coll 1982-; mem Amer Soc of Training & Dev 1982-; 1st vice pres Fulton Co Employees Assoc 1983-. **HONORS/ACHIEVEMENTS:** Charter mem Amer Muslim Mission 1974; editor Fulton Co Employees Assn 1982, 1983.

RASPBERRY, WILLIAM J.
Columnist. **PERSONAL:** Born Oct 12, 1935, Okolona, MS; married Sondra Dodson; children: Patricia D, Angela D, Mark J. **EDUCATION:** Indiana Central Coll, BS 1958; Indiana Univ, additional study; George Washington Univ. **CAREER:** The Indianapolis Recorder, reporter, editor 1956-60; WTTG Washington, TV commentator 1973; Howard Univ, instr journalism 1971-; Washington Post, columnist 1962-. **ORGANIZATIONS:** Mem Grid Iron Club, Capitol Press Club, Wash Assoc of Black Journalists, Kappa Alpha Psi. **HONORS/ACHIEVEMENTS:** Winner of several awds for interpretive & reporting; served on Pulitzer Prize Jury 1975-79; mem Pulitzer Prize Bd 1980-86. **MILITARY SERVICE:** AUS 1960-62. **BUSINESS ADDRESS:** Columnist, Washington Post, 1150 15 St NW, Washington, DC 20071.

RATES, NORMAN M.
Clergyman. **PERSONAL:** Born Jan 01, 1924, Owensboro, KY; married Laura Lynem; children: Sondra, Shari. **EDUCATION:** KY State Coll, AB 1947; Lincoln Univ, BD 1950; Oberlin Coll, MDiv 1952; Yale Univ, MAR 1961; Vanderbilt Univ, DMin 1974; Oberlin Coll, STM 1953; Harvard Univ, independent study 1968-69. **CAREER:** Camac Comm Ctr Phila, student counselor 1947-48; Philadelphia Gen Hosp, asst to protestant chaplain 1948-49; St Paul Bapt Ch W Chester PA, asst to pastor 1949-50; Div of Home Missions Natl Council for Ch of Christ in USA NY FL DE, missionary to agricultural migrants 1948-56; Morris Coll, minister dean of men tchr 1953-54; Morehouse Spelman Coll Pre-Coll Prog summers, counselor & minister 1966-67; Central Brooklyn Model Cities Summer Acad Spelman Coll summer, couns 1972; Interdenom Theol Ctr, guest lectr & part-time tchr 1971; Westhills Presb Ch GA summer, interim pastor 1963; Spelman Coll GA Dept of Religion, coll minister & chmn 1954-. **ORGANIZATIONS:** Mem Natl Assn of Coll & Univ Chaplains; mem Ministry to Blacks in Higher Educ; mem Amer Assn of Univ Profs; mem Natl Assn of Biblical Instr; memUniv Ctr in GA Div of Tchr of Religion; Petit Juror Fulton Co Superior Ct 1971, 1973; grand juror Fulton Co Superior Ct 1972; ministerial standing The United Ch of Christ; Fellow Conf on African & African-Amer Studies Atlanta Univ Campus; bd mem Camping Unlimited Blue Star Camps Inc; bd dir Planned Parenthood Assn of Atlanta; chmn Religious Affairs Com Planned Parenthood Assn of Atlanta; mem Com on the Ministry The United Ch of Christ; mem The Metro Atlanta Christian Council; mem GA-SC Assn of the United Ch of Christ SE Conf; mem Alpha Phi Alpha Frat. **HONORS/ACHIEVEMENTS:** C Morris Cain Prize in Bible Lincoln Univ 1949; Samuel Dickey Prize in New Testament Lincoln Univ 1949; Campus Christian Worker Grant Danforth Found 1960-61; Atlanta Univ Ctr Non-Western Studies Prog Grant for Travel & Study Ford Found 1968-69. **BUSINESS ADDRESS:** Coll Minist/Chmn Dept Religion, Spelman College, 350 Spelman Lane SW, Atlanta, GA 30314.

RATLIFF, JOE SAMUEL
Minister. **PERSONAL:** Born Jul 24, 1950, Lumberton, NC; married Doris Gardner. **EDUCATION:** Morehouse Coll, BA 1972; Interdenominational Theol Ctr Atlanta, MDiv 1975, DMin 1976. **CAREER:** Cobb Memorial Church Atlanta, pastor 1971-78; Morehouse Coll, prof 1974-77; Brentwood Bapt Church Atlanta, pastor 1980-. **ORGANIZATIONS:** Mem Urban League Bd 1985-; co-chairman Anti-Defamation League Black-Jewish Comm 1985-; mem bd of trustees Interdenominational Theol Ctr Atlanta 1986-. **HONORS/ACHIEVEMENTS:** 1986 Minister of the Year Natl Conf of Christians and Jews. **HOME ADDRESS:** 8202 Frontenac Dr, Houston, TX 77071. **BUSINESS ADDRESS:** Pastor, Brentwood Baptist Church, 13033 Landmark St, Houston, TX 77045.

RATTLEY, JESSIE M.
Councilwoman, educator. **PERSONAL:** Born May 04, 1929, Birmingham, AL; widowed; children: Florence, Robin. **EDUCATION:** Hampton Inst, BS 1951; grad courses; IBM Data Processing School; LaSalle Extension Univ. **CAREER:** Huntington HS Newport News, established Business Dept (the first Black High School in Newport News to offer business training to its students); Newport NewsCity Council, 1st Black & 1st woman councilman elected 1970, 1974, 1978, 1982; City of Newport News, vice-mayor 1976; 1st black & 1st woman mayor 1986-88; Peninsula Bus Coll, dir. **ORGANIZATIONS:** Vchmn State Dem Party 1972,76,80; pres Peninsula Coord Comm; mem Carver Memorial Presb Ch; hon mem Natl Assn of Negro Bus & Professional Women's Clubs;former basileus Lambda Omega Chap Alpha Kappa; mem Mental Health Bd; mem VA Peninsula Chaplaincy Svc; mem Southeastern Business Coll Assn; life mem NAACP; sponsor Delta Mu; chmn Revenue Sharing Task Force; mem City Policy Leadership Issues Task Force; mem Women in Municipal Govt Steering Comm; mem Infrastructure Task Force; appt by Gov to Criminal Justice & Crime Prevention Task Force; comm on Volunteerism; mem Special Task Force to study VA Jails; mem bd dir Public Admin Adv; vice pres bd of dir Whittaker Meml Hosp; mem bd of dir Natl Inst of Publ Mgmt; mem adv comm Inst of Govt VA; appt by Gov to Commiss on Future of VA. **HONORS/ACHIEVEMENTS:** Listed in the Natl Register of Prominent Amers 1975-77; Sojourner Truth Awd Natl Assn of Negro Business & Professional Women's Clubs 1978; Intl Woman of the Year Radio Sta WRAP-Norfolk VA 1979; Unique Achiev Awd for Polit Serv by Dubois Circle of Baltimore MD 1981; second annual Martin Luther King Jr Meml Awd Old Dominion Univ in recognition of lendership in social justice 1986. **BUSINESS ADDRESS:** Dir, Peninsula Business College, 2901 Jefferson Ave, Newport News, VA 23607.

RAULLERSON, CALVIN HENRY
International organization executive. **PERSONAL:** Born Dec 18, 1920, Utica, NY; son of Calvin T Raullerson and Cora White Raullerson; married Olive Lewis; children: Cheryl G, Earl Henry, Kevin Greer. **EDUCATION:** Lincoln Univ, AB 1943; Harvard Univ, post grad 1947; NY Univ, MPA 1949. **CAREER:** Asst to exec dir Civ Educ Services, United Negro Coll Fund 1952-61; Amer Soc African Culture Lagos Nigeria, dir 1961-64; Amer Soc African Culture, exec dir 1964-66; E & So African Peace Corps, chief 1966-69; Kenya Peace Corps, dir 1969-71; Africa Peace Corps, reg dir 1971-73; Intl Ctr for Arid & Semi-Arid Land TX Tech Univ, exec asst to dean, asst prof Health Org Mgmt 1973-78; Bur Pvt Devel Coop, asst admin Agency for Intl Devel 1978-81; African Amer Inst, vice pres 1981-85; Keene Monk Assocs, assoc 1985-86; One America Inc, dir intl programs 1987-88; Labat-Anderson, Inc, pres, Intl Div, 1988-. **ORGANIZATIONS:** Rockefeller travel grantee E & Central Africa 1960; del Intl Conf on African Hist Univ Ibadan Nigeria 1962; del Intl Conf on African Affairs Univ Ghana 1963; Treasurer US Planning Comm 1st World Festival Negro Art Dakar 1965-66; mem inform resources con group on business affairs Assn Amer Med Colls; mem adv com on desentification AAAS 1976-78; clubs, Harvard (Washington); Monroe & Plaza (Chicago). **HONORS/ACHIEVEMENTS:** Del UN Conf on Desertification Nairobi 1977; mem Career Ministers Selection Bd Dept of State 1980; asst ed & dir of rsch, Who's Who in Colored Amer; assoc ed, Who's Who in the UN; contributor Negro Yearbook; Woodrow Wilson Scholar 1978-80; head of US delegation Comm on Food Aid and Policy World Food Program Rome Italy 1980. **MILITARY SERVICE:** AUS 1942-44. **BUSINESS ADDRESS:** Pres, Intl Div, Labat-Anderson, Inc, 2200 Clarendon Blvd, Arlington, VA 22201.

RAVELING, GEORGE HENRY
Coach. **PERSONAL:** Born Jun 27, 1937, Washington, DC; married Vivian James; children: Mark. **EDUCATION:** Villanova U, BS 1960. **CAREER:** University of Iowa, head basketball coach; WA State U, head basketball coach; VillanovaUnivUniv MD, asst basketball coach; Sun Oil Co, marketing analysis sales rep; Converse Rubber Co, promotions rep; has syndicated newspaper column which appears in various Pacific NW & newspapers; TV & Radio Show; conducts annual basketball coaches clinic. **ORGANIZATIONS:** Mem Nat Spkrs Assn; Sports Illustrated Spkrs Bur; mem Nat Assn of Basketball Coaches; Am Humor Studies Assn; adv bd Uniroyal Corp Spaulding Corp Joseph P Kennedy Found for Mentally Retarded Letterman Coach & Athl Mags. **HONORS/ACHIEVEMENTS:** Mem black hall of fame Nat Black Sports Found; hon cert of citizenship from Kansas City & New Orleans; voted Pac-8 Coach of Year 1975; voted UPI w coast coach of year 1975; voted natl coll coach of year 1977; disting alumnus & humanitarian awards Villanova U; cert of merit outstanding sales Pub Rels & Marketing from Philadelphia Tribune Newspaper; Who's Who in Basketball. **BUSINESS ADDRESS:** Head Basketball Coach, US C University Park, 101A Heritage Hall, Los Angeles, CA 90089.

RAVENELL, JOSEPH PHILLIP
Clergyman. **PERSONAL:** Born Jan 20, 1940, Pinesville, SC; married Mary Jane Frazier; children: Joseph, Phillip, Byron. **EDUCATION:** St Peters Coll, BS Hist 1973; Princeton Theol Sem, MDiv 1976. **CAREER:** NJ St Prison, institutional chpln; Samaritan Bapt Ch, pastor 1979-; Trenton St Coll, coll chpln 1975-78; US Postal Svc, letter carrier 1966-75. **ORGANIZATIONS:** Pres of NJ Chap St Chpln Orgn 1978-; dir Com Network Proj 1979-; mem AUS Nat Guard Assn 1978-; mem Mil Chplns Assn 1978-; mem Am Correctnl Chplns Assn 1978-. **HONORS/ACHIEVEMENTS:** Good Conduct Medal AUS 1963. **MILITARY SERVICE:** AUS qsp/4 served 2 yrs. **BUSINESS ADDRESS:** New Jersey State Prison, Third Federal St, Trenton, NJ 08625.

RAVENELL, MILDRED
Educator. **PERSONAL:** Born Dec 01, 1944, Charleston, SC; married William Ravenell; children: William Samuel, Teressa Emlynne. **EDUCATION:** Fisk Univ, BA 1965; Howard Univ, JD 1968; Harvard Univ, LLM 1971. **CAREER:** IBM, systems engr 1968-70, marketing rep 1970; Boston Univ, asst dean for admissions & financial aid 1971-72; FL State Univ, assoc prof of law 1976-84; Univ of VA, visiting assoc prof of law 1984-85. **ORGANIZATIONS:** Mem Phi Beta Kappa; mem Amer Bar Assn; mem MA Bar Assn; mem Bethel AME Church; mem Delta Sigma Theta Sor; mem Jack & Jill of Amer Inc; former mem bd of dirs Terrell House at Tallahassee; mem bd of trustees Law Sch Admission council; former mem Bd of Bus Regulation FL.

RAVENELL, WILLIAM HUDSON
Attorney. **PERSONAL:** Born May 31, 1942, Boston, MA; son of William S Ravenell and Isabella T Ravenell; children: William Samuel, Teresa Emlynne. **EDUCATION:** Lincoln Univ PA, BA 1963; State Coll at Boston, MEd 1965; Howard Univ Sch of Law, JD 1968. **CAREER:** John Hancock Ins Co, analyst 1968-71; Housing Inspection Dept, admin 1971-72; State Dept of Comm Affairs, dep sec 1972-75; FL Dept of Comm Affairs, sec 1975-79; FL A&M Univ, prof 1979; FL Office of the Atty Gen, special asst 1979-80; US Dept of Transportation Fed Hwy Admin, chief counsel 1980-81; State of FL, asst attorney general 1982-85; Florida A&M Univ, attorney, professor 1985-. **ORGANIZATIONS:** Chmn FL Commn on Human Relations 1975-77; chmn FL Manpower Serv Council 1975-80; FL, DC, VA, Natl, Amer Bar Assns; mem Phi Alpha Delta, Omega Psi Phi, FL Council of 100. **BUSINESS ADDRESS:** Attorney/ Professor, Florida A&M University, Tallahassee, FL 32303.

RAWLES, ELIZABETH GIBBS
Manager public relations. **PERSONAL:** Born Dec 19, 1943, Roxbury, MA; children: Lewis Frederick. **EDUCATION:** Univ of CT, BA Sociology 1965; Univ of Hartford, MA Applied Communications 1984. **CAREER:** Urban League of Greater Hartford, prog asst 1969-73, prog dir 1970-73; WHNB TV West Hartford, minority programming 1973-76, comm affairs dir 1976-79; WVIT TV West Hartford, dir public affairs 1979-84; UConn Health Ctr, asst dir inst relations 1984-85, dir inst relations 1985-. **ORGANIZATIONS:** Mem Women in Communications, Natl Broadcast Assoc for Comm Affairs, Amer Mktg Assoc, Academic Medical Ctr Mktg Group, Assoc of Amer Medical Colls; partner in Hartcom Inc; adjunct prof Univ of Hartford Dept of Communications 1983-85, Hartford Coll for Women Oral Communication Presentation Skills 1986-. **HONORS/ACHIEVEMENTS:** Emmy Awd Natl Acad of TV Arts & Scis Boston New England Chap 1977; UPI Awd 1st place documentary 1977, citations of excellence 1975,78; CEBA Awd World Inst of Comm to Black Audiences Awd of Distinction 1979, Awd of Excellence 1980; IRIS Awd Natl Assoc of TV Prog Execs Natl Awd Documentary Category 1983; MATRIX Awd Women in Communications 1983; Women in Leadership Awd Hartford YWCA 1984. **HOME ADDRESS:** 145 Palm St, Hartford, CT 06112.

RAWLINGS, MARILYN MANUELA
Electronics company executive. **PERSONAL:** Born Feb 29, 1956, Baltimore, MD; daughter of Prince H Rawlings and Edwina M Rawlings (deceased). **EDUCATION:** Frostburg State Univ, Frostburg MD, BS, 1977. **CAREER:** Walper, Smullien & Blumenthal, Towson MD, tax acct, 1978-80; Lincoln Natl Life, Baltimore MD, exec sec for sales, 1980-81; Cameo Electronics Co Inc, Owings Mills MD, pres, 1981-. **ORGANIZATIONS:** Chairman of Minority Input Committee, MD/DC Minority Purchasing Council. **HONORS/ACHIEVEMENTS:** One of 50 Outstanding Business Leaders in MD, Baltimore Sun, 1988; Product/Supplier of the Year, MD/DC Minority Purchaing Council, 1987; Outstanding Achievement Award, MD/DC Minority Purchasing Council, 1988; Certificate of Appreciation, Minority Business Committee/Federal Exec Board, 1985; Speaker to the Black Student Body of Frostburg State Univ, 1987; Speaker for Elementary School System, Baltimore MD. **BUSINESS ADDRESS:** President, Cameo Electronics Co Inc, 11 Gwynns Mill Court, Owings Mills, MD 21117.

RAWLINGS, MARTHA (NEE MORSE)
Educator. **PERSONAL:** Born Jul 08, 1942, Baltimore, MD; married Gilbert Bruce; children: Tonya. **EDUCATION:** Towson St Coll, BS 1969; Syracuse U, MA 1974; OH St U, Post Grad. **CAREER:** Denison Univ, asst dean of students; Columbus Area Comm Mental Health Center, family crisis counselor 1973-; Dept of HEW, psych 1972; MD Res Manpower Center, mental health coordinator, counseling psych 1972; Univ of MD, psych 1970; Dept of Def, job counselor 1969; Johns Hopkins Hospital, psych research tech 1969; Frnds of Pshycist Research, research asst 1965-68; Dept of Educ, teachers aid 1965; Dept of Public Welfare, Dept of Social Serv, social worker asst 1964. **ORGANIZATIONS:** Mem adv bd Nat Counc of Blk Studies; mem APGA; mem Subcom ANWC & ACPA; bd dir Plnd Prnthd 1976. **HONORS/ACHIEVEMENTS:** Cert of training for stat sci US Civil Serv Commn 1972; "Curriculum Prop for Tchng Race Awareness in Primary & Scndry Sch" 1966; thesis "The TranstnlSit of Revse Integration & the Sit of Integratn in 2 MD Coll" Towson St Coll 1967; "Socio-Psychol Causes of Riots" SyracruseUniv 1969; "Prop to Facilitate Rltnshp Between Comm & Police" 1974; coretta king award Am Assn ofUniv Wm 1969-70; Maxwell CSch of Citznshp & Pub Afrs Flw 1969-70; Maurice Falk med fnd flw Maurice Falk Med Fnd 1970-71; deans list Towson St Coll 1966; pres Soc Club Towson St Coll 1967-68; Soc Hon Soc Alpha Kappa Delta 1969-71. **BUSINESS ADDRESS:** Denison Univ, Granville, OH 43023.

RAWLINS, ELIZABETH B.
Educator. **PERSONAL:** Born Nov 25, 1927, Cambridge; married Keith W Jr; children: Paul, Pattie E. **EDUCATION:** Salem St Coll, BS 1950; Simmons Coll, MS 1967; Tufts U, grad study; Harvard U, grad study. **CAREER:** Dorman School, teacher 1950-52; Narimasu Elem School Japan, 1953-54; Buckingham School, 1952-62; Hingham MA Public Schools, 1964-67; Simmons Coll, instr lectr 1967-75, asst prof 1975-79, assoc prof of educ 1979; Simmons Coll, assoc dean 1976-79, assoc dean of coll, assoc prof of educ. **ORGANIZATIONS:** Exec com pres MA Assoc for Mental Health 1970-; rsch com Legis Task Force Natl Assoc Mental Health; exec comm Natl Mental Health Assoc; gov task force Determination of Need; chmn Children's Adv Com MA Dept Mental Health; bd of regents for Higher Educ MA 1980-82, reapptd 1983-88; mem Educ Commn of the States 1982, reapptd 1985-. **HONORS/ACHIEVEMENTS:** Disting Alumna Awd Salem State Coll 1982; Educ Awd Boston Branch NAACP 1986.

RAWLINS, SEDRICK JOHN
Dentist. **PERSONAL:** Born May 29, 1927, NYC, NY; married Alyce Taliaferro; children: Wayne, Mark. **EDUCATION:** Lincoln U, AB 1950; Meharry Med Coll, DDS 1954. **CAREER:** E Hartford CT Dentist, pvt prac 1956-; CT Savs & Loan, incorporator 1969-70; Manchester Meml Hosp, 1969-72. **ORGANIZATIONS:** Mem Manchester Hum Relat Com 1959-; CT St Bd Parole 1959-, chmn 1966-68; CT Govt Plng Com Crmnl Adminstrn, chmn correction com 1967-69; mem CT House of Del 1970; mem Nat Dental Assn st vice pres 1968-70; Am & CT Dental Assn; CT Counc on Nat Paroling Authorities; mem Phi Beta Sigma; NAACP pres 1959-60; Dem; Bapt; mem High Noon Club Hartford CT. **HONORS/ACHIEVEMENTS:** Recip hum relat award E Hartford 1970; serv award NAACP 1960. **MILITARY SERVICE:** USAAF Dental Corps 1944-46; AUS 1954-56. **BUSINESS ADDRESS:** 183 Burnside Ave E, Hartford, CT 06108.

RAWLS, GEORGE H.
Surgeon. **PERSONAL:** Born Jun 02, 1928, Gainesville, FL; married Lula; children: Yvonne, Bettye, Sherri. **EDUCATION:** FL A&M Univ, 1948; Howard Univ Sch Med, 1952. **CAREER:** VA Hosp Dayton, surg resd 1955-59; OH State Univ, clinical instr surgeon 1957-59; Am Bd Surgery, diplomate 1961; Private Practice, surgeon. **ORGANIZATIONS:** Fellow Amer Coll Surgeons 1963; guest examiner Amer Bd Surgery 1977; co-chmn life mem NAACP; life mem bd Natl NAACP; prs Marion Co Med Soc; mem Alpha Phi Alpha; bd of dirs Urban League; Children's Mus; past bd dir Flanner House clinical asst prof surg IN Sch Med. **HONORS/ACHIEVEMENTS:** Citizen of the Yr Omega Psi Phi 1971; Citizen of the Yr Federated Clubs 1976; several articles publ in surgical journals. **MILITARY SERVICE:** AUS 1st lt 1953-55. **BUSINESS ADDRESS:** 3231 N Meridian, Indianapolis, IN 46208.

RAWLS, LOU
Singer. **PERSONAL:** Born Dec 01, 1936, Chicago, IL. **CAREER:** Lou Rawls & The Golddiggers, performer 1969; 77 Sunset Strip, Bourbon St Beat, The Big Valley, Mannix Fall Guy, Fantasy Island, actor; Stormy Monday, Lou Rawls & Strings, Tobacco Rd, Black & Blue, Nobody But Lou, singer; Dick Clark Show, Tonight Show, Steve Allen Show, performer; Uptown A Tribute to Apollo Theatre, singer 1980; Sam Cooke Pilgrim Travelers, singer 1962-; TV Program, Rhythm and Rawls 1982; vocals in two animated Garfield specials; featured on the Garfield soundtrack album; classic song hits You'll Never Find, Natural Man, Lady Love, Deadend Street, Love is a Hurtin' Thing; current album Love Your Blues Away. **ORGANIZATIONS:** Natl spokesman Anheuser-Busch 1976; hon chmn United Negro Coll Fund 1979; organized The Lou Rawls Parade of Stars Telethon to benefit UNCF; 1983 Christmas tour of military bases in Korea, Japan and the Phillipines. **HONORS/ACHIEVEMENTS:** Grammy Awds, 1967,71,77,78; 1 Platinum album "All Things In Time", 5 Gold albums "All Things In Time", "Lou Rawls Live", "Soulin'", "Unmistakably Lou", "When You Hear Lou"; Gold single "You'll Never Find". **MILITARY SERVICE:** AUS 1956-58. **BUSINESS ADDRESS:** The Brokaw Co, 9255 Sunset Blvd, Los Angeles, CA 90069.

RAWLS, LOUIS
Clergyman. **PERSONAL:** Born Jul 16, 1905, Johns, MS; married Willia J Lowe; children: Lou, Samuel B, Julius. **EDUCATION:** Moody Bibile Inst, Grad 1932; Rodger Williams U, BS 1932; No Bapt Theol Sem, BTh 1938; NorthwesternUniv Garrett Biblical Isnt, BD 1945, MD 1961;Cntrl St U, LLD, Hon DD 1957; MS Coll, 1954; Geo Williams Coll, MS 1961; Ideal Bible Coll, Hon DD 1968; Natchez Coll, Hon HHD 1975; Universal Bible Inst, PhD 1977. **CAREER:** Tabernacle Bapt Ch, pastor 34 yrs; Caanan Bapt Ch, 10 yrs; Var Businesses, funeral business, real est; car wash, ins, printing, Finan since 1932; Cook Co Jail, 1st black chpln; Chicago Bapt Inc, tchr 38 yrs; Notary 31 years. **ORGANIZATIONS:** Orgnzd Tabernacle Bapt Ch; fdr Tbrncl Comm Hosp & Hlth Ctr; helped rgn Progsv Nat Bapt Conv; only survivng orgnzr Chicago Bapt Inst; past presBapt St Conv 4 yrs; mem Arabic Temple; pres Bapt St Conv of IL; trustee Chicago Bapt Inst; Chicago C of C; Chicago Conf of Brthrhd; Met C of C; trustee Moorehouse Sch of Rel; trustee NAACP; Oper PUSH; SCLC; pres Tbrncl Bapt Ch Found; Tbrncl Bapt Ch Comm Ctr; United Bd Coll Devel for the 70 Predominately Black Coll in USA; Urban Leag; Wash Park YMCA; Wisdom Lodge; founder 7 bd EB Devel 1934, Community Hosp 1971, PHB Comm 1968; Erected the Willa Rawls Senior Citizens Complex 1981. **HONORS/ACHIEVEMENTS:** Recip award of merit Men Benevolent Serv Club 1958; cert of merit Bapt St Conv 1960; cert of commndtn Chicago Area Counc 1967; brthrhd award Chicago Conf for Brthrhd 1967; testimnl award Dr CO Cartlstrom Comm 1973; cert of recog Chicago Bapt Inst Alumni Assn 1973; Prog Nat Bapt Cong of Chris Educ 1973; apprctn award Pilgrim Bapt Mission 1973; humanitrn award Nat Sor Mu Chap 1975; industrl comm award Spiegel Inc. **BUSINESS ADDRESS:** 5421 S Morgan, Chicago, IL.

RAWLS, RALEIGH RICHARD
Attorney. **PERSONAL:** Born Jun 12, 1925, Gainesville, FL; married Annie R Robinson; children: Regina D, Rene N, Renard A, Rodney P. **EDUCATION:** Howard U, BA 1950, LLB 1956. **CAREER:** City of Ft Lauderdale, pub defender 1973-; Atty, pvt prac 1957-. **ORGANIZATIONS:** Mem Braward Co Bar Assn; Nat Bar Assn; life mem Alpha Phi Alpha; NAACP. **MILITARY SERVICE:** UUSN 1943-46. **BUSINESS ADDRESS:** 1018 1/2 NW 6 St, Fort Lauderdale, FL.

RAWLS, RODNEY ALAN
Economist. **PERSONAL:** Born May 13, 1956, Philadelphia, PA; son of Ceasar Octavious Rawls and Beatrice Brenda Bredell Rawls. **EDUCATION:** Cheyney State Coll, BA Biology 1979; Cheyney-Hahnemann, 6 yr BA, MD Prog; Temple Univ, MBA Econ 1987, PhD Prog Econ 1987-. **CAREER:** Liberty Mutual Ins Co, safety consul 1980-82; Mayberry Rigger, 1982-83; VR Business Broker, salesman 1983-84; Taco Bell, mgr 1984-86; US Dept of Labor, Philadelphia PA, student economist 1987-88. **ORGANIZATIONS:** Mem Alpha Phi Sigma Natl Sch Frat Xi Chapt, Beta Kappa Chi Scientific Soc Cheyney Chapt; mem Assoc of MBA Execs 1984-, Amer Economic Assoc 1985, 1987,Natl Black MBA Assoc 1985,87; volunteer UNICEF 1989-. **MILITARY SERVICE:** AUS Reserves 2nd lt 2 1/2 yrs; Honorable Discharge. **HOME ADDRESS:** 6015 Limekiln Pike, Apt #10, Philadelphia, PA 19141.

RAWLS, WILLIAM D., SR.
Insurance executive. **CAREER:** Golden Circle Life Insurance Co, Brownsville TN, chief executive. **BUSINESS ADDRESS:** Golden Circle Life Insurance Co, 39 Jackson Ave S, Brownsville, TN 38012. *

RAY, ANDREW
Educator. **PERSONAL:** Born Feb 04, 1948, Centreville, MS; son of Perry and Ruby. **EDUCATION:** Southern Univ, BS Economics 1969; State Univ of NY, MS Educ 1970; Univ of Buffalo MS Admin 1982. **CAREER:** Dept of State, intern 1968; US Congress, intern 1974; Urban League, career educator 1983; Adolescent Vocational Exploration Prog NY, dir; CSD, instructor/dean 1985-; admin vice pres 1988-. **ORGANIZATIONS:** Chair of brd Budon Federal Credit Union 1978-; comm mem YMCA 1979-; first vice dist rep Omega Psi Phi 1984, dist rep 1986; founder Black Educators Assoc. **HONORS/ACHIEVEMENTS:** Foreign Affairs Scholar Dept of State Wash DC; Presidential Fellow Wash DC; Teacher of the Year city of Rochester 1974; Distinguished Citizen Urban League 1980; Administrator of the Year 1989. **BUSINESS ADDRESS:** Dean of Students, CSD, 1801 E Main St #F317, Rochester, NY 14609.

RAY, AUSTIN H.
Marketing manager. **PERSONAL:** Born Aug 23, 1943, Lexington, MO; married Geneva Green; children: Keith, Krista. **EDUCATION:** Pittsburg State Univ, BA 1965; Western Michigan Univ, MBA 1973. **CAREER:** Case Western Reserve Univ, rsch assoc 1967-70; General Foods Corp, buyer/distribution supr 1970-73; Xerox Corp, dist plnr/mktg & prog mgmt 1973-83, plng mgr/quality mgr 1983-87, mgr future products marketing. **ORGANIZATIONS:** Life mem Kappa Alpha Psi Frat (polemarch/bd dir Roch Alumni); adv bd Finger Lakes Health Systems Agency 1976-78, Baden St Settlement (Rochester) 1978-83; dir for Junior Achievement Xerox Mgmt Assoc 1978-81; prog chmn Boys and Girls Club of Rochester 1980-83; mem Rochester Chamber of Commerce 1981-83; chmn Finance Commn Comm Congregational Church. **HONORS/ACHIEVEMENTS:** Disting Serv Kappa Alpha Psi Roch Alumni 1974-83; Disting Svc/Leadership Xerox Mgmt Assoc for Junior Achievement 1978-81; Outstanding Young Men in Amer US Jaycees; Outstanding Serv Urban League Rochester; Leadership/Disting Serv CARI Inc Rochester NY. **MILITARY SERVICE:** AUS 1st lt 2 yrs; Army Commendation Medal, Vietnam Serv Awd 1967. **HOME ADDRESS:** 4888 Elder Ave, Seal Beach, CA 90740. **BUSINESS ADDRESS:** Marketing Manager, Xerox Corp, 701 Aviation Blvd, ESCP304, El Segundo, CA 90245.

RAY, DAVID BRUCE
Education. **PERSONAL:** Born May 15, 1953, Somerville, NJ; married Christine Lindgren. **EDUCATION:** Middlesex County Coll, AA 1977; Rider Coll, BA 1979; George Washington Univ, MA 1984. **CAREER:** Natl Institute of Independent Colleges and Universities, research associate 1983. **ORGANIZATIONS:** Big Brothers of America, big brother. **HOME ADDRESS:** 16 8th Street, NE, Washington, DC 20002. **BUSINESS ADDRESS:** Research Associate, NIICU, 122 C St NW #750, Washington, DC 20001.

RAY, GILBERT T.
Attorney. **PERSONAL:** Born Sep 18, 1944, Mansfield, OH; married Valerie Jeanne; children: Tanika N, Tarlin B. **EDUCATION:** Ashland Coll, BBA 1966; Univ of Toledo, MBA 1968; Howard Univ School of Law, JD 1972. **CAREER:** Gen Foods Corp White Plains, personnel mgmt, mktg 1968-69; O'Melveny & Myers LA, partner attny. **ORGANIZATIONS:** Mem Amer Bar Assoc, Natl Bar Assoc, Langston Law Club; exec com Bus Law Sect State Bar 1979-, LA Cty Bar Assoc; ed-in-chief Howard Law Jrnl 1972; exec chmn Natl Conf of Law Reviews 1972; exec commLA Barrister 1976-78; vchmn CA Bus Law Sect 1980-82. **HONORS/ACHIEVEMENTS:** Listed in Who's Who in Amer Coll & Univ 1966, Outstanding Sen Awd 1966; Grad Honor Roll 1968.

RAY, JACQUELINE WALKER
Educator. **PERSONAL:** Born May 14, 1944, Buffalo, NY; married Lacy Ray Jr. **EDUCATION:** SUNY at Buffalo, BA 1965, MSW 1967; NY Univ, PhD 1975. **CAREER:** Columbia Univ Coler Proj, social worker 1967-68; NY City Housing Auth Model Cities Prog, field suprv 1968-70; Jersey City State Coll, asst prof of psych 1970-71; York Coll of CUNY, assoc prof of psych. **ORGANIZATIONS:** Amer Psychological Assn; bd of dir Comm Mediation servs; Queens Cty Mental Health Soc; Alpha Kappa Alpha Sorority; League of Women Voters, Region II Mental Health Consultant, Job Corps. **HONORS/ACHIEVEMENTS:** Articles publ Jrnl of Gen Ed 1979-, Jrnl of Intergroup Tensions 1983, Jrnl of Coll Student Personnel; Urban Ed Rsch Trainee CUNY Fellowship 1982-83; Ford Found Study Grant 1980, CUNY Faculty Fellow, 1989-90. **HOME ADDRESS:** PO Box 22, Old Westbury, NY 11568. **BUSINESS ADDRESS:** Assoc Professor of Psychology, York College of CUNY, Jamaica, NY 11451.

RAY, JAMES DEWITT
Professional athlete. **PERSONAL:** Born Jul 27, 1957, Clarksdale, MS; married Phyllis Jones. **EDUCATION:** Jacksonville Univ, BS Phys Ed 1980. **CAREER:** Denver Nuggets, forward 1980-83. **HONORS/ACHIEVEMENTS:** Conf Plyr of Yr as sr.

RAY, JOHNNY
Professional athlete. **PERSONAL:** Born Mar 01, 1957, Chouteau, OK; married Tammy; children: Johnny Jr. **EDUCATION:** Northeastern A&M Jr Coll; u of AR. **CAREER:** Pittsburgh Pirates, infielder. **HONORS/ACHIEVEMENTS:** 2nd highest avg of any NL Switch-hitter 1984; 6th Pirate 2nd baseman in history to reach 300 level in a single season 1984; 4 consecutive game-winning RBI 1984; most consecutive games to set NL record & tie the Major League with GWRBI; named NL Player of the Week 2 times in 1984; Set career highs in RBI & walks; recep of NL Silver Slugger Award 1983; Rookie Player of the Yr The Sporting News 1982; mem TOPPS AAA All-Star Team 1981; Top AAA 2nd baseman by All-Am Baseball News 1981; AR Professional Athlete of the Yr 1982. **BUSINESS ADDRESS:** Pittsburgh Pirates, Three Rivers Stadium, 600 Stadium Cir PO Box 7000, Pittsburgh, PA 15212.

RAY, JUDITH DIANA
Educator, researcher, amateur athlete. **PERSONAL:** Born Sep 14, 1946, St Louis, MO; daughter of Arthur Charles Ray Sr and Pauline Malloyd Ray. **EDUCATION:** Harris Stowe Teachers Coll St Mo, ABEd 1968; WA Univ MO, MAEd 1972; WA State Univ Pullman WA, MS 1979. **CAREER:** St Louis Bd of Ed, teacher 1968-72; WA Univ, St Louis, WA State, Univ Pullman, grad teaching, rsch asst 1970-79; ARC Milwaukee Pierre Marquette Div, natl field rep 1972-73; York Coll CUNY Jamaica Queens, lectr 1973-75; WA State Univ Sch of Vet med, equine rschr; West Chester Univ, asst prof 1978-. **ORGANIZATIONS:** Life mem Amer Alli of Health PE & Rec & Dance 1968-80; vol & mem Amer Soc of Testing & Matls 1978-89; mem Intl & Amer Soc of Biomechs 1978-89; vol teacher ARC 1960-80; faculty adv Gamma Sigma Sigma Natl Serv Sor 1978-80; mem Phi Delta Kappa W Chester 1978; Intl Soc of Biomechanic in Sport; Alpha Kappa Alpha, US Fencing Coaches Assn, life mem US Tennis Assn; US Prof Tennis Assn. **HONORS/ACHIEVEMENTS:** Co-author "EEG Analysis of Equine Joint Lameness" 1977; The Effects of Different Ground Surfaces of Equine Joint 1980; Motion As Analyzed by EEG, Journal of Biomechanics, Vol 13 pages 191-200, 1980. **BUSINESS ADDRESS:** Assistant Professor, West Chester University, 307 South Campus, West Chester, PA 19383.

RAY, MARY E.
Organization chairman. **PERSONAL:** Born Jul 06, 1911, Toones, TN; children: Janice Marie White, Mary Alice Crowder. **CAREER:** Macon Co Policy Bd Sr Cit IL, chmn 1975-. **ORGANIZATIONS:** Mem sec NAACP Mounds IL 1952-56; pres PTA Madison IL 1955-56; instituted nutrition prgm Sr Cit Macon Co 1974-; chmn Family Plng Adv Coun 1970-74;mem Planned Parenthood; mem New Salem Bapt Ch; mem vol outreach wrkr Ofc Aging Decatur IL; pres Mother's Bd of New Salem MBC Brother Dr SW BywarmCharlotte NC.

RAY, MERCER Z.
Retired insurance executive. **PERSONAL:** Born Feb 28, 1911, Roxboro, NC; son of James Ray and Alberta Ray; married Grace Mauney; children: Alice, Mercedes, Consuelo, John. **EDUCATION:** A&T State Univ, BS 1939. **CAREER:** NC Mutual Life Ins Co, agent 1939-40; Golden State Mutual Life Insurance Co, business exec 1941-76 (retired). **ORGANIZATIONS:** Mem NAACP, Urban League, Alpha Phi Alpha Frat, BSA; elder Presbyterian Church. **HONORS/ACHIEVEMENTS:** Order of Merit BSA 1959.

RAY, MOSES ALEXANDER
Dentist. **PERSONAL:** Born Sep 25, 1920, Clinton, NC; married Helen Bettina Jones; children: Shelia Anne, Ernest Alexander. **EDUCATION:** Shaw U, BS 1941; Howard U, DDS 1945. **CAREER:** Dentistry, Tarboro, pvt prac 1946-; Edgecombe Gen Hosp, mem staff. **ORGANIZATIONS:** Mem NC Dental Soc; Am Dental Assn; pres fdr Ranola Hgts Housing Devel Corp Inc 1970-; dir Nash Edgecombe Econ Devel Corp Tarboro; pres E Tarboro Citizens Leag 1965; councilman Tarboro 1967-; mem NC Govs Counc Occupational Hlth 1968-71; trustee Edgecombe Econ Devel Corp; mem Omega Psi Phi. **MILITARY SERVICE:** USAF 1951-53. **BUSINESS ADDRESS:** 409 Panola St, Tarboro, NC 27886.

RAY, RICHARD REX
Air force officer. **PERSONAL:** Born Apr 10, 1942, Dover, OH; married Vernell Lynette Cain; children: Richard Rex Jr, Rolland. **EDUCATION:** Kent State Univ, BBA 1967; Univ of MO Kansas City, MPA 1974. **CAREER:** Maxwell AFB AL, air force reserve officers training corps headquarters chief western resource branch 1976, student air command and staff coll 1979-80; Personnel Ctr Randolph AFB TX, resource mgr 1980-82, chief special assignments branch 1982-83, commander squadron sect 1983-85; USAF Recruiting Squadron St Louis, commander 1985-. **ORGANIZATIONS:** Coach/manager Little League/Amateur Baseball 1973-84; adjunct faculty Troy State Univ Montgomery AL 1977-80; life mem Air Force Assoc. **HONORS/ACHIEVEMENTS:** Outstanding Young Men of Amer 1974; publ "The Headquarters Squadron, The Junior Officer as Leader" Air Univ Review 1975; speaker NAACP Freedom Fund Banquet Dover OH 1978. **MILITARY SERVICE:** USAF lt col 20 yrs; Meritorious Serv Medal 4 Oak Leaf Clusters, Air Force Commendation Medal, Outstanding Unit Awd, Air Force Organizational Excellence Awd. **HOME ADDRESS:** 204 E Losey St, #2W, Scott AFB, IL 62225-1714. **BUSINESS ADDRESS:** Commander, 3545th USAF Recruiting Squad, 405 So Tucker, St Louis, MO 63102.

RAY, SANDY FREDERICK
Clergyman. **PERSONAL:** Born Feb 03, 1898, Marlin, TX; married Cynthia; children: Sandy, Jr, Dorothy. **EDUCATION:** AR Bapt Coll, DD 1936; Morehouse Coll, DD 1958. **CAREER:** Nat Bapt Conv USA, vp; Empire Missionary Bapt Conv NY St, pres; Cornerstone Bapt Ch Brooklyn, pastor. **ORGANIZATIONS:** Apptd NY St Counc on Yth 1967; Gov Task Force Deserting Fathers 1972; mem St Commn Against Discrimintn; chmn Brklyn Adv Counc of NY St Commn for Hum Rights; bd mem SCLC; Martin Luther King Meml Ctr for Soc Change; Morehouse Coll; Andover-Newton Theol Sem; Carver Fed Savs & Loan Assn. **HONORS/ACHIEVEMENTS:** Recip hon LLD Bishop Coll. **BUSINESS ADDRESS:** 562-74 Madison St, New York, NY 11213.

RAY, WALTER I., JR.
Business executive. **PERSONAL:** Born Sep 02, 1923, Newburgh, NY; married Rosemary

White; children: Rosalind R, Walter I III. **EDUCATION:** WV State Coll, 1941-43; Howard U, BS 1949. **CAREER:** Anheuser Busch, Inc, sales/sales supr 1958-70, branch mgr 1971-81; Esoray Publ/Business & Mkt, consultant 1983-85; Game Prod Inc (DC Lottery) vice pres 1982-83; John N Miller Assoc, assoc vice pres 1983-; Esoray Publ Co, pres 1983-. **ORGANIZATIONS:** Bd dir Syst Supp Corp 1984-85; writer Broadcast Music Inc; consultant DC Gov Multex Inc, Purcell Office Prod; DC Chamber Comm; mem NAACP; mem Masons Shriners Consi; mem Omega Psi Phi; mem Natl Assoc Mkt Devel. **HONORS/ACHIEVEMENTS:** Black Achievers of Industry 1972; Natl Capital Parks 1973; Leadership Mem BSA 1979; United Black Fund 1979; Walter I Ray Jr Day proclaimed in District of Columbia 1981. **MILITARY SERVICE:** AUS s/sgt 3 Yrs; USA. **HOME ADDRESS:** 1205 Morningside Dr, Silver Spring, MD 20904.

RAY, WILLIAM BENJAMIN
Educator, opera singer. **PERSONAL:** Born in Lexington, KY; son of Mason Ray and Beatric Clifton Smith; married Carrie Walls Kellogg, Sep 01, 1949; children: Alexander Pierre, William Benjamin Jr. **EDUCATION:** Attended Acad of Music Vienna Austria; KY State Coll, attended 1946-47; Oberlin Coll, BA 1952; Western Reserve Univ, attended 1953; Univ of Heidelberg Heidelberg, Germany, attended 1980-81; Boston Univ, MEd 1982. **CAREER:** De Paur's Infantry Chorus, featured soloist 1953-54; Karamu Theater, opera singer 1954-56; Cleveland Playhouse, opera singer 1954-56; Frankfurt Opera Frankfurt, Germany, opera singer 1957; actor/singer appeared in 14 different roles in Germany and Austrian Film and Television, in the German language; Decca, Intercord, Marcato, BBC, CBS, recording artist 1960-78; Concert Tour of Europe, concert/opera singer 1978-81; Concert Appearances, concert/opera singer 1982; Concert Appearances in Europe, concert/opera singer 1983-; Peabody Conservatory of Music, professor of voice 1982-. **ORGANIZATIONS:** Founder/pres Black Theater Productions 1974-85; mem Alpha Phi Alpha Frat 1946-; appointed exclusive Amer rep to select operatic talent for the Kaleidoscope Production Co Munich Germany. **HONORS/ACHIEVEMENTS:** Recip Gold Medal Lions Club of Italy 1978; listed in Blacks in Opera by Eileen Southern; Amer Fluegel Hubert Giesen; Berlin Opera Yearbook by Walter Felsenstein; Black Americans in Cleveland by Russell Davis. **MILITARY SERVICE:** Engr Sgt 1942-44; Bronze Medal, Purple Heart, Good Conduct, Excellent Marksmanship, ETO Medal, PTO Medal. **BUSINESS ADDRESS:** Professor of Voice, Peabody Conservatory of Music, 1 East Mt Vernon Place, Baltimore, MD 21202.

RAY-GOINS, JEANETTE
Educational executive. **PERSONAL:** Born Dec 08, 1933, St Louis, MO; daughter of Gene Ray and Alma Ray; children: Denise Alma, Maria Josette. **EDUCATION:** Bradley Univ, BA 1955; St Louis Univ, M of Urban Affairs 1972. **CAREER:** Chicago & St Louis Public Schools, teacher 1956-69; Yeatman Comm Corp, deputy executive dir 1970-79; R-G Group, Inc, businesswoman; CO Dept of Education, equity supervisor 1979-. **ORGANIZATIONS:** Pres/owner R-G Group, Inc 1981; mem CO Black Elected Officials 1981-85; vice-pres Aurora School Dist Bd of Ed 1981-85; pres/co-founder Western States Black Women and Business Enterprises, Inc 1984; natl consultant Educational Institutions, Natl Black Women Groups 1983-; owner Black Women West Products 1985; mem Delta Sigma Theta; Natl Coalition of Black School Board Members; exec adv bd CO Network. **HONORS/ACHIEVEMENTS:** Danforth Fellowship Danforth Found 1978-79; Tribute to Outstanding Woman in Politics Award by Co Black Women for Political Action Organization 1982-83; Consultant Award AWARE West Phoenix AZ 1983; Award, Womens Bank of Denver, 1988. **HOME ADDRESS:** 14751 E Tennessee Dr #224, Aurora, CO 80012. **BUSINESS ADDRESS:** Equity Supervisor, Colorado Dept of Education, 201 E Colfax Ave, Rm 206, Denver, CO 80203.

RAYBON, IRMA JULIAN (IRMA JULIAN COOPER)
Retired social worker. **PERSONAL:** Born Nov 14, 1912, Montgomery, AL; married Jesse D; children: Irma Julianne Cooper, Carole E. **EDUCATION:** DePauw Univ, BA 1933; Columbia Univ, MA French 1937; Columbia Teacher Coll, MA Vocational Guidance & Rehab 1950-59. **CAREER:** NY State Dept of Labor Brooklyn, counselor 1950-60; NY State Dept of Social Svc, voc rehab counselor for blind 1960-68; MO State Dept of Educ St Louis, rehab counselor for handicapped 1970-78. **ORGANIZATIONS:** Dir of employment & counseling office Harlem Br YMCA 1941-48; vice pres Brooklyn Links 1958; mem Natl Voc Rehab Assn 1960-78. **HONORS/ACHIEVEMENTS:** Fellowship Grant Soc of Crippled Children for Study at Inst of Phys Med & Rehab NY 1959; Who's Who Women of Amer 1966-67; Who's Who in MO Educ 1975.

RAYBURN, WENDELL GILBERT
Educational administrator. **PERSONAL:** Born May 20, 1929, Detroit, MI; son of Charles J Rayburn (deceased) and Grace Winston Rayburn (deceased); married Gloria Ann Myers; children: Rhonda Renee, Wendell Gilbert, Mark K Williams. **EDUCATION:** Eastern MI Univ, BA 1951; Univ of MI, MA 1952; Wayne State Univ Detroit, EdD 1972. **CAREER:** Detroit Public Schools, teacher, admin, 1954-68; Univ Detroit, asst dir to dir special projects 1968-72, assoc dean acad support programs 1972-74; Univ Coll Univ Louisville, dean 1974-80; Savannah State Coll GA, pres 1980-88; Lincoln Univ, pres 1988-. **ORGANIZATIONS:** Dir 1st Bank of Savannah; trustee Telfair Acad Arts Savannah 1980-; vice pres West Broad YMCA Savannah 1980-, Coastal Empire Council Boy Scouts Amer 1981-; bd dirs Savannah United Way 1981-, Savannah YMCA 1981, West Broad YMCA Savannah 1980, Candler Gen Hosp 1982-; mem Amer Assn Higher Educ, Amer Assn State Colls & Univs, Natl Assn Equal Oppty in Higher Educ, Kappa Alpha Psi, Sigma Pi Phi; mem, bd of governors, Memorial Community Hospital; dir Jefferson City Area Chamber of Commerce, Jefferson City Rotary Club. **HONORS/ACHIEVEMENTS:** Recipient Whitney M Young Jr Award Lincoln Found 1980; Distinguished Citizens Award City of Louisville 1980; Communicator of the Year (Mid-Missouri Chapter), Public Relations Soc of Amer 1988; United Way of the Coastal Empire 1988; Savannah Port Authority, Savannah GA 1982-87; West Broad Street YMCA 1986. **MILITARY SERVICE:** AUS 1952-59. **BUSINESS ADDRESS:** President, Lincoln University, 201 Young Hall, Jefferson City, MO 65101.

RAYE, JIMMY
Offensive coordinator. **PERSONAL:** Married Edwina; children: Robin, Jimmy. **EDUCATION:** Attended, Michigan State Univ. **CAREER:** LA Rams, defensive back; MI State, assistant 1972-75, receivers coach; San Francisco 49ers', receivers coach 1977; Detroit Lions, receivers coach; Atlanta Falcons, receivers coach; Tampa Bay Buccaneers, offensive coordinator.

RAYE, VANCE WALLACE
Attorney. **PERSONAL:** Born Sep 06, 1946, Hugo, OK; son of Edgar Allen Raye and Lexie Marie Raye; married Sandra Kay Wilson; children: Vanessa. **EDUCATION:** Univ of OK, BA 1967, JD 1970. **CAREER:** US Air Force, judge advocate 1970-74; CA Attorney General, deputy atty general 1974-80, sr asst atty general 1980-82, deputy legislative scty 1982-83; Governor of CA, legal counsel. **ORGANIZATIONS:** Mem State Bar of CA 1972-; vice chair CA Exec Emergency Council 1984-; mem CA Assn of Black Lawyers, Natl Bar Assn, NAACP, Urban League; mem CA State Bar Commn on Malpractice Insurance; chmn Staff Adv Council Natl Governors Assn Comm on Criminal Justice and Public Protection. **MILITARY SERVICE:** USAF capt 4 yrs; Air Force Commendation Medal. **BUSINESS ADDRESS:** Legal Counsel, Governor George Deukmejian, Governor's Office, State Capitol, Sacramento, CA 95814.

RAYFORD, BRENDA L.
Director, social worker. **PERSONAL:** Born Apr 03, 1940, Dayton, OH; married Kent A; children: Blake Nyette, Valdez Kamau. **EDUCATION:** Cntrl St U, BA 1962; Wayne St U, MSW 1971. **CAREER:** Detroit Black United Fund Inc, exec dir 1971-; Comp Hlth Svc, soc wkr 1969; Highland Park Pub Sch Spl Proj, soc work supr 1967-69; Travelers Aid Soc, soc wkr 1966-67; Montgomery Co Wlf Dept, soc wkr-intake 1962-66. **ORGANIZATIONS:** Consult Creative Strategies Inc 1970-; 3rd vice pres Nat Black United Fund Inc 1974-; field work supr Wayne StUniv Sch of Soc Work 1980-; chwm Fund Raising Com Bus & Professional Wmn Inc New Metro Chap 1975-; adv commn Detroit Pub Sch 1980-; co-author "The Guy Who Controls Your Future" 1970. **HONORS/ACHIEVEMENTS:** Outst commun ldrshp St Rep Barbara Rose Collins 1978; wmn of yr Negro Bus & Professional Wmn-New Metro 1978; commun serv award World of Islam in W Commun 1978; St of MI tribute MI St Sen 1979. **BUSINESS ADDRESS:** Executive Dir, Black United Fund of MI, 2187 W Grand Blvd, Detroit, MI 48208.

RAYFORD, FLOYD KINNARD
Professional athlete. **PERSONAL:** Born Jul 27, 1957, Memphis, TN; married Mary Luvenia Hawkins. **CAREER:** Baltimore Orioles, 1980; Baltimore Orioles, 1982; St Louis Cardinals, 1983; Baltimore Orioles, infielder 1984. **ORGANIZATIONS:** Signed for CA by Larry Himes; Best year was '78 at El Paso, hit 313, was 2nd in TX League in doubles (36). **BUSINESS ADDRESS:** Baltimore Orioles, Memorial Stadium, Baltimore, MD 21218.

RAYFORD, LEE EDWARD
Government official. **PERSONAL:** Born Nov 17, 1935, Fordyce, AR; married La Neal Lucas; children: Vickie, Celese. **EDUCATION:** Agr Mech & Normal Coll Pine Bluff AR, BS 1961;Univ of AR, M 1963; E TX St U, edD 1979. **CAREER:** St of NV Equal Rights Commn Las Vegas, exec dir 1979-80; Econ Oppor Bd Las Vegas, ESAA prgm dir 1974; Clark Co School Dist Las Vegas, research teacher 1973, adult educ teacher 1969-74; CCSA Las Vegas, site admin 1970-72. **ORGANIZATIONS:** Bd dir Westside Commun Devel; treas bd dir OIC/A; mem NAACP Las Vegas; mem SW Equal Employment Oppor Ofcrs (SWEEOA); mem Intl Assn of Hum Rghts Agy(IAOHRA); mem Prsnnl Adv Commn (Pac) St of NV; mem Kappa Alpha Psi Las Vegas; Phi Delta Kappa Las Vegas; Kappa Delta Psi Las Vegas. **HONORS/ACHIEVEMENTS:** Publ "Criteria for the Selection of Pub Elemntry Sch Princ of the St of NV" 1979. **MILITARY SERVICE:** USAF a/2c 1955-59. **BUSINESS ADDRESS:** 1515 E Tropicana #590, Las Vegas, NV 89158.

RAYFORD, PHILLIP LEON
Educational administrator. **PERSONAL:** Born Jul 25, 1927, Roanoke, VA; married Gloria Geraldine Kimber. **EDUCATION:** A&T State Univ, BS 1949; Univ of MD, MS 1970, PhD 1973; USDA Grad Sch, chemistry & math; A&T State Univ, Hon Doc Humanities 1985. **CAREER:** NIH Bethesda MD, super biologist endocrinology branch 1955-62, super biol Ghana radiobiol & biochem lab 1962-64, super biologist radioimmunoassayist endocrinology branch 1964-70, super biologist bio-radioimmunoassayist reproduction rsch branch 1970-73; Univ of TX Med Branch, asst prof dir surgical biochemistry lab dept of surgery 1973-76, assoc prof dir surgical biochemistry lab dept of surgery 1976-77, prof dir surgical biochemistry lab dept of surgery prof div of biochem human biological chem & genetics 1977-80, asst dean of medicine 1978-80; Univ of AR Coll of Medicine, prof & chmn dept of physiology and biophysics 1980-. **ORGANIZATIONS:** Mem Omega Psi Phi Frat 1946; mem F&AM Prince Hall 1977; editorial bd Peptides Soc for Exptl Biology & Med 1979-; site visitor NIH Bethesda MD various times; scientific reviewer Gastroentology Endocrinology Peptides various times; exec comm Univ of AR for Med Scis 1982-; deans adv comm Univ of AR for Medical Scis 1984-; study section General Med A NIH 1985-89; mem Amer Assn for the Advancement of Scis; mem Amer Assn of Univ Profs; mem Amer Federation for Clinical Rsch; mem Society of Sigma Xi; mem Amer Gastroenterology Assn; mem Natl Assn of Minority Medical Educators. **HONORS/ACHIEVEMENTS:** District Man of the Yr Omega Psi Phi Frat 1975,85; Adelphi Club Man of the Yr Galveston TX 1978; Omega Psi Phi Award for 25 yrs of Outstanding Serv 1982; Cosmos Club Washington DC 1984; Numerous publications including Rayford PL JA Jones and JC Thompson Gastrointestinal hormones In, Basic Clinical Endocrinology PO Kohler (ed) John Wiley, NY;Chowdhury P K Inoue and PL Rayford Effect of Nicotine on Basal and Bombesin Stimulated Canine Plasma Levels of Gastrin, Cholecystokinin and Gastrin in Rats Peptides; Baba N P Chowdhury K Inoue M Ami and PL Rayford Ileo-Caecal Resection Induced Pancreatic Growth in Rats Peptides; J C Thompson, GG Greely, PL Rayford and CW Townsend "Gastrointestinal Endocrinology, McGraw Hill, 1986. **MILITARY SERVICE:** AUS tech 5 1946-47. **BUSINESS ADDRESS:** Chmn Dept Physiology, Coll of Medicine, Univ of Ark for Med Sci, 4301 W Markham, Little Rock, AR 72205.

RAYFORD, ZULA M.
Educator. **PERSONAL:** Born Aug 05, 1941, Memphis, TN. **EDUCATION:** Langston U, BA 1964;Univ WI, Grad Work 1969-71. **CAREER:** YWCA, program counselor 1964-68; Holy Angels Catholic School, teacher 1968-70; Milwaukee Public School, teacher 1970-. **ORGANIZATIONS:** Mem NEA; WI Educ Assn; United Milwaukee Edn; Milwaukee Tchrs Assn; United Tchrs; mem Northside Nghbrhd Action Grp; Recording Sec; Black Educators. **HONORS/ACHIEVEMENTS:** Rep NEA Minority Ldrshp Conf & WI St Delegate NEA Convntn. **BUSINESS ADDRESS:** Brown St School, 2029 N 20th St, Milwaukee, WI 53206.

RAYMOND, HENRY JAMES
State government official. **PERSONAL:** Born Apr 29, 1957, Fort Meade, MD; married Cauldia Ann Murray. **EDUCATION:** NC A&T State Univ, BA 1979; Univ of Baltimore, MPA 1980; Bowie State Coll, MBA 1986. **CAREER:** MD Dept of Natural Resources, admin specialist 1981-84, admin officer 1984-. **ORGANIZATIONS:** Mem Omega Psi Phi Frat 1976-, Natl Black MBA Assoc 1985-, Amer Soc of Public Admin 1986-; mem NAACP, Natl Urban League. **HOME ADDRESS:** 4920 Lindsay Rd, Baltimore, MD 21229. **BUSINESS ADDRESS:** Administrator of Budgets, MD Dept of Natural Resources, Annapolis, MD 21401.

RAYMOND, PHILLIP GREGORY
Designer. **PERSONAL:** Born Jul 31, 1957, Berkeley, CA. **EDUCATION:** Univ of CA Berkeley, AB Arch 1975-80; CambridgeUniv England, 1979. **CAREER:** Lawrence Berkeley Lab, engr asst 1978-; Chem DeptUniv CA Berk, illustrator 197-78; Free Lance Designer, self employeed 1975-. **ORGANIZATIONS:** Mem Stdt Chap AIA 1975-; mem No CA Solar Enrgy Assn 1978-; mem Am Assn of Blacks in Enrgy 1979-; pres No Area NAACP Yth Counc 1979-; del Statehouse Conf on Chldrn & Yth 1980. **HONORS/ACHIEVEMENTS:** Artist of tomorrow award Gamma Phi Delta Sor Inc 1977. **BUSINESS ADDRESS:** Lawrence Berkley Lab, 1 Cyclotron Rd, Berkeley, CA 94720.

RAYON, PAUL E., III
Real estate manager. **PERSONAL:** Born Apr 15, 1950, Chicago, IL; married Freddie M Parr; children: Anjela N; Paul E IV. **EDUCATION:** TN State Univ, BS Criminal Justice 1976. **CAREER:** Thornton Twp Youth Comm, family counselor 1976-78; Cook Cty Housing Authority, housing mgr 1978-; Robbins Park Dist, commiss. **ORGANIZATIONS:** Parlimentarian Robbins Comm Agency Council 1983-; mem United Way of Robbins 1984; chmn Mayor's Office of Community Affairs Village of Robbins 1984. **HONORS/ACHIEVEMENTS:** Cert Natl Assoc of Housing & Re-Devel Officials 1979; Cert Robbins YMCA 1980; Cert Cook Cty Sheriff's Youth Serv 1983. **HOME ADDRESS:** 13800 Kedvale, Robbins, IL 60472.

REAGINS, ANN LOUVINA
Association executive. **PERSONAL:** Born Mar 07, 1955, Knox Co, TX. **EDUCATION:** E TX State Univ, BS (Hon) Journalism & Engl 1976. **CAREER:** ETSU Mach III Prog Commerce TX, grad asst 1976; Dallas Weekly Newspaper Dallas, office mgr 1977; NAACP Reg Office Dallas, reg VI youth field dir 1977-;NAACP, asst to dir of natl publ rel 1979-81, prog dir 1981-. **ORGANIZATIONS:** Mem Natl Council of Negro Women 1980, Bus & Professional Womens Club, Order of the Eastern Star. **HONORS/ACHIEVEMENTS:** Listed in Who's Who in HS 1973, Who's Who in Amer Coll & Univ 1976, Ebony Mag Fifty Future Leaders of Black Amer 1978.

REAMS-WHITMIRE, VERNETTA MARIA
Business executive. **PERSONAL:** Born Dec 28, 1930, Kansas City, KS; married Earl J Whitmire; children: 2 adult children. **EDUCATION:** Western Baptist Bible Coll, 1948; Blair Bus Coll, 1953; UCA Kansas City, MO, doctoral fellow 1984. **CAREER:** MO Div of Employment Security, social work; Central Amer Bible Coll, prof social serv; Wise Council House Inc, exec dir. **ORGANIZATIONS:** Mem Natl Black Council Alcohol 1984; mem Natl Halfway House Assn 1974; mem MO Assn Alcoholism Couns 1980; Natl "Historical" Mutual Musicians Found KC, MO; life mem NAACP; secy Natl Assn Campus Exec 1984. **HONORS/ACHIEVEMENTS:** Community Award Black United Appeal 1976; Community Award Salvation Army 1975; Community Vol Award Urban League Kansas City 1980. **BUSINESS ADDRESS:** Executive Dir, Wise Council House, Inc, 3005 Benton Blvd, Kansas City, MO 64128.

REARDEN, SARA B.
Attorney. **PERSONAL:** Born in Edgefield, SC; married Nigel Lauriston Haynes. **EDUCATION:** Howard Law Sch, JD 1969; NC St A&T U, BS Bus Adm with hons 1964. **CAREER:** US Merit Systems Protection Bd, sr appellate atty 1979-; George Wash Law Cntr Wash DC, part-time asst prof 1978-; Equal Employ Opport Com, supr atty 1974-79; Equal Empl Opp Comm, atty adv 1973-74; Neighborhood Legal Serv Wash DC, mang atty 1971-73; Reginald H Smith Comm Law Fellow Prog; Fellow NLS, prog staff 1969-71. **ORGANIZATIONS:** Adm to the Bars sup ct of SC 1971, DC 1973, us dist ct for DC 1973, us ct of appeals for the DC 1973; ch-chmn bd of dir Neighborhood Legal Serv Prog Wash DC; mem NBA, ABA; Nat Conf of Black Lawyrs; Natl Assn of Black Women Attys vice pres Howard Law Alumni Assn; Natl Couns of Negro Women; Howard Law Journ 1968-69; pres 1st & 2nd yr law class. **HONORS/ACHIEVEMENTS:** Wnr Constance Baker Motley Scholar 1968.

REASON, JOSEPH HENRY
Retired librarian. **PERSONAL:** Born Mar 23, 1905, Franklin, LA; son of Joseph Reason (deceased) and Bertha Peoples Reason (deceased); married Bernice Chism, Jun 24, 1931; children: Barbara Butler, J Paul. **EDUCATION:** New Orleans Univ, AB 1928; Howard Univ, AB 1932; Univ of PA, AM 1933; School of Library Serv Columbia Univ, BS 1936; Catholic Univ of Amer, PhD 1958. **CAREER:** Gilbert Acad New Orleans, language teacher 1928-29; FL A&M Coll, language teacher, l929-31, 1934-35, chief libarian l936-38; Howard Univ, reference librarian 1938-46, Univ librarian 1946-57, dir Univ library 1957-71; FL State Univ School of Library Sci, visiting prof 1972-73 (retired). **ORGANIZATIONS:** Library adv Univ of Rangoon Burma 1961-62; exec sec Assn of Coll & Rsch Librarians 1962-63; pres Assn of Coll & Rsch Librarians 1971-72; consultant Coll of the Sacred Heart 1972; trustee Eckerd Coll 1976-82; mem Sr Social Planning Council 1977; vice chmn Legislative Task Force State Library of FL 1977; mem bd of trustees Leon County Public Libr 1979-86; mem bd of dir Area Agency for Aging of Northern FL 1979-85, vice pres 1980-81. **HONORS/ACHIEVEMENTS:** Author of "An Inquiry Into the Structure, Style & Originality of Crestien's Yvain"; Fellowship Gen Ed Bd 1935-36; published articles Library Professional Journal.

REASON, JOSEPH PAUL
Nuclear engineer, naval officer. **PERSONAL:** Born Mar 22, 1941, Washington, DC; married Dianne L Fowler; children: Rebecca Lynn, Joseph Paul Jr. **EDUCATION:** US Naval Acad, BA 1965; US Naval Postgrad Sch, MS 1970; Swarthmore Coll, undergrad study; Lincoln U; howard U. **CAREER:** USS Bainbridge Guided Missile Cruiser; USS Missisippi, exec officer; Pres J Carter, naval aide 1977-79; Bur of Naval Personnel, personnel mgr 1976; sea duty 1966-76; completed naval nuclear propulsion training prgm 1966. **ORGANIZATIONS:** Commd as ofcr in USN 1965; Navy Mut Aid Assn 1967-69, 71-76; USN Acad Alumni Assn; qualified as ngr for nuclear powered ships 1969; designated surface warfare ocr USN 1971. **HONORS/ACHIEVEMENTS:** Rcvd Admiral Arleigh Burke Award for professional excellence 1972; decoratons; Navy Commendation Medal; rep of Vietnam Hon Med. **MILITARY SERVICE:** USN 1965-.

REAVES, BENJAMIN FRANKLIN
Educator. **PERSONAL:** Born Nov 22, 1932, New York, NY; son of Ernest McKinley Reaves and Lella Brinson Reaves; married Jean Manual, Sep 04, 1955; children: Terrilyn Reaves Jackson, Pamela, Benjamin. **EDUCATION:** Oakwood Coll Hunsville AL, BA, 1955; Andrews Univ, MA, M Div; Chicago Theological Seminary. **CAREER:** MI Conference of Seventh-Day Adventist, pastor, 1956-68; Westside Hospital, Chicago IL,counselor, 1968-72; Andrews Univ, Berrien Springs MI, youth pastor, 1972-73, assoc prof, 1973-77; US Army, instr for Homeletics, 1977-85; Oakwood Coll, Huntsville AL, pres, 1985-. **ORGANIZATIONS:** Mem, Advisory Board of Andrews Univ; mem, Advisory Board of Loma Linda Univ; mem, United Negro College Fund; mem, Natl Assn for Equal Opportunity in Higher Educ; mem, Council for the Advancement of Private Colleges in AL; mem, Huntsville Chamber of Commerce Board; mem, Vision 2000; mem, Rotary club; mem, Urban Ministries Program. **HONORS/ACHIEVEMENTS:** Distinguished Alumnus Award, Oakwood Coll, 1973; Teacher of the Year, Oakwood Coll, 1983; Music Humanitarian Award, Oakwood Coll, 1984; Outstanding Leadership Award, Oakwood Coll, 1986; author of articles in numerous journals such as: Message, The Review and Herald, Ministry, The Adventist Laymen, Collegiate Quarterly, South African Signs of the Times. **BUSINESS ADDRESS:** President, Oakwood College, Oakwod Road, Huntsville, AL 35896.

REAVES, E. FREDERICKA M.
Educator. **PERSONAL:** Born Nov 07, 1938, Washington, DC; married Robert (deceased); children: Reginald, Ricardo. **EDUCATION:** Morgan State U, BS 1960. **CAREER:** Sosa Jr High School, math teacher 1961; Goam Public Schools, math teacher 1964; San Diego City School, math teacher 1966; Alameda Unified School, math teacher 1967-83; Oakland Unified School Dist 1984-86. **ORGANIZATIONS:** Mem Natl Ed Assn 1967-; sec Alameda NAACP 1967-; brd mem Alamedans HOPE 1967-70; advisor Youth NAACP 1968-75; brd mem Am Red Cross 1970; chrpr Multicul Ins to Impl Article 33% CA Ed Code Training Grp 1970-74; mem Natl Coul Tchr Math 1970-82; mem Phi Delta Kapna 1973-. **HONORS/ACHIEVEMENTS:** Article publ Math Tchr 1973; PTA schlshp Fairmont Hgts High 1956; Morgan state u Merit Schlshp 1957. **HOME ADDRESS:** 762 Santa Clara Ave, Alameda, CA 94501.

REAVES, FRANKLIN CARLWELL
Business executive. **PERSONAL:** Born Aug 07, 1942, Mullins, SC; married Willie Dean White; children: Kathy Juanita, Jacquelyn C, Frankie Diana, Anthony "Kenny", Ron, Randy, Dexter, Branden. **EDUCATION:** Fayetteville State Univ, BS 1968; A&T State Univ, MS 1974; LaSalle Ext Univ, LLB 1978; A&T State Univ, MS 1982; Allen Univ, Hon Dr of Humanity 1984; Univ NC Greensboro, candidate for PhD; Attended, Lutheran Theology Seminary. **CAREER:** Columbus Co Bd of Educ, teacher 1968-; Operation HELP, president/founder 1968-. **ORGANIZATIONS:** Pres Columbus Co Unit for NC Assn of Educators; pres NC Region V Leadership Prevocational Planning Council; pres Black Educators Leadership Council 1984-;pastor African Methodist Episcopal Church 1968-; pres & founder Help the Economic Linkage of the Poor 1971-; pres Marion Co Chap of NAACP 1973-76; pres SC Affiliate of ACLU 1979-82; mem Amer Friends Serv Comm 1978-84; mem Natl Bd of Directors of ACLU 1982-; mem Southern Regional Council; pres & organizerof The Store Inc 1984-. **BUSINESS ADDRESS:** President, Operation HELP, PO Box 534, Mullins, SC 29574.

REAVES, GINEVERA N.
Educator. **PERSONAL:** Born Jan 21, 1925, Greenwood, MS; married Henry Eugene Sr; children: Henry Eugene, Jr, Naomi Normene (dec). **EDUCATION:** Rust Coll, BA 1951;Univ of Chgo, MA 1954;Univ of Tn; VA St; TX So; TN St; SoUniv of New Orleans; Ball St IN. **CAREER:** MS Public School, teacher 1942-64; Rust Coll, asst prof 1964, dir of teacher educ. **ORGANIZATIONS:** Mem Phi Delta Kappa; Am Assn of Univ Wmn; MS Tchr Assn; Historian Phi Delta Kappa 1976-77; mem US Commin on Civil Rghts 1976-77; 3rd Vice Pres MS Assn of Higher Edn; Delta Sigma Theta Sor; mem Benton Co NAACP; chpn First Congrsnl Dist Dem Party MS 1972; alt del Dem Nat Mid-Term Conf 1974; st exec bd Dem Party of MS; mem MS Affirmative Action Com 1975. **HONORS/ACHIEVEMENTS:** Runner-uo tchr of yr Rust Coll 1966; Sargent Shriver Award for alleviating poverty in rural Am 1966; Miss Finer Wmnhd award Zeta Phi Beta 1968; tchr of yr Rust Coll Zeta Phi Beta 1972; ginevera Reaves Day Benton Co NAACP 1975. **BUSINESS ADDRESS:** Rust Coll, Holly Springs, MS 38635.

REAVIS, JOHN WILLIAM, JR.
Educator. **PERSONAL:** Born Oct 30, 1935, Nyack, NY; son of John Reavis and Frances Reavis; married Catherine Smith (divorced); children: Dawn, John, III, Timothy. **EDUCATION:** London Arts of Applied Sci, Hon LHD 1973; NYU, MA 1965; Fayetteville St NC U, BS (cum laude) 1959. **CAREER:** SUNY-Farmingdale, Educ Oportunity Center, dean 1981-86, prof; SUNY A&T Coll, asst to pres for affirmative action 1980-81, dean; State Univ of NY, asst dean 1972-80, coord special programs 1969-72; Farmingdale, 1978-; EDPA Grant Garnett Patterson Jr HS, consultant 1972-73; Montgomery St School, principal 1968-69, elem guidance counselor 1962-67; Grand St School, asst principal 1967-68, tchr 1959-61; Elem English Negro Hist, adult educ teacher 1961-62; Continental Can Co, machine tender, packer 1953-55, part-time 1956-59; minority youth groups sports consultant; college dormitory asst; sports statistician; newspaper public relations writer; mgr of athletic teams. **ORGANIZATIONS:** Mem Natl Assn for Supervision & Curriculum Devel 1969-; life mem Omega Psi Phi Frat Inc; NY State Assn for Supervision & Curriculum Devel; Phi Delta Kappa; Natl Alliance of Black School Educators; comm mem Natl Legislative Comm; NY State Teachers Assn; NY State Guidance Assn; Fayetteville St Coll Alumni Assn; NY Alumni Assn; pres bd dir Schenectady Carver Comm Ctr 1976-78; steward Schenectady's Duryee AMEZ Ch; life mem PTA; pres Grand-Montgomery St Schools; mem adv council Suffolk Co BOCES Dist III 1978-; mem draft bd US Selective Serv for Suffolk Cty 1983-. **HONORS/ACHIEVEMENTS:** Cited local Omega Man of Yr 1977; Notable Amer 1976-77; Presidential Citation to Distinguished Alumni NAFEO 1987. **HOME ADDRESS:** 64 S Clinton Ave, #3A, Bay Shore, NY 11706.

REDD, GEORGE N.
Educator. **PERSONAL:** Born Apr 04, 1903, Baltimore; married Ruth Dryscoll. **EDUCATION:** Columbia U, BS 1925, MA 1930, EdD 1939. **CAREER:** Fisk Univ, dean, prof Emeritus 1970-, dean, prof educ 1951-70, prof, educ dir summer session 1939-51; Dillard Univ, dist vis prof 1970-71; TX Coll, dean, prof educ 1930-38; NYC, teacher public school system 1927-29. **ORGANIZATIONS:** Exec sec Grand Boule Sigma Pi Phi Frat 1953-79; mem exec com Counc of Grad Schs US; Conf of Acad Deans; consult Ctr for So Educ Studies George Peabody Coll. **HONORS/ACHIEVEMENTS:** Recip gen educ bd fellow ColumbiaUniv 1935-36, 1938-39; Kappa Delta Pi Hon Soc in Edn; res grant Carnegie Found for Advmnt of Tching. **BUSINESS ADDRESS:** Fisk Univ, Nashville, TN 37203.

REDD, M. PAUL, SR.
Affirmative action program executive. **PERSONAL:** Born Aug 11, 1928, Martinsville, VA; married Orial Banks; children: M Paul, Jr, Paula A. **EDUCATION:** A&T Coll Greensboro NC, 1953-55. **CAREER:** Owner of floor waxing company 1955-66; Wechsler Coffee Co, salesman, sales manager, 1966-69; MA Life Insurance Co, agent, 1972-74; Westchester-Putnam Affirmative Action Program Inc, president/chief operating officer, 1974-; Westchester County Press, president/publisher, 1986-. **ORGANIZATIONS:** Mem, 1964-, first vice pres, NY State Conference, 1966-70, legislative chmn, NY State Conference, 1977-, NAACP; founding mem, Black Democrats of Westchester, NY, 1966-; vice chmn, Rye City Democratic Comm, 1966-; vice chmn, Westchester County Democratic Comm, 1967-; mem, 1967-70, chmn Personnel Comm, 1968-70, Urban League of Westchester; mem of Task Force of the County Exec, Westchester Coalition, 1968-70; bd of dirs, United Way of Westchester, 1970-86; mem, 1970-, vice pres, 1972-, Council of Black Elected Democrats of NY State; chmn Region III, NY State Division of Human Rights, 1985-88; first vice chmn, 1987, chmn, 1988, Hudson Valley Economic Development District. **HONORS/ACHIEVEMENTS:** Eugene T Reed award NY St NAACP 1978. **MILITARY SERVICE:** AUS m sgt 1950-52. **BUSINESS ADDRESS:** President/Chief Operating Officer, Westchester-Putman Affirmative Action Program, Inc, 61 Mitchell Place, White Plains, NY 10601.

REDD, ORIAL ANNE
Government official. **PERSONAL:** Born in Rye, NY; married M Paul Redd, Sr; children: Paula A, M Paul Jr. **EDUCATION:** Bennett Coll, AB 1946; Wmn of Yr, Daughters of Isis 1981; Woman of the Year, Shrine of the New Covenant Church 1981; Mercy Coll, PhD (Honorary) 1983. **CAREER:** Westchester County, Asst to county exec, 1974-83; Urban League, Westchester prog dir, 1972-74; Urban League housing spec 1970-72; The Westchester County Press, vp/editor. **ORGANIZATIONS:** Mem, NY State Historical Records Advisory Bd, 1984-; mem NY State Historical Docum Inv Adv Comm 1985-; mem Westchester 2000 Adv Coun 1984-; assoc mem NY State Assn County Clerks 1984-; bd United Way Of Westchester 1984-; bd Carver Center Port Crester 1981-; vice pres Woman Auxilary Control Hudson Baptist Assn 1983-86; Pres Women's Auxilary Central Hudson Baptist Assn 1986. **HONORS/ACHIEVEMENTS:** Comm Serv, NAACP 1963; Comm Serv, United Hospital 1979; Ernest Lindsay Award Blk, Dem Westchester 1979; comm serv Westchester Comm Opportunity Program, 1978; govr achievement, Natl Assn Minority Banks 1975; Comm Serv, Operation Push, Westchester 1976. **HOME ADDRESS:** Rye Colony, Rye, NY 10580.

REDD, THOMASINA A.
Educator. **PERSONAL:** Born Aug 04, 1941, Montgomery, WV; daughter of Thomas Z Atwater and Catherine C Atwater; married Dr Bruce L Redd; children: Paul F, Stephen E. **EDUCATION:** West Virginia Univ, AB 1963, MS 1969, PhD 1986. **CAREER:** West Virginia Univ, lab tech 1962-63; Alderson-Broaddus College, instructor 1969-71, asst prof 1962-85, chairperson Div of Natural Sci 1985-, assoc prof 1985-. **ORGANIZATIONS:** Member Philippi Baptist Church 1964-; member WV Acad Science 1970-; trustee Barbour Library Board 1978-; trustee WV Foundation for Campus Ministry 1980-; member Allegheny Branch Amer Soc Microbiol 1983-; member Amer Soc of Microbiol 1983-; College Sci Teachers Assn 1982-; Amer Inst of Biological Sci 1982-; Southeastern Assn of Biology, 1989. **HONORS/ACHIEVEMENTS:** Grant Educ DKG Intl Assn Women Educ 1981. **BUSINESS ADDRESS:** Associate Professor of Biology, Aiderson-Broaddus College, PO Box 518 A-B College, Philippi, WV 26416.

REDD, WILLIAM L.
Attorney. **PERSONAL:** Born Sep 03, 1950, Wilcoe, WV; married Marie E; children: Le Marquis, D'Ann. **EDUCATION:** Marshall Univ, BA 1972; NC Central Univ Law Sch, JD 1976. **CAREER:** Marshall Univ, instructor 1976; Henderson & Redd, attorney 1976-82; Law Office, sole practitioner attorney 1982-. **ORGANIZATIONS:** Mem Grad Chap Omega Psi 1971; past pres Black Alumni Inc 1978-81; past pres Mountain State Bar Assn 1980-82; former sec Cabell Co Commission on Crime & Delinquency 1982-83; chmn bd of dirs Green Acres Found 1982-84; mem Marshall Univ Memorial Tournament Comm 1984; Little League Baseball coach 1984-85; NAACP Legal Redress Officer Huntington Branch NAACP 1976-; Legal Redress Comm WV Conference 1976-; pres Cabell Co Deputy Sheriff's Civil Serv Comm 1981-; vice pres Green Acres Mental Retardation Center 1981-; trustee First Baptist Church Huntington 1981-; chmn Scottie Reese Scholarship Bd First Baptist Church 1982-; mem Big Green Scholarship Fund Marshall Univ 1982-; mem adv counsel Licensed Practical Nurses Cabell Co 1982-; chmn Minority Recruitment Comm for Faculty & Staff at Marshall Univ NAACP 1984-. **HONORS/ACHIEVEMENTS:** Prentice Hall Awd NCCU Sch of Law 1976; Omega Man of the Year Omega Psi Phi Nu Beta Chap 1978; Outstanding Black Alumni Black Alumni Inc Marshall 1979; Recognition Awd Adbul Temple 1981; Outstanding Leadership Mt State Bar Assn 1982. **MILITARY SERVICE:** USAR sp-4 6 yrs. **BUSINESS ADDRESS:** Attorney, 530 Fifth Ave, Huntington, WV 25701.

REDDICK, ALZO JACKSON
Educator. **PERSONAL:** Born Nov 15, 1937, Alturas, FL; married Elouise Williams; children: Nesper, Tausha, Alzo J Jr, Jason. **EDUCATION:** Paul Quinn Coll, BS 1960; FL A&M, mEd 1971; Nova U, EdD 1977. **CAREER:** Rollins Coll, asst dean 1970-; HS, teacher; Valencia Comm, asst to vice pres of planning; State of FL, state rep. **ORGANIZATIONS:** Pres-elect SABAP; chmn FL Caucus Black Dems; consult FL Drug Abuse Trust; adv Crimnl Justice Task Force; bd dir Yth Prgms Inc; bd dir Additions Orange Co Inc; bd dir Mid-FL Ctr for Alcoholism; bd dir Channel #24 Pub TV; mem FL Bur of Hist Mus; youth comm, chmn dep majority leader Dem natl Comm 1984-86; chmn Affirmative Action Comm FL Dem Party Orlando Single Mem Dist Task Force; mem Amer Assoc of Higher Educ, Southern Coll Placement Assoc; bd dir Orange County Additions; bd dir Betty Bus Bureau, Brookwood Comm Hosp, Guardian Care Nursing Home; mem Alpha Phi Alpha, Phi Delta Kappa; chmn Mercy Drive Neighbors in Action; exec comm 1976,82, chmn 1980-81 Orange County Dem; mem FL Police Standards Comm 1980-81; chmn United Negro Coll Fund. **HONORS/ACHIEVEMENTS:** Comm Serv Awd WA Shores Assn for Recreation; Cited for Historical Presentations of the Black Cowboys Orange County Dem Exec Comm Community Serv Awd 1981; Cited for Community Contribs WASAR, The Additions Inc, Modern Majestic Club First Black Leg Awd 1982; Law Enforcement Most Effective Freshman 1983; JonesHS Serv & Leadership Awd 1983; Natl Dem Comm Appreciation Awd 1983. **MILITARY SERVICE:** AUS 1961-64. **BUSINESS ADDRESS:** State Representative, State of Florida, 725 S Goldwyn, Orlando, FL 32805.

REDDICK, LINDA H.
Retired educator. **PERSONAL:** Born Dec 20, 1916, Bronwood, GA; married Booker T. **EDUCATION:** Spelman Coll; Wiley Coll, AB 1935; NY U; Stetson U. **CAREER:** Edgewater HS, tchr; Jones HS Orlando, head of English Dept. **ORGANIZATIONS:** 1st black to serve as pres Co of Orange Tchr of English 1965; Reader & Adjudicator of English Written Composition Natl Council Teachers of English 1965; mem FL Council Teachers of English; am Assn of Univ Wmn; past area chmn So Area Links Inc 1963-67; vice-chmn City's Minimum Standards Bd of Adjmts & Appeals; mem Delta Sigma Theta Sor Inc; mem Orange Co Bd of Comm Svc; mem adv bd Orange County Council of Sci & Arts; bd of directors, Florida Symphony Orchestra; bd of directors, Metropolitan Orlando Urban League; first committee, First Academy, A First Baptist of Orlando Ministry; immediate past pres, founder, Orlando Chapter, Girl Friends Inc; mem, First Baptist/Orlando. **HONORS/ACHIEVEMENTS:** Greater Orlando Chamber of Commerce's Community Award 1988.

REDDICK, THOMAS J., JR.
Judge. **PERSONAL:** Born Jan 04, 1919, Sarasota, FL; divorced; children: Conrad R, Cedrick J, Thomas J, III. **EDUCATION:** FL A&M U, BS; Howard U, LLB. **CAREER:** St of FL, circuit judge, ct of record judge 1971-72, asst municipal judge 1970-71; Broward Co FL, pub defender 1965-67. **ORGANIZATIONS:** Mem Am Bar Assn; FL Bar Assn; Nat Bar Assn; fdr mem Judicial Counc of Nat Bar Assn; Broward Co Bar Assn; Alpha Kappa Mu Hon Soc; trustee Mt Hermon AME Ch; mem Elks; Omega Psi Phi Frat; Mason Sat on 4th Dist Ct of Appeals St of FL 1975. **MILITARY SERVICE:** M sgt 4 yrs. **BUSINESS ADDRESS:** 201 SE 6 St, Fort Lauderdale, FL 33301.

REDDING, LOUIS L.
Attorney. **PERSONAL:** Born in Alexandria, VA; married Gwnedolyn Kiah; children: Ann Holmes, Rupa R Lallinger, Judith R. **EDUCATION:** Brown Univ, AB, LLD Hon 1973; Harvard Law Sch, LLB 1928. **CAREER:** Fessenden Acad Ocala FL, vice principal 1923-24; Morehouse Coll, tchr 1924-25; State of DE, public defender 1965-84; Attorney at Law. **ORGANIZATIONS:** Mem Amer Bar Assn; mem Natl Bar Assn. **HOME ADDRESS:** 158 Locksley Rd, Glen Mills, PA 19342. **BUSINESS ADDRESS:** Attorney, 1200 Mellon Bank Building, Wilmington, DE 19801.

REDMAN, JAMES W.
Union official—retired. **PERSONAL:** Born May 07, 1915, Yardley, PA; son of William Redman and Jennie Lee Redman; married Louise Jones; children: Virginia L Gunnel, Wilbertine Collins. **EDUCATION:** Cheney Training 1936-37. **CAREER:** Acme Rubber, insp; Eastern Aircraft, lead man bench hand, 1942-46; Gen Motors Fisher Body Div, Trenton, NJ, shop dist committeeman 1975-80; retired UAW official; New Jersey State Assembly, staff member. **ORGANIZATIONS:** Vice chairman, board of deacons, Friendship Baptist Church; Aaron Lodge #9 F&AM Masons; organized Capital City Golf Club, serving Black Golfers, Mercer County, NJ, 1961; 1st vice president, Eastern Golf Assn, 1972; member, Princeton Country Club; president, Mercer County Senior Golfers Assn; chairman of the board, Concerned Citizens of Ewing Township; Ewing Township Senior Citizen's Advisory Board; Ewing Township Election Board; NAACP, Trenton Chapter, 1975—; secretary, Ewing Twp Lions Club, 1979—; AARP, 1980—. **HONORS/ACHIEVEMENTS:** Tied for 1st place, United Golf Assn Srs, Pittsburgh, 1971; runner-up, Mercer Co Srs Golf Tourney, Princeton Country Club, 1972; winner, Postal Customer Council Golf Tourney, Yardley, PA, Country Club 1974; Male Senior Citizen of the Year, 1986. **HOME ADDRESS:** 10 New Trent St, Trenton, NJ 08638.

REDMON, ANN LOUISE See ALI, FATIMA

REDMOND, EUGENE B.
Poet, educator. **PERSONAL:** Born Dec 01, 1937, East St Louis, IL; son of John Henry Redmond and Emma Hutchinson Redmond; children: Treasure. **EDUCATION:** Southern Illinois University, BA, 1964; Washington University, St Louis MO, MA, 1966. **CAREER:** East St Louis Beacon, East St Louis IL, associate editor, 1961-62; Monitor, East St Louis IL, contributing editor, 1963-65, executive editor, 1965-67, editorial page and contributing editor, 1967—; Southern Illinois University at Edwardsville, East St Louis IL branch, teacher-counselor in Experiment in Higher Education, 1967-68, poet in residence and director of language workshops, 1968-69; Oberlin College, Oberlin OH, writer in residence and lecturer in Afro-American studies, 1969-70; California State University, Sacramento CA, professor of English and poet in residence in ethnic studies, 1970-85; Eugene B. Redmond Writers Club, East St Louis IL, founder and director, 1985—; East St Louis Public Schools, East St Louis IL, special asst superintendent for cultural and language arts, 1 985—. Wayne State University, Detroit MI, Martin Luther King Jr-Cesar Chavez-Rosa Parks Visiting Professor, 1989; founder and publisher, Black River Writers Press; coordinator, Annual Third World Writers and Thinkers Symposium, 1972—; director, Henry Dumas Creative Writing Workshop, 1974—. **ORGANIZATIONS:** Congress of Racial Equality; American Newspaper Guild; Natl Newspaper Publishers Assn; Natl Assn of African American Educators; African Assn of Black Studies; California Assn of Teachers of English; California Writers Club; Northern California Black English Teachers Assn. **HONORS/ACHIEVEMENTS:** Washington Univ Annual Festival of the Arts first prize, 1965; Free Lance magazine first prize, 1966; Literary Achievement Award, Sacramento Regional Arts Council, 1974; Best of the Small Press Award, Pushcart Press, 1976; Poet Laureate of East St Louis IL, 1976; California State Univ, Sacramento, faculty research award, 1976; California Arts Council grant, 1977; Illinois Arts Council grant, 1977-78; National Endowment for the Arts fellowship, 1978; author of Sentry of the Four Golden Pillars, Black River Writers, 1971; author of In a Time of Rain and Desire: Love Poems, Black River Writers, 1973; author of Drumvoices: The Mission of Afro-American Poetry, A Critical History, Anchor, 1976. **MILITARY SERVICE:** US Marines, 1958-61. **HOME ADDRESS:** 8304 Carol Dr, East St Louis, IL 62203. *

REDMOND, JANE SMITH
Educational administrator. **PERSONAL:** Born Jul 20, 1948, Cleveland, TN; daughter of V. Campbell Smith and Earnestine Smith; children: Gyasi. **EDUCATION:** Knoxville Coll, BS 1970; Univ of TN, MS 1979; Ph.D. Student Ohio State Univ Columbus, Ohio. **CAREER:** UTK Program Office, prog advisor; UTK Women's Ctr, dir; Office of Minority Student Affairs Univ TN, dir. **ORGANIZATIONS:** Mem officer Alpha Kappa Alpha Sor Inc; bd of dirs United Way of Knoxville 1984-; bd of dirs Knoxville Inst for the Arts 1985-. **HONORS/ACHIEVEMENTS:** Knoxville's 10 Most Eligible Career Women 1983. **HOME ADDRESS:** 5544 Mesa Ridge, Columbus, OH 43229.

REDRICK, VIRGINIA PENDLETON
Mathematician. **PERSONAL:** Born May 09, 1945, Dallas Co, AL; married Phillip L; children: Phillip Lamont, Ponchitta Phillippya. **EDUCATION:** AL A&M, BA math 1967. **CAREER:** AUS Missile Command Redstone Arsenal, mathematician; various postions with above employer 1967. **ORGANIZATIONS:** Mem Fed Employed Women; Nat Council Of Negro Women; Am Montessori Soc; alpha Kappa Mu; Bta Kappa Chi; mem Delta Sigma Theta Huntsville Alumnae Pres 1973-75; NAACP; bd dir Huntsville Sickle Cell Cntr; bd mem Huntsville Group Home for Girls. **HONORS/ACHIEVEMENTS:** Outs young women of women 1973; outstanding comm ser award Delta Sigma Theta; pres cup for scholastic achievement 1964-65; Who's Who Among Students 1966-67. **BUSINESS ADDRESS:** Morehouse College, c/o Dr Philip Redrick, 830 Westview Dr SW, Atlanta, GA 30314.

REDUS, GARY EUGENE
Professional athlete. **PERSONAL:** Born Nov 01, 1956, Limestone Co, AL; married Minnie Diggs; children: Lakesha, Manesha, Nakosha. **CAREER:** Cincinnati Reds, outfielder 1982-. **HONORS/ACHIEVEMENTS:** Earned MVP honors for Tampa 1980; MVP of team Indianapolis named to the Amer Assc all-star team and Topps Class AAA all-star team 1982; leading all NL rookies in stolen bases, triples, runs and game-winning RBIs 1983.

REECE, AVALON B.
Educator. **PERSONAL:** Born Oct 10, 1927, Muskogee, OK. **EDUCATION:** Langston U, Bachelors Degree 1948;Univ Southern CA Los Angeles;; M Music Ed 1954; Pepperdine Clg Los Angeles CA; Vander Cook Sch Music Chicago, IL; Northeastern OK State U, Standard Cert Phys Ed 1963, Standard Cert HS Cnslr 1967; Southwestern OK State U. **CAREER:** Manuel Trainging HS, band directress 1948-66, girls physical educ instructor 1953-67, activity dir 1967-70, counselor 1967-70; EASP, secondary activity coordinator 1971-73; Muskogee HS, counselor 1971-. **ORGANIZATIONS:** Life mem Natl Ed Assc; mem Am Prsnl & Guid Assc; mem Am Sch Cnslr Assc; mem Profsnl Recgntn Com Am Sch Cnslr Assc; mem Assc Non White Concern; mem OK Prsnl & Guid Assc; mem Midwest Reg Brnch Assbly OK Prnsl & Guid Assc; mem OK Ed Assc; mem Human Relations Cmsn OK Ed Assc; mem Eastern Dist Deans & Cnslr OK Ed Assc; mem Muskogee Ed Assc; mem Natl League of Cities; mem OK Muncipal League; mem Professional Standards Bd StateBd of Ed; mem Natl Black Caucus of Local Elected Ofcrs; mem Women in Municipal Govt; mem Area VI Rep Bd of Dir; mem Citizens Advsry Cncl on Goalsfor OK Higher Ed; mem OK UN Day Com IWY; mem Human Resource Com NLC; parlimentarian southwest region Natl Sorority of Phi Delta Kappa- Delta Omicron Chptr; mem Assc Governing Bd; mem Real Estate Sales Assc; mem Muskogee City Cncl; mem Mayor's City Chrtr Revison; mem bd dir Muskogee Cty Cncl ofYouth Serv; Mayor's Cncl Drug Abuse; mem WIBC; mem Juvenile Prsnl Training Pgm; mem AAUW; mem Alpha Epsilon Omega Chap of Alpha Kappa Alpha Sor. **HONORS/ACHIEVEMENTS:** First black city cnclwmn State of OK; distgshd women Muskogee Serv League; woman of the yr Zeta Phi Beta Sorortity 1975; demo presdtl elector 1976; patriot of the month Muskogee Bicentennial Com 1976; key to the city Gary, IN 1976; key to the city Kansas City, MO 1979; delegate to the Demo Natl Conv 1980;honorable order of Kentucky Colonel; distgshd pblc serv awrd OK Clg of Osteopatic Medicine & Surg 1985; ambassador of good will awrd Governor Nigh 1982;disting public serv awd The OK Coll of Osteopathic Medicine & Surgery 1985; Awd 35 yr pin Muskogee Educ Assoc; apptd as Hon Atty General by OK StateAtty Genl Michael C Turpen 1986. **BUSINESS ADDRESS:** Regent, Muskogee High School, 3200 E Shawnee St, Muskogee, OK 74401.

REECE, STEVEN
Business executive. **PERSONAL:** Born Sep 12, 1947, Cincinnati, OH; son of Edward Reece and Claudia Reece; married Barbara Howard, Sep 12, 1970; children: Alicia Michelle Reece, Steven Reece Jr, Tiffany Janelle Reece. **EDUCATION:** Xavier Univ, BS Communication 1970; Ohio Business Coll BA 1985; Amos Tuck/Dartmouth Coll, MBA 1987. **CAREER:** WCPO-TV, TV director; Motown Records, road mgr for Supremes, Temptations, Stevie Wonder; Cincinnati's 1st Black Mayor Theodore M Berry, exec asst; Communiplex Services, pres/founder; Reece & Reece Enterprise, Cincinnati OH, pres/founder. **ORGANIZATIONS:** Pres Operation PUSH; co-chmn Rev Jesse Jackson's Presidential Campaign in Hamilton County; first Black elected to Cincinnati Advertising Club; radio program (WCIN-AM) "What Are the Issues?"; local chmn Operation PUSH Intl Trade Bureau; mktg chmn Greater Cincinnati Chamber of Commerce; jr grand warden Prince Hall Masons; promotion dir Prince Hall Shriner's Free & Accepted. **HONORS/ACHIEVEMENTS:** Certificate of Honor Central State Univ; CEBA Awd; Feature stories Jet, Time, Cincinnati Magazine, Nip Magazine and Natl TV Stations; Local School Chmn, Withrow High School; Cum Laude Honor Society, Withrow High School; America's Best and Brightest Young Business and Professional Men Dollars & Sense Magazine, 1987; Chmn, Communiplex Natl Women's Hall of Fame. **BUSINESS ADDRESS:** President/Founder, Communiplex Serv, PO Box 37973, Cincinnati, OH 45222.

REED, ADDISON W.
Educator. **PERSONAL:** Born Apr 22, 1929, Steubenville, OH; married Sylvia A; children: 1 Child. **EDUCATION:** Kent St U, AB 1951; MA & BS 1953 & 1957; Univ NC Chapel Hill, PhD 1973. **CAREER:** St Augustine's Coll, Raleigh NC, chmn music dept, div humanities; Albany St Coll, dir choral activities 1965-69; St Augustine's Coll, asst prof 1961-65; Booker HS, Sarasota, FL, instr music (choral) 1958-61; Henderson Inst, Henderson NC, instr music (choral) 1953-54. **ORGANIZATIONS:** Mem Musicological Assn; Music Educators Nat Conf; Nat Assn of Tchrs of Singing; Raleigh Chamber Music Guild; Am Musicological Soc; bd of dir NC Symphony Orch; Mu Beta Psi Outstdg Educator of Am 1973. **HONORS/ACHIEVEMENTS:** Dist Young Black American, 1973; Ford Dissertation Fellowship, 1972; Dissertation Topic the life and works of scott joplin; article on scott- joplin in VI edof Grove's Dict of Music and Musicians. **MILITARY SERVICE:** Pfc 1954-56. **BUSINESS ADDRESS:** Chrmn, Div of Hum & Mus Dept, St Augustines College, 1315 Oakwood Ave, Raleigh, NC 27611.

REED, ADOLPHUS REDOLPH
Expediter. **PERSONAL:** Born May 18, 1912, Pittsburg, TX; married Ernestine; children: 1 Child. **CAREER:** GD Convair, expediter 1975-. **ORGANIZATIONS:** Pres United Comm Dem Club 1975-; past v chmn Co Counc Dem Clubs; elect Co Dem Dent Comm by popular vote 8 terms (16 yrs) v chmn 4 times still serv; v chmn of Unit Comm Dem Club 6 terms; chmn United Comm Dem Club nine 1 yr terms pres Serv; apptd club chart chmn Co Dem Cent Comm 5 terms; v chmn NAACP 2 terms; city commn to elim litter; past mem San Diego Civic League; state Dem Cent Com; cau chmn 79th Assem Dist; com pres Kenn & Pres Johnson visit to San Diego. **HONORS/ACHIEVEMENTS:** Rec awds from Sen Pro-Tem of 4th Dist on 2 occas; awds NAACP; Black Fed of San Dieago; spon beauty cont more than 50 girls recd schol. **BUSINESS ADDRESS:** GD Convair, San Diego, CA.

REED, ALFONZO
Attorney. **PERSONAL:** Born Jun 05, 1938, Bessemer, AL; son of Rev. Scieb C. Reed and Willie Mae Taylor Reed. **EDUCATION:** Talladega Coll Talladega AL, BA 1958; Atlanta U, MS 1964; Howard Univ Washington DC, JD 1975. **CAREER:** Private Practice, atty 1976-; Wien Lane & Malkin NYC, legislative asst 1975-76; Greenwich CT, tchr 1966-72; Atlanta GA, tchr 1965-66; Groton CT, tchr 1965-65; Calhoun AL, tchr 1959-63. **ORGANIZATIONS:** Parliament Delta Theta Phi Law Frat 1975-75; bd of dir Urban League SW Fairfield Co CT 1975; mem CT Bar Assn 1976; mem Greenwich Bar Assn; chmn Black Awareness Comm Grnwch 1968-69; chmn Org of Black Studies Grnwch 1968-69; pres Grnwch Educ Assn 1970-71; mem Alpha Phi Alpha Frat Inc. **HONORS/ACHIEVEMENTS:** Man of the yr distinguished Serv awd Grnwch Jaycees 1971; Earl Warren scholarship NAACP Legal Def & Educ fund 1972-75; scholarship Howard Univ Sch of Law 1973; student of the yr Howard Univ Sch of Law 1975. **BUSINESS ADDRESS:** Attorney, A Reed Atty/Counselor at Law, 270 Greenwich Ave, Greenwich, CT 06830.

REED, ALLENE WALLACE
College administrator. **PERSONAL:** Born in Harpersville, AL; daughter of Waymon L Wallace, Sr and Eula B Davis Wallace; married Jesse Reed, Jr; children: Jesse III, Gwenderlyn Carol. **EDUCATION:** Univ of Cincinnati, BS 1972, EdM 1975, PhD 1980. **CAREER:** Ben Siegel Realtor, real estate sales assoc 1956-72; Cincinnati Public Schools, teacher 1968-72; Univ of Cincinnati, assoc to the dean 1973-75; asst to the dean 1972-73; asst dean dir div of social science 1975-. **ORGANIZATIONS:** Mem Natl Assn for Women Deans, Administrators and Counselors; mem Ohio Assn for Women Deans, Administrators, and Counselors; The Assn for Continuing Higher Educ; Natl Univ Contining Educ Assn; The Ohio Conf on Issues Facing Women, Black Faculty and Administration in Higher Educ; Rainbow Coalition; Natl Political Congress of Black Women NAACP; The Southern Poverty Law Center; Citizen's Cable Communication Bd of Cincinnati; Citizen's Comm on Youth; Woman's City Club of Greater Cincinnati; former chair Univ of Cincinnati City of Cincinnati Police Consortium; vice pres Charter Committee of Greater Cincinnati, Ohio Psychological Assn; Delta Sigma Theta; Psi Chi; Natl Political Women's Caucus 1988-89. **HONORS/ACHIEVEMENTS:** Outstanding Woman's Awd NAACP Natl Office 1981; Outstanding Contribution to the Black Commimotu UBAFAS 1981; Image Maker Radio Station WCTN 1984; Honorary Societies, Psi Chi; Alpha Sigma Kappa; Alpha Sigman Lambda; Citizen for the Day; 200 Univ of Cincinnati Alumni, Univ of Cincinnati 1988; Enquirer Woman of the Year, Cincinnati Enquirer l987; 200 Greater Cincinnatians, Cincinnati Bicentennial Commn 1988; Portraits of Excellence: 100 Black Cincinnatians, Cincinnati Bicentennial Commn l988. **HOME ADDRESS:** 3931 Wess Park Drive, Cincinnati, OH 45217. **BUSINESS ADDRESS:** Asst Dean, Dir Div Soc Ser, Univ of Cincinnati, 102 Hanna-McMicken Hall, M L #19, Cincinnati, OH 45221.

REED, BEATRICE M.
Real estate broker. **PERSONAL:** Born Jan 05, 1916, St Georges, Grenada;children: 1 Daughter. **EDUCATION:** HowardUniv Wash DC, BA 1967. **CAREER:** Beat M Reed RE Co, own brok 1951-; Unit Pub Wkrs of Am CIO, intnl rep 1946-48; DC Br NAACP, admin asst 1944-46; War & Product Bd USGovt, asst supr stat sec 1942-44; NC Mut Ins Co, ins agt 1940-42. **ORGANIZATIONS:** Cam mgr Camper for Congr 4th Congress Dist MD 1948; pres Bymarc Inc 1975-; past pres Wash R E Brok Assn 1975-76; chmn const & by-laws com Nat Assn of R E Brok 1979-; past pres Cent Club Nat Assn of Negro Bus & Professional Wom Clubs Inc 1968-71; chmn natl hous com Nat Assn of Neg Bus & Professional Wom Clubs Inc 1978-; bd of dir Sub MD Bd of Dir 1978-; pres Carib Am Intercul Orgn 1980. **HONORS/ACHIEVEMENTS:** 1st Black Civ Serv employ to serve as civ serv exam US Civ Serv Commn 1943; 1st Black Wom to be Intnl Rep Labor Un Unit Pub Wrkrs of Am CIO 1946-48; feat in HUD Chal Mag Intnl Wom Yr iss Dept of Hous & Urb Devel 1975; pres of the yr awd Nat Assn of RE Est Brok Inc 1976; pion wom in RE Nat Wom Counc of Nat Assn of RE Brok Inc 1979; awd of recog Nat Assn of RE Brok Inc 1980. **BUSINESS ADDRESS:** Beatrice M Reed Real Estate Co, 9320 Greyrock Road, Silver Spring, MD 20910.

REED, CORDELL
Vice president. **PERSONAL:** Born Mar 26, 1938, Chicago, IL; married Ora Lee; children: Derrick, Brian, Steven, Michael. **EDUCATION:** Univ of IL, BSME 1960. **CAREER:** Commonwealth Edison, vice pres nuclear operations; des op coal-fired generator Sta, 7 yrs; des construction oper nuclear power generator sta, 13 yrs. **ORGANIZATIONS:** Mem Amer Nuclear Soc; mem West Soc of Engineers; Natl Technical Assn; trustee Metropolitan Comm Church; trustee Abraham Lincoln Center; dir Independent Bank of Chicago. **HONORS/ACHIEVEMENTS:** Black Achievers of Industry, recognition award, YMCA. **BUSINESS ADDRESS:** One First Nat Plaza, Box 767, Chicago, IL 60690.

REED, DAISY FRYE
Educator. **PERSONAL:** Born in Washington, DC; married James S Reed Sr; children: James Jr, Kristel. **EDUCATION:** DC Teachers Coll, BS 1953-56; George Washington Univ, MA 1957-61; Teachers Coll Columbia Univ, MEd, EdD 1973-75. **CAREER:** Washington DC Publ Schools, teacher 1956-73; Teachers Coll Columbia Univ, asst prof, dir of teacher corps proj 1975-76; Teacher Corps Support Svc, consult 1976-80; Publ School Syst VA, consult 1976-85; Midwest Rsch Inst "Tech Asst to Guam" in Agana Guam, consult 1977; School of Ed VA Commonwealth Univ, assoc prof 1976-. **ORGANIZATIONS:** Speaker Chicago Principals Assoc, KS City MO School Dist 1977-78; mem ASCD, ATE, AERA, Zeta Phi Beta Sor Teacher. **HONORS/ACHIEVEMENTS:** Innovation Awd DC Publ Schools Washington; Minority Student Scholarship Teachers Coll Columbis Univ; Rsch Grants "Assessing Teacher Needs in Rural Schools", "Teacher Incentives in Rural Schools" articles publ in English Jrnl, The Rural Ed, The New England Jrnl of Black Studies, Instr

Mag, The VA English Bulletin, Reading in VA. **BUSINESS ADDRESS:** Associate Professor, VA CommonwealthUniv, School Of Education, Richmond, VA 23284.

REED, DAVID
Dentist. **PERSONAL:** Born Nov 15, 1949, Batesville, MS; son of Robert L T Reed and Coloms Brooks Reed; married Paula;; children: Valerie, Damany. **EDUCATION:** Jackson State Univ, BS chem 1972; Howard Univ School of Engrg, MS 1976; Baltimore Coll of Dental Surgery, DDS 1983. **CAREER:** Claiborne Health Center, dental dir; private practice, Vicksburg MS 1987-. **ORGANIZATIONS:** Mem Phi Beta Sigma 1969-; sec Upper Northwest Group Minority 1978-79; mem Acad of General Dentistry 1980-, Retired Officers Assn of Amer 1983-; vice pres 1985-86, pres 1986- Capitol Dental Soc; dir Habitat for Humanity 1986-; mem Mississippi Dental Assn 1987-, Amer Dental Assn 1987-, Mississippi Dental Soc 1986-, Paragon Lodge #7 1989-. **HONORS/ACHIEVEMENTS:** Hercules Cash Awd Hercules Chem Co 1970; Atomic Energy Fellowship Awd Atomic Energy Commn 1971. **MILITARY SERVICE:** Public Health Serv lt. **BUSINESS ADDRESS:** Dentist, 17170 Cherry St, Vicksburg, MS 39180.

REED, DERRYL L.
Marketing executive, insurance company executive. **PERSONAL:** Born in Chicago, IL; daughter of Jesse A Reed Jr; married Rhonda Bass Reed, Nov 20, 1982; children: Nicole Reed. **EDUCATION:** Southern IL Univ, BS Math 1970; Univ of Chicago, MBA Marketing/Finance 1976. **CAREER:** Chicago Bd of Educ, substitute teacher 1970-77; American Can Co, sales rep 1970-73, account mgr, 1973-75, area mgr, 1975-77, assoc product mgr, napkins, 1977-78, asst product mgr, Aurora Bathroom Tissue, 1978-80; Tetley Inc, product mgr soluble tea products, 1980-83, product mgr tea bags, 1983-85, sr product mgr tea bags, 1985-86, sr product mgr tea products, 1986-87; Heublein Inc, dir of marketing prepared drinks; Teachers Insurance & Annuity Assn of Amer, asst vice pres of insurance services, currently. **ORGANIZATIONS:** Mem bd of dirs Chicago NAACP 1975; consulting partner Reed & Reed Assocs; bd of dirs Natl Black MBA Assn; assoc bd of dirs Tea Assoc of the USA Inc; past chmn NY Corp Matching Gift Fund for Lou Rawls Parade of Stars Telethon for United Negro Coll Fund; life mem Kappa Alpha Psi Frat; mem, Consumer Promotion Comm, Assn of Natl Advertisers. **HONORS/ACHIEVEMENTS:** A Black Achiever in Industry Awd Amer Can Co; Outstanding Service & Achievement Awd Kappa Alpha Psi Frat; MBA of the Year, 1988; featured in Oct 1985 issue of Black Enterprise magazine; participant in 2 TV programs hosted by Phil Donahue; guest speaker, Connecticut Public Television; guest lecturer at the Univ of CT and Atlanta Univ. **HOME ADDRESS:** 5 Creeping Hemlock Dr, Norwalk, CT 06851.

REED, E. See EVANS, MARI

REED, EDDIE
Educator. **PERSONAL:** Born May 31, 1945, Jemison, AL; son of Curtis and Ola Mae; married Clarissia Smitherman. **EDUCATION:** Daniel Puyne Coll, BS 1967; Auburn Univ, 1971; Univ of Montevallo, MEd 1973. **CAREER:** City of Jemison, councilman 1976-; Curtis-James Patio Furniture, pres 1987-. **ORGANIZATIONS:** Mem NEA & AEA 1967-; worshipful master F&AM of AL 1971-85; mem Park & Rec Bd Town of Jemison. **HONORS/ACHIEVEMENTS:** Awd State of AL for Outstanding Achievement 1984; awd Chilton Improvement Assn Outstanding Services 1985; commissioner Election Law Comm State of AL 1980-. **HOME ADDRESS:** P O Box 267, Jemison, AL 35085. **BUSINESS ADDRESS:** President, Curtis-James Patio furniture, R L Langston Dr, Jemison, AL 35085.

REED, FLORINE
Clergyman. **PERSONAL:** Born Dec 11, 1905, Turlton, OK; married Eugene H. **EDUCATION:** Boston, BTh 1959. **CAREER:** Non-Denom Ch, pastor; Temple Christ Chs Inc, overseer; Dorchest MA & San Anton TX Chs, pastor. **BUSINESS ADDRESS:** 115 Connelly St, San Antonio, TX 78203.

REED, FLOYD T.
Clergyman. **PERSONAL:** Born Feb 04, 1915, Leavenworth, KS; married Lorene B; children: 3 children. **CAREER:** Resurrection Church of God in Christ, Kansas City MO, founder and pastor 1975-. **MILITARY SERVICE:** AUS 1st sgt 1941-49. **BUSINESS ADDRESS:** 2608 E 59 St, Kansas City, MO 64130.

REED, GREGORY J.
Attorney. **PERSONAL:** Born May 21, 1948, Michigan; son of Bertha Mae; married Verladia T; children: Arian Simone, Ashley Sierra. **EDUCATION:** MI State Univ, BS 1970, MS 1971; Wayne State Univ, JD 1974, LLM 1978. **CAREER:** Gregory J Reed & Assocs PC, attorney specializing in corporate, taxation and entertainment law; Wayne State Univ, Detroit MI, prof 1988-89; AHR Packaging Consultant Corp, Detroit MI, pres/developer 1987-. **ORGANIZATIONS:** Bd of dirs MI Assn of Community Arts Agencies; mem Natl Bar Assn; comm mem of entertainment sports, taxation, corp and real estate sects Amer Bar Assn; mem Amer Bar Assn; mem Accounting Aide Soc of Metro Detroit; bd comm New Detroit Inc; tax and corp advisor BUF; mem MI State Bar Taxation and Corporate Div; mem Amer Arbitration Assn; bd of dir BELA Entertainment Law Assn; bd of dirs MI Assn of Community Arts Agencies; mem State Bar Law Media Comm; first black attorney adv bd mem US Internal Revenue Serv; founder Advancement Amateur Athletics Inc 1986; first black chmn in US State Bar of MI Arts Communication Sports and Entertainment Sect 1987; speaker, lecturer US & foreign countries. **HONORS/ACHIEVEMENTS:** Graduate Professional Scholarship 3 consecutive years; Distinguished Alumni of the Yr Awd MI State Univ 1980; Resolution for Achievement State of MI Senate, City of Detroit; one of the top ten blacks in the law profession Detroit News 1985; implemented Gregory J Reed Scholarship Foundation 1986; author of Tax Planning & Contract Negotiating Techniques for Creative Persons, Professional Athletes & Entertainers (first book of its kind cited by the Amer Bar Assn), This Business of Boxing & Its Secrets publ 1981, This Business of Entertainment & Its Secrets 1985, Negotiations Behind Closed Doors 1987, The Progressive Business Cleric 1989; Award for Contributions to the arts Black Music Month State of MI House of Rep 1987; govt appointment Martin Luther King Commn of Michigan 1989-. **BUSINESS ADDRESS:** Attorney, Gregory J Reed & Assocs PC, 225 Garfield, Detroit, MI 48201.

REED, ISHMAEL SCOTT (EMMETT COLEMAN)
Writer, educator. **PERSONAL:** Born Feb 22, 1938, Chattanooga, TN; son of Henry Lenoir and Thelma Coleman; married Priscilla Rose, Sep 1960 (divorced 1970); children: Timothy, Brett; married Carla Blank; children: Tennessee Maria. **EDUCATION:** State Univ of NY at Buffalo, 1956-60. **CAREER:** Yardbird Pub Co Inc, Berkeley CA, cofounder, 1971, ed dir, 1971-75; Reed, Cannon & Johnson Commns Co, Berkeley, cofounder, 1973; Before Columbus Fdn, Berkeley, cofounder, 1976; Ishmael Reed & Al Young's Quilt, Berkeley, cofounder, 1980. Guest lecturer at num US colls and univs; Regents lecturer at Univ of CA, Santa Barbara, 1988; judge of literary competitions, 1980-81; chpn of Berkeley Art Commn. **ORGANIZATIONS:** Mem, chmn of bd of dir, 1975-79, adv bd chmn, 1977-79, Coordinating Coun of Lit Mags; mem Authors Guild of Amer, PEN, Celtic Found. **HONORS/ACHIEVEMENTS:** Awd Natl Inst Arts & Letters 1974; Awd ACLU 1978; Michaux Awd 1978; Natl Endowment for Arts writing fellow 1974; Guggenheim Fellow 1975; author Mumbo Jumbo 1972, The Last Days of Louisiana Red 1974, Flight to Canada 1976, The Terrible Twos 1982; poetry Catechism of the Neo-Amer HooDoo Church 1970, Conjure 1972,Chattanooga 1973, Sec to the Spirits 1978; essays Good Made Alaska for the Indians 1981, Shrovetide in Old New Orleans 1978; editor anthology 19 Necromancers From Now 1970; collaborator w/Carla Blank & Suzushi Hanayagi in multi-media Bicentennial mystery The Lost State of Franklin-winner Poetry in Publ Places contest 1975. **HOME ADDRESS:** 1446 6th Street, Apt C, Berkeley, CA 94710. *

REED, JAMES
Educational consultant. **PERSONAL:** Born Oct 01, 1935. **EDUCATION:** Grambling Coll, BS; Colum Univ Teachers Coll, MA; New York Univ Dir coll based second prep prog, additional study. **CAREER:** NY & LA HS & Elem School, teacher 1958-66; Hunter Coll, supr; NY Univ, curr supr consultant to fed funded program 1967-71; School of Educ Hofstra Univ, consultant early childhood 1971-. **ORGANIZATIONS:** Consultant, hosp hms for mentally retarded public school special educ prog; mem, NY Mayor's Task Force Rec for Hand; Phi Delta Kappa; Intern Read Assn; PTA Urban League NAACP. **HONORS/ACHIEVEMENTS:** Author, "Music is Fun for Children," Play School Assn; co-author, "Play With A Difference," Play School Assn. **BUSINESS ADDRESS:** Ed Consultant, PO Box 26, Lincolnton Station, New York, NY 10037.

REED, JAMES W.
Medical educator. **PERSONAL:** Born Nov 01, 1935, Pahokee, FL; son of Thomas and Chineater; married Edna; children: David M, Robert A, Mary I, Katherine E. **EDUCATION:** WV State Coll, BS (Summa Cum Laude) 1954; Howard Univ, MD 1963; resident/internal medicine Tacoma, WA 1966-69; post doctoral research fellowship Univ of California, San Francisco 1969-71. **CAREER:** Madigan Army Medical Ctr, resident/internal 1966-69; US Army Med Dept, chief of medicine 1978-81; Univ of TX at Dallas, dir of internal medical educ 1982-84; State of WA Med Asst Prog, int med consultant 1984-85; Morehouse School of Medicine, prof/chmn dept of medicine 1985-. **ORGANIZATIONS:** Cons-med Tuskegee VA Hospital 1982-; med dir MMA Inc 1982-; mem Amer Med Assoc, Amer Diabetic Assoc, Amer Endocrine Soc; mem bd of dir Intl Indisciplinary Soc of Hypertension in Blacks; vice pres Intl Society of Hypertension in Blacks 1987-. **HONORS/ACHIEVEMENTS:** Fellow American College of Physicians; Natl Alumnus of the Year W.VA St Coll 1987; Distinguished Alumni Award NAFECO 1989; Course Direction 2nd Intl Conf on Hypertension in Blacks 1987. **MILITARY SERVICE:** AUS col 1962-81; Meritorious Service Medal, Legion of Merit. **BUSINESS ADDRESS:** Prof/Chmn Dept of Medicine, Morehouse School of Medicine, 720 Westview Drive SW, Atlanta, GA 30310.

REED, JASPER PERCELL
Educator. **PERSONAL:** Born Mar 02, 1929, Centenary, SC; married Sandra Lee; children: Rosalyn Jackson, Rene Jackson, Valerie Linette. **EDUCATION:** SC State Coll, bS Bio 1957; PA State U, MEd Bio Sci 1968; PA State U, DEd Bio Sci 1977. **CAREER:** Comm Coll of Philadelphia, prof of bio 1965-; Temple Univ of Med, asst instr 1957-65; City Univ System NY, evalu 1970; Educ Testing Serv CLEP, test prod 1970-73. **ORGANIZATIONS:** Life mem Kappa Alpha Psi Frat 1956-; mem Beta Kappa Chi 1957; bd of deac White Rock Bapt Ch 1962-; mem Am Soc Allied Hlth Profn 1979. **HONORS/ACHIEVEMENTS:** Recpt Bronze Star Combat Medic Badge Good Conduct AUS 1948-54; ann achvmnt awd Philadelphia Kappa Alpha Psi 1974; cert Allied Hlth Admin Am Assn of State Coll &Univ 1979. **MILITARY SERVICE:** AUS sgt 1948-54. **BUSINESS ADDRESS:** 1600 Spring Garden St, Philadelphia, PA 19130.

REED, JOANN
Educator. **PERSONAL:** Born Mar 28, 1939, Flint, MI; married Willie C Reed; children: Kim F, George, Troy M. **EDUCATION:** Eastern MI Univ, BS 1960, MA 1982. **CAREER:** Carman-Ainsworth Schools, teacher of educable mentally impaired 1963-73; Bassett Sch Dist, inst for prog inst lab 1973-74, teen mother prog coord 1973-74; Metro Day Care Ctr, admin 1975-76; Ken MacGillivray Buick, salesperson 1976-77; Flint Bd of Educ, vice pres bd of ed teach consultant 1977-; pres Flint Bd of Educ 1985-86; treasurer Flint Board of Educ 1988-89. **ORGANIZATIONS:** Mem Natl Assn of Negro Business & Prof Women's Club Inc; asst sec treas Flint Bd of Educ 1981; prog development Mott Comm Coll 1984; vice pres Flint Bd of Educ 1984; mem Alpha Kappa Alpha Sor; mem Adahi-Hon Soc; mem Carman Educ Assn; mem Natl Roster of Black Elected Officials; Greater Flint Afro-American Hall of Fame 1985-. **HONORS/ACHIEVEMENTS:** Educators Awd Zeta Phi Beta Sorority Flint 1981; Appreciation Awd Natl Assn Negro Business & Professional Women 1982. **BUSINESS ADDRESS:** Teacher Consultant, Carman-Ainsworth School Dist, 1591 S Graham, Flint, MI 48504.

REED, JOE LOUIS
Executive secretary. **PERSONAL:** Born Sep 13, 1938, Evergreen, AL; married Mollie; children: Irva, Joe, Steven. **EDUCATION:** AL State U, BS 1962; Case West Resv U, MA 1966. **CAREER:** AL Educ Assn Inc, asso sec 1969-; AL State Tchrs Assn, exec sec 1964-69; AL State U, stud act 1963; Trenholm HS, tchr 1962. **ORGANIZATIONS:** Mem loc st & natl professional assn; life mem NEA; mem exec bd NCSEA 1969-75; coord vice pres NCSEA 1975; pres NCSEA 1976-; consult AL Educ Assn Professional Rts & Resp Commn; chmn DuShane Com Tchrs Rights NEA 1971-; stf advsr Unit Tchng Prfsn; delg NEA Conv & Rep Assemb; pres AL Leag for the Advncment of Educ Chrm AL Dem Conf 1970-; mem AL Advsry Com on Civil Rts; v chrm Mnrty Afrs AL Dem Pty 1974-; chm NAACP Com on Ecn 1969-; del DemNat Conv 1968; natl co-Chm Com of Edctrs for Humphrey-muskie pres tkt 1968; city cnclmn City Of Montgomery 1975-; mem Masons; mem Omega Psi Phi Frat. **HONORS/ACHIEVEMENTS:** Received Abraham Lincoln Award, Natl Educ Assn; ad-

dressed Democratic Natl Conv, 1972; initial report, Alabama League for Advancement of Educ, "The Slow Death of the Black Educator in Alabama; pres, jr class, Alabama State Univ 1960-61; pres, student body, Alabama State Univ, 1961-62. **MILITARY SERVICE:** AUS 1956-58. **BUSINESS ADDRESS:** 422 Dexter Ave, Montgomery, AL 36101.

REED, KATHLEEN RAND
Sociologist. **PERSONAL:** Born Feb 06, 1947, Chicago, IL; daughter of Kirkland James Reed and Johnie Viola Rand Cathey; divorced. **EDUCATION:** San Francisco State Univ, BA. **CAREER:** IL Supreme Ct Comm on Character and Fitness/(IICLE) Chicago, IL, investigator/rsch consultant 1970; ETA Public Relations Chicago, IL, acct exec 1970-72; WTVS TV 56 (Public TV) Detroit, MI, public relations & promotion dir 1972; WJLB Radio Detroit, MI, public affairs dir 1972-74; KH Arnold (self-employed) San Francisco, CA, business resource and resource consult 1974-80; The Headquarters Co Subsidiary of United Techn, special proj coord 1980-81; Natl Alliance of Business San Francisco, CA, administration mgr 1981-83; Michael St Michael/Corp Leather (self-employed), manufacturing exec/ pres 1983-. **ORGANIZATIONS:** Symposium Women in the News Media 1975; Natl Conf Public Relations Founder Am Futurists for Educ of Women; AFTRA; BMI Inc; documentary 1977; NANBPW; 1st vice pres SF Chapter NANBPW; Public Relations Soc of Amer 1972-; Amer Women in Radio & TV; Women's Bd Provident Hosp; World Affairs Council of N CA; commr Commn on Status of Women SF; chmn New Detroit Inc; mem Acad of Independent Scholars, Soc for the Study of Women in Legal History OH State Univ Coll of Law, Inst for Historical Study; pres Amer Futurists for the Educ of Women; mem World Future Soc, NOW, Women's Inst for Freedom of the Press, World Affairs Council, Bay Area Urban League, League of Women Voters, Natl Women Studies Assn, Natl Council of Negro Women, Commonwealth Club of CA 1977; Intl Aff Com; Women in Commn; aptd by Mayor of SF to C ommn on Status of Women 1977-80; Media & Public Info Com; consult & contrib to "Black Esthetics" 1972; bd of dirs San Francisco Convention and Visitors Bureau 1987-90, Urban Coalition West, Phoenix AZ 1987-93. **HONORS/ACHIEVEMENTS:** Major photo exhibit 1972; Western Region Volunteer Award Natl Assn of Negro Business and Prof Women 1977; Publications/Productions, "Femininity" Book Review Women's Review of Books 1984; "San Francisco Government, The City, The Citizen and Technetronics" 1978; "Back on the Track" Neighborhood Education Project Writer/Producer 1972; Lectures/ Speeches, Univ of CA Davis "The Black Female in Contemporary Society" Afro-American Studies and Women's Studies Combined Session 1984; Univ of San Francisco Lecturer "Women and the Working World" 1978; Lecturer "Reassessing Clerical Skills" Lockheed Missiles and Space Co 1978. **BUSINESS ADDRESS:** Principal, Necronomics Group, PO Box 6666, Stanford, CA 94309-6666.

REED, LAMBERT S., II
Coach. **PERSONAL:** Born May 31, 1937, Douglas, GA; married Melvynne Joyce Clark; children: Lambert III, La Jean Rooszon, Lamont. **EDUCATION:** Morris Brown Coll, BA 1959; FL A&M U, addl studies;Univ of Miami. **CAREER:** Morris Brown Coll, head football coach 1978;Univ of FL, 1st black coach 1975-77; Axe Handle Beer & Wine, owner; SEC, 1st black coach;Univ of Miami; 1st black coach 1972-74; miami killian sr hs, head varsity football coach, athletic dir, asst to prin 1966-72; mays hs, head football coach 1965; GW Carver HS, defensive football coach, head basketball coach 1962-65. **ORGANIZATIONS:** Mam exec com Greater Miami Athletic Conf 1971; pres-elect Greater Maimi Athletic Conf 1972; mem Alpha Phi Alpha; mem Citizens Rating Bd 1969-71; Big Bro & Sis of Greater Miami Adv Bd 1971-74; bd dir Greater Miami Boys Club; charter mem Bapt Hosp Comm Liaison Comm. **HONORS/ACHIEVEMENTS:** Coach of yr S Dade News Leader 1968; coach of yr Alpha Phi Alpha 1971; coach of yr S Dade News Lealder 1972; Miami Herald Athletic Hall of Fame 1973; 1st black coach in state of FL to be head coach in integrated sch 1966. **BUSINESS ADDRESS:** Axe Handle Beer & Wine, 1839 Hollywood Rd NW, Atlanta, GA 30318.

REED, LARITA D.
Convention center controller. **PERSONAL:** Born Sep 26, 1960, Chicago, IL; daughter of Henry Reed and Joyce Hinton Reed; married Gregory A Clark, Jun 18, 1988. **EDUCATION:** Loyola Univ, Chicago IL, BBA, 1982. **CAREER:** Peat Marwick Mitchell, Chicago IL, auditor, 1982-84; McCormick Place, Chicago IL, asst controller, 1982-84, controller, 1984-. **ORGANIZATIONS:** Mem, Natl Assn of Black Accountants, 1980-; mem, Amer Institute of CPA's, 1983-; mem, IL CPA Society, 1983-; mem, Unity Fellowship MB Church, 1983-; mem, Government Finance Officers Assn, 1984-. **HONORS/ACHIEVEMENTS:** Named among top black business & professional women, Dollars & Sense Magazine, 1988. **BUSINESS ADDRESS:** Controller, McCormick Place, 2301 S Lake Shore Drive, Chicago, IL 60616.

REED, LLOYD H.
Corporate attorney. **PERSONAL:** Born Jul 31, 1922, Washington, DC; married June E Moore; children: Rebecca C, Lloyd A. **EDUCATION:** Howard Univ, BA 1943; Harvard Law School, LLB 1949; Columbia School of Bus, 1977. **CAREER:** Mutual of NY, attny, asst counsel, assoc counsel, counsel, asst gen counsel, assoc gen counsel, vice pres real estate investment counsel 1949-; Mony Financial Services, vice pres corporate relations. **ORGANIZATIONS:** Mem Amer Bar Assoc, The Assoc of Life Ins Counsel, INSCOLAW; life mem NAACP; former mem School Bd of Greenburgh NY; founder, dir Westchester Comm Oppty Prog; gen couns Black Lawyers of Westchester Inc; dir Minority Interchange Inc. **BUSINESS ADDRESS:** Vice Pres Corporate Relations, Mony Financial Services, 1740 Broadway, New York, NY 10019.

REED, LOLA N.
Librarian. **PERSONAL:** Born Nov 27, 1923, Sneads, FL; widowed; children: Emmitt Jr, Gwendolyn, Bettye, Reginald, Ronald, Michael. **EDUCATION:** FL A&M Univ, BS Bus Ed 1946, BLS 1948; Rutgers State Univ, MLS 1960. **CAREER:** FL A&M Univ Dean of Ed, admin sec 1949-59; Mommouth Cty Library Freehold NJ, childrens librarian 1960-63; W Orange Free Publ Library, childrens librarian 1963-71, acting dir to dir 1971-. **ORGANIZATIONS:** Mem Amer Library Assoc, NJ Library Assoc, Essex Cty Directors Group, SW Essex Dir Council, FL A&M Univ Alumni Assoc, Rutgers Univ Alumni Assoc, Comm Serv Council of the Oranges & Maplewood, Natl Council of Univ Women. **BUSINESS ADDRESS:** Dir, W Orange Free Publ Library, 46 Mt Pleasant Ave, West Orange, NJ 07052.

REED, MAURICE L.
Mathematician. **PERSONAL:** Born Jan 03, 1924, Chgo; married Betty E; children: Verna O, Pamela C, Maureen R. **CAREER:** City of Sprngfld OH, data proc supr; Ops Res Analyst Sys Simu Br Wright Patter AFB, act br chief 1974-79; Sys Simu Br, math 1968-74; Adv Res & Techn Sec Plans & Mgmt Br, math 1966-68; Data Reduct Div Dir of Test Data Dep for Test & Support, math 1961-66. **ORGANIZATIONS:** Past pres OH Urban League Bd of Dir 1967; chmn resltns com Alpha Phi Alpha Frat 1969-74; educ counc Nat Urban League 1969-75; past v chmn bd of dir Clark Tech Coll 1971-74; mem Nat Assn of Parliam 1975; mem Am Inst of Parliamentarians 1977; bd Of dir Nat Counc of YMCAs of the US 1980; memnum other orgns. **HONORS/ACHIEVEMENTS:** Outstdg reg alumni brot of yr Alpha Phi Alpha Frat 1974; natl outstdg alumnus of yr Alpha Phi Alpha Frat 1974; cit of yr awd Front Intnl 1975. **MILITARY SERVICE:** USMC 1943-46. **BUSINESS ADDRESS:** Police Dept, City of Springfield, Springfield, OH 45501.

REED, RODNEY J.
Educator. **PERSONAL:** Born May 16, 1932, New Orleans, LA; son of Edgar J Reed and Ursul C Desvignes Reed (deceased); married Vernell M Auzenne, Aug 05, 1961; children: Karen, Ursula. **EDUCATION:** Clark Coll, BA 1951; Univ of MI, MA 1956; Univ of CA, Berkeley, PhD 1971. **CAREER:** Southern Univ Baton Rouge LA, asst prof/asst cond bnds 1956-61; Oakland CA Unified Sch District high sch tchr/vice prin 1961-68; Univ CA Berkeley, asst, assoc prof and prof 1970-; Univ CA Berkeley, faculty asst chancellor, affirmative action 1980-82. **ORGANIZATIONS:** Mem Am Ed Res Assoc 1970-; mem editorial bd Educ and Urban Soc 1972-86; pres Fornax, Inc Edtl Consult 1975-88; life mem NAACP 1975-; mem Assoc CA Schl Admin 1976-; mem editorial bd, Policy Studies Review Annual 1976-; mem Nat'l Conf Prof Edtl Admin 1977-; vice chair & mem brd Bay Area Urban Leag 1980-; chair Edtl Comm Bay Area Blk United Fund 1979-82; mem editorial bd, Educational Researcher 1982-; mem editorial bd, Natl Forum of Educ Admin & Supervisors 1983-; mem, Omega Psi Phi Fraternity; mem Sigma Pi Phi Frat 1983-; mem Amer Assoc of Sch Admin 1986-; mem, Phi Delta Kappa, 1971-; mem, Amer Educ Research Assn, 1974-. **HONORS/ACHIEVEMENTS:** Otstdng Man Yr Omega Psi Phi Frat Sigma Iota 1966; urban fellowship Univ CA Berkeley 1968-70; Bronze awd Bay Area Blk United Fund 1982; co-author (W/ James W Guthrie) Edtl Admin Policy Ldrshp Am Ed 1985; mem Order of the Golden Bear Univ of CA Berkeley 1985-; author, School & College Competency Testing Programs: Perceptions of African-Amer Students in Louisiana & North Carolina; author, Expectations & Student Achievement. **MILITARY SERVICE:** AUS specialist 3 1953-55. **BUSINESS ADDRESS:** Prof of Educ Admin, Univ of California, Berkeley, School of Educ, 3527 Tolman Hall, Berkeley, CA 94720.

REED, THERESA GREENE
Physician, government official. **PERSONAL:** Born Dec 09, 1923, Baltimore, MD; daughter of William James Greene and Theresa Greene Evans; divorced. **EDUCATION:** VA State Coll, BS 1945; Meharry Med Coll, MD 1949; The Johns Hopkins Univ, MPH 1967. **CAREER:** Homer G Phillips Hosp, staff physician, public health physician 1950-58; Private practice, physician 1950-65; Homer G Phillips Hosp, asst clinic dir 1958-66; Johns Hopkins Univ Sinai Hosp, preventive med fellow 1966-68; FDA med epidemiology officer 1968-, lecturer clinical pharmacology 1983-; Howard Univ, assoc prof comm med 1972-; FDA supvr Medical Officer 1975-79, 1987-. **ORGANIZATIONS:** Mem Amer Coll of Epidemiology; fellow Amer Coll of Preventive med; mem Soc for Epidemiological Rsch, Amer Soc for Microbiology; Amer Med Womens Assn, Amer Publ Health Assoc; vice pres of the medico Chirurgical Soc of DC; mem Assoc of Teachers of Preventive med, Amer VD Assoc; fellow Cty Med Soc; mem Intl Epidemiological Assoc, Alpha Kappa Alpha; sec, treas Daniel Hale Williams Med Reading Club; mem Protestant Episcopal Church; Natl Med Assn; chairman of the Committee on Admin & Financial Affairs of the Natl Medical Assn 1987-. **HONORS/ACHIEVEMENTS:** Author of numerous papers in med jrnls 1st pres Mound City Women Physicians; 1st Black Female Med Epidemiologist; Public Health Serv Special Recognition Award 1985; Outstanding Serv Award, Natl Medical Assn 1986-87; Food and Drug Administration Commendable Serv Award 1985; Devel directory of 1100 Black Physicians i the Metropolitan DC area; completed 4 years of outstanding serv as chairperson of Region II of the Natl Medical Assn. **HOME ADDRESS:** 11516 Patapsco Dr, Rockville, MD 20852.

REED, THOMAS J.
Legislator. **PERSONAL:** Born Sep 17, 1927, Brookhaven, MS; married Sereeta; children: Thomas, Jr, Ava, Evelyn. **EDUCATION:** MS Tuskegee Inst, BS. **CAREER:** Mem, AL Legislature. **ORGANIZATIONS:** Chmn, Black Elected & Appointed Officials of AL; state pres NAACP. **HONORS/ACHIEVEMENTS:** First black to serve as rep in AL state legislature since Reconstruction; Instrumental in getting legislature to hire first black page; pres over public hearing on maltreat Of AL prison inmates; pres Dept of Public Safety to hire 350 blacks in various positions; filed charges against 17 fed agencies in the state demand that blacks be given 25% of all federal jobs in AL. **BUSINESS ADDRESS:** Drawer EE, Tuskegee Inst, Tuskegee, AL 36088.

REED, VINCENT EMORY
Educator. **PERSONAL:** Born Mar 01, 1928, St Louis, MO; married Frances Bullitt. **EDUCATION:** WV State Coll Inst, BS Educ 1952; Howard Univ, MA 1965; Wharton School of Finance and Comm Univ of PA, completed inst on collective negotiations; VA State Coll, Guidance NDEA Scholarship; Iowa Univ. **CAREER:** WV State Coll, football coach 1955; Jefferson Jr HS, teacher 1956; Anacostia HS, Cardozo HS, Jefferson Jr HS, counselor 1963; Manpower Devel Training Program DC Public Schools, asst dir 1964; Dunbar HS, Wilson HS, asst principal; Woodrow Wilson Sr HS, first Black principal 1968-69; DC Public School, asst supt personnel 1969-70; DC Public School, asst supt safety & security 1970, exec asst 1970-71, asst supt 1971-74, assoc supt office of state admin 1974-75, supt 1975-80; President of US, asst sec for elem and secondary educ 1981-82; The Washington Post, vice pres for communications 1982-. **ORGANIZATIONS:** Mem NAACP, mem Jr Achievement (bd dir) Washington, DC; bd dir Stonewall Athletic Club; bd dir YMCA; bd dir Natl Conf of Christians and Jews; bd trustees Univ of DC; bd trustees Southeastern Univ; bd trustees Gallaudet Coll; bd trustees Amer Univ; found trustee WV State Coll; exec comm Convention and Visitors Center; Howard Univ Charter Day Comm; bd dir Big Brothers Inc; chmn Sch and Summer Jobs Board of Trade Washington, DC; bd dir Girl Scouts; bd dir Boy Scouts; bd dir Boys' and Girls' Club DC Police Dept; Merit Select Panel for US Magistrates; DC chmn United Way; past mem Amer Assn of Sch Personnel Admin; Amer Personnel and Guidance Assn; past chmn Area Supts Study Seminar; past bd dir Goodwill Industries. **HONORS/ACHIEVEMENTS:** Comm Serv Award SE Citizens Assn 1970; Superior Serv Award DC Bicentennial Assembly 1976; Outstanding Achievement Award WV State Coll 1976; Out-

standing Comm Serv Award NAACP 1977; Distinguished Serv Award Phi Delta Kappa Intl George Washington Univ 1979; Keynote Speaker NY State Urban League Convention; Keynote Speaker Natl Head Start Conf; Keynote Speaker Seven-State Conf of the PTA; mem of a comm evaluation qualifications of private school to admin vocational training for DC public schools; Principal Speaker at Commencement Exercises of Univ of DC, Southeastern Univ, etc; Honoarary degrees, WV State Coll, HHD; Southeastern Univ, Doctor of Public Admin; Georgetown Univ, Doct of Humane Letters; Univ of DC, Doctor of Laws; Strayer Coll, Doctor of Humane Letters; Harris-Stowe Univ, Doctor of Humane Letters. **MILITARY SERVICE:** AUS 1st Lt. **BUSINESS ADDRESS:** VP for Communications, The Washington Post, 1150 15th St NW, Washington, DC 20071.

REED, WILBUR R.
Government official. **PERSONAL:** Born Mar 13, 1936, St Louis, MO; married Bettye Freeman; children: Delecia, LaDonica, Durleon. **EDUCATION:** Univ of Toledo, BE 1960, MA 1968; School of Mediation Amer Arbitration Assoc, Graduate 1974. **CAREER:** Lott Day Sch, teacher 1960-61; Child Study Inst, probation counselor 1063-67; City of Toledo, dir delinquency div 1967-69; Univ of Toledo, lecturer 1967-69; Denver Juvenile Ct, probation officer 1969-, probation supervisor 1969-72; Comm Coll of Denver, instructor 1969-75; US Dept of Justice, mediator 1972-. **ORGANIZATIONS:** Bd of dirs Urban League 1978; commissioner Aurora Civil Service Commn 1980-82. **HONORS/ACHIEVEMENTS:** Special Appreciation Awd Denver Urban League 1982; publication "Crime and Delinquency, A Study of Toledo and Lucas County Ohio". **MILITARY SERVICE:** AUS 1st lt 2 yrs. **HOME ADDRESS:** 2027 S Ironton Ct, Aurora, CO 80014. **BUSINESS ADDRESS:** Mediator, US Dept of Justice, 333 W Colfax, Denver, CO 80204.

REED, WILLIS
Professional basketball coach. **PERSONAL:** Born Jun 25, 1942, Hico, LA; divorced; children: Carl, Veronica. **EDUCATION:** Grambling Coll, attending. **CAREER:** NY Knicks NBA Team, center, forward 1964-74, team capt, coach 1977; Creighton Univ, head basketball coach; Atlanta Hawks, assistant coach 1985-. **ORGANIZATIONS:** Mem All Star Team 1965-71,73, NBA, World Championship Team 1970,73. **HONORS/ACHIEVEMENTS:** Most Valuable Player Awd for Reg Season Playoffs & All Star Games 1970; Most Valuable Player Playoffs; Author w/Pete Pepe "The View from the Run 1971; mem Basketball Hall of Fame. **BUSINESS ADDRESS:** Assistant Coach, Atlanta Hawks, The Omni, 100 Techwood Drive, NW, Atlanta, GA 30303.

REED-MILLER, ROSEMARY E.
Businesswoman. **PERSONAL:** Born Jun 22, 1939, Philadelphia, PA; married Paul E Miller (deceased); children: Sabrina E, Paul D. **EDUCATION:** Temple Univ, BA 1962. **CAREER:** US Dept Agriculture, information specialist 1966-67; jewelry design, crafts development, journalism, Jamaica, WI, & Washington, DC (Womens Wear Daily, Afro-American, et al); Toast & Strawberries Inc Boutique, owner & oper 1967-. **ORGANIZATIONS:** Pres Task Force on Educ & Training for Minority Bus Enter 1973-74; bd mem Interracial Council on Bus Oppor 1973-; pres Howard Univ Faculty Wives Assn 1973-; mem founding group Assn Women Bus Owners 1974; del White House Conf on Small Bus 1980; mem Dupont Circle N Bus Assn; mem DC Barristers WivesAssn; DC Govt Economic Development Commission bd mem 1983-86; Woodley House bd mem1986; TV shows, Eye on Washington, maternity fashions 1985, Black Dressmakers in History 1986, America's Black Forum, fashion business, 1986; radio show, Fashion Business, Capital Edition WUSA, News WJLA, Inaugural Dress-up. **HONORS/ACHIEVEMENTS:** Bus Awd Century Club Natl Assn Negro Bus & Prof Women's Clubs 1973; Bus Awd for Serv Washington Black Econ Devel Corp 1973; Businesswoman of Yr Natl Council for Small Bus Dev Eastern Region 1974; Black Academic Development Alpha Kappa Alpha Sor 1975; Appreciation Plaque Awd Bus & Prof Women's League 1980; Black Women in Sisterhood Calendar Honoree 1982; Bus Serv Awd Century Club Club 20 1983; bd mem Economic Develop Bd-Mayor's Office 1983; Serv Awd Howard Univ, Institute of Urban Affairs 1984; Bus Serv Awd Blacks Within Govt 1984; Comm Serv Awd RSVP Club 1984; delegate White House Conf on Sm Bus. **BUSINESS ADDRESS:** Toast and Strawberries, 2009 R St NW, Washington, DC 20009.

REEDE, JAMES WILLIAM, JR.
Educational administrator. **PERSONAL:** Born Sep 14, 1952, Chicago, IL. **EDUCATION:** US Military Acad, 1971; Univ of San Francisco, BS 1981. **CAREER:** General Elec Nuclear San Jose, quality cont engr 1974-81; GE3 Windfarms San Jose, 1981-84; CA Publ Utilities Commn, quality cont consultant 1984-85; Cityof San Jose Housing Commn, commissioner 1981-; Mt Pleasant Sch Dist, vice pres bd of educ 1983-; US Dept of Defense DCASMA San Diego, production branchchief 1987-. **ORGANIZATIONS:** Mem Amer Assn of Blacks in Energy 1981-; mem (1st Black) Amer Wind Energy Assn 1981-; mem/founder CA Wind Energy Assn 1982-; strategus Kappa Alpha PSI San Jose Alumni 1985-; sr deacon Scottish Rite Masons AFAM 1984-; mem NAACP San Jose, Urban League San Jose. **HONORS/ACHIEVEMENTS:** Congressional Apptmnt US Military Acad 1970; Natl Merit Scholar 1970. **MILITARY SERVICE:** USAF; Honorable Discharge 1974. **HOME ADDRESS:** 3456 Chapala Drive, San Jose, CA 95148. **BUSINESS ADDRESS:** Production Branch Chief, Dept of Defense DCASMA, 4327 Pacific Coast Hwy, San Diego, CA.

REEDER, WILLIE R., JR.
Educator. **PERSONAL:** Born Jul 30, 1923, Minden, LA; married Charlesetta Bedford; children: Karen Michelle. **EDUCATION:** So Univ, BS 1947; StateUniv IA, MA 1957; LA TechUniv NW StateUniv &Univ MO At KC, Masters plus 30. **CAREER:** Webster Trade School Minden LA, dir 1947; Central HS Dubberly LA, math teacher & asst princ 1947-60; Union Elem School, prin 1960-. **ORGANIZATIONS:** Mem Unit Tchg Prof (WEA LEA NEA); 3 times pres Webster Educ Assn; mem NAESP; wrote syllabus In "New Math" for Webst Par Tchrs Workshop in 1964; mathcons in Area Workshop LA State Dept Educ 1964; mens Day Speaker for area chs yrly; consult spec prob in educ At LEA Ann Conv 1974; prin Web Par "Right to Read Sch Mem Title VII Adv Comm Read Imp Act For LA; life mem LA PTA 1977; mem Exec Counc LA Educ Assn; mem Lee Lodge #221 Prince Hall Masons; So Univ Alum Fed; NAACP Minden Fed of orgns; PTA; Web Unit Fed Credit Un; W Side Civ Club; chmn bd of Deacons & gen supt Sun Ch & Sch New Light Bapt Ch 1969. **HONORS/ACHIEVEMENTS:** Omega man of yr 1970, 1974; "Educator of Yr" (Adminstr) 4th Dist LEA & Shreveport Times 1965, 1973; elect del NEA Ann meet 3 times; serv plaque WEA pres 1970; one of 10 tchrs of distinc in LA LA State PTA 1976; serv awd (10 yrs) Web Unit Fed Cred Un 1968; WEA pres 1977-78. **MILITARY SERVICE:** AUS pvt 1943-44. **BUSINESS ADDRESS:** Webster Prsh Dist 9, 505 Morrow St, Minden, LA 71055.

REESE, DELLA
Singer, actress, composer. **PERSONAL:** Born Jul 06, 1931, Detroit, MI; married Franklin Thomas Lett Jr; children: Della Jr. **EDUCATION:** Wayne State Univ, attended. **CAREER:** Tonight Show, Merv Griffin Show, Ed Sullivan, McCloud, Police Woman, Mike Douglas Show, num game shows,TV spec, performed; Mahalia Jackson Troupe, performed1945-49; Sahara-Tahoe, Caesar's Palace, Coconut Grove, Mr Kelly's, Caribe Hilton, Flamingo, performed; Let's Rock 1958, The Last Minstrel Show 1978, actress; Jubilee, RCA, Victor Records, ABC Paramount, recording artist; Della Variety Show, hostess 1969-70; McCloud, Twice in a Lifetime, Police Woman, Petrocelli, Chico & The Man, actress 1977; solo recording artist 1957-. **HONORS/ACHIEVEMENTS:** Num gold records; Most Promising Girl Singer 1957. **BUSINESS ADDRESS:** William Morris Agency, 151 El Camino, Beverly Hills, CA 90212.

REESE, DON (THE UNDERTAKER)
Professional athlete. **PERSONAL:** Born Sep 04, 1951, Mobile, AL; married Paulette; children: Jean Paul, Phillip Charles. **EDUCATION:** Jackson State. **CAREER:** New Orlean Saints, football player; Dolphins, player 1974. **BUSINESS ADDRESS:** New Orleans Saint, 6928 Saints Avenue, Metairie, LA 70003.

REESE, FREDERICK D.
Pastor, educator. **PERSONAL:** Born Nov 28, 1929, Dallas County, AL; married Alline Toulas Crossing; children: Frederick, Jr, Valerie, Marvin, Christa, Alan. **EDUCATION:** Alabama State Univ, BS; Atlanta Bible Inst Clark Coll, adv study; Southern Univ; Selma Univ; Univ of Alabama; Livingston Univ, MEd. **CAREER:** Ebenezer Bapt Church, Selma AL, pastor; Eastside Jr High & High School, principal; city councilman. **ORGANIZATIONS:** Mem Natl Educ Assn; Alabama Educ Assn; dist VI Educ Assn; Phi Beta Sigma; bd dir YMCA; pres Dallas County Voters League. **HONORS/ACHIEVEMENTS:** Local leader in 1965 Voters Rights Move, Selma; organized black teachers for the right to vote; led demonstrations against local newspaper; resp for black clerks and cashiers in stores and banks; organized black citizens for position on Dallas County Dem Exec Comm; Abraham Lincoln Award; outstanding leadership educ NEA Detroit 1971; Teacher of the Year Award, Selma City Teachers Assn; Good Guy Award chmn Unit Appeal; numerous plaques & certificates for outstanding leadership in education and civil rights. **BUSINESS ADDRESS:** Eastside Jr High School, Selma, AL 36701.

REESE, MAMIE BYNES
Educator. **PERSONAL:** Born Sep 03, Gibson, GA. **EDUCATION:** Spelman Coll, BS 1933; Drake U, MS 1948; OH State U, adv study;Univ So CA; Simmons Coll; Boston U. **CAREER:** Center HS, teacher; Des Moines Tech HS; Baker & Burke Counties, home demon agnt; Albany State Coll, asso prof dean women. **ORGANIZATIONS:** Mem GA State Bd Pardons & Pardons; past pres Nat Assn Colored Wom Club Inc; mem GA Assn Educat; NEA; Sigma Rho Sigma Honor Sor; aux GA Osteop Med Assn; Nat Health Assn, Delta Sigma Theta Sor; Assn Parol Author; Am Correct Assn; World Fedn Meth Wom; Hines Memorial Butler St Meth Episco Chs; Albany Urban League & Guide; Albnay C Of C; Govs Spl Counc on Fam Plan; bd dir; Semper Fidel Club; GA Div Am Canc Soc; com mem Girl Scouts Am; num off NAACP. **HONORS/ACHIEVEMENTS:** Couple of yr Albany Chap Zeta Phi Beta Sor Inc 1958; cit Spelman Coll 1966; outstndg Citizen Albany State Coll Comm Relat Com 1966; women of conscience awd Nat Counc Wom USA 1969. **BUSINESS ADDRESS:** 800 Peachtree St NE, Atlanta, GA 30309.

REESE, MILOUS J.
Chiropractic physician. **EDUCATION:** Emory U, Postgrad Work in Internal Medicine; McCormick Medical Med Coll, MD; Nei Ching Intrl Chinese Healing Arts, Doctor of Philosophy; Univ AL, Spec Study of Alphine Culture Art & Lang. **ORGANIZATIONS:** Mem AL State Chiropractic Assn; mem Jefferson County Chiropractic Soc; mem Acupuncture Soc AL; mem Acupuncture Soc Amer Kansas City, MO; mem Ctr Chinese Med Los Angeles, CA; mem US Acad Acupuncture; mem Traditional Acupuncture Found Columbia, MD; mem First Black Appointed US Bd Acupuncture; mem Kappa Phi Sigma Med Frat; mem Natl Med Soc Assn Chicago, IL 1945; mem Intl Soc Naturopathic Physicians 1945; mem Amer Coll Chiropractic Orthopedist 1979; mem Natl Coll Alumni Assn 1949; mem Council Nutrition to the Amer Chiropractic Assc Inc; mem Orthopedic Class 1979; mem AL State Chiropractic Assn Cert 1958; cert mem Natl Chiropractic Assc 1945; crt mem Amer Council on Chrpctc Orthopedics of the ACA 1979; mem Natl Psychiatric Assn 1978; mem, Big Brothers Club 1975; honorary mem, Beta Psi Accounting Honor Society, Booker T Washington Business College 1972; founder, Alabama College of Drugless Therapy (medicine) 1950. **HONORS/ACHIEVEMENTS:** Recogn Dinner & Plaque in Recogn for Exemplary Serv in Field of Med for Humanitarian Serv and Dedicated Professional Leadership from Univ of Montevallo 1985; Doctor of Humane Letters, Miles College 1989; Certificate of Membership Gold Lapel Pin-50 years, The National College of Chiropractic 1989. **BUSINESS ADDRESS:** 2117 18th St Ensley, Birmingham, AL 35218.

REESE, VIOLA KATHRYN
Social service administrator. **PERSONAL:** Born Aug 23, 1953, Lexington, TN; daughter of Rev Billy Frank Dabbs and Willie Mae Smith Dabbs; married J Monroe Reese, Jr; children: Idesha, James III. **EDUCATION:** TN State Univ, BS 1975; Washington Univ, MSW, 1977. **CAREER:** Children's Ctr for Behavioral Devel, therapist 1977-80, satellite coord 1980-82, interim clinical dir 1982-83, family therapist/coordinator 1983-84; RDS Foundation Inc, exec dir 1986-. **ORGANIZATIONS:** Mem Natl Assoc of Social Workers 1972-, Natl Assoc Black Social Workers 1972-, IL Assoc Sch Social Workers 1976-; mem St Clair Co Comm on Difficult Children 1980-84; mem bd of dirs Council House 1981-84; sec bd of dirs 1980-83, pres bd of dirs 1983-84 Big Brothers/Big Sisters; private consultant 1981-; Optimist Intl Lexington Charter Board Member, 1989-; Caywood PTO, sec, 1988-89. **HONORS/ACHIEVEMENTS:** Outstanding Black College Female, Essence Magazine, 1975; TN State Alumni Assn, 1975-; University Scholar TN State Univ 1975; Washington Univ Alumni Assn 1977-; MADD, 1980-; League of Women Voters, deputy registar, 1980-84; Spanish Lake Democratic Party, 1980-86; Storman Stufflin PTA, 1981-86; Outstanding Achievement Big Brothers/Big Sisters 1982, 1984; Certificate of Achievement CCBD 1984; Montgomery High Alumni Assn, 1986-; Living Life on Wheels Par Limentarian, 1987-; Outstanding Parent Volunteer, Caywood PTO, 1989; Natl Spinal Cord Assn, 1989-; Henderson County Democratic Party, 1989-. **BUSINESS ADDRESS:** Executive Dir, RDS Foundation Inc, PO Box 1084, Lexington, TN 38351.

REEVES, ALAN M.
Automobile dealer. **CAREER:** Quality Ford Sales Inc, Columbus GA, chief executive; Spalding Ford-Lincoln-Mercury Inc, Griffin GA, chief executive. **BUSINESS ADDRESS:** Quality Ford Sales Inc, 1541 First Ave, Columbus, GA 31901. *

REEVES, JULIUS LEE
Engineer. **PERSONAL:** Born Nov 10, 1961, Detroit, MI; son of Troy Reeves, Sr and Delores Reeves. **EDUCATION:** Wayne State Univ, BS Industrial Engineering, 1986. **CAREER:** Midwest Aluminum Corp, engrg asst 1983; Kelsey-Hayes, mfg engr 1984-85; Electronic Data Systems, systems engr 1985-86; GM Warren Hydramatic, assoc industrial engr 1986-88. **ORGANIZATIONS:** Mem Phi Delta Psi 1979-, Inst of Industrial Engrs 1983-, Engrg Soc of Detroit 1984-; chapter pres Phi Delta Psi Fraternity 1984-85. **HONORS/ACHIEVEMENTS:** College of Engrg Deans List Wayne State Univ 1984-85; Natl Dean's List 1984-85; Fellowship, General Motors, 1989.

REEVES, LOUISE (MRS. CHARLES MITCHELL)
Government administrator. **PERSONAL:** Born Aug 13, 1944, St Louis, MO; married Charles B Mitchell. **EDUCATION:** St Louis U, BA Polit Sci 1976; Webster Coll, MA Pub Admin 1980. **CAREER:** St Louis Agency on Training & Employment, dep dir 1977-; St Louis Met YWCA, dir housing & counsel 1976-77; Consul Nghbrhd Serv Inc, asso dir 1965-76; MOState Housing Devel Commn , commr 1978-; Freedom of Res Inc, pres 1978-79. **ORGANIZATIONS:** Chmn Monsignour John Schocklee Scholarship Com 1979-; mem YMCA & YWCA; mem St Louis Wom Polit Caucas 1975-; Council Negro Women 1976. **HONORS/ACHIEVEMENTS:** Fellowship SIU Edwardsville Il 1974; YWCA serv (vol) awd St Louis Met YWCA; 70001 support awd St Louis Chap 70001 Youth Orgn 1979. **BUSINESS ADDRESS:** St Louis Agency on Training & Employme, 3800 Lindell Blvd, St Louis, MO 63108.

REEVES, LUCIUS V.
Army officer. **PERSONAL:** Born Feb 14, 1938, Magnolia, MS; married Florence Larry; children: Lynda Vaniece, Lydia Vee. **EDUCATION:** WV State Coll, BA Pol Sci 1963; Pacific Luth Univ, MA 1979. **CAREER:** 101st ABN Div, platoon leader & co exec officer 1963-66; 1st Brigade 101st Airborne Div, company commdr Vietnam 1966-67; WV State Coll, asst pms 1967-69; Vietnamese Ranger Command, sr adv 1970; III Corps HQ Vietnam, G-3 training officer 1970-71; HQ 6th AUS, operations/training staff officer 1971-73; HQ 4th ROTC Reg Ft Lewis Wash, maj operations/staff training officer 1973-; USAR 100th Div MTC, active 1980-; Container Corp of America, production supervisor. **ORGANIZATIONS:** Participated in various progs to inform minority comm of career & educ oppors thru ROTC prog; mem Omega Psi Phi. **HONORS/ACHIEVEMENTS:** Who's Who Among Students in Amer Univs & Colls 1960. **MILITARY SERVICE:** AUS career; Bronze Star Medal W/V & 2 Oak Leaf Clusters 1966-67; Meritorious Serv Medal 1973; various other medals connected w/the military service. **BUSINESS ADDRESS:** Production Supervisor, Container Corp of America, 12200 Westport Rd, Louisville, KY 40241.

REEVES, MARTHA ROSE
Entertainer. **PERSONAL:** Born Jul 18, 1941, Eufaula, AL. **CAREER:** Professional singer, 16 yrs; Martha Motown Records, leader 10 yrs. **ORGANIZATIONS:** Mem AFTRA; AGUA; SAG; attended Lee Strassberg's Thtr Ins; Johnny Carson; Mike Douglass; Merv Griffin; Ed Sullivan; Midnight Spl; Don Kirchner Rock Concerts; mem Negro Women's Assn; Mt Zion Bapt Ch. **HONORS/ACHIEVEMENTS:** Recpt 7 gold singles; Grammy nom; 12 albums. **BUSINESS ADDRESS:** Network Talent International, Box 82, Great Neck, NY 11022.

REEVES, MICHAEL S.
Business executive. **PERSONAL:** Born Oct 02, 1935, Memphis, TN; son of William Reeves (deceased) and Grace Reeves (deceased); married Patricia; children: Michael, Michelle. **EDUCATION:** Roosevelt U, BA 1964; NW U, MBA 1972. **CAREER:** Peoples Gas, mktg mgr 1972-73; customer rel supt 1973-74, office of the pres admin asst 1974-75; customer relations dept genl supt 1975-77, vice pres 1977-; exec vice pres 1987. **ORGANIZATIONS:** Dir Better Bus Bureau 1978-; chmn and trustee St Bernard Hosp; mem Business Adv Cncl Univ of IL at Chicago; mem, Exec Leadership Council. **MILITARY SERVICE:** USNA Signal Corp speclt 1958-60. **BUSINESS ADDRESS:** Exec Vice President, Peoples Gas Co Public Utility, 122 S Michigan Ave, Chicago, IL 60603.

REEVES, WILLIE LLOYD, JR.
Attorney/elected govt. official. **PERSONAL:** Born Apr 17, 1949, Portsmouth, VA. **EDUCATION:** Howard Univ, BA 1971, JD 1974. **CAREER:** Fed Communications Comm, trial atty 1976-; FCC Chap 209 NTEU Union, pres 1979-. **ORGANIZATIONS:** Chmn Adv Neighborhood Comm 2D 1981, 1982, 1984, 1985; vice chmn ANC-2D 1980,83,86,87; vice pres Labor Sect Natl Bar Assn 1984-85; mem Natl, American, Washington Bar Assns; mem Natl Conf of Black Elected Officials; mem Omega Psi Phi Frat; bd of dirs Southwest Neighborhood Assembly 1983-; MUSCLE 1980-; mem Phi Alpha Delta Legal Frat, NCBL; pres Southwest Neighborhood Assembly 1986. **HONORS/ACHIEVEMENTS:** Who's Who Among Colleges & Univs 1974; Outstanding Young Men of Amer 1983, 1984; Spec Achievement Awd Capital South Improvement assn 1983, 1984, 1985. **HOME ADDRESS:** 1100 6th St SW #213, Washington, DC 20024. **BUSINESS ADDRESS:** Trial Attorney, Federal Communications Commiss, 1919 M St NW, Washington, DC 20554.

REGGANS, JOHN
Automobile dealer. **CAREER:** North Star Dodge Center Inc, Brooklyn Center MN, chief executive. **BUSINESS ADDRESS:** North Star Dodge Center Inc, 6800 Brooklyn Blvd, Brooklyn Center, MN 55429. *

REGISTER, JASPER C.
Educator. **PERSONAL:** Born Jan 15, 1937, Valdosta, GA; divorced. **EDUCATION:** Morehouse Coll, AB (with Honors) 1959; Univ of KY, MA 1969, PhD 1974. **CAREER:** Stillman Coll, instr 1966-67; Baldwin-Wallace Coll, asst prof 1971-73; East Carolina Univ, assoc prof sociol. **ORGANIZATIONS:** Mem Amer Sociol Assoc 1974-, Southern Sociol Soc 1974-, Human Relations Council 1980-83; mem bd of dir Mental Health Assoc 1984-87, 1989-92. **HONORS/ACHIEVEMENTS:** Research Awd Social Sci Rsch Council 1968; Assoc Danforth Found 1981-86. **MILITARY SERVICE:** AUS capt 3 yrs; Occupation Medal 1962-65. **HOME ADDRESS:** 104 Fairwood Ln, Greenville, NC 27834. **BUSINESS ADDRESS:** Associate Professor, Sociology, East CarolinaUniv, Brewster Bldg, Greenville, NC 27834.

REID, BENJAMIN F.
Clergyman, college administrator, author. **PERSONAL:** Born Oct 05, 1937, New York City, NY; son of Noah Reid and Viola Reid; married Anna Pearl Batie; children: Benjamin Jr, Sylvia, Angela, Kathy, Judith, Stephanie. **EDUCATION:** Univ of Pittsburgh, attended; No Bapt Theol Sem, attended; Amer Bible Inst, DD 1971; CA Western Univ, PhD 1975; Ctr for Pastoral Studies Anderson IN School of Theol, 1980; CA Grad School of Theol, LD 1981; Anderson Coll, DD 1982; Univ of So CA, Diploma Continuing Educ Ctr 1982-86; World University, DTheol 1988. **CAREER:** Springfield IL, pastor 1958-59; Junction City KS, pastor 1959-63; Detroit MI, pastor 1963-70; LA 1st Church of God, pastor 1971-. **ORGANIZATIONS:** Mem Natl Bd of Ch Ext & Home Missions of the Church of God 1968-80; police chpln Inglewood CA 1973-84; founder, pres So CA Assoc of Holiness Chs 1977-79; dir West Coast Effective Ministries Workshop 1975, 1977-84; vice-chmn General Assembly of the Ch of God 1977-79; pres Partners in Ecumenism SW USA Reg 1979; pres LA Council of Chs 1980; presiding bishop 1st Ch of God Nigerian Conf Africa 1980-; mem bd of trustees Anderson College 1982-; pres So CA School of Ministry LA 1984-; elected Sr Bishop The Interstate Assoc of the Ch of God 1985; chmn Ministerial Assembly of the So CA Assoc of the Ch of God 1986; mem Natl Black Evangelical Assoc 1988-; founding mem Black Ecumenical Task Force Los Angeles CA 1988-; mem bd dir LA Urban League; gen chmn Interstate West Coast Assoc of the Ch of God; mem Council of Churchmen School of Theol Azusa Pacific Univ; mem LA Council of Chs, So Christian Leadership Conf, LA Met Learning Ctr, Ecumenical Ctr for Black Ch Studies of LA, USC Comm Advs Bd. inisterial Assembly of the Southern CA Assoc of the Church of God 1986. **HONORS/ACHIEVEMENTS:** Author "Confessions of a Happy Preacher" 1971, "Black Preacher Black Church" 1975, "Another Look at Glossalalia" 1977, "Another Look at Other Tongues" rev ed 1982, "Glory to the Spirit" 1989; Mayor's Awd (LA) for community serv 1986; Outstanding Bishop's Awd LA Awds Dinner; "Excellence in Preaching Awd Disciples of Christ Indianapolis IN 1986; Inglewood Mayor's Awd 1987; CA Senate Awd 1987; Los Angeles City Council Awd 1987; Compton Mayor's Awd 1987; Los Angeles County Supervisor's Awd 1987; named by Los Angeles Times as "One of Southern California's Twenty Outstanding Preachers"; Los Angeles Mayor's Award 1988; Honored Service Award City of Inglewood CA 1988. **BUSINESS ADDRESS:** Pastor, LA 1st Church of God, 9550 S Crenshaw Blvd, Inglewood, CA 90305.

REID, CHARLES E.
Deputy director, public health. **PERSONAL:** Married Sonja R Reid; children: Charles E, Loretta Yvonne, Kenneth O, Chandra S. **EDUCATION:** TX, BA; San Diego State Univ & Univ of CA, graduate work. **CAREER:** San Diego Co Dept of Public Welfare, dep dir. **ORGANIZATIONS:** Mem Natl Assn Comm Coll Trustees (pres-elect); Urban League; Port Commn Kiwanis Intl of San Diego; mem CA Transportation Comm; Econ Opportunity Comm; past pres NAACP 1970. **HONORS/ACHIEVEMENTS:** Outstanding Young Men Yr Harley E Knox Sch Past PTA 1965. **BUSINESS ADDRESS:** Deputy Dir, San Diego Co Dept Pub Welfare, 1255 Imperial Ave, San Diego, CA 92101.

REID, CHARLES H.
Business executive. **PERSONAL:** Born May 09, 1934, Dayton, OH. **EDUCATION:** Central State U, BS 1969-70; Wharton Sch of Finance;Univ PA; Temple U. **CAREER:** Nat Conf of Black Mayors Inc, exec dir 1975-; OH Office of Min Bus Enterp, asst bur chief 1973-75; Western Reg of Nat Progress Assn, reg dir 1971-73; Progress Assn For Econ Devel, exec dir 1969-71; Greene Co OI,C, stud serv dir 1968-69; OH Soldiers & Sailors Orphan Home, Engl instr social coord 1968. **ORGANIZATIONS:** Resp for plan & implem of 2nd Ann Conv for S Conf of Black Mayors 1976; major involve in plan & implem 2 Statewide Minor Bus Conf in OH; resp for packgng & provid mgmt & tgch asst to bus; mem NAACP; Nat Urban League; YMCA; mem Capital Devel Sub-com of Cincin MBOC; procure sub-orgn of Cincin (Mboc; rep OH OMBE Bur of Fed Exec Bd in Cinin & Columb; actively invol in orgn of a minor bk for cincin area. **HONORS/ACHIEVEMENTS:** Scholar Ford Found 1969-70; devel a complete minor bus direct for Dayton area; plan for establish of an Entrep Devel Training Ctr & bus devel libr inDayton. **BUSINESS ADDRESS:** 1422 W Peachtree St NW, Atlanta, GA 30309.

REID, CLARICE WILLS (NEE WILLS)
Physician, government official. **PERSONAL:** Born Nov 21, 1931, Birmingham, AL; daughter of Noah Edgar Wills, Jr and Willie Mae Brown; married Arthur Joseph Reid, Jr, Jun 11, 1955; children: Kevin, Sheila, Jill, Clarice. **EDUCATION:** Talladega Coll, BS 1952; Meharry Med Coll, med tech 1954; Univ Cincinnati Sch Med, MD 1959. **CAREER:** US Natl Institutes of Health, Sickle Cell Program, natl coord; Sickle Cell Program Health Serv Admin, dep dir 1973-76; Dept Pediatric Jewish Hospital, dir 1968-70; Jewish Hospital med tchr 1954-55; OH Dept Health, pediatric consultant 1964-70; DHEW, med consultant 1972-73. **ORGANIZATIONS:** Mem Natl Med Assn; AAAS; asst clinical prof Univ Cinnati School of Medicine 1965-70; mem Altrusa Intl; Amer Acad of Pediatrics; Amer Public Health Assn; mem Hamilton Co Adoption Agency 1966-69; Visiting Nurse Assn 1968-70; Amer Bridge Assn; mem NY Acad of Sci, Amer Soc of Hematology, Asst Clinical Prof Pediatrics, Howard Univ Coll of Medicine. **HONORS/ACHIEVEMENTS:** Co-author chapter "Family Care" Wms & Wilkins Co 1973; Outstanding Student Faculty Awd Meharry Med Coll 1954; NIH Dir Awd; NIH Merit Awd; co-author "Management & Therapy in Sickle Cell Disease"; PHS Special Recognition Award 1989.

REID, EDITH C.
Cardiologist. **PERSONAL:** Born in Atlantic City, NJ; married John L Edmonds. **EDUCATION:** Hunter Coll, BA; Meharry Med Coll, MD. **CAREER:** St Albans NY, pvt practice; Flower & 5th Ave Monroe, clin asst; clinical instr & asst physician; New York City Dept Health, physician chest clinic Jamaica Hosp, asst visiting physician; assoc attend med; Carter Community Health Ctr, chief med. **ORGANIZATIONS:** Mem Queens Clinical Soc Inc; Natl Amer Med Assn; Med Soc Queens & NY State; NY Heart Assn; Empire State Soc; Ad Hoc Com; NY Trudeau Soc; Amer Geriatric Soc; Ethics Comm; Civic Assn; NAACP; Neighborhood Health Council; Med Adv Comm NY Univ Bd Regents. **HONORS/ACHIEVEMENTS:** Quest hon wives club lunch 1973; achievement award Omega Psi Phi 1974; friends York Coll 1974; outstanding serv Delta Sigma Theta Sor. **BUSINESS ADDRESS:** Carter Community Health Center, 97 04 Sutphin Blvd, Jamaica, NY.

REID, ELLIS EDMUND
Attorney. **PERSONAL:** Born May 19, 1934, Chicago, IL; married Barbara A Kline; children: Ellis Edmund IV, David E. **EDUCATION:** Univ of IL, BA 1956; Univ of Chicago, JD 1959. **CAREER:** IL Bar, admitted 1959; Circuit Court of County, judge; Mccoy Ming & Black Chicago & Predecessor Firm, practice law 1959-, partner 1964-; Ofc Econ Opportunity Legal Serv Program, cons; real state borker; Cook County IL, states atty spl asst; Fair Employment Practices Commn, hearing examiner. **ORGANIZATIONS:** Mem Nat IL Chicago & Cook County; pres Bar Assns; Bar Assn 7th Fed Circuit; Am Am Arbitration Assn; mem Nat Panel Arbitrators; mem Phi Delta Phi; Kappa Alpha Psi; bd dir Better Boys Found; dir Highland Comm Bank; vice pres Chatham Avalon Park Comm Council; vice pres Chatham-avalon Pk Comm Council 1963-65,67. **MILITARY SERVICE:** AU capt 1957. **BUSINESS ADDRESS:** Judge, Circuit Court of Cook County, Richard J Daley Center, Room 310, Chicago, IL 60602.

REID, ERIC WILLIAM
Radio & TV executive. **PERSONAL:** Born Aug 30, 1952, Jamaica, NY; children: Eric William Jr. **EDUCATION:** SUNY at Albany, BA 1980. **CAREER:** Campus Ctr Univ MA at Amherst, dir of mkting 1984-85; McRei Enterprises Inc, pres 1980-.

REID, F. THEODORE, JR.
Psychiatrist, educator. **PERSONAL:** Born Nov 22, 1929, New York, NY; married Diane; children: Lynne, Frank. **EDUCATION:** Columbia Coll Columbia U, BA 1950; McGill Univ Montreal, CAN, MD faculty of med 1954; King Co Hosp Brooklyn, intern 1955, psychiatry resident 1957; VA Rsch Hosp Chicago, chf resident psychiatry 1960. **CAREER:** Private Practice, psychiatry 1960-; Pritzker Sch of Med Univ of Chicago, clinical assoc prof psychiatry 1975-76; Camelback Hosp, assoc 1977-; Maricopa Co Hosp AZ State Hosp, instr; psych residency 1976; Scottsdale Memorial Hosp Family Practice Residency, instr 1977; Phoenix Indian Hosp, consultant 1977-80; Northwestern U, assoc dept of psych neurology 1966-72; Michael Reese Hosp, coor group therapy training 1969-76; Adult Outpatient Psychiatric Clinic 1967-69; Madden Zone Ctr, dir ct referral unit 1966-67; M Reese Hosp Serv ISPI, chf 1961-66; Mental Health Assoc, owner. **ORGANIZATIONS:** Mem Comm on Emerging Issues APA 1978-80; bd of dirs Camelback Hosp Found 1979; dir Amer Group Psychotherapy Assn 1979-82, 1983-; co-chmn Inst Comm Amer Group Psychotherapy Assn 1974-78; fellow Amer Orthopsych Assn 1974-80; mem exec comm Amer Group Psych Assn 1973-75, 1977-79, 1984-86. **MILITARY SERVICE:** USNR lt med corps 1957-59. **BUSINESS ADDRESS:** Owner, Mental Health Associates, 7119 E First Ave, Scottsdale, AZ 85251.

REID, GOLDIE HARTSHORN
Educator. **PERSONAL:** Born Mar 17, 1913, Laredo, TX; married Dr Herbert; children: Gail, Hadley. **EDUCATION:** Tillotsen Coll Houston, BA; Tx S U, MA. **CAREER:** Houston Independent School Dist, asst prin; Blackshear School, teacher. **ORGANIZATIONS:** Mem Nat Merit Schl Qual Comm Sel Comm; mem New York City Coll Ent Exam Bd; Nat Educ Assn; Houston Prin Assn; mem Comm of Admin Blue Triangle YWCA; Links Inc; Alpha Kappa Alpha Sor. **HONORS/ACHIEVEMENTS:** Publ "A mini course in Vocational Edn". **BUSINESS ADDRESS:** 1906 Cieburne, Houston, TX 77004.

REID, INEZ SMITH
Attorney. **PERSONAL:** Born Apr 07, 1937, New Orleans, LA. **EDUCATION:** Tufts Univ, BA 1959; Yale Univ Law Sch, LLB 1962; UCLA, MA 1963; Columbia Univ, PhD 1968. **CAREER:** Barnard Coll Columbia Univ, assoc prof 1969-76; NY State Div for Youth, genl counsel 1976-77; Dept of Health Educ & Welfare, deputy genl counsel 1977-79; Environmental Protection Agency, inspector genl 1979-80; Dist of Columbia Govt, corp counsel. **ORGANIZATIONS:** Past bds Antioch Univ Bd of Trustees, United Ch of Christ Bd for Homeland Ministries. **HONORS/ACHIEVEMENTS:** Numerous articles published; numerous awds. **BUSINESS ADDRESS:** Corporation Counsel, Dist of Columbia Govt, Dist Bldg Ofc of Corp Coun, Room 329, Washington, DC 20004.

REID, JANIE ELLEN
Administrator. **PERSONAL:** Born Feb 15, 1950, Pelzer, SC. **EDUCATION:** SC State Coll, BS Bus Admin (Honor Grad) 1972. **CAREER:** SC Assoc of Student Financial Aid Admin, mem 1973-87, sec/treas 1975-77; JE Sirrine Scholarship Advisory Bd, mem 1974-75, chmn 1980-82; SC Commiss on Higher Ed, adv bd mem 1975-78; US Dept of Ed Bureau of Student Financial Aid, inst appl review panel mem 1976; Greenville Tech Coll, fin aid dir. **ORGANIZATIONS:** Instr New Financial Aid Officer Workshop Southern Assoc of Student Fin Aid Admin 1978,79; charter mem Greenville Urban League's Early Leadership & Confidence Training 1978-79; advisory bd SC Student Loan Corp 1981-83; chmn adv bd Greenville Urban League's Ed Talent Search Prog 1982-84; minister of ed Shady Grove Baptist Church 1983-85; ed advisory comm SC Appalachian Council of Governments 1983-89; chmn Greenville Cty Human Relations Comm 1985. **HONORS/ACHIEVEMENTS:** Citizenship Awd Greenville Civitan Club 1968; mem Iota Phi Lambda, Delta Eta Chap 1971-; Listed in Who's Who Among Students in Amer Univ & Coll 1972, Outstanding Young Women of Amer 1980; Annual Pastor's Awd Shady Grove Baptist Church 1981,82,83. **HOME ADDRESS:** 405 Old Hundred Rd, Pelzer, SC 29669. **BUSINESS ADDRESS:** Dir of Financial Aid, Greenville Technical College, PO Box 5616 Station B, Greenville, SC 29606.

REID, JOEL OTTO
Educator. **PERSONAL:** Born May 17, 1936, Newark, NJ; children: Joel II, Nicol. **EDUCATION:** NYUniv Sch of Ed, BS 1959; Montclair State Coll, MA 1965; Claremont Grad Sch Claremont CA, PhD 1973. **CAREER:** Elizabeth Public School System Elizabeth NJ, teacher; White Plaines HS, counselor, teacher 1962-65; White Plaines Bd of Educ, professional recruiter 1965-67; Natl Teachers Corps Migrant Univ So CA, teacher leader 1967-68; Claremont Grad School, staff mem 1971-72; Soc Sci Dept, prof 1978; Pasadena City Coll, dean of continuing educ 1968-78, prof of social sci 1978-. **ORGANIZATIONS:** Mem Pasadena Educ Assn; Pasadena City Coll Faculty Assn; NEA; LA Co Adult Educ Adminstrs Assn; chmn Eval Com for Western Assn Schs & Colls 1969,1970, 1974; mem bd dir Urban League Com for Educ Fund Dr; Fair Hsg Com of Westchester Co NY; Am Friends Ser Com on Hsg Pasadena; counseled Neighborhood Youth Cent; worked with economically educationally deprived areas; lectured at ednl, civic & religious orgns; consult to schs, pvt groups & Comm agencies . **HONORS/ACHIEVEMENTS:** Two yr schlrshop hs to Coll; Kiwanis Rotary Club Schlrshp; Valely Settlement Hse Schlrshp W Orange NJ; Womens Aux Schlrshp W Orange NJ; nom Who's Who Comm Ldrs of Am 1971. **MILITARY SERVICE:** AUS sp5 1959-62. **BUSINESS ADDRESS:** Professor of Social Science, Pasadena City College, 1570 E Colorado Blvd, Pasadena, CA 91106.

REID, JOHN DANIEL
Educator. **PERSONAL:** Born May 17, 1924, Columbus, GA; married Verna Anne Billingslea; children: John Daniel, Millicent. **EDUCATION:** Morehouse Coll, BA 1948; Atlanta U, MA 1948;Univ of Chgo, PhD 1956. **CAREER:** Howard U, grad prof of sociol 1979-; Bur of Census & Nat Cntr for Hlth Serv Research, vis schol res 1977-79; Atlanta U, prof chmn dept of sociol 1971-77; Mcmurray Coll Il, prof & chmn dept of sociol 1970-71; Albion Coll MI, prof of sociol 1968-70; Atlanta U, edit Phylon 1971-77; WEB Du Bois Inst for Study of Am Black, found & dir 1974-. **ORGANIZATIONS:** Fellow Soc for Applied Anthropol 1974; trust Popul Ref Bureau Inc 1976-; mem adv com Nat Com on Vital & Health Statis. **HONORS/ACHIEVEMENTS:** Bronze star AUS 1943-46, 1950-52; Carnegie Grant In Aid Research AtlantaUniv 1948; Alpha Kappa Delta Hon Sociological Frat AtlantaUniv 1948; NIMH fellowshipUniv of CA 1959; serv awd Hungry Club Atlanta 1963. **MILITARY SERVICE:** Aus m sgt 5 Yrs served.

REID, LESLIE BANCROFT
Dentist educator. **PERSONAL:** Born Nov 07, 1934, Clarendon, Jamaica;son of Walter B Reid; married Norma A Morris; children: Donovan, Diane. **EDUCATION:** Howard Univ, BS 1968, DDS 1972. **CAREER:** Govt Bacteriological Lab Jamaica, med tech 1953-59; Tia Maria Ltd Jamaica, chemist 1959-64; Cafritz Hosp Washington DC, med tech 1966-72; Howard Univ Dental Sch, faculty mem 1972-. **ORGANIZATIONS:** Dir Reid-& Yip Young DDS PA 1973-; consult Ministry of Health Jamaica 1974; consult Ministry of Health Guyana 1976; partner Eastover Dental Serv 1979-; consultant Ministry of Health Belize Central Amer 1984; bd of trustees Hospice of Charles County 1985-; staff Greater Southeast Comm Hosp 1986-; clinician numerous dental conventions; bd of trustees, Charles County Comm Coll 1969-76; bd of trustees, Warner Pacific Coll 1989-. **HONORS/ACHIEVEMENTS:** Co-author (paper) "Adaptability of Several Amalgam to Enamel Surface" Journal of Dental Rsch 1985; co-author A Manual of Fixed Prosthodontics Howard Univ 1986; Outstanding Faculty, Howard Univ Coll of Dentistry Student Council 1989; Laboratory Manual of Dental Anatomy and Occlusion 1988. **BUSINESS ADDRESS:** Faculty Member, HowardUniv Coll of Dentistry, 600 W St NW, Washington, DC 20059.

REID, MAUDE K.
Retired administrator. **PERSONAL:** Born in Georgetown, SC; divorced; children: Kennedy. **EDUCATION:** FL A&M Univ, BS 1936; Columbia Univ, MA; studied at Univ of Miami. **CAREER:** Negro Progs of FL Tuberculosis & Health Educ Agy, first field sec; Bethune-Cookman Coll & FL A&M Coll, summer workshop cons; Pittsburgh Courier, social columnist; FL State Dept of Educ, teacher trainer in home econ; Dade Co Public School System Miami, retired supr adult home educ 1965-. **ORGANIZATIONS:** Mem, Amer Vocational Assn; mem Natl Educ Assn; mem Amer Home Econ Assn; mem FL Educ Assn; mem Amer Assn of Univ Women; mem League of Women Voters; pres Council of United Fund Women; past pres Greater Miami Urban League Bd; mem Natl Council of Urban League Guilds; mem Links Inc; Greater Miami Urban League Guild; bd dir YMCA sr citizen; mem League of Women Voters; exec comm Natl Council of Jewish Women. **HONORS/ACHIEVEMENTS:** Recipient Woman of the Yr Awd Links Inc; Meritorious Achievement Awd FL A&M Univ.

REID, MILES ALVIN
Educational administrator. **PERSONAL:** Born Oct 23, 1931, West Point, VA; son of William E Reid and CeCelia Whiting Reid; married Alice Lee, Aug 14, 1966; children: Alice Mia. **EDUCATION:** Morgan State Coll, BA 1953; Hampton Inst, MA 1968. **CAREER:** King & Queen Central High School, tchr 1957-64; King & Queen Elem School Shanglai, VA, principal 1964-72; Hamilton Holmes Elem School King William VA, principal 1972-78; King William West Point Schools, dir federal prog 1978-83, assoc supt. **ORGANIZATIONS:** Mem VA Assn School Admin 1978-; mem Assoc Supvn Curric Devel 1980-; mem VA Assoc Federal Educ Prog 1978-; mem West Point Bi-Racial Comm 1968-; mem West Point Bd Zoning Appeal 1971-80; gen supt Mt Nebo Baptist Church School 1964-84; prog chmn Pamumkey Baptist Literary Union 1970-85; trustee Pamunkey Baptist Assoc 1985; Teacher, Mt. Nebo Baptist Church School 1985-. **HONORS/ACHIEVEMENTS:** Appreciation Award Mt Nebo Baptist Church 1972; Area Appreciation Award VA Peninsula Clubs Negro Business and Professional Womens Clubs 1982; honored, State Farmers Degree, VA Future Farmers of Amer 1976; honored, Chapter Farmers Degree King William HS Chapter FFA; Man of the Year Third Union Baptist Church 1985; Man of the Year Awd VA Peninsular Clubs Negro Business & Professional Women's Clubs Inc 1985. **HOME ADDRESS:** 216 16th St Box 103, West Point, VA 23181. **BUSINESS ADDRESS:** Associate Superintendent, King William, P O Box 185, King William, VA 23086.

REID, MILTON A.
Minister, publisher. **PERSONAL:** Born Jan 26, 1930, Chesapeake, VA; son of Rev Moses Annias Reid (deceased) and Mary M Reid (deceased); married Marian Elean Todd, Aug 18, 1952; children: Maravia Nse Ebong, Humphrey T, Michelle A Brown, Milton A Jr. **EDUCATION:** Virginia Union Univ, AB 1958; Virginia Union Univ School of Religions, MDiv, 1960; Boston Univ School of Theology, DMin, 1980. **CAREER:** Minister, Gideons Missionary Baptist Church; Guide Publishing Co, publisher/pres, 1974-87, publisher emeritus, 1987-. **ORGANIZATIONS:** Former mem, STOIC Natl Newspaper Publishers Assn; life mem, SCLC; founder, organizer, & past pres, Virginia State Unit, SCLC; past moderator, Bethany Baptist Assn; life mem, Norfolk Branch, NAACP, 1982-; bd of dirs, Interreligious Found for Community Org, 1972-; chmn, bd of dirs, Gideon Family Life Center, 1985-. **HONORS/ACHIEVEMENTS:** Doctor of Divinity Degree, Virginia Seminary & Coll, 1960; Distinguished Leadership Award, Virginia State Conf of NAACP, 1974; Meritorious Serv Award 1974-87 Journal & Guide Citizens Award; recipient of numerous other awards & citations; civil rights activist with Southern Christian Leadership Conf & mem of bd, 1963-70; dir, TRUST Inc; dir, NNPA, 1975-81. **MILITARY SERVICE:** US Army 82nd Airborne Div, corporal, 1948-52; numerous awards. **HOME ADDRESS:** 1909 Arlington Ave, Norfolk, VA 23523. **BUSINESS ADDRESS:** Gideon's Missionary Baptist Fellowship, 2709 Campostella Rd, Suite F, Chesapeake, VA 23324.

REID, OSWALD HUTTON
Manufacturing executive. **PERSONAL:** Born Jan 01, 1951, Georgetown, Guyana;married Barbara E Bishop; children: Felicia Alexis, Bryan Alan. **EDUCATION:** RCA Institutes,

AOS Electronic Tech 1974; Pratt Inst, BSEE 1977; Univ of Pgh, MSIE 1983. **CAREER:** Gen Elec Co, mfg process engr 1977-79, mfg proj engr 1979-80, mgr matls & prod control 1980-83, mgr mfg engrg 1983-85, General Electric Co Space-Craft Oper, mgr production meas, project control. **ORGANIZATIONS:** Adv bd member Earli Burks Associates 1983-; chmn Region II adv bd Natl Soc of Black Engrs 1985; indus counsellor Carnegie Mellon Univ 1984-; mem Greater Cleveland Urban League 1985. **HONORS/ACHIEVEMENTS:** GE Glass-Metall Prods Dept Go for Gold Awd 1980, Managerial Awd 1981. **BUSINESS ADDRESS:** Manager Production Meas, General Electric Co, Space-Craft Operations, PO Box 8555 Bldg 100 Rm UZ 626, Philadelphia, PA 19101.

REID, ROBERT
Professional athlete. **PERSONAL:** Born Aug 30, 1955, Atlanta, GA; married Donna; children: Robert, Keva Rachel. **EDUCATION:** St Mary's Univ, 1973-77. **CAREER:** Houston Rockets, forward 1977-. **ORGANIZATIONS:** Rec the NBA Humanitarian of the Year Awd in 1981; works with Spec Olympics, Big Brothers, hospital groups. **HONORS/ACHIEVEMENTS:** Was a first team NAIA All-Amer st St Mary's of San Antonio which twice finished 4th place in the NAIA finals. **BUSINESS ADDRESS:** Houston Rockets, The Summit, Houston, TX 77046.

REID, ROBERT DANIEL
Educator. **PERSONAL:** Born May 12, 1914, Selma, AL; married Ellen Irene Scott; children: Roberta Irene, Robert Daniel, Gussie. **EDUCATION:** Talladega Coll, AB 1935;Univ of MI, AM 1936;Univ of MN, PhD 1942. **CAREER:** Stillman Coll Tuscaloosa AL, social science instr 1936-37; Tuskegee Inst, faculty mem 1937-64; chmn div gen studies prof History 1949-55; dir self study prog 1955-58; dean of students 1957-63; history prof 1963-64; AL State Univ, dean summer 1964; Savannah State Coll, dean faculty 1964-66; Tuskegee Inst, self study prog 1966-68; Summer School, dean graduate programs Dir 1968-69; AL State Univ Montgomery, vice pres acad affairs 1969-72; Auburn Univ, prof history 1972-. **ORGANIZATIONS:** Mem Am Historians; Assn Higher Edn; Nat Educ Assn; Am Hist Assn; Am Historians; life mem Tuskegee Civic Assn; gen educ bd fellow 1941; mem AlphaPhi Alpha; Phi Alpha Theta; dem; meth trustee. **HONORS/ACHIEVEMENTS:** Author; sect yearbook, contr articles Jours revs; asst editor Journ Negro History 1945-48.

REID, ROBERT DENNIS
Retired educator. **PERSONAL:** Born Nov 09, 1924, Atlanta, GA. **EDUCATION:** Clark Coll of Atlanta, 1941-43; Art Inst of Chicago 1946-48; Parson's School of Design, NY City 1948-50 diploma in illustration. **CAREER:** SUNY, instr painting 1975; Drew Univ, instr painting 1978; Dordogne Coll France, lecturer 1978; Parsons School of Design, instr of drawing 1978-83, assoc prof of drawing 1970-89. **ORGANIZATIONS:** Lecturer Drew Univ 1969; instructor of painting Summit Art Center 1970-74. **HONORS/ACHIEVEMENTS:** Childe Hassam Purchase Amer Acad of Arts & Letters 1969; MacDowell Colony Fellow. **MILITARY SERVICE:** USN pttm 3/c 3 yrs. **HOME ADDRESS:** 309 Mott St #2-C, New York, NY 10012.

REID, ROBERT EDWARD
Clergyman. **PERSONAL:** Born Sep 13, 1903, Como, MS; married Clara A Humphress; children: Orien E. **EDUCATION:** Lane Coll, BA 1941; Gammon Seminary, MDiv 1971; Univ of MO & Kansas Univ, additional studies. **CAREER:** Covington GA Murray Chapel, Lane Chapel, Holsey Temple, Phillip's Temple, Bower Memorial, pastor; CME Church, dir visual aid 1940; Paseo Leadership Training School, dean 1959; CME Church, presiding elder 1959-69, admin asst sr bishop. **ORGANIZATIONS:** Attended one week's seminar Hebrew Univ Jerusalem, Israel 1964; vice pres Council on Religion & Race Kansas City, MO; chmn com which drew up resolution to establish Kansas City Council on Religion & Race 1964. **HONORS/ACHIEVEMENTS:** Cited by Kansas-Missouri Annual Conf for Civic Work in Kansas City, MO Area 1963; God & Man Award Council of Religion & Race 1969. **HOME ADDRESS:** 5201 Spruce, Kansas City, MO 64130.

REID, ROBERTO ELLIOTT
Educator. **PERSONAL:** Born Nov 12, 1930, Panama, Panama;son of Exley Reid and Ettie Reid; married Joyce. **EDUCATION:** NY U, AB 1954; Western Res Univ Sch Med, MD 1958; Philadelphia Gen Hosp, 1958-59; Bronx Municipal Hosp. **CAREER:** Assoc prof urology 1973; asst prof urology 1965-73; Albert Einstein Coll Med, assoc prof of urology 1963-85, prof of urology, 1985-; Bronx Municipal Hosp, dir urology 1973. **ORGANIZATIONS:** Coun Amer Coll Surgeons 1975-77; mem NY sec rep AVAA 1976; mem Sigma Pi Phi. **BUSINESS ADDRESS:** Albert Einstein Coll Medicine, 1300 Morris Park Ave, Bronx, NY 10461.

REID, RUBIN J.
Real estate agent. **PERSONAL:** Children: 2 Children. **EDUCATION:** VA, Grad Coll Bus 1963; BS Business Admnstrn. **CAREER:** Glenarden, mayor; Gitelson Neff Asso Inc, real estate agent; Glenarden, vice mayor. **ORGANIZATIONS:** Chmn Town Council. **HONORS/ACHIEVEMENTS:** Recip Korean Serv Medal; Good Conduct Medal; Nat Defense Serv Medal & W Bronze Star; United Ntns Serv Mdl; ROK Prsdntl Unit Citation; Certif of Merit US Govt; Spl Achvmnt Awd US Govt Certif of Merit United Supreme Cncl. **MILITARY SERVICE:** Sgt AUS.

REID, SELWYN CHARLES
Attorney. **PERSONAL:** Born Apr 19, 1944, Los Angeles, CA; married Beverly A Washington. **EDUCATION:** LA City Coll, AA 1970; CA St U, BA 1970-71; Univ So CA, JD, MPA 1971-74. **CAREER:** LA Co Dist Atty, dep dist atty; Legal Aid Found of LA, atty 1975-76; LA Dist Attys Ofc, law Clk 1972; US Post Ofcx, 1966-69. **ORGANIZATIONS:** State & Bar CA; LA Co Bar Assn; Langston Law Clb; Phi Alpha Delta Law Frat; USC Alumni Assn. **MILITARY SERVICE:** USMC corpl 1962-65. **BUSINESS ADDRESS:** 417 S Hill St, Los Angeles, CA 90013.

REID, SINA M.
Business executive. **PERSONAL:** Born Feb 08, 1944, Marion, NC; married Harold G Reid; children: Derek, Deren. **EDUCATION:** Univ of NC, BA 1965; Antioch Univ, MA 1978. **CAREER:** NTL Educ Assn, admin asst 1965-67; Hope Ctr for Retarded, dir of social serv 1967-70; NTL Educ Assn, admin mgr 1970-76; Broadway-Payne Inc, exec vice pres 1976-85; SMR Ltd, pres 1980-. **ORGANIZATIONS:** Mem Natl Assoc of Bus & Professional Women; hon bd of dir mem Natl Black McDonalds Opers; bd dir MD Ed Oppty Ctr 1985; mem Gr Baltimore Dialogue Group 1985; life mem NAACP, Delta Sigma Theta, Continental Soc Inc; mem President's Roundtable; bd of dirs Boy Scouts of Amer; sec bd of dirs Associated Black Charities. **HONORS/ACHIEVEMENTS:** Disting Serv VA Union Univ; Cert of Merit for Outstanding Serv Hope Ctr; Selected to attend McIver Conference Univ of NC; Bus Woman of the Year Natl Assoc of Negro Bus & Professional Women Inc. **HOME ADDRESS:** 102 Charlesbrooke Rd, Baltimore, MD 21212.

REID, TIM
Actor, director, producer. **PERSONAL:** Born Dec 19, 1944, Norfolk, VA; married 1962 (divorced 1975); children (previous marriage): Tim Jr, Tori; married Daphne Maxwell, 1982. **EDUCATION:** Norfolk State College, BS. **CAREER:** Dupont Corp, sales representative; member, "Tim and Tom" comedy team, 1971-75; actor in "WKRP in Cincinnati," beginning 1978; actor in "Simon & Simon," beginning 1983; actor and producer, "Frank's Place," 1987-88; actor in and director of numerous television programs and motion pictures. **ORGANIZATIONS:** Directors Guild of America; Academy of Motion Picture Arts and Sciences. **HOME ADDRESS:** 16540 Adlon Rd, Encino, CA 91436. **BUSINESS ADDRESS:** Perry & Neidorf, 315 S Beverly Dr, Beverly Hills, CA 90212. *

REID, VERNON H.
Retired state employee. **PERSONAL:** Born Nov 06, 1904, Columbus, OH; divorced. **EDUCATION:** BS Educ 1927; MA Spanish 1928. **CAREER:** Penn Transfer Co, mgr; Semi-retired; St OH, deputy asst gov; State of OH, retired asst to gov of OH. **ORGANIZATIONS:** Mem OH St Civl Svc.

REID, WILFRED
Clergyman. **PERSONAL:** Born Oct 09, 1923, Detroit; married Loretta Adams; children: Paul Wilfred, Lorna Joyce, Stephen Wilfred, Patricia Lorene. **EDUCATION:** Roosevelt Univ, BS; Northwestern University Garrett Theological Seminary, MA; Monrivia University, DDiv; Edwards Waters College, Jackson, FL, DHum. **CAREER:** Bethel AME Ch Muscatine IA, pastor 1956-57; Allen & Chapel AME Ch Galesburg IL, 1957-60; Bethel AME Ch Evanston IL, 1960-64; St Stephen AME Ch Chicago, 1964-85; 4th Dist African Meth Episcopal Ch, dir of evangelism 1969-71; Chicago ConfArcn Meth Episcopal Ch, dir christian educ 1969-74; Grant Memorial AME Ch Chicago IL, pastor, 1985; 4th Dist African Meth Episcopal Ch, dir ministerial training. **ORGANIZATIONS:** Mem Youth Div NAACP 1946-48; pres Student Univ of IL 1948-49; mem Mayor's Comm Human Relations Galesburg IL 1958-60; chmn N Suburban Coord Council & Social Rights Group 1963-64; mem Chicago Urban Legislative Investigative Comm 1964-65; Midwest Comm Council Exec Bd 1964-74; organizer Control W Shng & Neighborhood Com 1965-74; exec comm Neighborhood 13th Dist Police Workshop 1968-74; mem adv council Malcolm X College 1971-72; ex-official & mem bd trustees Garrett Theol Seminary 1972; chmn Ft Dearborn BSA 1972; exec bd dir Church Federation Grtr Chicago 1972; mem adv council Evangelical Child Welfare 1973; pres Chicago Chapter Operation PUSH 1974; mem Chicago Com Black Churchmen 1974; pres St Stephens Terrace Corp Chicago IL; mem Chicago Bd of Educ Chicago IL; mem bd dir Du Sable Museu; mem adv comm Chicago City Colleges Chicago IL; mem Midwest Community Council; mem bd dir Mile Square Community Org and Medical Center; mem bd dir Martin Luther King Boy's Club; mem adv council Provident Hospital; mem bd dir South Shore YMCA; comm mem Chicago Urban League Chicago IL. **HONORS/ACHIEVEMENTS:** Award of Excellence coll debate 1948; Awd of Merit coll debate 1948; recog partcptn Douglas Debate Centennial 1958; YMCA Achievmnt Recog 1955; Certif Appntmnt Bi-centennial Celebrtn Afrcn Meth Epscpl Ch 1960; Pastor Yr Awd 1961; Chicago Com Urbn Opprtnty Certif Comm Srv 1967; Cert Merit ChicagoCom Urbn Opprtnty 1968; Utstndng Srv Nghbrhd Yth Corp 1968; Christian Debutante 1972; BSA Ldrshp Awd 1972; Who's Who in Relgs Am 1972; edit Silver Beaver Awd BSA 1973; Humanitarian Awd St Matthew AME Ch Argo IL Man Dstnctn 1973; Chicago Area Almanac & Ref Book 1st edit 1973. **MILITARY SERVICE:** AUS 1943-46. **BUSINESS ADDRESS:** Grant Memorial AME Church, 4017 South Drexel Blvd, Chicago, IL 60653.

REID-BOOKHART, PATRICIA ANN
Educator. **PERSONAL:** Born Oct 31, 1950, Philadelphia, PA; daughter of Curtis Reid (deceased) and Etrulia Reid; divorced; children: Christina, Brahim. **EDUCATION:** Cabrini College, BA 1973; Temple Univ, M Social Work 1975; Univ of Pennsylvania, Advanced Certificate Social Work Educ 1979, D Social Work 1984. **CAREER:** Philadelphia General Hospital, psychiatric social worker 1975-76; Natl Assn of Black Social Workers, natl interim exec 1984-85; Lawnside Public Schools, school social work consultant 1980-; Stockton State College, prof and coord of social work. **ORGANIZATIONS:** Founder/artistic dir Afro-One Dance Drama and Drun Theatre 1975-; human serv task force chair New Jersey Black Issues Convention 1984-; co-founder pres Willingboro Black Business & Professional Assoc 1985-89; co-founder/chair Burlington County Interorganizational Black Leadership Council 1986-; bd of dirs Assn of Black Women in Higher Educ 1986-88, Black United Fund of NJ Burlington County 1986-; founder/pres Natl Assn of Black Social Workers South Jersey; founding pres Assnc of Black Women in Higher Educ Greater Philadelphia 1986-88. **HONORS/ACHIEVEMENTS:** 100 Philadelphia Women Philadelphia Publishing Group 1983; Citizen of the Yr NJ State Council Black Social Workers 1983; Youth Role Model Award Lawnside Bd of Educ 1984; Commitment to Black Youth Award Bd of Dirs Afro-One 1984; Distinguished Alumni Achievement Award Cabrini College 1986; Certificate of Honor Temple Univ General Alumni Assoc 1987; Civic Award, Links, Inc, Eastern Area Conference, 1989; Outstanding Achievement Award, Council of Black Faculty and Staff, 1989 . **BUSINESS ADDRESS:** Prof/Coord Social Work, Stockton State College, Jimmy Leeds Rd, Pomona, NJ 08240.

REINHARDT, JOHN EDWARD
Educator. **PERSONAL:** Born Mar 08, 1920, Glade Spring, VA; married Carolyn; children: Sharman, Alice, Carolyn. **EDUCATION:** Knoxville Coll, AB 1939; Univ of WI, MS 1947, PhD 1950. **CAREER:** VA State Coll, prof eng 1950-56; USIS Manila Philippines, cultural affairs officer 1956-58; Amer Cultural Ctr Kyoto Japan, dir 1958-63; USIS Tehran Iran, cultural attache 1963-66; Office E Asia & Pacific USIA, dep asst 1966-68; Nigeria, ambassador 1971-75; Washington DC, asst sec state 1975; Intl Comm Agency, dir 1976-81; Smithsonian Inst, asst sec for history & art 1981-84; Smithsonian Inst, dir, directorate of intl activities 1984-. **ORGANIZATIONS:** Mem, Amer Foreign Serv Assn, 1969-, Modern Language Assn, Intl Club, Cosmos Club. **MILITARY SERVICE:** AUS officer 1942-46. **BUSINESS ADDRESS:** Dir Intl Activities, Smithsonian Inst, USICA, 1750 Pennsylvania Ave NW, Washington, DC 20547.

REMBERT, EMMA WHITE
Educator. **PERSONAL:** Born in Quincy, FL. **EDUCATION:** FL A&M Coll, AB 1945; FL A&M Univ, MEd 1958; Syracuse Univ, EdD 1972. **CAREER:** Pinellas Co, supr & teacher 1954-67; Mobilization for Youth NYC, supr/clinician 1963-64; Charles E Merrill Pub, educ consul 1967-72; FL Intl Univ, prof 1972-. **ORGANIZATIONS:** State organizer Natl Council of Negro Women; mem Phi Delta Kappa; mem Kappa Delta Pi; mem Pi Lambda Theta; consult & lecturer Ministry of Educ-Commonwealth of Bahamas 1973-; dir adult vet ed Okeechobee Schs Ed & prof consul Textbook Series C E Merrill Co 1975; pub com Intl Reading Assn 1976-; manuscript reviewer McGraw Hill & Allyn & Bacon Co 1977-; dir Hemispheric Women's Cong 1977-; chairperson Delta Sigma Theta FL Council 1978-80. **HONORS/ACHIEVEMENTS:** Competence Awd State of FL 1965-66; Intl Scholarship-Leadership Awds Delta Sigma Tehta 1967 1972 & 1977; EPDA Fellow Syracuse Univ 1970-72; "Alternative Strategies" Kendall Hunt Pub Co 1976; FL Outstanding Teacher/Educator 1981. **BUSINESS ADDRESS:** Professor/Acting Dean, FL IntlUniv, Tamiami Tr, Miami, FL 33199.

REMSON, ANTHONY TERENCE
Physician. **PERSONAL:** Born Dec 17, 1952, Anniston, AL. **EDUCATION:** KY State Univ, BS 1975; Meharry Medical Coll, MD 1980; MI State Univ, Int Med Specialization 1983. **CAREER:** Northwest Roanoke Physicians Assoc, president. **ORGANIZATIONS:** Mem North Central TX Independent Practice Assoc 1984; teaching faculty Roanoke Mem & Community Hospitals 1984-; bd dirs Roanoke Chap Amer Heart Assoc 1984-86; mem Salem Chap NAACP 1985; consultant Roanoke Div Amer Red Cross 1985; bd dirs Harrison Cultural Ctr 1985-86; bd dirs Hunton Livesaving Group1985; mem Amer, Natl Medical Assocs; mem Amer Coll of Physicians; bd dirs Natl Bus Coll. **HONORS/ACHIEVEMENTS:** MI Medical Soc Resident Phys Section Delegate 1982-83; participant McNeil-Lehrer Report 1983; Outstanding Young Men of Amer 1984-85; Honors Convocation apeaker KY State Univ 1986; Leadership Honoree Roanoke Valley Chamber of Commerce 1986; NAFEO Disting Corporate Alumni of the Year 1986. **MILITARY SERVICE:** USNR lt cmdr, mc 1981. **BUSINESS ADDRESS:** 2701 Melrose Ave NW, Roanoke, VA 24017.

REMUS, EUGENE
Association executive. **PERSONAL:** Married Gloria Benson; children: Marvin, Barbara, Billy, Eugene Jr, Tina Ray. **CAREER:** Fleetwood Mbl Homes MS, skilled carpenter engineer. **ORGANIZATIONS:** Pres Lexington MS Br NAACP. **HONORS/ACHIEVEMENTS:** Spl achvmnt cmmndtns MS NAACP.

RENDER, SYLVIA LYONS
Literary & social historian. **PERSONAL:** Born Jun 08, 1913, Atlanta, GA; widowed; children: Frank Wyatt II. **EDUCATION:** TN State Univ, BS 1934; Univ of Chgo, 1934-35; The OH State Univ, MA 1952; Univ of WI, 1954-56; George Peabody Coll for Teachers, PhD 1962. **CAREER:** US Emp Svc, interviewer, stat, analyst 1939-50; FL A&M Univ, dir out of state scholarship aid prog, instr-asst prof-assoc prof-prof english 1950-64; NC Central Univ, prof of english 1964-75; Library of Congress, spec in afro-amer history & culture, manuscript div 1973-82; freelance lecturer & writer. **ORGANIZATIONS:** Mem MLA, CLA, NCTE, NC Folklore Soc, NC & VA Engl Assoc, SAMLA, Soc for Study of So Lit, Assoc for Study of Afro-Amer Life & History, LC Prof Assoc;founder Murray Afro-Amer Culture Club; mem NAACP, NUL, UNO, YMCA, YWCA, ARC, United Nations Org, Alpha Kappa Alpha, Assoc for Documentary Editing, Afro-Amer Historical & Genealogical Soc, Trust for Historic Preservation, Cub Scouts, Hopkins House Assoc Alexandria VA. **HONORS/ACHIEVEMENTS:** Rsch & Writing Awds Amer Philos Soc; Duke UNC Coop Prog in the Humanities; NCCCU Faculty Rsch Comm Ford Found, NEH; Outstanding Educator Theta AlphaChap of Kappa Delta Pi; publ "Short Fiction of Charles W Chesnutt" 1974,81, "Charles W Chesnutt" 1980; articles in scholarly jrnls.

RENDER, WILLIAM H.
Physician. **PERSONAL:** Born Feb 09, 1950, LaGrange, GA; son of Elizabeth Render; married Barbara Jean; children: Eric, Keyiana. **EDUCATION:** Emory Univ, A Medicine 1974; GA State Univ, Pre-med; Meharry Medical Coll, MD 1984. **CAREER:** Dr James B Palmer Atlanta GA, physician asst 1975-80; Emory Univ Affiliated Hosp, medical resident 1984-87; private practice, Internal Medicine 1987-; Fulton County Jail, physician 1987-. **HONORS/ACHIEVEMENTS:** Honor Medical Soc Alpha Omega Alpha 1984. **MILITARY SERVICE:** USN E-3 4 yrs. **BUSINESS ADDRESS:** Physician, 970 Martin Luther King Jr Dr # 305, Atlanta, GA 30314.

RENFRO, MEL
Coach. **PERSONAL:** Born Dec 30, 1941, Houston, TX; children: 4 children. **EDUCATION:** Attended, Univ of Oregon. **CAREER:** Dallas Cowboys, all pro defensive back, scout; Miller Beer Dallas, account mgr; Los Angeles Express, defensive secondary coach; St Louis Cardinals, defensiveback coach. **ORGANIZATIONS:** Involed in various charitable activies. **HONORS/ACHIEVEMENTS:** All-America running back in coll; All-Pro at both safety and cornerback; selected to the Pro Bowl 10 straight seasons; voted an All-Pro five times; inducted into Dallas' Ring of Honor at Texas Stadium 1981 (only one of six Cowboys to gain such distinction); inductee Football Hall of Fame; High School All-Amer Football & Track; MVP East/West Game 1960 HS OR; MVP Natl Golden West Track Meet HS 1960; MVP Pro-Bowl NFL 1971; 4 Super Bowls Dallas Cowboys. **BUSINESS ADDRESS:** Coach, St Louis Cardinals, 200 Stadium Plaza, St Louis, MO 63102.

RENFROE, EARL W.
Orthodontist, educator. **PERSONAL:** Born Jan 09, 1907, Chicago, IL; married Hilda Forte; children: Earl Jr, Diane L, Stephen P. **EDUCATION:** Univ IL, DDS 1931, MS 1942. **CAREER:** Univ of IL, prof emeritus orthodontics 1982-. **ORGANIZATIONS:** Life mem IL & Chicago Dental Socs; mem Amer Dental Assn; mem Amer & Chicago Assns Orthodontists; mem IL State Soc Orthodontists; author 2 textbooks "Ed H Angle Soc of Orth"; mem Chicago Coun Foreign Rel; Intl Visitors Ctr Chicago; Alpha Phi Alpha; Druids Soc Club; 1st black amer to receive Commercial Air License IL 1936; Fellowship Amer Coll Dentists; 1st Black person certified by Amer Bd Orthodontics; pres Chicago Assn of Orthodontists 1963-64; bd of dir Council on Foreign Rel 1963-68, vice pres 1968-69; Socio-honorario Sociadade Paulista de Ortodontia Sao Paulo Brazil. **HONORS/ACHIEVEMENTS:** IL NG 1932-40; ORC 1940-41; Alumni Loyalty Awd Univ IL 1971; 1st black full prof Univ of IL Med Campus; 1st black dept head Univ of IL Med Campus; Distinguished Alumnus Award, Dental Alumni Assn Univ of IL 1988. **MILITARY SERVICE:** AUS col (first black col) 1941-46; AUS brigadier general 1984-. **BUSINESS ADDRESS:** Prof Emeritus of Orthodontics, University of Illinois, 801 So Paulina St, Chicago, IL 60612.

RENFROE, IONA ANTOINETTE
Attorney. **PERSONAL:** Born Feb 13, 1953, New Orleans, LA; daughter of George Renfroe and Leona "Maude" Madison Renfroe. **EDUCATION:** Loyola Univ, New Orleans LA, BA, 1975; Loyola Law School, New Orleans LA, JD, 1978. **CAREER:** TANO Inc, New Orleans LA, technical writer, 1975; Chevron USA Inc, New Orleans LA, landman, 1979-81; LP&L/NOPSI, New Orleans LA, corporate counsel, 1981-. **ORGANIZATIONS:** Mem, Louisiana State Bar Assn, 1980-; mem, Louis Martinet Soc, 1980-; New Orleans Assn of Black Women Attorneys, 1984-; corporate dir, Sec Riverland Credit Union, 1985-; US Dist Court, Eastern Dist of Louisiana, 1986-; counsel to bd, Natl Forum for Black Public Admin, New Orleans Chapter, 1986-; mem, New Orleans Pro Bono Program, 1987-; mem, Louisiana State Bar Assn Continuing Legal Educ Theme Subcommittee 1988-; dir, New Orleans Children's Bureau, 1988-; counsel to bd, New Orleans Birthright Soc Inc, 1988-.

RENICK, JAMES C.
Educator. **PERSONAL:** Born Dec 08, 1948, Rockford, IL; married Peggy Gadsden; children: Karinda. **EDUCATION:** Central OH State Univ, BA 1970; KS Univ, MSW 1972; FL State Univ, 1980. **CAREER:** Univ of West FL, prof 1975-81; Univ of So FL, prof 1981-83, asst to pres 1983-85, asst dean & educ chmn 1985-. **ORGANIZATIONS:** Trustee Univ Psy Ctr 1984-; chmn Amer Assoc for Higher Educ Black Caucus 1985-; mem FL Leadership Network, FL C of C 1985-; mem FL Inst of Govt Policy Council 1986-89; exec comm Council of Fellows Amer Council on Educ 1987-89. **HONORS/ACHIEVEMENTS:** Outstanding Young Men in Amer 1982; Leadership Florida FL C of C 1985; Vstg Prog Assoc Smithsonian Inst 1987; Up and Comers Awd Price Waterhouse 1987. **BUSINESS ADDRESS:** Assistant Dean, Educ Chmn, Univ of South Florida, The Grad School, FAO 126, Tampa, FL 33620.

RENTIE, FRIEDA
Actress. **PERSONAL:** Born Dec 29, 1932, Chicago, IL. **EDUCATION:** Attended Wayne Univ Detroit. **CAREER:** Free-lance actress beauty consult model NY & Detroit; actress various feature motion pictures network TV shows; Financial Mgmt Co, pres. **ORGANIZATIONS:** Bd mem New Frontier Democrats; mem NAACP; mem Urban League; treas exec bd NAACP Beverly Hills Hollywood Br. **HONORS/ACHIEVEMENTS:** Outstanding Mem of Yr Awd New Frontier Democrats 1973. **BUSINESS ADDRESS:** President, F R Financial, 3500 W Manchester Blvd #255, Inglewood, CA 90305.

REUBEN, LUCY JEANETTE
Educator. **PERSONAL:** Born Dec 15, 1949, Sumter, SC; married Dr John A Cole; children: Kwame Odell Oliver, John Akayomi Cole. **EDUCATION:** Oberlin Coll, AB 1971; The Univ of MI, MBA 1974, PhD 1981. **CAREER:** Ford Motor Co, financial analyst 1974-75; Duke Univ, asst prof 1981-83; Bd of Governors Fed Res, vstg prof 1983-84; Financial Rsch Assoc Inc, vice pres 1984-; George Mason Univ, assoc prof of finance. **ORGANIZATIONS:** Mem adv bd Hayti Develop Corp 1982-84; mem Washington DC Urban Bankers Assoc 1984-; mem Washington DC Women Economists 1984-; consultant natl Bankers Assoc 1984-; consultant US Dept of Commerce 1984-; mem bd dirs Metropolitan Washington Planning & Housing Assoc 1986-; mem Amer Finance Assoc, Eastern Finance Assoc, Natl Black MBA Assoc, Natl Economic Assoc, Natl Assoc for Female Execs, Natl Assoc of Urban Bankers, Southern Finance Assoc, Southwestern Finance Assoc. **HONORS/ACHIEVEMENTS:** Earhart Foundation Fellowship 1978; Outstanding Young Women of Amer 1979; Ayres Fellow Stonier Grad Sch of Banking 1982; Who's Who of Amer Women; 12 publications including "Black Banks, A Survey and Analysis of the Literature" (with John A Cole, Alfred L Edwards, and Earl G Hamilton) Review of Black Political Economy Fall 1985. **BUSINESS ADDRESS:** Assoc Prof of Finance, George MasonUniv, 4400 University Dr, Fairfax, VA 22030.

REVELLE, ROBERT, SR.
Government administrator. **PERSONAL:** Born Jan 06, 1947, Harrellsville, NC; son of Hugh L Revelle (deceased) and Carrie Moore Revelle (deceased); married Annie M (Adams) Revelle, Dec 09, 1969; children: Sharon Marie, Robert Jr. **EDUCATION:** Goldey Beacom Business College, AA/Mgmt 1969-71; Natl Graduate University, Certificate 1973; Wilmington College, BBA 1973-78; Eastern Theological Seminary, Certificate 1989. **CAREER:** CDA, Wilmington, planner/consultant 1971-73, admin chief 1973-74; Community Affairs, dept dir 1974-75; Community Center, superintendent 1975-84; City of Wilmington, director, minority business prog 1984-87; deputy personnel director 1987-. **ORGANIZATIONS:** Member YMCA Resource Center 1983-84; pres vice-pres member Amer Cancer Society 1973-; pres vice-pres member Price Run Child Center 1976-; mem NAACP; mem Natl Forum for Black Public Administrators 1984; mem Wilmington Small Business Develop Ctr; mem DE Minority Business Med Week/Trade Fair Comm 1984-87; Delaware Private Industry Council, 1988-. **HONORS/ACHIEVEMENTS:** US Army Personnel School of Personnel Mgmt 1967; honor certificate Freedom Foundation of Valley Forge 1970; certificate of merit American Cancer Society 1975; certificate of appreciation West Center City Community Ctr 1980; member/chmn organ comm Police/Community Council Wilmington 1983-. **MILITARY SERVICE:** AUS spec E-5 1966-69; Outstanding Soldier 1966. **BUSINESS ADDRESS:** Director, Minority Bus Prog, City of Wilmington, DE, 800 French St, Wilmington, DE 19801.

REVELY, WILLIAM
Clergyman, social worker. **PERSONAL:** Born Jan 20, 1941, Charlottsville, VA; son of William Revely, Sr (deceased) and Reaver E Carter Revely (deceased); children: Christina. **EDUCATION:** Howard Univ, BA 1964; Howard Univ, M Div 1967; Howard Univ, MSW 1971; Howard Univ, D Min, 1982. **CAREER:** Mt Gilead Baptist Church, pastor 1979; Union Baptist Church, pastor 1965-79; Nara II Aftercare Unit Bureau Rehabilitation, chf 1973-76; Shaw Residence III (Hlfway House) Bureau Rehabilitation, dir 1976-77; Howard Univ School of Social Work, 1977-79. **ORGANIZATIONS:** Mem NAACP; SCLC; ACA; NABSW; Natl Progressive Baptist Convention; Natl Baptist Convention USA Inc; Middle Atlantic St Conf Correction; Intl CB Radio Assn; chmn Talbot Action Group; bd of trustees, Shaw Divinity School. **HONORS/ACHIEVEMENTS:** Vernon Johns Preaching Award, School of Religion Howard Univ 1967; NIMH Fellowship 1967-71. **BUSINESS ADDRESS:** Pastor, Missiah Bptist Church, 8100 W Seven Mile Road, Detroit, MI 48221.

REVIS, NATHANIEL W.
Educator. **PERSONAL:** Born Jul 27, 1939, Glenridge, NJ; married Sheena. **EDUCATION:** Fairleigh DickinsonUniv NJ, BS 1962;Univ of Louvain Belgium, MD 1968;Univ of Glasgow Scotland, PhD 1972. **CAREER:** Univ of TN, asso prof 1980; Oak Ridg Nat Lab, sr sci 1977;Univ of TN, asst prof 1974-80;Univ of Glasgow Dept Cardiology, asst prof 1972-74. **ORGANIZATIONS:** Mem Intl Soc Biochemistry 1972; mem Am & Intl Soc of Cardiology 1975; advsr (brain trust) Congressional Black 1978; advsr (Grant review S) NCI1979. **BUSINESS ADDRESS:** Dir, Oak Ridge Research Institute, 113 Union Valley Rd, Oak Ridge, TN 37830.

REYNOLDS, ANDREW BUCHANAN
Government official. **PERSONAL:** Born Jun 29, 1939, Winston-Salem, NC; son of Andrew B Reynolds and Florence Terry Reynolds; divorced. **EDUCATION:** Lincoln Univ PA, BA 1960; NC A&T Greensboro, BS 1962; Columbia Univ NY, Certificate of Journalism 1970. **CAREER:** Andy Reynolds & Assoc, owner, principal; Washington State Lottery Commission, chair; King Broadcasting Co, TV news reporter; New Day Inc, prod, dir 1975; September & Assoc, prod, dir 1973-75; WCAU-TV, reporter, prod 1970-71; PA Advancement Sch, curriculum & devel specialist 1967-70; NC Advancement School, counselor, tchr 1966-67; AUS Madigan General Hospital Ft Lewis WA, radioisotope tech 1964-65; Bowman Gray Sch of Med Dept of Pharmacology, research asst 1962-63; CORE, dir 1963; manager, public relations, Seattle Parks & Recreation. **ORGANIZATIONS:** Mem NAACP 1978; dir, co-chmn CORE 1963; pres, bd of trust Educ Opportunity Prog Univ of WA; chmn, editor, Leadership Tomorrow; former chmn WA State Lottery Commn; prog chmn UNCF Telethon Comm; former mem Public Defender Assn; mem Northwest Aids Foundation, Marketing Commn, Seattle/King Co Red Cross. **HONORS/ACHIEVEMENTS:** Honorable Mention Sigma Delta Chi Features 1973; first place Sigma Delta Chi Spot News 1975; third place Sigma Delta Chi Documentary 1977; Humbolt Award, first place for News Documentary 1978. **MILITARY SERVICE:** AUS E-4 1963-65. **BUSINESS ADDRESS:** Owner, Principal, Andy Reynolds & Assoc, 10311 20th Ave NE, Seattle, WA 98125.

REYNOLDS, AUDREY LUCILE
Educator. **PERSONAL:** Born Jul 19, Weatherford, OK; daughter of John Reynolds and Josephine Barbee-Reynolds; divorced. **EDUCATION:** Wichita Univ, BA 1932; KS State Univ, USC, graduate studies; Langston Univ, Langston OK; City Coll of Los Angeles. **CAREER:** Los Angeles CA, elementary school teacher 1948; Booker T Washington High School, Sapulpa OK, prof English; Bennett Coll, Greensboro NC. **ORGANIZATIONS:** Mem Iota Phi Lambda 1947; natl pres 1973-77. **HONORS/ACHIEVEMENTS:** AME Church Certificate Outstanding Elementary Teacher 1973; Golden Bell Award 1970; 25 Year Award Iota Phi Lambda; nom Outstanding Teacher of the Year Main St School 1973-74; Life Mem PTA; Cit Gov dedicated serv Children & Com 1974; Life Membership NAACP; participated in First Vice President's Conference on Civil Rights under President Nixon, also under Vice President L B Johnson.

REYNOLDS, BRUCE HOWARD
Dentist. **PERSONAL:** Born Oct 07, 1935, Chicago, IL; married Ellen Barnes; children: Bruce Jr, Jana. **EDUCATION:** Dillard U, BS 1959; Howard U, DDS 1963. **CAREER:** Dentist, pvt prac. **ORGANIZATIONS:** Am Dntl Assn; Nat Dntl Assn; Am Endodontic Soc; Evanston Dntl Assn; Dntl Consult IL Dentl Srv NAACP; bd Op PUSH; The Cheesmen Inc. **HONORS/ACHIEVEMENTS:** AUS, medic 1957-59; USAF DDS 1963-65. **BUSINESS ADDRESS:** 1310 Hartrey Ave, Evanston, IL 60202.

REYNOLDS, CHARLES MCKINLEY, JR.
Business executive. **PERSONAL:** Born Jan 11, 1937, Albany, GA; married Estella Henry; children: Eric Charles, Gregory Preston. **EDUCATION:** Morehouse Coll, BA 1954; Wayne State Univ, mortuary sci cert 1962; Albany State Coll, middle grades cert 1964. **CAREER:** Southside Jr HS, teacher & chmn dept of social studies 1962-65; US Treasury Dept, asst examiner 1965-69, natl bank examiner 1969-71; Citizen Trust Bank, vice pres 1971, pres 1971; Atlantic Natl Bank, pres and ceo 1975-. **ORGANIZATIONS:** Bd of dir Atlantic Natl Bank; bd dir Norfolk C of C; mem Jr Achievement of Tidewater Inc; mem Tidewater Area of Minority Contractors; exec comm Greater Norfolk Develop Corp; treas Norfolk Investment Co Inc; bd of visitors James Madison Univ; treas bd of dirs Norfolk State Univ Foundation; corpbd mem & chmn Audit Comm SCI Systems Inc; adv bd mem Norfolk State Univ Business and Social Work; gerontology adv cncl Hampton Inst; life mem Alpha Phi Alpha Frat; mem Sigma Pi Phi Frat, Guardsman Inc, Rotary Club, Old Dominion Univ Exec Adv Cncl. **HONORS/ACHIEVEMENTS:** Outstanding Achievement Awd Alpha Phi Alpha Gamma Omicron Lambda Chap 1966; listed in Outstanding Young Men of Amer 1969; Congress of Racial Equality 1975;CORE Publs & Camaro Publ Co; 100 Black Am A1/C 1956-60; Minority Advocacy of the Year Awd 1984; Natl Assoc of Minority Contractors 1984; US PresidentialCitation White House Conf on Small Business; Metro Atlanta Rapid Transit Auth Commendation; Comm Serv Awd Madison Secondary Sch 1985; Disting LeadershipAwd United Negro Coll Fund 1985; McDonald's Black Achievement Awd 1986; Old Dominion Univ First Black Student Awds Banquet 1986; Delicados Inc Awd for Blazing New Horizons in Banking 1986. **BUSINESS ADDRESS:** President and CEO, Atlantic Natl Bank, 415 St Paul Blvd, Norfolk, VA 23501.

REYNOLDS, EARL THOMAS
Attorney. **PERSONAL:** Born Sep 26, 1900, Topeka, KS; married Dora. **EDUCATION:** h. **CAREER:** Coffeyville KS, asst city atty 1974; Atty, pvt prac 1939; KS Hwy Commn, asst atty 1937-39; Topeka, atty 1924-39. **ORGANIZATIONS:** Mem Calvary Bapt Ch; Enterprise Ldg; SE KS Consistory; Human Rels Commn.

REYNOLDS, EDWARD
Educator. **PERSONAL:** Born Jan 23, 1942; children: Joel. **EDUCATION:** Wake Forest Univ, BA 1964; OH Univ, MA 1965; Yale Univ, MDiv 1968; London Univ PhD 1972. **CAREER:** Christ United Presby, assoc pastor 1982-; Univ of CA San Diego, asst prof 1971-74, assoc prof 1974-83, prof 1983-. **HONORS/ACHIEVEMENTS:** Books-Trade and Economic Change on the Gold Coast 1974; Stand the Storm A History of the Atlantic Slave Trade 1985. **BUSINESS ADDRESS:** Prof of History, Univ of CA San Diego, Dept of History C-004, La Jolla, CA 92093.

REYNOLDS, GRANT
Attorney educator, educational administrator. **PERSONAL:** Born Jul 29, 1908, Key West, FL; married Lillie Hobby. **EDUCATION:** Eden Seminary, BD 1936; Fenn Coll, AB 1940; Columbia Univ Law Sch, JD 1948. **CAREER:** Atty private practice 1951; Republican Natl Comm Chief of Minority Div, counsel to chmn 1962; US Dept Housing & Urban Develop, asst regional admin reg II 1970, dep reg admin region II 1972; Nova Univ Law Sch, prof of law & dir of minority affairs. **ORGANIZATIONS:** Mem Grace Congregational Church, White Plains Bar Assoc, Westchester Cty Bar Assoc, NY State, Amer Natl Bar Assoc, Amer Trial Lawyers Assoc, Amer Legion, Amer Vet Comm, NAACP, Urban League of Westchester, Omega Psi Phi, Masons Imperial Shrine 32nd Degree, US Power Squadron; asst grand legal adv IBPOEW; Westchester Club Men Inc, Lions Club; pres White Plains-Greenburgh NAACP; chmn Council Republican Organs; pres Natl Negro Republican Assembly; pres NY State Chap Natl Negro Republican Assembly; vice chmn Republicans for Progress; founder & co-leader of org that secured from Pres Truman the order banning segregation in the Armed Forces. **MILITARY SERVICE:** AUS capt. **BUSINESS ADDRESS:** Prof of Law-Dir of Minor Afrs, NovaUniv Law School, 3100 SW 9th Ave, Fort Lauderdale, FL 33315.

REYNOLDS, HARRY G.
Educator. **PERSONAL:** Born Nov 06, 1915, Baldwin, LA; married Ada Woodson; children: Harry Gjr. **EDUCATION:** Rust Coll MS, BA 1935; Columbia U, MA Tchr Coll 1947;Univ of TX, Completed Course Work For EdD 1962. **CAREER:** Public School New Albany MS, math teacher, band dir 1936-39; Conroe TX, 1939-42; TX Southern Univ, educ psychology summer 1947-48; Wheatley HS, math Teacher 1947-52; EO Smith Jr HS, 1952-57; Kashmere Jr & Sr HS, counselor 1957-69; Francis Scott Key Jr HS, 1969; Houston Independent School Dist, chmn guid dept. **ORGANIZATIONS:** Mem Houston Cnslrs Assn; bldg rep United Fund; United Negro Coll Fund; mem BSA; tchr Adult Bible Class, Trinity E Meth Ch; Trinity Grdns Cvl Leg. **HONORS/ACHIEVEMENTS:** Contbd articles related to adolescent devel to TX St Tchr Journal, 1952-57; presently working on original tapes for cnslng Pupils on Secondary Level; srvd with 731 Military Police & Core Area. **MILITARY SERVICE:** AUS 1942-46. **BUSINESS ADDRESS:** 4000 N Loop, Houston, TX 77026.

REYNOLDS, IDA MANNING
Appointed government official. **PERSONAL:** Born Sep 08, 1946, Hines, FL; daughter of James Westley Manning and Catherine Mosley Manning; married Wilfred Reynolds Jr, Sep 08, 1984; children: Ronald Jr, Katrina, Joseph Hayes Rawls, Tina, Wilfred Reynolds III. **EDUCATION:** Lincoln Technical Inst, Computer Science 1963-66. **CAREER:** Alachua Cty FL, benefit & payroll supvr 1963-73, personnel specialist 1973-79, personnel mgmt analysis 1979-81, dir of equal opportunity div, 1981-. **ORGANIZATIONS:** Sec Local Chapter Amer Soc Personnel Admin 1979; 1st vice pres Central FL Conf Women Missionary 1980-; state coord Amer Assoc Affirmative Action 1982; mem adv bd Fe Comm Coll Human Serv 1982-; mem bd of dir, FL Assn Comm Professionals, 1983-; chairperson area XIV FL Church Women United 1984-; regional pres FL Assoc Comm Relations 1984-; bd of dir/chair, Alachua County MKL Fund, 1984-; bd of dir, One Church One Child Black Adoption, 1986-; mem Natl Forum of Black Public Administrators, Natl Assn of Human Rights Workers, The Governor's Comm on Martin Luther King Commemorative Celebration 1986, Amer Assn of Public Admin and Conf of Minority Public Adminis; bd of dirs Gainesville/Alachua Co Marfin Luther King Fund Inc; bd of dirs, United Gainesville Comm Develop Corp, 1984-; mem Alachua County Black Adoption Bd. **HONORS/ACHIEVEMENTS:** Future Business Leaders of Amer 1981; Appreciation Awd Amer Cancer Soc 1981; Outstanding Contrib Reg IV Amer Assoc Affirm Action 1982; Outstanding Contrib Gainesville Job Corps 1984; Certificate of Recognition and Certificate of Appreciation Governor of the State of FL 1986; Distinguished Service Award Alachua County, 1989; Developed, implemented and coordinated private and public participation in Countywide Annual Conference on Human Rights and Equal Opportunity Law. **HOME ADDRESS:** 2405 NE 65th Terrace, Gainesville, FL 32609. **BUSINESS ADDRESS:** Director, Equal Oppty Div, Alachua Cty Florida, 21 East University Ave, 3rd Floor, Gainesville, FL 32602.

REYNOLDS, JAMES F.
Director. **PERSONAL:** Born Aug 29, 1914, Winston-Salem, NC; married Alice Gertrude Rausch; children: Lanell Rhone, Alice Owens, Micaela Jones, John. **EDUCATION:** Univ of Denver, BA 1960-62, MA 1962-63; Met State Coll, D of PA 1980. **CAREER:** City & Co of Denver, race consult 1963; Univ of CO, tchr 1967-75; Univ of Denver, teacher 1970-74; United for Progress Headstart, pres 1967-; CO Civil Rights Comm, dir 1963-80. **ORGANIZATIONS:** Pres Black Dir Council 1980; pres People to People/Sister Cities Intl 1980. **HONORS/ACHIEVEMENTS:** Man of the Yr Awd Delta Psi Lambda 1967; Whitehead Awd ACLU CO Chap 1978; Martin Luther King Awd Martin Luther King Found 1980; Awd Intl Assn of Ofcl Human Rights Agency 1980. **MILITARY SERVICE:** USAF maj 24 yrs. **BUSINESS ADDRESS:** CO Civil Rights Comm, 1525 Sherman St, Denver, CO 80203.

REYNOLDS, JAMES VAN
Actor. **PERSONAL:** Born Aug 10, 1946, Kansas City, MO; son of Leonard Reynolds and Dorothy J Cotton Reynolds; married Lissa Layng, Dec 21, 1985; children: Jed. **EDUCATION:** Washburn Univ, Topeka KS, BFA, 1970. **CAREER:** Los Angeles Repertory Theater, managing artistic dir, 1975-82; LaFamille Enterprises, pres, 1987-; South Pasadena Repertory Theater, managing artistic dir, 1989-. **ORGANIZATIONS:** Mem, advisory bd, Topeka Performing Arts Center, 1989-. **HONORS/ACHIEVEMENTS:** Man of the Year, Natl Jewish Hospital, Natl Asthma Center, 1985, 1986, 1987; Volunteer of the Year, Dir of Volunteers in Amer, 1987; Honorary Citizen, Wichita KS, 1988; Honorary Citizen, Kansas City KS, 1988; I, Too, Am Amer (a one man play performed nationally), 1988-89; Time Express, Burbank CA, actor, 1979; "Days of Our Lives," Burbank CA, actor, 1981-; other acting roles include, "Highway to Heaven," "Different Strokes," "The Incredible Hulk," Hound of Hell, Nero Wolfe, Keeper of the Wild, The Magic of Lassie, Hotline, Mr Majestyk. **MILITARY SERVICE:** US Marine Corps, 1964-66.

REYNOLDS, MILTON L.
Development programmer. **PERSONAL:** Born Nov 06, 1924, Winton, NC; married Anne; children: Rei, Jeneata, Camillejan, Richard. **EDUCATION:** NC Central Univ, BS 1948, MS 1950. **CAREER:** Winton NC HS, 1948-49; Durham NC HS, instr 1949-53; Univ MD, math instr 1953-56; IBM Corp, systems programmer 1956-81; SUNY, math instr 1963-64; Ulster Co Comm Coll, asst prof data processing & computer sci 1981-, dept chair 1984-. **ORGANIZATIONS:** Mem NAACP 1947-; Soc of Applied Mathematicians 1959-; Assn of Computing Machines 1959-; Amer Assn of Photogrammetry 1960-; mem Lion's Club 1966-;

Mid-Hudson Patterns for Progress Planning Group 1967-73; NY State Sch Bd Assn 1966-, dir 1972-79, exec com 1974-79, vice pres 1975-77, pres 1978; vice chmn Natl Sch Bd Assn NE Region 1978-80; chmn Natl Sch Bd Assn NE Region 1980-; mem Kingston Bd Educ 1966-72; mem Ulster Co Bd Coop Educ Serv 1968-, pres 1974-; mem bd of trustees Wilson Coll Chambersburg PA 1981-. **HONORS/ACHIEVEMENTS:** Beta Kappa Chi Natl Hon Soc; mem Coll Council SUNY 1970-80. **MILITARY SERVICE:** AUS corpl 1942-45. **BUSINESS ADDRESS:** Asst Prof Data Processing, Ulster County Comm Coll, Stone Ridge, NY 12484.

REYNOLDS, NANETTE LEE (NEE SMITH)
Educator. **PERSONAL:** Born Feb 22, 1946, Oberlin, OH; married Murphy L Reynolds; children: Malika, Michon Imani. **EDUCATION:** Howard Univ, BA 1967; S IL Univ at Carbondale, MS Educ 1969; Harvard Univ, EdD 1978. **CAREER:** MIT, asst dean for student affairs 1970-72; Brown Univ, asst dean of academic affrs 1972-74; RI Consortium for Continuing Educ in Human Serv & Comm Welfare, exec dir 1977-78; The Reynolds Group Human Resources Consultants, managing editor 1980-82; Federated Council of Domestic Violence Progs, exec dir 1982-83; Office of MI's Governor, prog specialist in educ and civil rights 1983-85; MI Dept of Civil Rights, exec asst to the dir 1985-. **ORGANIZATIONS:** Acting dir MI Women's Comm 1984; acting treas MI Women's Assembly 1984-85; chair Educ Adv Comm of Detroit Head Start Prog 1981-83; Delta Sigma Theta Sor Inc Second Vice Pres 1966-67; mem on sev natl comms; pres Boston Alumnae 1970-72; pres Providence RI Alumnae 1973-74; sec & vice chair & hon bd mem Project Transition 1979-; co-chair Intl Black Peoples Found 1980-81. **HONORS/ACHIEVEMENTS:** Ford Fellowship for Black Americans 1975-78. **HOME ADDRESS:** 1126 Sunset Lane, East Lansing, MI 48823. **BUSINESS ADDRESS:** Exec Asst to the Dir, MI Dept of Civil Rights, 303 West Kalamazoo 4th Floor, Lansing, MI 48913.

REYNOLDS, PAMELA TERESE
Journalist. **PERSONAL:** Born Dec 10, 1963, Los Angeles, CA; daughter of Mr & Mrs Theodore Reynolds; married Philip G Roth, Feb 13, 1988. **EDUCATION:** Univ of MO Columbia School of Journalism, BJ (magna cum laude) 1985. **CAREER:** The Boston Globe, feature writer, reporter; national reporter, 1987-89. **ORGANIZATIONS:** Mem Sigma Delta Chi 1984, Boston Assoc of Black Journalists 1986, Young Black Journalists Under 30 1985; tutor Literacy Volunteers of MA 1987. **HONORS/ACHIEVEMENTS:** Natl Achievement Scholar 1981; Reynolds Scholar Donald W Reynolds Found 1983; Kappa Tau Alpha Hon Journalism Soc 1985; Best Student Journalist New England Women's Press Assoc 1985. **BUSINESS ADDRESS:** Feature Writer, Reporter, The Boston Globe, 135 Morrissey Blvd, Boston, MA 02107.

REYNOLDS, ROBERT JAMES
Professional athlete. **PERSONAL:** Born Apr 19, 1960, Sacramento, CA; children: Fawn Rashelle, Robert IV. **EDUCATION:** Sacramento City Coll; Cosumnes Jr Coll. **CAREER:** Los Angeles Dodgers, Outfielder 1983-. **HONORS/ACHIEVEMENTS:** First major league hit was a three-run home run; named to TX League All-Star team. **BUSINESS ADDRESS:** Los Angeles Dodgers, 1000 Elysian Park Ave, Los Angeles, CA 90012.

REYNOLDS, VIOLA J.
Educator. **PERSONAL:** Born Feb 04, 1925, Savannah; widowed; children: LaVerne, Freddie Mae, Fred Jr, Janice, Marcia, Felicia, Tonia. **EDUCATION:** Nat Sch of Bus, 1946; Comm Devel Seminar, 1967-69. **CAREER:** US Dept of Labor, cost of living survey 1946; Univ of GA, nutrition Aide 1969-74; Univ of GA, nutrition Ldr aide & Coopertive extension serv 1974. **ORGANIZATIONS:** Chatham Cit Dem Clb 1946; mem PTA 1953-74; Girl Scout Ldr 1954-59; Y Teen Ldr 1961-63; YWCA Bd 1961-63; adv bd Savannah St Coll Emrgncy Sch Aid Act Prog 1974; crrspndng sec Chatham Co Coun PTA 1973-75. **HONORS/ACHIEVEMENTS:** Mem, seminar on rural hlth, Am Med Assn 1971; honorary Life Mem PTA 1968; natl honors for wrk Expanded Foods & Nutrition Educ Prog 1974; Cit Day, Savannah 1974. **BUSINESS ADDRESS:** US PO Wright Sq Br, Savannah, GA.

RHEA, MICHAEL
Association executive. **PERSONAL:** Born Oct 03, 1946. **EDUCATION:** UCLA; UCLA, MBA; Memphis St U, Tokyo U, LA Wrtrs Wrkshp, Postgrad. **CAREER:** Met Manpwr Commn, Indianapolis, dept admnstr 1973; WLWI TV "Here & Now", host 1970-74; Econ Devel Corp , mgr 1970-73; Thomas Ryan Inc Mgmt Cons, reg mgr 1969-70. **ORGANIZATIONS:** Mem Gov's Commn Status & Women 1973; chmn bd dirs Yth Market Pl 1973; pres & chmn bd People Better Brdcstng 1973; Jaycees; adv Black Stdnt Union; adv Black Arts Wrkshp; Mayor's Task Force Improve City Govt; Indianapolis Cable Steering Com; Adult Educ Coun Central IN; New World Cmmnctns; bd City & State Black Caucus; CORE; Young Rep; Nat Assn Execs & Mgr; Professional Mgrs Clb; Artist Am; Midwst Poet's Orgn; adv Boys Clb Am. **BUSINESS ADDRESS:** 2101 N College Ave, Indianapolis, IN 46202.

RHETTA, HELEN L.
Physician. **EDUCATION:** Univ MI, AB; Univ MI Med Sch, MD; Univ MI Sch of Pub Health US Dept HEW, MPH 1968-76. **CAREER:** Provident Hosp, intern & resident 1938-39; physician 1939-. **ORGANIZATIONS:** Mem IL State, Chicago, Med Soc; AMA; Amer Pub Health Soc; Delta Sigma Theta; Amer Physicians Art Assn. **HONORS/ACHIEVEMENTS:** USPH Fellowship 1966-67; Superior Serv Awd US Dept HEW 1972; Natl Assn of Coll Women Awd; Amer Physicians Recognition Awd; Zeta Phi Beta Woman of the Year.

RHINEHART, JUNE ACIE
Publishing executive. **PERSONAL:** Born Jul 01, 1934, Mckeesport, PA. **EDUCATION:** Wilson Jr Coll, AB 1962; Roosevelt U, Chicago, BA 1968; Northwestern U; LoyolaUniv Chicago, Grad Sch of Bus 1972; LoyolaUniv of Chicago Sch of Law, JD 1980. **CAREER:** Johnson Pub Co Inc, Chicago, vp; Ebony, Jet, Black Stars, & Ebony Jr Mags, asst to pub 1971, sec, adminstrv asst to pres & edtr 17 yrs; Atlass Cmmnctns RADIO Statn WJPC) Chic, corp sec. **ORGANIZATIONS:** Mem adv bd exec prog Stanford U; mem RooseveltUniv Alumni Bd; mem bd of trustees Chic StUniv Found; mem Alpha Kappa Alpha Sor; Chicago Network; Women's Div Oprtn PUSH; Chicago Focus. **HONORS/ACHIEVEMENTS:** Achievement Awd Nat Counc of Negro Women 1973; listed in Who's Who in Am; 1,000 Successful Blacks. **BUSINESS ADDRESS:** Vice President/Genl Counsel, Johnson Publishing Co, Inc, 820 S Michigan Ave, Chicago, IL 60605.

RHINEHART, VERNON MOREL
Attorney. **PERSONAL:** Born Sep 27, 1935, Kansas City, KS; son of Thomas A Rhinehart, Sr and Anna P Pennyman Rhinehart; married Carmen M Melendez-Rhinehart, Oct 01, 1983. **EDUCATION:** Howard Univ, Schl Of Law, LLB/JD 1966; Boston Univ Coll of Lib Arts, BA 1958; Chicago Tchrs Coll; The Univ of Chgo. **CAREER:** Elliot Donnelley Youth Cntr, group worker 1959; Cook Cnty Dept of PA, social worker 1959; Internatl Hrvstr Co, indstrl rel emplyee Rel Staff 1967; Off of Economic Opprtnty, 1967; Brunswick Corp, mngr 1967-68; Comm on Human Rel, human rel ofcr 1968-69; First Natl Bank of Chicago , ofcr cand comm lending 1969-70; Rivers, Cousins, Lawrence & Clayter, assoc 1972-74; Herman, Glazer, Rhinehart, Waters & Kessler, partner 1974-79; Clayter, Wood & Rhinehart, partner 1979-82; Law Offices of Vernon M Rhinehart, princple 1982-. **ORGANIZATIONS:** Mem IL Trial Lawyers Assoc, Natl Bar Assoc, Amer Bar Assoc, Cook Cnty Bar Assoc, IL State Bar Assoc, Alpha Phi Alpha Frat Inc, Amer Judicature Soc, Boston Univ Alumni Club of Chicago, Howard Univ Chicago Alumni, City Club of Chicago, Chicago Urban League, NAACP, bd Woodlawn/Yancey Units, Chicago Boys Club; mem Black Caucus of Health Workers, Amer Assoc of Blacks in Energy, Amer Soc of Hosp Attorneys of the Amer Hosp Assoc, Chicago Assoc of Black Journalists, Amer Arbitration Assoc, Natl Assoc of Health Services Execs, Amer Soc of Law & Med, Comprand (Comprehensive Research & Development). **HONORS/ACHIEVEMENTS:** Bancroft-Whitney Company's Award; Amer Jurisprudence Prize for Excellence in Fed Jurisdiction; Commissioner City of Chicago Health Systems Agency (appointed by Harold Washington, Mayor of Chicago, 1985); Recognition Award, Alpha Phi Alpha Frat Inc, XI Lambda Chap, 1987. **HOME ADDRESS:** 9400 S Forest Ave, Chicago, IL 60615. **BUSINESS ADDRESS:** Attorney & Commissioner, Law Ofc Atty Vernon Rhinehart, Marmon Bldg, 39 S LaSalle St Ste 200, Chicago, IL 60603.

RHINES, JESSE ALGERON
Business executive. **PERSONAL:** Born Jul 30, 1948, Washington, DC. **EDUCATION:** Antioch Coll, BA 1974; Yale Univ, MA 1983; UCLA, MA 1986. **CAREER:** Fides Neighborhood House, dir of comm 1973-74; Congressman RV Dellius, admin aide 1975-76; Mayor's Office New Haven CT, legislative affairs officer 1978-80; IBM, systems engr 1981-83; RC Squared, president 1984-. **ORGANIZATIONS:** Coord, Umoja Extended Family, New Haven, 1982-83; world ambassador, State YMCA of Michigan, 1985; Africa group leader, Operation Crossroads to Africa, 1985; photographer/mem, Black Filmmakers Found, 1985-; mem 21st Century Political Action Comm 1985-. **HONORS/ACHIEVEMENTS:** Ideals of the Center Award, Yale Afro-Amer Cultural Center, 1981; Outstanding Young Man of Amer, Jaycees, 1982; exhibited photographs taken in Mali, West Africa, at Yale Univ. **HOME ADDRESS:** 219 W 16th St, #1A, New York, NY 10011.

RHOADES, SAMUEL THOMAS
Educational administrator. **PERSONAL:** Born Aug 11, 1946, Raleigh, NC; children: Audria Michelle Humes. **EDUCATION:** NC Central Univ, BA Psych 1967; NC Central Univ, JD 1973. **CAREER:** Durham Coll, counseling & cooperative ed 1973-77; St Paul's Coll, spec asst/fed programs 1977-. **ORGANIZATIONS:** Treas Phi Alpha Delta Law Frat 1975; parliamentarian Natl Assoc of Title III Admin 1978; mem Amer Legion, Omega Psi Phi Frat, Beauty of Dunn Lodge of F&A Masons. **HONORS/ACHIEVEMENTS:** Law Jrnl NC Central Univ 1972; Honor Grad NC Central Univ 1972; Omega Man of the Year Omega Psi Phi Frat 1977. **MILITARY SERVICE:** AUS sgt E-5 2 yrs. **BUSINESS ADDRESS:** Special Asst to the President, St Pauls College, 406 Windsor Ave, Lawrenceville, VA 23868.

RHODEMAN, CLARE M.
Educator. **PERSONAL:** Born Jul 21, 1932, Biloxi, MS; married Thomas Johan; children: Rennee Maria, Thomas Johan, Nichole Irene. **EDUCATION:** Xavier U, New Orleans, BA 1953; Xavier U, MA 1957. **CAREER:** Elementary, Jr High & Sr High teacher & Sr High counselor; Nicholas Jr HS Biloxi Municipal Separate School System, Jr HS counselor; MTA BEA, coordinator 1973-74. **ORGANIZATIONS:** Mem MS Prsnl & Guid Assn; prof Stndrds Com; chmn guid Com 6th dist MS Tchr Assn; Nat Educ Assn; Cath 67, sec 67-71, vice pres 1971-72 Biloxi Interparochial Sch Bd; mem Our Mother Sorrows Cath Ch; Parish Cncl; MS Gulf Coast Alumnae Chpt, Delta Sigma Theta Sor; Biloxi NAACP; mem bd dir Harrison Co Devl Commn; Harrison Co Comm Action Prog; Harrison Co Untd Fnd; Dem Party; vol wrkr, Mothers March Birth Defects, Heart Fnd & PTA. **BUSINESS ADDRESS:** 950 Bellman St, Biloxi, MS 39530.

RHODEN, RICHARD ALLAN
Health scientist. **PERSONAL:** Born May 08, 1930, Coatesville, PA; son of Dorothy Rhoden; married Kathryn Vernice Coursey; children: Richard A Jr. **EDUCATION:** Lincoln Univ, AB 1951; Drexel Univ, MS 1967, PhD 1971. **CAREER:** Naval Air Devel Ctr, rsch chemist 1972; Environmental Protection Agency, environ scientist 1972-75; Natl Inst for Occupational Safety & Health, rsch pharmacologist 1975-82; Natl Insts of Health, health scientist administrator 1982-89; American Petroleum Institute, health scientist 1989-. **ORGANIZATIONS:** Exec sec subcomm on toxicology, exec comm, science adv bd US Environ Protection AGency 1979; sr policy analyst Office of Science & Tech Policy Exec Office of the President 1980-81; mem Environmental Studies Inst Adv Comm Drexel Univ 1980-84; rapporteur WHO Study Group on Recommended Health Based Limits in Occup Exposure to Pesticides Geneva Switzerland 1981. **HOME ADDRESS:** 12 Vallingby Cir, Rockville, MD 20850. **BUSINESS ADDRESS:** Health Scientist, American Petroleum Institute, 1220 L Street NW, Washington, DC 20005.

RHODES, ANNE L.
Retired human services director. **PERSONAL:** Born Oct 09, 1935, Richmond, IN. **EDUCATION:** Whittier Coll, BA Polit Sci 1957; Fresno State Coll, MSW Sch of Social Work 1968; CA Scholarship Fed. **CAREER:** San Bernardino Co Dept of Pubic Social Svcs, social worker 1959-62, social serv supvr I 1962-63, social serv super II 1963-68, social serv supr III 1968-71; Univ of CA Ext at Riverside, instr 1969; San Bernardino St Coll, lectr 1971-72; City of San Bernardino, mgmt analyst 1972-74; Chaffey Coll, instr 1973; City of San Bernardino, supt of comm serv dir human svcs; St Bernardine Med Cntr, medical social worker 1987. **ORGANIZATIONS:** Consult prog developer self employed; trained Head Start Staff of Econ Oppor Bd of Riverside Co 1970; served as trainer, consult Parents for Progress del agency of San Bernardino Co Dependency Prevention Commn; lifetime Comm Coll Teaching Cert; mem San Bernardino Co Affirmative Action Task Force 1972; City of San Bernardino EEOC 1973-; pres San Bernardino NAACP 1960-61; bd dirs San Bernardino Family Serv Agency 1971-74; Inland Empire Adolescent Clinic 1970-71; consult mem Local Welfare Rights Orgn; bd dirs Inland Area Urban League 1970-71; current mem NASW, ACSW, NOW, League of Women Voters, Urban League, Natl Cncl of Negro Women, NAACP; Zonta Intnl 1986-.

HONORS/ACHIEVEMENTS: Cert of Recog for Outstanding Support of San Bernardino Black Athletes Hall of Fame 1975; Cert Los Padrinos in recog for contrib to betterment of youth comm 1974; Cert in recognition San Bernardino Westside Comm Devel Corp 1974; first Black Dept Head in history of City of San Bernardino; German Minority Professional Exchange Prog 1979; mem State Com of Credentials 1980; commendation Common Council City of San Bernardino 1986.

RHODES, BESSIE M. L.
Business executive. **PERSONAL:** Born Nov 14, 1935, Hodgenville, KY. **EDUCATION:** KY St Coll, BA 1956; StUniv of IA, MA 1957; Nthwstrn U, PhD 1972. **CAREER:** Forrestville Elem School, Chicago, teacher 1957-62; Kindergarton Center, teacher; Foster Elem School, team leader 1962-70; Northwestern Univ, Evanston, IL, asst prof 1971- 72; Miller Elem School, Evanston, prin 1972-74; School Dist 65, Evanston, dir academic studies; Tupelo MS Schools, consultant 1967-68; New Albny MS Proj, coordinator 1968-70; The Amer School Project, Mexico City, consultant 1969; Office of Equal Opportunity, consult 1970. **ORGANIZATIONS:** Mem advsry com Amer Coll Tstng; mem advsry bd Tit III Proj; mem bd dir NWUniv Alum Assn; mem Dist 65 Edctrs Cncl, IL Ed Assn; Nat Ed Assn; Nat All Blk Schl Edctrs; IL Prin Assn; mem Alpha Kappa Alpha; Alpha Kappa MU; Evnstn Nrth Sub Com for Urbn Leg; NAACP. **HONORS/ACHIEVEMENTS:** Tchr of Yr 1968, Grade Tchr Mag; Wmn of Yr 1969; Ebenezer AME Ch; Comnty Contr Awd 1973, Delta Sigma Theta. **BUSINESS ADDRESS:** Xerox Corporation, 2200 E McFadden, Santa Ana, CA 92711.

RHODES, C. ADRIENNE
Marketing chairman, communications director. **PERSONAL:** Born Jul 16, 1961, Camden, NJ; daughter of Adele Clark Polk. **EDUCATION:** State Univ of NY at F I T, AAS 1984, BS 1989. **CAREER:** The New York Times Magazine Group, circ/prom serv asst 1980-82; Diane Von Furstenberg Inc, public relations mgr 1982-84; United Negro Coll Fund, mgr of media relations 1984-85, asst dir of communications 1985-89, dir of com 1989-. **ORGANIZATIONS:** Senator Student Govt Assoc Pratt Inst 1979-80; mem PRSA Young Profls Comm NY Chap 1983-84; assoc mem NY Assoc of Black Journalists 1986; mem Public Relations Soc of Amer Natl Chap 1987-89; marketing chmn Natl Assn of Black Journalists 1989. **HONORS/ACHIEVEMENTS:** CEBA Awd of Merit World Inst of Black Comm 1986. **BUSINESS ADDRESS:** Dir of Communications, United Negro College Fund, 500 East 62nd St, New York, NY 10021.

RHODES, DUPLAIN
Company executive. **PERSONAL:** Children: Edith, Sandra, Joan, Stephanie, Kathleen, Duplain III. **EDUCATION:** Attended, Creighton Univ Omaha NE. **CAREER:** Central Funeral Home Carrollton LA, partner w/CL Dennis; The Duplain W Rhodes Life Insurance Co, United Fidelity Life Insurance Co, Duplain W Rhodes Insurance Company of Alabama, owner.

RHODES, EDWARD
Government official. **PERSONAL:** Born Apr 05, 1943, Taylor, LA; married Mattie Jean Hemphill; children: Keith Edward, Treva LaShelle. **EDUCATION:** Grambling Coll, AA; FBI Supr Sch, Cert; Intl Assn Chfs Police Schl, Cert; AK St Troopers Acad, cert. **CAREER:** AK St Troopers, lt 1966. **ORGANIZATIONS:** Bd mem Anchorage Muncpl Schl; Nat Assn Black Law & Enfrcmnt Exec; Rotary Internat; Untd Supreme Cncl 33rd Degree Masons; Nat Assn Pub Info Offcrs; Anchorage Black Caucus; NAACP; AK Peace Offcrs Assn; AK St Troopers Life Saving. **HONORS/ACHIEVEMENTS:** Commend, Outstndng Law Enfrcmnt Offcr in AK, US Jaycees. **MILITARY SERVICE:** USAF sgt 1962-66. **BUSINESS ADDRESS:** PO Box 6188, Anchorage, AK 99502.

RHODES, EDWARD THOMAS, SR.
Transit authority administrator. **PERSONAL:** Born Mar 20, 1933, Cumberland, MD; son of John Henry Rhodes and Ella Harrison Burger Rhodes; married Ovetta Lyles Williams; children: Shari, Edward Jr. **EDUCATION:** Kenyon Coll, BA 1955. **CAREER:** W-PAFB, contract negotiator 1958-61; GSFC, sr procurement analyst 1961-64; FWPCA Dept of the Int, dir div of general serv 1964-71; EPA, dir contract mgmt div 1971-75, dep asst admin 1975-78; HEW dep asst sec grants & procurement mgmt 1975, dep asst sec grants & procurement 1978-80, deputy assoc dir/admin group Office of Personnel Mgmt 1980-86; Office of Procurement, Washington Metro Area Transit Authority, director. **ORGANIZATIONS:** Mem Natl Bd of Advisors Natl Contract Mgmt Assn; mem Bd of Regents Institute of Cost Analysis; pres Natl Assn of Black Procurement Professionals. **HONORS/ACHIEVEMENTS:** Meritorious Serv Award, Dept of Int, 1967; Distinguished Serv Award, Dept of Interior, 1967; Award for Achievement in Public Admin Wm A Jump Mem Found 1969; Silver Medal for Sup Service EPA 1972; Meritorious Serv Award OPM. **MILITARY SERVICE:** AUS sp-4 1955-57.

RHODES, JEANNE (NEE SIMMONS)
Business executive. **PERSONAL:** Born in Monongahela, PA; widowed; children: Joseph Simmons Scott, Margaret Herndon. **EDUCATION:** Duffs Bus Sch;Univ Pitts; Duquesne U. **CAREER:** Philadelphia Tribune, vice pres pub rltns. **ORGANIZATIONS:** Bd mem Am Red Cross; life mem, exec com, Grad Hosp Aux; bd mem Inglis Hse Home for Incurables; bd mem Philadelphia Tribune Co; bd trustee Ruth W Hayre Schlrshp Fnd; mem Spnsrs Schlrshp Clb; La Cabaneetas Estrn Seabrd Dinner Clb; Finesse Brdg; DCR Birthday Clb; bd mem Philadelphia 76; bd trustee Dowingtown Agr & Indsl Sch; spec Dept of Labor; p pres, p sec, Pitts Br, NAACP; p chmn bd Lemington Home Aged; p natl pres Iota P Hi Lambda; mem bd Cvl Light Opera Pittsburgh; hon bd mem Tribune Charities; Adv com Afro-am Mus; bd mem YWCA Belmont Br; Philadelphia Bicentennial Commn; Cenntennial Com for Lucretia Mott 1980; mem Bethesda United Presbyterian Ch; adhoc com for Floyd Logan Archives Temple U; treas S St W Bus Assn 1979; lay mem Fee Disputes Com Philadelphia Bar Assn 1979. **HONORS/ACHIEVEMENTS:** Serv Awd Philadelphia Tribune Charities 1973; Decision Maker, Nat Assn of Media Women, 1974; Bi-centennial Achvmt Awd, AME Ch 1976; Nat Assn ofUniv Women; Apprctn Awd Bicentennial Commn of PA; Police Athletic Leg, recog awd 1977; Serv Awd ARC 1978; Distngshd Serv Awd, Downingtown A&I Sch 1979; 50th Anniversary Ldrshp Awd Iota Phi Lambda Sor 1979. **BUSINESS ADDRESS:** 520-26 16th St, Philadelphia, PA 19146.

RHODES, JOSEPH, JR.
Consultant. **PERSONAL:** Born Aug 14, 1947, Pittsburgh, PA. **EDUCATION:** CA Inst of Tech, BS 1969; Harvard Univ, jr fellow 1969-72. **CAREER:** HEW, consult ofc of the sec 1968-70; Sch of Educ Univ of MA, lecturer 1969-70; pres comm on Voluntary Serv 1969; pres commn on Campus Unrest 1970; CA State Coll, lecturer 1971; Univ of Pgh Dept of History, lecturer 1972; PA House of Reps, state rep 1972-80; Sch of Social Work Univ of Pgh, lecturer 1974;Westinghouse, consultant corporate planning. **ORGANIZATIONS:** Mem Natl Bd Amer Civil Liberties Union; mem Natl Steering Comm Natl Urban Coalition; bd trustees Penn State Univ. **HONORS/ACHIEVEMENTS:** Recipient Extraordinary Serv CA Tech 1969; ADA Natl Youth Awd 1970; Time Magazine 200 Young Leaders of Amer 1974; Three Outstanding Young Men Awd of PA Jaycees 1975.

RHODES, LELIA G.
Library administrator. **PERSONAL:** Born Oct 21, Jackson, MS; married John D; children: Marilyn Latson, John D. **EDUCATION:** Jcksn St U, BS 1944; AtlntUniv Sch of Lbry Serv, MLS 1956; FL St U, PhD 1975. **CAREER:** Jcksn St U, dir of lbry serv 1976-, dir of lbry 1973-76, asso hd & ctlg lib 1965-73, ctlg lib 1957-65; Jcksn Pub Sch, lib 1952-57. **ORGANIZATIONS:** Pres MS Libry Assn 1980; vis team consult So Assn of Coll & Sch; ACRL Plng Com Am Lbry; mem SW Libry Assn; mem Am Assn ofUniv Prof; Am Assn ofUniv Wmn; YMCA; Alpha Kappa Alpha Sor; Grl Scts Mddl MS. **HONORS/ACHIEVEMENTS:** Univ Acad Fellow FL StUniv 1973-75; 1st blk & only wmn to rcv PhD in Libry Sci St of MS 1975; author Jcksn StUniv 1877-1977, 1st Hndrd Yrs 1979; ctzn of the yr Omega Psi Phi Frat 1979. **BUSINESS ADDRESS:** John R Lynch St, Jackson, MS 39217.

RHODES, LORD CECIL
Dentist. **PERSONAL:** Born May 26, 1920, Norfolk, VA; married Muriel; children: Lord Cecil Jr. **EDUCATION:** Shaw Univ, Raleigh, NC, BC 1941; Howard Univ Sch Denistry, DDS 1951; Univ IA, IA; HowardUniv Grad Sch; dept pharmacology. **CAREER:** Howard Univ Sch of Med, WA, resch Asst; City Dental Clinic, Ports VA, staff Den; Rhodes Dental Hosp, Norfolk, VA, admstr; Norfolk Comm Hosp, Norfolk, VA, staff Den; Bayside Hosp VA Bch, VA, staff Den. **ORGANIZATIONS:** Mbr John L McGritt Dental Soc; chrmn normel Amer Acad Imp Dent; mem Bioclectromagnetic Soc. **HONORS/ACHIEVEMENTS:** Phi Delta Kappa Disting Achievement in Dentistry 1969; Recognition Appreciation & Commendation for Education & Humanitarian Contribution to Children Young People and World at Large Natl Sor of Phi Delta Kappa 1969; Man of the Year Awd Omega Sigma 1972; Merit Awd Natl Med Assoc 1977; FRSH Royal Soc Health;FAAID Amer Acad Implant Dent; author "The Adjunctive Utilization of Diapulse Therapy (Pulsed High Peak Power Electromagnetic Energy) In Accelerating Tissue Healing in Oral Surgery" The Quarterly of Natl Dental Assoc 1981; "Boucher's Dental Terminology" 1984. **MILITARY SERVICE:** AUS staff sgt. **HOME ADDRESS:** 748 Stanwix Sq, Norfolk, VA 23502. **BUSINESS ADDRESS:** 501 E Brambleton Ave, Norfolk, VA 23501.

RHODES, PAULA R.
Educator. **PERSONAL:** Born Jul 18, New Orleans, LA; daughter of Leroy Rhodes and Marie Richard. **EDUCATION:** Amer Univ, BA 1971; Harvard Univ, JD 1974. **CAREER:** Legal Serv Corp, atty 1977-79; Mid Atlantic Legal Educ, prof 1980; Univ of San Diego Law School, visiting prof 1983-84; Howard Univ School of Law, assoc prof 1979-; Univ of Bridgeport, adjunct prof 1985. **ORGANIZATIONS:** Univ Budget Comm 1979-83, Senate Comm on Comm 1979-83; Ad Hoc Skills Comm 1981-82; Cncl of Univ Senate 1981-82; Acad Affairs Cncl 1982-83; DC Solar Task Force 1982-83; DC Comm on Women Legislative Comm 1983; Ad Hoc AALS Accred Comm 1983; mem Dist of Columbia Bar Assn, LA Bar Assn, Fed Bar Assn, & Amer Bar Assn; mem Inter Wolsa; bd of dir, numerous committees, Amer Friends Serv Comm; Pesticides Action Network Intl; Afr Amer United Nations Comm; So Others May Eat; Transafrica; legal comm Natl Rainbow Coalition; Debt Crisis Network; bd dir World Hunger Educ Serv; mem Quaker United Nations Comm; Haverford Col Corp; Friends Comm on Natl Legislation General Comm; bd of trustees Friends Mtg of Washington; Ad Hoc Comms 1984-85, 1986-87; bd of dir, Intl Third World Legal Studies Assn. **HONORS/ACHIEVEMENTS:** Various conferences including Amer Friends Serv Committee Consultation on Korea, Los Angeles, CA 1983, Inst for Policy Studies/Transnatl Inst Intl Conf on "Meeting the Corporate Challenge" Washington DC 1984; publications include "Devel of New Business Opportunities for Minorities in the Synthetic Fuels Program", Rsch & Legislative Narrative 1981; "Energy Security Act and its Implications for Economic Devel", Howard Law Journal 1981, "We the People and the Struggle for a New World, WSA Constitution on Human Rights 1987, and "Regulation of Multinational Corporations Intl Codes of Conduct", 1988; Assoc Ed Fed Bar Assn Forum 1982-83; Outstanding Young Women of Amer 1982; featured in Lisa Jones, The Path, Six Women Talk About Their Religious Faith Essence vol 16 #9 Jan 1986; Phi Delta Phi Legal Fraternity. **BUSINESS ADDRESS:** Associate Professor of Law, Howard University, 2900 Van Ness St NW, Washington, DC 20008.

RHODES, RAY
Defensive backfield coach. **PERSONAL:** Born Oct 20, 1950, Mexia, TX; married Carmen; children: Detra, Candra, Tynesha, Raven. **EDUCATION:** Attended, Texas Christian Univ. **CAREER:** NY Giants, wide receiver/defensive back; San Francisco 49ers', defensive back 1980, asst secondary coach, defensive backfield coach.

RHODES, ROBERT SHAW
Physician. **PERSONAL:** Born Mar 03, 1936, Orangeburg, SC; son of John Rhodes and Emma Rhodes; widowed; children: Robin, Robert Jr. **EDUCATION:** Meharry Med Coll, MD 1962; Hubbard Hosp, Internship 1962-63; Meharry Med Coll, Resident 1963-67; Vanderbilt Univ School of Med, Fellowship 1967-70; Univ of MI School of Public Health, MPH 1981-83. **CAREER:** Meharry Med Coll, head div of hematology 1972-78; Multiphasic Screening Lab, dir 1973-78; Hubbard Hosp, med dir 1975-78; Hydra-matic Div of GMC, assoc med dir 1978-80, med dir 1980-82; Health Serv and Safety, div dir 1982-87; General Motors Corp, Detroit West Medical Region, regional med dir 1988-. **ORGANIZATIONS:** Mem ed comm Natl Sickle Cell Found 1981-; chairperson Sickle Cell Adv Comm 1977-81; pres elect 1984-, vice pres 1983-84 MI Occupational Med Assoc; chmn Med Audit Comm Beyer Hosp 1980-83; exec bd Wolverine Council BSA. **MILITARY SERVICE:** USMC major 1967-70; US Army Commendation Medal 1970; AFIP Certificate of Meritorious Achievement 1970. **BUSINESS ADDRESS:** Regional Medical Director, Hydra-matic General Motors Corp, Medical Dept, M/C 340, Ypsilanti, MI 48198.

RIBBINS, GERTRUDE
Singer, writer. **PERSONAL:** Born Dec 28, 1924, Memphis, TN; daughter of James Pugh and Annie W Pugh; married John W (deceased); children: Anne Sylvia, John, Mark. **EDUCATION:** Lmyn Coll; Kent St. **CAREER:** Detroit SS Assn, guest soloist; Gr Chicago SS Assn, guest soloist; Wmn Alv Ont Can, conf soloist; Faith at Wrk Ont, conf slst; The Old Stn Ch Cleveland Lntn Srs, concerts 1973-74; E Stanley Jones St James AME Church, ashrm soloist; USA & Can, speaking & sngng tours. **ORGANIZATIONS:** Mem Adv Com Str for Hmn Serv 1974. **HONORS/ACHIEVEMENTS:** Author of articles on Negro Mus & Dvtnls for Periodicals; Ftrd in The Gospel Herald; Union Gospel Press 1973; Clubdate Magazine 1988; Sojourner Truth Award, NANBPWC-Cleveland 1989; MTV Certificate of Commendation 1988; Cleveland Federation for Community Planning. **BUSINESS ADDRESS:** Ribbins Book Store, 3612 East 116th, Cleveland, OH 44105.

RIBBS, WILLIAM THEODORE, JR. (WILLY T. RIBBS)
Racing driver. **PERSONAL:** Born Jan 03, 1956, San Jose, CA; son of William T. Ribbs, Sr. and Geraldine Henderson-Ribbs; married Suzanne Hamilton-Ribbs, Nov 22, 1979; children: Sasha Wanjiku. **EDUCATION:** San Jose City Coll San Jose, CA 1973-75. **CAREER:** Formula Ford Circuit, driver 1977; Formula Atlantic events; Sports 2000 events; Neil Deatley Trans-Am Team, driver 1983; Ford Motors Sports, 1984-85; Digard & Brooks Racing, 1986; racing driver Dan Gurneys All American Racers Santa Ana, CA, 1987. **HONORS/ACHIEVEMENTS:** Dunlop Star of Tomorrow Champion Europe 1977; Intl Driver of the Yr Europe 1977; British Sports Writers Awd Europe 1977; Trans-Am Rookie of the Year 1983; winner of 45 percent of races entered since 1983; winner of 1985 Trans-Am series opener in Phoenix (10 victory in 25 Trans-Am starts); 17 victories in 39 Trans-Am starts; 5 Intl Motor Sports Assn victories; 3 time 1986 Norelco Driver Cupt Awd winner; Proclamation Willy T Ribbs Day City of Miami 1984, City of Atlanta 1984, City of St Petersburg 1987; Interamerican Western Hemisphere Driving Champion 1984; Motorsports Press Assoc All Amer Drivers Awd 1984-85; Phillips Business systems 1987 Norelco GTO Driver of the Year, Phillips Business systems 1988 Norelco GTO Driver of the Year; S.C.C.A. Trans Am All Time Money Earner 1988.

RIBBS, WILLY T. See RIBBS, WILLIAM THEODORE, JR.

RICANEK, CAROLYN WRIGHT
City official. **PERSONAL:** Born Mar 10, 1939, Washington, DC; married Karl Ricanek; children: Lloyd O Taylor, Carooq M Taylor, Carmen T Harris, Demetrius A, Karl II. **EDUCATION:** Federal City Coll, 1972-76; George Mason Univ 1976-79. **CAREER:** K&R Plumbing Heating Co, vice-pres 1969-87; ANC Commissioner 7C, 1st elected 1976-85, chairperson 1986-87; Phelp Career Center, chmn 1982-87; Marshall Heights Comm Devel Corp, asst treasurer 1983-85, financial sec 1983-87; Advisory Neighborhood Comm, vice-chmn. **ORGANIZATIONS:** Chmn HD Woodson Athletic Booster Cl 1976-79; mem Deanwood Civic Assn 1970-85; mem Metropolitan Women Democratic Club 1980-85; asst coord Garden Resource Org 1983-85; mem Majestic Eagles Minority Entrepreneur Inc. **HONORS/ACHIEVEMENTS:** Cert of appreciation Houston Elem School 1979; Outstanding Citizen Coun Willie Hardy 1979-80; cert of award HD Woodson Sr High/Comm Services 1982; cert of appreciation Phelps Car Dev Cent 1983-84; First Elected Comm Mayor Marion Barry 1985. **HOME ADDRESS:** 1220 47th Place NE, Washington, DC 20019.

RICARD, JOHN H.
Auxiliary bishop. **PERSONAL:** Born Feb 29, 1940, Baton Rouge, LA; son of Maceo Ricard and Albanie St Amant Ricard. **EDUCATION:** Tulane Univ, New Orlenas, LA, M.A. 1970-72; The Catholic Univ Washington, D C, PhD, 1985. **CAREER:** Archdiocese of Baltimore, auxiliary bishop 1984-. **BUSINESS ADDRESS:** Auxiliary Bishop, Archdiocese of Baltimore, 320 Cathedral St, Room 710, Baltimore, MD 21201.

RICE, CONSTANCE WILLIAMS
Business executive. **PERSONAL:** Born Jun 23, 1945, Brooklyn, NY; daughter of Elliott Williams and Beulah Marshall Williams; married Norman B Rice; children: Mian. **EDUCATION:** Queens Coll, BA 1966; Univ of WA, Masters Public Admin 1970, PhD Higher Educ Admin 1974; Carnegie Mellon Univ, Sr Exec Mgmt 1983. **CAREER:** State Bd, prog asst; Shoreline Community Coll, chairperson; Corporate Comm METRO, mgr; Public Relations/Mgmt Firm, pres 1984-; asst exec dir Washington Educ Assoc 1987-88. **ORGANIZATIONS:** Pres-Elect Seattle Chapter 101 Black Women 1984-85; trustee Seattle Fdn 1984-; bd mem Amer Soc of Public Admin 1984-; pres-elect Seattle Chap LINKS 1985-86; past vice pres Seattle King County United Way 1983-84; pres 101 Black Women, Links Inc 1986-87; bd of governors Shoreline Comm Coll Foundation; bd mem Fred Hutchinson Cancer Research Foundation; vice chair King County Open Space Commn 1989; bd mem King County Chamber of Commerce 1989. **HONORS/ACHIEVEMENTS:** NY State Regents; Natl Sci Foundation Traineeship; Ed Professional Dir Award; Kellogg Grant; NW Outstanding Young Woman 1983-86; Women Entrepreneur of The Year runner-up 1985; White House Small Business delegate 1986; Top 25 Influential Women (Seattle) The Seattle Weekly 1986. **HOME ADDRESS:** 1711 Lake Washington Blvd S, Seattle, WA 98144. **BUSINESS ADDRESS:** President, CWR Inc Publ Relations, 1326 Fifth Ave, Seattle, WA 98101.

RICE, CORA LEE
Business executive. **PERSONAL:** Born Jun 18, 1926, Edenton, NC; divorced; children: 5 children. **EDUCATION:** Elizabeth City St Teachers, 1946; NYU, BA 1948. **CAREER:** Professional Answering Serv Inc, pres 1976-80; Commu Grfnckls, dir 1973-76; Ctrl Chrg Serv, training dir 1970-72. **ORGANIZATIONS:** Exec bd SCLC Metro Wash 1974-80; exec dir Prnc Grgs Untd Blk Fund 1976-80; pres Blk Wmns Assmbly 1978-80; exec bd NAACP MD 1969-80; pres PrncGrgs NAACP 1969. **HONORS/ACHIEVEMENTS:** Outstanding leadership Pres L B Johnson 1964; hon awd Human Rights & Justice NAACP 1967; outstanding achievement Prsnlts of the S 1973; Human Rights SCLC 1979. **BUSINESS ADDRESS:** President, Professional Answering Serv, 2833 Georgia Ave #4, Washington, DC 20001.

RICE, DAVID EUGENE, JR.
Trade, business and professional association executive. **PERSONAL:** Born Jul 01, 1916, Greenwood, SC; son of David E Rice, Sr and Mamye Elizabeth Johnson Rice; married Beryl Lena Carter, Jun 05, 1971. **EDUCATION:** Ohio State Univ, Columbus OH, BA, 1937; Northwestern Univ, Evanston IL, JD, 1941; Yale Law School, New Haven CT, Master of Law, 1950. **CAREER:** Lincoln Univ School of Law, St. Louis MO, assoc prof & editor Natl Bar Journal, 1946-48; Texas Southern Univ School of Law, Houston TX, dean, 1950-55; IL Federal Savings & Loan Assn, Chicago IL, savings officer, 1956-65; Chicago Small Business Opportunities Corp, Chicago IL, assoc dir, 1965-67; Natl Business League, Washington DC, dir Project Outreach, 1967-68, asst to the pres, 1969-83, dean of Certificate Institutes, 1977-87, resident historian, 1981-, vice pres for Const Aff, 1984-86, executive vice pres, 1987-. **ORGANIZATIONS:** Liaison, Natl Student Business League, 1975-87; chair, Rules Committee, DC Black Republican Council, 1985-; attorney, DC Black Republican Scholarship Fund, 1985-; mem, Screening Committee, KOOL Achiever Awards, 1987-; mem, Natl Bar Assn 1987-; mem, Coalition of Prof Organizations, 1988-; mem, Sub-Comm on Trade & Commerce; trustee bd, Metropolitan AME Church; mem, Fact Finding Committee, The Coalition to Protect Black Business. **HONORS/ACHIEVEMENTS:** Published articles in Journal of Criminal Law & Criminology, 1939, Illinois Law Review, 1941; Award of Recognition, Natl Student Business League, 1978, 1981; composer of musical compositions, "Night Songs," 1979-80; Presidental Citation, Natl Business League, 1985; 50 Year Certificate of Service, Kappa Alpha Psi Fraternity, 1986; Hunamitarian Award, Natl Student Business League, 1988; frederick Douglass Patterson Award, Natl Business League, 1988. **MILITARY SERVICE:** Counter Intelligence Corps, agent, 1943-45; Corps of Military Police, 2nd Lieutenant, 1945-46. **BUSINESS ADDRESS:** Executive Vice President, National Business League, 4324 Georgia Ave, NW, Washington, DC 20011.

RICE, EDWARD A.
Educator. **PERSONAL:** Born Apr 08, 1929, Richmond, VA; married Josie Wigfall; children: Patricia, Edward, Audrey. **EDUCATION:** VA Union U, BS 1949; Columbia U, MA 1952; Univ CT, MBA 1963. **CAREER:** Central State Univ, Wilberforce OH, asst prof, chmn business admin 1967-; USAF Nuclear Engineering Center, Wright-Patterson AFB, asst dir 1966-71; Aerospace Medical Div, Wright-Patterson AFB, rsch sci 1956-61; Air Force Units, admin 1951-56. **ORGANIZATIONS:** Mem Rsch Faculty & School of Aerospace Medicine, San Antonio 1962-66; mem Ohio Business Teachers Assn; pres Green County Joint Vocational School Bd 1973-74; Miami Valley Consortium; Midwest Business Admin Assn; Amer Nuclear Soc; Alpha Phi Alpha 1948-; Amer Assn of Univ Professors; Yellow Springs Bd Educ 1972-. **HONORS/ACHIEVEMENTS:** USAFR Medal; Natl Defense Serv Medal; Krn Serv Medal; UN Serv Medal; AF Commendation Medal. **MILITARY SERVICE:** USAF maj ret 1951-71. **BUSINESS ADDRESS:** Asst to Vice Pres for Acad Affairs, Central State University, Brush Road, Wilberforce, OH 45384.

RICE, EMMETT J.
Government official. **PERSONAL:** Born in Florence, SC. **EDUCATION:** CCNY, BBA 1941, MBA 1942; Univ of CA Berkeley, PhD 1955. **CAREER:** Univ of CA Berkeley, rsch asst in econs 1950-51, teaching asst 1953-54; Cornell Univ, asst prof econ 1954-60; Fed Reserve Bank, economist 1960-62; Central Bank of Nigeria Lagos, advisor 1962-64; Office Developing Nations Dept Treasury, dep dir, acting dir 1964-66; World Bank, exec dir 1966-70; Mayor's Econ Devel Comm Washington, 1970-71; Natl Bank Washington, sr vice pres 1972-79; Fed Reserve Bank Washington, gov 1979-. **BUSINESS ADDRESS:** Governor, Federal Reserve Board, Fed Reserve Bldg, Room B-2064, Washington, DC 20551.

RICE, FRED
Superintendent police. **PERSONAL:** Born Dec 24, 1926, Chicago, IL; married Thelma Martin; children: Lyle, Judith. **EDUCATION:** Roosevelt Univ, BS 1970, MS Pub Admin 1977. **CAREER:** Chicago Police Dept, mem 1955 promoted to sgt 1961, lt 1968, capt 1973, dist comdr 1970-78, dep chief patrol Area Four 1978-79, chief patrol div 1979-83, supt police 1983-. **HONORS/ACHIEVEMENTS:** Num awds for contribs to community. **MILITARY SERVICE:** AUS 1950-52.

RICE, HAYNES
Business executive. **PERSONAL:** Born Jan 10, 1932, Knoxville, TN; son of Haynes Rice (deceased) and Eddie Rice (deceased); married Eva McAllister; children: Robin, Rahn. **EDUCATION:** WV State Coll, BS 1953; Univ of Chicago, MBA 1964. **CAREER:** Kate Bitting Reynolds Hospital, acting admin, asst admin, accountant 1955-60; Jubilee Hospital, admin 1960-64; FL A&M Univ Hospital, admin 1964-66; Norfolk Comm Hospital VA, admin 1966-70; New York City Health & Hospital Corp, asst comm, exec asst to comm 1970-74; HUH, asst admin for spec proj 1976, dep dir 1976-79; School of Business Admin Howard Univ, prof; lecturer at numerous insts. **ORGANIZATIONS:** Dir Natl Work Study Recruitment Program for minorities interested in health care mgmt New York City 1970-74; task force Prison Reform United Presbyterian Church of USA 1971; natl adv comm New England Bd of Higher Ed; mem Natl Assoc of Health Serv Exec 1972; Comm on Natl Health Inst 1972-73; mem bd of trustees Amer Hosp Assoc 1989; mem Kappa Alpha Psi; chmn comm on health planning, pres 1982-83 DC Hospital Assoc; past pres Council of Teaching Hospital Assn of Amer Med Coll 1983-84; mem Natl Adv Comm for RW Johnson Found Faculty Fellowship Program Center for Hospital Finance & Mgmt Johns Hopkins Med Inst; mem task force Health on Health Costs/Policies United Presbyterian Church of the USA; mem mayors comm on maternal health and infant mortality; past pres washington regional organ procument agency. **HONORS/ACHIEVEMENTS:** Alpha Kappa Mu Hon Soc 1952; Mary H Bachmeyer Award Outstanding Student Hospital Admin Program Univ of Chicago 1959; Natl Assoc of Health Serv Exec 1973. **MILITARY SERVICE:** AUS 1st lt 1953-55. **BUSINESS ADDRESS:** Hospital Dir, HowardUniv Hospital, 2041 Georgia Ave, Washington, DC 20060.

RICE, JAMES EDWARD
Professional athlete. **PERSONAL:** Born Mar 08, 1953, Anderson, SC; married Corine Gilliard; children: Chauncy Brandon, Carissa Jacinda. **CAREER:** So Bank & Trust Co Greenville SC, pub relations rep; Boston Red Sox, player 1974-. **HONORS/ACHIEVEMENTS:** Named MVP & Rookie of Yr Intl League 1974; only player to ever have 3 straight 35 HR-200 Hit years 1977-79; named AL Player of the Year by The Sporting News 1978; MVP Amer League 1978; co-winner Joe Cronin Awd 1978; first AL player to get 400 TB since 1937; named to Amer League All-Star Team 1977, 1978, 1979, 1985, 1986; co-winner Tucson Pro-Am Gold Tournament 1977; T A Yawkey Awd as Sox MVP by Boston Writers 1983; named AL Player of Week June 4-10 1984; UPI & AL All Star Team 1984; Sporting News Silver Bat Team; mem All Star Team 1977, 1978, 1979, 1983, 1984, 1985, 1986. **BUSINESS ADDRESS:** Boston Red Sox, Fenway Park, Boston, MA 02215.

RICE, JERRY
Professional athlete. **PERSONAL:** Born Oct 13, 1962, Starkville, MS. **EDUCATION:** Attended, MS Valley State Univ. **CAREER:** San Francisco 49ers, wide receiver 1985-.

HONORS/ACHIEVEMENTS: Played in Blue-Gray game and Senior Bowl; named to most All-America teams as sr in coll; selected to Pro Football Weekly's all-rookie team; named UPI NFC Rookie of the Year 1985; NFLPA NFC Offensive Rookie of the Year 1985; mem 1987 Pro Bowl team. **BUSINESS ADDRESS:** San Francisco 49ers, 711 Nevada St, Redwood City, CA 94061.

RICE, LINDA JOHNSON
President/chief operating officer. **PERSONAL:** Born Mar 22, 1958, Chicago, IL; son of Mr and Mrs John H Johnson; married Andre Rice. **EDUCATION:** Univ of So CA Los Angeles, BA Journalism 1980; Northwestern Univ Evanston, MMgmt 1987. **CAREER:** Johnson Publishing Co, vice pres, president/chief operating officer. **ORGANIZATIONS:** Exec producer Ebony/Jet Showcase; dir Fashion Fair Fashions; aux bd The Art Inst of Chicago; bd trustees Museum of Contemporary Art; women's bd Boys & Girls Club of Chicago; mem Natl Assn of Black Journalists; bd of directors Continental Bank Corp; bd of dir of Magazine Publishers America. **BUSINESS ADDRESS:** Pres, Chief Operating Officer, Johnson Publishing Company, 820 S Michigan Ave, Chicago, IL 60605.

RICE, LOIS DICKSON (NEE DICKSON)
Administrator. **PERSONAL:** Born Feb 28, 1933, Portland, ME; married Alfred B Fitt; children: Susan E, Emmett John Jr. **EDUCATION:** Radcliffe Coll, AB1954; Columbia U, Woodrow Wilson Fellow. **CAREER:** Natl Scholarship Serv Fund for Negro Students, dir 1955-58; Ford Foundation, specialist 1963-64; Coll Entrance Exam Bd, dir 1971-73, dir 1973-74, vice pres 1974-; Control Data Corp, sr vice pres for govt affairs 1986-. **ORGANIZATIONS:** Bd dir Beauvoir Sch 1970-76; bd dir Childrens TV Workshop 1970-73; bd dir Fund for Improvement of Postsec Educ 1972-75; bd trustees Urban Inst Potomac Sushtuts; mem Carnegie Council on Policy Studies in Higher Edn; mem Commn on Acad Afrs Am Council on Educ 1974-76; mem DC Commn On Postsec Educ 1974-76; mem, natl adv bd Inst for Study of Educ Policy 1974; chmn, vis com Afro-Am Studies HarvardUniv 1974-77; mem Gov Temporary State Commn on Future of Postsec Educ in NY 1976-77; trustee Stephens Coll1976-78. **HONORS/ACHIEVEMENTS:** Disting Serv Awd HEW 1977; mem Phi Beta Kappa; numerous publications. **BUSINESS ADDRESS:** Senior Vice President, Control Data Corp, 1201 Pennsylvania Ave NW, Ste 370, Washington, DC 20004.

RICE, LOUISE ALLEN
Educator. **PERSONAL:** Born Nov 21, 1940, Augusta, GA; daughter of Willie Allen and Elnora Allen; married Wilson L Rice; children: Wilson L Jr, Robert Christopher. **EDUCATION:** Tuskegee Univ, BS 1963; Columbia Univ Teachers Coll, MA 1964-69 (summers); Univ of GA, PhD 1979. **CAREER:** Washington High Sch, English teacher 1963-66; Lucy Laney High School, English Teacher 1966-68; Paine Coll, instructor/reading specialist 1968-71; Lansing School Dist, instructor/reading specialist 1971-72; Paine Coll, assoc prof/asst academic dean 1972-77, 1979-81; Lamar Elem Sch, instructional lead teacher 1981-84; Augusta Coll, assoc dir of admissions 1984-88; asst prof of educ and reading 1988-. **ORGANIZATIONS:** Adv bd Richmond Co Bd of Educ 1982-; bd dirs CSRA Economic Opportunity Authority Inc 1984-; dir Southern Region Delta Sigma Theta Sor Inc 1986-; Educ Comm Augusta Human Relations Comm, 1989-. **HONORS/ACHIEVEMENTS:** Black Womanhood Speaker's Awd Paine Coll 1983; Distinguished Serv Awd Augusta Pan-Hellenic Council 1984; Urban Builders Awd Augusta Black History Comm 1985; Outstanding Comm Svcs, Leadership and Achievement Certificate Amer Assoc of Univ Women 1986, Educ of the Year, Lincoln League, Atlanta, 1988. **BUSINESS ADDRESS:** Department of Development Studies, Augusta College, 2500 Walton Way, Augusta, GA 30910.

RICE, MITCHELL F.
Educator. **PERSONAL:** Born Sep 11, 1948, Columbus, GA; son of Joseph Rice and Clarice Rice; married Cecelia Hawkins Rice; children: Colin C Rice, Melissa E Rice. **EDUCATION:** LA City Coll, AA 1969; CA State Univ LA, BA 1970, MS 1973; Claremont Grad Sch, PhD 1976. **CAREER:** Bonita Unified Sch Dist, public sch teacher 1971-76; Prairie View A&M Univ, asst prof 1976-77; Southwest TX State Univ, assoc prof of pol sci 1977-85; LA State Univ, prof of publ admin, pol sci. **ORGANIZATIONS:** Vice pres, chair-elect, natl chair Conference of Minority Pub Admn; Mem Amer Political Sci Assn; mem Natl Conf of Black Pol Scientists; mem Amer Soc for Public Admin; pres/owner Mgmt Develop & Training Consulting Serv 1980-; mem Amer Public Health Assn. **HONORS/ACHIEVEMENTS:** Amer Council on Educ Fellowship in Academic Admin 1983-84; Natl Rsch Council Ford Found Postdoctoral Fellowship for Minorities 1984-85; co-author of Contemporary Public Policy Perspectives and Black Amers Greenwood Press 1984; Rockefeller Found Postdoctoral Fellowship for Minorites 1985-86; co-author "Health Care Issues in Black America," Greenwood Press 1987; "Black Health Care, An Annotated Bibliography," Greenwood Press 1987; co-author, Blacks and American Government, Kendall Hunt 1987. **BUSINESS ADDRESS:** Prof Publ Admin/Pol Sci, Louisiana StateUniv, Public Admin Inst, Baton Rouge, LA 70803.

RICE, NORMAN BLANN
City council member, director. **PERSONAL:** Born May 04, 1943, Denver, CO; son of Otha P Price and Irene Price; married Dr Constance; children: Mian A. **EDUCATION:** Univ of WA, BA Commun 1972; Univ of Washington, MA Publ Admin 1974. **CAREER:** KOMO TV News, news asst, editor 1971-72; Seattle Urban League, asst dir, media action proj monitor 1972-74; Puget Sound Council of Govts, exec asst, dir of govt serv 1974-75; Rainier Natl Bank, mgr of corp contribs soc policy coord 1976-78; City of Seattle, council mem 1978-83, pres 1983-. **ORGANIZATIONS:** Chap mem, pres NW Min Commun Assoc, mem Amer Soc of Publ Admin, Natl acad of TV Arts & Sci, Sigma Delta Chi, Municipal League of Seattle & King Cty; bd of dirs Allied Arts; pres Mt Baker Comm Club 1977-78; bd of dirs Planned Parenthood 1978; mem Human Serv Comm 1978; life mem NAACP. **BUSINESS ADDRESS:** City Council Member, City of Seattle, 1116 Seattle Municipal Bldg, Seattle, WA 98104.

RICE, PAMELA ANN
Juvenile counselor. **PERSONAL:** Born Jun 27, 1956, Baltimore, MD; daughter of Edward Rice and Shirley Carrington. **EDUCATION:** VA State Univ, BS 1977; Coppin State Coll, MEd 1980; The Johns Hopkins Univ, Advanced degree 1982; The Amer Univ, Washington, DC, Ed.D, 1982, 1988. **CAREER:** Baltimore City Govt, worksite supervisor 1978; State of MD, juvenile counselor 1978-. **ORGANIZATIONS:** Mem VA State Alumni Assoc Baltimore Metro Chapter 1980-, Amer Assoc for Counseling & Develop 1980-, Alpha Kappa Alpha Sorority 1982-. **HOME ADDRESS:** 3708 Campfield Road, Baltimore, MD 21207. **BUSINESS ADDRESS:** Juvenile Counselor, State of Maryland, 242 So Hilton St, Baltimore, MD 21207.

RICE, ROBERT C.
Elected official. **PERSONAL:** Born Aug 27, 1923, Birmingham, AL; married Susie Leon; children: Brenda Wright. **EDUCATION:** Southern Univ, BS 1946; OH State Univ, MA 1949; Kent State Univ, Cert in Guid 1953. **CAREER:** Cleveland Public Schools, teacher 1955-60, supv voc educ 1960-83; Woodmere Village, mayor. **ORGANIZATIONS:** Life member Alpha Phi Alpha 1965-. **HOME ADDRESS:** 3707 Avondale Rd, Woodmere Village, OH 44122. **BUSINESS ADDRESS:** Mayor, Woodmere Vlg, 27899 Chagrin Blvd, Woodmere Village, OH 44122.

RICE, SUSIE LEON
Elected official. **PERSONAL:** Born Dec 28, 1922, Corona, AL; married Robert Calvin Rice; children: Brenda Sue Wright. **EDUCATION:** OH State Univ, BS Education 1948; Western Reserve Univ, MA Education 1953; John Carroll Univ, Certificate Elem Admin & Guid 1968; Cleveland State Univ, continued studies 1975. **CAREER:** Cleveland Bd of Educ, elem teacher 1948-69, jr/sr high guidance counselor 1969-78; Woodmere OH, councilwoman 1978-. **ORGANIZATIONS:** Bd of mgmt Glenville YWCA 1962-68; bd of dirs Valley YMCA-YWCA 1969-75; pres Lambda Phi Omega Chap Alpha Kappa Alpha Sor Inc 1980-81. **HONORS/ACHIEVEMENTS:** Outstanding Volunteer Serv Valley YM-YWCA bd of dirs 1975; Professional Honors Achievements Pi Lambda Theto Cleveland State Univ 1977. **HOME ADDRESS:** 3707 Avondale Rd, Woodmere Village, OH 44122.

RICE, WILLIAM E.
Government employee. **PERSONAL:** Born Dec 18, 1933, Huntsville, AL; married Delores; children: Duane, Donald, Marvin. **EDUCATION:** AL U, BS 1955; DePaul U, Grad Stud 1971. **CAREER:** Bur Lbr Ststcs, regl commr 1971-, dep regl dir 1970-71, asst regl dir 1967-70, regl empl ana 1962-65; OEO Chgo, asst regl mgr admin 1965-67; MI Empl Sec Commn, prog coord 1955-62. **ORGANIZATIONS:** Mem Am Ststcl Assn; Am Soc for Pub Admin; Chicago Guid Assn; Indstrl Reltns Rsrch Assn; mem Exec Club of Chgo; chmn Adv Com RsvltUniv Sch ofPub Admin; chmn Ecnmc & Mnpwr Devel Adv Com Chicago Urban Leag; chmn Rsrch Com for Chicago Cnstrctn Coord Com; mem Adv Com Curr Devel; YMCA Coll. **HONORS/ACHIEVEMENTS:** Recip otstndng vc awd Chicago US Dept of Lbr 1964; auth num artcls on regl lbr mkt ana. **MILITARY SERVICE:** AUS 1956-58; USAR 1958-62. **BUSINESS ADDRESS:** 230 S Dearborn, Chicago, IL 60604.

RICH, STANLEY C.
Police official. **PERSONAL:** Born Feb 25, 1920; married Coralie. **EDUCATION:** Morris Brown Coll, AB; Wayne State U, MA. **CAREER:** Detroit, MI Police Dept, second dep commr; Detroit Hlth Dept, former pvt acctnt a jr acctnt 1947-50; Mayor's Com for Human Resources Devel, sr acctnt 1964-65; Small Bus Devel Center, adminstr 1965-67; Mayor's Com for Human Resources Devel 1967; chmn police trial bd equal employ officer small & minor bus enter ofcr for police dept. **ORGANIZATIONS:** Mem Kappa Alpha Psi Frat; United Comm Serv of Met Detroit; bd dir St Peter Claver Comm Cntr.

RICH, WILBUR C.
Educator. **PERSONAL:** Born Sep 28, 1939, Montgomery, AL; son of Savage Rich and Lydia Rich; married Jean; children: Rachel, Alexandra. **EDUCATION:** Tyskegee Inst, BS 1960; Univ IL, EdM 1964, PhD 1972. **CAREER:** Columbia Univ, asst prof of political science; Univ IL Urbana, vis asst prof; Wesleyan Univ Middletown CT, vis asst prof; Dept Mntl Hlth St IL, cnslr asst admin 1965-67; Mntl Hlth CT, asst st dir 1969-72. **ORGANIZATIONS:** Mem Am Soc Pub Admin; Nat Conf Blk Pol Sci; Am Pol Sci Assn; Alpha Phi Alpha; Chi Gamma Iota; Phi Delta Kappa. **HONORS/ACHIEVEMENTS:** Career Devel Chair Award, Wayne State Univ, 1989; publications: The Politics of Urban Personnel Policy, 1982; Coleman Young & Detroit Politics, 1989. **MILITARY SERVICE:** USAF 1961-65. **BUSINESS ADDRESS:** Assoc Professor, Wayne StateUniv, 856 Mackenzie Hall, Detroit, MI 48202.

RICHARD, ALVIN J.
Educator. **PERSONAL:** Born Oct 14, 1932, New Orleans, LA; married Arlene Lecesne; children: Terrence, Kent, Wendy. **EDUCATION:** Univ of IL, EdD 1972; XavierUniv of LA, MA 1967, BS 1955; Fellow Ford Found, 1972. **CAREER:** Orleans Preschool School Bd, teacher 1957-65; Xavier Univ, asst dean of men 1965-66, dean of men 1966-70, dir univ administration 1972-75, dir rcrtmnt prprtn for ald hlth cars pro 1972-, dean of admsns & fncl aid 1975-; Univ of IL, staff asst 1970-72; So Univ in New Orleans, asso prof 1973-. **ORGANIZATIONS:** Mem Am Assn of Collgt Reg & Admsns Ofcrs; So Assn of Collgt Regs & Admsns Ofcrs; LA Assn of Collgt Regs & Admsns Ofcrs; Nat Assn of Coll Deans Regs & Admsns Ofcrs; Am Soc of Ald Hlth Profs; bd mem Yng Adlts Sprts Assn; mem Met Area Com; mem Strng Com Am Found of Negro Afrs;cons Mtn Cnsrtm on Admsns & Fncl Aid 1974-; prtcptn as pnlst spkr conf chmn for num agency 1972-74. **BUSINESS ADDRESS:** 7325 Palmetto St, New Orleans, LA 70125.

RICHARD, ARLENE CASTAIN
Physician. **PERSONAL:** Born Mar 01, 1955, St Martinville, LA; married Donald Ray Richard; children: Dawnia, Donald Jr, Sterlyn. **EDUCATION:** Univ of Southwestern LA, BS, BA (Cum Laude) 1977; Howard Univ Coll of Medicine, MD 1983. **CAREER:** Earl K Long Memorial Hosp, internship 1983-84; Univ Medical Ctr, LSU staff physician 1985; Howard Univ Hosp, family practice resident 1985-87. **ORGANIZATIONS:** Mem Alpha Kappa Alpha Sor 1974-, Amer Medical Assoc. **BUSINESS ADDRESS:** Staff Physician, Teche Action Clinic, 1115 Weber St, Franklin, LA 70538.

RICHARD, FLOYD ANTHONY
Physician ob/gyn. **PERSONAL:** Born May 05, 1952, Opelousas, LA; married Robin; children: Keiana, Floyd II, Jonathan. **EDUCATION:** Southern Univ, BS 1973; Meharry Medical Coll, MD 1981. **CAREER:** Conoco Oil, process control chemist 1973-74; The Upjohn Co, asst rsch chemist 1976-77; Meharry Medical College, asst prof dept ob/gyn 1985; Central North Alabama Health Svcs, chief dept ob/gyn. **ORGANIZATIONS:** Chairman youth div Second Ward Voters League 1976. **HONORS/ACHIEVEMENTS:** Uphohn Awd in Ob/Gyn 1981; Outstanding Young Men of America 1982; Gynecologic Laparoscopist Awd 1984; AOA Med Hon Soc. **HOME ADDRESS:** 6520 Willow Springs Blvd, Huntsville, AL

35806. **BUSINESS ADDRESS:** Chief Dept Ob/Gyn, Central North AL Health Serv, PO Box 380, Madison, AL 35758.

RICHARD, HENRI-CLAUDE
Physician. **PERSONAL:** Born Feb 12, 1944, Port-au-Prince, Haiti;son of Theophile and Christiane; children: Maurice. **EDUCATION:** Howard Univ Coll of Liberal Arts, BS 1968; Howard Univ Coll of Medicine, MD 1972. **CAREER:** Ireland Army Hospital, radiologist 1977-; Breckenridge Memorial Hospital, radiologist 1980-; Private Practice, radiologist. **ORGANIZATIONS:** Mem American Medical Association; Kentucky Medical Association; Hardin County Medical Association; Radiological Society of North America; American College of Radiology; American Institute of Ultrasound in Medicine; Falls City Medical Society; Inter-American College of Physicians and Surgeons. **BUSINESS ADDRESS:** Henri-Claude Richard MD, 650 W Lincoln Trail Blvd, Radcliff, KY 40160.

RICHARD, JAMES L.
Clergyman. **PERSONAL:** Born Aug 24, 1917, Lake Creek, TX; married Carolyn E Bunche; children: Jacqueline L, James L. **EDUCATION:** Conroe Nrml & Indsl Coll Ext Sch Theol, BTh 1957; Cntr of Urbn Blk Stds, DD 1978. **CAREER:** Evrgrn Msnry Bapt Ch, mnstr 1980-; Bapt Mnstrs Un of Oklnd & Bay Cts, pres 1967-80; Mt Zion Msnry Bapt Assn, mdrtr 1963-80. **ORGANIZATIONS:** Consult to M Luther King Pr Ppls Cpgn; pres CA Chap of So Ldrshp Con 1968; mem exec com No CA B Graham Crsd 1971; pres org St Luke's Soc Clergy & Med Drs 1977-78; bd of dirs Cmp Frct Inc; Sbsdry of the CA Bapt St Conv; chmn of fgn msn bd CA Bapt St Conv; stat Nat Bapt Conv ofAm 180; mem adv cncl Mayor Lionel Wlsn Oklnd 1980; bd of dirs City Cntr Ecn Devel Corp 1980. **HONORS/ACHIEVEMENTS:** Recip vcs of Evrgrn Radio Brdcst Rsltn; dvtd serv awd hon John Miller 13th Assmbly Dist 1976; otstndng serv Cltrl & Hist & Achv Coop 1980. **BUSINESS ADDRESS:** 408 W Mac Arthur Blvd, Oakland, CA 94608.

RICHARD, R. PAUL
Lawyer. **PERSONAL:** Born Jul 24, 1950, Washington, DC; son of Robert J and Adele (Mitchell). **EDUCATION:** Brown Univ, AB 1972; Georgetown Univ Law Center, JD 1976. **CAREER:** Georgetown Univ Law Center, asst dean 1976-78; Assoc of Amer Law Schools, assoc dir 1979-82; Law School Admin Council/Law School Admin Services, dir of special projects 1983-84, deputy exec dir 1984-86, consultant 1986-; Goldfarb & Lipman, associate 1986-. **ORGANIZATIONS:** Council mem Council on Legal Educ Opportunity 1984-, member exec comm 1985-87; mem Bar Assn of San Francisco, Comm on Minority Hiring. **HONORS/ACHIEVEMENTS:** Natl Merit Scholar 1968; Law Fellow Georgetown Univ Law Center 1974-75; mem Barristers' Council Georgetown Univ Law Center 1975-76. **BUSINESS ADDRESS:** Goldfarb & Lipman, 1 Montgomery St, Telesis Tower, 23rd Floor, San Francisco, CA 94104.

RICHARDS, ARTHUR A.
Educational administrator. **PERSONAL:** Born Sep 08, 1924, St Croix, VI; married Myrna V Todmann; children: Anthony, Pamela, Duane. **EDUCATION:** Howard U, BS 1948; Hmptn Inst, MA 1961; NY U, EdD 1965. **CAREER:** Virgin Islands Dept of Educ, hs prin 1950, asst commr 1963, commr of educ 1966; College of the Virgin Islands, prvst dean 1969, vice pres prvst 1978, pres. **ORGANIZATIONS:** Mem Rotary Club of St Croix 1963; mem VI Cncl on the Arts 1966; mem VI Adv Cncl on Voc Tech Educ 1977; mem VI Health Coord Cncl 1979; mem VI Rural Afrs Cncl 1980; exec comm mem Caribbean Univs & Rsch Insts. **HONORS/ACHIEVEMENTS:** Admin Fellow Fund for the Advanc of Educ 1955; Flbrght Fellow Intl Inst on Cmprtv Educ 1962. **BUSINESS ADDRESS:** President, College of the Virgin Islands, St Thomas, Virgin Islands of the United States 00801.

RICHARDS, BEAH
Actress. **PERSONAL:** Born in Vicksburg, MS; married Hugh Harrell. **CAREER:** First Broadway play A Raisin in the Sun; Take A Giant Step Bdwy, actress 1956; Miracle Worker Broadway featured roles in The Miracle Worker, Purlie Victorious, The Little Foxes, The Amen Corner; playwright One Is A Crowd; films Hurry Sundown, In the Heat of the Night, The Great White Hope, Guess Who's Coming to Dinner. **ORGANIZATIONS:** Mem NAACP; Cngrs Racial Eqlty; mem AEA; mem SAG. **HONORS/ACHIEVEMENTS:** Acad Awd nomination for Best Supporting Actress in Guess Who's Coming to Dinner; recip All-Amer Press Assoc Awd 1968; Black Filmmakers Hall of Fame 1974;poetry published "A Black Woman Speaks and Other Poems".

RICHARDS, EDWARD A.
Military career man. **PERSONAL:** Born Dec 15, 1930, Trenton, NJ; married Barbara; children: Edward, Jr, Denise. **EDUCATION:** Univ of California at Los Angeles; Washburn Univ; Bellvue Coll; Univ of Maryland; Management Schools; USAF Sr NCO Academy. **CAREER:** USAF, chief mgmt & prcdrs branch, enlisted, and with exception of seven months, remained on active serv 1950. **ORGANIZATIONS:** Life mem AF Sgt Assn; mem Human Relations Council; Enlisted Adv Council; servd Cmplnts NCO. **HONORS/ACHIEVEMENTS:** Has received numerous decorations most important AF Cmmndtn 1962; two Oak Leaf Clusters 1968, 1974. **MILITARY SERVICE:** USAF chf m/Sgt 1950-. **BUSINESS ADDRESS:** 26 Supply Squad, Box 1512 APO, New York, NY 09860.

RICHARDS, HILDA
Educational administrator. **PERSONAL:** Born Feb 07, 1936, St Joseph, MO; daughter of Togar Williams and Rose Avalynne (Williams) Young-Ballard. **EDUCATION:** St John's Sch of Nursing St Louis, diploma 1956; Hunter Coll City U, BS 1961; Tchrs Coll Columbia U, MEd 1965; NY U, MPA 1971; Tchrs Coll Columbia U, EdD 1976; Fellow in Acad Admin Amer Council on Educ 1976-77; Inst for Educ Mgmt Harvard Univ, Cert 1981. **CAREER:** Dept of Psych Harlem Hosp Center, coord clinical serv div of rehab serv 1965-69; Harlem Rehab Center Dept of Psych Harlem Hosp Center, dep chief 1969-71; Medgar Evers Coll, assoc prof, dir nursing prog 1971-73; Medgar Evers Coll, prof dir nursing prog 1973-76; CUNY, assoc dean acad affairs 1976-69; OH Univ Coll of Health & Human Svc, dean 1979-86; IN Univ of PA, provost, vice pres for acad affairs 1986-. **ORGANIZATIONS:** Mem Mental Health Settins & Appleton Century Crofts 1972; bd mem Natl Black Nurses Assn 1974-77; mem Nominating Comm Psychiatric Nursing/Mental Health Sect ANA 1978-80; mem AVANTA Network 1979-; mem Athens/Vinton/Hocking Co Mental Health & Mental Retardation Bd 1980; 1st vice pres Natl Black Nurses Assn 1984-88; mem IN County Comm Action 1986-, Econ Devel Comm 1986, PA Nurses Assn 1986-; Council on Educ 1976-77; editor Jrnl of Natl Black Nurses Assn; extensive work comm orgns; implications for nursing in the training of paraprofessional workers in the comm; Citizens Ambulance Service of Indiana County 1987-; Zonta Club of Indiana County 1987-; Indiana Chapter, NAACP Executive Committee (Education) 1989-; editor, Black Conference on Higher Education Journal 1988-. **HONORS/ACHIEVEMENTS:** Natl Inst of Mental Health Public Health Trainee Awd for Grad Educ 1963-65; Martin Luther King Grant for Study in Public Admin 1969-70; Rockefeller Found Awd for Amer Council on Educ Fellow in Acad Admin 1976-77; co-authored Imput of CAI for Remediating Basic Skills Deficiencies of Open Admissions Students Conf Proceedings 1978. **BUSINESS ADDRESS:** Provost/Vice Pres Academic Affairs, Indiana University of PA, 205 Sutton Hall, Indiana, PA 15705.

RICHARDS, JOHNETTA GLADYS
Educator. **PERSONAL:** Born Jul 18, 1950, Bronx, NY. **EDUCATION:** Virginia State Coll, BA 1972; Univ of Cincinnati, MA 1974, PhD 1987. **CAREER:** Trinity Coll, asst prof of history 1979-; Univ of California Santa Barbara, lecturer Afro-Amer history 1977-78; Univ of Cincinatti, lecturer Amer history 1976-77; Northeastern Univ, adjunct instructor Afro-Am history 1971; Women's Studies California State Univ at Fresno, assoc prof 1984-88; San Francisco State Univ, assoc prof Black Studies 1988-. **ORGANIZATIONS:** Mem Assn for the Study of Afro-Am Life & History 1978-; mem Phi Alpha Theta Natl Honorary Frat of Historians 1974-; mem NAACP Hartford CT 1979-80; mem Assn of Black Women Historians 1983-; chair Far Western Region of the Assn of Black Women Historians 1986-88; Amer Historical Soc, Pacific Coast Branch. **HONORS/ACHIEVEMENTS:** Doctoral Fellowship, Natl Fellowship Fund, Atlatna GA 1978-79; Dissertation Fellowship, Center for Black Studies Univ of California 1977-78; Graduate Research Grant, Univ of Grad 1977; Danforth Fellowship, Univ of Cincinnati 1972-73; Mellon Research Grant 1981.

RICHARDS, LAVERNE W.
Educational administrator. **PERSONAL:** Born Jun 19, 1947, Gaffney, SC; divorced; children: Brant, Jerrel. **EDUCATION:** San Jose State Coll, BA 1969; Univ of CA Berkeley, Teach Certificate 1970; Univ of Houston TX, MEd 1974, Mid-Management Administrator 1981. **CAREER:** Oakland Unified Sch Dist, teacher 1969-72; Delta Sigma Theta Inc, prog asst 1972; El Paso ISD, teacher 1974-76; Houston ISD, teacher 1972-74, 1977-85, asst principal 1985-. **ORGANIZATIONS:** Fine arts chmn Delta Sigma Theta Ft Bend 1984; coord United Way Clifton Middle Sch 1985,86,87; coord United Negro Coll Fund 1985,86,87; finance comm Houston Assoc of School Administrators 1985-; mem TX Assoc of Secondary School Principals 1985-; mem Phi Delta Kappa, Assoc of Supervision & Curriculum 1985-;mem Urban League Guild 1986-; scholarship chmn Human Enrichment of Life Prog 1987; Human Enrichment of Life Prog 1986-. **HONORS/ACHIEVEMENTS:** Exec bd mem Windsor Village Elem Vanguard Parents Assoc 1983-85; HISD Instructional Adv Comm Houston 1984; Young Black Achiever of Houston Human Enrichment of Life Programs Inc 1986. **HOME ADDRESS:** 12211 Preakness Way, Houston, TX 77071.

RICHARDS, LLOYD G.
Director, educator. **PERSONAL:** Born in Toronto, Ontario, Canada;married Barbara Davenport; children: Scott, Thomas. **EDUCATION:** Wayne State Univ, BA 1944; Yale Univ, MFA 1980. **CAREER:** Yale Univ Sch of Drama, dean; Yale Repertory Theatre, artistic dir; Hunter Coll, prof dept of theatre & cinema; O'Neill Ctr Nat Playwrights Conf, artistic dir 1969-; Natl Theatre Inst, teacher 1970-. **ORGANIZATIONS:** Mem pres Soc Stage Dirs & Choreographers 1970-; charter fellow Black Acad Arts & letters; co-chmn Theatre Panel Natl Endowment Arts; pres bd dirs Theatre Dev Fund; Rockefeller Found Playwrights Selection Com; former adv bd VISIONS KCET-TV Los Angeles; dir teacher lecturer actor announcer advisor foundmem These Twenty People Co Detroit; Actor's Co Repertory Detroit; Greenwich Mews Theatre NY; consultant to various founds; mem professional adv groups, task forces; mem Soc Stage Dirs and Choreographers, Actors Equity Assoc, AFTRA, Dirs Guild Amer. **MILITARY SERVICE:** USAAF 1944-45. **BUSINESS ADDRESS:** 222 York St, New Haven, CT 06520.

RICHARDS, LORETTA THERESA
Religious educator. **PERSONAL:** Born Apr 08, 1929, New York, NY; daughter of David A Richards and Mary Cornelius Richards Edwards. **EDUCATION:** College of Mt St Vincent, New York NY, BA, 1954; Catholic Univ, Washington DC, MA, 1960; Catechetical Institute, Yonkers NY, MRS, 1984. **CAREER:** St Aloysius School, New York NY, teacher, 1954-55, 1957-61; St Thomas School, Wilmington NC, teacher, 1955-57; Cathedral High School, New York NY, teacher, 1961-64; FHM, New York NY, supervisor of schools, 1964-74, president of congregation, 1974-82; St Aloysius Parish, New York NY, pastoral assoc, 1982—. **ORGANIZATIONS:** President of National Black Sisters Conference, 1985-89; vice president of National Black Catholic Congress, 1989—. **HONORS/ACHIEVEMENTS:** Doctor of Pedagogy, New York College of Podiatric Medicine, 1981. **HOME ADDRESS:** 15 West 124th St, New York, NY 10027.

RICHARDS, ROOSEVELT
President/owner. **PERSONAL:** Born Apr 21, 1933, Magnolia, MS; children: Stanley. **EDUCATION:** Rsvlt U, BS; Chicago St U; Tufts U. **CAREER:** The Bhrds Pub Co, pres owner; Hghtn Mfln Pub Co, dist sales mgr rep edtrl mgr; Addsn Wsky Pub Co, rep consult mktg rsch; Chicago Pub Sch, tchr. **ORGANIZATIONS:** Nat Alli of Blk Sch Edctrs; frmr treas mem exec bd NAACP; Urban Leag; ASCD IRA Assn of Am Publ. **HONORS/ACHIEVEMENTS:** Prsntd papers Nat Rgnl Lcl Conf. **MILITARY SERVICE:** AUS 1953-55. **BUSINESS ADDRESS:** 600 N McClurg Ct, 501A, Chicago, IL 60611.

RICHARDS, SANDRA LEE
Director. **PERSONAL:** Born Dec 31, 1946, Boston, MA. **EDUCATION:** Brown Univ, AB 1968; Stanford Univ, PhD 1979. **CAREER:** Amer Conservatory Theatre San Francisco, dir 1974-77; Oakland Ensemble Theatre, artistic dir 1978-; Black Actor's Workshop New Plays Prog, coord. **ORGANIZATIONS:** Co-founder Comm on Blk Performing Arts, Stanford Univ 1972-73; founding dir West Coast Black Repertory Theatre 1973-77; mem Theatre & Dance Adv Panel, San Francisco Arts Commn 1976-77; Performing Arts Serv 1978-80; bd of dir California Confederation of the Arts 1979-80; rprtr theatre prog Natl Endowment for the Arts 1979-80. **HONORS/ACHIEVEMENTS:** Eva A Mooar Prize, Brown Univ 1968; Mbll McLeod Lewis Memorial Fellow, Stanford Univ 1971-72; Black Theatre in San Francisco Bay Area Black World 1974; dissert Fellow Ctr for Black Studies, Univ of California Santa Barbara 1977-78; He Left Them Laughing B Williams San Francisco Theatre Mag 1978. **BUSINESS ADDRESS:** Asst Drama Dir, Stanford University, Stanford, CA 94305.

RICHARDS, WILLIAM EARL
Architectural design and engineering company executive. **PERSONAL:** Born Oct 19, 1921, New York, NY; son of John E. Richards, Jr. and Camily Deravaine Richards; married Ollun Sadler; children: William Jr. **EDUCATION:** Washburn Univ, BA; NY Univ, Additional Study; Officer Cand School, attended; AF Spec Weapons School, attended. **CAREER:** Lipsett Steel Co, gen supt 1946-49; Progressive Life Insurance agent 1949-51; NAACP, staff dir, legislative agent 1972; KS Comm on Alcoholism 1972-73; KS Dept of Soc & Rehabilitation Svcs, commn income maintenance & med asst 1973-83 retired; Richards Et Cie, pres; Myers and Stauffer CPA's, sr consultant; exec vice pres Cottonwood Technology Corporation, Kansas City KS Dec. 1988-. **ORGANIZATIONS:** Mem Washburn Alumni Assn, Amer Public Welfare Assn, Retired Officers Assn, Amer Defense Preparedness Assn, Assn of AUS, Alpha Phi Alpha; life mem NAACP, Euclid Lodge #2 F&AM, Kaw Valley Consistory #16, Oasis Temple #29; mem KS Corrections Ombudsman Bd; mem Topeka Knife & Fork Club. **HONORS/ACHIEVEMENTS:** Asiatic-Pacific Campaign Medal; Natl Defense Medal Oak Leaf Cluster; Korean Serv Medal; 2 Battle Serv Starr; AF Expeditionary Serv Medal; Vietnam Serv Medal; Battle Star; Armed Forces Res Medal 10 yr Device; United Nations Serv Medal; KS Governor Certificates for Meritorious Service. **MILITARY SERVICE:** AUS lt col 27 yrs; Legion of Merit, Army Commend Ribbon with Pendant; 1st Oak Leaf Cluster; Good Conduct Medal; Amer Campaign Medal; Battle Service Star. **BUSINESS ADDRESS:** Executive Vice President, Cottonwood Technology Corporation, 400 State Avenue, Tower Two - Suite 307, Kansas City, KS 66101.

RICHARDS-ALEXANDER, BILLIE J.
Consultant, company president. **PERSONAL:** Born Mar 20, Austin, TX; daughter of Roy A Bacon and Johnnie M Barber Bacon; married Castomal Alexander Sr, Jun 06, 1987; children: Roy, Dianne, Reginal. **EDUCATION:** Huston Tillotson Coll Austin, TX, BS 1962; Univ of TX Austin, attended 1963; Scarritt Coll Nashville, attended 1966; Univ of TX Arlington, MA 1974; London School of Business, London England, 1986. **CAREER:** Ebenezer Bapt Ch Austin, dir educ 1960-61; Dumbar High Sch Temple, TX, tchr 1961-64; Bethlehem Ctr, asst dir 1965-66, dir 1966-73; Fed Home Loan Bank Bd Center for Exec Devel, urban program coord 1962-73; Neighborhood Housing Serv of Dallas Inc, exec dir 1973-78; Dallas Fed Svngs & Loan Assn Urban Lending Dept, vice pres/dir 1978-80, sr vice pres 1980-87; Billie Richards Associates, pres, 1987-; Dallas County, housing officer, 1988. **HONORS/ACHIEVEMENTS:** Woman of the Year United for Action Women's Affiliate of the Dallas Black C of C 1978; Comm Affairs Award Com of 100 1978; Trailblazer Award S Dallas Bus & Professional Women's Orgn 1979; International Business Fellow 1986. **BUSINESS ADDRESS:** President, Billie Richards & Associates Inc, 1517 Bar Harbour Drive, Dallas, TX 75232.

RICHARDSON, ALFRED LLOYD
Consulting geotechnical engineer. **PERSONAL:** Born Jan 17, 1927, Kerens, TX; married Georgia E Murphy; children: Paul G, Yllona, Victor. **EDUCATION:** Prairie View A&M U, 1950;Univ of So CA, 1952. **CAREER:** Pcfc Sls Engrng Inc, vice pres copr tech servs, dir fnd tech servs 1971-76, proj engr 1963-71; LACFCD, ce asso ce asst 1952-65; CA Div of Hwys, jr civil engr 1950-52. **ORGANIZATIONS:** Pres LA Cncl of Blk Professional Engrs 1969-71; Lic Professional Engr CA; Engrs Cncl for Professional Devel 1970-84; ASCE Nat Com on Mnrty Progs 1975-79; asso mem Strctrl Engrs Assn CA; mem Engrng Professional Adv Cncl CA St U; mem Intl Soc of Soil Mech & Fnd Engrs; chmn ASCE LA Sect Hmn Rsrcs Devel Com 1971-77; So CA Engrng Soc Com Mnpwr Training 1970-71; adv Nat Soc of Blk Engrng Stud 2nd Anl Nat Conf CA PolyUniv Pmn 1975-76. **HONORS/ACHIEVEMENTS:** Fellow Am Soc of Civil Engrs; fellow Inst for Advnc of Engring. **MILITARY SERVICE:** Mltry serv 1946-47; commd ofcr 1947-53. **BUSINESS ADDRESS:** 1402 W 240th St, Harbor City, CA 90710.

RICHARDSON, ANTHONY W.
Dentist. **PERSONAL:** Born Mar 15, 1957, New York, NY; son of Archie Richardson and Harriet Boyd Richardson. **EDUCATION:** Bucknell Univ, BS 1979; Fairleigh Dickinson Univ Coll of Dental Medicine, DMD 1983. **CAREER:** Montefiore Hospital & Medical Center, general practice resident 1983-84; Fairleigh Dickinson Univ Coll of Dental Medicine, asst dir of minority affairs 1984-86, asst prof 1984-87, asst dir of admissions 1986-87, asst dir program for grads of non-approved dental schools 1986-87; dir of minority affairs 1986-87. **ORGANIZATIONS:** Charter mem Phi Beta Sigma Fraternity Iota Gamma Chap 1977; mem Amer Assoc of Dental Schools 1981-, Acad of General Dentistry 1982-, Natl Dental Assoc 1983-, NJ Commonwealth Dental Soc 1983-; advisory bd mem Health Careers Program Montclair State Coll 1983-; chapter advisor Phi Beta Sigma Fraternity Xi Omicron Chap 1984, 1985; graduate mem Phi Beta Sigma Frat Epsilon Sigma Chap 1984-. **HONORS/ACHIEVEMENTS:** New York State Governor's Citation 1975; New York State Regents Scholarship 1975; Women's League of Science and Medicine Scholarship 1980, 1981; Outstanding Service Certificate Student Natl Dental Assoc 1982, 1983; NJ Society of Dentistry for Children Award 1983; NJ Commonwealth Dental Soc Award 1983; bd of trustees, Natl Dental Assn, 1989. **HOME ADDRESS:** 3 Fordham Hill Oval, Ste 5F, Bronx, NY 10468. **BUSINESS ADDRESS:** Con-Court Dental Associates, 840-11 Grand Concourse, Suite 1BB, Bronx, NY 10451.

RICHARDSON, CHARLES H., JR.
Business executive. **PERSONAL:** Born Aug 30, 1948, New York, NY; married Suzanne Jackson; children: Tiombe, Dequan. **EDUCATION:** New York City Community College, AAS 1970; Medgar Evers College, BS cum laude 1976; Bernard M Baruch College, MS 1980; The Consultants Inst, Cert Prof Consult (CPC) 1984. **CAREER:** RCA Record Division, auditor 1968-69; Bache & Company, Inc, accountant 1970-71; Medgar Evers College, asst bus manager 1972-79; Inner City Broadcasting Corp, asst controller 1979-81, dir of administration 1981-. **ORGANIZATIONS:** Member Natl Assoc of Accountants 1983-; consulting CHR Management Consultant 1983-; assoc member CA Assoc of Fin Aid Admin 1984-; president Student Athletic Advisement Service 1984-; charter member American Consultants League 1985-. **HONORS/ACHIEVEMENTS:** Outstanding service Medgar Evers College-CUNY 1979; Youth Motivation Task Force/Natl Alliance of Business 1980-81; Information for the Student Athlete/OaklandPost 1985; Meritorious Achievement Urban League of Greater New York. **BUSINESS ADDRESS:** Dir of Admin Western Region, Inner City Broadcasting Co, 601 Ashby Ave, Berkeley, CA 94710.

RICHARDSON, CHARLES RONALD
University admissions director. **PERSONAL:** Born Jun 08, 1949, Bartow, FL; married Karen Janine Hill; children: Ericka, Charles Jr, Elden. **EDUCATION:** Univ of MD-Eastern Shore, 1967-70; Univ of MD-College Park, BGS 1976-77, MEd 1984. **CAREER:** Haven Connuty Ctr Inc, executive dir 1974-76; Univ of MD-College Park, program & resident dir 1977-78, academic advisor 1978-80, admissions counselor 1980-84; Minority Student Education, community liaison and info coord 1984-86; Drew Univ, asst dir of admissions 1986-. **ORGANIZATIONS:** Urban Resources Consultants, consultant 1980-86; Kappa Alpha Psi, keeper of records 1980-84; UMCP Black Alumni Assoc, president 1984-86; UMCP Black Faculty Staff Assoc, president 1984-86. **HONORS/ACHIEVEMENTS:** Winter Haven, FL Boys Club, "Man of the Year" 1976; Univ of MD-College Park, other race fellowship 1977-80; Zeta Phi Beta, "Zodiac Man of the Year" 1978; Goddard Space Flight Center, NASA-SHARP humanitarian award 1983-86. **HOME ADDRESS:** 45 Lafayette Ave #D, Chatham, NJ 07928. **BUSINESS ADDRESS:** Asst Dir of Admissions, Drew University, 36 Madison Ave, Madison, NJ 07940.

RICHARDSON, CLINT DEWITT
Professional athlete. **PERSONAL:** Born Aug 07, 1956, Seattle, WA; married Vicki; children: Tiffany Jade. **EDUCATION:** Univ of Seattle, 1979. **CAREER:** Philadelphia 76er's, guard 1979-. **HONORS/ACHIEVEMENTS:** Noted for his hard style of play and defensive prowess. **BUSINESS ADDRESS:** Philadelphia 76er's, Veterans Stadium, Ste 510, Philadelphia, PA 19141.

RICHARDSON, CORDELL
Educator. **PERSONAL:** Born Nov 10, 1946, Pittsburgh, PA; married Linda Turner. **EDUCATION:** Lincoln U, BS 1968;Univ of Pitts, MS 1970, PhD 1974. **CAREER:** Carnegie Mellon U, conslr asst dir & dir of upwrd bnd dir of Stud servs; Exclnc Prgm PUSH, natl dir. **ORGANIZATIONS:** Mem Omega Psi Phi Frat; Am Soc for Engr Educs; Am Prpsychl Rsrch Fnd; Prince Hall Masons. **BUSINESS ADDRESS:** 5000 Forbes, Pittsburgh, PA 15213.

RICHARDSON, DAVID PRESTON, JR.
State representative. **PERSONAL:** Born Apr 23, 1948, Philadelphia, PA. **CAREER:** St of PA, st rep 1972-. **ORGANIZATIONS:** Exec dir grtr Germantown Yth Corp 1968-73; bd dir Germantown Stlmnt; adv cncl E Germantown; cncl City-Wide Black Comm; urb studies bd LaSalle Coll; Germantown Br Yng Afro-Ams; mem Black Guard; Black People's Unity Mvmnt; mem RAM. **BUSINESS ADDRESS:** State Representative, PA House of Representatives, 6345 Germantown Ave, Philadelphia, PA 19144.

RICHARDSON, DELROY M.
Attorney/utility executive/corporate secretary. **PERSONAL:** Born Jun 26, 1938, Chicago, IL; son of Roy Richardson; married Greta M; children: Gayle L, Monique N. **EDUCATION:** UCLA, AB 1962; Univ of San Diego, JD 1969; Natl Univ, MBA 1975. **CAREER:** IRS, officer 1962-64; US Navy, legal officer 1964-67; Gen Dynamics, chief labor relations 1968-71; San Diego Gas & Electric Co, atty 1971-83, asst corp sec 1983-86, corp sec 1986-. **ORGANIZATIONS:** Mem Natl Bar, California State and San Diego County Bar Assns, NAACP, Navy League, Rotary Club, Black Atty Assn of San Diego County. **HONORS/ACHIEVEMENTS:** Outstanding Young Man of the Year Finalist, Jr Chamber of Commerce 1973; Outstanding Alumnus of USD Law School 1978. **MILITARY SERVICE:** USN 1964-67; Captain USNR. **BUSINESS ADDRESS:** Corporate Secretary, San Diego Gas & Elect Co, PO Box 1831 101 Ash St, San Diego, CA 92112.

RICHARDSON, DERUTHA GARDNER
Educator. **PERSONAL:** Born May 03, 1941, Muskogee, OK; married Alfred; children: Allyn Christopher, Adrian Charles. **EDUCATION:** Muskogee Jr Coll, Muskogee OK, AA 1960; NE State Coll, Thlqh OK, BS 1962, masters degree 1964. **CAREER:** Muskogee High School, first black business dept head and teacher coord 1967-; Taft St Children's Home Mtn School, exec sec ged teacher 1966-67; Central High School, first black secondary business teacher 1965-66; Mtn High School, secondary business teacher 1963-65; L'Ouverature High School, teacher sec 1962-63; Atty C P Kimble, part-time private legal sec 1955-70; Muskogee County Head Start, sec bookkeeper 1966-68; YWCA Cnnrs St Coll, adult business teacher 1975-77. **ORGANIZATIONS:** Natl Grmmts Zeta Phi Beta Sorority Inc WA 1973-74; treas Alpha Lambda Zeta Sorority 1975-80; pres Eastern Dist Oklahoma Educ Assn 1977-78. **HONORS/ACHIEVEMENTS:** First black teacher of the year, Muskogee Educ Assn 1977; teacher of the year finalist, Oklahoma Educ Assn 1977; Black Heritage Hon, Mt Calvary Baptist Church Muskogee 1977; Who's Who Among Noteworthy Americans, Raleigh Inst, Raleigh NC 1978; first black fourth place and second runner-up plaques, Oklahoma Teachers 1978-80; outstanding teachers plaque, DuBois School Reunion 1980; author Dear Teacher, Carlton Press NY 1980. **BUSINESS ADDRESS:** Assistant Principal, West Junior High School, 6400 Mathew Dr, Muskogee, OK 74401.

RICHARDSON, EARL STANFORD
Administrator. **PERSONAL:** Born Sep 25, 1943, Westover, MD; son of Mr and Mrs Phillip Richardson; married Sheila Bunting; children: Eric. **EDUCATION:** Univ of MD Eastern Shore, BA 1965; Univ of PA, MS 1973, EdD 1976. **CAREER:** Univ of MD, Eastern Shore, dir of career planning & placement 1970-72, acting dir admiss & reg 1970-71; Univ of PA; grad asst sch study council 1973-74; Univ of MD, Eastern Shore, dir of career planning & placement 1974-75, exec asst to chancellor 1975-82; Univ of MD System, assistant to pres 1982-84; Morgan State Univ, pres 1984-. **ORGANIZATIONS:** Consult Coll Placement Serv 1979; pres, bd of dir, mem Somerset Cty Head Start Prog 1974-; chap pres Alpha Phi Alpha Frat Inc 1976-79; pres Panhellenic Council of the Eastern Shore 1977-79, Alpha Kappa Mu Honor Soc Intl 1964-65; Sigma Pi Phi Fraternity Gamma Boule. **HONORS/ACHIEVEMENTS:** Fellowship Ford Found NY 1972-75; Phi Kappa Phi Hon Soc Intl 1979-; Fellow Kellogg Found NY 1980-83. **MILITARY SERVICE:** USAF capt 4 yrs; Commendation Medal 1970. **BUSINESS ADDRESS:** President, Morgan State University, Cold Spring La & Hillen Rd, Baltimore, MD 21239.

RICHARDSON, ELISHA R.
Dentist, educator. **PERSONAL:** Born Aug 15, 1931, Monroe, LA; married Pattye Whyte; children: Scott, Jonathan, Mark. **EDUCATION:** Sthrn U, BS 1951; Meharry Med Coll, DDS 1955;Univ of IL Med Ctr, MS 1963;Univ of MI, 1973; Harvard U, 1973; NY Acad of Sci. **CAREER:** SOD, asso dean chmn dept orthdntc; Meharry Med Coll, dir of rsrch sch of dent 1969-78, pres med & dent staff hbrd hosp 1971-72, rsrchr lectr cons; Univ of Colorado, prof and chairman div of orthodontics 1985-. **ORGANIZATIONS:** Chrmn Orthodonitc

Amer Assoc Dental Sch 1972-73; pres Craniofacial Biology 1978-79; pres elect chmn bd of tst Nat Dental Assn 1980; mem Am Assn Orthdntst; Nat Dental Assn; Am Dental Assn; Am Soc of Dent for Chldrn; Intl Assn for Dental Rsrch; Am Assn for Dental Schs; Am Assn for Advanc of Sci; Crnfcl Bio Grp; Meharry Almn Assn;Univ of IL Orthdntc Almn Assn; Am Pub Hlth Assn; Am Coll of Dntsts; mem Alpha Phi Alpha; NAACP; Nshvl Urban Leag; YMCA; Nshvl Symphny Assn; Civitan Internat; pres Natl Dental Assoc 1981; chrmn Council on Education American Assoc of Orthodontists 1987. **HONORS/ACHIEVEMENTS:** Beta Kappa Chi 1950; Kappa Sigma Phi 1954; Physio Soc of Upper 1/10th 1955; Omicron Kappa Upsilon 1955; Otstndng Prsnlts of So 1970-74; listed in Am Men & Wmn of Sci 11th Ed, Who's Who in So SW 1971-72; named one of the 100 Most Influential Black Americans by Ebony Mag 1981; Commissioned an Arkansas Traveler by Governor Frank White 1981; listed in Who's Who in the World 1982-83 & Who's Who in American 1982. **MILITARY SERVICE:** USAF capt 1955-60. **BUSINESS ADDRESS:** Univ of Colorado HlthSci, 4200 East 9th Ave, Box C284, Denver, CO 80262.

RICHARDSON, ERNEST A.
Consultant. **PERSONAL:** Born Aug 02, 1925, NYC, NY; married Olive; children: Brenda. **EDUCATION:** Columbia Univ NY city B.A. 1952; NY Univ NY City M.B.A. 1958. **CAREER:** Schnly Indst, accountant 1952-60; Intl Pearl Corp, controller 1960-66; St Regis Paper Co, mgr minority affairs. **ORGANIZATIONS:** Bd chmn New York City Task Force on Youth Motivation; natl chmn Nat Urban Afrs Cncl; indst chmn Fisk Univ Cluster; mem bd adv TN St Univ Cluster; mem adv com Nat Task Force Youth Motivation; mem Blk Corp Caucus; adv com Nat Urban Leag Skills Bank. **HONORS/ACHIEVEMENTS:** Hon Jacksonville FL Urban League 1972; hon Fisk Univ 1973; hon TN St Univ 1972; Exec of the Year, Assn of Meeting Planners 1983; Crusade Award, Amer Cancer Soc 1985; Merit Award, St Regis 1985; Natl Urban Affairs Council Appreciation 1987. **MILITARY SERVICE:** USMC staff sgt 1943-46, 1950-51. **HOME ADDRESS:** 186-30 Mangin Ave, St Albans, NY 11412.

RICHARDSON, F. C.
Educator. **PERSONAL:** Born Sep 22, 1936, Whitehaven, TN; children: 3 children. **EDUCATION:** Rust Coll, BA 1960; Atlanta Univ, MS 1964; Univ of CA Santa Barbara, PhD 1967. **CAREER:** Atlanta Univ, tchr asst 1962-64; Univ of CA Santa Barbara, tchr asst 1964-66; IN Univ, asst prof of Botany 1967-71, chrmn dept of Biology 1971-72, assoc prof of Botany 1971-83, prof of Botany 1983-84; Jackson State Univ, vice pres for Academic Affairs 1984-. **ORGANIZATIONS:** Sec IUN Faculty Orgn 1970-71, chmn 1972-73; chmn Faculty Salary Com 1971-72; faculty adv to Black Caucus IUN 1969-; adv com Black Studies Faculty 1970-73; participant in tutoring programs by Black Studies Program & Spl Serv IUN 1970-73; mem bd dir Spl Serv Project 1970-; exec counc Arts & Sci 1971-72; mem IU Pres Ad Hoc Com on Wage/Price Freeze 1971-72; mem Human Rel Com 1967-72; bd dir Lake Co Assn for Retarded Children 1969-; bd dir Gary Neighborhood House 1968-72, pres 1971-; bd dir Gary Methodist Hosp 1974; bd dir Gary Med Cntr Inc; adv bd Black Studies Program IUN 1969-74; Clean Air Coord Com chmn of Tech adv sub-com 1970-73; Air Pollution Cont Adv Bd City of Gary 1970-; dir Gary Youth Gardens Project 1971-72; mem Amer Inst of Biol Sci; mem Botanical Soc of Amer; mem Intl Soc of Plant Morphologists; mem IN Conf of Higher Edn; mem sub com "Environmental Health Task Force" 1971-;mem Selection Comm to Screen Candidates for Martin Luther King, Jr Fellowship Program Woodrow Wilson Natl Fellowship Found 1969-. **HONORS/ACHIEVEMENTS:** Author of numerous publns in field of botany & Black experiences; Recipient full scholarship Rust Coll 1955-56 & 1959-60; Univ Scholarship Atlanta Univ 1962-64; Honor Cert Rust Coll for fourth highest position in class of 60; Nat Sci Found Summer Fellowship for tchr asst 1966; Univ Doctoral Fellowship Univ of CA 1966-67. **MILITARY SERVICE:** Military Serv 1960-62. **BUSINESS ADDRESS:** Vice Pres for Academic Affairs, Jackson StateUniv, Jackson, MS 39217.

RICHARDSON, FRANK (MR. FRANK)
Artist. **PERSONAL:** Born Jan 14, 1950, Baltimore, MD. **EDUCATION:** Comm Coll of Baltimore; MD Inst Coll Art, AA; Towson St Coll Baltimore, BFA. **CAREER:** News Amer, 1976-; Baltimore's Black Art's Museum, dir 1976; 3rd World Prep Sch of Art, headmaster, 1975; Enoch Pratt Free Library Branch 17, painted mural interior & Exterior; Phase's Gallery, 1977; Ebony Collective, 1977. **ORGANIZATIONS:** Black Cultural Endowment 1974; Artist Fellowsihp Program MD Arts Council, 1977; Natl Soc of Public Poets. **HONORS/ACHIEVEMENTS:** African-Amer Day Parade, 1976; advertisement, United Fed of Black Comm Org; Art show, Univ of Ife Bookshop Ltd Nigeria; stroy Cape Herald & So Afrcn Newppr; reviews of work Colorful Mural Baltimore Sun 1967, Mr Richardsons Beautiful Wall Baltimore Afro-Amer, 1972, Mus Unit to Expand New Amer 1975, NY Times Intl Exp Imp Trd Opportunity Metro Magazine, 1977. **BUSINESS ADDRESS:** 552 Baker St, Baltimore, MD 21217.

RICHARDSON, GEORGE C.
Legislator. **PERSONAL:** Born Feb 19, 1929, Newark, NJ. **EDUCATION:** USAF Adminstrv Sch, grad; Jersey City Tech. **CAREER:** NJ St Assembly, asst minority ldr 1961-. **ORGANIZATIONS:** Chmn NJ Black Legsl Caucus; served on NJ St Narcotics Div Com on Inst & Agy; Com on Transp & Pub Utilities Sub-com on Hwy & Com on Taxation; pres Periscope Asso. **MILITARY SERVICE:** USAF korean war.

RICHARDSON, GILDA FAYE
Elected government official. **PERSONAL:** Born May 08, 1926, Wichita Falls, TX; married James Richardson; children: Linda Moore, Michael Cooper. **EDUCATION:** Southern Univ, 1943-45; Lansing Bus Univ, 1945-46; MI State Univ, 1972. **CAREER:** Beurmann/Marshall Adv Agency, commercial photographer 1965-68. **ORGANIZATIONS:** Bd mem YWCA 1967-85; bd mem/guild chairperson Lansing Urban League 1968-77; mem bd Lansing Family Health Ctr 1972, Housing Asst Found 1973-74, Office of Econ Opportunity 1973-74, Capital Area United Way 1973-78; sec/bd United Negro Coll Fund 1974-77; mem/sec Lansing Bd of Ed 1975-85. **HONORS/ACHIEVEMENTS:** Community Serv Natl Assn Negro Bus Professional Women 1967; Dedicated Serv Awd Lansing Urban League 1973; Dedicated Serv Awd Ingham Cty Commiss 1979; Diana Awd Comm Serv YWCA 1980; Multicultural Awd Lansing School Dist 1982. **HOME ADDRESS:** 3024 Colchester, Lansing, MI 48906. **BUSINESS ADDRESS:** Elected Official Secretary, Lansing School Dist, 519 W Kalamazoo, Lansing, MI 48933.

RICHARDSON, GLOSTER V.
Educator, athlete. **PERSONAL:** Born Jul 18, 1941, Clarksdale, MS; son of Rev. Willie Richardson, Sr. and Mary Alice Tompkins; married Bettye Neal, Dec 27, 1966; children: Glasetta, Maury. **EDUCATION:** Jackson State Coll, 1965. **CAREER:** Kansas City Chiefs, Dallas Cowboys, Cleveland Browns, professional football player; instr phys ed; athletic director Chicago Public Schools. **ORGANIZATIONS:** Mem Better Boys Found Benefit; works with young boys & the handicapped in many areas; Team Up, NFL Retired Players Assn; Mt. Carmel H.S. Father's Assn. **HONORS/ACHIEVEMENTS:** Played in 3 Super Bowl Championships; Football Hall of Fame, Jackson State Univ.

RICHARDSON, HAROLD EDWARD
Retired city official. **PERSONAL:** Born Dec 14, 1922, Portland, ME; son of Edward Richardson; married Helen J; children: Haroldeane, Lura, Carol, Robert. **EDUCATION:** Portland HS, 1941. **CAREER:** Portland Boys Club, dir 1982; ME Lions Sight & Hearing Assn, chmn 1981-84; Box 61 Inc, pres 1983-84; Grant Committee, dir 1985-90; Portland Water & SewerDist, trustee. **ORGANIZATIONS:** Chmn Civic Serv Police & Fire 1982; treasurer Kippy Serv Inc 1985. **HONORS/ACHIEVEMENTS:** Certificate of Recognition the Jefferson Awards 1984, 1985.

RICHARDSON, HENRY J., III
Educator. **PERSONAL:** Born Mar 24, 1941, Indianapolis, IN. **EDUCATION:** Univ de Besancon France, Cert en Hist 1962; Antioch Coll, AB 1963; Yale Law Sch, LLB 1966; UCLA Sch of Law, LLM 1971. **CAREER:** Temple Univ, prof of law; Govt Of Malawi Central Africa, intl leg ad 1966-68; African Studies Center UCLA, faculty africanist in law 1969-71; School of Law IN Univ, asst prof 1971-74, asso prof 1974-; Northwestern Univ School of Law, visiting asso prof of law 1975-76. **ORGANIZATIONS:** Chmn Nat Conf of Black Lwyrs Task Force on Intrntl Affairs; former rep UN NGO; mem, exec cncl Am Soc of Intrntl Law 1975-; various panels, presentations, pro mtg including NCBL Annual Mtg & panels at asil Annual Mtg; mem IN Bar; Nat Conf of Black Lwyrs; Am Soc of Intrntl Law; World Peace Thro Law Ctr, Sect of Intrntl Legal Ed; mem AID Rsrch Team on Law & Soc Chng 1971; World Peace Thro Law Con, Abidjan Ivory Cst; chmn panel on Intrntl Legal Ed in Africa 1973; mem NCBL del to Cuba to study legal inst 1974; mem, adv com ITT Intrntl Flwshp Prog; mem Am Soc of Intrntl Law Wrkng Grp onInfo Sys. **HONORS/ACHIEVEMENTS:** Author of numerous pblctns in various legal jrnls on Intrntl Law, African Law, Legal Ed, Law & Black People; recip Maxwell Afro-Asian Flwshp 1966-68; Maxwell Wrtng Flwshp 1968-69; UCLA Ford LLM Flwshp 1969-71; Fclty Rsrch Flwshp INUniv 1973. **BUSINESS ADDRESS:** Temple University, 1719 N Broad St, Philadelphia, PA 19122.

RICHARDSON, JOHNNY L.
Company executive. **PERSONAL:** Born Jul 14, 1952, Cleveland, MS; married Mary Goins; children: Teria D; Rapahelle K. **EDUCATION:** Ripon Coll WI, BA Econ 1974. **CAREER:** Miller Brewing Co, pricing analyst 1974-75, merchandising rep 1975-77, area mgr 1977-82, reg merchandising mgr 1982-. **ORGANIZATIONS:** Mem Natl Urban League; vice pres 1981-82; mem Chicago Merchandiser Exec Club 1982-; grad instructor Dale Carnegie Inst 1984; dir Park Ridge Jaycees 1984-85,Ripon Coll Alumni Bd 1984-87. **HONORS/ACHIEVEMENTS:** Dir of the Year Chicago South End Jaycees 1980; Pres Awd of Merit Chicago South-End Jaycees 1982. **BUSINESS ADDRESS:** Regional Merchandising Manager, Miller Brewing Co, 500 Park Blvd, Itasca, IL 60143.

RICHARDSON, JOSEPH
Owner, president. **PERSONAL:** Born Apr 23, 1940, Kansas City, MO; son of Joseph and Genevieve; married Jacquel. **EDUCATION:** Lincoln U, BA sociology 1964; MA Leadership, Augsburg Coll, Minneapolis, MN 1989. **CAREER:** JR & Assocs Inc, pres 1980; The Toro Co, dir employees relations mgr 1979-80, corp mgr manpower planning 1978-79, corp training mgr 1977-78, corp employment mgr 1976-77; Mgmt Recruiters, account exec 1973-76; John Tschohl & Assocs, VP 1972-73; Butler Mfg Co, div employee relations mgr 1970-72; Butler Mfg Co, copr employment rep 1968-70; Pan Hellenic Council, pres 1978-; MN Council of Ex-offender Employment, pres 1979-. **ORGANIZATIONS:** Mem Twin City Personnel Assn Vietnam Serv; Gamma Xi Lambda Alpha Phi Alpha Frat, VP 1977. **HONORS/ACHIEVEMENTS:** Medal-AUS Commedation Medal/Pres Citation/Oak Leaf Cluster AUS. **MILITARY SERVICE:** AUS captain 1964-68. **BUSINESS ADDRESS:** J R & Associates Inc, 101 W Burnsville Pkwy Ste 10, Burnsville, MN 55337.

RICHARDSON, LACY FRANKLIN
Social worker, clergyman. **PERSONAL:** Born Apr 08, 1937, Lynhurst, VA; son of Lacy Richardson and Roxie Richardson; married Regina L Crick, Mar 01, 1980; children: Darnel, Tina, Dori, Alexander. **EDUCATION:** OH Christian Coll, BTh (Summa Cum Laude) 1972; Univ of Pittsburgh, BA (Cum Laude) 1976, MSW 1977; Intl Bible Coll & Seminary, PhD (Summa Cum Laude) 1985. **CAREER:** Auburn Assoc Engrs, design draftsman 1964-68; Kaiser Engrs, design draftsman 1968-72; Mon-Yough CMH/MR Serv Inc, dir of consul educ 1972-77, dir of personnel 1984-. **ORGANIZATIONS:** Bd of dirs Aurborle Home for Boys 1980-; pastor Metropolitan Baptist Church 1981-; dir/coord Citizens Advisory Bd 1982-, Parents for Adult Mentally Ill; Bd of Dir, McKeesport Youth Service Corps, 1988. **HONORS/ACHIEVEMENTS:** Humanitarian Award Parents for Adult Mentally Ill 1986, Mon-Yough CMH/MR Serv Inc 1986; Outstanding Employee Award, Mon-Yough/MR, 1985; Outstanding Service Award, Auberle Homes for Boys, 1987. **BUSINESS ADDRESS:** Personnel Director, Mon-Yough CMH/MR Serv Inc, 500 Walnut St, 3rd Floor, Equibank Bldg, McKeesport, PA 15132.

RICHARDSON, LEO
Government official. **PERSONAL:** Born Dec 19, 1931, Marion, SC; son of Isiah Richardson and Ethel Richardson; married Mary Jane Frierson; children: Sandra Jane, Alfred Leo, Beverley Lynette:. **EDUCATION:** Morris Coll, BS 1954; Tuskegee Univ, MA 1961; SUNY at Buffalo, PhD 1985. **CAREER:** Morris Coll, head football & basketball coach 1961-64; Savannah State Coll, head football & basketball coach 1964-71; SUNY at Buffalo, head basketball coach & administrator 1972-84; SC Dept of Social Services, asst to commissioner 1984-86; Deputy Commissioner, 1986-. **ORGANIZATIONS:** Natl Assoc of Basketball Coaches, mem 1971-78; Natl Assoc of Basketball Coaches Clinic Committee, mem 1974-76; Buffalo Urban Caucus, mem 1974-78; Black Educator Assoc of Buffalo, mem 1975-76; PUSH Inc, mem 1976; Natl Assoc of Basketball Coaches Research Comm, mem 1976-78; Committee Action Organization, educational task force committee 1977-84; Buffalo Public Schools, task force on discipline chairman 1979, sports advisory committee chairman 1979-80; NAACP, board of directors 1979-82; Board of Directors Housing Assistance Center of Niagara Frontier, Inc, pres 1979-82; Dept of Education, chairman - advisory comm for single parents/

homemakers & sex equity prgms 1985; Francis Burns United Methodist Church, board of trustees 1985; Leadership Columbia, 1986; Alpha Phi Alpha Frat; Morris College Board of Trustees; Leadership SC Board of Regents. **HONORS/ACHIEVEMENTS:** University at Buffalo Community Advisory Council, Community Service Staff Award 1983; Black Educators of the Niagara Frontier, Community Service Award 1984-85; Man of the Year Award, Alpha Phi Alpha, 1987. **MILITARY SERVICE:** US Army, specialist third class. **HOME ADDRESS:** 241 King Charles Rd, Columbia, SC 29209. **BUSINESS ADDRESS:** Assistant to Commissioner, SC Dept of Social Services, PO Box 1520, Columbia, SC 29202.

RICHARDSON, LINDA WATERS
Fundraising consultant. **PERSONAL:** Born Nov 21, 1946, Philadelphia, PA; married Albert J Pitts; children: Aissia, Tarik, Monifa, Mariama. **EDUCATION:** Overbrook HS, Business 1964; New Hampshire College, Masters Candidate 1988-89. **CAREER:** BEDC Inc, asst dir 1971-73; Peoples Fund, coord 1973-74; Philadelphia Clearing House, dir 1974-81; Black United Fund, exec dir 1982-89, pres/ceo, 1989-. **ORGANIZATIONS:** Mem Natl Black United Fund 1983-89; mem Willingboro Home & Sch 1986; mem adv comm Episcopal Comm Svcs; mem Interfaith Revolving Loan Fund; mem, Women in Philanthropy, Assn of Black Foundation Executives. **HONORS/ACHIEVEMENTS:** Merit Chapel of 4 Chaplains 1985; Comm Leadership Awd Comm Leadership Seminars 1985; Minority Mental Health Advocacy Task Force Award 1989. **BUSINESS ADDRESS:** President/CEO, Black United Fund of Pa Inc, 4601 Market St, Philadelphia, PA 19139.

RICHARDSON, LOUIS M.
Government official, minister. **PERSONAL:** Born Nov 07, 1927, Johnstown, PA; married Allie; children: April, Louis III, Emmett, Alan T, Hope C, Peter, Holly A. **EDUCATION:** Livingstone Coll, AB 1952-55; Hood Theological Seminary NC, bD 1958. **CAREER:** City of Paterson City Hall, affirmative action coordinator 1976-; Paterson CETA Program, dir 1973-76; Martin Luther King Comm Center, dir 1970-73; NJ StateEmployment Serv, counselor 1967-70; First AME Church, minister 1964-; OIC, pres 1970-71; Paterson Bd of Ed, vP 1969-74. **ORGANIZATIONS:** Mem Paterson Rotary #70 1970-74; pres Alpha Phi Alpha Frat. **HONORS/ACHIEVEMENTS:** 1976-77; Citizenship Award Paterson Teachers Assn 1971. **BUSINESS ADDRESS:** City of Paterson, City Hall Ellison, Paterson, NJ 07505.

RICHARDSON, LUNS C.
Educator. **PERSONAL:** Born Apr 29, 1928, Hartsville, SC. **EDUCATION:** Bendict Coll, AB 1949; Columbia Univ Teachers Coll, MA 1958. **CAREER:** Denmark Tech Educ Ctr, dean 1949-64; St Helena HS, prin 1964-66; Wilson HS, prin 1966-67; Benedict Coll, staff/acting pres 1967-73; Voorhees Coll,vice pres, 1973-74; Morris Coll, pres 1974-. **ORGANIZATIONS:** Chmn Com on Rsch & Special Proj, Southern Assoc of Colls & Schs; bd of dirs SC State C of C; mem bd of dir Sumter C of C; mem Wateree Comm Actions Bd; adv bd Citizens & Southern Bank of Sumter; mem Omega Psi Phi Frat, NAACP, NEA, AAHE, Amer Acad of Polit & Social Sci, SC Educ Assoc, SumterCo Econ Develop Admin Com, Sumter Human Relations Cncl. **HONORS/ACHIEVEMENTS:** Mem Alpha Kappa Mu Honor Soc, Phi Delta Kappa; Hon Ped D Benedict Coll; Hon LHD Morris Coll; Outstanding Educators of Amer 1973; Citation Links Inc 1973; Citation Voorheez Coll BD of Trustees 1974; Personalities of the South 1974; Diction of Intl Biog 1975. **BUSINESS ADDRESS:** President, Morris College, North Main St, Sumter, SC 29150.

RICHARDSON, MADISON FRANKLIN
Surgeon. **PERSONAL:** Born Dec 26, 1943, Prairie View, TX; son of William Richardson; married Constance; children: Kelly, Kimberly, Karen. **EDUCATION:** Howard Univ, BS 1965, MD 1969. **CAREER:** Walter Reed Hosp, chief, head & neck surgery 1974-76; Martin Luther King Hosp, chief head & neck surgery 1977-. **ORGANIZATIONS:** Bd chair Los Angeles Urban League 1984-87; pres Charles Drew Med Soc 1984-85; chief surg serv Daniel Freeman Hosp 1986-87; pres bd chair Natl Urban League 1986; mem CA Medical Bd 1987-; bd dir Charles Drew Medical School 1988; bd dir Salerni Collegium; Alpha Omega. **HONORS/ACHIEVEMENTS:** Mem of Distinction Los Angeles AME Church 1982; Meritorious Awd LA NAACP 1983; dist alumnus Howard University 1987. **MILITARY SERVICE:** USA ltcol 1968-77. **BUSINESS ADDRESS:** Surgeon, 6200 Wilshire Blvd, Ste 908, Los Angeles, CA 90048.

RICHARDSON, MARY MARGARET
Educator. **PERSONAL:** Born Feb 19, 1932, Christian Co, KY. **EDUCATION:** KY Comm Coll Hopkinsville KY, AA 1970; Valdosta State Coll, BSN 1973; Med Coll of GA Mental Health/Psych Nursing, MSN 1974. **CAREER:** Brooks Hosp, ofc nurse 1952-72; Western KY State Mental Hosp, clin nurse 1956-71; Jennie Stuart Meml Hosp, private duty nurse 1970-71; Col Manor Hosp, part time head nurse 1974-75; School of Nursing Univ of N AL Florence, asst prof 1974-75; Grad School of Nursing Med Coll of Augusta GA, asst prof 1975; Valdosta State Coll, asst prof nursing 1975-78, assoc prof nursing 1978-80, asst dir nursing 1980-, dept head undergrad studies. **ORGANIZATIONS:** Mem Natl League for Nursing, Amer Nursing Assoc, GA League for Nursing, GA Nurses Assoc, KY Fed of LPN, Amer Assoc of Univ Prof, Amer Assoc of Univ Women, Task Force Leader Faculty Devel Proj, SREB at Valdosta State, Sigma Theta Tau Epsilon Pi Chap PDK, ODK. **HONORS/ACHIEVEMENTS:** Listed in Who's Who in Amer Coll & Univ Students, Outstanding Ed in Amer 1974, Personalities of the South; Fed Traineeship Scholarship 1973. **BUSINESS ADDRESS:** Dept Head Undergrad Studies, Valdosta State Coll, Div of Nursing, Valdosta, GA 31601.

RICHARDSON, MICHAEL CALVIN
Professional athlete. **PERSONAL:** Born May 23, 1961, Compton, CA. **EDUCATION:** Arizona St Univ, BS 1983. **CAREER:** Chicago Bears, cornerback 1983-. **HONORS/ACHIEVEMENTS:** 4-yr all-PAC 10 at ASU; All-Am at Compton (CA) High; first defensive player to win CA "Player of Year" Awrd. **BUSINESS ADDRESS:** Chicago Bears, Halas Hall, Lake Forest, IL 60045.

RICHARDSON, NOLA MAE
Medical administrator, poet. **PERSONAL:** Born Nov 12, 1936, Los Angeles, CA; daughter of Oscar Smith and Jessie Mae Anderson Smith; divorced 1969; children: Nolan, Virgil, Anthony, Julie, Dawn. **EDUCATION:** Compton Junior College, Compton CA, certificate in management, 1973. **CAREER:** North American Rockwell, Downey CA, administrative secretary, 1954-70; Drew Postgraduate Medical School, Los Angeles CA, administrative assistant, 1970-73, 1974—; Central Medical Group, Los Angeles CA, executive secretary and supervisor, 1973-74; poet. **HONORS/ACHIEVEMENTS:** Author of When One Loves: The Black Experience in America, Celestial Arts, 1974; author of Even in a Maze, Crescent, 1975. **HOME ADDRESS:** 10426 Crenshaw Blvd, #1, Inglewood, CA 90303. **BUSINESS ADDRESS:** Drew Postgraduate Medical School, 12012 Compton Ave, Los Angeles, CA 90059. *

RICHARDSON, NOLAN
Educator. **PERSONAL:** Born Dec 27, 1941, El Paso, TX; married Rose; children: Madalyn, Bradley, Nolan III, Yvonne, Sylvia. **EDUCATION:** Univ of TX at ElPaso, BA 1964. **CAREER:** Univ of AK, head basketball coach. **ORGANIZATIONS:** American Red Cross, bd of dir; Easter Seal, chairman. **HOME ADDRESS:** 2779 Joyce, Fayetteville, AR 72701.

RICHARDSON, ODIS GENE
Educator, free lance writer. **PERSONAL:** Born Nov 29, 1940, Lakes Charles, LA; son of Lucky Sip and Estella Scott Richardson; children: Ron Pressley, Odis G II. **EDUCATION:** Univ of Tampa, BS 1965; Chicago State Univ, MA 1971; Roosevelt Univ, MS 1983; Northwestern Univ, post graduate studies. **CAREER:** Boy Scouts of Amer, executive 1965-66; Dept of Public Assistance, social caseworker 1966-67; Chicago Public Schools, teacher 1967-; free lance writer. **ORGANIZATIONS:** Public relations chmn IL Speech & Theatre Assoc 1985-86; pres bd of dirs Maranatha Youth Ministries 1985-87; fellow Northwestern Univ 1986; mem IL Council on Exceptional Children; dir Richardson Special Educ Consultants; mem Phi Beta Sigma, Phi Delta Kappa, Chicago Urban League, NAACP; deacon South Shore Bible Baptist Church; mem Emergency Land Fund; bd of dirs Chicago Citizens Schools Committee 1987-89; fellow Foundation for Excellence in Teaching 1986-89; research linker Chicago Teacher's Union, Educational Research & Development; volunteer Project Image, Man-Boy Conference 1988-89; precinct captain, Fourth Ward Regional Democrats 1981-; teacher sponsor PAPPA Club, Pan African Pen Pal Assn 1988-89. **HONORS/ACHIEVEMENTS:** DuSable Man of the Year DuSable High School Chicago 1985; South Shore Outstanding Community Volunteer 1986; Golden Apple Awd 1986; Leadership, Illinois Council on Exceptional Children 1989; Volunteer, DuSable Museum of African-American History 1987; Volunteer Award, Pace Institute, Cook County (Jail) Dept of Corrections 1979. **MILITARY SERVICE:** USAF A/2C admin spec 4 yrs; Distinguished Airman Award. **HOME ADDRESS:** 7138 S Bennett, Chicago, IL 60649. **BUSINESS ADDRESS:** Chicago Public Schools, DuSable High School, 4934 So Wabash, Chicago, IL 60609.

RICHARDSON, PAUL E. L.
Physician. **PERSONAL:** Born Dec 08, 1957, Paget, Bermuda;married Michele Y Halyard-Richardson; children: Hamilton Prescott Alexander. **EDUCATION:** Oakwood Coll, BA Chem 1979; Howard Univ Coll of Medicine, MD 1983. **CAREER:** Howard Univ Hosp Dept of Urology, resident physician 1985-. **ORGANIZATIONS:** Pres Greater Metro Adventist Medical-Dental Group 1978-79; academic vice pres United Student Movement Oakwood Coll Huntsville AL 1978-79; pres Howard Univ Hosp House Staff Assoc 1986-87. **HONORS/ACHIEVEMENTS:** Who's Who Among Students in Amer Univs & Colls 1979; Outstanding Young Men of Amer 1980; Papers presented "The Effects of Intraspinal Opiates on the Urinary Trace," presented at the Urologic Sct of the Natl Medical Assoc 1986, "Nephrogenic Adenoma in the Female Urethral Diverticulum," presented at the Urologic Sct of the Natl Medical Assoc 1986.

RICHARDSON, RALPH H.
Attorney. **PERSONAL:** Born Oct 12, 1935, Detroit, MI; son of Ralph Onazime Richardson (deceased) and Lucinda Fluence Richardson (deceased); divorced; children: Traci, Theron. **EDUCATION:** Wayne St U, BA 1964; Wayne St Law Sch, JD 1970. **CAREER:** City of Detroit, clerk, public aid worker 1956-65; Ford Motor Co, sr labor rel rep 1965-70, wage admin 1966, labor rel rep 1967; Citizens Urban Opportunity Fund, dir 1970; Brown Grier & Richardson PC, sr partner 1970-71; Richardson & Grier PC, sr partner 1971-73; Stone & Richardson PC, labor arbitrator, sr partner 1973-. **ORGANIZATIONS:** Mem Am MI Natl Wolverine Bar Assns; Am Arbitration Assn; MI Trial Lawyers Assn; Am Judicial Soc; MI Criminal Defense Lawyers; Phi Alpha Delta, Kappa Alpha Psi; Smithsonian Inst; Natl Geographic Soc; mem Recorder's Ct Bar Assn; Labor Arbitrators; Am Arbitration Assn; Mason; mem Grtr Detroit Chamber of Commerce; Palmer Woods Assn; Econ Club of Detroit; Renaissance Club; mem Detroit Bar Assn, Natl Bar Assoc, State Bar of MI, Amer Bar Assn, Amer Trial Lawyers Assoc, MI Assn of the Professional, Boy Scouts of Amer, Jr Vice Polemarch Northern Reg; appointed by Gov to serve on bd of appeals for Hosp Bed Reduction in Southeastern MI 1982; appointed special asst atty general by Frank J Kelley, Atty General for the State of MI 1984; mem Executive Bd Detroit Golden Gloves Inc.; mem Bd of Directo rs Legal Aid & Defenders Assoc. 1985; Hiram Lodge #1 1986; Wolverine Consistory #6 1988; Marracci Temple #13 (Shriners) 1988; David Leary Lodge #6 (G.E.M.) 1989. **HONORS/ACHIEVEMENTS:** Cert of Appreciation Native Amer Strategic Serv 1976; MI State Bar Young Lawyers Sect Prison Proj Serv Awd 1977; Awd of Merit Mother Waddles Perpetual Mission 1979; Distinguished Recognition Awd Detroit City Council 1081; Spirit of Detroit Awd Mayor Coleman Young 1981; Honored Citizen Awd Mayor Coleman Young 1981; Distinguished Detroit Citizen Awd Office of the City Clerk James Bradley 1981; life membership NAACP 1983; contributing supporter Golden Heritage (NAACP) 1989; appointed to committee on Child Care Homes by City Council member Mehaffey 1988-89. **MILITARY SERVICE:** AUS sp4 1958-60. **BUSINESS ADDRESS:** Labor Arbitrator, Sr Partner, Stone & Richardson PC, 1500 First Natl Building, Detroit, MI 48226.

RICHARDSON, ROBERT EUGENE
Attorney. **PERSONAL:** Born Jul 16, 1941, Kansas City, MO; son of Joseph Richardson and Genevieve Richardson; married Shirley Ann Durham; children: Kerri L, Patrick G. **EDUCATION:** Rockhurst Coll, KC, MO, 1959-62; Georgetown Univ, Washington, DC, AB 1972; Georgetown Univ Law School, JD 1975. **CAREER:** US Dept of Justice, special asst to the asst atty gen 1978; Georgetown U, asst to the exec vice pres 1970-74; US General Service, asst legal policy coordinator 1975-76; US Dept of Justice, trial atty 1976-78; Civil Div US Dept of Justice, sr trial atty 1979-85; Howard Univ, exec asst to vice pres for legal affairs & general counsel 1985-86; private practice, atty. **HONORS/ACHIEVEMENTS:** Academic Fellow Whitney M Young 1973-75. **MILITARY SERVICE:** AUS captain 1963-70; USAR 1970-84. **HOME ADDRESS:** 1371 Underwood St NW, Washington, DC 20012. **BUSINESS ADDRESS:** Attorney, 655 15th St NW, Ste 320, Washington, DC 20005.

RICHARDSON, RUPERT FLORENCE
Director. **PERSONAL:** Born Jan 14, 1930; divorced. **EDUCATION:** Southern Univ Baton Rouge, BS Educ 1952; McNeese State Univ, MEd Counseling & Guidance 1964. **CAREER:** Various positions as High School classroom teacher, 1952-64; LA Dept of Employment Security, master counselor 1965-74; Office of Medical Assistance Policy, health planning officer 1974-75; Div of Health Planning and Develop, dir of plan develop 1975-78; LA Div of Health Planning & Develop, asst dir 1978-81; Office of Mental Health and Substance Abuse, planning consultant 1981-85; State Office of Prevention and Recovery from Alcohol and Drug Abuse, dir div of special svcs/support svcs. **ORGANIZATIONS:** Mem Women in Politics; founder LA Chap Negro Business and Professional Women's Clubs; mem Alpha Kappa Sor Inc founder of Zeta Chap at McNeese State Coll; mem state organizer Top Ladies of Distinction Inc; mem Mayor-President's Commn on Needs of Women; mem NAACP Task Force on Excellence in Educ, NTE Validation Comm, LA Assoc of Business & Industry Educ Task Force; treas LA Employment Counselors Assoc; mem Amer & LA Personnel & Guid Assoc; mem Natl Voc Guid Assoc, Natl Employment Counselors Assoc, LA Conf of Social Welfare, LA Assoc of MH/SA Administrators; trustee Special Contribution Fund and Natl Housing Corp NAACP; mem Governor's Learning Adv Cncl; governor's appointee LA Endowment for the Humanities; mem Natl & LA Parliamentarians Assoc, State Mental Health Adv bd; natl vice pres NAACP; chairperson LA Citizens Comm on Solutions to Crime; organizer & chief staff mem LA Medical Care Adv Comm; chairperson bd of dirs Baton Rouge Assoc for Comm Action; mem LA Public Health Assoc, LA Conf of Social Welfare. **HONORS/ACHIEVEMENTS:** First black female to enter professional serv in LA Dept of Labor; first black to complete a Masters' prog at McNeese State Univ; first professional black female to work as counselor in a male prison; first female editor of a black newspaper in Lake Charles LA; listings Outstanding Minority Women Fisk Univ 1977,79,81,82; Intl Biographies London England 1978; Who's Who Among Amer Women 1978; World Personalities 1978; Who's Who in Black LA 1982; listed in Governor's Book "A New Committment to Black Louisianians" 1982; Community Service Awds Baton Rouge Chap Assoc of Black Social Workers 1978, Comm Assoc for Welfare of School Children1980, Alpha Kappa Alpha 1981; LA NAACP Champion of the Cause Awd 1979 (highest internal awd) 1979; Unsung Heroine Awd 1980; Woman of the Year Awd NAACP Women's Conference (Natl) 1981; selectged as Citizen Ambassador to Europe and Soviet Union People to People Inc 1983; Hon Faculty Member Nicholls State Univ 1983; Outstanding Alumnus Southern Univ 1984; 50 Women of Achievement 1900-1984 LA Pavillion 1984 World Exposition; Black Leadership Awd New Mexico State Conf NAACP. **BUSINESS ADDRESS:** Dir Div of Special/Support Serv, Ofc of Prevention & Recovery, from Alcohol & Drug Abuse, 2744-B Wooddale Blvd, Baton Rouge, LA 70305.

RICHARDSON, SCOVEL
Judge. **PERSONAL:** Born Feb 04, 1912, Nashville; married Inez; children: Elaine (Harrisingh), Alice Inez, Mary Louise (johnson), Marjorie Linda (Forsythe). **EDUCATION:** Univ of IL, AM 1936; Howard U, JD 1937; Lincoln U, LlD 1973. **CAREER:** US Customs Ct, judge 1957-; 3d Div, presiding judge 1966-70; US Bd of Parole Washington, chmn 1954-57; OPA Washington, sr atty 1943-44; dean prof law 1944-53; Lincoln U, asso prof law 1939-43; Lawrence Richardson Chgo, atty 1938-39. **ORGANIZATIONS:** Mem Am Law Inst; am Bar Assn; Am Judicature Soc; Inst of Judicial Adminstrn; Nat Bar Assn; Fed Bar Assn; MO Bar Assn; Bar Assn of St Louis; judiciary mem Assn of Bar of the City of New York 2nd vP Bd of Govs New Rochelle Hosp Med Center; trustee ColgateUniv HowardUniv Nat Council on Crime & Delinquency. **HONORS/ACHIEVEMENTS:** Recip Cit Urban League St Louis 1953; Alumni Award HowardUniv 1958; Nat Bar Assn 1967; Wisdom Award of Honor 1970; Intl Trade Serv Award 1973; cert in Appreciation of Merit Serv Standing Com Customs Law of Am Bar Assn 1974. **BUSINESS ADDRESS:** US Customs Ct 1 Fed Plaza, New York, NY 10007.

RICHARDSON, TIMOTHY
Clergyman. **PERSONAL:** Born Jul 18, 1942, Pittsburgh. **EDUCATION:** Franciscan Friar. **CAREER:** Black Catholic Sch Harlem, tchr religious edn. **ORGANIZATIONS:** Mem Black Catholic Clergy Caucus. **HONORS/ACHIEVEMENTS:** Featured Ebony Mag work in Isral 1972; Jerusalem & Bethlehem 1968-73.

RICHARDSON, WALTER P.
Dental surgeon. **PERSONAL:** Born Apr 16, 1907, Suffolk, VA; married Thelma; children: Joyce A, Walter P Jr. **EDUCATION:** VA State Coll, 1928; Meharry Med Coll, DDS 1932. **CAREER:** Franklin VA, self-employed dental surgeon 1932-. **ORGANIZATIONS:** Mem bd dir Turner Peanut Corp Capron VA; mem adv bd City of Franklin 1964-65; chrmn Franklin Redevel Housing Auth 1973, mem 1966-74; past master Holland Lodge #256 F&A Masons; past pres Epsilon Iota Lambda Chap Alpha Phi Alpha; past pres Old Dominion Dental Soc; trustee, mem New Hope Bapt Ch. **HONORS/ACHIEVEMENTS:** Recipient of Certificate of Appreciation from pres of US 1943; Certificate of Award Southampton Co Training Sch 1954; Distinguished Service Certificate City of Franklin 1974.

RICHARDSON, WAYNE MICHAEL
Attorney. **PERSONAL:** Born Sep 22, 1948, Philadelphia, PA. **EDUCATION:** Cheyney State Coll, BA 1970; Temple Univ Law Sch, JD 1976. **CAREER:** PA Dept of Education, regional legal counsel 1976-83; PA State System of Higher Education, chief legal counsel 1983-. **ORGANIZATIONS:** Mem Natl Assn of Coll & Univ Attys 1977-; mem Alpha Phi Alpha Frat 1968-; trustee PA Faculty Health & Welfare Fund. **BUSINESS ADDRESS:** Chief Legal Counsel, Penn State Syst Higher Educ, 301 Market St, Harrisburg, PA 17108.

RICHARDSON, WILLIAM J.
Spirits & wine importer executive. **PERSONAL:** Born Apr 30, 1933, Suffolk, VA; married Gertrude Flood; children: Traci L. **EDUCATION:** VA State Coll, BS 1954. **CAREER:** Schieffelin & Co, metro sales mgr 1981-84, sales serv dir 1984-85, dir urban market develop 1985-87, vice pres urban market development 1987-. **ORGANIZATIONS:** Bd of dirs Prince Hall Day Care 1971-, United Mutual Insurance Co 1977-; mem Natl Assoc Mktg Developers, NY Sales Executive Club. **HONORS/ACHIEVEMENTS:** NAACP Freedom Awd; Man of the Year Negro Business & Professional Women; Achievement Awd Amer Cancer Soc; Black Achievers Awd Harlem YMCA; Support to Youth Awd New York City. **HOME ADDRESS:** 144 Stuyvesant Rd, Teaneck, NJ 07666.

RICHIE, LEROY C.
Automotive executive. **PERSONAL:** Born Sep 27, 1941, Buffalo, NY; son of Leroy C Richie and Mattie Allen Richie; married Julia C Thomas, Jun 10, 1972; children: Brooke, Darcy. **EDUCATION:** City Coll of New York, BA 1970; New York Univ Sch of Law, JD 1973. **CAREER:** White & Case NY, attorney 1973-78; Federal Trade Commn, dir NY regional office 1978-83; Chrysler Corp, asst general counsel 1983-84, assoc general counsel 1984-86, vice pres/general counsel. **ORGANIZATIONS:** Chmn, Visiting Nurse Association; chmn, Highland Park Development Corporation; bd mem, Marygrove College; bd mem, St Josephs Hospital, Pontiac; bd mem; Detroit Bar Foundation. **HONORS/ACHIEVEMENTS:** Valedictorian, City College of New York 1970; Arthur Garfield Hays Civil Liberties Fellowship, New York Univ Law School 1972. **MILITARY SERVICE:** AUS sp4e4 4 yrs. **HOME ADDRESS:** 1900 West Lincoln, Birmingham, MI 48009.

RICHIE, LIONEL BROCKMAN
Singer/songwriter. **PERSONAL:** Born Jun 20, 1949, Tuskegee, AL; son of Lionel B Richie, Sr and Alberta Foster Richie; married Brenda Harvey, 1975. **EDUCATION:** Tuskegee Univ, Econ. **CAREER:** Mem of musical group The Mystics (name later changed to The Commodores); Brockman Music, Los Angeles, CA, pres; songwriter, composer of theme song for movie "Endless Love," "Lady," "All Night Long," "Truly," "Can't Slow Down," "Say You, Say Me," and "Dancing on the Ceiling.". **ORGANIZATIONS:** Mem UNCF, Amer Soc of Composers Authors and Publishers, Natl Acad of Recording Arts and Sciences, Amer Acad of Motion Picture Arts & Sciences, Natl Assoc of Songwriters. **HONORS/ACHIEVEMENTS:** 3 Platinum Albums; 4 Gold Albums; Grammy nominee 18 times; Amer Music Award, 1979, 1982(2), 1983(2), 1984, 1985(2), 1987(4); People's Choice Award for best song, 1979, 1980, 1982, 1983, 1986, and for best composer, 1981; Natl Music Publications award, 1980, 1981, 1984; Best Young Artist in Film, 1980; Grammy Award, 1982(2), 1985, 1986; Amer Movie Award, 1982; NAACP Image Award, 1983(2), NAACP Entertainer of Year Award, 1987; Black Gold Award, 1984(3); ASCAP Writer of Yr, 1984, 1985, 1986, ASCAP Publisher of Year, 1985, ASCAP Pop Award, 1987; Man of Yr, Children's Diabetes Foundation, 1984; Alumnus of Yr, United Negro Coll Fund, 1984; 1985 ABAA Music Awd for efforts in conceiving and giving leadership to USA and Africa, producing the album and video "We Are the World"; honorary DMus, Tuskegee Univ, 1986; Academy Awd (Say You, Say Me), 1986; Golden Globe awd, 1986; American Music Academy Awd, 1987(2). **BUSINESS ADDRESS:** The DeMann Entertainment Co, 9200 Sunset Blvd, Suite 915, Los Angeles, CA 90069.

RICHIE, SHARON IVEY
Military nursing. **PERSONAL:** Born Dec 14, 1949, Philadelphia, PA; daughter of William Joseph Richie Sr and Helen L Oglesby Richie (deceased); married Paul A Henri. **EDUCATION:** Wagner Coll, BS Nursing 1971; Univ of TX Grad Sch of Nursing, MSN 1976; military educ, AMEDD Officer Basic Course 1971, Psychiatric Mental Health Clinician Course 1972, Clinical Head Nurse Course 1973, Alcoholism Orientation Course 1977, AMEDD Officer's Adv Course 1979, Combat Psychiatry Course 1980, Command and Genl Staff Coll 1982, Field Combat Nursing Course 1984; US Army War College, Carlisle PA, Diploma 1987-88. **CAREER:** Walter Reed Army Medical Ctr, clinical staff nurse 1971-72, clinical ICU staff nurse 1972, asst head nurse 1972-74; Brooke Army Med Ctr, asst head nurse 1974-75; 5th Gen Hosp Germany, hospital psychiatric nurse consul & head nurse 1976-77; Alcoholism Treatment Facility, psychiatric clinical nurse specialist 1977-79; The Pentagon Office of Drug & Alcohol Abuse Prevention, asst dir educ & rehab 1980-82; The White House, White House fellow of-fice of intergovtl affairs 1982-83; 8th Evacuation Hosp, PROFIS chief nurse 1984-86; Letterman Army Med Ctr, chief ambulatory nursing serv 1984-86; Ft George G Meade Med Dept Activity, chief dept of nursing; Walter Reed Army Medical Center, Washington DC, Clinical Nursing Service, chief 1988-. **ORGANIZATIONS:** Sec White House Fellows Assn; mem Sigma Theta Tau, Natl Black Nurses Assn, Amer Nurses Assn, Drug & Alcohol Nurses Assn, Assn of the US Army, Assn of Military Surgeons of the US; regional comm White House Fellowship Comm; vice pres The Rocks Inc; vice pres, White House Fellows Alumni Assn and Foundation Board 1989-. **HONORS/ACHIEVEMENTS:** 12 presentations including "Racism in Psychiatry" 1975; "Psychological & Emotional Aspects of the Rape Victim" 1976; "Alcoholism Workshop" 1977-78; "Combat Nursing Are You Ready?" 1984; Alumni of the Yr Awd Wagner Coll 1983; White House Fellowship 1983; Sec of Defense Meritorious Medal; Sec of Defense Identification Badge; Martin Luther King Memorial Awd Wagner Coll; publications "Drug Abuse in the Military, An Adolescent Misbehavior Problem" 1983; "Nurses and Policy Making, Washington Fellowships" Nursing Economics 1983; publication, Combat Nurses: You Won't Be Alone, Military Review Vol LXIX No 1 1989 p65-73. **MILITARY SERVICE:** AUS Nurse Corps colonel 18 yrs; 3 Army Meritorious Serv Medals; Army Commendation Medal; Natl Defense Ribbon; Army Serv Ribbon; Overseas Ribbon; Secretary of Defense Meritorious Serv Medal. **HOME ADDRESS:** 1763 Albert Dr, Mitchellville, MD 20716. **BUSINESS ADDRESS:** Chief, Clinical Nursing Service, Walter Reed Army Medical Center, Department of Nursing, Washington, DC 20307.

RICHIE, WINSTON HENRY
Dentist. **PERSONAL:** Born Sep 18, 1925, Jersey City, NJ; son of Dr William F Richie and Celeste Strode Richie; married Beatrice, Sep 05, 1953; children: Winston, Jr, Beth E, Laurel L, Anne C. **EDUCATION:** Adebert Coll Western Reserve Univ, BS 1948; Western Reserve Univ, DDS 1952. **CAREER:** East Suburban Council for Open Communities, exec dir 1952-86; Winston H Richie DDS Inc , retired dentist (35 years). **ORGANIZATIONS:** Mem American Dental Assn; Cleveland Dental Soc; Ohio State Dental Assn; Elder Fairmount Presbyterian Church 1972-75; pres Fair Housing Inc; Shaker Heights City Council 1972-; Shaker Heights City Council 1972-84, vice mayor 1977. **HONORS/ACHIEVEMENTS:** Distinguished Service in Open Housing Award given by Cuyahoga Plan of Cleveland; invited to Australia to represent the Ford Foundation & Harvard Univ discussing racial integration in the USA. **MILITARY SERVICE:** USN seaman 2nd cl 1944-46. **BUSINESS ADDRESS:** Executive Dir, East Suburban Council, 5010 Mayfield Rd #201, Lyndhurst, OH 44124.

RICHMOND, DELORES RUTH
Executive relocation director, broker associate, realtor. **PERSONAL:** Born May 28, 1951, Chicago, IL; daughter of Arthur Lee Freeman and Mamie Elizabeth McBride Freeman; married Larson Richmond, Oct 18, 1980 (divorced); children: Tesha Elizabeth, Dwayne L, Nicole L'Nae. **EDUCATION:** Chicago College of Commerce, Chicago, IL, 1975-76; Prairie State College, Chicago Heights, IL, 1980-81; Real Estate Education School, South Holland, IL, certificate, 1985; Real Estate Education School, Homewood, IL, realator broker's certificate, 1989. **CAREER:** US Federal Government, Chicago, IL, Administrator, 1970-79; Continen-

tal Bank, Matteson, IL, assistant supervisor, 1981-84; TV 38 Christian Station and Radio, Chicago, IL, studio audience coordinator, 1984-87; Century 21 Dabbs & Associates, Homewood, IL, broker, associate relocation director, 1985-. **ORGANIZATIONS:** Member, Homewood Full Gospel Church, 1981-; member, NAACP, 1982-; president, Today Is Your Day, 1984-, member of board of directors, Century 21 Dabbs & Associates, 1986-; member, Jack and Jill, 1988-; publicity director, Women's Council of Realators, 1988-. **HONORS/ACHIEVEMENTS:** Bronze, Silver, and Gold medals, Illinois Association of Realtors, 1986-89; Centurian Award, National Century 21, 1987, 1988; appreciation award, Ford Motor Company, 1987, 1988, 1989; Kizzy Award, Kizzy Scholarship Fund Foundation, 1989; has received hundreds of other real estate awards. **HOME ADDRESS:** 18850 Morgan Street, Homewood, IL 60430. **BUSINESS ADDRESS:** Broker Associate-Relocation Director, Century 21 Dabbs & Associates, 17804 South Halsted, Washington Park Plaza, Homewood, IL 60430.

RICHMOND, HAROLD O.
Business executive, engineer, lawyer. **PERSONAL:** Born Apr 21, 1938, NYC; married Carole W Vaugh; children: Jenniffer Cynthia, Matthew. **EDUCATION:** City Coll NY, BEE 196i; Wayne State U, MBA 1973, JD 1978. **CAREER:** Ralph M Parsons Co, mgr engrng & support, corp dir quality assurance 1979-; Detroit Edison Co, asst vice pres 1975-79, dir eng dept 1971-73; Ralph M Parsons Co, LA, proj mgr 1968-71, 1956-71. **ORGANIZATIONS:** Pres Econ Devel Corp, Greater Detroit 1973-; mem State Bar of MI; reg prof engr NY, MI; mem Eng Soc Detroit; Am Nuclear Soc; Inst E & E Engrs; Nat & MI Soc Professional Engrs; MI Inter-assn Black Bus & Eng Students; Am Mgmt Assn; Econ Club Detroit; Booker T Washington Businessmen's Assn; chmn Sch Adv Bd 1972-73; served Mayor's 10 Pt Prgm Devel Task Force 1973; TV appearances.

RICHMOND, ISABEL See SANFORD, ISABEL G.

RICHMOND, MYRIAN PATRICIA
City official. **PERSONAL:** Born Sep 28, 1942, Birmingham, AL; divorced; children: Brian, Kevin. **EDUCATION:** Lane Coll, BA 1965; Atlanta Univ, 1971-72. **CAREER:** Beauford Cty Schools, teacher 1967-69; WAOK Radio, writer/reporter 1973-76, news dir 1976-78; Fulton Cty Govt, info officer 1978-. **ORGANIZATIONS:** Consult The Onyx Corp 1973-75; alumna Leadership Atlanta 1980-;TV show host GA Public TV 1981-84; consult Martin L King Ctr 1982-84; mem Atlanta Assoc of Black Journalists 1984-85; bd mem Neighborhood Arts Ctr 1984-85. **HONORS/ACHIEVEMENTS:** Who's Who Among Students Lane Coll 1965; Media Woman of the Year Natl Assoc Media Women 1975; Essence Woman Essence Mag 1975; SCLC Achievement Awd Natl SCLC 1983; GA Black Women Honoree GA Coaltion of Black Women 1984-85. **BUSINESS ADDRESS:** Information Officer, Fulton County Government, 165 Central Ave SW #409, Atlanta, GA 30303.

RICHMOND, NORRIS L.
Educator, dentist. **PERSONAL:** Born Jun 19, 1931, Gary, IN; married Conden L Green; children: Taiyan, Tish. **EDUCATION:** IN U, BS 1959, DDS 1963, MSD 1965. **CAREER:** IN Univ School of Dentistry, full prof 1963-; IN Girl's School, staff dentist 1964-; private practice, Indianapolis 1963-66. **ORGANIZATIONS:** Mem Psi Omega; IN Dental Assn; Am Dental Assn; Indianapolis Dist Dental Soc; IN Pub Health Dentists Orgn; Am Assn of Pub Health Dentists; Am Academy of Gold Foil Operators; mem Student Affairs Com IN U; consult IN Health Careers; mem Housing Oppor Multiplied Ecumenically; Amateur Organists Assn Internat; couns to dental students; mem Hygienist Adm Com; mem Omicron Kappa Upsilon Theta Theta Chpt. **HONORS/ACHIEVEMENTS:** Best Dress Instr, INUniv 1973; "Cool Breeze" award, INUniv 1975; Golden Hatchet Award, INUniv 1977. **MILITARY SERVICE:** USAF ssgt 1952-56. **BUSINESS ADDRESS:** 1121 W Michigan St, Indianapolis, IN 46202.

RICHMOND, TYRONZA R.
Educator. **PERSONAL:** Born Jan 27, 1940, Memphis, TN; married Carol Kelly; children: Mark, Kelly. **EDUCATION:** Fisk Univ, BA (Cum Laude) 1962; American Univ, MA 1967; Purdue Univ, PhD 1971. **CAREER:** US Naval Weapons Lab, math/oper rsch 1962-72; Howard Univ, assoc dean business 1972-77; NC Central Univ, dean sch of business 1977-86, chancellor 1986-. **ORGANIZATIONS:** Consultant Federal Insurance Admin 1974, Alcoa 1974-76, EPA 1979; mem bd of dirs INROADS, Amer Assembly Coll & Schs. **BUSINESS ADDRESS:** Chancellor, North Carolina Central Univ, 1801 Fayetteville St, Durham, NC 27707.

RICKETTS, DAVID WILLIAM
Professional athlete. **PERSONAL:** Born Jul 12, 1935, Pottstown, PA; son of Richard John Ricketts and Margaret Lewis Ricketts; married Barbara Boswell, Aug 17, 1957; children: Marie Candace Ricketts-Powell. **EDUCATION:** Duquesne U, BA. **CAREER:** St Louis Cardinals, catcher 1967-69; Pittsburgh Pirates, catcher/bullpen coach 1970-73; St Louis Cardinals, coach 1974-; John Fisher Coll, coached basketball. **ORGANIZATIONS:** World Series 1967 & 1968; coach, World Series 1971, 1982, 1985, 1987. **HONORS/ACHIEVEMENTS:** Pennsylvania (Keystone) Hall of Fame; Duquesne Univ Hall of Fame. **MILITARY SERVICE:** AUS 1st Lt. 1957-59. **BUSINESS ADDRESS:** St Louis Cardinals, 250 Stadium Plaza, St Louis, MO 63102.

RICKMAN, LEWIS DANIEL, SR.
Business executive. **PERSONAL:** Born Aug 20, 1900, Middleport, OH; married Odella McCoy; children: Duana Johnson, Lewis, Cassandra, Earl, Dellria, Eileen Ramsey, Marcel Alexander, James. **EDUCATION:** Wilberforce Univ, BS (Cum Laude) 1944; Meharry Med Coll, MD 1947. **CAREER:** Wright-Patterson Air Force Base Allison Motor Parts, suprv 1941-43; Rickman Med Clinic, owner. **ORGANIZATIONS:** 1st black on med staff St Joseph Hosp Mt Clemens 1949; charter mem & bd dir Mt Clemens YMCA 1958-60, Macomb Clinic Guid Clinic 1964-66; pres Macomb Cty NAACP 1966-70; sec med staff St Joseph Hosp 1968-70; consult Camall Co 1968-76; bd of dir MI Cancer Soc 1968-76; med examiner Mt Clemons City 1970-73; exec comm St Joseph Hosp 1974-76; dep med examiner Macomb Cty 1974-79. **HONORS/ACHIEVEMENTS:** Beta Kappa Chi Natl Hon Sci Frat 1943; 1st black professional Macomb Cty 1949; bd of trustees 1950, chairperson 1968-, treas 1968-71, Turmer Chapel; 1st blackelected official 1960, pres 1982-84, Mt Clemons Bd of Ed; 1st black mem 1970, chairperson 1972-76 Macomb Cty Selective Serv Bd #52; Most Outstanding Black Bicentennial Celebration Mt Clemons 1976; Brother & Sister Awd Macomb Cty Interfaith 1982; Pres Detroit Dist CME Church Bd of Trustees 1984-; Comm on Mortgages Abstracts & Deed MI-IN Conf CME Church 1984-; Alpha Phi Alpha; Master Mason 32 Degree; Shriner; Macomb Cty Med Soc; MI State Med Soc; Amer Med Soc; Natl Med Soc. **MILITARY SERVICE:** ASTP ROTC pfc 18 mo. **HOME ADDRESS:** 158 Clemens St, Mount Clemens, MI 48043.

RICKMAN, RAY
State official. **PERSONAL:** Born Nov 25, 1948, Galatin, TN; son of James Bailey Rickman. **EDUCATION:** Eastern Michigan Univ, Ypsilanti MI, attended 1967-68; Wayne State Univ, Detroit MI, BA 1971. **CAREER:** US Congressman John Conyers, Detroit MI, chief asst 1971-74; Jeff Chalmers Non-Profit Corp, exec dir 1974-77; Harmony Village Non-Profit Corp, exec dir 1977-79; MA Medicaid Handicapped Program, dir 1979; Police Abuse Housing Issues, lecturer; Providence Human Relations Commn, exec dir 1979-; Affirmative Action, cons; MA Housing Finance Agency, equal opportunity officer 1982-85; Cornerstone Books, owner 1985-; General Assembly of RI, state rep 1986-; Shades-Talk Show, host, producer 1986-. **ORGANIZATIONS:** Pres Friends of Belle Isle, Detroit MI, 1974-78; bd mem ACLU of RI 1979-80; bd mem NAACP RI Chapter 1980-82; commr Providence Historic Dist Commn 1986-; mem Rhode Island Historical Soc 1989-. **HONORS/ACHIEVEMENTS:** Numerous awards City of Detroit, County of Wayne, State of MI & Civ Org; City of Providence-Resolution 1987; Talk Show Host of the Year 1988; many op-ed articles in Detroit Free Press, Detroit News, Providence Journal, Maine Times 1971-. **HOME ADDRESS:** 19 Pratt St, Providence, RI 02906.

RICKS, ALBERT WILLIAM
Clergyman. **PERSONAL:** Born Jul 10, 1900, Jonesburg, MO; married Lillian Evelyn Thomas. **EDUCATION:** Ward Grad Sch; Stone Coll; Smith Coll; Hampton Inst; NWHS. **CAREER:** Missionary Coffee Mission, W Africa 1936-41; pastor in Can, US. **ORGANIZATIONS:** St Luke AME Zion Ch; NAACP; Urban League; pres Florence Critten Homes for Unwed Mothers; Emancipation Assn; mem Ch Missionary Dept Gen Missionary Bd Coun Nat Voters League; Intl Minsterial Alliance; counclmn Pine Bluff, AR, Jefferson Co; Minister Assn; YMC Assn. **BUSINESS ADDRESS:** 3937 12th Ave N, Birmingham, AL 35204.

RICKS, GEORGE R.
Educator, administrator, applied behavio. **PERSONAL:** Born Oct 09, 1924, Washington, DC; divorced; children: Lynne L, Jeanne M. **EDUCATION:** Northwestern U, BMEd 1948, MA 1949, PhD 1960;Univ of ME, grad Studies 1969;Univ Cape Coast, Ghana, 1970;Univ Ibadan, Nigeria, 1970; Howard U,Univ of CT, Nat Coll of Ed, additional studies. **CAREER:** Chicago Public School, teacher 1953-59; Chicago City Coll, instr 1960-63; Northeastern IL State Coll, asst prof 1963-64; Chicago State Coll, asso prof 1964-65; Northwestern Univ NDEA Summer Inst for Advanced Study for Teachers of Disadvantaged Youth, appointed to faculty 1965; Northeastern IL State Coll, instr grad studies in disadvantagement 1966-69; Dept of Human Relations, Chicago Public School, dir human relations 1961-. **ORGANIZATIONS:** Mem Soc for Applied Anthropology; Am Anthropology Assn; Phi Delta Kappa; Am Soc for Training & Devel; Orgn Devel Network of NTL, Orgn Renewal Inc; Aesthetic Dynamics Inc; rsrch spl IL Comm on Human Rel; inst bilingual prgm Spanish Speaking Students, Chicago StateUniv 1974; EEO planner spl IL Sch Dist; Samuel B Stratton Educ Assn; mem Am Red Cr; mem bd dir & chmn Youth Serv; jr warden vestry Trinity Epis Ch; hearing bd Univ Civil Serv Sys of IL; Nat Urban League; NAACP; Assn for Study of Negro Life & History; Afro-Am Music Opportunities Inc; Alpha Phi Alpha. **HONORS/ACHIEVEMENTS:** NorthwesternUniv Alumni Assn recip Rockefeller Fam/African Am Inst Study Grant 1970; Who's Who in the Midwest 1972-73; Intl Men of Achvmt Award, Cambridge England 1974; author of numerous publs. **MILITARY SERVICE:** AUS 1942-45. **BUSINESS ADDRESS:** 228 N La Salle St, Chicago, IL 60601.

RICKSON, GARY AMES
Artist. **PERSONAL:** Born Aug 12, 1942, Boston, MA; married Kianga, Tianee, Alea;; children: Kianga Akua, Tiance Rayna, Alea Sekua. **EDUCATION:** Ministry Degree, 1964. **CAREER:** Boston African Amer Artist, pres 1964-68; Harvard Radio Brdcst Corp, artist-poet 1974-84. **ORGANIZATIONS:** Cultural advsr Roxbury YMCA 1984-85; pub reltns Boston African Amer Artists 1985-; mem Boston Urban Gardeners 1984-; -Roxbury Boys Club 1970. **HONORS/ACHIEVEMENTS:** Began Mural Mvmnt in Boston 1968; Outstanding Roxbury Cit Awd Black Bros Assoc 1970; Natl Endwmnt Grant 1970; Champ of Black Youth Award-Roxbury Boys Club 1970. **HOME ADDRESS:** 111 Dewitt Dr, Roxbury, MA 02119.

RIDDICK, EUGENE E.
Business executive. **PERSONAL:** Born Jan 23, 1938, Lee Hall, VA; son of James Wesley Riddick and Gertrude (Burks) Reid; married Evelyn G McNeese, Sep 08, 1962; children: Eric. **EDUCATION:** Howard Univ, BSME 1961; State of NJ, Prof Engrs License 1970. **CAREER:** Gibbs & Cox, Inc, asst engr 1963-64; MW Kellogg, sr engr 1964-70; Badger Engrs, Inc, mgr, fired heaters 1970-74, mgr, piping engrg 1974-79, mgr engrg aux 1979-82, mgr heat transfer 1982-. **ORGANIZATIONS:** Mbr ASME 1972-; chmn API Manuf & Contractors S/C on Fired Heaters 1984-; treas First Parish Unitarian Church 1980-82, chrmn, Art Comm 1980-87. **HONORS/ACHIEVEMENTS:** Black Achiever of 1989, Boston YMCA 1989. **MILITARY SERVICE:** AUS first lt 2 yrs. **HOME ADDRESS:** 31 Juniper Brook Rd, Northboro, MA 01532. **BUSINESS ADDRESS:** Manager, Badger Engineers Inc, One Broadway, Cambridge, MA 02142.

RIDDICK, LOUISE K.
Educator. **PERSONAL:** Born Dec 09, 1917, Slabfork, WV; married George E Riddick. **EDUCATION:** WV St Coll, BA 1941; NY U, M 1956; NY U, 6th yr cert adv study 1964. **CAREER:** Greenbrier Cnty, prin teacher 1941-49; US Gvmt Serv, 1948-49; relief prin teacher 1949-60; Roanok Cty Public School, educ specialist 1966-. **ORGANIZATIONS:** Mem Natl Council Negro Wmn; pres Coun Exceptional Chldrn Chap 134; pres Spl Ed Dept Dist P VA Ed Assoc; NEAVEAREA Roanoke Council Retarded Ctzns; reg dir Delta Sigma Theta Inc Amer Assoc Mental Deficiency. **HONORS/ACHIEVEMENTS:** ARC vol Delta Yr Awd 1970; Jennie Brewer Awd outstnd tchr handicapped chldrn 1973; Notable Am of the Bicentennial Era 1976; outstnd ldr in Elen & Second Sch 1976; Comm Ldr & Noteworthy Am 1976, 77; Notable Am 1976-77; World Who's Who of Women 1976; Personalities of the S 1977; Dictionary of Intl Biography 1977. **BUSINESS ADDRESS:** 3601 Ferncliff Ave NW, Roanoke, VA 24017.

RIDDLE, BEDFORD NEAL
Physician. **PERSONAL:** Born Nov 06, 1899, York, SC; married Winifred Harvey. **EDUCATION:** Howard U, BS 1924; Howard U, MD 1927. **CAREER:** Akron Gen Med Ctr, Akron City Hosp, hon staff of St Thomas; Soc of Akron OH, past pres ob-gyn; St Thomas & Akron Gen Med Ctr, privl staff; Akron City Hosp, sr staff ob-gyn. **ORGANIZATIONS:** NAACP; past pres Akron Chap of Frontiers Internat; 100 Men Club of Am; mem Wesley Temple AME Ch; bd trst past treas. **HONORS/ACHIEVEMENTS:** 53 yrs serv in prac of med awd HowardUniv Med Alumni 1977; recog awd 50 yrs parc of med & serv from med colleagues patients & friends. **BUSINESS ADDRESS:** 157 W Cedar St, Akron, OH 44307.

RIDGEL, GUS TOLVER
Educator. **PERSONAL:** Born Jul 01, 1926, Poplar Bluff; son of Herford S Ridgel and Lue Emma Davis Ridgel; married Gertrude Cain Ridgel; children: Betty Bolden. **EDUCATION:** Lincoln Univ, Jefferson City, MO, BS, 1947-50; Univ of MO, Columbia, MO, MA, 1950-51; Univ of WI, Madison, WI, Ph.D., 1956. **CAREER:** Fort Valley State Coll, Ft Valley, GA, head dept of business, 1952-58; Wiley Coll, Marshall, TX, dean academic affairs, 1958-60; Kentucky State Univ, Frankfort, KY, dean, School of Business, 1960-84; Central State Univ, Wilberforce, OH, vice pres, academic affairs, 1972-74; Southern Univ, Baton Rouge, vice pres academic affairs, 1985. **ORGANIZATIONS:** Mem of advisory bd, Republic Savings Bank, 1983-86; mem of LA Univ, Marine Consortium Council, 1986-. **HONORS/ACHIEVEMENTS:** Univ of Missouri-Columbia, The Gus T Ridgel Minority Graduate Fellowship, 1988. **MILITARY SERVICE:** Army, CPL, 1945-46. **HOME ADDRESS:** 4929 Parkoaks Dr, Baton Rouge, LA 70816.

RIDGES-HORTON, LEE ESTHER
Physician. **PERSONAL:** Born Jan 27, 1951, Bennettsville, SC; married Michael Earl Horton; children: Steven Bernard Ridges. **EDUCATION:** NIH Rsch Spelman Coll, trainee 1974-75; Spelman Coll, cum laude BS biology 1975; Meharry Med Coll, MD 1980. **CAREER:** GA Ave Southside Day Care, teacher's asst 1975-76; Martin Luther King Gen Hosp, pediatric intern 1980-81; USA, med officer 1981-86; Fed Civil Svc, med officer 1987-. **ORGANIZATIONS:** Mem Amer Med Assoc, Southern Med Assoc; youth instr Amer Red Cross 1987-, Amer Acad of Family Physicians. **HONORS/ACHIEVEMENTS:** Listed in Who's Who in Amer Coll & Univ 1974-75; mem Beta Kappa Chi Scientific Honor Soc. **MILITARY SERVICE:** USA capt 5 yrs; Army Serv Ribbon 1982. **BUSINESS ADDRESS:** Medical Officer, US Government Europe, 536th Gen Dispensary, APO New York, NY 091773494.

RIDGEWAY, BILL TOM
Zoology educator. **PERSONAL:** Born Aug 26, 1927, Columbia, MO; married Leta M Baker; children: Mark B, Myra Chesser, Beth A. **EDUCATION:** Freidns Univ of Wichita KS, AB 1951; Wichita Univ KS, MS 1958; Univ of MO Columbia, PhD 1966. **CAREER:** Wichita State Univ Wichita, grad rsch asst 1956-58; SW Coll Winfield KS, asst prof of zoology 1958-66; Univ of MO Columbia, asst prof of zoology 1966; IL Dept of Conservation, contract rsch sci 1970-; Univ of MD, visiting prof 1976; E IL Univ, prof of zoology 1966-. **ORGANIZATIONS:** Regional dir Alpha Phi Alpha 1969-77; dir Afro-Amer Studies Prog Eastern IL Univ 1971-73; rsch assoc 1974, vstg prof 1975, Natural Resources Inst Univ of MD 1974; treas Concerned Citizens of Charleston Assoc NAACP 1975-; prog officer 1981, presiding officer 1985, Midwest Conf of Parasitologists; mem spec ministries commn 1982, soc concerns commn Episcopal Diocese of Springfield; pres Rotary Club of Charleston 1986. **HONORS/ACHIEVEMENTS:** Graduate Fellowship in Zoology Wichita State Univ 1957; NSF Fellowship Univ of WA Marine Sta 1960; NSF Fellowship Univ of MI Biol Sta 1961-62; Rsch Fellowship in Zool Univ of MO Columbia 1963-66. **MILITARY SERVICE:** AUS 1945-47. **BUSINESS ADDRESS:** Professor of Zoology, E Illinois University, Department of Zoology, Charleston, IL 61920.

RIDGEWAY, WILLIAM C.
Business executive. **PERSONAL:** Born Sep 24, 1942, Selma, AL; married Charlotte A Nicholson; children: Traci L, Kristina L. **EDUCATION:** TN St U, BSEE 1965. **CAREER:** Chevy Motor Div, auto engr 1965-67; IBM Corp, jr component eng 1967-68; IBM Corp assoc component eng 1968-69; IBM Corp, sr assoc component eng 1969-72; IBM Corp, staff component eng 1972-73; IBM Corp, proj eng 1973-76; proj mgr 1976-. **ORGANIZATIONS:** IBM Golf Club; mem IEEE; vice pres Sr Class TN St U. **BUSINESS ADDRESS:** 555 Bailey Ave, PO Box 50020 Dept H83 Bldg G13, San Jose, CA 95150.

RIDLEY, ALFRED DENIS
Educator. **PERSONAL:** Born Jun 23, 1948, Kingston, Jamaica;married Pamela; children: Andrew, Jon. **EDUCATION:** Univ of the West Indies, MSc 1977; Clemson Univ, PhD 1982. **CAREER:** Jamaica Public Serv Co, mgr system planning 1970-79; Clemson Univ, lecturer 1979-82; George Mason Univ, prof 1982-84; Howard Univ, prof of information systems & analysis. **ORGANIZATIONS:** Pres Engineering Mgmt Consultants 1983-. **HONORS/ACHIEVEMENTS:** Jamaica Industrial Govt Scholarship 1965; JPS Co Scholarship 1974; Intl Atomic Energy Agency Fellowship 1977; paper "Economic conductor size under load growth conditions, constrained by load limited life times" 1978; OAS Fellowship 1980; paper "A spectgral analysis of the power market in South Carolina" 1981; monograph "Fourcast-multivariate spectral time series analysis & forecasting" 1984; review "Promoting Management Science" PBS TV course 1986. **HOME ADDRESS:** 10430 Collingham Dr, Fairfax, VA 22032.

RIDLEY, CHARLES ROBERT
Educator. **PERSONAL:** Born Aug 06, 1948, Philadelphia, PA; married Iris Rochelle Smith; children: Charles, Charliss. **EDUCATION:** Taylor Univ, BA 1970; Ball State Univ, MA 1971; Univ of MN, PhD 1978. **CAREER:** VA Hosp, psychology intern 1974-76; IN Univ, asst prof 1977-79; Univ of MD Coll Park, asst prof 1979-80; Personnel Decisions Inc, consult psych 1980-83; Fuller Theol Sem Grad School of Psych, asst prof of psych. **ORGANIZATIONS:** Bd mem Urban League Marion IN 1971-73; mem Amer Psych Assoc 1977-; consult Private Practice 1983-. **HONORS/ACHIEVEMENTS:** Rsch Grant Spencer Found 1978; "Clinical Treatment of the Nondisclosing Black Client, A Therapeutic Paradox" Amer Psych 1984. **BUSINESS ADDRESS:** Asst Prof of Psychology, Fuller Theological Seminary, 177 N Madison Ave, Grad Schl of Psychology FTS, Pasadena, CA 91101.

RIDLEY, HARRY JOSEPH
Educational administrator. **PERSONAL:** Born Oct 08, 1923, Baton Rouge, LA; married Yvonne F Bozonier; children: Alexander J, Harry M. **EDUCATION:** Spaulding Bus Coll, bus mgmt 1949-50; Southern U, BA Educ 1953; SoutherUniv & LA State U, MaA Educ plus 30 hrs 1967. **CAREER:** E Baton Rouge Parish Comm School, adminstr supr 1970-; E Baton Rouge Parish Adult Educ Prog, intgr spl 1953-70; Wilbert Elem School, prin 1957-58; New Roads High Sch, athl coach 1953-57; Exxon USA Baton Rouge Refinery, supr testing 1975-80; EBR Parish Continuing Educ Prog, pub rel spl 1970-80; Head Start Prog, educ tech asst 1976-80. **ORGANIZATIONS:** Active mem Phi Delta Kappa LSU Chap 1975-80; active mem Nat Educ Assn 1953-80; active mem Nat Comm Educ Assn 1970-80; mem LA Assn for Pub Continuing Adult Edn; mem E Baton Rouge Parish Supr Assn. **HONORS/ACHIEVEMENTS:** Outstnd personality awd SouthernUniv 1953; outstnd tchr awd EBR Parish Educ Assn 1967; head start awd Comm Action Inc 1972-77; outstnd citz awd key to city City of Baton Rouge 1978; LUTC & CLU awd Ins Underwriters Assn 1979; 1st registered supr of comm sch in LA; plaques comm serv awds & letters ofappre from numerous orgn & Assn; 5 battle stars good conduct & army of occupation awd AUS. **MILITARY SERVICE:** AUS sgt 1943-49. **BUSINESS ADDRESS:** E Baton Rouge Parish Comm Schs, 2928 College Dr, Baton Rouge, LA 70808.

RIDLEY, MAY ALICE
Educational director. **PERSONAL:** Born in Nashville, TN; widowed; children: Donald G Jr, Yvonda P. **EDUCATION:** TN State Univ, BS 1959, MS 1967; Univ of Pittsburgh, PhD 1982. **CAREER:** Metro Public Schools, tchr 1962-84; Univ Pittsburgh, asst prof 1975-76; TN State Univ, adjunct prof 1982-; Dept of Ed, State, dir of staff 1984; Tennessee Dept of Educ, exec admin asst to the commr of educ. **ORGANIZATIONS:** Mem TN State Bd of Ed 1981-; chr of special schls Comm TN State Bd of Ed 1982-83; mem Metro Nashville Human Rel Comm; mem St Vincent de Paul Church, Alpha Kappa Alpha Sor, Phi Delta Kappa Ed Frat; pres Parthenon Chapter of the Links Inc. **HONORS/ACHIEVEMENTS:** Alumnus of Year, TN State Univ 1978-79, Phi Alpha Theta Honor Soc, TN Colonel State Honor, Award of Appreciation from Nashville Mayor 1979; Humanitarian Award, TN State Univ 1985. **HOME ADDRESS:** 2027 Clintondale Dr, Nashville, TN 37218.

RIER, JOHN PAUL, JR.
Educator. **PERSONAL:** Born Apr 10, 1925, Boyce, VA; married Nadine Smith; children: John III, David. **EDUCATION:** VA State Coll, BS 1947; Howard U, MS 1950; Harvard U, AM 1958; Harvard U, PhD 1960. **CAREER:** Graduate prof 1974-; Graduate School Howard Univ, prof asso dean 1971-74; Rutgers Coll, prof 1968-71; Howard Univ, 1959-68. **ORGANIZATIONS:** Mem Am Soc Botany Soc of Devel & Biologists; Sci Adv Bd; Ecology Adv Com Environ Protection Agency 1976-; Nat Med Flwsp for Grad Study. **HONORS/ACHIEVEMENTS:** 10 rsrch articles; distgsd serv awdUniv Without Walls; awd of distinction Howard Grad Sch. **BUSINESS ADDRESS:** Dept Botany, HowardUniv, Washington, DC 20059.

RIGBY, EDWARD H.
Educator. **PERSONAL:** Born Jul 29, 1943, Gadsden, AL; married Marilyn Evans; children: Shawn M, Duane E. **EDUCATION:** A&MUniv AL, BS 1966; Case Western Reserve U, MA 1971. **CAREER:** Case Western Reserve Univ, dir youth devel prog; Urban League St Acad, teacher; Cleveland Bd Educ Cuyahoga County Welfare, social worker. **ORGANIZATIONS:** Adv Vet's Club; Task Force Comm; Proj Am Assoc Comm & Jr Coll; NAACP.

RIGGINS, LESTER
Educator, administrator. **PERSONAL:** Born Dec 08, 1928, Marshall, TX; son of John Riggins and Effie Riggins; married Marvell; children: 6. **EDUCATION:** FSC, BA 1951, IN Univ, MBA 1962; Fed City, MA 1974; USC, DPA prog. **CAREER:** Advocate Newspaper, owner pres bd 1976; State of CA, dept of genl serv dir; counselor Grank Skill Center; Askia World Game System Inc, secty/treas KA2 prods. **ORGANIZATIONS:** Mem Amer Personal & Guidance Assn 1971-75; senator CSUF 1971-75; coord Ethnic Studies CSUF 1971-76; mem Amer Legion Post 511; Bass-Black Advocates in State Serv 1977-83; Educators to Africa Assn; Reserve Officer Assn; Woodlin Lodge #30 Prince Hall Masons; mem Black Polit Council; mem Sacto Chap NAACP; central vice pres BAPAC 1979-; mem Victoria Consistory #25, Menelik Temple #36; mem CA Dem Council Black Caucus, Phi Gamma Mu; mem Fresno Dem Coalition; mem Affirmative Action Comm Sacto Unified Sch Dist; mem Affirmative Action Comm City of Sacto; pres Fannie Lou Hamer Democratic Club 1987-; mem AARP. **HONORS/ACHIEVEMENTS:** Outstanding ROTC Cadet 1951; Blue Key Honor Soc 1950-51; Troy Awd 1974; Advocates Awd 1977; LABBA Presidents Awd 1979-81; Alpha Man of the Year 1985; Outstanding Democratic Activist 1988; lifetime mem Urban League, Sacto 1987; nominee Community Award Human Rights, Fair Housing Commn of Sacramento CA. **MILITARY SERVICE:** USAF lt col 1951-71. **BUSINESS ADDRESS:** Secty/Treas, Askia World Game System Inc, 1033 Fairweather Drive, Sacramento, CA 95833.

RIGGS, ELIZABETH A.
Attorney. **PERSONAL:** Born Jan 02, 1942, Camden, NJ; children: Luke, Michael, Adam. **EDUCATION:** Bennett Coll, BA 1963; Rutgers Univ Sch of Law, JD 1973. **CAREER:** San Diego Co Prog, dep dist atty; State of CA, deputy atty gen 1977-79; El Cajon Judicial Dist, judge municipal ct 1979-84, presiding judge 1984-. **ORGANIZATIONS:** Dir YWCA Greensboro NC 1964-65; Camden City OEO; Neighborhood Youth Corp Coord; dir Head Start 1966-68; Rutgers Univ Proj Talent Search 1968-70; Citizens Adv Bd Rutgers Univ 1970-73; mem CA State Bar 1974-; chmn Min Affairs Comm San Diego City Bar 1978-79; bd of dirs Black Atty Assn; Legal Aid SocLawyers Club 1977-79; mem San Diego Co Black Atty's Assn 1974-; mem CA Assn of Black Lawyers 1976-; mem Dimensions 1977-; mem Speakers Bur San Diego Co Natl Conf of Negro Women; Mayors Comm on Status of Women; dimensions & charter 100 Professional Womens Associations; mem Natl Assn of Women Judges; mem CA Judges Assn; mem Co Women's Network; mem Soroptimist Intl. **HONORS/ACHIEVEMENTS:** Woman of the Yr San Diego Tribune 1974; CA Women in Govt Law & Justice Awd; Earl B Gillian Bar Assn Comm Appreciation Awd 1984; Disting Service Awd 1982; Women's Criminal Defense Appreciation Awd 1983; Disting Serv Awd Black Student Union Grossmont Coll 1981; San Diego Superior Court Valuable Serv Awd 1983; Black Achievement Awd In Law 1980; Delta Epsilon Chap Kappa Alpha Psi Awd in Law 1980. **BUSINESS ADDRESS:** Presiding Judge, El Cajon Municipal Court, 250 Main St, El Cajon, CA 92020.

RIGGS, ENRIQUE A.
General dentist. **PERSONAL:** Born Jun 03, 1943, Panama City, Panama;son of Eric Riggs

and Winifred Riggs; married Carol S Morales DDS; children: Myra Christine. **EDUCATION:** Central State Univ, BA Psychology 1968; State Univ of NY at Albany, MS Counseling 1971; Howard Univ Coll of Dentistry, DDS 1978; Sydenham Hosp NFCC, Certificate 1980. **CAREER:** State Univ of NY Albany, eop counselor 1968-71; Hudson Valley Comm Coll, EOP dir 1971-72; Private Practice, general dentist 1978-; New York City Health & Hosp Corp Sydenham Hosp, resident 1979-80; NYSA-ILA Medical Ctr, general dentist 1980-84; NYS Dept of Corrections, dental dir 1984-. **ORGANIZATIONS:** Mem Alpha Phi Alpha 1964-; mem Natl & Amer Dental Assocs 1974-; bd of dirs Uptown Chamber of Commerce 1978-; dir Central State Univ General Alumni Assoc 1978-, Health Systems Agency 1979-82; mem Acad of General Dentistry 1980-; dir Save Amateur Sports 1981-82; mem, sec bd of gov Amer Small Business Stock Exchange 1983-; mem 100 Black Men 1983-; pres/ceo C&E Assocs 1983-; nominating comm Howard Univ AA 1985; mem exec comm Howard Univ AA 1985; chmn Central State Univ Centennial Football Classic Comm 1986; dir NY Urban League 1986-; mem NYUL Finance Comm 1986-; pres Central State Univ Gen Alumni Assoc 1987-; bd of dirs 100 Black Men; pres Amer Small Business Stock Exchange; bd of dir Amer Small Business Stock Exchange Development Corp; bd of dirs Amer Assn of Securities Dealers; Sigma P i Phi Frat; Prince Hall F&AM. **HONORS/ACHIEVEMENTS:** Table Clinic Awd DC Dental Soc and Howard Univ Coll of Dentistry 1974; Oral Cancer Fellowship Memorial Sloan-Kettering Hosp 1976; Distinguished Alumni Award, NAFEO 1988; Alumnus of the Year, Central State Univ 1988. **MILITARY SERVICE:** AUS Reserve major 15 yrs. **HOME ADDRESS:** 25 Kathwood Rd, White Plains, NY 10607.

RIGGS, HARRY L.
Physician. **PERSONAL:** Born Sep 29, 1914, Birmingham; married Nancy M. **EDUCATION:** Wayne U, BS 1936; HowardUniv Med Sch, MD 1940. **CAREER:** Pvt Pract, physician; Randolph Field, flight surg. **ORGANIZATIONS:** Mem Oakland Co & MI State Med Socs; AMA; Nat & Detroit Med Assns Wolverine Med Soc; Am Coll Emergency Physicians; life mem NAACP; past pres Oakland Acad Gen Prac; past pres Urban Leag; life mem Alpha Phi Alpha; dep coroner Oakland Co. **HONORS/ACHIEVEMENTS:** Cert apprec Pontiac Sch Bd; Oaklan Co Ministerial Fellowship. **MILITARY SERVICE:** USAF capt 1942-47. **BUSINESS ADDRESS:** 149 Franklin Blvd, Pontiac, MI 48053.

RIGSBY, ESTHER MARTIN
Educational administrator. **PERSONAL:** Born in Port Gibson, MS; daughter of Rev. Alex L. Martin (deceased) and Annie M. Wilson Martin (deceased); married Dr John D Rigsby; children: Dr Reginald, Atty Delbert, Mark, Kenneth. **EDUCATION:** Alcorn State Univ, BS 1954; IN Univ, MS 1959; MS State Univ, Doctoral study 1980-83; Univ of MS, additional study 1980; Univ of So MS, doctoral study1985. **CAREER:** Jackson Public Schools, teacher 1960-; chmn, English & journalism teacher 1960-, Alcorn State Univ, adjunct instructor 1965. **ORGANIZATIONS:** MS Ed Assoc 1960-, NEA 1975-, mem NAACP 1975-, Natl Council of Negro Women 1977-, liaison coord Jackson Council & Natl Council of English Teachers 1979; Jackson Urban League 1980-; admin bd New Hope Bapt Church 1982-85; natl bd mem Alpha Kappa Alpha 1982-; supt adv council Jackson Public Schools 1984-85;mem YWCA 1985, Opera South Guild 1985; Links Inc, 1987. **HONORS/ACHIEVEMENTS:** Personalities of the South 1970; Awd Loyal Alumnae Alcorn State Univ 1977; Serv Awd Natl Council of Negro Women 1981; Serv Awd Women for Progress 1981; Serv Awd Alpha Kappa Alpha Sor Inc 1975-85. **HOME ADDRESS:** 3647 Westchester Dr, Jackson, MS 39213.

RILES, WILSON CAMANZA
Business executive. **PERSONAL:** Born Jun 27, 1917, Alexandria, LA; married Mary Louise Phillips;; children: Michael, Mrs Narvia Bostick, Wilson Jr, Phillip. **EDUCATION:** Northern AZ Univ, BA 1940, MA 1947. **CAREER:** CA State Dept of Ed, consultant, chief 1958-70; State of CA, supt Public Instr 1971-82; Wilson Riles & Assoc, Inc, pres 1983-. **ORGANIZATIONS:** Exec saec Flwshp of Reconciliation 1954-58; elem sch tchr, admnstr 1940-54; dir Wells Fargo Bank 1977-; dir Pacific Gas & Elec Co 1980-; mem Cleveland Conf, Nat'l Assoc for the Advancement of Colored People, Phi Beta Kappa, Nat'l Adv Council, Assoc of CA School Admin, American Assoc of School Admin; bd of dir Wells Fargo Bank and Wells Fargo Co, bd of trustees Foundation for the Teaching of Economics; mem Nat'l Committee on US-China Relations, Inc; bd of dir Pacific Gas and Electric Co; mem Save the Redwoods League Council; bd of dir Marshall McLuhan Center on Global Communications; bd of adv CAAssoc of Student Councils. **HONORS/ACHIEVEMENTS:** Berkeley Citation Distinguished Achievement and Notable Serv to the Univ of CA 1973; Springarn Medal Ntatl Assoc for the Advncmnt of Colored People 1973; dist Alumnus Award Amer Assoc of State Coll & Univ 1978; distinguished serv awd Harvard Club of San Francisco 1978; Robert Maynard Hutchins Awd 1978; medal for distinguished serv Columbia Univ 1979; distinguished alumnus awd American Assoc of State Coll & Univ 1979; 6 Honorary Doctor of Law Degrees; 3 Honorary Doctor of Humane Letters. **MILITARY SERVICE:** USAAC WWII. **BUSINESS ADDRESS:** President, Wilson Riles & Associates Inc, 555 Capitol Mall, Ste 740, Sacramento, CA 95814.

RILEY, BARBARA P.
Librarian. **PERSONAL:** Born Nov 21, 1928, Roselle, NJ; married George Emerson (deceased); children: George Jr, Glenn, Karen. **EDUCATION:** Howard Univ, AB 1950; NJ Coll Women, BS 1951; Columbia Univ, MS 1955; Further Study, Catholic Univ, Jersey City State Coll, Rutgers Univ, Kean Coll. **CAREER:** FL A&M Univ, asst librarian 1951-53; Morgan, asst librarian, 1955; US Dept of Defense, lib 1955-57; SC State Coll, asst librarian 1957-59, 1960; Univ WI, asst lib 1958-59; Atlanta Univ, circulation acquisitions librarian, 1960-68; Union Co Tech Inst, lib 1968-82; Union Co Coll, librarian scotch plains campus 1982-. **ORGANIZATIONS:** Asst dir, Union Co Anti-Poverty Agency 1968; Just-A-Mere Literary Club; ALA Black Lib Caucus; mem Alpha Kappa Alpha Sor; mem Bd of Educ Roselle NJ 1976-78; bd dirs Union Co Psychiatric Clinic 1980-83; mem Urban League of Eastern Union Co; mem NAACP; bd dirs Roselle NAACP 1984-; bd of dirs Pinewood Sr Citizens Housing 1982-85; NJ Coalition 100 Black Women 1983-; NJ Black Librarians Network 1983-, bd of dir 1986; bd of dir Black Womens History Conf 1986-. **BUSINESS ADDRESS:** Librarian, Union County College, Scotch Plains Campus, 1033 Springfield Ave, Cranford, NJ 07016.

RILEY, CHARLES WILBUR, SR.
Food products executive. **PERSONAL:** Born Dec 04, 1950, Bartow, FL; son of James F Riley, Sr and Flossie B Harvey Riley; married Avis Monica Bolden, May 21, 1983; children: Damonic Robertson, Charles Riley, Jr, Latara Riley, Terrence Riley. **EDUCATION:** Florida A&M Univ, Tallahassee, FL, BS-Accounting, 1968-72; Central MI Univ, Mt Pleasant, MI, MBA, 1977-79. **CAREER:** General Motors Co, Pontiac, MI, sr auditor, sr cost analyst, 1972, plant analyst, property accountant 1979; Miller Brewing Co, Milwaukee, WI, mgr of operations analysis, 1979-82, mgr of budgets & forcasting 1982-83; Adolph Coors Co, Golden, CO, mgr of plant operations finance, 1983-88, mgr of planning, 1989-. **ORGANIZATIONS:** Treasurer, Grandville Heights, Homeowners Assn, 1980-83; sec, bd of dir, Wisconsin Mesbic Finance Inst, 1981-83; treasurer & bd of dir, Colorado Business League, Business League, 1987-; bd of dir, Zion Baptist Church, 1987-. **BUSINESS ADDRESS:** Mgr of Planning, Coors Brewing Co, Mail #BC 330, Golden, CO 80401.

RILEY, CLAYTON
Writer, educator, journalist. **PERSONAL:** Born May 23, 1935, Brooklyn, NY; married Nancy; children: Hagar Lowine, Grayson. **CAREER:** Ebony, NY Times, The Liberator, Chicago Sun-Times & other publications, free-lance journalist; Fordham Univ Grad Sch of Educ & Sarah Lawrence Coll, tchr; former performer tech theater film; Nothing But A Man, production asst. **ORGANIZATIONS:** Mem Drama Desk; Harlem Writers Guild. **BUSINESS ADDRESS:** 523 W 112 St, New York, NY 10025.

RILEY, EMILE EDWARD
Physician. **PERSONAL:** Born Jul 30, 1934, New Orleans, LA; son of Emile E Riley Sr and Mercudell Riley; married Jacqueline; children: Wayne, Debra, Steven, Monique, Michelle. **EDUCATION:** Univ of MI, BS Zoology 1957; Meharry Medical Coll, MD 1960. **CAREER:** Flint-Goodridge Hospital New Orleans, medical staff 1967-81; Private Practice New Orleans, general surgery 1967-82; NASA, staff physician 1969-70; Orleans Parish LA, asst coroner 1979-82; US Post Office New Orleans, medical dir 1981-82; Private Practice, general surgery and medicine Opelousas LA 1982-85; St Landry Parish LA, deputy coroner 1983-85; LSU School of Medicine, clinical instructor in general surgery. **ORGANIZATIONS:** Bd mem Kingsley House 1973-; mem NAACP 1974-; exec comm New Orleans Drug Abuse Adv Council as apptd by Mayor 1979; founder New Orleans Sickle Cell Anemia Foundation; mem Southern Medical Assoc, Soc of Abdominal Surgeons, LA State Medical Soc, St Landry Parish Medical Soc, John D Rives Surgical Soc, Prince Hall Mason, Knights of Peter Claver, Opelousas Chamber of Commerce; life mem Alpha Phi Alpha Frat, Michigan Alumni Assoc. **HONORS/ACHIEVEMENTS:** Certificate of Achievement for Outstanding Work as Chief of Outpatient Clinic US Army; American Legion Awd Joseph S Clark Sr High School New Orleans; Honorary Colonel, Ambassador and Sec of State of Louisiana; publication "Effects of Freezing of the Common Bile Ducts," w/A Gage Amer Coll of Surgeons 1966. **HOME ADDRESS:** #7 Everglades, Kenner, LA 70065.

RILEY, KENNETH J.
Professional athlete. **PERSONAL:** Born Aug 06, 1947, Bartow, FL; married Barbara Moore; children: Kimberly, Ken II, Kenisha. **EDUCATION:** FL A&M Univ, BS Health & Phys Ed 1969; Univ of North FL, MEduc Administration 1974. **CAREER:** Cincinnati Bengals, def back 1969-83; Green Bay Packers, secondary coach 1984-. **ORGANIZATIONS:** Bd dir Big Brothers of Polk County; mem Alpha Phi Alpha Frat; mem Mt Gilboa Bapt Church; consult FL A&M Natl Alumni. **HONORS/ACHIEVEMENTS:** Inducted FL A&M's Hall of Fame Tallahassee, FL 1982; AFC Alltime Interceptor NFL 1983; NFL 4th Alltime Interceptor NFL 1983; Ken Riley Day at Riverfront Stadium (retired #13 jersey) 1983. **MILITARY SERVICE:** AUS Reserves Sgt served 6 yrs. **BUSINESS ADDRESS:** Coach, Florida A&MUniv, c/o Athletic Dept, Tallahassee, FL 32307.

RILEY, NEGAIL R.
Clergyman. **PERSONAL:** Born Sep 15, 1930, Oklahoma City, OK; married Gwendolyn Maurine; children: Beryl E. **EDUCATION:** Howard U, BA 1952; Perkins SMU, BD 1955; Boston U, ThD 1967. **CAREER:** GBGM Natl Div, exec secretary of dept of urban ministries 1968-75, AGS minority concerns 1970-72, AGS Mission Leadership 1974-79, asst general secretary parish ministries 1979-83, asst general secretary for Natl Div. **ORGANIZATIONS:** Dir Morgan Mem Youth & Children's Settlement House 1958-62; interim dir Brooks Meml Comm Center 1955; dir of Xn Educ Ch all Nations 1955-57; field staff City Dept natl Div Meth Bd of Missions 1967-68; exec sec Dept of Urban Ministries Meth Bd of Missions 1968-; chmn coord Policy Com of Black Comm Developers Prog 1969-; mem Urban Ind Missions Adv Core Group of the World Council of Ch 1970-; consult Urban Ministry devel in local ch conf dists jurisdictions 1967-; consult Govt Secular & Ecumenical urban & issue centered ministries 1968-; pres Interreligion Found for Comm Orgn; mem Alpha Phi Alpha Frat;adv bd Am Soc for Sickle Cell Anemia 1972-; chmn exec comm Nat Black United Fund 1974-; Racial Justice Working Group Nat Council of Ch. **HONORS/ACHIEVEMENTS:** Who's Who in the Meth Ch; Dictionary of Intl Biography; contribution to papers & articles, The Christian Advocate, Together, Choice & Chance, Engage, Power, World Outlook, Response. **BUSINESS ADDRESS:** Asst General Secretary, Genl Bd of Global Ministries, 475 Riverside Dr, Room 300, New York, NY 10115.

RILEY, ROSETTA MARGUERITTE
Automobile company executive. **PERSONAL:** Born Oct 25, 1940, Kansas City, MO; divorced; children: Courtney Elizabeth Riley. **EDUCATION:** California State Univ, Los Angeles, BS, 1968; UCLA, MA, 1969. **CAREER:** Bendix Corporation, Detroit MI, manager of business planning, marketing manager; General Motors, Detroit MI, Product Team, manager quality, Rochester NY Products Division, quality improvement mgr, Buick Oldsmobile Cadillac Group, Detroit MI, manager operations planning, Cadillac Motor Car Division, Detroit MI, director. **ORGANIZATIONS:** Amer Society for Quality Control; General Motors Key Executive to Tennessee State Univ; life mem, NAACP, 1984-89; mem, Detroit Institute of Arts, 1987-; Zeta Phi Sorority, 1964-; mem, United Foundation, 1984-. **BUSINESS ADDRESS:** Director of Customer Satisfaction, Cadillac Motor Car Division, General Motors Corporation, 2860 Clark Street, Detroit, MI 48232.

RILEY, SUMPTER MARION, JR.
Clergyman. **PERSONAL:** Born Jun 10, 1903, Greenwood, SC; married Varina Lone; children: Phyllis M. **EDUCATION:** DePauw U, AB 1926; Garrett Theological Seminary, BD 1930; BostonUniv Sch Theology, STM 1938; Philander Smith Coll, DD 1952; OH Northern U, HHD 1974. **CAREER:** Princeton, preacher 1927; S Park, Chicago, asst pastor 1928-29; Negro Work, asst dir 1930-31; Akron Centenary, 1931-32; Denver, 1932-34; Des Moines, 1934-36; St Louis, 1936-37; Boston, 1937-42; Columbus, 1942-43;Detroit, 1943-45; Chicago, Gorham, 1945-51; Chicago Dist, district supt 1951-57; Cory, 1957-68; Lima District, 1968-74. **ORGANIZATIONS:** Pres NAACP Chicago Branch; past pres Interdenominational Minis-

ters Alliance, Cleveland; active civic & youth groups; mem Gen Conf Union; mem World Meth Council; mem General & Uniting Conf; mem World Meth Conf.

RILEY, WAYNE JOSEPH
Government official. **PERSONAL:** Born May 03, 1959, New Orleans, LA; son of Emile E Riley Jr, MD and Jacqueline C Riley. **EDUCATION:** Yale Univ, BA 1981; Morehouse School of Medicine, MD (candidate); Tulane Univ, New Orleans LA, MPH Health Mgmt 1988. **CAREER:** City of New Orleans, administrative asst to the mayor 1981-86, exec asst to the mayor 1986; State of Louisiana, Office of Pulbic Health, health serv planner 1987-88. **ORGANIZATIONS:** Mem Kingsley Trust Assoc Yale Univ 1981-, Yale Alumni Assoc of LA 1981-; bd of dirs LA Youth Seminar 1984-; mem NAACP, Amer Medical Student Assn, Amer Medical Assn, Student Natl Medical Assn; exec dir Louisiana Independent Fedn of Electors Inc 1985-88; sec, treasurer Yale Alumni Assn of Louisiana 1988; Yale Club of Georgia 1989-; mem Eta Lambda Chapter, Alpha Phi Alpha Fraternity Inc. **HONORS/ACHIEVEMENTS:** Hall of Fame Inductee, Louisiana Youth Seminar 1986; participant, Metropolitan Leadership Forum, New Orleans 1987; President, Tulane Univ Black Professional Student Assn 1987-88; Lecturer, Adolescent Health Concerns Project, Emory Univ 1989-. **HOME ADDRESS:** 720 Westview Dr, SW, Box 271, Atlanta, GA 30310-1495.

RILEY, WILLIAM SCOTT
Police officer. **PERSONAL:** Born Sep 24, 1940, Chester, PA; son of Benjamin Riley and Leanna Riley; married Deloris L; children: Kimberly, Kelly, William S Jr. **EDUCATION:** Eastern Carolina Coll, attended 1960-61. **CAREER:** City of Chester, police officer. **ORGANIZATIONS:** Sec William Penn Lodge # 19 FOP 1987; bd mem Delaware Co Selective Serv Bd 1987; bd mem (1st Black) Delaware Co Democratic Exec Bd 1987. **HONORS/ACHIEVEMENTS:** Outstanding Comm Serv Awd Chester Scholarship Comm 1983; Eva Lou Winters Johnson Freedom Awds Chester Branch NAACP 1985. **MILITARY SERVICE:** USMC corpl 3 yrs. **HOME ADDRESS:** 918 Lloyd St, Chester, PA 19013. **BUSINESS ADDRESS:** Police Officer, City of Chester Police Dept, 4th & Welsh Sts, Chester, PA 19013.

RINGGOLD, FAITH
Artist/writer. **PERSONAL:** Born Oct 08, 1930, New York, NY; daughter of Andrew Jones and Willi Jones; married Burdette; children: Michelle Wallace, Barbara Wallace. **EDUCATION:** City Coll of NY, BS 1955; City Coll of NY of Grad Sch, MA 1959. **CAREER:** Artist & writer; Univ of CA at San Diego, prof of art 1984-. **HONORS/ACHIEVEMENTS:** Sculpture Fellowship Amer Assn of Univ Women 1976; Sculpture Fellowship Natl Endowment for the Arts 1978; Wonder Woman Foundation Awd 1983; 20 yr retrospective exhibition at Studio Museum in Harlem 1984; Warner Communications Candace Awd 100 Black Women 1984; Moore Coll of Fine Art, honorary doctor of fine art 1986; Wooster Coll, doctor of fine art 1987; John Simon Guggenheim Foundation Award 1987; numerous shows & exhibitions at natl & intl museums and universities. **BUSINESS ADDRESS:** Bernice Steinbaum Gallery, 132 Greene Gallery, New York, NY 10012.

RINSLAND, ROLAND D.
Educator, university official. **PERSONAL:** Born Apr 11, 1933, Low Moor, VA; son of Charles H and Lottie Parks. **EDUCATION:** VA State Univ, AB with Distinction 1954; Columbia Univ Tchrs Coll AM 1959, Professional Diploma 1960; Columbia Univ Tchrs Coll, EdD 1966; Co Officers Sch, diploma mil 1954; Post Graduate Study, Columbia Univ, Tchrs Coll 1982-83. **CAREER:** VA State Coll, student asst dean of men 1952-54; Glyco Products Co NYC, asst purchasing agt 1956-57; Columbia Univ, sec to sr clk registrar's office 1957-60, professional asst registrar's office 1960-66, registrar 1966-72, asst dean for student affairs & registrar & dir office of doctoral studies 1972-. **ORGANIZATIONS:** Amer Acad of Polit & Social Sci; Amer Assn Advancement of Sci; Assn for Institutional Rsch; Amer Assn Collegiate Registrars & Admissions Officers; Amer Assn Higher Educ; Amer Educ Rsch Assn; Amer Coll Personnel Assn; Assn of Records Exec & Adminstr; Natl Educ Assn;Natl Soc of Scabbard & Blade; Natl Soc Study Edn; Middle State Assn of Collegiate Registrars & Officers of Admission; Soc for Applied Anthropology; NY State Personnel & Guidance Assn; Intl Soc of Applied Psychology; Kappa Delta Pi; Kappa Phi Kappa; Phi Delta Kappa; Tchrs Coll Columbia Univ Faculty Exec Com; Coll Policy Council ex officio 1972-; Com on Instr & Rsch 1972-; subcom on Student Petitions for Exemptions from Degree Requirements 1972-; resource person to Com on Institutional Rsch 1968-; subcom on Student Petitions for Exemptions from Degree Requirements; rep to New York City Selective Serv 1966-; rep New York City Supt's Adv Com 1966-; Affirmative Action Comm 1981-83; Metro New York City Chap Assn of Records & Exec & Adminstr; Tchrs Coll Century Club 1970-; Tchrs Coll Devel Council 1974-76; Amer Assn of Collegiate Registrars & Officers of Admission; Amer Assn of Counseling & Devel. **HONORS/ACHIEVEMENTS:** Distinguished Military Student 1953; Disting Mil Grad 1954; Blanche B Carter Trophy & Key for Scholarship in ROTC VA State Coll 1954; charter mem & pres Beta Omicron Chap Kappa Phi Kappa 1953-54; Leah B Sykes Awd of Life; mem NEA VA State Coll 1954; charter mem New York City Chap Assn Records Exec & Adminstr 1967; designated as an important and valuable Human Resource of USA by Amer Heritage Rsch Assn of First Amer Bicentenium. **MILITARY SERVICE:** AUS 1st lt 1954-56; USAR 1956-62. **BUSINESS ADDRESS:** Asst Dean for Student Affairs, Registrar & Dir Doctoral Studies, Columbia Univ, Teachers Coll, Ofc of Registrar, 525 W 120th St, New York, NY 10027.

RISBROOK, ARTHUR TIMOTHY
Physician, businessman, administrator. **PERSONAL:** Born Dec 21, 1929, Brooklyn, NY; son of Belleville Timothy Risbrook and Ruby Isolene Risbrook; married Ida Marie, Jun 08, 1957; children: Donna Michelle, Deborah Nicole. **EDUCATION:** City Coll of NY, BS 1955; Meharry Med Coll, MD 1961; Meharry Med Coll, attended 1961; Bank Dir's Sch Montreal, attended 1973; CW Post Coll, nursing home admin course 1980. **CAREER:** Hempstead Sch Dist, chief physician; Nassau Co Drug Abuse & Addiction Center, founder dir med servs; Nassau Co Med Center, intern, resd; Physician, Mercy Hosp, A Holly Patterson Home for Aged, Hempstead Genl Hosp, Nassau Co Med Ctr 1965-; Chapin Nursing Home, medical director; A Holly Patterson Geriatric Center, medical director. **ORGANIZATIONS:** Mem AMA; Natl Med Assn; Empire State Med Assn; Nassau/Suffolk Clinical Assn; Clinical Soc NY Diabetes Assn; Amer Thoracic Soc; Nassau Co Med Soc; Amer Cancer Soc; fndr Topic House Drug Abuse Prog 1966; trustee Bd of Rehab Inst Mineola 1970; consult City Bank of NJ, 21st Century Bank NY, Queens AlliBank Chicago, Prospect Bank NJ 1972-73; fndr P&R Advertising Co 1974; med dir Grtr Harlem Nursing Home 1976; Marcus Garvey Manor Nursing Home 1977; adminstr Marcus Garvey Manor 1977; past sec treas vice pres chmn bylaws & com/pres Nassau Co Med & Dntl Staff 1975-79; mem Amer Geriatric Soc 1978; med dir Concord Nursing Home 1979; mem Med Malprac Panel Mineola 1979; fndr Belleville Med Grp 1979; owner Trida Travel Serv; W End Med Bldg; life mem NAACP; Kappa Alpha Psi Frat 1961; Alpha Sigma Boule of Sigma Pi Phi Frat 1977; mem NY State Bd Professional Med Conduct; NY Statewide Advisory Cncl; dep Soc Serv; bd dir Nassau Professional Rev Orgn; chmn sub-comm medicaid serv NY Statewide Adv Com Soc Svcs; mem Caduceus Med Hon Soc; mem at large, Executive Comm, Nassau County Medical Center. **HONORS/ACHIEVEMENTS:** Mayor's Com, Trail Blazer Award for Founding Vanguard Natl Bank; fndr chmn Vanguard Natl Bank 1969-74; Man of Yr Award Westbury Business & Professional Women; Brooklyn Business & Professional Women, Achievement Award 1973; Meharry Medical College President's Award. **MILITARY SERVICE:** AUS capt 1955; Purple Heart; 3 Battle Stars. **HOME ADDRESS:** 629 Oxford St, Westbury, NY 11590. **BUSINESS ADDRESS:** A Holly Patterson Geriatric Center, Jerusalem Ave, Uniondale, NY 11554.

RISHER, JOHN R., JR.
Law partner. **PERSONAL:** Born Sep 23, 1938, Washington, DC; son of John R Risher and Yvonne G Jones Peniston; married Carol Adriane Seeger; children: David, Michael, Mark, Conrad. **EDUCATION:** Morgan State Univ, BA 1960; Univ of S CA, JD 1962; John F Kennedy Sch, Harvard U, postgrad 1977. **CAREER:** US Dept of Justice, staff attorney 1965-68; US Dept of Justice, special asst US attorney 1966-68; Dist of Columbia Govt, corp cnsl 1976-78; Arent, Fox, Kintner, Plotkin & Kahn, partner 1975-76, 1978-. **ORGANIZATIONS:** Mem exec comm Nat Capital Area Civil Liberties Union 1969-71; chmn Montgomery Co Civil Liberties Union 1970-71; chmn Nominating Comm DC Bd Elections & Ethics 1974-76; mem DC Jud Conf 1975-; bd dir DC Pub Defender Serv 1975-76; bd dir , chm DC Comm on Licensure to Practice Healing Arts 1976-78; mem Jud Conf DC Cir 1976-; mem Adv Comm on Rules & Evidence Superior Ct DC 1976; DC Law Revision Comm 1976-78; mem Jud Planning Comm 1976-81; dir & sec Jewish Social Serv Agncy 1979-; mem DC Bar AD-Hoc Comm on Transfer of Felony Prosecutorial Jurisdiction 1979-81; dir Dist of Columbia Comm Ctr 1982-; dir Amer Jewish Comm, DC Chptr 1981-; pres DC Jewish Comm Ctr 1985-87; bd dir DC Jewish Community Center 1986-; bd dir United Jewish Appeal Fedn; mem District of Columbia commn on Admissions 1986-. **MILITARY SERVICE:** AUS capt 1963-65. **BUSINESS ADDRESS:** Attorney, Arent Fox Kintner Plotkin/Kahn, 1050 Connecticut Ave NW, Washington, DC 20036.

RISON, FAYE RISON
Educator. **PERSONAL:** Born Feb 25, 1942, Nacogdoches, TX; daughter of Archie and Rebecca; children: Sondra R Scott. **EDUCATION:** Univ of CO, MA 1970, PhD 1984. **CAREER:** Univ of CO Med Ctr, psychiatric nurse 1965-67; NW Team Dept of Health Hosp Denver, CO, psychiatric nurse 1967-71; Metro State Coll, asst prof 1971-82, assoc prof 1982-, prof of human serv. **ORGANIZATIONS:** Treas Natl Orgn of Human Serv, bd mem 1980-84; Amer Civil Liberties Union; Delta Sigma Theta; Black Womens Network; Denver Sister Cities; Black Women Completing Advanced Degrees. **HONORS/ACHIEVEMENTS:** Doct Fellowship Univ of CO 1980-82; Outstanding Faculty Award Human Serv 1979-82. **HOME ADDRESS:** 8792 E Kent Pl, Denver, CO 80237. **BUSINESS ADDRESS:** Professor of Human Services, Metro State Coll, 1006 11th St Box 12, Dept of Human Services WC 236, Denver, CO 80204.

RIST, SEWARD
Business executive. **PERSONAL:** Born Apr 13, 1943, Chicago, IL; married Beonca E Milton; children: Phillip. **EDUCATION:** Roosevelt Univ, BS, Bus Admin 1965; IL Assn of Realtors, 1979; Realtors Natl Mktg Inst, CRS Designation 1980; numerous courses, seminars & institutes. **CAREER:** Walgreen Drug Co, fin analyst 1965-67; Chicago Public Schools, teacher 1967-73; Real Estate Inst, instr 1976-77; United Way of Metro Chgo, bd mem new applicants comm 1981-83; Rist Realty & Bldg Inc, owned & administered real estate 1974-80; Rist Devel Corp/Real Estate Devel, pres 1979; UPI Real Estate Inc, pres 1983-. **ORGANIZATIONS:** Mem Inst of Real Estate Mgmt, Natl Assoc of Realtors; life mem NAACP; pres Kinectications 1978-; gen partner South Apts 1980-, Rist Property Offering III 1981-. **HONORS/ACHIEVEMENTS:** Feasibility Analysis Rist Property Offering III 1982; Market Analysis World Headquarters Site Selection 1983; Exec Dir of Congress of Racial Equality (CORE) South Side Chicago Chap 1963-65. **HOME ADDRESS:** 749 Goodpasture Terrace, Nashville, TN 37221. **BUSINESS ADDRESS:** President, UPI Real Estate Inc, 750 Old Hickory Blvd, Brentwood Commons 1 Ste 240, Brentwood, TN 37027.

RITCHEY, MERCEDES B.
Educator. **PERSONAL:** Born Sep 23, 1919, Washington, DC; married Alfred S. **EDUCATION:** UCLA, AB 1941; LA City Coll, AA; USC Berkeley tchr cred 1943; u of so cA, grad studies; san diego st u, ma 1963. **CAREER:** Douglas HS & Jr Coll El Centro CA, Teacher 1943-46; Gompers Jr HS San Diego, teacher 1955-59; O'Farrell Jr HS San Diego, teacher 1959-63; Jr HS Dist San Diego City School, resource teacher 1963-65; Lewis Jr HS San Diego, vice-prin 1965-68; Lincoln HS San Diego, vice-prin 1968-70, acting prin 1970-71, prin 1971-74; San Diego Unified School Dist, dir sec school div 1974-. **ORGANIZATIONS:** Mem San Diego Admin Assn; ACSCA; NASSP; past pres Delta Kappa Gamma Hon Ed Soc; mem Am Assn ofUniv Wmn; Nat Cncl of Admin Wmn in Ed; mem, past pres Alphas Kappa Alpha Sor; Braille Trnscrbrs Guild; YWCA; Urb Leag; past pres Las Munecas; NAACP; SW Involvement Proj; adv com to Cnclmn; Pres Cncl; corr sec Lincoln Booster Club; proj adv com Comm Ctr for Std Dev. **HONORS/ACHIEVEMENTS:** Hon life mem PTA Lewis Jr HS; Tchr of Wk 1963; Begro Bus & Pro Women of SD Ed 1966; 10 yrs Srv Awd Childrens Hm Soc Las Munecas Aux 1966; Wmnof Dstnctn Ed Wmn Inc 1966; Black Fed Outst Contrib to Black Comm 1973; Nat Assn of Negro Bus & Pro Wmn's Club Nat Sojourner Truth Meritorious Srv Awd 1974; Pacific St Assn IBPOE of W Abners Awd of Valor 1974; Outst Edctrs of Am 1974-75; San Diego Comm Ldrshp Rsltn Awd CA St Asmbly; Wmn of Achiev 1975. **BUSINESS ADDRESS:** San Diego City Schools, c/o Mrs Betty Ormsbee, 4100 Normal St, San Diego, CA 92103.

RITTER, THOMAS J.
Business executive. **PERSONAL:** Born Dec 24, 1922, Allendale, SC; married Betty Davis; children: Eva, Jephrey. **EDUCATION:** E Bapt Coll, BS 1959; Morris Coll, DD honorary 1968; E Bapt Coll, DD 1969; Dr Humane Letters, Pentecostal Theol Sem 1970. **CAREER:** Ritter Bros Med Equip Sales Co, partner 1947-49; ins 1949-55; Second & Macedonia Bapt Ch, pastor 1958; Dept of Welfare, PA, caseworker 1959-60; N Philadelphia Youth Community & Employment Serv, exec dir 1960-63; Opportunities Industrialization Cntr Inc, exec dir 1963-. **ORGANIZATIONS:** Bd mem Franklin Inst; Philadelphia Nat Bank; E Bapt Coll; Albert Einstein Med Cntr; Pathway Sch; Area Manpower Planning Coun; PA Industrial

Devel Auth; Contact Philadelphia; pres Coun of Am Inst of Mgmt; Acad for Career Educ Mem, Philadelphia Partnership; Mayor's Com of Twelve; Bapt Ministers Conf of Philadelphia & vincinity; Greater Philadelphia C of C; Governor's adv coun on Housing; Crime Commn of Philadelphia; adv Coun Vocational Educ Sch Dist of Philadelphia; Am Inst of Mgmt; Philadelphia Bapt Keystone Assn; Lower KY Environmental Cntr. **HONORS/ACHIEVEMENTS:** Cit com No-fault Ins; recipient OIC, Decade of Progress Award 1974; distinguished cit award US Civil Serv Commn 1972; outstanding serv award BronzeAssn for Cultural Advancement 1971; humanitarian award World Alliance of Holiness 1970; award of achievement Philadelphia Tribune Charities 1967; outstanding alumni award E Bapt Coll 1964; Margaret Van Dyne Award for outstanding scholarship & christian devotion 1959. **MILITARY SERVICE:** AUS 1942-45. **BUSINESS ADDRESS:** 1231 N Broad St, Philadelphia, PA 19122.

RIVERA, EDDY
Attorney. **PERSONAL:** Born Jul 23, 1938, St Croix, Virgin Islands of the United States;son of Adelo Rivera and Margot M Rivera; married Gloria Maria Rojas, Feb 26, 1967; children: Lisette M, Julia I, Eddy Jr, Vanessa M. **EDUCATION:** Interam Univ San German PR, 1960; Univ of PR San Juan, BBA (Cum Laude) 1963, JD 1972. **CAREER:** VI Properties Inc, chief accountant 1966-69; Govt of VI, asst attny gen 1973-76; Govt of VI, senator 1979-80; Private practice, attny 1976-. **ORGANIZATIONS:** Mem Amer Bar Assoc, PR Bar Assoc 1973, VI Bar Assoc 1976; bd mem CAMP ARAWAK Youth Serv Org 1974-76; pres Hispanos Unidos VI Inc 1974-78; bd of ed Govt of VI 1976-78; mem The Assoc of Trial Lawyers of Amer 1980-; pres Full Gospel Business Men's Fellowship Intl 1981-86. **MILITARY SERVICE:** AUS pfc 1963-65. **BUSINESS ADDRESS:** Attorney, 38 King St, Christiansted, St Croix, Virgin Islands of the United States 00820.

RIVERO, MARITA JOY (MARITA MUHAMMAD)
Vice chair & general manager. **PERSONAL:** Born Nov 25, 1943, West Grove, PA; married Askia Muhammad; children: Raafi Muhammad. **EDUCATION:** The Wharton School, Univ of PA, Mgmt Seminar 1982; Harvard Univ, School of Educ Work on M, Educ, 1970-71; Tufts Univ, MA, BS, Psychology 1964; Lincoln Univ, PA, Phi Beta Kappa Deans List transfer award. **CAREER:** WGBH Educ Found, TV Producer 1970-76; Consultant, Comm on Black Higher Educ,1977-80; Public Broadcasting Syst, 1977-80; KY Educational Broadcastint Systm, cnsltnt 1977-80; NSF, 1977-80; Nguzo Saba Films, Inc, 1977-80 natl black united fund, 1977-80 communictins taks force, 1977-80; Griot Productions Co, 1977-80; natl comm for responsive philanthropy, assoc dir 1978-79; WPFW-FM Pacifica, dir of Developmnt 1980-81. **ORGANIZATIONS:** Exec committee Capital Press Club, Natl Press Club, WA Area Broadcasters Assoc, Nat Conf of Black Lawyers, Amer women in Radio & TV, Natl Federation of Comm Broadcasters; officer The Pacifica Federation; mem DC Chamber of Commerce Advisory Bd, Festival of Black Storytelling 1985; bd of dir DC YWCA; Tech/distribution committee, bd of dir Natl Public Radio. **HONORS/ACHIEVEMENTS:** YMCA Black Achievement Award, 1976; Exec Producer, Natl Radio Program; The March on Washington for Jobs, Peace, & Freedom, 1983; The Washington Informer Community Serv Award, 1982; Toast & Strawberries Recognition Award, 1983; Capital Press Club; The Natl Press Club; Washington Area Broadcasters Assn; Communications Task Force; Natl Conf of Black Lawyers; YMCA Black Achievement Award. **BUSINESS ADDRESS:** Vice Chair & General Manager, WPFW-FM Pacifica, 700 H St NW, Washington, DC 20001.

RIVERS, ALFRED J.
Business executive. **PERSONAL:** Born Sep 18, 1925, Crisp Co, GA; married Vera Stripling; children: Gwendolyn Thrower, Gregory Rivers, Glenda. **EDUCATION:** LUTC, 1976; Grad Sch, 1976; TN State U. **CAREER:** NC Mutual Ins Co, 1946-; Gillespie Selden Comm Devel Ctr, dir vice pres 1972-77; Middle Flint Planning APDC, dir 1973-77; Crisp Cordele & C of C, dir 1973-77; Cordele City Commn, v chmn 1972-77. **ORGANIZATIONS:** Mem NAACP; mem Local Am Legion; Cancer Soc. **MILITARY SERVICE:** AUS capt 1943-46. **BUSINESS ADDRESS:** PO Box 1077, Cordele, GA 31015.

RIVERS, CLARENCE JOSEPH
Priest. **PERSONAL:** Born Sep 09, 1931, Selma, AL. **EDUCATION:** BA 1952; MA 1956; St Mary's Sem, Cincinnati; English Lit Xavier U; CathUniv of Am; Union Grad Sch, PhD; Institut Catholique, Paris. **CAREER:** Archdiocese of Cincinnati, priest 1956-; Purcell HS, tchr engl Lit 1956-66; St Joseph's & Assumption Parishes, asso pastor 1956-66; recorded publishes "An Am Mass Prog"" 1963; Dept of Culture & Worship Nat Ofc of Black Cath, founder first dir 1972, spl cons; Stimuli Inc, "Newborn Again", pres; authorbooks on worship; CBS Network, spripted/co-prod/starred "Freeing the spirit" 1971; CBS Network Easter Special, prod cons/narrator/composer "The Feast of Life". **ORGANIZATIONS:** Mem bd dir Nat Liturgical Conf; N Am Academy of Liturgy; Martin Luther Kings Fellows; pub "Turn Me Loose"; mem worship comm Archdiocese of Cincinnati. **HONORS/ACHIEVEMENTS:** Recipient pub serv awards; 1966 Gold Medal of Cath Art Assn for "An Am Mass Prog". **BUSINESS ADDRESS:** PO Box 20066, Cincinnati, OH 45220.

RIVERS, DAVID EUGENE
Appointed governmental official. **PERSONAL:** Born Jun 07, 1943, Monks Corner, SC; divorced; children: Darwin. **EDUCATION:** GA State Univ, BS 1971, MA 1975; Yale Univ, 1974; GA State Univ, 30 hrs toward PhD. **CAREER:** City of Atlanta, budget policy 1974-79; US Dept of energy, dir city & cty relations 1979-80; Under Sec DHHS, spec asst 1980-81, dep dir 1981-83, dir 1983-. **ORGANIZATIONS:** Mem steering comm Urban Consortium 1974, Alpha Phi Alpha Frat 1975, Master Mason Prince Hall 1979; bd of dir Community Design Ctr GA 1979; mem ResurgensAtlanta 1979, US Conf of City Human Serv Officials 1985, Amer Soc for Publ Admin 1985. **HONORS/ACHIEVEMENTS:** Publ "Atlanta's Planning Process, Comprehensive, Coordinated" 1968,79,82; Listed in Outstanding Young Men of Amer 1975. **MILITARY SERVICE:** AUS E-5 personnel mgmt spec 3 yrs; Hon Discharge 1966. **BUSINESS ADDRESS:** Dir, DC Dept of Human Services, 801 N Capitol St NE, Washington, DC 20002.

RIVERS, DAVID LAWRENCE
Technical representative. **PERSONAL:** Born Jun 18, 1944, Pittsburgh, PA; married Victoria A Mosley; children: Caryn Staci, David Lawrence II. **EDUCATION:** Cheyney St Coll, BS 1967; Wharton Schl of Bus, MBA 1972. **CAREER:** Hercules Inc, tech rep 1977; E I DuPont Co, chemist 1967; RCA Corp, acct supr. **ORGANIZATIONS:** Mem PA Soc for Coatings Tech; mem 52nd Ward Exec Comm 1972; cand PA House of Rep 1974; former mem bd Wynnefield Res Assn. **MILITARY SERVICE:** AUS res. **BUSINESS ADDRESS:** 91/ Market St, Wilmington, DE 19899.

RIVERS, DENOVIOUS ADOLPHUS
Judge. **PERSONAL:** Born Feb 02, 1928, Chicago, IL; married Loretta Brown; children: Donald Adolphus. **EDUCATION:** Wilson Jr Coll, Cert 1948; John Marshall Law School, JD 1951. **CAREER:** IL Supreme Court, admitted IL Bar 1951; US Dist Court, Northern Dist IL, admitted 1958; US Dist Court, Northern Dist IN, admitted 1960; Circuit Court Cook Cnty, IL, assoc judge 1984. **ORGANIZATIONS:** Mbr Cook Cnty Bar Assoc, Natl Bar Assoc 1954-; mem Chicago Bar Assoc 1968-, IL State Bar Assoc 1982-; mbr, asst sec 1984-; mem IL Judges Assoc 1984-; trste Abraham Lincoln Cntr 1968-84; vstrymn & treas St Bartholomew Episcopal Church 1960-76; mem Messiah-St Bartholomew Episcopal Church 1976-; mem & frmr treas Omega Psi Phi Frat 1948-; gvnrg brd & treas The Chicago Asmbly, Chicago Steering Comm, NAACP Legal Def & Ed Fund 1967-84; brd mbrHarvard St George Schl 1971-80. **HONORS/ACHIEVEMENTS:** FBI Commendation 1971; Meritorious Serv BIG BUDDIES YOUTH SERV, INC 1972; Judicial Awd Cook Cnty Bar Assoc 1984; outstanding serv Phoenix Park Dist 1984. **MILITARY SERVICE:** IL Nat Guard, Infantry 1st lt 20 yrs. **HOME ADDRESS:** 6947 Cregier Ave, Chicago, IL 60649. **BUSINESS ADDRESS:** Associate Judge, Circuit Court Cook County, Richard J Daley Center, Chicago, IL 60602.

RIVERS, DOROTHY
Administrator. **PERSONAL:** Born Aug 14, 1933, Chicago, IL; divorced. **EDUCATION:** John Marshall Law Sch, 1950-51; Nrthwstrn U, BA 1959. **CAREER:** Michael Reese Hosp & Med Ctr, exec adminstr, dept of psychtry; Nelson Prods Inc, vp. **ORGANIZATIONS:** Fndr, chrwmn Women's Div Chicago Ec Dev Corp; fndr, mem The XXI of Michael Reese Hosp; chrwmn 1st, 2nd & 3rd Mdwst Rgnl Conf on Bus Opport for Women; vp, bd dir Chicago Ec Dev Corp; bd dir Chicago Fin Dev Corp; chrprsn Vanguard of Chicago Urban Leag; chrprsn, exec adv bd Big Buddies Yth Serv 1964-; mem Bravo Chap Lyric Opera; bd dir Operation PUSH Found; wmns bd United Negro Coll Fund; mem Chicago Chap of Links. **HONORS/ACHIEVEMENTS:** Recip Vol Serv Awd Chicago Ec Dev Corp 1973; Vol Serv Awd Gov of IL 1967; Lady of the Day Awd Radio Sta WAAF & WAIT; cert of ldrshp Met YMCA 1975;cert of merit Chicago Heart Assn 1975; M F Bynun Comm Serv Awd 1975. **BUSINESS ADDRESS:** Michael Reece Hosp & Med Cnt, 2959 S Cottage Grove, Chicago, IL 60616.

RIVERS, GARY C.
Fundraiser. **PERSONAL:** Born Jan 06, 1951, Hardeeville, SC. **EDUCATION:** New York Univ, BA Biology 1973. **CAREER:** Boy Scouts of Amer, dist exec 1973-75; West Point Pepperell, institutional salesman 1975-78; Westvaco, fine papers salesman 1978-79; Boy Scouts of Amer, finance dir 1979-80; David M Winfield Foundation, exec dir. **ORGANIZATIONS:** Dir of develop Congressional Black Caucus Foundation 1980-85; bd mem Natl Coalition of Black Meeting Planners 1986; mem-at-large Natl Soc of Fund Raising Execs 1986-; mem 100 Black Men 1986-; bd mem Amer Cancer Soc. **HOME ADDRESS:** 19 Tributary Plaza, Englewood, NJ 07631.

RIVERS, GRIFFIN HAROLD
Deputy secretary. **PERSONAL:** Born Aug 21, 1939, Mobile, AL; married Freya Anderson; children: Monica, Shariba, Sanford. **EDUCATION:** Dillard Univ, BA 1966; MI State Univ, MS 1973; 1973; Orleans Parish Prison, spec asst sheriff 1973-74; So Univ Law Enforcement Baton Rouge, prof 1974-75; City of New Orleans, dep dir treatment alter. **CAREER:** Juvenile probation officer 1966-68; Total Comm Action, field rep 1968-69; US Equal Employment Oppty Comm, investigator 1969-72; MI State Univ, head resident adv 973; Orleans Parish Prison, spec asst sheriff 1973-74; So Univ Law Enforcement Baton Rouge 1974-75; City of New Orleans, dep dir treatment alternative to street crime 1974-76; LA Dept of Corrections, dep sec 1976-82; Dept of Public Safety & Corrections, dep sed 1984-. . **ORGANIZATIONS:** Mem Amer Correctional Assoc; consult Natl Assoc of Blacks in Criminal Justice 1976, So Gov Conf 1977; lectr Dominican Coll, Tulane, Loyola, So Dillard, Xavier Univ; bd dir Corrections Comm Svc; mem Coalition of Black Officials, Natl Counc on Crime & Deliquency, Treme Cultural & Enrichment Prog; mem Kappa, NAACP, Comm Org for Urban Politics, Comm for Racial Justice, Natl Assoc of Pretrial Serv Agency, Amer Soc of Criminology, Amer Law Enforcement Officers Assoc, Amer Jud Soc; asst dept Affirm Action & Consumer Affairs LA Dept of Ins 1983-84. **MILITARY SERVICE:** AUS spec E5 1963-76. **BUSINESS ADDRESS:** Deputy Secretary, Dept of Public Safety & Corr, PO Box 94304 Capitol Sta, Baton Rouge, LA 70804.

RIVERS, JOHNNY
Recording artist. **PERSONAL:** Born Nov 07, 1942, New York, NY. **CAREER:** Rivers Music, pres; Imperial Records, rcrdng artst 1963-; Soul City Records, LA, owner 1967-; Soul City Prods, Johnny Rivers Mus. **ORGANIZATIONS:** Firsthit Record Memphis 1964.

RIVERS, JOHNNY
Executive chef. **PERSONAL:** Born Oct 05, 1949, Orlando, FL; married Shirley Capers; children: Johnny Jr, Djuan, Dwain, Tanya, Zina. **CAREER:** Flountainbleu Miami FL, chef 1968; Mission Inn Country Club, chef 1963-64; Palmer House Chicago IL, chef 1969; Walt Disney World Co, exec chef 1970-. **ORGANIZATIONS:** Pres Central FL Chef Assoc 1974-75; host World Chef Congress 1984; publ relations Amer Culinary Fed 1984-85; mem Orange Cty School Bd 1985. **HONORS/ACHIEVEMENTS:** Acad of Chefs Amer Culinary Fed 1976-77; Award of Gratitude Brown Coll 1979; Chef of the Year Central FL Chef Assoc 1980; Listed in Personalities of Amer1985. **BUSINESS ADDRESS:** Executive Chef, Contemporary Resort Hotel, Walt Disney World Co, PO Box 10,000, Lake Buena Vista, FL 32830.

RIVERS, LOUIS
Educator. **PERSONAL:** Born Sep 18, 1922, Savannah, GA; married Ligia Sanchez; children: Luisa, Liana, Loria, Leigh. **EDUCATION:** Savannah State Coll, BS 1946; New York Univ, MA 1951; Fordham Univ, PhD 1975. **CAREER:** WV State Coll, instructor 1951-52; Southern Univ, instructor 1952-53; Tougaloo Coll, asst prof 1953-58; New York City Tech Coll, professor 1970-. **ORGANIZATIONS:** Mem Natl Writers Club, Dramatist Guild, Speech Communication Assoc, College Language Assoc, Phi Delta Kappa, Kappa Delta Pi. **HONORS/ACHIEVEMENTS:** John Hay Whitney Theater 1957; Outstanding Teacher

Plaque from Kappa Delta Pi 1983; Andrew Mellon Creative Writing Fellowship 1984. **MILITARY SERVICE:** US Corps of Engrs pvt 1942. **BUSINESS ADDRESS:** Professor of Writing/Speach, New York City Tech College, 300 Jay St, Brooklyn, NY 11201.

RIVERS, MICKEY MILTON
Professional athlete. **PERSONAL:** Born Aug 30, 1948, Miami, FL. **CAREER:** Calif Angels, outfielder 1973-75; New York Yankees, outfielder 1976-79; Texas Rangers, outfieldr 1979-85. **HONORS/ACHIEVEMENTS:** Named Rangers Player of the Yr 1980. **BUSINESS ADDRESS:** Texas Rangers, Arlington Stadium, Arlington, TX 76010.

RIVERS, ROBERT JOSEPH, JR.
Physician. **PERSONAL:** Born Nov 14, 1931, Princeton, NJ; married Ruth Lewis; children: Michael, Scott, Wendy, Robert D. **EDUCATION:** Princeton Univ, AB (Cum Laude) 1953; Harvard Medical School, MD 1957. **CAREER:** Private practice, vascular surgery 1965-86; Univ of Rochester School of Medicine & Dentistry, prof of clinical surgery 1984-89; assoc dean for minority affairs 1984-89. **ORGANIZATIONS:** Trustee Princeton Univ 1969-77; bd of trustees Rochester Savings Bank 1972-83; chief Div of Vascular Surgery The Genesee Hosp 1978-85; mem Alpha Phi Alpha Frat. **HONORS/ACHIEVEMENTS:** President's Citation Medical Soc of the State of NY 1971. **MILITARY SERVICE:** USN lt USNR 1959-61. **HOME ADDRESS:** 86 Great Oak Road, Orleans, MA 02653.

RIVERS, VALERIE L.
Appointed official & attorney. **PERSONAL:** Born Nov 25, 1952, Birmingham, AL; daughter of Eddie Rivers. **EDUCATION:** Tuskegee Inst, BS 1975; Southern Univ School of Law, JD 1980. **CAREER:** Wayne County Community Coll, Asst Dir Human Resources 1976; Gov Office of Consumer Protection State of LA, investigator 1979-80; B'ham Area Legal Service, staff atty candidate 1981; City of Birmingham, city council admin-first Black and first female to hold this position. **ORGANIZATIONS:** Mem Phi Alpha Delta Law Frat Intl 1978-; big-sister 1981-, adv comm 1983-, minor recruit 1983-, bd of dir 1985-88 Big Bros/Big Sisters of Gr Birmingham; mem Amer Soc Public Admin 1981-; mem natl Forum Black Admin 1983-. **HONORS/ACHIEVEMENTS:** First & past justice of AP Tureau Chapter of Phi Alpha Delta Law Frat intl & founding mem of Chapter 1978; Reginald Heber Smith Comm Lawyer Fellowship 1980-81; Hon Mayor of Pritchard, AL 1980; exec in residence Birmingham-Southern Coll 1983; Govt & Politics Black Women Business & Professional Assn 1984. **HOME ADDRESS:** 1908 Huntington Circle, Birmingham, AL 35214. **BUSINESS ADDRESS:** Council Administrator, Birmingham City Council, 710 North Nineteenth St, Birmingham, AL 35203.

RIVERS, VERNON FREDERICK
Educational administrator. **PERSONAL:** Born Jul 25, 1933, Peekskill, NY; married Audrey Cherry; children: Gregory, Pamela, Karen. **EDUCATION:** State Univ of NY, BS Ed 1955; Teachers Coll Columbia Univ NY, Grad Work 1960; City Coll of NY, Grad Work 1963; State Univ of NY New Paltz, MS Ed 1971. **CAREER:** Peekskill NY School Syst, 1st black teacher 1957-61; Irvington NY School System, 1st black teacher 1961-68; Elmsford NY School System, 1st black principal 1968-72; Elmsford School System, fed funds coord 1971-72; Ossining NY School Syst, teacher adult ed 1975; Brewster School Syst, 1st black principal 1972-. **ORGANIZATIONS:** Mem Assoc of Suprv & Curriculum 1975, Natl Assoc for Ed of Young Children 1975, sr warden Church of the Good Shepherd Granite Springs NY 1975; adv comm United Fund Yorktown Hts NY 1976; keeper of records/polemarch New Rochelle/White Plains Kappa Alpha Psi Alumni 1977-80; vice pres Lions Club of Yorktown 1978; school admin Assoc of NY/Natl Assoc of Elem Scoool Principals 1979-80; commr Girls Basketball Mohansic Boys Club 1979; bd of dir Beaverridge Housing DevelFund 1980; v chmn Yorktown Recreation Comm 1980. **HONORS/ACHIEVEMENTS:** Vanguard Awd Peekskill NAACP 1959; Cert of Apprec Elmsford Comm 1972; Cert of Apprec Lions Club of Yorktown & Rotary Club of Brewster NY 1974; Cert of Apprec Yorktown Area Jaycees 1978; Cert of Safety & Good Medal. **MILITARY SERVICE:** AUS pfc 1955-57. **BUSINESS ADDRESS:** Principal, Brewster School System, Garden St, Brewster, NY 10509.

ROACH, DELORIS
Public relations manager. **PERSONAL:** Born Apr 15, 1944, Pine Bluff, AR; children: Yvette Guyton, Frank, Anthony, Monica. **EDUCATION:** Univ of CA Berkeley, BA Journalism 1975; San Francisco State Univ, MA Radio/TV 1979. **CAREER:** KQED-TV Educ TV, admin asst 1979-81; KQED-TV Educ Films, rschr 1981-82; New Images Prod Inc, production coord 1982-84; Fleming Co Inc advertising coord; Emery Unified School Dist, mem, bd of trustees. **ORGANIZATIONS:** Consult CA Schools Bd Assoc 1979; mem CA School Bds Assoc, Alameda Cty School Bds Assoc 1979, CA Black School Bd Mem Assoc 1981. **HONORS/ACHIEVEMENTS:** Outstanding Citizen Award Emeryville Neighborhood Assoc 1981; Disting Serv Awd Alameda Cty School Bds Assoc 1984. **BUSINESS ADDRESS:** Emery Unified Sch Dist, 4727 San Pablo Ave, Emeryville, CA 94608.

ROACH, LEE
Association executive. **PERSONAL:** Born Jan 03, 1937, Rock Hill, SC. **EDUCATION:** Lincoln U, BA 1960; Bryn Mawr, MSW 1969; Cornell U. **CAREER:** Health Adminstr Program, 1972; Regional Comprehensive Health Planning Council Inc, sep asso dir 1969-; Grad Sch of Soc Work, Bryn Mawr, comm organization instr 1970-71; Health & Welfare Council, asst dir 1966-67; tchr, Math & Sci 1960-66; owner-mgr restaurant 1955-74; Equestrian Academy. **BUSINESS ADDRESS:** Dir of Planning, The Graduate Hospital, One Graduate Plaza, Philadelphia, PA 19146.

ROACH, MAX
Musician, composer, educator. **PERSONAL:** Born Jan 10, 1924, Elizabeth City, NC; married Mildred Wilkinson; children: Daryl, Maxine. **EDUCATION:** Manhattan School of Music, Composition. **CAREER:** Jazz clubs, drummer; Univ of MA Dept of Music & Dance, faculty. **ORGANIZATIONS:** Mem Jazz Artists Guild. **HONORS/ACHIEVEMENTS:** Winner Down Beat poll 1955,57,58,59,60,84. **BUSINESS ADDRESS:** c/o Willard Alexander Inc, 101 Park Ave, New York, NY 10178.

ROACHES, CARL
Professional football player. **PERSONAL:** Born Oct 02, 1953, Houston, TX. **EDUCATION:** TX A&M Univ. **CAREER:** Houston Oilers, professional football player 1980-. **ORGANIZATIONS:** Owns a cleaning serv and lawn maintenance company; active with Salvation Army and Leukemia Society. **HONORS/ACHIEVEMENTS:** Coll, in sr yr at TX A&M returned 38 punts for 238 yds, 5 kickoffs for 145 yds and added 8 receptions for 109 yds; profl, trails Billy "White Shoes" Johnson closely in most punt returns (151 to 155) and most kickoff returns (150 to 158); most punt returns season 47 in 1980; tied with Johnson for most career touchdowns on kickoff return 2; third and fourth longest touchdown runs on kickoff returns in club history; in 1981 topped the AFC with 275 avg on KORs en route to Pro Bowl and many other All-AFC honors.

ROAF, CLIFTON G.
Dentist. **PERSONAL:** Born Feb 10, 1941, Pine Bluff, AR; married Andree Layton; children: Phoebe, Mary, William, Andrew. **EDUCATION:** MI State U, BS 1963; HowardUniv Coll of Dntsty, DDS 1969. **CAREER:** Jeff Comp Care Ctr, Dir Dntl Unit, dentist 1973-76; private practice 1969-. **ORGANIZATIONS:** Mem Am Dntl Assn; Nat Dntl Assn; Acdmy Gen Dntstry; AR Med Dntl & Phrmctcl Assn; mem Pine Blf Schl Bd 1973-; mem Alpha Phi Alpha Frat; mem bd of visitorsUniv of AR Pine Bluff 1977-; Pine Blf Plng Comm 1971-74; mem AR Bd of Higher Educ 1980-; mem AR Council on Humanities 1986-; advisory bd Simmons 1st Nat'l Bank 1984-. **BUSINESS ADDRESS:** 1310 Linden St, Pine Bluff, AR 71601.

ROANE, GLENWOOD P.
Attorney. **PERSONAL:** Born Jul 26, 1930, Virginia; married Lucie Porter; children: Karen, Glenwood Jr, Rosemary. **EDUCATION:** VA State Coll, BS 1952; Howard Univ, JD 1957; Fletcher School of Law, Postgrad 1970-71. **CAREER:** Teacher 1957-59; USVA, adjudicator & attny rev 1960-62; USN, negotiator 1962-65; USAID/Liberia, officer 1966-68; USAID/Ghana, asst dir 1968-70; Reg Population Office, dir 1971-73; USAID/Vietnam, asst dir 1974-75; USAID Cairo, officer 1976; Agency for Intl Devel Office Equal Oppty Prog dir 1977-78; USAID Kenya, dir; VSU, diplomat in residence 1980-83; Roane & Everett Law Firm, sr partner attny. **ORGANIZATIONS:** Former pastor 1st Bapt Church Vienna VA 1977-; assoc pastor Purity Bapt Church 1976-; pres Devel Consult Intl; org Comm Against Crime 1975. **HONORS/ACHIEVEMENTS:** Superior Performance Awd 1962; Merit Honor Awd EOE Efforts 1976; Fulbright Nom 1957. **MILITARY SERVICE:** AUS 1st lt 1952-54. **BUSINESS ADDRESS:** Attorney, Roane & Everett Law Firm, Box 202, APO, New York, NY 09675.

ROANE, PHILIP RANSOM, JR.
Educator, virologist. **PERSONAL:** Born Nov 20, 1927, Baltimore, MD; son of Philip Ransom Roane, Sr and Mattie Brown Roane; married Vernice Haynes, Aug 01, 1981; children: Crystal Reed, Donald H Reed. **EDUCATION:** Morgan State Coll, BS 1952; Johns Hopkins, ScM 1960; Univ MD, PhD 1970. **CAREER:** Johns Hopkins, asst Microbiology 1960-64; Microbiol Assocs Inc, virologist 1964-72, dir quality control 1967-72; Howard Univ, prof microbiology 1972-79; Howard Univ, asst prof oncology 1977-, assoc prof microbiology 1979-. **ORGANIZATIONS:** Mem Amer Assn Immunologists; Virology Study Sect NIH; Amer Soc Microbiology; mem NIH Virology Study Sect 1976-80; mem Dept of Army Viral & Rickettseal Diseases Review Grp 1979-81; mem Sigma Xi; rsch publs in field of virology. **HONORS/ACHIEVEMENTS:** Kaiser Permanente Award for Distinguished Teaching 1979; Inspirational Leadership Award, Pre-Clinical Professor 1982. **MILITARY SERVICE:** USAAF 1946-47. **BUSINESS ADDRESS:** Associate Professor, Howard University-College of Medicine, Department of Microbiology, Pre-Clinical Bldg, 520 W St, NW, Washington, DC 20059.

ROBBINS, ALFRED S.
Judge. **PERSONAL:** Born Nov 09, 1925; married Louise; children: Daryl Lynn, Alfred. **EDUCATION:** Brooklyn Coll, BA; Brooklyn Law Sch, JD. **CAREER:** Nassau Hosp, dir; Supreme Ct, State of NY, justice 1979-; Dist Ct Nassau County, admin judge 1974-78; Legal Aid Soc, trial atty NY State Liquor Authority; private practice; Dist Atty's Office of Nassau County, asst dist atty 1967; Dist Ct Nassau County, judge 1971, admin judge 1974. **ORGANIZATIONS:** Pres Bd Judges; mem Nassau County Bar Assn; NY State Dist Atty Assn; Natl Dist Atty Assn; former dir Sheltering Arms Children's Aid Serv; former New York City Protestant Placement & Adoption Agency; former arbitrator Amer Arbitration Assn; former mem chmn Council of the State Univ of NY at Old Westbury Elder Presbyterian Church; commr Commn on Religion & Race; mem Hempstead Lion's Club; NAACP; former Eagle Scout Review Bd; Nassau County Council BSA; mem exec bd Nassau County Council of Boy Scouts. **MILITARY SERVICE:** USN. **BUSINESS ADDRESS:** Supreme Court Bldg, Supreme Ct Dr, Mineola, NY 11501.

ROBBINS, HERMAN C.
Educational administrator. **PERSONAL:** Born Jul 23, 1928, Ft Gibson, OK; children: Kelly, Beverly, Carol, Jacquelyn Shirley, Gerald, Ronald, Herman Jr. **EDUCATION:** Langston U, BS 1947-51; OK State U, MS 1951-52;Univ of Tulsa, post grad study 1968-69. **CAREER:** Tulsa Jr Coll, vice pres bus & aux svcs; Tulsa Jr Coll, asso dean evening programs 1974-75; Tulsa Jr Coll, chmn bus serv div 1971-74; Tulsa Jr Coll,mid-mgmt coordinator, bus instr 1970-71; Hanna Lumber Co, mgr 1965-70; Nanna Lumber Co, dept head gen hardware 1960-65; Hanna Lumber Co, floor salesman 1953-60; Hanna Lumber Co, bldg engr 1947-53; Hanna Lumber Co, dir 1965-70; Multi Fab Mfg Corp, dir 1968-71; Tulsa Jr Coll Found Inc, financial agt 1976-. **ORGANIZATIONS:** Turstee, treas First Bapt Ch 1965-; bd mem Hutcherson Br YMCA 1965-; exchequer Kappa Alpha Psi Frat 1970-; bd mem ARC 1976-; bd mem Childrens Med Center 1978-; mem Gov Council on Physical Fitness 1980-; mem Nat Conf of Christians & Jews 1980-. **BUSINESS ADDRESS:** 909 S Boston, Tulsa, OK 74119.

ROBBINS, MILLARD D.
Insurance broker. **PERSONAL:** Born Oct 07, 1919, Columbus, OH; son of Millard and Martha; married Alma Williams; children: Elizabeth Jones, Millard M, Jean M Brown, John J. **EDUCATION:** Roosevelt Univ, BA 1954. **CAREER:** Robbins Ins Agcy, Inc, pres 1947; Robbins Mortgage Co, pres 1962-72; BMJ Co, spres 1981; Robbins Ins Agcy, Inc, broker. **ORGANIZATIONS:** Dir Peoples Energy Corp 1972; dir Independent Bank 1965; dir Chicago Met Mutual Assn Co 1980; dir TR Auto Handling Co 1981; trustee DePaul Unv 1981; bus adv comm Chicago Urban League 1970; co-chmn mem comm Chicago Econ Club 1970; mem Univ Club 1970. **HONORS/ACHIEVEMENTS:** Am Mem Lloyds of London 1978. **MILITARY SERVICE:** AUS 1st sgt 1943-46. **BUSINESS ADDRESS:** Robbins Ins Agcy Inc, 8224 S King Dr, Chicago, IL 60619.

ROBBINS, ROBERT J.
Attorney. **PERSONAL:** Born Jun 13, 1924, Flint, MI; married Beryl Edith Claytor; children: Kevin Frederick. **EDUCATION:** Univ MI, BA 1952; Detroit Coll of Law, JD 1956. **CAREER:** MI Bar Grievance Bd, legal counsel; MI Civil Rights Commn, hearing referee; Private Practice, attorney. **ORGANIZATIONS:** Mem MI, Detroit, Wolverine, Amer Bar Assns; Amer Trial Lawyers Assn; Amer Judicature So; legal adv comm grps; appointed Detroit Bd Educ Com Desegregation & Speakers Bur 1975-; candidate US Congress 1960; precinct delegate rep 1960-64; pres Blaine Ave Block Club 1960-69; vice pres & org Wolverine Rep Orgn 1965; chmn Miller Jr HS Comm Council 1972; mem bd dir Hyde Park Coop Inc; Calvary Presb Ch 1960-, sunday sch tchr & supr, ruling elder bd trustees; mem Bills & Overtures Com & Judicial Bus Com Detroit Presbytery; former mem Interpretation & Stewardship Com Detroit Presbytery; precinct del 5th Precinct Detroit-Rep 1978-80; parliamentarian Rep 13th Congressional Dist Com; mem Issues Com-Rep State Central Com; admitted to practice US Ct of Appeals 6th Judicial Cir 1979; apptd spl counsel State of MI Atty Grievance Comm 1980; elected to membership Detroit Econ Club. **MILITARY SERVICE:** AUS corp 1943-45. **HOME ADDRESS:** 2092 Hyde Pk Dr, Detroit, MI 48207.

ROBERSON, DALTON ANTHONY
Judge. **PERSONAL:** Born May 11, 1937, Mount Vernon, AL; son of Drue Roberson and Sarah Ann Williams-Roberson; married Pearl Janet Stephens; children: Portia, Dalton Jr. **EDUCATION:** MI State Univ, BA, JD; Detroit Coll of Law, BA, JSD. **CAREER:** State of MI, soc worker 1964-68; Wayne Cty, asst prosecutor 1969-70; US Dist, atty 1970-71; Harrison Friedman Roberson, criminal defense lawyer 1970-74; City of Detroit Recorders Court, judge, alternate chief judge. **ORGANIZATIONS:** Mem MI State Bar Assn 1969, Wolverine Bar Assn 1969, Criminal Defense Lawyers Assn 1970-74, MI Civil Rts Commn 1972-73; chmn MI Civil Rts Commn 1973-74; mem MI Judges Assn 1974-; chmn Assn of Black Judges of MI; former bd mem Detroit Branch NAACP; mem exec comm Combines Wayne Circuit/Recorders Court; former mem exec comm MI Judges Assn; bd mem State of MI 1989-. **MILITARY SERVICE:** USAF a/1c 1954-58. **BUSINESS ADDRESS:** Alternate Chief Judge, City of Detroit, Recorders Court, 1441 St Antoine Rm 502, Detroit, MI 48226.

ROBERSON, EARL
College president. **CAREER:** Carver State Technical College, Mobile AL, president. **BUSINESS ADDRESS:** Carver State Technical College, Mobile, AL 36617. *

ROBERSON, F. ALEXIS H.
Administrator. **PERSONAL:** Born Sep 20, 1942, Aiken, SC; daughter of T A Hammond and F M Gomillion Hammond; divorced; children: Alan. **EDUCATION:** Howard Univ, Washington DC, BA, 1963, Masters in Educ, 1974; Univ of the District of Columbia, Washington DC, Post Graduate. **CAREER:** Opportunities Industralization Center, Washington DC, dir remedial educ, 1967-70, curriculum specialist, 1970-73, deputy dir, 1973-80; Washington DC Government, Washington DC, Dept of Recreation, deputy dir, 1980-82, dir, 1983-86, Dept of Employment Serv, dir, 1987-. **ORGANIZATIONS:** Commr, Washington DC Bd of Appeals and Review, Commn of Post-Secondary Educ; chairperson, bd of dir, US Youth Games; mem, The Links Inc, The Girl Friends Inc, The Washington Chapter NAACP, Zion Baptist Church, Washington DC; Govt Representative, The Washington DC Wage-Hour Bd, The Private Industry Council; pres, Washington Metropolitan Area Chapter, Natl Forum for Black Public Admn, 1987-. **HONORS/ACHIEVEMENTS:** Creator, Neighborhood Arts Acad Program, 1984; oraganizer, Ppotomac Riverfest, 1984; organizer, The Mayor's Amateur Boxing Tournament, 1985; The President's Award, Washington NAACP, 1986; Tribute from US House of Representatives, 1987; organizer, Project Success, Washington DC, 1987; Top 100 Black Business & Professional Women, Dollars & Sense Magazine, 1988; Public Serv, Natl Coalition of 100 Black Women, 1989; Public Serv, Washington Urban League, 1989; organizer, Design-A-Youth Program, 1989.

ROBERSON, GARY
Bank executive. **CAREER:** Berkley Federal Savings Bank, Norfolk VA, chief executive. **BUSINESS ADDRESS:** Berkley Federal Savings Bank, 101 Granby St, Norfolk, VA 23510. *

ROBERSON, LAWRENCE R.
Certified financial planner. **PERSONAL:** Born Aug 26, 1946, Birmingham, AL. **EDUCATION:** Alabama A&M Univ, BS 1967; Indiana Univ, MBA 1970; College for Financial Plng, CFP 1986. **CAREER:** IBM, systems engr 1967-68, financial analyst 1969; Ford Motor Co, supervisor financial analysis 1973-83; Wealth Management Group Inc, pres. **ORGANIZATIONS:** Mem Inst for Certified Financial Planners 1983-, Internatl Assoc for Financial Plng 1984-; dir Intl Exchange Cncl 1986-. **HONORS/ACHIEVEMENTS:** White House FEllowship Prog Regional finalist 1983-84; Outstanding Young Men in Amer; Who's Who in the Midwest. **BUSINESS ADDRESS:** President, Wealth Management Group Inc, 400 Renaissance Ctr, Ste 500, Detroit, MI 48243.

ROBERSON, SANDRA SHORT See SHAKOOR, WAHEEDAH AQUEELAH

ROBERTS, ALFRED LLOYD
Educator. **PERSONAL:** Born Dec 18, 1942; married Billie Kert; children: Alfrelynn, Latasha. **EDUCATION:** Prairie View A&M U, BS 1963; TX A&M U, MEd 1966, PhD 1973. **CAREER:** Dallas Independent Sch Dist, music coordinator 1965-69, elem prin 1969-71, dir community relations 1971-; E Oak Cliff Sub Dist, dep asst supt. **ORGANIZATIONS:** Mem Am Research Assn; Nat Elem Sch Prins; Nat Educ Assn; Phi Delta Kappa; Dallas Sch Administrs Assn; TX Sch Pub Relations Assn; Nat Sch PubRelations Assn; mem Alpha Phi Alpha; mem St Luke Comm United Meth Ch; mem Historic Preservation League; mem Com of 100; YMCA. **HONORS/ACHIEVEMENTS:** Dallas Negro C of C nominee; Ford Found Urban Educ Adminstr fellow 1970. **BUSINESS ADDRESS:** Administrator, Dallas ISD, 3700 Ross Ave, Dallas, TX 75204.

ROBERTS, ANN F.
Food service administrator. **CAREER:** Royal Ridge Management Co, Cleveland OH, chief executive. **BUSINESS ADDRESS:** Royal Ridge Management Co, 440 Leader Bldg, Cleveland, OH 44114. *

ROBERTS, BLANCHE ELIZABETH
Bank executive. **PERSONAL:** Born Apr 23, 1955, Chicago, IL; daughter of Dr Leroy Edison Jones and Alexandra Mary Hoover Johnson; married Charles Scott Roberts, Nov 23, 1985; children: Alexis Cleo. **EDUCATION:** Univ of Iowa, Iowa City IA, attended, 1972; Dartmouth Coll, Hanover NH, BA, 1977; DePaul Univ, Chicago IL, MBA, 1983. **CAREER:** Universidad de Granada, Granada, Spain, Spanish teaching asst, 1978; Instituto Chileno Norte Am, Santiago, Chile, English instructor, 1978-79; Charles of the Ritz, Chicago IL, commn sales, 1979-80; Freedom Systems, Chicago IL, exec asst, 1980-82; Northern Trust Company, Chicago IL, intl officer, 1982-85; First Natl Bank of Chicago, Chicago IL, asst vice pres, 1985-87; Exchange Natl Bank, Chicago IL, vice pres, 1987-. **ORGANIZATIONS:** Volunteer, Recording for the Blind, 1980; mem, State Microscopical Soc of Illinois, 1971; jr mem, Soc of Cosmetic Chemists, 1976-78; mem, Beta Gamma Sigma, Natl Honor Soc, 1983, Natl Corporate Cash Mgmt Assn, 1985-; dir, Visiting Nurse Assn of Chicago, 1988-, VNA Ventures (for profit company), 1988-. **HONORS/ACHIEVEMENTS:** First Place Winner (Outstanding), Chicago Science Fair, 1971, 1972, 1973; Semi-Finalist, Westinghouse Science Talent Search, 1973; First Place Winner (Outstanding), State Science Fair, 1973; Outstanding Sr in Science, Math Kenwood Acad, 1973; Vice President, Senior Class, 1973; Varsity Letter Winner, Dartmouth Coll, 1974, 1975, 1976; Willard Tostman Mmemorial Scholar, Dartmouth Coll, 1975; Chicago's Up and Coming, Dollars and Sense Magazine, 1988. **HOME ADDRESS:** 5448 South Cornell Ave, Chicago, IL 60615.

ROBERTS, BOBBY L.
Manufacturing executive. **PERSONAL:** Born Sep 19, 1938, Windom, TX. **EDUCATION:** Prairie View A&M Univ, BS 1960; Fairleigh Dickinson Univ, MBA 1978. **CAREER:** Plantation Foods Corp, supervisor 1960-62; Houston Lighting-Power Co, aux engr 1965-70; Anheuser-Busch Inc, operations engr 1970-72; Johnson & Johnson, chief engr 1972-86. **ORGANIZATIONS:** Mem NB MBA Assn Inc 1982-; mem sec Amer Inst of Plant Engrs 1984-. **HONORS/ACHIEVEMENTS:** Chicago Metropolitan Black and Hispanic Achievers of Industry Recognition Awd YMCA 1980; Plant Engineer of the Year Amer Inst of Plant Engrs Fox Valley Chap 1986. **MILITARY SERVICE:** AUS specialist 4th class 2 yrs. **HOME ADDRESS:** 1609 Signal Dr, Naperville, IL 60565. **BUSINESS ADDRESS:** Director of Operations Engineering, Wesley - Jessen Corporation, 400 West Superior Street, Chicago, IL 60610.

ROBERTS, CHARLES L.
Executive director. **PERSONAL:** Born May 25, 1943, Farmerville, LA; married Charlesetta Shoulders; children: Traci, Channa. **EDUCATION:** KY State U, BS;Univ of Louisville, MS;Univ of GA. **CAREER:** City of Louisville, dir of sanitation; Met Parks & Recreation Bd, asst dir 1970-74; Louisville Sch Dist, tchr 1964-70. **ORGANIZATIONS:** Mem Am Pub Works Assn; Mgmt Planning Council; State Reg Crime Council; NAACP; Omega Psi Phi. **HONORS/ACHIEVEMENTS:** Outstanding citizen award 1973. **BUSINESS ADDRESS:** 400 S 6 St, Louisville, KY.

ROBERTS, CHERYL DORNITA LYNN
Educator. **PERSONAL:** Born Jul 31, 1958, Martinsburg, WV; daughter of Shelby L Roberts Sr (deceased) and Dorothy J Davenport Roberts. **EDUCATION:** Shepherd Coll, BS 1980; Univ of DC, MA 1984. **CAREER:** Edgemeade of MD, recreation specialist 1980-81; Univ of DC, asst coach men's basketball 1981-85; Veterans Admin Med Ctr, recreation therapist 1985-87, vocational rehabilitation specialist 1987-88, asst chief, Domiciliary Operations 1988-. **ORGANIZATIONS:** Mem Amer Assn for Adult & Continued Ed 1983-, Delta Sigma Theta Sor Inc 1984-, mem Shepherd College Alumni Assn. **HONORS/ACHIEVEMENTS:** TV Appearances Good Morning Amer 1981, 1982; NY Times Feature Article Sports World Specials 1984. **BUSINESS ADDRESS:** Asst Chief, Domiciliary Operations, Domiciliary Operations (13B), Bldg 217 Room 37, Martinsburg, WV 25401.

ROBERTS, DONALD LEE
General manager. **PERSONAL:** Born Dec 20, 1929, South Orange, NJ; married Margaret Robinson. **EDUCATION:** WV State Coll, BS 1952. **CAREER:** Amalgamated Publishers Inc, vice pres gen mgr 1975-, gen mgr 1966-75, bus mgr 1958-66; Internal Revenue, agt 1955-58; Friendly Fuld Neighbrhd Ctr, pres. **ORGANIZATIONS:** Life mem NAACP; interim aud of accts natl office Kappa Alpha Psi Frat; life mem Kappa Alpha Psi Frat; mem 100 Black Men; mem Essex Co Urban League; mem Civil Liberties Union; mem Nat Bus League; mem Nat Assn of Mkt Develrs. **HONORS/ACHIEVEMENTS:** Kappa Alpha Psi Award, Northeastern Province 1977. **MILITARY SERVICE:** AUS 1st lt 1952-54. **BUSINESS ADDRESS:** 293 E Hazelwood Ave, Rahway, NJ 07065.

ROBERTS, EDWARD A.
Educational administrator. **PERSONAL:** Born Jun 17, 1950, Brooklyn, NY; married Yuklin B John. **EDUCATION:** City Coll of NY, BA 1979. **CAREER:** 902 Auto Inc, asst dir 1980-; City Univ of NY, bd of trustees 1976-80; Univ Student Senate City Univ of NY, chmn 1976-80; CCNY Office of the Dean of Students, asst higher educ officer 1975-76. **ORGANIZATIONS:** Exec mem Com for Pub Higher Educ 1977-79; mem NY State Higher Educ Servs Corp 1978; mem Gov's Task Force on Higher Educ 1979; mem City Coll Pres Policy Adv Com 1976-77; pres Carter's Action Review Commn 1977. **HONORS/ACHIEVEMENTS:** Outstanding Enlisted Man Award AUS 1972; "Who's Who in Am U" 1978; award of merit Bronx Comm Coll 1979, Queens Coll 1978, City Coll NY 1978. **MILITARY SERVICE:** AUS E-5 1971-73. **BUSINESS ADDRESS:** 535 E 80th St, New York, NY 10021.

ROBERTS, ELLA S.
Occupancy supervisor. **PERSONAL:** Born Aug 30, 1927, New Castle, KY; widowed; children: 5 children. **EDUCATION:** Lincoln Inst of Kentucky, 1945; Business School, 1946; Univ of Louisville, certificate. **CAREER:** Housing Authority of Louisville, Jefferson County School Dist Title I ESEA Parent Advisory Council, occupancy supervisor chmn. **ORGANIZATIONS:** Mem Citizens Team for Schools Eval Study Youth Dir Mt Olive Bapt Ch; asst dir Central Dist Young People of WMU; financial sec Central Dist Sun School & BTU Conv. **BUSINESS ADDRESS:** 420 S Eighth St, Louisville, KY 40203.

ROBERTS, EVELYN HOARD
Educator, consultant. **PERSONAL:** Born Nov 02, 1920, McAlester, OK. **EDUCATION:** Stowe Teachers Coll, BA 1940; Teachers Coll, Columbia Univ, MA 1946, EdD 1977. **CAREER:** St Louis Public Schs, teacher 1941-60; Harris Teachers Coll, instr English dept

1961-63; author Amer Literature & the Arts incl Black Expression, 1977; St Louis Comm Coll Meramec, prof English dept 1963-. **ORGANIZATIONS:** Dir, Back to School/Stay in School Program, 1989, past pres 1963-66, St Louis NAACP, natl bd dir 1966-; mem MO Adv Comm to US Civil Rights Commn 1965-75; mem Natl Assoc for Supr & Curriculum Develop 1976-; adv bd The Roy Wilkins Foundation 1983-; trustee NAACP Special Contribution Fund 1984-; pres The Crisis Magazine NAACP 1984; trustee The Missouri Historical Soc 1985; mem Intl Modern Language Assn of Amer; Natl Council of Teachers of English; Conf on Coll Composition & Communication; Midwest Modern Language Assn; lifemem NEA; MO Assn of Comm Jr Coll; Natl Soc Literature & the Arts; St Louis Coun Teachers English; life mem Alpha Kappa Alpha Sor. **HONORS/ACHIEVEMENTS:** Service Award St Louis Argus Newspaper 1957; appointed John Hay Fellow in Humanities 1960; Outstanding Comm Serv St Louis Assoc of Colored Women's Clubs Inc 1964; Woman of Achievement in Human Relations St Louis Globe-Dem Newspaper 1966; Citizen of the Week WRTH Radio 1966 Region IV NAACP Distinguished Serv Award 1975; appionted Smithsonia Natl Assn 1976; hon fellow Harry S Truman Library Inst 1977; St Louis Comm Coll Serv (15 Yrs) 1978; MTCNI, NAACP Awd 1978; awarded scholarship American Forum for Intl Study in Africa 1979; Outstanding Serv Awd Natl Women's Conf 1980; St Louis Sentinel Newspaper Awd Educ & Civic Work 1984; St Louis Comm Coll Serv Awd 1985 and prior years; Author, Amer Literature and the Arts Including Black Expression, 1977, 407pp; Article, "Tom Weatherly.". **BUSINESS ADDRESS:** Professor of English, St Louis Comm Coll at Meramec, 11333 Big Bend Blvd, St Louis, MO 63122.

ROBERTS, GRADY H., JR.
University educator, administrator. **PERSONAL:** Born Feb 08, 1940, Pittsburgh. **EDUCATION:** Central State Univ, Wilberforce OH, BS 1963; Univ of Pittsburgh, MSW 1965, MPH 1971, PhD 1974. **CAREER:** Univ of Pittsburgh School of Social Work, dir of admissions, asst prof 1969-; Western Psychiatric Inst & Clinic, psychiatric social worker 1967-69; Madigan Gen Hosp Tacoma WA, clinical social work officer, social work serv 1965-67. **ORGANIZATIONS:** Mem Assn of Black Soc wrkrs; Cncl on Soc wrk Ed; Nat Assn of Soc Wrkrs; mem Alpha Phi Alpha; NAACP. **MILITARY SERVICE:** AUS capt 1965-67; AUSR maj 1985. **BUSINESS ADDRESS:** University of Pittsburgh, School of Social Work, 2103 Cathedral of Learning, Pittsburgh, PA 15260.

ROBERTS, HARLAN WILLIAM, III
Systems engineer, consultant. **PERSONAL:** Born Jan 12, 1931, Wilmington, DE; divorced; children: Teala Jeanne, Harlan David. **EDUCATION:** Univ of PA, BS, MSW 1976. **CAREER:** United Methodist Action Program, suprv 1968-69; Family Serv Northern DE, counselor 1969-74; Univ of PA Family Maintance Org, coord 1975-76; Mental Health-Child Protective Serv of MD, clinical therapist. **ORGANIZATIONS:** Bd mem Delaware OIC 1970-74; bd mem Family Assoc of Amer 1971-74; exec bd Wilmington DE Chap NAACP 1971-82; 1st vice pres Wilmington United Neighborhood 1973-74; vice pres & pres Red Clay Consolidated Sch Bd 1981-85. **HONORS/ACHIEVEMENTS:** Harriet Tubman DE Chapter Harriet Tubman 1984. **MILITARY SERVICE:** AUS capt 8 yrs; US Ranger, Counted Intellegent Corp. **HOME ADDRESS:** 221 N Cleveland Ave, Wilmington, DE 19805.

ROBERTS, HERMAN
Business executive. **PERSONAL:** Born Jan 21, 1924, Beggs, OK; married Sonja Williams; children: Stephan, Herman, Fredric, Ewan, Rodne. **CAREER:** Taxicab Co, owner; Roberts Show Club, 1954-61; Roberts Motels Inc, pres 1961-. **ORGANIZATIONS:** Active in various comm endeavors; mem IL Citizens Found. **HONORS/ACHIEVEMENTS:** Disting Publ Serv Awd; Spec Recognition Awd Washington Pk YMCA; Man of the Year FFAF & Amer Guild Variety Artists Awd; Cert of Appreciation BSA; Honoree Annual Brotherhood Banquet. **BUSINESS ADDRESS:** President, Roberts Motels Inc, 301 E 63rd Dr, Chicago, IL 60637.

ROBERTS, HERMESE E.
Retired educator. **PERSONAL:** Born Sep 22, 1913, Panama Canal Zone, Panama;son of Jonathan Johnson and May Johnson; married Edwards J Roberts, Sr; children: Edward James Jr, Hermese Edwina. **EDUCATION:** Hunter Coll of NY, BA 1934; Atlanta Univ Atlanta, GA, MA 1941; Nova Univ Ft Lauderdale, FL, EdD 1975; Columbia Univ, Univ of Chgo, Advanced Stds. **CAREER:** Atlanta Univ Lab Sch, tchr 1934-39; Peach Cty Tr Sch Ft Valley, prin 1939-45; Southern Univ, reading program dir, 1945-46; Univ of Chicago Reading Clinics, reading clinician, 1946-49; Chicago Pub Sch, clin psych 1949-54; Dartmouth Coll, reading specialist, 1964; Amer Book Co, consultant, 1965-71; Mayo Elem Sch Chgo, IL, prin 1955-83. **ORGANIZATIONS:** Mem, Natl Educ Assn 1957; mem Intl Reading Assn; mem Chicago Princpals Assn. **HONORS/ACHIEVEMENTS:** Author, Dandy Dog Early Learning Program, Am Book Co 1966; co-author, Amer Book Co Basic Readers 1970; author, The Third Ear, English Language Inst 1970; "Don't Teach Them to Read" Elementary English NCTE 1970; editor, The Glories of Christ, by H J Heijkoop (translated from the German), Believers Bookshelf, Ontario, Canada, 1989.

ROBERTS, JAMES E.
Physician. **PERSONAL:** Born Jul 27, 1903, Mt Pleasant, PA; married Sylvesta R; children: Karen, Lisa. **EDUCATION:** Howard U, BS 1931, MS 1933, MD 1937. **CAREER:** Physician surgeon Ob-gyn; HowardUniv Med Sch, clinical instr, Obs-gyn 1941-75; MD Fair Housing Inc, Montgomery Co MD, founder vice pres 1961-; Montgomery Co Gynecological Soc, founder vice pres 1962-; Am Cancer Soc Metro Comm, Metropolitan Area Wash, pres 1974-75; Am Cancer Soc Div State of MD, pres elect 1976-77. **ORGANIZATIONS:** Mem Chi Delta Mu 1937-; chmn serv com Montgomery Co Unit Am Cancer Soc 1962-70, vice pres 1970-72, pres 1972-75; bd dir MD Div Am Cancer Soc 1964-. **HONORS/ACHIEVEMENTS:** Certificate of appreciation Pres Harry S Truman 1953, Dwight Eisenhower 1958, Lyndon B Johnson 1963; volunteer of year Am Cancer Soc 1972; citation 21 yrs serv treas of Assoc of Former Interns & Residents of Freedman's Hosp, Wash, DC; outstanding serv award White Oak Civic Assn; Father of Yr, Jack & Jill of Am Inc 1973. **BUSINESS ADDRESS:** 2328 Georgia Ave NW, Washington, DC 20001.

ROBERTS, JAMES T. L.
Physician. **PERSONAL:** Born Oct 30, 1954, Atlanta, GA. **EDUCATION:** Luther Coll, BS 1976; GA State Univ, MA 1980; Meharry Medical Coll, MD 1985. **CAREER:** Cook Co Hosp Dept of Ob/Gyn, physician 1985-. **ORGANIZATIONS:** Mem Phi Beta Sigma Inc Frat 1984-; group dir Big Brother of Amer 1985; mem Black Physicians Assoc of Cook Co Hosp 1985-; junior fellow Amer College of Ob/Gyn 1985-, Chicago Medical Soc 1985-. **HONORS/ACHIEVEMENTS:** Mem Alpha Omega Alpha Honor Medical Soc 1986; Certificate of Mutual Child Health Meharry Medical Coll 1983. **MILITARY SERVICE:** AUS Reserves 2nd lt 1983-. **BUSINESS ADDRESS:** Cook County Hospital, Ddpt of Ob/Gyn, 720 So Wolcott #1214, Chicago, IL 60612.

ROBERTS, JOHN B.
Business executive. **PERSONAL:** Born Mar 23, 1912, Dublin, GA; married Helen; children: John Jr. **CAREER:** Stunt bicycle rider 1930's; Cleveland Area Bicycle Dealers Assoc, org 1946; Roberts Enter, owner 1940-. **ORGANIZATIONS:** Bd mem Cleveland Bus League 25 yrs; mem Minority Econ Council, Comm Businessmen Credit Union, LERTA. **HONORS/ACHIEVEMENTS:** Awd of Hon Cleveland Bus League 1948. **MILITARY SERVICE:** AUS pvt 1943. **BUSINESS ADDRESS:** Roberts Enterprise, 7703-5-7 Cedar Ave, Cleveland, OH 44103.

ROBERTS, LESLIE J.
Executive director. **PERSONAL:** Born Jan 13, 1927, Flint, MI; children: 's Aid & Family Ser, present; Asst. **EDUCATION:** Wayne State U, BA 1954, MSW 1960. **CAREER:** Children's Aid Soc, exec dir; Sch of Soc Work, Wayne State, asst prof 1967-72; Neighborhood Ser Orgn, casework supr 1963-67; Children's Aid & Family Ser of Macomb Co, social worker 1959-63; Detroit Pub Welfare Dept, social worker 1956-59. **ORGANIZATIONS:** Mem Nat Assn of Social Workers; charter mem Assn of Black Social Workers; appointed Gov Welfare Study Comm; vice pres MI Fedn of Child & Family Agencies. **MILITARY SERVICE:** USN seaman 1/C 1945.

ROBERTS, LILLIAN
Business executive. **PERSONAL:** Born Jan 02, 1928, Chicago, IL; daughter of Henry Davis and Lillian Henry Davis; divorced. **EDUCATION:** Wilson Jr Coll; Univ of IL, attended 1944-45; Roosevelt Univ, Labor School 1958-60; Coll of New Rochelle, Honorary Degree LittD 1973. **CAREER:** Lying-In Hospital Chicago, nurse's aide/techn/employee organizer 1945-65; AFSCME Chicago & NYC, labor rep Hosp Div dir DC-37 1965-67; District Cncl 37 AFSCME NYC, assoc dir 1967-81; NYS Dept of Labor Albany, commr of labor 1981-87; Total Health Systems, sr vice pres. **ORGANIZATIONS:** Mem of numerous soc welfare and cultural orgn; hon adv bd of Natl Medical Fellowships; natl exec bd, Jewish Labor Comm Amer Jewish Congr; adv bdof Resources for Children with Special Needs Inc, A Philip Randolph Inst; bd of trustees of the Coll of New Rochelle, Amer for Democratic Action, NAACP NY Branch, Alvin Ailey/City Center Dance Theater, Kingston Artists Group, Delta Sigma Theta Sorority, NOW. **HONORS/ACHIEVEMENTS:** Roy Wilkins Award NAACP; Benjamin Potoker Award NYS Employees' Brotherhood Comm; Westchester Minority Contr Assn Achievement Award for Industry; Histadrut Humanitarian Award the Amer Trade Council for Histadrut; Good Govt Award NYS Careerists; Adam Clayton Powell Govt Award the Opport Indust Center 1982; the Hispanic Women's Center (NYC) Honorary Award; Friends of Educ Award the Assn of Black Educators of NY 1983; Frederick Douglass Award NY Urban League; Labor Award for Leadership Adjunct Faculty Assn of Nassau Comm Coll 1984; A Salute to America's Top 100 Black Business and Professional Women 1985.

ROBERTS, LORRAINE MARIE
Educator. **PERSONAL:** Born May 12, 1930, Philadelphia, PA; children: Kevin M, Harlan K. **EDUCATION:** Hampton Inst, Hampton VA, BS 1952; Bucknell Univ, Lewisburg, PA, exchange student; Columbia Univ NY, MA 1954. **CAREER:** Bowling Green Bd of Educ VA, teacher 1952-53; Rochester City School Dist, teacher 1956-64; NYS Univ System State Educ Dept, adj prof; Poughkeepsie NY City School Dist, coordinator, Business Educ, teacher, chairperson, Occupational Educ, 1966-. **ORGANIZATIONS:** Mem BTA; EBTA; PPSTA; NYSUT; AFL-TA Bd of trustees YWCA, Dutchess Co 1970-75; bd of dir (sec/mem) United Way of Dutchess County 1973-; chrpn Central Alloc Div United Way of Dutchess Co 1979-80; basileus/mem Iota Alpha Omega Chap Alpha Kappa Alpha Sor 1969-; mem Bethel Missionary Bapt Ch; mem NAACP; mem AFS of Poughkeepsie Comm Serv Awards, Am Legion; United Way; 4-h Clubs; NAACP. **HONORS/ACHIEVEMENTS:** Who's Who Am Coll Students 1952; Outstanding Educators in Am 1973-74; Area 10 leader/consultant/regents com; mem Bus Educ Div NYS Educ Dept. **BUSINESS ADDRESS:** Chairperson Occupational Educ, Poughkeepsie High School, May & Forbus St, Poughkeepsie, NY 12601.

ROBERTS, LOUIS WRIGHT
Government transportation official. **PERSONAL:** Born Sep 01, 1913, Jamestown, NY; son of Louis Lorenzo Roberts and Dora Catherine Wright; married Mercedes Pearl McGavock, Jun 08, 1938; children: Louis M, Lawrence E. **EDUCATION:** Fisk Univ, AB 1935; Univ of MI, MS 1937; MIT, PhD candidate, 1946. **CAREER:** Fisk Univ, teaching asst, physics dept, 1935-36; St Augustine's Coll, instructor, 1937-40, assoc prof of physics & mathematics, 1941-42; Howard Univ, assoc prof of physics, 1943-44; Sylvania Electric Products Inc, mgr, tube div, 1944-50; MIT Research Laboratory for Electronics, tube consultant, 1950-51; Microwave Assocs Inc, founder & pres, 1950-55; Bomac Laboratories Inc, engineering specialist & consultant, 1955-59; METCOM Inc, founder, vice pres & dir, 1959-67, Elcon Laboratories, pres, 1962-66; Addison-Wesley Press, consultant, 1963-67; NASA Electronics Research Center, chief, microwave laboratory, 1967-68, chief, optics & microwave laboratory, 1968-70; MIT, visiting sr lecturer, 1979-80; US Dept of Transportation, Transportation Systems Center, deputy dir, office of technology, 1970-72, dir, office of technology, 1972-77, dir, office of energy & environment, 1977-79, deputy dir, 1979, dir, office of data systems and technology, 1980-82, dir, office of admin, 1982-83, assoc dir, office of operations engineering, 1983-84, acting deputy dir, 1984, acting dir, 1984-85, dir, 1985-. **ORGANIZATIONS:** Mem Marine Electronics Comm Panel of the US-Japan Natural Resources Commn 1969-; mem adv bd Coll of Engrg Univ of MA 1972-; mem bd of trustees Univ Hosp Boston Univ 1973-; mem President's Adv Bd Bentley Coll 1974-; corporator Wakefield Svgs Bank 1975-; life fellow IEEE; mem AAAS, AAAA, Soc of Automotive Engrs. **HONORS/ACHIEVEMENTS:** Life Fellow Inst of Electrical and Electronic Engrs 1964-; Apollo Achievement Awd NASA; Outstanding Achievement Awd Univ of MI 1978; Letter of Appreciation AGARD/NATO 1979; Certificate of Appreciation Chelsea Kiwanis Club 1979; Order of the Engr Awd Univ of MA 1980; Sr Exec Service Bonus Awd 1983; Presidential Rank Meritorious Exec 1984; Doctor of Laws Fisk Univ 1985; Sr Exec Serv Bonus Awds 1985, 1986, 1987, 1988; author of 15 journal articles & about 120 company, univ & govt reports; editor, author, Handbook of Microwave Measurements, McGraw-Hill; holder of 9 patents. **HOME ADDRESS:** 5 Michael Rd, Wakefield, MA 01880. **BUSINESS ADDRESS:** Dir, Transportation Systems Ctr, 55 Broadway, Cambridge, MA 02142.

ROBERTS, MICHAEL V.
Attorney. **PERSONAL:** Born Oct 24, 1948, St Louis. **EDUCATION:** Lindenwood Coll, BS; St Louis Univ Law Sch, JD; Hague Acad Intl Law, Hague Holland, cert; Intl Inst Human Rights, Strasbourg France, cert. **CAREER:** Wayman F Smith III, Margaret Bush Wilson, asso atty. **ORGANIZATIONS:** Mem Kappa Alpha Psi Frat; Phi Delta Phi Legal Frat; MO Athletic Club; St Louis Council on World Affairs; pres St Louis Ebony Ski Club; mem cert PADI Scuba Diver's Assn; pres, fdr Hague Acad Com for Human Rights; fdr, mem 3rd Dimensional Alliance for Human Rights; bd mgr YMCA Jr Kind; mem All Saints Epis Ch; tchr, leader Am Youth Found; alt commnr St Louis Land Reutil Auth. **HONORS/ACHIEVEMENTS:** JCCA tennis champ; Danforth Found Fellowship.

ROBERTS, NARLIE
Business executive, owner. **PERSONAL:** Born Apr 14, 1931, Martin, SC; married Ann F Bush; children: Yvonne Pierce Moore, Michael. **EDUCATION:** Adult Educ Courses & Bus Seminars. **CAREER:** Royal Ridge Mgmt Co-McDonald Restaurants, pres 1970-; R & B Lathing & Plastering Inc, Cleveland, pres 1953-70. **ORGANIZATIONS:** Bd dirs Cleveland Growth Assn; bd dirs Rainey Inst of Music; bd dirs Superior-Euclid Devel Corp. **HONORS/ACHIEVEMENTS:** Award for Leadership in Humanitarian Activities, Mayor of E Cleveland; Cit of Merit, Muscular Dystrophy Assn; Outstanding Leadership in Student Training & Devel, E Cleveland Dept of Comm Devel; Top 10 McDonald Restaurant Award, Ohio region. **BUSINESS ADDRESS:** Royal Ridge Mgmt Co, 650 Leader Bldg, Cleveland, OH 44114.

ROBERTS, PAQUITA HUDSON
Educator. **PERSONAL:** Born Mar 02, 1938, Andrew, SC; children: Craig, Tali, Paquita. **EDUCATION:** South Carolina State Coll, BA 1961; Newark State Coll, MA 1967. **CAREER:** Hospital Center of Orange, speech pathologist 1964-67; Newark Bd of Educ, 1968-69; Mt Carmel Guild, prog dir 1969-75; NJ Dept of Educ, educ program specialist 1979-. **ORGANIZATIONS:** Consultant Orange Head Start, Intercoastal Business Associates, Barnett Hosp Speech and Hearing Div, CH Aston Assocs; adv bd RAP NY Univ Council forExceptional Children 1979-; vice pres chairperson bd of educ Christian St Marks AME Church. **HONORS/ACHIEVEMENTS:** Special Education Fellowship NJ Dept of Educ; Professional Recognition NJ Div for Early Childhood Awd 1986. **HOME ADDRESS:** 29 Burchard Ave, East Orange, NJ 07017. **BUSINESS ADDRESS:** Education Program Specialist, NJ Department of Education, 225 West State St, Trenton, NJ 08625.

ROBERTS, ROY J.
Educator. **PERSONAL:** Born Jul 01, 1940, Carthage, TX; married Brown; children: William, Ronan. **EDUCATION:** Willey Coll, BS 1964; Yeshiva U, atnd 1967-69; StateUniv of NY at Stony Brook, 1969-70; Adelphi, 1973-74. **CAREER:** Upward Bound Affirmative Action Com, dir proj; Dowling Coll, chairperson 1970-; Bellport NY, mathematics teacher 1967-70; E Islip NY, mathematics teacher 1966-67; John Marshall HS, physics instr 1964-66; Long Island Assn of Black Counselors, treas 1969. **ORGANIZATIONS:** Mem Minority Educators Assn of Long Island 1974-; Cits United for the Betterment of Educ 1967-; NEA 1968-; treas Assn fr Equality & Excellence in Educ 1979-; mem Bayshore Cntrl Islip NAACP 1966-; vol Bellport Ambulance Co 1968-; Bellport Fellowship 1968-. **BUSINESS ADDRESS:** Proj Upward Bound Dowling Coll, Oakdale, NY 11769.

ROBERTS, ROY S.
Vice president of personnel. **EDUCATION:** Western Michigan Univ, Business grad. **CAREER:** GM Assembly Plant North Tarrytown NY, mgr; General Motors Detroit, vice pres of personnel.

ROBERTS, SALLY-ANN See CRAFT, SALLY-ANN ROBERTS

ROBERTS, SAMUEL KELTON
Educator. **PERSONAL:** Born Sep 01, 1944, Muskogee, OK; married Valerie Hermoine Fisher; children: Samuel Kelton Jr, Franklin. **EDUCATION:** Univ de Lyon France, Diplome 1966; Morehouse Coll, BA 1967; Union Theol Sem, MDiv 1970; Columbia Univ, PhD 1974. **CAREER:** New York City Mission Soc, summer proj dir 1967-70; S Hempstead Congregational Church, pastor 1972-73; Pittsburgh Theol Sem, asst prof 1973-76; Union Theol Sem, asst prof religion & soc 1976-80; VA Union Univ, dean 1980-. **ORGANIZATIONS:** Mem Amer Acad of Rel; mem Soc for the Scientific Study of Rel; mem Soc for the Study of Black Relition. **HONORS/ACHIEVEMENTS:** Merril Overseas Study Award Morehouse Coll 1965-66; Protestant Fellow Fund for Theol Educ 1967-70; Fellow Columbia Univ 1970-72; author "George Edmund Haynes" 1978. **BUSINESS ADDRESS:** Dean, VA Union University, 1500 N Lombardy St, Richmond, VA 23220.

ROBERTS, STEVEN C.
Government official. **PERSONAL:** Born Apr 11, 1952, St Louis, MO; married Eva Louise Frazer. **EDUCATION:** Clark Univ, AB 1974; Washington Univ, LLM - JD 1977. **CAREER:** Roberts-Roberts & Assoc, business consult 1974-; private practice attorney 1980-; City of St Louis, alderman 1979-. **ORGANIZATIONS:** Mem Kappa Alpha Psi 1971-; bd dir N St Louis Amer Cancer Soc 1976-; bd dir Nursery Found of St Louis 1978-, Conf of Educ St Louis City & County 1978; mem Natl Bar Assn 1980, Amer Bar Assn 1980; bd dir Providence Prog Inc, St Louis Metro Urban League. **HONORS/ACHIEVEMENTS:** Fellowship Danforth Foundation 1974-77; Undergrad Achievement Award Kappa Alpha Psi Frat 1974; Bethune Grad Student Award Washington Univ 1977; "Dynamic Duo" Ebony Mag 1979. **BUSINESS ADDRESS:** Alderman Ward 20, City St Louis Bd of Aldermen, City Hall, Room 230, St Louis, MO 63103.

ROBERTS, TALMADGE
Business executive. **PERSONAL:** Born Feb 16, 1931, Ozark, AL; married Mary Elizabeth. **EDUCATION:** Howard Univ, BS 1957. **CAREER:** Food & Drug Admin, biochemist 1966-68; Paine Webber, stockbroker 1968-. **ORGANIZATIONS:** Bd dir/chrperson corp comm Bd of Pension of United Methodist Ch 1980-; bd dir Pax World Fund 1985; mem Capitol Press Club 1983-; mem NAACP 1980-; mem Urban League 1982-; bd of dirs Wesley Theological Seminary 1986. **MILITARY SERVICE:** USAF Corpl 1949-53. **HOME ADDRESS:** 5332 28th St NW, Washington, DC 20015. **BUSINESS ADDRESS:** Account Vice President, Paine, Webber, 1120 20th St NW, Washington, DC 20036.

ROBERTS, THOMAS L.
Educator. **PERSONAL:** Born Apr 17, 1932, Key West, FL; children: Kevin D, Garrett L. **EDUCATION:** Trinity Univ San Antonio, TX, MS 1961; Talladega Coll Talladega, AL, BS 1957; Clark Univ Worcester, MA, PhD 1965; Walden Univ Naples, FL, PhD 1977. **CAREER:** Univ TX Med Branch Galveston, rsch asst 1957-59; USAF Sch Aerospace Med, San Antonio, TX, microbiolgst 1959-63; MELPAR Inc, Falls Church, VA, scientist-microbiolgst 1963; Worcester State Coll, Worcester, MA, prof 1965-88; Univ MA Med Sch Worcester, adj prof nuclear med 1976-88. **ORGANIZATIONS:** Consultant Kane Med Labs Worcester, MA 1965-76; editoral bd Science of Biology Journal 1977-81; visiting prof Univ Liberia, WA 1972; bd dir Worcester Co-op Council Inc 1968-72; bd of dir Worcester Model Cities Inc 1967-70; pres Rehab Ctr of Worcester Inc 1978-81; chmn bd of trustees/dirs Rehab Ctr Worcester Inc 1979-81; mem Corp of Bermuda Biological Rsch Station. **HONORS/ACHIEVEMENTS:** John Hay Whitney Foundation Fellow Clark Univ Worcester, MA 1964-65; Teaching Fellow Clark Univ, MA 1963-65; Post-Doc Fellow Clark Univ, MA 1965-68; 20 research articles & comm; Fellow Soc of Sigma XI; Amer Inst of Chemists; New York Academy of Sciences. **MILITARY SERVICE:** AUS cprl 1952-55; USNR cmdr 1964-83.

ROBERTS, VIRGIL PATRICK
Business executive. **PERSONAL:** Born Jan 04, 1947, Ventura, CA; son of Julius Roberts and Emma Roberts; married Brenda Cecelia Banks; children: Gisele Simone, Hayley Tasha. **EDUCATION:** Ventura Coll, AA 1966; UCLA, BA 1968; Harvard Univ, JD 1972. **CAREER:** Pacht, Ross, Warne, Bernhard & Sears Law Firm, assoc 1972-76; Manning & Roberts Law Firm, sr partner 1976-81; Dick Griffey Prod, pres 1981-. **ORGANIZATIONS:** Judge pro tem Beverly Hills & L A Municipal Courts 1979-; pres Beverly Hill Bar Scholarship Found 1980; bd of govs Beverly Hills Bar Assn 1975-76; bd of govs Beverly Hills Brstrs & LA Cnty Brstrs 1975-77; bd mem LA Educ Partnership 1983-; bd mem CORO Found 1984-; treas bd mem Museum of African-Amer Art LA 1982-86; commr State of CA Comm Tchr Cr 1981-84. **HONORS/ACHIEVEMENTS:** Comm Serv Awrd LA Urban League 1978; Image Awrd Hollywood Beverly Hills NAACP 1980; Foreign Affairs Schlr Ford Found/Howard Univ 1968-69; "Discourage on Black Nationalism" Amer Behavorial Scientst 1969; "Minority Interest in Value & Power & Power Conflicts" Chapter of Book 1969. **BUSINESS ADDRESS:** President, Dick Griffey Prod/Solar Records, 1635 N Cahuenga Blvd, Hollywood, CA 90028.

ROBERTS, WESLEY A.
Educator & clergyman. **PERSONAL:** Born Jan 03, 1938, Jamaica, WI; son of Ignatius Roberts and Rayness Roberts; married Sylvia Y Forbes; children: Paul, Carolyn, Suzanne, Michael. **EDUCATION:** Waterloo Lutheran Univ, BA 1965; Toronto Baptist Seminary, MDiv 1965; Westminster Theological Seminary, ThM 1967; Univ of Guelph, MA 1968, PhD 1972. **CAREER:** Gordon-Conwell Theological Seminary, asst prof of black studies 1972-73, asst prof of christian thought 1974-75, assoc prof of church history, 1977-84, asst dean for acad prog 1980-84, prof of church history 1984-85. **ORGANIZATIONS:** Mem Soc for the Study of Black Religion, Amer Soc of Church History, Conf of Faith & History; interim pastor Peoples Baptist Church of Boston 1980-82; mem exec comm The Assoc of Theological Schools in the US & Canada 1980-84; pastor Peoples Baptist Church of Boston 1982-. **HONORS/ACHIEVEMENTS:** Articles published in Eerdman's Handbook of Amer Christianity, Eerdman's Handbook of the History of Christianity Fides et Historia; Ontario Grad Fellowship Government of Ontario 1968-70; Canada Council Doctoral Fellowship Government of Canada 1970-72. **HOME ADDRESS:** 1 Enon Rd, Wenham, MA 01984. **BUSINESS ADDRESS:** Senior Pastor, Peoples Baptist Church of Boston, 134 Camden Street, Boston, MA 02118.

ROBERTS, WILMOTH FITZGERALD
Psychologist. **PERSONAL:** Born Sep 01, 1934, Millburn, NJ; children: Craig, Tali, Hollie. **EDUCATION:** Morgan State Univ, AB 1956; NY Univ, MA 1968; Rutgers Univ, MA 1977; Union Grad School, PhD 1980. **CAREER:** Sheltered Wkshp Occupational Ctr of Essex Cty, vocational counselor 1962-65; Ctr for Youth Leaguers Inc, dir 1967-68; Ed Oppty Prog Kean Coll of NJ, dir 1968-77; Alcohol Extended Care Prog Coll of Med & Dentistry, psych 1976-77; Crisis Intervention Coll of Med & Dentistry, asst chief 1977-80; New York City Bur of Alcoholism Svc, sr consult 1980-82; Clinic for Mental Health Svcs, sr psych 1982-84; Contemporary Counseling & psychotherapy Inst, psychotherapist 1984-; Coll of Med & Dentistry Comm Mental Health Ctr, dir alcohol rehab. **ORGANIZATIONS:** Mem Natl Rehab Counselor Assoc 1964-, Assoc of Black Psych 1971-, Omega Psi Phi Frat; consult psych Elizabeth NY Headstart Prog 1978, Protective Serv Child Abuse Prog 1978-80, Family Violence Prog of Essex Cty 1979-80. **HONORS/ACHIEVEMENTS:** Outstanding Cont as Adv Third World Org Kean Coll 1969-76; Outstanding Citizen-Amin NJ Unit-Natl Assoc of Negro Bus & Professional Women 1970; Appreciation Awd Boy Scouts of Amer Troop # 154 1970; Comm Serv Awd Sigma Gamma Rho 1985. **MILITARY SERVICE:** AUs 2nd lt 1956-58.

ROBERTSON, ALAN D.
Banker. **PERSONAL:** Born Sep 10, 1958, Chicago, IL; son of Carl T Robertson and Gloria D Sadberry-Robertson; married Julia M Southern, Jun 19, 1983; children: Jessica Marie. **EDUCATION:** DePaul Univ, BSC Accounting (Sum Cum Laude) 1980; Certified Public Accountant Univ of IL Urbana 1980; Northwestern Univ, MM Finance and Marketing 1983. **CAREER:** Arthur Andersen, auditor 1980-81; Continental Bank, banking officer 1983-87; First Chicago, asst vice pres 1987-; DePaul Univ, Chicago IL, part-time faculty 1988-. **ORGANIZATIONS:** Bd mem Inroads Inc 1980; mem ILCPA Soc 1980-; mem AICPA Soc 1981-; treas Inroads Alumni Assoc 1983; mem Urban Bankers Forum 1983-; mem Natl Black MBA Assoc, Natl Assoc of Black Accountants; bd of dir, Chicago Children's Chour 1988-89. **HONORS/ACHIEVEMENTS:** Beta Alpha Psi, Delta Mu Delta; Natl Dean's List 1980; Johnson & Johnson Leadership Awd 1981; Outstanding Young Man in Amer 1983. **BUSINESS ADDRESS:** Asst Vice President, First Chicago Credit Corp, Mail Ste 0087, Chicago, IL 60670.

ROBERTSON, ALVIN ANTHONY
Professional athlete. **PERSONAL:** Born Jul 22, 1962, Barberton, OH. **EDUCATION:** Arkansas, studied crmnl justc 1984. **CAREER:** San Antonio Spurs, guard 1984-. **HONORS/ACHIEVEMENTS:** US Gold Medal-winning Olympic team; post-season Aloha and Hall of Fame classics; all-tournament & voted top defensive plyr in the Aloha; All-Plains by Bsktbl Weekley; MVP when Razorbacks won Southwest Conf tournmnt 1981-82. **BUSINESS ADDRESS:** San Antonio Spurs, HemisFair Arena, Ste 510, San Antonio, TX 78292.

ROBERTSON, ANDRE LEVETT
Professional athlete. **PERSONAL:** Born Oct 02, 1957, Orange, TX; married Lanier Herbert. **EDUCATION:** Univ of TX. **CAREER:** New York Yankees, shortstop 1981-84. **ORGANIZATIONS:** Played baseball football basketball track; All-State twice; all-American baseball; played Little League, Babe Ruth & Amer Legion baseball in Orang e. **BUSINESS ADDRESS:** New York Yankees, Yankee Stadium, Bronx, NY 10451.

ROBERTSON, BENJAMIN W.
Clergyman, educational administrator. **PERSONAL:** Born Apr 06, 1931, Roanoke, VA; son of Clarence Robertson (deceased) and Anna Mary Robertson (deceased); married Dolores Wallace; children: Benjamin W Jr. **EDUCATION:** VA Theol Seminary, BTh 1951; VA Union Univ, AB 1954; VA Seminary & Coll MDiv 1956, DD 1959, DMin 1968; Union Baptist Seminary, LLD 1971; Richmond VA Seminary LLD 1982. **CAREER:** Cedar St Memorial Bapt Ch of God, pastor 1955-; Radio Station WLEE, radio preacher 1961-; Natl Progressive Bapt Cong, tchr 1962-; Radio Station WANT, 1965-; Robertson's Kiddie Coll, pres 1968-; First Union Bapt Ch Chesterfield, pastor; Piney Grove Bapt Ch, pastor; Richmond VA Seminary, pres. **ORGANIZATIONS:** Bd dirs Commonwealth of VA Girl Scouts 1960-69, Brookland Branch YMCA 1963-75, Rich Met Blood Serv 1963-68, Rich Br NAACP 1964-68, vice pres Lott Carey Bapt Foreign Miss Conv 1976-83; treas Baptist Ministers Conf 1960-70; founder Progressive Natl Bapt Convention 1961; dean of preaching VA Theological Seminary 1965-75; pres VA Seminary & Coll 1980-81; Xi Delta Lambda Chap of Alpha Phi Alpha Frat Inc; tchr of leaders PNBC 1961-81; Founder and First Pres of Richmond VA Seminary 1981-. **HONORS/ACHIEVEMENTS:** Afro-Amer Awd for Superior Public Serv without Thought of Gain 1981; Minister of Yr Hayes-Allen VTS&C 1975; Rich Com Hosps Humanitarian Awd 1975; Beta Gamma Lambda Chap Alpha Phi Alpha Frat Inc 1968. **HOME ADDRESS:** 8901 Strath Road, Richmond, VA 23231. **BUSINESS ADDRESS:** President, Richmond VA Seminary, 801 N 23rd St, Richmond, VA 23223.

ROBERTSON, EVELYN CRAWFORD, JR.
Educational administrator. **PERSONAL:** Born Nov 19, 1941, Winchester, TN; son of Evelyn Robertson and Pearl Robertson; married Hugholene Ellison; children: Jeffrey Bernard, Sheila Yvette. **EDUCATION:** TN State Univ, BS 1959-62, MA 1969; Southwest MO State Univ, NDEA Cert 1970. **CAREER:** Allen White HS, teacher/coach 1962-68; Allen White Elem Sch, principal 1969; Central HS, asst principal 1970-74; Western Mental Health Inst, asst super 1974-79; Nat T Winston Develop Center, supt 1979-83; Western Mental Health Inst, supt 1983-. **ORGANIZATIONS:** Pres Harden Co Teachers Assn 1973; chmn Whiteville Civic League 1976-79; chmn of bd Harden Co Developmental Service Ctr 1977-78; pres Bolivar Civitan Club 1981; vice-pres Whiteville Bus Enterprise, Inc 1982; chmn Admin Div SEAAMD 1983; consultant Hardeman Mental Health Assn 1983; bd mem Amer Heart Assn affiliate 1980-. **HONORS/ACHIEVEMENTS:** Outstanding Young Educator Hardeman Co Jaycees 1976; EC Robertson Day given by citizens in my honor 1983. **HOME ADDRESS:** Rt 1 Box 178, Whiteville, TN 38075.

ROBERTSON, GERTRUDE
Educator. **PERSONAL:** Born Feb 11, 1924, Waskom, TX; daughter of Chesley Harris and Estella Spillman Harris; married Rev L E Robertson, Jan 25, 1947 (deceased); children: Elkins Renee. **EDUCATION:** Bishop Coll, Dallas, TX, BS, 1949; N TX State Univ, Denton, TX, MS, 1967. **CAREER:** Dallas Independent School Dist, teacher, 1950-. **ORGANIZATIONS:** Southwestern regional dir, The Natl Sorority of Phi Delta Kappa; pres, The Baptist Ministers' Wives, Dallas, TX; teacher of Adults at D. Edwin Johnson Bible Inst Dallas. **HONORS/ACHIEVEMENTS:** Teacher of the year, Thomas J. Rusk, Middle School and N Dallas, Chamber of Commerce; The Sorority of the year, The Natl Sorority of Phi Delta Kappa Inc. **HOME ADDRESS:** 3929 Kiest Meadow Dr, Dallas, (214)330-6848, 75233.

ROBERTSON, ISIAH, JR. (BUTCH)
Professional football player. **PERSONAL:** Born Aug 17, 1949, Covington, LA; married Jill. **EDUCATION:** So U, BS 1970. **CAREER:** Buffalo Bills, professional ftbl player 1980; LA Rams, professional ftbl player 1971-79. **HONORS/ACHIEVEMENTS:** Rookie of Yr NFL All-Pro 1971, 73-76; Pro Bowl 1973-77.

ROBERTSON, JAMES B.
Civil engineer. **PERSONAL:** Born Sep 05, 1940, Roanoke, VA; married Marjorie N Morris; children: James II, Cheryl, Bradley. **EDUCATION:** Howard U, BSCE 1963. **CAREER:** AZ Proj Office Water & Power Resource Serv, chief operations div, 1978-; US Bur of Reclamation, supr hydraulic engr 1972-78; Channing Co Inc, registered rep 1970-72; US & Bur of Reclamation, civil engr 1966-70; Omega Psi Phi Frat 1960-. **ORGANIZATIONS:** Sec Ancient Free & Accepted Mason 1970-; budgetary panel United Way 1976-77. **HONORS/ACHIEVEMENTS:** Meritorious serv awards Dept of Interior 1970&72; Mgrs Devel Prog Dept of Interior 1977. **MILITARY SERVICE:** AUS capt 1963-66. **BUSINESS ADDRESS:** 201 N Central Ave, Phoenix, AZ 85073.

ROBERTSON, JOHN GILBERT
Retired marketing manager. **PERSONAL:** Born Sep 04, 1932, E St Louis, IL; son of Linder Robertson and Nettie Robertson; married Delores W (divorced). **EDUCATION:** Univ of MI, BA; AM & N Coll, attended 1951-53; Univ of MI Med Ctr, School of Inhalation Therapy 1959-60. **CAREER:** AC Spark Plug Div, sales analyst 1974-88, prod control supr planner 1972-74, safety engr; Flint Public Schools, Flint MI, teacher 1962-65, substitute teacher 1988-; Hurley Hosp, inhalation therapist 1960-65; life ins debit mgr 1958-59. **ORGANIZATIONS:** Mem Eureka Lodge #16; Prince Hall Masons; 32nd Degree Mason Consistory #71; Shriner 1966; Basileus Omicron Rho Chap of Omega Psi Phi Frat, 1968-71; Industrial Exec Club of Michigan Club Leadership, 1976; NAACP; Urbam League; Inner-City Lions Club; mem Flint Human Relations Commn; grad of LEADERSHIP Flint Prog 1976; mem bd Flint Environmental Action Team FEAT 1977; couns vol Genesee Co Jail Treatment Prog 1972-73; mem bd of dirs Model Cities Devel Corp 1971-72; mem bd of dirs Inner City Lions Club 1976-77. **HONORS/ACHIEVEMENTS:** Omega Man of Yr Award 1975-76; pioneered 1st Civil Rights suit charging AC Spark Plub & Gen Motors Corp with racism in hiring & mobility practices won the case 1965. **MILITARY SERVICE:** AUS pfc 1953-55. **HOME ADDRESS:** 3315 Hampshire Dr, Flint, MI 48504.

ROBERTSON, JON H.
Music conductor. **PERSONAL:** Born Dec 03, 1942, Kingston; married Florence Bellande; children: Nadege, Sabine, Beranger. **EDUCATION:** Juilliard School of Music, BM 1954, MS 1966, DMA 1972; Private piano study with Ethel Leginska, 13 yrs; Paris Conserv of Music with Jean-Marie Darre; Juilliard School of Music, choral conducting with Abraham Kaplan 3 yrs; New England Conserv of Music, orchestral conducting with Richard Pittman; San Francisco Symphony, orchestral conducting with Herbert Blomstedt. **CAREER:** Oakwood Coll, chmn 1967-71, assoc prof of music 1969-71, chmn humanities 1971-72; Thayer Conservatory of Music, chmn, prof 1972-76; Atlantic Union CollIntl Orchestral Conducting Festival Loma Linda Univ, asst to Maestro Herbert Blomstedt 1976-; Orchestral Workshop Chgo, dir; private teaching & master classes nationally & internationally; Univ of Redlands, vstg adj prof 1982; Kristiansand Symphony Orch, music dir, conductor. **ORGANIZATIONS:** Exec dir, chmn of bd BENASA Found 1976-; conductor, music dir Redlands Symphony Orch 1981-; bd mem The Haitian Inst of CA 1983-; mem CA Arts Councils Panel of Org Grants Panelists 1985-86; bd mem Aldrich Library of Music; principal guest-conductor NE Chamber Orchestra; guest conductor Natl & Intl Orch; sec, exec bd Claremont Cultural Found. **HONORS/ACHIEVEMENTS:** Performed for 29 yrs as concert pianist toured in US, Europe, Scandinavia, Latin Averm, Carribean Isles; Walt Disney Prod as child pianist in "Mickey MouseTV Show"; CA Young Peoples Concert Audition Contest Winner 1951; Julliard School of Music Scholarship Winner 6 consecutive yrs; Found Found Scholars Fellowship 1970-72; Doctoral Teaching Fellowship Juilliard 1971-72.

ROBERTSON, LETHIA
Educational administrator. **PERSONAL:** Born May 10, 1940, Columbia, NC; married Jesse; children: Dean, Karen. **EDUCATION:** Pratt Inst, BFA 1977; NYU, MA Museum Studies 1981. **CAREER:** The Studio Museum, Harlem, curator of educ 1980-; The Brooklyn Museum, coordinator internship program 1977-79; Lethia Robertson Gallery, mgr 1969-80; Tracy Schernikow Gallery, art restorer 1962-69; Brooklyn Children's Museum, instructor, 1970-74; Brooklyn Coll, instructor, 1972-74; Metro Museum of Art, instructor, 1976-77. **ORGANIZATIONS:** Mem, Natl Conf of Artist 1977-80; lecture Hunter Coll; NYU; Univ of DC The Fence Art Show, The Brooklyn Museum, 1973; FESTAC 1976. **HONORS/ACHIEVEMENTS:** Black Women in the Arts Medgar Evers Coll 1977; Langston Hughes-Elton Fax Awd 1977.

ROBERTSON, LYNN E.
Clergyman. **PERSONAL:** Born Jun 18, 1921, Franklin, TX; married Gertrude Harris. **EDUCATION:** BA 1949. **CAREER:** Alta Mesa Mesa Pk Bapt Ch, Pastor; Inter-racial Bible Inst, instr; So Dallas Br NaAACP, pres. **ORGANIZATIONS:** Mem Bapt Min Union of Dallas; mem Interdenominational Ministerial All of Gr Dallas; mem Min All W Dallas. **MILITARY SERVICE:** AUS sgt 1942-46. **BUSINESS ADDRESS:** 2939 Palo Alto Dr, Dallas, TX 75241.

ROBERTSON, OSCAR PALMER
Chemical company executive. **PERSONAL:** Born Nov 24, 1938, Indianapolis, IN; son of Henry Bailey Robertson and Mazell Bell Robertson; married Yvonne Crittenden, Jun 25, 1960; children: Shana Robertson Shaw, Tia, Mari. **EDUCATION:** Cincinnati Univ, BBA 1960. **CAREER:** Cincinnati Royals NBA, guard 1960-70; Milwaukee Bucks NBA, player 1970-74; TV sports announcer; ORCHEM Inc, Cincinnati, OH, pres/CEO, 1981-; pres, Oscar Robertson & Assocs, 1983-. **ORGANIZATIONS:** Pres, Natl Basketball Players Assn, 1964-74; mem, NAACP Sports Bd, 1987; trustee, Indiana High School Hall of Fame, 1984-89; trustee, Basketball Hall of Fame, 1987-89; natl dir, Pepsi Cola Hot Shot Program. **HONORS/ACHIEVEMENTS:** Mem State Dept Tour Africa 1971; High Sch All-Amer; set 14 major collegiate records at Univ of Cincinnati; Recip All Star Game's Most Val Player Award 1961; NBA Most Valuable Player Award 3 times; Rookie of the Yr Award 1961; co-capt US Olympic Gold Medal Team 1960; mem World Championship Team 1971; Ranked 2nd only to Wilt Chamberlain as All-Time NBA Scorer with 26,710 points 1980; 4th Infield Goals (9058); 5th Field Goals Attempted (19620); 3rd Most Minutes Played (43,886); 1st Most Free Throws (9,887); First Milwaukee Buck to be inducted into Basketball Hall of Fame 1979; widely recognized as one of the greatest all around players in game history; mem Basketball Hall of Fame, 1979; mem, Olympic Hall of Fame, 1984; Natl Award, Boys Clubs of Amer, 1987; developer, Avondale Town Center, Cincinnati, 1981; developer/owner, Oscar Terrace (affordable housing units), Indianapolis, IN, 1989. **MILITARY SERVICE:** US Army, private first class, 1960-67. **BUSINESS ADDRESS:** Pres & CEO, ORCHEM Inc, 10925 Reed Hartman Hwy, #314, Cincinnati, OH 45242.

ROBERTSON, QUINCY L.
Educational administrator. **PERSONAL:** Born Jul 30, 1934, Wedowee, AL; son of Jessie Robertson and Viola Wilkes Robertson; married Dollie Williams; children: Stephanie. **EDUCATION:** TN State Univ, BA 1955, MA 1957. **CAREER:** Richmond County Bd of Ed, guidance counselor 1959-68; Paine Coll, dir of upward bound 1968-69, business mgr 1970-83, vice pres admin & fiscal affairs 1983-. **ORGANIZATIONS:** Bd of dir USO 1964-68; commiss Richmond Cty Personnel Bd 1973-78; chmn Thankful Baptist Church Trustee Bd 1977-85; vice pres Frontiersman 1984-85; bd of dir EIIA 1985-; bd of dir Univ Hosp. **HONORS/ACHIEVEMENTS:** Man of the Year Thankful Baptist Church 1969; Admin of the Year Paine Coll 1973-74; Citizen of the Year Alpha Phi Alpha Frat 1984. **MILITARY SERVICE:** AUS spec 4 1957-58; Good Conduct Medal, Expert Rifleman, Honorable Discharge. **HOME ADDRESS:** 3219 Tate Rd, Augusta, GA 30906. **BUSINESS ADDRESS:** VP Admin & Fiscal Affairs, Paine College, 1235 15th St, Augusta, GA 30910.

ROBERTSON, QUINDONELL S.
Educator. **PERSONAL:** Born Jan 28, Dallas, TX; married J William. **EDUCATION:** BA 1954, MA 1970. **CAREER:** Dallas Indus School Dist & School Sec, educator 1957-58, education cluster coordinator 1984-. **ORGANIZATIONS:** Mem NEA, TX State Teacher Assoc, Classroom Teachers of Dallas, TX Classroom Teacher, TX Assoc Teacher Ed, Amigos, Sigma Gamma Rho, TX Coll, TX So Univ Alumni Assoc; life mem YWCA; charter mem Dallas Urban League Guild; pres Top Ladies of Distinction Inc; bd dir Dallas Pan Hellenic Council; mem Phi Delta Kappa; master educator, Amer Board of Master Educators, 1987; mem, Amer Assn of Univ Women, 1986. **HONORS/ACHIEVEMENTS:** 9 plaques for leadership & svc; 1 silver tray for leadership & svc; Gavel for leadership; 2 trophies for leadership & svc, Medallion for YWCA Quota Buster; Gold Cup for chartering Arlington TX Sigma Gamma Rho 1983; Gold Charm for serving 3 yrs as pres of Sigma Gamma Rho, 1985-88. **HOME ADDRESS:** 1588 N Atoll Dr, Dallas, TX 75216.

ROBEY, LOUIS REED
Physician. **PERSONAL:** Born Jul 05, 1922, Galveston, TX; married Mary; children: Marla, Don. **EDUCATION:** Fisk U, 1945; Meharry Med Coll, 1949. **CAREER:** Pvt Prac, physician; St Elizabeth Hosp, past pres, med staff. **ORGANIZATIONS:** Mem Houston Med Forum; Lone Star State Med Soc; Harris Co Med Soc; TX Med Assn; AMA; Nat Med Assn; chtr mem TX Soc of Athletic Team Physician Diplomate; Am Bd Surgeons; flw Am Coll Surgeions; Intl Coll Surgeons; Am Coll Sports Med; Am Geriatrics Soc; clinicial instr Baylor Coll Med; asst dir hlth Houston Ind Sch Dist; commn doc Professional Wrestlers; past pres Vocational Guidance Serv; bd dir United Negro Coll Fund; tournament dir United Negro Coll Fund. **HONORS/ACHIEVEMENTS:** Past Father Yr. **BUSINESS ADDRESS:** 4120 Lyons Ave, Houston, TX 77020.

ROBICHAUX, JOLYN H.
Business executive. **PERSONAL:** Born May 21, 1928, Cairo, IL; widowed; children: Sheila, Joseph. **EDUCATION:** Chicago Teachr Coll, AB 1960; PA State Univ Ice Cream Tech, Cert. **CAREER:** State Dept Tour of Africa, spec nutritions consult 1956; Betty Crocker Home Serv Dept of Gen Mills, 1960-65; Cook Cty, jury comm 1971-72; Baldwin Ice Cream-Co, owner 1971-. **ORGANIZATIONS:** Bd of dir Chicago United Way 1984. **HONORS/ACHIEVEMENTS:** Elected 1 of 10 Outstanding Black Bus Leaders Black Book 1973; Comm Serv Awd Chicago S End Jaycees 1973; Black Excellence Awd in Bus by PUSH 1974,75; Achievement Awd So IL Council 1974; Achievement in Bus World of Black Women, Iota Phi Lambda 1974; Bus Woman of the Year Cosmopolitan C of C 1976; Disting Alumna Awd Chicago State Univ 1984; Par Excellence Awd PUSH Bus Woman of the Year 1984; Natl Minority Entrepreneur of the YearUniv S Dept of Commerce presented by Vice Pres George Bush 1985. **BUSINESS ADDRESS:** President, Baldwin Ice Cream Co, 4825 S Indiana, Chicago, IL 60615.

ROBIE, CLARENCE W.
Electrical parts distributor. **CAREER:** B & S Electric Supply Co, Atlanta GA, chief executive. **BUSINESS ADDRESS:** B & S Electric Supply Co, 610 Wendell Ct, SW, Atlanta, GA 30336. *

ROBINET, HARRIETTE GILLEM
Author. **PERSONAL:** Born Jul 14, 1931, Washington, DC; daughter of Richard Avitus Gillem and Martha Gray Gillem; married McLouis Joseph Robinet, Aug 06, 1960; children: Stephen, Philip, Rita, Jonathan, Marsha, Linda. **EDUCATION:** College of New Rochelle, BS, 1953; Catholic University of America, MS, 1957, PhD, 1962. **CAREER:** Children's Hospital, Washington DC, bacteriologist, 1953-54; Walter Reed Army Medical Center, Washington DC, medical bacteriologist, 1954-57, research bacteriologist, 1958-60; Xavier University, New Orleans LA, instructor in biology, 1957-58; US Army, Quartermaster Corps, civilian food bacteriologist, 1960-62; free-lance writer, 1962—. **ORGANIZATIONS:** American Orchid Society. **HONORS/ACHIEVEMENTS:** Author of Jay and the Marigold, Childrens Press, 1976; author of Ride the Red Cycle, Houghton, 1980. **HOME ADDRESS:** 214 South Elmwood, Oak Park, IL 60302. **BUSINESS ADDRESS:** 214 South Elmwood, Oak Park, IL 60302. *

ROBINSON, ADELINE BLACK
Educator. **PERSONAL:** Born Mar 07, 1915, Columbia, TN; married Phillip Edward Robinson. **EDUCATION:** TN State Univ, BS Eng & Educ 1935; Fisk Univ, MA Educ 1950; Teachers Coll Columbia Univ, EMR Prof Diploma in Educ 1955; Peabody Coll, post grad study 1960-62. **CAREER:** Metropolitan Nashville School, teacher 39 yrs, 20 yrs teaching EMR Classes, 8 summer sessions as Demonstration Class teacher in coop with TSU & Kennedy Center. **ORGANIZATIONS:** Mem law enforcement com Citizen's Goals 2000 Com; rep Diocesan Ecumenical Commn; Coord Council on Legislative Concerns 1975-76; recorder for League of Women Voters Unit Mtgs; monitor TN Legislature; reporter & asst with mailing CCLC Legislative Newsletter 1975; life mem NEA, Council for Exceptional Children; mem NEA Black Caucus; bd of dir Grace M Eaton Day Home; mem NAACP, natl Council of Negro Women YWCA, Common Cause, League of Women Voters, Holy Trinity Episcopal Ch, Natl Sor of Phi Delta Kappa Alpha Beta Chap tamias for 1975-76; mem Federation of Colored Womens Clubs; Garden Lovers Club; bd dirs St Luke Comm Ctr; mem of Ecumenical Action Comm of Church Women United. **HONORS/ACHIEVEMENTS:** Grad Cum Laude TSU; Awd of Merit Inst on Mental Retardation & Intellectual Devel; George Peabody for Tchr Nashville TN in recog of significant contribto behavioral sci by serving as an experimental tchr in EMR Lang Devel Proj 1965-67; Educ Fellowship Gift named in Honor of AAUW Nashville Br; Certificate of Recognition for Disting Leadership NCNW 1983; Woman of the Yr Natl Assn of Negro Bus & Professional Womens Clubs Inc 1984.

ROBINSON, ALBERT ARNOLD
Salesman. **PERSONAL:** Born May 02, 1937, Lawrenceville, VA; married Mary Elizabeth Wright; children: Terence, Todd, Trent, Tevis, Lisa. **EDUCATION:** VA State Univ, BS with distinction 1958; Central State Univ BS with distinction 1965-68; East Carolina Univ, 1976-77. **CAREER:** US Army, commissioned officer 1958-78; Ford Motor Co, manufacturing super 1978-80; Bechtel Power Corp, super fo reprographics 1980-84; Natl Reproductions Corp, sales rep 1984-85; Eastern MI Univ, mgr service operations 1985-. **ORGANIZATIONS:** Trustee Second Baptist Church 1979-; mem Ypsilanti/Willow Run Br NAACP 1980-; councilman Ypsilanti City Council 1981-; mem Ann Arbor/Ypsilanti Bus & Prof League 1982-; mem Emanon Club 1983-. **HONORS/ACHIEVEMENTS:** Who's Who Among Black Students in Amer Colleges & Univs 1957-58; mem Beta Kappa Chi Honorary Scientific Frat 1958; mem Kappa Phi Kappa Hon Educational Frat 1958. **MILITARY SERVICE:** AUS lt col 20 yrs; Legion of Merit, Bronze Star, Meritorious Serv Medal, Army Commendations, Parachutist Badge 1958-78. **HOME ADDRESS:** 918 Pleasant Dr, Ypsilanti, MI 48197. **BUSINESS ADDRESS:** Manager of Sales Operations, Eastern MI University, Physical Plant EMU, Ypsilanti, MI 48197.

ROBINSON, ALBERT M.
Association executive. **PERSONAL:** Married Jane B Carter; children: Albert Jr, Kimberly. **EDUCATION:** VA State Coll, BS; Rutgers U; Rider Coll. **CAREER:** United Progress Inc, exec dir; Dept Comm Affairs NJ, relocation ofcr; Trenton Hous Auth, mgr; Lockerman High Sch Denton, tchr; Trenton Br NAACP, pres. **HONORS/ACHIEVEMENTS:** Brotherhood award Jewish Fedn; outstanding & comm serv award 1970; Trenton Pub Serv Award 1968; outstanding achiev comm affairs NAACP 1971; pol action council award 1967. **MILITARY SERVICE:** AUS 1942-46. **BUSINESS ADDRESS:** 401 03 Pennington Ave, Trenton, NJ.

ROBINSON, ALCURTIS
Insurance company vice president. **EDUCATION:** Harris Teachers College, St Louis, MO, 1958-60; Purdue University, Professional Management Institute, West Lafayette, IN, 1976. **CAREER:** Mutual of Omaha-United of Omaha, St Louis, MO, salesman, 1967-69, sales training instructor, 1969-70, district manager, 1970-73; Mutual of Omaha-United of Omaha, Omaha, NE, associate director of management training, 1973-75, assistant vice president in career development and management training, 1975-77, second vice president, 1977-82, vice president in career development and public affairs, 1982-85, vice president in public service and minority affairs, 1985-, vice president in minority and community affairs, 1988-. **ORGANIZATIONS:** Member, NAACP, Baltimore, MD; board member, National Association for Sickle Cell Disease, Inc, Los Angeles, CA; member of Black Executive Exchange Program, National Urban League, Inc, New York, NY; member, National Alliance of Business, Washington, DC; member of career development advisory committee, National Urban League, New York, NY; development director, United Negro College Fund Drive, New York, NY; chairman of public employees retirement board, State of Nebraska, Lincoln, NE; chairman of board of directors, Christian Urban Education Services, Omaha, NE; member, Urban League of Nebraska, Omaha, NE; vice president of board of directors, Omaha School Foundation, Omaha, NE; member of board of directors, YMCA of Omaha, Omaha, NE. **MILITARY SERVICE:** US Army, 1963-65. **HOME ADDRESS:** 1411 North 128th Circle, Omaha, NE 68154.

ROBINSON, ALFREDA P.
Administrator. **PERSONAL:** Born May 07, 1932, Charlotte, NC. **EDUCATION:** Upsala Coll, BA 1954; Rutgers Sch of Social Work, additional study 1957; Union Grad Sch, doct cand. **CAREER:** Rutgers Graduate School of Mgmt, dean in charge of student servics; Rutgers Univ Graduate School of Bus & Adminstrn, asst dean in charge of student services; Financial Aid Douglass & Cook Coll of Rugers Univ, dir; Essex Co Probation Dept, sr probation officer; NJ Bureau of Children Serv Natl, case worker. **ORGANIZATIONS:** Proj com mem Delta Sigma Theta Inc; Nat Scholarship & Standards Com NJ Alumnae Chpt; Eastern Assn of Student Financial Aid Adminstr; councilman Nat Council on Student Financial Aid; NJ Assn of Student Financial Aid Adminstrn; corr sec & editor of Eastern assn of Student Financial Aid Adminstr; councilman Coll Entrance Exam Bd; Middle States Regfional Councilman Pub & Guidance Com; Upper Div Scholarship Nreview; Financial Aid; computation work shops, seminars & trainer, gen cons; mem N Jersey Alumnae Chpt; chmn coll Career & Day 1969-; past chairperson Direct Search for Talent Prog Trio Prog 1976-79; past pres N Jersey Chpt; vice pres bd trustees St Timothy House. **HONORS/ACHIEVEMENTS:** Com serv award Sigma Gamma Rho 1979; serv award Rutgers Black MBA Assn 1979. **BUSINESS ADDRESS:** Rutgers Grad Sch of Mgmt, 92 New St, Newark, NJ 07102.

ROBINSON, ALVIN J.
Business executive. **PERSONAL:** Born May 25, 1936, Chicago, IL. **EDUCATION:** No IL Univ, BS. **CAREER:** Cosmopolitan C of C, assoc dir 1961-63; Lever Bros Co 1963-66; Charles P Pfizer Co 1966-69; Great A&P Tea Co 1969-72; Borg-Warner Corp 1972-77; Chicago Area Pub Affairs, pres 1976; Gov James Thompson, special asst 1977-80; Med Accounting & Consulting Co 1980-83; Insurers Review Services Inc, pres. **ORGANIZATIONS:** Mem Assn Black Found Execs 1974-; mem Chicago Forum 1975-; consult WYNR Radio 1965-66; pres Provident Hosp Chicago 1972-; pres Big Bros/Big Sisters 1975-;dir Donors Forum of Chicago 1975-; dir Corp Responsib Group to Greater Chicago; mem trustee Foundry Educ Found; co-chmn Chicago United 1976-. **HONORS/ACHIEVEMENTS:** Great Guy Award WGRT; "One Person Does Make A Difference" Award from Save Our Neighborhoods, Save Our City Coalition 1985. **MILITARY SERVICE:** AUS 1959-61. **BUSINESS ADDRESS:** President, Insurers Review Serivces Inc, 6 North Michigan, Chicago, IL 60602.

ROBINSON, ANDREW
Educator. **PERSONAL:** Born Feb 16, 1939, Chicago. **EDUCATION:** Chicago State U, BA 1966; Roosevelt U, MA 1970; Northwestern U, PhD 1973. **CAREER:** Univ of KY, asst prof, asso dir Cntr for urban educ 1975-; Chicago City Colls, adminstr 1974-75; Urban & Ethnic Edn, Asst dir; Pub Inst Chicago, supt 1973-74; Chicago Urban League, educ dir 1970-73; Univ IL, visiting instr 1972-73; Chicago Pub Schs, tchr 1966-69. **ORGANIZATIONS:** Mem Phi Delta Kappa; Am Assn Sch Adminstrs; Am Assn of Tchr Edn; Nat Alliance Black Sch Educators; Prog Planning Comm Am Assoc of Coll Tchr Edn. **MILITARY SERVICE:** Mil serv 1962-63. **BUSINESS ADDRESS:** Coll of Educ Asst Dean, U of KY, Lexington, KY.

ROBINSON, ANN GARRETT
Educator. **PERSONAL:** Born Jun 08, 1934, Greenville, NC; married Charles Robinson; children: Angela Carol, George Carl. **EDUCATION:** NC Central Univ, BA 1954; Wayne State Univ, MA 1957; Nova Univ, EdD 1975; Yale Univ, Research Fellow 1986. **CAREER:** Robinson Robinson Behavioral Sci Consult New Haven, co-owner; NC Bd of Corrections, 1956-57; Central State Hosp, LaRue Carter Hosp, Augusta State Hosp, clinical psych 1958-64; Yale Univ Child Study Ctr, rsch asst 1968-70; Trinity Coll Hartford, asst prof psych 1970-72; Co Central Comm Coll, prof of psych; freelance writer 1983-; New Haven Register, newspaper columnist 1985-; South Central Comm Coll, prof of psychology, project coord life review/life history analysis. **ORGANIZATIONS:** Bd dir S Central CT Mental Health Plnng Reg 1974-77; mem NEA, Amer Psychol Assoc; bd of deaconnesses Immanuel Bapt Church, Alpha Kappa Alpha, Black Educators Assoc, Afro-Amer Hist Bd, Jack & Jill of Amer Inc; regional vice pres North East Psi Beta Inc The Natl Honor Soc in Psychology; pres-elect Natl Cncl Psi Beta Inc Natl Honor Soc in Psychology; chairlady Immanuel Baptist Church Bd of Deaconesses 1985-. **HONORS/ACHIEVEMENTS:** Outstanding Educator of Amer 1973; Nannie H Burroughs Awd Outstanding Black Educator of New Haven 1974; listed in Who's Who of Women of the World; Presidential Citation Awd SCCC 1977; Comm Serv Awd New Haven; author "Clouds & Clowns of Destiny", "Behind Krome Detention Ctr Walls", "Are the Doors to Higher Ed Starting to Close", "Heroic Women of the Past, The Three Wives of Booker T Washington"; Church of Christ Natl Yough Conference Awd 1986; SCCC Most Scholarly Awd 1987; Most Influential Prof SCCC Student Govt Awd 1987; Professional Woman of the Year Elm City Business and Professional Women. **BUSINESS ADDRESS:** Professor of Psychology, So Central Comm Coll, 60 Sargent Drive, South, New Haven, CT 06511.

ROBINSON, AUBREY EUGENE, JR.
Judge. **PERSONAL:** Born Mar 30, 1922, Madison, NJ; married Doris A Washington; children: Paula Elaine Robinson Collins, Sheryl Louise, Jacqueline C Washington. **EDUCATION:** Cornell Univ, BA 1943, LLB 1947. **CAREER:** Practiced with various law firms in WA, 1948-65; Amer Council Human Rights, gen counsel 1953-55, dir 1955; Juvenile Court DC, assoc judge 1965-66; US Dist Court, judge 1966-82, chief judge 1982-. **ORGANIZATIONS:** Bd dir 1954-63, vice pres 1958-61 Family and Child Services, Washington, DC; bd dir Family Services Assn of America 1958-68; bd trustees United Planning Organization, Washington, DC, 1963-66; exec comm, bd dir 1964-66, Citizens for Better Public Educ, Washington, DC; exec comm Interreligious Comm on Race Relations 1966-67; bd dir Eugene & Agnes E Meyer Foundation 1969-85; Cornell Law School Adv Council 1974-80; mem Comm on the Admin of the Criminal Law 1977-83; adj prof WA Coll of Law, Amer Univ 1975-84; bd mem Fed Judicial Center 1978-82; bd trustees Cornell Univ, Judicial Conf of the US 1982-; mem Amer Bar Assn. **HONORS/ACHIEVEMENTS:** Cornell Law School Distinguished Alumnus Award 1986. **MILITARY SERVICE:** USA 1943-46. **BUSINESS ADDRESS:** Chief Judge, US District Court of DC, US Ct House, Washington, DC 20001.

ROBINSON, BARRY LANE
Government official. **PERSONAL:** Born Jun 05, 1943, White Plains, NY; divorced; children: Two children. **EDUCATION:** State Univ of Buffalo, BA 1980. **CAREER:** Johnson & Johnson, salesman 1974-75; Attica Correction Ctr, corrections officer 1975-79; Masten Park Secure Ctr, child care worker 1979-; Erie Co, co legislator 1982-. **ORGANIZATIONS:** Mem NAACP 1985; mem Ellicott Dist Concerned Taxpayers 1985; mem Operation PUSH. **HONORS/ACHIEVEMENTS:** Mr Black America 1981; Dale Carnegie Awd Public Speaking/Univ; training course NY State Police. **MILITARY SERVICE:** AUS sp/5 trans 1966-80; Honorable Discharge. **BUSINESS ADDRESS:** County Legislator, Erie Co Dist 3, 25 Delaware Ave, Buffalo, NY 14202.

ROBINSON, BILL
Professional athlete. **PERSONAL:** Born Jun 26, 1943, McKeesport, PA; married Mary Alice Moore; children: William III, Kelly Ann. **CAREER:** Atlanta Braves, outfielder 1966; New York Yankees, outfielder 1967-69; Philadelia Phillies, outfielder 1972-74; Pittsburgh Pirates, outfielder 1975-82; Philadelphia Phillies, outfielder 1982-83; New York Mets, batting coach, 1st base coach 1983-. **ORGANIZATIONS:** Each Christmas plays Santa Claus for the kids in his neighborhood; chm of Lupus Soc which fights Lupus Erythematosus; last winter ran a highly successful Bill Robinson Hitting Club for youngsters aged 8-18 in Cherry Hill, NJ. **HONORS/ACHIEVEMENTS:** 14 yr major league veteran; 258 career batting average in 1,472 games had 1,127 hits with 229 doubles, 29 triples, 166 home runs and 641 RBI; tied Natl Leagbue record in 1977 hitting 2 grand slam homers in one week; Signed by Braves an hour after his graduation from Elizabeth Forward HS; 1978 recd Natl George Washington Carver Awd for his community work. **BUSINESS ADDRESS:** New York Mets, Shea Stadium, Flushing, NY 11368.

ROBINSON, BRENDA EVETTE
Military officer. **PERSONAL:** Born Sep 29, 1956, Philadelphia, PA. **EDUCATION:** Dowling Coll, BS Aeronautics 1978. **CAREER:** USN, C-1 aircraft carrier pilot 155 traps (shiplandings) 1980-83, C-12 pilot/instr twin engine Guam & Orient 1983-84, T-34 flight instr 1984-. **HONORS/ACHIEVEMENTS:** First & only Black Female Aviator in the Navy 1980-. **MILITARY SERVICE:** USN lt 6 yrs; Naval Aviator Wings 1980. **BUSINESS ADDRESS:** Naval Aviator Flight Instr, U S Navy, VT-6 NAS Whiting Field, Milton, FL 32570.

ROBINSON, BRENDA M.
Government official. **PERSONAL:** Born in Washington, DC. **EDUCATION:** Howard Univ Coll of Liberal Arts, BA 1967; Howard Univ Law Sch, JD 1970. **CAREER:** NAACP Legal Defense Fund NY, NY, Earl Warren fellow 1970-71; Goodwin & Goodwin Tulsa, OK, mng atty 1971; Legal Aid Tulsa, OK, atty 1972; Natl Labor Relations Bd (Reg 25), lit specialist 1972-79; Fed Labor Relations Authority (Reg V), reg atty 1979-80; Fed Labor Relations Authority, chf counsel 1980-81; Atlanta Univ School of Business Admin, lectr 1981; Fed Labor Relations Authority (Reg IV), reg dir. **ORGANIZATIONS:** Pres Midwest Chapter Soc Federal Labor Relations Prof, 1980; pres Natl Labor Relations Bd Union Local 25, 1975; mem Natl Bar Assn; mem NAACP; mem Intl Assn Personnel Women, 1984. **HONORS/ACHIEVEMENTS:** Public Serv Award, Atlanta Univ Public Admin Student Assn, 1984.

ROBINSON, CARL CORNELL
Attorney. **PERSONAL:** Born Sep 21, 1946, Washington, DC; son of Louis W Robinson and Florence A Robinson. **EDUCATION:** Univ of Michigan, BS Aero Eng 1969; Golden Gate Univ, MBA 1974; UCLA, JD 1977. **CAREER:** O'Melveny & Myers, attorney 1977-84; Robinson & Pearman, partner 1984-. **ORGANIZATIONS:** Dir San Fernando Valley Neighborhood Legal Serv 1981-; dir UCLA Public Interest Law Foundation 1982-89; vice pres Natl Black MBA Assoc Los Angeles 1985; mem Legal Serv Trust Fund Commn CA 1985, Judicial Evaluation Comm Los Angeles County Bar Assoc 1986, 1988; dir Natl Assoc of Securities Profls 1986-, dir, John M Langston Bar Assoc 1987-; dir, Western Center on Law and Poverty, Inc. **MILITARY SERVICE:** USAF capt 1969-74. **HOME ADDRESS:** 3924 So Sycamore Ave, Los Angeles, CA 90008. **BUSINESS ADDRESS:** Partner, Robinson & Pearman, 3460 Wilshire Boulevard, Suite 800, Los Angeles, CA 90010.

ROBINSON, CARL DAYTON
Pediatrician. **PERSONAL:** Born Jun 14, 1942, Tallulah, LA; son of Bernie Dayton Robinson and Emily Parker Robinson; married Sandra Lawson, Aug 14, 1965; children: Michael, Carla. **EDUCATION:** Howard Univ, BS 1964, MD 1968; Tulane Univ Sch of Public Health, MPH 1977. **CAREER:** Letterman Army Med Ctr, chf prenatal/infant serv 1971-73; Flint Goodridge Hospital, dir sickle cell pgm 1973-78; Natl Sickle Cell Adv Comm, mem 1976-78; Reg Med Pgm, LA, mem 1976-78; LA Commsn on Prenatal Care, mem 1977-81; Genetic Disease Ctr, med dir 1978-81; Tulane Univ Med Sch, cln asst prof pediatrics 1973-; Robinson Med Grp, pres 1978-; Childrens Hospital of New Orleans, pres medical staff 1986-88. **ORGANIZATIONS:** Consultant to sec Dept of Health & Human Resources LA 1984; vice pres Southeast LA Med Qlty Review Found 1979-81; pres APTECH Inc 1978-; pres LA Health Corp 1984-; life mem Alpha Phi Alpha; mem Amer Public Health Assn. **HONORS/ACHIEVEMENTS:** Fellow Amer Acad of Pediatrics; fellow Intl Coll of Pediatrics; elected to Orleans Parish School Bd 1989. **MILITARY SERVICE:** AUS major 1971-73. **BUSINESS ADDRESS:** President/CEO, Robinson Medical Group, 2600 Ursuline Ave, New Orleans, LA 70119.

ROBINSON, CATHERINE (NEE STROWN)
Educator. **PERSONAL:** Born Sep 11, 1904, Petersburg, VA; widowed; children: Lynne, McDonald II, Valarie. **EDUCATION:** RI Coll, atnd,Univ of RI. **CAREER:** So Prov ProjUniv of RI Coop Exten Serv, asst home econ ldr 1963-75; Family & Bus Relo Serv, field interviewer 1959-63; TV Series in Home Econ & Other Areas, hostess 2 yrs. **ORGANIZATIONS:** Mem bd dir Oppor Ind Ctr; mem Women's Counc of United Way; mem Civil Rights Commn RI Adv Commn of US Commn on Civil Rights; mem bd dir BlackHeritage Soc; fndr Scitamard Players 1937. **HONORS/ACHIEVEMENTS:** Comm ldr award United So Providence Block Club 1971; comm serv award 1973; cit for disting servUniv of RI Coop Exten Serv 1974; RI Heritage Hall of Fame 1975; hon PdD RI Coll; schlrshp Nat Conf of Christians & Jews Rutgers U.

ROBINSON, CECELIA ANN
Educator. **PERSONAL:** Born May 28, 1948, Dallas, TX; married Kenneth E. **EDUCATION:** Prairie View A&M U, BA 1969;Univ of MO Columbia, MEd 1970;Univ of MO, ed spec 1971. **CAREER:** William Jewell Coll, instr of english 1979-; Maple Woods Community Coll, instr of english 1979; Penn Valley Comm Coll, instr of engish 1976-79; Oak ParkHS, instr of english 1972-79; Prairie View A&M U, instr of english 1972. **ORGANIZATIONS:** Mem Sigma Tau Delta English Honro Soc 1972-; mem Nat Council Tchr of English 1972-; mem MO State Tchr of English 1972-; mem MO State Tchr of English Assn 1979-; mem William Jewell Woman's Com 1974-80; corr sec & journalist Delta Sigma Theta Sorority 1976-; bd of dir Mid-continent Council of Girl Scouts Kansas City 1979-. **HONORS/ACHIEVEMENTS:** Who's Who Among Students in Am Coll &Univ 1969; EPDA FellowshipUniv of MO 1970-71; English Speaking Union FellowshipUniv of Oxford Eng 1976; MO Writer's Proj GrantUniv of MO 1979. **BUSINESS ADDRESS:** Asst Prof of English, William Jewell College, Dept of English, Liberty, MO 64068.

ROBINSON, CHARLES
Educational administrator. **PERSONAL:** Born Mar 19, 1940, Philadelphia, PA; married Bernice Ann Baker; children: Deborah Ann, Lesly Denise. **EDUCATION:** Cheyney State Univ, BS 1966. **CAREER:** Philadelphia Dept of Recreation, dec leader 1962-66; Philadelphia Public Schools, teacher 1966-75, admin asst 1975-84, teacher 1984-85; NJ School Bd Assn, vice pres. **ORGANIZATIONS:** Scout master Troop 713 1968-74; chmn Edgewater Pk Twp Juvenile Conf Comm 1970-85; bd of educ Edgewater Pk Twp 1977-87; adv bd Burlington Co Voc Tech 1978-85; pres bd of trustees Edgewater Pk Football Assn 1981-83; vice pres Burlington Co Sch Bds Assn 1982-86; vice pres NJ Sch Bd Assn 1984-85. **MILITARY SERVICE:** AUSR sgt E-5 6 yrs. **BUSINESS ADDRESS:** Vice President, NJ Sch Bds Assn, 22nd & Chestnut St, Philadelphia, PA 19103.

ROBINSON, CHARLES E.
Psychiatric social worker. **PERSONAL:** Born Aug 31, 1926, Indianapolis, IN; married Ann Garrett; children: Angela, George. **EDUCATION:** IN Univ, BS 1950, MSW 1952. **CAREER:** Robinson & Robinson Behavioral Sci Cons, co-partner; Hallie Q Brown Settlement House St Paul, group soc worker 1952-54; Central State Hosp, psychiatric social worker 1954-64; IN Bd of School Comm, school social worker 1964-68; CMHC, dir of social work; Yale Univ Dept of Psychiatry, asst clinical prof of soc work in psychiatry. **ORGANIZATIONS:** Bd of deacons Immanuel Baptist Church; IN Alumni Assoc; Jr C of C; Acad of Cert Soc Workers; Natl Assoc of Soc Worker; treas, bd of dir Newhallville Comm Action 1971-73; natl bd mem Family Serv Assoc 1973-; pres New Haven Family Serv Assoc of Amer 1974-78. **HONORS/ACHIEVEMENTS:** Outstanding Human Serv Professional of Amer; Outstanding Comm Serv Awd, United Newhallville Org. **MILITARY SERVICE:** AUS 1945-47. **BUSINESS ADDRESS:** Assistant Clinical Professor, YaleUniv, Dept of Psychiatry, 34 Park St, New Haven, CT 06510.

ROBINSON, CHARLOTTE L.
Educator. **PERSONAL:** Born Jun 13, 1924, Long Island, NY; widowed; children: Barry, Cherylyn. **EDUCATION:** BA 1948; MA 1967;Univ of PA, dr degree 1976. **CAREER:** Philadelphia Pub Sch Sys, asst dir curriculum & instr multimedia instructional resources; CityUniv of NY, cons; Sears Roebuck & Co Phila, cons. **ORGANIZATIONS:** Mem Phi Delta Epsilon; Am Women in Radio & TV; Media Adv Com for Commonwealth of PA; Assn for Educ Communications & Tech; PA Learning Resources AssnPhiladelphia Unique Communications Project July-aug 1974. **BUSINESS ADDRESS:** 21 Pkwy, Philadelphia, PA 19103.

ROBINSON, CLARENCE B.
Legislator. **PERSONAL:** Born Feb 04, 1911, Chattanooga, TN; married Lillian D; children: Marie Robinson. **EDUCATION:** TN State Univ, BS; Atlanta Univ, MED; Univ of WI, post graduate. **CAREER:** Orchard Knob Baptist Church, trustee, chmn, bd of dirs; real estate broker self-employed; Alton Park Jr HS, Calvin Donaldson, principal; House of Reps TN, legislature, 1974-. **ORGANIZATIONS:** chmn emeritus, House Black Caucus; vice chmn, House Democratic Caucus; mem Natl Business League Bd; pres Chattanooga Chap of TN Voters Council; life mem NEANAACP NAASP Kappa Alpha Psi Fraternity; founder & co-chmn State TN Voters Council; mem Adv Bd of Human Relations; mem, Democratic Platform Adv Comm 1980. **HONORS/ACHIEVEMENTS:** Certificate, Chattanooga Ambassador of Good Will 1968; Achievement Award, Natl Assn for the Study of Afro-Amer Life & History 1977; Distinguished Serv Award, TN State Univ, 1981; Meritorious Serv Appreciation Award, Chattanooga City Coll; Distinguished Serv Plaque, Chattanooga Chapter, NAACP; CB Robinson Bridge named in his honor. **HOME ADDRESS:** 1909 E 5th St, Chattanooga, TN 37404. **BUSINESS ADDRESS:** State Rep/TN House of Reps, TN State Govt Dist 28, RM 113 War Memorial Bldg, Nashville, TN 37219.

ROBINSON, CLARENCE G.
Chief surgeon. **PERSONAL:** Born Sep 19, 1920, Chicago, IL; son of Dr Clarence G Robinson, Sr and Mary T Robinson; married Dr Thelma Lennard; children: David, Michael, Mary. **EDUCATION:** Univ of Chicago, BS 1942; Meharry Med Coll, MD 1945. **CAREER:** Coney Island Hosp, chief ambulatory care serv 1967-72; City of NY, police surgeon 1970-73; New York City Police Dept, 1st black chief surgeon 1973-80, 1st full-time police surgeon, suprv chief surgeon 1980-85; Intl Assn of Chiefs of Police, chmn police physicians section

1986-89. **ORGANIZATIONS:** Assoc mem 1955, Fellow 1964, Amer Coll of Physicians; assoc attending physician Maimonides Med Ctr certified 1955, recertified 1974 Amer Bd of Intl Med; clinical instr med SUNY Downstate Med Ctr 1962-69; dir, med ed Coney Island Hosp 1967-70; pres med bd 1970-72, sec 1969-70 Coney Island Hosp; clinical asst, prof of med SUNY Downstate Med Ctr 1969-; vice chmn 1970-71, chmn 1971-72 Adv Council of Med Bds of Municipal Hospitals; assoc attending physician Kings Cty Hosp Ctr 1971-. **HONORS/ACHIEVEMENTS:** Founding mem & pres-elect Amer Acad of Police Medicine 1976-80, pres 1981-85; certificate of advanced achievement in Internal Medicine, Amer Bd of Internal Medicine, 1987. **MILITARY SERVICE:** USAFR capt 1953-55.

ROBINSON, CLEVELAND L.
Trade union executive, civil rights leader. **PERSONAL:** Born Dec 12, 1914; married Doreen. **CAREER:** UAW Dist 65, 1st black officer 1950, past vp, sec/treas. **ORGANIZATIONS:** Founder, past pres Distrib Workers of Amer; admin chmn March on Washington 1963; founder, pres Natl Afro-Amer Labor Council; founder, 1st vice pres Coalition of Black Trade Unionists; labor adv Dr Martin Luther King Jr; past mem, bd of dir So Christian Leadership Conf; mem bd of dir Dr Martin Luther King. **HONORS/ACHIEVEMENTS:** Jr Ctr for Soc Change; past commiss New York City Comm for Human Rights. **MILITARY SERVICE:** Recipient of many awds giving testimony to the high esteem in which he is held. **BUSINESS ADDRESS:** Secretary, Treasurer, UAW Dist 65, 13 Astor Place, New York, NY 10003.

ROBINSON, CLIFF ANTHONY
Professional athlete. **PERSONAL:** Born Mar 13, 1960, Oakland, CA. **EDUCATION:** Southern Cal, 1981. **CAREER:** Washington Bullets, forward 1984; New Jersey Nets, 1979; Kansas City Kings, 1981. **HONORS/ACHIEVEMENTS:** Ranked 8th in League in rebounding; 23 points against the Bullets Mar 6, 1980 for a Nets club record; first team All-Conf selection; Bsktbl Weekly's Freshmn All-Am team; named to All-League Team. **BUSINESS ADDRESS:** Washington Bullets, One Harry S Truman, Ste 510, Landover, MD 20785.

ROBINSON, CURTIS
Educator. **PERSONAL:** Born May 12, 1934, Wilmington, NC; married Joan Elenor Williams; children: Debra D, Milton C, Cheryl A. **EDUCATION:** Morgan State U, BS 1960; Howard U, MS 1968;Univ of MD, PhD 1973. **CAREER:** Edinbroro State Coll, asso prof 1973-; Radiation Biology Lab Smithsonian Instn Rockville MD, research biologist 1962-69; Williston Sr HS NC, sci/math tchr 1961-62; Lincoln HS NC, sci/math tchr 1960-61. **ORGANIZATIONS:** Mem Am Soc of Plant Physiologists 1970-; mem Nat Educ Assn 1973-; mem Am Assn ofUniv Prof 1978-; mem Alpha Pha Alphga Frat 1959-; mem Assn of PA State Coll 19 Biologists 1973-; mem NAACP 1975. **MILITARY SERVICE:** AUS spec-3 3 yrs. **BUSINESS ADDRESS:** Edinboro State Coll, Edinboro, PA 16444.

ROBINSON, DANIEL LEE
Business owner, chef. **PERSONAL:** Born May 07, 1923, York County, SC; married Evelyn Young; children: Daniel Jr, Robert, Marilyn. **EDUCATION:** Friendship Jr Coll, attnd. **CAREER:** Desales Hall Theol Sem, chef 1977; Colonial Villa Manor Care, kitchen mgr 1965-74; Fed Cab Co, taxicab owner, operator 25 yrs; Taxicab Ind Assn, rep 1972; NIH, 1953-63; PTA & Emery Sch, pres 1967; Langley Jr HS PTA, pres 1972; McKinley Sr High School PTA, vice pres 1974. **ORGANIZATIONS:** Mem DC Dem Central Com 1973-76; bd mem Ctr City Comm Corp 1967-; vice pres Three A Area Counc Cong of Parents & Tchrs 1973; pres adv counc Emery Comm Sch 1975; Ward 5 campaign coord Mayor Walter E Washington 1974; chmn 5th Ward Dem 1973-77; 1st vice pres Edgewood Civic Assn 1977; commr Single Mem Dist 5c-06; Adv Neighbrhd Commn DC Govt 1976; active in sch bd campaigns 1972; worked in CORE & ACT 1950'‡; ward coord Barbara Sizemore Campaign 1977; trstee Franklin P Nash United Meth Ch; chrpsn area of Christian Soc Concerns. **HONORS/ACHIEVEMENTS:** Serv award Mattie G Taylor 1973; serv & award Ward 5 Counc William Spaulding 1976; grass roots hon DC Fdn of Civic Assns 1976; ten yr serv cert US Govt 1963. **MILITARY SERVICE:** AUS staff-sgt 1943-47. **BUSINESS ADDRESS:** 5001 Eastern Ave, Hyattsville, MD.

ROBINSON, DAPHNE MCCASKY See MCCASKEY, DAPHNE THEOPHILIA

ROBINSON, DEANNA ADELL
Convention service manager. **PERSONAL:** Born Jul 31, 1945, Chicago, IL; married Willie. **EDUCATION:** MI State Univ, BS 1967. **CAREER:** Hilton Hotels, 20 yrs serv with a wide range of positions, currently convention service mgr Palmer House Hotel. **ORGANIZATIONS:** Mem Natl Coalition of Black Meeting Planners 1986. **BUSINESS ADDRESS:** Asst Dir Convention Serv, Palmer House-Hilton Hotel, 17 E Monroe St, Chicago, IL 60690.

ROBINSON, DENAUVO M.
Director of special services. **PERSONAL:** Born Apr 10, 1949, Quincy, IL. **EDUCATION:** Northeast MO St U, BS 1971; MA 1971; Northern IL U, EdD 1977. **CAREER:** Drexel U, dir of Specl Srv; Northern ILUniv CHANCE Dekalb, IL, assoc dir 1974, counselor 1972-74; Western IL U, Macomb, counselor 1971-72. **ORGANIZATIONS:** Mem APGA; ANWC; IGPA; IANWC; NIU; APGA; NAACP; Civil Liberties Union. **BUSINESS ADDRESS:** Drexel University, 32nd & Chestnut Streets, Philadelphia, PA 19104.

ROBINSON, DONALD LEE
Dentist. **PERSONAL:** Born Jul 25, 1930, Indianapolis, IN; married Juanita Cook; children: Carmaletus F, Donald L II, Kimberly P. **EDUCATION:** AB 1955; DDS 1960; IN U. **CAREER:** Private Practice, dentist. **ORGANIZATIONS:** Mem, Am Dental Assn; Nat Dental Assn; IN Dental Assn; Indianapolis Dist Dental Soc; Indianapolis Dental Study Club; IN Branch, Natl Dental Assn; life mem, NAACP; life mem, Kappa Alpha Psi Fraternity, Mt Zion Baptist Church; bd mem, Indianapolis Alumni of Kappa Alpha Psi Frat. **MILITARY SERVICE:** AUS 1952-54. **BUSINESS ADDRESS:** 3721 N ILL St, Indianapolis, IN 46208.

ROBINSON, EDDIE
College football coach. **PERSONAL:** Married Doris. **CAREER:** Grambling Univ LA, football coach 1941-. **HONORS/ACHIEVEMENTS:** Holds record of most college football victories. **BUSINESS ADDRESS:** Coach, Grambling University, PO Box 868, Grambling, LA 71245.

ROBINSON, EDITH (NEE BROWN)
Business executive. **PERSONAL:** Born Dec 31, 1924, Buffalo, NY; married James C. **EDUCATION:** Wilberforce U, BS 1946; StateUniv NY, MSW. **CAREER:** Erie Co Dept of Social Svcs, asst dep commr; Pub Welfare, caseworker, sr caseworker, unit supr, dist supr 1947-77; StateUniv Coll SEEK Prgm, adj prof 1969-70. **ORGANIZATIONS:** Past pres Nat Assn of Social Workers ACSW; exec bd NY State Welfare Conf 1970-72; chmn Nat Field Adv Cncl Alexandria Am Red Cross 1977-78; vice-chmn Greater Buffalo Chap ARC 1971-; Resolutions Com ARC 1978; publicity chmn Am Lung Assn of NY 1977; Zonta Club of Buffalo 1970; YWCA 1972; Links Inc; Comm Adv Council StateUniv NY at Buffalo. **HONORS/ACHIEVEMENTS:** Alumna of year WilberforceUniv 1967; outst serv award Bronze Damsels 1968; 1st disting womans serv award Buffalo Urban Ctr 1971; comm serv award Buffalo Urban League 1975. **BUSINESS ADDRESS:** 95 Franklin St, Buffalo, NY 14202.

ROBINSON, EDSEL F.
Clergyman, real estate broker. **PERSONAL:** Born May 05, 1928, Wrightsville, GA; son of Rev Jasper Robinson and Tressie Robinson; married Pearlie Haynes; children: Edsel, Jr, Desiree. **EDUCATION:** Morris Brown Coll, 1959; Turner Theological Seminary, BD; Interdenominational Theological Center; Turner Theological Seminary of Interdenominational Theological Center Atlanta, Honorary DD candidate 1980. **CAREER:** EF Robinson Realty Co, pres; Mt Carmel AME Church, minister. **ORGANIZATIONS:** Mem NAACP, YMCA, AME Ministers' Union, SCLC, Empire Real Estate Bd, Operation Breadbasket, Natl Assn Real Estate Brokers 1974; mgmt broker Veterans Admin 1970-73; organizer Doraville Community Org 1974. **HONORS/ACHIEVEMENTS:** Salesman of the Year 1971-72; Special Award for Outstanding Serv to AME Church; recipient E F Robinson Day Proclamation for Outstanding Contribution to the city & poeople of all races, City of Doraville GA 1976. **HOME ADDRESS:** 3322 Rabun Dr SW, Atlanta, GA 30311. **BUSINESS ADDRESS:** Broker, E F Robinson Realty Co, Inc, 195 Auburn Ave, NE, Atlanta, GA 30303.

ROBINSON, EDWARD A.
Educator. **PERSONAL:** Born Jun 13, 1935, Gary, IN; married Lavada Hill; children: Edward Allen, Arlen Yohance. **EDUCATION:** Howard Univ, BA, 1959; Univ of Chicago, MAT 1970; Northwestern Univ, PhD, 1974. **CAREER:** Northeastern IL Univ, asst prof; Lake Forest Coll IL, English instr 1970-72; Chicago Bd of Educ, HS English consult 1970-72; Wendell Phillips & Summer HS Chicago,instr 1961-64; English Dept Harlan HS Chicago, instr & chmn 1960-69; Carver HS Chicago, instr 1959-60; Emmy Award Winning TV Prog "The Giants", "The Common Men", narrator 1967; "Like It Was the black man in Amer", teacher host 1969; midwest modern language assn conv, presented paper 1973; NDEA Inst Univ of Chicago, participant in summer 1965. **ORGANIZATIONS:** Mem S Shore Valley Comm Orgn 1969-74; Faulkner Sch Assn 1974-75; Faulkner Sch Father's Club 1974-75; Nat Urban League 1968-74; Operation PUSH 1972. **HONORS/ACHIEVEMENTS:** Recipient experienced tchr fellowshipUniv of Chicago 1969-70; ford found fellowship for black am 1973-74; author of numerous publications. **MILITARY SERVICE:** Served in AUS 1953-55. **BUSINESS ADDRESS:** Northeastern IL Univ, Bryn Mawr Ave at St Louis Ave, Chicago, IL 60625.

ROBINSON, EDWARD ASHTON
Attorney. **PERSONAL:** Born 1949, Hammond, LA. **EDUCATION:** Grambling U; State Univ NY; Rutgers U. **CAREER:** Private Practice, atty 1979-; Baton Rouge LA, chf adminstr, state atty gen. **HONORS/ACHIEVEMENTS:** Outsdng yng man LA Jaycees 1977. **BUSINESS ADDRESS:** PO Box 3131, 4962 Florida Blvd, Baton Rouge, LA 70821.

ROBINSON, EFFIE
Social worker. **PERSONAL:** Born Jan 07, Healdsburg, CA. **EDUCATION:** San Francisco State Coll, aB MAGNUM cum laude 1944;Univ of CA at Berkeley, mSW 1945; postgrad spl courses various schs. **CAREER:** Sr Cit Social Serv, dir, clin social worker 1968-; Human Relat & Social Serv San Francisco Housing Auth, dir 1964-; dir, case work 1960-64; Family Serv & Agency San Francisco, 1944-64. **ORGANIZATIONS:** Mem Groves Conf 1971-; Mayor's Com on Status of Women; bd dir Performing Arts for the 3rd Age; Nat Campire Girls; League Women Voters; life mem NAACP; fdr Friends JFK Ctr for Performing Arts; sponsors; links; sloroptimists. **HONORS/ACHIEVEMENTS:** Named one of ten distng women in bay area San Francisco Examiner 1961; Woman Of Yr Zeta Phi Beta 1967; Woman Of Month Ladies Home Journal 1975; nom Woman Of Yr 1976; Koshland Award for creative programming for elderly 1974; apptd State Housing Bd CA Housing Fin Agency 1975. **BUSINESS ADDRESS:** 440 Turk St, San Francisco, CA 94102.

ROBINSON, ELLA S.
Educator. **PERSONAL:** Born Apr 16, 1943, Wedowee, AL; daughter of Less Scales and Mary Ella MacPherson Scales; married John William Robinson, May 09, 1980 (deceased); children: John William, Jr. **EDUCATION:** AL State Univ, BS 1965; Univ of NE, MA 1970, PhD 1976. **CAREER:** Univ of IL, assistant prof 1975-77; Atlanta Univ, assistant prof 1977-79; Univ of Nebraska-Licoln, lecturer of English, 1979-. **ORGANIZATIONS:** Mem MLA 1974-87; chair afro-lite session MMLA 1985-86; life time mem NAACP 1986-; ALA; African Amer Poet for the Heritage Room, Bennet Martin Library, 1989. **HONORS/ACHIEVEMENTS:** Travelled throughout Nigeria in order to do research for poetry, paintings and articles. **BUSINESS ADDRESS:** Lecturer, English Dept, University of Nebraska-Lincoln, Andrews Hall, Lincoln, NE 68588.

ROBINSON, ERNEST PRESTON, SR.
Motivational consultant, sales trainer. **PERSONAL:** Born Aug 15, 1947, Detroit, MI; son of Andy "Pop" Brown and Willie B Robinson; married Sheila M Boswell, Aug 09, 1980; children: Ernie Jr, Eric. **EDUCATION:** Detroit Coll of Business, Dearborn MI, BS Mktg, 1971. **CAREER:** J L Hudson Co, Detroit MI, sales supvr, 1971-72; Allstate Insurance Co, Southfield MI, mktg sales mgr, natl sales trainer, 1972-88; Self-Employed, Farmington Hills MI, president, owner, 1988-. **ORGANIZATIONS:** Mem, Natl Assn of Life Underwriters, 1972-, Life Underwriting Training Council, 1978-, Veterans Boxing Assn, Ring 32, 1983-, Southern Christian Leadership Conf, 1987-, NAACP, 1987-, Thursday Luncheon Group, 1988-, Greater West Bloomfield Chamber of Commerce, 1988-, Michigan Coalition for Human Rights, 1988-; dir, Drama Soc of St John CME Church, 1988-. **HONORS/**

ACHIEVEMENTS: Author of poem, "Detroit Fate Train on the Move," 1967; Master Speech Award, Dale Carnegie, 1980; Key Mgr, Allstate Insurnce Co, 1985, 1986; Natl Sales Trainer Award, Allstate Insurance Co, 1987; Speaker of the Year, Southern Christian Leadership Conf, 1988; Actor of the Year, St John CME Church, 1988; Producer/Director/Actor in the dramatization, The Resurrection of the Spirit of Dr Martin Luther King Jr, 1988-. **BUSINESS ADDRESS:** Business Motivational Consultant, MoDrama Enterprises, 32651 Northwestern Hwy, Suite 316, Farmington Hills MI 48018.

ROBINSON, EUNICE PRIMUS
Counselor. **PERSONAL:** Born Oct 17, 1935, Hardeeville, SC; married DeWitt T, Jr; children: Janice, De Witt III, Glenn. **EDUCATION:** Savannah State Coll, BS Elem Educ 1953;Univ of SC, MEd 1972. **CAREER:** Midlands Tech Coll, couns; Benedict Coll, dean women, couns 1968-71; Rosenwald Elem Sch, tchr 1965-67; Allen U, couns, dir student activities 1959-63; SC State Coll, couns 1955-59; Hardeeville Elem Sch, tchr 1953-55. **ORGANIZATIONS:** Mem Zeta Phi Beta Sor; SC Pers & Guid Assn 1975; Nat Dirs Orientation Assn; fdr, adv Afro-Am Club of Midlands Tech Coll 1972-; mem Scholarship Found, Booker T Washington 1975; sec Fairwald Elem Sch PTA 1974-; treas Fairwald Middle Sch PTA; sec Altar Guild, St Luke's Epis Ch 1974-; sec Omega Psi Phi Frat Wives 1974-75; team mother Pony League, Dixie Youth League Baseball Prgm 1972-75. **HONORS/ACHIEVEMENTS:** Chosen by survey Counselor Most Seen by Students, Midlands Tech Coll 1973; Mother of Yr, Zeta Phi Beta Sor 1959; Mother of Yr, Afro-Am Club, Midlands Tech Coll 1975. **BUSINESS ADDRESS:** Midlands Tech Coll, PO Drawer Q, Columbia, SC 29250.

ROBINSON, FRANK
Professional baseball manager. **PERSONAL:** Born Aug 31, 1935, Beaumont, TX; married Barbara Ann Cole; children: Frank Kevin, Michelle. **CAREER:** Cincinnati Reds farm system teams, 1953-56; Cincinnati Reds major league team, 1956-65; Santurce Cangrejeros PR, mgr 1968-; Baltimore Orioles, outfldr 1965-71; LA Dodgers, 1972; CA Angels, 1973-74; Cleveland Indiana, mgr 1975-77; Rochester Red Wings, mgr 1978; San Francisco Giants, mgr 1981-84; Baltimore Orioles, coach. **HONORS/ACHIEVEMENTS:** Natl League Rookie of Yr 1956; Baseball Writers Assn 1956; Most Valuable Player 1961; Amer League Triple Crown 1966; Most Valuable, AL 1966; tied world series record for most times hit by pitcher 1961; appeared in 11 All Star games; author (with Al Silverman) "My Life is Baseball" 1968; elected to Hall of Fame at Cooperstown 1982. **BUSINESS ADDRESS:** c/o Baltimore Orioles, Mimi Stadium, Baltimore, MD 21218.

ROBINSON, FRANK J.
Educator, clergyman. **PERSONAL:** Born Nov 18, 1939, Montgomery, TX; married Reecie (deceased); children: Lady Robinson Nelson, Portia Elaine, Frank J Jr, Gusta Jovon. **EDUCATION:** TX So U, BS 1964. **CAREER:** Pleasant Home Bapt Ch Clat, TX, pastor; Bowid Dance Studio, Houston, instr of dramatics; Houston Comm Coll, instr; Urban Theatre, tech dir; Assured Blessing Ministry Ch 39, tech dir; treas Central Convention of TX Brotherhood; Greater St Matthews BC, clergyman. **ORGANIZATIONS:** Chmn Comm Coord TX State Conf of Br NAACP; vice pres Alpha Mu Omega; mem West End Civic Club. **MILITARY SERVICE:** USMCR 1957-68. **BUSINESS ADDRESS:** Clergyman, Greater St Matthews BC, 7701 Jutland, Houston, TX 77027.

ROBINSON, G. BRUCE
Retired judge. **PERSONAL:** Born Jun 02, 1907, Washington, DC; married Beryl Yancey. **EDUCATION:** Williams Coll, AB 1928; Boston Univ School of Law, LLB 1936. **CAREER:** Livingstone Coll, prof, dept head english dept 1928-33; Governor's Cncl of MA, exec sec 1947-48; Boston Juvenile Ct, spec justice, judge 1948-77. **ORGANIZATIONS:** Past mem bd of dir Roxbury YMCA, New England Home for Little Wanderers, Boston Br NAACP, Boston Urban League. **HONORS/ACHIEVEMENTS:** Citation for Disting Serv from Urban League of Boston, MA Black Lawyers Assoc, Greater Boston YMCA, MA Bar Assoc, Boston Univ Sch of Law.

ROBINSON, GARY O.
Director. **PERSONAL:** Born Aug 22, 1935, Boston, MA; married Diane Dismont; children: Michele, Dane, Kim. **EDUCATION:** Harvard Univ Grad Sch of Bus Admin, attended; Natl OIC Mgmt Training Prog, attended; Northweatern Univ, attended; Friendship Jr Coll Rockhill, attended. **CAREER:** Roxbury N Dorchester Area Planning Action Council MA, dir 1966-68; OIC of Greater Boston, exec dir 1968-71; Office of Human Serv, com of MA asst sec proj mgt exec office 1971-75; OIC Intl Inc, dep dir 1975, exec dir 1975-. **ORGANIZATIONS:** Dir Council for Intl Visitors Philadelphia 1980; dir Opportunities Acad of Mgmt Training Phila; dir OXFAM Am; mem YMCA, NAACP, Urban League, Big Brothers Assn. **BUSINESS ADDRESS:** Executive Dir, OIC Intl Inc, 240 W Tulpehocken St, Philadelphia, PA 19144.

ROBINSON, GENEVIEVE
Educator. **PERSONAL:** Born Apr 20, 1940, Kansas City, MO; daughter of James L. Robinson and Helen Williams Robinson. **EDUCATION:** Mt St Scholastica Coll, BA History 1968; New Mexico Highlands Univ, MA History 1974; Catholic Univ of Amer, History 1978-79; Boston Coll, PhD History 1986. **CAREER:** Lillis HS, History teacher 1969-73, 1974-75, History dept chairperson 1970-73, admin/curriculum dir 1974-75; Donnelly Comm Coll, instructor 1976-78; Boston Coll, instructor 1983; Rockhurst Coll, instr 1985-86, asst prof 1986-. **ORGANIZATIONS:** Mem Phi Alpha Theta, Kappa Mu Epsilon, Organization of Amer Historians, Immigration History Soc, Pi Gamma Mu; mem Ethical Review Board l988-. **HONORS/ACHIEVEMENTS:** Gasson Fellowship Boston Coll 1984-85; Natl Endowment for the Humanities Coll Teachers Summer Seminar Grant 1987, Presidential Grant, Rockhurst Coll, 1988. **BUSINESS ADDRESS:** Assistant Professor, Rockhurst College, 5225 Troost, Kansas City, MO 64110.

ROBINSON, GEORGE ALI
Analyst. **PERSONAL:** Born Apr 16, 1939, Americus, GA; children: Ali, Omari, Khalid. **EDUCATION:** Shaw Univ, AB 1965, MDiv 1975; Neotarian Coll, DD 1976; ITC, DMin 1977; Metanoia Univ, PhD 1981. **CAREER:** Ed Black Bus Awareness Mag; comm rel spec US Dept Justice Col writer "Moving On"; pastor Ridgeway Baptist Church; social worker Raleigh; prog analysisDHEW; pres A&G Enterprises Raleigh; consult MKT Pol Camp; HEW, soc sci analyst. **ORGANIZATIONS:** Consult AMEC Press; lecturer Chris Ed in Black Religion Conv, Black Theol Mason, PUSH, ASPA; author "Metanoia Conv, The need for the Black Church". **HONORS/ACHIEVEMENTS:** Listed in Personalitites of S Amer Biog Inst 1976-77; Comm Leaders & Noteworthy Amer 1977. **MILITARY SERVICE:** AUS sgt 1957-62. **BUSINESS ADDRESS:** Social Science Analyst, HEW, PO Box 2381, Raleigh, NC 27602.

ROBINSON, GEORGE L.
Educator. **PERSONAL:** Born in Memphis, TN; married Ida; children: Georgette, Seymour. **EDUCATION:** Lemoyne Coll, BS 1947; Memphis State Univ, MA 1964. **CAREER:** Natl Defense Cadet Corps, teacher 1939-59, dir, 1959-64; ROTC, dir 1964-70; Memphis City School Dept of Plant Mgmt, asst supt 1975-. **ORGANIZATIONS:** Mem Assoc of School Bus Officials, vice pres USO Council, United Way Budget Comm; bd dir Greater Memphis State Univ; mem, bd of dir Vstg Nurses Assoc; mem Phi Delta Kappa, Alpha Phi Alpha, Assoc of Safety Engrs, Better School Comm; trustee 1st Baptist Church Lauderdale. **HONORS/ACHIEVEMENTS:** Author & head of OSHA Prog for Memphis City Schools; Org school of month prog & contest for all city schools. **MILITARY SERVICE:** AUS Engrs capt 1942-46, maj 1950-52. **BUSINESS ADDRESS:** Assistant Superintendent, Memphis City School, Dept of Plant Mgmt, 2597 Avery Memphis, Memphis, TN 38112.

ROBINSON, GERTRUDE RIVERS
Educator. **PERSONAL:** Born Jun 30, 1927, Camden, SC; daughter of W Napoleon Rivers Jr, PhD and Gertrude Burroughs Rivers, PhD; married Spencer M Robinson, Sep 07, 1950 (deceased); children: Spencer, Jr, Gail Rivers (dec). **EDUCATION:** Cornell Univ, Mortar Bd, BA 1947; Univ of CA at Los Angeles, MA 1972, CPh 1977. **CAREER:** Music Dept Loyola Marymount Univ, assoc prof 1970-, chmn 1984-87; Semester at Sea, Univ of Pittsburgh, prof 1987; Univ of CA at Los Angeles, res asst 1963-67; Sark Studios, musical dir 1954-57; Lestor Horton Studios, 1951-53; Cornell Univ, instructor 1951-53. **ORGANIZATIONS:** Advisory bd Folk Arts Panel of California Council of the Arts 1985, 1986; composers music fellowship panel Natl Endowment for the Arts 1988, 1989; first vice pres League of Allied Arts Inc 1989-91; Mem, bd dirs Am Soc for Eastern Arts 1974-; bd dirs Soc for Ethnomusicology 1976; council mem, com chmn Soc for Ethnomusicology 1973-75; bd mem Design for Sharing, UCLA affiliate fine arts prod 1971-; chmn Arts & Letters, Delta Sigma Theta Inc, LA Alumnae Chapter 1976-77; mem Children's Serv Auxilary, Mental Health Center 1973-; publ Bali South, ie records, Inst of Ethnomusicology, UCLA; composer Bayangan for Western Septet & Balinese Octet 1962 & 1972; first-time recording & notes on compositions of traditional Balinese composer Wajan Gandera; mem Mortar Bd 1947. **HONORS/ACHIEVEMENTS:** US Office of Educ Res Study Grant, India 1976; Natl Fellow Grant 1977; Community Service Aeard, Assemblywoman Theresa Hughes 1988; publication "Moods for Flute and Piano I & II," Festsheift for Kwabena Nketia 1989. **BUSINESS ADDRESS:** Associate Professor, Loyola Marymount University, Loyola Blvd at W 80th, Burns 104, Los Angeles, CA 90045.

ROBINSON, GILL DONCELIA (GILL D. DANIELS)
Entrepreneur, educator, personnel administrator. **PERSONAL:** Born Mar 28, 1948, Baltimore, MD; divorced; children: Kimberly Frances. **EDUCATION:** Univ of Denver, BA 1970; Univ of Cal Los Angeles, MPA 1973; Univ of So Cal, PhD 1978. **CAREER:** City of Inglewood, CA, admin intern 1971-72, admin assist 1972-73; Office of the Chancellor CA State Univ & Coll, personnel analyst 1973-76; Ontario-Montclair Sch Dist, dir of classified personnel 1976-77; The Rodeo Rainbow for Children, owner 1984-85; CA State Univ Dominguez Hills, dir of staff personnel 1977-79, prof 1979-. **ORGANIZATIONS:** Vice chairwoman Com on Women in Pub Administration 1975-76; council mem Amer Soc for Pub Administration LA Chap 1977-84. **HONORS/ACHIEVEMENTS:** A Better Chance Scholarship Windsor Mt Sch 1964-66; Univ of Denver Acad Scholarship 1969; Grad Advancement Prog Fellowship UCLA 1970-72; Soroptimist Club Recognition Award Soroptimist Club Los Angeles, CA 1974. **BUSINESS ADDRESS:** Professor, California StateUniv, Dominguez Hills, 1000 E Victoria St, Carson, CA 90747.

ROBINSON, HAMILTON
Police executive. **PERSONAL:** Born Oct 25, 1930, Brooklyn, NY; married Irma J Ritchie. **EDUCATION:** John Jay Coll, BS 1972; FBI Nat Acad, 1976. **CAREER:** Intelligence Div Police Dept, City of NY, exec ofcr; New York City Police Dept, num positions. **ORGANIZATIONS:** Am Acad of Professional Law Execs; memshp com Nat Orgn of Black Law Enforcement Execs; 100 Black Men; FBI Nat Asso John Jay Coll Alumni Assn; NAACP;designed & adminstered study course for promotion to sgt New York City Police Dept 1968; lectr num police & comm relat; num TV & radio appearances; dir pre-svcentrance Civil Serv study courses for young men & women from educ disadv comm 1966-67. **BUSINESS ADDRESS:** NY City Police Department, 1 Police Plaza, New York, NY 10038.

ROBINSON, HARRY G., III
Educator, architect, city planner. **PERSONAL:** Born Jan 18, 1942, Washington, DC; son of Harry G Robinson Jr and Gwendolyn Herriford Robinson; married Dianne O Davis; children: Erin K, Leigh H, Kia L. **EDUCATION:** Howard Univ, BArch 1966, MCity Plng 1970; Harvard Univ, MUrban Design 1972. **CAREER:** DC Redevel Land Agency, arch, plnr 1968-72; Univ of the DC, prof 1969-70,71-74; Morgan State Univ, chmn, prof 1971-79; Howard Univ, dean arch & plng. **ORGANIZATIONS:** Principal Robinson & Assoc 1976-; pres DC Bd of Exam & Reg of Arch 1983-; mem Amer Inst of Arch 1976-, Amer Inst of Cert Plnrs 1974-; trustee Natl Building Museum; dir, Natl Council of Architectural Registration Bds. **HONORS/ACHIEVEMENTS:** Lasker Fellow in City Plng Lasker Found 1969-70; Martin Luther King Jr Fellow Woodrow Wilson Found 1969-70; Urban Transp Rsch Fellow US DOT 1969-70; Faculty Gold Medal in Design Howard Univ 1965; Silver Medal, Tau Sigma Delta, 1988. **MILITARY SERVICE:** AUS 1st lt 2 yrs; Ranger Tab; Bronze Star; Purple Heart 1966-68. **BUSINESS ADDRESS:** Dean, HowardUniv, Sch of Architecture & Planning, 2366 6th St NW, Washington, DC 20059.

ROBINSON, HENRY
Mayor. **PERSONAL:** Born Oct 02, 1936, Port Royal, SC; married Jannie Middleton; children: Elizabeth, Tracy, Stephanie. **CAREER:** Town of Port Royal, council & mayor protem, mayor. **ORGANIZATIONS:** Pres, Comm Ctr Port Royal; 2nd vice pres Dem Party Port Royal Prec. **HONORS/ACHIEVEMENTS:** Outstanding Comm Svc. **BUSINESS ADDRESS:** Mayor, Town of Port Royal, Drawer 8, Port Royal, SC 29935.

ROBINSON, HERBERT A.
Psychiatrist. **PERSONAL:** Born Feb 19, 1927, Burkeville, VA; divorced; children: Laura, Paul, Nancy, David. **EDUCATION:** Syracuse U, BA 1950; Howard U, MD 1957; Orange Co Gen Hosp, intern; Metro State Hosp, Qpsychiatric resident. **CAREER:** Mental Health Servs Los Angeles Co Dept Health, psychiatrist, acting dir; Mental Health Servs LA Co, 1965; Camarillo State Hosp, dir aftercare clin1963-65; Day-Treatment Clinic Metro State Hosp, dir 1961-63. **ORGANIZATIONS:** Diplomate Am Bd Psychiatry & Neurology 1964; fellow Am Psychiatric Assn 1974; mem, com Task Force Poverty Manpower Com; mem Ins & Malpractice Review Com; Am Psychiatric Assn. **HONORS/ACHIEVEMENTS:** Alumnus of Yr 1974. **MILITARY SERVICE:** USAF. **BUSINESS ADDRESS:** 1127 Wilshire Blvd, Los Angeles, CA 90017.

ROBINSON, HUBERT NELSON
Clergyman. **PERSONAL:** Born Apr 29, 1909, Urbana, OH; married Mary Isley. **EDUCATION:** OH State U, AB; Hamma Div Sch Wittenberg U, BD;Univ of Pittsburg & Chicago Theol Sch, addl grad studies. **CAREER:** 11th Episcopal Dist AME Ch, bishop; Edward Waters Coll Jacksonville, chmn of bd trustees; 18th Episcopal Dist, bishop 1964-68; 9th Episcopal Dist, 1968-72; various AME Chs, pastor 1934-64. **ORGANIZATIONS:** Gov Commn of Moral Ethics; Gov Commn on Traffic Safety State of MI; bd dir Met YMCA; adv bd Foster Home Children's Agy; pres Council of Bishops AME Ch; chmn Gen Conf Commn; chmn Commn on Youth Affairs; chmn Com on Haitian Refugees; past pres Detroit Pastors Union; Alger PTA; mem Kappa Alpha Psi; Urban League; Lambda Mu; PUSH; life mem NAACP. **HONORS/ACHIEVEMENTS:** Pub & edited in three native dialects hymnals for Mozambigue; outstanding serv to Advancement of Christian Educ Daniel Payne Coll 1974; outstanding support in area of life mem Jacksonville Br NAACP 1974; religion award Jacksonville Chap SCLC 1974; annual award-merit field of human relations Pi Lambda Sigma 1967. **BUSINESS ADDRESS:** 1658 Kings Rd, Jacksonville, FL 32209.

ROBINSON, HUGH GRANVILLE
Business executive. **PERSONAL:** Born Aug 04, 1932, Washington, DC; son of James and Wilhelmina; married Matilda; children: Hugh G Jr, Mrs Susan Gardner, Mia Turner. **EDUCATION:** US Military Acad West Point, BS 1954; MIT, MS 1959; Williams Coll, hon LD 1983. **CAREER:** Tetra Group, chmn & CEO, currently; Grigsby Brandford Powell Inc, sr vice pres, 1988-. **ORGANIZATIONS:** Bd dir Federal Reserve Bank of Dallas; bd dir Baylor Univ Med Cntr Found; bd dir Museum of African-Amer Life & Culture; bd trustees Dallas Museum of Fine Arts; bd mem TACA; bd dir exec com Dallas Civic Opera; bd mem Keep Amer Beautiful; adv council Clean Dallas Inc; bd dir Amer Red Cross, Dallas Power and Light, The Belo Corp, Lomas & Nettleton. **HONORS/ACHIEVEMENTS:** Fellow, Soc of Amer Military Engineers. **MILITARY SERVICE:** US Army Corps of Engineers, major general, 1955-83; Distinguished Serv Medal; Legion of Merit (with Oak Leaf Cluster); Bronze Star (with Oak Leaf Cluster); Meritorious Serv Medal; Air Medal (with two Oak Leaf Clusters); Joint Serv Commendation Medal; Army Commendation Medal (with Oak Leaf Cluster); Vietnamese Cross of Gallantry (Gold Star); Vietnamese Serv Medal; Vietnam Campaign Medal; Amer Defense Medal. **BUSINESS ADDRESS:** Chmn & CEO, Tetra Group, 4140 Office Parkway, Dallas, TX 75204.

ROBINSON, IRA CHARLES
Educator. **PERSONAL:** Born Aug 27, 1940, Webster, FL; married Clarice E James; children: Ira II, Patricia Clarice, Kirshwin Amicus, Charmalyn Elan. **EDUCATION:** Univ FL, PhD 1966; FL A&M U, BS 1961. **CAREER:** Howard U, prof 1973-; Nat Pharm Found Inc, exec dir 1973-; Howard U, dean 1973-76; FL A&M U, dean, prof 1969-73; Proj Leader of Pharm Rsrch, tech asst to vp; Med Products Rsrch & Devel Div Pfizer Inc, sr rsrch sci 1966-69;Univ FL, mfg pharmacist 1963-66; FL & AL, registered pharmacist,asst mgr pharm intern 1961-63. **ORGANIZATIONS:** Mem, editorial bd Evaluation & the Health Professions 1977-; dir Attucks Corp 1977-; dfir Fed Labs Inc 1977-; mem APHA Acad of Pharm Scis 1967-; asso fellow Am Coll of Apothecaries 1977-; fellow Am Soc of Consult Pharmacists 1970-73; Am Pharm Assn 1966-; Nat Pharm Assn 1969-; Collegio FarmaceuticoNatl de Cuba 1972-; Wash DC Pharm Assn 1973-; FL Pharm Assn 1969-73; hon mem FL Soc of Hosp Pharmacists 1970-; mem, bd dir FL A&MUniv Found Inc 1970-; Sigma Xi Sci Soc 1967-; AAAS 1967-; fellow NY Acad of Scis 1976-; mem Wash DC Pharm Assn Cont Educ Com 1976-. **HONORS/ACHIEVEMENTS:** US Patent #3577514 1971; Who's Who in Am 1972; Outst Personalities of S 1971; Leaders in Educ 1971; Am Men of Sci 1969; Outst Young Men of Am 1966; Who's Who Among Students in Am Colls & U's 1960; Hon Soc Alpha Kappa Mu; Rho Chi Hon Pharmacy; Sigma Xi Hon Sci Soc; num publs.

ROBINSON, ISAIAH E.
Association executive. **PERSONAL:** Born Feb 17, 1924, Birmingham; married Sylvia. **EDUCATION:** Tuskegee Inst Flying Sch, 1944. **CAREER:** New York City Bd of Edn, pres 1971-72; Borough Pres of Manhattan, educ cons; Delmar-Raywind Lithographers, art dir; US PO 1944-54. **ORGANIZATIONS:** Mem Conf of Large City Bds of Educ of NY; dir Ex-Officio; bd dir NY State Sch BdS Assn; NY State Del to the Nat Sch Bds Assn; mem Fed Rel Network of Nat Sch Bds Assn; Tchrs Retirement Sys of NYC; Leg Advocacy Com Council of Great City Bd of Edn; past chmn Harlem Parents Com; past assoc dir of Harlem Freedom Sch for study of Afro-Am Hist & Culture; past trustee Pub Educ Assn; pres Harlem Commonwealth Council for Econ Devel; Progressive Ninety-Niners Investing Club; chmn bd Commonwealth Holding Corp. **HONORS/ACHIEVEMENTS:** NY Assn of Black Educators Comm Ser Award Kappa Beta Sigma Chap 1973; Carter G Woodson Award African-Am Hist Assn; Pub Ser Award NY Br of NAACP 1958; Intl Elec Workers Union Aweard 159th St Block Assn 1966; Pub Ser Award Martin Luther King Dem Club. **MILITARY SERVICE:** USAAF 1943-46. **BUSINESS ADDRESS:** 110 Livingston St, Brooklyn, NY 11201.

ROBINSON, JACK, JR.
Attorney. **PERSONAL:** Born Mar 20, 1942, Chicago, IL; son of Jack Robinson and Clara L Robinsin; married Flora G; children: Jacqueline, Craig, Christopher. **EDUCATION:** Chicago Teachers Coll, BE 1963; Chicago Kent Coll Law, JD 1970. **CAREER:** Argonne Natl Lab, atty 1971-; Miller & Pomper, atty 1970-71. **ORGANIZATIONS:** Natl Bar Assn; Mem Natl Cook Co Bar Assn; Omega Psi Phi Fraternity. **BUSINESS ADDRESS:** Attorney, Argonne Natl Laboratory, 9700 S Cass, Argonne, IL 60439.

ROBINSON, JACK E.
Editor, publisher. **PERSONAL:** Divorced; children: Jacqueline, Errol, Sarah. **EDUCATION:** Boston U, AA, BS, grad study. **CAREER:** Washington Globe, editor, publisher; Park Dale Nursing Home; Burton Nursing Home; Compact Advt; Burton Realty Trust; Amer Business Mgmt; Consolidated Liquors; Amer Beverages Corp; Robinson Construction Corp; Universal Distributing; Compact Corp. **ORGANIZATIONS:** Pres Commonwealth Rep Club; Boston NAACP; Sportsmen Tennis Club; State Enterprises; Nat Assn Minority Contractors; Real Estate Owners Assn; bd dirs Voluntary Action Center; ABCD; Circle Assos; pres Am Motorist Assn; mem Omega Psi Phi Frat; Phi Epsilon Kappa Frat; Bay State Golf Club; pres Oak Bluffs Tennis Club; Alliance for a Safer Greater Boston. **HONORS/ACHIEVEMENTS:** Civil Liberties Union Adv Com Man of Yr Construction Engineering News Mag; Man of Yr Boston Bldg Dept; Savenergy Award Dir US Dept Commerce. **MILITARY SERVICE:** AUS. **BUSINESS ADDRESS:** President, Bulletin Corporation, 61 Arborway, Boston, MA 02130.

ROBINSON, JACK E.
Construction executive. **CAREER:** Apex Contruction Co, Chicago IL, chief executive. **BUSINESS ADDRESS:** Apex Construction Co, 2100 South Indiana Ave, Chicago, IL 60616. *

ROBINSON, JACQUELINE J.
Communications business executive. **PERSONAL:** Born Jun 18, 1919, Boston; married Alvin F; children: Alvin T, II, Jacqueline. **EDUCATION:** RN 1942; Assoc degree Spanish 1953; MEd 1975. **CAREER:** Radio WYCB, exec vp, part owner 1977-; Jack & Jill Am Found, natl pres 1968-75; Gil Friends Inc, natl pres 1972-76. **ORGANIZATIONS:** Mem Arlington Links; Minimum Wage Bd; past pres Faculty Wives HowardUniv 1954-56; dir Scholarship Bd Building Laborers 1965-; sec Wash Community Broadcasting Sys 1965-; organizer Wmn's Investment Group 1954-; mem Delta Sigma Theta Inc; trustee Lincs Inc; found annual scholarship. **HONORS/ACHIEVEMENTS:** Named Jacqueline Robinson Regional Competition Jack & Jill Am Found 1974; feature Black Enterprise Mag 1974, 1975; Key Cities KC MO 1970; St Louis 1974;Baltimore 1975. **BUSINESS ADDRESS:** WYCB Radio, 529 14th St NW, Washington, DC 20004.

ROBINSON, JACQUI See VAUGHN, JACQUELINE BARBARA

ROBINSON, JAMES EDWARD
Business executive. **PERSONAL:** Born Aug 31, 1943, Asheville, NC; married Shirley Byrd; children: Geno Nigel, Tajuana Yvette, Tanya, Aisha Monique. **EDUCATION:** Taylor Sch of Broadcast Tech, AA 1969; Elkins Inst of Broadcasting, certificate 1971. **CAREER:** Model Cities Agency, public info asst 1971-74; City of Asheville, public info officer 1974-76; Radio Station WBMU-FM, pres/gen mgr 1975-. **ORGANIZATIONS:** Mem Natl Assn of Black Owned Broadcasters; mem NC Soc of Public Relations Dirs. **HONORS/ACHIEVEMENTS:** Rec'd Awds for, Principles of Supervision, Supervisory Comm, Effective Mgmt NC State Univ at Raleigh, Comm Develop NC Dept of Natl & Economic Resources; Comm Broadcaster of the Year Optimist Intl; Asheville Chap NAACP Cert of Merit; Asheville Chap Sickle Cell Anemia Comm Svcs; W Carolina Univ Cert of Appreciation. **MILITARY SERVICE:** AUS 82nd airborne div 9 yrs.

ROBINSON, JAMES L.
Architect, real estate developer. **PERSONAL:** Born Jul 12, 1940, Longview, TX; son of W. L. Robinson and Ruby Newhouse Robinson; married Danie Annabell, Sep 10, 1985; children: Kerstin G, Maria T, Jasmin Marisol, Ruby Nell, Kenneth. **EDUCATION:** Southern Univ, B Arch 1964; Pratt Inst, MCP 1973. **CAREER:** Herbst & Rusciano AIA, architect 1964; Carson Lundin & Shaw, architect 1965; Kennerly Slomanson & Smith, architect 1966-68; Carl J Petrilli, architect 1968-69; American Arbitration Assn, arbitrator 1979; James L Robinson PC, architect 1970-84; Robinson Architects PC, architect 1984-. **ORGANIZATIONS:** Mem, Independent Platform Assn; Bd of Dirs, Boys Clubs of Amer. **HONORS/ACHIEVEMENTS:** Martin Luther King Fellow Pratt Inst 1972-74; Natl Housing Award Design & Environ 1976; AIA Design Citation Stuyvesant Height Christian Church; Bard Award Fulton Ct Complex 1977; Knighthood, Order of St Johns, Knights of Malta. Designer the Nehemiah Plan, NYC, 1985-present. **MILITARY SERVICE:** AUS Pfc 1966; Good Conduct Medal 1966. **BUSINESS ADDRESS:** Architect, Robinson Architects PC, 5 Beekman St, New York, NY 10038.

ROBINSON, JAMES WAYMOND
Physician. **PERSONAL:** Born Nov 06, 1926, Wilmington, NC; son of Sam Robinson and Addie Best Robinson; married Carol Blackmar. **EDUCATION:** NC Coll at Durham, BS 1950; Meharry Med Coll, MD 1960; internship 1960-61; resident 1961-65. **CAREER:** Joint Disease N General Hospital, asst attending physician 1979-; Beth Israel's Methadone Maintenance Treatment Prgm, assoc chief 1975-; Beth Israel's Methadone Maintenance Treatment Program Harlem Unit, unit dir 1965-75; Arthur C Logan Memorial Hospital, assoc attending physician 1965-79; Harlem Hospital, asst attending physician 1965-. **ORGANIZATIONS:** Med Soc of State & Co of NY; Omega Psi Phi Frat; mem ASIM; NYSSIM; NYCSIM. **HONORS/ACHIEVEMENTS:** Publ, "Methadone Poisoning, Diagnosis & Treatment"; "Methadone Treatment of Randomly Selected Criminal Addicts". **MILITARY SERVICE:** Military serv corporal 1945-46. **BUSINESS ADDRESS:** 2186 5th Ave, New York, NY 10037.

ROBINSON, JANE ALEXANDER
Clinical psychologist. **PERSONAL:** Born Jan 17, 1931, Chicago, IL; divorced; children: David, Amorie, Richard. **EDUCATION:** BS 1952, MS 1963, PhD 1978. **CAREER:** Detroit Publ Schools, elem teacher 1957-63; Southfield Bd of Ed, school psych 1964-68; Detroit Bd of Ed, school psych 1968-70; Private practice, clinical psych. **ORGANIZATIONS:** Mem, founder, sec 1968-70, pres 1975-76 MI Assoc Black Psych; consult Rape Counseling Ctr Detroit Receiving Hosp; mem Psi Chi Natl Hon Soc Psych Univ of Detroit Chapt. **HONORS/ACHIEVEMENTS:** Natl Assoc of Black Psych Awd for Org Leadership 1976; dissertation "Self-Esteem, Racial Consciousness & Perception of Difference Between the Values of Black & White Amers" 1977. **BUSINESS ADDRESS:** Clinical Psychologist, 28336 Franklin Road, Southfield, MI 48034.

ROBINSON, JASON GUY
Actor, stuntman, director, poet. **PERSONAL:** Born Aug 08, 1934; son of John Robinson and Mabel Walker Robinson; married Jean Wentz, Jan 30, 1977; children: Michelle. **EDUCATION:** Philadelphia Coll, BA 1961. **CAREER:** Actor, model, artist, disc jockey, poet

under professional name of Jason Guy; has appeared in movies, numerous plays, TV shows; WHAT & WXPN, disc jockey; Third WorldNews WXPN, editor, newscaster; model in various advertisements; Japanese Karate Assn, instr Marshall Arts; R & J Prod, partner; two albums "Jason Roars", "Jason Reads in the Lion's den". **ORGANIZATIONS:** Founder Drama III Theatre Projects Co Inc; mem Philadelphia Jazz Soc; Positive Thinking Parents Assn; East Coast Stuntmens Assn; AFTRA-SAG; founder, dir Citizens Against Drugs (CAD). **HONORS/ACHIEVEMENTS:** Holder of Black Belt (Nidan). **MILITARY SERVICE:** USMC sgt 1953-57. **BUSINESS ADDRESS:** Substance Abuse Prevention Specialist, Philadelphia Anti-Drug Anti-Violence Network, 121 N Broad St, 6th Floor, Philadelphia, PA 19107.

ROBINSON, JAYNE G.
Educator. **PERSONAL:** Born Aug 22, 1912, Freeport, TX; daughter of Ernest Glenn and Rachel Rebecca Bush Glenn; married Clarence Arthur Robinson, Jun 02, 1934. **EDUCATION:** TX Southern Univ, 1938; KS State Univ, 1939; NY Univ Drexel Inst, additional study; Univ of IL; TX Women's Univ. **CAREER:** TX Southern Univ, asst prof 1939-75; Riverside Hospital, 1941-45; NYA Center Houston TX, teacher 1940-41. **ORGANIZATIONS:** Mem Am Dietetic Assn; Am Home Econ Assn; TX Dietetic Assn; TX Home Econ Assn; Am Pub Health Assn; TX Pub Health Assn; Assn of Sch of Allied Health Professions; life mem YWCA; life mem Zeta Phi Beta; elder, mem of serv comm, Pinecrest Presb Church; mem, Fifth Ward Housing Corp of The Metropolitan; mem, Fifth Ward Area Planning & Advisory Council, Health & Human Serv Dept; mem, trustee bd, Fifth Ward Community Devel Corp; mem, Texas Southern Univ Recruitment Council; bd mem, St Elizabeth Hospital, 1977-87. **HONORS/ACHIEVEMENTS:** Texas Assn of Coll Teachers Service Award, Texas Southern Univ, 1975; Certificate of Recognition for Excellence in Humanitarian Achievement, 1982. **HOME ADDRESS:** 5202 Arapahoe, Houston, TX 77020.

ROBINSON, JESSE LEE
Management consultant. **PERSONAL:** Born Jan 17, 1912, Hattiesburg, MS; married Myrtle E Comfort; children: 1 Dau. **CAREER:** Avalon Med Mgmt Inc; Robinson's Resrch, pres 1967-77; LA PO, training dir 1956-67; 10th Dist Nat Alliance of Postal Emp, pres 1941-46; Enterprise Saving & Loan, chmn of bd 1963-77; Grtr LA Urban Coalition, co-chmn 1970-76; Compton Union HS, treas 1960; E LA Coll, prof bus dept 1955-70. **ORGANIZATIONS:** Pres So Pacific Assn; Amateur Athletic Union 1973-75; foreman LA Grand Jury 1974-75; pres Compton Br NAACP 1954-57; rotarian 1972-77. **HONORS/ACHIEVEMENTS:** LA Co Suprs Award 1969; Disting Award of Yr Interracial Counc Bus Oppty 1970. **BUSINESS ADDRESS:** President, Robinsons Research, 1702 N Wilmington Ave, Compton, CA 90222.

ROBINSON, JIM C.
Educator. **PERSONAL:** Born Feb 09, 1943, Ackerman, MS. **EDUCATION:** CA St, BA 1966; CA St, MA 1968; Stanford U, MA 1972; Stanford U, PhD 1973. **CAREER:** CA St Univ Long Beach, assoc prof Black Studies; CA St, spec asst vice pres acad affrs; CA St, dean faculty & staff affairs; San Jose St Coll, teacher. **ORGANIZATIONS:** Mem, Nat Alliance of Black Sch Educators; Am Assn ofUniv & Prof; dir of Reg Programs in W for Am Assn for Higher Edn; chmn Assn of Black Faculty &Staff of So CA; mem Mayor's Task Force Fiscal Mgmt & Cntrl, Compton. **BUSINESS ADDRESS:** Calif State University, 1250 Bellflower Blvd, Long Beach, CA 90840.

ROBINSON, JOHN E.
Insurance administrator. **PERSONAL:** Born Jul 12, 1942, Hollywood, AL; son of John Karie Robinson; children: Dana L. **EDUCATION:** Clark Coll, BA 1979; Atlanta Univ, MBA 1979. **CAREER:** Soc for Savings Bank, asst branch mgr 1964-69; Wesleyan Univ, asst personnel dir 1969-73; WSC Corp, admin vice pres 1973-77; Aetna Life & Casualty, administrator 1980-. **ORGANIZATIONS:** Past pres Beta Sigma Lambda Chapter Alpha Phi Alpha 1981-; mem Sigma Pi Phi 1983-; mem Univ Club of Hartford 1983-; producer/host 30 min talk show WVIT Channel 30 1983-; bd mem Greater Hartford Business Develop Ctr 1984-; mem Hartford Area Mediation Prog 1985, YMCA of metropolitan Hartford Central Branch Business &Finance Comm 1985; bd mem Trinity Coll Comm Child Center 1986-. **HONORS/ACHIEVEMENTS:** Outstanding Young Man of Amer Jaycees 1978; Outstanding Business Student Clark Coll 1979; Leadership of Greater Hartford Chamber of Commerce 1982; founded a network group F-200 1983. **HOME ADDRESS:** 485 High Street, Unit E, New Britain, CT 06053. **BUSINESS ADDRESS:** Administrator, Aetna Life & Casualty Co, 151 Farmington Ave MP31, Hartford, CT 06156.

ROBINSON, JOHN F.
Business executive. **PERSONAL:** Born May 03, 1944, Brooklyn, NY; children: Timothy. **EDUCATION:** AAS; BBA; New York City Community Coll; Baruch Coll Office Serv. **CAREER:** F Chusid & Co, office serv dupr 1966-68; Cancer Care Inc, dupr 1968-76; NY Educ & Training Consortium Inc, pres, exec dir; Natl Minority Business Inc, pres & CEO. **ORGANIZATIONS:** Mem Amer Mgmt Assn; mem Soc for Advancement of Mgmt; chmn Alliance of Minority Business Organizations Inc; bd of Harlem YMCA. **HONORS/ACHIEVEMENTS:** Published several mgmt articles in the monthly and quarterly journals of the Amer Mgmt Assn; minority business advocate Small Business Admin 1986 & Minority Business Developmemt Agency 1986; pres Minority Business Exec Prog; admin assoc Tuck Business School; mem, Small Business Admin Advisory Council. **BUSINESS ADDRESS:** President and CEO, Natl Minority Business Council, 235 E 42nd St, New York, NY 10017.

ROBINSON, JOHN L.
Retired television broadcaster. **PERSONAL:** Born Dec 15, 1930, Atlantic City, NJ; married Louise J Lambert; children: Jeffrey Oliveira, David Oliveira, Tracy R Crew, Jefrey L. **EDUCATION:** Lincoln Univ, 1948-49; Xavier Univ, 1949-50; TV Workshop of NY, 1955. **CAREER:** Crosley Broadcasting Corp, film librarian 1955-62; WTEV-TV, film dir 1962-65, prod mgr 1965-68, prg mgr 1968-79. **ORGANIZATIONS:** Corporator New Bedford Five Cents Savings Bank 1970-; mem RI Broadcasters Assn 1970-79, treas 1975-76; mem MA Broadcasters Assn 1970-79; mem Natl Assn TV Prg Execs 1970-79; mem Human Relations Comm New Bedford, MA 1975-76; mem Govs Council on Civil Rights RI; vice pres New Bedford Branch NAACP; mem NAACP. **HONORS/ACHIEVEMENTS:** Humanitarian Award NAACP New Bedford, MA 1970. **MILITARY SERVICE:** USAF stf/sgt 1951-55. **HOME ADDRESS:** 111 Brandt Island Rd, Mattapoisett, MA 02739.

ROBINSON, JONATHAN N.
Clergyman. **PERSONAL:** Born May 18, 1922, Emelle, AL; married Ethel M; children: 4 Children. **EDUCATION:** TX Coll;Univ CA; Worsham Coll Mortuary Sci; Morehouse Coll, AB 1961; Columbia Theol Sem, BD1965; MDiv 1971. **CAREER:** Sch tchr; embalmer; Rhodes Fun Home New Orleans, mrg; US Govt, ID splst; Minority Bus EnterpriseUniv of KY, prog officer; pastor 22 yrs; ch builder& organizer; Plymouth Congregational Ch United Ch Christ, pastor. **ORGANIZATIONS:** Mem SCLC; comm educator Alcohol Abuse-Alcoholism; chaplain PTA; bdF mem Camp Fire Girls; mem Met Blind Assn; Inner-City Council Presbyterian Ch US; Gen Assembly Causes Com; chmn bd Plymouth Settlement House; mem NAACP; Kappa Alpha Psi; YMCA; Urban League; Religious Pub Relations Council. **MILITARY SERVICE:** AUS sgt. **BUSINESS ADDRESS:** 1630 W Chestnut St, Louisville, KY 40203.

ROBINSON, JONTYLE THERESA
Educator. **PERSONAL:** Born Jul 22, 1947, Atlanta, GA. **EDUCATION:** Clark Coll, BA 1968; Univ of Georgia, MA 1971; Univ of Maryland, PhD 1983. **CAREER:** Cuban Art, writer, dir 1960-; Univ of Maryland, instr of humanities & art history; Fed Arts Project Field Research, Little Rock, 1972; Dept of Art, Philander Smith Coll, chmn 1971-72; Atlanta Univ, instr, summer 1971, 1972; Emory Univ, instr 1979-83, asst prof 1983-86; Smithsonian Inst Archives of Amer Art, visiting faculty. **ORGANIZATIONS:** Mem, natl exec sec of Natl Conf of Artists, 1971-72; Delta Sigma Theta; Natl Conf of Artists; Phi Kappa Phi Natl Hon Soc.

ROBINSON, JOSEPH
Clergyman. **PERSONAL:** Born Jul 28, 1940, Orangeburg, SC; married Lizzie Miller; children: Jonathan, Joseph, Jason. **EDUCATION:** Claflin Coll, Orangeburg, SC, BA 1964; Interdenominational Theological Center, Atlanta, BD 1967, MDiv 1973. **CAREER:** Morris Brown Coll, chaplain 1965-66; Turner Theo Sem, tchr 1966-67; Woodbury, NJ, campbell AME Ch 1967-68; St of NJ, soc wrkr 1967-68; St Johns AME Church, Brooklyn, minister, 1968-72; Grant AME Church Boston, minister 1972-78; Bethel AME Church Freeport NY, minister 1978-86; Macedonia AME Church Flushing NY, minister 1986-. **ORGANIZATIONS:** Phi Beta Sigma; mem bd dir Mass Cncl of Chs; mem Family Serv Div Prof Couns Staff Boston; pres bd dir Brightmoor Terr Inc Boston; mem Minstl All Grtr Bstn; v chmn trustee bd New England Annual Conf AME Ch; delegate Gen Conf AME Ch Atlanta 1976; pres NAACP Freeport/Roosevelt Branch 1978-79; commnr Human Relations Cncl of Freeport; trustee NY Annual Conf; mem bd of examiners NY Annual Conf; coord of 1st dist Episcopal Headquarters; bd of dirs Liberty Park Housing; chmn of bd, Paul Quinn Federal Credit Union; trustee, New York Annual Conf, AME Church, 1976-; mem, Self Help, First Episcopal District, 1989. **HONORS/ACHIEVEMENTS:** Phi Beta Sigma Schl Awd 1964; Jackson Fisher Awd 1964; Intrdenmntl Theol Ctr Schlrshp Awd 1966-67; Turner Memorial Awd 1967; Mortgage Reduction Citation; 19 years ahead of time Leadership Awd Macedonia AME Church 1986. **BUSINESS ADDRESS:** Pastor, Macedonia AME Church, 37-22 Union St, Flushing, NY 11354.

ROBINSON, KENNETH
Financial administrator. **PERSONAL:** Born Dec 10, 1947, Chicago, IL; son of Henry Lee Robinson and Seayray Govan Robinson; married Etta D Clement, Jun 07, 1987. **EDUCATION:** IL State Univ, BA Bus Admin 1975. **CAREER:** Amer Hosp Supply Corp, tax accountant; Abbott Labs, staff tax admin; IL Dept of Revenue, revenue auditor; Lake Co Comm Action, economic develop coord, administrative director. **ORGANIZATIONS:** Bd mem Lake Co Urban League 1981-; bd mem N Chicago Plan Comm 1982-; sch bd mem Dist # 64 No Chicago 1984-. **MILITARY SERVICE:** AUS sp/4 2 yrs. **HOME ADDRESS:** 1317 Broadway, North Chicago, IL 60064. **BUSINESS ADDRESS:** Administrative Dir, Lake Co Comm Action, 102-6 So Sheridan Rd, Waukegan, IL 60085.

ROBINSON, KENNETH EUGENE
Educator. **PERSONAL:** Born Mar 09, 1947, Hannibal, MO; married Cecilia. **EDUCATION:** William Jewell Coll, BS; Northwest MO State U, Ms Ed;Univ of MO Kansas City, Ed Spec 1980. **CAREER:** Liberty Sr HS, psychology/sociology instr 1972-80; Moberly Pub Schs, social studies instr 1969-71; Liberty Pub Schs, asst football & head track coach1972-80; Clay Co Juv Justice Center, detention officer 1977-78; Franklin Life Ins, ins agent 1979-80. **ORGANIZATIONS:** Mem Parks & Recreation Bd Liberty MO 1977-80; pres Liberty Tchrs Assn 1979-80; Minority Studies Task Force William Jewell Coll 1979-80; pres elect Libert CTA 1978-79; campaign chmn United Way Liberty Pub Schs 1979; mem Pub Relations Com MSTA 1980. **HONORS/ACHIEVEMENTS:** Listed Who's Who in Am Coll &Univ 1969. **BUSINESS ADDRESS:** Agent, State Farm Insurance, 7211 NW 83rd St, Kansas City, MO 64152.

ROBINSON, KITTY (WILLIE MAE KIDD)
Educator. **PERSONAL:** Born Jan 07, 1921, West Point, MS; widowed. **EDUCATION:** TN St U, BS 1942; DePaul U, M Supvis & Admin 1960; NW U, PhD 1974. **CAREER:** Chicago St U, asst dean; Chicago St U, early child educ 1967-76; Chicago Pub Sch, pr tchr 1956-66. **ORGANIZATIONS:** Chrmn Assn for Child Educ 1974; pan mem Coop Urban Tchr Educ Wrkshp; mem Amer Assoc ofUniv Prof; Natl Educ Assoc Intl; Assn for Child Educ Intl; IL Assn for Supvis & Curr Devel; Nat Coun of Tching Engl Res Assn; bd mem Assn of Mammequins; mem Nat Reading Conf; mem Chicago Urban League; S Shore Comm Serv; Women Mobil for Change; PUSH; Assn of Mannequins; Trophy Schol Fund Bd Jeffery-Yates Neigh; base oper Shore Patrol; past pres 79th St Block Club; mem Widows Club. **HONORS/ACHIEVEMENTS:** Cit sch comm Phi Delta Kappa Educ Honors Soc; recip Indep Wrkshp FellowshipUniv of Chicago 1967; award IL Assn for Supvis & Curric Devel 1974; Who'sWho Among Child Devel Profl; publ dissert "A Descrip Eval of the Disting Coop Tchr Prgm at Chicago & St U"; poetry Ebony Jr Magz Johnson Publ Co; pub coll text "Putting It All Together"Univ Press of Am 1977. **BUSINESS ADDRESS:** 95th & Kings' Dr, Chicago, IL 60628.

ROBINSON, LAWRENCE B.
Educator. **PERSONAL:** Born Sep 14, 1919, Tappahannock, VA; married Laura G Carter; children: Lyn, Gwen, Lawrence Jr. **EDUCATION:** VA Union U, BS 1939; Harvard U, MA 1941; Harvard U, PhD 1946; VA Union U, ScD 1968. **CAREER:** Univ of CA LA, prof engineering 1962-; asso prof 1960-62; part time lecturer 1957-60; Technische & Hochschule Aachen Germany, visiting prof 1966-67; BrooklynColl, asst prof physics 1954-56; Howard U, asso Prof 1948-51, asst prof 1946-47;Univ of Chicago, instr 1947-48; Ramo-Woolridge Corp

& Space Tech LabInc, mem tech staff 1956-60; Naval Research Lab Washington DC, research physicist 1953-54; N Am Aviation Downey CA, research engr 1951-53; US NavalResearch Lab, 1954; Lockheed Aircraft Corp, consult 1955; Aerospace Corp, 1960-66. **ORGANIZATIONS:** Charter mem LA Co Art Museum 1963-; mem SW Museum Highland Park 1963-; Buffalo Bill Hist Cntr Cody WY 1963-; Whitney Gallery of Western Art Cody WY 1963-; Westerners LA Corral 1969-; memshp NY Academy of Sci 1965. **HONORS/ACHIEVEMENTS:** Hon DSc VA UnionUniv 1968. **MILITARY SERVICE:** AAC WWII. **BUSINESS ADDRESS:** Sch of Engineering & Applied Sci, U of CA, Los Angeles, CA 90024.

ROBINSON, LAWRENCE D.
Physician, educator. **PERSONAL:** Born Sep 20, 1942, Baltimore, MD; children: one. **EDUCATION:** Univ Pittsburgh, BS 1964; Howard U, MD 1968. **CAREER:** Allergys & Immunology, asst prof pediatrics, dir; Martin L King Jr Hosp; Charles R Drew Postgrad Med Sch UCLA Immunology Fellowship 1973-; US Army Ped Dir Sicle Cell Dis Prog 1971-73; Johns Hopkins Hosp, intern 1968-69; res 1969-70; Sinai Hosp Baltimore, chief res 1970-71. **ORGANIZATIONS:** Nat Med Assn; Scien Adv Com of Nat Assn for Sickle Cell Dis; Bd Cert by Am Bd of Ped; Bd of Allery & Immunology 1975; mem Am Thoracic Soc; mem Am Acad of Ped; mem bd Am Lung Assn LA; Immunization Action Com 1978-80; co-chmn Nat Immunization Prog LA. **HONORS/ACHIEVEMENTS:** Who's Who in CA; has written & present many pub at meet of Am Ped SocAtlantic City, Am Ped Soc Wash; contributing editor Essence Mag; presented papers to Am Acad of Allergy; Who's Who in the W 1978.

ROBINSON, LEARTHON STEVEN
Attorney. **PERSONAL:** Born May 08, 1925, Pittsburgh, PA; married Beulah Beatrice Brown; children: Deborah L Flemister, Learthon S Jr, Iris R Rodgers, Michael J, Denise E. **EDUCATION:** Univ of Pittsburgh, BA 1948; Univ of WI, Grad Study 1950; Cleveland-Marshall Sch of Law/Cleveland State U, JD 1952. **CAREER:** Ohio Cvl Rgts Commsn, jdcl hrng ofcr 1964-65; Warren, OH Law Dept, city prsctr 1967-71, 1st dpty law dir 1971-87. **ORGANIZATIONS:** Pres PA-oH Blk Lwyrs Assn Inc 1981-; pres Shenango Vly Svcs, Inc 1985; comm mem Pblc Rels Spkrs Bureau Trumbull Co Bar Assn 1985; mem OH Bar, Amer Bar, DC Bar, Natl Bar Assocs; bd of trustees Goodwill Industries Warren/Youngstown Area 1986-89. **HONORS/ACHIEVEMENTS:** Congressional Citation and Proclamation for Exemplary Professional Serv City of Warren OH 1971-87; State of OH Citation and Proclamation for Exemplary Professional Serv City of Warren OH 1971-87; City Council of Warren Citation and Proclamation for Exemplary Professional Serv City Council of Warren OH 1971-87; Man of Yr Urban League Warren/Trumbull Chptr 1976; Cmnty Serv Trumbull Co NAACP 1982; Who's Who in Am Law 1982; Outstanding Leadership 17th Congressional Dist Caucus 1984. **MILITARY SERVICE:** USMC gnry sgt 1942-46; Hnrbly Dschrgd; 4 mjr cmpgns, Awrd 4 battle stars 1942-46; Pres Unit Citation; WWII Vctry Medal; 2 Purple Hrts. **HOME ADDRESS:** 4119 Chevelle Dr SE, Warren, OH 44484. **BUSINESS ADDRESS:** First Deputy Law Dir, City of Warren Law Dept, 391 Mahoning Ave NW, Warren, OH 44483.

ROBINSON, LEONARD (TRUCK)
Professional athlete. **PERSONAL:** Born Oct 04, 1951, Jacksonville, FL; children: Leonard Jr, Alisha. **EDUCATION:** TN State Univ, attended. **CAREER:** Washington Bullets, basketball player; Atlanta Hawks, basketball player; Utah Jazz, basketball player; NY Nicks, basketball player. **ORGANIZATIONS:** NBA's All-Star 1st team 1977-78; Eastern Conference All-Star 1978; Western Conference All-Star team 1981; Named to AP, UPI, NCAA Coaches' First Team All-Amer squads; Leading scorer & rebounder for US team which toured Soviet Union in summer of 1974. **BUSINESS ADDRESS:** New York Nicks, Madison Square Garden, 4 Pennsylvania Plaza, New York, NY 10001.

ROBINSON, LEONARD HARRISON, JR.
Association executive. **PERSONAL:** Born Apr 21, 1943, Winston-Salem, NC; son of Leonard H Robinson and Winnie Cornelia Thomas Robinson; divorced; children: Kimberly Michelle, Rani Craft. **EDUCATION:** OH State Univ, BA 1964; SUNY Binghamton, Grad Work 1966-67; Amer Univ, MA, PhD Candidate 1982-. **CAREER:** Peace Corps India & Washington DC, 1964-71; ATAC, econ & mgmt analyst 1971; Inner City Comm Prog EPA, dir 1971-72; FPIA, Africa reg dir 1972-78; US Congress, task force dir 1977-78; Office of Pop AID, chief Africa div 1978-79; HARC Battelle, dir intl devel study 1979-83; Dept of State for African Affairs, deputy asst sec of state 1983-85; African Devel Found, pres 1984-. **ORGANIZATIONS:** Mem Kappa Alpha Psi 1963-, APHA 1978-80, Mayors Task Force on Intl Affairs 1978-81; adv to bd family plnng Population Resource Ctr 1978-82; advisor on population OTA Congress 1979-80; adv to bd of dir Chamber of Commerce 1979-82; vstg adv Intl Prog for Training & Health Univ of NC 1980-83; bd mem DC Interagency Cncl on Family Planning 1981-82; New Directions Task Force Mont Co 1982-83; bd mem Soc for Intl Devel 1982-84, Washington Ballet 1982-85, 1986-;Men's Republican Club Montgomery Cty 1982-;bd of trustees Museum of African Art-Smithsonian 1983-85; bd of dir Coalition for Equitable Representation in Government Montgomery County 1985-; mem Sigma Pi Phi 1984-; bd of dir JACC 1985-86; bd mem Academy Review Bd, State of MD, Sen Chas Mc C Mathias 1986-; bd of visitors Shaw Univ 1986; dir Sevin Devel Group 1986; bd mem The Mont Co Bd of Social Serv 1986-; vice pres, Washington Ballet Board. **HONORS/ACHIEVEMENTS:** Le Droit d'Honneur OH State Univ 1963; Outstanding Black Amer Contrib Sears Roebuck & Co 1971; Doctor of Laws Degree Shaw Univ 1983; many publ & papers incl "Assessment & Analysis, Tanzania Battelle Mem Inst 1981, "Non-Academic Careers for Minority Scientists" Natl Inst of Health 1982, "Battelle PDP Draft India Country Strategy" w/James E Kocher Office of Population Agency for Intl Devel Battelle Mem Inst 1982; Commandeur de l'Ordre National du Niger (highest honor given by the Republic of Niger) 1988. **BUSINESS ADDRESS:** President, African Development Foundation, 1625 Massachusetts Ave NW, Ste 600, Washington, DC 20036.

ROBINSON, LOUIE, JR.
Free-lance writer, editor. **PERSONAL:** Born Oct 04, 1926, Dallas, TX; married Mati Walls; children: 6 children. **EDUCATION:** Lincoln Univ, 1943-45; George Williams Coll, 1959. **CAREER:** Tyler Tribune, reporter & editor 1948-50; Dallas Star-Post, reporter & editor 1950-51; Baltimore Afro-Amer, reporter 1952-53; Jet Mag assoc editor 1953-56; Ebony Mag, assoc editor 1956-59; Tan Mag, mgr 1956-59; Johnson Publ, w coast editor 1960-70; Claremont Coll, lecturer 1970-74; Ebony Mag, contrib editor 1972-81. **ORGANIZATIONS:** Member Cath Broadcasters Assn. **HONORS/ACHIEVEMENTS:** Author TV play "The Secret Weapon" 1965; Gabriel Award & TV Emmy nomination for drama "The Invincible Weapon" 1965; socio-political columnist Berkeley Daily Gazette under pen name James Wyatt 1965-66; author of "Arthur Ashe, Tennis Champion" 1967; co-author "The Nat King Cole Story" 1971; author "The Black Millionaires 1972. **MILITARY SERVICE:** AUS 1945-46.

ROBINSON, LOUIE M.
Dentist. **PERSONAL:** Born Sep 26, 1925, Chattanooga; married Lorena; children: Calvin, LaDonna, Louis III, Lori. **EDUCATION:** Morehouse Coll, AB 1950; Meharry Med Coll, DDS 1958. **CAREER:** Pvt pract dentist; Meharry Med Coll, asso prof of fixed prosthondontics. **ORGANIZATIONS:** Mem Nat Dental Assn; Myotronica Study Grp; LA Dental Study Grp. **MILITARY SERVICE:** USN. **BUSINESS ADDRESS:** 2500 W Florence, Pasadena, CA.

ROBINSON, LUTHER D.
Physician, superintendent. **PERSONAL:** Born Dec 22, 1922, Tappahannock, VA; married Betty Boyd; children: Jan, Barry, Vance. **EDUCATION:** VA State Coll, BS 1943; Meharry Med Coll, MD 1946. **CAREER:** St Elizabeths Hosp Washington, supt 1975-; St Elizabeths Hosp, staff 1955-; Mercy Hosp Phila, intern 1946-47; Lakin State Hosp Lakin WV, staff 1947-49; Freedmen's Hosp Washington, psychiatric residency 1953-54; St Elizabeths Hosp, 1954-55; HowardUniv Coll Med, clin instr 1956-68; vis lectr 1974-; Gallaudet Coll, lectr 1968-; GeorgetownUniv Sch Med, fac mem 1974-; Geo Washington U, clin assoc prof 1969-. **ORGANIZATIONS:** Mem Medico Chirurgical Soc; Med Soc DC; Washington Psychiatric Soc; AMA; natl chmn Commn Med & Audiology 7th World Cong; World Fedn Deaf Originated-Mental Health Prog Deaf St Elizabeths Hosp 1963; co-founder AA Prog St Elizabeths Hosp. **HONORS/ACHIEVEMENTS:** Hon DSc Gallaudet Coll 1971; Edw Miner Gallaudet Award 1974. **MILITARY SERVICE:** AUS capt 1949-52.

ROBINSON, MANUEL
Business executive. **PERSONAL:** Born Mar 08, 1931, Atlantic City, NJ; married Ernestina Gaiter. **EDUCATION:** Rutgers U, BA 1954; Columbia U, Graduate in Psychology. **CAREER:** Robinson Research Svcs, pres; Earl G Graves Marketing & Rsrch, proj dir; New York City Human Resources Adminstrn, survey research dir; Doyle Dane & Bernbach Advt, resrch proj dir; Foote, Cone, Belding Advt, accnt rsrch supr; McCann Erickson, resrch asst. **ORGANIZATIONS:** Mem Am Marketing Assn Ten of NY Inc; bd of advisors, Boys Harbor; mem Studio Mus in Harlem. **HONORS/ACHIEVEMENTS:** African-am Inst Directed a comprehensive study of minority attitudes, toward the mil svcs; Author of numerous reports on research among minorities. **BUSINESS ADDRESS:** Robinson Research Services, 241 West 97th St, New York, NY 10025.

ROBINSON, MARILYN PATRICIA
Journalist. **PERSONAL:** Born Dec 31, 1946, Washington, DC; married Richard H Ringell; children: Kassia,Case. **EDUCATION:** Howard Univ, BA 1968. **CAREER:** John F Kennedy Center for Performing Arts, public relations specialist, 1968-69; WRC/NBC News, reporter 1969-75; NBC, news correspondent, 1975-78; Labor News & Views, freelance journalist, syndicated radio columnist 1978-. **ORGANIZATIONS:** Mem Amer Federation of TV & Radio Artists 1969-, Natl Acad of TV Arts & Science 1969-, Radio & TV Correspondent Assn, Ledroit Park Pres Soc 1975-; AFTRA/SAG; The Natl Press Club; The Washington Assn of Black Journalists; The Washingtonians. **HONORS/ACHIEVEMENTS:** Best News Film Pkg Natl Acad of TV Arts & Sci "Emmy", "Hobson" 1972; Natl Healniers Award "Boston" 1974; Frederick Douglass Award Truth & Excellence in TV Journal, 1974; TV Excellence Award Egyptian Woman Assn, 1975; Outstanding TV Journal DC City Govt 1972; Best News Film Pkg Natl Acad of TV Arts & Science "Emmy", "Hobson" 1972; Outstanding TV Journal, Black United Front 1974; TV Excellence Award Iota Phi Lambda 1973; Outstanding Citizen DC Dem Comm 1977. **BUSINESS ADDRESS:** Freelance Journalist, 4434 Lowell St NW, Washington, DC 20016.

ROBINSON, MARTHA DELORES
Public relations director. **PERSONAL:** Born Sep 19, 1956, Halls, TN. **EDUCATION:** TN State Univ, BS 1978; Memphis State Univ, MA. **CAREER:** TN State Univ, production asst 1976-78; Lau-Fay-Ton, teacher 1978; Lauderdale Cty Enterprise, reporter 1978-790; Lane Coll, dir of publ relations. **ORGANIZATIONS:** Mem Comm Advisory Bd WLJF-TV 1985, Public Relations Soc of Amer 1985, TN Coll Public Relations Assoc, Council for the Advancement & Support of Educ, Natl Assoc for Advancement of Colored People, Tau Beta Sigma Natl Hon Band Sor, TSU Natl Alumni Assoc, Alpha Kappa Alpha Sor Inc. **HONORS/ACHIEVEMENTS:** Honor Student TN State Univ 1975-78; Plaque Disting Serv Lane Coll Pre Alumni 1980; Cert of Awd Alpha Kappa Alpha Sor 1980-82; Outstanding Serv Lane Coll Student Gov Assoc 1982; Guest of the White House by Pres Reagan 1983. **BUSINESS ADDRESS:** Dir of Public Relations, Lane College, 545 Lane Ave, Jackson, TN 38301.

ROBINSON, MARY ELIZABETH (NEE WILDER)
Attorney. **PERSONAL:** Born Feb 16, 1946, Sallis, MS; divorced; children: Deatra Rochelle, Regina Ann, Ftonella Elaine. **EDUCATION:** Wartburg Coll Waverly IA, BA 1972; Univ of IA Coll of Law Iowa City, JD 1977-78. **CAREER:** Mary E Robinson Law Office, atty 1979-; Coll of Law Univ of IA Iowa City, asst to dean of law 1977-79; Coll of Law Univ of IA, dir acad asst prog 1976-77; Martin Luther King Center for Vocational & Educ Training Waterloo IA, acting dir 1972-74; Educ Opportunity Prog Univ No IA Ceader Falls, dir on campus 1972-73. **ORGANIZATIONS:** Gov appointed bd mem IA State Dept of Pub Instr 1979-85; mem Nat Conf of Black Lawyers; mem Assn of Trial Lawyers of IA & Am; founder & pres Black Womens Civil Orgn Cedar Rapids IA 1978-; commr Human Rights Commn Cedar Rapids 1978-; dep IA-nENAACP Legal Redress Commn; IA rep Nat Task Force tothe White House Conf on Families 1980; IA del White House Conf on Families Minneapolis 1980; bd mem United Way of Linn Co Acad Ascholarship & Dean's List Wartburg Coll Waverly IA 1970-72; offered inte*Rnship Washington Interns in Educ Inst for Educ Leadership Washington DC 1974-75. **HONORS/ACHIEVEMENTS:** Outstanding Black Grad Student Award; AG Clark Award Water Loo 1976; Acieevement Award NAACP Cedar Rapids Chap 1979; One of Top 10 Black Women Ldrs State of IA US Dept of Labor. **BUSINESS ADDRESS:** Higley Bldg, Ste 315, Cedar Rapids, IA 52401.

ROBINSON, MAUDE ELOISE
Nursing educator. **PERSONAL:** Born Jan 18, 1927, New York, NY. **EDUCATION:** St John's Episcopal School of Nursing, RN 1955; Jersey City State Teachers Coll, BA, BS 1970; Hunter Coll CUNY, MS, MPH 1974; Walden Univ, PhD 1976; Hunter Coll, CUNY, BSN

1982, postgraduate, gerentology 1985; PhD program, Grambling State Univ, 1987-present. **CAREER:** Hospital in Brooklyn, supvr operating room 1960-65; Church of Christ Bible Inst NYC, health educator 1968-80; Nursing/Health/Safety ARC, intl instructor 1968-present; BRAVO/youth groups/church groups/BC/BS March of Dimes & Nat Council of Negro Women, lecturer/prof comm health educ 1970-; consultant various natl comm health agencies, 1970-; Nursing Resources Journal Nursing Admin, consultant 1978-80; St Joseph's Coll, prof 1978-, preceptor-counselor; Hunter Coll, coordinator health science & nursing 1974-; Coll of New Rochelle, prof, consultant, 1988-present. **HONORS/ACHIEVEMENTS:** Faculty of the Year Award, St Johns School of Nursing Brooklyn 1965-67; pub health/nursing articles NY Amsterdams News 1972; co-authored health career textbook Bd of Educ NY 1975; "Women in Am" 1977-present; Impact Remediation Nursing Aspirants Nat Black Nurses Assn Newsletter 1977; Laurel Wreath Doctoral Assn NY Educators 1977; health/nursing articles Everybody's Journal 1979; appeared on "News Center 5 Live at Five" Channel 4 WNBC-TV 1980; Top Ladies of Distinction Award 1983; Nurses Sorority Chi Eta Phi Inc, 1984-present. **BUSINESS ADDRESS:** Coordinator, Health Science & Nursing, Hunter Coll, Rm EB 1309, New York, NY 10021.

ROBINSON, MAURICE C.
Attorney. **PERSONAL:** Born Mar 04, 1932, St Andrew, Jamaica;son of Dr Herbert Ulysses Robinsin (deceased) and Mildred Anastasia Magnus Robinson (deceased); widowed; children: Mark Wayne, Janet Marie, Wade Patrick. **EDUCATION:** Univ Coll of West Indies, BA 1951-54. **CAREER:** Manton & Hart, co-dir 1959-64 partner 1964-77; Myers, Fletcher, Gordon, Manton & Hart, partner 1977-. **ORGANIZATIONS:** Dir Victoria Mutual Bldg Soc, Stresscon Jamaica Ltd, Eric Fong-Yee Engrg Co Ltd, Crop Culture (Jamaica) Ltd, Intl Trust of Washington (Jamaica) Ltd; chmn Public Utility Comm 1972-76; legal officer Air Jamaica Ltd 1970-; sec Air Jamaica Ltd 1968-69; dir Olds Discount Co Jamaica Ltd; dir Aerocon Constr Ltd; dir Travel Planners Ltd; Dyoll/Wataru Coffee Company Limited; KIW International Limited; dir Security Advisory & Management Services Ltd; dir Victoria Mutual Investments Ltd; mem Inst of Trade Mark Agents. **HONORS/ACHIEVEMENTS:** Full Univ Colours for Field Hockey 1953. **BUSINESS ADDRESS:** Attorney, Myers, Fletcher, Gordon, Manton & Hart, 21 East St, Kingston, Jamaica.

ROBINSON, MELVIN P.
Entrepreneur. **PERSONAL:** Born Feb 12, 1935, Atlantic City, NJ; son of Warren Robinson and Marcella Perry Robinson; children: Michael Ribano. **EDUCATION:** Villinova Univ, Villinova PA, 1952-54. **CAREER:** Self-Employed, 1965-. **ORGANIZATIONS:** Mem, Amer Inst of Organbuilders, 1978-. **HOME ADDRESS:** 12 Irving Pl, Mount Vernon, NY 10550.

ROBINSON, MILTON BERNIDINE
Clergyman, editor. **PERSONAL:** Born Jun 29, 1913, Forest City, NC; married Lois Mosley; children: Evelyn Mercer, Essie McDaniel, Connie Foust, Milton Bernidine, Arthur, Charles, Annie Evans, Bettie McKesson, Priscilla Hodge, Phylias, Kenneth. **EDUCATION:** Johnson Comm Coll, AB 1963; A&T State Univ Greensboro NC, MS 1967. **CAREER:** Former school bus driver, farmer, pullman porter, builder, brick mason, editor; AME Zion Church, ordained to ministry 1949; Rutherford Cty Carver HS, teacher 1965-69; Star of Zion, editor 1969-80; St John AME Zion Church, pastor 1965-76; Isothermal Community Coll, Hindale, NC, teacher, 1984-86 (retired). **ORGANIZATIONS:** Del Gen Conf AME Zion Church 1960, 1964, 1968, 1972, 1976, 1980, 1984; conn mem bd christian ed home-ch div 1968-; del World Meth Conf 1971; mem gov bd Natl Council Church Christ in USA 1972-; chmn Rutherford Cty Human Relations Council; 2nd vchmn Rutherford Cty Dem Exec Comm 1970-74; trustee Winston-Salem State UnivClinton Jr Coll Rock Hill SC; mem NAACP, Mason; presiding elder York-Chester Dist SC Conf African Meth Episcopal Zion Church 1981-87; trustee Isothermal Comm Coll Spindale 1983-91; chmn trustees, Doggett Grove AME Zion Church, Forest City, NC. **HONORS/ACHIEVEMENTS:** Honorary DD, Livingston Coll, 1973; Lincoln Univ Award for helping famine-struck people in Africa in the 1970's.

ROBINSON, MILTON J.
Appointed government official. **PERSONAL:** Born Aug 16, 1935, Asbury Park, NJ; married Sadie Pinkston; children: Valerie, Patricia. **EDUCATION:** Univ of MI, BS 1958; Columbia Univ, MA 1962; Univ of MI, MSW 1966, PhD 1980. **CAREER:** Battle Creek Urban League, exec dir 1966-69; Flint Urban League, exec dir 1969-70; Dept of Civil Rights State of MI, exec dir 1970-72; State of MI, parole board member 1972-; Wayne State Univ Sch of Social Work, adjunct prof 1975-, GMI Engineering & Mgmt Inst, admissions & corporate relations consultant 1985-; State of Michigan, exec sec parole and review bd. **ORGANIZATIONS:** Mem Kappa Alpha Psi Frat; bd mem United Neighborhood Cntrs of Am 1972-; pres Cath Youth Orgn 1978-; mem Lions Intl 1979-; bd mem Detroit Metro Youth Program 1985-. **HONORS/ACHIEVEMENTS:** Comm Serv Award City of Battle Creek 1969; Outstanding Professional Serv Award Flint Urban League 1978; Outstanding Contrib to Continuing Judicial Educ MI Judicial Inst 1979; Meritorious Serv Awd Catholic Youth Org 1984; Certificate of Achievement Natl Cncl of Juvenile & Family Court Judges 1986. **MILITARY SERVICE:** AUS Sp 4 1958-60. **BUSINESS ADDRESS:** State of Michigan, 1200 6th St, Detroit, MI 48226.

ROBINSON, MURIEL F. COX
Medical doctor. **PERSONAL:** Born Nov 06, 1927, Columbus, OH; daughter of Henry W. Cox and Veola Isbell Cox; divorced. **EDUCATION:** Attended, Ohio State Univ 1945-48; Meharry Medical Coll, MD 1952. **CAREER:** Homer G Phillips Hospital Affiliated w/ Washington Univ Sch of Medicine, psychiatry resident 1953-56; St Louis Municipal Child Guidance Clinic, staff psychiatrist 1956-57; Napa State Hosp, staff psychiatrist 1958; Richmond Mental Health Center, staff psychiatrist 1959-75; East Oakland Mental Health Center, staff psychiatrist 1976-79; Private Psychiatric Practice, psychiatrist 1960-79; CA Youth Authority, staff 1979-. **ORGANIZATIONS:** Former mem advisory bd Contra Costa Mental Health Advisory Bd; former mem bd of dirs North Richmond Neighborhood House; mem American Psychiatric Assn 1957-; member Black Psychiatrists of America; mem NAACP Sacramento 1987-. **HOME ADDRESS:** PO Box 28097, Sacramento, CA 95828. **BUSINESS ADDRESS:** Staff Psychiatrist, State of CA Dept of Youth Auth, Northern Reception Ctr/Clinic, 3001 Ramona Ave, Sacramento, CA 95826.

ROBINSON, NOAH R.
Construction executive. **CAREER:** Precision Contractors, Inc, Chicago IL, chief executive. **BUSINESS ADDRESS:** Precision Contractors Inc, 10842 South Michigan Ave, Chicago, IL 60628. *

ROBINSON, NORMAN R.
Attorney. **PERSONAL:** Born May 16, 1909, Nokomis, IL; married Olivette Peters; children: & Family Serv. **EDUCATION:** John Marshall Law Sch Chicago, LLB 1951; John Marshall Law Sch Chicago, JD 1972. **CAREER:** Gen prac of law 1952-69; asst atty gen of IL 1969-71; Cook Co, asst states atty 1972. **ORGANIZATIONS:** Pres 3rd Ward Regular Rep Orgn of Chicago 1962-64; candidate for judge of circuit ct of Cook Co 1974; mem IL State Bar Assn; Cook Co Bar Assn; Chatham Lions Orgn; Mem Pub Policy Com; Community Council of Met Chicago. **HONORS/ACHIEVEMENTS:** First black pres IL Federation of the Blind 1964-66; first black mem bd dir Am Council of the Blind 1972-; first black mem bd dir Am Blind Lawyers Assn 1972-; Blind Serv Award 1974; elected to Bd of Dir Nat Accreditation Counc for the Blind 1976; elected chmn of AdvF Counc of Commn Serv for the Blind & IL Visually Handicapped Inst Dept of Family Serv of IL 1976; elected to Bd of Dri Blind Serv Org of Chic 1977; elected to Bd of Dir Chic Lighthouse for the Blind 1977; Chicago Assn for Visually Handicapped Award 1974; Spl Award Action Magazine Chicago 1974.

ROBINSON, NORMAN T., JR.
Educator, clergyman, business executive. **PERSONAL:** Born Aug 31, 1918, Bennettsville, SC; married Mayme Adams; children: Norman III, Mansel, Lyndon. **EDUCATION:** SC State Coll, BSA 1939, MS 1964; Columbia Univ, post grad study. **CAREER:** Chesterfield-Marlboro EOC OEO, exec dir; Society Hill SC, teacher; Smith Elem School, principal; Shawton HS, teacher of vets; Dale SC, teacher; Petersburg Elem School Pageland SC, principal; Stuckey HS Johnsonville SC, teacher; St James Baptist Church Bonnettsville, pastor; Mt Tabur Bapt Church Clio SC, pastor; Marlboro Branch of SCLG, vice pres; Fine Print News, publisher; Marlboro Co Dist 4, councilman. **ORGANIZATIONS:** Vice pres Cherow Alumni Chap Kappa Alpha Psi Frat; mem NAACP, Marlboro Betterment League; mem SC Comm Action Agy; moderator Marlboro Union; sec exec bd Borea Assn; vice pres BTU Conv; chmn bd dir BTU Rest Home. **HONORS/ACHIEVEMENTS:** Comm Leader of Amer 1969; Certificate of Awd Leadership Inst for Comm Devel. **MILITARY SERVICE:** AUS 1943-46. **BUSINESS ADDRESS:** Councilman, District 4 Marlboro Co, 514 Cherad St, Bennettsville, SC 29512.

ROBINSON, PETER LEE, JR.
Fine artist, graphics designer, consultant. **PERSONAL:** Born Jan 16, 1922, Washington, DC; married Romaine Frances Scott. **EDUCATION:** Howard Univ, AB 1949. **CAREER:** USN, supr illustrator 1957-62; Natl Aeronautics & Space Admin, dir, visual info officer 1962-77; Self employed, fine artist, graphics designer, consultant. **ORGANIZATIONS:** Dir, founder HEM Rsch Inc Past Inc; pres, treas DC Art Assn; past vice pres Soc of Fed Artists & Designers, Fed Design Council; exhibits at the Corcoran Gallery of Art, Atlanta Univ Gallery, Smithsonian Inst, The Artists Mart, Howard Univ Gallery, Barnett Aden Gallery, Collectors Corner, The Potters House Gallery, The Smith-Mason Gallery, The Anacostia Nghbrd Mus, Univ of PA, Martin Luther King Jr Gallery, The Art Barn; US State Dept "Arts for the EmbassiesProg"; speaker Rice Univ 1969, 16th Intl Tech Comm Conf 1969, Morgan State Coll 1969, 19th Intl Tech Comm Conf 1970, NAIA 1971, 19th Intl Tech Comm Conf 1972, 1st Indust Graphics Intl Conf 1974, 4th Tech Writing Inst 1974, Natl Conf of Artists 1980. **HONORS/ACHIEVEMENTS:** Award of Excellence in Visiting Comm Soc of Fed Artists & Designers 1961; Meritorious Civilian Serv Award 1960; Apollo Achievement Award 1969; NASA Exceptional Serv Medal 1973; NASA Outstanding Performance Award 1975; NASA Spaceship Earth Award 1975. **MILITARY SERVICE:** USAAC 1943-46. **BUSINESS ADDRESS:** Fine Artist, Graphics Designer, 1900 Tulip St NW, Washington, DC 20012.

ROBINSON, PREZELL RUSSELL
Educator, edcuational administrator. **PERSONAL:** Born Aug 25, 1922, Batesburg, SC; married LuLu Harris; children: JesSanne. **EDUCATION:** St Augustine's Coll Raleigh NC, AB 1946; Bishop Coll, LLD 1951; Cornell Univ NY, MA 1951, EdD 1956. **CAREER:** Voorhees School & Jr Coll Denmark SC, instructor of French/math/science, 1948-54; Univ of Nairobi Kenya, visiting prof, 1973; Univ of Dar es Salaam Tanzania, vstg prof, 1973; Haile Selassie I Univ Addis Ababa Ethiopia, vstg prof, 1973; Univ of Guyana, vstg prof, 1974; Cornell Univ Ithaca NY, fellow, 1954-56; St Augustine's Coll, prof of sociology 1956-, dean 1956-64, exec dean 1964-66, acting pres 1966-67, pres 1967-. **ORGANIZATIONS:** Mem Phi Kappa Phi, Delta Mu Delta, Alpha Kappa Mu, Phi Delta Kappa, Amer Social Soc, NC Social Soc, Amer Acad of Political Sci, So Social Soc, AmerAssn for Advancement of Sci, Study of Negro Life & History, Amer Acad of Pol & Soc Sci; mem bd of dir Wachovia Bank & Trust Co; state bd of ed NC;exec comm NC Assn of Coll & Univ; bd of dir Natl Assn for Equal Oppty in Higher Ed; bd dir Tech Asst Consortium to Improve Coll Svc; pres United Negro Coll Fund, 1978-80; bd of dir Occoneechee Cty BSA; pres Natl Assoc for Equal Oppty in Higher Educ, 1981-84; bd dir C of C; pres Cooperating Raleigh Colls, 1981, 1986-88; mem exec comm Assn of Episcopal Coll, Omega Psi Phi. **HONORS/ACHIEVEMENTS:** Recipient Fulbright Fellow to India 1965; Tar Heel of the Week Raleigh News & Observer 1971; Recognition for Services Rendered Awd 2nd highest Awd from Liberia 1971; Outstanding Service Award, Alpha Phi Alpha, 1977; Citizen of the Year Award, Omega Psi Phi, 1979; Silver Anniversary Award, N Carolina Community Coll System, 1989; author of more than 21 articles in professional journals. **MILITARY SERVICE:** AUS. **BUSINESS ADDRESS:** President, St Augustine's College, 1315 Oakwood Ave, Raleigh, NC 27611.

ROBINSON, R. DAVID
Professional athlete. **PERSONAL:** Born May 03, 1941, Mt Holly, NJ; married Elaine Burns; children: Richard, David, Robert. **EDUCATION:** PA State U, BS 1963. **CAREER:** Schlitz Brewing Co Younstown OH, dist sales mgr; Washington Redskins, linebacker 1973-74; Green Bay Packers, 1963-72; Green Bay Packers, capt def 1972. **ORGANIZATIONS:** Mem NFL Players Assn; NFL Player rep 1967-70; vice pres Players Assn 1968-70; YMCA; Big Bros. **HONORS/ACHIEVEMENTS:** Liberty Bowl 1960; Gator Bowl (1st Black) 1961; 62 MVP; All Amer 1962; Hula Bowl 1962; All Star Game 1963; All Pro 1965-69; World Champions 1965-67; MVP ProBowl1968; 1st Black Linebacker NFL; starting linebacker NFL Hall Fame 1969. **BUSINESS ADDRESS:** Schlitz Brewing Co, Youngstown, OH.

ROBINSON, RANDALL
Executive director. **PERSONAL:** Born in Richmond, VA; children: Anikie, Jabari. **EDUCATION:** Virginia Union Univ,, Grad 1967; Harvard Law School, Grad 1970. **CAREER:** Rep Diggs, administrative asst; TransAfrica, executive dir. **HONORS/ACHIEVEMENTS:** Ford Fellowship. **BUSINESS ADDRESS:** Dir, TransAfrica, 545 8th St SE, Washington, DC 20003.

ROBINSON, RANDALL S.
Associate professor. **PERSONAL:** Born Nov 26, 1939, Philadelphia; married Janice Whitley; children: Randall, Ginger. **EDUCATION:** OH St U, BS 1961;Univ of PA, MS 1965; Temple U, EdD 1972. **CAREER:** Philadelphia Bd of Educ, teacher 1961-65; Glassboro St Coll NJ, assoc prof; Egg Harbor School System NJ, consultant Summer School Improvement Project 1967; Educational Materials Co, project coord, resrearch & devel 1668-69; Templ Univ, adjunctive prof 1968-69; Temple Univ, consult & Group Leader annual summer workshop in lang arts; Tioga Community Youth Council, educ consultant for disruptive youth 1971. **ORGANIZATIONS:** Mem Curriculum Revision Com; Glassboro St Coll early childhood educ & curriclum devel com; pub reltns com; com for entrance to profession; dept Tenure & Recontracting Com Urban Educ Curriculum Devel Com ; All Coll Promotion Com 1969-71; Human Resources Com 1973-75; faculty adv Black Cultural Leg ; cnslr & Adv Upward Bound Students; cnslr & adv Martin Luther King Schjolars Faculty; adv bd memUniv Year of Action 1973-75; guest spkr Elem social studies; mem Glassboro St Fdrtn of Coll Tchrs; mem Nat Council for the Social Studies; mem Washington Township Bd Educ 1973-76; mem Negotiations Com, Washington Township of Edn; mem Curriculum Com; Washington Township Bd of Edn; chmn Policy Com Washington Twnship Bd of Edn; me M Balanced Grp of WashingtonTownship. **HONORS/ACHIEVEMENTS:** Recip Plaque Tioga Community Youth Council 1973. **BUSINESS ADDRESS:** Glassboro State College, Elementary Education Dept, Glassboro, NJ 08028.

ROBINSON, RAY CHARLES See CHARLES, RAY

ROBINSON, RENAULT A.
Government official. **PERSONAL:** Born Sep 08, 1942, Chicago, IL; married Annette Richardson; children: Renault Jr, Brian, Kivu, Kobie. **EDUCATION:** Roosevelt Univ, BS 1970, MS Urban Studies 1971; Northwestern Univ, Urban Fellow 1972-73. **CAREER:** Chicago Police Dept, police officer & vice detective 1965-83; Chicago Housing Authority, chmn bd of commrs 1983-. **ORGANIZATIONS:** Chmn bd dir Afro-American Police League 1983-; exec dir Afro-American Police League 1968-83; mem NAACP; Chicago Urban League; Natl Forum for Black Public Admin. **HONORS/ACHIEVEMENTS:** Author "The Man Who Beat Clout City" 1977; Renault A Robinson Award Natl Black Police Assn 1979; Youth Award John D Rockefeller III Found 1979. **BUSINESS ADDRESS:** Chairman, Bd of Commissioners, Chicago Housing Authority, 22 W Madison St, Chicago, IL 60602.

ROBINSON, ROBERT LOVE, JR.
Certified public accountant. **PERSONAL:** Born Apr 21, 1961, Madera, CA; son of Robert L Robinson, Sr and Evelyn Barnes Robinson. **EDUCATION:** The Univ of Pacific, BS 1982. **CAREER:** Price Waterhouse, auditor 1982-85; Sun Diamond Growers of CA, internal auditor 1985-86; The Grupe Co, sr accountant 1986-; Grupe Co, Stockton, CA, Asst mgr Operations l989-. **ORGANIZATIONS:** Mem CA State Soc of CPA's 1985-; advisor Sacramento Valley Chapter Natl Assn of Black Accountants 1985-; mem UOP Alumni Assn 1986-. **BUSINESS ADDRESS:** Sr Accountant, The Grupe Company, 2291 W March Lane, Stockton, CA 95207.

ROBINSON, ROGER
Actor. **PERSONAL:** Born May 02, 1940, Seattle, WA. **CAREER:** Broadway/Off-Broadway, actor; TV, actor; Films, actor; Reportory, actor. **BUSINESS ADDRESS:** Agent, Bauman Hiller & Assoc, 250 W 57th St, 9200 11 Sunset Blvd, New York, NY 10019.

ROBINSON, RONNIE W.
Apparel company executive. **PERSONAL:** Born Dec 26, 1942, Louisville, KY; son of Lawrence Robinson and Donetta L Robinson; married Veronices Gray, Jul 14, 1973; children: Kelli, Ronnie, Jr. **EDUCATION:** Kentucky State Univ, Frankfort KY, BS, 1964. **CAREER:** ICI Americas Inc, Charlestown IN, mgr ballistics lab, 1965-71, mgr EEO, 1971-73, mgr employment, 1973-77; Johnson & Johnson, Chicago IL, mgr personel admin, 1977-82; Hart Schaffner & Marx, Chicago IL, dir human resources administration 1982-88, vice pres of human resources 1988-. **ORGANIZATIONS:** Bd mem, Society of Human Resources Professionals, 1982-83; bd mem, Cosmopolitan Chamber of Commerce, 1983-; mem, Chicago Urban Affairs Council, 1983-; chairman, Human Resources Committee, IL State Chamber of Commerce, 1986-87; mem personnel comm, Chicago Youth Centers, 1986-; bd mem, Duncan YMCA, 1987-. **BUSINESS ADDRESS:** Vice President of Human Resources, Hart Schaffner & Marx, 101 N Wacker Drive, Chicago, IL 60606.

ROBINSON, ROOSEVELT V.
Automobile dealer. **CAREER:** Robinson Cadillac-Volkswagen-Lotus, Inc, East Point GA, chief executive. **BUSINESS ADDRESS:** Robinson Volkswagen, 1734 West Washington Ave, East Point, GA 30344. *

ROBINSON, ROSALYN KAREN
Attorney. **PERSONAL:** Born Dec 05, 1946, Norristown, PA. **EDUCATION:** Dickinson Coll Carlisle, PA, AB 1968; Boston Coll Law Sch Newton, MA, JD 1973. **CAREER:** Chemical Bank NY, NY, mgmt trainee/ofcr's asst 1968-70; Hon Doris M Harris, Crt of Common Pleas, law clrk 1973-74; Philadelphia Dist Atty's Ofc, asst dist atty 1974-79; PA Dept of Aging, chf cnsl 1979-83c of Gen Cnsl, dpty gen cnsl 1983-. **ORGANIZATIONS:** Treas Brstrs Assn 1973-; mem Philadelphia Bar Assn 1973-; mem PA Bar Assn 1982-; mem Am Bar Assn 1979-83; cls chmn Dickinson Coll Annl Giving 1984; vice pres Dickinson Coll Alumni Cncl 1974-80; mem PA Coalition of 10 Black Women 1984-, Harrisburg Chap of Links Inc 1984-, Dickinson Coll Bd of Trustees1985-. **HONORS/ACHIEVEMENTS:** One of 79 to watch in 1979 Philadelphia Mag January 1979. **BUSINESS ADDRESS:** Deputy General Counsel, Office of General Counsel, 17th Flr Harristown II, 333 Market St, Harrisburg, PA 17108.

ROBINSON, ROSCOE, JR.
Brigadier general. **PERSONAL:** Born Oct 11, 1928, St Louis, MO. **EDUCATION:** US Military Acad, BS Milit Engrg; Univ Pittsburgh, MPIA; Infantry Sch, grad; AUS Command and Gen Staff Coll; Natl War Coll; Commnd 2nd Lt AUS advanced through grades to Commndg Gen 1975. **CAREER:** Infantry Br Ofc of Personnel Ops, personnel mgmt officer 1965-67; 7th Cavalry Div AUS Pacific-Vietnam, comdg ofcr 2nd bn 1968; 2nd Brigade 82nd Airborne Div Ft Bragg, NC, plans officer, SE Asia spl actions ofcr 1972-73; AUS Garrison Okinawa Base Comm, dep comdg gen 1973-75, comdg gen 1975-78; SeventhArmy, 1978-; NATO Mil Com, US Rep 1982-. **HONORS/ACHIEVEMENTS:** Decorated Silver Star with oak leaf cluster Legion of Merit with 2 oak leaf clusters; DFC; Bronze Star; Air Medal (10 awards); Army Commendation Medal; Combat Infantryman Badge (2nd award); Disting Flying Cross; Master Parachutist Badge.

ROBINSON, ROSE MILES
Administrator. **PERSONAL:** Born Oct 04, 1939, Baltimore, MD. **EDUCATION:** VA Union Univ, BA 1960; VA Commonwealth Univ, MS 1972; Univ of S CA, MPA. **CAREER:** US Dept of HEW, social sci analyst 1967-73; US Civil Serv Comm, coord fed exec dev 1973-75; Pub Admin Howard Univ, asst prof 1975; Natl League ofCities Proj on Unemploy Ins, coord 1976; Amer Consort for Intl Pub Admin, exec dir 1976; AID, spec asst to the asst adm tch asst, asst dir office of intl training. **ORGANIZATIONS:** Mem Amer Vocational Assn; mem Natl Assn for Foreign Student Affairs; corp sec N VA Chap Natl Coalition of 100 Black Women; mem Alfred St Baptist Church; mem Amer Soc for Pub Adm; chmn Liberal Studies Comm, USDA Grad Sch; Amer Acad of Pol & Soc Science; pres bd of dir Friendship HouseAssn Inc; mem bd of dir Unit Black Fund; mem Alpha Kappa Alpha Sor. **HONORS/ACHIEVEMENTS:** Outstanding Young Women of Amer 1972; Ed for Pub Mgmt Fellowship 1971; art publ Pub Adm Rev 1974. **BUSINESS ADDRESS:** Asst Dir Ofc of Intl Training, AID, 214 SA-18, State Department, Washington, DC 20523.

ROBINSON, RUTH
Educator. **PERSONAL:** Born Dec 17, 1949, Chicago, IL. **EDUCATION:** No IL Univ DeKalb, BA Elem Educ 1971; Pacific Oaks Coll, MA Child Develop 1974; Univ of CA Berkeley, PhD 1980. **CAREER:** Pacific Oaks Coll & Children's School, faculty/head teacher 1972-73; Harold E Jones Child Study Center, teacher 1976-77; CA State Polytechnic Univ, lectr 1974-75, 1977-78; IN State Univ, asst prof, assoc prof early childhood educ, asst dean school of educ 1984-. **ORGANIZATIONS:** Curriculum consult Merced Co Region III Child Develop & migrant Child Care Prog 1978; curriculum consult Oakland Comm Sch 1975-76; mem Natl Assn Educ of Young Children 1979-; bd of dir Stage Seven Inc Black Perspective in Early Childhood Educ 1973-80. **HONORS/ACHIEVEMENTS:** Grad Minority Fellowship UC Berkeley 1977-79; Doctoral Fellowship Carnegie Corp 1975-76; Collective Monologues I Toward a Black Perspective in Educ Stage Seven Inc Pasadena CA 1976. **BUSINESS ADDRESS:** Asst Dean School of Education, IN StateUniv, Statesman Towers West, Terre Haute, IN 47809.

ROBINSON, S. BENTON
Business executive. **PERSONAL:** Born Jun 05, 1928, Parsons, KS; married Dymple O McIntyre; children: Benton, Karen, Arthur. **EDUCATION:** WV St Coll, BS 1950;Univ of Chgo, MBA 1970. **CAREER:** Supreme Life Ins Co, dist mgr 1950-54, field auditor 1954-55, mgr field accounting 1955-62, vice pres controller 1962-70, first vice pres 1970-73 sr vice pres 1973, exec vp/sec 1980; Bass Foundation, Inc, controller. **ORGANIZATIONS:** Asso Life Ofc Mgmt Assn; vice pres United Charities of Chgo, bd dir; Exec Prog Club; sec, bd dirUniv of Chgo; memUniv of IL Citizens Com; Alpha Phi Alpha Frat; 1971-72 co-chmn United Negro Coll Fund. **MILITARY SERVICE:** USN 1946-48. **BUSINESS ADDRESS:** Controller, Brass Foundation, Inc, 7022 S Shore Drive, Chicago, IL 60649.

ROBINSON, S. YOLANDA
Program coordinator. **PERSONAL:** Born Oct 01, 1946, Gilliam, WV; daughter of Rudolph V Robinson and Lucy Robinson; children: Chad Heath. **EDUCATION:** Univ of MA, Med 1980; Franklin Univ, Columbus OH 1966. **CAREER:** OH State Univ Coll of Educ, admn asst 1971; Inst for Black Community Rsch & Devel, researcher 1979-80; Dept of Blk Stds admn sec; Natl Council for Black Studies, conf chr 1977-; OH State Univ, admn sec. **ORGANIZATIONS:** Conf chr Natl Council for Black Studies 1978-; mem CWA Clrcl Org Comm OSU 1982-83; mem OSU Affirmative Action Comm 1985; 1st v pres OH Black Political Assembly; sec Inst Black Community Rsch & Devel; mem OSU WISE 1984-85; pres Cardinal Chap Nine to Five 1986-87; bd mem, Call UAC 1988-92; bd mem, Ohio State Univ AIDS Task Force 1988-. **HONORS/ACHIEVEMENTS:** Serv Natl Council for Black Studies 1977-78; serv Natl Black Political Assembly 1976; serv Comm on Institutional co-op 1983; grant Affirmative Action, OSU 1985; Progressive Secretary of the Year 1986; Honorable Mention, Avery International 1987; OSU Distinguished Affirmative Action Award, The Ohio State Univ 1988; conference coordinator, The Black Woman Challenges and Perspectives For The Future 1989; conference coordinator, Health Issues Crisis and The Black Community 1989. **HOME ADDRESS:** 2960 E 11th Ave, Columbus, OH 43219. **BUSINESS ADDRESS:** Program Coordinator, The Ohio StateUniv, 905 Mt Vernon, Columbus, OH 43203.

ROBINSON, SAMUEL
Educational administrator. **PERSONAL:** Born Dec 18, 1935, Memphis, TN; married Hugh Ella Walker; children: Debra, Charlotte. **EDUCATION:** TN State Univ, BS 1956, MS 1958; IN Univ, EdD 1974. **CAREER:** Lincoln Inst, dean of ed 1964-66; Lincoln School, principal 1967-70; Shawnee High School, principal 1970-73; Lincoln Found, exec dir 1974-. **ORGANIZATIONS:** Matl exec dir Phi Beta Sigma Ed Found 1980-; mem Sigma Phi Phi 1983-; bd mem Presbyterian Health Ed & Welfare Assoc 1982-, Black Achievers Assoc 1980-, Assoc of Black Found Exec 1974-, Louisville Presbyterian; chmn KY Humanities Council 1984-. **HONORS/ACHIEVEMENTS:** Recipient Outstanding Young Man Awd Louisville C of C 1963; Outstanding Young Educator Awd Shelbyville Jr C of C 1966; Disting Serv Awd Zeta Phi Beta 1974; Outstanding Citizen Awd Louisville Defender 1975; Comm Serv Awd Alpha Kappa Alpha 1976; Social Action Awd Phi Beta Sigma; Outstanding Black Achiever Awd Louisville 1980; Disting Citizen Awd Alpha Kappa Alpha 1980; Man of the Year Sigma Pi Phi 1986; Achiever of the Year Black Achievers Assn 1987. **MILITARY SERVICE:** AUS sp4 1958-60. **BUSINESS ADDRESS:** Executive Dir, Lincoln Inst, 233 W Broadway, Louisville, KY 40202.

ROBINSON, SANDRA LAWSON
Secretary. **PERSONAL:** Born Mar 22, 1944, New Orleans, LA; married Carl Dayton Robinson; children: Michael David, Carla Marie. **EDUCATION:** HowardUniv Clg Liberal Arts Washingon, DC, BS 1965; HowardUniv Clg Medicine Washington, DC, MD 1969; Hlth Care Admn TulaneUniv Sch Pblc Hlth & Tropical Medicine New Orleans, LA, MPH 1977; Pediatric Intrnshp Childrns Hosp Natl Med Ctr Dist Columbia, 1969-70; Pediatric Resdnc Chldrns Hosp Natl Med Ctr Dist Columbia, 1970-71; Pediatric Residency Flwshp Ambulatory CareUniv CA San Francisco San Francisco Gen Hosp, 1971-72. **CAREER:** Neighborhood Health Clinics New Orleans, med dir 1973-77; Ambulatory Care/Outpatient Serv Charity Hosp, dir 1977-81; Minority Afrs LA State Med Ctr, coordinator 1979; Ambulatory Care Serv Childrens Hosp, dir 1981-84; LA StateUniv & TulaneUniv Sch of Medicine, clncl asst prof of peds; TulaneUniv Sch Pblc Hlth & Tropical Med, adjunct asst prof; Dept of Hlth & Human Resources, sec 1984-. **ORGANIZATIONS:** Med cnsltnt to Lrng Disabilities Teams Pilot Proj Mission Area Sch Unified Sch Dist San Francisco 1971-72; team pedtrcn Family Clncs San Francisco Gen Hosp; mem Med Advsry & Sickle Cell Anemia Rsrch Found San Francisco; med cnsltnt of Sch & Behavoir Unit Mt Zion Hosp San Francisco, CA; Prvt Practice of Peds San Francisco 1972-73; Proposal Dev Comprehensive Hlth Serv New Orleans Parish Prison Inmates 1974; Common Hlth Problem Manual Neighborhood Hlth Clncs 1974; Coordination Preventive Medicine Pgm Natl Med Assc Convention 1974; mem Ross Roundtable Upper Respiratory Disease 1974; Project Analysis Paper New Orleans Neighborhood Hlth Clncs 1975; bd mem Kingsley House 1976-79; bd mem Family Serv Soc 1976-79; cnsltnt Westington Corp Headstart Pgm 1976-80; bd mem New Orleans Area Bayou River Hlth Systms Agcy 1977-82; mem Plan Dev Com Hlth Systms Agcy 1978-82; mem Com Use of Human Subjects TulaneUniv 1974-; bd mem Urban League of Greater New Orleans 1967-82; bd mem Isidore Newman Sch 1978-. **HONORS/ACHIEVEMENTS:** Who's Who In Am Clg &Univ 1965; Outstndg Young Women of Am 1978; Who's Who in Black Am 1981; HowardUniv Alumni Region V Awrd; Black Orgnztn for Ldrshp Dev Outstndg Comm Serv Awrd. **HOME ADDRESS:** 4601 Owens Blvd, New Orleans, LA 70122.

ROBINSON, SHERMAN
Business executive. **PERSONAL:** Born Sep 16, 1932, Piqua, OH; married Bever!y J Clark; children: Tod, Tina, Tracy. **EDUCATION:** Central St Coll, 1952-53; OH U, 1953-56, 58-59. **CAREER:** Sherman Robinson Inc, pres 1970-; Saylor, Rhoads Equip Co, designer, draftsman 1969-70; JG Richards & asso, draftsman, designer, vice pres 1961; Western Fixture Co, equip dealer 1959. **ORGANIZATIONS:** Consult Food Facilities Soc; asso mem AIA Rippledale Optimist Club; past pres Keystone Optimist Club 1972-73. **HONORS/ACHIEVEMENTS:** Instns VF Awd 1975. **MILITARY SERVICE:** AUS sp3 1956-58. **BUSINESS ADDRESS:** 708 Bungalow Ct, Indianapolis, IN 46220.

ROBINSON, SMOKEY **See ROBINSON, WILLIAM, JR.**

ROBINSON, SPOTTSWOOD WILLIAM, III
Judge. **PERSONAL:** Born Jul 26, 1916, Richmond, VA; married Marian B Wilkerson; children: Spottswood IV, Nina. **EDUCATION:** VA Union Univ, 1932-34,35-36; Howard Univ, LLB (Magna Cum Laude) 1939; VA Union Univ, LLD (Hon) 1955. **CAREER:** Richmond, attny 1943-60; Howard Univ, prof of law 1945-64; NAACP Legal Defense & Ed Fund, legal rep 1948-50; NAACP SE, reg counsel 1951-60; Howard Univ Law School, dean 1960-64; US Dist Court WA, judge 1964-66; US Court of Appeals WA, judge 1966-. **ORGANIZATIONS:** Mem Howard Faculty 1939-49; vp, gen counsel Consolidated Bank & Trust Co of Richmond 1963-64; mem US Civil Rights Comm on Civil Rights 1961-63; vestryman Episcopal Church; mem VA Bar Assoc, Old Dominion Bar Assoc, Bar Assoc DC, Natl Lawyers Club, Episcopalian. **HONORS/ACHIEVEMENTS:** Named to Richmond Afro-Amer Honor Roll 1946; Testimonial of Merit in Jurisprudence Phi Phi Chap Omega Psi Phi 1946; Annual Alumni Awd Howard Univ 1951; Annual Non-Mem Citizenship Awd Beta Gamma Lambda Chap Alpha Phi Alpha 1951; Social Action Achievement Awd Phi Beta Sigma 1953; Citation Beta Theta Sigma Chap Delta Sigma Theta 1954; Richmond Chap Frontiers of Amer 1954; Awd MD Conf NAACP 1959; Testimonial of Merit ABA, Natl Bar Assoc 1948. **BUSINESS ADDRESS:** Judge, US Court of Appeals, US Ct House, Washington, DC 20001.

ROBINSON, THELMA MANIECE
Educator. **PERSONAL:** Born May 01, 1938, Tuscaloosa, AL. **EDUCATION:** AL St U, BS 1960;Univ of AL Tuscaloosa, MA 1970, currently working toward EdS. **CAREER:** TVA, personnel clk, examining officer; Florence Bd of Edn, presently guidance counselor. **ORGANIZATIONS:** Mem Am Personnel & Guidance Assn; Am Sch Counselor Assn; AL PGA & AL SCA; st sec for AL PGA; mem NEA; AEA; Florence Educ Assn; pres Delta Sigma Theta Sor; AL Assn of Univ Women; Florence League of Women Voters; mem Lauderdale Co Chpt, ARC, treas; vice pres Muscle Shoals Assn for Mental Hlth. **HONORS/ACHIEVEMENTS:** Chosen Outstanding Secondary Educator 1974. **BUSINESS ADDRESS:** Senior Guidance Counselor, Coffee High School, North Cherry St, Florence, AL 35630.

ROBINSON, THEODORE PAUL
Educator. **PERSONAL:** Born May 28, 1941, Buffalo, NY. **EDUCATION:** FL StateUniv Tallahassee, BS 1974; FL State U, MS 1975, PhD 1977. **CAREER:** Univ of OK, asst prof of polit sci 1977-; Met Advertising Co NY, asst vice pres treas 1962-72. **ORGANIZATIONS:** Mem Nat Conf of Black Polit Scientists 1974-; mem Am Polit Sci Assn 1975-; recruiting com So Polit Sci Assn 1978-; mem NAACP 1958-; exec counc Nat Hi-Y Assn of the YMCA 1965-. **HONORS/ACHIEVEMENTS:** Congressional Intern Sen Lawton Chiles State of FL 1974; Regents Flwshp State of FL 1975-77; "Black Represen on City Councils" Soc Sci Quarterly 1978. **BUSINESS ADDRESS:** 455 Elm, Norman, OK 73069.

ROBINSON, THOMAS DONALD
Chief executive officer. **PERSONAL:** Born Aug 18, 1941, West Virginia; son of George Will Robinson and Mattie Henderson Robinson; married Bonnie Bennett; children: Thomas D II, Brooke DeAnna. **EDUCATION:** Marshall Univ, BBA 1964; Georgia State Univ, MHA 1977. **CAREER:** Welch Emergency Hosp, administrator 1977-80; Parkway Regional Medical Ctr, asst administrator 1980-84; Newport News General Hosp, administrator 1984-85; Tyrone Hosp, chief exec officer 1985-; Pennsylvania State University, Continuing Education Faculty, 1988-. **ORGANIZATIONS:** Mem Amer Coll of Health Execs 1981-; bd Tyrone Salvation Army 1986-, pres Tyrone Rotary Club 1986-; pres Tyrone Area Chamber of Commerce 1987-; bd Blair County United Way 1987-; public affairs comm Hospital Assoc of Western PA 1987-. **HOME ADDRESS:** One Oak Hill Lane, PO Box 26, Tyrone, PA 16686. **BUSINESS ADDRESS:** Chief Executive Officer, Tyrone Hospital, Clay Avenue Extension, Tyrone, PA 16686.

ROBINSON, WALTER F.
Business executive. **PERSONAL:** Born Jan 08, 1950, Sabetha, KS; married Thelma J Fuqua; children: Joy. **EDUCATION:** KS State Univ, BS Comp Sci 1972; Xavier Univ, MBA Mgmt 1976. **CAREER:** Procter & Gamble Co, marketing systems mgr 1972-78; Intl Paper Co, systems planning mgr 1978-80; Chemical Bank, AVice Pres mgr of world banking systems 1980-82;Credit Suisse; vice pres 1982-85; Mincron SBC Corp Integrated Financial Software, pres 1985-. **ORGANIZATIONS:** Proj bus coord Jr Achievement 1977; mem ACM 1977-85; dir Urban Bankers Coalition 1980-85; mem One Hundred Black Men Inc 1984-85. **HONORS/ACHIEVEMENTS:** Outstanding Young Men of Amer 1983; Who's Who in Computer Mgmt 1984. **BUSINESS ADDRESS:** President, Mincron SBC Corp, Integrated Financial Software, 350 Fifth Ave, New York, NY 10118.

ROBINSON, WALTER G.
Educator. **PERSONAL:** Born Oct 16, 1928, Chgo; married Jean Dorsett; children: Walter III, Waddell Craig, Keith Jones. **EDUCATION:** Lincoln U, BS 1955;Univ of MO Social Work, MSW 1965; So IL U, PhD 1976. **CAREER:** Rehabilitation Institute Southern IL Univ, asst prof, asst to dir, former dir Black Amer Studies, asst to pres, asst to chancellor, asst to vice pres for Area & Internatl Serv Coordinator Univ Serv to Carbondale & Environs 1968-73; Neighborhood Youth Corp St Clair, Madison Co, dir; Social Work Serv, Child Welfare Serv, MO Div of Welfare, St Louis, supvr 1962-68. **ORGANIZATIONS:** Mem bd dirs Nat Council on Aging; bd dirs So IL Instrctl TV Assn; elected Jackson Bd of Comm; Certified IL Social Worker; cert rehab couns & mem NASW; AAVP; Nat Rehab Assn; Nat Assn Black Social Workers; Nat Assn Non-white Rehab Workers; Assn Black Psychologist; African Assn Black Studies; African Heritage Studies Assn; Buc Merit Acad; IL Council Educ Svc; Nat Caucus on Black Aging; IL St Adv & Council Title I Higher Act 1965; memNAACP; Omega Psi Phi Frat; Phi Delta Kappa Frat. **HONORS/ACHIEVEMENTS:** Recip Merit Comm Serv Awd E St Louis 1968; Merit Awd for Youth Prog E St Louis 1967; listed Comm Ldrs & Noteworth Ams 1973-74. **MILITARY SERVICE:** AUSR capt 1968. **BUSINESS ADDRESS:** Rehabilitation Inst, So IL Univ, Carbondale, IL 62901.

ROBINSON, WILBUR R.
Pharmacist. **PERSONAL:** Born Jan 02, 1916, Selma, AL; son of William D. Robinson and Minnie Craig Robinson; married Barbara G Battle; children: Wilbur Jr, John Preston, Alfonso Gomez. **EDUCATION:** Xavier U, BSPh 1954. **CAREER:** Tuskegee Inst, asst purchasing agent 1947-52; John A Andrew Meml Hosp Tuskegee Inst, chief pharmacist 1954-61; Robinson's Drug Store Tuskegee AL, owner, pharmacist 1961-. **ORGANIZATIONS:** Mem AL Pharm Assn; Nat Pharm Assn; Am Pharm Assn; Nat Assn of Retail Druggist; Tuskegee Civic Assn Tuskegee Inst; mem NAACP; Alpha Phi Alpha Frat; Chi Delta Mu Honor Soc; Sigma Pi Phi Frat Phi Boule. **MILITARY SERVICE:** USAF ret major 1941-47. **BUSINESS ADDRESS:** Robinson's Drug Store, 502 Fonville, Tuskegee, AL 36083.

ROBINSON, WILHELMENA S.
Historian. **PERSONAL:** Born Nov 12, 1912, Pensacola, FL; married Collins H. **EDUCATION:** TN A&I U, BS 1933; ColumbiaUniv NY, MA 1934; OH State, 3 yrs residence on PhD 1958. **CAREER:** Edward Waters Coll FL; AL State, teacher 1934-40; LeMoyne Coll, 1946; Central State Univ, 1947-74; Wright State, adjunct prof 1974; Brown, Cunningham & Robinson Man in Amer, author 1974; Let Freedom Ring 1980, Silver Burdett Publishers, 1976; The Library Co, Robinson historical Afro-Am biographies 1976; Central State Univ Wilberforce OH, author, lecturer, cons, prof emeritus of history; Univ of MI Ann Arbor, visiting prof 1966; Catherine Spalding Louisville, 1967; Univ of Louisville, 1968; Wright State Univ Dayton, 1974. **ORGANIZATIONS:** Life mem bd trustees OH Historical Soc 1971-77; mem Nat Educ Assn; Assn for Study of Afro-Am Life & History; League of Women Voters; Alpha Kappa Alpha; OH Acad of History; Am Historical Assn; So Historical Assn; Orgn Of Am Historian. **HONORS/ACHIEVEMENTS:** Recipient Governor's Award for Community Action 1974; OH House of ep Citation 1974; Distinguished Prof Award 1973; Shriners Award 1974; Masonic Award 1974.

ROBINSON, WILLIAM
Civil service management. **PERSONAL:** Born Jun 30, 1920, Harrisburg, PA; son of Earnest Robinson and Saddie Robinson; married Beatrice S; children: Paula, Evelyn, Nancy. **EDUCATION:** Lincoln Univ, BA; Pennsylvania State Extension Courses, accounting; Air Force & Army, management courses. **CAREER:** US Civil Service Air Force & Army, supply & logistics management; real estate sales. **ORGANIZATIONS:** Former mem Harrisburg City Council; former mem Vestry St Stephens; Cathedral Dioces of Central PA; mem Bd of Realtors PA & Natl Assn of Realtors; mem Harristown Bd of Directors; Comm on Ministry Episcopal Dioces of Central PA; life mem NAACP and Omega Psi Phi; lay deputy 1985/1988 Gen Natl Convention of Episcopal Church; bd mem PA Council of Churches, trustee, Lincoln Univ, PA. **BUSINESS ADDRESS:** PO Box 10466, 2309 Edgewood Rd, Harrisburg, PA 17105.

ROBINSON, WILLIAM, JR. (SMOKEY ROBINSON)
Musician, business executive. **PERSONAL:** Born Feb 19, 1940; son of William Robinson Sr; married Claudette (divorced 1985); children: Berry William, Tamla; children: Trey. **EDUCATION:** Attended Jr Coll. **CAREER:** Detroit Nightclub, performer; Smokey Robinson & The Miracles, recording artist 1957-72; Big Time, exec producer 1977; Motown Record Corp, vice pres; author of "Smokey: Inside My Life," 1989. **BUSINESS ADDRESS:** Vice President, Motown Record Corp, 6255 Sunset Blvd, Los Angeles, CA 90028. *

ROBINSON, WILLIAM ANDREW
Physician. **PERSONAL:** Born Jan 31, 1943, Philadelphia, PA; son of Colonial and Lillian; married Jacqueline E Knight; children: William Jr, David. **EDUCATION:** Hampton Inst, BA 1964; Meharry Medical Coll, MD 1971; Johns Hopkins School of Hygiene & Public Health, MPH 1973. **CAREER:** George W Hubbard Hosp Nashville, emergency room physician 1972; Food and Drug Admin, reviewing medical officer 1973-75; Health Resources & Services Admin, medical officer 1975-80, deputy bureau dir 1980-87, chief medical officer 1987-89; Public Health Service, Office of Minority Health, dir 1989-. **ORGANIZATIONS:** Mem Amer Public Health Assn, Sr Executives Assn, Federal Physicians Assn; Amer Acad of Family Physicians, National Medical Assn, American Medical Assn. **HONORS/**

ACHIEVEMENTS: Temporary health consultant US House of Representatives; Diplomate Natl Bd of Medical Examiners; Special Recognition Awd Public Health Serv 1980; Sr Exec Service US Govt 1984; HRSA Administrator's Awd for Excellence 1987. **MILITARY SERVICE:** AUS Medical Service Corps capt 1964-67; Natl Defense Medal, Army Commendation Medal 1967. **HOME ADDRESS:** 16608 Frontenac Terrace, Rockville, MD 20855. **BUSINESS ADDRESS:** Chief Medical Officer, Health Resource/Serv Admin, 5600 Fishers Lane Rm 14-39, Rockville, MD 20857.

ROBINSON, WILLIAM EARL
City official. **PERSONAL:** Born Nov 18, 1940, Morton, MS; son of P B Robinson and Gladys Robinson; married Estelle Nobles; children: Jacqueline, William E II. **EDUCATION:** MS Valley State Univ, Soc Sci & Pol Sci 1958-62. **CAREER:** North Las Vegas Chamber of Commerce, hon dir 1972-82; City of North Las Vegas, councilman 1983-91; School Success Monitor Clark County School Dist. **ORGANIZATIONS:** Pres North Las Vegas Jaycees 1973; natl dir NV Jaycees 1975; mem chmn North Las Vegas Democratic Club 1979, 1980; gaming policy comm State of NV 1973-81; life mem US Jaycees, NV Jaycees, North Las Vegas Jaycees; hon dir North Las Vegas Chamber of Commerce 10 yrs; second vice pres NV League of Cities; first vice pres NV League of Cities; pres, NV League of Cities, 1987-88; chairman of the board, NV League of Cities, 1988-89; chairman, North Las Vegas Housing Authority 1988-89. **HONORS/ACHIEVEMENTS:** Jaycee of the Year North Las Vegas Jaycees 1972, 1974, 1975; Appointed to the State Gaming Policy Comm by Gov of NV 1973; JCI Senate 28596 1976; One of the Hundred Most Influential Blacks in NV 1984-87. **HOME ADDRESS:** 1400 Pontiac Ave, North Las Vegas, NV 89030.

ROBINSON, WILLIAM HENRY
Educator. **PERSONAL:** Born Oct 24, 1922, Newport, RI; son of Julia W. S. Robinson; married Doris Carol Johnson, Jun 08, 1948. **EDUCATION:** New York Univ, BA, 1951; Boston Univ, MA, 1957; Harvard Univ, PhD, 1964. **CAREER:** Prairie View Agr & Mech Coll, Prairie View TX, English instructor, 1951-53; NC Agr & Tech State Univ, Greensboro, mem of English faculty, 1956-61, 1964-66; Boston Univ, MA, assoc prof of English & humanities, 1966-68; Howard Univ, Washington DC, prof of English, 1968-70; Rhode Is Coll, Providence, prof of English and dir black studies, 1970-85; vis prof of Amer & English lit, Brown Univ, 1987—. **ORGANIZATIONS:** Bd mem, RI Commn on the Humanities; Bd mem, RI Black Heritage Soc; Intl Lecture Platform Assn; mem, NSLCAH; Nat Com on Black Studies; NAACP; Urban League; Coll Language Arts Assn; Assn for Study of Negro Life & Culture. **HONORS/ACHIEVEMENTS:** Editor of Early Black American Poets, W.C. Brown, 1969, Early Black American Prose, W.C. Brown, 1970, Nommo: An Anthol of Modern Black African & Black American Lit, Macmillan, 1972, Critical Essays on Phillis Wheatley, G.K. Hall, 1982; author of Phillis Wheatly in the Black American Beginnings, Broadside, 1975, Phillis Wheatley: A Bio-Bibliography, G.K. Hall, 1981, Phillis Wheatley and Her Writings, Garland, 1984; also autho of num TV, stage, radio scripts; contr to journals. **MILITARY SERVICE:** US Army, 1942-45. **BUSINESS ADDRESS:** English Dept, Rhode Island College, 600 Mt Pleasant Ave, Providence, RI 02908. *

ROBINSON, WILLIAM J. (BISHOP BILLY ROBINSON)
Clergyman. **PERSONAL:** Born Feb 24, 1933, New Rochelle, NY; son of Thomas Robinson and Millie Royster Robinson; divorced; children: Daryl Anderson. **EDUCATION:** Pillar of Fire College & Penecostal Seminary, York, England, DCnL, 1970; Trinity College & Seminary, Sprinfield, IL, DDiv, 1972. **CAREER:** Bronx Dist, surp; E NY Mass Choir, minister of music; Milinary Shop, owner; The Garden of Prayer Ch of God in Christ, bishop. **ORGANIZATIONS:** Vice pres Bronx Shepherds Restoration Corp 1989; pres Fourth Saturday Conference 1st Jurisdiction Eastern NY Churches of God in Christ Inc; bd of dirs, Tremont Day Care Center; mem United Black Church Appeal; mem bd Intl Home & Foreign Mission; professional gospel singer for 30 years; 8 religious music albums; active in police & comm relations in 48th precinct; founder Garden of Prayer Church of God in Christ; composer of "Come and Stroll down Blessing Boulevard"; author of Come Stroll down Blessing Boulevard; latest record-composer "Ooh Whee.". **HONORS/ACHIEVEMENTS:** Largest Pentecostal Church in the Bronx; Awd for Best Choir of 1984 Gospel Acad Awds by ballots; award Bronx Shepherds Restoration Corp 1986; proclamation from Borough president 1988. **HOME ADDRESS:** 1281 E 223 St, Bronx, NY 10466-5801. **BUSINESS ADDRESS:** Garden of Prayer Ch of God, PO Box 79, Bronx, NY 10457.

ROBINSON, WILLIE C.
Educator. **PERSONAL:** Born Dec 13, 1934, Dunn, NC; married Ojetta Dowdy; children: William, Kevin, Lewis. **EDUCATION:** Agr & Tech Coll, BS; Univ of Bridgeport, MA; Tchrs Coll Columbia NY, EdD, LHD. **CAREER:** Yale Univ, dir mid-career prog in city school admin 1971-74, acting dir of teaching prep prog 1974-75; Yale Child Study Prog, research assoc 1975-76, special asst to pres 1976-77; FL Meml Coll Miami, pres. **ORGANIZATIONS:** Bd of govs & exec comm Gr Miami C of C 1979-80; vice chairman Gr Miami C of C 1983-84; vice pres exec bd Miami Dade Co Water & Sewer Auth 1979-80; bd of dirs Dade Co United Way 1979-80; past pres bd dir Urban League of Greater New Haven; dir & mem exec bd United Negro Coll Fund; dir Eastern Airlines Inc, Southeast Bank Holding Co, Southeast Bank NA, Sharon Steel Corp, assoc mem Orange Bowl Comm; past pres Alpha Phi Alpha Frat Inc Eta Alpha Lambda Chapt; dir NVF Co. **HONORS/ACHIEVEMENTS:** Outstanding Young Men of Amer Natl Jr C of C 1967; consult Tchrs Coll Columbia Univ Tchrs Corps; Outstanding Leadership Awd Dade Co NAACP; OutstandingCom Serv Awd Greater Miami Chap Alpha Phi Omega; Silver Medallion for serv to brotherhood Natl Conf of Christians and Jews 1985; Dr Willie C Robinson Day April 17 1982 City of Hialeah. **BUSINESS ADDRESS:** President, Fl Meml Coll, 15800 NW 42nd Ave, Miami, FL 33054.

ROBINSON-BROWN, JEANNETTE
Educational administrator. **PERSONAL:** Born Jul 08, Atlanta, GA; daughter of Reginald Robinson and Mary Robinson; married Gregory M Brown; children: Yolanda C Wade. **EDUCATION:** Essex Co Coll Newark, AS 1975; Rutgers Univ, BS 1977; Fairleigh Dickinson Univ, MBA 1980. **CAREER:** Newark Educational Inst, administrator 1973-80; Dept of Planning & Economic Development Div of Employment Training, contract mgmt supvr 1980-83; director of special programs Essex County Coll Nwk, N.J. 1983-88. **ORGANIZATIONS:** Business administrator IEE 1976-; pres Management Business Advisors 1980-; arbitrator Better Business Bureau NJ 1982-; mem NJ Educ Assoc, NJ Assoc for Equality and Excellence in Educ, Assoc of Black Women in Higher Educ, Delta Sigma Phi Frat, Natl Assoc of Veterans Program Administrators. **HONORS/ACHIEVEMENTS:** Publications "People Just Like You: A Guide for the Employer of the Handicapped" 1982, "People Just Like You: A Guide for the Teacher of the Handicapped" 1982. **HOME ADDRESS:** 91 Court St, Newark, NJ 07102. **BUSINESS ADDRESS:** Dir of Personnel, Personnel Dept Essex County College, 303 University Ave, Newark, NJ 07102.

ROBINSON-WALKER, MARY P.
Administrative assistant. **PERSONAL:** Born in Pittsburgh, PA; daughter of William Robinson and Eula Robinson; divorced. **EDUCATION:** Iron City Coll, Rose Demars Legal Sec School, French Inst. **CAREER:** Amer Comm on Africa, sec 1960-64; Artist Civil Rights Asst Fund, special projects dir 1965-66; Savings Bank Assoc of NY, sec 1967-68; Metro Applied Rsch Ctr, sec 1968-70; Black Economic Rsch Ctr, admin asst 1970-76; Pearl Bailey Review, Phillip-Fort Dancers, former professional dancer, dance instr; Ctrs for Reading and Writing of the New York Public Library. **ORGANIZATIONS:** Emcee Comm on Discrimination in Housing; performed by New York City Youth House, New School for Soc Rsch, US Naval Hosp, Western PA Psych Hosp; mem of bd of dir Harlem Philharmonic Soc 1969-; admin asst 21st Century Found; co-chmn ARC Harlem Div 1974-.

ROBY, REGGIE
Professional athlete. **PERSONAL:** Born Jul 31, 1961, Waterloo, IA. **EDUCATION:** Univ of IA. **CAREER:** Miami Dolphins, punter 1983-. **ORGANIZATIONS:** Post Season Honors included Pro Football Digest All-AFC in Pro Bowl; Charity Work for Special Olympics and for Shriners Hosp natl drug awareness prog for (Ncaa. **BUSINESS ADDRESS:** Miami Dolphins, 2269 NW 199 St, Opa-Locka, FL 33056.

ROCHA, JOSEPH RAMON, JR.
Educator. **PERSONAL:** Born Dec 04, 1925, Boston, MA; son of Joseph R. and Odie L.; married Enid Josephine Terrelonge; children: Ramona J Wilbun, Roxana L, Jeffrey R. **EDUCATION:** Northeastern Univ, BS 1948; New York Univ, MBA 1954; Howard Univ, JD 1960; Univ of IA, PhD 1966. **CAREER:** Morgan State Univ, asst to pres & asst prof 1963-65; Ball State Univ, assoc prof of econ 1965-73; Univ of Rhode Island, special asst to pres 1973-76; Chicago State Univ, prof of econ & chmn 1976-77; Univ of Lowell, prof of mgmt. **ORGANIZATIONS:** Labor arbitrator AAA & FMCS Natl Panels 1969-; training consultant City of Lowell, MA 1977-81; bd of dir Wilbun Entrepreneurs Inc Memphis 1984; mem Kappa Alpha Psi Frat 1947; pres Community Action Agency Delaware Co, IN 1969-71; mem IRRA; bd of dirs Elder Serv of the Merrimack Valley Inc Lawrence MA 1986-. **HONORS/ACHIEVEMENTS:** Delivered papers at various professional meetings; published articles on mgmt, labor relations & training. **MILITARY SERVICE:** AUS corporal 1950-52. **BUSINESS ADDRESS:** Professor of Management, Univ of Lowell, OneUniv Ave, Lowell, MA 01854.

ROCK-BAILEY, JINNI
Personnel administrator. **PERSONAL:** Born in Long Beach, NJ. **EDUCATION:** Howard Univ, BS Liberal Arts 1974; Rutgers Univ, MA Labor Relations 1977; SUNY Buffalo, AA Manpower Admin 1977. **CAREER:** The EDGES Group Inc, recording sec 1983-; the Greater NY Chap Natl Assn of Market Developers, president 1984-; Natrl Urban Affairs Cncl, parlimentarian; Sterling Drug Inc, corporate eeo mgr. **ORGANIZATIONS:** Comm chair Natl Urban Affairs Council 1984-; consultant OIC 1984-; consultant NUL-Summer Intern Prog 1985-. **HONORS/ACHIEVEMENTS:** Good Corporate Citizen Patterson OIC 1984. **BUSINESS ADDRESS:** Corporate EEO Manager, Sterling Drug Inc, 90 Park Ave, New York, NY 10016.

ROCKETT, DAMON EMERSON
Elected official & business executive. **PERSONAL:** Born Nov 13, 1938, Chicago, IL; married Darlene Sykes; children: Deborah, Sean Damon. **EDUCATION:** Drake Univ, BS/BA 1960. **CAREER:** Allstate Ins Co, claims super 1964-69; City of Harvey, comm public health & safety; IL Bell Telephone Co, bus office mgr 1969-80, phone ctr mgr 1980-81, staff-assessment ctr 1981-82, comm relations mgr. **ORGANIZATIONS:** Pres Harvey Rotary Club 1971-80; mem S Suburban Human Relations Comm 1973; bd mem & policy comm chmn Thornton Comm Coll 1975-79; bd mem CEDA 1980; YMCA Task Force 1984; mem Rotary Club of Park Forest 1984-; mem S Suburban Assn of Commerce & Industry 1984-; mem S Suburban Mayors & Mgrs Assn 1984-; bd mem Red Cross 1985; chmn African Relief Campaign 1985; mem NAACP. **HONORS/ACHIEVEMENTS:** Ten Outstanding Young People Harvey Jaycees 1975; Outstanding Citizen UHURU Black Student Org Thornton Comm Coll 1979; Outstanding Citizen S Suburban Chamber of Commerce & Industry 1979. **HOME ADDRESS:** 113 E 144th Court, Harvey, IL 60426. **BUSINESS ADDRESS:** Community Relations Manager, Illinois Bell Telephone, 646 Chicago Rd, Chicago Heights, IL 60411.

RODDY, HOWARD W.
Health administrator. **PERSONAL:** Born Feb 28, 1950, Nashville, TN; son of Howard W. Roddy and Marie B. Roddy; married Donna Norwood Roddy; children: Howard Carthie, John Travis. **EDUCATION:** Austin Peay State Univ, BS 1971; East TN State Univ, MS Environ Health Admin 1974. **CAREER:** Chattanooga-Hamilton Co Health Dept, environmentalist & dir of vector control project 1971-76; Alton Park/Dodson Ave Comm Health Ctrs, asst admin for planning/evaluation 1976-81; Chattanooga Hamilton Co Health Dept, administrator 1981-. **ORGANIZATIONS:** Mem Amer Public Health Assn 1977-; mem TN Public Health Assn 1981-; bd mem Chattanooga-Hamilton County Air Pollution Control Bureau 1983-; steering comm mem Natl Assn of Counties Energy & Environment 1983-; finance comm chmn Alton Park/Dodson Ave Comm Health Ctrs Governing Bd 1984-; treas Leadership Chattanooga Alumni Assoc 1985-; bd mem exec comm Chattanooga Area Urban League 1986-; bd mem United Way of Greater Chattanooga 1987. **HONORS/ACHIEVEMENTS:** Omega Man of the Year Kappa Iota Chapter of Omega Psi Phi Frat Inc 1981; Honorary Staff Mem State of TN 28th Dist Adv Comm 1982. **BUSINESS ADDRESS:** Administrator, Chattanooga-Hamilton Co Hlth, 921 E Third St, Chattanooga, TN 37403.

RODEZ, ANDREW LAMARR
Chief of police. **PERSONAL:** Born Oct 09, 1931, Chicago, IL; married Patricia Lander; children: Angelina, Andy, Rita. **EDUCATION:** VA Union Univ, AB; NE IL State Univ, MA; MI State Univ, PhD; FBI Natl Acad NW Traffic Inst, Diploma. **CAREER:** Off-The-Street-Boys Club, group worker 1956-57; Cook County Welfare Dept, case worker 1957-58; Evanston Police Dept, police officer 1958; Chicago Bd of Educ, teacher 1958-64; Benton Har-

bor, chief of police 1973-79; Benton Harbor Area School Dist, asst principal 1979-82; Maywood Police Dept, chief of police 1982-. **ORGANIZATIONS:** Charter mem Natl Org Black Law Enforement Reg IV, vice pres NOBLE 1984; adj prof Triton Coll; mem Kappa Alpha Psi, NW Univ Traffic Inst Alumni, ChessmenSocial/Civic Org, FBI Natl Acad Alumni Assoc, Phi Delta Kappa Ed, IL Assoc Chiefs of Police, West Suburban Chiefs of Police, VFW, NAACP; pres Task ForceYouth Motivation 1970. **HONORS/ACHIEVEMENTS:** Outstanding Citizen Awd NAACP 1970; Model Cities Awd 1974; Outstanding Alumni Awd Kappa Alpha Psi 1968; Bicent Awd Lake MI Coll 1976; All CIAA Football &Track 1951-52; Negro Coll All-Amer 1952. **BUSINESS ADDRESS:** Chief of Police, Maywood Police Dept, 125 S 6th Ave, Maywood, IL 60153.

RODGERS, ANTHONY RECARIDO, SR.
Deputy sheriff. **PERSONAL:** Born Apr 02, 1951, Jacksonville, FL; son of Clarence Rodgers and Clara Lee Maddox Washington; married Pharis Yvonne Hagans Rodgers, May 01, 1972; children: Anthony Jr, Martisha, Edward, Eric. **EDUCATION:** Florida Jr Coll, Jacksonville, FL, 1971-72; Northeast Florida Criminal Justice Educ & Training Center, 1973. **CAREER:** Duval County Sheriffs Office, Jacksonville FL, School Attendance Officer, Abandoned Property Officer, Certified Radar Operator, Field Training Officer, Deputy Sheriff, 1973-. **ORGANIZATIONS:** Mem, Jacksonville Urban League, 1973; president, Jacksonville Brotherhood of Police Officers, Inc, 1978; President Bliss Sertoma Club, 1979; treasurer, Viking Athletic Booster Club of Raines High School, 1980; mem, Jacksonville Job Corps Community Relations Council, 1983; lst vice pres, Jacksonville Branch NAACP, 1984; mem, Moncrief Improvement Assn, 1984; treasurer, Southern Region of Natl Black Police Assn, 1985; JUST US Comm on Community Problems, 1986; mem, FL Community Coll at Jacsonville Advisory Bd on New Direction, 1987. **HONORS/ACHIEVEMENTS:** Community Service Award, Operation Respect, 1981; Outstanding Sec Northwest Jacksonville Sertoma Club, 1984; Community Service Award, Northeast FL Community Action Agency, 1984; Achievement Award, Natl Black Police Assn Southern Region, 1985; Charlie Sea Police Officer of the Year, Jacksonville Brotherhood of Police Officers, 1988. **HOME ADDRESS:** 5720 Oprey St, Jacksonville, FL 32208.

RODGERS, CAROLYN MARIE
Author, lecturer. **PERSONAL:** Born Dec 14, 1943, Chicago, IL; daughter of Clarence and Bazella Colding. **EDUCATION:** Univ of Illinois, Navy Pier, 1960-61; Roosevelt Univ, Chicago, IL, BA, 1981; Univ of Chicago, MA, 1984. **CAREER:** Columbia, Coll, Chicago, IL, Afro-Amer lit instructor, 1969-70; Malcolm X Coll, Chicago, IL, writer-in-residence, 1971-72; Indiana Univ, Bloomington, IN, visiting prof of Afro Amer lit, 1973; Roosevelt Univ, Chicago, IL, writer-in-residence, 1983; Chicago State Univ, Chicago, IL, lecturer, 1985; Eden Press, Chicago, IL, editor/publisher, currently. **HONORS/ACHIEVEMENTS:** Author of Paper Soul, Third World Press, 1969; author of Songs of a Blackbird, TWP, 1970; Soc of Midland Authors Poet Laureate, 1970; Natl Endowment of the Arts, 1970; author of How I Got Ovah, Doubleday Anchor, 1975; author of The Heart as Evergreen, Doubleday, 1978; PEN, 1987; author of Echoes, From a Circle Called Earth, Eden Press, 1988; author of A Little Lower Than The Angels, Eden Press, 1988.

RODGERS, CHARLES
Clergyman. **PERSONAL:** Born Jul 28, 1941, Memphis, TN; married Gloria Dickerson; children: Adrian, Victor, Allison, Carlos. **EDUCATION:** Attennded LeMoyne Owen Coll. **CAREER:** Memphis Press-Scimitar, staff writer 1969; Memphis Publ Co, recruiting & job counseling 1973; Central TN Jurisdiction of Church of God in Christ, second asst to Bishop 1982-. **ORGANIZATIONS:** Pres State Evangelist Bd; vice pres Tipton Co Min Alliance; bd dir Memphis Teen Challenge; intl bd test Ch of God in Christ; mem Intl Bd of Trustees of Church of God in Christ 1972-84; asst dist elder Covington Dist COGIC; mem Shelby United Neighbors 1973-74; dir of News Serv for Church of God in Christ Intl Convention 1981-. **HONORS/ACHIEVEMENTS:** Listed in Who's Who in Amer in Religion 1976; Who's Who in Amer Jour 1976; Man of Yr Congressman H Ford 1976; cert Outstanding & Meritorious Serv mayor W Chandler 1976. **BUSINESS ADDRESS:** Pastor, 409 Haynie St, Covington, TN 38019.

RODGERS, DEL
Professional football player. **PERSONAL:** Born Jun 22, 1960, Salinas, CA. **EDUCATION:** Univ of Utah. **CAREER:** Green Bay Packers, professional football player (running back) 1982-. **ORGANIZATIONS:** Owns and operates Rodgers Auto Retailing Salt Lake City. **HONORS/ACHIEVEMENTS:** Coll, first 1,000 yard rusher in Utah's history; profl, in 1984 sixth ranking kickoff returner in NFC averaging 126 yds for 39 runbacks; valued contrib asrookie in 1982 helping Packers gain a Super Bowl Tournament berth. **BUSINESS ADDRESS:** Green Bay Packers, 1265 Lombardi Ave, Green Bay, WI 54303.

RODGERS, EDWARD
Judge. **PERSONAL:** Born Aug 12, 1927, Pittsburgh, PA; married Gwendolyn; children: 3 Children. **EDUCATION:** Howard U, BA 1949; FL A&M U, LLB 1963. **CAREER:** Palm Beach Co Sch Sys, tchr; asst co Solicitor; Cities of W Palm Beach & Riviera Beach FL, prosecutor ad litem; City of W Palm Beach, judge ad litem; Private Atty; Palm Beach Co Bd, presently co ct judge. **ORGANIZATIONS:** Bd dir Cancer & Soc; mem Masons; mem Visiting Nurses Assn; mem Mental Hlth Assn; mem Big Brothers; mem Legal Aid Soc; mem Palm Beach Co Bar Assn; mem Nat Bar Assn. **MILITARY SERVICE:** USN pharmacist mate 3/c 1944-46. **BUSINESS ADDRESS:** Judge, Palm Beach County Courthouse, Rm 419, West Palm Beach, FL.

RODGERS, HORACE J.
Attorney. **PERSONAL:** Born Dec 10, 1925, Detroit; married Yvonne Payne; children: Kimberly, Pamela. **EDUCATION:** Univ of MI, BA 1948;Univ of MI Sch of Law, JD 1951. **CAREER:** Rodgers & Morgenstein, Attys, partner present; asst US Atty; Fed Housing Adminstrn, reg atty; Standard Mortgage Corp & Bert L Smokler & Co, vp; Premier Mortgage Corp, founder & chmn bd. **ORGANIZATIONS:** Mem adv bd Govt Nat Mortgage Assn; mem Com of Visitors,Univ of MI Law Sch; past adv bd mem Fed Nat Mortgage Assn; Nat Corp for Housing Partnerships; chmn Nat Urban Affairs Com MBA; dir Nat Bank of Southfield; life mem NAACP; Alpha Phi Alpha; mem Sigma Pi Phi; chm Class Officers & Ldrs Council,Univ of MI Alumni Assn; dirUniv of MI Alumni Assn; trustee & v Chancellor Episcopal Diocese of MI. **MILITARY SERVICE:** AUS 1944-46. **BUSINESS ADDRESS:** 26011 Evergreen, Ste 315, Southfield, MI 48076.

RODGERS, JAMES R.
Manager. **PERSONAL:** Born Mar 15, 1947, Little Rock, AR; married Claudia A Dennis. **EDUCATION:** Univ of AR Little Rock, BS Accounting 1973; So MethUniv Grad Sch of Banking, 1976. **CAREER:** Little Rock Regional Airport, mgr 1979-; gen asst mgr 1979; adminstrv asst 1977; First Nat Bank of Little Rock, comm loan officer 1975; br mgr 1973. **ORGANIZATIONS:** Charter mem Coalition of Urban Bankers at Little Rock 1976; charter mem Nat Assn of Urban Bankers 1976; mem Am Assn of Airport Exec 1978; chmn budget rev United Way of Pulaski Co 1977; mem NAACP 1978-; exec bd mem Quapaw Council Boy Scouts 1978-. **HONORS/ACHIEVEMENTS:** Good Turn Awd, Quapaw Council Boy Scouts of Am 1978; Ldrshp Mem Awd, uapaw Council Boy Scouts of Am 1978; Outstanding Young Man Awd 1979; Motivation AwdUniv of AR Pine Bluff 1980. **MILITARY SERVICE:** USAF sgt e-5 1967-71. **BUSINESS ADDRESS:** Little Rock Regional Airport, #1 Airport Dr, Little Rock, AR 72202.

RODGERS, JOHNATHAN A.
Manager, journalist. **PERSONAL:** Born Jan 18, 1946, San Antonio, TX; married Royal Kennedy; children: David. **EDUCATION:** Univ of CA-Berkeley, BA 1967; Stanford Univ, MA 1972. **CAREER:** Newsweek Magazine, assoc editor 1968-73; KCBS-TV, news dir 1978-82, station manager 1982-83; CBS News, exec producer 1983-86. **ORGANIZATIONS:** Alpha Phi Alpha, mem. **MILITARY SERVICE:** US Army, sergeant. **BUSINESS ADDRESS:** Vice Pres/Gen Manager, WBBM-TV/CBS, Inc, 630 Mc Clurg Ct, Chicago, IL 60611.

RODGERS, JOSEPH JAMES, JR.
Educator. **PERSONAL:** Born Nov 22, 1939, Hopewell, VA; son of Joseph J Rodgers Sr and Mary Rodgers. **EDUCATION:** Morehouse Coll, BA 1962; Univ de Grenoble France, Cert d'etudes 1960; Univ of WI, MA 1965; Univ of So CA, PhD 1969. **CAREER:** Los Angeles City Coll, lecturer 1966-67; Univ of So CA, instr 1968-69; Occidental Coll, asst prof 1968-73; VA State Coll, prof & chmn 1970-71; Intl Curriculum Devel Program Phelps-Stokes Fund, reg coord 1975-; Carib-Amer School to Dominican Republic, 1975; Lincoln Univ, chmn, prof 1973-. **ORGANIZATIONS:** Pr tutor Stanley Kramer's son 1966-67; mem African Ethnic Herit Sem 1974, 1975. **HONORS/ACHIEVEMENTS:** Merrill Travel Study Group to Europe 1959-60; W Wilson Fellowship to Harvard 1962-63; NDEA & Oakley Fellow Univ of So CA 1965-69; numerous articles in Maghreb Digest 1966-67; Distinguished Teaching 1974; "African Leadership Ideology" (w/Ukandi Damachi) Praeger 1976; "Sacrificing Qual Lang Learn for Pol Exped" 1977; Lindback Awd Pi Delta Phi Frat Honor Soc; Alpha Mu Gamma Natl Foreign Language Honor Soc; Honored Nominee, CASE Professor of the Year 1989. **BUSINESS ADDRESS:** Professor, Lincoln University, Lincoln University, PA 19352.

RODGERS, ROD AUDRIAN
Performing arts. **PERSONAL:** Born Dec 04, 1937, Cleveland, OH; son of Ernest Rodgers and LaJune Rodgers; divorced; children: Jason Delius, Kalan Windsor, Kaldar Audrian, Jamal Kenmar. **EDUCATION:** Detroit Society of Arts & Crafts; Scholarships at several major professional dance studios in New York City; considers training rcvd as member of family of performing artists operating a theatrical booking and producing agency to be one of the most important aspects of preparation for later profession. **CAREER:** Free lance community arts cnslr, tchr, lecturer; Rod Rodgers Dance Co; fndr-artistic dir - principal choreographer; staged & directed "The Black Cowboys" comm by the Afro-Amer Singing Theatre; choreographed "The Prodigal Sister"; choreograph & act in ABC-TV spec "Like It Is"; choreographed & dir CBS-TV spec "Journey Into Blackness" & Martin Luther King for the Voices Inc Co; Rog Rodgers Dance Co has had ext natl tours & served as cult emmissaries for US, touring Africa, Portugal, & Syria for US Intl Comm Agency; orig dance theatre works incl Percussion Suite, Tangents, Rhythm Ritual, Ictus, Langston Lives, Box 71, Echoes of Ellington, the Legacy, Against Great Odds, In Hi-Rise Shadows, El Encounter. **ORGANIZATIONS:** Rod Rodgers Dance Co celebrated 20th anniversary in 1987-88 via natl & intl tour featuring poets & peacemakers with thematic tributes to Langston Hughes, Martin Luther King & other landmark figures from Black History. **HONORS/ACHIEVEMENTS:** Recipient of an AUDELCO Award; recipient of a John Hay Whitney Fellowship; commissions from numerous state and federal agencies including the NY State Council on the Arts, the Natl Endowment for the Arts, and the Rockefeller Foundation. **BUSINESS ADDRESS:** Artistic Dir/Prin Choreog, The Rod Rodgers Dance Company, 62 East 4th St, New York, NY 10003.

RODGERS, SHIRLEY MARIE
Administrative assistant. **PERSONAL:** Born Dec 29, 1948, Saginaw, MI. **EDUCATION:** MI State Univ, 1966-70, BA 1984. **CAREER:** Blue Cross of MI, serv rep 1970-71; MI State Univ, tutor for athletic dept 1970-71; Lansing School Dist, comm relations liaison 1972, tutor 1972; MI State Univ, prog coord Teach-a-Brother 1972-73; Meridian 4 Theaters, cashier 1973; MI State Univ, prog coord Natl Jr Tennis League 1973; Lansing School Dist, clerk Personnel Dept 1975-76, payroll clerk IV 1976-81, lead sec V to dir of adult & continuing educ 1981-82, unclassified sec to the asst supt for support serv 1982-. **ORGANIZATIONS:** Zeta Pi Beta Sor Inc MI State Univ 1970; mem Lansing Assn of Educ Sectys 1976-82 (held various positions); mem MI Democratic Party 1980-; mem Ingham Co Democratic Party 1980-; mem MSU Black Alumni Inc 1980-84; mem Ingham Co Sch Officers Assn 1981-; mem MSU Alumni Assn 1984; mem Gr Lansing MSU BlackAlumni Chap 1983-84; State Adv Council for Voc Educ 1983-84; mem NAACP 1985; Lansing Comm Coll bd of trustees six yr term beginning 1981; mem State Council for Vocational Educ 1985. **HONORS/ACHIEVEMENTS:** Citizen of the Year in Educ Phi Beta Sigma Frat Inc 1985. **BUSINESS ADDRESS:** Lansing Sch District, 519 W Kalamazoo St, Lansing, MI 48933.

RODGERS, WILLIAM M., JR.
Engineer. **PERSONAL:** Born Dec 22, 1941, Friars Point, MS; son of William M Rodgers, Sr and Leanna Felix (deceased); married Venora Ann Faulkerson; children: William III, Melita Elizabeth, Steven Eric. **EDUCATION:** Tennessee State Univ, BS 1963; Dartmouth Coll, MS 1970. **CAREER:** Natl Institutes of Health, Maryland, mathematician, 1963-64; Electronic Data Processing Div, Honeywell Inc, Virginia, systems analyst, 1964-66; Data Analysis Center of Itek Corp, Virginia, senior scientific programmer, 1966-67; Bell Telephone Labs, New Jersey, technical staff mem, 1968; Exxon Refinery TX, systems analyst 1970-75; Lockheed Elect Co Inc TX, staff engr 1975-77; Xerox Corp, mgr computer graphics requirements & appl 1977-82, proj mgr CAD/CAM acquisition 1982-83, mgr CAD/CAM acquistion & integration 1983-87, CAD/CAM strategy and planning, 1987-88, principal engr 1988-. **ORGANIZATIONS:** Mem Assn of Computing Machinery; Soc for Professional Engrs; Dart-

mouth Soc of Engrs; mem Dartmouth Alumni Orgn; Dartmouth Soc of Engrs Student Exec Comm 1969-70. **HONORS/ACHIEVEMENTS:** Univ Scholar Awd; Univ Counselor Tennessee State Univ 1961-62; Sears Roebuck Scholarship 1959;conducted presentation on large scale CAD/CAM Acquisitions, NCGA, 1989; conducted presentation on CAD/CAM system acquisition and related topics, Univ of Wisconson 1985, Rochester Inst of Tech 1987. **BUSINESS ADDRESS:** Principal Engineer, Advanced Systems Tools for Prduct Devel, Xerox Corp, 800 Phillips Rd, Mail Code 147-59C, Webster, NY 14534.

RODNEY, KARL BASIL
Publisher. **PERSONAL:** Born Nov 29, 1940, Kingston, Jamaica;married Faye A; children: Michele, Denine, Karlisa. **EDUCATION:** Hunter Coll CUNY, BA 1966, MA 1970. **CAREER:** Equitable Life Assurance Soc of US, analyst/project mgr/div mgr 1967-82; New York Carib News, publisher. **ORGANIZATIONS:** Chmn Caribbean Education & Cultural Inst 1976-; dir Martin Luther King Jr Living the Dream Inc NY 1985-. **HONORS/ACHIEVEMENTS:** Community Serv Award 1980; WA Domingo Award 1980; Excellence in Ethic Journalism Harlem Week 1985; Black Journalist Award, Pepsi-Cola NY 1986. **BUSINESS ADDRESS:** Publisher, New York Carib News, 28 West 39th St, New York, NY 10018.

RODNEY, MARTIN HURTUS
Dentist. **PERSONAL:** Born Mar 04, 1909; married Olga Eskimo Hart. **EDUCATION:** Howard Univ Wash DC, Pre-Dental 1934; Meharry Med Coll, DDS Honors 1938. **ORGANIZATIONS:** Mem, Amer Natl Dental Assns; mem Baltimore City Dental Assn; past pres MD Dental Assn; mem Fellow Acad of General Dentistry; mem Chi Delta Mu Fraternity; mem Omega Psi Phi Fraternity; mem, OKU Natl Hon Soc; life mem NAACP; mem Douglass Memorial Church, Baltimore City; bd mem and past pres AARP. **HONORS/ACHIEVEMENTS:** Louise Charlotte Ball Awd Ball Fdn 1938; Guggenheim Dental Scholarship Guggenheim Found 1938-39; Dentist of Yr Awd MD Acad of Gen Dentistry 1973; various articles pub Dental Digest; Gov's Citation State of MD 1975; Recognition Awd MD Dental Soc 1975.

RODRIGUEZ, DORIS L.
Association executive. **PERSONAL:** Born Mar 08, 1927, New York City; married Jules S; children: Anna, Julio, Louis. **EDUCATION:** Queens Coll. **CAREER:** Orginals of Jamaica Inc Urban Ctr, exec dir; Private Nurse, 1948-51; Manhattan Gen Hosp, obstet nurse 1951-58; Litman Dept Store NY, comparison shopper,interpretor 1946-48; Bilingual Adv Dists 27 & 28. **ORGANIZATIONS:** Mem bd dir Youth Consultation Serv 1972-; Concerned Parents Day Care Ctr 1969; Queensboro Council for Soc Welfare 1971; exec bd mem PTA Manlius Mil Acad; 103rd Precinct Comm Council 1969; mem Musical Art Group 1950; asso St Marys Sch for Girls & Convent 1950; adv council for Reimbursable Funds, Dist 27& 28 Citywide; queens Child Guidance Commn; mem founding com Ida B Wills Sch; mem Christ Ch Sag Harbor NY.

RODRIGUEZ, LYNNE ROXANNE
Community activist. **PERSONAL:** Born Nov 05, 1954, Bronx, NY; married Gregory Gilliam (deceased); children: Kendall Gilliam, Heath. **EDUCATION:** Pace Univ, attended 1978-79; John Jay Coll CUNY, attended 1981. **CAREER:** Women Educ the Bronx, founder/consultant 1984-; AFRAM Assoc Inc, consultant 1984-86; People Educating People Inc, exec dir 1985-. **ORGANIZATIONS:** Sec Concourse Jefferson Local Develop Corp 1984; co-founder Gospel Against Apartheid 1985; co-founder Morrisania Kwanzaa Cultural Comm 1985; treasurer Bronx Chap Natl Organization for Women 1986. **HONORS/ACHIEVEMENTS:** Comm Serv Awd Bronx Unity Democratic Club 1984; Comm Serv Awd Council of Baptist Churches 1985; Sponsor Annual African-Amer Day Festival Bronx 1985,86,87; Proclamation to Gov Colon of Puerto Rico from Mayor Koch & Gov Cuomo of New York City & NYS for July 1986 Festival; Elder Hawkins Humanitarian Awd NY Urban League 1987.

ROE, AUDREY R.
Educator. **PERSONAL:** Born Nov 04, 1946, New York, NY; divorced. **EDUCATION:** Fed City Coll, BA 1971. **CAREER:** DHS, commr social servs present; CPB dir Womens Activities; Natl Yough Alternative Proj, cons; Child Defense Fnd, education specialist/child advocate; Natl Welfare Rights Org, spec asst to ex dir 1972; Proj New Hope, ed dir 1972-72; SASA House Sum Prog, consult 1969; Pupil Inctv Prog NAACP, asst dir 1967-68; Natl Womens Pol Caucus, Natl vice chairperson 1973-75; natl Chairperson 1975-77; Natl Commn on Observance of Intl Womens Year, commr; Womans Adv Com to Sec Lbr 1973. **ORGANIZATIONS:** Mvmt for Econ Jstc pres of bd 1974; mem 1965; sec of bd; mem Nat Cncl Negro Womn 1967; chrprsn Juvenile Justice Adv Grp of DC (apptmnt of mayor); fndr DC Wmns Pol Caucus 1972; bd mem rep Womens Task Force; bd mem Womens Campaign Fund; DC Comm Mgmtn. **HONORS/ACHIEVEMENTS:** Org Awd DC Black Econ Union Comm; nom Sojourner Truth Awd 1974. **BUSINESS ADDRESS:** 122 C St NW, Washington, DC 20004.

ROEBUCK, JAMES RANDOLPH, JR.
State representative. **PERSONAL:** Born Feb 12, 1945, Philadephia, PA. **EDUCATION:** VA Union U, BA cum laude 1966;Univ of VA, MA 1969;Univ of VA, PhD 1977. **CAREER:** Drexel Univ, lect history 1970-77, asst prof history 1977-84; City of Philadelphia, leg asst Office of the Mayor 1984-85; Commonwealth of PA, rep in thegen assembly 1985-. **ORGANIZATIONS:** Mem bd dir SE PA Chap Amer Red Cross; mem Southern Home Svcs, Univ of VA Alumni Assoc, Mt Olivet Tabernacle Baptist Church; chmn bd of deacons Foreign Affairs Scholars Prog Wash DC; mem Southern Fellowships Fund Scholar Atlanta GA; mem Mutual Educ Exchange Grant US Office of Educ & Fulbright Prog Wash DC; mem Natl Endowment for the Humanities Grant, German Fed Republic Grant. **HONORS/ACHIEVEMENTS:** United Negro Coll Alumni Recognition Awd 1978; Chapel of the Four Chaplians Legion of Honor Awd 1980; Boy Scouts of Amer, Conestoga Dist Awd of Merit 1983, Silver Beaver Awd 1986; VA Union Univ Alumni Achievement Awd in Public Serv 1986; Natl Assoc for Equal Oppty in Higher Educ Citation 1987. **BUSINESS ADDRESS:** Representative in Gen Assem, Commonwealth of Pennsylvania, 211 South Office Bldg, Harrisburg, PA 17120.

ROEBUCK-HOARD, MARCIA VERONICA
Editor. **PERSONAL:** Born Jan 18, 1950, Colon, Panama;children: Turia. **EDUCATION:** Natl Coll of Educ, BA with Honors 1975, Postgraduate 1975; Book Mfg Seminar, 1979; AAP Book Manufacturing Seminar 1979. **CAREER:** Scott Foresman & Co, editor 1976-79, quality control mgr 1979-80; Ebony Jr Johnson Publication, managing editor 1980-. **ORGANIZATIONS:** Bd of dir Chicago UNICEF, Literacy Volunteers of Chgo; exec council of WTTW; bd of dir, treas Chicago Assn of Black Journalists; mem Alpha Kappa Alpha; IL-Black Writers Conf; Children's Reading Round Table; Minorities in Cable & New Tech; bd dir Metro Chicago Council of Camp Fire. **HONORS/ACHIEVEMENTS:** IL State Scholarship 1975; Natl Endowments of the Arts Fellow 1977; Outstanding Young Women of America 1981.

ROGERS, ALFRED R.
Business executive. **PERSONAL:** Born Apr 07, 1931, Hartford, CT; married Alice. **EDUCATION:** Univ of CT, BA 1953, JD 1963; Amer Inst of Real Estate Appraisal; Rensselar Polytechnic Inst of CT; Univ of MI, Public Utilities Exec Program 1982; Edison Electric Inst, Public Utilities Exec Program. **CAREER:** Bureau of Rights of Ways CT Dept of Transp, chief public utilities sect 1957-64; Hartford Elec Light Co Legal & Real Estate Dept, sr land agent 1964-69; Hartford Electric Light Co, mgr 1970-85; Northeast Utilities Central Region, vice pres 1985-. **ORGANIZATIONS:** Pres & sec Bd of Educ Hartford 1965-73; mem bd dir YMCA 1965-; state treasurer CT Assn of Bds of Educ 1966-69; Gov Advisory Council on Vocational Educ 1967-71; Gov Clean Air Task Force 1967-69; pres NE Hartford Devel Comm 1970-; exec bd Long River Council BSA 1973-; advisory bd Salvation Army 1973-; corporator Newington Childrens Hospital 1975-; pres Better Business of Greater Hartford 1977-79; dir Hartford Hospital 1982-; dir Greater Hartford Chamber of Commerce; trustee Boys Club of Hartford; dir Hartford Public Library; mem AABE; dir Mechanics Savings Bank Hartford; trustee Wadsworth Antheneum Hartford; mem Bradley Field Airport Commn. **HONORS/ACHIEVEMENTS:** Commendation Medal AUS. **MILITARY SERVICE:** AUS 2nd lt 1953-56. **BUSINESS ADDRESS:** VP Central Region, Northeast Utilities, 410 Sheldon St, Hartford, CT 06146.

ROGERS, BERNARD ROUSSEAU
Physician. **PERSONAL:** Born Jan 17, 1944, Winston-Salem, NC; married Linda Hargreaves. **EDUCATION:** NC Central Univ, BS 1966; Meharry Medical Coll, MD 1971. **CAREER:** Youngstown Hosp, intern and resident in pathology 1971-72; Private Practice, physician. **ORGANIZATIONS:** Mem Amer Medical Assoc 1976-, Amer Coll of Radiology 1977-. **BUSINESS ADDRESS:** Central Maine Medical Ctr, 300 Main St, Lewiston, ME 04240.

ROGERS, CHARLES CALVIN
Clergyman, major general. **PERSONAL:** Born Sep 06, 1929, Claremont, WV; son of Clyde Rogers Sr and Helen Rogers; married Margarete Schaefer Rogers, Jan 04, 1956; children: Jackie, Linda Rogers Peters, Barbara Rogers Sapolis. **EDUCATION:** WV St Coll, BS Gen Math; Shippensburg St Coll, MS Vocational Educ Guide; Shippenburg St Coll; Field Arty Sch; AUS Arty & Missile Sch; AUS Command & Gen Staff Coll; AUS War Coll; Ludwigs Maximillian Univ, Munich West Germany, MS Theology. **CAREER:** Over 33 yrs active commd svc; promoted from 2d Lt, 1951 to Major Gen, Sept 1975; dep & Chief of Staff ROTC Hdqrs Training & Doctrine Command, Ft Monroe VA; deputy commandng gen V Corps, Europe 1978-80, deputy chief of staff, Personnel, HQ US Army Europe 1980-84, commanding gen, VII Corps Arty Europe 1973-75; command offcr, 42d Fld Arty Group, Europe 1972-73; dep commander, V Corps Artillers, Europe, 1971-72; staff officer, Readiness Div Washington 1969-70; operations chief, J-3 US Mil Assist Command, Vietnam, Jan-Jul 1969; commanding officer, 1st Infantry Div Arty, Vietnam, Nov, 1969-Feb 1968; commanding officer, 1st Battalion, 2d Brigade, Ft Lewis, Washington, June, 1966-Nov, 1967; S-4, Later. **HONORS/ACHIEVEMENTS:** Recipient of Congressional Medal of Hon; Distinguished Service Medal, Legion of Merit with Oak Leaf Cluster; Distinguished Flying & Cross; Bronze Star Medal With V Device (with 3 Oak Leaf Clusters); Air Medal 10 Awds; Joint Serv Commendation Medal; Army Commendation Medal with 3 Oak Leaf Clusters; Purple Heart; Parachutist Badge; Grand Service Award with Star, Bundes Republic, Germany.

ROGERS, CHARLES D.
Educator. **PERSONAL:** Born Jan 05, 1935, Cherokee, OK. **EDUCATION:** CA State Coll, BA 1963; OH State U, MA 1974. **CAREER:** Johnson C Smith Univ Charlotte NC, asst prof of art educ 1972-; Bennett Coll Greensboro NC, produced Harlem Renaissance 1972; Vanguard Studios Van Nuys CA, commercial designer 1970; Watts Summer Festival Watts CA, co-dir 1967-69; Artcraft Studios Los Angeles, commercial designer 1964-69. **ORGANIZATIONS:** Mem Black Arts Council Los Angels CA; works displayed in numerous oneman group shows. **HONORS/ACHIEVEMENTS:** Author of Prints by Am Negro Artists & Black Aprtists On Art.

ROGERS, DAVID WILLIAM
Broadcast journalist. **PERSONAL:** Born Feb 02, 1959, Cleveland, OH; son of David Louis Rogers and Thelma Elizabeth Grahma. **EDUCATION:** Temple Univ, Philadelphia, PA, journalism, 1983. **CAREER:** WCAU-TV, Philadelphia, PA, news producer, 1979-85; WBBJ-TV, Jackson, TN, news anchor, 1985-86; WTVR-TV, Richmond, VA, 1986-87; WJBK-TV, Detroit, MI, weather anchor, 1987-. **ORGANIZATIONS:** Mem, YMCA, 1979; NAACP, 1989; mem, Natl Assn of Black Journalists, 1985; project coord, United Negro Coll Fund, 1986; mem, Westland Cultural Soc, 1987; mem, Muscular Dystrophy Assn, 1987. **HONORS/ACHIEVEMENTS:** Various articles published in the Philadelphia Inquirer, 1979-81; Award of Outstanding Achievement, United Negro Coll Fund, 1986; Barrier Awareness Award, Amer Assn of Handicapped Persons, 1987; Award of Appreciation, Amer Cancer Soc, 1988. **BUSINESS ADDRESS:** Weather Anchor, WJBK-TV News, PO Box 2000, Southfield, MI 48037.

ROGERS, DECATUR
Educational administrator. **CAREER:** Tennessee State University, School of Engineering, Nashville, TN, dean. **BUSINESS ADDRESS:** Tennessee State University, School of Engineering, 3500 John Merritt Blvd, Nashville, TN 37209. *

ROGERS, DIANNA
Educator. **PERSONAL:** Born in Baltimore, MD; children: Marcus. **EDUCATION:** Univ of MD Eastern Shore, BA 1969; Coppin State Coll, MEd 1972; Johns Hopkins Univ,

MS 1984. **CAREER:** Baltimore City Public Schools, teacher 1969-77, guidance counselor 1978-. **ORGANIZATIONS:** Mem Delta Sigma Theta Sor, NAACP, Black Mental Health Alliance, Inter-Alumni Council of Black Colls & Univs; consultant MD State Dept of Educ; governor'sappointee Baltimore City Foster Care Review Bd 1984-. **HONORS/ACHIEVEMENTS:** Congressional Fellow US House of Representatives 1983. **HOME ADDRESS:** 3700 Glen Ave, Baltimore, MD 21215. **BUSINESS ADDRESS:** Guidance Counselor, Baltimore City Public Schools, 501 Althol Ave, Baltimore, MD 21229.

ROGERS, EARLINE
State representative. **PERSONAL:** Born Dec 20, 1934; daughter of Earl Hicks Smith and Robbie Hicks Smith; married Louis C Rogers Jr, 1955. **EDUCATION:** Indiana University-Northwest; Indiana University, Bloomington IN, BS, 1957, MS, 1971. **CAREER:** Gary Common Council, member, 1980-83; General Assembly, state representative, 1983-86. **ORGANIZATIONS:** Mem, League of Women Voters; mem, NAACP; mem, National Council of Negro Women; mem, Indiana Women's Political Caucus. **BUSINESS ADDRESS:** 3636 West 15th Ave, Gary, IN 46404. *

ROGERS, ELIJAH BABY
Government officer. **PERSONAL:** Born Nov 02, 1939, Orlando, FL; married Jean Doctor. **EDUCATION:** SC State Coll, BA 1962; Univ of SC, 1965; Howard Univ, MSW 1967, MA 1972. **CAREER:** SC Dept of Corrections, suprv soc work serv 1967-69; WA Bur Natl Urban League, asst dir 1968-70; Natl Urban League, sr field rep 1969; Bowie MD, asst mgr, chief of staff 1970-71; Richmond VA, asst city mgr 1972-74; Berkeley CA, asst city mgr, mgr 1974-76; Grant Thornton, asst managing partner 1983-88. **ORGANIZATIONS:** Mem Natl Assn of Soc Workers, Acad of Cert Soc Workers, Incl City Mgmt Assoc, Young Professional Task Force 1971-72, Special Task Force on Minorities 1973-74; chairperson Minority Exec Placement Bd 1975-; mem Comm on Mgmt Labor Rel 1976; adv comm Econ Devel Natl Inst of Advanced Studies 1977; transp steering comm Natl League of Cities 1977; bd of dirs Met Wash Council of Govts 1980; bd of dir Gr Richmond Transit Co 1973-74; mem adv comm School of Soc Work 1972-73; adj prof Urban Studies 1973-74; fellow Intl City Mgmt. **HONORS/ACHIEVEMENTS:** Outstanding Serv Awd Gavel Club #29 1969; "ICMA/COG Minority Internship Prog Dept of Urban Studies Howard Univ Reflect" ICMA Newsletter 1971; "A Career in Municipal Govt for Blacks-Why Not?" Publ Mgmt 1972; "The Minority Exec-Which Way ICMA" Publ Mgmt 1975. **BUSINESS ADDRESS:** Chief Operating Officer, Delon Hampton and Associates, Chartered, 111 Massachusetts Ave NW, Suite 400, Washington, DC 20001.

ROGERS, FREDDIE CLYDE
Mayor. **PERSONAL:** Born Feb 15, 1922, Sumter Co, AL; son of Eddie and Corean; married Pearlie; children: Jocelyn, Belinda, Eric, Karen, Brian, Emily. **EDUCATION:** Fairfield Industrial, grad 1945. **CAREER:** Pyramid Sporting Goods Inc, co-owner; Ad hoc Comm NAACP, business mgr. **ORGANIZATIONS:** Mayor Roosevelt City Vice Pres Roosevelt Voters League; vice pres security investments & past pres Roosevelt Branch NAACP; mem Jefferson Co Mayors Assn; mem Nat League of Cities; mem Black Mayors Assn; mem Civic League; Roosevelt Civic League; Roosevelt Chamber of Commerce. **HONORS/ACHIEVEMENTS:** Sr Citizen Inc Outstanding Citizen Award Alpha Phi Alpha Fraterity; AL Beauticians Citation. **MILITARY SERVICE:** USN 1949. **BUSINESS ADDRESS:** 4543 Bess Super Hwy, Roosevelt City, AL.

ROGERS, GEORGE
Educator. **PERSONAL:** Born Sep 23, 1935, McKeesport, PA; married Emalyn Martin; children: Cheryl Jeanne Mincey, Rhea Avonne, Emalyn Cherea. **EDUCATION:** Langston Univ, BS Educ 1961; Central State Univ, MS Educ 1968; Univ of KS, EdD 1971. **CAREER:** AL A&M Univ, asst prof 1968-71; Wichita State Univ, assoc prof 1971-83; Langston Univ, vice pres academic 1983-86, prof special asst to the president 1986-. **ORGANIZATIONS:** Mem Phi Delta Kappa 1969; mem Alpha Phi Alpha Frat 1970; pres George Rogers & Assocs 1972-; mem Sigma Pi Phi Frat 1986. **HONORS/ACHIEVEMENTS:** Ford Foundation Fellow 1969-70; Honor Graduate Univ of KS 1971; Disting Young Black Amer Incentive Assoc Tallahasse, FL 1972. **MILITARY SERVICE:** AUS SP-3 3 yrs. **HOME ADDRESS:** 10201 C N Finely Rd, Oklahoma City, OK 73120. **BUSINESS ADDRESS:** Prof Special Asst to Pres, Langston University, Langston, OK 73050.

ROGERS, GEORGE, III
Educator. **PERSONAL:** Born Jan 08, 1947, Chicago, IL; son of George Rogers, Jr and Gertrude Ellington Rogers; married Rita F Guhr; children: Tara M, Bret Z. **EDUCATION:** Wilson City Coll, AA 1967; Bethel Coll, BS 1969; Wichita State Univ, MEd 1969-72; Univ of AR, PhD Candidate 1979-. **CAREER:** Bethel College, track coach 1969, dir of athletics, asst to coach, assoc prof of phys ed. **ORGANIZATIONS:** Mem Newton Jaycee's 1970; bd of dir FARM House (Alcohol & Drug Rehabilitation) 1975; mem adv bd First Step Industries; president, USD #373 School Board, 1987-; pres, Harvey County Rural Water District #3, 1987-. **HONORS/ACHIEVEMENTS:** Coach of Yr NAIA Area 3 Track Coach 1975; grad asst Track Coach Univ of AR 1979. **HOME ADDRESS:** 15 Royer West Drive, Newton, KS 67114. **BUSINESS ADDRESS:** Director/Associate Professor, Bethel Coll, Hwy, K 15 & 27th St, North Newton, KS 67117.

ROGERS, JAMES E.
Public administrator. **PERSONAL:** Born Jun 11, 1935, Warren, OH. **EDUCATION:** Pacific Coll, BA, LA 1966; Case Western Res U, MSLS 1972; Case Western Res U, PhD 1976. **CAREER:** So Area Boys Club of Am LA, phy educ dir 1958-59; LA Times Boys Club, social recreation dir 1959-60; Cath Youth Orgn LA, social group worker 1960-61; Watts Comm Cntr, CYO, LA, Ca, br exec 1961-65; So Area Boys Club of Am LA, asst exec dir 1965-67; State Assemblyman LA , adminstrv asst 1967-68; Orachard Place Des Moines, cottage coordinator 1969-70; 21st Congressional Dist Caucus Cleveland, exec dir 1970-71; Cleveland Public Library Cleveland, dir of urban serv 1971-76; East Cleveland Public Library, dir 1977-; Kent StateUniv Syracuse U, adjunct pro. **ORGANIZATIONS:** Professional memberships American Lib Assoc; American Society for Information Science; oh Lib Assoc; mem Froniters Internat; Cleveland Urban Forum; Certified Professional Boys Club Worker; grad senator Case Western ResUniv Library Sch; adjunct faculty extended learning prog OH U; local dir for Neighborhood Information Ctr Proj; chmn membership com Urban League of Cleveland 1972; Spanish Cultura Com, OH State Reformatory; Academic Master Plan Com; Cleveland State U; Cleveland Urban League; Afro-am Cultural Soc; Library Tech Adv Com of Cuyahoga Coll; Lee-harvard Comm Assn; 21st Congressional Dist Caucus Selected for Buckeye Boys State Clarence Hyde Post 278 1952; chmn Nat Foot Health Wk 1972. **HONORS/ACHIEVEMENTS:** Cited twice in Congressional Record; Lubizol Found Award Sch of Library Information Science 1972. **MILITARY SERVICE:** USMC. **BUSINESS ADDRESS:** 14101 Euclid Ave E, Cleveland, OH 44112.

ROGERS, JIMMY
Professional athlete. **PERSONAL:** Born Jun 29, 1955, Earle, AR; married Rhonda; children: Jimmy Jr. **EDUCATION:** OK Univ, Journalism, Public Rel. **CAREER:** New Orleans Saints, wide receiver 1979-. **HONORS/ACHIEVEMENTS:** Led Saints in rushing with 366 yards 1980.

ROGERS, JOHN W.
City official. **PERSONAL:** Born Sep 03, 1918, Knoxville, TN; divorced; children: John Jr. **EDUCATION:** Chicago Tchr Coll, BA 1941;Univ of Chicago, JD 1948. **CAREER:** Circuit Ct of Cook Co, judge 1976-. **ORGANIZATIONS:** Mem bd trustees Met Sanitary Dist of Greater Chicago; treas gen counsel Sivart Mortgage Co Chicago Admitted to IL Bar 1948; admitted to practice US Supreme Ct mem bd dir Chicago Council on Human Relations Ada S Mckinley Comm. **MILITARY SERVICE:** 2nd lt 99th Pursuit Squadron Ww Ii. **BUSINESS ADDRESS:** Juvenile Court, 1100 S Hamilton, Chicago, IL 60612.

ROGERS, LAWRENCE F.
Association executive. **PERSONAL:** Born Mar 18, 1937, Nashville; divorced; children: Robin. **EDUCATION:** Fisk U, BA 1967. **CAREER:** Environ Planning & Mgmt Prof, lic gen contr, cons; World Book Ency, salesman; Fish U, dir alumni fund 1969-70; Metro Action Commn, field rep 1969-70; JW Thompson Adv Agcy NYC, acct exec 1967-68. **ORGANIZATIONS:** Mem Middle TN Bus Assn; NAACP; life mem Kappa Alpha Psi 1st black appointed Davidson Co Election Commn 1971-73 reg 10000 in one day to vote; IL NG 1960-66.

ROGERS, MICHAEL CHARLES
Legal administrator. **PERSONAL:** Born Nov 12, 1949, Atlanta, GA. **EDUCATION:** Clark Coll, BA 1967-70; Univ of Nice France, Cert 1970-71; Univ of MI, MA Publ Policy 1971-73; Georgetown Univ Law Ctr, JD 1982. **CAREER:** Ann Arbor MI, asst city admin 1971-76; Intl City Mgmt Assoc asst to exec dir 1976-80; Financial Oversight Comm, assoc dir 1980-81; Washington Convention Ctr, dep gen mgr 1981-. **ORGANIZATIONS:** Mem Intl City Mgmt Assoc 1971-, Amer Soc of Publ Admin 1976-; vice pres Clark Coll Alumni Assoc 1979-85; mem Intl Assoc of Auditorium Mgrs 1981-; vpDC Urban Mgmt Assoc 1984-85; mem Amer Bar Assoc 1984, Natl Bar Assoc 1984. **BUSINESS ADDRESS:** Deputy General Manager, Washington Convention Center, 900 9th St NW, Washington, DC 20001.

ROGERS, NORMAN
Physician, educator. **PERSONAL:** Born Oct 14, 1931, Cairo, GA; married Juanita L Slack; children: Saundra, Norman III, Robert. **EDUCATION:** A&M U, BS 1957; Howard U, MS 1959; HowardUniv Coll of Med, MD 1963. **CAREER:** Howard Univ, clinical asso prof 1985; private practice of surgery & teaching 1969-; Tumor Clinic Howard Univ Dept of Surgery Freedmen's Hosp, clinical cancer fellow 1968-69; Howard Univ Freedmen's Hosp, surg resd 1964-68; Howard Univ Coll of Med, instr surgery 1968; Howard Univ Coll of Med, asst prof surgery 1971-; VA Hosp, vis prof 1973. **ORGANIZATIONS:** Nat Med Assn 1968; AMA 1968; Medico-Chirurgical Soc of DC 1968; DC Med Soc 1968; Diplomate Am Bd of Surgery 1969; fellow Am Coll of Surgeons 1971; The Assn of Acad Surgery 1972; fellow Intl Coll of Surgeons 1974; Soc of Sigmz Xi 1959; Beta Kappa Chi 1959. **HONORS/ACHIEVEMENTS:** Recpt Charles R Drew Nat Med Assn Fundamental Forum Award 1967; Congressional Citation for Breat Cancer Proj 1974; Who's Who in the E 1977; Dictionary of Intl Biography Vol XV 1978-79; Good Conduct Medal; United Natl Medal; Korean Serv Medal; Nat Def Serv Medal. **MILITARY SERVICE:** USAF s/sgt 1951-55; USPHS lt comdr 1965-66. **BUSINESS ADDRESS:** 601 Eastern Ave NE, Ste 101, Washington, DC 20019.

ROGERS, OSCAR ALLAN, JR.
College president. **PERSONAL:** Born Sep 10, 1928, Natchez, MS; married Ethel Lee Lewis; children: Christopher, Christian, Christoff. **EDUCATION:** Tougaloo Coll, AB (Summa Cum Laude) 1950; Harvard Divinity Sch, STB 1953; Harvard Univ, MAT 1954; Univ of AR, EdD 1960; Univ of Washington, Postdoctoral study 1968-69. **CAREER:** Natchez Jr Coll, dean/registrar 1954-56; AR Baptist Coll, pres 1956-59; Jackson State Univ, dean of students/prof of social science 1960-69, dean of the grad school 1969-84; Claflin Coll, pres. **ORGANIZATIONS:** Pastor Bolton-Edward United Methodist Church 1961-84; dir Orangeburg Chamber of Commerce 1987-90. **HONORS/ACHIEVEMENTS:** "My Mother Cooked My Way Through Harvard With These Creole Recipes," 1972; "Mississippi, The View From Tougaloo," 1979. **MILITARY SERVICE:** USN stm 3/c 1946-47. **BUSINESS ADDRESS:** President, Claflin Coll, College Ave NE, Orangeburg, SC 29115.

ROGERS, PEGGY J.
Educator. **PERSONAL:** Born Aug 19, 1951, Starkville, MS; son of David Rogers and Irene Jones Rogers. **EDUCATION:** Rust Coll, Holly Spring, MS, BS, 1969-73; MS State Univ, State Coll, MS, MA, 1975; MS State Univ, State Coll, MS, Spec, 1988. **CAREER:** Clay County Schools, West Point, MS, counselor, 1984-84; Oktibbeh County Schools, Starkville, MS, supt of educ, 1987; E Jasper Schools, Heidelberg, MS, curriculum coord, 1988; Oktibbeha County Schools, Starkville, MS, counselor, teacher. **HONORS/ACHIEVEMENTS:** NAACP; MS Assn for Educator; Phi Delta Kappa; Delta Sigma Theta; MS/Natl Assn of School Administrators; Teacher of the Year, Clay County Teacher Assn, vice chmn of the Democratic Party Oktibbeha County; approved, MTAI, MPAI, MPPI for the MS State Dept of Educ; consultant for Educ Equity Technical Assistance. **BUSINESS ADDRESS:** Curriculum Dir, E Jasper Consolidated School Dist, PO Drawer E, Heidelberg, MS.

ROGERS, TIMMIE
Entertainer, comedian, dancer, singer, composer. **PERSONAL:** Born in Detroit, MI; married Barbara; children: Joy, Gaye. **CAREER:** CBS TV Network, Sugar Hill Times 1948; dancer, singer, composer. **HONORS/ACHIEVEMENTS:** Launched first all black show; made TV apperances Sammy Davis, Jr, Melba Moore, Jackie Gleason, Ed- Sullivan, Merv Griffin, Johnny Carson; appeared in Las Vegas, Can & London, Vietnam, NY & Miami; composer, Nat King Cole, Tommy Dorsey, Sarah Vaughan, Appeared in Movin "Sparkle" 1976;

Referred to as dean of black comedians, has inspired such black entertainers as Nipsey Russell, Dick Gregory, Redd Foxx, Slappy White.

ROGERS-BELL, MAMIE LEE
Public relations/development. **PERSONAL:** Born Sep 10, 1954, Alston, GA; married Emery Argene Bell Jr; children: Latonya Renee, Emery Argene III. **EDUCATION:** Attended, Marsh-Draughon Coll 1972-74, Amer Inst of Banking 1980. **CAREER:** First Natl Bank of Atlanta, money mgmt teller 1979-80; Parks Jackson & Howell PC, legal sec 1980-83; Midtown Atlanta YWCA, branch mgr 1983-85; Development Asst, 1985-. **ORGANIZATIONS:** Registrar Fulton County Voter Registration; salute comm Salute to Women of Achievement 1987. **HONORS/ACHIEVEMENTS:** Woman of Achievement Honoree Midtown YWCA 1985. **BUSINESS ADDRESS:** Financial Develop Assistant, YWCA of Greater Atlanta, 100 Edgewood Ave NE, Atlanta, GA 30303.

ROGERS-GRUNDY, ETHEL W.
Insurance company executive. **PERSONAL:** Born Dec 03, 1938, Macclesfield, NC; daughter of Russell Wooten and Martha Pitt Wooten; married Sherman Grundy; children: Duane A Rogers, Angela S. **EDUCATION:** St Augustines Coll, BA 1960; Temple Univ, MEd 1970; Catholic Univ of Amer, additional study; Univ of MD. **CAREER:** DC Bd of Educ, coordinator office; Fed City Coll Washington, adj prof 1975; Woodson St HS, chmn, bus dept 1972-74; Johnston Co Sch Smithfield NC, asst dir of headstart 1966-67; St Augustines Coll NC, asst dean of students 1965-66. **ORGANIZATIONS:** Mem Eastern Bus Tchr Assn; Nat Bus Educ Assn; DC Bus Educ Assn; charter pres Prince Georges Co Alumnae Chap Delta Sigma Theta Inc; pres MD Council of Deltas; sec St Augustines Coll Nat Alumni Assn; mem bd of dir Lung Assn of So MN Inc; mem Alpha Zeta Chap Delta Phi Epsilon; Prince Georges Co MD NAACP; Womens Polit Caucas of Prince Georges Co MD; Pan Hellenic Council of Prince Georges Co MD; elected to Membership in Delta Phi Epsilon 1969. **HONORS/ACHIEVEMENTS:** Female Business Leader of the Year, Maryland Chamber of Commerce, 1976; Female Business Leader of the Year, Franklin Life Insurance Co, 1981, 1983. **HOME ADDRESS:** 11111 Lochton St, Upper Marlboro, MD 20772.

ROGERS-LOMAX, ALICE FAYE
Physician, educator. **PERSONAL:** Born Jan 20, 1950, Darlington, SC; daughter of James Rogers and Alice McCall Rogers; married Michael W Lomax, May 05, 1979; children: Lauren, Whitney. **EDUCATION:** Holy Family Coll, BA 1972; Philadelphia Coll of Osteopathic Med, DO 1976; HPCOM, Pediatric Residency 1977-79. **CAREER:** Philadelphia Coll of Osteopathic Medicine, asst prof pediatrics 1979-80; NY Coll of Osteopathic Medicine, visiting lecturer 1980; Philadelphia Coll of Osteopathic Medicine, chmn div ambulatory pediatrics 1981-; School of Nursing of the Univ of PA; adjunct clinical preceptor 1981-; Osteopathic Medical Center of Philadelphia, chmn div of ambulatory pediatrics 1981-89; Lomax Medical Associates, Philadelphia PA, private pediatric practice 1989. **ORGANIZATIONS:** Mem Amer Osteopathic Assn 1976-, Amer Coll of Osteopathic Ped 1977-, PA Osteopathic Med Soc 1979-, Student Admissions Comm 1982-, Philadelphia Pediatrics Soc 1983-, Ambulatory Pediatrics Assn 1983-, Student Admissions Comm, Osteopathic Medical Center 1982-86, Medical Soc of Eastern Pennsylvania 1987-. **HONORS/ACHIEVEMENTS:** Mem Beta Beta Beta Natl Biology Honor Soc 1972; Legion of Honor Mem Chapel of the Four Chaplains Philadelphia 1983. **BUSINESS ADDRESS:** Lomax Medical Associates, 300 N 52nd St, Philadelphia, PA 19139.

ROHADFOX, RONALD OTTO
Business executive. **PERSONAL:** Born Mar 12, 1935, Syracuse, NY; married Barbara; children: Renwick, Rodderick, Reginald, Rebecca. **EDUCATION:** IN Inst of Tech, BSCE 1961; Woodbury Univ, MBA 1980; Century Univ, PhD 1984. **CAREER:** Genge Comm Cons, vice pres; Baxtor Labs, engr; Construction Control Serv Corp, pres. **ORGANIZATIONS:** Mem Kappa Alpha Psi 1960, Amer Soc of Civil Engrs 1969, Amer Public Works Assoc 1977, Soc for Mktg Professional Serv 1982; assoc mem Urban Land Inst 1983;mem Natl Assoc of Minority Contractors 1985. **HONORS/ACHIEVEMENTS:** One of the Top 100 Black Successful Businessmen Black Enterprise Mag 1974; mem Republican Inner Circle 1985. **BUSINESS ADDRESS:** President, Construction Control Serv Corp, 115 W Main St, Durham, NC 27701.

ROHR, LEONARD CARL
Retired business executive. **PERSONAL:** Born Sep 29, 1921, Kimball, WV; son of David Rohr and Irma Rohr; married Katherine Whitman; children: Ronald, Carol, Steven. **EDUCATION:** Univ Denver, BS, ME 1950. **CAREER:** Leonard C Rohr Assocs Consulting Mech Engr, owner 1962-87; Koebig & Koebig Inc, chf mech engr 1957-62; Co Los Angeles, commr mech bd. **ORGANIZATIONS:** Mem Am Soc Mech Engr; Am Soc Heating Refrigeration & Air Conditioning Engr. Consulting Engineers. **HONORS/ACHIEVEMENTS:** Silver Star. **MILITARY SERVICE:** AUS 1st lt 1942-46.

ROKER, ROXIE
Actress. **PERSONAL:** Born Aug 28, Miami, FL; married Sy Kravitz; children: Leonard. **EDUCATION:** Dramatic Arts Howard U, BA; Shakespeare Inst Stratford on Avon, Stuied Shakespearean & Elizabethan Drama. **CAREER:** The Jefferson CBS, actress starring as helen willis; The River Niger, stage performance; The Blacks; Other TV Appearances, roots, kojak; coord of pub serv announcements NBC; Performed w/Negro Ensemble Co; Appeared in Ododo & Rosalee Pritchett. **ORGANIZATIONS:** Recpt Obie Award for "River Niger" 1973; Tony Awar Nomination.

ROLAND, BENAUTRICE, JR.
Staff supervisor. **PERSONAL:** Born Dec 11, 1945, Detroit, MI; married Brenda Thornton; children: Michele S, Michael L. **EDUCATION:** Univ of Detroit (cum laude), BS Finance 1972; Wharton Grad SchUniv of PA, MBA Finance 1974. **CAREER:** MI Bell Tele Co, staff supr 1979-; Ford Motor Co, financial analyst 1975-79; Morgan Guaranty Trust of NY, eurocurrency trader 1974-75. **ORGANIZATIONS:** Bd of dirsUniv of PA Alumni Club of MI; co-chmn Secondary Sch ComUniv of PA Alumni Club of MI. **MILITARY SERVICE:** USAF sgt 1964-67. **BUSINESS ADDRESS:** 444 Michigan Ave, Detroit, MI 48226.

ROLAND, JOHNNY E.
Businessman. **PERSONAL:** Born May 21, 1943, Corpus Christi, TX; son of Vernon L Roland and Willie Mae Roland; children: Johnny Jr, James E, Cynnamon Aisha. **EDUCATION:** Univ of MO, BS Bus Admin, Personnel Mgmt 1966. **CAREER:** St Louis Football Cardinals, player 1966-72; NY Giants, player 1973; Green Bay Packers, asst coach spec assignments 1974; Univ of Notre Dame Wide Receivers, asst coach 1975; Philadelphia Eagles Runnings Backs, asst coach 1976-78; Chicago Bears Running Backs, asst coach 1983-; Bronco Broadcasting Co Inc KIRL-AM Radio, pres and owner 1979-. **ORGANIZATIONS:** Mem Kappa Alpha Psi, Natl Football League Players Assn, Natl Football League Alumni St Louis Chap, Univ of MO Alumni Assn; bd mem United Way 1980-83; bd mem St Louis Children's Hospital Devel Fund 1980-83; St Louis Advertising Club 1979; Kiwanis Club 1970-73. **HONORS/ACHIEVEMENTS:** 1st black capt Univ of MO Football team 1965; mem TX Football Hall of Fame; Running Back All State TX 1960; Parade HS All Amer Team 1960; All Big Eight 1962, 1964-65; Walter Camp, Sporting News, AP, UPI, Kodak Coll All Amer 1965; NFL Pro Bowl 1966,67; NFL Rookie of the Year 1966; St Louis Cardinals Rookie of the Year 1966; St Louis Cardinals MVP 1967. **BUSINESS ADDRESS:** Coach, Chicago Bears, 250 N Washington Rd, Lake Forest, IL 60061.

ROLARK, CALVIN W.
Editor, publisher. **PERSONAL:** Born May 18, 1927, Texarkana, TX; son of Ross and Beatrice; married Wilhelmina; children: Calvin W Rolark, Jr, Denise Rolark Barnes. **EDUCATION:** Prairie View Coll, attended 1947; TN State Univ; MI State Univ; Cornell Univ. **CAREER:** Washington Informer Newspaper, verbal ed, publisher 1985; United Black Fund, founder, pres 1969-; Delegate Agency Coord Br United Planning Org, chief 1973-74; United Planning Org, contract coord 1971-73; Mst Police Dept Recruiting, consult 1969-70; Home Office Inspector Richmond Beneficial Ins Co, chief 1964-69; The New Observer Newspaper Co, ed 1961-64; Mutual United of Omaha, life ins underwriter 1960-61; Richmond Beneficial Life Ins Co, asst agency dir 1953-60; Home Ofc Inspector Universal Life Ins Co, chief 1948-50. **ORGANIZATIONS:** Pres Capital Press Club; chmn Natl Black Media Found; mem Professional Standard Review Org; pres Washington Highland Civic Assn; pres Anacostia Branch Amer Cancer Soc; pres bd mem, sec Washington Planning & Housing Assn; bd mem Frederick Douglas Comm Center; mem Officer Numerous Other Professional & Civic Orgs. **HONORS/ACHIEVEMENTS:** Recipient Citizen of Yr DC Federation of Civic Assn; Writer of Yr The Capitol Press Club 1969; Five Yr Serv Award Amer Cancer Soc; Federation of Civic Assn NAACP Award; Numerous Other Awards & Citations; co-author "Know Your DC Government". **MILITARY SERVICE:** US Airborn Infantry Regiment s/sgt 1950-52. **BUSINESS ADDRESS:** 1012 14th St NW, Washington, DC 20005.

ROLARK, M. WILHELMINA (NEE JACKSON)
Attorney. **PERSONAL:** Born Sep 27, Portsmouth; married Calvin W. **EDUCATION:** Howard U, AB 1936, MA 1938; Terrell Law Sch, LLB 1944. **CAREER:** Pvt practice 1947-; Elected to DC City Counc Dem Ward 8, mem 4 yr; Nat Assn Black Wmn Attorneys Inc, pres 1973-; Nat Bar Assn, asst sec; DC Human Rights Commn, commr. **ORGANIZATIONS:** Bd mem Legal Aid Aoc; gen counsel United Black Fund; mem Wash & DC Bar Assn Vice Pres DC Bi-Centennial Assembly; bd mem Wash Organization Wmn; Early Childhood Devel Cntr; DC Bd of Labor Rels. **HONORS/ACHIEVEMENTS:** Distinguished Serv Award Phyllis Wheatley 1966; Citation United Black Fund; Grassroots Award.

ROLLE, ALBERT EUSTACE
Surgeon. **PERSONAL:** Born Aug 03, 1935, Miami, FL; son of Jerod and Bessie Rolle; married Josephine James; children: Allyson, Jonathan. **EDUCATION:** FL A&M Univ, AB 1954; Univ of Pittsburgh, BS 1960; Univ of Pittsburgh Sch of Med, MD 1965. **CAREER:** Georgetown Univ Med Ctr, clin asst prof of surgery 1972-; DC Board Police/Fire Surgeons, surgeon 1973-78; Capital Area Permanent Med Group, general surgeon 1985. **ORGANIZATIONS:** Fellow Amer Coll of Surgeons 1973-; mem DC Med Soc 1970-; mem Washington Acad Surgery 1975-; past master Fellowship Lodge 26, F & AM, PHA 1973-; mem Kappa Alpha Psi Frat 1952-. **HONORS/ACHIEVEMENTS:** Outstanding Performance Award Metro Police Dept Bd of Police Surgeons 1977; Physicians Recognition Award Amer Med Assn 1972. **MILITARY SERVICE:** USAFR lt col Med Corps. **BUSINESS ADDRESS:** Surgeon, Kaiser Permanente Medical Group, 4200 Wisconsin Ave NW, Washington, DC 20016.

ROLLE, ESTHER
Actress. **PERSONAL:** Born Nov 08, Pompano Beach, FL. **EDUCATION:** Attended, Spellman Coll, Hunter Coll, New School for Social Rsch. **CAREER:** "The Blacks", off-broadway debut 1962; "God is a (Guess What?)", London stage debut 1969; Shogala Obola Dance Co, dancer; numerous stage appearances; toured Australia/New Zealand with Black Nativity/US w/Purlie; numerous films; "Maude",TV actress leading role; "Good Times", starred in own series; performed in several stage productions including, Nevis Mountain Dew, Dame Lorraine, The River Niger, Member of the Wedding, A Raisin in the Sun; TV guest star on, Flamingo Road, Up and Coming, Darkroom, The New Odd Couple, Love Boat, Fantasy Island; performed one woman show "Ain't I A Women"; feature films include, "Petaluma Pride", "A Fools Dance", "Grand Baby". **ORGANIZATIONS:** Grand marshall Cherry Blossom Festival Washington 1975; hon chmn President's Comm on Employment of Handicapped. **HONORS/ACHIEVEMENTS:** Hon Chmn Pres's Com on Employment of Handicapped; Woman of the Yr 3rd World Sisterhood 1976; NAACP Image Awd; first Black woman to serve as Grand Marshall of the Annual Cherry Blossom Festival in Washington DC; Emmy Awd 1979; Third Avenue renamed Esther Rolle Blvd. **BUSINESS ADDRESS:** c/o Traid Artist Inc, 10100 Santa Monica Blvd, Los Angeles, CA 90067.

ROLLINS, AVON WILLIAM, SR.
City official. **PERSONAL:** Born Sep 16, 1941, Knoxville, TN; son of Ralph Kershaw and Josephine Rollins Lee; married Sheryl Clark, Sep 28, 1974; children: Avon Jr, Avondria F. **EDUCATION:** Knoxville Coll; Univ of TN. **CAREER:** Student Nonviolent Coord Comm, natl exec; Southern Christian Leadership Conf, spec asst; TN Valley Authority, mgr minority econ devel. **ORGANIZATIONS:** One of co-founders, former natl exec SNCC Raleigh NC 1960; asst to the late Rev Dr Martin Luther King Jr; mem, bd of dir Mgmt Comm Knoxville Intl Enrgy Exposition 1982; chmn Magnolia Fed Savings & Loan Assoc; adv, former chmn & founder TVA Employees Minority Investment Forum, mem Chancellors Assoc The Univ of TN, mem Pres Round Table Knoxville Coll; chmn emeritus, former chmn of bd, founder, Greater Knoxville Minority Business Bureau Inc; former chmn, pres Knoxville Comm Coop, former mem Natl Rural Cable TV Task Force; co-founder Greater Knoxville Urban League; co-founder, former mem of bd of dir Knoxville Oppty Indust Ctr Inc. **HONORS/ACHIEVEMENTS:** Developed & produced periodical TV prog "Insight" & radio prog "In Touch-Insight-The Black Experience"; Natl Bus League Awd; Booker T Washington Awd forLeadership & Outstanding Serv Achievment Awd in the Field of Commmunity Serv pres-

ented by the Ancient Egyptian Arabic Order Noboes of the Mystic Shrine of North & South Amer Knoxville Coll Awd for Outstanding Contrib & Serv to the Coll; TN Black Caucus of State Legislators Awd; Authored numerous articles & poems on the civil rights struggle; Most recent publ are "Minority Econ Devel/Problems & Oppty", "The Black Consumer-The Myth & Reality", "The State of the Black Economy 1973", "Why We Can't Wait", "The State of TN Black Econ 1984"; "The State of Tennessee Black Economy 1986"; honored with resolution by the TN House of Reps with the Senate concurring during 94th Genl Assembly for untiring Service to Humanity. **BUSINESS ADDRESS:** Manager, TVA OCH 3B4B-K, Knoxville, TN 37902.

ROLLINS, CAL EDWARD
Research specialist, teacher. **PERSONAL:** Born Aug 01, 1936, Tucson, AZ; married Inge S; children: Birgit Ruhiyyih, Vanessa Bahiyyih. **EDUCATION:** Univ of AZ, BA;Univ of NM, MA 1973. **CAREER:** US Commission on Civil Rights, cvl rghts analyst rsrch 1977; Bur of Indian Affrs, humanities chmn 1970-77; Bur of Indian Affrs, lang arts supv 1965-70; Bur of Indian Affrs, tchr; Bur of Indian affrs, consult 1963-77. **ORGANIZATIONS:** Poet in residence NM Arts Commn Nat Endow for the Arts 1975-77. **HONORS/ACHIEVEMENTS:** Outstanding Contribution to Black Comm, Albuquerque Black Econ Leg 1976.

ROLLINS, ETHEL EUGENIA
Social worker. **PERSONAL:** Born Feb 16, 1932, Paris, TX; daughter of Elisha Grant and Julia Grant; married Edward C Rollins; children: Vyla LeJeune, Rojeune Bali. **EDUCATION:** Jarvis Christian Coll, BA 1954; Univ of Pittsburgh, MSW 1958. **CAREER:** Dayton Children Psych Hosp & Child Guidance Clinic, psych soc worker 1958-62; Family & Childrens Serv Assoc Dayton, psych soc worker 1964-65; Denver Cty Publ School Psych Svc, school social worker 1965-68; Denver Univ, assoc prof soc work 1975-80; Ft Logan Mental Health Ctr Denver, psych soc worker 1972-84. **ORGANIZATIONS:** Mem CO Christian Home Bd, CO Christian Home for Children Denver 1970-75; human svcs, adv bd Metro State Coll Denver 1979-84; week of compassion comm Christian Ch Disciples of Christ Indianapolis 1975-80; adv bd Mother to Mother Ministry 1978-80; bd & comm mem Habitat for Humanity 1979-80; leg & social concerns CO Council of Church 1980-82; sec CO Council of Churches 1981-82; chmn Outreach Christian Church Disciples of Christ CO, WY Reg Outreach on Reg Needs 1982-83; activist Peace/Justice Movement/Nuclear Freeze Movement 1982-84. **HONORS/ACHIEVEMENTS:** Hon Awd for Leadership State Fair of TX 4-H Club 1949; author "Changing Trends in Adoption" Natl Conf Social Welfare 1971; Rojeune, Edward & Ethel appeared as family on KCNC NBC Affil Denver CO 1983 discussing film "The Day After" results of nuclear war. **BUSINESS ADDRESS:** Psychiatric Social Worker, Ft Logan Mental Health Ctr, 3520 W Oxford Ave, Denver, CO 80236.

ROLLINS, HOWARD E., JR.
Actor. **PERSONAL:** Born Oct 17, 1950, Baltimore, MD; son of Howard E Rollins and Ruth Rollins. **EDUCATION:** Towson State University, Baltimore, MD. **CAREER:** Cast member of "Our Street" public television series, 1969-73; actor in numerous other plays, films, and television productions. **HONORS/ACHIEVEMENTS:** Actor in Public Broadcasting System production of "Eliza: Our Story," 1975; actor in films "Ragtime," 1981, and "A Soldier's Story," 1984; actor in theatrical productions of "Streamers," "Medal of Honor Rag," "G R Point," and "The Mighty Gents"; appeared in television productions of "King," "Roots: The Next Generation," "My Old Man," and "Doctor's Story.". **BUSINESS ADDRESS:** c/o National Broadcasting Co, Inc, 30 Rockefeller Plaza, New York, NY 10020. *

ROLLINS, LEE OWEN
Business executive. **PERSONAL:** Born Dec 22, 1938, Kansas City, KS; married Rosalie D; children: Lori, Linda, Larry, Lonny, Lyle. **EDUCATION:** Univ of NE, psychology 1956-63. **CAREER:** San Diego Gas & Elec, mgr employment 1979-, employment rep 1968-78, license negotiator 1966-68; Flintkote Co Los Angeles CA, marketing rep 1963-66. **ORGANIZATIONS:** Bd mem Western Coll Placement Assn 1975-80; chmn Affirmative Action Com WCPA 1975-78; vice pres campus relations Soc for Advancement of Mgmt 1979-; vice pres transportation SD Jr C of C 1970-74; dir Southeast Rotary 1974-79; dir Amigos del Ser 1979-80; Outstanding Kappa Man ETA ChapUniv of NE 1960. **HONORS/ACHIEVEMENTS:** Community Serv Award Nat Alliance of Businessmen 1968; Outstanding Serv Award Urban League 1979. **BUSINESS ADDRESS:** 101 Ash St, San Diego, CA 92101.

ROLLINS, RICHARD ALBERT
Educator. **PERSONAL:** Born Nov 30, 1927, Philadelphia, PA; married Audrey J King. **EDUCATION:** Lincoln Univ, AB 1952; Union Theological Seminary, MDiv 1955; Boston Univ School of Theology, STM 1960; Claremont School of Theology, RelD 1969. **CAREER:** Bishop Coll, chmn div of rel 1958-67, assoc dean/admin 1969-70, dean of the college 1970-77, vice pres for pme/prof of religion 1977-83, exec asst to pres dean of chapel 1983-. **ORGANIZATIONS:** Mem Goals for Dallas, Natl Urban League, NAACP, Natl Campus Ministry Assoc, Acad of Religion, TX Alcohol/Narcotics Assoc; bd of dirs Dallas YMCA; chmnMoorland Branch YMCA 1969-85. **HONORS/ACHIEVEMENTS:** Danforth Foundation Teacher Awd 1960-62; Ford Foundation Fellowship Awd 1967; Dallas Citizenship Awd Radio Station KNOK 1970. **MILITARY SERVICE:** AUS corpl 2 yrs. **HOME ADDRESS:** 630 Woodacre Dr, Dallas, TX 75241. **BUSINESS ADDRESS:** Exec Asst to the President, Bishop Coll, 3837 Simpson Stuart Rd, Dallas, TX 75241.

ROLLINS, SONNY See ROLLINS, WALTER THEODORE

ROLLINS, WALTER THEODORE (SONNY ROLLINS)
Composer, musician. **PERSONAL:** Born Sep 07, 1930, New York City, NY; married Lucille. **CAREER:** Recording career started in 1949, involved in modern jazz movement; now into more electric current sounds; travelling & rec band. **HONORS/ACHIEVEMENTS:** Numerous trade mag awds abroad & in US; Guggenheim Fellow 1972; Hall of Fame Downbeat Mag. **BUSINESS ADDRESS:** 310 Greenwich St, New York, NY 10013.

ROMAR, LORENZO ANTHONY
Professional athlete. **PERSONAL:** Born Nov 13, 1958, Compton, CA; married Leona; children: Terra. **EDUCATION:** Univ of Washington. **CAREER:** Golden State Warriors, guard 1980-83; Milwaukee Bucks, guard 1984-. **HONORS/ACHIEVEMENTS:** Scored a season high 17 points vs the Knicks in the Arena Feb 8; passed the 1,000 assist mark and the 200 plateau in steals; needs 16 more rebounds to reach400 career. **BUSINESS ADDRESS:** Milwaukee Bucks, 901 Fourth St, Ste 510, Milwaukee, WI 53203.

ROMES, CHARLES LEE
Professional athlete. **PERSONAL:** Born Dec 16, 1954; married Redalia; children: Twila Redalia. **EDUCATION:** NC Central, BA 1978. **CAREER:** Buffalo Bills, prof ath. **HONORS/ACHIEVEMENTS:** Has a string of 108 consult starts at right cornerback which includes three playoff games; led the Bills in interceptions last year with 5 which was a career best; since becoming a starter, he has at least one theft in each of the last seven seasons.

RONEY, RAYMOND G.
Educator. **PERSONAL:** Born Jul 26, 1941, Philadelphia, PA; son of Wallace Roney and Rosezell Harris Roney; married Ruth A Westgaph; children: Andre. **EDUCATION:** Central State Univ, BA Pol Sci 1963; Pratt Inst, MS Library Science 1965; Catholic Univ, PhD Cand 1980. **CAREER:** Howard Univ Library, supr ref dept 1965-66; Natl League of Cities/US Conf Mayors, dir library serv 1966-70; Washington Tech Inst, dir documentation ctr 1970-78; Wash Tech Inst, chmn med tech dept 1971-78; Univ of the District of Columbia, deputy dir learning resources, 1978-83; El Camino Coll, assoc dean learning resources 1984; El Camino Coll, dir learning resources, 1984-; El Camino Coll, dean instructional serv 1988-. **ORGANIZATIONS:** Pres Cncl on Lib/Media Tech 1983; bd mem COLT 1978; mem ALA, ACRL, AECT, COLT 1970; mem Phi Delta Kapa 1980; pres Shepherd Park Citizens Assn (DC) 1972-74; exec bd Paul Comm School 1974-83; United Way Advisory Board 1988-; dir California Library Employees Assn 1988; publisher Library Mosaics Magazine 1989-; Advisory Board, Afro-American Museum of CA 1989-. **HONORS/ACHIEVEMENTS:** Outstanding Achievement Bright Hope Baptist Church 1963; Grass Roots Award DC Fed Civic & Citizens Assn 1975; Outstanding Achievement Shepherd Park Citizens Assn 1975; Book Intro to AV for Tech Assts 1981; Book Classification Index for Urban Collections 1969; Book Job Descriptions for Library Support Personnel, 1986; Audiovisual Technology Primer, Libraries Unlimited 1988. **BUSINESS ADDRESS:** Dir Learning Resources, El Camino Coll, 16007 Crenshaw Blvd, Torrance, CA 90506.

ROOKS, CHARLES SHELBY
Theologian. **PERSONAL:** Born Oct 19, 1924, Beaufort, NC; son of Shelby A Rooks and Maggie Hawkins Rooks; married Adrienne Martinez; children: Laurence Gaylord, Carol Ann. **EDUCATION:** VA State Coll, AB 1949; Union Theol Sem, MDiv 1953; Coll of Wooster, DD 1968; Interdenominational Theol Ctr, DD 1979; VA Union Univ, DD 1980; Howard Univ, LHD 1982; VA State Univ, LHD 1984; Dillard Univ, LLD 1986; Teachers Coll, Columbia Univ, attended; Huston-Tillotson Coll, LittD 1989; Talladega Coll, LHD 1989. **CAREER:** Shanks Vill Protestant Church Orangeburg, pastor 1951-53; Lincoln Meml Temple United Church of Christ Washington, pastor 1953-60; Fund for Theol Educ Princeton, assoc dir 1960-67, exec dir 1967-74; Chicago Theol Sem, pres 1974-84; United Church Bd for Homeland Ministries, exec vice pres. **ORGANIZATIONS:** Pres Commun Recruitment & Training Inc; chmn bd of dir Office of Comm United Church of Christ; bd of dir Soc for the Study of Black Religion; bd dir Africa Fund; mem bd of dir The Interchurch Center, New York NY 1989-90. **HONORS/ACHIEVEMENTS:** Author of Rainbows and Reality, Atlanta, The ITC Press 1984; The Hopeful Spirit, New York, Pilgrim Press 1987. **MILITARY SERVICE:** AUS s/sgt 1943-46. **BUSINESS ADDRESS:** Executive Vice President, United Church Bd Homeland Min, 132 W 31st St, New York, NY 10001.

ROPER, BOBBY L.
Educator. **PERSONAL:** Born in Chicago, IL; son of William Roper; children: Reginald. **EDUCATION:** Chicago Teachers Coll, BEd 1959; Chicago State Univ, MS 1966. **CAREER:** Chicago Public School master teacher 1962-64, adjustment teacher 1965-68, asst principal 1968-71; Lawndale Comm Acad, principal. **ORGANIZATIONS:** Mem bd of dir Lawndale Homemakers 1970-75; mem bd of dir Chicago Youth Center 1975-; mem bd of dir Marcy Newberry Center 1982-83. **MILITARY SERVICE:** AUS corpl 1954-56. **BUSINESS ADDRESS:** Principal, Lawndale Community Acad, 3500 W Douglas Blvd, Chicago, IL 60623.

ROPER, GRACE TROTT
Librarian. **PERSONAL:** Born Sep 08, 1925, New York, NY; married Ivan Roper; children: James, Eric, Johanna, Robert. **EDUCATION:** City Coll of NY; Newark St Coll. **CAREER:** NY Public Library, asst to children lib 1950-54; Belmar Public Library, library dir 1962-. **ORGANIZATIONS:** Chmn Monmouth Council of Girl Scouts 1974-76; mem & sec The Vestry 1975; mem Belmar Bd of Educ 1976-; mem bd dir Monmouth Coun of Girl Scouts 1976; rec sec Monmouth Cty Lib Assn 1976-77; vice pres Monmouth Cty Lib Assn 1977-; mem Belmar Wom Club; mem Jersey Ctrl Bus Prof Wom Club; mem St Agnes Guild St Augustine's Epis Ch; Art on Belmar in Am Ency; pres of Belmar Bd of Educ 1983-84 & 1984-85. **HONORS/ACHIEVEMENTS:** Biog Who's Who of Amer Women; biog Comm Ldrs & Noteworthy Amer; wrote and published book on Belmar history, copywright 1978. **BUSINESS ADDRESS:** Library Dir, Belmar Public Library, 517 10th Ave, Belmar, NJ 07719.

ROPER, PATRICIA ANDERSON
Business executive. **PERSONAL:** Born Dec 23, 1945, Tulsa, OK; children: Lark Nanette, Thomas Bradford. **EDUCATION:** Lincoln Univ, BA 1966; PRSA, accreditation 1977. **CAREER:** US Senate Cand, dir research & policy info 1970-71; Blue Cross Hosp Serv St Louis, pub rel spec 1971-73; Western Elect Co St Louis, managing ed/comm aff spec 1973-77; Philip Morris Indsl Milwaukee, mgr communications 1977-78; Transatlantic Link, founder; TRB (Only Black Professional Speakers Bureau in US), director; The Roper Report/RHOPAR, pres/publisher. **ORGANIZATIONS:** Panel of judges Coro Found St Louis 1976; mem Pub Rel Soc of Amer 1977-80; bd dir Chicago Forum 1979; dir of pub rel/adv bd mem UNCF OIC Sherwood Forest St Louis 1974-77; bd of adv Lincoln Univ Jefferson City, MO 1975-77; chmn steering com Comm Pride Expo Milwaukee 1977; Tour of South Africa to establish professional networking ties 1985; bd Winnie Mandella Women's Ministries 1987. **HONORS/ACHIEVEMENTS:** Spl Citation for Documentary on Pre Con-Con OK Hist Soc 1970; Disting Serv Awards UNCF/OIC/Lincoln Univ/Milwaukee Journal/Jus Frens Milw/Coro Found 1974-79;producer/moderator WYMS (A Woman's Place); KJLH (Focus on Black Bus Woman); KACD (Ask Me) 1977-80; honored by Black Business and Prof Women of Los Angeles County at Fifth Annual Directory Reception; profiled in The Los Angeles Black Book 1985-86 edition; Key Speaker at the CA Governor's Conf 1985; host of radio show "Living Positively"; CA Governor honored Woman of the Year 1985; book

"Public Relations for Small Business". **BUSINESS ADDRESS:** Publisher/Lecturer, 14902 Preston Rd, Rm 212, Suite 184, Dallas, TX 75240.

ROPER, RICHARD WALTER
University administrator. **PERSONAL:** Born Sep 20, 1945, Deland, FL; son of Henry Roper and Dorothe Roper; married Marlene Peacock; children: Jelani, Akil. **EDUCATION:** Rutgers Univ, BA 1968; Princeton Univ, MPA 1971. **CAREER:** NJ Department of Higher Education, Trenton, NJ, asst to the vice chancellor, 1968-69; Dept of Transportation and Planning Greater London Council, London, England, research asst, 1971; Mayor's Education Task Force, Office of Newark Studies, Newark, NJ, staff coordinator, 1971-72; NJ Dept of Institutions and Agencies Div of Youth and Family Services, Trenton, NJ, 1972-73; Greater Newark Urban Coaltion, NJ Education Reform Project, Newark, NJ, director, 1973-74; Mayor Kenneth A Gibson, Newark, NJ, legislative aide, 1974-76; Office of Newark Studies, Newark, NJ, director, 1976-78; US Dept of Commerce, Office of the Secretary, Washington, DC, director, 1979-80; Woodrow Wilson School of Public and Intl Affairs, Program for NJ Affairs, Princeton University, Princeton, NJ, director, 1980-88, asst dean for graduate career services and governmental relations, 1988-. **ORGANIZATIONS:** Bd of dirs, 1982-, pres 1983-87, Assoc for Children of NJ; chmn bd trustees, Newark Public Radio, 1984-; bd of trustees, Center for Analysis of Public Issues, 1984-; bd trustees, Community Foundation for NJ, 1984-; mem Governor's Taskforce on Chid Abuse and Neglect, 1984-; chmn, NJ Child Life Protection Comm; bd dirs, NJ Public Policy Research Institute; bd trustees, Boys' & Girls' Clubs of Newark, NJ; mem NJ Comm, Regional Plann Assoc; vice chmn, Comm on Delinquency Causes and Prevention for the NJ Supreme Court's 1989 Judicial Conference. **HOME ADDRESS:** 12 Rutgers St, Maplewood, NJ 07040. **BUSINESS ADDRESS:** Assistant Dean for Graduate Career Services and Governmental Relations, Princeton University, Woodrow Wilson School of, Public & International Affrs, Princeton, NJ 08544.

ROSCOE, WILMA J.
Association executive. **PERSONAL:** Born Aug 24, 1938, Kershaw, SC; daughter of Chalmers Harris and Estelle Harris; married Alfred D Roscoe, Jr, Jul 06, 1963; children: Alfred D Roscoe III, Jenae V, Jeneen B. **EDUCATION:** Livingstone College, Salisbury, NC, BS, 1960. **CAREER:** Howard University, Washington, DC, admissions assistant, 1963-69; Fayetteville State University, Fayetteville, NC, director of tutorial program, 1969-74; National Association for Equal Opportunity in Higher Education, Washington, DC, 1975-. **ORGANIZATIONS:** Member, American Personnel and Guidance Association; member, National Coalition of Black Meeting Planners; member, Delta Sigma Theta. **HONORS/ACHIEVEMENTS:** Distinguished service award, National Association for Equal Opportunity in Higher Education, 1986; DHL, Livingstone College, Salisbury, NC, 1989; National Business League Award. **HOME ADDRESS:** 6001 Joyce Drive, Camp Springs, MD 20748. **BUSINESS ADDRESS:** Vice President, National Association for Equal Opportunity in Higher Education, 400 12th Street, NE, Lovejoy Building, Washington, DC 20002.

ROSE, ALVIN W.
Educator. **PERSONAL:** Born Feb 14, 1916, New Haven, MO; married Helen Cureton. **EDUCATION:** Lincoln U, BA 1938;Univ of IA, MA 1942;Univ of Chicago, PhD 1948; Sorbonne Paris, post-doctoral study 1952. **CAREER:** Fisk Univ, prof of Sociology 1946-47; NC Coll, prof 1948-56; Wayne State Univ, prof 1956-72; Dept of Sociology Wayne State Univ, chmn 1968-72; Univ of Miami, prof 1972-; visiting prof & lectr at numerous coll & univ. **ORGANIZATIONS:** Mem Am Social Assn; Soc for Study of Social Problems; Am Assn of Univ Prof; Intl Soc for Scientific Study of Race Relations; So Social Soc; AmAcad of Political & Social Sci; Phi Delta Kappa Social Sci Soc; Alpha Kappa Delta Social Soc; Nat Assn of Intergroup Relations Officials; FL Social Soc; African Studies Assn; NAACP; mem bd of Govs Museum of Sci; bd dir United Nations Assn; chmn Intergroup Relations Sect Soc for Study of Social Problems; memUniv of Miami Com on Salaries Rank & Promotion; memUniv of Miami Grad Com on Degrees & Acad Prog;Univ of Miami Faculty Com for Afro-Am Studies; mem exec com Univ Cntr for Urban Studies; Author of Numerous Publications. **BUSINESS ADDRESS:** Ashe Adminstrn Bldg, U of Miami, Coral Gables, FL 33124.

ROSE, ARTHUR
Artist, educator. **PERSONAL:** Born May 26, 1921, Charleston; married Elizabeth; children: 4. **EDUCATION:** Claflin Coll, BA 1950; NYU, MA 1952; IN Univ, post graduate, 1966-68. **CAREER:** Claflin Coll Orangeburg SC, head of art dept 1952-; Holmes Elem School, teacher, 1950-51. **ORGANIZATIONS:** Mem, Natl Conf Artists; SC Assn School Art; Smithsonian Assn; AAUP. **HONORS/ACHIEVEMENTS:** Best in Show Award JO Endris & Sons Jewelers 1967; Second Award Nat Conf Artists 1970. **MILITARY SERVICE:** USNR ship serviceman 3rd class 1942-45. **BUSINESS ADDRESS:** Art Dept, Claflin Coll, Orangeburg, SC 29115.

ROSE, RACHELLE SYLVIA
Licensed clinical social worker. **PERSONAL:** Born Aug 19, 1946, Chicago, IL. **EDUCATION:** District of Columbia Teachers Coll, BS Educ 1974; Howard Univ Grad Sch of Social Work, MSW 1976. **CAREER:** Kaiser Permanente Hospital, licensed clinical social worker. **ORGANIZATIONS:** Past mem Kappa Delta Pi Natl Teachers Honor Soc; mem Amer Cancer Soc Service & Rehab Comm 1981-; mem Natl Assoc of Social Workers 1981-, Natl Assoc of Oncology Social Workers 1986-; Natl Assoc Black SW Chief Chapter; Howard Univ Alumni. **HONORS/ACHIEVEMENTS:** Outstanding Young Women of Amer 1980. **HOME ADDRESS:** 4587 Don Tomaso Dr, Los Angeles, CA 90008. **BUSINESS ADDRESS:** Clinical Social Worker, Kaiser Permanente Hospital, 4733 Sunset Blvd, Los Angeles, CA 90027.

ROSE, RAYMOND E.
Engineer, scientist, manager. **PERSONAL:** Born Jul 17, 1926, Canton, OH; married Jessica Mack; children: Sharon, Critchett, Dan, Tim. **EDUCATION:** Univ MN, PhD 1966; Univ of MN, MS 1956; Univ of KS, BA 1951. **CAREER:** NASA Headquarters, aerospace engr, prgm mgr 1976-; Honeywell Inc, proj staff engr scientist 1974-76, sr prin res scientist prog mgr 1972-74, sr prin res scientist 1966-72;Univ of MN, res fellow 1962-66;Univ of MN Rosemont Aeronautical Labs, jr engr to scientist 1951-62; Edo Corp Coll Point NY, consult 1961-62; Pillsbury Corp Minneapolis MN, consult 1963-64. **ORGANIZATIONS:** Mem Am Helicopter Soc; Am Inst of Aeronautics & Astronautics; mem hon engineering frats Tau Beta Pi, Sigma Gamma Tau, Sigma Tau; patent Control Apparatus-Shock Swallowing Air Data Sensor for Aircraft 1971; 22 Publications 1953-73; 12 Presentations at Tech Conf Symposiums Univs etc 1971-75. **MILITARY SERVICE:** USAAF 1945-46. **BUSINESS ADDRESS:** Nat Aeronautics & Space Adm (N, Code RJA, Washington, DC 20546.

ROSE, SHELVIE
Educator. **PERSONAL:** Born Jan 05, 1936, Covington, TN; married Odessa White; children: Delores, Shelvie Jr, Saundra, Kelda La Trece, Kenny. **EDUCATION:** TN State U, BS; Memphis StateUnivUniv of TN, Grad Study. **CAREER:** Tipton Co Bd of Educ, health & driver educ instr; Aquatics, pro boy scout instr 1959-63; Tipton Co Pub Sch System, instr 1959-; Tipton Co, commr ofdist 1. **ORGANIZATIONS:** Mem Tipton Co Planning Commn; Tipton Co Reapportionment Com; Tipton Co Ins Com; Salary Com Mem Tipton Co Pub Works; bd of control; mem Legal Serv Assn of Sheby Co Memphis TN Tipton Co Lauderdale Co Fayett Co; chmn Tipton Co Voters Council; bd mem Tenn Voters Council. **BUSINESS ADDRESS:** Brighton HS, Brighton, TN 38011.

ROSEMOND, JOHN H.
Physician. **PERSONAL:** Born Oct 17, 1917, Jacksonville, FL; married Rosalie Edge; children: John Jr, Janith, Ronald. **EDUCATION:** FL A&M Univ, BS 1941; Howard Univ, MD 1951; DC General Hosp, intern 1951-52. **CAREER:** AUS Fort Belvoir VA, civilian phy one yr; Ohio Univ Coll Med, instr; physician private practice; Columbus OH Mem Soc Tchr Family Med 1985. **ORGANIZATIONS:** Mem med staff Grant St Anthony Mt Carmel Childrens &Univ Hosp; Flying Phy Assn; Fellow Am Acad Family Phy; pres bd trustees Columbus Tech Inst; chmn Freedom Fund; OH N AACP; Basileus Omega Psi Phi Frat 1970; mem bd dir Beneficial Acceptance Corp; exec bd Central OH Council; Boy Scouts Am 1968; chmn Columbus UN Festival; city councilman 1969-; chmn Service & Airport Com; mem Columbus Airport Commn & Council Rep Columbus Bd Health; elder Bethany Presb Ch; bd trustees Nat Med Assn; diplomate Am Bd of Family Practice; pres pro-team Columbus City Council; mem Min Affairs Com Am Acad of Family Physicians; Columbus Acad of Medicine; Ohio State Medical Assn; Central Ohio Acad of Family Physicians; Amer Acad of Family Physicians; Natl Medical Assn. **HONORS/ACHIEVEMENTS:** Frontiers Man Yr Columbus Chap Frontiers Intl 1969; Omega Man Yr 1970; Gen Practitioner Yr Nat Med Assn 1970; Layman Yr United Presb Ch 1973; Family Phy Yr OH Acad Family Phy 1974. **MILITARY SERVICE:** USAAF navigator-bombardier WWII 1st lt discharged 1946. **BUSINESS ADDRESS:** 1314 Mount Vernon Avenue, Columbus, OH 43203.

ROSEMOND, LEMUEL MENEFIELD
Physician. **PERSONAL:** Born Jan 23, 1920, Pickens, SC; married Gloria Gardner; children: Reginald, Wanda, Lisa. **EDUCATION:** Benedict Coll Columbia SC, BS 1941; Meharry Med Coll Nashville TN, MD 1950. **CAREER:** Physician private practice 1985; Cherokee, chief of staff. **ORGANIZATIONS:** Mem Hosp 1969-71; Cherokee Med Soc; Am Med Assn 1955-80; Nat Med Assn 1955-80; Am Acad of Family Physicians 1970-80; sec/treas Cherokee Co Med Soc 1973-76; pres Palmetto Med Dental Pharmaceutical Assn SC 1977; adv bd Salvation Army 1970-76; C of C 1974-78; adv bd Bank of Gaffney 1975-78. **HONORS/ACHIEVEMENTS:** Omega Man of the Year Omega Psi Phi Frat 1974; Twenty Five Year Award Meharry Med Coll 1975; Twenty Five Year Serv Award Palmetto Med Dental & Pharm Assn 1979. **MILITARY SERVICE:** AUS 1st lt 1941-46. **BUSINESS ADDRESS:** 313 W Meadow St, Gaffney, SC 29340.

ROSEMOND, MANNING WYLLARD, JR.
Dentist. **PERSONAL:** Born May 20, 1918, Toccoa, GA; married Edrose Smith; children: Manning III. **EDUCATION:** Claflin Univ, AB 1940; Atlanta Univ, MS 1949; OH State Univ, DDS 1956. **CAREER:** Private practice, dentist. **ORGANIZATIONS:** Mem Pres Adv Bd; pres 1973,74, chmn bd, pres elect 1972-73, vice pres 1971,72, exec bd 1967-71 NCA; pres Forest City Dental Study Club 1973-74; founder Buckeye State Dental Assoc 1974; dir Jane Adams Dental Clinic 1977-; pres CRC Enterprises; pres Romac Cty; mem Omega Psi Phi, NAACP, Frontiers Intl; holder, pvt pilots license; mem Aircraft Owners & Pilots Assoc; mem Amer Central Assoc, OH Dental Assoc; pres Max's Aerial Photographic Svcs. **MILITARY SERVICE:** AUS 1st lt 1942-46,50-52; Bronz Star. **BUSINESS ADDRESS:** 1296 Hayden Ave, Cleveland, OH 44112.

ROSENTHAL, ROBERT E.
Business executive. **PERSONAL:** Born Apr 09, 1945, Phillips, MS; children: Robert E Jr. **EDUCATION:** Univ of FL, 1967; Jackson State Univ, BS 1971; Jackson State Univ, Grad Work 1973. **CAREER:** Whitten Jr High Jackson, teacher 1972; PO Jackson, EEO couns 1974; PO Dist Jackson, EEO spec 1976; PO Edwards MS, postmaster 1978; Mid-South Records Inc Jackson, vp, co-owner 1978; mgmt & mktg consult for artists & record co's; Who's Who in Black Music, editor 1986; Who's Who in Music, editor 1987; Programming Ratio, editor 1987; Rosenthal & Maultsby-Music Research Intl, natl public relations mgr for The Young Black Programmer Coalition & The Black Music Assn; Philadelphia International Records, natl public relations manager; Philadelphia Intl Records,natl public relations mgr. **ORGANIZATIONS:** Mem MS Teachers Assoc, Natl Bus League, Natl Assoc of Postmasters, NAACP, NAREB Realist, Urban League, Jackson State Univ Alumni, Natl Counsel on Affirm Action; mem Minority Bus Brain Trust for the Congressional Black Caucus 1982-83,1984,1986,1987-; Rock Music Assoc; Young Black Programmers Coalition. **HONORS/ACHIEVEMENTS:** Best All Around Student Awd, Rosa Scott HS Madison MS 1963; Music Scholarship Jackson State Univ 1964; Good Conduct Medal. **MILITARY SERVICE:** USAF 1968. **BUSINESS ADDRESS:** Equal Empl Oppty Officer, Corps of Engrs, Lower MS Valley Div, PO Box 80, Vicksburg, MS 39180.

ROSS, ANTHONY ROGER
Educational administrator. **PERSONAL:** Born Jan 28, 1953, Jamaica, NY; son of Abram and Esther; married Deanna; children: Jamal, Shama. **EDUCATION:** St Lawrence Univ, BA Sociology 1971-75, MEd Counseling 1976-78; Northern AZ Univ, EdD Ed Admin 1981-84. **CAREER:** Utica Coll of Syracuse Univ, counselor higher educ opportunity prog 1975-76; St Lawrence Univ, dir higher educ opportunity prog 1976-81; St Lawrence Univ, asst basketball coach 1977-80; Northern AZ Univ, asst/assoc dean 1983-84, dean of students 1985-. **ORGANIZATIONS:** Mem Amer Coll Personnel Assoc 1978-, Amer Assoc for Counseling & Devel 1978-; pres Higher Educ Opportunity Prog Professional Org 1976-81; mem Natl Assoc of Student Personnel Admin 1980-, NAACP 1982-, Coach, Youth League Basketball & Soccer 1982-, Big Brothers of Flagstaff 1983-, Buffalo Soldiers of Flagstaff 1984-; bd of dirs, Coconino Community Guidance Ctr 1986; Commissioner on Flagstaff Cty Parks and Recreational Commission, 1986-. **HONORS/ACHIEVEMENTS:** Varsity Football 1971-75; Varsity Basketball 1972-75, captain 1975; pres Black Student Union St Lawrence Univ 1973-

74; Athlete of the Year St Lawrence Univ 1975; Outstanding Young Man of Amer Jaycees 1980,1983; pres, Higher Education Opportunity Program 1979-80. **BUSINESS ADDRESS:** Dean of Students, Northern ArizonaUniv, NAU Box 4095, Flagstaff, AZ 86011.

ROSS, CATHERINE LAVERNE
Educator. **PERSONAL:** Born Nov 01, 1948, Cleveland, OH; married Dr Thomas Daniel. **EDUCATION:** Kent St U, BA History/Sociology 1971; Cornell U, M of Regnl Plnning 1973; Cornell U, PhD City & Reg Plnning 1979. **CAREER:** GA Inst of Tech, asst prof 1976; Atlanta U, asst prof 1977-79; Cornell U, rsrch asst offc of transport 1975-76; Daton Dalton Little Newport Shaker Hgts, OH, transp planner 1973-74; Reg Planning Commn Cleveland, grad Asst 1972; GA Tech Engineering Experiment Sta, consult 1979; Comm Serv Admin Atlanta, consult resrchr 1979. **ORGANIZATIONS:** Mem N At Assn for the Advncmnt of Sci 1978; mem Black Women Academicians 1979; policy analyst, Am Planning Assn Wash DC 1979. **HONORS/ACHIEVEMENTS:** Ford found flwshp Am Soc of Plng Ofcls 1971-73; outstndg women Essence Mag 1974; sci & tech del Six Pan-African Congress Tanzania 1974; rockefeller found flwshp CornellUniv 1975. **BUSINESS ADDRESS:** Georgia Inst of Technology, College of Architecture, Graduate City Planning Program, Atlanta, GA 30332.

ROSS, CHARLES
Government official. **PERSONAL:** Born Aug 01, 1918, Summerville, SC; married Ida Brown. **CAREER:** Town of Lincolnville, mayor 1967-. **ORGANIZATIONS:** Mem Reg Plng Council Charleston Cty; bd mem Municipal Assoc SC; 1st vice pres Org of the So Conf of Black Mayors, Natl Conf of Black Mayors, Charleston Cty Assoc; founder So Conf of Black Mayors; mem State Municipality of SC; mem Council of Govt, Ebenizer AME Church of Lincolnville. **BUSINESS ADDRESS:** Mayor, Town of Lincolnville, PO Box 536, Lincolnville, SC 29483.

ROSS, CHARLES C.
Business executive. **PERSONAL:** Born Sep 06, 1914, Mound Bayou, MS; widowed. **EDUCATION:** Hampton Inst, BS 1936. **CAREER:** CC Ross Decorating Bus, owner 1946-; WV State Coll, tchr 1938-43; Atkins HS, tchr 1936-38; Winston-Salem, city alderman 1965-, mayor pro tem. **ORGANIZATIONS:** Mem Winston-SalemUniv 1969; chmn bd trustee Winston-Salem U; organizer dir Forsyth Bank & Trust Co 1973; Greater Winston-Salem C of C Omega Psi Phi; KC. **MILITARY SERVICE:** AUS staff sgt 1943-46. **BUSINESS ADDRESS:** 814 Bruce, Winston-Salem, NC 27101.

ROSS, CURLEE
Physician. **PERSONAL:** Born May 21, 1929, Dubach, LA; married Zoe Louse Wise; children: Carolyn Louise, Lisa Anne, David Michael. **EDUCATION:** Univ So CA, BS 1953; Univ So CA Sch of Med, MD 1957; Univ W Los Angel Sch of Law, JD 1972. **CAREER:** Pvt Prac LA, ob gyn 1964-; Univ So CA Sch of Med, asst clinical prof 1965-; Arroyo Vista Family Health Ctr, medical dir. **ORGANIZATIONS:** NAACP; LA Urban League. **MILITARY SERVICE:** AUS med Corps capt 1958-61.

ROSS, DIANA
Singer, entertainer. **PERSONAL:** Born Mar 26, 1944, Detroit, MI; married Arne Naess; children: 3 children. **CAREER:** The Temptations formerly The Primes, Marvin Gaye, Mary Wells, back-up singer; Diana Ross & The Supremes, lead singer; Diana Ross Enterprises Inc, pres; Lady Sings the Blues, The Wiz, star; TV Specials An Evening with Diana Ross 1977, Diana 1981. **HONORS/ACHIEVEMENTS:** Citation Vice Pres Humphrey to Efforts on Behalf of Pres Johnsons Youth Oppty Prog; Citation from Mr Mmartin Luther King Jr, Rev Abernathy for contribs to SCLC Cause; Billboard Awd; Cash Box Awd; Record World Awd as Worlds Outstanding Singer; Nominee Best Actress of the Year Motion Picture Acad Arts & Sci; Image Awd NAACP 1970; Grammy Awd 1970; Female Entertainer of the Year NAACP 1970; CUE Awd Entertainer of the Year 1972; Awarded star on Hollywood Walk of Fame; Antoinette Perry Awd 1977. **BUSINESS ADDRESS:** RTC Management, PO Box 1683, New York, NY 10185.

ROSS, DORIS A.
Govt. official. **PERSONAL:** Born Jan 30, 1923, Fitzgerald, GA; married JD Ross; children: Anthony, Michael R, Darryl, Marvetta, John, Robert. **EDUCATION:** Bethune-Cookman Coll, attended; Lee Johnson School of Business, Cert. **CAREER:** CT Housing Investment Fund, asst to dir 1965-72; State Comm on Human Rights & Oppty, comm relations spec 1978-; Norwalk Common Council, councilwoman 1977-. **ORGANIZATIONS:** Bd of dir CT Fed Black Dem 1972-80, Greater Norwalk Black Dem Club 1976-, Norwalk Econ Oppty Now 1977-, Norwalk Area Improvement League Inc 1080-; advcomm Fairfield Cablevision Inc 1980-81. **HONORS/ACHIEVEMENTS:** Disting Serv State Fed of Black Dem 1974; Outstanding Serv Alpha Phi Alpha & Norwalk Black 1976; Disting Achievement Norwalk Area Improvement League 1981; Achievement Recognition Norwalk Heritage Wall Comm 1985. **HOME ADDRESS:** Bldg 22 Apt 1D Roodner Ct, Norwalk, CT 06854. **BUSINESS ADDRESS:** Councilwoman, City of Norwalk, 41 N Main St, Norwalk, CT 06854.

ROSS, EDWARD
Cardiologist. **PERSONAL:** Born Oct 10, 1937, Fairfield, AL; son of Horace Ross and Carrie Ross; married Catherine I Webster; children: Edward, Ronald, Cheryl, Anthony. **EDUCATION:** Clark Coll Atlanta, GA, BS 1959; IN Univ Schl of Med, MD 1963. **CAREER:** Edward Ross, MD, Inc, pres (CEO) 1970-; Medical Cardiovascular Data, Inc, pres (CEO) 1982; Private Practice, Cardiologist. **ORGANIZATIONS:** Qualify exam Amer Brd of Internal Med 1969; diplomate Amer BrdK of Internal Med 1970; schlstc hnry soc Alpha Kappa Mu; scntfc hnry soc Beta Kappa Chi; hnr mdcl soc Alpha Omega Alpha; Cntrl IN Comprehensive Health Plng Cncl; Comprehensive Health Plng Cncl Marion Cnty 1972-73; Marion Cnty Medcl Soc; IN State Mdcl Assoc; Royal Soc for the Promotion of Health (London); Amer Soc of Internal Med; Aesculapean Mdcl Soc; NMA pres Hoosier State Mdcl Assoc 1980-86; Natl Mdcl Assoc; Amer Coll of Cardiology; Amer Coll of Angiology; clncl asst prfsr IN Univ Schl of Med 1970-75; sec Div Natl Mdcl Assoc 1972-73; pres elec Mdcl-Dental Serv Inc 1971-78; brd dir Cntrl IN TB & Resp Diseases Assoc 1971-74; apt Natl Cntr for Health Serv Rsch & Dvlpmnt 1970; med dir Martindale Health Cntr 1968-71; dir Multiphasic Screening 1968-71; rep IN Univ Medcl Schl Sesquicentennial Comm 1970; pres 1986, bd of dir 1979 Ind Society Internal Med; chairman Internal Medicine Section, IN State Medical Assn; Council on Scientific Assembly; Intl Platform Assn; consumer advisor, US Food & Drug Admin Radiologic Devise Panel, 1988-. **HONORS/ACHIEVEMENTS:** Fellowship Woodrow Wilson 1959, IN Heart Assoc 1961-62; Dept of Cardiology, Research Fellow in Cardiology Dept of Med 1968-70; chief fellow int med IN Univ 1969-70; Certificate of Merit Scientific Achievements in Biology 1959; natl Fdn Health Schlrshp 1955; Fellow Royal Soc for the Promotion of Health, 1974; Fellow, Amer Coll of Angiology; Fellow, Amer Coll of Cardiology. **MILITARY SERVICE:** USAAF, captain, Certificate of Appreciation SAC 1966-68. **BUSINESS ADDRESS:** Private Practice, 3171 N Meridian St #201, #201, Indianapolis, IN 46208.

ROSS, FRANK KENNETH
Certified public accountant. **PERSONAL:** Born Jul 09, 1943; son of Reginald Ross and Ruby Ross; married Cecelia M Mann; children: Michelle, Michael. **EDUCATION:** Long Island Univ, BS 1966, MBA 1968. **CAREER:** Peat, Marwick, Mitchell & Co CPA, partner 1966-73; Ross, Stewart & Benjamin, PC, CPA, pres/owner 1973-76; KPMG Peat Marwick, partner 1976-. **ORGANIZATIONS:** 1st natl pres/founder Natl Assn of Black Accountants 1969-70; mem Amer Inst of CPA's 1969-; tresurer Ellington Fund 1982-; mem Bd of Councilors, Coll of Business & Public Mgmt, Univ of the District of Columbia 1983-; treas Washington Urban League 1986-; bd mem Iona House; vice pres, treasurer Washington Project for the Arts 1986-; visiting prof Howard Univ 1982-. **HONORS/ACHIEVEMENTS:** Black Achievers in Industry YMCA of Greater NY 1980; Outstanding Achievement Award Washington DC Chapter NABA 1984; Distinguished Serv Awd NABA 1985. **BUSINESS ADDRESS:** Partner, KPMG Peat Marwick, 2001 M St, Washington, DC 20036.

ROSS, GLADYS MERRITT
Educator. **PERSONAL:** Born Nov 17, 1903, Jersey City, NJ; widowed. **EDUCATION:** NJ State, BS 1951; Seton Hall, MA 1953; FL U, PhD 1971. **CAREER:** Los Amigos School Schertz-Cibolo-Universal Independent School Dist, adult Educ dir 1985; Nigerian Methodist School 1966; Mexico City School of Guides 1965; speech therapist 1951-64; Child Develop Centers Jersey City, oeo dir; Bd of Educ 1923-64; E School Travel Agents 1967; Relax-a-Tours Montclair, travel rep 1967-68. **ORGANIZATIONS:** Supreme founder Nat Sority Phi Delta Kappa; past membership chmn & educ chmn League of Women Voters 1956-; mem Universal City Charter Revision Com; Mayors Adv Com; Crim Justice Commn. **HONORS/ACHIEVEMENTS:** Universal City TX Citizen Com; WNRI Radio Comm Award 1964; Woman of Achievement 1967; Afro-Founder of Yr 1960; Intl Womens Soc of Enugu 1966; Papal Audiences Pope Pius XII 1956 & Pope John XXIII 1962.

ROSS, JOANNE A.
Association executive. **PERSONAL:** Born Jun 24, 1929, East Falmouth, MA; children: Margo Ross, Nathan G, Armond. **CAREER:** Univ Yr for ActionUniv MS Boston Harbor Campus, dir 1985; BostonUniv Sch of Urban Studies & Planning, visiting lectr 1974-75; Tufts Experimental Coll Sociology Dept, faculty 1966-69; Commonwealth Serv Corps Boston, dir regional; Orgn for Social & Tech Innovations, consult 1968-71; Mustang Industrial Cleaners Inc, pres 1974-. **ORGANIZATIONS:** Mem Review Com Nation Cntr for Health Svcs; incorporating mem Elma Lewis Sch of Fine Arts MS; chrprsn Statewide Council Ofc for Children 1974-; interimchrprsn TCHUBA Cape Verdean Am Releif Orgn 1975; vol Lobbyist Welfare Rights & Civil Libs. **HONORS/ACHIEVEMENTS:** Recip NASW Comm Serv 1965; Columbia Point Civic Assn Comm Serv 1963, 1965, 1966; Lambda Kappa Contrib of Pub Serv 1968. **BUSINESS ADDRESS:** U MA, Boston Harbor Campus, Dorchester, MA 02125.

ROSS, JOY BELLE
Retired educational administrator. **PERSONAL:** Born Jul 04, 1910, Oklahoma City, OK; married Carl E; children: Mattye B, Ojirika, Carl E II. **EDUCATION:** Prairie View State Coll Prairie View TX, BS 1934; KS StateUniv Manhattan, MS 1939; TX Woman'sUniv Denton, PhD 1969. **CAREER:** TX Coll, head home econ dept 1969-80; TX Coll, prof 1949-68; Prairie View Univ, educator 1942-43; Tillotson Coll Austin, educator 1940-42, 1944-46; Smith Co Tyler TX, home dem agent 1935-38; Ft Bend & Angleton Cos TX, teacher public schools 1929-31. **ORGANIZATIONS:** Jeanses supr Nacogdoches & Sabine Cos TX 1939-40; pres PTA Council Smith Co Tyler TX 1955-68; procedure book chmn PTA State & E TX Dist 1956-69; memNat Assn Educ of Young Children Tyler & State Assn Educ of Young Children 1969-80; mem TX & Am Dietetic Assn 1973-80. **HONORS/ACHIEVEMENTS:** Cert & Plaque Local & State PTA 1956-68; Annual Plaque of Merit United Negro Coll Fund 1975-79; Annual Plaque of Merit YMCA Tyler 1975-79; Cert of Merit Tyler-Smith Co Mental Health 1976-78.

ROSS, KEVIN ARNOLD
Attorney, association executive. **PERSONAL:** Born Apr 22, 1955; married Gornata Lynn Cole; children: Kelly Alexis, April Whitney. **EDUCATION:** Dartmouth Coll, BA 1973-77; Emory Law School, JD 1977-80. **CAREER:** Kilpatrick & Cody, summer legal clinic 1979; Long & Aldridge, assoc attny 1980-. **ORGANIZATIONS:** Staff lawyer Volunteer Lawyer for the Arts 1981-84; sec, vp, pres elect, pres Gate City Bar Assoc 1982-85; vice pres Amer Diabetes Assoc 1982-84; mem StateLicensing Bd of Used Car Dealers 1984-89. **HONORS/ACHIEVEMENTS:** Leader Under 30 Ebony Mag 1985. **BUSINESS ADDRESS:** President, Gate City Bar Assn, 134 Peachtree St #1900, Atlanta, GA 30043.

ROSS, MARY OLIVIA
President. **PERSONAL:** Born in Georgia; married Rev Solomon D Ross (deceased). **EDUCATION:** Spelman Coll Atlanta, Graduate; Wayne State Univ, Univ of MI, Grad Studies. **CAREER:** The Natl Baptist Convention USA Inc, pres the women's convention aux. **ORGANIZATIONS:** Mem bd of trustees Amer Baptist Theol Seminary; mem bd of mgrs Church Women United; mem Women's Planning Comm Japan Intl Christian Univ Foundation; mem exec comm North Amer Baptist Women's Union; mem bd of trustees Morehouse School of Religion Atlanta; dir minister's wives div Natl Bapt Congress ofChristian Educ; mem Natl Sor of Phi Delta Kappa; life heritage mem NAACP; golden life mem Delta Sigma Theta Sor Inc; mem Top Ladies of Distinction Inc; mem bd of trustees Lewis Business Coll Detroit; guest lecturer/seminar leader First Asian Baptist Congress Hyderabad India; delegate 6th Assembly of the World Cncl of Churches Vancouver BC Canada; mem central comm World Cncl of Churches. **HONORS/ACHIEVEMENTS:** Admitted to the Order of African Redemption w/rank of Dean Grand Commander Monrovia Liberia 1972; DHL Spelman Coll Centennial Commencements 1981; Hon DDInterdenominational Theol Ctr Atlanta 1982; Founder's Day Speaker Spelman Coll 1983; authored "The Minister's Wife" and "New Women for a New World for Christ"; co-author "The Natl Missionary Study Guide"; editor "The Mission"; also has written several brochures and contributed to numerous religious journals and magazines; apptd by Gov of MI to Dr Martin Luther King Jr Holiday Commn 1985;

Living Legacy Awd 1986. **BUSINESS ADDRESS:** President, Womens Convention & Auxiliary, Nat'l Baptist Conv USA Inc, Detroit, MI.

ROSS, PHYLLIS HARRISON
Educator, psychiatrist. **PERSONAL:** Born Aug 14, 1936, Detroit, MI; married Edgar. **EDUCATION:** Albion Coll Albion MI, BA 1956; Wayne StateUniv Detroit 1959, MD; Kings Co Hosp Brooklyn, internship 1959-60. **CAREER:** NY Med Coll, prof of Psychiatry 1972-; Metropolitan Hosp Comm Mental Health Cntr, dir 1972-; physician pediatrics adult & child psychiatry 1959-; Jacoby Hosp Albert Einstein Coll of Med, residency-adult & child psychiatry 1962-66; NY Hosp/Cornell Med Coll, residency-pediatrics 1960-62. **ORGANIZATIONS:** Bd of dir Empire State Coll of StateUniv of NY 1972-79; bd of dir Bank St Coll 1972-79; bd of dir Children's TV Workshop 1976-; pres Black Psychiatrists of Am 1976-78; mem Med Review Bd NYS Commn of Corrections 1976-; mem Minority Adv Comm to Sec of HEW & Adminstr ADAMHA 1978-; author "Getting It Together A Psychology Textbook" plus Tchng Guide 1972; author "The Black Child A Parents Guide" 1973. **HONORS/ACHIEVEMENTS:** Achievement Award Greater NY Links 1973; Distinguished Alumnus Award Albion Coll 1976; Leadership in Med Award Susan Smith McKinney Steward Med Society 1978; Award of Merit Pub Health Assn of New York City 1980. **BUSINESS ADDRESS:** Met Hosp CMHC, 1900 Second Ave, New York, NY 10029.

ROSS, RALPH M.
Educator, clergyman. **PERSONAL:** Born Dec 23, 1936, Miami, FL; son of Leroy Ross and Effie Mae Ross; married Gertrude; children: Sharlene, Lydia, Ralph, Ray, Simona, Randall. **EDUCATION:** AB 1961; BD 1965; MDiv 1970; l988 DMin. **CAREER:** Beth Salem United Presb Ch Columbus, GA, minister 1965-66; Eastern Airlines Atlanta, ramp agt 1965-66; Mt Zion Baptist Church Miami, asso minister 1966-68; Urban League Miami, field rep 1967-68; Knoxville Coll, campus minister 1968-70; UT Knoxville, lecturer/religious dept 1969-; Knoxville Coll, dean of students; NC A&T State U, dir religious activities 1978-86, asst dean student devel 1986-. **ORGANIZATIONS:** Mem bd dir Ministries to Blacks in Higher Edn Knoxville; Knoxville Interdenominational Christian Ministeral Alliance; life mem Alpha Phi Alpha; NAACP, Pulpit Forum of Greensboro and Vicinity, ROA. **HONORS/ACHIEVEMENTS:** YMCA Best Blocker Award Knoxville Coll 1959; Rockefeller Fellowship Award 1964; Theta Phi Hon Soc 1965. **MILITARY SERVICE:** USNR Chaplains Corps commander. **BUSINESS ADDRESS:** Asst Dean of Student Dev, NC A&T State University, 1601 E Market St, Greensboro, NC 27411.

ROSS, REGINA D.
Educational administrator. **PERSONAL:** Born Jul 20, 1948, Harlem, NY. **EDUCATION:** City Coll NY, BA 1973; Columbia Univ Sch of Social Work, MSSW 1975. **CAREER:** Wiltwyck School, social worker 1976-77; Union Settlement E Harlem Outreach, psychiatric soc wk sup 1978-80; East Harlem Council for Comm Improvement, dirof planning 1980-81; Comm Sch Dist 12, deputy dir 1981-. **ORGANIZATIONS:** Instructor Malcom-King Harlem Coll Ext 1976-79; mem Assn of Black Soc Wkrs 1973-; pres Comm Sch Bd #4 1977-; mem Natl Assn for School Desegration 1979-; mem Comm Adviser Bd Met Hosp 1985-. **HONORS/ACHIEVEMENTS:** Columbia Univ School Soc Work 1973-75; Natl Urban Fellowship alternate 1982; Disting Serv East Harlem Boys Choir 1982; Outstanding Young Women of Amer 1982-83. **HOME ADDRESS:** 1735 Madison Ave, New York, NY 10029. **BUSINESS ADDRESS:** Deputy Dir, Board of Education, 1000 Jennings St, Bronx, NY 10460.

ROSS, ROBERT P.
Business executive. **PERSONAL:** Born Nov 27, 1934, Richmond, IN; married Norma J; children: Robert P Jr, Jenell. **EDUCATION:** General Mts Dealer Devel, 1972-73; Univ of Detroit, Assoc Degree 1973. **CAREER:** Wright-Patterson AFB, computer programmer 1956-62; Shannon Buick Co, sales 1962-72; Bob Ross Buick Inc, pres 1974-79; Bob Ross Buick Inc, pres 1979-. **ORGANIZATIONS:** Bd of dir Chamber of Commerce Crime Stoppers, United Way; mem Rotary Club, Natl Auto Dealers Assoc; bd of dir Dayton Auto Dealers Assoc; mem Gen Motors Pres Adv Council; chmn fund raising dr Boy Scouts of Amer. **HONORS/ACHIEVEMENTS:** #70 of 100 of Nations Leading Black Businesses Black Enterprise Mag 1976; 20th Top Black Business in the US Black Enterprise mag 1983; Outstanding OH Minority Bus of the Year Minority Purchasing Council 1983; Small Bus Person of the Year Univ of Dayton Small Bus Devel Ctr 1984; 1 of 5 Buick Dealerships of the 250 of the Midwest Region. **BUSINESS ADDRESS:** President, Bob Ross Buick, Inc, 85 Loop Road, Centerville, OH 45459.

ROSS, WILLIAM A.
Business executive. **PERSONAL:** Born Aug 17, 1929, Milford, DE; married Pinnig L; children: William, Jr, Rae, Dion. **EDUCATION:** DE State Coll, BS 1951;Univ of MD, EEd, Cert 1963. **CAREER:** Ryland Group Inc, vp/div mgr; Nat Urban League Devel Found, exec vice pres 1970-74; Ofc of Manpower Devel & Employment Oppor US Dept HUD, dir 1969-70; HOPE Inc, exec/vp 1967-69; Marketing Info Network, lectr; Kappa Alpha Psi Housing & Econ Devel Corp, exec vp; Urban Housing Comm Devel, lectr; League of New Comm Developers, asso. **ORGANIZATIONS:** Mem Kappa Alpha Psi; founder/1st pres Columbia Alumni Chpt; founder Concerned Black Men of Columbia. **HONORS/ACHIEVEMENTS:** Numerous awards presented in the area of Housing & Urban Devel & New Town Planning & Devel. **MILITARY SERVICE:** AUS 1951-53.

ROSS, WILLIAM ALEXANDER JACKSON
Physician. **PERSONAL:** Born Nov 26, 1937, Detroit, MI; married Etna; children: William Jr, Peter, Benjamin, Roxanne. **EDUCATION:** Univ MI, Wayne State Univ, 1956-60; Meharry Med Coll, MD 1964. **CAREER:** Private practice, orthopedic surgeon; Childrens Hosp, teacher; USN, intern 1964-65; USN, resident 1969-73; USN Hosp, physician 1969-73; W Oak Health Ctr, ortho cons; Herrick Hospital, chief of orthopedics; Arlington Medical Group, orthopedic surgeon. **ORGANIZATIONS:** 1st black submarine officer USN 1966; Qualified Submarine Med Officer 1966; mem Arlington Med Group, Natl Med Assoc, AMA, Alpha Phi Alpha, NAACP; mem, Sigma Pi Phi. **MILITARY SERVICE:** USN commander 1964-74. **BUSINESS ADDRESS:** Orthopedic Surgeon, Arlington Medical Group, 5709 Market St, Oakland, CA 94608.

ROSS, WINSTON A.
Social service director. **PERSONAL:** Born Dec 02, 1941; son of Reginald Ross and Ruby Swanston Ross; married Rosalind Golden. **EDUCATION:** NY City Commnty Coll, AAS 1961; NYU, BS 1963; Columbia Univ Sch of Social Work, MS 1971; Adelphi Univ Sch of Social Work, Doctorial Candi. **CAREER:** New York City Dept of Social Svcs/Preventive Svcs/Bureau of Child Welfare, caseworker/supr 1966-73; St Dominic's Home, Blauvelt NY, exec supr 1973-74; Graham Home & Sch, Hastings NY, social work supr 1975-76; The Wiltwyck Sch, Yorktown NY, unit dir 1976-78; Westchester Commnty Opportunity Pgm, Inc, exec dir. **ORGANIZATIONS:** Chmn Westchester Div, NYS Chap NASW 1979-80, & secy 1981-83; chmn Minority Affairs Com, NYS NASW 1979-84; co-chmn 5th Annual Whitney M Young Conf on Racism & Del of Human Svcs, NASW 1978-83; chairperson Nat Nominations & Leadership Com, NASW 1984-; pres Yonkers, NY Branch NAACP 1971-78; dir Westchester Regnl NYS Conf NAACP 1977-; chmn trustee bd Metropolitan AME Zion Ch 1969-; chmn Career Guidance Advisory Council, Educ Oppor Cntr of Westchester 1979-85; mem Statewide Advisory Council, NYS Div of Human Rights 1984-; mem New York State Bd of Social Work 1987-. **HONORS/ACHIEVEMENTS:** Freedom Fighter Award Yonkers NAACP 1978; Eugene T Reed Medalist, NYS Conf NAACP 1983; Social Worker of The Yr West Div NASW 1982; Citizen of The Yr Omega Psi Phi Frat, Beta Alpha Alpha Chap 1983; delegate Nat Delegate Assemblys NASW, Portland 1977 & Philadelphia 1981. **MILITARY SERVICE:** AUS sp 4th class 1963-66. **HOME ADDRESS:** Rt 2 Box 327, Yorktown Heights, NY 10598. **BUSINESS ADDRESS:** Executive Dir, Westchester Comm Opportunity Pgm, 172 S Broadway, White Plains, NY 10605.

ROSS-BARNETT, MARGUERITE
Educator. **PERSONAL:** Born May 21, 1942, Charlottesville, VA; married Walter King; children: Amy. **EDUCATION:** Antioch Coll, AB 1964; Univ of Chicago, AM 1966, PhD 1972. **CAREER:** Princeton Univ, asst prof 1970-76; Brookings Inst, guest scholar 1974-75; Howard Univ, prof (tenured) 1976-80, chairperson dept of pol sci 1977-80; Columbia Univ, prof 1980-83; City Univ of NY, vice chancellor for acad affairs 1983-; Univ of MO St Louis, chancellor 1986-. **ORGANIZATIONS:** Mem adv bd Rabinowitz Found 1972-77; mem exec comm Amer Pol Sci Assoc; mem exec council New Pol Sci; mem bd of dir, exec council Natl Council of Black Pol Sci; mem Assoc for Asian Studies, Soc for S India Studies, Assoc for Study of Afro-Amer Life & History. **HONORS/ACHIEVEMENTS:** Appt James Madison Bicent Perceptor 1974-76; Awd for Dist Rsch & Scholarship Howard Univ Grad School of Art & Sci 1976; author "The Politics of Cultural Nationalism in S India" Princeton Univ Press 1976; co-ed "Public Policy & the Black Comm, Strategies & Perspectives" Alfred Press 1976; Amer Political Science Assoc Awd 1981. **BUSINESS ADDRESS:** Chancellor, Univ of Missouri-St Louis, 8001 Natural Bridge, St Louis, MO 63121.

ROSSER, JAMES M.
President. **PERSONAL:** Born Apr 16, 1939, East St Louis, IL; married Carmen Rosita Colby; children: Terrence. **EDUCATION:** Southern IL Univ, Carbondale, BA 1962, MA 1963, PhD 1969. **CAREER:** Holden Hospital, diagnostic bacteriologist 1961-63; Health Educ & Coordinator of Black Amer Studies, instructor 1962-63; Eli Lily & Co, research Bacteriologist 1963-66; Southern IL Univ, mem graduate faculty 1966-70; Univ KS, ten assoc prof & assoc vice chancelor 1971-74; Dept of Higher Educ, acting vice chancelor 1974-79; Dept of Higher Ed, acting chancelor 1977; State Univ, Los Angeles, pres Health Care Mgmt 1979-. **ORGANIZATIONS:** Chr plng comm Dev of th Black Amer Studies Prog 1968; mem Academic Admnstrve Comm 1970-72; cnsltnt Rsch Cncl, Assoc for Supvrsn & Cirr Devlpmnt1970; mem Gen Advsry Pblctn Comm 1970; mem Cncl of Dir of Univ Div 1970-74; stf mem Resch Training Session "The Research Componet of Black Studies" 1971; mem State Coll & Univ Coordntg Comm KS State Brd of Regents 1971-72; cordntr Schl Health Workshop, Annual Mtg of Amer Assoc of Health, Physcl Ed & Rec 1971; mem Edtrl Brd Univ Press of KS 1971-74; v chrmn Edtrl Brd Univ Press KS 1972-74; chair Univ Computing Comm & Exec Comm for Computing, Univ KS 1971-73; cordntr New Faculty Orientation Prog Univ of KS 1971-74; cnsltnt Ottawa Univ KS 1972, KS Rgnl Med Prog 1972; cnsltnt HUD Seminar for Comm Dvlpmnt Specialists 1972; chr Comm. **HONORS/ACHIEVEMENTS:** Listed Outstanding Young Men Of Amer 1971, Outstanding Educators of Amer 1974, Who's Who Among Black Amer 1976, Men of Achievement 1977, Who's Who in Health Care 1977, Who's Who in Amer, 42nd Ed 1981-82; published "Biological & Physcl Characteristics of an Oncolytic Agent Isolated from Mouse Ascites Cells" 1965, "A Formulation Process for a Master Plan for Higher ed in KS" 1970, "Population & Envirnment, A Minority Perspective 1970; "Student Opinions & Black Studies" 1971, "Values and Health" 1971, "Is Health Science Ed Dvlpng Socially Conscious Practitioners" 1972, "Higher Ed and the Black Amer, An Overview" 1974, "Reflections, Black Studies-Black Ed" 1973, "A Student-Initiated Minority Engrng Prog, The Univ of KS" 1973, "A Factorial Study of Health Values" 1973, "The Consumer, Health, and the Health Professional" 1975, "Case Study and Postscript on Jersey" 1977, "Access and Student Aid, The New Jersey Approach" 1977, "After Bakke" 1979, "Identifying Urban Comm Coll Needs, The Role of Trustees" 1979, "A Court of Last Resort" 1980, "Who Controls Admissions Policies? The Role of Govrnmnt, The Rights of Institutions" 1980; W Coast Father of Year 1981; Black Achieve History Award 1981; Boy Scouts, LA area president 1985; bd mem, KCET-TV, LA Ch of Comm, LA Philharmonic, Southern CA Edison, Urban League. **BUSINESS ADDRESS:** President, CA StateUniv Los Angeles, 5151 State University Dr, 5151 State Univ Dr, Los Angeles, CA 90032.

ROSSER, PEARL (NEE LOCKHART)
Physician. **PERSONAL:** Born Dec 27, 1935, Miami, FL; married Dr Samuel B Rosser; children: Charles. **EDUCATION:** Howard Univ, BS 1956, MD 1960. **CAREER:** Freedman's Hosp, intern 1960-61, pediatric resd 1961-63; Howard Univ Coll of Med, prof of pediatrics 1964-; Retired 1985; consultant in Developmental pediatrics. **ORGANIZATIONS:** Consult Natl Headstart Prog 1969-76; consult Abt Asso 1976; Proj Thrive Adv Comm Natl Urban League 1976; mem Amer Acad of Pediatrics; bd dir Eugene & Agnes E Meyer Found 1977; fellow Amer Acad of Pediatrics; Amer Pediatric Soc; Soc for Rsch in Child Develop; Prof Adv Bd; Assn for Children with Learning Disabilities; Natl Council on Black Child Develop; over 10 journals published; over 5 chapts in prof books. **HONORS/ACHIEVEMENTS:** Co-editor "The Genetic Metabolic & Devel Aspects of Mental Retardation" 1972. **HOME ADDRESS:** 2222 Westview Dr, Silver Spring, MD 20910.

ROSSER, SAMUEL BLANTON
Physician, educator. **PERSONAL:** Born Jul 13, 1934, Tallapoosa, GA; married Pearl; children: Charles. **EDUCATION:** Clark Coll, BS 1954; Wayne State Univ, MS 1956; Howard Univ Coll Med, MD 1960. **CAREER:** Freedmen's Hospital, resident general surgeon 1961-66; Children's Hospital Natl Medical Center, resident 1970-72; Howard Univ Coll Med Pedi-

atric Surgery, assoc prof 1972-. **ORGANIZATIONS:** Pres 1976-77, mem Assoc of Former Interns & Residents of Howard Univ Hosp; fellow Amer Coll Surgeons;, mem Amer Acad Pediatrics, Amer Pediatric Surg Assoc. **MILITARY SERVICE:** AUSNG maj. **BUSINESS ADDRESS:** Associate Professor of Surgery, HowardUniv Coll of Medicine, 2041 Georgia Ave NW, Washington, DC 20060.

ROTAN, CONSTANCE S.
Educator, attorney. **PERSONAL:** Born Apr 19, 1935, Baton Rouge, LA; married James Rotan Jr; children: Kevin, Michael. **EDUCATION:** Southern Univ,BA (Cum Laude) 1956; Howard Univ Grad School, 36 hrs toward MA 1968; Howard Univ School of Law, JD (Hon Grad) 1967. **CAREER:** US Dept of Justice, gen trial atty 1968-70; United Planning Org, asst gen consultant 1970-72; Howard Univ School of Law, asst dean, asst prof 1972-75; Howard Univ, exec asst office vice pres for admin 1975-. **ORGANIZATIONS:** Mem Natl Bar Assoc 1970-, Kappa Beta Pi Intl Legal Sor 1965-, Alpha Kappa Alpha 1977-, Assoc of Amer Law Schools, Natl Assoc of Coll & Univ Attnys,US Dist Ct for DC, US Ct of Appeals for DC; dean Howard Univ Chap Kappa Beta Pi Intl Legal Sor 1963-64; co-chmn Comm on Age of Majority of DC; mem DC Bar, Phi Sigma Alpha; founding mem, officer Waring/Mitchell Law Soc; mem Public Mem Assoc of Foreign Svc. **HONORS/ACHIEVEMENTS:** Public Mem of USIA Selection Bd 1986. **HOME ADDRESS:** 9216 Creekbed Ct, Columbia, MD 21045. **BUSINESS ADDRESS:** Executive Assistant, HowardUniv, 2400 6th St NW Rm 440, Howard Univ, Washington, DC 20059.

ROULHAC, EDGAR EDWIN
Educational administrator. **PERSONAL:** Born Sep 28, 1946, Chicago, IL; son of Edgar Elijah Roulhac and Portia Goodloe Roulhac; married Patricia Gayle Johnson. **EDUCATION:** Southern IL Univ Carbondale, BS 1969, MS 1970, PhD 1974; Johns Hopkins Univ School of Public Health, MPH 1975, postdoctoral studies 1974-75; Harvard Univ, Inst for Educ Mgmt, 1987. **CAREER:** Southern IL Univ School of Medicine, prof of health care planning 1972-74; Towson State Univ, prof of health science 1975-78; Provident Hospital, Baltimore MD, dir 1978-82; Johns Hopkins School of Public Health, dean of students 1978-86, asst provost 1986-. **ORGANIZATIONS:** Mem Kappa Alpha Psi Fraternity 1965-; MD Soc for Medical Research, dir, vice pres 1981-84; mem Sigma Pi Phi Fraternity 1986-, AAHE, ACPA, APHA, BCHW, NAPW, NASPA, SOPHE. **HONORS/ACHIEVEMENTS:** Hon Educ Phi Delta Kappa 1972-; Hon Educ Kappa Delta Pi 1972-; postdoctoral fellow Johns Hopkins Univ School of Public Health 1974-75; Hon Public Health Delta Omega 1982-; Sigma Pi Phi 1986-. **HOME ADDRESS:** 9314 Edway Cir, Randallstown, MD 21133.

ROULHAC, JOSEPH D.
Judge. **PERSONAL:** Born Aug 18, 1916, Selma, AL; married Frances; children: Delores. **EDUCATION:** Stillman Coll, cert 1936; Lincoln Univ, AB 1938; Univ of PA, MA 1940, JD 1948. **CAREER:** Lincoln Univ, instr 1938-39; Ft Valley St Coll, instr 1940-41; Summit Cty OH, asst city pros 1957-63; Akron Municipal Ct, judge. **ORGANIZATIONS:** Mem OH, Natl, Amer Bar Asoc; mem Amer Judic Soc, OH Mun Judges Assoc; trustee Baldwin Wallace Coll & Stillman Coll; mem NAACP, VFW, Amer Leg, PhiBeta Sigma Dist Serv Chapt, Phi Beta Sigma. **MILITARY SERVICE:** M sgt 1942-46. **BUSINESS ADDRESS:** Judge, Akron Municipal Court, City Cty Safety Bldg, Akron, OH 44308.

ROULHAC, NELLIE GORDON
Educator. **PERSONAL:** Born Jun 05, 1924, Washington, DC; daughter of Dr Levi Preston Morton Gordon and Agnes Pauline Lee Gordon; married Dr Christopher M Roulhac Jr, Aug 01, 1944; children: Christopher M III, Dr Yvonne Agnes Roulhac Horton. **EDUCATION:** Cheyney State Univ, BA; Teachers Coll, Columbia Univ, MA; Temple Univ Post Grad, Cert Special Educ; Univ of Sarasota, EdD 1978; Univ of Pennsylvania, Post Grad Studies. **CAREER:** Westmoreland County, VA, principal sch 1945; Albany State Coll, Albany GA, instructor engl 1949; Memphis Public Sch, classroom tchr 1954; Sch Dist of Phila, supvr special educ 1971-83. **ORGANIZATIONS:** Chair Personnel Comm Delta Sigma Theta Sor Inc; chrmn fund-raising Jack & Jill of Am Found Bd of Trustees 1980-; commr Mayor's Commn for Women 1984-; past pres Bd of Trustees Pennhurst Cntr, Spring City, PA 1970-80; past pres Natl Jack & Jill of Amer 1954-58; past pres Jack & Jill of Am Found 1975-78; bd of trustees The Free Library of Philadelphia 1985-; founder Thirty Clusters; mem The Links Inc Philadelphia Chapter; former chair Eastern Area Links Inc; chair Services to Youth Comm; organizer Friends of Combs Coll of Music 1978; bd of trustees, Combs Coll of Music 1979-83; natl sec Delta Sigma Theta Sorority Inc 1954-58. **HONORS/ACHIEVEMENTS:** In Recognition of Outstanding Contribution Field of Special Educ/Mainline Comm Philadelphia Grand Opera Co; Continued Distinguished Serv to Jack & Jill of Amer Found 1972, 1974; Outstanding Serv Field Special Educ Div Philadelphia PA 1982; Recognition Serv to Youth YMCA Memphis, TN, Philadelphia PA; author, "Seventeen Days of Jimmie" 1981; Fund Raisers From A-Z 1984; Sadie T M Alexander Award, Philadelphia Alumnae Chapter, Delta Sigma Theta Sorority Inc 1988; In Recognition of Your Contribution to Pennhurst's History of Service, Pennhurst State School & Hospital 1987; Outstanding Service Award, Jack & Jill of Amer, 1988; author History of Jack and Jill of America Inc 1990. **HOME ADDRESS:** 7137 Lincoln Dr, Philadelphia, PA 19119.

ROULHAC, ROY L.
Administrative law judge. **PERSONAL:** Born Mar 27, 1943, Marianna, FL; son of J Y Rolack (deceased) and GeHazel Gibson Roulhoc (deceased); children: Sheryl LaSonya McGriff. **EDUCATION:** Wayne State Univ, Detroit MI, BS Business Mgmt, 1970; Univ of Detroit School of Law, Detroit MI, JD, 1975. **CAREER:** Wayne County Prosecutor's Office, Detroit MI, asst prosecutor, 1976; Michigan Dept of State, Detroit MI, admin law judge, 1977-79; Michigan Dept of Labor, Detroit MI, admin law jude, 1979-. **ORGANIZATIONS:** Pres, Michigan Assn for Admin Law Judges, 1982-84; bd of dir, Natl Alliance Against Racist & Political Repression, 1985-; treasurer, Amer Assn of Jurist, 1987-; mem, Omega Psi Phi Frat Inc, 1987-; pres, Assn of Black Judges of Michigan, 1988-89; pres-elect, Admin Law Section, State Bar of Michigan, 1988-89; bd of dir, Music Hall Center of Detroit, 1988-, Fred Hart Williams Genealogical Soc, 1988-. **HONORS/ACHIEVEMENTS:** Admin Law Judge of the Year, Michigan Assn of Admin Law Judes, 1986; Certificate of Appreciation, Office of Governor, 1989; Senate Concurrent Resolution #277, Michigan Legislature, 1989; Testimonial Resolution, Detroit City Council, 1989; Testimonial Resolution, County of Wayne & Office of County Executive, 1989. **MILITARY SERVICE:** US Army Reserves, Washington DC Natl Guard; 1st Lieutenant, 1964-70. **BUSINESS ADDRESS:** Administrative Law Judge, Michigan Department of Labor, Office of Hearings, 1200 6th St, 14th Floor, Detroit, MI 48226.

ROUNDFIELD, DANNY THOMAS (ROUNDS)
Professional athlete. **PERSONAL:** Born May 26, 1953, Detroit, MI; married Bernadine Owens; children: Corey, Christopher. **EDUCATION:** Central MI U, BS Bus 1975. **CAREER:** Atlanta Hawks, professional basketball player 1978-; Fulton Fed Sav & Loan, loan ofcr 1980, bank teller 1979. **HONORS/ACHIEVEMENTS:** 1st Team All-Pro 1980, 1st Team All-Defense 1980, 30th Team All-Star 1980 all in the NBA. **BUSINESS ADDRESS:** Atlanta Hawks, 100 Techwood Dr, Atlanta, GA 30303.

ROUNDTREE, EUGENE V. N.
Business executive. **PERSONAL:** Born Dec 19, 1927, Roxbury, MA; married Jacqueline Marie; children: Gene Jr, Nicholas, Nancy, Christopher, Phillip, Stephen, Anne Marie, Mary. **EDUCATION:** Bates Coll ME, BS 1951. **CAREER:** Black Corporate Pres of New Eng, dir; All-Stainless Inc, pres 1951-. **ORGANIZATIONS:** Dir New Eng Iron & Hardware Assn; past natl dir MA Jaycees; mem S Shore Cit Club; dir Nat Minority Prchsg Cncl; mem Hingham Rotary Club; past pres S Shore C of C; bd mem Mayor's Adv Cncl; dir Rockland Credit Union, Scoot, MA Mental Health Assoc. **BUSINESS ADDRESS:** President, All Stainless Inc, 75 Research Rd, Hingham, MA 02043.

ROUNDTREE, NICHOLAS JOHN
Marketing manager. **PERSONAL:** Born May 04, 1956, Quincy, MA. **EDUCATION:** Northeastern Univ, BS 1979, Bus Admin, Marketing Rsch 5 yrs. **CAREER:** Gillette, mfg planning 1975; Merriman Corp/Litton Ind, inside sales expediting 1976; Boston Globe, merchandising/promo 1977; Gen Elec, sales rep 1977; IBM, sales rep 1978-79; All-Stainless Inc, natl sales mgr 1979-. **ORGANIZATIONS:** Mem So Shore Chamber of Commerce 1979-. **BUSINESS ADDRESS:** Natl Sales Manager, All-Stainless, Inc, 75 Research Road, Hingham, MA 02143.

ROUNDTREE, RICHARD
Actor. **PERSONAL:** Born Jul 09, 1942, New Rochelle, NY; divorced; children: Kelly, Nicole. **EDUCATION:** So IL Univ, 2 yrs. **CAREER:** Barney's, suit salesman; model; Shaft 1971, Shaft's Big Score 1973; Negro Ensemble Co, Kongi's Harvest, Man, Better Man, Mau-Mau Room, performed; The Great White Hope, Shaft in Africa, Roots, actor; recorded several songs; What Do You Say To A Naked Lady? 1970, Parachute to Paradies, Embassy 1972, Charley One-Eye, Earthquake 1974, Man Friday 1974, Diamonds 1974, Escape to Athena 1979, The Merv Griffin Show, Search for Tomorrow, The New Yorkers, Inside Bedford-Stuyvesant, The Dean Martin Show, series Shaft 1973-74, Firehouse, actor; The Man From Shaft, recorded album; St Brother, recorded single. **BUSINESS ADDRESS:** Agency Performing Arts Inc, 9000 Sunset Blvd, Los Angeles, CA 90069.

ROUNSAVILLE, LUCIOUS BROWN, JR.
Senior specialist transportation. **PERSONAL:** Born Apr 14, 1954, Atlanta, GA. **EDUCATION:** GA State Univ, BBA 1977; Atlanta Univ, MBA 1983. **CAREER:** Colonial Pipeline Co, various positions clerk, analyst, staff analyst, sr staff analyst 1977-86, sr specialist property tax 1987-. **ORGANIZATIONS:** Mem Alpha Phi Alpha Frat 1976-, Natl Black MBA Assoc 1979-; treas Colonial Pipeline Co Employees Club 1981-83; mem The Atlanta Exchange Foundation 1983-, LA Assoc of Tax Representatives 1983-; mem The Atlanta Tax Club 1984-; treas Natl Black MBA Assoc Atlanta Chap 1984-85, exec comm 1987-; 2nd vice pres bdof dirs Yard Wide Federal Credit Union 1987-; pres Atlanta Univ Sch of Business Admin Alumni Assoc Atlanta Chap 1987-88; mem Cosmopolitan AME Church. **HONORS/ACHIEVEMENTS:** Mortar Board Outstanding Leadership Awd GA State Univ 1977; 5 Year Serv Awd 1982, 10 Year Serv Awd 1987 Colonial Pipeline Co; Outstanding Young Men of Amer US Jaycees 1984. **HOME ADDRESS:** 486 Spencer St NW, Atlanta, GA 30314. **BUSINESS ADDRESS:** Sr Specialist Property Tax, Colonial Pipeline Co, 3390 Peachtree Rd NE, Atlanta, GA 30326.

ROUNTREE, ELLA JACKSON
Educator. **PERSONAL:** Born Feb 27, 1936, Griffin, GA; widowed. **EDUCATION:** Ft Valley State Coll, BS 1957; Western CT State Coll, MS 1973. **CAREER:** Grassy Plain School, teacher 1963-; Moore Elem School, 1960-63; AL St Elem School, 1957-60. **ORGANIZATIONS:** Mem Bethel Educ Assn; Danbury City Cncl 1973-77; CT Educ Assn; Nat Educ Assn; Phi Lambda Theta; Nat Hon & Professional Assn in Edn; mem NAACP; AlphaKappa Alpha Sor; Black Dem; Waterbury Chap LINKS; Mt Pleasant AMEZ Ch; cnclpers Danbury City Cncl 6th Ward 1973-. **HONORS/ACHIEVEMENTS:** Outstand Elem Tchr of Am 1974. **BUSINESS ADDRESS:** 241 Greenwood Ave, Bethel, CT 06810.

ROUNTREE, LOUISE M.
Retired librarian. **PERSONAL:** Born Aug 16, 1921, Barnwell, SC; daughter of Clarence C Rountree and Mary M Rountree. **EDUCATION:** Morris Coll, AB 1941; Atlanta Univ, BLS 1950; Syracuse U, MLS 1956; Columbia Univ 1961; W Africa, ethnic heritage seminary 1974. **CAREER:** Estill HS Estill, SC, librarian; Allendale Co HS SC, librarian 1948-51; Livingstone Coll, asst librarian 1951-, acting head 1969-70, head librarian 1970-87, assoc prof 1978-87. **ORGANIZATIONS:** Mem Southeastern Library Assn; NC Lib Assn; sec 1972; cood ICDP 1976-; mem Mayor's Historic Commn 1975-77 & 1978-80; mem/bd mem Amer Assn of Univ Women 1971, topic chmn 1973, historian 1971-73; Rowan Historical Properties Commn 1972; Rowan Bicentennial Commn 1974-76; special events com RCCM 1974; Dial Help Back Up 1972-; chairperson Centennial Program Commn 1978 & 1980; chmn JC Price Marker Com 1978; rededication comm Dodge Hall 1981-82; chairperson for Inauguration of the 7th pres of Livingstone Coll 1984; mem NC Afro-Amer Genealogical Soc 1985-; mem Arts in Public Places Panel 1986-. **HONORS/ACHIEVEMENTS:** Recip Jennie Smallwood Price Award 1970; Dedication Coll Yearbook 1971; Plaque for 25 yrs of serv Friends of Livingstone Coll Library 1977; Scholarship in Honor of Louise M Rountree for Significant Serv AAUW Salisbury Chapter 1977; Certificate of Appreciation Rowan Public Library 1977; Certificate of Appreciation Athletic Dept 1979; Centennial Recognition Plaque for 25 plus yrs 1979; DAR Comm Serv Award 1983; Minority Woman of the Yr Award Zeta Phi Beta Sor 1985; Athletic Dept Serv Award for Preservation of Records 1985; apptd State Baptist Historian 1985; research editor State Baptist History (women) 1985; Livingstone Coll Alumni Meritorious Serv Award 1986; An Appreciation Award, Livingston College 1989.

ROUSE, BISHOP CLAUDE, JR.
Business executive. **PERSONAL:** Born Dec 04, 1948, Atlanta, GA; married Minnie Loney; children: Claudia, Bishop III, Kafi, Adam. **EDUCATION:** Allen U, BS Chem 1968-71; Argonne Nat Lab, CSUI Hon Stdnt 1971. **CAREER:** Federal Paper Co, chemist 1971-72;

Ohio State U, teaching asso 1972-73; Celanebe, engr 1973-82; Duracell, engr 1982-84, mgr 1984-. **ORGANIZATIONS:** Pres Burns Jr High PTO 1983-84; mem Advisory Cncl Cleveland Cnty Sch 1980-; chrmn Cleveland Cnty Commn for Women 1981-82. **HONORS/ACHIEVEMENTS:** Citizenship Award NC Assn Educators 1981; Cert of Appreciation & Outstand Serv to Cub Scouts Piedmont Cncl 1981; Outstand Serv to PTO Award Waco Elem Sch1981; missionary to HI SC United Methodist Ch 1968. **HOME ADDRESS:** Rt 1 Box 230a, Shelby, NC 28150.

ROUSE, DONALD E.
Educator. **PERSONAL:** Born May 30, 1932, Philadelphia, PA; married Barbara Miller; children: Wendy, Claire. **EDUCATION:** BS; MS; MEd; PhD Educ Admin. **CAREER:** New Teacher's Elementary & Secondary Coordinator, Intergroup Educ, teacher/consultant; principal; assoc prof educ; educ consultant; Elementary Summer School Program, original instructor; Adult Educ Germany, instructor; New Teachers Clinic, coordinator; reading consultant; Urban Centers, dir. **ORGANIZATIONS:** PSEA; NEA; Amer Assn of Univ Profs; Coll Grad Council; Natl AAU; Phi Delta Kappa; Philadelphia Assn of School Admins; bd dir Tribune Charities; Interested Negroes Inc; Am Assn, Afro-Amer Educators; NAACP; Masons; Amer Found Negro Affairs. **HONORS/ACHIEVEMENTS:** W Philadelphia Comm Award 1972; Landreth Man Yr Award 1971; St Thomas Church Awd; Schoolmen's Club 1986. **MILITARY SERVICE:** AUS lt 1955-57. **BUSINESS ADDRESS:** Dir, University Cheyney, Urban Center, Philadelphia, PA 19139.

ROUSE, GENE GORDON, SR.
Assistant district manager. **PERSONAL:** Born Apr 23, 1923, Mt Vernon, OH; son of Horace Rouse and Louise Rouse; married Estelle Lewis Rouse, Jun 04, 1949; children: Gene G Jr, Eric V. **EDUCATION:** Central State Univ OH, BS 1951; Chicago State Univ, 1960-61. **CAREER:** US Post Office, clerk 1952-60; Chicago bd of Ed, teacher 1960-65; Dept of Human Resources (Comm on Youth Welfare), neighborhood Worker 1966-68; Dept of Human Resources, unit dir 1968-80. **ORGANIZATIONS:** Chmn Englewood Inter Agncy Cnsl 1975-; selecting brd NROTC 1971-73; mem NACD 1969-; mem Kappa Alpha Psi 1974-75; pres Mendel Booster Club 1974-75; blood donor Kenglewood Hosp 1979-. **HONORS/ACHIEVEMENTS:** Hnry mem Puerto Rican Congress 1972; Great Guy Award-Radio Sta WGRT 1971; Midwest All-conference Football 1950; Athletic Acmplshmnt Award Austin Town Hall 1971; Certificate of Appreciation Englewood Hosp 1974; Outstanding Serv from 17th Ward Young Dem Org 1974; Certificate of Appreciation Natl Found for Cancer Rsch 1983; services rendered Dept Ag Univ of IL Circle Campus 1983. **MILITARY SERVICE:** AUS sgt 1943-45; Good Conduct Medal, ETO Ribbon. **HOME ADDRESS:** 1054 W 109th Pl, Chicago, IL 60643. **BUSINESS ADDRESS:** Assistant-District Manager, Dept of Human Services, 6201 S Halstead St, Chicago, IL 60621.

ROUSE, JACQUELINE ANNE
Educator. **PERSONAL:** Born Feb 01, 1950, Roseland, VA; daughter of Fannie Thompson Rouse. **EDUCATION:** Howard Univ, Washington, DC, 1968-72; Atlanta Univ, Atlanta, GA, MA, 1972-73; Emory Univ, Atlanta, GA, Ph.D., 1979-83. **CAREER:** Pal, Beach Jr Coll, Lake Worth, FL, sr instructor, 1973-80; Georgia Inst of Teachers, Atlanta, GA, guest lecturer, 1983; Morehouse Coll, Atlanta, GA, assoc prof, 1983-; Amer Univ/Smithsonian Inst, Landmarks prof of history, 1989-. **ORGANIZATIONS:** Asst editor, Journal of Negro History, 1983-89; advisor/reference, Harriet Tubman Historial & Cultural Museum, Macon, GA, 1985; panelist, Amer Association Univ of Women, 1985-; principal scholar/mem, Steering Comm, Natl Conf Women in Civil Rights Movement; 1988; panelist, Jacob Javits Fellowship, Dept of Educ, 1989; natl vice dir, Assn of Black Women Historians, 1989-; first vice pres, Assn of Social & Behavorial Scientists, 1989-; consultant/advisor, Atlanta Historical Soc, 1989; historian consultant, Apex Collection of Life & Heritage, 1989. **HONORS/ACHIEVEMENTS:** FIPSE, Curriculum on Black Women's History, Spellman Coll, 1983-84; NEH Summer Grant for Coll Teachers; 1984; UNCF Strengthening the Humanities Grant, 1985. **BUSINESS ADDRESS:** Assoc Prof of History, Morehouse Coll, 830 Westview Dr SW, Brawley Hall 208, Atlanta, GA 30314.

ROUSE, TERRIE
Museum director. **PERSONAL:** Born Dec 02, 1952, Youngstown, OH; daughter of Eurad Rouse and Florence Rouse. **EDUCATION:** Trinity Coll, BA 1974; Cornell Univ, Master Professional Studies 1977; Columbia Univ School of Intl Affairs, Cert 1979; Columbia Univ, MA 1979. **CAREER:** School of Intl Affairs, rsch asst 1977; Special Serv Project Hunter Coll, coord 1978-79; Adam Clayton Powell Jr State Office Bldg, mgr, curator 1979-81; Studio Museum in Harlem, sr curator; New York Transit Museum, museum dir. **ORGANIZATIONS:** Bellevue Hosp Art Bd; Literary Society; mem African Amer Museum Assn, Amer Museum Assn. **HONORS/ACHIEVEMENTS:** Honor Civil Rights Awd Trinity Coll 1974; Graduate Fellow Columbia Univ 1977, 1978; Graduate Fellow Cornell Univ 1974, 1976; Unit Citation, New York Transit Authority. **HOME ADDRESS:** 409 Edgecombe Ave #7 F, New York, NY 10032.

ROUSSELL, NORMAN
Educator. **PERSONAL:** Born Jul 11, 1934, New Orleans, LA; married Dorothy McCullum; children: Michael K. **EDUCATION:** Dillard Univ, BA 1960; Fisk Univ, MA 1965; Wayne State Univ, EdD 1974. **CAREER:** Orleans Parish School Systems, chmn science dept 1960-66; Dillard Univ, assoc dean of students 1969-75; Loyola Univ, dir title III 1976-79, exec asst to the pres 1979-86, vice pres for administration 1986-. **ORGANIZATIONS:** Mem bd of trustees NO Museum of Art 1973-86; mem Amer Assoc of Higher Educ 1977-86. **HONORS/ACHIEVEMENTS:** Charles S Mott Fellowship 1972; Danna Faculty Improvement Grant Dillard Univ 1973; Academic Scholarship Wayne State Univ 1973. **MILITARY SERVICE:** USAF staff sgt 4 yrs; Korean Serv Medal, Good Conduct Medal. **HOME ADDRESS:** 7441 Bullard Ave, New Orleans, LA 70128. **BUSINESS ADDRESS:** Vice Pres for Administration, Loyola University, 6363 St Charles Ave, New Orleans, LA 70118.

ROUTT, THOMAS H.
Judge. **PERSONAL:** Born Mar 05, 1930, Grimes Co, TX; son of James Scurry and Annie Roberts Johnson; married Ritchie Wilson, Dec 22, 1954; children: Lora Dean, Thomas Jr. **EDUCATION:** Prairie View Univ Prairie View, TX, 1945-47; TX Southern Univ, 1950-52; TX Southern Univ Law Sch, JD 1961; Annual Advocacy Inst Ann Arbor, MI, 1967; Amer Acad Judicial Ed Univ AL, Grad 1970; TX Coll for the Judiciary Austin,TX, Grad 1974; Natl Coll Judiciary Reno, NV, Grad 1975; New Trends Law Natl Coll State Judiciary Reno, NV, Post Grad 1977; Natl Judicial Coll, Evidence Grad Course 1983, Crmnl Law Grad Course 1983, Search & Seizure Spclty Course 1983, Grad Courses, 1985, 1987. **CAREER:** Private Practice 1961; Routte Harper & McDonald, sr prtnr 1963-64; Tillman & Hannah, associated 1964-65; Office of the Atty Gen TX, apptd to staff 1965-66; Neighborhood Law Ofc Houston Legal Found, managing atty 1966-68; Municipal Ct Number Six City of Houston, TX, aptd judge 1968-72; Ofc of the Atty Gen TX as Asst Chief Enfrcmnt Div, apptd to staff 1973; Cty Crmnl Ct Law Number Six Harris Cty TX, judge 1973-77; 208th Dist Ct Harris Cty TX; judge 1977-. **ORGANIZATIONS:** Admitted State Bar TX 1961, Bar of Fed Dist Ct for Southern Dist TX Houston Div 1965, Bar to Fed Dist Ct Eastern Dist TX Tyler Div 1965, Bar of Fed Dist Ct Western Dist TX Austin Div 1966, Bar of US Ct of Appeals for Fifth Circuit 1966, Bar of Supreme Ct US 1967, Bar of Fed Dist Ct Northern Dist TX Dallas Div 1973; mem State Bar TX, Amer Bar Assn, Amer Judicature Soc, Amer Judges Assn, Houston Bar Assn, Houston Lawyers Assn; mem Amer Correctional Assn; former vice pres bd mgr South Cntrl Brnch YMCA; mem bd dir Houston Urban League, TX Southern Univ Ex-Students Assn, TX Southern Univ Law Found; mem chmn bd dir Riverside General Hospital; mem advsry cncl Riverside General Hospital; mem bd dir Wesley Comm Center; mem bd trustee Houston Legal Found; mem budget panel com United Fund of Houston-Har ris Cty; mem bd dir Gre ater Houston Cncl of Camp Fire Girls Inc; mem Citizens for Good Sch; mem bd of governors Natl American Red Cross; mem bd of dirs Methodist Hospital, grand master, MWPHGL of Texas, Masons. **HONORS/ACHIEVEMENTS:** Citizen of Yr, Omega Psi Phi Frat Nu Phi Chptr 1969; Comm Serv Award, Delta Sigma Theta Sorority 1970; Distinguished Serv Award, Frontiers Intrl 1973; Man of Yr, Masonic Lodge 1976; Outstanding Comm Serv Award, Pleasantview Civic Clb 1976; Outstanding Vol Award, Houston-Harris Cty Chptr Amer Red Cross 1977; Outstanding Comm Serv Award, Heights Sect Natl Cncl Negro Women 1979; Achievement Award, Phi Alpha Delta Frat Greener Chptr 1979; Recognition Award, Houston Lawyers Assn 1980; Comm Achievement Award, State Conf NAACP Branches 1983; Outstanding Alumnu,s Thurgood Marshall Sch of Law 1984; Achievement Award, Black Women Lawyers Assn 1984; Achievement Award, Natl Bar Assn Area V 1984; Outstanding Achievement, Ethel Ransom Art Club 1984. **MILITARY SERVICE:** USAF; Hon Dischrg 1950, 14 Mnths Overseas, 3 Yrs Active Reserve 1953-56, Hon Discharged. **HOME ADDRESS:** PO Box 8175, Houston, TX 77288.

ROUX, VINCENT J.
Physician. **PERSONAL:** Born Apr 27, 1937, New Orleans, LA; son of John Roux and Beatrice Grammer Roux; married Lois Milton; children: Bridgette, Vincent Jr, Denise. **EDUCATION:** Xavier Univ, BS 1961; Howard Univ Coll of Med, MD 1965; Natl Bd of Med Bd of Examiners, Diploma 1966; Amer Bd Surgery, Cert 1971; Amer Coll of Surgeons, Fellow 1975. **CAREER:** Howard Univ Hosp, med dir 1972-; Howard Univ Coll of Med, assoc dean/clinical affairs 1972-75; Dept of Comm Health Practices, clinical instr 1972; Dept of Surg, asst prof 1971-; chief resident 1969-70; resident gen surgeon 1966-70; Freedmen's Hosp, intern 1966; Montreal Neurol Inst, extern 1964. **ORGANIZATIONS:** AMA; Natl Med Assn; Amer Coll of Surgeons; Med Chirurgical Soc of DC; chmn/bd dir DC Chap United Way 1974-76; mem/bd dir Natl Cap Med Found 1975-; mem DC C of C 1976-. **HONORS/ACHIEVEMENTS:** Publ, "The Stimulation of Adenosine 3', 5' Monophosphal Prodn by Antidiuretic Factors", "The CV Catheter, An Invasive Therapeutic Adj" 1977; Daniel Hale Williams Award 1966; Physician's Recog Award AMA 1969; Charles R Drew Meml Award 1965; 1st Annual Clarence Sumner Green Award 1965. **MILITARY SERVICE:** AUS specialist 3rd cl E-4 1955-58. **BUSINESS ADDRESS:** Medical Dir, Howard University Hospital, 2041 Georgia Ave, Washington, DC 20059.

ROWAN, ALBERT T.
Pastor. **PERSONAL:** Born May 15, 1927, Kansas City, MO; son of Albert Thomas Rowan and Florence Marion Diggs; married Carrie Mae McBride; children: Richard, Brenda Moore, Stephen, Allana Wheeler, Allan. **EDUCATION:** MI State U, 1946; Western Baptist Bible Coll, BRE, BTh 1955-59; Am Bible Inst, DD 1969; VA Seminary & Coll, DD 1975; Ashland Theological Sem, MDiv 1976; Trinity Theol Sem, DMin 1987. **CAREER:** 1st Baptist, Quincy IL, pastor 1955-60; Zion Baptist, Springfield IL, pastor 1960-61; Salem Baptist, Champaign IL, pastor 1961-64; Bethany Baptist, Cleveland OH,pastor 1964-. **ORGANIZATIONS:** 1st vice pres Baptist Minister's Conf of Cleveland; pres Northern OH Dist Congress 1955-60; past pres Cleveland Baptist Assn 1983-; mem exec bd OH General Baptist State Convention; mem Cleveland City Planning Commn; mem Exec Com Cleveland NAACP; mem Cleveland Library Bd of Trustees 1976-78. **HONORS/ACHIEVEMENTS:** Proclamation "Rev Albert T Rouan Day" Mayor Carl B Stokes 1970; Certificate of Appreciation Champaign County Urban League 1963; elected to Lincoln High School Hall of Fame 1981; Hon Dr of Div Am Bible Inst 1969; Hon Dr of Div VA Seminary & Coll 1975. **MILITARY SERVICE:** AUS Specialized Training Corps cadet student 1944-45. **HOME ADDRESS:** 3716 Langton Rd, Cleveland, OH 44121. **BUSINESS ADDRESS:** Pastor, Bethany Baptist Church, 10508 Hampden Ave, Cleveland, OH 44108.

ROWAN, CARL THOMAS
Journalist. **PERSONAL:** Born Aug 11, 1925, Ravenscroft, TN; son of Thomas David Rowan and Johnnie Bradford Rowan; married Vivien Louise Murphy, Aug 02, 1950; children: Barbara, Carl Thomas Jeffrey. **EDUCATION:** Tennessee State Univ, 1942-43; Washburn Univ, 1943-44; Oberlin Coll, AB 1947; Univ of Minnesota, MA 1948. **CAREER:** Minneapolis Tribune, Minneapolis MN, copywriter 1948-50, staff writer, 1950-61; US Dept of State, Washington DC, deputy asst sec for public affairs 1961-63; US ambassador to Finland, based in Helsinki, 1963-64; US Information Agency, dir 1964-65; Chicago Sun-Times (formerly Chicago Daily News), Chicago IL, columnist for Field Newspaper Syndicate (formerly Publishers Hall Syndicate), 1965-; natl affairs commentator on "The Rowan Report," heard nationally on radio five days a week; Post-Newsweek Broadcasting Co, Washington DC, political commentator for radio and television stations; "Agronsky & Co," nationally syndicated public affairs television show, regular panelist; "Meet the Press," frequent panelist; lecturer. **ORGANIZATIONS:** Dir DC Natl Bank; mem Comm of 100 Legal Def Fund; NAACP 1964-; chmn adv comm Natl Comm Against Discrimination in Housing 1967; mem Sigma Delta Chi. **HONORS/ACHIEVEMENTS:** Author, "South of Freedom" 1953, "The Pitiful & The Proud" 1956, "Go South to Sorrow" 1957, "Wait Till Next Year" 1960; Sidney Hillman Found Award 1952; Amer Teamwork Award, Natl Urban League 1955; Distinguished Achievement Award, Regents of Univ of Minnesota 1961; Golden Ruler Award, Philadelphia Fellowship Commn 1961; Communications Award in Human Relations, Anti-Defamation League of B'Nai B'Rith 1964; Distinguished Serv Award, Capital Press Club 1964; Natl Brotherhood Award, Natl Conf of Christians & Jews 1964; Elijah P Lovejoy Award 1968; numerous honorary degrees. **MILITARY SERVICE:** US Navy Res. **BUSINESS ADDRESS:** 1101 7 St NW, Washington, DC 20036. *

ROWE, ALBERT P.

Minister. **PERSONAL:** Born Sep 22, 1934, Columbia, SC; married Dorothy Collins. **EDUCATION:** Morgan St Coll, BA 1958; Crozer Theol Sem, 162; Princeton Theol Sem, 1969. **CAREER:** Central Bapt Ch, pastor 1962-68; Adult Basic Educ Prog, chief recruiter; Wilmington Brd Ed, 1966-68; Calvary Bapts Ch, pastor 1968-; Calvary Bapt Ch Day Care Ctr, advisor/cons; Voc Exploration Ctr & Progressive Reading & Rec Prog, 1972-. **ORGANIZATIONS:** Pres PUADA; bd of trustees Barnert Meml Hosp; commnr Paterson Bd of Edn; chmn Fund Renewal; bd dir/chrmn Civic Organ; vice pres Wilmington NAACP 1966-68. **HONORS/ACHIEVEMENTS:** Paterson NAACP Comm Serv Award 1974; Nominated Young Man of the Yr Wilmington JC'S 1967; Disting Serv Award Calvary Bapt Ch 1973. **MILITARY SERVICE:** AUS 1st lt 1958-59. **BUSINESS ADDRESS:** 575 E 18th, Paterson, NJ 07504.

ROWE, JASPER C.

Attorney. **PERSONAL:** Born Aug 27, 1945, Kilgore, TX; married Susan Adams. **EDUCATION:** Univ of TX, BA Physics 1968; Univ of TX, BA Math 1968; Univ of TX Sch of Law, JD 1971. **CAREER:** Texas Instrument Electronics Inc, elec engr & physicist 1965-68; US Army Corps of Engrs, constrn unit comdr 1970-74; AUS Judge Advocates Gen Corps, atty 1974-; US Dept of HHS Dallas, atty. **ORGANIZATIONS:** Bd dirs NBA 1968; vice pres HEW Employees Assn 1973; mem pres Dallas Ft Worth Black Lawyers Assn 1977; pres Black United Dallas Govt Employees Assn 1977-79; secty-treas bd of dirs Dallas Legal Serv Inc 1978; exec comm mem bd of dirs Dallas Legal Serv Inc 1978; membership chmn Dallas FedBar Assn; chmn Admin Law Sect NBA 1978; mem ABA, TX Bar Assn, Dallas Black C of C; mem Natl Urban League, NAACP, Fed Bus Assn; mem Reserve Officers Assn; mem 1st Baptist Church of Hamilton Park, Alpha Phi Alpha, Alpha Kappa Mu. **HONORS/ACHIEVEMENTS:** Listed in Who's Who in TX 1973-74; Who's Who in S & SW 1975-76; Men of Achievement 1976; Outstanding Am 1976-77; Who's Who in Amer Law 1979. **MILITARY SERVICE:** AUS corps of engrs 1st lt 1972. **BUSINESS ADDRESS:** Attorney, US Dept of HHS, HHS Office of Reg Atty, Ste 1300 1200 Main St, Dallas, TX 75202.

ROWE, JIMMY L.

Association executive. **PERSONAL:** Born Dec 06, 1932, Haskell, OK; children: Dianna, Leonardo, James, Kimberly, Michael. **EDUCATION:** SC St Coll, BA Industrial Educ 1956. **CAREER:** Sons Watts Own Recog Proj, dir 1971-74; Trans Oppor Prog Pico Rivera, CA, acting dir 1971-72, asst dir 1968-71, training coord 1967-68. **ORGANIZATIONS:** Tulsa Personnel Assn; Nat Assn Pretrial Release Assn; Comm Rel Commn Employment Com; dir coalition Los Angeles Model Ctys; mem Tulsa Urban League; asst pastor/minister christian ed St Luke Bapt Ch; youth minister Doublerock BC Compton, CA; Truevine BC Hawthorne, CA; NAACP; Black Econ Union Los Angeles; Mexican Am Political Assn. **HONORS/ACHIEVEMENTS:** Received Resolution Los Angeles City Cncl Outstand Leadership. **MILITARY SERVICE:** AUS Signal Corp 1956-58. **BUSINESS ADDRESS:** 240 E Apache, Tulsa, OK 74106.

ROWE, MARILYN JOHNSON

Government consultant. **PERSONAL:** Born Nov 09, 1954, Batesburg, SC; married Thaddeus E Rowe, Jr; children: Brandolyn. **EDUCATION:** Univ South Carolina, BA Educ 1977. **CAREER:** SC Human Affairs Commission, equal employment oppty consultant. **ORGANIZATIONS:** Member Amer Assoc Affirmation Action 1979- ;member Nat'l Assoc Hmn Rgts Wrkr 1979- ; Tau Beta Sigma USC 1976. **BUSINESS ADDRESS:** Equal Emplymt Opp Consultant, South Carolina Hmn Affrs Comm, 2611 Forest Drive, Columbia, SC 29202.

ROWE, NANSI IRENE

Business executive. **PERSONAL:** Born May 06, 1940, Detroit, MI; children: Leslie Anikaayoka. **EDUCATION:** Detroit Inst of Tech, BBA 1965; Wayne State U, Juris Doctorate 1973. **CAREER:** City of Detroit Corp, corp counsel, dep corp counsel 1974-78; Detroit Econ Growth Corp, vp, gen counsel, sec to bd of dir 1979-82; EO Constructors Inc, pres, chairperson of the bd 1980-; Nansi Row & Assoc PC, pres, chief counsel, partner 1982-. **ORGANIZATIONS:** Secy, treas Wayne Cnty Com Coll Found; secy, genl cnsl Detroit Eco Growth Corp; bd mem Southeastern MI Transit Auth; bd mem Brent Genl Hosp; bd mem Homes for Black Chldrn; bd mem United Community Serv 1978-81; mem bd Brent Hosp, State Bar of MI, Amer Arbitration Assoc; NAACP; bd dir Inner-City Bus Improvement Forum, Southeastern MI Bus Devel Ctr; mem Amer Bar Assoc, Detroit Bar Assoc; life mem Natl Bar Assoc, Wolverine Bar Assoc. **HONORS/ACHIEVEMENTS:** Woman of the Yr United Cncl of Churches 1981; Bus Woman of the Yr Nat Assn of Professional Women 1976. **BUSINESS ADDRESS:** President/Chief Counsel, Nansi Rowe & Assoc PC, 1101 Washington Blvd, Ste 600, Detroit, MI 48226.

ROWE, RICHARD L.

Executive. **PERSONAL:** Born Sep 21, 1926, New York, NY; married Mercedes L Walker; children: Delena Pugh, Patricia Anderson, Richard Jr. **EDUCATION:** City Coll, B Industrial Mgmt; City Univ, MBA. **CAREER:** Port Authority of NY & NJ, asst mgr operating personnel personnel dept 1968-70, mgr equal opportunity prog personnel 1970-72, mgr operating personnel 1972-76, mgr employee relations 1976-78, asst dir aviation dept 1978-83, general mgr JFK Intl Airport 1983-. **BUSINESS ADDRESS:** General Manager, John F Kennedy International, Port Authority of NY & NJ, Building 141, Jamaica, NY 11430.

ROWE, WILLIAM LEON

Business executive. **PERSONAL:** Born Dec 31, 1915, St Matthews, SC; married Isadora Viola Smith. **EDUCATION:** Southern U, SC, PhD. **CAREER:** New York City Police Dept, deputy police commr 1951; WW II, sr war corr; Interstate Tattler/Harlem News/Pittsburgh Courier, theatre editor; MGM & 20th Century Fox,press agent/pr Cons; Mayor of New Rochelle, cons; Nat Newspaper Publishers Assn; Inner City Broadcasting Corp; Amer Magazine, New York Bureau chief; Natl Photo News Svcs, founder/exec editor; Organizational Publishing Co, founder/pres; Louis-Rowe Enterprises, pres. **ORGANIZATIONS:** Capital Press Club Press Organ; Publicity Club of NY PR Organ; EDGES Organ of Corporate Exec; Nat Assn of Black Police Officers; exec bd mem/chrmn pr com Ed Newsletter New Rochelle NAACP; 2nd vice chrmn Black Demo of Westchester; pres Afro-Amer Guild of Performing Artists; bd of dirs Natl Dropout Prevention Fund; adv bd Natl Inst Against Prejudice and Violence; founding mem 100 Black Men Inc. **HONORS/ACHIEVEMENTS:** Half Century Award Nat Newspaper Pub Assn 1985; Appreciation Award Sickle Cell Diease Found of Greater NY 1985; Who's Who in Intl Public Rel; Northside Center for Child Devel;

1986 Ken Knight Awd given in Recognition for total involvement in Black Radio and Black Music at the Family Affair. **BUSINESS ADDRESS:** President, Louis-Rowe Enterprises, 455 Main St, Ste 103 & 105, New Rochelle, NY 10801.

ROWLAND, JAMES H.

Attorney. **PERSONAL:** Born Jan 09, 1909, Adairsville, GA; married Clara B Braswell; children: James H, William H II. **EDUCATION:** Cheyney State Normal, 1929, BS Ed 1932, MEd 1934; OH State Univ; Howard Univ, LLB 1944; Howard Univ, JD 1954. **CAREER:** CCC, ed adv 1934-35; Bluefield State Coll WV, teacher, coach 1935-41; Howard Univ Washington, teacher, coach 1941-44; Bluefield State, 1944-45; Beckley WV, prac atty 1944-55; Harrisburg PA, atty 1955-. **ORGANIZATIONS:** Mem State Bd of Ed WV 1953-55, State Bd of Ed PA 1963-79; pres Natl Assoc of State Bds of Ed 1970-71. **HONORS/ACHIEVEMENTS:** James H Rowland Intermediate School (Harrisburg, PA) named in honor 1986.

ROWLAND, LEON FLOYD

Asst. to the mayor. **PERSONAL:** Born Jul 07, 1945, Atlantic City, NJ. **EDUCATION:** Merced City Coll, AA 1972; Chapman Coll, BA 1975; Gonzaga Univ, MS 1978. **CAREER:** Kincheloe AFB, crew chief 1966-68; Yokota AFB Japan, maintenance supr 1968-71; Castle AFB CA/Fairchild AFB WA, race/human Relations supr 1971-77; Comm Mental Health of Spokane, physchiat therapist 1977-78; Central Comm Ctr City of Spokane WA, dir 1979-84; City of Spokane, asst to Mayor James E Chase 1984-. **ORGANIZATIONS:** Consult drug & alcohol abuse Merced City Coll CA 1973-74; supr minority mental health prog & race relations Comm Mental Health of Spokane 1974-77; mem Intl City Mgr Assn 1979; Natl Mgmt Assoc 1983-; mem Wash Dept Soc & Health Serv Adv Com 1976-; sec NAACP Spokane WA Br 1979-; sec Spokane Sch Dist 81 Citizen Adv Com 1980; mem Spokane OIC Bd of Dir 1980; Omega Psi Phi Frat Inc; Prince Hall Masons. **HONORS/ACHIEVEMENTS:** Cert of Service City of Merced 1975; Omega Psi Phi Citizen of the Yr 1983; Human Relations Council Awd Fairchild AFB WA 1976; Eastern Washington Univ BSW Service Awd 1983; producer Spokane Cultural Mini Festival Spokane Comm Mental Health Ctr 1976; Cert of Appreciation Spokane Comm Mental Health Ctr 1979. **MILITARY SERVICE:** USAF staff sgt 1966-78; Good Conduct Serv Awd. **BUSINESS ADDRESS:** Assistant to Mayor JE Chase, City of Spokane, Office of the Mayor, W 808 Spokane Falls BLvd, Spokane, WA 99201.

ROXBOROUGH, MILDRED (NEE BOND)

Association executive. **PERSONAL:** Born 1927, Brownsville, TN; married John W II. **EDUCATION:** Howard Univ; New York Univ, AB 1947; Columbia Univ, MA 1953; Univ of Paris; Univ of Mexico. **CAREER:** Natl NAACP, asst dir 1975-, exec asst, admin asst to exec dir 1963, natl staff field sec 1954, 1st woman admin asst, exec asst & asst dir. **ORGANIZATIONS:** Life mem, NAACP, 1958-. **BUSINESS ADDRESS:** Deputy Dir Corp Dev, NAACP, 260 5th Avenue, 6th Floor, New York, NY 10001.

ROY, AMERICUS M.

Clergyman. **PERSONAL:** Born Apr 12, 1929, Baltimore; married Doris Johnson. **EDUCATION:** Credits in sociology & polit sci. **CAREER:** Archdiocese of Balto, cath clergyman/permanent deacon; US PO Balto, distrib clerk 1968-72; Dept of Educ Balto, stationary engr 1960-68; counsels pre-trial releases & ex-offenders; St Ambrose Cath Ch, asso pastor. **ORGANIZATIONS:** Mem Black Cath Clergy Caucus; pres St Vincent DePaul Soc; co-chmn Balto Alliance Against Racist & Polit Repression; pres NW Emergency Needs Assn; pres St John's Cncl on Criminal Justice; mem Coalition to End Med Experimentation of Prisoners. **HONORS/ACHIEVEMENTS:** 1st Black Permanent Deacon in US ordained June, 1971. **MILITARY SERVICE:** AUS 1948-50. **BUSINESS ADDRESS:** 4502 Park Hgts Ave, Baltimore, MD 21215.

ROY, JASPER K.

Behavior management specialist. **PERSONAL:** Son of J W Roy; married Barbara Miller; children: 13. **EDUCATION:** Denver Ctr for Grad Studies, MBA 1978; Loyola Univ of Chicago, MPS 1986. **CAREER:** Roys Food Prod Inc Mfg Canned Chitterlings, vice pres 1945-62; Co-op League of the USA, cooperative consult 1967-68; IL Migrant Council, co-op spec 1968-71; Arch of Chicago, ordained perm deacon 1974; Cook County Dept of Corrections, volunteer Catholic chaplain 1974-; Penn Diaconate, assoc dir 1985-89, behavior management specialist 1979-. **ORGANIZATIONS:** Deacon, St Martin DePorres Catholic Church; American Red Cross, Finance Committee. **HOME ADDRESS:** 125 S Waller, Chicago, IL 60644.

ROY, JESSIE H. (NEE HAILSTACK)

Educator. **PERSONAL:** Born Oct 29, 1895, Warrenton, VA; widowed; children: Mrs Marilyn R Robinson. **EDUCATION:** Miner Normal, 1914-16; Howard U, AB 1919. **CAREER:** MI Park Christian Church, consultant day care center; Public School, teacher/retired 1959, sub teacher 1959-65, tutor. **ORGANIZATIONS:** Educ bd The Negro Hist Bull; ASNLH; initiated Alpha Chap AKA 1918; ed Ivy Leaf 1929-33; mem Am AssnUniv Women; mayor's com Food Nutrition Hlth Status of Women; del White House Conf on Aging 1971; hon sch bd Brooklyn Civic Assn; AKA 1966-; Inst for Urban Affairs & Research at Howard U. **HONORS/ACHIEVEMENTS:** Co-ed bibliographic survey, "The Negro in Print" 1965-70; co-author with Mrs Geneva Turner, books for black elem sch children; Honored by Comm Action Prgm Mntl Hlth Research & Devel Ctr; Salute to Black Women of DC Metro Area; symposium HowardUniv Chapel Dunbarten Campus; Cert of Merit Disting Contrib in the observance of Intl Women's Yr.

ROY, JOE EDDIE, SR.

Educator. **PERSONAL:** Born in Clarksdale, MS; married Gladys; children: Joe II, James, Jerry. **EDUCATION:** Alcorn State U, BS 1948; SoUniv & A&M Coll, BS 1963;Univ of IL, MS 1957; CO State U, MS 1979. **CAREER:** Jefferson County Public School Dist R-1, personnel teacher/special assignment; USGS, surveyor 1967-68; Denver Public School, 1965-67; Portsmouth, VA, teacher 1964-65; Edgard, LA, teacher/asst football coach 1963-64; Capitol Sr HS Baton Rouge, LA, teacher 1961-62; Southern Univ Baton Rouge, LA, instructor 1957-61; Franklin Co & Pike County School, teacher/band dir 1955-57; Forest, MS, teacher/band dir 1948-50. **ORGANIZATIONS:** Jefferson Co Educ Assn; CO Educ Assn; Nat Educ Assn; CO & Nat Bio Tchrs Assn 1968-; pres CO, WY St Conf of NAACP Brs 1969-; 1st vp/ed chmn/mem Mile High NAACP Brs 1968-; vol coun Denver Co Prob Serv 1966-; NAACP

Radio Show "Black Profile" 1973-; comdr Bonnette-Harrison Post Am Leg 1963-64; 100 Mem Club NAACP 1976;Univ of No CO 1969;Univ of IN 1970;Univ of WY 1971; Phi Beta Sigma Phi Delta Kappa. **HONORS/ACHIEVEMENTS:** Cert of Apprec Park Hill Br 1977; Cert of Apprec Long & Merit Denver Ct & Co Prob Serv 1974; Fellow Nat Sci Foun Tuskegee Inst 1963-64; Serv Award Region IV NAACP 1978. **MILITARY SERVICE:** AUS 1941-45, 1950-51. **BUSINESS ADDRESS:** Jefferson Co Pub Schs Dist R-1, 1215 Quail St, Lakewood, CO 80215.

ROY, WELTON J., JR.
Appointed official. **PERSONAL:** Born May 26, 1939, San Diego, CA; married Vivienne I Graham; children: Deborah A, Michelle M. **EDUCATION:** San Diego State Coll, BS Accounting 1964; Stanford Univ Graduate School of Business, MBA Finance 1968. **CAREER:** Exxon Corporation, financial/systems advisor 1968-85. **ORGANIZATIONS:** Member Natl Assoc of Accountants 1969-85; member Financial Executives Institute 1975-80; executive board member New Brunswick Branch NAACP 1979-84; chairperson-curriculum committee Franklin Twp Board of Educ 1984-85. **HOME ADDRESS:** 2 Cedar Brook Dr, Somerset, NJ 08873. **BUSINESS ADDRESS:** School Board Member, Exxon Corporation, PO Box 153, Florham Park, NJ 07932.

ROYAL, C. CHARLES, SR.
Auto dealer executive. **CAREER:** Royal Lincoln-Mercury-Merkur, Inc, Peoria, IL, chief executive; Royal Carriage Buick, GMC-Jeep Eagle, Oxnard, CA, chief executive, 1988-. **BUSINESS ADDRESS:** Carriage Buick-GMC-Jeep-Eagle, 2121 North Oxnard Blvd, Oxnard, CA 93030. *

ROYAL, JAMES E.
Maintenance. **PERSONAL:** Born Aug 07, 1941, Nashville; children: Lanita, Angela, Quaddrus. **CAREER:** Trailmobile Div of Pullman Inc, maint. **ORGANIZATIONS:** Mem Beautiful Zion Bapt Ch; originator mgr Beautiful Zion Ensemble; Mason; former sec asst sec Lodge #455; former mem bd dir Wonder City Boys Club; former sec Wonder City Boys Club; former income tax consult Wonder City Boys Club; exec dir Sickle Cell Anemia Assn; bd mem Headstart Sch; former asst scout master Troop #150; prog com chmn W Memphis Counc of Orgns; mgr coach Afro's Baseball Team; mem Quorum Ct; mem NAACP chmn Voters League; former exec dir Young People's Voters League; former bd mem W Memphis Headstart; former pres PTA, LR Jackson Elem Sch. **BUSINESS ADDRESS:** 360 W Mallory, PO Box 9007, Memphis, TN 38109.

ROYSTER, DON M., SR.
Business executive. **PERSONAL:** Born Mar 12, 1944, Baltimore, MD; married Vertie M Bagby; children: Don M Jr, Denise C. **EDUCATION:** Morgan State Univ, attended 1962-63; Agr & Tech Univ of NC, attended 1963-64; Natl Coll, BA 1970; Amer Coll, CLU 1976; Life Office Mgmt Assoc, FLMI 1977. **CAREER:** Johnson & Johnson Corp, prodn analyst 1967; Washington Natl Ins Co, claim adjustor 1967-72, proj dir 1976-79, adminis 1979-81, asst vice pres & adminis 1981-. **ORGANIZATIONS:** Mem Chicago Chap Chartered Life Underwriters 1976-; mem Chicago Chap Fellow Life Mgmt Inst 1977-; mem Chicago Assn of Health Underwriters 1979-; vicepres/dir Mental Health Assoc of Evanston 1981-83; chmn/commr Evanston Human Relations Commn 1981-84. **HONORS/ACHIEVEMENTS:** Featured in Speaking of People section Ebony Mag 1979; Chicago YMCA Black & Hispanic Achievement Awd 1980; featured in 1984 edition of Dollars & Sense Mag. **BUSINESS ADDRESS:** Asst Vice Pres & Adminstr, Washington Natl Ins Co, 1630 Chicago Ave, Evanston, IL 60201.

ROYSTON, LLOYD LEONARD
Educational administrator. **PERSONAL:** Married Marion Grant; children: Sharon, William, Jayston. **EDUCATION:** Talladega Coll, AB 1958; Tuskegee Inst, MEd 1971; Univ of AL, EdD 1980. **CAREER:** Tollapoosa County Bd Educ, classroom teacher 1959-63; New York City Dept of Soc Services, caseworker 1963-65; Tuskegee Inst, continuing educ dir 1965-74, assoc dir Human Resource Center 1974-77 & 1979-80; Univ of AL, dir Teaching Learning Center; Pensacola Jr Coll, district dean of continuing education 1982-88; Continuing Education, educational consultant; AL A&M Univ assoc dean continuing/extended educ 1988-. **ORGANIZATIONS:** Consultant Multi-Racial Corp 1972; consultant USAID 1979; mem advisory bd Univ West FL Inst of Gov 1982-86; bd mem Wedgewood Homeowners Assoc 1982-86; bd member PUSH, local chapter 1982-86; mem State Continuing Ed Standing Comm 1982-86; mem Gannett Found Scholarship Comm 1983-86; bd mem Private Indus Council 1983-86; mem Chamber of Commerce 1985-86; mem Amer Council on Educ 1987; mem Amer Assn of Adult & Continuing Educ 1987; mem Amer Assn of Community/Junior Colleges 1987. **HONORS/ACHIEVEMENTS:** First exec dir AL Migrant Workers Program 1974; Certificate of Appreciation Youth Services Council 1979; Planning Proct at Black Coll 1980; first black dean Pensacola Jr Coll 1982; first black coordinator Minority Student Services PJC 1983; Community Serv Awd Private Industry Council Pensacola 1983-86; Continuing Education Service Award 1987. **BUSINESS ADDRESS:** Educational Consultant, Continuing Education, 611 Royston St, Dadeville, AL 36853.

ROZIER, GILBERT DONALD
Executive officer. **PERSONAL:** Born Oct 19, 1940, West Palm Beach, FL; married Juanella Miller; children: Ricardo. **EDUCATION:** Benedict Coll, AB 1963. **CAREER:** Urban League of S Weston, exec dir; Urban League of CO, pres 1974; Urban League of S Weston Fairfield, asso dir 1970-74; Stamford Neighborhood Youth Corp, dir 1967-74; W Main St Comm Ctr, prog dir 1966-67; W Side YMCA NYC, youth worker 1963-66. **ORGANIZATIONS:** Sec CT State Fed of Demo Clubs 1974; pres AFLO Am Dem Club 1979. **HONORS/ACHIEVEMENTS:** Outstand Young Man of the Yr; outstand Young Men of Am 1973; Outstand Citizen Union Co NJ Human Resources 1979; Outstand Citizen St John Lodge #14 Stamford, CT 1980. **BUSINESS ADDRESS:** Urban League of S Weston, 36 Atlantic St, Stamford, CT 06901.

RUCKER, NANNIE GEORGE
Educator. **PERSONAL:** Born Apr 21, 1914, Murfreesboro, TN; married James I. **EDUCATION:** TN State U, BS Elem Educ 1950, MS Educ Psych 1958; Fisk U; George Peabody Coll; Middle TN State U; Tuskegee Inst. **CAREER:** Middle TN State Univ Campus School, lab teacher. **ORGANIZATIONS:** Mem Middle TN Tchrs Assn; Sigma Gamma Rho; Rutherford Co Tchrs Assn; Am Assn ofUniv Women; pres/sec Tchrs Assn; Pub Serv Comm Panel; sec State Fed of Dem Women 1975; mem State Dem Exec (2nd term); Steering Com of Intl Women's Yr 1975; League of Women Voters; Women's Round Table; 1st v chrprsn Dem Party for Middle TN 1976; mem TN State Bd of Edn/State Bd for Voc Educ 1979; mem admin & policy com State Bd of Edn/State Bd for Voc Educ 1979; bd dir Wee Care Day Care Child Devel Ctr 1980; mem 1st Bapt Ch; mem Delta Kappa Gamma; Alpha Kappa Mu; del Intl Reading Assn 1965; Dem Nat Conv(served as sec of TN Delegation 1972); NEA. **HONORS/ACHIEVEMENTS:** "Nannie G Rucker Day" Doylestown PA; Elected Del-at-Large Nat Dem Conv 1980. **BUSINESS ADDRESS:** Middle TN State Univ, Campus Sch, Murfreesboro, TN 37130.

RUCKER, REGINALD J. (REGGIE)
Sportscaster. **PERSONAL:** Born Sep 21, 1947, Washington, DC; divorced; children: Derek, Shannon, Sean. **EDUCATION:** Boston U, BS 1969. **CAREER:** Dallas Cowboys, player WR 1969-71; New England Patriots, player WR 1971-74; Cleveland Browns, player WR 1975-82; WUAB TV-43, Bsebll Cleveland, sports analyst 1983-84; WZAK Radio, sports-talk Cleveland 1986; WVIZ TV Cleveland, basketball analyst 1987; NBC, sports analyst 1983-, sportscaster. **ORGANIZATIONS:** Pr/mrktg consult Cleveland Coca-Cola Bottling Co 1981-; Sports Talk Show WGAR Cleveland 1985-; telethon host United Negro Coll Fund 1983-; chrmn United Black Fund 1985; spokesman Foster Parents 1984; spokesman Black History Media Cleveland 1981-; speaker Gov Celeste (Ohio) Just Say No Prog; UBF chmn Fund Raising Event Cleveland; UNCF chmn Celebrity Golf Tournament Cleveland. **BUSINESS ADDRESS:** Sportscaster, NBC, 3705 Carnegie, Cleveland, OH 44115.

RUCKER, ROBERT LOUIS, JR.
Artist, educator, manager. **PERSONAL:** Born Jan 19, 1947, Houston, TX; married Debra Ann. **EDUCATION:** LA City Coll, 1965-66; Dawson Coll/Sir George Williams U, 1970-72. **CAREER:** Valley Div of Educ Recreational Serv Inc, mgr 1979-, mgmt trainee 1979; MOVE Inc LA, gen mgr 1977-78; LA Unified School Dist, special educ proj asst 1975-78; Soul & Jazz Publ LA, art dir 1975-76; free-lance artist 1974-75; agric asst 1973-74; Inst of Soc Studies, res asst 1973-74; GA Prison Sys, comm work with prisoners & families 1972-73; comm proj dealing with youth 1970-72; Dawson Coll Summer Childrens Day Camp Montreal, art teacher/tutor 1970-72. **ORGANIZATIONS:** Cote Des Neiges Project (Youth Ctr) Montreal 1971; GA Prison Observers Comm; Comm for Prisoners Assist 1972-73; mem SCAG Para-Transit Task Force; mem So CA Assn of Govt; mem steering com/coord of transp Action 504 Atlanta, GA Watts Summer Festival 1974. **HONORS/ACHIEVEMENTS:** Black Art Award for Graphics; Publ, "Regional Transp Plann & Considerations for the Design & Implementation of Com Level Transit in SCAG Region" 1979. **MILITARY SERVICE:** USAF sgt 1966-70.

RUCKS, ALFRED J.
Engineer. **PERSONAL:** Born Oct 20, 1935, Bellwood, TN. **EDUCATION:** TN A&I State Univ, BSEE 1958. **CAREER:** Defense Atomic Support Agency, 1958-62; White Sands Missile Range, electronics engr, 1962-, EEO counselor 1973-85, chief safety engrg branch 1985-. **ORGANIZATIONS:** Mem IEEE 1959-; assoc mem NSPE; trustee N mesquite St Church of Christ 1962-; chmn Minority Housing Bd City of Las Cruces NM 1968-80; pres NM State NAACP 1970-86; chmn Reg VI NAACP 1974, 1979; bd of dir NAACP 1981-. **HONORS/ACHIEVEMENTS:** Achievement Awd NM State Conf NAACP 1972; Natl Merit Acad Awd 1973; Commanders Awd White Sands Missile Range 1975. **BUSINESS ADDRESS:** Electronics Engineer, White Sands Missile Range, STEWS-NR-CE, White Sands Missile Range, NM 88002.

RUDD, AMANDA S.
Library administrator. **PERSONAL:** Born Apr 09, 1923, Greenville, SC; daughter of Wesley Sullivan and Delarion Moore Sullivan; divorced; children: Lt Cmdr Grover Randle USN, Mrs Loretta Randle O'Brien. **EDUCATION:** FL A&M Univ, BS Ed; Western Reserve Univ, MLS. **CAREER:** SC, AK, FL, OH, school librarian, elem teacher; Cleveland Public Schools, asst suprv of libr 1965-70; Field Enterprises Educ Corp, consultant educ serv dept 1970-75; The Chicago Publ Library, asst chief librarian comm rel & special prog of serv 1975, dep commissioner 1975-81, commissioner 1981-85; currently library consultant. **ORGANIZATIONS:** Mem Amer Library Assn Planning Comm 1985, ALA Intl Relations Comm, ALA Legislative Comm Amer Library Trustee Assoc 1983-85, ALA Conf Comm, Metro Library Sect, Public Library Assoc 1984; chairperson Local Arrangements Comm Gen Conf, Intl Fed of Library Assoc & Inst 1985; mem, adv bd Grad School of Library & Info Sci Rosary Coll; mem Citizens Adv Bd of Channel 20 WYCC-TV Chicago, IL Literacy Council; ad hoc comm Plan for Implementation of Multitype Library Syst, IL Library Assn; mem visiting comm, Bd of Overseers for the School of Library Sci, Case Western Reserve Univ; mem Chicago Educ & Cultural Cable TV Consortium; mem bd of dir, Chicago Metro History Fair; mem Truman Coll Adv Bd Chicago; mem adv comm, The Stages of Shakespeare; mem adv comm, IL State Library; mem Read IL Comm, IL State Library; mem adv comm, Future of IL Publ Library; mem bd of dir, Human Serv Prov ider Tech Serv Inst; mem Women's Comm, 1982 Worlds Fair Chicago; chair Intl Relations Comm, ALA; treas North Shore Chap of Links Inc. **HONORS/ACHIEVEMENTS:** Marshall Bynum Humanitarian Awd for Civic & Social Achievement by Dress Horsemen Inc; Bethune Tubman Truth Awd for Community Serv & Professional Accomplishment by Black Women, Hall of Fame Found; Vivian C Harsh Awd, Afro-Amer Genealogical & Historical Soc of Chicago; "Profile in Accomplishments" A Salute to Black Amer on Black Entertainment TV Cable Network; Tribute for Outstanding Contrib in the Field of Library Serv, South Suburban Chicago Chap, Links Inc; Beta Phi Mu, Natl Library Sci Hon Soc; Alpha Gamma Pi Sor for Civic & Soc Achievement; numerous speaking engagements incl, "The Perfection of the Process of Living" Case Western Reserve Univ, "Challenges & Pleasures of Library Serv in the 1980's" Chicago Library Club, "The Chicago Publ Library, Reaches Out to its Youth, Public Library & School Cooperate in Chicago" Intl Assn of Metro City Libraries; "Traditional & Nontraditional Career Options in the Public Library" Univ of IL Champaign. **BUSINESS ADDRESS:** Library & Management Consultant, The Chicago Public Library, 5100 N Marine Dr, Suite 6A, Chicago, IL 60640.

RUDD, JAMES M.
Logistics manager. **PERSONAL:** Born Dec 19, 1916, Granite Springs, VA; married Rebecca Ryan; children: Dorothy Rudd Moore, Jacqueline May, Rosalind, James, Simone, Carolyn. **EDUCATION:** DE State College/Univ of DE, Certificates Council Effectiveness Training 1981/82; Natl Acad and Institute of Corrections Univ of CO, Certificate 1986. **CAREER:** US Civil Service, served in various supervisory capacities with the US Army electronics command, logistics administration and management field 1941-73 (retired); Bd of Educ Millside

School Dist, pres 1947-50; Dept of Corrections State of DE, mem council on corrections 1982-. **ORGANIZATIONS:** Mem Citizen Adv Council Colonial School Dist 1982-; chairperson Citizen Adv Council William Penn HS; mem State Adv council for Adult and Community Educ; mem bd of dirs Delaware Assn for Adult and Community Educ; mem Benevolent Order of Elks Philadelphia, Kiwanis Club of New Castle Hundred, Assn of the United States Army; pres bd of dirs New Castle Comm Progressive Club; mem Governor's Task Force on Correction Security 1986-. **HONORS/ACHIEVEMENTS:** Outstanding Performance US Army Matl Readiness Cmd Washington DC; Commendation US Aviation Systems Command St Louis, MO,. **HOME ADDRESS:** 15 Holcomb Ln, New Castle, DE 19720.

RUDD, WILLIE LESSLIE
Business executive. **PERSONAL:** Born Sep 22, 1944, Sardis, MS; married Barbara A; children: Jacqueline Yvette, Lynda Yvonne, Anita Michelle, Leslie Ann. **EDUCATION:** Booker T Washington HS, 1963. **CAREER:** NBFI Furniture Co, upholster 1964-72; United Furniture Workers AFL-CIO, intl rep 1972-76; United Furniture Wokers Intl Union AFL-CIO, intl vice pres 1976-;United Furniture Workers Local 282 AFL-CIO, pres 1976-. **ORGANIZATIONS:** Mem A Phillip Randolph Org 1970-, Union Valley MB Church 23 yrs; mem NAACP 1964, Union Valley Bapt Church 1964; 1st vchmn A Phillip Randolph Inst Memphis Chap 1978-; bd of dir Girls Clubs of Amer Memphis 1978. **HONORS/ACHIEVEMENTS:** Outstanding Youn Man of Amer Natl C of C 1980; Hon Sgt-at-Arms John Ford State Senator 1976; Key to Shelby Cty Commiss 1977. **BUSINESS ADDRESS:** President, United Furniture Workers of Am, 1254 Lamar Ave, Memphis, TN 38104.

RUDD-MOORE, DOROTHY
Composer. **PERSONAL:** Born Jun 04, 1940, New Castle, DE; married Kermit Moore. **EDUCATION:** Howard Univ Sch of Music, B Music (Magna Cum Laude) 1963; American Conservatory Fontainebleau France, diploma 1963. **CAREER:** Harlem School of the Arts, teacher piano & music theory 1965-66; NY University, teacher music history appreciation 1969; Bronx Comm Coll, teacher music history appreciation 1971; Private Instructor, voice theory piano; composer, singer-performer. **ORGANIZATIONS:** Founder Society of Black Composers 1968; bd mem 1986, mem Amer Composers Alliance 1972-; mem Broadcast Music Inc 1972-; composer mem of recording panel Natl Endowment for the Arts 1986,87. **HONORS/ACHIEVEMENTS:** Lucy Moten Fellowship Howard Univ; grant from NY State Council on the Arts 1985, Amer Music Ctr 1985; compositions include "From the Dark Tower" for voice orchestra, "Frederick Douglass" full length opera, "Dirge and Deliverance" for cello and piano, "Three Pieces" for violin and piano, Piano Trio No 1, "Dream andVariations" for piano, "Weary Blues" for voice, cello and piano. **HOME ADDRESS:** 33 Riverside Dr, New York, NY 10023.

RUDOLPH, WILMA
Athlete. **PERSONAL:** Born Jun 23, 1940, St Bethleham, TN. **ORGANIZATIONS:** TN StateUniv Runner Olympic Teams 1956, 60; Held Women's World Records in 100-M, 200-M, & Anchored 2 World Record 400-M Relay Team; Tied 100-M Record in Prelim Heat 1960. **HONORS/ACHIEVEMENTS:** Became first am woman to Win Both Sprint Gold Medals 1960; won gold medal With 240; Anchored US 400-M Relay Team to World & Record for Gold Medal; asst dir athletics Mayor Daley's Yth Found; winner helm world trophy awrd N Am 1960.

RUFFIN, BENJAMIN S.
Association executive. **PERSONAL:** Born Dec 11, 1941, Durham Co, NC. **EDUCATION:** NC Cntrl U, BA. **CAREER:** NC Mutual Ins Co, sr vice pres & spl asst to the pres. **ORGANIZATIONS:** Vp UDI; consult John Avery Boys Club; comm org Opera Breakthrough; dir United Organ for Comm Improv; mem Congress of Racial Equality; Nat Assn forComm Dev; Durham Com of Negro Affairs; sec Durham Homes Inc; Low-Income & Hsng Dev Inc; NAACP; Nat Welfare Rights Mvmt; Nat Bus Leag; Durham Bus & Prof Chain; sec Durham Legal Aid Soc; People's Ath Concern Com; treas REMCA Hsg Inc; Coordng Council for Sen Citzns. **BUSINESS ADDRESS:** Dir Public Affairs Prog, RJR Nabisco, Co, P O Box 2959, Winston-Salem, NC 27102.

RUFFIN, HERBERT
Educator. **PERSONAL:** Born Feb 13, 1940, Hammond, IN; married Arlene Harris; children: Kristin, Bradley. **EDUCATION:** Wichita State U, BA 1963, MEd 1970;Univ of KS, EdD 1973. **CAREER:** El Centro Coll Dallas Co Comm Coll Dist, dean of instructional serv 1979-; Dallas Co Comm Coll Dist, asst to Chancellor 1978-79; Bishop Coll Dallas, dean of academic affairs 1977-78; Univ of TN Knoxville, asst prof of educ 1973-77; Univ of KS Lawrence, KS, teaching assc 1970-73; East HS Wichita, KS, social studies teacher 1964-70. **ORGANIZATIONS:** Mem So Conf of Deans of Faculties & Acad V Pres; mem Am Assc of Higher Ed; mem Assc of Supervision & Curriculum Dev; mem Alpha Phi Alpha Frat 1968-; mem Optimist Clb Knoxville, TN 1975-77; bd dir Winston Sch Dallas 1978-; Ldrshp Dallas Dallas C of C 1979-; bd dir Dallas Urban League 1979-. **HONORS/ACHIEVEMENTS:** Honors/doctoral Oral ExamsUniv of KS 1972; Acad Admn Flw Am Cncl on EdUniv of TN 1975-76; "Supervision for Inner & City Sch"; TN Assc for Supervision & Curriculum Dev 1976; "Accountability & Urban Ed Gap of Shame" TN Ed 1977. **BUSINESS ADDRESS:** Main & Lamar, Dallas, TX 75202.

RUFFIN, JAMES E.
Publisher. **PERSONAL:** Born Jun 30, 1937, Wichita, KS. **EDUCATION:** BA 1959; BMEd 1963; Bethel Clg N Newton, KS; Yankton ClG Yankton, SD;Univ NE, Cert Extemperaceous Spch 1967. **CAREER:** Everybody Mag & Ruffin Publ Inc, pblshr advertising pub; First AME Ch Kansas City, KS, youth mus dir 1972-; Dominic HS Omaha, NE, mus instr 1969-70; Omaha Pub Schs Omaha, NE, mus instr 1963-64; Giltner Pub Schs Giltner, NE, engl & mus instr 1963-64; Yankton Pub Schs, mus instr 1962. **ORGANIZATIONS:** Bd dir Negro Press Assc; Omaha Ad Clb 1974; mem NE Hist Soc; KS Hist Soc; MW Prince Hall Grand Lodge; F&AM of NE; Malone Com Ctr Ambas Clb; AME Ch Layman's Organ; Youn Rep; Youth Mus Supvr; AME Ch 5th Episcopal. **HONORS/ACHIEVEMENTS:** Dist pub of yr Omaha Chap Am Red Cross 1969; field asst to Sen Robt Dole 1974; outst citizen Pi Beta Kappa 1968; attended White Hse Conf Status of Am Press 1973; ed of yr AME Ch Bishops Cncl 1974. **BUSINESS ADDRESS:** 845 Minnesota Ave, Kansas City, KS 66117.

RUFFIN, JANICE E.
Psychologist, psychiatric nurse. **PERSONAL:** Born Dec 06, 1942, Cleveland, OH. **EDUCATION:** Ohio State Univ, School of Nursing, BS 1964; Rutgers The State Univ Coll of Nursing, MS Psychiatric Nursing 1967; CUNY Grad Ctr, MPhil 1984, PhD Clinical Psychology 1985. **CAREER:** CT Mental Health Ctr New Haven, dir of nursing 1974-77; Yale Univ Sch of Nursing, asst prof grad prog in psychiatric nursing, assoc prof 1975-77; City Coll CUNY, lecturer dept of psychology 1978-80; Bronx Psychiatric Ctr, psychologist highbridge outpatient clinic 1980-85; Baruch Coll Office of Counseling & Psychological Svcs, psychologist 1985-, dir 1986-. **ORGANIZATIONS:** Mem Adv Com on Conf for Nurses in Comm Mental Hlth 1969-70; ANA NLN Com on Nursing Careers; 1971-72; past vice pres mem bd dir NY Black Nurses' Assn 1971-74; adv bd Nat Commn for Study of Nursing & Nursing Educ 1971-73; adv bd Breakthrough to Nursing 1971-73; chmn 1969-71 mem 1971-72 Com on Nursing in a Soc in Crisis; Affir Action Task Force 1972-76; mem editorial bd Perspectives in Psychiatric Care 1973-83; historian Natl Black Nurses Assoc 1972-82; bd dir Nat Black Nurses' Assn 1972-74; chmn 1971-72 & vice pres 1972-73; Operation Success in Nursing Educ mem Inst for Comm Organ & Personal Effectivesness bd dir 1974-77; mem Nurse Training Review Com NIMH 1974-78; mem AK Rice Inst 1979-; mem Sigma Theta Tau 1986-; certification and licensure as psychologist NY State Educ Dept 1986. **HONORS/ACHIEVEMENTS:** Certificate and Gold Medal OH State Univ Sch of Nursing 1970; Certificate of Excellence in Psychiatric Nursing Amer Nurses' Assoc 1975; Certificate in Psychiatric Mental Health Nursing by Amer Nurses Assoc 1975; Awd Natl Assoc Negro Business & Professional Women's Clubs Inc 1977; Dedicated Professional Service Awd Natl Assoc of Negro Business and Professional Womens Clubs Inc 1977; excellence in psychology, City Coll, CUNY, 1987. **BUSINESS ADDRESS:** Dir, Baruch Coll CUNY, 17 Lexington Avenue, P O Box 304, New York, NY 10010.

RUFFIN, JOHN
Educator. **PERSONAL:** Born Jun 29, 1943, New Orleans, LA; married Angela Beverly; children: John Wesley, Meeka, Beverly. **EDUCATION:** Dillard Univ, BS 1965; Atlanta Univ, MS 1967; KS State Univ, PhD 1971; Harvard Univ, Post Doctoral 1975-77. **CAREER:** Southern Univ Baton Rouge, biol instructor 1967-68; Atlanta Univ, asst prof 1971-74; AL A&M Univ, assoc prof 1974-75; NC Central Univ, prof biol, 1978-86, chmn biol, dean coll of arts & sciences 1986-. **ORGANIZATIONS:** Consult Natl Inst of Health Governor 1978-; consult Bd of Sci & Tech 1983-; consult ADAMHA, Natl Inst Mental Health 1984. **HONORS/ACHIEVEMENTS:** Beta Beta Beta Natl Hon Soc 1965-; Natl Sci Found Fellowship 1969; Natl Inst Health Fellowship 1974; Cabot Rsch Fellow Harvard Univ 1975. **BUSINESS ADDRESS:** Dean, Coll of Arts & Sciences, North Carolina CentralUniv, 1801 Fayetteville St, Durham, NC 27707.

RUFFIN, JOHN WALTER, JR.
Radio broadcasting management. **PERSONAL:** Born Jun 15, 1941, Moncure, NC; son of John Ruffin, Sr and Theima Harris Ruffin; married Dorothy L Walton; children: Jonathan, Jihan. **EDUCATION:** Morgan State Univ, BA 1963; Cornell Univ, MS 1970. **CAREER:** Pantry Pride Inc, vice pres 1980-85; Paradies Airport Shops, partner/consultant; JD Ruffin Assoc, pres chief exec officer; Sunao Broadcasting Co Inc, pres & gen mgr 1986-; Business Equipment Co, pres, CEO, 1988-. **ORGANIZATIONS:** Chmn of the bd Urban League Broward 1984-87; mem adv bd Barnett Bank 1985-87; chmn Broward Employ & Training 1986. **HONORS/ACHIEVEMENTS:** Special Recognition by US Congress 1985; Sen Lawton Chiles Commendation Outstanding Citizen City of Fort Lauderdale 1986; Great Achievement NAACP Broward 1986; State Top Ten Awds Natl Business League. **BUSINESS ADDRESS:** President & General Manager, Sunao Broadcasting Co Inc, 4431 Rock Island Rd, Fort Lauderdale, FL 33319.

RUFFIN, RICHARD D.
Physician. **PERSONAL:** Born Jul 07, 1924, Cairo, IL; son of Edward David Ruffin (deceased) and Alpha Curtis Ruffin (deceased); married Yvonne White; children: Richard David Jr, Patti Yvonne, Kenneth George. **EDUCATION:** Northern IL Univ Dekalb IL, 1940-41; IL State Univ Bloomington Normal, 1941-43; Univ of IL, 1946-47; Coll of Mortuary Sci, St Louis, B of Mortuary Sci 1948; Meharry Med Coll Nashville TN, MD 1953. **CAREER:** Homer G Phillips Hosp St Louis, MO, internship 1953-54, residencies surgery 1954-55, residencies urology 1955-58; private practice, urologist 1959-. **ORGANIZATIONS:** Chmn Section of Urology, St Anthony Hospital 1975-78; urological consultant State of OH, Dept of Rehabilitation & Correction 1975-78; secy/treas Central OH Urological Soc 1964-65, pres 1967-68; vice chief Med & Dental Staff, St Anthony Hosp 1973-76; Columbus Acad of Med 1958-; OH State Med Assn 1958-; Am Med Assn 1958-; Central OH Urological Soc 1959-; N Central Sect; Am Urological Assn 1961-; Am Urological Assn 1961-; Columbus Assn for Physicians/Dentists 1971-. **HONORS/ACHIEVEMENTS:** Citation Citizenship City of Columbus, OH Div of Police 1971; Outstanding Am Bicentennial Ed 1975; President's Award; Meharry Med Coll Nashville 1978; The Blue Book of Franklin County 1980-82; Children's Hosp Award 1984. **MILITARY SERVICE:** AUS 1943-45. **HOME ADDRESS:** 3236 E Livingston Ave, Columbus, OH 43227. **BUSINESS ADDRESS:** Urologist, 1829 E Long St, Columbus, OH 43203.

RUFFIN, ROBERT
Business executive. **PERSONAL:** Born Mar 04, 1936, Birmingham, AL; married Patricia A Ellis; children: Charleton, Darron. **EDUCATION:** Bus Admn, BS 1965. **CAREER:** Indsl Relations Bendix Corp Hydraulics Div, dir 1975-; Chrysler Corp Indianapolis Foundry, prsnl mgr 1972-75; Chrysler Corp Huber Ave Foundary, res prsnl mgr 1971-72; Chrysler Corp Indianapolis Foundry, labor & Relations Supr 1969-71; Chrysler Corp Huber Ave Foundry, lbr relations rep 1966-69; ChryslerCorp, prsnl intrvwr qlfr 1965-66. **ORGANIZATIONS:** Mem Prsnl Assc; mem C of C; professional adv com State of IN. **HONORS/ACHIEVEMENTS:** Recipient boss of yr awrd Natl Bus Woman Assc 1975. **MILITARY SERVICE:** AUS sp4 1958-61. **BUSINESS ADDRESS:** General Manager, Allied Automotive, 3737 Red Arrow Hwy, St Joseph, MI 49085.

RUFFINS, REYNOLDS
Illustrator, designer. **PERSONAL:** Born Aug 05, 1930, New York, NY. **CAREER:** Cooper Union, 1951; Dept Visual Communications Coll Visual & Performing Arts Syracuse Univ, visiting adjunct prof 1973-; School Visual Arts, instructor, 1967-70. **ORGANIZATIONS:** Designer illustrator 7 Books for Children; Annual Riddle Calender; Charles Scribners's Sons; Family Cir Mag. **HONORS/ACHIEVEMENTS:** Best illus awrd NY Times Book Rev 1973; Bologna (Italy) Children's Book Fair 1976; Am Inst Graphic Arts Art Dir Clb; CA mag awrd; soc illus awrd;profl achvmt awrd Cooper Union 1972; 200 Yrs Am Illus NY Hist Soc.

RUFFNER, RAY P.
Insurance executive. **PERSONAL:** Born Aug 11, 1946, Washington, DC; married Patricia Smith; children: Damien Earl. **EDUCATION:** Washington Lee HS, Grad 1964; Acct Correspondence Course, 1966-67. **CAREER:** Larry Buick Ar/VA, body & fender mech 1969-71; United Co Life Ins Co, ins sales 1971, ins sale & mgmt 1971-77; Ruffner & Assoc, ins sales & mgmt, sole proprietor 1977-. **ORGANIZATIONS:** Investor Real Estate 1973-. **HONORS/ACHIEVEMENTS:** Renovating homes for low income, 5 town homes currently in progress 1985; Public Service to High School & Coll 1984. **MILITARY SERVICE:** USMC E-5 4 yrs; NCO Awd 1966. **HOME ADDRESS:** 10605 Shadow Ln, Fairfax Station, VA 22039. **BUSINESS ADDRESS:** President, Ruffner & Assocs, PO Box 290, Lorton, VA 22079.

RUMPH, ANNIE ALRIDGE
Elected official. **PERSONAL:** Born Oct 05, 1917, Ellaville, GA; widowed. **EDUCATION:** Fort Valley State Coll, BS 1950; Albany State Coll, 1951; Tuskegee Inst, 1953-54. **CAREER:** St Peter AME Church, lay organization sec 1977-84, steward bd vice pres 1981-83; Operation Cure, co-chmn 1983-84; Peach County Chap of GA Coalition of Black Women, pres 1984-85; Peach County Bd of Com, county commissioner. **ORGANIZATIONS:** Mem State & County Retired Teachers Assoc 1977-85. **HONORS/ACHIEVEMENTS:** Certificate of Appreciation Citizenship Educ Com 1981; Distinguished Serv Fort Valley State Coll 1982; Community Serv Awd Delta Pi Sigma Chapter Sigma Gamma Rho Sor 1982-83; Outstanding Achievement End Zoners Club 1984.

RUNDLES, JAMES ISAIAH
Government official. **PERSONAL:** Born Jul 09, 1920, Jackson, MS; married Mattie Singleton. **EDUCATION:** Tougaloo So Christian Inst, bA 1940;Univ of HI Honolulu, 1944-45; Johnson Sch of Bus, Bus Ed 1948-49. **CAREER:** City of Jackson, MS, exec asst to mayor 1977-; Gov of MS (First Black), exec asst 1972-76; Pittsburg Courier/Chicago & Defender, civil rights rprtr 1960-71. **ORGANIZATIONS:** Fndr Rundles & Assc Pub Relations Consult 1960-71; natl pub affairs dir Montford Point Marines Assc 1960-66; news dir Radio WOKJ/JaCKSON, MS 1954-60; assc edtr The Jackson Advocate/Newspaper 1946-50; bd dir MS Bar Legal Assc 1973-76; adv comm relations Div US Justice Dept 1972-76; bd dir Am Red Cross 1973-; bd dir Boys Clubs of Am 1977-. **HONORS/ACHIEVEMENTS:** Black journalism awrd Nat Proj Media Assc 1975; Humanitarian Endeavors MS Independent Beauticians Assc 1975; outst & dedicated serv Gov Cncl for Minority Afrs 1975; efforts achvmt in the humanities Nine Iron Golf Assc SE 1979. **MILITARY SERVICE:** USMC sgt maj 1942-45; Prsidential Unit Citation (Iwo Jima) 1945. **BUSINESS ADDRESS:** PO Box 288, Jackson, MS 39205.

RUNNELS, BERNICE
Educational administrator. **PERSONAL:** Born Aug 29, 1925, Memphis, TN; daughter of Ben Bradd and Susie Bradd; married Ike (deceased); children: Patricia Teague, Isaac Jr, Reginald, Maurice. **CAREER:** Pembroke District 259, president 9 years, board mem 1963-84. **ORGANIZATIONS:** Mem Three Rivers Division of the Ill Board Assn 1975-83. **HOME ADDRESS:** PO Box 149, Hopkins Park, IL 60944.

RUSH, SONYA C.
Manufacturing executive. **PERSONAL:** Born Aug 23, 1959, Columbia, LA; daughter of Walter C Rush and Shirley Cross Rush. **EDUCATION:** GA Inst of Tech, BChE 1981; Univ of MI, MBA 1983. **CAREER:** Philip Morris USA, operations analyst 1983-88; superintendent-manufacturing 1988-. **ORGANIZATIONS:** Chmn economic develop Alpha Kappa Alpha Sor 1985-; allocations mem United Way; advisor Junior Achievement; recruiter Univ of MI Grad Sch of Business; mem Natl Coalition of 100 Black Women 1989-; mem Alpha Kappa Alpha Sor Inc 1979-; mem The Friends of Art 1989-. **HOME ADDRESS:** 5825-D Willow Oaks Dr, Richmond, VA 23225.

RUSHING, BYRON D.
Representative. **PERSONAL:** Born Jul 29, 1942, New York, NY; son of William Rushing and Linda Turpin Rushing; children: Osula. **CAREER:** Northern Student Movement, community organizer 1964-65; Community Voter Registration Project, dir 1964-66; Commn on Church & Race MA Council of Churches, field dir 1966-67; Ctr for Inner-City Change, administrator 1969-70; Museum of Afro-American History, pres 1972-84; Commonwealth of Massachusetts, mem house of representatives 1983-. **ORGANIZATIONS:** Pres Roxbury Historical Soc 1968-; lay deputy General Convention of Episcopal Church 1974-; treas St John's/St James Episcopal Church 1975-; hearings coord Urban Bishops Coalition 1977-78; past pres Episcopal Urban Caucus 1981-85; co-chair citizens adv comm Roxbury Heritage Park 1985-; treas Ward 4 Democratic Comm. **HONORS/ACHIEVEMENTS:** Author "I Was Born" Black Power Revolt 1968; author "Afro-Americana" Museum News 1982, The Lost and Found Paintings of Allan Rohan Crite 1982; Kellogg Lecturer Episcopal Divinity School 1985; "Black Heritage Trail" Walking Tour Brochure Boston African Amer Natl Historic Site; numerous articles on historic archaeology; Awd Human Rights Campaign Fund 1985; Bay State Banner 20th Anniversary Celebration 1985; Public Official of the Year Boston Teachers Union 1987; honorary degree Roxbury Community Coll 1989; author of "A Justice That Is Real," Plumbline 1987; author of "An Ideology of Struggle," Forward Motion 1988. **BUSINESS ADDRESS:** MRM House of Representatives, Commonwealth of Massachusetts, State House, Boston, MA 02133.

RUSHING, GEORGE A.
Bank executive. **CAREER:** Community Bank of Nebraska, Omaha, NE, chief executive. **BUSINESS ADDRESS:** Community Bank, 5180 Ames Ave, Omaha, NE 68104. *

RUSSELL, AUGUST WAYNE
Business executive. **PERSONAL:** Born Sep 10, 1942, San Antonio, TX; married Katie M; children: Wayne Jr, Damon, Jennifer Kay. **EDUCATION:** San Antonio Clg. **CAREER:** Esteban Equipment Co, pres; Wayne Russell Ford Inc, pres; AJ Foyt Chev, sls mgr 1973-75; Jack Criswell Lincoln-merc, new car sls 1966-73; Riverside Natl Bk, head teller 1963-66. **ORGANIZATIONS:** Fndr pres Greenfield Investment & Dev Corp 1968-77; past pres Brazoria Co Orgn for Unity 1975-77. **HONORS/ACHIEVEMENTS:** Lincoln-mercury inner cir awrd; Top 100 Bus in US Black Enterprise Mag. **BUSINESS ADDRESS:** Wayne Russell Ford, 901 S Velasco St, Angleton, TX 77515.

RUSSELL, BEVERLY A.
Librarian. **PERSONAL:** Born Jan 15, 1947, Riverside, CA; daughter of James H Russell (deceased) and Dr Hazel M Hawkins-Russell. **EDUCATION:** CA State Coll, BA 1971; CA State Univ, MS 1973. **CAREER:** Riverside Public Library, library asst 1974; CA State Dept of Rehab, librarian 1978; Magnavox Rsch Labs, library tech 1978-84; Burbank Unified Sch Dist, bookroom librarian 1986-. **ORGANIZATIONS:** Mem Alpha Kappa Alpha 1973-; mem/treasurer Intl Black Writers and Artists 1983-. **HONORS/ACHIEVEMENTS:** Co-author of Bearers of Blackness, poetry published February 1987 by Guild Press MN; co-author of Three Women Black, Guild Press 1987; published in Roots and Wings, An Anthology of Poems for African-American Children, published by New York City Schools 1988. **HOME ADDRESS:** 5730 Case Ave #3, North Hollywood, CA 91601.

RUSSELL, CAZZIE
Professional basketball player. **PERSONAL:** Born Jun 07, 1944, Chicago, IL. **EDUCATION:** Univ of MI, Grad 1966. **CAREER:** PhiladeLphia Kings, player-coach; NY Knicks 1966-71; Golden State Warriors 1971-73; Los Angeles Lakers 1974-. **HONORS/ACHIEVEMENTS:** 1st draft choice "NY Knicks" 1966. **BUSINESS ADDRESS:** Los Angeles Lakers Prof Basket, PO Box 10, Inglewood, CA 90306.

RUSSELL, CHARLIE L.
Director, playwright, educator. **PERSONAL:** Born Mar 10, 1932, Monroe, LA; children: Michael R, Katheryn K. **EDUCATION:** Univ of San Fran, BS eng 1959; NY U, MSW 1967. **CAREER:** Afro-Am Theater Conta Costa Coll, dir; NY U, asst prof 1975-77; City Coll NY, asst prof 1969-74; Am Place Theatre, writer in resid 1976. **HONORS/ACHIEVEMENTS:** Image Awd Best Filmscript NAACP 1975; Playwright Awd Rockefeller Found 1976; publ plays five on the Blacj Hand Side", "The Incident at Terminal Ecstasy Acres", filmscript "Five on the Black Hand Side"; publ novellas, short stories. **MILITARY SERVICE:** AUS pfc 1953-55.

RUSSELL, DOROTHY DELORES
Newspaper circulation classified manager. **PERSONAL:** Born Sep 11, 1950, Hayti, MO; daughter of Jimmie Russell, Sr and Carrie Vianna Lewis Russell. **EDUCATION:** Southeast MO State Univ, attended; Three Rivers Comm Coll, attended; Lincoln Univ, attended. **CAREER:** Univ of AR CES, clerk steno I 1973-76; Dept of Natural Resources, clerk steno II 1976-78; MO Exec Office, sec receptionist 1978-79; MO Patrol State Water,admin sec 1979-80; Pemiscot Publishing Co, copysetter, circulation/classified manager, 1989-. **ORGANIZATIONS:** Former asst 4-H Leader; former bd mem/vice pres Community Review Paper expired 1983-84; editor/writer/photographer Community Review Newspaper 1983-; estab 1st minority newspaper with paid ads in southeast MO; estab 1st minority chamber of commerce in Southeast MO & Northeast AR area; organized 4-H Club in Hayti/Hayti Hts; promoted minority interest in the print media in three city area; writer of "Jussilo Salvo" a satirical column; missionary Church of Jesus Christ Congregation; organized Southeast Missouri Black Writer's Club, 1989. **HONORS/ACHIEVEMENTS:** Achievement Award in English, Central HS, 1968; 4 Yr Pin/Leader 4-H Extension Serv, 1985. **HOME ADDRESS:** PO Box 383, Hayti, MS 63851.

RUSSELL, EDWIN R.
Chemist. **PERSONAL:** Born Jun 19, 1913, Columbia, SC; married Dorothy Nance; children: Vivian, Martin. **EDUCATION:** Benedict Clg, BS 1935; Howard U, MS 1937; Benedict Clg, DSc 1974. **CAREER:** EI DuPont Savannah River Lab, retired stf chemist 1953-76; Allen U, prof of chemistry 1947-53;Univ of Chgo, assc rsrch chemist 1942-47; Howard U, inst in chem 1938-42. **ORGANIZATIONS:** Chmn bd trustee Aiken Co Serv Cncl; trustee Friendship Jr Clg; New Ellenton Bldg Commn. **HONORS/ACHIEVEMENTS:** Hon dr of sci degree Benedict Clg 1974; spec serv awrd Manpower Commn; eleven patents on Atomic Energy Processes.

RUSSELL, ERNEST
Administrator. **PERSONAL:** Born Feb 16, 1933, Massillon, OH; son of Ernest Russell and Alzater (Carter) Russell; married Signe Hippert; children: Robert, Koren. **EDUCATION:** Attended Western Reserve Univ Cleveland 1951-53; Univ of KS Lawrence, BA 1958; attended Harvard Univ summer 1978. **CAREER:** KS State Employment Serv, employment interviewer 1959-60; Topeka KS Commn on Civil Rights, educ dir 1960-62; Des Moines Commn on Human Rights, exec dir 1962-65; Charlotte NC Bur of Employment Training & Placement, dir 1965-66; DC VISTA/OEO, vocational training officer 1966-67; CA VISTA Office of Econ Oppor, sr prog analyst 1967-69; NY VISTA Office of Econ Oppor, regional admin 1969-70; DC VISTA Office of Econ Oppor, natl dept dir 1970-71; Office of Econ Oppor, assoc dir for admin 1971-73; Natl Inst of Educ DHEW, assoc dir/admin & mgmt 1973-76; Natl Labor Relations Bd Washington, dir of admin 1976-. **ORGANIZATIONS:** Guest lectr numerous progs sponsored by coll & univ labor/mgmt groups; mem Amer Soc for Pub Admin; supr group training for individuals & groups CSC CA; labor mgmt & super training tchr CSC Washington; tchr managing mgmt time DHEW/USDA Washington; mem NAACP 1950; mem Natl Urban League 1950; mem Operation PUSH 1977; mem Gov's Commn on Human Rights IO; mem Amer Educ Inst Valpraiso IN; mem Inst on Human Relations Fisk Univ. **HONORS/ACHIEVEMENTS:** Human Rights Awd KS & IO 1960 & 1964; Awd Natl Assn of Equal Housing Oppor 1962; Awd for Work with Juveniles Natl Assn of Colored Women's Clubs 1963; Awd NAACP 1964; Meritorious Serv Awd Settlement House Des Moines 1965; Outstanding Performance Awd 1970; Outstanding & Sustained Superior Performance Awd OEO 1971; Quality Increase Awd OEO 1972; Highest Awd for Exceptional Serv OEO 1973; Boss of the Yr Awd L'Enfant Chap Amer Bus Women's Assn Wash DC 1973; Sustained Superior Performance Awd NLRB 1977; Quality Within-Grade Awd NLRB 1977; Recommendation for the Career Serv Awd Natl Civil Serv League NLRB 1978; EEO Outstanding Contribution Awd NLRB 1978; Special Achievement Awd NLRB 1978; Recommendation for Roger W Jones Awd for Exec Serv NLRB 1979; Sr Exec Serv Cash Bonus Awd 1980, 1984, 1985, 1987; Special Act Award for Exceptional Contributions by the Chmn, NLRB, 1987; Presidential Rank Award: Meritorious Exec, NLRB, 1988. **MILITARY SERVICE:** US Army, private first class, 1953-55. **BUSINESS ADDRESS:** Dir of Admin, Natl Labor Relations Bd, 1717 Pennsylvania Ave NW, Room 400, Washington, DC 20570.

RUSSELL, GEORGE A.
Composer, music theoretician, teacher. **PERSONAL:** Born Jun 23, 1923, Cincinnati; son of Joseph Russell and Bessie Sledge Russell; married Alice Norburry, Aug 04, 1981; children: Jock Russell Millgardth. **EDUCATION:** Wilberforce University, OH, 1940-43. **CA-**

REER: New England Conservatory of Music, Boston, MA, instructor in jazz studies, 1969-; George Russell Living Time Orchestra, musician, 1977-; lecturer at Harvard Univ, Tufts Univ, New Music Gallery in Vienna, Sibelius Academy in Helsinki, and others. **ORGANIZATIONS:** School Jazz Lenox MA 1959-60; Swedish Labor Org 1965; Festival of the Arts Finland 1966-67; Univ of IN Music School 1967; Lund Univ Sweden, Vaskilde & Summerschule 1971; apprenticed to panel of Natl Endowment for the Arts Washington DC 1975; mem Intl Society of Contemporary Musicians; Norwegian Society of New Music; American Federation of Musicians Local 802; adv council MA State Council on the Arts; adv bd Third Street Music School Settlement. **HONORS/ACHIEVEMENTS:** Author of "George Russell's Lydian Chromatic Concept of Tonal Organization" 1953; outstanding composer award Metronome Mag 1958; Natl Endowment for the Arts Award 1969; Guggenheim fellowship 1972; natl music award 1976; composition fellowship Natl Endowment for the Arts 1976, 1979, 1980, 1981; George Russell Day proclaimed by Gov of MA, 1983; two Grammy nominations, 1985; Jazz Master Award, Afro-American Museum Philadelphia PA, 1985. **HOME ADDRESS:** 40 Shepard St, Cambridge, MA 02138. *

RUSSELL, GEORGE ALTON, JR.
Financial administrator. **PERSONAL:** Born in Boston, MA; married Faye Sampson; children: Martin Bakari. **EDUCATION:** Clark Univ, BA 1972; NY Univ, MBA 1974. **CAREER:** Urban Bus Assistance Corp, pres 1972-74; State St Bank & Trust Co, vice pres 1979-84; City of Boston, collector-treas. **ORGANIZATIONS:** Dir Dimock Comm Hlth Ctr 1983-; bd mem Boston Indus Develop Finance Auth 1984-; treas-custodian State Boston Retirement System 1984-; comm Boston Arson Comm 1984-; custodian Boston Public Sch Teachers Retirement Fund 1984-; mem Business Assoc Club 1984-; mem Govt Finance Officers Assn 1984-; mem MA Collector-Treas Assn 1984-; trustee Boston Concert Opera; mem of corp Boston Science Museum; dir Organization for a New Equality 1985-; trustee United Methodist Church 1985-. **HONORS/ACHIEVEMENTS:** Prof Achievement Awd Boston Urban Bankers Forum 1984; Ten Outstanding Young Leaders Awd Boston Jaycees 1985; Professional Achievement Awd Boston Urban Banker's Forum 1985. **BUSINESS ADDRESS:** Collector-Treasurer, City of Boston, One City Hall Square, Boston, MA 02201.

RUSSELL, HARVEY CLARENCE
Business executive. **PERSONAL:** Born Apr 14, 1918, Louisville, KY; married Jacqueline Denison; children: Harvey, John. **EDUCATION:** KY State U, AB 1939; IN & MI U, 1939-41. **CAREER:** Pepsico Inc, vice pres 1965-; Pespi-Cola Co, vice pres 1950-65; Rose-Meta Cosmetics, sls mgr 1948-50; WB Graham Assc 1946-48. **ORGANIZATIONS:** Mem NY State Bd Soc Welfare 1969-79; Afrcn Am & Inst 1968; US State Dept Adv Cncl on Afrcn Afrs 1967-69; OEO Adv Cncl 1967-69; US Dept LaborManpower Adv Com 1970-72; vice pres Natl Alliance Busmn 1969-70; mem Arden House Steering Com on Welfare 1967-69; UNA Com on S Africa 1970-72; co-chmn ICBO 1963-69; tst Tougaloo Clg 1966-70; mem NY Cncl Crime & Delinquency 1962-66; Yonkers Family Serv 1963-65; NY State Comm Aid 1964-; Natl Mun League 1969-; Bus Adv Cncl NAACP 1973-; Spl Contrib Fund Exec Commn 1975-; NAACP Legal Def Fund Bd & Exec Com 1974-; exec bd Natl Assc Study Afro-am Life & Hist 1975-; Kappa Alpha Psi; Alpha Kappa Delta; Sigma Pi Phi; natl pres Hudson River Mus Bd 1978-80; rep African-Am Dialogues Tunisia 1970, Lesotho 1975,The Sudan 1977. **HONORS/ACHIEVEMENTS:** Achvmt awrd Alpha Kappa Alpha 1962; Natl Bus League 1963; KY state alumni awrd 1964; am jewish cong awrd 1965; Natl Assc Mkt Dev 1966; ICBO 1967; hon DHL Livingston Clg 1975. **MILITARY SERVICE:** USCG lt 1942-46.

RUSSELL, HERMAN JEROME
Builder, land developer. **PERSONAL:** Born Dec 23, 1930, Atlanta, GA; married Otelia; children: Donata, Michael, Jerome. **EDUCATION:** Tuskegee Inst, attended. **CAREER:** City Beverage Co Inc Atlanta GA, pres, chmn bd; Atlanta Enquirer Newspaper Inc, chmn bd dir; Enterprise Investments Inc, chmn bd; Concessions IntlInc, pres, chmn bd; GA Southeastern Land Co Inc, pres chmn bd; Paradise Apts Mng Co Inc, pres; HJ Russell Plastering Co & Constr Co, pres, owner, chmn bd; JH Russell & Co's Atlanta, pres, owner. **ORGANIZATIONS:** Chmn of bd DDR Intl Inc Atlanta GA; bd of dir World Congress Ctr Auth Atlanta GA; chmn bd dir Cit Trust Co Bank; mem bd dir YMCA; mem bd of trustees Morris Brown Coll Atlanta GA; life mem NAACP; mem natl adv bd GA Inst of Tech; mem African Meth Episcopal Church; mem bd of trustees AfricanEpiscopal Church; chmn bd Russell/Rowe Commun Inc; bd dir Prime Cable Inc; mem bd dir 1st Atlanta Corp; past pres Atlanta C of C; mem bd dir GA C of C, Central Atl Prog, Tuskegee Inst. **HONORS/ACHIEVEMENTS:** Natl Assoc of Market Developers Awd 1968; Meritorious Bus Achievement Awd Atlanta Comm Relations Comm 1969; Equal Oppty Day Atlanta Urban League 1972; African Meth Episcopal Outstanding Bus of the Year 1973; Winter Conf Awd Affiliate Contractor of Amer Inc 1973; Disting Serv Awd Empire Real Estate Bd 1973; Black Enterprise Mag Annual Achievement Awd 1978; Jr Achievement Awd (Bus & Youth) 1979; Natl Alumni Awd Tuskegee Inst. **BUSINESS ADDRESS:** President, Russell Rowe Communications, WGXA-TV 24, Macon, GA 31297.

RUSSELL, JAMES A., JR.
Educator. **PERSONAL:** Born Dec 25, 1917, Lawrenceville, VA; son of Dr. J. Alvin Russell and Nellie P. Russell; married Lottye J Washington; children: Charlotte R Coley, James A III. **EDUCATION:** Oberlin Coll, BA 1940; Bradley Univ, MS 1950; Univ of MD, EdD 1967; St Paul's Coll LLD 1984. **CAREER:** Norfolk Naval Shipyard, electrician 1941-42; US Naval Training School, instructor 1942-45; St Paul's College, asst prof 1945-50; Hampton Univ, prof & div dir 1950-71; St Paul's Coll, pres 1971-81; VA Comm Coll Sys, dir of instr prog 1981-82; WV State Coll, prof & div chmn 1982-86, Interim President 1986-. **ORGANIZATIONS:** Pres Peninsula Council on Human Relations 1962-65; mem Richmond Metro Authority 1981-82; sen warden & vestryman St James Episcopal Church 1982-. **HONORS/ACHIEVEMENTS:** Space scientist McDonnell Douglas Astronautics 1968; NAFEO Study Group Republic of China Taiwan 1979; Hon Degree LLD St Paul's College 1984; Distinguished Alumnus Award Bradley Univ 1984. **HOME ADDRESS:** 811 Grandview Dr, Dunbar, WV 25064.

RUSSELL, JOHN PETERSON, JR.
Educational administrator. **PERSONAL:** Born Aug 26, 1947, Cora, WV; married Gail P Davis; children: Kim, Janelle. **EDUCATION:** Bluefield State Coll, BS 1970; WV Coll of Grad Studies, MA 1975; VPI & SU, CAGS 1978. **CAREER:** Nathaneil Macon Jr HS, secondary teacher 1970-71; Omar Jr & Logan HS, secondary teacher 1971-74; Southern WV Comm Coll, counselor 1974-76, dean of students 1979-81, asst to dean of students. **ORGANIZATIONS:** Chmn, bd of dir New Employment for Women Inc 1981-; mem appt Amer Friends Serv Comm Relation Comm 1982-; mem elected Amer Friends Serv Exec Comm 1983-. **HONORS/ACHIEVEMENTS:** Outstanding Young Man 1979. **HOME ADDRESS:** PO Box 246, Logan, WV 25601. **BUSINESS ADDRESS:** Asst to Dean of Students, Southern WV Comm Coll, Dempsey Br, Logan, WV 25601.

RUSSELL, JOSEPH D.
Educator. **PERSONAL:** Born Aug 11, 1914, Richmond, KY; married Josie Marie Ruffin; children: Joseph III, Cirus, Candace. **EDUCATION:** Wilberforce Univ, BS 1937; OH State Univ, MA 1939; Univ of WI, Univ of IL, IL State Univ, attended. **CAREER:** Mounds Douglass HS, teacher basketball & track coach 1939-42; Attucks HS, teacher athletic coach 1943-57; Eisenhower HS Decatur IL, teacher basketball-tennis coach 1957-69; Bradley Univ, past asst prof 1960-80. **ORGANIZATIONS:** Mem bd YMCA 1963-65; bd mem Garden Angel Home for Dependant Boys & Girls 1975-76; multimedia instr ARC 1977-80. **HONORS/ACHIEVEMENTS:** Partic black coaches & principal giving black school the ability to partic in state tournaments 1945; 1st black coach of a predominantly white school in IL 1957-69; Coach of the Year Southern IL 1969; Hall of Fame Coach IL Hall of Fame 1976. **BUSINESS ADDRESS:** Bradley University, Peoria, IL 61614.

RUSSELL, JOSEPH J.
Educator. **PERSONAL:** Born Apr 11, 1934. **EDUCATION:** VA State Clg, BS 1960; IN U, MS 1968, EdD 1970. **CAREER:** IN Univ, chmn 1972-, dir 1970-72; Richmond Public School, visiting teacher 1964-67; Richmond Social Serv Bur, social worker 1960-64. **ORGANIZATIONS:** Chpn Dept of Afro-Am Studies; exec dir Natl Cncl for Black Studies; adv com Urban Affairs 1973-; adv comUniv Div 1974-; standing com Blo Omington Campus 1974-; faculty hearing ofcr 1974-; chmn Afro-Am Conf Grp IHETS 1974-; mem Stdnt Life Study Commn 1977; mem IN State Adv Bd 1974-. **HONORS/ACHIEVEMENTS:** Comm serv awrd 2nd Bapt Ch 1976; outst educator awrd Phi Beta Sigma 1976; serv appreciation plaque NM Black Studies Consortium 1977; natl Dev & ldrshp awrd Natl Cncl for Black Studies 1977; 100 Most Influential Friends for 1977; Black Jour 1977; Num Presentation & Papers. **MILITARY SERVICE:** USAF airman 1954-58.

RUSSELL, KAY A.
National account executive. **PERSONAL:** Born Jul 12, 1954, Charleston, SC; daughter of John Henry Russell and Mary Forrest Russell. **EDUCATION:** Trident Technical Coll, Charleston, SC, 1974; Univ Dist of Columbia, Washington, DC, BA Marketing, 1979. **CAREER:** Marriott, Washington, DC, sales mgr, 1980-82; Omni Shoreman, Washington, DC, sales mgr. 1982-83; Westin Hotel Detroit, Detroit, MI, natl sales mgr. 1983-88; Minneapolis Convention Bureau, Minneapolis, MN, natl account mgr, 1988-. **ORGANIZATIONS:** Mem, Exec Women Intl, 1983-85; mem, Coalition Black Meeting Planners, 1984-; mem, NAACP, 1985-. **HONORS/ACHIEVEMENTS:** Golden Egg Award, Natl Assn of Media Women, 1987; Sales Manager of the year, The Westin Hotel Detroit, 1988; Imperial Potentate Achievement Award, AEOANMS, 1988. **BUSINESS ADDRESS:** Natl Accounts Mgr, Greater Minneapolis Convention & Visitors Assn, 1219 Marquette Ave, Suite 300, Minneapolis, MN 55403.

RUSSELL, KEITH BRADLEY
Curator. **PERSONAL:** Born Aug 13, 1956, Augusta, GA; son of John Raphael Russell and Barbara Elaine Tullerson. **EDUCATION:** Cornell Univ, Ithaca NY, BS, 1977; Clemson Univ, Clemson SC, MS, 1981. **CAREER:** Academy of Natural Sciences, Philadelphia PA; collection mgr, 1982-. **ORGANIZATIONS:** Mem, Delaware Valley Ornithological Club, 1973-, Soc for the Preservation of Natural History Collections, 1988-. **HONORS/ACHIEVEMENTS:** Coordinator, Philadelphia Mid-winter Bird Census, 1987-. **BUSINESS ADDRESS:** Collection Manager-Exhibit Collection, Academy of Natural Sciences of Philadelphia, 19th & Benjamin Franklin Pkwy, Philadelphia, PA 19103.

RUSSELL, LEON W.
Affirmative action/EEO officer. **PERSONAL:** Born Nov 03, Pulaski, VA. **EDUCATION:** East TN State Univ, BS 1972; East TN State Univ Sch of Grad Studies, attended 1972-74. **CAREER:** TN State House of Reps, legislative intern and asst 1973; East TN State Univ Dept of Political Science, grad teaching asst 1972-73; TN Municipal League, mgmt intern and rsch asst 1974; KY Commission on Human Rights, field rep 1975-77; Pinellas County Govt Office of Human Rights, affirmative action/eeo officer 1977-. **ORGANIZATIONS:** Charter mem Beta Zeta Alumni Chap Alpha Kappa Lambda Frat; mem natl bd dirs Natl Assoc of Human Rights Workers; mem Intl City Mgmt Assoc; bd dirs OIC of the Suncoast; asst sec Clearwater Branch NAACP; mem FL State NAACP Conf of Branches; mem East TN State Univ Alumni Assoc; bd dirs Alternative Human Svcs; allocations comm bd dirs United Way of Pinellas Co; bd dirs FL Assoc of Comm Relations Profls. **HONORS/ACHIEVEMENTS:** Who's Who in Amer Colls and Univs 1971; Pi Gamma Mu Natl Social Science Honor Soc. **BUSINESS ADDRESS:** AA/EEO Officer, Pinellas County Government, 315 Court St, Clearwater, FL 34616.

RUSSELL, LEONARD ALONZO
Dentist. **PERSONAL:** Born Dec 27, 1949, Paris, KY. **EDUCATION:** Easter KY, BS Indust 1971; Central State, BS Biology 1978; Case Western Reserve Univ, DDS 1982. **CAREER:** Private Practice, dentist. **ORGANIZATIONS:** Natl parliamentarian Student Natl Dental Assoc 1981-82; mem Acad of General Dentistry 1981-; mem Ohio Dental Assoc 1982-; pres Forest City Dental Soc 1986-87. **HONORS/ACHIEVEMENTS:** Leonard A Russell Awd Kappa Alpha Psi Frat 1971; Kenneth W Clement Awd Cleveland City Council 1981; Outstanding Young Man of Amer US Jaycees 1984. **BUSINESS ADDRESS:** 2204 South Taylor Rd, Cleveland Heights, OH 44118.

RUSSELL, MAURICE V.
Educator. **PERSONAL:** Born May 07, 1923. **EDUCATION:** Temple U, AB 1948; Columbia U, MSW 1950; Columbia U, edD 1964. **CAREER:** NY Univ Med Center, prof 1973-; Social Serv Dept, dir 1973-; Amer Public Health Assc, pres 1976-77; Einstein Med Center, prof 1970-73; Bronx Municipal Hospital Center, dir; Columbia Univ School of Public Health, assc prof 1965-70. **ORGANIZATIONS:** Vis prof Case Western Res 1971; lectr New Sch for Soc Rsrch 1974-75; chmn bd St Philips Comm Ctr; St Philips Day Care Ctr 1973-; Am Cncl emigres in Profn 1970-; Cancer Care & Am Cancer Found 1974-; tres Robert Popper Found 1968-; past pres Soc for Hosp Soc Work Dirs 1972; past chmn ColumbiaUniv Sch of Soc Work 1975; past chmn Training Com Natl Inst of Mental Hlth 1974; chmn Tech

Advy Com New York City Hlth Dept 1968-73; flwshp Natl Inst of MentalHlth 1950. **HONORS/ACHIEVEMENTS:** Outst comm serv awrd Natl Urban League 1965; outst soc worker Hlth Care in State of NY NY State Welfare Conf 1972; Ida M Cannon Awrd Am Hosp Assc 1973; Num Publ.

RUSSELL, MICHAEL (CAMPY)
Professional athlete. **PERSONAL:** Born Jan 12, 1952, Jackson, TN; married Robyn; children: Oyin, Mandisha Iman. **EDUCATION:** MI 1974. **CAREER:** Cleveland Cavaliers, professional bsktbl forward. **HONORS/ACHIEVEMENTS:** Athlete of yr Pontiac-Waterford Times 1978-79; pro of yr Cleveland Touchdown Clb 1978-79.

RUSSELL, NATHANIEL S.
Business executive. **PERSONAL:** Born Mar 16, 1930, Long Branch, NJ; married Frances L Tynes; children: Richard, Rosanne, Michael, Sharon, David, Gary, Nathaniel. **EDUCATION:** Manmouth Clg NJ, AA 1950;Univ AZ Tucson, 1963; Natl Hsg Spec Inst Am U, 1971. **CAREER:** Builders Urban Dev Co Inc, proj dir exec vp; PB Dev Co Inc, proj dir qlfyg heavy constr consult ; RE Broker 1938; Russell Realty & Ins Tucson, ins broker 1963. **ORGANIZATIONS:** Can status IREM CPM 1972; consult Natl Corp of Hsg Partnerships 1971; cert FHA Fee Appraiser 1967; pres Builders Urban Consult & Appraisers; pres Russell Realty & Ins 1958; mem Natl Inst of RE Mgmt; Natl Assc Realtors; AZ Assc Realtors; Tucson Bd Realtors; Natl Assc Hsg Cons; Natl Assc Min Con; bd dirs Natl Assc Homebldrs; Southern AZ Homebldrs Assc; bd dirs Com for Econ Opp; chmnUniv Heights Area Cncl; pres Tucson Bd Realtors; mem Multiple Listing Serv. **MILITARY SERVICE:** USAF t/sgt 1950-54. **BUSINESS ADDRESS:** 1320 E 22nd St, Tucson, AZ 85713.

RUSSELL, NIPSEY
Comedian, actor. **PERSONAL:** Born in Atlanta, GA. **EDUCATION:** Univ Cincinnati, 1946. **CAREER:** Formerly headlined at Harlem's Small's Paradise; Dean Martin Show, TV appearances; Barefoot in the Park; Les Crance Show, co-host; reg on several TV game shows. **HONORS/ACHIEVEMENTS:** Movie appearance The Wiz 1978; 1st black regularly employed as MC on natl TV program. **MILITARY SERVICE:** AUS capt WWII. **BUSINESS ADDRESS:** c/o Joseph Rapp Enterprises, 1650 Broadway, SUite 705, New York, NY 10019.

RUSSELL, WESLEY L.
Engineer. **PERSONAL:** Born Nov 06, 1938, Camphill, AL; married Geraldine K; children: Derek, Dante, Deirdre, Derwin. **EDUCATION:** Tuskegee Inst, BS 1963; San Diego State Univ, attended. **CAREER:** General Dynamics Electronics, assoc engr 1963, electrical engr 1964, sr electrical engr 1968, hw mgr, tactical system, section head 1984-. **HONORS/ACHIEVEMENTS:** Letter of Commendation in support of initial operational evaluation of P5604 Secure Telecommun Terminals Tinker AFB OK 1974. **BUSINESS ADDRESS:** Section Head, General Dynamics Electronics, PO Box 85468, MZ 6105-E, San Diego, CA 92138.

RUSSELL, WILBERT C.
Executive director. **PERSONAL:** Born Jun 02, 1926, Middlesex Co, VA; married Eleanor Shell; children: Tanya, Todd. **EDUCATION:** VA Union U, BD; Case Western Reserve U, MA;Univ of VA, EdD; NY U; Knox Clg. **CAREER:** Univ of DC, pres 1974; DC Occuptnl Info Coord Com Under DC Labor Employment Serv, exec dir; VA State Clg, pres 1970-74; Am Can Co, dir of pub affairs 1970, asst to vice pres for pub relations & advertising 1970, rsrch mgr pub relations & advertising 1969-70; VA Union U, dean of clg 1963-69, dean of stdnt 1957-63, instr 1956-57; Benedict Clg, asst prof & dir pub relations 1951-56; Child Welfare Bd OH, case worker 1950-51. **ORGANIZATIONS:** Past bd mem Natl Laboratory for Higher Ed; past chmn adv com Ofc for Advancement of Pub Negro Clg; chmn DC Commn on Postsec Ed; chmn Manpower Serv Planning Adv Cncl; mem Commin on Licensure to Prac the Healing Art in the DC; mem bd of dir Natl Ctr for Higher Ed Mgmt Systems & Futures Com; mem bd dir Downtown Progress; past mem exec com So Regional Ed Bd; past mem adv com VA State Conf on Sch Age Parents; past mem adv bd VAState Commn for Title III Higher Ed; past consult Dept of HEW; mem Phi Delta Kappa Ed Frat; mem Omega Psi Phi Frat; mem NEA; past Army Adv Com Ft Lee, VA; past mem Commn on City-co Relations; past mem Gov Manpower Planning Cncl; past mem State Water Control Bd; past mem exec com Ft Lee Army Adv Com; past mem bd trustee Friends Assc of Richmond; past mem bd of trustee Richmond Area Comm Cncl; past dir of pub relations Greenwich, CT Comm Chest. **MILITARY SERVICE:** AUS sgt 1945-46.

RUSSELL, WILLIAM FENTON (BILL)
Sportscaster, professional athlete, coach. **PERSONAL:** Born Feb 12, 1934, Monroe, LA; married Didi Anstett. **EDUCATION:** San Francisco State Coll, 1956. **CAREER:** Seattle Times, weekly columnist; Seattle Supersonics, 1st black head coach 1973-77; Boston Celtics, basketball player, coach; "Cowboy in Africa", performed; ABC-TV, sportscaster 1969-; Sacramento Kings, head coach 1987-. **ORGANIZATIONS:** Mem Natl Basketball Assoc 17 yrs; served as a network NBA color analyst for 13 yrs incl serv at ABC, CBS & WTBS. **HONORS/ACHIEVEMENTS:** Podoloff Cup as MVP 1957-65; MVP US Basketbll Writers 1960-65; author "Second Wind, Memoirs of an Opinionated Man" 1979; Gold Medal US Olympic Basketball Team 1956; mem Basketball Hall of Fame. **BUSINESS ADDRESS:** Head Coach, Sacramento Kings, 1515 Sports Drive, Sacramento, CA 95834.

RUSSELL-MCCLOUD, PATRICIA A.
Attorney. **PERSONAL:** Born in Indianapolis, IN; married Errenous Earl Jr. **EDUCATION:** KY State U, BA 1968; Harvard Univ Sch of Law, 1968; Howard Univ Sch of Law, Juris Doc 1973. **CAREER:** Fed Communicative Commn Mass Media Bureau, Wash DC, chief, complaints branch 1973-83; Patricia A Russell Consultants, pres/consulting. **ORGANIZATIONS:** Sup parliamentarian Alpha Kappa Alpha Sor Inc 1978-82; The Links, Inc 1976-85; Nat Bar Assn 1975-85; mem US Supreme Court Bar 1979; mem DC Bar Assn 1978; mem IN Bar Assn 1973. **HONORS/ACHIEVEMENTS:** Speach, "If Not You, Who, If Not Now When" listed in free Congressional Record 1981; Honorary Doc of Laws Bethune Cochran Coll 1983; NAACP Legal Defense & Educ Fund Award 1981.

RUTHERFORD, HAROLD PHILLIP, III
Educational administrator. **PERSONAL:** Born Sep 03, 1951, New York, NY; married Vancenia Dowdell; children: Paitra. **EDUCATION:** John Carroll Univ, AB 1974; Kent State Univ, MA 1977. **CAREER:** Kent State Univ, asst to the dean 1976-80; City of East Cleveland, vice-city mgr 1980-83; RDR Mgmt Consultants, exec dir 1982-85; Fort Valley State Coll, dir of develop 1985-. **ORGANIZATIONS:** Consultant East Cleveland Sch Bd 1980-83; consultant City of Maywood, IL 1982-85; mem Sigma Pi Phi Frat 1983; mem Portage County NAACP 1984; bd mem Reccord & Associates 1984-86. **HONORS/ACHIEVEMENTS:** Woodrow Wilson Natl Fellowship 1985-86; Management Develop Program Harvard Univ 1986; Management Awd Certificate The Wharton School 1986. **HOME ADDRESS:** 4923 B Friar Rd, Stow, OH 44224.

RUTLAND, WILLIAM G.
Deputy director. **PERSONAL:** Born Jun 28, 1918, Cherokee, AL; married Eva E Neal; children: Elsie, Billy, Patty Jo, Ginger. **EDUCATION:** Morehouse Clg, BS; Wayne State U; Grad; MI Clg; Bergamo Ctr. **CAREER:** Sacramento Air Logis Ctr McClellan AFB, deputy chief dir of plans & pgms; USAF, dir of material mgmt operations elect sys & div. **ORGANIZATIONS:** Pres Sacramento Unified Sch Dist Bd of Ed 1970, 77; mem Rotary Intrntl Sacramento Symphony; Mental Hlth Assc; Am Red Cross. **BUSINESS ADDRESS:** Mc Clellan AFB, Sacramento, CA.

RUTLEDGE, ESSIE MANUEL
Educational administrator. **PERSONAL:** Born Oct 01, 1934, Midway, AL; daughter of Algie L Manuel Sr (deceased) and Ollie M Jordan Jones; married Albert C Rutledge; children: Jeffrey A. **EDUCATION:** FL A&M Univ, BA 1958; Univ of WI Madison, MA 1965; Univ of MI, PhD 1974. **CAREER:** 16th Street Jr HS, St Petersburg, social studies teacher 1958-61; Gibbs & St Petersburg Jr Coll, instr 1961-67; Macomb County Comm Coll, asst prof of sociology 1968-71; Univ of MI Flint, asst prof of sociology 1974-76; Western IL Univ, assoc prof & chairperson of Afro-Amer Studies 1976-84, prof 1984, prof of Sociology 1985-. **ORGANIZATIONS:** Mem Amer Sociological Assn 1967-; mem & membership chmn Assn of Black Sociologists 1970-84; pres Assoc of Black Sociologists 1985-86; mem Com on Status of Women of the Amer Sociological Assn 1978-80; mem IL Council of Black Studies 1979-; adv bd McDonough Co Health Dept 1979-81; mem Ch Women United 1980; mem Pi Gamma Mu Natl Social Sci Honor Soc A&M Univ FL 1965. **HONORS/ACHIEVEMENTS:** Post-doctoral Fellow, Program in Applied Gerontlogy 1989; Inducted into the College of Arts and Sciences Gallery of Distinction at Florida A&M Univ 1987; Summer grants Natl Sci Found 1965-67; Rackham Fellowship Univ of MI 1971-74; Awd for Serv to Enhance Position of Women Western Orgn for Women Western IL Univ 1979; pub articles on Black Women, Role Knowledge, Black Husbands & Wives, Separatism, Black Families, racism, socialization in "The Black Woman", "ERIC Documents", "Reflector", "Genetic Psychology Monograph"; "Journal of Negro History", "Marriage and Family Therapy", "Contemporary Sociology, "Journal of Comparative Family Studies", "Minority Voices" 1970-. **BUSINESS ADDRESS:** Prof of Sociology, Western ILUniv, 900 W Adams, Macomb, IL 61455.

RUTLEDGE, JENNIFER M.
Management consultant. **PERSONAL:** Born Sep 12, 1951, White Plains, NY; son of James Rutledge and Elizabeth Rutledge. **EDUCATION:** MI State Univ, BS industrial psych 1973; Pace Univ Lubin School of Business, MBA 1980. **CAREER:** Allstate Ins, personnel 1973-76; NAACP Legal Defense & Educ fund, dir of personnel 1976-79; Natl Council of Negro Women, natl coord work exp prog 1979-80; Girls Clubs of Amer Inc, partner northeast serv ctr 1983-86; Delphi Consulting Group Inc, partner. **ORGANIZATIONS:** Bd mem Westchester Urban League 1976, Afro-Amer Cultural Assn 1976; bd mem, vice pres Afro-Amer Civic Assn 1978; mem Natl Assn Female Exec, Natl Assn MBA's; guest lecturer Business & Professional Women's Clubs; mem Meeting Planners Intl; bd mem Lubin Grad School of Bus Alumni Assn, Pace Univ; bd mem Support Network Inc 1988-. **HONORS/ACHIEVEMENTS:** Business Woman of the Year, Afro-Amer Civic Assoc 1987; contributing writer Human Resources Development Review 1988-. **BUSINESS ADDRESS:** Partner, Delphi Consulting Group, Inc, 5 Corporate Park Dr, Ste 311, White Plains, NY 10604.

RUTLEDGE, PHILIP J.
Educator. **PERSONAL:** Born Oct 15, 1925, Dawson, GA; son of John Rutledge and Bessie Perry; married Violet Eklund; children: Phyllis, Janet, Edward, Patricia. **EDUCATION:** Roosevelt Univ, BA 1952; Univ of MI, MPH 1958; additional graduate study, Wayne State Univ, Rackham Graduate School, Univ of MI; IN Univ, LLD 1980. **CAREER:** Detroit Dept of Health, sr health inspector 1955-60, dir bur of health ed 1960-64; Mayor Comm for Human Resources Devel, dir 1965-67; US Dept of Labor, exec dir, acting dep manpower admin 1967-69; Stanley H Ruttenberg & Assoc, sr assoc 1969; Comm for Human Resource Programs, asst to mayor 1969-70, dir human resources 1970-71; SRS Dept of HEW, dep admin 1971-73; School of Business & Public Admin Howard Univ, prof/chmn public admin 1973-80; Natl League of Cities US Conf of Mayors, dir office of policy analy; Natl Inst of Public Mgmt, pres; IN Univ Northwest, dir, prof div of public & environmental affairs, dir Great Lakes Center for Public Affairs, int programs coordinator 1982-; IN Univ Center for Global Studies, special asst to pres and dir 1989. **ORGANIZATIONS:** SMem Lake Cty Crime & Criminal Justice Task Force, Lake Cty Comm Devel Comm, Lake Cty Private Indust Council, Rotary Club; pres Gary Redevelopment Commiss, Lake Cty Job Training Corp, Gov's Task Force on Welfare & Poor Relief, NAACP; chmn SSI Study Group 1975-, Com on Evaluation of Employment & Training Programs, Natl Rsch Council, Natl Acad of Science; consultant Dept of HEW, Law Enforcement Asst Admin; pres Gr WA Rsch Center; adjunct prof public admin Fairleigh Dickinson Univ; gov bd Center for Public Affaris & Admin Nova Univ; advisory bd Salvation Army; mem World Future Soc, AAAS, Amer Political Science Assoc, Amer Sociology Assoc, Natl Council on Employment Policy, Harvard Univ Bd of Overseers Visiting Comm to JFK School of Gov, Intl City Mgmt Assoc, Natl Planning Assoc, Amer Public Welfare Assoc, Amer Acad of Political & Social Science; bd trustees DC Inst of Mental Hygiene; bd dir Natl Center for Public Serv Internships; fellow Amer Public Health Assoc; mem bd of dir ARC DC Chapter; advisory comm Evaluation of Urban Transportation Alternative natl rsch; chmn Urban League of Northwest IN; pres World Affairs Council NW IN; vice pres IN Council on World Affairs; bd dir Mid-west Univ Consortium for Intl Activities; vice chair Lake Co Private Industry Council; Indianapolis Comm on Foreign Relations. **HONORS/ACHIEVEMENTS:** Fellow Institute of Politics Harvard Univ; pres Amer Soc Public Admin; elected to Natl Acad Public Admin; international lecturer US State Dept; numerous citizen of the year awards. **BUSINESS ADDRESS:** Office of the President, Indiana University, Bryan Hall, Bloomington, IN 47405.

RUTLEDGE, WILLIAM LYMAN
Surgeon. **PERSONAL:** Born Jun 27, 1952, Little Rock, AR; married Marilyn Faye Woolfolk; children: Rodney B, Estelle A, Jessica M. **EDUCATION:** TX Southern Univ, BA

(Cum Laude) 1975; Meharry Medical Coll, MD (w/Honors) 1979. **CAREER:** Arkansas Surgical Assocs, pres 1984-. **ORGANIZATIONS:** Mem Alpha Omega Alpha Honor Medical Soc 1978-, Natl Medical Assoc 1979-; dist commnr Boy Scouts of Amer 1986; sec Scott Hamilton Drive Medical ClinicInc 1986. **BUSINESS ADDRESS:** President, Arkansas Surgical Assocs, 5800 West 10th Ste 405, Little Rock, AR 72204.

RYAN, AGNES C.
Attorney. **PERSONAL:** Born Sep 17, 1928, Houston, TX; widowed; children: 3 Children. **EDUCATION:** Howard U, BA 1947; Fordham U, Juris Doc 1950. **CAREER:** Legal Aid Bureau, vlntr lawyer 1951-52; Private Prac, lawyer 1952-53; Legal Aid Bureau, staff lawyer 1955-, supervisory lawyer. **ORGANIZATIONS:** Mem Chicago Bar Assn 1968-, bd of mgrs 1976-78; mem Am Bar Assn 1971-; bd mem Bartelme Homes 1977-. **HONORS/ACHIEVEMENTS:** Educ Award Elks 1971; consult to author of "Consumers in Trouble". **BUSINESS ADDRESS:** Supervisory Lawyer, Legal Aid Bureau, 14 E Jackson Blvd, Chicago, IL 60604.

RYAN, MARSHA ANN (NEE NEUSTADTER)
Business executive. **PERSONAL:** Born Mar 12, 1947, New Orleans, LA; married Cecil James; children: Michelle, Marisa. **EDUCATION:** Fisk U, BA 1968; TN State U, Tchr Cert 1970. **CAREER:** OR Adult & Fam Serv Dir Multnomah Reg Off, pgm exec bd/supr pre-admsn screening/resource unit 1980-; OR Dept of Hmn Resources Dir Ofc, pgm anls 1979-80; OR Motor Vechicles Div, pgm dev 1978-79; OR Dept of Transp, afrmtv action & ofcr 1977-78, career dev anlyst 1975; Singer, area sls mgr1974; Xerox Ed Products Div, area sls rep 1973; Gen Elec Co, data processing instr 1971; Neely's Bend Jr H, tchr 1970-71. **ORGANIZATIONS:** Mem Am Assc of Affirmative Action; Gov Tri-Co Affirmative Action Assc; Affirmative Action Ofcrs Assc dev for state gov publ "oR dept of Transp's Oral Interviewers Manual The ODOT Employee Orientation Pgm". **BUSINESS ADDRESS:** Multomah Regional PAS/Resource, 821 SE 14th St, Portland, OR.

RYAN-WHITE, JEWELL
Public relations/promotions coordinator, producer. **PERSONAL:** Born May 24, 1943, Columbus, MS; daughter of L A Ryan, Sr and Martha Ryan; divorced; children: Donald. **EDUCATION:** Attended Alcorn A&M Coll, Joliet Jr Coll, Olive Harvey Coll, IL State Univ. **CAREER:** IL Bell Tel Co, opr investigator dial serv clerk 1967-76; Comm Wkrs of Amer Loca 5011, pres 1972-86; American Cablesystems Midwest, comm TV 1986-87, public relations/promotions coord 1987; California School Employees Assn, CBS program analyst. **ORGANIZATIONS:** Credentials Com Intl Conv for Comm Wrkrs of Amer 1977; del CWA Natl Conv Detroit 1979, LA 1980; chmn bd of dirs Joliet Will Co Comm Action Bd 1982; State of IL Comm Serv Black Grant Bd 1982-83; chmn labor div Joliet Chap Amer Cancer Soc 1982; chmn of bd Joliet Catholic HS adv bd 1983-85; bd of dirs Big Brothers 1984; mem Black Trade Unionists, Urban League, Oper PUSH, Vol Parent Guardian Angel Home; mem St John Vianney Cath Church; mem SCLC; mem Cath Educ Assn; Smithsonian Assoc; mem Personnel & Public Policy Comm Natl Campaign Human Dev Washington DC 1985-87; mem Joliet Jr Coll Minority/Intercultural Affairs Bd of Dir 1985-87; mem Women in Cable 1986-87; commnr 1986, chair of bd 1987 Housing Authority of Joliet; mem Natl Assoc of Housing & Redevelop Officials 1986-87; bd of dir Sr Serv Ctr 1987, Sr Companion Prog 1987; chmn EOC Comm, Natl Federation of Local Cable Programmers 1988-90; sec of bd of dir, arbitrator, Natl Bd of Arbitrators 1989; mem NAACP, Beverly Hill/Hollywood Chap 1989-90; mem Los Angeles Urban League 1989-90. **HONORS/ACHIEVEMENTS:** Schlrshp in Clothing 1961; Awd Salesclerking RE Hunt HS 1961; Awd Newly Elected Officers Training Sch CWA 1973; Cert of Merit IL Bell Tele Co 1974; Awd of Appreciation CWA 1976; United Way of Will Co 1977; City of Hope COPE 1977; Pace Setter Awd City of Hope 1979; Crusade Awd Amer Cancer Soc 1980; Citizen of the Month City of Joliet 1982; Certificate of Achievement Pro-Skills 1986, Achievement Awd 1986, American Ambassador Awd 1986 American Cablesystems; Awd of Appreciation Campaign Human Develop Joliet Catholic Diocese 1986; Awd of Appreciation Natl Campaign Human Dev Washington DC 1987; Awd for Cable Excellence, Cable Television Administration and Marketing Society 1987; 3 awds for overall contribution to field of adult educ/illiteracy, Jolliet Junior College 1987; public speaking awd, American Cable Systems 1987; named to Natl Bd of Consumer Arbitrators 1989. **BUSINESS ADDRESS:** California School Employees Association, CBS Program Analyst, 5601 East Slauson #203, Los Angeles, CA 90040.

RYDER, GEORGIA ATKINS
Educational administrator. **PERSONAL:** Born Jan 30, 1924, Newport News, VA; daughter of Benjamin F Atkins, Sr and Mary Carter Atkins; married Noah Francis (deceased); children: O Diana Jackson, Malcolm E, Aleta R. **EDUCATION:** Hampton Inst, BS Music (Summa Cum Laude) 1944; Univ of MI, MusM 1946; NY Univ, PhD Music 1970. **CAREER:** Alexandria VA Public Schools, music resource teacher 1945-48; Norfolk State Univ, music prof 1948-79, dept head of music 1969-79; NY Univ, lecturer 1968-69; Norfolk State Univ, dean school of arts & letters 1979-86 (retired). **ORGANIZATIONS:** Mem Alpha Kappa Mu 1943-; past pres Intercollegiate Music Assoc 1975-78; commissioner Norfolk Commission on the Arts & Humanities 1978-; council mem Coll Music Soc 1980-82; panelist Natl Endowment for the Arts 1980-83; exec commn mem Natl Colloquim of Arts & Letters 1983-; dir of finance Southeastern VA Arts Assoc 1983-; panelist VA Commn for the Arts 1984-; trustee Bank St Memorial Baptist Church 1984-; judge Governor's Awards for the Arts in VA 1985; bd mem Center for Black Music Research, Columbia Coll, Chicago 1984; bd mem Natl Consortium of Arts & Letters for Historically Black Coll 1983. **HONORS/ACHIEVEMENTS:** Grant Southern Fellowships Fund 1967-69; Founders Day Awd for Distinguished Scholarship NY Univ 1979; Citation Distinguished Serv Norfolk Comm for Improvement of Educ 1974; Citation Leadership in Teacher Educ Norfolk State Coll 1977; Distinguished Service in the Performing Arts, City of Nortolk, VA, 1986; Service to Community, State, Nation, Southeastern VA Arts Assn, 1986; published articles in professional publications 1973-82; contributor to Black Music and the Harlem Renaissance S A Floyd 1989. **HOME ADDRESS:** 5551 Brookville Rd, Norfolk, VA 23502.

RYDER, MAHLER B.
Educational administration. **PERSONAL:** Born Jul 07, 1937, Columbus, OH; son of Mahler Ryder and Virginia Ryder; divorced; children: Ulli Kira. **EDUCATION:** Coll of Art and Design, Columbus, OH, 1955-58; Artillery School Ft Sill OK, 1960; OH State Univ, 1963; Provincetown Workshop, 1964; Art Students League NY 1965-66; School of Visual Arts NY 1967-68; RI School of Design, 1978. **CAREER:** Project Turn-On NY Board of Ed, part-time faculty/asst admin 1969; SOMSEC Art Program New York City Board of Ed 1969; New School for Soc Research, part-time faculty 1969; Providence School Dept 1969-72; RI School of Design, instructor 1969-70, asst prof 1970-81, assoc prof 1981-88, prof 1988-; Providence Pub Lib, dir Special Children's Art Program 1972-73; USA, CAN, Germany, Italy, exhibited artwork; visual artist, has exhibited 14 one-man and 50 group shows in Germany, Canada, and USA. **ORGANIZATIONS:** Mem comm to establish the Studio Museum in Harlem 1967; mem Comm Talented & Gifted Children RI Dept of Educ 1977; exec comm Conference of Christians and Jews 1977; council mem RI State Council on the Arts 1978-82; mem of bd RI Volunteer Lawyers for the Arts 1978-80; chmn RI Governors Arts Awards Comm 1981; New England Foundation for the Arts 1981-83; juror Newport Art Assoc 1983; juror Arts Fellowship Boston MA 1988; juror, Manchester Art Assoc 1988; juror RI State Council for the Arts 1989; project dir JAZZ devoted to jazz music featuring established artists and musicians. **HONORS/ACHIEVEMENTS:** Lectures including, Univ of Saarbruecken, Germany 1962; Wheeler School, Providence, RI 1982; Natl Center of Afro-Amer Artists 1983; Smithsonian NEH Grant Afro-Amer Art Symposium 1985; nom Loeb Fellowship for museum concept for jazz Harvard Univ 1984; solo artist Pugilist Series as part of the kick off for 1988 World Trade Ctr New York City 1984; artwork selected for office of Sen Robt Kennedy; Artists Against Apartheid UN Sponsored Exhibit 1984; org exhibit, Artists in Uniform Germany US Diplomatic Serv & Germany Gov 1962, JF Kennedy Performing Arts Ctr. **MILITARY SERVICE:** Airborne Artillery PFC 1960-63; Good Conduct, Expert Rifle, Machine Gun, European Service Ribbon. **BUSINESS ADDRESS:** Professor Illustration, Rhode Island School of Design, 2 College St, Providence, RI 02903.

S

SAAR, BETYE I.
Artist, designer, educator. **PERSONAL:** Born Jul 30, 1926, Los Angeles, CA; daughter of Jefferson Brown and Beatrice Brown; divorced; children: Lesley, Alison, Tracye. **EDUCATION:** UCLA, BA 1949; attended Amer Film Inst 1972. **CAREER:** Artist; numerous exhibits; Whitney Museum Modern Art, solo exhibit 1975; Studio Museum in Harlen, solo exhibit 1980; Monique Knowlton Gallery NY, solo exhibit 1981; Jan Baum Gallery LA, solo exhibit 1981; Quay Gallery San Francisco, 1982; WAM & Carnbena School of Art Australia, solo exhibit 1984; Georgia State Univ Gallery, 1984; Museum of Contemporary Art LA, solo exhibitions in context 1984; MIT Center Gallery 1987; exhibitions Tai Chung Taiwan, Kuala Lumpur Malaysia, Manila Philipines, 1988. **HONORS/ACHIEVEMENTS:** Awd Natl Endowment of Arts 1974 & 1984; "Spirit Catcher-The Art of Betye Saar"; film featured on women in the Art series WNET-TV NYC.

SABOURIN, CLEMONCE
Clergyman. **PERSONAL:** Born Oct 06, 1910, New Orleans, LA; married Glenice Thelma James; children: Clemonce James. **EDUCATION:** Immanuel Lutheran Sem, 1935; Johnson C Smith Univ, 1939. **CAREER:** Mt Zion Lutheran Church, pastor. **ORGANIZATIONS:** Pres Luth Human Relations Assn Am 1960-70; past pres Gen conf Negro Luth Chs; founder, dir The School on the Hill; lectr numerous bds coms in field; pres Union Free Pub School Dist #12. **HONORS/ACHIEVEMENTS:** Hon LLD Valparaiso Univ 1963; Mind of Christ Award Luth Human Relations Assn Amer 1969; Servant of Christ Award Concordia Coll 1972. **HOME ADDRESS:** 1168 W Wythe St, Petersburg, VA 23803.

SABREE, CLARICE SALAAM
Program administrator. **PERSONAL:** Born Oct 25, 1949, Camden, NJ; divorced; children: Zahir, Anwar, Ameen, Hassan. **EDUCATION:** Rutgers Univ Camden, BA 1978. **CAREER:** Lawnside Bd of Educ, teacher 1978-80; Camden Bd of Educ, elem teacher 1980-82; DMC Energy Inc, office mgr 1983-87; CAPEDA, energy analyst 1987-88; project specialist 1988-; NJ Dept of Community Affairs, Division of Community resources, Office of Low-Income Energy Conservation. **ORGANIZATIONS:** Researcher/collector/lecturer Intl Black Dolls 1979-; steering comm Camden Coalition for a Free South Africa & Nambia 1980-; vocalist/songwriter/musician Maximum Persuasion 1984-89. **HONORS/ACHIEVEMENTS:** Outstanding Volunteer Headstart Camden 1978; Cultural Awareness Council for the Preservation of African-Amer Culture 1985-87. **HOME ADDRESS:** 1476 Mt Ephraim Ave, Camden, NJ 08104. **BUSINESS ADDRESS:** Department of Community Affairs, Div of Community Resources, Office of Low-Income Energy Conservation, 101 S Broad St, CN 814, Trenton, NJ 08625.

SADDLER, WILLIAM E.
Consultant. **PERSONAL:** Born Jun 08, 1915, Ft Worth, TX; married Audrey; children: Yolandia Tatum, Kawanie, William Jr, Karen. **EDUCATION:** TX So Houston, BA 1948. **CAREER:** SW Drug Co Ft Worth, liquor warehouse mgr 1941-43; Billy's Restaurant & Club Ft Worth, owner & mgr 1945-49; Ajax Distr Co Houston, field rep 1959-62;Lone Star Cty Dallas, publ relations 1963-73; Penland Distr Co, consult 1963-80. **ORGANIZATIONS:** Mem Masons 1941; treas Elks Lodge 1941; mem YMCA 1941; mem TX Restaurant Assoc 1941; treas NAMD 1962; mem Urban League 1964; mem Pylon Salesmanship Club. **HONORS/ACHIEVEMENTS:** 15 Yrs Serv in Sales Mktg & Publ Relations Awd NAMD Dallas 1966; Man of the Year in Publ Relations Awd TX State Assoc BCL Dallas 1969; Marketeer of the Year E Stoke Marshall Dallas 1973; Marketeer Serv Awd TX State Assoc & BCL League #47 Dallas 1977. **MILITARY SERVICE:** AUS tech sgt 1942-45. **BUSINESS ADDRESS:** Consultant, Penland Distributors Inc, 2730 Irving Blvd, Dallas, TX 75207.

SADLER, KENNETH MARVIN
Dentist. **PERSONAL:** Born Oct 12, 1949, Gastonia, NC; son of Edward Dewitt Sadler Sr and Mildred Jackson Sadler; married Brenda Arlene Latham, MD; children: Jackson Lewis Ezekiel Sadler. **EDUCATION:** Lincoln Univ, BA 1971; Howard Univ Coll of Dentistry, DDS 1975; Golden Gate Univ, MPA 1978. **CAREER:** Howard Univ Coll of Dentistry, instructor/coordinator 1972-76; US Army Dental Corps, captain/dentist 1975-78; Winston-Salem Dental Care Plan, coordinator of quality assurance and professional referral serv 1978-. **ORGANIZATIONS:** Omega Psi Phi, life mem 1969; Natl Dental Assn, mem 1975-; Amer Dental Assn, mem 1975-; Academy of General Dentistry, mem 1976-; Lincoln Univ, bd of trustees 1983-; Old North State Dental Soc, chmn peer review comm 1986; presentations DC Dental Soc, Post-graduate Seminar Howard Univ, Pellican State Dental Soc, Natl Dental Assoc, NC Dental Soc, Forsyth Co Dental Asst Soc, Lincoln Univ Chemistry Dept, Amer Acad of Dental Group Practice, Palmetto State Dental Medical Pharmaceutical Assoc; bd of dir Old Hickory Council Boy Scouts of Amer 1988-. **HONORS/ACHIEVEMENTS:**

Omicron Kappa Epsilon, mem 1975-; Intl Coll of Dentistry Award 1975; The Amer Assn of Endodontics Award 1975; US Army, dental diploma-general practice 1976; Academy of Gen Dentistry, fellow 1982; Journal of Natl Dental Assn- Article, resin bonded retainers 1984; Recognition Cetificate, Chicago Dental Soc, 1989; Plaque-Appreciation, Fifth Dist Dental Soc, 1989; Lecture/Table Clinic, Chicago Mid-winter Meeting, 1989; Table Clinic, Thomas P Hinman Dental Meeting, 1989. **MILITARY SERVICE:** US Army, major, commendation medal. **BUSINESS ADDRESS:** Coord of Quality Assurance, Winston-Salem Dental Care, Inc, 201 Charlois Blvd, Winston-Salem, NC 27103.

SADLER, WILBERT L.
Educator. **PERSONAL:** Born Nov 17, Atlanta, GA; married Carolyn Johnson; children: Anthony Lee, Wilbert Bryant, Crystal Yolanda. **EDUCATION:** Paine Coll, BS 1970; Morgan State Univ, MS 1972; Boston Univ, EdD 1981; Univ of Pennsylvania, Post Doctorate study 1981. **CAREER:** Morgan State Coll, instructor 1970-74; Boston Univ, grad asst 1974-76; Livingstone Coll, asst prof 1976-82; Winston-Salem State Univ, assoc prof 1982-. **ORGANIZATIONS:** Mem Pinehurst Comm Club 1976-; mem Salisbury Rown Symphony Guild; mem Optimist Club; mem Assoc of Coll & Univ Profs, Assoc for Educ Comm & Tech, Natl Council of Teachers of English, Assoc for Supervision & Curriculum Develop, Coll Reading Assoc, Intl Reading Assoc, Alpha Kappa Mu Hon Soc; mem Beta Mu Lambda, Alpha Phi Alpha Frat Inc. **HONORS/ACHIEVEMENTS:** Natl Endowment for Humanities Fellowship; Published 2 books, 3 articles. **MILITARY SERVICE:** AUS sp/4 2 yrs. **BUSINESS ADDRESS:** Associate Professor, Winston-Salem StateUniv, Education Dept, Stadium Dr, Winston-Salem, NC 27110.

SAFFEL, E. FRANK
Business executive. **PERSONAL:** Born Jan 25, 1923, Knoxville, TN; son of Huse and Elsie; married Bloneva (deceased); children: Candance Frye, Beverly Jackson. **CAREER:** Oprtv Plstrs & Cmnt Masons Intl Assn, vice pres 1970-, org 1966-70. **ORGANIZATIONS:** Mem Cmnt Masons Un Lcl 524 Cncnti 1952-; bd of trst Nat Plstrng Inds Jnt Apprntcshp Trst Fund 1979; sec Nat Jnt Cmnt Msnry Apprntcshp & Trng Com 1980; bd of trst Prep Ins 1980; Lcnsd Real Est Slsmn Cinci, MD, DC; co-chair Natl Trust Fund, Cement Masons Training 1989. **HONORS/ACHIEVEMENTS:** Labor Temple bldg dedicated in my name Cincinnati OH 1983. **MILITARY SERVICE:** Army Corp of Engineers corpl 1942-44. **HOME ADDRESS:** 3512 28th St, NE, Washington, DC 20018. **BUSINESS ADDRESS:** Vice President, Plasterers & Cement Masons, 1125 17th St, NW, Washington, DC 20036.

SAFFOLD, OSCAR E.
Physician. **PERSONAL:** Born Feb 20, 1941, Cleveland, OH. **EDUCATION:** Fisk U, BA 1963; Meharry Med Coll, MD 1967. **CAREER:** Grg W Hbbd Hosp, intern 1967-68; TaftsUniv Sch Med, asst resd derm 1968-72; Boston City Hosp, chf resd derm 1972-73; Case Wstrn Res Med Sch, asst derm dept med 1974-, clncl instr 1973-. **ORGANIZATIONS:** Sec Derm Sect Nat Med Assn 1975-; dir Medic-Scrn Inc 1975-; staff St Vncnt Chrty Hosp; Shkr Med Hosp;Univ Hosp Cleve 1973-; mem MA St Bd; OH St Bd; Am Bd Derm 1974; mem Am Acad Derm; Am Soc for Derm Srgry Inc; AMA; Cleve Acad of Med; Cleve Derm Assn; Nat Med Assn; OH St Med Assn. **HONORS/ACHIEVEMENTS:** Publ Gundala Schmbrg Lever MD, Histlgy & Ultrstrctr of Herpes & Gstns, Fred S Hirsh MD, Oscar E Saffold MD, Mycbctrm Kansasii Infctn With Derm Mnfstns; Arch Derm 1973, 1976. **BUSINESS ADDRESS:** Central Med Arts Bldg, 2475 E 22nd St, Cleveland, OH 44115.

SAGERS, RUDOLPH, JR.
Marketing representative. **PERSONAL:** Born Feb 14, 1955, Chicago, IL; married Carol Hillsman; children: Ryan Christopher. **EDUCATION:** Univ of IL, BS 1978; Univ of Cincinnati, MS 1980. **CAREER:** Veterans Administration, mgmt analyst trainee 1979-80, mgmt analyst 1980-81, health systems specialist 1981-84; Intl Business Machines, marketing rep 1984-. **ORGANIZATIONS:** Mem Amer Coll of Hospital Administrators 1982, MI Health Council 1982, Amer Health Planning Assoc 1983, Soc for Hospital Planning 1983, Black Data ProflAssoc 1986-. **HONORS/ACHIEVEMENTS:** Outstanding Young Man of Amer Awd 1983; Veterans Admin Achievement of Service Awd 1983; Veterans Admin Superior Performance Awd 1983; Veterans Admin Special Contribution Awd 1984; Medical Ctr Director's Commendation of Excellence Awd; Intl Business Machines Branch Mgr Awd 1985,86; Intl Business Machines Natl 100% Sales Club Awd 1985,86. **HOME ADDRESS:** 2737 Tarpon Ct, Homewood, IL 60430. **BUSINESS ADDRESS:** Marketing Representative, Intl Business Machines, One IBM Plaza, Chicago, IL 60611.

ST. JOHN, PRIMUS
Associate professor of English. **PERSONAL:** Born Jul 21, 1939, New York, NY; son of Marcus L St John Hall and Pearle E Hall; divorced; children: Joy Pearle, May Ginger. **EDUCATION:** University of Maryland; Lewis and Clark College. **CAREER:** Mary Holmes Junior College, West Point, MS, teacher; University of Utah, teacher; Portland State University, Portland, OR, associate professor of English, 1973-; Portland Arts Commission, member, 1979-81; educational consultant. **HONORS/ACHIEVEMENTS:** National Endowment for the Arts fellow, 1970, 1974, 1982; author of Skins on the Earth, 1976; author of Love Is Not a Consolation; It Is a Light, 1982. **HOME ADDRESS:** 3275 Fairview Way, West Linn, OR 97068. **BUSINESS ADDRESS:** Department of English, Portland State University, Portland, OR 97207. *

ST. MARY, JOSEPH JEROME
Union official. **PERSONAL:** Born Oct 27, 1941, Lake Charles, LA; married Elaine Guillovy; children: Jennifer Ann, Lisa Rene, Joseph J. **EDUCATION:** Sowela Tech Inst, business 1968; Loyola Univ, labor course 1984. **CAREER:** Plasterers & Cement Mason #487, recording sec 1962-69, fin sec & bus mgr 1970-; Calcasieu Parish Police Jury, vice-pres 1979-80, pres 1981-82. **ORGANIZATIONS:** Exec bd Southwest Central Trades Council 1974-; vice-pres Southwest LA Bldg Trades Council 1974-; fin sec A Phillip Randolph Inst 1974-; vice pres LA AFL-CIO 1975-. **HOME ADDRESS:** 414 N Simmons St, Lake Charles, LA 70601. **BUSINESS ADDRESS:** Police Juror, Calcasieu Prsh, 118 N Enterprise Blvd, Lake Charles, LA 70601.

ST. OMER, VINCENT V. E.
Educator, consultant. **PERSONAL:** Born Nov 16, 1934, St Lucia, St. Lucia;married Margaret Muir; children: Ingrid, Denise, Jeffrey, Raymond. **EDUCATION:** Ontario Vet Coll, DVM 1962; Univ Manitoba, MSc 1965; Ontario Vet CollUniv Guelph, PhD 1969. **CAREER:** Hamilton & Dist Cattle Breeders Assn, field vet 1962-63; ON Vet CollUniv Guelph, lecturer 1965-67; Univ KS, res assoc bur of child rsch 1968-71, adj prof 1970-73; adj rsch assoc bureau child rsch 1972-74, asst prof coll vet med 1972-74; Sch of MedUniv MO, prof; Dept Vet Biomedical Sciences, prof. **ORGANIZATIONS:** Mem Optimist Intl 1970-; mem Soc Sigma Xi, Amer Soc of Vet Physiologists & Pharmacol, Soc for Neuroscience, MO Vet Med Assn; Conf of Rsch Workersin Animal Disease NY Acad of Scis; rsch interests, Neuropharmacology & Neurotoxicology. **HONORS/ACHIEVEMENTS:** Fellow of the Amer Acad of Veterinary Pharmacology and Therapeutics. **BUSINESS ADDRESS:** Professor, Dept Vet Biomedical Sciences, Coll Vet MedUniv MO, Columbia, MO 65201.

SAINTE-JOHNN, DON
Communications. **PERSONAL:** Born Jul 09, 1949, Monroeville, AL; married Brenda L Hodge; children: W Marcus, J'Michael Kristopher. **EDUCATION:** LA City Coll, 1968; Cal-State Long Beach, 1969. **CAREER:** XEGM Radio San Diego, prog dir 1968-69; KWK St Louis, prog dir 1969-71; KYUM Yuma AZ, sports dir 1969; Aradcom Prod of St Louis, pres 1970-71; WJPC Radio Chgo, am air personality 1971-74; KFRC RKO Broadcasting Inc, air personality. **ORGANIZATIONS:** Mem Natl Assoc Radio-TV Ammoun; lic CA Real Estate; mem bd E Bay Zoological Soc; mem Bay Area March of Dimes Superwalk, Natl Acad TV Arts & Sci, Amer Fed TV & Radio Art, Alpha Epsilon Rho, SC Broadcaster Assoc,; mem bd of dir Paul J Hall Boys Club; spear-headed on air int WJPC Chicago to support black boxers; athletic dir St Davids School; bd mem Diocesan Boys Athletic Council of Oakland; former basketball coach Richmond Police Activities League, El Sobrante Boys Club, St Davids Schools. **HONORS/ACHIEVEMENTS:** Billboard Air Personalities of the Year 1973,74; Prod Special on Sickle Cell Anemia Channel 26 Chicago 1971; Hon as Concerned Spon for Chicago Pin-Killers Bowl Club 1974; Most Outstanding Radio Student at LA City Coll 1967; Hon for Cont in Law Enf St Louis MO 1971; Air Personality of the Year Billboard Mag 1974,75; air Personality on Pop Radio Awd Black Radio Exclusive Mag 1980. **BUSINESS ADDRESS:** KFRC RKO Broadcasting Inc, 415 Bush St, San Francisco, CA 94108.

SALAAM, ABDUL (LEO MCCALLUM)
Dentist. **PERSONAL:** Born Aug 18, 1929, Newark, NJ; son of Roosevelt McCallum and Katie Allen McCallum; married Khadijah, May 14, 1954; children: Sharonda Khan, Valerie Best, Robert, Darwin, Abdul II. **EDUCATION:** Wash Sq Coll, NYU, BS 1952; ColumbiaUniv Sch of Oral/Dental Surgery, DDS 1956; Acad of Genl Dentistry, FAGD 1973. **CAREER:** NYU Wrestling Team, capt 1950; Jarvie Hon Soc, Columbia U, mem 1954; Lincoln Dental Soc Bulletin, editor 1972; Guaranty Bank, Chicago IL, bd of dir 1976. **ORGANIZATIONS:** Post grad instructor Inst for Grad Dentists 1966-; pres Commonwealth Dental Soc of NJ 1964; pres Specialty Promo Co Inc Import Export 1959-; organ pres Nation of Islam 1976; pres bd of dir New Earth Child Care Community Network 1984-88; teachers certificate in general semantics from Inst of General Semantics Englewood NJ 1986; pres-elect Kenwood Hyde Park Br of Chicago Dental Soc 1987-88; bd of dir Masjid Al' Fatir 1987-; treasurer Muhammad Ali Investment Corp 1988-; guest lecturer Inst for General Semantics 1988-; newspaper columnist Amer Muslim Journal; mem bd of dirs Amer Muslim Journal; rep Chicago Dental Soc in Dialogue in Dentistry an agency for helping employers to understand dental ins programs. **HONORS/ACHIEVEMENTS:** Man of the Yr Commonwealth Dental Soc of NJ 1966; fellow The Acad of Genl Dentistry IL 1973. **MILITARY SERVICE:** AUS Medical Corp pvt 1st class 1947-48. **BUSINESS ADDRESS:** Self Employed, 640 E 79th St, Chicago, IL 60619.

SALES, RICHARD OWEN
Business executive. **PERSONAL:** Born Aug 12, 1948, New York, NY; married Dorethye Ann; children: Doricha, Brandy. **EDUCATION:** Rochester Inst of Tech, BS, Printing Mgmt 1970; Northeastern Univ, Boston MA, MBA 1985-89. **CAREER:** MIT Press, Cambridge MA, prod mgr 1970-72; Williams Graphic Serv Wakefield MA, prod mgr 1972-74; Houghton Mifflin Co, Boston MA, vice pres, dir production 1974-. **ORGANIZATIONS:** Secy bd mem Soc of Printers 1983-; past pres Bookbuilders of Boston 1982-83; mem of partnership, Boston Fellows 1988-. **HONORS/ACHIEVEMENTS:** Black Achievers Award Greater Boston Black Achievers 1979. **BUSINESS ADDRESS:** Vice Pres/Dir of Production, Houghton Mifflin Co, One Beacon St, Boston, MA 02108.

SALLEY, COLUMBUS
Educator. **PERSONAL:** Born Apr 10, 1943, Chicago, IL; children: Jennifer, Christopher. **EDUCATION:** Univ of PA, Ed D 1974; Loyola U, MEd 1970; Chicago State U, BS 1965. **CAREER:** IRC Univ of Chicago, sr research assoc dir staff devel; Consortum for Educ Leadership, exec sec; Harcrt Brc Jvnvch, consult ed & hmnts prog 1971-72, consultant 1973-74, lecturer 1965-; Univ City HS Philadelphia, admin asst 1971-72; Chicago, instructor 1967; Trinity Coll Deerfield IL, instructor 1969-70; HBJ NY, asso eng educ 1969-70; HBJ Chicago, sales rep 1967-69. **HONORS/ACHIEVEMENTS:** Author Your God is Too White 1970, White Racism in American 1972; other artcls.

SALMON, JASLIN URIAH
Educator. **PERSONAL:** Born Jan 04, 1942, Darliston, Jamaica;son of Leaford Salmon and Jane Sylent Salmon; divorced; children: Janet Felice, Jennifer Renee. **EDUCATION:** Olivet Nazarene Univ, BA 1969; Ball State U, MA 1970; Univ of IL Chicago, PhD 1977. **CAREER:** Ball State U, teaching asst 1969-70; George Williams Coll, asst prof of sociology 1970-76; Triton Coll, prof of sociology 1976-77; Human Resource Devel Govt of Jamaica, dir 1977-79; Triton Coll, prof of soc 1979-, dir center for parenting 1985-. **ORGANIZATIONS:** Social worker Dept of Mental Health IL 1968-69; dir HOP 1973-75; dir & mem Chicago Forum 1971-72; chmn Academic Senate George Williams Coll 1974; consult Parenting/Women & Minorities at the work place; pres, NAACP Oak Park IL Branch 1989-. **HONORS/ACHIEVEMENTS:** Teacher of the Year George Williams Coll 1973; author, "Black Executives in White Business" 1979. **HOME ADDRESS:** 713 S Humphrey, Oak Park, IL 60304. **BUSINESS ADDRESS:** Prof Soc, Dir Parenting, Triton Coll, 2000 5th Ave, River Grove, IL 60171.

SALMON CAMPBELL, JOAN MITCHELL
Clergywoman. **PERSONAL:** Born Mar 31, 1938, St Louis, MO; daughter of David Andrew Mitchell and Corleda Brady Mitchell; married James Campbell, Jr, Jan 17, 1977; children: Rebecca, David, Jeanne Salmon Stowe, Peter, Paul. **EDUCATION:** Univ of Rochester Eastman School of Music, Rochester NY, BM, 1959; Inter-Met Theological Center, Washington DC, Master of Divinity, 1977. **CAREER:** Piano and voice teacher, concert singer, Rochester NY, 1959-66; asst pastor, St Mark Presbyterian Church, Rockville MD,

1974-77; interim pastor, Arlington Prsbyterian Church, Arlington VA, 1976-78; co-pastor, Linwood United Church, Kansas City MO, 1978-80; pastor, St Paul Presbyterian Church, Kansas City MO, 1978-82. **ORGANIZATIONS:** Chairman of bd, Sickle Cell Anemia, Kansas City MO Chapter, 1980-82; basileus, Delta Nu Omega Chapter, Alpha Kappa Alpha Sorority, 1963; pres, Ujoma Consultant Network, Kansas City MO, 1980-82; pres, chairman of bd, Shalom Ministries Inc, Exton PA, 1982-89. **HONORS/ACHIEVEMENTS:** Black Folks Legacy to America, History of Black Religious Music, 1966; Doctor of Divinity, Central American Univ, 1981; Vice Moderator of Presbyterian Church, Reunion Assembly, 1983; Moderator of 201st GA Presbyterian Church, 1987.

SALTER, KWAME S.
Business executive. **PERSONAL:** Born Jan 31, 1946, Delhi, LA; son of Samuel L and Reva Daniels Salter; married Phyllis V Harris; children: Kevin Jamal, Keri JeMelda. **EDUCATION:** WI State Univ Whitewater, EdB (magna cum Laude) 1968; Univ of WI Madison, MA Ed Admin 1970; Univ of WI, PhD candidate. **CAREER:** Milwaukee Pub Sch Bd of Edn, teacher 1968-69; WI State Univ Whitewater, acad counselor 1968-70; Univ of WI Madison, project asst 1969-70; UW Madison Afro-Amer Cultural Ctr, exec dir 1970-73; Dane Co Parent Council Inc, exec dir 1976-86; Bd of Educ Madison Met Sch Dist, president 1982-86; Oscar Mayer Foods Corp, corparate human resources mgr 1986-. **ORGANIZATIONS:** Pres Exec Council for Cultural Interaction & Awareness Inc 1973; vice pres NAACP Madison Chap 1974-75; mem Madison Downtown Optimist Serv Club 1977; pres Common Touch Inc 1977-; mem Admin Mgmt Soc 1978-; vice pres Madison Met Sch Dist Bd of Educ 1980; mem Phi Delta Kappa 1980-; chrmn WI State Advisory Comm to US Civil Rights Commission 1985-87. **HONORS/ACHIEVEMENTS:** Fellow in Educ Ford Found (UW Madison) 1970; Outstanding Leader/Educator WI Omega Psi Phi-Kappa Phi Chap Milwaukee 1979; State Leaders for the 80's WI, The Milwaukee Journ Newspaper 1980; Outstanding Recent Alumni UW-Whitewater 1986. **BUSINESS ADDRESS:** Corporate Human Resources Mgr, Oscar Mayer Foods Corporation, 910 Mayer Ave, Madison, WI 53704.

SALTER, ROGER FRANKLIN
Business executive. **PERSONAL:** Born Jul 15, 1940, Chicago, IL; married Jacqueline M Floyd; children: Dawn, Roger J, Marc CPres, Sanmar Fin. **EDUCATION:** Chicago Tchrs Coll, BE 1962; DePaul U. **CAREER:** Sanmar Fin Plng Corp, pres; Blkbrn Agency Mut Benft Life, asst gen agt 1970-74; Mut Benfit Life, agt 1965-70; Ins Sales, asst mgr 1964; Chicago MetAsrnc Co, 2nd ldng agt 1962-63. **ORGANIZATIONS:** Dir sec 2nd vice pres 1st vice pres S Side Br Chicago Assn of Life Undrwrtrs; exec dir Fin for S Shore Comm; pres Ekrsll Nghrs Comm Grp; bd dir Mile Sqr Hlth Ctr; mem NAACP; Chicago Urban League; Nat Bus League; Chicago Area Cncl Boy Scts of Am; Omega Psi Phi Frat; life mem Mlln Dllr Rnd Tbl 1972-; 4th Blk in US. **HONORS/ACHIEVEMENTS:** 10 Outst Bus Awd Jycs 1972; Nat Qulty Awrd Ins Sales 1971; Man of Yr 1965-67. **BUSINESS ADDRESS:** 9730 S Western, Evergreen Park, IL 60642.

SAMKANGE, TOMMIE MARIE
Educational psychologist. **PERSONAL:** Born Aug 01, 1932, Jackson, MS; daughter of Harry Anderson and Marie Hughes Anderson; widowed 1989; children: Stanlake, Jr, Harry M. **EDUCATION:** Tougaloo Coll, BS 1953; Indiana Univ, MS 1955, PhD 1958. **CAREER:** Tougaloo Coll, assc prof 1955-56; Tuskegee Inst, assoc prof 1964-67; Tennessee State Univ, prof 1967-71; Afro-Amer Studies Dept Harvard Univ, lecturer head tutor 1971-74; Stnlk Smkng, prof; Salem State Coll, asst dir minority affairs; Tufts Univ, asst prof 1979; Northeastern Univ, lecturer 1979; chief educ psychologist, Ministry of Educ, Zimbabwe 1981-. **ORGANIZATIONS:** Mem Amer Psychological Assn; mem League Women Vtrs, Health Professions Council of Zimbabwe (Psychologist); Zimbabwe Psychological Assn; vice chmn Ronche House Coll of Citizenship. **HONORS/ACHIEVEMENTS:** Mellon Found Grant 1977; Fellow Amer Assn Advncmnt Science. **HOME ADDRESS:** The Castle, PO Hatfield, Harare, Zimbabwe. **BUSINESS ADDRESS:** Chief Educational Psychologist, Ministry of Primary and Secondary Education, Box 8022, Causeway, Harare, Zimbabwe.

SAMPLE, WILLIAM AMOS
Professional athlete. **PERSONAL:** Born Mar 02, 1955, Roanoke, VA; married Debra Evans; children: Nikki, Ian. **EDUCATION:** James Madison U, BS Psychology 1977. **CAREER:** Texas Rangers, outfielder 1978-. **ORGANIZATIONS:** Outfielder Topps Major League All-Rookie Team; selected as 1st team NCAA Div II All-Am at 2nd base 1976. **BUSINESS ADDRESS:** Texas Rangers, Arlington Stadium, Arlington, TX 76010.

SAMPLER, MARION
Art director. **PERSONAL:** Born Jun 30, 1920, Anniston, AL; married Georgianna. **EDUCATION:** Art Acad of Cincinnati; Jepson Art Inst; Art Center School; Chouinard Art Inst; Univ of Southern CA, BFA, 1955. **CAREER:** Gruen Assn, graphic designer; Fremont HS, teacher; LA Valley Coll, art instructor. **ORGANIZATIONS:** Design consultant LA Co Museum of Art; Am Inst of Arch; Pacific Design Center; Jack Lenor Larsen; LA City School; Central City Comm Mental Health Facility. **HONORS/ACHIEVEMENTS:** Art work exhibit LA Co Museum of Art; Long Beach State Univ; CA State Univ, Northridge. **MILITARY SERVICE:** USAF sgt. **BUSINESS ADDRESS:** 6330 San Vicente Blvd, Los Angeles, CA 90048.

SAMPLES, BENJAMIN NORRIS
Judge. **PERSONAL:** Born Aug 05, 1935, Baton Rouge, LA; married Tobortha M; children: Benjamin N II. **EDUCATION:** Bishop College, BA Pol Sci 1965; St Mary's Univ School of Law, JD 1970. **CAREER:** Bexar Co Legal Aid, staff atty 1970-71, private practice 1971-78; San Antonio Civil Service Commission, chmn 1975-78; Bexar Co Juvenile Dept, judicial referee 1976-78; City of San Antonio, municipal court judge 1978-81; Bexar Co TX, judge 1981-. **ORGANIZATIONS:** Bars admitted to, State Bar of TX 1970, US Dist Court Western Dist of TX 1972, US Court of Appeals 5th Cir 1971, US Supreme Court 1973; mem San Antonio, American Bar Assns; mem San Antonio Trial Lawyers Assn; mem Judicial Section State Bar of TX. **HONORS/ACHIEVEMENTS:** Delta Theta Phi Fraternity 1969; bd of dirs Bexar Co Easter Seals 1972; chmn trustee bd St James AME Church 1972; bd of dirs St Mary's Univ AlumniAssn 1983. **BUSINESS ADDRESS:** Judge County Court, Bexar Co, Bexar Co Courthouse, San Antonio, TX 78205.

SAMPSON, ALBERT RICHARD
Clergyman. **PERSONAL:** Born Nov 27, 1938, Boston, MA; son of Paul Sampson and Mildred Howell; divorced. **EDUCATION:** Shaw Univ, BA 1961; Governor's State Univ, MA 1973; McCormick Theological Seminary, DIV 1977. **CAREER:** Newark NJ Poor People's Campaign, project director; Zion Baptist Church Everett MA, pastor; Fernwood United Methodist Church, pastor. **ORGANIZATIONS:** Community org consultant for poverty programs in Syracuse NY, Wilmington DE, Indianapolis IN, Boston MA; pres Council of Black Churches; spokesman Ministers Action Comm for Jobs 1985-92; intl vice pres for training of Allied Workers Intl Union; vice chmn Mayor Harold Washington's First Source Task Force; vice pres Roseland Clergy Assoc; traveled extensively in Europe to study industrialized Housing Systems as SCLC Natl Housing Director; pres, United Westland Food Proram, linking black farmer black consumer in chicago. **HONORS/ACHIEVEMENTS:** Featured in Jet Magazine, Minority Builders Magazine, Chicago Sun-Times, Chicago Tribune; Christian Award 1981; Westside People for Progress Award 1983, South Shore Chamber of Commerce Award 1983; Martin Luther King Jr Award Intl Black Writer's Assn 1983; organized Dr Martin Luther King's low income cooperative housing program entitled 221d3, the only one of its kind in the nation; traveled fact finding mission to Angola, South Africa, Israel, Lebanon, Kenya, Tahzania. **HOME ADDRESS:** 10056 S Parnell, Chicago, IL 60628.

SAMPSON, CALVIN COOLIDGE
Educator. **PERSONAL:** Born Feb 01, 1928, Cambridge, MD; son of Robert H Sampson and Hattie M Sampson; married Corrine Delores Pannell; children: Cathleen Dale, Judith Gail. **EDUCATION:** Hampton Inst U, BS Chem 1947; Meharry Med Coll, MD 1951. **CAREER:** Episcopal Hosp Philadelphia PA, asst dir of lab 1956-58; Freedmen's Hosp Howard U, dir of lab 1958-75; Howard Univ Coll of Med, asst prof of Path 1958-, prof of Pathology. **ORGANIZATIONS:** Vp bd of trustees Hosp for Sick Children Washington DC 1979-1985. **HONORS/ACHIEVEMENTS:** Editor Journal of The Nat Med Assn Washington DC 1978-; 80 scientific articles published in med journals. **MILITARY SERVICE:** AUS col 1953-76. **HOME ADDRESS:** 1614 Varnum Pl NE, Washington, DC 20017. **BUSINESS ADDRESS:** Professor of Pathology, Howard Univ, 520 West St NW, Washington, DC 20059.

SAMPSON, DOROTHY VERMELLE
Attorney. **PERSONAL:** Born Aug 04, 1919, Sumter, SC; daughter of William B Sampson and Bessie Moore Sampson. **EDUCATION:** Hampton Inst, BS 1941; Atlanta Univ, MSW 1952; North Carolina Central Univ, LlB 1963, JD 1969. **CAREER:** Private Practice, atty 1964; Veteran's Admim, psychologist, social worker 1956. **ORGANIZATIONS:** Mem US Supreme Court 1967; 4th Circuit Court of Appeals 1966; Head Start Org 1965; IPAC 1949-53; ind sec Baltimore Urban League 1947; Natl Aux Epis Women 1941-42; bd of dir YWCA; candidate South Carolina Senate 1968; bd of dir South Carolina Farm Migrants Commn 1967-70; subscrib life mem NAACP. **HONORS/ACHIEVEMENTS:** Award United Found 1968-69; Leadership Award, Marry Coll; Leadership Award, Youth Council 1977; Leadership Award, Mount Pisjah AME 1966; Martin Luther King Jr Civil Rights Award, Martin Luther King Jr Birthday Comm 1987. **BUSINESS ADDRESS:** 204 W Oakland Ave, Sumter, SC 29150.

SAMPSON, HENRY THOMAS
Engineer. **PERSONAL:** Born Apr 22, 1934, Jackson, MS; divorced; children: Henry III, Martin. **EDUCATION:** Purdue Univ, BS 1956; MSc Univ of IL 1965; UCLA, MSc 1961; Univ of IL, PhD 1967. **CAREER:** US Naval Weapons Ctr, rsch chem engr 1956-61; rsch consult several documentary films; Pioneer Black Filmmakers, lecturer; Aerospace Corp, proj engr spaceflight S81-1 1967-. **ORGANIZATIONS:** Mem AAAS, Amer Nuclear Soc, Omega Psi Phi; fac adv comm Nuclear Eng 1976-. **HONORS/ACHIEVEMENTS:** Author "Blacks in Black & White-A Source Book on Black Films 1910-50"; US Naval Ed Fellowship 1962; AEC Fellowship 1962-67; several patents engrg devices 1957-65; Scarecrow Press 1977; author "Blacks in Blackface, A Source Book on Early Black Musical Shows" Scarecrow Press 1980, "The Ghost Walks, A Chronological History of Blacks in Show Business 1863-1910" Scarecrow Press 1987, "Blacks in Black and White" Scarecrow Press. **BUSINESS ADDRESS:** Director, Planning STP, Aerospace Corp, 125/1270 PO Box 92957, Los Angeles, CA 90274.

SAMPSON, MARVA W.
Director. **PERSONAL:** Born Sep 04, 1936, Hamilton, OH; married Norman; children: Raymond, Anthony. **EDUCATION:** Miami Univ; Univ of Dayton, Pub Adm 1976. **CAREER:** Hamilton OH City School System, priv sec 1954-58, ofc mgr 1958-59; Citizens Council on Human Relations, coor sec 1966-70; City of Middletown, dept of comm dev relocations officer 1964-66, dir dept of human resources 1971-. **ORGANIZATIONS:** Bd dir YMCA 1971; mem OH Mncpl Leag 1978; bd of trust ASPA 1978; pres Pi Alpha Alpha 1979; pres Ctr for Frnsc Psychiatry 1979-80; choir dir, pianist 2nd Bapt Church; exec bd mem Arts in Middletown; bd of trustees Central Ohio River Valley Assn; exec comm mem Butler County Children Services Bd; pres Middletown Area Safety Council; sec/coord Middletown Job Opportunity Inc; exec comm mem Middletown Area United Way; Natl Assn for Social Workers; Ohio Public Health Assn; Human Services Council; Friends of the Sorg; Ohio Parks and Recreation Assn; Natl Parks & Recreation Assn. **HONORS/ACHIEVEMENTS:** Certs of Merit Serv C of C 1968; Lady of the Week Woman of the Year WPFB Radio Sta 1970; Red Triangle Award YMCA 1971-76; Outstanding Citizens Awd Knights Social Club 1972. **BUSINESS ADDRESS:** Dir Dept of Human Resources, City of Middletown, One City Centre Plaza, Middletown, OH 45042.

SAMPSON, RALPH
Professional athlete. **PERSONAL:** Born Jul 07, 1960, Harrisonburg, VA; married Aleize Rena Dial. **EDUCATION:** Univ of VA, BA Speech Comm 1983. **CAREER:** Univ of VA, center basketball player; Houston Rockets, basketball player. **HONORS/ACHIEVEMENTS:** 3 times NCAA Player of the Year; 4 times All Amer; Rookie of the Year; MVP 1985 All Star game; mem 36th & 37th NBA All Star Teams. **BUSINESS ADDRESS:** Houston Rockets, c/o Tim Foley, 10 Greenway Plaza, Houston, TX 77046.

SAMPSON, ROBERT R.
Pharmacist. **PERSONAL:** Born Oct 17, 1924, Clinton, NC; son of Frank J Sampson and Annie Curry Sampson; married Myrtle B; children: Frank R Sampson. **EDUCATION:** Fayetteville State Univ, Fayetteville NC 1942-43; Howard Univ, Washington DC BS Pharmacy 1946-50. **CAREER:** Sampson's Pharmacy, owner. **ORGANIZATIONS:** Pres NC Old

N St Pharm Soc; mem-at-large NPhA; Incorp Chtr Stockholder Gtwy Bank; mem Amer Pharm Assn; Natl Assn of Retail Druggists; mem Greensboro Med Soc; Greensboro Soc of Pharm; Omega Psi Phi Frat; Natl Pharm Assn; UMLA; Greensboro C of C. **MILITARY SERVICE:** AUS combat infantry. **HOME ADDRESS:** 4608 Splitrail Ct, Greensboro, NC 27406.

SAMPSON, RONALD ALVIN
Business executive. **PERSONAL:** Born in Charlottesville, VA; married Norvelle Johnson; children: David, Cheryl. **EDUCATION:** DePaul U, BS Commerce 1956. **CAREER:** Ebony Mag, adv sales rep 1958-63; Foote Cone & Belding Advert, merchandising supr 1963-66; Tatham Laird Kudner Advert, partner/mgmnt supr 1966-78; Burrell Advert, exec vice pres 1978-81; D'Arcy MacManus Masius Advert, sr vp. **ORGANIZATIONS:** Advisor Am Assoc of Advert Agencies 1972-. **HONORS/ACHIEVEMENTS:** Vp bd of dir Community Renewal Soc 1973-; mem Chicago Forum 1978-. **MILITARY SERVICE:** AUS sp 4 1956-58. **HOME ADDRESS:** 6715 S Oglesby, Chicago, IL 60649.

SAMS, ERISTUS
Government official. **PERSONAL:** Children: 3 Children. **EDUCATION:** Tuskegee, BA; Prairie View, MS. **CAREER:** Prairie View, mayor 1969. **BUSINESS ADDRESS:** City Hall, Prairie View, TX.

SAMUEL, FREDERICK E.
Government official. **PERSONAL:** Born Jan 22, 1924. **EDUCATION:** McGill U, BS 1949; NY U, MA 1949; Fordham U, LLB 1953. **CAREER:** NY City, city ofcl; Atty, pvt prac. **ORGANIZATIONS:** Mem NY City Counc 1974; chmn bd Haryou Act Dist Ldr Dem Party 1971; chmn NY Co Dem Com 1973; NY Bar 1954; mem Harlem Lawyers Assn 1966-68. **BUSINESS ADDRESS:** 2315 7th Ave, New York, NY 10030.

SAMUEL, LOIS S.
Educator. **PERSONAL:** Born May 26, 1925, Boston, MA; widowed; children: David, Judith. **EDUCATION:** Simmons Coll, BS; ColumbiaUniv Sch, SSW Soc Wrk. **CAREER:** Leake & Watts Chgldrns Home, social worker 1947-49; Youth Consultant Serv, Social Worker 1949-51; New York City Bd Educ Bureau, child guidance 1955-73, suprv 1973-; Drug Abuse Prevention & Educ Prog Academy of Certified Social Workers, dir dist 29 1971-. **ORGANIZATIONS:** Mem Nat Assn Soc Wrkrs; Nat Assn Blk Soc Wrkrs; mem NAACP Br Pres 1972-74; Com Adv Cncl; Hmpstd Sch Bd; bd mem Wndhm Chldrns Svc; trstCongreg Ch S Hmpstd; mem Delta Sigma Theta Sor; past pres Nassau Alm Chpt. **HONORS/ACHIEVEMENTS:** Simmons Honor Soc Num Publs in Field. **BUSINESS ADDRESS:** Drug Abuse Prevention & Educ Pr, PS 136 201 15 115 Ave St, St Albans, NY 11412.

SAMUEL, MINOR BOOKER
Judge. **PERSONAL:** Born Feb 29, 1904, Wilkinson Co, MS; married Everleaner Chambere. **EDUCATION:** Wilknsn Co Dist 2, jdg jstc ct; Clntn Bnd Cdr Saw Mill, frmn 1951-52. **CAREER:** Rec sec St John Bapt Ch 1924-80; rec sec GMBSS Assn 1959-80; rec sec Ft Adam Msnc Ldg No 622 1958-80; supt St John BCSS 1930-75; sec Bnlnt Soc Care Home Peo Un 1930-70; chr ofc dcn St John No 2 Bapt Ch 1941-80. **BUSINESS ADDRESS:** Wilkinson Co Dist 2, Rt 2 Box 795, Woodville, MS 39669.

SAMUELS, ANNETTE JACQUELINE
Communications. **PERSONAL:** Born Jul 17, 1935, New York, NY; divorced; children: Linda, Shelly, Angelique, Micheal, Douglas, Melvin. **EDUCATION:** New York U; New Sch for Soc Rsrch; Sch of Visual Arts; Amer U. **CAREER:** Essence Mag, fashio editor 1969-70; Family Circle Mag, asst fashion editor 1970-71; Tuesday Publ, sr editor 1972-73; Continental Group, coor envir affairs 1973-74; Community News Svc, exec ed 1974-76; free-lance & jrnlst 1976-77; Women's Div NYS Exec Chamber, assoc dir pub info 1977-79; The White House, asst presidential press sec 1979-81; The Mayor's Office, press sec to the mayor. **ORGANIZATIONS:** Mem of bd Richard Allen Center for Culture & Art; mem Women in Comm Inc; mem Coalition of 100 Black Women; bd dir, mem Big Sisters of WMA Inc; mem Natl Press Club, Public Relations Soc of Amer. **HONORS/ACHIEVEMENTS:** Who's Who of Am Women 10th edit; Comm Serv Awd Nat Assn Media Women 1976. **BUSINESS ADDRESS:** Press Secretary to the Mayor, The Mayor's Office, District Bldg Room 532, Washington, DC 20004.

SAMUELS, CHARLOTTE
Educator. **PERSONAL:** Born May 27, 1948, Philadelphia, PA. **EDUCATION:** Central State Univ, BS Educ 1969; Temple Univ, MEd 1973. **CAREER:** School District of Philadelphia, mathematics chairperson. **ORGANIZATIONS:** Mem Assoc for Supervision & Curriculum Development, Natl Council of Teachers of Math, Assoc of Teachers of Math of Philadelphia and Vicinity, Black women's Educ Alliance, Assoc of Professional & Exec Women, Joint Center for Political Studies, COBBE; mem NAACP, Big Sisters of America, Campaign Comm for State Rep Dwight Evans; volunteer Victim of Crime Program; mem Natl Forum for Black Public Administrators Philadelphia Chapt. **MILITARY SERVICE:** AUS Reserves Sp5 3 yrs; Civil Affairs Awd for Disting Svcs. **HOME ADDRESS:** 4000 Gypsy Lane #340, Philadelphia, PA 19144.

SAMUELS, EVERETT PAUL
Sports & entertainment manager. **PERSONAL:** Born Aug 27, 1958, Tulsa, OK; son of Chester R Samuels and Gwendolyn Verone Busby; married Patricia Ann Harris Samuels, Sep 04, 1982; children: Everett Paul II. **EDUCATION:** Central State Univ, BS 1980. **CAREER:** Xerox Corp, sr marketing rep 1983-84, marketing exec 1984-85, account exec 1985-86; Progressive Mgmt Assocs, exec vice pres 1985-. **ORGANIZATIONS:** Mem, tutor Tulsa Public Schools 1982-; bd dirs 1984-, pres 1987-89 Tulsa Economic Dev Corp; asst treasurer Bd of Trustees 1985-, assistance sec Deacon Bd 1986-, Friendship Baptist Church; mem Phi Mu Alpha Fraternity, NAACP; volunteer United Negro College Fund; bd mem Sickle Cell Anemia Foundation 1987-; bd mem Gilcrease Hills Homeowners Assoc 1989-. **HONORS/ACHIEVEMENTS:** Inter-Univ Counsel/State of OH. **HOME ADDRESS:** 904 N Zenith Pl, Tulsa, OK 74127. **BUSINESS ADDRESS:** Executive Vice President, Progressive Management Assocs, 16 East 16th St, Ste 401, Tulsa, OK 74119.

SAMUELS, JAMES E.
Business executive, land developer. **PERSONAL:** Born Jun 09, 1928, Detroit; married Eleanor M; children: 6. **EDUCATION:** Brooklyn Coll. **CAREER:** VI Civil Rights Commission, exec dir 1982-; V I Trnscrbn Arwys, dir 1968-70; V I Pt Auth, asst to exec dir 1966-68; V I, asst to atty gen 1961-66; radio TV 1961-; Rltns Inc, self emplyd pub rltns advrtsng cmmnctn splst. **ORGANIZATIONS:** Pres Tmrnd Ntch Ltd St John; vice pres bd dirs USVI Nat Assn TV & Radio Announcers 1966-72; Cubmaster BSA 1972-74; mem Prsch Club Am; Early Fd V8 Club Am. **HONORS/ACHIEVEMENTS:** Cubmaster of Yr 1973; Apprctn & Excellnce Awd Nat Assn TV & Radio Announcers 1969. **MILITARY SERVICE:** AUS sgt 1950-52.

SAMUELS, LESLIE EUGENE
Government official. **PERSONAL:** Born Nov 12, 1929, St Croix, Virgin Islands of the United States;son of Henry Francis Samuels and Annamartha Venetia Ford; married Reather James; children: Leslie Jr, Venetia, Yvette, Philip. **EDUCATION:** NY Univ/Carnegie Hall Music Sc, BM 1956; Blackstone Sch of Law, LLB, JD 1969-75; Columbia Pacific Univ, MBA, PhD 1981-85. **CAREER:** Van Dyke Studios, concert artist 1956-66; Samuels & Co Inc, pres/CEO 1985-; NY Dept of Housing Preservation & Develop, dir of city serv 1966-; New York State, bandmaster 1967-76. **ORGANIZATIONS:** Comm bd mem Astor Home for Children 1975-; mem Amer Mgmt Assoc 1984-; bd chmn Samuels & Co Inc 1985-; mem NY/NJ Minority Purchasing Cncl 1986, Natl Black MBA Assoc 1986-; Harvard Business Review Harvard Grad Sch of Business Admin 1987; mem Intl Traders 1988-90; task force mem Republican Presidential Task Force 1989; natl mem The Smithsonian Associates 1989-90. **HONORS/ACHIEVEMENTS:** Performance Role of Dr Herdal in Henrik Ibsen's Master Builder 1950; Concert Artist Tenor Carnegie Hall 1951-; mem of cast in Langston Hughes', Simply Heavenly 1957; Marketing Thesis Columbia Pacific Univ 1984; Presidential Merit Award, Republican Presidential Task Force 1989. **MILITARY SERVICE:** AUS pvt 1st class 2 yrs. **HOME ADDRESS:** 2814 Bruner Ave, Bronx, NY 10469. **BUSINESS ADDRESS:** Dir, Dept of Housing Preservation, 100 Gold St, New York, NY 10007.

SAMUELS, OLIVE CONSTANCE
Educator, nurse manager. **PERSONAL:** Born Aug 30, 1926, Montclair, NJ. **EDUCATION:** Attended, Harlem Hosp Ctr Sch of Nursing; Seton Hall Univ So Orange NJ, BSN 1965, MA 1972; Columbia Univ Post Grad courses; Montclair State Tech Coll, Post Grad courses. **CAREER:** Possaic Co Comm Coll NJ, prof 1979-; Newark Beth Israel Med, pen nurse spec 1978-79; Bell Lab Mrry Hill NJ, ind nursing 1977-78; Long Island U, asst prof 1974-79; Essx Co Comm Coll Newark, instr of nurses 1970-74; Hrlm Hosp Cntr, inst of nurs stud 1959-70, head nurse 1952-58, staff nurse 1950-52. **ORGANIZATIONS:** Mem AKA Omicron XI Omega NJ 1989-; basil Omicron Chap Chi Eta Phi Sor Inc 1978-80; mem Tau Chi Chapter NJ Nursing Sorority Chi Eta Phi Inc 1981-; mem ANA NY Bus Prof Women; mem Alumni Assoc Seton Hall Univ, Harlem Hosp Ctr School of Nursing; mem YWCA, The Sickle Cell Disease Foundation of Greater NY; choir mem Trinity Episcopal Church. **BUSINESS ADDRESS:** Clinical Coordinator, St Mary's Hospital, 211 Pennington Ave, Passaic, NJ 07055.

SAMUELS, ROBERT J.
Business executive. **PERSONAL:** Born Aug 14, 1938, Philadelphia, PA; son of Hubert Samuels and Lorraine Samuels; divorced; children: Robert Jr, Anthony, Christopher. **EDUCATION:** Attended Amer Inst of Banking, NY Inst of Credit, NY Univ; graduate Stonier Graduate School of Banking. **CAREER:** Manufacturers Hanover Trust Co, NY, credit investigator, 1969-71, asst sec, 1971-73, asst vice pres, 1973-75, vice pres, 1975-; 1st Pennsylvania Bank, former loan mgr. **ORGANIZATIONS:** Pres Natl Assn of Urban Bankers; dir NY Urban League; chmn United Negro Coll Funds NY Corp Matching Gifts Program; visiting prof, Natl Urban League Black Exec Exchange Program; trustee, NY State Higher Educ Serv Corp, 1987; chair, HESC Audit Comm; bd member, Aaron Davis Hall; chair, NYC Bd of Educ Adopt-a-Class Corp advisory comm. **HONORS/ACHIEVEMENTS:** Named Philadelphia's Outstanding Jaycee, 1968; Robert J Samuels Founder's Award established by Natl Assn of Urban Bankers, 1984; Outstanding Citizen Award, United Negro Coll Fund, 1987; Roy Wilkins Humanitarian Award, NAACP, 1988. **MILITARY SERVICE:** USAF 1956-60. **BUSINESS ADDRESS:** Vice President, Manufacturers Hanover Trust, 270 Park Avenue, New York, NY 10017.

SAMUELS, RONALD S.
Attorney. **PERSONAL:** Born Jun 17, 1941, Chicago, IL; son of Peter and Leng; married Melva; children: 4. **EDUCATION:** Chicago State Univ, BA 1964; John Marshall Law Sch, JD 1969. **CAREER:** Chicago Bd Educ, teacher 1964-69; Attorney, 1969-70; Leadership Council for Metro Open Housing, chief trial lawyer 1970-73; Cook Co States Atty Office, chief fraud div 1974-77; Ronald S Samuels and Associates, partner/attorney. **ORGANIZATIONS:** Mem Natl, Cook Co, Chicago, IL State, Amer Bar Assns; dir Legal Oppor Scholarship Prog; chmn Consumer Task Force; mem Chicago Urban League, Kappa Alpha Psi Alumni Chapt, CSU Alumni Assn, PUSH. **HONORS/ACHIEVEMENTS:** Amer Jurisprudence Awd; William Ming Award; Richard E Westbrooks; PUSH Outstanding Public Service; Distinguished Service Award, Natl Bar Assn. **BUSINESS ADDRESS:** Attorney, Ronald S Samuels & Associates, 123 W Madison, Chicago, IL 60602.

SANCHEZ, SONIA BENITA
Author, educator. **PERSONAL:** Born Sep 09, 1934, B'ltam, AL; divorced; children: Morani, Mungu, Anita. **EDUCATION:** Hunter Coll, BA 1955; NY Univ, 1957. **CAREER:** San Francisco State Coll, instr 1966-67; Univ of Pittsburgh, instr 1968-69; Rutgers Univ, asst prof 1969-70; Manhattan Comm Coll, asst prof 1970-72; Amherst Coll, assoc prof 1973-75; Temple Univ, poet, prof. **ORGANIZATIONS:** Mem PA Council on the Arts; contributing editor to "Black Scholar" and "Journal of African Studies"; adv bd SISA, MADRE and WILPF. **HONORS/ACHIEVEMENTS:** Author of 13 books incl, "Homegirls and Handgrenades", "Under a Soprano Sky", "I've Been a Woman", "A Sound Investment", "Love Poems", "Homecoming", "It's a New Day"; PEN Writing Awd New York City 1969; Natl Inst of Arts & Letters Grant 1970; Hon HHD Wilberforce Univ 1972; author of play "Sister Sonji" Joseph Papps Publ Theatre NY; contrib ed "Black Scholar"; edited "We Be Word Sorcerers, 25 Stories by Black Amer", "360 Degrees of Blackness Comin' at You"; NEA Recipient Washington DC 1978-79; Amer Book Awd for "Homegirls and Handgrenades". **BUSINESS ADDRESS:** Professor, TempleUniv, English Dept, Philadelphia, PA 19122.

SANDERLIN, JAMES B.
Judge. **PERSONAL:** Born Jan 02, 1929, Petersburg, VA. **EDUCATION:** Howard U, BS 1950; Boston U, 1957, JD 1962; Nat Coll of the St Jdcry, 1973. **CAREER:** Cir Ct St of FL, co jdg; Fed Dist Ct, jdg 1965; US Ct of Appeals 50th Cir, jdg 1966. **ORGANIZATIONS:** Past chmn Civil Ser Comm City of St Ptrsbrg; past pres St Ptrsbrg Cncl on Hum Rel; mem FL Adv Comm to US Comm on Cvl Rghts; past bd mem Fam & Chldrns Serv Inc; Adult Mtl Hlth Clnc; 1st pres Pnlls Co Hdstrt Inc. **MILITARY SERVICE:** USAR 2nd lt 1950-53. **BUSINESS ADDRESS:** Judge, 2nd District Court, 801 Twiggs St, Tampa, FL 33602.

SANDERS, ARCHIE, JR.
Councilman. **PERSONAL:** Born Sep 06, 1937, Hughes, AR; married Bernice Dawkines; children: Tommy, Willie C, Bonnie, Archie III, Theresa, Diann. **EDUCATION:** Kansas Comm Jr Coll, attended. **CAREER:** Adult educ adv council, 1972-73; Bonner Springs KS, councilman. **ORGANIZATIONS:** Mem Jaycees, Police Reserve, Fire Dept; bd dir C&D Ctr; treas NAACP. **HONORS/ACHIEVEMENTS:** NAACP Achievement Awd 1971.

SANDERS, AUGUSTA SWANN
Health services. **PERSONAL:** Born Jul 22, 1932, Alexandria, LA; daughter of James Swann and Elizabeth Thompson Swann; divorced. **EDUCATION:** Provident Hospital School of Nursing/Morgan State Coll, nursing 1953-56. **CAREER:** Dept of Mental Health, program coordinator. **ORGANIZATIONS:** Pres MD State Student Nurses 1955-56; sec Mu Chi 1975; mem Sen Diane Watson's Comm on Health Problems 1980-; mem CA State Board of Medical Quality Assurance 1981-; mem Assemblyman Mike Roos' Comm on Women's Issues 1982-; pres Wilshire Bus and Professional Women 1982-83; comm LA Unified school board 1985; pres Los Angeles Sunset Dist CA Fedn of Bus and Professional Women 1988-89. **BUSINESS ADDRESS:** Augusta Sanders, R N, Mental Health Services Coordinator, Augustus F Hawkins Comprehensive Mental Health Ctr, 1720 E 120th St Room 1084, Los Angeles, CA 90059.

SANDERS, BARBARA A.
Automotive company executive. **PERSONAL:** Born in New Orleans, LA; daughter of Otis Miles and Arma L Atkins Miles; married Joe Sanders Jr. **EDUCATION:** Southern Univ, BS 1969; Rutgers Univ, MS 1972; Indiana Exec Program, Certificate 1981-82; Harvard Univ PMD Program, Certificate 1985. **CAREER:** General Motors Corp, composites materials dept head 1979-81, composites processing manager 1981-83, CAD/CAM dir 1983-85, artificial intelligence dir 1985-87, advanced manufacturing engineering dir 1987-. **ORGANIZATIONS:** Mem Engrg Soc of Detroit 1981-86; mem Soc of Mfg Engrs 1983-86; key executive GM/Southern Univ Key Inst Program 1984-86; chairperson entrepreneurs comm Minority Tech Council of MI 1985-89; class sec Harvard Univ PMD-49 1985-87; mem Women Economic Club. **HONORS/ACHIEVEMENTS:** Outstanding Alumni Southern Univ Alumni Detroit Chap 1982, 86; Disting Alumni NAFEO 1986; numerous articles/presentations in Tech Area, Lasers, CAD/CAM, AI, Composite Materials 1979-86; Honorary Doctorate, Southern Univ 1988. **BUSINESS ADDRESS:** Dir, General Motors Tech Center, Advanced Engrg Staff, 30300 Mound Rd A/MD-23, Warren, MI 48090.

SANDERS, CHARLES LIONEL
Educator. **PERSONAL:** Born Aug 10, 1936, Lakeland, FL; son of Willie A Sanders and Eleather Sanders; divorced. **EDUCATION:** Howard Univ Coll of Liberal Arts, Bachelor 1959, Schl of Social Work, Masters 1961; NY Univ Grad Schl of Public Admin, Doctorate 1972. **CAREER:** NYCB Radio Wash DC, dir of pub affairs 1978-86; McKinley-Penn Comm Schls, prog dir 1982-84; DC Pub Schls, spec asst supr of schls 1982-84; pres Natl Capital Radio Corp 1983-; Amer Council of Educ, consult 1984-; Univ of DC, professor, College of Business and Public Management 1985-. **ORGANIZATIONS:** Consult, Control Data Inst Arlington VA 1984-85, Amer Council on Educ Wash DC 1984-85, Opport Advertising Inc Wash DC 1984; Amer Soc of Pub Admin Howard Univ Alumni 1984; Amer Mgmt Assc Capital Press Club 1984; Natl Black Media Coalition NY Univ Alumni Assc 1984; bd of dirs, Metropolitan Boys & Girls Club, Natl Capital Radio Corp; pres Natl Capital Broadcast 1985. **HONORS/ACHIEVEMENTS:** Mental Health Ach Award Psych Inst 1982; CEBA Award 1981; Man of the Year, Annual Love Club Awd 1986; Fellow, Center for Applied & Urban Research Univ of DC 1988-89; Fellow, Amer Assn of State Coll and Univ-Japanese Studies Inst 1989. **MILITARY SERVICE:** AUS Med Srv Corp cpt 1962-64. **HOME ADDRESS:** 2801 New Mexico Ave NW #1212, Washington, DC 20007.

SANDERS, DELBERT
Association executive. **PERSONAL:** Born Jun 08, 1931, Demopolis, AL; married Mae; children: 6 Children. **EDUCATION:** Akron Univ, BS 1960, MS 1967; Univ of Mich, doctoral candidate. **CAREER:** Juvenile Ct Ctr School, dir 1961-66; NEC Proj Wide Math, dir 1969-71; Berry School, asst principal 1969-72; Guyton Elementary School, principal 1972-74; Region 8 Detroit Public Schools, Title I admin. **ORGANIZATIONS:** Mem Metropolitan Detroit Soc Blk Educ Admin; Natl Assn Elementary School Principals; Orgn School Admin & Supr; Akron Univ Alumni Assn; Wayne State Univ Alumni Assn; mem Detroit Chap NAACP; consultant numerous publications. **HONORS/ACHIEVEMENTS:** Outstanding Citizens Award Akron; numerous community serv awards. **MILITARY SERVICE:** AUS 1951-66. **BUSINESS ADDRESS:** 8131 E Jeffersn, Detroit, MI 48214.

SANDERS, ELLA J. **See TEAL, ELLA S.**

SANDERS, GEORGE L.
Physician. **PERSONAL:** Born Jul 04, 1942, Vidalia, GA; son of Felton Sanders and Eva Mae Sanders; married Frances; children: G Eldridge, Cleaver. **EDUCATION:** Morehouse Coll, 1965; Univ Miami Sch Med, 1969; Jackson Meml Hosp, intern 1970, resd 1974, flw cardiology 1976. **CAREER:** Private Practice, phy internal med & cardiology; Cedars of Lebanon Hosp, consult cardiologist; N Shore Hosp. **ORGANIZATIONS:** Mem Phi Beta Sigma Frat; Phi Delta Epsilon; bd dir Spectrum Prog Inc 1977; asst clinical profUniv Miami Sch Med; vice pres Greater Miami Heart Assoc; mem American College of Physicians; medical dir North Shore Medical Center Cardiology. **HONORS/ACHIEVEMENTS:** Univ FL Commendation Med AUS 1972; diplomate Am Bd of Internal Med; Student of Yr Phi Beta Sigma 1966; Student Nat Med Assn Awd 1976; flwshp Nat Med Found 1965-69. **MILITARY SERVICE:** AUS capt 1970-72. **BUSINESS ADDRESS:** Owner, GL Sanders MD PA, P O Box 380696, Miami, FL 33238-0696.

SANDERS, GLENN CARLOS
Data base analyst. **PERSONAL:** Born May 24, 1949, Bastrop, TX; son of Charles Sanders, Sr and Marjorie Sanders; married Catherine McCarty; children: Chandra, Brian. **EDUCATION:** Texas Southern Univ, attended 1967-69; California Baptist Coll, BS 1987. **CAREER:** Zales Jewelers Inc, asst mgr 1973-76; TRW Information Svcs, Programmer analyst 1976-80; Riverside Co Data Processing, data base analyst 1980-83; Transamerica Life Companies, data base analyst 1983-. **ORGANIZATIONS:** Mem Phi Beta Sigma 1968-, Planetary Soc 1985-; vice pres Southwestern Information Mgmt Users Group 1986-88; bd mem Parents Against Gangs 1989-. **HONORS/ACHIEVEMENTS:** Natl Student Merit Qualifying Test Commended Candidate; Who's Who in Amer High School Students 1967; Deans List Freshmen Year TX Southern Univ 1968; Top DivSales Zales Jewelers 1973; 1st Place State Extemporaneous Speaking Competition 1967; 2nd Place State Debate Competition 1967. **MILITARY SERVICE:** USN machinist mate 3rd class 2 yrs. **BUSINESS ADDRESS:** Data Base Analyst, Transamerica Life Companies, 1150 So Olive, Rm B808, Los Angeles, CA 90015.

SANDERS, GWENDOLYN W.
Educational administrator. **PERSONAL:** Born Dec 17, 1937, St Louis, MO; daughter of Adolph Fisher and Burnett Harris; married Gordon B; children: Darrell F, Romona R Sanders Fullman, Jocelyn M. **EDUCATION:** St Louis U, BS 1956; Harris Tchrs Coll, BA 1962; St Louis U, MEd 1967; Nova Univ, EdD; Univ of DE & Glassboro St Coll, undergrad work; graduate inst, Harvard. **CAREER:** DE Tech & Comm Coll, dean of student serv 1973-;Univ of DE, instr 1973-75; DE Tech & Comm Coll, plng coord 1972-73; Cty Demonstration Agy, educ cons-planner 1969-72; St Peters Cathedral-Wilmington Pub Sch, tchr dir 1968-70; Oppor Indust Cntr, tchr 1969-70; Lincoln Pub Sch, tchr 1966-68; St Louis Pub Sch, master tchr 1962-68; Harris Tchrs Coll St Louis, lab asst 1959-62; Pvt Phy St Louis, med tech 1956-59. **ORGANIZATIONS:** DE Comm Coord Child Care Comm; mem DE Lib Counc; mem Beta Beta Beta; Headstart Adv Bd; vice pres Educ Com NAACP; consult US Dept of Justice; mem Urban Youth Devel Proj-meth Action Prog; pres, Northeast Council Black Amer Affairs; bd mem, Natl Council Black Amer Affairs, AACJC; consultant, NJ Dept of Higher Educ, Middle States Commn Higher Educ; reader/evaluator, US Dept of Higher Educ; vice pres, Brandywine Professional Assn, AACD, 1980-; DCPA; NAFSA; AAHE; ACPA; People to People Intl; exec bd, Delaware Academy for Youth, 1988. **HONORS/ACHIEVEMENTS:** Developed bi-lingual bi-cultural day care center, 1970; developed and initiated ESL Prog, Delaware Tech, 1976; Outstanding Achievers Award-Education, BPA, 1989; Outstanding Community Service Award, Alliance of Ministers Businesses and Agencies, 1988; Outstanding Community Service Award, Delaware Head Start, 1988. **BUSINESS ADDRESS:** Dean of Student Services, Delaware Technical & Community Coll, 333 Shipley St, Wilmington, DE 19801.

SANDERS, HANK
State senator, attorney. **PERSONAL:** Born Oct 28, 1942, Baldwin Co, AL; son of Sam Sanders and Olamae Sanders; married Rose M Gaines; children: Malika A, Kindaka J, Ainka M, Charles, Maurice. **EDUCATION:** Talladega Coll, BA 1967; Harvard Law School, JD 1970. **CAREER:** Stucky Lumber Co, saw mill worker 1960-61; Honeywell, elec tech 1962-63; Chestnut Sanders Sanders Turner & Williams, attorney 1972-. **ORGANIZATIONS:** Co-founder, former pres AL Lawyers Assn 1973; co-founder, former Pres Campaign for a New South 1982; bd mem Claude C Brown YMCA 1976-85; pres, Alabama New South Coalition 1988-. **HONORS/ACHIEVEMENTS:** Middle East & Africa Fellowship Ford Found 1970-71; Reginald Heber Smith Fellowship Legal Service Corp 1971; 2nd Annual Awd for Outstanding Service Natl Assn of Landowners 1979; Outstanding Senator, 1986; New South Leadership Award, 1989. **BUSINESS ADDRESS:** Senator, Alabama State Senate, P O Box 1305, Selma, AL 36701.

SANDERS, HOBART C.
Physician, surgeon. **PERSONAL:** Born Aug 19, 1929, Boley, OK; son of Hobart M Sanders and Thelma Sanders; married Maurine Lee; children: Thelma, Alice, Hobart, Jr. **EDUCATION:** Lincoln Univ, AB 1949; Meharry Med Coll, MD 1954; Gen Hosp KC MO, Jr Internship Ob & Gyn Res. **CAREER:** Physician, private practice, Tulsa 1958-. **ORGANIZATIONS:** Mem Oklahoma Med Dental Pharm Assns; Natl Med Assn; Tulsa County Ob Gyn Soc; Tulsa County Med Soc; Amer Med Assn; Amer Bd Observ & Gyn; Central Assn of Ob & Gyn; YMCA; Tulsa Urban Leage; Alpha Phi Alpha; Tulsa Bd Educ 1972-; life mem NAACP; Tulsa Grnwd Bly OK C of C; fld faculty Meharry Med Coll & Univ of Oklahoma School of Med; asst state dir, Amer Assn of Retired Persons, Ok. **HONORS/ACHIEVEMENTS:** Fellow Amer Coll Observ & Gyn. **BUSINESS ADDRESS:** 114 S Main St, PO Box 217, Boley, OK 74829.

SANDERS, ISAAC WARREN
Educator. **PERSONAL:** Born Aug 09, 1948, Montgomery, AL; married Cora Allen; children: W Machion, Christin Machael. **EDUCATION:** Tuskegee Univ, BS 1971; Cornell Univ, MS 1973; KS State Univ, PhD 1984; Columbia Univ, New York NY, post doctoral certificate 1988. **CAREER:** Ft Valley State Coll, instructor/rsch assoc 1973-75; Claflin Coll, federal relations officer 1975-76; AL State Univ, dir fed relations 1976-82; Woodrow Wilson Natl Fellowship Found, vice pres 1984-86; Natl Action Council for Minorities in Engrg, dir 1986-89, vice pres 1989-. **ORGANIZATIONS:** Mem Natl Soc for Fundraising Execs 1980-; bd mem Greater Trenton NJ Mental Health 1984-; vice pres and bd mem Optimist Club Lower Bucks PA 1985-; vice pres Blanton and Assocs 1986-; pres Tuskegee Univ Philadelphia Area Alumni Assn 1986-; assoc dir Northeast Region Tuskegee Alumni Assoc 1986-; mem Kappa Alpha Psi; bd of dir NAACP Bucks Co PA 1989. **HONORS/ACHIEVEMENTS:** United Negro College Fund Mind Fire Award 1982; Phi Delta Kappa KS State Univ 1983. **HOME ADDRESS:** 1041 Muscony Lane, Bensalem, PA 19020. **BUSINESS ADDRESS:** Vice President, Resource Development, NACME, 3 West 35th St, New York, NY 10001.

SANDERS, JAMES WILLIAM
Clergyman. **PERSONAL:** Born Sep 17, 1929, Union, SC; married Ruby Lee Corry; children: Jewette LaVernae, James William Jr, Ruzlin Maria. **EDUCATION:** Benedict Coll Columbia SC, BA 1951; A&T State Univ Greensboro NC, MEd 1961; Friendship Coll Rock Hill SC, DD 1973. **CAREER:** Union SC, elementary school prin 1961-65, HS asst prin 1965-72; Union Co Educ Assn, treas 1964-69; Union SC Adult Educ Prog, co coord 1970-72; Bethel Baptist Church, minister. **ORGANIZATIONS:** Pres Cherokee Co Black Ministers Alliance 1965-79; mem Planning & Zoning Comm for City of Gaffney 1980-; mem Election Comm of Cherokee Co 1980-; chmn Area Agency for the Aging for 6 county region 1979-; mem Gov's Task Force to Study Health Needs of the State of SC; bd mem Habilitation Serv

for Cherokee Co Inc 1981-; vice chmn Cherokee Co Comm of the Food & Shelter Emergency Fund 1984-; moderator Co Bapt Assn 1973-; finance committeeman Natl Baptist Conv of Amer 1979-; pres NAACP of Cherokee Co Gaffney SC 1962-68; exec bd mem Appalachian Council of Govts 1972-; mem Mayor's Human Relations Comm of Gaffney SC 1972-; vice pres Cherokee Co Dem Party 1978-. **HONORS/ACHIEVEMENTS:** Leadership Awd Boy Scouts of Amer 1960; Human Serv Awd Comm Action Prog 1971; Who's Who Among Black Ams in the S 1972; Citizen of the Yr Awd Phi Alpha Chap Omega Psi Phi Frat Inc 1975. **BUSINESS ADDRESS:** Minister, Bethel Baptist Church, 332 W Meadow St, Gaffney, SC 29340.

SANDERS, JOSEPH STANLEY
Attorney. **PERSONAL:** Born Aug 09, 1942, Los Angeles, CA; son of Hays Sanders and Eva Sanders; children: Edward Moore, Justin Hays, Alexandria, Chelsea. **EDUCATION:** Whittier Coll, BA 1963; Magdalen Coll Oxford Univ, BA/MA 1965; Yale Law Sch, LLB 1968. **CAREER:** Yale Univ Transitional Year, dir pro tem & instr 1967-68; Western Center on Law & Poverty Los Angeles, staff atty 1968-69; Lawyer's Com for Civil Rights Under Law LA, exec dir 1969-70; Wyman Bautzer Finell Rothman & Kuchel Beverly Hills, assoc 1969-71; Rosenfeld Lederer Jacobs & Sanders Beverly Hills, partner 1971-72; Sanders & Tisdale LA, partner 1972-77; Sanders & Dickerson Los Angeles, atty partner 1978-. **ORGANIZATIONS:** Co-founder Watts Summer Festival 1966; coord CA Conf of Black Atty 1969; mem Amer Bar Assn 1969-; co-chmn Whittier Coll Alumni Fund 1970-71; mem bd of dirs W LA United Way 1970; mem LA World Affairs Council 1971-; mem Yale Law Alumni Com on Curriculum Reform 1971; chmn membership drive BSA LA Dist 8 1971; mem Com on Foreign Affairs Los Angeles 1972; trustee Ctr for Law in the Pub Interest 1973-80; mem bd of trustees Whittier Coll 1974-; bd of dir Econ Resoures Corp 1974-; mem Mayor's Citizens Com on Rapid Transit 1975; mem Mayor's Com on Cultural Affairs 1975-; mem bd of dir Amer Red Cross LA 1975-; bd of dir Arthritis Found So CA Chap 1976-; mem CA Postsecondary Educ Comm 1976; co-chmn CA Dem Party Rules Comm 1976-; vice pres LA Recreation & Parks Comm 1980-; mem LA Memorial Coliseum Comm 1980-; dir Black Arts Council; mem Langston law Club LA Co Bar Assn; chmn United Way Task Force on Minority Youth Employment 1985-. **HONORS/ACHIEVEMENTS:** Pub "I'll Never Escape the Ghetto" Ebony Mag 1967, "Rhodes Scholar Looks at South Africa" Ebony Mag 1970; Rhodes Scholarship; 1st Team NAIA All-Amer Football 1961; Small Coll NAIA Discus Champsion 1963; Ten Outstanding Young Men of Amer Awd 1971; Fifty Disting Alumni Awd Los Angeles City Sch Bicentennial 1976. **BUSINESS ADDRESS:** Attorney, Sanders & Dickerson, 3580 Wilshire Blvd #1440, Los Angeles, CA 90010.

SANDERS, LAURA GREEN
Operations manager. **PERSONAL:** Born Nov 14, 1942, Victoria, TX; daughter of Cluster Green and Althea McNary Green; married Willie Sanders; children: Laresee Sanders Harris. **EDUCATION:** Victoria Junior Coll, attended 1968; TX State Management Develop Ctr, Managers Program 1986. **CAREER:** TX Employment Commn, clerk, interviewer, supervisor, asst mgr 1969-. **ORGANIZATIONS:** Mem Intl Assoc of Personnel in Employment Svcs; bd of dirs Victoria Co Adult Literacy Council, Victoria Co Sr Citizens Assoc; adv comm Victoria Public School Voc Educ Prog; exec dir Victoria Co Extension Svcs; mem Victoria Co Black Historical Soc; co-owner Willie Sanders Registered Quarter Horses; mem Mt Nebo Baptist Church; dir Mt Nebo Senior Choir; pres, Women in Partnership for Progress 1988-89. **HONORS/ACHIEVEMENTS:** Editor "Success Profiles of Black Victorians"; co-host and awds organizer for "Black Honors Fest" a sesquincentennial celebration. **HOME ADDRESS:** PO Box 175, Nursery, TX 77976.

SANDERS, LINA (NEE MCCULLERS)
Educator. **PERSONAL:** Born Apr 09, 1937, Johnston Co; children: Gary, Gretchen. **EDUCATION:** Fyttvl St U, BS 1964; NC St U; E Crln U; UNC-G. **CAREER:** John Co Bd of Edn, tchr; Smthhfld Jr HS, tchr; John Tech Inst Sec, prt-tm instr. **ORGANIZATIONS:** Sec Lcl Nat Assn ofUniv Wmen; past pres Lcl NC Assn of Ed; NC Assn of Ed; NEA; Assn of Clsrm Tchrs; chrpsn Polit Act Com for Ed; prlmntrn Dist 2 ACT; NCAE Commn on Frng Bnfts & Spl Serv; NCAE Professional Negoti Com; Civic Mdrntts Club; apptd commmnd to serv on bd of dir Atlntc & NC Rr; mem Galilee Bapt Ch; mem Mizpah Ct 79 Dau of Isis; mem NAACP; mem NCACT-NCAE Women's Ccs. **HONORS/ACHIEVEMENTS:** Outstn Elem Tchr of Am 1973; Tchr of the Yr Smthfld Jr HS 1975-76; NCAE Hum Rel Nom 1977; inttd 1st Sal Sup for Tchrs John Co.

SANDERS, MICHAEL ANTHONY
Professional athlete. **PERSONAL:** Born May 07, 1960, Vidalia, LA; married Crystal Tate. **EDUCATION:** UCLA, BA 1982. **CAREER:** Phoenix Suns, forward 1983-; San Antonio Spurs, 1982-83. **HONORS/ACHIEVEMENTS:** Named CBA Rookie of Yr; 1st Team All-CBA; 2nd team hnrs on the CBA All-Defensive Team; team capt 2 yrs; twice named All-PAC 10; MVP soph yr; Westrn RegNCAA MVP. **BUSINESS ADDRESS:** Phoenix Suns, P O Box 1369, Ste 510, Phoenix, AZ 85001.

SANDERS, ROBER LAFAYETTE
Engineer/scientist. **PERSONAL:** Born Feb 14, 1952, Raleigh, NC. **EDUCATION:** NC State Univ, BSEE 1973; Univ of AZ Phoenix, MBA 1983. **CAREER:** Black Engrs of Amer, pres 1971-73; State NAACP, pres 1983-87; Branch NAACP, pres 1983-87; Optimist Club, vice pres 1985-87; IBM, chief architecture. **ORGANIZATIONS:** Mem vice pres IEEE 1973, 86; mem ACME 1973-87, Amer Physicists 1973-87; basileus Omega Psi Phi Frat 1982-87; prs Scholastic Aptitude 1983-87; treas Tucson Black Forum 1985-87; treas Tucson Democratic Party 1986-87. **HONORS/ACHIEVEMENTS:** Outstanding Young Man Jaycees 1985,86; Engineer of the Yr BEA 1986; Omega Man of the Year Omega Psi Phi 1986. **HOME ADDRESS:** 429 "N" St SW #S702, Washington, DC 20024. **BUSINESS ADDRESS:** Chief Architecture, IBM, 9500 Godwin Dr, Manassas, VA 22110.

SANDERS, ROBERT B.
Educator. **PERSONAL:** Born Dec 09, 1938, Augusta, GA; son of Robert Sanders and Lois Jones Sanders; married Gladys Nealous; children: Sylvia, William. **EDUCATION:** Paine Coll Augusta GA, BS 1959; Univ of MI Ann Arbor, MS 1961, PhD 1964; Univ of WI Madison, Post Doctorate 1966. **CAREER:** Battelle Memorial Inst, visiting scientist 1970-71; Univ of TX Med Schl Houston, visiting assoc prof 1974-75; Natl Science Found, prog dir 1978-79; Univ of KS Lawrence, asst prof, assoc prof, full prof 1966-, assoc dean, The Graduate School 1987-. **ORGANIZATIONS:** Mem bd dir United Child Devl Ctr 1968-; consult Natl Sci Fnd 1983-87, Dept of Educ 1983, Natl Inst of Health 1982, Interx Research Corp 1972-80, Natl Research Councl 1973-77, mem Bd of Higher Educ United Meth Church 1976-80; mem American Soc for Biochemistry and Molecular Biology; Amer Soc for Pharmacology and Experimental Therapeutics, American Assoc of Univ Prof, and Sigma Xi. **HONORS/ACHIEVEMENTS:** Postdoctoral Fellowship Natl Inst of Health 1974-75, Amer Cancer Soc 1964-66; fellowship Battelle Mem Inst 1970-71; about 50 scientific articles; about 30 research grants. **MILITARY SERVICE:** AUSR e-4 1955-62. **BUSINESS ADDRESS:** Professor Biochemistry, University of Kansas, Dept of Biochemistry, Lawrence, KS 66045-2106.

SANDERS, SALLY RUTH
Registered nurse. **PERSONAL:** Born Jun 01, 1952, Tyler, TX; married Donald Ray Sanders; children: Carla, Candace, Christopher. **EDUCATION:** TX Eastern Sch of Nursing, Tyler Jr Coll, diploma in nursing asst 1973-75, 1972-74; Univ of TX at Tyler, BSN 1982-84. **CAREER:** Relief Health Care Svcs, dir 1985-86; Triage, head nurse; Progressive Health Care, asst adminis 1986-. **ORGANIZATIONS:** Historian Diabetes Assoc 1984-85; asst dir Marche Incorp 1986-; mem Negro Business & Professional Women's Org; mem Rose Bud Civitan Club, Civitan. **HONORS/ACHIEVEMENTS:** Woman of the Year UTHCT 1985. **BUSINESS ADDRESS:** Nurse Clinician/Asst Adminis, Progressive Health Care, PO Box 2003, Tyler, TX 75710.

SANDERS, THELMA
Educator, business executive. **PERSONAL:** Born in Tougaloo, MS; married Dr IS Sanders; children: IS Jr. **EDUCATION:** Tougaloo Coll, BS; Univ of So MS, attended; MS Coll, attended. **CAREER:** State of MS, hs teacher; Sanders Women Apparel Store, owner, mgr 1950-. **ORGANIZATIONS:** Mem bd trustees Tougaloo Coll 1969-; bd mem FCC Interim Bd WLBT 1971-73; exec bd Natl Bus & Professional Women Clubs Inc 1968-; exec bd Rust-Tougaloo UNCF 1972-; grad Top Models of Amer Ltd 1976; life mem Natl Council of Negro Women, Natl Bus & Professional Womens Clubs Inc, NAACP; mem League of Women Voters, MS Council on Human Relations, Jackson Urban League, YWCA; partic in various fund raising drives; supv donations made by Natl Assoc of Bus & Professional Womens Clubs Inc to Delta Area of MS & Gulf Coast; org 8 Bus & Professional Womens Clubs in MS. **HONORS/ACHIEVEMENTS:** Cert of Appreciation, March of Dimes, NAACP, United Negro Coll Fund, YWCA, Bus & Professional Women Club; Alumnus of the Year Tougaloo Coll 1964; Outstanding Serv Awd Natl BPW Clubs Inc 1969; Bus Woman of Distinc Awd Natl BPW Clubs Inc 1970; listed in Black Women "Making It", Bus Black Enterprises Mag 1970, Outstanding Cit of MS Beta Delta Omega Chap Alpha Kappa Alpha Sor 1972; Past Pres Awd Jackson BPW Club 1970; Past Pres Awd Jackson-Tougaloo Alumni Club 1971; Cert Govs of MS 1975; listed in Notable Amer 2nd Ed 1976-77, Who's Who's Who of Women 1977, Outstanding MS Black Women, MS St Fed of Colored Womens Club 1976, Personalities of the South 1972, Ebony's Best Dressed Women Ebony Mag 1967. **BUSINESS ADDRESS:** Manager, Sanders Women Apparel Store, 1224 West Capitol St, Jackson, MS 39202.

SANDERS, VICTORIA LYNN
Business executive. **PERSONAL:** Born in Aurora, IL; divorced. **EDUCATION:** Drake U, BS; Bradley U, MBA;Univ of Chigo. **CAREER:** First Womens Corp, resrch analyst; Stock Broker; Iknvestment Adv; established A Hlth Servs & Consult Orgn composed of 5 Cos Hot Line, Womens Care Ltd, Chic Womens Ctr Found Servs; has Co which supports First Womens in the investor info & finan plng for the individual; prod Money Talk TV Prgm for investor info; Great Talent Mgmt, assists promising entertainers with their careers; instr Marion Bus Coll Operation PUSH. **ORGANIZATIONS:** Cosmo C of C; Chicago C of C; Links; Alpha Kappa Alpha Sor; Phi Gamma Nu Bus Sor; NAACP; prog com Duncan UMCA; Black Exec Exzchange Prgm; bd of regents; mem Daniel Hale Williams U; finan edtr Chicago Post; author Victoria Letter; varius Educ Radio & TV prgms First Annual Top Rung Citation, Chicago Opptys Indusltn Ctr 1970; Achvmt Awd Cosmo C of C 1971; Black Bus Otst Serv Rendered to Profession & Comm Blackbook 1974; Black Women in Bus in NY, Black Enterprise 1974. **HONORS/ACHIEVEMENTS:** We Need More of You Awd Kennedy & Co Channel 7, 1974; Women With Real Power Who Cal Help Hou, Cosmo 1975; Intl Womens Yr Awd PUSH, Spl Marketing Consult TIFCO Fiberglass Pool Renovation. **BUSINESS ADDRESS:** 2nd Office, 185 N Wabash 1806, Chicago, IL 60611.

SANDERS, WENDELL ROWAN
Physician. **PERSONAL:** Born Dec 12, 1933, Vicksburg, MS. **EDUCATION:** Morehouse Coll, BS (summa cum laude) 1954; Meharry Med Coll, MD (cum laude) 1958. **CAREER:** Wayne StUniv Sch of Med, instr psych 1978-; Pvt Prac, 1978-; Harreld Ctr for Yng Adlts, dir 1972; Comm Mntl Hlth, agency dir 1973; Wayne Co Gen Hosp, psych 1965-68; MS St Hosp, psych 1960-62; Gen Prac, 1959-60. **ORGANIZATIONS:** Clncl dir SE Oakland Prgm 1971-73; psych consult various cts in Met Rgn for yng adlts; guest lctr Wayne St U; lctr Oakland Co Comm Coll; prsnl analysis 1965-70; Pres MI Soc ofr Study of Adolscnts 1973-74; pres Med staff Northville St Hosp 1975-77; mem APA; MI Soc for study of adolscnts; MI Soc of Adolscnt Psych; MI Assn of Tchrs of Emtnly Dstrbd Chldrn; NAACP; NRA; mem Detroit Educ TV Network. **HONORS/ACHIEVEMENTS:** Papers "Trtmnt Plan for Adolscnts at Wayne Co Gen Hosp"; "A Trtmnt Plan for Black Patients"; "Trtmnt of Black Yng Adlts". **BUSINESS ADDRESS:** Northville State Hosp, Northville, MI 48167.

SANDERS, WESLEY, JR.
City official. **PERSONAL:** Born Feb 07, 1933, Los Angeles; married Benrice Jackson; children: Malinda Gale, Douglas Edward, Wesley III, Kenneth Wayne, Derlwyn Mark, Jeffery. **EDUCATION:** Harbor Coll, 1952. **CAREER:** Triple Quality Meats, founder 1961; John Morrell Meat Co, salesman 1966-71; City of Compton, reserve police officer, city treas 1973-. **ORGANIZATIONS:** Mem Compton C of C; Negro Bus & Prof Mens Assn; BF Talbot #8 Prince Hall Masons; welfare Planning Council, mem Nat Municipal Treas Assn; CA Municipal Treas Assn; NAACP. **HONORS/ACHIEVEMENTS:** Otstndng Salesman Awd, John Morrell Meat Co 1966-67-68; Otstndng Reserve Police Officer Awd 1974; Achievement Awd, Model Cities; Otstndng Awd Block Central. **MILITARY SERVICE:** USAF; sgt; 1952-56. **BUSINESS ADDRESS:** 600 N Alameda, Compton, CA.

SANDERS, WILLIAM MAC
Educator. **PERSONAL:** Born Dec 11, 1919, Cheraw, SC; married Velora Scott; children: Samuel Bret. **EDUCATION:** KY State Univ, BS; Univ of KY, MS; Univ of MI, MPH; Univ of MI, EdD. **CAREER:** KY State Coll, coach 1948-50; Grambling State Univ; Chairman, Secondary Educ; 1970-72; Health & Physical Educ, 1972-75; Dir, Sports Admin, 1975-. **ORGANIZATIONS:** Mem Assn of Teacher Educ, Assn of Higher Educ, Amer Assn of Univ Profs, Phi Epsilon Kappa, Omega Psi Phi, Pub Health Traineeship, LA Health Adv Council;

mem Amer Alliance HPERD. **MILITARY SERVICE:** AUS sgt 1942-45. **BUSINESS ADDRESS:** Administrator, Grambling State Univ, 130 Adams Hall #118, Grambling, LA 71245.

SANDERS, WOODROW MAC
Educator. **PERSONAL:** Born Aug 04, 1943, Luling, TX; married Estella Gonzales; children: Rodrigo. **EDUCATION:** Univ of AK;Univ of ND, 1964-66; TX A&I UKingsville, BA 1970; TX A&IUniv Corpus Christi, MS 1977. **CAREER:** Bee Co Coll, counselor/instructor 1978-; Nueces Co Mental Health/Mental Retardation Center, dir of outpatient serv 1972-78; Gateway Wholesale Sporting Goods, asst mgr 1971-72; USN Counseling & Asst Cntgr Corpus Christi, TX, consult asso psychologist 1973-78; Univ of TX Austin, inst of Alcohol Studies 1977; S TX Housing Corp, bd pres 1978. **ORGANIZATIONS:** Adv bd mem Nueces House TX Yough Council 1977-78; bd mem Coastal Bend Bus & Indsl Devel Inc 1977-; life mem NAACP; mem US Rifle Marksmanship TeamUSAF 1962-64. **HONORS/ACHIEVEMENTS:** Presidential Unit Citation USAF 1965; Republic of Viet Nam Medal of Valor USAF 1966; Youth Serv Awd Corpus Christi Police Dept 1967; Awd for Ser in Drug Abuse - Prevention, Coastal Bend Council of Govts Drug Abuse Adv Com Corpus Christi 1976-77; flwshp TX Research Inst of Mental Sci Houston 1977. **MILITARY SERVICE:** USAF; staff sgt; 1961-66.

SANDERS-WEST, SELMA D.
Consultant. **PERSONAL:** Born in Farrell, PA; daughter of Henry K Sanders and Rev Martha J (Wiley) Sanders; married Rev Robert M West, Sep 13, 1986; children: Phebe Joy West. **EDUCATION:** Pennsylvania State Univ, Univ Park PA, 1970-71; Univ of Massachusetts, Amherst MA, MA, Regional Planning, 1986. **CAREER:** Mercer County Community Action Agency, Farrell PA, program coord, 1980-81, economic devel specialist, 1981-84; Chicago Bd of Educ, Chicago IL, special asst to gen supt, 1985-86, consultant, 1986-87, press officer, 1987-88; West & Assoc, Sharon PA, pres, 1988-. **ORGANIZATIONS:** Bd of dir, Mercer County Branch, NAACP, Farrell PA, 1980-; former bd mem, newsletter editor, National Urban/Rural Fellows, 1986-88, mem, 1986-; Farrell Area School Bd, Farrell PA, 1989-93. **HONORS/ACHIEVEMENTS:** Natl Rural Fellow, Natl Urban/Rural Fellows Inc, 1985-86; contributing editor, Beautiful for Him Magazine, a Chicago-based Christian women's magazine, 1986-87. **HOME ADDRESS:** 538 Sharon-New Castle Rd, Farrell, PA 16121. **BUSINESS ADDRESS:** President, West & Associates, PO Box 865, Sharon, PA 16146.

SANDERSON, RANDY CHRIS
Assistant controller. **PERSONAL:** Born Dec 23, 1954, St Louis, MO; married Toni M Harper. **EDUCATION:** Univ of MO at St Louis, BS 1977. **CAREER:** May Dept Stores, staff/sr accountant mgr plans 1977-81, dir capital/pland/expense analysis 1984-87; May Company CA, dir adv acctg/financial plans 1981-84; Caldor Inc, assistant controller 1987-. **ORGANIZATIONS:** Chmn Natl Alumni Assoc Inroads 1985-87. **HONORS/ACHIEVEMENTS:** John C Willis Awd Natl Assoc of Black Accountants 1976; CPA State of MO. **BUSINESS ADDRESS:** Assistant Controller, Caldor Inc, 20 Glover Ave, Norwalk, CT 06850.

SANDIDGE, KANITA DURICE
Administrative services director. **PERSONAL:** Born Dec 02, 1947, Cleveland, OH; daughter of John R Sandidge and Virginia L Sandidge. **EDUCATION:** Cornell Univ, BA 1970; Case Western Reserve Univ, MBA 1979. **CAREER:** AT&T Network Systems, acting section chief 1970-72, section chief cost control 1972-78, dept chief data processing and accounting 1978-79, dept chief account analysis 1979-80, administration mgr 1980-83, sales forecasting and analysis mgr 1983-86, planning and devel mgr 1986-87, admin serv dir, 1987-. **ORGANIZATIONS:** Mem Beta Alpha Psi Accounting Honorary, Amer Mgmt Assn, The Alliance of AT&T Black Mgrs, Natl Black MBA's, Natl Assoc for Female Executives; life mem NAACP; black executives exchange prog NUL 1986-; bd of dir, East-West Corporate Corridor Assn (Illinois), 1987-, Quad County Urban League (Illinois), 1988-. **HONORS/ACHIEVEMENTS:** Harlem YMCA Black Achiever in Industry 1981; Tribute to Women & Industry Achievement Award YWCA 1985. **BUSINESS ADDRESS:** Administrative Services Director, AT&T Network Systems, 2600 Warrenville Rd, Lisle, IL 60532.

SANDIFER, JAWN A.
Judge. **PERSONAL:** Born Feb 18, 1919, Greensboro, NC; married Laura; children: 1 Child. **EDUCATION:** C Smith Univ, AB 1938; Howard Law Sch, LlB 1941; Johnson, Hon LlD. **CAREER:** PRIVATE PRACTICE, 1 Child Atty; Civil Ct NYC, 10 Yr Term Judge 1964; NY Supreme Ct, term justice 1969; Criminal Br Supreme Ct, appted supr judge 1973; Criminal Branch NYC, dep admin judge 1974; Equal Employ Ofcr Unified Cy Sys State of NY; US History, Globe Press, NY, gen ed Afro-Am In; Minorities USA Globe Press, NY, co-author. **ORGANIZATIONS:** Mem Am Nat Bar Assns; Harlem Lawyers Asn; NY County Trial - Lawyers Assn; New York City Bar Assn; US Supreme Ct Bar Assn; mem Alpha Phi Alpha Frat; bd trustees Harlem Eye, Ear, Nose Hosp; gen counsel, NY State Conf N Aacp, past pres, NY Br; former mem Adv Com NY State Dept Edn; former bd mem, sec HARYOU ACT; mem Steward's Bd, St Marks Meth Ch ; former bd dirs, Hope Day Nursery & Windham Children's Svc; mem Resource Com, Bd Edn, NYC. **MILITARY SERVICE:** USAF. **BUSINESS ADDRESS:** Supreme Ct State NY, 100 Centre St, New York, NY.

SANDLE, FLOYD LESLIE
Educator. **PERSONAL:** Born Jul 04, 1913, Magnolia, MS; son of Leslie Sandle and Essie Sandle; married Marie Johnson; children: Gail Synette, Ava Leslie, Wanda Marie, Floyd Leslie, Anthony Wayne. **EDUCATION:** Dillard Univ, AB, 1937; Univ of Chicago, MA, 1947; NY Univ, postgraduate, 1951-52; LA State Univ, PhD, 1959. **CAREER:** Grambling State Univ, prof emeritus, 1985; Grambling Coll, instructor, prof, dept head, speech & dean, div general studies, 1951-78; Dillard Univ, prof, Speech & Drama, chair, Humanities Div, 1978-86. **ORGANIZATIONS:** Mem, South Speech Assn; Natl Assn Dramatic & Speech Arts; Am Educ Theatre Assn; mem, Theta Alpha Phi, Kappa Delta Phi, Omega Psi Phi; author "The Negro in the American Education Theatre", 1964; Orientation "An Image of the College" 1967; contributed articles to professional journals; pres Assn of LA Coll & Univs, 1977; mem, LA State Literacy Task Force, LA Council on Aging, GSU Foundation, pres, Lion's Club, Grambling, LA. **HONORS/ACHIEVEMENTS:** Inducted to Hall of Fame, Grambling State Univ, 1986. **MILITARY SERVICE:** USN boatswain's mate 2/c 1943-45; instructor USAFEI Prog South Pacific 1944-45.

SANDLER, JOAN D.
Association executive. **PERSONAL:** Born Oct 02, 1934, NYC, NY; divorced; children: Eve, Kathe. **EDUCATION:** Attended, City Coll of NY, Univ of Mexico. **CAREER:** Bloomingdale Family Svc, tchr dir 1963-66; Metro Applied Rsch Ctr, researcher 1966-68; Dept Cultural Affairs, prog specialist 1968-72; Black Theatre Alliance, exec dir 1972-77; The Senghor Found, 1977-80; Metro Museum of Art, assoc museum educ in charge of comm educ. **ORGANIZATIONS:** Panelist & consult Natl Endowment of Arts 1971-74; consult NY State Council for Arts 1972-; adv VISIONS KCET/TV Pub Broadcasting Corp 1974; theater panel The Theater Develop Fund; bd dirs Natl Council of Women; bd dirs Children Arts Carnival; Oppor Resources; adv Gov's Task Force; lecturer Scripps Coll, BankSt Coll, Rutgers Univ, Baruch Coll, The Inst of Contemporary Arts, Hunter Coll, Princeton Univ; bd of dirs 1st Amer Congress of Theatre, NSINGHA; mem Natl Coalition of 100 Black Women, The Amer Museum's Assn, Museum's Educators Roundtable. **HONORS/ACHIEVEMENTS:** American Biographies; Kellogg Fellow Smithsonian Inst; Audelco Awd 1973. **BUSINESS ADDRESS:** Assoc Museum Educ-Comm Educ, Metropolitan Museum of Art, 1564 Broadway, New York, NY 10036.

SANDOVAL, DOLORES S.
Educator. **PERSONAL:** Born Sep 30, 1937, Montreal, Quebec, Canada. **EDUCATION:** Institute of Chicago, Art 1956-58;Univ of MI, BSD 1958-60; IN U, MS 1968; INUniv PhD 1970. **CAREER:** Univ of Vt, prof of educ 1977-; Human Resources & Asso, asst to pres 1972-77; Univ of VT, prof of educ with tenure 1971-72; State Univ Coll At Buffalo, assoc prof 1970-71; IN Univ, spec grad asst to Dr Annie L Butler prof of Early Childhood Educ 1967; Educ Materials Center, grad asst to dir of educ materials 1967-70; Lake Ridge Schools Gary, IN, elem school teacher 1963-66; Vice Pres Western Girl Inc New York City & LA, pers coun & asst to Vice Pres 1960-63; Childhood Edu Inter, chairperson ref book comm 1974-77. **ORGANIZATIONS:** Mem Nat Coun of Tchrs of English; Intern Reading Assn; The Am Assn for Higher Edn; bd trustees, RI Sch of Design 1976-; part Inst for Educ Mgmt,Harvard 1975; Soc for Psycho Study of Social Issues; Comm for the Concerns of Women in New England Coll and U; Minority Women Admins Appted to Governor&S Comm on Status of Women in New England Coll and U;Minority Women Admin Appted to Governor's Comm on Status of Women 1972-74 & 1974-76; Governor's Task Force on Women in Gov 1974. **HONORS/ACHIEVEMENTS:** Women's Honary in Edu Pi Lambda Theta; Anna M Held Scholarship Art Inst of Chicago; NDEA Fellow IN U; Dean's List IN U; US Ofc of Edu Fellowship INU; Nom to Leaders of Black Am, Leaders in Edn; Publs - Doctoral Dissertation, Responses to the Language Experience Approach to - Reading by Black, Culturally Different, Inner-city Students, Experiencing Reading Disability in Grades Five & Eleven; The Ghetto Child Can Relate to the Graffiti Fence, Phi Delta Kappan1971. **BUSINESS ADDRESS:** Professional Educ & Curriculum Devel D, U of VT, Burlington, VT 05405.

SANDS, DOUGLAS BRUCE
Government official, minister. **PERSONAL:** Born Mar 01, 1934, Cooksville; son of Alexander Sands and Bess Sands; married Barbara Jean Corpening; children: Dellyne Ivy Monroe, Douglas B, Jr, Curtis O, Cecelia O. **EDUCATION:** Morgan State Coll, BS (with High Honors/Distinguished mil student/Cadet Comdr/Student govern pres) 1956; Howard Univ School of Divinity, Masters of Divinity. **CAREER:** Minority & Affairs State of Maryland, exec asst to gov and dir of office 1979-; Robert Clay Inc Contracting Co, vice pres proj mgr 1977-79; High Ridge Land Devel Co, pres 1973-79; AlasKa Asso Arctic Pipeline Constrn, gen mgr 1975-77; Maryland Minority Contractors Assn Inc, founder, pres 1975-79. **ORGANIZATIONS:** Founder/Dir New Community Inc Community Devel Corp 1971; bd of dirs Workhorse Club Community Serv 1971; exec dir Washington DC Metro Area Southern Christian Leadership Conf 1973-79; program dir Volunteers in Tech Asst 1974-75; mem Alpha Phi Alpha Frat Inc 1953-; organ com Cantonville Community Coll & Howard Community Coll 1963-72; lay speaker & local pastor United Methodist Church 1975. **HONORS/ACHIEVEMENTS:** Outstanding Commendations AUS 1957-58; Outstanding Community Serv Omega Psi Phi Frat Award 1962; Superior Public Serv Maryland State Conf of NAACP Branches 1966; Public Serv Award Washington DC Metro SCLS 1974; Outstanding Public Serv Award Maryland Minority Contractors Assn. **MILITARY SERVICE:** AUS 1st lt 1956-58. **BUSINESS ADDRESS:** State House, Annapolis, MD 21401.

SANDS, GEORGE M.
Management consultant/trainer. **PERSONAL:** Born Jan 15, 1942, Port Chester, NY; married Mary Alice Moxley; children: Jeffrey, Kenneth. **EDUCATION:** Western MI Univ, BS 1964; Hunter Coll Sch of Social Work, MSW 1970. **CAREER:** Cage Teen Center Inc, exec dir 1972-78; Empire State Coll, lecturer 1981-; Westchester Comm Coll, adjunct prof 1973-; Sands Assocs, owner/dir 1978-. **ORGANIZATIONS:** Educ chmn Middletown NAACP; mem Amer Soc for Personnel Admin; bd of dirs Michael Schwerner Found 1970-72; personnel chmn Middletown Bd of Educ 1976-82; consultant/trainer Stony Brook Univ 1977-; bd mem Orange Co Private Indus Council 1983-; trainer Cornell Univ School of Industrial Labor Relations. **HONORS/ACHIEVEMENTS:** Teacher of the Yr Westchester Comm Coll 1982; Service Awd Middletown Bd of Educ 1982. **BUSINESS ADDRESS:** Dir, Sands Associates, PO Box 352, New Hampton, NY 10958.

SANDS, HENRY W.
Attorney. **PERSONAL:** Born Aug 24, 1933, New York, NY; children: Jay, Clinton, Kenyatta, Tisa. **EDUCATION:** Morgan State Coll, BS 1959; Univ of MD, JD 1963. **CAREER:** Private practice, attorney 1964; Sands, Mason, Laidley & Lawson Lawyers, partner, presently. **ORGANIZATIONS:** Mem US Supreme Court, LA Chamber of Commerce 1972, Black Business Assn 1972, CA State Bar Atty, SCLC, Compton NAACP, Black Truckers Assoc, Black Business Assn, Black Petroleum Retailers, United High Blood Pressure Found, Sickle Cell Disease Rsch Found, CORE; chmn CORE MD 1961-62. **HONORS/ACHIEVEMENTS:** 5 Natl Honor Socs. **MILITARY SERVICE:** USAF 1950-54. **BUSINESS ADDRESS:** Attorney, 2116 S Arlington Ave, Ste 201, Los Angeles, CA 90018.

SANDS, MARY ALICE
Educator. **PERSONAL:** Born Oct 20, 1941, Indianapolis, IN; daughter of Frank O Moxley and Velma Goodnight Moxley; married George M Sands; children: Jeffrey, Kenneth. **EDUCATION:** State Univ of IA, 1959-60; Western MI Univ, BS 1964; Bank St Coll of Ed, MSEd 1982. **CAREER:** Bronx Municipal Hosp Ctr, asst chief OT Dept 1965-70; Harlem Hosp OT Dept, supervisor Clinical Ed 1971; Rockland Community Coll, chair OTA Prog 1973-77; Orange Cty Community Coll, chair OTA Prog 1977-; 1987 Founder & Co-Owner Occupational Therapy Plus. **ORGANIZATIONS:** Mem NAACP, Alpha Kappa Alpha, Amer O T Assoc; program evaluator Amer OT Assoc 1979-; adv bd mem Upjohn Health Care Services

1980-; vice-chair NY State Bd for OT 1981-; mem AOTA Program Adv Comm 1983-86; mem bd of directors Orange Cty Cerebral Palsy Assoc 1984-87; ot consult Middletown Park Manor SNF & HRF 1982-. **HONORS/ACHIEVEMENTS:** Awd of Merit for Practice NYS O T Assoc 1985; contributing author Service Learning in Aging, Implications for Occupational Therapy; Contributing Author Target 2000; chair, Amer Occupational Therapy Assn Commn on Educ 1989-92. **HOME ADDRESS:** 16 Ross Lane, Middletown, NY 10940. **BUSINESS ADDRESS:** Chairperson-OTA Program, Orange County Community Coll, 115 South St, Middletown, NY 10940.

SANDS, ROSETTA F.
Nurse education administrator. **PERSONAL:** Born Sep 21, 1931, Homestead, FL; daughter of John H Ford and Annie Pickett Ford; married Charles H Sands, Jun 09, 1956 (divorced); children: Michael H Sands. **EDUCATION:** Harlem Hospital School of Nursing, New York NY, Diploma, 1954; Univ of Maryland School of Nursing, Baltimore MD, BSN, 1966, Univ of Maryland-College Park, MS, 1970; Johns Hopkins Univ, Baltimore MD, post-graduate study, 1970-77; The Union Graduate School, Cincinnati OH, PhD, 1980. **CAREER:** Univ of MD School of Nursing, Baltimore MD, instructor of medical/surgical, nursing, 1970-71, asst prof of registered nursing prog, 1971-83, team coordinator, 1971-74, asst dean, 1974-79; Wayne NJ, Tuskegee Univ, Tuskegee Inst AL, dean & assoc, 1983-87; The William Paterson Coll, dean & prof, 1987-. **ORGANIZATIONS:** Mem, 1968, trustee of Natl Sorority House, 1976-79; Chi Eta Phi Sorority for Nurses; mem, Sigma Theta Tau Intl Honor Society for Nursing, 1969; mem, Peer Review Panel, Special Project Grants, Dept of Health and Human Services, 1976-83; mem, Task Force on Teaching Culturally Diverse Students, 1977-82; mem, Phi Kappa Phi Honor Society, 1977; pres, bd of trustees, Provident Hospital, 1978-81; mem, bd of dir, Maryland Blue Cross, 1980-83; mem, Maryland Advisory Committee, US Civil Rights Committee, 1981-83; pres, Maryland Nurse Assn, 1981-82; mem, bd of dir, Amer Assn of Colleges of Nursing, 1986-88; mem, Zeta Phi Beta Sorority, Inc. **HONORS/ACHIEVEMENTS:** Author of Consumer Perception of the Expanded Role of the Nurse, Glowing Lamp, 1973; Certificate of Recognition of Leadership in Nursing, Univ of MD Nursing Faculty, 1976; Community Service and Nomination for Mary E Mahoney Award, Resolution, MD Senate, 1979; Professional Leadership in Nursing, Award, Chi Eta Phi Sorority, Gamma Chapter, 1980; Superior Leadership as President of Board of Trustees, Provident Hospital Board of Trustees, 1981; Finer Womanhood Award for Work with Youth in Health Careers, 1981; author of The 1985 Resolution and the Nursing Shortage, MD Nurse, 1981; author of Cultural Conflict in Nurse, Client Interactions, Videocassette, 1983; Excellence in Professional Achievements Award, Black Nurses Assn of Baltimore, 1983; author of Enhancing Cultural Sensitivity in Clinical Practice, 1987; author of The Predictive Potential of Social Variables for Black Students, Performance on NCELX, 1988. **BUSINESS ADDRESS:** Dean, School of Health Professions and Nursing, The William Paterson College of New Jersey, 300 Pompton Road, Room 120 Hunziker Wing, Wayne, NJ 07470.

SANFORD, ISABEL G. (ISABEL RICHMOND)
Actress. **PERSONAL:** Born Aug 29, New York, NY; married Wm E Richmond (deceased); children: Pamela Richmond Ruff, William Eric Richmond, Sanford Sanford. **CAREER:** Embassy TV "The Jeffersons", actress 1969-. **ORGANIZATIONS:** Corr sec Kwanza Found 1973. **HONORS/ACHIEVEMENTS:** Trouper Awd "Y" Drama Guild YMCA New York City 1965; Best Actress in Comedy Role, Image Awd NAACP 1975; 20 Grand Salutes "Outstanding Actress" 1976; Best Actress in TV Image Awd NAACP 1978; Best Actress in a Comdey Series Emmy Awd for "The Jeffersons" 1981. **BUSINESS ADDRESS:** The Jeffersons, c/o Sharp/Lemack Pub Relations, 9157 Sunset Blvd #200, Los Angeles, CA 90069.

SANFORD, LORETTA LOVE
Corporate human resource manager. **PERSONAL:** Born May 16, 1951, Chicago, IL; divorced. **EDUCATION:** Howard Univ, BS 1972; Univ of Chicago, MBA 1983. **CAREER:** Sears Roebuck & Co, programmer 1972-74, office mgr 1974-78, consumer rsch serv mgr 1978-80, survey consultant 1980-81; Continental Bank, commercial lending1981-83, coll relations 1983-84; Kraft Inc, corporate recruiter. **ORGANIZATIONS:** Mem Natl Black MBA Assoc 1980-; pres 1986-, mem Minority Economic Resources Corp Council 1984-; seminar dir Werner Erhard & Assoc 1985-; vice pres 1987, Career Mgmt Comm Univ of Chicago Women's Business Group mem 1985-; secty/treas and bd of dirs Northern Cook Co Private Industry Cncl 1986-. **BUSINESS ADDRESS:** Corporate Recruiter, Kraft Inc, One Kraft Court, Glenview, IL 60025.

SANFORD, MARK
Business executive. **PERSONAL:** Born Nov 24, 1953, St Louis, MO; son of Mr & Mrs Levi Sanford; married Kathleen Danner; children: Tifani Iris, Marcus L Alexander. **EDUCATION:** Washington Univ, BA (Magna Cum Laude) 1975; St Louis Univ, MHA 1981. **CAREER:** St Louis Univ Med Ctr, staff assoc 1981-82; St Mary's Hospital, admin asst lab 1982-83, admin asst human resources 1983-84, vice president 1984-. **ORGANIZATIONS:** Mem Amer Coll Healthcare Execs 1981-; bd mem Explorer Post 400/401 Boy Scout 1985-; mem Urban League, St Louis Chap Black MBA's 1985-, loaned exec 1982 United Way Campaign; bd mem E St Louis C of C; bd mem, Target 2000, Promise Center for the Developmentally Disabled, Catherine Kasper Center; vice chmn Illini District Boy Scouts; pres National Black MBA Association St Louis Chapter. **HONORS/ACHIEVEMENTS:** MBA of the Year, St Louis Chapter, Natl Black MBA Assn, 1988. **HOME ADDRESS:** 5103 Washington, St Louis, MO 63108. **BUSINESS ADDRESS:** Vice President, St Mary's Hospital, 129 No 8th St, East St Louis, IL 62201.

SANTIFUL, LUTHUR L.
Business executive. **PERSONAL:** Married Wilhelmia D Flythe. **EDUCATION:** Univ VA, Cert. **CAREER:** Naval Air Rework Fac, machinist, engr tech, deputy EEO off; Golden Comb Beauty Salon, owner. **ORGANIZATIONS:** Mem Manpower Adv Com; Human Resources Inst; bd dir Movon Corp; pres Hampton NAACP; mem Hampton Rds Jaycees; bd dir Citizens Boys Clb; mem Mayor'sMinrty Affrs Com. **HONORS/ACHIEVEMENTS:** Spec achvmnt US Navy; Mayor's Awd; Am City Awd. **BUSINESS ADDRESS:** Naval Air Rework Facility, Norfolk, VA 23511.

SANTOS, HENRY J.
Educator, pianist. **PERSONAL:** Born Aug 29, 1927, Lewistown, ME; married Leola Waters. **EDUCATION:** BostonUniv Sch of Fine & Appl Arts, BMus; Harvard U, Grad Stdy; Boston U, pvt study piano Alfredo Fondacaro 1952-60; Arturo Benedetti Michaelangli Lugano, Switzerland, study 1969; Boston U, condctng Allan Lanom 1972, piano Edith Stearns 1975, study theor wrk Dr H Norden 1975. **CAREER:** Bridgewater St Coll, asst prof music 1970-75; Perkins School for Blind, 1956-70. **ORGANIZATIONS:** Mem Music Ed Nat Conf; Nat Entmnt Conf Am; Assn for the Instru for the Blind; Adv Bd Fuller Art Museum. **HONORS/ACHIEVEMENTS:** Piano recitals chamber mus progs in major cities of NE US & Europe; chosen instr perf Albert Schweitzer Fest 1950; rec cits Ach Awd Cape Verdean Benef Soc 1968; semi-fin 1st Louis Moreau Gottschalk Intl Compet for Pianists & Comp DillardUniv 1970; perf of classical mus for piano by Afro-Am Cmpsers;TV prog Say Bro 1971; prog WGBH "Perf European & Afro-Am Cmpsers for Piano 1972; lectr recital St Estrn Reg Conf Music Educ Nat Conf 1973; aptd Ethnic Herit Task Force of Commnwlth of MA by Gov Francis Sargent 1974; grant MA Council on Arts & Humanities for Trad Europ & Afro-Am music progsfor elem & sec sch child Bridgewater St Coll 1974. **MILITARY SERVICE:** AUS 1946-47. **BUSINESS ADDRESS:** Music Dept, Bridgewater State Coll, Bridgewater, MA 02324.

SARMIENTO, SHIRLEY JEAN
Educator. **PERSONAL:** Born Nov 28, 1946, Buffalo, NY; daughter of Mr & Mrs John C Laughlin; married William Sarmiento; children: Tolley Reeves. **EDUCATION:** Medaille Coll, BS 1980; Canisius Coll, attended 1980-83; NY State Univ at Buffalo American studies/women's studies 1988-. **CAREER:** Offender Aide & Restoration, coord family support mgr 1982-83; Night People (homeless), worker 1985-86; Buffalo Bd of Educ, sub teacher; Jesse Nash Health Ctr, family life prog; Cowanda Psychiatric Ctr, WNY Peace Ctr, rep/peace educator; NY State Univ at Buffalo, lecturer 1989. **ORGANIZATIONS:** Organizer/active mem Sister-Hood Assoc; mem NAACP, WNY Peace Ctr, Natl Women's Studies Assoc, Educators for Social Responsibility, Christian Ministeries Prison Prog; panel mem Peace Women & Employment. **HONORS/ACHIEVEMENTS:** Certificate Head Start; Certificate Offender Aid & Restoration. **MILITARY SERVICE:** AUS Reserves sp 4 3 yrs; 2 Appreciation Awards 1977-80. **HOME ADDRESS:** 205 Marine Dr #4D, Buffalo, NY 14212. **BUSINESS ADDRESS:** Director, St Anns Community Center, 472 Emslie St, Buffalo, NY 14212.

SARREALS, E. DON
Scientist. **PERSONAL:** Born Sep 22, 1931, Winston-Salem, NC; married Florence B Coleman; children: Cheryl Lynn, Esquire. **EDUCATION:** City Coll of NY, BS Meteorology 1957; New York Univ, MS Meteorology 1961. **CAREER:** Natl Weather Serv Forecast Office, NYC, supr radar meteorologist 1961-69; WRC TV Natl Broadcasting Co, TV meteorologist 1969-75; Storm Finders Inc , pres/cons meteorologist 1969-76; Natl Weather Serv Headquarters, dissemination meteorologist 1976-80; MD Center for Public Broadcasting, TV meteorologist 1976-81; NEXRAD Project, NOAA/NWS, chief, oper. **ORGANIZATIONS:** Lecturer/meterology City Coll of NY 1957-69; chmn bd dir 157th St & Riverside Dr Housing Co Inc 1966-68; mem Natl Acad of Sci Committee on Common Disasters & Media 1977-75; mem Natl Telecommunications Info Agency's Teletext Comm 1978-80; prof mem Amer Meteorological Soc 1955-; mem Natl Weather Assn 1980-; lecturer Smithsonian Inst Washington DC 1972; mem Montgomery Center School Comm on Secondary School 1976-78; bd mem D Rumaldry Homes Assn 1984-. **HONORS/ACHIEVEMENTS:** Ward Medal Meteorology City Coll of NY 1957; Teaching Fellowship CCNY 1957; Community Serv River Terrace Men's Club New York City 1969; Service Awards NWS 1964-65, 1980, 1984; publ NWS Forecasting Handbook #2 NWS 1978; Next Generation Weather Radar (NEXRAD) Operators Concept 1983, Product Description Document 1984, second edition 1987; "NEXRAD Products" 23rd Amer Meteorological Soc Con on Radar Meteorology 1986; "NEXRAD Operational Capability" proceedings of 1987 annual meeting of the Natl Weather Assoc; "NEXRAD Products and Operational Capability" proceedings of 25th Aerospace Sciences meeting Amer Inst of Aeronautics & Astronautics 1987. **MILITARY SERVICE:** AUS cpl; Natl Defense Serv Ribbon; Good Conduct Medal 1953-55. **HOME ADDRESS:** 6300 Contention Ct, Bethesda, MD 20817. **BUSINESS ADDRESS:** Chief of Operations, NEXRAD Project, NOAA/NWS, Natl Weather Serv, 8060 13th St, Silver Spring, MD 20910.

SATCHELL, ELIZABETH
Communications. **PERSONAL:** Born in Eastville, VA; daughter of Alice Watson Satchell; children: Troi Eric. **EDUCATION:** Drake Coll of Business, graduate 1969; Temple Univ; Charles Morris Sch of Adv & Journalism; Union Co Coll; Amer Acad of Broadcasting. **CAREER:** CBS/WCAU-TV Channel 10, sales asst 1970-75, news prod asst 1975-77, newswriter/reporter 1977-79; WNJR Radio, dir pub rel/news editorials 1979-80, prog dir 1980-81, vp/prog dir 1981-82, vp/station mgr 1982-; Realty World Professional Associate, Scotch Plains NJ realtor assoc 1989. **ORGANIZATIONS:** dir Board of Dir Future Devel Group 1986; dir Board of Dir ANYMRAD, (NY Market Radio Braodcasters Assn) 1989; Natl Assn of Broadcasters; Natl Assn of Black Owned Broadcasters; Radio Advertising Bureau; Greater Newark Chamber of Commerce. **HONORS/ACHIEVEMENTS:** Black Achiever/Business and Education YM-YWCA Neward & Vicinity 1982; diploma Radio Sales Univ, Radio Advertising Bureau 1988; diploma NJ Realty Institute 1989; NJ Real Estate License 1989. **HOME ADDRESS:** 948 West 8th St, Plainfield, NJ 07060.

SATCHELL, ERNEST R.
Educator. **PERSONAL:** Born Jul 29, 1941, Exmore, VA; married Elsa Martin; children: Kwame, Keita. **EDUCATION:** Towson St Coll, MEd 1971; MD St Coll, BS; St Joseph's Coll Phil, adv study. **CAREER:** Univ of MD Eastern Shore, chmn art educ dept, instr of ceramics; Boeing Vertol Corp Phil, commercial art dir; VA Hosp Phil, art the rapist. **ORGANIZATIONS:** Mem Nat Conf of Artists; Ant Art Educ Assn; MD St Tchrs Assn; NEA; Alpha Phi Alpha; mem bd dir Somerset Co Art Assn; mem Union Bapts Ch mem Com on Higher Edn. **HONORS/ACHIEVEMENTS:** One-man show Acad of the Arts Easton MD 1974; exhib Towson St Coll 1974; PA StUniv 1971. **MILITARY SERVICE:** USS Forrestal 1968.

SATCHER, DAVID
Physician. **PERSONAL:** Born Mar 02, 1941, Anniston, AL; married Nola; children: Gretchen, David, Daraka, Daryl. **EDUCATION:** Morehouse Coll, BS 1963; Case Western Reserve Univ, MD, PhD 1970. **CAREER:** Strong Meml Hosp Univ Rochester, resd 1971-72; King-Drew Med Ctr, dir 1972-75; Charles Drew Postgrad Med School, Macy faculty fellow 1972-75; King-DrewSickle Cell Ctr, assoc dir 1973-75, asst prof, interim chmn 1974-75; UCLA School of Med, asst prof 1974-76, resd 1975-76; King-Drew Med Ctr, prof, chmn, dept of family med; Morehouse Coll School of Med, pres. **ORGANIZATIONS:** Chmn Dept Comm Med & Fam Practice, Dept of Fam Med King-Drew Med Ctr LA; dir King-Drew

Sickle Cell Ctr; med dir 2nd Bapt Free Clinic, Amer Acad of Family Physicians, Amer Soc of Human Genetics; bd of dir Soc of Teachers of Fam Med, Joint Bd of Family Practice of GA, Phi Beta Kappa chap Delta 1977; mem Alpha Omega Alpha Hon Medical Soc, Amer Assn for the Advancement of Science, Amer Cancer Soc, AMA, Amer Health Assn, Natl Medical Assn; life mem NAACP; mem Urban League; mem Soc of Teachers of Family Medicine; bd dir Friends of the Natl Library of Medicine; mem Natl Adv Rsch ResourcesCouncil; adv comm Robert Wood Johnson Prepaid Health Plan; adv comm Commonwealth Academic Health Center Project. **HONORS/ACHIEVEMENTS:** Outstanding Morehouse Alumnus Awd 1973; Awd for Med Ed for Sickle Cell Disease 1973; Macy Found Faculty Fellow Comm Med 1972-73; Dudley Seaton Meml Awd Outstanding Alumnus Case Western Res Univ 1980-; numerous publications. **BUSINESS ADDRESS:** President, Meharry Medical College, 1005 D B Todd Blvd, Nashville, TN 37208.

SATCHER, ROBERT LEE, SR.
Educational administrator. **PERSONAL:** Born Sep 19, 1937, Anniston, AL; son of Wilmer Satcher and Anna Curry Satcher; married Marian Hanna; children: Serena, Robert Jr, Rodney, Robin. **EDUCATION:** AL State Univ, BS 1959; AZ State Univ, MS 1963; OR State Univ, PhD 1971; further studies at Univ of Missouri, Oklahoma Univ, Tufts Univ, TX A&M Univ, MIT. **CAREER:** Booker T Washington HS, instructor, 1959-62; AL State Univ, instructor, chem, phys science, 1963-65; Hampton Inst, chief planning officer, instructor to assoc prof, chem, 1965-79; Tororo Girl's Coll Uganda E Africa, prof chem, sci adv, 1973; Voorhees Coll, exec vp, prof of chem 1979-83; Fisk Univ, interim pres 1984, acad dean/provost 1982-88; Acting Pres, Provost, St Paul's Coll, 1988-. **ORGANIZATIONS:** Consult USOE/AIDP, Univ Assoc, Washington, DC, 1975-78, Moton Inst Capahosic VA 1977, Comm on Colls SACS Atlanta GA 1978-; mem, Operation PUSH, NAACP, SCLC, Amer Nuclear Soc, BKX Natl Hon Sci Soc, Natl Inst Sci, AAAS, Soc of Coll & Univ Planning, AIR; external evaluation, TN State Univ 1977-81, Norfolk State Univ 1980-83; eval Title III US Dept Ed WA 1983; Alpha Kappa Mu Honor Soc, 1988. **HONORS/ACHIEVEMENTS:** Seven articles Natl Inst of Sci Journal of Photochem Intl Congress Photobiology, 1968-75; fellowship grants, US Atomic Energy Comm Ford Found, 1968-71; seven articles, Higher Educ Condenses Assn of Inst Rsch, 1974-78; fellow, acad admin Amer Council on Educ, 1975-76; Citizen of the Year Zeta Omicron Chap Omega Psi Phi 1977; Change Mag 1978; co-author, Photochem of Thymine 1972; author, Long Range Planning, 1978; NIH grantee, 1972-77; Ford Found fellow 1969-71; Silver Beaver, BSA, 1988; Paper, Photochem of Thymine in Bochum, Germany, 1977. **BUSINESS ADDRESS:** Acting Pres/Provost, St Paulis Coll, 406 Windsor Ave, Lawrenceville, VA 23868.

SATTERFIELD, FLOYD
Artist. **PERSONAL:** Born Jun 12, 1945, Orange, TX; married Marsha Robinson. **EDUCATION:** LSU, MFA 1972; Southern Univ Baton Rouge, BFA 1968. **CAREER:** Southern Univ, asst prof 1971-72; Young Adult Project, teacher 1972-73; Chabot Special School, San Leandro, CA, instructor, 1973-74; Berkeley Art Gallery, special artist. **ORGANIZATIONS:** Mem Nat Conf Artst & Crdntr; Berkeley Select Fine Arts Com; consult Berkeley Recreation & Parks Dept. **MILITARY SERVICE:** AUS e-4 1969-71. **BUSINESS ADDRESS:** 1275 Walnut St, Berkeley, CA.

SATTERWHITE, FRANK JOSEPH
Business executive. **PERSONAL:** Born Oct 03, 1942, Akron, OH; son of Arthur Satterwhite and Ethel Gindrow Satterwhite; divorced; children: Frank Jr, Kuntu, Onira, Kai. **EDUCATION:** Howard Univ, BA Educ 1965; Southern IL Univ, MS Coll Admin 1967; Stanford Univ, PhD Coll Admin 1975. **CAREER:** College Entrance Exam Bd, asst dir 1968-71; Oberlin Coll, assoc dean 1971-72; Ravenswood School Dist, asst to the supt 1972-76; Comm Develop Inst, pres 1978-. **ORGANIZATIONS:** Councilman EPA Municipal Council 1974-78; mem Narobi Secretarat 1979-85; planning comm SMC Planning Comm 1980-83; mem BAPAC 1981-85; mem Mid-Peninsula Urban Coalition 1982-85; councilman EPA City Council 1983-85. **HONORS/ACHIEVEMENTS:** Comm Serv EPACCI 1983; Comm Serv EPA Chamber of Comm 1983; Champion OICW 1985; Kellogg Natl Fellowship (1986-89). **HOME ADDRESS:** 2275 Euclid Ave, East Palo Alto, CA 94303. **BUSINESS ADDRESS:** President, Comm Develop Institute, P O Box 50099, East Palo Alto, CA 94303.

SATTERWHITE, JOHN H.
Educator. **PERSONAL:** Born Jan 01, 1913, Newberry, SC; married Lucille C Mills; children: Joan Cecille, John Mills. **EDUCATION:** Benedict Coll, AB; Oberlin Grad Sch Theol, BD, STM; BostonUniv Sch Theol, ThD; Johnson C Smith U, DD; Benedict Coll, DD. **CAREER:** Livingstone Coll, instr 1938-40; Hood Theol Sem, dean, prof 1940-57; Wesley Theol Sem, prof 1958-74; AME Zion Ch Phila-Balti Conf, clrgymn; AME Zion Qrtrly Rev, edtr. **ORGANIZATIONS:** Gen Sec Consult on Ch Union Adv 4th Asmbly World Coun of Chs Sweden 1968; mem Fllwshp of Profs of Missions & Ecumncs; N Am Acad Ecumncs; Inter-Relg Com on Race Rel; Oxford Theol Sem; Wrld Meth Coun; Div of Chrstn Unity; Nat Coun Chs; past pres Am Soc of Christian Ethics; dir Gastave Weigel Soc Cont Edn. **BUSINESS ADDRESS:** 228 Alexander St, Princeton, NJ 08540.

SAULSBERRY, GUY O.
Physician. **PERSONAL:** Born Jul 15, 1900, Greenville, KY; married Essell McConico; children: Guy G, Gaylord F. **EDUCATION:** HowardUniv Med Sch Washington, MD 1927. **CAREER:** Kirwood Gen Hosp, fundr & med dir; Kirwood Ment Hlth Cntr, fundr & coord. **ORGANIZATIONS:** Mem Omega Psi Phi; Seminar Soc; Sigma Ph Phi Frat Iota Chap Boule; NAACP; Nat Med Assn; Detroit Med Assn; Wolverine Med Assn; Econ Clb of Detroit;Greater Detroit C Of C; Brooker T Washington Bus Assn. **HONORS/ACHIEVEMENTS:** Honorary Dr of Humane Letrs Deg Shaw Coll of Detroit 1972; Flight for Freedom Awd; NAACP; River Rouge Ecorse Br 1967; Physician of the Yr Awd Detroit Med Soc 1968; Outstng ach awd Detroit Coun of Insur Exec 1967; Gen Practr of the Yr Aw Nat Med Soc 1972; Outstndg Citz Aw Omega Psi Phi Frat 1976. **BUSINESS ADDRESS:** 4059 W Davison Ave, Detroit, MI 48238.

SAULTER, GILBERT JOHN
Senior executive. **PERSONAL:** Born Apr 20, 1936, Seattle, WA; son of Gerald Saulter and Bernice Saulter; married Frances; children: Bradford, Melonie, Daryl. **EDUCATION:** Univ of WA, BSEE 1962; UCLA & Univ of WA, Postgrad; Registered Professional Engr. **CAREER:** Boeing Co, engr aid 1958-62; Inst of Elect & Electron Engr, engr aid 1962-; Aerospace Ind, engr 1962-71; US Dept of Labor, saf engr 1971-74, area dir 1974-76; US Dept of Labor, reg admin Boston, MA 1976-1978; US Dept of Labor; Sr Executive official, Dallas, TX 1978-. **ORGANIZATIONS:** Mem adv comm Gov Job Injury 1984; reg professional engr elect & safety; past vp, charter mem NW Council of Black Professional Engr; chmn YMCA Youth Comm & Indin Prog, Parents Comm, sr adv BSA; mem NAACP 1966; mem Kappa Alpha Psi; mem Bd dirs, opportunity Industrialization Center 1985-; Bd dirs, Classical Guitar Society 1986-; Chief US Delegate to the Internat'l Labor Organ, Geneva, Switzerland, 1986; US Delegate to Petroleum Conference in Lagos, Nigeria, 1985. **HONORS/ACHIEVEMENTS:** Hon Roll Univ of WA 1961; Merit Awd Northrop Corp 1963,65; Merit Awd ITEK Corp 1967; Publ "Act Network Compen for Adap Cont Syst"; Trail Blazer Awd, SO Dallas Business and Professional Women's Club, 1983; Outstanding Sr Executive Awd 1985. **MILITARY SERVICE:** Nat'l Guard, 8 yrs, Honorable Discharge 1962. **BUSINESS ADDRESS:** Regional Administrator, OSHA Reg 6 Dept of Labor, 555 Griffin Sq Bldg, Dallas, TX 75202.

SAUNDERS, BARBARA ANN (NEE PARKS)
Public relations manager. **PERSONAL:** Born Jun 05, 1950, Roanoke, VA; married Byron Creighton Saunders. **EDUCATION:** Hampton Univ Hampton, VA, BA Fine Arts 1972. **CAREER:** Amer Security Bank WA DC, cust serv rep 1973-75; GA Film & Videotape Office, pr specialist 1976-80; freelance writer; freelance commerical voiceover talent 1985-; GA Dept Ind & Trade, acct asst 1975-76, pr prog coord 1980-. **ORGANIZATIONS:** Bd dir Women In Film-Atlanta 1977-79; pres Sigma Gamma Nu Social Club (Hampton Univ) 1971. **BUSINESS ADDRESS:** Public Relations Program Coord, GA Dept Industry & Trade, PO Box 1776, Atlanta, GA 30301.

SAUNDERS, DORIS E.
Educator, editor. **PERSONAL:** Born Aug 08, 1921, Chicago, IL; daughter of Alvesta Stewart Evans and Thelma Rice; divorced; children: Ann Camille, Vivian, Vincent E III. **EDUCATION:** Roosevelt U, BA 1951; Boston U, MS Journ 1977, MA Afro-Am Studies 1977; ABD History, Vanderbilt Univ 1984. **CAREER:** Johnson Publishing Co Chicago, org dev ed sp library 1949-60, org developer book div 1960-66 1972-78; Chicago Daily Defender, columnist 1966-70; The Plus Factor/Inf Inc, pres 1966-72; Chicago State Univ, dir comm relations 1968-70; Univ of IL Chicago Circle, chancellor 1970-72; Chicago Courier Newspaper,columnist 1970-72; Jackson State Univ, prof coord print journalism 1978-, staff assoc Office of Chancellor, prof mass communications 1985-. **ORGANIZATIONS:** Mem adv com Fed Reserve Bd 1968-71; mem adv com Dept of Labor Bureau of the Census 1972-80; consultant Lilly Endowment 1978-; pres Publishing Dir Special Libraries Assoc 1958-59; pres IL Chap Special Librarians Assoc 1959-60; prof Mass Communications 1985; mem Sigma Delta Chi; Natl Assoc Black Journalists; pres Ancestor Hunting. **HONORS/ACHIEVEMENTS:** Edited numerous books Johnson Publishing Co 1961-66, 1972-80; co-author w/Gerri Mayer "Black Society" Johnson Publishing Co 1976; in progress biography William L Dawson of (D.Ill) 1886-1970; editor, Kith and Kin newsletter. **BUSINESS ADDRESS:** Prof Coord Print Journalism, Jackson StateUniv, PO Box 18067, Jackson, MS 39217.

SAUNDERS, EDWARD HOWARD
Physician. **PERSONAL:** Born Aug 16, 1926, Pittsburg, PA. **EDUCATION:** Morehouse Coll, BS 1949; HowardUniv Coll of Med, MD 1957. **CAREER:** Freedmans Hosp, chief res urol 1962-63; private practice, physician. **ORGANIZATIONS:** Mem Am Plat Com, Nat Med Assn, Am Med Assn, DC Med Soc, Med & Chirug Soc of DC, Diplomate Am Bd of Urol 1966. **BUSINESS ADDRESS:** 715 Florida Ave, NW, Washington, DC 20001.

SAUNDERS, ELIJAH
Physician. **PERSONAL:** Born Dec 09, 1934, Baltimore, MD; married Monzella Smith; children: Kevin, Donna, Monzella. **EDUCATION:** Morgan State Coll, BS 1956;Univ of MD Sch of Med, 1960;Univ of MD Hosp, intern 1960-61, asst res 1961-63;Univ of MD Hosp, flwshp 1963-65. **CAREER:** Provident Hosp, chief of cardiol 1966-84, act chief 1973-, dir 1968; MD Gen Hosp, asso cardiol 1965-; Univ of MD, instr 1965-; Provident Hosp, chief 1969-71; Private Practice, 1965-; Univ of MD Sch & Hosp, assoc prof of medicine, head hypertension div 1984-. **ORGANIZATIONS:** Num pos Am Heart Assn; Cntrl MD Chpt; MD Affil; NY Dallas; chmn Nat Schlarshp Fund; Unit Ch of Jesus Christ Apost; mem Med & Chirurgi Fac of MD; mem Am Med Assn; chmn cardiopul resusc com Provident Hosp 1966-; admsns comUniv of MD 1970-75; mem Edtl Bd Spirit; trste bd 1st Un Ch of Jesus Christ Apost; steer com Hyperten Contr Prgm; subcom target grp Hyperten Contr Prgm; mem MD Soc of Cardiol; Am Coll of Physic; Am Coll of Cardiol; Am Coll of Angiol; num other assns & com. **HONORS/ACHIEVEMENTS:** Author num film strips; num appear on TV & radio; num lect; Bronze Serv Medall; Pres Awd; Am Heart Assn 1975; Pres Plaque Cntrl MD Heart Assn 1975; House Resol 15 Del Webs 1976; fdr Heart House; Silver Disting Serv Medal Am Heart Assn 1976; fellow Am Coll of Cardiol 1976; Disting Leadership Plaque MD High Blood Pressure Coordinating Cncl 1982; Outstanding Achievement in Health Care Awd Black Nurses Assoc of Baltimore 1985. **MILITARY SERVICE:** Army NG maj 1960-66. **BUSINESS ADDRESS:** Assoc Prof of Medicine, University of MD Hospital, School of Medicine, 22 S Greene St, Baltimore, MD 21201.

SAUNDERS, ELIZABETH A.
Educator. **PERSONAL:** Born Apr 12, 1948, Centralia, IL. **EDUCATION:** Freed-Hardeman Coll, AA 1967; Memphis State U, BS 1969; Memphis State U, masters plus 30 1979. **CAREER:** Freed-Hardman Coll Henderson TN, acad adv & instr 1978-; Haywood High School Brownsville TN, instr of English & reading 1977-78; Anderson Grammar School Brownsville, instr of reading 1976-77; Haywood High Jr Div Brownsville, instru of English & read lab 1970-76. **ORGANIZATIONS:** Mem HEA/WTEA/TEA/NEA 1970-78; mem TN Assoc for Super & Curric Devel 1978-; mem Intern Reading Assoc 1979-; mem Am Pers & Guid Assoc 1980; mem NAACP Alpha Kappa Sor 1969-; comm chmn FHC Wom Club & Stud Rel Comm Fac Self-study Comm 1979-; tchr Lucyville Ch of Christ. **HONORS/ACHIEVEMENTS:** High schl valed Vincent HS Henderson 1966; valed schlrshp Freed-Hardeman Coll Henderson 1966; elec rep TN Educ Assoc Gen Assem 1975; cert as spec in devel educ Appalach StateUniv Boone NC 1980. **BUSINESS ADDRESS:** Freed Hardeman Coll, Henderson, TN 38340.

SAUNDERS, JAMES WARREN (CHOPPY)
Steel company executive (retired). **PERSONAL:** Born Jan 07, 1919, MIddletown, OH; married LaVerne Burden; children: Nancy L Saunders Smith. **EDUCATION:** Attended, Miami Univ OH, West Virginia State Univ, Howard Univ. **CAREER:** Armco Steel Corp, 1939-84; City of Middletown, city commissioner 1972-86, mayor 1982-86. **ORGANIZA-**

TIONS: Pres bd of trustees 1976, first vice pres 1981 Ohio, Kentucky, Indiana Regional Cncl on Govts; mem medical serv planning activities CORVA; pres Middletown Bdof Health; bd mem Middletown Regional Hosp; mem bd of dirs Middletown City Sch Dist Educ Fund; dist commissioner Boy Scouts of Amer; pres Middletown Rotary, Middletown Area United Way. **HOME ADDRESS:** 805 11th Avenue, Middletown, OH 45044.

SAUNDERS, JOHN EDWARD, III
Government official. **PERSONAL:** Born Jan 17, 1945, Bryn Mawr, PA; son of John Edward Saunders and Eleanor Smith Saunders; married Vivian E Williams; children: John Edward IV, Jason Elliott. **EDUCATION:** Central State Univ, BS Business Admin 1968; LaSalle Coll & Univ of PA, Social Serv Agency Mgmt Educ & Develop Prog certificate 1982; IBM Comm Exec Seminar, certificate 1982; Lincoln Univ, MA Human Serv Admin 1983. **CAREER:** Dun & Bradstreet Inc, credit analyst 1972-76; Urban League of Philadelphia, prog dir 1976-78, sr vice pres 1978-83; Urban League of Greater Hartford Inc, pres & ceo 1983-88; State of Connecticut, deputy labor commissioner 1988-. **ORGANIZATIONS:** Mem Hartford Rotary Club; mem Assn of Black Social Workers; mem CT Civil Rights Coordinating Comm; chmn Hartford Health Network Inc 1984-88; exec bd mem Long Rivers Council Boy Scouts 1984-86; bd mem Hartford Area Private Indus Council 1984-86; bd mem Almada Lodge Times Farm Camp Corp 1985-; chmn, Operation Fuel Inc 1986-; bd mem, Science Museum of Connecticut 1988-; trustee, Watkinson School 1988-; bd mem, Connecticut Law Enforcement Foundation 1987-; bd mem, Connecticut Prison Assn 1986-. **HONORS/ACHIEVEMENTS:** ML King Jr Awd Hand in Hand Inc Philadelphia 1984; Fellow Amer Leadership Forum Hartford 1985. **MILITARY SERVICE:** AUS specialist 6 3 1/2 yrs; Bronze Star; Army Commendation w/OLC; Air Medal; Vietnam Serv & Campaign Medal. **BUSINESS ADDRESS:** Deputy Labor Commissioner, Department of Labor, State of Connecticut, 200 Folly Brook Blvd, Wethersfield, CT 06109.

SAUNDERS, KENNETH PAUL
Navy lieutenant. **PERSONAL:** Born May 15, 1948, Philadelphia. **EDUCATION:** Univ of Dayton, BEE 1970; OCS USN, 1971; Armed Forces Air Intel Training Ctr Denver, 1975; Naviga Flight Training Pensacola 1975. **CAREER:** NYC, minor affairs off 1972-74; Small Combat Norfolk, weap off 1971-72; Gen Elec Philadel, systems & Analys 1970. **HONORS/ACHIEVEMENTS:** Art public Am Contemp Artist Bicent Issue; gall Ligoa Duncan Gall New York City 1973; Bros Two Gall of New Mast TX 1975; Gall Ray Duncan Prix De Paris France 1975. **MILITARY SERVICE:** USN lt. **BUSINESS ADDRESS:** Lt Saunders AFAITC, Lowry AFB, Denver, CO 80003.

SAUNDERS, MARY A.
Educator. **PERSONAL:** Born Feb 19, 1937. **EDUCATION:** CCNY, MS 1971. **CAREER:** Dist 9 New York City Bd of Educ, asst dir sites & bldgs; SS New York City Bd of Educ, teacher; Educ & Employ Prog, dir; teacher computer language oper of different program machines; Reg Atty for Fed Housing Administration, admin asst. **ORGANIZATIONS:** Mem Protest Tchrs Assn; FordhamUniv Sch Adminstrs Assn; Black Tchrs Assn; Nat Blak Caucas of Sch Bd Mem; vice pres Comm Sch Bd 6 NYC; mem Comm Plann Bd 9; Borough Pres Commn to imp the Waterfront; v chmn Area 145, Comm Corp; Hamilt Grange Bd Dirs; NAACP. **HONORS/ACHIEVEMENTS:** Recpt Good Cit Awds 1967, 1969, 1972 Hamilton Grange Day Care Cntr & Bd of Edn. **BUSINESS ADDRESS:** 620 W 150 St, New York, NY 10031.

SAUNDERS, MAUDERIE HANCOCK
Educator. **PERSONAL:** Born Jun 13, 1929, Bartlesville, OK; children: Cheryle M Crawford, Leonard Anthony. **EDUCATION:** LangstonUniv Langston OK, BA 1947;Univ of OK Norman, MEd 1950;Univ of OK, PhD 1961;Univ of Chgo, 1965. **CAREER:** Howard Univ, coordinator special educ prof of educ 1979-, chmn & prof of educ psychoednl studies dept 1976-79, prof dir special educ 1974-76; Howard Univ Center for the Study of Handicapped Children, asst dir 1973-74; Eastern Il Univ Charleston IL, prof 1970-73; WV State Coll Inst, prof 1966-70; Minot State Coll Minot ND, prof 1963-66; So Univ Baton Rouge, asso prof 1960-62; OK City Public Schools, visiting counselor school psychology 1950-59; Child Serv State Dept of Welfare Minot ND, psychol 1963-66; WV State Dept Mental Health, psychology consultant 1966-70; WV St Dept of Health. **ORGANIZATIONS:** Mem Am Psychol Assn 1961-; mem Alpha Kappa Alpha 1972; sponsor Chartered Chap Eta Gamma East IL campus 1972; spons Charter Chap #253 Counc of Except Child HowardUniv 1976. **HONORS/ACHIEVEMENTS:** Listed in black OK res guide Archives of OK 1950; first black wom to rec PhDUniv of OK Norman 1961; "Teach the Educ Mental Retard Reading" Curr ThePointer 1964; outst W Virginians 1969; analys of cult diff Jour of Negro Educ 1970. **BUSINESS ADDRESS:** 2400 6th St NW, Washington, DC 20059.

SAUNDERS, MEREDITH ROY
Ophthalmologist. **PERSONAL:** Born Apr 15, 1930, Mason City, IA; daughter of Albert J Saunders and Edna M Saunders; divorced; children: Meredith Jr, Desda C, Brita B, Alaire M. **EDUCATION:** Mason City Jr Coll, AA 1949; Univ of Iowa, BA 1952, MD 1956. **CAREER:** Private Practice, ophthalmologist. **BUSINESS ADDRESS:** Ophthalmologist, Meredith R Saunders MD,PC, 1422 Woodland Ave, Des Moines, IA 50309.

SAUNDERS, RAYMOND JENNINGS
Educator. **PERSONAL:** Born Oct 28, 1934, Pittsburgh, PA. **EDUCATION:** Carnegie Inst of Tech, BA 1950-53 1959-60; PA Acad of Fine Arts, 1953-57; Univ of PA, 1954-57; CA Coll of Arts & Crafts, MFA 1961. **CAREER:** RI School of Design, adjunct prof 1972; PA Acad of Art, visiting artist 1975; Hunter Coll NYC, distinguishe prof 1981; Univ of TX Austin, visiting artist 1983; CA State Univ Hayward, prof dept of art. **ORGANIZATIONS:** Bd mem CA Arts Council 1984. **HONORS/ACHIEVEMENTS:** Fellowsship, Natl Endowment for the Arts 1977, 1984, Guggenheim Fellowship, 1976, Prix de Rome 1964, 1966; award Natl Inst of Arts and Letters 1963. **HOME ADDRESS:** 6007 Rockridge Blvd, Oakland, CA 94618.

SAUNDERS, ROBERT WILLIAM, SR.
Retired government official. **PERSONAL:** Born Jun 09, 1921, Tampa, FL; son of Willard Saunders and Christina Rogers Saunders; married Helen S Strickland, Jan 20, 1954; children: Robert W Jr. **EDUCATION:** Bethune Cookman Coll, AA 1942; Univ of Detroit Coll of Law, 1952; Detroit Inst of Tech, AB 1951. **CAREER:** NAACP, field dir 1952-66; US Govt, chief office of civil rights CSA 1966-1976; Hillsborough Cty, dir equal opport office 1976-87, executive asst to Hillsborough County admin 1987-88; retired. **ORGANIZATIONS:** Gov appt Tampa Bay Reg Planning Cnsl 1984-86; mem FL Assc Prof Comm Human Rights Wrkr 1978-, Natl Assc of Human Rights Wrkr 1960-; vice pres FL State Conf NAACP Branches 1978-85,exec bd; mem Tampa Urban League 1960-,exec bd, 1989-; steward St Paul AME Church 1964-. treasurer, Hillsborough Co Democratic Exec Comm, 1986-; Omega Psi Phi Frat. **HONORS/ACHIEVEMENTS:** Ruthledge H Pearson FL NAACP State Conf 1979; Whitney M Young, Jr Urban League Tampa FL 1982; Meritorious Award US Dept of Housing Urban Dev 1983; Nathan W Collier Award FL Memorial and Industrial Coll 1961; Outstanding Service Awrd Council of Handicapped Organizations; Gwendolyn Cherry Mem Freedom Fighters Awrd; Kentucky Colonel Commission 1974; "The Order of the Palmetto 1971"; President's Council, Univ of South FL; Bob's Corner, Column, Natl Assn of Intergroup/Human Rights Workers 1988-89. Whitney Young Memorial Award, 1986. **MILITARY SERVICE:** AAC sgt 1942-46. **HOME ADDRESS:** PO Box 4292, Tampa, FL 33677-4292.

SAUNDERS, THEODORE D. (RED)
Theatrical agent, musician. **PERSONAL:** Born Mar 02, 1912, Memphis, TN; children: Theodore, Jr, Edmund, Deneen. **CAREER:** Chicago's top theatres and night clubs, entertainer 1958-; Club Delisa Chicago, band leader 1937-58; assoc with such stars as Count Basie, Duke Ellington, ed Skelton, Tommy Dorsey, Benny Goodman, Glenn Miller, numerous others; Annex Club, music 1935-36; Walk A Thon Band, Music 1928-33; theatrical agent 1955-. **ORGANIZATIONS:** Mem NAACP. **HONORS/ACHIEVEMENTS:** Recipient Mahalia Jackson Award; Dick Gregory Award; Chicago Historical Soc Award; Record Music of Amer Award; Best Tune of the Year Award for "Hambone" (2 million rec seller) 1952; other recordings include "Stop Pretty Baby Stop," "Boot Em Up," "The Laraspa," "Advent in HiFi," "I Got Rhythm"; Ency of Jazz Award.

SAUNDERS, WILLIAM BURNETT
Retired attorney. **PERSONAL:** Born Mar 03, 1895, DeLand, FL. **EDUCATION:** Morehouse Coll, AB; Baldwin-Wallace Coll, LlB; Cleveland State Law Sch, LlD. **CAREER:** Attorney (retired) Atty General's Offce Cleveland, prosecutor; OH, rep 1940-44. **ORGANIZATIONS:** Served on many bds various orgns; NAACP; YMCA; Phillis Wheatley Assn; Cleveland Church Federation; exec & com Rep Party; Cleveland Urban League; spec Com Bar Assn. **MILITARY SERVICE:** Military Service WWI.

SAUNDERS-HENDERSON, MARTHA M.
Educational administrator. **PERSONAL:** Born Dec 18, 1924, Spartanburg, SC; daughter of Alex Pinky Saunders and Milderd Ruth Clemons Saunders; married Mark Henderson Jr; children: Sondra JoAnn Jones, Woodrene Ruth, Markette Harris, Mark III, Alexis Lillian Marion. **EDUCATION:** Burlington Cty Coll, AA 1978, AS 1979; Southern IL Univ, BS 1982; Central MI Univ, MBA 1983; Rutgers Univ, Doctorial. **CAREER:** Governer Island Nursery School, dir 1963; Girls Scouts Far East Okinowa, coord 1965; NJ, PA Dept of Ed, consult 1970; Merabash Museum, dir of program teaching spec sch 1986-87, pres, vp, museum exec 1970-; Burlington County Coll, Pemberton NJ Instructor, Museum 1989. **ORGANIZATIONS:** Bd of trustee Merabash Museum 1969-85; commiss Burl Co Cultural & Heritage NJ 1975-890; consult NJ Art Assoc NJ 1977-78, Burlington Cty Coll NJ 1980-84; instr Spec Serv School NJ 1983-84; instr Beverly City School NJ 1984; consultant Burlington Co Cultural & Heritage Ft Dix for Black History Prog; mem Burlington Coll Alumni Hall of Fame; mem Union Co Coll Fund Raising; mem Community Alert a service of WNET/Thirteen Comm Affairs Dept; mem African Amer Museum Assoc, Contemporary Educ in the Arts and Culture Rsch of Black Children. **HONORS/ACHIEVEMENTS:** Outstanding Serv NJ Dept of Ed 1979; Recognition NJ Commiss 1980, Black Arts & History 1981; Hall of Fame Burlington Cty Coll 1984; listed in Who's Who inthe East, Who's Who of Amer Women, Who's Who in Amer, The World Who's Who of Women, The Directory of Disting Amers; Hall of Fame for Contribs as a Museum Dir; Hon Mem Sigma Gamma Rho Sor 1986; NJ Historical Commn Awd of Recognition; Certificate for Outstanding Service to Public Natl Business and Professional Women's Club of NJ; Special Recognition Award Afro-One Dance, Drama and Drum Theatre Inc 1989. **HOME ADDRESS:** 59 Emerald Lane, Willingboro, NJ 08046. **BUSINESS ADDRESS:** Dir of Programs, Merabash Museum, PO Box 752, Willingboro, NJ 08046.

SAVAGE, ARCHIE BERNARD, JR.
Educational administrator. **PERSONAL:** Born Nov 12, 1929, Memphis, TN; children: Carl, Karen DeBow, Barbara Whitaker. **EDUCATION:** Marquette Univ, 1955; Talladega Clge, 1949; Lemoyne-Owen Clge, 1950; Univ of WI, 1951; Univ of Denver, BA 1966; Univ of MD, MEd 1971; Univ of Denver, PhD 1976. **CAREER:** US Counterintelligence Spec Agent, 1951-73; Coord of Inst Research Univ of Denver, 1973-76; UT State Univ, asst dir affirmative action prog 1976-79; Univ of CT Health Center and Central CT State Univ, dir affirmative action prog. **ORGANIZATIONS:** Pres ABS Enterprises 1980-; dir New Britain United Comm Srvs 1982-; consult Higher Educ Admin 1979-; mem Assc of Black Cardiologists 1984-; dir New Britain YMCA 1985; corp New Britain Gen Hosp 1981-; chrmn NB Comm On Human Rights and Opport 1984-; coord CT Unit of Amer Assc for Aff Action 1984-. **HONORS/ACHIEVEMENTS:** Keynoter Hartford Alumni Kappa Alpha Psi 1985, New Britain Black History Month 1983; flwshp award Univ of Denver 1974-76; mem Kappa Delta Pi Hnry Educ Soc 1984-. **MILITARY SERVICE:** AUS cw3; Army Bronze Star 1971; Army Navy and Air Force Commendation Medal 1973. **HOME ADDRESS:** 503 Commonwealth Ave, PO Box 877, New Britain, CT 06050. **BUSINESS ADDRESS:** Dir Affirmative Action Prog, Univ of CT Health Center, 263 Farmington Ave, Farmington, CT 06032.

SAVAGE, AUGUSTUS A.
Editor. **PERSONAL:** Born Oct 30, 1925, Detroit, MI; married Eunice King (deceased); children: Thomas James, Emma Mae. **EDUCATION:** Roosevelt Univ, BA 1950; Chicago Kent Clge of Law, grad study 1953. **CAREER:** Westside Booster, newspaper editor & publ 1958-60; Woodlawn Booster, newspaper editor 1961-64; Bulletin, newspaper editor 1963-64; Citizen, newspaper editor &publ 1965-79; Chicago Weekend, newspaper editor & publ 1973-79; US House of Rep, rep 2nd dist IL. **ORGANIZATIONS:** US Rep 2nd Dist IL Publ Works & Transp Small Bus 1981-; US Rep 2nd Dist IL Post Off & Civil Srv Comts 1981-83. **HONORS/ACHIEVEMENTS:** Award of Merit Oper PUSH Chicago IL 1976; Merit Award Best Columnist Natl Newspaper Publ Assc 1979; Freshman of the Year NAACP Evanston IL 1981; Pres Award Cook Cty Bar Assc Chicago IL 1981; Ach of the Year Chicago South Cokc Chicago IL 1981. **MILITARY SERVICE:** AUS 1943-46. **BUSINESS ADDRESS:**

Representative 2nd Dist IL, US House of Rep, 1121 Longworth NOB, Washington, DC 20515.

SAVAGE, DENNIS JAMES
Marketing research manager. **PERSONAL:** Born Aug 21, 1925, Dancy, AL; married Augusta A. **EDUCATION:** Jr Coll. **CAREER:** Cit Newspapers, gen mgr. **ORGANIZATIONS:** Mem A Flight Club Winner1970-77; Chicago-women Golf Club 1970; Midwest Dist UGA 1971; Ebony Ladies Golf League 1973; chmn Jr Golf Club "Bob O'Link" Sponsored By Chicago & Women Golf Club 1971-74. **BUSINESS ADDRESS:** St of DE Dept of Comm Afrs Eco, DE St Bldg 820 N French St, Wilmington, DE 19801.

SAVAGE, EDWARD W., JR.
Physician. **PERSONAL:** Born Jul 07, 1933, Macon, GA; married Carole Avonne Porter; children: Cheryl, Racheal, Edward III. **EDUCATION:** Talladega Coll, AB 1955; Meharry Med Coll, MD 1960; St Louis Univ, postgrad 1955; State Univ of NY, USPHS Flwsp Downstate Med Ctr 1967-69. **CAREER:** State Univ of NY Downstate Med Ctr, asst instr 1964-66, instr 1966-69; Univ of IL Med Ctr, asst prof 1969-73, assoc prof 1973; Charles R Drew Postgrad Med Sch, assoc prof 1973-80; Univ of CA, adjunct assoc prof 1977; Charles R Drew Postgrad Med Sch, prof 1980, vice chmn clinical serv 1983; Private Practice, physician 1973-. **ORGANIZATIONS:** Numerous hospital apptmnts; mem various committees Univ of IL, Martin Luther King Hosp, Chas Drew Postgrad Med Sch; mem Task Force on the Assessment of Quality Health Care Amer Coll of Ob/Gyn 1977-80; consult ob/gyn Albert Einstein Eval Unit Dept of Health Educ & Welfare 1973-76; consult ob/gyn Drew Ambulatory Care Review Team Dept Health Educ & Welfare 1973-76; consult ob/gyn State of CA Health Care Evaluation Sect Alternative Hlth Systems Div 1975-77; consult The Albert F Mathieu Chrioepithelioma Registry S CA Cancer Ctr 1975; consult Dept of Health & Human Serv 1980; consult Ob/Gyn Natl Inst of Health 1981; certified Amer Bd of Obstetrics & Gynecology 1969; certified Special Competence in Gynecologic Oncology 1974; mem editorial bd Journal of the Natl Med Assn1981; specl reviewer Ob/Gyn The Journal of the Amer Med Assn CHEST. **HONORS/ACHIEVEMENTS:** Dean's list Meharry Med Coll 1960; USPHS Postdoctoral Fellowship Gynecologic Cancer 1967-69; Who's Who in the West 15th 17th 18th Eds; US Medical Directory 4th 5th 6th Eds; Personalities of the West and Midwest 1977-78 & 7th Eds; Notable Amers 2nd & 3rd Eds; Intl Who's Who in Comm Serv 3rd Ed; Dictionary of Intl Biography Vols XV XVI XVII; Directory of Med Specialists 19th 20th Eds; Personalities of Amer 10th Ed; Who's Who in Amer 41st 42nd Eds; Intl Register of Profiles 5th Ed; Best Doctors in Amer 1st Ed; Men of Achievement 7th Ed; Who's Who in the World 5th Ed; Who's Who in CA 13th Ed; numerous publsabstracts & presentations including Savage EW Matlock DL Salem FA & Charles EH "The Effect of Endocervical Gland Involvement On the Cure Rates of Patients with CIN Undergoing Cryosurgery" Gynecol Oncol 14, 194-198 1982; Savage E W "Cesarean Hysterectomy Abstracts of Semelweiss Waters" OB Conf Dec 30 1981;"Treatment of Cervical Intraepithelial Carcinoma" Meharry Med Coll Ob/Gyn Grand Rounds Nashville TN June 16 1983. **MILITARY SERVICE:** USAF medical corps capt 1961-63. **HOME ADDRESS:** 28521 Covecrest Dr, Rancho Palos Verde, CA 90274. **BUSINESS ADDRESS:** Professor, King/Drew Medical Center, 12021 S Wilmington Ave, Los Angeles, CA 90059.

SAVAGE, HORACE CHRISTOPHER
Business executive, clergyman. **PERSONAL:** Born Jul 30, 1941; children: Christopher, Nicholas, Carter. **EDUCATION:** VA State Coll, BA 1968; NorthwesternUniv Evanston Il , MA & PhD 1968-77. **CAREER:** George MasonUniv Fairfax VA, asso prof clinical psychology; Pvt Practice, 1973; HowardUniv Wash DC, lectrasst vice pres & dir of research & evaluation 1972; EMarie Johnson & Assoc Chicago, 1970-72; Lake Forest Coll IL, lecturer in psychology 1971-72; NW Univ, visiting lecturer in ed 1971-72; Chicago-read MentalHealth Cntr Chicago, 1971-72; spur of teaching interns 1970-71; Northwestern U, teaching asst 1969-70; Northwestern U, research asst 1968-69; Sesame St Evalutation Proj Ed Testing Serv 1969; USN Naval Shipyard 1968-70 Past, personnel mgt spec. **ORGANIZATIONS:** Eastern region chmn, Nat Assn of Black Psychologists; mem Am Psychological Assn; Am AssnUniv Profs; International Transactional Analysis Assn; Am Correctional Assn; Am Ed Research Assn; Nat & Counc for Blck Child Devel; Phi Delta Kappa Professional Ed Frat; Am Assn for the Advancement of Science; MD Pry Assn; DC Assn of Black Psychologists; DC Psychological Assn; Am Mgt Assn; mem bd of psychologists Examiners Wash DC. **HONORS/ACHIEVEMENTS:** Has written—many papers and publications in his field and conducted many workshops;Univ Scholarship; NorthwesternUniv 1970; summer research fellowship Princeton1970; Martin Luther King Jr Wodrow Wilson Fellowship 1970; WEB Dubois Award 1968; listed in Who's Who in AmUniv & Coll 1967-68; alpha mu gamma Nat Foreign Language Honor Soc; beta kappa chi Nat Scientific Honor Soc; Who's Who Amg Blk Am 1976; Personalities of & The S 1976; Outstanding Young Men of Am 1973. **MILITARY SERVICE:** USAF 3 yrs. **BUSINESS ADDRESS:** 548 A N Cumberland St, Jackson, TN 38301.

SAVAGE, JAMES EDWARD, JR.
Psychologist. **PERSONAL:** Born Jul 30, 1941, Norfolk, VA; son of James Savage and Thelma; divorced; children: Jeffrey, Itayo, James. **EDUCATION:** VA State Coll Norfolk, VA, BA 1968; Northwestern Univ Evanston, IL, MA 1970, PhD 1971. **CAREER:** Institute for Life Enrichment, dir 1979-; pres James E Savage, Jr & Assoc Ltd 1978-. **ORGANIZATIONS:** Mem Intl Transactional Analysis Assn 1972-; mem Amer Psychological Assn 1972-; past Eastern Reg chmn Natl Assn of Black Psychologists 1971-. **HONORS/ACHIEVEMENTS:** Martin Luther King Jr Woodrow Wilson Fellowship Woodrow Wilson Fellowship Found 1968-70; Educational Testing Serv Summer Research Fellowship Princeton, NJ 1970. **MILITARY SERVICE:** USAF E-3 served 3 1/2 yrs; Good Conduct Medal. **HOME ADDRESS:** 1600 Myrtle St NW, Washington, DC 20012. **BUSINESS ADDRESS:** Dir, Institute for Life Enrichment, 7852 16th St NW, Washington, DC 20012.

SAWYER, ALFRED M.
Business executive. **PERSONAL:** Born Aug 08, 1934, Enterprise, OK; married Bertha L; children: Alfred Jr, Allen M, Alecia M. **EDUCATION:** USAF Inst, 1959; Eastern NMUniv Jr Coll, 1965-66. **CAREER:** Gen Serv Dept, dir of EO; NM Human Rights Com, dpty dir 1969-; Albuquerque Black Econ Leag, exec dir 1976-79; EEO NM State Plng Ofc, spl asst to gov 1971-74; NM State Office of Econ Oppor, econ devel 1970; NM Human Rights Commn, civil rights investigator 1969. **ORGANIZATIONS:** Bd mem Albuquerque Black Econ Leag 1975-77; bd of dir Albuquerque C of C 1977-79; orgnzr consult NM Human Rights Citzns Com 1979-; pres Chaves Co Nghbrhd Assn 1966-67; vice pres Roswell Br NAACP 1966; pres Roswell Br NAACP 1967; mem Roswell Urban Renewal Housing Com 1967-68; sec Chaves Co Emplyng the Handicapped Com 1968-69; pres Roswell Youth Rsrc Devel 1968-69; panel of judges 17th Annual State DECA Ldrshp Conf 1971; adv com Title I Secondary Educ 1970-71; recruitment com mem Upward Bound Proj 1970-71; steering com mem Chaves Co Red Cross 1970-71; adv com mem Home Educ Livelihood 1971; bd mempres Sickle Cell Counc of NM 1971-72; modrtr Black Ldrshp Conf 1971-73; mem Minority Bus Oppor Com 1973-78; mem Black Merit Acad 1974; 1st vice pres NMConfs of Brs NAACP 1975-76; pres Albuquerque Br NAACP 1975-76; bd mem Gov's Black Task Force 1976; past 2 vice pres NM NAACP 1976; bd mem Albuquerque Fedn of Orgn 1977; mem Job Corps Friends Com 1977. **HONORS/ACHIEVEMENTS:** Cert outstndg achvmnt black comm Black Merit Acad AL Chap 1973; col aide de camp Gov NM 1973; ctzn of the yr award NM Black Ldrshp Conf 1974; cert of achvmnt in econ devel Albuquerque Black Con Leag 1974; cert of nobility Sec of State of NM 1975; cert of apprec Black Student UnionUniv of AL 1976; col aide de camp Lt Gov NM 1979; USAF longevity serv award USAF ; cert of nobility Sec of State of NM 1980. **MILITARY SERVICE:** USAF a 2/c 1956-60. **BUSINESS ADDRESS:** Dir of EO, General Services Dept, State of New Mexico, Santa Fe, NM 87503.

SAWYER, BROADUS EUGENE
Educator. **PERSONAL:** Born May 04, 1921, Pinnacle, NC; married Iva. **EDUCATION:** A&T State Univ, BS 1943; Univ of PA, MBA 1948; NY Univ, PHD 1955; CPA 1960; Univ of MI, post doctoral study 1960. **CAREER:** A&T Univ, asst prof 1948-50, assoc prof 1955-56; Prairie View A&M Univ, assoc prof 1954-55; Morgan State Univ School of Bus, prof, dean 1956-83, prof emeritus 1984-. **ORGANIZATIONS:** Mem Sharp St Memorial UM Church, NAACP, Urban League, MD Assoc of CPA's, AICPA. **HONORS/ACHIEVEMENTS:** Pres Gamma Tau Chap Alpha Kappa Mu 1943; co-founder, treas Adv Fed Savings & Loan 1956; Founders Day Cert of Achievement NYU 1956. **MILITARY SERVICE:** AUS tech 4th gr 1943-46. **BUSINESS ADDRESS:** Professor Emeritus, Morgan StateUniv, Sch of Bus, Morgan StateUniv, Baltimore, MD 21239.

SAWYER, GEORGE EDWARD
Attorney. **PERSONAL:** Born May 07, 1919, Mobile, AL; married Maxine; children: Cynthia, Donald, Geoffrey, Michael. **EDUCATION:** A&I State Coll, AB 1947;Univ of So CA, MA 1952, PhD 1955. **CAREER:** TX So U, pres 1968-; Huston-Tillotson Coll, form dean 1947-56, prof speech drama; TN A&I State Univ Bd dir & Nat Space Hall of Fame, form vp; Counc of Pres of TX Sr Coll & U, v chmn; So Assn of Coll & Sch, trust; Fed Facilities & Equip Grants Prog of TX Coll & Univ sys, adv com. **ORGANIZATIONS:** Bd mem Standard Savs Assn; pub articles on blk acad & stud dissent on blk coll campuses. **BUSINESS ADDRESS:** 206 Reed Bldg, Richmond, IN 47374.

SAYERS, GAYLE E.
Executive/retired profl football player. **PERSONAL:** Born May 30, 1943, Wichita, KS; married Ardythe Elaine Bullard; children: Gale Lynne, Scott Aaron, Timothy Gale, Gaylon, Guy, Gary. **EDUCATION:** Attended, Kansas Univ, NY Inst Finance. **CAREER:** Chicago Bears, running back 1965-72; Kansas Univ, asst to athletic dir; Southern IL Univ, athletic dir 1981; Computer Supplies by Sayers, vice pres marketing 1984-. **ORGANIZATIONS:** Co-chmn legal defense fund sports com NAACP; coord Reach Out prog Chicago; columnist Chicago Daily News; hon chmn American Cancer Soc; commnr Chicago Park District. **HONORS/ACHIEVEMENTS:** Received numerous awds for playing; holder of numerous NFL records; named to Natl Football Hall of Fame 1977; mem Kappa Alpha Psi. **BUSINESS ADDRESS:** Vice President Marketing, Computer Supplies by Sayers, 550 Frontage Rd, Ste 2010, Northfield, IL 60093.

SCAGGS, EDWARD W.
Management consultant. **PERSONAL:** Born Mar 04, 1932, East St Louis, IL; children: Jonathan, Gregory, Helen, Keith, Edward Jr, Patricia Jean. **EDUCATION:** IL St Normal Univ, BS 1956; Univ of IL, MS 1958; Kansas State Univ, PhD 1975. **CAREER:** Self employed, consultant; PATCO, spec exec dir; Ten Cities DOL-HEW, exec dir; Univ of KS, asst prof; Training Corp of Amer, exec dir; Social Dynamics Inc; Poland Springs Eco Sys Corp, lang dir; St Paul Sch of Midwest Theol Sem; Western Auto Co; Milgrams Food Chains; Builder's Assoc; Impact Studies Inc; Wichita Fallas TX Govt. **ORGANIZATIONS:** Mem KS City C of C, KS City Human Rel Menorah Med Ctr, Skill Upgrading Inc, Al Nellum Assoc, Al Andrews & Co; dir KC Sch Dist Bd; exec bd MO Sch Bds Assoc; adv bd MO Voc Educ Bd; adv bd Urban League; adv bd YMCA Careers; adv bd Niles Home for Children. **HONORS/ACHIEVEMENTS:** Published numerous articles and manuals.

SCALES, ALICE MARIE
Educator. **PERSONAL:** Born Nov 03, 1941, Darling, MS. **EDUCATION:** Rust Coll, BS 1963; So U, MEd 1966;Univ of MA, EdD 1971. **CAREER:** Univ of Pitts, asso prof;Univ of Pgh, assoc prof of indructional studies 1972-77; IN U, 1971-72; Westfield State Coll, instr 1970-71; Hadley Sch Sys, rdg splst 1969-70; Ware Sch Sys, 1966-69; remedial rdg tchr 1966-67; John Hyson Elem Sch, tchr 1963-65. **ORGANIZATIONS:** Consult Carnegie-Mellon Action Proj Carnegie Mellon U; ESAA Sch; Banneker Contracted Curriculum Ctr; mem Intl Rdg Assn; Am Prsnl & Guid Assn; NAACP; Nat Assn of Black Psy; Alpha Kappa Alpha Sor Inc; Nat Alliance of Black Sch Edcr; Am Educ Rsrch Assn; Nat Cncl of Tchrs of English; AAUP; Black Women's Assn Inc. **HONORS/ACHIEVEMENTS:** Publ "Efficient Reading for Minorities implications for counselors", "strategies for humanizing the testing of minorities", "coll rdg & study skills An Asses-Perscriptive Model", "A Comm Operated After Sch Rdg Prgm", "Preparing to Assist Black Children in the Rdg Act". **BUSINESS ADDRESS:** Assoc Prof of Education, Univeristy of Pittsburgh, 4H01 Forbes Quadrangle, Pittsburgh, PA 15260.

SCALES, ERWIN CARLVET
Business executive. **PERSONAL:** Born Dec 24, 1949, Eden, NC; son of Irving L Scales and Gwynzetta V Strong Scales; married Diana L Guster, Apr 02, 1983; children: Edwin David. **EDUCATION:** Univ NE Lincoln, 1971; Harper Comm Coll, 1979; Wichita State Univ, 1977; Insurance School of Chicago, 1981-86. **CAREER:** Sears Roebuck & Co, various retail store controller assignments, asst mgr financial budgets and projections, corporate auditor, natl risk mgr; Winster Mgmt Svcs, pres. **ORGANIZATIONS:** mem Risk Mgmt & Insurance Soc, Natl Assoc of Black Accountants, Black Exec Support Team; advisor Junior Achievement; PHA; Mason; budget comm chmn Homeowners Assn; vice pres, County Affairs/Civic Assn. **HONORS/ACHIEVEMENTS:** Jr Achievement Company of the Year Award; dir, Risk Mgmt & Insurance Soc. **HOME ADDRESS:** 1824 Clearlake Trace, Stone Mountain, GA 30088.

SCALES, MANDERLINE ELIZABETH
Educator. **PERSONAL:** Born Mar 14, 1927, Winston-Salem, NC; daughter of Shakepeare Pitts and Roxanne Pitts; married Robert Albert Scales, Apr 09, 1955; children: Albert Marvin Scales. **EDUCATION:** Spelman Coll, AB 1949; Univ Pittsburgh, MEd; Univ of Valencia, Spain; Univ of NC at Greensboro, doctorate. **CAREER:** Winston-Salem State U, prof Soc Sci Spanish; The Winston-Salem Forsyth Co Schs Forsyth Tech Inst, tchr; Assn of Classroom Tchrs, past Pres; Dist & State Levels of Foreign Lang Tchrs In NCTA, chmn; Forsyth PTA Enrich Proj, chmn; Forsyth Co WYCA, dir on bd; Winston-Salem Natl Council of Negro Women, pres. **ORGANIZATIONS:** Past Loyal Lady Ruler Golden Circ, past Commandress Daughters of Isis; mem OES; Delta Sigma Theta Sor; The Delta Fine Arts Proj bd of dirs; trust Shiloh Bapt Ch; pres Union RJ Reynolds Flwshp to study in Spain; dir, Shilohian St Peter's Corp Family Center 1984-89; pres, Top Ladies of Distinction, Inc, 1986-89. **HONORS/ACHIEVEMENTS:** Recip Outstanding Woman in Civic & Comm Winston-Salem 1974; hon by 1972 class of Winston-Salem State U; Commandress of Yr Nat Organ of Daughters of Isis; Com on the Forsyth County Hall of Justice in Winston-Salem; Relationships of Members and Non-Members of Fraternities & Sororities, 1982. **HOME ADDRESS:** 4000 Whitfield Road, NE, Winston-Salem, NC 27105. **BUSINESS ADDRESS:** Assistant Vice-Chancellor for Student Affairs/Devel, Winston-Salem StateUniv, 601 Martin Luther King, Jr Dr, Winston-Salem, NC 27110.

SCALES, PATRICIA BOWLES
Construction executive. **PERSONAL:** Born Dec 13, 1939, Matinsville, VA; daughter of Tommy B Bowles and Irene Martin Bowles; married Vesharn Nathaniel Scales, Sep 27, 1969. **EDUCATION:** VA State Univ, BS 1963; Trinity Coll, MA 1975; George Washington Univ, EdD 1984. **CAREER:** MTI Const Co Inc, vice pres 1978-83; Liberty Constr Inc, pres, ceo 1983-. **ORGANIZATIONS:** Vp Torchbearers Circle Shiloh Baptist Church 1981-89; chair, bd of dir Liberty Constr Inc 1983-; life mem Natl Council of Negro Women 1983-; treas Friends of Juanita Miller 1986-; alt del White House Conf on Small Bus 1986; mem MD Productivity Awd Comm 1986-89; MD Apprenticeship & Training Council 1986-87; mem Board of Directors for Africare, Inc 1989. **HONORS/ACHIEVEMENTS:** Achievement Awd Natl Council of Negro Women 1986; Achievement Awd for Being one of Amer Top 100 Bus & Professional Women Dollars & Sense Mag 1986; Proclamation for Achievment from Prince George's Cty Council MD 1987; dir of Capital Stewardship Campaign Shiloh Baptist Church 1989. **HOME ADDRESS:** 12506 Pleasant Prospect Rd, Mitchellville, MD 20716. **BUSINESS ADDRESS:** President & CEO, Liberty Construction, Inc, 6029 Dix St NE Ste 201, Washington, DC 20019.

SCALES, ROBERT L.
Politician. **PERSONAL:** Born Sep 14, 1931, Wedeowee, AL; married Marcia. **EDUCATION:** Allied Inst Tech, master machinist;Univ IL, num courses. **CAREER:** Maywood, vill trust 4th dist; Tool & Die Maker Am Can Co, 25 yrs; AFL-CIO, workmen's compen rep; United Steel Workers Am, grieve com 1972. **ORGANIZATIONS:** Mem bd dir Proviso Day Care Cntr; past bd mem Proviso-Leyden Counc Comm Action; Asso Dean Polit Educ Operation PUSH, mem Oper PUSH; mem Nat Blk Caucas Loc Elected Ofc; Polit organ in voter regis & Voter Edn; mem First Bapt Ch Melrose Pk; organ over 100 Vol Maywood Comm 1972 pres elec; demon vote splitting; initiated comm wide newsletter Black Men Pushing, oper PUSH. **MILITARY SERVICE:** AUS 1952-54.

SCALES-TRENT, JUDY
Attorney. **PERSONAL:** Born Oct 01, 1940, Winston-Salem, NC; daughter of William J Trent Jr and Viola Scales Trent; children: Jason B Ellis. **EDUCATION:** Oberlin Coll, BA 1962; Middlebury Coll, MA 1967; Northwestern Univ Sch of Law, JD 1973. **CAREER:** Equal Empl Opp Commn, spec asst to vice chmn 1977-79, spec asst to gen counsel 1979-80, appellate attorney 1980-84; SUNY Buffalo Law Sch, assoc prof of law 1984-. **ORGANIZATIONS:** Consult Buffalo Bd of Educ May-June 1985; mem DC Bar; US Ct of Appeals for the Fourth, Fifth, Sixth, Seventh, Ninth and Eleventh Circuits; mem Amer Bar Assn; Natl Conf of Black Lawyers; Law and Society Assn; Soc of Amer Law School Tchrs; mem bd dir Park School of Buffalo (1985-88 term); mem, bd of dirs, National Women and the Law Assn 1987-91. **HONORS/ACHIEVEMENTS:** Articles published, "Comparable Worth, Is This a Theory for Black Workers" 8 Women's Rights L Rptr 51 (Winter 1984); "Sexual Harassment and Race, A Legal Analysis of Discrimination" 8 Notre Dame J Legis 30 (1981); with Leroy D Clark "Affirmative Action in Recessionary Periods, The Legal Strictures" 7 Adherent 3,54 1980; publication, Black Women and the Constitution: Finding our Place, Asserting our Rights, 24 Harvard Civil Rights-Civil Liberties Law Review 1989. **BUSINESS ADDRESS:** SUNY Buffalo Law School, O'Brian Hall, Amherst Campus, Buffalo, NY 14260.

SCARBOROUGH, CHARLES S.
Educator. **PERSONAL:** Born May 20, 1933, Goodman, MS; married Merion Anderson; children: Charles II, James II. **EDUCATION:** Rust Coll, AB 1955; Northwestern U, MS 1958; MI State U, PhD 1969. **CAREER:** Alcorn A&M Coll, instr 1957-59; MI State Univ, graduate teacher asst 1959-63, instr 1963-69, asst prof 1969-72, asst dir 1971-73, asso prof 1972-, dir 1973-. **ORGANIZATIONS:** Mem Am Men & Women of Sci; Acad Affairs Admin; Sigma Xi hon; Am Assn for Advance Sci; Assn Gen & Liberal Studies; mem Consumer Infor Com MI StateUniv Employ Credit Union 1972-; chmn elect MI StateUniv Blck Faculty & Admins Grp. **BUSINESS ADDRESS:** Michigan State University, U Coll Student Affairs, Office 109 Brody Hall, East Lansing, MI 48824.

SCHENCK, FREDERICK A.
Senior vice president. **PERSONAL:** Born May 12, 1928, Trenton, NJ; married H Quinta Chapman. **EDUCATION:** Attended Howard Univ 1948-50; Rider Coll, BS Commerce 1958, MA 1976. **CAREER:** NJ Dept of Labor & Industry, personnel officer 1960-64; NJ Office of Econ Oppor, chief admin serv 1966-68; NJ Dept of Comm Affairs, chief pub employment career devel prog 1966-68, dir of admin 1967-72; NJ Dept of Inst & Agy, dir div of youth & family serv 1972-74; NJ Dept of Treas, dep dir admin Div of purchase & property 1974-77; US Dept of Commerce, reg rep sec of commerce 1977-78, dep under sec 1978-79; Resorts Intl Casino Hotel Atlantic City NJ, sr vice pres admin. **ORGANIZATIONS:** Mem adv bd Rider Coll; mem 100 Black Men of NJ Inc; bd of dir Atlantic Co Chap ARC; mem Atlantic City Chap Rotary Intl. **BUSINESS ADDRESS:** Senior Vice President Admin, Resorts Intl Casino Hotel, N Carolina Ave & Boardwalk, Atlantic City, NJ 08404.

SCHEXNIDER, ALVIN J.
Educational administrator. **PERSONAL:** Born May 26, 1945, Lake Charles, LA; son of Mr & Mrs Alfred Schexnider; married Virginia Y Reeves. **EDUCATION:** Grambling State Univ, BA 1968; Northwestern Univ, MA 1971, PhD 1973. **CAREER:** Owens-IL Inc, asst personnel 1968; So Univ, asst prof 1973-74; Syracuse Univ, asst prof 1974-77; Fed Exec Inst, sr prof 1977-79; VA Commonwealth Univ, assoc dean; Univ of NC Greensboro, asst vice chancellor; assoc vice pres VA Commonwealth Univ 1987-. **ORGANIZATIONS:** Mem Amer Pol Sci Assoc, Amer Soc for Publ Admin, Natl Conf of Black Polit Sci, Alpha Phi Alpha 1965-; fellow Inter-Univ Seminar on Armed Forces &Soc 1975-; consult VA Municipal League 1980; pres VA Chap Amer Soc for Public Admin 1983-84; gov commiss VA Future 1982-84; adv bd Greensboro Natl Bank 1986-; bd of visitors VA State Univ 1986-. **HONORS/ACHIEVEMENTS:** Norman Wait Harris Fellow Northwestern Univ 1971-72; Ford Found Fellow Ford Found 1972; Fellow Woodrow Wilson Found 1973; Outstanding Young Men of Amer US Jaycees 1978; J Sargent Reynolds Awd Amer Soc for Publ Admin 1980. **MILITARY SERVICE:** AUS sgt 1968-70. **BUSINESS ADDRESS:** Assoc Vice Pres, Virginia Commonwealth Univ, Richmond, VA 23284.

SCHIESLER, MARY ANTOINETTE
Educational administrator. **PERSONAL:** Born Dec 13, 1934, Chicago, IL; married Robert Alan Schiesler. **EDUCATION:** Coll of Notre Dame of MD, BA 1967; Univ of TN, MS 1968; Univ of MD at Coll Park, PhD 1977. **CAREER:** Mt Providence Jr Coll, academic dean, registrar 1968-72; Univ of MD, lecturer, lab coord 1973-76, dir of minority affairs 1976-78; Univ of State Boardfor Higher Education, staff specialist 1978-79; Natl Science Foundation, prog manager 1979-80; Eastern MI Univ, dir of research 1981-85; Villanova Univ, dir of research & sponsored project 1985-. **ORGANIZATIONS:** Van Buren Bd of Education, trustee 1982-85; Episcopal Diocese of MI, trustee 1982-85; trustee Episcopal Community Serv PA 1986-89. **HONORS/ACHIEVEMENTS:** A Model for Cultivating the Habit of Research in Black Grad Students for the Journal of the Society of Ethnic and Special Studies 1984. **BUSINESS ADDRESS:** Dir of Research, Villanova University, Office of Research, Villanova, PA 19085.

SCHMOKE, KURT LIDELL
Mayor of Baltimore. **PERSONAL:** Married Patricia; children: Gregory, Katherine. **EDUCATION:** Yale Univ, BA; Oxford Univ, attended; Harvard Univ, law degree 1976. **CAREER:** Piper and Marbury Baltimore, attorney, 1976-; White House Domestic Policy Staff, appointed by Pres Carter as asst dir, 1977; City of Baltimore, asst US atty, 1978, elected state's atty 1982, elected mayor, 1987-. **ORGANIZATIONS:** Admitted MD Bar 1976-; served on Governor's Commn on Prison Overcrowding, MD Criminal Justice Coord Council, Task Force to Reform the Insanity Defense; involved in a variety of civic and community associations. **HONORS/ACHIEVEMENTS:** Rhodes Scholar; Honorary degrees from Western MD Coll, Univ of Baltimore. **BUSINESS ADDRESS:** Mayor, City of Baltimore, 250 City Hall, 100 N Holliday St, Baltimore, MD 21220. *

SCHOOLER, JAMES MORSE, JR.
Educator. **PERSONAL:** Born Mar 22, 1936, Durham, NC; married Mignon Miller; children: Wesley, Vincent. **EDUCATION:** Wittenberg Coll, AB 1957;Univ of WI, MS 1959;Univ of WI, PhD 1964. **CAREER:** NC Central Univ, prof & chmn of chem; Duke Univ, asst prof of physiology 1970-; Tuskegee Inst, asst prof 1966-70; Dept of Physiology Harvard Med School, research fellow 1964-66. **ORGANIZATIONS:** Mem Am Chem Soc; An Assn for Advancement of Sci; Am Physiological Soc; mem BSA; Durham Com on Negro Affairs Educ Subcom; trst White Rock Bapt Ch; Sigma Xi; Beta Kappa Chi; Phi Lambda Upsilon; Phi Alpha Theta. **HONORS/ACHIEVEMENTS:** Hillside HS Alumni Award 1970. **BUSINESS ADDRESS:** Chairman of Chemistry Dept, North Carolina CentralUniv, 1801 Fayetteville St, Durham, NC 27707.

SCHULTZ, MICHAEL
Director. **PERSONAL:** Born Nov 10, 1938, Milwaukee, WI; married Lauren Jones. **EDUCATION:** Attended, Univ of WI, Marquette Univ. **CAREER:** Song of the Lusitanian Bogey, Negro Ensemble Co New York City 1968, Negro Ensemblo Co, London, Kongi's Harvest, God Is a (Guess What?), Does a Tiger Wear a Necktie?, Broadway debut The Reckoning 1969, Every Night When the Sun Goes Down 1969, dir; Eugene O'Neill Meml Theatre 1969, Oper Sidewinder, Dream on Monkey Mountain 1970, Woyzeck 1970, The Three Sisters 1973, Thoughts 1973, The Poison Tree 1973, What the Winesellers Buy 1974, playwright; To Be Young, Gifted & Black 1971, Cooley High 1974, Car Wash 1976, Greased Lightning 1977, Which Way Is Up? 1977, Sgt Pepper's Lonely Hearts Club Band 1978, Scavenger Hunt 1979, Carbon Copy 1981, Benny's Pl 1982, For Us, the Living 1983, dir.

SCHUMACHER, BROCKMAN
Educator. **PERSONAL:** Born Aug 26, 1924, St Louis; married Doris Goodman; children: Brockman Jr, Douglass William. **EDUCATION:** StateUniv of IA, BA 1949; Washington U, MAEd 1952, PhD 1969. **CAREER:** So IL U, coord rehab couns training prog rehab inst 1968-; Human Devel Corp, dir comprehen manpower progs 1966-68; St Louis State Hosp, dir of reha serv 1957-66; Halfway House for Psychia Patients, dir res & demon 1959-62; Webster Coll, asst prof soc scis 1966-67; Counc on Rehab, pres 1971-. **ORGANIZATIONS:** Mem bd dir Nat Rehab Assn 1971-; IL bd of Mental Hlth Commnrs 1974-; IL Mental Hlth Plann Bd 1970-73; chmn com on Accreditation of rehab couns training progs Am Rehab Couns Assn 1972-. **HONORS/ACHIEVEMENTS:** Recip St Louis Mental Hlth Assn Citation for comm serv in mental hlth 1963; awd for serv Human Develop Corp 1968; NRA Cert of apprec for serv on bd of dirs 1971-73; Am Rehab Couns Assn; Nat Assn of Non-White Rehab Wkrs; Nat Task Force for Rehab of the mentally ill Dept of Health Educ & Welfare;Ed Problems Uniue to the Rehab of Psychia Patients St Louis Hosp 1963; Intens Serv for the Disadvataged IL Div of Voc Rehab 1972. **MILITARY SERVICE:** USAF 1943-46. **BUSINESS ADDRESS:** Rehabilitation Inst, SIU, Carbondale, IL 62901.

SCHUTZ, ANDREA LOUISE
Business executive. **PERSONAL:** Born Feb 15, 1948, Natchez, MS; married Simuel. **EDUCATION:** Tougaloo Coll, BA; Tuskegee Inst, 1966; Yale U, 1967; Princeton U, M 1971. **CAREER:** Mathematica Inc, vice pres 1978-84, personnel dir 1975-77; Princeton U, asst to dean of grad sch 1972-75; Urban Opinion Surveys Mathematica Inc, rsrch asso 1971; Adams-Jefferson Improve Corp, tutorial dir 1969; Educ Found, consult 1970; DC Redevel Land Agy, urban renewal asst 1970; NJ Municipal & Co Govt Study Com, researcher interviewer 1971; Alpha Kappa Alpha Sor Tougaloo Coll, pres 1966-67; Lenox Inc, dir of human resources

1984-88; Educational Testing Services, Human Resources, vice pres 1988-. **ORGANIZATIONS:** Adv bd mem Professional Women's Roster Princeton NJ 1979-; mem Assn of Black Princeton Alumni 1979-; mem Tougaloo Coll Alumni Assn 1979-; bd mem, Princeton NJ YMCA; NAACP Legal Defense & Education Fund. **HONORS/ACHIEVEMENTS:** Hon mention Danforth Found 1969; hon mention Woodrow Wilson Found 1969; "Admin Issues in Establishing & Operating a Natl Cash Assistance Program" Joint Econ Com US Congress Princeton, NJ 1972. **BUSINESS ADDRESS:** Vice Pres, Human Resources, Educational Testing Servies, Rosedale Rd, Princeton, NJ 08540.

SCHWEICH, ANDERSON M.
Insurance executive. **PERSONAL:** Born Jun 12, 1923, Chicago, IL; married Mary. **EDUCATION:** Loyola Univ, BS 1951; Northwestern & Stanford Univ, attended. **CAREER:** Chicago Met Mutual Assur Co, office mgr, data processing mgr, asst sec in charge of systems & procedures, vp, controller, exec vice pres 1951-71, pres 1971-. **ORGANIZATIONS:** Bd dir Independence Bank of Chgo, Chicago Alliance of Businessmen, Joint Negro Appeal; chmn of the bd, ceo Chicago Metro Mutual Assurance Co 1978; bd of dir Jr Achievement of Chgo; mem Natl Insurance Assoc, Natl Insurance Assoc Corp, Chicago Econ Devel Corp; bd of trustee DePaul Univ Chgo, Natl Assoc of Accountants. **BUSINESS ADDRESS:** President, Chicago Met Mutual Assur Co, 4455 S King Dr, Chicago, IL 60653.

SCIPIO, LAURENCE HAROLD
Physician/urologist. **PERSONAL:** Born Aug 15, 1942; married JoAnn Wilson; children: Kia Nicole, Courtney Lauren. **EDUCATION:** Howard Univ, College of Liberal Arts BS 1970, School of Medicine MD 1974. **CAREER:** Vocational Rehabilitation, physician 1979-82; Birt & Howard PA, physician/urologist 1979-80; Constant Care Comm Health Ctr, urology consultant 1984-; Private Practice, physician/urologist 1980-; Northwest Community Health Care, urology consult 1983-. **ORGANIZATIONS:** Attending staff Liberty Medical Ctr Inc, Maryland General Hospital, Bon Secours Hosp, Mercy Hosp, North Charles General Hosp; mem MD Urology Assoc, Medical & Chirurgical Faculty of the State of MD, Baltimore City Medical Soc, Monumental City Medical Soc, all 1980-; urology consultant Northwest Comm Hlth Ctr 1983-, West Baltimore Comm Hlth Ctr 1984-, Care First 1986-. **HONORS/ACHIEVEMENTS:** Asst Chief of Urology MD General Hosp 1985-86.

SCONIERS, DARYL ANTHONY
Professional athlete. **PERSONAL:** Born Oct 03, 1958, San Bernardino, CA. **EDUCATION:** Orange Coast Clge. **CAREER:** CA Angels, infielder 1981-84. **ORGANIZATIONS:** Fontana HS played one year varsity first base; made second-team All-CIF; named to All-South Coast Conf team at Orange Coast Clge. **HONORS/ACHIEVEMENTS:** Voted Angels "Rookie of Year" by Anaheim-Los Angeles Chapter of BBWAA in 1983; tied club record by hitting pair of grand slam home runs in r ookie season.

SCOTT, ALBERT NELSON
Elected official. **PERSONAL:** Born Nov 27, 1916, Richmond, VA; married Annie Mae Smith; children: Maxine Gill, Albert N Jr, Luana Webster, Duane, Leona, Barbara, Charlene Jones, Eugene, Cynthia Henry. **EDUCATION:** Fayette Co Schools WV. **CAREER:** Local Union 2325 Coal Mine, vice pres 1971; Mine Comm, chmn 1971-79; Beckley City Council, city councilman 1979-. **ORGANIZATIONS:** Mem Raleigh Co Commitment Comm for Democratic Party 1970; mem Recreation Bd 1971; mem Citizens Adv Comm 1972; mem WV Planning Assn 1979-84; mem Amer Legion Post 70 1982; mem St Comm 1982-84; head deacon Holiness Church of Jesus 1965-; mem NAACP 1985; appt mem Beckley Urban Renewal Auth 1985. **HONORS/ACHIEVEMENTS:** Working With Youths Beckley City Youth 1981-82; Cert of Appreciation Quad Counties OIC Inc 1982; ground breaking Water Pollution Control Project 1984. **MILITARY SERVICE:** AUS staff sgt 1941-45; Good Conduct Medal. **HOME ADDRESS:** 212 Antonio Ave, Beckley, WV 25801.

SCOTT, ALFRED J.
Bishop. **PERSONAL:** Born Oct 30, 1913, Gordon, AL; married May E Hollaway; children: Scylance B, Rubbeanuion. **EDUCATION:** Theo Cntr Atlanta, GA, cert religious educ 1970. **CAREER:** Triumph The Ch & King of God in Christ, bishop; Interdenom Ministerial Alliance, pres 1972-73; Evangelical Min Alliance, pres 1962-63; Savannah Transit Auth, sec. **ORGANIZATIONS:** Mem Dem Exec Com; Star of Firebell in the Night 1971; NAACP Adv Counc mem; founder Tricakogic Inc; licenced Master Barber Dist Bishop of diocee, SC,NC, NY; NJ Del Com MA; chmn gen bd of trust; mem exec bd NAACP chmn Legis Com.

SCOTT, ALICE H.
Librarian. **PERSONAL:** Born in Jefferson, GA; daughter of Frank D. Holly and Annie Colbert Holly; married Alphonso Scott; children: Christopher, Alison. **EDUCATION:** Spelman Clge Atlanta GA, AB 1957; Atlanta Univ Atlanta GA, MLS 1958; Univ of Chicago, PhD 1983. **CAREER:** Brooklyn Publ NY, libr I, Brooklyn Pub Libr 1958-59; Chicago Publ Libr, libr I, Woodlawn Branch 1959-61, libr Hall Branch 1961-67, libr Woodlaw n Branch 1968-73, dir Woodson Regl Libr 1974-77, dir comm rel 1977-82, deputy comm 1982-1987, assistant commissioner, 1987-. **ORGANIZATIONS:** Council mem Amer Libr Assc 1982-85; mem IL Library Assc, DuSable Museum. **HONORS/ACHIEVEMENTS:** Beta Phi Mu Libr Hnr Soc 1958-; CIC Doctoral Flwshp Univ of Chicago and Consortia 1974. **BUSINESS ADDRESS:** Assistant Commissioner, Chicago Publ Library, 1224 W. Van Buren, Chicago, IL 60607.

SCOTT, ALVIN EUGENE
Professional athlete. **PERSONAL:** Born Sep 14, 1955, Cleveland, TN; married Rochelle; children: Tonya; Erica; Stephanie. **EDUCATION:** Oral Roberts U, 1973-77. **CAREER:** Phoenix Suns, forward 1977-. **BUSINESS ADDRESS:** Phoenix Suns, P O Box 1369, Ste 510, Phoenix, AZ 85001.

SCOTT, ARTHUR BISHOP
Company executive. **PERSONAL:** Born Jul 12, 1938, Denver, CO; married Frazier Marie. **EDUCATION:** Univ of CA, MA 1970; CA St U, BS 1969; Merritt Coll, AA 1967. **CAREER:** Log cont Office, postal clerk 1960-65, supv mgmt asst 1965-68; CA State Univ, dir inst 1969-79; Kass Mgmt Serv Inc Food Servs, chmn of bd, pres, janitorial & landscape maintenance control, 1977-. **ORGANIZATIONS:** Bd mem 24 Hr Adult Parent Child Ctr; bd mem OCCUR; bd mem Proj on Inst Racism; Prof Assn; Stud Serv Pers Assn; CA St Employ Assn; mem & found Niagara Move Dem Club; Nat Naval Ofcr Assn; Alhpa Phi Alpha Frat; Educ Oppor Prgm Assn; Nat Coord Coun for Educ Oppor; NAACP; Comm Asst Coun Navy Rec; AD HOC Com on Ethnic Stud; AD HOC Com on Minor Stud Support Serv; AD HOC Com for Learn Asst Ctr; Educ Consort Com; Spec Adm Com; Task Force Com on Env Stud. **HONORS/ACHIEVEMENTS:** Dean's List Merritt Coll 1967, CSCH, 1969; graduate fellowship of CA, 1969-70; Faculty advisor, Black Student Union, 1969-76. **MILITARY SERVICE:** USNR ledr. **BUSINESS ADDRESS:** President, Kass Mgt Services, Inc, 1807 Martin Luther King Jr Way, Oakland, CA 94612.

SCOTT, AUNDREA ARTHUR
Performing arts director, educator. **PERSONAL:** Born Sep 05, 1942, Washington, DC; son of Rev. Willie A Scott and Florence C Coles Scott Phillips. **EDUCATION:** American Univ, attended 1966; Natl Spiritual Science Center, Minister, 1979-84. **CAREER:** Up With People, sound lighting/recruitment, 1967-68; John Hancock Life, agent/salesman/consultant, 1968-72; Zodiac Enterprise Inc, co-founder, vice pres, treasurer, 1972-75; The Club House, co-founder, vice pres, treasurer, light/sound technician, 1975-; Lemaze Restaurant, co-founder, treasurer, light-sound technician, 1983-; Z.E.I. Social Club, Washington, DC, owner/mgr, 1975-; Inner City Aids Network, director, 1989-. **ORGANIZATIONS:** Trainer/instr Club House Ltd, 1975-; coordinator of talent, ZEI Social Inc, 1978; producer, promoter, mgr, Chasse Band & Show, 1978; chmn, coordinator, The Children's Hour Social Club, 1976-; mem, Black Music Assn, 1978-; bd of dir, Pyramid Communications Intl, 1986; clergy, Natl Spiritual Science Center, 1984-; co-founder & pres, Us Helping Us People into Living 1988-; co-founder & co-chmn, Melvin Boozer Leadership Roundtable 1989-; mem, AIDS Advisory Comm, DC Commn of Public Health, 1988-. **HONORS/ACHIEVEMENTS:** Certificate of Merit, Eagle Scout, 1965; Achievement Award, Casablanca Records, 1977; #1 Dance Club Owner, Creative Concepts in Music, 1979; Best Sound/Lighting Club, Seemingly Better Product Record Pool ,1979; Special Commendation for Assistance for Voter Rights, Mayor Marion Barry, 1979; Platinum Record, CBS, Thriller-Michael Jackson, 1984. **MILITARY SERVICE:** USAF staff sgt 1962-65. **BUSINESS ADDRESS:** Dir, Inner City Aids Network, 1707 7th St, NW, 2nd floor, Washington, DC 20001.

SCOTT, BASIL Y.
Educational administrator. **PERSONAL:** Born Jan 18, 1925, Barbados, WI; son of James Scott and Iris Scott; married Luna Lucille Edwards; children: Karen, Brian Y. **EDUCATION:** CCNY, BA 1948; Columbia Univ, MA 1949; Siena Coll, MBA 1952; Syracuse Univ, PhD 1962. **CAREER:** NY State Dept of Motor Vehicles, various positions 1960-70, admin dir 1970-77, deputy commissioner 1977-78; NY State Dept of Educ, dep commiss 1978-83; Kutztown Univ, vice pres for admin & financial aid. **ORGANIZATIONS:** Adjunct prof Siene Coll 1959-68, State Univ of NY 1968-70; mem bd of dir Blue Shield of Northeastern NY 1971-81; mem bd of governors Albany Med Ctr 1975-81; chmn bd of dir Blue Shield of Northeastern NY 1978-81; mem bd of dir Kutztown Univ Found 1983-; adjunct prof Kutztown Univ 1984-. **HONORS/ACHIEVEMENTS:** Elected to Phi Beta Kappa 1948; Pres Appt Natl Hwy Safety Advisory Comm 1969-72, 1977-80; Sec of Transportation Appointed to Natl Motor Vehicle Safety Advisory Council 1975-77. **MILITARY SERVICE:** AUS corpl 1943-46. **HOME ADDRESS:** 1927 Meadow Lane, Wyomissing, PA 19610. **BUSINESS ADDRESS:** Vice Pres/Admin & Finance, Kutztown University, 302 Administration Bldg, Kutztown, PA 19530.

SCOTT, BENJAMIN
Chief executive. **PERSONAL:** Born Nov 30, 1929, Maringouin, LA; married Doretha; children: Benjamin E Scott Jr, Daryl D. **EDUCATION:** Pasadena City Coll, AA 1954; Pacific St Univ, BS 1959; UCLA, MS 1969. **CAREER:** US Naval R&D Lab, electrical engr 1959, proj engr 1974; Benjamin Scott Assoc & Co, Inc, consult engr 1974, chief cons. **ORGANIZATIONS:** Chmn Pasadena NAACP 1967; Chmn, Watts Comm Action Comm 1970; Chmn, Pasadena Urban Coalition 1968. **HONORS/ACHIEVEMENTS:** Medal of Freedom, NAACP Pasadena Urban Coalition & Core 1966; Medal of Achievement by Pres Wm Tolbert, Jr 1972; Congratule Achievement by Pres Richard M Nixon 1972. **MILITARY SERVICE:** AUS m/sgt 5 Yrs; Silver Star 1950. **BUSINESS ADDRESS:** Consultant, Benjamin Scott Assoc & Co Inc, 2007 Wilshire Blvd, Los Angeles, CA 90057.

SCOTT, BEVERLY ANGELA
Government official. **PERSONAL:** Born Aug 20, 1951, Cleveland, OH; daughter of Nathaniel H. Smith and Winifred M. Jones Smith; married Arthur F. Scott, Dec 31, 1986; children: Lewis K. Grisby, III. **EDUCATION:** Fisk Univ, Nashville TN, BA, 1972; Howard Univ, Washington DC, PhD, 1977. **CAREER:** Tennessee State Univ, Nashville TN, asst prof, 1976; Metropolitan Transit Authority, Harris Co TX, asst gen mgr, 1978-83; Minority Contractors Assoc, Houston TX, exec dir, 1983-84; A. O. Phillips & Associates, Houston TX, consultant, 1984-85; New York City/Metropolitan Transit Authority, asst vice pres, 1985-89, vice pres, administration/personnel, 1989—. **ORGANIZATIONS:** American Public Transit Association. **HONORS/ACHIEVEMENTS:** Ford Foundation fellow, 1972-76; Carnegie Foundation fellow, 1977-78; Outstanding Black Woman award, Black Media (Houston TX), 1984.

SCOTT, BYRON LAVELLE
Professional athlete. **PERSONAL:** Born Mar 28, 1961. **EDUCATION:** AZ State Univ. **CAREER:** Los Angeles Lakers, guard. **HONORS/ACHIEVEMENTS:** AZ State all time scoring leader with 1,572 points; 2nd in steals & 3rd in assists & career scoring ave at ASU; Pac-10 Rookie of the year 1980; 2-time Fiesta Classic MVP; MVP of Aloha Classic 1982; led LA Lakers rally in game 6 of championship series with 11 points in 17 min. **BUSINESS ADDRESS:** Los Angeles Lakers, P O Box 10, Ste 510, Inglewood, CA 90306.

SCOTT, C. WALDO
Physician. **PERSONAL:** Born Apr 22, 1916, Atlanta, GA; son of C Waldo Scott, Sr and Eva P Scott; married Mae E Hamlin; children: Charles Jr, Robert, Jon, Valerie. **EDUCATION:** Howard Univ, BS (cum laude) 1936, MS 1937, MI Med Sch, MD (cum laude) 1941; Cleveland City Hosp, internship & surgical residency 1941-44; Cook Co Grad Sch of Med, post-grad 1951, 1976, 1977; NY Univ Grad Sch of Med, post-grad 1961; Harvard Univ Grad Sch of Med, post-grad 1962. **CAREER:** Howard Univ Med Sch, asst in thoracic surgery 1945-46, instr surgery 1946-48; Newport News VA, private practice 1948; Amer Bd of Surgery, diplomate 1948; Whittaker Meml Hosp, med dir/acting chief surgeon 1948-58; Vet Admin Hosp Hampton VA, consult thoracic surgery 1949-57; Hampton Gen Hosp, surgeon

1949-; Whittaker Meml Hosp, chief surgeon 1958-70; Mary Immaculate Hosp, surgeon 1964-; Peninsula Surgical Assoc, Inc; Whittaker Meml Hosp, surgeon 1970-. **ORGANIZATIONS:** Fellow Amer Coll of Surgeons 1952; Old Dominion Med Soc, pres 1955-56; assoc mem Amer Coll of Chest Physicians 1955-; mem Natl Med Assn; mem & past pres Peninsula Med Soc; mem Hampton Med Soc; mem TB Assn Sch Bd Newport News 1952-58 & 1962-66; mem Omega Psi Phi Frat; mem Sigma Pi Phi Frat; master mason Hiram Abiff Lodge No 90 F & AM Masons; exec bd Peninsula Comm Servs, planning council 1953-63; bd of dirs VA Council on Human Relations 1955-; vestry St Augustine's Episcopal Ch 1956-60; chmn Peninsula Coord Comm 1961-64; bd of vis VA State Coll 1964-69; bd of vis Norfolk State Coll 1969-75; bd of trustees Hampton Gen Hosp 1976-; mem Boy's Club VA Peninsula 1980-; bd of dir Hampton Rds Chap ARC 1972-75, 1976-; mem Inst of Med of the Natl Acad of Sciences 1974-77; life mem NAACP. **HONORS/ACHIEVEMENTS:** Published several articles 1951-53; Outstanding Brother in Newport News Omega Psi Phi Frat 1950-52; Distinguished Serv Awd VA Tchrs Assn 1957; Man of the Yr Peninsula Jr C of C 1957; Man of the Yr Dorie Miller Teen Age Council 1957; Brotherhood Awd Peninsula Chap Natl Conf of Christians & Jews 1978. **BUSINESS ADDRESS:** Retired Surgeon, Peninsula Surgical Assoc Inc, 2010 27th St, Newport News, VA 23607.

SCOTT, CARSTELLA H.
City official. **PERSONAL:** Born Apr 06, 1928, Thomasville, AL; married Percy Scott Sr; children: Rosia B Grafton, Percy Jr, Maxine , Veronia, Geraldine, Katherine Y Parham, Christine, Roderick. **EDUCATION:** Ruth's Poro Beauty Coll, BS; Southern Beauty Congress, MA; Southern Beauty Congress, PhD 1984. **CAREER:** Englewood Elementary Fairfield, pres 1957-67; Law Comm of AL, mem 1980-; AL Governor's Comm, mem 1983-; Fairfield Democratic Women, vp; AL Voter Ed, mem 1985; Fairfield City Council, councilwoman; Fairfield AL PTA, pres. **ORGANIZATIONS:** Mem NAACP, Zeta Phi Lambda Sor for Christian Women of Amer 1980; mem & exec bd mem AL Modern Beauticans, Chamber of Commerce Fairfield 1982. **HONORS/ACHIEVEMENTS:** Nominating comm Women's Missionary Council; Mother of the Year Fairfield School Syst; pres missionary circle Shady Grove CME Church 1973-; Nine Year Svc Awd CME Church-Birmingham Conf 1984. **HOME ADDRESS:** 3913 Court G, Fairfield, AL 35064.

SCOTT, CHARLES E.
Realtor. **PERSONAL:** Born Dec 04, 1940, Macon, GA; married Francenia D Hall; children: Erica, Derek. **EDUCATION:** Morris Brown Coll, BS 1963. **CAREER:** Atlanta Bd of Educ, music teacher 1963-65; IBM Corp, sales rep 1968-71; Charles E Scott Real Estate, realtor/appraiser 1971-. **ORGANIZATIONS:** Assoc mem Soc of Real Estate Appraisers 1977-; pres Natl Soc of Real Est Appraisers Inc Local Satellite Chap 1980; sec Children's Psychiat Ctr 1979-; vice pres Comm Mental Health; sec Allapattah Comm Action Agency; special master Prop Appraisal Adjustment Bd Dade Co. **MILITARY SERVICE:** AUS e-4 1966-68. **BUSINESS ADDRESS:** Realtor/Appraiser, Charles E Scott Real Estate, 931 NE 79th St, Miami, FL 33138.

SCOTT, CHARLOTTE HANLEY
Educator. **PERSONAL:** Born Mar 18, 1925, Yonkers, NY; daughter of Edgar Hanley and Charlotte Hanley; married Nathan A Scott Jr; children: Nathan A III MD, Leslie Ashamu. **EDUCATION:** Barnard Coll, AB 1947; Amer Univ, attended 1949-53; Univ of Chicago Sch of Business, MBA 1964; Allegheny Coll, LLD 1981. **CAREER:** Natl Bureau of Economic Rsch NY, rsch assoc 1947-48; RW Goldsmith Assoc, rsch assoc 1948-55; Univ of Chicago Sch of Business, economist 1955-56; Federal Reserve Bank of Chicago, economist 1956-71, asst vice pres 1971-76; Univ of VA McIntire Schl of Commerce, Curny School of Educ, prof 1976-. **ORGANIZATIONS:** Mem bd dirs Sovran Bank NA 1977-; mem 1980-82, vice chmn 1981, chmn 1982 Consumer Advisory Bd Fed Reserve 1980-82; mem Gov's Commn on VA Future 1982-84;mem VA Commn on Status of women 1982-; pres Women's Bd Chicago Urban League 1967-69; trustee Barnard Coll Columbia Univ 1977-81; treas VA Women's Cultural History Project 1982-85. **HONORS/ACHIEVEMENTS:** Outstanding Woman Alpha Gamma Pi Chicago 1965; Alumni Medal Columbia Univ 1984. **BUSINESS ADDRESS:** Prof of Commerce & Education, Univ of VA, Monroe Hall, Charlottesville, VA 22903.

SCOTT, CLARENCE RAYMOND, JR.
Retired professional athlete, real estate executive. **PERSONAL:** Born Apr 09, 1949, Atlanta, GA; married Regina Barnett; children: Kawana Chanelle, Chimere Monet, Armond Raymond. **EDUCATION:** KS State Univ, 1967-71; John Marshal Law School, attending. **CAREER:** NS All Star Game, pro athlete 1970; Coll All Star Game, athlete 1971; All Amer Game, pro athlete 1971; Sr Bowl, pro athlete 1971; Cleveland Browns, cornerback retired 1984; Royal Ackerman, real estate 1974-; Mighty Clean Svcs, owner; Clarence Scott Travel Agency, owner/pres. **ORGANIZATIONS:** Volunteer Boy's Club; All Rookie Team 1971; UPI All Conf 1972; AP & UPI All Pro 1973; All Pro Bowl Game 1973; mem DeKalb Co NAACP, Atlanta Jaycees, Conf of Minority Transportation Officials. **HONORS/ACHIEVEMENTS:** Cleveland Touchdown Club Awd Outstanding Browns Def Play 1973; All Time Interception Record 12 yrs 1968-71; All Big Eight Conf 1970; Look Mag All Amer 1970; All Amer Football Writers Assoc 1970; Collegiate Def Play of the Year 100% Wrong Club 1970; Trophy Helping Beat Every Team in the Big 8 during career & putting KSU football on the map 1970. **BUSINESS ADDRESS:** Owner/President, Clarence Scott Travel, 5254 Memorial Dr, Stone Mountain, GA.

SCOTT, CLIFFORD ALVA
Attorney. **PERSONAL:** Born Feb 08, 1908, Edwards, MS; married Ruth. **EDUCATION:** Morris Brown Coll; Morehouse Coll; Univ KS. **CAREER:** WA Scott, admin estate 1934-; Atlanta Better Bus Bur, bd dir 1970-77. **ORGANIZATIONS:** Mem Fulton Co Dept Family & Child Serv 1965-69; Acad Sci Columbia U; bd dir Nat Newspaper Pub Assn; Mutual Fed Bldg Loan Assn; George Washington Carver Boys' Club; tst Warren United Meml Ch; exec com Fulton Co; Nat Conf Christian & Jews; Capital City Press Club 1975; Atlanta Med Assn 1976; Cancer Soc 1975; YMCA Centruy Club; United Appeal; Marta 1975. **HONORS/ACHIEVEMENTS:** Recip Frontiers External Awd rep party 1972; Silver Arch Key to city StLouis, MO; citation GA C of C; Accolade of Apprct 1959; Citz Awd 1975. **BUSINESS ADDRESS:** 100 Centre St, New York, NY 10007.

SCOTT, CORNEALIOUS SOCRATES, SR.
Clergyman, educator. **PERSONAL:** Born Mar 25, 1909, Camden, AR; married Willie Mae Matthews; children: William McKinley, Wanda Joyce, Grace Louise, Cornealious Socrates, Jr, StevenEmerson. **EDUCATION:** Western Baptist Seminary, BSEd 1952; Central Mo State Coll, MSEd 1970, Certificate for Admin, 1972; Central Baptist Theology Seminary, 1984. **CAREER:** St Convention MO Youth Dept, guidance & counselor 1951-56, 1981; Era Baptist Dist Assn KC, MO, pastor masonry Baptist; KS City, MO School Syst, teaching 1963-81; E Comm Cncl, pres Moderator New 1970-72; US Dept HEW, 1970-74; E Side Masonry Baptist Church, pastor. **ORGANIZATIONS:** Vice pres, KC MO Branch NAACP 1953-58; comm mem KC MO Human Relations Dept L1954-58; mem of Municipal Comm on UNICEF of KC Mo 1956-54; mem Natl Comm to Preserve SS & Medicare 1984-; mem KC MO Ministers Un; Annually Renewals bd mem of the New Era Masonry Baptist Dist Assn Gamma Tou Theology Fraternity 1949. **HONORS/ACHIEVEMENTS:** Honorary lifetime mem, Reserve Officers Training Corps, Lincoln Univ, Jefferson, MO, 19774; 20 Club mem, cert J C Nichol Co, KS, MO, 1974; Women Comm Serv Inc, 1968. **HOME ADDRESS:** 2400 Norton Ave, Kansas City, MO 64127. **BUSINESS ADDRESS:** Pastor, East Side Missionary Bapt Ch, 2303 Cleveland Ave, Kansas City, MO 64127.

SCOTT, CORNELIUS ADOLPHUS
Publisher. **PERSONAL:** Born Feb 08, 1908, Edwards, MS; married Ruth Perry; children: Jocelyn Scott Walker, Portia A. **EDUCATION:** Morehouse Coll, attended; Univ of KS, attended; Morris Brown Coll, attended. **CAREER:** Atlanta Daily World, publisher 1934-. **ORGANIZATIONS:** Bd mem NAACP Atlanta Chap over 30 yrs, Mutual Fed Savings & Loan Bank over 30 yrs, Carver Home Boys Club 1950's-; mem Republican Party 1955-; vchmn Atlanta Bi-Partisan Voters League; chmn of bd of dir Atlanta Consumers Club. **HONORS/ACHIEVEMENTS:** Cited for numerous media awds & bus awds by org & agencies. **BUSINESS ADDRESS:** Publisher, Atlanta Daily World, 145 Auburn Ave NE, Atlanta, GA 30335.

SCOTT, DEBORAH ANN
Physician. **PERSONAL:** Born Oct 02, 1953, New York, NY; married Ralph C Martin II. **EDUCATION:** Princeton Univ, BA 1975; Howard Univ, MD 1979. **CAREER:** Howard Univ Hosp, dermatology fellow 1982-83; Roger Williams General Hosp, dermatology fellow 1983-86; MIT, staff physician 1986-. **ORGANIZATIONS:** Mem MA Medical Soc 1983-87, Amer Acad of Dermatology 1986, New England Medical Soc 1986, New England Dermatological Soc 1987. **HONORS/ACHIEVEMENTS:** Alpha Omega Alpha Hon Soc 1979. **BUSINESS ADDRESS:** Dermatologist, 110 Francis St, Boston, MA 02215.

SCOTT, ELSIE L.
Organization administrator. **PERSONAL:** Born in Lake Providence, LA; daughter of John H Scoot and Alease Scott; divorced. **EDUCATION:** Southern Univ, BA, 1968; Univ of IA, MA, 1970; Atlanta Univ, PhD, 1980. **CAREER:** NC Central Univ, asst prof, 1979-80; Howard Univ, rsch assoc, asst prof, 1981-83; Natl Org of Black Law Enforcement Execs, program mgr, 1983-86; exec dir, 1986-. **ORGANIZATIONS:** Pres, Natl Conf of Black Political Scientists, 1980-81; sec, John H Scott Memorial Fund, 1981-; advisory bd, Natl Inst Against Prejudice & Violence, 1985-; panel mem, Comm on the Status of Black Amers Natl Rsch Council, 1986-. **HONORS/ACHIEVEMENTS:** Award for Best Paper, Natl Conf of Black Political Scientists, 1978; author, Violence Against Blacks in the US, 1979-81, 1983; co-author, Racial & Religious Violence, 1986. **BUSINESS ADDRESS:** Exec Dir, Natl Org Black Law Enforcement Executives, 908 Pennsylvania Ave SE, Washington, DC 20003.

SCOTT, GLORIA DEAN RANDLE
Educational administrator. **PERSONAL:** Born Apr 14, 1938, Houston, TX; married Dr Will Braxton Scott. **EDUCATION:** IN Univ, AB, MA, PhD 1959, 1960, 1965, LLD 1977. **CAREER:** Inst for Psych Research, research assoc in Genetics 1961-63; Marian Coll, coll prof 1961-65; Knoxville Coll, prof 1965-67; NCA TSU, prof 1967-76; NCATSU, asst to pres 1967-68; TSU, 1977-78; Natl Inst of Educ, hd postsecondary research 1973-75; NCATSU, dir of Plng & Inst Research 1973-76; TX Southern Univ, prof 1976-78; Clark Coll, prof 1978-86, vice pres 1978-86; Grambling State Univ, prof 1987; Bennett Coll, pres. **ORGANIZATIONS:** Bd of dirs Southern Educ Foundation 1971-76; pres G Randle Serv 1975-; co-owner Scotts Bay Courts 1972-; consult Ford Fndtn, Southern Edctn Fndtn 1967-72, 76; sec Corp PREP 1966-82; pres Girl Scouts USA 1975-78, 1st vice pres 1972-75; bd of dir Nat Urban League 1976-82; mem & chw Defense Comm on Women in theServices 1979-81; chair of bd of dirs Natl Scholarship Fund for Negro Students 1984-85; delegation head 1985 UN Decade for Women Intl Forum Nairobi Kenyua 1985; contributing editor Good Housekeeping 1985. **HONORS/ACHIEVEMENTS:** Woman of Year, Past Standard Houston YMCA, 1977; Honorary degree, DHL Farleigh Dickinson Univ, 1978; Kizzie Image Award, Chicago, 1979; YWCA Acad of Women Achievers, Atlanta YWCA, 1986; In Exhibit, "I Dream A World, 75 Black Women Who Changed America". **HOME ADDRESS:** Rt 1 Box 53, Riviera, TX 78379. **BUSINESS ADDRESS:** President, Bennett College, 900 E Washington St, Greensboro, NC 27420.

SCOTT, HAROLD RUSSELL, JR.
Director, performer, educator. **PERSONAL:** Born Sep 06, 1935, Morristown, NJ; son of Harold Russell Scott MD and Janet Gordon Scott. **EDUCATION:** Harvard Univ, BA 1957; studied acting with Robert Lewis, William Ball, Michael Howard; studied under the direction of Elia Kazan, Harold Clurman, Jose Quintero; studied voice and speech with Arthur Lessac, Kristin Linklater, Alice Hermes, Graham Bernard; studied dance with Anna Sokolow, Alvin Ailey. **CAREER:** Professional actor in commercial theatre, 1958-71; created roles in original New York productions for Jean Genet's Deathwatch (1958), Edward

Albee's The Death of Bessie Smith (1961), Arthur Miller's After the Fall (1964) and Incident at Vichy (1965), Wole Soyinka's The Trials of Brother Jero and The Strong Breed (both 1967), Jack Gelber's The Cuban Thing (1968), and Lorraine Hansberry's Les Blancs (1970); appeared in approximately 50 other Broadway, off-Broadway, regional and stock theatre productions; Eugene O'Neill Theatre Center, New London CT, staff dir, 1970-76; Cincinnati Playhouse in the Park, artistic dir, 1972-74; Natl Theatre Inst, guest lecturer, 1975; Univ of North Carolina, artist-in-residence, 1974-75; Duke Univ, guest lecturer, 1975; North Carolina Central Univ, guest lecturer, 1975; Amer Coll Theater Festival, Washington DC, guest lecturer, 1975; Henry St Settlement Urban Life Center, acting teacher, 1976-77; Amer Coll Theater Festival Howard Univ "A Dialogue with Hal Scott" 1978; directed numerous stage productions including The Mighty Gents, Ambassador Theatre, NYC, and Kennedy Center Eisenhower Theatre, Washington DC (1978), A Raisin in the Sun 25th Anniversary Production, Roundabout Theatre, NYC, and Kennedy Center Eisenhower Theatre, Washington DC (1986), Paul Robeson (starring Avery Brooks), Golden Theatre, NYC (1988) and Kennedy Center, Washington DC (1989), and Member of the Wedding, Roundabout Theatre, NYC (1989); directed television productions including Monkey, Monkey, Bottle of Beer, How Many Monkeys Have We Here?, Theatre in America (PBS-TV, 1974) and The Past Is the Past (CBS Cable, 1981); Design Inst Natl Arts Consortium NYC, artistic dir, 1979-81; Peterborough Players, New Hampshire, staff dir, 1981-85, assoc dir, 1985-88, acting artistic dir, 1989-; Rutgers Univ, Mason Gross School of the Arts, co-adjunct 1980-81, assoc prof 1981-83, assoc prof and head of directing program 1983-87, prof and head of directing program 1987-; Crossroads Theatre, New Brunswick NJ, assoc artist, 1988-. **ORGANIZATIONS:** Mem, Signet Soc-Harvard, 1956-; mem YMCA, 25 years; elected dir, Associated Harvard Alumni, 1976-79; professional theatre panel, Natl Endowment for the Arts, 1985-87; mem, Harvard Club of New Jersey; mem, Ensemble Studio Theatre; bd of dir, Non-Traditional Casting Project, 1987-; bd of dir, Theatre Communications Group, 1988-; mem, Soc of Stage Directors and Choreographers, Actors Equity Assn, and Amer Fed of Television and Radio Artists. **HONORS/ACHIEVEMENTS:** Obie Award for distinguished performance in Deathwatch, 1959; Special Award for Excellence as Actor, Director, and Teacher, New England Theater Conf, 1972; Exxon Award, 1974; nominee for Black Image Award, NAACP, 1985; Black Theatre Award for A Raisin in the Sun 25th Anniversary Production, 10 awards including best director, NAACP, 1988; Scott production of A Raisin in the Sun 25th Anniversary was produced for Amer Playhouse, PBS-TV, 1989; has made spoken word recordings of A Raisin in the Sun (Caedmon), After the Fall (Mercury), Incident at Vichy (Mercury), and God's Trombones (United Artists); recorded over 30 "Talking Books" for Amer Found for the Blind Inc, Library of Congress. **HOME ADDRESS:** 276 Delavan Ave East, Newark, NJ 07104. **BUSINESS ADDRESS:** Prof/Hd of MFA Professional Directing Prog, Rutgers Univ, Mason Gross School of the Arts, Levin Theatre, Douglass Campus, New Brunswick, NJ 08901.

SCOTT, HERBERT
Professional athlete. **PERSONAL:** Born Jan 18, 1953. **EDUCATION:** VA Union. **CAREER:** Dallas Cowboys, professional football guard 1975-. **HONORS/ACHIEVEMENTS:** First team All-NFC UPI 1978-79; Pro Bowl 1979.

SCOTT, HOSIE L.
College executive. **PERSONAL:** Born May 31, 1943, Clopton, AL; married Ruth. **EDUCATION:** Kean Coll, BA, MA; Brookdale Community Coll; Lincroft. **CAREER:** Brookdale Community Coll Lincroft NJ, coor of affirm action & personnel admin 1972-; Red Bank YMCA, exec youth program dir 1970-72; NC Mutual Life InsCo Newark NJ, life underwriter counselor & debit mgr 1968-70; Jersey Central Power Co Sayreville NJ, techn 1967-68. **ORGANIZATIONS:** Mem NJ Coll & Univ Personnel Assn; Monmouth Ocean Co Prof Personnel Dir Assn; dir on affirm action NJ Prof; Nat Coun on Black Am Affairs; Am Assn Comm Jr Coll; past mem Life Underwriters Assn 1968-70; Assn of Professional Dir YMCA 1970-72; BAN-WY'S YMCA 1970-74; Am Soc of Notaries; mem Greater Red Bank NAACP; bd dir Union Co Urban League NJ; chmn Affirm Action Adv Com Brookdale Coll NJ; chmn Matawan Twp Drug Coun NJ; adv bd EOF Brookdale Coll; mem State Com Persnnl Resrcs Urban League; mem Dept of Higher Educ Affirm & Action Com; adv com mem for Inst of Applied Humanities Brkdl Comm Coll; mem Dr M Luther King Obsrvnc Com; exec com mem Monmouth Co NJ Bicentennial; past pres Tri-Comm Club Matawan NJ. **HONORS/ACHIEVEMENTS:** Recipient Matawan Twp Tri-Community Club Distinguished Serv Award 1973; service award Greater Red Bank NAACP 1973; fitness finders award Nat YMCA 1972; outstanding leadership award New Shrewbury NJ Kiwanis 1972; outstndng cert of ldrshp & achie award Dept of Army 1967. **BUSINESS ADDRESS:** Brookdale Community College, 765 Newman-Springs Road, Lincroft, NJ 07738.

SCOTT, HUBERT R.
Business executive. **PERSONAL:** Born Sep 24, 1919, Athens, GA; married Betty DuMetz; children: Hubert, Wayne. **EDUCATION:** Morehouse Coll, BS 1942; Atlanta U, MS 1947;Univ of MI, Addl Stud. **CAREER:** Pilgrim Health & Life Ins Co, 2nd vice pres & sec treas 1968-, actuary 1947-68. **ORGANIZATIONS:** Mem tech sect chmn actuary statistician Nat Ins Assn 1953-59; treas NAACP 1958-66; mem bd dir chmn Personnel Com YMCA 1956-; mem bd dir Shiloh Orphanage 1956-; Civil Serv Commn 1968-73. **HONORS/ACHIEVEMENTS:** Citizen of yr YMCA 1956; citizen of yr Kappa Alpha Psi 1968. **MILITARY SERVICE:** AUS s/sgt 1942-45. **BUSINESS ADDRESS:** 1143 Gwinnett St, Augusta, GA.

SCOTT, HUGH J.
Educator. **PERSONAL:** Born Nov 14, 1933, Detroit, MI; married Florence I Edwards; children: Marvalisa, Hugh. **EDUCATION:** Wayne State Univ, BS 1956, MEd 1960; Wayne State Univ, Educ Spec 1964; MI State Univ, EdD 1966. **CAREER:** Detroit Great Cities School Improvement Project, asst dir 1965; City of Detroit, teacher 1956-65, asst principal 1966-67, asst deputy supt school comm relations 1967-68; MI State Univ, instruct 1965-66; Washington, supt schools 1970-73; Howard Univ, prof 1973-75; Hunter Coll & City Univ NY, dean progs in educ 1975-. **ORGANIZATIONS:** Mem Phi Delta Kappa 1960-; mem NAACP 1967-; mem Detroit Soc Black Educ Admins (bd dirs 1968-70); mem Amer Assn Sch Admins 1969-; mem Natl Alliance Black Sch Educators 1970-; mem Natl Eval Comm Univ WI Cognitive Devel Ctr 1972-75; mem Natl Acad Sch Execs 1972. **HONORS/ACHIEVEMENTS:** Dist Serv Cert Phi Delta Kappa 1969; Dist Alumni Awd MI State Univ 1970. **MILITARY SERVICE:** AUS pfc 1956-58. **BUSINESS ADDRESS:** Dean, Programs in Education, Hunter Coll CUNY, 695 Park Ave, New York, NY 10021.

SCOTT, J. IRVING ELIAS
Author. **PERSONAL:** Born Jan 13, 1901. **EDUCATION:** Lincoln U, AB; Wihenburg, AM;Univ of Pittsburgh, PhD. **CAREER:** Retired author of num books "Living with Others"; "Finding My Way"; "Negro Students & Their Coll"; "Getting Most Out of HS"; "The Educ of Black People in FL" Dorrance & Co 1974. **ORGANIZATIONS:** Found & editor-in-chief Negro Educ Rev; pres Cit Invest Corp. **HONORS/ACHIEVEMENTS:** Listed in Who's Who In Am; Who's Who in the World; Who's Who in the S & SW; Contemp Authors; Royal Blue Book; Com Leaders.

SCOTT, JACOB REGINALD
Executive. **PERSONAL:** Born Jun 02, 1938, New York, NY; widowed; children: Elaine Beatrice, Lisa Anne. **EDUCATION:** Lincoln Univ, BSc Psych 1960; Inst African De Geneve, Geneva Switz, diploma African studies 1971. **CAREER:** US State Dept Foreign Svc, econ/comm officer Ethiopia 1966-68; Seagram Africa, sales, mktg dir 1971-82; Seagram Overseas Sales NY, mktg dir Africa 1980-84, vice pres Africa 1984-. **ORGANIZATIONS:** Founding mem Montclair Alumni Chap Kappa Alpha Psi 1981-83; dir, vice pres Intl Distillery Dev Ltd 1982-; dir United Distillers & Vintners Logos Nigeria 1983-; dir Fermencam Douala Cameroun 1986-; dir Nigeria/Amer C of C 1986-. **BUSINESS ADDRESS:** Vice President, Seagram Overseas Sales Co, 375 Park Ave, New York, NY 10152.

SCOTT, JAMES
Professional athlete. **PERSONAL:** Born Mar 28, 1952, Longview, TX. **EDUCATION:** Henderson JC. **CAREER:** Chicago Bears, football player-wide recvr 1976-; NY Jets, player 1975; WFL Chicago Fire, player 1974. **HONORS/ACHIEVEMENTS:** All-Conf Recvr at HC JC (was leading WFL recvr when injured) 1971. **BUSINESS ADDRESS:** Chicago Bears Halas Hall, 240 N Washington Rd PO Box 204, Lake Forest, IL 60045.

SCOTT, JAMES F., SR.
Physician. **PERSONAL:** Born Jul 29, 1903, Porter, OH; married Muriel Goings; children: June, James Jr, Robert. **EDUCATION:** BS; MD. **CAREER:** Physcian, priv prac; Hlth Dept, dir, coroner. **ORGANIZATIONS:** Mem Am Med Assn; OH State Med Soc; Scioto Co Med Soc; Intl Assn of Coroners & Med Examr; OH State Coroners Assn; mem & past master of Trinity Lodge #9 Masons; mem & past pres Scioto Co Crime Clinic. **HONORS/ACHIEVEMENTS:** First black Coroner elected in USA; Family of Yr.

SCOTT, JAMES HENRY
Business executive. **PERSONAL:** Born Dec 22, 1942, St Louis, MO; married Cora Sabeta Dillon; children: James H. **EDUCATION:** Villanova Univ, BEE 1965; Washington Univ, St Louis, MBA 1970. **CAREER:** Bank Morgan Labouchere NY, vice pres & dep 1979-; Morgan Guaranty Trust Co of New York, vice pres 1973-; The White House, White House fellow 1978-79; Gulf & Western Ind Inc, asst to vice pres fin 1972-73; Citibank, acct officer 1970-72; Guyana, South Amer, Peace Corps volunteer 1966-68. **ORGANIZATIONS:** Editor-in-chief, The Circuit, 1964-65; co-found & sec, AFRAM Enterprises Inc 1968-73; asst treas, Greater New York Coun Boy Scouts of Amer, 1976-; mem, New York Urban League, 1977-; mem, Acad of Polit Sci, 1977-. **HONORS/ACHIEVEMENTS:** HT scholarship HT Dyett Found Rome Cable Corp 1960; Natl Rugby Football Team, Guyana, South Amer 1967; Outstanding Young Men of Amer, Jaycees 1979. **BUSINESS ADDRESS:** Tesselschadestraat 12, Amsterdam, Netherlands.

SCOTT, JEAN SAMPSON
Genealogist, educator. **PERSONAL:** Born Jan 31, 1925, Zanesville, OH; daughter of Charles Theodore Sampson and Alyce Stotts Sampson; married Osborne E. Scott, Dec 29, 1947; children: Osborne E., Jr., Michael David. **EDUCATION:** Hampton Institute, Hampton VA, BS, 1948; Columbia Univ, New York NY, 1968. **CAREER:** US Govt, Tokyo, Japan, recreation, 1954-56; New York Board of Education, New York NY, elementary teacher, 1958-59; US Dependent Schools, Germany, teacher, 1960-62; Mamaroneck Board of Education, Larchmont NY, teacher, 1964-80; College of New Rochelle, New Rochelle NY, teacher, 1972-86. **ORGANIZATIONS:** Founding member and executive board president of Afro-American Historical and Genealogical Society, Association of Black Women Historians, Association for Study of Afro-American Life & History. **HOME ADDRESS:** 323 Egmont Ave, Mt Vernon, NY 10553.

SCOTT, JOHN H.
Clergyman. **PERSONAL:** Married Alease Truley; children: 8. **EDUCATION:** So U, BTh. **CAREER:** E Carroll Bapt Assn, minstr present; N Star Bapt Church, pastr. **ORGANIZATIONS:** Pres E Carroll Bapt Sunday Sch Con; chaplain 5th Dist PTA; pres NAACP; bd mem LA Voter Educ Proj; vice pres LA Bapt State Conv; chmn E Carroll Biracial Com; mem E Carroll Library Bd. **HONORS/ACHIEVEMENTS:** Cert of mer LA State Conf NAACP & Youth Counc Lake Prov Br 1972.

SCOTT, JOHN P.
Retired. **PERSONAL:** Born Dec 17, 1907, Harrisburg, PA; married E Louise; children: Stephanie Scott Williams, David W. **EDUCATION:** Hampton Inst, cert 1930; Hampton Inst, BS 1932; Harvard U, EdM 1957. **CAREER:** Dept Commerce VI, commr 1971-74; Bur Rec St Thomas VI, dir 1959-62; Dept Educ St Thomas VI, prin high school 1950-59; Dept Educ St Thomas VI, tradeteacher 1933-41; owner commer poultry farm 1941-60; Scott Hotel, owner-mgr 1962-79; Harris Enter Real Estate, pres 1962-79. **ORGANIZATIONS:** Pres St Thomas Rotary 1964; bd of dir VI Nat Bank 1968-71; chmn Citzns Crime Prevntn Counc 1979-; bd of dir Discover Am Tourist Orgn 1972-74. **HONORS/ACHIEVEMENTS:** Cit one of seven rotarians Intl Mag 1973; hon chmn Regional Expansion Counc 1973; outstndg alumni awd Hampton Inst 1979.

SCOTT, JOHN SHERMAN
Educator, writer. **PERSONAL:** Born Jul 20, 1937, Bellaire, OH; son of George Scott and Beauta Scott; married Sharon A Riley, 1982; children: Jon-Jama Scott, Jasmin Evangelene Scott. **EDUCATION:** SC State U, BA 1961; Bowling Green U, MA 1966; PhD 1972.

CAREER: Bowling Green State Univ OH, prof ethnic studies & resident-writer 1970-; director, Ethnic Cultural Arts Program. **ORGANIZATIONS:** Consultant Toledo Model Cities Prog 1969-72; consult Toledo Bd Edn; mem NY Dramatists League 1971-; Speech Comm Assn 1966-73; Eugene O'Neill Memorial Theatre Center 1970-; Frank Silvera Writer's Wrkshp 1973-. **HONORS/ACHIEVEMENTS:** Pub articles Players Black Lines; plays performed, Off-Broadway, NYC; Ride a Black Horse, Negro Ensemble Company 1972; Karma and The Goodship Credit, Richard Allen Center 1978-79. **MILITARY SERVICE:** AUS pfc 1961-64. **BUSINESS ADDRESS:** Prof of Ethnic Studies & Resident-Writer, Bowling Green State Univ, Shatzel Hall, Bowling Green, OH 43402.

SCOTT, JOHN T.
Educator. **PERSONAL:** Born Jun 30, 1940, New Orleans, LA; married Anna Rita Smith; children: Maria Laland, Tyra Lurana, Lauren Rita, Alanda Judith, Ayo Yohance. **EDUCATION:** Xavier Univ, BA 1962; MI State Univ, MFA 1965. **CAREER:** Xavier Univ of LA, prof of art 1965-85. **ORGANIZATIONS:** Mem, Galerie Simonne Stern New Orleans, LA 1984; mem Harris Brown Gallery, Boston, MA 1984; bd mem New Orleans Arts Council; bd mem vice chmn, LA State Arts Council 1984-. **HONORS/ACHIEVEMENTS:** Artist of the Yr New Orleans Mayors Awd 1979; Hand Hollow Fellow Hand Hollow Fndtn G Rickey 1983. **HOME ADDRESS:** 3861 Pauger St, New Orleans, LA 70122. **BUSINESS ADDRESS:** Professor of Art, XavierUniv of LA, 7325 Palmetto St, New Orleans, LA 70125.

SCOTT, JOSEPH WALTER
Sociology educator. **PERSONAL:** Born May 07, 1935, Detroit, MI; son of William F. Scott and Bertha Colbert Scott; divorced; children: Victor, Valli, Velissa. **EDUCATION:** Central MI U, BS 1957; IN U, MA 1959; IN U, PhD 1963. **CAREER:** Uuniv prof & chair of American Ethnic Studies Dept, prof of Sociology Dept, Univ. of Washington 1985-; Univ of Notre Dame, prof soc/anthro 1970-85;Univ of Toledo, prof of soc 1967-70;Univ of KY, prof of soc 1965-67. **ORGANIZATIONS:** Mem Amer Sociol Assn 1958-; vstg lectr num colls; mem NAACP; consult War on Poverty Prog in IN; mem CORE; Sunday school teacher Braden Meth Church inToledo; bd mem Mt Zion Baptist Church Ethnic School; mem Rainbow Coalition Organizer in SB IN; elected del State Dem Convention. **HONORS/ACHIEVEMENTS:** ldrshp awd Mil Police Offcrs Basic Sch 1963; various rsrch grants various assn 1966-72; Fulbright Scholar Argentina 1967 & 69; fellow Rockefeller Fellow 1972-73; fellow Am Council on Educ 1975-76; pub num books & arts on sociol topics 1966-. **MILITARY SERVICE:** USMPC capt 1963-65; ROTC Disting Military Student 1956-57. **BUSINESS ADDRESS:** Professor, Chairman, Univ of Washington, GN80, Seattle, WA 98118.

SCOTT, JUANITA SIMONS
Educator. **PERSONAL:** Born Jun 13, 1936, Eastover, SC; married Robert L Scott; children: Robert vincent, Felicia C, Julian C. **EDUCATION:** Clinton Jr Coll, AA 1956; Livingstone Coll, BS 1958; Atlanta Univ, MS 1962; Univ of SC, EdD 1979. **CAREER:** Benedict Coll, minority biomedical researcher; Area Health Educ Center Med Univ SC, consultant; Benedict Coll, minority pre-med advisor, instructor biology 1963-64, instructor 1965-69, asst prof biology 1969-72, asst prof of biol dir of biol study project 1972-80, prof biology 1972-81; Morris Coll, instructor 1964-65; Benedict Coll, prof biology head dept of biol science 1981-. **ORGANIZATIONS:** Past pres PTA UNCF Faculty Fellowship 1979; mem Central Midlands Reg Planning Coun, Zeta Phi Beta, Antioch AME Church. **HONORS/ACHIEVEMENTS:** NSF Awd 1960-61; Outstanding Educators Am 1971; YWCA Career Women's Recognition Awd 1980; Beta Kappa Chi Hon Soc. **BUSINESS ADDRESS:** Head Dept of Biological Scis, Benedict College, Horden & Blanding Sts, Columbia, SC 29204.

SCOTT, JUDITH SUGG
Lawyer, executive. **PERSONAL:** Born Aug 30, 1945, Washington, DC; daughter of Irvin D. Sugg and Bernice Humphrey Sugg; married Robert C. Scott, Jan 02, 88; children: Carmen, Nichole. **EDUCATION:** Virginia State Coll, Petersburg VA, BS; Swarthmore Coll, Swarthmore PA, post-baccalaureate degree; Catholic Univ School of Law, Washington DC, JD,. **CAREER:** Virginia Housing Devel Authority, Richmon VA, sr counsel in real estate and bond financing; office of Gov Charles Robb, sr counsel in policy and legislative devel and implementation; Systems Mgmt American Corp, corp vice pres and gen counsel in corp affairs, corp sec. **ORGANIZATIONS:** Mem, American Bar Assn, Virginia State Bar, Norfolk and Portsmouth Bar Assn; chmn, Governor's War on Drugs Task Force. **HONORS/ACHIEVEMENTS:** Rockefeller Foundation fellow; outstanding woman award from Iota Phi Lambda; named Virgina Woman of Achievement in Govt and Virginia's Outstanding Woman Atty. **BUSINESS ADDRESS:** Systems Mgmt Amer Corp, 254 Monticello Ave, Norfolk, VA 23510.

SCOTT, JULIUS S., JR.
Educational administrator. **PERSONAL:** Born Feb 26, 1925, Houston, TX; son of Julius Sebastian Scott and Bertha Bell Scott; married Ianthia Ann; children: Julius III, David K, Lamar K. **EDUCATION:** Wiley College, Marshall TX, AB, 1945; Garrett Theological Seminary, Evanston IL, BD, 1949; Brown Univ, Providence RI, AM, 1964; Boston Univ, Boston MA, PhD, 1968. **CAREER:** Massachusetts Institute of Technology, Cambridge MA, Meth campus minister, 1960-61; Wesleyan Foundation, Houston TX, chair of united ministries, 1961-63; Southern Fellowships Fund, Atlanta GA, asst dir, 1967-69; Spelman College, Atlanta GA, special asst to pres, 1972-74; Paine College, Augusta GA, pres, 1970-82; Division of Higher Education, Board of Higher Education, Nashville TN, assoc gen secy, 1982-88; Paine College, Augusta GA, pres, 1988—. **ORGANIZATIONS:** American Sociological Assn, American Assn Univ Professors, Black Methodists for Church Renewal, Society for Educational Reconstruction. **HONORS/ACHIEVEMENTS:** Citizen of Year Award, Augusta Chapter Association of Social Workers, 1982; distinguished alumnus award, Boston Univ, 1987; Alumni Hall of Fame, Wiley College, 1988.

SCOTT, LARRY B.
Actor. **PERSONAL:** Born Aug 17, 1961, New York, NY. **EDUCATION:** John Bowne, diploma 1978. **CAREER:** Films, Extreme Prejudice, Space Camp, Iron Eagle, Inside Adam Swit, That Was Then This Is Now, Revenge of the Nerds, Karate Kid, A Hero Ain't Nothing But a Sandwich, Theives; TV, The Liberators, Children of Time Square, Grand Babies, All for One, Rag Tag Champs, Roll of Thunder Hear My Cry, The Jerk Too, One in a Million, Siege, Wilma, Magnum PI, The Jeffersons, St Elsewhere, Hill St Blues, Trapper John MD, Benson, Quincy, Lou Grant, Teachers Only, Rightous Apples, Barney Miller; Theater, 227, Back to Back, Eden, The Wizard of Oz. **HONORS/ACHIEVEMENTS:** Best Supporting Actor Virgin Islands Film Festival movie "A Hero Ain't Nothing But a Sandwich"; Outstanding Achievement in Theatre for play "Eden" Ensemble Perf 1980; LA Drama Critics Awd. **BUSINESS ADDRESS:** 6834 Hollywood Blvd, Ste 303, Los Angeles, CA 90028.

SCOTT, LEON LEROY
Certified public accountant. **PERSONAL:** Born Aug 08, 1941, Charleston, SC; married Veryl J Wells; children: Leon L Jr, Helen E, Woodrow L, Frederick W. **EDUCATION:** Howard Univ, BA 1968. **CAREER:** Ernst & Whinney CPA's, sr accountant 1967-72; Howard Univ, internal audit mgr 1972-74, asst to the comptroller 1974-75; Lincoln Univ, vice pres 1975-76; Metropolitan Comm Colls, comptroller/dir of accounting 1976-80; Norfolk State Univ, vice pres for finance and business 1980-. **ORGANIZATIONS:** Mem Amer Inst of Certified Public Accountants, Assoc of Coll and Univ Auditors, Dist of Columbia Inst of Certified Public Accountants, Norfolk Council Hampton Roads Chamber of Commerce, Inst of Internal Auditors, Natl Assoc of Black Accountants, Natl Assoc of Coll & Univ Business Officers, MO Assoc of Comm and Jr Colls, Financial Execs Inst, VA Exec Inst. **MILITARY SERVICE:** USMC corpl 5 yrs; Good Conduct Medal; Marksman Awd. **BUSINESS ADDRESS:** VP for Finance & Business, Norfolk State University, 2401 Corprew Ave, Norfolk, VA 23504.

SCOTT, LEONARD LAMAR
Educator. **PERSONAL:** Born Aug 09, 1924, Cherokee Cty, AL; married Velma J Turner; children: Patricia Ann Lee, Bernard Lewis, Brenda Louise Stallworth, Curtis Lamar. **EDUCATION:** Tuskegee Inst, BS 1951; Univ of PA, 1963; UCLA, 1972; Northwestern, 1974; Tuskegee Inst Grad Study 28 hrs 1979. **CAREER:** High School Coach;, basketball, track, tennis, volley ball 1951-55; Little League, coach 1954-63; Scout Master, 1954-63; Natl Rehab Assoc, liaison officer; South East Chap Amer Corrective Therapy Assoc, pres 1974-75; Mt Olive Baptist Church, supt of sunday school 1976-; vice chmn Deacon Bd; AFGE #110 pres 1964-; VAMC Rehab Med, suprv clinical training, chief corrective therapy. **ORGANIZATIONS:** Registrar Civil Serv Reg & Voter's Act 1965; mem Tuskegee Civic Assoc 1966; rep VA Council 1980-83; sgt at arms AL State Council AFGE 1980-81; chaplain AFGE 5th Dist 1982-; mem NAACP, KAY, Kappa Delta Pi; life mem DAV; mem Minuteman Society, Natl SS Society. **HONORS/ACHIEVEMENTS:** Disting Serv Awd Scouting 1963; Professional Article publ by ACTA Jrnl "Corrective Therapy as Profession" 1975-76; Curriculum Unpubl for Maj in Phys Ed & Corrective Therapy; Compiled Clinical Training Handbook for VAMC Tuskegee AL Rehab Svc; pres AL Res Officers Minute Man Award recorded in the Res Officers Hall of Fame State Capital Montgomery, AL 1977; Presenters Awd for Delivery of Speech to HS AL 1983; Stanley H Wertz Awd for Achievement in Corrective Therapy1986; Outstanding Performance Awd 1986. **MILITARY SERVICE:** AUS tech sgt 2 1/2 yrs; USAF maj 21 yrs; Good Conduct Medal, Asiatic Campaign & Serv Medal, WWII Victory Medal, European Middle East Medal. **HOME ADDRESS:** 904 Howard Road, Tuskegee Institute, AL 36088. **BUSINESS ADDRESS:** Clinical Trainee Superv VAMC, VAMC, Corrective Therapy Dept, Tuskegee, AL 36083.

SCOTT, LEONARD STEPHEN (STEVE)
Dentist. **PERSONAL:** Born Feb 28, 1949, Indianapolis, IN; married Christine Tyson; children: John, Bryant, Nathan, Leonard, Lynna, Melanie, Katherine. **EDUCATION:** IN Univ Med Ctr, attended 1976; IN Univ Sch Dentistry, DDS 1973. **CAREER:** Leonbea Inc, pres; Tyscott Inc Recording Co, pres; Scott Manor Nursing Home Inc, pres; Private Practice, LS Scott DDS. **ORGANIZATIONS:** Mem Amer Dental Assn; mem Indianapolis Dist Dental Soc; IN State Health Facility Admin; mem IN Dental Assn; mem Natl Dental Assn; mem Omega Psi Phi Frat; mem NAACP; tst Christ Ch Apostolic; bd dir sec Christ Ch Apostolic; bd dir Wheeler's Boy's Club; mem AO Dental Frat; vice pres Gospel MusicAssn; mem Natl Acad of Recording Arts & Sciences; pres Circle City Records; pres Gospel Excellence Ministries Inc. **HONORS/ACHIEVEMENTS:** Fellow Acad Gen Dentistry. **BUSINESS ADDRESS:** Dentist, 3532 N Keystone Ave, Indianapolis, IN 46218.

SCOTT, LEVAN RALPH
Educational administrator. **PERSONAL:** Born Jun 26, 1915, Muncie, IN; son of John Scott and Fay Scott; married Ogretta M Clemens; children: Diana, Lavonne Floyd. **EDUCATION:** Ball St U, BS 1958, MS 1963, EdD 1973. **CAREER:** Mammoth Life Ins Co, mgr 1948-53; Intl Harvester, ind rltns 1954-56; Ft Wayne Comm Schls, tchr 1958-62, elem prin 1965-76, reg dir elem ed 1977-80, asst supt 1980-87 (retired). **ORGANIZATIONS:** Bd of dir Parkview Hosp; Am Red Cross; bd of Dir Summet Bank; bd of dir Ft Wayne Chamber of Com; Kappa Alphi Pi; Phil Delta Kappa; Am Asso of Sch Adm; Natl Ed Asso. **HONORS/ACHIEVEMENTS:** Liberty Bell Awd Allen Co Bar Asso 1970; Public Citizens Awd Natl Soc Wrkrs 1974; Allen Co United Way Dist Serv 1975; Dist Alum Awd Ball St Univ 1971; honarary degree Doctor of Human Letters IN Univ 1988. **HOME ADDRESS:** 1922 Hazelwood Dr, Fort Wayne, IN 46805. **BUSINESS ADDRESS:** Assistant Superintendent, Fort Wayne Community Schools, 1230 S Clinton, Fort Wayne, IN 46802.

SCOTT, LEWIS NATHANEL
Government official, business executive. **PERSONAL:** Born Mar 06, 1938, Eastover, SC; married Julia Louise Woodard; children: Brenda, Anthony, Gwendolyn, Casaundra, Gretta. **CAREER:** Football player 1953-57; night club, restaurant mgr 1962-71; Robinson & Son & Milligan funeral Home, mgr 1965-; Richland Cty Election Commun, poll mgr 1976-; Town of Eastover, mayor 1972-. **ORGANIZATIONS:** Exec comm Natl Conf of Mayors 1973, C of C 1974-; supr Richland Cty Publ Works 1971-; chmn deacon bd Mt Zion Bapt Church 1974, State of SC Criminal Justice Acad 1974, SC Water Assoc 19877, Midland Reg Plng Council 1974-, Gov Beautification Com 1974-. **HONORS/ACHIEVEMENTS:** Cert of Appreciation Richland Cty Dem party 1969-70. **BUSINESS ADDRESS:** Mayor, Town of Eastover, PO Box 36, Eastover, SC 29044.

SCOTT, LINZY, JR.
Physician. **PERSONAL:** Born Jul 04, 1934, Newark, NJ; son of Linzy Scott and Ruby Scott; divorced; children: Gina Ann, Linzy III. **EDUCATION:** Lincoln Univ PA, BA 1957; Fisk Univ, MA 1959; Howard Univ, MD 1963. **CAREER:** NJ NG, hdqtrs phys 1964-68; NJ Coll of Med, instr 1968-70; Crippled Children's Hosp, lectr phys 1968-70; Holy Family Hosp, phys 1970-75; SW CommHosp, chairperson disaster prog 1970-76; Hughes Spalding Pav, phys 1970-76; SW Comm Hosp, initiator pain clinic 1977; GA State Med Assn, clinical studies 1977; SW Comm Hosp, chief of ortho 1970-78; NJ Rehab Commn, ortho consul 1973-;

Social Security Admin, phys 1973-; Gen Motors Corp, phys 1975-; GA Rehab Commn, phys 1976-; SW Ortho Asso, orthopedic surg 1970-, pres. **ORGANIZATIONS:** Mem Amer Med Assn, Atlanta Med Assn, Atlanta Ortho Soc, Eastern Ortho Soc, Natl Med Assn; diplomate Amer Bd of Orthopedic Surgeons; fellow AmerAcad of Orthopedic Surgeons; fellow Amer Acad for Cerebral Palsy; mem Gladden Mem Orthopedic Soc; certified by Amer Bd of Orthopedic Surgery; licensed in MD 1963, NJ 1965, CA 1968, OR 1968, GA 1970; fndr Pastoral Prog Southwest Comm Hosp. **HONORS/ACHIEVEMENTS:** Amer Acad for Cerebral Palsy Fellowship 1967-68; Olympic Team Physician 1981; physician for Gold Medalist Natl Amateur Basketball Team 1983; Benjamin E Mays Appreciation Awd 1983; Amer Med Assn Negotiation Awd; Howard Univ Alumni Soc; Amer Acad of Family Physicians 1983; inventor Scott Spiral Knee Brace 1980; numerous presentations. **MILITARY SERVICE:** NJ NG capt med corps 1964-68. **BUSINESS ADDRESS:** President, SW Ortho Associates, 2085 Campbelton Rd SW, Atlanta, GA 30311.

SCOTT, MARVIN BAILEY
Management consultant. **PERSONAL:** Born Mar 10, 1944, Henderson, NC; son of Robert Scott and Gertrude (Bailey) Scott; married Carol A Johnson, Oct 15, 1967; children: Robert B, Cinda P. **EDUCATION:** Attended Univ of Allahabad, India, one yr; Johnson C Smith U, BA Psych 1966;Univ of Pittsburgh, MEd 1968, PhD 1970. **CAREER:** Boston Univ Sch of Ed, assoc prof dean 1970-79; Boston U, asst to Provost 1979-80;Univ of MA Office to Pres, ACE fellowship 1979-80; ATEX Computers, dir of human rsrs 1980-82; St of MA, asst to chancellor prof, 1983-86; St Paul's Coll, Lawrenceville, VA, pres, 1986-88; Marvin B Scott Assoc, pres, 1988-. **ORGANIZATIONS:** Vice pres, Bd of Intl Visitors; NAACP Sch Desegration Cases 1981-84; vice pres Minuteman Cncl BSA; bd dir Black Media Coalition Wash DC.; mem, Old Dominion Area Coun of Boy Scouts of Amer; sec and exec bd mem, Central Intercoll Athletic Assn; mem, Comm Adv Bd, Brunswick Correctional Ctr, Lawrenceville. **HONORS/ACHIEVEMENTS:** Kappa Alpha Psi Dist Serv Awd 1978; Am Cncl on Ed Flwshp in Acdmc Adm 1979-80; Silver Beaver Awd, Boy Scouts of America, 1984; host of radio talk show, WRKO, Boston, 1982-86; host of "Central VA Focus" TV program, WPLZ, Richmond, VA, 1987-88; author of books The Essential Profession, Five Essential Dimensions of Curriculum Design, and Schools on Trial; author of chapter in The Future of Big-City Schools. **HOME ADDRESS:** 8 Springdale Rd, Lexington, MA 02173. **BUSINESS ADDRESS:** Consultant, Marvin B Scott Associates, 8 Springdale Rd, Lexington, MA 02173.

SCOTT, MARVIN WAYNE
Educator. **PERSONAL:** Born Jan 21, 1952, Philadelphia, PA; son of Albert Scott and Maloy Scott; married Marcia Annette Simons, Nov 23, 1973; children: Thembi L, Kori A. **EDUCATION:** East Stroudsburg Univ, BS 1973; OH State Univ, MA 1974; Univ of NC, Greensboro, EdD, 1986. **CAREER:** Miami Dade Community Coll, asst prof, 1974-78; Howard Comm Coll, assoc prof, 1979-87; Univ of Maryland, asst prof, 1987-. **ORGANIZATIONS:** Scholarship Comm, MD Assn for Health, Physical Educ, Recreation & Dance, 1980, 1984; Comm to investigate greater involvement, EDA Amer Alliance for Health, Physical Educ, Recreation & Dance 1981; Nom Comm, Natl Assn for Sport & Physical Educ, 1982; curriculum consultant, Hampton Inst, 1982, MD State Dept of Ed, 1982; program evaluator, Univ of MD, Batlimore, 1984. **HONORS/ACHIEVEMENTS:** Published, "Miami Dade South Basketball Motion Offense" 1978, "In Persuit of the Perfect Job, A Philosophical Fable" 1979. **BUSINESS ADDRESS:** Asst Professor, Univ of Maryland, Little Patuxent Pkwy, Columbia, MD 21044.

SCOTT, MARY SHY
Educator, music consultant. **PERSONAL:** Born Jul 19, Atlanta, GA; daughter of Robert Shy; married Alfred Scott; children: Alfredene Scott Cheely, Arthur Robert, 1st Lt Alfred Jr. **EDUCATION:** Spelman Coll, AB 1950; NY Univ, MA 1969; post grad study, NY Univ and GA State Univ. **CAREER:** Pres, Scott Assoc; Atlanta Public Schs, music specialist beginning1950; Alpha Kappa Alpha Sor Inc, S Atlantic regional dir, 1st Natl VP, natl pres, 1990-. **ORGANIZATIONS:** Natl arts chairlady Alpha Kappa Alpha Sor Inc 1980-82; arts chairlady LINKS Inc 1984-; mem Music Educators Natl Conf 1985; mem GA Music Educs Assn 1985; mem/steward Allen Temple AME Church 1985; Peachtree Chapter of LINKS, Inc, pres 1987; SCLC, bd mem 1987; member, Top Ladies of Distinction Inc. **HONORS/ACHIEVEMENTS:** Basilius Award, Alpha Kappa Alpha, 1978; Golden Dove Award, Kappa Omega Chapter, Alpha Kappa Alpha, 1980; Negro Heritage Bronze Woman of the Year Fine Arts Iota Phi Lambda Sor 1980; World Who's Who of Women 1980; meritorious serv award, Omega Psi Phi, 1987; Keys to the cities of Pansacola, Thomasville, Columbus, GA, Orlando, Augusta, Selma, Long Beach, and Kansas City; Mary Shy Scott Day in Kansas City, Macon, Fulton County, Charleston, SC, and Miami; honorary citizen of Columbus, GA, Huntsville, Jacksonville, Little Rock, Baltimore, and State of AL; honorary lt, State of Alabama, 1988; drama "And These Came Forth" co-author 1980; "Kappa Omega Chorus In Concert" recording Mark label 1980. **HOME ADDRESS:** 2781 Baker Ridge Dr NW, Atlanta, GA 30318. **BUSINESS ADDRESS:** President, Scott Associates, 2781 Baker Ridge Dr NW, Atlanta, GA 30318.

SCOTT, MELVINA BROOKS
Insurance agent, us congressional caseworker. **PERSONAL:** Born Mar 19, 1948, Goodman, MS; daughter of Shed Brooks and Sabina Walker Brooks; divorced; children: Johnny F Jr, James T, Kateea P. **EDUCATION:** Hawkeye Inst of Tech, grad life underwriting assn tng; Univ of Northern IA, BA Social Work 1976; Wartsburg Coll, Cert, Mgmt By Objective, Community Law, Affirmative Action Substance Abuse 1985. **CAREER:** Prudential Insur Co, dist agt 1977-; Black Hawk Co Dept of Corr Svc, probation ofcr 1976-77; Minority Alcoholism Counc, 1975-76; Area Educ Agency VII, media clerk 1968-75; political consult 1978-86; Cutler for Congress, political cons; All State Ins, 1981-85; Waterloo Comm Schools, 7th grade basketball coach 1985-; Nagle for Congress, political cons 1986; Congressman David Nagle, caseworker/staff asst, currently. **ORGANIZATIONS:** Polit acton counc mem Life Underwriters Assn 1978-; vice pres of bd Logandate Coop Daycare 1977-; youth adv, vice pres Black Hawk Co NAACP 1976-80; chair dem party Black Hawk Co 1974-78; civic com memberships C of C Com Delta Sigma Theta 1977-79; Comm Devel Com Funding Layman Orgn Payne AME Ch; mem Payne AME; com mem Minority Drug Counc Intl Women's Yr Com Del to Houston; co mem Third Dist Affir Action Com; ward leader Dem Party Central Com 1980-; vchair IA Black Caucus; bd treas NHS 1983-86; Mayor Review Committee on Streets 1988-89; Mayor Review Committee on Area Economic Devel 1989. **HONORS/ACHIEVEMENTS:** Nat Sale Achvmt Awd 1978, 80; Personality of Midwest & West Am Biog Inst 1978; Serv Awd Boy's Club of Waterloo 1977; Outstdg Young Women of Am, Outstdg Student, Culture of GhettoUniv of No IA 1975. **HOME ADDRESS:** 413 Oneida St, Waterloo, IA 50703. **BUSINESS ADDRESS:** Congressional Caseworker, Congressman Dave Nagle, 524 Washington St, Waterloo, IA 50703.

SCOTT, MONA VAUGHN
Educator. **PERSONAL:** Born in Jackson, MS; married Dr Richard; children: Monika, Sean, Malaika. **EDUCATION:** Coll of Pacific, BA;Univ of Pacific, MA; Stanford U, PhD 1977. **CAREER:** Scotts Intl Research & Educ Consultant Organ, exec dir researcher; Univ of CA Dental School, teacher; Natl Med Assn, research cons; Golden State Med Assn, research cons; Black Repertory Group, research cons; WA Sch of Psychiatry & George Wash Univ, dir of research on soc servs 1966; Univ of CA Dental School on Minority Admissions Comm, consultant 1969; Gen Admissions Com Dental School of Univ of San Fran, consultant 1969; MAHLCOM (Min Allied Hlth League Concentration on Motivation), founder dir consultant 1970-75; Family Background & Family Lifestyles of Minorities in San Fran, dir of research 1971-73. **ORGANIZATIONS:** Mem CATESOL CA Assn of Tchrs of Eng as a Second Lang; dir SIRECO; mem BAABP Bay Area Assn of Blk Psychologists; mem NAACP; mem ORCHESIS; mem HonorSoc Nat Modern Dance. **HONORS/ACHIEVEMENTS:** Tulley Knowles Schlrshp Philosophy Inst; Mary R Smith Schlrshp; outstdg Nat Meth Student Schlrshp; 2 time winner Nat Meth Schlrshp; Ambassadors AwdsComm Serv Wash, DC; Women of Yr Awd Delta Theta Nu 1964; Dept of Behavioral Tech Awd Westinghouse; pub "The Efficacy of Tuition-Retention Progs for Minorities" Westinghouse Div of Behavioral Tech 1967-68; "White Racism & Black Power" pub by Meth Pub House TN 1969; co-author "Algerian Interview with Kathleen Cleaver" Black Scholar Mag 1972; co-author "Institutional Racism in Urban Sch" pub by StanfordUniv Center for Educ Rsrch 1975; num other publ.

SCOTT, NATHAN A., JR.
Educator. **PERSONAL:** Born Apr 24, 1925, Cleveland, OH; son of Nathan Alexander Scott and Maggie Martin Scott; married Charlotte Hanley; children: Nathan A, III, Leslie Ashamu. **EDUCATION:** Univ of MI, BA 1944; Union Theol Sem, MDiv 1946; Columbia Univ, PhD 1949. **CAREER:** VA Union Univ, dean of the chapel 1946-47; Howard Univ, assoc prof of humanities 1948-55; Univ of Chicago, prof of theology and literature 1955-76; Univ of VA, Wm R Kenan prof of religious studies, prof of English 1976-. **ORGANIZATIONS:** Amer Philosophical Assn; Amer Acad of Religion; Modern Language Assn; Soc for Values in Higher Educ; advisory editor, The Virginia Quarterly Review, Callalloo, Modernist Studies (Univ of Alberta); mem of bd of consultants and co-editor The Journal of Religion; mem advisory bd, Religion & Literature, Religion and Intellectual Life, The Journal of Literature and Theology. **HONORS/ACHIEVEMENTS:** LittD, Ripon Coll, 1965; LHD, Wittenberg Univ, 1965; DD, Philadelphia Divinity School, 1967; STD, Gen Theological Seminary, 1968; LittD, St Mary's Coll Notre Dame, 1969; LHD, Univ of DC, 1976; LittD, Denison Univ, 1976; LittD, Brown Univ, 1981; LittD, Northwestern Univ, 1982; DD, Virginia Theological Seminary, 1985; HumD, Univ of Michigan, 1988; LittD, Elizabethtown Coll, 1989; LittD, Wesleyan Univ, 1989; fellow, Amer Acad of Arts and Sciences, 1979; author, 25 books; contributor, 42 books; Amer Acad of Religion vice pres 1984, pres-elect 1985, pres 1986. **HOME ADDRESS:** 1419 Hilltop Rd, Charlottesville, VA 22903. **BUSINESS ADDRESS:** Prof Religious Studies & English, Univ of Virginia, Dept of Religious Studies, Charlottesville, VA 22903.

SCOTT, NIGEL L.
Attorney. **PERSONAL:** Born Aug 23, 1940; married Monica Chasteau; children: Duane, Omar, Rion. **EDUCATION:** Howard U, BS Chem 1970; Howard Univ Sch of Law, JD 1973. **CAREER:** Scott & Yallery-Arthur, atty 1980-; Atty, pvt prac 1975-79; Eastman Kodak, patent atty 1973-75. **ORGANIZATIONS:** Mem DC PA & US Patent Bars 1975-; exec dir Nat Patent Law Assn 1979-; adv mem Hum Rghts Commn Montgomery Co 1980; pres Trinidad & Tobago Assn of Wash DC 1977-79. **BUSINESS ADDRESS:** 7603 Georgia Ave NW, #304, Washington, DC 20012.

SCOTT, OSBORNE E.
Educator. **PERSONAL:** Born Feb 05, 1916, Gloucester, VA; married Jean Sampson; children: Osborne, Jr, Michael D. **EDUCATION:** Hampton Inst, BS 1938; Oberlin Grad Sch of Theol, BD 1941; Tchrs Coll Columbia U, MA 1951. **CAREER:** Dept of Black Studies City Coll of NY, prof 1972-; Dept of Urban & Ethnic Studies, prof & chmn 1964-71; Am Leprosy Missions, exec vice pres 1964-69; Hampton Inst, asst to pres 1941. **ORGANIZATIONS:** Sr asso Ldrshp Res Inc 1970-; bd dir Ch World Serv Nat Council of Chs; mem N Am Proj Comm Org; World Counc of Chs; NY State Welfare Assn; sr asso ldrshp Res Inc WA; bd dir Cncl for Econ Devel & Empowerment Black People; co-chmn African Academy of Arts & Rsrch Inc; minstr Trinity Bapt Ch Brooklyn NY; chmn fac sen City Coll of NY 1980. **HONORS/ACHIEVEMENTS:** Outstndg alumnus Hampton Inst 1948; Who's Who in the East 1974-79; Dictnry of Intl Biog 1975-79. **MILITARY SERVICE:** AUS lt col 1941-64. **BUSINESS ADDRESS:** Professor, City College of New York, 138 St & Convent Ave, New York, NY 10031.

SCOTT, OTIS
Educator, county councilman. **PERSONAL:** Born Sep 19, 1919, Lynchburg, SC; son of Ed Scott and Emma Green Scott; married Wilhelmenia Dennis; children: Myrtle Scott Johnson, Otis Jr, Linda Scott Norwood. **EDUCATION:** Morris Coll, BA; Columbia U, MA; Univ of SC. **CAREER:** Sumter County School District #2, teacher, county councilman; Vet on the Job Training, instructor; Lower Lee School, teacher, basketball coach; Delaine Elementary School, teacher; Ebenezer Jr High School Sumter County Educ Assn, teacher. **ORGANIZATIONS:** Assn of Classroom Teachers; SC Educ Assn; bd dir NEA Boylan Haven-Mather Acad; mem bd dir Proj T Sq; Sumter County Econ Opportunity; Day Care Ctr; Sumter County Democratic Party; pres Voters Precinct #1; Notary Public; master mason Prince Hall Affil; mem NAACP; Shriner; pastor Mt Nebo Bapt Church Jerusalem Baptist & Barnettesville Baptist Church 1952-70; pastor Mt Moriah Baptist Church 1970-; field worker Morris Coll; clerk Wateree Assn LD; moderator Lynches River Union; clerk Sunday School Conv; instructor Ann Inst Mt Moriah Assn; mem Natl Prog Conv; helped establish & build day care centers Rembert Horatio Comm; built churches Lee Co Clarendon Do; councilman, Natl Assn of Counties, 1984-; councilman, South Carolina Assn of Counties, 1984-; bd mem, Hillcrest High School Foundation, 1988-; bd mem, Minority Scholarship Comm, Sumter School District 17, 1989-. **HONORS/ACHIEVEMENTS:** Distinguished Alumnus Award, Morris College, 1988; Special Recognition Award, Morris College, 1989. **MILITARY SERVICE:** Served 4 yrs in AF; 1 yr in US, 3 yrs in Asiatic Pacific 1941-45.

SCOTT, PORTIA ADELE (A. THOMAS)
Business executive. **PERSONAL:** Born Nov 01, 1946, Port Chester, NY. **EDUCATION:**

Pace U; NY U; Katherine Gibbs Sch Bus, 1974. **CAREER:** Atlanta Daily World, assoc edtr; Mutual Broadcasting Sys, mgr spl projs; ABC Leisure Mags NYC, advertising rep 1978; ABC Inc, exec asst, rsrchr corp affairs 1974-78; ABC News, admin asst pres 1969-74; ABC News, exec sec 1965-69. **ORGANIZATIONS:** Chmn Minority Emplyes Assn 1976-78; pres NAACP Yth Chap Port Chester 1962-64; mem Am Women in Radio & TV; mem NAACP; Urban Leag; Nat Cncl Negro Women; Nat Hookup of Black Women. **HONORS/ACHIEVEMENTS:** Winner oratorical contest BPOE Mamaroneck; singer Westchester Co All-Country Choir 1963-64; nightclub singer 1974-; collaborated with dir off- b'way Show.

SCOTT, R. LEE
Dist manager/utility. **PERSONAL:** Born Oct 08, 1943, Hollywood, AL; married Mae Frances Kline; children: Ronald, Lynne. **EDUCATION:** Univ of CT, BA 1966; Univ of Hartford, MBA 1977; Cornell Univ, Exec Dev Prog 1984. **CAREER:** Aetna Life & Casualty Ins, sr underwriter 1966-70; So New England Telecom, district staff mgr int auditing 1970-. **ORGANIZATIONS:** Mem Alpha Phi Alpha Frat 1968-; adjunct prof Univ of Hartford 1978-; mem Sigma Pi Phi Frat 1981-; pres Scott & Assocs 1983-; mem HFD Child & Family Serv 1984-; mem New Britain NAACP; bd dir Indian Hills Country Club Newington CT. **HONORS/ACHIEVEMENTS:** Certificate of Recognition Natl Alliance of Businessmen 1973; Outstanding Young Man of Amer Natl Jaycees 1978,80; Disting Minority Grad Univ of CT 1984; article "Make Your Class Room Time Count," Minority Educ Philadelphia 1980, preprinted by Northern MI Univ in career newsletter 1980; case study Personnel Assessment Ctrs in Collaboration in Organization, Alternatives to Hierarchy by William A Kraus, Human Sciences Press NY 1980. **HOME ADDRESS:** 87 Little Brook Dr, Newington, CT 06111.

SCOTT, RACHEL LORAINE
Business executive. **PERSONAL:** Born Jun 05, 1954, Bristol, TN; daughter of Melton Scott and Elizabeth Gose Scott. **EDUCATION:** Radford Univ, BS 1976. **CAREER:** Bank of VA, admin asst 1976-77; Central Fidelity Bank NA, asst vice pres 1977-82; Citizens & Southern Natl Bank, vp/domestic funding mngr 1982-. **ORGANIZATIONS:** Advisor Jr Achievement of Richmond 1977-82; mem Natl Assoc of Bank Women 1980-, Jr Chamber of Commerce 1981, Career Ed Committee; mem Atlanta Urban Bankers Assoc, Atlanta Assoc of Women in Securities, Natl Assoc of Securities Professionals. **BUSINESS ADDRESS:** Vice President, Citizens & Southern Natl Bk, 34 Broad St, Atlanta, GA 30302.

SCOTT, RICHARD ELEY
Judge. **PERSONAL:** Born Dec 25, 1945, Kilgore, TX. **EDUCATION:** Prairie View A&M U, BA 1968; Univ of TX, JD 1972. **CAREER:** Travis Co TX, justice of the peace 1975-; Austin Comm Coll, part-time instr 1973; TX Stdte Rep Eddie B Johnson, legal asst 1973; Priv Prac, law 1972. **ORGANIZATIONS:** NAACP; Travis Co Jr Bar Assn 1973; State Bar TX 1972; sponsoring com Austin Urban League 1977; com chmn on adm State Bar of TX 1976; Rishon Lodge # 1 1977; E Austin Youth Found Coach 1976; Nat Bar Assn 1975; Del Dem Nat Conv 1972; floor whip US Sen Humphrey 1972. **HONORS/ACHIEVEMENTS:** Who's Who in Am Politics 1974; Who's Who in Politics in the S & SW 1974;Outstdg Young Men of Am 1974. **BUSINESS ADDRESS:** 3230 E Martin Luther King, Austin, TX 78721.

SCOTT, ROBERT CORTEZ
Attorney. **PERSONAL:** Born Apr 30, 1947, Washington, DC; son of C Waldo Scott and Mae H Scott. **EDUCATION:** Harvard Coll, BA 1969; Boston Coll Law Sch, JD 1973. **CAREER:** Atty at law 1973-; VA Gen Assembly, delegate 1978-83; Senate of Virginia, senator 1983-. **ORGANIZATIONS:** Mem Newport News Old Dominion Bar Assn 1973-; pres Peninsula Bar Assn 1974-78; golden herit life mem NAACP 1976-; pres Peninsula Legal Aid Cntr Inc 1976-81; chmn 1st Congressional Dist Dem Com 1980-85; vchmn VA Dem Black Caucus 1980; del Nat Dem Convention l980; mem Hampton Inst Annual Fund Com; bd mem Peninsula Assn Sickle Cell Anemia & Peninsula Coun Boy Scouts of Am; mem March of Dimes, Alpha Phi Alpha, Sigma Pi Phi. **HONORS/ACHIEVEMENTS:** Outstanding Leader Hampton Roads Jaycees 1976; Man of the Year Zeta Lambda Chap Alpha Phi Alpha Frat 1977; Distinguished Comm Serv Kennedy-Evers-King Meml Found 1977; Outstanding Achievement Peninsula Nat Assn Negro Business & Professional Women 1978; Brotherhood Citation Natl Conf of Christians & Jews 1985; Public Health Recognition Award, VA Public Health Assoc, 1986; Outstanding Legislator Award, VA Chpt/Amer Pediatric Soc, 1986, honorary doctorate of Govt Science Degee, Commonwealth Coll, 1987. **MILITARY SERVICE:** MA Army Natl Guard 1970-73; AUSR 1973-76. **BUSINESS ADDRESS:** Senator, Senate of Virginia, PO Box 251, Newport News, VA 23607.

SCOTT, ROBERT L.
College executive. **PERSONAL:** Born Oct 22, 1935, Eastover, SC; married Juanita Simons; children: Robert Vincent, Felicia C, Julian C. **EDUCATION:** Blayton's Bus Coll, A 1955; Benedict Coll, BS 1968; Atlanta Univ, MBA 1969; Univ of SC, EdD 1980. **CAREER:** YMCA Atlanta, physical clerk 1954-58, night supvr 1961-62; Allied Chem Co, process controller 1962-66; Benedict Coll, admin asst to pres, dir of personnel & purchasing 1969-71, asst pres dir of personnel 1971-85; faculty dev dir 1985-. **ORGANIZATIONS:** Notary public State of SC; constable State of SC; mem Coll & Univ Personnel Assn; Gr Columbia C of C; United Way Vol Staff Richland Lexington Cos; Mason; Phi Bet Sigma; pres Corporate Bd of Greater Columbia Boys Club,. **HONORS/ACHIEVEMENTS:** Full Scholarship Atlanta Univ for one yr; grad from Benedict with high honors; Sigma Man of the Year 1986. **MILITARY SERVICE:** AUS spec E-4 1958-61. **BUSINESS ADDRESS:** Dir of Faculty Devlopmnt, Benedict College, Harden & Blanding Sts, Columbia, SC 29204.

SCOTT, ROLAND B.
Physician, educator. **PERSONAL:** Born Apr 18, 1909, Houston, TX; married Sarah Rosetta Weaver; children: Roland B Jr, Venice S Carlenius, Estelle Irene Scott. **EDUCATION:** Howard Univ, BS 1931, MD 1934; KS City Genl Hosp, internship 1934-35; Provident Hosp, pediatric residency 1935-36; Univ of Chicago, genl educ bd fellow in pediatrics 1936-39. **CAREER:** Howard Univ, faculty 1939-;, prof pediatrics 1952-77; sabbatical leave July 1, 1950 'thru June 30, 1951 for study Pediatric Allergy Inst of Allergy RooseveltHosp NYC; Skin & Cancer Hosp, courses in pediatric dermatology 1956-59; Howard Univ, dir ctr for sickle cell disease 1973-, dist prof of ped & child health 1977-, disting prof of ped & child health 1977-. **ORGANIZATIONS:** Mem editorial bd Clinical Pediatrics 1962-80; mem editorial bd Jour Natl Med Assn 1978-; consult editor Med Aspects of Human Sexuality; editorial bd Annals of Allergy 1977-80; mem Mayor's Developmental Disabilities Council of DC Re-apptd 1984; mem Corporate Bd Children's Hosp Natl Med Ctr 1984; mem Cosmos Club Washington DC 1985; participated in numerous foreign ed travel & med meetings abroad including Children's Hosp Montreal Canada, hospitals & univs in Caribbean Area, Univ of the West Indies Hosp, Children's Hosp Havana Cuba, Lisbon Portugal, Quito Ecuador; chmn Sect on Pediatrics of the Natl Medical Assn 1952-65; mem bd trustees Hospital Serv Agency of Washington; mem Med Adv Comm of the United Cerebral Palsy Assn 1951-55; mem Maternal & Child Health Comm of the Public Health Adv Council 1964-; mem Drug Experience Adv Comm & Consultant to Bureau of Medicine Public Health Serv HEW 1969-; mem Scientific Adv Comm of Natl Assn for Sickle Cell Disease Inc 1972-; mem Rsch Comm Children's Hosp Natl Medical Ctr Washington DC 1982-83. **HONORS/ACHIEVEMENTS:** Percy L Julian Awd Phi Beta Kappa Sigma Xi Howard Univ 1977 1979; Fellow Distinguished Awd Amer Coll of Allergists 1977 1985; numerous publications; GoldAwd Outstanding Employee Support United Natl Capital Area 1978; plaque Outstanding & Dedicated Serv in Fighting Sickle Cell Disease 1980; Noteworthy Serv &Illustrious Career in Sickle Cell Education & Rsch; Distinguished Serv to Health Awd Natl Assn of Med Minority Educators 1982; Who's Who in America; Who's Who in the World; Who's Who in the S & SW; Who's Who in the World; Who's Who in the United Stated; Who's Who in Community Svcs; Men of Achievement; Intl Biographical Cambridge England; Dictionary of Intl Biography Cambridge England; Notable Americans-Bibliographical Inst; People Who Matter; Plaque Section Council on Pediatrics of the AMA 1985; Amer Acad of Pediatrics Jacobi Awd 1985; One of 17 Washingtonians of the Year named by Washingtonian magazine 1986; Hon DS Howard Univ 1987. **BUSINESS ADDRESS:** Dir, Howard Univ Ctr for Sicle Cell, 2121 Georgia Ave NW, Washington, DC 20059.

SCOTT, RUTH
Government official, educator, company executive. **PERSONAL:** Born Aug 13, 1934, Albion, MI; daughter of Robert Holland and Edna Holland; married William G Scott; children: Greg, June, Chrystal. **EDUCATION:** Albion Coll, BA Social Work 1956; Kent State Univ, ME Counseling 1961; Buffalo State, 6 hrs toward EdD 1968. **CAREER:** Valley Central School NY, teacher 1961-62; Arcade Central School NY, teacher 1964-66; Educ Serv BOCES Cattaraugus Co, consultant 1966-70; City School Dist Rochester, counsultant to nursing program 1971; Wilson Jr High School, reading lab coord 1974; City School Dist Rochester, adv specialist/human relations 1975-77; The Ford Found, consultant 1976-78; Community Savings Bank of Rochester, personnel compliance coord 1977-; Rochester Community Savings Bank, regional mgr; City of Rochester, city councilwoman-at-large, council pres 1986-; Scott Assoc Consulting, pres 1989-. **ORGANIZATIONS:** Mem WXXI bd of dirs 1976-; mem Friends of Rochester Public Library 1976-; mem adv council of Women's Career Center 1977-; mem Phi Delta Kappa; exec sec Rochester Area Found; bd dir WHEC TV-10; chairperson Natl League of Cities Community & Economic Devel 1987; mem bd of dir NLC's Women in Municipal Govt, New Futures Initiative; bd vice pres Rochester Community Found. **HONORS/ACHIEVEMENTS:** Championship Debater Albion Coll 1952; Outstanding Alumni Award Albion Coll 1975; Outstanding Citizen-Politician-Christian Worker Black Student Caucus of local coll of Divinity; Honored by YWCA as one of their Women Builders of Communities and Dreams; honored as one of five businesswomen by prestigious Athena Award committee for significant conbributions in business & community; received Volunteer Serv Award Certificate from Martin Luther King Jr Greater Rochester Festival Commission. **BUSINESS ADDRESS:** Council President, Rochester City Council, 30 Church St, Rochester, NY 14614.

SCOTT, SAMUEL
Engineer. **PERSONAL:** Born Feb 02, 1946, San Francisco, CA; married Christine Mary Harrington; children: Stephany, Sybil. **EDUCATION:** Wayne State U, 1964-68. **CAREER:** Off of Film & TV Serv MI Dept of Commerce, dir present; Detroit Free Press, photo/jazz critic 1972-79; Optek Potographic, dir/photo 1971-72; Detroit News, photo 1969-71; Studio Theaters of Detroit, supr 1968-69;Univ of MI Soc Rsrch Study, coor of persnl 1967-68. **ORGANIZATIONS:** Mem MI Press Photo Assn 1972-80; exec off MI Film & TV Coun; mem Nat Assn of Film Commissions 1980. **HONORS/ACHIEVEMENTS:** 1st/2nd/3rd & hon ment MI Press Photo 1976-79; pub serv awd Wayne Co Bd of Commissioners 1979. **BUSINESS ADDRESS:** 2021 Jefferson Davis Hwy, Crystal City, Arlington, VA 22202.

SCOTT, STANLEY S.
Corporate business executive. **PERSONAL:** Born Jan 31, 1933, Bolivar, TN; married Carrie Delores Lyles; children: Kenneth, Susan, Stanley S II. **EDUCATION:** Lincoln Univ, BS Journalism 1959. **CAREER:** Memphis World, editor-general manager; Atlanta Daily World, reporter; United Press International, news reporter; NAACP, ast dir of public relations; Westinghouse Broadcasting Corp, radio newsman; White House Staff, asst dir of communications; State Dept's Agency for Intl Development, asst administrator; Philip Morris USA, vice president public affairs. **ORGANIZATIONS:** Mbr bd dirs St Luke's/Roosevelt Hospital Center; mem bd dirs Jacob K Javits Convention Center of NY; mem bd visitors NC Central Univ School of Law; vice chmn New York City Fire Safety Foundation; mem bd dirs Citizens' Rsch Foundation. **HONORS/ACHIEVEMENTS:** Apptd in 1982 by Pres Ronald Reagan as mem Adv Committee on Small and Minority Business Ownership; mem President's Commission on White House Fellowships; apptd by Gov Mario Cuomo as mem of Martin Luther King, Jr Commission; Pulitzer nomination while at UPI for eye-witness account of the assassination of civilrights advocate Malcolm X; Russwurm Awd for Excellence in Journalism; Silurians Awd, New York Newsmen; Lincoln Univ Distinguished Alumni Awd. **MILITARY SERVICE:** Served AUS 1954-56. **BUSINESS ADDRESS:** VP & Dir of Corp Affairs, Philip Morris Companies, Inc, 120 Park Ave, New York, NY 10017.

SCOTT, TIMOTHY VAN
Medical doctor-specialist-ophthalmology. **PERSONAL:** Born Jul 12, 1942, Newport News, VA; son of William H Scott and Janet H Scott; married Karen Hill Scott; children: Van, Lanita, Kevin, Amara. **EDUCATION:** Fisk U, BA 1964; Meharry Med Coll, MD 1968; Hubbard Hosp Nashville Ophthalmology Res, rotating intrnshp 1968-69; Thomas Jefferson Univ Hosp Philadelphia 1969-72; HEED Ophthalmic Found Fellow Glaucoma Jules Stein Eye Inst UCLA 1972-73. **CAREER:** Private practice; Ophthalmology Martin Luther King Jr Gen Hosp, chief div 1973-82; Glaucoma Serv Jules Stein Eye Inst UCLA Los Angeles CA, consult 1973-; Glaucoma Serv Harbor Hosp Torrance CA, 1973-79; Ophthalmologist Kaiser Hosp Torrance CA, staff 1972-73; Am Bd Ophthalmology, dip 1973-; Charles R Drew Postgrad Med Sch, asst prof surgery; Ophthalmology UCLA Sch Med, assoc prof. **ORGANIZATIONS:** Amer Assn Ophthalmology; Natl Assn Res & Interns; Soc HEED Fellows;

Omega Psi Phi Frat. **HONORS/ACHIEVEMENTS:** Outstanding Young Men of Amer 1974. **BUSINESS ADDRESS:** 323 N Prairie Ave #201, Inglewood, CA 90301.

SCOTT, VERONICA J.
Educator, physician. **PERSONAL:** Born Feb 08, 1946, Greenville, AL. **EDUCATION:** Howard U, BS 1968; Albert Einstein Clg of Med, MD 1973; UCLA Sch of Publ Hlth, MPH 1978. **CAREER:** Beth Israel Hosp Boston, MA, intern res med 1973-75; UCLA Wadsworth VA Med Ctr LA CA, fellow geriatric med 1978-80; VA Med Ctr, chief geriatrics sect 1980-; UAB Med Ctr, asst dir Center for Aging 1980-; VA Medical Ctr dir of home care 1984-86, dir of team training in geriatrics 1982-86; UAB Geriatric Educ Ctr, co-dir 1985-. **ORGANIZATIONS:** Mbr Am Ger Soc 1978-; mem Ger Soc 1978-; mem Western Ger Soc 1978-; mem Am Pub Hlth Assoc 1978-; comm mem Jeff Co Long Term Care 1982-84; chp Ombudsman Comm Visiting Nurs Assoc Prof Adv Comm 1983; co-chp VNA Med Adv Comm 1983-; comm Mayors Comm on the Status of Women 1984-. **HONORS/ACHIEVEMENTS:** Gov Awd ITTG Gov G C Wallace 1984; Natl Sci Fndtn Rsrch Awd 1965-68; Ger Med Acdmc Aws Nat Inst on Aging 1982-87; Assoc Inv Awd VA 1980. **HOME ADDRESS:** 1202 Springcreek Dr, Nashville, TN 37209. **BUSINESS ADDRESS:** Assistant Professor of Med, UAB/VA Medical Centers, 700 S 19th St, Birmingham, AL 35233.

SCOTT, WESLEY E.
Physician. **PERSONAL:** Born Mar 23, 1925, Memphis, TN; married Virginia Smith; children: Tom, Stephany. **EDUCATION:** Lemoyne Coll; Meharry Med Coll, MD 1950; NYUniv Bellevue Med Ctr, 1955. **CAREER:** Stony Brook Sch Med, clinical prof ortho 1974-; Freeport Hosp, chf ortho 1958-63; Mitchel AFB Hosp 1951-53. **ORGANIZATIONS:** Mem Am Coll Surgeons 1957; Intl Coll & Surgeons 1957; Am Bd Ortho Surgery; Am Acad Ortho; Nassau Surg Soc; Nassau Co Med Soc; NY State Med Soc; NY State Ortho Soc; Pan-Am Med Soc; Life mem NAACP; mem Negro Airmen Internat; vice pres Roosevelt NY Sch Bd 1966-69; mem Omega Psi Phi Frat. **HONORS/ACHIEVEMENTS:** Man of yr NAACP 1966. **MILITARY SERVICE:** USAF capt 1951-53.

SCOTT, WILLIAM EDD
Business executive. **PERSONAL:** Born May 12, 1944, Somerville, TN; married Melba L Winston; children: Drew, Makisha, Tauros. **EDUCATION:** Alma Coll, attended 1964-65; Wayne State Univ, attended 1965-68. **CAREER:** Crest Lincoln Mercury Inc, sales consul 1970-72; Tae Kwan Do-Ji Do Kwan Inc, vice pres 1971-78; Bob Maxey Lincoln Mercury Inc, sales consul 1972-78; Ford Motor Co, dealer trainee 1978-80; Conyers Ford Inc, gen mgr 1980-82; Bill Scott Oldsmobile Inc, pres. **ORGANIZATIONS:** Bd mem Amer Lung Assn; comm mem Sports Comm Chamber of Comm; bd mem Boy Scouts of Amer; diac candidate Archdiocese of Syracuse. **HONORS/ACHIEVEMENTS:** Top 100 Black Business' in the Nation Black Enterprise Magazine (ranked #43) 1983. **BUSINESS ADDRESS:** President, Bill Scott Oldsmobile, Inc, 6123 N Sixty First St, Paradise Valley, AZ 85253.

SCOTT, WINDIE OLIVIA
Attorney. **PERSONAL:** Born in Mobile, AL; daughter of Clifford A Scott and Vivian Pugh Scott. **EDUCATION:** California Polytechnic Univ, BA, Political Science, 1970-74; Univ of CA, Juris Doctor, 1974-77. **CAREER:** State of California, Office of State Controller, sr staff counsel, 1987-present; Wiley Manuel Bar Assn, pres, 1984; CA Assn of Black Lawyers, bd mem, 1984-85; Centro de Legal-Sacramento, bd mem, 1984-85. **ORGANIZATIONS:** Pres, Women Lawyers of Sacramento, 1989; vice pres, California Assn of Black Lawyers, 1989; treasurer, Pan Hellenic Council, 1982-84; parlimentarian, Alpha kappa Alpha Sorority, 1984-89; mem, City Bar of Sacramento, 1984-85; mem, State Bar of CA, 1979-; mem, Natl Bar Assn, 1980-; mem, Black Women's Network. **HONORS/ACHIEVEMENTS:** Sacramento 100 Most Influential Blacks, 1984; Past President Award, Wiley Manuel Bar Assn, 1985; Ernest L Robinson Jr Award, McGeorge Black Law Students Assn, 1985; Outstanding Women Award, Natl Council of Negro Women, 1988. **BUSINESS ADDRESS:** Sr Staff Counsel to the State Controller Gray Davis, State of California, 1020 N St, Suite 128, Sacramento, CA 95814.

SCOTT, YOLANDA MADDEN
Business executive. **PERSONAL:** Born May 10, 1946, Taclobam Leyte, Philippines;children: Jo Ann, Yolanda, Charles, Joe L Jr. **EDUCATION:** Pace Univ, BBA (cum laude) 1972-76; Amer Inst of Banking, certificate 1976; New York Credit Inst, credit analysis certificate 1976; Columbia Univ, MBA (honors) 1980. **CAREER:** Xerox Corp, admin asst to pres 1967-69, credit & mgmt trainee 1976-77; Manufacturers Hanover Trust, marketing officer 1977-80; First Interstate Bank LA, asst vice pres marketing 1980-81; Union Bank LA, vice pres marketing. **ORGANIZATIONS:** Mem, Women in Finance, 1976; vice pres & sec, Urban Bankers Coalition of New York, 1977-78; bd mem Natl Assn of Urban Bankers, 1978; mem, Amer Marketing Assn, 1979-; comm chairperson, Urban Bankers Coalition of LA, 1981-; mem, Southern California Jr Ice Hockey League, 1982-; mem, Wilson High School Football Boosters, 1982-; counselor/facilitator, St John Vianney Youth Group, 1984-; mem, Bank Marketing Assn, 1984-. **HONORS/ACHIEVEMENTS:** Natl Honor Soc, Pace Univ, 1976; Pace & Columbia Univ Scholarships, 1974-80; Outstanding Trainee, Manufacturers Hanover Trust, 1976; Discretionary Award, Union Bank, 1984. **BUSINESS ADDRESS:** Vice President, Union Bank, 445 S Figueroa St, Los Angeles, CA 90071.

SCOTT-HERON, GIL
Musician, poet. **PERSONAL:** Born Apr 01, 1949, Chicago, IL; son of Bobbie Scott. **EDUCATION:** Attended Fieldston School of Ethical Culture, Lincoln Univ, 1967; Johns Hopkins Univ, MA, 1972. **CAREER:** Creative Writing Fed City College, Washington DC, teacher; formed musical grp Midnight Band; film Baron Wolfgang Von Tripps (score) 1976; recordings include Small Talk at 125th & Lenox, The Revolution Will Not Be Televised, Winter in America, It's Your World, No Nukes, and Sun City; composer, writer, 1970-. **HONORS/ACHIEVEMENTS:** Johns Hopkins Univ Fellowship; author of novels The Vulture, World Publishing, 1970, and The Nigger Factory, Dial, 1972; author of poetry collections, Small Talk at 125th & Lenox, World Publishing, 1970, and So Far, So Good, 1988. **BUSINESS ADDRESS:** Mister E, PO Box 11639, Alexandria, VA 22312. *

SCOTT-JOHNSON, ROBERTA VIRGINIA
Elected govt. official, educator. **PERSONAL:** Born in West Virginia; married Jesse; children: Robert Jerome Patterson, Rex Lenear Patterson, Carolyn Marie Patterson, Terrence Jerome. **EDUCATION:** Bluefield Coll, BS Bus Admin attended; Univ of MI, MA Guidance & Counseling 1966; Univ of Edinborough, 1979. **CAREER:** Elkhorn HS WV, dir of commercial ed; Saginaw City School Dist, teacher, counselor; Econ Devel Corp Buena Vista Twp, directorship, township trustee, twp treasurer. **HONORS/ACHIEVEMENTS:** Outstanding Serv Jessie Rouse School 1970-80; Outstanding Political Serv Six yrs at Twp Trustee 1978-84; Honorary Awd Buena Vista Twp 1980. **HOME ADDRESS:** 4636 S Gregory, Saginaw, MI 48601.

SCRANAGE, CLARENCE, JR.
Emergency physician. **PERSONAL:** Born Mar 16, 1955, Richmond, VA. **EDUCATION:** VA Commonwealth Univ, BS Biology 1977; Meharry Medical Coll, MD 1982. **CAREER:** Howard Univ Hosp, emergency resident 1985; State of VA, medical examiner 1986-; Virginia EMS, medical dir 1986-. **ORGANIZATIONS:** Life mem Kappa Alpha Psi 1980-; regional dir VA Amer Coll of Emergency Physicians 1986-; chmn Southside Emergency Medical Serv 1986; mem Amer Medical Assoc, VA Medical Assoc. **HONORS/ACHIEVEMENTS:** Outstanding Young Men in Amer Awd. **HOME ADDRESS:** 219 W Danigren Rd, King George, VA 22485. **BUSINESS ADDRESS:** Dir Emergency Unit, Community Memorial Hospital, 126 Buena Vista Circle, South Hill, VA 23970.

SCRIBNER, ARTHUR GERALD, JR.
Senior systems analyst, engineer. **PERSONAL:** Born Nov 19, 1955, Baltimore, MD; son of Arthur Gerald Scribner Sr and Elizabeth Worrell Scribner; children: Lamara Chanelle. **EDUCATION:** Univ of MD Baltimore, BA (Magna Cum Laude) 1981, BS (Magna Cum Laude) 1981; Johns Hopkins Univ School of Engineering, MS (Cum Laude) 1987. **CAREER:** Scribner Consulting Inc, pres 1985-; MD Medical Laboratories, pathology asst 1986-; Inner Harbor Sounds Inc, producer 1986-; US Dept of Defense, sr systems analyst/engr 1982-; A G Scribner & Associates, pres 1988-; The Consortium Inc, pres/CEO 1988-. **ORGANIZATIONS:** Tenor & soloist Univ of MD Chamber Choir 1978-81; public relations consultant Vivians Fashions of NY 1980-; asst instructor Univ of MD 1980-81; talent coordinator Baltimore Citywide Star Search 1985-86; vice pres Metropolitan Entertainment Consortium Inc 1985-. **HONORS/ACHIEVEMENTS:** Superior Achievement Award Interprofessional Studies Inst Univ of MD 1982. **HOME ADDRESS:** 6820 Parsons Ave, Baltimore, MD 21207. **BUSINESS ADDRESS:** Asst Dir of Special Projects, US Dept of Defense, 9800 Savage Rd, Fort Meade, MD 20755.

SCRUGGS, ALLIE W.
Psychologist, educator. **PERSONAL:** Born Feb 13, 1927, Akron, OH. **EDUCATION:** Boston U, BSEd 1958, EdD 1971. **ORGANIZATIONS:** New Eng reg chmn Human Rights Am Pewrsonnel & Guidance Assn 1972; acting dir AIDUniv of Lowell 1973-77; chmn Task Force One Conf Minorities in Higher Educ MA Sec Ed Affairs Ofc 1975; mem Am Psychol Assn 1979; mem Adv Count of racial imbalance MA Bd of Educ 1965-66; consult METCO Boston; Educ Dev Corp Cambridge 1972; chmn sub-com Higher Educ Adv Coun MA Off Educ Affairs 1976-79; mem Educ Testing Corp Princeton 1980. **HONORS/ACHIEVEMENTS:** Schlrshp BostonUniv 1958; Schlrshp Jewis Anti-defamation League 1963; Flwshp Grant Nat Def Educ Act 1964; Flwshp Grant Ford Found 1970. **MILITARY SERVICE:** Univ of Lowell, prof/chairperson psy dept 1979-, prof 1974-79; Lowell St Coll, asst prof/asso prof 1966-74; Boston Univ, instr/psy 1965-66; Ayer Public School,teacher/counselor guid dir Asst Prin 1959-64. **BUSINESS ADDRESS:** Professor of Psychology, University of Lowell, One University Ave, Lowell, MA 01854.

SCRUGGS, BOOKER T., II
Educational administrator. **PERSONAL:** Born Oct 02, 1942, Chattanooga, TN; son of Booker T Scruggs I and Mabel Humphrey Scruggs; married Johnnie Lynn Haslerig, Oct 26, 1968; children: Cameroun. **EDUCATION:** Clark Coll, BA 1964; Atlanta Univ, MA 1966. **CAREER:** Howard High School, science teacher 1966; Community Action Agency, coordinator research & reporting 1966-70; WNOO Radio, program moderator 1973-82; Univ TN Chattanooga, asst dir Upward Bound 1970-. **ORGANIZATIONS:** Mem Alpha Phi Alpha, Big Brothers, Adult Educ Counselor; former mem bd Chattanooga Elec Power Bd 1975-85; mem Natl Kidney Foundation, Amer Lung Assoc; tv host "Point of View"; TV public affairs producer "Point of View"; mem Chattanooga Gospel Orchestra; bd mem Methodist Neighborhood Centers; choir mem Wiley Methodist Church; bd mem Arts & Education Council 1976-; chmn Constitutional Committee, TN Assn of Special Programs 1980-; vice pres Brainerd High School PTA 1989-90. **HONORS/ACHIEVEMENTS:** Jaycees Presidential Award Honor 1974; Alpha Phi Alpha Man of the Year 1986. **BUSINESS ADDRESS:** Upward Bound Program Director, The University of Tennessee at Chattanooga, 615 McCallie Ave, 213 Race Hall, Chattanooga, TN 37403.

SCRUGGS, CLEORAH J.
Educator. **PERSONAL:** Born Aug 20, 1948, Akron, OH; daughter of Mr & Mrs C Scruggs. **EDUCATION:** Univ of Akron OH, BA Elem Ed 1970, MA Ed 1977, Admin Cert 1984; Professional Devel & Personnel Trng, Professional Cert 1981; Personal Dynamics Inst Inc, attended. **CAREER:** Akron Bd of Educ Akron OH, summer rec suprv 1970-73; Flint Bd of Educ, summer recreational supvr, 1974-80; Mott Adult HS Flint MI, GED instr 1974; Charles Harrison Mason Bible Coll, instr 1975-76; Flint Bd of Ed, instructor, 1970-. **ORGANIZATIONS:** Mem, United Teachers of Flint, Natl Educ Assn, Michigan Educ Assn, Urban League, NAACP, Natl Alliance of Black School Educ, Alpha Kappa Alpha Sorority Inc, Business & Professional Assn; Chair, Flint Community Schools Superintendent's Advisory Council, Human Relations Comm, United Way, United Negro Coll Fund; pres Young Women's Christian Council; former pres Usher Bd; founder, dir, Actress, Christian Drama Guild. **HONORS/ACHIEVEMENTS:** Comm Serv Awd Floyd J McCree Theatre & other civic & religious assns; Masters Thesis, "Identification of Beginning Teachers' Problems" Univ of Akron 1970. **HOME ADDRESS:** 605 W Baker, Flint, MI 48505. **BUSINESS ADDRESS:** Instructor, Flint Board of Education, 923 E Kearsley, Flint, MI 48505.

SCRUGGS, OTEY MATTHEW
Educator. **PERSONAL:** Born Jun 29, 1929, Vallejo, CA; son of Otey and Maude; married Barbara Fitzgerald; children: Jeffrey. **EDUCATION:** Univ of CA Santa Barbara, BA 1951; Harvard U, MA 1952, PhD 1958. **CAREER:** Univ of CA Santa Barbara, instr to asso prof 1957-69; Syracuse Univ, prof of history 1969-86, chmn dept of history 1986-. **ORGANIZATIONS:** Mem Assn for Study of Afro/Am Life & Hist; editl Bd Afro-ams in NY Life & Hist 1977-; mem Orgn of Am Historians; mem bd of dir Onondaga Historical Assn 1988-. **MILITARY SERVICE:** USNR 1948-57. **BUSINESS ADDRESS:** Chairman Department of History, Syracuse University, Maxwell 320, Syracuse, NY 13210.

SCRUGGS, SYLVIA ANN
Educator. **PERSONAL:** Born Jun 18, 1951, Akron, OH. **EDUCATION:** Univ of Akron, BS 1976. **CAREER:** Univ of Akron, clerk typist 1974-77; Akron Children's Medical Center, ward secretary 1977-78; Akron Urban League, educator 1978-82; Hwakins Skill Center, educator 1983; Department of Human Services, income maint II 1984-. **ORGANIZATIONS:** Counselors asst South High School 1969; big sister & tutor Univ of Akron 1970; precinct committee Community Third Wrd 1981; youth leader Youth Motivation Task Force 1982; mem committee NAACP 1981-82. **HOME ADDRESS:** 1066 Orlando Ave, Akron, OH 44320.

SCRUTCHIONS, BENJAMIN
Educator. **PERSONAL:** Born Aug 13, 1926, Montezuma, GA. **EDUCATION:** Roosevelt U, BS; DePaul U, MS;Univ of Florence, Italy, further study; Northwestern U;Univ of Chicago. **CAREER:** Chicago Bd of Educ, dir Comm & Human Relations Dept; past positions as cons, supt of schools, asst prin & instr. **ORGANIZATIONS:** Mdm Kappa Alpha Psi; Phi Delta Kappa; mem various Professional & civic orgns. **HONORS/ACHIEVEMENTS:** Recipient Dist Serv Awd; Alumni Awd, Roosevelt U; 1st Black Supt of Schs in IL. **MILITARY SERVICE:** AUS. **BUSINESS ADDRESS:** 1750 E 71 St, Chicago, IL 60649.

SCURRY, FRED L.
Attorney. **PERSONAL:** Born Dec 16, 1942, London, OH; married Shelia. **EDUCATION:** Central St U, BS 1966; Howard Univ Law Sch, JD 1969. **CAREER:** Atty, pvt prac 1974-; London, city solic 1976-79; IRS, 1972-74; Clarence J Brown MC, staff 1967-69. **ORGANIZATIONS:** Mem Columbus OH Bar Assn; Madison Co Bar Assn; bd of dir Madison Co Comm Action; bd of dir Madison-Union-Delaware Co Comm Action; London Lions Club. **MILITARY SERVICE:** AUS capt 1970-72. **BUSINESS ADDRESS:** 100 W 2nd, London, OH 43140.

SEABROOK, LEMUEL, III
Bank administrator. **PERSONAL:** Born Aug 21, 1952, Augusta, GA; married Michele J Hooper. **EDUCATION:** Univ of Chicago, AB Business 1974, MBA Finance 1975; Augusta College 1973; Univ of Michigan 1982. **CAREER:** Continental Illinois Natl Bank, vice president 1975-84; Harris Bank, vice president. **BUSINESS ADDRESS:** Vice President, Harris Bank, 111 West Monroe St, Chicago, IL 60690.

SEABROOKS-EDWARDS, MARILYN S.
Government official. **PERSONAL:** Born Mar 03, 1955, Allendale, SC; married Ronald Burke Edwards. **EDUCATION:** University of South Carolina Saik Regional Campus, summer session 1974-75; Georgia Southern College, AB 1977; US Department of Agriculture, evening graduate studies 1984; Baruch College/City Univ of NY, MPA 1984. **CAREER:** City of Savannah Housing Department, special projects coordinator 1981-83; Department of Human Services, special assistant to the dir 1983-84; City of Savannah Housing Department, program coordinator 1984-85; Department of Human Services, program analyst 1985-; Exec Office of the Mayor Office of the Sec of the District of Columbia, chief admin officer 1987-. **ORGANIZATIONS:** Secretary WVGS Radio Board Georgia So College 1976 & 1977; social studies teacher Jenkins County School System 1977-78; financial counselor City of Savannah Housing Department 1978-81; instructor YMCA 1983; membership YMCA 1983-85; membership Washing Urban League 1984-85; membership Natl Forum for Black Public Admin 1984-85; membership Intl City Management Assn 1984-85; sec Wash DC Chap natl Forum for Black Public Admin; bd mem Notary Public Bd for the Dist of Columbia; hearings compliance officer Exec Office of the Mayor. **HONORS/ACHIEVEMENTS:** John Phillip Sousa Award 1973; Psi Alpha Theta Georgia So College 1975-77; Outstanding Young Women of America 1982 & 1983; Natl Urban Fellowship 1983-84; Who's Who Among Amer Women 1986; Who's Who Among Emerging Leaders 1987. **HOME ADDRESS:** 2352 Glenmont Circle #201, Silver Spring, MD 20902. **BUSINESS ADDRESS:** Chief Office of Admin, Exec Office of the Mayor, 1350 Pennsylvania Ave, Room 508 Dist Bldg, Washington, DC 20001.

SEAGEARS, MARGARET JACQUELINE
Administrator. **PERSONAL:** Born Jan 01, 1927, Baltimore, MD; married M Thomas Seagears; children: George, Gary. **EDUCATION:** NJ State Teacher's Coll, BS; Columbia Univ, MA (cum laude); Univ of Puerto Rico, MS (cum laude); Cornell Univ, AMS Montessori Teacher Training Cert Cornell Univ; VA Polytechnic Inst & State Univ, EdD; Rutgers Univ, Post Grad Fellow; Glassboro State Teacher's Coll, Post Grad Fellow; Harvard Univ, Post Grad; Mary Mount College, Post Grad. **CAREER:** Passaic, NJ, kdg primary tchr; Montessori Teacher Training Coll San Juan, pres; Escuelas Las Nereidas Montessori Ctr Puerto Rico, dir & chief admin officer; US Dept of Educ, deputy asst sec for institutional support & intl educ, dir Title III developing institutions program, exec dir office of external relations; Office of Postsecondary Education Dept of Educ, exec dir White House Initiative on Historically Black Colleges & Univs. **ORGANIZATIONS:** Coord of Curriculum & Inst Las Nereidas 1964-70; pres Montessori Tchr Training Coll PR 1973; prof & dir Intrnshp Training Montessori Tchr Coll PR 1974-77; consultUniv Sagrado Corazon PR 1976; consult Dept of Inst San Juan 1976; lecturer Career Image Garfinkles Wash DC 1977-78; conf coord US Off of Educ Dept of Hlth Educ & Welfare 1978-79; cond wkshps seminars mgmt skills Dept of the Interior Fed Women's Prog 1979; maj addr/commencemnts, fndrs day/ tech asst seminars wkshps conf symposiums for White House & US Dept of Educ 1981-85; Amer Assoc of Univ Women; Foreigh Pol Assoc; Amer Pol Sci Assoc; Natlsoc for Child Dev; Interntl Schl Assoc; vice pres Business & Prof Women;s Club Passaic, NJ; bd mem Cmmty Chest, Red Cross, GSA, Cancer Soc, Pablo Cassels Fest PR; Natl Urban League; fndr PR Children's Theatre; fndr Fest of Arts PR; dir CARE; vice pres Acad Affairs. **HONORS/ACHIEVEMENTS:** Fellow Vassar Family Inst 1949; Fellow Rutgers Univ 1951; Fellow Glassboro State Teacher's Coll 1952; Cum Laude Columbia Univ 1953; Civic Awd for Comm Serv St Thomas Virgin Islands 1960; Girl Scout Awd of Excellence for Outstanding Leadership & Serv 1965; Cum Laude Univ of Puerto Rico 1967; Kiwanis Awd forOutstanding Contribution 1972; Outstanding Serv Awd Soc for Mental Retardation 1973; CARE Awd for Distinguished Serv 1974; Woman of the Year Intl Year of the Woman 1975; chairperson Puerto Rico Bicentennial 1975-77; listed as one of Washington DC's Ten Outstanding Career Women Washington Star 1978; Who's Who ofAmerican Women 1979; Personalities of the South Amer Biographical Inst 1980; World's Who's Who of Women 1980; Who's Who in Intl Women Cambridge England 1980; Phi Delta Kappa Honor Soc 1981; Sec Bell's (USDOE) Outstanding Awd 1982; Honorary Degrees, Dr of Humanities Shaw Coll; Dr of Humanities FL Memorial College; Dr of Humanities St Augustine's College Raleigh; Dr of Laws Edward Waters Coll; 1 of 10 Most Elegant Women Washington Dossier 1985; Presidential Awards for Outstndg Serv to HBCU's, Morehouse Med Sch 1985; VA Union 1984; Spellman Coll 1984; Savannah State 1983; TX Southern 1983; Fayetteville State Tchrs Coll 1982; St Augustine 1982; Natl Assn Equal Oppty 1982. **BUSINESS ADDRESS:** Executive Dir White Hse HBCU, US Dept of Education, Room 3682 ROB 3 7th & D Sts SW, Washington, DC 20202.

SEALE, BOBBY
Political activist. **PERSONAL:** Born Oct 22, 1936, Dallas, TX; married Artie. **EDUCATION:** Merritt Coll. **CAREER:** Black Panther Party for Self-Defense, chmn, former minister of infor, co-organizer 1966; Seize the Time, author. **MILITARY SERVICE:** USAF 3 yrs. **BUSINESS ADDRESS:** Youth Employment Strategies, 6117 Germantown, Philadelphia, PA 19144.

SEALS, CONNIE C.
Business executive. **PERSONAL:** Born Sep 01, 1931, Chicago, IL; daughter of Mary Lee Wade; married Jack Hollis; children: Theodore, Victor, Michelle, Philip. **EDUCATION:** Daniel Hale Williams Univ, BA, Public Admin, 1976. **CAREER:** Bulletin Comm Newspaper, asst editor, 1962-63; Chicago Urban League, dir, Communications, 1963-73; IL Comm on Human Relations, exec dir, 1973-80; C-BREM Comm Corp, pres. **ORGANIZATIONS:** APR Chair, Minority Affairs Comm, Public Relations Soc of Amer, 1985; mem, Public Club of Chicago, 1985; Chair, Minority Affairs Comm PRSA, Chicago, 1984-85; Chair, IL Consultants On Ethnicity in Educ, ICEE, 1984-85; mem, exec comm, Chicago Tourism Council, 1985-. **HONORS/ACHIEVEMENTS:** Hon LLD, 1977; Merit Award Beatrice Caffrey, Chicago 1981; Amer Pluralism Award, ICEE, 1982; Certificate of Appreciation, NAACP, 1984. **HOME ADDRESS:** 7228 S Rhodes Ave, Chicago, IL 60619. **BUSINESS ADDRESS:** President, C-BREM Communications Corp, 7228 S Rhodes Ave, Chicago, IL 60619.

SEALS, GEORGE E.
Business executive. **PERSONAL:** Born Oct 02, 1942, Higginsville, MO; married Cecelia McClellean. **EDUCATION:** Univ of MO. **CAREER:** Trader, Chicago, bd of trade; WA Redskins, Chicago Bears, & KC Chiefs, former football player; Chicago Bd Options Exchange Bd, mem. **ORGANIZATIONS:** Mem Better Boys Found; Chicago PUSH; bd of regents Daniel Hale WilliamsUniv 1967; All Pro Team. **BUSINESS ADDRESS:** 141 W Jackson, Chicago, IL.

SEALS, GERALD
Appointed government official. **PERSONAL:** Born Sep 22, 1953, Columbia, SC; son of Janet K Seals; married Carolyn E Seals; children: Gerald II, Jelani-Akil. **EDUCATION:** Univ of SC, BA 1975; Univ of Denver, MA 1976; Southern IL Univ Carbondale, MS ABT 1978. **CAREER:** City of Carbondale IL, admin intern 1977-78; Village of Glen Ellyn IL, asst to village admin 1978-81; Village of Glendale Heights, asst village mgr 1981-82; Village of Glendale Heights, village mgr 1982-84; City of Springfield, asst city mgr 1984-86, city manager 1986-88; City of Corvallis, city manager, 1988-. **ORGANIZATIONS:** Vice chmn of bd Intergovt Risk Mgmt 1982-83; chmn DuPage Reg IV Sub-Region Regionalization Comm 1982-84; chmn of bd Intergovt Risk Mgmt Agency 1983-84; bd mem Springfield Civic Theatre 1985-88; bd mem Springfield OIC 1985-; bd of Clark County Transportation Coordinating Comm 1985-88; State of Oregon Structural Code Advisory Board, 1988-; Corvallis/Benton County United Way, 1989-; bd mem, Natl Forum for Black Public Administrators, 1989-. **HONORS/ACHIEVEMENTS:** Acad Fellowship Univ of Denver 1975-76; Acad Fellowship Southern IL Univ 1976-78; Image Awd Fred Hampton Scholarship Fund 1983; Cert of Conformance GovtFinance Officers Assoc 1984; A Face of 1984 Article Springfield News Sun 1984. **HOME ADDRESS:** 230 NE Powderhorn Drive, Corvallis, OR 97330. **BUSINESS ADDRESS:** City Manager, City of Corvallis, 501 SW Madison Avenue, Corvallis, OR 97339.

SEALS, MAXINE
Educational administration. **PERSONAL:** Born in Trinity, TX; married Frank Seals; children: Thaddeus, Cedric. **EDUCATION:** Houston Comm Coll, attended; TX Southern Univ, attended. **ORGANIZATIONS:** Mem, sec Fontaine Scenic Woods Civic Club; bd of dir Gulf Coast School Bd 1984-85; pres TX Caucus Black School Bd Mem 1984-85. **HOME ADDRESS:** 5106 Nolridge, Houston, TX 77016.

SEALS, R. GRANT
Administrator. **PERSONAL:** Born Aug 06, 1932, Shelbyville, KY; married Georgetta Angela Lynem; children: Rupert La Wendell, Rori LaRele, Regan Wayne, LaRita Angela. **EDUCATION:** Florida A&M U, BS with honors 1953;Univ of KY, MS 1956; Washington State U, PhD 1960. **CAREER:** Coll of AgrUniv of NV Reno, asso dean 1976-; US Dept of Agr, coord spl prog SEA/CR 1974-76; FA A&M U, dean prof sch of agr of agr-home econ 1969-74; IA State U, asst prof food tech 1966-69; IA State U, research asso food tech 1964-66; TN State U, asso prof dairy chem biochem 1959-64; Wash State U, research asst dairy mfg 1955-59; FL A&M U, instr dairying 1954-55. **ORGANIZATIONS:** Mem expt sta com on policy NASULGC 1971-73; mem overseas liaison com Am Counc on Educ Wash DC 1971-77; dir FAMU agr research & educ ctr Inst of Food & Agr SciUniv of FL 1972-74; mem Alpha Kappa Mu Honor Soc FL A&MUniv 1951; memSigma Xi Wash StateUniv 1958; chmn Ames Fair Housing Bd Ames IA 1967-69; pres Meth Men First Meth Ch Ames IA 1967-68; mem Alpha Phi Alpha; mem Gamma Sigma Delta Honor Soc 1979. **HONORS/ACHIEVEMENTS:** Pub 28 sci papers/Articles/Abstracts 1958-; Outstdng Young Men of Am 1965; Am Men of Sci 1966; Personalitites of the South 1971; Who's Who in Am 1972. **MILITARY SERVICE:** USAR e-6 8 yrs served;5. **BUSINESS ADDRESS:** University of NV, Reno, NV 89557.

SEALY, JOAN R.
Physician. **PERSONAL:** Born Apr 23, 1942, Philadelphia, PA; divorced; children: Desa, Denice. **EDUCATION:** Univ of Chicago, BA 1964; George Washington Univ, MD 1968; Med Washing Hosp Ctr, intership 1968-69; Yale Univ Med Ctr, res psychiatric 1969-72. **CAREER:** Private practice, psychiatrist; George Washington Univ Med School, asst clinical prof.

SEARLES, CHARLES R.
Artist, educator. **PERSONAL:** Born Jul 11, 1937, Philadelphia; married Kathleen; children: Vanessa, Gregory. **EDUCATION:** Europe, cresson meml traveling scholarship 1971; Africa, ware meml traveling scholarship 1972; PA Acad Fine Arts, grad 1972. **CAREER:** ILE-IFE Center, asst orng art dept 1970; Peal Galleries PA Acad, mem exhibition com 1971; Philadelphia Coll Art, instr; Philadelphia Museum Art Studio Classes, artist; Brooklyn Museum Art School, instr 1983-. **ORGANIZATIONS:** Comm US Gen Serv Admin Interior 1976; mural "Celebration" Wm J Green Fed Bldg; "Play Time" Malory Publ Playground 1976; Smithsonian Inst 1976; "Festac77"; collection NY St Off Bldg 1977; Philadelphia Museum of Art, Fed Railroad Admis, Ciba-Gigy Inc; exhibits, one person show Sande Webster Gallery Philadelphia PA 1984,86; group shows, Charlottenborg Museum Denmark 1986, Port of History Museum 1987. **HONORS/ACHIEVEMENTS:** Commission Newark NJ Amtrak Station Wall Sculpture "Rhythmic Forms" 1985. **BUSINESS ADDRESS:** Instructor, Brooklyn Museum Art School, 115 S 5 Ave, Broad & Pine Sts, Maywood, IL 60153.

SEARS, ARTHUR, JR.
Manager. **PERSONAL:** Born Jul 01, 1928, Pittsburgh; married Bettie Jean S; children: Norma Jean, Arthur, III, Galana, Jory, Ryan. **EDUCATION:** Univ Pittsburgh, BA, 1954; Univ of WI, attending 1951. **CAREER:** Norfolk Journal & Guide, reporter 1954-57; Cleveland Call & Post, dist mgr ed reporter 1957-58; Ebony & Jet, assoc ed 1959-64; Jet & Ebony, NY ed & assoc ed 1964-66; Nat Urban League, asso dir public relations, 1966-67; Wall St Journal, reporter 1967-69; Business Environment Analysis & Comm General Electric Co, consultant 1969-72; Corp Educ Comm, consultant 1972-76; New York City Export Sales & Serv Div Gen Electric Co, mgr public affairs. **ORGANIZATIONS:** Lecturer, Plainfield HS Middlesex Coll Rutger Univ for Minority Journ Workshops; past mem, Plainfield Library Bd; Plainfield Area Comm Bd; Plainfield Mayor's Adv Com on Economic Devel; mem, Alpha Phi Alpha Fraternity; Scoutleader; PTA pres. **HONORS/ACHIEVEMENTS:** Meyer Berger Awd ColumbiaUniv Grad Sch Journ 1970; plaque 1967; GE Nom plaque Gerald L & Phillippe Awd for Pub Serv 1980; conrbr chap "Malcom X A Man & His Times" 1968. **MILITARY SERVICE:** Sgt maj 1950-52.

SEARS, BERTRAM E.
Educator. **PERSONAL:** Born Sep 28, 1930, Atlanta, GA; married Frances; children: Sheryl, Kay, Bertram Jr. **EDUCATION:** Morehouse Coll, BS 1951; Meharry Med Coll, MD1958; Hurley Hosp, internshp;Univ OK Hlth Sci Ctr, res 1959-61, 63-64. **CAREER:** Univ of OK Hlth Sci Ctr, prof 1964-; Cardiorespiratory Sci, prof schrm 1969; OK Children's Mem Hosp, chief of anthes 1964; Amer Bd of Anesth, dipl 1967; Amer Coll of Anesth, fellow 1967. **ORGANIZATIONS:** Amer Med Assoc 1967; Amer Assoc ofUniv Prof 1965; OK Co Med Soc 1961; Amer Acad of Pedia 1968; OK Soc of Anesth 1961; Am Assn for Respiratory Therapy 1969; OK Assoc for Respir Ther 1969; Intl Anesth Res Soc 1965; Natl Med Assoc 1971; YMCA; NAACP; Kappa Alpha Psi; trst Avery Chap AME Ch. **HONORS/ACHIEVEMENTS:** Pub "Omplic of Ketamine" Anesth 32231 1971; "exper with ketamine anesth" journ of natl med assoc 6732 1975; "pneumothorax from an obstructed Vent Port" Anesthesiology 7311 1977. **MILITARY SERVICE:** AUS med corps capt 1961-63. **BUSINESS ADDRESS:** PO Box 26901, Oklahoma City, OK 73190.

SEARS-COLLINS, LEAH J.
Judge. **PERSONAL:** Born Jun 13, 1955, Heidelberg, Federal Republic of Germany;daughter of Thomas E Sears and Onnye Jean Rountree Sears; married Love Sears-Collins III, Jul 03, 1976; children: Addison, Brennan. **EDUCATION:** Cornell Univ, Ithaca NY, BS, 1976; Emory Univ School of Law, Atlanta GA, JD, 1980; Natl Judicial Coll, Reno NV, MJS, 1987. **CAREER:** Columbus Ledger Newspaper, Columbus OH, reporter, 1976-77; summer associate for law firm, 1979; practicing atty, 1980-85; City Court of Atlanta, GA, judge pro hac vice, 1982-85; judge, 1985-88; Superior Court of Fulton County, Atlanta GA, judge, 1989—. **ORGANIZATIONS:** Mem, Amer, Natl, Georgia, Atlanta, and Gate City Bar Assns; mem, Natl Assn of Women Judges; founding pres, comm mem, Georgia Assn of Black Women Attys; mem, exec comm, Greater Atlanta Club of Natl Assn of Negro Business & Professional Women; bd mem, Georgia Assn for Women Lawyers; bd mem, American Red Cross, Atlanta Chapter; mem, Natl Assn of Alcoholism and Drug Abuse Counselors; mem, Amer Business Women's Assn. **HONORS/ACHIEVEMENTS:** NAACP Award (Atlanta Chapter) Award for Community Service; Distinguished Leadership Award for Outstanding Service in the Judiciary, 1988; founder of Battered Women's Project of Columbus, Georgia. **BUSINESS ADDRESS:** Superior Court of Fulton County, 136 Pryor St SW, Rm 805, Atlanta, GA 30303.

SEATON, SHIRLEY MARIE SMITH
Educator. **PERSONAL:** Born in Cleveland, OH; daughter of Kibble Clarence Smith and Cecil Stone Wright Smith; married Lawrence Seaton, Oct 05, 1965; children: Eric Dean. **EDUCATION:** Howard Univ, Washington DC, BA, 1947, MA, 1948; Case Western Reserve Univ, Cleveland OH, MA, 1956; Institute Universitario di Studi Europei, Turin, Italy, cert. advanced study, 1959; Univ of Akron, Akron OH, PhD, 1981; Beijing Normal Univ, Beijing, China, 1982. **CAREER:** Cleveland Board of Education, Cleveland OH, teacher, 1950-58, asst principal, 1959-65, principal, 1966-67; US Govt, Washington DC, educational specialist, 1965; WEWS-TV, Cleveland OH, television teacher, 1963-67; Cleveland State Univ, Cleveland OH, univ supervisor, field service office, 1977-85; Basics and Beyond Education Consultants, Cleveland Heights OH, currently director. **ORGANIZATIONS:** National Alliance of Black School Educators, National Council for Social Studies, National Association of Secondary School Principals, Association for Supervision & Curriculum Development, Metropolitan Cleveland Alliance of Black School Educators. **HONORS/ACHIEVEMENTS:** Fulbright grant to Italy, 1959, and to China, 1982; Martin Luther King Outstanding Educator Award, 1989; outstanding educator awards from Cleveland City Council and Ohio State Legislature. **BUSINESS ADDRESS:** Director, Basics and Beyond, Educational Consultants, 3680 Bendemeer Rd, Cleveland Heights, OH 44118.

SEAVERS, CLARENCE W.
Business executive. **PERSONAL:** Born Aug 13, 1919, Sandusky, OH; married Juanita Jackson. **EDUCATION:** Attended, Bowling Green Extension, Univ of HI. **CAREER:** Erie Co Health Dist, bd mem, 1968-; Erie Huron CAC, treasurer, 1969-; Erie County Bd of Elections, bd mem, 1981-; Seavers License Bureau, owner 1986-. **ORGANIZATIONS:** mem, OH Office of the Consumers Counsel, 1989; trustee, Providence Hospital, 1989; trustee, YMCA, 1989; mem, LEADS (Chamber of Commerce affiliate) 1984; chmn, Goodwill Industries, 1984; chmn, Youth Advisory Comm, 1985; mem, Downtown Merchants Inc, 1986; mem, Chamber of Commerce 1987. **HONORS/ACHIEVEMENTS:** Outstanding & Dedicated Serv to the Community, Sandusky Branch, NAACP, 1982; Outstanding Citizen's Award, State of Ohio, 1983; Community Srv Award Progress Lodge # 85, 1985; Gold Award, United Way, 1989. **MILITARY SERVICE:** AUS tech 5 sgt 4 yrs, Good Conduct Medal, 1943, Asiatic Pacific Medal, 1944. **HOME ADDRESS:** 1490 Dixon Dr, Sandusky, OH 44870. **BUSINESS ADDRESS:** Owner, Seavers License Bureau, 1437 Sycamore Lane, Sandusky, OH 44870.

SEAY, LORRAINE KING
Educator. **PERSONAL:** Born Jun 20, 1926, Switchback, WV; married John T Seay; children: Yvonne D, Sean V. **EDUCATION:** Bluefield St Clge, BS 1949; WV Univ, MS 1960. **CAREER:** Cheerleader coach 1950-71; Stratton Jr High, girls basketball/volleyball track coach 1960-78; gymnastic coach 1971-83, phyicial educ teacher 1950-85 (retired). **ORGANIZATIONS:** City Council Woman City of Beckley 1971-79; Phys Educ instr 1950-; coach cheerleader bsktbl vlybl track; recr bd City of Beckley 1979-85; life mem NEA;life mem NAACP; Amer Red Cross Bd of Raleigh Co; Raleigh Cty Assc Classroom Tchrs; Bluefield State Clge Alumni; TV Bd for Station WSWP/TV; mem Maids & Matrons Soc Study Club; ch clerk & sr usher bd mem Central Bapt Church; golden life mem Delta Sigma Theta Sor; bd dir Amer Cancer Soc Raleigh Co;mem Adv Commin, WV Hlth Agcy; summer recr dir City of Beckley; assc dir acrobatics Jerry Rose Dance Studio; WV Extention Agent bd dir; mem AAVW; mem Delta Kappa Gamma Intl Soc; mem WVEA Civil Serv Commn for Firemen. **HONORS/ACHIEVEMENTS:** Silver Cup Vol Heart Fund Wrkr; Woman of the Year Raleigh Co Woman's Club; Outstanding Comm Work Mountainer State Bar Assc; World Who's Who of Wmn 1978, 1980; Intl Who's Who in Comm Srv 1979; Who's Who Among Black Amer 1980-81. **HOME ADDRESS:** 315 G St, Beckley, WV 25801.

SEAY, NORMAN R.
Educational administrator. **PERSONAL:** Born Feb 18, 1932, St Louis, MO. **EDUCATION:** Stowe Tchrs Coll, BA 1954; Lincoln Univ, MEduc 1966. **CAREER:** Dept of Health, Educ and Welfare, Equal Employment Opportunity specialist; Social Serv, proj dir 1971-73, dep gen mgr 1970-71; Concentrated Employment Prog, dir 1967-70; Dist OEO Ofcs, dir 1965-67; Work-Study Coord St Louis Bd Edn, tchr 1954-65. **ORGANIZATIONS:** Mem Bd of Adult Welfare Serv; MO Assn for Soc Welfare, exec Bd; Pub Improv Bond Issue Screening Comm; Yeatman-Central City Foods Inc, chmn bd dirs; Patrolman CC Smith's Children Educ Trust Fund Comm, numerous other civic affiliations; co-chair, Racial Polarization Task Force 1988-; co-chair, Education Advisory Committee, VP Fair 1989-. **HONORS/ACHIEVEMENTS:** Distinguised Citizen Awd St Louis Argus Newspaper 1974; Oustanding Comm Serv Gamma Omega Chap Alpha Kappa Alpha; Outstanding & Dist St Louis Blk Police Assn; serv to all comm of Greater St Louis bd of mgmt Sheldon Memorial Ethical Soc of St Louis; Valiant Leadership Alpha Zeta Chap Iota Phi Lambda Sor Inc; Certificate of Achievement United Front of Cairo, IL; Comm Serv Radio Sta KATZ; Outstanding Aid to Law Enforcement St Louis Police Dept; Concern & Comm to Metro St Louis Youth St Louis Mayor's Council on Youth; comm serv St Louis CORE; Police Affairs St Louis NAACP; Gr Contrib for 1972 Natl Conf of Blk Policemen; Outstanding Comm Serv Northside Church of Seventh-Day Adventists; Outstanding civic work True Light Baptist Church; merit serv HDC Credit Union; Most Distinguished Alumni Award, Harris-Stowe State College 1989. **MILITARY SERVICE:** AUS 1955-57.

SEBHATU, MESGUN
Educator. **PERSONAL:** Born Jan 06, 1946, Eritrea, Ethiopia;married Almaz Yilma; children: Emnet M Sebhatu. **EDUCATION:** Haile Selassie I Univ, BSc Physics 1969; Clemson Univ, PhD Physics 1975. **CAREER:** Clemson Univ, grad TA 1970-75; NC St Univ, vis asst prof Physics 1975-76; Pensacola Jr Coll, asst prof Physics 1976-78; Winthrop Coll, asst prof Physics 1978-84, assoc prof of Physics 1984-. **ORGANIZATIONS:** Mbr Catholic Ch 1946-; mem Am Physical Soc; mem Am Assoc of Physics Tchrs. **HONORS/ACHIEVEMENTS:** Grantee Rsrch Corp; published articles in Il Nuovo Cimento, Acta Physica Polonica, Physics Tchr Etc; rec'd physical science book for Prentice Hall, Inc. **BUSINESS ADDRESS:** Associate Professor Physics, Winthrop Coll, 101 Sims, Winthrop College, Rock Hill, SC 29733.

SECHREST, EDWARD AMACKER
Manager, oceanographic programs. **PERSONAL:** Born Oct 12, 1931, Washington, DC; married Margaret Ann Thomas; children: Edward Jr, Kim Ann, Lisa Marie Sechrest Ehrhardt. **EDUCATION:** Lincoln University, 1948-50; US Naval Academy, BS 1952-56; US Naval Postgraduate School, BSEE 1962-64; Geo Washington Univ, MS 1966-67. **CAREER:** US Navy, officer 1956-85; AT&T Technologies, account executive 1985-86; Magnavox Govt & Ind Electronics Co, mgr advanced navy programs 1986-. **ORGANIZATIONS:** US Naval Academy, instructor marine & electrical eng 1967-70; USS Barry (DD-933) US Atlantic Fleet, commanding officer 1971-73; Navy Recruiting Command, special asst for minority affairs 1974-77; Military Organizations, annual speaking engagements 1974-85; Institute of Electrical & Electronics Engineers, mem 1979-86; Northern VA Special Olympics, chairman 1980-83; Alexandria-Fairfax Alumni, Kappa Alpha Psi, polemarch 1981-83; Natl Security Industrial Assoc, consultant 1986. **HONORS/ACHIEVEMENTS:** Naval War College, "Communism in Tanzania" publication 1966; US Navy, bronze star, meritorious service, joint service commendation, navy commendation 1969-85. **MILITARY SERVICE:** US Navy, Capt 1956-85. **HOME ADDRESS:** 8103 Touchstone Terrace, McLean, VA 22102.

SECRET, PHILIP E.
Administrator/educator. **PERSONAL:** Born in Omaha, NE; son of Roscoe Secret and Louise Secret; married Tijiuana R Smith; children: Sheila, Philip Jr, Marcus. **EDUCATION:** Univ of Nebraska, BS 1969, PhD 1978. **CAREER:** Univ of Nebraska Omaha, prof 1972-, assoc dean coll of public affairs and comm serv. **HONORS/ACHIEVEMENTS:** "Sex, Race & Political Participation " Western Political Quarterly Mar 1981; "Race & Political Protest" Journal of Black Studies Mar 1982, "Impact of Region on Racial Differences in Attitudes Toward Abortion,"; "Political Efficacy, Political Trust & Electoral Participation," Western Journal of Black Studies Summer 1985; "Attitudes Toward The Court's Decision on Prayer in Public Schools" Social Science Quarterly, 1986; "The Supreme Court and Race-Conscious Seniority Systems," Howard Law Journal, 1988. **MILITARY SERVICE:** USAF Honorably Discharged. **HOME ADDRESS:** 11536 Spaulding St, Omaha, NE 68164. **BUSINESS ADDRESS:** Prof, Political Sci/Criminal Justice, University of Nebraska Omaha, 60th Dodge St, Omaha, NE 68182.

SECUNDY, MARIAN GRAY
Educator. **PERSONAL:** Born Oct 20, 1938, Baton Rouge, LA; married Robert; children: Susan, Joel. **EDUCATION:** Vassar Coll, AB 1960; Bryn Mawr Sch Social Work, MSS 1962. **CAREER:** Howard Univ Coll Med, instr dept of comm health & family prac 1971-; Coll Allied Health, asst prof 1974; Reston Counsel Serv Inc, partner 1971-; Psychiat Inst, 1972-; Montgomery Co Housing Auth, consultant 1970-71; No VA Mental Health Inst, psychiat caseworker 1968-69; Gulf-Reston Inc, consultant 1968; Urban Systems Inc, asso prg dir 1967; Amer Friends Serv Com, asso dir & dir 1965-67; Redevel Auth Phila, relocation spec comm rel rep urban renewal caseworker 1962-65; Dept Social Work & Social Research, research asst 1961. **ORGANIZATIONS:** Mem Reston Chap Links 1976-; Vassar Coll Bd Tst 1971; Bassar Club WA 1966; Nat Assn Social Workers 1962; Reston Black Focus 1969; Soc Hlth & Human Values 1974; Nat Cncl Negro Women 1974; Social Tchrs of Family Med memsp com educ com; Assn Behavioral Sci Med Educ 1973; bd dir Wider Oppt for Women1975; mem Fairfax Hosp Tst 1975; past mem Soc Friends Yrly Meeting Race Rels Com 1962-63; Am Friends Serv Com 1962-69; Columbia Br YWCA 1964-65; Vassar Club Philadelphia 1960-65; Alumnae Assn Vassar Coll 1968-71; Fairfax Co Leag Women Voters 1967-71; bd dir Reston VA Comm Assn 1968-71. **HONORS/ACHIEVEMENTS:** Recip $1,200 grant Nat Endowment For Humanities Study Med Ethics 1975; publ "Clinical Experiences for Frshmn & Sphmr Med Students" Journ Nat Med Assn 1974; "Factors in Patient/Dr Comm A Commun Skills Elective" Journ Med & Educ 1975; "The Social Worker as Humanist" 1976; "Bereavement the role of the Family Physician" Journ Nat Med Assn 1977. **BUSINESS ADDRESS:** HowardUniv College Med, 520 "W" St NW, Washington, DC 20059.

SEE, LETHA ANNETTE
College professor. **PERSONAL:** Born Jan 23, 1930, Poteau, OK; married Colonel Wilburn R See; children: Terry L. **EDUCATION:** Langston Univ, BA 1956; Univ of OK, EdM 1957; Univ of AR, MSW 1972; Univ of WI, Post Masters 1976; Bryn Mawr Coll, PhD 1982. **CAREER:** Univ of AR, asst prof 1972-77; Child Welfare Svcs, agency dir 1977-80; Atlanta Univ, assoc prof 1982-83; Univ of GA, assoc prof 1983-. **ORGANIZATIONS:** Pres 1986, consultant Natl Assoc Social Work; delegate to Soviet Union World Congress of Women 1987. **HONORS/ACHIEVEMENTS:** Article "Migration and Refugees" Natl Assoc Human Rights 1986-87; editor Gerontological SW 1986; Title III Fellowship Univ WI-Madison 1987; author "Tensions & Tangles" 1987. **HOME ADDRESS:** 909 Otter Way, Marietta, GA 30067. **BUSINESS ADDRESS:** Associate Professor, Univ of Georgia, 3001 Mercer University Dr, Atlanta, GA 30301.

SEIBERT-MCCAULEY, MARY F.
Educator. **PERSONAL:** Born Jun 21, 1930, Louisiana; daughter of Frank Seibert and M Seibert; widowed. **EDUCATION:** TN State Univ, BS 1952, MA 1961; Northwestern Univ, attended 1957; Vanderbilt, attended 1966, 1967, 1977; George Peabody Vanderbilt, PhD 1983. **CAREER:** Future City Sch, teacher 1952-57; Roosevelt HS, english teacher 1957-62; Bruce HS, english teacher 1963-69; Dyersburg Comm Coll, assoc prof 1969-, chmn of English 1974-84; prof of English 1985, chmn of humanities 1976-84. **ORGANIZATIONS:** Mem Delta Sigma Theta Sor 1951-; disc-jockey First Black Stations WJRO WDSG 1953-57; pres NAACP Dyersburg Chap 1963-64; pres Math Inc Construction Co 1977-; mem 1st Woman Dyer Co Bd of Educ 1977-; bd mem Dyer Co Mentally Retarded Assoc 1980-; bd mem Dyer Co Cancer Assoc 1982-; mem Tabernacle Bapt Ch; real estate holdings; mem of Kiwanis Club 1988-; part owner of Union City Ford, Lincoln, Mercury Inc 1988-; first black Dyersburg City Bd of Educ 1988-. **HONORS/ACHIEVEMENTS:** Outstanding Teacher Awd, TN Governor's Comm on Handicapped 1966; First Black Teacher Dyersburg HS & DSCC 1966-; Certificate Outstanding Educator of Amer 1975; Stipend Natl Endowment for Humanities 1976. **BUSINESS ADDRESS:** Chmn of Humanities, Dyersburg State Comm Coll, Dyersburg, TN 38024.

SEIDEL, JOHN C.
Automobile dealer. **CAREER:** Seidel Chevrolet Inc, Landover, MD, chief executive. **BUSINESS ADDRESS:** Seidel Chevrolet Inc, 7610 Central Ave, Landover, MD 20785. *

SEIDENBERG, MARK
Bank executive. **CAREER:** Time Savings and Loan Association, San Francisco CA, chief executive. **BUSINESS ADDRESS:** Time Savings and Loan Association, One Daniel Burnham Court, San Francisco, CA 94109. *

SELBY, CORA NORWOOD
Retired educator. **PERSONAL:** Born Jul 15, 1920, Nassau, DE; daughter of Clarence Page Norwood and Martha L Maull Norwood; widowed; children: Paul MN, Clarence PN, Clyde LN, Adrian Selby LeBlanc, Terence RN. **EDUCATION:** Delaware State Coll, BS (Valedictorian) 1940; Univ of DE, MEd 1959; Delaware State Coll, Dover, DE, BS, 1933-40; Univ of Delaware, Newark, DE, MED 1948-59. **CAREER:** Ross Point School Dist, teacher 1941-64, reading teacher 1964-65, special educ teacher 1965-66, 2nd grade teacher 1966-69; Headstart Followthrough Prog, faculty advisor 1969-80; Laurel Sch Dist, gifted & talented teacher 1980; Migrant Educ Program, teacher (tutor) 1981-87; State Bd of Educ, Dover, Laurel teacher specialist 1941-87; Indian River School Dist, Millsboro, ABE Inst, 1968-. **ORGANIZATIONS:** LEA, DSEA, NEA Teacher Educ Org 1941-; sec DE State Coll 1980-; pres Laurel Sr Ctr 1987-; vice pres Peninsula Conf Council on Ministries UM Church 1985-; chaplain Alpha Delta Kappa State Chap 1986; mem Phi Delta Kappa; sec bd dirs Carvel Garden Housing; mem Laurel Historical Society; lay leader Peninsula Conference UM Church; state and natl PTA youth counselor; mem, Commn of Archives & History, Peninsula Conf Member Comm on Area Episcopacy - Peninsula Conf 1988-; Delaware Div of Literacy 1988-; AARP-DRSPA, SCRSPA 1987-. **HONORS/ACHIEVEMENTS:** President's Awd for Volunteer Serv DAACE 1982; First Lady of Year Psi Chap Beta Sigma Phi 1983; Outstanding Educator in DE Natl Assoc of Univ Women 1983; Teacher of the Year Laurel School Dist 1985-86; Outstanding Alumnus DE State Coll NAFEO 1985-86; Doctor of Letters, Delaware State Coll, 1987; Alumni Queen, Delaware State Coll, 1988. **HOME ADDRESS:** Rt 2 Box 343, Laurel, DE 19956.

SELBY, RALPH IRVING
Attorney. **PERSONAL:** Born Feb 16, 1930, Omaha, NE; son of Ralph L. Selby and Georgia M. Selby; married Archie Mae; children: Ralph Earl, Myra Consetta, Karen Lynn, George Franklin. **EDUCATION:** Univ Omaha, BA;Univ MI, LLB. **CAREER:** Baker & Selby, atty. **ORGANIZATIONS:** Mem An Nat Wolverine Bay Co Bar Assn; Am Trial Lawyers Assn; bd dirs MI Trial Lawyers Assn; referee MI Civic Rights Comm; vice pres Bay City Jaycees; pres Boys Club Bay City; state chmn MI Area Council; bd mem Bay Co Comm Mental Health Serv Bd; vice pres Bay City Chap NAACP; pres United Way Bay Co; mem Bay-Midland Legal Aid Soc; Bay Co C of C; MI Chap Am Civil Liverties Unoin; Omicron Delta Kappa; Alpha Phi Alpha; bd mem United Way of MI; trst Delta Coll. **BUSINESS ADDRESS:** Attorney, Baker & Selby, 508 Bay City Bank Bldg, P.O. Box 718, Bay City, MI 48707.

SELLERS, MARY E.
Data processing sales. **PERSONAL:** Born Feb 19, 1950, Springfield, IL. **EDUCATION:** Andrews U, BA 1971; Ford Doc Fellowship Finalist, hon grad. **CAREER:** IBM, Asso mktg rep data proces div & application mktg mgr for nah fed mktg; IBM, mktg trainee 1973; Spfld & Sangamon Co Comm Agy, field oper dir 1972; Cty of Spfld Hsng Relocation Ofc, relocation ofcr 1971. **ORGANIZATIONS:** State of IL Mktg Team.

SELLERS, THERESA ANN
Accounting analyst. **PERSONAL:** Born Jul 24, 1954, Eutawville, SC; daughter of George William Sellers and Aslee Murray Sellers. **EDUCATION:** South Carolina State, BS 1976. **CAREER:** Standard Oil of IN, sr acct clerk 1979-81; SC State Coll, administrative asst 1982-85; Compton Unified School District, elementary teacher 1985-86; Great Amer Life Insurance Co, accounting analyst 1986-; Maxicare Health Plan, Los Angeles CA, assoc acct 1987-88; US Dept of Commerce, Compton CA, asst mgr admin 1989-. **ORGANIZATIONS:** Asst state coordinator Operation PUSH 1981-83; assoc matron SC Eutaw Chapter No 324 OES PHA 1982-84; vice pres SC State Rainbow Coalition 1984; mem Crenshaw-LaTijera BPW Org USA 1986-; mem NAACP, Black Women Forum, Natl Rainbow Coalition, Iota Phi Lambda Sorority, Brookins Community AME Church, Los Angeles CA, Mary M Kidd Missionary Society, Los Angeles CA. **HONORS/ACHIEVEMENTS:** Humanitarian/Leadership Eutaw Chapter No 324 OES PHA 1982, Orangeburg Calhoun Allendale Bamberg Comm Action Agency 1983. **HOME ADDRESS:** PO Box 2354, Los Angeles, CA 90051-0354.

SELLERS, THOMAS J.
Retired educator. **PERSONAL:** Born Mar 17, 1911, Charlottesville, VA; son of Thomas Sellers and Rachel Seller; married Eleanora E Brown; children: Thomassine E. **EDUCATION:** VA Union U, AB 1938; NY U, MA 1958, post grad study 1959. **CAREER:** Dist 11 Bd of Educ City of NY, spl asst to comm supt, dir, pub rels & educ inform svc; Journal & Guide Norfolk, VA, suprv edtrl positions 1941; Afro Am Newspapers Baltimore, 1956; Amsterdam News NYC, 1953-56; Richmond Ben Life Ins Co, dist mgr; New York City Priv & Pub Schs, tchr 1957-64; Bd of Educ NYC, comm rels coor 1964-65; consult & freelance writer since retirement from Bd of Educ City of NY. **ORGANIZATIONS:** Mem Council of Supervisors & Admins, NAACP, Protest Tchrs Assn NYC, Nat Sch Pub Rel Assn, Ed Writers Assn.

SELLERS, WALTER G.
Administrator. **PERSONAL:** Born Jul 25, 1925, Ann Arbor; son of Walter and Leona; children: Victoria, Walter III, Ronald. **EDUCATION:** Central State Univ, BS 1951. **CAREER:** Central State Univ, various admin positions, 1951-present; currently, special asst to the pres. **ORGANIZATIONS:** Mem, Xenia City Bd Educ, 1968-; past pres, Xenia Kiwanis Club, 1971-72; bd dirs, Amer Alumni Council, 1972-73; mem, OH Sch Bds Tenure Study Comm, 1973; lt governor, Kiwanis Intl, 1974-75; bd trustees, Amer Alumni Council/Amer Coll Pub Relations Assn, 1974-; past pres, OH Assn Colleges Admissions Counselors; Council Admissions Officers State Assisted Colls Univs OH; mem, OH HS Coll Relations Comm; Midwestern Adv Panel Coll Entrance Exam Bd; mem, OH School Bds Assn Comm; OSBA Governance Comm; exec bd, Xenia YMCA; bd dirs, Xenia Sr Citizens; pres, OH Sch Bd Assn, 1981-82; governor, OH Dist Kiwanis Intl, 1984-85; comm chmn, Kiwanis Intl. **HONORS/ACHIEVEMENTS:** Alumnus of Year, CSU General Alumni Assn, 1972; Hon mem, SW Region OH School Bds Assn, 1973; FM Torrence Award for Outstanding Community Service, 1980; Hon LND, Central State Univ, 1988; Alumni Bldg, Central State Univ, named the "Walter G Sellers Alumni Center", 1988. **MILITARY SERVICE:** USN, 1944-46. **BUSINESS ADDRESS:** Special Asst to the Pres, Central StateUniv, Wilberforce, OH 45384.

SELLS, MAMIE EARL
Journalist, field representative. **PERSONAL:** Born Feb 15, Moundville, AL; divorced; children: Marcia Lynn, Stephen Charles. **EDUCATION:** Mary Manse Coll Toledo OH, BA 1956; Kellogg Found Leadership Training, cert 1979; Univ of Cincinnati, grad work on MA. **CAREER:** Cincinnati Herald, woman's editor 1977-; Neighborhood Reinvestment Corp of Fed Home & Loan Bank Bd, field rep 1980; City of Cincinnati Mayor, comm rel asst 1978-79; Central Comm Health Bd Cincinnati, prog coord 1977-78; Cincinnati Public Sch System, tchr 1965-75; Cincinnati Call-Post, woman's editor 1974-77; WGUC-; Univ of Cincinnati Radio Station, contrib interviewer 1976; Natl Newspaper Pub Assn to Nigeria, journalist special assignment 1979. **ORGANIZATIONS:** Bd of trst Cincinnati Comm Chest Council; comm chmn Comm Resources Div Chest Council; bd mem NAACP; Adv Bd Council on World Affaris; adv CincinnatiTech Coll; past pres Cincinnati Chap Alpha Kappa Alpha Sorority; mem Top Ladies of Distinction; Friends of Ballet; Women Alliance; former trst YWCA; vpPlayhouse in Park; mem Cincinnati Found 1979-94; co-chmn opening night gala Cincinnati Symphony Orchestra 1975; c/-chmn Alvin Ailey City Center Ballet Co Benefit Cincinniat Arts Consortium 1976. **HONORS/ACHIEVEMENTS:** Media awd Cincinnati Federated Colored Women's Club 1975; hon doc of tech letters Cincinnati Tech Coll 1977; feature story series of articles Cincinnati Enquirer 1977; cover story NIP Mag Cincinnati 1979. **BUSINESS ADDRESS:** Cincinnati Herald, 863 Lincoln Ave, Cincinnati, OH 45206.

SELMON, DEWEY WILLIS
Professional athlete. **PERSONAL:** Born Nov 19, 1953, Eufavia, OK; married Katnryn. **EDUCATION:** Oklahoma, BS. **CAREER:** Tampa Bay Buccaneers, professional football player. **HONORS/ACHIEVEMENTS:** MVP St Petersburg Times 1978. **BUSINESS ADDRESS:** Tampa Bay Buccaneers, 1 Buccaneer Pl, Tampa, FL 33607.

SELMON, LEE ROY
Professional athlete. **PERSONAL:** Born Oct 20, 1954, Eufaula, OK; married Claybra; children: Brandy, Lee Roy Jr, Christopher. **EDUCATION:** Attended Oklahoma. **CAREER:** Tampa Bay Buccaneers, football player. **ORGANIZATIONS:** Chmn United Negro Coll

Fund Sports Comm. **BUSINESS ADDRESS:** Tampa Bay Buccaneers, One Buccaneer Place, Tampa, FL 33607.

SENECA, ARLENA E.
Educator. **PERSONAL:** Born Sep 09, 1919, Laurel, MS; daughter of Mr & Mrs Benjamin Seneca. **EDUCATION:** Talladega Coll, BS, 1939; Atlanta Univ, MS, 1941; Univ of KS, Lawrence; Teachers Coll, Columbia Univ, 1946-48, 1952, 1954, 1965; Lincoln Univ, 1958; Harvard Univ, 1955; Univ of IN, 1959, 1960, 1962, 1966; Univ of CO, BSCS, 1960; Univ of AZ, 1956-67, 1958-59; Columbia Univ of the United Kingdom, Birmingham England, PhD, 1983. **CAREER:** Carver High School, sponsor student council, instructor, 1945-53; Atlanta Univ, dir sci workshop 1946; Columbia Univ, panelist guest lecturer 1947; Carver High School, pres CTA 1950; Natl Science Teachers Assn, consultant, 1956; S Mt HS, head sci dept 1957; Sussex Co Chapter, Amer Cancer Soc Inc, resource person, 1957; AZ Educ Assn, panelist/demonstrator 1957; TX So Univ, guest lecturer 1958; Biol Sci Curric Study, participant, 1960-62; S Mt HS, dir adult educ program 1961-62; Sci Workshop, Sheraton Park Elementary School, dir 1965; Educ Tour, Europe 1966, Mexico 1967; Sky-Y-Camp AZ, adv 1968; Phoenix Union HS Syst, consult human relations; Dir/ConsDesert Services. **ORGANIZATIONS:** Treasurer, South minister United Presbyterian Church, 1965-; state dir Science, Amer Assn of Univ Women & Testing Values in a Changing Soc 1966-69; bd dir YWCA 1967-70; co-sponsor Group Assn for Progress 1966-; mem Anytown Advisory Com 1967-70; dir/cons Desert Consultant Serv 1981-; consultant Home & Comm Com Gov Com on Status of Women 1967-68; mem, Gov Human Resource Bd 1968; mem LEAP Commn Phoenix 1968-76; chmn bd dir Proj Uplift 1967-; mem Delta Kappa Gamma Soc Intl; pres Amer Assn Univ Women 1972-74; bd dir Big Sisters Intl 1972-; bd dir Samaritan Health Serv 1973-; vice chmn Human Resources Citizens Bond Com 1974-; fellow Intl Inst of Comm Serv 1974; mem Governors 7 Mem Com to Select Future Prison Sites for the State of AZ 1979-80; Delta Sigma Theta Sorority Inc. **HONORS/ACHIEVEMENTS:** Co-author, The Evolution of Susan Prim, 1945; Mental Health & the Teacher, Clearing House & the Phoenix Magazine 1957; Curriculum Guide for Biology 3 & 4 Phoenix Union HS Syst, 1958; Whack that Quack, Amer Biology Teacher, 1961; Science Dept Carver HS, The Phoenix Magazine 1963; A Spark for Johnny S Mountain HS Phoenix Rep 1966; Neurohumoral Changes w/Respect to Color Pattern in Ameiurus Nebulosus 1969; Root Pressure Science Teacher Workshop 1969; Mitosis 1969; Phoenix Woman of the Yr 1954, 1958; Natl Science Teacher Achievement Recognition Award, 1956; Charles D Poston Award 1957; achievement certificate Natl Science Teacher 1960; Silver Tray Urban League Guild 1964; 1st Annual Citizens Award for Outstanding Serv to Comm Daughter Elks 1965; Phoenix Woman Yr Phoenix Advertising Club Inc 1967-68; Woman of Achievement Awa rd AAUW 1969; 1st vice pres AZ State Div of AAUW, 1969; Outstanding Mem, Certificate Soc of Women Engrs, 1973; Outstanding Comm Serv, Delta Sigma Theta Sor Inc, 1975; Certificate of Appreciation, Mayor of Phoenix, 1975; Diploma of Honor Award, Intl Inst of Comm Serv, London, EN, 1975; NAACP Image Award, 1983; Leadership Award, AZ State Univ, 1986; Comm General Assembly, Presbyterian Church, 1987. **BUSINESS ADDRESS:** System/Dsrt Consult Services, Phoenix Union High School, 3421 N 51st St, Phoenix, AZ 85018.

SENEGAL, CHARLES
Public affairs manager. **PERSONAL:** Born May 08, 1930, Gary, IN; married Phyllis J; children: Greg Spencer, Gary Spencer, Guy Spencer, Tamara J. **EDUCATION:** IN Univ Bloomington, BS 1957; attended Pepsi-Cola Mgmt Inst 1978. **CAREER:** Chicago Met Mut, ins salesman 1958-60; US Steel, mgmt trainee 1960-62; Pepsi-Cola Gen Bottlers Inc, route salesman 1962-66, spl markets mgr 1966-70, safety dir/pub affairs mgr 1970-. **ORGANIZATIONS:** Bd mem Urban League NW IN 1975; bd mem Lake Co Econ Oppor Council 1978; mem Frontiers of Gary Serv Club 1978; bd mem Gary Neighborhood Serv Inc chmn building & prop comm 1982. **HONORS/ACHIEVEMENTS:** Comm Serv Awd Lake Co Econ Oppor Council 1979. **MILITARY SERVICE:** USAF sgt 4 yrs; Battle Star & Good Conduct Medal. **BUSINESS ADDRESS:** Safety Dir/Pub Affairs, Pepsi-Cola Genl Bottlers Inc, 9300 Calumet Ave, Munster, IN 46321.

SENEGAL, PHYLLIS J.
Lawyer. **PERSONAL:** Born Apr 28, 1930, Cleveland, OH; married Charles; children: Gregg Spencer, Guy Spencer, Gary Spencer, Tamara. **EDUCATION:** Western Reserve U; Cleveland Marshall Law Sch, LLB 1966. **CAREER:** Legal Aid Soc Gary, exec dir 1969-75; Gary, city atty 1968-69; asst city atty 1967-68, arbitrator 1976-; private practice, general counsel for Gary Regional Airport Authority 1988-. **ORGANIZATIONS:** Mem Gary Bar Assn; Am Bar Assn; James Kimbrough Law Assn; mem Urban League; League of Women Voters; Am Assn of Univ Women; Gary Commn on Status of Women; mem Lake County Bar Assn, IN State Bar Assn. **HONORS/ACHIEVEMENTS:** Conn Serv Award City of Gary 1975. **BUSINESS ADDRESS:** Executive Plaza, 5429 Broadway, Merrillville, IN 46410.

SENGSTACKE, JOHN H.
Business executive. **PERSONAL:** Born Nov 25, 1912, Savannah, GA; divorced; children: Robert. **EDUCATION:** Brick Jr Coll, Grad 1929; Hampton Inst, BS Bus Admin 1934; Mergenthaler Linotype School, attended; Chicago School of Printing, attended; Northwestern Univ, attended; OH State Univ, attended; Elmhurst Coll, LLD (Hon) 1969; Bethune-Cookman Coll, Allen Univ, LLB. **CAREER:** Robert S Abbott Publishing Co, vice pres, gen mgr 1934; Robt S Abbott Publishing Co, pres 1940; Amalgamated Publishing Inc, pres; New Pittsburgh Courier Publishing Co, pres; FL Courier Publishing Co Miami, pres; MI Chronicle Publishing Co Detroit, pres; Tri-State Defender Memphis, pres; Sengstacke Enterprises, Inc, pres. **ORGANIZATIONS:** Dir Natl News Paper Publ Assoc; founded Negro Newspaper Publ Assoc 1940; elected 3 yr term bd dir Amer Soc of Newspaper Ed 1970; mem AF Acad Publ Affairs Adv Com 2 yr term 1970; elected mem The Econ Club of Chicago 1970; mem bd dirs Cosmopolitan C of C, IL Fed Savings & Loan Assoc, Golden State Mutual Life Ins Co; appointed by pres Lyndon Johnson mem Natl Alliance of Bus Exec Bd 1968; appointed by Pres Johnson bd of govs USO 1965,68; appointed by Pres Johnson mem US Assay Comm 1964; appointed by Gov Kerner mem IL Sesquicentennial Comm 1965 yr term; mem Pres John F Kennedy's New Adv Com on Equal Oppty in the Armed Forces 1962; chmn Selec Com for Comp Cook Cty Hosp governing Comm; chmn, bd trustees Provident Hosp; mem bd dir Jr Achievement, Bethune-Cookman Coll, Washington Park YMCA, Royal Order of Snakes, Mason, Elk, Chicago Pres Club; chmn Club Publ Com, Rotary Club of Chgo, Original Forty Club of Chgo; appointed by Pres Truman comm to integrate Armed Serv 1948. **HONORS/ACHIEVEMENTS:** 1st recipient Amer Jewish Com mass media Awd; Commander Star of Africa bestowed by Pres Tubman of Republic of Liberia 1958; Honored by Pres Paul Magloire of Haiti 1953; Two Friends Awd 1954; YMCA Serv Awd; Chicago Urban League, Freedom Fighter Awd; 20 Yrs Bd Serv Awd Washington Park YMCA. **BUSINESS ADDRESS:** President, Sengstacke Enterprises, Inc, 2400 S Michigan, Chicago, IL 60616.

SENGSTACKE, WHITTIER ALEXANDER, SR.
Retired publisher. **PERSONAL:** Born Aug 16, 1916, Savannah, GA; son of Herman Alexander Sengstacke and Rose Davis Sengstacke; married Mattie Pryor; children: Astrid Jones, Whittier Jr, Herman Fredrick, Ethel Marie Mitchell. **EDUCATION:** Hampton Inst 1936-37; Wilson Jr Coll, 1939; Mdeill School of Journalism, attended 1939-40. **CAREER:** Chicago Defender, advertising mgr 1947-59, treasurer 1957-59; City Serv Advertising, pres 1947-59; Fashion Enterprises, mgr; Beale St Records United Music Heritage, consultant. **ORGANIZATIONS:** Managing editor Memphis Tri-State Defender 1959-75; vice pres Chicago Daily Defender 1959-77; dir Chickasaw Boy Scout Council 1963-69; bridge commiss Hernando Desoto Bridge Comm 1964-; crime commiss Mayoral Appointments 1965-67. **HONORS/ACHIEVEMENTS:** School Bell TN Educ Assoc 1963,65,68,70-73; Resolution Union 1965; Good Neighbor 2nd Congregational Church 1965; Community Serv Heritage Tours 1986; Humanitarism Awd St Paul AME Church 1987. **BUSINESS ADDRESS:** Consultant, Beale St Records, PO Box 1618, Memphis, TN 38101.

SEON, GERALD HAMILTON
Dentist. **PERSONAL:** Born Oct 28, 1899, Brooklyn, NY; widowed. **EDUCATION:** ColumbiaUniv Dental & Oral Surgery, 1924. **CAREER:** Kings Co Hosp, clinical asst vis dentist 1957-67. **ORGANIZATIONS:** Mem Kings Co Dental Soc; life mem Second Dist Dental Soc; Dental Soc NY State; Am Dental Assn; past pres finc sec Ocean Hill Dental Soc; mem Omega Psi Phi Frat; Chi Delta Mu Med Frat.

SERAILE, JANETTE
Attorney. **PERSONAL:** Born Oct 24, 1945, New York; daughter of Maurice W Grey and Sarah Edwards Grey; married William; children: Garnet Tana, Aden Wayne. **EDUCATION:** Col Law Schl, gread 1972; Lake Fores Coll, 1967. **CAREER:** Bedford Stuyvesant Restoration Corp, atty 1972-; Chance & White, law asst 1970-72; Edwards Sisters Realty Assn, asst mgr 1967-70; self-employed 1974-. **ORGANIZATIONS:** Mem NY co lawyers assn. **BUSINESS ADDRESS:** 740 St Nicholas, New York, NY 10031.

SERGENT, ERNEST, JR.
Scientist. **PERSONAL:** Born Feb 09, 1943, New Orleans, LA; married Claudette Ruth Brown; children: Sandra Michelle, Ernest III, James Richard. **EDUCATION:** So Univ New Orleans, BS Math & Physics 1970; Univ of MI Ann Arbor, MS Physics 1972. **CAREER:** Univ of MI Geology Dept, rsch assoc 1972-74; Gen Motors Rsch Ctr, jr physicist 1973; 3M Company, advanced physicist 1974-75, adv product control engr1975-79, sr physicist 1979-. **ORGANIZATIONS:** Pres & vice pres Afro-Amer Art Soc of 3M Co 1978-80; bd dir Cottage Grove Jaycees 1978-79; commn mem Cottage Grove Human Serv Commn 1980-; chmn Cottage Grove Human Svcs/Human Rights Comm 1981-. **HONORS/ACHIEVEMENTS:** Special Physics Fellowship Univ of MI 1970-72; Outstanding Young Men of Amer US Jaycees 1979. **MILITARY SERVICE:** AUS sp-4 1961-64; Good Conduct Medal. **BUSINESS ADDRESS:** Senior Physicist, 3 M Company, 3 M Center, St Paul, MN 55101.

SERIKI, OLUSOLA OLUYEMISI
Real estate development executive. **PERSONAL:** Born Jul 12, 1958, Lagos, Nigeria;son of Olumuyiwa Seriki, MD and Olapeju Ajayi Seriki; married Angela Kristen Jenkins, Dec 16, 1980; children: Joseph Olatunde, Oluyemisi Haniel, Angele Olufeyisayo. **EDUCATION:** Howard Univ Washington DC, BArch 1979. **CAREER:** Tradex Corp Washington, project dir 1979-83; The Rouse Co Columbia MD, associate devel dir 1983-89. **ORGANIZATIONS:** Vp Natl Assoc of Black Developers 1985/86; mem Intl Council of Shopping Centers 1985-87; assoc mem Urban Land Inst 1986-89; mem Natl Assoc of Corporate Real Estate Execs 1986-89; dir Metropolix Company 1987-89; consultant Extended Family Inc 1988-89; chairman Extended Family Day Committee 1988; advisor Crossroads Afrique 1988-89. **HONORS/ACHIEVEMENTS:** Housing for Nigerians with low income considerations 1982; a constraint to accelerated housing development in Nigeria 1982; Leadership Award, Extended Family 1988. **BUSINESS ADDRESS:** Associate Development Dir, The Rouse Co, 10275 Little Patuxent Parkway, Columbia, MD 21044.

SERVICE, RUSSELL NEWTON
Appointed official. **PERSONAL:** Born Sep 03, 1913, Boston, MA; married Dorothy; children: Russell N Jr, Michael B. **EDUCATION:** Univ of Buffalo, BA 1938, MEd 1946. **CAREER:** YMCA of Buffalo & Erie Co NY, exec dir 1938-59; Bedford YMCA Brooklyn, exec dir 1959-64; YMCA of Greater NY, assoc exec vice pres for urban affairs 1964-74; Nassau Co CETA Prog, commissioner 1978-82; Nassau Co, deputy co exec 1974-77, 1982-. **ORGANIZATIONS:** Mem Nassau Co Village Officials 1974; life mem Hempstead Chamber of Comm 1981; deputy mayor Village of Hempstead 1967-; chairperson Hempstead Black & Hispanic Voters League 1975-; mem Natl Assn Black Elected Officials 1975-; mem Long Island Area Develop Agency 1980-; chairperson Nassau Co Affirmative Action Prog 1982-; life mem NAACP; vice chmn exec comm Nassau County Republican Comm. **HONORS/ACHIEVEMENTS:** Achievement Awd Intl Key Women of America 1974; Selected Public Servant Hempstead Chamber of Comm 1981; Distinguished Serv Awd Hofstra Univ 1983; Serv Awd Afro-Amer Heritage Assn 1984. **BUSINESS ADDRESS:** Deputy Co Exec of Nassau Co, Nassau Co Govt, One West St, Mineola, NY 11501.

SESSING, TREVOR W.
National sales manager. **PERSONAL:** Born Jul 29, 1943, Kingston, Jamaica. **EDUCATION:** LIU (New York), BA Communications 1966; McGill Univ, grad courses 1968; Carleton Univ, grad courses 1969-70. **CAREER:** Maclaren Advertising of Canada, copywriter/acct supvr 1967-68; Ministry of Multiculturalism Ottawa, Ontario, Canada, PRO Spec Asst to the Minister for Multiculturalism 1977; Greater Miami Vis & Conv Bureau, natl sales mgr. **ORGANIZATIONS:** Mem Sigma Delta Chi (profl journalism soc) 1962-; mem North Miami Forum. **HONORS/ACHIEVEMENTS:** Sigma Delta Chi Natl Chap 1962-; Canada Council Award Scholar Ottawa, Ont, Canada 1970-72; Ontario Arts Council Award Scholar Toronto, Ont, Canada 1970-72. **BUSINESS ADDRESS:** Natl Sales Manager, Grtr Miami Vis & Conv Bureau, 4770 Biscayne Blvd, Penthouse A, Miami, FL 33137.

SESSION, JOHNNY FRANK
Government official. **PERSONAL:** Born Mar 02, 1949, Panama City, FL; son of Jake Ses-

sion and Karetta Baker Alexander; married Linda Tibbs, May 11, 1969; children: Tameka, Johnny Frank, Jr., Marcus. **EDUCATION:** Gulf Coast Jr College, Panama City FL, AA, 1970; Florida A&M Univ, Tallahassee FL, BS, 1973. **CAREER:** Deloit Haskins and Sells, Ft Lauderdale FL, staff accountant, 1973-75; City of Hollywood, Hollywood FL, staff accountant, 1975-77, senior accountant, 1977-81, controller, 1981-84; City of Tallahassee, Tallahassee FL, controller, 1984—. **ORGANIZATIONS:** American Institute of CPA, National Govt Finance Officers Association, National Association of Black Accountants, Florida Institute of CPA. **HONORS/ACHIEVEMENTS:** Award for financial reporting, Govt Financial Officer Assn, 1985; WORD Award, Florida A&M Univ Alumni Assn, 1987; distinguished service award, NABA Tallahassee Chapter, 1988. **HOME ADDRESS:** 2806 Sweetbriar Dr, Tallahassee, FL 32312.

SESSOMS, FRANK EUGENE
Physician. **PERSONAL:** Born Oct 24, 1947, Rochester, PA; son of Frank L Sessoms and Catherine Sessoms. **EDUCATION:** Harvard Univ, Intensive Summer Studies program 1968; TN State Univ, BS 1970; Meharry Medical Coll, MD 1974; Bradley Univ 1965-66. **CAREER:** Procter & Gamble, food products technical brand specialist 1969; US Dept of Agriculture, summer researcher animal hlth div 1970; Procter & Gamble Miami Valley Labs, summer researcher 1971; Meharry Medical Coll, student rscher 1971-74; St Margaret's Memorial Hospital, internship and residency in family practice 1974-77; St John's General Hosp, dir of emergency serv 1977, Diplomate of Amer Board of Family Practice 1977, 1983; medical consultant psychiatric dept; Private Practice, physician 1979-. **ORGANIZATIONS:** Vice pres student council TN State Univ 1969-70; class pres Meharry Med Coll 1970-71; vice pres Pre-Alumni Cncl Meharry Med Coll 1973-74; mem Congressional Black Caucus Health Brain Trust 1974-; mem of bd Homewood Brushton YMCA 1979-83; chmn of bd Pittsburgh Black Action Methadone Maint Ctr 1985,86; mem Natl Medical Assoc; medical dir Bidwell Drug & Alcohol Program; life mem Alpha Phi Alpha, NAACP; mem Urban League, Amer Medical Assoc, PA Medical Soc, Frogs Club, Undersea Med Soc, Natl Assoc of Health Serv Executives; host of weekly radio show entitled "You and Your Health"; mem Pgh Chap 100 Black Men; mem Frontiers Intl; bd of governors TN State Univ Student Union; mem Univ Counselors TN State Univ; mem Alumni Bd of Mgmt Meharry Medical Coll; elected 1st vice pres mem Frogs Club of Pittsburgh; mem Chi Delta Mu Fraternity. **HONORS/ACHIEVEMENTS:** Fellow New York Acad of Science; patent holder High-Portein Fruit-Flavored Fat Stablized Spread 1969; Who's Who Among Students in Colls & Univs 1970-71; Samuel Goldwyn Foundation Fellowship 1971-74; Pre-Alumni Council Awd 1974; Honorary Sgt-at-Arms of TN House of Representatives 1974; Outstanding Young Men of Amer 1974,77,76,79; Who's Who in the East 18th Ed 1981-82; Presidential Citation Natl Assoc for Equal Oppor in Higher Educ 1984; Fellow Amer Acad of Family Practice; paper published "Effects of Ethane 1,1 Dihydorxy Diphospanate "EHDP" on the Collagen Metabolism in the Rat" 1971 (Proctor & Gamble Rsch Lab); scientific articles "Uses of the Soybean and Their Prospects for the Future," TN State Univ Dept of Bio-Chemistry 1970. **MILITARY SERVICE:** USAF Awd for Valor and Heroism 1968. **HOME ADDRESS:** 5868 Douglas St, Pittsburgh, PA 15217. **BUSINESS ADDRESS:** 211 N Whitfield St, Pittsburgh, PA 15206.

SETTLES, CARL E.
Psychologist. **PERSONAL:** Born Jul 23, 1948, Houston; son of Paul Silas Settles and Lena Epps Settles; married Carol H; children: Carl, Jr, Corey. **EDUCATION:** Prairie View Univ, BS 1970, MEd 1971; Univ of Texas, PhD 1976. **CAREER:** Waller Indep School Dist, teacher 1970-71; Austin Indep School Dist, 1971-73; Upward Bound Huston-Tillotson Coll, prog coord 1973-74; Dept Educ & Psychol, acad asst 1973-74; Center for Public Schools Ethnic Studies, group leader 1972-74; Univ TX, research assoc II 1974; 1st practicum student, advanced practicum student teaching asst 1973-; Prairie View A&M Univ, dir, counseling center; USA Ft Lewis Wash, div psychologist; BSD Ft Sam Houston, chief psychopathology sect; USAMEDDAC Japan One Stop Counseling Center, dir. **ORGANIZATIONS:** Mem, Austin Assn Teachers Inc, 1972-73; mem, Texas Classroom Teachers Assn, 1972-83; mem, Austin Group Therapy Assn; mem, Black Grad Student Assn, 1973; mem, Amer Psychol Assn, 1974-; chairperson, Ethnic Minority Affairs Comm, Div 19, Amer Psychol Assn, 1989-. **HONORS/ACHIEVEMENTS:** Dr A I Thomas Award, 1969-70; T K Lawless Award, 1969-70; Outstanding Coll Athlete, 1970; Henderson Found Fund Fellow, 1974-75; Fellow, Univ of Texas, 1974-75; Grad Fellow, Natl Fellowship Fund, 1975-76; Outstanding Young Men of Amer, 1977; scholarship, Texas Center & Natl Conf of the A K Rice Inst, 1977. **MILITARY SERVICE:** AUS Medical Serv Corp major clinical psychologist 1981-. **BUSINESS ADDRESS:** Family Therapy Fellow, Letterman Army Medical Center, Dept of Psychiatry, Presidio of San Francisco, CA 94129.

SETTLES, ROSETTA HAYES
Educator. **PERSONAL:** Born Nov 16, 1920, Little Rock, AR; married Dan. **EDUCATION:** Wiley Coll, BA 1948; Harvard U, EdM 1951; Walden U, PhD 1977; Oakland U, Grad Study 1970; Summer Sch, Overseas Study 1971; Great Britain Sch, TourStudy 1973. **CAREER:** Oakland Univ, asso prof 1969-; Garden City Public School, rdng supr 1967-, first black teacher 1967-; Clintondale Public School, rdng spec, clinician 1965-67; Little Rock, remedial rdng elem teacher 1945-56; Harvard Boston Summer School Prog, team teacher 1965; Summer School Prog, asst dir; Detroit Public School, rdng consultant 1972; Garden City Summer School Prog, prin, dir 1974. **ORGANIZATIONS:** Fdr org Nat Dunbar HS Alumni Reunion of Classes; vice pres Detroit Chap Dunbar High Alumni 1980-; mem Nat Bd of Dir Dunbar HS Alumni Assn 1977-; mem IRA; NCTE; MRA; del NEA; mem NAACP. **HONORS/ACHIEVEMENTS:** Originator, sponsor Lena D Hayes Schlrshp Award 1950; HarvardUniv Schlrshp 1951; Top Ten Outstndng Dunbar HS Alumni Nation 1973; Tribute Award 1977; Top Ten Outstndng Dunbar HS Alumni Nat, Little Rock AR Conv 1979; article "Reading & Rhythm" 1970. **BUSINESS ADDRESS:** 31753 Maplewood St, Garden City, MI 48135.

SEVILLIAN, CLARENCE MARVIN
Educator. **PERSONAL:** Born Apr 23, 1945, Buffalo, NY; married Madeline Carol Cochran; children: Clarence II, Nicole Ren. **EDUCATION:** FL A&M U, BS 1966; Estrn MI U, MEd Admin 1974. **CAREER:** Northwestern HS, Flint, staff spec; Bryant Jr HS, instrumental Music teacher 1970-74; Saginaw Foundries, purch agent 1968-70; Hoxey Job Corp Center, Catillac, resident, counselor 1966-68. **ORGANIZATIONS:** Records keeper Saginaw Alumni, Kappa Alpha Psi; mem MI Ed Assn; NEA; United Tchr of Flint; MI Sch Band & Orch Assn; Music Educators Nat Conf; adv Bryant Band & Orch Parents Assn; first vice pres Unity Urban Comm Dev & Rehab Corp. **HONORS/ACHIEVEMENTS:** Outs Secondary Educator of Am 1974; Outs Young Man of Am 1974. **BUSINESS ADDRESS:** Deputy Principal, Beecher Community Schools, 1020 W Coldwater Road, Flint, MI 48505.

SEWELL, EDWARD C.
Business executive. **PERSONAL:** Born Aug 18, 1946, Hanover, MD. **EDUCATION:** IN U, MBA (magna cum laude); Bowling Green U, BA (magna cum laude) Omicron Delta Kappa. **CAREER:** Xerox Corp, fin anlyst 1970-72; Irwin Mgmt Co, asst to pres real est dvlpr 1972-75; Crocker Natl Bank, vice pres real est plng 1975-78; J P Mahoney & Co, real est Dvlpr 1978-; Prof Sports Ctr, pres sports agent 1983-. **ORGANIZATIONS:** V chm & fndr Judge Joseph Kennedy Fndtn Schlrshp Fndtn for Bay Area Mnrts; flwshp Consortium for Grad Study in Mgmt 1968-70. **HONORS/ACHIEVEMENTS:** Whos Who in Coll & Univ. **HOME ADDRESS:** 201 Telegraph Hill Blvd 4, San Francisco, CA 94133. **BUSINESS ADDRESS:** Executive Vice President, J P Mahoney & Co, 505 Sansome Ste 1500, San Francisco, CA 94111.

SEWELL, ISIAH OBEDIAH
Government official. **PERSONAL:** Born Nov 20, 1938, Lexington, SC; married Julia Smith; children: Kevin, Kendra, Keith. **EDUCATION:** SC State Coll, BSEE 1961; George Washington Univ, attended 1969-72. **CAREER:** US Dept of Navy, elec engr 1964-71, head utilities 1971-75; US Dept of Energy, general engr 1975-84, hbcu liason 1984-. **ORGANIZATIONS:** Mem Federal Task Force Natl Power Grid Study 1979; mem Alpha Phi Alpha, Alpha Kappa Mu; Lawrence Berkeley Natl Lab/Mendez Educ Foundation Science Consortium 1986-; chmn Federal Agency Sci and Tech Bd 1986-; past pres Athenians Inc Washington DC; past pres Washington Chap SC State Coll Natl Alumni. **HONORS/ACHIEVEMENTS:** Who's Who Among Students in Amer Colls and Univs 1960-61; Disting Military Grad 1961; Congressional Fellow nominee US Dept of Navy 1974. **MILITARY SERVICE:** AUS 1st lt 3 yrs. **HOME ADDRESS:** 7000 97th Ave, Seabrook, MD 20706. **BUSINESS ADDRESS:** Black Colls & Univs Liaison, US Department of Energy, 1000 Independence Ave SW, Washington, DC 20585.

SEWELL, LUTHER JOSEPH
Business executive. **PERSONAL:** Born Aug 09, 1936, Chattanooga, TN; son of Luther Sewell and Minnie P Sloan; married Wilma Johnson, Jan 19, 1968; children: Luther J III, Lela J. **EDUCATION:** Attended Tennessee A&I Univ 1954-56, Duquesne Univ 1956-58, Monterey Peninsula Coll 1960, Allegheny Community Coll, Univ of Arizona 1969; Trinity Hall Coll & Seminary, graduate 1971. **CAREER:** Talk Magazine, publisher 1962-; Luther J Sewell Inc, founder 1962-; Mellon Natl Bank, consult 1965-71; Business & Job Devel Corp, consultant, market analyst, community devel coor 1964-70; Allegheny County Civil Serv Commn, sec 1973-; Trans World Airlines, Pennsylvania Lottery, consultant. **ORGANIZATIONS:** Mem Business & Job Devel Corp 1963; mem Amer Marketing Assn 1968-72; former vice pres Loendi Literary & Social Club 1969; mem review comm Community Chest Allegheny County 1971-73; bd dirs Pittsburgh Goodwill Industries 1972-; Mendelssohn Choir 1972-; former partner, vice pres A&S Securities Systems Inc 1973-74; bd dirs Pittsburgh Chapter NAACP 1973-; mem Pittsburgh Press Club, Gateway Center Club. **HONORS/ACHIEVEMENTS:** Young Businessman of Year, AME Gen Conf 1965; Economic Devel Award, Urban Youth Action Inc 1972; Communications Award, Pittsburgh Club United 1972; Martin Luther King Award, Music & Arts Club of Pittsburgh 1972; Red Cross Volunteer Award 1973; Black Achievers Award, Centre Ave YMCA 1973; Publishers Award, Black Political Action Assn 1988; Business Award, Federal Executive Bd 1989. **MILITARY SERVICE:** AUS sp4 1958-62. **BUSINESS ADDRESS:** LJS Publishing Inc, 3423 Webster Ave, Pittsburgh, PA 15219.

SEWELL, RICHARD HUSTON
Executive director. **PERSONAL:** Born Nov 01, 1946, Bowling Green, KY; married Iris Jean Jones; children: Rhonda Beth, Erica Jordon. **EDUCATION:** Bowling Green State Univ, BS 1968; Univ of OK, MPH 1974. **CAREER:** Health Planning Assoc of Northwest OH, dir med care div 1971-76; Council for Comm Serv in Metro Chgo, sr planner 1976-77; Suburban Health Systems Agency, dir of planning 1977-80; Hay Assoc, consult 1980; Suburban Health Systems Agency, exec dir. **ORGANIZATIONS:** Mem Alpha Phi Alpha 1964-; treas IL Assoc of Health Systems Agencies 1983-85; pres natl Black Health Planners Assoc 1984-86; bd of dir & exec comm Amer Health Planning Assoc 1984-87; vice chmn United Way Membership Comm 1984-; pres Men's Fellowship Trinity United Church of Christ 1984-85. **HONORS/ACHIEVEMENTS:** Invited to testify health subcommittee Inst of Med of the Natl Acad of Sci 1979. **HOME ADDRESS:** 5304 S Cornell, Chicago, IL 60615.

SEWELL, TOM EUGENE
Professional athlete. **PERSONAL:** Born Mar 14, 1962, Pensacola, FL. **EDUCATION:** Lamar Univ, 1984. **CAREER:** Washington Bullets, guard 1988; Philadelphia 76er's. **HONORS/ACHIEVEMENTS:** Southland Plyr of Year 1983-84 after leading club to 6th League Chmpnshp; led Lamar to Natl Invtnl Tournmnt. **BUSINESS ADDRESS:** Washington Bullets, One Harry S Truman Dr, Ste 510, Landover, MD 20785.

SEXTON, EDWIN T., JR.
Association executive. **PERSONAL:** Born Jul 12, 1923, Wichita, KS; married Dorothy Hellen; children: Telana Denise, Darcel Yvette. **EDUCATION:** Univ Wichita KS, 1923. **CAREER:** Off Minority Bus Enterprise, staff asst, dir 1973-; Rep Nat Comd consult 1967-73; enlightener nwspr, wichita, ed, pub 1960-68. **ORGANIZATIONS:** Mem NAACP; found Wichita Urban Leag; dep grand master Prince Hall Grand Lodge KS F&AM; dir Vet Affairs Elks; Am Leg; ARC; C of C; Frontier's Intrntl. **HONORS/ACHIEVEMENTS:** Outstndng Comm Srv Award YMCA; Hon KY Col; adm Great Navy NE; plainsman CO; traveler AR; Nat Man Yr Award 1973; Keys to City, Wichita, Birmingham, Hopkinsville KY, Tuskeege AL, E St Louis IL; Hon LlD Daniel PayneUniv Birmingham; Who's Who Wichita; hon citizen OK. **MILITARY SERVICE:** AUS 1943.

SEYMOUR, CYNTHIA MARIA
Account representative. **PERSONAL:** Born Sep 01, 1933, Houston, TX; married Oliver W Seymour; children: Michael Dwight Sweet, Wendell Raynard Sweet, Eugene LaValle Sweet Jr. **EDUCATION:** John Adams School of Business, Business certificate 1965. **CAREER:** Gamma Phi Delta Sor, supreme anti-grammateus 1986-. **ORGANIZATIONS:** Vice pres San Francisco 49ers Toastmistress 1981-83; financial grammateus Gamma Phi Delta Sor Regional 1982-86; mem NAACP, Natl Council of Negro Women; mem Jones Memorial

United Methodist Church; advisor Young Adult Fellowship; sec Joseph P Kennedy Foundation; bd of dirs Eleanor R Spikes Memorial; sec Finance Comm Jones Memorial United Meth Church 1986-. **HONORS/ACHIEVEMENTS:** Outstanding Salesperson Lion's Club 1976,82; Certificate of Appreciation Gamma Phi Delta Sor 1983; Certificate of Appreciation Jones Memorial United Meth Church 1984,86; Certificate of Honor City and County of San Francisco 1985; Woman of the Year for Western Region Gamma Phi Delta Sor 1987; Certificate of Appreciation City of Detroit. **HOME ADDRESS:** 2535 Ardee Ln, South San Francisco, CA 94080.

SEYMOUR, LAURENCE DARRYL
Surgeon. **PERSONAL:** Born Feb 01, 1935, Memphis, TN; married Janet A Arnold; children: Lauren Juanita, Eric Lawrence. **EDUCATION:** TN St U, BS 1957; Howard U, MD 1961. **CAREER:** City of St Louis Hosp, intern 1961-62; resident 1962-66; Boston U, instr urology 1966-68; Univ TN Memphis, clin asso urology 1969-; Med Clinic Inc, vp 1971-. **ORGANIZATIONS:** Trustee Collins Chapel Hosp Memphis 1972; mem Am Bluff City Med Assns; mem Alpha Kappa Mu; Beta Kappa Chi; Omega Psi Phi; Mason; bd dirs Boys Club Memphis 1969-. **MILITARY SERVICE:** USNR lt comdr 1966-68. **BUSINESS ADDRESS:** 701 E Mallory St, Memphis, TN 38106.

SEYMOUR, ROBERT F.
Physician. **PERSONAL:** Born Apr 08, 1926, Yonkers, NY; married Flora; children: Marc, Stephen, Lauren, Leslie. **EDUCATION:** Howard Univ, BS 1948, MD 1952. **CAREER:** Cleveland Veteran's Admin Hosp, Case Western Reserve Univ, combined program urology specialty trng; Harlem Hospital, internship 1952-53; Private Practice, physician. **ORGANIZATIONS:** Mem Natl Medical Assoc, Cleveland Medical Assoc, Amer Urolog Assoc. **MILITARY SERVICE:** AUS 1st lt 2 yrs. **BUSINESS ADDRESS:** Urologic Surgeon, Cleveland Urologists Inc, 11201 Shaker Bl No 118, Cleveland, OH 44104.

SEYMOUR, STANLEY
Information systems professional. **PERSONAL:** Born Jul 02, 1951, Bronx, NY; son of Charles B. Clark and Ertha M. Reese Seymore; married Julia A. Williams, Feb 12, 1977; children: Kadeem Toure. **EDUCATION:** Brooklyn College, Brooklyn NY, BA, 1980. **CAREER:** Blue Cross Blue Shield, New York NY, operational auditor, 1974-79, systems coordinator, 1979-81, programmer, 1981-84; Morgan Guaranty Trust, New York NY, programmer analyst, 1984-86; New York Times, New York NY, systems analyst, 1986—. **ORGANIZATIONS:** National Black Data Processing Associations, American Payroll Association. **HONORS/ACHIEVEMENTS:** Member of Year, NY chapter of Black Data Processing Associates, 1987. **MILITARY SERVICE:** US Air Force, sergeant, 1970-74. **HOME ADDRESS:** 60 East 17th St, #2G, Brooklyn, NY 11226.

SHACK, WILLIAM A.
Educator & educational administrator. **PERSONAL:** Born Apr 19, 1923, Chicago, IL; son of William Shack and Emma McAvoy Shack; married Dorothy Nash, Sep 01, 1961; children: Hailu. **EDUCATION:** Sch of the Art Institute Chicago, BAE 1955; Univ of Chicago, MA 1957; London Sch of Economics, PhD 1961. **CAREER:** Northeastern IL State Coll, asst prof 1961-62; Haile Sellassie I Univ, asst prof 1962-65; Univ of IL, assoc prof 1966-70; Univ of CA Berkeley, prof 1970-. **ORGANIZATIONS:** Fellow Intl African Inst 1959-; fellow Royal Anthropoligical Assoc 1961-; fellow Amer Anthropological Inst 1961-; mem The Athenaeum London 1978-; pres N Amer Comm Royal Anthropological Inst 1982; vice chmn, exec council Intl African Inst 1984-; chairman Intl African Inst 1987-. **HONORS/ACHIEVEMENTS:** Fellow Amer Assn for the Advancement of Science 1984-; Chevalier l'ordre Nationale du Merite, Republic of France, 1987. **MILITARY SERVICE:** USCG ETM 2/c 3 yrs; American Campaign Medal; Asiatic-Pacific Medal; WWII Victory Campaign Medal. **BUSINESS ADDRESS:** Professor of Anthropology, University of CA Berkeley, 232 Kroeber Hall, Berkeley, CA 94720.

SHACK, WILLIAM EDWARD
Business executive. **PERSONAL:** Born Feb 04, 1943, Woodward, AL; married Lois D Webster; children: William Edward III, Vincent W. **EDUCATION:** Clark Coll, 1961-62. **CAREER:** Thrifty Drug & Discount, mgr 1966-72; Ford Motor Co, mgr 1972-75; B & W Rent A Car, owner 1974-75; Miramar Lincoln-Mercury San Diego, Future Ford Banning, pres, owner 1983-; Miramar Lincoln Mercury Yucca Valley Ford Future Ford, pres owner. **ORGANIZATIONS:** Pres, Black Ford Lincoln Mercury Dealer Council, 1979, 1982, 1985; dir United Way 1977-83; mem Yucca Valley Lions 1977-84; dir Inland Area Urban League 1977-83; pres PUSH Intl Trade Bureau 1985; dir Jackie Robinson YMCA San Diego; commissioner San Diego City & County Intl World Trade Commission. **HONORS/ACHIEVEMENTS:** Distinguished Achievement Award, Ford Motor Co 1977-84; Gold Award Urban League 1980-82; Gold Award United Way 1979-80; Founder Milligan Mem Scholarship 1980; Johnson Publishing Distinguished Businessman Award 1984. **MILITARY SERVICE:** USAF e-4 1961-64. **BUSINESS ADDRESS:** President, Miramar Lincoln Mercury, 6006 Miramar, San Diego, CA 92121.

SHACKELFORD, GEORGE FRANKLIN
Capital investment manager. **PERSONAL:** Born Jun 03, 1939, Baltimore, MD; son of George Shackelford and Doris Shackelford; married Barbara Janice; children: Shawn, Terrence, Kymberly. **EDUCATION:** Univ MD, prog for mgmt devel; Harvard Univ. **CAREER:** Capital Investment, mgr; mgr advertising & consumer affairs, dir mktg rsch, dir mktg strategies, manager special account, Amoco Oil Co, dist mgr, mgr mdsg, spl proj devel, pricing spec, fld sls mgr, term mgr, terr mgr, equip clk, mail boy 1965. **MILITARY SERVICE:** AUS 1962-65. **HOME ADDRESS:** 2307 Appleby Dr, Wheaton, IL 60187.

SHACKELFORD, LOTTIE H.
City director. **PERSONAL:** Born Apr 30, 1941, Little Rock, AR; daughter of Curtis Holt (deceased) and Bernice Linzy Holt; divorced; children: Russell, Karen, Karla. **EDUCATION:** Broadway Sch of Real Est, Diploma 1973; Inst of Politics, Fellow 1975; Philander Smith Clg, BA (cum laude) 1979; JFK Sch of Govt Harvard Univ, Fellow 1983. **CAREER:** Urban League of Greater Little Rock, educ dir 1973-78; AR Regional Minority Council, exec dir 1982-. **ORGANIZATIONS:** Bd mem Natl League of Cities 1984-86; vice chm AR Democratic St Comm 1982-; reg dir Natl Black Caucus Locally Elected Official; pres S Reg Cncl 1980-; bd of dir Urban League; bd mem Womens Pol Caucus; mem Delta Sigma Theta Sor; vice chmn Democratic National Comm 1989-92; mem Links Inc. **HONORS/ACHIEVEMENTS:** Outstanding citizen Philander Smith Alum Awd 1982; outstanding community serv HOPE NLR 1977; trailblazer awd Delta Sigma Theta Sor 1977; outstanding citizen Bus & Prof Women 1984; Honorary Doctorate of Human Letters, Philander Smith College 1988; Honorary Doctorate of Humane Letters, Shorter College 1987. **BUSINESS ADDRESS:** Mayor, City of Little Rock, City Hall, Little Rock, AR 72201.

SHACKELFORD, WILLIAM G., JR.
Educator. **PERSONAL:** Born Mar 30, 1950, Chicago; married Renee Nuckols; children: Dionne Deneen, Lenise Yvone, Andre' Tarik. **EDUCATION:** Clark Coll, BS 1971; GA Inst of Tech, MS 1974. **CAREER:** Babcock & Wilcox Navl Nclr Fuel Div of VA, quality control engr 1972-73; Clark Coll, assoc rschr physics dept 1973-74, coop gen sci prog phys dept; Natl Center for Atmospheric Rsch CO, vstg rschr 1975; Central Intelligence AGency, analyst 1975-77; Nuclear Assurance Corp, project mgr 1977-79; Atlanta Univ Center, dir dual degree engrg prog 1980-86; Knox Consultants, mktg mgr 1986-. **ORGANIZATIONS:** Mem chmn Spectrum Club Com 1974; Leadershp GA Participant 1982; mem Natl Conf Local Plng Comm Natl Action Council for Minorities in Engrg Inc; reg pres, natl membership chmn Natl Assoc of Minority Engrg Prog Admins; recording sec Amer Nuclear Soc; mem Atlanta Council of Black Professional Engrs. **HONORS/ACHIEVEMENTS:** Beta Kappa Chi Natl Hon Soc Joint Mtng 1971; Judge DeKalb Co Dist Sci Fair 1974,75,78-84; listed on roster Blacks in Physics Scnd Awds Ceremony for Outstanding Black Physics 1975; recip first prize paper presented at Natl Sci Found.

SHADE, BARBARA J. (NEE ROBINSON)
Educator. **PERSONAL:** Born Oct 30, 1933, Armstrong, MO; married Oscar DePreist; children: Christina Marie, Kenneth E, Patricia Louise. **EDUCATION:** Pittsburg StUniv Pittsburg KS, BS 1955;Univ of WI Milwaukee, MS 1967;Univ of WI Madison, PhD 1973. **CAREER:** Univ of WI, asst prof dept Afro-am Studies 1975; Dane Co Head Start, exec dir 1969-71; Milwaukee WI Pub Schs, tchr 1960-68; Consult parent Devel Regn V, 1973-75; Dept of Pub Instr WI, urban ed consult 1974-75; Univ of WI Parkside, assoc prof/chair div of educ. **ORGANIZATIONS:** Mem Delta Sigma Theta Sor 1952-; mem Am Psychol Assn; bd pres St Mary's Hosp Med Cntr 1978; vice pres priorities Dane Co United Way 1979; mem Assoc of Black Psychologists, Amer Educ Rsch Assoc. **HONORS/ACHIEVEMENTS:** Postdoctorial Fellow, Nat Endwmnt for Hmnties 1973-74; Publ Jour of Psychol Jour of Social Psychol; Negro Educ Rvw; Review of Educational Rsch; Journal of Negro Educ; Journal of School Psychology. **BUSINESS ADDRESS:** Associate Professor, University of Wisconsin, Box 2000, Kenosha, WI 53141.

SHADE, OSCAR D.
Educator. **PERSONAL:** Born Sep 05, 1931. **EDUCATION:** Coffeyville Jr Coll KS, 1950-52; KS State Coll Pittsburgh, KS, BS 1956;Univ Denver, CO, MS 1958, part time Grad Stdnt Dept Educ Policy Studies 1972-. **CAREER:** Univ WI, clin prof 1972-; New Concepts Handicapped Fnd Inc, exec dir 1971-72; Bureau Mental Retardation Dept Health & Soc Svc, asst dir 1970-71; Univ WI Madison, WI, clin prof 1967-70; WI Dept Pub Welfare, soc worker 1958-67; Univ Extension, summer workshop 1971, summer inst 1970; Marshfield WI, follow through proj 1972; Jewish Voc Serv Milwaukee, consult structured comm serv 1965-67, 1958-. **ORGANIZATIONS:** Nat Assn Soc Workers; Acad Cert Soc Workers; Southeast WI Assn Soc Workers; Am Assn Mntl Dfcncy; WI Pub Welfare Cncl 1973-; commn mem Gov Commn UN; bd mem Dane Co Mntl Hlth Ctr Inc; City Madison Mayors Sys & Procedures Comn; pres WI Conf NAACP 1972-73; bd mem Family Serv Assn Madison 1970-; adv com Nat Alliance Businessmen JOBS 1970-; admissions comUniv WI 1969-70; treas WI Assn Retarded Chldrn 1968-70; mem CORE Clin ComUniv WI 1968-70; pres Madison Br NAACP; bd mem northside YMCA Milwaukee 1965-67; pres WI Assn Soc Workers Retarded 1965-67. **HONORS/ACHIEVEMENTS:** Numerous publ. **MILITARY SERVICE:** AUS 1953-55.

SHAKIR, ADIB AKMAL
Educational administrator. **PERSONAL:** Born Jun 15, 1953, Richmond, VA; married Dr Annette Goins; children: Ameenah N, Yusuf S. **EDUCATION:** Morehouse Coll, BA (Cum Laude) 1976; Norfolk State Univ, MA 1980; Florida State Univ, PhD 1985. **CAREER:** Florida A&M Univ, instructor of psychology 1981-83; Bethune-Cookman College, dir counseling ctr 1983-85, asst to the pres for govtl affairs 1985-86, intvp acad afrs/dean of faculty 1986-. **ORGANIZATIONS:** Mem East Central FL Consortium for Higher Educ/Industry; mem Natl Council for Black Studies; mem Natl Assoc of Black Psychologists; mem North FL Chaptof the Assoc of Black Psychologists. **HONORS/ACHIEVEMENTS:** Merrill Study/Travel Scholarship Morehouse College 1973; Psychology Dept Honors Morehouse Coll 1976; McKnight Jr Faculty Develop Fellowship McKnight Foundation 1984-85. **BUSINESS ADDRESS:** Interin Vice Pres Acad Afrs/Dean Fac, Bethune-Cookman Coll, 640 Second Ave, Daytona Beach, FL 32014.

SHAKOOR, ADAM ADIB
Judge. **PERSONAL:** Born Aug 06, 1947, Detroit, MI; married Nikki Haleema Graves; children: Shair, Lateef, Keisha, Malik, Khalidah, Koya, Kareena, Jelani. **EDUCATION:** Wayne State Univ, Univ of MI Labor Sch, certificate 1969; Wayne State Univ, BS 1971, MEd 1974, JD 1976; King Abdul Aziz Univ Saudi Arabia, certificate 1977. **CAREER:** Wayne County Comm Coll, Detroit MI, prof bus law & black studies, 1971-; Marygrove Coll, Detroit MI, prof real estate law, 1984; 36th Dist Court, Detroit MI, chief judge; City of Detroit, deputy mayor, 1989-. **ORGANIZATIONS:** Consult in comm affairs New Detroit Inc 1973-74; pres Black Legal Alliance 1975-76; founding mem Natl Conf of Black Lawyers Detroit Chap 1975-; com memNew Detroit Inc 1977-81; com mem The Econ Club of Detroit; hon club pres Optimist Club of Renaissance Detroit 1982-83; pres Assoc of Black Judges of MI1985-86; life mem Kappa Alpha Phi. **HONORS/ACHIEVEMENTS:** Grnd Fellowship HUD 1971-73; Grad Fellow SE MI Council of Govt 1971-73; Wolverine Bar Assn Scholarship Natl Bar Assn 1975; Cert of Distinction Com for Student Rights 1979; Certificate of Merit for Exceptional Achievement in Govt Affairs MI State Legislature 1980; Resolution of Tribute MI State Legislature 1981. **BUSINESS ADDRESS:** Deputy Mayor, City of Detroit, City-County Bldg, 2 Woodward Ave, Detroit, MI 48226. *

SHAKOOR, WAHEEDAH AQUEELAH (SANDRA SHORT ROBERSON)
Education administrator, elected official. **PERSONAL:** Born Feb 11, 1950, Washington, DC; children: Barella Nazirah. **EDUCATION:** Wilberforce Univ, 1968-71; Univ of Cincinnati, BS 1973; Univ of DC, MEd 1980; Trinity Coll, 1977-84. **CAREER:** Cincinnati Recreation Commiss, prog dir, mentally retarded 1973; Cincinnati Public Schools, teacher spec ed 1973-74; Univ of Islam, teacher, elem ed 1974-75; Charles Cty Schools, teacher spec ed 1976-

79; Dist of Columbia Public Schools, teacher, dept chairperson spec ed 1979-85. **ORGANIZATIONS:** Mem Council for Exceptional Children 1971-84; coach Spec Olympics 1974-77; mem Marshall Hts Civic Assoc 1981-84; adv neighborhood commiss DC Govt 1981-83; mem Capitol View Civic Assoc 1981-85; consult bd of ed Sis Clara Muhammad School 1981-85; exec bd mem Marshall Hts Comm Devel Org 1981-84; ed, pr Washington Saturday Coll 1982-85; pres Bilal Entr Inc 1983-85; mem Friends of the DC Youth Orchestra 1985-. **HONORS/ACHIEVEMENTS:** Dedication to Spec Olympics 1974; Serv Handicapped Parent Assoc Learning Disabled 1978; Outstanding Serv DCPS Eastern HS 1981; Serv Title I DCPS Title I Private School 1982; coord Far NE, SE Coalition for Mayoral Forum 1982; Serv to Community Marshall Hts Community Devel Org 1983; Hajij Rep Amer Muslim Mission 1984. **HOME ADDRESS:** 5340 East Capitol St, Washington, DC 20019. **BUSINESS ADDRESS:** Chairperson Spec Ed, DCPS-Anacostia High, 2406 21st Pl NE, Washington, DC 20018.

SHAMWELL, JOE
Radio executive. **PERSONAL:** Born Aug 29, 1944, District of Columbia; married Marcia L; children: Kenneth, Jehad, Ayanna, Ebay, Aisha. **EDUCATION:** Jackson State Univ, Mass Communications. **CAREER:** Songwriter/Producer/Recording Artist, 1966-; East Memphis Music Inc, professional mgr 1974-76; Groovesville Music Inc, dir of operations 1977-79; Lee King Productions, dir publicity & promotion 1976-84; J Shamwell Creative Svcs, pres 1977-; Jackson State Univ, adjunct prof mass comm 1980-84; WOKJ/WJMI, acct exec 1983-85; WACR AM/FM, genl mgr 1985-. **ORGANIZATIONS:** Vp Golden TRiangle Advertising Federation 1987-88; chmn Comm Affairs & Hospitality Columbus/Lownoes Chamber of Commerce 1987-88; acting pres Regional Assoc of Radio Execs 1987; mem NAACP, Main St Adv Bd Columbus 1987, Natl Black Media Coalition 1987. **HONORS/ACHIEVEMENTS:** Jingle of the Year Jackson Music Awds 1978-84; Songwriter of the Year Jackson Music Awds 1978,80,84; Disting Sales Awd SME 1984; Employee of the Year WOKJ/WJMI 1984; Outstanding Volunteer Serv Awd Governor of MS. **MILITARY SERVICE:** AUS personnel mgmt specialist 1969-72. **HOME ADDRESS:** 2705 5th St No #147, Columbus, MS 39701. **BUSINESS ADDRESS:** General Manager, WACR AM/FM, PO Box 1078, Columbus, MS 39703.

SHAMWELL, RONALD L.
Executive director. **PERSONAL:** Born Nov 08, 1942, Philadelphia; married Jean; children: Nathan, Monique. **EDUCATION:** Winston-Salem St U, BS 1969; Temple U, MSW 1973. **CAREER:** Philadelphia Schs, tchr 1970-71; asst Exec dir 1973; Antioch Coll, instr 1974; Wharton Cntr, exec dir 1974-. **ORGANIZATIONS:** Mem Assn Balck Social Wrkrs; Nat Fed Settlements; bd mem Urban Priorities; chmn bd North Central Dist Ylth an Dwelfare Coun; mem Delaware Valley Assn Dirs Vol Prog; bd mem Comm Concern #13; mem Rotary Club; consult TempleUniv Massiah Coll, Antioch Coll; chmn Yth Task Force North Central Phila; mem Philadelphia Chp Operation Breadbasket. **HONORS/ACHIEVEMENTS:** Honor awd Temple U; merit awd Antioch Coll. **BUSINESS ADDRESS:** 1708 N 22 St, Philadelphia, PA 19121.

SHANDS, FRANKLIN M., SR.
Business executive, educator. **PERSONAL:** Born Aug 11, 1920, Cincinnati; married Colleen Suel; children: Sharon Adell, Franklin, Jr. **EDUCATION:** Miami U, BFA 1946. **CAREER:** DePorres HS, teacher coach 1947-64; Purcell HS, teacher Coach 1964-69; Princeton HS, 1970-; artist illustrator 1944-46; Republic Natl Life Ins Co, agent. **ORGANIZATIONS:** Pres SW OH Track Coach Assn 1968-70; fndr dir Viking Relays; pres fndr Rembrandt Const Co and Shands Inc Builders 1947-70; contrib numerous art collections. **HONORS/ACHIEVEMENTS:** Coach of yr "A" OH St 1961, 63, Nt Dist 2 1969; Miami-Univ Track Hall of Fame 1970; Fred Hutchinson Meml Awd 1972; dinstgd serv awd Miami-Univ 1971; Bishop Alumni Medal 1971. **BUSINESS ADDRESS:** 11080 Chester Rd, Ste 215, Cincinnati, OH 45246.

SHANGE, NTOZAKE
Poet, playwriter. **PERSONAL:** Born Oct 18, 1948, Trenton, NJ. **EDUCATION:** Barnard Coll, BA am studies (cum laude) 1970;Univ so CA, MA 1973;"For Colored Girls Who Have Considered Suicide When the Rainbow is Enuf", poet author 1976; negros 1977; a photograph-Lovers in Motion 1977; Sounds in Motion Dance Co; performed in various jazz poetry Collaborations; Sonoma State U, mem faculty 1973-75; Mills Coll, mem faculty 1975; CCNY, mem faculty 1975; Douglass Coll, mem faculty 1978; lectr in field. **CAREER:** Mem of numerous soc including Poets & Writers Inc, NY Feminist Art Guild, Women's Inst for Freedom of Press. **ORGANIZATIONS:** Recip award Outer Critics Circle 1977; Obie Award 1977; Audelco Award 1977; Frank Silvera Writers Workshop Award 1978. **BUSINESS ADDRESS:** Assoc Prof of Drama, Univ of Houston, 4800 Cullen Dr, Houston, TX 77004.

SHANKS, JAMES A.
Mayor. **PERSONAL:** Born Feb 07, 1912, Tutwiler, MS; son of T.A. and Dora; married Willye B Harper. **EDUCATION:** MS Valley State Coll, BS Ed 1958;Univ of St Louis, 1961; MS State U, 1964-65. **CAREER:** Town of Jonestown, mayor 1973-, alderman 1973; Coahoma Co Sch Sys, tchr 1938-77. **ORGANIZATIONS:** Sec & treas NAACP 1944; exec com Dem Party for the Co & Dist 1974; deacon/supt & tchr Met Bapt Ch 1942; mem MACE 1944; mem Elks Club 1946; asst to prgms Elderly Hsng Inc/Manpower Proj Clarksdale MS 1978. **HONORS/ACHIEVEMENTS:** Outstdng Achvmnt in Pub Serv MS Vly State Coll Itta Bena 1977; MS Intrnl Dev Sys Gov of MS 1978. **BUSINESS ADDRESS:** Town of Jonestown, PO Box 110, Jonestown, MS 38639.

SHANKS, WILHELMINA BYRD
Retail executive. **PERSONAL:** Born Jul 19, 1951, Atlanta, GA; daughter of T. J. Watkins, Sr. and Annie Beatrice Byrd Watkins; married Harold Jerome Shanks, Sep 14, 1978; children: Harold Jerome, Jr.. **EDUCATION:** Morris Brown College, Atlanta GA, BA, 1973; Georgia State Univ, Atlanta GA, 1973-74. **CAREER:** Rich's, Atlanta GA, sales mgr, 1973-75, buyer, 1975-78; Jordan Marsh, Fort Lauderdale FL, divisional mgr, 1978-80; Macy's South, Atlanta GA, merchandise mgr, 1980-84, store mgr, 1984—, vice pres, 1986—. **ORGANIZATIONS:** American Business Women's Association. **HONORS/ACHIEVEMENTS:** English Award, Teachers Guild, 1973; Outstanding Leadership Award, Junior Achievement, 1974. **HOME ADDRESS:** 505 Trailside Court, Roswell, GA 30075.

SHANKS, WILLIAM COLEMON, JR.
Physician. **PERSONAL:** Born May 10, 1917, Burlington, NC; married Mary Louise Lorits; children: William DeWitt MD, Elissa Stewart. **EDUCATION:** Shaw Univ Raleigh NC BS 1939; Meharry Med Coll Nashville TN, MD 1943. **CAREER:** Meml Hosp of Alamance mem staff 1970-; Dept of Gen Pract, chief 1975-78; Alamance Co Hosp, staff mem 1955-80 Sharks Clinic. **ORGANIZATIONS:** Pres Old N State Med Soc 1957-58; 1st black mem Burlington City Bd of Educ 1964-87; bd mem Alamance-Caswell Reg Mntl Hlth Bd 1968-80 v chmn Burlington City Bd of Educ 1972-87; exec bd hlth & sfty chmn Boy Scouts of Am Cherokee Cncl 1972-74; life mem Alpha Phi Alpha. **HONORS/ACHIEVEMENTS:** Recipient 3 bronze stars & A-P Ribbon AUSMC 1945; Silver Beaver Awrd BSA 1974; Award of Merit Alamance Co Commn on Civic Afrs 1979. **MILITARY SERVICE:** AUSMC capt 1944-46. **BUSINESS ADDRESS:** Sharks Clinic, 532 Shepard St, Burlington, NC 27215

SHANNON, DAVID THOMAS
Educator. **PERSONAL:** Born Sep 26, 1933, Richmond, VA; married Shannon P Averett children: Vernita, Davine, David Jr. **EDUCATION:** VA Union Univ, BA 1954; VA Union Sch of Relig, BD 1957; Oberlin Grad Sch of Theo, STM 1959; Vanderbilt Univ, DMin 1974 Univ of Pgh, PhD 1975. **CAREER:** Antioch Baptist Church, stud asst 1957-59; Fair Oaks Baptist Church, pastor 1954-57; Oberlin Graduate School of Theo, grad asst 1958-59; VA Union Univ, lectr 1959-69; VA Union Univ, Univ pastor 1960-61; Ebenezer Baptist Church pastor 1960-69; Howard Univ Div School, visiting lecturer 1968; Amer Baptist Bd of Educ & Public, dir 1969-71; St Mary's Sem, visiting prof 1969-72; Bucknell Univ, prof & dir 1971-72; PA Theo Sem, dean of faculty 1972-; Hartford Sem Found, disting prof of biblical stud 1979; VA Union Univ, pres 1979-1985; Inter Denominational Theo Ctr, vice pres for academic affairs 1985-. **ORGANIZATIONS:** Chairperson Baptist Task Force of the World Baptist Alliance for Dialogue with the Secretariat of the Roman Cath Church; mem Soc for Biblical Lit; unit comm Natl Coun Ch; comm on theol concerns Amer Bapt Conv; coun comm United Presby Ch USA; bd of dirs First & Merchants Natl Bank of Richmond; BaptWorld Alliance gen bd of Amer Baptist Ch USA; mem Amer Assn Higher Educ; mem Amer Acad of Religion, Richmond Rotary Club, Soc for Biblical Lit, Soc for Study of Black Religion; broadcast series Amer Baptist Conv 1973-74; mem scholarship selection com Phillip Morris New York City 1980-; dir Sovran Bank Richmond 1980-; bd dirs Urban Training Atlanta 1985-; mem Deans & Registrars Atlanta Univ Ctr 1985-; life mem NAACP; mem Alpha Kappa Mu, Phi Beta Sigma. **HONORS/ACHIEVEMENTS:** Who's Who in Religion 1977; Dictionary of Intl Biog 1977; named Man of Year NCCJ 1981; numerous publs including "Theol Methodology & The Black Expereince,"The Future of Black Theol 1977; "The Old Testament Exper of Faith," Judson Press 1977; "Roots, Some Theol Reflections," Journal of Interdenom Sem 1979. **BUSINESS ADDRESS:** VP for Academic Affairs, Inter Denominational Theo Ctr 671 Beckwith Street, SW, Atlanta, GA 30314.

SHANNON, GEORGE A.
Mayor. **PERSONAL:** Born Sep 17, 1918, Pleasant Hill, LA; son of Wilkin Shannon and Elma Jones Shannon; children (previous marriage): W Ronald; married Elvera Ricks, Apr 19, 1984; children: Michael K. **EDUCATION:** Southern Univ, Baton Rouge LA, BS, 1949 Bishop College, Marshall TX, MS, 1955. **CAREER:** Sabine Parish School Board, Many LA, principal, 1949-79; currently mayor of Town of Pleasant Hill LA. **ORGANIZATIONS:** Carver Civic Org. **MILITARY SERVICE:** US Army, 1st sergeant. **HOME ADDRESS:** 409 Texas St, PO Box 127, Pleasant Hill, LA 71065. **BUSINESS ADDRESS** Mayor, Town of Pleasant Hill, 100 Pearl St, PO Box 125, Pleasant Hill, LA 71065.

SHANNON, JOHN W.
Government official. **PERSONAL:** Born Sep 13, 1933, Louisville; children: one child. **EDUCATION:** Central State Univ, BS 1955; Shippenburg Coll, MS 1975. **CAREER:** Office of Sec Army Washington, congressional liaison officer 1972-74; Dept of the Army Washington, deputy dir for manpower and res affairs 1978-81; Office of the Asst Sec of Defense Legislative Affairs, special asst for manpower res affairs/logistics 1978-81, deputy under sec 1981-84 asst sec for installations/logistics 1984-. **MILITARY SERVICE:** AUS col; Legion of Merit, Bronze Star, Combat Infantry Badge, others.

SHANNON, MARIAN L.H.
Counselor. **PERSONAL:** Born Oct 14, 1922, Escambia Co, FL; married TJ. **EDUCATION:** Hampton Inst, BS 1944, MEd 1964; Ewd Waters Coll, Hon Doc deg 1954. **CAREER:** Dade Co Public School, school counselor chairperson Student Serv Guid & Tstng Booker T Washington Jr HS; Curr Writer Fed Proj, "Self Concept", Images in Black" & "Counseling the Minority Student"; Business Educ Courses Social Studies Courses, teacher **ORGANIZATIONS:** Pres FL State Tchrs Assn 1965-66; pres Dade Co Persnl & Guid Assn 1973-74; mem Professional Prac Council of FL 1965-71; NEA Resolutions Com 1966-72; Nat Council of Tchr Educ Evaluation Bd 1973-76; Am Assn ofUniv Women; past Nat trustee Educ of Nat Mag ARCHON Zeta Phi Beta Sor 1963-70; Nat dir Pub Rels Zeta Phi Beta Sor Inc; corr sec HERSTORY Inc Pblshrs of Dade Co Women in Hist; guild chrprsn Miami Chap March of Dimes Fnd. **HONORS/ACHIEVEMENTS:** Cited in Outstndng Personalities of South 1968; Who's Who of Am Women 1970-73; recip Outstndng Cit Omega Psi Phi Frat 1967; Meritorious Serv Awrd Outstndng Zeta, Zeta Phi Beta Sor 1965, 1970; Outstndng Serv Awrd professional orgns 1971-73. **BUSINESS ADDRESS:** 1200 NW Sixth Ave, Miami FL 33136.

SHANNON, ODESSA M.
County government official. **PERSONAL:** Born Jul 04, 1928, Washington, DC; divorced children: Mark V, Lisa S. **EDUCATION:** Smith Coll, BA 1950. **CAREER:** EEOC, dep dir field serv 1979-81, dir prog planning & evaluation 1981-82, prog dir 1982-84, ex asst Of of Research; Bureau of Census, comp syst analyst; Baltimore Public School, teacher; special asst to county exec 1984-86; Montgomery County MD, dir human serv coord & planning 1986-. **ORGANIZATIONS:** Mbr bd of ed Montgomery Co, MD 1982-84; reg bd of dir Nat Conf of Christians & Jews 1980-; Local Council; United Way; mem Alpha Kappa Alpha Sor NAACP; bd dir Regional Inst for Children & Adolescents; bd dir MT Co Arts Council; chmn of bd Coalition for Equitable Representation in Govt 1986-. **HONORS/ACHIEVEMENTS:** Am Assoc Pub Adm Outstand Pub Serv 1984; NAACP Legal Def & Ed Fund Excptnl Achvmnts 1984; Outstand Pub Serv AKA 1984; Kappa Alpha Psi 1982; AlphaPhi Alpha 1978; Omega Psi Phi 1977; Outstanding Achievements in Human Rights TX State NAACP, 1983. Intl Book of Honor 1986. **HOME ADDRESS:** 13320 Bea Kay Dr, Silver Spring, MD 20904.

SHANNON, ROBERT F.
Educator. **PERSONAL:** Born Jul 15, 1920, Montgomery, AL; married Eloise Wynn; children: Robert, Yolanda, Valerie, Charles. **EDUCATION:** AL State Tchrs Coll, BS 1940; Wayne State U, MA 1955, EdS 1974. **CAREER:** Detroit Bd Educ In-School Neighborhood Youth Corps, proj dir; Detroit Bd Educ, admin 1968-, elem staff coord 1967-68, job upgrading & Couns 1965-67, teacher1964-65; Neighborhood Serv Org, group worker 1954-64. **ORGANIZATIONS:** Mem educ com Detroit Urban League 1972-73; trustee Detroit Counc for Youth Serv Inc 1971-; subcom on Juvenile Delinq State of MI 1968-71; pres bd trust Afro-Am Museum of Detroit 1974; deacon Tabernacle Bapt Ch 1961; mem bd dir Met Detroit Soc of Black Educ Adminstrs 1971. **HONORS/ACHIEVEMENTS:** Outstanding serv to sch & comm Wash Sch PTA 1963; Outstndng Man of Year Tabernacle Bapt Ch 1964; Youth Serv Awrd Hannan Br YMCA 1969-71; Crisis Team Intervention in Sch-Comm Unrest Social Casework 1971. **MILITARY SERVICE:** AUS pfc 1943-46. **BUSINESS ADDRESS:** 10100 Grand River, Detroit, MI 48204.

SHARP, CHARLES LOUIS
Business executive. **PERSONAL:** Born May 19, 1951, Madisonville, KY. **EDUCATION:** General Motors Scholar, 1969-73; Millikin Univ, BS 1973; Washington Univ, MBA 1975. **CAREER:** RJ Reynolds Tobacco USA, brand asst 1975-77, brand mgr 1978-81, planning mgr 1982-86, group mgr 1986-. **ORGANIZATIONS:** Big brother Big Brother/Big Sister 1983-87; mem YMCA 1984-; treas Civic Devel Council 1987. **HONORS/ACHIEVEMENTS:** Appreciation Cert Black Exec Exchange Prog. **HOME ADDRESS:** 7624 Penland Dr, Clemmons, NC 27012. **BUSINESS ADDRESS:** Group Manager, RJ Reynolds Tabacco Co, 401 N Main St, Winston-Salem, NC 27102.

SHARP, JAMES ALFRED
Mayor. **PERSONAL:** Born May 28, 1933, New York, NY; married Tessie Marie Baltrip; children: Owen, Jacqueline A, James A III, LaTanya M. **EDUCATION:** Univ of CA San Diego, attended; Harvard Univ, attended. **CAREER:** US Marine Corps, retired 1st sgt 20 yrs; US Senate; Senator Donald Riegle Jr, mgr state serv 11 yrs; City of Flint MI, mayor. **MILITARY SERVICE:** USMC 20 yrs; Served in Korea, Cuba, Vietnam; Vietnam Cross of Gallantry; 3 Navy Commendation Medals for Valor; Purple Heart. **BUSINESS ADDRESS:** Mayor, City of Flint, 1101 S Saginaw St, Flint, MI 48503.

SHARP, JEAN MARIE
Educational administrator. **PERSONAL:** Born Dec 31, 1945, Gary, IN. **EDUCATION:** Ball State U, BA 1967; IN U, MA Tchng 1969; ColumbiaUniv Tchrs Coll, EdM 1975, EdD 1976. **CAREER:** Montclair Bd of Educ, dir of pupil 1978-, asst supt for admin serv 1978; Office for Human & Devel Serv, special asst to asst sec 1977; Gen Asst Center Columbia Univ, field specialist 1976; W Side HS Gary IN, dept chmn/teacher 1969-72; Froebel HS Gary IN, teacher 1966-68. **ORGANIZATIONS:** Mem Am Assn of Sch Admnstrs 1980; mem Black Child Dev Inst 1980; mem Kappa Delta Pi 1980; coord 1st & 2nd Annual Black Representation Org Symposiums1973-74; tchr (vol) Uhuru Sasa Sch Brooklyn 1975; vice pres Nu Age Cntr of Harlem 1979-. **HONORS/ACHIEVEMENTS:** Outstndng Yng Women of the Yr United Fedn of Women 1971; Doctoral Prgm in Educ Ldrshp Flwshp Ford Fdn 1973-76; Student Sen Awrd of Merit & Serv ColumbiaUniv New York City 1974; Human Resources Flwshp Rockefeller Fnd 1977. **BUSINESS ADDRESS:** Montclair Board of Education, 22 Valley Road, Montclair, NJ 07042.

SHARP, LAWRENCE N., JR.
Realtor. **PERSONAL:** Born Jan 23, 1959, Knoxville, TN. **EDUCATION:** Jacksonville State Univ, BA 1979, BS 1981, MBA 1982. **CAREER:** Paschal Realty Co, sales mgr 1983-85; Re/Max East Inc, realtor/marketing consultant 1985-. **ORGANIZATIONS:** Mem Atlanta Exchange; bd of dirs Natl Black MBA; mem Jr Entrepreneur Traders Assoc, DeKalb Co Meals on Wheels, New Birth Missionary Baptist Church, DeKalb Bd of Realtors, Young Realtors Council, GA Assoc of Realtors, Natl Assoc of Realtors; comm mem GA Assoc of Minority Entrepreneurs; co-chairman public relations GAME; chairman United Negro College Fund Comm for Natl Black MBA's; mem Kiwanis Intl 1985-; pro business project Atlanta Exchange 1985-. **HONORS/ACHIEVEMENTS:** Outstanding Young Men in Amer 1981,84,85,86,87; President Club Re/Max of GA 1985; Executive Club Re/Max of GA 1986; Agent of the Month Re/Max East Inc 1986. **HOME ADDRESS:** 1922 Corners Circle, Lithonia, GA 30058.

SHARP, SAUNDRA
Writer, actress, filmmaker. **PERSONAL:** Born Dec 21, 1942, Cleveland, OH; daughter of Clarence McIntyre and Faythe McIntyre. **EDUCATION:** Bowling Green State Univ, Bowling Green OH, BS, 1964; attended Los Angeles City Coll, Los Angeles CA, 1980-84, 1989. **CAREER:** Actress in film, "The Learning Tree," and in plays "Black Girl," "To Be Young, Gifted, and Black," and "Hello, Dolly!"; appeared in TV movies "Hollow Image," "Minstrel Man," "One More Hurdle: The Donna Cheek Story" and in TV series "Wonder Woman," "Knots Landing," "St. Elsewhere"; films include "Back Inside Herself," "Life Is A Saxophone" (documentary), "Picking Tribes"; assoc editor of Black Film Review; former editor of Black Anti-Defamation Coalition newsletter. **ORGANIZATIONS:** Mem, Black American Cinema Society; found mem, Reel Black Women; mem, Atlanta African Film Society. **HONORS/ACHIEVEMENTS:** Author of poetry volumes From the Windows of My Mind (1970), In the Midst of Change (1972), Soft Song (1978); author of stageplay "The Sistuhs"; publisher of Blood Lines by Robert Earl Price, 1978, and Directory of Black Film/TV Technicians and Artists, West Coast, 1980; 1st place, Black American Film Society, 1984, 1989, for film production; 1st place, San Francisco Poetry Film Festival, 1985; Heritage Magazine Award for outstanding journalism, 1988; Paul Robeson Award, Newark Black Film Festival, 1989; film awards for "Picking Tribes" from Women in Film, Black American Cinema Society, and National Black Programming Consortium. **BUSINESS ADDRESS:** PO Box 75796, Sanford Sta, Los Angeles, CA 90075.

SHARPE, AUDREY HOWELL
Educator. **PERSONAL:** Born Dec 14, 1938, Elizabeth City, NC; daughter of Simon Howell and Essie Griffin Howell; married Willie M, Aug 07, 1964; children: Kimberly Y. **EDUCATION:** Hampton Inst, BS 1960; Northwestern Univ, MA 1966; Ball State Univ, EdD 1980. **CAREER:** State of IN Ft Wayne, speech & hearing therapist 1960-62; State of IL Dixon, hearing & speech specialist 1962-64; Ft Wayne, speech & hearing therapist 1964-65; Univ of MI Children's Psychiatric Hospital Ann Arbor, educational diagnostician language pathic asst prin 1965-68; E Wayne State Center Ft Wayne, Headstart dir 1968-69; Purdue Univ, lecturer in educ 1968-69; Village Woods Jr High, asst principal 1980-81; Village Elementary School, principal 1981-; East Allen Co School, Title I teacher 1973-74, Title I coordinator 1974, principal. **ORGANIZATIONS:** Mem Amer Speech & Hearing Assn 1961-74; Assn for Children with Learning Disabilities 1968; mem bd dir Three Rivers Assn for Children with Learning Disabilities 1969-72; mem Delta Sigma Theta, Alpha Kappa Mu, Kappa Delta Pi, Natl Assn of Elementary Schools Principals, IN Assoc of Elementary & Middle School Principals, Assoc for Supervision & Curriculum Devel; Public Library of Ft Wayne & Allen Co; bd dir Allen Co Child Care Commn; bd dir YWCA 1984-87; mem Jr League of Ft Wayne; Natl Assn of Elementary School Principals; Indiana Assn of Elementary and Middle School Principals; Natl Assn for Supervision and Curriculum Devel; Phi Delta Kappa; Intl Reading Assn; Ft Wayne Alliance of Black School Eductors. **HONORS/ACHIEVEMENTS:** Woman of Year Delta Sigma Theta 1973; Florene Williams Service Award 1986; Phi Beta Sigma Educator of the Year 1987; Kappa Alpha Psi Fraternity Serv Award 1984-85; Educational Service Award, Phi Beta Sigma Fraternity 1988; publications: "Another View of Affective Education: The Four Hs-Honesty, Humaneness, Humility, and Hope," Principal, Fall 1985, guest columnist for "Fort Wayne News-Sentinel," "Frost Illustrated," "Language Training in Headstart Programs," ISHA, Spring 1969, "Pass Me That Language Ticket," Principal, Spring 1986, "Physical Education, A No Frills Component to the Elementary Curriculum," Principal, Fall 1984. **HOME ADDRESS:** 6727 Lakecrest Ct, Fort Wayne, IN 46815. **BUSINESS ADDRESS:** Principal, East Allen County Schools, 4625 Werling Dr, Fort Wayne, IN 46806.

SHARPE, CALVIN WILLIAM
Educator, arbitrator. **PERSONAL:** Born Feb 22, 1945, Greensboro, NC; daughter of Ralph David and Mildred Johnson Sharpe; married Janice McCoy Jones; children: Kabral, Melanie, Stephanie. **EDUCATION:** Clark Coll, BA 1967; Oberlin Coll, Post-Baccalaureate 1968; Chicago Theological Seminary, attended 1969-71; Northwestern Univ Law Sch, JD 1974. **CAREER:** Hon Hubert L Will US District Court, law clerk 1974-76; Cotton Watt Jones King & Bowlus Law Firm, assoc 1976-77; Natl Labor Relations Bd, trial attorney 1977-81; Univ of VA Law School, asst prof 1981-84; Case Western Reserve Univ, prof of law (tenured) 1964-. **ORGANIZATIONS:** Mem labor panel Amer Arbitration Assoc 1984-; bd of trustees Cleveland Hearing & Speech Ctr 1985-; mem OH State Employment Relations Bd Panel of Neutrals 1985-; chair-evidence section Amer Assoc of Law Schools 1987; exec bd Public Sector Labor Relations Assoc 1987-89; Federal Mediation and Conciliation Serv Roster of Arbitrators 1987-; Permanent Arbitrator Ohio Office of Collective Bargaining, OH Health Care Employees Assoc Dist 1199 1987-; AFSCME/OCSEA 1987-; State Council of Professional Educators OEA/NEA 1989-; Youth Services Subsidy Advisory Bd of Commissioners, Cuyahoga County Ohio. **HONORS/ACHIEVEMENTS:** Publications "Two-Step Balancing and the Admissibility of Other Crimes Evidence, A Sliding Scale of Proof" 59 Notre Dame Law Review 556 1984; "Proof of Non-Interest in Representation Disputes, A Burden Without Reason" 11 Univ Dayton Law Review 3 1985; "Fact-Finding in Ohio, Advancing the Pole of Rationality in Public Sector Collective Bargaining," Univ of Toledo Law Review 1987; "NLRB Deferral to Grievance-Arbitration, A General Theory," 48 Ohio St LJ No 3 1987; Introduction, The Natl War Labor Bd and Critical Issues in the Development of Modern Grievance Arbitration, 39 Case W Res L Rev No 2 1988. **HOME ADDRESS:** 2350 Ardleigh Dr, Cleveland Heights, OH 44106. **BUSINESS ADDRESS:** Prof of Law, Case Western ReserveUniv, 11075 East Boulevard, Cleveland, OH 44106.

SHARPE, RONALD M.
Law enforcement executive. **PERSONAL:** Born Apr 16, 1940, Philadelphia, PA; son of Cornelius Wendell Sharpe and Elizabeth Morgan Sharpe; married Jessie L. Sowell, May 01, 1965; children: Martin, Tracey, Jennifer. **EDUCATION:** Northwestern Univ, Evanston IL, Police Admin Trng, 1968; Elizabethtown College, Elizabethtown PA, BA, 1975; St Francis College, Loretto PA, MA, 1978; additional graduate study at Temple Univ. **CAREER:** Pennsylvania State Police, Hershey PA, 1962, Harrisburg PA, corporal, 1969, Washington PA, sergeant, 1976, Lancaster PA, lieutenant, 1977, Milesburg PA, captain, 1985, Harrisburg PA, major, 1986, deputy commissioner, 1987, commissioner, 1987—. **ORGANIZATIONS:** International Association of Chiefs of Police, National Org of Black Law Enforcement Executives, Pennsylvania Chiefs of Police Association, NAACP. **HONORS/ACHIEVEMENTS:** Law Enforcement Oscar, Philadelphia Housing Police & International Union of Police Assn; achievement awards from Optimist Club, Lions Club, 5th Masonic District, and 111th Tactical Air Support Group. **BUSINESS ADDRESS:** Commissioner, Pennsylvania State Police, 1800 Elmerton Ave, Harrisburg, PA 17110.

SHARPP, NANCY CHARLENE
Social service administrator. **PERSONAL:** Born in Pine Bluff, AR; married Tilmon Lee Sharpp; children: Tilmon Monroe. **EDUCATION:** Wayne St Univ, BA 1961; Governors St Univ, MA 1976. **CAREER:** IL Dept of Corrections Juvenile Div, supervisor, admin 1966-79; IL Dept Children & Family Services, manager for support services 1979-81, case review admin 1981-; West Maywood Park Dist, pres bd of commrs. **ORGANIZATIONS:** Panelist Panel of American Women 1968-72; founder/past pres Chicago Area Club-Nat'l Assoc of Negro Business & Prof Womens Clubs, Inc 1977-82; founder Ascension to Manhood, Inc 1982; life mem Nat'l Assoc of Negro Business Prof Womens Clubs, Inc; appointed commr of West Maywood Park Dist 1981; elected to 2 yrunexpired term 1983; elected to 6 yr term 1985. **HONORS/ACHIEVEMENTS:** Nat'l Presidents Award Nat'l Assoc of Negro Business & Prof Womens Clubs, Inc 1977; Sperry-Hutchins Comm Service Award Sperry-Hutchins Corp/NANBPW, Inc 1981; Comm Image Award Fred Hampton Mem Scholarship Fund, Inc 1983. **BUSINESS ADDRESS:** President Bd of Commissioners, West Maywood Park District, 16th and Washington, Maywood, IL 60153.

SHARRIEFF, OSMAN IBN
Journalist. **PERSONAL:** Born May 09, 1935, Corinth, MS; son of Osman Sharrieff and Maryam Bankhead Sharrieff; married Gloria Howard Sharrieff, May 07, 1989; children: Sabakhan, Laela. **EDUCATION:** Univ of Bordeux France, Journalism 1958-59; Chicago Loop Jr Coll, Polit Sci 1960-62; Univ of Chicago, Linguistics 1961; Al-Azhar Univ Egypt, Islamic Culture 1970-71. **CAREER:** Tri-City Journal, publisher. **ORGANIZATIONS:** Chmn Black Media Reps 1974; vice pres Black Media Inc 1975-87. **HONORS/ACHIEVEMENTS:** Black Media Rep Serv 1974; Best Feature Article NNPA 1976; Best News Picture NNPA 1977. **MILITARY SERVICE:** AUS pfc 2 yrs. **BUSINESS ADDRESS:** Publisher, Tri-City Journal, 8 South Michigan, Chicago, IL 60603.

SHAVERS, CATHERINE
Commissioner. **PERSONAL:** Born Feb 22, 1928, Montgomery; divorced; children: Adell, Vickie, Brenda, Kenneth. **CAREER:** Wayne Co, cnty commr; Detroit Labor Action Council, coord 1969-70. **ORGANIZATIONS:** Fdr & past pres Westside Teen Dems & Westside Youth Inc; Organized Webber Jr HS Comm Council; exec mem Greater OIC of Detroit; mem Local 174 & UAW; TULC-MDLCA Gen Council; United Black Trade Unionist; mem Dem Party; Dem Council of Precinct Delegates; MI Fed Dem Club; James Europe Post 3080 Womens Aux; Beulah Lan Temple IBPOE. **HONORS/ACHIEVEMENTS:** Appreciation Awrd from Grtr OIC of Metro Detroit 1975; Humanitarian of Year Neighborhood Leg Serv 1971; Humanitarian of Yr Lidranso Soc & Civ Club 1969; Humanitarian Awrd Cancer Fnd 1968. **BUSINESS ADDRESS:** 726 City Co Bldg, Detroit, MI.

SHAW, ALVIA A.
Clergyman. **PERSONAL:** Born May 07, 1915, Duarte, CA; married Ruth; children: Alvia, Jr, Wendell. **EDUCATION:** Univ of So CA;; BA; Pacific Sch of Religion, MDiv. **CAREER:** St James AME Ch Cleveland, pastor 1968-; St Paul AME Ch Columbus OH, former pastor; First AME Ch, former pastor 1951-56. **ORGANIZATIONS:** Mem OH AME Conv; consult Nat Council of Ch; mem NAACP. **HONORS/ACHIEVEMENTS:** Recipient hon DD Payne Theol Sem. **MILITARY SERVICE:** AUS chaplain 1942-46. **BUSINESS ADDRESS:** St James AME Church, 8401 Cedar Ave, Cleveland, OH 44103.

SHAW, ANN
Executive. **PERSONAL:** Born Nov 21, 1921, Columbus, OH; daughter of Pearl Daniel White and Sarah Roberts White; widowed; children: Valerie, Leslie Jr, Rebecca, Dan. **EDUCATION:** Univ of Redlands, LHD 1971;Univ So CA, MSW 1968; OH State U, MA 1944;Univ Redlands, AB 1943. **CAREER:** UCLA, tchr; LA Job Corps Ctr Women, exec asst 1965-66; LA City Sch, tchr 1949-51; Central St Coll, asst prof 1946-48; VA Union U, instr; Founders Savings & Loan Assoc, chmn of the bd. **ORGANIZATIONS:** Bd mem, The California Community Found, The California Medical Center Found, The Cathedral Corp of the Episcopal Church; appointed to serve on California Joint Select Task Force on the Changing Family; alumni assn; Univ So CA; OH State & Redlands U; PTA; Nat Council Negro Women; NAACP; appointed by Gov of CA 1st Black 1st Women to serve on State Commn on Judicial Performance 1976; mem YWCA World Serv Council; pres Wilfandel Club; mem Awds & Recognition Comm; sec corporate bd, United Way Inc; mem bd of visitors UCLA School of Med, Loyola Law School. **HONORS/ACHIEVEMENTS:** Agency leadership awards & com Womens Div United Way; certificate merit Assn Study Negro Life & Hist 1964; Univ Redlands 1964; Woman of the Year LA Sentinel Newspaper 1964; Mother of the Year CA State Assn Colored Women Clubs 1967; Royal Blue Book; NAACP Legal Defense & Educ Fund Award Black Women of Achievement 1985; Big Sisters of Los Angeles Awd 1986; CA Senate Woman of the Year Awdfor Senatorial Dist 30, 1987; United Way's Highest Honor The Gold Key Award; The Athena Award, YWCA, 1989; Community Serv Award, YWCA, 1989; The Key Council Award, California Afro-Amer Museum, 1989.

SHAW, BERNARD
Television news anchor. **PERSONAL:** Born May 22, 1940, Chicago, IL; son of Edgar Shaw and Camilla Murphy Shaw; married Linda Allston, Mar 30, 1974; children: Amar Edgar, Anil Louise. **EDUCATION:** University of Illinois at Chicago Circle, 1963. **CAREER:** WYNR/WNUS-Radio, Chicago IL, reporter, 1964-66; Westinghouse Broadcasting Co, Chicago IL, reporter, 1966-68; correspondent in Washington DC, 1968-71; Colum bia Broadcasting System (CBS), Washington DC, television reporter, 1971-74, correspondent, 1974-77; American Broadcasting Co (ABC), Miami FL, correspondent and chief of Latin American bureau, 1977-79; Cable News Network (CNN), Washington DC, television news anchor, 1980—. **ORGANIZATIONS:** National Press Club; Sigma Delta Chi. **HONORS/ACHIEVEMENTS:** Honorary doctorate, Marion College, 1985; distinguished service award, Congressional Black Caucus, 1985; named to top ten outstanding business and professional honorees list, 1988. **MILITARY SERVICE:** US Marine Corps, 1959-63. **BUSINESS ADDRESS:** Cable News Network, Turner Broadcasting System, 111 Massachusetts Ave NW, 3rd Floor, Washington, DC 20001. *

SHAW, BOOKER THOMAS
Judge. **PERSONAL:** Born Sep 14, 1951, St Louis, MO; married Laine C. **EDUCATION:** Southern IL Univ Carbondale, BA Govt 1973; Catholic Univ of Amer, JD 1976; MO Bar, 1976. **CAREER:** Fed Trade Commiss, law clerk 1974; Columbus Comm Legal Svcs, law clerk 1975-76; Circuit Attny Office, asst circuit attny 1976-83; MO 22nd Circuit Court,assoc circuit judge 1983-. **ORGANIZATIONS:** Mem Mound City Bar Assoc, Metro Bar Assoc; trustee St John AME Church. **HONORS/ACHIEVEMENTS:** Southern IL Univ Scholarship Awd in Music 1970-72; Spirit of St Louis Scholarship Awd 1975; Disting Serv Mound City Bar 1983; Disting Serv Circuit AttnySt Louis 1983. **BUSINESS ADDRESS:** Judge Assoc Circuit Court, Missouri Circuit Court, Civil Courts Bldg, St Louis, MO 63101.

SHAW, CHARLES A.
Judge. **PERSONAL:** Born Dec 31, 1944, Jackson, TN; married Kathleen Marie Ingram; children: Bryan Ingram. **EDUCATION:** Harris-Stowe Coll, BA, 1966; Univ of Missouri, MBS, 1971; Catholic Univ of Amer, JD, 1974. **CAREER:** Berlin Roisman & Kessler, law clerk, 1972; Dept of Justice, Law Enforcement Asst Admin, law clerk, 1972-73; Office of Mayor, DC, assigned to DC publ school, hearing officer, 1973-74; Natl Labor Relations Bd (enforcement litigation div DC), attorney, 1973-76; Lashly-Caruthers-Thies-Rava & Hamel (law firm), attorney, 1976-80; Dept of Justice, E Dist of Missouri, asst US attorney, 1980-87; State of Missouri, circuit judge, current. **ORGANIZATIONS:** Chairperson, labor mgmt relations comm, Amer Bar Assn Young Lawyers Div, 1976-77; MO state vice chairperson, Econ of Law Section Amer Bar Assn, 1976-77; comm mem, Lawyers Fee Dispute Comm, St Louis Met Bar Assn, 1979-80; mem, Am Bar Assn, MO Bar Assn, DC Bar Assn, MO State & Corporate Comm, United Negro Coll Fund, 1978-80, NAACP, Catholic Univ Law School Alumni Assn, Harris-Stowe Coll Alumni Assn; bd mem, St Louis Black Forum, 1979-80, bd of trustees, St Louis Art Museum, 1979-80. **HONORS/ACHIEVEMENTS:** St Louis Leadership Fellow, Danforth Found, 1978-79; Distinguished Serv Citation, United Negro Coll Fund, 1979. **BUSINESS ADDRESS:** Civil Courts Bldg, 10 N Tucker Blvd, St Louis, MO 63101.

SHAW, CURTIS E.
Association executive. **PERSONAL:** Born Dec 31, 1944, Jackson, TN; married Kathleen Marie. **EDUCATION:** Harris-Stowe Coll, BA 1966;;Univ of MO, MBA 1971; CathUniv of Am, JD 1974. **CAREER:** E Dist of MO Dept of Justice, asst US atty; Lashly-Caruthers-Thies-Rava & Hamel (Law Firm), atty 1976-80; Nat Labor Rels Bd, atty enfrcmnt lit div DC 1973-76; Mayor DC assigned to DC Pub Sch, hearing officer 1973-74; Law Enforc Asst Admin Deptg of Justice, law clk 1972-73; Berlin Roisman & Kessler, law clk 1972. **ORGANIZATIONS:** Chrprsn Labor Mgmt Rels Com Am Bar Assn Young Lwyrs Div 1976-77; MO State v-chrprsn Econ of Law Sect Am Bar Assn 1976-77; com mem Lawyers Fee Dispute Com St Louis Met Bar Assn 1979-80; mem Am Bar Assn, MO Bar Assn, DC Bar Assn; MO State & Corp Com United Negro Coll Fund 1978-80; bd mem St Louis Black Forum 1979-80; bd of trustees St Louis Art Museum 1979-80; mem NAACP CathUniv Law Sch Alumni & Assn Harris Stowe Coll Alumni Assn St Louis Ldrshp Flw Danforth Fnd 1978-79. **HONORS/ACHIEVEMENTS:** Distngshd Serv Citation United Negro Coll Fund 1979. **BUSINESS ADDRESS:** 11821 Euclid Ave, Cleveland, OH 44106.

SHAW, CURTIS MITCHELL
Attorney. **PERSONAL:** Born Apr 13, 1944, Jacksonville, TX; married Ann; children: Caja, Curtis Jr, Kendra, Alexis. **EDUCATION:** Univ of NM, BS 1967; Loyola Univ of LA, JD 1975. **CAREER:** Priv Prac, atty; Musical Entertainers & Motion Picture Personalities, rep; Denver Public Schools, educator; LA Unified School Dist Bd; Hollywood Chamber of Commerce; LA Co Bar Assn; Langston Law Club; Amer Bar Assn; Beverly Hills Bar Assn. **ORGANIZATIONS:** Dir num motion picture & prod cos. **BUSINESS ADDRESS:** 6255 Sunset Blvd, Ste 1005, Hollywood, CA 90028.

SHAW, DAVID CALVIN
Professional athlete. **PERSONAL:** Born May 27, 1957, Norco, CA. **EDUCATION:** California. **CAREER:** Oakland Invaders, lb 1982. **ORGANIZATIONS:** Owner Reliable Building Serv Oakland. **HONORS/ACHIEVEMENTS:** Had 4 1/2 quarterback sacks for 23 1/2 yds; totaled 90 tackles; started all 18 games at outside linebacker; voted the Bears' Defensive MVP as a sr; also played in Japan Bowl.

SHAW, DENISE
Attorney. **PERSONAL:** Born Feb 19, 1949, Los Angeles, CA. **EDUCATION:** Bard Coll, AB 1971; Univ of PA Sch of Law, JD 1974. **CAREER:** US Dept of HUD Ofc of Reg Couns, atty; Texaco, law clk 1972; Yvonne Burke Asmblywmn, legis intern 1970. **ORGANIZATIONS:** Mem PA Bar Assn; bd dir Bishop RR Wright Meml Hlth Ctr; civ rghts com PA Bar Assn; Legal Educ Com Nat Bar Assn; Hous Com; Civ Rghts Com;adminstrv law com Fed Bar Assn. **HONORS/ACHIEVEMENTS:** Prfrmnc awd Ofc of Gen Couns Dept of HUD. **BUSINESS ADDRESS:** Brad College Alumni Office, c/o Susan Mason, Annandale Hudson, NY 12504.

SHAW, FERDINAND
Executive. **PERSONAL:** Born May 30, 1933, McDonough, GA; children: Mark, Gail. **EDUCATION:** OH State U, BS Nursing 1955; Boston U, MS 1957; Union Grad Sch, PhD cand 1980. **CAREER:** OH StateUniv Sch of Nursing, asso prof 1973; OH State U, instr/asst prof 1957-73; Cincinnati Gen Hosp, staff nurse/asst head nurse 1955-56. **ORGANIZATIONS:** Adv com Am Nrs Assn RN Maternity Flwshp Prog 1973-; 2nd vice pres Am Nrs Assn 1974-76; chrprsn Am Nrs Assn Com on Human Rights 1976-; consult & review panel mem Div of Nrsng Dept of HEW 1965-74; bd mem Sex Info & Educ Council of US 1971-74; consult Womens Rsrch Staff Nat Inst of Educ Dept of HEW1975. **HONORS/ACHIEVEMENTS:** Recipient Mortarboard Awrd OH StateUniv 1970; Centennial Awrd OH StateUniv Sch of Nursing 1970; awrd for Contrib to Orgn Nat Black Nurses Assn 1974-77; Flwshp Am Acad of Nursing Am Nurses Assn 1979. **BUSINESS ADDRESS:** 830 K St Mall, Sacramento, CA 95814.

SHAW, FREDERICK B.
Association executive. **PERSONAL:** Born Dec 08, 1935, St Louis. **EDUCATION:** So IL U, BS 1959, MA 1966. **CAREER:** Curative Workshp of Milw, counselor 1961-62; Milwaukee Schs, tchr cnslr 1962-64; Jewish Voc Serv of Milw, counselor 1964; State CA, rehab counselor 1964-66; Dept Rehab CA Patton State Hosp, program supr 1966-69; State CA Dept Rehab, asst dpty dir fld oper; Chapman Coll, lectr 1971-72;Univ So CA, 1970-71; Pub Afrs Radio Show "Rap Line", host moderator. **ORGANIZATIONS:** Mem Nat Rehab Assn; exec bd So CA Chap NRA 1972-75; mem CA Coor Council NRA Nat; pres Nat Assn Non-White Rehab Wrkrs 1975. **HONORS/ACHIEVEMENTS:** Outstndng Leadership Awrd staff Dept Rehab Downey Dist 1974. **BUSINESS ADDRESS:** 22 N Front St, Ste 626, Memphis, TN 38103.

SHAW, JULIUS FENNELL
Director. **PERSONAL:** Born Dec 28, 1942, Waco, TX. **EDUCATION:** Jarvis Christ Coll, BS 1965. **CAREER:** IN Dept of Pub Instr, per dir; US Congr Off, spec asst 1972-74; City of Indianap, pub info off 1970-72; City of Indianap, dir cit partic 1968-70. **ORGANIZATIONS:** Ind Chamb of Comm; Afro Amer Inst & Martin Ctr; Indianap Greater Hsing Devel Corp; couns IN Black Repub ; in Conf on Black Pol. **BUSINESS ADDRESS:** Room 224 Statehouse, Indianapolis, IN 46204.

SHAW, LEANDER J., JR.
Judge. **PERSONAL:** Born Sep 06, 1930, Salem, VA; son of Leander J. Shaw and Margaret W. Shaw; married Vidya B Shaw; children: Sean, Jerry, Sherri, Dione, Dawn. **EDUCATION:** WV State Coll, BA 1952; Howard Univ, JD 1957; WV State Coll, honorary doctor of laws degree 1986. **CAREER:** FL A&M Univ, asst prof 1957-60; Private Practice, attorney 1960-69; State of FL, asst pub defender 1965-69, asst state atty 1969-72; Private Practice Duval Co, attorney 1972-74; FL Industrial Relations Comm, comm 1974-79; State of FL 1st Dist Court of Appeal, judge 1979-83; FL Supreme Ct, Justice. **ORGANIZATIONS:** Chmn, bd of elections Amer Bar Assoc, FL Bar Assoc, Natl Bar Assoc, FL Gov Bar Assoc; dir FL Bar Found; adv Judicial Admin Commiss, State Traffic Courts Review Comm; chmn State Courts' Restructure Commiss; mem FL Assoc of Volunteer Agencies for Caribbean Action, Most Worshipful Union Grand Lodge Free & Accepted Masons of FL PHA Inc, Alpha Phi Alpha. **HONORS/ACHIEVEMENTS:** Dedication to Justice FL Chap Natl Bar Assn 1977; Comm Service Jacksonville Bar Assn 1978; Exemplary Achievement in Judicial Serv State of FL Natl Bar Assn 1984. **MILITARY SERVICE:** AUS artillery lt 2 yrs. **BUSINESS ADDRESS:** Justice, FL Supreme Court, Supreme Ct Bldg, Tallahassee, FL 32301.

SHAW, MARIO WILLIAM
Retired administrator. **PERSONAL:** Born Jan 09, 1929, Montgomery, AL; son of James

H Shaw Sr and Alma E Page Shaw. **EDUCATION:** St Johns Univ Collegeville, MN, AB 1954, STB 1956; Univ of Ottawa Can, STL 1960, STD (Cand). **CAREER:** St Maurs Sem, prof of Scripture 1956-59; Univ of Ottawa, inst in Rel 1960-61; St Maurs Sem, prof of Scripture 1960-65; Cath Sem Found of Indianapolis, adm 1965-75; St Augustine Manor, adm. **ORGANIZATIONS:** Comm Peoria Housing Auth 1980; mem Pres Cncl Diocese of Peoria 1984-88; Clg of Cnsltrs 1984-88; vice pres Natl Black Catholic Clergy Caucus 1972-76; exec bd mem Crossroads of Amer Council BSA 1973-75; mem Sr Citizens Found 1977-80; chm Peoria Housing & Rehab Comm 1978-80. **HONORS/ACHIEVEMENTS:** Rev & the Bible "Focus on Faith" (Wkly TV Prog) Channel 6 Indianapolis 1969-71; Rsrch Stds "Buffalo, NY, A Study of Dem Change 1940-70" 1974, "Christian Anti-Jewish Polemic" 1973. **BUSINESS ADDRESS:** Administrator, St Augustine Manor, 1301 NE Glendale, Peoria, IL 61603.

SHAW, MARY LOUISE
Educator. **PERSONAL:** Born Mar 07, 1928, Oklahoma; married Ellis. **EDUCATION:** Marinello Comer Beauty Sch 1964. **CAREER:** Bakersfield City School Dist, comm contact aide; Lincoln Jr HS, instructional aide; Fremont School, aide to school counselor. **ORGANIZATIONS:** Mem Bakersfield City Sch Dist Title I-SB 90, adv com; Region IV Parent Dir of CA Assn of Compensatory Educ 1975; mem Coalition ESEA Title I Parents 1975; conf seminar leader CACE Leadership Inservice 1975; mem Nat Cncl of Negro Women; CA State Assn of Colored Women's Club Inc; chmn Central Dist Parliamentarian CA State Assn of Colored Women's Club Inc 1968; pres Golden W Federated Women's Club Inc; pres Parent-Tchr Assn. **BUSINESS ADDRESS:** Educ Center, 1300 Baker St, Bakersfield, CA 93305.

SHAW, MELVIN B.
Educational administration, assoc admin. **PERSONAL:** Born Dec 23, 1940, Memphis, TN; married Gwendolyn; children: Remel, Dana, Randall, Renee. **EDUCATION:** Lane Coll, BS 1962; Memphis State Univ, MB Ed 1968; Harvard Business School, Ed Mgmt 1970. **CAREER:** Shelby Cty Bd of Ed, teacher 1962-68; Lane Coll, dir of devel 1968; TX Assoc of Coll, dir of devel 1970, exec dir 1973; United Negro Coll Fund, natl dir spec promos. **ORGANIZATIONS:** Mem Omega Psi Phi 1959. **BUSINESS ADDRESS:** Natl Dir Spec Promo, United Negro College Fund Inc, 500 E 62nd St, New York, NY 10021.

SHAW, MICHAEL DENNIS
Neonatologist. **PERSONAL:** Born Jun 29, 1949, Hartford, CT; married Patricia W; children: Lauren Denise. **EDUCATION:** Fisk Univ, BA 1971; Meharry Medical Coll, MD 1977. **CAREER:** George Hubbard Hosp, resident in pediatrics 1976-77; Cardinal Glennon Hosp for Children, 1978-80; USAF Hosp Scott AFB, staff pediatrician 1980-84; Magee Women's Hospital Pittsburgh PA, fellow in neonatology 1984-86; St John's Mercy Medical Ctr, assoc dir of neonatology. **ORGANIZATIONS:** Mem Alpha Phi Alpha Frat Inc 1968-. **MILITARY SERVICE:** USAF major 1980-84. **BUSINESS ADDRESS:** Assoc Dir of Neonatology, St John's Mercy Medical Ctr, 615 So New Ballas Rd, St Louis, MO 63146.

SHAW, NANCY H.
Executive director. **PERSONAL:** Born Sep 24, 1942. **EDUCATION:** Jarvis Christian Coll Hawkins TX, BA 1965. **CAREER:** Human Rights Commn Indianapolis & Marion Co, exec dir 1971-; IN Civil Rights Commn, dep dir 1970-71; Bd Fundamental Edn, spl asst pres 1969-70, mgr adminstrv servs 1968-69, adminstrv asst dir & educ 1967-68; Manpower Training Prog, employment counselor 1966-67; VISTA Training Prog, couns 1966; Flanner House, research asst 1965-66; Indianapolis Bus Dev Fndtn, vp; Comm Action Against Poverty, vp. **ORGANIZATIONS:** Mem Comp Health Planning Coun; Citizens Com Full Employment; bd dirs Comm Serv Coun Gr Indpls; racism com Episcopal Diocese So IN; All Saints Epis Ch.

SHAW, RICHARD GORDON
Government official. **PERSONAL:** Born Jul 25, 1943, Clemson, SC; married Patricia A Friday; children: Sylvia, Richard, Raphael. **EDUCATION:** SC State Coll, BS 1964; Coll of Ins, cert 1977. **CAREER:** State of WV, ins commr; Aetna Life & Casualty, controller 1973-77, supt 1968-73; Charles B Lifflander & Co, adminstrv asst 1964-65. **ORGANIZATIONS:** Mem Am Mgmt Assn Bd; dir Civitan Sheltered Workshop; bd dir Wheeling WV Area Transp Auth; exec com Wheeling OH Co NAACP; vol Wheeling CrisisHotline Ctr. **MILITARY SERVICE:** USAF sgt 1965-68. **BUSINESS ADDRESS:** 1800 Washington St E, Charleston, WV 25305.

SHAW, SPENCER GILBERT
Librarian, educator. **PERSONAL:** Born Aug 15, 1916, Hartford, CT; son of Eugene D. Shaw and Martha A. (Taylor) Shaw. **EDUCATION:** Hampton Univ, BS 1940; Sch of Librarianship Univ WI, BLS 1941; Univ Chicago, Grad Library Sch, advanced studies, 1948-49. **CAREER:** Hartford CT, br librarian 1940-43, 1945-48; Brooklyn Public Library, prgm coord/storytelling spec 1949-59; Nassau Co NY Library System, consult pub librarysvc to children 1959-70; Visiting Faculty, Queens Coll 1958-60, Drexel Univ 1962, Syracuse Univ 1964, Kent State Univ 1965, Univ MD 1968, Univ of IL 1969; Univ HI 1969-70, Univ WA 1961, Univ AK Anchorage 1974; Univ WI Madison 1979; Univ WA, prof 1970-86, prof emeritus, 1986-. Lecturer in Australia, New Zealand, Cyprus, Japan, Hong Kong, Canada, Mexico, England. **ORGANIZATIONS:** Mem Editorial Adv Bd World Book Childcraft Intl Inc 1972-86; radio &TV 1945-; mem Prog Planning Comm WA State Gov's Conf on Lib & Info Serv 1978-79; consult lecturer insts for educ library inst & professional orgns 1949-; mem Amer Library Assn 1950-; pres Assn for Library Serv to Children 1975-76; mem Assn of Amer Library Schs 1970-; WA Lib Media Assn 1970-; Pacific Northwest Lib Assn 1978; WA Library Assn 1970-; NY Library Assn 1949-78; CT Library Assn 1941-48; Natl Council of the Tchrs of English 1970-; Intl Soc for Educ Through Art 1978-82; Child Study Assn of Amer 1965-70; Beta Phi Mu 1949. **HONORS/ACHIEVEMENTS:** Carnegie Fellowship 1940; Friends of the Library Awd Brooklyn Public Library 1955; Dist Alumni Awd Hampton Univ 1960; Amer Library Assn rep White House Conf on Children 1970; Keynote Speaker 23rd World Congress Intl Soc for Educ through Art S Australia 1978; Disting Amer participating in Australian Observance of Ams Bicentennial 1976; guest narrator Sydney (New S Wales Australia) Symphony Orch 1976; author; raconteur; film narrator 1945-; mem People to People European Good Will Tour 1975; Spencer G Shaw Research, Storytelling Collection established at Invergargill Pub Library, NZ, 1978; Who's Who in Library and Info Serv, 1983; Grolier Found Award, 1983; profiled in TV series "Upon Reflections," 1984, and "Faces of Amer," 1985; Spencer G Shaw honor lectureship series established Univ of WA, 1986; certif of apprec, Univ of WA, Grad School of Library and Info Sci, 1986; Black Librarians of Puget Sounc plaque, 1986; Pres Award, WA Library Assn, 1986; recog certif, King County Coun, Seattle, 1986; Amer Library Assn hon member for life, 1988; disting serv award, Black Caucus, Amer Library Assn, 1988. Author of articles in Arts in Cultural Diversity, Holt, Rinehart, 1980, Recreation Leadership, Prentice-Hall, 1987, The Day When the Animals Talked by William Faulkner, Follett, 1977. Narrator of films: "Ashanti to Zulu: African Traditions," Weston Woods Studio, 1976, "Why the Sun and Moon Live in the Sky," ACI Films, 1977. Recording: "Sounds of Childcraft," Field Enterprises, 1974. f WA, 1986; certif of apprec Univ of WA, 1986; Black Librarians of Puget Sound plaque, 1986; Pres Award, WA Library Assn, 1986; recognition certif, King County Coun, Seattle, 1986; Amer Library Assn hon member for life, 1988; disting serv award, Black Caucus, Amer Library Assn, 1988. **MILITARY SERVICE:** AUS lt 1943-45. **HOME ADDRESS:** 2714 Fairview Ave E, Seattle, WA 98102.

SHAW, STAN
Actor. **PERSONAL:** Born Jul 14, 1952, Chicago, IL. **CAREER:** Actor in Broadway shows "Hair," "The Me Nobody Knows," "Via Galactica"; actor in motion pictures "The Great Santini," "Bingo Long and the Traveling Allstars and Motor Kings," "The Boys in Company C," Rocky," "Trucker Turner," "TNT Jackson"; TV actor, "The Buffalo Soldiers," "Roots II," "St Killing," "Money Changers," "Scared Straight: Another Story," "Lucan," "The Day JFK Died.". **BUSINESS ADDRESS:** Henderson-Hogan Agency, 247 S Beverly Dr, Beverly Hills, CA 90212.

SHAW, TALBERT OSCALL
Educator. **PERSONAL:** Born Feb 28, 1928; married Lillieth H Brown; children: Patrick Talbert, Talieth Andrea. **EDUCATION:** Andrews U, BA 1960, MA 1961, BD 1963;Univ of Chgo, MA 1968, PhD 1973. **CAREER:** Coll of Lib Arts Morgan State Univ Baltimore, dean 1981-; School of Religion Howard Univ, acting dean/asso prof of ethics 1972-81; Bowie State Coll, visiting prof 1974; Princeton Theo Sem, visiting prof 1975; Cath Univ of Amer, visiting prof 1973-74; Oakwood Coll, prof of chris ethics 1965-72, dean of students. **ORGANIZATIONS:** Mem exec bd Nat Com for the Prevention of Alcoholism; exec com Washington Theo Consortium; exec com Howard U; faculty mem Soc for the Study of BlackReligions; Am Acad of Religion; Am Socof Chris Ethics 1972. **HONORS/ACHIEVEMENTS:** Voted distin tchr of yr HowardUniv Sch of Religion 1974. **BUSINESS ADDRESS:** Sch of Religion, Howard Univ, Washington, DC 20059.

SHAW, WILLIE G.
Athletic director. **PERSONAL:** Born Mar 29, 1942, Jackson, TN; married Brenda Joyce Robinson; children: Stacey Alexis, Daricus. **EDUCATION:** Lane Coll, BS 1964; Univ of TN Knoxville, MS 1968; Middle TN State Univ, DA 1975; Memphis State Univ 1984. **CAREER:** New York Astronauts, professional basketball player 1964-65; Lane Coll, asst football coach 1965-71, basketball coach 1976-79; City of Jackson TN, gymnastics instr 1976-79; Lane Coll Natl Youth Sports Prog, proj activity dir 1976-80; Lane Coll, dir of athletics. **ORGANIZATIONS:** Chmn south reg Natl Collegiate Athletic Assoc Div III Basketball Comm 1977-; athletic dir Lane Coll 1979-; mem Natl Coll Athletic Assoc Comm on Committees 1979-81; proj admin Lane Coll Natl Youth Sports Prog 1980-; bd mem Jackson-Madison Cty Airport Auth Bd of Dir 1980-; natl chmn Natl CollAthletic Assoc Div III Basketball comm 1981-; bd chmn Jackson Housing Auth Anti-Crime Comm 1982. **HONORS/ACHIEVEMENTS:** Coll div Basketball Scoring Leading Natl Assoc of Intercoll Athletic Natl Coll Athletic Assoc 1962,64; Basketball All Amer Natl Assoc of Intercoll Athletics Assoc Press United Press Intl 1963-64; Who's Who in Amer Coll & Univ 1964; Outstanding Young Men in the South 1971; State Fellow Middle TN State Univ 1972,73. **HOME ADDRESS:** 149 Commanche Trail, Jackson, TN 38305. **BUSINESS ADDRESS:** Athletic Dir, Lane College, 545 Lane College, Jackson, TN 38301.

SHAWNEE, LAURA ANN
Human resources management. **PERSONAL:** Born Sep 18, 1953, Merced, CA. **EDUCATION:** Univ of Santa Clara, BA (Cum Laude) 1975. **CAREER:** NASA Ames Rsch Ctr, coll recruitment coord 1975-83, personnel mgr 1975-84, handicapped program mgr 1982-84, deputy chief eop office 1984-. **ORGANIZATIONS:** Cumming Temple Christian Meth Episcopal Church admin asst 1975-, church treas 1975-, pres missionary soc/ 1985; mem NAMEPA 1985-; mem Comm of Life & Witness 1986; mem comm on life & witness Christian Meth Episcopal Church, NAMEPA 1985, mem bd of dir and imperative comm to eliminate racism 1987; Mid Peninsula YWCA. **HONORS/ACHIEVEMENTS:** Bank of Amer Achievement Awd 1971; Agency Group Achievement Awd Summer Med Student Intern Program NASA 1976; Special Achievement Awd for College Recruiting Program NASA 1980. **BUSINESS ADDRESS:** Deputy Chief, EOP Office, NASA Ames Research Ctr, Mail Stop 241-7, Moffett Field, CA 94035.

SHEARES, REUBEN A., II
Pastor. **PERSONAL:** Born Sep 03, 1933, Charleston, SC; married Ora Myles; children: Reuben, III, Bradley, Craig. **EDUCATION:** Talladega Coll, BA 1955; Colgate-rochester Div Sch, BD 1959; Roosevelt U, MPA 1972; Chicago Theol Sem, DMin 1973; Defiance Coll, DHL 1977. **CAREER:** Office for Ch Life & Leadership United Ch of Christ, exec dir; Comm Renewal Soc, assoc & exec dir 1967-74; Urban Ch Dept United Ch Bd for Homeland Ministries United Ch of Christ, sec 1965-67; So CA & SW UCC, min of met mission 1963-65; Howard United Ch Nashville, pastor 1963-65; Blackwell Chapel Ch Jamestown NY, pastor 1959-61; Tougaloo Coll, trustee; United Theol Sem, trustee. **ORGANIZATIONS:** Mem Am Soc for Pub Adminstrn; mem Alpha Phi Alpah Frat; UCC Black Churchman; chaplain UCC Eighth Gen Synod Grand Rapids 1971. **BUSINESS ADDRESS:** United Church of Christ, Ofc for Church Life/Ldrshp, 105 Madison Ave, New York, NY 10016.

SHEEN, ALBERT A.
Attorney. **PERSONAL:** Born Jul 14, 1920, StCroix, VI; married Ada Mae Finch; children: Albert Jr, Nicole. **EDUCATION:** Lincoln Univ, BA 1964; Howard Univ, JD 1968. **CAREER:** Virgin Islands, senator 1972-74; Antilles Petro Indus, pres gen counsel 1974-76; US Bankruptcy Judge Virgin Islands 1972-84; US Magistrate 1984-; Hodge& Sheen, attorney 1969-. **ORGANIZATIONS:** US Dist Ct DC 1969; US Ct of Appeals 3rd Circuit 1969; VI Bd of Educ 1970-72; Judicial Conf of 3rd Circuit 1973-74; VI Bar 1974-; Coll of VI 1975-; Peoples Broadcasting Corp; Rubin Bros Intl. **BUSINESS ADDRESS:** Attorney, 46-47 Company St, Christiansted, St Croix, Virgin Islands of the United States 00821.

SHEFFEY, FRED C.
Major general. **PERSONAL:** Born Aug 27, 1928, McKeesport, PA; son of Fred Culmore Sheffey and Julia B Richardson; married Jane Hughes, Dec 27, 1952; children: Alan C, Steven C, Patricia C. **EDUCATION:** Central State Coll, BS 1950; OH State U, MBA 1962; George Washington U, MS 1969; Command & Gen Staff Coll, 1965; Natl War Coll, 1969. **CAREER:** AUS Quartermaster Cntr & Ft Lee, commanding general, AUS Quartermaster Sch Ft Lee VA, comdt; served various duties as military career man; LTV Missiles & Electronics Group, dir admin & prog support. **ORGANIZATIONS:** Chmn of the bd Dallas Urban League; deputy dir, Sunbelt Natl Bank 1982-86. **HONORS/ACHIEVEMENTS:** Legion of merit with 2 oak leaf clusters; bronze star medal; merit serv medal; army commend medal with one oak leaf cluster; Purple Heart; army of Occup Medal; United Nations Serv medal; Nat Devense Ser Medal with One Oak Leaf Cluster; Korean Serv Medal with Three Battle Stars; Vietnamese serv medal; rep of Vietnam Campaign medal with 60 device; combat infantry badge; Hall of Fame Central State Univ, 1989; Productivity With Quality Publication, 1988. **MILITARY SERVICE:** AUS major general 1973; retired from active duty 1980.

SHEFFEY, RUTHE G.
Educator. **PERSONAL:** Born in Essex Co, VA; married Vernon R Sheffey; children: Illona Sheffey Rawlings, Renata Gabrielle. **EDUCATION:** Morgan State Univ, BA 1947; Howard Univ, MA 1949; Univ of PA, PhD 1959. **CAREER:** Howard Univ, graduate asst in English, 1947-48; Claflin Coll, instructor, English, French, 1948-49; Morgan State Coll, asst prof, 1959-64, assoc prof, 1964-70; chairperson, English dept, 1970-74, prof, dept of English, 1975-. **ORGANIZATIONS:** Mem, Coll English Assn, Coll Language Assn, Modern Language Assn, Natl Council of the Teachers of English, Eighteenth Century Studies Assn, Middle Atlantic Writers Assn; vice pres, Langston Hughes Soc; founder/pres, Zora Neale Hurston Soc; editor, Zora Neale Hurston Forum; mem, Assn for the Study of Afro-Amer Life & Culture; bd of christian educ, Enon Baptist Church; mem, New Essenes Guild Enon Baptist Church; Progressive Neighborhood Assn, Woodmoor Parent-Teacher Assn; mem, Mayor's Council on Women's Rights; delegate, White House Conf on Women as Economic Equals; mem, Morgan State, Howard Univ & the Univ of PA Alumni Assns; communications comm, United Fund of MD, 1972-74; commnr & vice chair, Baltimore Co Human Relations Commn; MD state delegate, Paula Hollinger's Scholarship Award Panel. **HONORS/ACHIEVEMENTS:** Coll Language Assn Creative Achievement Award, 1974; United Fund Award for Community Serv, 1975; Community Serv Award, Jack & Jill of Amer, 1979; Distinguished Alumni Citation, Natl Assn for Equal Opportunity, 1980; Faculty Rsch Grants for studies in Shakespearean Production, 1983; Achievement Award for Preservation of Higher Educ Standards & Contributions to African Amer History & Culture 1984; Morgan State Univ Women Award, 1985; Citation for Outstanding Serv to Scholarly and Literary Communities; Numerous book, articles and reviews published. **BUSINESS ADDRESS:** Professor of English, Morgan StateUniv, Coldspring & Hillen Rds, Baltimore, MD 21239.

SHEFFIELD, HORACE L., JR.
Association executive. **PERSONAL:** Born Feb 22, 1916, Vienna, GA; widowed; children: 4 children. **EDUCATION:** Detroit Inst of Tech, attended; UCLA, attended; Wayne State Univ, DDL (Hon) 1972. **CAREER:** Detroit News, past columnist; UAW, various positions incl natl org, natl staff rep citizenship-legislative dept, admin asst to Pres Leonard Woodcock; WCHB, moderator 1961-. **ORGANIZATIONS:** Pres W Detroit NAACP Youth Council; mem A Philip Randolphs WWII March on Washington Comm; 1st exec sec MI State CIO Civil Rights Comm; co-organizer of reg & voting campaign Birmingham AL 1955; co-org MI Non-Partisan Voter Reg League; chmn, bd of trustees Detroit Gen Hosp; vchmn bd trustees Wayne State Univ Clinics Bldg; vice pres Detroit Med Ctr Corp; dir United Found; dir Comm on Hosp Gov Eds, Amer Hosp Assoc; dir Wayne State Univ Higher OpptyComm; columnist MI Chronicle; dir Legal Aid & Defender Assoc, Detroit Sickle Cell Detection & Info Ctr, Childrens Hosp, Detroit Br NAACP, Natl Coalition of Black Trade Unionist, Detroit Zoological Soc, Blue Cross & Blue Shield Sr Adv Comm, US Dist US Court Monitoring Comm, PBS, WTVS TV Channel 56, A Philip Randolph Inst; pres Detroit Assoc of Black Orgs; exec vice pres Trade Union Leadership Council; pres Detroit CBTU; life mem Kappa Alpha Psi, Golden Heritagge; mem NAACP. **BUSINESS ADDRESS:** Moderator, WCHB Radio, 4450 Oakman Blvd, Detroit, MI 48204.

SHEFTALL, WILLIS B., JR.
Educational administrator. **PERSONAL:** Born Dec 12, 1943, Macon, GA. **EDUCATION:** Morehouse Coll, BA 1964; Atlanta Univ, MA 1969; GA State Univ, PhD 1981. **CAREER:** AL State Univ, instructor in econ 1969-71; Atlanta Univ, rsch assoc 1978-80; Morehouse Coll, asst prof of econ 1976-81; Hampton Univ, chmn econ dept 1981-82, dean school of business. **ORGANIZATIONS:** Consult to various agencies/official bodies of City of Atlanta, State of GA, Commonwealth of VA, General Serv Admin 1977-82; mem Amer Econ Assoc, Natl EconAssoc, Intl Assoc of Black Bus Ed, Assoc of Social & Behavorial Sci; mem past & pres Natl Urban League, NAACP. **HONORS/ACHIEVEMENTS:** Published articles in the areas of local public finance & urban economics; Merrill Foreign Study Travel Scholar 1968-69; Southern Fellowships Fund Fellow 1972-75. **MILITARY SERVICE:** USN quartermaster 3rd class 1964-66. **BUSINESS ADDRESS:** Dept of Economics, Moorhouse College, Atlanta, GA 30314.

SHELBY, REGINALD W.
Physician. **PERSONAL:** Born Jul 06, 1920, Memphis, TN; son of Charles H Shelby and Grace Irving Shelby; married Jay; children: Cathi, Reginald Jr. **EDUCATION:** LeMoyne-Owen Coll Memphis TN, BS 1940; Meharry Medical Coll, 1950; NY City Hosp, Post-Grad Training 1950-57; Intl Coll Surgeons, Fellow 1959; American Brd Surgery Chicago Illinois Member 1967; American Brd Surgery Chicago Illinois re-Certified 1980. **CAREER:** Ashtabula County Med Center, chief surgery 1987; private practice, 1959-. **ORGANIZATIONS:** Bd dir Western Reserve Health Plan, Ashtabula County Health Serv 1987; past pres Ashtabula County Med Soc; past chief of staff Ashtabula County Med Ctr;past mem Ashtabula City Bd of Health; mem Ashtabula C of C; bd dir Mary Chatman Comm Center; past asst coroner Ashtabula County; mem Comm Action County-wide Sickle-Cell Screening; fellow Pan-Amer Soc Med; mem OH State Med Assoc, Ashtabula County Med Assoc, Kappa Alpha Psi; legal defense contrib NAACP; Ashtabula County Health Dept medical dir 1987-. **MILITARY SERVICE:** AUS 1952-56; WWII Pacific Theatre m/sgt New Guinea, Philippines, Japan. **BUSINESS ADDRESS:** Physician, Reginald W Shelby MD Inc, 524 West 24th St, Ashtabula, OH 44004.

SHELBY, REGINALD W.
Dentist. **PERSONAL:** Born Mar 29, 1948, Laurel, MS; son of Milton and Hester; children: Jibril Muhammad. **EDUCATION:** Flint Comm Coll, AA 1968; N MI Univ, BA 1970; Howard Univ, DDS 1975. **CAREER:** Private Practice, dentist 1976; Arthur Capper Dental Clinic, team leader 1981; self-employed. **ORGANIZATIONS:** Photographer; founder and pres Universal Peace 1983; videographer. **HONORS/ACHIEVEMENTS:** Awd of Excellence DC Government 1983; produced video documentary of 1984 march on Washington 1984. **BUSINESS ADDRESS:** 1616 18th St NW, Washington, DC 20009.

SHELL, ARTHUR
Athlete. **PERSONAL:** Born Nov 26, 1946, Charleston, SC; married Janice; children: two children. **EDUCATION:** MD State Eastern Shore Coll, BS 1968. **CAREER:** Oakland Raiders, offensive tackle, mem coaching staff. **BUSINESS ADDRESS:** Offensive Line Coach, Los Angeles Raiders, 332 Center St, El Segundo, CA 90245.

SHELL, DONNIE (NECK)
Professional athlete. **PERSONAL:** Born Aug 26, 1952, Whitmire, SC; married Paulette E Richardson; children: April Nicole, Dawn Patricia, Donnie Lamont. **EDUCATION:** SC State Coll, BS 1974, MA 1977. **CAREER:** Off Season, manages commercial properties; Pittsburgh Steelers, defensive capt 1974-. **ORGANIZATIONS:** Mem Groove Phi Groove Soc Fellowship Inc; mem Block "S" Club SCSC; mem Natl Fellowship of Christian Ath; mem NFL's Players Assn; vol special groups &progs. **HONORS/ACHIEVEMENTS:** Pgh Courier All Amer Team 1973-74; Kodack All Amer 1973-74; NFL Honors include AL, Pro Football Writers, Pro Football Weekly, Football News; MVP 1980. **BUSINESS ADDRESS:** Pittsburgh Steelers, Three Rivers Stadium, 300 Stadium Circle, Pittsburgh, PA 15212.

SHELL, JUANITA
Psychologist & educator. **PERSONAL:** Born Apr 21, 1940, Winston Salem, NC; married Alonza Peterson; children: Lisa, Jason. **EDUCATION:** CCNY, BA 1971; Grad Ctr City Univ of NY, PhD 1977; NY Univ Postdoctoral program Psychoanaly & Psychotherapy. **CAREER:** Brooklyn Com Counsel Ctr, staff psychologist 1976-84; Brooklyn Coll, adj prof 1976-78; NYU Bellevue Med Ctr, clinical instructor/staff psych 1978-. **ORGANIZATIONS:** Mem Amer Psych Assoc 1975-, Mayors Advisory Sub-com of Mental Retard & Dev Disabil 1978-; chairperson Health Com of Community Bd #4 1979-81; 1st vpmetropolitan Chap of Jack & Jill of Amer 1984; consult Shelter & Arms Child Serv 1984; mem NYAS 1981-. **HONORS/ACHIEVEMENTS:** Grantee NIMH 1971-74; fellow Black Analy Inc 1975-76; article Shell, Juanita, Campion, John "A Study of Three Brothers with Infantile Autism" Jrnl of the Amer Acad of Child Psych 1984. **HOME ADDRESS:** 906 Gerard Ave, Bronx, NY 10452. **BUSINESS ADDRESS:** Clinical Instr Staff Psych, NYU Bellevue Med Center, 550 1st Ave, Dept of Psychiatry Rm E615, New York, NY 10016.

SHELL, THEODORE A.
Dentist. **PERSONAL:** Married Juanita Hamlin; children: Gail, Theodore Jr. **EDUCATION:** Miles Mem Coll, AB; Wayne State Univ, MBA; CLU Am Coll of Life Underwriters. **CAREER:** Great Lakes Mutual Ins Co, debit mgr asst mgr & mgr 1934-44; Great Lakes Mutual Life Ins Co, exec vice pres 1944-59; Golden State Minority Foundation, various offices, pres; Golden State Mutual Life Ins Co, v chm of Bd 1960-. **ORGANIZATIONS:** Mem bd dir Family Savings & Loan Assn; mem Nat Assn Life Underwriters; Life Mgrs Assn; Town Hall; Chartered Life Underwriters; bd mem SCLC West; LA Urban League LA; NAACP; trustee bd Second Bapt Ch; bd of govs Town Hall; comm mem CA C of C Statewide Welfare Comm; So CA Research Comm; Community Skills Cntr Advisory Comm; chmn CA Job Creation Prog Bd; bd of commr Muncpl Auditorium; citz mngmt review comm LA Sch System; chmn sub-com on budget & finance LA Sch System; bd of trustees Pitzer Coll; bd of dir Joint Ctr Comm Studies; Grantsmanship Ctr; Fundraising Sch; develop Comm Town & Hall; United Way Study Comm; top vice pres agency dir Nat Ins Assn 1964-72. **HONORS/ACHIEVEMENTS:** Olive Crosthwait Award Chicago Ins Assn; Spec Ser Award Nat Ins Assn 1973; Who's Who in the W; Personalities of W & midwest; Am Biographical Inst CommLdrs & Noteworthy Americans. **BUSINESS ADDRESS:** 1931 15th St NW, Washington, DC 20009.

SHELL, WILLIAM H.
Medical social worker. **PERSONAL:** Born Aug 22, 1910, Cartersville, GA; married Ethel Margaret Moore. **EDUCATION:** Morehouse Coll, AB 1933; Atlanta Univ, AM 1935, certificate in indus statistics 1943. **CAREER:** Natl Youth Admin, asst state dir 1935-38, state adv on Negro affairs 1938-42; Ft Valley State Coll, instr social studies & workshop consult 1940-41; US Post Office, railway post clerk 1943; YMCA Butler St Br, prog membership sec 1944; War Manpower Comm Region 7, placement specialist 1944-47; VA Hosp, exec sec bd of US civil serv examiners 1947-49, med social worker 1949-50; US Dept of Agriculture, admin officer 1950-53; Natl Found for Infantile Paralysis, asst Brooklyn & Manhattan dir 1953-54; New York City Health & Hosp Corp, med social worker 1954-75. **ORGANIZATIONS:** Consultant to many organizations; bd dir House of Friendship Comm Ctr NY; Cornerstone Baptist Church Day Care Ctr Inc mem bd trustees 1970-84; genl supt of church sch; mem Friendship Baptist Church, Nineteenth St Baptist Church, Mt Zion Baptist Church; mem Admin Com Natl Office March on Washington for Jobs & Freedom; mem Acad of Certified Soc Workers, NAACP, Amer Assn of Retired Persons; mem Atlanta Univ Alumni Assn, Morehouse Coll Natl Alumni Assn; charter mem Natl Assn of Social Workers. **HONORS/ACHIEVEMENTS:** Awd of Merit Tuskegee Inst 1949; plaque for Disting Serv as Comm Leader Am Biog Inst; Herbert F Rawll Mem Awd; Pres Awd Ebony Mag 1959.

SHELTON, CHARLES E.
Sales director. **PERSONAL:** Born Oct 05, 1945, New York, NY; son of Edward Shelton and Fredrine Bolden Shelton; married Sylvina Robinson, Oct 10, 1964; children: Helen, Charmaine, Mia. **EDUCATION:** Northeastern Univ, Boston MA, 1963-65; Pace Univ, 1984. **CAREER:** New York Times, New York NY, budget analyst, 1967-79, consumer marketing rep, 1979-81, city circulation mgr, 1981-83, metropolitan circulation mgr, 1983-87, metropolitan home delivery dir, 1987-88, single copy sales dir, 1988-89, dir of NY edition, 1989—. **HONORS/ACHIEVEMENTS:** Black Achiever Award, Harlem YMCA branch, 1982. **BUSINESS ADDRESS:** Director, New York Edition Circulation, New York Times, 229 West 43rd St, New York, NY 10036.

SHELTON, CORA R.
Counselor. **PERSONAL:** Born Mar 05, 1925, Monroe, MI; married Jean C Mitchell; children: Deborah, Mark, Janice. **EDUCATION:** Wayne StateUniv Detroit, attended 1944-60; Wayne Co Community Coll, attended 1969;Univ of MI Extension Detroit, 1972. **CAREER:** Kent Barry Eaton Connecting Ry Inc, pres/gen mgr 1979-; Met Life Ins Co, sales rep 1973-79; Detroit St & Rys, transp equipment operator 1946-73. **ORGANIZATIONS:** Corp dir Kent Barry Eaton Connecting Ry 1979-; mem Nat Fedn of Independent Bus1979; mem Southcentral MI Transp Planning Com 1980; dist rep Div 26Streetcar & Bus Operators 1960-62; v chmn City-Wide Polit Action Group 1961-63; pres St Cecelia Ch Dad's Club 1968-70. **HONORS/ACHIEVEMENTS:** Man of the year award Nat Life Underwriters 1974. **BUSINESS ADDRESS:** Lexington Childrens Cntr, 115 E 98 St, New York, NY 10029.

SHELTON, EDWARD E.
Association executive. **PERSONAL:** Born Jun 17, 1946, Baltimore, MD; married Sharynne. **EDUCATION:** Morgan State U, BS 1969;Univ MD Sch Dentistry, DDS 1974. **CAREER:** Provident Hosp, dentist self flw anesthesia 1975, gen resd 1974. **ORGANIZATIONS:** Mem Am Dental Assn; MD State Dental Assn; MD State Dental Soc; Chi Delta Mu Serv Frat; Am Dental & Soc Anesthesiology Inc; Acad Gen Dentistry; Nat Dental Assn; mem Alpha Phi Omeg Serv Frat; Prince Hall Masonic Masons. **HONORS/ACHIEVEMENTS:** Certificate of award One on One Hlth Proj 1976. **BUSINESS ADDRESS:** 18 & C St NW, Washington, DC 20040.

SHELTON, HAROLD TILLMAN
Physician. **PERSONAL:** Born May 04, 1941, Lake Charles, LA; married Dolores Hayes; children: Keith, Sherry, Stephanie. **EDUCATION:** McNeese State Univ, BS 1970; LA State Univ Med Sch, MD 1974; LA State Univ Med Cntr, internship 1975; LSU Med Cntr New Orleans, residency in general surgery, 1975-79. **CAREER:** Private Practice, General surgery, 1979; LA State Univ, Med Center, Clinical Instructor, 1980. **ORGANIZATIONS:** Regional dir, Region III Center Natl Med Assn 1973; mem, cand group Am Coll of Surgeons 1979-; diploma, Am Bd of Surgery 1980; mem, Amer Med Assn; LA State Med Soc; Calcasieu Parish Med Soc 1979; staff mem Lake Charles Memorial Hosp & St Patrick Hosp 1979. **HONORS/ACHIEVEMENTS:** Pub "Evaluation of Wound Irrigation by Pulsatile Jet & Conventional Methods" Annals of Surg Feb 1978. **BUSINESS ADDRESS:** 511 Hodges St, Lake Charles, LA 70602.

SHELTON, HARVEY WILLIAM
Administrator. **PERSONAL:** Born Jan 18, 1936, Charlottesville, VA; married Delores Manly; children: Renee, Harvey Jr. **EDUCATION:** VA State Coll, BS 1960; NC State U, cert pub policy 1967; NC State U, MEd Adult Educ 1969; VPI&SU, EdD Adult & Continuing Educ 1976. **CAREER:** Pittsylvania Co VA, extension agent 1963-69; VPI&SU, area resource devel agent 1969-70; Comm Resource Devel VPI&SU, program leader 1970-78; Comm Resource Devel & Energy MD Coop Ext Serv, asst dir 1978-86; MD Cooperative Extension Service, asst to the dir 1986-. **ORGANIZATIONS:** Kellogg Found, fellow 1966-67; Big Brothers Assoc, big brother 1971-73; mem Adult Educ Assn of USA 1972-80; Ford Found, fellow 1974-75; mem Phi KappaPhi Honorary Soc 1975-80; bd mem Boy Scout Council 1976-78; treas & bd mem Roanoke NAACP1976-78; chmn professional improvement com Comm Devel Soc of Amer 1979-80, bd mem 1981-83; mem MD Assoc of Adult Educ 1980. **HONORS/ACHIEVEMENTS:** Epsilon Sigma Phi Outstanding Achievement Award; VA Pol Inst & StU 1978; Army Commendation Medal; US Senator MacMathis awd 1983; Community Development Soc service awd 1985. **MILITARY SERVICE:** AUS first lt 1961-63. **BUSINESS ADDRESS:** Asst to the Dir, Cooperative Extension Service, University of Maryland, Symons Hall, College Park, MD 20742.

SHELTON, JEWELL VENNERRIE
Educational administrator. **PERSONAL:** Born Oct 09, 1928, St Louis, MO; married Robert Louis; children: Robbin M. **EDUCATION:** Pitzer Coll Claremont CA, BA sociology 1973. **CAREER:** San Bernardino City Unified Sch Dist, pres bd of edn, Office of Comm Devel City of San Bernardino, sr proj coor 1975-; Proj Understanding, human relations specialist 1973-75;Univ of CA, staff asst/nutrition Educ 1969-71; KUCR-TV San Bernardino Vly Coll, consult comm resource 1967-79; Home Econs EducUniv CA Riverside, consult 1969-71. **ORGANIZATIONS:** Bd of dirs GSA 1966-67; bd mem San Bernardino Pub Library 1972-75; pres NCNW Inland Empire 1974-75. **HONORS/ACHIEVEMENTS:** Martin Luther King Scholarship San Bernardino Valley Coll 1968; S & H Found Award/Scholarship Claremont Coll 1970; Woman of Achievement award Nat Council Negro Women1974; Citizen of Achievement award League of Women Voters Inland Empire 1975. **BUSINESS ADDRESS:** 777 N F St, San Bernardino, CA 92410.

SHELTON, LEE RAYMOND
Director, hospital emergency services. **PERSONAL:** Born Oct 25, 1927, Pittsburgh, PA; son of Lee Shelton and Mable Shelton; married Delores; children: Marva, Fawn, Gia, Raymond. **EDUCATION:** Howard U, BS 1951; Howard Univ Med Sch, MD 1955; General Surgery Residency Certified 1973. **CAREER:** General Surgeon, 1961-77; SW Hospital & Med Ctr, dir emergency svcs; Morehouse Coll of Medicine, clinical asst prof surgery; Atlanta Southside Comprehensive Health Ctr, dir health svcs; vice pres and dir of Health Services, dir Health lst Foundation. **ORGANIZATIONS:** Bd dir Health 1st (HMO); life mem NAACP; mem Montford Point Marine Assoc; vestry St Paul's Episcopal Church; mem Omega Psi Phi Frat, Urban League, Common Cause, ACLU, Atlanta Med Assoc, GA State Med Assoc, MAG, NMA, Howard Univ Med Alumni Assoc; St Andrew's School, YMCA, ACEP. **MILITARY SERVICE:** USMC sgt 1946-49; AUSR MC capt. **BUSINESS ADDRESS:** 725 Lynhurst Dr SW, Atlanta, GA 30311.

SHELTON, O. L.
Elected official. **PERSONAL:** Born Feb 06, 1946, Greenwood, MS; son of Obie and Idell; married Linda Kay; children: Eric, Shron, Jaimal, Kianna, Ryan. **EDUCATION:** Lincoln Univ, AB 1970. **ORGANIZATIONS:** Chmn Freedom St Louis Inc, Ville Area Neighborhood Housing Assn Inc; bd mem Early Child Care Devel Corp, Williams Comm School. **HOME ADDRESS:** 1803A Cora, St Louis, MO 63113.

SHELTON, REUBEN ANDERSON
Attorney. **PERSONAL:** Born Dec 06, 1954, St Louis, MO; son of Sedathon Shelton and Elizabeth Shelton; married D'Anne Tombs; children: Christan, Heather. **EDUCATION:** Univ of KS, BS journalism 1973-77; St Louis Univ School of Law, JD 1978-81. **CAREER:** Legal Serv of Eastern MO, atty 1980-81; US District Court, law clerk 19781-83; Husch, Eppenberger, Donohue et al, litigation atty 1983-84; Union Electric Co, in house atty 1984-. **ORGANIZATIONS:** Mem Kappa Alpha Psi 1974-; chair of att comm United Negro Coll Fund 1983-; task force dir Bar Assoc of Metro St Louis 1984-; pres Mound City Bar Assoc 1985-86; dir Childhaven Autistic Childcare 1986-, YMCA 1986-. **HONORS/ACHIEVEMENTS:** Academic All Amer Univ of KS Basketball Team 1975-76; Law Student of the Year St Louis Chapter of Black Amer Law 1981. **BUSINESS ADDRESS:** Attorney, Union Electric Co, PO Box 149 Mail Code 1320, St Louis, MO 63166.

SHELTON, S. MCDOWELL
Evangelist. **PERSONAL:** Born Apr 18, 1929, Philadelphia, PA; children: Marion, Fincourt, Arthur, Roddy, Erik, W Edward, Kenneth. **EDUCATION:** Rutgers Univ, BS; Univ of Lisbon Portugal, grad studies; Berlitz Sch of Languages. **CAREER:** WT Publishing & Broadcasting Agency, exec vice pres; nightly radio prog, The Whole Truth Radio Prog; Church of the Lord Jesus Christ of the Apostolic Faith, author, educator, spiritual head, evangelist. **ORGANIZATIONS:** Editor ch monthly magazine The Whole Truth; hon consul gen State of PA for the Kingdom of Lesotho. **HONORS/ACHIEVEMENTS:** Bishop Shelton rec 1972 awd from Phila's Commn on Human Relations; rec'd by several world leaders Emperor Haile Selassie, Mrs Indira Gandhi, late Pres Georges Pompidou, Pres Wm Tolbert of Liberia, King Hussein of Jordan; speaks many languages fluently.

SHELTON, ULYSSES
State legislator. **PERSONAL:** Born Jul 01, 1917; married Pearl; children: Charles, Frederick. **EDUCATION:** Mastbaum Vocational Sch. **CAREER:** PA House of Rep 181 Dist, retired dem Mem 1960-80; US Congressman Bradley, former magistgrate's clk, dept of records, clk, aide; beer Distributor; Yorktown Civic Assn, club owner. **ORGANIZATIONS:** N Philadelphia Model City Prog. **MILITARY SERVICE:** USAF. **BUSINESS ADDRESS:** 1132 W Jefferson St, Philadelphia, PA 19122.

SHEPARD, HUEY PERCY
Director. **PERSONAL:** Born Jun 19, 1936, Jefferson, TX; married Elaine Blanks; children: Dawn V, Huey Jr. **EDUCATION:** CA State Univ Long Beach, BA 1957; UCLA Law School, LLB 1960. **CAREER:** LA Cty Superior Court, juvenile court referee 1965-68, commr 1968-71; Compton Mun Court, judge 1971-75; LA Cty Superior Court, judge 1975-81; Court Arbitration Ctr, dir 1981-. **HONORS/ACHIEVEMENTS:** Resolution of Commendation City Council Compton 1973; Resolution of Commendation City Council Long Beach 1974; Honor Grad of the Year Long Beach Unified School Dist 1975; Outstanding Alumnus CA State Univ Alumni Long Beach 1975. **BUSINESS ADDRESS:** Dir, Court Arbitration Center, 18411 Crenshaw Blvd, Ste 250, Torrance, CA 90504.

SHEPARD, JOAN
Reporter. **PERSONAL:** Born in Philadelphia, PA. **EDUCATION:** The NY Daily News, reporter; NBC, consumer reporter 1975-76; WINS Radio, consumer reporter 1969-73; Women's Wear Daily, editor feature writer 1964-69. **BUSINESS ADDRESS:** Cultural Affairs Editor, Daily News, 220 E 42nd St, New York, NY 10019.

SHEPARD, LINDA IRENE
Consultant. **PERSONAL:** Born Dec 13, 1945, St Louis, MO; daughter of Woodie McCune and Dorothy Alice McCune; widowed; children: Monica Shepard, Adrienne Fitts, Alton Fitts III. **EDUCATION:** Merritt College, Oxford CA, AA, 1972; Mills College, Oakland CA, BA, 1975. **CAREER:** Assemblyman Bill Lockyear, San Leondio CA, district secy, 1975-76; Jimmy Carter for President, Atlanta GA, dir of campaign operations, 1976; BART, Oakland CA, affirmative action officer, 1976-85; Mayor Lionel Wilson, Oakland CA, campaign mgr, 1985-86; Superior Consultants, owner, 1985—. **ORGANIZATIONS:** National Council of Negro Women, NAACP. **HONORS/ACHIEVEMENTS:** Special recognition, Metropolitan Transportation Commission, 1985, for Bay Area Rapid Transit District summer program; outstanding business achievement award, National Council of Negro Women, 1987.

SHEPARD, RAY A.
Educational publishing. **PERSONAL:** Born Jun 26, 1940, Sedalia, MO; married Kathy Crisman; children: Jon, Alice, Austin, Semantha. **EDUCATION:** Univ of NE, BS 1967; Harvard Grad School of Educ, MAT 1971. **CAREER:** Scholastic Inc, editor 1972-83; Houghton Mifflin Co, vp, editorial dir 1983-87; Globe Book Co, pres 1987-. **MILITARY SERVICE:** AUS sp4 1954-61. **BUSINESS ADDRESS:** President, Globe Book Co, 50 W 23rd St, New York, NY 10010.

SHEPARD, SAMUEL, JR.
Educator. **PERSONAL:** Born Jul 02, 1907, Kansas City, MO; married LaDoris Bibb; children: Ethelyn, Willard. **EDUCATION:** Univ of MI, BS 1928, MA 1940, PhD 1954. **CAREER:** E Chicago Hghts IL Bd of Educ, supt of schools 1970-79 retired; Stowe Teachers Coll, teacher; Kansas City MO, hs teacher 1928-30; St Louis Public Schools, 1931-70; Banneker Dist, prin/dir elem edn/asst supt. **ORGANIZATIONS:** Mem bd Comm Serv City of St Louis; scholar athlete Adv com St Louis Post Dispatch; Woodrow Wilson Nat Flwsp Fnd; Sci Rsrch Asso Educ Adv Bd; Educ Testing Serv; mem NAEB 1967; White House Conf on Children 1970; v chmn Right to Read; NABSE. **HONORS/ACHIEVEMENTS:** Prairie State Coll Found Citz of Yr Mound City Press Club 1959; Page One Awd St Louis Newspaper Guild 1960; Comm Serv Award Educ Alpha Kappa Alpha Sor 1964; Distgshd Ldrsp Award Maryville Coll 1964; Hall of Fame St Louis Athletic Assn 1964; Big Bro of Yr Big Ro Orgn 1965; Hon LLDUniv of Mi 1965; Cit for Distgshd Serv to EducUniv of MO 1966; Margaret E Simms Award Jack & Jill of Am 1970; Cit for Comm Serv Human Dvl & Corp St Louis MO 1970; receptEach One-Reach One St Louis Nat Cncl of Negro Women 1970; Hon LLD LincolnUniv 1971; Resolution of Appreciation IL Lake Co Chicago 1976.

SHEPHERD, BENJAMIN A.
Educator. **PERSONAL:** Born Jan 28, 1941, Woodville, MS; married Ann Marie Turner; children: Benjamin III, Amy Michelle. **EDUCATION:** Tougaloo Coll MS, BS 1961; Atlant U, MS 1963; Kansas State U, PhD 1970. **CAREER:** Grad Atlanta Univ, teacher 1962-63; Tougaloo Coll, instr 1963-65; Kansas State Univ, teacher asst 1966-69; SIU, asst prof 1970-73; Asso Prof 1973-; Asst Dean Grad School 1973-74; SIUC, asst chmn zoology 1976-79; Prof Zoology 1979; SIUC, asso vice pres academic affairs & research 1979. **ORGANIZATIONS:** Pres Local Chap Omega Psi Phi; mem Amer Soc Zoologists; mem Am Assn of Anatomists;

mem IL Acad of Sci; mem NY Acad of Sci; mem Am Assn for the Advancement of Sci (AAAS); Sigma Xi; Soc for Study Reproduction. **HONORS/ACHIEVEMENTS:** Mason Sr Achievement Award Bio Tougaloo Coll 1961; Reg Fellow AtlantaUniv 1962; Best Grad Tchr Asst Kansas StateUniv 1968; Runner-up Best Tchr of Yr SIU 1972; Omega Man of the Year Tau Upsilon Chap 1979; ACE Fellowship LSU Baton Rouge 1978-79; Numerous Publications in Field. **BUSINESS ADDRESS:** Assoc Vice Pres Academic Affairs, Southern IL University, Anthony Hall #106, Carbondale, IL 62901.

SHEPHERD, BERISFORD (SHEP)
Musician. **PERSONAL:** Born Jan 19, 1917; married Pearl E Timberlake; children: Roscoe, Synthia, Keith. **EDUCATION:** Studied percussion instruments pvt then majoring Music Mast-Baum Cons. **CAREER:** Jimmy Gorham's Orchestra Phila, drum & arr 1932-41; Benny Carter 1941-42; recorded Artie Shaw Lena Horne; AUS Bands 1943-46; short tour Cab Calloway 1946; Buck Clayton Sextet 1947; 3 yrs Earl Bostic Philadelphia 1950-52; free lancing Bill Doggett Combo 1952-59; played & transcribed several broadway shows Mr Kicks & Co,Am Be Seated, Jerico Mim Crow, Here's Love; Sy Oliver Orchestra; 1964 played "here's Love" SF Drumming Show "Club Finocchio"; co-writer Honky-Tonk; Berisford of San Francisco, owner, designer, builder fine furniture.

SHEPHERD, GRETA DANDRIDGE
Educational administrator. **PERSONAL:** Born Aug 15, 1930, Washington, DC; daughter of Philip J Dandridge and Bertha Johnson Dandridge; married Gilbert A Shepherd (deceased); children: Michele M Murchison. **EDUCATION:** Miner Teachers Coll Washington DC, BS 1951; DC Teachers Coll Washington DC, MA 1961. **CAREER:** DC Publ Schools, teacher 1951-66, asst principal, principal 1966-72; E Orange Public Schools, NJ, supt, 1980-82; Plainfield NJ, supt of schools 1982-84; NJ State Dept of Educ, cty supt of schools; mem Phi Delta Kappa 1987-; supt Essex County Vocational Schools NJ, currently. **ORGANIZATIONS:** Mem Alpha Kappa Alpha Sor 1950; assoc CFK Ltd Found 1971; pres elect CADRE Found 1975-; bd of dir YWCA of the Oranges 1975-78; mem, bd of trustees East Orange Public Library 1981-83; bd of trustees Mercer Co Comm Coll 1984-; fed policy comm mem Amer Assoc of School Admin 1984-; mem, PhimDelta Kappa, 1987-. **HONORS/ACHIEVEMENTS:** Fulbright/Hayes Fellow Intl Christian Univ 1965; Woman of the Year No Jersey Chap Zeta Phi Beta 1983; 5 Point Awd Educ No Jersey Chap Delta Sigma Theta Sor 1984; Awd of Recognition Congressional Black Caucus Educ Braintrust 1984; Educator of The Year, Northeast Coalition of Educational Leaders Inc 1988. **BUSINESS ADDRESS:** Superintendent, Essex County Vocational School District, 68 S Harrison St, East Orange, NJ 07018.

SHEPHERD, MARIAN E.
Business executive. **PERSONAL:** Born Mar 25, 1947, Norfolk, VA. **EDUCATION:** Norfolk State Coll, BS 1970; Trenton State Coll, MEd 1976; MA Inst of Tech, MS 1983. **CAREER:** AT&T Bell Labs, organizational consult 1974, group supv affirmative action/EEO training 1976; exec asst rsch 1978, head, affirmative action 1979, dir personnel 1983, mgr human resources planning. **ORGANIZATIONS:** Bd mem BUF-NJ 1983-85, Advisory Council of Kean Coll 1983-85; vice pres Committee 1985; mem ASPA 1985, Natl Assoc of Femal Execs. **HONORS/ACHIEVEMENTS:** Gatson-Robeson Awd Norfolk State Coll 1970; included in Who's Who in the East 1978. **BUSINESS ADDRESS:** Manager Human Resources Plnng, AT&T Technologies, 650 Liberty Ave, Motorized Mail H, Union Hills, NJ 07083.

SHEPHERD, ROBERT
Educator. **PERSONAL:** Born Aug 07, 1932, Kinston, NC; married Aredell Meadows; children: Ingrid. **EDUCATION:** North Carolina A&T State Univ,BS 1955; Columbia University, MA 1965;Southern Illinois University, PhD 1974. **CAREER:** Shaw College Detroit MI, Vice Pres Academic Affrs; 1976-77; Institute for Services to Education, Dir Inst Planning 1979-81; Livingstone College, Assoc Academic Dean 1978-83; Knoxville College, Acting President 1985-86. **ORGANIZATIONS:** Member, Post Doctoral Academy in Higher Educ; Higher Educ Support Serv; Higher Education Group; American Council on Ed Minority Affrs; Phi Beta Sigma; 1986Phi Delta Kappa; Kappa Delta Pi. **HONORS/ACHIEVEMENTS:** Academic Excellence Alumni Awd North Carolina A&T Univ;Mayors Citation for Performance on NATO Cultural Tour; Directors Award; RJReynolds Fellowship Awdfor study. **MILITARY SERVICE:** Army;Spec 2yrs. **BUSINESS ADDRESS:** President, Knoxville College, 901 College St NW, Knoxville, TN 37921.

SHEPHERD, ROOSEVELT EUGENE
Educator. **PERSONAL:** Born Oct 31, 1933, Elkridge, WV; married Cora Mae Stallworth; children: Melba Jean Edmonson, Prisca Pineda Heard, Nathetha Chamelle Shepherd. **EDUCATION:** KY State Coll, BS Bus Admin (w/high distinct/dept honors) 1955; Univ of Louisville, Cert in Police Sci So Police Inst 1969; MI State Univ, MS Criminal Justice 1971; Univ of PA, MGA Govt Admin 1979; Univ of MD, Univ of Cincinnati, Temple Univ, Shippensburg Univ, PA State Univ, course work. **CAREER:** Cincinnati Div of Police, police officer (patrolman specialist sgt lt) 1956-71; Cincinnati OH, security consult 1971-72; PA Dept of Comm Affairs Harrisburg,comm serv consult (police mgmt) 1972-76; Shippenburg Univ, assoc prof of criminal justice/dept chairperson 1976-. **ORGANIZATIONS:** Prog chmn Harrisburg-Riverside Optimist Club 1977-79; mem Acad of Criminal Justice Sci 1978-; mem City of Harrisburg PA Civil Serv Comm; dist dir PA Black Conf on Higher Educ 1979-80; mem sec Dauphin Co Pretrial Serv Agency (DCPSA) Bd of Dirs; mem Omega Psi Phi Frat Inc 1953-; mem Reserve Officers Assn ROA 1968-; mem Phi Delta Kappa Intl 1977-; consult PA Dept of Community Affairs, MD Transportation Auth, PA Human Relations Commiss. **HONORS/ACHIEVEMENTS:** Who's Who Among Students in Amer Univs & Colls 1955; Law Enforcement Exec Devel Fellowship LEAA US Dept of Justice 1970; Who's Who in Amer Law Enforcement 1976. **MILITARY SERVICE:** AUS spec 4 1956-58; Good Conduct Medal; Soilder of the Month Awd; AUS Reserves chief warrant officer 1958-. **BUSINESS ADDRESS:** Assoc Prof Criminal Justice, ShippensburgUniv, Criminal Justice Dept, Shippensburg, PA 17257.

SHEPHERD, SAUNDRA DIANNE
Physician. **PERSONAL:** Born Jul 16, 1945, New York, NY; daughter of Archibald E Shepherd and Sylvia M Allman Shepherd; married Dr Peter JP Finch; children: Abi Jean Shepherd-Finch. **EDUCATION:** City Coll of CUNY, BS 1968; Hunter Coll of CUNY, MA 1972; Yale Univ School of Medicine, MD 1975. **CAREER:** New York Univ Bellevue Med Center, internship & residency 1975-78, fellowship 1978-79; Columbia Presbyterian Med Center, fellowship & staff assoc 1979-81; St Luke's-Roosevelt Hospital, attending physician 1981-; Harlem Hospital Center, attending physician 1982-86; Sophie Dan's School of Biomedical Education CUNY, adjunct faculty; Montefiore Hospital, asst prof of pediatrics 1984-, residency program in social medicine pediatric faculty 1984-86, dir of pediatric training 1986-. **ORGANIZATIONS:** Consultant pediatrician Legal Aid Soc, Legal Serv Corp; advisor Legal Aid on medical issues for homeless families, neglect & abuse, foster care system problems; supervised delivery of medical relief to Mozambique on behalf of United Methodist Church; bd of dirs United Methodist City Soc 1984-; mem Bronx Boro President's Advisory Comm on the Homeless 1986-87; junior fellow Amer Acad of Pediatrics; mem NY Acad of Sciences, Amer Assoc of Univ Women, Amer Assoc of Women in Medicine, Physicians for Social Responsibility, The Black Caucus of Health Workers of the APHA; APHA, Amer Orthopsychiatric Assn. **HONORS/ACHIEVEMENTS:** NIH training grant in Pediatric Hematology-Oncology 1979, 1980; participant 1st US/Nicaragua Medical Colloquium on Health 1983; advisor to United Methodist Church Relief to Mozambique 1985-. **MILITARY SERVICE:** NY State Natl Guard medical consultant 1981-82. **HOME ADDRESS:** 59 West 94th St, New York, NY 10025. **BUSINESS ADDRESS:** Dir of Social Pediatric Training, Montefiore Hospital, Residency Prog in Social Med, 111 East 210th St, Bronx, NY 10467.

SHEPP, ARCHIE VERNON
Saxophonsit. **PERSONAL:** Born May 24, 1934, Ft Lauderdale, FL; married Garth Jill Gardoze; children: Pauel Glahn, Accra Patrice. **EDUCATION:** Goddard Coll Plainfield UT, BA 1959. **CAREER:** NY Pub Sch Jr HS, tchr eng 1961-63; Moblzn For Youth Mus, artist-in-residence 1963. **ORGANIZATIONS:** Appeared in concert at Goddard Coll 1960, The Connection by Jack Gelber at Living & Theatre 1960, Five Spot Cafe 1961, Judson Hall Concert 1924, Village Gate Concert 1965, Newport Jazz Fest 1965; Chicago Jazz Fest 1965, European tour 1962, Scand tour 1963; Mem Jazz Composers Guild. **HONORS/ACHIEVEMENTS:** Recipient New Star Downbeat Mag Award 1965. **BUSINESS ADDRESS:** 27 Cooper Sq, New York, NY 10003.

SHEPPARD, RONALD JOHN
Educational administrator. **PERSONAL:** Born Apr 13, 1939, New Rochelle, NY; married Shirley C; children: Jeffrey Brandon, Mark Justin. **EDUCATION:** Rensselaer Polytech Inst, PS Physics 1961; Howard Univ, MS PhD Physics 1962-65; Rochester Inst of Tech, MBA 1974; Detroit Clg of Law, Toward JD. **CAREER:** Booz Allen Hamilton Inc, mgmt cnslnt 1966-69; Xerox Corp, group prog mgr 1971-77; Ford Motor Co, prod plg mgr 1977-79; Gen Motors, dir strategy anlys 1979-82; Imperial Clevite, mgr New Market Devel 1983; Univ of Toledo, dir Center for Bus/Ind. **ORGANIZATIONS:** Pres of bd Rochester Montessori Sch Sales & Mkt Exec Club 1983; bd mem Marrotta Montessori Sch 1983; bd mem Easter Seal Soc 1975-77; Rotary Club 1975-77; New Detroit, Inc 1973-75. **HONORS/ACHIEVEMENTS:** Human Relations Awd B-Nai Brith 1957; comm serv Lawrence Inst of Tech 1975; Grad Student Tech Awd Harry Diamond Lab 1963. **HOME ADDRESS:** 19521 Burlington Dr, Detroit, MI 48203. **BUSINESS ADDRESS:** Director, Ctr for Bus/Ind, University of Toledo, 2801 W Bancroft, Toledo, OH 43606.

SHEPPARD, STEVENSON ROYRAYSON
City official & educational administrator. **PERSONAL:** Born Jan 10, 1945, Bunkie, LA; married Diana Lewis; children: Stephen, Steven. **EDUCATION:** Grambling State Univ, BS 1967; Southern Univ, MEd 1974; Northwestern State Univ, MA 1976. **CAREER:** Rapides Parish School System, teacher 1967; Aroyelles Parish School System, teacher & coach 1968; Aroyelles Progress Action Com, athletics dir 1968; Sheppard& Jones Reading Clinic, dir; Town of Bunkie, alderman-at-large. **ORGANIZATIONS:** Dir, vice pres Zach & Shep's Skate-Arama Inc 1983. **HONORS/ACHIEVEMENTS:** Wm Progressive Lodge #217 1975; chmn of bd Amazon Baptist Church 1982. **HOME ADDRESS:** 312 Hickory St, Bunkie, LA 71322. **BUSINESS ADDRESS:** Alderman at Large, Town of Bunkie, Walnut St, Bunkie, LA 71322.

SHEPPHARD, CHARLES BERNARD
Educator. **PERSONAL:** Born Sep 26, 1949, Port Gibson, MS; married Brenda Joyce Stone; children: Charles Kwami, Tenopia Mekda, Ashanta. **EDUCATION:** Alcorn State Univ, BS 1970; Southern Univ, JD 1973; MS College, Doctorate of Jurisprudence 1977. **CAREER:** Shepphard & Assoc, complete consulting svcs; Alcorn State Univ, prof of history/polit sci 1977-; MS House of Rep, 1984-88. **ORGANIZATIONS:** Member Amer Historical Assn; member Southern Growth Policy Bd; member Amer Management Assn; member Intl Affairs Assn; chmn NAACP-Fair Share Committee; chmn Local Political Party Activities; coordinator Political Sci Internship Program Black Political Sci Soc. **HONORS/ACHIEVEMENTS:** Outstanding Young Men Award; Progressive Young Legislator of MS. **HOME ADDRESS:** PO Box 254, Lorman, MS 39096.

SHERMAN, EDWARD FORRESTER
Photographer. **PERSONAL:** Born Jan 17, 1945, New York, NY; married Audrey Johnson; children: Edward F. **EDUCATION:** Amsterdam Photographic Workship 1960; Bronx Comm Coll 1962-64;Univ S Marine Corps 1966; New Sch Soc Research Spring 1969; Brooklyn Coll 1970-73. **CAREER:** NCA New Journal, asso ed 1973-; Freelance Photographer 1969-; New Dimensions Assoc, dir 1968-; Comm Corp Lower W Side, art instr 1972; Photographic Prog, dir June-Sept 1970; Photo-Lab Tech 1968-69; Still Photographer USMC, 1965-67; freelance photographer 1962-65. **ORGANIZATIONS:** Co-chmn Collective Black Photographers 1971; chmn Benin Enterprises Inc 1975-. **MILITARY SERVICE:** USMC sgt. **BUSINESS ADDRESS:** 240 W 139 St, New York, NY 10030.

SHERMAN, MARCUS HARVEY
Government official. **PERSONAL:** Born Jun 09, 1917, Pittsburgh, PA; married Evelyn Gurkoff; children: 3 Children. **EDUCATION:** Los Angeles Jr Coll, AA 1937;Univ of CA at Berkeley, BA 1938; MA 1939;Univ of Chicago, postgrad 1939-41. **CAREER:** Univ of Chicago, research asst 1939-41; US Bur Budget, orgn & methods analyst adminstrv mgmt div 1946-48, staff asst to dir 1948-49, budget & planningofficer 1949-51; US Tech Corp Adminstrn, dir pub adminstrn staff 1951-53; Near E Africa S Asia US FOA, pub adminstr adviser 1953-55; Port of NY Authority NYC, acting personnel dir 1964-65; Orgn & Procedures Dept, dis 1955-73; Terminals Dept, acting dir 1970-71; Budgeting Syracuse U, vis lectr 1951, 1956; US Dept Agr Grad Sch, tchr 1949-51; Gov't City Coll NY, instr 1957-59. **ORGANIZATIONS:** Mem Conf on Pub Serv 1965-68; mem adv bd to com on Gov Improvement Com on Econ Devel 1965-68; Mayor's Citizen's Adv Com on Comm Devel Englewood,NJ 1968-69; Educ Task Force NY Urban Coalition 1968-71; mgmt adv Panel NASA 1968-69; vice-chmn

Englewood NJ Adult Sch Bd 1970-; mem, natl pres Am Soc Pub Adminstrn 1964-65; Am Polit Sci Assn; Nat Acad Pub Adminstrn; mem Phi Beta Kappa. **HONORS/ACHIEVEMENTS:** Author, It All Depends, A Pragmatic Approach to Orgn 1966; Contrib Articles to Professional Jours. **MILITARY SERVICE:** AUS capt 1941-46. **BUSINESS ADDRESS:** 111 8 Ave, New York, NY 10011.

SHERMAN, ODDIE LEE
Clergyman. **PERSONAL:** Born in Jacksonville, TX; married Edna Othenia; children: John Oliver Davis, Mary Etta Gipson. **EDUCATION:** Jackson Theol Sem TX Coll. **CAREER:** Retired Bishop; AME Ch, elected bishop 1956; Paul Quinn Coll Waco TX, former chancellor. **ORGANIZATIONS:** Mem Nat Council of Ch; The World Meth Conf; Am Bible Soc. **HONORS/ACHIEVEMENTS:** Recipient Honorary DD WilberforceUniv Shorter Coll & Monrovia Coll Liberia. **BUSINESS ADDRESS:** 2525 Chester St, Little Rock, AR 72206.

SHERMAN, THOMAS OSCAR, JR.
Engineering programs manager. **PERSONAL:** Born May 29, 1948, Elberton, GA; son of Thomas O Sherman, Sr and Edna Murray Sherman; married Joyce Chestang, May 12, 1973; children: Alfred, Morris, Katherine. **EDUCATION:** NC A&T State Univ, BSEE 1971; Golden Gate Univ, MBA Mgmt 1979. **CAREER:** USAF ATC, capt ewo instructor 1976-80; Ford Aerospace sr systems engr 1980-83, mgr computer systems 1983-84, mgr TREWS engrg 1984-88, SDDS/TREWS Program Manager 1988-. **ORGANIZATIONS:** Mem Assoc of Old Crows 1976-; mem Natl Guard/Air Force Assoc 1980-; opers officer (capt) 129th Communications Flight CA ANG 1980-83; commander (major) 129th Information Systems Flight CA ANG 1983-87; Choirmember Union Baptist Church 1986-; mem Union Baptist Church Ridgecrest CA; commander (lieutenant colonel) 129 Mission Support Squadron CA ANG 1987-; adult bible teacher, 1987, chairman, 1986-, Union Baptist Church. **HONORS/ACHIEVEMENTS:** Distinguished ROTC Graduate NC A&T State Univ 1971. **MILITARY SERVICE:** USAF/ANG, lieutenant colonel, 1971-; AF Commendation Medal (1 cluster); Natl Defense Ribbon; Coast Guard Outstanding Unit Ribbon (1 cluster); AF Outstanding Unit Ribbon; Longevity Service Ribbon (3 clusters). **BUSINESS ADDRESS:** Deputy Director of Electronic Warfaer Programs, Ford Aerospace Corp, 1127 W Reeves, Ridgecrest, CA 93555.

SHEROW, DON CARL
Clergyman. **PERSONAL:** Born Apr 15, 1949, Gilmer, TX; married Hazel June Smith; children: Don Jr, Shuna, Kenan, Brecca. **EDUCATION:** Tuskegee Inst, BA English 1971; Covenant theological Seminary, MDiv 1976. **CAREER:** Tuskegee Inst, instructor 1971-72; Berachah Comm Church, pastor 1976-78; Westminster Schools, teacher 1978-81; Madison Ave Christian Reformed Church, minister & pastor. **ORGANIZATIONS:** Bd mem Covenant Theological Seminary 1979-85; bd mem Dawn Treader Sch 1983-85; consultant and seminar leader "Racism & Reconciliation" 1983-85; chmn family select comm & bd mem Paterson Habitat for Humanity 1984-85. **HONORS/ACHIEVEMENTS:** Who's Who in Amer Colls & Univs 1972; composer/arranger Religious music 1963-85; consultant the revision of The Psalter Hymnal 1983-84; article "The Black Connection" published in The Banner 1984. **BUSINESS ADDRESS:** Minister, Madison Ave Christn Refrmd Chr, 494 Madison Ave, Paterson, NJ 07514.

SHERRELL, CHARLES RONALD, II
Broadcasting executive. **PERSONAL:** Born May 10, 1936, Gary, IN; son of George Wesley Sherrell, Jr. and Beatrice Mariner Sherrell; married Trutie Thigpen, Nov 25, 1969. **EDUCATION:** Mexico City Coll, Mexico, BA, 1958; Roosevelt Univ, Chicago IL, MA, 1963; Univ of Chicago, PhD, 1975. **CAREER:** Gary Public Shools, Gary IN, foreign language tchr, 1961-65; United States Steel, Gary IN, foreman, 1965-67; Globe Trotter Commns, Chicago IL, sales mgr, 1967-71; Bell & Howell Schools, Chicago IL, vice pres, 1971-74; Mariner Broadcasters Inc, Chicago IL, pres, 1974—. **ORGANIZATIONS:** Mem, Radio Advertising Bureau, 1974—; pres, Amer Soc of Linguists, 1978-80; chmn of memshp comm, Black Hispanics Assoc, 1979-84; mem of reading educ comm, New Fronteirs Inc, 1981-82; chmn, Natl Assn of African-Amer Anthropologists, 1983-85; chmn of cable TV comm, 901 Condo Bd Assn, 1987-89; pres, Natl assn of Black-owned Broadcasters Inc, 1988—. **HONORS/ACHIEVEMENTS:** Distinguished Alumnus Award, Univ of Chicago Alumni Assn, 1979; Humanitarian Award, American Linguists Soc, 1980; Humanitarian Award, New Frontiers Inc, 1981. **MILITARY SERVICE:** US Army, 1959-61. **HOME ADDRESS:** 1098 North Ave, Highland Park, IL 60035.

SHERRILL, VANITA LYTLE
Educator. **PERSONAL:** Born Feb 23, 1945, Nashville, TN. **EDUCATION:** Fisk U, BA 1966; Fisk U, MA 1971; Vanderbilt U, 1985. **CAREER:** Volunteer State Comm Coll, instr/field supr 1973-; Vocational Diagnostic Component Nashville CE Program, coord 1973; Metro Health Dept, social worker consult 1971-72; TN State Planning Commn, research asst 1970-71; Hubbard Hosp MeHarry Med Center, asst proj adminstr 1966-69; Gerontology TN State U, instr 1977; Univ of TN, educ intern 1977; Vanderbilt Univ Com for the Behavioral Sci, review bd 1985; Dede Wallace Center, treas 1985; Samaritan Center, sec bd of dirs, 1985; Nashville Urban League, bd of dirs 1985. **ORGANIZATIONS:** Mem Delta Sigma Theta Soc 1985; mem Intl Curr Devel Prog; mem Am Personnel & Guidance Assn; mem Am Psychol Assn; mem Nat Assn of Black Social Wkrs; mem Jack & Jill Inc Nashville Chap 1985; mem Hendersonville Chap of Links Inc 1985; bd of dirs Alive-Hospice 1985; bd of dirs Council of Comm Servs 1985. **HONORS/ACHIEVEMENTS:** Outstanding Yng Women of Am 1976; Grant Educ & Research Tour of W Africa Phelps-Stokes Found 1979; Commr Century III 1985; Charter Mem Leadership Nashville 1985; Listed Personalities of S 1976; Who's Who in S & SW 1980. **BUSINESS ADDRESS:** Associate Professor, Volunteer State Comm Coll, Nashville Pike, Gallatin, TN 37066.

SHERRILL, WILLIAM HENRY
Educator. **PERSONAL:** Born Dec 06, 1932, North Carolina; married Gloria; children: William Jr, Adrienne Budd, Erick, Sharon, Karen. **EDUCATION:** Shaw U, AB 1954;Univ PA 1959;Univ MI, MA 1960;Univ CA, PhD 1961-72; SF State Coll 1965. **CAREER:** Howard Univ, dean 1972-; Univ CA, dir 1968-72; Univ CA 1968-69; Univ CA, dir 1967-68; SF State Coll, lectr 1965-69; Berkeley HS, teacher counselor 1960-67; LH Foster HS, teacher 1954-59. **ORGANIZATIONS:** Mem Afro-Am Educators Assn; Am Assn of Collegiate Registrats & Admissions Officers; Am Council on Higher Edn; Am Personnel & Guidance Assn; CA Counseling & Guidance Assn; CA Tchrs Assn; Coll Entrance Exam Bd; Berkeley Tchrs Assn; No CA Counseling & Guidance Assn; Nat Assn of Berkeley Councelors;Nat Assn of Coll Deans Registrars Admissions Officers; Nat Assn of Coll Admissions Counselors; Nat Assn of Fgn Students Affairs; Consortium ofUniv of the WA Metro Area; WA Area Admissions Assn; DC Orgn of Admissions & Financial Aid Personnel; Proj BOOST 1968; Upward Bound 1968; Monterey Co Counselors Assn 1968; Am Coll Test Adv Bd 1968-72; Educ Testing Serv 1969; Educ Oppty Prgms 1968-72; Coll Entrance Exam Bd Proj Acess 1969; Nat Merit Scholarship Selection Com 1971-72; Nat Achvmt Scholarship Selection Com 1969-70; Nat Teamsters Scholarship Selection Com 1973-; W Reg Scholarship Selection Com 1972. **HONORS/ACHIEVEMENTS:** Num Professional Confs Attended; Publ 'counseling in the Absence of Intergration", "A Comparative Study of Selected Psychol & Soc Perception of Negro & Mexican-Am Adolescents".

SHERROD, CHARLES M.
Clergyman. **PERSONAL:** Born Jan 02, 1937, Petersburg, VA; son of Raymond Sherrod and Martha Walker Sherrod Gibson; married Shirley M Sherrod; children: Russia, Kenyatta. **EDUCATION:** VA Union Univ, AB 1958; VA Union Univ School of Religion, BD 1961; Union Theological Seminary, STm 1967; Univ of GA, Certificate of Comm Development. **CAREER:** Interdenominational, minister 1956-; SNCC, Field Sec 1961-67; SW GA Project, dir 1961-87; New Comm Inc, dir 1968-85; City of Albany, city commissioner 1977-. **ORGANIZATIONS:** 1st SNCC Field Organizer 1961; mem Freedom Ride Coordinating Comm 1963; US Govt OEO 1974; Fellow Inst for Policy Studies 1974; consultant Natl Council of Churches 1978; pres SW GA Project 1967-85; bd NAACP 1970-85; bd Slater King Center 1975-85; bd SW GA Planning Comm 1978-85; bd mem Fed of Southern Coop 1979-87; GA Coalition of Housing 1983-85. **HONORS/ACHIEVEMENTS:** Omega Man of the Year Lambda Chapter Richmond 1958; Honors in Civil Rights Natl Lawyers Guild 1985; Delegate Natl Democratic Party Convention 1984; song writer, poet, singer. **BUSINESS ADDRESS:** Commissioner Wd 6, City of Albany, New Communities Inc, Leesburg, GA 31763.

SHERROD, EZRA CORNELL
Data processing facility manager. **PERSONAL:** Born Jul 25, 1950, Wilson, NC; married Charlotte Pye; children: Derrick Cornell. **EDUCATION:** Lear Siegler Inst, AA 1971; Univ District of Columbia, BA 1977; Project Management Seminars, 1977-80; People and Resources Mgmt Seminars, 1983-86. **CAREER:** Woodard and Lothrop, computer specialist 1970-72; Intl Business Serv Inc, project mgr 1972-80; Automated Datatron Inc, project mgr 1980-86; Sherrod Security Co, pres/owner 1986; Wilkins Systems Inc, facility mgr 1986-. **ORGANIZATIONS:** Pres history club Univ DC 1974-76; mem Univ District of Columbia Alumni 1984; mem Minority Business Commn 1986; active mem Evangel Assembly Church Camp Springs MD; mem Business Network of Washington DC; mem Physical and Mental Self-Improvement Programs. **HONORS/ACHIEVEMENTS:** Top Five Mgrs of Year Automated Datatron Inc 1985; author letter of intro "Saga of Sidney Moore," 1985; top candidate for major exec position involving a major computer network w/Wilkins Systems Inc 1987. **HOME ADDRESS:** 808 Kirkwood Rd, Waldorf, MD 20601.

SHERVINGTON, E. WALTER
Physician. **PERSONAL:** Born Jul 23, 1906, Antigua, WI; son of Ashley Shervington and Ethel Julian M.; married Charlotte; children: Anne, Walter, Carol. **EDUCATION:** Howard U, BS 1931; HowardUniv Coll Med, MD 1934. **CAREER:** retired physician internal med; VD Clinics Baltimore City Hlth Dept, dir 1954-76; Baltimore City Hosp, chf med clinic 1960-70; Johns Hopkins Sch MedMed, instr med 1964-80; instructor Emeritus, l980-89, Epidemiology Sch Hlth & Hygiene Johns Hopkins U; Consult Med Ch Hosp, staff; Soc Security Medicare consultant. **ORGANIZATIONS:** Mem AMA; Baltimore Med Soc; MD Med Soc; Chi Delta Mu Med Frat; Flw Royal Soc Hlth; Am Coll Angiology; Am Geriatric Assn; Intl Coll Angiology; mem Am Pub Hlth Assn; Clinical Cncl Am Heart Assn. **MILITARY SERVICE:** AUS MC capt 1950-52. **BUSINESS ADDRESS:** Physician, 2301 Harlem Ave, Baltimore, MD 21216.

SHERWOOD, O. PETER
Attorney. **PERSONAL:** Born Feb 09, 1945, Kingston, Jamaica;son of Laopold Sherwood and Gloria Sherwood; married Ruby Birt; children: 1. **EDUCATION:** Brooklyn Coll, BA 1968; NYU Sch of Law, JD 1971. **CAREER:** NY Civil Court, law sec to Hon Fritz W Alexander II l971-74; NAACP Legal Def & Educ Fund Inc, atty l974-84; NY Univ School of Law, adj asst prof of law l980-87; State of NY, solicitor general. **ORGANIZATIONS:** Trustee NY Univ Law Ctr Found; co-chmn Compliance & Enforcement Comm NY & St Bar Assn; Taskforce on NY St Div on Human Rights 1977-80; mem bd dir New York City Comm Action Legal Serv l971-75; mem Metro Black Bar Assn, Natl Bar Assn, Fed Cts Comm, Assn of the Bar of the City of NY. **BUSINESS ADDRESS:** Solicitor General, State of New York, 120 Broadway, New York, NY 10271.

SHERWOOD, WALLACE WALTER
Attorney, professor of law and criminal justice. **PERSONAL:** Born Oct 06, 1944, Nassau, Bahamas. **EDUCATION:** St Vincent Coll, BA 1966; Harvard Univ, LLM 1971; George Washington Univ, JD 1969. **CAREER:** Legal Svcs, staff atty 1969-71; MA Comm Against Discrimination, commnr 1971-73; Roxbury Pub Def, dir 1971-73; OEO, gen counsel 1973-74; Lawyers Comm for Civil Rights under Law, exec div 1974-76; Private Practice, attorney 1976-; NE Univ Coll of Criminal Justice, assoc prof. **ORGANIZATIONS:** Mem MA Bar Assn 1969-; mem Boston Bar Assn 1969-; mem MA Council for Pub Justice. **HONORS/ACHIEVEMENTS:** Dulles Fulbright Awd Natl Law Ctr 1969; Teacher of The Year, 1987 Coll of Criminal Justice. **BUSINESS ADDRESS:** Associate Professor, NEUniv Coll Criminal Justice, 360 Huntington Ave, Boston, MA 02115.

SHIELDS, KAREN BETHEA (KAREN GALLOWAY SHIELDS)
Attorney. **PERSONAL:** Born Apr 29, 1949, Raleigh, NC; daughter of Bryant W Bethea and Grace Parrish Bethea; married Linwood B Shields, Dec 31, 1984. **EDUCATION:** E Carolina Univ Greenville NC, AB 1971; Duke Univ School of Law Durham NC, JD 1974; 14th Judicial Dist Durham Cty, judge 1980-1985; attorney at law 1986-89. **CAREER:** Paul Keenan Rowan & Galloway, partner 1974-77; Loflin Loflin Galloway & Acker, partner 1977-80; 14th Judicial Dist Durham Cty, judge 1980-1985; sole practitioner in firm of Karen Bethea-Shields 1986-; attorney and counselor at law Durham, NC. **ORGANIZATIONS:** Mem Amer Bar Assoc, Natl Conf of Black Lawyers, Jud Council of Natl Bar Assoc, Amer Civil Liberties Union; faculty mem Natl Inst of Trial Advocacy; mem Trial Practice Instr for the Training of Lawyers, Natl Coll for Criminal Defense Lawyers of NACDA, Natl Judicial Coll of Natl Bar Assoc, Natl Assoc of Women Judges, Amer Judicature Soc, Natl Judicial

Coll Search & Seizure & Grad Evidence Spec Sessions 1983; faculty mem Women Trial Lawyers Advocacy Clinic San Francisco CA 1984; guest lecturer & workshop panel mem Natl Acad of Trial Lawyers Toronto Canada 1982; Intl Platform Assn, 1988-89. Natl Council of Negro Women, 1989; Vice chair Educ Comm, Durham Comm on Affairs of Black People, 1989-; bd of dir, Edgemont Community Ctr, 1989. **HONORS/ACHIEVEMENTS:** Lawyer of the Year Natl Conf of Black Lawyers 1976; Outstanding Serv Awd Raleigh Chap of Delta Sigma Theta 1977; Outstanding Young Woman of the Year 1983; NAACP Distinguished Achievement Awd 1981; Runners-up in NEXT Mag 100 Most Powerful People for the 80's; NC Juvenile Court Judges Cert for 1982, 1984; Cert of Appreciation NC State Assoc of Black Soc Workers 1979; 1st black female, 1st female Dist Court Judge in Durham Cty; 2nd black female judge in NC; member of Joann Little Defense Team 1974-75; Outstanding Service for Community Service and Excellence in Education, Sister Clara Muhammad Schools Education Fund for NC 1989. **HOME ADDRESS:** 3525 Mayfair Rd Apt 205, Durham, NC 27707. **BUSINESS ADDRESS:** Attorney, 3525 Mayfair St #205, Durham, NC 27707.

SHIELDS, LANDRUM EUGENE
Clergyman. **PERSONAL:** Born Mar 17, 1927, Winston Salem, NC; son of Samuel J Shields and Joanna Berry Shields; married Marjorie, Jun 11, 1955; children: Landrum Jr, Sharyn, Laurita, Andrea. **EDUCATION:** Lincoln Univ, AB 1949; Oberlin Grad Sch of Theol; Howard Univ Sch of Religion, BD 1954; Christian Theol Sem, MRE 1960. **CAREER:** Witherspoon Presbyterian Church, clergyman; United Presb Ch 1985; Central State Hosp, dir tng; IN U, asso faculty; IN Central Coll, instr; Indpls YMCA, youth & adult sec; Howard U, chaplain; 1st Congregational Ch, pastor. **ORGANIZATIONS:** Vp pres bd commrs Indianapolis Pub Schs; bd dir Comm Serv Cncl; Whitewater Presbytery of United Presb Ch; Marion Co Tax Adjustment Bd; Indianapolis Mayor's Task Force on Communications; UNICEF Indianapolis Com; Num Other Affiliations. **HONORS/ACHIEVEMENTS:** Human Rels Roll of Honor Indpls; Recorder Newspaper 1968; Award of Merit So Cross #39 F & A M; Award for Outstanding Ldrshp & Dedication to Am Cancer Soc City of Indianapolis 1972-73; 59th Ann Distinguished Alumni Award Christian Theol Sem; 1976 Father of Yr Award Greyhound Corp; Chaplain for A Day US Senate 1977. **BUSINESS ADDRESS:** Clergyman, Witherspoon Presbyterian Ch, 5136 N Michigan Rd, Indianapolis, IN 46208.

SHIELDS, VAREE, JR.
Editor, publisher. **PERSONAL:** Born Feb 19, 1935, Huntsville, TX; son of Varee Shields and Robbie Hagan Shields; married Johnnie Wright Shields, 1986; children: Ronald Victor Shields. **EDUCATION:** TX Southern Univ, Houston, TX, BA 1956. **CAREER:** Houston Informer, gen assigments reporter 1959-60; Forward Times, Houston, TX, reporter, managing editor, 1960-86; The Houston Flame, editor & publisher 1986-. **ORGANIZATIONS:** Pres Vartrom Inc; chmn of bd J Wright & Associates Inc; mem bd Fannie Lou Hamer Memorial Found Inc, mem, Natl Newspaper Publisher Assn, 1963-86; pres, Huntsville, TX, Sam Houston High School, ex-students assn, 1982-84; mem, Metropolitan Transit Authrity Northeast Houston Transit Task Force, 1985-88; mem, Texas Publishers Assn, 1987-. **HONORS/ACHIEVEMENTS:** Outstanding Media Award, Texas Black Media Coalition, 1977, Community Service, PABA Lynn Eusan Award, 1979. **MILITARY SERVICE:** AUS Security Agency, specialist 5, 1956-59. **HOME ADDRESS:** 7401 Jay St, Houston, TX 77028.

SHIELDS, VINCENT O.
Director civil rights. **PERSONAL:** Born Feb 20, 1924, Chillicothe, MO; married Edna Gilbert. **EDUCATION:** Lincoln U, Attended 1946-48. **CAREER:** Chillicothe MO, us post office, fireman, laborer 1948-73; Fed Hwy Adm, equal oppor; Ofc of Civil Rights Fed Hwy Adm Reg 7, dir 1985; Mayor's Citizen Adv Com on Minority Housing Chillicothe, ch 1970; Chillicothe Housing Authority, 1st vp; MO State Conf NAACP, pres 1968-73. **ORGANIZATIONS:** Bd mem Hope Haven Ind 1968; pres Livingston Ct Human Dev Corp 1969-73; mem Amer Legion Post 25 Veterans of Foreign Ward; pres KC Chillicothe Br 1954-73; ch EEO Adv Com Green Hills Comm Action 1970-71. **HONORS/ACHIEVEMENTS:** Award for Outstanding Serv Green Hill Human Dev Corp 1971; Outstanding Contribution to Improvement Social Justice Health & Welfare for People of MO MO Assn for Social Welfare 1973; Award Reg IV NAACP 1976; Bd Mem KS City Br NAACP; Plaque for Outstanding Dedicated & Loyal Leadership as Pres; MO State ConfNAACP & Branches 1973. **MILITARY SERVICE:** US Army Inf 1943-45. **BUSINESS ADDRESS:** Federal Highway Administration, PO Box 19715, Kansas City, MO 64141.

SHIFFLETT, LYNNE CAROL
Communications journalist. **PERSONAL:** Born in Los Angeles, CA; daughter of James H. Shifflett and Carolyn Larkin Shifflett. **EDUCATION:** Govt, Political Sci, Los Angeles State Coll, BA; Univ of WI, MA. **CAREER:** NBC, admin; Neighborhood Adult Participation Project, Watts Center Dir; Sch for Workers, Univ of WI, instructor; Communcations Relations-Social Devel Commn, Milwaukee Co, urban planner, 1969-71; KMOX-TV (CBS), news writer, 1971-72, news producer, 1972-73; Columbia Univ Summer Program in Broadcast Journalism for Minority Groups, consultant and teacher 1973; WNBC-TV NewsCenter 4, weekend news producer, 1973-75, NBC Loan to Comm Film Workshop, training dir & teacher, 1975, WNBC-TV news field producer/writer, 1975-85; Shifflett Gallery, dir, 1985-; Sr news writer, KCOP Television News, 1989-. **ORGANIZATIONS:** Fellowship Operations Crossroads Africa; delegate 8th Natl Conf US Natl Com for UNESCO 1961; Cert Comm Leadership Sch of Public Admin USC 1966; bd of dir Triad Inc 1977; bd of dir Henry St Settlement 1978; adv comm Edwin Grould Serv for Children 1985; Golden Life Mem, Delta Sigma Theta Sorority; Amer Women in Radio & TV; Natl Acad of Television Arts & Sciences; Natl Assn of Black Journalists. **HONORS/ACHIEVEMENTS:** Outstanding Young Woman in Amer, Missouri, 1973. **BUSINESS ADDRESS:** Shifflett Gallery, PO Box 19159, Los Angeles, CA 90019.

SHINE, TED
Drama professor. **PERSONAL:** Born Apr 26, 1931, Baton Rouge, LA; son of Theodis Wesley Shine and Bessie Herson Shine. **EDUCATION:** Howard University, Washington, DC, BA, 1953; University of Iowa, MA, 1958; University of California, Santa Barbara, CA, PhD, 1971. **CAREER:** Dillard University, New Orleans, LA, instructor in drama and English, 1960-61; Howard University, Washington, DC, assistant professor of drama, 1961-67; Prairie View A & M University, Prairie View, TX, professor and head of department of drama, 1967-; Texas Non-Profit Theatres, Inc, board member. **ORGANIZATIONS:** Member, American Theatre Association; member, Southwest Theatre Conference; member, Texas Educational Theatre Association. **HONORS/ACHIEVEMENTS:** Brook-Hines Award for Playwriting, Howard University, for "Morning, Noon, and Night," 1970; author of "Plantation," 1970; author of The Woman Who Was Tampered with in Youth, 1980; author of Going Berserk, 1984; author of over sixty television scripts for series "Our Street.". **HOME ADDRESS:** 10717 Cox Lane, Dallas, TX 75229. **BUSINESS ADDRESS:** PO Box 2082, Prairie View, TX 77445. *

SHIPE, JAMESETTA DENISE HOLMES
Journalist. **PERSONAL:** Born May 30, 1956, Knoxville, TN; daughter of James Edward Holmes and Lavonia Thompson Holmes; married Abie Shipe, Jr, Oct 10, 1987. **EDUCATION:** Univ of TN, BS Commun/Journalism 1980; Cooper Business School, AS (Cum Laude) Bus 1982; TN Institute, Electronics 1989-. **CAREER:** FBI Office of Congressional & Public Affairs, writer, public relations rep 1982-83; Martin-Marietta Energy Systems Inc Elect Electron Svcs, customer relations rep 1983-. **ORGANIZATIONS:** Mem Sigma Delta Chi Soc of Prof Journalists 1975-, Public Relations Soc of Amer 1977; public affairs/press consult Knoxville Women's Ctr 1979-80; mem Phi Beta Lambda Soc of Bus 1982; mem Smithsonian Institution 1987-89; mem NAACP 1988-. **HONORS/ACHIEVEMENTS:** PTA Scholarship Knoxville Chap 1974-75; Minority Scholarship Amer Newspaper Publ Assoc 1976-78; Dean's List Univ of TN 1980. **HOME ADDRESS:** 821 W Vanderbilt Drive, Oak Ridge, TN 37830.

SHIPLEY, ANTHONY J.
Clergyman. **PERSONAL:** Born May 19, 1939, New York, NY; son of Oscar Shipley and Lillian Shipley; married Barbara McCullough, Sep 03, 1960; children: Cornelia Jean. **EDUCATION:** Drew Univ, BA 1961; Garrett Sem, MDiv 1964; Adrian Coll, DD 1974. **CAREER:** United Methodist Church, supt Detroit West Dist 1982-; Scott Church, pastor. **ORGANIZATIONS:** Metro Comm UMC NY; St Matthews UMC Chicago; Metro Duane UMC NY; consultant to Natl Young Adult Project; exec dir Head Start Prog Brooklyn; pastor Union UMC Brklyn; assoc prog dir NY Conf of United Methodist Church; prog dir Detroit Conf of United Methodist Church; consultant to Liberia Annual Conf of United Methodist Church; pres Interfaith Community Serv Brooklyn; NAACP; mem Natl Council of Black Churchmen; Black Methodists for Church Renewal; New York City Urban Coalition; bd dir NY Project Equality; chmn Devel Commn of the Ctr for Parish Development; chmn Church Resourcing Project of the Inst for Advanced Pastoral Studies; consultant NCJ Urban Network; adjunct prof Garrett Evangelical Theol Sem; bd of dir Adrian Coll; vice chmn Devel Commn for Detroit Black United Fund; mem President's Assn of the Amer Mgmt Assn; delegate Gen Conf of the United Methodist 1980; lecturer Church Admin at N MS Pastors School; Inst for Adv Pastoral Studies; Oppor Indus Ctr; pres Natl Fellowship Conf Council; dir mem Detroit Council of Churches; MI State Council of Churches; MI State United Ministries in Higher Educ; Natl Bd of Higher Educ & Min; mgmt consultant Charfoos Christenson Law Firm; bd dir Methodist Theol School in OH. **HONORS/ACHIEVEMENTS:** Published "The Care & Feeding of Cliques in the Church" Interpreter Magazine 1975; "The Self Winding Congregation" Interpreter Magazine 1975; "The Council on Ministries as a Support System" Letter Ctr for Parish Devel; "Everybody Wants to Go to Heaven But Nobody Wants to Die" Christian Century 1976; "Long Range Planning in the Local Church" MI Christian Advocate; "Something for Nothing" MI Christian Advocate; "Fable of Disconnection" MI Christian Advocate. **BUSINESS ADDRESS:** Pastor, Scott Church, 10372 W Chicago Blvd, Detroit, MI 48204.

SHIPMON, LUTHER JUNE
Clergyman/social worker. **PERSONAL:** Born Sep 24, 1932, Clarkton, NC; married Daisy Lindzy; children: Krishmu J. **EDUCATION:** Shaw Univ, AB 1954, MDiv 1955, DD 1956; Friendship Coll, DD 1957. **CAREER:** LJ Shipmon Found Inc, pres 1972-85; Youngstown UN Day, chmn 1980; United Nations of YO Chapt, mem 1982; Northside Coalition YO, mem 1983; Regional Council on Alcoholism Inc, chmn bd dirs 1983. **ORGANIZATIONS:** Mem Mahoning Co Amer Cancer Soc 1980-; mem Health System Agency 1979-80; statistician Lott Cary Bapt Foreign Mission Coun USA 1965-81; chmn United Negro Coll Fund Inc 1979-82; clerk Steel Valley Assn Souther Bapt Con 1983; chmn NAACP membership drive 1975; minister Univ Park Bapt Ch 1962; minister Second Bapt Ch 1964; coord Mahoning Co Social Serv EPSDT 1981-83; minister First Calvary Bapt Ch YO 1965; minister/fndr St John's Bapt Temple YO 1982-85; Civil Rights Coord mahoning Co Welfare Dept YO 1974-80; delegate World Bapt Alliance in Stockholm Sweden 1975; coordinator 1st Nat'l Holiday Celebration for Martin Luther King Jr 1986; chiarman/bd dir Youngstown Food to Gleeners Inc 1986; pres Baptist Ministers Conference & Vicinity Youngstown OH 1986-88. **BUSINESS ADDRESS:** Minister, 2801 Market St, Youngstown, OH 44503.

SHIPP, E. R.
Journalist. **PERSONAL:** Born Jun 06, 1955, Conyers, GA; daughter of Johnny W Shipp Sr and Minnie Ola (Moore) Shipp. **EDUCATION:** Georgia State Univ, BA Journalism 1976; Columbia Univ, MA Journalism 1978. **CAREER:** The New York Times, natl correspondent, legal correspondent; asst metropolitan editor. **ORGANIZATIONS:** Mem Chicago Assoc of Black Journalists 1983-86; mem Natl Assoc of Black Journalists 1983-; New York Assn of Black Journalists 1986-. **BUSINESS ADDRESS:** Asst Metropolitan Editor, New York Times, 229 W 43rd St, New York, NY 10036.

SHIPP, HOWARD J., JR.
Educator. **PERSONAL:** Born Oct 02, 1938, Muskogee, OK; married Jeanetta Combs; children: Jackie. **EDUCATION:** Langston U, BS 1962; Northeastern State Coll, MS 1966; OK State U, post grad. **CAREER:** Univ Counseling Serv OK State Univ, counselor; Muskogee Public Schools, teacher football coach; Douglas HS Oklahoma City, teacher football coach; Northeast HS Oklahoma City, asst principal; Professional Baseball Player 1958-59; Professional Barber 1966-71. **ORGANIZATIONS:** Mem Oklahoma City Classroom Tchr Assn; Oklahoma City C of C; OK Educ Assn; Nat Assn of Edn; APGA NAACP; mem OCPA Bd Community Action Prog Stillwater OK; treas Mid Scope; chmn Minority Scholarship Com9; mem Institutional Scholarship Com; faculty advisor OSU Afro-Am Soc; sponsor Kappa Alpha Phi. **HONORS/ACHIEVEMENTS:** Recipient Black Gold Award Alpha Phi Alpha Epsilon Epsilon Chap 1972-73; Co-coordinated Book "Techniques for the Low-Achiever in Science". **BUSINESS ADDRESS:** Oklahoma StateUniv, Univ Counseling Serv, Stillwater, OK 74074.

SHIPP, MAURINE SARAH
Realtor & appraiser. **PERSONAL:** Born Mar 06, 1913, Holiday, MO; widowed; children: Jerome Reynolds, Patricia R England. **EDUCATION:** Lasalle Ext IL Univ, Ext Course Completed 1956; IL Bus Clg, Completed 1963. **CAREER:** Natl Conf Min Women, charter

mem; Dept Agr St of IL, supv; Comm Dev Prog, appraiser; Urban League, mbr; NAACP, mem; Sppfld Pub Bldg, mbr; Shipp Real Estate Agcy, real est broker appraiser. **ORGANIZATIONS:** State appraiser st of IL; bldg comm by the Mayor of Spfld 1984. **HONORS/ACHIEVEMENTS:** Hnry degree CO Christian Clg. **HOME ADDRESS:** 831 Bellerire Road, Springfield, IL 62704. **BUSINESS ADDRESS:** Real Estate Broker Appraiser, Shipp Real Estate Agency, 1115 E Ash St, Springfield, IL 62703.

SHIPP, MELVIN DOUGLAS
Educational administration. **PERSONAL:** Born Aug 10, 1948, Columbus, GA; married Dr Michele Pierre-Louis; children: Gael, Elizabeth. **EDUCATION:** IN Univ School of Arts & Sci, BS 1970; IN Univ School of Optometry, OD 1972; Harvard Univ School of Public Health, MPH 1980. **CAREER:** Naval Hosp Port Hueneme, chief optometry serv 1972-76; School of Optometry Univ of AL, dir optometric tech prog 1976-79, asst dean for clinical serv 1980-. **ORGANIZATIONS:** Consult Med Info System via Telephone 1976-; panalist, consult Ophthalmic Devices Panels 1980-; chmn, exec comm Ed Manpower Div Amer Optometric Assn 1983-; chmn Continuing Ed Comm Natl Optometric Assn 1983-; participant, guest Channel 10 PBS-TV Advances in Health 1983. **HONORS/ACHIEVEMENTS:** Listed in Outstanding Young Men of Amer 1978,81; Commiss Spec Citation Food & Drug Admin 1983. **MILITARY SERVICE:** USN Reserve comm 14 yrs; Natl Defense Medal, Armed Forces Reserve Medal, Meritorious Mast 61st Marine Amphibious Unit USCM 1978, Bell Ringer Awd REDCOMNINE. **BUSINESS ADDRESS:** Assistant Dean Clinical Serv, Univ of Alabama, School of Optometry, Birmingham, AL 35294.

SHIPP, PAMELA LOUISE
Psychotherapist. **PERSONAL:** Born Feb 18, 1947, St Louis, MO; daughter of Mall B Shipp and Lovia L Falconer-Shipp. **EDUCATION:** Colorado Coll, BA 1969; George Washington Univ, MA 1973; Denver Univ, PhD 1985. **CAREER:** Irving Jr HS, dean of students 1975-77, counselor 1977-83; Southern IL Univ Counseling Ctr, therapist 1983-84; Palmer HS, counselor 1984-85; Colorado Coll, therapist 1985-; Pikes Peak Psychological Ctr, therapist 1985-. **ORGANIZATIONS:** Alumni Kappa Kappa Gamma Sor 1966-87; mem Amer Psychological Assoc Div 16 1985-87; consultant Ctr for Creative Leadership 1986-; pres Assoc of Black Psychologists Denver/Rocky Mtn Chap 1986-87; bd of dirs, Boys & Girls Club of Pike Peaks Region 1988-91; bd of dirs, World Affairs Council-Colorado Springs 1988-91. **HONORS/ACHIEVEMENTS:** Publication "Counseling Blacks, A Group Approach," The Personnel and Guidance Journal 1983. **BUSINESS ADDRESS:** Psychotherapist, Pikes Peak Psychological Ctr, 1414 N Nevada Ave, Colorado Springs, CO 80906.

SHIRLEY, CALVIN HYLTON
Physician. **PERSONAL:** Born Jan 28, 1921, Tallahassee, FL; married Jeanette Lindsey; children: Calvin H Jr, John W, Jasmin Denise, Cedric H, Carmen Anita. **EDUCATION:** FL A&M Coll Tallahassee, pre-med 1942; Boston Coll of Physicians & Surgeons, MD 1947. **CAREER:** JC & SB Property Development Corp, owner/mgr; Private Practice, physician 1947-. **ORGANIZATIONS:** Pres Broward Co Med Dental & Pharm Assn of FL 1955-59; adv exec bd mem FL State Bur of Comprehensive Med 1969; state med dir 1977, present Grand Asst Medical Dir IBPO Elks of the World; asst med dir FL State Sickle Cell Found 1979; active mem FL Med Assoc, Natl Med Assoc; past pres Kappa Alpha Psi Alumni Chapt; solo accompanist playing trumpet with St Christopher Episcopal Church Choir; 1st trumpet player with the Broward Comm Coll Symphony Orchestra. **HONORS/ACHIEVEMENTS:** FL State Distinguished Serv Awd Gov of FL 1976; Personalites of the S Awd Editorial Bd of Amer Biog Inst 1976-77; So Provincial Achievement Awd So Provincial of Kappa Alpha Psi Frat Inc 1977. **MILITARY SERVICE:** USN hosp corpsman 1944-45; Asiatic Pacific Campaign. **BUSINESS ADDRESS:** 720 NW 22nd Rd, PO Box 9767, Fort Lauderdale, FL 33310.

SHIRLEY, EDWIN SAMUEL, JR.
Surgeon/physician. **PERSONAL:** Born Dec 13, 1922, Tallahassee, FL; son of Edwin S. Shirley, Sr. and Stella Gertrude Young Shirley; married Iris Mays, Jul 03, 1954; children: Edwin, John, Michael, Donald. **EDUCATION:** FL A&M U, BS 1942; HowardUniv Grad Sch, MS 1948; Coll of Med Howard U, MD 1952; HowardUniv & USPH Staten Island, surgical residency 1953-57. **CAREER:** Dade Monroe Co Lung Assoc, rep dir 1966-; Chirs Hosp Miami, chief of staff 1968-; Dade Co Sickle Cell Council, chmn 1971-; Jackson Memorial Hosp, vicechmn bd trustees 1973-; Public Health Trust Miami, chmn exec com; Emergency Medicine Univ of Miami Family Practice Residents, instructor 1975-84; Ambulatory Walk-In Serv for Comm Health Inc, dir 1977-; Floral Park Med Ctr Miami, owner/director 1966-; instructor emergency medicine U of Miami Jackson Hospital Miami Florida, 1975-; Floral Park Medical Center owner 1966-. **ORGANIZATIONS:** Mem Nat Med Assn; FL State Med Assn; Am Thoracic Soc; Dade Co Acad of Med; chmn Educ Task Force Model Cities; mem Chi Delta Mu Phi Beta Sigma Sigma Pi Phi Frats; mem Amer College of Medicine; Floral Park Medical Center owner 1966-. **HONORS/ACHIEVEMENTS:** Oaths Honors Award in Pediatrics 1952; Merit Achievement Award FL A&MUniv 1968; Soc Action Award Phi Beta Sigma Frat 1970; Dean's Adv ComUniv of Miami Sch of Med; Disting Serv Awd Howard Univ 1975; Special Meritorious Awd Comm Health Inc 1983; the emergency room of Comm Hlth Inc of Miami re-named "The Edwin S Shirley, MD Ambulatory Walk-In Service" 1985; Ambulatory Walk-In Service C.H.I., Inc dir 1978-. **MILITARY SERVICE:** UAS capt 1943-46. **HOME ADDRESS:** 2000 NW 56 St, Miami, FL 33142. **BUSINESS ADDRESS:** Floral Park Medical Center, 1521 B NW 54 St, Miami, FL 33142.

SHIRLEY, J. L., SR.
Physician. **PERSONAL:** Born Dec 15, 1878, Jamaica; widowed; children: Gladys. **EDUCATION:** Christian Inst 1906; Meharry Med Coll 1910. **CAREER:** Physician. **ORGANIZATIONS:** Mem Sardis Bapt Ch Fifty Yrs Serv to Mankind Meharry Med Coll 1960. **HONORS/ACHIEVEMENTS:** Award for Comm Med GA State Med Assn 1975.

SHIVERS, S. MICHAEL
Elected city official. **PERSONAL:** Born Mar 20, 1935, Madison, WI; married Jacklyn Lee Gerth; children: Steven Michael, David Wallace, Julie Ann. **EDUCATION:** Univ of WI, BS 1958. **CAREER:** WI Soc of Professional Soil Scientists, mem 1958-78; City of Madison, alderman 17th dist. **ORGANIZATIONS:** Former comm Equal Opport Commiss, Bd of Public Works, City Parks Commiss, Transp Commiss, Legislative Comm; present comm Madison Water Utility, HealthCommiss, Dane Cty Parks Commiss, Common Council Org Comm; City-County Bldg Comm; mem NAACP, Urban League. **HONORS/ACHIEVEMENTS:** Disting Serv Awd North Madison Jaycees 1977-78; sr mem Madison Common Council; Re-elected to 7 two yr terms by a constituency that is 97% white. **BUSINESS ADDRESS:** Alderman District 17, City of Madison, City County Bldg, Madison, WI 53709.

SHOCKLEY, ALONZO HILTON, JR.
Educator. **PERSONAL:** Born Sep 30, 1920, Milford, DE; married Kay Marilyn Falke; children: Novella Shockley Randolph, Cheryl Shockley Durant, Alonzo Hilton III. **EDUCATION:** DE State Coll, BS 1943; MI State Univ, MA 1947; NY Univ, advance cert ad/supv 1956, candidate doctoral degree; (NY Univ). **CAREER:** Brooks HS, science tchr 1948; Dept of Public Instruction, prin elem/jr high 1948-58; DE State Coll, rsch assoc 1958-60; Central Sch Dist #4, tchr 6th grade 1960-62; Union Free Sch Dist, prin 4-6 grades 1962-63; NY State Educ Dept, assoc adminstr 1964-65; Nassau Co Health & Welfare Cncl, educ coord 1965-66; Freeport Public Schs, dir state fed progs 1966-; Retired-Education Consultant 1985. **ORGANIZATIONS:** Pres 1984-85 bd dirs 1973- NY Univ Alumni; allocation comm United Way of Long Island 1977-; NY State Cncl of Superintendent Fed Legislation Comm 1976-. **HONORS/ACHIEVEMENTS:** Who's Who in Amer 1984-85; Who's Who in the East 1984-85; Comm Leaders & Noteworthy Amer Awd 1974 1975; Afro Amer Republican Cert Awd Long Island Cncl 1973; Meritorious Serv Awd Black Educators Comm of Freeport 1974; Serv Above Self Rotary Club of Westbury LI; Recog of Dedicated Serv Adminstrs in Compensatory Educ NY State 1972; Dictionary of Intl Biography Cambridge England 1974; Who's Who In The East 1986-87; Pres Mid-Long Island Chapter United Nations Assoc-USA 1983-; Member Board of Dir Southern NY ST Div-United Nations Assoc of the USA 1978-; Board of Dir (member) Long Island Science Congress 1976-; Board of Directors-Alumni Federation of NYU Inc, and NYU Alumni Assoc- School of York Univ Alumni Assoc Health Nursing and Arts Profession 1984-85; Alocation Committee-United Way of Long Island-1976-; US Army 37th Special Service Co 10/30/42 to 11/09/45 (Retired). **HOME ADDRESS:** 49 Gaymore Road, Port Jefferson Station, Long Island City, NY 11776.

SHOCKLEY, ANN ALLEN
Librarian, writer. **PERSONAL:** Born Jun 21, 1927, Louisville, KY; daughter of Henry Allen and Bessie Allen; divorced; children: William L, Tamara A. **EDUCATION:** Fisk Univ, BA 1948; Case Western Res Univ, MSLS 1959. **CAREER:** Del State Coll, freelance writer asst lib 1959-60, asst lib 1960-66, assoc lib 1966-69; Univ of MD East Shore, lib 1969, assoc lib pub serv, dir oral history; Fisk Univ, assoc lib for special collections & univ archivist, assoc prof lib sci 1970-. **ORGANIZATIONS:** Authors Guild; Feminist Writers Guild; Oral History Assn; Soc of American Archivists; Tennessee Literary Arts Assn; Amer Library Assn Black Caucus; Women's Studies Assn; Tennessee Archivists; Assn of Black Women Historians; College Language Assn. **HONORS/ACHIEVEMENTS:** Research Grant Del State Coll; Short Story Award, AAWW, 1962; Faculty Research Grant, Fisk Univ, 1970; Fellow, Univ of Maryland Library Admin Devel Inst, 1974; ALA Black Caucus Award, 1975; Martin Luther King Black Author's Award, 1982; First Annual Hatshepsut Award for Lit, CVOBW, 1981; Susan Koppelman Award for Best Anthology of 1989 (for book Afro-Amer Women Writers 1746-1933), Popular and American Culture Associations; published works include Living Black American Authors 1973, Loving Her, Bobbs-Merrill Inc 1974, A Handbook for Black Librarianship 1977, Say Jesus and Come to Me, Avon Books 1982, The Black and White of It, Naiad Press 1980, and Afro-American Women Writers 1746-1933: An Anthology and Critical Guide, G K Hall 1988. **HOME ADDRESS:** 5975 Post Road, Nashville, TN 37205.

SHOCKLEY, GRANT S.
Educator, education administrator. **PERSONAL:** Born Sep 03, 1919, Philadelphia, PA; son of Andrew Caleb Shockley and Mattile Blanche Sneed Shockley; married Doris V Taylor; children: Muriel E. **EDUCATION:** Lincoln Univ PA, BA 1942; Drew Univ NJ, BD 1945; Union Theol Sem, Columbia Univ, MA 1946, EdD 1952. **CAREER:** St Mark's United Methodist Church NYC, assoc pastor 1942-46; Clark Coll Atlanta GA, assoc prof bible & religion 1946-49; Gammon Theol Sem Atlanta, profreligious ed 1949-51; Whatcoat Meml UMC Dover DE, pastor 1951-53; Janes Meml UMC Brooklyn NYC, pastor 1953-59; Garrett Theol Sem Northwestern Univ CampusEvanston IL, prof rel ed 1959-66; Exec sec Interboard Com Christian Ed Overseas Bd Global Ministries UMC New York City 1966-70; Emory Univ Atlanta, prof christian ed 1970-75; Interdenom Theol Ctr, pres 1975-79; Philander Smith Coll, pres 1980-83; Duke Univ Divinity School, prof christian ed 1983-89. **ORGANIZATIONS:** Mem Profs & Rschrs in Religious Educ; mem Religious Educ Assoc of US & Canada; mem Alpha Phi Alpha, Sigma Pi Phi, Phi Delta Kappa; mem bd of trustees Methodist Coll Fayetteville NC; mem Univ Senate, The United Methodist Church; mem Christian Educators Fellowship; mem United Methodist Assoc of Profs of Christian Educ; mem NAACP. **HONORS/ACHIEVEMENTS:** Awd for Disting Serv IL Human Relations Council 1961; Hon Alumni Awd Outstanding Achievement Berean Inst Philadelphia 1967; author "New Generation in Africa"; co-author "Black Pastors and Churches in Methodism"; contributing writer Christian Education volumes, dictionaries, encyclopedias, journals and curriculum resource materials. **HOME ADDRESS:** 3423 Revere Road, SW, Atlanta, GA 30331.

SHOCKLEY, THOMAS EDWARD
Educator. **PERSONAL:** Born Mar 15, 1929, Rock Island, TN; married Dolores Janet Cooper; children: Thomas Jr, Beverly, Kimberly, Janet. **EDUCATION:** Fisk U, BA 1949; OH St U, MSc 1952; OH St U, PhD 1954. **CAREER:** Meharry Med Coll, prof chmn dept of micribiology 1971-; OH St Univ, researcher fellow 1952-54; OH St Univ, grad asst 1951-52; OH St Univ, researcher & teacher 1951. **ORGANIZATIONS:** Mem Soc of Sigma Xi; Am Soc for Microbiology; Placement Com of Am Soc for Microbiol 1975-78; bd of tst Assn of Med Sch Microbiology chmn 1975-78. **HONORS/ACHIEVEMENTS:** Rockefeller Found Flw 1959-60; Sclr of Am Cancer Soc 1960-61.

SHOEMAKER, VERONICA SAPP
Clergyman, elected official. **PERSONAL:** Born Jun 23, 1929, Ft Myers, FL; daughter of Rev Henry Sapp and Lillian Sapp; married Bennie Shoemaker (deceased); children: Mattie, Bennie, Duane E. **EDUCATION:** Edward Waters Coll Jacksonville FL, 1950-51; Edison Comm Coll Ft Myers FL, 1971-72. **CAREER:** FL Health & Rehab Svcs, foster care home 1974-83; Sunland Deve Ctr, residenttraining instr; City of East Ft Meyers, city councilwoman-at-large 1982-90; Veronica Shoemaker Florist, woner/designer 1974-. **ORGANIZATIONS:** Pres Lee Cty Branch of NAACP 1972-82; bd of dir Lee Cty Assoc for Retarded Citizens 1980-84; area dir Southwest FL State Conf of NAACP; volunteer progLee Cty RSVP Comm; mem Hispanic Amer Soc; mem bd Lee Cty Cemetary; school bd mem Lee Cty School Bd ESAA Comm; bd mem, charter mem Dunbar Merchants' Assoc Inc; mem Greater Ft Myers Chamber of Comm, FL Conf on Children & Youth, Lee Cty Charter Comm, Lee Cty

Hosp Study Comm, Lee County Human Relations Comm; past chmn Lee Cty Bi-Racial Comm, Lee Cty Mental Health Assoc; past pres Dunbar HS & Elem PTA; past mem Lee Cty Council PTA; past pres & charter mem Dunbar Little League; past charter mem Ebony Parent Club; past mem Dunbar Easter Club; past charter mem, vice pres FL Women's Political Caucus; past charter mem Southwest FL Women's Political Caucus; past mem Lee Cty League of Women Voters, Overall Econ Devel Comm; pres & charter mem Dunbar Improvement Assoc 1979-; bd dir Natl League of Cities, Goodwill Indust, Metro Org, SW FL League of Cities, Women in Municipal Govt; dir, founder Food Bank; Mayor Pro-Tem City of Ft Myers FL 1988-90; Southwest FL Regional Planning Counsel 1989-91; chairman of Public Works of City of Ft Myers 1989-90. **HONORS/ACHIEVEMENTS:** Woman of the Year Zeta Phi Beta; SROP for Comm Serv Plaque; Natl Assoc for the Advancement of Colored People Awd FL; Natl Historical Soc Awd for Personalities of the South NC; Pres Awd Dunbar Little League; Honor & Awd Edison Comm Coll Black Student Union; Easter Club; Dunbar Coalition; Lay Man in Ed AwdPhi Delta Kappa; High Honor Heart of Gold Gannett Found. **HOME ADDRESS:** 3054 Mango St, East Fort Meyers, FL 33916.

SHOFFNER, CLARENCE L.
Dentist. **PERSONAL:** Born Dec 13, 1921, Greensboro, NC; son of Ira B Shuffner and Lelia B Shuffner; married Carrie Carter; children: Selia L, Annah Y. **EDUCATION:** A&T State Univ, BS 1942; attended PA Univ 1946-47; Howard Univ Coll of Dentistry, DDS 1951. **CAREER:** Howard Univ Coll of Dentistry, asst clin prof 1976-; Dr of Dental Surgery 1975-. **ORGANIZATIONS:** Past pres Old North State Dental Soc & Rocky Mount Acad Med Dentistry & Pharmaceutical Soc; past baselius Alpha Omicron Chap Omega Psi Phi; mem Intl Platform Assn; Master Mason; pres Hillcrest Realty Subdivision Roanoke Rapids NC; mem Amer Endodontic Soc; mem Amer Dental Assn & various dental socs; life mem Omega Psi Phi, Chi Delta Mu, Alpha Phi Omega; bd trustees Halifax Comm Coll; mem K of C; bd of ed Weldon City Schools; bd of trustees NC Community Coll System 1986-. **HONORS/ACHIEVEMENTS:** Omega Man of Yr Alpha Omicron Chap 1961; Pres's Alumni Pacesetter Awd A&T State Univ 1967; NC Dental Soc 5th Dist Scholar Awd continuing educ 1973-74; Howard Univ Coll Dentistry Alumni Awd 1974; Fellow Acad of Gen Dent 1976; Fellow Acad of Dentistry Intl; Masters of Acad of Gen Dentistry; Fellow of Amer Coll of Dentists. **MILITARY SERVICE:** USAF corpl 1942-45.

SHOFFNER, JAMES PRIEST
Chemist. **PERSONAL:** Born Jan 14, 1928, New Madrid, MO; married Cornelia Dow; children: Stuart, Karen, Andrew. **EDUCATION:** Lincoln U, BS 1951; DePaul U, MS 1956;Univ IL, PhD 1965. **CAREER:** UOP Inc, rsrch chemist 1963-; CPC Internat, rsrch chm 1956-61. **ORGANIZATIONS:** Mem Am Chem Co; Catalysis Soc; Chicago Chem Club; IL Acad of Sci; Nat Councilor Am Chem Soc; chmn Chicago ACS 1976-77; bd mem NW Suburban SCLC; Dist 59 Sch Comm Council; Omega Psi Phi; Black Achievers Award YMCA 1975; pub Papers in Num Sci Jours Patents. **MILITARY SERVICE:** AUS tech-5 1946-47. **BUSINESS ADDRESS:** 10 UOP Plaza, Des Plaines, IL 60016.

SHOOK, PATRICIA LOUISE
Dentist. **PERSONAL:** Born Feb 25, 1919, Chicago, IL. **EDUCATION:** Fisk Univ, AB 1939; Meharry Med Clg, Cert of Dental Hygiene 1941, DDS 1951. **CAREER:** Bethune Cookman Clg, tchr 1941-42; WAC, Armed Services 1942-46; Self Employed, dentist (retired) 1951-86. **ORGANIZATIONS:** Amer Dental Assoc; Amer Assoc of Women Dentists; Western Dental Assoc; CA Dental Assoc. **MILITARY SERVICE:** WAAC & WAC 1st lt 2 1/2 yrs. **HOME ADDRESS:** 4268 Mt Vernon Dr, Los Angeles, CA 90008.

SHOPSHIRE, JAMES MAYNARD
Educator/seminary professor. **PERSONAL:** Born Oct 07, 1942, Atlanta, GA; married Berlinda Kay Brown; children: James Jr, Anika Diara, Ekerin Ayobami. **EDUCATION:** Clark Coll, BA 1963; Interdenominational Theological Ctr Gammon Seminary, BD 1966; Northwestern Univ, PhD 1975. **CAREER:** Interdenominational Theol Ctr, asst prof 1975-80, chair of church & soc dept 1978-80; Wesley Theological Seminary, assoc prof 1980-83, assoc dean 1980-85, prof 1983-. **ORGANIZATIONS:** Minister Bethlehem United Methodist Church 1964-66, Burns United methodist Church 1966-71, Ingleside-Whitfield United Meth Church 1974-75. **HONORS/ACHIEVEMENTS:** Rockefeller Doctoral Fellowship Fund for Theol Educ 1971-72; Crusade Scholarship United Methodist Church 1973-74. **HOME ADDRESS:** 6215 Sligo Mill Rd, NE, Washington, DC 20011. **BUSINESS ADDRESS:** Prof of Sociology of Religion, Wesley Theological Seminary, 4500 Massachusetts Ave NW, Washington, DC 20016.

SHORT, BOBBY (ROBERT WALTRIP)
Entertainer. **PERSONAL:** Born Sep 15, 1924, Danville, IL. **CAREER:** Specializes in songs of the 1920's & 1930's by composers such as Duke Ellington, Cole Porter, George & Ira Gershwin; appeared in Broadway productins 1956-; appeared almost nightly at New York City Cafe Carlyle 1968-; performed for a yr in Paris & London; teamed up with Mabel Mercer for concert in New York City Town Hall 1968 & rec of concert was a best seller; appeared at White House 1970; appeared inTV movie "Roots, The Next Generation" 1979; produced DancEllington; appeared in motion picture "Splash" 1984. **ORGANIZATIONS:** Life mem NAACP. **HONORS/ACHIEVEMENTS:** Laureate of the Lincoln Acad State of IL; author "Black and White Baby," 1971; also articles. **BUSINESS ADDRESS:** c/o Betty Lee Hunt Assoc, 444 E 57th St, New York, NY 10022.

SHORT, JAMES EDWARD
Elected official. **PERSONAL:** Born Sep 21, 1914, Washington, DC; married Harriette Barksdale. **EDUCATION:** Juliard School of Music,; Coast Guard Acad, Sonarman 1943-44. **CAREER:** Ward 4 Dem, elected treas; Bureau of Rehab, Prison Corrections,, voc counselor; Intl Rev NYC, subject chief 1944-45; DC Congressional Dist Ward, vice chmn 1971-72; Sen Kennedy's Cong Dist 2 DC, co-ord 1982; Postal Transp Railway Mail, 33 yrs; DC Ward 4C, ANC Commissioner retired. **ORGANIZATIONS:** Mem Holy Name Soc, St Vincent De Paul 1955-; 4th degree Knights of Columbus 1972-; mem Reading is Fundamental DC 1975-; usher St Gabriels Catholic Church 25 yrs, Shrine of the Immaculate Conception; mem NW Boundry Civic Assoc; treas CCD St Gabriels Cath Church; mem Commiss Youth Council, Mental Health Assoc of DC; sec mandatory sentencing DC City Councilman John Ray. **HONORS/ACHIEVEMENTS:** Superior Accomplishment Postal Trans 1964; Dist & Fed Govt; appt to ANC Task Force by 1st City Council Chmn Arrington Dixon Ward 4. **MILITARY SERVICE:** USCG Platoon Leader 1943-44; Hon Serv Button 1944. **BUSINESS ADDRESS:** ANC Commissioner (retired), DC Ward 4C, 4020 8th St NW, Washington, DC 20011.

SHORT, KENNETH L.
Educator. **PERSONAL:** Born Aug 21, 1943, Chicago, IL. **EDUCATION:** Howard U, BSEE 1966; SUNY At Stony Brook, MS 1969; SUNY at Stony Brook, PhD 1972. **CAREER:** State Univ of NY at Stony Brook, asst prof 1985. **ORGANIZATIONS:** Mem of faculty Dept of Elec Scis StateUniv of NY at Stony Brook 1968; consult Several Industries in NY Area Specializing in Design of Instumentation & Digital Sys; research in design of microprocessor Based Digital Sys Reg Professional Engr NY 1970-; mem NY State Soc of Professional Engrs 1970-; Inst of Elec & Electronic Engrs 1964-; mem NY Karate Assn 1970-. **HONORS/ACHIEVEMENTS:** Recip Schmitt Scholar Fellowship Nat Engring; Consortium Inc 1974. **BUSINESS ADDRESS:** Dept of Electrical Sciences SU, Stony Brook, NY 11794.

SHORT, TED
Business executive. **PERSONAL:** Children: Tod, Toi Lynne. **EDUCATION:** BA; AA; MBA; mgmt & personnel certs. **CAREER:** Cunningham Short Berryman & Assos Inc, pres chmn bd 1968-; Whittaker Corp, personnel mgr 1966-68; N Am Rockwell, adminstrv asst 1966; Home Sav& Loan, mgmt trainee 1965-66. **ORGANIZATIONS:** Mem Am Arbitration Assn CA Minority Employment & Coun; Urban & Transp Sys Grp; Inst Human Eng Scis; Foothill Free Clinic; Personnel & Indus Rel Assn; Valley Professional Emplymt Coun; Pacoimaskills Cntr; Altadena/Pasadena Bus Asso Carnegie Flwshp. **HONORS/ACHIEVEMENTS:** Adminstrv mgmt award Indus Educ Inst; personnel mgmt award Am Mgmt Assn; outstndg yng man yr award 1972; comm ldrs Am 1972; Personalities of West& Midwest 1972.

SHORTER, KENNETH LIVINGSTON
Judge. **PERSONAL:** Born Aug 09, 1915, New York, NY; son of James Wilfred Shorter and Lillian O Giffin; married Muriel Louise Reid; children: Elliot, Ann. **EDUCATION:** City Coll NY, BA 1934; Columbia Univ, MA 1938; Fordham Law Sch, BLL 1942. **CAREER:** Civil Court NY, judge 1973-82; Supreme Court NY, judge. **ORGANIZATIONS:** Bd mem Natl Lawyers Guild 1960-62; chmn of bd Amer Bridge Players Assn 1968-73; bd mem Harlem Lawyers Assn 1980-82; library comm NY Co Lawyers; bd mem Comm Serv Council; bd mem Townsend Harris Alumni. **BUSINESS ADDRESS:** Judge State Supreme Court, New York State, 60 Centre St, New York, NY 10007.

SHORTY, VERNON JAMES
Mental health executive. **PERSONAL:** Born Dec 17, 1943, New Orleans, LA; son of Earl Shorty (deceased) and Adries Shorty; divorced; children: Angelique, Chyna. **EDUCATION:** Southern Univ in New Orleans, BA History 1972, BA Sociology 1973; Tulane Univ New Orleans, Fellowship Certificate 1974; Admin of Drug Abuse Prgms, entered Southern Univ in Baton Rouge Master in Ed 1983. **CAREER:** Desire Narcotic Rehabilitation Ctr, Inc Exec Dir, 1970- ; Southern Univ System; Instructor 1973- ; LA State Univ; adjunct instructor 1970-72; CADA Desire Florida outreach Admin Asst 1970-72. **ORGANIZATIONS:** Consultant technician Veterans Administration 1973-; co-chmn First Natl Drug Abuse Conference 1974; chmn LA Assoc of Program Directors 1974-86; mem Phi Alpha Theta Soc. **HONORS/ACHIEVEMENTS:** Social Justice Awd Natl Black Policemen Assoc; HTLV III Study Rsch Triangle Inst 1985-86; published "A Situation of Desire" Org & Adm of Drug Treatment Prog 1974; American's Unsung Heroes 1988; Kool Achiever Awards Nominee; frequent isolation and moleculas identification of human T-Cell Leukemia Virus Type-2 1988; High rate of HTLV-II infection in Seropositive IV Drug Abusers in New Orleans 1989. **MILITARY SERVICE:** USN E-4 2 yrs; USN Reserves 4 yrs. **HOME ADDRESS:** 4760 Franklin Avenue, New Orleans, LA 70122. **BUSINESS ADDRESS:** Executive Dir, Desire Narcotic Rehab Ctr Inc, 3307 Desire Parkway, New Orleans, LA 70126.

SHOTWELL, ADA CHRISTENA
Educator. **PERSONAL:** Born Sep 05, 1940, Helena, AR; married Roy Edward. **EDUCATION:** SoUniv Baton Rouge, BA 1961;Univ of CA at Berkeley, tchg cert 1962; Memphis State U, edM 1976. **CAREER:** State Tech Inst at Memphis Correctional Center, div head correctional educ 1978-; State Tech Inst, dept head Developmental studies 1976-78; State Tech Inst, teacher 1975; Memphis City School, teacher 1968-75; Clover Park School Dist, teacher 1964-67. **ORGANIZATIONS:** Mem AVA 1976-; mem TVA 1976-; mem ATEA 1976-; mem TTEC 1976-; mem WTEA 1976-; mem MACBE 1976-; mem sec Nat Assn of Black Am in Vocational Educ 1979-80; chap mem bd of dir Black on Black Crime Task Force 1985; mem NAACP 1985; mem PUSH 1985. **HONORS/ACHIEVEMENTS:** Outstanding Young Woman of Am 1976; Citizen of the Week WLOK Radio State 1978; Tchr of The Year Correctional Educ Assn Region III 1978; TN Correctional Educator of Year TN Assn 1978; Professional of Quarter Quarterly Jour of Corrections. **BUSINESS ADDRESS:** Professor Develop Studies, State Tech Inst at Memphis, 5983 Macon Cove, Memphis, TN 38134.

SHOULTZ, RUDOLPH SAMUEL
Clergyman. **PERSONAL:** Born Jul 24, 1918; married Vera Pearson; children: Tony E, Michele V. **EDUCATION:** Moody Bible Inst; Chicago Bapt Inst, BTh 1961; Ministerial Inst & Coll, DD 1967. **CAREER:** Bapt Gen State Cong Christian Edn, dir gen; Woodriver Bapt Dist Assn Bd, treas; St Paul Bapt Ch Freeport IL, asst pastor 1952; Second Bapt Ch Dixon IL, pastor 1956; Union Bapt Ch Springfield IL, pastor 1968-. **ORGANIZATIONS:** Mem IL Housing Devel Authority; bd mem Mayor's Adv Council (Dept of Community Devel & Prog); bd mem Adv Council Comprehensive Employment Act; elected bd mem Springfield Metro Exposition Auditorium Auth. **BUSINESS ADDRESS:** Pastor, Union Baptist Church, 1405 E Monroe, PO Box 2193, Springfield, IL 62705.

SHOWELL, HAZEL JARMON
Educator. **PERSONAL:** Born Apr 05, 1945, Macon, GA; children: Angela, Patrick. **EDUCATION:** DE State Coll, BA Eng 1968;Univ of Bridgeport, MA Guidance 1973. **CAREER:** Dept of Pub Instrn, state supr adult educ 1976-; Wm Henry Middle School Dover DE, asso prin 1973-76; Wm Henry Middle School Dover DE, teacher of humanities 1968-73; Univ of DE, consultant for staff leadership 1975; State of VA, cons/evaluator 1978; State of DE, cons/police training 1979. **ORGANIZATIONS:** Mem Delta Sigma Theta Sor 1968; pres Peninsula Sect of Nat Counc of Negro Women 1976-79; chairperson Social Justice Com (NAPCAE) 1978; tchr of the Yr Award Capital Sch Dist Dover DE 1972; Women of Vision

Daring to Venture Delta Sigma Theta Sor Dover DE 1974. **HONORS/ACHIEVEMENTS:** Outstanding Yng Women in Am State of DE 1978; White House Conference on Families State of DE 1979-80. **BUSINESS ADDRESS:** State Supervisor Adult CommEd, STDept of Public Instruction, PO Box 1402, J C Townsend Blvd, Dover, DE 19903.

SHOWELL, MILTON W.
Military officer. **PERSONAL:** Born Apr 19, 1936, Baltimore; married Alberta Graves; children: Keith, Kimberly. **EDUCATION:** Morgan State Coll, BS 1958. **CAREER:** Logistic Vietnam, mgr med serv 1966-67; Korea 1971-72; US Army Europe, implemented race relations prog; Seminars Drug Abuse; Author Book; Dept Def RaceRelations Inst, grad; Patrick AFB FL 1974. **ORGANIZATIONS:** Mem Toastmasters Am; Intl Winner Toastmaster's Inernat; European Speech Contest 1975; All Europe Winner Toastmaster's Dist Speech Contest 1975 (1st American); mem First Apostolic Faith Ch Baltimore. **HONORS/ACHIEVEMENTS:** AUS maj 1961. **MILITARY SERVICE:** AUS maj 1961-.

SHROPSHIRE, ARTHUR C.
Educator. **PERSONAL:** Born Feb 02, 1909, Hunnewell, MO; married Grace A Steward; children: Jacqulyn, Arthur, Jr. **EDUCATION:** LincolnUniv Jefferson City, MO, BS 1930;Univ of NE Lincoln, MA 1941;Univ of NE, PhD 1951. **CAREER:** Lincoln Univ, coordinator of teacher corps 1973-; Langston School Desoto, MO, prin 1930-39; Festus Coop HS Festus, MO, prin 1939-40; Bartlett HS, prin & supt of elem school 1944-51; Langston Univ Langsto, OK, dir of div ed 1951-63; Kinloch Schools Kinloch, MO, supt 1963-73; State Coll Orangeburg, SC Sum, visiting prof 1949; Tuskegee 1950; So Univ Baton Rouge 1957; Prairie View Prairie View, TX 1958-60. **ORGANIZATIONS:** Omicron Chap Phi Delta Kappa NE Chpt; Beta Beta Beta; Bio Hon Soc Delta Delta Chap 1963; Okla Acad of Sci 32nd Deg Mason St Louis Co Human Rel Com 1965-71; Human Dev Corp Bd St Louis; Adv Bd Sen Cit St Louis Area; life Mem NAACP; Steward Ward Chapel AME Ch Kinloch, MO. **HONORS/ACHIEVEMENTS:** Curators awrd LincolnUniv of MO 1967; Org Festus Coop HS Which Pros HS Ed for All of East & Cen MO for Blacks; pres of MO Assc Negro Tchrs.

SHROPSHIRE, CLAUDIUS NAPOLEON, JR.
Surgeon. **PERSONAL:** Born Jan 10, 1925, Texarkana, AR; son of Rev Claudius N Shropshire Sr and Eulah Brinker Shropshire; married Jane Frances Moore; children: Claudius N III, Kenneth Leroy. **EDUCATION:** Johnson C Smith Univ, BS (Cum Laude) 1947; Meharry Medical Coll, MD 1951. **CAREER:** Madigan Army Hospital, internship 1951-52; Wadsworth General Hospital, residency genl surgery 1953-57; UCLA School of Medicine, asst clinical prof of surgery 1963-; Private Practice, surgeon. **ORGANIZATIONS:** Mem Los Angeles County Medical Assn 1977-; mem CA Medical Assn; bd of dirs Charles R Drew Medical Soc 1977-; mem Golden State Medical Soc; fellow Amer College of Surgeons; mem Los Angeles Surgical Soc; sustaining mem Graduate Surgeons of LA County, Orange County Surgical Soc, Matthew Walker Surgical Club; mem Amer Geriatrics Soc, Amer Soc of Abdominal Surgeons; bd of dirs Amer Cancer Soc; bd of medical advisors Colostomy Club; mem Kappa Alpha Psi Frat; Sigma Pi Phi Frat, Xi Boule; mem Johnson C Smith University Alumni Los Angeles Chapt; mem Natl Alumni Assoc Meharry Medical Coll; mem exec comm Charles R Drew Postgraduate Medical College; mem Urban League, Westminster Presbyterian Church; mem 100 Black Men of Los Angeles; mem bd of trustees Johnson C Smith Univ; mem bd of dirs CA Medic al Review Inc. **HONORS/ACHIEVEMENTS:** Mem Beta Kappa Chi Natl Scientific Honor Soc, Kappa Pi Natl Medical Honor Soc, Alpha Omega Alpha Honor Medical Soc, Alpha Kappa Mu Natl Honor Soc; Distinguished Alumnus in Medicine Meharry Medical Coll 1981. **MILITARY SERVICE:** AUS 1943-46, USAR 1946-51, USAF 1951-53, USAFR capt 1953-57; Bronze Star, Purple Heart 1944-45. **BUSINESS ADDRESS:** 1828 S Western Ave, Ste 6, Los Angeles, CA 90006.

SHROPSHIRE, HARRY W.
Financial administrator. **PERSONAL:** Born Apr 13, 1934, Asbury Park, NJ; married Kathleen Rae Nelson. **EDUCATION:** Moravian Coll, BS Econ & Bus Admin 1957; Advanced Training, Mgmt 1972, Foreign Affairs Exec Studies Prog 1974, Financial and Economic Analysis 1976. **CAREER:** Emerson Radio & Phonograph Corp NJ, accountant 1957-62; Hess Oil & Chemical Corp NJ, accountant 1962-65; US Dept of State AID, auditor 1965-70, acctng divchf 1970-75, foreign serv controller 1975-86; Self-employed, financial mgmt consultant 1986-. **ORGANIZATIONS:** Mem Assn of Govt Accountants 1966-; mem Am Mgmt Assns 1976-. **HONORS/ACHIEVEMENTS:** Cert of Apprec for Coop in Equal Oppor Prog Dept of State AID 1974. **MILITARY SERVICE:** USNR 1952-60. **HOME ADDRESS:** 592 Trout Lake Drive, Bellingham, WA 98226.

SHROPSHIRE, JOHN SHERWIN
Educational administrator. **PERSONAL:** Born Sep 06, 1938, Pittsburgh, PA; son of John Shropshire and Willa Shields; married Jamie Nagle; children: Philip, Christopher, Alicia. **EDUCATION:** Clarion Un of PA, BS 1961; Yale Un, Grad; Shippensburg Un, Grad; Penn St Un, Grad. **CAREER:** Central Dauphin East HS Hgh PA, tchr/coach 1961-72; Hgh Nwspr, Black History Nwspr wrtr 1962-65; Am Red Cross, bd of dir Clarion Co 1979-; Rotary Club, bd of dir 1980-; PA Un Adm Assoc, pres 1979-82; Am Asso of Collegiate Reg & Adm Officers, comm mbr; Hgb Hospital, bd of dir; Clarion Univ of PA, dean of admissions & reg, dean of enrollment mgmt and academic records. **ORGANIZATIONS:** Exec bd PA Un Adm Asso; bd of dir Clarion Co Red Cross 1979- judge of elections Paint Twshp 1980-; bd of dir, pres Clarion Co Rotary Club 1983-; exec bd PA Un Adm Assoc; elected Township Supervisor Paint Township (6 yr term). **HONORS/ACHIEVEMENTS:** NDEA Grant to Study African History Yale Un; Many Articles in Black History. **BUSINESS ADDRESS:** Dean Enrollment Mgmt/Acad Rec, Clarion University of PA, Clarion, PA 16214.

SHROPSHIRE, THOMAS B.
Retired business executive. **PERSONAL:** Born Oct 15, 1925, Little Rock; son of William B Shropshire; married Jacqulyn Calloway; children: Terilyn, Tom, Jr. **EDUCATION:** Lincoln U, BS 1950; NY Univ Grad Sch of Business Admn, MBA 1951. **CAREER:** Philip Morris Inc, corporate vice pres 1978; Miller Brewing Co (Sub of Philip Morris Inc), sr vice pres tres 1978. **ORGANIZATIONS:** Vp Mkt Plng Miller Brewing Co; mem bd dir 1972; dir Fin Holding Co; chmn & managing dir Phillip Morris Nigeria 1968 sales mgr tropical Africa 1963; coll supr 1953; sales rep Philip Morris Inc 1952; life mem NAACP; Alpha Phi Alpha; Am Mktg Assc; Intl Adv Assn; Natl Assc of Mkt Dev; tres Milwaukee Urban League; mem Cncl of Trustees Univ of WI Hosps; adv cncl of W Paul Stillman Sch of Business Seton Hall U; bd of trustees Howard Univ 1982-; bd of trustees Winthrop Rockefeller Foundation 1984-; bd of trustees Natl Urban League 1984-; bd of dir Key Banks Puget Sound 1988-89. **HONORS/ACHIEVEMENTS:** Distnguished alumni award Lincoln Univ Jefferson City, MO; Dr of Law, Lincoln Univ 1980; Dr of Humane Letters, Houston-Tilloston Coll 1982; Dr of Humane Letters, Miles Coll 1984; Dr of Humane Letters, Philander Smith Coll 1985; Dr of Humane Letters, Talladega Coll 1987. **MILITARY SERVICE:** USN 1944-46.

SHUFFER, GEORGE MACON, JR.
Military clergyman. **PERSONAL:** Born Sep 27, 1923, Palestine, TX; son of George Macon Shuffer, Sr. and Johnnie D'Ella Butler Shuffer; married Maria Cecilia Rose; children: Gloria, David, George III, Marlene Kuhn, Rita Lloyd, Monica Thomas, Rosemary McQuillan, Joseph, Maria Wallace, Anita Bayler, Peter. **EDUCATION:** Monterey Peninsula Clg, AA 1953; Un of MD, BS 1956; Un of MD, MA 1959. **CAREER:** 2nd Inf US Army, battalion commander 1964-66; US Army & Sec of Def, Pentagon staff off 1967-70; 193rd US Army, brigade cmdr 1970-71; 3rd Inf Div, asst div cmdr 1972-74. **ORGANIZATIONS:** Deacon Roman Catholic Ch 1977-. **HONORS/ACHIEVEMENTS:** US Armored Force 1916-40 Univ of MD 1959; "Finish Them With Firepower" Military Review 1967; "An Appropriate Response" Military Review 1969. **MILITARY SERVICE:** AUS brigadier gen 35 yrs; Dist Serv Medal; 3 Silver Stars; 3 Legions of Merit 1944-75; 3 Bronz Stars; 6 Air Medals; Purple Heart. **BUSINESS ADDRESS:** Hospital Chaplain, Wm Beaumont, AMC, WBAMC, El Paso, TX 79920.

SHUFORD, HUMPHREY LEWIS
Educational administrator. **PERSONAL:** Born Nov 18, 1945, Wetumpka, AL; divorced; children: M:Shondia, Monique. **EDUCATION:** AL A&M Univ, BS, 1969; Troy State Univ, advanced studies, 1973; Univ of So AL, advanced studies 1974; Auburn Univ, advanced studies 1975-76; AL State Univ, MS 1978. **CAREER:** Atmore State Tech Coll, coord of student personnel; Jefferson Davis St Jr Coll; part time Sociology Inst. **ORGANIZATIONS:** mem, AL Coll Personnel Assn 1980-86, AL Counselsor Assn 1980-86; Atmore State Tech Coll Educ Assn vice pres, 1982-84, pres 1984-86; vice pres, pres, Progressive Civic Club 1982-83; vice pres, pres Atmore Alumni Chapter, Kappa Alpha Psi 1983, 85; bd mem, Atmore Chamber of Commerce; mem, AL Educ Assn, 1986, Natl Educ Assn, 1986, Amer Assn for Counseling 1986, AL Democratic Conf, Hermon Lodge No 260. **HONORS/ACHIEVEMENTS:** Achievement Awd Progressive Club 1979; Polemarch Awd 1981, Achievement Awd 1981 Atmore Alumni Chap Kappa Alpha Psi; Achievement Awd State Testing Program 1982; Special Service Awd Atmore Alumni Chap Kappa Alpha Psi 1982; Southern Province Achievement Awd Kappa Alpha Psi 1986; Chapter of the Yr Awd Kappa Alpha Psi Frat 1986. **HOME ADDRESS:** PO Box 902, Atmore, AL 36502. **BUSINESS ADDRESS:** Coord of Student Personnel, Atmore State Tech College, PO Box 1119, Atmore, AL 36502.

SHUMAN, JEROME
Attorney, educator. **PERSONAL:** Born Sep 24, 1937, St Augustine, FL; married Christine. **EDUCATION:** Trenton Jr Coll, AA 1958; Howard Univ, BA 1960, LLB 1963; Yale Univ LLM 1964. **CAREER:** Howard Univ, prof of law 1964-69; Amer Univ, adj prof law; Univ TN, Rutgers Univ, visiting adj prof law; Georgetown Univ, prof law 1968-78; US Dept Agriculture, dir office equal oppor 1971-74; Howard Univ, prof law. **ORGANIZATIONS:** Chmn bd of dirs District of Columbia Housing Finance Agency. **BUSINESS ADDRESS:** Prof of Law, HowardUniv, 2900 Van Mess St NW, Washington, DC 20008.

SHUMATE, GLEN
Community relations manager. **PERSONAL:** Born Sep 09, 1958, Sandusky, OH; son of John Wesley Shumate and Annie Ruth (Henson) Shumate; children: Darrin Wesley. **EDUCATION:** Univ of Toledo, Toledo OH, BS Student Services, 1982. **CAREER:** Univ of Toledo, Toledo OH, activities coord, 1980-82, counselor asst, 1982-83; Burlington Northern, Holland OH, operations agent, 1983-84; Cimmaron Express, Genoa OH, operating mgr, 1984-86; Landscape Outlet, Cleveland OH, admin coord; Hillcrest Hospital, Mayfield OH, mgr patient support serv, 1986-88. **ORGANIZATIONS:** Mem, Big Brothers/Big Sisters, 1988-; bd mem, Cleveland Food Basket, 1988-, Citizens Mental Health Assembly, 1988-, Cleveland State Univ Coll of Urban Affairs-Recruitment & Placement, 1989-. **HONORS/ACHIEVEMENTS:** Glen Shumate Award, Black Faculty/Staff at Univ of Toledo, 1981; Leadership Award, Black Student Union, 1981; Unemployment in the 9th Congressional Dist, Congressional Record, 1982; Eastern Campus Honors List, Cuyahoga Community Coll, 1987. **BUSINESS ADDRESS:** Manager, Community Relations, Cleveland Indians, Cleveland Stadium, Cleveland, OH 44120.

SHUTTLESWORTH, FRED L.
Clergyman. **PERSONAL:** Born Mar 18, 1922, Montgomery, AL; widowed; children: Patricia, Ruby, Fred, Jr, Carolyn. **EDUCATION:** Selma U, AB; AL State Clg, BS 1955; Birmingham Bapt Clg, LlD 1969. **CAREER:** Greater New Light Bapt Ch Cincinnati, fndr pastor 1966-. **ORGANIZATIONS:** Bd mem 1st sec SCLC; former aide to Dr Martin Luther King, Jr; fndr AL & Christian Movement for Human Rights 1956-69. **HONORS/ACHIEVEMENTS:** Recipient hon DD Cincinnati Bapt Bible Clg 1971; russwurm awrd Natl Nwspr Pub Assc 1958; fdr awrd SCLC 1977; ml king civil rights awrd ProgressiveNatl Bapt 1975; rosa parks awrd SCLC 1963; spec awrd Back Our Brothers Inc 1963; spec cit Natl Com for Rural Sch 1961; excellence awrd PUSH 1974; human rel awrd Press Clb 1962. **BUSINESS ADDRESS:** Grtr New Light Baptist Church, 710 N Crescent, Cincinnati, OH 45229.

SIBLEY, ELLEN C.
Librarian. **PERSONAL:** Born Sep 21, 1918, Forrest City, AR; married Rev T E Sibley. **EDUCATION:** Ft Valley State, BS 1961; Atlanta U, MLS 1962; Wayne State U, 1970. **CAREER:** Ft Valley State Clg, asst libr 1962-65; Detroit Pub Lib, children's libr 1965-70; lib neighborhood consult 1970-73; Duffield Lib, chief div 1973-75; Learing Resources & Ctr Wayne Co Comm Clg, coord 1975-. **ORGANIZATIONS:** Mem Alpha Kappa Mu Hon Soc 1959-; Delta Sigma Theta 1960-; ch Lib Tribute to Black Am 1973-; mem Natl Cncl Negro Women Detroit Sect; cncl FL State Lib 1971; MI State Lib 1972. **HONORS/ACHIEVEMENTS:** Knox awrd Ft Valley State Clg 1961; awrd Detroit Pub Lib; co-author series Biographical Calendars. **BUSINESS ADDRESS:** Rosary Cntr, 8551 Greenfield, Detroit, MI 48221.

SIDBURY, HAROLD DAVID
Minister/pastor. **PERSONAL:** Born Sep 15, 1940, Hampstead, NC; married Vivian Ann Radd; children: Timothy, Channeta, Felicia, Colette, Harold Jr, Jarvis, Ingar. **EDUCATION:** Attended, Cape Fear Tech 1960, Kittrell Coll 1966. **CAREER:** African Methodist Episcopal Church, pastor 1966-87; General Contractor, owner 1974-87. **ORGANIZATIONS:** Chmn Counsel Bd of Educ Pender co 1960-85; mem East Gate Masonic Lodge # 143 1965-; chmn bd of trustees Grand United Order of Salem 1978-85; chmn bd ofdirs Grand United Order of Salem 1985-87. **HONORS/ACHIEVEMENTS:** Appreciation Awd Neighborhood Housing Develop Wilmington Chap 1979; Designing & Building Awd Grand United Order of Salem Building 1982; Most Outstanding Minister of Year Black Caucus Robeson Co 1984. **BUSINESS ADDRESS:** Manager & Owner, General Construction, 419 North 7th St, Wilmington, NC 28401.

SIGLER, I. GARLAND
Business executive. **PERSONAL:** Born Dec 07, 1932, Bessemer, AL; married Bertha; children: Glenn Garland, Ennis Stevenson. **EDUCATION:** Pennsylvania State U; Temple U. **CAREER:** SE PA Transportation Authority, ino agent 1960-; Philadelphia HS for Girls, instr 1967-; Sigler Travel Serv & Ticket Agcy, pres; Comm Serv Ctr, exec dir1970-; Teamster Local 161 Intl Brotherhood Teamster, vice pres 1972-. **ORGANIZATIONS:** Chldren's pgm dir Natl Med Assc 1971; pres Transit Roundtable of Philadelphia; pres York 15 Home Assc; life mem NAACP; dir N Philadelphia Br 1972-73. **HONORS/ACHIEVEMENTS:** Mason of yr Prince Hall Mason Tuscan Morning Star Lodge 48 1968; comm serv awrd NAACP 1971; serv awrd Natl Dairies Corp. **BUSINESS ADDRESS:** 1330 W Olney Ave, Philadelphia, PA 19141.

SIKES, MELVIN PATTERSON
Retired psychologist, educator. **PERSONAL:** Born Dec 24, 1917, Charleston, MO; son of Kimmie Sikes and Dorthy Sikes; married Zeta Lorraine Bledsoe. **EDUCATION:** NC Clge Durham, BA (cum laude) 1938; Univ of Chicago, MA 1948, PhD 1950. **CAREER:** Wilberforce Univ OH, dean 1950-52; Bishop Clge Marshall TX, dean, admin 1952-55; VA Hosp Houston TX, clinical psych 1960-1969; Univ of TX at Austin, prof educ psych 1969-Ret; Zeta Assc Inc, dir. **ORGANIZATIONS:** Life mem Amer Psych Assc 1950-, Natl Educ Assc, TX Psych Assc; mem Intl Psych Assc, NAACP, Kappa Alpha Psi, 32 Deg Mason, Shriner. **HONORS/ACHIEVEMENTS:** Meritorious Srv Award Amer Psych Assc for work in Area of Psych; book Haper and Rowe The Admin of Injustice; research grant. **MILITARY SERVICE:** USAF 2nd lt 1943-45; Amer Theatre Medal Sharpshooter. **BUSINESS ADDRESS:** Dir, Zeta Assc Inc, 8703 Point West Dr, Austin, TX 78759.

SILAS, DOLORES IRENE
Educational administrator. **PERSONAL:** Born Apr 03, Elkhart, IN. **EDUCATION:** Tuskegee Inst, BS 1948;Univ of AZ, MEd 1962; US Intrntl U, PhD 1977. **CAREER:** Tacoma Public School, prin 1971-, asst asst 1970-71, team Leader/teacher corp 1969-70, teache, 1953-69. **ORGANIZATIONS:** Mem Phi Delta Kappa 1975-; chmn of bd Allenmore Comm Hosp 1979-80; mem Downtown's Boys Clb 1979-80; mem Alpha Kappa Alpha 1970-; mem Tacoma Urban League 1975-; pres Tacoma Br NAACP 1978-80. **HONORS/ACHIEVEMENTS:** Schlrshp Delta Kappa Gamma 1975-76; schlshp Soroptimist Intrntl 1976-77; doctoral theses Comm Ed & Its Rlthnshp to Comm Clg Non-degree Pgm 1977; invtd to White House Pres Carter 1979. **BUSINESS ADDRESS:** 1229 Moorlands Dr, South Tacoma, WA 98405.

SILAS, JACQUELINE ANN
Attorney. **PERSONAL:** Born Aug 20, 1959, Middletown, OH; married Lawrence Berry Butler Jr. **EDUCATION:** The OH State Univ, BA 1981; Univ of Akron School of Law, JD 1984. **CAREER:** Parms, Purnell, Stubbs & Gilbert, law clerk 1982-83; Jones Day Reavis & Poque, law clerk 1983-84; Akron Metro Housing Auth, legal intern & Hearing officer 1983-84; Parms Purnell Gilbert & Stidham, assoc 1985-86; Summit Co Prosecutor's Office, asst prosecuting atty 1984-; Robinson Smith & Silas Law Firm, attorney/partner 1986-. **ORGANIZATIONS:** Vice pres Black Law Students Assoc 1981-84; mem Delta Sigma Theta Sor 1984-; pres 1987-, mem Akron Barristers Club 1984-; third vice pres Akron Branch NAACP 1985-87; vice chairperson young lawyers comm 1986-, mem Akron Bar Assoc 1986-; mem Natl Bar Assoc 1986-, Natl Assoc of Black Women Attys 1986-, The OH State Bar Assoc 1986-, Business Network Connection 1986-; bd mem & sec East Akron Comm House 1986-. **HONORS/ACHIEVEMENTS:** Outstanding Young Woman of Amer 1983-86; Member of the Year 1984, Senior Awd 1984 Black Law Students Assoc; Whose Who Among American Law Students 1984. **BUSINESS ADDRESS:** Partner, Robinson Smith Silas Law Firm, 680 East Market St Ste 309, Akron, OH 44304.

SILCOTT, WILLIAM L.
Psychiatrist. **PERSONAL:** Born Jan 10, 1899. **EDUCATION:** TN St, BS 1942; Meharry Med Coll, MD 1935. **CAREER:** Harlem Vly St Hosp, supr psychtrst 1955-74 (ret), sr psychtrst 1954-55; Meharry Med Coll, asso prof 1945-50, asst prof 1936-39. **ORGANIZATIONS:** Mem Am Psychia Assn. **HONORS/ACHIEVEMENTS:** Kappa Pi Hon Soc cert Am Bd of Psychtry 1954; Hon Nat Bd of Med Examiners Highest Grade in Pathology 1936; Cngrsnl Slctv Srv Awd for Faithful & Loyal Srv Meharry Med Coll. **MILITARY SERVICE:** WW II. **BUSINESS ADDRESS:** PO Box 363, Pawling, NY 12564-0363.

SILER, BRENDA CLAIRE
Public relations director. **PERSONAL:** Born Oct 03, 1953, Washington, DC; daughter of Floyd Howard Siler and Helen Siler. **EDUCATION:** Spelman Coll, BA, English, 1975. **CAREER:** Natl Center for Voluntary Action, resource specialist, 1978-79; United Way of Metro Atlanta, comm assoc, 1979-82; Rafshoon Shivers Vargas & Tolpin, acct exec, 1982; Siler & Assocs, owner/pres, 1982-83; Amer Red Cross Metro Atlanta Chapter, asst dir, public rel, dir, chapter communication, dir, external communications, 1983-89; AARP, assoc area rep, public relations, 1989-present. **ORGANIZATIONS:** producer, host, WCLK-FM, weekly jazz program, 1974-78, 1980-; special events coordinator, Special Audience Inc, 1976-79; publicity Comm Natl Council of Negro Women, 1979; membership chairperson, Atlanta Assn of Black Journalists, 1980; mem, adv comm, WIGO radio, 1980; guest lecturer, Clark Coll Mass Communications Dept, 1981-82; public comm Minority Business Awareness Week 1982; mem, Bronze Jubilee Task Force, WETV, 1982-83; chaplain, Natl Assn of Media Women, Atlanta, 1983; publicity chair, Atlanta Assn of Black Journalists, 1983; mem, United Way's Volunteer Atlanta Advisory Council, 1983-; prof standards chair, Atlanta Assn of Black Journalists, 1984; 2nd vice pres, Natl Assn of Media Woman, 1984-85; team captain, High Museum Membership Comm 1985; bd mem, Atlanta Women's Network, 1985-86; vice pres, Atlanta Women's Network, 1987; mem Natl Assoc of Market De velopers; vice pres/mem International Assn of Business Communicators, Atlanta Chapter 1981-82. **HONORS/ACHIEVEMENTS:** Gold Awd for Annual Report Writing United Way 1980; Outstanding Achievement in Public Relations Natl Assn of Media Women 1980; Outstanding Young Women in Amer 1981; President's Awd Natl Assn of Media Woman 1983-85; Chairman's Awd Atlanta Assn of Black Journalists 1984; honorable mention for Annual Report Writing, Amer Red Cross Communications Excellence 1987; honorable mention for Exhibits Amer Red Cross Communications Excellence 1989. **BUSINESS ADDRESS:** Associate Area Representative, Public Relations, AARP-Region IV Office, 2965 Flowers Rd South, Suite 233, Atlanta, GA 30341.

SILER, JOYCE B.
Educator. **PERSONAL:** Born Aug 01, 1945, Siler City, NC; married Lloyd G Flowers; children: Rashad Flowers. **EDUCATION:** NC Central Univ, BS 1967; Hunter Coll, MS Ed 1976; Manhattan Coll, MBA 1983. **CAREER:** Barnard Coll, secretary 1967-68; NY City Housing Authority, housing asst 1968-70; Model Cities Admin, principal program spec 1970-74; Medgar Evers Coll, asst prof 1974-. **ORGANIZATIONS:** Vice pres programs, Delta Pi Epsilon Alpha Xi Chap 1988-91; historian, Coll Business Educators Assoc BEA 1989-90; sec John W Saunders Scholarship Comm Conv Church 1985-; mem, Women's Auxiliary Bd M L Wilson Boys' Club of Harlem. **HONORS/ACHIEVEMENTS:** Article "Advice for Business Women," Everybody's Magazine 1985; co-author, several articles about income tax. **BUSINESS ADDRESS:** Assistant Professor, Medgar Evers College, 1150 Carroll St, Brooklyn, NY 11225.

SILLAH, MARION ROGERS
Educator. **PERSONAL:** Born Aug 07, 1945, Cuthbert, GA; daughter of Mary Nell Rogers; married Samba, Samouri, Amie (divorced). **EDUCATION:** Tuskegee Inst, Tuskegee AL, BS, 1967; Morgan State Coll, Baltimore MD, attended 1065-66; Univ of Michigan, Ann Arbor MI, MBA, 1969; Univ of South Carolina, Columbia SC, PhD, 1986. **CAREER:** W R Grace & Co, New York NY, exec asst, 1969-71; IT & T, New York NY, compensation analyst, 1971-72; Bloomingdale's, New York NY, asst dept mgr, boys' clothing, 1972-74; Tuskegee Univ, Tuskegee AL, instructor, asst prof, 1974-78, 1985-87; New Horizons Realty, Tuskegee AL, licensed agent, 1977-78; Tuskegee Univ Human Resource Devel Center, consultant, 1985; independent consultant, 1985-; Morehouse Coll, Atlanta GA, assoc prof, 1987-. **ORGANIZATIONS:** Mem, Amer Real Estate and Urban Economics Assn, 1979-, Rho Epsilon Frat (real estate), 1980-85, Amer Real Estate Soc, 1985-, Young Advisory Council, Soc of Real Estate Appraisers, 1985; mem, chmn, Educ Comm, Natl Soc of Real Estate Appraisers, 1988-; mem, Urban Land Inst, 1988-, Intl Council of Shopping Centers, 1989-. **HONORS/ACHIEVEMENTS:** First Black Female MBA, The Univ of Michigan, 1969; United Negro Coll Fund Fellow, United Negro Coll Fund, 1983; First Black Female PhD Graduate in Real Estate, Univ of Southern California, 1986; Faculty Award in Research, Tuskegee Univ, 1987. **BUSINESS ADDRESS:** Associate Professor, Morehouse College, 830 Westview Dr, SW, Wheeler Hall, Room 221, Atlanta, GA 30314.

SILLS, GREGORY D.
Administrator. **PERSONAL:** Born Mar 02, 1950, Newport, AR; married Wanda Lou Brown; children: Brian Keith, Phillip Lawrence. **EDUCATION:** Crowley's Ridge Jr Clg Paragould AA 1969; HardingUniv Searcy, AR, BA 1971. **CAREER:** White River Voc Tech School, asst dir 1975-; AR State Juvenile Servs Div, youth serv cncl 1972-75; Jackson Co & Family & Children Serv, juvenile probation officer 1971-72. **ORGANIZATIONS:** Adv bd mem Retired Sr Citizens Vol Pgm 1977-; adv bd mem AR Educ TV Network 1979-; area plng bd mem State Div of Employment Dev 1980-; past pres vice pres Newport Jaycees 1973-75; mem Newport Urban League 1978-. **HONORS/ACHIEVEMENTS:** Citizen of the yr WF Br HS 1965-66; outst jaycee of the yr Newport Jaycee Chap 1973-74; nominated personalities of Am Am Biographical Inst 1978-79;nominated intrntl youth in achvmnt Am Biographical Inst 1979-80. **BUSINESS ADDRESS:** Dir of Student Services, White River Voc Tech Services, P O Box 1120, Newport, AR 72177.

SILLS, MARVIN G.
Educator. **PERSONAL:** Born Apr 09, 1949, Rocky Mount, NC. **EDUCATION:** Glassboro State Clg, BA 1970, MS 1975. **CAREER:** Glassboro State Coll, asst dean admin, asst dir of admin 1972; Glassboro, asst to dir 1970; Clearview Reg HS, sub-teacher 1970; Glassboro State Coll, asst football coach 1970, research dir 1970; E Orange Bd of Recreation, recreation supvr 1968; Glassboro State Coll, dorm proctor & counselor 1967. **ORGANIZATIONS:** Mem Am Pers & Guid Assc; APGA Assc of Non-White Concerns; NJ Am Clg Admsn Cnslrs; NJACAC Human Rel Com; NJ Admissions Assc ; NJ Assc of Black & PR Admissions Cnslrs; Natl Bank Alliance; Leaguer's Inc; adv bd mem NJ Assc of State Clg Admnstr; mem Admissions & Transfer Com 1973; EOF Selec Com1971-; Fin Aid Review & Appeal Com 1975; Fin Aid & Schlarship Com 1972-74; Human Resources Com 1970-; Inst Plg Com 1969-71; Inter-collegiate Athletic &Com 1973; Puertorrequenos Associados for Comm Orgn 1973-; Salary Ranges Com 1973. **HONORS/ACHIEVEMENTS:** Recip several local awrds & accomendations as Stdnt Athlete, Ftbl Coach, Athletic Recruiter, Cnslr, Recruiter of Disadvantage Stdnts. **BUSINESS ADDRESS:** Ofc of Admissions, Glassboro State Coll, Glassboro, NJ 08028.

SILLS, THOMAS ALBERT
Artist. **PERSONAL:** Born Aug 20, 1914, Castalia, NC; married Jeanne Reynal; children: Mickael, Kennith. **CAREER:** Museum Collections, Metro Museum of Art Fordham U; Whitney Museum of Amer Art; Mus of Modern Art; Finch Clg Museum; Rose Museum Brandeis Coll; Syracuse Univ Mus; Sheldon Meml Gallery; Williams Coll Museum; Phoenix Art Museum; Norfolk Museum of Arts & Science; LA & Co Museum; Krannert Art Museum Chase Manhattan Collection; Rockefeller Univ; Hofstra Univ; Fisk Univ; San Francisco Museum of Art; Wichita State Univ; Ciba-Geigy Collection; Greenville Co Museum of Art; Johnson Pub Co; St Lawrence Univ; Tougallo Coll; Univ of NC. **ORGANIZATIONS:** 1st PA Bnkg & Trust Co; Brooklyn Mus; High Mus of Art; Trevor Farnet Lib;Univ Art Mus; Studio Mus in Harlem Exhibits, Betty Parsons Gallery 1955, 57, 59, 61, Paul Kantor Gallery 1962, Bodley Gallery 1964, 67, 70, 72; Fine Arts Gallery 1967; The Cushing Gallery; Artists Annual Stable Gallery 1955; New Sch for Soc Rsrch 1956; Artist Grp 1956; Whitney Mus of Am Art Annual 1959-60, 71, 72;Univ of CO; Fairleigh DickinsonUniv 1964; Dord & Fitz Gallery; Mus of Modern Art 1969; Stdnt Ctr Art Gallery 1969; Afro-Am Artists 1969; Wilson Clg 1968; Mt Holyoke Clg 1969;Univ Art Mus; Mus of Fine Arts; Minneapolis Inst of Art St Paul's Clg; Everson Mus of Art; Betty Parson Pvt Collection; Sidney Wolfson Gallery; PVI

Gallery; CIRCAL The Art Gallery Mag Jay Jacobs 1970; The Flowering of Thomas Sills Art News 1972; The Afro Am Artist Elsa Honig Fine 1973; Sills William & Noma Copley Found 1957; Landmark Gallery Exhibits 1980.

SILVA, ARTHUR P.
Auto dealer executive. **CAREER:** Team Ford, Inc, Sioux City, IA, chief executive. **BUSINESS ADDRESS:** Team Ford, Inc, 900 Dakotah Ave, Sioux City, IA 51109. *

SILVA, HENRY ANDREW
Government & association executive. **PERSONAL:** Born Aug 26, 1924, Worcester, MA; married Celeste; children: Cherryle Goode, Kimberly. **EDUCATION:** Howard Univ, BA, 1975; George Washington Univ; Amer Univ; Natl Anthology of coll Poetry; Howard Univ School of Divinity, MDiv 1983, Doctor of Ministry 1985. **CAREER:** EEO Natl Labor Relations Bd, dir 1974-80; EEO Food & Drug Admin, dep dir 1971-74; EEO US Naval Oceanographic Office, coordinator 1965-71; St Marks United Methodist Church, pastor; SCLC, natl bd mem; Natl vice pres, SCLC assigned North Atlantic Region pres; Dorcestor Community Assn, chmn, Baltimore Support Group Community for Non-Violence. **ORGANIZATIONS:** Past pres, DC Metro Area EEO Council, 1970-75; Pres, DC Chapter, SCLC; Natl bd mem, SCLC; Regional vice pres, Natl N Atlantic SCLC; Past pres/founder, Natl Union of Security Officers; Montgomery Improvement Assn, Montgomery Bus Boycott, AL; Founder, Tent City Rangers (used as security in march on WA Resurrection City Charleston Hospital Strike, Memphis Rally; War Against Repression Atlanta GA); March Forsyth GA Commr DC Human Rights Commission 1980; participant of most major rallys & marches throughout the country for the last 30 years. **HONORS/ACHIEVEMENTS:** Mayor's Award Testimonial Dinner 1975; plaques SCLC, HEW, NLRB, USNAU, DC Metro EEO Council 1943-46; SCLC, CK Steele Award, 1984. **MILITARY SERVICE:** US Army Air Force 1943-46. **BUSINESS ADDRESS:** Pastor, St Marks UMC, 1029 E Monument St, Baltimore, MD 21202.

SILVA, OMEGA C. LOGAN
Physician. **PERSONAL:** Born Dec 14, 1936, Washington, DC; daughter of Louis Jasper Logan and Mary Ruth Dickerson Logan; married Harold B Webb; children: Frances Cecile. **EDUCATION:** Howard Univ, BS (Cum Laude) 1958, MD 1967. **CAREER:** Veterans Admin Medical Ctr, intern 1967-68, resident 1968-70, rsch assoc 1971-74, clinical investigator 1974-77, asst chief endocrinology 1977-; Howard Univ, prof of oncology 1985-; George Washington Univ, univ assoc prof medicine 1980-; Veterans Admin Medical Ctr, asst chief endocrinology. **ORGANIZATIONS:** Consultant FDA Immunology Panel 1981-; pres Howard Univ Medical Alumni 1983-; mem VA Adv Comm on Women Veterans 1983-; general rsch support review comm NIH 1984-; vice pres Amer Medical Womens Assoc 1986-87. **HONORS/ACHIEVEMENTS:** First woman president Howard Univ Medical Alumni; Letter of Commendation from the Pres of the United States 1984; pres Howard University Alumni Assn 1983-88; pres American Medicial Women's Assn 1987-88. **HOME ADDRESS:** 354 N St SW, Washington, DC 20024. **BUSINESS ADDRESS:** Asst Chief Endocrinology, Veterans Admin Medical Ctr, 50 Irving St NW, Washington, DC 20422.

SILVER, HORACE WARD MARTIN TAVARES
Pianist, composer, business executive. **PERSONAL:** Born Sep 02, 1928, Norwalk, CT; children: Gregory. **CAREER:** Pianist; Composer, nica's dream the prchr snr blues doodlin' enchntmnt home ckin' slvl 1956, ckn' at the cntntl moon rays 1957, sis sadie peace come on home 1959, strln' 1960, flthy mcnsty 1961, the tokyo blues 1962, slvr's srnd 1963, que pasa sngs for my fthr 1965; Horace Slvr Quintet, ldr 1955-. **ORGANIZATIONS:** Pres Ecaroh Mus Inc New York City 1955-; mem ASCAP; pres Silveto Records, Emerald Records. **HONORS/ACHIEVEMENTS:** Bud Mus Exclnc Awd Am Fedn Mus Recip 1958; Slvr Rcrd Awd Blue Note Rcrds 1959; Cit Call Entrtnmnt Awd 1960. **BUSINESS ADDRESS:** Pianist, Bridge Agency, c/o Joanne Jimenez, 106 Fort Greene Place, Brooklyn, NY 11217.

SILVEY, EDWARD
Educational administrator. **PERSONAL:** Born Oct 28, 1937, Jersey City, NJ; married Joan Drane; children: Adrienne, Marc. **EDUCATION:** St Paul's Coll, BS Sec Ed 1959; NC State Univ. **CAREER:** New York City Dept of Soc Svcs, soc worker 1959-61, 1963-66; Harnett Cty Bd of Ed, supr 1966-68; NC Dept of Admin, dir of manpower 1968-69; Shaw Univ, asst to the pres 1969-75; Wake Tech Coll, dir of dev & inst rsch 1975-76, dean of students 1976-. **ORGANIZATIONS:** Pastor Pleasant Grove UCC 1982-; state advisor NC Student Govt Assoc; pers advisor State Pres NC Student Govt Assoc; task forces state level Minority Recruit, Career Caucus, Student Devel; chmn Christian Soc Ministries Comm, Southern Conf UCC; pres Ministers for Racial & Soc Justice, Eastern NC Assoc. **HONORS/ACHIEVEMENTS:** Outstanding Educator Omega Psi Phi 1976. **MILITARY SERVICE:** AUS E-4 2 years. **BUSINESS ADDRESS:** Dean of Students, Wake Technical College, 9101 Fayetteville Rd, Raleigh, NC 27603.

SIMKINS, GEORGE CHRISTOPHER
Dentist. **PERSONAL:** Born Aug 23, 1924, Greensboro, NC; son of Dr. George C. Simkins, Sr.; married Anna; children: George III, Jeanne. **EDUCATION:** Attended Herzel Jr Coll 1942, Talladega Coll 1944; Meharry Dental Sch, DDS 1948; Jersey City Med Ctr, intern 1949. **CAREER:** Dentist general practice 1954-. **ORGANIZATIONS:** Mem Guilford Co Health Dept 1949-54; mem Amer Dental Assn, NC Dental Soc, Old N State Dental Soc, Greensboro Med Soc, Natl Dental Assn; staff memL Richardson Mem Hosp; pres Greensboro Br NAACP; mem Gillespie Park Gold Assn; bd mem NAACP Legal Def & Educ Fund; mem Greensboro Men's Club; mem NC Guardsman. **HONORS/ACHIEVEMENTS:** Certificate of Merit Alpha Phi Alpha Frat 1964; Dentist of Yr Old N State Dental Soc 1964; Scroll of Hon Natl Med Assn 1964; 25 yrs Serv to Mankind Meharry Med Coll 1973. **BUSINESS ADDRESS:** Doctor of Dental Surgery, 500 S Benbow Rd, Greensboro, NC 27401.

SIMMELKJAER, ROBERT T.
Educational administrator. **PERSONAL:** Born Feb 12, 1942, New York, NY; married Gloria J Foster; children: Robert Jr, Mark Allen. **EDUCATION:** CCNY, BS Pol Sci 1962, MA Pol Sci 1964; Columbia Univ Teachers Coll, EdD Ed Admin 1972; Columbia Univ Business School, MBA Bus Admin 1977; Fordham Univ School of Law, JD 1978. **CAREER:** Inst for Ed Devel, exec asst to pres 1969-71; NY City Bd of Ed, principal 1971-74; CCNY, prof ed admin 1974-79, dean school of gen studies 1979-, vice provost for acad admin. **ORGANIZATIONS:** PERC, OCB 1977-; minority school fin network Urban League & NAACP 1980-83; bd of dir Inst for Mediation & Conflict Resolution 1980-84; consult Ford Found, Natl School Fin Proj, NY Task Force Equity & Excellence, Urban Coalition Local School Devel 1980-83; vice chmn Personnel Appeals Bd US Acctg Office 1981-84; speaker, consult US Info Agency 1981-84; consult NY Univ School of Bus 1982-83. **HONORS/ACHIEVEMENTS:** NY State Regents Scholarship 1957; US OE Ed Fellowship 1969-70; Great Cities Rsch Fellow 1971; Chap in "A Quest for Ed Oppty in a Major Urban School District, The Case of Washington DC" 1975; Article "From Partnership to Renewal, Evolution of an Urban Ed Reform" The Ed Forum 1979. **BUSINESS ADDRESS:** Vice Provost for Acad Admin, City College of New York, 138th St & Convent Ave, New York, NY 10031.

SIMMONS, ALBERT BUFORT, JR.
Social service administrator. **PERSONAL:** Born Feb 01, 1943, Chicago, IL; son of Albert Simmons and Arnetta Woodhouse Simmons; divorced; children: Vera. **EDUCATION:** Anderson Univ, Anderson IN, AB, 1968; Indiana Univ School of Law, Indianapolis IN, 1970-71. **CAREER:** Urban League of Madison County, Anderson IN, pres & CEO, 1967-; Indiana Health Careers, Indianapolis IN, dir of counseling, 1970-71; Action Inc, Muncie IN, exec dir, 1971-72; Equal Employment Opportunity, Washington DC, mgmt official, 1972-84; Equality Profits, Washington DC, pres & CEO, 1984-87. **BUSINESS ADDRESS:** President & CEO, Urban League of Madison County Inc, 1210 W 10th St, PO Box 271, Anderson, IN 46015.

SIMMONS, ALTHEA T.L.
Administration. **PERSONAL:** Born Apr 17, 1924, Shreveport, LA; daughter of M M Simmons and Lillian Littleton Simmons; divorced. **EDUCATION:** So U, BS 1945; Univ IL, MS 1951; Howard U, JD 1956. **CAREER:** Washington Bureau NAACP, dir 1979-; Br & Field Serv NAACP, assc dir 1977-79; NAACP natl ed dir 1974-77, natl training dir 1965-74, legis adv & field dir 1961-65; WJ Durham Law Ofcs, 1956-61. **ORGANIZATIONS:** Natl Manpower Adv Com USDL 1969-74; Filer Commn on Pvt Philanthropy & Pub Needs 1973-75; vice pres Am Soc for Training & Dev 1973; vice pres NOW Legal Def & Ed Fund Inc 1974-77; Natl Adv Cncl Hogg Found for Mental Hlth 1973-76; edtr adv bd Integrated Ed; Jour of Afro-Am Issues; US Cenusus Adv Com Black Populations 1980 Census 1975-; consult ofc of Fed Contract Compliance Natl Adv Cncl; Equally of Ed Oppty; bd of trustee Tchrs Clg United Seamen's Serv 1976-; mem, Gen Bd of Pensions, United Methodist Church, 1988-; mem, Natl Bd & Co-Chair Social Action Commn, Delta Sigma Theta Inc, 1988-. **HONORS/ACHIEVEMENTS:** President's Award, Washburn Univ, 1975; Leadership Award, 1988, Alumni Award for Postgraduate Achievement in Law & Public Service, Howard Univ, 1987; Distinguished Alumni Award, 1987, Leadership Award, 1988, Natl Assn for Equal Education Opportunity; 1988, one of 75 women featured in "I Dream a World: Portraits of Black Women Who Changed America" photography exhibit, 1988. **HOME ADDRESS:** 3001 Veazey Terrace NW, Washington, DC 20008. **BUSINESS ADDRESS:** Dir, NAACP, 1025 Vermont Ave, Suite 730, Washington, DC 20005.

SIMMONS, ANNIE MARIE
Educator. **PERSONAL:** Born Jul 25, 1949, Henderson, TX; children: Shirley N Lawdins. **EDUCATION:** North TX State Univ, BA Psychology 1970, MEd 1972, Post Grad Studies 1972-74; TX Southern Univ 1975, 1979. **CAREER:** NTSU Counseling Center, counselor 1970-72; Favor's Pre-School, asst dir 1970-72; Geary Elem School, para prof 1972-74; Galveston Coll, prof. **ORGANIZATIONS:** Psi Chi 1968-; TX Jr Coll Teacher's Assn 1974-; League of Women Voters 1976-; Electa Chapter Order Eastern Star 1979-; pres Black Ladies of Distinction 1980-81; pres Alpha Kappa Alpha Sor 1983-85. **HONORS/ACHIEVEMENTS:** Outstanding Grammateus-Beta Phi Omega Chap of Alpha Kappa Alpha 1978; Outstanding Achieve in Galveston Comm 1979; cert of appreciation Epsilon Mu Chap of Alpha Kappa Alpha Outstanding Alumni 1972-82; Galveston Fire Dept Training Acad most popular visiting instructor 1979-81; pres BLOD 1980-81; Distinguished Service Awd Galveston Jaycees 1981; Sigma Gamma Rho Outstanding Black Galvestonian 1982; cert of appreciation Noon Optimist Club of Galveston 1982; NTSU/TWU Black Alumni Assn Quality of Life 1982; Outstanding Citizen of the Year Gamma Phi Lambda Chap of Alpha Phi Alpha Frat 1982; elected to Galveston Independent School Dist Bd of Trustees 1982-85; NAACP Galveston Br Juneteenth Image Awd 1983; Outstanding Women of Amer 1983; appointed to Gov's Commn for Women 1983-85 by Gov of TX Mark White. **HOME ADDRESS:** 3525 Avenue O, Galveston, TX 77550. **BUSINESS ADDRESS:** Prof Developmental Studies, Galveston College, 4015 Avenue Q, Galveston, TX 77550.

SIMMONS, ARTHUR HUGH
Physician. **PERSONAL:** Born Jun 01, 1899, Washington, DC; married Ethel M Alexander. **EDUCATION:** Howard U; Harvard U; Howard Med Sch, MD 1925. **CAREER:** Freedmen's Hosp, ret dep med dir; Howard Univ Clg of Med, clncl asst prof of med; Positions Held chief phys med 1927-38, chief of stf outpatient clinics 1927-70. **ORGANIZATIONS:** Mem Am Med Assc; Natl Med Assc ; wash Heart Assc; Am Heart Assc; Soc of Harvard Chem; chtr mem Mid Eastern Chap Soc of Nuclear Med; life memDC Med Soc; made plans & worked with arch for the bldg of Hosp Auditorium & Tuberculosis Annex & the New Howard Hosp. **MILITARY SERVICE:** AUS Med Corp lt col 1942-46.

SIMMONS, BELVA TERESHIA
Journalist. **PERSONAL:** Born Jul 02, 1927, Jacksonville, FL. **EDUCATION:** Spelman Coll, 1946-47; Lincoln Univ, BJ 1949-52. **CAREER:** St Louis Argus, feature editor; US Senate Constitutional Rts, prof staff 1955-69; Amer Natl Red Cross, public relations writer 1970-73; KMOX-TV, community relations coord 1973-78; Anne Beers Elem Sch Journalism, dir/instructor 1981-83; ANC 7B Newsletter, editor/writer 1981-; DC Comm Schs, editor Sound Off. **ORGANIZATIONS:** Mem League of Women Voters; mem NAACP. **HONORS/ACHIEVEMENTS:** Alumni Achievement Awd Lincoln Univ Sch of Journalism 1975; Distinguished Serv Human Develop Corp 1978; Comm Serv Awd ANC & Southeast Neighbors Inc 1981. **HOME ADDRESS:** 3604 Austin St SE, Washington, DC 20020.

SIMMONS, CHARLES WILLIAM
Educator. **PERSONAL:** Born Jun 17, 1938, Baltimore, MD; son of Floyd Simmons and Vivian Jordan Simmons; married Brenda Leola Hughes; children: Dominic, Natalie Bohannan, Wanda Williams, Anthony, Kojo, Rashida, Tacuma. **EDUCATION:** Antioch Univ, Baltimore MD, AB, 1972; Union Graduate School, Cincinnati OH, PhD, 1978; Harvard Univ, Cambridge MA, 1984. **CAREER:** International Brotherhood of Teamsters, Baltimore MD, field rep, 1964-67; Baltimore City Health Department, Baltimore MD, dir of health, education & community org, 1967-74; Antioch Univ, Baltimore MD, co-dir, 1972-80;

Sojourner-Douglass College, Baltimore MD, president, 1980—. **ORGANIZATIONS:** NAACP, African-American Empowerment Project. **HONORS/ACHIEVEMENTS:** President's Award, Black Women's Political Leadership Caucus, 1988; leadership award, Historically Black Colleges & Universities, 1988; Pace Setter Award, African-American Heritage Inc, 1989. **MILITARY SERVICE:** US Marine Corps, sergeant, 1955-60. **BUSINESS ADDRESS:** President, Sojourner-Douglass College, 500 North Caroline St, Baltimore, MD 21205.

SIMMONS, CLAYTON LLOYD
Retired supervising probation officer. **PERSONAL:** Born Sep 11, 1918, New York, NY; son of William Arthur Simmons and Florence Forde Simmons; married Angela L Petioni; children: Janet, Sandra, Angela, Rene. **EDUCATION:** Columbia Univ, BS 1954, MS 1969. **CAREER:** New York City Dept of Probation, held various assignments as probation officer, supervising probation officer, project coord, eeo officer 1960-82; freelance pianist & keyboardist 1983-; Upjohn Health Care Svcs, contract social worker 1984-85; ABC Home Health of Florida Inc, social work consultant 1987-; Best Western Hotel, pianist 1988-. **ORGANIZATIONS:** Mem Natl Council on Crime & Delinquency 1962-83; mem Rockland Co NY Bd of Commissioners of Sewer Dist No 1 1974-78; mem bd dirs Columbia Univ Sch of Social Work 1977-80; mem Rockland Co NY Bd of Governors for Health Facilities 1977-79; jr warden St Paul's Episcopal Ch 1977-82; vice chmn Spring Valley NY Democratic Comm 1978-80; mem bd trustees Village of Spring Valley NY 1979-82; pres Martin Luther King Jr Multi-Purpose Ctr Inc 1980-82; chmn bd dirs Youth Activities Comm Inc 1972-82; mem Vestry of St Stephen's Episcopal Ch Silver Spring Shores FL 1984-88; mem Commn on Church in Soc in the Central FL Episcopal Diocese 1984-88; 2nd vice commander Post 284 American Legion 1987-88. **HONORS/ACHIEVEMENTS:** Certificate of Merit Roberto Clemente Social & Cultural Club Inc 1974; plaque Carlton & Surrey Apts for serv to tenants 1977; Guardsman Award for patriotic service to Natl Guard Bureau 1977; Plaque for Outstanding Leadership and Intensified Struggle for Minorities, First Baptist Church, 1978; Distinguished Serv Awd Rockland Co 1977 1979 1982; Cert of Appreciation Office of the Dist Attorney Rockland Co 1980; plaque Club Personality for Magnificent Job as Pres of Spring Valley NAACP 1973-79; NY State Senate Achievement Awd 1981; NY State Assembly Cert of Merit 1981; plaques Outstanding Serv to Village of spring Valley NY 1982; plaque Outstanding & Dedicated Serv to NAACP & Comm NAACP 1982; plaque Haitian-Amer Cultural & Social Orgns for Serv to Comm 1982; Cert of Appreciation 26th Congressional Dist 1982; Cer tificate of Awd Spring Valley NY Youth Council of NAACP 1982; Awd clock from Bla r King Jr Multi-Purpose Ctr Inc 1982; plaque Black Political Caucus of Rockland Co NY for Years of Dedicated Serv 1984; Certificate of Participation Amer Legion Post 284 Bellview FL 1986; Certificate of Appreciaton Office of the Governor State of FL 1986. **MILITARY SERVICE:** AUS staff sgt 1942-45. **HOME ADDRESS:** 4 Palm Run - SSS, Ocala, FL 32672.

SIMMONS, DONALD M.
Business executive. **PERSONAL:** Born Jul 03, 1935, Muskogee, OK; married Barbara Jean Ford; children: Annamarie, Donna Rose, Barbara Elaine. **EDUCATION:** OK State Univ, BS & Grad Study 1961. **CAREER:** Phillips Petroleum Co, Regional Mgr 1963-67; US Sen J Howard Edmondson, Legis Asst 1962; Harlem Commonwealth Council, exec dir 1967-70; Simmons Royalty Co, pres 1970-. **ORGANIZATIONS:** Life mem NAACP; life mem Alpha Phi Alpha Frat; mem Centennial Comm OK State Univ; mem Natl Petroleum Council 1981-; mem Bd of Trustees Musk Reg Med Ctr 1981-; mem Interstate Oil Compact Comm 1981-; gov's apptmt mem Prof Respon Tribunal 1982-. **HONORS/ACHIEVEMENTS:** Business Awd NAACP. **HOME ADDRESS:** 402 N 17th St, Muskogee, OK 74401. **BUSINESS ADDRESS:** President, Simmons Royalty Co, 323 W Broadway, Manhattan Bldtg, Ste 404, Muskogee, OK 74401.

SIMMONS, EARL MELVIN
Doctor. **PERSONAL:** Born Feb 20, 1931, Brooklyn, NY; son of Isaac and Iris; married Elena; children: Erin, Erlan, Elissa, Erik. **EDUCATION:** Brooklyn Coll, 1949-53; Howard Univ, BS Chem magna cum laude 1958; Howard Univ Med Coll, MD 1962; Meadowbrook Hosp, surg cert 1964; Mt Sinai Hosp, otolaryngol cert 1967. **CAREER:** Cook Cty Hosp, intern cert 1963; Mt Sinai Med School, clin instr 1966; East Orange NJ Gen Hosp, chief dept otolaryngol 1967-79; Newark Eye & Ear Infirmary & NJ Med School, att phys 1967-79; USAF Hosp, chief dept otolaryngol 1979-81; Encinitas CA, pvt practice 1981-. **ORGANIZATIONS:** Mem Council of Otolaryngology, Deafness Rsch Found, Med Soc of San Diego, AMA, NMA, Undersea Med Soc, Assn of Military Plastic Surgeons, YMCA, UNICEF, NAACP. **HONORS/ACHIEVEMENTS:** AMA Phys Recog Awd 1978-80; 6 books of poetry Turn Hourglass 1977, Eagle Spree 1979; Spirit Flesh and Circles 1984, Songs of Sunset 1988, Sonnets and Such 1989. **MILITARY SERVICE:** USA pfc 1953-55; PHS surgeon 1963-79; USAF lt col 1979-81. **BUSINESS ADDRESS:** Otolaryngologist, 285 N El Camino Real 215, Encinitas, CA 92024.

SIMMONS, ELLAMAE
Physician. **PERSONAL:** Born Mar 26, 1919, Mt Vernon, OH; daughter of G L Simmons and Ella C Simmons; children: Delabian, Diana, Daphne, Debra (stepchildren). **EDUCATION:** Hampton Inst, RN 1940, MA 1950; Meharry Med Coll, grad student 1955; Howard Univ, MD 1959; Ohio State Univ, B.S., l948; Ohio State Univ, M.A., l958. **CAREER:** Practiced nursing at various hosps, 1940-42, 1950-51; Bellevue Hosp, med social worker 1951-53; Wayne Co Hosp, intern; Univ Co Med Ctr, resident 1962-63; Natl Jewish Hosp, resident chest med & allergy 1963-65; Kaiser Found Hosp, allergist 1965-. **ORGANIZATIONS:** Mem AMA; Admissions Com Univ of CA Sch of Med 1974-; CA & San Francisco Med Soc; John Hale Med Soc; Amer Acad Allergy; Amer Med Womens Assn No CA Chmn; Mutual Real Estate Investment Trust; mem No CA Med Dental Pharmaceutical Assn 1974-; mem Univ of CA San Francisco Sch of med Admissions Com 1974-; mem Amer Civil Liberties Union, NAACP, Urban League. **MILITARY SERVICE:** Army Nurse Corps 1942-46. **BUSINESS ADDRESS:** Kaiser Permanente Medical Group, 2200 O'Farrell St, San Francisco, CA 94115.

SIMMONS, EMMETT BRYSON, III (SLIM)
Administrative assistant. **PERSONAL:** Born Apr 06, 1953, Chicago, IL. **EDUCATION:** Univ of WI, Cert 1976; IL State Univ, BA 1977; Performing Arts Soc of LA, Cert 1979; Kiis Broadcasting Prof'l Workshop, Cert, 1980. **CAREER:** IL State Univ Bloomington/Normal, IL, TV 10 anchorman/WGLT radio talk show host/Viddette newspaper columnist 1971-75; CBS TV Network, accountant/performer 1978-80; Columbia Pictures Ind Inc, admin asst/actor 1981-. **ORGANIZATIONS:** Mem AFTRA 1979-; del Natl Black Polit Convs Gary/Cincinnati/Little Rock 1972-76; mem PUSH; mem Urban League; mem NAACP; mem SCLC; mem CORE. **HONORS/ACHIEVEMENTS:** Natl & IL State Speech/Drama Champion Natl Forensics Assn 1970-75; Who's Who in Amer Univs 1973-74; VIP Award Wash, DC Forensics 1971; Letters of Recognition from Presidents Ford (1973), Carter (1977), Reagan (1984); Distinct Award Town of Normal, IL 1974-75; Who's Who Among Black Americans 1980; Ebony Mag Bachelor of the Year 1980; 90 Life Time Awards. **HOME ADDRESS:** 3221 W 109th St, Inglewood, CA 90303. **BUSINESS ADDRESS:** Administrative Assistant, Columbia Pictures Ind, 2901 W Alameda Blvd, Ste 3005, Burbank, CA 91505.

SIMMONS, ERIC
Businessman. **PERSONAL:** Born Dec 23, 1920, New York, NY; son of Alexander and Glady; married Nora Mae Nellons; children: Eric Alexander, Frederick Leroy, Chester Russell. **CAREER:** General Elec Co, 1941; Dek Tool Co, tool maker 1941; E Simmons Mov & Wreck Contract, pres/owner 1942-. **ORGANIZATIONS:** Organ & founder Central City Bus Assn 1950; promo dir Syracuse Celebrators Club 1960-; mem NAACP 1962-; past dir Better Bus Bur 1972-76; bd dir Syracuse C of C 1973-; treas Bethany Baptist Church Mens Fellowship 1973-; mem Coun of Negro Women 1973-; mem Citizens for Concerned Comm 1976; organ fdr pres Fedn of Black Orgn 1976. **HONORS/ACHIEVEMENTS:** Small Bus Admin Awd recog of outst comm serv since 1974; Lamma Kappa Mu Awd for Outst serv for 15 yrs as promo dir; Syracuse Celebrators Club Awdfor 5 yrs serv Small Bus Admin 1976. **BUSINESS ADDRESS:** President, E Simmons Mov & Wreck Contr, 901 Emerson Ave, Syracuse, NY 13204.

SIMMONS, ESMERALDA
Attorney. **PERSONAL:** Born Dec 16, 1950, Brooklyn, NY; children: Marques Akinsheye, Ewansiha Elias. **EDUCATION:** Hunter Coll CUNY, BA 1974; Brooklyn Law School, JD 1978. **CAREER:** New York City Law Dept, honors attorney (civil rights employment unit) 1978-79; US Dist Ct US Dist Judge Henry Bramwell, law clerk 1979-80; US Dept of Educ Office of Civil Rights, regional civil rights atty 1980-82; NY Dept of Law Atty General's Office, asst attorney general 1982-83; NY State Div of Human Rights, first deputy commissioner 1983-85; Medgar Evers Coll Ctr for Law and Social Justice, dir 1985-. **ORGANIZATIONS:** Mem Natl Conf Black Lawyers 1975-, Natl Bar Assoc 1979-; vice chair bd of dirs Vannguard Urban Improvement Assoc Inc 1979-; pres Bedford Stuyvesant Lawyers Assoc 1981-84; legal comm chair/mem Coalition for Community Empowerment 1983-; vice chair bd dirs Metro Black Bar Assoc 1984-. **HONORS/ACHIEVEMENTS:** Partner in Educ Awd NY City Bd of Educ 1981; Appreciation Awd Central Brooklyn Mobilization 1982; Lawyer of the Year Bedford Stuyvesant Lawyers Assoc Inc 1984; Imani Awd Weusi Shule Parents Council 1984; Professional of the Year Natl Assoc of Negro Business and Professional Womens Clubs Inc 1986. **BUSINESS ADDRESS:** Dir, Medgar Evers College, Cetner for Law/Social Justice, 1150 Carroll St, Brooklyn, NY 11225.

SIMMONS, GERALDINE CROSSLEY
Attorney. **PERSONAL:** Born Feb 17, 1939, Chicago, IL; daughter of Hosea H Crossley Sr and Ivey Moore Crossley; divorced; children: Stacey Elizabeth. **EDUCATION:** Roosevelt Univ, BA; John Marshall Law School, JD 1981. **CAREER:** Scott Foreman & Co, dir copyrights, permission contracts 1966-81; IL Appellate Court, judicial law clerk 1981; US Court of Appeals 7th Circuit, staff atty 1981-83; Roosevelt Univ Paralegal Program, instructor 1985-86; Salone Salone Simmons Assoc, attorney. **ORGANIZATIONS:** Mem chair Up South Chicago Land Fund 1981-84; past pres bd of dir Womens Law Group 1981-87; panel atty MBELDEF 1984-; 3rd vice pres Cook County Bar Assn 1985-87, pres 1989-90; vice chair bd of dir Chatham Business Assn 1985-; exec dir Small Business Devel Center 1986-87; bd mem John Marshall Law School Alumni Bd 1988-90, Parkway Community Home 1988-. **HONORS/ACHIEVEMENTS:** Nathan Burkan Copyright Competition John Marshall Law School 1979; Law Review John Marshall Law School 1981; Distinguished Serv Awdar Cook County Bar Assn 1985; Businesswoman of the Year Parkway Community Center 1986. **BUSINESS ADDRESS:** Attorney at Law, Salone, Salone, Simmons Assoc, 737 E 93rd St, Chicago, IL 60619.

SIMMONS, HAZEL FORROW
Educator. **PERSONAL:** Born Jun 21, 1927, Houston, TX; married Jerrimiah Simmons; children: David, James. **EDUCATION:** Attended Prairie View A&M Coll 1945-46; TX So Univ, BA 1954, MA 1974. **CAREER:** BH Grimes Elem School, teacher 1954-59; J R Reynolds Elem School, teacher 1959-68; Camp Fire Girls, field dir 1960-68; Fort Worth Independ Public School, Maude I Logan Elem, first Black coordinator reading improvement center 1972-; Ft Worth Public School, teacher 1968-. **ORGANIZATIONS:** So reg sir Amicae 1960-64; charter mem Houston League Negro Bus & Prof Women's Club 1962-68; exec sec Houston Classroom Teachers Assn 1964-66; dir so region Zeta Phi Beta 1965-72; natl trust Zeta Phi Beta 1972-76; chairperson Zeta Phi Beta So Reg Exec Bd 1972-78; charter & 1st vice pres Gr Ft Worth Area Negro Bus & Prof Women's Club 1975-81; natl dir Stork's Nest Proj Zeta Phi Beta 1976-; pres Kappa Silhouettes 1976-80; life mem NEA TX State Teachers Assn, TX Classroom Teacher's Assn, Ft Worth Classroom Teachers Assn; mem YWCA, YMCA; life mem Zeta Phi Beta; reg chairperson March of Dimes, Muscular Dystrophy, Leukemia So of Amer; ruling elder St Peter Presb Church 1980-83, 1984-86, 1987; pres Psi Zeta Chap Zeta Phi Beta Sor 1981-; pres Greater Fort Worth Area Negro Business & Professional Women 1981-84; sponsor Zeta Amicae 1981-. **HONORS/ACHIEVEMENTS:** Outstanding Serv Awd TX So Univ 1962, 1963; Zeta of Yr 1964; 5 yr Serv Awd Zeta Amicae 1965; Outstanding Serv as dir Zeta Phi Beta 1965-72; So Reg Zeta of Yr 1974; So Reg 2nd place Undergrad sponsors 1975; March of Dimes Vol Serv Awd 1974-75; Ombudswoman S Cent Negro Bus & Prof Women 1976; 1st Natl Zeta Phi Beta Legacy Awd 1976; Psi Zeta's Zeta of the Year Awd 1987. **BUSINESS ADDRESS:** Teacher, Ft Worth Public Sch, 3207 Hollis, Fort Worth, TX 76111.

SIMMONS, HERBERT
Councilman. **PERSONAL:** Born Nov 24, Washington, PA; married Margaret Smith; children: Barbara Simmons Vashon, Herbert, Roberta Simmons Scott, David, Leonard. **EDUCATION:** Penn State, Cert; Morturary Sch; Tailoring Sch, Grad. **CAREER:** Self Employed, tailor 1971; Borough Norristown, PA, vice pres cnclmn. **ORGANIZATIONS:** Past exalted ruler Elks Lodge; mem YMCA; Mt Pisgah Lodge; Bi-Racial Study; C of C Bd; Salvation Army; mem NAACP; Monitg Ct Boro's Assc; pres Boro Cncl 1976; Black Political Caucus; AFL-CIO; Amalgamated Clothing Am. **HONORS/ACHIEVEMENTS:** Man of yr NAACP 1974; 1st meml awrd; man of yr Norristown Recreation Awrd 1970; man of yr Mt Pisgah 32 1968; Samuel B Bersch Brotherhood Awrd 1966. **BUSINESS ADDRESS:** City Hall Airy St, Norristown, PA 19401.

SIMMONS, HOWARD L.
Educational administrator. **PERSONAL:** Born Apr 21, 1938, Mobile, AL; son of Eugene Simmons and Daisy Simmons. **EDUCATION:** Spring Hill Coll, BS 1960; IN Univ, MAT 1965; FL States Univ, PhD 1975. **CAREER:** Lake Shore High School, Florida, Spanish/English instructor 1960-61; Central High School, Alabama, Russian/Spanish instructor 1961-63; Forest Park Community Coll, Missouri, chmn foreign language dept 1964-69; Northampton County Area Community Coll, Pennsylvania, dean of instrnl serv 1969-74; Comm on Higher Educ, Middle States Assn, assoc dir 1974-88, exec dir 1988-. **ORGANIZATIONS:** Consultant to various US coll & univ 1969-; staff assoc Amer Assn of Community & Jr Coll 1972-73; bd of dirs Amer Assn for Higher Educ 1974-75; bd mem St Louis Teachers Credit Union 1965-69; mem Phi Delta Kappa 1972-; mem Kappa Delta Phi 1974-; sr researcher/visiting scholar Natl Ctr for Postsecondary Governance and Finance Rsch Ctr at Arizona State Univ 1986-87; consultant Assn of Dominican Univ Chancellors, Santo Domingo, 1987-; exec bd Amer Assn for Higher Educ Black Caucus 1989-. **HONORS/ACHIEVEMENTS:** NDEA Fellowship, Indiana Univ, 1963-64; Outstanding Young Men of Amer Award, 1972; ACE/AAIP Fellow, Amer Council on Educ, 1972-73; EPDA Fellowship, Florida State Univ, 1973-75; keynote speaker on future of higher educ in Puerto Rico, Angel Ramos Found 1987; published study "Involvement and Empowerment of Minorities and Women in the Accreditation Process," 1986; Grad Made Good (Distinguished Alumnus), Florida State Univ, 1988. **BUSINESS ADDRESS:** Associate Dir, Comm on Higher Educ, 3624 Market St, Philadelphia, PA 19104.

SIMMONS, ISAAC TYRONE
Computer manager. **PERSONAL:** Born Aug 09, 1946, Birmingham, AL; married Jamesena Hall. **EDUCATION:** Knoxville Coll, BS Math 1968; Univ of TN, MS Math Ed 1970. **CAREER:** Robertsville Jr HS, teacher 1970-71; Atlanta Area Tech School, part time teacher 1978-83; City of Atlanta, syst & programming mgr. **ORGANIZATIONS:** Mem Data Processing Mgr Assoc 1979-85; pres City of Atlanta Toastmasters 1980-85; mem Amer Mgmt Assoc 1983-85; vice pres Ben Hill UMC Santuary Choir 1983. **HOME ADDRESS:** 3611 Heritage Valley Rd SW, Atlanta, GA 30331. **BUSINESS ADDRESS:** Systems & Programming Mgr, City of Atlanta, 1201 City Hall, Atlanta, GA 30335.

SIMMONS, JAMES E.
Educational administrator. **PERSONAL:** Born Aug 24, 1927, New York, NY; married Cecilia Wyche-Simmons; children: Keith, Robert, Andreas. **EDUCATION:** Hampton Inst, BS 1955; Harvard Univ, MEd 1963; Univ CA Berkeley, PhD, ABD 1975-76. **CAREER:** Stanford Univ, asst pres 1968-74; Univ MA Amherst, staff asst 1976-80; Simmons and Assc, consult 1980-83; Stanford Univ, financial Adv 1983-. **ORGANIZATIONS:** Exec dir Contac Hartford CT 1967-68, ABC Boston MA 1963-67; deputy dir OEO Upward Bound DC 1965; Alpha Phi Alpha. **HONORS/ACHIEVEMENTS:** Ford Fellow Harvard 1962-63. **MILITARY SERVICE:** USN tm; Pacific Theater Victory Medal 44-49. **HOME ADDRESS:** 23 Capewell Drive, Bloomfield, CT 06002. **BUSINESS ADDRESS:** Financial Advisor, StanfordUniv, Old Union Bldg, StanfordUniv, Stanford, CA 94305.

SIMMONS, JAMES O.
Association executive. **PERSONAL:** Born Oct 21, 1935, Murfreesboro, TN; married Mabel A; children: Gail D, James O, III. **EDUCATION:** TN A&I U; Hillsborough Comm Clg;Univ S FL. **CAREER:** Tampa-hillsborough Co Manpower Consortium Tampa, manpower dir 1972-; HRDP, mgr 1971-72; MNA Res Stf Dev Pgmr, coord 1970-71; Model & Cities, housing Cnslr 1969-70; FL State, job adv 1968-69; FL State ES, comm worker 1967-68; USAF, admntr supr 1954-66. **ORGANIZATIONS:** Pres Village Civic Cncl 1967-72; mem NAACP; Urban League; Cub Scouts of Am; chmn Police Athletic League; trustee First Bapt Ch of Progress Village. **HONORS/ACHIEVEMENTS:** Squadron airman of month Nov 1955; AF Good Conduct Medal; commendation meda 1965; outst unit awrd 1965; presidential citation; named in Hon Simmons-bowers. **MILITARY SERVICE:** USAF t/sgt 1954-66.

SIMMONS, JAMES RICHARD
Administrator. **PERSONAL:** Born Mar 01, 1939, Chicago, IL; son of Oscar Lee and Phyllis Isbell Jones; married Judith Marion Albritton; children: James Jr, David. **EDUCATION:** Grinnell Clg, BA 1961; Univ of Chicago Sch of Social Serv Admn, MA 1964; Brandeis Univ Heller School of Advanced Social Policy, MM 1984. **CAREER:** IL Youth Commn, caseworker/team moderator 1964-66; IL Children's Home & Aid Soc, caseworker & psychotherapist 1966-69; Volunteers of Amer, state & exec dir, dir of children's serv 1969-71; Chicago United Inc, vice president-admin 1984-. **ORGANIZATIONS:** Mem Natl Assn of Soc Workers 1964-72; mem Acad of Certified Soc Workers 1966-72; mem Natl Assn of Black Soc Workers 1973-75; vice pres Grinnell Coll Alumni Bd 1973; bd mem Planning Consortium for Children 1973-75; bd mem IL Child Care Assc of IL 1975-76; Natl Soc Welfare Sec Vol of Am 1980; Delegatefrom IL White House Conf Children 1970; Nat'l Assoc of Black MBA's 1986; pres Hellen School Alumni Brandeis Univ 1986-. **HONORS/ACHIEVEMENTS:** Minority advocate - IL, US Small Business Admin 1989. **BUSINESS ADDRESS:** Vice President, Chicago United, Inc, 116 S Michigan Ave, Chicago, IL 60603.

SIMMONS, JOHN EMMETT
Educator. **PERSONAL:** Born Feb 06, 1936, St Petersburg, FL. **EDUCATION:** Morehose Clge, BS 1957; Syracuse Univ, MS 1961; CO State Univ, PhD 1971. **CAREER:** Western Clge for Women, asst prof of biology 1965-68; Research Fnd Washington Hosp Cntr, research assoc 1968-70; CO State Univ, asst prof of physiology 1971-72; Trinity Coll, assoc prof of biology 1972-82, prof of biology 1982-. **HONORS/ACHIEVEMENTS:** Elected to membership The Endocrine Soc 1972; Fulbright Schlr Gezira Univ Wad Medani Sudan 1982-83. **BUSINESS ADDRESS:** Professor of Biology, Trinity Clge, Biology Dept Trinity College, Hartford, CT 06106.

SIMMONS, JOSEPH
Auto dealer, attorney. **PERSONAL:** Born Oct 26, 1923, Ogden, UT; married Naomi; children: Patricia, Peggy, Barry, Michael. **EDUCATION:** Golden Gate Univ Law Sch, LlB 1961. **CAREER:** Capital Olds Inc, pres; Am Arbitration Assc, panel arbitrators 1971-; San Leandro-Hayward Municipal Ct, judge pro-tem 1972; Oakland-Piedmont Municipal Ct 1975. **ORGANIZATIONS:** Tres Charls Houston & Law Clb 1969-74; spec consult to pres Natl Bar Assc 1973-74; mem Civic Rights 3 Responsibilitities Com & Client Relations Com; Alameda Co Bar Assc 1973-75; mem Charles Houston Bar Assc 1976; co-chmn Ad Hoc Com Opposing Boycott Black Liquor Retailers 1972; co-chmn Lawyers Com For Civil Rights Under Law Oakland Br 1970-71; grad Gen Motors Minority Dealer Dev Acad 1974. **HONORS/ACHIEVEMENTS:** Awrd Cal State Package Store & Tavern Owners Assc 1972. **BUSINESS ADDRESS:** 1700 K St, Sacramento, CA 95814.

SIMMONS, JOSEPH JACOB, III
Government official. **PERSONAL:** Born Mar 26, 1925, Muskogee, OK; married Bernice Elizabeth Miller; children: Joseph Jacob IV, Bernice Garza, Mary Agnes Bursick, Jacolyn Reade, Eva Frances. **EDUCATION:** Univ of Detroit, 1942-44, 1946-77; St Louis Univ, BS 1949. **CAREER:** Dept of the Interior, under sec 1983-84; Interstate Commerce Commn, commissioner 1984-85, vice chmn 1985-86, commissioner 1987-. **ORGANIZATIONS:** Professional Amer Assoc of Petroleum Geologists 1958-; vice pres govt relations Amerada Hess Corp 1970-82; commissioner Statue of Liberty Ellis Island Commn 1983-; mem Natl Acad of Sci Bd of Mineral and Energy 1984-; mem Dept of the Interior Outer Continental Shelf Adv Bd 1984-. **HONORS/ACHIEVEMENTS:** Special Act of Service Awd, Outstanding Performance Awd, Disting Serv Awd all from Dept of the Interior; Public Service Awd Amer Assoc of Petroleum Geologists 1984. **MILITARY SERVICE:** AUS sgt 2 yrs. **HOME ADDRESS:** 2736 Unicorn Lane NW, Washington, DC 20015. **BUSINESS ADDRESS:** Commissioner, Interstate Commerce Commission, 12th & Constitution Ave NW, Washington, DC 20423.

SIMMONS, JOYCE HOBSON (JOYCE ANN HOBSON-SIMMONS)
Accountant. **PERSONAL:** Born Aug 01, 1947, Port Jefferson, NY; daughter of Nathan Edward Hobson Sr and Ada Rebecca Townes Hobson; married Leroy Simmons, Jr, Feb 21, 1978; children: Leroy III (stepson), Victor. **EDUCATION:** Essex Cty Comm Coll, 1971; Indian River Comm Coll, AA 1973; Amer Inst of Banking, Basic Cert 1973; FL Atlantic Univ, BBA 1975. **CAREER:** Port of NY Authority, personnel dept, police recruitment, world trade ctr, bldg constr dept, toll collector 1969-71; First Natl Bank & Trust Co, auditor-commercial loan dept, supv proof & bkkp dept 1971-75; Homrich Miel & Mehlich, staff acct 1976-77; Westinghouse Comm Dev Group, staff supv 1977; JA Hobson Acct & Tax Svc, sole proprietor 1978-. **ORGANIZATIONS:** Dir United Way of Martin Cty, Stuart/Martin Cty Chamber of Comm 1980-82; pres Amer Bus Women's Assoc 1981-82; chairperson Martin Cty School Bd 1982-86; dir Girl Scouts of Amer Palm Glade Council 1982-86; FAU Alumni Assoc 1982-, IRCC Advisory Council Acct & Fin 1984-, Martin Cty 4-H Found 1984-; mem Martin Memorial Found Hosp Comm Council, Amer Accounting Assn; bd of trustees, IRCC, 1987; dir, Children's Serv Council, 1988. **HONORS/ACHIEVEMENTS:** Women of the Year Amer Business Women's Assoc 1982; Outstanding Serv as Chmn Legislative Subcomm FL Sch Bd's Assoc. **HOME ADDRESS:** PO Box 784, Port Salerno, FL 33992.

SIMMONS, JULIUS CAESAR
Clergyman, counselor. **PERSONAL:** Born Nov 24, 1925, New Rochelle, NY; son of Charles Simmons and Precilla Dilgard; married Alma Alexander; children: Patricia Diane, Julius Caesar Jr. **EDUCATION:** VA Union Univ, AB 1952; VUU School of Religion, MDiv 1955; Ft Valley State Coll, Additional Study. **CAREER:** Dayton Christian Center Dayton OH, work with boys 1955-57; Ft Valley State Coll, dean of men 1957-69, dir of financial aid 1969-73, counselor 1973-. **ORGANIZATIONS:** Chmn Peach Cty Hospital Authority 1965-; Natl Dove of Peace Phi Beta Sigma Fraternity Inc; mem Citizen Educ Comm, optimist. **HONORS/ACHIEVEMENTS:** Citizenship Award Citizen Educ Comm 1980; Devoted Serv To Roesh Cty Alumni Assn FVSC 1977; Serv to FVS Coll Area Alumni Chapter 1983. **MILITARY SERVICE:** USN stewart 2c 1944-46; Honorable Discharge WWII Victory Medal. **BUSINESS ADDRESS:** Counselor, Dept Devel Studies, Fort Valley State College, State College Dr, Fort Valley, GA 31030.

SIMMONS, KENNETH H.
Architect-planner. **PERSONAL:** Born Jun 28, 1933, Muskogee, OK; divorced; children: Margot Eva, Kenneth II, Annette, Jalia. **EDUCATION:** Harvard Clg, AB 1954;Univ CA Berkley, BArch 1964. **CAREER:** Housing & Community Dev, pgm coor; San Francisco Econ Opportunity Cncl 1964; Bay Grp Arch & Plnrs San Francisco, prin 1965; Arch Renewal Com Harlem,co-dir 1966; Hunts Point Nghbrhd Project for Urban Am Inc Bronx, exec dir 1967; Com Design Collaborative Arch & Plnrs, prin;Univ CA, assc prof; Comm Design Collaborative Architects & Urban Planners, partner. **ORGANIZATIONS:** Bd dir Dock of the Bay Inc; mem Amer Planning Assoc; mem Am Inst of Cert Plnrs; mem Bethel AME Ch; bd dir East Bay Munic Utility Dist; mem Architects Designers and Planners for Social Responsibility; mem African Studies Assoc; mem Assoc of Concerned African Scholars; mem TransAfrica; mem Washington Office on Africa. **BUSINESS ADDRESS:** Partner, Comm Design Collab Arch, 630 20th St 3rd Fl, Oakland, CA 94612.

SIMMONS, LEONARD (BUD)
Public official. **PERSONAL:** Born May 02, 1920, Goldsboro, NC; married Claudia; children: Patricia, Leonard Jr, Gloria, Dennis, Jeffrey, Pamela, Zeno. **EDUCATION:** Browne Bus School NYC, 1941. **CAREER:** State of NJ, commissioner, civil service 1972-. **ORGANIZATIONS:** Former city councilman, pres of council & police commiss City of Roselle; former pres, mem Roselle Bd of Ed 13 yrs; original & only black mem NJ Lottery Commiss; former mem, pres Union Cty NJ Vocational & Comm Coll; former comm clerk NJ Leg; former vice pres NJ Vocational School Bd Assoc; org, past presRoselle Br NAACP; former congressional aide to congresswoman Florence P Dwyer 21st Dist NJ. **HONORS/ACHIEVEMENTS:** 1st black policeman in Roselle NJ; 1st black in history of NJ to be named to State Civil Serv Comm. **BUSINESS ADDRESS:** Commissioner, Civil Service, State of New Jersey, 1019 Chandler Ave, Roselle, NJ 07203.

SIMMONS, MAURICE CLYDE
Marketing management. **PERSONAL:** Born Feb 15, 1957, Washington, DC; son of Clyde T Simmons and Ada Blaylock Simmons; married Vicki Baker, Sep 1988; children: Marcus Simmons. **EDUCATION:** Dartmouth Coll, AB 1979; Univ of Pennsylvania Wharton Sch, MBA 1986. **CAREER:** Procter & Gamble, sales rep 1979-81, dist field rep 1981-82, unit mgr 1982-84; McNeil Consumer Products Co, asst prod dir 1986-; McNeil Consumer Products Co, Ft Washington PA, product dir 1986-. **ORGANIZATIONS:** Mem Natl Black MBA Assoc Philadelphia Chap 1984; regional coord Black Alumni of Dartmouth 1984,87; pres Wharton Black MBA Assoc 1985; co-chmn prog develop Natl Black MBA 1987 Conf Comm. **HOME ADDRESS:** 3601 Conshohocken Ave #203, Philadelphia, PA 19131.

SIMMONS, PAUL A.
Judge. **PERSONAL:** Born Aug 31, 1921, Monongahela, PA; married Gwendolyn; children: Paul Jr, Gwendolyn, Anne. **EDUCATION:** Univ of Pgh, 1946; Harvard Law Sch, 1949. **CAREER:** PA RR, employee 1941-46; SC Coll Law, prof of law 1949-52; NC Coll Law, prof of law 1952-56; general practice 1956-58; Clyde G Tempest, 1958-70; Hormell Tempest Simmons Bigi & Melenyzer, law partner 1970-73; Common Pleas WA Co PA, judge 1973-78; US Dist Court for the W Dist of PA, judge 1978-. **ORGANIZATIONS:** Mem Amer Bar Assn, Amer Trial Lawyers Assn, Amer Judicature Soc, PA Bar Assn, WA Co Bar Assn, NC State Bar; mem NAACP, Ind Benevolent Protective Order Elks of World, PA Human Rel Comm, Commonwealth PA Minor Judiciary Educ Bd; bd dir Mon Valley United Health Serv; mem Bethel AME Church; past grand atty State of PA for Most Worshipful Prince Hall Grand Lodge F&AM PA; mem Alpha Phi Alpha Soc Frat Mon Lodge. **HONORS/ACHIEVEMENTS:** Two Human Rights Awds NAACP; Meritorious Comm Serv Awd the Most Worshipful Prince Hall Grand Lodge. **BUSINESS ADDRESS:** Judge, US Dist Ct for the W Dist PA, Room 620, US Post Office & Court House, Pittsburgh, PA 15219.

SIMMONS, S. DALLAS
Educational administrator. **PERSONAL:** Born Jan 28, 1940, Ahoskie, NC; son of Mary A Simmons; married Yvonne Martin; children: S Dallas, Jr, Kristie Lynn. **EDUCATION:** North Carolina Central Univ, BS 1962, MS 1967; Duke Univ, PhD 1977. **CAREER:** North Carolina Central Univ, dir data processing 1962-64; Norfolk State Univ, dir data processing 1964-66; North Carolina Central Univ, asst prof business admin 1967-71, asst to the chancellor 1971-77, vice chancellor for univ relations 1977-81; St Paul's College, pres 1981-85, VA Union Univ, pres 1985-. **ORGANIZATIONS:** Mem Durham C of C 1971-81; liaison officer Moton Coll Serv Bureau 1972-; competency testing commiss NC State Bd of Educ 1977-81; exec comm 1981-, council of pres 1981-, fin comm 1984-85, bd of dir 1981-, Central Intercollegiate Athletic Assoc; bd dir VA Polytech Inst & State Univ 1982-83; bd trust NC Central Univ 1983-85; conf comm, 1983, chmn leadership awds comm 1984-85, bd of dir 1985 Natl Assoc for Equal Oppty in Higher Educ; exec comm mem bd of trust NC Central Univ 1983-85; exec com mem bd of dir UNCF; mem Amer Mgmt Assn, Kappa Alpha Psi, Brunswick C of C 1981-85; mem bd dir Pace Amer Bank 1984-; mem US Zululand Educ Found 1985; exec bd John B McLendon Found Inc 1985; Data Processing Mgmt Assoc, Doric Lodge No 28 of Free & Accepted Masons, Durham Consistory No 218 32 Degree, Zaffa Temple No 176 Shriner, Kappa Alpha Psi, Tobaccoland Kiwanians, Sigma Pi Phi Frat Alpha Beta Boule', Optimist club, Amer Assoc of School Admin, Amer Assoc of Univ Admin, The Downtown Club. **HONORS/ACHIEVEMENTS:** Kappa of the Month Kappa Alpha Psi Fraternity 1981; Citizen of the Year Omega Psi Phi Fraternity 1983-84; Black Amer Achievers 1983-84; Business Associate of the Year B&G Charter Chapter, ABWA 1984; Intl Book of Honor, Personalities of the South. **BUSINESS ADDRESS:** President, Virginia Union University, 1500 N Lombardy St, Richmond, VA 23220.

SIMMONS, SAMUEL J.
Association executive. **PERSONAL:** Born Apr 13, 1927, Flint, MI; married Barbara Lett; children: David Clay, Robert Allen. **EDUCATION:** Western MI Univ, BA 1949. **CAREER:** US Dept of Housing and Urban Dev, asst secr 1969-72; Natl Ctr for Housing Mgmt, pres 1972-81; Fed Natl Mortgage Assc, dir 1978-; Natl Housing Conf, dir 1979-; Natl Comm Against Discrimination in Housing, treas 1980-; Natl Caucus and Ctr on Black Aged Inc, pres. **ORGANIZATIONS:** Life mem NAACP and Urban League. **HONORS/ACHIEVEMENTS:** Honorary Doctor of Pub Srv Western MI Univ 1970. **BUSINESS ADDRESS:** President, Natl Caucus & Ctr Blk Aged, 1424 K St NW 500, Washington, DC 20005.

SIMMONS, SHIRLEY DAVIS
Elected official. **PERSONAL:** Born Sep 03, 1941, Vaughn, MS; married Princeston G Simmons; children: Brenda S Gooden, Vernadette S Gipson, Princeston Jr, Katrina, Makeba. **EDUCATION:** Tougaloo Coll, certificate AA; Jackson State Univ, certificate; Mary Holmes Coll, certificate. **CAREER:** Natl Council of Negro Women, 1st vice pres 1978; NAACP, chmn of redress 1980-82; Women for Progress, publicity chmn 1982; Madison-Yazoo-Leake Health Clinic,chmn of personnel 1984; Madison Co Schools, bd member. **ORGANIZATIONS:** Coord Summer Feeding Program 1979; coord Energy Assistance 1984; mem Project Unity 1985; mem Madison Co School Bd 1984-. **HONORS/ACHIEVEMENTS:** Outstanding Contribution to Youth Awd Project Unity 1983. **HOME ADDRESS:** Rte 3 Box 327, Canton, MS 39046.

SIMMONS, SYLVIA J.
Educator. **PERSONAL:** Born May 08, 1935, Boston, MA; daughter of Lorenzo C Quarles and Margaret Thomas Quarles; married Herbert G Simmons Jr, Oct 26, 1957; children: Stephen, Lisa, Allison. **EDUCATION:** Manhattanville Coll, BA 1957; Boston Coll, MED 1962. **CAREER:** ABCD Headstart Program, soc serv suprv 1965; Charles River Park Nursery School, montessori teacher 1965-66; Boston Coll, reg school of mgmt 1966-70; HarvardUniv, assoc dean of admissions & financial aid, faculty arts & sci 1974-76; Radcliffe Coll, assoc dean of admissions, financial aid & womens educ, dir financial aid 1972-76; Univ of MA Central Office,; assoc vice pres academic affairs 1976-81; MA Higher Educ Asst Corp, sr vice pres 1982-. **ORGANIZATIONS:** Past mem Exec Council Natl Assoc of Student Financial Aid Admin; past 1st vice pres Eastern Assoc of Financial Aid Admin; mem MA Assoc of Coll Minority Admin; consult Dept of HEW Office of Educ Reg I; consultant Coll Scholarship Serv, MA Bd of Higher Educ; past mem Rockefeller Selection Comm Harvard Univ; mem Delta Sigma Theta Natl; bd mem Family Serv Assoc Boston, Wayland Fair Housing, Concerts in Black & White, past pres Newton Chapter of Jack & Jill Inc, Boston Chapter Links Inc, Boston Manhattanville Club; mem bd of trustees Manhattanville Coll; past bd trustees Rivers Country Day School; past bd mem Cambridge Mental Health Assn; past bd trustees Simons Rock Coll; North Shore CC, chmn bd of trustees; William Price Unit of American Cancer Soc, pres; bd of dir Amer Cancer Soc MA Div 1988-. **HONORS/ACHIEVEMENTS:** Women in Politics; Outstanding Young Leader Boston Jr Chamber of Commerce 1971; Boston Coll Bicentennial Award 1976; Black Achiever Award 1976; President's Award, Massachusetts Educ Opportunity Program 1988; Human Rights Award, Massachusetts Teachers Assn, 1988; Educator of the Year, Boston Chapter Assn of Negro Business & Professional Women's Club, 1989; Recognition of Contributions to Higher Educ, Boston Coll Club, 1988. **BUSINESS ADDRESS:** Senior Vice President, MA Higher Ed Asst Corp, 250 Stuart St, Boston, MA 02116.

SIMMONS, THOMAS M.
Attorney. **PERSONAL:** Born Feb 25, 1932, Chicago, IL; children: Karen, Paul. **EDUCATION:** Loyola Univ, Chgo, BS (History) 1953; Boston Coll Law Schl, JD 1956; Suffolk Univ (Boston), Grad Studiess (Business). **CAREER:** Private Practice, lawyer 1956-; Boston Coll Law Schl, instr 1974-72; attorney. **ORGANIZATIONS:** Mem Student Cncl Coll of Arts & Sci, Loyola Univ Extrnl Rel Comm of Student Union; sr del Natl Fed Catholic Coll Stdnts; mem Univ Debating Soc; pres Univ Ushers; admtd MA Bar 1956, Fed Dist Court 1957, Supreme Court of US 1973, US Tax Court, Examiner of Titles in Land Court of Commonwealth of MA Supr Court 1975; apptd by Mayort Kevin H White to Brd of Examiners 1969-83, "Fair Hearing Officer" in US Dept of Health, Ed & Welfare Med Progfor MA 1974; Tchr Boston Coll Schl of Law 1973-75, Lowell Univ Eve Div Lowell MA 1975-76; elec Brd Dir Rath & Strong, Inc 1975-82; apptd as resource to US Fed Exec Brd Min Bus Optrnty Comm Sterling Comm 1975-76; mem brd trustees of Fdn for Co-op Housing 1974 -1981, mem Exec Comm 1981; chrmn Spcl Comm on Condo Conversion for City of Newton 1974; apptd Natl Panel Arbitration 1964, Boston Area Advsry Cncl of AAA 1970, Boston Advsry Brd ofNatl Cntr for Dispute Stlmnt 1975, Comm Disputes Serv Panel of AAA 1975; chrm Internatl Relations Comm. **HONORS/ACHIEVEMENTS:** USO Award for Service to Armed Forces 1977; USO Brd Gvnrs Award 1979; NAACP Gen Cnsl Advocacy Award 1974; Names to Who Is Who in East 1976, Black Amer 1981, Catholic Church 1976; St Thomass Moor Award 1970; Names in the Catholic Who is who Bicentennial Edtn 1976.

SIMMONS, WILLIE, JR.
Bank executive. **PERSONAL:** Born May 23, 1939, Meridian, MS; son of Willie Simmons (deceased) and Gussie Simmons (deceased); married Vernocia Neblett; children: Michael Anthony, Kevin Lawrence. **EDUCATION:** Military Police Officer, advanced course 1970; Univ of Tampa, BS (sr honors) 1975. **CAREER:** AUS, police officer 1958-78; Ingalls Memorial Hosp, dir of security 1978-80; First Chicago Security Serv Inc, chmn CEO 1985-; First Natl Bank of Chicago, mgr of protection & security 1980-85, dir of corporate security 1985-. **ORGANIZATIONS:** Pres IL Security Chiefs Assoc 1982; speaker Project We Care 1982-; chmn Deacon Bd Truevine MB Church 1982-; mem Amer Soc for Industrial Security 1984-; chmn Bd of Christian Educ Truevine MB Church 1985-; vice chmn, Crime Stoppers Plus 1986-; mem, Intl Org of Black Security Executives. **HONORS/ACHIEVEMENTS:** Outstanding Serv Awd Hospital Security 1980; Outstanding Serv Awd IL Security Chiefs Assoc 1980, 1981; Award of Excellence, 1986, First Chicago Corp; Appreciation Award, 1988, Natl Assn of Asian-Amer Professionals, 1986. **MILITARY SERVICE:** AUS major 20 yrs; Bronze Star, Meritorious Svcs, Vietnam Serv 1958-78. **BUSINESS ADDRESS:** Director/Vice President, First Natl Bank of Chicago, One First Natl Plaza, Chicago, IL 60670.

SIMMONS-EDELSTEIN, DEE
Business executive. **PERSONAL:** Born Jul 01, 1937, NYC; divorced. **EDUCATION:** City Coll of NY. **CAREER:** Ophelia DeVore Assn, vp; mistress of ceremonies; fashion commentator; Grace Del Marco, professional commercial model; WNJR-AM, NJ, Dee Simmons Radio Show; Nat Shoes, NYC, statistical bookkeeper; mag cover girl; lectr. **ORGANIZATIONS:** Mem Am Fedn of TV & Radio Assn; mem Nat Assn of Women in Media; 100 Coalition of Black Women; Affairs Com for Freedom Fund Drive; NAACP; Nat Drive Cerebral Palsy Telethon. **HONORS/ACHIEVEMENTS:** Spl Achvmt Award 1973; Pharmaco Products Award for first model of color to do TV commercial 1962; Ms Empire State 1962; Model of the Year 1963; Ms Beaux Arts for Schaefer Brewery 1962-63; hon award United Negro Coll Fund; Comm Serv Award for anti-narcotic rehab Prgm.

SIMMS, ALBERT L.
Clergyman. **PERSONAL:** Born Jan 21, 1931, Claremont, WV; divorced; children: Div. **EDUCATION:** Appalachian Bible Inst, grad; So Baptist Sem Ext Sch, 1973; Hilltop Baptist Ext Sem, grad 1976; North Gate Bible Coll, BA. **CAREER:** First Baptist Church Harlem Heights, pastor. **ORGANIZATIONS:** Past treas New River Valley Missionary Baptist Assn; asst dir Hill Baptist Ext Seminary; historian New River Valley Bapt Assn; mem Hist Comm WV Baptist State Conv; ch Dist Assn new River Educ Com; Hill Top Baptist Ext Sem adv bd; mem WV Baptist Minister Conf; past vice pres Fayette Ct Com Action; mem Crippled Children Div Assn Huntington; active in Bible Integratged camps & 4H camps as youth counselor. **HONORS/ACHIEVEMENTS:** Awd of Merit Profiles of a Christian 1972.

SIMMS, CARROLL HARRIS
Artist, educator. **PERSONAL:** Born Apr 29, 1924, Bald Knob, AR. **EDUCATION:** Cranbrook Art Acad, BFA 1950, MFA 1960. **CAREER:** Toledo State Mental Hosp, 1948-49; Detroit Art Inst Art Sch, 1950; TX So Univ, prof art 1950-87. **ORGANIZATIONS:** Pub numerous books articles illustrations periodicals; numerous exhibitions and sculpture commissions; assoc life mem Inst African StudiesUniv Ibadan Nigeria; TX So Univ Group Study Abroad Project Natl Univ of Haiti Port-au-Prince/Heriquez Padre Urena Natl Univ Santo Domingo Dominican Republic West Indies 1981 East/West, Contemporary American Art July 1984; mem Houston Municipal Art Comm Houston TX 1984; Dallas Mus Fine Arts 1952, 1953; mem Amer Soc African Culture; assoc life mem Inst African CultureUniv Ibadan Nigeria; life mem Inst Intl Educ; life mem Slade Soc Univ Coll London England; mem TX Assn Coll Tchrs; adv panel TX Comm on Arts & Humanities 1972-79; Natl Humanities Fac 1975-77; Houston Municipal Art Commn Houston TX 1986-87; Sec, The Houston Municipal Art Commission 1988-89. **HONORS/ACHIEVEMENTS:** 1st Awd Toledo Mus Fine Arts 1949-50; Purchase Awd Cranbrook Mus Art 1953; Fulbright Fellow 1954-56; Scholarship Swedish Inst Stockholm Survey Contem Ceramic Pottery 1964; TX So Univ Awd; Cert of Recog for Exemplory Representing Afro-Amer Artistic & Cultural Expression Second World Black & African Festivalof Arts 1977; contrib author "Black Art in Houston, The TX Southern Univ Experience" TX A&M Univ Press 1978; "Black Artists/South 1800-1978" Huntsville Museum of Art AL 1979; Carroll Sims Day Mayor of City of Houston 1977; exhibition "African-Amer Artists" 1978; Griot Awd Southern Conf on Afro-Amer Studies IncHouston 1984; "He's Got the Whole World In His Hands" bronze sculpture permanent collection the new CA Afro-Amer Museum LA CA; Alpha Kappa Omega Chap Alpha Kappa Alpha Sor Inc Educator and Outstanding Achievement in Visual Arts; Sculpture bronze permanent collection Texas Southern Univ title "A Tradition of Music" 1986.

SIMMS, ERNEST S.
Educator. **PERSONAL:** Born Jun 24, 1917, New Orleans; married Virginia; children: Marsha, Phillip. **EDUCATION:** Lewis Inst Chgo;Univ MN. **CAREER:** Homer Phillips Hospital, serologist 1940-43; Aloe Scientific Co, chemist 1947-49; Washington Univ Med School, research asst 1949-72; Microbiology Washington Univ Med School St Louis, assc prof 1972-. **ORGANIZATIONS:** Mem Am Assc & Immunologists 1969; Am Soc for Microbiology 1957;

Sigma XI. **BUSINESS ADDRESS:** WashingtonUniv, Dept of Microbiology, Box 8093, St Louis, MO 63110.

SIMMS, GREGORY FRAME
Business executive. **PERSONAL:** Born Dec 07, 1928, Newton, KS; divorced; children: Gabrielle Elise, Christian Michael David, Claudia Alison, Monica Maria, Liimu Afua. **EDUCATION:** Univ of KS, BMusic 1950; Sorbonne Univ of Vienna; Univ Perugia; Jean Tennyson Fellowship, 1950; John H Whitney Fellowship, 1954. **CAREER:** New Approach Method Inc, exec dir pres of bd; New Ed Methods Pub Co Inc, pres; Medgan Evers Comm Coll Brooklyn NY, instr 1977-; Bucks Co Comm Coll, instr 1972-73; NJ Comm Action Training Inst, dep dir 1965-69; Harlem Domestic Peace Corps, dir 1963-65; US Peace Corps Dominican Rep, dep dir 1962-63. **ORGANIZATIONS:** Dir Marlboro Houses Comm Ctr 1961-62; teen grp wrkr New York City Yth Bd 1958-60; soloist Siena Opera Fest Italy 1956-57; bass soloist Am Concert Chr 1953-54; bd mem AFRAM Inc; past bd mem Trenton NAACP; fdng bd Escuela Hispana Montessori. **HONORS/ACHIEVEMENTS:** Co-authored NAM Britannica Reading Program 1977; author Don't Wait Till You're Ready; publ in Day Care & Early & Educ; Phi Alpha Mu Hon Music Fraternity 1976; Young Amer artist of the Year Natl Assn of Negro Musicians 1948. **MILITARY SERVICE:** USAF 1952. **BUSINESS ADDRESS:** 40 Parkside Ave, Trenton, NJ 08618.

SIMMS, JAMES EDWARD
Educational admin. & clergyman. **PERSONAL:** Born Dec 14, 1943, Richmond, VA; married Emmajane Miller; children: Rachael, Eboni, James. **EDUCATION:** VA Union Univ, BA 1967; Pgh Theological Seminary, MDiv 1972, Dr of Ministry 1974. **CAREER:** Pgh Human Relations Comm, exec dir 1972; Allegheny Co Comm Coll, student serv coord 1973; Chatham Coll, instructor 1974; Comm Release Agency, exec dir 1974; Comm Action Pgh Inc, neighborhood admin 1977; City of Pittsburgh, asst exec sec office of the mayor. **ORGANIZATIONS:** Chmn United Negro College Fund Telethon 1983; pastor St Paul Baptist Church; pres Amer Baptist Theological Seminary; chmn Municipal Campaign United Way; mem Natl Forum of Black Public Admin; pres Homer S Brown Alumni Assn of VA Union Univ; pres bd of dirs Hill House Comm Serv Inc; mem bd of dirs Hill House Assn; mem bd of dirs Volunteer Action Center; mem bd of dirs Action Housing; mem Bd of Garfield Jubilee Housing Inc. **HONORS/ACHIEVEMENTS:** Varsity Letters Inter-Collegiate Football VA Union Univ 1965-67; Distinguished Serv Awd Conf of Minority Public Admins 1978; Political Awareness Awd Young Republican Council 1979; Civil Rights Awd Hand in Hand Inc 1980. **BUSINESS ADDRESS:** Asst Exec Secretary, Office of The Mayor, 517 City County Bldg, Pittsburgh, PA 15219.

SIMMS, MARGARET CONSTANCE
Economist. **PERSONAL:** Born Jul 30, 1946, St Louis, MO; daughter of Frederick T Simms and Margaret E Simms. **EDUCATION:** Carleton Coll, Northfield, MN, BA 1967; Stanford Univ, MA 1969; Stanford Univ, PhD 1974. **CAREER:** Univ of CA, Santa Cruz, acting asst prof 1971-72; Atlanta Univ, asst prof School of Business 1972-76; Atlanta Univ, Econ Dept, assoc prof & dept chair 1976-81; The Urban Inst, sr rsch assoc 1979-81, dir minorities & social policy prog 1981-86; The Joint Center for Political Studies, dep dir of rsch, 1986-. **ORGANIZATIONS:** Edtr The Review of Black Political Econ 1983-; mem Natl Economic Assoc 1971-, pres 1978-79; bd mem Council on Economic Priorities 1979-85; bd mem Women's Equity Action League 1984-; mem Fed Advsry Panel on Financial Elem & Secondary Ed 1979-82. **HONORS/ACHIEVEMENTS:** Selected Publs ed. "Black Economic Progress: An Agenda for 1990s" with Julianne M Malveaux, Slipping Through the Cracks, The Status of Black Women 1986, with Kristin A Moore & Charles L Betsey, Choice & Circumstance, Racial Differences in Adolescent Sexuality & Fertility (New Brunswick, NJ, Transaction Books, 1985) "The Economic Well-Being of Minorities during the Regean Years," Urban Inst Paper 1984; "The Impact of Chgs in Fed Elem & Secondary Ed Policy," Urban Inst Discussion Paper 1984. **BUSINESS ADDRESS:** Deputy Dir of Research, Joint Ctr for Political Study, 1301 Pennsylvania Ave NW, Ste 400, Washington, DC 20004.

SIMMS, ROBERT H.
Company executive, consultant. **PERSONAL:** Born Oct 02, 1927, Snowhill, AL; son of Harry and Alberta; married Aubrey Watkins, Nov 27, 1953; children: Leah Aliece Simms-Graham, David Michael. **EDUCATION:** Xavier Univ, BS 1949; Tuskegee Inst NY Univ, Advanced Study; Univ of Miami; Univ of MA. **CAREER:** Bob Simms Assoc Inc, pres/CEO; Comm Rel Bd Metro Dade Co, exec dir; Small Business & Development Center, exec dir 1965-66; Dade Co Bd of Educ, teacher 1953-65; Macon Co Bd of Educ, teacher 1949-50, 1952-53. **ORGANIZATIONS:** Pres Bob H Simms & Assoc Inc; mem Amer Soc for Public Admin; founder Miami Varsity Club; Natl Assn of Human Rights Workers; mem Orange Bowl Com; mem Greater Miami Philharmonic Soc; mem Kappa Alpha Psi; mem Sigma Pi Phi; mem Sigma Pi Designer; Creator of Inner City/Minority Experience for Defense Dept's Race Relations Inst 1972; dir Beacon Council; mem Greater Miami Chamber of Commerce. **MILITARY SERVICE:** AUS sgt e5 1950-52. **BUSINESS ADDRESS:** President-CEO, Bob Simms Assoc, Inc, 300 Biscayne Blvd Way, Dupont Plaza, Suite 616, Miami, FL 33131.

SIMMS, STUART OSWALD
Attorney. **PERSONAL:** Married Candace Otterbein; children: Marcus. **EDUCATION:** Harvard Law School, 1975. **CAREER:** US Attny's Office US Courthouse, attny 1978-. **ORGANIZATIONS:** Pres Black Alumni Assoc 1979-81. **BUSINESS ADDRESS:** Attorney, US Attorneys Office, US Courthouse, 101 West Lombard St, Baltimore, MD 21201.

SIMMS, WILLIAM E.
Insurance company executive. **PERSONAL:** Born Aug 23, 1944, Indianapolis, IN; son of Frank T Simms Sr (deceased) and Rosa Lee Smith Simms (deceased); married Maxine A Newman Simms, Jul 03, 1971; children: Terry Denise Reddix-Simms, Randall L. **EDUCATION:** Univ of Southern California, Los Angeles CA, BS Business Admin, 1971, MBA Marketing, 1976. **CAREER:** Transamerica Occidental Life, Los Angeles CA, mgr, 1969-77; Lincoln Natl Reinsurance Co, Fortwayne IN, second vice pres, 1977-80; Transamerica Occidental Life, Los Angeles CA, vice pres reinsurance mktg, 1980-84, vice pres sales/admin, 1984-86, vice pres reinsurance, 1987, sr vice pres reinsurance, 1988-. **ORGANIZATIONS:** California Life Insurance Companies Assn; Los Angeles Jr Chamber of Commerce; Natl Urban Leauge; bd of trustees, Los Angeles Summer Games Found; Los Angeles Open Gulf Found; advisory bd, United Negro Coll Fund. **MILITARY SERVICE:** US Air Force, staff sergeant, 1963-67. **BUSINESS ADDRESS:** Senior Vice President-Reinsurance, Transamerica Occidental Life Insurance Company, 1150 S Olive, Tower 2817, Los Angeles, CA 90015.

SIMON, ELAINE
Cosmetologist. **PERSONAL:** Born Nov 30, 1944, St Johns, Antigua-Barbuda;daughter of Hubert Phillips and Rosalyn Richards Jarvis; divorced; children: Denise, Francine, Sheldean. **EDUCATION:** Bay Coll of Baltimore, Baltimore MD, AA, 1976; Univ of Baltimore, attended, 1977-78; Natl Beauty Culturist League, Washington DC, Doctorate, 1987; Catinsville Community Coll, Certificate, 1982; Central State Univ, Columbus OH, Certificate, 1985; Coppin State Coll, Certificate, 1985. **CAREER:** Bay Coll of Maryland, lounge mgr, 1985-76; Johnsons Product Co, lecturer, technician, 1979-85; Touch of Paris Coiffure, owner, mgr, 1978-. **ORGANIZATIONS:** Natl Beauticulturist League, Baltimore MD, public relations dir, 1978-89; exec dir, Natl Black Women Consciousness Raising Assn, 1980-89; public relations dir, Master Beautician Assn, 1982-89; educ dir, Maryland State Beauty-Culture Assn, 1982-89; public relations dir, Theta Mu Sigma Natl Sorority, Zeta Chapter, 1985. **HONORS/ACHIEVEMENTS:** Civil Rights Humanitarian Award, Maryland Special Inaugural Comm, 1981; Governor's Citation, Governor of Maryland, 1983; Resolution, City Council of Baltimore 1989; Booker T Washington Citation Honor, Business League of Baltimore, 1989; Economic Stress Threaten Black Salon (shop talk magazine), 1983; "Pocket News Paper," 1983. **HOME ADDRESS:** 20 N Kossuth St, Baltimore, MD 21229.

SIMON, FABRICE JULE (FABRICE)
Fashion designer. **PERSONAL:** Born Jan 29, 1951, Petion-Ville, Haiti;married Andre Simon. **EDUCATION:** Fashion Inst of Tech, fashion & textile 1971. **CAREER:** Cohama Textile, colorist 1971-73; Concord Fabrics, designer 1973-74. **HONORS/ACHIEVEMENTS:** Awds rec'd from Coty 1981, Harvey's Bristol Cream 1981. **BUSINESS ADDRESS:** President, Apparels, 226 5th Ave, New York, NY 10001.

SIMON, JEWEL WOODARD
Artist. **PERSONAL:** Born Jul 28, 1911, Houston, TX; daughter of Mr & Mrs C A Woodard; married E L Simon (deceased); children: Edward L Jr, Margaret Jewel. **EDUCATION:** Atlanta Univ, AB (summa cum laude) 1931; Commercial Art, grad cert 1962; Atlanta Coll Art, BFA 1967. **CAREER:** Jack Yates High School, math dept head 1931-39; artist, many one-man shows. **ORGANIZATIONS:** Mem High Museum, Theater Guild, Atlanta Coll Art; past pres Mosolit Literary Cir, life mem AKA Sor; mem Amer Assn Univ Women, Natl Council of Negro Women, GA Council Arts; past bd mem YWCA; past mem Atlanta Civic Design Comm; past pres Jack & Jill of Amer Atlanta Chapt; past natl serv proj chmn Jack & Jill of Amer; past pres Grady Metro-Atlantic Girls Club; past pres E R Carter School PTA; Girls Clubs of Amer; life mem Church Women United; mem Amer Assn Univ Women; 1st Congregational Church; vice pres Assn Emory Sch of Nursing; past treas, Black Artist Atlanta; works included in Carver Museum, DuSable Museum, Kiah Museum, Educ Dept Ringling Museum, Atlanta Univ, Clark Coll, many private collections in US and abroad; slide collections in Natl Archives, Carnegie Inst, Atlanta Univ, Chicago Univ, Alabama Univ, Portland State Univ and many other universities & colleges in US and Canada; in books, Amer Negro Art Cedric Dover, Black Dimensions in Contemp Amer Art, Women Artists in Amer, Amer Printmakers; leading Comtemporary American Artists Les Krantz; chrm deaconess bd First Congregational Church; bd dir "Special Audiences" Judge Fortheir Handicapped Artist Show. **HONORS/ACHIEVEMENTS:** NCA Awds Mental Health Assn 1958; Atlanta Univ Alumni Awd 1966; WSB Beaver Awd 1968; Recognition Awd Simon Family Natl Conf of Christians & Jews 1971; Outstanding Leadership Awd 1975; Amer Assn Univ Women; Distinguished Serv March of Dimes; Mother of the Yr Awd; Bronze Woman Yr Fine Art; 8 purchase awds; Golden Dove Heritage Awd; First Pres Alumni Awd for Outstanding Achievement Artist Teacher Humanitarian 1984; Valiant Woman Award CWU 1987; Lifetime Deputy Governor, ABIRA.

SIMON, JOSEPH DONALD
Clergyman. **PERSONAL:** Born Jun 30, 1932, Natchitoches, LA. **EDUCATION:** Attended Divine Word Seminary Epworth IA 1955; Divine Word Sem Bay St Louis, BA 1961; Gregorian Univ Rome Italy, MA Eclec Hist 1963. **CAREER:** Divine Word Sem Bay St Louis, prof ch hist 1963-66; Divine Word Coll Epworth, dir of develop 1975-80; Divine Word Coll Epworth, asst prof history 1966-81, academic dean/vice pres 1981-87, pres 1987-. **ORGANIZATIONS:** City council Epworth IA 1976-85; chmn Area Council of Govts Dubuque Co 1976; chmn E Central Intergovernmental Assn 1977; bd of trustees Divine Word Coll 1975-80; bd of dirs League of Iowa Municipalities 1979-80; exec comm East Central Intergovtl Assoc 1980-; chmn E Iowa Regional Housing Auth 1982; chmn Eastern Iowa Regional Housing Auth 1983-; chmn East Central Intergovtl Assoc Business Growth Inc 1985-. **BUSINESS ADDRESS:** Assistant Professor History, Divine Word College, Center Ave, Epworth, IA 52045.

SIMON, KENNETH BERNARD
General surgeon. **PERSONAL:** Born Sep 29, 1953, San Francisco, CA. **EDUCATION:** Univ of AZ-Tucson, BS RN 1976; Meharry Medical Coll, MD 1980; American Bd of Surgery, Specialty Certification 1986. **CAREER:** DC General Hosp, staff surgeon/instructor in surgery 1985-86; Univ of Alberta Hospitals, resident in cardiac surgery 1986-87. **HONORS/ACHIEVEMENTS:** Kim Meche Scholar Univ of AZ 1974-75. **HOME ADDRESS:** 7710 Maple Ave, #501, Takoma Park, MD 20912. **BUSINESS ADDRESS:** 8210 111st St, Suite 2209, Edmonton, Alberta, Canada.

SIMON, LONNIE A.
Clergyman. **PERSONAL:** Born Mar 23, 1925, East Mulga, AL; son of William Simon and Tempie; married Florence, May 14, 1949; children: Janet Ellis, Lonita Ross, Kenneth, Cynthia. **EDUCATION:** Central Bible Coll, 1963; Amer Baptist Theol Sem, 1975; Trinity Theological Seminary, enrolled master of theology program, Newburgh IN 1983-; Youngstown Coll, 1959. **CAREER:** Eastern OH Baptist Assn, moderator 1968-76; New Bethel Baptist Church, 1962-; Jerusalem Baptist Church 1960-62; Elizabeth Baptist Church 1954-59; US Post Office Youngstown OH, letter carrier 1955-65. **ORGANIZATIONS:** Song leader exec bd mem Lott Carey Bapt Foreign Mission Conv; mem Youngstown Bd of Ed 1972-75; missionary Guyana South Amer 1968, 76; registrar & instr Yo Ext Unit of the Amer Baptist Theol Seminary; vice pres Intl Ministerial Alliance; coord Eastern Dist of OH Leadership Conf; past pres Youngstown Council of Churches; past pres Youngstown Urban League; past vice pres Youngstown Br NAACP; Youngstown Black Polit Assembly; former Mem Health & Welfare Council; former mem Mayor's Human Relations Commn; Downtown Kiwanis;

2nd vice moderator Northern OH Baptist Assn 1985-; vice pres Partners In Ecumenism, Natl Council of Churches of christ Program; commissioner Human Relations Commission 1986-; advisory committee member Northeastern Educational Television of OH Inc 1989-. **HONORS/ACHIEVEMENTS:** Received ten week Ford Found grant to attend Urban Training Ctr Chicago 1967; Natl Inst of Mental Health four-week grant to attend Case Western Res Univ 1969; observer All African Council of Churches, Partners in Ecumenism, 1987; Jesse Jackson delegate Natl Democratic Convention 1988. **MILITARY SERVICE:** USN 3rd class officers & steward 1943-46. **BUSINESS ADDRESS:** Rev, New Bethel Baptist Church, 1507 Hillman St, Youngstown, OH 44507.

SIMON, ROSALYN MCCORD
Consultant. **PERSONAL:** Born Dec 02, 1946, Baltimore, MD; children: Monica Lynnette. **EDUCATION:** Coppin State Coll, BS 1973; Morgan State Univ, MS 1981. **CAREER:** Admin on Develop Disabilities, consultant 1982-84; Amer Assoc of Univ Affiliated Progs, project dir 1984-86; Natl Information Ctr for Handicapped Children & Youth, consultant 1986-. **ORGANIZATIONS:** Consultant Developmental Disabilities Law Project Inc 1980-82, DC Commn on Public Health DC District Govt 1986. **HOME ADDRESS:** 6800 Liberty Rd #313, Baltimore, MD 21207.

SIMON, WALTER J.
Business executive. **PERSONAL:** Born Dec 01, 1941, New Orleans, LA; married Margaret Peay; children: Christopher. **EDUCATION:** Benedict Coll, BS 1963; Hunter Coll, 1967. **CAREER:** Bronx State Hosp, chief therapist 1963-67; NY Nets ABA, pro basketball player 1967-70; Wise Planning of NY, reg rep, stockbroker 1969-70; KY Colonels ABA, pro basketball player 1970-75; KY Fried Chicken Corp, vice pres bus devel 1975-. **ORGANIZATIONS:** Mem Intl Franchising Assoc 1976; bd mem, comm Jud Nominating Comm State of KY 1979; comm KY v comm on Human Rights 1980. **HONORS/ACHIEVEMENTS:** All Amer Coll Basketball NCAA-NAIA 1961; All Star All Pro NY Nets ABA Basketball 1968; Outstanding Young Man of KY Louisville Jaycees 1975. **BUSINESS ADDRESS:** Vice President Business Devel, Kentucky Fried Chicken Corp, 1441 Gardiner Ln, Louisville, KY 40232.

SIMONE, NINA
Singer, composer, pianist. **PERSONAL:** Born Feb 21, 1940, Tryon, NC; daughter of John D Waymon and Kate Waymon; children: Lisa Celeste. **EDUCATION:** Julliard Sch of Music (Carl Freidberg), student 1954-56; Curtis Inst Music (Vladimir Sokoloff), student 1950-53; Malcolm X College, DH; Amherst College, DMusic; Private Study, with Clemens Sandresky, Grace Carrol. **CAREER:** Private Lessons, teacher 1954; Composer, Mississippi Goddam 1963; Four Women 1964 (with Langston Hughs); Backlash Blues 1966; recording for RCA Victor Records; accompanist for vocal student Arlent Smith Studio Phila; Film, actress "Someone to Watch Over Me" 1987; Composer, "Young, Gifted & Black" was named Natl Anthem of Black America by CORE, composed 500 songs, made 56 albums. **ORGANIZATIONS:** Mem ASCAP, AFTRA, Amer Federation Musicians, SAG. **HONORS/ACHIEVEMENTS:** Albums incl, Silk & Soul, Emergency Ward, It Is Finished, Here Comes the Sun, Young Gifted & Black; Recip YMCA Life Award for Fund Raising; Named Woman of the Year Jazz at Home Club Philadelphia 1966; Hits from albums are "Porgy" from Porgy & Bess, "Life" from Rock Opera Hair, My Baby Just Cares For Me; Awarded keys to 7 major US cities. **BUSINESS ADDRESS:** Sibongile Music & Publishers, Mail Boxes USA, 9095 Hollywood Blvd, Hollywood, CA 90046.

SIMONS, GAIL DERESE
Hospital administration. **PERSONAL:** Born Dec 31, 1959, Columbia, SC. **EDUCATION:** Univ of SC, BS Acctg 1981; Harvard Grad Sch of Business, MBA 1985. **CAREER:** Scana Corp, junior accountant 1981-83; American Medical Intl, management assoc 1985-86, mktg dir Atlanta 1986, admin dir of opers & financial analysis 1987-. **ORGANIZATIONS:** Bd of dirs Harvard Business Sch Black Alumni Assoc 1985-88; exec comm Natl Black MBA Assoc 1987. **HONORS/ACHIEVEMENTS:** Outstanding Senior Awd; Achievement Awd NBMBA Assoc; Omicron Delta Kappa; Beta Alpha Psi. **HOME ADDRESS:** 111 Newberry Ave, Irmo, SC 29063.

SIMPKINS, J. EDWARD
Educator. **PERSONAL:** Born Oct 18, 1932, Detroit, MI; married Alice Marie Mann; children: Edward, Ann Marie, Evelyn. **EDUCATION:** Wayne St U, BA 1955, edM 1961; Harvard U, CAS 1969, edD 1971. **CAREER:** Coll of Educ, Wayne St Univ, dean 1974-; Center for Black Student, Wayne St Univ, 1972-74; PA Public Schools, chief negotiator 1971-72; Fac & Exec Dir of Center for Urban Student at Harvard Graduate School of Educ, asst & dean 1970-71; Hist Dept, Tufts Univ, Lecturer 1968-71; Detroit Fed of Teachers, ex-vice pres 1965-68; HS English Journ History, teacher 1956-65. **ORGANIZATIONS:** Mem Am Arb Assc; mem Ind Rel Res Assc; mem Phi Delta Kappa; pres Assc for the Study of Afro Am Life & Hist St of MI; mem Phi Delta Kappa. **HONORS/ACHIEVEMENTS:** Human rights awrd 1968; spirit of detroit awrd 1974; Martin Luther King Awrd; Woodrow Wilson Foundation; HarvardUniv Flw. **MILITARY SERVICE:** USNA pvt 1956-58. **BUSINESS ADDRESS:** Coll of Educ Wayne State Univ, Detroit, MI 48202.

SIMPKINS, WILLIAM JOSEPH
Military. **PERSONAL:** Born Dec 30, 1934, Edgefield, SC. **EDUCATION:** NC A&T State Univ, BS 1952-56; Attended, Univ of MD; Baylor Univ, MHA 1969. **CAREER:** 121 Evc Hosp Repub of Korea, exec officer 1969-70; Mcdonald Army Hosp Ft Eustis VA, exec officer 1970-71; HQ AUS Ofc of Surgeon Genl, asst chief personnel serv 1971-75; Eisenhower Med Ctr Ft Gordon, chief/personnel div troop comdr 1975-78; AUS Med Command Korea, exec officer 1978-79; Walter Reed Army Med Ctr, col AUS dir of personnel & comm activities 1979-83; US Army Medical Dept Personnel Support Agency Office of the Surgeon Genl, commander 1983-. **ORGANIZATIONS:** Mem Natl Assn of Health Serv Exec 1971-80; mem US Military Surgeons Assn; mem Amer Hosp Assn; mem Keystone Consistory #85 Free & Accepted Masons; mem NAACP; life mem Alpha Phi Alpha Frat Inc. **HONORS/ACHIEVEMENTS:** Who's Who Among Students in Amer Colls & Univs 1955; Legion of Merit Office of Surgeon Gen HQ AUS; Bronze Star Medal Republic of Vietnam; Meritorious ServMedal Ft Gordon GA; Meritorious Serv Medal Repub of Korea. **MILITARY SERVICE:** AUS col 1956-. **BUSINESS ADDRESS:** AUS Med Dept Personnel Sup Agency, Office of the Surgeon Genl, 1900 Half St SW, Washington, DC 20024.

SIMPSON, CAROLE
Journalist. **PERSONAL:** Born Dec 07, 1940, Chicago, IL; married Jim Marshall; children: Mallika. **EDUCATION:** Univ of MI, BA; Univ of IA, MA. **CAREER:** Voice of Amer, stringer corr; Tuskegee Inst, editor of info bur, jrnl instr, adv to coll newspaper; WBBM Radio, reporter; WCFL Radio Chgo, reporter; USIU Radio Station IA; WMAQ-TV, news corr 1970-74; Northwestern Univ, instr of journalism 1971-74; NBC Midwest Bur & NBC News WA, news corr 1974-82; ABC News, corr 1982-. **BUSINESS ADDRESS:** Correspondent, ABC News, 1717 DeSales St NW, Washington, DC 20036.

SIMPSON, DAZELLE DEAN
Physician. **PERSONAL:** Born Aug 28, 1924, Miami, FL; married George Augustus Simpson Sr MD; children: George Jr, Gregory, Gary. **EDUCATION:** Fisk Univ, BA magna cum laude 1945; Meharry Med Coll, MD highest honors 1950. **CAREER:** Private practice physician. **ORGANIZATIONS:** Bd trustees Meharry Med Coll 1977-; diplomate Amer bd of Pediatrics 1957; fellow Amer Acad of Pediatrics; Alumnus of Year Meharry Coll 1974; chmn (pediatric sec) Natl Med Assn 1975-77; natl pres Meharry Alumni Assc 1976-77; life mem NAACP; mem Delta Sigma Theta Sor Head Start Consult Force on Pediatric Educ 1974-78; Task mem Amer Acad of Ped; mem bd of dirs, Miami Childrens Hospital 1988-. **HONORS/ACHIEVEMENTS:** Contributing editor Current Therapy 1980. **BUSINESS ADDRESS:** Physician, 1001 NW 54th St, Ste C, Miami, FL 33127.

SIMPSON, DIANE JEANNETTE
Social worker. **PERSONAL:** Born Sep 20, 1952, Denver, CO; daughter of Arthur H Simpson (deceased) and Irma Virginia Jordan Simpson. **EDUCATION:** NE Wesleyan Univ, BS 1974; Univ of Denver Grad School of Social Work, MSW 1977. **CAREER:** Girl Scouts Mile Hi Council, summer asst 1971-77; Univ of Denver Grad School of Soc Work, field instr 1984-; Denver Public Schools, social worker asst 1974-75, social worker 1977-. **ORGANIZATIONS:** Mem Natl Assoc of Black Soc Workers 1980-86, Natl & CO Assn of Ed 1980-; sec of bd of trustees Warren Village Inc 1982-83; nominations & personnel comm Christ United Methodist Church 1981-84; mem Denver Chap Black Geneology Org 1981-87; chairperson of minority adult recruitment team Girl Scouts Mile Hi Council 1982-84; mem Black Women's Network 1983-86; natl council delegate Girl Scouts 1984-87; chairperson planning comm Creative Ctr for Children 1984, adv bd 1984-86, Christ United Meth Church; mem traveler Denver Sister Cities Inc 1984; admin bd, staff, parish relations, Council of Ministries Christ United Methodist Church 1984-87. **HONORS/ACHIEVEMENTS:** Selectee to Ghana West Africa Girl Scouts of the USA/Oper Crossroads Africa 1974; Crusade Scholar Bd of Global Ministries, United Methodist Church 1976-77; Spec Mission Recognition United Methodist Women, United Methodist Church 1982; Elizabeth Hayden Award for Outstanding Serv Girl Scouts Mile Hi Council 1983; Young Alumni Loyalty Awd NE Wesleyan Univ 1985; Woman of the Year Award Aurora Area Business & Professional Women's Org 1986. **HOME ADDRESS:** 6865 E Arizona Ave#D, Denver, CO 80224.

SIMPSON, DONNIE
Radio & tv host. **PERSONAL:** Born Jan 30, 1954, Detroit, MI; son of Calvin Simpson and Dorothy Simpson; married Pamela; children: Donnie Jr, Dawn. **EDUCATION:** Univ of Detroit, BA Communications. **CAREER:** WJLB Detroit, air personality 1969-77; Black Entertainment TV Host of Video Soul, prog dir & morning personality of WKYS Radio in DC. **ORGANIZATIONS:** Supporter United Negro Coll Fund, Big Brothers, Easter Seals. **HONORS/ACHIEVEMENTS:** Program Dir of the Year, Billboard Magazine 1982; Superstar of the Year, The National Urban Coalition 1989. **BUSINESS ADDRESS:** Video Soul Host, Black Entertainment TV, 4001 Nebraska Ave, NW, Washington, DC 20016.

SIMPSON, FRANK B.
Educator. **PERSONAL:** Born Dec 21, 1919, Jewett, TX; married Estelle Martin; children: Rosetta L. **EDUCATION:** KY State Univ, BS 1942; Univ KY, MS 1956; Univ KY & Univ Louisville, postgrad. **CAREER:** Jefferson Co Bd Educ, area supt 1969-; Hopkinsville Bd of Educ, asst supt 1967-69; HS prin. **ORGANIZATIONS:** Mem KEA; mem NEA; mem KASA; past pres 3rd Dist Tchrs Assc; 2nd Dist Prins Assc; KY HS Athletic Assc; past mem Gov Commn of High Educ; mem Gov Adv Commn on Local Govt; life mem NAACP; mem Urban League; mem Alpha Phi Alpha Frat; Mason; mem Gov State Com on Educ Improvement 1978-82; mem Sigma Pi Phi Frat Bolue Louisville Chpt; bd mem USO; steward Miles Meml CME Ch. **HONORS/ACHIEVEMENTS:** Man of Year Alpha Ph Alpha Gamma Epsilon Lambda 1966; distg KY State Univ Alumni Award 1971; the Lucy Hart Smith-Atwood S Wilson Award KY Educ Assc 1975. **MILITARY SERVICE:** AUS sgt 1942-46. **BUSINESS ADDRESS:** 3332 Newburg Rd, Louisville, KY 40218.

SIMPSON, GREGORY LOUIS
Physician. **PERSONAL:** Born Feb 16, 1958, Columbus, OH; married Alena M Baquet-Simpson MD; children: Gregory II, Nathaniel. **EDUCATION:** VA Union Univ, attended 1976-79 (achieved early acceptance into 2 medical schools without BS); Meharry Medical Coll, MD 1983. **CAREER:** Martin Luther King Jr General Hosp, internship 1983-84, residency 1984-86, chief resident 1984-86; Los Angeles Co Court System, medical expert on call list 1984-; Los Angeles Co Dept of Hlth Svcs, medical expert panel for child abuse 1984-, medical expert witness for child abuse 1984-; Private Practice, pediatrician 1986-; Martin Luther King Jr General Hosp, fellow child abuse/child develop 1986-. **ORGANIZATIONS:** Mem NAACP 1976-, Amer Medical Student Assoc 1979-83, Student Natl Medical Assoc 1979-83; assoc minister Southfield Comm Missionary Bapt Church ColumbusOH 1979-; licensed baptist minister 1979-; mem Los Angeles Pediatric Soc 1983-, Amer Medical Assoc 1983-, Physician Housestaff Educ Comm ML King Genl Hosp 1984-86; mem Suspected Child Abuse and Neglect Team ML King Jr Genl Hosp 1984-; mem Patient Care Fund 1984,85; mem Joint Council of Residents and Interns 1985-; mem Los Angeles Co Medical Assoc 1987-. **HONORS/ACHIEVEMENTS:** Mem Alpha Kappa Mu Natl Honor Frat 1978, Beta Kappa Chi Natl Honor Frat 1978; Student Rsch Fellowship Natl Insts of Health Washington DC 1979; Outstanding Young Man of Amer 1981; Housestaff of the Year Awd Dept of Pediatrics Charles R Drew Medical Sch Martin Luther King Jr Genl Hosp 1985,86. **HOME ADDRESS:** 2301 West 115th Place, Inglewood, CA 90303. **BUSINESS ADDRESS:** Child Abuse Consultant, Martin Luther King Genl Hosp, 12021 So Wilmington Ave, Los Angeles, CA 90059.

SIMPSON, JAMES ARLINGTON See SIMPSON, NORVELL J.

SIMPSON, JOYCE MICHELLE
Account executive. **PERSONAL:** Born Oct 09, 1959, Philadelphia, PA. **EDUCATION:**

Temple Univ, BA 1981. **CAREER:** Ron Lucas & Assocs, freelance media consultant; Nutri/System Inc, advertising coord 1982-83; Bernard Hodes Adv, account coord 1981-82, 1983-84; Ogilvy & Mather Advertising, asst acct exec 1985-; Warner Bros Inc, admin of intl advertising. **ORGANIZATIONS:** Treas Assoc of Black Journalists (student chapt) 1978-81; sec FSO Elite 1982-84; mem Natl Assoc of Female Execs 1985. **HONORS/ACHIEVEMENTS:** Most Valuable Staffer Award Burlington Co Times 1977; Student Writing Awd Newspaper Fund 1977; Guest Soloist (Natl Anthem) NBA 1983, 1984; On The Move Black Enterprise Magazine 1984. **BUSINESS ADDRESS:** Admin of Intl Advertising, Warner Bros Inc, 4000 Warner Blvd, Los Angeles, CA 91522.

SIMPSON, JUANITA H.
Retired educator. **PERSONAL:** Born Aug 27, 1925, Terre Haute, IN; daughter of Will Hatchett and Cornelia Williams Hatchett; married William Simpson, May 15, 1949; children: Barton A, Cathy L MD, Capt Dorothy E. **EDUCATION:** Northwestern Univ, Evanston IL, BA Music Educ, 1947; Roosevelt Univ, Chicago IL, MA Music Educ, 1964, MA Arts, 1973. **CAREER:** Chicago Bd of Educ, Chicago IL, teacher, 1947-86, asst principal, 1980-85. **ORGANIZATIONS:** Bd mem, School Dist 163, Park Forest IL, 1973-75; pres, Illinois State Conference NAACP Branches, 1986-89. **HOME ADDRESS:** 403 Wilshire, Park Forest, IL 60466.

SIMPSON, MERTON DANIEL
Artist, business executive. **PERSONAL:** Born Sep 20, 1928, Charleston, SC; married Beatrice Houston; children: Merton Daniel Jr, Kenneth Charles. **EDUCATION:** NYU, Attended; Cooper Union Art School. **CAREER:** Merton D Simpson Gallery Inc, pres & owner. **ORGANIZATIONS:** Mem Curatorial Counc Studio Mus Harlem 1977-; Red Cross Exchange Exhibit Paris & Tokyo 1950; Intercultural Club 1951; SC Cultural Fund 1951; Gibbes Art Gallery 1956. **HONORS/ACHIEVEMENTS:** Publ Young Amer Painters 1954; Amer Negro Art 1960; comtemporary Artists of SC 1970; The Afro Amer Artist 1973; numerous exhibits, permanent collections. **MILITARY SERVICE:** USAF artist 1951-54. **HOME ADDRESS:** 1063 Madison Ave, New York, NY 10028.

SIMPSON, NORVELL J. (JAMES ARLINGTON SIMPSON)
Human relations administrator. **PERSONAL:** Born Mar 25, 1931, Rochester, NY; son of Frank Douglas Simpson and Martha Perlina Jentons Simpson; married Alice Saxton, Jul 11, 1953; children: Gary A, Sharon R, Leslie A. **EDUCATION:** Park Clge, BA Econ and Bus 1970; Univ of CO, MA Cand Guid and Couns 1981. **CAREER:** USAF, sr mstr sgt 1949-71; Pikes Peak Comm Action Prog, exec dir 1972-74; El Paso Cty CO, dir comm serv dept 1974-79; TRW/EPI, prop mgr 1980-86; Colorado Springs Public Schools Dist 11, human relations adminstrator 1986-. **ORGANIZATIONS:** Dir United Way Pikes Peak Reg 1978-; Schl Dist 11 1975-85; CO Assc of Schl Bd 1983-84; comm Colo Sprngs Human Rel 1973-79. **HONORS/ACHIEVEMENTS:** Citizen of the Year Alpha Phi Alpha 1979 1981 1982; Omega Psi Phi 1978; Comm Ldr of Amer 1979-81; TRW Leadership Award TRW 1979; The Norvell Simpson Community Center, The Colorado Educ Assn Lion II Award. **MILITARY SERVICE:** USAF sr mstr sgt 1949-71. **HOME ADDRESS:** 4880 Topaz Dr, Colorado Springs, CO 80918.

SIMPSON, O. J. See SIMPSON, ORENTHAL JAMES

SIMPSON, ORENTHAL JAMES (O. J. SIMPSON)
Professional athlete, sports commentator. **PERSONAL:** Born Jul 09, 1947, San Francisco, CA; married Nicole; children: Arnelle, Jason, Sydney. **EDUCATION:** San Francisco City Coll, 1965-67; Univ of So Cal, 1967-69. **CAREER:** Buffalo Bills, halfback 1969-78; San Francisco 49'ers 1978; actor in, The Towering Inferno 1974, The Clansman 1974, Killer Force 1975, Cassandra Crossing 1976,Capricorn I 1977, Firepower 1978, Hambone & Hilly 1983; appeared on variousTV productions; Orenthal Productions, owner, exec producer of severalTV productions; ABC-TV Sports 1969-77; competed in an won the 1975 Superstars Competition; 1976 Summer Olympics, color commentator; NBC-TV Sports 1978-82; ABC-TV, sports color commentator Mon Night Football 1983-86, Rose Bowl color commentator 1979, 1980; 1984 Summer Olympic Sports special events; several TV commercials. **HONORS/ACHIEVEMENTS:** Coll of San Francisco, All American 1965-66; USC, All American 1967-68; world record 440 yd relay team 1967; Heisman Trophy winner 1968; UPI & AP, college athlete of the year 1968; voted coll player of the decade ABC Sports 1970; Named Amer Football League All Star Team 1970; named collegiate athlete of the decade1972; Most yds gained in a season 2,003 1973; Most games in a season with 100 yds or more 11 1973; Most rushing attempts in a season 332, 1973; Hickok Belt recipient 1973; NFL most valuable player 1975; AFC most valuable player 1972, 1973, 1975; Most yds gained rushing in a game 273, 1976; Record holder for most yds rushing gained in a season; Most yds rushing gained in a game; Pro Bowl 1972,74,75,76; Named NFL Player of the Decade 1979; College Football Hall of Fame inducion 1983; 2nd leading rusher in NFL history; Pro Football Hall of Fame induction 1985.

SIMPSON, RALPH DEREK
Professional athlete. **PERSONAL:** Born Aug 10, 1949, Detroit, MI; married Joyce McMullen. **EDUCATION:** MI State, attd 1973. **CAREER:** NJ Nets, prof bsktbl guard; Denver Nuggets, prof bsktbl plyr 1977-78; Detroit Pistons, prof bsktbl plyr 1976-77; Philadelphia 76'ers, prof bsktbl plyr; Chicago Bulls, prof bsktbl plyr 1972. **BUSINESS ADDRESS:** NJ Nets, 185 E Union Ave, East Rutherford, NJ 07073.

SIMPSON, SAMUEL G.
Clergyman. **PERSONAL:** Born Dec 06, 1931; married Lola Campbell; children: Erica, Stephen, Kim. **EDUCATION:** BRE 1967; student of MDiv. **CAREER:** Jamaica, civil servant treas 1955-59; Bronx Bapt Ch NY, pastor 1964-74; So Bapt Chs Bronx, pastor dir. **ORGANIZATIONS:** Pres East Tremont Ch Coun; vice pres Counc of Ch Bronx Div; vice pres Met NY Bapt Assc; vice pres Bapt Conv of NY; chmn Nominating Com of Council of Chs New York City Sec Comm Planning Bd No 6 Bronx; treas Twin Parks Urban Renewal Bronx; 46 pct exec bd mem Alumni of Year 1974; of Northeastern Bible Clge. **HONORS/ACHIEVEMENTS:** Award Bapt Conv of MD. **BUSINESS ADDRESS:** 331 E 187, Bronx, NY 10458.

SIMPSON, STEPHEN WHITTINGTON
Attorney. **PERSONAL:** Born Mar 14, 1945, Philadelphia, PA; married Audrey C Murdah; children: Stephen Jr, Christopher Lindsey. **EDUCATION:** Harvard Univ, AB 1966; Univ of PA, JD 1969. **CAREER:** ARA Serv Inc, asst gen counsel; Goodrs Greenfield, atty 1973-77; Dechert, Price & Rhoades, atty 1970-73; PA Superior Ct, law clerk 1969-70. **ORGANIZATIONS:** Amer Bar Assc; Philadelphia Bar Assc; Barristers Club; Ex Comm Philadelphia Indsl Devel Corp; Metro Bd YMCA; United Way; Germantown Hist Soc; W Mt Airy Neighbors; tste William Penn Chtr Sch.

SIMPSON, VALERIE
Singer, songwriter. **PERSONAL:** Born in New York, NY; married Nicholas; children: Nicole. **CAREER:** Songwriter/singer with Nick Ashford, worked for Motown Records; wrote songs for, Diana Ross, Marvin Gaye & Tammi Terrell, Ray Charles, Chaka Khan, Gladys Knight & the Pips. **HONORS/ACHIEVEMENTS:** Songs incl, So, So Satisfied, Send It, Reach Out and Touch, Ain't Nothing Like the Real Thing, Your Precious Love, It's My House, Ain't No Mountain High Enough. **BUSINESS ADDRESS:** c/o Patty Keller, 1260 Avenue of the Americas, New York, NY 10020.

SIMPSON, WALTER
Business executive. **PERSONAL:** Born Apr 17, 1941, New York City; married Patricia Deas. **EDUCATION:** Clark Clge, BA Sociology cum laude 1963; CCNY, MS 1970. **CAREER:** Xerox Corp, mgr employee resources 1973-; Equal Opportunity Hazeltine Corp Greenlawn NY, dir; Kennecott Copper Corp NY, prof employment; Bulova Watch CoJackson Hghts NY, personnel assc. **ORGANIZATIONS:** Mem EDGES Group 1972-; NY State & GA State Teaching Licenses; Licenses to sell life & health ins in NY; former bd chmn Harlem Prof Inc; sec Harlem Prof Inc 1970-. **MILITARY SERVICE:** NY Army Natl Guard sgt 1963-69. **BUSINESS ADDRESS:** 445 Hamilton Ave, White Plains, NY 10601.

SIMPSON, WILLA JEAN
Child development coordinator. **PERSONAL:** Born May 15, 1943, Little Rock, AR; married Earl Henry Simpson; children: Desiree, Jill, Earla. **EDUCATION:** Kennedy King Clge, AA 1969; Chicago State Univ, BS 1974; Governors State Univ, MA 1975; Fielding Inst, PhD 1981. **CAREER:** Golden Gate Cons, child family therapist 1981-; Malcolm X Coll Chicago IL, instr 1981-84; Dept of Army Savanna IL, educ spec 1984; BCDI Chicago affiliate, rec secr 1982-85; AUS Dept Defense Rock Island Arsenal, child devel serv coord; Fort Hood Army Base, child develop serv coord 1987-. **ORGANIZATIONS:** Handicap coord Dept Human Srv Chicago IL 1982-1983; spec needs mgr Ebony Mgmt Assc Chic 1980-82; deputy dir CEDA Chicago 1976-78; rec sec Black Child Dev Inst 1982-85; mem Natl Phi Delta Kappa Inc 1983; pres Golden Gate Bd of Dir 1971-81; mem Pi Lam Theda 1985-. **HONORS/ACHIEVEMENTS:** Biog study of Black Educ PhD Dissertation GGDCC Pub 1981; Srv Award Harris YWCA Chic 1974, Holy Cross Child Care Ctr 1984, Gldn Gate Day Care Ctr Chic 1984; Special Act Awd Rock Island Arsenal 1985; Exceptional Performance Awd Rock Island Arsenal 1986.

SIMPSON-WATSON, ORA LEE
Educator. **PERSONAL:** Born Jul 07, 1943, East Chicago, IN; children: Ronald Damon, Kendyl Joi. **EDUCATION:** Ball State Univ, BA 1965; Purdue Univ, MA 1969, PhD 1977. **CAREER:** Dallas Independent School District, dir learning 1977-80, dean of instruction 1981-83; Dallas County Comm College, div chair North Lake College 1983-. **ORGANIZATIONS:** School bd trustee Dallas Independent School Dist; mem Natl Assn Black School Educators; mem Alpha Kappa Alpha; mem Links, Texas Assn of School Boards; consultant Republic of Suri Name 1986, Child Care, Dallas 1986. **HONORS/ACHIEVEMENTS:** Hon mem Dallas Regional NABSE 1986. **BUSINESS ADDRESS:** Div Chair Humanities/Comm, North Lake College, 5001 N Mac Arthur Blvd, Irving, TX 75038.

SIMS, ADRIENNE
Educator. **PERSONAL:** Born Apr 01, 1952, Tacoma, WA; daughter of Alfred Sims and Mary Sims. **EDUCATION:** Univ of CA-Irvine, BA 1974; CA State Univ-Los Angeles, MS 1978; Pepperdine Univ, EdD 1987. **CAREER:** LA Comm Coll Dist, student/comm serv rep 1976-77; Long Beach Comm Coll Dist, student advisor coord 1978-81; Univ of Phoenix, dir of admissions 1981-84; Univ of Redlands, asst dean of admissions 1985-. **ORGANIZATIONS:** Mem Pacific Assoc of College Registrars/Admission Officers 1981-, Phi Delta Kappa 1983-, Natl Assoc of Coll Admission Counselors 1985-, mem Natl Assoc for Foreign Student Affairs 1985-, mem Third World Counselors Assoc 1985-, mem CA Coll Personnel Assoc 1985-; pres CA Counselors for Minority Success 1986; Natl Assn of Women Administrators. **HONORS/ACHIEVEMENTS:** Outstanding Young Women of Amer Awd 1985.

SIMS, BARBARA M.
Judge. **PERSONAL:** Born in Buffalo, NY; married William Sims; children: Frank William, Sue Cynthia. **EDUCATION:** State Univ Clge at Buffalo, BS; State Univ of NY at Buffalo Law Sch, JD. **CAREER:** City Ct of Buffalo, city ct judge 1977-; City of Buffalo Parking Violations Bur, hearing ofcr 1975-77; State Univ of NY Buffalo, asst to pres 1969-74; State Univ of NY Buffalo Law Sch, lectr; Erie Co DA Office, asst da 1964-68. **ORGANIZATIONS:** Mem Natl Bar Assc; Women's Polit Caucus; natl vice pres Natl Assc of Black Women Attys 1975-80; mem Erie Co Bar Assc; former pres Women Lawyers of W NY; numerous law assc; mem NAACP; mem bd dir NAACP; bd dir BC/BS of W NY; mem United Fund Natl Fnd for Birth Defects; mem Natl Assc of Negro Bus-Prof Women Buffalo Chpt. **HONORS/ACHIEVEMENTS:** Recipt Comm Srv Award 1968; Fight for Freedom Award 1968; Distg Achievement Award 1968; chosen One of 100 Black Women Chicago Conv 1972; del Natl Women's Year Conf Houston 1977; Distg Srv Award Grand United Order of Oddfellows 1978; listed Who's Who of Amer Women. **BUSINESS ADDRESS:** 50 Delaware Ave, Buffalo, NY 14202.

SIMS, BILLY (THE SILVER STREAK)
Professional athlete. **PERSONAL:** Born Sep 18, 1955, St Louis, MO; married Brenda; children: Billy Jr, Brent. **EDUCATION:** OK Univ, Deg Rec Therapy. **CAREER:** Detroit Lions, running back 1980-. **HONORS/ACHIEVEMENTS:** Heisman Trophy 1979; NFL Rookie-of-the Year 1980; Offensive MVP of the Lions 1980,82,83; All-Amer at OK 1978,79. **BUSINESS ADDRESS:** Running Back, Detroit Lions, 1200 Featherstone Rd, Box 4200, Pontiac, MI 48057.

SIMS, CARL W.
Newspaper editor. **PERSONAL:** Born Apr 29, 1941, Washington, DC; married Barbara

Lindsey; children: 1 son. **EDUCATION:** Howard Univ, 1960-62; Univ of MN, 1987-. **CAREER:** Peace Corps Sierra Leone, vol 1962-63; WA Post, reporter 1965-70; Boston Globe, copy editor 1970; Bay State Banner Boston, editor 1970-72; Newsweek, assoc editor 1973-74; Minneapolis Star & Tribune, editor 1974-. **ORGANIZATIONS:** Mem Capital Press Club 1966-69, MN & Press Club 1974-, Harvard Club of MN. **HONORS/ACHIEVEMENTS:** Nieman Fellow Harvard Univ 1972-73. **BUSINESS ADDRESS:** Editor, Minneapolis Star & Tribune, 425 Portland Ave, Minneapolis, MN 55488.

SIMS, CONSTANCE ARLETTE
Educational administrator. **PERSONAL:** Born Nov 26, 1940, Detroit, MI; married Dr Joseph William Sims; children: Andre-Marc, Nicole Danielle. **EDUCATION:** MI State Univ, BA 1962; Univ of MI Flint, MA 1970; Nova Univ, EdD 1983. **CAREER:** Flint Primary School, teacher 1962-66, title I reading spec 1966-68; MI Coord of Early Childhood Genesee Comm Coll, project dir 1968-70, coord 1970-72; Univ of MI, coord of student teaching 1971-75; Unified School Dist Oakland CA, reading resource teacher 1975-76, tech asst; Park Forest School Dist 163, title vii spec 1976-77; Dogwood Elementary School, principal 1977-82; Lakewood School, elem sch principal 1982-84; Pine Bush Schls, dir of continuing educ 1984-85; Netherwood Elem School, principal 1985-. **ORGANIZATIONS:** Mem IL Principal's Assoc 1977-84, Phi Delta Kappa 1983-; Urban League, NAACP, Second Baptist Church ASCD 1985-, Mid-Hudson Reading Assoc 1986-. **BUSINESS ADDRESS:** Principal, Netherwood Elementary School, Netherwood Rd, Hyde Park, NY 12538.

SIMS, EDITH R.
Educator. **PERSONAL:** Born Dec 24, 1932, Marion, LA; married Samuel C Davis; children: Cynthia Laverne, William, Jr. **EDUCATION:** AM&N Coll, BS (cum laude) 1955; Tuskegee Inst, MS 1960; Univ Buffalo, post grad study 1960-61. **CAREER:** Merrill HS, teacher 1955-59; Englewood HS, 1961-66, counselor 1966-68; Fenger HS, 1968-69, Calumet HS, asst prin, acting prin 1969-71; Caldwell & McDowell Schools, prin 1971-82; Corliss HS, prin 1982-. **ORGANIZATIONS:** Mem Chicago Bd Educ, SE Comm Org, IL Prin Assn; Chicago Prin Assn; Ella Flagg Young Chap Natl Alliance of Black Sch Edns; Natl Council of Admin Women in Educ; Delta Sigma Theta Sor; Crerar Presb Ch; Chicago Urban League; mem Beta Kappa Chi Sci Frat. **HONORS/ACHIEVEMENTS:** Univ of AR Alumni Assn at Pine Bluff "Miss Alumni" 1955; Alpha Kappa Mu Natl Honor Soc; listed in Who's Who Among Students in Amer Colls & Univs 1955; Who's Who of Amer Women 10th ed; Roseland Comm Grit Awd 1986; Outstanding Chicago Principal Awd Dist 33 1986; Disting Alumni Awd Univ of AR Pine Bluff 1987. **BUSINESS ADDRESS:** Principal, Corliss High School, 821 E 103rd St, Chicago, IL 60628.

SIMS, EDWARD HACKNEY
Physician/surgeon. **PERSONAL:** Born Sep 05, 1944, Atlanta, GA; children: Jessica Carolyn. **EDUCATION:** Morris Brown Coll Atlanta, BS 1965; Meharry Medical Coll, MD 1972. **CAREER:** King/Drew Medical Ctr, chief of general surgery 1983-87. **MILITARY SERVICE:** USAF E-4 3 yrs. **BUSINESS ADDRESS:** Chief of General Surgery, King/Drew Medical Ctr, 3611 E Century Blvd #8, Lynwood, CA 90262.

SIMS, GENEVIEVE CONSTANCE
Lawyer. **PERSONAL:** Born Nov 04, 1947, Baltimore, MD; daughter of Joe Sims and Fannie Sims. **EDUCATION:** North Carolina State Univ, BA, 1969; Univ of Southern California, MPA, 1976;North Carolina Central Univ, JD, 1986. **CAREER:** Lawyer, Law Offices of Genevieve C. Sims, 1987-; Merit Sys Protection Bd, special asst, 1979-81; US Civil Serv Commn, special asst commr, 1977-78; Office of Mgmt & Budget Exec Office Pres, mgmt analyst, 1976-77; US Civil Serv Commn, personnel mgmt spec, 1972-76; Office of State Personnel, North Carolina State Govt, econ analyst 1969-72; North Carolina State Univ, Raleigh, NC, asst professor, 1982-; North Carolina Central Univ, Durham, NC, visiting instr, 1982-89. **ORGANIZATIONS:** Chairperson, bd of dir, Shelley School; bd of dir, North Carolina Assn Black Lawyers; North Carolina Academy of Trial Lawyers, North Carolina Bar Assn; bd of dir, United Black Fund of Washington, 1976-81. **HONORS/ACHIEVEMENTS:** Award, North Carolina Special Olympics, 1982. **BUSINESS ADDRESS:** 3203 Woman's Club Dr, Suite 229, Raleigh, NC 27612.

SIMS, HAROLD RUDOLPH
President sound radio. **PERSONAL:** Born Jul 25, 1935, Memphis, TN; married Lana Joyce Taylor; children: Douglass D, Kimberly J. **EDUCATION:** Southern Univ, BR, LA, BA 1957; Univ of Poona, Poona, India, certf 1956; Geo Washington Univ, MS 1967; John Hopkins Univ, Baltimore, Grad Study 1961-62. **CAREER:** Ofc Econ Oppor Exec Ofc Pres White House, exec sec 1967-69; Johnson & Johnson, vice pres 1972-79; Sims & Assoc/Sims Intl, pres 1979-; Soung Radio WNJR, chmn/pres 1983-85; NJ Jr Commn Office of Governor, exec dir 1985-86; Ebony Magazine, sr account exec 1986-. **ORGANIZATIONS:** Ores Sims-Sutton Indstrl Dev Group 1982-; natl advsry brd Natl Science Fdn 1977-82; exec v pres Gibson-Wonder Film Co/Jos P Gibson Fdn 1983-; comsnr NJ Milk Jr Commerative Comsnr 1984-; brd dir Martin Luther King Jr Ctr 1972-; intl brd advsr African-Amer Inst 1976-; advsry brd (Soc) Princeton Univ 1971-82. **HONORS/ACHIEVEMENTS:** Spcl citation Martin L King Jr Cntr for NVSC, Atlanta 1981; spcl citation/comm Congrsnl Black Caucus Inc (DC) 1973; spcl citation Friends of Harold R Sims, Waldorf Astoria 1972; spcl citation/Resolution Natl Urban Bd of Dir 1971; numerous articles, Artistic Acmplshmnts, Awards, Citations, etc. **MILITARY SERVICE:** AUS maj 1957-67; Bronze Star, Commendation Medal (2), Purple Heart Vietnam Campaign, Army Pard Badge, Joint Staff Champaign, Cert of Achvmnt 1957-67. **HOME ADDRESS:** 1274 Carlisle Rd, New Brunswick, NJ 08902. **BUSINESS ADDRESS:** President, Sims & Assoc, 1700 Union Ave, Union, NJ 07083.

SIMS, JOHN LEONARD
Computer company executive. **PERSONAL:** Born Jul 01, 1934, Wilmington, DE; son of Thomas A Sims and Ella Gibbs Sims; married Shirley (Horton) Sims, Jun 14, 1962; children: John Jr, Kevin, Joe. **EDUCATION:** Delaware State Coll, Dover DE, BS, 1962; Ohio State Univ, Columbus OH, Graduate Work; Columbia Univ, New York NY, Mgmt Training Courses. **CAREER:** E I Du Pont de Nemours Co Inc, mgmt positions, chemist; Champion Intl Corp, mgmt positions, govt relations; Digital Equipment Corp, Maynard MA, corp mgr EEO/AA, 1974-75, dir of manf personnel, 1975-81, corporate staff mgr, 1981-84, vice pres personnel, 1984-87, vice pres strategic resources, 1987-. **ORGANIZATIONS:** Mem, Natl NAACP, The Boston Private Industry Council, Guardsmen of Boston, Northeast Human Resources Assn, Exec Leaderhsip Council; bd of trustees, The Natl Urban League; bd of dir, Mainstream; SBI Roundtable at Florida A&M; vice chmn, Boston Bank of Commerce, 1983-; bd of dir, AB&W Manufacturing Co, 1983-; bd of governors of ASTD, 1987-; chmn, Freedom House, Project Reach,1987-; bd of dir, Cambridge Medical Technology, 1988-. **HONORS/ACHIEVEMENTS:** Top 25 Most Powerful Black Managers, Black Enterprise Magazine, 1988; Award for Service, Freedom House; Award for Service, Alpha; Award for Contributing, Natl Urban League, 1988; Award for Achievements, Several Colleges and Minority Organizations. **MILITARY SERVICE:** US Army Corps, 1955-57. **BUSINESS ADDRESS:** Vice President, Strategic Resources, Digital Equipment Corporation, 146 Main St, ML012-1/A51, Maynard, MA 01754.

SIMS, JOHN THOMAS
Educational admin. **PERSONAL:** Born Nov 29, 1956, New York, NY. **EDUCATION:** Wagner College, BS 1979; Brooklyn College, MA 1982. **CAREER:** Hospital for Joint Diseases, teacher's Aid 1980-81; Ottille Home for Children, childcare worker 1981-82; Adelphi Institute, financial aid counselor 1983-84, academic counselor 1984-. **ORGANIZATIONS:** Founder Sigma Phi Rho 1978; tutor Black Concern-Heritage House 1978-79; volunteer coord March of Dimes 1981; fundraising co-chairman Sickle Cell Anemia Foundation 1984; natl pres Sigma Phi Rho 1981-85; asst chairman New York Region Coalition of Fraternities and Sororities 1984-85; advisor to the president Sigma Phi Rho 1985. **HONORS/ACHIEVEMENTS:** New York City Mayor's Scholarship 1978; Outstanding Leadership Award Sigma Phi Rho 1983; Outstanding Young Men of America 1984; Distinguished Volunteer ServiceMarch of Dimes Birth Defect Foundation Greater New York Chapter 1984. **MILITARY SERVICE:** USMC corporal 2 yrs. **HOME ADDRESS:** 411 Vanderbilt Ave Apt 24, Staten Island, NY 10304.

SIMS, JOSEPH WILLIAM
Educational administrator. **PERSONAL:** Born Feb 14, 1937, Detroit, MI; married Constance A Williams; children: Nicole, Andre. **EDUCATION:** MI State Univ, BA 1961, MA 1962; Univ of MI, PhD 1972. **CAREER:** Prairie State Coll Chicago Heights IL, vice pres student serv 1976-83; Oakland & Berkeley School Dist CA, Rockefeller intern 1975-76; Flint Community School Flint MI, asst principal/deputy principal/principal 1968-75; Southwestern High School Flint MI, French teacher 1967-68; AC Spark Plug Flint MI, supvr 1965-67; Southwestern High School, French & Spanish teacher 1962-65. **ORGANIZATIONS:** Mem Amer Assn for Higher Educ; mem Natl Assn of Student Personnel Admin; mem Alliance of Black School Educ; mem IL Council Community Coll Admin; mem IL Coll Personnel Assn Natl Defense Educ Act Grant US Govt 1968; Mott Found Grant Charles S Mott Found Flint MI 1970-71. **HONORS/ACHIEVEMENTS:** Superintendency Training Grant Rockefeller Found NY 1975-76; Distinguished Serv Award City of Detroit 1975. **MILITARY SERVICE:** USAF s/sgt 1954-58.

SIMS, LAURA MACK
Owner. **PERSONAL:** Born Aug 17, 1914, Charleston County, SC; married William Sims; children: Clarence, Lula ?, Wade, Elizabeth Staten, Sarah Brown. **EDUCATION:** Bethune-Cookman Clge, PhD; Woods-Morgan Barber & Beauty Cult Clge, grad; Poro Beauty Clge; Miriam Charage Sch of Beauty Cult Paris. **CAREER:** House of Beauty #1 & #2, owner & oper; The Ebony Beauty School & Buchanan Barb Coll, fdr oper; elem grade teacher; Cosmet, teacher. **ORGANIZATIONS:** Past natl pres United Beauty Sch Owners & Tchrs Assc; Interest Counc St Bd of Cosmet Exam; past 1st vice pres SC Cosmet Assc; mem Cosmet Art Bd; mem Const Sch Bd Dist; mem YMCA; Bus & Prof Club of Charleston; Natl Coun of Negro Women Club; past reg dir SE Reg Alpha Chi Pi Omega Sor; orgnr Rho Alpha Chap Alpha Chi Pi Omega Sor; past Basileus Rho Alpha Chpt; orgnr Teenage Love-In Club Dedic. **HONORS/ACHIEVEMENTS:** Woman's Award Bethune-Cookman Clge; merit award SC Vocat Dept of Educ; Fed Women & Girl's Club Award; listed Who's Who Among Amer Educ; one of Ten Most Trav Tchrs SC Award; Tchr of Year Burke HS 1967.

SIMS, LOWERY STOKES
Curator. **PERSONAL:** Born Feb 13, 1949, Washington, DC. **EDUCATION:** Queens Coll, BA 1970; Johns Hopkins Univ, MA 1972. **CAREER:** Metro Museum of Art, asst museum educ 1972-75; Queens Coll Dept Art, adjunct instructor 1973-76; Sch Visual Arts, instructor 1975-76, 1981-86; Metro Museum of Art, assoc curator. **ORGANIZATIONS:** Mem grants comm, Metro Museum Art, 1975-77; museum aid panel, NY State Council on Arts, 1977-79; visual arts panel, Dept of Cultural Affairs of City of NY, 1977; mem, Art Table, College Art Assn 1983-, Assn of Art Critics, Amer Sect Intl Art Critics Assn 1980-, Natl Conf of Artists; visual arts panel, New York State Council on Arts 1984-86; bd mem, project commitee, Public Art Fund. **HONORS/ACHIEVEMENTS:** Fellowship for Black Dr Students, Ford Found, 1970-72; Employee Travel Grant, Metro Museum Art, 1973; numerous publications; Amer Artists & Exhibition Catalogs; Hon Doctor of Humane Letters, Maryland Inst Coll of Art, 1988. **BUSINESS ADDRESS:** Associate Curator, Metro Museum of Art, Dept of 20th Century Art, New York, NY 10028.

SIMS, LYDIA THERESA
Retired city administrator. **PERSONAL:** Born Nov 18, 1920, Pennsgrove, NJ; daughter of Clifton Williams (deceased) and Helen Hoskins Williams (deceased); married James M Sims, Sr; children: James M Jr, Ronald C, Donald C. **EDUCATION:** NY Business Sch, attended 1941; WA State Univ, attended 1971; E WA State Coll, attended 1974-77. **CAREER:** YWCA/Spokesman Review Newspaper, stenographer/sec 1951-66; Eastside Neighborhood Ctr, dep dir 1968-70; Comm Action Council, manpower training specialist/personnel 1970-73; City of Spokane, affirmative action dir 1975-. **ORGANIZATIONS:** Pres Spokane Br NAACP 1976-80; mem OIC Bd of Dirs 1978-80; pres NAACP Northwest Area Conf of Branches 1980-82; mem WA State Adv Com US Commn on Civil Rights 1978-84; mem League of Women Voters 1970-; mem Amer Assn of Affirmative Action 1978-; precinct comm mem Spokane Co Central Com 1980-; mem NW Women's Law Ctr 1980-; Amer Mgmt Assn 1983-; Amer Soc for Personnel Directors 1980-; YWCA Spokane Bd of Dir vice pres chrp Mutual World Serv Comm 1981-88; vice chrpsn Interstate Task Force on Human Relations 1979-; mem Women in Municipal Govt 1982-88; mem Citizen Adv Comm Pinelodge Correctional Ctr 1980-86; mem Blacks in Govt; Black elected and appointed officials Treasurer Amer Assn of Affirmative Action Region X 1985-present Life member NAACP Life member Lincoln Univ PA Women's Auxiliary Chairp task force on Minority aged, Eastern WA Area Agency on Aging; member Greater Spokane Women's Commission 1986-87; Magnuson Democratic Club 1986-; Spokane Fall AARP Chpt 1989; mem Spokane Chpt United Nations 1978-; WA State Commissioner, Martin Luther King Celebration 1985-; exec committee Spokane Branch NAACP 1982-. **HONORS/ACHIEVEMENTS:** First black hired Spokesman Review Newspaper 1964; first black personnel officer Spokane Comm Ac-

tion Council 1972; first female pres NAACP NW Conf of Branches 1980; first female pres Spokane NAACP 1976; Human Relations Awd Fairchild AFB 1977; 1983 NAACP Awd NW Area Conf of Branches; rsch & devel dir "Brief History Black Americans in Spokane Co 1878-1978" 1979; Awd of Appreciation Kiwanis; First Black Female Adminstr City of Spokane 1979; Governing Board East Central Comm Center Award of Appreciation 1979-81; 1982 Spokane Co Black Students Awd of Appreciation; 1980 Awd of Appreciation Black Students Lewis & Clark HS; Amer Assoc for Affirmative Action Award for Dedication 1985; Outstanding Leadership Award in Government and Politics YWCA 1986; Cert of Appreciation, Eastern WA Univ 1986; BSO Certificate of Appreciation, City Univ 1987. **HOME ADDRESS:** E 1218 5th Ave, Spokane, WA 99202.

SIMS, MICHAEL S.
Business executive. **PERSONAL:** Born May 29, 1943, Muncie, IN; married Marianna Poole; children: Michael S. **EDUCATION:** IN U, BS (math/economics) 1965; Ball State U, MBA (mgmt) 1967; Purdue U, 1967-68; George Washington U, 1969-71;Univ of Pitts, 1972. **CAREER:** Johnson Products Co & Inc, exec vp; Westinghouse Electric Corp, various positions 1965-74. **ORGANIZATIONS:** Deacon Chicago United; mem Chicago StateUniv Bus Adv Counc; mem The NY Acad of Scis; mem Opera PUSH; mem Nat MBA Assn; mem Intl Toastmasters; mem Nat Cosmetics, Toiletry, Fragrance Assn. **HONORS/ACHIEVEMENTS:** Ten outstndg yng people of Chicago award 1976; achvmnt award IN Black Expo 1977; key to the cty of Indianapolis 1977.

SIMS, NAOMI R.
Author, business executive. **PERSONAL:** Born Mar 30, 1949, Oxford, MS; married Michael Alistair Findlay. **EDUCATION:** Fashion Inst Tech NY; NYU, 1967. **CAREER:** Fashion Model, 1967-73; Fashion & Beauty, freelance writer, many articles; Naomi Sims Collection, owner founder bd chmn chief exec. **ORGANIZATIONS:** Mem, bd dirs Northside Center Child Devel Harlem; NAACP; mem, Womens' Firm Inc 1977; panel mem lecturer; Sickle Cell Anemia Dr; NY St Drug Rehabilitation Program; Play Schools Assn NY. **HONORS/ACHIEVEMENTS:** Model of the Year Award, 1969, 1970; Modeling Hall of Fame Intl Mnqns 1977; Intl Best Dressed List 1971-73, 1976, 1977; Women of the Country Intl Mnqns 1977; proclaimed Sept 20 Naomi Sims Day Gov Walker, IL 1973; Women of Achievement Lds Home Jour 1970; Women of Achievement Amer Cancer Soc 1972; Ebony Success Library; Top Hat Award New Pitts Courier 1974; Key to City Cleveland 1971; NY City Bd Educ Award 1970; devel new fiber for wigs 1973-. **BUSINESS ADDRESS:** Chairman, Naomi Sims Beauty Products Ltd, 435 W 57th St, New York, NY 10019.

SIMS, PAUL A.
Educational administrator. **PERSONAL:** Born Nov 07, 1922, Parsons, KS; married Naomi. **EDUCATION:** Univ of KS, BA 1948; Jarvis Christian Coll, HHD 1976; Brite Div Sch TX Christian U, Grad Study; WilberforceUniv OH;Univ of CA Santa Barbara;Univ of Chgo;Univ of Florence Italy. **CAREER:** Jarvis Christian Coll, asst to Pres 1979-; Jarvis Christian Coll, coord of institutional advancement 1976-79; Brite Div School TCU, adj instr 1973-77; Comm Christian Church, exec min 1971-77; TX Christian Univ, instr evening coll 1971-72; Greater Ft Worth & Tarrant Co Comm Action Agency, dep dir & dir of Planning 1966-71; TX Assn of Christian Churches, dir negro work 1956-66; TX Christian Missionary Conv, exec sec 1956-66; Dallas, Topeka, Atchison & KS City, pastorates 1950-56; Westvaco Chemical Co Lawrence KS, chief chem oper, purchasing agent 1948-48. **ORGANIZATIONS:** Ofcr dir trst Jarvis Christian Coll; Intl Conv of Christian Chs; Nat Christian Educators Flwshp; Nat Conv of Christian Chs; Julliete Folwer Homes; fdr & pres Ft Worth Minority Bus & Comm Ldrs Counc; ofcr bd com mem Ft Worth Literacy Counc; Child Welfare Adv Bd; Travelers Aid Bd; Comm Counc; Town Hall Comm Plng & Devel Com; Jr Coll Devel Com; Mayor's Comm Rela Com; Comm Action Prog Com; Ft Worth Affil So Christian Ldrshp Conf; NAACP; Plnd Prnthd Adv Com; Interdenom Ministerial Alli; Youth Oppor Cntr Bd; Nat Conf of Christian & Jews; United Fund Campaign Area Ldr; FtWorth Sch Bd Minoirty Adv Counc; Tarrent Co Commn for the Hearing Impaired; Tarrant Co Youth Servs Bur; Fed Correctional Adv; Christian Ch in TX; Ft Worth Bd of Adjust; Ft Worth Trans Adv Com; Compreh Alch Prog Bd of Mgrs; Tarrant Co Heart Fund Assn; trst The Sch of Theol for the Laitry Dallas; mem Comm Christian Ch; mem Kiwanis; mem Kappa Alpha Psi Frat; mem YMCA; mem CASC. **HONORS/ACHIEVEMENTS:** Paul Sims Day proclaimed Mayors of Lawrence KS & Ft Worth; bronze star medal in combat WWII 92nd Inf Div Europe; recip Numerous Civic & Outstndg Citzn Awards. **MILITARY SERVICE:** AUS operations ofcr.

SIMS, PETE, JR.
Business executive. **PERSONAL:** Born May 11, 1924, El Dorado, AR; widowed. **EDUCATION:** Atlnt Coll of Mrtry Sci, 1950. **CAREER:** Sims Mrtrty Inc, pres; El Dorado Hsng Athrty, pres 1970-; NFDMA AR St Fnrl Dirs, past pres dist gov; Sims-Shaw Burial Ins Assn, sec; Sims Entrprs, pres 1973-; AR Fun Dirs & Mrtcns Assn, pres 1974. **ORGANIZATIONS:** Mem Nat Mrtcns & Fun Dirs Assn 1969-75; op supvr El Dorado Cmtry 1973-74; exec bd mem De Soto Boy Scts Cncl 1971-; mem 1st Bapt Ch; mem El Dorado C of C 1964; mem City Hlth Plng Cncl 1973-75; mem NAACP 1960-; mem Epsln Nu Delta Mrtry Frat 1969-; chmn Fin & Bdgt Com. **HONORS/ACHIEVEMENTS:** Who's Who in AR 1974. **MILITARY SERVICE:** AUS m/Sgt WW II. **BUSINESS ADDRESS:** Sims Mortuary, PO Box 967, El Dorado, AR 71730.

SIMS, PHILLIP C.
Business executive. **PERSONAL:** Born Dec 24, 1932, Muncie, IN; married Chalonie Livingston; children: Dante', Blake. **EDUCATION:** Wayne State U, BS 1961; Detroit Coll of Law, 1967-68;Univ of MI & MI State, postgrad; US Dept of Commerce, export mgmt cert. **CAREER:** OSA Intl Inc, pres; Phillip Sims Assoc, 1965-77; Sch of Labor & Indus Relat, Wayne State U,Univ of MI, Eastern MI U, joint faculties 1965-68. **ORGANIZATIONS:** Chmn Wayne Co Small & Min Bus Advis Com 1978-86; chmn Wayne Co Overall Econ Devel Comm's Econ Dev Sub Com; mem Detroit Water & Sewerage Dept; Citz's Advis Com; mem exec com & full com MI House of Rep House Agr Com; mem Nat Commercial & Construction Panel Am Arbitration Assn 1977-80; elected del White House Conference On Small Bus 1980; mem Intl Assn for the Advancement of Appropriate Tech for Devel Countries Inc; adv Detroit Cty Counc's Intl Trade Com; full fledged chf (Uzo Eghelu) & mem of tribal counc Awka Etiti Anambra State Nigeria; mem MI Dist Export Council via Appointmentof US Sec of Commerce; chmn Jefferson-Chalmers Citizens Dist Council; pres Jefferson-Chalmers Non Profit Housing Corp; bd dir Consortium for Belizian Central Amer Develop. **HONORS/ACHIEVEMENTS:** Numerous awards & citations locally nationally & internat; Most Notable Am 1976-77; Intl Biography Dictionary London Eng; guest lectr on Am Pub Policy & Doing Bus in Africa Detroit Houston Benton Harbor MI Dearborn MI & TheUniv of Windsor Ontario Canada. **MILITARY SERVICE:** USAF sr acro-med spec, flight crew mem 1952-56.

SIMS, RIPLEY SINGLETON
Educator. **PERSONAL:** Born Jul 05, 1907, Mobile, AL; married Dorothy Revalion. **EDUCATION:** Talladega Clge, AB 1931; Northwestern Univ, MA 1939; Univ of Chicago, postgrad 1940-42. **CAREER:** Teacher math 1931-32; private hs prin 1932-38; Univ of Chicago, research asst 1940-42; USAAF, math-electricity instr 1942-46; USAF Inst, educ spec 1946-54, head educ div 1954-68; assoc deputy dir for acad prog 1968-; Educational Consultant. **ORGANIZATIONS:** Mem Amer Assc Higher Educ; Adult Educ Assc; Amer Educ Research Assc. **HONORS/ACHIEVEMENTS:** Contrb articles to prof jours; author "An Inquiry into Correspondence Educating Processes"; Univ Extension Assoc Awd for Achievement. **MILITARY SERVICE:** USAAF civilian instructor 1942-46.

SIMS, THEOPHLOUS ARON, SR.
Pharmacist. **PERSONAL:** Born Mar 17, 1939, Jefferson, TX; married Nancy Jayne Wattley; children: Theophlous Jr, Shannon D'Lynne, Stephanie Racquel. **EDUCATION:** TX Southern Univ, BS Pharm 1961. **ORGANIZATIONS:** Mem Natl Assoc of Retail Druggist; life mem Kappa Alpha Psi Frat; mem A Ph A 1983; bd mem TX Enterprise Found 1984; advisory comm TX Girls Choir 1984, Natl Inst of Health (Sickle Cell) 1984-. **HONORS/ACHIEVEMENTS:** Black Achievers Awd Ft Worth/Dallas 1980; Outstanding Business Awd Fannie Brooks/Heath Club 1984; TSU Shining Star TSU Houston TX 1985; Quest for Success Awd Dallas TX 1985. **HOME ADDRESS:** 4421 Kingsdale Dr, Fort Worth, TX 76119. **BUSINESS ADDRESS:** School Board Member, Secretary, Fort Worth Isd 4, 944 E Berry St, Fort Worth, TX 76110.

SIMS, WILLIAM
Attorney, judge, businessman. **PERSONAL:** Born May 28, 1922, Hughes, AR; son of John Sims and Sephronia Sims; married Barbara Merriweather; children: Sue Cynthia, Frank William. **EDUCATION:** Univ of Buffalo BA 1947; Univ of Buffalo, LLB 1950; Suny at Buffalo, JD 1966. **CAREER:** Law Office Buffalo, sole proprietor 1976-; Robinson Sims Gibson & Green, law partner 1971; Sims & Purks, law partner 1968; Buffalo Cty Ct, assoc judge 1966; Sims & Sims Law Firm, partner 1956; Law Office, sole proprietor 1951. **ORGANIZATIONS:** Pres Buffalo Chap NAACP 1953; ofcr dir Ellicott Lanes Inc 1959-; dir vice pres Heart Assn of Western NY 1967-73; natl atty Grand United Order of Oddfellows 1974-; dir Nghbrhd House Assn 1975-; mil judge USMC Reserve. **HONORS/ACHIEVEMENTS:** Recip 3 battle stars for overseas duty ETO USMC 1942-45; merit award for comm serv P Ballantine & Sons 1966; founding mem Judicial Counc NBA 1971; regional dir NBA 1973; dir at Large NBA 1972 & 74. **MILITARY SERVICE:** US Army (SGT) 1942-45, 1973-80 major USMCR, military judge. **BUSINESS ADDRESS:** 280 Humbolt Parkway, Buffalo, NY 14214.

SIMS, WILLIAM E.
Educator, administrator. **PERSONAL:** Born Mar 28, 1921, Chickasha, OK; married Muriel. **EDUCATION:** Lincoln Univ MO, AB 1949; CO State Clge, MA 1952, DEd 1963; KS Univ, addt study. **CAREER:** Langston Univ OK, pres 1970-, acting pres 1969-70, dean of acad affairs 1965-69, chmn dept of music 1963; Tulsa OK, prof of music & band dir 1953-63, teacher public school 1945-53. **ORGANIZATIONS:** Mem Adult Educ Assc; Kappa Delta Pi; Phi Delta Kappa; mem OK Humanities Task Force. **MILITARY SERVICE:** USN musician 2nd class 1942-46. **BUSINESS ADDRESS:** Langston Univ, Langston, OK 73050.

SINCLAIR, CLAYTON, JR.
Attorney. **PERSONAL:** Born Jul 04, 1933, Wadesboro, NC; married Jeanette B. **EDUCATION:** Univ ME, BA 1955; Howard Univ Law Sch, LLB 1960. **CAREER:** Sinclair & Dixon, sr partner 1976-; Patterson Parks & Franklin Atlanta, atty 1971-76; Goodis, Greenfield & Mann Phila, atty 1970-71; Scott Paper Co, 1969-70; NY State Banking Dept NYC, asst coun 1968-69; O'Donald & Schwartz NYC, atty 1960-68. **ORGANIZATIONS:** Mem Bar States NY, PA, GA; US Fed Dist Ct; So & Eastern Dist NY; US Sup Ct; Amer Bar Assc; Natl Bar Assc; Atlanta Bar Assc; GA Trial Lawyers Assc. **BUSINESS ADDRESS:** Sinclair & Dixon Ste 301, 100 Peachtree St, Atlanta, GA 30303.

SINDLER, MICHAEL H.
Executive director. **PERSONAL:** Born May 15, 1943, District of Columbia; married Louise Bates. **EDUCATION:** Georgetown Sch Foreign Srv, BS 1965; Georgetown Law Sch, JD 1968; further study. **CAREER:** DC Legislation & Opinions Div, asst corp counsel 1969-73; Motor Vehicles DC, asst dir 1973-74, spl asst to dir 1974-. **ORGANIZATIONS:** Mem numerous offices, coms & Washington Bar Assc; DC Bar Assc; Fed Bar Assc; mem DC Municipal Officers Club 1973-. **HONORS/ACHIEVEMENTS:** Amer Jurisprudence Award. **BUSINESS ADDRESS:** 301 C St NW, Washington, DC 20001.

SINDOS, LOUISE KING
Educator. **PERSONAL:** Born Jan 28, 1930, Franklinton, NC; married Dr Henry Sindos; children: Anthony, Maria, Steven, Catherine. **EDUCATION:** AB 1950; MSW 1952; Columbia Univ, PhD candidate. **CAREER:** Westchester Baccalaureate Social Work Consortium, prof; White Plains Child Day Care Assoc, social serv dir; Columbia Univ School of Social Work, asst prof; EDU-CAGE, founder dir. **ORGANIZATIONS:** Mem Assc of Black Social Workers; fellow Amer Orthopsychiatric Assc; mem Natl Assc of Social Workers; mem Delta Sigma Theta; Dist Ldr Dem Party New Rochelle. **BUSINESS ADDRESS:** Mercy College, 555 Broadway, Dobbs Ferry, NY 10522.

SINGH, RAJENDRA P.
Educator. **PERSONAL:** Born May 06, 1934, Mnagar; married Sneh P; children: Ram C, David A. **EDUCATION:** Agra Univ, BScI 1952; King George's Dental Coll & Hosp, BDS 1964; Guggenehim Dental Ctr, Cert Clinical Dentistry 1966; Univ of Pittsburgh, Grad Studies in Endodontics 1975. **CAREER:** King George's Dental Hosp, house surgeon 1964-65; Murry & Leonie Dental Clinic, fellow of the dental staff 1965-66; Howard Univ Coll of Dentistry, instr 1969-77, asst prof 1977-. **ORGANIZATIONS:** Rsch assoc in oral surgery NJ Coll of Dentistry 1966-69; mem Amer Dental Assoc 1970-, Amer Assoc of Endodontists 1975-; lecturer Adv in Sci 1978-79, Black Brotherhood Week Key Jr High 1983; nom judge Montgomery County Debating Contest 1985; mem, Washington DC Dental Society 1977;

mem, Edward C Penne Endodontic Club 1978; official delegate, Citizen Ambassador Program-People to People International (visited People's Republic of China). **HONORS/ACHIEVEMENTS:** Outstanding Clinical Teacher Student's Council Coll of Dentistry 1973-74; Louise C Ball Fellowship Awd Coll of Dentists 1974-77; Theses, "Evaluation of Optimal Site Maxi Teeth" Library of Congress 1977; article "Endodontic Considerations of Tricanaled Mand Premolar" Jr of Maryland Dental Assoc 1987; Outstanding Faculty Award, Student Council of Dentistry 1973, 1989. **HOME ADDRESS:** 8822 Sleppy Hollow Ln, Potomac, MD 20854.

SINGLETARY, INEZ M.
Government administrator. **PERSONAL:** Born in New York, NY; married Samuel P Singletary; children: Shauna K Singletary Alami, Samuel P III. **EDUCATION:** Hunter Clge, BA, MA. **CAREER:** PS 99 Bronx, school teacher 1947-64; Ferris Ave Neighborhood Center, exec dir 1965-68; White Plains Comm Action Prog Inc, exec dir 1968-69; Day Care Council Westchester Inc, exec dir 1969-81; West County Dept Comm Mental Health, dir comm rel. **ORGANIZATIONS:** Prof Grad Schl of Educ Clge of New Rochelle; secr Day Care Council of Westchester Inc; co fndr past pres NY St Child Care Coord Cncl Inc; bd mem Oak Lanes Child Care Ctr Inc; The Children's Place at the Plaza Albany NY; chrpsn Westchester Women's Council; Task Force on Worship; mem of Admin Bd Platteville United Meth Church. **HONORS/ACHIEVEMENTS:** Outstanding Srv to Humanity Church of our Savior United Meth Church Yonkers NY 1971; invaluable srv to comm Yonkers Child Care Assc Yonkers NY 1975; Womanof the Year Cty of Westchester 1979; Sojourner Truth Award Natl Assn of Negro Bus and Prof Women Inc West Cty Club 1981. **BUSINESS ADDRESS:** Dir of Community Relations, West Cty Dept Comm Mental, 112 E Post Rd, White Plains, NY 10601.

SINGLETARY, MIKE
Professional athlete. **PERSONAL:** Born Oct 09, 1958, Houston, TX; married Kim; children: Kristen Nicole. **EDUCATION:** Baylor Univ, BA 1981. **CAREER:** Chicago Bears, middle linebacker 1981-. **ORGANIZATIONS:** Involved in Fellowship of Christian Athletes; Brian Piccolo Cancer Rsch; Sports TEams Organized for Prevention of Drug Abuse. **HONORS/ACHIEVEMENTS:** SWC Player of Year in 1979,80; set school record with 232 tackles in 1978; played in Hula and Japan Bowls; Finalist 1980 Lombardi Trophy voting; First-team allNFL choice by Sporting News PFW Football Digest AP, NEA, PFWA; UPI all NFC; played in second straight Pro Bowl as starter; Piccolo Award Winner as rookie; Consensus SWC "Player of the Yr" 1979-80 at Baylor; AP & UPI Defensive Player of the Year 1985; served as defensive captain and isgnal-caller for 3 straight years;Mayor Daley Awd for Community Serv 1985 Red Cloud Banquet; mem NFL Pro Bowl teams 1986,87. **BUSINESS ADDRESS:** Chicago Bears, 55 E Jackson, Ste 1200, Chicago, IL 60604.

SINGLETARY, REGGIE CALVIN
Professional athlete. **PERSONAL:** Born May 03, 1962, Tampa, FL; married Delice. **EDUCATION:** Kansas State. **CAREER:** Oakalnd Invaders, nose tackle 1984-. **HONORS/ACHIEVEMENTS:** Named All-Big 8 three times; enjoys fishing & boating.

SINGLETON, BENJAMIN, SR.
Duputy sheriff. **PERSONAL:** Born Dec 17, 1943, Summerville, SC; son of Clement Addison Singleton Sr and Catherine Fludd; married Dorothy Abraham, May 02, 1964; children: Benjamin Jr. **EDUCATION:** Vocational Training, Columbia SC, Certificate, 1977-81; Atlanta Univ Criminal Justice Institute, Miami FL, Certificate, 1985. **CAREER:** Dorchester County Sheriff's Dept, St George SC, lieutenant, deputy sheriff, 1971-; Knightsville Dry Cleaners, Summerville SC, owner, 1986-. **ORGANIZATIONS:** Life mem, Cannan United Methodist Church, United Methodist Mens Club; mem, New Eden Lodge #32, 1984-, NAACP, 1985-, The Upper Dorchester Civic Club, 1985-; vice pres, Palmetto State Law Enforcement Office Assn, 1985-87, pres, 1987-89; mem, The First Congressional Dist Black Caucus, 1986-; bd mem, South Carolina Attorney General Advisory Bd for State Grand Jury, 1988-92, Univ of South Carolina Police Census, 1988-92. **HONORS/ACHIEVEMENTS:** Sponsor, Annual Senior Citizens Dinner for the Tri-County; Co-Sponsor, Dixie League Baseball Team for the Community, 1967-; Co-Founder, The Berkeley-Dorchester Chapter of PSLEOA, 1977; Outstanding Services, Palmetto State Law Enforcement, 1982; Sponsor, Dixie League Baseball Team, 1984; Speaker to varied church youth groups on law enforcement, 1985-; Community Service, Berkeley-Dorchester Chapter, 1989. **HOME ADDRESS:** 406 E Old Orangeburg Rd, Summerville, SC 29483. **BUSINESS ADDRESS:** Owner, Knightsville Dry Cleaners, 1580 Central Ave, PO Box 515, Summerville, SC 29483.

SINGLETON, HAROLD DOUGLAS
Retired clergyman. **PERSONAL:** Born Dec 10, 1908, Brunswick, GA; son of Joseph Singleton and Annie King Singleton; married Mary; children: Mercedes, Harold Jr, Alvin, Kenneth, Marilyn, Dwight. **EDUCATION:** Oakwood Coll, 1928; Union Coll, attended; 7th Day Advent Sem, attended. **CAREER:** Pastor 1932-42; S Atlanta Conf SDA, pres 1946-54; NE Conf SDA, pres 1954-62; N Amer Black SDA Prog, dir 1962-75; retired clergyman.

SINGLETON, HARRY M.
Attorney/consultant. **PERSONAL:** Born Apr 10, 1949, Meadville, PA; son of G T Singleton and Rose Fucci Singleton; divorced; children: Harry Jr, Leah. **EDUCATION:** The Johns Hopkins Univ, BA 1971; Yale Law School, JD 1974. **CAREER:** Houston & Gardner Law Firm, assoc 1974-75; Office of General Counsel/Fed Trade Commiss, attny 1975-76; Covington & Burling Law Firm, assoc 1976-77; Comm on the Dist of Columbia/US House of Reps, dep minority counsel 1977-79, minority chief counsel & staff dir 1979-81; Office of Congressional Affairs/US Dept of Commerce, dep asst sec 1981-82; US Dept of Ed, asst sec 1982-85; Harry M Singleton & Assocs Inc, pres 1986-. **ORGANIZATIONS:** Consult Amer Enterprise Inst 1975; pres, bd of trustee Barney Neighborhood House 1978-80; mem bd of dir Childrens Hosp Natl Med Ctr 1984-88. **HONORS/ACHIEVEMENTS:** Disting Hon Alumnus Awd Langston Univ 1984. **BUSINESS ADDRESS:** President, Harry M Singleton & Assocs, 604 Butternut St NW, Washington, DC 20012.

SINGLETON, HERBERT
Investment. **PERSONAL:** Born Jul 21, 1947, Jacksonville, FL; son of Henry Baker, Sr. and Henrietta Singleton Wallace; married Brenda Ann Oliver; children: Wanda Y, Chante L. **EDUCATION:** Morris Brown Coll, BA 1969; St Francis Coll, MBA 1979, MSBA 1978. **CAREER:** Lincoln Natl Corp,programmer 1974-1978, mgr professional dev & training 1978-

80, data processing devel mgr 1980-83; Lincoln Natl Investment Mgmt Co, dir invest sys 1983-84, asst vice pres 1984-. **ORGANIZATIONS:** Mem Assoc of MBA Exec 1980-83; chap pres Alpha Phi Alpha 1984-86. **HONORS/ACHIEVEMENTS:** Computer Programmer Cert 1970; Cert Teacher CA Commun Coll Syst 1974; Outstanding Coll Alumnus Morris Brown Coll 1983. **MILITARY SERVICE:** USAF staff sgt 1970-74; Outstanding Airman of the Month 1973,74. **BUSINESS ADDRESS:** Assistant Vice President, Lincoln Natl Invest Co, 1300 S Clinton St, Fort Wayne, IN 46801.

SINGLETON, ISAAC, SR.
Pastor. **PERSONAL:** Born Mar 31, 1928, Tallulah, LA; married Pearl B; children: Gloria Hayes, Isaac Jr, Charles, Barbara Edward, Valerie Gaffin, Willie D. **EDUCATION:** Lincoln Christian Coll, BA 1962; Bearea Sem, M Div 1983. **CAREER:** Lebanon Bapt Dist Assoc, moderator 1963-75; Joliet Chptr Oper PUSH, pres 1974-; Joliet Reg Chmbr of Comm, v pres 1978-80; Operation Push, natl brd 1979-. **ORGANIZATIONS:** Pres PUSH 1974-; adv bd Children & Family of IL 1980-, chmn 1986-; vice pres Bapt Gen Congress of Chris Ed 1980-; chrmn rgnl brd Children & Family 1983-. **HONORS/ACHIEVEMENTS:** Dr of Divinity Miller Univ Plainfld, NJ 1969; comm ldr of Amer 1969; Who's Who Black Amer 1976-77; Hon Citizen of New Orleans 1978. **MILITARY SERVICE:** USAAF sgt 1945-47; Good Conduct. **BUSINESS ADDRESS:** Pastor, Mt Zion Baptist Church, McKinley & Erie, Joliet, IL 60436.

SINGLETON, JAMES BENJAMIN, JR.
Retired dentist. **PERSONAL:** Born Aug 17, 1902, Nashville, TN; married Charlie May Malone; children: Velma (dec), Gloria JB III. **EDUCATION:** Attended, Fisk Univ, Meharry Med Coll Sch of Dentistry, OH State Univ, Univ of Pittsburgh Dental Coll. **CAREER:** Meharry Med Sch, prof oral surgery 1934-71, head oral surgery 1935-70; Private Practice, dentist. **ORGANIZATIONS:** Pres Pan-TN Dental Assn; pres Natl Dental Assn 1961-62; tst bd past reas First Bapt Ch; mem Omega Psi Phi 1924-77; Sigma Pi Phi; life mem NAACP; mem Agora Assembly; trustee First Baptist Church Capitol Hill. **HONORS/ACHIEVEMENTS:** Clinic named in The J B Singleton Oral Surgery Clinic Meharry 1971; Prof Emeritus School of Dentistry.

SINGLETON, JAMES LEROY
Physician. **PERSONAL:** Born Jul 20, 1944, Beaufort, SC; married Maxine; children: Daphne, Andrea, Krystal. **EDUCATION:** VA Union Univ, BS 1967; VA State Clge 1969; OH Clge Podiatric Med, DPM 1973; Sidney A Sumby, resd 1973-74. **CAREER:** Richmond Pub Sch System, physician self tchr. **ORGANIZATIONS:** Mem Amer Podiatry Assc; MI State Podiatry Assc; diplomate Natl Bd Podiatry Exmnr; VA Podiatry Soc; staff mem Sidney A Sumby Mem Hosp; Norfolk Comm Hosp; Med Ctr Hosp; Chesapeake Gen Hosp; mem Noble Mystic Shrine; 32nd degree Mason; OH Royal Arch Mason; Eureka Lodge 52 Most Worshipful Prince Hall; Alpha Phi Alpha Frat; bd dir Jamson Bible Inst. **HONORS/ACHIEVEMENTS:** Christian Physician Award Jamson Bible Inst 1975; OH Clge Podiatric Award 1973; Natl Fed March of Dimes 1974; PA Podiatry Assc Surg Seminar 1972; Pres's Award 1966. **BUSINESS ADDRESS:** PO Box 5402, Chesapeake, VA 23324.

SINGLETON, JAMES MILTON
Government administrator. **PERSONAL:** Born Aug 10, 1933, Hazelhurst, MS; married Allie Mae Young; children: James Jr, Jacquelyn. **EDUCATION:** So Univ of Baton Rouge LA, BS; Xavier Univ New Orleans, Health Plnng; Loyola Univ, attended; Univ of OK, attended. **CAREER:** Orleans Parish School Bd, teacher 1956-70; Natl Urban Health New Orleans, consult 1970-71; City of New Orleans Mayors Office, spec consult on health 1971-78; City of New Orleans, city councilman 1978-. **ORGANIZATIONS:** Pres Central City Econ Corp 1965-78, Total Comm Action Inc 1975; chmn Dryades St YMCA; chmn Heritage Aq Adv Comm, Bd of LA Health Plan, Total CommAction Inc. **HONORS/ACHIEVEMENTS:** Past Pres Awd Total Comm Action Inc 1976; Past Pres Awd Dryades St YMCA 1977. **MILITARY SERVICE:** AUS lt col 16 yrs. **BUSINESS ADDRESS:** City Councilman, City of New Orleans, 1300 Perdido St, Room 2 E09, New Orleans, LA 70125.

SINGLETON, KENNETH WAYNE
Athlete. **PERSONAL:** Born Jun 10, 1947, New York, NY. **EDUCATION:** Hofstra Univ. **CAREER:** Minor Leagues, baseball player 1967-70; NY Mets, baseball player 1970-71; Montreal Expos, baseball player 1972-73; Baltimore Orioles, professional baseball player 1974-79; The Sports Network Canada, analyst. **HONORS/ACHIEVEMENTS:** Led FL State League batters in walks (87) 1967; led CA League in sacrifice flies (6) 1968; tied NL record most home runs switch hitting 1 month 1973; played in All Star Game 1977-79; played in AL Championship Series 1979; played in World Series 1979; named rightfielder Sporting News AL All Star Team 1979. **BUSINESS ADDRESS:** Sports Analyst, The Sports Network, c/o Montreal Expos, PO Box 500Station M, Montreal, Quebec, Canada.

SINGLETON, LEROY, SR.
Mayor. **PERSONAL:** Born Oct 08, 1941, Hempstead, TX; son of Oscar Singleton, Sr. and Rosie Lee Moore Singleton; married Willie E. Franklin, Apr 24, 1977; children: LaRonda, Leroy, Jr., Kaye, Erica, Kareen, Gerard. **EDUCATION:** Prairie View A&M College, Prairie View TX, BS, 1969; Prairie View A&M Univ, Prairie View TX, MEd, 1971; Commonwealth School of Mortician, Houston TX, cert, 1982. **CAREER:** Dallas ISD, Dallas TX, teacher, 1968-69; Prairie View A&M Univ, Prairie View TX, associate teacher, 1970-75, Singleton Morot Line, Hempstead TX, owner/driver, 1975-82; Singleton Funeral Home, Hempstead TX, owner/mgr, 1982—; mayor of Hempstead TX, 1984—. **ORGANIZATIONS:** Independent Funeral Directors Assn, Texas Independent Funeral Directors Assn. **MILITARY SERVICE:** US Navy, 1962-65; unit citation. **HOME ADDRESS:** 606 7th St, Hempstead, TX 77445.

SINGLETON, ROBERT
Association executive. **PERSONAL:** Born Jan 08, 1936, Philadelphia, PA; married Helen Singleton; children: Robby, Damani, Malik. **EDUCATION:** Univ of CA, BA 1960, MA 1962, PhD 1983. **CAREER:** Pacific Hist Review Univ CA, asst editor 1958-60; Univ of CA, rsch asst 1961-63; Inst Indus Relations Univ CA, chief rscher 1963-64; US Labor Dept,rsch economist 1964-66; Educ Assoc Inc Wash, consul; Univ of CA, rsch economist 1967-69; Afro-Amer Studies Ctr Univ CA, dir & Prof 1969-70; Univ of CA, economist 1969-71; Robert Singleton & Assoc, pres 1979-; Loyola Marymount Univ, economics prof 1980-. **ORGANIZATIONS:** Past pres UCLA-NAACP; past chmn Santa Monica Venice Congress Racial Equali-

ty; mem Chancellors Adv Com Discrimination, Amer Civil Liberties Union, Soc Science Rsch Council Com Afro-Amer Studies; consultant staff Senate Select Subcom, OP-EN; HEW; Urban Educ Task Force; Natl Urban League Educ Task Force; mem Natl Assn Planners; founder & chmn Journal Black Studies; founding dir UCLA Ctr Afro-Amer Studies,. **HONORS/ACHIEVEMENTS:** John Hay Whitney Fellowship 1963; US Dept Labor Grant support dissertation 1966; Order Golden Bruins Chancellors Secret Hon Soc 1963-; Outstanding Young MenAmer 1972; John Hay Whitney Grant problems Black Educ 1972; Who's Who Marquis 1972-73; Dictionary Intl Biography; Who's Who Comm Serv; Comm Leaders & Noteworthy Amers; Assembly Rules Com CA Legislature Resolution 1974. **BUSINESS ADDRESS:** Economics Prof, Loyola Marymont University, 80th St & Loyola Blvd, Los Angeles, CA 92045.

SINGLETON, WILLIAM MATTHEW
Clergyman, educator. **PERSONAL:** Born Oct 12, 1924, Conway, SC; married Florence Revels; children: Margaret, Elizabeth, William Jr. **EDUCATION:** VA Union Univ, BA 1946; Howard Univ Sch of Religion, BD 1949; Drew Univ, MRE 1951; Western Bapt Bible Clge, DD 1959. **CAREER:** Western Bapt Bible Clge, pres 1965-, tchr dean 1954-61; 1st Bapt Ch, pastor 1951-52; Butler Clge, dean of chapel 1947-50; 2nd Bapt Ch Miami MO, pastor 1964-69; 2nd Bapt Ch Columbia MO, interim pastor 1969-71; Ward Memorial Baptist Church Sedalia MO 1982-87. **ORGANIZATIONS:** Mem Inst of Religion Howard Univ; mem KS City Theol Soc; mem Natl Bapt Conv USA Inc; mem NAACP; Urban League; Omega Psi Phi Frat; KS City Bapt Ministers Union. **HONORS/ACHIEVEMENTS:** Num publ 1946-71. **BUSINESS ADDRESS:** 2119 Tracy, Kansas City, MO 64108.

SINGLEY, ELIJAH
Assistant librarian. **PERSONAL:** Born Jan 29, 1935, Bessemer, AL; married Yvonne Jean; children: Jennifer. **EDUCATION:** Miles Coll, AB 1958; Atlanta Univ, MS in LS 1963; Sangamon State Univ, MA 1980. **CAREER:** VA State Coll, asst ref librarian 1960; AL State Univ, library dir 1963-71; Lincoln Land Comm Coll, asst librarian 1971-. **ORGANIZATIONS:** Mem Alpha Phi Alpha Frat; mem Amer Numismatic Assn; mem Natl Urban League; mem IL Sociological Assn; mem IL Library Assn; mem White House Conf on Library & Info Serv 1978-79. **HONORS/ACHIEVEMENTS:** Sports Hall of Fame Miles Coll Birmingham, AL, 1981. **MILITARY SERVICE:** AUS spec 4th class 1960-63; Good Conduct Medal; Natl Defense Serv Medal. **HOME ADDRESS:** 2301 Noble Ave, Springfield, IL 62704. **BUSINESS ADDRESS:** Assistant Librarian, Lincoln Land Comm College, Shepherd Rd, Springfield, IL 62708.

SINGLEY, YVONNE JEAN
Analyst. **PERSONAL:** Born Jun 18, 1947, Gary, IN; daughter of Edgar Williams and Mary Williams; married Elijah Singley, May 24, 1980; children: Jennifer. **EDUCATION:** Memphis State Univ, BA 1969; Univ of IL, MUP 1974. **CAREER:** IN Univ-Northwest, rsch assoc 1970-72; Opportunities Indus Ctr, educ dir 1974-75; Dept of Rehab Serv Methods, proc adv 1975-79; IL Bd of Higher Educ, asst dir 1979-87; IL Community College Board, dir Academic Programs 1987-. **ORGANIZATIONS:** Pres Access to Housing 1979; consultant Amer Med Assoc 1982-, Assoc of Indpnt Colls & Schools 1984-, US Dept of Educ 1986/87; bd mem Jr League of Springfield 1984. **HONORS/ACHIEVEMENTS:** Univ of IL Fellowship 1974/75; several presentations at univs & confs 1979-; Outstanding Young Women 1984; Educ Policy Fellowship George Washington Univ Inst 1982; "Minority American Women, A Biographical Directory," Fisk Univ Nashville 1983; Recognition Award - Illinois Community College Faculty Association,1989. **HOME ADDRESS:** 2301 Noble Ave, Springfield, IL 62704. **BUSINESS ADDRESS:** Director, Academic Programs, Illinois Community College Board, 509 South 6th Street, Room 400, Springfield, IL 62701.

SINKLER, GEORGE
Educator. **PERSONAL:** Born Dec 22, 1927, Charleston, SC; married Albertha Amelia Richardson; children: Gregory, Kenneth, Georgette. **EDUCATION:** Augustana Coll (RI, IL), AB 1953; Columbia Univ (Tchrs), MA 1954; Columbia Univ (Tchrs), Ed D (History) 1966. **CAREER:** Bluefield State Coll, instr 1954-55; Prairie View A&M Coll, instr assoc prof 1955-65; Morgan State Univ, prof history 1965-. **ORGANIZATIONS:** Visiting prof Jackson State Coll 1969; visiting prof Amherst 1969, Baltimore Comm Coll 1972, Frostburg State Univ 1969, Youngstown State Univ 1969, Univ of NE (Omaha) 1971, Catonsville Comm Coll 1971; mem Govans United Meth Church 1967-; cncl mem Govans Comm 1967-79; mem York Road Plng Comm 1967; Amer Assoc of Univ Profs; Amer Hist Assoc; Orgn of Amer Historians. **HONORS/ACHIEVEMENTS:** Phi Beta Kappa, Phi Alpha Theta, Kappa Delta Augustiana Coll 1953; Mr Friednship 1953; Who's Who Among Stdnts, Augustana Grad Flwshp 1953; Post Doctoral Flw Johns Hopkins Univ 1972-73; NEH Summer Stipend for Coll Tchrs 1980; book Racial Attitudes of Amer Pres, Doubleday 1971; articles in OH Hist, Vol 77 1968; IN Magazine of Hist Vol 65 1969; newspapers Afro-Amer (Batimore 1972; Amsterdam News 1976; publications incl, "What History Tells Us About Presidentsand Race" Afro-American Feb 19, 1972; "Blacks and American Presidents" New York Amsterdam News Summer 1976. **MILITARY SERVICE:** USN 1st class stewards mate 1946-49; Partcptd Navy Golden Gloves; Good Conduct Medal. **HOME ADDRESS:** 821 Beaumont Ave, Baltimore, MD 21212. **BUSINESS ADDRESS:** Professor of History, Morgan State University, Cold Spring Lane & Hillen Rd, Baltimore, MD 21239.

SINNETTE, CALVIN HERMAN
Physician. **PERSONAL:** Born Aug 30, 1924, New York, NY; son of Norman J Sinnette; married Elinor Kathleen DesVerney; children: Caleen S Jennings, Darryle S Craig. **EDUCATION:** City Coll of New York, BS 1945; Howard Univ Coll of Medicine, MD 1949. **CAREER:** Univ of Ibadan & Zaria Univ, prof pediatrics 1964-70; Columbia Univ, prof pediatrics 1970-75; Univ of Nairobi Kenya, prof pediatrics 1975-77; School of Medicine Morehouse Assoc, dean clin affairs 1977-79; Howard Univ, asst to vice pres health affairs 1979-88, asst vice pres health affairs, 1988-. **ORGANIZATIONS:** Mem Natl Medical Assoc 1977-; bd of dirs TransAfrica 1981-89. **MILITARY SERVICE:** USAF capt 1 1/2 yrs. **BUSINESS ADDRESS:** Asst Vice Pres for Health Affairs, Howard University, Freedmen's Square Annex 2, Washington, DC 20059.

SIRMANS, MEREDITH FRANKLIN
Educator, physician. **PERSONAL:** Born Aug 22, 1939, New York, NY; son of Booker Tariaffero Sirmans and Audrey Elizabeth Gray Sirmans; divorced; children: M Franklin Jr, Meryl D, Traci D. **EDUCATION:** Lincoln Univ, AB (Cum Laude) 1961; Meharry Medical Coll, MD (Cum Laude) 1965. **CAREER:** Presbyterian Hospital, asst attending Ob-Gyn 1972; Harlem Hospital Center, assoc attending Ob-Gyn 1975; Med Serv for Women PC, med dir 1975-; Coll of Physicians & Surgeons Columbia Univ, asst prof clinical Ob-Gyn. **ORGANIZATIONS:** Exec comm NAACP 1984-85; pres Manhattan Center Med Soc 1983-85; lecturer graduate program, nurse midwifery Columbia Univ 1971-74; rsch clerk Tissue Bank Natl Naval Med Center 1963; lecturer Human Sexuality Program NY, Amer Coll of Ob-Gyn, Amer Coll, Coll of Surgeons, Amer Assoc of Gyne Laparscopists, Amer Fertility soc, Amer Assoc of Sex Educs Counselors & Therapists; physician advisor NY City Health Science Review Org, 369th Veterans Assoc, Omega Psi Phi; pres Black Caucus of Harlem Health Workers; diplomate Amer Bd of Ob-Gyn, Natl Bd of Med Examiners; rschr, fellowship biochem Meharry Medical Coll 1962-63; panelists, sex therapy NY Assoc of Black Psychologists 1977; mem Rotary Club; chmn Region I Natl Medical Assn 1988-89. **HONORS/ACHIEVEMENTS:** Acad Scholarship Meharry Med Coll 1962-65. **MILITARY SERVICE:** USN, MC, LCDR 1966-69; Vietnam Serv Medal, Natl Defense. **BUSINESS ADDRESS:** Medical Director, President, Medical Services for Women, PC, 449 E 58th St, New York, NY 10022.

SISNEY, RICARDO
Educational administrator. **PERSONAL:** Born Feb 18, 1939, Henderson, KY; married Shirley Ann Pace. **EDUCATION:** KY State Univ, BS 1962; Western KY Univ, MA 1965; Western KY Univ, Rank I 1967. **CAREER:** Bowling Green City Bd of Educ, 1st black asst prin sr high 1971-; Western KY Univ, asst dir teacher corps 1970-71; Bowling Green Bd of Educ, teacher corps, team leader 1968-70, classroom teacher, science 1962-68. **ORGANIZATIONS:** Mem KY Educ Assc 1962-; mem Natl Educ Assc 1962-; mem Bowling Green Educ Assc 1962-; vice pres Alpha Phi Alpha Grad Chap 1973; commr KY Commn on Human Rights 1973-; past mem Masonic Lodge 1973-; mem NAACP/PHI Delta Kappa/Jaycees 1973-75; bd dir United Way/Red Cross/Council on Com Hlth/Girls Club. **HONORS/ACHIEVEMENTS:** Outst Young Educ Tchr Corps Team Ldr Bowling Green Bd of Educ 1968; Merit Award US Jayees 1971; KY Colonel 1971; Comm Ldrshp Award 1975. **BUSINESS ADDRESS:** Bowling Green Sr High, 1801 Rockingham Ln, Bowling Green, KY 42101.

SISTRUNK, MANUEL (MANNY)
Athlete. **PERSONAL:** Born Jun 16, 1947, Montgomery, AL. **EDUCATION:** AR AM&N Clge, BS Comm Rec. **CAREER:** Wash Redskins, 1970-75; Philadelphia Eagles, defensive end 1976-. **HONORS/ACHIEVEMENTS:** NFC & NFL Championship Game 1972. **BUSINESS ADDRESS:** Philadelphia Eagles, Vet Stad Broad St & Pattison A, Philadelphia, PA 19148.

SISTRUNK, OSCAR, JR.
Dentist. **PERSONAL:** Born Feb 01, 1930, Winter Park, FL; married Elouise Cynthia King. **EDUCATION:** Lincoln Univ, BA 1952; Howard Univ, DDS 1956. **CAREER:** Self-employed dentist. **ORGANIZATIONS:** Mem Liason Com Amer Dental Assc; Natl Dental Assc Speaker Hse of Dels; mem Commonwealth NJ Plainfield Dental Socs; Amer Soc Dentistry for Children; Amer Soc for Preventive Dentistry; amer Inst for Prevention & Eradication of Dental Diseases Inc; mem Franklin Township Kiwanis Club; Franklin Township Bd Educ 1963-69, pres 1968-69; mem bd dir Raitan Valley YMCA; Hamilton Park Youth Dev Proj; mem Alpha Phi Alpha Frat Grad Chpt; mem com Boy ScoutsAmer; trustee Mason Gross Educ Fund Rutgers Univ fndr & dir state bank manville; dental consult somerset county action Prog; mem Mu Boule Sigma Phi Phi Frat; bd trustees Rutgers Prepartory Sch; mem Rutgers Univ Med Sch Minorities Admission Com; adv bd Rutgers Psychology Dept. **MILITARY SERVICE:** AUS capt 1956-58.

SISTRUNK, OTIS
Athlete. **PERSONAL:** Born Sep 18, 1946, Columbus, GA. **CAREER:** Oakland Raiders, def tckl 1980; LA Rams, athlete 1972. **HONORS/ACHIEVEMENTS:** Pro Bowl 1974; ACF Champ Game 1973-75; NFL Champ Game 1976. **BUSINESS ADDRESS:** Los Angeles Raiders, c/o Cheryl Nichols, 322 Center St, El Segundo, CA 90245.

SIZEMORE, BARBARA A. (NEE LAFFOON)
Educator. **PERSONAL:** Born Dec 17, 1927, Chicago, IL; daughter of Sylvester W Laffoon and Delila Mae Alexander; married Jake Milliones, Jr; children: Kymara Spikes, Furman Sizemore, Beatena Milliones, DuBois Milliones,Momar Milliones, Marimba Milliones. **EDUCATION:** Northwestern Univ Evanston IL, BA 1947, MA 1954; Univ of Chicago IL, PhD 1979. **CAREER:** Chicago Pub Schl Chicago IL, tchr, elem prin, hs prin dir of Woodlawn Exper Schl Proj 1947-72; Amer Assc of Schl Admin, assc sec 1972-73; Washington DC, supt of schls 1973-75; Univ of Pittsburgh, assc prof 1977-. **ORGANIZATIONS:** Consult PEO Univ of MI 1975-; Race and Sex Desegregation Ctr KS State Univ Manhattan KS 1975-; mem Delta Sigma Theta; Natl Alliance of Black Schl Educ; bd mem Journal of Negro Educ 1974-83. **HONORS/ACHIEVEMENTS:** Honorary Doctor of Letters Central State Univ 1974; Honorary Doctor of Laws DE State Coll 1974; Honorary Doctor of Humane Letters Baltimore Coll of the Bible 1974; Northwestern Univ Merit Alumni Awd 1974; United Nations Assoc of Pittsburgh Human Rights Awd 1985; The Ruptured Diamond: The Politics of the Decentralization of the DC Public Schools, Lanham, MD: Univ Press of America, 1981. **HOME ADDRESS:** 3510 Iowa St, Pittsburgh, PA 15219. **BUSINESS ADDRESS:** Associate Professor, Univ of Pittsburgh, Forbes Quad 3T18, 230 S Bouquet, Pittsburgh, PA 15260.

SKEENE, LINELL DE-SILVA
Physician. **PERSONAL:** Born Nov 06, 1938, Brooklyn, NY. **EDUCATION:** Temple U, BA 1959; Meharry Med Coll, MD 1966. **CAREER:** Maimonides Med Ctr, atdng surg 1973-; Metro Hosp, 1971-72; NY Med Coll, instr surg 1971-72. **ORGANIZATIONS:** Mem AMA; Am Med Women's Assn; NY St Med Soc; mem Nat Cncl of Negro Women; NAACP. **HONORS/ACHIEVEMENTS:** Outstdng Yng Women of Am 1974. **BUSINESS ADDRESS:** 25 Dunhill Rd, New Hyde Park, NY 11040.

SKERRETT, PHILIP VINCENT
Pathologist. **PERSONAL:** Born Aug 10, 1923, Lincoln Univ, PA; son of William D. Skerrett; married Dolores Evon Barksdale; children: Philip V II, Donna L Tabrizi, Stephanie M. **EDUCATION:** Lincoln Univ, AB 1947; Meharry Medical Coll, MD 1951. **CAREER:** Mercy-Douglas Hospital, internship 1951-52; T Jefferson Med Sch, instruction in pathology 1958-66; Univ of PA Med Sch, asst prof pathology 1964-76; Medical Coll of PA, assoc prof of pathology 1976-; Veterans Admin Hospital Philadelphia, asst chief lab serv 1957-64, chief

lab serv 1964-78; chief anatomic pathology 1978-1988; dir Blood Bank/Hematology Labs 1988-. **ORGANIZATIONS:** Mem Alpha Phi Alpha Frat 1946-, AMA, PMS, PCMC, NMA, MSEP 1956-; diplomate AM Bd of Pathology Coll AM Pathology 1956; mem Int Acad Pathology Philadelphia PathSoc 1957-; diplomate AM Bd of Clinical Pathology 1964; mem Med Lab Tech Adv Commn Comm Coll of Phila. **HONORS/ACHIEVEMENTS:** Beta Kappa Chi Hon Scientific Soc Lincoln Univ 1943; Kappa Phi Hon Soc Meharry Medical Coll 1950; pres Philadelphia Alumni Lincoln Univ PA 1960-64; presidentMeharry Medical College Alumni Philadelphia 1982-. **MILITARY SERVICE:** AUS staff sgt 3 yrs. **BUSINESS ADDRESS:** Director Blood Bank & Hematology Labs, VA Medical Center, University & Woodland Aves, Philadelphia, PA 19104.

SKINNER, BYRON R.
University president. **CAREER:** Univ Maine Augusta, pres 1983-. **BUSINESS ADDRESS:** President, University of Maine at Augusta, University Heights, Augusta, ME 04330.

SKINNER, CLEMENTINE ANNA
Retired educator. **PERSONAL:** Born Feb 09, 1916, Birmingham, AL; married Herbert Skinner Sr (deceased); children: Herbert Jr, Kenneth C. **EDUCATION:** Wilson Jr Coll, AA 1959; Chicago Teachers Coll, BE 1961, ME 1963; Univ of Chicago, Loyola Univ, graduate work 1964-74; Nova Univ, EdD 1976. **CAREER:** Manley Vocational High School, school library clerk 1950-53; Wadsworth Elementary School, teacher/librarian 1960-68; Kenwood Acad, teacher/librarian 1968-70; South Shore High School, special asst principal in charge of curriculum 1970-82. **ORGANIZATIONS:** Elder former clerk of session Sixth Grace Presbyterian Church 1939-; sec United Presbyterian African Methodist Episcopal Conf Inc 1969-; former chmn Woodlawn Adv Council DHS 1970-80; bd mem YWCA of Metro Chicago, YWCA Harris Center; chmn bd of dirs Plano Child Devel Center; mem Exec Serv Corp Chicago; bd mem exec council Assoc for Study of Afro-Amer Life and History; past moderator Presbytery of Chicago 1987. **HONORS/ACHIEVEMENTS:** CRRT Award Childrens Reading Round Table 1976; Soror of the Year Natl Sorority of Phi Delta Kappa Mu Chapter 1976; honoree Alpha Gamma Pi Sorority 1976; Ralph Metcalfe Award Plano Child Devel Center 1980; Sr Citizens Hall of Fame City of Chicago 1983; Hall of Fame Wendell Phillips High School 1983; Distinguished Serv Award ASALH-Chicago Branch 1989; Connectional Humanitarian Award, MDC-African Methodist Episcopal Church 1989. **MILITARY SERVICE:** WAC tech/cpl 2 yrs; Good Conduct Medal, American Theatre. **HOME ADDRESS:** 8245 So Champlain Ave, Chicago, IL 60619.

SKINNER, EUGENE W.
Educator. **PERSONAL:** Born Jul 25, 1935, Bristow, VA; married Rosamond Anderson; children: Inez India, Eugene Jr, Carl Edward, Paul Wesley. **EDUCATION:** VA Union Univ, BS 1957; Howard Univ, MS 1967; Advance Studies at Amer Univ of MD, Univ of VA, Hampton Univ, Old Domion Univ, Madison Univ, VA Tech &ST Univ, VA ST Univ, William & Mary, Nova Univ, Montgomery Coll MD, OK ST Univ. **CAREER:** Fairfax County School Bd, science supvr VA Union Univ, asst coach 1958; Luther Jackson HS, chmn, science dept 1959-60; Vernon HS, chmn science 1960-67; Fort Hunt HS, asst principal 1981-1985; 1987 Hayfield Secondary Sub School Principal. **ORGANIZATIONS:** Mem NAACP, Urban League, Fairfax Hosp Assoc; pres Randall Civic Assoc 1969-; founder, pres Psi Nu Chap Omega Psi 1971; pres VA Union Athletic Alumni Assoc; Manassas Elks; Focus Club; mem Dept Progressive Club Inc,. **HONORS/ACHIEVEMENTS:** Outstanding Sci Teacher 1961; Omega Man of the Year Psi Nu Chap 1971; Top Ten Class Leadership School; Listed Who's Who Among Black VA 1974; Cert of Awd in Recog of Dedication in Ed to Young People, Outstanding Serv to Prof of Teaching & Guidance in Sci & Math The Joint Bd of Sci & Engrg Ed of Greater WA Area 1975; Scroll of Honor for Outstanding Serv to the Chap & the Comm Psi Nu Chap 1981. **MILITARY SERVICE:** AUS sfc 1953-55.

SKINNER, HOLLIS W.
Industrial specialist. **PERSONAL:** Born May 29, 1941, Trenton, TN; married Beverly A Johnson. **EDUCATION:** Lane Coll, BA 1970;Univ TN Martin. **CAREER:** Dept AUS, Milan Army Ammo Plnt, indstrl spec 1985; Sears, Jackson TN, salesprsn 1970-72. **ORGANIZATIONS:** Elected City Cnclmn-at-Large Trenton 1971, re-elected 1973; mem Light & Water Dept; sun sch tchr Recreational Com; Kappa Alpha Psi Frat 1968; mem Bi-racial Sch Bd. **HONORS/ACHIEVEMENTS:** Recip Outstndng Study in Field of Sociology, Lane Coll 1970; Outstndng Young Men of Am 1974; Man of Yr, Trenton 1973. **MILITARY SERVICE:** AUS spl 4th class.

SKINNER, ROBERT L., JR.
Airline executive. **PERSONAL:** Born Oct 05, 1941, Chicago, IL; son of Robert L Skinner Sr and Willie Louise Jemison Skinner. **EDUCATION:** Chicago City Coll, Chicago IL, attended, 1959-61; Univ of Wisconsin, Madison WI, attended, 1963; Northeastern Univ, Boston MA, attended, 1978-79. **CAREER:** American Airlines, Chicago IL, passenger serv representative, 1965-66, passenger serv mgr, 1966-69, sales representative, 1969-77, Boston MA, supvr flight serv, 1977-80, Chicago IL, account exec, 1980-88, mgr convention and company meeting sales, 1984-88, Rochester MN, gen mgr, 1988-. **ORGANIZATIONS:** Bd of dir, Rochester Convention and Visitors Bureau, 1989-. **MILITARY SERVICE:** US Air Force, Airman First Class, 1961-64. **BUSINESS ADDRESS:** General Manager, American Airlines Inc, Rochester Municipal Airport, Rochester, MN 55902.

SKLAREK, NORMA MERRICK (NORMA MERRICK-FAIRWEATHER)
Architect. **PERSONAL:** Born Apr 15, 1928, New York, NY; daughter of Walter Merrick and Amy Willoughby Merrick; married Cornelius Welch, MD, Oct 12, 1985; children: Gregory Ransom, David Fairweather, Susan. **EDUCATION:** Columbia Univ NYC, BArch 1950. **CAREER:** Skidmore Owings Merrill, architect 1955-60; Gruen Assoc, dir of arch 1960-80; Welton Becket Assocs, vice pres 1980-85; Own architectural firm, 1985-89; Siegel-Sklarek-Diamond, AIA Architects; The Jerde Partnership, principal, 1989-. **ORGANIZATIONS:** Arch faculty mem New York City College 1957-60; commr California Bd of Arch Examiners 1970-; arch faculty mem UCLA 1972-78; dir LA/AIA & CC/AIA 1973-; dir USC Arch Guild 1984-87. **HONORS/ACHIEVEMENTS:** First Black Woman Licensed Architect in New York, California, USA; First Black Woman Fellow of AIA; Fellow of Amer Inst of Architects 1980. **BUSINESS ADDRESS:** Principal, The Jerde Partnership Inc, 909 Ocean Front Walk, Suite 200, Venice, CA 90291.

SLADE, PHOEBE J.
Educator, sociologist. **PERSONAL:** Born Oct 17, 1935, New York; married Robert H; children: Robert, Paula. **EDUCATION:** Columbia U, EdD 1976, MA 1960; Jersey City St Coll, BS 1958; Bellevue Nrsng Sch, RN 1957; Hunter Coll, 1954. **CAREER:** Jersey City St Coll, asso prof 1975-, asst prof 1963-74; chmn dept 1968-69; asst dir dorm 1966-67; Hunter Coll, lecturer 1965-71; NJ St Dept Health, consultant 1961-63; NY City Dept Health, public health nurse 1959-61. **ORGANIZATIONS:** Mem Jersey City St Coll Faculty Assn 1963-; mem Assn NJ Coll Faculties 1963-; Delta Sigma Theta Sor 1953; Am Pub Hlth Assn 1962-; Nat Cncl Family Rels 1966-; Tri-St Cncl Family Rels 1968; Royal Soc Hlth, London England 1969; Nat Ed Assn 1972-; mem, Bd of Ethics, Teaneck 1976-; Jersey St Coll 1975-; mem Archdiocean Bd of Ed 1976-; vice pres Hawthorne's PTA 1977; Afro-Am Com Political Act 1985; Mayors Spl Task Force Resrch, Teaneck 1985; bd Teaneck & Together 1973-; Mayors Task Force Ed, Jersey City 1972-; Jersey City Bd Ed 1971-74; bd Jersey City Pub Lib 1970-74; Jersey City Com Criminal Justice1970-75. **HONORS/ACHIEVEMENTS:** Comm Ldrs & Noteworthy Ams 1976-77; Outstndng Young Wmn Am 1970; Who's Who E 1968-69; Who's Who Am Amn 1966-67; Dictionary Intrntl Biography 1966; PiLamda Theta, Nat Schlstc Org for Women in Ed 1967; Citation Award, Com Civil Rights Met NY 1963; Srv Award, Jersey City Pub Lib 1975. **BUSINESS ADDRESS:** Professor, Jersey City State College, 2039 Kennedy Blvd, Jersey City, NJ 07666.

SLADE, WALTER R., JR.
Physician. **PERSONAL:** Born Nov 11, 1918, Knightsdale, NC; son of S Walter R Slade and Blonnie Pair Slade; married Ruth D Sims. **EDUCATION:** St Augustine's Coll, BS tchrs cert 1939; Meharry Med Coll, MD 1947. **CAREER:** Brooklyn VA Med Ctr, staff Neurologist 1954-59, staff psychiatrist 1960-1962, staff neurologist 1963-1970, chief neurology 1970-. **ORGANIZATIONS:** Attending neurologist Kingsbrook Jewish Med Ctr 1966-; Kings Cty Hosp Ctr 1967-; clinical prof Downstate Med Ctr 1980-; consult Baptist Hosp of Brooklyn 1973-80; bd trustees Kingsbrook Jewish Med Ctr 1976-77; vice pres Midwood Dev Corp 1980-; Amer Coll of Angiology 1978-; chmn of the bd Midwood Devel Corp 1985. **HONORS/ACHIEVEMENTS:** Doctor of the Year Award TAN Magazine 1952; Family of the Year Award Brooklyn Council of Churches 1982; Distinguished Brotherhood Award William Moss Brotherhood 1979; living treas View from the Torch 1986; editor, Geriatric Neurology, 1980; editor, Angiology (journal) more than 30 publications 1950-88. **BUSINESS ADDRESS:** Chief Neurology Service, Brooklyn VA Med Ctr, 800 Poly Place, Brooklyn, NY 11209.

SLASH, JOSEPH A.
Business executive, cert. public acctnt. **PERSONAL:** Born Aug 25, 1943, Huntington, WV; married Meredith. **EDUCATION:** Marshall Univ, BBA 1966. **CAREER:** Sears Roebuck & Co, comptroller asst 1966; Arthur Young & Co, audit mgr 1968-78; city of Indianapolis IN, dep mayor 1978-. **ORGANIZATIONS:** Bd of dir 1972, treas 1974-, Indianapolis Urban League 1972-; bd of dir 1975, vice pres 1977 Indianapolis Bus Devel Found; mem, allocations sub-comm 1975,United Way Greater Indianapolis; mem IN Assoc CPA's Adv Forum 1976-78, Amer Inst CPA, IN Assoc CPA's; bd of dir Indianapolis Chap IN Assoc CPA's; mem Kappa Alpha Psi, Alpha Eta Boule, Sigma Pi Phi, Planning Comm NAACP Natl Conv 1973. **BUSINESS ADDRESS:** Deputy Mayor, City of Indianapolis, 2501 City County Bldg, Indianapolis, IN 46204.

SLATER, HELENE FORD SOUTHERN
Public relations counsel. **PERSONAL:** Born in Philadelphia, PA; daughter of William B Southern (deceased) and Henrietta B Ford-Southern (deceased); married Chester E Slater (divorced). **EDUCATION:** New School for Social Rsch, BA, 1955, MA 1959; Howard Univ, Temple Univ, City Coll of NY, Yeshiva Univ, Fordham Univ, Bank State Coll of Ed, Postgraduate. **CAREER:** Various newspapers, reporter, columnist, feature writer 1940-; New York City Bd of Ed, teacher retired; Southern-Slater Enterprises Public Relations, pres, 1955-. **ORGANIZATIONS:** Editor, The Acorn, LKM House Org, 1960-65, 1978-81; mem of bd, 1963-65, 1977-81, NW regional dir, 1967-68, NE regional dir, 1968-70 Lambda Kappa Mu Sor Inc, Natl Epistoleus; natl publ relations dir, 1969-71, 1973-75, 1978-83, 1984; Natl Assn of Media Women Inc; chmn, Natl Const 1971-73; public relations specialist, publicity dir, 1970-85; Shirley Chisholm Comm Action Assn, 1972; pres, Howard Univ Alumni Club of New York City, 1975-79; public relations dir, UNCF/Arthur ASHE Tennis Benefit, 1978-82; mem, Amer Social Soc, Natl Assn of Univ Women, Negro Business & Professional Women's Club, 100 Black Women, Bd of New Harlem YWCA. **HONORS/ACHIEVEMENTS:** Outstanding Person in Comm Radio Station, WWRL, 1965; Oustanding Soror of the Year, Lambda Kappa Mu, 1967; Achievement Award, Lambda Kappa Mu, 1971; Pres Award, Natl Assn of Media Women Inc, 1971, 1979; Citation of Merit, Lambda Kappa Mu Sor, 1973; Founders Cup, Natl Assn of Media Women Inc, 1974; Certificate of Merit, Howard Univ Alumni Club of New York City, 1975; Distinguished Serv Key Lambda Kappa Mu Sorority, 1977; Achievement Award, Howard Univ Alumni Club of New York City, 1980; Outstanding Person in Communications, WNYE-FM Medgar Evers Coll Comm Radio 1983; Prizes for Excellence in Latin & Greek upon grad from HS; Citation-Honorary Barbadian, Barbados Bd of Tourism, 1983; Special Recognition Award for Excellence in Public Relations and Editorial Ability, Lambda Kappa Mu Sorority, 1987. **BUSINESS ADDRESS:** President, Southern-Slater Enterprises, 360 W 22nd St, Suite 11-K, New York, NY 10011.

SLATER, JACKIE
Professional athlete. **PERSONAL:** Born May 27, 1954, Jackson, MS; married Annie; children: Matthew. **EDUCATION:** Attended, Jackson State. **CAREER:** Los Angeles Rams, player 1976-. **ORGANIZATIONS:** Active in Rams Speakers Bureau in off-season. **HONORS/ACHIEVEMENTS:** All-American (Pittsburgh Courier) at Jackson State; played in College All-Star game after sr season; first recipient of Walter Payton Physical Educ Awd at Jackson State; selected by UPI All-NFC and All-NFL (second team) 1983; named All-NFC by the Football News and UPI All-NFC (second team) 1985; mem Pro Bowl team 1986 and 1987. **BUSINESS ADDRESS:** Los Angeles Rams, 2327 Lincoln Ave, Anaheim, CA 92801.

SLATER, RODNEY E.
State government administrator. **PERSONAL:** Born Feb 23, 1955, Tutwiler, MS. **EDUCATION:** Eastern MI Univ, BS 1977; Univ of AR, JD 1980. **CAREER:** State Atty General's Office, asst atty 1980-82; AR Gov Bill Clinton, staff special assistant 1983-85, exec asst 1985-87; AR Hwy & Transportation, commissioner; AR State Univ, dir of govt relations 1987-. **ORGANIZATIONS:** Campaign mgr Gov Bill Clinton's Staff 1982,84,86; pres W Harold Flowers Law Soc; founding mem AR Children's Hosp Comm for the Future; former bd mem GW Carver YMCA of Little Rock; mem John Gammon Scholarship Found of AR,

former bd mem United Cerebral Palsy of Central AR; appointed by Fed Judge Henry Woods to serve as mem ofEastern District of AR Comm on the Bicentennial of the US Constitution; volunteer & supporter of Boy Scouts of Amer, Gyst House, March of Dimes, Sickle Cell Anemia Found, Thurgood Marshall Scholarship Fund, United Negro Coll Fund; mem Eastern Arkansas Area Council bd of dir of the Boy Scouts of Amer; mem AK Advocates for Children and Families Bd of Dir; Sec-Treasurer of the AK Bar Assn; mem Commission on AK's Future. **HONORS/ACHIEVEMENTS:** Elton Rynearson Grid Scholar Awd 1976; EMU Top Ten Student Awd 1977; Eastern MI Univ natl Championship Foresnics Team 1977; Univ Political Science Hon Soc of Phi Sigma Alpha; listed in Who's Who in Amer Coll & Univ, Outstanding Young Men of Amer 1986;. **BUSINESS ADDRESS:** Dir of Govt Relations, Arkansas State Univ, PO Box 249, State University, AR 72467.

SLAUGHTER, CAROLE D.
Testing expert. **PERSONAL:** Born Jul 27, 1945, Chatanooga, TN; son of Preston Jones and Rebecca Jones; married Thomas F Slaughter Jr; children: Kelli, Eric. **EDUCATION:** Douglass Coll-Rutgers Univ, AB 1972; Princeton Univ, MA 1975. **CAREER:** Educ Testing Services, assoc examiner 1974-79, grad record exams assoc program dir & dir develop 1979-86, coll & univ programs prog dir 1986-87, Office of Corp Secretary, dir, 1987. **ORGANIZATIONS:** Chairperson ETS Comm on Personnel Equity 1983-85; chairperson League of Women Voters Women's Rights Study Group; mem Highland Park NJ School Bd. **HONORS/ACHIEVEMENTS:** Ford Foundation Fellowship 1972-76; Test Preparation Specialist. **BUSINESS ADDRESS:** Dir, Office of Corp Sec, Educational Testing Service, Rosedale Rd, Princeton, NJ 08541.

SLAUGHTER, DIANA T.
Psychologist/educator. **PERSONAL:** Born Oct 28, 1941, Chicago, IL; daughter of Gwendolyn Malva Armstead and John Ison Slaughter. **EDUCATION:** BA (with Honors) 1962, MA 1964, PhD 1968. **CAREER:** Univ of Chicago Grad School of Educ, rsch assoc 1966-67; Howard Univ School of Med, instr in psychiatry 1967-68; Yale Univ School of Med, asst prof psych 1968-70; Univ of Chicago, asst prof behavioral sci human devel, educ 1970-77; Northwestern Univ, asst prof 1977-80, assoc prof 1980-. **ORGANIZATIONS:** Mem African Seminar sponsored by Inst for Intl Educ in New York & Inst for African Studies Univ of Ghana 1972; elected chairperson Black Caucus of the Soc for Rsch in Child Devel 1979-81; appt Natl Adv Bd of Child Abuse & Neglect 1979-81; elected mem Governing Council Soc for Rsch in Child Devel 1981-87; mem Soc Rsch Child Devel Study Tour to the Peoples Republic of China 1984; mem Amer psych Assn, Soc for Rsch in Child Devel, Amer Educ Rsch Assn, Natl Assn Black Psych, Groves Conf on the Family, Delta Sigma Theta, Natl Assoc Educ of Young Children; mem Bd of Ethnic and Minority Affairs Amer Psychological Assn 1986-88; mem Committee on Child Development Research and Public Policy, National Research Council, 1987-; bd of dir, Ancona School, Chicago IL, 1989-. **HONORS/ACHIEVEMENTS:** First Pi Lambda Distinguished Rsch Awd for Most Outstanding Thesis conducted by women in educ 1969; first Black Scholar Achievement Award, Black Caucus of the Society for Research in Child Development, 1987-; published books, Visible Now: Blacks in Private Schools (Greenwood Press) 1988,and Black Children and Poverty: A Developmental Perspective (Jossey-Bass Press) 1988. **BUSINESS ADDRESS:** Associate Professor, NorthwesternUniv, School of Educ & Social Policy, 2003 Sheridan Rd, Evanston, IL 60208.

SLAUGHTER, FRED LEON
Educator, attorney. **PERSONAL:** Born Mar 13, 1942, Santa Cruz, CA; married Kay Valerie Johnson; children: Hilary Spring, Fred Wallace. **EDUCATION:** UCLA, BS 1964, MBA 1966; Columbia U, JD 1969. **CAREER:** Practicing atty 1970-; School of Law, UCLA, asst dean, lecturer 1971-; real est broker 1974-; assoc campus advocate 1971-72; spec asst to chnclr 1969-71. **ORGANIZATIONS:** Mem LA Co, CA St Am Bar Asn; licensed to prac law before the US Supreme Ct, US Fed Cts, CA St Cts; life mem UCLA Alumni Assn. **BUSINESS ADDRESS:** 1224 Law Bldg, 405 Hilgard Ave, Los Angeles, CA 90024.

SLAUGHTER, JOHN BROOKS
Educational administrator. **PERSONAL:** Born Mar 16, 1934, Topeka, KS; married Ida Bernice Johnson; children: John, Jacqueline. **EDUCATION:** KS State Univ, BSEE 1956; UCLA, MS Engr 1961; Univ of CA San Diego, PhD Engr Sci 1971; 13 Hnry Doctorate Degrees. **CAREER:** Naval Elec Lab Center, dept head 1960-75; Applied Physics Lab Univ of WA, dir 1975-77; Natl Science Fnd, asst dir 1977-79; WA St Univ, acad vice pres and provost 1979-80; Natl Science Fnd, dir 1980-82; Univ of MD Coll Park, chancellor. **ORGANIZATIONS:** Pres Zeta Sigma Lambda Chap of Alpha Phi Alpha 1956-60; mem San Diego Urban League 1962-66; mem San Diego Transit Corp 1968-75; mem Amer Assoc Adv ofSci 1984-; mem Baltimore Gas and Elec Co 1984-; bd dir Comm Credit Co 1983-; bd of dirs Sovran Bank 1985; Medical Mutual Liability Insurance Soc of MD 1986; Martin Marietta Corp 1987. **HONORS/ACHIEVEMENTS:** Who's Who in Engrg 1977; Fellow Amer Assoc for Adv of Sci 1978; Fellow Inst of Elec and Electrnc Engrs 1977; election to Natl Acad of Engrs Washington DC 1982; Who's Who in Frontiers of Science and Technology 1985. **BUSINESS ADDRESS:** Chancellor, Univ of MD Clge Park, 1101 Main Administration, Univ of Maryland, College Park, MD 20742.

SLAUGHTER, JOHN ETTA
Educator. **PERSONAL:** Born Nov 03, 1929, Beaumont, TX; married Murray L Slaughter; children: JoAnne Brunson, Beverly Janine. **EDUCATION:** Howard Univ, BA, MA 1946-51. **CAREER:** San Antonio Independent School Dist, teacher 1957-69; St Philip's Coll, prof history 1969-, chmn soc sci 1978-. **ORGANIZATIONS:** Faculty senate pres St Philips Coll 1978-80; proj dir grants NEH, TCH, TCA 1980-85; mem Phi Delta Kappa, Delta Kappa Gamma, TX Jr Coll Teachers Assn; scholarship chmn Delta Sigma Theta; mem NAACP; pres San Antonio Alumnae Chap Delta Sigma Theta; mem Bexar County Historical Commiss; mem Martin Luther King Memoiral City County Commiss. **HONORS/ACHIEVEMENTS:** Grad Scholarship in History Howard Univ; Master Teacher Award from Univ of TX at Austin. **BUSINESS ADDRESS:** Chairman, Soc Sciences Dept, St Philips College, 2111 Nevada St, San Antonio, TX 78203.

SLAUGHTER, PETER
Physician. **PERSONAL:** Born May 15, 1928, Detroit; married Geraldine; children: Chevon, Karen, Tracy. **EDUCATION:** Wayne U, BS 1955;Univ of MI, MD 1963. **CAREER:** Samaritan, medical dir; Clinical Operations, Dmic Prescad, dir. **ORGANIZATIONS:** Mem Detrt Ped Soc. **HONORS/ACHIEVEMENTS:** Felw Am Acad of Ped 1973; Spec Acvmnt Galen's Hon Soc 1961. **MILITARY SERVICE:** AUS sfc 1950-52. **BUSINESS ADDRESS:** Midical Dir, Samaritan, 10201 E Jefferson, Detroit, MI 48226.

SLAUGHTER, VERNON L.
Business executive. **PERSONAL:** Born in Omaha, NE. **EDUCATION:** Univ of NE Lincoln, BA 1972. **CAREER:** CBS Records Washington DC, local promo mgr 1973-76; CBS Records NY, assoc dir album prmo 1976-77, dir jazz/prog mktg 1977-79. **ORGANIZATIONS:** Mem Country Music Assoc 1976-80; mem exec council Black Music Assoc 1980. **HONORS/ACHIEVEMENTS:** Black Achievers Awd Harlem YMCA New York City 1980. **BUSINESS ADDRESS:** Dir Jazz/Prog Marketing, CBS Records, 51 W 52nd St, New York, NY 10019.

SLEET, MONETA J., JR.
Photographer. **PERSONAL:** Born Feb 14, 1926, Owensboro, KY; married Juanita Harris; children: Gregory, Lisa, Michael. **EDUCATION:** NYU, MA 1950; KY St Coll, BA 1947. **CAREER:** Johnson Pub Co, photog 1955-; Our World Mag, photog 1950-55; Amsterdam News, NYC, reporter 1950; Maryland St Coll, instr photog 1948-49. **ORGANIZATIONS:** Mem bd dir Assn for the Help of Retarded Children; mem NAACP; mem Black Acad Arts & Letters. **HONORS/ACHIEVEMENTS:** Pulitzer Prize in Feature Photog 1969; Citation for Execll, Overseas Press Club of Am 1957; One Man Shows in Detroit & St Louis Art Museum; First Black Artist to have One Man Show at Museum 1970; featured in Black Photog Annual 1973. **MILITARY SERVICE:** AUS s/sgt 1944-46. **BUSINESS ADDRESS:** Johnson Publ Co, 1270 6 Ave, New York, NY 10020.

SLIE, SAMUEL N.
Educator, clergyman. **PERSONAL:** Born Jun 08, 1925, Branford, CT; son of Robert Slie and Anne Brown Slie. **EDUCATION:** Springfield Clge, BS 1949; Yale Div Schl, BD 1952, STM 1963; NY Theological Seminary, Dr of Ministry 1985. **CAREER:** Natl Student Council YMCA, southern area staff 1952-55; Student Christian Movement, United Church of Christ staff 1955-63; Yale Univ, assoc pastor and lecturer in higher educ 1965-; Southern CT State Univ, dir united ministry in higher educ 1976-86; coordinator Downtown Coopertive Ministry, New Haven 1986-. **ORGANIZATIONS:** Mem United Church of Christ Task Force on World Hunger 1972-73; corp mem United Church Bd World Ministries 1973-81; past pres Natl Campus Ministers Assn 1973-74; mem Theological Comm Worlds Alliance of YMCA's 1981-86; treas CT United Nations Assn USA 1984-; adv council Natl Ecumenical Student Christian Council 1984-86. **HONORS/ACHIEVEMENTS:** Distinguished Serv Awd Alpha Phi Omega Gamma Eta Springfield Coll 1949; Intl Distinguished Serv Awd Natl YMCA Boston 1981; article The New Natl Ecumenical Journal 1981; Elm-Ivy Awd for Contributions to Town-Govt Relations by Mayor of New Haven and Pres of Yale Univ 1985; distinguished educational service Dixwell Community House 1989. **MILITARY SERVICE:** AUS Infantry staff sgt 1943-46; Mediteranean and European Theatre Medals 2 Battle Stars, Combat Infantry Medal. **HOME ADDRESS:** 188 W Walk, West Haven, CT 06516. **BUSINESS ADDRESS:** Associate Pastor, Church Christian YaleUniv, 404 A Yale Station, New Haven, CT 06520.

SLOAN, DAVID E.
Attorney. **PERSONAL:** Born Apr 23, 1923, Baltimore, MD; married Jo Rogers; children: one child. **EDUCATION:** St Coll, AB 1944; Howard Univ, JD 1950; Temple Univ, Grad Cert 1970. **CAREER:** DC law practice 1954-65; Afro-Amer News Baltimore, sr ed 1966-71; Private practice, 1971-; Baltimore Contractors, house counsel 1971-. **ORGANIZATIONS:** Org Urban Task Force BS Amer, Amer Bar Assoc, DC Bar Assoc, NAACP, Urban League, Alpha Phi Alpha, Baltimore City Bar Assoc, MD Bar Assoc. **MILITARY SERVICE:** USNR 1944-46. **BUSINESS ADDRESS:** House Counsel, Baltimore Contractors, Ste 1153 Mondawmin Concourse, Baltimore, MD 21215.

SLOAN, EDITH BARKSDALE
Attorney. **PERSONAL:** Born Nov 29, 1940, New York, NY; married E Ned Sloan; children: Douglass Ned. **EDUCATION:** Hunter Coll, BA 1960; CathUniv of Am, JD 1974. **CAREER:** Cncl on Std Travel, mgr of info office 1960-61; US Peace Corps Philippines, 1962-64; Eleanor Roosevelt Human Rel NY Urban League, intern 1964-65; US Commn on Civil Rights, pub info spce 1965-68; Natl Com on Household Emp, exec dir/cnsl 1969-75; DC Office of Consumer Protection, dir 1976-77; US ConsumerProduct Safety Commn, 1978-. **ORGANIZATIONS:** Mem PA Bar 1974, DC Bar 1977; mem Community Adv Com HowardUniv Cancer Rsch Ctr, Women's Div Nat Bar Assn, Inst on Women Today; adv com Natl Ctr Policy Rev; mem bd dir The Lupis Fndtn; fndr Black Am Law Stds Assoc; Catholic Univ; Delta Sigma Theta Inc; bd mem Greater Washington Rsch Ctr, Natl Consumers League, Public Voice. **HONORS/ACHIEVEMENTS:** Adam Clayton Powell Award 1974; named One of 75 Outstndng Black Women in Pub Srv 1974; subject of NBC-TV Documentary "a woman is " 1974. **BUSINESS ADDRESS:** Attorney at Law, 1200 29th St NW, Washington, DC 20007.

SLOAN, MACEO ARCHIBALD
Business executive. **PERSONAL:** Born Aug 10, 1913, Newport, AR; married Charlotte Kennedy; children: Sylvia S Black, Maceo K. **EDUCATION:** Attended, Prairie View State Coll, Wharton Sch Univ of PA, Temple Univ, CLU Seminars Univ of WI. **CAREER:** NC Mutual Life Ins Co, agent, asst mgr, exec asst mgr, asst agency dir, vice chmn prod, exec vp, vice chmn bd of dirs 1938-86 (retired). **ORGANIZATIONS:** Bd mem Salvation Army Natl Adv Cncl, Salvation Army Boy's Club Adv Bd; bd govrs Univ of NC; bd mem Natl Bus League, Fund fopr the Advancement of Sci & Math Educ in NC; vice pres Natl Ins Assn Found; bd mem Duke Power Co, Durham Chamber of Commerce; immediate past chmn bd Fed Reserve Bank of Richmond; mem Amer Soc Chartered Life Underwriters, Amer Mgmt Assn; former pres & chmn bd Natl Ins Assn; mem Durham Comm on the Affairs of Black People; vice pres NC Cncl on Economic Educ; mem Alpha Phi Alpha, Sigma Pi Phi. **HONORS/ACHIEVEMENTS:** Cert of Achievement Prairie View State Coll 1955; Cert Quarter Million Dollar Round Table Natl Ins Assn; Speaker of the Yr 1975 Zion Chapel Bapt Ch Cleveland; Honrary Dr of Laws, Livingstone Coll, 1977.

SLOAN, MACEO KENNEDY
Investment manager. **PERSONAL:** Born Oct 18, 1949, Philadelphia, PA; son of Maceo Archibald Sloan and Charlotte Kennedy Sloan; married Melva Iona Wilder; children: Maceo S, Malia K. **EDUCATION:** Morehouse Coll, BA 1971; Georgia State Univ, MBA (w/

Honors) 1973; NC Central Univ Law School, JD (w/Honors) 1979. **CAREER:** NC Mutual Life Insurance Co, investment analyst trainee 1973-75, investment analyst 1975-77, asst to treasurer 1977-78, asst vice pres 1978-83, treasurer 1983-85, vice pres/treasurer 1985-86; NCCU School of Law, adjunct visiting prof 1979-86; Study Seminar for Financial Analysts, workshop review leader 1980-; Moore & Van Allen Attorneys at Law, of counsel 1985-86; NCM Capital Mgmt Group Inc, president/CEO 1985-86. **ORGANIZATIONS:** Mem Financial Analysts Federation 1974-; mem Durham Chamber of Commerce 1974-; mem, vice pres 1977-78 NC Soc of Financial Analysts 1974-; bd of visitors NCCU School of Law 1979-86; mem NC State Bar 1979-; bd of dirs Mechanics & Farmers Bank 1979-; bd of dirs Natl Insurance Assoc 1980-; bd of dirs United Way of Durham 1980-89; vice chmn/treas Urban Ministries of Durham 1983-88; mem Univ Club 1986-, The Georgetown Club 1988-; founder & pres Natl Investment Managers Assn. **HONORS/ACHIEVEMENTS:** Resolution in Appreciation The Durham City Council; Certificate of Service City of Durham; Outstanding Service as Pres Better Business Bureau 1980; Freedmon Guard Award, Durham Jaycees 1981; Outstanding Leadership Award, United Way Durham 1984. **BUSINESS ADDRESS:** President/CEO, NCM Capital Mgmt Group Inc, Two Mutual Plaza, 501 Willard St, Durham, NC 27701.

SLOSS, MINERVA A.
Retired educator. **PERSONAL:** Born Jun 02, 1921, Waco, TX; daughter of Earnest Grantt and Ruby M Jones; married Curley L Sloss, Sr; children: Curley L Jr. **EDUCATION:** Wiley Coll, Marshall, TX, AB, 1942; Univ of Oklahoma, Norman, OK, Master Sec Educ, 1953; Central State Univ, Edmond OK, Certificate, Guidance and Counseling, 1970. **CAREER:** Oklahoma City Public School, attendance secretary, 1947-49, English and journalism teacher, 1949-69, sec guidance counselor, 1969-75, language arts consultant, 1975-77; Rose State Coll, english instructor, 1977-1986 (retired); Part-timeEnglish teacher, Rose State Coll, 1988-. **ORGANIZATIONS:** Pres Okalahoma City Minority Pol Assc Women, 1984-; area I chairperson, Okalahoma Conf WMS 12th Epis Dist AME; 1st vice pres Avery Chapel AME Church WMS 1978-; workshop coord Oklahoma Delta Sigma Theta's Membership Seminar, 1984; regl dir Central Region Delta Sigma Theta Inc 1961-66; parliamentarian Blanche M Bruner Order of the Eastern Star, 1982-86; mem Natl Council of Teachers of English, Rose State Coll Faculty Assn; chairperson Tenure Comm Rose State Coll Humanities Div, 1983-84; rep Annual Scholastic Contest Humanities Div; mem North Central State Cert Team Putnam City JHS, 1983-84; mem sponsor Phi Theta Kappa Honorary Soc Rose State Coll; mem Oklahoma City Set Club Inc, Links Inc; part time english teacher, Rose State Coll, 1988; bd of dir, Sunbeam Home Serv, 1987; equity comm, Oklahoma City Public Schools, 1988; area I chairperson, Oklahoma, Conf, WMS,12th African Methodist Episcopal. **HONORS/ACHIEVEMENTS:** Fellowship Grant Wall St Journal, 1961; articles pub in The Black Chronicle The Former Black Dispatch, Oklahoma Today, Oklahoma Educ Journal For English Teachers, Oklahoman and Times, Oklahoma Sage, Pittsburg Courier and Kansas City Coll. **HOME ADDRESS:** 12120 NE 50th Street, Spencer, OK 73084.

SLUBY, TOM EUGENE
Professional athlete. **PERSONAL:** Born Feb 18, 1962, Washington, DC. **EDUCATION:** Notre Dame, 1980-84. **CAREER:** Dallas Mavericks, guard 1984-. **HONORS/ACHIEVEMENTS:** Drafted by Dallas on 2nd round in 1984 (41st overall). **BUSINESS ADDRESS:** Dallas Mavericks, Reunion Arena, Ste 510, Dallas, TX 75207.

SMALL, ISADORE, III
Sales engineer. **PERSONAL:** Born Apr 27, 1944, Pontiac, MI; married Earline Olivia Washington; children: Michael, Brian, Vanessa. **EDUCATION:** Univ of MI, BS Elect Engr 1967; Wayne State Univ, Masters Bus Admin 1981. **CAREER:** Cutler-hammer Inc Milwaukee WI, design engr 1967-74; Detroit MI, sales engr 1974-82; Eaton Corp Southfield MI, sales mgr 1982-83; Eaton Corp Grand RapidsMI, sr sales engr 1984-. **ORGANIZATIONS:** Mem Soc of Automotive Engr 66-67; Assc of Iron and Steel Engr 1974-; Elect Manuf Rep Assc 1979-; state youth dir Churchs of God WI 1969-74; Alpha PiOmega Frat 66-67; chrmn bd of trustees Metropolitan Church of God 1974-84; chrmn Bus Assembly. **HONORS/ACHIEVEMENTS:** Electronic Patent US Patent Office 1972, 1974; mem Eaton Soc of Inventors 1980. **BUSINESS ADDRESS:** Senior Sales Engineer, Eaton Corp, 733 Alger St SE, Grand Rapids, MI 49507.

SMALL, ISRAEL G.
Administrator. **PERSONAL:** Born Feb 26, 1941, Rincon, GA; married Jenetha Jenkins. **EDUCATION:** Savannah St Coll, BS 1963; GA S Coll, Grad Study; Ft Valley St Coll;Univ of GA; Comm Planning & Evaluation Inst, Washington DC. **CAREER:** Bur of Pub Dev, Savannah, dir, hum serv 1985; City of Savannah, model cities admin; Model Cities Prog, served in various capacities 1970. **ORGANIZATIONS:** Mem Kappa Alpha Psi; past mem GA Tchrs Ed Assn; Nat Ed Assn; Am Tchrs Assn; YMCA; Savannah Drug Abuse Adv Cncl; mem NAACP; mem People United toSave Humanity; completed training in Municipal & Comm Plng. **MILITARY SERVICE:** AUS e-5 1966-68.

SMALL, KENNETH LESTER
Strategic planner and researcher. **PERSONAL:** Born Oct 01, 1957, New York, NY; son of Julius Small and Catherine Johnson Small; married Patricia A Cooper, 1988. **EDUCATION:** Fordham Univ at Lincoln Center, BA 1979; Long Island Univ at Brooklyn Center, MA 1981. **CAREER:** Long Island Univ, rsch asst 1979-80; US Dept of Labor, economist 1980-81; The New York Public Library, information asst 1981-84; Natl Urban League, New York, NY, program evaluator, 1984-86; Natl Urban League, Inc, asst dir, 1985-86, exec asst 1986-, strategic planner, 1986-. **ORGANIZATIONS:** Mem Amer Economic Assoc, Amer Evaluation Assoc 1985-, Regional Plan Assoc, New York Urban League, Natl Economic Assoc, Co-op Amer, Friends of the Black Scholar; bd mem, Eastern Evaluation Research Soc, 1987-. **HONORS/ACHIEVEMENTS:** Graduate Fellowship, Long Island Univ, 1979. **BUSINESS ADDRESS:** Exec Asst for Strategic Plng, Natl Urban League Inc, 500 East 62nd St, 11th Floor, New York, NY 10021.

SMALL, LAWRENCE MALCOLM
Business executive. **PERSONAL:** Born Sep 14, 1941, New York, NY; married Sandra. **EDUCATION:** Brown U, BA 1963. **CAREER:** First Nat City Bk, vp, sr vice pres 1964-. **ORGANIZATIONS:** Trustee Moorehouse Coll. **MILITARY SERVICE:** AUS 1963-64. **BUSINESS ADDRESS:** 399 Park Ave, New York, NY 10022.

SMALL, LILY B.
Educator. **PERSONAL:** Born Sep 01, 1934, Trelawny, Jamaica;married Sylvester; children: Dale Andrew, Donna Marie. **EDUCATION:** CA St U, Fresno, bA 1970, MA 1971;Univ of Pacific Stockton CA, EdD 1976. **CAREER:** CA St Univ, Fresno CA, asso prof, affirm action coord 1975-; Stockton Univ School Dist, Stockton CA, reading spec 1973-74; Ministry of Ed, Kingston Jamaica, teacher. **ORGANIZATIONS:** Mem Am Assn for Affirm Act; mem Am Assn ofUniv Women; mem San Joaquin Rdng Assn; mem, chap sec Phi Kappa Phi 1978-80; tchr, supr Sun Sch Ch of God; mem Black Faculty & Staff Assn. **HONORS/ACHIEVEMENTS:** Who's Who in W & Mid W 1971; nominated mem Phi Kappa Phi UOP, Stockton CA 1976. **BUSINESS ADDRESS:** California State Univ Maple, Shaw Ave, Fresno, CA 93740.

SMALL, STANLEY JOSEPH
Educational administrator. **PERSONAL:** Born Jun 01, 1946, Weeks Island, LA; married Dorothy Collins; children: Keith V, Keisha L, Kory K. **EDUCATION:** Southern Univ Baton Rouge, BS Math & Sci 1968, MS Admin & Super 1973. **CAREER:** New Iberia Middle Sch, teacher 1968-70; Anderson St Middle Sch, teacher 1970-81; Iberia Parish Council, elected parish official 1984-88; New Iberia Middle Sch, asst principal. **ORGANIZATIONS:** Mem Natl Educ Assn 1969-85; pres Neighborhood Comm Serv Coalition 1978-85; mem LA Assn of Ed/Pol Action Comm 1979-85; chmn Human Serv Comm Iberia Parish Council 1984; mem NACO Human Serv Steering Comm 1984; mem Parish Bd (SMILE) Comm Action Agency 1984. **HONORS/ACHIEVEMENTS:** Outstanding Teacher of the Yr Assn of Classroom Teachers 1978; developed and implemented motivation prog for students New Iberia Middle Sch 1981. **HOME ADDRESS:** 816 Francis St, New Iberia, LA 70560. **BUSINESS ADDRESS:** Asst Principal, New Iberia Middle Sch, 415 Center St, New Iberia, LA 70560.

SMALL, SYDNEY L.
Business executive. **PERSONAL:** Born Feb 18, 1941, Brooklyn, NY. **EDUCATION:** Pace U, BA 1961. **CAREER:** Unity Broadcasting Network Inc, exec vice pres & co-found; Nat Black Network NYC, vice chairman 1973; Unity Broadcasting Network PA Inc WDAS AM/FM Phila, PA; ABC, bus mgr 1963-69; Time, Inc, 1969-71; Unity Broadcasting Network Inc, exec vp; Queens Inner Unity Cable Systems NYC, pres; NBN Broadcasting Inc, pres. **ORGANIZATIONS:** Mem Intl Radio & TV Soc; Nat Assn of Bdcstr; Nat Assn of Black-Owned Bdcstr; mem NAACP; NY Urban League; bd of dir World Insto of Black CommInc 1978; mem New York C of Comm Com 1979; pres World Inst of Black Commun 1986; pres Natl Assoc of Black Owned Broadcasters 1987. **HONORS/ACHIEVEMENTS:** AUS 1961-63. **MILITARY SERVICE:** AUS 1961-63. **BUSINESS ADDRESS:** Chairman, NBN Broadcasting Inc, 10 Columbus Circle, Tenth Fl, New York, NY 10019.

SMALL, WILLIAM
Administration. **PERSONAL:** Born Dec 05, 1940, Elizabeth, NJ; married Carolyn; children: William, Michael. **EDUCATION:** Howard U, AB 1962; Howard U, JD 1965. **CAREER:** Contract Adminstrn, dir 1975-; William Paterson Coll, dir acad serv 1971; William Patterson Coll, asso prof 1970; Newark State Coll, instr 1970; CAFEO, dep dir, acting exec dir 1969; Union Co Legal Serv Corp, chf investigator 1968-69; Domar Buckle Mfg Corp, laborer 1959; Astro Air Products Corp,laborer 1960-61; Western Elec Corp, laborer 1962; Union Co Legal Serv Corp, 1968-69; Polit Sci Soc; The Promethean Vice Pres Summer of Serv Corp, publicity & circulation mgr 1969; Title 1, asv com; Plans for Progress Task Force on Youth Motivation, part; Mayors Task Force o. **ORGANIZATIONS:** Bd trustees Urban League of Eastern Union Co; Concern Inc; adv various comm-based youth groups. **HONORS/ACHIEVEMENTS:** Outst Achvmt Award in Fed Jurisdiction; Outst Serv Award William & Paterson Coll Student Govt Assn; Serv Award Nat Headquarters Boy Scouts of Am 1974-75; Outst TraineeUniv Co 3re BCT Bde; Outst Trainee postwide competition; Nat Def Serv Medal; Vietnamese Serv Medal; Vietnamese Campaign Medal; Good Conduct Medal; Army Commedation Medal. **MILITARY SERVICE:** Military Serv #E-5 1956-67. **BUSINESS ADDRESS:** 300 Pompton Rd, Wayne, NJ 07470.

SMALLEY, PAUL
Relations manager. **PERSONAL:** Born Dec 08, 1935, Gay Head, MA; children: Polly, Patrick. **CAREER:** Comm Rel NE 1969-; Gen Dynamics 1958-69; Adv Com OIC Nat Tech V. **ORGANIZATIONS:** Chmn OIC Reg I; Deep River Dem Town Chmn 1980-82; v chman Reg Bd of Ed #4 1973-79; CT NAACP St Bd of Fin; mem bd of dir Urban League of Gr Hartford; min adv bd chmn WFSB-TV-3. **MILITARY SERVICE:** USMC #E-4 1954-75. **BUSINESS ADDRESS:** PO Box 270, Hartford, CT 06101.

SMALLS, CHARLEY MAE
Scientist. **PERSONAL:** Born Oct 22, 1943, Charleston, SC; daughter of Charles A Smalls Sr and Ida Mae White Smalls (deceased). **EDUCATION:** Knoxville Coll, BS 1965; Univ of MD, MS 1972. **CAREER:** Medical Univ of S Carolina Dept of Anatomy, lab technician, 1965-68; Johns Hopkins Univ Dept of Pathology, research technician, 1968-70; Dept Zoology Univ of MD, grad asst 1970-72; Dept Anatomy Milton S Hershey Med Ctr, research asst 1973-79; US EPA, EPA asst 1980-81, environmental scientist 1981-88, HMC/EPA Environmental Monitoring Lab, environmental radiation specialist, 1988-. **ORGANIZATIONS:** Capital Presb Church, deacon; Electron Microscopy Soc of Amer; Amer Microsopical Soc; Alpha Kappa Alpha; NY Acad of Sci; Susquehana Valley Health Physics Soc. **HONORS/ACHIEVEMENTS:** Bronze Medal US EPA 1980; CM Smalls & MD Goode 1977 "Ca2 Accumulating Components in Dev Skeletal Muscle" J Morph 1977; Bronze Medal, US Environmental Protection Agency, 1988. **HOME ADDRESS:** 1901 Herr St, Harrisburg, PA 17103. **BUSINESS ADDRESS:** Environmental Radiation Specialist, HMC/EPA Environmental Monitoring Laboratory, Milton S Hershey Medical Center, 100 Brown St, Middletown, PA 17057.

SMALLS, CHARLIE E.
Business executive, performer. **PERSONAL:** Born Oct 25, 1943, New York, NY; divorced. **EDUCATION:** Julliard School of Music. **CAREER:** Self-employed Charlie Smalls & Co; film score The Wiz 1977; film score Drum 1976; A&M recording artist, composer-lyrical Broadway The Wiz 1974; performer, theme composer, film Faces 1960; musical dir club The Scene 1960; musical dir Club Improvisation 1960; Air Force Band 1960. **ORGANIZATIONS:** Mem BMI. **HONORS/ACHIEVEMENTS:** Show of the Month Award The Wiz 1976; Drama Desk Award 1974-75; Outst Achvmt The Wiz; Grammy Award, Best Cast Show Album The Wiz 1976; Tony Award Best ScoreLyrics Musical Play The Wiz 1975; Tony

Award Best Score Music The Wiz 1975. **MILITARY SERVICE:** USAF. **BUSINESS ADDRESS:** 924 W End Ave, Apt 55, New York, NY 10025.

SMALLS, DOROTHY M. (NEE MAYHAMS)
Educator. **PERSONAL:** Born Jan 02, 1920, Georgetown, SC; divorced; children: Eleanor J, Carla S, Lois D. **EDUCATION:** SC State Coll, BS 1940; SC State Coll, MS 1960;Univ of SC;Univ of Chgo. **CAREER:** Bd End Georgetown, english teacher; JB Beck Elem Georgetown, elem school teacher; Kensington School Georgetown, reading consultant; Wm C Reavis School Chicago, teacher; Beck Jr HS Georgetown, teacher english, reading. **ORGANIZATIONS:** Mem United Tchng Profession; Pee Dee Reading Council; Nat Council of Reading; past pres SC State Alumni; past sec GC Educ Assn; past pres Dis Missions; mem NAACP; Voter Registration; Home Missions.

SMALLS, JACQUELYN ELAINE
Speech-language pathologist, consultant. **PERSONAL:** Born Nov 16, 1946, Charleston, SC; daughter of Charles Augustus Smalls Sr and Ida Mae White Smalls (deceased). **EDUCATION:** Hampton Inst, BA 1968; Penn State Univ, MEd 1976; Howard Univ, MS 1980, PhD 1984. **CAREER:** Blast IU #14, coordinator 1975-76; York City Public Schools, speech pathologist 1968-78; Public School Program, consultant program evaluator 1982; DC Public Schools, speech pathologist 1982-, Mentally Retarded Children and Adults, consultant 1987-. **ORGANIZATIONS:** Consult Natl Educ Assn 1975; Philadelphia Public Schools 1982; mem Amer Speech Language and Hearing 1982-; Sargent Memorial Presbyterian Church 1983-. **HONORS/ACHIEVEMENTS:** Distinguished Amer; Rec Graduate Fellowship Penn State Univ 1970, 1971, 1973; Fellowship Howard Univ 1978-83. **BUSINESS ADDRESS:** Speech, Language, Pathology Consultant, District of Columbia Public Schools, 100 Gallatin St NE, Washington, DC 20011.

SMALLS, MARCELLA E.
Account executive. **PERSONAL:** Born Sep 30, 1946, McClellanville, SC; children: Marcus. **EDUCATION:** Voorhees Coll, 1963-65; Durham Coll, BA 1968. **CAREER:** South Santee Germantown Action Group, fin sec 1980-83; SC Charleston Chap Natl Sec Assoc, name tag comm 1982; South-Santee Comm Ctr, bd of dir 1983; Howard AME Church, asst sec 1982-; Amoco Chem Corp, accountant. **ORGANIZATIONS:** Treas Amoco Chem Recreation Club 1983; secty/trustee Bldg Fund for Howard AME Church; financial advisor for Jr Achievement Cainhoy HS 1986-87. **HOME ADDRESS:** 1940 Hill Rd, McClellanville, SC 29458.

SMALLS, O'NEAL
Business executive, educator. **PERSONAL:** Born Sep 07, 1941, Myrtle Beach, SC. **EDUCATION:** Tuskegee Inst, BS 1964; Harvard Law Sch, JD 1967; Georgetown Univ, LLM 1975. **CAREER:** Amer Univ, assoc prof 1969-76; Systems & Applied Sci Corp, bd of dirs 1974-; George Washington Univ Sch of Law, prof law 1976-79; American Univ, prof of law 1979-. **ORGANIZATIONS:** Mem Harvard Law Sch Res Com 1966-67; asst dir Harvard Law Sch Summer Prog for Minority Students 1966; dir of admissions & chmn of Com Admissions & Scholarships Amer Univ 1970-74; mem DC, Natl, Amer Bar Assns; chmn bd dir Skyanchor Corp; exec bd DC Bapt Conv; Services Com & bd trustees Law Sch Admissions Coun Princeton 1972-76; adv com Leg Serv Plan Laborers' Dist coun of Washington DC 1973-75; bd dir Systems & Applied Sci Corp 1974-85. **HONORS/ACHIEVEMENTS:** Articles "Class Actions Under Title VII" Amer Univ Law Review 1976; "The Path & The Promised Land" Amer Univ Law Review 1972; booklets "New Directions, An Urban Reclamation Program for the Dist of Columbia" July 1982; "Manhood Training An Introduction to Adulthood for Inner City Boys Ages 11-13" April 1985. **MILITARY SERVICE:** AUS capt 1967-69. **BUSINESS ADDRESS:** Professor of Law, AmericanUniv Law Sch, MA & NE Aves NW, Washington, DC 20016.

SMALLWOOD, OSBORN TUCKER
Educator. **PERSONAL:** Born Aug 12, 1911, Hillhouse, MS; married Hazel Demouy; children: Angela Cockfield, Osborn Jr, Glenn Hazelton, Carl. **EDUCATION:** NC A&T Univ, BS 1937; Howard Univ, MA 1939; NY Univ, PhD 1948. **CAREER:** Samuel Huston Coll, chmn dept of English 1939-42; Office of Price Admin, History rsch specialist 1942-44; St Mathews Lutheran Church, pastor 1944-46; Howard Univ, instructor, assoc prof 1947-61; Foreign Serv Office W Germany, cultural officer consultamt 1961-70; OH State Univ, dir intl program, asst vice pres, prof of comm 1970-80, prof emeritus 1980-. **ORGANIZATIONS:** Chmn OH Fulbright Hayes Scholarship Comm 1970-72; mem advisory comm Inst for Intl Educ, mem bd of dir Columbus Area Intl Program Tau Kappa Alpha Forensic Honor Soc, Speech Communications Assoc, NAACP, Urban League, Natl Assn of Foreign Student Affairs, Torch Intl; pres Intl Educ Assn of OH Coll & Univ 1973-74, United Nationas Assoc, Phi Beta Sigma. **HONORS/ACHIEVEMENTS:** Citizen of the Year Woodridge Civic Assoc 1954; Fulbright Guest Prof Anatolia Coll Salonica Greece 1955-57; Merit Serv Award US Info Agency 1967; Outstanding Serv Award Intl Educ Assoc of OH Coll & Univ 1975; Merit Serv Award Inst of Intl Ed 1977. **BUSINESS ADDRESS:** Professor Emeritus, Ohio StateUniv, 154 N Oval Mall, Columbus, OH 43210.

SMART, EDWARD BERNARD, JR.
Clergyman. **PERSONAL:** Born Jun 23, 1949, Dothan, AL; children: Belinda. **EDUCATION:** Fisk Univ 1967; Harrisburg Area Comm Coll, AA 1969; PA State Univ, BA 1975; Shipperburt Univ, attended. **CAREER:** HBE Redevel, relocation office 1970-72; Warner Lambert, sales rep 1972-79; St John AME Church, pastor 1979-80; Scotland School for Vet Children, chaplain 1982-; St James AME Church, pastor 1980-86; St Stephena Comm AME Church, pastor 1986-. **ORGANIZATIONS:** Councilman Borough of Chambersburg 1981-85; past pres Chambersburg Black Ministry 1982; chaplain Scotland School for Vet Children 1982-, Franklin Cty Migrant Ministry 1983-85; pres Chambersburg Comm Improve Assoc 1983-; bd of dir South Central Comm Action Program 1983-; past pres Chambersburg Ministry 1984;trustee Philadelphia Annual Conf 1984,85,86; mem Mayor's Task Force on Racism 1986; trustee NY Annual Conference 1986-87. **HONORS/ACHIEVEMENTS:** Fisk JS Fisk Univ 1967; Father of the Year Daughters of Fkd Co 1982; Outstanding Young Man of Amer 1983. **HOME ADDRESS:** 1065 East 226th St, Bronx, NY 10466. **BUSINESS ADDRESS:** Pastor, AME Church, 2139 Frederick Bouglas Blvd, New York, NY 10026.

SMILEY, EMMETT L.
Dentist. **PERSONAL:** Born Jun 14, 1922, Montgomery, AL; married Mary Jo; children: Lynn Elise, Karen, Kim, George. **EDUCATION:** AL State Univ, BS 1945; Prairie View Univ Hempsted TX; Univ of Florence Florence Italy; Meharry Med Coll, DDS 1950. **CAREER:** Den Practice since 1950. **ORGANIZATIONS:** Pres AL Dental Soc 1964-66; exec bd AL Dental Soc 1966-; pres Capitol City Med Soc 1968-70; Nat Dental Assn; Mid-century Dental Assn; Ewell Neil Dental Soc; Delta Dental Care Inc; adv bd Urban League; mem Montgomery Area C of C; Mayors Com on Comm Affairs 1964-70; Montgomery Improvement Assn; eecbd mem Sigma Pi Phi Frat; Alpha Phi Alpha Frat past pres; Cligue Social Club past pres; Cleveland Ave Branch YMCA; Century Club mem. **HONORS/ACHIEVEMENTS:** Listed in Whos Who in the S & SE; Am Biographical Insts Personalities of the S; Dic of Intl Biography; AL Dept of Archives History under "Men ofProminence". **MILITARY SERVICE:** Served in military from 1942-1945. **BUSINESS ADDRESS:** 1031 Oak St, Montgomery, AL 36108.

SMILEY, JAMES WALKER, SR.
Retired postal director. **PERSONAL:** Born May 19, 1928, Selma, AL; son of David Smiley, Sr. and Sophia Deanna Bonner Smiley; married Lillian; children: James W Jr, Gloria Jean, Jacqueline, Carolyn Smiley-Robinson. **EDUCATION:** Evening Coll, 1964-68; Univ of Cincinnati. **CAREER:** US Postal Serv, line foreman 1967-69, gnl foreman 1969-74, operations mngr 1974-78, mngr mail distrib 1978-81; US Postal Service Cincinnati, OH dir mail processing 1981-85; Village of Woodlawn Woodlawn, OH admin 1989-. **ORGANIZATIONS:** NAACP; Natl Assoc of Postal Spvsrs; councilman Woodlawn, OH 1981-81 & 1983-; natl vice pres Natl Phoenix Assoc of Postal Mgrs 1983-1985; Board of Directors Cincinniti Hypertension Education pres 1989-; Ideal Investment Club pres. **HONORS/ACHIEVEMENTS:** Dedicated Service Cint Local NAPFE 1981; Outstanding/Dedicated Service Natl Phoenix Assoc Postal Mgrs 1983; Superior Accomplish Award US Postal Serv 1969. **MILITARY SERVICE:** AUS sfc 5 years; WW II Victory, Good Conduct 1946-52. **HOME ADDRESS:** 1122 Prairie Ave, Woodlawn, OH 45215.

SMILEY, KAREN JO
Family physician. **PERSONAL:** Born May 13, 1957, Montgomery, AL; married Douglas Blair Edwards. **EDUCATION:** Auburn Univ, BS 1978; Meharry Medical Coll, MD 1983. **CAREER:** Private Practice, family physician. **BUSINESS ADDRESS:** 1005 DB Todd Jr Blvd, Nashville, TN 37208.

SMILEY, WILLIAM L.
Physician. **PERSONAL:** Born Nov 14, 1912, Alabama; married Adella; children: Michele, Nina. **EDUCATION:** OH State U, BA 1933; OH StateUniv Med Sch, MD 1937. **CAREER:** City of St Louis Div of Health & Hosp, deputy asst health commr; Homer Phillips Hosp, acting path & chief of Labs 1944-46; Homer Phillips Hosp, assoc chief dept ob-gyn 1946-47. **ORGANIZATIONS:** Dir Cancer Screening Prog 1953-57; co-dir Sch for Continued Educ & Med Care of Pregnant Girls 1968-; chmn bd St Louis Comprehensive Health Ctr 1969-70; FACS, FACOG. **BUSINESS ADDRESS:** 1421 N Jefferson, St Louis, MO 63106.

SMILEY-ROBERTSON, CAROLYN
Systems analyst. **PERSONAL:** Born Aug 26, 1954, Cincinnati, OH; daughter of James W Smiley and Lillian Anderson Smiley; married Tommie L Robertson, Nov 19, 1983; children: Kevin James Robertson, Michael John Robertson. **EDUCATION:** Wellesley Coll, BA 1976. **CAREER:** Western Southern Life Ins, programmer 1976-78; AT&T, systems devel spec 1978-83; Village of Woodlawn, councilmember 1978-84; AT&T Commun, mgr syst analyst 1984-85, mgr information mgmt 1985-. **ORGANIZATIONS:** Mem Woodlawn Bd of Zoning Appeals 1978-82, Woodlawn Planning Comm 1978-84; trustee Woodlawn Comm Improvement Corp 1981-; economic consult Village of Woodlawn 1984-. **HONORS/ACHIEVEMENTS:** Ambassador Village of Woodlawn 1980; vice mayor Village of Woodlawn 1982; YMCA Black Achiever Cincinnati OH 1983. **BUSINESS ADDRESS:** Manager & Information Mgmt, AT&T Communications, 221 East Fourth St, Cincinnati, OH 45202.

SMIRNI, ALLAN DESMOND
Attorney. **PERSONAL:** Born Aug 27, 1939, New York City, NY; son of Donald and Ruby; divorced; children: Amie. **EDUCATION:** Brooklyn Coll CUNY, BA 1956-60; Law Sch Univ of CA Berkeley, JD 1968-71. **CAREER:** Brobeck Phleger & Harrison, asso atty 1971-74; Envirotech Corp, asst gen cnsl/asst sec 1974-81; TeleVideo Systems Inc, chief cnsl & sec 1982-86; Memorex Corp vice pres general counsel & secretary 1987-. **ORGANIZATIONS:** Mem State of CA Job Training/Devel 1970-72; trustee Envirotech Found 1978-81; trustee TeleVideo Found 1983-; mem State Bar of CA 1972-; mem Am Soc of Corporate Sec 1976-; mem Charles Houston Bar Assn 1972-; mem Amer Assn of Corporate Counsel 1982-. **MILITARY SERVICE:** USAF capt; AF Commendation Medal 1966. **HOME ADDRESS:** 1090 Michaelangelo Dr, Sunnyvale, CA 94087.

SMITH, A. MACEO
Assistant administrator. **PERSONAL:** Born Apr 16, 1903, Texarkana, TX; married Fannie. **EDUCATION:** Fisk U, AB; NY U, MBA; Columbia U, post grad. **CAREER:** US Dept HUD, asst reg admin; Sterling Enterprises, exec vP; S Maceo Smith & Asso, prop; Harlem Adv Agency, co-prop; Universal Life Ins Co, state mrg; Smith & Daniels Realty Co, co-owner; Western Mutual Life Ins Co, organizer; Dallas Pub Sch, educator 1935; Dallas Express Newsp, publ; Dalls Negro C of C, exec dir; Alpha Phi Alpha Frat, pres 1951-54. **ORGANIZATIONS:** Nat bd mem NAACP 1953-59; vP NaT Bus League; pres Pres Fisk Alumni Assn; pres SW Area Counc YMCA 1970-71; pres Dallas Urban League; mem bd Trustees Bishop Coll; bd mem "United Way"; life mem NAACP; trustee New Hope Bapt Ch; Nat bd mem Nat Assn Human Rights Workers; bd mem TX Assn Developing Colleges; mem TX Com on Human Rel; mem Greater Dallas Planning Coun; life mem Alpha Phi Alpha Inc; mem bd trustees DAME; mem Dallas Rotary Club; 33 Deg Mason; Shriner; Knights of Pythias; Am Woodmen; bd mem Greater Dallas Coun of Chs; bd mem Dallas Negro C of C; bd mem NCCJ; co-chmn Dallas Bi Racial Comm; Advisory bd mem Natl Security Bk Ryler ;Tx; chr TX Council of Urban Leagues. **HONORS/ACHIEVEMENTS:** Civic Leader Award Asso Pub 1968; Fisk Alumni Award 1949; Dist Serv Award NAACP 1955; Dist Serv Award SW Area Coun YMCA 1962; Award for Dist Serv in Housing Prairie View A&M Coll 1958; Dist Serv Award Alpha Phi Alpha 1964; Spec Serv Award Ft Worth Fed Bus Assn 1969; Cert of Merit Award HUD 1973; Dist Serv Award Dallas Co Home Builders Assn 1973; listed in Outstanding Civic Leaders of Am 1968.

SMITH, A. WADE
Educator, researcher. **PERSONAL:** Born Aug 29, 1950, Newport News, VA; son of A Wade Smith and Eunice Gray Smith; married Elsie Gloria Jean Moore; children: Arthur Wade, Aaron Webster, Allen Weldon. **EDUCATION:** Dartmouth Coll, AB 1972; Univ of Chicago, MA 1976, PhD 1977. **CAREER:** Univ of SC, asst prof 1977-80; Natl Opinion Rsch Ctr, rsch assoc 1977-86; Ctr for the Study of Youth Develop, vstg rsch scientist 1980; AZ State Univ, asst to assoc prof 1980-. **ORGANIZATIONS:** Membership chmn Assoc of Black Sociologists 1984-88; mem AZ Law Enforcement Adv Council 1986-; assoc editor Journal of Marriage and the Family 1986-; assoc editor Amer Sociological Review 1987-90. **HONORS/ACHIEVEMENTS:** Articles "Racial Tolerance as a Function of Group Position" 1981, "Cohorts, Education, and the Evolution of Tolerance" 1985, "Sex and Race Differences in Mathematics Aptitude" 1986, "Problems & Progress in the Measurement of Black Public Opinion" 1987; "Maintaining the Pipeline of Black Teachers for the 21st Century", 1988; "Racial Insularity at the Core: Contemporary American Racial Attitudes, 1988; "Finding Subgroups for Surveys", 1989. **BUSINESS ADDRESS:** Assoc Prof of Sociology, Arizona StateUniv, Dept of Sociology, Tempe, AZ 85287-2101.

SMITH, A. Z.
Association executive. **PERSONAL:** Born Jun 16, 1938, Grand Junction, TN; married Mattie Lou Peterson; children: Burnett, Azell, Wanda, Jovernia. **EDUCATION:** Air Conditioning Training Co, Inc, degree 1961; Rust College 1961-62. **CAREER:** Church Deacon Board, deacon 1969; Hardaways MB Church, choir president 1971-84, superintendent sunday school 1971-; Carrier A/C Inc Co, machine set-up and operator. **ORGANIZATIONS:** General staff Mississippi Governor's Colonel 1976-80; school board Benton Cty MS Bd of Education 1981-; member NAACP. **HONORS/ACHIEVEMENTS:** Best all-around for religious activities, Old Salem School 1960; Golden Circle Club Collerville 1985. **BUSINESS ADDRESS:** Carrier A/C Inc Co, 97 South Byhalia Road, Collierville, TN 38017.

SMITH, ALBERT E.
University president. **PERSONAL:** Born Oct 24, 1932, Sioux Falls, SD; son of Calvert Smith and Ethel Johnson Smith; married Sadie Burris, Jan 27, 1956; children: Albert Clayton, Robbin Renae, Angela E. **EDUCATION:** North Carolina A&T State Univ, Greensboro NC, BS, 1956; George Williams Coll, Downers Grove IL, MS, 1963; Univ of Pittsburgh, Pittsburgh PA, PhD, 1984. **CAREER:** Knoxville Coll, Knoxville TN, dir of student center & head baseball coach, 1964-66; North Carolina A&T State Univ, Greensboro NC, dir of intercollegiate athletics & the memorial student union, 1968-71; Univ of Pittsburgh, Pittsburgh PA, exec asst dir of intercollegiate athletics & lecturer, 1971-75; Eastern Michigan Univ, Ypsilanti MI, dir of intercollegiate athletics & assoc prof of educ, 1975-76; North Carolina A&T State Univ, Greensboro NC, vice chancellor for devel & univ relations, 1976-86; South Carolina State Coll, Orangeburg SC, pres, 1986-. **ORGANIZATIONS:** Chmn, council of presidents, South Carolina State Colleges & Universities; mem, advisory comm, Office of Advancement for Public Black Colleges; mem, advisory bd, Governor's Agricultural & Rural Economic Devel Task Force; commr, Commn of the Future of South Carolina; bd of dir, South Carolina Heart Assn, First Natl Bank of Orangeburg, City Industrial Devel Commn, South Carolina Business Week. **HONORS/ACHIEVEMENTS:** North Carolina A&T Sports Hall of Fame, North Carolina A&T State Colleges & Universities, 1988; Hall of Fame, Mid-Eastern Athletic Conf; 2nd Annual Golden Achievement Award, Afro-Amer History Club, George Washington Carver High School; Inventor, Combined Clock & Advertising Display, 1984; Inventor, Desk Ornament, 1982; "A Plan for the Development of the Afro-American Cultural and Entertainment Complex, Univ of Pittsburgh, Pittsburgh PA," 1974; "Reach for Progress," Greensboro Business, (Greensboro Chamber of Commerce Publication) Greensboro NC, 1968; Weekly Sports Column, Carolina Peacemaker, Greensboro NC, 1968. **MILITARY SERVICE:** US Army, 2nd lieutenant. **BUSINESS ADDRESS:** President, South Carolina State College, 300 College St, NE, Orangeburg, SC 29117.

SMITH, ALFRED J., JR.
Educator. **PERSONAL:** Born Jul 09, 1948, Montclair, NJ; married Judith Moore. **EDUCATION:** Boston U, BFA 1970; Boston U, MFA 1972. **CAREER:** Howard Univ, assoc art 1972-; Norfolk Correct Inst, inst art 1970-72; Boston U, asst inst 1970-72; Boston Univ Afro-Amer Center, dir cult affrs 1970-71; NatlCenter Afro-Amer Art, inst art 1969-72; prof pntr sculp & crafts. **ORGANIZATIONS:** Mem Nat Conf of Art. **HONORS/ACHIEVEMENTS:** "Educ to Africa Assn" Afric Am Inst Tchrs Assist grant BostonUniv 1970-72; art awd BostonUniv 1967-68, 1970; comm from City of Boston in "Grtr Walls & Spaces" compet 1972; partic in num exhib; recpt Nat Endow grant for crafts 1975. **BUSINESS ADDRESS:** Howard University, College of Fine Arts, 6th & Fairmont Streets NW, Washington, DC 20059.

SMITH, ALICE
Education administration. **EDUCATION:** Ft Valley State Coll, BA French Lit 1968; Atlanta Univ, MA French Lit 1969; Yale Univ New Haven CT, Intensive Lang & Lit 1970; MI State Univ, French Lit 1971-72; Sorbonne, Paris, France, Modern French Lit 1972-73; Columbia Univ NY, German Lang 1973; Univ of MA, PhD French Lit 1978. **CAREER:** Hawkinsville HS, instr 1967; Ft Valley State Coll, instr 1969-71; Univ of MA, teaching asst 1973-77; Univ of MA, placement counselor 1979-80, dir resource ctr 1979-81, asst dir placement serv 1979-. **ORGANIZATIONS:** Mem Alpha Kappa Mu Natl Hon soc, Alpha Kappa Alpha, Phi Delta Kappa 1980. **HONORS/ACHIEVEMENTS:** Acad Scholarship Paris France 1966; Natl Defense Scholarship Ft Valley State Coll 1964-68; The Atlanta Univ Fellowship 1968-69; Natl Fellowships Fund 1976-78; listed in Who's Who Among Amer Coll & Univ, World's Who's Who of Women 1979.

SMITH, ALLEN JOSEPH, SR.
Educational administrator. **PERSONAL:** Born Mar 10, 1936, Chicago, IL; divorced; children: Allen J Jr, Wendy M, Anthony R. **EDUCATION:** Roosevelt Univ, BA 1960, MA 1966; Nova Univ, EdD 1981. **CAREER:** Chicago Bd of Educ, teacher 1960-67, adult educ teacher 1964-67, counselor 1967-69, guidance coord 1969-82, dir bureau of guidance 1982-. **ORGANIZATIONS:** Bd of dirs Parliamentarian Assoc for Multicultural Counseling and Development 1978-82, 1985-86; bd of dirs Human Resource Develop Inst 1984-. **HONORS/ACHIEVEMENTS:** Disting Volunteer Awd UNCF 1984; 1984 Educator of the Year Phi Delta Kappa 1984; Special Appreciation Awd ANWC 1985; Certification of Appreciation Natl Beta Club 1985. **BUSINESS ADDRESS:** Director, Bureau of Guidance, Chicago Public Schools, 1819 W Pershing Rd 6th Fl, Chicago, IL 60609.

SMITH, ALONZO NELSON
Educator. **PERSONAL:** Born Oct 11, 1940, Washington, DC; married Susan T Cramer; children: Anne Marie, Alexander. **EDUCATION:** Georgetown Univ, BS Foreign Service 1962; Howard Univ, MA African Hist 1967; UCLA, PhD Afro-Amer Hist 1978. **CAREER:** Black Studies Center of the Claremont Colleges, lecturer 1970-75; Cal Poly State Univ, inst history 1976-77; Univ of NE, asst prof 1978-. **ORGANIZATIONS:** Mem Omaha NAACP 1985; mem Central Comm NE State Democratic Party 1985. **HONORS/ACHIEVEMENTS:** Article Afro-Americans and the Presidential Election of 1948-Western Journal of Black Studies 1984. **MILITARY SERVICE:** Peace Corps W Africa 1962-64. **HOME ADDRESS:** 2048 N 54th St, Omaha, NE 68104.

SMITH, ALPHONSO LEHMAN
Educational administrator. **PERSONAL:** Born Feb 27, 1937, Memphis, TN; divorced; children: Angela, Anthony, Audrey. **EDUCATION:** Fisk U, 1955-57; OH State U, BS 1964. **CAREER:** Wright State Univ, dir affirmative action programs 1973-; Wright State Univ, asst dir of affirmative action for faculty 1972-73; Wright State Univ, math instr 1964-68; asst prof of computer & sci 1970-. **ORGANIZATIONS:** Mem Am Math Soc 1961-; mem & former chmn OH Affirmative Action Officers Assn 1973-; mem Yellow Springs Title IX Adv Com 1976-77; Nat Sci Found Fellow 1956-72; mem Pi Mu Epsilon Math Hon 1958-; hon mem Phi Beta Kappa 1960-. **BUSINESS ADDRESS:** Wright State Univ, Col Glenn Highway, Dayton, OH 45435.

SMITH, ALVIN
Educator. **PERSONAL:** Born Nov 27, 1933, Gary, IN; divorced. **EDUCATION:** Teachers Coll, Columbia Univ, EdD 1973; Univ of IL, AM 1960; State Univ of IA, BA 1955. **CAREER:** Marymount Manhattan Coll, assc prof; Queens Coll, asst prof 1966-76; Amherst Coll, assoc prof 1974-75. **ORGANIZATIONS:** Artist in residence, Natl Art Educ; Intl Soc for Educ Through Art; Coll Art Assn; Univ Council on Art Educ; Phi Delta Kappa. **HONORS/ACHIEVEMENTS:** Natl Endowment for the Arts Visual Arts Grant 1973; NY State Council on the Arts CAPS Grant 1972; Amherst Coll Faculty Rsch Grant 1974; One Man Art Exhibitions, Amherst Coll 1975; Union Coll Schemectady NY 1973; Collegiate School, NY 1972; Living Arts Ctr Dayton 1968; Teachers Coll, Columbia Univ 1967; Dayton Art Inst Dayton 1961. **MILITARY SERVICE:** AUS sp4 1957-59.

SMITH, ANDREW W.
Performer. **PERSONAL:** Born Aug 24, 1941, Lexington, KY; married Yvonne Bransford; children: Antron W. **EDUCATION:** KY StateUniv Frankfort, KY, BS 1964; RooseveltUniv Chicago, MM 1970. **CAREER:** Opera Orch of NY 1979-; Met Opera, opera singer 1976-; Markham Roller Rink Markham IL, asst mgr/co-owner 1972-76; City of Markham, acting city mgr 1972-73, dir urban dev 1971; Chicago Bd of Ed, tchr 1964-70. **ORGANIZATIONS:** Opera singer New York City Opera 1977-79/Houston Grand Opera/MI Opera/Boston Opera/Atlanta Symphony/Grand Park Summer Festival/Art Park Music Festival/Chicago Sinai Congregation Cantorial Soloist 7 Yrs; mem Masonic Lodge; mem Kappa Alpha Phi. **HONORS/ACHIEVEMENTS:** Winner Of Chicagoland Music Festival 1965; WGN Audition of the Air Met Audition; emmy award for One of prin soloists for Best Opera Rec 1977; toni awrd Principal Soloist on Recording of "Porgy & Bess"; Natl Acad of Rec Arts & Sci 1977. **BUSINESS ADDRESS:** Lincoln Center, New York, NY.

SMITH, ANN ELIZABETH
Educator, insurance salesperson, manager. **PERSONAL:** Born Aug 17, 1939, Poplar Bluff, MO. **EDUCATION:** Lincoln Univ, BA 1960; Univ of IA, MA 1962; Union Graduate School, OH, PhD, 1974. **CAREER:** Prudential Ins Co, sales mgr 1978-; Acad Affairs (acting), vp; Speech & Performing Arts NE IL Univ, assc prof 1975-77; NE IL Univ, asst to pres 1969-75; instr 1966-69; Univ of IN Black Theatre, lecturer 1971; Theatre E IL Univ, instr 1962-66; English Central HS, instr 1960. **ORGANIZATIONS:** Consultant Dramatic Art; Chicago Pub Sch 1967, 68 , 71; consult for Women's Pgm Regnl Office of HEW & HUD 1972-73; announcer Our People WTTW Channel 11 1968-71; Chicago Film Festival Judge 1971, 1972; prod coordinator, Org of Black Am Culture 1967-; bd mem League of Black Women 1976-80; Delta Sigma Theta Sorority, 1957, natl policy bd mem 1972-75; chairperson, 1974-75; Union Graduate School Public Coll in the City, Commuters & Comm Houses; Improving Coll & Univ Teaching 1974. **HONORS/ACHIEVEMENTS:** Outst young women of am 1967; Who's Who of Am Women 1977; NE ILUniv Intrntl women's yr awrd 1975; PUSH excellance awrd 1977; World's Who's Who of Women1978; leginare awrd Prudential Ins Co 1978-79; pres citation Prudential Ins Co 1979; Million Dollar Roundtable Prudential Ins Co 1980. **BUSINESS ADDRESS:** Vice-President, Endow, Inc, 180 N LaSalle #1700, Chicago, IL 60601.

SMITH, ANTHONY EDWARD
Operations manager. **PERSONAL:** Born Nov 14, 1961, Harvey, IL. **EDUCATION:** Univ of IL at Urbana, BS Engrg 1983. **CAREER:** Owens-Corning Fiberglas, engrg intern 1981-82; IL Bell Telephone Co, asst mgr 1983-86, area mgr 1986-. **ORGANIZATIONS:** Mem Amer Youth Foundation 1978-; pres Black Student Union Univ of IL 1980-81; mem IL Soc of General Engrs 1982-83; mem Rotary Intl Harvey Club 1986-; mem Natl Black MBA Assoc. **HONORS/ACHIEVEMENTS:** Larson Awd for Creative Solutions to Complex Engr Problems Univ of IL 1983; featured in US Black Engr High Tech Jobs in Midwest 1987.

SMITH, ARTHUR D.
Educational administrator. **EDUCATION:** Kent State Univ, BS 1957, MA 1962; Yale Univ, PhD 1973. **CAREER:** Transitional Program Yale Univ, dir 1968-70; Baldwin-King Program Yale Child Study Center, dir 1970-73; Yale Univ, asst dean 1973-74; Northwestern Univ, assoc prof 1974-78; Northeastern Univ, dean 1978-80, assoc provost 1981-86, dir of planning 1986. **ORGANIZATIONS:** Educ consultant Amer Friends 1974-; chmn of bd Northcare 1976; assoc provost Northeastern Univ 1980-; program volunteer evaluator United Way Boston 1979-80. **HONORS/ACHIEVEMENTS:** John Hay Fellow John Hay Whitney Found 1964; Branford Coll Fellow Yale Univ 1972. **BUSINESS ADDRESS:** Dean, NortheasternUniv, 360 Huntington Ave, Boston, MA 02115.

SMITH, ARTHUR D.
Retired educator, business executive. **PERSONAL:** Born Feb 05, 1913, Sailes, LA; married Lucille T Walton; children: Arthur D Jr, Billy C, Lonnie B, Cassandra. **EDUCATION:** Leland Coll, AB 1939; Western Reserve Univ, MA 1949; further study Western Reserve, Univ of SC, Univ of CO, LA State Univ. **CAREER:** Teacher, 1939-42; Grambling Coll, assoc

prof ed 1946-70; Smith Ins, owner/oper 1961-77; A D Smith Insurance Inc, principal owner/pres 1978-. **ORGANIZATIONS:** Mem Phi Delta Kappa Prof Frat, Amer Assn Univ Prof, Natl Educ Assn, Natl Assn Teacher Educ, Natl Assn Sec Sch Prin, Natl Bus League, Natl Assn Ins Agents; mem Grambling Town Council (retired 1985 after 20 yrs svcs); mem bd dir two bus corps; 33rd Deg Mason; deacon & fin sec Mt Zion Bap Church; mayor-protem of Grambling; mem NAACP; pres Grambling Voters League. **HONORS/ACHIEVEMENTS:** Grad High Hon Leland Coll 1939; Citizen of Yr Awd of Grambling by Phi Beta Sigma Frat 1965; Citizen of Yr Awd of Grambling by Phi Beta Sigma Frat 1965; Hon 33rd Deg 1972; Silver Beaver Awd serv to Scouting 1974. **MILITARY SERVICE:** Chief warrant off 1942-46. **BUSINESS ADDRESS:** President, AD Smith Insurance Co, 102 W Grand Ave, PO Box 628, Grambling, LA 71245.

SMITH, ARTHUR L., JR. See ASANTE, MOLEFI KETE

SMITH, ASHBY GORDON, JR.
Association executive. **PERSONAL:** Born 1932. **EDUCATION:** Univ Chgo; Roosevelt U. **CAREER:** Bureau of Emplymnt Security, rsrch analyst; Chicago Urban Leag, asst to dir 1964-71; State IL, manpower plng splst; IL State Emplymnt Svc, supt.

SMITH, BARBARA
Writer. **PERSONAL:** Born Nov 16, 1946, Cleveland, OH. **EDUCATION:** Mount Holyoke Coll, BA 1969; Univ of Pittsburgh, MA 1971. **CAREER:** Univ of MA, instructor 1976-81; Barnard Coll, instructor 1983; NY Univ, instructor 1985; Univ of MN, vstg prof 1986; vstg prof Hobart William Smith Coll, 1987; Kitchen Table Women of Color Press, director. **ORGANIZATIONS:** Mem/founder Combahee River Collective 1974-80; artist-in-residence Hambidge Ctr for the Arts & Sci 1983, Millay Colony for the Arts 1983, Yaddo 1984, Blue Mountain Ctr 1985; bd of dir NCBLG 1985-; mem NAACP. **HONORS/ACHIEVEMENTS:** Outstanding Woman of Color Awd 1982; Women Educator's Curriculum Awd 1983; Books, "Conditions, Five The Black Women's Issue," co-editor 1979; "But Some of UsAre Brave, Black Women's Studies," co-editor 1982; "Home Girls, A Black Feminist Anthology," editor 1983; "Yours in Struggle, Three Feminist Perspectives on Anti-Semitism and Racism," co-author 1984. **BUSINESS ADDRESS:** Dir, Kitchen Table Women of Color, PO Box 908, Latham, NY 12110.

SMITH, BENJAMIN FRANKLIN
Educator. **PERSONAL:** Born in Martinsville, VA; married Dorothy P; children: Pamela Elizabeth. **EDUCATION:** VA Union Univ, BS 1940; Univ of IL, BS 1941, MS 1945; NY Univ, MA 1949, PhD 1951. **CAREER:** NC Coll, prof of psychology 1947-64; Univ of IL, vis prof grad sch 1964; Towson State Univ, part-time prof 1966, 1967; Jessup State Hosp, psychologist 1969-70; Howard Univ, part-time prof 1970-72; Morgan State Univ, prof, Educ Psychology. **ORGANIZATIONS:** Talent scout, Amer Legion State of NC 1960-63; dir Off-Duty Educ Prog for Enlisted Men AUS 1942-45; Amer Psychol Assn; MD Psychol Assn; chmn human resources com MD Psychological Assn 1977; Amer Educ Rsch Assn; Phi Delta Kappa; NAACP; elder Grace Presbyterian Church; Amer Acad of Social Sciences; pres NC Library Assn; elected vice commander, Amer Legion State of NC. **HONORS/ACHIEVEMENTS:** Omega Man of the Yr; elder & clerk of sessions Grace United Presby Ch; mem evaluation teams for the State Dept of Pub Instr So Assn of Schs & CollsNatl Council for the Accreditation of Tchr Edn; mem Prgm Com of Div 16 APA 1975-77. **MILITARY SERVICE:** AUS. **BUSINESS ADDRESS:** Professor of Psychology, Morgan StateUniv, 315 Jenkins Bldg, Baltimore, MD 21239.

SMITH, BENNETT W., SR.
Clergyman. **PERSONAL:** Born Apr 07, 1933, Florence, AL; married Marilyn J Donelson, Dec 29, 1985; children: Debra T, Bennett W Jr, Lydia R Matthew T. **EDUCATION:** TN State Univ, BS 1958; Cinn Bapt Theo Sem, DD 1967; Medaille Clge, LLD 1979. **CAREER:** Oper Breadbasket Cinn OH, dir 1967-70; Oper PUSH Buffalo NY, pres 1973-; Oper PUSH, Natl bd mem 1973-; VA MI Housing Co, bd chrmn 1981-; Pres Oper PUSH Buffalo, pastor St John Baptist Ch. **ORGANIZATIONS:** Life mem NAACP 1978-, Kappa Alpha Psi Frat 1979-; vice pres Prog Natl Bapt Conv 1984-. **HONORS/ACHIEVEMENTS:** Medgar Evers NAACP Buffalo NY 1982; Outstanding Bl Ach 1490 Enterprise 1981. **MILITARY SERVICE:** USAF s/sgt. **BUSINESS ADDRESS:** Pastor, Pres Oper PUSH Buffalo, 184 Goodell St, Buffalo, NY 14204.

SMITH, BERNICE LEWIS
Educational administrator. **PERSONAL:** Born in St Louis, MO; married Thomas Peter (deceased); children: Karla Denyce. **EDUCATION:** Stowe Tchrs Clge, AB 1948; Univ of IL, MA 1951; St Louis Univ, 1963; Univ of Chicago, 1952; SE MO State Univ, 1972; Harris-stowe State, 1976; Univ of MO, Post Grad 1980. **CAREER:** Riddick School, teacher 1948-51; Riddick Branch School, teacher 1950-51; Clark Elem School, principal 1956-58; Clark Branch 1 School, teacher 1958-67; Clark Branch 2 School, principal 1967-84; Arlington Elem School, principal 1984-. **ORGANIZATIONS:** Bd mem MO Kidney Fnd 1976-83; courtesy comm Elem Schl Admin 1978-; corr secr Sigma Gamma Rho Sor Inc 1982-84; lecturer and TV appearances Kidney Fnd 1976-; pres Wayman AME Church Schlrshp Council 1984-. **HONORS/ACHIEVEMENTS:** Mother of the Year Sigma Gamma Rho 1982; Apple for the Teacher Iota Phi Lambda 1983; Outstanding Comm Srv St Louis Ambassadors 1983; 1988 Bould Hostess Sigma Gamma Rho Sor Inc. **BUSINESS ADDRESS:** Principal, Arlington School, 1617 Burd Ave, St Louis, MO 63112.

SMITH, BETTIE M.
Educator. **PERSONAL:** Born Apr 26, 1914, Knoxville; married David L. **EDUCATION:** TN A&IUniv Nashville, BS; NY U, MA, EdD. **CAREER:** Catoosa & Whitfield Cts GA, teacher; Emory St HS Dalton, GA, teacher coach; Stephens School Calhoun, GA, prin; Harrison HS West Point, prin; NY Univ, instr; FL A&M, assc prof; School Food Serv Program GA State Dept of Educ, instr; Twin Cities Ext Am Theol Sem Nashville, instr; Stillman Coll Tuscaloosa, AL, prof. **ORGANIZATIONS:** Mem Natl Assc; GA Cncl Scndry Sch; prins Natl Ed & GA Assc Ed; Am Assc AL Assc For Hlth, Phy Ed & Recreation; Am Sch Food Assc; Am SchHlth Assc; Schlmstrs Clb GA; GA State Bd Am Cancer Soc; GA Chap Pi Lambda Theta; Alpha Kappa Mu; Alpha Kappa Alpha; former Mem GA Textbook Selection Com; rep NYUniv at World Hlth Orgn Helsink, Finland; mem GA Com White House Conf on Ed. **HONORS/ACHIEVEMENTS:** Woman of yr Dalton GA. **BUSINESS ADDRESS:** Box 4901, Stillman Coll, Tuscaloosa, AL 35401.

SMITH, BEVERLY EVANS
Association executive. **PERSONAL:** Born Apr 12, 1948, Massillm, OH; daughter of Louie Edward Evans and Willa Dumas Evans; married Stephen J Smith, Aug 28, 1971; children: Brian S, Stacy N. **EDUCATION:** Bowling Green State Univ, Bowling Green OH, BS, 1970; Kent State Univ, Kent OH, MEd, 1973; Babson Coll, Wellesly MA, Exec Devel Consortium, 1987. **CAREER:** Kent State Univ, Kent OH, asst dir, Financial Aids, 1972-74, dir, Upward Bound, 1974; Georgia State Univ, Atlanta GA, asst dean, Student Life, 1976-78; Southern Bell, Atlanta GA, staff manager, 1978-83; AT&T, Atlanta GA, dist mgr, 1984-88; Delta Sigma Theta, Washington DC, exec dir, 1988-. **ORGANIZATIONS:** Past officer, mem, Delta Sigma Theta Sorority Inc, 1967-; past pres, Jack & Jill Inc, North Suburban Atlanta Chapter, 1981-84; state commr, Georgia Clean & Beautiful Commn, 1984-88; chair, Adult Educ, St Catherine's Episcopal Church, 1986-88; mem, Leadership Cobb, Cobb County Georgia Selection, 1987-88, Project Mgmt Inst, 1987-89, Assn Chief Exec Council, 1988-89; bd mem, Women for a Meaningful Summit, 1989. **HONORS/ACHIEVEMENTS:** Outstanding Freshman & Senior Woman, Bowling Green State Univ, 1967, 1970; Mortar Bd Honor Soc, 1969; Omicrom Delta Kappa Honor Soc, 1977; Georgia Woman of the Year in Business, Cobb County Georgia, 1984; Outstanding Business Professional, Washington DC Business Professional Assn, 1988. **BUSINESS ADDRESS:** National Executive Director, Delta Sigma Theta Sorority Inc, 1707 New Hampshire Ave NW, Washington, DC 20009.

SMITH, BOBBY ANTONIA
Government official. **PERSONAL:** Born Feb 12, 1949, West Palm Beach, FL; daughter of Will Smith and Ida Mae Smith; divorced; children: Antonia, Erika. **EDUCATION:** Florida A&M Univ, Tallahassee FL, BS, 1970; Florida State Univ, Tallahassee FL, MPA, 1972; Nova Univ, Ft Lauderdale FL, 1983—. **CAREER:** Broward County School District, Pompano Beach FL, instructor, 1970-73; Florida Dept of Community Affairs, Tallahassee FL, local govt spec II, 1973-75; Florida WPB, asst county administrator, 1975—. **ORGANIZATIONS:** NAACP, Urban League of Palm Beach County. **HONORS/ACHIEVEMENTS:** Public service award, Florida A&M Univ, 1979. **BUSINESS ADDRESS:** Assistant County Administrator, Palm Beach County Board of County Commissioners, 301 North Olive, Governmental Center Complex (11th Floor), West Palm Beach, FL 33402.

SMITH, BUBBA
Former professional athlete, actor. **PERSONAL:** Born 1947; divorced. **EDUCATION:** MI State, Sociology. **CAREER:** Baltimore Colts, defensive lineman 1967-71; Oakland Raiders; defensive lineman 1972-74; Houston Oilers, defensive lineman 1975-77; Actor, Blue Thunder 1984, Half Nelson 1985, Police Academy, Police Academy II, Black Moon Rising, The Fun Buch; Video, Until It Hurts; Miller Beer Co, spokesman 1976-. **ORGANIZATIONS:** Vol Young People in LA Area. **HONORS/ACHIEVEMENTS:** All American MI State 1965, 1966; All American Team Sporting News 1966; First Player selected NFL Draft 1967; AFC All Star Team Sporting News 1970, 1971; player Super Bowl 1969, 1971; player AFC Championship 1973, 1974. **BUSINESS ADDRESS:** Spokesman, Miller Beer, 3939 West Highland Blvd, Milwaukee, WI 53201.

SMITH, CALVERT H.
College president. **CAREER:** Morris Brown College, Atlanta, GA, president. **BUSINESS ADDRESS:** Morris Brown College, Atlanta, GA 30314. *

SMITH, CALVIN MILES
Dentist. **PERSONAL:** Born Dec 11, 1924, Atlanta, GA; son of Harvey Smith and Stella Smith; married Margaret Odessa Nixon; children: Calvin Miles, Stephen LaCoste, Lynne LaVada, Kim Clarice. **EDUCATION:** Morehouse Coll, BS 1948; Howard Univ, DDS 1953. **CAREER:** Ballard HS Macon, teacher 1948-49; Atlanta Res Manpower Training Ctr, den consul; Dentistry, Atlanta 1953-. **ORGANIZATIONS:** Mem Amer Den Soc; pres GA Den Soc 1964-65; pres N GA Den Soc 1963-64; mem N Dist Den Assn; mem house del GA Den Assn; sports comm chmn Natl Den Assn; panel chmn Atlanta Comm Chest 1966-67; pres Atlanta NAACP 1963-64, treas 1962, 1965-66; Atlanta Comm Coop Act 1961-; Mayor's Comm Hot & Res Deseg 1961; mem Atlanta C of C; Gr Atlanta Hous Dev Coop; mem Exec Atlanta Model Cities Prog vice chmn 1967-75; Atlanta Youth Coun 1968; vice pres Fulton Co Dem Club 1963-71; chmn bd Sadie G Mays Mem Inst Care Nurs Home 1953-; 32nd Degree Mason. **HONORS/ACHIEVEMENTS:** Citizen Yr 1964; Ach Awd from Guardsmen 1964; Pgh Civic League Awd for Ded Serv in Model Cities 1974; Dist Serv Awd Morehouse Club 1961; listed in Marquis "Who's Who in S & SE 1973-74; Natl Social Directory 1977; Unheralded Citizens Awd Atlanta Job Corps 1977; Outstanding Achievement Awd Radio Station WLTA-100 1979; Disting Alumnus Achievement Awd Morehouse Coll 1976; 25th Anniversary Awd Howard Univ Alumni Assn 1978; Appreciation Awd North GA Dental Soc 1979; Appreciation Awd Atlanta Guardsmen 1980; Atlanta Magazine as one of Atlanta's City Shapers; Harper Awd & Procalmation for COntributions NAACP; AB Cooper Awd & Past Pres Awd 1983 from N Ga Dental Soc; honorable fellow awd GA Dental Assoc 1983. **MILITARY SERVICE:** USMCR pto 1944-46. **BUSINESS ADDRESS:** Dentist, 2380 B E Mays Dr, SW, Atlanta, GA 30311.

SMITH, CARL REGINALD (REGGIE SMITH)
Athlete. **PERSONAL:** Born Apr 02, 1945, Shreveport, LA. **EDUCATION:** Compton Comm Clg. **CAREER:** LA Dodgers, plyr 1976; St Louis Cardinals 1973-76; Boston Red Sox 1966-73. **ORGANIZATIONS:** Am League All Star 1969, 72, 74, 75, 77, 78; Natl League All Star 1974. **BUSINESS ADDRESS:** LA Dodgers, Dodger Stad 1000 Elysian Pk Ave, Los Angeles, CA 90012.

SMITH, CARL WILLIAM
Administrator. **PERSONAL:** Born Jun 08, 1931, Raleigh, NC; married Pearl Mitchell Wilson; children: Wanda, Wendi. **EDUCATION:** St Augustine Coll, BA (Honors) 1954; NC Central Univ, MSC 1962; Univ of WI-Madison, attended 1965; The Exec Program Univ NC-Chapel Hill, Certificate1981. **CAREER:** CE Perry HS, asst principal/teacher 1954-55; St Augustine's Coll, administrator/instructor 1955-60; NC Central Univ, asst chmn/faculty 1961-72; Univ NC-Chapel Hill, asst to the provost 1972-. **ORGANIZATIONS:** Consultant PPG Industries 1969, 70, 71; mem Amer Mgmt Assoc, Amer Marketing Assoc, Amer Assoc of Higher Educ. **HONORS/ACHIEVEMENTS:** Alpha Phi Alpha Frat Inc; Alpha Kappa Mu; Fellowship Natl Urban League 1968. **MILITARY SERVICE:** USAF airman 1949. **HOME ADDRESS:** 1310 Oakwood Ave, Raleigh, NC 27610. **BUSINESS ADDRESS:** Asst to the Provost, University of North Carolina, 104B South Bldg UNC-CH, Chapel Hill, NC 27514.

SMITH, CAROL BARLOW
City empolyee. **PERSONAL:** Born Mar 09, 1945, Atlanta, GA; married Douglas Smith; children: Eric Douglas. **EDUCATION:** AK Business College, attended 1965. **CAREER:** Gr Anchorage Area Comm Action Agency Northwest Rep of Women's Caucus, public information specialist; BLM Anchorage, asst to chief br of field surveys; City of Anchorage, eeo officer; Municipality of Anchorage, affirm action adm, safety officer. **ORGANIZATIONS:** Mem Intl Assn of Official Human Rights Agencies; bd dir AK Presswomen; Council on Drug Abuse; Council for Planned Parenthood; bd dir Citizens for Consumer Protection; YWMU; pres New Hope Bapt Ch; mem bd commrs AK State Human Rights Commn; past 2nd vice pres NAACP; AK Presswomen; Anchorage Bicentennial Commn; chmn AK State Human Rights Comm 1976; Anchorage Equal Rights assn; chairperson NAACP Freedom Fund Banquet 1972; vice chairperson AK State Human RightsCommn. **HONORS/ACHIEVEMENTS:** Business Leader of the Day 1974. **BUSINESS ADDRESS:** Safety Officer, Municipality of Anchorage, 550 West 8th Ave, Ste 202, Anchorage, AK 99501.

SMITH, CAROL J. (CAROL J. HOBSON)
Private consultant. **PERSONAL:** Born Dec 24, 1923, Houston, TX; daughter of Richard T Andrews, Sr and Julia Augusta Somerville Andrews; divorced; children: Julius W Hobson Jr, Jean M Hobson Tilley. **EDUCATION:** Prairie View, BA 1944; Howard Univ, MA 1948. **CAREER:** US Office of Education, deputy acting asst commn for spec concern 1971-74; US Dept of Educ Office of Postsecondary Educ, liaison for minorities & women in higher educ 1974-84, prog delegate natl adv committee on black higher educ & black colls & univs 1976-82; US Dept of Educ Office of Higher Educ Progs, dir Div of Student Serv 1984-86; private practice, consultant. **ORGANIZATIONS:** Bd mem Jr Achievement of Washington DC; elder Church of the Redeemer Presbyterian; mem adv consult NAFEO's Rsch Adv Bd; bd mem Talent Search Univ of MD Coll Park Campus; mem Mayor's Advisory Comm on Elem, Secondary School and Postsecondary Educ Committees; Consultant, Educ Braintrust, Congressional Black Caucus; vice pres B May's Research Center. **HONORS/ACHIEVEMENTS:** Graduate Fellowships Howard Univ 1944-45 1947-48; Superior Serv Awd US Office of Educ 1970; Cert for Outstanding Performance US Dept of Educ Office of the Postsecondary Educ 1979; Achievement Awd Natl Alliance of Black Sch Educators 1982; Leadership Awd in Higher Educ Natl Assn for Equal Oppor in Higher Educ 1983; Honored by Natl Council of Educ Oppor Assoc 1986. **BUSINESS ADDRESS:** Consultant, 4801 Queens Chapel Terr NE, Washington, DC 20017.

SMITH, CAROLYN LEE
Business executive. **PERSONAL:** Born Nov 14, 1942, Lakewood, NJ; daughter of Davis Lee and Arline Erwin; married Vernon; children: Sonia, Angela. **EDUCATION:** Howard U, BA 1965; Am U, 1972. **CAREER:** DC Dept of Fin & Revenue, dir govt dc, tres 1977-79; Cooper & Lybrand, audit mgr 1971-77; natl inst for comm dev, vice pres fin mgmt 1972-73; United Plng Orgn, bkpng methods speclst 1965-66; Coopers & Lybrand, audit mgr 1982-85, dir, mgmt consult 1985-86, partner 1986. **ORGANIZATIONS:** Mem Natl Assoc Black Accts; past pres Met Wash DC Chapt; mem Greater Wash Bd of Trade 1983-; treas Public Access Bd 1985-87; chmn DC Bd of Accountancy 1985-88; bd of gov DC Inst of CPAs 1985-87; mem DC Retirement Bd 1988-92. **HONORS/ACHIEVEMENTS:** DC CPA 1969; Meritorious Service Awds from DC Govt 1979,80; Outstanding Achievement Awd Natl Assoc of Minority CPA Firms 1979; Key to the City of Cleveland 1981; Proclamation from the Mayor of the District of Columbia for Outstanding Service 1982. **BUSINESS ADDRESS:** Partner, Coopers & Lybrand, 1800 M St NW, Washington, DC 20036.

SMITH, CARSON EUGENE
Education administration. **PERSONAL:** Born Dec 23, 1943, Louisville, KY; married Gleneva McCowan; children: Mark, Shanna, Angela, Andrew. **EDUCATION:** KY State Univ, BA History & Pol Sci 1965; Univ of KY, MA Pol Sci 1972, Dissertation Stage 1973. **CAREER:** Office for Policy & Mgmt State Govt, policy adv for higher educ 1973-74; Council on Higher Educ, coor for fin planning 1974-77; Univ of KY, asst budget dir 1977-80; Univ of MO, asst dir budget 1980-83; KY State Univ, vice pres business affairs. **ORGANIZATIONS:** Mem Central Assoc of Coll & Univ Bus Officers, Southern Assoc of Coll & Univ Bus Officers, Natl Assoc of Coll & Univ Bus Officers, Alpha Phi Alpha 1962-. **MILITARY SERVICE:** USAF capt 4 yrs. **HOME ADDRESS:** 169 Bellemeade Dr, Frankfort, KY 40601. **BUSINESS ADDRESS:** VP For Business Affairs, Kentucky State University, 261 Academic Serv Bldg, Frankfort, KY 40601.

SMITH, CHARLES
Retired county official. **PERSONAL:** Born Oct 04, 1914, Lowndes, AL; son of Nathaniel Smith and Odell Pradd Smith; married Ella Mae Timmon Smith, Oct 26, 1936; children: Jess C, Charles E, Mary Lu Allen, Doris Collier, Lonnie, Josephos, El oise, Ferlonia Davis, Eli B, Jeremiah, Theo. **EDUCATION:** Univ WI, Cert from Flwng Inst 1968; Penn Comm Ctr 1968; Lowndes Co Training Sch. **CAREER:** Shipyard Mobile, AL, erector 1942-45; Farmer 1945-65; Lowndes Co Bd Deacons Mt Calvary Bapt Ch, co commr; Lawndes Co State of AL, county commissioner. **ORGANIZATIONS:** Chmn Lowndes & Co Christian Movement; mem adv coun of Title I Pgm in Lownde Co; bd dir Lowndes Co Hlth Serv Assc. **HONORS/ACHIEVEMENTS:** Awrd Natl Urban League for Equal Opportunity 1969; Ford Fellowhship 1970-71; Citation of Merit Award Auburn Univ AL. **HOME ADDRESS:** RFD 1 Box 271, Letohatchee, AL 36047.

SMITH, CHARLES EDWARD (TANK)
Athlete. **PERSONAL:** Born Jul 26, 1950, Monroe, LA; married Bernice. **EDUCATION:** Grambling State U, BS 1973. **CAREER:** Philadelphia Eagles, wide receiver 1974-; LA Rams, 1973; Monroe LA, sub tchr.

SMITH, CHARLES F., JR.
Educator. **PERSONAL:** Born Jan 05, 1933, Cleveland, OH; son of Charles Frank Smith, Sr and Julia Anna Worthy; married Lois Thompson; children: Carolyn Adelle, Charles Frank III. **EDUCATION:** Bowling Green State Univ, BS 1960; Kent State Univ, EdM 1963; Harvard Univ Grad School Ed, CAS 1965; MI State Univ, EdD 1969. **CAREER:** Elementary School Teacher Lorain OH 1960-62; Peace Corps Field Trgn Ctr Puerto Rico, dir 1962-63; Peace Corps, spec asst 1963; Flint Publ Schools, asst dir elem ed 1965-66; MI State Univ, instr ed 1966-68; Boston Coll, assoc prof ed 1968-. **ORGANIZATIONS:** Mem adv task force MA Comm Crim Justice; adv council MA Council Bilingual Ed; adv comm MA Comm Minority Higher Ed; bd of dir School Vols Boston; adv task force, implement phase I deseg Boston Publ School; chmn Area Welfare Bd; vice pres Black Citizen of Newton; chmn Black Faculty Staff and Administrators Assoc of Boston Coll; mem Curriculum Comm Natl Cncl for the Social Studies; bd of dir MA Council of the Social Studies; bd of dir, Natl Council for the Social Studies. **HONORS/ACHIEVEMENTS:** Phi Delta Kappa Teaching Fellow Harvard Univ Grad School Ed 1963-65, Danforth Assoc 1974; Traveling Fellowships Cameroons & Nigeria, Africa, 1958,60, Canada 1957, Germany 1954, Jamaica 1953; Visiting Scholar Univ of MI 1988. **MILITARY SERVICE:** US Army medic 1954-56. **BUSINESS ADDRESS:** Associate Professor Education, Boston College, Campion Hall, 140 Commonwealth Ave, Chestnut Hill, MA 02167.

SMITH, CHARLES J.
Business executive. **PERSONAL:** Born Feb 07, 1935, New York, NY; children: Charles Jr, David. **EDUCATION:** Fordham Univ, BA. **CAREER:** Natl Broadcasting Co, asst mag editor press & publ dept 1953, sr mag editor 1962; RCA Corp News & Info Dept, admin, radio &TV news, staff writer, dir publ relations 1968-. **HONORS/ACHIEVEMENTS:** Color TV Pioneer Awd 1974.

SMITH, CHARLES JAMES, III
Educational administrator. **PERSONAL:** Born Oct 07, 1926, Savannah, GA; married Wilma Anis; children: Donna, Charles IV. **EDUCATION:** TN State Univ, AB 1947; St Univ of IA, MA 1948; Univ of MN, Postgrad; FL A&M Univ, attended. **CAREER:** Savannah State Coll, dir publicity & publ 1948-50; FL A&M Univ, dir publ rel, assoc prof 1950-63; Royal Crown Cola Co, dir, spec mkts 1963-71; TheGreyhound Corp Phoenix, asst to vice pres special mkts 1971-78; TX So Univ, dir media relations. **ORGANIZATIONS:** Art on black consumer mkt Annual Emphasis 1966-87; pres 1970-71, bd chmn 1971-75 Natl Assoc of Mktg Dev; mem Sigma Delta Chi Prol Jrnl Soc, Publ Rel Soc of Amer, Amer Mkt Assoc, Delta Phi Delta Natl Jrnl Soc; former bd mem, vice pres 1973-75, budget comm chmn 1974-76 Phoenix Scottsdale United Way; bd mem Valley Big Bros; past bd mem Phoenix Urban League & Lead Conf on Civil Rights; former mem adv comm US Census Bur for Accurate Black Count 1980. **HONORS/ACHIEVEMENTS:** Newspaper Fund Fellow Mass Media Univ of MN 1971; author A Guide to Total Mkt Penetration 1968. **BUSINESS ADDRESS:** Dir Media Relations, Texas SouthernUniv, 3100 Cleburne, Houston, TX 77004.

SMITH, CHARLES LEBANON
Administrator. **PERSONAL:** Born Apr 30, 1938, Neptune, NJ; married Muriel Lyle; children: Stacey, Romy, Kecia. **EDUCATION:** Albright Coll Reading PA, BA psychology 1960. **CAREER:** US Dept of Labor Labor Mgmt Svc, reg adminstr; US Dept of Labor Labor Mgmt Serv Adminstrn, asst reg adminstr 1977-78; US Dept of Labor Labor Mgmt Serv Adminstrn, dep asst reg adminstr 1975-77; US Dept of Labor Labor Mgmt SvcAdminstrn, field liason officer 1974-75; US Dept of Labor Labor Mgmt Serv Adminstrn, sr compliance officer 1970-74; US Dept of Labor Labor Mgmt Serv Adminstrn, compliance officer 1966-70. **ORGANIZATIONS:** Mem So of Fed Labor Relations Professional 1972-; mem Indsl Relations Research Assn 1978-; mem Omega Psi Phi Frat Inc 1974-; former chmn NJ Black HeritageFestival 1978-79. **HONORS/ACHIEVEMENTS:** Secretary's Spl Commendation US Dept of Labor 1973. **BUSINESS ADDRESS:** US Dept of Labor Labor Mgmt Sr, Room 3515 1515 Broadway, New York, NY 10036.

SMITH, CHARLES U.
Educator. **PERSONAL:** Born in Birmingham; children: Shauna. **EDUCATION:** Tuskegee Inst, BA 1944; Fisk Univ, MA 1946; WA State Univ, PhD 1950; Univ of MI, postdoctoral study 1958. **CAREER:** FL A&M Univ, grad dean 1974-. **ORGANIZATIONS:** Pres So Sociol Soc; mem Amer Sociol Assn 1960-; Natl Soc Study Educ 1973-; Amer Acad Polit Soc Sci 1969-; WFSU TV adv Com 1973-; edit bd Journal Soc & Behavioral Sci 1973-; adj prof sociol FL State Univ 1966-; state committeeman 1975; mem Leon Co Dem exec comm 1969-; bd dir Leon Co CAP 1972-; bd of advisors FL Mental Health Inst; pres Conf of Deans of Black Grad Schs; mem Council of Grad Schls in US; Conf of So Grad Schs; editoral bd Negro Ed Review 1976-; editor FL A&M Rsch Bulletin 1960-; consul SC Comm on Higher Educ 1984. **HONORS/ACHIEVEMENTS:** Honor Societies, Alpha Kappa Delta, Pi Gamma Mu, Alpha Kappa Mu, Phi Delta Kappa, Sigma Rho Sigma, Phi Kappa Phi, Lambda Alpha Epsilon; plaque Serv Dept Sociol 1970; Coll Athletics 1966; Cert Serv State FL 1965 1972; Silver Mental Health Serv 1966; Gold Medallion 1970; FL delegate White House Conf 1960 1965 19701971; DuBois Awd Scholarship Serv 1973; FL A&M Univ Merit Achievement Awd 1973; plaque Sociol 1974; listed in numerous publs. **BUSINESS ADDRESS:** Graduate Dean, FL A&MUniv, PO Box 895, FLA&M Univ, Tallahassee, FL 32302.

SMITH, CHARLIE CALVIN
Educator. **PERSONAL:** Born Jun 12, 1943, Brickeys, AR; son of Charlie Smith and Estella Smith; married Earline Williams. **EDUCATION:** AM & N Coll Pine Bluff AR, BA history 1966; AR StateUniv Jonesboro, MSE social science 1971;Univ of AR Fayetteville, PhD US history 1978. **CAREER:** AR State Univ, asst prof of History 1978-; AR State Univ, instructor in History 1970-78; Lee Co Pubic School Marianna AR, Social Studies teacher, asst football coach 1966-70; Arkansas State Univ, assoc prof of History, 1982-86, asst dean 1986-. **ORGANIZATIONS:** Comm mem AR Endowment for the Humanities 1975-77; govs appointee bd mem AR Student Loan Assn 1975-76; govs appointee bd mem AR Historic Preservation Program 1979-84; mem Jonesboro Rotary Club, 1987-; pres Southern Conference on Afro-Amer Studies, 1988-. **HONORS/ACHIEVEMENTS:** Published "The Oppressed Oppressors Negro Slavery among the choctaws of OK" red river valley history review vol 2 1975; published "the civil war letters of John G Marsh" Upper OH Valley History Review 1979; published "The Diluting of an Inst the social impact of WWII on the AR family" AR history quarter (spring) 1980; published biographical sketches of AR Governors J Marion Futrell & Homer M Adkins AR Ednowment for the Humanities 1980; Presidential Fellow, Arkansas State Univ, 1982; Outstanding Black Faculty Member/Teacher, Black Student Body ASU, 1984-86, 1988; War and Wartime Changes; The Transformation of Arkansas, 1940-45, Uof A Press, 1987. **BUSINESS ADDRESS:** Assistant Dean, College of Arts & Sciences, Professor of History, Arkansas State University, PO Box 1030, State University, AR 72467.

SMITH, CHESTER B.
Government official. **PERSONAL:** Born Jul 01, 1954, Mound Bayou, MS. **EDUCATION:** Tufts Univ, BA 1976; Northwestern Univ, MBA 1977, JD 1980. **CAREER:** Delta Capital Corp, vice-pres 1980-84; Pro-Mark Inc, financial consultant 1984-85; Private Practice, attorney 1983-86; US Dept of Commerce Minority Business Dev Agency, asst dir 1986-. **ORGANIZATIONS:** Vstg prof Black Exec Exchange Program 1981-83; former dir New Memphis Dev Corp 1981-84; founder Ctr for Economic Growth 1982; mem MS State Bar

Assoc 1982-87; consultant Project Business 1982-85; consultant TN Valley Authority 1985-86. **HONORS/ACHIEVEMENTS:** Junior Achievement 1983-85; Disting Serv Awd Natl Business League 1986; Executive Forum Dept of Commerce 1987. **HOME ADDRESS:** PO Box 2746, Arlington, VA 22202. **BUSINESS ADDRESS:** Assistant Dir, US Dept of Commerce, 14th & Pennsylvania Ave, Room 5096, Washington, DC 20230.

SMITH, CLEVELAND EMANUEL
Physician. **PERSONAL:** Born Oct 05, 1924, Panama; married Beatrice; children: Nancy, Cleveland Jr, Clifford. **EDUCATION:** Howard U, BS 1950; Howard U, MD 1955; resd 1961; cert ob gyn. **CAREER:** Dept Ob Gyn Howard Univ Coll Med, asst prof 1961-75; Ob Gyn Serv Columbia Hosp for Women, chf; Cleveland E Smith Flw Am Coll Ob Gyn, pres. **ORGANIZATIONS:** Mem Nat Med Assn; Med Chirurgical Soc DC; Dist Med Soc; Med Bd Dir Planned Parenthood. **BUSINESS ADDRESS:** 29 Grant Cir NW, Washington, DC 20011.

SMITH, CONRAD P.
Attorney. **PERSONAL:** Born Feb 15, 1932, Detroit, MI; son of Alfred Smith and Minnie J Smith; married Elsie May Smith, Nov 27, 1957; children: Judy E Smith, Conrad W Smith. **EDUCATION:** Howard Univ, BS 1962; Howard Univ, JD 1969. **CAREER:** US Justice Dept, statistical analyst 1962; US Dept of Labor, manpower research analyst 1962-64; US Comm on Civil Rights, soc sci analyst 1964-66; US Comm on Civil Rights, asst gen counsel 1969-73; private practice law. **ORGANIZATIONS:** Chmn Ward 1 Dem Comm Wash DC; mem ACLU; NAACP; Urban League; People's Involment Corp; Civic Assn; DC Bar Assn; Danford Fellow 1961; candidate DC City Council 1974; mem DC Bd of Educ 1976-; pres DC Bd of Educ 1978; chmn DC Parent-Child Center Wash DC 1980-85. **MILITARY SERVICE:** AUS. **HOME ADDRESS:** 722 Fairmont St NW, Washington, DC 20001.

SMITH, DANIEL H., JR.
Attorney. **PERSONAL:** Born Apr 27, 1933, Chicago, IL; married Joyce; children: David, Robin. **EDUCATION:** Howard Univ, BA 1959, JD 1966. **CAREER:** Urban Renewal, consultant; Robin Shore Realty & Ins Agency, pres; Self-Employed, attorney. **ORGANIZATIONS:** Mem Amer Bar Assn, Natl Bar Assn; past vice pres Cook Co Bar Assn; mem Chicago, IL State Bar Assns; bd dir Legal Assit Found of Chicago; panelistfor Amer Arbitration Assn; mem The Amer Judicature Soc; Natl Assn of Real Estate Brokers; mem Dearborn Real Estate Bd; mem S Shore Gardens Comm Org; mem Phi Alpha Delta Law Frat; mem bd dirs Media Inc; mem J Leslie Rosenblum Chicago Boys Club, South Shore YMCA, Kuumba Comm Theater, VIP Associates. **MILITARY SERVICE:** USAF 1st lt 1952-56.

SMITH, DAVID R.
Attorney. **PERSONAL:** Born Sep 27, 1946, Loveland, OH; son of William E Smith and Mamie Robinson Smith; married Wessylyne French Smith, Apr 12, 1969; children: Kimberly K. **EDUCATION:** Central State Univ, Wilberforce OH, BA, 1969; DePaul Univ Coll of Law, Chicago IL, JD, 1974. **CAREER:** US Dept of Energy, Argonne IL, asst chief counsel, 1972-83; Cole & Smith, Chicago IL, partner, 1983-85; The MAXIMA Corp, Rockville MD, corporate sr vice pres, gen counsel sec, 1985-. **ORGANIZATIONS:** Alpha Phi Alpha Frat, 1969; Amer Bar Assn, Maryland Bar Assn, Natl Bar Assn, Illinois Bar Assn, Admitted to practice: US Supreme Court, US Claims Court, Federal Trial Bars for Illinois, Marland and the District of Columbia. **HONORS/ACHIEVEMENTS:** Outstanding Young Men of America, 1979; publications: "Contracting with The Federal Government: 10 Key Areas; Chicgo Bar Assn, 1984; Small Business and Technology Devel Contract Mgmt Magazine; Sphinx Magazine, 1983; "Exploring The Energy Frontier"; Natl Bar Assn, 1982.

SMITH, DAWN C. F.
Associate brand manager. **PERSONAL:** Born Dec 23, 1960, London, England;daughter of George Smith and Mavis Smith. **EDUCATION:** Brown Univ, BA 1982; Univ of MI, MBA 1985. **CAREER:** General Mills, market rsch intern 1984; Colgate Palmolive, asst brand mgr 1985-87; Kraft Inc, assoc brand mgr 1987-88; Jacobs Suchard, brand mgr 1988-. **ORGANIZATIONS:** Mem Natl Black MBA Assoc 1983-. **HONORS/ACHIEVEMENTS:** Co-managing editor Black Student's Guide to Colleges 1982; MBA Consortium Fellowship 1983-85; Natl Black MBA Scholarship 1984. **HOME ADDRESS:** 4800 S Lake Shore Dr, #2506-S, Chicago, IL 60615. **BUSINESS ADDRESS:** Brand Mgr, Jacobs Suchard, One Tower Ln, Oak brook Terrace, IL 60181.

SMITH, DEHAVEN L.
Attorney. **PERSONAL:** Born Aug 10, 1928, Baltimore, MD; married Gertrude Jackson; children: Rubye. **EDUCATION:** VA Union Univ, AB 1949; Univ MD School of Law, JD 1958. **CAREER:** Williams, Smith & Murphy, attorney. **ORGANIZATIONS:** Mem Am Bar Assn, Nat Bar Assn, Monumental City Bar Assn, Baltimore City Bar Assn Judicature Soc; World Peace through Law Comm; NAACP. **MILITARY SERVICE:** AUS 1950-52. **BUSINESS ADDRESS:** Attorney, Williams, Smith & Murphy, 34 Market Pl, Ste 324, Baltimore, MD 21202.

SMITH, DENNIS
Professional athlete. **PERSONAL:** Born Feb 03, 1959, Santa Monica, CA; married Andree; children: Tiffany Diamond, Armani Joseph. **EDUCATION:** Attended, Southern California. **CAREER:** Denver Broncos, safety 1981-. **HONORS/ACHIEVEMENTS:** Played in Rose Bowl, Bluebonnet Bowl; named All-NFL Pro Football Weekly, College and Pro Football Newsweekly 1984; All-AFC Pro Football Weekly UPI second team 1985; named All-NFL Coll and Pro Football Newsweekly; All-AFC UPI second team 1985; mem Pro Bowl teams 1986,87. **BUSINESS ADDRESS:** Denver Broncos, 5700 Logan St, Denver, CO 80216.

SMITH, DENNIS RAE
Engineer. **PERSONAL:** Born Oct 23, 1961, Lewisville, AR; son of Lannie A Smith and Ardenia L Smith; married Penny Harris Smith. **EDUCATION:** Southern Methodist Univ, BSEE 1985. **CAREER:** Rockwell International, test engineer. **ORGANIZATIONS:** Vice pres student chap Natl Soc of Black Engrs 1984-85; natl mem at large NAACP 1987; sec Hewlett-Packard Users Group 1987-88; volunteer Big Brothers & Sisters 1988-. **HONORS/ACHIEVEMENTS:** Featured in article "The Pulse-First Jobs" The Minority Engr Magazine 1986. **BUSINESS ADDRESS:** Test Engineer, Rockwell International, 1200 N Alma Rd, Richardson, TX 75081.

SMITH, DEREK EUGENE
Professional athlete. **PERSONAL:** Born Nov 01, 1961, Lagrange, GA; married Monica. **EDUCATION:** Louisville, 1982. **CAREER:** Los Angeles Clippers, guard 1983-; Golden State, 1982-83. **HONORS/ACHIEVEMENTS:** Was a 1st Team Metro Conf All-Tournmnt selection in each of his last 3 seasons at Louisville; also selected Co-Metro Conf Player of Year in 1980-81 as jr. **BUSINESS ADDRESS:** Los Angeles Clippers, 3939 S Figueroa St, Ste 510, Los Angeles, CA 90037.

SMITH, DOLORES J.
Human resources management consultant and trainer. **PERSONAL:** Born Feb 10, 1936, Lockport, IL; daughter of Ernest Gill Jones (deceased) and Mira Ellen (Jones) Sprinks; married Paul R Smith; children: Kathleen Lindsay, Robert, Debra, Alan, Paul II, Dolores II. **EDUCATION:** Roosevelt Univ, BS 1979; Ohio Univ Athens OH, MA 1983; Gestalt Inst of Cleveland, Post-Graduate Studies in Organization and Systems Devel 1989. **CAREER:** Smith's Office Serv, owner/mgr 1959-65; Suburban Echo Reporter, advertising mgr 1965-67; Jewel Cos Inc, area Personnel mgr 1967-79; Bausman Assocs, mgmt consultant 1979-80; WTTW Chicago, dir admin serv 1980-82; Ohio Univ, instructor/grad asst 1982-83; Columbia Coll Chicago, instructor 1983-; NBC WKQX Radio, producer/host 1983-86; DJ Smith Enterprises, pres 1983-. **ORGANIZATIONS:** Exec comm bd of dir Midwest Women's Ctr 1977-; mem NAACP, Amer Soc for Personnel Admin, Amer Soc for Training and Devel; trustee Wieboldt Found 1982-; bd of dirs Women and Foundations Corp Philanthropy 1984-; exec comm bd of dir Lambda Alpha Omega Chap Alpha Kappa Alpha Sor 1986-. **HONORS/ACHIEVEMENTS:** Appointed to Governor's Adv Council on Employment and Training 1977-82; Corporation for Public Broadcasting Scholar at Ohio Univ 1982-83; lecturer, moderator and panelist appearing before profl, univ and TV audiences on selected topics. **HOME ADDRESS:** PO Box 1083, Maywood, IL 60153. **BUSINESS ADDRESS:** President, DJ Smith Enterprises, PO Box 1083, Maywood, IL 60153.

SMITH, DONALD HUGH
Educator. **PERSONAL:** Born Mar 20, 1932, Chicago, IL; son of William and Madolene; divorced. **EDUCATION:** Univ of IL, AB 1953; DePaul, MA 1959; Univ of WI, PhD 1964. **CAREER:** Baruch Coll, prof, chairman, dept of educ; Chicago Pub Sch, tchr 1956-63; Cntr for Inner City Studies Northeastern IL U, asst prof asso prof dir 1964-68; Univ Comm Educ Prgms Univ of Pitts, prof dir 1968-69; Nat Urban Coalition Washington DC, exec asso 1969-70; Educ Devel Baruch Coll Cty of NY, prof dir 1970-. **ORGANIZATIONS:** Exec dir Chancellor's Task Force on SEEK Cty Univ of NY 1974-; Nat Adv Counc Voc Educ 1968-70; adv Doctoral Prgm in Educ Adminstrn Atlanta Univ 1975; Black Faculty of Cty Univ of NY 1970-; mem InterAm Congress of Psychology 1972-; advisor Martin Luther King Jr Ctr for Social Change; mem Nat Study Commn of Tchr Educ 1972-75; chmn task force NY State Dropout Problem; bd of dir NY Serv to Older People; consult to numerous schools & univs; pres Natl Alliance of Black School Educators 1983-85; chmn task force NY State Dropout Problem; bd dir NY Serv to Older People; consult to numerous schools & univs. **HONORS/ACHIEVEMENTS:** Recip Chicago Bd of Educ Flwshp 1962; Univ of WI Flwshp 1963; del White House Conf on the Disadvantaged 1966; Disting Leadership Awd Natl Alliance of Black School Educators 1986; Awd for Distinguished Serv NY State Black & Puerto Rican Legislation; Natl Alliance of Black School Educators Awd for Distinguished Leadership 1986; NY State Black & Puerto Rican Legislators Awd for Distinguished Svc. **MILITARY SERVICE:** AUS 1954-55.

SMITH, DONALD M.
Business manager. **PERSONAL:** Born Jul 12, 1931, Elgin, IL; married Martha L Smith; children: Tracy, Tiffany. **EDUCATION:** Purdue Univ, BA 1956, MA 1961. **CAREER:** Hills McCanna, shop supt 1960-69; Hemmenns Auditorium, gen mgr 1969-80; Rockford Metro Centre, oper mgr 1980-. **ORGANIZATIONS:** Mem Intl Assoc of Aud Mgr 1964, Amer Legion 1969-, Prince Hall Masons 1980-. **HONORS/ACHIEVEMENTS:** Founder of the Performing Arts for Young People 1969-80; Founder of the Elgin Area Arts Council 1969-80. **MILITARY SERVICE:** AUS, USAF sgt 5 yrs; Bronze Star, Korean Service Medal, Far East Campaign Medal 1949. **BUSINESS ADDRESS:** Operations Manager, Rockford Metro Centre, 300 Elm St, Rockford, IL 61101.

SMITH, DOROTHY J.
Educator. **PERSONAL:** Born Jun 24, 1948, Greenville, MS. **EDUCATION:** Tufts Univ, BA 1970, MEd 1971; Southern IL Univ, PhD 1981. **CAREER:** Southern IL Univ Office of Student Develop, coord of student develop 1979-81;MS Valley State Univ, asst prof & dir academic skills parlor 1971-. **ORGANIZATIONS:** Bd mem NAACP 1982-84; mem Post Doctoral Acad of Higher Ed 1979-; sec Les Modernette Social Club 1981-; mem Teacher Ed Comm MS Valley St 1983-; mem Intl Reading Assn 1985; mem Southern IL Univ Alumni Assn; mem Concerned Educators of Black Students; mem Southeast Regional Reading Conf; anti grammetus Alpha Kappa Alpha Sor Inc; mem Progressive Art and Civic Club, MS Reading Assoc, Natl Assoc of Develop Educators, MS Assoc of Develop Educators. **HONORS/ACHIEVEMENTS:** Clark Doctoral Scholar Awd for Rsch S IL Univ 1981; NAACP Education Awd MS 1981; Education Achievement Awd Progressive Art & Civic Club 1982; OutstandingYoung Women of America 1979-. **HOME ADDRESS:** 326 E Alexander St #12, Greenville, MS 38701. **BUSINESS ADDRESS:** Assistant Professor, MS Valley StateUniv, P O Box 247-MVS, Itta Bena, MS 38941.

SMITH, DOROTHY LOUISE WHITE
Educator. **PERSONAL:** Born Sep 28, 1939, Memphis, TN; daughter of Theodore Everett White and Ellie Mae Turner White; married Dr Carl Smith, Nov 26, 1958; children: Dr Carlton Edward Smith, Miss Sharian Shalon Smith. **EDUCATION:** Philander Smith Coll, Natl Methodist Scholar 1957-59; Cuyahoga Comm Coll 1963-64; California State Univ, MA English 1968-69; Case-Western Reserve Univ, BA English (summa cum laude) 1964-66; Univ of Southern California, EdD candidate. **CAREER:** Glenville High School, instructor of English 1966-67; Millikan High School, instructor of English 1969-70; Long Beach City Coll, instructor of English 1970-73; instructor of Afro-Amer literature and English San Diego City Coll 1973- (professional study leave); San Diego Unified Sch Dist, mem bd of Educ 1981-88; San Diego State Univ School of Teacher Educ, 1989-. **ORGANIZATIONS:** Mem Alpha Kappa Alpha Sorority 1958-; mem Women Inc 1974-; adv comm mem Allensworth State Historic Park 1977-; mem Assn of CA Urban School Dist 1982-87; mem CSBA Curriculum & Rsch Task Force 1983-85; mem Delegate Assembly CA School Bds Assn 1981-88; mem Delegate Assembly, Natl School Bds Assn 1983-85; mem Steering Comm Council of Urban Bds of Educ 1985-88; adv comm San Diego State Univ Teacher Educ 1986-89; mem CA Middle Grades Task Force. **HONORS/ACHIEVEMENTS:** Distinguished School Bd Award

1984; Distinguished Public Serv Award Alpha Kappa Alpha 1985; Woman of Achievement Award 1985; Woman of the Year Award 1984; Community Service Award; Achievement in Politics Award 1982; Salute to Black Women Achievement Award 1984; Honorary Life Mem Lincoln Council PTA; Certificate of Merit for Outstanding Contribution to San Diego Community 1983; Outstanding Contribution in Educ Award 1983; Career Women Assoc Outstanding San Diego Woman Award 1983; City of San Diego Proclamation of Community Serv 1984; Rotary Club of SE San Diego for Service Above Self 1981; Outstanding Leadership as President of Board of Educaton; Women in Govt Tribute to Women, 1985; Phi Delta Kappa Community Serv Award, 1988; Samaritan of the Year Award, 1988; Intl Reading Assn Literacy Award, 1989; Magnet Schools Leadership Award, 1989. **HOME ADDRESS:** 2650 Blackton Dr, San Diego, CA 92105. **BUSINESS ADDRESS:** San Diego State University, Lecturer, School of Teacher Education, Suite 152A, San Diego, CA 92182.

SMITH, DOROTHY O.
Mayor. **PERSONAL:** Born May 28, 1943, Lawrence County, AL; daughter of James Samuel Owens Sr (deceased) and Cornelia Swoope Owens; divorced; children: Derra S Warren, Leo Smith Jr, Kathleen R Smith. **EDUCATION:** John C Calhoun, Decatur AL, Business, 1969. **CAREER:** South Central Bell, Decatur AL, network, 1971; City of Hillsboro, Hillsboro AL, mayor, 1989. **ORGANIZATIONS:** Sec, Black Mayors Conf, 1988; mem, Natl Black Women Mayors Caucus, 1988; Martin Luther King Jr Profiles in Courage, ADC, Lawrence County Chapter, 1988. **HONORS/ACHIEVEMENTS:** Award for Church Sec, 1987; Award from The Lawrence County Extension Serv, 1989; Award from The Lawrence County Chamber of Commerce 1989; numerous community serv awards for speaking.

SMITH, EARL BRADFORD
Social worker. **PERSONAL:** Born Sep 28, 1953, St Louis, MO; married Treva Talon Smith. **EDUCATION:** Thiel Coll, BA Psych, Sociol 1977; Marywood Coll, MSW 1979; Univ of Pittsburgh, PhD Candidate Ed. **CAREER:** Vet Admin Hospital, social work assoc 1976-78; Susquehanna Human Serv, human resources spec 1979-; Lackawanna Cty Child & Youth Serv, social worker II 1979-82; Pittsburgh Bd of Educ, school social worker 1982-. **ORGANIZATIONS:** Mem Natl Assoc of Social Workers 1979-; lector St Peters Cathedral Soc 1977-82; lector St Benedicts & St Marys Lectureship Soc 1982-. **HONORS/ACHIEVEMENTS:** Outstanding Male Model NE PA Model's Assoc 1979; Dance Awds Acquired from various Modern Dance-Jazz Performances; All Amer In Football & Track Pres Athletic Conf 1974-77. **MILITARY SERVICE:** USMC corpl 2 yrs; Expert Rifleman 1972-74. **HOME ADDRESS:** 741 Chautauqua Court, Pittsburgh, PA 15214.

SMITH, EDDIE D.
Attorney. **PERSONAL:** Born Apr 10, 1920, Vicksburgs, MS. **EDUCATION:** AB; ML. **CAREER:** Pvt prac; Henry Smith Sabbath & Dillard. **ORGANIZATIONS:** Mem Am Bd Arbitrators; State Legal Adv; IBPOEW; Masons; Trial Lawyers Am changed many MI state laws. **MILITARY SERVICE:** USN quartermaster 2C 1943-46. **BUSINESS ADDRESS:** 2211 E Jefferson, Ste 610, Detroit, MI.

SMITH, EDDIE D., SR.
Clergyman. **PERSONAL:** Born Jun 08, 1946, Macon, GA; married Verlene Fields; children: Charlitha S Austin, Edwanna L, Eddie Jr, Corey, Alvy. **EDUCATION:** Ft Valley State Coll, BS 1968, MS 1971. **CAREER:** Bibb Co Sch, tchr 1968-82; City of Macon, councilman 1975-78; Bibb Co, bd of educ 1985-; Macedonia MB Ch, pastor 1972-. **HONORS/ACHIEVEMENTS:** Minister of the Day GA State Legislature 1981; 3 Yr Serv Award for City Cncl City of Macon 1979; Medgar Malcolm Martin's Award SCLC 1979; Dr ED Smith DayProclamation City of Macon 1977; dir Disting Am 1981; Men of Achievemnt Intl Biographical Ctr Cambridge, Engl; Who's Who Among Personalities of The South 1978; Who's Who Among Outstand Negros 1977; Nat Alumni Cert of Achievement Ft Valley State Coll 1978; Cert of Appreciation Bibb Co Voter's League 1977;Citizens Award Macon Courier 1977. **BUSINESS ADDRESS:** Pastor, Macedonia MB Church, 928 Anthony Rd, Macon, GA 31204.

SMITH, EDDIE GLENN, JR.
Educator, health care administrator, dentist. **PERSONAL:** Born Nov 13, 1926, Palatka, FL; married Callie Glasby; children: Katressia M, Katherine J. **EDUCATION:** BS 1952; DDS 1959; FACD 1972. **CAREER:** Private Practice, dentist 1960-80; Howard Univ Coll of Dentistry, asst prof 1969-80; Comm Group Health Found Washington, exec dir Health Center 1970-77; Coll Med, staff 1974; dentist. **ORGANIZATIONS:** Pres Howard Univ Dental Alumni Assn 1967-69; pres Robt T Freeman Dent Soc 1968-71; spl consult Sec HEW 1968-72; chmn DC Med Care Adv Com 1974-80; mem Nat Dental Assn (pres 1972); NAACP; Urban League; YMCA; Intl Platform Assn; ARC; Am Dental Assn; DC Dental Soc; Natl Assn Neighborhood Health Cntrs; Am Pub Health Assn; consult Howard Univ Cntr Sickle Cell Anemia; bd adv Urban Health Mag; adv com TB & Respiratory Diseases Assn; consult Robert Wood Johnson Found; consult Am Fund Dental Health; Omega Psi Phi; President's bd regents Nat Lib Med Nominee. **HONORS/ACHIEVEMENTS:** Dentist of the Year Award 1969; Speaker's Award 1970; Keys to City Miami Beach 1971, New Orleans 1972; President's Award 1972; Civil Rights Award 1972; aide decamp Gov Dunn, TN 1972; Keys to City of Detroit 1973; Listing "100 Most Influential Black Americans" Ebony 1973; President's Award Nat Dental Assn 1973; Freedom Award NAACP 1974; Dentist of the Year Natl Dental Assoc 1986. **MILITARY SERVICE:** USAAF 1945-47. **BUSINESS ADDRESS:** 740 Sixth St NW, Washington, DC 20001.

SMITH, EDGAR E.
Educator. **PERSONAL:** Born Aug 06, 1934, Hollandale, MS; son of Sam and Augusta; married Inez O; children: Edwin D, Anthony R, Stephen S, Gregory S. **EDUCATION:** Tougaloo Clg Tougaloo, MS, BS 1955; PurdueUniv Lafayette, IN, MS 1957; PurdueUniv Biochemistry, PhD 1960. **CAREER:** Dept of Biochemistry Purdue Univ Lafayette, IN, rsrch asst 1955-58; Dept Biochemistry Purdue Univ Lafayette, IN, tchg asst 1958-59; Harvard Med Sch Boston, MA, rsrch flw surg biochemistry 1959-61; Beth Israel Hosp Boston, MA, assc surg rsrch 1959-68; Harvard Med Sch Boston, MA, rsrch assc surg biochemistry 1961-68; BostonUniv Sch Med Boston, MA, asst prof surg chem 1968-70; Natl Cancer Inst, rsrch career dev awrdee 1969-74; Boston Univ Sch Medicine Boston, MA, assc prof surg chem 1970-73; Univ of MA Med Center Provost/Assoc Prof 1974-83; Univ MA Vice Pres 1983-. **ORGANIZATIONS:** Trustee Alcohol Bev Med Rsrch Found 1982-; mem governing bd Rob Wood Johnson Hlth Policy Flwshp Pgm 1978-; mem Am Soc Biological Chemists; cnsltnt Natl Inst Hlth; trustee Morehouse Sch Medicine 1976-; trustee Tougaloo Clg 1968-; trustee Metro Schlrshp Fund 1979-; mem bd dir Planned Parenthood MA 1984-; mem Am Assc Higher Ed; mem Natl Forum Systm Chief Acad Ofcr; mem NASULGC Cncl on Acad Afrs mem am soc biological Chemist; mem Am Chem Soc Div Biological Chem; mem Am Assc Advncmnt Sci; mem NY Acad Sci; mem Am Assc Cancer Rsrch; mem Flw Am Inst Chem; mem Boston Cancer Rsrch Assc; mem Sigma Xi; mem Phi Lambda Upsilon Natl Chem Hon Soc; mem Am Pol Sci Assc; mem NAMME Natl Assc Minority Med Edctrs; chrmn Dean's Ad Hoc Com Black Grad Stdnts; admsn com Sch of Medicine; chrmn Black Faculty Caucus; edtrl bd Centerscope; com Am Cancer Soc Inst Grant; liaison Div Med Sci Biochemistry; joint com Admission to Six Yr Pgm; promotion com Six Yr Pgm. **HONORS/ACHIEVEMENTS:** Res cancer dev awrd Natl Cancer Inst 1969-74; alumnus of yr Tougaloo Clg 1969; NAACP hlth awrd NAACP Boston Brnch 1977; Rbt Wood Johnson Hlth Policy Flwhsp Inst of Medicine 1977; awrd outstndg achvmnt Field Biochemisty Natl Consortium Black Profsnl Dev 1976; human relations awrd MA Tchrs Assc 1977; old master Purdue Univ 1978; distngshd alumnus Natl Assc Equal Opportnty Higher Ed; natl foud flw Purdue Univ Lafayette, IN 1958-59; Distgnshd Ldrs Hlth Care 1978; Directory Distngshd Am 1981; Honorary Doctor of Science, Morehouse School of Medicine 1989. **BUSINESS ADDRESS:** Vice President for Acad Aff, U of MA System, 250 Stuart St, Boston, MA 02116.

SMITH, EDWARD CHARLES
City official. **PERSONAL:** Born Jan 21, 1949, Pueblo, CO; married Gwendolyn F Creighton; children: Damon, Marcus. **EDUCATION:** KS State Univ, BS 1971. **CAREER:** City of Kansas City, manpower program (CETA) 1974; manpower serv coord 1975; asst dir mgmt coord City Planning Dept 1975; comm devel coord 1976; dir comm devel div 1977-. **ORGANIZATIONS:** Mid Am Reg Cncl 1975; bd of dir United Way of Wyandotte Co 1975-77; United Comm Serv Inc 1975-77; mem KS League of Municipalities 1976-77; Nat Assnfor Comm Devel 1977; Nat Assn of Housing & Redevel Ofcl 1977; Nat Comm Devel Assn 1977; Legislative Comm mem Natl Comm Devel Assn 1978-80; Natl Urban Affairs Council 1978-80; mem bd of governors United Way 1980; sec Minority Municipal Employees Organiz 1980; pres of Region VIII Nat Comm Develop Assn 1982; first vice pres of Nat Comm Develop Assn 1982; past pres Natl Assn for Comm Development 1983-84; dir Neighborhood Preserv Dept City of Kansas City, Kansas 1983. **BUSINESS ADDRESS:** City of Kansas City, 701 N 7th Municipal Ofc Bldg, Kansas City, KS 66101.

SMITH, EDWARD NATHANIEL, JR.
Physician. **PERSONAL:** Born Jul 28, 1955, Elizabeth City, NC; son of Edward Nathaniel Smith Sr and Georgia Long Smith; married Mona LaMothe, Nov 26, 1983; children: Edward N III. **EDUCATION:** Morehouse Coll, BS 1976; Howard Univ Coll of Medicine, MD 1980. **CAREER:** US Public Health Svcs, medical officer 1980-82; Emory Univ Sch of Medicine, clinical assoc 1982-84; Howard Univ Hospital, radiology resident 1984-87, asst prof of radiology 1988-. **ORGANIZATIONS:** Mem Omega Psi Phi Frat 1974-; mem Amer Cancer Soc 1980-; bd of dirs Omega Diversified Investment Corp 1982-; mem Piney Branch Sligo Civic Organization 1984-; mem Natl Medical Assoc Radiology Sect 1985-, Radiological Soc of North America 1985-; mem American Roentgen Ray Society 1988-. **HONORS/ACHIEVEMENTS:** Phi Beta Kappa, Delta of GA 1976; mem Alpha Omega Alpha Howard Univ College of Medicine Chap 1980-. **HOME ADDRESS:** 9119 Sudbury Rd, Silver Spring, MD 20901. **BUSINESS ADDRESS:** Asst Professor of Radiology, Dept of Radiology, Howard Univ Hospital, 2041 Georgia Ave NW, Washington, DC 20060.

SMITH, ELAINE MARIE
Government employee. **PERSONAL:** Born Nov 30, 1947, Mobile, AL; children: Vernon Leon York Jr. **EDUCATION:** AL A&M Univ, BS; Merced Coll, AA 1972. **CAREER:** USAF, staffing asst 1976-77, personnel staffing specl 1977-78; US Army Corps of Engrs, staffing asst 1978, affirmative action recruiter 1978-. **ORGANIZATIONS:** Mem Youth Motivation Task Force 1980-86; vice pres sec Blacks in Govt 1980-86; sec Carver State Tech Coll Adv Bd 1982-86; mem Southern College Placement Assoc 1982-86; mem Southeastern Federal Recruiting Council 1982-86; mem Black Execs Exchange Program 1986. **HONORS/ACHIEVEMENTS:** Outstanding Young Woman of Amer 1981; Quality Salary Increase US Corps of Engrs 1984; Sustained Superior Performance Awd US Corps of Engrs 1982, 86. **BUSINESS ADDRESS:** Affirmative Action Recruiter, US Army Corps of Engineers, Personnel Office, P O Box 2288, Mobile, AL 36628.

SMITH, ELEANOR JANE
Dean of institutional affairs. **PERSONAL:** Born Jan 10, 1933, Circleville, OH; son of John A Lewis (deceased) and Eleanor Dade Lewis; married Paul M Smith, Jr, Dec 27, 1972; children: Teresa Marie Banner. **EDUCATION:** Capital Univ, BSM 1955; Ohio St Univ, 1966; The Union Graduate School/UECU, PhD 1972. **CAREER:** Board of Ed,Columbus, OH 2nd-6th grd tchr 1956-64; Board of Ed, Worthington OH 6 & 7th grd tchr 1964-69; Univ of Cinn, prof, Afro-Am Studies 1972-82; vice provost Faculty & Acad Affairs; Smith Coll, dean of institutional affairs, currently. **ORGANIZATIONS:** Assoc of Black Women Historians, natl co-founder & co-director 1978-80; mem Natl Council for Black Studies 1982-; mem Natl Assn Women Deans, Admin & Counselors 1986-. **HONORS/ACHIEVEMENTS:** Historical Presentation " Black Heritage, History, Music & Dance written & produced 1972- ; numerous publications; YWCA Career Women of Achievement 1983; Capital Univ, Alumni Achiev Awd 1986. **HOME ADDRESS:** 58 Paradise Road #1, Northampton, MA 01060. **BUSINESS ADDRESS:** Dean of Institutional Affairs, College Hall #31, Smith College, Northampton, MA 01063.

SMITH, ELIJAH (WYRE SMITH)
Clergyman. **PERSONAL:** Born Dec 28, 1939, Peach County, GA; son of Samuel Lee Smith and Ola Mae Johnson Smith; married Janet Broner, Jun 07, 1987; children: Audrey Maria Diamond, Elijah Jr, Sonja A, Avice D, Richard A, Mark A; stepchildren: D'ete Smith, LaShaunda R Thomas, Velecia Thomas. **EDUCATION:** Turner Theol Seminary, diploma in Theol 1975. **CAREER:** Blue Bird Body Co, utility man 1964-66; Robins Air Force Base GA, electronic repairman 1966-75; Eastman Circuit Eastman GA, pastor 1967-71; Allen Chapel & Mountain Creek AME Chs, pastor 1971-84; D&S Florist, owner 1974-76; St John AME Church, pastor. **ORGANIZATIONS:** Mem Columbus & Phoenix City Ministerial Alliance 1984-; mem Masonic Lodge 134 Powersville GA 1965-; mem Columbus Branch NAACP 1984-; mem Public Affairs Cncl of Columbus 1984-; mem AME Church Ministers Alliance of Columbus; mem South Columbus Exchange Club 1989. **HONORS/ACHIEVEMENTS:** Oscar Maxwell Awd Man of the Yr Americus Boy Scouts 1978; Minister of the Yr Black Youth in Action 1979; Tomorrow's Leaders Awd Georgia Power 1979; Outstanding Pub Serv Awd Sumter Co Bd of Gov of C of C 1980; Outstanding Serv & Dedication Awd Kent Hill Youth Develop Prog 1984; Disting & Devoted Serv Awd Americus-Sumter

Co NAACP 1984; Comm Serv Awd Mayor City of Americus 1984; Serv Awd Chief of Police Americus GA 1984; Outstanding & Dedicated Serv AwdAmericus Police Dept & Comm of Americus & Sumter Co 1984. **HOME ADDRESS:** 3625 Montrose Drive, Columbus, GA 31906. **BUSINESS ADDRESS:** Pastor, St John AME Church, 1516 Fifth Avenue, Columbus, GA 31901.

SMITH, ELMER G., JR.
Physician. **PERSONAL:** Born May 22, 1957, Chicago, IL; son of Elmer and Joyce; married Ingrid SP, Jun 04, 1983; children: Brittany Francoise, Harrison Monfort. **EDUCATION:** Univ of IL-Chicago, BS 1980; Howard Univ Coll of Medicine, MD 1983. **CAREER:** Norwalk Hosp, resident physician 1983-86; Mount Sinai Hosp, adjunct attending physician; Cook County Hospital, Chicago IL, consultant in medicine 1988-. **ORGANIZATIONS:** Mem Alpha Phi Alpha Frat Inc 1980-, Amer Medical Assoc 1980-, Amer Coll of Physicians 1985-, IL State Medical Soc 1986-, Chicago Medical Soc 1986-; pres American Cancer Society, Illinois Division, Austin Unit, 1987-. **HONORS/ACHIEVEMENTS:** Vice President, Public Relations, Senior Class, Howard Univ 1982-83; Psychiatry Rsch Awd Howard Univ Coll of Medicine 1983; Diplomate Amer Bd of Internal medicine 1986; Chicago's Caring Physicians Award, Metropolitan Chicago Health Care Council 1987; Acute Pharyngitis, Cook County Hospital 1989. **BUSINESS ADDRESS:** 4909 W Division St, Ste 202, Chicago, IL 60651.

SMITH, EMMITT MOZART
Educator. **PERSONAL:** Born Jun 06, 1905, Homer, LA; married Naomi L Malone. **EDUCATION:** Philander Smith Coll, BA 1934; Fisk U, MA 1936; NM State U, educ splst degree 1947; Reed Coll of Religion, DDiv 1969. **CAREER:** Retired prin; Carlsbad NM, prin 1957-73; elem sch prin & asst to supt 1953-57; hs prin 1949-52; hs tchr & basketball coach 1934-35; Rice Meml Meth Ch, pastor 1962-74. **ORGANIZATIONS:** Presiding elder in CME Ch; council delegate to NM Educ Assn 1956-64; past vice pres Carlsbad Educ Assn 1952; past coord for persons working toward advance degrees from NM StateUniv & tching in Carlsbad 195057; past sec S Eddy Co Red Cross 1958-63; mem Lion's Club 1964-; City Park & Recreation Bd 1964-74. **BUSINESS ADDRESS:** 2601 S Carver St, Carlsbad, NM.

SMITH, ERNEST HOWARD
Physician. **PERSONAL:** Born Nov 09, 1931, Bethlehem, PA. **EDUCATION:** Lincoln U, AB cum laude 1953; Howard U, mD 1957; Children Hosp Philadelphia DC Gen Hosp, studied pediatrics; Childrens Hosp Philadelphia, Henry FordHosp Detroit, pediatric cardiology. **CAREER:** US Pub Health Cheyenne Sioux Reservation Eagle Butte SD, med officer in charge 1958-61; Henry Ford Hosp, staff pediatric cardiologist 1965-71; Detroit, priv prac pediatric cardiology 1964-68; Drew Med Sch Los Angeles CA, asst prof pediatrics, pediatric cardiologist head of community pediatrics 1972-. **ORGANIZATIONS:** Mem Catalytic Community Assn Detroit 1968-70; South Central Planning Coun Los Angeles 1973-; Southeast Mental Health Liason Coun 1973-; Cit for Youth Employment 1973-; organist Pilgrim Congregational Ch Eagle Butte SD; Christ United Ch of Christ Detroit; Hartford Ave Bapt Ch Detroit; First Bapt Ch Warrenton VA; St Pauls Bapt Ch Bethlehem PA; accompanist LincolnUniv Glee Club PA. **HONORS/ACHIEVEMENTS:** Recipient Quinland Prize Biology LincolnUniv 1953; Kappa Alpha Psi Award Mu Chap 1953; Cheyenne Sioux Tribal Citation 1961; President's Award South Central Planning Coun 1974; Educ Frat Award for So CA outstanding contrib in field on scndry educ Phi Delta Kappa 1975. **BUSINESS ADDRESS:** 12021 S Wilmington Ave, Los Angeles, CA.

SMITH, ESTRELLA W.
Bank executive. **CAREER:** Heritage National Bank, Pittsburgh, PA, chief executive. **BUSINESS ADDRESS:** Heritage National Bank, 401 Smithfield, Pittsburgh, PA 15222. *

SMITH, ESTUS
Educator. **PERSONAL:** Born Oct 13, 1930, Crystal Springs, MS; married Dorothy Triplett; children: Donald Gregory. **EDUCATION:** Jackson State Univ, BS 1953; IN Univ, MME 1960; Univ of IA, PhD 1970; Eastman Sch of Music, addl studies. **CAREER:** Michens HS Dade City, band dir 1953-58; Burglund HS McComb MS, band dir 1958-61; Brinkley HS Jackson, band dir 1961-62; Jackson State Univ, dir bands 1962-68; Jackson State Univ, dean sch of liberal studies 1969-73, vice pres acad affairs prof of music 1973-84; Kettering Found, fellow. **ORGANIZATIONS:** Mem IN Univ, Jackson State Coll, Univ of IA Alumni Assns; fellow Amer Coun Higher Educ 1969; chmn MS Com for the Humanities; bd trustees Dept of Archives & Hist State of MS; past pres, vice pres So Conf Deans of Faculty & Acad; past chmn bd dir State Mutual Fed Savings & Loan Assn; past pres Opera/S Co; mem, Natl Assn for Humanities Educ, Mississippians for Educ Television, Federation for Public Programs in the Humanities (Natl), Jackson Metro Boys Clubs (local), Univ of MS Engineering Sch Bd of Advisors (Regional), NAACP, Omega Psi Phi, Phi Delta Kappa, Phi Kappa Phi, Beta Beta Beta. **HONORS/ACHIEVEMENTS:** Episcopalian Outstanding Amer, 1970; Outstanding Alumni & Scholar 1970; Outstanding Educ of South. **MILITARY SERVICE:** AUS 1953-55.

SMITH, EUGENE
Business executive. **PERSONAL:** Born Aug 13, 1938, Alquippa, PA; married Jacquelyn; children: Charmaine, Deborah, Carlton. **EDUCATION:** Geneva Coll;Univ Duquesne. **CAREER:** Aliquippa Water Authority, ast mgr. **ORGANIZATIONS:** Bd mem, vice pres Alquippa Pub Sch Dist; bd mem Beaver Co Hosp Authority; mem bd of dir PA Minority Bus Devel Commn; mem US Mil Selection Com; mem Zion Hope Lodge #72; St Cyprian Consistory #4; Sahara Temple #2. **HONORS/ACHIEVEMENTS:** Man Yr Award Negro Bus Professional Women Beaver Co. **BUSINESS ADDRESS:** 160 Hopewell Ave, Aliquippa, PA 15001.

SMITH, EUGENE
Business executive. **PERSONAL:** Born Sep 01, 1929, Miami, FL; married Josephine Scott; children: Michael, Milton Brown (foster). **EDUCATION:** FL A&M Univ, BS 1954-58. **CAREER:** HUD, asst dir mgmt, north central dist dir. **ORGANIZATIONS:** Deacon 1972, Sunday school teacher, business mgr Glendale Baptist Church; mem NAHRO 1979-. **MILITARY SERVICE:** AUS pfc 2 yrs. **BUSINESS ADDRESS:** North Central Dist Dir, HUD, 325 NW 62 St, Miami, FL 33150.

SMITH, FRANCES C.
Funeral director. **PERSONAL:** Born Jun 21, Williamston, NC; daughter of Leo Cherry and Omenella Riddick Cherry; married Alfred J Smith Jr; children: Randy, Trent. **EDUCATION:** Attended, McAllister Sch of Embalming; Amer Acad Sch of Embalming, grad studies. **CAREER:** Smith Funeral Home, owner/funeral director. **ORGANIZATIONS:** Mem NJ State Bd of Mortuary Science; mem Elizabeth Development Co; mem Garden State Funeral Dirs; past pres Urban League Guild; past matron Lincoln Chap OES; pres Union Co Unit of Natl Assn of Negro Bus & Professional Womens Clubs; past pres Womens Scholarship Club of Elizabeth; mem Elizabeth Bd of Educ; mem Soroptimist Intl of Eliz; mem National Caucus of Blk School Bd Members - Bd of Directors; mem Union County Association of Women Business Owners. **HONORS/ACHIEVEMENTS:** Achievement Awd Urban League of Eastern Union Co; Professional Woman of Yr Awd N Jersey Unit of Natl Assn of Negro Bus & Professional Womens Clubs; first Black bd mem Egenolf Day Nursery in Elizabeth presently on adv bd of nursery; Honored by receiving Key to City by Mayor 1st Black woman to receive such honor; Appreciation Awd Elizabeth Br NAACP 1980; Business Woman of Yr Awd Union Co NANBPW.

SMITH, FRANK
Clergyman, educational administrator. **PERSONAL:** Born Dec 03, 1910, Camden, AL; married Etta Pearl Martin; children: Carolyn S Taylor, Gwendolyn Geraldine, Jesse J, Larry Whittie. **EDUCATION:** AL State Univ, BS 1955, MS 1971; Selma Univ, Hon Dr of Divinity 1977. **CAREER:** Elem School AL, GA, OH teacher 1941, 1967, 1968, 1977; Rock Hill Bapt Church, pastor 1945-50; Star Hope Sunday School/BTU Congress, dean 1955-65; Lower Peach Tree Troup #171, scout master 1957. **ORGANIZATIONS:** Principal Lower Peach Tree Jr High 1951-55; chmn Human Relation Comm 1971; chaplain 5th St Intl W's Men Club 1976; youth advisor NAACP 1976-77; pastoral Marengo, Clarke, Dallas, Wilcox Counties 1977-85; counselor & supervisor Selma Univ 1978-79; mem Wilcox Cty AL School Bd 1980. **HONORS/ACHIEVEMENTS:** Teacher of the Year Green Cty Ed Assn GA 1968; Leadership Awds Boys' Scouts of Amer; Protest Articles Southern Courier Montg Advertiser; Citation OH Ed Assn Comm on Human Relations; Citation Robert A Taft Inst of Government. **HOME ADDRESS:** Rt 1 Box 178-A, Lower Peach Tree, AL 36751.

SMITH, FRANK JUNIUS
Management consultant. **PERSONAL:** Born Oct 21, 1937, Richmond, VA; married Shirley E Carter; children: Monica T, Frank J Jr, Leah F. **EDUCATION:** Hampton Inst, BS 1960; Amer Univ, MBA 1967; Rensseleaer Polytechnic Inst, certificate 1972. **CAREER:** Melpar Inc, methods engr, 1962-64; Vitro Corp of Amer, staff specialist 1964-67; Pratt & Whitney Aircraft, staff indus engr, 1967-69; CT Gen Ins Co, supr 1969-74; Travelers Insurance Co, 2nd vice pres agency mgmt consult 1974-. **ORGANIZATIONS:** Sr mem, Am Inst of Indus Engrs 1962-; professional mem Assn for Systems Mgmt 1975-; Professional mem Assn of Intl Mgmt Consultant 1976-; Incorporator Manchester Mem Hosp 1979; dir CT Savs & Loan Assn 1980. **HONORS/ACHIEVEMENTS:** Ujima Award Ujima Inc 1977; Chap Pres Award Am Inst Indus Engrs 1978; Distinguished Alumni Award Hampton Inst 1980. **BUSINESS ADDRESS:** 2nd Vice President, Travelers Insurance Co, 1 Tower Sq, Hartford, CT 06115.

SMITH, FREDDIE A.
Surgeon. **PERSONAL:** Born Sep 29, 1924, Athens, GA; married Mary W. **EDUCATION:** FL A&M Univ, BS 1949; Meharry Med Coll, MD 1950. **CAREER:** General Practice Sanford, FL 1952-57; Central Life Insurance Co, med officer 1964-; General Surgeon self-employed. **ORGANIZATIONS:** Diplomate Amer Bd of Surgery 1963; fellow Amer Coll of Surgeons 1966; mem Hillsborough County Med Assn; mem FL Med Assn; mem Amer Med Assn; mem Natl Med Assn; FL Med, Dental & Pharmaceut Assn; NAACP; Tampa Urban League; Alpha Phi Alpha; past pres FL Med, Dental & Pharmaceut Assn; Bellmen-Waiters Club. **HONORS/ACHIEVEMENTS:** Citizen of the Year 1967; Achievement Award Frontiers of Amer 1972. **MILITARY SERVICE:** USAF 1943-46. **BUSINESS ADDRESS:** Surgeon, 2605 N Howard Ave, Box 4375, Tampa, FL 33677.

SMITH, FREDERICK D.
Chief of courts. **PERSONAL:** Born Mar 29, 1917, Ellsworth, KS. **EDUCATION:** Univ of IA, BA; Hastings Coll of Law, 1954. **CAREER:** Pub Defenders Ofc San Francisco, chief of cts; chief trial atty. **MILITARY SERVICE:** AUS capt 1942-45. **BUSINESS ADDRESS:** Chief Trail Attorney, 850 Bryant St, San Francisco, CA 94103.

SMITH, FREDERICK ELLIS
Dentist. **PERSONAL:** Born Oct 23, 1928, Dayton, OH; married Dolores J Miles; children: Frederick M, Katherine D. **EDUCATION:** OH State U, BS 1950; OH State U, DDS cum laude 1958;Univ Detroit, orthodontia 1977-78. **CAREER:** Dentist pvt prac 1958-; Tempora Mandibular Joint Clinic Miami Valley Hosp, co-dir 1973. **ORGANIZATIONS:** Mem Am Dental Assn; AR Weprin Maxillo Facial Study Grp; Nat Dental Assn; Am Acad Craniomandibular Ortho; OH Commn Dental Testing; pres Western OHAcad of Dental Practice Adminstrn 1979-81; mem NAACP; Urban League; Alpha Phi Alpha Frat; mem Pierre Fauchard Acad 1977; Aca. **HONORS/ACHIEVEMENTS:** Recipient Outstanding Table Clinic Dayton Dental Soc 1969; Golden Award for Teaching OH State Med Assn 1969. **MILITARY SERVICE:** AUS 1951-53. **BUSINESS ADDRESS:** 133 N Gettysburg, Dayton, OH 45417.

SMITH, FREDRICK E.
Educator. **PERSONAL:** Born Oct 27, 1935, Mound City, IL; married Mary L; children: David E, Melissa L. **EDUCATION:** LincolnUniv of MO, AB 1960; AtlantaUniv Sch of Social Work, MSW 1962; St Louis U, PhD 1976. **CAREER:** Washington Univ St Louis, asst prof 1969-; Med Security Inst St Louis, dir of social serv 1967-69; Urban League St Louis, dist coord 1965-67; Health Welfare & Housing MN Urban League, asso dir 1963-65; Kingdom House St Louis, dir of children's prog 1962-63. **ORGANIZATIONS:** Consult Jeff-Vander-Lou Corp; Nat Urban Coalition; pres Nat Com on Neighborhoods; adv Nat Urban League's Coop Energy Educ Proj; Congresional Black Caucus Energy Adv Braintrust; chmn Nat Assn of Black Social Workers Energy/Envir Com; bd mem, chmn St Louis Chap NABSW Energy/Environment Com; Counc onSocial Welfare Edn; Midwest Coord Project 80 Coalition forblack Coll 1980. **HONORS/ACHIEVEMENTS:** Conduct med; pres citation; parachutist badge; Strivers Community Leadership Award Narcotics Serv Council 1970; St Louis Met Found Fellow Award Danforth Found St Louis 1970-74; Community Leaders & Noteworthy Americans Award 1976-77; "Task Force on Energy Final Report" Nat Assn

of Black Social Workers 1980; "Energy/Environment & the Black Community" Proud Mag 1980; Fellowship Award Nat Inst for the Study of Race in the Mil 1980; hon mem 9th & 10th Cavalries "The Buffalow Soldiers". **MILITARY SERVICE:** AUS 1953-56. **BUSINESS ADDRESS:** Washington Univ Campus, Box 1196, St Louis, MO 63130.

SMITH, GARLAND M., JR.
Elected educational administrator. **PERSONAL:** Born Nov 26, 1935, Kansas City, KS; married Ruby D Bailey; children: Etta M, Jerome A, Margie J, Harold C, Gregory L. **EDUCATION:** Sumner HS grad 1954; Legal serv workshops all across the country dealing with legal rights for poor people 1968-81; Ed workshops 1975-85. **CAREER:** KS Natl Client Council, chairperson 1976-79; KS Legal Serv vice pres 1979-81; Wyandotte Cty Legal Aid Soc, pres 1978-81; Painter Mobil Oil Corp; self employed as sign painting & decorating. **ORGANIZATIONS:** Bd mem Unied Way, KS City KS Comm Coll Endowment Found; bd mem White Eagle Credit Union 1988-90. **HONORS/ACHIEVEMENTS:** Volunteer of The Year Award; United Way Wyandotte 1988. **MILITARY SERVICE:** NG spec3 class 6 yrs. **BUSINESS ADDRESS:** Painter, Mobil Oil Corp, 1100 Sunshine Rd, Kansas City, KS 66112.

SMITH, GENE EUGENE
Professional athlete. **PERSONAL:** Born Aug 20, 1962, Washington, DC. **EDUCATION:** Georgetown, 1984. **CAREER:** Indiana Pacers, guard 1984-. **HONORS/ACHIEVEMENTS:** Capt of the Georgetown team that won the NCAA chmpnshp; had 66 steals to rank among natl ldrs. **BUSINESS ADDRESS:** Indiana Pacers, Two West Washington St, Ste 510, Indianapolis, IN 46204.

SMITH, GEORGE BUNDY
Judge. **PERSONAL:** Born Apr 07, 1937, New Orleans, LA; married Alene Jackson; children: George Jr, Beth. **EDUCATION:** Inst d'Etudes Politiques Paris, CEP Inst 1958; Yale Univ, BA 1959; Yale Law School, LLB 1962; NYU, MA 1967, PhD 1974. **CAREER:** New York City Civil Court, judge 1975-79; Supreme Court State of NY, justice 1980-87; Supreme Court Appellate Div State of NY, assoc justice 1987-. **ORGANIZATIONS:** Past Admin of Model Cities NYC; admitted to NY State Bar Assn 1963. **BUSINESS ADDRESS:** Associate Justice, New York State Supreme Court, Appellate Division, 27 Madison Ave, New York, NY 10010.

SMITH, GEORGE S.
Government administrator. **PERSONAL:** Born Jan 06, 1940, Terry, MS; children: George Jr, Tosha, Eric, Carol. **EDUCATION:** Utica Jr Coll, AA; Jackson State Univ. **CAREER:** State Bldg Comm, suprv 1979; Governor of MS, sr staff 1966; State Medicaid Comm, comm mem 1966; Hinds Cty Dist Five, suprv 1979,83, pres 1984-. **ORGANIZATIONS:** Mem TC Almore Lodge #242, Jackson Chap of Natl Business League, Jackson Urban League, Natl Assoc for the Advancement of Colored People; mem bd of dir Smith-Robertson Comm, Metropolitan Young Men Christian Assoc, Goodwill Indust, Central MS Planning & Devel Dist Advisory Council on Aging, Centre South Industrial Devel Group, Jackson Chamber of Commerce. **HONORS/ACHIEVEMENTS:** Appointed 1st black to the State Bldg Comm; 1st black to be sr staff mem to Gov of MS, 1st black to be appointed as commiss mem of State Med Commiss; One of two blacks to be elected suprv of Hinds Cty Dist Five 1979, re-elected suprv 1983; 1st black to serve as pres of Hinds Cty Bd of Suprvs 1984. **BUSINESS ADDRESS:** President, Hinds Cty Bd of Suprvs, PO Box 686, Jackson, MS 39170.

SMITH, GEORGE V.
Businessman. **PERSONAL:** Born Mar 19, 1926, Livingston, TX; married Evie Lee Flournoy; children: Charles, George Jr, Jacquelyn Eastland. **CAREER:** Smith Pipe Supply Inc, pres/owner 1974-; Seaboard Pipe Testers, vp/gen mgr 1970-74; Atlans Bradford Co (pipe co), field supr 1952-70. **ORGANIZATIONS:** Bd of dir Houston Regnl Minority Purchasing Coun 1976-78; bd of dirs Am Business Coun 1978; bd of trustees St Elizabeth Hosp 1978-; bd of dirs TX Occupational Safety Bd 1979; bd of dirs Houston Br Fed Res Bank of Dallas 1980. **HONORS/ACHIEVEMENTS:** Named in Top 100 Black Businessmen Black Enterprise 1977-78; Outst Achvmnt by a Vendor Co Houston Regnl Minority Purchasing Coun 1978; Excel in Achvmnt Awd TX SoUniv 1979; Bus Achvmnt Awd Houston Citizens C of C 1980; Top Hat Awd Pittsburgh Courier 1980; Distng Achvmnt Awd Nat Assn of Black Acctnts Inc 1980. **MILITARY SERVICE:** USAF t5 1945-47. **BUSINESS ADDRESS:** 12615 E Freeway, Ste 410, Houston, TX 77015.

SMITH, GEORGE WALKER
Clergyman. **PERSONAL:** Born Apr 28, 1929, Hayneville, AL; married Elizabeth; children: Anthony, Carolyn, Joyce. **EDUCATION:** Knoxville Coll, BS 1951; Pittsburgh Theol Sem, MDiv. **CAREER:** Golden Hill United Presby Ch, minister; Nat Sch Bd Assn, 1st vp. **ORGANIZATIONS:** Appt to serve on CA Ad Hoc Comm; sec treas Nat Sch Bd Assn; apptd CA Savs & Loan Leag; past pres Council of Great City Schs; mem San Diego Bd Edn; one of fndrs dir vice pres Pacific Coast Bank; served in various capacities on various org; Kappa Alpha Psi; Soclia Club; chrtr mem San Diego Chap Alpha Pi Boule; Sigma Pi Phi. **HONORS/ACHIEVEMENTS:** Received various honors & awards. **BUSINESS ADDRESS:** 2130 Market St, San Diego, CA 92102.

SMITH, GERALDINE T.
Social worker, educator. **PERSONAL:** Born Sep 14, 1918, Cave Spring, GA; daughter of Dallas C Turner and Cora Johnson Turner; divorced; children: Karen T. **EDUCATION:** Hunter Coll, BA 1943; Columbia Univ, MA 1947; Smith Coll Sch for Social Work, MSS 1952. **CAREER:** Bureau Child Welfare, social worker 1952-57; Pgh Public Schs, sch social worker 1957-58; Western Psychiatric Inst, sr psychiat social worker 1958-68; Univ of Pgh, asst prof 1965-; Neighborhood Psychiat Unit & Counseling Serv 1966-68; Western Psychiatric Inst Univ of Pgh, dir social work 1968-75, asst dir of educ CMH/MRC 1975-78; Dixmont State Hosp Social Serv, consult 1973-74; Pgh Model Cities Agency, 1968-69; WPIC Hill Satellite Ctr Western Psych InstUniv of Pgh, dir 1979-87. **ORGANIZATIONS:** Sec adv bd New Opportunities for the Aging (NOFA) 1984, adv bd mem 1981-; mem Natl Assn of Social Workers; Acad Certified Social Workers; Council on Social Work Educ; Natl Conf Social Welfare; Soc for Hosp Social Work Dirs; United Mental Health of Allegheny County. **HOME ADDRESS:** 1710 Swissvale Ave, Pittsburgh, PA 15221.

SMITH, GLENN R.
Educator. **PERSONAL:** Born Jul 14, 1945, Topeka, KS; married Judy; children: Glenn, II, Marla. **EDUCATION:** Adams State Coll, BA 1968;Univ CO, MA 1971;Univ CO, PhD 1975. **CAREER:** Community Coll Denver, instr; Met State Coll, asst dir financial aid; Urban Educ Prog, asst dir. **ORGANIZATIONS:** Mem Am Educ Studies Assn; Black Eductors Denver; phi Delta Kappa; mem & Greater Park Hill; US Civil Serv Commn CU FellowshipUniv CO 1972-74. **BUSINESS ADDRESS:** 250 W 14 Ave, Denver, CO 80204.

SMITH, GLORIA R.
Nurse, educator. **PERSONAL:** Born Sep 29, 1934, Chicago, IL; married Leroy. **EDUCATION:** Wayne U, BS 1955; Mich U, MPH 1959;Univ CA, cert 1971;Univ of OK, MA 1977; Union for Experimenting Coll & U, phD 1979. **CAREER:** Detroit Visiting Nurse's Assn, public health nurse 1955-56; sr public health nurse 1957-58; asst dist office supr 1959-63; Tuskegee Inst, asst prof 1963-66; Albany State Coll, 1966-68; Okla State Health Dept, dist nurse supr 1968-70; medicare nurse consultant 1970-71; Univ Okla, coor asst prof 1971-73; interim dean asso prof 1971-73; dean & prof 1975-83; MI Dept Public Health, dir 1983-. **ORGANIZATIONS:** Mem & officer Am Assn of Coll of Nursing; comm & Am Academy of Nursing; mem past officer Nat Black Nurses Assn; mem steering Com & first bd of dirMidwest Alliance in Nursing 1977-80; Nat Student Nurses Assn; bd of dir Nat League for Nursing; OK State Nurses Assn; officer Am Nurses Assn; Okla Pub Health Assn; Wayne State Alumni & Nursing Alumni Assns; Sigma Gamma Rho Sor Sigma Theta Tau; Inter Greek Council; Interagency Com Health Serv Task Orce;bd dirs YMCA 1972-; steering com Human Relations Council Greater Okla City; bd dirS St Peter Claver Community Credit Union 1961-63; Mayor's Com to Study In-migrants Detroit 1963. **HONORS/ACHIEVEMENTS:** Outstanding Serv Awd Franklin Settlement Detroit 1963; Outstanding Sigma of the Year 1963; Outstanding Young Woman of Amer 1966; Outstanding Educ of Amer 1973; Cert OK State Nurses' Assn Black Nurses' Caucus 1973; Key to the City Miami Beach 1974; 1st Speaker Katherine Faville Disting Lecturer Series Wayne State Univ 1975; Leaders in Educ 1975; Who's Who in OK 1975; Cert of Recognition NBNA 1976; Cert & Plaque Sigma Gamma Rho 1977; Hall of Fame Sigma Gamma Rho Sor 1974; The World Who's Who of Women in Educ 1978; Community Serv Awd for Leadership; Soul Bazaar Coord Clara Luper 1980; Who's Who in Health Care 1982 Dictionary of Intl Biography 1983; Plaque of Appreciation presented by Pres Banowsky Univ of OK 1983; Plaque of Appreciation presented by Assoc of Black Personnel 1983; Hon Mem Chi Eta Phi Sor 1984; Hon Recognition Awd OK Nurses' Assoc 1984; Disting Alumni Awd Wayne State Univ 1984; Disting Scholar Amer Nurses Found 1986. **BUSINESS ADDRESS:** Dir, Michigan Dept of Public Health, 3500 N Logan, PO Box 30035, Lansing, MI 48909.

SMITH, GORDON ALLEN
Educational administrator. **PERSONAL:** Born May 08, 1933, Detroit, MI; married Patricia Evon Ware; children: Dorel, Gordon, Brian, Stephanie. **EDUCATION:** Wayne State U, BS 1966; No IL U, MS 1969; No IL U, EdD 1977. **CAREER:** IL Office of Educ, affirmative action officer 1975-; No IL Univ, asst to pres 1973-75; No IL Univ, counselor 1970-73; Detroit & Public School, teacher 1965-68; Detroit, public aid worker 1968; Inland Steel Recruitment Com; Natl Assn Affrm Act Officers; IL Affrm Action Officers Assn Commr Dekalb Human Rel, 1973-75; commr IL Commn on Human Rel, 1974. **MILITARY SERVICE:** AUS 1954-56. **BUSINESS ADDRESS:** 100 N 1st St, Springfield, IL 62777.

SMITH, GRANVILLE L.
Insurance executive. **CAREER:** Benevolent Life Insurance Company, Inc., Shreveport, LA, chief exwcutive officer. **BUSINESS ADDRESS:** Benevolent Life Insurance Company, 1624 Milan, Shreveport, LA 71103. *

SMITH, GRANVILLE N.
Clergyman. **PERSONAL:** Born Jan 03, 1927, Tillatobia, MS; married Hazel Brock. **EDUCATION:** Midwestern Bible Coll, BRE 1968; Am Bapt Theo Sem, BA 1969; United Theo Sem, BTh 1973. **CAREER:** Mt Calvary Missionary Bapt Ch, pastor. **ORGANIZATIONS:** Chmn bd dirs Ops Industrialization Cntr 1973-75; first vice pres Gr Lakes Dist Congress of Religious Edn; vice pres Wolverine Bapt State Conv; Dir United TheoSem Ext Cntr; instr Greek Homiletics New Testament Theo United Theo Sem Ext; instr Gr Lakes Dist Congress of Rel Edn; Wolverine St Congress of Rel Edn; Nat Sunday Sch & GTU Congress; mem Concerned Pastors for Social Action; chmn Black Enterprise Com CPSA; Fin Sec CPSA; sec-treas Chris Busnessmen's Assn bd mem Mt Morris Cable TV. **HONORS/ACHIEVEMENTS:** Recip hon doc united theo sem 1973; lectr World Bapt Youth Alliance 1974; rated fourth among natl bapt conv chs in foreign mission contrib Mt Calvary Bapt Ch 1973. **MILITARY SERVICE:** USN steward 2 class 1944-46. **BUSINESS ADDRESS:** 4801 N Saginaw St, Flint, MI 48505.

SMITH, GREGORY ALLEN
Obstetrician/gynecologist. **PERSONAL:** Born Sep 12, 1952, Detroit, MI; married Jennifer; children: Amber, Camille. **EDUCATION:** MI State Univ, BS 1974; Howard Univ, MD 1978. **CAREER:** Wayne State Univ, resident ob/gyn 1978-82; AMI Doctors Medical Ctr, chief ob/gyn 1987-88; Associated Women's Care of Tulsa, pres. **ORGANIZATIONS:** Mem Natl & Amer Medical Assocs, OK State Medical Soc, Tulsa Co Medical Soc; adv bd Sickle Cell Anemia Rsch Foundation of OK. **HONORS/ACHIEVEMENTS:** Diplomate Amer Bd of Obstetrics-Gynecology. **BUSINESS ADDRESS:** President, Associated Women's Care Tulsa, 2325 So Harvard No-502, Tulsa, OK 74114.

SMITH, GWENDOLYN G.
Social service. **PERSONAL:** Born Oct 30, 1945, Gary, WV. **EDUCATION:** AL State Univ, BA 1967; Univ of Chicago, MSW 1973. **CAREER:** Clinton Jop Corps Ctr, advisor 1967-68; Children Serv Bd, caseworker 1968-71; Vanderbilt Univ, dir in patient social serv 1973-86; Private Practice, clinician. **ORGANIZATIONS:** Mem Zeta Phi Beta 1966-; pres Smith & Assocs 1986-87; mem NAACP 1986-87, NASW 1987. **HONORS/ACHIEVEMENTS:** Academy of Certified Social Worker 1978; Outstanding Young Women of Amer 1979; book published "Why Stand Up?" 1986. **HOME ADDRESS:** 2621 Wyandotte St #64, Las Vegas, NV 89102-5449. **BUSINESS ADDRESS:** Clinician/Author, PO Box 158214, Nashville, TN 37215.

SMITH, HALE
Editor, educator, composer. **PERSONAL:** Born Jun 29, 1925, Cleveland, OH; son of Hale Smith and Jimmie Anne Clay Smith; married Juanita R Hancock; children: Hale Michael, Marcel Hancock, Robin Alison, Eric Dale. **EDUCATION:** Cleveland Inst of Mus, BM

1950; Cleveland Inst of Mus, MM 1952. **CAREER:** Composer of music; Univ of CT, prof emeritus of music; freelance composer-arranger 1945-; Edward B Marks Mus Corp, ed-consult 1962-63; Frank Mus Corp, 1963-65; Sam Fox Music Publ, 1967-71; CF Peters Corp, 1962-; CW Post Coll, adj assoc prof of mus 1969-70. **ORGANIZATIONS:** Freelance consult to Performers, Composers, Diverse Music Publishing Firms; consult Copyright Infringement; lectr numerous coll throughout the US; former mem Bd of Gov of the Am Comp All; former pres Freeport Arts Counc; mem Freeport Bd of Ethics. **HONORS/ ACHIEVEMENTS:** BMI Student Composers Awd 1952; Cleveland Arts Prize 1973; Distinguished Scholar Xavier Univ of New Orleans LA; Amer Academy Institute of Arts and Letters Award 1988; Honorary Doctorate of Music, Cleveland Institute of Music 1988; numerous commns maj perf & publ. **MILITARY SERVICE:** Military Serv private 1943-45. **HOME ADDRESS:** 225 Pine St, Freeport, NY 11520.

SMITH, HEMAN BERNARD
Attorney, educator. **PERSONAL:** Born Aug 20, 1929, Alexandria, LA; son of Heyman Smith and Rosa Smith; married Ina Jean Washington, Dec 26, 1952; children: Heman III, Lanie C, Paula Barnes. **EDUCATION:** Univ of Maryland (Far East Div), attended, 1958-60; Univ of Pacific, McGeorge School of Law, JD, 1971. **CAREER:** Smith, Hanna, de Bruin & Yee, Sacto CA, partner, sr attorney, 1971-78; Smith & Yee, Sacto CA, partner, 1978-84; Smith & Assoc, Sacto CA, sr attorney, 1984-88; Univ of Northern California, L P School of Law, Sacto CA, exec dean, 1988. **ORGANIZATIONS:** Bd mem, Amer Red Cross, Sacto CA, 1980-87; mem, Minority Steering Comm California Youth Authority, 1985-87, Sacto Urban League, presently, Sacto NAACP, presently; pres, Zeta Beta Lambda, 1987-88, Wiley Man Bar Assn, 1988-. **MILITARY SERVICE:** US Air Force, 1948-69. **HOME ADDRESS:** 6370 Havenside Dr, Sacramento, CA 95831. **BUSINESS ADDRESS:** Executive Dean, Univ of Northern CA, Lorenzo Patino School of Law, 816 H Street, Suite 108, Sacramento, CA 95814.

SMITH, HENRY R., JR.
Judge. **PERSONAL:** Born Feb 06, 1917, Philadelphia, PA; son of Henry R. Smith and Julia Black Smith; married Margaret Marshall Smith, Nov 28, 1941; children: Leslie R., Daryl H., Camille E.. **EDUCATION:** Pennsylvania State Coll, BA, 1939; Duquesne Univ Law School, LLB, 1949. **CAREER:** Pennsylvania State Employment Service, investigator, 1943-44; Housing Authority of the City of Pittsburgh, PA, asst mgr, mgr, 1944-51, asst gen counsel, 1951-53; Allegheny County PA, asst dist atty, 1951-52; private practice of law; Allegheny County Planning Commn, planning analyst, 1964; Allegheny County Office of Economic Opportunity, director, 1964-69; elected judge of Ct of Common Pleas, 1969, served two ten-yr terms; consultant to Imo State, Nigeria, on implementation of constitutional govt, 1981. **ORGANIZATIONS:** Mem, Pennsylvania Bar Assoc, Allegheny Bar Assoc, Amer Judicature Soc, Pennsylvania State Trial Judges, Homer S. Brown Law Assn. **HONORS/ ACHIEVEMENTS:** Pittsburgh Courier Civil Rights Award, 1962; Pennsylvania NAACP Human Rights Award, 1969; New Pittsburgh Courier Top Hat Award, 1981. **HOME ADDRESS:** 220 N Dithridge St, Apt 603, Pittsburgh, PA 15213. **BUSINESS ADDRESS:** Hon. Henry R. Smith, Court of Common Pleas of Allegheny County, 535 Court House, Pittsburgh, PA 15219.

SMITH, HENRY THOMAS
Physician. **PERSONAL:** Born Mar 31, 1937, Portsmouth, VA; married Diane; children: Robert, Alicia. **EDUCATION:** Howard Univ, BS 1957; Univ of Rochester, MD 1961. **CAREER:** MN Gen Hosp, intern 1961-62; Hennepin Co Gen Hosp, resd 1964-67; Hennepin Co Med Ctr, asst dir chronic dialysis unit 1967-69; Pilot City Hlth Ctr,physician 1969; Modern Med Jour, assoc editor 1970-72; Geriatrics Jour, abstract editor 1970-72; Nephrology Modern Med Jour, consult 1975-77; St Louis Park Med Ctr 1977; Univ of MN Sch Med, clinical assoc prof. **ORGANIZATIONS:** Sister Kenny Inst 1972-75; MN Heart Assn 1974-76; president Natl Kidney Foundation of Upper Midwest 1982-84; mem Amer Med Assn; mem Minneapolis Soc ofInternal Med; mem Natl Med Assn; Am Soc Nephrology fellow; Am Coll Physicians. **HONORS/ACHIEVEMENTS:** Cert Internal Med 1969, Nephrology 1974; Nephrolog advisor for modern medicine. **MILITARY SERVICE:** AUS Capt 1962-64; Cert Achievement Kenner Army Hosp. **BUSINESS ADDRESS:** Park Nicollet Medical Ctr, 5000 W 39th St, Minneapolis, MN 55416.

SMITH, HERALD LEONYDUS
Clergyman, printer. **PERSONAL:** Born Apr 20, 1909, Smithfield, OH; married Dorothy Irene Mcclinton; children: Herald, Verl, Rosalie, David. **EDUCATION:** Wilberforce, b of theology 1945; Monrovia W Africa, d of divinity 1955; Wilberforce Dept of Christian Edn, honors 1959. **CAREER:** AME Church, clergyman; Cleveland Clinic, chapel organist 1978-80; Smith Typing-mimeograph & Multigraph, owner 1963-; Quinn Chapel AME Cleveland, church builder & pastor 1963-; St Mathews Lorain OH, pastor 1967; "The Herald", ditor 1959-80; Boyd Funeral Home & House of Wills & Others, eulogist/sermon builder 1957-80; Rotary Club Ironton OH, speaker 1952; St John AME Cleveland, asst pastor 1962-66; St James AME Cleveland Branch of Payne Theol Seminar of Wilberforce OH, theol tchr 1965. **ORGANIZATIONS:** Pres AME Ministers Fellowship Cleeland 1971-80; vice pres NAACP Cincinnati Br; adult educ tchr Smithfield OH; master mason; mem Alpha Phi Alph Frat Wilberforce U. **HONORS/ACHIEVEMENTS:** Cert Kiwinis Club of Cleveland 1963; invited to attend inaugural Pres Jimmy Carter; communication from King of Saudi Arabia in response to Article & invitation to visti Saudi Arabia 1979; cert of Honor St Paul AME Ch Cincinnati; plaque The Clevelanders Musical Group; letter of congratulations upon building church Gov Rhodes; respones to articel "Extending the Pulpit" Gov Wallace. **BUSINESS ADDRESS:** Episcopal HeadquartersUniv Ci, 2767 Halleck Dr, Columbus, OH.

SMITH, HERMAN TALLIFERRIO
Attorney. **PERSONAL:** Born Oct 06, 1915, Fulton, AR; married Celestine Reed; children: Herman T; Reginald (dec). **EDUCATION:** Prairie View Univ, BA 1937; Southwestern Univ, JD 1954. **CAREER:** 55th Assembly Dist State of CA, LA, rep nominee 1958; US Congress 23rd Congr Dist State of CA, LA, rep nominee 1962; Smith & Glasco, LA, atty. **ORGANIZATIONS:** Mem LA Cnty Judicial Procedure Comm 1962-; coop atty Legal Def Fund NAACP 1960-; chmn Watts Br NAACP Legal Redress Comm 1965-69; chmn LA Br NAACP Legal Redress Comm; pres LA Chap Prairie View Alumni Assn; mem bd of Trustees Bel Vue Comm United Presb Ch 1958-61 & 1975; Orgn & Ext Chmn BSA 1956-61; mem CA State Bar Assn; Natl Black Lawyers Assn. **HONORS/ACHIEVEMENTS:** Who's Who in The West 1960, 1963, 1972; Who's Who in Amer Law (Marquis) 1st & 2nd editions; co-author "CA Politics & Policies"; pub serv awards LA Cnty, City of LA, LA City Council, State Leg Rules Comm; Who's Who in Amer Law 1982-84.

SMITH, HOWARD C.
Banking executive. **CAREER:** Unity State Bank, Dayton, OH, chief executive. **BUSINESS ADDRESS:** Unity State Bank, 1158 West Third St, Dayton, OH 45407. *

SMITH, HOWLETT P.
Musician. **PERSONAL:** Born Feb 29, 1933, Phoenix, AZ; married Judith Celestin; children: Juliette, Rachel, Mark, April, Sandra, Peter. **EDUCATION:** Univ Ariz, BM 1955. **CAREER:** Composer, pianist, singer, arranger, vocal coach, numerous public appearances. **ORGANIZATIONS:** Lectr & demonstrations concerning use of jazz in church; life mem Psi Mu AlphaUniv Ariz Alumni Asn; Kappa Kappa Psi Mr Newmanite 1955. **HONORS/ ACHIEVEMENTS:** Musical dir "Me & Bessie mark taper forum vol title i program la city unified dist.

SMITH, ISAAC DIXON
Professional soldier. **PERSONAL:** Born May 02, 1932, Wakefield, LA; married Mildred L Pierre; children: Debra, Ronald. **EDUCATION:** S Univ A&M Coll, BA 1954; Command & Gen Staff Coll, 1969; Army War Coll, 1973; Shippensberg State Coll, MA 1973. **CAREER:** 5th Bn 83rd Artillery, battery comm 1964-67; 8th Bn 4th Artillery, battalion comm 1969-72; 23rd Vietnamese Infantry Div, adv 1971; Army's Equal Oppor Prog, dep dir 1974; DIVARTY 1st Infantry Div, comm 1975-78; Second ROTC Region, comm gen 1981-83; lst Armored Div, asst div comm 1983-. **ORGANIZATIONS:** VFW Post 10592. **HONORS/ACHIEVEMENTS:** Silver Star; Legion of Merit w/Oak Leaf Cluster; Bronze Star; meritorious Serv medal; Army Commendation Medal. **MILITARY SERVICE:** AUS field artillery maj gen 30 yrs. **BUSINESS ADDRESS:** USAREUR & 7th/A, HQ USAREUER & 7th Army, Office of the DCSPER, APO New York, NY 09403.

SMITH, ISABELLE R.
Educator. **PERSONAL:** Born Jun 08, 1924, Woodstown, NJ; married Daniel; children: Brenda, Roger, Debra, Karen, Randall, Douglas. **EDUCATION:** Wayne State U, BS 1946;Univ KS Med Ctr, 1947; W MI U, MS 1965. **CAREER:** Univ KS, sub dietitian 1947; Rochester Gen Hosp, floor dietitian 1947-48; Receiving Hosp, diabetic dietitian 1948-50; Battle Creek HS, instr 1964-68; W MI Univ, instr 1968-70; asst prof 1970-74; dept chmn 1974. **ORGANIZATIONS:** Mem Am AssnUniv Women 1959-63, 1974-; MI Home Economics Assn 1965-; Am Home Economics Assn 195-; Am AssnUniv Profs 1969-72; MI Home Economics Scholarship Com 1972-74; com chmn 1974-; State Scholarship Com 1971-74; dept rep Affirmative Action 1974-; vice pres Urban League Guild 1973; mem Urban League & Urban League Guild 1950-; Denatl Auxiliary; Goodwill Industry Auxiliary 1973. **HONORS/ ACHIEVEMENTS:** Placque Urban League 1973. **BUSINESS ADDRESS:** Dept Home Economics W MI Univ, Kalamazoo, MI.

SMITH, J. ALFRED, SR.
Clergyman. **PERSONAL:** Born May 19, 1931, Kansas City, MO; son of Amy Smith; married Joanna Goodwin; children: J Alfred Jr, Craig, Anthony, Amy Jones, Shari Rigmaiden, Ronald Craig. **EDUCATION:** Western Baptist Coll, BS, Elementary Educ, 1952; Missouri School of Religion, Univ of MO, Columbia, BD, 1959; Pacific School of Religion, Berkeley, CA, 1962; Inter-Baptist Theological Center, TX, Church & Community, ThM, 1966; Amer Baptist Seminary of the West, 1970, ThM 1972; Golden Gate Baptist Theological Seminary, DM 1975. **CAREER:** American Baptist Convention, area rep 1968-70; Bishop Coll, asst to the pres 1963-65; American Baptist Seminary of the West, acting dean and prof 1975-87;Golden Gate Theol Seminary, adjunct prof 1976-; Allen Temple Baptist Church Oakland CA, pastor; pres Progressive Natl Baptist Convention Inc 1986-88. **ORGANIZATIONS:** Lecturer and instructor Laney Coll, Merritt Coll 1969-71; pres Baptist Pastors/Ministers Conf of Oakland and the Easy Bay 1986-; pres Progressive Natl Baptist Convention 1986-88; bd of dirs Metropolitan YMCA, Natl Cncl of Churches, Council of Natl Black Churches, Bread for the World; bd of dirs Natl Cncl of Churches, Congress of Natl Black Churches, Bread for the World, Natl Conf of Black Seminarians, Howard Thurman Educ Trust, Bishop Coll Renaissance campaign. **HONORS/ACHIEVEMENTS:** Published numerous articles 1960-76; Man of the Year Award Golden West Mag LA 1976; Award for Outstanding Accomplishments at Grass Roots Level New Oakland Com 1976; Man of the Year Award Sun-Reporter/Metro Reporter 1976; Recognition for Distinguished Serv, Boy Scouts of Amer 1986; Bishop Coll Renaissance Campaign; Ebony Magazine 1987; 100 Most Influential Blacks in Amer; recipient of over 100 local & natl awards, three awards named in his honor; featured in numerous magazines & newspapers; Earl Lectures, Pacific School of Religion, 1989; Hay Lecturer, Drake Univ, 1989; Addressed United Nations on South African Apartheid, 1989; Lecturer, Hampton Univ, 1979; Included in Ebony's 100 Most Influential People list. **BUSINESS ADDRESS:** Pastor, Allen Temple Baptist Church, 8500 A St, Oakland, CA 94621.

SMITH, J. C.
Clergyman, carpenter. **PERSONAL:** Born Jul 08, 1930, Montgomery, AL; married Willie Mae Myrick; children: Jennifer, Jonathan, Jeffrey, Jerold, Jacques. **EDUCATION:** Chic Bapt Inst, BTh 1971. **CAREER:** Bethlehem Temple Bapt Ch, pastor 1969-; Self-Employed, carpenter 1963-; ins salesman 1958-62; wkr glass plant 1953-58; Dr Martin Luther King Jr MontgomeryBus Boycott, worked with 1955-56. **ORGANIZATIONS:** Past pres Prog Min Assn of Chic; pres Harvey Min Assn; sec & mem Schl Bd Schl Dist 147; vpres Nat Black Caucus of Schl Bd 1977; chm GSU #147 Comm Council; policy bd GSU #147 Comm Council; adv com Harvey Police Commr 1980; moderator So Suburban Bapt Dist Assn. **MILITARY SERVICE:** AUS corpl 1951-53. **BUSINESS ADDRESS:** W Harvey-Dixmoor Sch Dist 147, 15028 S Ashland St, Harvey, IL 60426.

SMITH, J. CLAY, JR.
Government official attorney. **PERSONAL:** Born Apr 15, 1942, Omaha, NE; son of J Clay Smith, Sr and Emily V Williams; married Patti Jones; children: Stager Clay, Michael Laurel, Michelle Lori, Eugene Douglas. **EDUCATION:** Creighton Univ Omaha, NE, AB 1964; Howard Law Sch Washington, DC, JD 1967; George Washington Law Sch Washington, DC, LLM, 1970, SJD 1977. **CAREER:** US Army Judge Advocates Gen Corp, capt lyr 1967-71; Arent Fox Kintner Plotkin & Kahn Washington, DC, assc 1971-74; Fed Commctn Cmsn, deputy chf cable TV bureau 1974-76; Fed Cmnctn Cmsn, assc gen cnsl 1976-77; Equal Emplymnt Opprtnty Cmsn, us cmsnr apptd by Jimmy Carter 1977-82, actng chrmn apptd by Ronald W Reagan 1981-82; Howard Univ Sch of Law, prof of law 1982-86; dean & prof of law, Howard University Sch of Law 1986. **ORGANIZATIONS:** NE Bar Assoc 1967; mem Howard Law Sch Alumni Assc 1967-; Dist of Columbia Bar 1968; pres bd dir Washington

Bar Assc 1970; US Supreme Court 1973; advsr pres Natl Bar Assc 1973-; mem NAACP 1975-; mem Urban League 1975-; natl pres mem Fed Bar Assc 1979; utlty spec Pblc Serv Cmsn 1982-; Editorial Board ABA Compleat Lawyer 1984; Advisory Committee, DC Bar Exam; bd mem Natl Lawyers Club; planning committee for Task Force on Black Males AM Psyh Assn 1986-; mem Am Law Inst 1986-88; chair Natl Bar Assn Comm on History of Blk Lawyers; legal counsel for the Elderly Policy Bd 1986-88. **HONORS/ACHIEVEMENTS:** Frst blck elected natl pres fed bar assc in 60 yr hstry Fed Bar Assc 1980-81; founder jurisart movement Washington Bar Assc 1978; am bar assc found Am Bar Assc 1982-; order of the coif hon George Washington Law Sch 1978-; many publications including Fed Bar Assc Natl Pres Messages, Fed Bar News,CIVICS LEAP, Law Reason & Creativity, Mgng Multi-ethnic Multi-racial Workforce Criminal, Chronic Alcoholism — Lack of Mens Rea — A Dfns Pblc Intoxication13 Howard Law Journal, An Investment in a new century, Wash Afro Am; The BlackBar Assn & Civil Rights; A black lawyers response to the Fairmont Papers; Memoriam: Clarence Clyde Ferguson, Jr, Harvard Law Rev; Forgotten Hero: Charles H Houston, Harvard Law Rev; OllieMay Cooper Award, 1986; The C Francis Stradford Award 1986. **BUSINESS ADDRESS:** Professor of Law, Howard Univ Sch of Law, 2900 Van Ness St NW, Howard Univ Sch of Law, Washington, DC 20008.

SMITH, J. HARRY
Educator. **PERSONAL:** Born Aug 22, 1922, Newport News, VA; married Marilyn Horton; children: Danielle, Stephanie, Judith. **EDUCATION:** Seton Hall U, LLD, MA, BA. **CAREER:** Essex Co Coll, pres, vp, chf exec officer 1969-. **ORGANIZATIONS:** Mem Commn on Higher Educ of Middle States; Assn of Coll & U; pres Assn of Comm Coll; pres NJ Assn of Coll &Univ 1976; bd tsts Seton Hall U; dirYorkwood Savings & Loan Assn; mem Cncl for Ocptnl Edn; Am Assn of Comm & Jr Coll; chmn Govtl Affairs Commn; NJ State Schlrsp Commn Bd of Tsts; Grtr Newark Hosp Fund; mem 4th Degree KC; past mem Nat Adv Cncl on Adult Edn; mem Commission for the Prison Complex in the State of NJ; past chmn Newark-Essex Chap of Congress of Racial Equality; Nat Ass of Negro Bus & Professional Women's Club 1975; trustee Cancer Inst of NJ; mem trustee bd Blue Cross of NJ; rep Amer Assn of Comm and Jr Colls and Amer Council on Educ before Subcomm on Educ of the Senate Commn on Labor and Public Welfare. **HONORS/ACHIEVEMENTS:** President's Medal for Distgshd Serv Seton Hall U; Man of Yr Award So Ward Boy's Clubs of Newark NJ 1975; Leadership Award B'nai B'rith Career & Cnslg Serv; Educator of Yr Award NJ GOP Heritage Found Inc; apptd to Pres Nixon's Adv Cncl on Adult Educ; Brotherhood Awd Natl Conference of Christians and Jews; Service Awd Citizens for All People; Educator of the Yr New Jersey GOP Heritage Foundation, Inc; Achievement Awd Frontiers Intl; Man of the Yr Awd North Jersey Unit Natl Assn of Negro Business and Professional Women's Clubs; numerous articles published in professional journals. **MILITARY SERVICE:** USAF capt. **BUSINESS ADDRESS:** Chairman, Galaxy Personnel Forum, 50 Park Place, Newark, NJ 07102.

SMITH, JACK ELLIOTT
Journalist. **PERSONAL:** Born Jul 16, 1947, Los Angeles, CA. **EDUCATION:** LA City Coll, AA (broadcasting radio) 1969-72; Brown Univ, 1975-77. **CAREER:** CBS News NY, assoc producer 1978-; WSBE TV-36 Providence RI, producer, reporter writer, anchor 1977; KNXT (CBS) LA, research reporter 1972-73; Columbia Univ Summer Journalism Program for Minority Groups NY, instr 1972; Ken Minyard Show KABC Radio LA, asst producer 1970-71. **HONORS/ACHIEVEMENTS:** Assoc Press Award for best news feature program, WSBE TV-36 Providence 1978; USN Vietnam Serv Medal with 4 Bronze Stars; Navy Unit Commendation Ribbon (third); Natl Defense Serv Medal; rep of Vietnam Campaign Medal eith Device; Armed Forces Expeditionary Medal (Korea). **MILITARY SERVICE:** USN petty officer 3 1/2 yrs. **BUSINESS ADDRESS:** 524 W 57th St, New York, NY 10019.

SMITH, JAMES, JR.
Personnel director. **PERSONAL:** Born Nov 10, 1932, Beckley, WV; married V Anne Smith; children: Byron A. **EDUCATION:** Spokane Falls Comm Coll, AAS 1978; Fort Wright Coll, BS Mgmt 1981. **CAREER:** USAF, security police 1953-70, training admin 1970-75; City of Spokane, personnel tech 1978-81, asst personnel dir 1981-83, personnel dir 1983-. **ORGANIZATIONS:** Pres WA Council of Public Admin 1987-; chmn of the bd Natl Mgmt Assn 1983-87; mem Natl Forum for Black Public Admin 1983-; mem Alpha Phi Alpha Frat 1983-; pres Pine State Athletic Club 1984-87; bd dir NFBP 1985; mem bd dir Assn of Negotiators & Contr Administrators. **HONORS/ACHIEVEMENTS:** Superior Serv Awd City of Spokane 1985. **MILITARY SERVICE:** USAF msgt 1953-75; Commendation Medal; Good Conduct Medal. **BUSINESS ADDRESS:** Personnel Dir, City of Spokane, W 808 Spokane Falls Blvd, Spokane, WA 99201.

SMITH, JAMES A.
Association executive. **PERSONAL:** Born Oct 05, 1927, Ruther Glen, VA; married Katherene Stucky; children: Sherley, Willette. **EDUCATION:** Empire State Coll, BA 1975. **CAREER:** Human Resources Devel Inst AFL-CIO, area rep. **ORGANIZATIONS:** Mem New York City Taxi Drivers Union 1963-66; financial sec Black Trade Unionist Leadership Committee, NYC Central Labor Council AFL-CIO 1966-; area rep New York City Central Labor Council Job Placement Prog 1968-73; sec New York City Taxi Drivers Joint Industry Bd; elected mem Comm Sch Bd Dist 3 Manhattan; Industry Educ Coord Com NY; Chancellors Com promote equal opportunity prevent sex discrimination employment; New York City Bd Edn; mem of NAACP 125th St Manhattan Branch, Chairman of Selective Services Board 125th St NYC. **MILITARY SERVICE:** AUS 24th inf regt 1946-48; recalled Sept 1950-52. **HOME ADDRESS:** 65 W 96 St, Apt 22C, New York, NY 10025.

SMITH, JAMES ALMER, III
Psychiatrist. **PERSONAL:** Born May 24, 1950, St Louis, MO; married Sandra Wright; children: Anthony, Jason, Brian. **EDUCATION:** Howard Univ, BS 1972, MD 1976. **CAREER:** Harlem Hosp Ctr, intern 1976-77; Walter Reed Army Medical Ctr, resident 1977-80; US Army Ft Bragg, in-patient chief psych 1980-81, out-patient chief psych 1981-82; Central Prison Dept of Corrections, staff psych 1982-85, clinical dir 1985-87; NC Dept of Corrections, clinical dir of mental health. **ORGANIZATIONS:** Out-patient psych Wake Co Alcoholism Treatment Ctr 1983-87; mem bd dirs Drug Action of Wake Co 1986-87. **MILITARY SERVICE:** AUS major 9 yrs; US Army Commendation Medal 1986. **HOME ADDRESS:** 5100 N Hills Dr, Raleigh, NC 27612. **BUSINESS ADDRESS:** Clinical Dir of Mental Hlth, NC Dept of Corrections, 1300 Western Blvd, Raleigh, NC 27606.

SMITH, JAMES ALMER, JR.
Physician. **PERSONAL:** Born May 30, 1923, Montclair, NJ; son of James A Smith and Carrie Elizabeth Moten Smith; married Elsie, Oct 15, 1949; children: James III, Roger, Margo, Melanie. **EDUCATION:** Howard Univ, BS 1947, MD 1948. **CAREER:** Homer G Phillips Hosp, intern 1948-49, resd psychiat 1949-51; Washington Univ, child psychiat 1952-53; Mental Hygiene Clinic Group Co, co 1953-55; Hartley Salmon Child Guidance Clinic, staff psychiat 1955-60; Children Serv of CT, 1956-60; Juv Ct Hartford, consult 1956-61; Bay State Med Ctr, asst vis psychiat 1960; Childrens Study Home, consultant 1960-; Kolburne Sch New Marlborough medical dir 1968-; Springfield Child Guidance Clinic, assoc psychiatrist 1960-83; Tufts Sch Med, asst clinical prof 1977-. **ORGANIZATIONS:** Mem Human Rel Commn Springfield 1961-62; mem Am Psychiat Assn; fellow Am Ortho Psychiat Assn; Am Assn of Psychoanalytic Physicians Inc; Amer Society of Physician Analyst Fellow 1965-; Bd Negro Catholic Scholarship fund 1980-. **HONORS/ACHIEVEMENTS:** Am Acad Human Serv Award 1974-75; "Who's Who in the East" 1977-78; community leaders and noteworthy americans awd 1978; Int'l Directory of Distinguished Psychotherapists 1981/82; Dr Anthony L Brown Award WW Johnson Center 1987. **MILITARY SERVICE:** AUSR MC Capt 1953-55. **HOME ADDRESS:** 96 Dartmouth St, Springfield, MA 01109.

SMITH, JAMES DAVID
Practicing artist, educator. **PERSONAL:** Born Jun 23, 1930, Monroe, LA; married Ruth Johnson. **EDUCATION:** So U, BA 1952;Univ CA, 1954-55;Univ So CA, MFA 1956; Chouinard Art Inst, 1962; CO Coll, 1963;Univ OR, PhD 1969. **CAREER:** Univ CA, full prof 1969-; Univ OR, vis asst prof 1967-69; Santa Barbara HS, instr 1966-67; So Univ, asst prof 1958-66; Prairie View Coll, instr 1956-58; So Univ, vis prof 1954-55; Santa Barbara Co Schools, consult 1970, 1974, 1975; Univ CA, chmn 1969-73; Dept of Studio Art Univ of CA, grad adv 1969-. **ORGANIZATIONS:** Nat Art Educ Assn 1963-; past pres CA Art Educ Assn 1977-79; mem Kappa Alpha Psi; Phi Delta Kappa; NAACP; bd dir Self Care Found of Santa Barbara 1974-; bd dir Children's Creative Proj Santa Barbara 1975-; pres CA Art Educ Assn 1975-77; co-orgnr Spl Art Exhibition for Hon Edmond Brown Jr 1975. **HONORS/ACHIEVEMENTS:** Several awards selected John Hay Whitney Fellow in the Humanities 1963; exhibited in Dallas Mus of Art; Santa Barbara Mus of Art 1973; numerous shows in galleries throughout US. **MILITARY SERVICE:** AUS capt. **BUSINESS ADDRESS:** Dept of Studio ArtUniv of Cal, Santa Barbara, CA 93106.

SMITH, JAMES ODELL
Professional boxer. **PERSONAL:** Born Apr 03, 1953, Magnolia, NC; married Reba Sloan; children: Raymond, Jamie. **EDUCATION:** Kenansville NC, AA Business 1973; Shaw Univ Raleigh NC, BA Business 1975. **CAREER:** NC Dept of Corrections, officer/counselor 1979-82; professional boxer. **HONORS/ACHIEVEMENTS:** Heavyweight Champion of the World WBA 1986. **MILITARY SERVICE:** AUS sgt 3 yrs; Commendation Medal 1975-78. **HOME ADDRESS:** Route 2 Box 273, Lillington, NC 27546.

SMITH, JAMES OSCAR (JIMMY)
Musician. **PERSONAL:** Born Dec 08, 1928, Norristown, PA; married Edna Joy Goins; children: Jimmy, Jr, Jia. **EDUCATION:** Hamilton Sch of Mus; Ornstein Sch of Music, 1946-49. **CAREER:** Edmy Music Pub Co, owner, dir 1962; jazz organist who heads his own jazz group The Jimmy Smith Trio; began mus career 1952; playing piano with Don Gardner & His Sonotones; began performing as a single act during intermissions at the Harlem club in Atlanta City 1954; composer num organ pieces; compiler organ books. **HONORS/ACHIEVEMENTS:** Qrecipient 1st place in Downbeat Mag Jazz Poll catagory for Organ 1964; has won recognition in the poll every yr since; won Playboy Jazz Poll 1969; has been listed in that poll every yr since; Grammy Award for album The Cat 1964; other albums includ Got My Mojo Working 1966; In A Plain Brown Wrapper 1971. **BUSINESS ADDRESS:** 6355 Topanga Canyon Blvd, Ste 307, Woodland Hills, CA 91364.

SMITH, JAMES RUSSELL
Elected official. **PERSONAL:** Born May 02, 1931, Tupelo, MS; married Madie Ola; children: Rickey Young, Robert Young, Anita Young, Bonita Tate, Valeria Wedley, Richard. **EDUCATION:** Jackson State Jr College, AB 1979. **CAREER:** Communication CGN (USAF), supervisor 1951-72; Air Refueling Tech (USAF), supervisor 1951-72; Golden Circle Life Ins Co, salesman 1972-85. **ORGANIZATIONS:** President Humboldt Chapter NAACP 1975-80; board member Humboldt City Schools 1982-85. **MILITARY SERVICE:** USAF tsgt 1951-72; Air Medal 2 oak leaf clusters 1967; USAF oak leaf cluster 1968; retired 1972. **HOME ADDRESS:** 301 S 3rd Ave, Humboldt, TN 38343. **BUSINESS ADDRESS:** Sales Rep, Golden Circle Life Insurance, 39 S Jackson St, Brownsville, TN 38012.

SMITH, JANICE EVON
Public relations. **PERSONAL:** Born Feb 21, 1952, Warsaw, NC. **EDUCATION:** NC A&T State Univ, BS 1974; The OH State Univ, MA 1975. **CAREER:** Greensboro Daily News-Record, reporting intern 1974; The Charlotte News, daily newspaper reporter 1975-79, reporter/editor 1980; Natl Urban League Washington Opers, comm assoc 1981-83; DC Office of Human Rights, special asst to the director. **ORGANIZATIONS:** Dist III Chair NC Press Women's Assoc 1977; publicity chair/bd dirs Charlotte Mecklenburg Afro-Amer Cultural Ctr 1978-80; forum coord Washington Assoc of Black Journalists 1982; mem Capital Press Club 1982-85; mem Washington Urban League 1982-; mem NAACP 1983-84; comm chair Natl Capital Chap Public Relations Soc of Amer 1986-87. **HONORS/ACHIEVEMENTS:** Freelance articles published Essence magazine 1977-78; George Edmund Haynes Fellow Natl Urban League 1980; Outstanding Young Women of Amer 1982; Service Cert of Recognition Natl Capital Chap Public Relations Soc of Amer 1986. **BUSINESS ADDRESS:** Special Asst to Dir, DC Office of Human Rights, 2000 14th St NW, Third Floor, Washington, DC 20009.

SMITH, JEAN M.
Public relations officer. **PERSONAL:** Born Sep 14, 1943, Indianapolis, IN; daughter of William E. McAnulty and Ann L. Moss McAnulty; children: Kelly Moss. **EDUCATION:** Jrnslm Butler U, BA 1965. **CAREER:** INB Natl Bank, asst vice pres 1977-; The Indianapolis Star, reporter 1972-77; WISH-TV, dir of comm affairs reporter 1971-72; Indianapolis Urban League, dir of comm educ 1970; IN Gov Branigin, press sec 1966-69; Indianapolis News, reporter 1963-66; INB Financial Corp, first vp 1988-, dir of public relations. **ORGANIZATIONS:** Various committees United Way of Central IN 1978-; bd of trust Butler Univ 1981-; mem 1981-, vice pres 1986-87 Indianapolis Chap of Links; vchair Wilma Rudolph

Found 1982-85; mem Circle City Classic Football Weekend 1984-89; mem Jr League of Indianapolis 1974-; mem NBA All Star Game 1986; bd dir Indianapolis Symphony Orchestra 1985-1987. **HONORS/ACHIEVEMENTS:** Writing award Hoosier State Press Assn 1974; writing award Indianapolis Press Club 1976; most outstanding sr in jrnslm Butler U; most outstanding sr Woman in Jrnslm Butler U; Brown Scholarship Hilton U; Outstanding Woman in Business Awd Center for Leadership Devel 1981. **BUSINESS ADDRESS:** First Vice President, INB Financial Corp, 540 INB Tower, Indianapolis, IN 46266.

SMITH, JERALDINE WILLIAMS
Attorney, business executive. **PERSONAL:** Born Jan 14, 1946, Tampa, FL; married Dr Walter L Smith; children: Salesia Vanette, Walter Lee II. **EDUCATION:** Univ of FL, BS Journalism 1967; Atlanta Univ, MBA 1970; FL State Law School, JD 1981. **CAREER:** Freedom Savings, bank mgr 1973-75; Digital Equip Corp, admin mgr 1975-77; FL Dept of Ins, lawyer 1983-; Capital Outlook Weekly Newspaper, publ 1983-. **ORGANIZATIONS:** Mem Amer Bar Assoc, FL Bar Assoc, Natl Newspaper Publ Assoc, FL Press Assoc. **HONORS/ACHIEVEMENTS:** William Randolph Hearst Natl Newspaper Awards Winner 1967; Businesswoman of the Year Iota Phi Lambda 1971. **HOME ADDRESS:** 2122 E Randolph Circle, Tallahassee, FL 32312. **BUSINESS ADDRESS:** Publisher-Attorney, Capitol Outlook Newspaper, PO Box 11335, Tallahassee, FL 32302.

SMITH, JESSIE CARNEY
Educator, librarian. **PERSONAL:** Born in Greensboro, NC; daughter of James Ampler Carney and Vesona Bigelow Graves; divorced; children: Frederick Douglas Smith Jr. **EDUCATION:** NC A&T Univ, BS home economics, 1950; Cornell Univ, 1950; MI State Univ, MA child devel, 1956; George Peabody Coll for Teachers, MA library science 1957; Univ of IL, PhD library admin, 1964. **CAREER:** Nashville City Schs, teacher, spring 1957; TN State Univ, head cataloger & instr 1957-60, coord of library serv, asst prof, 1963-65; Univ of IL, tchng asst, 1961-63; Fisk Univ, univ librarian, prof, 1965-; univ lib, prof fed rel officer, dir of fed progs 1975-77; Dept of Lib Sci, Vanderbilt Univ, lectr 1969-, visiting prof, 1980-84 (part-time); AL A&M Univ, assoc prof, consultant 1971-73; Univ of TN Sch of Lib Sci, visiting lec 1973-74; Workshop Intern Prog for Librarians in Predominately Negro Coll, Atlanta Univ, assoc dir 1969, 1970; Inst on Selection Organization & Use of Materials by & About Negro, Fisk Univ, dir 1970. **ORGANIZATIONS:** Mem Am Lib Assn; TN Lib Assn; SE Lib Assn; Assn of Coll & Research Lib ALA; Lib Admin Div ALA; Lib Edu Div ALA; Am Assn of Univ Profs; Nom Comm Coll & Univ sec SE Lib Assn 1965-66; Ad Hoc Comm on Opps for Negro Students in Lib Profes Am Lib Assn 1966-67; Assn of Coll & Res Lib, Comm on Appointments 1968, Nom Comm 1969, Comm on Grants 1968-70; Special Comm on Natl Manpower Progs Am Lib Assn 1967-69; TN Adv Coun on Libs 1971-75; TN Lib Recruit Network 1965-69; chmn of Jury Halsey W Wilson Recruit; vchmn Chmn-elect Coll & Univ Sec TN Lib Assn 1968-69, chmn 1969-70; Choice Editorial Bd 1969-72, 1972-75; Am Lib Assn Coun 1969-71; TN Rep Lib Recruit Network 1969-71; Ref & Sub Books Review Comm ALA 1969-71, 1971-73; Adv Comm ALA Ofc for Recruit 1969-72, 1972-73; Advisory Council Martin Luther King Jr Cntr 1970-72; sec COSATI Sub-comm on Negro Res Libs 1970-73; African Studies Assn; ALA Resources & Tech Serv Div Cataloging & Class Sec 1971-74; mem, Episcopacy Comm, United Methodist Church, 1984-88, Metropolitan Historical Commn, Nashville, 1984-88, Natl Comm on the Bicentennial Scholars Prog, United Methodist Church, 1985-87, bd of dir, Children's Intl Educ Center, 1986-, bd of dir, Historic Nashville, 1986-89. **HONORS/ACHIEVEMENTS:** Fellowship, Council on Library Resources, 1969; Martin Luther King Jr Black Author's Award, 1982; Academic or Research Librarian of the Year Award, Assn of Coll and Research Libraries, Amer Library Assn, 1985; Distinguished Scholars Award, United Negro Coll Fund, 1986; Distinguished Alumni Award, Dept of Library Science, Peabody Coll of Vanderbilt Univ, 1987; numerous writings, including: A Handbook for the Study of Black Bibliography, 1971, Ethnic Genealogy: A Reseaarach Guide, 1983, Images of Blacks in Amer Culture: A Reference Guide to Information Sources, 1988. **BUSINESS ADDRESS:** Office of the Librarian, Fisk University, 17th Ave North, Nashville, TN 37208.

SMITH, JOCK MICHAEL
Attorney. **PERSONAL:** Born Jun 10, 1948, Manhattan-NYC, NY; married Yvette Smiley Johnson; children: Janay M. **EDUCATION:** Tuskegee Inst, BS History 1970; Univ of Notre Dame Law School, JD 1973. **CAREER:** US Customs Court, clerk 1970; Police Youth Involvement Prog, instructor 1972; Natl Urban League, legal asst 1972-73; NAACP Civil Rights Project, general counsel 1973; attorney private practice. **ORGANIZATIONS:** Vice pres Student Govt Assn 1969-70; chmn Notre Dame Law Sch Chap Black Amer Law Students Assn 1972-73; pres AL Lawyers Assn 1983-84; mem Alpha PhiAlpha Frat 1968-; mem AL Trial Lawyers Assn 1983-; mem Natl Bar Assn 1983-. **HONORS/ACHIEVEMENTS:** Awded Honor Roll Cert of 3 consecutive yrs 1967-70; Tuskegee Inst Dept of History Citation for Achieving Highest Average in Major 38 1968-70; listed in Natl Student Register 1968-70; Luther H Foster Awd for Outstanding Performance 1969-70; listed in Who's Who in Amer Colls & Univs 1969-70; Alpha Phi Alpha Awd for academic achievement 1969-70; co-authored Summer Youth Education Legal Rights Career Guidance Citizen Awareness 1972; awded 3 yr scholarship for continuing academic achievement; 3 yr academic scholarship to Notre Dame Law Sch on the basis of undergrad achievements; in 1st yr participated in the Moot Court Prog. **BUSINESS ADDRESS:** Attorney, PO Box 1162, Tuskegee, AL 36088.

SMITH, JOE ELLIOTT
Physician. **PERSONAL:** Born Jan 28, 1938, Little Rock, AR; married Mary; children: Sharol, Gary, John. **EDUCATION:** Philander Smith Coll, BS, 1959; Univ AR Med School, MD 1963. **CAREER:** VA Hospital, Univ AR Med School, chief asst ophtholmology 1969-71; Private Practice, physician. **ORGANIZATIONS:** Diplomate Amer Bd Ophthalomology 1971. **MILITARY SERVICE:** USAF captain, 1964-66. **BUSINESS ADDRESS:** 7107 W 12th, Little Rock, AR 72204.

SMITH, JOE LEE
Educational administrator. **PERSONAL:** Born May 29, 1936, Cocoa, FL; married Altamese Edmonson; children: Chyrell, Trina, Sharon, Twila. **EDUCATION:** FL A&M Univ, BS 1959, MEd 1963; Univ of FL, Rank 1-A Ed S 1973, Doctorate Ed Admin & Supv Higher Ed 1974. **CAREER:** Brevard Cty Public Schools, instr 1959-63; Ft Lauderdale Broward Cty Public Schools, instr 1963-67; Miami Dade Comm Coll, instr 1967-69; Cocoa HS, asst principal 1969-70; Brevard Comm Coll, dir of student activities 1970-72; Univ of FL, rsch asst to assoc dir of inst rsch council 1972-73; Brevard Comm Coll, dir of placement 1974-75, dir of coop ed placement & follow-up 1975-77, dean of student serv 1977-. **ORGANIZATIONS:** Mem Phi Delta Kappa 1963, Omega Psi Phi Frat 1969; vice chmn Rockledge City Council 1972-; mem FL Assoc of Comm Coll 1974; sunday school teacher Zion Orthodox Primitive Baptist Church. **HONORS/ACHIEVEMENTS:** Citizen of the Year Alpha Phi Alpha Frat 1972; recreation ctr named Joe Lee Smith Recreation Ctr 1973; Outstanding Ed of Amer 1975; Article "27 Steps to Better Discipline" 1974. **HOME ADDRESS:** 918 Levitt Pkwy, Rockledge, FL 32955. **BUSINESS ADDRESS:** Dean of Student Services, Brevard Comm College, 1111 North US 1, Titusville, FL 32796.

SMITH, JOHN ARTHUR
Physician. **PERSONAL:** Born Aug 25, 1937, Cincinnati, OH; divorced; children: Ann, Janis, Gwen, Jill. **EDUCATION:** Miami Univ, AB 1958; Univ of Cincinnati, MD 1964. **CAREER:** SUNY Downstate, physician 1971-72; Harvard Univ, visiting prof 1978; Indiana Univ Sch of Medicine, professor 1972-. **ORGANIZATIONS:** Mem/delegate NMA 1969-; bd Indianapolis Boys Club 1979-85; Alpha Eta Boule 1979-; mem chmn Soc for Pediatric Radiology 1983. **HONORS/ACHIEVEMENTS:** 1-2-3 Contact PBS Feature 1985; contributor 3 books; numerous articles in professional journals. **MILITARY SERVICE:** USAF capt 2 yrs; USAFE consultant radiologist 1968-70. **BUSINESS ADDRESS:** Professor, IndianaUniv Sch of Medicine, 702 Barnhill Dr, Indianapolis, IN 46223.

SMITH, JOHN THOMAS
Educational administrator. **PERSONAL:** Born Jun 14, 1919, Lexington, KY; married Josephine Estelle Fleming; children: Thomas H. **EDUCATION:** KY State Coll, AB eng & soc 1940;Univ of KY, MA admin 1958;Univ of KY, EdD adminstrn 1961. **CAREER:** Univ KY, vice pres minority affairs 1975-; Jefferson Comm Coll Univ KY, asso dir, dir 1968-75; Ashland Comm Coll Univ KY, asso prof psy & educ 1965-68; Lexington Public School, prin 1961-65; Lexington Public School, asst prin 1954-58; Lexington Public School, instr of Eng 1946-54. **ORGANIZATIONS:** Mem Phi Delta Kappa 1954-; mem Alpha Kappa Delta 1956-; mem Omicron Delta Kappa 1976-. **HONORS/ACHIEVEMENTS:** Recipient Marksman Award AC; Order of State Performance YMCA 1964; Kiwanis Award 1965. **MILITARY SERVICE:** AC corpl 3 yrs. **BUSINESS ADDRESS:** University of Kentucky, Rm 207 Administration Bldg, Lexington, KY 40505R.

SMITH, JOHNNIE M.
Business executive. **PERSONAL:** Born Jan 31, 1934, Pelham, GA; married Sandral E; children: Johnnie, Jr,Mark Alan. **CAREER:** Evangelistic Temples Inc, bishop & founder; BONT Cultural Cncl, pres; Yurika Foods Corp, independent distributor; Godason Corp Food Warehousing & Distribution, pres; Smith Enterprises, pres. **ORGANIZATIONS:** Bd of dirs Phillis Wheatley Assoc 1974-76; bd of commissioners Greenville Tech Coll 1974-76; adjustments, appeals code revision comm City of Greenville Hous8ing Bd 1974-75; bd of dirs Metropolitan Arts Cncl 1976-78; counties bd of dirs County Councilman SCAC 1977-84; piedmont subscriber cncl Blue Cross/Blue Shield 1978-79; Mgmt Assoc; Rotary Intl 1979-83; appalachian cncl of govt bd of dir, secty/treas NARC 1979-84; mem St Soc Serv Adv Commn 1982-83; mem JTPA 1982-83; vice chmn, mem CETA. **HONORS/ACHIEVEMENTS:** Leadership Evangelistic Temple Church 1969-76; housing board City of Greenville 1974; first class Leadership Greenville 1975; Invauluable Support RSVP 1976; Citzen of the Year Omega Psi Phi Fraternity 1976; Service and Outstanding Leadership Greenville Tech Coll 1976; Professor for a Day Award Clemson Univ 1982; Humanitarian Award Rutledge Coll 1984; Distinguished Services Award SC Assoc of Counties 1984; Community Services Award Pentecostal Temple Church 1984; Distinguished Service Award Natl Assoc of Black County Officials 1984; Outstanding Service Award Office of the Governer 1984; Community Service Award Gower Assoc 1984; Human Relations Commn Award 1985. **BUSINESS ADDRESS:** President, Smith Enterprises, PO Box 16269, Greenville, SC 29606.

SMITH, JOSCELYN E.
Judge. **PERSONAL:** Born Feb 09, 1918, New York, NY; daughter of Joscelyn E Smith and Ethel Jackson Henderson; married Marion A Pinckney; children: Barbara C, Diane M, Joscelyn E. **EDUCATION:** Howard Univ Wash DC, 1940-41; Long Island Univ Brooklyn, 1946-48; Brooklyn Law Sch, LLB 1948-50. **CAREER:** Atty pvt prac 1951-76; NY State Assembly, counsel to maj leader 1965-69; NY State Senate, legislative asst 1963-65; Borough of Queens NYC, borough sec 1958-60; City of New York, asst corp counsel 1956-58; Allied Real Estate Bd Queens Co, organizer, sponsor 1955-63; Civil Court, City of New York, judge, 1978-87; Supreme Ct State of NY, Supremem Ct Justice 1987-. **ORGANIZATIONS:** Cofndr Macon B Allen Black Bar Assn 1970-; pres Queens Co Yth Athl Centre 1955-63; pres Queens Child Guidance Centre 1970-76; pres Mens Club Queen Co 1972-76. **HONORS/ACHIEVEMENTS:** Plaque Inst Better Living 1976; plaque Women of Distinction 1976; plaque Natl Assn of Negro Business & Professional Women 1977; plaque Macon B Allen Black Bar Assn 1978. **MILITARY SERVICE:** AUS lt col 1941-46; AUSR 35 yrs.

SMITH, JOSEPH EDWARD
Educator. **PERSONAL:** Born Jan 22, 1925, Terre Haute, IN; son of Lemuel L Smith and Etila Smith; married Betty J Wright; children: Joseph Jr, Floyd P, Andrea I. **EDUCATION:** IN State Univ, BS 1950, MS 1955; MO Univ, Further Study. **CAREER:** Benedict Clge, art dept chr 1951-61; Lincoln Univ, instr 1961-65; Lemoyne Clge, assc prof 1965-69; Southern IL Univ, assc prof 1969-. **ORGANIZATIONS:** Mem Masonic Ldg; Omega Psi Phi Frat deacon trustee Mt Joy Bapt Ch of Edwardsville; mem Natl Conf of Artist; Am Assc of Univ Prof; Danforth Assc Prog; organizer Black Artist of Memphis Annual Exhibit 1965. **HONORS/ACHIEVEMENTS:** Consult SC State Audio Visual Wrkshp 1951-61; artist demonostrater Childrens Hour TV Prog Memphis State Univ 1968-69; creator and dir Comm Art for Ghetto Children of Memphis 1969; researcher 3D Sculptured Painting Complexities Approved Proj 1978-84; consult Art Wrkshps East St Louis 1982-84. **MILITARY SERVICE:** AUS sgt; Game Theater Ribbon; Bronze Stars; Victory Medal WWII; Am Theater Ribbon; Asiatic-Pacific Theater Ribbon; Good Conduct Medal 1943-46. **HOME ADDRESS:** 1916 Vassar Dr, Edwardsville, IL 62025. **BUSINESS ADDRESS:** Associate Professor, Southern ILUniv, PO Box 1764, Bldg III Room 3126, Edwardsville, IL 62026.

SMITH, JOSEPH EDWARD
Chemist. **PERSONAL:** Born Sep 13, 1938, Jacksonville, FL; married Mildred; children: Daryl, Ivan, Jomila. **EDUCATION:** Allen U, BS 1960; HowardUniv Coll Dentistry, DDS 1970. **CAREER:** Dentist self; Jacksonville Hlth Ctr, 1974-76; Boston Univ Grad Sch Dentistry, asst prof 1970-74; Roxbury Hlth Ctr, chemist 1966-67. **ORGANIZATIONS:** US Bur of Mines 1964-66; sec, treas Denticare Prepaid Dental Plan of FL 1976-77; dir Denticare Prepaid Dental Plan 1976-77; Small Busmens Serv Assn 1976-77; mem Nat Dental Assn; Am

Dental Assn; FL Dental Assn; VI Dental Assn; mem New Bethel AME Ch; stewart, pres Kenneth White Gospel Chorus; 3rd Sunday supt Sunday Sch; dir Northside Boys Club; bd mem Yth Congress Sickle Cell Anemia Prgm; life mem NAACP; mem Jacksonville Opt Ind Ctr 1976-77; Ribault Jr HS 1975. **MILITARY SERVICE:** AUS E-5 1961-63. **BUSINESS ADDRESS:** 1915 N Pearl St, Jacksonville, FL 32206.

SMITH, JOSEPH F.
Business executive. **PERSONAL:** Born Aug 22, 1945, Jacksonville. **EDUCATION:** T Valley State Coll, BA 1967; Howard U, JD 1970. **CAREER:** WRC/NBC "Consumer Guidelines", moderator 1971-74; Consumer Liason Div Office of Consumer Affairs Dept of HUD, formerly dir; Nat Consomer Inf Ctr, producer, exec dir; WRC/NBC IT's Your World", exec producer, moderator; Am & Howard Us, prof; numerous consumer manuals, economic & political articles, editor, lct pub. **ORGANIZATIONS:** Mem consult Office Consumer Affairs 1969-; mem Cong Staff; Black Caucus; Fed Trade Commn 1968-; Housing & Urban Dev; Soical Rehab Serv; OEO 1970-; Consumer Adv Com Fed Enery Office 1972-74; Cost of Living Council Assn 1974; Nat Assn Attorney Generals; Assn Home Appliances Mfgs 1974; Nat Legal Aid & Defender's Assn 1972; Nat Inst Educ in Law & Poverty 1970; Office of Gov 1973-; Atty Gen Offices of MA DC WI 1970-74; NY NV Consumer Offices 1973-74; OhioC of C 1973; Am Bar Assn 1971; mem Alpha Phi Alpha; NAACP; Consumer Fedearation Am; Nat Conf Black Lawyers; HowardUniv Law Sch Alumni Assn. **HONORS/ACHIEVEMENTS:** Numerous honors, awards, achievements in field. **BUSINESS ADDRESS:** Dept of HUD, 451 7th St, SW, Washington, DC 20410.

SMITH, JOSHUA ISAAC
Business executive. **PERSONAL:** Born Apr 08, 1941, Garrard Co, KY; married Jacqueline Jones; children: Joshua I II. **EDUCATION:** Central State Univ, BS Biology/Chemistry 1963; Univ of Akron Sch of Law, grad studies 1967-68; Univ of Delaware, association management 1975; Central MIUniv, grad studies business mgmt 1977. **CAREER:** Plenum Publishing Corp, mgr databook div 1969-70; Amer Soc for Information Science, exec dir 1970-76; Herner & Co, vice pres 1976-78; The MAXIMA Corp, pres & ceo 1978-. **ORGANIZATIONS:** Chmn 1984 United Way Fundraising Campaign; chmn of the bd Natl Business League of Montgomery Co; mem bd of dirs Intl Assn of Students in Business Mgmt & Economics; mem Minority Business Enterprise Legal Defense & Educ Fund; mem Natl Urban Coalition; dir TN Tech Foundation; mem Citizens Adv Comm forCareer & Vocational Educ; mem Corporate Round Table; mem adv bd Grad Sch of Library & Info Science Univ of TN; mem adv bd NC Central Univ Sch of Library Scis; mem Amer Assn for the Advancement of Scis; mem Amer Library Assn; mem Amer Soc for Info Sci; mem Black Presidents Roundtable Washington; mem Engineering Index Inc; mem Info Industry Assn Long Range Planning Comm; mem Natl Business League of Montgomery Co. **HONORS/ACHIEVEMENTS:** Minority Businessperson of the Yr Small Business Admin; Distinguished Corporate Awd US Dept of Commerce Minority Business Develop Agency; Special Recognition Awd for Valuable Commitment US Dept of Commerce Minority Business Develop Agency; numerous publications including "Library and Information Service for Special Groups" 1974; "The ERIC Clearinghouse on Library & Information Sciences (ERIC/CLIS)" The Bowker Annual Library & Book Trade Information 1973.

SMITH, JOSHUA L.
Educational administrator. **PERSONAL:** Born Dec 11, 1934, Boston, MA; son of Joshua Smith and Lorina A Henry Smith. **EDUCATION:** Boston Univ, BA 1955; Harvard Graduate School of Educ, MAT 1959, EdD 1967. **CAREER:** Pittsburgh PA, admin asst to supt of schools/acting vice principal 1966-68; Ford Found New York, program officer/asst program officer/project specialist 1968-74; City Coll City Univ of New York, prof of Educ 1974-76, dean school of educ 1976-77; Borough of Manhattan Community Coll, acting pres 1977-78; Borough of Manhattan Community Coll, pres 1978-85; State of California Community Colls, chancellor 1985-87; Brookdale Community Coll, Lincroft NJ, pres, 1987-. **ORGANIZATIONS:** Bd trustees Public Educ Assn 1974-; bd trustees Museums Collaborative Inc 1974-; bd trustees Natl Humanities Faculty 1974-; chmn NAACP Task Force on Quality Educ 1977-; mem AACJC Commn on Govt Affairs 1978-; repr CUNY to Big City Comunity Colls Pres & Chancellors AACJC 1978-; mem New Yorl Co Local Devel Corp Inc 1980; bd dir AACJC 1980; vice chair Joint Comm on Fed Relations AACJC/ACCT 1982, chair 1983; bd dir vice chair 1983-84, bd dir chair 1984-85 AACJC; bd of overseers Univ of the State of New York Regents Coll Degrees & Examination 1985-; golden heritage membership NAACP; bd of deacons Riverside Church, New York NY, 1977-82, bd of trustees, 1988-. **HONORS/ACHIEVEMENTS:** Phi Delta Kappa Award of Achievement for Outstanding Serv to the Field of Educ AL A&M Univ 1972; Distinguished Serv Award Bilingual Vol of Amer 1973; Distinguished Serv Award Harlem Preparatory School 1973-75; Award of Appreciation Support of the Devel of the S Leadership Devel Program So Region Council 1974. **MILITARY SERVICE:** USAF capt 1955-58. **HOME ADDRESS:** PO Box 576, Lincroft, NJ 07738. **BUSINESS ADDRESS:** President, Brookdale Community Center, Newman Springs Rd, Lincroft, NJ 07738.

SMITH, JUANITA JANE
Retired librarian. **PERSONAL:** Born Jun 11, 1923, Muncie, IN. **EDUCATION:** Ball State Univ, BS Educ 1945, post grad work 1946-48; Univ of MI, AMLS 1951, grad work 1958. **CAREER:** Indianapolis Pub Schools, teacher 1945-46; Ball State Univ, sec to dean/sec to dir of grad studies 1946-49, catalog & ref libr 1949-75, special collections librarian 1975-83; Steinbeck Quarterly & Steinbeck Monograph Series, asst editor 1978-82, assoc editor 1983; retired librarian 1983. **ORGANIZATIONS:** Mem Am Lib Assn; mem IN Lib Assn; mem Soc of Am Archivists; mem Soc of IN Archivists; mem Am Assn of Univ Profs; mem Delta Kappa Gamma Soc; mem Am Assn of Univ Women; mem League of Women Voters; mem YWCA. **HONORS/ACHIEVEMENTS:** Contributed articles Steinbeck Quarterly & Steinbeck Monograph Series 1978-80. **BUSINESS ADDRESS:** Ball StateUniv, University Avenue, Muncie, IN 47306.

SMITH, JUANITA SMITH
Elected official. **PERSONAL:** Born Jun 28, 1927, St Petersburg, FL; daughter of Ruffin Smith and Annabelle Momoan Smith; married Thomas H; children: Carl Tracey,. **EDUCATION:** Gibbs Jr Coll, elem educ; Tuskegee Inst, Industrial Arts 1947; Florida Intl Univ, BS Political Science 1974, extensive studies in counseling, social work, law, and criminal justice. **CAREER:** AL Lewis Elem School, teacher; Homestead Jr HS, teacher; Dade Co Bd of Pub Instruction, teacher 1967-; Florida City, vice mayor elected 2nd term 1984. **ORGANIZATIONS:** Mem Dade Co Crime Comm Court Aide; mem Amer Red Cross; mem United Heart Fund; mem Dade Co Cancer Soc; mem March of Dimes; mem Dade Co Comm Action Ctr; mem Dade Co Dept of Public Health; mem Hillsborough Co Juvenile Home; vice pres Dade Co Voters League; vice pres A L Lewis PTA; adv bd Protestant Christian Comm Serv Agency; adv bd FL City Parks & Rec; chairperson Public Relation Bd A L Lewis Elem School; mem Comm Block Club; mem Natl Council of Negro Women; mem Crime Stoppers; mem Children's Library Club; mem Sunshine Skating Club; mem, youth leader, welfare worker Seventh Day Adventist Church; member of board, urban league of Greater Miami 1986-; member of board, Community Health Inc Dade County 1987-; bd mem, Dade League of Cities, 1987-; mem NAACP, 1986-. **HONORS/ACHIEVEMENTS:** Woman of the year Links Inc 1985; awd of appreciation Naval Security Group Activity 1985; certificate and award of service Dade County Community Action Ser 1985; woman of the year Zeta Phi Beta 1985; woman of the year Bethel Seventh Day Adventist Church. **HOME ADDRESS:** 526 NW 14th St, Florida City, FL 33034.

SMITH, JUDITH MOORE
Educator. **PERSONAL:** Born Aug 03, 1948, Tallahassee, FL. **EDUCATION:** Hampton Inst, BS summa cum laude 1970; Boston U, MA 1971. **CAREER:** Univ of DC, asst prof of communicative & performing arts 1978-; Univ of DC Van Ness Campus Faculty Senate, chairperson 1977-78; Cambridge High & Latin School, instr eng, comm 1971-72; WAMU-FM Radio, prod, writer, series host 1977-78; Natl Public Radio-Radio Netherlands UDC, independent prod 1978-; Univ of DC FM Radio Proj, communications cons; bd mem's newsletter 1978-80; lead dancer African Heritage Dancers & Drummers 1973-. **ORGANIZATIONS:** Bd of dir Friendship House 1975-; mem Nat Coun of Negro Women 1977. **HONORS/ACHIEVEMENTS:** Fellowship Woodrow Wilson Doctoral 1970; fellowship Ford Found Doctoral 1970; faculty serv awardUniv of DC student body 1972-74; pr intrnsp Cong Black Caucus 1977; Outstanding Young Women of Am 1978; prod radio reports Nat Pub Radio 1979-. **BUSINESS ADDRESS:** 4200 Connecticut Ave, NW, Washington, DC 20008.

SMITH, KATRINA MARITA
Physician. **PERSONAL:** Born Oct 01, 1958, Kosciusko, MS. **EDUCATION:** Palmer Jr Coll, attended; East Carolina Univ, attended, Univ of Northern IA, attended, Palmer Coll of Chiropractic, DC 1984. **ORGANIZATIONS:** Mem Sigma Phi Chi 1984, Intl Chiropractic Assoc 1984, Amer Chiropractic Assoc 1984; sec Black Chiropractic Assoc 1984. **MILITARY SERVICE:** USMC corpl 4 yrs; Meritorious Mast, Good Conduct Medal 1st Awd. **BUSINESS ADDRESS:** Chiropractic Physician, 514 W Fortification, Jackson, MS 39203.

SMITH, KEITH DRYDEN, JR.
Educational administrator. **PERSONAL:** Born Jun 08, 1951, New York, NY; son of Keith D Smith Sr and Marion B Southerland Smith; married Sharon Anne Benson. **EDUCATION:** State Univ of NY, BA 1973; Syracuse Univ, MS 1978. **CAREER:** Red Creek Central Schools, science teacher 1974-75; Utica Coll of Syracuse Univ, HEOP counselor 1975-77, HEOP coord of academic and supportive serv 1977-79,HEOP dir 1979-81; State Univ of NY Plattsburgh, lecturer in Afro-Amer studies 1984-86, eop dir 1981-. **ORGANIZATIONS:** Mem Amer Assoc of Univ Prof 1975-81, United Univ Professors 1981-; affirmative action comm sec SUNY Plattsburgh 1983-; inst planning comm SUNY Office of Special Programs 1985-; human rights chair College Student Personnel Assoc of NY Inc 1986-87; certified mediator, Unified Court System of NY, Community Dispute Resolution Program, 1987-. **HONORS/ACHIEVEMENTS:** Dir of EOP Program with largest percentage of senior level students; conducted statewide survey of Minority Student Personnel Profiles 1985-; co-author, 1st comprehensive training activity for SUNY EOP Dirs, 1988. **HOME ADDRESS:** 57 Stoney Acres DrRD2, West Chazy, NY 12992. **BUSINESS ADDRESS:** Dir Educ Oppor Program, SUNY Plattsburgh, 103 Algonquin, Plattsburgh, NY 12901.

SMITH, KEVIN L.
Security guard company executive. **CAREER:** SC Security Inc, Charlottesville, VA, chief executive. **BUSINESS ADDRESS:** SC Security Inc, 125 Riverbend, Charlottesville, VA 22901. *

SMITH, LAFAYETTE KENNETH
Public administrator. **PERSONAL:** Born Dec 17, 1947, Memphis, TN; son of Joseph Smith and Elizabeth Berniece Hodge-Smith. **EDUCATION:** Howard Univ, Washington DC, BS, 1971; Bernard M Baruch Coll (CUNY), New York City NY, MPA, 1984. **CAREER:** Opportunities Industrialization Center, Washington DC, job placement specialist, 1972-75, job placement supvr, 1975-76, program supvr, 1976-78, branch mgr, 1978-81, program coord, 1981-82; Chicago Public Schools, Chicago IL, special asst to gen supt, 1982-83; Washington DC Govt, Dept of Human Serv, Washington DC, asst chief, Contracts Bureau, 1984-87, Youth Serv, contract admin, 1987-. **ORGANIZATIONS:** Mem, NAACP, 1970-, Howard Univ Alumni Assn, 1971-, Big Brothers, Washington DC, 1975-82, Prince Georges County, Private Indus Council, 1979-81, State of Maryland Occupational Information, 1980-81; tutor, Washington DC Public Schools, 1980-82; scout master, Boy Scouts of Amer, 1981-81; mem, Amer Soc of Public Admin, 1982-, Chicago Urban League, 1982-83, Barach Coll Alumni Assn, 1984-, Natl Forum of Black Public Admin, 1985-; bd mem, Natl Urban Fellows Alumni Assn, 1986-, Concerned Black Men Inc, 1986-. **HONORS/ACHIEVEMENTS:** Natl Urban Fellow, Natl Urban Fellows Inc, 1982; Natl OIC of Amer, 10 year Serv Award, OIC, 1982; Outstanding Young Men of Amer, US Jaycee, 1983; Enterprise Zones (Thesis), 1983. **BUSINESS ADDRESS:** Chief, Contracts and Monitoring Unit, DC Government, Youth Services Admin, Comm on Social Services, 817 14th St NW, 4th Floor, Washington, DC 20005.

SMITH, LEE
Professional athlete. **PERSONAL:** Born Dec 04, 1957, Jamestown, LA; married Diane. **CAREER:** Chicago Cubs, pitcher 1980. **ORGANIZATIONS:** Has shut out opponents in 124 of 170 outings, during which he registered 77 saves; 19 earned runs in 66 appearances in 1983; 29 saves a care er high. **HONORS/ACHIEVEMENTS:** 1984 ranks second in the NL in saves 33; tied Philadelphia's Al Holland for The Sporting News Fireman of the Year honors in 1983. **BUSINESS ADDRESS:** Chicago Cubs, 1060 W Addison St, Chicago, IL 60613.

SMITH, LEO GRANT
Educator. **PERSONAL:** Born Jun 21, 1940, Atlanta, GA; married Mildred Louise Holt; children: Wendy, Kimberly. **EDUCATION:** BA 1962, MA 1971; EdS 1982. **CAREER:** Hamilton HS, teacher 1962-68; Chamblee HS, asst principal 1968-72; Gordon HS DeKalb

Cty Bd of Ed, principal. **ORGANIZATIONS:** Vp GA Assoc of Secondary Principals 1973-74; mem DeKalb Assoc of Secondary School Principals, Gordon High PTA, Venetian Hills Elem PTA; vice pres DeKalb Admin Assoc 1975-. **HONORS/ACHIEVEMENTS:** ASCA administrator of the year. **BUSINESS ADDRESS:** Principal, Gordon High School, 2190 Wallingford Drive, Decatur, GA 30032.

SMITH, LEROI MATTHEW-PIERRE, III
Social service administrator. **PERSONAL:** Born Jan 11, 1946, Chicago, IL; children: Le Roi IV. **EDUCATION:** ID State Univ, BA 1969; WA State Univ, PhD 1977. **CAREER:** ID State Univ, lecturer 1969-70; WA State Univ, lecturer 1970-71; Evergreen State Coll, prof 1971-1981; Port of Seattle, equal employ manager. **ORGANIZATIONS:** Bd dir Thurston Mason Co Mental Health 1974-1981; Tacoma-pierce Co OIC 1979-1981; consult Seattle Pub Schls 1976-1985; mem Amer Soc for Personnel Admin1981-; Natl Assc of Black Psychologist 1974-1980; Amer Psychological Assc. **HONORS/ACHIEVEMENTS:** Flwshp Lilly Fnd 1981; Danforth Fnd 1978; Natl Sci Fnd 1976; US Dept of Educ 1969. **HOME ADDRESS:** 761 S 45th St, Tacoma, WA 98408.

SMITH, LEROY VICTOR
Football coach. **PERSONAL:** Born Aug 04, 1938, Lexington, KY; married Mary Levi; children: Darryl Victor, Angela Maria, Danee LaVon. **EDUCATION:** Jackson State Coll, BS 1958;Univ KY, MS 1963. **CAREER:** Lexington Recreation Dept, supr summers 1956-63; with MS Valley State Coll, 1958-59; Randolph HS, head football coach 1959-63; with Meigs HS Nashville,1963-64; Tuskegee Inst, head football coach 1964-70; KY State U, 1970-; Comm Educ Prog Tuskegee, consult 1966. **ORGANIZATIONS:** Mem Am Football Coaches Assn; author of articles; mem Kappa Alpha Psi; Alpha Kappa Mu.

SMITH, LILA
Scientist. **PERSONAL:** Born in Memphis, TN. **EDUCATION:** Lemoyne Coll, BS Math (high honor) 1957; Howard Univ, MS Physics 1959. **CAREER:** FL A&M Univ, asst prof of physics 1959-62; LeMoyne Coll, asst prof of Math 1962-63; US Atomic Energy Comm, scientific analyst 1963-76; Tech Info Ctr US Dept of Energy, chief conservation & solar branch 1976-83, chief nuclear engrg & physics Branch OSTI/USDOE. **ORGANIZATIONS:** Pres and charter mem Blacks in Govt Oak Ridge Chap 1984; 1st vice pres Region IV Blacks in Govt Inc 1984-; vice pres Xi Iota Omega Chap Alpha Kappa Alpha Sor 1985; mem Amer Solar Energy Soc Inc; mem Natl Forum of Black Public Admins; mem Altrusa Inc Oak Ridge Chpt; mem NAACP; mem Fed Employed Women Inc; mem Negro Bus & Professional Women's Clubs; mem TN Council on Human Relations; Oak Valley Baptist Church; Toastmasters Intl. **HONORS/ACHIEVEMENTS:** Sigma Pi Sigma Physics Soc; Equal Empl Opportunity (EEO); adv bd US Atomic Energy Comm Oak Ridge 1968-77; Personnel Security Bd US Dept of Energy 1974-81; Achievement Award for Outstanding Accomplishments in Sci & Civic Affairs Jack & Jill of Amer 1976; Spec Achievement Award for EEO US Energy Rsch & Develop Admin 1978; publications incl Geothermal Resources Bibliography 1975, 1976; Solar Energy Update Abstract Journal 1975. **HOME ADDRESS:** 114 W Lincoln Rd, Oak Ridge, TN 37830. **BUSINESS ADDRESS:** Chf Nuc Engrg & Physics Branch, US Dept of Energy Sci & Tech, PO Box 62, Oak Ridge, TN 37831.

SMITH, LONNIE
Professional athlete. **PERSONAL:** Born Dec 22, 1955, Chicago, IL; married Pearl; children: Yaritza LaVonne, Eric Tramaine. **CAREER:** Philadelphia Phillies, outfielder 1979-81; St Louis Cardinals, outfielder 1981-. **ORGANIZATIONS:** Successful on 30 of 36 stolen base attempts, 16 straight; led Cards in batting ave runs, hits, doubles, triples, and stolen bases, 2nd in Games played; on league level 4th in batting ave, 1st in runs, 2nd in stolen bases, 5th in hits and triples, 6th in doubles; stole fiv e bases in one Game tie a modern Natl League Record, reach the 100 career stolen base level and hitting his first grand slam home run and first inside-the-park round-tripper; batted 600 in the 1980 League Championship Series; 1982 elected to the Natl League's All-Star team. **HONORS/ACHIEVEMENTS:** Chosen Rookie of the Year 1980 by The Sporting News and Baseball Digest; St Louis BBWAA's Man of the Year 1982. **BUSINESS ADDRESS:** St Louis Cardinals, 250 Stadium Plaza, St Louis, MO 63102.

SMITH, LOUIS
Executive, government employee. **PERSONAL:** Born Nov 07, 1939, Ft Lauderdale, FL; married Bessie. **EDUCATION:** Morgan State, BS 1962; NYU, MA1970. **CAREER:** NY Dept of Mental Hygiene Kingsboro Psychiat Center, exec dir 1974-; Morrisania Hosp, asso dir 1973-74; Sydenham Hosp, asso dir 1971-73; NYUniv MedCenter, asst adminstr, 1968-71; Goldwater Meml Hosp, asst adminstr 1970-71; NYU Bellevue Hosp Center, liaison adminstr 1965-70; NYU Bellevue Hosp Center, asst liason adminstr 1968. **ORGANIZATIONS:** Mem Nat Assn of Health Exec; 100 Black Men of NYC; New York City Comprehensive Health Com; Assn of Mental Health Adminstr Asso; adj prof Long Island U; doctoral cand NYU Sch of Pub Adminstration; examiner NY State Dept of Civil Serv Nat In-Door Mile Relay Team 1959-61. **BUSINESS ADDRESS:** 681 Clarkson Ave, Brooklyn, NY 11203.

SMITH, LUTHER EDWARD, JR.
Educator clergyman. **PERSONAL:** Born May 29, 1947, St Louis, MO; son of Luther Smith and Clementine Smith; married Beth Mclaury; children: Luther Aaron, Nathan. **EDUCATION:** WA Univ, AB 1965-69; Eden Theological Sem, MDiv 1969-72; St Louis Univ, PhD 1973-79. **CAREER:** E St Louis Welfare Rgts Org, coord 1970-72; Educ for Blk Urban Mnstrs, exec coord 1972-79; Lane Tabernacle CME Church, asst pstr 1972-79; Black Church Ldrs Prog St Louis Univ, prog coord 1975-79; Candler Sch of Theology Emory Univ, prof of Church and Comm. **ORGANIZATIONS:** Bd chmn Northside Team Ministries 1973-79; 1st vice pres MO Assoc Soc Welfare St Louis Div 1973-79; prog coord Metropolitan Ministerial Alliance of St Louis 1975-79, Urban Churches in Community Dev Prog 1978-79; bd mem Urban Training Org of Atlanta 1980-; bd mem Inst for World Evangelism 1982-, Eden Tehological Sem. **HONORS/ACHIEVEMENTS:** Distg srv awards St Louis and Mid St Louis Cty Jaycees 1975; co author actor What's Black televised KETC 1970, Earth Day televised PBS 1970; Author of book Howard Thurman,the Mystic As Prophet 1981; member of Honor Society International Society of Theta Phi 1987. **BUSINESS ADDRESS:** Prof of Church & Community, Candler Schl of Theology, Bishops Hall EmoryUniv, Atlanta, GA 30322.

SMITH, LYNN STANFORD
Optometrist. **PERSONAL:** Born Sep 20, 1951, Oakland, CA; married Consuela McSterling; children: Galen Emerson. **EDUCATION:** Univ of CA Berkeley Sch of Optometry, BS 1974, OD 1976; Univ of IL Med Cntr Sch of Pub Health, MPH 1979. **CAREER:** Plano Child Devel Center, staff optometrist 1976-79; IL Coll of Optometry, asst prof of optometry 1978-80; private practice optometry Oakland, CA. **ORGANIZATIONS:** Bd dir Diversified Contract Serv Oakland, CA 1976-; region II trustee Natl Optometric Assn 1979-80; mem IL Optometric Assn 1979-80; mem Amer Optometric Assn; mem Amer Pub Health Assn 1979-; mem Seameda Contra Costa Cnty Optometric Soc; Rotary Toastmasters. **HONORS/ACHIEVEMENTS:** Publication "FDA Regulations Regarding Soft Contact Lens" Intl Contact Lens Clinic 1980; Outstanding Young Men of America 1982. **BUSINESS ADDRESS:** 1741 Broadway, Oakland, CA 94612.

SMITH, MARIE EVANS
Child psychologist. **PERSONAL:** Born Oct 21, 1928, Philadelphia, PA; married Charles N Smith; children: Dianne S Partee, Dionne S Jones, Deborah S Smith. **EDUCATION:** Temple Univ, BS 1972; Antioch Univ, MEd 1974; Kensington Univ, PhD 1985. **CAREER:** Greentree School, teacher 1960-65; The Inst of Human Potential, asst dir 1965-70; Parkway Day School, perceptual motor spec 1970-74; Hahnemann Medical Coll & John F Kennedy Mental Health Center, instructor and supervisor 1974-; John F Kennedy Mental Health/Mental Retardation Center, PA clinical psychologist 1974-, site director 1988-. **ORGANIZATIONS:** Founding mem1940-, women's day chairperson Providence Baptist Church 1986-87; pres Wellesley Civic Assoc 1965-; mem Temple Univ Alumni Assoc 1973-87, Antioch Univ Alumni Assoc 1974-87; mental health consultant Sch Dist of Philadelphia 1974-; mem Council for Intl Visitors Museum Civic Center 1983-87; mem Counseling Assoc of Greater Philadelphia 1985-, Natl Geographical Soc 1985-; mem at large NAACP 1985-; mem Afro-Amer Historical Cultural Museum 1985-87; bd mem Amer Black Women's Heritage Soc 1986-87; mem Zeta Phi Beta 1986-; consultant & child psychologist Minority Mental Health Advocacy Task Force; foundingmem Amer Legion Aux Henry Hopkins Post 881. **HONORS/ACHIEVEMENTS:** Legions of Honor Membership Chapel of Four Chaplains Awd 1965; Serv to Children Awd parkway Day School 1974; Certificate of Service Awd Hahnemann Medical Coll 1980; Certification of African Cultures Amer Forum for Intl Study 1981; Certificate of Merit Sch Dist of Philadelphia 1983; Recognition of Achievement Providence Baptist Church 1985; John F Kennedy Community Serv Awd Philadelphia PA 1985,86; Certificate of Achievement Behavioral Therapy Temple Univ; Womens History Month NJ Black Women's Educational Alliance 1989; Recognition of Service, John F Kennedy Mental Health/Mental Retardation Center 1988; Fellowship, Intl Biographical Assn 1989. **HOME ADDRESS:** 518 Wellesley Rd, Philadelphia, PA 19119. **BUSINESS ADDRESS:** Clinical Psychologist, Hahnemann Medical Coll & Hosp, 921 N 6th St, Philadelphia, PA 19122.

SMITH, MARIETTA CULBREATH
Education administrator. **PERSONAL:** Born Jul 11, 1933, Saulda, SC; married Sylvester Odellas Smith; children: Melvin, Darrion, Lorraine, Wardell, Sylvester Jr, Patricia Ann, Tryone. **EDUCATION:** New York Univ, Cert 1970; Washington Tech, Cert 1971; American Univ, Cert; Pre School Day Care Div, Cert 1971. **CAREER:** Change Inc, board of dir, vice chmn 1970-; Neighborhood Planning, counsellor, treasure 1984-; Ward One Council on Educ, chmn Ways & Means 1980-; Advisory Neighborhood Comm, vice chmn/educational aide 1984-85. **ORGANIZATIONS:** Asst treas Ward I Council of Educ; sec Ward I Democrats 1985-88; bd of dirs Teachers Ctr DC Public Schools; working on computer lab Terrell Jr HS; vice chair ANC 1986-88. **HONORS/ACHIEVEMENTS:** Presidential Awd 1970; Life time mem PTA Congress 1974; Appreciation Awd DC Congress 1960- & City Council 1974-88. **HOME ADDRESS:** 1351 Meridian Pl NW, Washington, DC 20010. **BUSINESS ADDRESS:** Educational Aide, Advisory Neighborhood Comm, 104 Spring Rd NW, Washington, DC 20010.

SMITH, MARION L.
Government official. **PERSONAL:** Born Apr 05, 1901, Atlanta, GA; married Alice; children: Marion Jr, Mayra. **EDUCATION:** Tuskegee Inst, 4 yrs; Chicago Real Estate Coll. **CAREER:** Robbins IL, mayor; Palad Triangle Dry Goods, owner; Pullman Repair Shop, machinist 20 yrs. **ORGANIZATIONS:** Mem Cook Co Housing Authority 22 yrs; mem Elks Club; Robins Celebration League; Good Shepard Luth Ch. **BUSINESS ADDRESS:** 3327 W 137th St, Robbins, IL 60472.

SMITH, MARLYN STANSBURY
Artist. **PERSONAL:** Born Jul 13, 1942, Philadelphia, PA; divorced; children: Najwa. **EDUCATION:** Univ of PA, MSW 1976; Musukeba Drammeh Banjul Gambia W Africa, Ibou Souare Dakar Senegal W Africa, Batik study 1982. **CAREER:** Originating from Smith Studio serving Public Schools & Community Activities, comm cultural activist; Horizon House Inst for Rsch & Devel, training coord1976-78; Comm Coll of Philadelphia, classroom instruction coordinator, 1978-80; Harrah's Hotel/Casino, supvr security trainer 1980-. **ORGANIZATIONS:** Mem Philadelphia Art Alliance 1977-, Artists Equity Assoc Inc 1978-; vice chairperson bd of dirs Natl Minority for Child Abuse Resource Ctr 1978-80; chairperson Philadelphia Chap Natl Conf of Artists 1979-80; life mem Atlantic City Art Ctr, Ocean City Art Ctr; chairperson Atlantic Co Mental Health Adv Bd 1986-87;art juror Marina Fine Art Show 1986 Harrah's Hotel/Marina Casino Craft Show 1987. **HONORS/ACHIEVEMENTS:** Art Awd Afro Amer Historical Cultural Museum 1980; First prize 20th Annual NJ State Juried Exhibition 1981; First prize Harrah's Hotel/Casino 1983; Fellowship Council on Social Work Educ 1984-; One Woman Shows, Johnson & Johnson New Brunswick NJ 1980, Comm Coll of Philadelphia 1981, Galerie Art Negre Dakar Senegal W Africa 1982, Franklin & Marshall Coll PA 1986; Credits, Artist Source Book PA, Council on the Arts, Atlantic City Magazine, Chicago Tribune. **HOME ADDRESS:** 2233 Kuehnle Ave, Atlantic City, NJ 08401.

SMITH, MARVETTE THOMAS
Educational administrator. **PERSONAL:** Born Jan 27, 1953, Montgomery, AL; daughter of Robert Marvin Thomas and Bernice Morgan Thomas; divorced; children: Janel Bernice Cobb. **EDUCATION:** Austin Peay State Univ, BS 1977; Murray State Univ, MS 1980; George Peabody Coll of Vanderbilt Univ, EdD 1984. **CAREER:** Northwest HS, spec ed teacher, chair spec ed spec needs counselor 1979-83; Vanderbilt Univ, teaching, grad asst 1981; Women in Nontraditional Careers WINC, dir proj 1986-; LA State Univ Eunice, counselor 1984, acting dir spec serv & devel ed, dir spec serv 1985-89; dir TRIO Programs 1989-. **ORGANIZATIONS:** Mem Natl Assoc of Univ Women, Amer Assoc of Counseling & Devel, Natl Council of Negro Women, Amer Coll Personnel Ass, LA Assoc for Devel Ed, Southwest Assoc of Student Asst Prog, Socialite Soc & Civic Club; sec Opelousas Alumnae Chap Delta Sigma Theta Inc; past pres Clarksville TN Alumnae Chapt Delta Sigma Theta; bd dir Eunice

C of C; mem bd of dir Bayou Girl Scout Council 1987-; mem bd of dir Moosa Memorial Hospital 1988-; pres LA Assn of Student Assistance Programs 1988-89; mem bd of dir Southwest Assn of Student Assistance Programs 1988-90; pres-elect LA Assn of Student Assistance Programs 1989-90. **HONORS/ACHIEVEMENTS:** Outstanding Young Woman of Amer 1976,81; Inductee Phi Delta Kappa 1979; Natl Cert Counselor 1983; Chi Sigma Iota 1985; Outstanding Woman of Eunice, The Eunice News 1987; mem President's Council Natl Council of Educ Opportunity Assn 1988. **BUSINESS ADDRESS:** Dir TRIO Programs, Louisiana StateUniv, PO Box 1129, Eunice, LA 70535.

SMITH, MARY LEVI
Educational administrator. **PERSONAL:** Born Jan 30, 1936, Hazlehurst, MS; daughter of Rev William Levi and Byneter Markham Levi; married LeRoy; children: Darryl, Angela Williams, Danee. **EDUCATION:** Jackson State Univ, BS 1957; Univ of KY, MA 1964, EdD 1980. **CAREER:** MS, AL, TN Elem Grade Schools, teacher 1957-64; Tuskegee Inst, asst dir of reading clinic 1964-70; KY State Univ, assoc prof of ed 1970-, chairperson dept of ed 1981-83; Coll of Applied Sci KY State Univ, dean 1983-88; vice pres for Academic Affairs 1988-89; interim pres of Kentucky State Univ 1989-. **ORGANIZATIONS:** Mem KY Assoc of Coll of Teacher Ed 1981-; inst rep Amer Assoc of Coll of Teacher Ed 1981-; coord Litte Miss Black Frankfort Pageant 1982,83; bd of dir Frankfort Arts Found 1984-. **HONORS/ACHIEVEMENTS:** Kent St Univ, outstanding faculty of the yr 1986; Outstanding Alumnus Award Jackson State Univ 1988; Torchbearers and Trailbearers Award in Education 1989. **BUSINESS ADDRESS:** Interim President, Kentucky State University, Hume Hall, Frankfort, KY 40601.

SMITH, MARZELL
Educator. **PERSONAL:** Born Aug 14, 1936, Conehatta, MS; married Albertine. **EDUCATION:** Piney Woods Jr Coll; 1952-56; Jackson State Coll, BS 1958; TN A&I State U, MEd 1964;Univ Miami, 1969;Univ Miami, EdD 1973. **CAREER:** FL Sch DesegregationUniv Miami, staff consult 1970-;Univ Miami, flw 1969-70; GN Smith Elem Sch, asst prin 1966-69; Jim Hill Jr Sr HS, tchr 1964-66; Allen Carver Jr Sr HS, 1958-64; Douglas Elem, coord 1971-72; Monreo Co Sch System; Alachua Co, 1972; Collier Co; Dept Found FL Atlantic U, 1975. **ORGANIZATIONS:** Mem Am Educ Rsrch Assn; Nat Assn Sch Adminstr; BSA; Nat Assn Secondary Sch Prin; College Hill Bapt Ch; Jackson Bd Certified Officials; Phi Delta Kappa; SW Officials Assn; Kappa Alpha Psi Frat; Urban League; MTA-JTA-CTA; Miami Chap Nat Alliance of Black Sch Edr; mem FL Assn Dist Sch Supt;So Asn Black Adminstrv Personnel;Univ Miami Black Faculty Adminstr; bd dir Miami Black Arts Gallery & Workshop; mem Dept Adminstr Curriculum & Instr; NEA; Nat Alliance of Black Sch Edr; Poverty Law Ctr; NAACP; unpubl papers "An OD Analysis of Aw Soc Serv Orgn"; "Discipline Problems in a Pub Jr HS blueprints for action"; "the polit action strategies of dr martin luther king jr implications & applications"; "the role of Hallucinogenic Plants in Early Am Colonial & European Witchcraft"; "Discipline Problems in Three Pub FL Sr HS implications & applications"; "Conflict Intervention Strategies in a Pub Sch System in FL; Applications". **MILITARY SERVICE:** AUS pvt. **BUSINESS ADDRESS:** PO Box 8065, Coral Gables, FL 33124.

SMITH, MAXINE ATKINS
Association executive. **PERSONAL:** Born in Memphis, TN; married Dr Vasco A Smith, Jr; children: Vasco III. **EDUCATION:** Spelman Clg Atlanta, GA, AB; Middlebury Clg Middlebury, VT, MA. **CAREER:** Prairie View A&MUniv Prairie View, TX, instr frnch 1950-52; FL A&MUniv Tallahassee, FL, instr frnch 1952-53; LeMoyne Clg Memphis, TN, asst prof frnch & english 1955-56; Memphis Branch NAACP, exec sec 1962. **ORGANIZATIONS:** Mem Delta Theta Sorority Inc Memphis Alumnae Chptr; mem Natl Smart Set Inc Memphis Chptr; mem Links Inc Memphis Chptr; mem bd of dir Democratic Voters Cncl; temporary chrmn Memphis Alliance Comm Organization; mem exec bd Memphis Com Comm Relations; bd dir Memphis Branch NAACP 1957; mem chrmn Memphis Branch NAACP 1958-61; coordinated & partcipated Freedmon Movement 1960-61; dir NAACP Annual Registration Campaigns; bd dir Voter Ed Proj Inc 1971; advsry bd Tri-State Defender 1983; hon chrprsn LeMoyne-Owen Clg 1983; bd dir Lorraine Civil Rights Museum 1984; bd trustee Ldrshp Memphis 1985; chairedNAACP's Natl Springarm Award Com 1985. **HONORS/ACHIEVEMENTS:** Woman of yr Trinity CME Chrch; achvmnt awrd Omega Psi Phi Frat; one of ten outstndg young am Pageant Mag; woman of yr Civil Rights YWCA; annual merit awrd Memphis Brnch NAACP 1960; humanitarian of yr Alpha Pi Chi Sorority Alpha Beta Chptr 1964; woman of action awrd Alpha Kappa Alpha Sorority 1969; outstndg citizen of yr Omega Psi Plhi Frat 1969; one of five citizens Natl NAACP Outstndg NAACP Ldrshp 1970; selected to appear in seventh edition Who's Who of Am Women; recipient of outstndg citizen awrd Frontier Intrl Inc 1970; recipient distngshd citizen awrd for contributions & ldrshp Mallory Knights 1960;outstndg ldrshp in field civil rights Longview Seventh Day Adventist Chrch; cited civil rights actvty Ward Chapel AME Church 1971; selected for biographical & pictorial inclusion in "Two Thousand Women of Achievement - 1972" Pblshd Melrose Press Ltd Londong England; plaque for outstanding comm serv Beta Epsilon Omega Chptr Alpha Kappa Alpha Sorority 1972; black histry week plaque of recognition Beulah Bapt Chruch 1972; recipient of Kappa Alpha Psi Plaque for Meritorious Serv to Comm Area Human Rights/. **HOME ADDRESS:** 1208 E Parkway S, Memphis, TN 38114. **BUSINESS ADDRESS:** Executive Secretary, Memphis Branch NAACP, 588 Vance Ave, Memphis, TN 38126.

SMITH, MELISSA ANN
Director of minority affairs. **PERSONAL:** Born Jul 30, 1962, Kansas City, KS; daughter of Francella E Hayes. **EDUCATION:** Univ of Kansas-Lawrence, BS Journalism 1984; Univ of MO - KC, working on MS in Higher Educ Administration. **CAREER:** RFC Intermediaries - Los Angeles, claims clerk 1984; St Mary College 2 Plus Two Prog, administrative asst 1985; Donnelly Coll, dir of publicity 1985-88; Longview College, dir of minority affairs 1989-. **ORGANIZATIONS:** America's Heart Co-Op, public relations consultant 1986; KCK Area Chamber of Comm, leadership 2000 participant 1986-1987; Freelance Writer and Layout Designer1986-. **HONORS/ACHIEVEMENTS:** Fundraising committee mem KCK Women's Chamber of Comm 1986; mem KCK NAACP 1985-86; mem organist Pleasant Valley Bapt Church. **HOME ADDRESS:** PO Box 3611, Kansas City, KS 66103. **BUSINESS ADDRESS:** Dir of Minority Affairs, Longview College, 500 Longview Rd, Lee's Summit, MO 64081.

SMITH, MILDRED B.
Educator. **PERSONAL:** Born Feb 03, 1935, South Carolina; divorced. **EDUCATION:** SC State Coll, BS; MI State U, MA; MI State U, PhD. **CAREER:** Curriculum Coordinator, elementary teacher; elementary dir; u vis lectr; conselor; Flint Bd Educ, elementary dir. **ORGANIZATIONS:** Mem bd dir First Independence Nat Bank of Detroit; mem bd of Regents for Eastern MI U. **HONORS/ACHIEVEMENTS:** Author "Home & Sch Focus on Reading" 1971; co-author "Reading Systems & Open Highways" 1971-74; numerous listings in Who's Who publ; The Nat Register Prominent Am; Dictionary of Intl Biography.

SMITH, MILLARD, JR.
US naval officer. **PERSONAL:** Born Jul 09, 1948, Lufkin, TX; son of Millard Smith Sr (deceased) and Gussie Mae Williams Smith; married Helen Jean Woodson Smith, Feb 14, 1969; children: Demethra Rochelle, Millard III. **EDUCATION:** National Univ, San Diego CA, BA, 1980. **CAREER:** US Navy, Great Lakes IL, commanding officer, 1970-. **ORGANIZATIONS:** Pres, San Diego Chapter, Natl Naval Officers Assn, 1987-88; grand chapter pres, Zeta Sigma Lambda Chapter, Alpha Phi Alpha, 1988-89. **MILITARY SERVICE:** US Navy, lieutenant/03E, 1970-; Navy Commendation, Navy Achievement 2 Awards.

SMITH, MORRIS LESLIE
Researcher. **PERSONAL:** Born May 29, 1933, Camden, NJ; son of William E Smith and Tamae A Smith; married Alice Marie Gray; children: Morris G, Wesley E, Stephen J. **EDUCATION:** MI State Univ, BS 1959; Temple Univ, MBA Program 1978. **CAREER:** Magna Bond Inc, rsch chemist 1959-61; EL Conwell Inc, analytical chemist 1961; Scott Paper Co Philadelphia, rsch chemist 1961-65, sr rsch project chemist 1965-74, sect leader 1974-78, sr rsch leader 1978-. **ORGANIZATIONS:** Study prog Mt Zion United Methodist Church 1972-; mem bd dir United Methodist Homes of NJ 1980-; mem bd dir St Peter's School Philadelphia 1970-88; mem bd dir Agape Day Care Center Marcus Hook 1982-; pres Echelon Branch Camden Co YMCA 1983-86; exec at large Intl Soc of African Scientists 1984-; mem bd of dirs Camden Co YMCA; mem TV Mins Comm Southern New Jersey Annual Conf of United Methodist Church; treas parade marshall Lawnside 4th of July Comm Inc. **HONORS/ACHIEVEMENTS:** US Patent #3,389,108 1968; use of fragrance in paper Talk publ Amer Soc of Perfumers 1973; Lay Panelist Administrative Court of NJ 1984; mem NJ School Bds Assn 1975-76; Commendation Ltr Martin Luther King Mem Library DC 1984. **MILITARY SERVICE:** AUS specialist 1955-57; Honorable Discharge. **BUSINESS ADDRESS:** Senior Research Leader, Scott Paper Company, Scott Plaza III, Philadelphia, PA 19113.

SMITH, NATHANIEL
Administrative executive. **PERSONAL:** Born Feb 23, 1929, Pittsburgh, PA; married Mini Lee Henderson; children: Renee, Sabrina, Nathaniel, Jr. **EDUCATION:** Carnegie Mellon U, hon HHD 1976. **CAREER:** Primary Care Hlth Ctr Inc, chmn 1977-; Sch of Pub Urban Affaird Carnegie Mellon U, consult 1977-; Tch Cris Mgmt & Carnegie Mellon U, 1971-72; Dept ofLabor Pittsburgh, exec liaison 1968-; DIG Pittsburgh, founder adminstr oper 1967-; IUOE Local 66, oper engr 1952-; prolf boxer 1945-59; ConsultUniv ofPittsburgh, 1967-73; NY World Trade Center, 1967-74; RTP NY, 1969; Carnegie Mellon U, 1970; Blk Constr Coalition, pres 1968-71;Univ of Buffalo, lectr 1969; Roosevelt Coll Chicago, 1969-73; Harvard-prinston Clb, 1969; Berkeley CA U, 1969; Carlow Coll Pittsburgh, 1970. **ORGANIZATIONS:** Bd mem Plan Comm for Health & Welfare; FACE; oper PUSH; Espisopalian Iocese; exec bd mem NAACP; NEED; dir Pittsburgh Br Operation PUSH; chmn Solidarity Fair; life mem NAACP; mem PTA; Drug Rehabilitation Prog Hill Cultural Center; Allegheny Conf. **HONORS/ACHIEVEMENTS:** Recipient citation of merit Co of Allegheny 1972; Man of Yr Talk Mag 1972-73; Man of Yr Women's Aux Orgn 1973; one of 100 most influential blacks in Am Ebony Mag 1973-76; Jesse Jackson Award Poor People's Conf 1974; Man of Yr Allegheny Co 1974; Man of Yr Pittsburgh Gardians 1974; bronze hat award Minor Trade Orgn 1975; proclamation from Gov of PA 1975; Lrockwell Intl Award 1975; serv & brotherhood award WZUM Radio 1975; nom man of yr Pittsburgh Jaycee's1976; Marquis' Who's Who in Am 1976. **MILITARY SERVICE:** Usnr 1942-44.

SMITH, NATHANIEL, JR.
Manufacturing executive. **CAREER:** Ver-Val Enterprises, Fort Walton Beach, FL, chief executive. **BUSINESS ADDRESS:** Ver-Val Enterprises, 91 Heill, PO Drawer 4550, Fort Walton Beach, FL. *

SMITH, NELLIE J.
Educator. **PERSONAL:** Born May 15, 1932, Meridian, MS; married Levi; children: Bobby, Paula, Perry, Joseph. **EDUCATION:** Rust Coll Holly Spring MS, BS 1954; KS State Teachers Coll Emporia, MS 1956; Univ of ND, PhD 1973. **CAREER:** Intl Brothers Teamsters, 1st black clerk 1960-62; Rust Coll, bus instr 1962-63; Harris Jr Coll, bus instr 1963-64; MS Valley State Coll, asst prof 1964-70; Rust Coll, chairperson div bus, assoc prof bus ed 1970-. **ORGANIZATIONS:** Mem So bus Ed Assoc, UMC 9142-, Acappella Choir Rust Coll 1950-55; voice recital MS Valley State Coll 1969; choral union Univ of ND 1971-73, Natl Bus Ed Assoc, Delta Pi Epsilon, Pi Omega Pi, Phi Beta Lambda. **HONORS/ACHIEVEMENTS:** Personalities of the South 1969,74; Publ poem "Life Its Mystery & Struggle" set to music 1969; publ 6 articles, 4 shorthand tests 1973, "How to use Fortran Arithmetic Operators" 1973, typewriting speed test 1973. **BUSINESS ADDRESS:** Associate Professor Bus Ed, Rust College, 1 Rust Ave, Holly Springs, MS 38635.

SMITH, NORMAN RAYMOND
Publisher. **PERSONAL:** Born Nov 17, 1944, New Orleans, LA; married Joyce Singleton; children: Corey Norman, Christopher Jude. **EDUCATION:** Commonwealth Coll of Science, Mortuary Science 1966; Attended, Southern Univ at New Orleans. **CAREER:** Treme Improvement Political Soc, pres/chmn of bd 1970-; Upper Pontalba Bldg Commn, mem 1980-; Treme Cultural Enrichment Progs, secty; LA Black CultureCommn, exec bd mem 1984-; Forget-Me-Knots Inc, pres/chmn of bd. **ORGANIZATIONS:** Mem New Orleans Embalmers Assoc 1966-; mem Armstrong Park Adv Comm 1983; grand knight Knights of Peter Claver-Thomy Lafon Council #240 1986-; treas Greater New Orleans Black Tourism Ctr 1986-. **HONORS/ACHIEVEMENTS:** Fellow Loyola Univ Inst of Politics 1979; publisher of "Etches of Ebony Louisiana," annual Black LA history caldenar since 1983 incl current issue 1987. **MILITARY SERVICE:** AUS sgt 1967-69; Good Conduct Medal, Vietnam Campaign Medal. **HOME ADDRESS:** 4653 Tulip St, New Orleans, LA 70126. **BUSINESS ADDRESS:** President, Forget-Me-Knots Inc, PO Box 7332, New Orleans, LA 70186.

SMITH, OSCAR SAMUEL, JR.
Business executive. **PERSONAL:** Born Aug 05, 1929, Raleigh, NC; married Mrs Gloria K; children: Mrs Robin Swinson, Oscar S III. **EDUCATION:** St Augustine's Coll Raleigh, BA 1955;Univ of MD, MA 1968;Univ of NC, Inst of Gov't 1978. **CAREER:** US Info Agency DC, info specIsts 1956-65; Urban Renewal Auth MD, asso dir 1965-68; Shaw U, dir u rel 1968-72; Capitol Broadcast Co, cap news anchor/reporter 1972-77; NC Dept of Ins, dir pub affairs 1977-85; Creative Communications, pres/chrmn of the bd. **ORGANIZATIONS:** Pub rel consult United Communities Against Poverty 1968; pub rel consult Wk Co Sr Citizens Office 1977; minority affairs advisor Am Coll Pub Rel Assn 1972; NC StateUniv Publ Rel Adv Bd 1977; mem NC Black Political Cacus; mem Wake Co Black Political Action Comm; mem St Paul's AME Ch. **HONORS/ACHIEVEMENTS:** Excell in Publications Am Coll Pub Rel Soc; Journalism Hall of Fame NC; Disting Serv Award St Augustine's Coll; Disting Serv Award Prince George's Co MD. **MILITARY SERVICE:** AUS splst 4th class 1953-55; Served in Armed Forces Radio Network 7th Inf Div Hdqtrs. **HOME ADDRESS:** 201 Clarendon Crescent, Raleigh, NC 27610. **BUSINESS ADDRESS:** President/Chairman of Board, Creative Communications, PO Box 26374, PO Box 26387, Raleigh, NC 27611.

SMITH, OSWALD GARRISON
Physician. **PERSONAL:** Born Sep 04, 1915, Vicksburg, MS; married Millie. **EDUCATION:** Meharry Med Coll, mD 1940. **CAREER:** Queens Hosp Ctr, asso atdng anesthesiologist; State Univ NY, asso clinical prof, Misericordia Hosp, acting dir anesth dept 1962; Bronx VA Hosp, resd anesth 1959-61; physician gen prac 1946-59. **ORGANIZATIONS:** Mem Alpha Phi Alpha & Frat NAACP; Am Soc Anesthes; AMA; Nat Med Assn Chmn PM Smith Meml Schlrsp Com Diplomat Am Bd Anesthes 1964. **HONORS/ACHIEVEMENTS:** Flw Am Coll Anesthes 1962; 1st black mem MS State Med Soc 1956. **MILITARY SERVICE:** AUS MC 1st lt 1942-46.

SMITH, OTIS BENTON, JR.
Clergyman. **PERSONAL:** Born Nov 05, 1939, Lexington, KY; son of Rev Otis B Smith Sr and Hattie Bibbs Smith; married Bertha Odessa Stevenson; children: Otis III, Patrick Tyrone, Kenise Lynette. **EDUCATION:** Central State Univ, BS 1960; So Baptist Theol Sem, MDiv 1969, Certificate of Merit 1984; Univ of North AL, Certificate of Continuing Educ 1985. **CAREER:** Natl Jewish Hosp Pediatric Sect, recreation supr & coun 1964-65; E Moline State Hosp, recreation supr 1965-66; WV Hosp Dayton, recreation spl 1966; Fifth St Baptist Ch Louisville, asst to pastor 1966-69; First Bapt Church, pastor 1969-. **ORGANIZATIONS:** Instr Sch of Religion N AL Bapt Acad-Courtland AL 1970-73; conv mem bd trustees Selma Univ 1973-; lecturer & Sect N AL Bapt Ministers Conf 1976-79; vice moderator Muscle Shoals Bapt Dist Assn of AL 1983-85; pres Muscle Shoals Bapt SS and BTU Congress 1981-; lecturer AL Bapt State Conv Ministers Seminar 1980-; exec mem bd dir Muscle Shoals Area Mental Health 1971-; vice chmn bd dir Muscle Shoals Area Mental Health Cen 1983-85; exec mem bd dir Colbert Lauderdale Comm Action Agency 1973-79; 1st Black mem bd dirs Shoals Hosp 1980-82; mem NAACP, Kappa Alpha Psi, AL Bapt State Conv, NBC Inc; chmn bd of dirs Muscle Shoals Area Mental Health Ctr 1985-87; advisory council Shoals Community College 1987-; asst sec, Natl Baptist Convention USA INC, 1988-. **HONORS/ACHIEVEMENTS:** Minister of the Yr NAACP Muscle Shoals AL 1976; Minister of the Yr Alpha Pi Chap Omega Psi Phi 1979; Spl Cert of Recog Tri County Branch of NAACP 1979; Citizen of the Yr Alpha Pi Chap Omega Psi Phi 1983. **MILITARY SERVICE:** AUS 1st lt 1960-64; Commendation Medal. **HOME ADDRESS:** 506 E 7th St, PO BOX 544, Tuscumbia, AL 35674. **BUSINESS ADDRESS:** First Baptist Church, 611 S High St, Tuscumbia, AL 35674.

SMITH, OTIS M.
Attorney. **PERSONAL:** Born Feb 20, 1922, Memphis, TN; son of Sam Smith and Eva Smith; married Mavis C Livingston; children: Vincent, Raymond, Anthony, Steven. **EDUCATION:** Fisk Univ, attended 1941-42; Syracuse Univ, attended 1946-47; Catholic Univ Amer, JD 1950; Western MI Univ, LLD 1973; Morgan State Coll, Hon LLD 1978; Syracuse Univ, Hon LLD 1978; Southwestern at Memphis, Hon LLD 1978; Univ Detroit, Hon LLD 1980; Univ of MI, Hon LLD 1983. **CAREER:** Mallory & Smith, 1950-57; Genesee Co, asst pros atty 1954, pub admin 1955-57; Flint Elec Bd, mem 1956-57; MI Pub Serv Comm, chmn 1957-59; MI, auditor gen 1959-61; Supreme Ct MI, justice 1961-66; General Motors Corp, legal sta 1967-83, asst gen counsel 1973-74, vice pres assoc genl counsel 1974-77,vice pres genl counsel 1977-83 (retired); Lewis White & Clay Law Firm, of counsel. **ORGANIZATIONS:** Mem Amer Judicature Soc 1968-76; trustee Oakland Univ 1971-; house of dels Amer Bar Assn 1972-76; vice pres United Found Detroit 1973-; mem Flint ARC,Red Feather Fund, YMCA, MI Children's Aid Soc, Flint Urban League, Cath Charities, MI Natl Urban League 1973; mem bd commrs State Bar of MI; bd dir/sec Natl Urban League 1973-, chmn bd 1972-74; trustee Fisk Univ 1973-79; trustee Henry Ford Hosp 1978-; trustee Catholic Univ Amer 1979-; bd of dir Kroger 1983-; bd of dir Detroit Edison 1984; mem DC/MI Bar; exec com MI United fund; bd dir MI Partners Alliance. **HONORS/ACHIEVEMENTS:** Disting Serv Awd Flint C of C 1956; Natl Alumni Awd for Govt Catholic Univ Amer 1961; Silver Beaver Awd Boy Scouts of Amer 1966; Fellow Amer Bar Found; Man of Yr Awd Omega Psi Phi 1962. **MILITARY SERVICE:** AUS 1942-46. **BUSINESS ADDRESS:** Retired Vice Pres General Counsel, General Motors, 1300 First Natl Bldg, Detroit, MI 48226.

SMITH, OTRIE (O. B. HICKERSON)
Psychiatrist. **PERSONAL:** Born Mar 17, 1936, Coffeyville, KS; married Robert A Sr; children: Claude, Donna, Robert Jr. **EDUCATION:** Howard U, BS 1958; HowardUniv Coll of Med, MD 1962; Kings Co Hosp, intnsp 1962-63; Menatl Hlth Inst, res 1963-66. **CAREER:** Jackson-hinds Comprehensive Hlth Ctr, dir mental 1970-; Am & Psychiat Assn, obsvr consult 1974-75;Univ Med Ctr, instr 1969-; Tougaloo Coll, 1969-72; VACtr, staff mem 1969-70; Area B Comm Hlth Ctr, chf 1967-69; Menninger Found, staff mem 1966-67. **ORGANIZATIONS:** Mem Minority Mental Hlth Ctr of the NIMH; Nat Med Assn; AMA; Am Psychiat Assn; Com of Black Psychiat; MS Med Assn; MS State Dept of Mental Hlth; Delta Sigma Theta Sor Consult Tougaloo Coll; friends of childredn of MS Head Start Proj; bd mem Hinds Co Proj Head Start; fld instr Jackson State U;Tougaloo Coll. **BUSINESS ADDRESS:** 1134 Winter St, Jackson, MS 39203.

SMITH, OZZIE
Professional athlete. **PERSONAL:** Born Dec 26, 1954, Mobile, AL; married Denise Jackson; children: Osborne Earl Jr, Dustin Cameron. **EDUCATION:** CA State Poly (San Luis Obispo), Graduate. **CAREER:** San Diego Padres, shortstop 1978; St Louis Cardinals, shortstop 1982-. **ORGANIZATIONS:** Worker for charity causes including Red Cross, Multiple Sclerosis, March of Dimes and Annie Malone Childrens Home; pres Cncl on Drug Abuse; natl spokesman for CPR. **HONORS/ACHIEVEMENTS:** Recognized as Natl Leagues Premier Shortstop on AP UPI; 6 Golden Glove Awds; elected Natl League All Star Teams 1981-82-83-84-85-86, named MVP 1984 series; voted to United Press Intl & Sporting News NL Post Season All Star Team in 1982; St Louis Baseball Man of Yr 1982; MVP; nominated NAACP Image Awd for Sportsmanship, Humanitariansim & Comm Activities 1983; "Operation Grandslam" introduced in St Louis, also San Diego Natl Campaign to Teach Children Living in Juvenile Halls Proper Baseball Skills & Techniques; Joined Group of Cardinal Reps in 1982-83 on Anheuser-Busch Promotional Tour of Japan; named 1986 Father of the Year by Natl Father's Day Comm; 1 of 24 major league All-Stars chosen to play 7 game series in Japan 1986; led NL shortstops for third straight year in fielding pct 1986; was rated League's Best Defensive Infielder and Smartest Player in League by NL managers; mem All Star Team 1981-86. **BUSINESS ADDRESS:** St Louis Cardinals, 250 Stadium, St Louis, MO 63102.

SMITH, PATRICIA G.
Telecommunications manager. **PERSONAL:** Born Nov 10, 1947, Tuskegee, AL; daughter of Douglas Jones Sr and Wilhelmina R (Griffin) Jones; married J Clay Smith Jr, Jun 25, 1983; children: Stager C, Michelle L, Michael L, Eugene Grace. **EDUCATION:** Wesleyan Coll, acad exchange prog 1964; Univ of MI, acad exchange prog 1965; Tuskegee Inst, BA English 1968 (upper 10th of class); Auburn Univ, compl grad courses masters prog English 1969-71; Harvard Univ Grad Sch of Bus Admin, Broadcast Mgmt Dev Course 1976; George Washington Univ, Telecomm Policy Course 1984. **CAREER:** Tuskegee Inst, instr dept of English 1969-71; Curber Assoc, program mgr 1971-73; Natl Assn of Broadcasters, dir of placement 1973-74, dir of community affairs 1974-77; Group W Westinghouse Broadcasting Co WJZ Television, assoc producer 1977, producer 1977-78; Sheridan Broadcasting Network, dir of affiliate relations and programming 1978-80; FCC Office of Public Affairs, chief consumer assist & small business div 1980-. **ORGANIZATIONS:** Trustee Natl Urban League 1976-81; vice chairperson Natl Conf of Black Lawyers Task Force on Communications 1975-; mem Communications Comm Cancer Coord Council 1977-84; mem Braintrust Subcommittee on Children's Prog Congress Black Caucus 1976-; mem Lambda Iota Tau Intl Hon Soc; mem Adv Bd Black Arts Celebration 1978-83; mem Journalism & Communications Adv Council Auburn Univ 1976-78; mem Amer Women in Radio and TV 1973-77; interim chairperson Intl Broadcasing Comm Natl Assn of Television and Radio Artists 1974; mem Natl Adv Comm Women in Communications Inc; mem Cert Prog in Communications Mgmt and Tech 1974-76; bd dirs The Broadcasters Club; mem AL State Soc 1984-; mem Washington Urban League 1983-; mem NAACP 1983-; mem DC Donor Project Natl Kidney Found of Natl Capital Area 1984-; mem Coalition of One Hundred Black Women of DC Inc 1985-. **HONORS/ACHIEVEMENTS:** Named Outstanding Young Woman of the Year 1975 & 1978; Sustained Superior Performance Awd 1981-88; commnr 1986-88, chair 1987-, District of Columbia Commn on Human Rights. **HOME ADDRESS:** 4010 16th St, NW, Washington, DC 20011. **BUSINESS ADDRESS:** Chief, Consumer Assistance and Small Business, Office of Public Affairs, Federal Communications Commission, 1919 M St NW Room 254, Washington, DC 20554.

SMITH, PAUL
Clergyman. **PERSONAL:** Born Sep 20, 1935, South Bend, IN; married Frances Irene Pitts; children: Kathleen, Heather, Krista. **EDUCATION:** Talladega Clge, AB 1957; Hartford Sem, MDiv 1960; Eden Theological Sem, DMin 1977. **CAREER:** WA Univ, assc vice chancellor 1974-78; Monehouse Coll, vice pres 1978-79; Columbia Theological Sem, adjunct prof 1979-; Candler School of Theology, adjunct prof 1979-; Hillside Presb Church, pastor. **ORGANIZATIONS:** Trustee Presby Schl of Christian Educ 1981-; consult Howard Thurman Educ Trust 1982; bd mem Child Srv Family Cnslng 1983-; Metro Fair Housing Srv Inc 1981-; Ldrshp Atlanta 1981; mem Council Atlanta Presb; former mem State Adv Comm US Civil Rights Comm 1977-1983. **HONORS/ACHIEVEMENTS:** NEH Recepient 1982; publ Unity, Diversity, Inclusiveness 1985; book J Knox Press Theology in a Computerized World 1985-86. **BUSINESS ADDRESS:** Pastor, Hillside Presb Church, 1879 Columbia Dr, Decatur, GA 30032.

SMITH, PAUL BERNARD
Priest. **PERSONAL:** Born Sep 29, 1931, Baltimore, MD. **EDUCATION:** Loyola Coll, BS 1956; Univ of Scranton, MA 1969. **CAREER:** Ordained priest 1962; Catholic Univ of Amer; Notre Dame Seminary; Malcolm X Coll, Chicago IL, English instr; Holy Angels School, Chicago, principal 1970-; Menard Central High School Alexandria, 1968-70; Holy Ghost Church & School & Marksville, asst curate & teacher 1962-67; Dept of Health & Welfare, 1955-56. **BUSINESS ADDRESS:** 545 E Oakwood Blvd, Chicago, IL 60653.

SMITH, PAUL M.
Educator. **PERSONAL:** Born Aug 10, 1920, Raleigh, NC; married Eleanor J Lewis; children: Cheryl O Christophe, Paul Byron. **EDUCATION:** St Augustine's Coll, BA 1941; NC Central Univ, BLS 1947; Univ IL, MS 1949; Indiana Univ, EdD 1957. **CAREER:** Albany State Coll, prof 1958-59; SC State Coll, prof 1959-60; NC Central Univ, prof 1960-69; Columbia Univ, adj prof 1969-70; Univ Cincinnati, prof Afro-Amer Studies/prof psychology. **ORGANIZATIONS:** Dir rsch Harlem Rehab Center 1969-70; dir NDEA Counseling Inst NC 1961; consult Workshop in Disadvantaged IN 1971; chf librarian A&T State Univ 1957-58; mem Assn of Black Psychologists 1980-85; ed bd mem Personnel & Guidance Journal 1969-72; trustee bd mem HUME Child Dev Cntr 1951-52. **HONORS/ACHIEVEMENTS:** Licensed Psychologist OH 1973-; publns in many nationally known journals. **MILITARY SERVICE:** USMC Pfc 1943-46. **BUSINESS ADDRESS:** Prof Afro-Amer Studies/Psych, University of Cincinnati, 22 McMicken Hall, Cincinnati, OH 45221.

SMITH, PEARLENA W.
Retired educator. **PERSONAL:** Born Apr 13, 1916, Greenwood, SC; daughter of David Williams and Margie Frances Owens; married Dr William N Smith, Jul 04, 1957 (deceased). **EDUCATION:** SC State Coll Orangeburg, BS & MS 1950-54; NYU, attended 1962-63. **CAREER:** Hudson Valley Community Coll, retired prof 1979-; Hudson Valley Community Coll, prof liberal arts 1970-78; Colonie Pub Sch NY, reading supr 1968-70; Teaneck Pub Sch NJ, reading supr 1964-68; Jersey City State Coll, asst prof 1962-64; NC Coll Durham, asst prof of educ 1959-62; Voorhees Jr Coll Denmark SC, asst prof of reading & dng 1957-59; FL Normal Coll St Augustine, dean of women & asst prof 1956-57; Columbia Pub Sch Sys SC, elementary tchr 1950-56. **ORGANIZATIONS:** Chmn Jr Red Cross Carver Elem Sch SCH SC 1950-56; mem of Pres Adv Com Hudson Valley Community Coll NY 1972-78. **HONORS/ACHIEVEMENTS:** Publ article on reading Jersey City State Coll 1963. **HOME ADDRESS:** 417 Magnolia Ave, Greenwood, SC 29646.

SMITH, PERRY ANDERSON, III
Pastor. **PERSONAL:** Born May 16, 1934, Mound Bayou, MS; son of Perry and Elease; married Elliece Saundle; children: I Russell. **EDUCATION:** Howard Univ, AB 1955, MDiv 1958. **CAREER:** Comm Action of PG County MD, exec dir 1965-69; Natl Civil Srv League, assc dir 1969-72; Univ of MD, chaplain 1975-82; First Bapt Church Inc, pastor1958-. **ORGANIZATIONS:** Treas Prog Natl Baptist Conv 1974-76, auditor 1978-80; bd dir NAACP Pricne George's Co MD, Min to Blacks in Higher Educ; vice pres Natl Conf of Black Churchmen. **HONORS/ACHIEVEMENTS:** Blk Ldrshp Phi Beta Sigma Frat Univ MD 1978; Metro Srv Iota Upsilon Lambda Alpha Phi Alpha 1979; Comm Srv Frontiers Intl Prince Georges Co; OutstndngSrv DC Women Ministers Assc 1975. **HOME ADDRESS:** 10312 Buena Vista Ave, Lanham-Seabrook, MD 20706. **BUSINESS ADDRESS:** Pastor, First Bapt Church Inc, 4009 Wallace Rd, North Brentwood, MD 20722.

SMITH, PHILIP GENE
Human rights specialist. **PERSONAL:** Born Mar 03, 1928, Chicago, IL; son of S David Smith and Ruth Smith McGowan; married Elaine J Kehrer; children: Philip G Jr, Kelyn M. **EDUCATION:** KY State Coll, BA 1949; Chicago Teachers Coll, BE 1953; Antioch School of Law, MA 1982. **CAREER:** Danville IL Human Relations Comm, dir 1976-77; Detroit Human Rights Dept, commn administrative coord 1977-86; Voters Organized to Educate, dir 1986-; Highland Park Community Coll, Highland Park MI, instructor political science 1987-. **ORGANIZATIONS:** Political editor Dollars & Sense Magazine 1976-; precinct delegate MI Democratic Convention 1980-88; mem Kappa Alpha Psi, MI Assoc Human Rights Workers; pres Ethnic Educ Rsch Corp. **HONORS/ACHIEVEMENTS:** Fred Hampton Scholarship Fund Image Awd 1986; 1st annual Frederick Douglass Award, Hope and Magnolia United Methodist Churches, Southfield MI, 1988; published article "One Step Forward/Two Steps Backwards-An Analysis of Progressive Politics", Independent Press, Detroit MI 1989. **MILITARY SERVICE:** AUS pvt E-II 1 yr. **HOME ADDRESS:** 19480 Stratford Road, Detroit, MI 48221.

SMITH, PHILIP MEEK
Business executive. **PERSONAL:** Born May 18, 1932, Springfield, OH. **EDUCATION:** OH State Univ, BS 1954, MA 1955. **CAREER:** US Natl Com for Intl Geophys Yr Natl Acad Sci, mem staff 1957-58; NSF, prog dir 1958-63, dir ops US Antarctice Rsch prog 1964-69, dep head divpolar prog 1969-73; Office Mgmt & Budget Exec Office of Pres, chief gen sci br 1973-74; NSF, exec asst to dir 1974-75, sci adv to pres 1974-76; Office Sci & Tech Policy Exec Office of Pres, assoc dir 1976-81; Natl Sci Bd, spec asst to chmn 1981; NRC Natl Acad Sci Washington, exec officer 1981-. **ORGANIZATIONS:** Corp mem Woods Hole Oceanographic Inst 1983-; pres Cave Rsch Found Yellow Springs OH 1957-63; chmn tech panels Fed Coord Council Sci & Engrg & Tech1976-80; bd dirs WA Project for the Arts 1983-, WA Sculptors Group 1983-; mem AAAS, Amer Mgmt Assoc, Antarctican Soc, Western River Guides Assoc Clubs,Cosmos Washington, Amer Alpine NYC. **HONORS/ACHIEVEMENTS:** Author "Defrosting Antarctice Secrets," 1962; "The Frozen Future, a Prophetic Report from Anartica," 1973; contrib numerous articles in professional journals. **MILITARY SERVICE:** AUS 1st lt Transp Corps 1955-57; Commendation Medal, Antarctice Serv Medal USN 1967; Meritorious Serv Medal NSF 1972. **BUSINESS ADDRESS:** Executive Officer, NRC Natl Academy of Science, 1012 Tenth St NW, 3rd Floor, Washington, DC 20001.

SMITH, PHILLIP M.
Humanist, educator. **PERSONAL:** Born Jan 24, 1937, Vulcan, WV; married Gloria J; children: Phillip Jr, Jeffrey M. **EDUCATION:** WV State Coll, BS 1958; CityUniv of NY, MA 1969; Educ Adminstrn, diploma edna; Hofstra U, permanent certification 1970. **CAREER:** Dept Welfare, Childrens counselor 1958-59; Dept Parks, recreation leader 1959-60; Dept Hosp, recreation & Dir 1960-; Wilkyck School for Boys, childcare specialist, supervisor 1962-66; Neighborhood Youth Corps, curriculum specialist 1965-66; Roos Jr & Sr HS, science teacher 1966-69; asst prin 1969-. **ORGANIZATIONS:** Dir Adult Ed 1969-70; dir Reading Prog 1969-70; principal Summer Reading & Math Prog 1969-70; dir Multi-level Alternative Prog 1973-; Nat Assn Sec Sch Adminstrn NY; Nat All of Black Sch Educators; Sch Adminstrv Assn; bd of dirs 21 Century Capital Corp 1969-70; coord of tennis work shops. **HONORS/ACHIEVEMENTS:** Cover photo for feature article "Black tennis" Tennis Mag Dec 1974; Who's Who Am Coll & U; 15 yrs serv awd Health & Hosp corp. **BUSINESS ADDRESS:** Principal, Roosevelt Jr Sr High School, 1 Wagner Ave, Roosevelt, NY 11575.

SMITH, QUENTIN P.
Educator. **PERSONAL:** Born Jul 30, 1918, Huntsville, TX; son of Paige and Ione; divorced. **EDUCATION:** Chicago U, MA 1947; IN U, MS 1956. **CAREER:** Gary Comm Sch Corp, exec dir of sec ed; W Side HS Gary, educator; guid cnsl, educator 1957-. **ORGANIZATIONS:** Past pres Urb Leag of IN 1967; comm of Pks Gary 1964; pres Gary Hum Rel Comm 1966; pres Gary City Cncl 1969; vice pres Am Fed of Tchrs 1957; Lk Co Bd Pub Wlfr 1973; IN Cncl of Ed 1974; Gary Redev Comm 1970-72; lctr in urb studies INUniv NW 1974; St Josephs Calumet Coll 1973; bd trust Calumet Coll 1968-; adv bd Bk of IN 1970-. **HONORS/ACHIEVEMENTS:** Recip Gary Jaycees Good Govt Awd 1971; NEA Tchr in Politics 1970. **MILITARY SERVICE:** USAF 1st lt 1942-45. **BUSINESS ADDRESS:** Exec Dir Secondary Education, Gary Community School Corp, 620 E 10th Place, Gary, IN 46402.

SMITH, QUENTIN PAIGE, JR.
Business executive. **PERSONAL:** Born Jun 18, 1951, Gary, IN; son of Questin P. Smith, Sr and Juanita Smith. **EDUCATION:** Purdue Univ, BS 1972; Pepperdine Univ, MBA 1976. **CAREER:** Hughes Aircraft Co, consult mgr 1975-77; MCA Universal, consult mgr 1977-79; Great Western Savings, data processing mgr 1979-80; Gottfried Consultants Inc, dir 1980-83; The Denver Group Inc, CEO and pres 1983-; Data Line Service Company, director and co-owner. **ORGANIZATIONS:** Bd mem LA Urban League 1982-; bd mem US Genl Serv Admin 1983-86; dir Armstrong Data Serv Inc 1984-; Center fro Educational Achievement, dir 1986. **HONORS/ACHIEVEMENTS:** Cert of Accomplishment Dunn & Bradstreet Financial Analysis 1974; Cert of Appreciation Youth Motivation Task Force 1980; Outstanding Young Man of America US Jaycees 1980. **BUSINESS ADDRESS:** President/Chief Executive Ofcr, The Denver Group Inc, 6222 Wilshire Blvd, Los Angeles, CA 90049.

SMITH, QUENTIN T.
University educator. **PERSONAL:** Born May 01, 1937, Seaford, DE; son of Carlton Smith and Elizabeth Smith; married Marjorie M Smith MD; children: Candace, Jason, Michael. **EDUCATION:** Fisk Univ, AB 1958-61; Howard Univ, MD 1963-1967. **CAREER:** WMHC Fulton Cty, dir 1974-75; Mental Health Grady Hosp, dir Outpatient Child and Adolescent 1977-82; Ridgeview Inst, assc dir adolescent srvs; Emory, assc prof, prof psychiatry Morehouse Medical School. **ORGANIZATIONS:** Fellow Amer Psychiatric Assoc 1971-, Amer Acad Child Psychiatry 1974-; secr treas Psychiatry Section Natl Med Assc 1984-85; mem Educ Comm GA Psychiatric Assc 1984-85; quality assurance comm Amer Psychiatric Assoc; peer reviewer for Amer Psychiatric Assoc; mem Child Psychiatry & Psychiatric Residency Comm Emory Univ Dept of Child Psychiatry; peer review subcommittee Ridgeview Inst; vice pres Ridgeview Medical Staff; consult Dept of Psychiatry Meharry Med Coll; student acad affairs & promotions comm Morehouse Med School; corresponding faculty Amer Ortho Psychiatric Assoc. **HONORS/ACHIEVEMENTS:** Phi Beta Kappa Fisk Univ Nashville TN 1961, Beta Kappa Chi 1961; Woodrow Wilson Fellowship Univ of Chicago IL 1961-62; Natl Med Fellowship Howard Univ Washington DC 1963-67; Man of the Year Awd Fisk Univ 1961. **BUSINESS ADDRESS:** Assoc Dir Child & Adolescent Services, Ridgeview Institute, 3995 S Cobb Dr, Ste 1008, Smyrna, GA 30080.

SMITH, REGGIE **See SMITH, CARL REGINALD**

SMITH, REGINALD B.
Business executive. **PERSONAL:** Born Feb 08, 1938, Austin; married Margaret A Jolly; children: Reginald II, Stephen, Eric. **EDUCATION:** Southeastern Univ, BA 1964-65; Temple Univ 1959. **CAREER:** Fast Food Services Ltd Kingston, chmn dir & shareholder 1971-; Besmar Co Inc, pres; Franchise Assn Diversified, general partner 1971-; All Pro & Enterprises Inc, dir & corp vice pres 1969-71; Brady Keys Kentucky Fried Chicken Inc, vice pres of operations 1970-71; Univ of Texas at Austin, purchashing & acct officer 1965-69; US Govt, acct & fin 1962-65. **ORGANIZATIONS:** Mem Detroit C of C; Natl Restaurant Assn; Michigan Restaurant Assn; exec Food Serv Assn; Booker T Washington Business Assn; Natl Business League; mem Big Brothers Inc; Kingston Jamaica Jaycees. **HONORS/ACHIEVEMENTS:** Business award Detroit C of C 1974; minority achievement Detroit Free Press 1973; minority business achievement Detroit News 1973. **MILITARY SERVICE:** AUS 1959-61.

SMITH, REGINALD D.
Educator. **PERSONAL:** Born Feb 21, 1918, Baltimore; married Euzelle Patterson; children: Andrea, Pamela, Patrice, Regi. **EDUCATION:** Hampton Inst, BS 1940; A&T Coll Greensboro NC StateUniv Raleigh, grad work. **CAREER:** Hampton Inst, staff 1940-42; Chapel Hill City Schools, teacher asst prin 1942-. **ORGANIZATIONS:** Mem NCAE; NEA; NASSP; NC League & Municipalities; Triangle J Council Govts 1970-74; Civitan Chapel Hill; Chapel Hill Planning Bd 1959-65; bdalderman 1965-74. **HONORS/ACHIEVEMENTS:** NC Hmaptonian of Yr 1969; Chapel Hill Father of Yr 1970; masonic distinguished serv award 1971; mayor pro-tem Chapel Hill 1969-74. **MILITARY SERVICE:** CAC sgt 1944-46. **BUSINESS ADDRESS:** Chapel Hill Sr HS, Chapel Hill, NC.

SMITH, RICHARD ALFRED
International health specialist. **PERSONAL:** Born Oct 13, 1932, Norwalk, CT; son of Julius Smith and Mabel Smith; married Lorna Carrier; children: Dirk Devi, Rik Balakrishna, Erik Dibnarine, Blake Andrew, Quinten Everett. **EDUCATION:** Howard Univ, BSc 1953, MD 1957; Columbia Univ, MPH 1960. **CAREER:** US Public Health Service, medical dir 24 yrs; Peace Corps Nigeria 1961-63; Washington DC, deputy medical dir 1963-65; Dept of Health & Human Serv Office of Intl Health, chief office of planning 1965-67; MEDEX Prog Univ of Washington, prof & dir 1968-72; The MEDEX Group, School of Medicine, Univ of Hawaii, dir 1972-. **ORGANIZATIONS:** Fellow Amer Coll of Preventive Medicine 1961-; mem Amer Public Health Assn 1963-; mem Inst of Medicine of the Natl Acad of Science 1972-; consultant World Health Orgn 1972-. **HONORS/ACHIEVEMENTS:** William A Jump Awd Dept of Health, Educ & Welfare; Gerard B Lambert Awd Lambert Foundation 1971; Rockefeller Public Service Awd Princeton Univ 1981. **BUSINESS ADDRESS:** Dir, The MEDEX Group, School of Medicine, University of Hawaii, 1833 Kalakaua Ave #700, Honolulu, HI 96815.

SMITH, ROBBIE
Business executive. **PERSONAL:** Born Jun 03, 1948, Monroe, LA; daughter of Evelyn Lovelady and Robert Lovelady. **EDUCATION:** Roosevelt Univ, BS Eng Journalism 1977, MS Marketing Communications. **CAREER:** Standard Oil Co Indiana, sec 1969-72, exec sec 1973-75; Enterprising Anchors-Public Relations Co, owner 1983-84; Standard Oil Co Indiana, coord of urban affairs 1977-86; pres and owner The Right Image, Inc 1986; co-founder, partner Ren Productions, 1989-. **ORGANIZATIONS:** Business adv bd Westside Cluster School 1977-84; mem League of Black Women 1977-84, Natl Assn of Media Women 1978-84; chmn business adv bd Career Guidance Ctr Chicago City Wide Coll 1979-84; treas Old Town Boys Club 1979-80; 1st vice pres Cosmopolitan C of C 1980; pres League of Black Women, Cosmopolitan C of C; vice pres Black Public Relations Soc Chicago Chap 1983-84; deacon Chicago United 1983-84; publ relations chairperson Chicago Blacks in Philanthropy 1983-84; pres Black Public Relations Soc Chicago Chapt; steering comm Inst for Athletics and Education; bd of dir Better Boys Found; mem Chicago Regional Purchasing Council. **HONORS/ACHIEVEMENTS:** Black Achiever of Indiana Awd YMCA of Metro Chicago 1977; Outstanding Serv Awd Natl Tech Assn, 1978; Kizzy Awd Womanfest Inc 1980; Serv Awd Black Contractors United; Media Woman of the Year Awd, Natl Assn of Media Women; "Up and Coming Black Business and Professional Women" Dollars & Sense Magazine 1985; outstanding achievement awd Chicago City-Wide Coll 1986; "We Care" Role Model, Chicago Police Department, 1988, 1989; Exemplary Service Black Public Relations Society, 1989; published booklet, Stepping Off On The Right Foot, 1988. **BUSINESS ADDRESS:** President, The Right Image, Inc, 30 W Washington, Ste 503, Chicago, IL 60602.

SMITH, ROBERT
Association executive, physician. **PERSONAL:** Born Dec 20, 1937, Terry, MS; married Otrie Hickerson Smith MD; children: 4 children. **EDUCATION:** Tougaloo Coll, BA; Howard Univ, MD; Cook County Hosp Chicago, rotating internship; Postgrad Courses, Univ of TN, Harvard Univ, Univ of MS. **CAREER:** Tufts Univ Coll of Medicine, instructor dept of preventive med 1967-69; Meharry Coll, preceptor dept of comm & family med, area dir; asst prof part-time Univ of MS Sch of Family Med; Univ of IA, preceptor Coll of Med & Continuing Educ; mem on staff Hinds Gen Hosp, MS Baptist Hosp, St Dominic-Jackson Mem Hosp; Brown Univ, guest lecturer, preceptor for school of medicine; MS Family Health Ctr, dir. **ORGANIZATIONS:** Charter bd Jackson Urban League; founder MS Com for Human Rights; mem Amer Cancer Soc MS Div, MS Med & Surgical Assn, Amer Med Assn, natl Med

Assn, MS Med & Surgical Assn, MS Med Assn; charter diplomate Amer Bd of Family Practice; very active as consult & participant in health programs with govt & various assns & groups; exec comm & delegate to MS State Med Assoc from Central Medical Soc local component of AMA; bd of dirs, membership chmn Arts Alliance of Jackson/Hinds County; former commnr MS Health Care Commn apptd in 1984 by Atty General Ed Pittman; bd of trustees Leadership Jackson Prog JacksonChamber of Commerce 1987; phys adv comm on Child Health with MS State Dept of Health Jackson MS 1987. **HONORS/ACHIEVEMENTS:** Cited by Time Mag & various other natl publs; 1st Solomon Carter Fuller Awd Black Psychiatrists of Amer; Disting Serv Awd of Med Com for Human Rights1965; Alumnus of Yr Awd Tougaloo Coll 1966; Physician Recognition Awd Amer Med Assn 1971; charter fellow Amer Acad of Family Physicians 1972; Physicianof the Yr 1974 MS Med & Surgical Assn; Honorary LHD Tougaloo Coll 1974; Disting Serv Awd MS Med & Surg Assoc 1977; Man of the Year Natl Cncl of Church of Christ Holiness 1981; Outstanding Serv rendered to the Comm Awd Natl Cncl of Negro Women 1981; Outstanding Serv Awd for Medicine Jackson Links Inc 1983; Expressions of Excellence Awd MS Cultural Arts Coalition 1984; Medgar Evers Awd MS NAACP Chap Freedom Awds Banquet 1984; Disting Serv Awd for Outstanding Contributions in Serv and Delivery of Health Care Natl Assoc of Med Minority Educators Southern Region 1985; Health Serv Awd Jackson Copncerned Officers for Progress Jackson MS 1986; Appreciation Awd Natl Caucus of Black Aged 1987; Role Model of the Year in the field of Medicine Citizens HS Student Develop Fund Inc 1987. **BUSINESS ADDRESS:** Dir, MS Family Health Ctr Ltd, 1134 Winter St, Jackson, MS 39204.

SMITH, ROBERT EDWARD
Flight officer. **PERSONAL:** Born Mar 07, 1943, Louisville; married Constance Evans; children: Dana M, Robert E, Jr. **EDUCATION:** Univ Louisville, BA 1966. **CAREER:** Eastern Airlines, dir & chief pilot 1972-; Phillip Morris, supvr 1966-72. **MILITARY SERVICE:** USAF capt 1966-71. **BUSINESS ADDRESS:** Atlanta Harsfield Intl Air, Atlanta, GA.

SMITH, ROBERT H.
University president. **CAREER:** Southern University at Shreveport, Shreveport, LA, president. **BUSINESS ADDRESS:** Southern University at Shreveport, Shreveport, LA 71107. *

SMITH, ROBERT J.
Physician. **PERSONAL:** Born Nov 21, 1929, Hayti, MO; married Dorothy; children: Anne, Robert Jr, Marie, Lisa, Elaina, Martin, Virginia. **EDUCATION:** So IL U, 1948-51;Univ MO Med Sch, 1951-53; Meharry Med Coll, 1953-55. **CAREER:** VA Hosp Little Rock, surgery cons;Univ AR Med Ctr, clinical asst prof; Meharry Med Coll, instr surgery 1966-; York VA Hosp, chief of surgery. **ORGANIZATIONS:** Pres Interested Citz for Voter Registration; mem Alpha Omega Alpha; 20th Century Club; life mem NAACP; Vchmn surgery sect Nat Med Asn. **MILITARY SERVICE:** AUS capt 1956-58. **BUSINESS ADDRESS:** Chief of Surgery, York VA Hospital, Murfreesboro, TN.

SMITH, ROBERT JOHNSON
Clergyman, educator. **PERSONAL:** Born Sep 26, 1920, Chicago, IL; married Jennie Mae; children: Estelle, Everett, Renee, Robert II. **EDUCATION:** Morehouse Coll, AB 1937; Theol Sch, BD, STM, DMin; Bryn Mawr Coll, MSW; Morehouse Coll & VA Coll, honarary DD. **CAREER:** Salem Baptist Church, minister 1956-; Philadelphia School Dist, counselor 1960-; Hill St Church & 1954-56; High St Church, minister 1946-54; VA Hosp, chaplain 1945-54; AUS, chaplain 1941-45. **ORGANIZATIONS:** Chmn bd of trustees Berean Inst; bd mem Abington Meml Hosp VA Coll; mem Rotary Internat; Omega Psi Phi; Acad of Certified Soc Workers. **MILITARY SERVICE:** AUS maj 1941-46. **BUSINESS ADDRESS:** Salem Baptist Church, 610 Summit Ave, Jenkintown, PA 19046.

SMITH, ROBERT L. T., SR.
Clergyman, writer, poet. **PERSONAL:** Born Dec 19, 1902, Hinds County, MS; married Annie Louise Mason (deceased); children: Ann, Louise, Roberta, Robert, Edward, Tresa, Charles, Gloria, Lawrence, Royce, Jerelyn. **EDUCATION:** Jackson Coll, Tougaloo Coll, Hon Doctorate of Humane Letters 1980. **CAREER:** Oak Grove Baptist Church, pastor. **ORGANIZATIONS:** Civil rights leader; mem United Negro Coll Fund, MS Free Press Assn, NAACP, The Urban League Bd of Dirs of Dirs Mississippi Action for Progress which administers head start progrms; started Head Start Programs in MS & elsewhere in US; started Job Corps Program in MS. **HONORS/ACHIEVEMENTS:** Man of the Year, Kappa Alpha Psi, Omega Psi Phi, Phi Beta Sigma; listed in Newsweek's 100 Most Influential Blacks in the US; chmn Civil Rights Movement State of MS; First Black to run for US Congress in MS since reconstruction by encouraging blacks to vote and political particiaption; Resolution Commending Outstanding Civic Leadership from MS State Legislature March 1985; Univ of MS, Award of distinction 1987; Omicron Delta Kappa, 1987; Struggle for Freedom for All, 1989. **BUSINESS ADDRESS:** Pastor, Oak Grove Baptist Church, 1253 Valley St, Ste 6, Jackson, MS 39203.

SMITH, ROBERT LONDON
Educator, administrator, scientist. **PERSONAL:** Born Oct 13, 1919, Alexandria, LA; married Jewel Busch; children: Jewel Smith Feist, Robert London Jr, Karl Busch. **EDUCATION:** Yale Univ, diploma 1944; Air Univ, diploma 1952; Coll of St Joseph, BA 1954; Univ of OK, MA 1955; The Amer Univ Wash DC, PhD 1964. **CAREER:** Hdqrs Office Aerospace Rsch Wash, asst dep chief of staff material 1960-62; Office of Sci Rsch Wash, asst exec dir 1963-65; Natl Acad of Sci, dir AFOSR post doctoral rsch prog 1964; Univ AK, assoc prof & dept head 1965-67; Univ AK, dean coll of bus econ & govt 1968-70, prof & head dept of polit sci 1970-80; Governor's Cabinet State of AK, commr dept of health & social serv 1983-84; Univ of AK, prof of polit sci emeritus 1984. **ORGANIZATIONS:** Mem Natl Acad of Polit Sci 1957; mem Natl Inst for Social & Behavioral Sci 1961; fellow and scientist AAAS 1964; mem Natl Inst for US in World Affairs 1964; mem Amer Polit Sci Assn 1965-80; educ commr AK C of C 1967; mem Men of Achievement Cambridge England 1974; mem Rsch & Advance Study Council Univ of AK 1968-70; mem Acad Council Univ of AK 1968-70; committeeman-at-large Natl Council Boy Scouts of Amer 1970-72; mem AK Govt Employment Commn; pres Fairbanks USO Council; bd dirs Artic First Fed Svgs & Loan Assn; corporator Mt McKinely Mutual Savs Bank. **HONORS/ACHIEVEMENTS:** Natl Polit Sci Honor Frat Pi Sigma Alpha 1962; Silver Beaver Awd Boy Scouts of Amer 1970; Outstanding Educ Awd NAACP 1970; Outstanding Prof Univ of AK 1974-75; Outstanding Educator of Amer 1975. **MILITARY SERVICE:** USAF lt col 25 yrs; Commendation Medal Meritorious Serv 1956. **BUSINESS ADDRESS:** Prof Political Sci Emeritus, Univ of Alaska, Dept of Polit Science, Fairbanks, AK 99709.

SMITH, ROBERT P., JR.
Emeritus professor. **PERSONAL:** Born Oct 12, 1923, New Orleans, LA; son of Robert and Leola; married Arlette Marie Carlton; children: 1. **EDUCATION:** Howard Univ, BA 1948; Univ of Chicago, MA 1950; DEU Univ of Bordeaux, France 1953; Univ of PA, PhD 1969. **CAREER:** Talladega Coll, instructor French Spanish German 1953-54; Fisk Univ, asst prof French & Spanish 1954-58; Rutgers Univ, instructor, asst prof, assoc prof, chmn of French Dept 1965-73; assoc dean for academic affairs 1973-79; full prof 1984-89; emeritus 1987-. **ORGANIZATIONS:** Mem Alpha Phi Alpha, Amer Assn of Univ Profs, Amer Assn of Teachers of French, Mod Lang Assn, African Lit Assoc; published articles in French Review, College Lang Assn Journal, Langston Hughes Review, Le Petit Courier, Celacef Bulletin, World Literature Today, Celfan Review. **HONORS/ACHIEVEMENTS:** Fulbright Fellowship to France DEU CEF Universite de Bordeaux France 1952-53; John Hay Whitney Found Fellowship 1958-59; NEH Summer Grant 1981. **MILITARY SERVICE:** USAF sgt 1943-45.

SMITH, ROBERT T., III
Center director. **PERSONAL:** Born Aug 31, 1949, Ft Lewis, WA; children: 's Hosp. **EDUCATION:** Univ of Ghana in Legon &Univ of Sci & Tech Kumasi Ghana W Africa, cert 1970; Morehouse Coll, BA 1971;Univ of Chgo, MA 1973. **CAREER:** Martin Luther King Jr Nghbrhd Hlth Cntr, cntr dir 1974-; Provident Hosp & Training Sch Assn Chgo, asst dir of planning 1973-74; Mid-Southside Hlth Planning Orgn Chgo, proj ofcr & training coord 1972-73; LaRabida Children's Hosp Chgo, physical therapy asso 1972; US Dept of Labor Rent-a-kid Inc Atlanta,prog tech 1971; Morehouse Coll Atlanta, instr 1970-71; Office of Econ Oppor, asst adminstr 1969-70. **ORGANIZATIONS:** Mem Am Pub Hlth Assn; mem IL Pub Hlth Assn; mem Black Caucus of Hlth Wrkrs; mem Am Soc pf Plng Ofcls; bd mem Midwest Assn of Hlth Cntrs Inc; mem Am Med Student Assn Adv Com; mem Gov's StateUniv Hlth Servs Adminstrn Adv Counc; mem Am Hosp Assn Com on Hlth Care for the Disadvantaged 3 yrs; mem Nat Assn of Hlth Servs Execs; mem Chicago Chap Nat Assn of Black Social Wrkrs; consult Catalyst for Youth Inc Chgo; consult Lassiter & Co Chgo; consult Nat Found March of Dimes Chgo; memUniv of Chicago Alumni Assn; mem (SSA) Black Alumni Schlrshp Com; mem Chgo-Area Morehouse Coll AlumniClub; mem Nat Norehouse Coll Alumni Assn; mem Chicago Urban Leag; bd mem The Film Symposium; mem St Frances Xavier Cabrini Follow-Through Proj; mem Intl Hosp Fedn; dist chmn Chicago Area Counc BSA; chmnUniv of Chicago Comprehensive Sickle Cell Cntr Adv Counc; consult Citizs Com on Youth Cincinnati; consult Nat Alliance of Businessmen Columbus GA; consult The Film Symposium Chgo. **HONORS/ACHIEVEMENTS:** Pub & presented numerous papers on Hlth Servs; recip comm serv award in hlth Chicago Suburban Chap 1976; so christian ldrshp award 1976; comm ldr & noteworthy Am Bicentennial Meml Edition Am Biog Inst 1976-77; outstndg serv award Martin Luther King Jr Nghbrhd Hlth Cntr Sr Citizs Club 1976; blackachievers recog award YMCA 1977; outstndg young adminstrs award Nat Assn of Hlth Servs Execs 1978.

SMITH, ROBERT W.
Auto dealer executive. **CAREER:** Bob Smith Chevrolet, Inc, Louisville, KY, chief executive. **BUSINESS ADDRESS:** Bob Smith Chevrolet, Inc, 10500 Westport Road, Louisville, KY 40222. *

SMITH, ROBERT W., JR.
Mathematician. **PERSONAL:** Born Apr 02, 1918, Philadelphia, PA; son of Robert W Smith, Sr and Henrietta Smith; married Helen C Harris; children: Robert III, Joyce Y, Derrick W. **EDUCATION:** Temple Univ, AB 1941; Univ PA, MA 1948; Univ of Pittsburgh, post graduate work. **CAREER:** ADP Systems Br Pittsburgh Energy Tech Ctr, chief spec design & super; Authorization Systems Inc, regional dir 1981-; Carnegie Mellon Univ Pittsburgh PA Senior Lecturer Math 1954-71; Robert W Smith Enterprises, pres, 1981-. **ORGANIZATIONS:** Mem Amer Assn Computing Machinery, Amer Assn for Advancement of Sci, Amer Soc of Pub Admin; mem & former vestryman Holy Cross Epis Ch Pittsburgh; past pres Homewood-Brushton YMCA; mem exec bd & bd mgmt Pittsburgh Metro YMCA; past vice pres Pittsburgh Chap Amer Soc of Pub Admin; mem Kappa Alpha Psi. **HONORS/ACHIEVEMENTS:** Black Achievers Awd Pittsburgh YMCA 1973; Distinguished Serv Awd Pittsburgh YMCA 1972; Kappa Alpha Psi Pittsburgh Man of Yr 1966; Outstanding Achievement in Sci Pittsburgh Courier Newspaper 1962; Serv Awd from Pittsburgh Bd Public Educ 1965. **MILITARY SERVICE:** AUS 1941-46. **BUSINESS ADDRESS:** Regional Dir, Authorization Systems Inc, 6011 Penn Circle South, Pittsburgh, PA 15206.

SMITH, ROGER LEROY
Electrical engineer. **PERSONAL:** Born May 15, 1946, New York, NY; divorced; children: Kim M, Lisa R, Shawnee L. **EDUCATION:** Criminal Justice Nassau Comm Coll, AA 1975. **CAREER:** Federal Aviation Adminstrn/Flight Inspec, electronic technician 1976-; FAA, air traffic controller 1974-76; US customs, sec/patrol off skymarshal ; US Customs Bur, 1971-74. **HONORS/ACHIEVEMENTS:** Comm pilot only black airborne tcchnician FAA Flight Inspec Div; mem 1st All Black Flight Insp Crew; vietnam serv medal USN. **MILITARY SERVICE:** USN 2nd class petty ofcr 1966-69. **BUSINESS ADDRESS:** Fed Aviation Adminstrn, FIFO NAFEC Bldg 301 Rm 407, Atlantic City, NJ 08405.

SMITH, ROLAND BLAIR, JR.
Educational administrator. **PERSONAL:** Born Mar 21, 1946, Washington, DC; married Valerie V Peyton; children: Rovelle Louise, Roland Blair III. **EDUCATION:** Bowie St Coll, BA Soc Anthro 1969; Univ of Notre Dame, attended 1969-70; IN Univ Sch of Pub & Environ Affairs, MPA 1976; Univ Notre Dame, Sociology 1978-80; Harvard Univ, EdD candidate 1983-. **CAREER:** Bowie St Coll, faculty asst sociology-anthro dept 1968-69; US Senate, intern/rsch asst 1970; PSC S Bend IN, dir of youth employment 1970-71; MAPC SBend IN, manpower systems coord 1971-73; Univ of Notre Dame Proj Upward Bound, asst dir 1973-76 dir 1976-80; Center for Educ Oppor, dir 1980-83; Harvard Grad Sch of Educ, academic counselor 1984-. **ORGANIZATIONS:** Field reader DHEW US Office of Educ (Reg 5) 1977; bd dirs Mid-Am Assn for Educ Oppor Prog Personnel 1979-81; pres IN Assn for Educ Oppor Prog Personnel 1979-80; editorial bd Harvard Educ Review 1984-; exec bd Youth Serv Bur of St Joseph Co IN 1972-77; pres S Bend Branch NAACP 1975-76; IN AdvCom US Civil Rights Commn 1979-. **HONORS/ACHIEVEMENTS:** MD State Senatorial Schol Awd 1968; mem Lambda Alpha Natl Anthropology Honor Soc 1969; Who's Who

Among Students in Coll & Univs 1969; Disting Serv AwdUnited Negro Fund 1974; Outstanding Achievement Awd Kappa Alpha Psi S Bend Alumni Chap 1976; Pres Citation Bowie State Coll 1977.

SMITH, ROULETTE WILLIAM
Educator. **PERSONAL:** Born Jan 19, 1942, New York, NY; married Norma Abe; children: Nicole Michelle, Todd Roulette. **EDUCATION:** Morehouse, BS 1961; Stanford, MS 1964; MS 1965; PhD 1973; Univ CA San Francisco 1976-80. **CAREER:** Stanford U, research asst 1966-70; asst prof 1970-75; Univ CA Santa Barbara; BERD Univ CA, specialist assoc dir 1970-74; Inst for Postgrad Interdisciplinary Studies, dir 1984-. **ORGANIZATIONS:** Pres Humanized Tech & Inc 1973-; editorial Instructional Sci 1971-83; asso editor Health Policy & Educ 1979-83; sales mgr Stanford European Auto 1970-74; Consulting Rand Corp 1970-74; Value Engineering Co 1973-. **BUSINESS ADDRESS:** Dir, Inst for Postgrad Interdisc, PO Box 60846, Palo Alto, CA 94306.

SMITH, RUFUS BURNETT, JR.
Educator. **PERSONAL:** Born May 13, 1943, Dallas, TX; son of Rufus B Smith, Sr. **EDUCATION:** George Washington Univ, BA 1971. **CAREER:** District of Columbia Economic Devel, chief exam branch occupational and professional licensing div 1971-74; Educational Testing Serv Princeton NJ, sr prog dirhealth programs ctr for occupational and professional assessment 1974-86; Intl Academy Sacramento CA, owner/director 1987-. **ORGANIZATIONS:** Exec officer Natl Bd of Podiatric Medical Exam 1985-87; mem NAACP 1985-; consultant Educ Testing Serv 1986-; licensed school owner CA State Bd of Cosmetology 1987-; mem adv bd Natl Youth Sports Project Sacramento State Coll; mem educ comm North Sacramento Chamber of Commerce; bus dir, bd of dir Sacramento Hairdressers Guild 1988-89; chmn, educ comm & treasurer, bd of dir, North Sacramento Chamber of Commerce 1988-89. **HONORS/ACHIEVEMENTS:** Outstanding Staff Mem Educ Testing Serv 1985; Delta Chi Honor Soc George Washington Univ. **MILITARY SERVICE:** AUS specialist 5 1966-68; Army Commendation Medal 1968. **HOME ADDRESS:** 200 P St B-32, Sacramento, CA 95814. **BUSINESS ADDRESS:** Director/Owner, International Academy, 920 Del Paso Blvd, Sacramento, CA 95815.

SMITH, RUFUS HERMAN
Government official. **PERSONAL:** Born Jun 23, 1950, Loudon, TN; married Patricia Ann House; children: Rufus H Jr, Courtney Danielle. **EDUCATION:** TN State Univ, BS 1972; Univ of TN Knoxville, MS 1978. **CAREER:** TN Valley Authority, equal opportunity staff 1978-83; USDept of Energy, equal opportunity manager 1983-. **ORGANIZATIONS:** Manager affirmative action program for Federal employees and direct minority educational assistance programs, including those specifically related to historically black colleges and universities. **HONORS/ACHIEVEMENTS:** Member Alpha Phi Alpha. **HOME ADDRESS:** 940 Brantley Drive, Knoxville, TN 37923. **BUSINESS ADDRESS:** Program Manager, Equal Opportunity, PO Box E, Oak Ridge, TN 37831.

SMITH, SALLIE P. (NEE PHILLIPS)
Educator. **PERSONAL:** Born Nov 15, 1880, Edgecombe County; widowed. **EDUCATION:** Hampton Inst; A NC Coll. **CAREER:** Retired teacher. **ORGANIZATIONS:** Mem NTA; Eastern Star; many church clubs.

SMITH, SAM
City government official. **PERSONAL:** Born Jul 21, 1922, Gibsland, LA; son of Stephen Kelly Smith; married Marion King Smith, Jan 29, 1947; children: Amelia, Carl, Anthony, Donald, Ronald, Stephen III. **EDUCATION:** Seattle Univ, Seattle WA, BSS, 1951; Univ of Washington, Seattle WA, BA, 1952. **CAREER:** State of Ashington, Olympia WA, state rep, 1958-67; City of Seattle, Seattle Wa, city councilman, 1967—. **ORGANIZATIONS:** Mem, Board of Mgrs, Amer Baptist Churches USA; mem, NAACP; mem, Seattle Urban League. **HONORS/ACHIEVEMENTS:** Legislator of the Year Award, WA State House of Reps, 1967; Seattle Urban League Annual Award, 1968; Distinguished Alumnus Award, Seattle Univ, 1976; selected most outstanding public official, Municipal of Seattle and King County, 1985; Nat'l Conf of Christians and Jews recognition award, 1986; Booker T. Washington Award, Natl Business League, 1987. **MILITARY SERVICE:** US Army, warrant officer jr grade, 1942-46; received Distinguished Service Award, Asiatic Pacific Medal. **BUSINESS ADDRESS:** President/Seattle City Council, City of Seattle, 600 4th Ave, 11th Fl, Seattle, WA 98104.

SMITH, SHERMAN
Manufacturing mgr. & elected official. **PERSONAL:** Born Apr 26, 1957, Earle, AR; married Odessa Pitchford; children: Margual, Sherman Jr. **EDUCATION:** Draughon Bus Coll, Assoc in Bus Mgmt 1977. **CAREER:** Earle Jr HS, sub-teacher 1977-78; Halstead Indus Prod, storeroom supervisor 1981-. **ORGANIZATIONS:** Alderman City of Earle 1983-; minister of the gospel Earle Church of God in Christ 1983-; youth dept pres Earle Church of God in Christ; pres Student Govt 1976-77. **HONORS/ACHIEVEMENTS:** Certified income tax preparer certificate from HR Block 1978. **HOME ADDRESS:** 215 Alabama St, Earle, AR 72331.

SMITH, SHIRLEY LAVERNE
Government recruitment coordinator. **PERSONAL:** Born Apr 02, 1951, Midlothian, VA; daughter of Walter Smith and Thelma Draper Smith. **EDUCATION:** Virginia Commonwealth Univ, BS 1973. **CAREER:** Internal Revenue Service, clerk/tax examiner 1974-79, tax rep/tax specialist 1979-81, eeo specialist 1981-84, eeo officer 1984-88, recruitment coordinator 1988-. **ORGANIZATIONS:** Northeast Region Undergrad Chap Coor Sigma Gamma Rho 1986-88; intl bd of dirs Sigma Gamma Rho Sor 1986-90; mem Federally Employed Women, Intl Training in Communication Clubs, Urgan League Guild, YWCA, NAACP, Richmond Jazz Soc, Assn for Improvement of Minorities-IRS, National Council of Negro Women; northeast regional dir, Sigma Gamma Rho Sorority Inc 1988-90. **HONORS/ACHIEVEMENTS:** IRS Communication Awd 1981; IRS Performance Awd 1984; Natl Achievement Awd Sigma Gamma Rho Sor 1984; Certificate of Appreciation Richmond Urban League 1982,84, Northeast Region Sigma Gamma Rho Sor 1984; Richmond Youth Serv Recognition Awd 1985; IRS Performance Award 1987, 1988. **HOME ADDRESS:** P O Box 935, Midlothian, VA 23113.

SMITH, STANLEY G.
Bank official. **PERSONAL:** Born Jul 21, 1940, Brooklyn, NY; married Ruth Grey; children: Craig, Carl. **EDUCATION:** Seton Hall U, JD 1970; Rutgers U, BA Actg. **CAREER:** Urb Dev Res Inc, pres; Newark Hsng Dev & Rehab Corp, pres, chief exec ofcr 1980-; City Newark NJ, asst corp cncl 1972; Fed Prog Newark Hsng Dev Corp, att; Fidelity Union & Trust Co, fed asst, code enfor, fin analyst 1968-70; RCA, 1964-68; Seton Hall Univ Sch of Law, prof 1972-; Lofton Lester & Smith, att law prtnr 1985. **ORGANIZATIONS:** Mem Nat Bar Assn; concerned legal asso mem, bd dirs Nghbrhd Hlth Serv Corp 1972; bd dirs Voice Nwspr 1971-72; vice pres Phi Sigma Delta 1960. **HONORS/ACHIEVEMENTS:** On dean's list RutgersUniv 1961-62; adjunct prof Seton HallUniv 1972-; St Schlrshp (4 yrs) RutgersUniv 1957; Hon Soc Seton Hall Law Sch 1967; Hon Schlrshp NJ Bell Elks Club. **BUSINESS ADDRESS:** Executive Vice President, City Natl Bank, 900 Broad St, Newark, NJ 07102.

SMITH, STEPHEN CHARLES
Industrial hygienist. **PERSONAL:** Born Feb 27, 1951, Newport News, VA; children: Lashunya. **EDUCATION:** Virginia State Univ, BS Chemistry 1973; Univ of Iowa, MBA 1983. **CAREER:** Alcoa, environmental engr 1974-78, industrial hygienist 1979-83, sr industrial hygienist 1983-84, staff industrial hygienist 1984-. **ORGANIZATIONS:** Bd of dirs 1983-84, pres 1984-85 Iowa-Illinois Sect AIHA; bd of dirs Iota Phi Theta Frat Inc 1983-; comm mem Natl Amer Industrial Hygiene Assoc 1985-; mem Natl Black MBA Assoc 1985; finance comm chmn bd of dirs Iota Phi Theta Frat Inc 1986-. **HONORS/ACHIEVEMENTS:** Certified industrial hygienist in the chemical aspect ABIH 1982; certified industrial hygienist in the comprehensive practice ABIH 1985; certified safety professional in the mgmt aspect BCSP 1986; published 2 hygienic guides "Cobalt" and "Dichlorodifluoromethane" AIHA 1986. **BUSINESS ADDRESS:** Staff Industrial Hygienist, Alcoa, PO Box 3567, Davenport, IA 52808.

SMITH, SUNDRA SHEALEY
Health services administrator. **PERSONAL:** Born Feb 09, 1948, Birmingham, AL; daughter of John Shealey and Eddie Griggs Harrell; married Marcellus L Smith Jr, Sep 09, 1978; children: Sonja Q, Stephanie M. **EDUCATION:** Tuskegee Inst, Tuskegee AL, BS, 1970; Southern Illinois Univ, Carbondale IL, MS, 1973; Univ of Alabama at Birmingham, Birmingham AL, MPH, 1984. **CAREER:** Progressive Enterprises, Birmingham AL, owner, 1976-80; Alabama Christian Coll, Birmingham AL, instructor, 1981-83; Lawson State Jr Coll, Birmingham AL, instructor, 1983-86; Univ of Alabama at Birmingham, Birmingham AL, medical researcher, School Public Health, 1982-84, coord, Geriatric Medicine, 1984-86; Birmingham Reg Plan Comm, Birmingham AL, manager, Medicaid Waivers, 1987-. **ORGANIZATIONS:** Mem, Natl Assn of Negro Business & Professional Women's Clubs Inc, 1974-, vice-governor, SE Dist; mem, Omicron Omega Chapter, Alpha Kappa Alpha Sorority; sec, Birmingham Rose Soc; arbitrator, Birmingham Better Business Bureau, 1981-; mem, Amer Public Health Assn, 1982-, Alabama Public Health Assn, 1986-, Alabama Gerontological Soc, 1986-, Brown & Williamson, Kool Achiever Awards Screening Comm, 1986-89, Birmingham News Advisory Bd, 1986-88, Birmingham League of Women Voters, 1988-. **HONORS/ACHIEVEMENTS:** Club Serv Award, Metro Birmingham Club, Natl Assn of Negro Business & Professional Women, 1986; Paper Presentation, Southern Gerontological Assn Mtg, 1986; Service Award, St Mark's Episcopal Church, 1987; District Service Award, Natl Assn of Negro Business & Professional Women, 1989; Appreciation Award, Better Business Bureau, 1989. **HOME ADDRESS:** 207 Stone View Trail, Birmingham, AL 35210.

SMITH, SYMUEL HAROLD
Executive director. **PERSONAL:** Born Jun 01, 1922, Port Tampa City, FL; divorced; children: Cynthia D, Celeste D, Carmen D. **EDUCATION:** WashingtonUniv St Louis, M of Hosp Admin 1965; WshingtonUniv St Louis, BS Bus Finance 1961; St LouisUniv St Louis, AA Pub Admin 1943. **CAREER:** Milwaudee Co Insts & Depts WI, dir 1978-; Detroit Gen Hosp, dir of hosps/Chf exec ofcr 1978; Wayne Co Gen Hosp MI, exec dir 1974-78; Morisania City Hosp Bronx, exec dir 1968-74; Edgecombe Rehab Cntr NY State Narcotic Addic Control Comm NYC, dir 1967-68; NY State Depart of Health NYC, hosp admin consul 1966-67; Bronx Muni Hosp Cntr Bronx, assist admin 1965-66; Flint-goodridge Hosp New Orleans, adminis resi & adminis assis 1964-65; Homer G Phillips Hosp St Louis, asst adminis 1952-63; City St Louis Depart Health 1950-52. **ORGANIZATIONS:** Mem Am Hosp Assn; Fellow Am Pub Health Assn; mem Am Coll of Hosp Adminis; mem Nat Assn of Health Serv Execs; past first vP Hosp Exec Club of NYC; mem exec com Grtr Detroit Area Hosp Counc; mem MI State Arbitrtn Com; chmn Client Intervention Servs Syst Subcom; hospadm consult City of St Louis MO; mem Naacp; mem Gov Coun Pub Gen Hosp Sec AHA mem Task Force on Nat Assess of Clinical Edu of Allied Health Manpwr Health Res Adminis DHEW Wash DC; mem Adminis Prac Comm Greater NY Hosp Assn; Cita Chi Eta Phi Sor Inc Omicron Chptr Oct 1970. **HONORS/ACHIEVEMENTS:** Cita Morrisania City Hosp Employees Coun Feb 1971; cita Morrisania City Hosp Comm Licensed Prac Nurses of NY Inc Feb 1971; cita Employees of Morrisania City Hosp Oct 1971; Man of Yr South Bronx Naacp Nov 1971. **MILITARY SERVICE:** AUS SSGT 1943-46. **BUSINESS ADDRESS:** Milwaukee Co Insts Depts, 8731 Watertown Plank Rd, Wauwatosa, WI 53226.

SMITH, TEASTHER WEST
Educator. **PERSONAL:** Born Dec 26, 1941, Carthage, MS; divorced. **EDUCATION:** Grand Rapids Jr Coll, AA 1961; Univ of MI, MA 1968; MI State Univ, BA 1965, MA 1973. **CAREER:** Grand Rapids Pub Schls, tchr 1963-75; Free Lance Writer, 1971-; Vietnamese Consultant 1976-; Women & Minority Concern, consultant 1973-. **ORGANIZATIONS:** Mem MEA Womens Task Force; mem MEA-NEA Women's Caucus; mem MEA Legis Comm, MEA Human Rel Comm; mem Dyer-Ives Found; mem Civ Theatre 1972-75; mem Alpha Kappa Alpha Sor; bd dir Bethel Day Care Ctr; mem bd dir Human Serv Agy; mem Kent CAP Counc; mem Art Gallery Guild; mem Leagueof Women Voters; mem NOW; MEA Women's Caucus; sec treas MEA Women's Caucus 1973-75; mem NEA Women's Caucus; Natl Women's Pol Caucus. **HONORS/ACHIEVEMENTS:** Coalition of Labor Union Women Natl Honor Soc 1958; Mensa Outstanding Young Educ 1975; Outstanding Young Women of Amer 1976; Who's Who 1976 Tchrs Vol; EDale Kennedy Awd for Human Relations 1975; art publ 1974-75. **BUSINESS ADDRESS:** Consultant, Women & Minority Concern, 4020 Eastern SE, Grand Rapids, MI 49508.

SMITH, THELMA J.
Savings & loan chief executive officer. **CAREER:** Illinois Service/Federal Savings and Loan Association of Chicago, Chicago, IL, chief executive, 1934—. **BUSINESS ADDRESS:** Illinois Service/Federal Savings and Loan Association of Chicago, 4619 South Dr. Martin Luther King Jr. Dr, Chicago, IL 60653. *

SMITH, TOMMIE
Athlete. **PERSONAL:** Born Jun 12, 1944, Clarksville, TX. **EDUCATION:** MS Phys Ed & Soc. **CAREER:** Olympic Team, sprinter 1968; Santa Monica; Coll, fac mem; Calohtex Inc LA, owner 1980. **HONORS/ACHIEVEMENTS:** Holds world 200-m straightway & 220-yd straightway; AAU Champ 220-yd & 200-m 1967-68; Won NCAA San Jose State 220 yd 1967; Top ranked 200-m, 220-ys Man inthe World Track & Field News 1967-68; World Olympic Record Mexico City 1968; Held more world records simultaneously (13) than any other athlete in track & field Hist San Jose State Univ; Still holds World Track & Field Records in 3 individual events; Currently working on book to preceed movie of his life to be viewed on CBS 1980-81.

SMITH, TOMMIE M.
Business executive. **PERSONAL:** Born Jun 19, 1919, Pulaski, TN; married Eugene W Smith; children: Joe W London. **EDUCATION:** Univ Louisville, 12 Hrs "Sucessful Mgmt of Indpendent Bus". **CAREER:** Tommie's Health Salon Inc, pres. **ORGANIZATIONS:** Mem Am Massage & Therapy Assc Inc 1965-; mem Urban League Louisville 1982-; chrmn Voter Registration NAACP 1963-64; precinct capt 141-A 1974-84; chrmn33rd Legislative Dist 1984-; chrmn Political Action Com NAACP 1972-76; life mem NAACP; mem Rivercity Bus & Profsnl Clb 1977-; mem Better Bus Bureau 1965; mem Commissioned KY Colonel 1974; mem Older Women's League 1982; pres KY Chap Massage Therapy Assocs 1983-87. **HONORS/ACHIEVEMENTS:** Cert of Merits & Apprections Louisville Urban League Comm Vol Serv 1961, Ketuckiana Recruiting Serv 1971, Jefferson Cty Bd of Ed 1974, Gornr Cmsn to State Hlth Plng Cncl; Woman of Achvmnt River City Bus & Profsnl Women's Clb 1979; Achvr Awd Achievers AKA 1980; 1986 Black Women for Political Action Awd; 1986 Jefferson County Democrat Awd. **BUSINESS ADDRESS:** President, Tommie's Health Salon Inc, 3932 Shelbyville Rd, Louisville, KY 40207.

SMITH, VASCO A.
Commissioner. **PERSONAL:** Born Aug 24, 1920, Harvard, AR; married Georgia Maxine Atkins; children: Vasco A III. **EDUCATION:** LeMoyne Coll, BS 1941; Meharry Med Coll, DDS 1945; TN Bapt Sch of Religion, LHD 1978; TX Coll, ScD 1983. **CAREER:** Private practice, dentist 1946-; Memphis Branch NAACP, bd mem 1955-; Tri-State Bank of Memphis, bd mem 1970; Shelby Co Govt, commr 1972-. **HONORS/ACHIEVEMENTS:** Civil Rights Award Natl Dental Assn 1980; Merit Award Tennessee A&I Univ 1979; Merit Award West Tennessee 1980; Public Serv Award Memphis Urban League 1975; Citizen of Year Omega Psi Phi Frat 1968; Pres Award Meharry Med Coll 1970; Leadership Award IBPOE of W (Elks) 1969; Achievement Award OIC 1973; Merit Award NAACP 1961; Citation Congressional Record 1975; Citation Mallory Knights 1969. **MILITARY SERVICE:** USAF cpt 1953-55. **HOME ADDRESS:** 1208 E Parkway S, Memphis, TN 38114. **BUSINESS ADDRESS:** Commissioner, Shelby Co Govt, 1952 Lamar Ave, Memphis, TN 38114.

SMITH, VERNEL HAP
City official. **PERSONAL:** Born Nov 12, 1924, Waycross, GA; divorced; children: Randy, Kevin. **EDUCATION:** OH State Univ, BS; OH State Univ, MA. **CAREER:** US & Overseas Social Welfare, admin, lecturer, teacher, trainer; City of Oakland CA, mgr recreation serv 1966-74, dir office of parks & recreation 1974-. **HONORS/ACHIEVEMENTS:** Outstanding & Dedicated Service Awd Natl Recreation & Park Assoc Ethnic Minority Soc 1984. **BUSINESS ADDRESS:** Dir, City of Oakland, Office of Parks & Recreation, 1520 Lakeside Dr, Oakland, CA 94612.

SMITH, VERNON G.
Councilman/educator. **PERSONAL:** Born Apr 11, 1944, Gary, IN; son of Albert Smith. **EDUCATION:** IN U, BS 1966, MS 1969, Ed D 1978. **CAREER:** Gary Urban League's Operation Jobs, asst dir 1966; OEO's Operation Sparkle, asst dir 1967; John Will Anderson Boys Clb, stf asst 1967-68; Gary, IN Pblc Sch Systm, tchr 1966-71, resource tchr 1971-72; Ivanhoe Sch Gary, IN, asst prncpl 1972-78; Nobel Sch Gary, IN, prncpl 1978-85; Williams School Gary IN, principal 1985-; 4th district councilman, City of Gary, IN, 1972-. **ORGANIZATIONS:** Pres tres Gary Downtown Merchants Assc; mem Gary Brnch NAACP; life mem INUniv Alumni Assc; life mem Omega Psi Phi Frat; founder pres IU Gents Inc;founder pres IU Dons Inc; founder spnsr Focus Hope; founder spnsr Young Citizens League; founder spnsr Youth Ensuring Solidarity; mem Phi Delta Kappa Frat; pres Gary Comm Mental Hlth Bd; mem past pres Elem Prncpl Assc; mem Med Ctr Gary; vice pres NW IN Urban Legue; mem deacon, trustee, and teacher Pilgrim Bapt Chrch; mem Gary's Ed Talent Srch Bd; mem Little League World Series Bd; mem Gary Young Demo; pres, Gary Common Coun, 1976, 1983-84, vice pres, 1985-. **HONORS/ACHIEVEMENTS:** GOIC Dr Leon H Sullivan Awrd 1982; gary comm mentl hlth Ctr 1981; outstndg serv ed awrd NAACP 1980; Mahalia Jackson Spec Achvmnt Awrd Field of Gospel Music; Omega Psi Phi Alpha Chi Chptr Citizen of Yr Awrd 1980; young democrat's outstanding serv awrd 1979; gary downtown merchants businessman of yr awrd 1979; LEFS Serv Awrd 1979; Who's Who in Am Pol 1979; club fab outstndg achvmnt citation 1978; Who's Who Among Blck Am 1978; distghsd & outstndg persnlties of the midwest 1978; Intrl Who's Who Comm Serv 1978; ebony mag most eligible bachelor 1977; gary jaycee good govt awrd 1977; listed in 9th edition comm ldrs notoble am 1977; three decades minority progess 1977; Who's Who Among Blck Am & Who's Who Am Pol 1977; listed notable am 1976; Who's Who Among Black Am & Who's Who Am Pol 1975; omega man yr 1974; better opportunity bldg legislative awrd 1974; carpetbaggers serv 1974; club progess outstndg achvmnt pol awrd 1974; listed blck ldrs am 1974; Who's Who Among Black Am & Who's Who in Am Pol 1974; omega psi phi 10th dist citizen of yr 1972; ldr am elem & scndry ed 1971; Gary Jaycees Youth Award, 1983; Outstanding Citizen of NW IN and Outstanding Educ Award, Info Newspaper, 1984; Blaine Marz Tap Award, Post Tribune, 1984; Gary Comm School Corp Speech Dept regoc award, 1984. **HOME ADDRESS:** PO M622, Gary, IN 46401.

SMITH, VINCENT D.
Painter, educator. **PERSONAL:** Born Dec 12, 1929, New York, NY; married Cynthia Linton, Jul 12, 1972. **EDUCATION:** Brooklyn Museum, 1954-56. **CAREER:** Painter oneman shows & exhibits; Whitney Mus Art Resource Ctr, instr 1967. **ORGANIZATIONS:** Illustrator "Folklore Stories from Africa" 1974; mem Natl Conf of Artists, African-Amer Museum Assoc, Audubon Artist, Natl Soc of Painters in Casein & Acrylics. **HONORS/ACHIEVEMENTS:** Scholarship Showhegan School of Painting & Sculpture 1955; Brooklyn Museum Art School 1955-56; Fellowship John Hay Whitney Found 1959-60; Artist-in-Residence Smithsonian Conf Ctr 1967; Natl Inst of Arts & Letters Grant 1968; Childe Hassam Purchase Prize Amer Acad of Arts & Letters 1973,74; Thomas B Clarke Prize Natl Acad of Design 1974; Commd for 4 murals for New York City Bd of Ed 1975, "Impressions-Our World" Portfolio of Black Artists 1975; Participant 2nd World Black & African Festival of Arts & Culture LAGOS Nigeria 1977; Artist-in-Resident Cite Des Arts Intl Paris France 1978; Mural Crotoma Ctr Human Resources Admin Bronx NYC; Collections Mus of Mod Art NYC, Newark Mus NJ, Brooklyn Mus NYC, Colum bus Gallery of Fine Art OH; Commn Mural Oberia D Dempsey Multi-Service Center for Central Harlem NYC 1989. **MILITARY SERVICE:** AUS pvt 1948-49. **BUSINESS ADDRESS:** Instructor, Whitney Music Art Resource Ctr, 264 E Broadway, New York, NY 10002.

SMITH, VIRGIL CLARK, JR.
State representative. **PERSONAL:** Born Jul 04, 1947, Detroit, MI; married Evelyn Owen; children: Virgil Kai, Adam Justin. **EDUCATION:** MI State Univ, BA Pol Sci 1969; Wayne State Law, JD 1972. **CAREER:** Justice Wade McCree US Appeals Ct, student clerk; Wayne Co Legal Svcs, legal advisor 1972-73; Model Cities Drug Clinic; Corporations Council City of Detroit; MI House of Reps, state rep. **ORGANIZATIONS:** Mem Natl Caucus of Black State Legislators; mem North Central Lions Club Detroit; vice chair Taxation Comm MI House of Reps 1977-; chmn Economic Develop & Energy 1985-; mem Comm on Judiciary & Elections; asst majority floor leader Legislative Black Caucus. **HOME ADDRESS:** 19450 Gloucester, Detroit, MI 48203. **BUSINESS ADDRESS:** State Representative, MI House of Representatives, RM-3-G Capitol Bldg, Lansing, MI 48913.

SMITH, VIRGINIA M.
Educator. **PERSONAL:** Born May 09, 1929, El Dorado, AR; daughter of Henry Burks and Annie Burks; children: Marcia Green Wilson, Gregory Green, Dana Paul Green. **EDUCATION:** Am&N Coll, BA 1950; Univ IL, MEd 1955; Univ AR, 1963; Henderson State U, 1968, 1972; AK State Univ 1979; program management trng, Title III 1983, 1985. **CAREER:** AR Pub Schs, tchr 1950-60; So U, asst prof 1963-65; El Dorado, counselor 1965-70; Henderson State U, personnel dean 1971-81; dir of special services for disadvantaged students 1982-86; retired 1986 from Henderson State Univ; teacher of English, AK Baptist Coll 1986-. **ORGANIZATIONS:** Delta Sigma Theta Sor; mem NAACP; mem Natl Coucil of Teachers of English; AK Coll English Teachers Assn; Arkadelphia Women's Devel Council. **BUSINESS ADDRESS:** Box 274, Arkadelphia, AR 71923.

SMITH, WALLACE CHARLES
Clergyman educator. **PERSONAL:** Born Nov 06, 1948, Philadelphia, PA; married G Elaine. **EDUCATION:** Villanova U, BA 1970; Eastern Bapt Sem, MDiv 1974; Eastern Bapt Sem, DMin 1979. **CAREER:** Eastern Bapt Sem, dir alumni affairs & asst dir field educ 1979-; Calvary Bapt Church, pastor 1974-; Prog Natl Bapt, home mission bd 1979. **ORGANIZATIONS:** Exec bd Chester Br NAACP 1974-; pres Chester Clergy Assn 1977-79; pres Chester Community Improvement Project 1979-. **BUSINESS ADDRESS:** City & Lancaster Ave, Philadelphia, PA 19151.

SMITH, WALTER L.
Educational administrator. **PERSONAL:** Born May 14, 1935, Tampa, FL; married Jeraldine Williams; children: John, Andre, Salesia, Walter II. **EDUCATION:** FL A&M Univ, BA Biology & Chem 1963, MEd Admin & Supv 1966; FL State Univ PhD Higher Ed Admin 1974. **CAREER:** Natl Educ Assn, assoc regional dir for NEA 1969-70; FL Educ Assn, admin asst 1970, asst exec sec 1970-73; Hillsborough Comm Coll, collegium dir 1973, dean employee relations 1973-74, provost 1974; Roxbury Comm Coll, pres 1974-77; FL A&M Univ, prof, president 1977-. **ORGANIZATIONS:** Chairperson FL Supreme Ct Judicial Nominating Comm 1980-83; FL Supreme Ct Article V Comm 1983; chmn State Bd of Educ US Dept of Interior 1984; bd of dirs Natl Assoc for Equal Opportunity HE 1982-; bd dir Amer Assn of State Colleges and Univs. **HONORS/ACHIEVEMENTS:** Red-X Awd Cape Kennedy IBM Corp 1966; Scholarly Distinction Awd Univs Urban League 1974; Meritorious Serv Awd Amer Assoc State Colleges & Univs 1984; Jackson Memorial Awd Assoc of Classroom Teachers 1984; Fulbright Senior Scholar 1985. **MILITARY SERVICE:** AUS sp-5 3 yrs; Commendation Medal; Natl Defense Medal; Good Conduct Medal 1953-56. **BUSINESS ADDRESS:** President, Florida A&M University, Office of the President, Room 307 FHAC, Tallahassee, FL 32307.

SMITH, WALTER T.
Dentist. **PERSONAL:** Born May 25, 1927, Huntsville, AL; married Maureen; children: Shawn, Walter. **EDUCATION:** Howard U, BS 1956; Meharry, DDS 1961. **CAREER:** Gary Ind, dentist private practice 1965-; Meharry Dental School, instr. **ORGANIZATIONS:** Mem Omega Psi Phi; ADA; Lincoln Dental Soc Chgo; NW Ind & IDA Dental Socs; NDA; Acad of Gen Dentistry; mem exec & adv Com NW Ind Sickle Cell Found; mem Gary Police Civil Serv Comm; mem United Fund. **MILITARY SERVICE:** USN 1945-47; AUS 1953-55. **BUSINESS ADDRESS:** 1706 Broadway, Gary, IN 46407.

SMITH, WAYMAN F., III
Vice president. **PERSONAL:** Born Jun 18, 1940, St Louis, MO; children: Kymberly Ann. **EDUCATION:** Attended, Washington Univ 1957-59; Monmouth Coll, BS 1962; Howard Univ, JD 1965. **CAREER:** Missouri Commn on Human Rights, dir of concilliation 1966-68; Law Firm Wilson Smith Smith & McCullin, partner 1969; St Louis City Council, three-term alderman; City of St Louis, municipal court judge 1973-75; Anheuser-Busch Companies Inc, vice pres of corporate affairs 1980-. **ORGANIZATIONS:** Mem bd alderman City of St Louis 1975-; mem bd of dirs Anheuser-Busch Companies Inc 1981-; coord Lou Rawls Parade of Stars fund-raising telethon which benefits The United Negro College Fund; mem bd of admissions US District Court for the Eastern District of MO; mem ABA, Natl Bar Assoc, Mound City Bar Assoc; Bar Assoc Met St Louis. **HONORS/ACHIEVEMENTS:** Distinguished Alumni Howard Univ 1983;, Monmouth Coll 1983. **BUSINESS ADDRESS:** VP, Corporate Affairs, Anheauser-Busch, One Busch Place, St Louis, MO 63118.

SMITH, WILBER GENE
Consultant director. **PERSONAL:** Born Mar 22, 1935, Orlando, FL; married Paula Gorenstein; children: Mona, Christopher, Scott, Stephan, Stacy, Adam. **EDUCATION:** Eastern CT State U, BA English 1976;Univ of CT Sch of Law, 4th Yr stdnt 1985. **CAREER:** Comm Renwl Team Grtr Htfd, dir, consmr ed 1961-65; NAACP CT State Conf, urban pgm dir 1965-68, 1967-71; State of CT Gen Assmbly, state sen 1971-77, 1981-85; Natl Assn Adv Col People, NY, dir, prison pgm 1976-78; Jonathan-Joseph Corp W Haven, CT, v pres gov & comm afrs 1985-. **ORGANIZATIONS:** Cnsltnt UPS Serv Mng Train 1966-68, 1972-75; cnsltnt Unity Cntrctrs (Minority Bsns Ent) 1975-77; bd dir Jonathan-Joseph Corp W Haven, CT; Cmptrzd

Telemrktng Sys 1985-; chrmn Jackson for Pres CT Commt 1983-84 ; chrmn CT Rainbow Coalition 1984-; bd NAACP Hrtfrd Brnch 1960-80; exec comm NAACP CT State Conf 1967-; pres NAACP CT State Conf 1967-68, 1975-76; mem Perm Comm Status of Wmn State of CT 1975-77. **HONORS/ACHIEVEMENTS:** Cvl Rghts Ldr Awrd CT Cncl on Human Rghts Hrtfrd 1968; Human Rghts Awrd W Indian Ann Indep Day 1973, 1978; Pol & Human Rgts Prgrs CT State ConfNAACP; Cvl Rgts Awrd Htfd Br, NAACP 1975; Correc in State Jaycees Somers, CT State Prison 1971; Outstndng Cntrbtns Prison Rfrm Lewisburg Fed Pen, NAACP 1977. **MILITARY SERVICE:** AUS cpl, 196 FA Battl 1954-57; Dstngshd Serv Awrd; Hnrbl Dschrg 1957. **HOME ADDRESS:** 196 Palm St, Hartford, CT 06112. **BUSINESS ADDRESS:** VP Gov & Comm Affairs, Jonathan-Joseph Corp, 215, Hartford, CT 06120.

SMITH, WILLIAM FRED
Business executive. **PERSONAL:** Born Mar 22, 1938, Savannah, GA. **EDUCATION:** Savannah State Coll; California State Univ. **CAREER:** Bunker Ramo Corp, lA mgr affirmative action 1980; Litton Date Systems, mgr affirmative 1978-80; EEO Computer Sci Corp, corp mgr 1976-78; Litton Guidance & Control Sys, research devel & affirmative action 1972-76; Pacoima MDTA, mgr affirmative action, skill center adv comm mem 1972-; Venice MDTA mem 1971-72; Assn Inc, personnel & industrial relations 1974-; Covina City, human relations comm 1970-74; Aztian, personnel mgmt assn 1974; Ad Hoc Comm, aerospace indus 1970-. **ORGANIZATIONS:** Merit employers Assn LA 1970-; mem Kappa Alpha Psi Frat; mem PMAA; mem LA Basin EEO; NAACP. **HONORS/ACHIEVEMENTS:** Comm Serv Award 1971; LA County Human Relations Commn Community Serv Award 1972; Natl Media Women Communication Award 1973; mem LA Dist Atty Comm Adv Council 1972; selective sys bd mem adv appointed by President 1971; appointed to CA Gov Comm for Employment of the Handicapped 1978; San Fernando Concerned Black Womens Award 1979; invited to White House by Pres Carter 1980; received award from Soc of Black Engineers CA State Univ Northridge 1980. **BUSINESS ADDRESS:** 31717 La Tienda Dr, Box 5009, Westlake Village, CA 91359.

SMITH, WILLIAM FRENCH
Environmental safety manager. **PERSONAL:** Born Nov 30, 1941, Bay City, TX; son of Smith and Perry; married Syl Morgan, Feb 04, 1977; children: William III, Maurice. **EDUCATION:** Tuskegee Univ, BS 1959-64; WA Univ St Louis MO, Graduate Study 1968-70. **CAREER:** Westinghouse Corp, safety engineer; EI DuPont, area engineer; St Louis County Govt, project engineer; McDonnal Douglas Corp, design engineer; The Boeing Co, equipment engineer; Denver Public Schools, engineer. **ORGANIZATIONS:** Bd dir Denver Opportunity Industrial Center 1979-80, Natl Comm on Future of Regis Coll; mem Mayor's Citizens Adv Comm on Energy 1980-; mem Amer Soc Safety Engineers, CO Assn School Energy Coords, Amer Assn Blacks in Energy, treas Denver Public Schools Black Admin & Supvs Assn; mem CO Environ Health Assn, Natl Asbestos Council, CO Hazardous Waste Mgmt Soc, CO Hazardous Materials Assn, Natl Assn Minority Contractors, Intl Hazardous Matls Assn, Tuskegee Univ Alumni Assn. **HONORS/ACHIEVEMENTS:** Recipient President's Natl Award for Energy Conservation 1980. **MILITARY SERVICE:** USNR 1978-80. **BUSINESS ADDRESS:** Engineer, Denver Public Schools, 900 Grant St, Denver, CO 80203.

SMITH, WILLIAM HOWARD
Engineer. **PERSONAL:** Born Dec 17, 1912, Talladega, AL; married Eva; children: Julius, Burton, Marianne, Kenneth, Harold, Patricia. **EDUCATION:** MI State Univ, BS 1937. **CAREER:** Hwy design engr retired. **ORGANIZATIONS:** Past office, current mem NAACP; past pres Model Cities Adv Bd; chmn Tri Cty Plnng Comm; adv comm, vice pres BASE; mem Black Assoc in State Employment, CDCH. **HONORS/ACHIEVEMENTS:** 39 Yr Cert & Roadside Park Name St Hwy & Transp comm; hon life mem Hwy Mens Club; AASHO 25 Yr Awd Pine & Cert.

SMITH, WILLIAM JAMES
Attorney. **PERSONAL:** Born Mar 05, 1946, Fresno, CA; married Alice; children: Danielle, Nicole. **EDUCATION:** UCLA, BA 1968; UCLA Sch of Law, 1972. **CAREER:** Trust Admin Union Bank, UCLA football; Nat Labor Relations Bd, atty; Brundage Reich & Pappy Labor Spec, atty. **ORGANIZATIONS:** Mem Nat Conf Black Lawyers; bd dirs Black Law Journ; mem LA Bar Assn; mem CA Bar Assn; mem Langston Law Club; Pro Bono Cases Labor Law. **BUSINESS ADDRESS:** 13130 L St Ste E, Fresno, CA.

SMITH, WILLIAM M., JR.
State official. **PERSONAL:** Born Sep 28, 1934, Chattanooga, TN; married Lola M Young; children: Wynton, Kimbilly. **EDUCATION:** IL Inst of Tech, BS Arch 1960, Master City/Reg Planning 1964. **CAREER:** Stanton & Rockwell, staff Planner 1959-61; Comm Renewal Prog, jr planner 1961-64; Comm Improvement Prog, sr planner 1964-66; Dept of Urban Renewal Chicago, sr planner 1966-68, southeast area coord 1968-70; Model Cities Natl Urban Coalition, asst reg dir 1970-71; Perkins & Will Planners, sr planner 1971-72; Andrew Heard & Assoc, vice pres planning 1972-74; Barton-Achman Consultants, sr assoc 1974-78; Baltimore City Planning, asst dir 1978-82; Mayor's Office of Human Develop, dir mayor's 1982-84; Maryland State Dept of State, asst secty. **ORGANIZATIONS:** Mem Amer Inst Certified Planners; mem Amer Soc of Planning Officials; mem Natl Assn of Housing & Redevelopment. **MILITARY SERVICE:** USMC sgt 1952-55. **BUSINESS ADDRESS:** Assistant Secretary, MD Dept of State Planning, 301 W Preston St Rm 1207, Baltimore, MD 21201.

SMITH, WILLIAM MILTON
Clergyman. **PERSONAL:** Born Dec 18, 1918, Stockton, AL; married Ida M Anderson; children: Eula C Goole. **EDUCATION:** Tuskegee Inst Livingstone Coll, SMU, Perkins School of Religion, BS; AL State Univ, BS Ed. **CAREER:** 2nd Episcopal Dist AME Zion Church, presiding bishop; African Methodist Epis Zion Church Mobile AL, sr bishop. **ORGANIZATIONS:** Bd dir Gulf Fed Loan Assoc, YMCA, Mobile Co United Fund, Mobile United, Mobile Cty Red Cross, Mobile Gen Hosp, Mobile Found for Med Care, Mobile Cty Men Health, Amer Jun Miss Pagent Inc, Legal Aid Soc, Mobile Cty Palsy Inc; natl com life mem NAACP; chmn Church Ext Bd AME Zion Church; trustee Liingstone Coll, Lomax-Hannon Coll, AL State Univ 1980-; mem Cty & State Exec Com Rep Party. **HONORS/ACHIEVEMENTS:** Ebony Magazine Awd 1980; various group awds. **BUSINESS ADDRESS:** Senior Bishop, African Meth Epis Zion Church, 3753 Springhill Ave, Mobile, AL 36608.

SMITH, WILLIAM PERNELL
Educator. **PERSONAL:** Born Oct 02, 1919, Birmingham, AL; married Dorothy; children: Barbara J, William Pernell, III, Eric B. **EDUCATION:** Tuskegee Inst, BS 1939; Rutgers U, MEd 1947; EdD 1959. **CAREER:** Tuskegee Inst, instr 1947-51; asso prof Educ 1960-69; VA Constrn Cos Newark NJ, clerk 1951-52; AL State Coll Montgomery, asst prof 1952-55; asso prof educ 1956-60; AL State Univ, prof educ, chmn, dir, teacher educ & psychology 1969-71; area coordinator, guidance E & psychology 1971-; Rutgers, visiting lecturer 1957-58; Stanford Research Inst, regl rep 1968-75; Office of Econ Oppor & other fed projects, consult in guidance & psychology 1964-75; AL State Univ, retired prof of education. **ORGANIZATIONS:** Mem AL Educ Assn; Am Personnel Guidance Assn; Nat Vocational Guidance Assn; Student Personnel Assn for Tchrs in Edn; Assn for Measurement & Evaluation in Guidance; NEA; life vP Com for Greater Tuskegee 1969-70; pres 1970-71; mem Phi Delta Kappa; Kappa Delta Pi. **MILITARY SERVICE:** AUS 1942-46.

SMITH, WILLIAM XAVIER
Banker. **PERSONAL:** Born Dec 09, 1934, Livingston, AL; married Ether Lee Jones (divorced); children: Molina, Xavier Gerard, Dianna, April. **EDUCATION:** Bryant Coll, BS 1960; AIB basic & standard certificates, certificates 1970-74; Univ of WI School for Bank Admin, diploma 1975. **CAREER:** Liggett Drug Co, jr accountant 1960-62; Wonstop Auto Service, accountant 1962-63; US Treas Dept, intl revênue agent 1963-67; GAC Corp, tax rsch supvr, 1967-70; Unity Bank & Trust, asst treasurer 1970-72; Peoples Bank of Virgin Islands, vice pres cashier 1972-77; American State Bank, vice pres operations 1977-82, pres & dir 1982-. **ORGANIZATIONS:** Dir/treas Boy Scouts of Amer Virgin Islands 1974-77; pres Greenwood Chamber of Commerce 1984-; dir Tulsa Comm Action Agency 1985-. **MILITARY SERVICE:** USAF airman 1st class 1954-57. **HOME ADDRESS:** 857 N 33 West Ave, Tulsa, OK 74127. **BUSINESS ADDRESS:** President/Dir, American State Bank, 3816 North Peoria St, Tulsa, OK 74106.

SMITH, WYRE See SMITH, ELIJAH

SMITH-GRAY, CASSANDRA ELAINE
City administrator. **PERSONAL:** Born Mar 07, 1947, Detroit, MI; married Charles A Gray; children: David Charles. **EDUCATION:** Wayne State Univ, BS 1971. **CAREER:** Detroit Public Schools, ed 1970-74; City of Detroit Youth Dept, dir 1974-76; City of Detroit Bd of Assessors, assessor 1976-82; City of Detroit Neighborhood Svc, exec dir 1982-. **ORGANIZATIONS:** Mem Natl Assoc Negro Business & Prof Women 1974-; campaign mgr Mayor Young's Re-election 1981; bd mem Mayor's Anti-Crime Project 1982; trustee Ctr for Humanist Studies 1983-; bd mem Wayne Cty Child Care Council 1983-; state central mem alternate MI Democratic Party 1982-; life mem NAACP; det campaign mgr Mondale-Ferrarro Campaign 1984. **HONORS/ACHIEVEMENTS:** Dir Youngest Dept Head in City's History 1974; assessor First Black Woman Assessor-Natl 1976; assessor 1st Black Woman Assessor Cert in MI 1979. **BUSINESS ADDRESS:** Executive Dir, Neighborhood Services, 5031 Grandy, Detroit, MI 48211.

SMITH-SURLES, CAROL DIANN
Educational administrator. **PERSONAL:** Born Oct 07, 1946, Pensacola, FL; children: Lisa Ronique, Philip. **EDUCATION:** Fisk Univ, BA 1968; Chapman Coll, MA 1971; The Univ of MI, PhD 1978. **CAREER:** Santa Barbara County, social worker 1968-69; Allan Hancock Coll, instructor 1971-72; The Univ of MI, personnel rep 1971-77; Univ of Central FL, dir of eeo1978-84, exec asst to the pres 1982-84, assoc vice pres 1984-. **ORGANIZATIONS:** Mem NAACP, Urban League; mem bd trustees WMFETV and FM radio 1984-; bd mem Orlando Human Relations Bd 1984-; pres Orlando Leadership Council Orlando Chamber of Commerce 1985. **HONORS/ACHIEVEMENTS:** Listed in Who's Who in the Midwest, Who's Who in the South and Southwest; Phi Lambda Theta Honor Soc 1977-; Outstanding Scholars Awd Delta Tau Kappa Intl Social Sci Hon Soc 1983. **BUSINESS ADDRESS:** Assoc Vice President, Univ of Central Florida, ADM-330, Orlando, FL 32816.

SMITH-WHITAKER, AUDREY N.
Educational administrator. **PERSONAL:** Born Mar 06, 1953, Chicago, IL; daughter of Erron Smith and Anita Smith; married Horace Edward Whitaker Jr. **EDUCATION:** Wellesley Coll, BA 1974; Univ of ME Orono, MEd 1978. **CAREER:** Zayre Corp, personnel admin exec recruiter 1974-76; Univ of ME Orono, intern teacher corps 1976-78; Wellesley Coll, admission counselor 1978-79, asst dir admission 1979-80, sr asst dir admission 1980-81, assoc dir of admission 1981-85; Natl Assn of Independent Schls, dir admission and financial aid serv 1985-87; Radcliffe College-Radcliffe Seminars, Cambridge MA, recruiter/academic advisor 1987-88; Sun Financial Group, Wellesley Hills MA, registered representative 1987-88; Massachusetts A Better Chance, The College Board-Northeast Regional Office, education consultant 1987-88. **ORGANIZATIONS:** Mem Natl Assoc Coll Admission Counselors 1978-, New England Assoc of Black Admission Counselors Inc 1978-, Assoc of Black Admission & Financial Aid Officers of the Ivy League & Sister Schools Inc 1976-, New England Assoc Coll Admission Counselors 1979-; Black achiever Black Achievers Inc Boston MA 1981-; founding mem Wellesley Black Alumnae Network 1981-; mem School Volunteers of Boston 1982-; eval team mem New England Assoc of Schools & Coll Secondary Schools 1983-; consult Tri-Lateral Council 1984; adv council The Educ Resources Inst 1985-; mem Urban League of Eastern MA 1986-; bd mem Girl Scouts Patriots Trail Council 1986-; adv council Educ Records Bureau; mem, Links Inc 1989-. **HONORS/ACHIEVEMENTS:** Black Achiever Black Achiever Assoc Inc Boston 1981; Outstanding Admin Black Grad Wellesley Coll 1982; rsch coordinator A Comparison of the Career Patterns of Black Grads of Two Selective Coll & Their Parents Morgan State Univ 1984. **BUSINESS ADDRESS:** Corporate Contributions Programs Manager, Digital Equipment Corporation, 111 Powdermill Rd M50/B14, Maynard, MA 01701.

SMITHERMAN, GENEVA
Educator. **PERSONAL:** Born in Brownsville, TN; daughter of Harry Napoleon; married Jeff R Donaldson; children: Robert Anthony. **EDUCATION:** Wayne State U, BA 1960, MA 1962; Univ of MI, PhD 1969. **CAREER:** Detroit Public Sch, tchr 1960-66; Eastern MI Univ & Wayne State Univ, instr 1965-71; Wayne State Univ, asst prof; Afro-Amer Studies Harvard Univ, lectr 1971-73; Univ of MI, adjunct prof 1973; Wayne State Univ, prof 1973-. **ORGANIZATIONS:** Mem Natl Coun Tchrs of English 1979-82; mem Exec Comm Conf Coll Composition 1971-73; chmn Black Lit Sect Midwest Lang Assn 1972; mem Modern Lang Assn Comm Minorities 1976-77; mem Oral Hist Comm Afro Museum 1967-68; judge Scholastic Writing Awrds Contest 1975; adv bd Ethnic Awareness Proj 1977-78; founding mem

African Amer Heritage Assn 1976. **HONORS/ACHIEVEMENTS:** Dean's List of Honor Students Wayne State Univ; Univ of MI Pre-Doctoral Fellowship; Award for Scholarly Leadership in Lang Arts Instruction 1980. **BUSINESS ADDRESS:** Prof, Speech Communication, Wayne StateUniv, 538 Manoogian, Detroit, MI 48202.

SMITHERS, ORAL LESTER, JR.
F-16 director of engineering. **PERSONAL:** Born Jul 12, 1940, Columbus, OH; son of O Lester Smithers Sr and Mildred H Smithers; married Priscilla; children: Sheila, Lisa. **EDUCATION:** Ohio State Univ, BCE 1963; Sacramento State Coll, MEngr Mech; Central Michigan Univ, MA 1982; Massachusetts Inst of Technology, Cambridge MA, MS 1985. **CAREER:** Aerojet Gen Corp, design engineer 1963-68; USAF, aerospace engineer 1968-85; Dept of Air Force, Wright Pallerson Air Force Base, F-16 dir of engineering, 1988-. **ORGANIZATIONS:** Mem OH Soc of Professional Engineers, USAF/FAA DC-10 Pylon Accident Damage Tolerance Assessment Team, Clark/Champaign Cty Soc of Professional Engineers, Springfield Schools Math Curriculum Study Comm Omega Psi Phi, Clark Cty/Springfield Planning Comm; past mem steward bd St Andrews AME Church. **HONORS/ACHIEVEMENTS:** Meritorious Civ Serv Award Air Force Sys Command; Civil Engineering Hon Chi Epsilon; Sloan Fellow MIT 1984-85; 4th Distinguished Man of the Year Omega Psi Phi 1984; Sr Engineer of the Year USAF Aeronautical Syst 1984.

SMITHERS, PRISCILLA JANE
Government official. **PERSONAL:** Born Jan 02, 1942, Parkersburg, WV; married O Lester Smithers, Jr; children: Sheila, Lisa. **EDUCATION:** Mtn State Coll, Prksbrg, WV, Exec Sec 1959-60; Am River Coll, Sacramento, CA, part time 1968; Clark Tech Coll, Spfld, OH, part time 1971-73. **CAREER:** Cont Cablevsn Spfld, OH, comm serv dir & prod & host of wkly TV show 1973-78; City of Spfld, OH, city clrk 1978-; United Way of Clark & Champaign Counties. **ORGANIZATIONS:** Mem League of Women Voters 1973-; past chmn Civil Serv Comm City of Springfield 1973-78; bd dir United Way 1976-; mem OH Municipal Clerks Assoc 1978-; mem Intl Inst of Municipal Clerks 1978-. **HONORS/ACHIEVEMENTS:** Prtcpnt Chmbr Comm "Ldrshp Acad" 1982; ctzn of Year (pltcl ctgry) Black Wmn Ldrshp Caucus, OH 1979; Ctzn of Year Frntr Intl Spfld, OH 1978; Saluteto Career Wmn Awrd YWCA of Spfld, OH 1982. **HOME ADDRESS:** 15 Bobwhite Dr, Enon, OH 45323. **BUSINESS ADDRESS:** United Way, 616 N Limestone St, Springfield, OH 45502.

SMITHEY, ROBERT ARTHUR
Educator. **PERSONAL:** Born Dec 18, 1925, Norfolk, VA; son of Phillip J Smithey and Lovie Jordan Smithey. **EDUCATION:** DePauw Univ Greencastle IN, AB 1950; Univ of WI Madison, AM 1953; Univ of WI, PhD 1968. **CAREER:** Talladega Coll Talladega AL, chmn lower div 1960-64; Univ of MO Kansas City, asst prof english 1968-70; Univ of Houston, assoc prof English 1970-72; Norfolk State Univ VA, prof English & Communications 1972-. **ORGANIZATIONS:** Exec comm Conf on Coll Composition & Comm 1964-67; dir Natl Council of Teachers of English 1968-70; reader Coll Bd of Exams 1970-72; lay reader St James Episcopal Church Houston 1970-72; editorial bd Four C's 1972-76; lay reader, chalicer, Grace Episcopal Church Norfolk 1972-. **HONORS/ACHIEVEMENTS:** IBM Fellow Univ of WI 1964-68; Vilas Fellow Univ of WI 1965-68; Univ Fellow Univ of WI 1966-68; Ford Fellow Univ of WI 1967-68; pres, National Youth Conf, NAACP 1944-45. **MILITARY SERVICE:** AUS cpl; USAF a1/c 5 yrs. **BUSINESS ADDRESS:** Professor of English & Commun, Norfolk StateUniv, 2401 Corprew Ave, Norfolk, VA 23504.

SMOOT, ALBERTHA PEARL
Elected official. **PERSONAL:** Born Oct 10, 1914, Society Hill, SC; daughter of Robert Antrum and Sally Antrum; married Clarence Smoot (deceased); children: Bruce Goldson, Jean Silva. **EDUCATION:** Ansonia HS, diploma 1932. **CAREER:** Macedonia Baptist Church, organist 1930-85; Lily of the Valley IBPOE of W, financial sec 1965-85; Second Ward, alderman. **ORGANIZATIONS:** Charter mem NAACP 1940-85; mem Ansonia Republican Town Comm 1947-85; mem Ansonia Recreation Comm 1983-85; first woman appointed to Bd of Public Works 1985 for 1 yr term, reappointed in 1986 for 2 year term, 1988 for 2 year term. **HONORS/ACHIEVEMENTS:** Serv rendered Macedonia Baptist Church 1965; serv rendered Lily of Valley IBPOE of W 1979; 50 yr member Macedonia Baptist Church 1984. **HOME ADDRESS:** Hunters Lane, Ansonia, CT 06401.

SMOOT, CAROLYN ELIZABETH
Corporate consultant, educational administrator. **PERSONAL:** Born Sep 24, 1945, Logan, WV; daughter of Mr & Mrs Edward Hickman; married Douglas B Smoot, Jan 27, 1967; children: Caroline Trucia. **EDUCATION:** WV State Coll Inst, BS, 1967; WV Coll of Graduate Study Inst, MPA, 1975. **CAREER:** Mgmt & Training Corp, dir of Education & Training, 1984-; mgmt consultant/researcher, 1983-84; WV State Coll, staff assoc, Office of Development, 1982-83; mgmt consultant, researcher, 1981-82; Nemderoloc/Medlock Co Inc, corporate consultant, 1979-80; WV Dept of Employment Security, commr, 1977-78; WV State Coll Inst, part-time instructor, 1975-77; Thiokol Corp, mgr placement & records dept, 1976-77; Teledyne Economic Devel Co, dept head placement serv, 1972-76; sr instructor, 1968-72; Packard Bell Electric Corp, residential advisor, 1967-68. **ORGANIZATIONS:** Co-chmn, Gov Commn on Employment of Handicapped; ex-officio mem, Commn on Aging; co-chmn, Veteran Employment & Training Advisory Council, 1977; Advisory Bd, Human Resources Devel Found, 1977; bd, Mt State Economic Assn, 1977; advisory bd, Regional Training Center, 1977; legislative Comm, Interstate Conf of Employment Security Agencies, 1977; Charleston Metro Advisory Bd, 1977; Advisory Bd, State Manpower Serv Council, 1977; Govs Human Resource Comm, 1977; Chamber of Commerce Lecturer, WV Coll of Graduate Study Placement as it relates to the disadvantaged, 1975; lecturer, Industrial Relation Class Industries Role in Hiring Minorities 1975; guest lecturer, various civic, social & comm org on topics relating to the Changing Role of Women Placement; several TV appearances; mem Delta Sigma Theta Sorority; Phi Delta Kappa Sor; mem Natl Womens Political Caucus & WV Women Political Caucus; asst, Durbar WV Chapter of Blue Birds Inc; homeroom mother, Dunbar Elementary School; bd dir, Multi-cap; NAACP; Amer Vocational Assn, 1984-present; WV Adult Educ Assn, 1984-present; WV Vocational Educ Assn, 1984-present; WV Human Resources Assn, 1984-87; Private Industry Council of Kanawha County, bd of dir, 1984-present; Charleston Business & Professional Club, pres & first Vice Pres, 1983-86; Shawnee Community Center, bd of dir, 1984-87. **HONORS/ACHIEVEMENTS:** Appointed WV Ambassador of Good Will, 1981; Participant in the first White House Conf on Balanced Natl Growth & Economic Devel, 1978; Featured in Ebony Magazine, "The Problems of Women Bosses", 1977; Participant in the White House Conf on Science & Technology, 1985. **HOME ADDRESS:** Box 222, Institute, WV 25112. **BUSINESS ADDRESS:** Dir of Educ & Training, Mgmt & Training Corp, Virginia & Summers Sts, Charleston, WV 25301.

SMOTHERS, RONALD
Restaurant executive. **CAREER:** Fastaurants, Inc, Los Angeles, CA, chief executive. **BUSINESS ADDRESS:** Fastaurants, Inc, 3700 Coliseum St, Los Angeles, CA 90016. *

SMOTHERS, RONALD ERIC
Reporter. **PERSONAL:** Born Sep 03, 1946, Washington, DC; married Brenda. **EDUCATION:** Hobart Coll, BA 1967. **CAREER:** Comm News Serv, editor 1969-72; Newsday, rptr 1968-69; WA Post, 1967-68. **BUSINESS ADDRESS:** The New York Times, 229 W 43rd St, New York, NY 10036.

SMOTHERSON, MELVIN
Minister. **PERSONAL:** Born Nov 06, 1936, Hattiesburg, MS; son of Melvin Smotherson and Estella S Rogers; married Geraldine Jackson, Jun 23, 1957; children: Charles, Bwayne, Pamela, Darren. **EDUCATION:** Brooks Bible Coll, Cert 1965; MO Bapt Coll, BA 1974; Webster Coll, MA 1980. **CAREER:** 1st Bapt Church of Creve Coeur, pastor 1963-71; Bapt State Sunday School & BTU Cong, historian 1974-75; Ministers Union of Greater St Louis, 1st & 2nd vice pres 1977-79; Washington Tabernacle Bapt Church, pastor 1971-80; Cornerstone Institutional Bapt Church, pastor 1980-. **ORGANIZATIONS:** Attended various conf & conv assoc with Bapt Church 1963-67; grand jr warden/grand chaplain, dep grand master Most Worshipful Prince Hall Grand Lodge; hon mem MI Grand Lodge F&AM; exec comm NAACP; deputy imperial chaplain Ancient Egyptian Arabic Order, Nobles of the Mystic Shrine of North & South Amer and its Jurisdiction 1985-; Most Worshipful Grand Master-MWPHGL of MO 1988-. **HONORS/ACHIEVEMENTS:** Various awds & certs NAACP & sororities 1965-74; Minister of the Year Awd Bapt Church 1973; Cert of Merit NAACP 1974; Doctor of Divinity Central Baptist Theological Seminary 1975; Citizen of the Year Awd George Washington Carver Assoc 1979; Citizen of the Year Awd Grand Chap OES; Knight Grand Commander of Humanity Republic of Liberia 1989; Chief of Bbandi Tribe Lofa District Monrovia Liberia; speaker in Trinidad West Indies, Seoul Korea, Rome Italy 1987-98.

SMYTHE-HAITH, MABEL MURPHY
Educator emerita, government official. **PERSONAL:** Born Apr 03, 1918, Montgomery, AL; daughter of Harry S Murphy and Josephine Dibble Murphy; married Hugh H Smythe, Jul 26, 1939 (deceased); children: Karen Pamela Smythe; married Robert Haith, Jr, 1985. **EDUCATION:** Spellman Coll, 1933-36; Mt Holyoke Coll, BA 1937, Northwestern Univ, MA, 1940; Univ of WI, PhD 1942. **CAREER:** NAACP Legal Defense & Educ Fund, deputy dir, non-legal rsch for school segregation cases 1953; Baruch School, adj prof 1959-60; Queens Coll, adjunct prof 1962; New Lincoln School, coord principal of high school, 1959-69; Encyclopedia Britannica Ed Corp, consult 1969-73; US Commn on Civil Rights, scholar-in-residence 1973-74; Phelps-Stokes Fund NY, dir rsch & publ 1970-72, vice pres 1972-77; United Republic of Cameroon, US ambassador 1977-80; Republic of Equatorial Guinea, US ambassador 1979-80; US Dept of State, dep asst sec for African Affairs 1980-81; Northwestern Univ Melville J Kerskovits, prof of African studies 1981-83, assoc dir African studies 1983-85, prof emerita 1985-. **ORGANIZATIONS:** Free-lance cons, speaker, writer 1950-; mem Council on Foreign Rel, Caucus of Black Econ; fellow African Studies Assoc; mem Amer Econ Assoc, The Smithsonian Inst, Museum of the Amer Indian, Cosmopolitan Club, Refugee Policy Group, Council of Amer Ambassadors, Assoc of Black Amer Ambassadors; trustee Spelman Coll 1980-; accompanied Ambassador Donald McHenry to Zimbabwe & Liberia to consult with their presidents 1980; US del Intl Conf to Asst Refugees in Africa 1981; Refugee Policy Group 1983-; US del to funeral of Sir Seretse Khama Pres of Botswana; US del So African Devel Coord Conf Maputo Mozambique 1980; bd dir Ralpha Bunche Inst on the United Natl CUNY 1986-. **HONORS/ACHIEVEMENTS:** Julius Rosenwald Fellow; Harriett Remington Laird Fellow; Nat Fellow; Disting Serv Awd, NY Chap of Links; Gran Dama D'Ino; LHD, Mount Holyoke Coll, 1977; LHD, Univ of Massachusetts at Amherst, 1979; Top Hat Awd Pittsburgh Courier 1979; LLD, Spelman Coll, 1980; Grand Officer Order of Valor United Republic of Cameroon 1980; Mary McLeod Bethune Women of Achievement Awd 1981; Ella T Grasso Awd Mt Holyoke Coll 1982; Decade of Serv Awd Phelps-Stokes Fund 1982; guest scholar Woodrow Wilson Intl Center for Scholars 1982; Alumna of the Year Awd Northwestern Univ 1983; Natl Coalition of 100 Black Women Awd 1984; Assoc of Black Amer Ambassadors' Study Mission to Japan 1985; African Seminar NAFEO 1985; US Info Agency Outstanding Serv Award, 1986. **HOME ADDRESS:** 700 New Hampshire Ave, Washington, DC 20037.

SNAGGS, CARMEN
Medford business executive. **PERSONAL:** Born Mar 28, New York, NY; married Bert. **EDUCATION:** City Coll, BBA 1944. **CAREER:** Carmen Medford, pub acct, priv prac 1944-. **ORGANIZATIONS:** Mem Met Soc of Acct; Empire State Assn of Acct Fin of Acct Fin sec treas N Bronx Section Nat Council of Negro Women Inc 1968-72; pres N Bronx Section Nat Council of Negro Women Inc 1972-; project dir Women in Comm Serv 1970-; oranizer & temporary chmn Black Concerned Citizens Com; fin sec bd dir Williamsbridge Sr Citizens Cntr 1972-; mem Sch Comm Adv Council Olinville Jr HS 1972-; Williamsbridge Br NAACP 1962-; Neighborhood Block Assn.

SNEAD, JOHN D.
Retired community official. **PERSONAL:** Born Nov 02, 1917, Paducah, KY; son of John P Snead and Mable Snead; widowed; children: Ronald, Jon, Jr, Marva. **EDUCATION:** AB, LUTC-IIAMA 1941; Purdue U, mardeting; KY State U, graduate 1961. **CAREER:** Gen Mtrs Lab, prof musician; UAW; committeeman; Great Lakes Mut Life Inst, insurance salesman, asst dist mgr, dist mgr, western MI mgr; Kent Co Dept of Soc Serv, caseworker, caseworker supervisor, supervisor of neighborhood ctrs & comm rel, supervisor of comm social svcs. **ORGANIZATIONS:** Com mem Nghbrhd Hlth Servs; Mnthl Hlth Servs; United Comm Servs Plng Com; mem Frankln-hall Adv Cncl; bd mem Hd Strt Par Advsy Com; Model Cities HEW Com; trste Kent Co Migrnt Affrs Cncl; mem Kent Co Jail Rehab Advsy Com; exec bdmem Grand Rapids Bus Opport; vice pres Comm Actn Prog Gov Bd; mem Urban Lgue Meth Comm Hse; bd dir Amer Red Cross. **HONORS/ACHIEVEMENTS:** Kentucky Colonel; NAACP Man of the Year Grand Rapids; Service Awd Grand Rapids Multifamily Svc; Achievement Awd Black Business & Professional Women's Club Inc; Service Awd Michigan Senate; Kent County Youth Companion Award, Service to abused & neglected children. **MILITARY SERVICE:** AUS capt.

SNEED, PAULA A.
Food and beverage executive. **PERSONAL:** Born Nov 10, 1947, Everett, MA; daughter of Thomas E Sneed and F Mary Turner Sneed; married Lawrence P Bass, Sep 02, 1978; chil-

dren: Courtney J. **EDUCATION:** Simmons Coll, Boston MA, BA Social Science, 1969; Harvard Business School Boston MA, MBA, 1977. **CAREER:** Outreach Program for Problem Drinkers, Roxbury MA, educ supvr, female coord, 1969-71; Ecumenical Center, Roxbury MA, dir of plans, Program Devel and Evaluation, 1971-72; Boston Sickle Cell Center, Boston MA, program coord, 1972-75; General Foods USA, White Plains NY, summer intern, Stove Top Stuffing, 1976, asst product mgr, Stove Top Stuffing, 1977-79, assoc product mgr, Coating Devel and Oven Fry, 1979-80, product mgr, Establish Coatings and Devel, 1980-82, sr product mgr, Shake 'N Bake and Oven Fry, 1982-83, product group mgr, Good Seasons Salas Dressing, 1983-86, category mgr, Dessert Enhancers and Ingredients, 1986-87, vice pres, Consumer Affairs, 1987-. **ORGANIZATIONS:** Consultant, Natl Inst of Alcohol and Alcohol Abuse, 1971-72; mem, Governor's Advisory Comm on Alcohol and Alcohol Abuse, 1971-72, Amer Assn of Univ Women, 1980-, Coalition of 100 Black Women, 1982-, Natl Assn of Negro Business and Professional Women, 1983-, Soc of Consumer Affairs Professionals, 1987-. **HONORS/ACHIEVEMENTS:** Black Achiever, Harlem YMCA, 1982; MBA of the Year Award, Harvard Business School Black Alumni Organization, 1987, Benevolent Heart Award, Graham-Windham, 1987. **HOME ADDRESS:** 303 Pershing Ave, Ridgewood, NJ 07450.

SNELL, JIMMY GREGORY
Manager, councilman. **PERSONAL:** Born Jan 17, 1927, Waco, TX; married Joanna Verdun; children: James, Jerald, Joseph, Juliette. **EDUCATION:** Wiley Coll, BA 1951. **CAREER:** Port Arthur Sch Dist, 1954-56; City of Austin, councilman 1975-; Co Commissioner, precinct 1 1981-84, 1985-88; Atlanta Life Ins Co, gen mgr 1952-. **ORGANIZATIONS:** Mem NAACP, Urban League, Natl Bus League; bd mem Child Guidance; bd of comm council; Anderson Jr HS Human Relations Bd; St Austin's Church Finance Bd; chmn of bd Child Inc; scoutmaster campaign mgr Rev Martin Griffen state rep Wilhelmina Delco. **HONORS/ACHIEVEMENTS:** Arthur DeWitty Awd NAACP 1974; Man of Yr Awd Omega Psi Phi 1976. **MILITARY SERVICE:** USAF sgt 1945-47. **BUSINESS ADDRESS:** Manager, Atlanta Life Ins Co, PO Box 1088, Austin, TX 78767.

SNELL, JOAN YVONNE ERVIN
Engineering administrator. **PERSONAL:** Born Apr 05, 1932, Waxahachie, TX; married Clarence L Sr; children: Tyrone, Clarence Jr. **EDUCATION:** Draughons Bus Coll, 1950; Prairie View A&M Coll, BA. **CAREER:** IBM Corp, field engineering adminstrn splst; Lubbock City Hall,. **ORGANIZATIONS:** Bd of dir YWCA 1956-66; exec sec NAACP 1973-75; mem, sec New Hope Bapt Ch 1952; sec NAACP; mem Gov's Com on Higher Edn; dir New Hope Bapt Ch Yth Dept; sec W TX Bapt Dist Assn; sec Women of BM & E Conv of TX; mem Mayor's Com & C of C. **HONORS/ACHIEVEMENTS:** First blk sec Lubbock City Hall 1954; first blk sec elem sch prin 1952; first blk IBM'eR hired to corp 1962; first blk elect offcl city of Lubbock 1970, 1972; 1st blk woman nomin Woman of the Yr 1969; Outstdng IBM Means Serv Aw 1968; spec hon guest to pres of corp; noble cit, gifts, & aw 1970. **BUSINESS ADDRESS:** 1602 10th, PO Box 1890, Lubbock, TX 79408.

SNELLINGS, ROLLAND See EL-TOURE, ASKIA MUHAMMAD ABU BAKR

SNIPES, KENNETH
Administrator. **PERSONAL:** Born Oct 13, 1938; married Jean; children: Kevin, Kyra, Julie. **EDUCATION:** Philadelphia Mus Coll, BFA 1962; Philadelphia Settlement Music Sch, studied voice 1958-63; Case-western Res U, attnd mgmt training seminar 1969; Harvard U, Inst in Arts Adminstrn Summer 1970. **CAREER:** Karamu House, exec dir 1969-; exec adminstr 1968-69; art dir 1956-68; Charton Center, dir 1964-65; Philadelphia Bd of Educ, extension prog art Teacher 1962-63; lecturer various coll & other instns; WKBF-TV Cleveland, former moderator-host; Fairfax Found Inc, many paintings exhibited, music, Cleveland & Philadelphia Pres. **ORGANIZATIONS:** Mem Mayor of Cleveland Council on Youth Opportunity; Cleveland Jr League Prog Com. **BUSINESS ADDRESS:** 2355 E 89 St, Cleveland, OH 44106.

SNOWDEN, CHARLENE G.
Manager. **PERSONAL:** Born Mar 31, 1941, Jeffersonville, IN; married Raymond. **EDUCATION:** MI State U, BA 1972; Wayne State U, MSW 1975. **CAREER:** MI Cancer Found, regional mgr 1977-; Family & Neighborhood Serv, group spec 1975-77; Huron Valley Child Guidance Clinic, psy social worker 1974-75; Family& Neighborhood & Serv, sch social worker 1973-74; Bishop Coll, counselor/instr 1972-73; Urban League of Flint, asst to exec 1962-70. **ORGANIZATIONS:** Mem Nat Assn of Social Workers; mem Assn of Black Social Workers; mem Am Personnel Guidance Assn; mem Assn of Nonwhite Concerns; mem Am Educ Communication Tech; mem Am Spl Educ Tech; mem Am Assn ofUniv Women; mem Urban League of Detroit; mem Black Causes & NAACP; mem Gamma Phi Delta Sorority; mem Womens Div of the Roundtable; mem Nat Conf of Christians & Jews; mem Health Care Inc; mem Church Women United; mem/Treas Mortor Bd Hon Soc forWomen MI StateUniv 1972. **HONORS/ACHIEVEMENTS:** Outstanding Employee Serv Urban League of Flint 1970; Scholarship Urban League of Flint 1970; Scholarship MI StateUniv 1970-72; Scholarship-garduate Professional Wayne StateUniv 1973-75; Outstanding Young Woman of Am Dallas 1973. **BUSINESS ADDRESS:** MI Cancer Foundation, 110 E Warren Ave, Detroit, MI 48201.

SNOWDEN, FRANK WALTER
Scientist. **PERSONAL:** Born Nov 05, 1939, New Orleans, LA; divorced. **EDUCATION:** XavierUniv New Orleans, BS 1960; HowardUniv Wash DC, 1960-63;Univ of New Orleans, PhD 1975. **CAREER:** Sr technical serv engr 3m;Univ of New Orleans, research & teaching 1970-73; US Dept of Agriculture So Reg Research Lab, chemist 1960-73; Howard U, teaching fellow 1960-63; US Dept of Agriculture So Reg Research Lab, student trainee 1957-60. **ORGANIZATIONS:** Mem Am Chemical Soc 1960-; mem Am Pub Transit Assn 1977-; Commr Mr Met Transit Commn Twin Cities 1977-; mem Alpha Phi Alpha Frat Inc Several; Patents/Research Publ & Presentations. **BUSINESS ADDRESS:** 3 M, 3 M Center, St Paul, MN 55144.

SNOWDEN, FREDRICK
Educator. **PERSONAL:** Born Apr 03, 1936, Brewton, AL; married Maye; children: Charles, Stacey. **EDUCATION:** Wayne State U, BS 1958; Wayne State U, MeE 1965. **CAREER:** Univ of AZ, asso prof, head basketball coach 1972-;Univ of MI, asst basketball coach 1968-72; NW HS, head basketball & baseball coach 1961-68; NW HS,asst basketball coach 1958-68. **ORGANIZATIONS:** Mem Nat Assn of Basketball Coaches of the US 1968-; mem bd dir Am Savings & Loan Assn 1973-; asso systems consult Multi-media Assn 1974-; mem bd dir Tucson Urban League 1973-75; co-chmn Easter Seal Campaign for AZ 1973-74; co-chmn March of Dimes Tucson 1974-75; chmn memshp com Nat Asn of BasketballCoaches 1973-75; Western Athletic Conf. **HONORS/ACHIEVEMENTS:** Coach of the Year 1972-73; Region 7 Coach of the Year 1973-74; Man of the Year Tucson 1973; Special Recog Award Tucson Conquistadors 1975; mem Environmental Protection Agency 1972; Fred Snowden Day in Detroit Dec 19 1976; 1st Black Am named head coach at a majorUniv in a major conference 1972; Key to City AchievementResolution from Mayor City Counc & MI Legislature. **BUSINESS ADDRESS:** Mc Kale Ctr, Room 242, Tucson, AZ 85721.

SNOWDEN, GAIL
Corporate officer. **PERSONAL:** Born Jul 05, 1945, New York, NY; children: Leigh Trimmier. **EDUCATION:** Radcliffe Coll, BA 1967; Simmons Coll Grad Prog in Mgmt, MB 1978. **CAREER:** First Natl Bank of Boston, br officer 1971-76, br credit officer 1977-79, loan officer 1980, asst vice pres 1981-. **ORGANIZATIONS:** Mem Natl Assoc of Bank Women 1971-; treas Radcliffe Club of Boston 1976; asst dir Boston Urban Bankers Forum 1979-80; conf steering comm Simmons Grad Prog in Man Alumnae Assoc 1979-80; steering comm of family Govt Comm on Children & Family 1980; vice pres Natl Assoc of Urban Bankers 1984-85. **BUSINESS ADDRESS:** Assistant Vice President, First Natl Bank of Boston, 100 Federal St, Boston, MA 02110.

SNOWDEN, RAYMOND C.
General agent. **PERSONAL:** Born Aug 05, 1937, McNary, AZ; son of Clarence Snowden and Loretta Hockett Banks; married Bettye; children: Joni, Brian, Eric, Angie. **EDUCATION:** AA Psychology, 1962. **CAREER:** Safeway Stores Inc LA, store mgr 1965-67; Continental Assurance Co, assoc mgr 1969; Transamerica Occidental Life, agent 1971-. **ORGANIZATIONS:** Pres Kiwanis Club SW LA 1976-77; mem Inglewood CA C of C; mem Salvation Army Youth Adv Council 1978; mem Life Underwriters Assn; dir Inglewood C of C 1978-80; pres Crenshaw-Imperial Sect of Inglewood C of C 1978-80; mem citizen adv com Centenila Hosp 1980-86; pres Inglewood C of C 1982-84; pres Imperial-Crenshaw Kiwanis Club 1982-83. **HONORS/ACHIEVEMENTS:** New Agency of Yr Awd Transamerica Occidental Life of CA 1972; first black general agent for Transamerica Occidental Life of CA 1971; featured in issue Sports Illus in Occidental Life's adver June 11, 1974; Kiwanis Intl Awd for Comm Serv 1974; Commendation Inglewood City Council for Comm Serv 1984. **BUSINESS ADDRESS:** Ray Snowden Insurance Agency, 2930 W Imperial Hwy, Ste 324, Inglewood, CA 90303.

SNYDER, EDD G.
Manufacturing executive. **PERSONAL:** Born Jun 01, 1947, Ann Arbor, MI; divorced; children: Aaron. **EDUCATION:** Western MI Univ, BS Comm 1970. **CAREER:** Kalamazoo MI Gazette, reporter 1972-74; Uphohn Co, public relations 1974-77; Ford Motor Co, press relations 1977-84; Ypsi Corp, vice pres 1983-; American Motors Corp, mgr news & info 1984-. **ORGANIZATIONS:** Publicist African-American Museum of Detroit 1981-83; dir Public Relations Soc of Amer Detroit Chap 1983-. **HONORS/ACHIEVEMENTS:** Wall of Distinction Western MI Univ Alumni 1984. **BUSINESS ADDRESS:** Mgr News & Fin Information, American Motors Corp, 27777 Franklin Rd, Southfield, MI 48034.

SNYDER, GEORGE W.
Journalist, writer. **PERSONAL:** Born Dec 06, 1944, New Orleans, LA. **EDUCATION:** MI St U, BA 1966. **CAREER:** San Francisco Chronicle, reporter; KPIX TV, KGO TV, writer, producer, reporter 1970; Yukon Terr British Columbia, licensed prospector 1968-70; The Canadian Press, Toronto, feature editor 1967-68. **ORGANIZATIONS:** Mem San Francisco & Black Media Assn; mem, Sonoma County Fish & Wildlife Advisory Board 1986-; vice pres, Urban Creeks Council Sonoma Chapter 1988-. **HONORS/ACHIEVEMENTS:** Author, "Peyote Moon" 1973; Comm Art Workshop. **HOME ADDRESS:** P O Box 464, Occidental, CA 95465. **BUSINESS ADDRESS:** Writer, San Francisco Chronicle, N Bay Bureau, 50 Old Courthouse Sq # 604, Santa Rosa, CA 95404.

SNYDER, WADELL D.
Personnel administrator, educator. **PERSONAL:** Born Sep 24, 1929, Steubenville, OH; married Myrtle; children: Rinee Sue Jette, Wadell D. **EDUCATION:** Kent StateUniv Kent OH, BS 1956; Kent State U, MEd 1961;Univ of OR-EUGENE, PhD 1973. **CAREER:** Central WA Univ, dir staff personnel 1974-; Lane Council of Govts, dir comm educ 1973-74; Univ of OR, research & asst 1971-73; Tongue Point Job Corps Center Univ of OR, dir 1971; Univ of OR Job Corps Center, dep dir 1969-71. **ORGANIZATIONS:** Chmn Personnel Officers Higher Educ State of WA 1974-80; asso prof Cent WAUniv Ethnic Studies 1977-; consult personnel Affirmation Action Ellensburg Sch Dist 1978-; mem Governons Manpower Com OR 1969-70; mem Kiwanis Club 1970-71; mem educ con March of Dimes 1978-; mem Phi Delta Kappa 1975-. **HONORS/ACHIEVEMENTS:** Received Korean Sector Medal; NDEA Fellowship MI StateUniv 1966; NDEA Felloswhip Ursuline Coll 1967; NFS traineeshipUniv of WA 1970; author Affirmative Action Plans & Progs An Intro 1974; pub Some Effects of Tchr Training on Tchr-student Interaction as Assessed by Flanders Categories 1975. **MILITARY SERVICE:** AUS sgt 1952-54.

SOARIES, RAYNES L., JR.
Administrator. **PERSONAL:** Born Jan 11, 1924, Chattanooga, TN. **EDUCATION:** Sch of Commerce NY U, BS 1972; Grad Sch of Pub Admin NYU, post grad 1973-74. **CAREER:** EEO Gen Motors Acceptance Corp, staff asst 1973-; Gen Motors Corp, analyst-stock 1963-73. **ORGANIZATIONS:** Mem Brooklyn Rotary Club 1974-; 1st vP Brooklyn Br NAACP 1974-; bd mem Brooklyn Br Urban League 1979-; bd mem Bedford Mental Health Clinic 1976-77; exec com mem The Edges Group Inc 1976-; treas Com Planning Bd #9 1978. **HONORS/ACHIEVEMENTS:** Recipient of 5 Battle Stars European Theatre 1944-45; Pub Serv Award Econ Devel Counc of New York City 1974; Black Achievers Award in Ind Harlem Br of YMCA 1974; Roy Wilkins Award Harlem NAACP New York City 1976. **MILITARY SERVICE:** AUS maj. **BUSINESS ADDRESS:** 767 5th Ave, New York, NY 10023.

SOBERS, AUSTIN W.
Association executive, educator. **PERSONAL:** Born Mar 21, 1914, Boston, MA; married Cora. **EDUCATION:** Howard Univ, BS 1940; Columbia Univ, MA 1942; NYU, post grad. **CAREER:** CSDA Bd of Educ NYC, dep exec dir div 1973-; Chancellor, spec asst 1972-73;

Bd of Educ, spec asst to pres 1971-72; Zoning, spec asst 1970-71; Planning & Rsch Div, asst prin 1966-67; Zoning Unit, zoning assoc cntrl 1962-66; Dist 16, comm coord 1954-62; J-35-K, teacher 1946-54. **ORGANIZATIONS:** Mem NY Soc for Exper Study of Educ; mem 100 Black Men; NY Urban League; chmn Brooklyn Adv Bd; Gateway; Amer Legion; mem Kappa Alpha Psi Frat. **MILITARY SERVICE:** AUS lt 1943-46. **BUSINESS ADDRESS:** 110 Livingston St, Brooklyn, NY 11201.

SOBERS, RICKY
Athlete. **PERSONAL:** Born Jan 15, 1953, Bronx, NY. **EDUCATION:** Coll of Southern Idaho; Univ of Las Vegas, 1975. **CAREER:** Chicago Bulls, basketball player 1979-; Indiana Pacers, player 1977-79; Phoenix Suns, player 1975-77; voted MVP Univ of Las Vegas, voted; second NBA career in free throw percentage 882. **BUSINESS ADDRESS:** Chicago Bulls, 333 N Michigan Ave, Chicago, IL 60601.

SOBERS, WAYNETT A., JR.
Automobile dealership owner/operator. **PERSONAL:** Born Feb 15, 1937, Bronx, NY; son of Waynett Sobers and Athlene Ghyll Sobers; married Yvonne C Barrett, Aug 23, 1969; children: Loren, Julian, Stephanie. **EDUCATION:** CCNY, BS 1959; Sobelsohn Sch of Ins, 1965; Baruch Coll, MBA 1972; Gen Motors Dealer Devel Acad 1987-88. **CAREER:** Meteorologist 1963-69; WA Sobers Assoc Inc, pres 1965-69; Johnson Publ Co, advertising rep 1969; Marketing Svc, mgr 1971-73; Advertising & Marketing, vice pres 1973; EGG Dallas Broadcasting Inc, vice pres 1977; BCI Marketing Inc, pres; Earl G Graves Ltd, exec vice pres 1980-87. **ORGANIZATIONS:** Former dir Equitable Variable Life Ins Co; Amer Mgmt Assn; Amer Marketing Assn; City Coll NY Alumni Assn; CCNY Black Alumni Assn; Bernard M Baruch Coll Alumni Assn; pres Chappaqua Ridge Assn 1977. **HONORS/ACHIEVEMENTS:** 100 Black Men; Salesman of the Year-Ebony 1971; Exemplary Serv Award St Luke's Epis Ch 1976; Broadcaster of the Year Natl Assn of Black-Owned Broadcasters 1984. **MILITARY SERVICE:** USNR 1963-66. **BUSINESS ADDRESS:** President, Sobers Chevrolet Inc, 156 N Broad St, PO Box 90, Mooresville, NC 28115.

SOCKWELL, OLIVER R., JR.
Chief executive officer. **PERSONAL:** Born Jul 27, 1943, Washington, DC; son of Oliver Sockwell and Janet Sockwell; married Harriet E; children: Kristine, Brian, Jason. **EDUCATION:** Howard Univ, BS Physics 1965; Columbia Univ, MBA Finance 1972. **CAREER:** Bell System, commun engr 1965-67; IBM, mktg rep 1967-70; Smith Barney & Co, investment banker 1972-74; Sallie Mae Student Loan Mktg Assoc, vice pres mktg 1974-83, sr vice pres operation 1983-84, exec vice pres finance 1984-87; Connie Lee (Coll Construction Loan Insurance Assn), pres and CEO 1987-. **ORGANIZATIONS:** Dir DC Govt Retirement Fund 1981-83; trustee Wilberforce Univ 1982-; dir WA Proj for the Arts 1985-; dir Washington Urban League 1986-; dir Connie Lee Insurance Co 1987-. **BUSINESS ADDRESS:** President & Chief Executive Officer, Connie Lee, 2445 M St NW, Washington, DC 20037.

SODEN, RICHARD ALLAN
Attorney. **PERSONAL:** Born Feb 16, 1945, Brooklyn, NY; son of Hamilton David Soden and Clara Elaine Seale Soden; married Marcia LaMonte Mitchell, Jun 07, 1969; children: Matthew Hamilton, Mark Mitchell. **EDUCATION:** Hamilton Coll, AB 1967; Boston Univ Sch of Law, JD 1970. **CAREER:** Hon Geo Clifton Edwards Jr US Court of Appeals for the 6th Circuit, law clerk 1970-71; Boston Coll Sch of Law, faculty 1973-74; Goodwin Procter & Hoar, assoc 1971-79, partner 1979-. **ORGANIZATIONS:** Mem Amer Natl MA & Boston Bar Assns; mem Cncl of the Boston Bar Assn 1983-; mem MA Black Lawyers Assn; trustee Judge Baker Guidance Ctr 1974-; dir Boston Municipal Rsch Bureau 1977-; pres United South End Settlements 1977-78; adv cncl Suffolk Univ Sch of Mgmt 1980-; faculty MA Continuing Legal Educ 1980-; pres Mass Black Lawyers Assn 1980-81; mem Adv Task Force on Securities Regulation Sec of State of the Commonwealth of MA 1982-; trustee Greater Boston Cncl Boy Scouts of Amer 1983-; mem adv comm on Legal Educ Supreme Judicial Ct of MA 1984-; mem Mass Minority Business Devel Commn; mem bd of visitors Boston Univ Goldman School of Graduate Dentistry. **BUSINESS ADDRESS:** Attorney, Goodwin Procter & Hoar, Exchange Place, Boston, MA 02109.

SOGAH, DOTSEVI Y.
Scientist, manufacturing researcher. **PERSONAL:** Born Apr 19, 1945, Tegbi, Ghana;married Monica Adzo Selormey; children: Senanu, Dodzie, Esinam. **EDUCATION:** Univ of Ghana, Legon Accra Ghana, BSc (First Class) 1970, BSc (Honors) 1971; UCLA Los Angeles CA, MS 1974, PhD 1975. **CAREER:** UC Santa Barbara, postdoctoral 1975-77; UCLA, rsch assoc 1977-80, vstg prof 1978-80; DuPont Co, rsch chemist 1981-83, group leader 1983-84, rsch suprv 1984-. **ORGANIZATIONS:** Mem bd of dir Intl Soc of African Sci 1982-84; chmn comm ACS Delaware Wilmington DE 1984-85; chmn proj comm ISAS 1985-; mem NY Acad of Sci, SigmaXi Rsch Soc; mem Amer Chem Soc; Amer Assn for Advancement of Sci; visit prof Columbia Univ Spring 1984. **HONORS/ACHIEVEMENTS:** AFGRAD Fellowship 1971-75; Commonwealth Fellowship British Commonwealth 1971; Wadel Prize Univ of Ghana Legon 1974; 100 Outstanding/Brightest Scientists in Amer Science Digest 1984; Plenary Lectureships, First and Second Techn Conferences of the ISAS; Seventh Intl Symposium Organosolicon Chem Kyoto, Japan 1984; First Symposium on New Dev in Organic Synthesis ACS 1984; Intl Symposium on Advances in Polymer Synthesis ACS 1984; Specialty Polymers Birmingham UK 1984. **HOME ADDRESS:** 2518 Channin Dr, Wilmington, DE 19810. **BUSINESS ADDRESS:** Research Supervisor, E I duPont de Nemours, Central Research & Development, Experimental Station, Bldg 328, Wilmington, DE 19898.

SOLANO, ROBERTO
Attorney. **PERSONAL:** Born May 02, 1940, Aguadilla, PR; married Donna Mae Young. **EDUCATION:** AZ St U, MA 1974; Univ Baltimore, JD 1963. **CAREER:** Defense Contract Adminstrn Svcs, rep 1966-72; Civil Rights Employment US EEOC, atty; AZ Job Coll, chmn bd Dir 1972-74; Image AZ, chmn bd; Bilingual Bicultural Assn Inc, adv consult 1973-74. **ORGANIZATIONS:** Mem Maricopa AZ chap NAACP; Nat Bar Assn 1972; adv Phoenix Indian Cntr, 1973-74; Nat Seasonal Farmworkers Coalition. **HONORS/ACHIEVEMENTS:** Vp Law School class 1963. **MILITARY SERVICE:** AUS Judge Advocates Office 1963-64.

SOLIUNAS, FRANCINE STEWART
Telecommunications manager. **PERSONAL:** Born Feb 14, 1948, Chicago, IL; daughter of Wilborn Stewart and Juanita Jeanette Harris Stewart (deceased); married Jonas Soliunas, Nov 17, 1973; children: Lukas, Mikah. **EDUCATION:** DePaul Univ, Chicago IL, BS Math, 1970; DePaul Univ Coll of Law, Chicago IL, JD, 1973. **CAREER:** State Appellate Defender, Chicago IL, staff attorney, 1974-76; Equal Employment Opportunity Commn, Chicago IL, supervising attorney, 1976-80; Illinois Bell Telephone Co, Chicago IL, sr attorney, 1980-88, sr dir labor relations, 1988-. **ORGANIZATIONS:** Mem, Cook County Bar Assn, 1972-, Iowa State Bar Assn, 1974-86, Sickle Cell Anemia Volunteer Enterprise, 1980-, Natl Bar Assn, 1982-; trustee, St Thomas Theological Seminary, 1985-88; vice pres, Sickle Cell Anemia Volunteer Enterprise, 1985-87; dir, DePaul Univ President's Club, 1986-; mem, Chicago Bar Assn Judicial Evaluation Comm, 1987-; bd of dir, DePaul Univ Coll of Arts & Sciences Advisory Council, 1987-; dir, South Central Community Services, 1988-. **HONORS/ACHIEVEMENTS:** Outstanding Corporate Achiever, YMCA-Chicago Tribune, 1987; Chicago's Up & Coming, Dollars and Sense, 1988; Distinguished Alumni, DePaul Univ, 1988; Black Rose Award, League of Black Women, 1988. **BUSINESS ADDRESS:** Senior Director-Labor Relations, Illinois Bell Telephone Company, 225 W Randolph, Floor 18B, Chicago, IL 60614.

SOLOMON, BARBARA J.
Educator. **PERSONAL:** Born Sep 10, 1934, Houston, TX; daughter of Willie Bryant and Malinda Edmond Bryant Stinson; married Donald; children: Hugo, Edmund, Jeffrey, Marcia. **EDUCATION:** Howard U, BS 1954; Sch of Social Welfare Univ of CA, MSW 1956; Univ of So CA, DSW 1966. **CAREER:** USC, prof 1966-; Univ of CA Los Angeles Sch of Social Welfare, field instr 1962-63; Univ of TX Sch of Social Work, field instr 1958-60; VA Hospitals Houston & Los Angeles, clinical social worker 1957-63; Alameda Co Medical Institution, clinical social worker 1956-57; vice provost for Graduate and Professional Studies and Dean of the Graduate School 1987-; professor School of Social Work. **ORGANIZATIONS:** Mem, Natl Assn of Social Workers; Council on Social Work Education; Council of Graduate Schools; Amer Assn of Higher Educ; mem, bd of dir Greater LA Partnership for the Homeless; Sickle Cell Foundation; CA Pediatric Center; United Way of LA; mem, Alpha Kappa Alpha; Links Inc. **HONORS/ACHIEVEMENTS:** Author "Black Empowerment social work in oppressed comms" NY Columbia Univ press 1976. **HOME ADDRESS:** 5987 Wrightcrest Drive, Culver City, CA 90232. **BUSINESS ADDRESS:** Univ of Southern California, Administration Building, Room 303, Los Angeles, CA 90089-4015.

SOLOMON, DENZIL KENNETH
Health services president. **PERSONAL:** Born May 05, 1952, Tucson, AZ; married Kathryn Jo; children: Christopher D, Alyxzander R. **EDUCATION:** AZ State Univ, attended 1971-75. **CAREER:** Non Invasive Diagnostic Lab Inc, chief technologist 1977-78; Good Samaritan Hosp, chief tech/cardiac ultrasound lab 1978-79; Cardiovascular Dynamics Inc, vice pres 1978-79; Advanced Diagnostic Tech, pres cardiovascular rsch & develop 1978-; Skylab Aviation Svcs, pres 1984-86; Hemodynamics, owner 1981-; Solomon Tech Corp, pres 1985-. **ORGANIZATIONS:** Designed and built prototype of all-electronic digital dashboard for automobiles 1975-79; art work currently displayed Reading Ctr AZ State Univ 1975-86; program bd mem Amer Heart Assoc 1986; mem Natl Soc for Cardiopulmonary Tech, Amer Inst of Ultrasound in Medicine, Amer Soc of Echocardiography, Amer Soc of Ultrasound Tech Specialists, AZ Soc for Cardiopulmonary Tech, Soc of Non-Invasive Vascular Tech, Natl Geographic Soc, Scottsdale Ctr for the Arts, Amer Registry for Diagnostic Medical Sonographers; registered diagnostic medical sonographer, cardiovascular tech, emergency medical tech. **HONORS/ACHIEVEMENTS:** Hemodynamics awarded Service Co of the Year US Dept of Commerce 1985; cert of copyright registration Abacus Ultrasound Computer Program 1985, Abacus Ultrasound Computer Program Rev I 1985, Abacus Ultrasound Computer Users Guide 1985; illustrated textbook "Tactics and Techniques"; Solomon Tech Corp awarded ServiceCompany of the Year Dept of Commerce 1986; keynote speaker at AZ Council of Black Engineers and Scientists 1986, Minority Business Enterprise Development Program Conf 1986; 6 papers submitted for publication; 4 newspaper articles published. **BUSINESS ADDRESS:** President, Hemodynamics/Solomon Tech, 2405 E Southern Ave No 10, Tempe, AZ 85282.

SOLOMON, DONALD L.
Business executive. **PERSONAL:** Born Feb 13, 1932, Birmingham, AL; married Clarice; children: Donald Jr, Walter Lynn, Gerald. **EDUCATION:** Miles Coll, BA; Life Ins Mgmt Course for Staff Mgrs, grad; LUTC, cert; OH State U, Savannah State Coll, US Armed Forces Inst,Univ of CA. **CAREER:** Booker T Washington Ins Co, promoted vP agency dir 1960. **ORGANIZATIONS:** Mem Indus Devel Bd Dirs Birmingham; mem Omega Psi Phi Frat; mem Triune Lodge #430 FAM Mngr of Yr 3 yrs Nat Ins Assn. **HONORS/ACHIEVEMENTS:** Blount Award Nat Ins Assn 1972-73; Merit Award Booker T Washington Ins Co. **MILITARY SERVICE:** Served military ssgt discharged 1958. **BUSINESS ADDRESS:** PO Box 697, Birmingham, AL 35201.

SOLOMON, EDDIE, JR. (BUDDY JAY-KING)
Professional athlete. **PERSONAL:** Born Feb 09, 1951, Perry, GA; married Gloria Moore. **CAREER:** Pittsburgh Pirates, professional baseball pitcher; Los Angeles Dodgers, professional baseball pitcher; Chicago Cubs, professional baseball pitcher; St Louis Cardinals, professional baseball pitcher; Tulsa Oilers, professional baseball pitcher; New Orleans Pelicans, professional baseball pitcher. **HONORS/ACHIEVEMENTS:** Dearie mulvey award Los Angeles Dodgers 1973; outstndg rookie Spring Training; al star team Dodgers 1971; all star team Dodgers Class AAA 1974.

SOLOMON, FREDDIE
Athlete. **PERSONAL:** Born Jan 11, 1953, Sumter, SC; married Delilah. **EDUCATION:** Attended Tampa. **CAREER:** Miami Dolphins, football player 1975-77; San Francisco 49ers, prof football player. **BUSINESS ADDRESS:** San Francisco 49ers, 711 Nevada St, Redwood City, CA 94061.

SOLOMON, JAMES DANIEL
Physician. **PERSONAL:** Born Jun 03, 1913, Georgia; son of Stephen Solomon and Amanda Solomon; married Effie O'Neal; children: Elaine E Comegys. **EDUCATION:** Cntrl YMCA Coll, Chgo, BS 1941; DePaul U, Chgo, MS 1943; Meharry Med Coll Nashvl, MD 1953; Univ of IL Chgo, PhD 1953. **CAREER:** Univ of IL, rsrch asst 1939-42; St Elizabeth Hosp (HEW), chf Cl Path 1954-58, dir labs 1958-83; Private Pract, physician. **ORGANI-**

ZATIONS: Pres St Elizabeth Hosp Med Soc 1977; mem Am Med Asso, Natl Med Asso 1985; mem New York Acad Sci 1985. **HONORS/ACHIEVEMENTS:** Soc of Sigma Xi 1946; Fellow Nutrition Foundation Univ of IL 1947-49; Superior Serv Awd Dept HEW, Wash, DC 1960; Outstanding Per Awd Dept of HEW,Washington, DC 1961. **MILITARY SERVICE:** USAF 1st lt 4 yrs. **HOME ADDRESS:** 1919 Ruxton Ave, Baltimore, MD 21216.

SOLOMON, WILBERT F.
Government official. **PERSONAL:** Born Dec 17, 1942, Littleton, NC; married Litisia R Smith; children: Roderic, Natalie, Jerold. **EDUCATION:** Clark Coll, BA 1965. **CAREER:** senior vice pres, Aurora Assn, Inc. 1983-87; director, Older Worker Programs U.S. Dept. of Labor 1987-; Job Corps US Dept of Labor, dep dir 1978-, ofc of youth prgms 1978; US Dept of Labor Chicago, dep regnl dir 1974-78; Job Corps US Dept of Labor Atlanta, GA, proj mgr 1968-74; Job Corps City of Atlanta, dir 1968; Econ Opportunity ATL Inc, apprentice couns 1965-67. **ORGANIZATIONS:** Mem Omega Psi Phi Frat 1963; Sunday sch supt Ch of Our Lord Jesus Christ 1974-80; pres International Congress, Church of our Lord Jesus Christ 1981-. **HONORS/ACHIEVEMENTS:** Recip Performance Awards, US Dept of Labor 1972, 77, 79. **BUSINESS ADDRESS:** US Dept of Labor, 200 Constitution Avenue N.W. - N -4643, Washington, DC 20010.

SOMERSET, LEO L., JR.
Mortgage executive. **PERSONAL:** Born Aug 27, 1945, Memphis, TN. **EDUCATION:** Memphis State Univ, BBA 1968; Indiana Univ, MBA 1973. **CAREER:** Citicorp Real Estate Inc & Citibank NA, vice pres 1973-83; Colwell Financial Corp, vice pres 1983-. **HONORS/ACHIEVEMENTS:** Noyes Fellow Consortium for Grad Study in Mgmt Indiana Univ 1971. **MILITARY SERVICE:** USAF 1st lt 3 yrs; Honorable Discharge. **BUSINESS ADDRESS:** Vice President, Colwell Financial Corp, 3223 West 6th St, Los Angeles, CA 90020.

SOMERVILLE, ADDISON WIMBS
Educator/psychologist. **PERSONAL:** Born Aug 06, 1927, Greensboro, AL; son of Ernest Somerville and Ellen Wimbs Somerville; married Carolyn Coffey; children: Laurene, Ernest, Christopher. **EDUCATION:** Howard Univ, BS Psych 1948, MS Psych 1950; IL Inst Tech, PhD Psych 1963. **CAREER:** Crownsvl State Hosp MD, cl psych intrn 1950; Tech Vly Frg Army Hosp PA, chf cl psych 1950-52; W Charlotte H Sch NC, gdnc dir 1953-54; Elgin State Hosp Elgin, IL, stf psychlgst 1954; IIT Inst for Psych Ser, cl & cnslng psych 1954-58; Dept of Pupil Aprsl Wash, DC, sch psych 1958-59; Francis W Parker Sch Chgo, chf sch psych 1959-64; Govt of Virgin Isls St Thomas, US Virgin, Isld, asst dir of plng for mntl hlth 1964-65; CA State Univ, Sacto, prof psych 1965-. **ORGANIZATIONS:** Cnsltnt Dept of Human Rsrcs & Dev 1966-71; training dir Dlnqncy Prvntn Unit Proj Sacto Police Dept 1971-72; instr/cnsltnt CA State Prsnl Bd 1972-80;instr CA Hwy Patrol 1966-79; prvt prct Somerville & Somerville Asso 1975-; pres Suicide Prvntn Serv 1971-72; bd dir Suicide Prvntn Serv 1968-75; pres/bd dir CA State Psych Asso; Sac Vly Chptr 1979-84; mem Wstrn Rgnl Bd Am Bd of Prof Psych 1981-. **HONORS/ACHIEVEMENTS:** Excptnl Merit Serv Awrd CA State Univ 1984; diplomate Am Bd of Professional Psych, Inc 1971; Apprvd Flw in Sex Educ in Intl Cncl of Sex Educ & Parenthd(FIC), Am Univ 1981; Cert Sex Thrpst & Sex Educ, Am Asso of Sex Edctrs, Cnslrs & Thrpst 1977-; over 20 articles pblshd in professional jrnls; Fellow and Diplomate American Brd of Medical Psychotherapists 1988; Diplomate American Board of Sexology 1989; Exceptional Merit Service Award for Outstanding Teaching and Service to the Community, California State Univ 1988. **MILITARY SERVICE:** AUS sgt 1950-52. **HOME ADDRESS:** 61 Grand Rio Cir, Sacramento, CA 95826. **BUSINESS ADDRESS:** Professor of Psychology, CA StateUniv, 6000 Jay St, Sacramento, CA 95819-2694.

SOMERVILLE, DORA B.
Retired administrator. **PERSONAL:** Born Nov 29, 1920, Greensboro, AL; daughter of Ernest Somerville (deceased) and Ellen Wimbs Somerville (deceased). **EDUCATION:** Ursuline Coll, BS Educ 1939; Catholic Univ of Amer, MA Child Study 1942; Loyola Univ, MA Social Work 1948. **CAREER:** IL Dept of Corrections, former correctional progs exec 1971-74; IL Dept of Corrections, statewide field placement & internship coord 1974-78; Municipal Court Psychiatric Institute, Chicago IL, dir of social services 1953-62; Illinois Youth Commission, Chicago IL, commissioner 1962-69. **ORGANIZATIONS:** First woman mem of IL Parole & Pardon bd; co-author "The Delinquent Girl" 1970, revised 1975; written papers for numerous prof journals; mem Amer Correctional Assn, Natl Assn of Social Workers, Women's Bd Loyola Univ of Chicago; mem Amer Fed of State Co & Municipal Retirees; mem Alpha Kappa Alpha Sor former mem bd of trustees Loyola Univ of Chicago; former mem Natl Council on Crime & Delinquency; tech consult White House Conf on Children & Youth 1970-; mem bd of dirs Halfway House Comm Inc; mem Alpha Gamma Pi Sor, Chicago Urban League, NAACP, Amer Assoc of Retired Persons, IL State Employees Assoc, Chicago Women's Golf Club, IL Acad of Criminology; dir, Sheil Guidance Clinic, Catholic Youth Organization 1946-50; program coordinator, Illinois State Training School for Girls 1950-53; mem, John Howard Assn. **HONORS/ACHIEVEMENTS:** Citation of Merit Ursuline Coll & Loyola Univ; Honor Roll Citation by Alpha Kappa Alpha Sor; Order of the Eastern Star Eureka Grand Chapter; Citation of Merit by radio station WAIT; A Special Award, Illinois Academy of Criminology 1988.

SOMERVILLE, ROBERT ALSTON
Physician. **PERSONAL:** Born Jan 11, 1920, Warren Co, NC; son of Solomon and Mary; married Jacqueline; children: Ronald, Gregory, Jeffrey, Robert Jr. **EDUCATION:** Lincoln Univ, AB 1946; Howard Univ, MD 1951. **CAREER:** physician, family practice, 1957; Queens Clinical Soc, general practice; Harlem Hosp, intern, 1951-52; Laguardia Hosp, Assoc attending physician, 1969-; LaGuardia Medical Group, medical coordinator 1980-. **ORGANIZATIONS:** AMA; mem, Comus Social Club Inc (frat org); NMA; Am Geriatrics Soc; bd mem, Chi Delta Mu Med Soc; Phi Beta Sigma Frat; NAACP; charter mem, Paedergaat Yacht Squadron; Societe De Medecine De Paris. **HONORS/ACHIEVEMENTS:** Published Anthology of Black Pioneers-children's Books. **MILITARY SERVICE:** AUS mc 1943-46; res corp 1942-43. **BUSINESS ADDRESS:** 112 18 Springfield Blvd, Queens Village, NY 11429.

SOMMERVILLE, JOSEPH C.
Educator. **PERSONAL:** Born Dec 28, 1926, Birmingham, AL; married Mattie Cunningham; children: Joseph, Jr, Barry C. **EDUCATION:** Morehouse Coll, BS 1949;Univ of MI, MS 1956, EdS, PhD. **CAREER:** Univ of Toledo, prof of educ, prof, dir of adminstrv internship 1970-75; Wayne Co Intermediate School Dist, The Assist Center, staff development specialist 1968-70; Woodson School Inkster, MI, prin 1965-68, teacher, prin 1949-65. **ORGANIZATIONS:** Mem OH Assn of Elem Sch Principals; Assn for Sch Curriculum Development; Phi Kappa Phi; Am Educ Research Assn; exec bd Nat Urban Educ Assn; pres bd trustees Toledo-Lucas Co Library; Westmoreland Assn; Phi Delta Kappa; Model Comm Sch Com; scholarship com chmn Omega Psi Phi. **HONORS/ACHIEVEMENTS:** Citation of Outstanding Serv to Wayne Co; speaker many natl & local professional confs; author several articles in natl & state journals & books publ by U. **MILITARY SERVICE:** AUS s/sgt 1945-46. **BUSINESS ADDRESS:** Dept of Adminstrn & Supervisio, Coll of Educ Univ of Toledo, Toledo, OH 43606.

SOREY, REVIE, JR.
Professional athlete. **PERSONAL:** Born Sep 10, 1953, Brooklyn, NY. **EDUCATION:** Univ of IL. **CAREER:** Chicago Bears, professional football guard 1975-. **HONORS/ACHIEVEMENTS:** Selected to play Sr Bowl & Blue-Gray & Am Bowl; All-Big Ten Pick; named to 2nd Team All NFC Squad, UPI 1979. **BUSINESS ADDRESS:** Chicago Bears, PO Box 204, Lake Forest, IL 60045.

SOSA, CATHERINE A. E.
Advertising executive. **PERSONAL:** Born Jan 14, 1956; married Fred Sosa. **EDUCATION:** State Univ of NY, BS 1977. **CAREER:** Earl G Graves Ltd, rschr 1978-81; Media Networks Inc, sr rschr 1981; Wells, Rich, Green, media planner 1982-83; Reiser, Williams, DeYong, media dir. **ORGANIZATIONS:** Mem, Nat'l Assn of Female Executives, American Management Assn, BPAA.

SOUTH, WESLEY W.
Newspaper editor. **PERSONAL:** Born Mar 23, 1919, Muskogee, OK; married Mildred. **EDUCATION:** Northwestern U, PhB. **CAREER:** Radio Sta WVON, 1961-; Chicago Courier, ed 1964-68; NOW Mag, pub, ed 1961-62; Chicago Am, columnist 1957-61; Ebony Mag, asso ed 1951-57; Chicago Defender, 1950-51. **ORGANIZATIONS:** Bd mem NAACP 1964-68; Chicago Urban League 1967-71; co-fdr People United to Save Humanity, PUSH, 1971-76; bd mem, v chmn PUSH; bd mem Afro-Am Patrolmen's League 1975-. **MILITARY SERVICE:** AUS corpl 1943-45.

SOUTHALL, CHARLES
Elected official. **PERSONAL:** Born May 10, 1937, Marion, AR; married Claudette; children: Cheryl, Charlotte, Mark. **EDUCATION:** Univ of Cincinnati, 1958-61. **ORGANIZATIONS:** Pres of bd of trustees Lincoln Heights Health Ctr 1980-85. **HOME ADDRESS:** 1440 Chicago Ave, Lincoln Heights, OH 45215. **BUSINESS ADDRESS:** Mayor, City of Lincoln Heights, 1201 Steffen St, Lincoln Heights, OH 45215.

SOUTHALL, GENEVA H.
Handy, educator. **PERSONAL:** Born Dec 05, 1925, New Orleans, LA; divorced. **EDUCATION:** Dillard U, BA 1945; Natl Guild Pianist, Artist Dipl 1954; Am Conserv of Mus, MusM 1956;Univ of IA, PhD 1966. **CAREER:** Univ of MN, prof Afro-amer Music Culture in New World 1970-; Grambling Coll, prof 1966-70; SC St Coll, asso prof 1962-64; Knoxville Coll, asst music prof 1959-61; US Info Serv, chamber pianist 1955. **ORGANIZATIONS:** Mem Am Stud Fac AssemUniv of MN; mem Womens Stud AssemUniv of MN; mem Field Res Activ, Haiti & Jamaica; grad fac Mus DeptUniv of MN; mem AfricanStudies CouncUniv of MN; memUniv Sen; music ed HowardUniv Press; mem bd dir Urban League; mem NAACP; bd of dir Urban Coalition of Mpls; life mem, bd dir Assn for the Study of Afro-Amer Life & Hist; Met Cultural Arts Ctr; mem adm bd Park Ave Unit Meth Ch; mem bd of dir Natl Women HelpingOffenders; mem Soc for Ethnomusicology; mem Am Musicol Soc; Crusade Scholar, Meth Ch 1961-62; mem Pi Kappa Lamda, Natl Hon Mus Soc. **HONORS/ACHIEVEMENTS:** Listed in Who's Who in Am 39th Edn; World's Who's Who of Women; Who's Who in Music & Musicians Dir; Who's Who of Am Women; Internatl Who's Who of Intell Outstanding Educators of Am 1973; Personalities of the S 1970-71; World's Who's Who of Music 1974; publ in Reflections in Afro-am Music, Black Perspectives in Music. **BUSINESS ADDRESS:** University of Minnesota, Dept of Afro American Music, Rm 827 Social Science, Minneapolis, MN 55455.

SOUTHALL, HERBERT HOWARDTON, SR.
Retired insurance executive. **PERSONAL:** Born Mar 07, 1907, Richmond, VA; son of Russell Southall and Evelyn M Sledd; married Louise P Southall, Jun 12, 1929; children: Louise Y Forrest; Herbert H Southall Jr. **EDUCATION:** VA State Univ, part 1 CLU 1951; TN A&I Univ, Cert 1951; Brookings Inst of Wash, DC & the Univ of Richmond, Cert 1964; Continuation Oas related to Richmond, Cert 1965. **CAREER:** So Aid Life Ins Co, Inc, stenographer 1925, asst to sec 1926; Natl Ins Asso, sec 1960; So Aid Life Ins Co, Inc, worked in all positions until pres 1964; Natl Ins Assn, 1st v pres 1965, pres 1966, chmn of bd 1967-68; Retired, 1974; Retired Sr Vlntr Pgm, dir 1974-77. **ORGANIZATIONS:** Former mem bd dir Greater Richmond Fndtn; former mem adv bd Cntrl VA Hlth Sys Agncy; adv bd Richmond Chptr #12, Serv Corp of Ret Exec; bd Richmond Chamberlayne Chptr #390 AARP; mem Kiwanis Club of Richmond 1972; frmr pres Astoria Beneficial Clb 1960; Oriental Beneficial Clb prior 1960; Phi Beta Sigma Frat 1960; Mason 320 1960. **HONORS/ACHIEVEMENTS:** Astorian of Year Astoria Beneficial Club 1965; Order of Merit Boy Scouts of Am 1966; Silver Beaver Boy Scouts of Am 1967; Outstndng Ldrshp 7-Up Co 1967; Outstndng Achvmnt in Field of Business James E Grant Award 1967; Distingushed Serv Award Natl Ins Assn 1970. **HOME ADDRESS:** 2723 Fendall Ave, Richmond, VA 23222.

SOUTHERLAND, ELLEASE
Professor, writer. **PERSONAL:** Born Jun 18, 1943, Brooklyn, NY; daughter of Monroe Penrose Southerland and Ellease Dozier Southerland. **EDUCATION:** Queens College of the City University of New York, BA, 1965; Columbia University, MFA, 1974. **CAREER:** Department of Social Services, New York City, caseworker, 1966-72; Columbia University, New York City, instructor in English, 1973-76; Borough of Manhattan Community College of the City Univ of New York, adjunct asst prof of black literature, 1973-; Pace University, New York City, poet in residence in African literature, 1975-; writer. **HONORS/ACHIEVEMENTS:** John Golden Award for Fiction, Queens College of the City University of New York, 1964; Gwendolyn Brooks Poetry Award, Black World, 1972; author of novella White Shadows, 1964, author of poetry collection The Magic Sun Spins, Paul Breman, 1975, author of autobiographical novel Let the Lion Eat Straw, Scribner, 1979; contributor of stories, essays, and poems to anthologies and periodicals. **HOME ADDRESS:** 160-27 119th

Dr, Jamaica, NY 11434. **BUSINESS ADDRESS:** Professor, Department of English, Pace University, 1 Pace Plaza, New York, NY 10038. *

SOUTHERN, CHARLES O.
Business executive. **PERSONAL:** Born Feb 24, 1920, Cincinnati, OH; married Ingerborg Moltke; children: Cheryle D, Charles O Jr. **EDUCATION:** Univ of Cincinnati, BSc 1948, Cert of Real Est 1959. **CAREER:** Wright Aeronautcl Corp Cincinnati, OH, mtrls hndlr 1941-42; US Army Air Corps, comm ofcr 1942-46; Univ of Cincinnati, 1946-48; Self-emplyd, elec eng 1948-56; Gen Elec Co Cincinnati, OH, aero eng 1956-82; Cincinnati Metro Hsng Auth, vice chmn bd of dir. **ORGANIZATIONS:** Mem Inst of Radio Eng 1943-48; mem Am Inst of Aeronautics & Astronautics 1966-76; bd mem Lincoln Hts Nghbrhd Serv 1970-76; bd mem Avondale Comm Cncl 1970-83; bd mem Cincinnati Metro Hsng Auth 1982-85. **HONORS/ACHIEVEMENTS:** Cert of Achvmnt Outstndng Comm Serv from Gen Electrc Co 1970. **MILITARY SERVICE:** AUS Air Corps cptn 1942-46. **HOME ADDRESS:** 6865 Cooper Rd, Montgomery, OH 45242.

SOUTHERN, EILEEN JACKSON
Educator. **PERSONAL:** Born Feb 19, 1920, Minneapolis, MN; married Joseph Southern; children: April Southern Reilly, Edward Joseph Southern. **EDUCATION:** Univ of Chicago, BA 1940, MA 1941; New York Univ, PhD 1961. **CAREER:** Prairie View State Coll, lecturer, 1941-42; Southern Univ, asst prof 1943-45, 1949-51; Alcorn Coll, asst prof 1945-46; Claflin Univ, asst prof 1947-49; City Univ of New York, asst full prof 1960-75; Harvard Univ, full prof 1975-87, prof emeritus. **ORGANIZATIONS:** Concert pianist Touring in USA, Haiti 1942-54; co-founder/editor, The Black Perspective in Music scholarly journal 1973-; mem, Assn for Study of Afro-Amer Life & History; mem, Alpha Kappa Alpha; bd, New York City YWCA, 1950; leader, Girl Scouts of Amer, 1950-1960. **HONORS/ACHIEVEMENTS:** Alumni Achievement Award, Univ of Chicago 1971; "Readings in Black American Music" WW Norton 1971, revised 1983; Achievement Award, Natl Assn Negro Musicians 1971; Citation Voice of Amer, 1971; Deems Taylor Awrd ASCAP 1973; Bd of Dir, Amer Musicological Soc, 1974-76; Honorary MA, Harvard Univ 1976; Honorary Phi Beta Kappa Radcliffe/Harvard Chapter 1982; The Buxheim Organ Book (Brooklyn, NY) 1963; The Music of Black Amer (New York) 1971, 2nd Ed 1983; "Anonymous Pieces in the Ms El Escorial IVa24" Hanssler-Verlag 1981; author, Biographical Dictionary of Afro-Amer & African Musicians (Westport) 1982; author of articles in The New Grove Dictionary of Music and Musicians (Macmillan) 1980 and The New Grove Dictionary of American Music (Macmillan) 1986; bd of dirs Sonneck Soc of Amer Music 1986-88. **BUSINESS ADDRESS:** Prof Music & Afro-Amer Studies, HarvardUniv, Cambridge, MA 02138.

SOUTHERN, HERBERT B.
Architect. **PERSONAL:** Born May 21, 1926, Washington, DC; married Mary Ann. **EDUCATION:** Howard U, BS Arch 1950; Catholic U, additional graduate architecture study. **CAREER:** Arch, private practice 1954-; Newark, NJ, draftsman 1951-53. **ORGANIZATIONS:** Mem Am Inst of Arch; NJ Soc of Arch; bd dir Harmonia Savings Bank; past pres Flying Arch Assn of Am 1970-71; past mem Rahway Planning Bd; mem NAACP, Urban League & other orgns. **HONORS/ACHIEVEMENTS:** Cit for archit design of Rahway Pub Library 1967. **MILITARY SERVICE:** AUS sgt 1943-46.

SOUTHERN, JOSEPH
Professor Emeritus. **PERSONAL:** Born Nov 21, 1919, Indianapolis, IN; married Eileen; children: April Southern Reilly, Edward Joseph. **EDUCATION:** Lincoln Univ, BS 1941; Univ of Chgo, MBA 1945. **CAREER:** Prairie View State Coll, asst rgstr 1941-42; Southern Univ, asst prof 1944-45; Alcorn Coll, bsns mgr 1945-46; Claflin Univ, bsns mgr 194 6-49; KY State Coll, prof 1950-53; Cmnty Fin Corp, NY, mgr/vice pres 1953-57; New York Pub Sch, tchr 1957-71; City Univ NY (LaGuardia Coll), prof 1971-85. **ORGANIZATIONS:** Co-fndr & pres Fndtn for Rsrch in Afro-Am Creative Arts, Inc 1971-; co-fndr & mgn edtr The Black Perspective in Music 1973-; Asso for Stdy of Afro-Am Life & Hist; Kappa Alpha Psi; life mem NAACP; scout ldr Boy Scouts of Am. **HONORS/ACHIEVEMENTS:** Awrd Boy Scouts of Am 1960. **BUSINESS ADDRESS:** Business Accounting, CityUniv of New York, P O Drawer I, 31 10 Thomson Ave, Cambria Heights, NY 11411.

SOWELL, MYZELL
Attorney. **PERSONAL:** Born Nov 16, 1924, Detroit, MI; married Robin Hamilton. **EDUCATION:** Wayne State Univ, BBA 1953; Detroit Coll, LlB 1952. **CAREER:** Gen law practice, specialist in criminal law 1953-67; Legal Aid and Defender Assn of Detroit, Defender Office, chief defender 1968-. **ORGANIZATIONS:** Mem Detroit Bar Assn; mem State Bar of Michigan; mem Wolverine Bar Assn; mem Natl Bar Assn; mem Amer Bar Assn; mem Natl Lawyers Guild; pres Michigan Assn of Criminal Defense Attys; mem Natl Legal Aid and Defender Assn; referee Civil Rights Comm; mem bd dir Homes for Black Children; life mem NAACP; mem bd dir Urban Alliance; mem Mayor's Comm on Civil Disturbance; mem Booker T Washington Businessmen's Assn; mem by-laws comm, Detroit-Wayne County Criminal Justice System Coord Co; mem Judiciary and Correc Comm, New Detroit Inc; mem Michigan Comm on Law Enforcement and Criminal Justice Task Force on Adjudication; mem adv comm Min Program, Comm of Visitors of Law School, Wayne State Univ Law School; mem bd dirs Wayne State Fund, Wayne State Univ; mem Wayne County Jail Adv Comm; lecturer ICLE; lecturer Prosecuting Attys Assn of Michigan; lecturer Natl Def Coll; lecturer Northwestern Univ Law School, Criminal Law; lecturer Yale Univ Law School; lecturer Natl Dist Atty's Coll; mem Bd Regents, Natl Coll of Criminal Defense Lawyers and Public Defenders. **MILITARY SERVICE:** AUS sgt 1943-45. **BUSINESS ADDRESS:** 462 Gratiot, Detroit, MI 48226.

SOWELL, THOMAS
Educator. **PERSONAL:** Born Jun 30, 1930, Gastonia, NC; married Alma Jean Parr; children: two. **EDUCATION:** Harvard Univ, Cambridge MA, AB, 1958; Columbia Univ, New York NY, AM, 1959; Univ of Chicago, IL, PhD, 1968. **CAREER:** US Dept Labor, economist 1961-62; Rutgers U, instr 1962-63; Howard U, lectr 1963-64; Am Tel & Telegraph Co, econ analyst 1964-65; Cornell Univ, asst prof, 1965-69; Brandeis U, assoc prof, 1969-70; UCLA, assoc prof, 1970-74, prof of econ, 1974-80; Urban Inst, Washington DC, project dir, 1972-74. **ORGANIZATIONS:** Consultant, Urban Coalition, Rockefeller Found, Urban Inst. **HONORS/ACHIEVEMENTS:** Author numerous works in field, incl Civil Rights: Rhetoric of Reality?, Morrow, 1985, Education: Assumptions versus History, Hoover Inst, 1986, Compassion versus Guilt, and Other Essays, Morrow, 1987, A Conflict of Visions: Ideological Origins of Political Struggles, Morrow, 1987; contr to numerous periodicals. **MILITARY SERVICE:** US Marine Corps, 1951-53. **BUSINESS ADDRESS:** Hoover Institution, Stanford, CA 94305. *

SPAIGHTS, ERNEST
Educator. **PERSONAL:** Born Sep 04, 1935, St Petersburg, FL; son of Marsellous Spaights and Sara Spaights; divorced; children: Ernest Van Spaights,II. **EDUCATION:** Central State Univ, BS 1960; OH State Univ, MA 1962, PhD 1965. **CAREER:** Columbus Public Schs, teacher counselor 1960-63; OH State Univ, coord asst prof 1963-65; Univ of WI, asso prof dir 1965-58, asst to chancellor 1968-72, asst chancellor assoc prof 1970-71, asst chancellor prof 1971-79; Leon H Sullivan prof social welfare & educ psychology 1979-. **ORGANIZATIONS:** Mem Amer Personnel & Guidance Assn 1962, Amer Educ Rsch Assn 1962, Amer Assn Univ Profs 1964, Integrated Educ Soc 1964, WI Counselor Educ Assn 1965, Amer Psychol Assn 1965, WI Psychol Assn 1965, NY Acad of Sci 1969; health & welfare comm Milwaukee Urban League 1969-71; mem Oppor Industrial Ctr 1969-71, WI Heart Assn 1971-, Milwaukee Advertising Council 1972-, WI Hosp 1972-, Family Serv Gr Milwaukee 1972-; mem Phi Delta Kappa, Phi Alpha Theta, Alpha Phi Gamma bd dirs; United Development Co pres 1974-89. **HONORS/ACHIEVEMENTS:** Edward & Rosa Uhrig Awd 1967; Disting Serv Awd WI Chap Natl Conf Christians & Jews 1970; Citation Achievement Grad Sch OH State Univ 1973. **MILITARY SERVICE:** AUS signal corps 1st lt 1954-57. **HOME ADDRESS:** 5275 N Lake Dr, Milwaukee, WI 53217. **BUSINESS ADDRESS:** Professor, Univ of Wisconson-Milwaukee, PO Box 413, Milwaukee, WI 53201.

SPAIN, HIRAM, JR.
Attorney, director. **PERSONAL:** Born Aug 22, 1936, Conway, SC; married Doris; children: Hiram, Nicole. **EDUCATION:** SC State Coll, BS 1961; Howard U, JD 1971. **CAREER:** Columbia Urban League, exec dir 1974-; Office of Gov of SC, proj dir 1972-74; legal intern, Greenville 1971-72; tchr 1961-68. **ORGANIZATIONS:** Nat Assn of Black Soc Workers; Delta Theta Phi Lavy Frat; Delta Psi Omega; consult HEW 1977; NABSW Bus Conf 1975; NAACP; Kappa Alpha Psi; Masons; Columbia Black Lawyers Assn; Notary Pub, SC; Delta Psi Omega; Health Policy Council, Gov John West 1974; Nat Council of Urban League. **HONORS/ACHIEVEMENTS:** Outst Employee Award, NCIC 1971; Who's Who in the SE 1976; Who's Who in Am Colls 1961; Outst Bus Student Award, UBEA 1961; Outst Young Men of Am 1974;Outst Soldier, Bussac, France 1956. **MILITARY SERVICE:** AUS 1954-57. **BUSINESS ADDRESS:** Exec Asst for Self Sufficiency, State Dept of Soc Services, 1520 Confederate Ave, Columbia, SC 29230.

SPAIN, JAMES S.
Business executive. **PERSONAL:** Born Aug 16, 1939, Glen Ridge, NJ. **EDUCATION:** Rutgers U, BA; Fordham U, LLB. **CAREER:** The Assn ofr the Integration of Mgmt Inc, exec dir; Western Electirc Co, mgr; Allied Chemical Corp, mgr. **HONORS/ACHIEVEMENTS:** Num articles on minority grp mgmt devel, publ over the last 15 yrs.

SPANN, NOAH ATTERSON, JR.
Commissioner. **PERSONAL:** Born Oct 13, 1938, E Chicago, IN; married Claudette; children: Dwayne, Darren, Tyrone. **EDUCATION:** IN State Univ. **CAREER:** Mayor's Office E Chgo, admin asst 1975; Bd of Commiss of Lake Cty IN, cty commiss. **ORGANIZATIONS:** Mem E Chicago Young Dem 1956-74, E Chicago Jaycees 1963-73, Frat Order of Masons Twin City Lodge 47 1974-; pres NW IN Reg Planning Comm, IL-IN Bi-State Comm, Tri-City Compr Mental Health, NW IN Sick Cell Found, NAACP; trustee Antioch Bapt Church; pres Five Cty Drainage Bd. **HONORS/ACHIEVEMENTS:** Outstanding Member Serv to Lake Cty Young Dem Ray J Madden Serv Awd; Minority Bus Ste Com for Outstanding Mem; Zion Christian Expo 1976; Awd E Chicago NAACP 1975-76. **MILITARY SERVICE:** USAR 1958. **BUSINESS ADDRESS:** County Commissioner, Bd of Commiss of Lake Cty, 2293 N Main St, Crown Point, IN 46307.

SPANN, THERESA TIEUEL
Educator. **PERSONAL:** Born Apr 21, 1918, Boley, OK; married Samuel Wayne Spann. **EDUCATION:** TX Coll, 1933-36; Langston Univ, BS 1941; OK State Univ, MS 1964. **CAREER:** Boley Public School, spec educ teacher 1974, grade sch principal 1984; Midway Dry Good Co, mgr & owner 1979-85; council member-at-large. **ORGANIZATIONS:** Supt of Sunday School Amos Temple CME Church 1970-84; mem Zeta Phi Beta Sor; sec, music dir Ladies Indust Club 1980-85; dir Christian Ed in the OK CityDist of the Okea-Muskogee Conf of the Christian Methodist Episcopal Church; pianist & organist, sec Amos Temple CME Church 1963-85; chmn ed comm NAACP 1985-86; deputy clerk Boley School Board, 1988. **HONORS/ACHIEVEMENTS:** Woman of the Year McAlester Dist of the CME Church 1968; Amos Temple Woman of the Year 1981; Inducted in Natl Christian Eds Council of Christian Methodist Episcopal Church 1983; del Gen Conf of Christian Methodist Edpiscopal Church 1982; Recognized for serv to ed Lampton Univ Dr Holloway pres 1983. **HOME ADDRESS:** PO Box 266, Boley, OK 74825.

SPARKS, EDWARD FRANKLIN
Dentist. **PERSONAL:** Born Nov 15, 1937, Tucson, AZ; married Vertie Mae; children: Keith James, Robin Hilda. **EDUCATION:** Univ of Arizona, 1959-61; Texas College, BS 1963; Howard Univ, DDS 1967. **CAREER:** Self-employed dentist; US Capitol Police, Washington, 1965-67; Kings Co Med Ctr, Brooklyn, intern oral surg 1967-98; Dr Floyd Thompson, Tucson, assoc dentistry 1968. **ORGANIZATIONS:** Bd dir Tucson Rotary Club 1968-; bd dir Tucson Urban League 1975-; Natl Analgesia Soc 1974-; Mason, Pima Lodge #10 1972-; mem Christ Methodist Episcopal Church Trinity Temple 1952-, treas 1968, trustee 1973-; Kappa Alph Psi 1960-; Texas College Hon Soc 1961-63; Oral Cancer Soc 1963-67; Chi Delta Mu 1965-; Natl Dental Assn; Amer Dental Assn; Southern Arizona Dental Assn 1968-; cert Armed Forces Inst Pathology 1968; pres Beau Brummel 1975-. **BUSINESS ADDRESS:** 368 E Grant Rd, Tucson, AZ 85705.

SPARROW, RORY DARNELL
Professional athlete. **PERSONAL:** Born in Paterson, VA. **EDUCATION:** Villanova Coll, BS Engrg. **CAREER:** N J Nets, bsktbl plyr; Scranton CBA, bksbl plyr; Atlanta Hawks, bskbl plyr; N Y Nicks, bskbl plyr. **ORGANIZATIONS:** Founder Rory D Sparrow Found. **HONORS/ACHIEVEMENTS:** Scored career high 30 points with Atlanta vs Chicago in 1982; all Big-5 First Team; US Basketball Writer's All-Dist Team; Eastern Atl Assoc All-Tour Team. **BUSINESS ADDRESS:** New York Nicks, Madison Sq Garden, 4 Pennsylvania Plaza, New York, NY 10001.

SPARROW, VICTOR HOWARD, III
Attorney. **PERSONAL:** Born Jan 06, 1945, Philadelphia, PA; married Martha Oeleon; children: Victor IV, Christopher. **EDUCATION:** Kenyon Coll, AB 1966; Harvard Law Sch, JD 1969. **CAREER:** The Wickes Corp, Intl Div, atty; Mobil Oil Corp Intl Div, Atty; Textron Inc, 1975-77; US Securities & Exchange Commn, 1975; IBM Corp 1970-74. **ORGANIZATIONS:** Mem White House Flw Assn; NY Bar Assn; PA Bar Assn; RI Bar Assn; md Bar Assn; DC Bar Assn. **HONORS/ACHIEVEMENTS:** Felix Frankfurter Flwsp, Harvard Law Sch 1966-69; White House Flwsp 1969-70; Proctor & Gamble Schlr 1974. **BUSINESS ADDRESS:** The Wickes Corp, 1010 2nd Ave, San Diego, CA 92101.

SPAULDING, AARON LOWERY
Investment banker. **PERSONAL:** Born Mar 16, 1943, Durham, NC. **EDUCATION:** Attended NC Central Univ Durham 1960-64; attended Wharton Grad Sch of Finance & Commerce Univ of PA Philadelphia 1966-68. **CAREER:** Re-Con Serv Inc, dir & co-founder 1968; JFK Center for the Performing Arts, comptroller 1972-74; Boyden Bd of Dirs Servs, exec dir 1974; B&C Assoc Washington, dir bus devel & consult 1974; Exec Office of the Pres The White House, assoc dir pres personnel office 1974-77; Salomon Brothers Inc, vice pres 1977-. **ORGANIZATIONS:** Pres Wharton MBA Assn; rsch asst Dept of Industry & the Placement Office (RE-CON Proj) Univ of PA. **HONORS/ACHIEVEMENTS:** Outstanding Acad Achievement Awd NC Central Univ 1964. **MILITARY SERVICE:** USN supply corps officer & mil social aide 1969-72.

SPAULDING, ASA T.
Retired insurance executive. **PERSONAL:** Born Jul 22, 1902, Columbus County, NC; married Elna B; children: Asa Jr, Aaron Lowery, Patricia A Spaulding Moore, Kenneth B. **EDUCATION:** NY Univ, BS Accounting (Magna Cum Laude) 1930; Univ of MI, MA 1932; Hon LLD's shaw Univ 1958, NC Coll 1960, Univ NC 1967, Duke Univ 1969; Morgan State Coll, Hon D Bus 1961; Andrews Presbyterian Coll, DHL 1972; Howard Univ, LLD 1975. **CAREER:** NC Mutual Life Ins Co, vice pres, actuary & controller 1930-59, president 1959-68 retired; Asa T Spaulding Consulting & Advisory Serv, president. **ORGANIZATIONS:** Dir NC Mutual Life Ins Co, Mechanics & Farmer Bank, Mutual Savs & Loan Assn, WT Grant Co NY; mem Amer Mgmt Assn NY; James F Shepard Mem Found; NAACP Legal Defense & Educ Fund; John Avery Boys Club; trustee Howard Univ, Johnson C Smith Univ, Shaw Univ, Washington Tech Inst; Amer Freedom From Hunger Found; Natl Conf of Christians & Jews; People-to-People Prog; White Rock Baptist Church; mem Visiting Comm Duke Univ Div Sch; bd gov Amer Acad Achievement; NC Tarheel Club; Gov Adv Coun, NC Tech Serv Prog; steering comm Natl Urban Coalition; NC State Parks & Forestry Commn; NC State Constitution Study Commn; Mayor's Human Relations Commn; City Bd Adjustment; Hon Admiral NC Navy; apptd by Pres Johnson to 9-member Bd of Washington Technical Inst. **HONORS/ACHIEVEMENTS:** Presidential Citation for Unselfish Devotion in Helping to Stabilize Our Economy; Frederick Douglass Achievement Awd; City of Philadelphia Tribute by Mayor James H J Tate; Amer Acad Golden Achievement Awd; Natl Urban League's Equal Opportunity Day Awd Key to City of Chattanooga TN; Cert American Ambassador of Good Will; Sesquicentennial Awd, Univ of MI; Durham Chamber of Commerce Honor Awd; Distinguished Citizen's Awd, NC Prince Hall Grand Lodge; listed in The Cyclopedia of Insurance in the US; publications "Negro Insurance in the US," "The Impact of the Changing World on Women's Organizations-Economically," "Discrimination and the Negro in the US," "Moral & Spiritual Values, America's Greatest Need"; North Carolina Business Hall of Fame, Junior Achievement of North Carolina, 1989.

SPAULDING, DANIEL W.
Business executive. **PERSONAL:** Born Oct 24, 1914, Whitesboro, NJ; married Hazel B; children: Donna, William. **EDUCATION:** Lincoln U, AB 1932; MDUniv &Univ of PA, grad studies. **CAREER:** Spaulding Realty Co Inc, owner, pres; NC Nutual Life Ins Co, 15 yrs; Morgan State Coll, tchr 3 yrs. **ORGANIZATIONS:** Pres Nat Assn of Real Estate Brokers Inc 1973-75; former exec vice pres Advance Fed Savs & Loan Assn of Baltimore; former chmn Mortgage Loan Dept, Adv Fed Savs & Loan Assn of Baltimore; bd dir Real Estate Brokers of Baltimore Inc; mortgage loan ofcr NC Mutual Life Ins Co; past bd dir Council for Bus Opportunity; negotiator for Baltimore Comm & Housing Devel Vacant House Prgm; chmn Pub Affairs Com, Nat Assn of Real Estate Brokers Inc; mem Legislative Narello Com of NAREB; vice pres Bus League of Baltimore City; chmn trustee bd Gbrace Presb Ch; chmn bldg com Grace Presb Ch; chmn Housing Com of Baltimore Br, NAACP; bd mem Baltimore Neighborhoods Inc; former bd dir Cit & Planning Housing Adminstr of Baltimore; past treas Urban Leage of Baltimore City; mem Omega Psi Frat; 33 degree Mason. **BUSINESS ADDRESS:** 1613 W North Ave, Baltimore, MD 21217.

SPAULDING, KENNETH BRIDGEFORTH
Attorney. **PERSONAL:** Born Nov 29, 1944, Durham, NC; married Jean Gaillard; children: Chandler, Courtney. **EDUCATION:** Howard U, BA 1967; Univ of NC Sch of Law, JD 1970. **CAREER:** Kenneth B Spaulding Atty at Law, court atty 1970-; Office of the Vice Pres of the US, intern 1968; Office of the US Atty Gen, intern 1967; Office of the NC Atty Gen, intern 1969; Office of the City Mgr Durham, NC, intern 1966. **ORGANIZATIONS:** Mem NC Acad of Trial Lawyers; mem Pi Sigma Alpha Hon Govt Soc Howard U; bd dirs Family Counseling Serv 1974; state rep, NC Gen Assembly; pres 1styear law class,Univ of NC Sch of Law 1968; chief justice of the honor court,Univ of NC Sch of Law 1970. **HONORS/ACHIEVEMENTS:** Outstanding Achvmt in Trial Advocacy, Darror Soc 1971. **BUSINESS ADDRESS:** Spaulding Attorney, 505 S Duke St, Durham, NC 27702.

SPAULDING, LYNETTE VICTORIA
Attorney. **PERSONAL:** Born Dec 21, 1954, Bronx, NY. **EDUCATION:** State Univ of NY Stoney Brook, BA 1976; Syracuse Univ Coll of Law, JD 1979. **CAREER:** Syracuse Univ Law School, sec 1976-79; Bristol Lab, law clerk 1977-79; Legal Aid Soc of Westchester Co, attny 1979-. **ORGANIZATIONS:** Youth dir Divine Light SDA Church 1973-; treas NAACP at Stony Brook 1975-76; comm chairperson Black Amer Law Students Assoc Syracuse 1976-79; justice Judicial Bd Syracuse Univ Coll 1976-79; bd of dir Natl Assoc of Black Women Attnys 1978-; mem Black Lawyers of Westchester Co 1979-, Coll of Law Moot Court Bd 1979; mem NY State Bar. **HONORS/ACHIEVEMENTS:** Spec Recog BALSA & Womens Law Caucus Law Day 1977; Frederick Douglass Moot Court BALSA Natl 1979; Reginald Heber Smith Comm Lawyer Fellowship Prog 1979. **BUSINESS ADDRESS:** Attorney, Legal Aid Soc of Westchester, 1 N Broadway 9th Fl, White Plains, NY 10601.

SPAULDING, WILLIAM RIDLEY
Elected city official. **PERSONAL:** Born in Clarkton, NC; married Dolores Hinton; children: Angelyn Flowers, Michelle, Deirdre. **EDUCATION:** Howard Univ, BS Mech Engrg 1947. **CAREER:** DC Public Schools, instructor 1947-52; Howard Univ, instructor 1950-60; Nat Security Agency, engr 1952-74; Univ District of Columbia, instructor 1980; City Council councilman. **ORGANIZATIONS:** Chair Ft Lincoln Found; bd mem Kidney Found; bd mem Amer Heart Assn; chair Talent Search Inc. **HONORS/ACHIEVEMENTS:** Producer Metro Talent Search 1978-85. **HOME ADDRESS:** 1905 Randolph St NE, Washington, DC 20018. **BUSINESS ADDRESS:** Councilman, City Council, 14th & E Sts NW, Washington, DC 20004.

SPEAR, E. EUGENE
Attorney. **PERSONAL:** Born Apr 18, 1938, Cinn; married Delois Jean; children: Lisa Dawn, Selena Marie. **EDUCATION:** Univ of CT, BA Econ 1960; Univ of CT Sch of Law, grad 1963. **CAREER:** Superior Ct, CT Judicial Dept, asst pub defender; Merchant Melville Spear & Seymour, Bridgeport & Stanford, practiced law 1967-73; Juvenile Ct, Brideport, ct advocate 1968-70. **ORGANIZATIONS:** Past mem bd dir Bridgeport Legal Ser Inc; mem bd dir Bridgeport C of C; Org CT Savings & Loan Assn; mem Bridgeport Bar Assn; Bd of Fire Commrs, Bridgeport; chmn Bapt Hous Site Agy; pres Hall Neighborhood House; Bridgeport Bd of Edn. **HONORS/ACHIEVEMENTS:** Man of Yr , Jr C of C 1968; Outs Young Man of CT, CT Jaycees 1968; Outs Young Man of New England, New England Jaycees 1968. **BUSINESS ADDRESS:** Superior Ct, 1061 Main St, Bridgeport, CT 06604.

SPEARMAN, LARNA KAYE
Engineer. **PERSONAL:** Born May 07, 1945, Kokomo, IN; married Sarah Jewell Busch; children: Angela, Derek. **EDUCATION:** Purdue U, BS 1967; INUniv Law Sch, 1969-71. **CAREER:** Eli Lilly & Co, personnel 1977-; Mayor, coord 1976-77; Eli Lilly & Co, supr 1971-76; Detroit Deisel-Allison, engr 1967-71. **ORGANIZATIONS:** Guest lectr, mem Nat Crime Prevention Inst; Sch of Police Adminstrn,Univ of Lousiville; v-chmn Human Rights Commn of Indianapolis & Marion Co 1973-; sec Indianapolis Settlements Inc 1974-; bd mem Indianapolis Chap NAACP 1969-; Indianapolis Black Rep Cncl 1975-; Indianapolis Police Merit Bd 1970-74; Minority Contractors Adv Cncl 1970-71. **HONORS/ACHIEVEMENTS:** Distshd Serv Award, Indianapolis Jaycees 1977; Outstdg Young Hoosier Award, IN Jaycees 1977; Citz Award, Police League Of IN 1977. **BUSINESS ADDRESS:** 307 E Mc Carty St, Indianapolis, IN 46204.

SPEARMAN, LEONARD HALL O'CONNELL
Educational administrator. **PERSONAL:** Born Jul 08, 1929, Tallahassee, FL; married Valeria Benbow; children: Lynn S McKenzie, Leonard Jr, Charles M. **EDUCATION:** FL A&M Univ, BS 1947; Univ of MI, MA 1950, PhD 1960; Beloit Coll Natl Sci Found, Post Doctoral Fellowship. **CAREER:** Lincoln HS, tchr biol scis 1949-50; FL A&M Univ, assoc prof of psych 1950-60; Lower Coll, prof psych/dean 1965-70; Southern Univ, prof of psych/dean 1960-70; Queens Coll of NY, visit prof of psych 1965; Rutgers Univ, Martin Luther King Scholar 1969; US Office of Educ Wash, DC, dir div of student spec serv 1970-72; Univ of DC, visit lectr 1971-80; US Ofc of Edn, dir div of student assist 1972-75, assoc commr for student asst 1975-78, assoc dep commr higher/cont educ 1978-80; US Dept Edn, assoc dep asst sec higher/cont educ 1980; TX Southern Univ, president 1980-. **ORGANIZATIONS:** Chmn Natl Adv Bd on Intl Educ Programs 1985 (mem 1982-85); mem Governor's Adv Comm on Equal Educ Oppty State of TX; mem Governor's Adv Comm on Women and Minorities State of TX; mem bd dirs Houston C of C 1985; mem Clean Houston Commn; founding mem bd Houston Lyceum; bd govs Houston Forum Club 1985; bd dirs Houston Chptr Natl Kidney Found 1985; bd mem Sam Houston Area Cncl Boy Scouts of Amer; mem bd dirs Houston Chptr Amer Red Cross; mem Houston Job Training Partnership Cncl; mem Neighborhood Adv Comm Freedmen's Town Assn Inc. **HONORS/ACHIEVEMENTS:** LLD Shaw Univ NC 1970; LLD Oakland Univ MI 1973; LLD Southern Vermont 1978; DHL Edward Waters Coll FL 1975; Meritorious Achievement Award FL A&M Univ 1972; Superior Serv Award Highest Honor in the US Office of Education 1975; Disting Serv Award Highest Honor in the Dept of Health, Educ & Welfare 1978;articles, The Key, Knowing Language The Houston Chronicle Nov 16, 1980; Quality Control Will Benefit Minorities, Too The Houston Chronicle June 26, 1983; On 'De-endangering' an Endangered Academic Species, Ruminations on the Status of an American Black College, Meeting of the Amer Cncl on Educ San Francisco Oct 9,1980; Federal Roles and Responsibilities Relative to the Higher Education of Blacks since 1967, Journ of Negro Education Vol 50 No 3 summer 1981. **HOME ADDRESS:** 4216 Fernwood Dr, Houston, TX 77021. **BUSINESS ADDRESS:** President, Texas Southern University, Office of the President, 3201 Wheeler Ave, Houston, TX 77004.

SPEARS, CHARLES
Educator. **CAREER:** US Steel Corp; Diamond City Shoe Store, co-owner. **ORGANIZATIONS:** Pres, vp, sec Contra Costa Co Bd of Educ 1975-77; co bd mem 1973-; mem CA Co Bd of Educ Nominating Com; Governance Com Sec Los Medanos Hosp Corp; bd chmn Lpittsburgh Drug Therapy Ctr; City of Pittsburgh Redevel Agy; mem Mt Diablo Unified Sch Dist Parents' Study Cncl; Pacifica HS Parents Club; mgr Woods Manor Low Cost Housing; past chmn Concerted Svc; orgzr W Pitts Pop Warner Football League; past pres Pitts Br NAACP; mem Eastern Contra Costa Hlth Com; chmn Hlth/Welfare Com; Local 1440 United Steel Workers of Am. **HONORS/ACHIEVEMENTS:** Man of Yr Award 1969; hon life mem Pittsburg CA Jaycees; Christian Ldrshp Award, CA Congress of Parents & Tchrs 1970; Cert of Appreciation, Meth & Epis Chs. **MILITARY SERVICE:** AUS sgt.

SPEARS, HENRY ALBERT
Insurance representative. **PERSONAL:** Born Jun 04, 1928, Montgomery, AL; married Kathleen Stanford; children: Vicki Regina Truitt, Henry A Jr, Kathy Evangeline Cobbs. **EDUCATION:** AL State Coll Lab School, Graduate (Valedictorian) 1946; AL State Univ, BS Sec Ed 1950, MEd 1955; Springfield Coll, Grad Study 1959; NY Life Career Course & NASD Regional Rep Course 1973-74. **CAREER:** St Jude's Educ Inst Montgomery AL, teacher auto mechanics 1949-50; G W Carver High School, sci & math teacher 1950-55; Carver Adult School, instr 1954-55; Montgomery YMCA, exec sec 1955-63, 1968-69; AL State Coll, dir coll relations 1963-68; AL State Univ, vice pres for devel 1969-72; NY Life Ins Co, regional rep 1973-, RHU designation 1979-, field underwriter 1972-. **ORGANIZATIONS:** Mem Montgomery Athletic Boosters Club 1973-; Montgomery & Natl Assoc of Health Underwriters 1973-; mem adv bd Central AL Home Health Serv Inc 1974-; mem bd of dir AL State Univ Found 1974-81, 1983-; bd mem Montgomery Co Bd of Educ 1976-; mem Red Cross Two Gallon Plus Donor Club 1976-; trustee bd mem Lomax-Hannon Jr Coll 1978-; mem bd of dir Goodwill Ind, Central AL Rehab Ctr 1983-; owner/mgr two student boarding houses 1983-85; bd mem Montgomery Metropolitan YMCA; Cleveland Ave Branch YMCA;

past pres Dist IV; former bd mem AL Assn of School Bds; life mem Omega Psi Phi; bd mem Life Mem Found; 1st vice dir 7th Dist; keeper of Finance of Sigma Phi Chapter; Alpha Kappa Mu; Beta Kappa Chi; Phi Delta Kappa; chmn trustee bd Mt Zion AME Zion Church Inc; life mem Natl Ed Assn; mem West Montgomery Masonic Lodge, Montgomery Chap NAACP, Democratic Party/Club, AL Democratic Conf. **HONORS/ACHIEVEMENTS:** Outstanding Young Men of Amer 1959; Outstanding Serv as Exec Sec Cleveland Ave YMCA 1963; 5 Yrs Meritorious Serv Plaque AL State Univ 1968; Alumnus of the Year Gen Alumni Assn AL State Univ 1969; Distinguished Serv & Prestige to the Univ AL State Univ 1972; Outstanding Serv to Montgomery Area United Appeal 1973; Outstanding Alumni Awardees AL State Univ Centennial 1974; Omega Man of the Year Awd Sigma Phi Chap 1976; Outstanding Leadership in the Montgomery Urban League 1979-81; qualified each year as a "Star Club Member" through a notable sales record with NY Life 1973-81; Health Ins Leader 5 yrs, RHU 1979; Citizen of the Year Awd Sigma Phi Chap 1982; 30 Yrs of Serv Plaque YMCA 1982; Natl Sales Achievement Awd 10 yrs; Natl Quality Awd 6 yrs; Health Ins Quality Awd 5 yrs; Leading Producers Roundtable Health Ins 3 yrs; Reg Prof Disability Income & Health Ins Underwriter. **HOME ADDRESS:** 2069 Wabash St, Montgomery, AL 36108. **BUSINESS ADDRESS:** Field Underwriter/Reg Rep, New York Life Insurance Co, 509 Interstate Park Dr, Montgomery, AL 36109.

SPEARS, MACK J.
Educational administrator. **PERSONAL:** Married Olga; children: Olga S Jones. **EDUCATION:** Dillard U, AB; Xavier U, MA; Harvard U, PhD 1954. **CAREER:** Dillard U, dean of students. **ORGANIZATIONS:** Mem Orleans Parish Sch Bd 1968-; bd of dir LA Sch Bd Assn 1973-; dir Nat Sch Bd Assn 1975-; pres Central Congregational Ch 1960-; bd of dir United Way 1971-75; pres LA Sch Bd Assn 1978-79; former vice pres United Ch Bd for World Ministries. **HONORS/ACHIEVEMENTS:** Pres Natl School Bd 1985-86. **BUSINESS ADDRESS:** Dillard University, 2601 Gentilly Blvd, New Orleans, LA 70122.

SPEARS-JONES, PATRICIA KAY
Poet/arts administrator. **PERSONAL:** Born Feb 11, 1951, Forrest City, AR; daughter of Lee Spears and Lillie B Dodd Spears Jones. **EDUCATION:** Rhodes Coll, BA Communications 1973; Vermont Coll, MFA candidate 1991. **CAREER:** Poet/Writer, 1974-; Samuel French Inc, mgr amateur leasing 1974-77; Coordinating Council of Literary Magazines, grants progs dir 1977-81; Heresies Collective Inc, managing coord 1982-83; Poetry Project at St Mark's Church, prog coord 1984-86; MA Council on the Arts & Humanities, program specialist 1987-. **ORGANIZATIONS:** Freelance journalist Essence The Village Voice Poetry Project Newsletter 1978-; vice pres Natl Assoc of Third World Writers 1979-82; consultant CCLM 1981; dir Mabou Mines 1984-86; mem Poetry Soc of Amer 1984-, NY Assoc of Black Journalists 1985-86. **HONORS/ACHIEVEMENTS:** Panelist CCLM, OH Arts Council, MA Artists Foundation 1976-85; Fellow in Poetry CAPS 1983-84, New York Foundation for the Arts 1986; publication, "Mythologizing Always," Telephone Books CT 1981; travel/research grant, Goethe Institute 1988; mem advisory bd Artgarden, Amsterdam the netherlands.

SPEEDE-FRANKLIN, WANDA A.
Educational administrator. **PERSONAL:** Born Aug 01, 1956, Bronx, NY; married Melvin L Franklin; children: Ihsan K. **EDUCATION:** Princeton Univ, BA 1978, certificate of prof in African-Amer Studies 1978; Northwestern Univ, MA 1980. **CAREER:** Princeton Univ, rsch asst computer ctr 1974-78, asst to dir third world ctr 1974-78; Chicago Metro History Fair, assoc dir for programs & operations 1980-82; Natl Assn of Independent Schools, minority affairs & info serv 1982-87; asst dir for admin, public affairs, Mass Bay Transportation Authority, 1987-88; dir, Newton Metco Program, 1988-. **ORGANIZATIONS:** Mem Natl Assn of Black School Educators; mem Amer Assn for Affirmative Action; mem Natl Assn of Negro Women; bd mem Metro Council for Equal Opportunity (METCO) 1985-; trustee Project Match Minority Student Talent Search Agency 1984-. **HONORS/ACHIEVEMENTS:** Graduate Fellowship Northwestern Univ 1978-79; contributing author of Visible Now: Blacks in Private Schools, Greenwood Press, 1988. **BUSINESS ADDRESS:** Director, Newton Metco Program, Newton Public Schools, 100 Walnut Street, Room 112, Newtonville, MA 02160.

SPEIGHT, EVA B.
Educator. **PERSONAL:** Born Dec 09, 1930, Snow Hill, NC; daughter of Eddie L Bess and Easter B Bess; married James Thomas Speight Jr, Aug 25, 1962; children: Sharon, Thomara, James T, III. **EDUCATION:** Howard Univ; DC Teacher Coll; Univ of NC; NC A&T State Univ, BS 1957; Trinity Coll. **CAREER:** Jr HS, Washington DC Bd of Educ, teacher of English 1962-; Jones County Bd of Educ, Trenton NC, teacher 1957-62. **ORGANIZATIONS:** Mem Washington Teacher Union; sec, principal advisory council Sousa Jr HS; advisor Natl Jr Honor Soc; charter mem Kinston Alumnae Chapter Delta Sigma Theta Sorority; Les Torchettes Social Club, NC 1957-62; pres Washington Alumnae Chapter Delta Sigma Theta Sorority Inc 1974-76; past pres Alpha Phi Alpha Wives of Washington DC 1969-71; mem choir Ebenezer Baptist Church, NC; Natl Council of Negro Women; PTA; NC A&T State Univ Alumni Assn; Penn Branch Civic Assn; NAACP; Urban League; sec Capitol Hill Montessori School Bd. **HONORS/ACHIEVEMENTS:** Pres Award, Alpha Wives of Washington, DC 1975; delegate to regional conf Delta Sigma Theta 1972 & natl convention 1975; Reclamation Award, Delta Sigma Theta, 4 yrs; Awardee Agnes G Meyer Found (one of five finalists); Citation/Plaque-Superintendent, Outstanding Teacher/Service Award. **BUSINESS ADDRESS:** Teacher of English, District of Columbia Public Schools, 415 12th St, NW, Washington, DC 20004.

SPEIGHT, VELMA R.
Educator. **PERSONAL:** Born Nov 18, 1932, Snow Hill, NC; daughter of John Thomas Speight and Mable Edwards Speight; divorced; children: T Chineta Kennedy Bowen. **EDUCATION:** A&T State Univ NC, BS 1953; attended Amer Univ; Morgan St Coll, NSF Fellow 1956; Univ of Maryland, NSF Fellow 1957, MEd Guidance 1965, PhD Counseling Personnel Serv 1976; Virginia State Coll, NDEA Fellow 1963. **CAREER:** Kennard High School, teacher 1954-60; Kennard High School, Queen Anne's County High School, counselor 1960-68, coordinator guidance dept 1966-68; NDEA Inst for Disadvantaged Youth, Univ of Maryland, Eastern Shore Br, staff consultant summer 1967; Family Life & Sex Educ, Caroline, Kent, Queen Anne's & Talbot Counties, curriculum research specialist 1969; Univ of Maryland, Johns Hopkins Univ, visiting prof, assoc prof; Equal Opportunity Recruitment Prog, Univ of Maryland, dir 1972; Maryland State Dept of Educ, asst supr compensatory urban & supplementary programs 1969-72, specialist guidance 1972-76, administrator 1976, asst state supt 1982-86; Univ of Maryland, Eastern Shore, Princess Anne MD, chair, dept of counseling educ, 1986-87; East Carolina Univ, Greenville NC, chair, dept of counseling and adult educ, 1987-. **ORGANIZATIONS:** Life mem, MD State Tchr Assn; Natl Educ Assn; first black pres, Queen Anne's County Tchr Assn and Educ Assoc; MD Assn for Counselor Educ & Supv; MD School Counselors Assn; Amer Personnel & Guidance Assn; mem, MD Assn of Curriculum Devel, Amer Assn of School Bus Officials; Delmarva Alumni Assn, A&T State Univ; Study Group Mothers Prevent Dropouts; tchr, Summer Courses for Black Students; organizer, chmn, Youth Group to Study Problems of Integration; Queen Anne's, Kent & Talbot Counties Comm Action Agency Bd; MD & Natl Congress Parents & Tchrs; NAACP; organizer, chmn, Parent Educ Group Communication Rather Than Confrontation; chmn, Christian Social Relations Comm, Weslyan Serv Guild; mem, Assn for Sup & Curriculum Devel, Amer Assn for Counseling & Devel, Assn for Counselor Educ & Sup, Natl Career Devel Assn, Amer School Counselors Assn, Amer Rehabilitation Counseling Assn; Assn for Meas & Evaluation in Counseling & Devel, Assn for Multicultural Counseling & Devel, MD Assoc for Counseling & Devel, MD Career Devel Assn, MD Assn for Multicultural Counseling & Devel; organizer, Black Churches for Educational Excellence, 1987-. **HONORS/ACHIEVEMENTS:** Woman of theYear, Negro Business & Professional Women's Orgn; A&T State Univ Alumni Achievement Awd 1974; Phi Delta Kappa; A&T State Univ Alumni Excellence Awd 1982; Natl Assn for Equal Opportunity in Higher Educ Presidential Citation to Distinguished Alumni 1985; Minority Achievement Award, Maryland State Teachers Assn, 1988; appointed by governor of Maryland to chair a comm to study sentencing alternatives for women convicted of crime, 1987; author of Improving the Status of the Culturally Different and Disadvantaged Minority Students in Gifted Programs, 1988-89. **HOME ADDRESS:** Rte 1, Box 106, Snow Hill, NC 28580.

SPEIGHTS, JOHN D.
Dentist. **PERSONAL:** Born Mar 05, 1926, Dickson, TN; son of Foster and Margaret; married Marian C Washington. **EDUCATION:** Meharry Dental Coll, Cert in Dental Tech 1948; Wilson Jr Coll, AA 1953; Chicago Tchrs Coll, B Educ 1957; Howard Univ Dental Coll, DDS 1963. **CAREER:** Dentist, pvt prac 1963-; Chicago Pub Schs, tchr 1957-59; Dr William J Walker, Sr, dental technician 1949-59. **ORGANIZATIONS:** Mem Lincoln Dental Soc; Nat Dental Assn; Am Dental Assn; Chicago Dental Soc; IL State Dental Soc; Howard Univ Dental Alumni Assn. **HONORS/ACHIEVEMENTS:** DH Turpin Award, outstanding perf in Prostodontia, Meharry Med Coll & Howard Dental Sch 1963. **MILITARY SERVICE:** US Navy S 1st class 1944-46. **BUSINESS ADDRESS:** 536 E 87th St, Chicago, IL 60619.

SPEIGHTS, NATHANIEL H.
Attorney. **PERSONAL:** Born Nov 24, 1949, Bellaire, OH; son of Nathaniel H Speights and Ollie Speights; married Grace E Speights; children: Ashley, Nathaniel IV. **EDUCATION:** Coll of Wooster, Ohio, BA, 1972; Univ of Miami, Florida, JD, 1975. **CAREER:** Speights & Michael, Washington DC, attorney, currently. **ORGANIZATIONS:** Pres, Washington Bar Assn, currently. **BUSINESS ADDRESS:** Attorney, Speights & Michael, 2000 L St, NW, Suite 810, Washington, DC 20036.

SPEIGINER, GERTHA
Business executive. **PERSONAL:** Born Apr 28, 1917, St Louis; married Louis Sol; children: Delores, Doris, Deborah, Darlene, Delanya, Desiree, Delicya, Dauphne Delauna. **EDUCATION:** Mt San Antonio Coll. **CAREER:** Studio Girl Cosmetic, rep; CA Polytechnic U, lecturer 1972-73; Mt San Antonio Coll Comm Cntr, dir 1970-74. **ORGANIZATIONS:** Pres Pomona Valley Branch NAACP; vice pres So Area Conf NAACP 1974-76; fdr, pres Pomona Parents Council 1965-68; past pres Parents for Understandin 1967-71; charter mem, treas, Pomona Day School; bd mem YWCA; Outreach Program YMCA; mem Pasadena Legal Aid Bd; Pomona Legal Aid; Nat Assn of Colores Women. **HONORS/ACHIEVEMENTS:** Plaque for outs Black comm ser 1971; cert of merit for continuous service to comm; plaque for dedicated ser to comm Pomona Valley Br. **BUSINESS ADDRESS:** 2243 Larchmont Ave, Pomona, CA 91767.

SPELLER, CHARLES K.
Orthopedic surgeon. **PERSONAL:** Born Feb 25, 1933, Windsor, NC; married Virginia. **EDUCATION:** NC Cent U, 1954; Meharry Med Coll, 1966. **CAREER:** Monmouth Med Cent Long Branch NJ; IL Masonic Hosp; Columbia Univ NY, internship. **ORGANIZATIONS:** Mem Harris Co Med Soc; Houston Med Forum; Nat Med Assn; Nat Trauma Soc Sovereign Grand Insp Gen of 33rd & last deg Ancient & Accept Scottish Riteof Freemasonry Adg Gen Corp 1954-56. **BUSINESS ADDRESS:** 5445 Almeda, Ste 302, Houston, TX 77004.

SPELLER, EUGENE THURLEY
Engineer, educator. **PERSONAL:** Born Jan 25, 1928, Charleston, MO; married Thelma; children: Barry, Bernnine, Michelle. **EDUCATION:** MI State U, BS 1955; MI State U, MA 1967; OH State U, PhD 1975. **CAREER:** Olive Harvey Coll, pres 1975-; Austin Comm Coll, dean 1973-75; OH State Univ, fellow 1971-73; Sundstrand Hydro-Transmission, engineer 1971-72; Ford Motor Co, 1964; Lansing Public School, teacher 1963-67; John Deere Tractor Works, engineer 1955-63. **ORGANIZATIONS:** Chmn Hydraulics & Preumatics Com Soc of Auto Engr 1969-71; Gen Interes Co 1975-; Engineering Educ Activity 1972-; mem Assn ofUniv Adminstr; Phi Delta Kappa; Am Assn of Comm & Jr Coll; Am Assn of Higher Educ Bd of Dir; Chicago S C of C; mem Calument Area Indsl Commn; Chicago Assn of Commerce & Ind; bd of dir 111th St YMCA; mem Nat Alliance of Black Sch Edcr; Assn for the Study of Afro-Am Life & Hist; Cncl on Black Am Affairs. **HONORS/ACHIEVEMENTS:** Jour Award Sparton Engr Mag; Distgsd Citz Civic Serv Award IL Valley C of C; flwsp Nat Prgm for Educ Ldrsp. **MILITARY SERVICE:** AUS 1956-58. **BUSINESS ADDRESS:** 10001 S Woodlawn Ave, Chicago, IL 60628.

SPELLER, J. FINTON
State official, physician. **PERSONAL:** Born Apr 13, 1909, Philadelphia; married Dorothy M Lynn; children: Sandra, Jeffrey, Marsha. **EDUCATION:** Lincoln Univ, AB 1932; Howard Univ, MD 1940; Univ Penn, postgrad 1945-46; Howard Univ, urologic fellow 1946-48. **CAREER:** Commonwealth of PA, former sec of health 1971-75. **ORGANIZATIONS:** With attendant memberships by virtue of office; numerous director appointments; previously pres Delaware Valley Council Churches; lay speaker New Hope Methodist Church; vice pres, advisory bd George School; pres advisory bd George School; treasurer Planned Parenthood Assn Bucks County; Med Advisory Bd Philadelphia Planned Parenthood Assn; mem PA Acad Fine Arts; Peale Club; Philadelphia Art Alliance; Poor Richard Club; Philadelphia Art

Museum; Amer Museum in Britain; Smithsonian Inst; Friends of Philadelphia Museum Art; World Affairs Council; Patron of Art of Haverford Coll; Philadelphia Grand Oper Co; PA Ballet Co. **BUSINESS ADDRESS:** 245 N Broad St, Philadelphia, PA 19107.

SPELLMAN, ALFRED B.
Writer, educator. **PERSONAL:** Born Aug 07, 1935, Nixonton, NC; son of Alfred Spellman and Rosa Bailey Spellman. **EDUCATION:** Howard Univ, BA, 1958. **CAREER:** Worked in bookstores and as disc jockey in New York, NY, 1958-67; taught poetry, writing, black literature, Afro-American culture, and jazz at Rutgers, Harvard, and other universities; writer-in-residence at Morehouse College and Emory University, both Atlanta, GA; music editor of periodical Kulchur; co-founder of journal Umbra. **ORGANIZATIONS:** Founder, Atlanta Center for the Black Arts, GA, 1969; affiliated with Natl Endowment for the Arts and Education; panel member, Rockefeller Foundation. **HONORS/ACHIEVEMENTS:** Author of poetry collection The Beautiful Days, Poets Press, 1965; author of Four Lives in the Bebop Business, Pantheon, 1966; co-author of Trippin': A Need for Change, Cricket, 1969; contributor of poetry and articles to anthologies and periodicals. **BUSINESS ADDRESS:** c/o Morehouse College, 223 Chestnut St SW, Atlanta, GA 30314. *

SPELLMAN, KAREN EDMUNDS
Educator. **PERSONAL:** Born Sep 09, 1943, San Antonio, TX; married A B. **EDUCATION:** Howard U, BA French 1964; Howard U, grad work. **CAREER:** So Educ Prog Inc Atlanta, dir; Student Non-violent Coordinating Com, research officer 1966. **ORGANIZATIONS:** Mem Assn for African Edn; bd dirs Atlanta Cntr for Black Art; Martin Luther King Scholarship Com of Woodrow Wilson Fellowships.

SPELLMAN, OLIVER B., JR.
City government official. **PERSONAL:** Born Sep 11, 1953, New York, NY; son of Oliver B Spellman and Iris Spellman Astwood; married Tara Jaye Wilson Spellman, Jul 11, 1989; children: Qiana Marie Spellman. **EDUCATION:** St Michael's Coll, Winooski VT, BA American Studies, 1975; Howard Univ School of Law, Washington DC, JD, 1978. **CAREER:** Ohio State Attorney General's Office, Columbus OH, law asst, 1978-79; Alabama State Univ, Montgomery AL, asst prof, Criminal Justice, 1979-82; New York City Criminal Justice Agency, New York NY, Bronx dir, 1982-84; New York City Dept of Parks, Brooklyn NY, enforcement dir, 1984-85, dir, Special Projects, 1985-87, park mgr, 1987-88, New York City, Urban Park Serv, chief, 1988-. **ORGANIZATIONS:** Alpha Phi Alpha Inc, 1983-. **BUSINESS ADDRESS:** Chief, Urban Park Service, New York City Dept of Parks and Recreation, 1234 5th AveArsenal North, New York, NY 10029.

SPENCE, DONALD DALE
Dentist. **PERSONAL:** Born Dec 06, 1926, Philadelphia, PA; married Theresa Seltzer; children: Kenneth, Donna, Rosalynn, Melanie. **EDUCATION:** Morris College Atlanta, attended 1950; Howard Univ Sch of Dentistry, DDS 1960. **CAREER:** Private Practice Pensacola, dentist. **ORGANIZATIONS:** Mem Staff Baptist, Univ, Sacred Heart Hosps; mem Gulf Coast, Natl, Santa Rosa-Escambia, Northwest FL, FL & AM Dental Assns; bd dirs So Fed Svgs & Loan; bd dirs Pensacola C of C; NAACP; Kappa Alpha Psi; Elks; Pensacola Jr Coll Found Bd; St Cyprians Epis Ch; pres NW FL Adv Counc Minority Affairs; Natl Guardsmen Inc FL Chapt; utility & zoning long-range planning com Pensacola City Coun 1974-; exec com Reg Planning W FL. **HONORS/ACHIEVEMENTS:** Apptd by Gov Reubin Asken to Escambia Co Sch Bd highest ranking Black ofcl in NW FL 1975.

SPENCE, JOSEPH SAMUEL, SR.
Lawyer, minister. **PERSONAL:** Born Dec 20, 1950, Kingston, Jamaica;son of Kenneth John Spence and Olive Maud Bambridge; married Sheila M Parrish-Spence; children: Joseph Jr, Joselyn Maria. **EDUCATION:** Pikes Peak Coll, AA 1979; Univ of MD, BSc 1980; Webster Univ, MA 1984; Washburn Univ Law School, Topeka, KS, JD, 1986-89. **CAREER:** Colorado Springs Police Dept, police officer 1973-75; DC Dept of Corrections, correctional officer 1976-78; H&R Block, tax consultant 1977-80; Century 21 Real Estate, realtor assoc 1978-80; United States Army, capt 1980-86; Riley County District Attorney's Office, 1987; City of Topeka Attorney's Office, 1988-89; Kansas State Senate, 1988-89. **ORGANIZATIONS:** Mem Daughters of Amer Revolution 1980; rep-at-large Frederick Douglass Ctr Manhattan KS 1986-87, WSBA Washburn Law Sch 1986-87; mem Kiwanis Intl 1986-87; marshall Phi Alpha Delta Law Frat 1986-87; founder & charter pres NAACP Manhattan KS 1986; founder & legal advisor, Lex Explorer, Washburn Law School, 1988; assoc minister Mt Carmel Missionary Baptist Church 1986-87; chairperson Legal Redress Comm NAACP KS 1987-; mem Manhattan Kansas Chamber of Commerce, Manhattan KS Amer Red Cross; Commissioner-at-large, Amer Bar Assn, 1987-; Christian Lawyers Assn, 1987-; Christian Legal Soc, 1987-; Americans United for Seperation of Church & State, 1987-. **HONORS/ACHIEVEMENTS:** Disting Military Student 1979, Disting Military Grad 1980 Howard Univ ROTC; Earl Warren Scholar NAACP Legal Defense Fund 1986-89; various awds for public speaking; Daughters of Amer Revolution Awd; Disting Grad Air Assault School; Disting Grad Logistics Automated Mgmt Sch; Expert Shooting Qualification; Jurcyk-Royle Oral Advocacy Competition; Certificate of Commendation, Amer Bar Assn, 1989; Certificate of Merit, Washburn Law Clinic, 1988; founder & chapter pres, Lambda Alpha Epsilon Criminal Justice Fraternity, 1985. **MILITARY SERVICE:** AUS company cmdr capt 8 yrs; Expert Infantry Badge, Airborne Air Assault Overseas Serv Ribbon, Army Achievement, NCO Develop, Army Svcs, Good Conduct; Natl Defense Ribbon; Command and General Staff Coll grad; Multi-Natl Force and Observer Ribbon. **HOME ADDRESS:** 2045 SW Macvicar #19, Topeka, KS 66604. **BUSINESS ADDRESS:** Captain, US Army Reserves, Fort Benjamin Harrison, IN 46216.

SPENCER, ANTHONY LAWRENCE
Government administrator. **PERSONAL:** Born Aug 10, 1946, New York, NY; married Jeanette Butler; children: Anthony. **EDUCATION:** City Coll of NY, 1970-75; Cmd & Gen Stf Coll, 1980-84. **CAREER:** Seattle Fire Department Fire Chief 1959-; Inst for Mediation & Cnflct Asso, special asst to pres 1972-75; State Charter Revision Comm for NYC, asst div of cmnty rels 1975-76; J P Stevens & Co, tech sales rep synthetic fbrcs div 1976-79; New York Dept of State, special asst to sec of state, exec asst to gov black affairs adv comm. **ORGANIZATIONS:** Mem Bd of Div/ML Wilson Boys Club of Harlem 1982-; 1st vice pres Community Bd 9 New York, NY 1983-84; pres student body City Coll of New York 1972-73; vice pres Christmas Tree in Harlem 1981; mem Men Who Cook; mem Intl Assn of Fire Fighters, Local 27 1959-; mem Intl Assn of Black Professional Fire Fighters 1968-; mem Seafair 1985-; mem Boy Scouts of Amer 1985-; mem Girls Club of Puget Sound 1985-; bd mem Intl Assn of Fire Chiefs/Metro Section 1986-. **HONORS/ACHIEVEMENTS:** Distinguished Serv Citation United Negro Coll Fund 1981; 125 Anniv Medal City Coll of New York 1972. **MILITARY SERVICE:** UASF; AUS mjr 21 yrs; NDSM/AFOUA/SOGB/AFGCM/ARCOM/ARCAM. **BUSINESS ADDRESS:** Executive Assistant, NY St Gov Adv Comm for Blk Afr, Executive Chamber, 2 World Trade Center, New York, NY 10047.

SPENCER, BRENDA L.
Industrial engineer. **PERSONAL:** Born Jul 07, 1951, Youngstown, OH; married Herbert Spencer; children: Ebony Ayana. **EDUCATION:** Kent State, BS Ind Engineering 1978. **CAREER:** General Motors, accountant 1973-76; BL Unlimited Engrg & Consult Corp, owner; Republic Steel, indus engr. **ORGANIZATIONS:** Natl youth leader Natl Assn of Negro Business and Prof Women 1978-80; natl dir Youth and Young Adults 1980-82; natl vice president Prof Women and Young Adults 1982-85; treasurer Kappa Nu Zeta 1983-85; treasurer Zeta Phi Beta 1983-85; membership chairman Amer Inst of Engineers 1983-84. **HONORS/ACHIEVEMENTS:** Voluntary Leader Natl March of Dimes 1980; Leadership Natl March of Dimes 1982; Good Housekeeping 100 Young Women of Promise 1985. **HOME ADDRESS:** PO Box 5814, Youngstown, OH 44504.

SPENCER, DONALD ANDREW
Broker. **PERSONAL:** Born Mar 05, 1915, Cincinnati, OH; married Marian; children: Donald, Edward. **EDUCATION:** Univ of Cincinnati, AB 1936;Univ of Cincinnati, BE 1937;Univ of Cincinnati, ME 1940. **CAREER:** Re broker 1945-; Cincinnati Public School, teacher 1936-54. **ORGANIZATIONS:** Pres bd dtrustees OHUniv 1974-; pres Housine Bd of Appeals 1970-77; Natl Assoc Real Estate Brokers; mem PAC Com 1967-75; orgnzr First Midwinter Conf;Estab Beta Eta Chptr of Kappa Alpha Psi Frat onUniv of Cincinnati Campus 1949; mem Admin & Fin Comm W OH & Lexington Conf of Meth Ch 1957-46; trustee OH Coun of Ch; orgnzr, 1st pres Comm on Relig & Race 1960-65. **HONORS/ACHIEVEMENTS:** Publ 1st Nat Song Book for Kappa Alpha Psi Frat 1951; pres Award Cincinnati Br NAACP 1975. **BUSINESS ADDRESS:** 940 Lexington Ave, Cincinnati, OH 45229.

SPENCER, JOAN MOORE
Librarian. **PERSONAL:** Born Feb 17, 1932, Henderson, NC; married Francis Herman; children: Francine Dejuanna, Christopher Columbus. **EDUCATION:** NC Central U, BSC 1950-54; NC Central U, MLS 1960; NC State U, 9 hrs on PhD 1978-79. **CAREER:** Wake Co Pub Libraries, young adult coordinator 1977-; Wake Co Pub Libraries, asst %Dir 1974-77; Wake Co Pub Libraries, head reference dept 1968-73; JR Faison High Sch Wadesboro NC, sch librarian 1954-64. **ORGANIZATIONS:** Chmn const bylaws NC Adult Educ Assn 1975-77; pub library dir NC Library Assn Pub Sect 1977-79; com mem Am Library Assn YASD Media & Usage 1979-80; dir RAYC St Paul AME Ch 1970-; bd mem Wake Co Mental Health Assn 1977-79; mem Raleigh Chap of Natl Epicureans 1979-, Boyer Assembly of the Golden Circle 1979-; ivy leaf reporter Alpha Theta Omega Chap Alpha Kappa Alpha Inc 1980; compiler of ofcl index NC Library Assn 1976-; WNCC Branch UPD dir AME Church 1984. **HONORS/ACHIEVEMENTS:** Mother of the Year Alpha Phi Alpha Frat Raleigh NC 1977; Pres Pin for Outstanding PTA Serv Aycock Sch PTA 1978; Woman of the Yr Zeta Phi Beta Sorority 1979. **BUSINESS ADDRESS:** Local History Librarian, Wake County Public Libraries, Wake Co Public Libraries, 1930 Clark Ave, Raleigh, NC 27603.

SPENCER, MARGARET BEALE
Psychologist. **PERSONAL:** Born Sep 05, 1944, Philadelphia, PA; married Charles L Spencer MD; children: Tirzah Renee, Natasha Ann, Charles Asramon. **EDUCATION:** Temple Univ Coll of Pharmacy, BS 1967; Univ of KS, MA Psychology 1970; Univ of Chicago, PhD 1976. **CAREER:** Univ of KS Medical Center, registered pharmacist 1967-69; Univ of Chicago, research project dir 1974-77; Morehouse School of Medicine, clinical assoc prof 1982-; Emory Univ, faculty mem 1977-. **ORGANIZATIONS:** Consultant/comm Foundation for Child Develop 1981-85; consultant Fulton Co GA Health Dept 1983-; bd exec comm Fulton Co Black Family Project 1983-; bdSouth DeKalb Co YMCA 1984-86; mem W T Grant Foundation 1986-, Natl Black Child Develop Inst 1986-, Ctr for Successful Child Develop 1986-; comm chmnSoc for Rsch in Child Develop 1987-. **HONORS/ACHIEVEMENTS:** Spencer Foundation Grant Rsch Support 1984-87; Awd for Service DeKalb Co YMCA 1985; Outstanding Serv Awd Delta Sigma Theta Sor 1986; book "Beginnings, The Affective and Social Development of Black Children," w/Brookin & Allen 1985. **HOME ADDRESS:** 3587 Greentree Farms Dr, Decatur, GA 30034. **BUSINESS ADDRESS:** Assoc Professor, EmoryUniv, Div of Educational Studies, Fishburne #201, Atlanta, GA 30322.

SPENCER, MARIAN A.
Elected official. **PERSONAL:** Born Jun 28, 1920, Gallipolis, OH; married Donald A Spencer; children: Donald, Edward. **EDUCATION:** Univ of Cincinnati, graduate. **CAREER:** Cincinnati City Council, councilmember. **ORGANIZATIONS:** Chairperson Human Resources Comm; mem Urban Develop Planning Zoning & Housing Comm; vice chairperson Law Committee; mem City Planning Comm; life mem NAACP; mem Alpha Kappa Alpha Sor; past pres Cincinnati Chap of Links Inc; past pres Woman's City Club. **HONORS/ACHIEVEMENTS:** First Black woman elected to City Council; only woman ever to serve as pres of the Cincinnati Branch NAACP; Brotherhood Awd Natl Conf of Christians & Jews;Woman of the Yr Awd Cincinnati Enquirer; Black Excellence Awd PUSH; Ethelrie Harper Awd Cincinnati Human Relations Comm; Disting Alumna Awd Alumna Assnof the Univ of Cincinnati; recognized by the Cincinnati Post as one of the 12 Most Influential Women in the City of Cincinnati; Career Woman of Achievement Awd YWCA 1984; recently inducted into the OH Women's Hall of Fame. **BUSINESS ADDRESS:** Councilmember, Cincinnati City Council, 354 City Hall, 801 Plum St, Cincinnati, OH 45202.

SPENCER, MICHAEL GREGG
Engineer, professor. **PERSONAL:** Born Mar 09, 1952, Detroit, MI; son of Thomas Spencer; divorced; children: Thomas Lewis. **EDUCATION:** Cornell Univ, Ithaca NY, BS, 1974, MEE, 1975, PhD, 1981. **CAREER:** General Electric, Syracuse NY, co-op engineer, 1972, 1973; Bell Laboratories, Whippany NJ, mem of technical staff, 1974-77; Howard Univ, Washington DC, asst prof, 1981-85, assoc prof, 1985—; Materials Science Research Center of Excellence, director, 1987—; SIMNET Laboratory, co-director, 1987—. **ORGANIZATIONS:** Mem, officer, National Soc of Black Engineers, 1977—; mem, Natl Science Found proposal review comm, 1984—, advisory council for Electrical Engineering and computer systems, 1988, advisory comm for materials research, 1989—; mem, Amer Vacuum Soc, 1985—; officer, Electron Device Soc of Inst of Electrical and Electronics Engineers, 1987—. **HON-**

ORS/ACHIEVEMENTS: Presidential Young Investigator Award, Natl Science Found, 1985; Allen Berman Research Publication Award, Naval Research Laboratory, 1986; Outstanding Faculty Award, White House Initiative on Historically Black Colls and Univs, 1988. **HOME ADDRESS:** 5133 8th St NE, Washington, DC 20011. **BUSINESS ADDRESS:** Dept of Electrical Engineering, Material Science Research Center of Excellence, Howard Univ, 2300 6th St NW - Downing Hall, Washington, DC 20059.

SPENCER, TIM CALVIN
Professional athlete. **PERSONAL:** Born Dec 10, 1960, Martins Ferry, OH; married Gilda. **EDUCATION:** Ohio State. **CAREER:** Arizona Wranglers, 1983; Chicago Blitz, 1984; Memphis Showboats, runningback 1985-. **HONORS/ACHIEVEMENTS:** Ranks as the No 3 all-time rusher in the USFL; led Big Ten in rushing (1,034 yds) & all-purpose running (1514 yd avg) in 1982; was All Big Ten & All-Am selection & appeared in 4 bowl games; 1981 Liberty Bowl against Navy. **BUSINESS ADDRESS:** Memphis Showboats, 3767 New Getwell Rd, P O Box 500 Sta M Montreal, Memphis, TN 38118.

SPICER, CARMELITA
Business executive. **PERSONAL:** Born Mar 14, 1946, Jacksonville, NC. **EDUCATION:** NC Central Univ, BS 1968; Rutgers Univ, MEd 1975. **CAREER:** Inner City Mktg, sales & merchandising; Johnson & Johnson Baby Products Co, mktg cons; J & J Div, consumer mktg; Personal Products Co, asst dir; Celanese Fibers Mktg Co, coord; Spicer & Assoc, president; Central City Marketing Inc, vice pres mktg dir. **ORGANIZATIONS:** Alpha Kappa Alpha Sor 1963; co-chmn mem Am Home Econ Assn 1971; Instrumental in opening 7 markets with an innovative health care radio prgm 1976-; InnerCity Merchandising Grp; Media Women; Nat Assn of Mktg Developers. **HONORS/ACHIEVEMENTS:** Jr Achievers Advisor Citation 1967; recpt Tuition Remission Grant Rutgers Univ 1975; Image Builder Award Operation PUSH 1977; Order of Flying Orchids Delta Airlines 1977; nominated Advertising Woman of the Year 1977. **BUSINESS ADDRESS:** Vice President Marketing Dir, Central City Marketing Inc, 1716 S Michigan Ave, Chicago, IL 60616.

SPICER, KENNETH, SR.
Government official. **PERSONAL:** Born Aug 21, 1949, Jacksonville, FL; married Patricia A Baker, Jun 25, 1972; children: Kenneth, Sherry, Michelle. **EDUCATION:** Bethune-Cookman Coll, Daytona Beach FL, BS Business Admin, 1971; Univ of Massachusetts, Boston MA, MPA, 1990. **CAREER:** South Florida Employment Training Consortium, Miami FL, dir public serv employment, 1980, dir of operations, 1980-81; Dade County JMH/Community Mental Health Center, Miami FL, dir of operations & finance, 1981; Dade County Haitian-Amer Community Health Center, Miami FL, exec dir, 1982-85; Office of City Manager, Tallahassee FL, dir of M/WBE, 1985-86; EOCD, Office of Secretary, Boston MA, dir of Affirmative Action, 1986-. **ORGANIZATIONS:** Alpha Phi Alpha Frat Inc, 1971-; pres, Boston Chapter, Natl Forum for Black Public Admin Inc; chmn, bd of dir, Massachusetts Municipal Assn Minority Mgmt Intern Program, Boston MA; Intl City Mgmt Assn, Conf of Minorities in Public Admin Inc; Amer Soc for Public Admin Inc; Governor's Civil Rights Working Group, Boston MA; Assn of Affirmative Action Professionals Inc, Boston MA; Amer Assn of Affirmative Action, Boston MA; Amer Soc of Pesonnel Admin Inc. **HONORS/ACHIEVEMENTS:** Appreciation Award, Boston Chapter, Natl Forum for Black Public Admin, 1989; Appreciation Award, State of Massachusetts, 1989. **BUSINESS ADDRESS:** Dir, Office of Affirmative Action, Office of the Secretary, Governor's Exec Office of Communities & Development, 100 Cambridge St, 14th Fl, Boston, MA 02202.

SPIGNER, DONALD WAYNE
Physician. **PERSONAL:** Born Feb 14, 1940, Tyler, TX; son of Kermit Spigner and Jessie Spigner; married Kathleen Hughes; children: Nicole Adeyinka, Danielle Khadeja. **EDUCATION:** Univ of CA Riverside, BS 1962; Univ of CA San Francisco, MD 1966; Los Angeles Cty Govt Hosp, Internship 1967; Board Certified Academy of Family Practice and Certified in Preventive Medicine. **CAREER:** US Peace Corps, physician 1967-69, med dir of Africa Div 1969-70; Pilot City Health Ctr, proj dir 1970-73; Univ of MN School of Med, assoc prof 1973-75; Univ of MN School of Publ Health, lecturer 1973-75; Hamilton Health Ctr; med dir 1975-87; Comm Med Assoc, pres; Univ of PA Hershey Med Cntr, assoc prof 1975-; City of Harrisburg, city health ofcr 1977-80; Keystone Peer Review, part-time reviewer 1986-; Blue Shield of PA, medical dir; Unicare Inc, pres, 1987-; High Quality Properties, sole proprietor, 1987-. **ORGANIZATIONS:** Consult Afric Care 1975-85; partner 3540 N Progress Assoc 1980-; mem Boys Club 1982-; partner Keystone Assoc 1984-; pres Dauphin Cty Med Soc 1984-; mem Dauphin Cty MH/MR Bd 1984-86; partner H Quality Prop 1985; mem St Paul Baptist Church, mem, Advisory Bd of PA State Univ, Harrisburg Campus. **HONORS/ACHIEVEMENTS:** Selected to represent Univ of CA Riverside on Project India 1961; mem PA State Bd of Podiatry; video tape on African/Amer Folk medicine, 1977. **MILITARY SERVICE:** US Public Health Serv Surgeon 1967-69;USPMS. **BUSINESS ADDRESS:** President, Community Medical Assoc, 3544 N Progress, Harrisburg, PA 17110.

SPIKES, DOLORES R.
University president. **CAREER:** Southern University, Baton Rouge, LA, president of univ system and interim president of univ at Baton Rouge. **BUSINESS ADDRESS:** Southern University System, Baton Rouge, LA 70813. *

SPINKS, MICHAEL
Professional boxer. **PERSONAL:** Born 1956; married Sandy (deceased); children: Michelle. **CAREER:** Professional Boxer, 1976-. **HONORS/ACHIEVEMENTS:** Gold Medalist 1976 Olympics; World Boxing Assoc Light-Heavyweight Champion 1981; World Boxing Cncl Light Heavyweight Champion 1983-85; Intl Boxing Federation Heavyweight Champion 1985.

SPIVA, ULYSSES VAN
Educator. **PERSONAL:** Born May 06, 1931, New Market, TN; married Olivia A; children: Vanessa, Valerie, Bruce. **EDUCATION:** Stanford U, PhD 1971; Case Western Reserve U, MA 1964; TN State U, BS 1954. **CAREER:** Old Dominion Univ, prof; FL Intl Univ, dir spnsrd research; School Health School Serv, exec asst pres, interim dean; School Educ FL & Internat, asst dean; Natl Follow Through Program, US Office Educ, spec asst dir; Stanford Univ Graduate School Educ, asst dean; Cleveland, OH Public School, evening school prin & math dept chmn; Union Graduate School, adj prof; Nova Univ, natl lecturer; US Office Educ, gen cons. **ORGANIZATIONS:** Mem NABSE, Stanford Alumni Assn, VA Beach School Bd; bd dir Southeastern Tidewater Oppty Proj, Appalachia Educ Lab, Norfolk Kiwanis Inc; bd of trustees VA Beach Arts Center; natl lecturer Nova Univ. **HONORS/ACHIEVEMENTS:** Alpha Phi Alpha Frat Publ, Ldrshp & Eagle Awd in Pedagogy, John F Kennedy HS 1969; Phi Delta Kappa Hon soc; publ 3 books & numerous papers. **BUSINESS ADDRESS:** Professor, Old Dominion University, 5215 Hampton Blvd, Norfolk, VA 23508.

SPIVEY, DONALD
Educator. **PERSONAL:** Born Jul 18, 1948, Chicago, IL; married Diane Marie; children: 2 children. **EDUCATION:** Univ of IL, BA History 1971, MA History 1972; Univ of CA, PhD History 1976. **CAREER:** Univ of IL, dept of elem educ rsch asst 1971-72; Univ of CA, dept of history teaching asst 1972-74; Sacramento CA, music instructor 1972-74; Univ of CA Davis, lecturer in history 1975-76; Wright State Univ, asst prof of history 1976-79; Univ of MI, vstg asst prof of history 1978-79; Univ of CT, assoc prof of history 1979-85; Univ of CT, prof of history 1985-. **ORGANIZATIONS:** Mem President's Comm on Human Relations at Univ of CT 1984-85; mem Assoc for the Study of Afro-Amer Life and History, Organization of Amer Historians, Amer Historical Assoc, Popular Culture Assoc, Southwest Social Science Assoc, Natl Council for Black Studies, Southern Historical Assoc, North Amer Soc for the History of Sport. **HONORS/ACHIEVEMENTS:** Publ Schooling for the New Slavery, Black Indust Educ 1868-1915 Greenwood Press 1978; Bolinga Dist Teacher-Scholar Awd Black Faculty Wright State Univ 1978; listed in Dir of Amer Scholars (History), Who's Who in the Midwest, Dir of Intl Biography, Amer Council of Learned Societies Rsch Grant 1980; Rsch Found Grant Univ of CT 1983-84; publ The Politics of Miseducation, The Booker Washington Inst of Liberia 1928-84 Univ of KY Press 1984, Sport in Amer Greenwood Press 1985. **BUSINESS ADDRESS:** Professor of History, University of Connecticut, Department of History, Storrs, CT 06268.

SPOONER, JOHN C.
Director of human relations. **PERSONAL:** Born Dec 26, 1950, Dayton, OH; married Pamela McNease; children: Candace. **EDUCATION:** Elmhurst Coll, BA Art 1973. **CAREER:** Harris Trust & Savings Bank, asst emp trust admin 1974-76; Consolidated Foods Corp, asst emp benefits supvr 1976-77; Harris Trust & Savings Bank, compensation spec 1977-80, comp officer 1980-81, asst vp, dir human rel 1981-86, vice pres 1986-. **ORGANIZATIONS:** Mem Elmhurst Coll Alumni Assoc 1973-85, Elmhurst Coll Athletic Assoc 1973-85, Amer Compensation Assoc 1979 & 1980, Urban Bankers Forum 1980-, Chicago Area Assoc for Affirm Action Compliance 1981-; exec bd mem Natl Assoc of Banking Affirm Action Dir 1982-, IL Sheriffs Assoc 1985; mem/contrib World Vision Child Care Partnership Prog 1985; mem Active Brothers for Christ 1984-; mem Wheaton Christian Center 1985-. **HONORS/ACHIEVEMENTS:** Numerous athletic awds NCAA Div III Football 1969-73; Coll Dorm Resident Advisor 1971,72,73; Num appt to Dean's List Elmhurst Coll 1971-73; Cert Hay Assoc Cert of Achievement 1978,79; Merit Awd Youth Motivation Awd 1979; Cert & Publ Bio Outstanding Young Man of Amer 1983; Chicago Assn of Comm & Ind. **HOME ADDRESS:** 1350 Rebecca Road, Lombard, IL 60148. **BUSINESS ADDRESS:** VP, Dir Human Rel, Harris Trust & Saving Bank, P O Box 755, Chicago, IL 60690.

SPOONER, RICHARD C.
Attorney. **PERSONAL:** Born Jul 03, 1945, New York, NY. **EDUCATION:** NY U, BA 1970; FordhamUniv Sch of Law, JD 1975. **CAREER:** Comm Devel Agency, dir of prog plan 1970-71; Human Resources Admin NYC, spl asst to gen counsel 1972-75; Carroll & Reid, assoc 1975-77; Chemical Bank, vice pres & sr counsel. **ORGANIZATIONS:** Mem Am Bar Assn 1977-; mem Urban Bankers Coalition 1978-, bd of dir 1980-84, gen counsel 1981-85, intl vice pres 1983; mem Nat Bar Assn 1979-; mem MetroBlack Bar Assoc 1985-, vice pres finance 1985. **BUSINESS ADDRESS:** Vice President & Counsel, Chemical Bank, 380 Madison Ave, New York, NY 10016.

SPOTTSVILLE, CLIFFORD M.
Retired judge/attorney. **PERSONAL:** Born Oct 11, 1911, Independence, KS; married Geraldine A Rice; children: Keslie Rochelle, Shelly Rochelle. **EDUCATION:** Univ KS, attended; Howard Univ School of Law, JD 1946; Natl Coll State Judiciary, further study. **CAREER:** US Coast & Geodetic Survey Commerce Dept, employee 1942-48; Private practice, atty 1948-53; Jackson Cty MO, asst prosecuting atty 1953-61; Western Dist MO, asst US atty 1961-67; Jackson Cty MO, 1st asst prosecuting atty 1967-70; Municipal Court KC, judge 1970-77; Private practice, atty 1977-. **ORGANIZATIONS:** Mem Kansas City MO, Amer, Jackson Cty Bar Assocs; mem Amer Judicature Soc; pres Municipal & Magistrate Judges Assoc MO 1974-75; bd dirs Boys Club, United Way; bd trustees Univ MO, Ottawa Univ Ottawa KS. **BUSINESS ADDRESS:** Attorney, 500 Traders Bank Bldg, 1125 Grand Ave, Kansas City, MO 64106.

SPRADLEY, MARK MERRITT
Consultant. **EDUCATION:** Howard Univ, BS 1983; Med Univ SC, MHSA 1986. **CAREER:** US Dept of State, consultant, 1979-84; Voice of Amer, consultant, 1983-84; Pres Private Sector Surveyon Cost Control, consultant, 1983-84; Mayor's Comm on Food Nutrition & Health Wash, comm, 1983-84; African Marketplace 1984 World's Fair, consultant, 1984. **ORGANIZATIONS:** Discussant Amer Enterprise Inst Religious & Econ Seminars 1984; chmn Charleston Co Young Republicans 1985-. **HONORS/ACHIEVEMENTS:** Several newspaper & magazine articles on health & political topics. **HOME ADDRESS:** PO Box 39212, Charleston, SC 29407.

SPRADLING, MARY ELIZABETH MACE
Librarian. **PERSONAL:** Born Dec 31, Winchester, KY; widowed. **EDUCATION:** KY State Coll, AB 1933; Atlanta Univ, BLS 1958; Rutgers Univ, certificate 1971. **CAREER:** Public Schs KY SC, tchr 1933-37; Shelbyville Sch, tchr lib 1944-47; Public Library, librn 1948-57; Kalamazoo Pub Lib, young adult dept 1957-76; Gale Rsch Co, bibliographer compiler. **ORGANIZATIONS:** Mem Family Serv Org Comm Cncl, Louisville Area Girl Scouts Bd, Kalamazoo Cncl on Human Relations, Kalamazoo YWCA Pub Affrs Comm, Kalamazoo Co Comm Serv Cncl, Kalamazoo Youth Comm, Kalamazoo Cncl Churches, Kalamazoo Co Library Bd, Mayor's Adv Comm on Problems of Law Enforcement, Kalamazoo Co Bi-Centennial Comms, King Meml Fund Bd Secty; Kalamazoo Branch NAACP; bd trustees Nazareth Coll; mem Delta Kappa Gamma Soc Epsilon Chapt; mem Kalamazoo Alumnae Chap Delta Sigma Theta Sor; asst supt Friendship Home; chmn Librarian's Sect KY Negro Educ Assn; KY mem chmn Assn of Young People's Librarians; mem MI Library Assn Recruiting Comm; mem YASD Comm "Recent Adult Books for Young People"; mem Book

Bait Comm ALA; guest lectr Dept of Librarianship Western MI Univ; mem bd dirs Young Adult Serv ALA; mem Amer Lib Assn Cncl; contributor PREVIEWS Magazine; keynote spkr IN Library Assn YART, Student Library Workshop Western MI Univ. **HONORS/ACHIEVEMENTS:** Listed in Who's Who in Library Serv 6th ed; Who's Who in Amer Women; Notable Black Women Nancy Ellin 1984; Citations Midwest Region, Delta Sigma Theta Sor Inc, Kalamazoo Alumnae Delta Sigma Theta Sor, Adero Sisterhood Awd, Black Educators Kalamazoo; Kalamazoo NAACP Freedom Fund Humanitarian Awd 1984; "There IsNo Such Book" Top of the News June 1965; Afro Amer Quiz 1976, In Black & White, Afro-Amers in Print, 2nd & 3rd edition supplement in preparation (a guide); "Black Librarians in KY" 1980. **BUSINESS ADDRESS:** Bibliographer/Compiler, Gale Research Company, 307 S Dartmouth, Kalamazoo, MI 49007.

SPRAGGINS, STEWART
Executive administrator. **PERSONAL:** Born May 17, 1936, Pheba, MS; married Jean Caldwell; children: Renee Ericka, Stewart II. **EDUCATION:** Mary Holmes Coll, AA 1958; Knoxville Coll, BA 1962; Fairfield Univ, MA 1972; Miles Coll, Dr of Human Letters 1983. **CAREER:** YMCA of Greater Bridgeport, exec mem & phys ed 1962-70; YMCA of Greater OK City, metro outreach exec 1970-72; YMCA of the Oranges, exec dir 1972-74; YMCA of Greater NY, exec dir 1974-77; JP Stevens & Co Inc, dir comm affairs 1977-. **ORGANIZATIONS:** Chmn Council of Concerned Black Execs; exec comm The Edges Group Inc; treas Natl Urban Affairs Council Inc; mem Corporate Coordinators Volunteers Council Inc; bd member Mary Holmes Coll 1983; bd mem NY March of Dimes 1983; bd member Accent Magazine 1984; bd mem Inst of NJ 1984. **HONORS/ACHIEVEMENTS:** Outstanding Blk Amer NAACP & City of Bridgeport 1968; past state pres Elks of N America & Can 1969; Board Member of the Yr OK City Comm Action Prog 1970; Dr of Humane Letters Miles Coll 1983. **MILITARY SERVICE:** AUS pvt 1 yr. **HOME ADDRESS:** 18 Maplewood Ave, Maplewood, NJ 07040.

SPRATLEN, THADDEUS H.
Educator, consultant. **PERSONAL:** Born May 28, 1930, Union City, TN; son of John B Spratlen (deceased) and Lela C Dobbins (deceased); married Lois Price, Sep 28, 1952; children: Pamela, Patricia, Paula, Thadd Price, Townsand Price. **EDUCATION:** OH State U, BS 1956; OH State U, MA 1957; OH State U, PhD 1962. **CAREER:** Howard Univ School of Business Administration, visiting research professor of marketing, 1986-87; Univ of WA, acting dir Afro-Amer Studies, 1980-81; Univ of WA, assoc dir Black Studies Program, 1979-80; Univ of WA, prof marketing 1975-; Univ of WA, assoc prof 1972-75; UCLA, 1969-72; W WA State Coll, 1961-69; author pubns; conference speaker; UCLA, consultant, adjunct assoc prof, 1972-75; Univ CA Berkeley, lecturer, 1965; Ethnic Studies Prog W WA State Coll, acting dir 1969; Black Economists Devel Proj, dir 1970-74. **ORGANIZATIONS:** Mem Natl Econ Assn; mem Caucus Black Economists; mem Amer Marketing Assn; mem WA State Adv Comm Minority Business 1974-76; mem Beta Gamma Sigma; mem US Census Adv Comm of Amer Marketing Assn 1975-81; United Negro Coll Fund Lecturer 1971, 1974. **HONORS/ACHIEVEMENTS:** John Hay Whitney Fellowship 1958-59; Frederick Douglass Scholar Award, Natl Council for Black Studies, Pacific Northwest Region, 1986. **MILITARY SERVICE:** AUSA 1st lt 1952-54; enlisted KT Corp, 1948-51. **BUSINESS ADDRESS:** Univ of Washington, School of Business Administration, DJ-10, Seattle, WA 98195.

SPRAUVE, GILBERT A.
Educator. **PERSONAL:** Born Jun 09, 1937, St Thomas, VI; married Alvara Eulalia Ritter; children: Masserae, Margaret, Janine, Singanu. **EDUCATION:** Brooklyn Coll, BA 1960;Univ of So CA, MA 1965; Princeton U, PhD 1974. **CAREER:** Coll of the VI, asso prof modern langs 1967-; LA City Schs CA, French, Spanish tchr 1963-67; Albert Acad Sierra Leone, French, Spanish tchr 1961-63; Lyce Donka Guinea, Span, Engl tchr 1960-61; Third Constitutional Conv of VI, del 1977; 14th Leg of Virgin Island, senator at-large, vp; candidate forlt gov on the runner-up Bryan/Sprauve ticket in 1986 general elections; Univ of Virgin Islands, prof of modern langs. **ORGANIZATIONS:** Mem VI Bd of Educ 1978-; adv bd mem Caribbean Fishery Mgmt Council 1979-; Rockefeller Foun Fellowship Grad Black Studies 1971-74. **HONORS/ACHIEVEMENTS:** Pub "The Queue" The Literary Review 1974; del Pres Conf on Libraries 1979; principal role Derek Walcott's "Marie La Veau" a world premiere workshop at Coll VI 1979. **BUSINESS ADDRESS:** Professor, Univ of the Virgin Islands, St Thomas, Virgin Islands of the United States 00801.

SPRIGGS, EDWARD S.
Museum executive. **PERSONAL:** Born Dec 06, 1934, Cleveland, OH; divorced; children: Tracey Lynne, Lisa Kelly. **EDUCATION:** San Francisco Art Inst, 1953-55; San Francisco State Coll, BA. **CAREER:** The Studio Mus of Contemporary Black Art in Harlem NY, exec dir; adminstr creative head of mus's progs, exhbn's, fund raising, pub relations 1969-; postal clk 1958-65; freelance graphic artist, caseworker, freelance sound tech, film editor 1965-69; pub poet; writer of articles; Black Dialogue Mag, editor; exhibited his works in numerous art shows. **ORGANIZATIONS:** Founder Bay Artists & Craftsmen United; vol art dir Negro Hist & Cultural Soc San Francisco Bay Area; instr silk screen design & processing; mem adminstrv staff Harlem's Black Arts Repertory Theater.

SPRIGGS, G. MAX
Educator. **PERSONAL:** Born Apr 24, 1925, Des Moines, IA; married Phyllis Joan Leadon; children: James Max, Lyna Ruth Spriggs-Hasenjager, Daniel Edward. **EDUCATION:** DrakeUniv Des Moines IA, 1947-49;Univ of MN, BS 1950; St Cloud State U, MS 1967;Univ of MN, EdD 1972. **CAREER:** Moorehead State Univ, asso prof of special educ 1978-; Univ of IL Urbana IL, chmn dept of special educ 1972-74; Roseville Area School St Paul MN, dir of special educ 1969-70; Highline School Dist Seattle WA, dir of special educ 1968-69; Minneapolis Public School, coordinator of MR program 1965-66. **HONORS/ACHIEVEMENTS:** Ideal tchrUniv of MN 1950; Ski-U-Mah service toUnivUniv of MN 1950. **MILITARY SERVICE:** NG capt 23 yrs. **BUSINESS ADDRESS:** Moorhead State Univ, Moorhead, MN 56560.

SPRIGGS, LARRY LAVELLE
Professional athlete. **PERSONAL:** Born Sep 08, 1959, Cheverly, MD. **EDUCATION:** San Jacinto TX Jr Coll; Howard Univ, 1981. **CAREER:** Los Angeles Lakers, forward. **ORGANIZATIONS:** Particip Ntnl Sports Festival 1979. **HONORS/ACHIEVEMENTS:** Broke personal career scoring-high twice during final week of reg season as he averaged 117 points and hit 16-19 FG's during the week; had 11 points, 5 rebounds and 24 minutes April 11 Vs portland, all career highs; erased those marks with 18 points, 8-9 fGs, and 6 rebounds in 30 minutes in the season finale April 15 vs Phoenix. **BUSINESS ADDRESS:** Los Angeles Lakers, P O Box 10, Ste 510, Inglewood, CA 90306.

SPRIGGS, RAY V.
Management consultant. **PERSONAL:** Born Oct 05, 1937, West Chester, PA; married Velva; children: Vashon. **EDUCATION:** Lincoln U, AB 1960;Univ of PA, Grad Sch of educ 1961;Univ of CA, Certif 1961;Univ of Ghana, Certif 1961. **CAREER:** DAMANS & Asso, assoc dir; Robert F Kennedy, proj coord 1977; Spriggs Assn, pres 1970; A L Nellum Assn Inc, trainer 1974; Unicorn Inc, consult 1974; Control Systems; Third World Arts 'n' Crafts, pres, owner. **ORGANIZATIONS:** Inter Res Assoc, 1972; lctr, "Black Am/Black African Rel"Univ of OK, 1972; exec dir, Comm Action Bd 1967; asst exec dir Cleveland NAACP 1965; tchr Philadelphia PA 1960; elected adv Neigh Commn 1976; pres Tenant Coun 1976; foun DC Tenants' Cong 1977; pres Oper Enlightenment Intl 1972; US Congressional Luncheon Speaker for Peace Corps 25th Anniv 1986. **HONORS/ACHIEVEMENTS:** Walter White Schol IBPOEW oratorical winner; Webster Meredith awd in oratory;Univ PA fellow; publ poetry US Peace Corps, 1961-63. **BUSINESS ADDRESS:** Owner, Third World Arts 'n' Crafts, 3649 New Hampshire Ave NW, Washington, DC 20010.

SPRINGER, ASHTON, JR.
Theatrical general manager. **PERSONAL:** Born Nov 01, 1930, New York, NY; married Myra L Burns; children: Mark, Chesley. **EDUCATION:** OH State U, BS 1954. **CAREER:** Theatre Mgmt Asso Inc, gen mgr; Bubbling Brown Sugar BR-wAY Musical, co-producer; No Place To Be Somebody, co-producer. **ORGANIZATIONS:** Pres Motor Car Asso 1966-70; mem League of NY Theatres & Prdcrs; mem Assn of Theatrical Press Agents & Mgrs. **HONORS/ACHIEVEMENTS:** One World Award No Place To Be Somebody NAACP 1971; Philadelphia Playgoers Award Special Achievement in Theatre 1977; Pulitzer Prize No Place To Be Somebody 1970. **BUSINESS ADDRESS:** President, Theatre Mgmt Associates, 240 W 44th St, New York, NY 10036.

SPRINGER, ERIC WINSTON
Attorney. **PERSONAL:** Born May 17, 1929, New York, NY; son of Owen W and Maida S; married Cecile Marie Kennedy; children: Brian, Christina. **EDUCATION:** Rutgers Univ, AB, 1950; NY Univ School of Law, LLB, 1953. **CAREER:** Justice NY State Supreme Court, law clerk, 1955-56; Univ of Pittsburgh, rsch assoc, 1956-58; asst prof of law, 1958-64, assoc prof of law, 1965-68, dir of compliance EEOC, 1967; Aspen Systems Corp Pittsburgh, vice pres, dir, publisher, 1968-71; Horty, Springer & Mattern PC Pittsburgh, partner, 1971-82, principal, 1982-. **ORGANIZATIONS:** Dir Presbyterian Univ Hosp 1967-; mem NY Bar (inactive) 1953, PA Bar 1975-; dir Duquesne Light Co 1977-; 2nd vice pres Urban League of Pittsburgh; mem ABA, NBA, Allegheny Cty Bar Assoc; life mem NAACP. **HONORS/ACHIEVEMENTS:** Honorary Fellow Amer Coll of Healthcare Execs 1978; author "Group Practice and the Law" 1969; editor "Nursing and the Law" 1970; "Automated Medical Records and the Law" 1971; contributing editor of monthly newsletter "Action-Kit for Hospital Law" 1973. **MILITARY SERVICE:** AUS 1953-55. **BUSINESS ADDRESS:** Executive Vice President, Horty, Springer & Mattern PC, 4614 Fifth Ave, Pittsburgh, PA 15213.

SPRINGER, GEORGE CHELSTON
Labor union administrator, educator. **PERSONAL:** Born Nov 09, 1932, La Boca, Canal Zone, Panama;son of Bertley Nimrod Springer and Edna Ethel Westerman-Springer; married Gerri Brown Springer, Oct 11, 1980; children: Rosina Francesca Springer Audette, Linda Inez Springer-Broderick, George C Jr. **EDUCATION:** Canal Zone Jr Coll, La Boca CZ, AA, 1952; Teachers Coll of Connecticut, New Britain CT, BS, 1954, Central Connecticut State Univ, New Britain CT, attended, 1955-75. **CAREER:** Fafnir Bearing Co, New Britain CT, hardener, 1955-57, 1959; US Army, occupational therapy tech, 1957-59; Consolidated School Dist, New Britain CT, teacher, 1959-79; Connecticut Fedn of Teachers, Berlin CT, pres, 1979-. **ORGANIZATIONS:** Mem, SDE Educ Equity Comm, 1979-; vice pres, Connecticut State AFL-CIO, 1979-; pres, New Britain Chapter NAACP, 1982-86; secretary, treasurer, Legislative Electional Action Program, 1982-; vice pres, United Labor Agency, 1983-; mem, advisory council, CSU Center for Educ Excellence, 1986-; mem, Connecticut Coalition for Literacy, 1986-; bd of trustees, Connecticut Law School Found, 1987-; bd of dir, Connecticut Civil Liberties Union, 1987-; bd of overseers, Regional Lab for Educ Improvement in the Northeast & Islands, 1988-; vice pres, Amer Fedn of Teachers, 1988-; fellow, Amer Leadership Forum, 1988-; co-chair, Sixth Dist Fed Priorities Project, 1988-. **HONORS/ACHIEVEMENTS:** Man of the Year, St James Baptist Church, 1984; John P Shaw Award (Outstanding Serv to Community), New Britain NAACP, 1984; Meritorious Serv Award, UNCF, 1987; Educators of Distinction Award, Connecticut Coalition of 100 Black Women, 1988; Carl Huroit Award (Grassroot Politics, Progressive Issues, Coalition Building), LEAP, 1989; Harriet Tubman Award (Achievement in Pursuit of Social Justice), Connecticut NOW, 1989. **MILITARY SERVICE:** US Army, Sp-4, 1957-59. **HOME ADDRESS:** 45 Glen Carlyn Rd, New Britain, CT 06053. **BUSINESS ADDRESS:** President, Connecticut State Federation of Teachers, AFT, AFL-CIO, 1781 Wilbur Cross Pkwy, Berlin, CT 06037.

SPRINGS, LENNY F.
Business executive. **PERSONAL:** Born Apr 25, 1947, Edgefield, SC. **EDUCATION:** Voorhees Coll, BS 1968. **CAREER:** Greenville Urban League, proj dir 1976-79, deputy dir 1979-82, exec dir 1982-83; Southern Bank, comm relations officer 1983-. **ORGANIZATIONS:** Vice pres Greenville Branch NAACP 1976-84; chmn Legal Redress Comm SC Conf NAACP 1978-; vice chmn SC Human Affairs Comm 1983-. **HONORS/ACHIEVEMENTS:** Outstanding Young Men of Amer 1973 & 1979; NAACP Legal Awd for SC 1980; Greenville Branch NAACP Awd 1984. **MILITARY SERVICE:** AUS sgt E-5 2 yrs; 2 Bronze Stars; Air Medal. **BUSINESS ADDRESS:** Asst Vice Pres/Comm Rela, Southern Bank, PO Box 1329, Greenville, SC 29602.

SPRINGS, RON
Professional athlete. **PERSONAL:** Born Nov 04, 1956, Williamsburg, VA; married Adriane. **EDUCATION:** Ohio State, Communications. **CAREER:** Rentex, owner; Dallas Cowboys, runningback 1979-. **HONORS/ACHIEVEMENTS:** Led NFL running backs in receiving & set club record with 73 catches 1983; Led the team in kickoff returns in 1979.

SPROUT, FRANCIS ALLEN
Artist, educator. **PERSONAL:** Born Mar 05, 1940, Tucson, AZ. **EDUCATION:** Univ of AZ Tuscon, BFA 1967; Univ of CA San Diego, MFA 1972, MA (in progress). **CAREER:**

Univ of Denver, CO, asst prof Art 1972-75; Univ of CO, Boulder, instr African & African Amer Vsl Traditions 1976-82; Metro State Coll Denver, CO, asso prof Art 1976-. **ORGANIZATIONS:** Mem African Studies Asso 1984; mem Chicano Hmnts & Art Cncl Denver 1982-; mem Alliance for Contmpry Art Denver Art Museum 1980; grant review pnl CO Cncl on the Arts & Humnts 1984-85. **HONORS/ACHIEVEMENTS:** Flwshp Inst on Africa, Hamline Univ 1978; CO Rep 74th Wstn Annual Denver Art Museum 1972; Flwshp Grad Stdy Ford Fndtn 1971-72. **MILITARY SERVICE:** USNG 1st lt 6 yrs. **BUSINESS ADDRESS:** Professor of Art, Metropolitan State Coll, Art Dept Box 59, 1006 11th St, Denver, CO 80204.

SPRUILL, ALBERT WESTLEY
Educational administrator. **PERSONAL:** Born Aug 05, 1926, Columbia, NC; married Pearl Floydelia Farrish; children: Albert Westley Jr, Ogden Bertrand, Ronald Conrad. **EDUCATION:** NC A&T State Univ, BS 1949; IA State Univ Ames, MS 1951; Cornell Univ, EdD 1958. **CAREER:** NC Agr Ext Svc, cty agent 1949-50; MS Voc Coll, act dir div of agr 1951-52; Tuskegee Inst, teacher trainer agr ed 1952-53; NC A&T State Univ, instr prof 1955-, dean grad studies 1970-. **ORGANIZATIONS:** Mem NAACP 1960-; deacon Providence Baptist Church 1970-; vice pres & pres Southern Conf of Grad Schools 1974-76; sec/treas Southern Assn Land Grant Coll & State Univ 1976-; bd of dir Council of Grad Schools in US 1985-. **HONORS/ACHIEVEMENTS:** Gate City Alumni Awd NC A&T State Univ 1949; Gen Ed Bd Fellow Gen Educ Bd 1953-54; Elected to Phi Delta Kappa Theta Chap Cornell 1954; Alumni Merit Awd IA State Univ Ames 1982. **MILITARY SERVICE:** AUS pfc 1946-47. **HOME ADDRESS:** 1303 Marboro Drive, Greensboro, NC 27406. **BUSINESS ADDRESS:** Dean, Graduate School, NC Agr & Tech StateUniv, 120 Gibbs Hall, Greensboro, NC 27411.

SPRUILL, JAMES ARTHUR
Educator. **PERSONAL:** Born Sep 28, 1937, Baltimore, MD; married Lynda; children: Robert, Joshua. **EDUCATION:** Goddard Coll, AB 1968; Boston Univ, MFA 1975. **CAREER:** Boston Univ School for Arts, asst prof; Emerson Coll, teacher 1970-74; Goddard Coll, visiting prof 1971-72; Boston State Coll, visiting prof 1972-75; Theatre Co of Boston, acted, production, dir, taught 1967-75. **ORGANIZATIONS:** Pres, New African Co Inc 1968-; co-founder New African Co Inc 1968-; mem bd trustees Metro Cultural All; mem New England Theatre Conf; sr mem ActorsAquity Assn; past mem Theatre Advis Panel MA Coun on Arts & Human Martin Luither King Fellow Boston Univ 1968; prod "The Blacks" Loeb Drama Center HarvardU 1969; reg cit New English Theatre Conf 1970; devel & taught course in Black Drama History Boston Coll, Emerson Coll, Boston State Coll; directed first play published in US (1858) by W W Brown World premiere Emersol Coll 1972; directed "The Escape or a Leap for Freedom" at BU 1977; Roxbury Action Program. **HONORS/ACHIEVEMENTS:** Insight award 1975. **BUSINESS ADDRESS:** Assoc Prof, Boston Univ, 855 Commonwealth Ave, Boston, MA 02115.

SPRUILL, ROBERT I.
Business executive. **PERSONAL:** Born Jul 10, 1947, New Bern, NC. **EDUCATION:** NC Cen U, BS 1970. **CAREER:** WAFRM FM Comm Radio Workshop Inc, pres & founder. **ORGANIZATIONS:** Mem Nat Assn of Educ Broadcasters; NC Assn Broadcasters. **HONORS/ACHIEVEMENTS:** First black owned & controlled educ radio station in Am; Featured in Ebony Magazine, 1973. **BUSINESS ADDRESS:** WAFR-FM, 2501 Fayetteville St, Durham, NC 27707.

SPURLOCK, CHARLES T.
Educator. **PERSONAL:** Born Mar 29, 1917, Richmond, VA; married LaVerne Beard. **EDUCATION:** VA Union U, BA1940; Columbia U, MA1948; Boston U,Univ of VA, further study. **CAREER:** Richmond Public Schools, middle schools prin; Richmond, past teacher, counselor, asst prin 1946-. **ORGANIZATIONS:** Mem NASSP; NEA; Richmond Assn for Sch Adminstrs; Chmn Search Comfor Ebenezer Bapt Ch; chmn Henrico Co Draft Bd; bd mem Tiny Angels Child Care Center; bd mem Salvation Army Boys Club; bd mem YMCA; mem Alpha Phi Alpha; CIAA football official. **HONORS/ACHIEVEMENTS:** Man & Boy Award Salvation Army Boys Club 1975; Merit Serv Award BSA Frederick Douglass Dist. **MILITARY SERVICE:** AUS warrant officer WW II. **BUSINESS ADDRESS:** 701 N 37 St, Richmond, VA 23223.

SPURLOCK, JAMES B., JR.
Industry executive. **PERSONAL:** Born Jan 20, 1936, Roanoke, VA; married Nancy H; children: James B III, Deborah G, Kenneth L. **EDUCATION:** A&t State Univ, BS (cum laude) 1959; Personnel Adm Personnel Mgmt, diploma 1960, 1962; Mgmt Training Course, grad 1968; Univ of MI, grad Advanced Mgmt Prog 1970. **CAREER:** Roanoke Valley Training & Devel Assn; VA Coll Placement Assn; S Coll Placement Assn, public relations assoc. **ORGANIZATIONS:** Mem VA State C of C; lectr Univ MI; A&T State Univ Career Convocation & Interview Clinic; SE Elec Exchange Fall Conf; mem Rotary Club Intl Salem VA; panelist for Natl Assn of Market Devel & WRFT-TV; Indus Mgmt Clubs of VA; VA Western Comm Coll; past chmn bd dir Roanoke Chap Oppty Indus Ctr Inc; bd of deacons First African Baptist Church; past mem bd trustees Sweet Union Baptist Ch; past mem Roanoke Jaycees; past mem bd dir Roanoke Valley Council of Comm Svcs; past mem bd dir Roanoke Valley Unit Amer Cancer Soc; past mem bd of Roanoke Valley Vol Bur; past mem Roanoke Selective Serv Bd; past mem Gainsboro Elec Mfg Co; past loan exec Roanoke Valley United Fund Campaign; past mem Roanoke City Sch Bd; various others. **HONORS/ACHIEVEMENTS:** Publ articles "Obsolescence or Change"; "Recruiting the Qualified Minority Grad"; Who's Who in Amer Colls & Univs 1958-59; treas Sigma Rho Sigma Natl Honor Soc; Outstanding Citizen's Awd 1973; Personality of the S 1973; Outstanding Serv on the Bd of Dir VA Coll Placement Assn 1972; Outstanding Comm LdrBurrell Meml Hosp 1974; Father of the Yr Inter-Faith Comm Choir 1971; Key to City of Roanoke 1975; Cert of Merit City Council of Roanoke for Serv on Roanoke Sch Bd 1974; Cert of Recog Natl Alliance of Busmn for Serv on Youth Motivation Task Force 1973-74; Cert of Appreciation State Dir of Selective Serv for Serv on Roanoke Selective Serv Bd; Awd of Apprec So Coll Placement Assn for Serv on Bd Dir; state chmn United Nations Day 1977; selected as one of VA Comm Ldrs; Who's Who of the Commonwealth's Comm Leaders 1976-77. **MILITARY SERVICE:** AUS capt 1960-68. **BUSINESS ADDRESS:** 4500 S Laburnum Ave, Richmond, VA 23231.

SPURLOCK, JEANNE
Physician, educator. **PERSONAL:** Born in Sandusky, OH. **EDUCATION:** Howard Univ Sch of Medicine, MD 1947; Chicago Inst for Psychoanalysis, completed post-grad study. **CAREER:** Meharry Med Coll, ch dept psych; Michael Reese Hosp Chicago, chief of child psychiatry clinic; tchr at numerous med schs across the country; Amer Psychiatric Assn; deputy med dir 1974-. **ORGANIZATIONS:** Mem Natl Med Assn, Amer Acad of Child Psychiatry; mem bd dirs Urban League. **HONORS/ACHIEVEMENTS:** 1st Black to receive Edward Strecker Awd Inst of PA Hosp for Outstanding Ability as a Clinician Educator & Comm Leader; listed in Who's Who in Med. **BUSINESS ADDRESS:** Deputy Medical Dir, Amer Psychiatric Assn, 1400 K St, NW, Washington, DC 20005.

SPURLOCK, LANGLEY AUGUSTINE
Government executive. **PERSONAL:** Born Nov 09, 1939, Charleston, WV. **EDUCATION:** WV State Coll, BS 1959; Wayne State Univ, PhD 1963. **CAREER:** Brown Univ, assoc prof of chemistry 1969-73; Amer Council on Educ, asst to pres 1973-76; US Dept of HEW, HEW fellow 1976-77; Natl Science Found, sr staffassoc 1977-82; Chemical Mfg Assn, dir CHEMSTAR Division. **ORGANIZATIONS:** Mem Amer Chem Soc; Amer Society of Assn Executives; Amer Assoc for the Advancement of Science; Phi Lambda Upsilon Hon Chem Soc; Soc of Sigma Xi; Beta Kappa Chi Hon Sci Soc; Alpha Kappa Mu Hon Schol Soc; Delta Phi Alpha Hon German Soc; Kappa Alpha Psi. **HONORS/ACHIEVEMENTS:** Certified Assn Executive 1989-; Alfred P Sloan Fellow 1973-75; NIH Postdoctoral Fellow Harvard Univ 1966; NIH predoctoral fellow Wayne State Univ 1961-63; Magna Cum Laude WV State Coll 1959; author 34 publications & 3 patents. **BUSINESS ADDRESS:** Director, CHEMSTAR Division, Chemical Manufacturers Assn, 2501 M St NW, Washington, DC 20037.

SPURLOCK, LAVERNE B.
Educator. **PERSONAL:** Born Feb 23, 1930, Richmond, VA; married Charles T. **EDUCATION:** VA State Coll, BS 1950; Columbia U, MA 1954;Univ of VA, advanced study 1974. **CAREER:** Richmond Public Schools, coordinator of Guidance dept 1970-; Maggie L Walker HS, counselor 1960; Maggie L Walker HS, teacher 1951. **ORGANIZATIONS:** Mem cochmn VA Assn for Non-White Concerns; past pres VA Sch Counselor Assn; past dir for educ & vice pres for educ Richmond Personnel & Guidance Assnb pres elect; APEA; VPGA; vol listener Youth Emergency Svcs; bd mem Richmond Area Psychiatric Clinic; past mem Bd of Christian Educ Ebenezer Bapt Ch; past mem Personnel Com Ebenezer Bapt Ch; past pres Richmond Chap Delta Sigma Theta. **BUSINESS ADDRESS:** 4225 Old Brook Rd, Richmond, VA 23227.

SPURLOCK-EVANS, KARLA JEANNE
College administrator. **PERSONAL:** Born Jun 30, 1949, Willimantic, CT; daughter of Kelly M Spurlock and Odessa Fuller Spurlock; married Booker Evans, Jul 01, 1978; children: Mariama Ifetayo. **EDUCATION:** Barnard Coll, AB (Magna Cum Laude) 1971; Emory Univ, MA 1972. **CAREER:** State Univ of NY at Albany, asst prof 1975-77; Haverford Coll, dir of minority affairs 1977-80; Lake Forest Coll, asst dean of students 1981-85; Northwestern Univ, assoc dean of students/dir Afro-Amer student affairs 1985-. **ORGANIZATIONS:** Bd mem Assoc for the Advancement of Creative Musicians 1981-83; mem IL College Personnel Assoc, IL Comm on Black Concerns in Higher Educ, Natl Assoc of Women Deans, Administrators and Counselors. **HONORS/ACHIEVEMENTS:** Phi Beta Kappa; Grad Fellowship John Hay Whitney Foundation 1971-72; Grad Fellowship Danforth Foundation 1971-75. **BUSINESS ADDRESS:** Assoc Dean/Dir, Northwestern University, 1914 Sheridan Rd, Evanston, IL 60201.

SQUIRES, MAUDEST KELLY
Retired educator. **PERSONAL:** Born Dec 18, 1903, Georgetown, SC; widowed; children: Kathryn White, Mae Walton. **EDUCATION:** Benedict Coll Columbia SC, attended; Hartshorn Mem Coll Richmond VA, attended; SC Coll Orangeburg, BS, MS; George Peabody Coll, attended; Howard UnivWashington DC, attended; Columbia Univ NY City, attended. **CAREER:** Howard HS, teacher 1923-27; Patterson Springs Elem School Shelby NC, teacher 1929-35; Whittemore HS Conway SC, teacher/suprv 1935-41; Felton Training School SC State Coll Orangeburg, principal 1941-43, assoc prof 1943-51; Rural Schools in Georgetown Cty, suprv 1951-57; Chopee High & Elem School Georgetown SC, principal 1957-74. **ORGANIZATIONS:** Sec Georgetwon Cty Bd of Ed; voting delegate State School Bd Convention; attended Natl School Bd Convention; mem Georgetown Cty Bd of Ed; mem Finance Committee; first steering comm Bond Referendum; mem SC Textbook Commiss; coord Committee for Ed Improvement; organizer Baruch Playground, Bus & Professional Women in Georgetown Cty; governors task force Citizen Partic in Ed; mem Bethesda Missionary Baptist Church, Youth Dir; pres BYPU; teacher Sunday School; mem Choir; substitute organist. **HONORS/ACHIEVEMENTS:** 1st Disting Svd Awd Georgetown Cty Chamber of Comm 1984; Royal Blue Book of England, Who's Who in Amer, Who's Who in the South & Southwest, Who's Who Among Women in Amer; recipient of Dreamkeepers Awd Comm for the Celebration of Agro-Amer History; Most Disting Alumni Awd SC State Coll; Honored by Omega Psi Phi Frat Inc; Delta Sigma Theta Sor Inc Silver Cert; Honored by Alpha Kappa Alpha Sor Inc; Publ "School Scrutiny", "Teaching Methods & Devices", "Carver", "Credit Where Credit is Due", "County Study of Dropouts Shows Progress Can Be Made"; Who's Who in American Education.

STAATS, FLORENCE JOAN
Educational administrator. **PERSONAL:** Born Nov 18, 1940, Newark, NJ; daughter of Jay M Staats and Florence Wheatley Staats. **EDUCATION:** Parsons Sch of Design cert 1961; new york univ, bs 1968; pratt inst, mfa 1970; columbia univ tchrs coll, edd 1978. **CAREER:** Newark Pub Lbry, exhibit artst 1965-68; Essex Co Coll, fine arts instr 1972-78, asst prof coord of Art pgm 1978-81; Dutchess Comm Coll, asst dean1982-84, asst to pres 1984-; Bloomfield Coll, associate dean 1985-86; Rockland Cmmty Coll, associate dean 1986-88; Acting Dir NY African American Institute SUNY 1988-. **ORGANIZATIONS:** Cnsltnt artst Pgm for Spcl Arts Fstvl 1981-81; cnsltnt Creative Arts Proj Dev 1982-83; bd dir Clearwater, Inc 1983-; rep ACE/NIP Instnl Am Cncl Education Mid Hudson Chptr 1983-; exec bd dir Ulster Co Cncl for Arts 1983-85; creative dir/pres The Arts Connection 1984-; pres Arts & Communication Network Inc 1985-; Bd of Dir Creative Research in African Amer Life 1986-; Executive Board/Chairperson Ulster County NAACP Education Committee. **HONORS/ACHIEVEMENTS:** NEH Grant Black Exprnc in Am 1977; OE Grant (Fullbright) G7 Cmnty Coll Smnr Poland 1974; CBS/EEC Awrd for Mrktng Pln 1984; Ldrshp 80'S Proj Am Asso of Wmn in Cmnty Coll 1985; Summer Research Grant NY African American Institute 1987. **HOME ADDRESS:** 501 Mossy Brook Rd, High Falls, NY 12440. **BUSINESS**

ADDRESS: Acting Director, New York African American Institute-SUNY, State University Plaza, Albany, NY 12246.

STACIA, KEVIN MAURICE
Senior human resources representative. **PERSONAL:** Born Nov 01, 1958, Baton Rouge, LA. **EDUCATION:** Southern Univ, BS (Magna Cum Laude) 1980; Atlanta Univ, Sch of Business, MBA 1982. **CAREER:** Fidelity Natl Bank Baton Rouge, bank teller 1977-80; General Dynamics Corp San Diego, intern 1979; Scientific-Atlanta Inc, human resource rep 1982-86; Hewlett-Packard Co, sr human resources rep 1987-. **ORGANIZATIONS:** Adv bd mem Atlanta Urban League 1985-; assoc deacon and chmn of brotherhood Ebenezer Bapt Ch 1985-; trustee Atlanta Exchange Inc 1986-; co-chair programs comm metro Atlanta High Tech Personnel Assoc 1986-; pres Atlanta Chap Natl Black MBA Assoc 1987-; mem outreach prog comm Alpha Phi Alpha Frat Inc 1987-. **HONORS/ACHIEVEMENTS:** Outstanding Serv Awd Natl Black MBA Assoc 1985; Professional in Human Resources Accreditation Amer Soc for Personnel Admin 1986; MBA of the Year Atlanta Chap Natl Black MBA Assoc 1986. **BUSINESS ADDRESS:** Sr Human Resources Rep, Hewlett-Packard Co, 2000 South Park Place, Atlanta, GA 30339.

STACKHOUSE, E. MARILYN
Public relations director. **PERSONAL:** Born Mar 09, 1955, Washington, DC; daughter of Braxton L Stackhouse and Esterlean Moody Stackhouse. **EDUCATION:** Shaw Univ, Raleigh NC, 1973-77; Univ of Pittsburgh, Pittsburgh PA, 1983-84. **CAREER:** US Dept of Agriculture, Alexandria VA, public affairs specialist, 1977-85; DC General Hosp, Washington DC, asst dir public affairs & marketing, 1985-87; MAXIMA Corp, Rockeville MD, dir of corp communications, 1987—. **ORGANIZATIONS:** International Assn of Business Communicators, National Black MBA Assn, Capital Press Club. **BUSINESS ADDRESS:** Director of Corporate Communications, MAXIMA Corp, 2101 East Jefferson St, Rockville, MD 20852.

STAES, BEVERLY N.
Savings and loan executive. **CAREER:** United Federal Savings & Loan Assn, New Orleans, LA, chief exec. **BUSINESS ADDRESS:** United Federal Savings & Loan Assn, 1501 Canal St, New Orleans, LA 70112. *

STAGGERS, FRANK EUGENE
Physician. **PERSONAL:** Born Aug 23, 1926, Charleston, SC; widowed; children: Frank Jr, Barbara, Michael. **EDUCATION:** VA State Coll, BS 1949; Meharry Med Coll, MD 1953. **CAREER:** Physician urology 1963-; USN Hosp, asst chf urology 1961-63; USN, resd 1957-60; USN Hosp, intern 1953-54. **ORGANIZATIONS:** Mem AMA; CMA; ACCMA; NMA; Western Sect AUA; Med Staff & Survey Com CA Med Assn; sr staff surveyor 1971-; mem CA Blue Shield Policy Com 1972-; Geriatrics Com 1970-; pres Golden State Med Soc; St Luke's Soc; Nursing Educ Adv Com Merrie & Laney Coll 1971-; Sigma Pi Phi Frat; Kappa Alpha Psi; Beta Kappa Chi Nat Hon Sci Coc; co-chmn Golden State Med Assn CA Med Assn Liasion Com Recpt Carcinoma of the Prostate Gland in CA 1977; Carcinoma of the Prostate UC Med Ctr 1973. **HONORS/ACHIEVEMENTS:** Publ "Treatment of the Underscended Testis With Especial Reference to Pathological Anatomy" Jour Urology 1960. **MILITARY SERVICE:** AUS comdr 1945-45; AUSNR 1947-53; USN 1953-63; USNR 1963-73. **BUSINESS ADDRESS:** 5900 Shattuck Ave, Ste 203, Oakland, CA 94609.

STAHNKE, WILLIAM E.
Bank executive. **CAREER:** First Texas Bank, Dallas, chief exec. **BUSINESS ADDRESS:** First Texas Bank, 2650 Royal Ln, Dallas, TX 75229. *

STALEY, VALERIA HOWARD
Librarian. **PERSONAL:** Born May 05, 1925, Georgetown, SC; married Frank Marcellus Staley Jr; children: Frank Howard, Elisa Claire. **EDUCATION:** Talladega Coll, BA 1945; Univ of Chicago, BLS 1946. **CAREER:** FL A&M Univ, ref librarian 1946-49; Howard HS, school librarian 1949-57; SC State Coll, reference and information specialist 1958-85 (retired). **ORGANIZATIONS:** Chmn Orangeburg Co Library Comm 1969-; bd dirs Orangeburg Co Arts Festival; mem Amer Library Assn; mem Southeastern Lib Assn; mem SC Library Assn; mem Amer Assn of Univ Profs; mem Phi Delta Kappa Frat; mem Black Caucus Amer Library Assn; Churchwomen United; Links Inc; mem past pres Delta Sigma Theta Sor; mem Jeddah Ct Daughters of Isis; mem Eastern Stars; mem VFW Auxiliary Post 8166; past pres Jack & Jill of Amer; past pres vice pres NAACP; mem Wm Chapel AME Ch.

STALKS, LARRIE W.
Public official. **PERSONAL:** Born Sep 28, 1925, Newark, NJ; married Frederick Stalks. **EDUCATION:** Rutgers U; NY U. **CAREER:** Essex Co, register of deeds Jan 1975-; Central Planning Bd City of Newark, former sec; Dept of Health & Welfare City of Newark, dir 1966-70; Central Planning Bd City of Newark, exec sec; Congressman Hugh J Addonizio, home dist sec. **ORGANIZATIONS:** Bd trustees Central Ward Girls Club; Edmund L Houston Found Rutgers Univ; Essex Co Youth House; pres Metro Urban Social Serv Inc; vice pres OMEGA InvestmentCorp (MESBIC Prog); counsellor Municipal Careerwomen of Newark; founder, sec Newark Comm Housing Corp; sec Peoples Devel Corp; former pres Esqui-Vogues of Northern NJ; past vice pres Shanley Ave Civic Assn; past life mem chrn NAACP (Newark Br); past state bd dir NAACP State Conf; past public affairs chrnNegro Bus & Prof Womens Club; past Ed Citizenship; chmn Newark Chapter Council of Negro Women; Nat Planning Assn; Am Soc of Planning Officials; various organizations; vice-chmn, past vice-chrn Newark Central Ward; co-chmn Newark Essex Co Meyner for Governor Club; Essex Co Rep Young Dem Conv; Newark Liaison All Co Campaigns; founder, organizer, advisor Central Ward Young Dem; Congressional Liaison Kennedy Air-Lift (Pres campaign); exec dir Hugh J Addonizio Civic Assn; Minorities Affairs; chrn Dem Party Co State. **HONORS/ACHIEVEMENTS:** Recipient Comm Serv Award Afro Am Newspaper 1952; Achievement Award Iota Phi Lamba 1956; Achievement Award Frontiers of Am 1957; Newark Br NAACP Serv Award 1960; Stephen P Teamer Civic Assn Serv Award 1962; Negro Business & Professional Women Achievement Award 1963; Metro Civic Assn Serv Awd 1965; ILA Local 1233 Serv Award 1965; Ballantine Award 1965; Laura Grant Award 1965; Deomart Enterprises Woman of the Yr 1965; Newark Br NAACP 1966; Central Planning Bd Appreciation Award 1967; Iota Phi Chapter Sorority Outstanding Women 1968; South Ward Little League Serv Award 1968; Am Negro Assembly Inc Achievement Award 1968; Municipal Careerwomen of Newark Achievement Award 1968; Abraham Yecies Award 1972; After Hours Magazine Serv Award 1974; first black dept head & cabinet mem in 300 yrs of Newark's municipal govt. **BUSINESS ADDRESS:** Office of the Register Hall of, Newark, NJ 07102.

STALLINGS, GREGORY RALPH
Educator. **PERSONAL:** Born Dec 28, 1957, Richmond, VA; son of Mr & Mrs Steward B Stallings, Sr; married Mitzi Keyes; children: Brittny Jean. **EDUCATION:** The College of William & Mary, BA 1980. **CAREER:** Boys Club of Richmond, unit dir 1980-81; Richmond Public Schools, teacher 1981-86, coord intervention progs 1986-88, instructional leader 1988-. **ORGANIZATIONS:** College advisor Theta Rho Chap Alpha Phi Alpha VA Commonwealth Univ; dir of educational affairs Xi Delta Lambda Alpha Phi Alpha 1985-87; treas, male user bd First Union Baptist Church; basketball coach Recreation Dept; pres Xi Delta Lambda Alpha Phi Alpha 1988-90; area dir VACAPAF; instructor for VA Center for Educational Leadership. **HONORS/ACHIEVEMENTS:** First Black "Golden Boy" Boy's Club of Richmond 1972; Outstanding Teaching Awd JL Francis Elementary School 1983-86. **HOME ADDRESS:** 5110 Boscobel Ave, Richmond, VA 23225.

STALLINGS, JAMES RAIFORD
Administrator. **PERSONAL:** Born Oct 09, 1936, Augusta, GA; married Geneva Butler; children: Sylvia B, James R. **EDUCATION:** Allen Univ, BS 1955-59; So IL Univ, MS 1966-68. **CAREER:** Richmond Co Bd of Educ, math teacher 1959-71; C&S Natl Bank, loan officer & asst branch mgr 1971-75; Augusta Coll, dir of financial aid 1975-. **ORGANIZATIONS:** Mem Alpha Phi Alpha; mem Natl Bankers Assn 1971-75; mem Bank PAC 1973; mem GASFAA 1975-; mem SASFAA 1975-; mem NASFAA 1975-. **HONORS/ACHIEVEMENTS:** Most Outstanding Teacher Glenn Hills HS Augusta 1970; Star Teacher Glenn Hills HS Augusta 1970; first black banking officer in SC C&S Bank 1973. **BUSINESS ADDRESS:** Dir, Augusta Coll, 2500 Walton Way, Augusta, GA 30910.

STALLS, MADLYN ALBERTA
Educator. **PERSONAL:** Born Oct 22, 1947, Metropolis, IL; daughter of Robert A. Stalls and Freda Mae Houston Stalls; children: Robert C Goodwin. **EDUCATION:** Southern IL Univ, BA 1970, MS 1976. **CAREER:** IL Dept of Children & Family Svcs, social worker 1970-75; IL Farmers Union, manpower coordinator 1976-78; SIU-C School of Tech Careers, researcher/service coord 1978-80; SIU-C Ctr for Basic Skills, coord of supple inst developmental skills specialist/instructor 1980-. **ORGANIZATIONS:** Founder/coord Black Women's Coalition 1983; mentor SIU-C Project Magic 1984-; consultant Jack Co Public Hous Initiatives Training Prog 1985; steering comm mem IL Comm on Black Concerns in Higher Educ 1985-; consultant SIU-C Women's Studies Film Project 1986-; mem American Assn. of Counseling and Devel; exec dir Star Human Serv Devel Corp Inc, 1987-. **HONORS/ACHIEVEMENTS:** Service Awd Eurma C Hayes Comp Child Care Services/PAC 1977; Fellow IL Comm on Black Concerns in Higher Educ 1984; Cert of Appreciation SIU-C HEADSTART Carbondale, IL 1986; Iota Phi Theta Quintessence Award 1984; SIU-C-BAC Academic Excellence Award 1987, Paul Robeson Award; Faculty Staff Award 1988; 5 Poems published in Literati 1989; coord Southern Region ICBCHE Regional Fall Seminar 1988. **BUSINESS ADDRESS:** Instruct/Devel Skills Spclst, Southern Illinois University, Center For Basic Skills, Woody Hall, C9B, Carbondale, IL 62901.

STALLWORTH, ALMA G.
Government official. **PERSONAL:** Born Nov 15, 1932, Little Rock; married Thomas; children: Thomas Jr, Keith. **EDUCATION:** Highland Park Jr Coll, 1948-49; Wayne State U, 1950-51; Merrill Palmer Inst, 1965. **CAREER:** Parent Involvement Program Headstart Archdiocesan Detroit, coor 1964-68; dir vol serv 1968-69; St John's Day Care Ctr, dir 1969-70; Oak Grove Day Care Ctr; state rep 1970-74; ran for state Senator 7th Dist 1974; Historical Dept City of Detroit, dep dir 1978; State of MI, rep 1982-; chair Public Utilities Committee. **ORGANIZATIONS:** Mem Oak Grove AME Ch; Birwood Block Club; Community Utilization of Jewish Community Ctr; chmn Finance Com; mem Demo Patry Century Club; Inner-City Inter Faith Council Racial Justice; Memford HS Parent's Club; Natl Assn Business and Pro Women's Club Inc; Nat Order Women Legislators; Mayor's Citizens Task Force; Nat Orgtn Women Detroit Sect; State Training Sch Adv Council; Nat Inst Women's Wrongs; Wayne County Juvenile Justice Commn; exec comm United Negro College Fund, Natl Conf of State Legislature; bd of dir of New Detroit Inc, honarary mem Alpha Kappa Alpha Soroity. **HONORS/ACHIEVEMENTS:** Legislator of the Year MI Assoc of Children's Alliance; Community Serv Awd Lula Belle Stewart Centr; Dedicated Serv & Support Awd United Negro Coll Fund 1985; Outstanding Personal & Professional Commitment Awd Planned Parenthood 1985; Blue Cross Blue Shield Health & People PAC Awd 1986; Cert of Achievement for Maternal & Child Health Progs Gov Blanchard & Dept of Health; Spirit of Detroit Awd Gentlemen of Wall St; Distinguished Serv Awd MI Public Health Assoc; Susan B Anthony Awd Detroit Chap of Natl Org of Women; Walter A Bergman Human Rights Award, Federation of Teachers; Women's Honors in Public Service, Nurses Assn; Distinguished Service Award, United Negro College Fund. **BUSINESS ADDRESS:** State Representative, State of Michigan, 114 Capitol Building, Lansing, MI 48913.

STALLWORTH, ANN P.
Elected government official. **PERSONAL:** Born May 15, 1932, DeKalb, TX; divorced; children: Maj Charles, Patricia Banks, Lilye Chaffin, Rachel, Allen Anthony Jr, Eric Darrel. **EDUCATION:** Langston Univ, Bus Admin; Delta Coll, unit in computer sci. **CAREER:** Pacific Telephone, asst traffic mgr 1963-83, employment interviewer 1968-72, mktg adm 1972-84; AT&T Info System, tech cast consult 1984-; Stockton Unified School, trustee area 2; tech consult 1984-85; Contract Reference Svcs, dir of oper 1987. **ORGANIZATIONS:** Bd of dir Stockton Police Youth Activity 1968-74; mem bd Dameron Hosp 1970-; mem Natl Assoc Advancement of Colored People 1970-; bd mem Dameron Hosp1970-; mem San Joaquin Cty Grand Jury 1971-72, sec, pres, Positive Ed Oppty 1971-73; bd of trustee 1973-, vice pres 1975, pres 1976,80, vice pres 1984, Stockton Unified School Dist; chairperson Delegate Assembly CSBA Task Force 1977-81; mem Desegragation Integration 1977-78, Nominating Comm 1977-78, Governance Task Force 1978-79, Legislative Net Work 1978-80; founder, pres Stockton Chap BAPAC, central reg v chair CA Chap Black Amer Political Assoc of CA 1979-80; v chairperson CA State BAPAC 1980-84; mem Facilities Task Force 1980-81; vice pres Coalition of Urban School Board 1986-87. **HONORS/ACHIEVEMENTS:** Hon Life Mem James Monroe PTA 1964; Commendation on Vocational Ed Dr Wilson Riles Supt of Public Instr State of CA 1974; Black Woman in Ed Stockton Comm 1974; Nominee Soroptimist Woman of the Year Awd 1978. **BUSINESS ADDRESS:** Dir of Operation, Contract Reference Services, San Francisco, CA.

STALLWORTH, CHARLES DEROTHEA
Retired educational administrator. **PERSONAL:** Born Nov 22, 1906, Buenavista, AL; married Annie Matt Horn; children: Charles Derothea Jr, Willie Lewis. **EDUCATION:** Payne U, 1927-30; AL State U, BS 1936; AL State U, MEd 1948. **CAREER:** Chatom Middle Sch, prin 1972-77; Washington Co Jr High Sch, prin 1969-72; N Central Hich Sch, prin 1962-69; Koenton High Sch, prin 1938-62; Ridge Sch, prin 1937; Vredenburgh Sch, prin 1936; Burnt Corn High Sch, prin 1934-35. **ORGANIZATIONS:** Pres Monroe Co Tchrs Assn 1936-37; pres Washington Co Tchrs Assn 1944-45; vista worker Fedn of So Coop 1977-80; pres Washington Co Athletic Assn 1939-40, 1945-55; life mem NEA; pres Dist IX PTA 1960-65. **HONORS/ACHIEVEMENTS:** Cited for superior procedures as supervising prin Civic Participation AL Tchrs Assn 1959; Tchr of the Yr Washington Co 1959; cited for vista work Minority Peoples Council on the TTW 1978-80.

STALLWORTH, JOHN LEE
Professional athlete. **PERSONAL:** Born Jul 15, 1952, Tuscaloosa County; married Florastein Caudle; children: Johnny Lee Jr, Natasha. **EDUCATION:** AL A&M Univ, BS, MBA. **CAREER:** Amer Amicable Ins, salesman 1975-; AL A&M Univ, part-time football coach; Pittsburgh Steelers, football player 1974-. **ORGANIZATIONS:** Involved with MS, Amer Lung Assn, Sheriff's Boy's Ranch. **HONORS/ACHIEVEMENTS:** SIAC All Confer Team 1972-73; Sr Bowl Squad 1974; All AL Football Squad 1973; Pittsburgh Courier All Am 1974; Honor Ment AP Little All Am 1974; Football Digest All Rookie Team 1974; nom Most Outstanding Young Huntsvillian; Super Bowl Winner 1975-76; AFC All-Stars Sporting News 1979; Pro Bowl 1979; NFL Championship Games 1974-75 & 1978-79; AFC Championship Game 1974-76 & 1978-79; Holds all-time NFL record for most postseason touchdown receptions (12) and most 100-yard games (5); Pro Bowl 1971 & 1982; Holds Super Bowl records for career average per catch (244); Alabama's "Professional Athlete of the Year" 1979; Dapper Dan "Man of the Year" 1984. **BUSINESS ADDRESS:** Pittsburgh Steelers, Three Rivers Stadium, 300 Stadium Circle, Pittsburgh, PA 15212.

STALLWORTH, OSCAR B.
Engineering manager. **PERSONAL:** Born Dec 05, 1944, Mobile; married Elsie Thigpen; children: Oscar, Jr, Brett. **EDUCATION:** BS mech ngring 1966. **CAREER:** Castings & Brake Components Motor Wheel Corp subsidary of Goodyear tire & Rubber Co, manager 1971-; prod engr passenger car brakes & wheels, motor wheel 1968-71; jr proj engr motor wheel 1967-68. **ORGANIZATIONS:** Mem Soc of Automotive Engrs 1967; Am Soc for Metals 1967; Am Foundryman's Soc 1967; mem, bd dirs Boys Club of Lansing 1971-; chmn Voter Regis A Phillip Randolph Inst 1972-; v chmn, Ingham Co Dem Party 1970-72; advisor, solicitor Jr Achievement 1968; Alpha Phi Alpha Frat 1964; mgr Field Operations Political Campaigns 1970-; pres Coland Inc. **HONORS/ACHIEVEMENTS:** Nominee Lansing Outstanding Person of Yr Lansing Jaycees. **BUSINESS ADDRESS:** 1600 N Larch St, Lansing, MI 48914.

STALLWORTH, THOMAS FONTAINE, III
Business executive. **PERSONAL:** Born Apr 14, 1985, Detroit, MI; married Sharon J; children: Thomas, Joseph. **EDUCATION:** MI State Univ, BA 1975. **CAREER:** Detroit Urban League, ed spec 1975-76; A&P, store mgr 1976-79; City of Detroit, admin asst to mayor 1979-84; Mich Con Gas Co, personnel spec 1984-. **ORGANIZATIONS:** Bd mem Leadership Detroit/Detroit Chamber of Commerce 1982-; exec bd mem Children's Aid Soc 1982-; vice pres Detroit Aff Natl Black Child Devel Inst 1983-; chmn resolutions comm MI School Bd Assoc 1983-84; bd mem Detroit Bd of Ed 1983-84; chmn of bd United Comm Serv 1984-. **HONORS/ACHIEVEMENTS:** Cert of Appreciation Mayor City of Detroit 1984; Cert of Merit MI Senate 1984; Letter of Commendation Governor State of MI 1984; Spirit of Detroit Awd Detroit City Council 1984. **BUSINESS ADDRESS:** Personnel Specialist, MichCon, 500 Griswold 2nd Fl, Detroit, MI 48226.

STALLWORTH, WILLIAM FRED
Government official. **PERSONAL:** Born Aug 12, 1954. **EDUCATION:** Jackson State Univ, BS Indus Arts 1975; Realtors Institute, graduate. **CAREER:** Biloxi Develop Comm, draftsman 1975, relocation adv 1975-77; Biloxi Public Schs, teacher 1978-79; Joint Ctr for Political Studies, comm develop specialist 1979-81; City of Biloxi, personnel officer 1981-83, voter registrar 1981-83, council member 1983-. **ORGANIZATIONS:** Pres Alpha & Omega Enterprises 1983-; pres BFS Serv 1984-; bd of dirs, Gulf Coast Job Corp Center; Coastal Family Health Clinic; Biloxi Economic DevelFoundation; Trustee, St John's AME Church. **BUSINESS ADDRESS:** Councilmember, City of Biloxi, PO Box 429, Biloxi, MS 39533.

STAMPER, HENRY J.
Financial executive. **CAREER:** First Federal Savings & Loan Assn of Scotlandville, Baton Rouge, LA, chief executive. **BUSINESS ADDRESS:** First Federal Savings & Loan Assn of Scotlandville, 7990 Scenic Hwy, Baton Rouge, LA 70807. *

STAMPLEY, GILBERT ELVIN
Attorney. **PERSONAL:** Born May 24, 1943, Baton Rouge, LA; married Ester J Francis. **EDUCATION:** Grambling State U, BA 1965; JD Tulane Univ Sch of Law, JD 1972. **CAREER:** Harris Stampley Mckee Bernard & Broussard, atty; Smith & Stampley, att 1972-75 EEO Commn, case analyst 1970-72; Men's Affaird Jarvis Christian Coll, dep dir 1965-67; Am Bar Assn; Martinet Soc; LA State Bar Assn; Nat Bar Assn; Nat Conf of Black Lawyers Exec Com NAACP; Palm-air Civil Improvement Assn; Orleans Parish Prog Voters League, vp; Young Dem of Am; Urban League; LA Assn for Sickle Cell Anemia Found. **ORGANIZATIONS:** Mem City Plng Commn of New Orleans 1976-81; mem LA State Dem Ctrl Com Dist 62; Earl Warren Fellow 1971-72. **MILITARY SERVICE:** AUS E-5 1968-70. **BUSINESS ADDRESS:** 1440 Canal St, Ste 1714, New Orleans, LA 70112.

STAMPS, HERMAN FRANKLIN
Dentist. **PERSONAL:** Born Jan 20, 1924, Washington, DC; son of Herman Stamps and Alice Stamps; married Ann Grigsby, Apr 04, 1987; children: Eric, Alisa. **EDUCATION:** Howard Univ, BS 1945, DDS 1948; Univ MI, MSc 1953. **CAREER:** Genl Practice, dentistry 1948-52; Diplomate American Board Endodontics 1953-; Coll of Dentistry, dir clinics 1967-70, prof 1969-, coord facilities systems & planning 1970-86; Montgomery Co Jr Coll, 1966; Washington Bd of Educ, 1963-65; Howard Univ, retired 1986. **ORGANIZATIONS:** Bd dirs Wash Urban League 1958-; mem Robert T Freeman Dental Soc (pres 1959-61); bd dirs COIN 1962-65; manpower bd Labor Dept 1964-67; chmn supervisory com Armstrong Neighborhood Fed Credit Union 1964-66; mem Natl, Amer Dental Assns, DC Dental Soc, Amer Soc History Dentistry (charter); mem Amer Assn Endodontics; author "Modern Prescription Writing" 1954; mem Omicron Kappa Upsilon; bd dirs American Diabetes Assn 1985-; Natl Comm ADA Minority Perspectives 1989-. **HOME ADDRESS:** 7541 16 St NW, Washington, DC 20012.

STAMPS, JOE, JR.
Elected official. **PERSONAL:** Born Dec 03, 1939, Houston, TX; married Eloise Grant; children: Jo-Ellen, Bernadette, Joe III. **EDUCATION:** Texas Southern Univ, 1959-62; Labor Studies, Linden-Hall Dawson, PA; 1979 & 1982. **CAREER:** Pct 371 Harris Co, election judge 1978-; United Steelworkers Local 7682, president 1979-82; Board of Education, legislation rep 1981-. **ORGANIZATIONS:** Member A-Philip Randolf Institution 1963-. **BUSINESS ADDRESS:** School Board Member, North Forest I S D, PO Box 2378, Houston, TX 77078.

STAMPS, LEON PREIST
City official & auditor. **PERSONAL:** Born Dec 29, 1953, Bronx, NY; married Barbara Logan. **EDUCATION:** Boston Coll, BS Acct 1975; Northeastern Univ, MBA Bus Policy 1976. **CAREER:** Arthur Anderson & Co, accountant 1977-79; Xerox Corp, equip control mgr 1979-81, ne reg control mgr 1981-84; City of Boston, city auditor/controller. **ORGANIZATIONS:** Bd of dir Boston Coll Alumni Assoc 1975-; accountant internship Continental Group Inc 1976; consult to dir of public serv Blue Cross & Blue Shield 1976; acctg prof Roxbury Comm Coll 1979; mem at large Natl Assoc of Black Accountants 1984-; mem Boston Black Media Coalition 1985. **HONORS/ACHIEVEMENTS:** Recip The Young Alumni Achievers Award Boston Coll 1985. **BUSINESS ADDRESS:** Auditor/ Controller, City of Boston, City Hall Room M-4, Boston, MA 02201.

STAMPS, LYNMAN A., SR.
Clergyman. **PERSONAL:** Born May 31, 1940, Utica, MS; married Margarett C Donaldson; children: Lynman A Stamps Jr. **EDUCATION:** Lane Coll Jackson, TN, BA 1968; Webster Univ, MAT 1972; US Dept Justice, Cert Jail Operations; Natl Inst of Correct Admin Studies; Western Interstate Comm for Higher Edn. **CAREER:** IL St Sch for Boys, cottage parent 1960-62; Chicago Parent Soc Adj Sch Boys, fam instr 1962-63; AUS, MP 1963-65; Trinity Temple CME Ch, 1964-66; Martin Tabernacle CME Ch, pastor 1966-69; Parkers Chapel CME Ch, pastor 1969-70; Clark Jr HS E St Louis, IL, civic tchr 1968-71; Pilgrim Temple CME Ch, pastor 1970-74; Radio Sta WESL E St Louis, mgr part owner 1972-78; E St Louis, civil serv commr 1971-74; St Louis Correc Inst, supt 1972-76; Coleman Temple CME Ch, pastor 1974-83; First Christian Methodist Church, paster/founder 1983-; Normandy Jr HS Normandy, MO, tchr 1981-84; Marion Comm, pastor/managing partner; St Louis Bd of Educ, Military Specialist 1988-89. **ORGANIZATIONS:** Life mem NAACP; mem The Amer Correct Assn; exec bd mem E St Louis Madison St Clair Co Urban League 1972-73; exec bd mem E St Louis Model City Agency 1972-73; vice pres Downtown Merchant Columbus, MS 1985. **HONORS/ACHIEVEMENTS:** Cert of Honor Utica Inst Jr Coll 1956; Man of the Yr Award Afro-Amer Club Columbus, MS 1985; Found/Pres Trenton Civic League Trenton, TN; Cert of Award for Outstanding Achievements to Jobs Workshop Ex Offender Prog of Human Dev Corp Prog Metro St Louis 1976; Cert of Apprec Gateway Jaycees and US Jaycees 1976; Award Plaque Offenders Chap of AA 1974. **MILITARY SERVICE:** AUS Spec 4th Class served 2 yrs; Good Conduct Medal 1963-65. **HOME ADDRESS:** 12031 Mereview Dr, St Louis, MO 63146.

STANBACK, THURMAN W.
Educator. **PERSONAL:** Born Mar 20, 1922, Washington, DC. **EDUCATION:** VA Union U, BA 1941; Columbia U, MA 1947; Cornell U, PhD 1953-. **CAREER:** FL Atlantic U, retired prof of theatre 1986; Bethune-Cookman Coll 1953-73 & 1953-70; Sterer Coll, 1947-49. **ORGANIZATIONS:** Mem Am Theatre Assn 1953-75; Speech Assn of Am 1953-75; Alpha Phi Alpha 1955-75; Nat Assn of & Dramatic & Speech Arts 1953-70. **HONORS/ACHIEVEMENTS:** Teacher of Yr Bethune Cookman Coll 1969; Distinguished Alumni in the Arts, Virginia Union University 1986; Distinguished Alumnus, National Assn for Equal Opportunity in Higher Education 1989. **MILITARY SERVICE:** AUS ssgt 1943-46.

STANCELL, DOLORES WILSON PEGRAM
Attorney. **PERSONAL:** Born Oct 26, 1936, New York, NY; married Vernon H; children: Timothy, Vernon. **EDUCATION:** Rutgers U, BA 1970; Rutgers Sch of Law, JD 1974; MI State U, Annual Regulatory Studies Prog 1976. **CAREER:** NJ Dept of Pub Adv Div of Rate Counsel, asst dep pub adv; Hon David D Furman Superior Ct Chan Div NJ, law sec 1974-75; Rutgers Univ Rutgers Jour of Comptrs & the Law, admin 1973; Jersey Shore Med Ctr, nurse 1972; Middlesex Cty Legal Svcs, legal intern 1970; Rutgers Urban Studies Ctr, rsch asst 1968; Head Start MCEOC, nurse 1967; Head Start, nurse 1966; Beth Israel Hosp, staff nurse 1958-62; Fordham Hosp, staff nurse 1957-58. **ORGANIZATIONS:** Am Bar Assn Sect on Legal Educ & Admissions to the Bar 1977-78; Forum Comm on Hlth Law 1977-78; Gen Practice 1976-77; Natl Bar Assn 1st vp, Women's Div 1977-78; vice pres Civil Trial Advocacy Sect 1977-78; Legislation & Uniform & State Laws Comm 1977-78; nom com Women's Div 1976-77; Fed Bar Assn; Garden State Bar Assn; NJ State Bar Assn; Hlth Leg & Hlth Plng Serv Com 1976-78; Monmouth Bar Assn; Crmnl Pract Com 1976-78; treas Assn Black Women Lawyers NJ 1977-78; Rutgers Law Sch Alumni Assn; RutgersUniv Alumni Assn; panelist MRC-TV NY Program, Medical Costs, The Breath of Life 1977; Am Nurses Assn; NJ State Nurses Assn; vol Ocean-Monmouth Legal Serv 1972; vol urban agt Rutgers Urban Studies Cen 1967-68; Pub Policy Forum on Civil Disorders & Forum on the Future of NJ RutgersUniv 1968; coord Rutgers-Douglass Coll Elem Sch Tutorial Prog 1967-68; trustee Unitarian Soc 1970-72; Acad Adv Com 1977-78; bd Parents Assn Rutgers Prep Sch 1970-71; New Brunswick YWCA; Urban League; NAACP. **HONORS/ACHIEVEMENTS:** Human Rels Awrd Fordham Hosp 1957; articles Wilson, Computerization of Welfare Recipients, Implications for the Individual & The Right to Privacy 4 Rutgers Journal of Computers and The Law 163 (1974); Minoritiy Workers 1 Womens Rights Law Reporter 71 (1972-73). **BUSINESS ADDRESS:** 10 Commerce Ct, Newark, NJ 07102.

STANDARD, RAYMOND LINWOOD
Physician. **PERSONAL:** Born May 20, 1925, Hartford, CT; son of V Linwood and Ruth Lee King; married Donna Ann Boddy; children: Kia Michalle, Gina Lynette, Darry Linwood. **EDUCATION:** Howard Univ Coll of Liberal Arts, BS 1948; Howard Univ Coll of Medicine, MD 1952; Johns Hopkins Univ Sch of Hygiene & Public Health, MPH 1967. **CAREER:** Intl Med Provident Hosp, clinical dir 1956-60; NW Central Clinic, chief clinical serv 1960-66; Bureau of Chronic Disease Control, chief adult health & geriatrics 1967-68, chief bureau of

chronic disease control 1968-69; DC Govt, dir pub health 1969-80; E of the River Health Assn, med dir 1980-81; clinical assoc prof Howard/Georgetown/GW Med Schs 1969-; Howard Univ Coll of Medicine, assoc prof. **ORGANIZATIONS:** Exec dir DC Office of Bicentennial Programs 1976; chmn med sub-com Pres Carter's Inaugural Com 1977; founder/past pres Standard Investment Co Inc; founder/past pres Century Limited Inc; bd of dirs United Natl Bank; published 45 health care admin articles local & Natl med journals 1969-. **HONORS/ACHIEVEMENTS:** Fellowship World Health Organ Norway & Sweden Health Systems 1976. **MILITARY SERVICE:** AUS pfc 1943-46; Bronze Star; Combat Medic Badge. **BUSINESS ADDRESS:** Dir Grad Educ Public Health, Howard University, 520 W St NW, Washington, DC 20059.

STANDIFER, BEN H.
Educator. **PERSONAL:** Born Aug 24, 1934, Itasca, TX; married Esther; children: Sonceria, Fawn, Ben, Jr, Corey. **EDUCATION:** Prairie View A&M Coll, BS 1959; TX Christian U, MA 1972; TX Christian U, certification supv 1973; N TX State U, certification adminstrn 1975; Carleton Coll, study 1965; Prairie View A&M Coll, 1966; N TX State U, 1967;Univ of TX 1968; IL Inst of Tech, 1969; Cornell U, 1970; TX Wesleyan Coll 1974. **CAREER:** Ft Worth Public School, math teacher 1959-73; FWISD, math instructional improvement specialist 1973-74; Ft Worth Public School, math improvement specialist 1974-; Dunbar Sr High School Fort Worth Indep School Dist, principal 1975-; Our Lady of Victory Priv School Bd, pres next 3 yrs. **ORGANIZATIONS:** Mem Ft Worth Classroom Tchr Assn; mem TX Classroom Tchr Assn; mem Nat Educ Assn; mem TX Industrial Educ Assn; mem Phi Delta Kappa Frat; mem FtWorth Area Council of Tchr of Math; mem Task Force Team Lay Acad United Meth Ch; d mem Ft Worth-tarrant Co Community Devel Fund Inc; steering com mem Conf for Advancement of Math Teaching; organized Parent Student Study Group Como High Community 1960; drew up Trigonometry Transparencies used in Ft Orth-Pub Sch System 1965. **HONORS/ACHIEVEMENTS:** Published book "A Practical Guide to Good Study Habits" 1969; created progarm at Western Hills HS in Audio Tutorial Instruction 1970; organized tutorial program to help students in Wester Hills Eidglea Como Arlington Heights Communities 1971; published book of Audio Tutorial Instruction 1972; vice pres PTA 1973; presHom E& Sch Assn; pilot program for emotionally disturbed children 1974; publication Success in Math 1974; publication Improvement of & Curricular/Instructional System 1974; sunday sch tchr & church lay leader Morningside Meth Ch; tchr & com mem task force team of Lay Acad of TX Wesleyan Coll; recip of numerous awards including outstanding tchr & tchr of yr awards & healdiner in educ award Ft Worth Press Club; apptd adminstrv trainee Ft Worth Pub Sch; layacademy recognition United Meth Ch W TX Conf S/Sgt. **MILITARY SERVICE:** USAF 1954-58. **BUSINESS ADDRESS:** Fort Worth Pub Sch, 3210 W Lancaster, Fort Worth, TX.

STANDIFER, LONNIE NATHANIEL
Entomologist. **PERSONAL:** Born Oct 28, 1926, Itasa, TX; divorced. **EDUCATION:** Prairie View A&M Coll, BS 1949; KS State Coll, MS 1951; Cornell Univ, PhD 1954. **CAREER:** Campus Pest Control, suprv; Tuskegee Inst AL, instr biol sci 1951-53; Cornell Univ, rsch asst 1953-54; So Univ Baton Rouge, asst prof biol sci 1954-56; US Dept of Agr Tucson AZ, rsch entomologist 1956-70, retired suprv rsch entomolgist, lab dir 1970-86. **ORGANIZATIONS:** Consult Dept Agr Biochem Univ of AZ 1963; mem Entomol Soc Amer, USDA, SEA, AR; tech adv Rsch Prog on Nutrition on Honey Bees; natl consult USA-AZ, Intl Bee Rsch Assoc, AZ Acad Sci; mem Sigma Xi, Beta Kappa Chi. **HONORS/ACHIEVEMENTS:** Outstanding Alumni Awd Prairie View A&M Coll 1967. **MILITARY SERVICE:** USAF WWII.

STANLEY, ARTHUR W.
Business executive. **PERSONAL:** Married Theodosia King; children: Theodore, Emily Carol. **CAREER:** Stanley's Enterprises, pres. **ORGANIZATIONS:** mem Darlington Co NAACP; sec 1952-54; pres 1955-; mem Darlington Co Bd Registration; mem Cresent Temple 148; mem SC Council Hum Rights; mem Am Legion Post 210; mem St James United Meth Ch & Recipient Beta Theta Chpt. **HONORS/ACHIEVEMENTS:** Award for promoting oustanding social action; outstanding bus achievement Phi Beta Sigma; james mcbride dabbs award State Coun for human relations. **MILITARY SERVICE:** AUS 1943-45. **BUSINESS ADDRESS:** 1004 S Main St, Darlington, SC.

STANLEY, COLUMBUS LANDON, SR.
City official, engineer. **PERSONAL:** Born Sep 10, 1922, Fayetteville, NC; married Dorothy Bradford; children: Joyce Stanley Johnson, Columbus Jr, Charles, Kirk, Brian. **EDUCATION:** NCA&T State Univ, attended 1945-46; SC State Univ, BS EE 1958; SUNY New Paltz NY, grad courses 1960-61. **CAREER:** IBM, staff engr 1955-; City of Poughkeepsie NY, asst mayor 1974-81, alderman 1967-87. **ORGANIZATIONS:** Life mem Kappa Alpha Psi 1958-; mem All-SIAC Football & Basketball team; mem All-CIAA Football & Basketball team; founder Poughkeepsie Area Golfers League; mem NY Conf of Mayors 1967-; mem Natl League of Cities 1967-; treas founder Hudson Valley OIC Inc 1967-77; founder bd mem Mid-Hudson Valley HABITAT/Humanity 1983-; mem Natl Black Caucus/Local Elected Officials. **HONORS/ACHIEVEMENTS:** Comm Serv Awd Key Women's Club Inc 1974; Comm Serv Awd Martin Luther King Commemorative Comm 1970; Alumni Achievement Awd NE Province Kappa Alpha Psi Frat Inc 1977; Comm Serv Awd Poughkeepsie Alumni Kappa Alpha Psi Frat Inc 1976. **HOME ADDRESS:** 168 N Clinton St, Poughkeepsie, NY 12601.

STANLEY, CURTIS E.
Educator. **PERSONAL:** Born Mar 26, 1917, Valdosta, GA; married Louise Murray. **EDUCATION:** Johnson C Smith U, AB 1939; Daniel Payne Coll, MA 1972. **CAREER:** Afro Amer Life Ins Co, dist mgr 1946-47; Darwin HS Cookeville TN, prin 1948-52; Washington HS Blakely GA 1952-60; AL State Univ Montgomery, freshman dean 1960-63; asso prof educ 1953-. **ORGANIZATIONS:** Mem & GA Tchrs & Educ Assn; Am AssnUniv Profs; NEA; Assn for Supervision & Curriculum Devel; AL Educ Assn Dir Am Cancer Soc 1954-56; AL StateU Credit Union 1961-69; mem Omega Psi Phi; AME Ch Steward 1960-; Elk; Mason 32 Degree Shringer.

STANLEY, ELLIS M., SR.
Government official. **PERSONAL:** Born Jun 13, 1951, Shallotte, NC; son of Lewis A Stanley and Mae Belle Bryant Stanley; married Iris M White Stanley, May 31, 1975; children: Ellis M Jr, Christopher J. **EDUCATION:** Univ of North Carolina, Chapel Hill NC, BA, 1973. **CAREER:** Brunswick County Govt, Bolivia NC, dir emergency mgmt, 1975-82; Durham County Govt, Durham NC, dir emergency mgmt, 1982-87; Atlanta-Fulton County Govt, Atlanta GA, dir emergency mgmt, 1987-; Universal Consultants Inc, exec vice pres, 1987-. **ORGANIZATIONS:** Vice pres, Natl Forum for Black Public Admin, 1983-87; pres Natl Coordinating Council on Emergency Mgmt, 1985, state representative, 1988-; mem, Fulton Red Cross Advisory Comm, 1987-, Red Cross Emergency Community Serv Comm, 1987-, Hazardous Material Advisory Council, 1988-, Leadership Atlanta, class of 1990. **HONORS/ACHIEVEMENTS:** Presidential Citation, US Civil Defense Assn, 1983; testified several times before the US Congress on Emergency Mgmt, 1985-86; lead Delegation to China to study Emergency Mgmt, 1988; presented at 1st Security Seminar in Caribbean, 1988. **BUSINESS ADDRESS:** Director, Atlanta-Fulton County Emergency Management Agency, 130 Peachtree St, SW, Atlanta, GA 30303.

STANLEY, EUGENE
Education administrator. **PERSONAL:** Born Nov 03, 1916, Rome, GA; married Dorothy P (deceased); children: Robert E, Dr William D. **EDUCATION:** Wilberforce Univ, BS 1939; OH State Univ, MA 1946, continued study 1947-48. **CAREER:** NC A&T Univ, asst prof of educ, asst dean of men 1946-47; Savannah State Coll GA, asst prof, dir of student teaching 1948-49, dean of coll 1949-50; Morgan State Coll, asst prof of educ 1950-57, dir of student teaching, acting head of educ 1958-60, asst dean, dir of lower div 1960-67; State Bd for Higher Educ, dir div of inst approval & eval 1967-80, retired. **ORGANIZATIONS:** Consult higher ed Benedict Coll 1962, Johnson C Smith Univ 1963, Southern Reg Ed Bd 1966; author report for Middle States Accreditation Team for Morgan State Univ 1968; mem Urban League, NAACP, Assoc for Higher Ed, AARP, Phi Delta Kappa, Alpha Phi Alpha, Zeta Sigma Tau. **HONORS/ACHIEVEMENTS:** Prominent Public Speaker in the Mid-West 1940's & 1950's; Articles publ in Bulletin of Negro History, Philos of Ed Society, Jrnl of Ed Sociology, School &Society; Authored studies for State of MD on need for School of Veterinary Med & Optometry; Cited as a living maker of Negro History 1950's. **HOME ADDRESS:** 2506 Overland Ave, Baltimore, MD 21214.

STANLEY, HILBERT DENNIS
Educator. **PERSONAL:** Born Feb 24, 1931, Cambridge, MD; children: Denise R, Guy Derek. **EDUCATION:** Morgan State Univ, BS 1952, MS 1970; Wayne State Univ, EdD 1978. **CAREER:** Edmondson HS, principal 1973-75; Rockefeller Found, fellow 1975-76; Lake Clifton HS, prin 1979-81; Office of Mayor Baltimore, educ liaison officer 1981-84; Southwestern HS, principal. **ORGANIZATIONS:** Vice basileus Pi Omega Chap Omega Psi Phi Frat 1978; pres Baltimore Chap Natl Alliance Black Sch Educators 1978-80; mem Board of Dirs Arena Players 1980-; mem Bd of Dirs Afro Amer Newspaper 1981-83; chmn Selective Serv Local Bd 1982-85. **HONORS/ACHIEVEMENTS:** Rockefeller Grant 1975; Man of the Yr Omega Psi Phi Frat 1980. **HOME ADDRESS:** 413 George St, Baltimore, MD 21201.

STANLEY, WOODROW
Govt. official. **PERSONAL:** Born Jun 12, 1950, Schlater, MS; married Reta Venessa James; children: Heather Venessa, Jasmine Woodrina. **EDUCATION:** Mott Comm Coll, 1969-71; Univ of MI, BA Polit Sci 1971-73; Univ of MI, Flint, MI, candidate for Master of Public Admin. **CAREER:** Whitney M Young St Acad, counselor 1974-77; Greater Flint OIC, asst services coord 1977-79, case mgt coord 1979-83, job club coord 1983-; Flint City Council, councilman 1983-. **ORGANIZATIONS:** Former bd mem Flint Human Relations Comm 1973-76; bd mem YMCA 1976-77; bd mem McCree Theatre & Fine Arts Centre 1975-; bd mem Valley Area Agency on Aging 1982-; bd mem Economic Develop Corp 1983-; adv bd mem Univ of MI Flint African-Afro Amer Studies Prog 1983-; steering comm Coalition of Greater Flint African Relief Fund 1984-; former adv bd mem/pres Ombudsman Adv Bd; former bd mem YMCA; chair bd of dirs Valley Area Agency on Aging; bd mem Foss Ave Christian Sch; alternate trustee Flint Retirement Bd; mem MI Municipal League's Legislative and Urban Affairs Comm; committe mem Natl Leauge of Cities Human Devel Steering Comm 1989-90; bd of dir MI Municipal League 1988-91. **HONORS/ACHIEVEMENTS:** Listed US Jaycees Outstanding Young Men of America publication 1975; cert of achievement Leadership Flint 1975-76; Vol Service Awd Urgan League of Flint 1981; Awd of Recognition Mott Adult HS 1982; Distinguished Comm Service Awd Foss Ave Baptist Church 1983; Comm Serv Awd Eureka Lodge F&AM 1986; Who's Who in Amer Politics 1987. **BUSINESS ADDRESS:** City Councilman, City of Flint, 1101 S Saginaw, Flint, MI 48502.

STANMORE, ROGER DALE
Medical doctor. **PERSONAL:** Born Jan 20, 1957, Alanta, TX. **EDUCATION:** Southwestern Union Coll, BS 1979; Meharry Medical Coll, MD 1984. **CAREER:** DC General Hosp, resident physician surgery 1984-85; Methodist Hosp/SUNY, resident physician 1985-86; Department of Justice, chief of medical staff. **ORGANIZATIONS:** Mem Amer & Natl Medical Assocs 1980-87; mem The Technology Transfer Soc 1982-87. **HONORS/ACHIEVEMENTS:** Amer Coll of Surgeons Scholarship 1983; representative Joint Commn of Medical Education 1983. **HOME ADDRESS:** 1713 Cherry Circle, Anniston, AL 36201.

STANSBURY, CLAYTON CRESVELL
Educator. **PERSONAL:** Born Mar 20, 1932, Havre de Grace, MD; married Catherine Laverne Posey. **EDUCATION:** Morgan Stateu, BS 1955; Howard U, MS 1962;Univ of MD, PhD 1972. **CAREER:** Student Services, vice-pres 1978-; Morgan State Univ, acting dean of student affairs, prof psychology; Lower Div, dir 1975-77. **ORGANIZATIONS:** Chmn Psychology Dept 1973-75; asst dean Freshman Prgm 1970-73; psychol Couns Morgan StateUniv 1967-70; instr Psychology HowardUniv 1965-67; tch asst PsychologyUniv MD 1963-65; instr Psychology HowardUniv 1962-63; mem Am Psychol Assn MD Psychol Assn; Psi Chi Nat Honor Soc; mem Alpha Phi Alpha Frat; Urban League; life mem NAACP; mem bd dir YMCA; mem Little League Baseball; football promotions; Boy Scouts of Am; United Meth Men; Proj Upward Bound; Morgan ROTC; hon mem PKT;Univ chief marshal; cert YMCA. **HONORS/ACHIEVEMENTS:** Author Portrait of a Colored Man; A Black Moses of Hartford Co MD 1977; 50 Years of Humanitarian Thoughts. **MILITARY SERVICE:** AUS 1955-57. **BUSINESS ADDRESS:** Cold Spring Ln & Hillen Rd, Baltimore, MD 21239.

STANSBURY, MARKHUM L., SR.
Manager community relations. **PERSONAL:** Born Apr 05, 1942, Memphis; married Lucy. **EDUCATION:** Lane Coll, BA 1966. **CAREER:** Jet & Ebony Mag, stringer-photographer reporter; Tri-state Defender, photographer; WJAK Radio, disk jockey; WDIA, announcer; Holiday Inns Inc, mgr comm relations. **ORGANIZATIONS:** Pres Memphis Chap PRSA;

mem Beale St Nat Historic Found; NAACP; Vollentine Boys Club; Omega Psi Phi Frat; Sr Citizens Inc; bd trustees St Andrew AME Ch; budget Com United Way Greater Memphis. **HONORS/ACHIEVEMENTS:** Who's Who Among Students AmUniv & Coll 1965-66; omega man yr award 1966; outstanding young men am 1967-78; merit award NAACP 1978; plaque outstanding serv lane Coll; certificate appreciation Shelby United Neighbors. **BUSINESS ADDRESS:** Agent, Cooper & Associates, 6063 Mt Moriah #9, Memphis, TN 38115.

STANSBURY, TERRENCE EUGENE
Professional athlete. **PERSONAL:** Born Feb 27, 1961, Wilmington, DE. **EDUCATION:** Temple Univ, BS 1984. **CAREER:** Dallas Mavericks, guard 1984-. **HONORS/ACHIEVEMENTS:** NBA Experience currently in 1st season; set an NCAA record as Jr when avgd 404 minutes, sitting out only 7 min all yr as Temple went 14-15 and Stansbury avgd 246 ppg; named to the Aloha Classic all-tourney team; 43-inch vertical jumper. **BUSINESS ADDRESS:** Dallas Mavericks, Reunion Arena, Ste 510, Dallas, TX 75207.

STANSBURY, VERNON CARVER, JR.
Corporate president. **PERSONAL:** Born Jul 13, 1939, Lexington, MS; divorced; children: Nicole Elaine, Vernon III. **EDUCATION:** Roosevelt Univ, BS 1962; Kent Coll of Law, attended 1964; Harvard Bus Sch, MBA 1973. **CAREER:** IBM, sr systems engr 1962-67; Exxon Intl, head fleet analysis 1967-71; Cummins Engine Co, gen mgr serv tools 1973-78; Dept of Commerce, dir export dev 1978-81; Scientific and Commercial Systems Corp pres 1981-. **ORGANIZATIONS:** Chmn AASU-Harvard Bus Sch 1972; chmn ERB-Sr Exec Serv 1979; pres DC Chap Harvard Black Alumni 1980; chmn William R Laws Found 1974; chmn ColumbusUnited Negro Coll Fund 1977. **HONORS/ACHIEVEMENTS:** Goldman Sachs Awd Harvard Bus Sch 1974; charter mem Sr Exec Serv of the US 1979; Outstanding Contrib White House Conf on Small Bus 1980. **MILITARY SERVICE:** USAR warrant officer 1962-70. **BUSINESS ADDRESS:** President, Scientific & Commercial Systms, 4651 King St, Alexandria, VA 22302.

STANTON, BEVERLY A.
Campus clergy. **PERSONAL:** Born Dec 06, 1944, Gettysburg, PA. **EDUCATION:** Coll Misericordia, BS 1966; Loyola Coll, MEd 1973. **CAREER:** Archdiocese of Baltimore, campus minister; Notre Dame U, instr ministry wrksp 1975; St Mary's New Oxford, tchr 1970-71; St Patrick's Harrisbrg, tchr sci 1968-69; Gate of Heaven Dallas, tchr sci math 1967; St Mary's Lancaster, tchr sci math 1967; Dallas, tchr biology 1966. **ORGANIZATIONS:** Mem bd sec MBHE; mem consult team CCMA; bd mem NOBC; vice pres bd mem NBSC 1973-75; spkr Ecumenical Campus Ministry Conf 1975; mem rsrc prsn Women's Campus Ministry Caucus 1973-; rsrc prsn Danforth Found Consult on Women in Campus Ministry 1975; mem YWCA Baltimore Cntrl Com 1974-; Morgan State Coll Women Orgn 1974-; Sisters of Mercy of Union 1966-. **HONORS/ACHIEVEMENTS:** Written articles in several mags journals on ministry. **BUSINESS ADDRESS:** Coppin State College, 2500 W North Avenue, Baltimore, MD 21216.

STANTON, JANICE D.
Elected government official. **PERSONAL:** Born Jun 26, 1928, Beaumont, TX; daughter of Joseph Dewey Splane and Myrtle Trimble Splane; married Rufus H Stanton Jr DDS, Mar 07, 1944; children: Rufus H III, Deborah Stanton Burke, Robert T. **EDUCATION:** Wiley Coll, 1942-44. **CAREER:** Galveston Coll, vice pres bd of regents. **ORGANIZATIONS:** Adv bd Galveston Co Coord Comm Clinics; adv bd City of Galveston Emergency Med Comm 1979; pres bd of trustees Gulf Coast Regional Mental Health-Mental Retardation Ctr 1980-82; bd of councilors St Mary's Hosp 1980-86; adv bd Galveston Historical Found 1984; vice pres United Way of Galveston 1985-87; mem Grievance Committee, District 5B, State Bar of Texas 1988-. **HONORS/ACHIEVEMENTS:** Image Awd Galveston Branch NAACP 1983; Comm Achievement Awd Zeta Phi Beta Sor 1983. **HOME ADDRESS:** 3615 Avenue O, Galveston, TX 77550.

STANWOOD, HELEN S.
Health service administrator. **PERSONAL:** Born Sep 21, 1935, New Orleans; divorced. **EDUCATION:** So Univ, BA 1966; Tulane Univ, grad study 1967; Loyola Univ, 1969; Harvard Univ, 1972. **CAREER:** New Orleans Health Dept, dep dir 1971-; Depaul Hosp, soc worker 1971; Epis Comm Svcs, prog dir 1969-71; LA Dept Pub Welfare, caseworker 1967-69; Soc Welfare Planning Coun, comm orgnr; Mental Retardation Prog Total Comm Action, part-time supr 1966-67; Welfare Dept New Orleans, couns 1960-66. **ORGANIZATIONS:** Mem New Orleans Sociological Assn; LA Pub Health Assn; Cen City Mental Retardation Com; assn Black Social Workers; Am Publ Health Assn; New Orleans Sickle Cell Anemia Found; various other civic & prof organizations. **HONORS/ACHIEVEMENTS:** Recipient honore certificate & service award So Univ in New Orleans; award for Volunteer Serv Total Comm Action; cert of merit City of New Orleans 1965&75;cert of honor Antioch Bapt Ch.

STANYARD, HERMINE P.
Retired teacher. **PERSONAL:** Born May 07, 1928, Charleston, SC; married George Dewey Stanyard Sr; children: Geormine Deweya, George Dewey Jr. **EDUCATION:** SC State Coll, BA 1949; New York Univ, MA 1952; Columbia Univ, Univ of SC, Adv Guid 1956,74,77; The Citadel Coll of Chas, Professional Certificate 1967, 1979-80. **CAREER:** Barnes Elem School Georgetown, teacher 1949-50; Wilson HS, english teacher 1952-56; Laing HS, english teacher 1956-59, guidance counselor 1959-67, english & reading teacher/reading coord 1967-85. **ORGANIZATIONS:** Mem campaigner Greater Chas YWCA 1966-86; pres Charleston Co Council Intl Reading Assoc 1977-79; chmn of nominating comm SC State Reading Assoc 1979-81; chmn Disting Teacher Membership 1981-85; volunteer teacher Morris St Bapt Church Tutorial Prog 1982,83,86; volunteer Laubach Reading Teacher. **HONORS/ACHIEVEMENTS:** Certificates of Appreciation & Mother of the Year Morris St Bapt Church 1979,84,85; Certificate of Appreciation Greater Chas YWCA 1983; Delta of the Year Delta Sigma Theta Sor Inc 1983; Scroll of Honor Omega Psi Phi Frat 1984. **HOME ADDRESS:** 17 Charlotte St, Apt A, Charleston, SC 29403.

STAPLES, ROBERT E.
Educator. **PERSONAL:** Born Jun 28, 1942, Roanoke, VA; son of John Staples and Anna Staples; divorced. **EDUCATION:** LA Valley Coll, AA 1960; CA State Univ Northridge, AB 1963; San Jose State Univ, MA 1965; Univ of MN, PhD 1970. **CAREER:** St Paul Urban League, dir of rsch 1966-67; CA State Univ, Hayward, asst prof Sociology 1968-70; Fisk Univ, asst prof Sociology 1970-71; Howard Univ, assoc prof Sociology 1971-73; Univ of CA, prof of Sociology. **ORGANIZATIONS:** Bd dir, Black World Found, 1980-; editor, Western Journal of Black Studies, 1978-. **HONORS/ACHIEVEMENTS:** Distinguished Achievement, Howard Univ 1979; Simon Bolivar Lecture Univ del Zulia, Maracaibo, Venezeula 1979; Distinguished achievement, Natl Council on Family Relations, 1982; Visiting Fellow Inst of Family Studies, Australia 1982; Marie Peters Award, Natl Council on Family Relations 1986. **BUSINESS ADDRESS:** Professor of Sociology, Univ of CA, San Francisco, CA 94143.

STARGELL, WILVER DORNEL (WILLIE)
Athlete. **PERSONAL:** Born Mar 06, 1941, Earlsboro, OK; children: Wendy, Precious, Dawn, Wilver Jr, Kelli. **EDUCATION:** Attended, Santa Rosa Jr Coll. **CAREER:** Pittsburgh Pirates, player, coach; Atlanta Braves, coach. **ORGANIZATIONS:** Mem Natl Adv Cncl on Sickle Cell Anemia; lectures at colls and univs in off-season; narrations to accompany symphony concerts around the country performing both at Carnegie Hall and the Kennedy Ctr. **HONORS/ACHIEVEMENTS:** Led Natl League HR - 48 1971; HR & RBI's 1973; All Star 1964-66 & 1971-73 & 1978; Sporting News and UPI Comeback Player of the Year 1978; Co-Most Val Player Natl League 1979; Sportsman of the Year Sports Illustrated 1979; Major League Player of the Year Sporting News 1979. **BUSINESS ADDRESS:** Coach, Atlanta Braves, PO Box 4064, Atlanta, GA 30302.

STARK, SHIRLEY J.
Sculptor. **PERSONAL:** Born May 27, 1927, New York, NY. **EDUCATION:** Univ Detroit; Wayne State Univ Sculptor. **CAREER:** Carnegie Mellon Univ, visiting Andrew Mellon prof, sculpture 1975; Butler Inst, exhibitions, 1962, 1968; So Sculpture 1967; Natl Traveling Exhibit; Detroit Inst of Arts,1968; Fall Invitational Roswell Museum, 1974; Carnegie Inst, 1975; Museum of & Albuquerque, 1976; 1st Natl Spring Exhibition, 1976; Ontario Art Gallery of Windsor, 1977; Consultant, Detroit Council of Arts, 1977; lectr Herbert A Lehman Coll CUNY 1975; Skidmore Coll 1977; numerous commissioned works; Sculpture Fels Macdowell Colony, numerous specialized lectures 1968, 1976; Wurlitzer Found, 1969, 1974, 1976; Mexico Taos Found, travel grant to 1970. **HONORS/ACHIEVEMENTS:** Nomination award Draco Found 1973-74; Jerome Fel Printing NY 1976; Exhibitions, Detroit Historical Museum 1980; Randall Galeries Ltd NY 1977; "Consult Cooperative School Prof of the Studio of Harlem 1977-78; nomination as academic of & Italy Accademia Italia Belle Arti e del Lavoro Parma Italy.

STARKE, CATHERINE JUANITA
Educator. **PERSONAL:** Born Apr 05, 1913, Charlotte, NC; married William Campbell. **EDUCATION:** Hunter Coll, BA 1936; Tchrs Coll, MA 1937, EdD 1963. **CAREER:** St Paul's Coll, 1938-46; Morgan State Univ, 1947-56; Jersey City State Coll, prof emeritus. **HONORS/ACHIEVEMENTS:** Publ "Symbolism of the Negro Coll" 1956; "Black Portraiture in Am Fiction, Stock Characters Archetypes & Individuals" 1971.

STARKE, GEORGE
Professional athlete. **PERSONAL:** Born Jul 18, 1948, White Plains, NY. **EDUCATION:** Columbia. **CAREER:** Washington Redskin, 1971-72; Kansas City Chiefs, 1972; Dallas Cowboys, 1972; Washington Redskins, 1972-. **ORGANIZATIONS:** Pres Starke-Reid Televideo & George Starke Commnctns; film on Boston Marathon Featuring Wheel Chair Participant; appears WTTG 10,00 O'Clock News Twice a WeekWith Comments on Games; puts together Wkly Segment Channel 5'S PM Mag; appeared Movie "The Imagemaker" & McDonalds TV Cmrcl; two main charit ities devotes much time Marthas Table & Soup Kitchen. **HONORS/ACHIEVEMENTS:** Tied second best NFC 1983.

STARKEY, FRANK DAVID
Personnel administrator. **PERSONAL:** Born Aug 06, 1944, Indianapolis, IN; married Gunilla Emilia Ekstedt; children: Michael, Julia. **EDUCATION:** Wabash Coll IN, AB 1966; Brown Univ, PhD Chem 1973. **CAREER:** IL Wesleyan Univ, prof 1971-80; General Elec Co, mgr equal oppor prog corp rsch & develop 1980-82, mgr human resource program 1982-. **ORGANIZATIONS:** Pres Wabash Council on Racial Equality 1965; chmn various comm Brown Univ Afro Amer Soc 1967-71; mem state council Amer Assn of Univ Prof 1972; memgrant rev panel NSF 1980; mem GE Found Minority Engrg Comm 1980-; comm mem to select the outstanding high school trainer of chemistry for the year Amer Chem Soc 1983-85; mem selection comm Outstanding State Biology Teacher Awd for Natl Assoc of Biology Teachers 1986. **HONORS/ACHIEVEMENTS:** Alfred P Sloan Scholarship Wabash Coll 1962-66; NSF Traineeship Brown Univ 1966-70; Tchr of the Yr IL Wesleyan Univ 1978; Outstanding Young Man of Amer 1979; GE Honoree for Black Achiever In Industry Harlem YMCA 1986. **BUSINESS ADDRESS:** Manager Human Resource Program, General Elec Co, PO Box 8, Schenectady, NY 12301.

STARKS, RICK
Community development specialist. **PERSONAL:** Born Apr 16, 1948, Scottsville, KY; son of L C Starks and Ruby Starks; married Saundra Harlin Starks, Nov 28, 1968; children: Derrick D, Shannon M. **EDUCATION:** Western KY Univ, BS 1971, MPS 1975; Univ of OK, Economic Development Institute 1986-88. **CAREER:** Barren River Area Devel Dist, recreation planner/proj splst 1972-80; Bowing Green Parks & Rec, cntr dir 1971-72; Mammoth Cave Nat Park, park tech 1971; TN Valley Authority, Bowling Green, KY, economic development representative 1989-. **ORGANIZATIONS:** Mem Nat Recreation Park Assn; mem KY Parks & Recreation Soc; vice pres Big Brothers/Big Sister 1978-79; v polemarch Kappa Alpha Psi Frat 1978-, keeper of records, 1989; chmn action Bowling Green NAACP 1979-, special projects advisor, 1988; chmn Bradd Economic Devel Committee, 1988; mem Ky Industrial Devel Council, 1989; bd dir UPPRE, Inc, 1989-. **HONORS/ACHIEVEMENTS:** Outstanding young man award 1978; past mem Bowling Green Human Rights Commn 1978; big brother of the year award Big Brothers Agency 1979; civitan service award Bowling Green Noon Civitan 1979; AWARE Meritorious Service award, 1980; developed NAACP Youth Improvement Grant, 1987, UPPRE Grant, 1988. **BUSINESS ADDRESS:** Economic Development Represemtatove, Tennessee Valley Authority, PO Box 20260, Bowling Green, KY 42101.

STARKS, ROBERT TERRY
Professor. **PERSONAL:** Born Jan 24, 1944, Grenada, MS; son of Lula Ella Starks; married Judith Ann Minor; children: Kenya Mariama, Robert Willis. **EDUCATION:** Loyola Univ, BS 1968, MA 1971. **CAREER:** Booz-Allen and Hamilton Inc, mgmt & consultant 1968-69;

Chicago Urban League, rsch specialist 1969-70; Northern IL Univ, dir black studies 1970-72; Northeastern IL Univ, assoc prof 1972-. **ORGANIZATIONS:** Council mem Natl Conf of Black Political Scientists 1979-81; mem DuSable Museum of Afro-Amer History 1980-; vice pres PUSH intl Trade Bureau 1981-82; issues consultant Rev Jesse L Jackson Natl Rainbow Coalition and Operation PUSH 1981-; issues consultant Mayor Harold Washington and the City of Chicago 1982-; founder/chmn Task Force for Black Political Empowerment 1982-; founder/chmn Free South Africa Movement in Chicago 1985-; fellow Leadership Greater Chicago 1986-87; bd mem Third World Conf Foundation 1986-; bd mem IL Chapter Amer Civil Liberties Union 1987; vice chmn IL Black United Fund 1987; DAAD Interdisciplinary German Studies seminar Phillips Univ 1987. **HONORS/ACHIEVEMENTS:** Univ of MI Vstg Scholar at the Horace H Rackham Sch of Grad Studies 1976; Kellogg Foundation Rsch Fellow Northeastern IL Univ 1978-80; Natl Endowment for the Humanities Coll Teachers Summer Seminar 1982; Goethe Inst Berlin Germany Language Fellow 1986. **HOME ADDRESS:** 1556 East Park Shore East Ct, Chicago, IL 60637. **BUSINESS ADDRESS:** Associate Professor, Northeastern IL University, 700 E Oakwood Blvd, Chicago, IL 60653.

STARLING, JOHN CRAWFORD
Physician. **PERSONAL:** Born Nov 16, 1916, Charleston, WV; married Anna; children: Nedra, Gayle, John. **EDUCATION:** WV State Coll, 1938; Meharry Med Coll, 1942. **CAREER:** Private Practice, physician; Parkside Hospital, resident; Harlem Hosp, intern 1942-43. **ORGANIZATIONS:** Mem AMA; NMA; OH State Med Soc; Cleveland Med Soc; Amer Soc Abdominal Surgeons; AAGP; Amer Geriatric & Soc; Catholic Physicians Guild; staff mem Huron Hospital; Polyclinic Hospital; Forest City Hospital All-Amer Football WV State Coll 1936; Kappa Alpha Psi Fraternity. **MILITARY SERVICE:** AUS major 1943-48. **BUSINESS ADDRESS:** 7916 Cedar Rd, Cleveland, OH 44103.

STARR-WHITE, DEBI See LIVINGSTON-WHITE, DEBORAH J. H.

STATHAM, CARL
Business executive. **PERSONAL:** Born Dec 09, 1950, Macon, GA; son of Carl Statham and Marie Statham; married Gloria Marie Long; children: Stephanie, Christopher. **EDUCATION:** Tuskegee Inst, BS 1973. **CAREER:** General Motors, business consultant 1973-77; Ford Motor Co, acct rep 1977-80, mgr acct reps 1980-83; Ford Motor Co, Southside Ford, acct general mgr 1983-84, pres 1984-. **HONORS/ACHIEVEMENTS:** Top 100 Black Businesses 1984-88 Black Enterprise; Top 300 Dealers Parts & Serv Volume Ford Motor Co 1984-88; Distinguished Serv Award Ford Motor Co 1984-87; Top 10 Nationally Ford Co Truck S/S, 1987; Co Ford Hwy Truck Dealer Council, 1989. **BUSINESS ADDRESS:** President, Southside Ford Truck Sales, 810-850 W 39th St, Chicago, IL 60609.

STATUM, HAYWARD S.
Businessman. **PERSONAL:** Born Oct 16, 1942, McCormick, SC; married Portia Johnson; children: Tammy, Hayward II. **EDUCATION:** A&T St U, undergrad; Gen Motors Dealers Dev Acad & Univ of Detroit Grad 1974. **CAREER:** Statum Chev Inc, pres; Tal Williams Traders Chev, rep & mgt 1968-74; Zone Pontiac, sales rep 1968; Charl-mont Rest & Sheraton Motel, rom serv capt 1965-67; Kirby Vacuum Cleaner Co, sales rep 1963-65. **ORGANIZATIONS:** Bd mem 5th Plan Dist Roanoke Valley; mem bd of dir Merchants Assn of Roanoke Valley; bus adv bd Roanoke Met Nat Alliance of Businessmen; mem bd of dir Tinker Mount Workshops. **HONORS/ACHIEVEMENTS:** Most enterprising business man of yr Roanoke Valley Bus League 1975; bus of yr awd Roanoke Valley Bus League 1976; awd of excellence VA St C of C & VA St of Minor Bus Enterprise; top 100 black bus in country 1975-76. **BUSINESS ADDRESS:** Friendly Lincoln-Mercury Inc, 1354 E Main St, Salem, VA 24153.

STAUPERS, MABEL KEATON
Nurse (retired). **PERSONAL:** Born Feb 27, 1890; daughter of Thomas Clarence Doyle and Pauline Lobo Doyle; married James Max Keaton, 1917 (divorced); married Fritz Staupers, 1931 (died 1949). **EDUCATION:** Freedman's Hospital Sch of Nursing, Graduated w/ Honors 1917. **CAREER:** New York City, Washington DC, private duty nursing; Booker T Washington Sanatorium, organized and served as administrator/director of nurses 1920-22; New York Tuberculosis Health Assoc Harlem Area, first exec sec, 1922-34; Natl Assn of Colored Grad Nurses, first nurse-exec, 1934-49, pres, 1949-51. **ORGANIZATIONS:** Lecturer, Howard Univ Coll of Nursing, 1969; former mem, adv comm on aging, NY City Dept of Welfare; charter and life mem, Natl Coun of Negro Women; founding mem, Manhattan Coun of Negro Women; Young Women's Christian Assn of NY, 44 year membership. **HONORS/ACHIEVEMENTS:** Sojourner Truth Awd, Natl Assn of Negro Business and Prof Women, 1947; Mary Mahoney Medal, Natl Assn of Colored Grad Nurses, 1947; Spingarn Medal, NAACP, 1951; Citation, Omicron Chap Chi Eta Phi, Natl Nursing Sor; Omicron Chap presents The Mabel Keaton Staupers Awd annually; Women's League of Science and Medicine Awd for Humanitarian Achievements in Health, 1961; Amer Caribbean Women's Assn award, 1961; Bethel Temple, Bronx, award, 1962; Natl Urban League Award, 1963; Democ Party Central Comm citation, 1964; Medgar Evans Human Rights Awd Capitol Press Club Washington DC, 1965; Citation of Appreciation from John V Lindsay Mayor of the City of New York, 1967; Howard Univ Alumni Awd, 1970; Caribbean-Amer Intercultural Org Award, 1972; Linda Richards Awd for Unique and Pioneering Contributions to Nursing, 1973; Amer Nursing Assn Award, 1974; Barbados Nurses Assn of Amer award plaque, 1985; Living Legacy Award, Natl Black Caucus, 1986; author of No Time for Prejudice, Macmillan, 1961.

STEANS, EDITH ELIZABETH
Government official. **PERSONAL:** Born Sep 04, 1929, Anderson, IN; daughter of Ernest J Downing (deceased) and Mary L Adams Downing (deceased); divorced; children: Bruce, Judith, Carol, Stacy. **EDUCATION:** Anderson Coll, BA 1976; Ball State Univ, MAS 1978. **CAREER:** Madison Co Dept of Public Welfare, caseworker 1969-72; Madison Co Superior Court II, chief juvenile probation officer 1973-79; State of Indiana, affirmativeaction dir 1979-82; City of Anderson, affirmative action/human relations dir 1982-. **ORGANIZATIONS:** Mem Urban League 1955-, NAACP 1955-, St Mary's Church; bd dirs Comm Justice Ctr 1970-, YWCA 1973-; mem Alpha Kappa Alpha Sor 1978-; instructor AndersonColl 1978-; commissioner Mayor's Economical Develop 1982-; bd dir St John's Hospital Chemical Dependency 1982-; bd dirs Enterprize Zone Assoc 1984-. **HONORS/ACHIEVEMENTS:** Outstanding Citizen NAACP 1983. **HOME ADDRESS:** 1619 W 15th St, Anderson, IN 46011. **BUSINESS ADDRESS:** Dir, City of Anderson, P O Box 2100, Anderson, IN 46018.

STEARNS, LILLARD G.
Business executive. **PERSONAL:** Born Jan 10, 1941, Boley, OK; married Janet K; children: Michelle, Sherry, Lillard Jr. **EDUCATION:** Tulsa U, BA 1964;Univ of CO, 1968-69. **CAREER:** Tulsa Urban League Inc, exec dir 1973-; USAF Prepatory Sch, exec officer 1969-73; Space Def Ctr, chief orbital analyst 1965-69; Inst USAF Acad Prep Sch 1969-73; bd of dir & BLG Enterprises 1976. **ORGANIZATIONS:** Mem Adv Council Manpower 1975-; tulsa Tennants Assn Bd 1973-75; bd mem Greenwood Chamber 1975-77; bd mem Tulsa NAACP 1975-; exec producer 30 minweekly TV show "Insight". **HONORS/ACHIEVEMENTS:** Author, newspaper articles,"Accenting the Positive" Comendation Medal USAF. **MILITARY SERVICE:** USAF capt 1964-73; USAFR maj.

STEBBINS, DANA BREWINGTON
Government official. **PERSONAL:** Born Nov 02, 1946, Baltimore, MD. **EDUCATION:** Howard Univ Washington DC, BA 1963-67; Howard U, MSW 1967-70; Howard U, JD 1972-75. **CAREER:** Small Bus Adminstrn, spl asst to the asso adminstr for minority small us 1980-; Nat Bar Assn, dir commercial law proj 1978-80; Commodity Futures Trading Commn, atty/adv/spl asst 1977-78; Superior Ct for DC, judicial clk 1975-77. **ORGANIZATIONS:** Mem Am Bar Assn; mem Nat Assn of Black Women Attys; mem Nat Bar Assn; mem Nat Assn of Black Social Workers; mem Delta Theta Phi Legal Frat ; mem Nat Assn of Social Workers; mem Nat Conf of Black Lawyers. **HONORS/ACHIEVEMENTS:** Who's Who Among Students in Am Coll &Univ HowardUniv 1967; outstanding young women in am 1978; Who's Who in Am Law The Marquis Who's Who Publ Bd 1978. **BUSINESS ADDRESS:** Small Bus Adminstrn, 1441 L St NW Room 317, Washington, DC 20416.

STEED, TYRONE
Insurance executive. **PERSONAL:** Born Aug 18, 1948, Norfolk, VA; married Irene; children: Kenyatta Uniquegu. **EDUCATION:** Newark School of Fine & Indust Art, Interior Design Diploma 1971-72; Fashion Inst of Tech AAS Interior Design 1973-75; Thomas Edison Coll, BA 1976-80;Kean Coll of NJ, MA Org Devel 1981-86. **CAREER:** New Horizons Inc, dist mgr, asst vice pres 1976-77; Girl Scouts of Amer, council field rep 1977-79; St Charles Kids School, teacher 1979-80; Newark Office onAging, sr commun relations spec 1980-; VA Med Ctr, chief voluntary svc, dir public relations. **ORGANIZATIONS:** Mem Amer Hosp Assoc 1981-, NJ Hosp Assoc 1981-, Amer Hosp Assoc Soc of PR Dir 1982-, Seton Hall Univ Gerontology Advisory Comm 1982-; NJ Assn Dir Volunteer Serv 1983. **HONORS/ACHIEVEMENTS:** 20 min film on girl Scouts Girl Scout Council of Greater Essex Cty 1977-79; 50 page thesis innovation & change in org Kean Coll of NJ 1981-85. **MILITARY SERVICE:** AUS sp4 3 yrs; Expert 45 Pistol 1965-68.

STEELE, CLAUDE MASON
Educator. **PERSONAL:** Born Jan 01, 1946, Chicago, IL; married Dorothy Munson; children: Jory, Claire, Claude, Benjamin. **EDUCATION:** Hiram Coll, BA 1967; OH State Univ, MA 1969; OH State Univ, PhD 1971. **CAREER:** Univ of UT, asst prof 1971-73; Univ of Washington, asst prof 1977, assoc prof 1977-85, prof 1985-. **ORGANIZATIONS:** Bd mem Black Student Psychology Assn 1968-71; mem Amer Psychology Assn 1968-; mem Psycho-social grant review panel Natl Institute of Alcohol Abuse and Alcoholism 1984-; assoc editor "Personality and Social Psychology Bulliten 1984-; 20 articles published in prof journals. **HONORS/ACHIEVEMENTS:** Dissertation Year Fellowship OH State Univ 1969-71. **BUSINESS ADDRESS:** Full Professor, University of WA, Seattle, WA 98195.

STEELE, CLEOPHAS R., JR.
Judge. **PERSONAL:** Born Jul 13, 1945, Dallas, TX; married Barbara; children: Sheri, Sharron, Cheronda. **EDUCATION:** Univ of Oklahoma, BA & BS 1967; Southern Methodist Univ, JD 1970. **CAREER:** City of Dallas, assoc judge 1974-76; Dallas County, justice of the peace. **ORGANIZATIONS:** Trustee/deacon Goodstreet Baptist Church; member Omega Psi Phi Fraternity 1965-; board member Dallas Alliance 1978-84. **HOME ADDRESS:** 1531 Cove Drive, Dallas, TX 75216. **BUSINESS ADDRESS:** Justice Of The Peace, Dallas Co Pct 8 Pl 2, 414 South R L Thorton, Dallas, TX 75203.

STEELE, PERCY H., JR.
Social service administrator. **PERSONAL:** Born Feb 04, 1920, Hopkinton, MA; children: Loretta Steele Chatmon. **EDUCATION:** NC Central Univ, AB 1944; Atlanta Univ Sch of Social Work, MSW 1946. **CAREER:** Washington Urban League, comm org sec 1945-46; Morris County NJ Urban League, prog dir 1946-47, exec dir 1948-53; College of St Elizabeth, sociology instructor 1951-53; San Diego Urban League, exec dir 1953-63; Bay Area Urban League, pres 1964-. **ORGANIZATIONS:** Bd of dirs Bay Area Black United Fund, Bay Area Assoc of Black Social Workers, Federation of Bay Area United Way Agencies; treas Council of Execs NUL, Black AGenda Council SF, Sigma Pi Phi Frat; mem Regional Planning Commn of Assoc of Bay Area Govts. **HONORS/ACHIEVEMENTS:** First black to be apptd to exec dir of local housing authority in the US; Social Worker of the Year Natl Assoc of Social Workers 1976; Robert C Kirkwood Awd San Francisco Foundation 1985. **BUSINESS ADDRESS:** President, Bay Area Urban League, Kaiser Ctr Mall Ste 211, 344 20th St, Oakland, CA 94612.

STEELE, WARREN BELL
Business executive. **PERSONAL:** Born Apr 14, 1923, Milledgeville, GA; married Victoria Kitchen; children: Holly Burns, Woody, William, Audrey Brown, Warren, Theresa Page, Frank. **EDUCATION:** Paine Coll, BA 1947; The Am U, MA 1965. **CAREER:** Columbus Consolidated Govt Columbus GA, personnel officer 1983-; Signature Mfg Co Nashville TN, minority owner 1981-83; Cummins Charleston Urban League Columbus GA, exec on loan 1979-81; Cummins Charleston Inc Charleston SC, personnel div mgr 1975-79; Frigiking Dallas, vice pres personnel 1973-75; Cummins Engine Co Columbus IN, dir personnel & adminstr 1970-73; Cummins Engine Co Columbus IN, personnel adminstr 1969-70. **ORGANIZATIONS:** Mem Am Soc of Personnel Adminstrs 1976-; mem Tri-Co Personnel Assn 1976-; chmn Dorchester Co (SC) Sch Adv Bd 1977-; bd mem King's Grant Home Owners Assn 1977-78; trustee Voorhees Coll Denmark SC; friend to Educ Dorchester Cnty Tchrs Assn; friend to Educ Dorchester Cnty Tchrs Assn 1979; mem bd Columbus GA C of C. **HONORS/ACHIEVEMENTS:** Bronza star; defense commen; Vietnam Def. **MILITARY SERVICE:** AUS lt col 23 yrs.

STEGALL, GILL CALVIN
Professional athlete. **PERSONAL:** Born Apr 30, 1961, Little Rock, AR. **EDUCATION:** Harding, Phys Educ Major 1983; AR State, 1980-82. **CAREER:** Denver Gold, slot back

1985;-. **HONORS/ACHIEVEMENTS:** 3 yr letterman AR State; 3 yr stats at AR State include 17 pass receptions for 187 yds and 2 touchdowns.

STEGER, C. DONALD
City official. **PERSONAL:** Born Aug 27, 1936, Huntsville, AL; son of Fred Steger and Lula Cliff Steger; married Elizabeth Sutton, Jun 01, 1966; children: Lisa Monique. **EDUCATION:** Bethune Cookman Coll, BA 1964; Gammon Theol Seminary, BD 1968; Univ South Florida, PhD 1972. **CAREER:** WOBS Radio Jacksonville, announcer 1960-64; Tampa Inner City Programs, dir 1968-71; McCabe Black Comm Develop, dir 1972-75; Pinellas County FL Schools, administrator 1975-77; City of St Petersburg FL, deputy city mgr 1977-79; City of Charlotte, asst city mgr 1979-. **ORGANIZATIONS:** Consultant US Civil Serv Commn 1969-78, General Electric Co 1972-74, Honeywell 1975-77; mem bd of dirs, Rotary Club of Charlotte 1975-; pres bd Bethlehem Ctr Charlotte 1985-86; chmn Campaign for Charlotte Meckenburg United Way 1986; dir, Foundation for the Carolinas, 1986-. **HONORS/ACHIEVEMENTS:** Doctoral Dissertation USF 1972; chmn, 1986 United Way Campaign, 1986. **MILITARY SERVICE:** USAR corpl 1956-62. **HOME ADDRESS:** 110 Dovershire Rd, Charlotte, NC 28226. **BUSINESS ADDRESS:** Assistant City Manager, City of Charlotte, 600 East 4th St, Charlotte, NC 28202.

STEIB, JAMES T.
Clergyman. **PERSONAL:** Born May 17, 1940, Vacherie, LA. **EDUCATION:** Ordained 1957. **CAREER:** Titular Bishop of Britonia; St Louis, auxiliary bishop 1983-. **BUSINESS ADDRESS:** Archdiocese of St Louis, 4445 Lindell Blvd, St Louis, MO 63108.

STENNETT, RENALDO ANTONIO (RENNIE)
Athlete. **PERSONAL:** Born Apr 05, 1951, Colon, Panama. **CAREER:** San Francisco Giants, professional baseball player 1979-; Pittsburgh Pirates, outfielder infielder 1971-79; Minor Leagues, baseball player 1969-71. **HONORS/ACHIEVEMENTS:** Led W Carolinas League outfielders double plays 5 1969; led Carolina Legue total bases 229 1970; played in NL Championship Series 1972, 74, 75, 79; tied modern NL record most hist 3 consec games 12 1975; tied modern major league records most times reacher 1st base safely 1 game 1975; most at bats 1 game 1975; tied major league record for most innings 2 or more hits 1 games 1975; set modern major league records most hits 1 game 7 1975; msot consec hits 1 game 1975; most hits 2 consec games 1975; played in World series 1979. **BUSINESS ADDRESS:** San Francisco Giants, Candlestick Pk, San Francisco, CA 94124.

STENNIS, WILLIE JAMES
Business executive. **PERSONAL:** Born Sep 08, 1923, Philadelphia, MS; married Zelma Miles; children: Roger, William, Kevin, Michael. **EDUCATION:** Central Inst, Archit Engr 1946-48; UCLA, bus courses; So CA Restaurant Assn, yearly seminars. **CAREER:** Dept of St Railways Detroit, driver cashier sta m 1948-57; formed chicken take-out restaurant, 1953; Golden Bird Inc LA, owner 1958-. **ORGANIZATIONS:** Pres Golden Bird Inc; So CA Restaurant Assn; mem Natl Restaurant Assn; trustee CA State Univ & Colls; dir City of LA; CA Educ Facilities Auth State of CA; mem LA Town Hall; Law & Justice Com; LA C of C; Rotary Intl adv bd Daniel Freeman Hosp. **MILITARY SERVICE:** USAF sgt 1942-46. **BUSINESS ADDRESS:** President, Golden Bird Inc, 4201 Wilshire Blvd, Ste 525, Los Angeles, CA 90010.

STENT, MADELON DELANY
Educator. **PERSONAL:** Born Sep 22, 1933, Wash, DC; married Theodore R Stent; children: Michelle, Nicole, Evan. **EDUCATION:** Sarah Lawrence Coll, BA; Wellesley Coll, MA; Columbia U, EdD 1965. **CAREER:** Teachers Coll, Columbia Univ, Queens Coll, CUNY, educator; Cultural Pluralism in Amer Higher Educ, author researcher co-author 1973; Minoprity Enrollment & Rep in Inst of Higher educ, dir author 1974; "Minorities in US Inst of Higher Educ", author 1976; Random House-Knopf Mag-journ, author ed of art, Div of Interdept Studies City Coll City Univ of NY, prof dir. **ORGANIZATIONS:** Fndr pres first black owned Educ Research Corp Urbanal Ed Inc 1967; educ con planner for Voices Inc 1966-; NE reg dir Right to Read Tech Ass Teams St Croix to Canada 1971-74; local sch bd Bronx NY 1965-70; Nat Asn Black Sch Educators 1971-; Am Educ Research Assn 1973-; natl chpsn Higher EdnComm Nat Alliance of Black Sch Educators; consult to numerous orgns & univs; HARYOU-ACT; US Off of Edn;Univ of P Rico;Univ of CA; etc. **HONORS/ACHIEVEMENTS:** Comm Serv Soc Awd 1964; vis prof FordhamUniv Sch of Educ 1969-71; Ford Found Research Grantee 1973; Ford Found Grantee 1974; Rockefeller Scholar in Re Bellagio Italy 1975; Kappa Delta Pi Honor Educ Soc; Student Amb Awd in Spanish to Spain 1952.

STENT, MICHELLE DORENE
Attorney. **PERSONAL:** Born Feb 04, 1955, New York, NY; daughter of Theodore R Stent and Madelon Delany Stent; married Steven Pruitt, Sep 24, 1988. **EDUCATION:** Univ of Puerto Rico, Certificate of Merit 1974; Univ of London, Certificate of Distinction 1975; Tufts Univ, BA 1976; Howard Univ School of Law, JD 1980. **CAREER:** Senator Edward W Brooke, intern 1976; Office of Civil Rights, public info consultant 1979; Congressional Black Caucus, graduate student intern 1979; Congressman Charles Rangel, legislative intern 1980; Comm on Educ and Labor US House of Reps, legislative counsel 1980-85; United Negro Coll Fund, dir govt affairs, assoc general counsel, Washington Office, vice pres 1989-. **ORGANIZATIONS:** Bd dirs Caribbean Action Lobby; consultant Natl Urban League; select comm Congressional Black Caucus Intern Program; mem Delta Theta Phi Law Fraternity, Natl Bar Assn; assn mem Congressional Black Assocs, NAACP, Natl Urban League, Natl Assn of Black Women Attorneys, Coalition of 100 Black Women; bd of dir, Natl Coalition Black Voter Participation 1985-; bd of dir, Capitol City Ballet, 1988-. **HONORS/ACHIEVEMENTS:** Articles published Black Issues in Higher Education, Point of View; honorary doctorate, Texas Coll, Tyler, TX, 1987; Title IX Award, Natl Assn for Equal Opportunity in Higher Educ, 1987; Newspaper Articles, NY Voice, Mississippi Memo Digest, Tyler Courier Times, editor/writer, Government Affairs Reports UUCF, 1985-. **BUSINESS ADDRESS:** Vice President-Washington Office, United Negro College Fund Inc, 2100 M St NW #405, Washington, DC 20037.

STENT, THEODORE R.
Radiologist, educator, musical producer. **PERSONAL:** Born Jan 07, 1924, Charleston, SC; married Madelon Delany; children: Michelle, Nicole, Evan. **EDUCATION:** Talladega Coll, AB 1944; Meharry Medical Coll, MD 1948; Sydenham Hospital, internship 1948-49. **CAREER:** AUS Hospital, chief radiology 1951-53; Bellevue Hospital, resident 1955; Amer Bd of Radiology, diplomat 1955; Workman Compensation NY, special radiology 1955; Bellevue Hospital, asstroent 1955-56; Private Practice NYC, radiology 1955-71; Bronx Hospital, adj attendingg roent 1956-64; Hospital for Joint Dist, adj radiologist 1955-57; Sydenham Hospital, radiologist 1955-60, phy chrg tumor clinic 1956-60; NY Medical Coll, asst prof radiology 1960-67; Columbia Univ, assoc prof radiology 1966-73; Intramer Life Insurance Co, medical dir, vice pres 1966-71; Harlem Hospital, dir School for Nuclear Medical Technology 1971; clinical coord Antioch Coll, Harlem Hospital Center 1972; Nursing Home on Hill, pres medical bd 1973-; Ebony Medex Inc, medical dir 1974. **ORGANIZATIONS:** Mem Medical Advisory Council Natl Urban League 1970-; mem Natl Medical Assn, NY Roent Soc, Amer Coll Radiology, Radiological Soc NY Medical Coll, Amer Inst Ultrasound Medicine, Amer Coll Nuclear Medicine, Soc of Nuclear Medicine; mem HANA Voices Inc, Symphony New World Tiffany Entertainment Corp, Phoenix Comm Group Inc NY Prof Center bd of dirs on all above; mem Urban League Greater NY; bd dirs Greater Harlem Nursing Home Corp; mem NAACP, YMCA, Mayor's Org Task Force, 100 Black Men NYC; mem Sigma Pi Phi Frat, Omega Psi Phi, Guardsmen Inc; numerous publications. **BUSINESS ADDRESS:** Dir Nuclear Medicine, Harlem Hospital, 506 Lenox Ave, New York, NY 10037.

STEPHENS, BOOKER T.
Judge. **PERSONAL:** Born Nov 03, 1944, Bluefield, WV; married Gloria M Davis; children: Ciara Midori, Booker Taliaferro. **EDUCATION:** WV State Coll, BA 1966; Howard Univ, JD 1972. **CAREER:** Asst prosecuting atty 1977-78; WV House of Delegates 1979-82; circuit court judge. **MILITARY SERVICE:** AUS sp5 2 yrs. **HOME ADDRESS:** Drawer E, Keystone, WV 24852. **BUSINESS ADDRESS:** Circuit Court Judge, PO Box 310, Welch, WV 24801.

STEPHENS, CHARLES RICHARD
Higher education administrator. **PERSONAL:** Born Mar 01, 1938, McIntosh County, GA; son of James A Stephens Sr and L R Frances Stephens; married E Delores; children: Chandra, Charlita. **EDUCATION:** Morehouse Coll, BA 1960; Atlanta Univ; Springfield Coll; New Orleans Univ. **CAREER:** Atlanta Univ, vice pres for devel; Dillard Univ, vice pres for devel 1977-79; Butler St YMCA, public relations sec asst gen exec 1961-70; United Negro Coll Fund, city campaign dir natl campaign dir 1970-76; School of Medicine Morehouse Coll, devel officer 1977; Butler Village Inc, 1970-73. **ORGANIZATIONS:** Mem Alpha Phi Alpha Frat 1958-; mem Natl Soc of Fund Raisers 1960-; mem Atlanta Jaycees 1965-69, Intl Com YMCA's 1966-68; bd Wright Jackson Brown Williams & Stephens 1969-71; support agency United Presbyterian Church; assn dir YMCA 1965-70, 1979-; mem Leadership Atlanta 1974; pres Natl Alumni Council UNCF 1982-86; bd mem United Negro Coll Fund 1982-86; bd mem Atlanta Urban League; bd mem Carrie Steele-Pitts Home; sec natl bd Natl Soc of Fund Raising Executives. **HONORS/ACHIEVEMENTS:** Outstanding Ind UNCF Perform Awd 1971; certificate of commendation. **MILITARY SERVICE:** AUS s/4 1962-64. **BUSINESS ADDRESS:** Vice Pres, Development & Institutional Relations, Atlanta University, 240 James P Brawley Dr SW, Atlanta, GA 30314.

STEPHENS, CYNTHIA DIANE
Government official. **PERSONAL:** Born Aug 27, 1951, Detroit, MI; daughter of Nathaniel Otis Stephens and Diane Shand Stephens; children: Imani Diane Stephens. **EDUCATION:** Univ of MI, BA 1971; Atlanta Univ, postgraduate 1971-72; Emory Law School, JD 1976. **CAREER:** Natl Conf of Black Lawyers, so regional dir 1976-77; Natl League of Cities, coord 1977-78; Pan-African Orthodox Christian Church, genl counsel 1978-82; Michigan Senate, assoc general counsel 1979-82; Wayne County Charter Commn, vice-chmn 1980-81; Law Offices of Cynthia D Stephens, attorney 1981-82; 36th District Ct, judge 1982-85; faculty Wayne County Community Coll 1985-; faculty Univ of Detroit Law School 1988-; Wayne County Circuit Court, judge 1985-. **ORGANIZATIONS:** Mem Wolverine Bar Assoc 1979; bd mem Wayne Co Neighborhood Legal Serv 1980; mem New Detroit Inc 1981-; bd mem Assoc of Black Judges of MI 1982-89, MI Dist Judges Assoc 1982-85, Greater Detroit Health Care Cncl 1983-85; guest lecturer Southern Univ Women and Leadership Symposium Baton Rouge LA 1983, Western MI Univ Dept of Women Studies Kalamazoo 1983; Univ of MI Symposium series for the Ctr for African and Afro-Amer Studies 1984; mem adv bd African Diaspora Project of the Delta Inst 1984-; mem City Wide Sch Comm Organization-at-Large 1984-86, Delta Manor LDHA 1984-, YMCA Downtown Detroit 1984; mem Amer Bar Assoc Comm on Judicial Evaluation 1984-85, Delta Sigma Theta Detroit Alumni 1984-85; mem adv bd MI Bar Journal 1985-; Amer Corporate Counsel Pro-Bono Adv Comm 1982-88; life mem Natl Bar Assoc; bd of commissioner, State Bar of MI 1986-. mem Natl Conference of Black Lawyers, Natl Assoc of Women Judges, MI Judges Assoc. **HONORS/ACHIEVEMENTS:** Outstanding Woman Awd Woodward Ave Presbyterian Ch 1982; Disting Serv Awd Region 5 Detroit Public Schools 1983; Wolverine Bar Member of the Yr 1984; Little Rock Baptist Ch Golden Heritage Awd for Judicial Excellence 1984; Outstanding Woman in Law Hartford Memorial Bapt Ch 1985; publication "Judicial Selection and Diversity", MI Bar Journal Vol 64 No 6 1985; Disting Alumni Awd Cass Tech HS 1987. **BUSINESS ADDRESS:** Judge, Wayne County Circuit Court, 1801 City County Bldg, Detroit, MI 48226.

STEPHENS, GEORGE BENJAMIN DAVIS
Physician. **PERSONAL:** Born Oct 12, 1904, Norfolk, VA; married Dolores Shirley Carr. **EDUCATION:** Hampton Inst Hampton VA, dip 1924; HowardUniv Washington DC, BS 1930; Howard U, MD 1935. **CAREER:** Priv Pract, physician 1935-; blank for box structure which folds into box or box with tray, inventor 1980. **ORGANIZATIONS:** Mem Phi Beta Sigma Frat. **HONORS/ACHIEVEMENTS:** Recip 50-Mile Swim Awd Hampton Inst ARC 1965.

STEPHENS, HERBERT MALONE
Judge. **PERSONAL:** Born Jul 10, 1918, Okmulgee, OK; married Lillian; children: Sydney, Sheri. **EDUCATION:** Morehouse Coll, BA 1938; Univ of Washington Law School, juris doctorate 1950. **CAREER:** King Co Seattle WA, deputy prosecuting atty 1952-56; Seattle Dist Court, judge protem 1968-73; WA State, supreme court judge. **ORGANIZATIONS:** Past mem Amer Bar Assn; Amer Judicual Soc 1961-62; mem WA State & Seattle-King Co Bar Assns; mem chmn Seattle Civil Serv Comm 1963-71; mem WA State Human Rights Com 1965-60; chmn bd dirs Neighborhood Inc. **MILITARY SERVICE:** USAF 1943-46. **BUSINESS ADDRESS:** Superior Court Judge, Washington Superior Court, King Co Courthouse, Seattle, WA 98104.

STEPHENS, HERMAN ALVIN
Physician. **PERSONAL:** Born Nov 19, 1914, Yazoo City, MS; married Kathryn; children:

Patricia, Herman, Edgar, Thelma, Benjamin, Nelda, Alva, Yvette. **EDUCATION:** Ferris Inst, PhC 1930;Univ Detroit, PhB 1932; Meharry Med Coll, MD 1936. **CAREER:** Stephens Nursing Home, fndr operator 1956-; VA Hosp, acting chf psychiatry 1966-71; VA Reg Off, psychiat 1964-66; Pvt Prac, 1942-64; VA Hosp, resd 1938-42; Provident Hosp Training Sch, intern 1936-37. **ORGANIZATIONS:** Mem bd dir Lexington YMCA; Meth Ch; Alpha Phi Alpha Frat; Pilgrim Bapt Ch; YMCA; flw Am Geriatric Soc; Nat Med Assn; AMA; mem Mil Surgeons US. **HONORS/ACHIEVEMENTS:** Two Cerr merit Commonwealth KY 1966; cit meritorious serv Pers Com 1966; physician yr State KY 1966. **BUSINESS ADDRESS:** PO Box 11786, Lexington, KY 40578.

STEPHENS, JAMES ANTHONY
City official. **PERSONAL:** Born Jan 02, 1914, McIntosh County, GA; married Lillie Mae; children: Charles Richard, James Anthony Jr, Herbert Clark. **EDUCATION:** Franklin Inst; Univ of GA, Cert Bnkng & Fin. **CAREER:** Brunswick Brnch Pstl Svc, ret pstl clrk 1940, ret equal opprtnty liason; Atlanta Life Ins, ret ins rep 1942-84; City of Brunswick, GA city cmmr 1978-. **ORGANIZATIONS:** Chmn bd dir CAPDC 1980-81; chmn Glynn Co Boys Clbs of Am; mem Glynn Co Chmbr Comm Bd; Tuesday coord & mem Christian TV Mnstrs 1976-84; bd dir United Way of Glynn Co; bd dir Coastal Area Tourism; mem Gvnrs Adv Bd Area Plng & Dev Comm; pres Zion Bptst Asso. **HONORS/ACHIEVEMENTS:** Ctzns Awrds GA Masonic Org; govnrs Adv Awrd State of GA 1984; Postal CmndtnsUniv S Postal Svc; Southern Personalities & Who's Who Amng Blck Am; Serv awrd The Coastal Area Plng & Dev. **HOME ADDRESS:** 2417 Johnson St, Brunswick, GA 31520.

STEPHENS, LEE B., JR.
Educator. **PERSONAL:** Born Oct 22, 1925, Atlanta, GA; married Betty S Stephens; children: Lee B III, Gary B, David B. **EDUCATION:** Morehouse Coll, BS 1947; Atlanta Univ, MS 1950; State Univ IA, PhD 1957. **CAREER:** Dillard Univ, instr biology 1950-53; NC Coll, instr biology 1953-54; So Univ, assoc prof biology 1957-59, prof biology 1959-62; CA State Univ, assocprof biology 1957-59, prof 1959-62, asst prof biology 1962-65, assoc prof biology 1965-70, assoc dean sch natl sci 1975-83, prof biology 1970-. **ORGANIZATIONS:** Mem Soc of Sigma Xi; Amer Soc Zoologists; Amer Microscopital Soc; Pre-doctoral fellowships; Natl Med Fellowship Inc; NSF grants to study at Hopkins Marine Sta of Stanford Univ; rsch & study grant Marine Biol Lab NSF; rsch grants NSF, Long Beach State Coll Found. **HONORS/ACHIEVEMENTS:** Author articles publ in sci jours, J Exp Zool, Ann Ent Soc Amer, Amer Zool, Trans Am Microscopical Socl J Histochem & Cytochem. **BUSINESS ADDRESS:** Prof of Biology, CA StateUniv, 1250 Bellflower Blvd, Long Beach, CA 90840.

STEPHENS, PAUL A.
Dentist. **PERSONAL:** Born Feb 28, 1921, Muskogee, OK; son of Lonny and Maudie; divorced; children: Marsha W Wilson, Paul A Jr, Derek M. **EDUCATION:** Howard Univ, BS 1942, DDS 1945. **CAREER:** Coll of Dentistry Howard Univ, instr 1945-46; Private Practice, dentist Gary IN 1946-. **ORGANIZATIONS:** Pres Gary IN Bd of Health 1973-79; pres Asso Med Cntr 1978-80; pres IN State Bd of Dental Exam 1978-80; mem IN Univ, Purdue Univ Adv Bd 1974-80; pres IN Acad Gen Dentistry 1980-81; vice pres Reg 7 OH-IN-Acad Gen Dentistry 1980-81; Chi Lambda Kappa; Amer Coll Dentistry. **HONORS/ACHIEVEMENTS:** Howard Univ Dentist of Yr Intl Coll of Dentists 1979; Alpha Phi Alpha Piere Fauchard Acad; life mem NAACP, Acad of Dentist Intl; rec of ASTP. **MILITARY SERVICE:** AUS pfc 1943-45. **HOME ADDRESS:** 1901 Taft St, Gary, IN 46404.

STEPHENS, PHYGENAU
Editor. **PERSONAL:** Born Jun 04, 1923, Ann Arbor, MI; widowed. **EDUCATION:** Wilberforce Univ, BA; Univ of Detroit, currently working on MA. **CAREER:** Kodday Prod & Control City Marketing Inc, natl publ; MI Challenger Newspaper, women's editor; The Weldon Group Ltd, pres; Detroit Courier, writer; WGPR-FM, comm 4 yrs; pub rel 7yrs; elem tchr; business coll tchr; newspapers women's editor; newspaper food editor; lecturer. **ORGANIZATIONS:** Mem Nat Assn of Market Devel; pub rel Booker T Wash Bus Assn; 2nd vice pres Nat Assn of Media Women Inc; Detroit Urban League Guild; United Coll Fund;League of Cath Women; African Art Com; Nat Assn of Negro Bus Prof Women; Enconta Doras Fisher YMCA; Fund Raiser; Downtown YWCA; Wolverrine Rep Assn; Detroit Round Table of Christ Jews; Am Women in Radio & TV; Interracial Cncl; Detroit Women's Advertising Club; Black Women's Pol Caucus Group; Speakers Bur of United Found; bd mem Delta Sigma Theta Home for Girls; reg dir Capital Formation for Nat Awds. **HONORS/ACHIEVEMENTS:** Pres awd NAMW; Gold Key Awd; Nat Boy's Club & Girl's Club of Am; wednesday luncheon awd BTWBA; Betty Jane Everett awd NAMWA; most outstng pub rel woman NAMW.

STEPHENS, VIVIAN
Social worker. **PERSONAL:** Born Oct 25, 1942, Enoree, SC; married Grover. **EDUCATION:** Deshazors Beauty Coll, atnd area colls. **CAREER:** Social Worker SC Resource Devel, manpower specialist; Laurens Co Comm Action Prog Br of The Ofc of Economic Opp, outreach worker 1971-74. **ORGANIZATIONS:** Mem Laurens Co NAACP; State Welfare Forum; bd dir Co Health Dept; bd of Voters Registration 1974-. **HONORS/ACHIEVEMENTS:** Cited for Outstanding Comm Leadershipawards Night NAACP 1973. **BUSINESS ADDRESS:** Rt 2 Denver Section, Anderson, SC.

STEPHENS, WALLACE O.
Engineering executive. **CAREER:** Stephens Engineering Co Inc, Greenbelt, MD, chief exec. **BUSINESS ADDRESS:** Stephens Engineering Co Inc, 6301 Ivy Lane, Suite 300, Greenbelt, MD 20770. *

STEPHENS, WARREN E.
Business executive. **PERSONAL:** Born Sep 26, 1933, Columbus, OH; divorced; children: Denise Jean, Warren E Jr, Rodeana Christina. **EDUCATION:** Attended, Tilloston Univ, Warner Sch of Music, OH State Univ. **CAREER:** J&S Ent Dir SMADA Artist Mgmt Intl, pres; John Levy Ent, personal mgr; Justin Mgmt Corp; pres; MGM Records, assoc producer; NJ Bd of Educ, tchr; Shaw Talent Artist Corp, talent agent; Queen Booking Corp, w coast dir; JH Grant Mgmt Inc, exec vice pres. **ORGANIZATIONS:** Mem AF of M; UAW-CIO; mem Jr Achievement Columbus. **HONORS/ACHIEVEMENTS:** Hon Sheriff Nashville TN 1976; Delcaration of Achievement in Entertainment Indus City Counsel LA 1974. **BUSINESS ADDRESS:** Executive Vice President, JH Grant Mgmt Inc, 6464 Sunset Blvd Ste 1030, Hollywood, CA 90028.

STEPHENS, WILLIAM HAYNES
Judge. **PERSONAL:** Born Mar 02, 1935, New Orleans, LA; son of William Stephens and Myrtle Stephens; children: Michael (deceased), Stuart, Patrick. **EDUCATION:** San Jose State Univ San Jose CA, BA 1956; Univ of California Hastings Coll of Law, JD 1967. **CAREER:** Municipal Court County of Marin CA, judge 1988-; law office of William H Stephens, atty at law 1972-79; Bagley/Bianchi & Sheeks, assoc atty 1969-72; Contra & Costa Co, deputy public defender 1968-69; Natl Labor Relations Bd, atty 1968; Marin Co Bar Assn, dir 1970-73; Marin Co Human Rights Commn, chmn 1977-79; Marin Co Dist, dist counsel 1977-79; Marin Co Superior Ct, arbitrator 1977-79; California Agr Labor Relations Bd, admin law officer 1978-79. **ORGANIZATIONS:** Dir; La Familia De Marin 1977-, Amer Heart Assn, 1985-; California Judges Assn, Natl Bar Assn, Amer Bar Assn. **BUSINESS ADDRESS:** Judge, County of Marin Hall Justice, Civic Center, San Rafael, CA 94903.

STEPHENSON, ALLAN ANTHONY
Government official. **PERSONAL:** Born Oct 27, 1937, New York, NY; married Deloris; children: Diane, Allan Jr. **EDUCATION:** Morgan St Coll, BA 1960; Ny CityUniv John Jay Sch of Crim Just, postgrad. **CAREER:** US Dept of Commerce Ofc of Minor Bus Enterprise, acting dir & dep dir for operations; reg dir 1973-77, br chief 1970-73; Assist Negro Bus, exec dir 1968-69; Urban League of Westchester Co, asso exec dir 1967-68; Urban League of Westchester Co, dir econ devel & employ 1966-67; Bus Educ Train Intgerracial Coun for Bus Oppor, asso dir 1965-66. **ORGANIZATIONS:** Bd mem exec com NY St Coun of Urban Leagues 1967-68; sec bd of dir Assn to Assist Negro Bus 1967-70; mem bd of dir Oakland Mills Youth Conf 1975-76; adv com Comp Statewide Plan for Vocation Rehab Serv 1967-69; mem bd of dir Sr Personnel Employ Com 1967-69; Statewide Manpwr Panel on Job Train Employ 1967-69; US Dept of Commerce Incent Awards Com 1975-77; Judo & Karate Club of Baltimore; Roots Asso Adv Com Comp Statewide Plan for VocatRehab Serv 1965. **HONORS/ACHIEVEMENTS:** Outst Perf Awd US Dept of Commerce 1974-75; Presidential Cit 1975. **MILITARY SERVICE:** AUS res 1964-67; NYNG 1961-64. **BUSINESS ADDRESS:** 14th Constitution Ave NW, Rm 5053, Washington, DC 20230.

STEPHENSON, CAROLYN L.
Educational administrator. **PERSONAL:** Born Jul 27, 1945, Brownsville, TN, daughter of James and Fannie Lee. **EDUCATION:** Univ of KY, AA, JCC Sociology 1974;Univ of Louisville, BS Guid & Cnslng 1976;Univ of Louisville Coll, MEd, student personnel 1978. **CAREER:** Univ of Louisville, couns Ath Dept 1977;Univ of Louisville, fncl aid & intern 1977;Univ of Louisville, couns W Louisville Educ Prog 1976; MD Sch of Art & Design, consult 1977. **ORGANIZATIONS:** Chrprsn Annual Conf on Black FamilyUniv of Louisville Pan African Study 1979-80; panel reader Talent Srch Prog Offc Educ Washington 1980; mem KY Assn of Stdnt Fncl Aid Adminstrn; KASFAA 1977-80; mem, So Assn of Student Financial Aid Adminstrn SASFAA Z1977-80. **HONORS/ACHIEVEMENTS:** Achievement awd New Aid Admstrn, So Assn of Student Fin Aid Adminstrn 1977-78; grad assistantship,Univ of Louisville 1977; spkr Fncl Aid Awrnes Wk Prsntatn WLOU Educ 1979. **BUSINESS ADDRESS:** Coordinator of Minority Student Services, University of Louisville, Office of Minority Services, Belknap Campus, Louisville, KY 40292.

STEPHENSON, CHARLES E., III
Fast-food executive. **CAREER:** Stepco of South Carolina Inc, Columbia, chief exec. **HOME ADDRESS:** 14 Upper Pond Rd, Columbia, SC 29223. **BUSINESS ADDRESS:** Stepco of South Carolina Inc, Columbia, SC. *

STEPHENSON, DWIGHT
Professional athlete. **PERSONAL:** Born Nov 20, 1957, Murfreesboro, NC; married Dinah; children: Dwight Jr. **EDUCATION:** Attended, Univ Alabama. **CAREER:** Miami Dolphins, center 1980-. **ORGANIZATIONS:** Involved in charity work in South FL including efforts for Baby House (Cerebral Palsy) and Boy Scouts. **HONORS/ACHIEVEMENTS:** Along with teammate Don McNeal received Silver Medal of Valor Miami-Dade Police Dept 1984 (highest awd that can be bestowed upon a civilian); Man of the YearHampton VA; named team's outstanding offensive lineman for 4 straight seasons; named to the AP, NEA and PFWA All-NFL squads; UPI All-AFC selection; Sporting News All-Pro; Pro Football Weekly All-Pro; Football News All-AFC; NFLPA Offensive Lineman of the Year; USA Today NFL Offensive Lineman of the Year; AFC Pro Bowl starter and AP First Team All-Pro; mem NFL Pro Bowl teams 1986,87. **BUSINESS ADDRESS:** Miami Dolphins, 2269 NW 199 St, Opa-Locka, FL 33056.

STEPHENSON, JERRY L.
Public administrator. **PERSONAL:** Born Feb 02, 1949, Jeffersonville, IN; married Rita Zenon; children: Margaret A, Nicole L, Jerry II, Lydia A. **EDUCATION:** Austin Peay State Univ, BA 1972; Dunn & Bradstreet, personnel mgmt training 1978; IN Univ, mgmt by objective course certificate 1979. **CAREER:** Home Credit Co, credit & loan officer 1972-73; Clark Co Comm Action Agency Inc, dep dir 1973-74; Midwest Church of Christ, 1984-; Hoosier Valley EconomicOppor Corp, exec dir 1974-. **ORGANIZATIONS:** Mem & past vice pres Jeffersonville Social Concerns Civic League; mem Natl Comm Action Agency Exec Dirs Assn, IN Comm Action Agency Dirs Assn; assoc minister Midwest Church of Christ; vice pres Clark Co NAACP; mem Rotary Club; pres bd of dirs New Hope Svcs; mem YMCA Bd of Dirs; admin JTPA Hoosier Falls Private Industry Council for 7 southern IN counties; mem Alumni 1st class of Leadership Clark Co; mem various sch bds, econ devel comms, manpower comms; Governor's Child Support Commission. **HONORS/ACHIEVEMENTS:** Jaycees Outstanding Boss Awd Jeffersonville Jaycees 1975; Gov's Commendation Awd office of the Gov of IN 1976; Citizen of the Day Awd radio sta WXVW Jeffersonville 1976; Outstanding Comm Serv Awd Jeffersonville Social Concerns Civic League 1977; Citizen of the Week radio station WCII for helping to save a lifein a suicide case 1984. **BUSINESS ADDRESS:** Executive Dir, Hoosier Valley Econ Oppor Corp, 510 Spring St PO Box 843, Jeffersonville, IN 47130.

STEPP, MARC
Association executive. **PERSONAL:** Born Jan 31, 1923, Versailles, KY; married Elanor. **EDUCATION:** Wolverine Trade Sch, 1949; Lewis Bus Sch, 1951;Univ of Detroit, BBA 1963. **CAREER:** Intl Union, vP; UAW Region 1b, asst dir; Common Pleas Ct, clerk; UAW Region 1b, intl rep; Comm Hlth Assn, asst dir. **ORGANIZATIONS:** Mem UAW Intl Exec Bd Dir UAW Soc Tech Educ Prgm; Job Devel Training Prgm, co-dir; UAW SE MI Comm Action Prgm, chmn; mem Dexter Ave Bapt Ch; vice-chmn bd trustees Detroit Gen Hosp; mem New Detroit bd of trustees; mem bd of Greater Detroit Area Hosp Counc; vP United Comm Svcs;

mem NAACP; mem MI Dept of Soc Svcs; Trade Union Ldrshp Counc; Coalition of Black Trade Unionists; mem Dem Black Caucus Streeing Com; mem Dem Nat Com. **MILITARY SERVICE:** AUS 1943-46. **BUSINESS ADDRESS:** 8000 E Jefferson Ave, Detroit, MI 48214.

STEPPE, CECIL H.
Probation officer. **PERSONAL:** Born Jan 31, 1933, Versailes, KY; married Evelyn Lee Elliott; children: Gregory, Russell, Steven, Cecily, Annette. **EDUCATION:** San Diego City Coll, AA 1961; CA Western Univ, BA 1964; Grossmont Coll, Teaching Credential 1972. **CAREER:** Grossmont Coll, instr criminology dept 1969-73; San Diego Cty CA, suprv probation officer 1968-73, dir juvenile intake 1973-75, asst supt of juvenile hall 1975, responsible for finalization of due-process system for adult inst 1975-76; dir Camp West Fork 1976-77, dir adult inst 1977-80, chief probation officer 1980-. **ORGANIZATIONS:** Mem Black Leadership Council 1980; co-covenor Black Cty Admin 1980; vice pres Chief Probation Officers of CA 1983; bd mem Amer Probation & Parole Assn 1984; chmn State Advisory Bd Victim/Witness Prog 1984; editor "Expense" Mag CA probation/Parole & Correctional Assn 1984; bd mem St Youth Prog; Mayors Crime Commiss, Criminal Justice Council; Interagency Youth Adv Comm; mem Natl Forum for Black Public Admin, CA Black Correction Coalition, Amer Probation & Parole Assoc, Chief Probation & Parole Assoc, Chief Probation Officers of CA, Black Leadership Council, San Diego Cty Exec Assoc. **HONORS/ACHIEVEMENTS:** Equal Oppty San Diego Urban League 1983; Valuable Serv San Diego Cty Foster Parent Assn 1984. **MILITARY SERVICE:** USAF a 1/c 1952-56. **BUSINESS ADDRESS:** Chief Probation Officer, San Diego Cty Probation Dept, 2901 Meadow Lark Dr, San Diego, CA 92123.

STEPTO, ROBERT BURNS
Educator. **PERSONAL:** Born Oct 28, 1945, Chicago, IL; son of Robert C Stepto and Anna Burns Stepto; married Michele A Leiss, Jun 21, 1967; children: Gabriel Burns Stepto, Rafael Hawkins Stepto. **EDUCATION:** Trinity Coll, Hartford CT, BA (cum laude), English, 1966; Stanford Univ, Stanford CA, MA, 1968, PhD, 1974. **CAREER:** Williams Coll, Williamstown MA, asst prof, 1971-74; Yale Univ, New Haven CT, asst prof, 1974-79, assoc prof, 1979-84, prof, 1984-. **ORGANIZATIONS:** Chair, MLA Commn on the Literatures & Languages of Amer, 1977-78; mem, Connecticut Humanities Council, 1980-82, trustee, Trinity Coll, 1982-92; assoc editor, Callaloo, 1984-88; advisor, Yale-New Haven Teachers Inst, 1985-, Anson Phelps Stokes Inst, 1985-; bd of editors, American Literature, 1987-88; advisor, Southern Connecticut Library Council, 1987; advisory editor, Callaloo, 1988-. **HONORS/ACHIEVEMENTS:** Woodrow Wilson Fellowship, Woodrow Wilson Found, 1966-67; Morse Fellowship, Yale Univ, 1977-78; From Behind the Veil: A Study of Afro-Amer Narrative, 1979; edited with M Harper, Chant of Saints: Afro-Amer Literature, Art, Scholarship, 1979; edited with D Fisher, D Fisher, Afro-Amer Literature: The Reconstruction of Instinction, 1979; Senior Fellowship, Natl Endowment for the Humanities, 1981-82; Alumni Medal, Trinity Coll, 1986; Ed, The Selected Poems of Jay Wright, 1987; contributor to the Columbia Literary History of the United States, 1987. **BUSINESS ADDRESS:** Professor,, English, American Studies, African-American Studies, Yale University, 3388 Yale Station, New Haven, CT 06520.

STEPTO, ROBERT CHARLES
Educator, physician. **PERSONAL:** Born Oct 06, 1920, Chicago, IL; son of Robert L. Stepto and Grace Williams; married Ann; children: Robert, Jan. **EDUCATION:** Northwestern Univ, BS 1941; Howard Univ Med Sch, MD 1944; Univ Chicago, PhD 1948. **CAREER:** Chicago Med Sch, prof chmn ob 1970-75; Cook Co Hosp, chmn dept ob 1972-76; Rush Med Sch, prof 1975-79; Univ of Chicago, chief of gynecology 1979-; Mt Sinai Hosp, chmn dept of ob-gyn 1969-1979. **ORGANIZATIONS:** Pres Intl Coll Surgeons 1978-79; Pres Chicago Bd Health 1988-; pres Chicago Gynecology Soc 1983; pres Assn of Gyn Oncologists 1983; pres Natl Med Fellowship; bd dir Children Home & Aid Soc; Fellow US PHS 1948-50; mem Natl Med Assn 1946-48; mem Amer Coll of Ob/Gyn; bd dir Gyn Urol Soc, Chicago Health Rsch Found; mem Sigma Pi Phi. **HONORS/ACHIEVEMENTS:** Fellow Amer Coll Surgeons; Hon Fellow Peruvian Surg Soc; Cent. Assn Ob/Gyn (Life). **MILITARY SERVICE:** AUS MC capt 1951-53. **BUSINESS ADDRESS:** Professor Ob/Gyn Dept, Univ of Chicago Medical Sch, 5841 S Maryland Ave, Chicago, IL 60637.

STEPTOE, JOHN LEWIS
Artist and author. **PERSONAL:** Born Sep 14, 1950, Brooklyn, NY; son of John Oliver Steptoe and Elesteen Hill Steptoe; children: Bweela, Javaka. **EDUCATION:** New York School of Art and Design, 1964-67. **CAREER:** Brooklyn Music School, Brooklyn, NY, teacher, 1970; author and artist of children's books. **ORGANIZATIONS:** Amnesty International. **HONORS/ACHIEVEMENTS:** Gold Medal, Society of Illustrators, 1970; Caldecott Honor Book, 1985, 1988; Coretta Scott King Award, 1988; author of Stevie, Harper, 1969; author of Jumping Mouse: A Native American Legend, Lothrop, 1984; author of Mufaro's Beautiful Daughters: An African Tale, Lothrop, 1987. **HOME ADDRESS:** 840 Monroe Street, Brooklyn, NY 11221. *

STEPTOE, ROOSEVELT
Educational administrator. **PERSONAL:** Born Nov 28, 1934, Liberty, MS. **EDUCATION:** SouthernUniv Baton Rouge, BS 1952;Univ of MA Amherst, phD 1966; CarnegiemellonUniv Pittsburgh, post doctorate study. **CAREER:** Couthern Univ, chancellor 1977-; Southern Univ, vice pres 1975-77; So Univ, dir of economic research & transp center 1967-75; So Univ, prof of econ 1966-67;Univ of MA, teaching assn 1963-66; FL A&M Univ, asst prof of econ 1961-63; US Office of Econ Oppor, consultant 1967-70; Fed of So Cooperatives Atlanta, consultant 1967-70; Amer Econ Assn; Caucus of Black Economists. **HONORS/ACHIEVEMENTS:** Govs Commn on priority issues pub "Mass Trans Demands of the Scotlandville Residents" Hwy Research Record; pub "Scotlandville Before the Hwy" US Deptof Trans Office of the Sec 1974; pub "The Trans Problem of the Aged & Physically Handicapped" The Baton Rouge Experience; pub "Community Planning for HwyImprovements a Case Study". **MILITARY SERVICE:** USAF a-1c 1953-57. **BUSINESS ADDRESS:** So Univ So Branch PO, Baton Rouge, LA 70813.

STERLING, CHARLES A.
Business executive, publisher. **PERSONAL:** Born Aug 17, 1932, Chicago, IL; son of Lott Sterling and Delelah Sterling; divorced; children: Dana Sterling Davis. **EDUCATION:** Lake Forest Coll, BA 1954; Northwestern Univ, Business Admin Grad; Marquette Univ, Business Admin Grad; Washington Univ, Business Admin. **CAREER:** Arnold & Assoc Memphis, vice pres 1959-60; Sterling & Assoc, head of firm 1960-63; Helene Curtis Inc Chicago, natl sales mgr special markets; Tuesday Publ Inc Chicago, acct exec 1965-66; P Lorillard Co New York, asst gen sales mgr 1966-68; Summit Lab Indianapolis Inc, gen sales mgr 1970-72; New York, dir devel council 1972-74; Black Sports Mag, vice pres mktg & devel 1974-75; Tuesday Mag, assoc publ 1974-76; Arasery Inc, vice pres sales 1976-78; Waters of Saratoga Springs Inc, pres & Chief exec 1978-84; Minority Business Exchange, vice pres 1984. **ORGANIZATIONS:** Pres Detroit & New York Chap Natl Assn Market Devel 1968-70; bd mem Council Concerned Black Exec 1968-70,72-75; lecturing prof Wharton Comm Coll Univ PA 1972-75; prof mktg Malcolm King Coll New York City 1974-75; Blair Mktg Assoc 1969-70; exec bd Boy Scouts of Amer Saratoga City 1979-83; mem Private Industry Council of Saratoga City 1979-; state dir Jr C of C; mem Alpha Phi Alpha; vice pres NAACP 1979-83; pres Men's Group of Northside Ctr 1972-74; former pres Chicago Pan-Hellenic Council; alumni bd gov Lake Forest Coll 1974-80; bd mem Saratoga City Private Indust Council 1980-84. **HONORS/ACHIEVEMENTS:** Distinguished Alumni Award Lake Forest Coll 1973; 2000 Men of Achievement Award England 1969; received recognition Natl Poetry Soc; Athletic Hall of Fame Lake Forest Coll 1976. **HOME ADDRESS:** PO Box 748, New York, NY 10113. **BUSINESS ADDRESS:** vice pres, Minority Supplier Devel, Minority Business Exchange, One Madison Ave, New York, NY 10010.

STETSON, JEFFREY P.
Educator. **PERSONAL:** Born Jun 05, 1948, New York, NY; son of John Stetson and Isabella Stetson; married Carmen Hayward. **EDUCATION:** Framingham State Coll, BA 1973; Boston Univ, EdM 1974, ABD 1976. **CAREER:** MA State Coll System, dir of affirmative action & alternatives for individual develop 1974-79; Univ of Lovell, dir of affirmative action 1979; CA State Univ, dean of faculty & staff 1979-86, dir of public affairs 1986-. **ORGANIZATIONS:** Pres & mem bd dirs Black Alliance for Scholarship & Educ 1981-84; pres & mem bd dirs Concerned Helpers of Inner Comm Endeavors 1984-; mem NAACP, Urban League, Amer Assoc of Affirmative Action, Dramatists Guild, Los Angeles Black Playwrights, Los Angeles Actor's Theatre Playwrights Lab; Writers Guild of Amer, West. **HONORS/ACHIEVEMENTS:** Whitney Young Jr Fellowship Boston Univ 1975; CHOICE Comm Serv Awd 1984; Louis B Mayer Awd for Outstanding Achievement in Playwrighting 1985; 8 NAACP Theatre Image Awards 1987; 6 NY Audelco Theatre nominations; Theodore Ward Theatre Award 1989; Production of The Meeting, Amer Playhouse, 1989; Natl Playwrights Conf 1988. **HOME ADDRESS:** 14005 Palawan Way #210, Marina Del Rey, CA 90292. **BUSINESS ADDRESS:** Dean Faculty & Staff Affairs, California StateUniv, 400 Golden Shore, Long Beach, CA 90802.

STEVENS, ALTHEA WILLIAMS
Educator. **PERSONAL:** Born Oct 23, 1931, Norfolk, VA. **EDUCATION:** CA StUniv Los Angeles, BS 1969; Rutgers U, MEd 1974; Rutgers U, doctoral Can. **CAREER:** Western Wyoming Coll, div chrmn, assoc prof; Bergen Co Comm Coll, prof bus admin 1977-78; Montclair State Coll, instr bus educ & off sys adm 1975-78; Camden HS, instr data processing 1970-75; Los Angeles Co Probation Dept, stat coor 196-68. **ORGANIZATIONS:** Consult comp Sweetwater Co WY Planning Bd 1978-79; gen prb mem WY Bd of Cert Pub Accts 1980-83; Assn Computer Mgmt AVA, NBEA,WBEA. **HONORS/ACHIEVEMENTS:** Omicron Tau Theta; Delta Pi Espilon; Who's Who Am Women 1978-80; Who's Who in the W 1980; World Who's Who of Women 1980. **BUSINESS ADDRESS:** Western Wyoming College, PO Box 428, Rock Springs, WY 82901.

STEVENS, CLEVELAND
Attorney. **PERSONAL:** Born Mar 25, 1927, Loris, SC; married Leola M Dewitt. **EDUCATION:** SC State Coll, AB, LLB 1953. **CAREER:** Legal Clerk 1953; Horry County, public defender; USAF Judge Adv Corp, 1955-59; Conway, SC, priv pract 1960-66; US Dept Agr DC, ofc gen coun 1966-70; Neighborhood Legal Assis Prog Inc & Charleston, dir 1972. **ORGANIZATIONS:** Mem SC Supreme Ct; US Dist Ct for SC; US Ct of Appeals, 4th Cir; US Supreme Ct. **HONORS/ACHIEVEMENTS:** Reginald Heber Smith Fellow 1970-72; mem Kappa Alpha Psi, Mason & Shriner; aptd by Gov of SC to Advi Coun for Consumer Protection, Aug 1972. **BUSINESS ADDRESS:** Horry County, PO Box 1666, Conway, SC 29526.

STEVENS, GEORGE L.
Administrative assistant. **PERSONAL:** Born Feb 06, 1932, Junction City, LA; married Brenda Washington; children: Marc, Michelle, Eric, Gary. **EDUCATION:** CA Comm Coll, AA, teacher credentials in ethnic studies; San Diego State Univ, BS, MA candidate. **CAREER:** San Diego Jr Coll & San Diego State Univ, instructor; General Dynamics, logistic analyst & engineering admin 1958-64; Lockheed Aircraft, engineering mgmt rep 1966; San Diego Urban League, dir job devel & placement 1967-68; Philco-Ford, dir of placement 1968-69; State of CA, job agent for state 1969-72; Co of San Diego, affirmative action officer 1972; Viewpoint News, dir of marketing & sales 1972-74; US Congressman Jim Bates, special asst. **ORGANIZATIONS:** Participant March on Montgomery w/Dr Martin Luther King 1964; Civil Rights March on San Francisco 1965; placed 512 black people on job without staff or financial assistance from agency in 1967 while working at Urban League; chmn of CORE, 1967-69; past chmn Congress of African People 1969-72; past city commr Model City Advisory bd, 1971-72; city commr San Diego Stadium Authority 1971-; pas mem bd dir NAACP; asst to pastor of Calvary Baptist Church. **HONORS/ACHIEVEMENTS:** Black Fed Award 1963; Black Man of Year, 1968 Black Congress; organized Black & Mexican Amer Convention 1968; Civic Contribution Award 1973; author City Ordinance paving way for the first black to be elected to bd of educ; Religious Leader Award 1980; Freedom Award Black Achievement 1982; Fredrick Douglass Award, 1986. **MILITARY SERVICE:** AUS 1953-55; Honorable Discharge.

STEVENS, HAROLD A.
Judge. **EDUCATION:** Boston Coll. **CAREER:** 1st Appellate Div, judge 1969-retirement; State Supreme Ct, 1956; NY State Legis, pvt 1947-50; Pvt Prac, atty 14 yrs. **BUSINESS ADDRESS:** Supreme Ct Appellate Div 1st D, New York, NY 10010.

STEVENS, JOHN THEODORE, SR.
Brewery marketing manager. **PERSONAL:** Born Feb 02, 1924, Detroit, MI; son of John Arthur Stevens (deceased) and Helen Valaria White Stevens (deceased); married Jimmie Rose Phillips, Jun 21, 1951; children: John T Jr, Sandra J. **EDUCATION:** Wayne State Univ, Detroit MI, attended, 1947-50; Univ of Detroit, Detroit MI, attended, 1954-56. **CAREER:** Anheuser-Bush Inc, Detroit MI, branch salesman, 1954-63, special representative, 1963-66,

regional representative, 1963-71, Los Angeles CA, dist mgr, 1971-81, Woodland Hills CA, mgr of special markets, Western Region, 1981-. **ORGANIZATIONS:** Life mem, NAACP; mem, Alpha Phi Alpha Frat, 1948-, Christ Good Shepherd Episcopal Church, 1971-, LA Chapter UNCF, 1973-; bd mem, Good Shepherd Manor, 1982-, Chas Drew Medical School, 1983-; mem, chmmr, Los Angeles County Fire Dept, 1983-87; bd mem, Golden State Minority Found, 1986-; mem, Los Angeles County Fire Dept Advisory Bd, 1988, Prince Hall of Masons, 1989-. **HONORS/ACHIEVEMENTS:** Honorary Doctorate of Humane Letters, Shorter Coll, Little Rock AR, 1987; Honorary Fire Chief, Compton CA Fire Dept, 1987. **MILITARY SERVICE:** US Navy, machinist mate 3rd class, 1943-46; Honorable Discharge. **BUSINESS ADDRESS:** Manager of Special Field Markets, Western Region, Anheuser-Bush Inc, 20970 Warner Center Ln, Woodland Hills, CA 91367.

STEVENS, MAXWELL MCDEW
Assistant dean of instruction. **PERSONAL:** Born Dec 03, 1942, Savannah, GA. **EDUCATION:** St Augustine Coll, BS 1964; Atlanta Univ, MBA 1970; Rutgers Univ, Ed D 1977. **CAREER:** Glenbrook Labs, chemist/Group Ldr 1964-68; Allied Chemical Corp, mktg Analyst 1970-72. **ORGANIZATIONS:** Pres Intrnl Coop Ed Assoc 1974; pres NJ Coop Ed Assoc 1974; pres Amer Mktg Assoc; advsry brd Mid-atlantic Training Cntr for Coop Ed, Temple Univ; advsry brd Somerset Cnty Day Care Cntr; advsry brd Ed Opptnty Fund Somerset Cnty Coll 1980; advsry brd Somerset Cnty Coll. **HOME ADDRESS:** 15 Llewellyn Pl, New Brunswick, NJ 08901. **BUSINESS ADDRESS:** Assistant Dean of Instruction, Somerset County College, P O Box 3300, PO Box 3300, Somerville, NJ 08876.

STEVENS, PATRICIA ANN
Education administrator. **PERSONAL:** Born Dec 16, 1946, Rochester, NY; daughter of Allee George Elliott and Alice Gray Elliott; married Dwight Morrow Russell; children: Kimberly, Kenneth. **EDUCATION:** Monroe Comm Coll, AS Liberal Arts 1968; State Univ of NY Brockport, BS History/Psychology 1970, MS Educ 1972, MS Higher Educ Admin 1979; Natl Bd for Certified Counselors Inc, certificate 1984. **CAREER:** Monroe Comm Coll, counselor 1970-76, asst dir 1976-81, dir 1981-89; EOC SUNY Brockport executive dir 1989-. **ORGANIZATIONS:** Chairperson Sch of Applied Indus Studies adv bd 1982-; bd mem Genesee Settlement House Inc 1982-; vice pres United Neighborhood Ctrs of Gr Rochester 1982-; chairperson Gr Rochester Area Spec Prog 1983-; mem Standing Comm on Blacks in Higher Educ; sec Ralph Bunche Scholarship Comm 1985-; mem UNCF Comm 1980-; adv to African Amer Student Assoc 1950; chrpsn Acad Standards Comm Monroe Comm Coll 1982; mem Amer Assoc of Jr & Comm Coll 1980; mem NADE, Ctr for Educ Develop; bd mem Catholic Youth Org; educational consultant. **HONORS/ACHIEVEMENTS:** Outstanding Serv & Dedication Gr Rochester Area Spec Progs 1983; Outstanding Admin Standing Comm on Blacks in Higher Educ 1984; Distinguished Service Award Council of EOP Directors 1989. **BUSINESS ADDRESS:** Dir Educ Opport Center, SUNY Brockport, 305 Andrews Street, Rochester, NY 14623.

STEVENS, REATHA J.
Association executive. **PERSONAL:** Born Jun 21, 1931, Quitman, GA; divorced; children: Elinda, Ronald, Lavon. **EDUCATION:** Savannah State Coll, BS;Univ GA, further studies. **CAREER:** Family Counseling Center Savannah, community organizer social serv visitor 1966-69; Dept Family & Children Svcs, caseworker 1969-70; Dept Family & Children Svcs, casework supr 1970-72; Wesley & Community Centers Savannah, exec dir 1972-. **ORGANIZATIONS:** Mem Social Planning Steering Bd Unted Way Chatham Ctny 1970-; GA Assn on Young Children 1974-75; Armstrong-Savannah State Coll Social Work Adv Counc 1974-75; den mother 1964-65; bd dirs Frank Callen Boys Club 1965-72; treas 1970-71; consult Savannah Assn for the Blind 1968-69; bd dirs Savannah Assn for the Blind 1969-; vice pres 1970-73; mem Chatham Counc on Human Relations 1973-74; hon mem Barons of Goodwill Rehab Club. **HONORS/ACHIEVEMENTS:** Cert recognition for Distinguished Achvmt in Humanitarianism 1974; plaque serv rendered to Blind of Savannah 1973; plaque outstanding serv to Frank Callen Boys Club 1972. **BUSINESS ADDRESS:** Executive Dir, Wesley Community Center, Inc, 1601 Drayton St, Savannah, GA 31401.

STEVENS, SHARON A.
Journalist. **PERSONAL:** Born Jun 14, 1949, Chicago, IL. **EDUCATION:** Northern IL Univ, BS Journalism 1971; Columbia Univ NYC, Fellowship 1972. **CAREER:** WBBM Radio Chicago IL, reporter/anchor 1971-75; NBC Radio NYC, reporter/anchor 1975-78; WGBH-TV Boston MA, news reporter 1978-82; KTVI-TV St Louis MO, news reporter/anchorwoman. **ORGANIZATIONS:** Mem Alpha Kappa Alpha Sor Inc 1968-, Amer Fed of Radio & TV Artists 1971-; pres Greater St Louis Assoc of Black Journalists 1985; mem Natl Assoc of Black Journalists. **HONORS/ACHIEVEMENTS:** Plexiglass Awd YMCA Black Achievers Awd 1974; Recognition Cert Outstanding Young Women of Amer Inc 1977; Emmy Nomination Natl Acad of TV Arts & Sci Boston Chap 1979, 1980; Spec Recognition Boston Mag 1979; Black Excellence Awd Best Series TV 1987, Political Coverage TV 1987. **BUSINESS ADDRESS:** Newsreporter/Anchor, KTVI-TV, 5915 Berthold Avenue, St Louis, MO 63110.

STEVENS, THOMAS LORENZO, JR.
Business executive. **PERSONAL:** Born Apr 09, 1933, Pine Bluff, AR; married Opal D Scott. **EDUCATION:** Univ of AR Pine Bluff, BS 1954;Univ of So CA Los Angeles, MBA 1975. **CAREER:** LA Trade-Tech Coll, pres 1976-; LA Comm Coll Dist, dir of budget 1973-76; LA Comm Coll Dist, mgr retirement serv 1969-73; LA Unified School Dist, accounting adminstr 1969; LA Unified School Dist, asst retirement systems mgr 1967-69; LA Unified Sch Dist, acct & finan mgmt supv 1961-67. **ORGANIZATIONS:** Bd mem vice pres Western Region Counc on Black Am Affairs 1977-80; mem commn of finance CA Comm & Jr Coll Assn 1977-80; mem pol action com Assn of CA Comm Coll Adminstr 1977-80; mem Commerce Asso 1975-80; mem Assn of MBA Execs 1975-80; bd of gov & dirs Goodwill Indust Inc 1978-80. **HONORS/ACHIEVEMENTS:** Comm serv Award Met Counc for Responsive Adminstrn 1976; citation of Appreciation for Comm Serv Mayor Tom Bradley 1976; notable Am Award Am Biographical Inst 1976-77; comm serv Award Assemblywomen Gwen Moore 1979. **MILITARY SERVICE:** USN storekeeper 3/c 1955-57. **BUSINESS ADDRESS:** 400 W Washington Blvd, Los Angeles, CA 90015.

STEVENS, TIMOTHY S.
Association executive. **EDUCATION:** Urban & Regional Planning, M; Political Science, BA. **CAREER:** Pittsburgn Br NAACP, exec dir 1970-; NAACP, youth dir 1969; Juvenile Ct, probation ofcr 1968; Humble Oil Co Wash, DC, dealer sales trainee 1967-68. **ORGANIZATIONS:** Mem ASCAP; mem AFTRA; mem AGVA; sec-treas Stebro Enter; vice pres Arkel Pub Co & Stebro Records; bd mem Hill Hse Assn; bd mem Hill Dist YMCA; host radio shows WAMO, WWSW 14k radio; mem Allegheny Co Manpwr Advis Coun; mem Mayor's Art Comm; guest Mike Douglas Show 1972. **HONORS/ACHIEVEMENTS:** Received Whitney Young Award Poor People's Dinner Pittsburgh 1974; outstanding young men of Am 1973; "He's a Black Man" Award 1973; comm award for Entertainmnt & Comm Award for Achieve in Youth Social Work in Black Comm Pittsburgh Clubs United 1970. **BUSINESS ADDRESS:** 2203 Wylle Ave, Pittsburgh, PA 15219.

STEVENS, WARREN SHERWOOD
Business consultant. **PERSONAL:** Born Jul 08, 1941, Urbana, OH; married Audrey Doreen Stevens, May 30, 1965; children: Warren D, Shanee A. **EDUCATION:** Ohio State Univ, BS Business Admin 1978. **CAREER:** USAF, admin clerk 1960-64; Juvenile Diagnostic Center, mail clerk 1964-65; Western Electric Co, cable former 1965-68 & 1971-73, tester 1968-71, Local IBEW union steward 1970-71, chief union steward 1971-73; Intl Harvester, employee interviewer 1973-74, industrial engineer 1974-80; St Regis Co, staff industrial engineer 1981-83; Urban Univ, dir of admin; City of Urbana, city councilman; Baumfolder Corp, time study & methods engineer 1984-85; Williams Hardware, salesman, clerk, cashier 1986-; Executive Fundlife Insurance Co, insurance agent 1987-89; Hoffman Wood Products, working supvr 1989-. **ORGANIZATIONS:** Mem MTM Assn 1974; coach Urbana City Baseball Program 1978; mem Champaign Co Amer Cancer Soc Bd 1980; pres Champaign Co Amer Cancer Soc Bd 1981; mem Kiwanis Club 1982; coach Urbana City Baseball pony league 1983; coach Urbana Baseball Boosters 1983; coach Urbana City Baseball pony league 1984; adv mem Public Educ Comm Amer Cancer Soc Bd; former mem Urbana Local Outdoor Educ Bd; former sec Urbana Men's Progressive Club; Democratic mem Champaign Co Central Comm & Exec Comm; one of three Black men to organize the first Black men's service organization (The Urbana Men's Progressive Club) in Urbana, OH; editor Urbana Lions Club Newsletter. **HONORS/ACHIEVEMENTS:** 1st Black Trainee & Indus Engineer Intl Harvester 1974; Co-Chmn 1981 Annual Crusade Amer Cancer Soc Champaign Co 1981; Tape Line Project Standard Labor Cost System St Regis Co 1981-83, Baumfolder 1984-85; Standard Labor Cost Savings Baumfolder 1984-85; held highest admin position of any Black ever Urban Univ; Only Black that presently sits on Urbana City Council. **MILITARY SERVICE:** USAF A/2C 4 yrs. **HOME ADDRESS:** 641 S Kenton St, Urbana, OH 43078.

STEVENSON, JAMES EARL
Director. **PERSONAL:** Born Jun 30, 1946, Bluefield, WV; children: Cory James, Craig Jerome. **EDUCATION:** Wilmington Coll, BA 1968; Loyla Univ, MSW 1971; Roosevelt Univ, MPA 1980. **CAREER:** City of Chicago Dept Human Resources, dir joint youth serv bureau 1972-74; Roosevelt Univ BA Social Work Prog, asst prof 1974-80; South Central Comm Center, dir 1980-82; ECHO, dir of alcoholism serv 1982-. **ORGANIZATIONS:** Bd gov's IL Alcoholism Counsl Cert Bd 1985-; conf chrperson Natl Black Alcoholism Counselor Inc 1983-; pres Chicago Chap Assn of Black Soc Workers 1977-79; pub rel chrperson Loyola Univ Minorities 1984-; recruitment comm Region II Alcoholism Coalition Sector III Del 1983-; bd mem Christian Womans Assn 1984-. **BUSINESS ADDRESS:** Dir Alcoholism Services, Englewood Comm Health Organiz, 945 W 69th St, Chicago, IL 60621.

STEVENSON, LILLIAN
Nurse. **PERSONAL:** Born Nov 27, 1922, Indianapolis, IN; daughter of George Brown and Jane Brown; divorced; children: John Austin Anthony, Phillip Kelly. **EDUCATION:** Indianap City Hosp Sch of Nurs, 1941-44; Mdme CJ Walker Coll of Cosmotol, 1958; Debbie's School of Cosmetology. **CAREER:** Nurs Serv Citz Ambulatory Health Ctr Neighborhood Hlth Care Facility, chg nurs; supvs head nurs staff nurs 36 yrs; cosmotol 1 yr; salesperson 1 yr; foot care specialist, manicurist. **ORGANIZATIONS:** Mem Natl Black Nurse Assoc; pres Black Nurse Assoc of Indianap Inc 1974-77; 3rd blk grad any sch of nurs in Indianap 1944; instr nurs Marion Co Gen Hosp; surg supr nurse St Monica's Hosp; Ladies Aux Knights of St Peter Claver Ct; #97 Indiana Christ Leadershp Confer; bd mem Indianap Chptr Oper PUSH; mem Nat Counc of Negro Women; bd mem Sub Area Counc Hlth Syst Agen; bd mem NE Unit Am Cancer Assn; past bd mem Model Cities Fed Cred Union; bd mem Hillside Cult Center; bd, Catholic Charities; pres, Archdiocesan Black Catholics concerned. **HONORS/ACHIEVEMENTS:** IN Black Assem Cert of Distinct 1975; IN Black Bicent Commn 1976; Black Lag Book 1st edit 1976; IN Confer of Women 1976 gold medal winner Natl Knights of St Peter Claver 1979; Drum Major Award, ICLC 1983; co-mem, Sisters of St Joseph-Trton IN, CSJ, 1986; Food Pantry Coordinator, 1985; bd mem, St Vincent dePaul Society, 1984.

STEVENSON, MORTON COLEMAN
State official. **PERSONAL:** Born in New York City, NY; married Edith M Thompson. **EDUCATION:** NY Univ School of Commerce, BA 1951; NY Univ Grad Sch Business, MBA 1955. **CAREER:** Urban League of Greater New York, asst indus rels sec 1951-53; NYS Banking Dept, admin asst 1957-62; NYS Career Dev Pgm, dpty dir 1967-71 ; City of Cleveland, OH, consultant 1970; NYS Dept of Civil Svc, dist supr. **ORGANIZATIONS:** Mem Intl Prsnl Mgnt Asso 1963-; mem NY Prsnl mgnt asso 1965; mem Intl Inst of Admin Sci 1974; mem 100 Blck Men 1974; mem Grand St Boys 1962; mem Oratorio Soc NY 1955; bd dir Oratorio Soc of NY 1966-69; adv comm OIC NY 1971. **HONORS/ACHIEVEMENTS:** Past Pres Awrd Estrn Reg Intl Prsnl Mgmt Asso 1983. **MILITARY SERVICE:** AUS port & prsnl sgt mjr 3 yrs. **BUSINESS ADDRESS:** District Supervisor, NYS Dept of Civil Service, Two World Trade Center, Room 5500, New York, NY 10047.

STEVENSON, RUSSELL A.
Educator. **PERSONAL:** Born Feb 17, 1923, Bronx, NY; married Dora L Anderson; children: Vanessa, Melanie. **EDUCATION:** Columbia Univ, MA 1961; New England Conservatory of Music, BM 1948. **CAREER:** Suffolk County Community Coll, dept head 1976-; asst prof, music 1971-; Copiague Public School, teacher/dir of music 1956-71; Bny City Dept of Parks, recreation leader 1949-56; concert pianist & accompanist, 1949-. **ORGANIZATIONS:** bd of dir Symphony of New World 1976-; charter mem NY St Admins of Music, 1963-; adjudicator NY Sch Music Assn; charter mem treas Rolling Hills PTA 1967-70; Alpha Phi Alpha; Phi Mu Alpha Sinfonia Frat; NYSSMA; SCMEA; MENC; NAJE; mem Rotary Intl. **HONORS/ACHIEVEMENTS:** 1st black secondary school music teacher, Suffolk Co; Company History for 238 QM WWII; solo Boston Pops 1949; solo concert Town Hall 1956; concert tour, Univ of MN 1950-51. **MILITARY SERVICE:** AUS s/sgt ETO 1943-45. **BUSINESS ADDRESS:** 533 College Rd, Selden, NY 11784.

STEVENSON, SYBIL JORDAN
Business executive. **PERSONAL:** Born Sep 01, 1944, Springfield, MO. **EDUCATION:**

Earlham Coll, BA 1966; Univ of Chgo, MST 1968; Columbia Univ Tchrs Coll, MEd 1982, Doctoral Cand 1987. **CAREER:** Social Security Payment Center, benifit examiner 1966-67; Louis Champlian Elem School Chicago, teacher 1968-69; Iona Coll, dir HEOP 1971-76, asst to dean A&S 1976-78, asst dean A&S 1978-84; GTE Corp, mgr corp contributions. **ORGANIZATIONS:** Bd dir New Rochelle Cncl of Comm Serv 1972-78; bd dir New Rochelle H Sch Schlrshp Fnd 1979-80; pres Soroptimist Intl New Rochelle 1981-82. **HONORS/ACHIEVEMENTS:** Educ Awrd New Rochelle NAACP 1978; Grad Flwshp Columbia Univ Tchrs Coll 1980-81; NSSFNS Schlrshp Natl Schlrshp Serv & Fnd for Negro Stdnts 1962-66; Freedmans Schlrshp Earlham Coll; Iona Coll Woman of Achievement Awd 1986. **BUSINESS ADDRESS:** Manager of Corp Contributions, GTE Corp, One Stamford Forum, Stamford, CT 06904.

STEVENSON, UNICE TEEN
Business executive. **PERSONAL:** Born Apr 07, 1950, Columbus, MS. **EDUCATION:** Univ of Akron, BS Education 1976; Lake Erie College, MBA 1985. **CAREER:** Alltel Corp, plant accountant 1969-72, accountant/bkpr 1972-73, admin asst 1973-76; commer asst 1976-79; Alltel Service Corp, gen acctg supr 1979-84, spec projects coord 1984-. **ORGANIZATIONS:** Mem Natl Assn of Negro Business and Prof Women's Club, Inc; mem Natl Assn of Black MBA's; mem Independent Telephone Pioneer Assn; mem OH Business Teachers Assn; mem NAACP; mem Mt Olive Baptist Church; mem Natl Council of Negro Women, Inc; past pres OH Natl Baptist Convention, Inc Youth Dept; past dir of mt Olive Baptist Church Young People's Dept; past pres Progressive Dist Young Peoples Dept. **HONORS/ACHIEVEMENTS:** Listed in Who's Who in Black Corporate America 1981 collectors edition. **HOME ADDRESS:** 5999 Bear Creek Drive, Ste 410, Bedford Heights, OH 44146. **BUSINESS ADDRESS:** Special Projects Coordinator, Alltell Service Corp, P O Box 2227, Hudson, OH 44236.

STEWARD, EMANUEL
Business executive. **PERSONAL:** Born Jul 07, 1944, Vivian, WV; married Marie Estelle Steel; children: Sylvia Ann, Sylvette Marie. **EDUCATION:** Henry Ford Community Coll, grad 1970; Detroit Edison's Electrician-Apprenticeship Prog, grad Master Electrician 1970. **CAREER:** Detroit Edison, master electrician 1966-71; Securities and Life Insurance, salesman 1971-76; Escot Boxing Enterprises Inc, pres. **ORGANIZATIONS:** Life mem NAACP; franchise holder Little Caesar's Pizza Chain; pres Scholarship Fund for Children; founder Emanuel Steward Athletic Scholarship. **HONORS/ACHIEVEMENTS:** Manager/Trainer of the yr Boxing Writers Assn 1980; Amateur Boxing Coach of the Yr USABCA (United States Amateur Boxing Coaches Assn) 1977; Natl Golden Gloves 119 lbs Champ 1963; Manager/Trainer of the Yr WBC (World Boxing Council) 1983; Life Enrichment Award-Focus Life 1984; SCLC Youth Devel Award 1983; champions unter tutelage, Thomas Hearns-WBC Super Welterweight Champion of the World; Milton McCrory-WBC Welterweight Champion of the World; Jimmy Paul-IBF (Intl Boxing Federation) Lightweight Champion of the World; Duane Thomas WBC Super Welterweight Champion of the World; Tony Tucker IBF Heavyweight Champion of the World. **BUSINESS ADDRESS:** President, Escot Boxing Enterprises Inc, 19600 W McNichols, Detroit, MI 48219.

STEWARD, LOWELL C.
Real estate appraiser. **PERSONAL:** Born Feb 25, 1919, Los Angeles; married Helen Jane Ford; children: Pamela, Lowell, Jr, Shelley. **EDUCATION:** Santa Barbara State Coll, BA 1942; UCLA, Real Estate Certificate 1952. **CAREER:** Lowell Steward Assoc, real estate appraiser. **ORGANIZATIONS:** Sr mem Soc of Real Estate Appraisers 1970; past mem bd dir Consolidated Realty Bd; mem bd dirUniv CA Santa Barbara Alumni Assn 8 yrs; past pres Tuskegee Airmen Western Region; mem Kappa Alpha Psi; life mem NAACP; natl chmn Tuskegee Airman Schlrsp Fund. **HONORS/ACHIEVEMENTS:** Recip Distinguished Flying Cross WWII. **MILITARY SERVICE:** Fighter pilot 332nd fighter group WWII major.

STEWART, ADELLE WRIGHT
Retired educator. **PERSONAL:** Born Sep 25, 1922, Ft Motte, SC; daughter of Walter Wright Sr (deceased) and Elnora Wilson Wright. **EDUCATION:** Morris Coll, AB 1945; SC State Coll, MS 1957; Univ of PA, MS 1961; Clemson Univ, PhD 1974. **CAREER:** Butler HS, teacher 1945-46; Morris Coll, teacher 1946-49; Palmetto HS, teacher 1949-50; John Ford HS, teacher 1950-59; Morris Coll, asst prof biology 1960-62; SC State Coll, asst prof biology 1962-74, assoc prof biology 1974-78, prof of biology 1978-87. **ORGANIZATIONS:** Mem Delta Sigma Theta Sor; participant Atomic Energy Comm Project Savannah River Lab Aiken SC 1967. **HONORS/ACHIEVEMENTS:** Summa Cum Laude Morris Coll 1945; Natl Science Found Fellowship 1959-60; Natl Science Found Fellowship summer 1965; first black female to earn a PhD at Clemson Univ; Ford Found Fellowship & Natl Fellowships Fund; Presidential Citation, National Assn for Equal Opportunity in Higher Education 1984; Oustanding Alumnus Award, Morris College 1975. **HOME ADDRESS:** 2715 Old Cameron Rd, Orangeburg, SC 29115.

STEWART, ALBERT C.
Educator, business executive. **PERSONAL:** Born in Detroit, MI; son of Albert Q. Stewart and Jeanne Kaiser Stewart; married Colleen M Hyland. **EDUCATION:** Univ of Chicago, BS 1942, MS 1949; St Louis Univ, PhD 1951. **CAREER:** St Louis Univ, instr chemistry 1949-51; Knoxville Coll, prof chem/physics 1953-56; John Carroll Univ Cleveland, OH, lecturer chem 1956-63; Union Carbide Corp, intl bus mgr 1973-77, dir sales 1977-79, natl sales mgr 1979-82, dir univ relations 1982-84; Western CT State Univ, assoc dean/profmktg. **ORGANIZATIONS:** Mem Rotary Cleveland/NY 1962-69; mem Oak Ridge, TN town cncl 1953-57; pres/chmn Urban League Cleveland/NY 1959-69; mem trustee NY Philharmonic Soc 1975-80. **HONORS/ACHIEVEMENTS:** Alumni Merit Award St Louis Univ 1958; Cert of Merit Soc of Chem Professions Cleveland 1962; Alumni Citation Univ of Chicago 1966; 2 US patents 1966. **MILITARY SERVICE:** USNR Lt (JG) 1944-56. **BUSINESS ADDRESS:** Acting Dean/Prof Marketing, Western CT State University, Ancell School of Business, 181 White St, Danbury, CT 06810.

STEWART, BERNARD
Cable broadcasting programmer. **PERSONAL:** Born Jul 03, 1950, Birmingham, AL; married Alice Faye Carr; children: Reginald, Anthony. **EDUCATION:** Ball State Univ, Muncie IN, BS, 1974; Southern Connecticut State Univ, New Haven CT, MS Urban Studies, 1977, MS Media Studies, 1979. **CAREER:** WBZ-TV, Boston MA, exec news producer; WTNH-TV, New Haven CT, producer; Independent, filmmaker, producer; ESPN Inc, Briston Ct, dir of program planning, currently. **HONORS/ACHIEVEMENTS:** Lapides Award, Center for Urban Studies; Outstanding Young Man of Amer, US Jaycees; Emmy Nominations (2), Natl TV Academy, 1978, 1979. **MILITARY SERVICE:** US Air Force, sergeant, 1971-75. **BUSINESS ADDRESS:** Director-Program Planning, ESPN, ESPN Plaza, Bristol, CT 06010.

STEWART, CARL L.
Doctor. **PERSONAL:** Born Oct 16, 1936, Trinidad, WI; married Annette; children: Patrice, Jomo. **EDUCATION:** HowardUniv Coll of Liberal Arts, BS 1960; HowardUniv Coll of Med, honorsmagna cum laude 1965. **CAREER:** Miami Valley Hosp Dayton, OH, intern 1965-66; Freedman's Hosp Wash, DC, resid 1966-69; Private Pract, 1969-; Carl L Stewart MD Inc, med corp 1973-. **ORGANIZATIONS:** Phi Beta Kappa; mem Oaks Found. **HONORS/ACHIEVEMENTS:** Listed in Who's Who in CA for 1974. **BUSINESS ADDRESS:** 1704 W Manchester Ave, Ste 210, Los Angeles, CA 90047.

STEWART, CHARLES J.
Fire prevention and control administration. **PERSONAL:** Born Mar 26, 1928, Chicago, IL; son of Roy Clinton and Helen Stewart (deceased); married Annette Stokes, Jun 04, 1985; children: Malcolm Rogers, Valarie, Ellie Rose Williams (Stewart). **EDUCATION:** Richard J Daley Coll, Chicago IL, AAS Fire Science, 1976; Southern Illinois Univ, Carbondale IL, BS Fire Science, 1978. **CAREER:** Chciago Fire Dept, Chicago IL, firefighter, 1962-67, engineer, 1967-78, lieutenant, 1978-79, captain, 1979-88, deputy dist chief, 1988-. **ORGANIZATIONS:** Past master, Kin David Lodge #100 F&AM, PHA, IL, 1951; mem, Operation PUSH, 1971, Chicago Urban League; consultant, Citywide Detective Agency, 1987-; life mem, NAACP, 1987; mem, Xi Lambda Chapter, Alpha Phi Alpha Inc, 1988. **HONORS/ACHIEVEMENTS:** Mason of the Year, MW Prince Hall Grand Lodge, Illinois, 1965; Award of Recognition, Illinois Council of Delibration 33 degree, 1980; Certificate of Achievement, Chicago Fire Dept, 1981; Distinguished Serv Award, Operation PUSH, 1988; Afro-Amer Symbol of Excellence, Life Center Church, 1988. **MILITARY SERVICE:** US Army, Tec 5, 1946-48, 1948-50, 1950-51. **HOME ADDRESS:** 9052 S Luella Ave, Chicago, IL 60617.

STEWART, DARNEAU V.
Clergyman. **PERSONAL:** Born Aug 21, 1928, Chicago, IL; married Christine. **EDUCATION:** Wilberforce U, BS; Payne Theol Sem, BD. **CAREER:** People's Comm Ch Detroit, pastor 1967-; asst pastor 1959-67; Bethel AME Ch Des Moines, pastor. **ORGANIZATIONS:** Mem bd trsts Nat Counc of Comm Chs; past pres Nat Counc of Comm Chs; mem Nghbd Hlth Planning Bd; Detroit Bd of Edn; mem Wayne Co Intermed Sch Dist; past pres Great Cities Research Counc; mem Kappa Alpha Psi; life mem NAACP. **BUSINESS ADDRESS:** Peoples Comm Church, 8601 Woodward Ave, Detroit, MI 48202.

STEWART, DAVID KEITH
Professional athlete. **PERSONAL:** Born Feb 19, 1957, Oakland, CA. **CAREER:** Texas Rangers, pitcher 1983-. **HONORS/ACHIEVEMENTS:** Set career highs with 27 games started, 1921 innings pitched & 119 Strikeouts, 4th on Rangers Staff. **BUSINESS ADDRESS:** Texas Rangers, Arlington Stadium, Arlington, TX 76010.

STEWART, DONALD MITCHELL
Educator. **PERSONAL:** Born Jul 08, 1938, Chicago, IL; son of Elmer Stewart and Ann Stewart; married Isabel Carter Johnston; children: Jay Ashton, Carter Mitchell. **EDUCATION:** Grinell Coll, BA (w/Highest Honors) 1959; Yale Univ, MA 1962; The Graduate Inst of Intl Studies Geneva Switzerland, studies in intl org and economics 1960-62; Harvard University Kennedy School of Government, MPA l969 DPA l975. **CAREER:** The Ford Foundation, asst to the rep for West Africa 1962-64, program asst Middle East Africa prog 1964-66, asst rep Cairo 1966-67, asst rep North Africa 1966-68, program officer Middle East Africa prog 1968-69; The Univ of PA, exec asst to pres 1970-72, Ford Foundation Study awd to conduct rsch in Washington DC 1972-73, dir comm leadership seminar prog 1973-75, assoc dean faculty of arts and scis, dir coll of general studies, counselor to provost, asst prof, rsch assoc & dir continuing educ sch of public and urban policy 1975-76; pres Spellman College l976-86; pres The College Board 1987-. **ORGANIZATIONS:** Mem Natl Acad of Public Admin; bd of trustees Martin Luther King Jr Ctr for Social Change; bd of dirs, bd of trustees Grinnell Coll; bd of dirs Principal Insurance Co of Iowa; mem The Council on Foreign Relations; trustee, Teachers College Columbia University; trustee, Markle Foundation; dir The New York Times Co. **HONORS/ACHIEVEMENTS:** Publication "The Not So Steady State of Governance in Higher Education," Aspen Inst for Humanistic Studies position paper. **BUSINESS ADDRESS:** President, The College Board, 45 Columbus Ave, New York, NY 10023.

STEWART, DOROTHY NELL
City official. **PERSONAL:** Born Sep 02, 1949, Centerville, TX; daughter of Murry B. Fortson III and Artince Houston-Fortson; married Craig G. Stewart, Oct 22, 1975; children: Craig G. II, Aretha R. Ferrell, Shannon L., Craig-Murry III. **EDUCATION:** Attended Tarrant County Junior Coll. **CAREER:** Fort Worth Police Dept, Fort Worth TX, public safety dispatcher, 1973-1980; City of Fort Worth Action Center, TX, administrative aide, 1980-82, administrative asst, 1982-84, coordinator, office of city mgr, 1984—. **ORGANIZATIONS:** Mem, Amer Soc for Public Administrators; program chpn, 1982-83, 1984-85, sec, 1983, North Texas Conf of Minority Public Administrators; vice chpn, 1985-86, co-chpn, 1986-87, Urban Mgmt Assts of North Texas; chapter public rel officer, 1986-88, Natl Forum for Black Administrators; Texas City Mgmt Assn. **BUSINESS ADDRESS:** Action Center Coordinator, City of Fort Worth, 1000 Throckmorton St #370, Fort Worth, TX 76102.

STEWART, ELIZABETH PIERCE
Educator. **PERSONAL:** Born Apr 18, 1947, Laurel, MS; married Valentine. **EDUCATION:** Stillman Coll, BS 1970;Univ of AL, MSW 1972; Univ of Pittsburgh, PhD School of Social Work 1986. **CAREER:** HEW Washington DC, mgmt analyst 1971; Crawford Co Bd of Assistance Meadville PA, housing specialist 1973; Edinboro State Coll, asst prof social work 1973, prof. **ORGANIZATIONS:** Past pres & treas PA Assn of Under Grad Social Work Educ 1978-80; bd mem Community Health Services 1978-82; bd mem United Fund Crawford Co 1979-80; pres Martin Luther King Scholarship Found 1980-82; pres Pennsylvania Assn of Undergraduate Social Work Educators; bd mem Erie County Mental Health Mental Retardation Adv Bd. **HONORS/ACHIEVEMENTS:** Whos Who in CollUniv Stillman Coll AL 1966-70; Outstanding Leadership in the Social Work Prof Local Chap NASW 1978-

80; JFK Nato Cntr Award Erie PA1978. **BUSINESS ADDRESS:** Professor of Social Work, Edinboro University of PA, 107 Hendricks Hall, Edinboro, PA 16444.

STEWART, EMILY JONES
Educator. **PERSONAL:** Born Oct 26, 1937, Welcome, LA; married Elliot. **EDUCATION:** So U, BS 1960; S U, MA plus 30 1969. **CAREER:** Iberville Middle School, teacher; Edward J Gay School, teacher 1971-74; Seymourville School, teacher 1967-71; Magnolia HS, teacher & sr sponser 1961, 67; St Tammany HS teacher & counselor 1960-61. **ORGANIZATIONS:** Pres Iberville Educ Assn 1974-; newly elec pres 6th Dist LA Educ Assn; exec coun woman LA Educ Assn; mem 100 Man Accountability Team of State of LA; mem Educ Div of JK Haynes Found & Legal Defense Fund; vice pres 6th Dist LA Educ Assn 1976-; pres Educ Com Iberville Fed Cred Union 1974-76; elected pres 6th Dist LEA 1977; exec cncl Women LEA 1977; mem bd dir Iberville Fed Cred Union 1977; mem Iberville Parish SoUniv Alumni Chpt; mem Misionary Mt Calvery Bapt Ch; tchr & vice spt Mt Zion No 1 Sun Sch; asso mem Mt Olive Bapt Ch.

STEWART, GREGORY
Educator. **PERSONAL:** Born May 28, 1958, Cincinnati, OH; married Pamela Jean Butler; children: Brandon. **EDUCATION:** Univ of Cincinnati, BSW 1981; Miami Univ (OH), MS 1982. **CAREER:** Denison Univ, asst dir of admissions 1982-84, asst to the dean 1984-85; Univ of Cincinnati, admissions officer 1985-86; OH Univer, asst dir of admissions Coll of Osteopathic Med 1986-. **ORGANIZATIONS:** Mem Natl Assoc of College Admissions Counselors 1982-, Natl Assoc of Medical Minority Educators 1986-, Natl Assoc of Student Personnel Administrators 1986-; mem Athens Chap Civitan 1986-; mem Natl Assoc of Advisors for the Health Professions 1986-. **HONORS/ACHIEVEMENTS:** Youth Leadership Awd Cincinnati Community Chest & Council 1976; presentor Educational Showcase Hofstra Univ 1978; authored article Synergist Journal 1981; presentor Natl Convention Natl Assoc of College Admissions Counselors 1985. **HOME ADDRESS:** 318 Carriage Hill Dr, Athens, OH 45701. **BUSINESS ADDRESS:** Asst Dir of Admissions, Ohio University, College of Osteopathic Med, 102 Grosvenor Hall, Athens, OH 45701.

STEWART, HORACE W. (NICK)
Theatre founder, producer. **PERSONAL:** Born Mar 15, 1910, New York, NY; married Edna Wortherly; children: Valarie, Roger, Christopher. **CAREER:** Ebony Showcase Theatre & Cultural Arts Cntr Inc, founder & managing dir 1950-; Eddie Cantor Show, Beulah Show, Rudy Valee Show Armed Forces Radio Show, radio performer; Irving Berlin's Louisiana Purchase, Carmen & Jones Midsummer Nights Dream, broadway performer 1939-; Louis Armstron, Cab Calloway Duke Ellington, Jimmy Lanceford, dancer & Comedian 1936-39; NY Cotton Club, chorus boy 1934; Amos & Andy (Lightnin), Milton Berle Show, Ramar of the Jungle Mr Ed, TV actor 1950-; Carmen Jones Cabin in the Sky, Dakota, Stormy Weather, Its a Mad Mad Mad Mad World, Silver Streak, film actor. **ORGANIZATIONS:** Founder Ebony Showcase Theatre (1st & longest existing black founded legitimate theatre in Am) 1950-; USO enterntained in Aleutian Islands 1947; LACity Counc Resolution City of LA 1966. **HONORS/ACHIEVEMENTS:** LA Dramam Critics Circle Award LA Drama Critics 1969; cert of Commendation State of CA Museum of Sci & Industry; Mayor's cert of appreciation City of LA; author & producer Carnival Island, Greaters Mouse That Ever Lived, Chris Columbus Brown. **BUSINESS ADDRESS:** Ebony Showcase Theatre & Cultu, 4718-4726 W Washington Blvd, Los Angeles, CA 90016.

STEWART, IMOGENE BIGHAM
Clergyman. **PERSONAL:** Born Jan 23, 1942, Dublin, GA. **EDUCATION:** Univ of DC, AA 1972. **CAREER:** Amer Women's Clergy Assn, natl chairperson. **BUSINESS ADDRESS:** Natl Chairperson, American Womens Clergy Assoc, 214 P St NW, Washington, DC 20001.

STEWART, JAMES A., III
Insurance executive. **BUSINESS ADDRESS:** Peoples Assured Family Life Insurance Company, 886 North Farish, Jackson, MS 39202. *

STEWART, JAMES BENJAMIN
Black studies educator. **PERSONAL:** Born Jul 18, 1947, Cleveland, OH; son of Reuben Stewart and Clora Stewart; married Sharon Lynn Sullivan; children: Kristin, Lorin, Jaliya. **EDUCATION:** Rose-Hulman Institute of Technology, BS 1969; Cleveland State Univ, MA 1971; Univ of Notre Dame, PhD 1976. **CAREER:** Cleveland Elec Illuminating Co, assoc tech studies engr 1969-74; Dyke Coll, part-time instructor 1972-73; Univ of Notre Dame, asst prof of economics and dir of black studies program; The Pennsylvania State Univ, assoc prof of economics, dir black studies program 1984-86, assoc prof of labor studies and industrial relations, dir of black studies program 1980-; tenured prof of labor and industrial relations 1989-; The Review of Black Political Economy, editor 1987-. **ORGANIZATIONS:** Mem Natl Cncl for Black Studies 1975-; vice chair Natl Cncl for Black Studies 1981-; mem Assn for Social Economics 1978-; mem Soc for Values in HigherEduc 1980-; mem Black History Adv Comm and Historic Preservation Bd; mem Amer Economic Assn 1983-; bd of trustees United Black Fellowship 1985-; advisor Comm for Justice in South Africa 1985-; mem OIC; Amer Archival Adv Comm 1986-; Black Fellowship 1985-88; mem Natl Economics Assn 1984-, Phi Delta Kappa 1988-, Opportunities Academy of Mgmt Training Inc Board 1989-. **HONORS/ACHIEVEMENTS:** Pennsylvania Black Book 1985; Outstanding Volunteer Award, Rockview State Correctional Institution 1987; Phi Delta Kappa 1988-; Omicron Delta Kappa 1982-; Delta Tau Kappa 1979-; Honorary Outstanding Black Delawarean by the Black Studies Prog & Student Government Assn of Delaware State Coll 1985; First Humanitarian Service Awd Forum on Black Affairs 1985. **BUSINESS ADDRESS:** Dir Black Studies Program, Pennsylvania State University, 236 Grange Bldg, University Park, PA 16802.

STEWART, JEWEL HOPE
Institutional research planner. **PERSONAL:** Born Oct 31, 1948, Petersburg, VA; daughter of Wilbert L Stewart (deceased) and Pearl Sally Stewart Bonner; children: Zanda Milan Stewart. **EDUCATION:** Morgan State Univ, BA 1970; Ohio State Univ, MA 1973; Indiana Univ, EdD 1980. **CAREER:** Benedict Coll, asst dir planning rsch eval 1973-74; Lincoln Univ, inst rsch off 1974-76; MO Coord Bd/Higher Educ, assoc dir planning & rsch 1978-81; NC A&T State Univ, dir inst rsch & planning 1982-. **ORGANIZATIONS:** Exec comm NC Assoc Inst Rsch 1985-87; mem Southern Assoc Inst Rsch, Assoc Inst Rsch. **BUSINESS ADDRESS:** Director, I/R Planning, North Carolina A&T StateUniv, 1601 East Market St, Greensboro, NC 27411.

STEWART, JOHN O.
Attorney. **PERSONAL:** Born Dec 19, 1935, Springfield, IL. **EDUCATION:** Univ CA, AB 1959; JD 1964. **CAREER:** US Atomic Energy Commn, contract adminstr 1965-66; Econ Opport Counc, gen counsel 1968-69; Housing Opport Div US Dept Housing & Urban Devel, reg dir 1969; San Francisco Legal Assist Found, dir 1970-74; Bechtel Corp, counsel. **ORGANIZATIONS:** Mem Com Bar Examiners State Bar CA; Charles Hoston Law Club; bd dirs San Francisco Gen Hosp; mem Com on Disadvantaged & the Law State Bar CA; judicary com San Francisco Bar Assn 1970-73. **MILITARY SERVICE:** AUS sp/4 1959-61. **BUSINESS ADDRESS:** Chief Counsel, Bechtel, Inc, Legal Dept, 50 Beale St, San Francisco, CA 94105.

STEWART, JOHN OTHNEIL
Educator, author. **PERSONAL:** Born Jan 24, 1933; son of Ernest Stewart and Irene Holder; married Sandra McDonald; children: John Malcolm, Ernest Jabali, Ruth Laini. **EDUCATION:** Stanford Univ, MA 1965; Univ of IA, MFA 1966; Univ of CA LA, PhD 1973. **CAREER:** Univ of IA, English instr; CA State Univ, prof of engl; Univ of IL, prof of anthrop/writer; OH State Univ, prof english 1984-. **ORGANIZATIONS:** Fellow Amer Anthropology Assn; mem Inst for Advanced Study Princeton 1979-80. **HONORS/ACHIEVEMENTS:** Winifred Holtby Prize for Novel Royal Soc of Lit London 1972. **BUSINESS ADDRESS:** Prof of English, OH StateUniv, English Department, Columbus, OH 43210.

STEWART, JOSEPH M.
Food company executive. **PERSONAL:** Born Dec 23, 1942, Marinqouin, LA; son of Willie Stewart Sr and Stella M (Patterson) Stewart; married Clara J (St Amant), 1967; children: Erick J, Kendra L. **EDUCATION:** Southern Univ, Baton Rouge LA, BA Foods & Nutrition, 1965. **CAREER:** Howard Univ, Washington DC, dir food serv, 1969-71; Washington DC Public Schools, Washington DC, dir of food serv & state dir child nutrition, 1971-80; Kellogg Company, Battle Creek MI, dir child feeding program, 1980-81, dir corporate communications, 1981-85, vice pres public affairs, 1985-88, sr vice pres corp affairs, 1988-. **ORGANIZATIONS:** Mem, past bd of dir, Amer School Food Serv Assn, 1971-; mem, IFMA, Intl Gold & Silver Plate Soc, 1971-; bd of dir, Battle Creek Area Urban League, 1983-88; bd mem, Battle Creek Area United Way, 1985-; bd of dir, PRIDE Inc, 1986-88; bd of governors, Public Affairs Council of Amer, 1987-; bd mem, Natl Agriculture-Users Advisory, 1988-, State of Michigan Food & Nutrition Advisory, 1988-; bd of trustees, Battle Creek Health System, 1988-. **HONORS/ACHIEVEMENTS:** IFMA Silver Plate Award, 1974; Battle Creek Area Urban League Central Region Award, Natl Urban League, 1988; Whitney M Young Jr Community Serv Award, 1989; auhor of the following articles: "American School Food Services Journal,"; "Congressional Record," 1973, 1975, 1976; "Jet Magazine," 1974; "School Food Service Journal," 1987. **BUSINESS ADDRESS:** Senior Vice President-Corporate Affairs, Kellogg Company, One Kellogg Square, Battle Creek, MI 49016.

STEWART, KENNETH C.
Clergyman,missionary. **PERSONAL:** Born Sep 28, 1939, Washington, DC. **EDUCATION:** St Joseph's Coll, BA 1964; Capuchin Sem of St Anthony, 1968. **CAREER:** NOBC Washington, DC, dir ch vocations 1974-; Queen of Angels Retreat Cntr Saginaw, retreat tm mem 1973-74; St Boniface Parish, Milwaukee, pastor 1970-73; Francis Comm Sch, Milwaukee, adminstr pub relations 1969-70; St Francis, St Elizabeth, Milwaukee, parish asso 1968-69. **ORGANIZATIONS:** A solemnly professed friar, St Joseph Province of the Capuchin Order 1963; mem Nat Black Cath Clergy Caucus; ordained priest 1967. **BUSINESS ADDRESS:** Prov of St Joseph-Capuchin, 1740 Mt Elliott, Detroit, MI 48207.

STEWART, LEON HOLMES
Business executive. **PERSONAL:** Born Jun 10, 1900, Springfield, IL; married Lucille C (divorced). **CAREER:** Peoples Natl Bank Springfield, co-organizer pres 1967-71, chmn bd of dirs 1971-74. **ORGANIZATIONS:** Mem St John's AME Church bd trustees 1954-79, treas 1969-; mem Frontiers Intl 1955-; mem YMCA 1959-; mem bd dirs Springfield Memorial Hosp 1969-; bd dirs Springfield Urban League 1969; pres Springfield Boys Club 1973-74; mem BSA; life mem NAACP; mem bd dirs Sangamon Co & Comm Chest Agency; memSpringfield Railroad Relocation Comm; mem Springfield C of C; mem United Supreme Council 33 Degree AASR of Freemasonary NJ Prince Hall affiliation Grandeast Phila. **BUSINESS ADDRESS:** Stewart's Service, 1731 E Cook St, Springfield, IL 62703.

STEWART, MAC A.
Educator. **PERSONAL:** Born Jul 07, 1942, Forsyth, GA; son of Alonzo Stewart and Zillia Stewart; married Ernestine Clemons; children: Bruce Kifle, Justin Che. **EDUCATION:** Morehouse Coll, BA 1963; Atlanta Univ, MA 1965; The Ohio State Univ, PhD 1973. **CAREER:** Jasper County Training School, teacher/counselor 1963-64; Crispus Attucks HS, teacher 1965-66; Morehouse Coll, dir of student financial aid 1966-70; The Ohio State Univ, asst dean 1973-75, assoc dean 1975-present. **ORGANIZATIONS:** Consultant KY State Univ 1978; mem bd dirs Buckeye Boys Ranch 1979-85; mem bd dirs Bethune Center for Unwed Mothers 1980-83; consultant Wilberforce Univ 1980; faculty mem Ohio Staters Inc 1982-; consultant The Ohio Bd of Regents 1986; mem Amer Personnel and Guidance Assoc, Amer Coll Personnel Assoc, Natl Assoc of Student Personnel Administrators, Mid-Western Assoc of Student Financial Aid Administrators, Alpha Kappa Delta Natl Hon Sociological Soc, Phi Delta Kappa Natl Hon Educ Frat, Phi Kappa Phi Natl Honor Soc, Amer Assoc of Higher Educ; bd mem, Human Subjects Research Committee Children's Hospital. **HONORS/ACHIEVEMENTS:** Distinguished Affirmative Action Awd The Ohio State Univ 1984; Outstanding Alumni Awd Hubbard School 1986. **HOME ADDRESS:** 6358 Stonebridge St, Columbus, OH 43229. **BUSINESS ADDRESS:** Associate Dean, The Ohio StateUniv, 154 W 12th Ave, Columbus, OH 43210.

STEWART, MAE E.
City commissioner. **PERSONAL:** Born Jun 04, 1926, Memphis; married Robert; children: Jacqueline, Robert Jr, Saundra, Ernest. **ORGANIZATIONS:** First black PTA pres, E-C Sch Dist 1962; co-fdr Rozelle Superior Civic Assn 1963; co-fdr E Cleveland Scholarship Fund; Huron Rd Hosp Asso; first black woman elected to E Cleveland City Commission; vice pres E Cleveland 2nd Ward Dem Club; bd trustees OH Municiple League; exec bd 21st Cong Dist

Nat League of Cities, Human Resources Pol Com; bd dir E Cleveland Police Athletic League; NAACP; Urban League. **HONORS/ACHIEVEMENTS:** E Cleveland Cit of Yr 1971. **BUSINESS ADDRESS:** 14340 Euclid Ave E, Cleveland, OH 44112.

STEWART, MALCOLM M.
Business executive. **PERSONAL:** Born Apr 29, 1920, Salem, VA; married Muriel; children: Michael, Paul, Malcolm. **EDUCATION:** Attended NYU, RCA Inst, Queens Coll. **CAREER:** FL A&M Coll, instr radio shop & theory 1942-43;TV & appliance serv contracting 1946-52; Sperry Rand Corp, engr writer 1952-68, eeo admin 1968-70, adminmgr devel & training 1971-72, eeo admin Sperry Div 1972-. **ORGANIZATIONS:** Prog mgr Econ Devel Council of New York City 1970-71; experimental bus/edn partnership prog Bushwick HS; treas Natl Urban Affairs Council Inc; sr mem Soc for Teach Comm; mem adv council New York City Task Force on Youth Motivation; mem EDGES Group Inc. **HONORS/ACHIEVEMENTS:** Natl Alliance of Businessmen Commendation Awds (4) 1971-75; Plans for Progress Certificate of Appreciation 1966; Bronze Plaque Econ Devel Council of NY. **MILITARY SERVICE:** USAF 1943-46. **BUSINESS ADDRESS:** EEO Adminis, Sperry Div of Sperry Rand, Great Neck, NY 11020.

STEWART, PAUL WILBUR
Curator. **PERSONAL:** Born Dec 18, 1925, Clinton, IA; son of Eugene Joseph Stewart and Martha L Moore Stewart; married Johnnie Mae Davis, 1986; children: Mark, Tracy, Linda, Earl. **EDUCATION:** Hampton Inst; Roosevelt Coll; Moler Barber Coll, certificate, 1947. **CAREER:** Black Amer W Found, curator; licensed barber, IL, WI, NY, CO; Black Am W Museum, dir; Met State Coll, instructor. **ORGANIZATIONS:** Musician, Consult Co; mem, Historical Records Advisory Bd for CO; co-producer, documentary, "Blacks Here & Now" on Educ TV, Ch 6, Denver, 1972; established Afro-Amer Bicentennial Corp of CO; Appointed Governor's Commn of Highways, Bi-Ways Committee, 1989-. **HONORS/ACHIEVEMENTS:** Interviewed by Denver TV & radio stations; featured in several magazines; Barney Ford Award, 1977; Black Educators United Award 1977; George Washington Honor Medal Achievement, Valley Forge, 1985; Featured in Smithsonian Magazine (front cover), 1989. **MILITARY SERVICE:** USN seaman 1st class. **BUSINESS ADDRESS:** 608-26th St, Denver, CO 80205.

STEWART, RICHARD E.
Clergyman. **PERSONAL:** Born Sep 23, 1932, Angleton, TX; married Jeanette Anderson; children: Janet, Richard E, Jr, Laiandrea. **EDUCATION:** Wiley Coll, AB 1954; So Meth U, MTh 1960; LI U, MS 1972. **CAREER:** Wiley Coll, dean men & chapel 1960-62; AUS, chaplain 1962-; Clinical Pastrl Educ Parkland Hosp, asst supr. **ORGANIZATIONS:** Mem Assn Clinical & Pastrl Educ 1972-; Military Chaplns Assn 1962-; Assn AUS 1965-; Mason; elder TX Conf United Meth Ch 1960-; mem Omega Psi Phi Frat; Alpha Phi Omega Serv Frat. **HONORS/ACHIEVEMENTS:** Bronze Star Medal 1969; Army Commndtn Medal 1969; with oak leaf cluster 1972; meritorious Serv Medal Walter Reed Army Med Ctr 1974. **MILITARY SERVICE:** AUSF 1954-58; AUS 1962-. **BUSINESS ADDRESS:** Parkland Meml Hosp, 5201 Harry Hines Blvd, Dallas, TX 75235.

STEWART, ROBERT L.
Accountant. **PERSONAL:** Born May 09, 1935, New York, NY; married Gloria Faye Brooks. **EDUCATION:** NY U, BS; Long Island U, MS; NY, CPA; NJ, CPA. **CAREER:** Stewart Benjamin & Brown, sec treas dir 1973-; Price Waterhouse Co, sr tax spec 1970-73; Warnaco Inc, tax accnt 1968-70; IRS, revenue agt 1963-68; Queens Coll CUNY, instr taxation 1977-; Long Island U, instr advance accntng 1975; Essex Co Coll, instr immediate accntng 1976; Hostos Com Coll, instr. **ORGANIZATIONS:** Am Inst of CPA; NY State Soc of CPA; Nat Assn of Minor CPA Firms; mem tax com NYS Soc of CPA; former vice pres dir Nat Assn of Black Accountants; NJ Soc of CPA Tax Articles NY Soc of CAP Jour. **MILITARY SERVICE:** USAF a/1c 1954-58.

STEWART, RONALD L.
Manager. **PERSONAL:** Born Apr 29, 1936, Philadelphia, PA; married Ardelia; children: Maitland, Adriane. **EDUCATION:** Cheyney St Coll, BS 1960;Univ of PA, MS 1963. **CAREER:** St Govt Relat Smith Kline & Fr Labs, mgr 1979-; Smith Kline Corp Person, mgr compens 1972-73, rel consul 1969-72; Natl. **ORGANIZATIONS:** Natl Urban Leag Black Exec Exch Prgm 1969-; mem Bd Educ Moorestown NJ Pub Sch 1969-78; mem Kappa Alpha Psi Frat; mem NAACP So Burlngtn Co NJ. **HONORS/ACHIEVEMENTS:** Publ Heil & Stewart "Key Role Awaits Comm Pharms" Am Pharm Assn 1974. **MILITARY SERVICE:** USMC 1959-61. **BUSINESS ADDRESS:** 1500 Spring Garden St, Philadelphia, PA 19101.

STEWART, RONALD PATRICK
Educator. **PERSONAL:** Born Nov 14, 1942, Birmingham. **EDUCATION:** Drake U, BFA 1966; OH U, MEd 1968;Univ Cincinnati, MA 1970. **CAREER:** Nat Tchr Corps, tchr 1966-68; Hammond Sch City, 1968-69; Englewood Community Theatre, dir 1969;Univ Cincinnati, instr 1969-71; Contemporary Arts Cntr, consult dir 1974;Univ Cincinnati, asst prof 1971. **ORGANIZATIONS:** Bd & dir Arts Cncl OH Rvr Vlly; exec dir Arts Consortium; co-convenor Cultural Task Force Cincinnati; consult Bicentennial Prgrms Queen City Met; adv com Beamon Hough Art Fund, Links Inc Steering Com; Individual Artist, The Arts Cncl OH Rvr Vlly; mem Nat Art Educ Assn; City Core Activity Commn; OH Art Educ Assn; Phi Delta Kappa. **HONORS/ACHIEVEMENTS:** Numerous honors, prizes, awds, juried & invited art exhibitions. **BUSINESS ADDRESS:** Arts Consortium, 1515 Linn St, Cincinnati, OH 45214.

STEWART, RUTH ANN
Library administrator. **PERSONAL:** Born Apr 04, 1942, Chicago, IL; daughter of Elmer Stewart and Ann Stewart; children: Allegra. **EDUCATION:** Univ of Chgo, 1961-62; Wheaton Coll Norton, MA, BA 1963; Simmions Coll Lbry Sch, 1963; Columbia Univ, MLS 1965; Harvard Univ, 1974; John F Kennedy School, 1987. **CAREER:** Philips Acad Andover MA, librarian 1963-64; Biology Library Columbia NY, head librarian 1965-68; Macmillan Co, prod mgr 1968-70; Schomburg Center for Rsch in Black Culture NY, asst chief 1970-80; New York Public Library, assoc dir for ext serv 1980-86; Library of Congress Washington DC, asst librarian for natl progs 1986-. **ORGANIZATIONS:** Consultant Long Island Hist Soc, Brooklyn Museum, Natl Endowment for Humanities, Natl Park Serv, Cathedral School, Baylor School, Studio Museum in Harlem; dir Natl Park Found 1978-84; trustee Wheaton Coll 1979-; mem Council Foreign Relations 1980-; mem Harvard Univ Library Visiting Comm 1976-; visiting comm MIT Library 1986-; Board of Visitors, School of Library and Information Science, Univ. of Pittsburgh, 1987-. **HONORS/ACHIEVEMENTS:** Intl Council of Museums Fellow 1974; Portia Published by Doubleday 1977. **BUSINESS ADDRESS:** Assistant Librarian for National Programs, Library of Congress, 1st St & Independence Ave, SE, Washington, DC 20540.

STEWART, W. DOUGLAS
Government administrator. **PERSONAL:** Born Apr 08, 1938, Paterson, NJ; married Norma; children: Giselle. **EDUCATION:** Fairleigh Dickenson Univ, BS 1970. **CAREER:** Wend Realty, pres; NJ Bank NA, asst treas; City of Paterson, dir div real estate & assessment; City of Orange Township, tax assessor, dir finance dept; City of Atlanta, tax assessor. **ORGANIZATIONS:** Mem Rotary; Jersey Ski; Intl Assn of Assessing Officers, Northeast Region Assn of Assessing Officers; Soc of Professional Assessors. **HONORS/ACHIEVEMENTS:** Distinguished Serv Award Passaic Co Planned Parenthood 1984; Past Officers Award Passaic Co Child Care Coordinator Agency 1978. **MILITARY SERVICE:** AUS 2 yrs. **BUSINESS ADDRESS:** Tax Assessor, City of Atlantic City NJ, 1301 Bacharach Blvd, Room 606, Atlantic City, NJ 08401.

STEWART, WARREN HAMPTON, SR.
Pastor. **PERSONAL:** Born Dec 11, 1951, Independence, KS; son of Jesse Jared Stewart and Jessie Elizabeth Jenkins Stewart; married Serena Michele Wilson, Jun 18, 1977; children: Warren Hampton, Jr., Matthew Christian, Jared Chamberlain, Justin Mitchell, Aaron Frederick Taylor. **EDUCATION:** Bishop Coll, Dallas TX, BA, 1973; Union Theological Seminary, New York NY, MDiv, 1976, MST, 1977; Amer Baptist Seminary of the West, Berkeley CA, DM, 1982. **CAREER:** Cornerstone Baptist Church, Brooklyn NY, assoc minister, 1973-78; First Institutional Baptist Church, Phoenix AZ, 1977—. **ORGANIZATIONS:** Life mem, NAACP; mem, evangelical bd, Natl Baptist Convention USA; mem, American Baptist Churches, USA; mem, Amer Baptist Churches of Arizona; bd mem, pres, Amer Baptist Churches of Pacific Southwest. **HONORS/ACHIEVEMENTS:** Image Award, NAACP; Amer Muslim Mission award; Reverend William Hardison Memorial Award; Roy Wilkins Memorial Award, NAACP (Maricopa County chapter); humanitarian award, Central Dist Congress of Christian Education; Martin Luther King Jr Justice Award, First Intl Baptist Church, 1988; distinguished service award, United Nations Assn (Greater Phoenix chapter); author of Interpreting God's Word in Black Preaching, Judson, 1984; established Samaritan House, emer shelter for homeless. **BUSINESS ADDRESS:** Pastor, First Institutional Baptist Church, 1141 E Jefferson St, Phoenix, AZ 85034.

STEWART, WILLIAM E. L.
Retired physician. **PERSONAL:** Born Jun 12, 1917; married Jeannette Alice Marie Tardif; children: Frank, David, Joan, William. **EDUCATION:** HS & Jr Coll Queen's Royal Coll Trinidad W Indies, 1928-34; Howard U, BS (magna cum laude) 1945-48; Albany Med Coll Albany NY, 1948-52. **CAREER:** Physician, pvt prac 1955-; New Britain Meml Hosp CT, mem med staff 1955-; New Britian Gen Hosp, mem med staff 1954-; Freedmen's Hosp Wash DC, med intrnshp 1952-53; Crownsville State Hosp MD, med rsdncy 1953-54. **ORGANIZATIONS:** Mem Hartford Co Med Assn 1961; AMA 1961; CT Med Soc 1961; License States of CT NY DC MD 1954. **HONORS/ACHIEVEMENTS:** Diplomate Nat Bd of Med Examnrs 1953; Trinidad W Indies diplomate Licentiate of Med Counc of Canada 1959; fellow Am Acad of Family Phys 1977. **HOME ADDRESS:** 447 Ellis St, New Britain, CT 06051.

STEWART, WILLIAM H.
Educator, paster, business executive. **PERSONAL:** Born Apr 18, 1935, Greensboro, NC; son of Harold W Stewart and Mildred Hancock; divorced; children: Candida. **EDUCATION:** NC A&T State Univ, BS 1957-60; Central MI Univ, MA 1972-73; Blackstone School of Law, D of Jurisprudence 1972-77; Western CO Univ, D Bus Admin 1977-80. **CAREER:** Coop League of the USA, demonstration prog 1966-69; General Elect Co Chicago, training dir 1969-70; City of Ann Arbor, dir model cities prog 1970-71; US Dept of Housing Urban Dev, div dir 1971-75; Exec Seminar Ctr US Civil Serv Commiss, assoc dir 1975-78; TN Valley Authority Div of Energy Use, mgr Community Conserv Proj 1978-86; The Eagle Companies, pres/CEO 1986-; Exec Dir, Mutual Housing Corp, 1987-present; Dir, Div of Business & Social Sciences, Knoxville Coll, 1987-present; Pastor, Mother Love Baptist Church, 1987-present. **ORGANIZATIONS:** Mem, Alpha Phi Alpha Fraternity 1959-; pres bd of dir The Stewart-Candida Co 1978-85; dean Chattanooga Baptist Bible Coll 1981-84; bd of dir Chattanooga Area Urban League 1981-; pres bd of dir Chattanooga Area Minority Investment Forum 1981-87; pres Rochdale Inst of Tech 1984-85; chmn bd dir Sun Belt Allied Industries 1985-86; chmn Seville-Benz Corp 1986-; pres, Operation PUSH, Chattanooga, TN, 1986-present. **HONORS/ACHIEVEMENTS:** Youth & Commun Serv Fredrick Douglass Chapter Hamilton Co 1981; Serv Award Lane Coll Jackson TN 1981; Distinguished Citizen City of Chattanooga TN 1981; Outstanding Mem Alpha Iota Alpha 1983; Distinguished Serv Sun Belt Assn Ind 1984; Humanitarian Award, Das B. Dudley High School Alumni Assn, 1988; Doctorate of Divinity, Laurence Univ, 1968; Doctor of Laws, Buckner Univ, 1970. **MILITARY SERVICE:** AUS sgt 3 years. **BUSINESS ADDRESS:** Dir, Div of Business & Social Sciences, Knoxville Coll, 901 College St, Knoxville, TN 37921.

STEWART, WILLIAM O.
Assistant principal. **PERSONAL:** Born Feb 08, 1925, Chicago, IL; son of James Stewart and Marvella Brewer Stewart; married Corinne Lucas, Jun 27, 1974. **EDUCATION:** TN State Univ, BS 1950; DePaul Univ, ME 1967; Univ of Sarasota, EdD 1980. **CAREER:** Chicago Bd of Educ, asst prinicpal 1951-; TN State Univ Alumni Asso, Mid-West vice chm 1961; Chicago Tchrs Union Dist 13 Chicago Bd of Educ, legislative coord 1976-85; Univ of Sarasota, Natl Bd of Schls & Univ, stdnt rep 1979; IL Republican St Cntrl Comm, vice chm. **ORGANIZATIONS:** Sec Daniel Hale Med Ctr 1985; chm bd Trustees Chicago Tchrs Union 1985; asst prin John Farren Elem Sch 1985; bd dir Beatrice Caffrey Yth Ctr 1985; adv Dist 13 Educ Cncl (Bd of Ed) 1985; area coord IL Fed of Tchrs 1985; vice pres Daniel Hale Medical Foundation. **HONORS/ACHIEVEMENTS:** People of Purpose Grass Roots Org 1981; Certificate of Honor Past Pres TN State Alumni 1980; Fclty Awrd John Farren Elem Sch 1976; Great Guy Awrd Radio Station WJPC 1974; Apple Award Chicago Bd of Educ 1988. **HOME ADDRESS:** 219 E 45th St, Chicago, IL 60653. **BUSINESS ADDRESS:** Assistant Principal, Chicago Board of Education, Farren School, 5055 S State Street, Chicago, IL 60609.

STICKNEY, JANICE L.
Biomedical consultant. **PERSONAL:** Born Jul 21, 1941, Tallahassee, FL; daughter of Wil-

liam H Stickney (deceased) and Nerissa Lee Stickney (deceased). **EDUCATION:** Oberlin Coll, AB 1962; Univ of Michigan, PhD 1967. **CAREER:** UCSF, postdoctoral fellow 1967-68, instructor 1968-69; Michicag State Univ, asst prof 1972-75, assoc prof 1975-81, prof 1981; GD Searle & Co, sr scientist 1981-83, assoc dir office of scientific affairs 1983-87, dir dept of medical and scientific information, 1987-88; Brokenburr Stickney Assoc, pres, 1988-. **ORGANIZATIONS:** Consultant law firms; serve on review comm NIH and NSF; consultant FDA 1971-80; mem Amer Assn for the Advancement of Science; mem Soc of Sigma Xi, Pharmacological Soc of Canada; mem Amer Soc of Pharmacology & Exper Therapeutics; elected to nominating comm 1978, membership comm 1981-84, councillor 1984-87; mem NY Acad of Scientists; adv council NIEHS 1979-83. **HONORS/ACHIEVEMENTS:** Author of more than 25 full length publications. **BUSINESS ADDRESS:** President, Brokenburr Stickney Associates, 1555 Sherman, Dept 142, Evanston, IL 60201.

STILL, ART BARRY
Professional football player. **PERSONAL:** Born Dec 05, 1955, Camden, NJ. **EDUCATION:** Univ of KY, BA 1978. **CAREER:** Kansas City Chiefs, defensive end 1978-. **HONORS/ACHIEVEMENTS:** Named to The Sporting News NFL All-Star Team 1980; played in Pro Bowl NFL All-Star Game following 1980-82,84 seasons. **BUSINESS ADDRESS:** Defensive End, Kansas City Chiefs, One Arrowhead Drive, Kansas City, MO 64129.

STINGLEY, DARRYL F.
Bus. exec., former professional athlete. **PERSONAL:** Born Sep 18, 1951, Chicago, IL; children: Darryl Jr, Derek. **EDUCATION:** Purdue Univ, 1969-73. **CAREER:** New England Patriots Football Club, wide reciever, exec dir player personnel. **ORGANIZATIONS:** Hon chmn Intl Spinal Cord Injury Found, Natl Spinal Cord Injury, Therapeutic Com Inc. **HONORS/ACHIEVEMENTS:** HS All State All-Amer 1969; HS Natl Hon Soc Knute Rockne Awd; Scholastic Athletic Achievement Chgo; HS Athlete of the Year 1968; Natl Football League Hall of Fame; NFL, AFC All Rookie Team 1973; Selected Coll All Amer Big Ten Team Purdue; directed activities toward humanitarian efforts after serious spinal cord injury & being paralyzed from neck down; established annual scholarship Marshall HS Chgo. **BUSINESS ADDRESS:** Exec Dir Player Personnel, New England Patriots, Sullivan Stadium, Route l, Foxboro, MA 02035.

STINSON, CONSTANCE ROBINSON
Realtor. **PERSONAL:** Born in Windsor, Ontario, Canada;married Harold N Stinson, Sr; children: Harold N Jr. **EDUCATION:** Barber Scotia Coll, BS 1949; Tchrs Coll Columbia Univ, MA 1962. **CAREER:** Burke Co GA Sch Sys, tchr 1940-67; Pearl H Sch Nashvl TN, tchr 1964-65; Engl Wrkshp So Univ Baton Rouge, LA, dir NDEA 1966; Elon Miller Realty, Tuscaloosa, AL, rltr 1971-. **ORGANIZATIONS:** Mem AL Asso of Rltrs, Natl Asso of Rltrs, Wmn's Cncl of Rltrs 1972-; mem Gen Asmbly Mission Bd Presby Chrch 1982-; mem bd of dir Presbyt AptsNorthport, AL 1982-; deacon Brown Mem Presbyt Chrch Tuscaloosa, AL 1972-. **HONORS/ACHIEVEMENTS:** Slsprsn of Year Tuscaloosa Bd of Rltrs 1979; life mem Million Dollar Rndtbl Bd of Rltrs Tuscaloosa, AL 1979-. **BUSINESS ADDRESS:** Realtor, Elon Miller Realty, 1410 McFarland Blvd E, Tuscaloosa, AL 35405.

STINSON, DONALD R.
Business executive, artist. **PERSONAL:** Born Jan 29, 1929, Detroit; married Clara Key. **EDUCATION:** E LA Jr Coll, 1948-49; Wayne U, 1950-51; Compton Jr Coll, 1960-62. **CAREER:** Owner, 3 homes for aged persons, mentally ill, mentally retarded adults, retired; Golden St Life Ins Co, field rep 1956-71; Vets Hosp Long Bch, retired prac nurse 1955-56; City of Berkeley CA, rec dir 1949-50. **ORGANIZATIONS:** Mem bd dir Adv Med Diag Labs LA; prgm dir bd mem Willing Worker for Mentally Retarded LA; exec bd Com for Simon Rodias Towers in Watts LA; mem Stewart Grant AME Ch LA; Out of Home Care Tech Adv Com LA; mem Hub City Optimist Club of Compton; Art W Assn Inc; Black Art Counc; mem CA Caretakers Orgn; owner Billees Liquor; mem Nat Conf of Artist. **HONORS/ACHIEVEMENTS:** Master enamelist award MaDonna Fest; Barnsdall all City Show LA; Watts Fest Art Show; CA Black Craftsman Show; Black Artisits in Am; won sev awards & hon while selling for Golden St Life Ins. **MILITARY SERVICE:** USAF A/1c 1951-54. **BUSINESS ADDRESS:** 315 S Tamarind Ave, Compton, CA 90220.

STINSON, JOSEPH MCLESTER
Physician, educator. **PERSONAL:** Born Jul 27, 1939, Hartwell, GA; married Elizabeth; children: Joseph Jr, Jeffrey, Julia. **EDUCATION:** Paine Coll, BS 1960; Meharry Med Coll, MD 1964; Hubbard Hosp, intern 1964-65. **CAREER:** Harvard Med School, research fellow physiology 1966-68; Meharry Med Coll, assoc prof physiology 1972-74; Vanderbilt Univ, fellow pulmonary diseases 1974-76; Meharry Med Coll, assoc prof dir pulmonary diseases 1976-81, chmn dept of physiology 1981-84, assoc prof med & physiology 1984-. **ORGANIZATIONS:** Consul pulmonary diseases VA Hosp 1976-; bd dir TN Lung Assn 1976-; TN Thoracic Soc, sec/treas 1977-; mem Amer Physiol Soc; mem Thoracic Soc SecSt Luke Geriatric Ctr; mem TN Heart Assn; pres TN Thoracic Soc 1985-87; mem Nashville Soc for Internal Medicine; bd of dirs Paine Coll Natl Alumni Assoc 1985-. **HONORS/ACHIEVEMENTS:** Outstanding Young Men of Amer 1970; 24 sci publ 1969-76; Macy Faculty Fellow 1974-77; Pulmonary Acad Awd NHLBI 1977-82; Alpha Omega Alpha Hon Med Soc; Who's Who in Amer 1984. **MILITARY SERVICE:** USAF maj 1968-72. **BUSINESS ADDRESS:** Associate Professor, Meharry Med Coll, 1005 18th Ave N, Nashville, TN 37208.

STITH, ANTOINETTE FREEMAN
Company supervisor. **PERSONAL:** Born Aug 10, 1958, Atlanta, GA; daughter of William A Freeman and Eva M Freeman; divorced. **EDUCATION:** Newport News Shipbuilding Apprentice School, Certificate 1981; Thomas Nelson Community Coll, Industrial Mgmt Trainee Certificate 1982. **CAREER:** Newport News Shipbuilding, supervisor. **ORGANIZATIONS:** Mem Apprentice Alumni Assn 1981-; public relations officer Coalition of 100 Black Women 1985-86; licensed real estate agent 1985-; public relations officer, charter mem The Peninsula Chapter Newport News-Hampton VA. **HONORS/ACHIEVEMENTS:** Real Estate Sales Assoc of the Month 5-Star Real Estate 1987. **HOME ADDRESS:** 636 27th St, Newport News, VA 23607.

STITH, CHARLES RICHARD
Clergyman. **PERSONAL:** Born Aug 26, 1949, St Louis, MO; married Deborah; children: Percy, Mary. **EDUCATION:** Baker Univ, BA 1973; Interdenominational Theol Ctr, MDiv 1975; Harvard Univ, ThM 1977. **CAREER:** Boston Coll, adjunct prof 1979-; Union United Methodist Church, sr pastor 1979-; Organization for a New Equality, pres. **ORGANIZATIONS:** Incorporator Boston Bank of Commerce 1984; bd mem WCVB-TV Editorial Bd; trustee MLK Ctr for Nonviolent Social Change; dir United Way Mass Bay until 1986. **HONORS/ACHIEVEMENTS:** Racial Harmony Awd Black Educators Alliance of MA 1984; Frederick Douglass Awd YMCA 1985; Ingram Memorial Awd Boston Urban Bankers Forum 1985. Paul Revere Bowl, City of Boston, 1989; book: Polical Religion, Beacon Pres, 1989; Esquire Magazine Register, 1988. **BUSINESS ADDRESS:** President, Org for a New Equality, 485 Columbus Ave, Boston, MA 02118.

STITH, MELVIN THOMAS
Educator. **PERSONAL:** Born Aug 11, 1946, Portsmouth, VA; married Patricia Lynch; children: Melvin, Jr, Lori, William. **EDUCATION:** Norfolk State Univ, Norfolk, VA, BA 1968; Syracuse Univ, MBA, PhD 1971-77. **CAREER:** Syracuse Univ, director, MBA program 1976-77; Univ of South Florida, asst dean/asst prof 1977-82, assoc dean/assoc prof 1982; Florida A&M Univ, assoc prof 1982-85; FL State Univ, dept chair marketing 1985-. **ORGANIZATIONS:** Polemarch Syracuse Alumni Kappa Alpha Psi Frat 1976-77; polemarch Tampa Alumni Kappa Alpha Psi Frat 1981; consulting Anheuser-Busch, Inc 1982-83; bd of directors Tampa Branch Urban League 1981; consulting The Drackett Co 1984; consulting Management Horizons 1984, Amer Hosp Supply 1985; FL Council of Educational Mgmt 1988-. **HONORS/ACHIEVEMENTS:** Scholarship AUS ROTC 1966-68; Fellowship School of Mgmt Syracuse Univ 1971-73; various awards (Service, Kappa Alpha Psi) 1977, 1982; various publ including,"Middle Class Values in Black & White" in "Personal Values and Consumer Psychology" 1984; "Black Versus White Leaders, A comparative Review of the Literature" (co-authored with Charles Evans and Kathryn Bartol), 1978; major program appearances including, Discussant, "Off-Price Retailers Spin the Wheel of Retailing", Mid-Atlantic Marketing Assn, Orlando, FL 1984; "The Importance of Values to the Black Consumer", 16th African Heritage Conf Tampa, FL 1984; Achievement Award Kappa Alpha Psi Fraternity 1989; Being There Award Div of Student Affairs, FL State Univ 1989; various publications, Black Consumer & Value Systems. **MILITARY SERVICE:** AUS Captain Military Intelligence 1968-71. **HOME ADDRESS:** 2588 Noble Drive, Tallahassee, FL 32312-2818.

STITT, E. DON (ELLIOTT D. STITT)
Zone sales manager. **PERSONAL:** Born Dec 17, 1942, Birmingham, AL; son of Wilner C Stitt and Niola (Johnson) Stitt; married E Lois (Lowe) Stitt, Oct 17, 1973; children: Nikoal C, Kelley L. **EDUCATION:** Central Michigan Univ, Mount Pleasant MI, BA, 1981. **CAREER:** Chrysler Motors, several positions from job setter to zone sales manager, 1965-. **ORGANIZATIONS:** Mem, Chamber of Commerce, Denver CO, Urban League of Metro Denver, Operation PUSH, Chrysler Minority Dealer Assn; life mem, NAACP. **HONORS/ACHIEVEMENTS:** Mentor of the Year, Natl Assn of Black Women Entrepreneurs, 1987; Award Plaque, Chrysler Black Dealer Assn, 1987; Life-time Membership, NAACP, 1988. **MILITARY SERVICE:** AUS, Sergeant, 1961-64. **BUSINESS ADDRESS:** Zone Sales Manager, Chrysler Motors Corp, 12225 E 39th Ave, Denver, CO 80239.

STITT, ELLIOTT D. See STITT, E. DON

STOCKS, ELEANOR LOUISE
Educator/administrator. **PERSONAL:** Born May 10, 1943, Taledigga, AL; married James A Stocks Jr; children: Kevin, Kim. **EDUCATION:** Central State Univ, BS Educ 1965; Ohio Univ, MEd 1971; Miami Univ, Post-grad 1976-78. **CAREER:** Dayton Public Schools, educator 1966-69; Ohio Univ, administrator 1970-72; Sinclair Comm Coll, assoc prof 1973-84; Springfield Urban League, president/CEO 1985-. **ORGANIZATIONS:** Vice pres Dayton Chap Jack & Jill of Amer 1984; bd mem Human Serv Adv Bd 1985-; pres Ohio Council of Urban League Executives 1986-; mem Natl Urban League Educ Iniative Comm 1986; mem NAACP 1986-87; pres/charter mem Black Women for Professional Development. **HONORS/ACHIEVEMENTS:** Publication education materials University Press Co 1978; Service Awd "Twinning Program" NCNW Dayton 1980; producer "Around Town with the Urban League," WIZE1985.

STOCKTON, BARBARA MARSHALL
Psychologist. **PERSONAL:** Born Oct 19, 1923, Rockville, MD. **EDUCATION:** Howard U, BS 1951, MS 1955; OxfordUniv UK, Certs 1966; NY Med Coll &Univ of Madrid, 1969;Univ of Athens Greece, 1970; Royal Acad London, 1971;Univ of Vienna, 1973;Univ of Bologna, 1974. **CAREER:** DC Pub Sch Ctr III, dir 1967-, clinical Psychlgst 1965-67; Crownsville St Hosp MD, psychlgy intrn 1957-59; AUS Dept of Defns, anlytcl stat 1955-57, suprvsy stat clk 1948-55, stat cdng clk 1943-58; US Dept of Comrce, sctn clk 1942-43. **ORGANIZATIONS:** Mem Am Psychol Assn; DC Psychol Assn; Nat Assn of Sch Psychol; Am Assn for Mentl Def; Am Acdmy of Pol & Soc Sci; the Counc for Excptnl Chldrn Bd of Gov DC 1972-75; pres Fed #524 1970-71, pres & trea Chap #49, chmn Spec Study Grp; mem Delta Sigma Theta chap pres 1972-74, chap trea sec cchpln; mem Psi Chi 1950; Women's Leag HowardUniv Assn Womn Admin in Edn; mem Women's Nat Dem Club; Archives Assn; Nat Trst for Hist Presvtn; pres Womn of St Mary's PE Ch 1959-67; Ch Vstrymn 1963-67; dir Ch Sch 1972-74; mem Bd Dir & Nom Com Eplpsy Found of Am; mem Bd Dir Chmn Spec Proj 1971-72; chmn Nom Com DC Mntl Hlth Assn; mem Mayor's Comm on Food Nutrtn & Hlth; chmn Child Feeding Subcom. **HONORS/ACHIEVEMENTS:** Merit civ award US Dept of Defns 1947; outst achvmt award Cncl for Excptnl Chldrn; 1972; hon Who's Who of Am Wmn 1972-74; Who's Who in S & SW 1973; 2 Thsnd Wmn of Achvmnt 1973. **BUSINESS ADDRESS:** 504 Kennedy St NW, Washington, DC 20011.

STOCKTON, CLIFFORD, SR.
Associate manager. **PERSONAL:** Born Sep 16, 1932, Memphis; married Lois J Hampton; children: Angela, Clifford, Jr, Brian. **EDUCATION:** TN St U, 1954;Memphis StUniv & TN St U, Grad Work; C of C Inst;Univ of GA. **CAREER:** Memphis Pub Schs, tchr 1956-68; Upward Bound Proj LeMoyne-Owen Coll, tchr 1967-68 summers; NAB Training Prgm Goldsmith's Dept Store, coord 1967-69; HumanResources C of C, asso mgr 1969-71, mgr 1971-72; Bus Resrce Ctr, exec dir 1972; Eco Dev Memphis Area C of C, asso mgr. **ORGANIZATIONS:** Bd dirs Boys Club of Am; OIC; Memphis Vol Plcmnt Prgm. **HONORS/ACHIEVEMENTS:** Received Outst Serv to Minority Bus; Booker T Wash Award 1972 NBL. **MILITARY SERVICE:** AUS spec 3rd class 1954-56. **BUSINESS ADDRESS:** PO Box 224, Memphis, TN 38101.

STODGHILL, RONALD
Superintendent. **PERSONAL:** Born Dec 21, 1939, White Plains, NY; divorced; children: Kimberly Denise Minter, Ronald Stodghill Iii. **EDUCATION:** Wayne State Univ, Education Doctorate 1981; Western MI Univ, Master of Art Degree Cirriculum Dvlmnpt & Coordntr 1961. **CAREER:** St Louis Public School, assoc supt 1976-79; St Louis Pub School, deputy supt 1979-82; St Louis Public School, interim supt of Schools 1982-83; St Louis Public Schools, deputy Supt of instr 1983-84; City Detroit-Dept of Parks/Rec, rec instr 1961; Detroit Bd of Educ, science & eng teacher 1963; Detroit Bd of Educ, biology teacher 1963-65; Western MI Univ Custer Job Corps, team leader 1965-67; US Ind Custer Job Corp, mtnce school ad admnstr 1967-68; MI-OH Regional Educ Lab, prog assoc 1968-68. **ORGANIZATIONS:** Dir ed New Detroit, Inc 1973-76; assoc dir assoc Suprvsn & Curr DvlMpt 1970-73; coordntr of comm MI-OH Rgnl Edctnl Lab 1968-69; exec cncl mem Assoc for Suprvsn & Curr Dvlpmt (ASCD) 1979; mem brd of dir Assoc for Suprvsn & Curr dvlmpt 1977-79; chrmn ASCD 1977 conf Assoc for Suprvsn & Curr Dvlpmt 1977. **HONORS/ACHIEVEMENTS:** Special Achiever 1979; St Louis Metro Sentinel Nwspr 1979; Who's Who Among Black Amer ALL EDITIONS; Who's Who in Edctnl Admin 1976-; Comm Recognition Award/Coca-Cola Btlng Co 1982; Eastern Airlines/MAJIC 108FM Radio Station. **BUSINESS ADDRESS:** Superintendent, Wellston School District, 6574 St Louis Ave, Wellston, MO 63121.

STODGHILL, WILLIAM
Labor union official. **PERSONAL:** Born Oct 07, 1940, Mount Vernon, NY; son of Joseph Stodghill and Marion (Wynn) Stodghill. **EDUCATION:** Wayne State Univ, Detroit MI, attended; Univ of Detroit, Detroit MI, attended. **CAREER:** Local 79 SEIU, Detroit MI, oranizer, 1966-74; Local 50 SEIU, St Louis MO, pres, 1978-; Serv Employees Intl Union, Washington DC, vice pres, 1979-. **ORGANIZATIONS:** Chmn, Local 50 Benefit Serv Trust and Pension, currently, Contract Cleaners Trust and Pension, currently; trustee, South African Freedom Fund, currently; mem, Advisory Comm on Civil Rights, currently; chmn, SEIU Health Care Div, currently; exec bd, A Philip Randolph Inst, currently; bd mem, United Way of Greater St Louis, currently, St Louis Branch NAACP, currently, Jewish labor Comm, currently; secretary/treasurer, Central States Labor Council, currently. **HONORS/ACHIEVEMENTS:** Proclamation, Mayor of St Louis, 1983; Isrel Solidarity Award, 1983; Martin Luther King Award, Martin Luther King Assn; Man of the Year, Minority Women, 1986; A Philip Randolph Award, A Philip Randolph Inst, 1986. **MILITARY SERVICE:** US Army, sergeant, 1962-64. **BUSINESS ADDRESS:** President & International President, Local 50, Service Employees Intl Union, AFL-CIO, CLC, 4108 Lindell Blvd, St Louis, MO 63108.

STOKES, BUNNY, JR.
Banking executive. **CAREER:** Citizen's Federal Savings Bank, Birmingham, AL, chief executive. **BUSINESS ADDRESS:** Citizen's Federal Savings Bank, 300 18th N, Birmingham, AL 35203. *

STOKES, CARL BURTON
Judge. **PERSONAL:** Born Jun 21, 1927, Cleveland, OH; son of Charles Stokes and Louise Stokes; married Raija Kostadinov; children: Carl Jr, Cordi, Cordell, Sasha Kostadinov. **EDUCATION:** West Virginia State Coll, 1947-48; Western Reserve U, 1948-50; Univ MN, BS Law 1952-54; Cleveland Marshall Sch Law, Juris Doctor 1954-56. **CAREER:** Law Firm of Minor McCurdy Stokes & Stokes, partner 1956-58; Cleveland OH, asst city prosecutor 1958-62; OH Gen Assbly, state rep 1962-67; City of Cleveland, OH, mayor 1967-72; WNBC-TV NY, news correspondent & anchorman 1972-80; Green Schiavoni Murphy Haines F& Sgambati, sr partner 1980-82; Stokes & Character, specializing labor law 1982-83; Cleveland Municipal Ct, presiding/admin judge 1983-86. **ORGANIZATIONS:** Intl advisory council African Amer Inst New York, NY; Cleveland Council World Affrs; pres elect Natl League of Cities 1970; advisory bd US Conf Mayors; steering comm Urban Amer Inc; life mem Natl Assn for Advancement of Colored People; Cleveland Cuyahoga County & OH Bar Assn; NY State Bar Assn. **HONORS/ACHIEVEMENTS:** Emmy Natl Acad TV Arts & Sci Outstanding Individual Craft in Feature Reporting; publications: "The Urban Crisis" Highlights 1968, "The Quality of the Environment" Univ Oregon Press 1968, "Summer Progress & Soc Progress" UUA, "Summer in the City" Tuesday Mag 1968, "What's Ahead in Race Relations" syndicated by Hearst Newspaper Inc Dec 1968, "The City" review of bk by Mayor John V Lindsay, Cleveland Press & Plain Dlr, "The Unheavenly City" Tuesday Mag 1968, "What's Ahead in Race Relations" synicated by Hearst Newspaper Inc Dec 1968, "The City" review of bk of Mayor John V Lindsay, Cleveland Press & Plain Dir, "The Unheavenly City: review of book by Edward Banfield, Boston Herald-Traveler Mar 1970, "Survival of a Nation" FL Presb Coll Forum St Petersburg, FL 1970, "How Cities Fight Progress" Heights Le Moyne Coll Syracuse, NY 1970, "Saving the Cities" Playboy 1971, "The Poor Need Not Always Be With Us" Soc Sci Quarterly Univ TX Spring 1971. **MILITARY SERVICE:** AUS cpl. **HOME ADDRESS:** 13714 Larchmer Blvd, Cleveland, OH 44120. **BUSINESS ADDRESS:** Judge, Cleveland Municipal Court, 1200 Ontario St, Cleveland, OH 44113.

STOKES, CAROL LYNN
Museum director. **PERSONAL:** Born Nov 10, 1962, Macon, GA. **EDUCATION:** Univ of GA, ABJ 1984. **CAREER:** WGXA-TV, news writer/editor 1984-85; Talking Book Center, talking book tech 1984-86; Macon Telegraph & News, staff reviewer 1985-86; Harriet Tubman Museum, museum dir 1986-. **ORGANIZATIONS:** Mem Delta Sigma Theta 1981-; youth dir NAACP 1985-; mem Macon Arts Alliance 1985-, C of C 1986-. **HONORS/ACHIEVEMENTS:** Cert of Appreciation NAACP 1986, Robins Air Force Base 1987. **BUSINESS ADDRESS:** Museum Dir, Harriet Tubman Museum, 340 Walnut St, Macon, GA 31201.

STOKES, CAROLYN ASHE
Organization/leadership consultant. **PERSONAL:** Born Nov 18, 1925, Philadelphia, PA; daughter of Charles Malcolm Ashe and Louisa Burrell Ashe Shelton; married Joseph H Stokes DDS, Oct 29, 1947; children: Michael, Monica, Craig. **EDUCATION:** Howard Univ, BA 1947, Univ of CA Berkeley, Grad Educ, 1948; John F Kennedy Univ, MA 1983, Management 1987. **CAREER:** Scott Air Force Thrift Shop, bookkeeper; Joseph H Stokes DDS, dental asst and office mgr; Citizen's for Eisenhower Congressional Comm Washington DC, dir of public relations in rsch dept; Dept of Commerce Immegration and Naturalization Serv Wage Price Admin Washington, numerous clerical and personnel positions; The Media Group, Art & the Handicapped, Inst of Arts & Disabilities Workshop, script writer; Clas Enterprises Art Consciousness & Well-Being Workshop, dir/founder; senior senator, CA Senior Legislature. **ORGANIZATIONS:** Annual mtg chair Mental Health Assoc of Contra Costa Co; mem-at-large Area Council on Aging; bd mem Ctr for New Amers; public relations comm Family Serv of the East Bay; health career assistance comm Alta Bates Hosp; bd Howard Thurman Educ Trust; life mem Natl Council of Negro Women; volunteer AAUW Diablo Intl Resource Ctr; consultant Council for Civic Unity of Irinda Lafayette Moraga; leadership comm United Way Opportunity West; mem West County Women's Forum, Amer Assoc of Univ Women, Inst of Art & Disabilities; bd member, Entrepreneurial Skills Ctr. **HONORS/ACHIEVEMENTS:** AAUW Distinguished Woman Awd; Howard Univ Outstanding Graduate; Delta Sigma Theta Comm Serv Awd; United Way Volunteer Awd; Amer Christian Freedom Soc Awd; Most Valuable Person Awd Ctr for New Americans; First Historical Awd Black Family Assoc of Contra Costa Co; Golden Poet Award, World of Poetry; Christian Sr's Extension, Admin Assts Senior Award; Contra Costa County Supvr commendation; George Miller Award; Congressman Ron Dellums Award; State Assemblyman Campbell Award; City of Richmond Award. **HOME ADDRESS:** 90 Estates Dr, Orinda, CA 94563.

STOKES, GERALD VIRGIL
Educator, scientist. **PERSONAL:** Born Mar 25, 1943, Chicago, IL; married Charlotte M Eubanks; children: Gordon K, Garrett K. **EDUCATION:** Wilson Jr Coll, AA 1965; Southern IL Univ, BA 1967; Univ of Chicago, PhD 1973. **CAREER:** Univ of CO, postdoc 1973-76; Meharry Medical Coll, asst prof 1976-78; George Washington Univ, asst/assoc prof 1976-. **ORGANIZATIONS:** Mem Assoc of Amer Med Coll 1977-; CSMM-chmn Amer Soc for Microbiology 1984-; pres elect Wash DC Branch Amer Soc for Microbiology 1986-87; mem review comm Minority Biomedical Rsch Support 1986-90. **HONORS/ACHIEVEMENTS:** ACS Fellow Univ of CO 1973-75; NIH PostDoc Fellow Univ of CO 1976; Sigma Xi George Washington Univ 1978-. **BUSINESS ADDRESS:** Assoc Prof of Microbiology, George WashingtonUniv, 2300 Eye St NW, Washington, DC 20037.

STOKES, JOHNNIE MAE
Educator. **PERSONAL:** Born Oct 15, 1941, Tuscaloosa, AL; married Julius; children: Salvatore, Zachary. **EDUCATION:** OH St U, BS Home Ec 1962; Portland St U, MS Educ 1974. **CAREER:** Mt Hood Comm Coll, couns instr 1975-; Good Samrtn Hosp & Med Ctr, clinical dietitian 1971-75; VA Hosp Vancouver WA, clin dietitian 1967-69; Chicago Bd of Hlth, mem & nutritionist 1966-67; VA Hosp Hines IL, clin diettn 1963-65; Bronx VA Hosp, dietetic intrnshp 1963. **ORGANIZATIONS:** Adv bd mem E Multnomah Co Leag of Women Voters; mem Am & OR Dietetic Assn; mem OR Assn of Sch Couns; vice pres Portland Chap of Links Inc 1979-81; mem Alpha Kappa Alpha Sor. **HONORS/ACHIEVEMENTS:** Home ec hon Phi Upsilon Omericon; educ hon Phi Lambda Theta; Outst Yng Wmn of Am 1975. **BUSINESS ADDRESS:** Mt Hood Community College, 26000 S E Stark, Gresham, OR 97030.

STOKES, LILLIAN GATLIN
Nurse, educator. **PERSONAL:** Born Feb 18, 1942, Greenville, NC; married Robert; children: Everett, Robyn. **EDUCATION:** Kate B Reynolds Sch of Nursing, diploma 1963; NC Central Univ, BS 1966; IN Univ, MSc 1969. **CAREER:** Norfolk Comm Hosp, staff nurse 1963-64; Silver Cross Hosp, staff nurse 1966-67; Purdue Univ, asst prof of nursing 1969-72; Natl Inst of Health, peer review spec proj grants 1977; IN Univ, assoc prof nursing. **ORGANIZATIONS:** Am Nurs Assn; IN St Nurs Assn; Natl Leag for Nurs; chpn Aud Nurs Com Home Care Agency of Gr Indnpls 1974-76; bd dir INUniv Sch of Nurs Alumni Assn 1973-; Chi Eta Phi Sor; Sigma Theta Tau; Alpha Kappa Alpha Sor; Wmn's Aux Indianapolis Dist Dental Soc; mem Jack & Jill of Amer Inc, Coalition of 100 Black Women; mem exec cncl IN Univ Alumni Assoc; bd of dir Girls Clubs of Greater Indianapolis. **HONORS/ACHIEVEMENTS:** Co-author "Adult & Child Care a Client Apprch to Nurs" CV Mosby Co 1973 1nd ed 1977; Lucille Petry Leone Awd Natl League for Nurs 1975; Special Achievement Awd Chi Eta Phi Sor 1975; chap "Delivering Health Serv in a Black Comm" publ in Cur Prac in Family Ctred Comm Nurs 1977; chap in "Growing Oldin the Black Comm" Current Prac in Gerontological Nursing 1979; Lillian G Stokes Awd given in my honor by IN Univ Sch of Nursing Alumni Assoc annually since 1980; included in Contemporary Minority Leaders in Nursing 1983; Outstanding Service Awd Jack & Jill of Amer Inc; Disting Serv Awd Girls Clubs of Greater Indianapolis Inc; co-author "Medical-Surgical Nursing, Common Problems of Adults and Children Across the Life Span," 1983 ed 2 1987. **BUSINESS ADDRESS:** 1100 W Michigan St, Indianapolis, IN 46202.

STOKES, LOUIS
Congressman, attorney. **PERSONAL:** Born Feb 23, 1925, Cleveland, OH; son of Charles Stokes (deceased) and Louise Stokes (deceased); married Jeanette Jay; children: Shelley, Louis C, Angela, Lorene. **EDUCATION:** Western Reserve Univ, attended; Cleveland Marshall Law School, JD; Hon Degrees, Wilberforce Univ, LLD, Shaw Univ, LLD, Livingstone Coll, LLD, OH Coll of Podiatric Med, LLD, Oberlin Coll, LLD, Morehouse Coll, LLD, Meharry Med Coll, LLD, Atlanta Univ, LLD; Howard Univ LLD; Morehouse Sch of Med, LLD; Central State Univ, LLD; Xavier Univ, LLD. **CAREER:** 21st Congressional Dist US House of Reps, rep 1968-; Private practice, attorney. **ORGANIZATIONS:** Bd of trustees Martin Luther King Jr Ctr for Social Change, Forest City Hosp, Cleveland State Univ; bd dirs Karamu House; vchmn, trustee bd St Paul AME Zion Church; fellow OH State Bar Assn; mem Cleveland Cuyahoga Cty, Amer Bar Assn, Pythagoras Lodge #9; exec comm Cuyahoga Cty Dem Party; exec comm OH State Dem Party; mem Urban League, Citizens League, John Harlan Law Club, Kappa Alpha Psi, Amer Civil Liberties Union, Plus Club, Amer Legion, African-Amer Inst Intl Adv Council; vice pres NAACP Cleveland Branch 1965-66; vice chmn Cleveland Sub-Com of US Comm on Civil Rights 1966; guest lecturer Cleveland Branch NAACP; chmn of House Intelligence Committee. **HONORS/ACHIEVEMENTS:** Publications in field; Distinguished Serv Award; Certificate of Appreciation US Comm on Civil Rights. **MILITARY SERVICE:** AUS 1943-46. **BUSINESS ADDRESS:** US House of Representatives, Room 2356, Rayburn Bldg, Washington, DC 20515.

STOKES, MARGARET SMITH
Social services. **PERSONAL:** Born Dec 26, 1950, Pittsburgh, PA; divorced; children: Nyna La Shele, Jared Paris. **EDUCATION:** Temple Univ, BSW 1973; Univ of MI, MSW 1975. **CAREER:** City of Pittsburgh, payroll supervisor 1975; West Philadelphia Mental Health Consort, dir of social serv 1975-76; Children's Serv Inc, social worker 1976-. **ORGANIZATIONS:** Mem Natl Assoc of Social Work 1975-, Acad of Certified Social Workers 1979-; block captain 9th St 49ers 1983-; sunday school teacher Friendly Bapt Church1985-; mem Philadelphia Housing Dev Corp Rental Rehab 1985-; steering comm City of Philadelphia Dept of Child & Youth 1986. **HOME ADDRESS:** 4954 No 9th St, Philadelphia, PA 19141.

STOKES, REMBERT EDWARDS
Educator, administrator. **PERSONAL:** Born Jun 16, 1917, Dayton, OH; married Nancy;

children: Linda, Deborah, Celeste. **EDUCATION:** Wilberforce U, BS Sacred Theol ; Boston U, STB, ThD. **CAREER:** African Episcopalian Church Rhodesia, bishop; Wilberforce Univ, pres 1956-76; Payne Theol Sem, dean; AME Church Jamestown Cambridge Canton, previously minister. **ORGANIZATIONS:** Mem Assn for Higher Edn; AAAS; mem OH Mntl Hlth Assn; trustee of Cleveland Chap of Nat Conf of Christns & Jews; mem Nat Counc of Chs. **HONORS/ACHIEVEMENTS:** Recip alumni award for distngshd pub serv BostonUniv 1966.

STOKES, STERLING J.
Auto dealer. **CAREER:** Bannister Lincoln-Mercury, Inc, Kansas City, MO, chief executive, 1983—. **BUSINESS ADDRESS:** Bannister Lincoln-Mercury, Inc, 6300 East 87th St, Kansas City, MO 64138. *

STONE, CHUCK
Journalist, university professor. **PERSONAL:** Born Jul 21, 1924, St Louis, MO; son of Charles Stone and Madalene Stone; married Louise; children: Krishna, Allegra, Charles III. **EDUCATION:** Wesleyan Univ, AB, 1948; Univ of Chicago, MA, 1951. **CAREER:** CARE, overseas rep, 1956-57; NY Age, editor, 1958-60; Am Com on Africa, assoc dir, 1960; WA Afro-Am Newspaper, White House corres editor, 1960-63; Columbia Coll, instructor, journalist, 1963-64; Chicago Daily Defender, editor-in-chief, 1963-64; Rep Adam Clayton Powell Jr, special asst, 1965-67; Rep Robert NC Nix, editoral rsch specialist; Educ Testing Serv Princeton NJ, dir minority affairs; Philadelphia Daily News, sr editor; Prof, English, Univ of Delaware, currently; sr editor, columnist, Philadelphia Daily News, currently. **ORGANIZATIONS:** Chmn, Natl Conf on Black Power; fellow, founding mem, The Black Acad Arts & Letters; council mem, Natl Conf Black Political Science; founding mem, 1st pres, Natl Assn of Black Journalists. **HONORS/ACHIEVEMENTS:** First prize, Best Column of Year, NNPA, 1960; Journalist of the Yr, Capital Press Club, 1961; Annual Distinguished Citizen Award, CORE, 1964; Award of Merit for Journalist, Alpha Phi Alpha 1965; Politician-in-Residence, Morgan State Coll, 1969; author of Tell It Like It Is, 1968, Black Political Power in America, 1968, King Strut, 1970; Honorary LittD, Rider Coll, 1985; Honorary LHD, Wilberforce Univ, 1977; Outstanding Prof, Univ of Delaware Honor Soc, 1986; Honorary Federal Warden, US Bureau of Prisons, 1983; 1st Place, column, Pennsylvania Newspaper Publishers Assn; Laubach Excellence in Teaching Award, Univ of Delaware, 1989. **MILITARY SERVICE:** USAF navigator 1943-45. **BUSINESS ADDRESS:** Senior Editor, Philadelphia Daily News, 2271 Bryn Mawr Ave, Philadelphia, PA 19131.

STONE, DANIEL M.
Social worker. **PERSONAL:** Born Dec 12, 1942, Martinsville, VA; married Charity L Hodge. **EDUCATION:** St Pauls Coll, BA 1965; Haverford Coll, post grad 1966; Bryn Mawr Sch Social Work & Social Res, MSS 1968. **CAREER:** Comm Mental Health Ctr Thomas Jefferson Univ, social worker 1968-69; NE Comm Mental Health Ctr Phila, dir comm educ 1970-71; Natl Council on Aging Phila, mid atlantic region rep 1971-73; Region III Dept of OHD Aging Serv Phila, reg rep 1973; Adult & Family Serv City of Philadelphia, dir; Philadelphia Dept Human Svcs, first dep commissioner 1986-. **ORGANIZATIONS:** Mem Nat Assn of Soc Wrks; Nat Caucas on the Black Aged; Nat Council on the Aging; pres bd dirs Stephen Smith Geriatric Cntr; vice pres bd trustees, Stephen Smith Towers. **HONORS/ACHIEVEMENTS:** Recip Nat Woodrow Wilson Fellowship Found Qualifing Yr Awd 1965; Thomas J Young Mem Awd 1975; Community Srvc Awd 1980. **BUSINESS ADDRESS:** Deputy Commissioner, Philadelphia Dept Human Serv, 1401 Arch St, UGI Bldg 3rd Fl, Philadelphia, PA 19119.

STONE, DOLORES JUNE
Union official. **PERSONAL:** Born Jun 16, 1939, Mount Clemens, MI; daughter of Charles K Dorsey and Annie R Dorsey; married Kenneth Eugene Stone, May 23, 1955; children: Don Rico, Joyce Graham Adams, Denise D Neal, Kenneth Jr. **EDUCATION:** Ford Motor, 240 Hrs Sewing 1966; UAW, Black Lake Labor Class 1971; MCCC, Speech 1981. **CAREER:** The Fawns Temple, pdr 1964; Local 400 UAW, joint council 1970, exec board 1971; V of New Haven p comm sec 1980; Ford Motor, floor inspector; mem Order of the Eastern Star Supreme Lodge Intnl ; mem bd of dir The New Haven Public Housing; mem of The New Haven HS Citzens Advisory Comm. **ORGANIZATIONS:** Trustee Village of New Haven 1982; sec EI Ford Motor 1983, leader 1984; prec delegate New Haven Democrate 1984; lioness sec New Haven 1984; historian Village of New Haven; bd of dir, Downriver Medical Facility 1987; vice pres, S E MCOGS City/Village Bloc, 1989. **BUSINESS ADDRESS:** Resident Agent, New Haven Historical Society, Reg 1989, PO Box 428, New Haven, MI 48048.

STONE, HAROLD ANTHONY
Marketing manager. **PERSONAL:** Born Aug 09, 1949, New Bedford, MA; married Elizabeth G Bates. **EDUCATION:** Univ of MA Amherst, BB 1969, BBA 1973; Atlanta U, MBA 1976-78. **CAREER:** Coca-Cola USA Cincnnti, cntrl/Mid-east area spl mrkt mgr 1976-; Maxwell House Div/Gen Foods, sales rep 1973-76. **ORGANIZATIONS:** Mem Nat Assn of Mrkt Devlprs; mem NAACP; mem Operation PUSH Inc. **MILITARY SERVICE:** USNR 1971-77. **BUSINESS ADDRESS:** Coca-Cola USA, 8180 Corporate Park Dr, Ste 300, Cincinnati, OH 45242.

STONE, HERMAN, JR.
Educator, administrator. **PERSONAL:** Born Dec 12, 1919, Tupelo, MS; married Mary Frances Houston. **EDUCATION:** Lane Coll, BS 1946; Howard U, MS 1950;Univ CO, PhD 1962. **CAREER:** Lane Coll Jackson, pres 1970-, prof & adminstr past 26 srvng as biology instr, chmn, div natl sci, dean of instrn. **HONORS/ACHIEVEMENTS:** Received many awards including- Prof of Yr 1963; Distngshd Serv Award 1972; Student Govt Assn Award for dedicated concern for students 1972. **BUSINESS ADDRESS:** Office of Pres, Lane Coll, Jackson, TN 38301.

STONE, JESSE NEALAND, JR.
Educational administrator. **PERSONAL:** Born Jun 17, 1924, Gibsland, LA; married Willia Dean Anderson; children: Michael (Deceased), Shonda D. **EDUCATION:** Southern Univ; Southern Univ Sch of Law, JD 1946-50. **CAREER:** LA Comm Human Rels Rgts & Respnsblts, asso dir 1966-70; Southern Univ Sch of Law, dean 1971-72; LA State Dept of Educ, asst supt of educ 1972-74; Southern Univ System, pres 1974-; 3rd Supreme Court Dist LA Supreme Court, assoc justc 1979. **ORGANIZATIONS:** Sec bd dir Am Cncl Educ 1985; mem bd dir Am Cncl Educ 1984; mem cncl of trustees Gulf So Rsrch Inst 1985; mem bd dir YMCA 1985 ; mem Unvrsl Grnd Lodge of LA 32nd Degree; mem Omega Psi Phi Frat. **HONORS/ACHIEVEMENTS:** "Top Hat" Awrd Pittsburgh-Courier 1978; Apprctn Awrd Am Natl Red Cross 1973; Dstngshd Serv Awrd LA Educ Assn 1969; LA Ctzn of Year Awrd Omega Psi Frat 1966. **MILITARY SERVICE:** AUS 1st sgt 1943-46; Asiatic Pacific Theatre Medal & Hnrbl Dschrg. **BUSINESS ADDRESS:** President, SouthernUniv System, Southern Branch Post Office, Baton Rouge, LA 70813.

STONE, JOHN S.
Obstetrician-gynecologist. **PERSONAL:** Born Jul 16, 1930, Tampa, FL; son of Mr & Mrs Edward W Stone; married Gertrude Jane Holliday Stone; children: Dr Faith Stone, Dr Enid Griner, John. **EDUCATION:** Talladega Coll, BS 1951; Meharry Medical Coll, MD 1956; Univ of TX St Joseph Hosp, 1969-72. **CAREER:** Houston Medical Forum, pres 1986-88; obstetrician-gynecologist. **ORGANIZATIONS:** Bd mem Central Life Ins Co of FL 1973-87; founder pres St Elizabeth Hosp of Houston Found 1974-78; mem United Fund Agency Operations Comm 1975; mem Amer Med Assoc, TX Medical Assoc, Harris County Med Soc; bd mem Catholic Charities, Central Life Ins Co of FL 1978-87; pres med staff Riverside General Hosp 1981-82; be mem Catholic Charities 1983-87; Houston Medical Forum 1986-87; mem Amer med Assoc, Lone State State Med Assoc, TX Med Assoc, Houston Med Forum, Harris County Med Soc, Houston Acad of medicine, Nu Boule'. **MILITARY SERVICE:** USAF capt 1957-59. **BUSINESS ADDRESS:** Obstetrician, Gynecologist, 5445 Almeda Rd, Ste 202, Houston, TX 77004.

STONE, KARA LYNN
Educator. **PERSONAL:** Born Nov 30, 1929, Richmond, KY. **EDUCATION:** BA Knoxvl Coll, BA 1949-53; Eastern Univ, MA 1960-62. **CAREER:** Louisville School for Blind, teacher 1954-55; Paris KY School Sys, teacher 1963-64; Talbot Co MD School Sys, teacher 1964-68; The Lincoln School for Gifted, dorm cnslr 1968-69; Eastern KY Univ, asst prof 1969. **ORGANIZATIONS:** Loan sec Eastern KY Credit Union 1978-; chrtr mem initiator Eastern Credit Union 1978-; bd mem Richmond League of Women Vtrs 1980-82; mem Zeta Phi Beta Sor Inc 1951; bd mem United Way of Madison Co 1978-79; pres Madison Co NAACP 1980-. **HONORS/ACHIEVEMENTS:** 1st Full Time Fclty Female Eastern KY Univ 1969-; Gov's Comm for Drug Abuse Educ Pgm EKU 1971; Centennial Awrd for Exc in Tchr EKU 1974; Gov's Comm for Ser To KY 1978. **MILITARY SERVICE:** WAC nco 1955-58. **BUSINESS ADDRESS:** Asst Prof, Eastern Kentucky, Richmond, KY 40475.

STONE, REESE J., JR.
Corporate communications executive. **PERSONAL:** Born Feb 1947, Dublin, GA; son of Reese J Stone Sr and Mildred Andrews Stone; married Jennifer S Eng, Aug 1979; children: Meris E. **EDUCATION:** Tennessee State Univ, Nashville TN, BS, 1966; Howard Univ, Washington DC, MPA, 1973. **CAREER:** Howard Univ, Washington DC, assoc dir student affairs, 1970-72; Natl Educ Assn, Washington DC, communications coord, 1972-79; Metropolitan Transit Authority, New York NY, dir public affairs, 1979-85; Planned Parenthood Fedn of Amer, New York NY, dir communications, 1985-87; Philip Morris Companies Inc, New York NY, mgr corporate communications, 1987-. **ORGANIZATIONS:** Mem, Natl Press Club, Washington DC, Overseas Press Club, New York NY, 100 Black Men; vice pres, principal, Commercial Real Estate-Sandstone Associates Inc, Newark NJ, 1981-; mentor, Columbia Univ Mentor Program, 1987-89. **HONORS/ACHIEVEMENTS:** PRSA Big Apple Award, Public Relations Soc of Amer, 1989. **MILITARY SERVICE:** US Army, Alaskan Command, Fairbanks, 1969-70; Honorable Discharge.

STONE, WILLIAM T.
Attorney, business executive. **PERSONAL:** Born Jan 08, 1931, Washington, DC; married Sara Cumber; children: William T, Jr, Jacquelyn E, Michael R, Christopher D. **EDUCATION:** Central State Univ, BS 1953; New Eng Inst Anatomy, attended 1956; Amer Univ, JD 1961. **CAREER:** Law Practice, 1962-; Williamsburg City & James City Co Cts, substitute judge 1968-; Whiting's Funeral Home, owner; Stone Bland & Pugh, sr partner. **ORGANIZATIONS:** Mem Old Dominion, PA, Amer, Williamsburg & Peninsula Bar Assns; VA Trial Lawyers Assn; Natl Funeral Dirs & Morticians Assn; VA Mortician's Assn; First Baptist Ch; Omega Psi Phi. **MILITARY SERVICE:** Served from 1953-55. **BUSINESS ADDRESS:** Attorney, 7345 Pocahontas Trail, Williamsburg, VA 23185.

STOREY, CHARLES F.
Dentist. **PERSONAL:** Born Jul 05, 1926, New York, NY; children: bd. **EDUCATION:** City Coll NY, BS 1950; Meharry Med Coll, DDS 1954. **CAREER:** Springfield, dentist 1957-73; Holyoke, dentist 1973-; Springfield Pub Sch Dntst 1961-. **ORGANIZATIONS:** Am Dntl Assn; 1st pres co-fdr Mt Calvary Brthrhd Fed Credit Union Sprngfld 1959; pres fdr Black Bus Assn Hampden Co Inc 1970; Phi Beta Sigma Frat; exalted ruler Harmony Lodge 1940 IBPOE of W 1963; Sprngfld Salvtn Army Adv Bd 1967; NAACP Bd Dir 1967-70; pres Comm Concern 1972; St Lukes Lodge 17 AF & AM; bd dir Holyoke Counc Chldrn 1974; Martin Luther King Jr Comm Ch. **HONORS/ACHIEVEMENTS:** Diplomate Nat Dental Bd 1954. **MILITARY SERVICE:** Dental Corps capt 1945-46, 55-56. **BUSINESS ADDRESS:** 225 High St, Holyoke, MA.

STOREY, ROBERT D.
Attorney. **PERSONAL:** Born Mar 28, 1936, Tuskegee, AL; married Juanita K Cohen; children: Charles, Christopher, Rebecca. **EDUCATION:** Harvard U, AB 1958; Western Reserve U, JD 1964. **CAREER:** East OH Gas Co, atty 1964-65; Legal Aid Soc of Cleveland, asst dir 1966; Burke Haber & Berick, atty 1967-. **ORGANIZATIONS:** Dir Capital Nat Bank; trustee Phillips Exeter Acad 1969-; vice pres Assn Harvard Alumni 1974-; trustee Cleveland StUniv 1971-; City Plng Commn Cleveland 1966-74; trusteeUniv Sch 1974-; mem bd dirs GTE Stamford, CT; mem bd dirs Moore McCormack Resources Inc Stamford, CT; mem bd dirs Courier-Journal; mem bddirs Louisville Times. **HONORS/ACHIEVEMENTS:** Top 10 yng men of yr Cleveland Jr C of C 1968. **MILITARY SERVICE:** USMC capt 1958-61. **BUSINESS ADDRESS:** 1500 Central Natl Bank Bld, Cleveland, OH 44114.

STORY, CHARLES IRVIN
Business executive. **PERSONAL:** Born Aug 10, 1954, Richmond, VA; married Deborah Ellis; children: Lachelle. **EDUCATION:** Fisk Univ, BA 1976; Univ of TN, TN State Univ, MPA 1978. **CAREER:** Fisk Univ, personnel dir 1977-78; INROADS, dir 1978-81, reg dir 1981-83, exec vice pres 1983-. **ORGANIZATIONS:** Alumni trustee Fisk Univ1976-79;

mem Leadership Nashville 1981-82; bd mem School of Bus TN State Univ 1982-83; bd mem Rochelle Training & Rehab Ctr 1982-83; chmn strategic plnng comm Child Guidance Ctr 1984-; vice chmn 1987, mem United Way Disabled Serv Panel 1984-; allocation comm United Way of Greater St Louis 1987; bd of dirs Life Crisis Serv St Louis MO 1987. **HONORS/ACHIEVEMENTS:** Ranked #1 in Coll Grad Class Fisk Univ 1976; Outstanding Young Man of Amer US Jaycees 1978; Alumni Apprec Awd INROADS 1983; Disting Serv Awd INROADS 1984. **HOME ADDRESS:** 8789 Boyce Pl, St Louis, MO 63136. **BUSINESS ADDRESS:** Executive Vice President, Inroads, Inc, 1221 Locust Ste 410, St Louis, MO 63103.

STOTTS, VALMON D.
Clergyman. **PERSONAL:** Born Oct 24, 1925, Detroit, MI; married Ethel; children: Valmon Jr, Angela, Valarie. **EDUCATION:** Detroit Bible Coll, 1957; Bible Sch Comm Coll, 1958; Wayne St U. **CAREER:** Unity Bapt Ch, pastor (over 2200 mmbrshp). **ORGANIZATIONS:** Cnslr Billy Graham Campaign 1954; bd dir Oppt Ind Corp; Big Bros Am; pres Sherrill Sch PTA; chaplain Detroit Gen Hosp 1969-70; 2nd vice pres Counc of Bapt Pastors; sec St Cong Evangelism; yth ldr inst ABOUTS. **BUSINESS ADDRESS:** Unity Bapt Ch, 7500 Tireman Ave, Detroit, MI 48204.

STOUT, JUANITA KIDD
Judge. **PERSONAL:** Born Mar 07, 1919, Wewoka, OK; daughter of Henry M Kidd and Mary Chandler Kidd; widowed. **EDUCATION:** Univ IA, BA 1939; IN Univ, JD 1948; LLM 1954. **CAREER:** FL A&M Univ & TX So Univ, tchr 1948-50; Hon W H Hastie US Ct Appeals for Third Circuit, Phila, admin asst 1950-55; Appeals Pardons & Paroles Divs DA Office Phila, chief 1956-59; City of Philadelphia, asst DA, 1956-59; Commonwealth of Pennsylvania, judge and justice, 1959-. **ORGANIZATIONS:** Amer Bar Assn, 1954; Pennsylvania Bar Assn, 1954-; Philadelphia Bar Assn, 1954-; bds of Hahnemann Hospital, Philadelphia Chapter Amer Red Cross. **HONORS/ACHIEVEMENTS:** Jane Addams Medal Rockford Coll 1966; Hon Doc Degs, Ursinus Coll PA 1965, Russell Sage Coll NY 1966, IN Univ 1966, Lebanon Valley Coll PA 1969, Drexel Univ Philadelphia 1972, Rockford Coll IL 1974, Univ of MD Eastern Shore 1980, Roger Williams Coll Bristol 1984; Inducted into OK Hall of Fame Nov 16 1981; Distinguished Daughter of Philadelphia, 1988; Gimbel Award, 1988; honorary doctor of laws degrees: Ursinus Coll, 1965, Indiana Univ, 1966, Lebanon Valley Coll, 1969, Drexel Univ, 1972, Rockford Coll, 1974, Univ of Maryland, 1980, Roger Williams Coll, 1984, Morgan State Univ, 1985, Fisk Univ, 1989; honorary doctor of humane letters degree, Russell Sage Coll, 1966. **HOME ADDRESS:** 1919 Chestnut St, Apt 2805, Philadelphia, PA 19103.

STOVALL, AUDREAN
Telecommunication specialist. **PERSONAL:** Born Sep 18, 1933, Lexa, AR; daughter of John F Rice and Fredonia Little John Rice; married Williard Stovall; children: Darryl Byrd. **EDUCATION:** Mercy Coll of Detroit, BS 1984; Wayne State Univ, 1984. **CAREER:** MI Bell Telephone Co, various positions 1953-83; Electronic Data Systems, telecommunication specialist; US Sprint, account consultant; A B Stovall Consulting, ITSI. **ORGANIZATIONS:** Mem business corporate comm ABWA 1963-; mem business corporate comm NBMBA 1985-86; mem AFCEA, Wayne State Univ MBA Assoc, Amer Business Women's Assoc,Women's Economic Club of Detroit, Urban League Guild, NAACP, Junior Achievement, Pioneers of Amer; mem founders soc Detroit Inst of Arts; mem admissions and fund comm Mercy College Alumni; mem telethon comm United Negro College Fund. **BUSINESS ADDRESS:** 18023 Forrer, Detroit, MI 48235.

STOVALL, MARY KATE
Director. **PERSONAL:** Born Dec 13, 1921, Uniontown, AL; children: Kathleen D, Audrey Y Stovall Coleman. **EDUCATION:** AL State Univ, BS 1949, MEd 1955; Atlanta Univ, MLS 1969. **CAREER:** Perry County Bd of Educ AL, teacher 1943-51; Russell Co Bd of Educ AL, teacher/librarian 1951-76; Stovall Funeral Home, director/owner. **ORGANIZATIONS:** Pres East AL Mental Health Bd Dirs; treas East AL Funeral Directors Assoc; chairwoman Hurtsboro Ladies Aux; mem AL Democratic Conference, State Democratic Exec Comm. **BUSINESS ADDRESS:** Director/Owner, Stovall Funeral Home, PO Box 154, Hurtsboro, AL 36860.

STOVALL, STANLEY V.
Anchorman, journalist. **PERSONAL:** Born Feb 24, 1953, Rochester, NY. **EDUCATION:** AZ State U, BS 1971-75. **CAREER:** KTVK-TV, anchorman, reporter, photographer 1970-75; KTAR-TV Phoenix, anchorman, reporter 1975; KSDK-TV St Louis, anchorman, reporter 1975-78, anchorman 1983-86; WBAL-TV Baltimore, anchorman 1978-83; WCAV-TV Philadelphia, news anchor, reporter. **ORGANIZATIONS:** Mem Greater & St Louis Assn of Black Journalist 1975-78; mem Assn of Black Media Workers Baltimore; mem NAACP Baltimore Br 1980-83, St Louis Br 1983-86. **HONORS/ACHIEVEMENTS:** First Black TV Anchorman in Phoenix, KTVK TV Phoenix 1970; Mr MD Bodybuilding Champ, Baltimore, 1980; Mr South Atlantic Bodybuilding Champ Baltimore 1980; Citizens Housing and Planning Assoc "Hard Hat" Awd Baltimore 1983; Baltimore City Council proclamation for Community Serv Baltimore 1983; Greater St Louis Assoc of Black Journalist & Journalist of the Year St Louis 1986; Emmy Awd for "Best News Anchor," St Louis 1986. **BUSINESS ADDRESS:** News Anchor/Reporter, WCAV-TV, City Ave & Monument Rd, Philadelphia, PA 19131.

STOWE, LOUISE PITTS
Educator. **PERSONAL:** Born Jun 14, 1932, Boston, MA. **EDUCATION:** New England Conservatory of Music, BMus; Boston Univ, MEd; Boston Coll, PhD. **CAREER:** Ridgerield Sch Sys CT, teacher 1965-68; Hull HS MA, teacher 1968-70; City of Boston, model cities admin 1971-73; WSC, dir alternatives for indiv devel 1973-75; Worcester State Coll, dir affirmative action 1975-. **ORGANIZATIONS:** Assoc mem MA Bar Assn; mem Amer Assn ofUniv Admins, Amer Assn of Higher Educ; bd mem Vis Nurses Assn of Worcester; bd mem St Vincent's Hosp Sch of Nursing; mem Intl Coun of Educ; presentation human rights Natl Adult Educ Conf 1979; presentation Spl progs & practices for handicapped coll & univ students New Eng Assn for Educ Oppor Progs 1980; pub "Affirmative Action Interview Procedures" Prentice-Hall publs 1980; workshop presentation Handicapped Students in Amer Higher Educ presented at univs in Spain, Czechoslovakia, Poland, Bulgaria, Romania & Hungary 1981; Handicapped Students in Higher Education, A Global Perspective Internatl Conf of ICET paper printed in Resources in Education by ERIC 1983. **HONORS/ACHIEVEMENTS:** Cert of Appreciation US Dept of Commerce 1980; Certificate of Appreciation The Media Council on Handicap Issues Inc. **BUSINESS ADDRESS:** Dir Affirmative Action, Worcester State Coll, 486 Chandler St, Worcester, MA 01602.

STRACHAN, JOHN R.
Manager, postmaster. **PERSONAL:** Born Aug 05, 1916, New York; children: JoAnn, Jacqueline, John, Jr. **EDUCATION:** NYU, BS 1959, MA 1961; Harvard, Adv Mgmt 1972; Brookings Inst, 1975. **CAREER:** New York City Dist US Postal Svc, dist mgr postmstr 1973-; Manhattan/Bronx Dist, mgr 1972-73, met ctr mgr 1971-72, postmstr, 1967-71, asst to regnl dir 1963-67; NYU, inst 1964; Secondary Sch, tchr 1962. **ORGANIZATIONS:** Mem Adv Com Educ Oppor Ctr Manhattan; mem Fed Exec Bd; Fed Bus Assn; mem Cath Interraciel Counc of NY; Gr NY Fund; NAACP; Urban Leag; Columbian Assn; Jewish Postal Employees Welfare Leag; Am Legion; 369th Vets Assn. **HONORS/ACHIEVEMENTS:** Recip Postmstr of Yr 1970; POD Spl Achvmt Award 1970; Harlem Prep Awards 1970 & 71; Regents Schlrshp Award. **MILITARY SERVICE:** AUS 4 yrs. **BUSINESS ADDRESS:** GPO 33 St & 8 Ave, New York, NY 10001.

STRACHAN, RICHARD JAMES
Educational administrator. **PERSONAL:** Born Jan 21, 1928, Miama, FL; married Lorraine Farrington; children: Denia, Richard II, Reginald, Regina, Lori. **EDUCATION:** Bethune-Cookman Coll, BS 1956; IN Univ, MS 1966; Barry Univ, MS 1972; Atlanta Univ, PhD Educ 1978. **CAREER:** North Dade Jr-Sr HS, teacher/athletic dir 1960-66; Miami Central, dept head/band dir 1966-72; Hialeah HS/Carol City/Norland, asst prin 1972-81; COPE School North, principal 1981-. **ORGANIZATIONS:** Bd mem NAACP; bd mem YMCA; bd mem Inner City Sch Dance; bd mem Dade Co Admin Assoc; bd mem FL Alternative Admin Sch Educators; bd mem Offc of Black Affairs 1981-86; bd mem Omega Psi Phi; bd mem youth Adv Council. **HONORS/ACHIEVEMENTS:** Rockefeller Grant 1975; Outstanding Bethune-Cookman Coll Exelloc Club 1975; Service Award Sigma Gamma Rho DLSSA-NABSE-YMCA-NCAO Atlanta Univ 1986. **MILITARY SERVICE:** USAF S/Sgt 1946-49; Soldier of the Yr 1947-48. **HOME ADDRESS:** 8841 NW 14th Ave, Miami, FL 33147.

STRAIT, GEORGE A.
Librarian. **PERSONAL:** Born Nov 20, 1914, Providence, RI. **EDUCATION:** Howard U, 1934-36; Suffolk U, 1940-42; LA St U, 1952-53; SuffolkUniv Sch of Law, LLB, JD 1949. **CAREER:** Social Law Lib Boston, 1946-49; SoUniv Sch of Law LA, lib asst 1950-53; Worcester Co Law Lib MA, law lib & inst of law 1953-58; HarvardUniv Law Sch Lib Cambrdg, law lib, asst lib 1958-67; NortheasternUniv Sch of Law, law lib & asso prof 1967-69; HarvardUniv Law Sch Lib, asso lib 1969-70, acting lib 1970-71, asso lib 1971-72, asso lib 1974-76; Antioch Sch of Law Lib, law lib & prof of law 1972-74;Univ of IA, law lib prof of law 1976-. **ORGANIZATIONS:** Boston Bar Assn, Com on Automation; Am Assn of Law Lib, com recruitmnt, former chmn, chptrs, nom, & certification; former pres law lib of New Eng;life mem NAACP; mem Am Field Svc; former Town Meeting mem Finan Com, Natick; Selectman (elected) Natick, MA 2 terms. **HONORS/ACHIEVEMENTS:** Recip alumni fellow SuffolkUniv 1973; publ biblio of the writings of Roscoe Pound 1940-60; hon by Intl Law Lib with trip to Rome 1972; Fclty Wrkshp for New Lib Lagos, Nigeria 1975. **MILITARY SERVICE:** WW II capt. **BUSINESS ADDRESS:** Harvard Law Sch Library Langde, Cambridge, MA 02138.

STRAIT, GEORGE ALFRED, JR.
Journalist. **PERSONAL:** Born Mar 24, 1945, Cambridge, MA; married Lisa Michelle McIver; children: Eric Mathew, Kevin Michael Angelo. **EDUCATION:** Boston Univ, BA 1967; Atlanta Univ, MS Prog 1968-69. **CAREER:** CBS News, Washington correspondent 1976-77, gen assign corresp 1977-81, White House corresp 1979-81, med corresp 1981-. **ORGANIZATIONS:** 1st black sports anchor WPVI Philadelphia 1972-74; charter mem Natl Assn Black Journalists; lay reader Episcopal Church of Amer 1984-. **HONORS/ACHIEVEMENTS:** Assoc of Science Writers Awd 1985; Harvard Univ Fellow 1986; Overseas Press Club Awd 1987. **BUSINESS ADDRESS:** Correspondent, ABC - News, 1717 Desales St, Washington, DC 20036.

STRANGE, ALONZO, JR.
Labor/industrial relations manager. **PERSONAL:** Born Nov 25, 1947, Littlerock, AR; married Renae Suelyn Biggers. **EDUCATION:** St Mary's Coll CA, BA Philo 1965-72; Golden GateUniv Sch of Law, JD In Progress 1978-82. **CAREER:** Qantel Corp, mgr of persnnl 1980-; Smith Corona Marchant Corp-Glidden Coating & Resins Div, reg persnnl mgr 1977-79; Kaiser Steel Corp-Steel ManufacDiv Fontana CA, labor relat rep 1975-77; Kaiser Ind Corp-Gen Ofcs Oakland CA, ind rela spec 1972-75. **ORGANIZATIONS:** Mem Am Comp Assn 1973-80; exec vice pres Black Persnnl Mgmt Assn 1975; mgmt consult Handy Consult Grp Inc 1979; finan sec Gamma Phi Lamda Chap Alpha Phi Alpha Frat Inc 1975-76; mem NAACP Berkeley Chap 1978; chmn student relat com & dir St Mary's Coll Alumni Assn 1979-80. **HONORS/ACHIEVEMENTS:** Boy of yr TX Coll Alumni Assn 1965; recip Bronze Star; Vietnamese Cross of Gallantry; Army Commndtn for Valor 1969. **MILITARY SERVICE:** AUS 1st lt 1967-70.

STRANGE, GERALD LEON
Orthopaedic surgeon. **PERSONAL:** Born Aug 03, 1931, Los Angeles, CA; divorced; children: Gerald J, Julie Patrice. **EDUCATION:** UCLA, AA, AB 1953; Howard U, MD 1960; StUniv of NY Upst Med Ctr Syracuse NY, orthopaedic Surg Resid 1966. **CAREER:** Orthopadic Surg, pvt prac 1968-; San Fran Pioneers Wmns Bsktbll Leag, ortho surg & team phys; CA St Univ Hayward, ortho surg & team phys 1975; Collof San Mateo, ortho surg & team phys 1970-76; Clifton Springs Hosp & Clinic NY, ortho surg 1966-68. **ORGANIZATIONS:** Mem diplomate Am Bd of Ortho Surgs 1971; mem Am Acad of Ortho Surgs 1972; clncl isntrUniv CA Med Ctr San Fran; mem Ama; NMA; CMA; San Fran Med Soc; mem Robert Gladden Ortho Soc; mem W Ortho & Leroy Abbott Ortho Soc. **HONORS/ACHIEVEMENTS:** Pelvic & Extremity Fractures in Dogs, Surg Gyn & Ob 1954; recip European Occupation Force 1954-56; "Ski Injuries" NY St Med Jour 1966; Vertebral Sarcoidosis Radiology 1976. **MILITARY SERVICE:** AUS E-3 1954-56. **BUSINESS ADDRESS:** 45 Castro St Ste 232, San Francisco, CA 94114.

STRATTON-MORRIS, MADELINE ROBINSON
Educator, author. **PERSONAL:** Born Aug 14, 1906, Chicago, IL; married Walter Morris (deceased). **EDUCATION:** Chicago Normal College, attended 1929; NW Univ, BE 1936, MEd 1941; Univ of Chicago, post grad 1942-62. **CAREER:** Chicago Public Schools, teacher

1933-68; introduced study of Afro-Amer Hist in Chicago Curr grades 1-8 entitled Supplementary Units in Social Studies 1941; Sheil School of Social Studies, bishop 1942-43; Family Relations Comm, chrprsn 1952; Triton Coll River Grove IL, teacher 1968-70; Mayfair City Coll, 1969-72; Chicago ST Univ 1972-75; Governor State Univ 1975-1981; Chicago Bd of Ed Human Rel Dept 1968-77. **ORGANIZATIONS:** Mem League of Women Voters; mem Alpha Kappa Alpha Theta Omega Chapt; Urban League mem 1940-; pres Natl Council of Negro Women Chicago Chap 1946-48; Basileus of Phi Delta Kappa Mu Chapter 1941-42-43; mem Amer Assn of Univ Women 1950-74; life mem NAACP, bd mem 1950-70; 1940-Chicago chapter of Links, Inc 1953-87; alpha gamma pi 1964-87; pres Chicago Br of Assn for the Study of Afro-Amer Life & Hist; founder Carter G Woodson 1970-76. **HONORS/ACHIEVEMENTS:** Author "Negroes Who Helped Build Amer" Ginn Social Science Enrichment Books 1965; "Strides Forward Afro-Amer Biographies" Xerox Ginn Co Jan 1973.

STRAUGHTER, EDGAR, SR.
Educational administrator. **PERSONAL:** Born Feb 08, 1929, Willis, TX; son of K J Straughter and Annie Lee Straughter; married Betty Harvey, Oct 22, 1954; children: Edgar, Lewis, Ernest, Johnnie, Sherman, Betty, Debra. **EDUCATION:** TX So Univ, 2 Yrs. **CAREER:** Willis Indus Public School Dist, pres (1st black); Quality Control supvr, Louisiana Pacific, presently; major, City of Willis, TX, presently. **ORGANIZATIONS:** Vp Montgomery Co Voters League; mem Willis Fire Dept 1965-; drill instructor 2 yrs; mem Willis City Planning Commn. **HONORS/ACHIEVEMENTS:** AUS corpl 1950-52. **HOME ADDRESS:** Philpot St, Rt 3 Box 190, Willis, TX 77378. **BUSINESS ADDRESS:** Mayor, City of Willis, TX, Quality Control Supvr, Lousania Pacific, New Waverly TX, New Waverly, TX.

STRAWBERRY, DARRYL
Professional athlete. **PERSONAL:** Born Mar 12, 1962, Los Angeles, CA; married Lisa Andrews. **CAREER:** NY Mets, professional baseball player 1980-. **HONORS/ACHIEVEMENTS:** Named 1st team of Class AA, All Star Team; John Murphy Awd; named MVP Texas League 1982, led the league in home runs (34) walks (100) and slugging percentage (604); Doubleday Award; led Mets in RBI (97) & homers (26); Tied a club record with three doubles; 3rd New York Met to be selected Natl League Rookie of the Year by the Baseball Writers Assoc of Amer 1983; The Sporting News Natl League Rookie Player of the Year; most homers for lefthanded batter (26; most homers, rookie (26); most RBI, rookie (74); selected to League All-Star game in mid-season & League's All-Star team; honored as NL Player of the Week twice in a four week span; mem NL All Star Team 1984-86. **BUSINESS ADDRESS:** New York Mets, Shea Stadium, Flushing, NY 11368.

STRAWN, AIMEE WILLIAMS
Educator. **PERSONAL:** Born Aug 05, 1925, Chicago, IL; daughter of Ross F Williams and Lillian Lattimer. **EDUCATION:** DePaul Univ, BA 1948; Chicago Teachers Coll, MEd 1956. **CAREER:** Chicago Boys Clubs, group worker 1945-51; Chicago Pub Schs, tchr librarian asst principal 1951-64; WGN-TV Chicago Tchrs Coll, instructor 1958-59; Chicago State Univ, instr & asst prof 1964-68; Univ of IL at Chgo, asst prof of educ 1968-. **ORGANIZATIONS:** Book promotion chmn & publicity chmn Children's Reading Round Table 1978-80; co-chairperson Children's Lit Conf 4 Children's Reading Round Table 1980; 1st vice pres 1980-82, pres 1982-84 Alpha Delta Chap of Delta Kappa Gamma Intl; "Sex Educ & the Schs or Whatever You Do Is Wrong (& Be Careful or You May Go Blind)" The Natl Elem Principal 1978, reprinted as "A Teachers Strong Views on Sex-Education for the Grade School Child" Woman's Day 1978. **HONORS/ACHIEVEMENTS:** Winner of Silver Circle Awd for Excellence in Teaching 1984, 1988. **BUSINESS ADDRESS:** Asst Prof of Educ, Univ of Illinois at Chicago, Box 4348, Chicago, IL 60680.

STRAYHORN, EARL CARLTON
Surgeon. **PERSONAL:** Born Aug 27, 1948, Bronx, NY; son of Rhudolphus Clemons Strayhorn and Lydia Strayhorn Blocker; married Louisa Sapp, Jun 1968 (divorced); children: Kharim, Jamal. **EDUCATION:** Harvard Univ, Cambridge MA, AB, 1971; Tufts Medical School, Boston MA, MD, 1975. **CAREER:** Beth Israel Hospital, Boston MA, intern, 1975, resident, chief resident, 1976-81; Massachusetts Gen Hospital, fellow in vascular surgery, 1982; Virgini Vascular Associates, Norfolk VA, vascular surgeon, transplant surgeon, 1983—; Norfolk Community Hospital, Norfolk VA, chief of vascular surgery, 1983—; Norfolk Gen Hospital, Norfolk VA, vice-chairman of surgery, 1988—; host of community health radio program on WTJZ-Radio, 1988—. **ORGANIZATIONS:** Mem, Urban League, National Medical Assn, American Medical Assn, all 1983—. **HONORS/ACHIEVEMENTS:** Natl Science Found grant, 1969-70; Ellis Memorial Award for Achievement in Surgery, Tufts Medical School, 1975; author of articles for medical journals. **HOME ADDRESS:** 4501 Mossy Cup Ct, Virginia Beach, VA 23462. **BUSINESS ADDRESS:** Virginia Vascular Associates, 6219 E Virginia Beach Blvd, Norfolk, VA 23502.

STRAYHORN, EARL E.
Circuit judge. **PERSONAL:** Born Apr 24, 1918, Columbus, MS; son of Earl E Strayhorn and Minnie Lee Davis Strayhorn; married Lygia E Jackson; children: Donald R, Earlene E. **EDUCATION:** Univ IL, AB 1941; DePaul Univ Coll Law, JD 1948. **CAREER:** Cook Co, asst states atty 1948-52; City of Chicago, civil serv commr 1959-63; Met Sanitary Dist Gr Chicago, vice pres bd of trustees 1963-70; Cook Co IL, circuit ct judge 1970-; Univ of IL Dept of Crim Justice, adj prof 1977-79; Natl Inst of Trial Advocacy, instr 1977-; Northwestern Univ Sch of Law, instr 1977; Natl Coll of Criminal Defense Attys, instructor 1980; Natl Inst of Trial Advocacy, instructor 1977-; Emory Univ Coll of Law, instructor 1980-; Natl Judicial Coll, discussion leader 1985; Benjamin Cardozo Sch of Law, instructor 1987; instructor trial advocacy Harvard Univ Coll of Law 1988-89. **ORGANIZATIONS:** Mem NAACP; former vice pres & bd mem Chicago Urban League; mem Kappa Alpha Psi; past pres PTA Howalton Day Sch; 6th Grace United Presbyterian Church; former mem Comm Race & Religion United Presby Church USA. **HONORS/ACHIEVEMENTS:** Parliamentarian Tuskegee Airmen Inc 1985-. **MILITARY SERVICE:** AUS 1st lt 1941-46; IL Natl Guard 1948 lt col 1968-69. **BUSINESS ADDRESS:** Circuit Judge, Cook Co Circuit Court, Rm 706, 2600 S California Ave, Chicago, IL 60608.

STRAYHORN, LLOYD
Numerologist/author/columnist. **CAREER:** Tree of Life Bookstore, teacher of numerology 1976-83; Big Red Newspaper, weekly columnist "Numbers and You" 1978-; NY Amsterdam News, weekly column "Numbersand You" 1979-; Project ENTER, teaching numerology to former drug/alchol abusers 1979-; Arts and Culture, teaching numerology to teenagers 1980-81; BMI Syndication, weekly column dist to over 100 newspapers "Astro/Numerology and You" 1980-. **ORGANIZATIONS:** Radio show host "Numbers and You" on WLIB-AM in New York. **HONORS/ACHIEVEMENTS:** Author of book "Numbers and You" 1980. **BUSINESS ADDRESS:** Numerologist, Abby Hoffer Enterprises, 223 1/2 E 48th St, New York, NY 10017.

STRAYHORNE, PAULINE (NEE ALLEN)
Business executive. **PERSONAL:** Born Nov 12, 1926, Birmingham, AL; divorced; children: Charlotte. **EDUCATION:** Chase Coll, attended 1946-47; Univ Cincinnati, attended 1961-63; Inst for Financial Educ, attended 1950-62. **CAREER:** Major Fed Svgs & Loan Assn, clerk 1947, elected to bd 1949, sec 1952, exec vice pres sec 1970-. **ORGANIZATIONS:** Trustee Svgs & Loan League 1966-68, 1972-74; 1st Black female bd of trustees Gtr Cincinnati C of C 1980-85; bd dirs Amer Svgs & Loan League 1969-74; Natl Soc Controllers & Financial Officers for Savings Inst; Amer Soc of Women Accountants; Credit Women Intl 1968-69; bd dirs Cincinnati Bus & Professional Womens Club 1975-78, 2nd vice pres 1975-76; Cincinnati Rehab Finance Corp; trustee Jennie D Porter Educ Fund; 1st Black female on bd dirs Jr Achievement Cincinnati; bd dirs Cincinnati Area Sr Serv Inc; Cincinnati bd dirs OIC; Lady Wonders Federated Club; treas Cosmopolitan Club 1964-73; bd dirs Beech Acres Genl Protestant Orphan Home 1984; bd dirs Greater Cincinnati Ctr for Economic Educ & 2nd vice pres 1984; bd trustees WCET Educ TV 1984. **HONORS/ACHIEVEMENTS:** Push Black Excellence Awd 1972; Outstanding Women Bus 1973; Comm Serv Awd NIP Mag 1975; Hall of Fame Temple Bible Coll 1977.

STREET, ANNE A.
Administrator. **PERSONAL:** Born Mar 19, 1942, Spartanburg, SC; daughter of Willie L Amos and Sallie McCracken Amos; divorced; children: Michael D. **EDUCATION:** Howard Univ, BA 1964, MSW 1969; Ctr for Group Stds, completed 1 yrof 2 yr Pgm 1974. **CAREER:** Dept of Human Rsrcs, social wrkr 1969-72; Howard Univ Hosp Psych & Social Serv Dept, social wrkr/instr 1972-80; Howard Univ Hosp Social Serv Dept asso dir 1980-; Howard Univ Hospital Washington DC, dir of social services 1986-. **ORGANIZATIONS:** Mem Gamma Sigma Sigma Natl Service Sorority 1963-; Realtor assoc Jackson Realty 1989-; corres sec bd dir Ionia R Whipper Home, Inc 1984-; rcrdng sec DC Hook-Up of Blck wmn 1980-84; mem Natl Asso of Social Wrkrs 1969-; mem Society of Hospital Social Work Dirs of the Amer Hospital Assn 1986-; mem Amer Public Health Assn 1986-. **HONORS/ACHIEVEMENTS:** Flwshp Grant Natl Endwmnt for Humanities 1980; Pres Meritorious Awrd DC Hook-Up of Blck Wmn 1983; Training Stdtn Natl Inst of Mntl Hlth 1967-6 9. **BUSINESS ADDRESS:** Director of Social Service, Howard Univ Hospital, 2041 Georgia Ave NW, Washington, DC 20060.

STREET, T. MILTON
Government official. **PERSONAL:** Born Apr 25, 1941, Norristown, PA. **EDUCATION:** Oakwood Coll of 7th Day Adventist, 1960-61; Temple U, 1966-67. **CAREER:** PA House of Reps, state rep; Street's Quality Wig Shop, organizer 1968-69; Street's Quality Food Serv, organizer-Mgr 1969-76; N Philadelphia Block & Devel Corp, founder organizer; Philadelphia Black St Vendors Assn, founder organizer. **HONORS/ACHIEVEMENTS:** Recipient award Nat Assn of Black Accountants; award Philadelphia Tribune; award Man of the Year 1980; award Main Line NANBPW. **BUSINESS ADDRESS:** Senate of Pennsylvania, Main Capitol BldgRm 186, Harrisburg, PA 17120.

STREET, VIVIAN SUE
Health care administrator. **PERSONAL:** Born Jun 21, 1954, Edgefield, SC; daughter of James Harry Bussey and Susie Bell Werts-Bussey; married Ronnie Street, Sep 24, 1978; children: Jermaine Toriano. **EDUCATION:** SUNY Coll at Brockport, Brockport NY, BS, 1976; Coll of New Rochelle, New Rochelle NY, MS (cum laude), 1981. **CAREER:** Westchester Devel Center, Orangeburg NY, special educ teacher, 1971-76; Westchester Devel Serv, White Plains NY, community residence supvr, 1977-78, Tarrytown NY, placement coord, 1978-82; Letchworth Village Devel Serv, Thiells NY, team leader, placement team, 1982-86; Westchester Devel Disabilities Serv, Tarrytown NY, program devel specialist, fiscal liaison, 1986-. **ORGANIZATIONS:** Vice pres, Black Caucus of PS&T Workers PEF, 1983-; convention delegate, Public Employees Fedn, 1985-; steering comm, Black Tennis & Sports Found, 1986-; treasurer, NAACP Spring Valley NY, 1988-; bd mem, Time for Tots Nursery School, 1989-. **HONORS/ACHIEVEMENTS:** Humanitarium, Public Employees Fedn, 1987; Community Serv, United Negro Scholarship Fund, 1988; Community Serv, Black Tennis & Sports Found, 1988.

STREET-KIDD, MAE
Legislator, public relations consultant. **PERSONAL:** Born in Millersburg, KY; married John Meredith III. **EDUCATION:** Lincoln Inst; Amer Univ, attended 1966-67. **CAREER:** Mammoth Life & Accident Ins Co, former supr policy issues/sales rep/pub rel couns 1935-64; KY House of Reps 41st Dist, mem 1968-; Continental Bank ofKY, dir prog & pub rel; free-lance mktg & pub rel cons. **ORGANIZATIONS:** Mem Banking & Ins Cities & Rules Comm; v chmn Elections Const Amendment Comm; sec Dem Caucus; deleg 1978 Dem Natl Party Conf; former bd mem YMCA; mem Natl Ins Assoc; charter mem Iota Phi Lambda; spearheaded fund-raising drives for GSA/NAACP Legal Fund. **HONORS/ACHIEVEMENTS:** Unsung Heroine Award Natl NAACP Women's Conf; Ten Top Outstanding Kentuckian Award; Honor Award Louisville Urban League; Outstanding Serv & Dedication Award Portland Area Councl; Recogn as Outstanding Producer in Ordinary Sales 3 consec years Mammoth Life & Accident Ins Co; Humanitarian Serv Award United Cerebral Palsy 1974; Dist Citz Award Black Scene Mag 1974; Cato-Watts Award 1976; Serv Award Mammoth Employ Credit Union 1977; Outst Serv & Dedication Award Portland Area Councl 1977; Recip Gold Plaque for qualifying as mem Half Million Dollar Club 1966. **BUSINESS ADDRESS:** Legislator/Pub Relations Consult, 2308 W Chestnut St, Louisville, KY 40211.

STREETER, ELWOOD JAMES
Dentist. **PERSONAL:** Born Jun 14, 1930, Greenville, NC; married Martha; children: Agnes, Nicole. **EDUCATION:** NC Coll, BS 1952; Howard U, DDS 1956; UCLA, cert 1969. **CAREER:** Perez & Streeter Dental Corp, dentist 1958-; LA Co USC Med Ctr, dental attending; Hollywood Presbyterian Med Center, attending staff. **ORGANIZATIONS:** Mem Am Dental Assn; CA Dental Assn; So CA Stomatognathic & Rsrch Seminar; pres So CA Acad Gen Denistry 1978; mem YMCA; NAACP; NC Coll Alumni Assn; LA Dental Soc Dental Care Com. **HONORS/ACHIEVEMENTS:** Fellowship Acad General Denistry

1972. **MILITARY SERVICE:** USN; USNR. **BUSINESS ADDRESS:** 1818 S Western Ave, Los Angeles, CA 90006.

STRICKLAND, ARVARH E.
Educator. **PERSONAL:** Born Jul 06, 1930, Hattiesburg, MS; son of Eunice Strickland and Clotiel Marshall Strickland; divorced; children: Duane Arvarh, Bruce Elmore. **EDUCATION:** Tougaloo Coll, Jackson MS, BA History, English, 1951; Univ of Illinois, Chicago IL, MA Educ, 1953, PhD History 1962. **CAREER:** Chicago State Coll, assoc prof,1965-68, prof, 1968-69; Univ of Missouri at Columbia, prof, 1969-, chmn dept of history, 1980-83, interim dir black studies program, 1986, Office of the Vice President for Academic Affairs, sr faculty assoc, 1987-88; interim assoc vice pres for academic affairs, 1989-, assoc vice pres for academic affairs, 1989-. **ORGANIZATIONS:** Amer Assn of Univ Prof; Chicago Historical Soc; bd of dir, Illinois Historical Soc, 1967-69; Amer Historical Assn, Org of Amer Historians, Comm on Nominations, 1973-75; Missouri Advisory Commn on Historic Preservation, 1976-80; Gen Bd of Higher Educ and Ministry, The United Methodist Church, 1976-80; mem exec comm commr, Columbia Planning and Zoning Comm, 1977-80; Assn for the Study of Afro-Amer Life and History Southern Historical Assn; bd of trustees, Historical Soc of Missouri; co-chmn, Mayor's Steering Comm for Commemorating the Contribution of Black Columbians (Columbia MO), 1980; mem, Fed Judicial Merit Selection Comm for the Western Dist of Missouri, 1982, Kiwanis Club of Columbia, 1985-88, Missouri Historical Records Advisory Bd; commr, Peace Officers Standards and Training Commn. **HONORS/ACHIEVEMENTS:** Kappa Delta Pi (education), 1953; Phi Alpha Theta (history), 1960; Kendric C Babcock Fellow in History, Univ of Illinois, 1961-62; Distinguished Serv Award, Illinois Historical Soc, 1967 Honor Soc of Phi Kappa Phi, Univ of Missouri, 1973; Assoc of the Danforth Found, 1973; Omicron Delta Kappa Natl Leadership Honor Soc, 1978; Martin Luther King Memorial Comm Award for Outstanding Community Serv, 1982; Faculty-Alumni Award, Alumni Assn of the Univ of Missouri, 1983; Serv Appreciation Award, Missouri Comm for the Humanities, 1984; Thomas Jefferson Award, Univ of Missouri, 1985; Office of Equal Opportunity Award for Exemplary Serv in Enhancing the Status of Minorities, Univ of Missouri, 1985; Distinguished Alumni Award (Tougaloo Coll), Natl Assn for Equal Opportunity in Higher Educ, 1986; Natl Endowment for the Humanities, Travel to Collections Grant, 1986; publications: History of the Chicago Uran League, Univ of Illinois Press, 1966; Building the United States, author with Jerome Reich and Edward Biller, Harcourt, Brace Jovanovich Inc, 1971; The Black American Experience, co-author with Jerome Reich, Harcourt, Brace Jovanovich Inc, 1974; Vol I, From Slavery through Reconstruction to 1877; Vol 11, From Reconstruction to the Present Since 1877; Edited with an Introduction, Lorenzo J Green, Working With Carter G Woodson, The Father of Black History: A Diary, 1928-30, Louisiana State Univ Press, 1989. **MILITARY SERVICE:** US Army, Sp-4, 1953-55; Honorble discharge from reserves, 1961. **BUSINESS ADDRESS:** Assoc Vice President for Academic Affairs and Prof of History, University of Missouri, 309 University Hall, Columbia, MO 65211.

STRICKLAND, CLINTON VERNAL, JR.
Educational administrator. **PERSONAL:** Born Dec 19, 1950, Elmira, NY; son of Clinton V. Strickland, Sr. and Grace Brooks; married Holly E Williams, Apr 21, 1973; children: Crystal V, Cicely V, Clinton III, Christopher V. Caitlyn V. **EDUCATION:** Univ of Rochester, BA 1974, MA 1975; SUNY Brockport, Cert Study of Ed Admin 1977; SUNY Buffalo, Doctoral Program. **CAREER:** Rochester City School Dist, teacher 1974-79, counselor 1979, dean of students 1980-82, jr high admin 1982-84, project mgr of schl environment prog 1984-85, vice principal Nathaniel Rochester Comm Sch 1985-. **ORGANIZATIONS:** Volunteer Urban League of Rochester NY Inc 1979-; bd of dir Office of Black Ministries Catholic Diocese of Rochester 1982-83; chmn Eureka Lodge #36 Ed & Charitable Trust, life mem Theta Omicron Chap Omega Psi Phi Frat; trainer/facilitator NYSCCT United Teachers; mem Phi Delta Kappa; pres founder Black Ed Assoc of Rochester. **HONORS/ACHIEVEMENTS:** Gen Electric Fellowship Boston Univ General Electric Co 1975; Summer Intern Industrial Mgmt Co 1981; Outstanding Volunteer Awd Urban League of Rochester 1982, 83, 84; Disting Serv Awd to Masons Eureka Lodge 36 Prince Hall Masons. **HOME ADDRESS:** 2 Brickston Drive, Pittsford, NY 14534.

STRICKLAND, DOROTHY S.
Educator. **PERSONAL:** Born Sep 29, 1933, Newark, NJ; daughter of Leroy Salley, Sr and Evelyn Daniels Salley; married Maurice R Strickland, Aug 27, 1955; children: Mark, M Randall, Michael. **EDUCATION:** Kean Coll, BS; NY Univ, MA, PhD, 1951-55; New York Univ, NY, MA, 1956-58, PH.D., 1967-71. **CAREER:** Kean Coll, prof 1970-80; NY Univ, adj prof; Jersey City State Coll, asst prof; Learning Disability Spec E Orange, teacher, reading consultant; Teachers Coll Columbia Univ, prof of Educ 1980-. **ORGANIZATIONS:** Teacher, East Orange, NJ, 1955-61; reading specialist, East Orange, NJ, 1961-66; Jersey City State Coll, Jersey City, NJ, 1966-70; bd of dir Natl Council Teachers English; Educ advisory bd Early Years Magazine; chmn Early Childhood Educ; mem Journal Reading Instructor, Websters New World Dictionary, commission Sprint Magazine; pres Intl Reading Assoc 1978-79; mem Natl Comm Ed Migrant Children; trustee, Research Found, Natl Council Teachers English, 1983-86. **HONORS/ACHIEVEMENTS:** Woman of the Year Zeta Phi Beta 1980; Natl Rsch Award Natl Council Teachers English 1972; Founders Day Recognition NY Univ 1971; Outstanding Teacher Educ Reading, Intl Reading Assn, 1985; Award for Outstanding Contribution to Ed, Natl Assn of Univ Women, 1987; emerging literacy, Intl Reading assn, 1989; admin & supvr, reading programs, Teachers Coll Press, 1989.

STRICKLAND, FREDERICK WILLIAM, JR.
Physician. **PERSONAL:** Born Aug 24, 1944, Kansas City, MO; son of Frederick William Strickland Sr and Ardene Strickland. **EDUCATION:** Southwestern Coll, BA 1966; Drake Univ, MA 1976; Coll of Osteopathic Medicine & Surgery, DO 1978. **CAREER:** Oklahoma City Public Schools, science teacher 1967-69; Des Moines Public Schools, science teacher 1969-74; Des Moines General Hosp, intern/resident 1978-80; UOMHS, prof family medicine 1980-; COMS, clinic dir student trainer 1980-. **ORGANIZATIONS:** Mem AOA 1978-; mem ACGP 1980-; mem corporate bd Des Moines General Hosp 1983-; mem Polk Co Democratic Central Comm 1984-; mem Des Moines Art Ctr 1984-; adv commn State of IA DUR Commn 1985-; mem Plan & Zoning Commn City of Des Moines 1985-; mem Still Nat Museum 1985-; mem bd of trustees Des Moines Genl Hosp 1986-; mem DMGH Foundation Des Moines Genl Hosp 1986-; mem Assoc for Retarded Citizens 1986-; mem Boys & Girls Club of Des Moines Board of Dirs 1988-; mem Bernie Lorenz Recovery House Board of Dirs 1987-. **HONORS/ACHIEVEMENTS:** The Moundbuilder Awd Southwestern Coll 1978; The DUR Awd Iowa Pharmacy Assoc 1986; "Alcohol-Induced Rhabdomyolysis," Hawkeye Osteopath Journal 1986; "Osteomyelitis of the Maxillary Antrum & Ethmoid Sinus in an Adolesent Male," Osteopath Medical News 1987. **MILITARY SERVICE:** AUS Medical Corps maj IA Army Natl Guard 9 yrs; Flight Surgeon, Iowa Army Commendation Awd 1983-85. **HOME ADDRESS:** 4910 Country Club Blvd, Des Moines, IA 50312.

STRICKLAND, R. JAMES
Business executive. **PERSONAL:** Born Feb 24, 1930, Kansas City, KS; married Deanna Cartman; children: James, Jay, Jeffrey, Deanna, Dori. **EDUCATION:** KS U, BS pharmacy 1954. **CAREER:** Strickland Drugs Inc, pres owner 1968-; Joslyn Clinic, mgr 1954-68. **ORGANIZATIONS:** Bd chmn Chatham Bus Assn 1676-77; bd mem Chicago Retail Druggist Assn 1977; pres Alpha Phi, Alpha Upsilon Chptr 1953-54; housing chmn W Sub NAACP 1965; vice pres NAACP West Sub Chap 1966; vice pres Met Improvement Assn 1971; bd chmn Met Improvement Assn 1972-73; vice pres Chicago Conf of Brothd 1977. **HONORS/ACHIEVEMENTS:** Award Chicago Conf for Brothd 1974. **BUSINESS ADDRESS:** 7900 S Cottage Gr, Chicago, IL 60619.

STRICKLIN, JAMES
Cameraman. **PERSONAL:** Born Mar 27, 1934, Chicago, IL; married Marita Joyce; children: Nicholas. **EDUCATION:** IL Inst of Tech, BS 1958; attended Art Inst of Chicago. **CAREER:** Univ of Chicago, lecturer film cinematography; Can Broadcasting Corp, cameraman 1964-67; NBC-News, cinematographer/cameraman 1967-. **ORGANIZATIONS:** Univ IL photos exhibited Smithsonian Inst 1962; co-author "With Grief Acquainted" 1963; IL Arts Council 1976-77; num documentary films. **HONORS/ACHIEVEMENTS:** Emmy Outstanding Cinematographer 1971-72. **BUSINESS ADDRESS:** Cinematographer/Cameraman, NBC-News, Merchandise Mart Plaza, Chicago, IL 60659.

STRIDER, MAURICE WILLIAM
Educator, artist. **PERSONAL:** Born Mar 18, 1913, Lexington, KY; married Mildred Goff. **EDUCATION:** Fisk Univ, AB; Univ of KY, MA 1960; Univ of Cinncinnati; Univ of KY; Morehead State Univ. **CAREER:** Morehead State Univ, asso prof of art 1966-; Louisville Defender & Pittsburgh Courier, correspondent/photographer 1935-66; Lexington KY Public School System, instr 1934-66. **ORGANIZATIONS:** Past pres Lexington Tchrs Assn; Lexington Educ Assn; delegate assembly Nat Educ Assn; KY Educ Assn; mem Phi Delta Kappa; Kappa Pi; Kappa Alpha Psi; mem Black History Com KY Human Rights Commn; adv bd KY Educ TV; honored past mem Fisk U; Fisk Jubilee Singers 1972. **HONORS/ACHIEVEMENTS:** John Hope Purchase Art Award Atlanta Univ 1960; represented exhibit "30 Years of Black Art" Chicago DuSable Museum 1975; exhibit Carnegie Inst KY State Univ, Lexington Public Library, Morehead State Univ, IL State Univ; award Southern Educ Assn fellowship, Univ of KY; Award, Fed rsch grants for rsch Afro-Amer Art. **BUSINESS ADDRESS:** Professor Emeritus, Morehead State University, Morehead, KY 40351.

STRINGER, C. VIVIAN
Head coach. **PERSONAL:** Born Mar 16, 1948, Edenborn, PA; married William Stringer; children: David, Janine, Justin. **EDUCATION:** Slippery Rock Univ, BS 1971, MEd 1972. **CAREER:** Cheyney State Univ, head coach basketball professor 1972-83; Univ of Iowa, head coach basketball 1983-. **ORGANIZATIONS:** Founder Natl Women's Basketball Coaches Assoc 1980; instructor Natl Kodak Basketball Clinics 1983; bd mem Amateur Basketball Assoc USA 1984-85; bd mem Nike Adv Bd 1986. **HONORS/ACHIEVEMENTS:** Head Coach Natl Sports Festival Indianapolis IN 1982; Natl Coach of the Yr NCAA 1982; Outstanding Alumni Hall of Fame Slippery Rock Univ 1985; District 5 Coach of the Yr Natl Collegiate Athletic Assoc 1985; Head Coach World Univ Games Kobe Japan 1985. **BUSINESS ADDRESS:** Head Coach, University of Iowa, Carver-Hawkeye Arena, Iowa City, IA 52242.

STRINGER, MELYIN, SR.
Business executive. **PERSONAL:** Born May 15, 1927, Princeton, LA; married Hazel Rayson; children: Melvin II, Norbert G. **EDUCATION:** De Paul U, BSC 1952; Northwestern U, 1951-53. **CAREER:** IRS, agent 1951-59; private practice acct 1960-62; Dept Ins State Ill, exam surp 1961-69; Supreme Life Ins Co, asst controller 1969, controller 1970, vice pres 1973, sr vice pres 1974-77, bd of dir 1977, sr vice pres treas/controller 1977. **ORGANIZATIONS:** Mem NAACP; Ins Accounting & Statistical Assn; charter mem Assn Black Accountants. **MILITARY SERVICE:** AUS sgt 1945-46. **BUSINESS ADDRESS:** 3501 S Dr Martin Luther King J, Chicago, IL 60653.

STRINGER, NELSON HOWARD, JR.
Physician. **PERSONAL:** Born Feb 07, 1948, Savannah, GA; married Denise. **EDUCATION:** Fisk U, BA 1969; Meharry Med Coll, MD 1973. **CAREER:** Cook Co Hosp, resd ob-gyn 1974-77, intern 1973-74; Presb St Lukes Hosp, atdg physician; Dept Ob-gyn Rush Med Coll, instr; Emergency Room Serv S Shore Hosp, dir 1974-77. **ORGANIZATIONS:** Mem AMA; IL Med Soc; Chicago Med Soc; Am Assn Gyn Laparoscopists. **HONORS/ACHIEVEMENTS:** Alpha Phi Alpha Frat flw; Jessie Noyes Smith 1968-73. **BUSINESS ADDRESS:** Rush Presb St Lukes Med Cntr, Chicago, IL.

STRINGER, THOMAS EDWARD, SR.
Circuit judge. **PERSONAL:** Born Jul 08, 1944, Peekskill, NY; son of Theordore and Fannie; married Lillian Jean Cooper; children: Thomas E Jr, Daryl Q, Rhonda E, Roderick E. **EDUCATION:** New York Univ (Washington Square Coll), BA 1967; Stetson Univ Coll of Law, JD 1974. **CAREER:** Hillsborough County State Atty's Office, staff atty 1974-76; Rosello & Stringer PA, staff atty 1976-84; Hillsborough County Court, county judge 1984-87; Hillsborough County, circuit judge 1988-. **ORGANIZATIONS:** Life mem Natl Bar Assoc 1974-; mem Hillsborough County Bar Assoc 1974-; mem bd of dirs Boys & Girls Clubs of Greater Tampa Inc 1976-; mem Omega Psi Phi Frat 1980-; mem bd of dirs Bay Area Legal Serv 1984-; mem bd of overseers Stetson Univ Coll of Law 1986-; mem Bay Area Chamber of Commerce 1986-. **HONORS/ACHIEVEMENTS:** Citizen of the Year Pi Iota Chap Omega Psi Phi Frat 1984; George E Edgecomb Awd Tampa Urban League 1984. **MILITARY SERVICE:** USAF capt 1967-71. **BUSINESS ADDRESS:** Hillsborough County Circuit Judge, State of Florida, Hillsborough County Courthouse, Room 296, Tampa, FL 33629.

STRIPLING, LUTHER
Educator. **PERSONAL:** Born Aug 25, 1935, Tignall, GA; son of Luther Stripling and Catherine Stripling; married Myrtice Jones, Nov 07, 1957; children: Cedric Ravel, Lloyd

Byron. **EDUCATION:** Clark Coll, AB 1957; Atlanta Univ, attended 1960-65; Univ KY, MMus 1968; Univ CO, DMus 1971. **CAREER:** Hamilton HS, teacher 1957-66, chmn music dept 1960-66; GA Interscholastic Assn, chmn vocal div 1964-66; Univ KY, instructor 1966-68; Univ CO, 1970-71; Macalester Coll, coordinator vocal activities 1971; So IL Univ at Edwardsville, assoc prof of music/dir of opera workshop; Tarrant County Jr Coll NE Campus, professor of vocal music/dir of opera workshop. **ORGANIZATIONS:** Pres MN chapter Natl Opera Assn Inc; general dir Macalester Coll Opera Workshop; assoc general dir Assoc Coll of the Twin Cities Opera Workshop; minister of music Pilgrim Baptist Church; pres St Louis Dist Chapter of Natl Assn of Teachers of Singing 1980-82; numerous performances orchestral appearances directing papers in field. **HONORS/ACHIEVEMENTS:** Outstanding Young Man of Yr 1967; contributor Burkhart Charles Anthology for Musical Analysis 3rd Ed NY Holt Rinehart & Winston 1978. **HOME ADDRESS:** 901 Woodcreek Ct, Euless, TX 76039.

STRODE, VELMA MCEWEN
Former senior executive. **PERSONAL:** Born Oct 19, 1919, Jackson, MS; daughter of Rev & Mrs B T McEwen; married James W (deceased); children: James C. **CAREER:** Office of Equal Employment Opportunity, US Dept of Labor, dir 1971-; Dept of Justice, Community Relations Serv, sr community relations specialist; Community Center in Utica NY, dir; The Velma McEwen Show, broadcaster. **ORGANIZATIONS:** Exec Urban League 1946-57; Acad of Certified Social Workers; Alumni Assn of Fed Exec Inst; Amer Women in Radio & TV; bd of trustees, St Augustine's Coll; United Way Bd of Dist of Columbia; rep Greater Metro United Way Bd; advisor Capit Tower Proj Home for Delinquent Young Women; Exec Women in Govt Org; Natl Urban League; NAACP; Social Action Commn Delta Sigma Theta Sor; Leadership Conf on Civil Rights; advisory bd, YWCA Tower. **HONORS/ACHIEVEMENTS:** Recognition for outstanding performance of duties, US Dept of Labor 1973; activist award, Cleveland OH 1974; outstanding serv to humanity, St Augustine Coll 1975; the Chapel of Four Chaplains Philadelphia 1975; the Conf of Minority Public Admin Award 1976; Amer GI Forum Award 1976; Equal Employment Opportunity Commn Award Dallas 1976; EEO award, Fed Women's Prog, Texas Region, Equal Employment Opportunity Commn 1976; hon citizen, Dallas TX 1976; labor mgmt award, Natl Black Women's Political Leadership Caucus 1976.

STROGER, JOHN HERMAN, JR.
Attorney. **PERSONAL:** Born May 19, 1929, Helena, AR; married Yonnie Rita Bachelor; children: Yonnie Lynn, Hans Eric, Todd Herman. **EDUCATION:** Xavier U, LA, BS 1952; DePaul Univ Law Sch, Chicago, JD 1965. **CAREER:** HS basketball coach 1952-53. **ORGANIZATIONS:** Mem Cook Co Bd of Commrs; committeeman 8th Ward Regular Dem Orgn 1968; personnel dir Cook Co Jail 1955-59; mem Cook Co Bar Assn; Chicago Bar Assn; IL Bar Assn; Am Bar Assn; bd dir Chicago Woodlawn Boys Club; mem BSA; Kiwanis Club; YMCA; Xi Lambda Chpt; Alpha Phi Alpha Frat Inc. **HONORS/ACHIEVEMENTS:** Recipient award of merit Chicago Inter Alumni Council of the United Negro Coll Fund; Cook Co Bar Assn Edward H Wright Award 1973; Kiwanis Club of SE Area, Chicago; Englewood Bus Promotions Award; S Chicago Organized for People's Efforts Award; Chicago Park Dist Award 1973. **BUSINESS ADDRESS:** 109 N Dearborn St, Ste 801, Chicago, IL.

STROMAN, CHERYL DELORES
Pharmacist. **PERSONAL:** Born Jan 12, 1956, Gaffney, SC; daughter of John H Parker, Sr and Ruby White Parker; married Joseph B Stroman, Sep 17, 1988; children: Radhiya Marjani Stroman. **EDUCATION:** Univ of North Carolina, Pre-pharmacy 1974; Howard Univ, BS Pharmacy 1979. **CAREER:** Hill Health Center, staff pharmacist 1979-80; Comm Health Care Cte Plan, pharmacy coordinator 1980-84; Eckerd Drug Gastonia, pharmacist mgr 1985-86; Kaiser Foundation Health Plan, pharmacy supervisor 1986-. **ORGANIZATIONS:** Mem Alpha Kappa Alpha Sorority Inc 1975-, Amer Pharmaceutical Assn 1979-, Amer Diabetes Assn 1984-, North Carolina Pharmaceutical Assoc 1985-; mem Little Rock AME Zion Church. **BUSINESS ADDRESS:** Pharmacy Supervisor, Kaiser Permanente, 5970 Fairview Rd, Bldg 3, Suite 100, Charlotte, NC 28210.

STROMAN, KENNETH
Eeo coordinator/sr exec recruiter. **PERSONAL:** Born Jun 19, 1948, New Rochelle, NY. **EDUCATION:** Atlantic Union College, BA History Psychology 1970. **CAREER:** Drug Abuse Control Commission, narcotic parole officer 1975-76; Manufacturers Hanover Trust, exec recruiter 1978-85; Merrill Lynch & Co Inc, sr exec recruiter 1985, eeo coord 1985-. **ORGANIZATIONS:** Steering comm mem Harlem Branch YMCA "Salute to Black Achievers in Industry" 1986-87; Jackie Robinson Foundation 1986; mem NAACP 1986, Natl Urban League1986. **HONORS/ACHIEVEMENTS:** Service Awd Southern Christian Leadership Conference 1985, 86. **HOME ADDRESS:** 65 West 96th St #9A, New York, NY 10025. **BUSINESS ADDRESS:** EEO Coordinator, Merrill Lynch & Co Inc, 165 Broadway, New York, NY 10080.

STRONG, AMANDA L.
Nursing coordinator. **PERSONAL:** Born Nov 22, 1935, Marvel, AR; daughter of Percy Watson and Earlie Mae Watson; widowed; children: Cheryl Beard, Pamela Tender, Jerilyn S. **EDUCATION:** St Vincents Hospital School Nursing, Diploma 1954-57; Indiana Univ, BSN 1973; ANA, Certificate 1980; Indiana Univ, MSN 1983; Family Nurse Practitioner, Certificate 1985-90. **CAREER:** Indiana Univ Med Center, asst head nurse 1959-64; Visiting Nurse Assn, supr 1964-72; Dept of Corr, family nurse practitioner 1974-80; Vets Admin Med Center Hospital Based Home Care Prog, nurse practitioner 1980-. **ORGANIZATIONS:** Bd mem Capitol Improvemnts Bd 1978-85; pres Holy Angels Parish Cncl 1979-83; comm ch & bd mem Coalition 100 Black Women 1980-; mem black & minority health task force Indiana State Bd of Health; mem standards comm Chronic Health Indiana State Bd of Health; bd mem Indiana State Bd Nurses & Nurse Practitioner Council; pres, Indiana Univ School of Nursing, 1988-91; sec, District 5 Alumni Assn Bd of Nursing, Indiana State Nurses Assn, 1987-89; facilitator, Hospital Based Home Care Support Group, 1989-. **HONORS/ACHIEVEMENTS:** Those Special People Sigma Phi Communications Award; Cert Amer Nurses Assn Adult Practitioner 1980-85; Martin Luther King Leadership Award SCLC; Citizen of Day WTLC Radio; chosen Hospital Based Home Care Nurse for 1985; Special Contribution to Nursing Veterans Admin Nursing, 1989; Minority Nurse Role Model, Indianapolis Star, 1989. **HOME ADDRESS:** 402 E 46th St, Indianapolis, IN 46205. **BUSINESS ADDRESS:** Veterans Adm Med Ctr, 1481 W 10th St, Indianapolis, IN 46202.

STRONG, BLONDELL MCDONALD
Consultant, real estate agent. **PERSONAL:** Born Jan 11, 1943, Fort Pierce, FL; daughter of Jeff McDonald (deceased) and Bertha McDonald; divorced; children: Stanford II, Jeff Bertram. **EDUCATION:** Tennessee State Univ, BS 1964; Geo Peabody Coll of Vanderbilt Univ, MLS 1967; Univ of Michigan, PhD 1983. **CAREER:** Lincoln Jr Coll, librarian & music instructor 1964-65; Indian River Jr Coll, librarian & asst cataloger 1965-67; Meharry Med Coll, library dir 1967-78; Univ of Michigan, post-doctorate fellow; Mamlika Enterprises Inc, pres 1989-; mgmt consultant; Bond Realty Inc, real estate agent 1986-88; Bordeaux Realty Plus, pres & co-owner. **ORGANIZATIONS:** Mem NAACP, Tennessee State Univ Alumni Assn. **HONORS/ACHIEVEMENTS:** Outstanding Young Women Amer 1973; Kappa Delta Pi Hon Soc; Beta Phi Mu Intl Library Science Hon Soc. **BUSINESS ADDRESS:** President, Bordeaux Realty Plus, PO Box 5745, Nashville, TN 37208.

STRONG, CRAIG STEPHEN
Judge. **PERSONAL:** Born Sep 05, 1947, Detroit, MI. **EDUCATION:** Howard Univ, BA 1969; Detroit Coll of Law, JD 1973. **CAREER:** Wayne Co Neighborhood Legal Serv, law intern & staff atty 1970-73; Terry Ahmad & Bradfield, assoc atty 1973; Elliard Crenshaw & Strong PC, partner 1974-76; Recorder's Court City of Detroit Traffic & Ordinance Div, referee 1978; City of Detroit Recorder's Court, judge 1979-. **ORGANIZATIONS:** Past pres Wolverine Bar Assn; regional dir Natl Bar Assn; former recorder's ct com chmn Detroit Bar Assn; vice chmn bd of dir Wayne Co Neighborhood Legal Svcs; rep assembly State Bar of MI; mem Prince Hall Masons 32nd Degree. **HONORS/ACHIEVEMENTS:** Man of the Yr Awd Detroit Urban Center 1979; Howardite of the Yr Awd Howard Univ Detroit Chap 1979; Resolution State of MI 1979; Disting Serv Awd Natl Council of Negro Women 1980; Renaissance Awd 13th Dist Democratic Party 1982; Outstanding Museum Serv Awd Afro-Amer Museum of Detroit 1983; Humanitarian Awd of Excellence Mother Waddles Perpetual Mission 1983; man of the year North End youth Improvement Council 1986; award of appreciation Boy Scouts of America Renaissance Cistrict 1988. **MILITARY SERVICE:** USNR lcdr. **BUSINESS ADDRESS:** Judge Recorder's Court, City of Detroit, 1441 St Antoine, Detroit, MI 48226.

STRONG, DOUGLAS DONALD
Physician. **PERSONAL:** Born May 31, 1938, Detroit, MI; married Helen Francine; children: Mark, Douglas Jr, Jennifer Anne, Stephen. **EDUCATION:** Univ of MI, BA 1959; Howard Univ, MD 1963. **CAREER:** Grace Hosp Detroit, intern 1963-64; Mt Carmel Mercy Hosp Detroit, surgery resident 1966-67; San Francisco VA Hosp Univ of CA, post-doctoral cand 1968-70; Otolaryn/physician present. **ORGANIZATIONS:** Mem Detroit Med Soc, Wayne Co Med Soc, Natl Med Soc, Acad of Ophthal & Otolaryn; mem Alpha Phi Alpha Frat, NAACP; hosp staffs Harper Hospital, SW Hospital, Mt Carmel Hosp, Childrens Hosp; chief of otolaryngology Hutzel Hosp; instr Otolaryngology Wayne State Univ. **HONORS/ACHIEVEMENTS:** Testimonial Resolution from Detroit City Council; Special Tribute from Senate of the State of MI. **MILITARY SERVICE:** AUS capt 1964-66. **BUSINESS ADDRESS:** 3800 Woodward, Detroit, MI 48201.

STRONG, HELEN FRANCINE (FRAN LANIER)
Attorney. **PERSONAL:** Born Mar 22, 1947, Detroit, MI; married Douglas Donald Jr; children: Douglas Jr, Jennifer Anne, Stephen. **EDUCATION:** Univ of Detroit, AB 1969; Univ of Detroit, JD 1972. **CAREER:** State of MI, asst attny gen; Detroit Edison Co, staff attny 1973-80; William C Gage PC, assoc 1980-81; Lewis White & Clay PC, sr assoc. **ORGANIZATIONS:** Mem Natl Bar Assoc, Fed Bar Assoc, MI Bar Assoc, Detroit Bar Assoc, Wolverine Bar Assoc, Amer Bar Assoc,; legal adv Delta Sigma Theta 1973-75; aux to Detroit Med Soc, Natl Med Soc; life mem NAACP; founder Soc Detroit Inst of Arts; mem Assoc of Trial Lawyers of Amer, MI Trial Lawyers Assoc; bd dir Founders Jr Council-Detroit Inst of Arts 1979-; sec bd dir Founders Jr Council Detroit Inst of Arts 1982-83; adv comm Detroit Inst of Arts Centennial Comm 1983-, Your Heritage House Inc 1983-84; bd dir Your Heritage House Inc 1984-; chmn Exhibition Treasures of Ancient Nigeria-Legacy of Two Thousand-Years Detroit Inst of Arts Founders Jr Council 1980; co-chmn Exhibition Opening Black Folk Art in Amer 1930-1980 Detroit Inst of Arts 1983. **HONORS/ACHIEVEMENTS:** Cert for Outstanding Scholarship in Intramural Moot Ct Compet 1970; Univ of Detroit Jr Natl Moot Ct Team 1970-71; Univ of Detroit Sr Natl Moot Ct Team 1971-72; Moot Ct Bd of Dir 1971-72; Univ of Detroit Law School Admiss Comm 1970-71; Cert for Outstanding Serv Univ of Detroit School of Law 1972; 1stblack attny, 1st woman attny empl by Detroit Edison Co; listed in Who's Who of Amer Women 14th Ed. **BUSINESS ADDRESS:** Senior Associate, Lewis, White & Clay PC, 1300 First Natl, Detroit, MI 48226.

STRONG, MARILYN TERRY
Retired educator. **PERSONAL:** Born Sep 10, 1929, Hartford, CT; daughter of George William Teryy and Odessa Callie Stewart Terry; married Edward M Strong (deceased). **EDUCATION:** Univ of CT, BA 1950, MA 1965. **CAREER:** Hartford Bd of Educ, elem physical educ teacher 1950-60, secondary physical educ teacher 1960-84; Weaver High School, physical educ dept head 1971-77, varsity basketball & softball coach 1972-86, continuing educ teacher 1984; retired 1989. **ORGANIZATIONS:** Mem AAHPER 1950-; vice pres 1971-72 CAHPERD 1950-85; mem CEA & NEA 1950-; Golden life mem, pres 1963-65 Hartford Alumnae Delta Sigma Theta Sor Inc 1951-; mem Order of Eastern Star Stella Chap #16 1957-; leader chairperson bd of dirs CT Valley Girl Scouts 1951-; pres 1985-87, treas 1989-90, Hartford Jazz Soc 1977-; mem CT Black Caucus/AFT 1985-; mem The Links Inc 1986-. **HONORS/ACHIEVEMENTS:** Delta Sigma Theta Comm Serv Awd 1965; Outstanding Secondary Educator 1973, 1976; Maharishi Educ Awd 1977; Hartford Teacher of the Yr Hartford Bd of Educ 1981; Comm Serv Awd Brass Key Inc 1982; Comm Serv Awd Natl Assoc Negro Business & Professional Women's Clubs Inc Hartford Chap 1986; Iota Phi Lambda, Beta Chapter Apple for the Teacher Award 1988. **HOME ADDRESS:** 42 Canterbury St, Hartford, CT 06112.

STRONG, OTIS REGINALD, III
Consumer affairs representative. **PERSONAL:** Born Sep 26, 1954, Norfolk, VA; son of Rev Thomas Smith (step-father) and Mallie Smith; married Gloria W; children: Cayce J. **EDUCATION:** Elizabeth City State Univ, BS 1976. **CAREER:** Delta Air Lines Inc, customer service support agent 1976-77, sr customer service agent 1978-83, sr passenger service agent 1983-84, consumer affairs rep 1984-. **ORGANIZATIONS:** Mem NAACP 1976-, JOHER-AAHPR 1976-; vice pres Uni-Time Inc 1984-; pres Alumni Chap ECSU 1985-, Atlanta Alumni Chap ECSU 1985-; coach/head, Fayette County Rec Assn 1987-; coach, Fayette County AAU Basketball-GA 1988-. **HONORS/ACHIEVEMENTS:** Distinguished Alumni Awd 1986. **BUSINESS ADDRESS:** Consumer Affairs Rep, Delta Air Lines Inc, Hartsfield Intl Airport, Atlanta, GA 30320.

STRONG, PETER E.
Dentist. **PERSONAL:** Born Apr 01, 1930, Detroit, MI; married Helen Rowe; children: Peter Christopher, Kent Alexander. **EDUCATION:** Univ of MI, DDS 1955. **CAREER:** Detroit Dept of Health, sr dentist 1957-58; pvt practice of gen dentistry 1958-; Staff Grace Hosp, 1965-; Delta Dental Plan of MI, consult 1974-. **ORGANIZATIONS:** Pres Wolverine Dental Soc 1972-73; NE Component Detroit Dist Dental Soc 1974-75; exec Council Detroit Dist Dental Soc 1973-75; bd of trustee Detroit Med Found 1972-; bd of trustee Nat Dental Assn 1965-67; mem MI Dental Assn 1957-; Am Dental Assn 1953-; charter mem Am Soc for Preventive Dentistry; mem Steering Com of MI Chap 1970-; Acad of Gen Dentistry 1973-; mem Alumni Visitation Com Adv on Curriculum ofUniv of MI Sch of Dentistry 1971-74; Med Com of Human Rights 1964-70; life mem NAACP; mem Am Civil Liberties Union; Alpha Phi Alpha Frat 1950-; The Moors; The Recess; Detroit Boat Club; Sch Health Council of Detroit Pub Sch System 1971-; Preventive Dental Health & Educ Program Detroit Pub Sch System; Clinician MI Dental Assn Conv 1972; Phi Eta Sigma Freshman Honor Frat. **MILITARY SERVICE:** AUS cpt Dental Corp 1955-57. **BUSINESS ADDRESS:** President, Peter E Strong, DDS PC, 4727 Saint Antoine, Ste 210, Detroit, MI 48201.

STRONG, WALTER L.
Educator/administrator. **EDUCATION:** Southern IL Univ-Carbondale, BA; Univ of NE-Lincoln, MA; Univ of IL, doctoral ABD; Golden Gate Univ, PhD. **CAREER:** Univ of CA Mgmt Inst, faculty mem; Univ of IL-Urbana, asst vice chancellor for academic affairs, political science faculty mem; Univ of CA-Berkeley, asst vice president for personnel development; Meharry Medical Coll, vice pres for institutional advancement; Florida Intl Univ, vice pres of univ relations/develop. **ORGANIZATIONS:** Cumberland Museum of Science Tech, board of membership; The Robertson Assoc; United Way of Nashville; NAACP, mem; Kappa Alpha Psi; Council for the Advancement and Support of Education; American Management Assoc. **BUSINESS ADDRESS:** Vice Pres for Development, Florida Intl University, PC230 TA Miami Campus, Miami, FL 33199.

STROUD, HOWARD BURNETT, SR.
Educator. **PERSONAL:** Born Mar 31, 1939, Athens, GA; married Victoria Lee Baker; children: Howard Jr, Kesha. **EDUCATION:** Morehouse Coll, BA 1956; Atlanta Univ, MA 1968; Additional Study, Univ of GA, Agnes Scott Coll, Appalachain State Boone NC. **CAREER:** Union Inst, teacher 1956; Burney Harris HS, teacher 1956-65; Lyons Middle School, guidance counselor asst prin teacher 1963-65; Lyons Middle School Clark Co, prin 1965-78; Clark Co School Dist, coord middle & secondary schools 1978-80, admin asst to supt 1980-81, acting supt 1981-82, assoc supt 1981-. **ORGANIZATIONS:** Mem CCAE/GAE/NEA; bd dir GA Assn of Educ Ldrs; mem Prin Rsch & Info Ctr; mem Editorial Bd Amer Middle Sch Educ Journal; mem Editoral Bd GA Assn of Middle Sch Prins Jour; bd dir GA Assn of Educ Ldrs 1976-; mem GA Assn of Curriculum & Instructional Supr; mem Natl Assn Secondary Sch Prins; Natl Educ Assn; GA Clarke Co Educ Assns; pres GA Middle Sch Prins; exalted ruler Classic City Elks Lodge; lay vice pres Athens-Clarke Cancer Soc;mem Clarke Co Charter Commn; state bd Cancer Soc; pres exec comm Cancer Soc; Optimists Club; mem Athens-Clarke C of C; Phi Delta Kappa, Kappa AlphaPsi; Mason; past polemarch Elks; charter mem Athens Area Oppors Indus Ctr; mem OIC bd of dir 1976-; mem Athens Council on Wellness 1982-; mem bd dirFamily Counseling; chmn steering comm Union Baptist Inst Inc; chmn Prestigious GA Professional Practices Comm 1984-; mem GA Secondary Comm Southern Assn of Colls & Schs 1984-; mem Hosp Auth Clarke Co 1983-; chmn bd deacons Mt Pleasant Baptist Ch 1980-. **HONORS/ACHIEVEMENTS:** Leadership Plaque YMCA 1959; Cert of Appreciation Amer Cancer Soc 1970; Tchr of Yr Awd Burney Harris HS 1960; Cert of Appreciation VFW 1961, 1962; Golden Awd Plaque GT/EA 1968; Presidential Citation Optimist Intl for Leadership as pres Athens Breakfast Optimist Club; Cert of Apprec Athens Rec Dept 1975; Personalites of the S; Who's Who in the S & SW; Cert of Achievement Kappa Alpha Psi Frat; Heritage Awd Optimist Intl; Who's Who in Amer 1974-75; Outstanding Educators Awd Lyons Fac 1977; This is Your Life Lyons Fac & Student Body 1977; Serv Awd Mosley Gospel Choir 1977; Dedication & Serv Plaque Lyons Fac & Student Body; Outstanding Ldrshp GA Assn of Middle Sch Prins 1978; Portrait unveiled Lyons Middle Sch 1978; Awd of Excel Pub Sch Admin Kappa Delta Pi 1978; Serv Awd GA Assn Educ Ldrshp 1977-78, 1978-79; Serv Awd Citizens Group of Athens 1979;Ldrshp Awd Phi Beta Sigma Frat 1982; Mkt Place Achiev Awd Milledge Bapt Ch 1982; Outstndg Ldrshp Awd Clarke Co Bd Educ 1981-82; Human Relations Awd GA Assn of Educs 1983; W Judicial Circuit Liberty Bell Law Day Awd 1984; Spec Recog Awd 100 Percenters 1982; Outstndg Serv Awd Athens Cntr Rec Ctr Day 1984; Outstndg Serv Awd Athens Tech Sch 1982. **MILITARY SERVICE:** AUS 1951-53. **BUSINESS ADDRESS:** Associate Superintendent, Clark Co Sch Dist, 500 College Ave, Athens, GA 30606.

STROUD, LAWRENCE LOWELL
Manager. **PERSONAL:** Born Apr 26, 1935, Macon, GA; married Elizabeth Ervin; children: Larren, Sherri, Calisse. **EDUCATION:** A&T U, Greensboro, NC, BS 1957; Glassboro State Coll, MA 1973. **CAREER:** US Govt, supr monitor prodn; FAA mgmt software respons nations air space environment. **ORGANIZATIONS:** Past pres Atlantic Co Citizens on Environment; Alpha Phi Alpha Frat; pres FAA Flying Club NAFFC; commr Pleasantville Housing Auth; adj coll prof; pastchmn personnel Pleasantville Bd of Edn; mem Toastmaster Internat. **HONORS/ACHIEVEMENTS:** Citation Metoriuos Serv to City of Pleasantville, Bd of Educ 1976. **MILITARY SERVICE:** USAR platoon leader.

STROUD, LOUIS WINSTON
Management consultant. **PERSONAL:** Born Nov 21, 1946, Cincinnati, OH. **EDUCATION:** Canisius Coll, AB Hist 1968; Harvard Grad School of Bus Admin, MBA Finance 1970; Univ of San Francisco School of Law, JD 1976. **CAREER:** Kaiser Aluminum & Chem Corp, merger acquisition specialist 1976; Mfrs Hanover Trust, product mgr disbursements 1974-76; Mfrs Hanover Trust, corp planner 1973. **ORGANIZATIONS:** Mem Harvard Bus School Club 1976-80; mem Harvard Club 1980. **BUSINESS ADDRESS:** Kuwait Petrol Corp, PO Box 26565, Safat, Kuwait.

STROUD, MILTON
Law enforcement supervisor. **PERSONAL:** Born Mar 11, 1936, Durham, NC; children: Monica Shafi, Dwayne Bland. **EDUCATION:** Queens Coll, BA 1965; Long Island Univ, MA 1967; New York Univ, PhD 1976. **CAREER:** New York State Division of Parole, supervisor. **ORGANIZATIONS:** Vice chmn Area Policy Bd Brooklyn 1980-; bd chmn Old 80 Precinct Council 1981-; exec vice pres Ebony Soc 1985-; exec bd mem Professional Employees Federation 1985-; mem Natl Assoc of Blacks in Criminal Justice, Natl Acad of Criminology, Amer Sociological Assoc, Natl Black Police Assoc; mem NY City Community Action Board. **HONORS/ACHIEVEMENTS:** Omega Psi Phi Man of the Year 1973; Certificate of Merit Natl Assoc of Black Counselors 1985; Delta Sigma Theta Comm Serv Awd 1985; Achievement Awd EbonySoc 1986; Humanitarian Awd Amer Federation of Police 1986. **MILITARY SERVICE:** NG 2 yrs. **HOME ADDRESS:** 1048 Union St, Brooklyn, NY 11225.

STROZIER, YVONNE IGLEHART
State official, educator. **PERSONAL:** Born Nov 14, 1938, Waco, TX; daughter of Bishop T D Iglehart and Dessie Mae Truitt Iglehart; married Arthur A Strozier, Oct 13, 1974; children: William Charles Wilborn, Thaddeus Iglehart Wilborn, Desi Artrice Iglehart Strozier. **EDUCATION:** Bishop Coll, Marshall TX, BS, 1959; Prarie View A&M, Prarie View TX, MA, 1965; San Diego State, San Diego CA, attended, 1968. **CAREER:** Conway Public Schools, Conway AR, teacher, 1959-60; Waco Independent School Dist, Waco TX, teacher 1961-65; El Dorado County Schools, Placerville CA, teacher, 1965-66; San Diego City Schools, San Diego CA, teacher, project dir, 1966-72; California Dept of Educ, Sacramento CA, consultant, 1972-. **ORGANIZATIONS:** Mem, Delta Sigma Sorority, 1955-, Jack & Jill Inc, 1970-; co-founder, California Alliance of Black School Educ, 1979-; exec bd, Natl Alliance of Black School Educ, 1985-; corporate bd mem, California Assn of Compensatory Educ, 1985-; admin, Strozier Youth Center, 1986-; coord, The Speaker's Educ Breakfast Club (Speaker of the House, California State Assembly), 1986-; meeting planner, Natl Alliance of Black School Educ, 1986-; mem, Coalition of Black Meeting Planners, 1987-; bd mem, C H Mason Found-Church of God in Christ, 1988-. **HONORS/ACHIEVEMENTS:** Coordinator, The Proficiency in Standard English Porgarm for African-Amer Students (the first and only program operated by a state educ agency), 1979; Outstanding Achievement, California Alliance of Black School Educators, 1980; Proclamation of Appreciation, Natl Assn of Black School Educ, 1980-; Outstanding Educator, California Dept of Educ, 1983; Outstanding Achievement, California Assn of Compensatory Educ, 1985, 1986; Proclamation of Appreciation, Inglewood School Dist, Inglewood CA, 1987. **BUSINESS ADDRESS:** Consultant, California Department of Education, 721 Capitol Mall, Sacramento, CA 95814.

STRUDWICK, LINDSEY H., SR.
Certified purchasing manager. **PERSONAL:** Born Aug 08, 1946, Durham, NC; son of London L Strudwick, Sr and Christine Alston Strudwick; married Gladys B Strudwick, Nov 09, 1968; children: Lindsey Howard Jr, Casandra Michelle. **EDUCATION:** Durham Business Coll, Durham NC, assoc degree in science/business admin; Shaw Univ, Raleigh NC, BA; Southeastern Univ, Greenville SC, MBA. **CAREER:** Intl Fertility Research, Chapel Hill NC, purchasing mgr, 1974-76; Northrop Corp, Research Triangle Pk NC, manager of purchasing and facilities, 1976-78; Gen Telephone Co, Durham NC, personnel asst, 1978-79; Northern Telecom Inc, Research Triangle Pk NC, group leader in purchasing, 1979-81; Scientific-Atlanta Inc, Atlanta GA, mgr of purchasing and contracts, 1982-86; Coors Brewing Co, Golden CO, dir of purchasing and materials, 1986—. **ORGANIZATIONS:** Mem, NAACP, 1978—; mem, Natl Assn of Purchasing Mgmt, 1978—; mem, Amer Prioduction and Inventory Control Soc, 1980—; mem, Amer Purchasing Soc, 1985—; mem, bd of dirs, 1986—, chmn, 1986-88, Rocky Mtn Regional Minority Supplier Develpment Council; mem, bd of dirs, Natl Minority Supplier Development Council, 1987—; mem, bd of dirs, Natl Minorities Business Directories, 1988—. **HONORS/ACHIEVEMENTS:** Named Man of the Year (regional), Natl Urban League, 1986; corporate citizenship award, United Indian Development Assn, 1988. **MILITARY SERVICE:** US Army, first lieutenant, 1966-69. **BUSINESS ADDRESS:** Director, Purchasing & Materials: Brewery, Coors Brewing Co, 12th and Ford Sts, BC500, Golden, CO 80401.

STRUDWICK, WARREN JAMES
Physician. **PERSONAL:** Born Dec 23, 1923, Durham, NC; married Dr Bette; children: Laura, Warren Jr, William. **EDUCATION:** Howard Univ, BS 1948, MD 1952. **CAREER:** Howard Univ, asst clinical prof; Washington DC, surgeon. **ORGANIZATIONS:** Mem Amer Coll Surgeons, Natl Med Assoc, Med Chirurgical Soc DC, DC Med Soc, Zion Bapt Church, Kappa Alpha Psi, Pigskin Club Inc, Produffers Golf Club, IN Springs Country Club. **MILITARY SERVICE:** USMCR 1943-46. **BUSINESS ADDRESS:** Surgeon, 513 Kennedy St NW, Washington, DC 20011.

STUART, IVAN I.
Military. **PERSONAL:** Married Dorthey M; children: Ivan, Jr, Connie, Selwyn, JoAnn, Desire. **CAREER:** 20 years military service retired; Floyd Co Branch NAACP, pres. **ORGANIZATIONS:** Mem bd of gov's New River Comm Action & Program; delegate Dem Com; VA Deacon Little River Bapt Ch Floyd; mem Masonic Lodge 146. **HONORS/ACHIEVEMENTS:** Letters of commendation military svc. **MILITARY SERVICE:** AUS 1943-64. **BUSINESS ADDRESS:** Rt 1 Box 62, Copper Hill, VA 24079.

STUART, MARJORIE MANN
Educator. **PERSONAL:** Born Nov 12, 1921, New Bern, NC; daughter of William Mann, MD and Clara Smith Mann; divorced; children: Sandra Stuart, R Sterling Stuart. **EDUCATION:** Hampton Inst, BS 1941; NY U, MA 1944; Universidad Inter-Americana, Mexico, PhD 1971;Univ Ghana Inst, 1971; OK Coll, 1972. **CAREER:** Hampton Inst, instr 1941-45; asso prof, cons, choreographer, performer, dance; dir childrens dance group Houston 1963-70; YMCA, instr 1952-68; consult headstart leadership devel 1966-; Univ of TX Sch of Edn, consult 1974-; choreographer educ TV series 1954; co-devel prog multi-ethnicity finearts 1974-75; TX Southern Univ professor,1948-83, retired 1983. **ORGANIZATIONS:** Mm Dance Panel of The TX Commn for the Arts & Humanities 1973-74; US Com Intl Orgn for Early Childhood Educ 1973-; Dance Adv Bd; HS Performing & Visual Arts, Houston 1972-; tech adv bd Hope Devel, Houston 1974-; exec dir Terpsilor Inc; mem Augustana Luth Ch Fellow; So Fellowshops Fund 1970. **HONORS/ACHIEVEMENTS:** Serv recognition awards TSU Chap TX Assn Coll Tchrs 1974, 175; hon mem Epsilon Phi Chpt; Sigma Delta Pi; Nat Spanish Soc; Houston Woman of Courage, Houston Woman of Courage Project and the Radcliffe Club 1985; TX Black Women's Hall of Fame, Museum of African-American Life and Culture Dallas 1986.

STUART, REGINALD A.
Reporter. **PERSONAL:** Born Nov 26, 1948, Nashville, TN; married Daryl Thomas. **EDUCATION:** TN State U, BS 1968; Columbia U, MJour 1971. **CAREER:** NY Times, business/finance news reporter 1974-; Jay Hay Whitney Found, NYC, consultant 1972-74; WSIX-AM-FM-TV, 1969-70; Nashville Tennessean, reporter 1968-69. **ORGANIZATIONS:** Mem NAACP; Big Bros; ACLU; CME. **HONORS/ACHIEVEMENTS:** Carter G Wood-

son Nat Educ Assn Award 1969; Outstanding Young Men Am 1970; Nat Headliners Award Best Team News Rpting 1970; Service Award NAACP 1974. **BUSINESS ADDRESS:** The Philadelphia Daily News, 700 National Press Building, Washington, DC 20045.

STUBBLEFIELD, JENNYE WASHINGTON
Educator, government official. **PERSONAL:** Born Mar 06, 1925, Jacksonville, FL; daughter of Marion Washington and Ira Johnson Washington; married Charles Stubblefield, Jun 26, 1954. **EDUCATION:** Tuskegee Inst, BS 1946; Rutgers State Univ, MS 1966. **CAREER:** Wm Jason H Sch, cafe mgr & voc foods tchr 1950-56; Helene Fuld Hosp Sch, 1964-70; St Francis Hosp Sch, nutritionist 1957-64; Middlesex County NJ Head Start Prog, dir food service 1966-67; Home Economics Hamilton Twp NJ, tchr 1967-71; Dept Health Recreation & Welfare Trenton, dir 1971-74; Aid to Low Income Alcoholics Trenton, dir 1974-76; Trenton Public Schools Bd of Educ, supervisor home economics & family life educ progs 1976-; City of Trenton, councilwoman 1976-. **ORGANIZATIONS:** Mem Amer Dietetic Assoc 1964-; mem Amer Home Economic Assoc 1967-; chmn County Democratic Comm Mercer County NJ 1984-85. **HONORS/ACHIEVEMENTS:** Plaques comm serv Carver Youth & Family Cntr 1983, Bilalian African Amer Conf 1983, Fairless Steel Black Caucus 1984, Mercer Co N Ward Dem Club 1984. **HOME ADDRESS:** 21 Alden Ave, Trenton, NJ 08618. **BUSINESS ADDRESS:** Supervisor-Home Economics & Family Life Education, Trenton Board of Education, 108 N Clinton Ave, Room 206, Trenton, NJ 08609.

STUBBLEFIELD, RAYMOND M.
Association executive. **PERSONAL:** Born Aug 03, 1945, Abilene, TX; married Pat. **EDUCATION:** NM Highland Coll, Taft Coll, San Diego State, BS & BA 1969. **CAREER:** United Food & Commercial Workers Union, asst dir; Comm Rel Dept Retail Clks Intl Assn, co-dir; Big Brothers, works correction officers. **HONORS/ACHIEVEMENTS:** Comm serv awd, San Diego Youth Leg 1970. **BUSINESS ADDRESS:** Assistant to Dir, UFCW, 4552 Valley View Lane, Dallas, TX 75038.

STUBBS, FRANKLIN LEE
Professional athlete. **PERSONAL:** Born Oct 21, 1960, Laurinburg, NC. **EDUCATION:** VA Tech. **CAREER:** Los Angeles Dodgers, first baseman/outfielder 1984-. **HONORS/ACHIEVEMENTS:** Named to All-Amer teams as soph at VA Tech; missed by 1 home run being 1st plyr in coll bsbl hist to hit 30 home runs & steal 30 bases; started for US bsbl squad that won 2 gold medals in internatl play 1981; 1982 winner of John Carey Award as most improved plyr in AZ Instructional League. **BUSINESS ADDRESS:** Los Angeles Dodgers, 1000 Elysian Park Ave, Los Angeles, CA 90012.

STUBBS, GEORGE WINSTON
Physician. **PERSONAL:** Born Sep 13, 1942, Brooklyn, NY; son of Connelius A Stubbs and Bernli Hinds Stubbs; married Joyce Kennedy; children: George W II, C David L. **EDUCATION:** Hunter Coll, AB 1964; Howard Univ, MD 1968. **CAREER:** Wills Em Hospital, asst srgn 1977; Med Clg of PA, asst prof of srgry 1979; G Winston Stubbs MD Ltd, pres 1982; Germantown Hosp, attndng opthlmgst. **ORGANIZATIONS:** Internatl Coll of Surgeon, flw 1979; Philadelphia Coll of Physicians, flw 1980; Amer Coll of Surgeon, flw 1981. **HONORS/ACHIEVEMENTS:** Physician recognition award 1981, 83, 87. **MILITARY SERVICE:** USPHS lt cmdr. **BUSINESS ADDRESS:** Ophthalmologist, 8121 1/2 Slenton Ave, Philadelphia, PA 19150.

STUBBS, HAROLD K.
Attorney. **PERSONAL:** Born Dec 08, 1940, FtLauderdale, FL; married Sandra Kay; children: Michele, Lisa, Malaika, Nouvelle. **EDUCATION:** Kent State Univ, BA 1963; Howard Law Sch, LLB 1966. **CAREER:** Parms Purnell Stubbs & Gilbert; atty; Criminal Div Summit Co, chief asst prosecutor; Akron Law Dept, asst prosecutor 1968-69; City of Akron, law director. **ORGANIZATIONS:** Bd mem East Akron Comm House; Akron Frontiers of Amer; mem Akron, OH, Amer Natl Bar Assns; pres Turf Builders Civic Group; bd mem Salvation Army; div chmn United Negro Coll Fund Dr 1973; West Akron YMCA 1973; chmn Akron Admin Com for the Akron Plan; bd trustees St Paul AME. **HONORS/ACHIEVEMENTS:** Who's Who in OH; Outstanding Young Americans; Kappa Alpha Psi Akron Alumni Chap Blue Key Men's Honorary; Scabbard & Blade Military Hon. **BUSINESS ADDRESS:** Law Dir, City of Akron, State Building, Akron, OH 44308.

STUBBS, LEVI
Singer. **PERSONAL:** Married Clineice; children: 5 children. **CAREER:** Member of singing group The Four Tops; voice of Audrey II in Little Shop of Horrors.

STULL, DONALD L.
Executive, architect. **PERSONAL:** Born May 16, 1937, Springfield, OH; son of Robert Stull and Ruth Stull; children: Cydney Lynn, Robert Branson, Gia Virginia. **EDUCATION:** OH State Univ, BArch 1961; Harvard Grad Sch of Design, MArch 1962. **CAREER:** George Mason Clark, architect designer 1958-62; Boston Federal Office Bldg, architects designer 1961-62; Samuel Glaser & Partners, proj dir 1962-66; Stull Assoc Inc Architects, pres 1966-83; Stull & Lee Inc Architects & Planners, pres 1984-. **ORGANIZATIONS:** Brunner Fellowship in Psychol 1961-62; bd dir Unity Bank & Trust 1968-73; mem Myer Comm Yale Univ 1970-71; Intl Platform Assn 1972-; chmn MA State Bldg Code Comm 1973-75; bd of trustees Boston Inst of Contemp Art 1973-74; visiting critic Harvard & Yale Univ; Amer Arb Assn 1973-; bishop ch in archt Yale Univ 1975; adv com Museum Sch of Boston Museum of Fine Arts 1975-77; past mem Boston Historic Landmarks Commn, Museum Afro-Amer History, Museum of Natl Ctr of Afro-Amer Artist; mem NAACP; mem Boston Art Comm; mem Presdtl Design Awds Jury 1984 and l988. **HONORS/ACHIEVEMENTS:** Ten Outstanding Young Men Boston 1970; Outstanding Young Men Amer 1970; Design Awd Jury Progressive Architr 1972; Design Awd Amer Inst Arch; Design Awd HUD Housing 1972; 100 Top Black Businesses 1973. **BUSINESS ADDRESS:** President, Stull & Lee Inc, 38 Chauncy St, Suite ll00, Boston, MA 02111.

STULL, ROBERT J.
Educator, artist. **PERSONAL:** Born Nov 04, 1935, Springfield, OH; married Bettye Joan. **EDUCATION:** OH State, BS 1962, MA 1963; Japanese Language Sch, NY U, 1964-65; Kyoto City Coll, Japan. **CAREER:** Black Studies, adj prof; OH State Univ, pres black faculty & staff caucus; Univ MI, assoc prof 1971, asst prof 1968; Kyoto City Coll of Fine Arts, lecturer 1966-67; Greenwich House Pottery, NYC, mgr 1963-65, 1967-68. **ORGANIZATIONS:** Chmn Ceramic DeptUniv MI 1969-70; chmn Grad Program Black Studies, OH StateUniv 1972-73; co-founder Gallery 7, Detroit 1968-; dir founder Gallery 7, Columbus; vice pres DARC Asso Consultants of Pub & Pvt Bus 1972-; C State dr Nat of OH Conf Artists 1973; bd dir Paul Lawrence Dunbar Cultural Center, Columbus; Eastside YMCA; consultantUniv MI Office of Minority Affairs. **HONORS/ACHIEVEMENTS:** Exhibitions; pub books. **MILITARY SERVICE:** USAF sgt. **BUSINESS ADDRESS:** Dept of Art OH State Univ, Columbus, OH.

STULL, VIRGINIA ELIZABETH
Physician. **PERSONAL:** Born May 07, 1939, Springfield, OH. **EDUCATION:** TX So U, BS 1960; Am U, 1960-61;Univ TX Med Br, MD 1966; Capital U, 1970-72. **CAREER:** Physician pvt Prac 1967-; Bur Voc Rehab, field med consult 1968-75; Columbus Bd Edn, sch phy 1968-73; ER phy 1967-71; Med Diagnostic Serv Inc, pres, owner 1975-; Dept Physical Med & Rehab, OH State Univ Med Sch, clinical prof; St Anthony Hosp. **ORGANIZATIONS:** Mem Am Med Women's Assn; AMA; Acad Med Columbus & Franklin Co; Alpha Kappa Alpha Sor; Sigma Xi Am Sci Soc. **HONORS/ACHIEVEMENTS:** Worlds' Who's Who of Women; Am Who's Who of Women; OH Who's Who; recpt Outsdng Yng Women Am Award 1975; Lambda Chi Outsdng Black Woman OH 1975; Flowers for Living Award 1975; Columbus Chpt, Nat Epicureans Inc. **BUSINESS ADDRESS:** 4656 Heaton Rd, Columbus, OH 43229.

STURDIVANT, JOHN NATHAN
Administrator. **PERSONAL:** Born Jun 30, 1938, Philadelphia, PA; children: Michelle T. **EDUCATION:** Attended Lord Fairfax Comm Coll 1974-76; Antioch Univ, BA Labor Studies 1980; attended Univ of MD 1979-80. **CAREER:** Amer Fed of Govt Employees (AFL-CIO), Local 1754 sec 1962-64, vice pres 1965-67, pres 1968-76; VA Council of Locals AFGE (AFL-CIO), vice pres 1970-73;N VA Central Labor Council (AFL-CIO), mem exec bd 1973-; Amer Fed of Govt Employees (AFL-CIO), admin asst to the exec vice pres 1980-84, exec vice pres 1984-. **ORGANIZATIONS:** Labor appointee-chmn PR subcom No Valley Manpower Planning Council CETA 1973-76; bd of dirs NW Workshop for the Physically Handicapped 1974-77; mem Soc of Fed Labor Relations Prof 1974-; mem Coalition of Black Trade Unionists 1975-; mem 8th & 10th Congress Dist Comm on Polit Educ COPE AFL-CIO 1976-; mem Fairfax Co Demo Com VA Demo State Central Comm 1977-. **HONORS/ACHIEVEMENTS:** Cert of Achievement AUS Interagency Communications Agency 1969; Cert of Recognition Gtr Wash Central Labor Council. **MILITARY SERVICE:** USAF A/2C 1956-60. **BUSINESS ADDRESS:** Executive Vice President, AFL-CIO, 1325 Massachusetts Ave NW, Washington, DC 20005.

STURGIES, CALVIN HENRY, JR.
Buisness executive. **PERSONAL:** Born Jan 13, 1933, Akron, OH. **EDUCATION:** Central State OH, BA Psychology 1959; Columbia Univ, MSc Clinical Social Work 1967, EdD Applied Human Devel 1977, Adv Prog in Org Devel & Human Resource Mgmt 1981; Yale Univ School of Med Dept of Psych, clinical internship 1973; NY Med Coll, Cert Post Grad Prog Group Psychotherapy & Psychoanalysis 1974. **CAREER:** Columbia Univ NYC, asst prof 1969-72; Commun Psych St Lukes Hosp NYC, dir 1972; Reality House Inc NYC, dep dir 1972-73; Boone Young & Assoc NYC, sr consult 1973-74; Private practice, consulting 1974-79; Levi Strauss & Co San Francisco, dir consulting serv 1979-86; Organization Planning, Analysis and Develpment Consultin Co, partner 1986-. **ORGANIZATIONS:** Faculty Univ of San Francisco 1979-; mem Amer Assoc of Univ Prof, Amer Soc for Group Psychodrama & Psychotherapy, Intl Soc for Non-Verbal Psychotherapy, Intl Registry of Organization Development Profls, Natl Org Devel Network, NY Org Devel Network, Natl Assoc of Social Workers, Acad of Certified Social Workers, Amer Personnel & Guidance Assoc, Amer Public Health Assoc. **HONORS/ACHIEVEMENTS:** The Daniel E Koshland Awd Levi Strauss & Co San Francisco 1983; "An Examination of the Relationship Between Locus of Control, Sociometric Choice, IndividualPerformance, & Group Effectiveness in Human Relations Training" unpubl doct dissertation Columbia Univ 1977; publs, "Of Races & Rights" 1976, "CompetenciesRequired of the Applied Human Devel Spec" 1976, "The Human Side of Counseling" 1974, "Humanistic Responses to Instnl Racism" 1971, "Group Work with Adolescents in a Pub Foster Care Agency" 1970, "On A Clear Day You Can See The Elevated" 1971, "The Unit Based Adolescent Couns Group, The Description & Eval of an Exper Model" 1969, " A View of Adolescence as a Devel Phonnomenon, Diagn & Treatment Implications" 1967; consulting staff on The AK Rice nine-day residential conf at Mount Holyoke Coll 1987,. **MILITARY SERVICE:** AUS sp3 Signal Corps 3 yrs. **BUSINESS ADDRESS:** OPAD, 7038 Sayre Drive, Oakland, CA 94611.

STYLES, FREDDIE L.
Artist. **PERSONAL:** Born May 12, 1944, Madison, GA. **EDUCATION:** Morris-Brown Coll, 1962-65; Atlanta School Art. **CAREER:** Artist freelance; Natl Urban League, org art Exhibition 1975; Black Artist, Carnegie Inst, lecturer 1969; Morris Brown Coll Drama Guild, costume set designer 1963-65; Expansion Arts Project Black Artists, co-dir. **ORGANIZATIONS:** Mem LA Watercolor Soc 1973-74; Cooperstown Art Assn 1974-75; High Mus of Art; Black Artists; Clarence White Contemporary Art Gallery. **HONORS/ACHIEVEMENTS:** Exhibitions, USA Artist I & II High Museum; Atlanta Univ Ann Exhibition; Johnsons Publishing Co; CTI Printing Co.

STYLES, JULIAN ENGLISH
Retired government employee. **PERSONAL:** Born Jun 18, 1924, Dallas, GA; son of Paul and Ruby; married Jennie Marine Sims; children: Gwenelle O'Neal, Teresa, Julian, Marty. **EDUCATION:** Attended, Atlanta Tailoring School, Clark College. **CAREER:** US Postal Service, distribution clerk 1950-65, window clerk 1965-83, information clerk 1983-84 (retired). **ORGANIZATIONS:** Mem NAACP, ACLU, Southern Poverty Law Ctr. **HONORS/ACHIEVEMENTS:** Service Awd US Postal Serv 1984; Certificate of Appreciation Children's Mercy Fund 1986. **MILITARY SERVICE:** AUS tech 5th grade 2 yrs; Europeak-African-Middle Eastern Theater Ribbon, Bronze Service Star, Asiatic Pacific Theater Ribbon, Philippine Liberation Ribbon, Good Conduct Medal, World War II Victory Medal, American Campaign Medal. **HOME ADDRESS:** 949 Jett St NW, Atlanta, GA 30314.

STYLES, KATHLEEN ANN
College counselor. **PERSONAL:** Born Aug 06, 1949, Baltimore, MD; daughter of Calvin P Styles and Minnie V Brown Styles. **EDUCATION:** Coppin State Coll, BS Elem Ed 1967-71, MS Special Ed/ED 1971-72; Univ of MD 1979-83. **CAREER:** Community Coll of Baltimore, employment counselor 1974-76, coll counselor 1976-76, Act dir student act 1979-80,

prof devel specialist 1981-, acting dir of off campus and ext centers 1986-. **ORGANIZATIONS:** Housing advisor US Dept Housing & Urban Devel 1972-73; instructor CETA Program 1971-72; founder Learning Intellectual Skills for Advancement 1988-; mem Natl Task Force of Career Educ 1978-80; mem of bd SSD Inc 1982-84. **HONORS/ACHIEVEMENTS:** Resolution Maryland Legislative Black Caucus 1984; sponsored workshop "Trading Places" 1984; resolution Maryland State Legislature 1978. **HOME ADDRESS:** 5709 Gwynn Oak Ave, Baltimore, MD 21207. **BUSINESS ADDRESS:** Assistant Dean, Community College of Baltimore, 2901 Liberty Heights Ave, Baltimore, MD 21215.

STYLES, MARVALENE H.
Educational administrator. **PERSONAL:** Born Feb 11, 1937, Eutaw, AL; married Dr David J Brinks. **EDUCATION:** FL St U, PhD 1969; Hrvrd U, Post-doc MLE Mgmt Inst 1979. **CAREER:** Center for Counselor Serv Career Planning & Placement San Diego St Univ, dir 1977-, prof counselor 1972-77; CA School of Professional Psychology, faculty 1974-76; FL Presby Coll St Petersburgh, dir of counselors 1969-70. **ORGANIZATIONS:** Mem Fclty Union Grad Sch 1978-; consult HEW 1970-80; Organ Cons; sntr Am Prsnnl & Gdnc Assn 1977-81; exec cncl mem Am Coll Prsnnl Assn 1977-; chrprsn Nat Prog Com Am Coll Prsnnl Assn 1979; pnlst Educ Tstng Ser Prnctn 1980; adv bd to mayor St Ptrsbrg 1971-72; chrprsn Affirm Actn AdvCom to Pres 1974-80. **HONORS/ACHIEVEMENTS:** Who's Who Amng Stdnts in Am Colls &Univ 1959; Who's Who in the So 1971; invtd mem Hon Soc of Phi Kappa Phi 1977-; pub Sevrl Artcls; natl & lcl spkr & prsntr. **BUSINESS ADDRESS:** College Ave, San Diego, CA 92182.

STYLES, RICHARD WAYNE
Clergyman. **PERSONAL:** Born Jun 22, 1939, Waterbury, CT; son of James Lawrence Styles, Sr and Helene Marie Copeland Styles; married Helen Penepole Horton; children: Richard Wayne Jr, Helene Rishae'. **EDUCATION:** Shaw Univ, AB 1965; Southeastern Baptist Theological Sem, M Div 1969; Yale Divinity Schl, further study in Continuing Education. **CAREER:** Burlington Housing Authority, bd of dirs 1977-; Burlington Christ Acad, bd of dir 1980-83; Access, bd of dir 1980-84; Allied Church of Alamance Cnty, vice chmn bd of dir 1983-; bd of dir Hospice of Alamanee County; bd of dir Fair Housing Committee; dean United Bible Inst; mem Ministeriel Fellowship Alliance of Alamanee Cnty. **ORGANIZATIONS:** Exec dir Alamance Cnty Headstart 1984-; exec comm N State Legal Aid 1980-; vlntr cnslr Alamance Cnty Court Sys 1979-83; dean of inst United Bible Inst 1980-; recruiter Crop Walk 1977-; chmn of religious activities Broadview Mid Schl 1984-; bd of dir Homecare Providers; bd of dir Care Ministry. **HONORS/ACHIEVEMENTS:** Continuing Ed Grant Yale Div Sch 1972; Good Shepherd Awd Boy Scouts of Amer 1979; volunteer counselor Awd Gov James Hunt of NC 1983; Honorary Doctorate by United Bible Inst. **HOME ADDRESS:** 612 Crestview Dr, Burlington, NC 27215. **BUSINESS ADDRESS:** Pastor, First Baptist Church, 508 Apple St, Burlington, NC 27215.

SUBRYAN, CARMEN
Educator. **PERSONAL:** Born Dec 30, 1944, Linden, Guyana;daughter of Lawrence Barclay and Sybil Allicock Barclay; divorced; children: Nicole, Natasha. **EDUCATION:** Howard Univ, Washingtn DC, BA, 1971, MA, 1973, PhD, 1983. **CAREER:** Univ of Washington DC, Washington DC, academic support, 1973-74; Howard Univ, Washington DC, instructor, program coord, 1974-. **ORGANIZATIONS:** Mem, Natl Council of Teachers of English, 1980-84, Coll Language Assn, 1981-86, Natl Assn of Developmental Educ, 1985-87, GUYAID, 1985-. **HONORS/ACHIEVEMENTS:** Phi Beta Kappa, Howard Univ, 1971; Magna Cum Laude, Howard Univ, 1971; Reprise, a book of poetry, 1984; "Walter Dean Myers," article in Dictionary of Literary Biography, 1984; "A B Spellman," article in Dictionary of Literary Biography, 1985; Woman's Survival, booklet, 1989. **HOME ADDRESS:** 11400 Pitsea Dr, Beltsville, MD 20705.

SUDARKASA, NIARA (GLORIA A. MARSHALL)
Educational administrator. **PERSONAL:** Born Aug 14, 1938, Ft Lauderdale, FL; married John L Clark; children: Michael Eric. **EDUCATION:** Fisk Univ, 1953-56; Oberlin Coll, AB 1957; Columbia Univ, MA 1959; Columbia Univ, PhD Anthropology 1964. **CAREER:** Comm for the Comparative Study of New Nations The Univ of Chicago, fellow 1963-64; NY Univ, asst prof 1964-67; Univ of MI, asst to full prof 1967-; Center for Afro-Amer & African Studies The Univ of MI, dir 1981-84; Univ of MI, assoc vice pres academic affairs, prof of anthropology; Lincoln Univ, president 1987-. **ORGANIZATIONS:** Mem African Studies Assn 1959-69, 1982-; fellow Amer Anthrop Assn 1964-; Fellow Amer Anthrop Assn Exec Bd 1972-75; chmn State of MI Comm on Minorities Women & Handicappers in Higher Ed 1984-; mem bd of dir Ann Arbor Comm Ctr 1983-; mem Assn of Black Anthropologists; mem American Assoc for HigherEduc 1986. **HONORS/ACHIEVEMENTS:** Ford Found Scholarship for Early Admiss to Coll 1953-57; Ford Found Foreign Area Training Fellowship 1960-63; John Hay Whitney Oppty Fellowship 1959-60; Carnegie Found Study of New Nation Fellowship 1963-64; Social Science Rsch Council Fellowship 1973-74; Sr Fulbright Rsch Scholarship 1982-83; Achievement Awds from Links, Alpha Kappa Alpha, Zeta Phi Beta, Elks, City of Ft Lauderdale; publications on African Women, West African Migration, Afro-Amer and African Family and Minorities Organization in higher education. **BUSINESS ADDRESS:** University President, Lincoln University, Lincoln University, PA 19352.

SUDBURY, LESLIE G.
Chemist. **PERSONAL:** Born May 11, 1939, Meridan, MS; married Audrey Faulkens; children: Leslie D, Pamela M, David G, Gloria M. **EDUCATION:** Xavier U, BSc Chemistry 1961; Notre Dame Grad School, Chemistry. **CAREER:** Whitehall Labs, pharm control chemist 1961-65; Miles Labs Inc, rsch chemist 1966-73, supervisor control chemist 1973-78, mgr div control 1978-82, mgr biological evaluation 1982-85; ICN Immuno; Operation Manager 1985- . **ORGANIZATIONS:** Mem Amer Chem Soc 1966-; sec & editor newsletter Amer Chem Soc St Joseph Valley Sec 1979-83; mem Amer Soc of Quality Control 1982-86; coach IYHLSoccer 1980-82; co-chmn BAC Inter Community Commn 1980-82; bd dirs NOBC & treas 1977-85; bd mem NBLCC 1976-85; mem Knights of Peter Claver 1984-85;Sec Council #251 KPC. **HONORS/ACHIEVEMENTS:** Outstanding Service Amer Chem Soc St Joe Valley Sec 1981; Outstanding Service NBLCC Midwest Regional 1978; Service St Augustine Parish South Bend IN 1974& 1976. **MILITARY SERVICE:** AUS spl 4th 1962-64. **HOME ADDRESS:** 220 Terrance, Naperville, IL 60565.

SUDDERTH, WILLIAM H.
Business executive. **PERSONAL:** Born Nov 29, 1924, Jersey City, NJ; son of William H Sudderth, Sr and Frankie Little; married Estelle McGaney; children: William III, Philip, June, Theresa. **EDUCATION:** Pace Univ, attended 1952-55; Monroe Flegenheimer Sch of Ins, attended 1957; Attended, Dale Carnegie Inst. **CAREER:** Gen Ins, agt broker. **ORGANIZATIONS:** Past pres Exchange Club of White Plains 1976-77; past pres NY State Dist Exchange Clubs 1983-84; Prince Hall Grand Lodge; Shriner; Mason; Eastern Star; firecommr Fairview Fire Dist; Greenburgh Housing Auth; NAACP; NYS Fire Chiefs Assn; Natl Assn of Housing & Redevel Officials; Ins Brokers of NYC; Pete Mete Chap 98 Disable Amer Vets Assn; received the 33 deg in Masonery Scotich Rite. **HONORS/ACHIEVEMENTS:** Asst & Dirs Awd Dale Carnegie Courses; Bugler Awd White Plains; NY State Senate Achievement Awd 1984; Westchester Co Exec Cert of Appreciation 1984; USA Awd The President of the United States of Amer Awds the Private Sector Initiative Commendation in recog of exemplary comm serv in the finest amer tradition 1984 signed by Pres Ronald Reagan. **MILITARY SERVICE:** Army SF Band & Engrs. **BUSINESS ADDRESS:** Agent/Broker, Genl Insurance, 32 Longdale Ave, White Plains, NY 10607.

SUGGS, ROBERT CHINELO
Educator. **PERSONAL:** Born Dec 23, 1943, Newport, RI; married Mary Louise Morrison; children: Lawrence, Sarah, Elizabeth, James. **EDUCATION:** Barrington Coll, BA 1967; State Univ of NY at Albany, MS 1971, EdD 1979. **CAREER:** Dept of Counselor Ed State Univ, asst prof 1972-80; Comm Bible Church, pastor 1974-80; Dept of Counselor Ed Millersville Univ, adjunct asst prof 1982-85; Psychophysiological Clinic Univ of MD, clinical asst prof 1983-85; Crossroads Counseling Assocs, therapist 1983-; Christian Assoc of Psych Studies, newsletter editor 1983-; Messiah Coll, assoc prof of psychology. **HONORS/ACHIEVEMENTS:** Doctoral fellow State Univ of NY at Albany 1971-73; outstanding teacher Messiah Coll 1981; Named to Top 500 High School Basketball Players in the US Dell Mag 1963. **BUSINESS ADDRESS:** Prof of Psychology, Messiah College, Dept of Behavioral Science, Grantham, PA 17027.

SUGGS, WILLIAM ALBERT
Educator, pastor. **PERSONAL:** Born Jun 01, 1922, Capleville, TN; married Carnelia Tate. **EDUCATION:** Tskg Inst, 1943; TN St U, 1949, MS 1955. **CAREER:** Rchlnd Vocational School, teacher supr 1949-53; Hamilton HS, teacher dept chmn 1955-; Friendship Bapt Church, pastor. **ORGANIZATIONS:** Mem Memphis W TN TN Nat Educ Assns; Nat & Cncl Soc Stds; pres Memphis & Shlby Co Almn Assn 1970; pres Suggs Entrprss; mem Hmltn PTA. **HONORS/ACHIEVEMENTS:** Cert of Merit Hmltn HS 1974; num publs in field. **MILITARY SERVICE:** QMC sgt 1943-45. **BUSINESS ADDRESS:** Friendship Baptist Church, 1355 Vollintine Ave, Memphis, TN.

SULLIVAN, ALLEN R.
Educational administrator. **PERSONAL:** Born Jul 15, 1941, Cambridge, MA; son of Fernando Sullivan and Dorothy Sullivan; married Deborah M Haywood; children: Raylene, Reginald. **EDUCATION:** NE Univ, BS 1965; Syracuse Univ, MS 1966, Ph D 1970. **CAREER:** New England Home for Little Wanders, assn spvr res 1962-65; Syracuse Public Schl, spcl ed tchr 1966-68; Univ of MN, dir training of tchrs 1971-75; Univ of MN, assoc prof psych ed studies 1970-75; Dallas Independent School District, asst supt instructional support services, executive director student services. **ORGANIZATIONS:** Advsry bd Ft Worth State Schl 1978-; bd dir CT Gen of N Amer Cigna 1984-; min advsry comm Cncl for Excptnl Chldrn 1984-; bd chmn Jr Black Acad Of Arts & Letters 1984-; bd Friends of the Art Dist 1984-86; bd of dirs Dallas County Mental Health & Mental Retardation; Omega Psi Phi Fraternity. **HONORS/ACHIEVEMENTS:** Who's Who Child Dvlmnt 1976; Who's Who South & Southwest 1980; Who's Who in MN 1975; Men of Achvmnt Intrnl Biog Cntr London England 1977. **BUSINESS ADDRESS:** Executive Director Student Services, Dallas Independent Sch Dist, 3700 Ross Ave, Dallas, TX 75204.

SULLIVAN, CARL CALVIN
Professional athlete. **PERSONAL:** Born Apr 30, 1962, San Jose, CA. **EDUCATION:** San Jose State. **CAREER:** Oakland Invaders, defensive end 1984-. **HONORS/ACHIEVEMENTS:** As a sr tight end was named honorable mention All-Am and All-PCAA.

SULLIVAN, EDWARD JAMES
Dentist. **PERSONAL:** Born May 07, 1932, Cleveland, OH; married Janet Grant; children: Kathi Ann, Steven, Alicia. **EDUCATION:** Ohio State Univ, PS 1956, DDS 1969. **CAREER:** Univ Hospitals Ohio State, pharmacist 1957-64; Columbus Health Dept, dentist 1969-73; Columbus State Inst, dentist 1973-79; Dept of Pedodontics OH State Univ, clinical instructor 1981-; Private Practice, dentist 1969-. **ORGANIZATIONS:** Bd mem South State Health Ctr 1975-77; mem bd of dirs Hilltop Health Ctr 1977; delegate Natl Assoc of Neighborhood Health Ctrs 1977-80; mem bd Columbus Area Comm Health Ctr 1978-81. **HONORS/ACHIEVEMENTS:** Certificate of Appreciation Hilltop Health Ctr 1977; Mayor's Voluntary Serv Awd City of Columbus 1980. **BUSINESS ADDRESS:** 1800 S Parsons Ave, Columbus, OH 43207.

SULLIVAN, J. CHRISTOPHER
Actor/performer. **PERSONAL:** Born Sep 15, 1932, Greenville, TX; son of Jack Sullivan and Veola Sullivan; married Eloise Hicks (divorced); children: Jerome. **EDUCATION:** Prairie View A&M Univ, BA 1953; Univ of TX, MA 1958, PhD 1964. **CAREER:** Abilene City Schools, teacher 1955-58; Dallas Ind Schools, teacher 1961-62; Prairie View A&M Univ, dir student acts 1962-63; Univ of TX, teacher 1963-64; Screen Actors Guild, professional actor. **ORGANIZATIONS:** Mem Screen Actors Guild 1968-, Amer Federation of TV & Radio Artists 1970-, Acad of TV Arts & Scis 1975-; exec bd 1980-87, interpreter French 1984 Los Angeles Olympics Org Comm; vice pres Beverly Hills/Hollywood NAACP 1984-87. **HONORS/ACHIEVEMENTS:** Distinguished Alumni Prairie View A&M Phi Beta Sigma Inc 1980; Phi Beta Kappa; Merit of Achievement Drama Univ of TX 1984; Image Awd/Best Actor NAACP Beverly Hills 1986. **MILITARY SERVICE:** Infantry capt 1953-57. **HOME ADDRESS:** 6326 Lexington Ave, Los Angeles, CA 90038.

SULLIVAN, JOHN CALVIN
Professional athlete. **PERSONAL:** Born Oct 15, 1961, Hartford, CT. **EDUCATION:** California, Pol Sci. **CAREER:** Oakland Invaders, safety 1984-. **HONORS/ACHIEVEMENTS:** Honorable mention All-Pac 10 as soph and jr.

SULLIVAN, LEON HOWARD
Clergyman, organization head. **PERSONAL:** Born Oct 16, 1922, Charleston, WV; married Grace Banks; children: Howard, Julie, Hope. **EDUCATION:** West Virginia State College, BA, 1943; Union Theological Seminary, 1945; Columbia Univ, MA, 1947; Virginia Union Univ, DD. **CAREER:** Zion Bapt Church Phila, pastor 1950-88; pastor emeritus, 1988-. **ORGANIZATIONS:** Founder/chmn Zion Home for Ret 1960-; founder, dir, bd chmn, Opp Indus Cntrs of Am Inc, 1964, Zion Investment Assoc Inc, Progress Aerospace Inc; dir Gen Motors Corp, Mellon Bank Corp; co-founder of Self-Help. **HONORS/ACHIEVEMENTS:** Russwurm Awd, Natl Publisher's Assn, 1963; Amer Exemplar Medal, 1969; Philadelphia Book Award, 1966; Philadelphia Fellowship Commn Awd, 1964; Leon Howard Sullivan Chair, School of Social Welfare, Univ of Wisconsin, 1976; Franklin D Roosevelt Four Freedom Medal Award, 1987; Leon Howard Sullivan Scholarship Fund established at Bentley Coll, Massachusetts, 1988; Hon LLD Dartmouth Coll, Princeton Univ, Swarthmore Coll; Bordoin Coll, Denison Univ, Gannon Coll, Temple Univ; Hon EdD, Judson Coll. **BUSINESS ADDRESS:** Progress Plaza Shopping Center, 1501 N Broad St, Philadelphia, PA 19122. *

SULLIVAN, LOUIS W.
Educational administrator, physician. **PERSONAL:** Born Nov 03, 1933, Blakely, GA; married Eva Williamson; children: Paul, Shanta, Halsted. **EDUCATION:** Morehouse Coll, BS (Magna Cum Laude) 1954; Bostun Univ, MD (Cum Laude) 1958. **CAREER:** Boston City Hosp, Boston MA, dir hematology, 1973-75; Boston Univ, Boston MA, prof medicine and physiology, 1974-75; Morehouse Coll of Medicine, Atlanta GA, dean 1975-; US Dept of Health and Human Services, Washington DC, head, 1989- . **ORGANIZATIONS:** Ad hoc panel on blood diseases Natl Heart Lung Blood Disease Bur 1973; mem sickle cell anemia adv com NIH 1974-75; mem Natl Adv Rsch Cncl 1977; mem Amer Soc of Hematology, Amer Soc Clin Investigation, Inst Medicine, Phi Beta Kappa, Alpha Omega Alpha. **HONORS/ACHIEVEMENTS:** Published over 50 articles in medical journals & magazines 1957-77; pub "The Education of Black Health Professionals," 1977; progress report The Sch of Medicine Morehouse Coll 1977; num professorships & attending physician positions. **BUSINESS ADDRESS:** Dean, Morehouse College, School of Medicine, 223 Chestnut St, Atlanta, GA 30314. *

SULLIVAN, MARTHA ADAMS (MECCA)
Social worker. **PERSONAL:** Born Jun 13, 1952, Philadelphia, PA; daughter of Leon H Adams and Lillie B Foster Adams; married James Pearley Sullivan; children: Mecca Jamilah, Malik Khalil. **EDUCATION:** NYU Washington Square College, BA 1974; Hunter Coll Sch of Social Work, MSW 1976; ABD 1989-. **CAREER:** Henry St Settlement Comm Consultation Ctr, supervising social worker/family therapist 1976-83; Private Practice, psychotherapist 1981-; Gouverneur Diagnostic & Treatment Ctr Dept of Psychiatry, asst dir 1983-. **ORGANIZATIONS:** Founder and mem Source, The Black Women Therapists' Collective 1978-; consultant Center for Women in Govt 1985-; mem Natl Assn of Social Workers 1985-; chairperson Manhattan Geriatric Comm 1986-; mem Natl Caucus and Center on the Black Aged. **HONORS/ACHIEVEMENTS:** Co-author "Women of Color & Feminist Practice," in Not For Women Only NASW Publ 1986. **BUSINESS ADDRESS:** Asst Dir of Psychiatry, Gouverneur Diag/Trtmt Center, 227 Madison St #329, New York, NY 10002.

SULLIVAN, RICHARD H.
Educator. **PERSONAL:** Born Apr 27, 1941, Laurens, SC; married Rubye Jones; children: Richard Ali, Jamal Obi. **EDUCATION:** SC St Coll, BS 1963; Howrd U, PhD 1972. **CAREER:** Navel Ordanence Sta Indn Hd MD, research chem 1966-71; Fyttvll St Univ, asst prof 1972-73; Jackson St Univ, asso prof 1973-; Inst of Ser to Educ Wash DC, prog assoc 1974; Clemson Univ, lecturer 1972; NC A&T, lecturer 1973; Jackson State Univ, dir marc/hurt prog 1977-, prof and chrmn of chemistry 1983-. **ORGANIZATIONS:** Prtcpnt in smmr phys sci Workshop of Inst for Serv to Edn; ACS SoEstrn Regn 1973; mem Am Chem Soc; Am Assn for Adv of Sci; Nat Inst of Sci; Beta Kappa Chi; Kappa Alpha Psi. **HONORS/ACHIEVEMENTS:** Super Ach Awd Nvl Ordnnc Sta 1970; Promted to Prog Assoc 1974. **MILITARY SERVICE:** AUS 1962-65. **BUSINESS ADDRESS:** Chemistry Dept Chairman, Jackson State University, PO Box 17636, Jackson, MS 39217.

SULLIVAN, ZOLA JILES
Educator, educational administrator. **PERSONAL:** Born Nov 05, 1921, Tallahassee, FL; married Dr William David; children: Yolands Someya, William David II. **EDUCATION:** FL A MUniv Tllhs, BS MS 1950; FiskUniv Nshvl;Univ of MI Ann Arbor; OxfrdUniv Engl, 1965;Univ of IL Urbn Champ, PhD 1970. **CAREER:** Broward Co Public School Sys Ft Lauderdale, teacher 1942-43; Palm Beach Co Elementary School, teacher 1943-50; FL A&M Univ, instructor 1950-53; Dade Co Public Sys, prin elementary teacher 1953-71; FL Intl Univ Miami FL, asst prof educ 1971-74, assoc prof educ 1974-. **ORGANIZATIONS:** Chmn Num Chldhd Educ Com; consult Num Educ Assn; spkr lectr Num Elmntry Schs; coor Num Educ Wrkshps; mem Num Educ Assns; spkr Num Ch Grps;mem Rchmnd Hghts Women's Club FL; mem Alpha Phi Alpha Frat; Iota Pi Lambda Chap Miami; mem bd of dirs Sickle Cell Anm Assn Dade Co 1978; mem FL Intl Task Force on Needs Assessment to Improve Educational Opportunities in Guinea. **HONORS/ACHIEVEMENTS:** Recip num schol & career opport cert; pub num papers on edn; NDEA FellwshpUniv of IL 1969-70; inttr various prog &Univ class; recip num plqs & cert for outstndng work; listed in Who's Who and Why of Successful FL Woman, 1985; FL Governor's Awd for Outstanding Achievement 1986; Outstanding Serv to African Educators Political Leaders and Students, recognized by FL Chapter of the Natl Council of Intl Visitors. **BUSINESS ADDRESS:** Assoc Professor of Education, FL International Unviersity, Tamiami Trail, Miami, FL 33199.

SULLY, IVORY ULYSSES
Professional athlete. **PERSONAL:** Born Jan 20, 1957, Salisbury, MD. **EDUCATION:** Delaware, BEd. **CAREER:** L A Rams, safety 1979.

SULTON, JACQUELINE RHODA
Physician/pediatrician. **PERSONAL:** Born Mar 27, 1957, Detroit, MI; daughter of Dr & Mrs Nathaniel Holloway; married Francis Arnold Sulton; children: Carmen Denease, Jonathan Francis. **EDUCATION:** Spelman Coll, BS 1978; Meharry Medical Coll, DM 1982. **CAREER:** Tulane Univ Sch of Medicine, internship/residency 1982-85; Robinson-Gouri Pediatric Group New Orleans, pediatrician 1984-85; Morehouse Sch of Medicine, student preceptor; Oakhurst Comm Health Ctr, staff pediatrician 1985-88; private practice Pediatric & Adolescent Medicine, Decatur GA. **ORGANIZATIONS:** Mem Amer Med Assoc, Alpha Kappa Alpha Sor, Atlanta Medical Assoc Inc. **HONORS/ACHIEVEMENTS:** Atlanta Univ Ctr Biology Honor Soc 1976; Outstanding Academic Performance in Biology 1977; life mem NAACP; Certificate of Merit Student Rsch 1980. **BUSINESS ADDRESS:** Private Physician, Pediatric and Adolescent Medicine, 1760 Candler Rd, Suite D, Decatur, GA 30032.

SULTON, JOHN D.
Business executive. **PERSONAL:** Born Aug 18, 1912, St George, SC; son of John Jacob and Daisey; married Kathleen Hunter; children: Linda N Wosu. **EDUCATION:** SC State Coll, BA 1934; KS State Univ, BA 1941. **CAREER:** Office of Hilyard R Robinson, architect 1941-42; US Fed Pub Housing Authority, 1943-44; Fed Works Agency, 1945; Hilyard R Robinson, 1946-63; Cassell-Gray-Sulton, partner 1963-64; Sulton Campbell & Assocs, 1965-71, pres 1971-80, chmn 1980-. **ORGANIZATIONS:** Mem Natl Tech Assn 1945; Nat Treas 1964-74; Corp mem Amer Inst Architects 1955; mem FAIA Amer Inst of Arch 1982; mem Washington Bldg Congress 1971; Washington Bd of Trade 1972. **HONORS/ACHIEVEMENTS:** Hon Mention Awd Ch Architectural Guild Am 1957; Prestressed Concrete Inst Awd; HUD's Operations Breakthrough 1981; KS State Univ Hon for Distinguished Serv in Arch & Design 1981. **BUSINESS ADDRESS:** President, Sulton Campbell & Assocs, 2901 Druid Park Dr, Suite 208B, Baltimore, MD 21215.

SUMLER-LEWIS, JANICE L.
College professor, attorney. **PERSONAL:** Born Aug 10, 1948, New York, NY; daughter of Ernest Sumler and Lucille Jones Sumler; divorced. **EDUCATION:** UCLA, Los Angeles CA, BA, 1970, MA, 1971; Georgetown Univ, Washington DC, PhD, 1978; UCLA School of Law, Los Angeles CA, JD, 1985. **CAREER:** Spelman Coll, Atlanta GA, visiting prof, 1980-81; Reginald Heber Smith Fellowship, legal aid of Los Angeles, 1985-86; Clark Atlanta Univ, Atlanta GA, assoc prof, 1986-. **ORGANIZATIONS:** Natl vice dir, Assn of Black Women Historians, 1986-88, natl dir, 1988-90; mem, Georgia Assn of Black Women Attorneys, 1987-; recruiter, Georgetown Univ, 1988-. **HONORS/ACHIEVEMENTS:** Lubic Memorial Law Scholarship, 1983-84; Southern Fellowship Fund Summer Research Award, 1988; "The Forten-Purvis Women and the Antislavery Crusade," Journal of Negro History, 1981; "Personhood and Citizenship: Black Women Litigants, 1867-1890," forthcoming.

SUMMER, DONNA ANDREA
Musician, singer. **PERSONAL:** Born Nov 30, 1948, Boston, MA; married Bruce Sudano; children: Mimi, Brook Lyn, Amanda Grace. **CAREER:** Casablanca Record & Filmworks, "Hair", Germany & Vienne, "Godspell" Vienne Germany Switzerland Musicals, recording artist, performer 1969-74; "Porgy & Bess" Vienne Folks Opera, "Showboat" Vienne Folks Opera Vienne Austria, "The Me Nobody Knows" Germany, "After Dark", "Love To Love Ya Baby", performer, recording artist;Theme for "The Deep", co-author. **HONORS/ACHIEVEMENTS:** Narm Awd Female Soul Artist 1977; Gold Albums, Love To Love You Baby, Love Trilogy, Four Seasons of Love; #1 Top New Female Vocalist 1975; #1 Top Female Vocalist; Record World Annual Directory Awds; Best Female Rock Vocalist 1979; named Favorite Female Pop Vocalist Amer Music Awds 1979; Favorite Female Vocalist of-Soul Music 1979; Favorite Pop Single 1979; named Best Selling Black Music album for Female Artist Natl Assoc Record Merchandizers 1979; Best Selling album for Female Artist 1980; Ampex Golden Reel Awd for Single On the Radio 1980, for album On the Radio, for album Bad Girls; best rock performance Best of Las Vegas Jimmy Awd 1980; Grammy Awd for Best Inspirational Performance 1984. **BUSINESS ADDRESS:** c/o Munao Mgmt, 1224 N Vine St, Los Angeles, CA 90038.

SUMMEROUR-PERRY, LISA
Spokesmodel. **PERSONAL:** Born Sep 05, 1962, Somers Point, NJ. **EDUCATION:** Howard Univ, attended 1980-82. **CAREER:** Prudential Realty Group, legal sec 1983-84; Sughrue Mion Zinn Macpeak & Seas, legal sec 1984; Lenox China/Crystal, sec 1985; Sands Hotel Casino, execsecty 1985-86. **ORGANIZATIONS:** USO participation toured the Mediterranean on the 1st Annual Miss USA USO/DOD Tour 1986, USO Show Fort Eustis Hampton VA 1986, USO Show Celebrating the commissioning of the USS Roosevelt 1986, USO Show 1987 Natl Salute to Hospitalized Veterans 1987. **HONORS/ACHIEVEMENTS:** Natl Quill & Scroll; Southern Univ Academic Achievement Awd. **HOME ADDRESS:** 101 Kensington Ave, Trenton, NJ 08618.

SUMMERS, DAVID STEWART
Physician, educator. **PERSONAL:** Born Feb 16, 1932, Canton, OH; son of William Summers (deceased) and Stuard Jordan Summers (deceased); married Ernestine Cumber, Nov 30, 1957; children: David S II, Timothy C. **EDUCATION:** VA State Univ, BS 1954; VA Union Univ (Electives only) 1954-55; Univ of VA Sch of medicine, MD 1959. **CAREER:** SUNY Upstate Med Ctr at Syracuse, intern resident & instr 1959-63; Univ Rochester Sch Med & Strong Meml Hosp Dept of Neurology, instr asst prof dir EEG labs 1967-72; McGuire VA Hosp, neurologist 1967; Univ Utah Coll Med Dept of Neurology, asst prof & electroencephalographer 1972-76; DHEW, natl cncl serv & facilities devel disabled 1974-77; State of Utah, gov's black policy cncl 1975-77; Univ of Utah, affirm action comm 1975-77; Hill AFB Hosp & SLC VA Hosp, neurology consult 1972-76; St Vincent Health Ctr, neurologist & electroencephalographer. **ORGANIZATIONS:** Mem Amer Acad of neurology 1962-; mem Erie Co & PA Med Socs 1976-; neurology consul Hamot Med Ctr Metro Hlth Ctr Millcreek Hosp 1978-, Great Lakes Rehab Hosp 1986-; lectr neurology Gannon Univ & Gannon-Hahnemann Med Prog 1977-; lectr neurology St Vincent Health Ctr CME Prog 1976-; mem E Assn of Electroencephalographers 1971-; mem Amer Epilepsy Soc 1971-; mem Epilepsy Found of Amer 1972-; mem Natl Med Assn 1977-; life mem Erie NAACP, Univ VA Alumni Assn 1976-; cncl mem Immanuel Lutheran Ch 1980-86; mem bd dir Natl Multiple Sclerosis Soc NW PA Chap 1986-. **HONORS/ACHIEVEMENTS:** Publs of Neurology topics 1964-81; Abby Aldrich Rockefeller Scholar, John D Rockefeller, 3rd 1951-54. **MILITARY SERVICE:** AUS Med Corps capt 3 yrs; Natl Def Serv Medal; Cert of Achievement-Germany 1967. **HOME ADDRESS:** 1520 Pasadena Dr, Erie, PA 16505. **BUSINESS ADDRESS:** Neurologist, 2314 Sassafras St, Suite 206, Erie, PA 16502.

SUMMERS, EDNA WHITE
Elected official. **PERSONAL:** Born Sep 04, 1919, Evanston, IL; married William J Summers; children: Michael, Stephen, Elizabeth, Jerome. **EDUCATION:** Roosevelt Univ, Univ of Wisc - Milw,. **CAREER:** City of Evanston, alderman 1968-81; State of Ill, social service 1974-85; City of Evanston, Township Supervisor 1985-. **ORGANIZATIONS:** Real estate Evanston-North Shore board; trustee Ebenezer Ame Church; lecturer Early Childhood De-

velopment; life mem Ill Parent-Teachers, NAACP - Evanston; mem Zonta-International. **HONORS/ACHIEVEMENTS:** Service Awd Evanston NAACP; Woman of the Year Delta Sigma Theta and Mens Social Club. **HOME ADDRESS:** 1941 Hartrey Ave, Evanston, IL 60201.

SUMMERS, JOSEPH W.
State representative. **PERSONAL:** Born Mar 08, 1930, Indianapolis, IN; son of Joe and Willie Mae Johnson; married Joyce Benson, 1948; children: 2. **EDUCATION:** Indiana University; Indiana College of Mortuary Science, Indianapolis, IN, graduate. **CAREER:** Precinct committeeman in Indianapolis, 1952; ward chairman; Summers Funeral Chapel, Indianapolis, IN, owner and operator, 1962—; Indianapolis Board of Public Safety, Indianapolis, IN, member, 1965-68; Marion County Government, IN, chief deputy coroner, 1967-78; Indiana State Government, Indianapolis, IN, state representative, 1977-86. **ORGANIZATIONS:** National convention chmn, NAACP, 1973; Better Business Bureau; Funeral Directors Assn; member of board, Alpha Home; member of board, Sicle Cell Center; member of board, Indianapolis-Scarborough Peace Games; member, African Methodist Episcopal Church; member, Indiana Black Legislative Caucus. **BUSINESS ADDRESS:** 1146 Brook Ln, Indianapolis, IN 46202. *

SUMMERS, RETHA
Consultant. **PERSONAL:** Born May 04, 1953, Goldsboro, NC; daughter of Harvey Summers (deceased) and Aletha Summers. **EDUCATION:** NC A&T State Univ, BS Bus Admin 1971-75; Campbell Univ, currently pursuing MEd Counseling & Guidance. **CAREER:** Employment Security Commission, employment interviewer 1976-77; Carolina Telephone, telephone co rep 1977-, engineering clerk, currently. **ORGANIZATIONS:** Past pres Amer Bus Women's Assoc 1984; mem Amer Assoc of Counseling & Development 1987; dir Future Christian Leaders of Amer 1987-. **HONORS/ACHIEVEMENTS:** Most Outstanding bus Student Awd North Lenoir High/Future Bus Leaders of Amer 1971; Banner Awd and Woman of the Year Awd Amer Bus Women's Assoc/Ram Neuse Chap Kingston NC 1984. **HOME ADDRESS:** PO Box 366, La Grange, NC 28551.

SUMMERS, RODGER
Educational administrator. **PERSONAL:** Born Jan 10, 1945, Philadelphia, PA; married Dr Pamela F; children: Megan KF. **EDUCATION:** Cheyney Univ, BS Ed, English 1968; Univ of VT, MA English 1972; IN Univ, EdD Higher Ed 1980. **CAREER:** Univ of VT, asst dean of students 1974-79, assoc dean of students 1979-81; North Adams State Coll, vice pres student affairs 1981-84; West Chester Univ, vice pres student affairs 1984-. **ORGANIZATIONS:** Mem Salvation Army Bd 1981; NASPA bd of dir, mem at large Natl Assoc of Student Personnel Admin 1983; bd mem YMCA 1985. **HONORS/ACHIEVEMENTS:** Co-author "Commuter Marriages" VT Journal 1981. **BUSINESS ADDRESS:** Vice President Student Affairs, West Chester University, Sykes Union Bldg, West Chester, PA 19383.

SUMMERS, TIMOTHY
Psychiatrist. **PERSONAL:** Born Sep 09, 1942, Jackson, MS; divorced; children: Rachael D, Stephanie N, William J, Timothy C, Zachary. **EDUCATION:** Tougaloo Coll, 1963-64;Univ of IL, 1964-66; Jackson State U, BS 1969;Univ of MS Sch of Med, MD 1974;Univ of MS Sch of Med, residen psychiatry 1974-76; Menninger Sch of Psych, 1976-77. **CAREER:** State Hosp of Whitefield MS, staff spych 1974; Psychiat Educ Br Natl Inst of Mental Health, consult 1977-78; Assem of Amer Psychiat Assoc, minor rep 1977-81; Menninger Found CF Menninger Hosp, staff psych 1977-; Human Care Inc, medical dir 1984-. **ORGANIZATIONS:** PresUniv of MS Sch of Med; chap stud Natl Med Assoc 1971-72; mem bd of dir MS Min Med Educ Found 1976-; mem bd of dir Jackson StateUniv Drug Alch and Abuse Prog; chrpsn Amer Psych Assoc Comm of Resid 1977-; liason Am Psych Assoc Assem Exec Comm 1976-; liason Am Assoc of Psych training dir 1975-77; chf consultUniv of MS Sch of Med 1972-; mem Am Psych Assn; Nat Inst of Ment hlth; flwsp select advis comm 1977; Urban Leag; NAACP; col Staff of Cliff Finch Gov of MS; MS Psy Assn; Am Med Assn; Assn of Psy Training dirs; Black Psys of Am; mem World Federation of Mental Health,Intl Soc for the Study of Pain, World Medical Soc. **HONORS/ACHIEVEMENTS:** Solomon Fuller flwsp award 1976. **MILITARY SERVICE:** USAF 1959-61. **BUSINESS ADDRESS:** Medical Dir, Human Care, Inc, 1058 Riverside Plaza, Jackson, MS 39208.

SUMMERS, WILLIAM E., III
Broadcast executive, pastor. **PERSONAL:** Born Oct 17, 1918; children: William, IV, Seretha, Sherryl. **EDUCATION:** KY St Coll; Coll of Scrip;Univ of Rome. **CAREER:** Summrs Brdcstng Inc, pres part owner; Radio Sta WLOU, gen mgr, sprts annouc 1951, num other pos 1972; St Pauls AME Ch Louis, pastor. **ORGANIZATIONS:** Mem bd KY Brdcstrs Assn; bd of dir Met YMCA; mem OvrsrsUniv of Louis. **BUSINESS ADDRESS:** 2549 S 3 St, Louisville, KY 40208.

SUMMERS, WILLIAM E., IV
City official. **PERSONAL:** Born Mar 11, 1943, Louisville, KY; son of William E Summers III and Sallie Sellers Summers; married Paulette Sweatt Summers, Jun 30, 1966; children: Kimberly, William, Anthony. **EDUCATION:** Central State Univ, Wilberforce OH, 1961-62; Univ of Maryland, Far East Extension, 1964-65; Univ of Louisville, Louisville KY, 1970-71; Kentucky State Univ, Frankfort KY, 1974-76. **CAREER:** City of Louisville, Louisville KY, admin asst to Mayor, 1968-74; State of Kentucky, Frankfort KY, civil rights compliance officer, 1974-76; City of Louisville, Louisville KY, Dept of Sanitation, dir, 1976-79; Mr Klean's Janitor & Maintenance Serv, Louisville KY, vice pres, 1979-82; Property Maintenance & Mgmt Inc, Louisville KY, pres, 1982-86; City of Louisville, Louisville KY, Internal Operations, chief of staff, 1986-. **ORGANIZATIONS:** Bd of dirs, NAACP, Louisville Urban League, Big Brothers/Big Sisters, Kentuckiana Girl Scout Council; bd of overseers, Bellermine Coll; mem, Urban Affairs Assn, 1986, Soc for Public Admin, 1986, Conference of Minority Public Admin, 1987; bd of dir, Humana Hospital-Audubon, 1988, Natl Forum for Black Public Admin, 1989; mem, Council on Higher Educ & Comm on Equal Opportunities. **HONORS/ACHIEVEMENTS:** Leadership Louisville, Louisville Chamber of Commerce, 1981; Leadership Kentucky, Kentucky Chamber of Commerce, 1987; People to Watch, Louisville Magazine; several training certificates. **MILITARY SERVICE:** AUS, E-5, 1963-65. **BUSINESS ADDRESS:** Chief of Staff, Internal Operations, Mayor's Office, City of Louisville, 601 W Jefferson St, Louisville, KY 40202.

SUMMERVILLE, TOMMIE LEWIS
Educator. **PERSONAL:** Born Jul 29, 1928, Aliceville, AL; married Delessie Willis; children: Lynn, Wendell, Evelyn, Tommie. **EDUCATION:** AL A & M, BS 1956; Wayne St U, MEd 1959. **CAREER:** Inkster Public School, teacher; Great Lakes Mutual Life Ins Co; Fltr Qun Hm Sntn Sys; Detroit Public School, sub teacher; Smmrvll Party Store, owner. **ORGANIZATIONS:** Pres Inkster Fedn of Tchr AFL-CIO; vice pres MI Fedn of Tchr AFL-CIO; mem NAACP; Dtrt Inkster Chpts; Inkster-Drbrn Hum Rel Cncl; chmn 8th Grd Prfrmnc Objctvs Com St Bd of Edn; Mddl Sch Task Frc Com St Bd of Edn, co-chmn MFT Resol Com, chmn MFT Pol Actn Fund Rsng Com; NAACP Resol Com Nat Conv St Bd of Educ 2yrs; org Summervll Ins Agy, Summervll Prty Str, Summervll Entrprs; del Am Fedn of Tchr Educ Surv Day Conf Wash 1973; Am Fedn of Tchr Resol Com 3 Nat & Conv; chmn Summervll & Krksy Nat Almn; past pres Dtrt Chap AL A&M Almn Club; vice pres Fllrth Mddl Sch PTA; vice pres exec dir MI St Cncl Blck Clubs; mem NoLwn Blck Club; Bgly Comm Cncl; Omega Psi Phi Frat; Crtr Met Meth Ch; asst tchr Sndy Sch; atnd Civil Rghts Conf; City Chrtr Rev Conf. **MILITARY SERVICE:** AUS 1948-52. **BUSINESS ADDRESS:** 18517 Northlawn Blvd, Detroit, MI.

SUMMITT, GAZELLA ANN
Educational administrator. **PERSONAL:** Born Feb 27, 1941, Wheatland, IN; daughter of John Ferrell Granger and Rhoda Gazella Howard Granger; married Paul O Summitt; children: Krista, Dana. **EDUCATION:** Vincennes Univ, AS 1964; St Mary-of-the-Woods Coll, BS 1983. **CAREER:** Vincennes Univ, sec to pres 1960-63, admin asst to pres 1963-80, asst to pres for admin and affirmative action officer 1980-. **ORGANIZATIONS:** Bd of trustees First Church of God Vincennes 1987-; dir & sec Vincennes Univ Foundation 1980-; state coord Amer Assoc Women in Comm & Jr Colls 1984-; co-chairperson Women's Div Knox Co United Fund 1985, 86; sec Region V Amer Assoc for Affirmative Action 1986-88; co-chair (founding mem 1984) Indiana Coalition of Blacks in Higher Educ 1986; mem Historic Review Bd City of Vincennes 1986; Steering Committee, March of Dimes Walk America 1986-; Steering Committee, Riley Children's Hospital Campaign 1986-; sec Amer Assn for Affirmative Action 1988-. **HONORS/ACHIEVEMENTS:** Women of the Yr ABWA 1974; (2) Stephen Bufton Memorial Grants Amer Business Women's Assoc 1982, 83; Vincennes Univ Blue and Gold Cord Award as Outstanding Prof Alumnus 1982; Greater Vincennes Area Church Women United Valiant Woman Award 1983; Martin Luther King Support Award 1988. **BUSINESS ADDRESS:** Assistant to the President, VincennesUniv, Admin & Affirmative Action, 1002 North First St, Vincennes, IN 47591.

SUMNER, THOMAS ROBERT
Attorney. **PERSONAL:** Born Dec 04, 1949, Louisville, KY; married Sherry Ann Beene; children: Nyshana, Rahman. **EDUCATION:** Univ of IL Chicago, BA 1971; John Marshall Law Sch, JD 1977. **CAREER:** Cook Co Pub Defender's Ofc, trial atty 1977-; Univ of IL Chicago, acad coun, 1971-77; Chicago Title Ins, title examiner 1977. **ORGANIZATIONS:** Gen sec Cook Co Bar Assn 1980; mem Am & Trial Lawyers Assn 1980-; mem IL State Bar Assn 1980; mem Chicago Bar Assn 1980; mem Am Bar Assn 1980; vol atty Chicago Vol Lelgal Servs Found 1980. **BUSINESS ADDRESS:** Cook Cty Bar Assoc, 25 E Washington St, Ste 150, Chicago, IL 60602.

SUNEJA, SUDHIR KUMAR
Radiologist. **PERSONAL:** Born Jul 13, 1954, Chandigarh, India;married Kumkum D. **EDUCATION:** Howard Univ Coll of Medicine, MD 1976. **CAREER:** Case Western Reserve Univ, intern 1977; Howard Univ Hospital Family Practice, resident 1977-80, diagnostic radiology 1980-83; Johns Hopkins Hospital, nuclear medicine resident 1983-85; Charity Hospital of New Orleans, assoc dir of nuclear medicine 1985-87; LA State Univ Medical Center, asst prof of radiology 1985-87; Howard Univ Hospital, asst prof of radiology 1987. **ORGANIZATIONS:** Mem Amer Coll of Radiology, Soc of Nuclear Medicine, Radiological Soc of North Amer, Amer Medical Assn, Southern Medical Assn; radiation safety comm LA State Univ Medical Center, NOLA; lecture presentations New Orleans Fall Radiology Conference "Neuroreceptor Imaging with Positron Emission Tomography", "Nuclear Cardiology"; case presentations New Orleans Radiology Soc. **HONORS/ACHIEVEMENTS:** Physicians Recognition Award Amer Medical Assn; bd mem Amer Bd of Family Practice 1982, Amer Bd of Radiology 1985, Amer Bd of Nuclear Medicine 1986. **BUSINESS ADDRESS:** Asst Prof of Radiology, HowardUniv Hospital, 2041 Georgia Ave NW, Washington, DC 20060.

SUTTLE, DANE LAVELLE
Professional athlete. **PERSONAL:** Born Aug 09, 1961, Los Angeles, CA. **EDUCATION:** Pepperdine Univ. **CAREER:** Kansas City Kings, guard. **HONORS/ACHIEVEMENTS:** Had 10 double figure scoring games; career high 26 points at Detroit 11/12; 1982-83 Co-Most Valuable palyer in the West Coast Ath Conf; All-Dist 15 and Assoc Press All-Amer hon mention 1982-83; ended career at Pepperdine as all-time leading scorer (1,702); ranked 14th in nation in scoring averaging 235 ppg for1982-83; All-West Coast Ath Conf rec 1981-82; touted a 814 career free throw shooting percentage.

SUTTON, CHARYN DIANE
Marketing communications executive. **PERSONAL:** Born Apr 06, Philadelphia, PA; children: Kamal Everett Hoagland. **EDUCATION:** Lincoln Univ, AB (magna cum laude) 1970; Temple Univ Grad Fellowship School of Communications & Theatre, 1977-79. **CAREER:** OIC's of Amer, communications dir 1976-77; Planned Parenthood Southeastern PA, communications dir 1978-79; Campbell Soup Co, product publicist 1979; Census Bureau US Dept of Commerce, regional public relations coord 1979-80; City of Philadelphia Employment & Training, community info dir 1980-84; Big Brothers/Big Sisters of Amer, dir mktg & communications. **ORGANIZATIONS:** Editor State of Black Philadelphia Philadelphia Urban League 1983-; exec editor GRIO Mag 1984-; exec bd, asst sec Philadelphia Urban League 1984-; trust Metro YWCA of Philadelphia 1985-; trust United Way of Southeastern PA 1987-. **HONORS/ACHIEVEMENTS:** Lincoln Univ Alumni Awd 1970; Leadership Awd Philadelphia Urban League 1987. **BUSINESS ADDRESS:** Dir of Marketing & Comm, Big Brothers/Big Sister Amer, 230 N 13th St, Philadelphia, PA 19107.

SUTTON, DIANNE FLOYD
Human resource developer. **PERSONAL:** Born Dec 06, 1948, Houston, TX; daughter of Dr Osborne English Floyd and Dorothy Woods Brown; married Ronald N Sutton, Sep 15, 1984 (died 1985); children: Anthony Specer Jones. **EDUCATION:** Harris Stowe State Coll, BA Educ 1970; Washington Univ, MA Educ 1974. **CAREER:** St Louis Public School System, math instructor 1970-76; US EEOC St Louis Dist Office, EEO investigator/conciliator 1976-79, trainer/course design 1979-85; Creations by Dyan, design silk flowers and floral ar-

rangements 1979-87; Sutton Enterprises, independent mgmt consultant 1980-; US Dept of Agriculture, employee develop specialist 1985-87. **ORGANIZATIONS:** Mem Natl Assoc for Female Execs 1976-; mem Training Officers Conf 1980-, DC Black Republican Council 1980-; mem Amer Soc of Trainers and Developers 1986, For My People Washington DC 1987, Missionary Soc Metropolitan Baptist Church Washington DC 1987; Delta Sigma Theta Sorority. **HONORS/ACHIEVEMENTS:** Experienced Teachers Grad Fellowship Washington Univ St Louis MO 1971; Special Achievement Award for Superior Performance US EEOC 1978,83; exec bd mem Training Officers Conf Washington DC 1980-; Distinguished Serv Award for EEO Training Progs Trainers Officers Conf 1982; Group Award for Organizational Needs Assessment, Training Officers Conference 1986. **BUSINESS ADDRESS:** President, Sutton Enterprises, 5702 Colorado Ave NW, Washington, DC 20011.

SUTTON, GLORIA W.
Librarian. **PERSONAL:** Born Feb 17, 1952, Kinston, NC; divorced; children: Dimitri. **EDUCATION:** Lenoir Comm Coll, AA 1972; East Carolina Univ, BS 1974; NC Central Univ, MLS 1987. **CAREER:** Lenoir Comm Coll, evening librarian 1974-75; Wayne Co Public Library, cataloguer 1975-76; Sampson Tech Coll, librarian 1976-81; Wake Technical Community Coll, librarian 1981-. **ORGANIZATIONS:** Mem NC Comm Coll Learning Resources Assoc 1977-; volunteer coord Garner Rd YMCA 1982-85; youth minister Wake Baptist Grove Ch 1983-; mem Shaw Div SchLibrary 1985-86, Wake Baptist Grove Ch Library 1985-, Capital Area Library Assoc 1985-, Professional Develop Comm Wake Tech Coll 1986-87, Church & Synagogue Library Assoc 1986-; bd of admin YWCA of Wake Co 1986-; church library consul NC Black Churches 1986-; vice chairperson ReHI Consortium 1986-. **HONORS/ACHIEVEMENTS:** Volunteer of the Year Garner Rd YMCA 1983; Gloria Sutton Scholarship Wake Tech Coll 1984-; Youth Radio Ministry WSES Radio 1984-86; Outstanding Young Women of Amer 1985; Wake Baptist Grove Church minister of Youth Services 1983. **HOME ADDRESS:** 917 Seventh Avenue A-l06, Garner, NC 27529. **BUSINESS ADDRESS:** Librarian, Wake Technical College, 9101 Fayetteville Rd, Raleigh, NC 27603.

SUTTON, JAMES CARTER
Purchasing manager. **PERSONAL:** Born Jan 06, 1945, Lynville, TN; son of Felton Sutton and Nannie Sutton Readus (deceased); married Joyce Roach Sutton, Mar 20, 1989; children: Kyra. **EDUCATION:** Wayne State Univ, BS Business Admin 1975; Univ of Detroit, MBA. **CAREER:** Eastman Kodak Co, supervising buyer 1984, admin asst to vice pres 1984-85, proj mgr business ed 1985-86, public affairs planning dir 1986-, Worldwide Corporate Sourcing, manager. **ORGANIZATIONS:** Bd mem Urban League of Rochester, Girl Scouts of Genesee Valley Geva Theatre Group, YMCA of Metro Rochester; mem Dept of Ed Ad Hoc Taskforce for Adult Literacy; minority supplier coord Eastman Kodak Co 1982-84; minority employee recruiter Eastman Kodak Co 1984-. **HONORS/ACHIEVEMENTS:** Features in company newspaper for involvement in Jr Achievement; featured in company Image Promotion for Community Involvement; Citation for involvement with Big Brother Program. **MILITARY SERVICE:** USAF e-5 4 1/2 yrs. **HOME ADDRESS:** 6 Sugarmills Cr, Fairport, NY 14450. **BUSINESS ADDRESS:** Manager, Worldwide Corporate Sourcing, Eastman Kodak Company, 343 State St, Rochester, NY 14650-0521.

SUTTON, MARY A. (NEE SWEET)
Senior software engineer. **PERSONAL:** Born Oct 12, 1945, LA. **EDUCATION:** Univ of Santa Clara, MS 1973; Prairie View A&M Coll, BS 1966. **CAREER:** Ford Aerospace & Communications, sr software engr; TRW Systems, proj mgr 1969-76; career lecturer for hs stud; Lockheed, asso engr 1967-69; Martin-marietta, asso engr 1966-67; Sunnyvale Employees Assn TRW, pres 1973-74. **ORGANIZATIONS:** Past mem Sunnyvale's TRW Affirmative Action Prog 1973-74; memUniv of Santa Clara Alumni Orgn 1973-. **HONORS/ACHIEVEMENTS:** First black, first woman mgr at TRW Sunnyvale; Who's Who Among The World of Women 1977; Who's Who Among Notable Am 1977. **BUSINESS ADDRESS:** 1145 E Arques Ave, Sunnyvale, CA 94086.

SUTTON, MOSES
Clergyman. **PERSONAL:** Born May 03, 1920, Morganfield, KY; married Emma Lou Forbes; children: Ethel Pierce, Alvin, Berthenia Hall, Stanley, Stephanie. **EDUCATION:** Lane Coll, attended 1940; Louisville Municipal Coll, attended 1943; Eastern NM State Coll, attended 1945; Univ of Louisville, attended 1951. **CAREER:** Miles Chapel, pastor 1939; Patterson Chapel, pastor 1945; Muir Chapel, pastor 1951; Louisville District, presiding elder 1970; Christian Methodist Episcopal Church, mem judicial council 1982-86. **ORGANIZATIONS:** Chmn grievance comm, recording sec UAW #1336 1953-55; pastor Brown Mem 1973; pastor Miles Mem 1975; chmn bd of dir Miles Mem Comm Ctr 1975-85; presiding elder Louisville District 1978; chaplain Lanite Alumni 1980-85; pastor Keas Tabernacle 1982-87. **HONORS/ACHIEVEMENTS:** KY Col Gov WH Ford 1973; Ambassador Gov JM Carroll 1976; KY Col Gov JM Carroll 1978; Key to Louisville Mayor HI Sloane 1984; Citizen Awd Co Judge M McConnell 1984; Christian Serv Awd Brown Mem Church 1984; Appreciation Awd Lanite Alumni 1984.

SUTTON, NORMA J.
Corporate attorney. **PERSONAL:** Born Jun 11, 1952, Chicago, IL; children: Edward. **EDUCATION:** Loyola Univ, BA 1974; Governor's State Univ, MA 1976; Loyola Univ Sch of Law, JD 1980. **CAREER:** Cemrel Inc, office mgr 1975-77; North Amer Co for Ins, legal asst 1977-80; Appellate Court, judicial clerk 1980-82; Soft Sheen Products, corporate counsel 1982-85; Digital Equipment Corp, managing attorney 1985-. **ORGANIZATIONS:** Sec 1986-87, vice chair 1987-88 Illinois State Bar Assoc YLD; mem Amer Bar Assoc, Cook County Bar Assoc; mem Digital Equipment Corp Comm Relations Council. **HONORS/ACHIEVEMENTS:** Leadership and Service Loyola Univ Sch of Law Chicago 1980; Outstanding Young Women 1981; Who's Who of Amer Women 1984; Who's Who in Amer Law 1986.

SUTTON, OLIVER CARTER, II
Attorney, entertainment executive. **PERSONAL:** Born Jan 31, 1948, San Antonio, TX; son of Oliver C Sutton and James Marcell Burley Heyward Sutton; married Cyrene Williams, Jun 05, 89; children: Oliver C Sutton III. **EDUCATION:** Texas Southern Univ, Houston TX, BA, 1970; St. Mary's Univ Law School, San Antonio TX, JD, 1976. **CAREER:** Bexar County, TX, criminal investigator, asst dist atty in criminal dist atty's office; State of Texas, asst atty gen; private law practice; St. Philips Community Coll, TX, political science instructor until 1982; Alamo Community Coll Dist, San Antonio TX, trustee, 1982-86; Inner City Broadcasting Corp, asst to chmn of the board, 1986—. **ORGANIZATIONS:** Bd mem, United Way of San Antonio, Boys Choir of Harlem. **BUSINESS ADDRESS:** Inner City Broadcasting Corp, 801 Second Ave, Suite 303, New York, NY 10037.

SUTTON, OZELL
Appointed government official. **PERSONAL:** Born Dec 13, 1925, Gould, AR; son of Charlie Sutton and Lula B Dowltrard Sutton; married Joanna Freeman, May 09, 1947; children: Angela Sutton-Martin, Alta Muhammad, Dietre Jo Sutton. **EDUCATION:** Philander Smith Coll, BA 1950, Hon D 1971; Fisk Univ, Nashville TN, attended, 1961. **CAREER:** AR Dem, staff writer 1950-57; Little Rock Housing Authority, relocations supervisor 1957-59; Winthrop Rockefeller, public relations 1959-61; AR Council on Human Relations, exec dir 1961-66; US Dept of Justice, field rep CRS 1966-68; Winthrop Rockefeller, special asst 1968-69; US Dept of Justice, state supervisor AR state dir CRS 1969-72, reg dir SE region comm 1972-. **ORGANIZATIONS:** Relocation supvr, Litle Rock Housing Authority 1959-61; dir Arkansas Council on Human Relations, 1971-66; exec bd Philander Smith Coll 1971; bd of trustees Friendship Baptist Church 1974-; exec bd Atlanta Branch NAACP 1976-; gen pres Alpha Phi Alpha Frat Inc 1980; exec bd Leadership Conf on Civil Rights; exec bd Black Leadership Forum; chairperson Council of Presidents of Black Greekletter Organs; pres Vater Educ Project; chair Forum Comm Metro-Atlanta Crime Commn; co-chair Atlanta Black-Jewish Coalition; pres Inter-Alumni Council. **HONORS/ACHIEVEMENTS:** Distinguished Serv Award NAACP 1978; Distinguished Serv Award Alpha Phi Alpha Frat 1979; Outstanding Performance Award US Dept of Justice 1979-80; Distinguished Alumnus Award Philander Smith Coll; more than 100 other awards from many orgs; 2 Special Achievement Awards US Dept of Justice; "The Black Experience in America," dramatic protrayal of black struggle; "Watch Your Language," commentary on impact of racial & ethnic slurs. **MILITARY SERVICE:** USMC corpl 1944-46. **BUSINESS ADDRESS:** Regional Dir, US Dept of Justice, Comm Relations Serv USDI, 75 Piedmont Ste 900, Atlanta, GA 30303.

SUTTON, PERCY E.
Business executive. **PERSONAL:** Born Nov 24, 1920, San Antonio, TX; married Leatrice; children: Pierre, Cheryl. **EDUCATION:** Prairie View Coll, Tuskegee Inst, Hampton Inst, Columbia Univ, attended; Brooklyn Law School, LLB; Morgan State Coll, LLD (Hon) 1969. **CAREER:** Private practice, attny; NY State Assembly, elected 1964-66; Borough of Manhattan, pres 1966-77; Inner-City Broadcasting Corp, chmn, bd of dir, owner 1977-. **ORGANIZATIONS:** Mem Martin Luther King Dems; dir NY Br NAACP, Amer Mus of Natural History, Mus of City of NY; natl dir Urban League, Oper PUSH. **MILITARY SERVICE:** USAF capt, combat intelligence officer, intelligence officer, judge advocate; Combat Stars for Serv in Italian & Mediterranean Theaters WWII. **BUSINESS ADDRESS:** Chairman, Inner City Braodcasting Corp, 801 2nd Blvd, New York, NY 10017.

SUTTON, PIERRE MONTE
Business executive. **PERSONAL:** Born Feb 01, 1947, New York, NY. **EDUCATION:** Univ of Toledo, BA 1968;Univ of KY, attended 1972. **CAREER:** Inner City Broadcasting, pres 1977-; Inner City Broadcasting Corp, vice pres 1975-77; WLIB Radio, pub affairs 1972-75; NY Courier Newspaper, exec editor 1971-72; Inner City Res & Analysis Corp, vice pres 1971. **ORGANIZATIONS:** Bd & mem Minority Investment Fund 1979-; first vice pres Nat Assn of Black Owned Broadcasters 1979-; chmn Harlem Oy Scouts 1975-; bd mem & exec com New York City Marathon 1979-; bd trustee Alvin Ailey Dance Found 1980-; bd mem Better Bus Bur Harlem 1972-77; bd mem Hayden Planetarium 1979-. **MILITARY SERVICE:** USMC E-4 3yrs. **BUSINESS ADDRESS:** President, Inner City Broadcasting, 801 Second Ave, New York, NY 10017.

SUTTON, SHARON EGRETTA
Educator. **PERSONAL:** Born Feb 18, 1941, Cincinnati, OH; daughter of Booker Johnson and Egretta Johnson. **EDUCATION:** Univ of Hartford, B Mus 1963; Columbia Univ, March 1973; City Univ of NY, M Phil 1981, MA Psychology 1982, PhD Psychology 1982. **CAREER:** As a musician, orchestras of "Fiddler on the Roof", "Man of La Mancha", the Bolshoi, Moiseiyev and Leningrad Ballet Companies 1963-68; As an architect, Pratt Institute, Visiting Asst Prof 1975-81; Columbia Univ, adj asst prof 1981-82; Univ of Cincinnati, asst prof 1982-84; SE Sutton Architect, private practice 1976-; Univ of MI, assoc prof of architecture; Art Exhibitions, The Evans-Tibbs Collection in Washington, DC 1985, Your Heritage House in Detroit, MI 1986, June Kelly Gallery in NYC 1987, Univ of MI Musuem of Art 1988; Art included in collections of, The Mint Museum, The Baltimore Museum of Art, Baltimore, MD, The Wadsworth Atheneum, Hartford, CT. **ORGANIZATIONS:** Mem Amer Institute of Architects; mem Amer Psychological Assn. **HONORS/ACHIEVEMENTS:** Rsch in black comm Metropolitan Applied Rsch Center 1970-71; grad & undergrad awd William K Fellows Columbia Univ 1971-73; Pamela Galiber Mem Awd rsch in black comm 1981; Design Rsch Recognition Awd Natl Endowment for the Arts 1983; group VII Natl Fellowship, WK Kellogg Foundation, 1986-1989; project director Natl Endowment for the Arts, "Design of Cities" Grant. **HOME ADDRESS:** 8071 Main St, Dexter, MI 48130. **BUSINESS ADDRESS:** Assoc Prof of Architecture, Univ of Michigan, 2000 Bonisteel Blvd, Ann Arbor, MI 48109.

SUTTON, STERLING E.
Business executive. **PERSONAL:** Born Sep 07, 1928, Oklahoma City, OK; children: Valera. **EDUCATION:** Alex Hamilton Inst, ABA 1949; Chicago Bd Underwriters, certificate 1964. **CAREER:** Unity Mutual Life Ins, agent 1949-52, mgr 1952-56, vice pres 1956-62; Sterling Sutton Assocs, pres 1962-. **ORGANIZATIONS:** Bd mem Neighborhood Housing Serv of Chicago 1979; mem Midwest Chicago Brokers Assns; bd mem Lake Grove Village; chmn trustee bd St Stephen AME Church; vice pres Professional Ins Agents & Brokers Assn; delegate Genl Conf of AME Churches 1980; vice pres Chicago Conf Laymen's Organ; pres Prof Ins Agents & Brokers Assoc of IL 1981-83, bd chmn to date. **HONORS/ACHIEVEMENTS:** Natl Ins Assn Serv Awd 1956; Serv Awd Chicago Urban League 1960; Serv Awd F&AM Prince Hall AFFL 1961; Mayor Daley's Youth Serv Awd 1962; Chicago Econ Dev Corp Man of the Yr 1971; Disting Serv Awd 1974. **BUSINESS ADDRESS:** President, Sterling Sutton Assocs, 5529 S Ashland Ave, Chicago, IL 60636.

SUTTON, THOMAS
Retired director. **PERSONAL:** Born Apr 07, 1918, Brookhaven, MS; divorced; children: Jacqueline Record, Peggy. **CAREER:** Mayfair Acad of Fine Arts Ret, pres 1979; The Dance Workshop, natl vice pres workshop dir found for the promotion of dance; one of top lead authority on instr & history of tap dance; Natl Dance Teachers Seminars & Workshops & Choreographer, sponsor, dir, perform various indus shows; lecturer, demonstr, various

dance subj varcoll; Child Revues for Comm, dir, producer; contributor, comm orgn, sch, ch groups; conduct career conf in pub sch; worked & interest in devel of handicapped child through dance educ. **HONORS/ACHIEVEMENTS:** Chmn of bd spl awd Take 5 Workshops 1973-74; Tchr of Yr LEO'S Advance Theatrical Co 1974; cultural awd YMCA 1977. **MILITARY SERVICE:** AUS ETO sgt 1942-46. **BUSINESS ADDRESS:** 1025 E 79th St, Chicago, IL 60619.

SUTTON, WALTER L.
Educator. **PERSONAL:** Born Jul 26, 1917, Woodbury, GA; son of Raymond Sutton and Carrie Sutton; married Sammie W; children: Walter L Sutton, Jr. **EDUCATION:** BA magna cum laude 1941; MS 1954. **CAREER:** Wiley Coll, asst prof hictory, phys edn, sociology, economics 1968-; coach football, basketball, baseball 1968-; TX Schs, hS tchr & coach 1945-68. **ORGANIZATIONS:** Mem NEA Southwestern HPER; TX State Assn HPER; TX State & Baseball Assn; TX State Tchrs Assn; Football & Basketball State Assn; Nat Economic Assn; Kappa Alpha Psi; Mason Regular Fellows Club; Railroad Union; Southwest Football Official; umpire Little League; referee Kiwanis Club All Conf & Al Dist Football & Basketball. **HONORS/ACHIEVEMENTS:** Awards NAIA Dit 8 Coach Of Yr 1974-75; Man of The Year Bethesda Baptist Church 1983; volunteer Harrison County Food Bank 1985-88; Hall of Fame Bethesda Baptist Church 1989; retired Wiley College Athletic Director. **MILITARY SERVICE:** AUS stt ETO 1943-45. **BUSINESS ADDRESS:** Wiley Coll, PO Box 7352, Marshall, TX 75670.

SUTTON, WILLIAM WALLACE
Educational administrator. **PERSONAL:** Born Dec 15, 1930, Monticello, MS; married Leatrice Eva Hubbard; children: William W Jr, Averell H, Sheryl Smith, Alan D, Allison M, Gavin J. **EDUCATION:** Dillard Univ, BA 1953; Howard Univ, MS 1959, PhD 1965. **CAREER:** DC Genl Hosp Washington, med Tech 1955-59; Dillard Univ, instr to prof of biology 1959-79, chair div of natl sci 1969-79; Chicago St Univ, vice pres/acad afrs & provost 1979-85, prof of biol sci 1982-85; Kansas State Univ, vice pres educ & student svcs, prof biol 1985-. **ORGANIZATIONS:** Mem Amer Council on Educ 1983-; past pres Natl Inst of Sci; mem Society of Sigma Xi; reg liaison off Danforth Assoc Prog Danforth Found 1975-79; consul US Dept of Educ 1977-81, 83, 84; consul Natl Res Cncl Natl Acad of Sci 1980, 82, 83; consul 16 Inst Health Sci Consortium 1974-; deacon Chicago United 1980-82; bd of trustees WYES TV New Orleans 1973-79; bd dirs Methodist Hosp New Orleans 1975-79; bd dirs Urban League of New Orleans 1970-78; bd dirs Natl Conf of Christians & Jews 1968-79; bd dirs Amer Heart Assoc LA 1977-79. **HONORS/ACHIEVEMENTS:** Disting Awd Dillard Univ 1982; Presidential Citation Natl Assn for Equal Oppor 1979 1980; Disting Alumni Awd Dillard Univ 1978; Silver Beaver Awd BoyScouts of Amer 1976; Man of the Middle South Changing Middle South Mag 1973; listed in Amer Men & Women of Sci, Who's Who in the S & SW, Outstanding Educators of Amer, Who's Who in Amer. **HOME ADDRESS:** C/O MVSU, 125 Washington Ave, Itta Bena, MS 38941. **BUSINESS ADDRESS:** Vice President, Professor, Kansas StateUniv, Anderson Hall, Manhattan, KS 66502.

SUTTON, WILMA JEAN
Business executive. **PERSONAL:** Born Nov 11, 1933, Murphysboro, IL; married Clarence E. **EDUCATION:** Univ of IL Urbana, cert of mgmt 1969;Univ of CT Storrs, cert 1970;Univ of IN Bloomington, cert 1976; RooseveltUniv Chicago IL, B 1978; Roosevelt U, M 1979. **CAREER:** Hyde Park Fed Savings & Loan Assn of Chicago, exec vice pres 1964-; Chicago Title Ins Co Chicago IL, preliminary & examiner 1951-64. **ORGANIZATIONS:** Bd of dirs Hyde Park Fed Savings & Oan Assn of Chicago; bd of dirs Hyde Park Nieghborhood Club; bd of dirs Loretto Adult Educ Ctr; mem Lambda Alpha Ely Chpt; mem UNICEF; mem US Savings & Loan League; mem Chicago Urban League; mem NAACP; mem IL Commn on the Status of Women; mem Museum of Sci & Industry; mem St Thaddeus Ch Appointment; mem Savings & Loan Adv Bd Gov Daniel Walker State of IL. **HONORS/ACHIEVEMENTS:** Cert of recognition Nat Alliance of Businessmen; editorial reviews Ebony Mag/Jet Mag/Chicago Sun Times/Chicgo Tribune/Real Estate News. **BUSINESS ADDRESS:** VP/Regional Supervisor, Comm Outreach Svgs of Amer, 2605 W 22nd St, Ste 25, Oak Brook, IL 60521.

SWAIN, ALICE M.
Educator. **PERSONAL:** Born Feb 03, 1924, Oklahoma City; married Robert; children: Robert A. **EDUCATION:** Famous Writer's Sch Westport, BS 1946, ME 1952. **CAREER:** Univ of Oklahoma, graduate teaching assoc 1978-80; Langston Univ, asst prof 1973-78; reading specialist 1970-73; elem tchr 1948-69; Sigma Gamma & Rho, org local chapter. **ORGANIZATIONS:** Pres, vice pres & sec; chmn of bd Youth Services; vice pres & sec Nat Pan-hellenic Council Inc; pres & owner of The Together Charm & Fashion Modeling Sch; owner & producer of OK'S Hal Jackson's Miss US Talented Teen Pagaent. **HONORS/ACHIEVEMENTS:** Soc columnist The Black Dispatch Weekly Grand Epistoleus Sigma Gamma Rho 1974-76; Nat Pub Rel Chmn Sigma Gamma Rho 1974-76; Sowest Region Sigma of Yr 1963; one of nation's ten outstanding women 1967; local sigma of yr 1970; Sigma's Hall of Fame 1974; award of merit Nat Pan Hellenic Cncl Inc 1976; 1st gradn anti basileus Sigam Gamma Rho Sor Inc 1976-78; congratulatory plaque local Omega Psi Phi 1974; cert of merit for distinguished serv in Youth & Comm. **BUSINESS ADDRESS:** 3016 Norcrest Dr, Oklahoma City, OK 73111.

SWAIN, HAMP
Radio broadcaster. **PERSONAL:** Born Dec 03, 1929, Macon; married Zenola Hardeman; children: Ronald Leo, Ouida Louise, Natalie Valencia, Jarvis Osmond. **CAREER:** Little Richard and The Hamptones, band leader, sax player 1949-56; WIBB, radio broadcaster, announcer; Record Production Co, owner, two retail record outlets;5th St Record Shop, 1963-; Record World Disccount, 1970-. **ORGANIZATIONS:** Mem local NAACP; co-sponsor Wendell Mcintosh Bowl; fighter for Human Rights. **BUSINESS ADDRESS:** 275 5 St, Macon, GA 31201.

SWAIN, JAMES H.
Attorney. **PERSONAL:** Born Jul 04, 1954, Philadelphia, PA; son of James P Swain and Alice Blake Swain; married Sharon Matthews, Sep 1985. **EDUCATION:** Univ of Bridgeport, BA 1975; Temple Univ School of Law, JD 1978; Univ of Pennsylvania Law School, LLM 1986. **CAREER:** US Atty So Dist of NY, summer intern 1977; Third Circuit Ct of Appeals, clerkship intern Hon A Leon Higginbotham 1978; US Dept of Labor, trial atty office of reg solicitor, 1978-88; US Dept of Justice, Philadelphia PA, asst US atty, 1989-. **ORGANIZATIONS:** Chmn, Legislation Review Comm, Barristers Assn of Philadelphia, 1978-; exec comm mem, Barristers Assn of Philadelphia, 1979-80, 1986-89; mem bd of dir, Community Legal Services, 1988-; mem bd of dir, Wynnfield Residents Assn, 1988-; mem, Federal Bar Assn Philadelphia Chapter, 1988-; mem, Philadelphia Bar Assn, 1989-. **HONORS/ACHIEVEMENTS:** Scholar of the Year Award, Omega Psi Phi Frat Inc, Rho Upsilon Chap 1975-76; Distinguished Serv Award, Black Amer Law Students Assn, 1977-78; Certificate of Appreciation, Barristers Assn of Philadelphia, 1978-79, 1979-80; mem, Omega Psi Phi Frat Inc, Mu Omega Chap; author of "Protecting Individual Employers: Is it Safe to Complain About Safety?" in Univ of Bridgeport Law Review, 1988. **BUSINESS ADDRESS:** Asst United States Atty, US Atty's Office, US Courthouse, Rm 3310, 6th and Market Sts, Philadelphia, PA 19106.

SWAIN, ROBERT J.
Dentist. **PERSONAL:** Born Jun 17, 1919, St Petersburg, FL; married Helen Scott; children: Lynette, Tanya, Kimberly, Robert, III, Shana, William. **EDUCATION:** FL A&M U, BS; Howard U, DDS 1944. **CAREER:** Pvt Prac, dentist; Bayfront Med Ctnr St Petersburg, staff. **ORGANIZATIONS:** Mem FL State Med Denatl Pharmaceutical Assn; Nat Dental Assn; Am Dental Assn; HowardUniv & Recruitment Com; HowardUniv Alumni Asn; Ambassadors Inc, Omega Psi Phi Frat. **HONORS/ACHIEVEMENTS:** Recip humanitarian serv award Nat Council of Negro Women; Who's Who in SE Am; Internatl Platform Assn. **MILITARY SERVICE:** AUS capt. **BUSINESS ADDRESS:** 2100 9 St So, St Petersburg, FL 33705.

SWAIN, RONALD L.
Minister educational administrator. **PERSONAL:** Born Oct 09, 1948, Macon, GA; son of Hampton and Evelyn; married Chrystle A Bullock; children: Ronald. **EDUCATION:** Duquesne Univ Pgh PA, BA 1970, M Ed 1972; The Shaw Divinity Schl Ral NC, M Div 1975; The Univ of NC at Chapel Hill, M Ed 1983; George Washington University, DC Ed D 1987. **CAREER:** Shaw Univ, dir of counsel 1975-78; Univ of NC at CH, dir grad stud ctr 1978-80; Shaw Univ, assoc dean of stdnt 1980-81, spec asst to pres 1981-84, dir of devel 1987-88, vice pres for institutional advancement and planning 1988-. **ORGANIZATIONS:** Bd of dir The Life Enrich Cntr 1983-; cnsltnt The UNC-CH Organ Dev Group 1979-82, Human Resources Consltnt 1978-82; bd of dir The Business Innovation Advancement Technology Center, Raleigh NC 1988-. **HONORS/ACHIEVEMENTS:** Flwshp Woodrow Wilson Natl Fellow Fdn Princeton, NJ 1984-84; proj dir NC Humanities Comm 120 yrs at Shaw Proj 1984-85; UNCF Fellowship for Doctoral Study 1985-87; publications: Case Study of the US Dept of Educ Institutional Devel Program, 1986; Strategic Planning for the Use of Computer Technology in HBCUs, 1987. **HOME ADDRESS:** 4123 Trotter Ridge Rd, Durham, NC 27707. **BUSINESS ADDRESS:** Vice President for Institutional Advancement and Planning, ShawUniv, 118 E South St, Raleigh, NC 27611.

SWAN, JOHN W.
Business executive, justice of the peace. **PERSONAL:** Born Jul 03, 1935; son of John N Swan (deceased) and Margaret E Swan; married Jacqueline; children: 3 children. **EDUCATION:** WV Wesleyan Coll, BA, LLD (Honorary) 1987; Univ of Tampa, LLD (Honorary) 1986. **CAREER:** Lloyds, underwriting mem; John L Swan Limited, founder/real estate; Justice of the Peace; Premier of Bermuda. **ORGANIZATIONS:** Trustee Bermuda Biological Station for Research; mem Young Presidents Orgns; mem Hamilton Rotary Club; elected to Parliament in 1972. **BUSINESS ADDRESS:** Premier of Bermuda, Cabinet Office, 105 Front St, W, Hamilton 12, Bermuda.

SWAN, L. ALEX
Education administrator. **PERSONAL:** Born Jan 17, 1938, Grand Turk, Turks and Caicos Islands;married Karla K. **EDUCATION:** West Indies Coll, AS 1963; Leg Aspects Bus (England), assoc cert 1964; Blackstone Law Sch, LLB 1966; Oakwood Coll, BS 1967; Atlanta U, MA 1969;Univ CA at Berkeley, MS PhD 1972. **CAREER:** Fisk Univ, chmn Dept Sociology; Univ CA at Berkeley & Sonoma State Coll, lectr; Miami-Dade Jr Coll & Dinthill Tech HS, instr. **ORGANIZATIONS:** Mem Am Sociological Assn; Am Soc Criminology; Black World Fndtn; NAACP cHMN leg redress com 1973-74). **HONORS/ACHIEVEMENTS:** Who's Who Amng Students; Who's Who in Caribbean.

SWAN, LIONEL F.
Physician. **PERSONAL:** Born Apr 01, 1909; children: Alfreda, Andrea, Virginia, Lionel Jr. **EDUCATION:** BS 1932; MD 1939. **CAREER:** Detroit Med & Surg Center, physician & pres; Nat Med Assn Fndtn, fndr; Nat Med Assn, past pres; Det Med Soc, past pres; Detroit Med News, edstaff. **ORGANIZATIONS:** Mem Nat Med Assn; Detroit Med & Soc; AMA; MI State Med Soc; Wayne Co Med Soc; MI Health Council; bd MI Health Maintenance Orgn; life mem NAACP; Phi Beta Sigma; Lions Club. **HONORS/ACHIEVEMENTS:** Dist serv award MI Health Council 1968; fellow Am of Fam Prac; lumnus o Yr 1964. **BUSINESS ADDRESS:** 8300 Mark Ave, Detroit, MI 48214.

SWAN, MONROE
Executive director. **PERSONAL:** Born Jun 02, 1937, Belzoni, MS; children: Rosalyn, Cheryl, Gwendolyn, Allyn. **EDUCATION:** Milwaukee Area Tech Coll; Univ of WI, BS. **CAREER:** Amer Motors Corp, material expeditor 1967-68; Local 75, head steward; Concentrated Employment Program, dir 1968-72; former WI state senator; FIRE HELP, exec dir. **ORGANIZATIONS:** Former pres orgn of Orgns (Triple "O"); chmn Senate Com Govtl & Vet Affairs; mem Senate Joint Com Review of Adminstrv Rules; former supt Ch God in Christ Sunday Sch NW WI; mem Frontiers Intl. **HONORS/ACHIEVEMENTS:** Mreitorious Award VFW; Damn Fine Legislator Award Vet Educ Com; Cert of Merit US Jaycees. **BUSINESS ADDRESS:** Executive Dir, FIRE HELP of Wisconsin, 5815 W Capitol Dr, Ste 404, Milwaukee, WI 53216.

SWANIGAN, JESSE CALVIN
Accountant, auditor. **PERSONAL:** Born Nov 18, 1933, Widner, AR. **EDUCATION:** Washington Univ St Louis, BS 1966; St Louis Univ, MBA 1977. **CAREER:** EB Koonce Mortuary Inc, supvr trainee 1961; Johnson Publishing Co, staff representative 1962; Mcdonnell Douglas Aircraft Corp, sr quality/productivity improvement consultant 1963-. **ORGANIZATIONS:** Ordained elder United Presbyterian Church in the USA 1976; life mem NAACP 1976; consultant United Negro Coll Fund Comm 1979; mem Natl Assn of Black Accountants 1977; mem Black Presbyterians United 1980; bd mem Natl Black MBA Assn; treasurer 100 Black Men of Amer Inc; bd mem Carver House. **HONORS/**

ACHIEVEMENTS: Black Leader for 1980 United Presbyterian Church in the USA 1979; Founder & Past Pres, St Louis Natl Black MBA Assn 1988; Honor of Appreciation, Amer Business Women's Assn 1989. **BUSINESS ADDRESS:** Sr Quality/Productivity Improvement Consultant, McDonnell Douglas Aircraft Crp, PO Box 516, Mail Code 0012711, St Louis, MO 63166.

SWANN, EUGENE MERWYN
Attorney. **PERSONAL:** Born Aug 01, 1934, Philadelphia, PA; children: Liana, Michael, Elliott. **EDUCATION:** Temple U, BS 1957;Univ of MA, MA Econ 1959;Univ of CA Berkeley, LLB 1962. **CAREER:** Contra Costa Co, dep dist atty 1963-67; Contra Costa Legal Svcs, dir 1967-77; Office of Citzens Complaints, dir 1983-84; SF Police Dept, 1984-85; Self Employed, lecturer/atty 1977-83; Economics-Univ of Calif, Berkeley, and Stanford Graduate Schl of Business. **HONORS/ACHIEVEMENTS:** Outstand Legal Serv Attorney in Nation 1974. **HOME ADDRESS:** 43 Donald Dr, Orinda, CA 94563.

SWANN, LYNN CURTIS
Athlete. **PERSONAL:** Born Mar 07, 1952, Alcoa, TN. **EDUCATION:** Univ So, 1974. **CAREER:** Pitts Steelers, Widereceiver 1974-. **ORGANIZATIONS:** Mem Screen Actors Guild; mem AFTRA All Pro 1977. **HONORS/ACHIEVEMENTS:** Most Valuable Player in Super Bowl X 1975. **BUSINESS ADDRESS:** Pittsburgh Steelers, Three Rivers Stad 300 Stad Cir, Pittsburgh, PA 15212.

SWANSON, CHARLES
Lawyer. **PERSONAL:** Born Aug 16, 1949, Camp Hill, AL; married Anne Elizabeth Fox; children: Tesfaye C, Tonya D, Tamara A, Charles Joseph. **EDUCATION:** Univ of WI-Madison, BA 1971; Univ of WI Law School, JD 1973. **CAREER:** Univ of WI-Madison, teaching asst afro-amer history 1970-73; Racine Co Public Defenders Office, asst public defender 1974-75; NAACP, legal redress 1978-; Private Practice, attorney. **ORGANIZATIONS:** Mem Racine County, Amer Bar Assocs; mem Natl Assoc of Criminal Defense Lawyers; mem bd dirs Racine NAACP; mem Racine Optimist Club. **HONORS/ACHIEVEMENTS:** Apptd Racine County Circuit Court Commissioner 1980; Outstanding Young Man of Amer 1984; Outstanding Dir Racine Jaycees. **MILITARY SERVICE:** ROTC-Army. **BUSINESS ADDRESS:** 1006 Washington Ave, Racine, WI 53403.

SWANSON, EDITH (NEE MAYS)
Educator. **PERSONAL:** Born Jul 16, 1934, Detroit, MI; married Charles; children: Kenneth, Charles, II. **EDUCATION:** E MI U, BS 1970; E MI U, MA 1975. **CAREER:** MI Educ Assn, full-time vice pres 1977-; Willow Run Comm Sch, tchr; Willow Run Educ Assn, pres 1972-75. **ORGANIZATIONS:** Bd of dir MI Educ Assn 1974-77; chpsn MI Educ Assn Minor Group & Task Force 1975; vice pres elect MI Educ Assn 1977; chairperson Coalition Against Parochaid 1977-; NEA Del World Confedtn of Orgns of Tchg Profession Jakarta Indonesia 1978; exec com MI Educ Assn; centr reg coord NEA Women's Caucus; mem Nat Alliance Blakc Sch Edctrs/MI Alliance Black Edctrs/Coalition of Labor Union Women/NAACP; pres Ypsilanti Palm Leaf Club 1973-75; Delta Sigma Theta Sor Grad Chap; v chpsn Washtenaw Co Black Dem Caucus 1974-77. **HONORS/ACHIEVEMENTS:** Trib to outst women NEA educ awd rep aay 1976; maurine wyatt feminist award MI Educ Assn 1978; 1 Of Most Inflntl Black Edctrs Ebony Mag 1980.

SWANSON, O'NEIL D.
Funeral director. **PERSONAL:** Born Apr 06, Birmingham, AL; children: O'Neil II, Linda E, Kimberly E. **EDUCATION:** Central State Univ, BS 1953; Cincinnati Coll of Embalming, Mortuary Science 1956. **CAREER:** Swanson Funeral Home Inc, president/CEO. **ORGANIZATIONS:** Exec bd dir & life mem NAACP; dir First Independence Natl Bank of Detroit 1970-80; dir Natl Alumni Assoc Central State Univ 1978, Natl Funeral Dirs & Morticians Assoc 1979. **HONORS/ACHIEVEMENTS:** 33rd Degree Ancient Egyptian Arabic Order of the Mystic Shrine 1974; Honorary Doctoral Degree Shaw Coll Detroit 1974; Honorary Doctoral Degree Central State Univ 1974. **MILITARY SERVICE:** AUS 1st lt 2 yrs. **BUSINESS ADDRESS:** President/CEO, Swanson Funeral Home Inc, 806 E Grand Blvd, Detroit, MI 48207.

SWANSTON, CLARENCE EUGENE
Organization executive. **PERSONAL:** Born May 15, 1947, New York, NY; son of Norman C. Swanston and Beryl Ina Swaby Swanston. **EDUCATION:** St John's Univ, Jamaica NY, BS, 1969; Metropolitan Training Institute, Queens College, Flushing NY, cert in counseling, 1973. **CAREER:** Sound of New York, Inc (CBS), New York NY, vice president finance, 1981-84; City University of New York, New York NY, budget officer, 1977-82; New Jersey Higher Education Authority, Trenton NJ, asst dir of finance, 1982-86; Planned Parenthood of America, New York NY, deputy grants dir, 1986-87; National Urban League, New York NY, asst dir, 1987-88; Urban League of the Albany Area, Inc, Albany NY, president, CEO, 1988—. **BUSINESS ADDRESS:** Urban League of the Albany Area, Inc, 93-95 Livingston Ave, Albany, NY 12207.

SWAYNE, STEVEN ROBERT
University administrator, clergyman. **PERSONAL:** Born Jan 25, 1957, Los Angeles, CA; son of Louis Swayne, Jr. and Lelia Catherine (Horton) Swayne. **EDUCATION:** Occidental Coll, BA (Summa Cum Laude, Phi Beta Kappa) 1978; Fuller Theological Seminary, MDiv 1983. **CAREER:** Lake Ave Congregational Church, adm Asst to sr pastor 1978-85; Seattle Pacific Univ, dir of campus ministries 1985-. **ORGANIZATIONS:** Ordained minister Conservative Congregational Christian Conf 1984-; lay pastor Westminster Chapel 1986-; member, executive committee, Alumni/ae Association, Fuller Theological Seminary 1987-. **HONORS/ACHIEVEMENTS:** Music published Fred Bock Music Productions; recital appearances (piano) on West Coast; articles published in various Christian periodicals; first prize, John Wesley Work III Composition Competition 1979. **BUSINESS ADDRESS:** Dir of Student Ministries, Seattle PacificUniv, Seattle, WA 98119.

SWEAT, SHEILA DIANE
Investment analyst. **PERSONAL:** Born May 08, 1961, New York, NY. **EDUCATION:** Hampton Inst, BS 1983. **CAREER:** Moody's Investors Svcs, credit analyst 1984-86; Irving Trust Co, investment analyst 1986-. **ORGANIZATIONS:** Mem Long Island Chap Hampton Alumni Assoc 1984-. **BUSINESS ADDRESS:** Investment Analyst, Irving Trust Company, One Wall St, New York, NY 10015.

SWEENEY, JOHN ALBERT
Educator. **PERSONAL:** Born Jun 03, 1925, Columbus, OH; married Veronica Khan; children: Dereck, Peitra. **EDUCATION:** NYU, BA 1949; Trinity Coll London, LTCL 1951; Amer Guild of Organists, AAGO 1953; NYU, MA 1953; State Coll of Music Munich Germany, graduate certificate, 1954; Free Univ West Berlin Germany, PhD 1961; Johns Hopkins Univ, Ed 1965; African Studies, Univ of Nairobi & Kenya E Africa, graduate certificate 1971. **CAREER:** Morgan State Univ, prof of music, instruments, theory, musicology, ethnumusicology 1962; Univ of MD Extension Prgm USAF Berlin Germany, teacher music theory 1955-60; W Germany, guest lectr musicology 1954-61; USA; 1962-; NYC St Mark's morgan State Univ, 1962-; NY Munich Baltimore, french hornist, bands orchestras 1945-70; Music Educs Nat Conf; Soc for Ethnomusicology; Morgan State Univ & Baltimore Area, adv intl studies. **ORGANIZATIONS:** Mem Ping Councl for Annual Black Music Week Morgan State U; mem adv counc Left Bank & Jazz Soc Baltimore; mem India Forum; dedicated to dissemination of Indian Culture; organist Union Baptist Ch Elected to following Honor Soc; Mu Sigms NYUniv 1968; Phi Beta Kappa NYUniv 1949; Phi Delta Kappa Dn Johns HopkinsUniv 1965. **HONORS/ACHIEVEMENTS:** Fulbright scholar to Germany 1953-54; Published anthem 134 th psalm 1951; Book the trumpets in the cntatas of js bach 1961; book reviews; article; Guyanea & the African Diaspora 1976. **MILITARY SERVICE:** USAF sgt 1944-46. **BUSINESS ADDRESS:** Morgan State Univ, Baltimore, MD 21239.

SWEENEY, ROBERT LUCIEN
Retired postal supervisor. **PERSONAL:** Born Nov 14, 1895, Highland, KS; widowed. **EDUCATION:** Kansas City Univ 1952-54. **CAREER:** Kansas City, MO Post Office, retired supvr 1926-64. **ORGANIZATIONS:** Mem bd dir Twin City Fed Savs & Loan; bd dir Douglas State Bank; adv dir Twin City Safety Fed Savs & Loan; Commr Land Clearance for Redevelopment Auth of KC, MO; mem bd dir of Model Cities; mem Commn to frame a charter for the govt of Jackson Co charter approved & adopted 1970; mem bd dir Martin Luther King Hosp; comdr Dept V State Comdr Tacitus Gaillard Post VFW #2069; charter mem Wayne Miner Post 149; pres Beau Brummel Club 1948; mem Dem party. **HONORS/ACHIEVEMENTS:** Appointed "Colonel" of Gov Hearnes staff; 1st Black Supr appointed in KC, MO Post Office 1948; Life Mem Hon Fellows Truman Libr Inst for Natl & Intl Affairs 1974; Life-long friend of Pres Harry S Truman; Life Mem Beta Lambda Chap Alpha Phi Alpha. **MILITARY SERVICE:** AUS 1918.

SWEET, CLIFFORD C.
Attorney. **PERSONAL:** Born Aug 03, 1936, W Palm Beach, FL; married Roxanna Thayer. **EDUCATION:** San Jose State, BA 1959; Lincoln U, LLB 1965. **CAREER:** Legal Aid Soc Alameda Co, exec atty 1971-; Sweet & Sweet San Jose, pvt pract; Lega Aid Soc, staff atty 1967-. **ORGANIZATIONS:** Mem Fed & Inter-am Bar Assns; State Bar CA; past bd mem Urban League; ACLU; Barrister's Club; Dem Lawyer's Club; legal couns Oakland Black Police Officer's Assns; Oakland Firefighter's Assn; Nat Orgn Women; NAACP; COYOTE. **BUSINESS ADDRESS:** 1815 Telegraph Ave, Oakland, CA 94612.

SWIFT, JAY JAMES
City official. **PERSONAL:** Born Jan 29, 1926, New York City, NY; married Diane; children: Susan, Jay. **EDUCATION:** Yale U, BA 1948; NY State U, CSW 1967. **CAREER:** NY City Environmental Control Bd, exec dir; NY, dep city adminstr 1973-74; NY City Addiction Serv Agy, 1st dep commr 1970-73; Ad Hoc Rev for DrugAbuse Treatment Prgm, spl consult 1970-73. **ORGANIZATIONS:** Mem NY & State Narcotics Addiction Control Control Comn Adv Cncl 1969-72. **BUSINESS ADDRESS:** 120 Wall St, New York, NY 10005.

SWIFT, LEROY V.
Police administrator. **PERSONAL:** Born Aug 11, 1936, Gause, TX; married Karen Ann Reece; children: Cheryl D, Matthew B, Darrylyn Z, Duane J. **EDUCATION:** Central MO State Univ, AA 1974; Univ of MO at Kansas City, BS 1975; Central MO State Univ, MS 1980. **CAREER:** Kansas City MO Police Dept, patrlmn 1958-67, sgt 1967-69, capt 1969-73, maj 1973-76; col dir admin 1976-. **ORGANIZATIONS:** Consultant police training KC MO Housing Authority Police 1969-77; mem Natl Orgn of Black LE exec 1984-, Inttl Assn of Chiefs of Police 1984; MO Police Chiefs Assn 1984. **MILITARY SERVICE:** AUS e-4 1955-58. **BUSINESS ADDRESS:** Colonel, Dir of Admin, Kansas City MO Police Dept, 1125 Locust Ave, Kansas City, MO 64106.

SWIGGETT, ERNEST L.
Religious administrator. **EDUCATION:** Drew Univ, NY Univ, Grad Courses; PA State Univ, BS; Columbia Univ, MA; Emory Univ Candler School of Theology, Cert UMCBA. **CAREER:** Unique NY Mag, comptroller 1974-76; Harkless & Lyons Inc, principal 1976-78; Salem United Methodist Church, bus admin 1978-87; Salem Home Care Serv Inc, dir 1980-87; NY Annual Conf of the United Methodist Church, bus admin, treasurer. **ORGANIZATIONS:** Cons, workshops NY & Eastern PA Conf of the United Methodist Church, Black Methodist for Church Renewal Inc, Drew & NY Theological Seminaries 1980-; mem 100 Black Men Inc, United Methodist Assoc of Church Bus Admins, AUDELCO, Methodist Church Home of NY, Black Methodist for Church Renewal Inc, Natl Assoc ofChurch Bus Admin; dir, Gen Bd of Global Ministries of The US Methodist Church; dir, United Methodist Devel Fund, Inc; Natl Chairperson, Black Methodists for Church Renewal, Inc; mem Assn of United Methodists Conf Treasurers, Inc. **HONORS/ACHIEVEMENTS:** Publ Unique NY Mag, Encore, Amsterdam News, New World Outlook, The Interpreter Mag; Pioneer Awd Salem Community Serv Council Inc; Service Award, Bethany United Methodist Church 1988. **HOME ADDRESS:** 135 Eastern Pkwy, Brooklyn, NY 11238. **BUSINESS ADDRESS:** Business Admin, Treasurer, New York Annual Conference of, The United Methodist Church, 252 Brant Ave, White Plains, NY 10605.

SWINDELL, WARREN C.
Director. **PERSONAL:** Born Mar 22, 1934, Kansas City, MO; married Monica Streetman; children: Warna Celia, Lillian Ann. **EDUCATION:** Lincoln Univ of MO, BS Music Educ 1956; The Univ of MI Ann Arbor, MM 1964; The Univ of IA, PhD Music Educ 1970. **CAREER:** Central High Sch Hayti MO, band and choir dir 1956-57, dir of musical act 1959-60; Hubbard High Sch, dir of music act 1960-61; Flint MI Public Schools, inst mus specialist 1961-67; KY State Univ, chair/prof of music 1970-79, prof of music 1979-80; Indiana State Univ, dir/prof ctr for afro-amer studies1980-. **ORGANIZATIONS:** Evaluator Natl Assoc of Schools of Music Accred 1977-78; screening panel KY Arts Commn Project 1977-79; chaired State, Div & Natl MENC meetings 1979-80. **HONORS/ACHIEVEMENTS:** Nu-

merous Service Awds NAACP 1978-85; NEH Summer Seminar for College Teachers Grant 1984; Faculty Rsch Grant Indiana State Univ 1985; IN State Univ Research Grant 1987-88; Amer Philosophical Society Research Grant 1988. **MILITARY SERVICE:** AUS spl 4th class 2 yrs. **HOME ADDRESS:** 14 Douglas Place, Terre Haute, IN 47803. **BUSINESS ADDRESS:** Dir, Indiana State University, Center Afro-American Studies, Stalker Hall 203, Terre Haute, IN 47809.

SWINER, CONNIE, III
Physician. **PERSONAL:** Born Sep 08, 1959, Washington, DC. **EDUCATION:** College of William and Mary, BS 1980; Howard Univ Coll of Medicine, MD 1985. **ORGANIZATIONS:** Mem Amer Medical Assoc 1982-; mem Black Physicians Assoc/Cook Co Hosp 1986-; mem Alpha Phi Alpha Frat Inc, Howard Univ Medical Alumni Assoc. **HONORS/ACHIEVEMENTS:** Who's Who in Amer Univs & Colls 1980; Outstanding Young Man of Amer 1982; mem Alpha Omega Alpha Honor Medical Soc Howard Univ 1985. **BUSINESS ADDRESS:** Resident, 840 So Wood St, Chicago, IL 60612.

SWINGER, HERSHEL KENDELL
Educational administrator. **PERSONAL:** Born Apr 16, 1939, Parsons, KS; married Sandra Marie Reese; children: Robbin D, Hershel K Jr. **EDUCATION:** CA State Univ Los Angeles, BA Psych 1966, MS Rehab Counseling 1968; Univ Southern CA, PhD Clinical Psych 1978. **CAREER:** LA Cty Occupational Health Svc, dir counseling 1970-74; Reg IX Ctr on Child Abuse/Neglect, dir 1975-80; Dept Counselor Ed CA State Univ, assoc prof 1979-; Reg IX Ctr on Children Youth & Families, dir 1981-84; Southern CA Child Abuse Prevention Training Ctr, dir, prof. **ORGANIZATIONS:** Consult Natl Ctr on Child Abuse/Neglect 1978-; mem Black Psych Assoc 1980-; dir family crisis ctr Childrens Inst Intl 1982-; vice pres South Central LA Reg Ctr 1982-; exec mem West Area Council on Alcoholism 1983-; cons, psych El Centro Comm Mental Health Ctr 1984-. **HONORS/ACHIEVEMENTS:** Outstanding Service LA Cty Supervising Soc Worker 1982; Roy Wilkins Ed Awd Inglewood South Bay NAACP 1984; Outstanding Alumni CA State Univ 1984; Outstanding Comm Service Black Soc Workers of LA 1984. **MILITARY SERVICE:** AUS spc 4 1963-65. **BUSINESS ADDRESS:** Director, Professor, So CA Child Abuse Prevent Ctr, 5151 State University Dr, Los Angeles, CA 90032.

SWINNEY, T. LEWIS
Physician. **PERSONAL:** Born Jun 03, 1946, Nashville, TN. **EDUCATION:** Benedict Coll, BS (w/Honors) 1970; Meharry Medical Coll, MD 1975. **CAREER:** Staten Island Hosp, internship/residency internal medicine 1975-78; United States Navy, chief of pulmonary medicine, chief of alcohol rehab unit, staff physician internal medicine 1978-81; Self-Employed, physician. **HONORS/ACHIEVEMENTS:** Physician of the Year Queens-Corona 1984. **MILITARY SERVICE:** USN lt commander 1978-81. **HOME ADDRESS:** 100 Washington St #5B, Hempstead, NY 11550. **BUSINESS ADDRESS:** 33 Front St Ste 306, Hempstead, NY 11550.

SWINTON, LEE VERTIS
Attorney, legislator. **PERSONAL:** Born Aug 09, 1922, Dardanelle, AR; married Grace Thompson. **EDUCATION:** Pittsburg State Coll, AB 1948; Univ MO Kansas City, JD 1954-. **CAREER:** Kansas City, acting municipal ct judge 1963-64; MO, spl asst atty gen 1965-67; Jackson County, asst county counselor 1967-72; 9th Dist Kansas City MO, state sen 1980; Private Practice, atty. **ORGANIZATIONS:** Mem MO Jackson County Bar Assns; past secUniv MO at Kansas City Law Alumni; vice pres Jackson County Bar Assn; past pres Kansas City NAACP 1960-67; past bd mem Uran League; YMCA; elder W Paseo Christian Ch; bd mem Freedom Inc. **MILITARY SERVICE:** AUS 1942-45. **BUSINESS ADDRESS:** 125 State Capitol, Jefferson City, MO 65101.

SWINTON, PATRICIA ANN
Clinical psychologist. **PERSONAL:** Born Feb 19, 1954, Washington, DC. **EDUCATION:** The Univ of the District of Columbia, BS 1970; Howard Univ, M 1973, PhD 1981; UCLA, Post-Doctoral Educ in Health Serv 1984-. **CAREER:** District of Columbia Public Schools System, counselor & educator 1970-80; Howard Univ, rsch and eval specialist 1980-82; Augustus F Hawkins Mental Health Ctr, staff psychologist 1983-84, asst ward chief 1984-86, psychiatric inpatient educ coord 1987-. **ORGANIZATIONS:** Mem Amer Personnel and Guidance Assoc 1981-, Natl Assoc for Mental Health Specialists 1981-; clinical psychology consultant Charles R Drew Postgraduate Med Sch HeadStart Prog 1982-, mem Amer Educ Rsch Assoc 1982-; clinical psychology consultant Child Youth and Family Serv 1983-; curriculum rsch specialist Computer Assisted Instructional Resources 1983-; mem Long Beach CA Psychological Assoc. **HONORS/ACHIEVEMENTS:** Educ Rsch Awd for Outstanding Work in the field of Rsch Amer Educ Rsch Assoc 1982; Recognition for Outstanding Achievement Los Agneles CA Sentinel 1983; Natl Social Work Awd for Outstanding Serv Dept of Social Serv Martin Luther King Jr General Hosp 1986; listed in Who's Who of Amer Women 15 edition 1987; Who's Who in the West 1987-88; Intl Dir of Disting Leadership 1987-88; The World Who's Who of Women 1987-88; Intl Who's Who of Professional and Business Women1988; Natl Social Work/Social Services Awd for Outstanding Service in the field of Social Work 1987. **HOME ADDRESS:** 2151 Locust Ave, Long Beach, CA 90806.

SWINTON, SYLVIA P.
Retired educator, consultant. **PERSONAL:** Born Oct 05, 1909, Hartsville, SC; married Toney Vance Swinton. **EDUCATION:** Allen Univ, AB (Cum Laude) 1931; IN Univ Bloomington, MS Ed 1942, EdD 1956. **CAREER:** Barber-Scolia Coll, chair dept educ 1961-62; Morris Brown Coll, dir tchr educ 1966-67; Allen Univ, dir tchr educ 1967-73; Morris Coll, dir tchr edn1974-78, spec consult to pres 1978-,fed relations ofcr 1979-80, dir media center 1980-81; Allen Univ, spec consult to pres 1982-84, interim pres 1983-84; Morris Coll, prof emeritus/consultant. **ORGANIZATIONS:** Pres SCATE SC Assn Tchr Educ 1970-71; pres SRATE Southeastern Assn Tchr Educ 1971-72; pres SCIRA SC Intl Reading Assn 1974; life mem NEA, NAACP,NCNW. **HONORS/ACHIEVEMENTS:** Allen Univ Alumni Award Allen Univ 1985; Reading Plaque SC State Coll; Allen Univ Athletic Hall of Fame; Living Legacy Award Natl Council of Negro Women; NY City Alumni Award. **HOME ADDRESS:** PO Box 61, Columbia, SC 29202.

SWITZER, LUCIOUS
Business executive. **PERSONAL:** Born Oct 12, 1948, Orangeburg, SC; married Ann Froelich; children: Gregory, Rhonda. **EDUCATION:** Pratt Inst Brooklyn NY, attended 1966-73. **CAREER:** The Switzer Group Inc, pres 1975-; LCL Desing Asso Inc NYC, partner 1973-75; WE Htton & Co NYC, asst dir of facilities 1971-73; Office Design Asso Inc & NYC, draftsman/designer 1970-71; Sherburne Asso Inc NYC, draftsman/designer 1966-70. **BUSINESS ADDRESS:** 515 Madison Ave, New York, NY 10022.

SWITZER, VERYL A.
Educator. **PERSONAL:** Born Aug 06, 1932, Nicodemus, KS; married Fern N Stalnaker; children: Teresa, Veryl, Jr, Calvin. **EDUCATION:** KS State U, 1954; Depaul U, grad work 1968-69; KS State U, MS 1974. **CAREER:** KS State Univ, dean for minority affairs special prgs 1973-; Minority & Cultural Programs KS State Univ, dir 1969-73; Chicago Public Schools, teacher 1959-69; Canadian, profl & football player 1958-60; Green Bay Packers, football player 1954-55. **ORGANIZATIONS:** Mem Faculty Senate Univ Loan Com; Univ Fair Practice & Housing Com; Phi Delta Kappa; Nat Assn of Student Personel Adminsitrs; mem bd Educ USD #383 Manhattan KS;cHMN KSUniv Athletic Counc. **HONORS/ACHIEVEMENTS:** Recipient Numerous awards including Kappa Alpha Psi Achievement Award; all-armed forces football team; all-am first team NFL 1953; all-am second team 1951-52; NEA & AP. **MILITARY SERVICE:** USAF 1st lt 1956-58. **BUSINESS ADDRESS:** Holtz Hall KS State Univ, Manhattan, KS 66506.

SWYGERT, HAYWOOD PATRICK
Educational administrator. **PERSONAL:** Born Mar 17, 1943, Philadelphia, PA; married Sonja E; children: Haywood Patrick Jr, Michael Branson. **EDUCATION:** Howard Univ, AB History 1965, JD (cum laude) 1968. **CAREER:** Temple Univ School of Law, asst prof of law 1972-77; US Civil Serv Commiss, gen counsel 1977-79; Merit Systems Protection Bd, spec counsel 1979-; Temple Univ School of Law, counsel 1980, prof of law 1980-, vice pres admin; law clerk, Ch. Judge William H. Hastie, Fed Ct of Appeals l968-69; admin asst, Cong Charles B. Rangel, l971-72; assoc Debevoise, Plimpton, New York, NY l969-71. **ORGANIZATIONS:** Mem bd of dir Wynnefield Residents Assoc 1973-75; exec committee Public Interest Law Ctr of Philadelphia 1973-77, 1980-; exec comm Legal Careers Proj Amer Fed for Negro Affairs 1974-77, Minority Affairs Assoc of Amer Law Schools 1974-77; vice chmn Public Serv Comm Philadelphia Bar Assoc 1975, l976; consult Univ Wide Affirm Action 1980; mem nominating comm United Way of SE PA 1981; apptd by Gov Robt P Casey as state rep on Bd of the Southeastern PA Transportation Authority; bd of dir, WHYY-TV and WHYY-FM; vice chmn, Philadelphia City Charter Revision Comm. **HONORS/ACHIEVEMENTS:** Commissioners Awd for Distinguished Serv 1978; Certificate of Appreciation HUD 1981; Black Law Students Awd Temple Univ School of Law Chap 1982; Pres Citation Natl Assoc for Equal Oppty in Higher Ed 1984, Outstanding Alumnus, Howard Univ, Washington DC, l986. **BUSINESS ADDRESS:** Executive Vice Pres, Temple University, Conwell Hall,, Philadelphia, PA 19122.

SYKES, ABEL B., JR.
Educational administrator. **PERSONAL:** Born Jun 01, 1934, Kansas City, KS; married Sylvia; children: Dawn, Daphne, Leslie. **EDUCATION:** Univ of MO Kansas City, BA 1959; Univ of MO, MA 1960; San Diego State Coll Univ of CA, grad studies 1960-68; UCLA Grad Sch of Edn, 1968-71; Univ of CA LA, EdD 1971; Harvard Bus Sch, cert 1976. **CAREER:** O'Farrell Jr HS, instr 1960-64; San Diego Evening Coll, instr 1962-64; Grossmont Coll, instr 1962-68; Compton Comm Coll, dean instr 1968-69, pres/supt 1969-; Kings River College, president. **ORGANIZATIONS:** Mem Amer Assn of Univ Profs; mem Assn of CA Comm Coll Adminst; mem Phi Delta Kappa; mem Chancellor's Adv Com. **HONORS/ACHIEVEMENTS:** Educator of the Year Phi Delta Kappa 1972. **BUSINESS ADDRESS:** President, Kings River College, 995 N Reed Avenue, Reedley, CA 93654.

SYKES, RAY
Business owner, president. **PERSONAL:** Born in LeCompte, LA; divorced; children: Tracey, Raymonda, Ray Anthony. **EDUCATION:** Attended, Santa Monica City Coll. **CAREER:** Douglass Aircraft, machinist; Jack in the Box Restaurant Los Angeles, owner; Superior Ford Minneapolis, pres/owner; Ray Sikes Buick Kingwood TX, president/owner. **ORGANIZATIONS:** Civil Service Commissioner City of Houston; exec bd of dirs Boy Scouts of Amer; bd of dir UNCF; vice pres Houston Buick Dealers Assoc; mem adv bd Sch of Business Texas Southern Univ. **HONORS/ACHIEVEMENTS:** Houston Area Urban League Small Business Awd. **MILITARY SERVICE:** AUS 1963-66; Purple Heart; Vietnam Veteran. **BUSINESS ADDRESS:** President/Owner, Ray Sykes Buick/Jeep-Eagle Inc, 22300 N Highway 59, Kingwood, TX 77339.

SYKES, RAYMOND A.
Business executive. **PERSONAL:** Born Oct 31, 1945, Meeker, LA; married Connie; children: Jon, Rayd, Tracy. **CAREER:** Superior Ford Inc, pres, owner; Bub Currie Ford, auto sales mgr 1973-75; auto sales rep 1972-73; Jack-in-the-box Restaurant, lessee 1970-72. **ORGANIZATIONS:** Mem Minneapolis Urban League; Minneapolis NAACP; Minnapolis C of C; Monitors Social & Charity Club. **HONORS/ACHIEVEMENTS:** Vietnam serv medal; purple heart; good conduct medal. **MILITARY SERVICE:** AUS 1963-66.

SYKES, ROBERT A.
Gas utility executive. **PERSONAL:** Born Dec 25, 1947, Gary, IN; son of Jasper Sykes and Mary Campbell Sykes; divorced. **EDUCATION:** Fisk Univ, Nashville TN, BA Philosophy, 1969. **CAREER:** Natural Gas Pipeline Co of Amer, Chicago IL, employment compliance admin, 1970-75; Fermi Natl Accerlerator Lab, Batavia IL, mgr EEO & community relations, 1975-78; General Mills, West Chicago IL, asst personnel mgr, 1978-79; Washington Gas Light Co, Springfield VA, vice pres human resources, 1979-. **ORGANIZATIONS:** Mem, Amer Gas Assn, Amer Soc of Personnel Admin, Amer Assn of Blacks in Energy; bd mem, Natl Capital Area Health Care Coalition, Melwood Horticultural Training Center. **HONORS/ACHIEVEMENTS:** Elected to Phi Beta Kappa, 1969.

SYKES, VERNON LEE
Economist, state representative. **PERSONAL:** Born Oct 02, 1951, Forrest City, AR; son of Walter Sykes and Louise Stewart Sykes; married Barbara Ann, Dec 25, 1975; children: Stancy; Emilia. **EDUCATION:** OH Univ Coll of Bus Admin, BBA 1974; Natl Assoc of Accountants, Operational Auditing 1977; Univ of Louisville School of Police Admin, 1978; Southwestern TX State Univ, Community Crime Prevention 1979; Wright State Univ Dayton OH, MS Economics 1980; Kent State Univ, MPA Mgmt 1985; public admin Harvard Univ Cambridge MA Masters l986; Wright State Univ, Dayton OH Masters Science l980. **CAREER:**

Akron Bd of Ed, sub teacher 1974-75; UNCI-Econ Devel Program, sr mgmt spec 1975-76; Summit Cty Criminal Justice Commiss, planner Rsch & Eval 1976-79; Akron City Council, chmn, vice chmn, mem 1980-83; Buckeye Coll, part time instr 1980-; Univ of Akron, part time instr 1980-; Interstate Coop, chmn; Clarence Allen Realty, salesman; Athenian Enterprises Inc; The Harvard Group; OH House of Rep, 42nd house dist 1983-; chmn Interstate Coop Comm; real estate salesman; Ohio House of Reps Columbus OH State Rep 3/1983-; instructor/economics Univ of Akron Akron OH 1/1980-. **ORGANIZATIONS:** Vice chmn Interstate Coop, Energy & Environ, Ways & Means Reference, State Govt, Pay Equity Advisory Comm, Travel & Tourism, High Speed Rail Task Force, Job Training Coord Council; chmn Audit Committee, Recycle Energy Comm, Health & Social Svcs; vice chmn Housing & Urban Devel, Downtown Redevel; mem Parks& Recreation Comm, Finance Comm, Annexation Comm, Akron Summit/Medina Private Ind Council, Summit Cty Human Serv Advisory Comm, Mayor Roy Ray's Citizen's Financial Adv Comm, Western Econ Intl, Alpha Homes; vice pres Alpha Library Comm Inc, chmn Ed & Scholarship Comm Alpha Phi Alpha; dir The Harvard Group 4/1987-. **MILITARY SERVICE:** USMC private 2 mos. **HOME ADDRESS:** 615 Diagonal Road, Akron, OH 44320. **BUSINESS ADDRESS:** State Representative Vernon Sykes, Ohio House of Representatives, 77 South High Street, Riffe Center Building, Columbus, OH 43215.

SYKES, WEATHERS Y.
Business executive. **PERSONAL:** Born May 13, 1927, Pond, MS; son of Weathers and Irene; married Carol E; children: Michael, Lori, Stephen. **EDUCATION:** Univ WI, BS 1950. **CAREER:** Chicago Metropolitan Mutual Assurance Co, dir 1977-, sr vice pres operations 1976-; Supreme Life Ins Co Am, sr vice pres 1970-76, vp/asst sec 1968-70, asst sec mgr 1965-68, asst claims mgr 1963-65; Emess Corp, dir 1969-72; Pullman Bank & Trust Co, dir 1971; Supreme Life Ins Co Am, dir 1972-76; Michael Reese Health Plan, pres/dir 1977-; Chicago State Univ Found, dir 1978-. **ORGANIZATIONS:** Dir/mem exec com Mental Hlth Assn of Gr Chicago 1978-80; mem Execs Club Chgo; Intl Claims Assn 1967-; Chicago Home Office Life Underwriters; trustee Michael Reese Med Ctr 1968-; vice pres Michael Reese Research Found; trustee Ravinia Festival Assn; IL Reg Med Prog 1972-75; dir Comm Renewal Soc 1970-74; Vis Com Div Sch Univ Chicago 1971; Sigma Xi; Scientific Research So NA; mem Kappa Alpha 1943-; mem Zeta Beta Tau/Phi Sigma Delta 1948; mem Original 40 Club of Chicago 1971-; mem edit bd The Chicago Reporter 1975-; deacon Chicago United 1976-; vp, dir Chicago Council Navy League of the US 1984-; dir Chicago Econ Devel Corp 1981-; mem Chicago Reg Adv Group 1986-; principal, Chicago United 1986-; vice pres, Chicago Council-Navy League United States 1985-; editor, Bullhorn, Newsletter, Chicago Council, Navy League 1987-; mem, CONDUCT (Committee on Decent Unbiased Campaign Tactics) 1988-. **MILITARY SERVICE:** AUS Pacific Theatre of Operations 1943-46. **BUSINESS ADDRESS:** Chicago Metropolitan Mutual Assurance Company, 4455 S King Dr, Chicago, IL 60653.

SYLVAS, LIONEL B.
Educational administrator. **PERSONAL:** Born May 10, 1940, New Orleans, LA; son of Junius and Iona. **EDUCATION:** Southern Univ, BS 1963; Univ of Detroit, MA 1971; Nova Univ, EdD 1975. **CAREER:** Ford Motor Co, indust rsch analy 1967-69, ed training spec 1969-71; Miami Dade Comm Coll, assoc acad dean 1971-74; Miami Dade Comm Coll, asst to pres 1974-77; Northern VA Comm Coll, campus provost. **ORGANIZATIONS:** Consult Southern Assoc of Coll & Schools Eval Team 1974-; mem advisory bd Black Amer Affairs, Natl School Volunteer Prog 1974-78; pres Southern Reg Couns 1977-88; field reader for Titles III & IV Office of Educ 1979-; mem advisory bd Amer Red Cross 1982-; consult advisory group VA Power Co 1983-87; panelist on the VA Commission of the Arts; mem Constitution Bicentennial Commiss VA. **HONORS/ACHIEVEMENTS:** Outstanding Educator Miami Dade Comm Coll 1975. **MILITARY SERVICE:** AUS 1st lt 1963-65. **HOME ADDRESS:** 6666 Old Blasksmith Drive, Burke, VA 22015. **BUSINESS ADDRESS:** Campus Provost, Northern Virginia Comm Coll, 15200 Neabscomille Rd, Woodbridge, VA 22191.

SYLVESTER, MELVIN R.
Educator. **PERSONAL:** Born Mar 25, 1939, New Orleans, LA; son of John Sylvester and Myrtle Sylvester; married Frances Modica; children: Lori Alaine, Kyle Eugene. **EDUCATION:** Dillard Univ, BA 1961; Long Island Univ, MSLS 1966, MEd 1973. **CAREER:** Dillard Univ, circulation lib 1961-62; CW Post Lib, head circulation dept 1962-64; Long Island Univ B Davis Schwartz Lib, head serials records 1964-; full profssor 1988. **ORGANIZATIONS:** Faculty & chap adv Tau Kappa Epsilon 1965-; mem ALA, NYLA, Nassau Co Lib Assn; mem, N Amer Serials Group for Libraries, 1987-; mem Greater NY Metro Area Chap ACRL 1983-; sec Coll & Univ Div Nassau Co Lib Assn 1973-75; Martin Luther King Higher Educ Oppor Prog Adv Bd 1974-78; mem Lib Faculty Personnel Comm 1974-78; mem Melvil Dui Marching & Chowder Assn 1975-; rep CW Post Ctr Faculty Council 1974-78; adv bd Friendship House Glen Core NY 1975-78; Space Utilization Com CW Post Ctr 1975-78; mem Pre-Medical Comm CW Post 1984-; chmn Space Utilization Com 1977-78; mem Comm on the Handicapped Glen Cove Sch 1978-80; bd of dir Boy's Club at Lincoln House Glen Cove NY 1978-85, Day Care Head Start Ctr Glen Cove NY 1979-89; student affairs appeal comm CW Post Ctr 1979-82; mem 100 Black Men Nassau/Suffolk Inc 1983-; Affirmative Action Task Force CW Post Ctr 1980-86, chairperson, 1984-86; mem, Lions Intl, 1983-; library bd of trust Glen Cove Public Library, 1984-; chairperson, Instruction Committee, CW Post, 1986-88; Freshman Mentor Programm, CW Post 1987-; Bd of Dir, Alliance Counseling Center, 1986-; mem, Career Advisor's Group, CW Post, 1986-; Bd of Trustees, Nassau Library System, 1988-; Campaign Committee & Youth & Family Services Panel of United Way of Long Island, 1988-89; mem Legislative Committee of Long Island Resources Council Inc (for libraries), 1988-; served on Univ Study Group V for Long Island Univ LIU Plan, 1988; mem Advisory bd, Nassau County Dept of Mental Health, 1988-. **HONORS/ACHIEVEMENTS:** Contr screenings Lib Journal & Sch Lib Journal 1971-; printed publs, "Negro Periodicals in the US 1826-1960" an annotated bibliography; "A Library Handbook to Basic Source Materials in Guidance & Counseling" 1973; Faculty Recog Awd Alpha Phi Alpha 1979; Serv Awd Glen Cove Public Schools Comm on the Handicapped 1980; Public Serv Awd Malik Sigma Psi 1981; Serv Awd African Student Convocation 1986; Student Govt Assoc Awd for Serv to Students CW Post Campus 1986.

SYLVESTER, ODELL HOWARD, JR.
Police official. **PERSONAL:** Born Nov 03, 1924, Dallas, TX; married Dorothy Lanning; children: Jennifer, Jon. **EDUCATION:** Univ Of CA, BDs 1948; Univ of So CA, MPA 1974; Harvard U, post grad. **CAREER:** Berkeley CA, apptd Chief of Police 1977; Oakland Police Dept Bur of Investigation, comdg ofcr 1971-77, dep chief 1971, capt 1963, lt 1961, sgt 1957, patrolman 1949; retired Berkley chief of police 1981; pres Urban Mgmt Assoc 1981-. **ORGANIZATIONS:** Participated in devel of Oakland Police Dept New Careers Prgm; Model Cities Intern Prgm; dir Bay Area Minor Recruit Proj; Am Soc for Pub Admin CA Peace Ofcrs Assn; Intl Assn of Chiefs of Police; exec com Nat Orgn of Black Law Enforcement exec bd of Dir Oakland Boys Club; bd of Gov Goodwill Ind; Lake Merritt Breakfast Club; Lions Intl Serv Club; Men of Tomorrow; Kiwanis Intl Serv Club; Oakland Central UMCA; chmn Fund Raising Camp for bd of dir of NW YMCA; Family Serv Agy; Nat Conf of Christ & Jews; NAACP; Alpha Phi Alpha; Sigma Pi Phi. **HONORS/ACHIEVEMENTS:** Awds for Outst Serv to Oakland Comm 1968, 1969, 1971, 1976, 1981, 1985, 1987,1989.

SYLVESTER, PATRICK JOSEPH
Educator. **PERSONAL:** Widowed. **EDUCATION:** St Franics Xavier Univ, BA 1960; Univ PA, MA 1967; Bryn Mawr College, PhD 1973. **CAREER:** St Lucia Natl Devel Corp Wisconsin, consultant; West Chester Univ, prof econ. **HONORS/ACHIEVEMENTS:** Honorary Consul General for St Lucia in New York. **BUSINESS ADDRESS:** Professor of Economics, West ChesterUniv, Dept of Business & Econ, West Chester, PA 19380.

SYPHAX, BURKE
Physician. **PERSONAL:** Born Dec 18, 1910, Washington, DC; married Juanita Jamerson. **EDUCATION:** Howard U, BS; HowardUniv Med Sch, MD 1936. **CAREER:** Howard Univ Coll of Med, prof surg 1970-, chf div 1952-70, acting chf div gen surg 1951-52, asso prof 1950-58, asst prof surg 1944-50, instr surg 1942-44, asst in surg 1940-41. **ORGANIZATIONS:** Kappa Pi Frat; Alpha Omega Alpha Hon Soc. **HONORS/ACHIEVEMENTS:** Outst Alumnus Awd; NY Alumni Assn; Student Cncl Awd; 1st Disting Prof Awd 1974; Rockefeller Fellow, Strong Meml Hosp,Univ of Rochester 1941-42. **BUSINESS ADDRESS:** 2041 Georgia Ave NW, Washington, DC 20060.

SYPHAX, MARGARITE R.
Business executive. **PERSONAL:** Born Feb 11, 1923, Pittsburgh, PA; married William Syphax; children: Carolyn (Young), William Jeffrey. **EDUCATION:** Dluff Iron City Business Coll PA; Washington Business Inst NYC; USDA Coll Studies, DC; Amer Univ, Inst of Property Mgmt; Howard Univ; Real Estate Mgmt Brokers Inst of Natl Assn of Real Estate Brokers Inc, cert Real Estate Mgr 1971. **CAREER:** Personnel Affairs Br Benefit Sect, correspondence unity supt Dept of Personnel 1948-54; Custom Built Homes & Property Mgr for Multi-Family Housing WT Syphax Mgnt Co, supr construction 1948-54. **ORGANIZATIONS:** Mem Natl Soc Prof Resident Mgrs; Natl Assn Real Estate Brokers Inc; Natl Assn Apt Owners; Apt House Council of Home Builders Assn of Suburban VA; Home Builders Assn of Suburban VA; DC Chap Natl Inst Real Estate Mgmt; exec council N Virginia Chap Natl Inst Real Estate Mgmt; former mem Arlington Health & Welfare Council; former Arlington rep to Metro Bd Dir Health & Welfare Council; former mem Adv Bd Mental Hygiene Clinic Arlington; mem N Virginia Mental Health Assn; Comm of 100 Arlington Co; C of C Arlington Co; mem bd dir Arlington Metro Chorus; Marymount Coll VA; mem Arlington Co Plumbing Bd; Arlington Co Tenant-Landlord Commn & Bicentennial Commn Arlington Co VA; prog dir N Virginia Chap Jack & Jill of Amer; financial sec Arlington Chap Links Inc; Eastern Regional Dir of Serv to Youth Links Inc; life mem NAACP; mem Natl Urban League; bd mem Vets Memorial YMCA; mem Arlington View Civic Assn; mem, treas, Sunday school teacher, Mt Olive Baptist Church; former pres Missionary Soc. **HONORS/ACHIEVEMENTS:** Plaques & tributes for outstanding serv to church & community 1974. **MILITARY SERVICE:** USMC headquarters. **BUSINESS ADDRESS:** 800 N Taylor St, Arlington, VA 22203.

SYPHAX, WILLIAM THOMAS
Business executive. **PERSONAL:** Born Jul 31, 1920, Arlington. **EDUCATION:** VA St Coll, BS 1942; George Wash U, MA 1964; Rutgers; Yale; Cath U. **CAREER:** Dept Def, empl 1943-64; Syphax Entrps, pres, chmn bd dirs. **ORGANIZATIONS:** Bd dir Hemisphr Nat Bank; mem Asso Bldrs & Cntrctrs; bd dir DC Bldrs Assn; mem Wash Area Contrctrs Assn; bd dirs Subrbn Home Bldrs; mem No VA Bd Realtors; No VA Apt Owners's Assn; mem Arlington Cnty Bldg Code Bd Appeals; arlngtn Cnty Drug Abuse Commn; bd dir Arlngtn Cnty Red Cross; mem Arlngtn Cnty C of C; legis adv bd rector bd vis VA St Coll; mem Com 100 Arlngtn Cnty; life mem NAACP; past pres VA Real Estate Brkrs Assn; Arlngtn View Civ Assn; mem Arlngtns for Better Cnty Cmpgn Com; life mem Alpha Phi Alpha Frat; mem Beta Kappa Chi Nat Sci Soc; Free & Accptd Masons Prince Hall; VA St Coll Alumni Assn; George WashUniv Alumni Assn; Mt Olive Bapt Ch. **HONORS/ACHIEVEMENTS:** Cert merit Subrbn Home Bldrs Assn 1969; commn serv awd Alpha Kappa Alpha 1968; man of merit awd Alpha Phi Alpha 1966; cert mertrs serv VA St Coll 1964; bldr of yr awd VA Real Est Brkrs Assn 1964; plaque Arlngtn Gridiron Club 1963; This is Your Life Plaque 1962. **MILITARY SERVICE:** USAF.

T

T, MR. See TERO, LAWRENCE

TABOR, LILLIE MONTAGUE
State employee. **PERSONAL:** Born May 13, 1933, Marianna, AR; married Norman. **EDUCATION:** Univ MI, MSW 1961; Western MI U, BA Tuskegee Inst. **CAREER:** Detroit, nursery sch tchr 1951-53; Bur Soc Aid Detroit, soc worker 1954-57; Oak Co Childrens Svc, child welfare worker 1957-60; MI, psyciat soc worker 1960-62; Dept Soc Svc, admin 1965-69; MI Civil Serv Lansing, dir new careers 1969-72; Soc Serv Region 9 Wayne Co Consult Serv State MI, dep dir 1963-65; Family Life Educ Merrill Palmer Inst Detroit, asso prof 1968-71;Univ MI, field instr soc 1972-74. **ORGANIZATIONS:** Child Welfare League Am reg elected com mem 1964-68; bd mem Neighborhood Serv Org 1969-; adv com Vista Marie Sch 1970-; NASW; NAACP; Nat Council Alcoholism Delegate 1970, White House Conf Children; Spl Review Successful Program 1970; Nat Inst New Careers Free press Frank Angelo Interesting Action People 1971. **BUSINESS ADDRESS:** MI State Plaza, 1200 6 St, Detroit, MI 48226.

TABORN, JOHN MARVIN
University professor. **PERSONAL:** Born Nov 07, 1935, Carrier Mills, IL; married Marjorie Campbell; children: John Gregory, Craig Marvin. **EDUCATION:** Southern IL Univ,

BS 1956; Univ of IL, MA 1958; Univ of MN, PhD 1970; Harvard Business Sch, Mgmt Certificate 1971. **CAREER:** Minneapolis Public Schools, psychologist 1966-70; Univ of MN, youth develop consultant 1971-73; J Taborn Assocs Inc, pres 1979-; Univ of MN, assoc prof 1973-. **ORGANIZATIONS:** Mem Natl Assoc of Black Psychologists 1970-; professional mem Amer Psychological Assoc 1972-; consultant State of MN 1973-82; bd of dirs Minneapolis Urban League 1974-80; consultant Honeywell Inc 1981-84; mem Sigma Pi Phi Frat 1983-; consultant Natl Assoc Black Police 1984-, State of CA Education 1986-. **HONORS/ACHIEVEMENTS:** Bush Leadership Fellow 1970; Monitor of the Year Monitors Minneapolis 1980; numerous scholarly publications. **MILITARY SERVICE:** USNR capt 1959-; Natl Defense, Armed Forces Reserve, Navy Expeditionary. **BUSINESS ADDRESS:** Assoc Professor, Univ of Minnesota, 808 Social Science Bldg, 167 19th Ave So, Minneapolis, MN 55455.

TALBERT, MELVIN GEORGE
Clergyman. **PERSONAL:** Born Jun 14, 1934, Clinton, LA; son of Nettles Talbert and Florence George Talbert; married Ethelou Douglas, Jun 03, 1961; children: Evangeline Violet. **EDUCATION:** Southern Univ, Baton Rouge LA, BA, 1959; Gammon Theological Seminary, Atlanta GA, MD, 1962. **CAREER:** Boyd Chapel/United Methodist Church, Jefferson TN, pastor, 1960-61; Wesley United Methodist Church, Los Angeles CA, assoc pastor, 1961-64; Hamilton United Methodist Church, Los Angeles CA, pastor, 1964-67; Southern California-Arizona Conf, Long Beach CA, district supt, 1968-73; General Board of Discipleship, Nashville TN, gen secy, 1973-80; United Methodist Church, Seattle WA, bishop, 1980-88; United Methodist Church, San Francisco CA, bishop, 1988—. **ORGANIZATIONS:** NAACP, Advisory Committee of Mayor of Seattle, member of board of Seattle United Way. **HONORS/ACHIEVEMENTS:** National Achievement Award, National Assn of Black Women, 1965, Doctor of Divinity, Huston-Tillston College, 1972; LLD, Univ of Pugent Sound, 1987. **BUSINESS ADDRESS:** Bishop, San Francisco Area, United Methodist Church, PO Box 467, 330 Ellis St, Suite 301, San Francisco, CA 94101.

TALBOT, ALFRED KENNETH, JR.
Educator. **PERSONAL:** Born Sep 01, 1916, New York, NY; married Hazel Grace Greene (deceased). **EDUCATION:** HamptonUniv VA, BS 1940, MA Educ Admin 1949; New York U, 1953-57; George Peabody Coll, 1955;Univ of KS, 1965; Coll of William & Mary VA, EdD 1985. **CAREER:** Laboratory School Hampton Univ VA, critic teacher/supv student teachers 1946-47; Carver Elem School Loudoun Co Public School VA, principal 1947-55; Bruton Hgts, School Williamsburg Jas City Co Pub School VA, asst prin 1955-63, prin 1963-67; Williamsburg Jas City Co Public School VA, supr elem school 1968-70 ; Salisbury State Coll, prof of sociology. **ORGANIZATIONS:** Mem Governor's Comm Study Merit Pay for Tchrs Commonwealth of VA 1964-66; mem bd of dir Williamsburg, VA Area Day Care Ctr Williamsburg Jas City Co Gov 1966-70; chmn bd dir VA Tchrs Assn (VTA) 1964-66, pres 1962-64. **HONORS/ACHIEVEMENTS:** Plaque for Disting Serv as Chmn Bd Dir VA Tchrs Assn 1964-66, Plaque for Disting Serv as Pres 1962-64; Plaque for Disting Serv & Leadership as Pres VA Congress of Colored Parents-Tchrs 1955-59; listed in Who's Who in Am Edn, Who's Who in The South & Southwest, The Intl Who's Who of Intellectual. **HOME ADDRESS:** Dept of Sociology, Salisbury State Univ, Salisbury, MD 21801. **BUSINESS ADDRESS:** Professor of Sociology, Salisbury State Coll, College & Camden Aves, Salisbury, MD 21801.

TALBOT, DAVID ARLINGTON ROBERTS, SR.
Educator. **PERSONAL:** Born Jan 25, 1916, Georgetown, Guyana;son of Dr David Patterson Talbot and Maud Huberta Roberts Talbot; married Phyllis S Willis, Jun 19, 1946; children: David A Jr, James P, Eric M. **EDUCATION:** Queens Coll of Guyana, Certificate 1934; Morris Brown Coll, BA (w/Honors) 1939; Columbia Univ, MA 1951; Univ of AR, EdD 1966. **CAREER:** Morris Brown Coll, instructor 1939-40; City of New York, social worker 1947-51; Shorter Coll, prof & admin 1952-57; Univ of AR Pine Bluff, assoc dir of student personnel 1957-60, dean of students/prof 1960-68; East TX State Univ, prof of counseling & guidance 1968-86, dir of counseling ctr 1974-82, special asst to pres 1982-87, prof emeritus 1987-. **ORGANIZATIONS:** Mem Omega Psi Phi 1936-; former treas Natl Assoc of Personnel Workers 1967-70; natl vice pres Society of Ethnic & Special Studies 1973-; mem Kiwanis 1985-. **HONORS/ACHIEVEMENTS:** Hon DD Jackson Theol Seminary 1960; DHL Morris Brown Coll 1976; Outstanding Alumnus Morris Brown Coll 1985; Centennial Awd Professor Shorter Coll 1986. **MILITARY SERVICE:** AUS 1943-45, Technical Seargent, Bronze Star Medal 1945. **HOME ADDRESS:** 3011 Tanglewood, Commerce, TX 75428.

TALBOT, GERALD EDGERTON
State official. **PERSONAL:** Born Oct 28, 1931, Bangor, ME; son of W Edgerton Talbot and Aruella (McIntyre) Talbot; married Anita J Cummings, Jul 24, 1954; children: Sharon Renee, Regina L Philips, Rachel A Ross, Robin M Landry. **EDUCATION:** Diploma lessons in printing 1970; ME State Apprenticeship Council, cert of apprenticeship for printing 1972. **CAREER:** Maine State Legis 1972 1974 1976; Portland Savings Bank, corporator 1975-; Guy Gannett Publ Co, state rep. **ORGANIZATIONS:** Mem City Mgrs Policy Adv Comm 1979; adv council State of ME Dept Manpower Affairs 1979; mem State Bd of Educ 1980; founder Black Educ & Cultural History Inc 1980; mem Natl Assn of State Bds of Educ (GAC) 1981; mem Educ Comm Task Force on Sex Equality 1982; Congressman McKernan's Task Force on Children Youth & Families 1983; mem Maine Congressional Citizens Educ Adv Comm 1983; mem State Bd of Educ 1980, v chmn 1981, chmn 1983-84; corporator ME Med Ctr 1984; mem Gr Portland Federated Labor Council, Portland Typographical Union Local 66; life mem NAACP; mem Rescue Inc; mem Dem City Comm 106 ME St Leg; mem ME Assn Blk Prog, ME Conf on Human Serv; corp Portland Svg Bank; bd of dir Epilepsy Fnd Amer ME; adv bd mem Fam Nrs Assn Proj; mem St Interim Adv Cncl Mental Hlth; Justice of Peace; mem Southern ME Area Agency on Aging 1986; bd trust ME Vocational Tech Inst 1986; bd dir Portland United Way Inc 1986, ME Project on Southern AFrica 1985; bd mem, US Selective Service System, Maine 1987. **HONORS/ACHIEVEMENTS:** First Black elected to ME Legislature in state history; Citizen of Week WLOB radio 1964; Golden Pin Awd NAACP Portland Br 1967; Hall of Fame Cert Laurel MS NAACP 1970-73; Outstanding Ser Comm & State Bangor NAACP 1974; Viva Cert of Recog & Appreciation 1974; Cert of Appreciation Natl Assn of Human Rights Workers 1979; Right-On Brother of Yr Awd; Cert of Appreciation ME Chap Multiple Sclerosis; Jefferson Awd Amer Inst for Public Serv WCSH-TV 1980; The Black History Maker of ME Awd 1984; Portland Branch NAACP Leadership Awd 1984; ME State Bd of Ed Awd 1984; Maine Martin Luther King Award, Maine Martin Luther King Commission 1988; 1st Place Certificate of Excellence, Maine Multicultural Festival 1987; Friendship Award, Portland West Neighborhood Planning Council 1989; Twenty Years, Portlan d Branch NAACP 1964-84, Souvenir Edition, Author 1985; Black Ethnic Collectibles, Writer (out of Hyattsville MD) 1987-. **MILITARY SERVICE:** AUS pfc 1953-56. **HOME ADDRESS:** 132 Glenwood Ave, Portland, ME 04103.

TALBOT, JAMES PATTERSON, SR.
Life insurance executive. **PERSONAL:** Born Nov 21, 1950, New York; son of Dr David A Talbot and Phyllis S Willis Talbot; married Cassaundra; children: James Jr, John David. **EDUCATION:** East Texas State Univ, BSc 1973. **CAREER:** G L Rutley & Assoc Insurance, sales 1975-78; Chapman Assocs/Protective Life, sales 1978-83; J P Talbot Insurance, pres/owner 1982-. **ORGANIZATIONS:** Mem Dallas Assn of Life Underwriters 1979-, Word of Faith 1981-, Dallas Estate Planning Council 1981-; CEO/pres Professional Sports Mgmt Inc 1985-; registered representative Mutual Benefit Life 1985-; mem Dallas/Ft Worth Minority Business Devel Council 1986-. **HONORS/ACHIEVEMENTS:** Mem Million Dollar Round Table several years; Natl Achievement Award, Natl Assoc Life Underwriters 1979-85; Natl Quality Award, Natl Assoc Life Underwriters 1985-.

TALBOT, THEODORE A.
Business executive. **PERSONAL:** Born Dec 22, 1923, Guyana; married Dorothy. **EDUCATION:** Coll of Lib Arts, BA 1949; Sch of Journalism Syracuse U, MA 1951; Baylor U, TX A&M U. **CAREER:** TX State Tch Inst, vP; TX State Tech Inst, sec bd of Regents; Div of Humanities Paul Quinn Coll, chmn; Prairie View A&M Coll, asso prof dept ofenglish. **ORGANIZATIONS:** Mem bd dir Am Tech Educ Assn; Nat Council of Tchrs of English; Conf of Coll Com Comm; S-contrl Modern Language Assn; So Council for the Humanities Monern Language Assn; Coll Language Assn; mem Edwards Chapel ANE Ch; Alpha Phi Alpha Frat; Rotary Internatl; Minority Contractors Assn of Waco Bd Dirs; Heart of TX Council of Govt; Mclennan Co Human Serv Delivery Sys Prog Hon Consul for State of TX Coop Republic of Guyana. **BUSINESS ADDRESS:** TX State Tech Inst, Waco, TX 76705.

TALIAFERRO, ADDISON
Government official. **PERSONAL:** Born Dec 20, 1936, Springfield, MA; married Gayle E Wanagar; children: Cheryl, Addison Jr. **EDUCATION:** Lincoln Univ, AB 1959; Columbia univ Sch of Pub Health, MPH. **CAREER:** NJ State Dept of Health, chief cancer registry. **ORGANIZATIONS:** Mem Upper Freehold Sch Bd; mem Mercer Co Comm Action Prog; mem Upper Freehold PTA, Upper Freehold Welfare Dir; chmn Check Mate Inc; mem Monmouth Co CAP 1983-84, treas CAP prog 2 yrs; pres PTA 1970-72. **HONORS/ACHIEVEMENTS:** First black elected to Bd of Educ 1974; first vice pres, pres Bd of Educ 1975-76. **BUSINESS ADDRESS:** Chief Cancer Registry, NJ State Dept of Health, Box 1540, CN 360, Trenton, NJ 08625.

TALIAFERRO, CECIL R.
Educator. **PERSONAL:** Born Feb 03, 1942, Pittsburgh, PA; divorced. **EDUCATION:** VA Union Univ, BA 1966; Univ of Pgh, MEd 1971, PhD 1975. **CAREER:** Wilkinsburg Public School, teacher 1967; NEED Negro Educ Emergency Dr, asst dir 1968; Comm Coll of Allegheny Co, counselor 1969-71; Chatham College, academic adminis higher educ. **ORGANIZATIONS:** Mem Amer Assn of Higher Educ; mem Amer Personnel & Guidance Assn; vice pres NEED Alumni Assn; bd mem FACE Inc; bd mem Black Campus Ministry Inc; pres elect Penn Hills Branch of NAACP; field reader US Dept of Education 1980-81. **HONORS/ACHIEVEMENTS:** HEW Fellowship to Howard Univ Grad of Educ 1966; Outstanding Young Man of America US Jaycees 1978. **BUSINESS ADDRESS:** Academic Administrator, IndianaUniv of PA, 105 Fayebern Dr, Verona, PA 15147.

TALIAFERRO, GEORGE
Athlete, educational administrator. **PERSONAL:** Born Jan 08, 1927, Gates, TN; married Viola; children: Linda T. **EDUCATION:** IN Univ Bloomington, BS 1951; Howard Univ Washington DC 1962. **CAREER:** Lafayette Square Community Center, Baltimore, dir 1957-59; Prisoners Aid Assn Shaw Residence DC, caseworker 1959-66; United Planning Org DC, dir com action progs 1966-68; Dico Corp Martin-Marietta Corp Washington DC, vice pres/general mgr 1968-70; IN Univ, special asst to pres 1972-; Morgan State Coll, dean of students 1970-72; Couns Center & Drug Abuse Authority of MD, exec dir 1970; Big Ten Athletic Conf Spl Adv Comm, chmn 1974-. **ORGANIZATIONS:** Mem Kappa Alpha Psi 1948-; bd of dirs Baltimore Big Bros & Druid Hill YMCA 1962-68; pres & founder Monroe Co Big Bros/Big Sisters 1973-. **HONORS/ACHIEVEMENTS:** Recipient All-Am All Big Ten & All State Awards Coll Football Writers & Coaches 1945-48; Football Hall of Fame. **MILITARY SERVICE:** AUS corpl 1946-47. **BUSINESS ADDRESS:** Indiana University, Bloomington, IN 47405.

TALIAFERRO, NETTIE HOWARD
Physician. **PERSONAL:** Born Jan 01, 1944, Washington, DC; children: Carole, Kermit II. **EDUCATION:** George Washington U, BSMT 1965; Howard U, MD 1974. **CAREER:** Boston City Hosp Boston, MA, intern/residency in internal med 1974-77; Mt Auburn Hosp Cambridge, MA, active staff 1972-; Santa Maria Hosp Cambridge, MA, courtesy staff 1977-; Private Practice Cambridge, MA, physician/internal med 1977-. **ORGANIZATIONS:** Clinical instructor in med HarvardUniv Coll of Med 1977-; mem Nat Med Assn; mem New England Med Soc; life mem NAACP S Middlesex Chap; mem, American Women Medical Assn, Massachusetts Branch. **HONORS/ACHIEVEMENTS:** Alpha Omega Alpha Med Honor Soc. **BUSINESS ADDRESS:** Physician, 300 Mt Auburn St, Cambridge, MA 02238.

TALIFERRO, MIKE CALVIN
Professional athlete. **PERSONAL:** Born Aug 23, 1961, Riviera Beach, FL. **EDUCATION:** TX Christian, Communications Major. **CAREER:** Denver Gold, defensive end 1984-.

TALL, BOOKER T.
Educator. **PERSONAL:** Born Dec 12, 1928, Hooker Bend, TN; son of Booker T. Tall, Sr and Julia MacFulton; married Carolyn; children: Reginald, Bruce, Victor, Christopher, Michael. **EDUCATION:** Akron Univ, BA 1952; Case Western Reserve Univ, MA 1956; Oxford Univ England, grad study 1953; Harvard Univ, Management, 1977; Case Western Reserve, Weatherhead School of Management, 1984. **CAREER:** Congressman Louis Stokes, admin asst 1978-80; Cuyahoga Comm Coll Afro-Amer Studies, dept chmn; Urban Studies, dir 1968-70; Cuyahoga Comm Coll, instructor 1956-68; Akron Urban League, 1947-52, founder OIC; Cleveland 1st Black Minority Business Directory, published 1971-73; 1st Black

Studies Directory, published 1972; Cit Participation Handbook, published 1972; Mt Pleasant Comm Council, pres; Minor Book Publishing Co, pres; US Conference of Mayors, Washington DC, business consultant, 1984; President Minority Franchise Assn, Cleveland Ohio, 1989. **ORGANIZATIONS:** Bd mem Bronze Marker Program for Distinguished Black Amer; mem N Cent Accredidation Team; mem NAACP; Greater Cleveland Cit League; VP Ludlow Assn; mem Nat Advisory Bd Assn for Study Afro-Amer Life & History; VP State of OH Assn for Study of Afro-Amer Life & History; bd mem Nigerian Sister City Program; mem, President's Bush Task Force/Inner Circle, 1989; pres, Western Reserve Historical Society, 1970-89; Black Archives Auxillary. **HONORS/ACHIEVEMENTS:** Man Yr Urban League 1973; Omicron Delta Men Leadership Award 1952; Adv Yr Cuyahoga Comm Coll 1973; Good Neighbor Year 1974; recipient Alpha Fraternity Comm Serv Award 1976; publr "Black Settlers in Cleveland" 1976; Achvmnt Award Fed Exec Bd Minority Business 1980; author of numerous articles on planning & urban revitalization; Life Achievement Award, Black Professional Assn, 1987; History of Black Entreprenuer, Cleveland Ohio, 1988; State of Black Cleveland 1988 Urban League, 1989. **MILITARY SERVICE:** Mil sgt 1954-56.

TALLEY, JAMES EDWARD
Educator. **PERSONAL:** Born Aug 22, 1940, Spartanburg, SC; married Barbara J Goins; children: James Carlton, Deidra Sharee. **EDUCATION:** Livingstone Coll, BS 1963; Converse Coll, 1968; SC State, 1972. **CAREER:** Bryson HS, teacher, coach 1967-68; Carver HS, teacher, coach 1968-70; WSPA-TV,TV show host 1973-75; WKDY Spartanburg, radio show host 1975-78; Wofford Coll, football coach; Spartanburg HS, teacher of math. **ORGANIZATIONS:** Mem LD Barksdale Sicle Cell Found 1975-85; chmn Bethlehem Ctr Trustees 1978-81; chmn Cammie F Clagget Scholarship 1979-85; basileus Epsilon Nu Chap of Omega 1980-82; councilman City of Spartanburg 1981-85; exec comm Spartanburg Devel Cncl. **HONORS/ACHIEVEMENTS:** Man of the Year Mt Moriah Baptist Church 1979; Omega Man of the Year Epsilon Nu Chap of Omega 1980; Human Relation Awd Spartanburg Cty Ed Assoc 1983. **MILITARY SERVICE:** USN radioman 2 4 yrs; Honorman, Navy Co 473 Man of the Year 1963-67; Honorable Discharge 1967. **HOME ADDRESS:** 325 Willow Oar Dr, Spartanburg, SC 29301.

TALLEY, JOHN STEPHEN
Educator. **PERSONAL:** Born Dec 12, 1930, Sterlington, LA; married Furman; children: Kimberly, Stephen. **EDUCATION:** Grambling Coll, BS 1954; Columbia, MA 1958; professional dipolma 1964. **CAREER:** Grambling Coll Nursery School, teacher 1954-56; dir teacher 1956-63; Coll teacher 1964-66; coordinator head start staff training progs 1966; Queens Coll Early Childhood Educ Center Flushing, head teacher, supervising teacher 1963-64; State of LA Office Econ Opportunity Grambling, regl training officer 1966-67; Grambling Coll, part-time teacher; Lincoln Parish, part-time supr kindergarten progs; S Central Regional Educ Lab Little Rock, cons; SW Region Office Child Devel, intl. **ORGANIZATIONS:** Mem LA Educ Assn; Assn for Childhood Edn; Intl So Assn for Children Under Six; Nat Assn for Educ Young Children; Am AssnUniv Profs; Am Home Econs Assn; Day Care & Child Devel Council Am; mem Alpha Kappa Alpha. **BUSINESS ADDRESS:** 360 W 13th St, Indianapolis, IN 46204.

TALLEY, OLGA ANN
Educational administrator. **PERSONAL:** Born Dec 02, 1934, Kansas City, KS; daughter of Ulysses G Plummer Jr and Bernadette Brummell Plummer; married Benjamin F Talley Jr, Nov 09, 1957; children: Karla, Stephanie, Benita Lynn Gilliard, Deanna, Benjamin F III. **EDUCATION:** Univ of Portland, BA Elementary Educ 1970; Portland State Univ, MS 1973, Standard Admin Certificate 1985; US Dept of Health & Human Serv Natl Mgmt Training School, attended 1989. **CAREER:** Portland Public Schools, teacher 1970-72; St Vincent de Paul Child Development Center, child devel coordinator 1973-78; Portland State Univ/Div Continuing Educ, child development specialist 1978-79; Portland Public Schools, supervisor of early childhood educ 1979-. **ORGANIZATIONS:** Mem Delta Sigma Theta Sorority 1954-; mem Natl State & Local Assn for the Educ of Young Children 1973-; mem Portland Chapter of Links Inc 1974; bd mem Parent Child Serv Inc 1982-; mem Natl & Local Associations of Black School Educ 1982-; mem Natl Black Child Development Inst 1985-; chairperson Natl Head Start Assoc Training Conf 1986; mem early childhood advisory comm Oregon Dept of Educ 1987; mem Natl Assn of Female Execs 1987; mem Urban League of Portland, NAACP; Assn for Area and Central Admin Personnel 1985-; Assn for Supervision and Curriculum Devel 1988-; Natl Assn for Female Exec 1987; Natl and Local Alliance of Black School Educator 1982-; Natl, State & Local Assn for the Educ of Young Children 1973-; Natl & State Head Start Assn 1979; Intl Montessori Soc 1986-; Natl Black Child Devel Inst Inc 1986-. **HONORS/ACHIEVEMENTS:** Fellowship Grant Portland State Univ Dept of Special Educ 1972; Certificate Portland Public Schools Career & Vocational Advisory Council 1984; Certificate District Chapter I Parent Advisory Council 1985; Kindergarten Guide Oregon Dept of Educ Participant and Review 1988; Oregon Mathematics Guilde, k-12 Reviewer & Writer 1978; Headstart Staff Policy & Personnel Handbook 1980-. **HOME ADDRESS:** 13740 NE Fremont Ct, Portland, OR 97230.

TALTON, ALMANDA R.
Educator. **PERSONAL:** Born Oct 29, 1950, Newport News, VA; married Alvin. **EDUCATION:** Spelman Coll Atlanta, BA 1973; Wash Coll of Law AmUniv Wash DC, JD 1975. **CAREER:** Youngstown State U, e mD law instr 1978-; Mason & Robinson Law Firm Norfolk VA, asso atty 1976-78; Booker T Washington Found Wash DC, spl asst to the pres 1975; VA Employment Comm Charlottesville, employment specialist 1974; VA State Bar Examiners, license to practice 1976; OH State Bar Examiners, license to practice 1979. **ORGANIZATIONS:** Mem Am Bar Assn; mem Old Dominion Bar Assn; mem Acad Criminal Justice Scis Legal Adv Exec Com Battered Womens Shelter 1979-; bd of trustees YWCA 1980-. **HONORS/ACHIEVEMENTS:** "Prosecutorial Discretion & Juveniles" presentation ACJS Cincinnati 1979; "Sentencing Dispartiy, Adult Female Offender" presentation ACJS OK City 1980.

TANDY, MARY B.
Publisher. **PERSONAL:** Born Jan 13, Louise, MS; daughter of Thomas McGee (deceased) and Florence Coleman (deceased); married OL Tandy (dec) (deceased); children: Bernice, Betty, Mary Ann, Alice M, Leroy Bryant. **EDUCATION:** Ivy Tech Coll, AA 1982; Indiana Univ, 1966. **CAREER:** Indiana Herald, owner/publisher. **ORGANIZATIONS:** SProgram chmn Amer Business Women Assn 1980-82; noble gov Household of Ruth 1980-82; Democratic precinct comm 25 yrs; publicity comm NAACP life mem; mem IDEA Ind Demo Editors 1975. **BUSINESS ADDRESS:** Publisher, Indiana Herald, 2170 N Illinois St, Indianapolis, IN 46202.

TANKERSON, RICHARD E.
Government executive, minister. **PERSONAL:** Born Mar 17, 1940, New Orleans; married Michele; children: Roderick, Dawn, Karen, Linda, Rhonda. **EDUCATION:** Dillard U, BS 1961; Howard U, MDiv 1967. **CAREER:** US Civil Serv Comm, prog analyst 1972-73; Redevelopment Land Agy, EEO spl 1970-72; DCRLA, employee rel spl 1969-70; DCRLA, coordinator 1968;DCRLA, urban renewal asst 1967-68; Simms Chapel, pastor; Ward Memorial 1968-72; Robinson AME Ch, 1962-68. **ORGANIZATIONS:** Mem Nat Council Ch; Nat Council Black Churchmen; mem Jaycees; NAACP; Nat Urban League; Am GI Forum; IMAGE; Operation SER; Black United Dallas GovtEmployees Parliamentarian. **HONORS/ACHIEVEMENTS:** Vernon Jones Award HowardUniv 1967; biography, Biographical Directory Negro Ministers; Black Leaders Am Harco Press. **MILITARY SERVICE:** AUS EEO officer.

TANNER, GLORIA TRAVIS
State official, real estate agent. **PERSONAL:** Born Jul 16, 1935, Atlanta, GA; daughter of Marcellus Travis and Blanche Arnold Travis; widowed; children: Terrance Ralph, Tanvis Renee, Tracey Lynne. **EDUCATION:** Met State Coll, BA Political Science (Magna Cum Laude) 1974; Univ of CO, Master Urban Affairs 1976. **CAREER:** Office of Hearings & Appeals US Dept of Interior, admin asst 1967-72; Denver Weekly News, reporter, feature writer 1972-76; 888 Real Estate Office, real estate salesperson 1976; Lt Gov of CO, exec asst 1976-78; Senator Regis Groff Comm Office, exec dir 1978, public admin 1978-; State of Colorado, state rep 1982-. **ORGANIZATIONS:** Mem & public chmn Delta Sigma Theta 1974; chairwoman Senatorial Dist 3 Dem Party 1974-80; mem Amer Soc Public Admin 1976, CO Black Women for Political Action CBWPA 1976-80; exec bd CO Comm on Women 1976-79; mem natl Assoc Real Estate Brokers; minority caucus chairperson. **HONORS/ACHIEVEMENTS:** Outstanding Woman of the Year Award Scott United Methodist Church Denver 1974; Denver Chamber Leadership Award Denver Chamber of Commerce 1975; Outstanding Woman of the Year Award Reginas Civic Club Denver 1976; Outstanding Comm Serv Award Barney Ford Comm Serv Award Denver 1977; Senator Groffs Comm Serv Award Senator Groff 1977; Democratic Caucus Chairperson, 2nd black elected to a leadership position in the Colorado General Assembly. **BUSINESS ADDRESS:** State Representative, State of Colorado, State Capitol, Denver, CO 80203.

TANNER, JACK E.
Federal judge. **PERSONAL:** Born 1919; married Alice M Powell; children: Maryetta J Greaves, Donnetta M Gillum. **CAREER:** Tacoma pvt practice, 1955-78; US Dist Ct WA Tacoma, judge 1978-. **ORGANIZATIONS:** Mem Natl Bar Assn. **BUSINESS ADDRESS:** Federal Judge, Washington Eastern & West Div, 304 Post Office Bldg, PO Box 2015, Tacoma, WA 98401.

TANNER, JAMES W., JR.
Educator. **PERSONAL:** Born Mar 18, 1936, Spartanburg, SC; married Priscilla; children: Tonya, Angela, James III. **EDUCATION:** SC State Coll, BSA 1958; SC State Coll, MEd 1969;Univ of SC, advanced 1974. **CAREER:** Johnsonville School Dist # 5 Bd, teacher coordinator dept head vo educ 1973-74. **ORGANIZATIONS:** Bd educ Florence Co 1973-74; Govs Commn; Florence Co Educ Assn pres 1973; vP 1971, dist rep 1970; bd dir SC Educ Assn 1974-; pres Florence CoVoters League 1970-; treas Congressional Dist 6 Voters Educ Proj 1973-74; mem Masonic Blue Lodge Master 1970; Am Vocation Assn 1962; Nat Council for Therapy & Rehab through Horticulture; Nat Vacation Agr Tchr Assn 1963; SC Vocational Assn 1962; Nat Educ Assn 1964; Nat Vo Agr Tchr Assn 1962; SC Vo Agr Tchr Assn 1962; bd dir Tri-co Health Clinic; Johnsonville-hemingway Drug Commn; Hickory Hill Comm Recreation dir; Johnsonville Devel Bd; BoyScout post adv; membership chmn Local NAACP; Boy Scout Master 1970-74. **HONORS/ACHIEVEMENTS:** Recipient Distinguished Serv Award Agr Educ 1969; a concurrent resolution by the SC Gen Assembly offering congratulations for being elected to SCEA bd dir & for Dedicated & inspiration serv to educ 1975; Sears Roebuck Scholarship 1953 in Agr Ed; Outstanding Secondary Educ of Am 1973. **MILITARY SERVICE:** Served in military 1958-62. **BUSINESS ADDRESS:** Dean of Student Services, Williamsburg Tech College, 601 Lane Rd, Johnsonville, SC 29556.

TAPPAN, MAJOR WILLIAM
Dentist. **PERSONAL:** Born Mar 18, 1924, Chester, PA; children: Eric Rowland, Ameedah Abdullah, Bobbi Jill Jennings. **EDUCATION:** HowardUniv Lib Arts, 1941-44; HowardUniv Dental Sch, DDS 1944-48; Columbia U, MPH 1965-66. **CAREER:** Roselle, NJ, private practitioner 1948-67; Denver Dept of Hlth & Hosp, dental dir 1967-70, dir public hlth dental svcs. **ORGANIZATIONS:** Dir Found for Urban & Neighborhood Devel Inc 1984; pres The Mage Corp 1983-; consult US Dept of Labor Job Corps 1973-; spcl consult Am Dental Assn 1976; mem Urban League of Denver; dir Denticare of CO Inc 1983-; mem CF Holmes Dental Soc Nat Dental Assn. **HONORS/ACHIEVEMENTS:** Diplomate Am Bd of Dental Pub Hlth; asso profUniv of CO Hlth Sci Ctr Dental Sch 1970-; mem Nat Ctr for Hlth Serv Research Study Sec 1976-79. **MILITARY SERVICE:** AUS 1st lt 1952-54. **BUSINESS ADDRESS:** Dir, Denver Dept of Hlth & Hosp, 605 Bannock St, Denver, CO 80204.

TAPPES, SHELTON
Business executive. **PERSONAL:** Born Mar 27, 1911, Omaha; married Louise. **CAREER:** Intl Union UAW, intl rep; Local 600 UAW, 1st recording sec worlds largest local Union; Workmens Compensation & Housing Dept, educ dir, dir;Nat UAW Ford Dept, intl rep. **ORGANIZATIONS:** Life mem NAACP; past treas Detroit Chap NAACP 1970-73. **HONORS/ACHIEVEMENTS:** Young Man of Yr Pittsburg Courier 1943; Outstanding Cit Award 1945; "Y" Man of 1942 St Antoine Br Detroit; Civic Award Fisher Br 1944; Detroit Spl Cit Mayors Award 1950. **BUSINESS ADDRESS:** 8000 E Jefferson Ave, Detroit, MI 48214.

TARDY, WALTER J., JR.
Psychiatrist, psychoanalyst, educator. **PERSONAL:** Born May 19, 1941, Verona, MS; married Louise; children: Angela, David. **EDUCATION:** TN State U, AB 1962;Univ of WI Med Sch, MD 1967; Queens Med Ctr Honolulu, internship 1968; Harvard Sch of Pub Health, MPH 1969; Coll of Physicians Surgeons Columbia U, residency, psychiatry 1975. **CAREER:** Queens Hosp Cntr Affiliation LI Jewish Hillside Med Cntr, dir of psychiatry; StateUniv of NY at Stony Brook, asst prof psychiatry dept of behavioralSci; research, pvt prac & consultations; Columbia Psychoanalytic Cntr, advanced candidate; Addiction Research & Treatment Corp, med dir 1972; Flight Med 13th AF, chief 1971; Clark AFB Philippines, chief

epidemiologist 1st med serv 1971; Preventive Med Pacific AF, consult 1971. **ORGANIZATIONS:** Mem Am Med Assn; Am Pub Health Assn; Assn of Psychiatrists in Africa; Am Psychiatric Assn; Royal Soc of Health Harvard Sch of Pub Health Alumni Assn; mem Harvard Club of NY mem Assn for Acad Psychiatry; mem Am Assn for Advancement of Sci; mem 100 Black Men; consult in psychiatry Nat Inst of Mental Health; pres Intl Psychoanalytical Students Org; bd dir Welfare Research Inc; consult United Nat Med Serv NYC; consult NY State Bd of Social Welfare; mem Black Psychiatrists of Am. **HONORS/ACHIEVEMENTS:** Recip Outstanding Young Men in Am 1971; Air Medal USAF 1972; Physicians Recog Award Am Med Assn 1972; Solomon Fuller Traveling Fellowship 1975; Nat Psychiatric Endowment Fund Award 1975. **MILITARY SERVICE:** USAF Med Corps major 1969-72. **BUSINESS ADDRESS:** Queen Hospital, Center 82-68 164th St, Jamaica, NY 11432.

TARRY, ELLEN
Author. **PERSONAL:** Born Sep 26, 1906, Birmingham, AL; daughter of John Baber Tarry and Eula Tarry; divorced; children: Elizabeth, Tarry Patton. **EDUCATION:** AL State; Bank St Coll, NYC; Fordham Univ Sch Com, NYC. **CAREER:** Journalist; Friendship House, NYC & Chicago, co-founder 1929-; Natl Catholic Comm Serv, staff mem during WWII; Support HUD, dir fld 1958-76; Com Center Public School NYC, dir 1968; Comm Relations St Charles School Fund, dir; Womens Activities NCCS-USO, dir. **ORGANIZATIONS:** Mem, Catholic Interracial Counseling Commr Black Ministry; Archdiocese of NY; Coalition of 100 Blk Women; Nat Assn of Media Women Inc. **HONORS/ACHIEVEMENTS:** Author of Janie Bell, Garden City Pub, 1940; Hezekiah Horton, Viking, 1942; My Dog Rinty, Viking, 1946; The Runaway Elephant, Viking, 1950; The Third Door: The Autobiography of an Amer Negro Woman, McKay, 1955; Katharine Drexel: Friend of the Neglected, Farrar Straus, 1958; Martin de Porres: Saint of the New World, Vision Bks, 1963; Young Jim: The Early Years of James Weldon Johnson, Dodd, 1967; The Other Toussaint: A Modern Biog of Pierre Toussaint, a Post-Revolutionary Black, St Paul Editions, 1981.

TARTABULL, DANNY
Professional athlete. **PERSONAL:** Born Oct 30, 1962, San Juan, PR; married Monica. **CAREER:** Seattle Mariners, infielder. **HONORS/ACHIEVEMENTS:** TOPPS/Natl Assoc Player of the Month for Sept. **BUSINESS ADDRESS:** Seattle Mariners, PO Box 4100, Seattle, WA 98104.

TARTER, JAMES H., III
Business executive. **PERSONAL:** Born Mar 06, 1927, NYC; married Marion; children: Krishna, Yasmin, Karim, James, Gamal. **EDUCATION:** NY U; St Johns U; Inst for Advanced Mktng Studies; Advtsng Club of NY Hon DD. **CAREER:** Tarter & Wetzel Co Inc, pres; NAACP Spl Contrib Fund, fund raising & pub relations natl dir of devel 1967-; Home Prods Corp, prodn mgr; F&M Schaefer Co, adv supvr; Fuller Brush Co, br mgr; So Delicious Bakeries, pres, gen mgr; NAACP Nat Dept of Tours, founder; NAACP Emergency Relief Fund, dir. **ORGANIZATIONS:** Mem Nat Soc of Fund Raisers; NY Soc of Fund Raising Dirs; Advtsng Club of NY; Knights of Columbus. **HONORS/ACHIEVEMENTS:** Recip Hon Cit of New Orleans; awarded Jeruselem Medl Govt of Israel; Cit of Cr CTM. **MILITARY SERVICE:** US Merchant Marine 1944-49. **BUSINESS ADDRESS:** 424 Madison Ave, New York, NY.

TARTER, JAMES H., SR.
Real estate broker. **PERSONAL:** Born Nov 17, 1904, Riceville, TN; married Elizabeth; children: Gloria, James, III, Roger, Jerome. **EDUCATION:** Columbia U, 1949; US Treas Dept Training Sch, cert. **CAREER:** James H Tarter Real Estate, real estate broker 1953-; Water Supply Mt Vernon, commnr bd 1964-67; Mt Vernon, deputy comptroller first black to be appointedto ofc; candidate Co Supvr on Dem ticket 1957; Sec to Comptroller 1954-56; Sec to Police Commnr 1952-54; first black to be appointed to position. **ORGANIZATIONS:** Mem Columbia Soc of Real Estate Appraisers; spl agent OPA Bur of Sp Investigation Currency protection div assigned to criminal cases 1942-47; held barious admin positions with New York City Dept of Welfare; spl investigator Mayros Commn on Conditions in Harlem 1935-36; mem Dem City Com of Mt Vernon; execbd Black Caucus Dem Party; Sacred Heart Cath Ch. **HONORS/ACHIEVEMENTS:** Recip OPA Award for Superior Accomplishment; commendation US Attys ofc in Chgo. **BUSINESS ADDRESS:** 37 Adams St, Mount Vernon, NY 10550.

TARTER, ROBERT R., JR.
Business executive. **PERSONAL:** Born Jul 11, 1948, Cleveland, OH; son of Robert Tarter and Edna Tarter; married June Robinson. **EDUCATION:** Univ of PA, BS Economics 1970. **CAREER:** Bankers Trust Co, asst treas 1971, asst vice pres 1973, vice pres 1976, sr vice pres 1985, managing dir 1986. **ORGANIZATIONS:** Dir United Bank for Africa 1985; trustee African-Am Inst 1984-; dir Black Alumni Soc Univ of PA 1984-; mem YMCA of New York City Bd of Dirs; mem 100 Black Men 1979-. **BUSINESS ADDRESS:** Managing Dir, Bankers Trust Co, 280 Park Ave, New York, NY 10017.

TARVER, ELKING
Government official. **PERSONAL:** Born Nov 28, 1953, East Liverpool, OH. **EDUCATION:** Gannon Univ, BS Accounting, 1976. **CAREER:** US Department of State, accountant 1976-78; US Dept of Agriculture, supervisory auditor. **ORGANIZATIONS:** mem, Assn of Black Accountants, 1979-81; Assn of Govt Accountants 1982-, Shiloh Baptist Church 1983-. **HOME ADDRESS:** PO Box 1727, Hyattsville, MD 20788. **BUSINESS ADDRESS:** Supervisory Auditor, US Dept of Agriculture, 6505 Belcrest Rd #422, Hyattsville, MD 20782.

TARVER, GREGORY W.
Business executive. **PERSONAL:** Born Mar 30, 1946, Shreveport, LA; divorced. **EDUCATION:** Grambling State U; Centenary Coll. **CAREER:** JS Williams Fun Home, pres; Royal Life of LA Ins Co, pres; lic fun dir. **ORGANIZATIONS:** Mem Shreveport Fun Dir Caddo Parish Police Juror; mem bd of dir LA Men Health Assn; mem Zion Bapt Ch; chrmn bd of Caddo Barber Coll; pres J SWilliams Inc Co; 33rd Degree Mason; Universal Grand Lodge; Shriner; mem United Dem Campaign Com; mem Shreveport Jr C of C; Shreveport C of C; NAACP; Shreveport Negro C of C; Adv Council of YWCA. **HONORS/ACHIEVEMENTS:** Army Accom Medal AUS. **MILITARY SERVICE:** AUS spec 5 E-5 1968-69. **BUSINESS ADDRESS:** 1104 Pierre Ave, Shreveport, LA 71103.

TARVER, MARIE NERO
Municipal government administrator. **PERSONAL:** Born Aug 29, 1925, New Orleans, LA; daughter of Charles L Nero Sr (deceased) and Daisy Lee Blackmore Nero; married Rupert J, Jr; children: Rupert J, III, Charles LN, Stanley J, Gregory T, Bernard J, Cornelius A. **EDUCATION:** Southern Univ Baton Rouge, BA Educ (cum laude) 1945; Univ of WI Madison School of Journalism, MA 1947. **CAREER:** New Orleans Informer Newspaper, women's editor 1945-46; Southern Univ Baton Rouge, English instructor 1947-49; Galesburg High School, Galesburg, IL, English teacher 1954-56; Dutchess Comm Coll Poughkeepsie, English instructor 1961-62; Marist Coll Poughkeepsie, English instructor 1963-68; Model City Agency, asst dir for planning 1968-70, deputy dir 1970-71, exec dir 1971-77; City of Poughkeepsie, NY, dir of social devel 1977-. **ORGANIZATIONS:** Pres & mem Bd of Educ Poughkeepsie City School Dist 1964-70; 1st vice pres natl Model Cities Comm Devel Assn 1975-77; bd of dirs Dutchess Co NY YMCA 1970-74; chr bd of dirs United Way of Dutchess Co NY Inc 1979; chr United Way Campaign 1982; Natl Antapokritis Zeta Phi Beta Sorority Inc 1948-52; commr chmn Poughkeepsie Housing Authority; exec com Dutchess-Putnam Private Indus Council; bd of dir Youth Resources Devel Corp; Mid-Hudson Reg Economic Devel Council; Dutchess Co Arts Council; trustee bd Vassar Bros Hospital; New York State Assn of Renewal and Housing Officials Inc; bd of dirs Dutchess County Child Devel Council, Hudson River Housing Inc; Dutchess/Dominica Partners of the Americas. **HONORS/ACHIEVEMENTS:** First Recipient Sepia Award for Comm Serv Alpha Phi Alpha Fraternity Inc Mid-Hudson Chapter 1976; Merit Award Black Women's Caucus Polk, NY 1979; Amer Assn of Univ Women "Woman of the Year" 1982; Alexis De Tocqueville Award, United Way of Dutchess County 1989. **BUSINESS ADDRESS:** Dir of Social Development, City of Poughkeepsie, Municipal Bldg, Poughkeepsie, NY 12602.

TASCO, MARIAN B.
Government official. **PERSONAL:** Born in Greensboro, NC; married Thomas Earle Williams; children: Charles III. **EDUCATION:** Bennett Coll, attended 1956-58; Temple Univ, BS Business Educ 1965. **CAREER:** City of Philadelphia, city commissioner, city council mem 1987-. **ORGANIZATIONS:** Mem Delta Sigma Theta Sor, Natl Political Congress of Black Women, Women's Way, Family Planning Council of Southeastern PA; trainer/consultant Natl Womens Campaign Fund, YWCA Leadership Inst; natl co-chair Geraldine Ferraro Campaign 1984; apptd delegate Democratic Convention 1984. **HONORS/ACHIEVEMENTS:** Government Awd Bright Hope Baptist Church 1980; Winners Awd Women's Alliance for Job Equity 1985; Martin Luther King Jr Awd Salem Bapt Church 1986; Achievement Awds United Negro Coll Fund 1986; Outstanding Serv & Committment Awd Philadelphia Affirmative Action Coalition. **BUSINESS ADDRESS:** City Council Member, City of Philadelphia, City Hall, Philadelphia, PA 19107.

TATE, ADOLPHUS, JR.
Business executive. **PERSONAL:** Born Aug 18, 1942, Turrel, AR; son of Adolphus Tate, Sr. and Ruth Lee Johnson Tate; married Patricia Dawson; children: Adolphus III, Cherie Levelle, Faith Elizabeth Ann. **EDUCATION:** LA City Coll, AA 1964. **CAREER:** Western & So Life Ins Co, assoc sales mgr 1968-75, dist sales mgr 1975-1985; sales manager Western Southern Life, 1988-. **ORGANIZATIONS:** Mem Bowen Un Meth 1969-; pres Gardena Interest Neighbor vice pres 1971-73; vice pres Un Meth 1976-86; mem Million Dollar Club Western & So Life Ins Co; mem Hollypary Comm Assn; co-chairperson Bolden United Meth; 3rd Degree Mason; chairperson Finance Comm Bowen Church 1983-85; sec United Methodist Men 1987; chairperson Trustee Bd Bowen Un Meth Church 1989-. **HONORS/ACHIEVEMENTS:** Policyholders Merit Awd 1971, 1976-79; Leader in the co field in given serv for past 6 yrs. **MILITARY SERVICE:** US Army 1964-1966 SP/4. **BUSINESS ADDRESS:** District Sales Manager, Western & So Life Ins Co, 4300 S Crenshaw Blvd, Los Angeles, CA 90008.

TATE, DAVID KIRK
Attorney. **PERSONAL:** Born Apr 20, 1939, Detroit, MI; son of Andrew G Tate and Izona Kirk Tate; married L Arlayne Carter, Nov 19, 1961; children: DeMarcus David Holland, Lisa Arlayne Tate. **EDUCATION:** Michigan State Univ, East Lansing MI, BS, 1962; Univ of Detroit School of Law, Detroit MI, JD, 1973. **CAREER:** Patmon, Young & Kirk, Detroit MI, associate, 1973-76; Detroit Edison Co, Detroit MI, staff attorney, 1976-77; R J Reynolds Tobacco Co, Winston-Salem NC, asst counsel, 1977-79, assoc counsel, 1979-82, counsel corporate and commercial, 1982-86, sr counsel and asst secy, 1986—. **ORGANIZATIONS:** American Bar Assn, North Carolina Bar Assn, Wolverine Bar Assn. **MILITARY SERVICE:** US Army Infantry, captain, 1963-68; received bronze star and air medal, 1968. **HOME ADDRESS:** 340 Lynhaven Dr, Winston-Salem, NC 27104. **BUSINESS ADDRESS:** Senior Counsel and Assistant Secretary, R J Reynolds Tobacco Co, 401 North Main St, Winston-Salem, NC 27104.

TATE, ELEANORA ELAINE
Author and journalist. **PERSONAL:** Born Apr 16, 1948, Canton, MO; daughter of Clifford Tate and Lillie Douglas Tate; married Zack E Hamlett, III, Aug 19, 1972; children: Gretchen Rae. **EDUCATION:** Drake University, Des Moines, IA, BA, 1973. **CAREER:** Iowa Bystander, Des Moines, IA, news editor, 1966-68; Des Moines Register, Des Moines, IA, reporter, 1969-76; Register, Des Moines, IA, reporter, 1969-76; Jackson Sun, Jackson, TN, staff writer, 1976-77; Memphis Tri-State Defender, free-lance writer, 1977; Kreative Koncepts, Inc, Myrtle Beach, SC, writer, 1979-81; free-lance writer, 1982-; Postive Images, Inc, Myrtle Beach, SC, president and owner, 1983-. **ORGANIZATIONS:** Member, Iowa Arts Council Artists in Schools/Community, 1970-; member, South Carolina Arts Commission Artists in Education, 1982-; member, NAACP, Georgetown chapter, Georgetown, SC, 1984-; member, Concerned Citizens Operation Reach-Out of Horry County, 1985-; member of board of governors, South Carolina Academy of Authors, 1986-; member of board of directors, 1987-, vice president of board of directors, 1988-, Horry Cultural Arts Council; member, Pee Dee Reading Council, Myrtle Beach, SC, 1987-88; member, Arts in Basic Currriculum Steering Committee, 1988-; board member, National Association of Black Storytellers, 1988-. **HONORS/ACHIEVEMENTS:** Unity Award, Lincoln University, 1974; Community Lifestyle award, Tennessee Press Association, 1977; author of Just an Overnight Guest, Dial, 1980; fellowship in children's fiction, Breadloaf Writers' Conference, 1981; Parents' Choice award, 1987; author of The Secret of Gumbo Grove, F Watts, 1987; Presidential Award, National Association of Negro Business and Professional Women's Clubs, South Carolina chapter, 1988; author of Thank You, Dr Martin Luther King, Jr!, F Watts, 1990. **HOME ADDRESS:** PO Box 483, Myrtle Beach, SC 29578-0483. **BUSINESS ADDRESS:** President, Positive Images, Inc, PO Box 483, Myrtle Beach, SC 29578-0483.

TATE, EULA BOOKER
Elected official, educational administrator. **PERSONAL:** Born Nov 17, 1948, Ypsilanti, MI; daughter of Leslie Davis Booker and Genia Webster Booker; married Ronnie G Tate; children: Ronald L, Donald D, Jennifer C, Stephen J. **EDUCATION:** Univ of MI, BS 1977. **CAREER:** Chrysler Corp UAW Local 630, 1st vice pres 1967-80; MI State Univ, labor ed; City of Ypsilanti MI, councilmember. **ORGANIZATIONS:** Exec comm delegate Council of Governments Southeast MI 1982-; active mem Second Baptist Church. **HONORS/ACHIEVEMENTS:** Awarded Cert of Employee Recognition YWCA Diana Dinner 1983-84; Nominated MI Chronicles Churchwoman of the Year 1984. **HOME ADDRESS:** 801 W Michigan Ave, Ypsilanti, MI 48197.

TATE, GRADY B.
Entertainer. **PERSONAL:** Born Jan 14, 1932, Durham, NC; married Vivian Tapp. **EDUCATION:** NC Central Univ, BA 1959; Amer Acad Dramatic Arts NY, studied. **CAREER:** Positions include studio musician; NBC Tonight Show, musician; performed numerous night clubs prisons TV commercials. **HONORS/ACHIEVEMENTS:** Special Awd Daytop Village Festival Music New York City 1968; Record World All Star Band New Artist New York City 1968; Awd for Outstanding Achievement in Area of Entertainment Hillside HS Durham NC 1971; 1st Humanitarian Awd NC Central Univ 1970-71; Overseas Jazz Club Awd 1971; Jazz Achievement Awd Jazz at Home Club Amer 1971. **MILITARY SERVICE:** USAF s/sgt 1952-55. **BUSINESS ADDRESS:** 185 E 85 St, New York, NY 10028.

TATE, HERBERT HOLMES, JR.
Prosecutor. **PERSONAL:** Born Feb 22, 1953, Karachi, Pakistan;son of Herbert H Tate Sr (deceased) and Ethel Harris Tate. **EDUCATION:** Wesleyan Univ, BA (Cum Laude) 1978; Rutgers Univ Sch of Law, JD 1978. **CAREER:** Essex Co Prosecutor's Office Appellate Sect, law clerk 1977-78; Hon Van Y Clinton, judicial clerk 1978-79; Carella Byrne Bain Gilfillan, assoc 1983-85; Private Practice, attorney 1985-86; Essex Co Prosecutor's Office, asst pros 1979-83, trial sect dir of juvenile trial sect 1982-83; Bloomfield Coll, adjunct prof 1985; Essex Co Prosecutor's Office, prosecutor 1986-. **ORGANIZATIONS:** Mem Kiwanis Intl Newark Chapt; mem NJ Bar, Federal Bar NJ Dist, Pennsylvania Bar; apptd by Gov Thomas Kean as mem of NJ Urban Enterprise Zone Authority1985-86; mem NJ State Bar Assoc Criminal Law Comm, Exec Comm for Criminal Law Sect; mem Essex Co Bar Assoc, Natl Bar Assoc, Natl District Attorney's Assoc, Natl Black Prosecutors Assoc, Natl Org of Black Law Enforcement Execs, Intl Narcotic Enforcement Officers Assoc; mem, State Youth Services Comm, State of New Jersey; mem, Supreme Court Task Force on Minority Concerns; mem, County Prosecutors Assn. **HONORS/ACHIEVEMENTS:** Commendation City of Newark Municipal Cncl; East Orange Optomist Intl Law Enforcement Awd 1987; Bronze Shields Inc Law Enforcement Awd 1987. **BUSINESS ADDRESS:** County Prosecutor, Essex County Prosecutor's Ofc, Essex County Courts Building, 50 W Market, Newark, NJ 07102.

TATE, HORACE EDWARD
Educator, state senator. **PERSONAL:** Born Oct 06, 1922, Elberton, GA; son of Henry Lawrence Tate and Mattie Beatrice Harper Tate; married Virginia Cecily Barnett, Dec 23, 1949; children: Calvin Lee, Veloisa Cecily Tate Marsh, Horacena Edwean Tate. **EDUCATION:** Ft Valley State Coll, BS 1943; Atlanta U, Masters 1951; Univ of KY, Doctorate 1961. **CAREER:** Georgia State Senate, senator, 1975-; GA Assn of Educators, exec sec 1977-; GA Assn of Educators, assoc exec 1970-77; GA Tchrs and Educ Assn, exec sec 1961-70; Ft Valley State Coll, assoc prof 1959-61; Fairmont High School, Griffin, GA, principal, 1951-57; Greensboro High School, Greensboro, GA, teacher & principal, 1945-51; Union Point High School, Union Point, GA, teacher & principal, 1943-45. **ORGANIZATIONS:** Life mem Nat Educ Assn; mem Mut Fed Savs & Loan-bd of Dirs; mem Atlanta Bd of Educ 1965-69; mem Nat Commn on Libraries and Information Sci 1978-82; vice chmn, Georgia Democratic Party, 1969-73. **HONORS/ACHIEVEMENTS:** Achievement & Serv Award The Atlanta Inquirer Newspaper 1969; Distinguished Mem Award Butler CME Ch 1969; delegate World Confederation of Orgns of the Teaching Profession Kenya Africa 1973; Most Illustrious Alumnus Award Ft Valley State Coll 1979; Distinguished Service Award, Fort Valley State Coll, 1982; Legislator of the Year Award, Mental Health Assn of Georgia, 1988; Trail Blaze Award, Antioch Baptist Church, 1988; Secular Educ Award, St Mark AME Church, 1989; author, "Equality & Opportunity," 1965; author, "Some Evils of Tolerated Tokenism," 1973. **HOME ADDRESS:** 621 Lilla Dr SW, Atlanta, GA 30310.

TATE, JAMES A.
Educational administrator. **PERSONAL:** Born Aug 07, 1927, Canton, MS; married Barbara; children: Lisa, Jayme. **EDUCATION:** Jackson State Coll Jackson MS, BS 1950; MI State U, MA 1970; PhD cand 1975-. **CAREER:** Admissions & Scholarships MI State Univ, asso dir 1971-; dir devel prgm for admissions Office of Admissions 1977; science teacher prin elem schools 1968-70; MI, elem teacher 1959-70; Detroit, elem teacher 1955-57; MS, elem teacher, asst prin 1950-55. **ORGANIZATIONS:** Mem exec bd Adminstrv Professional Orgn 1974-76; mem Career Planning & Placement Council; mem Black Faculty Adminstrs Assn; adv bd Ypsilanti Area Comm Servs; Phi Beta Sigma; Am Personnell Guid Assn; MI Counselors Assn; Nat Cong Parents & Tchrs; Nat & MI Educ Assns; mem MASSP; MACAC; MAAAO; MIAssn Collegiate Registrars & Admissions Officers; Orgn MI State U; YMCA; Urban League; NAACP; Amer Assn Collegiate Registrars B Admissions Officers; exec bd Admin Professional Orgn, MI Educ Assn. **MILITARY SERVICE:** AUS 1944. **BUSINESS ADDRESS:** Associate Dir, Michigan State University, Achievement Admissions Program, 250 Administration Bldg, Lansing, MI 48824.

TATE, LEONARD E.
Consultant, administrator. **PERSONAL:** Born Nov 01, 1943, Sandusky, OH; married Shirley; children: Kenyatta, Kambui. **EDUCATION:** Central State Univ, BA Pol Sci 1970; Harvard Univ, Mgmt Cert 1970; Jackson State Univ, MPA 1972; Cleveland State Univ, JD 1979. **CAREER:** MI State Senate Judiciary Comm, consult 1979; Legal Aid of Central MI, legal consult 1980; Ingham Cty Juvenile Court, referee, dir Ingham Cty Juvenile Court 1981-84; Jesse Jackson Delegation DNC, consult 1980-84; Jesse Jackson for Pres MI, mgr 1984; US Sen Howard M Metzenbaum, spec admin asst; OH Youth Comm, youth prog admin; Temple Univ, prog dir; city of Dayton OH, manpower admin; Excons Inc, cons; City of Dayton OH City Gov, mgmt cons; Natl Assoc of Stud Govts Natl Black Pol Assem, cons; State of GA, cons. **ORGANIZATIONS:** Chmn Lansing Assoc of Black Soc Workers 1982-84; assoc dir Lansing Black Lawyers Assoc 1982-84; pres Black Amer Law Students Assoc 1978-79; org NAACP, Urban League, Natl Black Pol Assembly 1972-74; del Natl Demo Convent. **HONORS/ACHIEVEMENTS:** Listed in Outstanding Young Men of Amer 1977, Who's Who in Amer Colls & Univs 1970; Disting Serv Lansing Assoc of Black Social Workers 1979; Serv Recog Awd Cleveland State Law School BALSA Ch 1979; Black Nationhood Awd Central State Univ Student Govt 1970; Woodrow Wilson Fellowship 1970; Martin Luther King-Fellowship 1971. **MILITARY SERVICE:** USMC corpl e-4 4 yrs; Bronze Star; Disting Serv Medal.

TATE, MATTHEW
Educational admin. **PERSONAL:** Born Sep 16, 1940, McComb, MS; married Rosemary Brymfield; children: Mathis Melone. **EDUCATION:** Southern Univ, BS 1963; Louisiana State Univ, additional work 1964; Southern Univ, Master of Ed in Administration 1969; Southeastern Louisiana Univ, Education Specialist 1974. **CAREER:** W S Young Constr Co, field coordinator; Fed Summer Nutritional Prog, bookkeeper; Louisiana Assn of Educators, representative 1978-82; Washington Parish Police Juror, juror 1984; Franklinton High School, assistant principal. **ORGANIZATIONS:** President of Washington Parish Ed Assn 1967; president Phi Delta Kappa 1974; chairperson Supervisory Committee Washington Parish Ed Fed Credit Union 1980; secretary Franklinton Area Political League; committee person local mental health assn; president Rural Franklinton Water Dist; boardmen Review Board Capitol Region Planning Comm, Louisiana; member Congressional Contact Team LAE/NEA. **HONORS/ACHIEVEMENTS:** Police Juror Washington Parrish Police Jury, Franklinton, LA. **HOME ADDRESS:** PO Box 368, Franklinton, LA 70438.

TATE, MERZE
Retired educator. **PERSONAL:** Born Feb 06, 1905, Blanchard, MI; daughter of Charles Tate and Myrtle K. Tate. **EDUCATION:** Western MI Univ, BA 1927; Columbia Univ, MA 1932; Oxford Univ, BLitt 1935; Harvard Univ & Radcliffe Coll, PhD 1941. **CAREER:** Crispus Attucks HS Indianapolis, hist tchr 1927-32; Barber-Scotia Coll, dean of women & hist 1935-36; Bennett Coll, prof of hist 1936-41; Morgan StateUniv, dean of women & prof polit sci 1941-42; Howard Univ & US Army, prof of hist/polit sci geopolitics 1942-77. **ORGANIZATIONS:** Phi Beta Kappa; Pi Gamma Mu; AAUW; Radcliffe Club of Wash, DC (vp for 6 years); Alpha Kappa Alpha; Phi Delta Kappa; Round Table Club of Wash, DC; Writers Club of Wash, DC; Amer Historical Assn; Assn for the Study of Afro-Amer Life & Hist; Amer Bridge Assn; Howard Univ Women's Club; Howard Univ Retirees; mem of Found & President's Club at Western MI Univ; The Associates at Radcliffe; President's Club at Howard Univ; mem Phi Beta Kappa Assoc of Wash DC, Harvard Club of Wash DC, Smithsonian Assoc. **HONORS/ACHIEVEMENTS:** Spirit of Detroit Awd of Merit 1978; The Amer Black Artist's Pioneer Awd 1978; The Radcliffe Coll Alumnae Achiev Awd 1979; The Promethean Plaque of Honor & Life Membership (the only woman) 1980; The Disting Alumnus Awd of the Amer Assn of State Colleges & Univs 1981; Howard Univ Doctor of Humane Letters degree l986; Num publs incl, "The Disarmament Illusion—The Movement for a Limitation of Armaments to 1970" McMillan 1942 (reprinted by Russell & Russell 1970); "Control of Atomic Energy" pamphlet in an UNESCO kit on Atomic Energy Paris 1952, The US & Armaments Harvard Univ 1947, The US & The Hawaiian Kingdom Yale Univ 1964, Hawaii, Reciprocity or Annexation, MI State, Diplomacy in the Pacific, Howard Univ Mineral Railways & Projects in Amer under contract Howard Univ Press. **HOME ADDRESS:** 1314 Perry St NE, Washington, DC 20017.

TATE, SHERMAN E.
Vice-president of community/consumer relations for gas company. **PERSONAL:** Born Oct 05, 1945, Marvell, AR; son of Rufus Tate, Jr. and Annie B. Tucker Tate; married Janet Davis Tate, Dec 25, 1966; children: Amber Nicole. **EDUCATION:** Smith College, Little Rock, AR, BA, 1970. **CAREER:** City of Little Rock, AR, consultant, 1970; Arkansas State Personnel Division, Department of Finance and Administration, Little Rock, AR, personnel analyst, 1970-73; Arkansas Legislative Council, Little Rock, AR, personnel and budget specialist, 1973-75; University of Arkansas at Little Rock, Little Rock, AR, director of personnel, 1975-77; Arkansas State Office of Personnel Management, Little Rock, AR, administrator, 1977-80; Arkansas Louisiana Gas Company, Little Rock, AR, assistant vice president of employee relations, 1980-83, vice president of community/consumer relations, 1983-. **ORGANIZATIONS:** Treasurer, American Association of Blacks in Energy; member of national energy committee, NAACP; member of national advisory council, National Alliance of Business; member of board of directors, One National Bank; chairman, Arkansas State Police Commission; member of board of directors, Centers for Youth and Families; chairman, Greater Little Rock Chamber of Commerce, 1989; member of board of trustees, Philander Smith College. **HONORS/ACHIEVEMENTS:** Distinguished alumnus of Philander Smith College, National Association for Equal Opportunity in Higher Education; Doctor of Humane Letters, Philander Smith College, Little Rock, AR, 1988. **MILITARY SERVICE:** US Army, sergeant; National Guard, major; received Bronze Star. **HOME ADDRESS:** 16 Windy Court, Little Rock, AR 72207. **BUSINESS ADDRESS:** Vice President, Community/Consumer Relations, Arkansas Louisiana Gas Company, 400 East Capitol, Little Rock, AR 72202.

TATEM, PATRICIA ANN
Physical chemist. **PERSONAL:** Born Aug 21, 1946, Wilmington, NC; daughter of Ozie T Faison Sr and Martha Smith Faison; divorced; children: Paul Hadley. **EDUCATION:** Bennett Coll, BS 1967; The George Washington Univ, MS 1970, PhD 1984. **CAREER:** The Naval Rsch Lab, tech editor 1967-72, rsch chemist 1972-. **ORGANIZATIONS:** Mem WA Chromatography Discussion Group, Amer Chem Soc, The Combustion Inst, Sigma Xi. **HONORS/ACHIEVEMENTS:** Summa Cum Laude Bennett Coll 1967; Co-recipient NRL Rsch Publ Awd for Applied Rsch, NRL, 1973; Recipient of Edison Meml Grad NRL 1978-81; Co-recipient NRL Rsch Publ Awd for Applied Rsch, NRL, 1983; Black Engr Awd, Professional Achievement, Morgan State Univ/US Black Engr Mag 1987. **BUSINESS ADDRESS:** Research Chemist, Naval Research Laboratory, 4555 Overlook Ave SW, Washington, DC 20375-5000.

TATMON, EUGENE
Engineer. **PERSONAL:** Born Jan 24, 1941, Oakland, CA; children: R. **EDUCATION:** Laney Coll, AA;Univ of San Francisco, BS. **CAREER:** Pacific Tel Co, engr 1970-, urban aff rep & person supv 1969, chief transmission man 1966-69; Golden St Trophy Co, owner; Positive Directions West, pres 1970-71. **ORGANIZATIONS:** Dir San Francisco Comm Fest & Found; st pres CA Jaycees 1976-77; chmn of Bd CA Jaycees; ACT Team mem US Jaycees; dir Jaycees; dir Bay Area UrbanLeague; adv bd ESCMT Future Tech. **HONORS/ACHIEVEMENTS:** Outst Young Men of Am 1976; Who's Who in Fin & Ind 1976; CA Most Outst Dist Gov 1974; CA Most Outst Nat Dir 1975; Col Hon Order of KY Col; senator Jaycees Intl St Assy Resol of Commendation 1976. **BUSINESS ADDRESS:** 2436 Bayshore Blvd, San Francisco, CA 94134.

TATUM, CAROL EVORA

Administrator. **PERSONAL:** Born Feb 07, 1943, Alabama; children: Charles, Maurice, Shelly, Lisa. **EDUCATION:** BA 1976. **CAREER:** Western Addition Project Area Comm, admin asst 1972-74; Model Cities, admin asst 1972-74; Bayview Hunter's Point Foundation Ctr for Problem Drinkers, dir 1974-87. **ORGANIZATIONS:** Sec SF Chap Natl Assoc Bus & Professional Women 1983-; vice pres CA Black Alcoholism Council 1984-86; sec San Francisco Business & Professional Women 1985-. **HOME ADDRESS:** 201 Ordway St, San Francisco, CA 94134. **BUSINESS ADDRESS:** Dir, Bayview Hunters Point Fdn, 5033 3rd St, San Francisco, CA 94124.

TATUM, EARL

Professional athlete. **PERSONAL:** Born Jul 26, 1953, Elizabethtown, NC; married Larena. **EDUCATION:** Marquette, BA Sociology 1976. **CAREER:** Cleveland Cavaliers, professional basketball guard; Detroit, professional Basketball Player 1978-79, Boston 1978-79, Indian 1977-78, Los Angeles 1976-78. **HONORS/ACHIEVEMENTS:** First four year letterman Marquette; All American.

TATUM, JERRY

Set director/freelance interior designer. **CAREER:** Universal Studios Hollywood CA, set decorator, has worked on the sets of the film Legal Eagles, as well as the sets of episodes of TV shows Amazing Stories, Murder She Wrote, Simon & Simon; also an experienced landscape artist and designer of floral arrangements.

TATUM, JOHN DAVID (JACK)

Athlete. **PERSONAL:** Born Nov 18, 1948, Cherryville, NC. **EDUCATION:** OH State U. **CAREER:** Oakland Raiders, defensive back 1971-. **HONORS/ACHIEVEMENTS:** Named to Sporting News Coll All Am Team 1969-70; AFL All Star Team 1975, 76, 77; Pro Bowl 1973-74 & 77. **BUSINESS ADDRESS:** Los Angeles Raiders, c/o Cheryl Nichols, 322 Center St, El Segundo, CA 90245.

TATUM, MILDRED CARTHAN

Elected official. **PERSONAL:** Born Mar 26, 1940, Grady, AR; married Charles Leon Tatum, Sr; children: Carl, Sharon, Charles, Jr, Gerald, Terrance, Edwin. **EDUCATION:** Voca Sewing Class, 1st place 1959; Sharter College NLR, Special Ed 1979. **CAREER:** PTA, president 1969; Federal Program, president 1980; Regional 6 Chapter 1 Program, treasurer 1981; State Dept of PAC, treasurer 1982; Pulaski Co Special School Dist, president of school board. **ORGANIZATIONS:** Owner 145 St Liquors 1969; owner grocery store 1981; board of dir for Metroplan 1984; natl board for AAS board 1984; Judge Wood appointee to internal board 1985; owner rental house. **HONORS/ACHIEVEMENTS:** Natl Honor Soc (1st Queen in college 10% of class) 1974; Key to City of LA Chapter PAC 1976; Outstanding Leader in School Dist 1983; 1st Black President School Board 1984.

TATUM, WILBERT A.

Business executive. **PERSONAL:** Born Jan 23, 1933, Durham, NC; married Susan Kohn. **EDUCATION:** Yale New Haven, MA 1972; Occidental Coll, MA 1972; Lincoln Univ Pennsylvania, BA. **CAREER:** Health Ins Plan, vice pres marketing; City of NY, commr 1974-78; Borough of Manhattan City of NY, dep pres 1973-74; Milbank & Frawley Urban Renewal Area City of NY, exec dir 1968-72; Stockholm Univ, journalist instr; Inner City Broadcasting Corp, major stockholder 1972-80; Amsterdam News Corp, major stockholder vice chmn sec treas 1972-80. **ORGANIZATIONS:** Chmn of bd Tatum Kohn Assoc 1979-80; mem bd of mgrs Sloane House YMCA 1968-80; vice pres Educ Alliance 1970-80; v chmn of bd Coll for Human Serv 1974-80; asst to commr dir of comm relations Dept of Buildings; asst dir housing Coalition; headed Mayor Beame's Apparel Ofc of Plng & Devel; vice pres mktg Health Ins Plan of NY. **HONORS/ACHIEVEMENTS:** Citation of merit B'Nai B'rith 1976; achievement award Nat Assn of Buying Offices 1976; Man of the Year Am Jewish Congress 1977; Man of the Year Fashion Nat & Urban Fellowship; US Conf of Mayors Black Retail Action Group 1977. **MILITARY SERVICE:** USMC corpl 1951-54. **BUSINESS ADDRESS:** Health Insurance Plan, 625 Madison Ave, New York, NY 10022.

TAYARI, KABILI

Legislation analyst. **PERSONAL:** Born Jun 26, 1950, Wilson, NC. **EDUCATION:** Jersey City State Coll, BA Media & Health Sci 1974; Seton Hall Univ, grad study 1974-76. **CAREER:** Hudson Co Welfare, analyst 1974-78; Vornado Inc, mgr 1974-79; Conrail Passenger Div, operations mgr 1978-80; freelance lecturer 1980-; Natl Black Independent Political Party, natl presiding officer. **ORGANIZATIONS:** Mem NAACP 1968; mem African Heritage Studies Assn 1970-; exec mem NJ Assn of Black Educators 1972-; mem Amer Federation of State Co & Municipal Emps 1974-76; mem coalition of Black Trade Unionists 1974-75; producer & critic Intl TV Assn 1978-; mem Amer Mgmt Assn 1978-; natl presiding officer Natl Black Independent Political Party 1980-; prog coord & tutor Title 20 Afterschool Recreation and Tutorial Prog of the Eastern Co YMCA 1980-84; mem Natl Title I/Chap I Adv Council; rep Natl Black Leadership Roundtable; sec Greenville Natl Little League; pres of Jersey City City Wide Parents Cncl May 1985-; mem NJ Black Issues Convention. **HONORS/ACHIEVEMENTS:** Comm Serv Awd Black Assn of Alumni Faculty Staff & Students Organ at Jersey City State Coll 1981; Comm Serv Award from Title I/Chapter I Dist Wide Parents Adv Cncl 1985. **BUSINESS ADDRESS:** Natl Presiding Officer, Natl Black Indepen Pol Party, PO Box N Lafayette Sta, Jersey City, NJ 07304.

TAYLOR, ALBERT, JR.

System analyst. **PERSONAL:** Born Feb 14, 1957, Fairfield, AL; son of Albert Taylor, Sr. and Voncile Taylor; married Christella Simpson Taylor, Aug 06, 1983. **EDUCATION:** AL State Univ, BS 1978; Samford Univ, MBA 1987. **CAREER:** John F Lawhon, data processing mgr 1978-80; Birmingham Bd of Educ, system analyst 1980-. **ORGANIZATIONS:** Mem Kappa Kappa Psi Hon Band Frat 1975-87, Alpha Phi Alpha Frat Inc 1975-87, Data Processing Mgmt Assoc 1982-87, Neighborhood Watch Assoc 1984-87, Natl Black MBA Assoc 1986-87, Boy Scouts of Amer 1987. **HONORS/ACHIEVEMENTS:** Outstanding Young Men of Amer 1984,86. **HOME ADDRESS:** 7620 4th Ave So, Birmingham, AL 35206. **BUSINESS ADDRESS:** System Analyst, Birmingham Board of Educ, 2015 Park Place, Birmingham, AL 35203.

TAYLOR, ANDERSON

Educator. **PERSONAL:** Born in Autaugaville, AL; married Virginia Burgohoy. **EDUCATION:** Tuskegee Inst AL, BS 1956; Bradley Univ Peoria IL, MS 1963; Atlanta Univ GA, 1965; GA Tech, 1968; Univ of GA, attended. **CAREER:** MS Voc Coll Itta Bena MS, teacher 1957-59; Douglass School, teacher 1959-65; Carver Voc HS Atlanta, teacher 1965-74; Walter F George HS, dct coord, teacher. **ORGANIZATIONS:** Mem Ed Lowndes Cty Christian Movement 1966, Overseas Teacher Aid Prog in Ethiopia NEA 1967, Are Ind Arts Addis Tech TTI Univ 1970; master Boy Scouts KeyWest 1962-64; deacon Bethel AME Church 1960-65; dir Anti-Pov Prog Haynesville AL; faculty rep Carver Voc School 1971-74; chmn Ind Arts Dept. **HONORS/ACHIEVEMENTS:** Awd for work in Ethiopia for Spec Summer Prog Univ of GA NEA 1967; Teacher of the Year 1974-75; Self-Study Career Ed Prog Univ of GA 6 yrs Cert in Ind Arts; Ed in Ethiopia & NEA Overseas Teach Aid Prog. **BUSINESS ADDRESS:** DCT Coordinator, Teacher, Walter F George High School, 800 Hutchens Rd SE, Atlanta, GA 30354.

TAYLOR, ANNA DIGGS

Judge. **PERSONAL:** Born Dec 09, 1932, Washington; daughter of V. D. Johnston and Hazel B. Johnston; married S Martin Taylor; children: Douglass Johnston, Carla Cecilia. **EDUCATION:** Barnard Coll, BA 1954; Yale Univ, LLB 1957. **CAREER:** Dept Labor, atty office solicitor 1957-60; Wayne Co MI, asst prosecutor 1961-62; Eastern Dist of MI, asst US atty 1966; Zwerdling, Maurer, Diggs & Papp, partner 1970-75; City of Detroit, asst corp counsel 1975-79; Eastern Dist Detroit, MI, US Dist judge 1979-. **ORGANIZATIONS:** Adj prof labor law Wayne State Univ 1976; trustee Receiving Hosp Detroit, Episcopal Diocese MI, Detroit Symphony, Neighborhood Service Orgn; mem Fed Bar Assn, Natl Lawyer's Guild, State Bar MI, Wolverine Bar Assn, Women Lawyers Assn; bd mem Delta Home for Girls; mem League of Women Voters; mem Women's Natl Dem Club; NAACP; Met Detroit YWCA; trustee United Foundation & Community Foundation for S Eastern MI. **BUSINESS ADDRESS:** US Dist Judge, Eastern District, 740 Federal Courthouse, Detroit, MI 48226.

TAYLOR, ARLENE M. J.

Systems analyst. **PERSONAL:** Born Aug 26, 1955, Baltimore, MD; daughter of Mack Christopher Jones and Glays Page Jones; married O Odell Taylor Jr, May 10, 1986; children: Michael O. **EDUCATION:** Univ of MD, BS Math 1977; OH State Univ, MS Math 1979. **CAREER:** OH State Univ, lecturer-mathematics 1980-81; NASA, intern programmer 1975-76; Western Elec, information systems design 1979-80; AT&T Tech, information system staff 1980-. **ORGANIZATIONS:** Treas, life mem Zeta Phi Beta Sor Inc 1974-; life mem Phi Kappa Phi Honor Soc 1976-; Alpha Kappa Mu Honor Soc 1976-; Natl Assn for Female Executives 1989; treasurer Ohio Oracle User's Group 1989. **HONORS/ACHIEVEMENTS:** Who's Who Among Students in Amer Univs & Colls 1976; Zeta of the Year (local chapt) Zeta Phi Beta Sor Inc 1976; Disting Corporate Alumni Natl Assoc for Equal Oppor in Higher Educ 1983; Outstanding Young Women of Amer 1984; Alumi of the Year Univ of Md Eastern Shore 1989. **HOME ADDRESS:** 5076 Chipman Dr, Columbus, OH 43232. **BUSINESS ADDRESS:** Information Systems Staff Mbr, AT&T, 5151 Blazer Memorial Pkwy, Dublin, OH 43017.

TAYLOR, ARNOLD H.

Educator. **PERSONAL:** Born Nov 29, 1929, Regina, VA. **EDUCATION:** VA Union U, BA cum laude 1951; Howard U, MA 1952; The CathUniv of Am, PhD 1963. **CAREER:** Howard Univ, prof History 1972-; Univ of CT at Sterrs, prof history 1970-72; NC Central Univ, prof History 1965-70; So Univ in New Orleans, prof history chmn div of soc sci 1964-65; Benedict Coll, instr to prof of history 1955-64. **ORGANIZATIONS:** Mem assn for the study of Afro Am Life & History; So Historical Assn; Am Historical Assn; Orgn of Am Historians; author Am Diplomacy & the Narcotics Traffic 1900-39, A Study in InternatlHumanitarian Reform DukeUniv Press 1969, "Travail & Triumph Black Life & Culture in the South Since the Civil War" Greenwood Press 1976; author several articles in scholarly journals Fulbright Hays Sr Lectr, Am Hist at JadavpurUniv Calcutta India 1967-68-. **HONORS/ACHIEVEMENTS:** Recip post doc res grants Nat Endowment on the Humanities 1968, Am Council of Learned Societies 1969, Ford Found 1969-70,Univ of CT res found 1971-72. **MILITARY SERVICE:** AUS corpl 1952-54. **BUSINESS ADDRESS:** Prof of History & Dept Chrmn, Howard University, History Department, Washington, DC 20059.

TAYLOR, ARTHUR DUANE

Educational administrator. **PERSONAL:** Born Jul 28, 1920, Buxton, IA; married Roberta Hudson; children: Rosylin, Roberta Elaine Lively, Arthur Duane Jr. **EDUCATION:** Coe Coll Rapids IA, AB; INUniv Bloomington IN, AM 1953; IN U, Supervision Credit. **CAREER:** Shasta Coll, dean of students 1969-80; Los Angeles School, dir multi-cultural leadership training 1968-69; Los Angeles School, consult intrgrp rltns 1966-69; Job Corps, pr, dept dir Educ & Guid 1965-66; HS IN & Denver, instr dir of phys ed, basketball coach 1950-65. **ORGANIZATIONS:** Commr CA Apprenticeshp Council 1970-74; p bd of dir Dynamics Rsrch Redding CA; pres Kiwanis Clb Redding 1978-79; NAACP; bd chmn Martin Luther King Cntr Redding; delegate Gov Conf Libraries 1979; del White House Conf 1979. **HONORS/ACHIEVEMENTS:** 1st vice pres NAACP. **BUSINESS ADDRESS:** Shasta Coll, 1065 N Old Oregon Trail, Redding, CA 96001.

TAYLOR, BRENDA L.

Business exec. **PERSONAL:** Born Sep 02, 1949, New Brunswick, NJ. **EDUCATION:** New Brunswick Sr High School, 1967. **CAREER:** Lofton, Lester & Smith, Esqs, legal secretary 1970-72; Irving Ostrow, Esq, legal secretary 1972-75; Engelhard Industries, Patent Dept, administrator 1975-77; City of East Orange, Law Dept, administrator 1978-81; Executype Inc, pres 1981-. **ORGANIZATIONS:** Mem Union Baptist Church, Elizabeth, NJ 1978-; board of directors Natl Urban Affairs Council, NJ Chap 1985-; mem The Edges Group 1986-. **HONORS/ACHIEVEMENTS:** Serv Awd Middlesex Central Baptist Assoc 1983 and 1984; Serv Awd Black Women's History Conference 1985. **BUSINESS ADDRESS:** President, Executype, Inc, 201-203 Washington St, Newark, NJ 07102.

TAYLOR, CAROLE LILLIAN

Educator. **PERSONAL:** Born in Pittsburgh, PA; children: Colette, Yvette. **EDUCATION:** BS 1971; MEd 1972; PhD 1973; sp dipl 1975. **CAREER:** EPIC Inc, exec fdr; Tolafr Acad Elem Sch 1978; EPIC Pitts Bd of Edn, exec 1973-77, tchr 1972-77; Akronite Mag, fashion editor 1967-68;Univ of PittsAm Assn ofUniv Profs, model instr. **ORGANIZATIONS:** Intl Platform Assn; Doctorate AssnUniv of Pitts. **HONORS/ACHIEVEMENTS:** Oustdng accomplishments in letters Delta Sigma Theta 1976; spkr Intl Platform Assn 1977; Rotary

club I Chicago Cleve 1978; Robert L Vann award Pittsburgh Courier; Lolette Wears a Patch 1975-77; ABC 1975-77; Essence Woman of the Year 1985, Essence Magazine 1985; Those Eyes, album (jazz) 1986; Speak and Read, text (instructional manual reading program) 1987. **BUSINESS ADDRESS:** Executive Director, Tolafr Academy-Epic Inc, 1112 N Negley Ave, Pittsburgh, PA 15206.

TAYLOR, CASSANDRA W.
National sales manager. **PERSONAL:** Born Oct 12, 1951, Franklin, TN; daughter of Frederick Douglas Williams and Mattie Lish Hughes Williams; married Wilbert H Taylor Jr, Apr 20, 1974; children: Frederick Delano, Kori Michelle. **EDUCATION:** Memphis State Univ, Memphis TN, BBA, 1973. **CAREER:** Sears Roebuck & Co, Nashville TN, credit sales rep, 1973-74; Goldsmith's Dept Store, Memphis TN, asst buyer, 1974-77; Center City Commission, Memphis TN, marketing & promotions spec, 1977-82; Board of Education, Memphis TN, marketing spec, 1982-83; Greetings, Memphis TN, owner, 1983-85; Memphis Convention & Visitors Bureau, Memphis TN, currently national sales mgr. **ORGANIZATIONS:** Mem, Natl Coalition of Black Meeting Planners; assoc mem bd of dir, Hotel Sales Marketing Assn Intl; mem bd of dir, Tennessee/Arkansas/Mississippi Girl Scout Council; mem, Amer Business Women's Assn, Whitehaven Chapter; chmn, Memphis in May Intl Festival; sec, Shelby State Community Coll, Parent Advisory Bd and Early Childhood Education Center. **HONORS/ACHIEVEMENTS:** Blues Lover Musician's Award, Beale Street Blues Foundation, 1980; Appreciation Merit Award, Memphis in May International Festival, 1980-82; Outstanding Young Women of American Award, 1981; Mother of the Year Award, Shelby State Early Childhood Education Center, 1981-82. **BUSINESS ADDRESS:** National Sales Manager, Memphis Convention & Visitors Bureau, 50 North Front St, Suite 450, Memphis, TN 38103.

TAYLOR, CHARLES AVON
Educational administrator. **PERSONAL:** Born in Baltimore, MD; son of Ellsworth Howard Taylor and Ursula Milden Taylor; married Scheherazade Reed Taylor, Mar 12, 1982; children: Sherri, Charles Jr, Charlana, Aaron. **EDUCATION:** Univ of Maryland, Baltimore MD, BA, 1973; Johns Hopkins Univ, Washington DC, 1976; Loyola Univ of Chicago, Chicago IL, EdD, 1984. **CAREER:** Univ of Maryland, Baltimore MD, counselor, resident life dept, 1971-73; Univ of Kentucky, Minority Affairs Accreditation Team, consultant, 1975; Catonsville Community Coll, Catonsville MD, student activities specialist, 1974-76; Loyola Univ of Chicago, Chicago IL, asst dean of students, 1976-86, instructor in counseling, psychology, and higher education, 1983-88, instructor in African American studies, 1984-88; Empak Enterprises, Inc, Chicago IL, educational consultant, 1985-88; Chicago State Univ, Chicago IL, dean of student development, 1986-88; Kellogg Community Coll, Battle Creek MI, vice pres for student services, 1988—. **ORGANIZATIONS:** Chmn, education committee, NAACP of Battle Creek MI; exec bd mem, Michigan Assn of Community Coll Student Personnel Administrators. **HONORS/ACHIEVEMENTS:** Advisor of the Year, Loyola Univ of Chicago, 1980; Community Leadership Award, Neighborhood Housing Services of Chicago, 1984; Black & Hispanic Achievers of Industry Award, YMCA of Metropolitan Chicago, 1984; Outstanding Young Men of America, 1985; Outstanding Citizens Award, Chicago Junior Assn of Commerce & Industry, 1986. **BUSINESS ADDRESS:** Vice President for Student Services, Kellogg Community College, 450 North Ave, Battle Creek, MI 49017.

TAYLOR, CHARLES E.
Company executive. **PERSONAL:** Born Jun 05, 1944, Columbus, OH; son of Robert Taylor and Catherine Taylor; married Judy Marshall; children: Enid, Antjuan, Jerome. **EDUCATION:** Ohio State Univ, Columbus OH, BA, 1967, MA, 1969, PhD, 1971. **CAREER:** South Side Settlement House, program dir, 1967-68; Ohio State Univ, Columbus OH, teaching research assoc, 1968-69; Columbus Metropolitian Area Community Action Org, dir, 1969-70; VISTA, program officer, 1969; Urban Resources, consultant, 1970; Battelle Memorial Inst, consultant, 1970; Washington Internships in Educ, intern, 1970-71; Inst for Educ Leadership, staff assoc, 1971-72; Acad for Contemp Problems, vice pres for operations, 1972-76; Wilberforce Univ, pres, 1976-84; Standard Oil Co, dir contributions & comm affairs, 1984-86; Standard Oil Co Marine Transport, general mgr, 1986-89; Brand Implementation & Control, USA, mgr, 1989. **ORGANIZATIONS:** Exec dir Columbus Area Leadership Program; dir Ohio Educ Sem Amer Educ Research Assn; Amer Assn of School Admin; Amer Mgmt Assn; Amer Acad of Political & Social Science; author producer Color Line WVKO radio; bd of dir, chmn, program com Columbus Urban League; bd of dir Blacks Against Drugs Uhuru Drug Treatment Facility; chmn Manpower Advisory Council for Columbus, Franklin Cos; steering comm Devel Comm of Greater Columbus 1974-76; bd of dir, chmn Govt Relations Comm Berwick Civic Assn 1974; bd of dir, treasurer Columbus Area Leadership Program 1974-75; bd of dir CARE Regional Resources Bd 1974-76; exec comm Franklin County Democratic Party 1974-76; bd of dir, chmn, personnel comm Neighborhood Devel Corp 1974-76; Full Employment Action Council; fellow, advisory bd Joint Center for Political Studies; bd of trustees Franklin Univ 1975-76; bd of dir Campus Free Coll 1970-72; faculty inst for Pract Politics ; exec staff Natl Policy Conf on Educ for Blacks 1972; part Educ Staff Seminar Japan 1972; bd of educ Shaker Heights OH 1985-89; bd of dir Ameritrust Devel Bank 1988-; bd of trustees Univ of Akron 1988-. **HONORS/ACHIEVEMENTS:** Community Serv Award, Columbus Urban League; talents, style & lead award Columbus Area Lead Program; Award for Asst to Acad for Contemp Problems, Battelle Memorial Inst; Award for Inspiration to Help Humanity, Assn of Black Sec; "Black Enterprise" top 25 black mgrs; Professional of the Year, Black Professionals Assn of Cleveland. *

TAYLOR, CHARLEY R.
Professional athlete. **PERSONAL:** Born Sep 28, 1942, Dallas; married Patricia Grant; children: Charles, Elizabeth. **EDUCATION:** AZ State Univ. **CAREER:** Washington Redskins, scout 1977-, halfback 1964-77, split end 1966-. **ORGANIZATIONS:** Charities No Greater Love; Special Olympics Mentally Retarded Bowls 1963. **HONORS/ACHIEVEMENTS:** Hula 1964; All-Amer 1964; Chicago All Star most valuable player 1964; NFL Rookie Yr 1964; Pro Bowl 1964-68; NFL pass receiving titles 1966-67; All Pro 1967 1974; No 1 Active Pass Receiver; outstanding citizen Grand Prairie TX 1964; rec Club's Offensive Player Yr 1974. **BUSINESS ADDRESS:** Washington Redskins, PO Box 17247, Dulles Intl Airport, Washington, DC 20041.

TAYLOR, CHRISTOPHER LENARD
Dentist. **PERSONAL:** Born Dec 21, 1923, Charlotte, NC; son of Russell B and Viola; children: Ballinger, Russell III. **EDUCATION:** Johnson C Smith Univ, BS 1945; Howard Univ Dental Sch, 1950; Jersey City Med Cntr, internship 1950-51. **CAREER:** Self-employed dentist, Los Angeles, 1951-. **ORGANIZATIONS:** Coast Dir Johnson C Smith Univ Alumni Assn 1954-; pres Pacific Town Club 1960; pres LA Chap NAACP 1962-64; gen chmn Com on Police Brutality; Rally 2nd Bapt Ch 1961; orgn gen chmn LA Civil Rights Rally 1963; 1st chmn United Civil Rights Comm; fdr chmn LA NAACP; life mem dinner 1963-65; num other affiliations; led num marches & boycotts; licensed to pract dentistry in CA, NJ, NY, NC; chmn bd Chris T RB III Corp; chmn bd T & T Dental Corp; charities, Johnson C Smith Univ, NAACP, CORE, Howard Univ, United Way, Urban League; Johnson C Smith Alumni Assn; Omega Psi Phi Frat; Alpha Kappa Mu Frat; Pacific Town Club; Amer Dental Assn; Natl Dental Assn; life mem NAACP; Intl Dental Soc; Angel City Dental Soc; Life mem Intl Anesthesiology Soc; Westminster Nghbrhood Assn; Howard Univ Alumni Assn. **HONORS/ACHIEVEMENTS:** Howard Univ Alumni Achievement Award for Civil Rights Leadership, 1966; Scroll for Civil Rights Achievement, Los Angeles City Council, 1969; Award, Church of the Advent, 1970; ANC Mothers' Award, 1972; holds patent #2,807,818. **MILITARY SERVICE:** WWII; Korean War. **BUSINESS ADDRESS:** 10209 S Compton Ave, Los Angeles, CA 90002.

TAYLOR, CLARENCE B.
Attorney. **PERSONAL:** Born Jan 16, 1937, Pineville, KY; son of William Morris Taylor and Frankie Love Taylor; married Bertha M Thaxton, Feb 01, 1964; children: Tonyah, Renate, Clarence, Jr. **EDUCATION:** OH State Univ, BA 1959; OH State Univ Coll of Law, LLB JD 1962. **CAREER:** US Atty's Off Cleveland, first asst US attorney 1972-1978; executive asst, US Attorney, 1978-; Veterans Admin Field Attorneys, supvr 1969-72; Judge Advocate General Corps & USAR, officer 1963-69(active duty); reserve officer, 1969-; grade lieutenant colonel. **ORGANIZATIONS:** Mem OH State Bar Assn; Alpha Phi Alpha; pres Cleveland Lawyers Assn 1973. **HONORS/ACHIEVEMENTS:** Special Achievement Award, Attorney General, US Dept of Justice, 1988. **MILITARY SERVICE:** Lieutenant Colonel, JAGC, USAR. **HOME ADDRESS:** 3307 Brainard Rd, Pepper Pike, OH 44124. **BUSINESS ADDRESS:** 1404 East 9th Street, Suite 500, Cleveland, OH 44114.

TAYLOR, CLEDIE COLLINS
Educational administrator, metal craftsman. **PERSONAL:** Born Mar 08, 1926, Bolivar, AR; daughter of Dallas Collins and Osie Gaines Collins; divorced; children: Paul Dallas. **EDUCATION:** Wayne State U, BS 1948, MA 1957; L'UNiversita Per Stranieri, Cert Etruscology 1968; Wayne State U, SP Cert Humanities/Art/Hist 1970; Union Grad Sch, PhD Art Hist 1978. **CAREER:** Detroit Pub Sch, art tchr 1979, supr of art 1980-; Metal Processes WSU, instructor fashion design 1981; Arts Extended Gallery Inc, dir; Pri Jewelry Design, practicing metal craftsperson; Detroit Pub Sch, supr of art; children's museum asst dir. **ORGANIZATIONS:** 1st chmn Detroit Cncl of the Arts 1977-81; 1st chmn Minority Arts Advisory Panel MI Cncl for the Arts 1982-; mem bd of trustees Haystack Mountain Sch of Crafts 1982-; mem Detroit Scarab Club 1983-; DPS advisor/liason Detroit Art Tchrs Assn 1983-; mem/art advisor Nat Assn of the African Diaspora 1980-; dir Art Simposium Surinam NAAD Conf 1982; mem Berea Lutheran Ch; mem Alpha Kappa Alpha Sor; dir Art Symposium Barbados; appointed Michigan Council for the Arts 1987-; Board of Michigan Arts Foundation, 1988-. **HONORS/ACHIEVEMENTS:** Contribution to Black Artist Nat Conf of Artist 1984; Spirit of Detroit Award City of Detroit 1983; book publ "Journey to Odiamola" 1978; "Words in a SketchBook" 1985; curator "African Tales in Words And Wood" 1984; curator "Tribute to Ernest Hardman" Exhibit Scarab Club 1985; award, Spirit of Detroit, City of Detroit for Small Business 1988; One Hundred Black Women for Art and Literature 1989. **BUSINESS ADDRESS:** Assistant Director Childrens Museum, Detroit Board of Education, 67 East Kirby, Detroit, MI 48204.

TAYLOR, COMER L., JR.
Business executive. **PERSONAL:** Born Oct 12, 1949, Ft Lauderdale, FL; married Crystal Bryant; children: Tracy Angelique, Tamara Kayaran. **EDUCATION:** AL A&M U, BS 1971, MS 1972;Univ of TN Knoxville, MS 1974;Univ of CA Berkeley, Cert 1980. **CAREER:** TN Valley Authority, pgm analyst 1978-79; TN Vly Ctr for Minority Eco Devel Inc, project mgr 1979-83; Metro Broadcasting Media Inc, pres 1980-; Real Estate First, managing partner 1983-84; Glamour Beauty Supplies Inc, pres. **ORGANIZATIONS:** Regnl planner TN Valley Authority 1972-78; urban planner Top of AL Cncl of Gov't 1971-72; trustee Middle Baptist Ch 1982-; life mem NAACP 1976-. **HONORS/ACHIEVEMENTS:** Article "Consequences of Displacement Caused by Urban Renewal" The TN Planner 1975; article "Partnership Planning for Rural Commercial Areas" Practicing Planner 1977; article "Planning and Energy Conservation" Practicing Planner 1978; article "Elkmont Rural Village" HUD Mag 1978. **BUSINESS ADDRESS:** President, Glamour Beauty Supplies Inc, 1277 Winchester Rd, Memphis, TN 38116.

TAYLOR, DAISY CURRY
Congressional aide. **PERSONAL:** Born Jul 24, 1948, Fort Lauderdale, FL; married Dr Theodore D Taylor; children: Tamila Annay, Tiffany Patrice. **EDUCATION:** Bethune-Cookman, Liberal Arts 1970; Nova Univ, MPA 1975; Cong Professional Devel Cert Congressional Asst 1984. **CAREER:** FL Mem Coll, rsch analyst 1970-71; City of Ft Lauderdale, admin aide 1971-74; City of Oakland Park, dir comm affairs 1974-84; Exquisito Serv of Ft Lauderdale Mgmt Consult Firm, chmn of the bd/pres; Congressman E Clay Shaw, congressional aide 1984-. **ORGANIZATIONS:** Bd of dir Area Agency on Aging 1974-, Early Childhood Devel 1978-81, Community Action Agency 1983-; mem Urban League, NAACP, Task Force on the Black Aged, Women in Business, Amer Soc of Public Admin The Forum Black in Public Admin; Urban League Guild; E Broward Med Assoc Fndn; bd mem Black Coalition of Broward; bd mem Cncl for African Amer Econ Devel. **HONORS/ACHIEVEMENTS:** Community Serv Area Agency on Aging 1979; Outstanding Citizen Community Partnership 1981; Outstanding Contribution to Broward Cty Mt Herman AME Church 1985; Women in Business 1986. **BUSINESS ADDRESS:** Congressional Aide, E Clay Shaw, 299 E Broward Blvd, Fort Lauderdale, FL 33301.

TAYLOR, DALE B.
Educator. **PERSONAL:** Born Jun 13, 1939, Topeka, KS; son of Wesley Taylor and Cassie Taylor; married Marguerite Davis, Mar 14, 1981; children: Shannon Michelle Davis (stepdaughter), Shawn Jeffery. **EDUCATION:** Coll of Emporia, KS, 1957-59; Univ of KS, BMusEd 1963, M of Music Educ 1971, Doc of Philosophy 1984. **CAREER:** Milwaukee County Mntl Hlth Ctr, music therapist 1963; Mendota State Hosp, dir music therapy 1964-67;Univ of WI Eau Claire, dir music therapy 1969-, assoc prof of music. **ORGANIZATIONS:** Co-founder WI Chap for Music Therapy 1973; visiting clinicianUniv of MO at Kansas City 1975; visiting clinician Mt Senario Coll 1975; assembly of delegatesNatl Assoc for Music Therapy Inc 1976-83, 1985-87; clinical facUniv of KS Dept of AMEMT 1979-80; exec bd of dir Taylor Inst Pasadena 1984-; grants review panelist WI Arts Bd 1984-; mem Eau

Claire Affirmative Action Review Comm 1984-; vice commodore 1978-80, commodore 1985-87 Lake Wissota Yacht Club, racing chmn1981-83; pres Great Lakes Region of the NAMT 1976-78; bd of dirs Intl Assn of Music for the Handicapped Inc 1986-; advisory comm, Univ of Wisconsin System Inst on Race & Ethnicity, 1988-; planning comm, Univ of Wisconsin System Design for Diversity Conf, 1989; conductor, accompanist, Eau Claire Gospel Choir, 1987-. **HONORS/ACHIEVEMENTS:** Pi Kappa Lambda Music Hon Soc; Honoree Martin Luther King Mem Lib Display 1985; US Deleg Intl Symposium on Music Ed for Handicapped 1980, 1983, 1985; Spcl Ambassador to Europe People-to-People 1962; Univ of KS Players, Univ of WI Players, Univ of WI-Stout Teleproduction Ctr actor/singer/dancer Madison Theatre Guild Mad Opera Co; US delegate Intl Study Group Theory of Music Therapy 1979; Biology of Music Making Intl Conference 1987; author of 13 publications in professional journals; 26 presentations at conferences. **BUSINESS ADDRESS:** Associate Professor, Univ of Wisconsin-Eau Claire, Eau Claire, WI 54702.

TAYLOR, DALMAS A.
Educator. **PERSONAL:** Born Sep 09, 1933, Detroit, MI; married Faye; children: Monique, Carla, Courtney. **EDUCATION:** Western Res U, BA 1959;Univ DE, PhD 1965; Howard U, MS 1961. **CAREER:** Univ MD, prof. **ORGANIZATIONS:** Dir minority flwsp prog Am Psychol Assn 1975-77; chmn asso prof dept psychology Fed City Coll DC 1969-70; rsrch psychologist Nat Naval Med Ctr1965-69; bd tst N VA Comm Coll 1973-77; bd dir Cncl Applied Soc Rsrch 1976-; Beacon Press 1971-; cncl rep soc psychol Study Social Issues 1977-; mem planning com Nat Conf Black Concerns with Pub Media Content; bd tst Unitarian Universalist Assn; bd dir Suburban Md Fare Housing Montgomery Co; chap Am Civil Liberties Union; pres Psi Chi Hon Soc Psychology 1961-62; Psi Chi 1964-65; postdoctoral flw Nat Acad Sci; biography Who's Who. **MILITARY SERVICE:** AUS 1956-58. **BUSINESS ADDRESS:** Dept PsychologyUniv MD Coll, Park, MD 20742.

TAYLOR, DAVID VASSAR
Administrator, educator. **PERSONAL:** Born Jul 13, 1945, St Paul, MN; married Josephine Reed. **EDUCATION:** Univ of Minnesota, BA 1967; Univ of Nebraska, MA 1971, PhD 1977; Harvard Univ, IEM Program 1985. **CAREER:** St Olaf Coll, Northfield MN, dir Amer minority studies program 1974=76; State Univ of New York New Paltz Campus, chairperson black studies dept 1977-78; Hubert Humphrey Collection Minnesota Historical Soc, curator 1978-79; Macalester Coll, dir minority/special serv program 1979=83; The Coll of Charleston, dean of undergraduate studies 1983-86; Minnesota State Univ System Office, assoc vice chancellor for academic affairs 1986-89; Univ of Minnesota Gen Coll, Minneapolis MN, dean 1989-. **ORGANIZATIONS:** Bd of dirs Hallie Q Brown Comm Center St Paul 1978-79; bd of advisors Perrie Jones Library Fund St Paul 1979-80, Minnesota Quality of Life Study 1979-80; vestry St Phillip's Episcopal Church 1978-81; bd of trustees Seabury Western Theological Seminary 1985-. **HONORS/ACHIEVEMENTS:** Research Fellow-Dissertation Fellowship Fund for Balck Americans 1975-77; consultant historian "Blacks in Minnesota" film for Gen Mills 1980; author bibliography/3 articles/chapter in book. **MILITARY SERVICE:** US Army, spec 5 1969-70; Bronze Star & several commendations. **BUSINESS ADDRESS:** Dean, General College, University of Minnesota, 128 Pleasant St SE, Minneapolis, MN 55455.

TAYLOR, DEFORREST WALKER
Chief of personnel. **PERSONAL:** Born Jan 12, 1933, Brooklyn, NY; son of Harold B. Taylor, Sr. and Francis A. Walker Taylor; married Myrna Fraser; children: DeForrest F Jr, Minnette G, Karla M. **EDUCATION:** John Jay Coll of Criminal Justice, BS 1972; FBI Acad, 1972; Univ of Va; John Jay Coll of Criminal Justice Masters Program. **CAREER:** New York City Police Dept, entered dept 1956, promoted to sgt 1965, promoted to Lt 1969, captain 1972, exec ofcr 79th Precinct, commanding ofcr 28th Precinct 1975-, deputy inspector 1977, inspector 1980, deputy chief 1982, assistant chief 1983; chief of Personnel 1989. **ORGANIZATIONS:** Intl Assn of Chiefs of Police; bd dir Captains Endowment Assn, NYCPD; Am Acad for Professional Law Enforcement; Nat Acad Assoc Guardinas Assn NYCPD; NAACP; NOBLE. **HONORS/ACHIEVEMENTS:** 100 Black Men; Omega Psi Phi Fraternity Inc. **MILITARY SERVICE:** AUS Pfc 1953-55. **BUSINESS ADDRESS:** Chief of Personnel, Personnel Bureau, One Police Plaza, New York, NY 10038.

TAYLOR, DELLA B.
Educator. **PERSONAL:** Born May 20, 1922, Charleston, WV; married Francis; children: Andrea Taylor (Coaxum), Francis, Jr, Faith. **EDUCATION:** WV State Coll, BS 1943; Boston U, MA 1945; MA Coll of Art, addl study; OH U, addl study. **CAREER:** Wv State Coll, asso prof 1956-; Real Estate Broker 1971-; Charleston Gazette & Gazette Mail, art critic 1965-73; Boston Pub Sch, art tchr 1954-56; Fogg Art Mus Cambridge 1950, photo dept asst; 1950. **ORGANIZATIONS:** Dir arts & crafts Cambridge Comm Cntr 1952; mem The Links Inc; Alpha Kappa Alpha; Mattie V Lee Home Coll Art Assn; Am Crafts Council; Nat Art Assn; chmn bd of trustees Charleston Art Gallery at Sunrise; various exhibitions & awards; various gallaries. **HONORS/ACHIEVEMENTS:** The Booklovers mother of Yr Alpha Phi Alpha; WV State Coll Alumnus of Yr 1969.

TAYLOR, DONALD FULTON, SR.
Educational administrator. **PERSONAL:** Born Jul 10, 1932, Charles Town, WV; married Phyllis Shirley Jackson; children: Donald Jr, Keith C, Pamela Jackson, Mark J, Christy A Butts. **EDUCATION:** Shepherd College, AB 1957; Johns Hopkins University, ScD 1971; Virginia Union University, MDiv Magna Cum Laude 1982. **CAREER:** Darby Twp HS, head, dept of science 1958-65; Cheyney State College, coordinator, health sciences 1970-75; Norfolk State Univ, dean 1975-. **ORGANIZATIONS:** Pastor Greater Mt Zion Baptist Church 1985; chairperson Eastern Virginia Health Education Consort 1985; bd of directors Society for Aid of Sickle Cell Anemia 1985; bd of directors Natl Society of Allied Health 1985; task force Medicaid, Organ Transplant 1985; bd of directors Norfolk Area Health Education Center 1985; mem Prince Hall Masons, Norfolk Rotary Club; bd dir, treas Norfolk Area Health Ed Ctr 1985; mem Amer Public Health Assoc 1985, VA Assoc of Allied Health Professional 1985, VA Public Health Assoc 1985, Tidewater Metro Ministers Assoc 1985; bd of dir Chesapeake Hosp Authority 1986-90; vice pres Norfolk Area Hlth Educ Cntr 1986-; mem advisory bd Juvenile Court Conf Comm 1986-. **HONORS/ACHIEVEMENTS:** Publication Allied Health Professions Admission Test 1984; Carl Haven Young Award American Corrective Therapy Assn 1984; Chapel of the Four Chaplins Award; Outstanding Educators of America-listing. **MILITARY SERVICE:** AUS pfc 3-5 yrs; Silver Star with Cluster 1948-51. **HOME ADDRESS:** 431 Ivy Crescent, Chesapeake, VA 23325. **BUSINESS ADDRESS:** Dean, Norfolk State University, 2401 Corpew Ave, Norfolk, VA 23504.

TAYLOR, EDWARD WALTER
Architect, business executive. **PERSONAL:** Born Jul 17, 1926, Baltimore, MD; son of Elbert Taylor and Rebecca Taylor; married Alene Lassiter. **EDUCATION:** Hampton Inst, 1950; Johns Hopkins Univ, Univ of Maryland 1974. **CAREER:** US Govt, chief drafting 1950-59; Henry L Lives Balt, archt mgr 1958-63; Westinghouse Electric, mech designer 1960-73; Edward Q Rogers Balt, archt 1964-67; Sultor Campbell Architects Balt, acht mgr 1968-73; Atti Consult Ltd, owner 1973-. **ORGANIZATIONS:** Mem Natl Tech Assoc, Comm Devel Adv Comm, Howard Park Civic Assoc, AIA, NW Outer Urban Coaltion, NAACP; tech adv Pan African Congress; dir Model Cities Housing Corp; chmn MD Comm Devel Comm 1973; tech consult E Baltimore Comm Corp; graphics advisor Voc Ed Baltimore Construction Specification Institute; mem Construction Specification Institute; vice chairperson Education Committee Concord Baptist Church. **HONORS/ACHIEVEMENTS:** Man of the Year Awd; Samuel Cheevers Awd; Tribute Awd Natl Tech Assoc; Service Award Concord Baptist Church 1987; Man of the Year Dunbar High School Baltimore; Baptist Educational Awardee 1988. **MILITARY SERVICE:** USAF 1944-46. **BUSINESS ADDRESS:** Atti Consultants Ltd, 2125 Harford Road, Baltimore, MD 21218.

TAYLOR, ELLIS CLARENCE
Staff engineer. **PERSONAL:** Born Feb 04, 1931, New Hebron, MS; son of Marva A Whitney. **EDUCATION:** Universal TV & Electronics Systems, diploma 1953; Cleveland Inst of Electronics, diploma 1954; Univ of Kansas City, 1959-62; Central Tech Inst 1968, Univ of Missouri Kansas City, video production studies 1977-82; received FCC First Class License 1955. **CAREER:** KPRS Radio, part-time engineer 1957-58; Taylors TV Serv & Sales 1957-63; AM-FM station KPRS, chief engineerr 1963-66; Freelance Music Producer & Contractor, 1967; KMBC TV, staff engineer 1968-. **ORGANIZATIONS:** 1st black licensing exam bd mem KC Radio & TV 1961-84; mem IBEW Exec Council 1977-79; mem NAACP 1974-77; founding bd mem United Minority Media Assn of Missouri; mem Black Music Assn 1980, Soc of Broadcast Engineers 1980-; life mem Univ of Missouri Kansas City Alumni Assn; mem Audio Engineering Soc Inc 1986-. **HONORS/ACHIEVEMENTS:** Commended by high level leaders for efforts to deter youth crime 1975-76; Leader Jazz & Cultural Arts Study by Black Kansas City Economic Union & The Ford Foundation concerning Kansas City Jazz; invited guest of Recording Industry Assoc of Amer White House Reception 1979; host 11th Cultural Awards presentation of the RIAA; founder People Involved in Public Entertainment Inc Productions (non-profit) 1980. **MILITARY SERVICE:** USN gunnery 1948-50. **HOME ADDRESS:** 1859 East 76th St, PO Box 17061, Kansas City, MO 64132.

TAYLOR, ERNEST NORMAN, JR.
Naval aviator. **PERSONAL:** Born Aug 19, 1953, Chester, PA; son of Ernest Norman Taylor Sr and Elizabeth Ann Derry Taylor; married Ines Emilia Pelayo; children: Randy, Kevin, Matthew. **EDUCATION:** Miami-Dade Comm Coll, AA 1973; Dillard Univ, BA (Cum Laude) 1975. **CAREER:** US Navy, 1975-, naval aviator 1976-. **ORGANIZATIONS:** Eastern region vice pres Natl Naval Officers Assn 1985-87; mem Tuskegee Airman Inc, Negro Airman Intl, NAACP, Aircraft Owners & Pilot Assn; Organization of Black Airline Pilots. **HONORS/ACHIEVEMENTS:** Dorie Miller Awd Natl Naval Officers Assn 1986. **MILITARY SERVICE:** USN LCDR/04 14 yrs; Navy Commendation Medal; Navy Achievement Medal; Meritorious Unit Commendation (3); Humanitarian Medal; Korean Presidential Unit Citation. **BUSINESS ADDRESS:** Patrol Squadron Forty-Nine, US Navy, (VP-49), FPO Miami, FL 34099-5922.

TAYLOR, ESTELLE WORMLEY
English professor. **PERSONAL:** Born Jan 12, 1924, Washington, DC; daughter of Luther Charles Wormley and Wilhelmina Jordan Wormley; married Ivan Earle Taylor, Dec 26, 1953. **EDUCATION:** Miner Teachers College, Washington, DC, BS, 1945; Howard University, Washington, DC, MA, 1947; Catholic University, Washington, DC, PhD, 1969. **CAREER:** Howard University, Washington, DC, instructor in English and Humanities, 1947-52; Langley Junior High, Washington, DC, English teacher, 1952-55; Easter Senior High, Washington, DC, English teacher, 1955-63; District of Columbia Teachers College, Washington, DC, English instructor, professor, 1963-76; Federal City College, Washington, DC, associate provost, 1974-75; District of Columbia Teachers College, Washington, DC, acting academic dean, 1975-76; Howard University, Washington, DC, English professor, chairman of department, 1976-85, associate dean of College of Liberal Arts, 1985-86, director of Graduate Expository Writing, 1988-. **ORGANIZATIONS:** Member, National Council of Teachers of English, 1955-; member, Modern Language Association of America, 1963-; member, College Language Association, 1963-; member, Shakespeare Association of America, 1965; member, Board of Higher Education of the District of Columbia, 1974-75; member, 1979-, vice president, 1979-81, Capital City Links, Inc, Washington, DC; member, 1979-83, vice chairman, 1983, University of the District of Columbia board of trustees, Washington, DC; member of executive committee, Folger Institute, 1982-; public member, US Department of State Foreign Service Selection Board, 1983; member, Commission on Higher Education, 1984-91; public member of Senior Threshold Foreign Service Appointments and Selections Board, Agency for International Development, 1984; member of research board of advisers, American Bibliographical Institute, Inc, 1985-; member, Women's National Democratic Club, 1987-; member, Malone Society, 1987-; member, National Council of Negro Women; member, District of Columbia Urban League; member, NAACP. **HONORS/ACHIEVEMENTS:** Author of Survival or Surrender: The Dilemma of Higher Education, 1975; author of The Ironic Equation in Shakespeare's Othello: Appearances Equal Reality, 1977; Rockefeller/Aspen Institute fellowship, 1978-79; Outstanding Teacher in College of Liberal Arts, Howard University, 1980; author of The Masking in Othello and the Unmasking of Othello Criticism, 1984; Outstanding Contribution to Higher Education award, University of the District of Columbia, College of Human Ecology, 1988. **HOME ADDRESS:** 3221 20th Street, NE, Washington, DC 20018. **BUSINESS ADDRESS:** Howard University, Graduate School of Arts and Sciences, Fourth and College Streets, NW, Annex 3, Washington, DC 20059.

TAYLOR, EUGENE DONALDSON
Physician. **PERSONAL:** Born Oct 10, 1922, St Louis, MO; married Carol; children: William, Eugene. **EDUCATION:** VA State Coll, BS 1947; Wilberforce Univ, 1948; Howard Univ Med Sch, MD 54. **CAREER:** Jewish Hosp, physician; Homer G Phillips, asso dir ob-gyn 1967-; St Louis Pub Sch System, tchr 1948-49; publ "Hazards of Labor in the Grand Miltipara"1968; "Complications of Teenage Pregnancies as seen in the Municipal Hosp" 1970; "Recession of the Near Point of Convergence in the Toxic Hypertensive Syndrome of Pregnancy" jour NMA 1958. **ORGANIZATIONS:** Mem FACOS 1977; FACOB-GYN 1962; Amer Bd Ob-gyn 1962; mem Amer Coll Ob-gyn 1959-61; St Louis Med Soc 1959-60; MO Med Soc 1960; Amer Med Soc 1960; St Louis Gyn Soc 1962; treas 1976-77; Amer Soc Abdom-

inal Surgeons 1961; NY Acad Sci 1971; Pan Amer Med Assn 1975; Mount City Med Soc 1959; Natl Med Assn 1959-; MO Pan Amer Med Assn 1959-; MO Ob-gyn Assn 1973-; Med Adv Com Planned Parenthood 1973-; Amer Coll Surgery 1977. **MILITARY SERVICE:** AUS S/Sgt 1943-46. **BUSINESS ADDRESS:** 2715 N Union, St Louis, MO 63113.

TAYLOR, FELICIA MICHELLE
Educator. **PERSONAL:** Born Feb 14, 1960, Concord, NC; daughter of Milton Lee Taylor and Shirley Alsbrooks Taylor. **EDUCATION:** Univ of NC Chapel Hill, BA 1982; Rowan Tech Sch, special training 1982; Private Pilot Ground Sch Salisbury, NC; Univ of NC Charlotte, MS 1984; The Florida State Univ Tallahassee Florida pursuing PhD 1987-. **CAREER:** Upward Bound UNC-Ch, tutor 1978; Woodrow Wilson Elem Sch, instr 1981; Social Security Admin, soc sec human serv aide 1981; Kannapolis Middle Sch, elemsch instr 1982; I Care Inc, youth counselor 1982; Cabarrus Cty Job Placement Asst, youth counselor 1983; Univ of NC Charlotte, admissions counselor 1983-84; Barber-Scotia Coll, admin asst 1984-85; Shaw Univ, instructor 1985-87; instructor The Florida State University, 1988-. **ORGANIZATIONS:** Mem Sweet Carolines 1980-82; mem Young Democrats 1982-83, Cloud Cappers Ltd Assn 1982-; Delta Sigma Theta 1985; CVAN (Volunteer Assn for Battered Women) 1985; volunteer (probation & parole) 1983-84; counselor Mecklenburg Co Charlotte; chmn UNICEF; Hall Rep 1980-81; UNC-Ch sec of dorm 1981-82; UNC Chapel Hillco-chmn 1st UNCF Tennis Tourn in Cabarrus Co; Advisor, Society of Criminal Justice 1985-87; mem Cooperative Colleges Task Force, 1986; Delta Sigma Theta, Inc. **HONORS/ACHIEVEMENTS:** Jonathan Awd South Rowan Sr HS 1976-77; mem Natl Honor Soc 1977-78, Honor Court UNC Chapel Hill 1980-82; 1st Grad of MS degree in criminal justice UNC Charlotte 1984; Latin Honor Soc 1976-77; In Beta Club 1974-76; Scholastic Acad Award 1978 Sandy Ridge Lodge #2; publication Southern Conference "Role Play" 1987. **HOME ADDRESS:** PO Box 45, Landis, NC 28088.

TAYLOR, GEORGE N., JR.
Retired personnel director. **PERSONAL:** Born Jul 07, 1945, Kansas City, MO; married Berry Jean Cody; children: Lisa C, Jonathan K, George N III. **EDUCATION:** Morehouse Coll Atlanta, GA, BA 1967;Univ of TN at Chattanooga, Grad Work in Bus Admin & Eco 1970-78. **CAREER:** City of Chattanooga, TN, asst personnel dir 1968-70, personnel dir 1970-83, retired. **ORGANIZATIONS:** Mem Am Soc for Personnel Admin; mem bd Catholic Social Serv Chattanooga, TN 1980-; mem Knights of Columbus Chattanooga, TN 1965-. **BUSINESS ADDRESS:** Catholic Social Service, 502 Biltmore Dr, Chattanooga, TN 37411.

TAYLOR, GILBERT LEON
Consultant. **PERSONAL:** Born May 05, 1937, Indianapolis, IN; children: Ernest, Francis, Sandy, Victor, James, Ezekiel, Chase. **EDUCATION:** IN Central U, BS 1958; IN U, MS 1969;Univ of MA, EdD Cand. **CAREER:** IN Pub Sch, tchr 1959-63; Liberia Presbyterian Sch, ed tchr consult 1963-66; Knoxville Coll, administrator 1966-68; IN U, administrator 1968-70; Coll of the Holly Cross, administrator 1970-74; The Children's Museum, administrator 1976-84; Assoc Editor for/Afrique Histoire Magazine; Private Practice, consult 1975-. **ORGANIZATIONS:** Bd mem Cncl for Intl Visitors 1982-86; pres Parent Centered Educ 1984-85; Long range plan comm African-Am Museum Assn 1983-85; coord Cncl for Black Exec 1984-85; long range plan comm Madame Walker Urban Life Ctr 1984-85; advisory comm Freetown Vlg 1984-85; advisory comm Training Inc 1984-85; Co-hostViews & Visions TY Pgm WTTV 1983-. **HONORS/ACHIEVEMENTS:** Ford FellowUniv of MA 1974-76; Featured Personality United Press Intl 1983; Recog Award Bahai Faith 1983; Key to the City Tuskegee City 1979; Ed & Human Rights Ind Tchrs Assn 1983. **BUSINESS ADDRESS:** Mentor Coordinator, Career Beginnings-Butler University, 4600 Sunset, Indianapolis, IN 46208.

TAYLOR, GLORIA JEAN
Elected official. **PERSONAL:** Married Lamond Charles Taylor; children: Clifford, Theresa. **EDUCATION:** Coll Graduate, Business Admin. **CAREER:** Harvey Park Dist, treas 1979-81, pres 1981-. **ORGANIZATIONS:** Asst area leader Harvey Democratic Org 1984-; work IL State Police Crime Lab, fingerprint tech & criminal history records processor. **HONORS/ACHIEVEMENTS:** Longest sitting commissioner Harvey Park Dist 1985; Public Service/Leadership Awd 1986 and 1988; 10 Year Public Service Award 1989. **HOME ADDRESS:** 15400 Claremont Ct, Harvey, IL 60426. **BUSINESS ADDRESS:** President, Harvey Park Dist, 15335 Broadway, Harvey, IL 60426.

TAYLOR, HAROLD LEON
Dentist. **PERSONAL:** Born Mar 07, 1946, Memphis, TN; married Madeleine. **EDUCATION:** Morehouse Coll, BS 1968; Howard U, DDS 1972; Howard U, cert oral surg 1975. **CAREER:** Dentist oral maxillofcaial surgery 1975-; TN Coll Denistry, asst prof 1975; DC Gen Hosp, chf resd 1972-74; Freedmen's Hosp, 1972; Howard U, lectr coll denistry; St Joseph Hosp, atdng oral surgeon; St Francis Hosp; Mid-S Hosp. **ORGANIZATIONS:** Bd Dir Memphis Chap Nat Bus League; Runaway House, Inc; house del Nat Dental Assn; mem Memphis Soc Oral Surgeons; mem Fndrs Club Boys Club Memphis; Alpha Phi Alpha Frat; Chi Delta Mu Frat; pres Shelby Co Dental Soc 1979; bd of dir Mason St Home for Boys 1979; mem Am Assn of Oral & Maxillofacial Surgeons 1978; Am Dental Assn; editonal bd Dental Students Mag 1972; Operations Crossroads Africa 1967; flwsp Meml Hosp Cancer 1971. **HONORS/ACHIEVEMENTS:** Deans Award HowardUniv 1972; Omicron Kappa Upsilon Nat Hon Soc. **BUSINESS ADDRESS:** 1411 Lamar Ave, Memphis, TN 38104.

TAYLOR, HENRY MARSHALL
Business executive. **PERSONAL:** Born Dec 24, 1932, Indianapolis, IN; married Marcella Jean Collins; children: Cynthia J, Timothy M. **EDUCATION:** IN Central U, BS 1959. **CAREER:** Crispus Attucks HS Indpls, teacher/coach 1959-68; Commnty Serv Cncl Metro Inpls, planner 1968-71; Indianapolis Bus Devel Found, pres 1971-. **ORGANIZATIONS:** Instructor Continuing Studies IU-PUI 1974-; pres HM Taylor & Asso 1983-; bd mem Ind Inst for New Bus Ventures 1984-; mem IN Dist SBA Adv Cncl; mem Omega Psi Phi Zeta Phi 1963-; commr Metro Dev Commn 1976-82; mem/treas bd Ind Export Adv Cncl US Doc Consortium for Urban Ed 1978-; sec Consumer Credit Cnslng Svc; chmn Cncl of Black Exec; exec chmn Central IN Bus Dev Coalition. **HONORS/ACHIEVEMENTS:** Bus Achievement Award Zeta Phi Chap 1984; Who's Who in Am Coll &Univ 1959; Delta Hall of Fame 1975; Disting Award Center for Leadership Dev 1981. **MILITARY SERVICE:** AUS sgt E-5. **HOME ADDRESS:** 3423 N Lesley Ave, Indianapolis, IN 46218. **BUSINESS ADDRESS:** President, Indianapolis Bus Dev Found, One Virginia Ave, Indianapolis, IN 46204.

TAYLOR, HERBERT CHARLES
Manufacturing company executive. **PERSONAL:** Born Feb 02, 1948, Red Jacket, WV; children: Herbert Jr, Holly. **EDUCATION:** Detroit Coll of Business, BA 1977; Central MI Univ, MA 1981. **CAREER:** General Motor Corp, purchasing mgr 1966-84; Bing Steel Inc, exec vice pres 1984-85; Superb Manufacturing Inc, pres 1985-. **ORGANIZATIONS:** Bd of dirs Bing Steel Inc 1984-, Superb Manufacturing Inc 1984-; mem Natl Black MBA Assoc 1985-; bd mem Natl Assoc of Black Auto Suppliers 1986-. **BUSINESS ADDRESS:** President, Superb Manufacturing Inc, 6100 15 Mile Rd, Sterling Heights, MI 48077.

TAYLOR, HERMAN DANIEL
Educator. **PERSONAL:** Born Feb 26, 1937, Yazoo City, MS; married Vivian Celestine Hicks; children: Alicia Danielle, Herman Daniel Jr, Kristin Nicole. **EDUCATION:** Chicago Musical Coll of Roosevelt Univ, BMus 1963; Univ of MI, MMus 1974, AMusD 1976. **CAREER:** Southern Univ, instr of music 1963-67; Dillard Univ, instr of music 1969-73; Prairie View A&M Univ, assoc prof of music 1976-77; Dillard Univ, prof ofmusic 1977-. **ORGANIZATIONS:** State chmn Amer Guild of Organists; volunteer for the Heart Fund 1978-; asst club scout master 1984-85. **HONORS/ACHIEVEMENTS:** Artist Fellowship Awd LA State Arts Council 1984; Performing from memory all the organ works of JS Bach in US & in Europe 1984-85; UNCF Disting Faculty Scholar 1985-86. **HOME ADDRESS:** 7570 Branch Dr, New Orleans, LA 70128. **BUSINESS ADDRESS:** Professor of Music, DillardUniv, 2601 Gentilly Blvd, New Orleans, LA 70122.

TAYLOR, HOWARD F.
Educator. **PERSONAL:** Born Jul 07, 1939, Cleveland, OH; married Patricia A Epps. **EDUCATION:** Yale, PhD 1966; Yale, MA 1964; Hiram Coll, AB 1961. **CAREER:** Princeton Univ, prof 1973; Syracuse Univ, 1968-73; IL Inst of Tech, 1966-68; Natl Acad of Scis, cons. **ORGANIZATIONS:** NAAS; Am Sociol Assn; E Sociol Soc; Am Assn ofUniv Profs; Assn of Black Sociologists. **HONORS/ACHIEVEMENTS:** Various grants; publ two books num articles. **BUSINESS ADDRESS:** Princeton University, Afro-Amer Studies Prog, Princeton, NJ 08544.

TAYLOR, HYCEL B.
Clergyman. **PERSONAL:** Born Apr 21, 1936, Columbus, OH; married Annie Bdallis; children: Chandra, Audreanna, Hycel, III. **EDUCATION:** Fields Bible Inst, 1960; Kent State U, BFA 1965; Oberlin Grad Sch of Theol; Vanderbilt Div Sch, MDiv 1969; Vanderbilt Div Sch, Doctorate Ministery 1970; Univ of Chicago Divinity Sch, Post Doctoral study. **CAREER:** Garret-Evangelical Theol Sem, assoc prof 1970-; Fisk U, appointed dean chapel; Fisk Univ, minister instr in religion 1969-70; Howard Congregational Ch,pastor 1966-69; Elizabeth Baptist Ch, pastor 1962-66; Union Baptist Ch, youth dir 1959; No Baptist Dist Assn Union Grove Baptist Ch, license preacher 1956; Martin Luther King, Jr, consultant lectr founder; The Church and the Black Experience Garrett-Eangelical Theol Seminary Evanston, founder/developer; Second Bapt Church Evanston IL, pastor. **ORGANIZATIONS:** Mem scholarship fund Vanderbilt Div Sch; prac artist painting sculpture Martin Luther King Fund; mem Ch & Ministry of SE Conf of Un Ch of Christ; mem Life & Work Com of Nashville Council of Chs; Nashville Urban & Ministers Cadre; Bapt Sem Devel Assn; bd trustees Nashville OIC; Nashville Council on Human Relations. **HONORS/ACHIEVEMENTS:** Recip TW Graham Award in Homiletics Oberlin Coll 1966. **MILITARY SERVICE:** USMC res 1953-59. **BUSINESS ADDRESS:** Pastor, Second Baptist Church, 1717 Benson Ave, Evanston, IL 60201.

TAYLOR, JACK ALVIN, JR.
University administrator. **PERSONAL:** Born Jul 15, 1949, Pittsburgh, PA; married Janet Victoria Bivins; children: Marcus, Matthew, Jack III. **EDUCATION:** California Univ of Pennsylvania, BA 1971, MEd 1975; Bowling Green State Univ, PhD 1985. **CAREER:** California Univ of Pennsylvania, dir counseling/spec serv 1972-75; Frostburg State Coll, asst dir minority affairs 1975-78; Bowling Green State Univ, student develop & spec serv 1978-85, asst vice pres for minority affairs 1985-. **ORGANIZATIONS:** Consultant Minority Affairs; consultant Educ Development Programs; mem Amer Assoc of Counseling & Develop; chairperson Legislative & Judicial Comm Cumberland MD Chap NAACP; mem Mid-Amer Assoc of Educ Oppor Program Personnel; mem Kappa Alpha Psi Frat Inc, PA Intercollegiate Athletic Assoc Championship Team 1970. **BUSINESS ADDRESS:** Assistant Vice President, Bowling Green StateUniv, Bowling Green, OH 43403.

TAYLOR, JAMES
Business executive. **PERSONAL:** Born Sep 08, 1922, Maywood, IL; married Margaret Caples. **EDUCATION:** IL Inst of Tech, Inst of Design, BS 1951. **CAREER:** Community Film Workshop of Chicago, exec dir 1971; Cinema Video Concepts Prod Inc, pres 1971; Ctr ofr New Sch, media specialist 1975-76; Columbia Coll, instr 1972; Studio 402, freelance photojournalist, cinematographer 1966-71; Astra Photo Serv, photo lat tech 1956-66. **ORGANIZATIONS:** Mem, exec bd dir Intl All of Theatre Stage Employment & Moving Picture Machine Operators Union 666; Cameraman's Chic; bd dir Chic Filmmakers; bd of adv Black Arts Celebration Pro & Con Screening Bd. **HONORS/ACHIEVEMENTS:** Union photographer feature film credits, "Am Dream" 1980; "Blue Bro" 1979; "The Duke" 1978; "The Awakening Land" 1977; "Moonbeam Rider" 1977; "Black Beauty" 1977; "Blue Collar" 1977; "FIST" 1977; "Piece of the Action" 1976; "Monkey Hustle" 1975; "Cooley High" 1975; "Lord Shango" 1974; "Cutter" 1972; prod & dir credits, "Ashes of Black" 1979; Fire Safety Films; Nation of Islam Saviors Day; Beacon House; Sea Scouts; Traffic Safety Commercials. **MILITARY SERVICE:** US Army Air Corps corpl 1943-45. **BUSINESS ADDRESS:** 441 N Clark St, Chicago, IL 60610.

TAYLOR, JAMES C.
State representative. **PERSONAL:** Born Feb 08, 1930, Crawfordsville, AR; married Ella; children: Richard, Cassaundra, Cynthia. **EDUCATION:** Univ of IL; Monticello Coll of IL. **CAREER:** State rep 4th term; asst supt of sanitation; ward committeeman 16th ward Chicago; hwy maintenance supt; professional prize fighter; hwy instructional equip operator; sanitation engr. **ORGANIZATIONS:** Mem Teamster Union Local 726; Ward Supt Assn; scoutmaster Troop 429 Southtown Dist; mem St Brendan's Cath Ch; mem IL Legislative Investigating Commn; mem exec com Personnel & Pensions of IL Ho of Rep; chmn Cities & Villages Com IL Ho of Rep; honor mem Boy Scouts Cherokee Tribe; mem S Town YMCA. **HONORS/ACHIEVEMENTS:** Recipient IL Fair Employment Practices Commn Spl Recognition Award; registered Sanitation Dept of Registration & Edn; achievement award US Dept of

Labor Bur of Labor Standard. **MILITARY SERVICE:** AUS corpl Korean Conflict. **BUSINESS ADDRESS:** 2104 State Ofc Bldg, Springfield, IL 62706.

TAYLOR, JAMES ELTON
Educational administrator. **PERSONAL:** Born Jul 06, 1947, Edenton, NC; married Catherine Ward; children: Kim A, Eric C, Angela Y, Pamela Y. **EDUCATION:** Univ of MI, Business Internship 1968; Shaw Univ, BA 1969; Atlanta Univ, attended 1968-69. **CAREER:** First Union Natl Bank, branch mgr 1969-73; Integon Life Ins Corp, sales rep 1973-74; Elizabeth City State Univ, fin aid admin 1974-. **ORGANIZATIONS:** NC Assoc of Student Fin Aid Admin consul 1976 & 1977, treas 1978-80, vice pres 1980-81; Edenton-Chowan Civic League first vice pres 1984, pres 1985-;mem Edenton-Chowan Bd of Educ 1980-86; mem NAACP 1985-. **HONORS/ACHIEVEMENTS:** Governor's Bulls Eye Awd NC Democratic Party 1980; Serv Awd NC Assn of Educators 1980-81; Valuable Serv Awd NC Assn of Student Fin Aid Admin 1983 & 1984; Dedicated Serv Awd Edenton-Chowan Civil League 1984. **HOME ADDRESS:** 206 W Church St, Edenton, NC 27932. **BUSINESS ADDRESS:** Financial Aid Administrator, Elizabeth City StateUniv, Parkview Dr, Elizabeth City, NC 27909.

TAYLOR, JANICE A.
Attorney. **PERSONAL:** Born May 23, 1954, Brooklyn, NY. **EDUCATION:** Coll of William and Mary, BA 1975; SUNY/Buffalo Sch of Law, JD 1978. **CAREER:** NY City Transit Authority, attorney 1978-81, assoc attorney 1981-86; District Council 37 AFSCME AFL-CIO, asst genl counsel 1986-87; Civil Court of the City of New York, small claims arbitrator 1987-; Macon B Allen Black Bar Assoc, pres. **ORGANIZATIONS:** Legal counsel Concerned Citizens of South Queens 1981-87; parliamentarian Delta Sigma Theta Inc Queens Alumnae Chap 1982; legal redress chairperson NAACP Jamaica Branch 1983-85, 1987-88, exec bd mem 1983-85, 1987-88; regional council mem Natl Bar Assoc 1983-87; deaconette Concord Bapt Church of Christ 1984-;bd mem Black Women in Transit 1985-86. **HOME ADDRESS:** 111-26 198th St, Hollis, NY 11412.

TAYLOR, JEFF EUGENE
Professional athlete. **PERSONAL:** Born Jan 01, 1960, Blythesville, AR. **EDUCATION:** TX Tech, 1978-82. **CAREER:** Houston Rockets, 1982-83; Phoenix Suns, guard 1983-. **BUSINESS ADDRESS:** Phoenix Suns, PO Box 1369, Ste 510, Phoenix, AZ 85001.

TAYLOR, JEROME
Educator. **PERSONAL:** Born Jan 26, 1940, Waukegan, IL; married Tommie Nell; children: Kim, Lisa, Jacques, Zwehla. **EDUCATION:** Univ of Denver, BA 1961; IN Univ, PhD 1965; Menninger Found, Postdoctoral Fellow 1965-67. **CAREER:** Mental Health Unit Topeka, dir 1968-69; Univ of Pittsburgh Clinical Psych Ctr, dir 1969-71; Univ of Pittsburgh, assoc prof ed & psych. **ORGANIZATIONS:** Mem Amer Psychol Assoc, Assoc of Black Psych, Omicron Delta Kappa, Sigma Xi, Psi Chi. **BUSINESS ADDRESS:** Associate Professor, Univ of Pittsburgh, Inst for the Black Family, Pittsburgh, PA 15260.

TAYLOR, JESSE ELLIOTT, JR.
Business executive. **PERSONAL:** Born in Powhattan, LA; divorced. **EDUCATION:** Case-Western Reserve Univ, BBA 1950; Univ of MI, graduate work; Air Univ; UCLA; Univ of CA Riverside, Univ Utah. **CAREER:** Ohio Dept of Liquor Control Columbus, permit examiner & enforcement ofcr 1947-51; USAF Ballistic Missiles Div, contracting ofcr br chief 1951-64; Long Beach Coll of Bus Inc, Van Nuys Coll of Bus Inc, 3rd St Properties Inc, pres, owner, chmn, bd dir, fdr 1964-; Long Beach Coll of Business Inc, pres. **ORGANIZATIONS:** Rotary Club 1968-; Downtown Long Beach Bus Assn; Long Beach C of C; Alpha Phi Alpha Frat; chmn bd trustees Cong Church of Christian Fellowship 1971-75; financial sec 1975-77; W Assn of Student Finan Aid Admin; CA Assn of Priv Educs; Nat Assn of Sch Adminstr; Data Proc Mgr Assn; mem NAACP; mem CAAssoc of Private Postsecondary Schools. **HONORS/ACHIEVEMENTS:** CA Dept of Vocational Rehab Assn Sustained Superior Perf Award; Air Force Cert of Appointment; Contracting Officer USAF; consult special review bd panelistfor 9th Regional Hdqts of Dept of HEW; Commendation for Outstnd contrib to City of Los Angeles for ch & comm serv from Mayor of LA; Outstnd Serv & Achievement Award for serv to comm & city City Council of LA 1976. **MILITARY SERVICE:** AUS Corpl 1942-45; awarded 3 campaign medals for N Africa & European Theatres of Operations. **BUSINESS ADDRESS:** President, Long Beach Coll of Business, PO Box 530, Long Beach, CA 90801.

TAYLOR, JOHN L.
Appointed government official. **PERSONAL:** Born May 07, 1947, Holly Springs, MS; son of Charlie E Taylor Sr and Cinderella Simms; married Naomi Ruth Thomas; children: Tony, Jonathan, Chere. **EDUCATION:** Rust Coll, BS 1969. **ORGANIZATIONS:** Deacon, clerk, Church Baptist. **HONORS/ACHIEVEMENTS:** Outstanding Young Man 1982; Teacher of the Day Radio Station Memphis TN 1984; Academic Career Day Univ of MS 1985. **HOME ADDRESS:** Rt 4 Box 107, Byhalia, MS 38611.

TAYLOR, JOSEPH T.
Educator. **PERSONAL:** Born Feb 11, 1913, Rolling Fork, MS; son of Joseph Taylor and Willie Ann (Price) Taylor; married Hertha Ward; children: Bruce T, Judith F, Joel H. **EDUCATION:** Univ of IL, AB 1936, AM 1937; IN Univ, PhD 1952; Berea Coll KY, LLD 1969; Marian Coll, LittD 1979; IN Univ, DHL 1984. **CAREER:** IN Univ assoc prof 1962-66; Indianapolis Regional Campus, asst dir 1965, acting dean 1966; Fisk Univ, tcher fellow, Rosenwald fellow; Flanner House Survey Indianapolis, field worker; Carnegie-Myrdal Study The Negro in Amer, field investigator; FL A&M Coll, instr; Natl Youth Admin, area dir; FL A&M Coll, asst to pres, acting dean grad div; Albany State Coll, dir arts & sci prof; Dillard Univ, chmn div of social sci prof, acting dean; Flanner House of Indianapolis, dir prog devel; IN Univ Purdue Univ, prof of sociology 1967-; IN Univ, Purdue Univ, Dean School of Liberal Arts, 1967-78, special asst,vp 1978-83 retired. **ORGANIZATIONS:** Spl appointee by Fed Dist Ct Judge Dillin to devel interim plan for Court ordered desegregation of Indianapolis Pub Sch 1973; author of numerous publications; bd dir Indianapolis YMCA & YWCA; bd dir United Way of Gr Indianapolis; bd dir Urban League of Gr Indianapolis; bd trustees Berea Coll KY; bd mem Comm Serv Coun of Indianapolis; bd mem Family Serv Assn of Indianapolis; bd mem Natl Conf of Christians & Jews; bd mem New Hope Found of IN; mem Christian Theological Sem Adv Coun; mem Comprehensive Health Planning Coun of Marion Co Inc; mem Federation of Asso Clubs adv com; mem Greater Indianapolis Housing Devel Corp; mem Indianapolis Prog Com; co-chmn Citizen Adv Comm Indianapolis Bd of Sch Commrs; mem Gr Indianapolis Prog Com; commr Indianapolis Housing Auth; mem Natl Bd of Higher Educ United Meth Church; mem Negro Coll Advance United Meth Ch; mem Rotary Intl, State of INDev Disabilities Adv Council; mem YMCA Natl Coun (Mid-Amer Region); Sigma Pi Phi, Alpha Phi Alpha Inc, Prince Hall Mason. **HONORS/ACHIEVEMENTS:** Black History & Fine Arts Festival Awd E St Louis Il 1974; Man of the Yr Awd Natl Coun Christians & Jews 1974; Disting Achievement Awd Fed of Assoc Clubs 1974; Indiana Academy Fellow 1989; Paul Harris Fellow, Rotary International 1989. **MILITARY SERVICE:** AUS 1942-46.

TAYLOR, JULIA W.
President, chief executive officer. **PERSONAL:** Born Apr 04, 1936, Durham, NC. **EDUCATION:** NC Central Univ, 1954-55; Stonier Grad School of Banking, 1967; LaSalle Extension Univ Chicago, attended; Amer Inst of Banking, attended. **CAREER:** Bank of Amer, employee 1960; Broadway Fed Savings & Loan Assoc, sr clerk 1961-62; Broadway Fed Savings & Loan Assoc, escrow officer 1962, asst sec 1962-63; Mechanics & Farmers Bank, note teller 1965-66, asst cashier 1966-67, vp, mgr 1967-78, sr vp, city exec 1978-83, pres, ceo 1983-. **ORGANIZATIONS:** Treas, bd mem Natl Bankers Assoc 1974-82; mem Raleigh Civic Ctr Auth 1976-80; bd mem, past 2nd vice pres Jr Achievement of Wake Cty 1976-; dir Mech & Farmers Bk Durham NC 1978-; mem, vchmn NC State Ed Asst Auth 1978-; bd mem, past treas Raleigh Wake Urban League 1978-; trustee St Joseph AME Church Durham 1980; mem adv bd Rutledge Coll; mem bd of dir, exec comm Mech & Farmers Bank; mem bd of dir NC Bankers Assoc, mem NC Central Univ Bd of Visitors, Greater Durham Comm found; mem bd of trustees Univ of NC Wilmington, Daisy E Scarborough Found Inc; mem bd of dir Greater Durham C of C; mem bd of dir Kaiser Found Health Plan of NC; mem NC State Banking Commission; assoc mem State Conf Bank Supervisors. **HONORS/ACHIEVEMENTS:** Named Tar Heel of the Week by News & Observer 1986; YMCA Women of Achievement Awd 1985. **BUSINESS ADDRESS:** President, Mechanics & Farmers Bank, 114 W Parrish St, Durham, NC 27701.

TAYLOR, JULIUS H.
Educator. **PERSONAL:** Born Feb 15, 1914, Cape May, NJ; married Patricia Spaulding; children: Dwight, Trena. **EDUCATION:** Lincoln Univ, AB; Univ PA, MS, PhD. **CAREER:** WV State Coll, dept head 1945; Morgan State Coll, assoc prof 1949, dept head & prof 1951-; publ & unpub work. **ORGANIZATIONS:** Mem Chesapeake Amer Assn Physics Tchrs; Natl Com Physics Secondary Educ; pres AAPT 1962-63; rep AAPT 1964-65; Natl Science Found; Travelers Aid Soc; Gov Science Adv Council; zone councillor Soc Physics Students Alumnus Yr Lincoln Univ 1963. **HONORS/ACHIEVEMENTS:** Research award; Julius Rosenwald fellow Univ PA 1943-44. **MILITARY SERVICE:** AUS 1953-57. **BUSINESS ADDRESS:** Morgan State Univ, Baltimore, MD 21239.

TAYLOR, KENNETH DOYLE
Engineer/scientist. **PERSONAL:** Born Nov 05, 1949, Hartford, CT; son of Frank K Taylor and Adelaide Tweedy Jordan; married Mattie Jane Dolphy; children: Jerome Daniel. **EDUCATION:** University of CT, BS 1971, MS 1974, PhD 1981; Rensselaer Polytechnic Institute (Hartford Graduate Center) Hartford CT, MBA 1988. **CAREER:** Picker Corp, design engr 1973-74; St Francis Hosp & Medical Ctr, mgr rsch lab 1974-79; Natl Institutes of Health, asst to the dir 1985-86; United Technologies Rsch Ctr, sr project engr 1979-; Trinity College, adjunct prof 1988-. **ORGANIZATIONS:** Lecturer Univ of CT Dept of Elec Engrg 1977-83; chmn/treas Family Federal Credit Union 1978-80, 1983-85; adjunct lecturer Hartford Grad Ctr 1982-; sr mem IEEE 1983-; vice pres Beta Sigma Lambda, Alpha Phi Alpha Frat 1983-85; mem Sigma Pi Phi Frat 1984-; bd of dirs, Connecticut Pre-Engineering Program 1989-; bd of dirs, Channel 3 Country Camp 1989-. **HONORS/ACHIEVEMENTS:** United Technologies Awd 1981; Univ of CT Disting Grad Awd 1982; AIAA Contribution to Society Awd 1985; President's Commn on Exec Exchange Class XVI 1985-86; Registered Professional Engineer, State of Connecticut 1977. **HOME ADDRESS:** 17 Gorski Dr, South Windsor, CT 06074. **BUSINESS ADDRESS:** Sr Project Engineer, United Technologies Rsch Ctr, MS 58 400 Main St, East Hartford, CT 06108.

TAYLOR, KENNETH MATTHEW
Business executive. **PERSONAL:** Born in Jersey City, NJ. **EDUCATION:** BS; MBA. **CAREER:** Witco Chem Corp NYC, sr auditor/financial analyst; Allied Chem Corp Morristown, NJ, sr auditor; Colgate-Palmolive Corp NYC, sr accountant; Philip Morris Inc NYC, sr analyst/auditor; Bache & Co Inc NYC, sr brokerage accountant. **ORGANIZATIONS:** Mem Am Mgmt Assn; Inst of Internal Auditors; Nat Assn of Black Accountants; Nat Assn of Accountants N Jersey Chpt; mem Omega Psi Phi Frat; chmn 2nd Dist Budget & Finance Com Newark 1972-74; mem Nat Budget & Financo Com 1973-74; keeper of finance Upsilon Phi Chap 1970-74. **HONORS/ACHIEVEMENTS:** Distinguished Award as Chmn Finance Com 1974. **MILITARY SERVICE:** USAF. **BUSINESS ADDRESS:** 277 Park Ave, New York, NY 10017.

TAYLOR, LAWRENCE JULIUS
Professional athlete. **PERSONAL:** Born Feb 04, 1959, Williamsburg, VA; son of Clarence Taylor and Iris Taylor; married Linda Cooley; children: four children. **EDUCATION:** Attended Univ of N Carolina, 1977-81. **CAREER:** New York Giants, linebacker 1981-. **HONORS/ACHIEVEMENTS:** All-American at North Carolina; Unanimous All NFL selection for 3 yrs; Pro Bowl starter 3 yrs; Top linebacker in NFL by Player's Assn for 3 yrs; 2 times named the Associated Press' Most Valuable Defensive Player in NFL; NFL'S Defensive Player of the Yr Award from Seagram's Computer Awards Pgm; consensus All-Am at NC; Atlantic Coast Conf Player of the Yr 1980; East-West Shrine Game; Japan Bowl; named to All NFL team; mem NFL Pro Bowl teams 1986, 87. **BUSINESS ADDRESS:** New York Giants, Giants Stadium, East Rutherford, NJ 07073. *

TAYLOR, LEONARD WAYNE
Management analyst. **PERSONAL:** Born Oct 02, 1946, Topeka, KS; children: Lisa G. **EDUCATION:** Kansas City Comm Coll, AA 1967; Pittsburg State Univ, BS 1969, MS 1970. **CAREER:** Osawatomie State Mental Hosp, psychiatric social worker 1970; City of Kansas City, program coord 1970-71, project mgt spec 1971-76; Kansas Dept of Human Resources, program & Eval spec 1976-78; Urban League of Greater KC, chief, rsch & dev 1979-84; US Dept of Agriculture, mgmt analyst 1986-. **ORGANIZATIONS:** Bd mem Mid-Amer Regional Council Citizen Adv Comm; comm mem USDA Handicapped Emp Advis Com EEO 1986-. **HONORS/ACHIEVEMENTS:** "Pluralistic and Elitist Structures as they Relate

to Conflict with the Black Movement," Sociological Abstract 1971. **HOME ADDRESS:** PO Box 1425, Kansas City, KS 66117.

TAYLOR, LINDA SUZANNA See TAYLOR, MARIE DE PORRES

TAYLOR, LYNNETTE DOBBINS
Administrator. **PERSONAL:** Born in Birmingham, AL; married Hobart Taylor Jr; children: Albert, Hobart III. **EDUCATION:** AL State Teachers Coll, BS 1939; Wayne State Univ, MS 1948. **CAREER:** Chicago Defender & Detroit Tribune, NY editor; Roosevelt Elem School Detroit, principal; Office of Econ Oppty WA, VA MD, prog analyst; Delta Sigma Theta, past exec dir; Taylor Enterprises, pres. **ORGANIZATIONS:** Past mem curriculum commiss, comm to select teachers & admin Detroit Publ School System; mem bd dirs Natl Friends of Publ Broadcasting Corp; mem Natl Ctr for Vol Action; dir Coll & Youth Activities ARC; mem bd Envoys on Main St; bd mem Ed Rsch Counc of Amer; mem bd Natl Capitol YMCA; mem bd Intl Wash; mem Child Health Ctr Bd; mem bd Council of the Arts; mem Publ Com on Truth in Lending Legislation; mem bd Wash Fed Savings & Loan; bd trustees Natl Urban League; pres Black Womens Agenda; commiss Natl Commiss for UNESCO; bd Boy Scouts of Amer; bd mem Delta Sigma Theta.

TAYLOR, MARGARET See BURROUGHS, MARGARET TAYLOR

TAYLOR, MARIE DE PORRES (LINDA SUZANNA TAYLOR)
Executive director. **PERSONAL:** Born May 27, 1947, Los Angeles, CA; daughter of James (Sam) Taylor and Isabel McCoy Taylor Clarke. **EDUCATION:** Marylhurst Coll, Marylhurst OR, BA, 1970; California State Univ, San Francisco CA, MA, 1976; Pacific Lutheran Seminary, Berkeley CA, 1982; California State Univ, Hayward CA, 1986—. **CAREER:** Holy Names High School, Oakland CA, chair home economics dept, 1969-77; St Benedict Church, Oakland CA, assoc pastor, 1977-82; Roman Catholic Bishop, Oakland CA, dir of Black Catholics, 1982-89; National Black Sisters Conference, Oakland CA, exec dir, 1982—; Oakland Private Industry Council, Oakland CA, program coordinator, 1989—. **ORGANIZATIONS:** Chmn, bd of dir, Bay Area Black United Fund; pres, bd of dir, Oakland Citizens Committee for Urban Renewal (OCCUR); pres, United East Oakland Clergy; mem, bd of dir, Holy Names College, Oakland CA; vice chmn, bd of dir, Oakland Police Activity League; mem, Mayor's Committee on Homeless, Oakland CA. **HONORS/ACHIEVEMENTS:** Image Builders Award, College Bounders of the Bay Area, 1981; Rose Casanave Service Award, Black Catholic Vicariate, Diocese of Oakland CA, 1982; Outstanding Leadership in Bay Area Award, Links Inc, 1982; Outstanding Young Women of America, 1983; Martin Luther King Jr Award, United East Oakland Clergy, 1984. **HOME ADDRESS:** 7871 Hillside St, Oakland, CA 94605.

TAYLOR, MARTHA
Transportation manager. **PERSONAL:** Born Jul 26, 1941, Shreveport, LA; daughter of Henry Taylor and Viola Harris Taylor; married Royal Odell Taylor, Feb 14, 1975; children: Valerie L Thompson, Debra L Benton. **EDUCATION:** Merritt College, Oakland, CA, AA, 1977; University of San Francisco, San Francisco, CA, BA, 1979, MPA, 1981. **CAREER:** Bay Area Rapid Transit District, Oakland, CA, police officer, 1973-77, police sergeant, 1977-81, police lieutenant, 1981-83, support and analysis manager, 1983-. **ORGANIZATIONS:** President, Black Managers and Professionals Association, 1981-; member, Conference Minority Transit Officials, 1985-; member, member of board of directors, East Oakland Youth Development Center, East Oakland, CA, 1986-87; second vice president, National Forum for Black Public Administrators, Oakland chapter, Oakland, CA, 1986-88; member of executive board, Black Women Organized for Political Action, 1986-; member of Youth Mentor Program, Oakland Public Schools, Oakland, CA, 1986-; chair of committee training, Women in Transit-American Public Transit Association, 1987-; bible instructor, Bethel Missionary Baptist Church, 1987-. **HONORS/ACHIEVEMENTS:** Certificate of recognition, American Public Transit Association, Western Confernce, 1985; certificate for outstanding contributions, American Public Transit Association, 1987; author of "The Challenge of Climbing the Organizational Ladder: A Matter Of Perspective," California Law Enforcement Association Police Recorder, 1988. **HOME ADDRESS:** 3828 Sequoyah Road, Oakland, CA 94605. **BUSINESS ADDRESS:** Manager, Support and Analysis, Bay Area Rapid Transit District, 800 Madison Street, Room 214, Oakland, CA 94605.

TAYLOR, MAURICE CLIFTON
Educator. **PERSONAL:** Born May 11, 1950, Baltimore, MD. **EDUCATION:** Juniata Coll, BA 1972; Bowling Green State Univ, MA 1974, PhD 1978. **CAREER:** Northampton Co Comm Coll, instructor of sociology 1974-76; Trenton State Coll, asst prof of criminal justice 1978-80; Hampton Univ, chairperson dept of sociology 1980-86, dir div of social sciences 1985-86. **ORGANIZATIONS:** Mem Assoc of Black Sociologists; big brother Big Brothers of the VA Peninsula 1982-84; mem VA Social Science Assoc 1984-86. **HONORS/ACHIEVEMENTS:** Outstanding Young Man of Amer 1981; numerous publications including "Academic Performance of Blacks on White Campuses," 1978, "Black Male-Female Suicide," West Jour of Blk Stud 1982, "Honor Among Thieves," Jour of Ethnic Studies 1984,. **BUSINESS ADDRESS:** Dir, Hampton University, Division of Social Science, Hampton, VA 23668.

TAYLOR, MICHAEL
Retail executive, consultant. **PERSONAL:** Born Oct 13, 1958, New York, NY; son of Donald Taylor and Patricia Taylor; married Sandy Jones, Sep 05, 1987. **EDUCATION:** Stanford Univ, MBA 1984; Harvard Univ, BA 1980. **CAREER:** Pacific Bell, systems analyst 1980-82; Ducommon, asst mgr corp develop 1983; Booz Allen and Hamilton, assoc 1984-86; Infotech Planning Group, principal, 1986-; Amer Pop Video, pres Inc, 1988-. **ORGANIZATIONS:** Mem Niagara Movement Democratic Club, Natl Black MBA Assoc; charter mem UJAMAA. **HOME ADDRESS:** 498 Jean St, Oakland, CA 94610. **BUSINESS ADDRESS:** Pres, American Pop Video, 505 14th St, Oakland, CA 94612.

TAYLOR, MICHAEL LOEB
Educator. **PERSONAL:** Born Jan 11, 1947, Houston, TX; children: Christopher Kirrinkai Parrish-Taylor, Jennifer Nichol Parrish-Taylor. **EDUCATION:** UCLA, BA 1970, MA 1972, MFA 1974. **CAREER:** Univ of Nairobi Nairobi, Kenya, lecturer 1972-73 & 1975-77; Western KY Univ, asst prof 1977-81; Lewis & Clark Coll, assoc prof 1981-. **ORGANIZATIONS:** Design consult African Heritage Ltd Nairobi, Kenya 1972-73 & 1975-77; mem/artist Blackfish Gallery Portland, OR 1984; mem Members Gallery 1982-83. **HONORS/ACHIEVEMENTS:** Fulbright Award (declined) Turkey 1981; Commission for Washington State Arts Commission 1989. **BUSINESS ADDRESS:** Associate Professor of Art, Lewis & Clark College, Portland, OR 97219.

TAYLOR, MICHAEL M.
Marketing manager. **PERSONAL:** Born Jan 24, 1956, Chicago, IL; married Delphine Brooks; children: Candace, Christopher, Constance. **EDUCATION:** Alliance Francaise Paris France, 1974; Wartburg Coll Waverly IA, BA 1975;Univ of Chgo, MBA 1980. **CAREER:** Hallmark Cards Inc, mgr, acct exec 1980-; Carpenter Tech Corp, sales rep 1975-80. **ORGANIZATIONS:** Bd of dir Christ Org to Promo Ed 1972-; fndng mem, bd of dir IA Intrclgt Black Alliance 1972-; staff asso Safer Found 1977-80. **HONORS/ACHIEVEMENTS:** Who's Who Amoung Am Coll &Univ Stds 1974-75; 1st Black Std Body Pres Wartburg Coll 1975; cngrsnl aide US Congress Hon R Metcalfe & Sen W Mondale 1975. **BUSINESS ADDRESS:** 4109 Maple St, West Des Moines, IA 50265.

TAYLOR, MILDRED D.
Writer. **PERSONAL:** Born 1943, Jackson, MS. **EDUCATION:** Graduated from University of Toledo; received master's degree from University of Colorado School of Journalism. **CAREER:** Peace Corps, taught English and history in Ethiopia, became recruiter in the US; University of Colorado, organizer of black studies program and study skills coordinator; writer. **ORGANIZATIONS:** Member, Univ of Colorado Black Students Alumni Group. **HONORS/ACHIEVEMENTS:** Author of Song of the Trees, Dial, 1975; author of Roll of Thunder, Hear My Cry, Dial, 1976; author of Let the Circle Be Unbroken, Dial, 1981; award from Council on Interracial Books for Children, 1975; New York Times outstanding book award, 1975; Children's Book Showcase award, 1976; Newbery Award, 1977; Horn Book honor award from Boston Globe; Coretta Scott King Award; honor from American Library Association, 1981. **BUSINESS ADDRESS:** c/o Dial Press, One Dag Hammarskjold Plaza, New York, NY 10017. *

TAYLOR, MILDRED E. CROSBY
Personnel specialist. **PERSONAL:** Born Dec 18, 1919, Centralia, IL; married David P. **EDUCATION:** LaSalle Ext Univ, 1939-41; US Dept of Agriculture Grad Sch, certificate; Exec Inst, exec devel training; US Dept of Labor, leadership devel courses; Catholic Univ Washington DC, grad study. **CAREER:** Women's Bur US Dept of Labor, conv planner ret social science advisor; Surgeon General's Office Dept of Army, personnel asst; Surgeon General's Office Dept of Air Force, personnel specialist; keynote speaker panelist moderator at meetings & seminars. **ORGANIZATIONS:** Women's Bur liaison to black women's orngs on employment; mem Sec of Labor's Vol Day Com; bd dir Dept of Labor Recreation Assn; charter mem Toastmasters Internat; vice pres Air & Cruise Travel Adminstrs Washington DC; charter mem DC Women's Commn on Crime Prevention; charter mem bd dir Trinity AME Zion Ch Housing Corp; past pres Century Club Nat Asnn of Negor Bus & Professional Women Inc; past loyal lady ruler Order of Golden Circle; past matron Order of Eastern Star; Urban League NAACP; past commandress Mecca Ct #2 Daughters of Isis (Women's Aux to Shriners); imperial conv directness Imperial Ct Daughters of Isis; vol worker for many charitable orgns. **HONORS/ACHIEVEMENTS:** Recipient outstanding serv award Prentiss Inst Hon KY Col Gov Nunn 1971; first woman to receive distinguished service award from Mecca Temple #10 Ancient Egyptian Arabic Order Nobles of Mystic Shrine (Press Release to Blak Press by Dept of Labor); World's Who's Who of Women 1977; honorary dr of humanities deg Ministerial Inst- Coll West Point MS 1977. **BUSINESS ADDRESS:** 1809 Kilbourne Pl NW, Washington, DC 20010.

TAYLOR, MYRON
Business executive. **PERSONAL:** Born in Washington, DC; married JoAnn. **EDUCATION:** Howard U, BS 1968. **CAREER:** Morgan Guaranty Trust Co, sr vice pres 1976-, vice pres 1974-76, asst vice pres 1973-74, asst treas 1970-73.

TAYLOR, NOEL C.
Clergyman, mayor. **PERSONAL:** Born Jul 15, 1924, Bedford City, VA; married Barbara Jean Smith; children: Sabrina T Law, Deseree Charletta. **EDUCATION:** Bluefield State Coll, BS(with honors) 1949; VA Sem & Coll, BD 1955, DD 1959; NY Univ, MA Religious Educ 1963; Ordained to Ministry of Baptist Ch. **CAREER:** Bedford City Pub Sch, teacher 1949, elem sch prin 1950-52; First Baptist Ch Clifton Forge, VA, pastor 1955-58; First Baptist Ch Norfolk, VA, pastor 1958-61; High St Baptist Ch, pastor. **ORGANIZATIONS:** Councilman Roanoke City Council 1970-; vice-mayor Roanoke, VA 1974-75; mayor Roanoke, VA 1975-; dir Dominion Bank; bd dir Local Arc & Blue Cross & Blue Shield So Western VA; bd dir Bapt Children's Home; bd dir Blue Ridge Mountains Council Boy Scouts of Amer; mem NAACP, mem VA Bapt State Conv Roanoke Ministers Conf; Valley Bapt Assn Amer Baptist Conv Nat'l Baptist Conv; Lott Carey Bapt Foreign Missions Conv; US Conf of Mayors; Nat'l Conf of Black Mayors; Nat'l League of Cities; Alpha Phi Alpha; 33rd degree Masons Mem United Supreme Cncl; mem Kiwanis;Brd of Directors-Blue Ridge Mountains Council of Boy Scouts of Am; Wlm A Hunton YMCA Family Ctr; Advisory Brd of Central YWCA, Virginia Coal Research and Dev; Roanoke Valley Chpter Amer Red Cross; Roanoke Mem Hospitals; Design 85 Steering Comm; First Vice Pres VA Municipal League; Brd of Dir Jobs for Virginia Graduates requested by Governor Robb. **HONORS/ACHIEVEMENTS:** Man of the Year twice Omega Phi Psi; Cert of Merit Natl Phi Delta Kappa; Cert of Apprec Roanoke Jaycees; Brotherhood Award NCCJ; Tri-Ominis Celebrity Award; Man of the Year Masons; Comm Serv Award Delta Sigma Theta; Nat'l Cncl of Christians & Jews Brotherhood Awd 1974; Northwest Jaycees Awd for Outstanding Comm Serv 1976; Lions Club Outstanding Serv Awd 1977; Ivy Bpt Church Newport News VA leadership awd 1978; Delta Sigma Theta Man of the Year 1978; Omega Phi Psi Man of the Year 1978; Nat'l Comm Educ Awd for Contributing to Community Educ 1979; Blue Cross/Blue Shield Dedicated Serv Awd 1979; Zeta Phi Beta Citizen of Year 1979;Booster Club Awd for Outstanding Serv 1979; Awd of Appreciation March of Dimes 1980; VA Educ Assoc Dist Service Awd 1981; Jackson Jr HS Apprec Awd 1981;Alpha Kappa Alpha Citizen of Year 1984;Univ S A F American Spirit Awd 1984; Int'l Mgmt Cncl Top Manager of the Year 1984-85. **MILITARY SERVICE:** AUS 1943-46. **BUSINESS ADDRESS:** Mayor, High St Baptist Church, 215 Church Ave SE, Roanoke, VA 24011.

TAYLOR, NORMAN EUGENE
Government official. **PERSONAL:** Born Nov 12, 1948, Newark, NJ; son of Edwin Alfred Taylor and Martha Small Taylor; married Theresa Singleton, Apr 26, 1980; children: Norman

Assaf, Todd Farrell, Norman Amman, Joy Jamillah, Autier Dawn. **EDUCATION:** Bethune-Cookman College, Daytona Beach FL, BA, 1970; Florida Atlantic Univ, Boca Raton FL, MPA, 1976. **CAREER:** October Center, Inc, Fort Lauderdale FL, director, 1973-80; Norman E. Taylor & Associates, Inc, Miami FL, president, 1980-83; Broward County Govt, Fort Lauderdale FL, public relations mgr, 1983-84, director, 1984—. **ORGANIZATIONS:** National Forum for Black Public Administrators, Council for Black Economic Development. **HONORS/ACHIEVEMENTS:** City and County awards, Fort Lauderdale chapter of NAACP, 1978, 1980; outstanding service award, October Center, Inc, 1980. **MILITARY SERVICE:** US Army, E-4, 1971-73; award for outstanding service in human relations, 1973. **BUSINESS ADDRESS:** Director, Office of Employment & Small Business Development, Broward County Board of County Commissioners, 115 South Andrews Ave, Governmental Center, Room 427, Fort Lauderdale, FL 33301.

TAYLOR, OCTAVIA G.
Educator. **PERSONAL:** Born Dec 17, 1925, Lake Charles, LA; married George E; children: Andrea M, George E, Jr, Nancy E. **EDUCATION:** SoUniv Baton Rouge, BA 1946; Columbiau, MA 1953; USC, Grad Study 1963. **CAREER:** Calcasieu Parish HS, eng instr 1975-; WO Boston HS Lake Charles, eng drama instr 1953-62; Mt Vernon Jr HS LA, eng instr 1963. **ORGANIZATIONS:** Pres Classroom Tchrs Assn St LA 1970; mem LA Coun Tchrs Eng; New Sunlight Bapt Ch Order Eastern Star; pres Beta Kappa Zeta Chap Zeta Phi Beta 1970; imperial directress Region III; Imp Dep St LA Daus Isis; bd mem Nat Counc christns & Jews. **HONORS/ACHIEVEMENTS:** Testimonial banquet LA Charities 1974; Daus of Isis aUX Shriners).

TAYLOR, ORLANDO L.
Educational administrator. **PERSONAL:** Born Aug 09, 1936, Chattanooga, TN; son of Leroy Taylor and Carrie Lee Sanders Taylor; married Loretta M, Jun 06, 1957; children: Orlando II, Ingrid Taylor-Boone. **EDUCATION:** Hampton Institute, Hampton VA, BS, 1957; Indiana Univ, Bloomington IN, MA, 1960; Univ of Michigan, Ann Arbor MI, PhD, 1966. **CAREER:** Indiana Univ, Bloomington IN, asst prof, 1964-69; Center for Applied Linguistics, Washington DC, senior research fellow, 1969-75; University of District of Columbia, Washington DC, prof, 1970-73; Howard Univ, Washington DC, prof, 1973—; dean of communications, 1985—. **HONORS/ACHIEVEMENTS:** Distinguished scholar award, Howard Univ, 1984.

TAYLOR, PATRICIA E.
Attorney. **PERSONAL:** Born Feb 17, 1942, New Haven; married Dr Howard F; children: Carla Y. **EDUCATION:** IL Inst Tech, BS 1967; Yale, JS 1971. **CAREER:** Commun Prog Inc, commun wrkr 1963-65; Summer Rec Prgm Com Urban Opport, area coord 1966-68; Onondaga Lega Svc, law clk 1971-73; Princeton U, vis lctr 1974-. **ORGANIZATIONS:** Mem NJ Bar Assn; US Sup Ct Bar; Nat Conf Black Lawyers; Yale Law Club; asst Gen Couns Educ Testing Serv Princeton NJ; bd dir ARC 1972-73. **HONORS/ACHIEVEMENTS:** Reginald Herber Smith Fellow 1971-73; Outst Yng Wmn Am 1974. **BUSINESS ADDRESS:** Educ Testing Serv, Rosendale Rd, Princeton, NJ 08540.

TAYLOR, PATRICIA TATE
Management consultant. **PERSONAL:** Born Jan 13, 1954, Cleveland, OH; daughter of John Henry Tate and Catherine Johnson Tate. **EDUCATION:** Case Western Reserve Univ, BA 1977; Harvard Business Sch, MBA 1985. **CAREER:** Standard Oil Co OH, acctg, mktg, human resources 1977-83; Deloitte Haskins & Sells, consultant 1984; Cresap McCormick & Paget, management consultant 1985-87; US General Accounting Office, Management Expert, 1987-. **ORGANIZATIONS:** Mem Black Professionals Assn 1979-83; industry adv bd Cornell Univ 1981-83; industry adv comm Natl Assn of Engr Prog Admin 1981-83; mem, American Management Assn 1985-; mem, Harvard Alumni Assn 1985-; mem, Natl Assn of Female Executives 1985-. **HONORS/ACHIEVEMENTS:** Scholarship, National Achievement 1972; Academic Fellowship Harvard Univ Council for Opportunity in Graduate Management Education 1985. **MILITARY SERVICE:** Army ROTC cadet sgt major 1973-75. **BUSINESS ADDRESS:** Management Expert, US General Accounting Office, 441 G Street NW, Washington, DC 20548.

TAYLOR, PAUL DAVID
Health services. **PERSONAL:** Born May 01, 1937, Lexington, TN; son of Ray Otis Taylor (deceased) and Jessie Mae Williams (deceased); divorced; children: Paul David Jr, Bentley Christopher. **EDUCATION:** Garden City Comm Coll, AS 1957; Univ of KS, 1958. **CAREER:** Univ of CO Health Sci Ctr, biol lab tech 1962-65, rsch assoc, 1965-67, sr instr 1969-, coord organ transplant prog 1967-. **ORGANIZATIONS:** Mem Knights of Pythagorus KS 1955, World's 1st Human Liver Transplant Team Denver CO 1963; past master Prince Hall Masons Denver 1967; chmn, jurisprudence Prince Hall Grand Lodge CO & Jurisdiction Denver 1970-; founding mem North Amer Transplant Coord Org 1975; bd of dir CO Soc to Prevent Blindness Denver 1977-; consult Eurotransplant Coord Org Leiden Holland 1983, Canadian Transplant Coord Calgary Alberta 1983, 10th Annual Meeting of Japanese Transplantation & Artificial Organ Soc Sendi Japan 1985, Cardiovascular Transplantation Seminar Osaka Japan 1985, Minister of Health & Welfare Tokyo Japan 1985; Right Worshipful Grand Trustee, MW Prince Hall Grand Lodge, Colorado and its Jurisdiction, 1987-90. **HONORS/ACHIEVEMENTS:** Author or Co-Author Scientific Paper 1965-; Citizenship Awd Prince Hall Masons CO & Jurisdiction 1982; Cover & Story Oddysey West Mag Denver 1983; Guest Lecturer Denver Public Schools Denver 1983-; Subject Stories Ebony Magazine Newspapers Denver 1984; Inaugural inductee High School Hall of Fame Garden City, KS May 1985; Citizenship Awrd Hattie Anthony Resource Center 1986; Man of Distinction, Lane Contempories of Lane College Alumni Assn, Denver Chapter, 1989. **HOME ADDRESS:** 507 S Magnolia Ln, Denver, CO 80224. **BUSINESS ADDRESS:** Coordinator Organ Transpl Prog, Univ of Colorado Health Centr, 4200 E 9th Ave, Denver, CO 80262.

TAYLOR, PAULINE J.
Curator. **PERSONAL:** Born Oct 20, 1911, Bessemer, AL; married Julius C; children: Barbara McCrary Saunders. **CAREER:** Detroit St Rys, conductorette 1942-46; The Edison Inst, Henry Ford Museum, Greenfield Village, housekeeper of decorative arts retired. **ORGANIZATIONS:** Pres Detroit Bridge League 1957-61; 1st female natl pres Amer Bridge Assn 1969-73; mem Hamilton Intl Corp, Health Soc of Wayne Cty 1962; past pres,exec bd mem Amer Bridge Assn 1974; mem NAACP, Urban League, Petite Bowling League, YWCA, Motor City Duplicettes, St Johns Christian Meth. **HONORS/ACHIEVEMENTS:** Citation for Bravery City of Detroit; Outstanding Serv Awd Amer Bridge Assn; Plaque, Trophy, Life Membership Amer Bridge Assn; Silver Bracelet for Serving with Excellence Women of Detroit 1974. **HOME ADDRESS:** 97 Arden Pk, Detroit, MI 48202.

TAYLOR, PRINCE ALBERT, JR.
Retired clergyman. **PERSONAL:** Born Jan 27, 1907, Hennessey, OK; son of Prince Albert Taylor, Sr and Bertha Ann; married Annie Belle Thaxton; children: Isabella M, Taylor Jenkins. **EDUCATION:** Samuel Huston Coll, AB 1931; Gammon Theological Seminary, BD 1931; Columbia & Union Theological Seminary, MA 1940; NY Univ, EdD 1948; Rust Coll, DD 1949; Gammon Theological Seminary, DD 1950; Philander Smith Coll, LLD 1956; Univ Puget Sound, LittD 1965; Dickinson Coll, DD 1967; Drew Univ, LHD 1972. **CAREER:** NC Conf, ordained pastor NC & NY 1931; St Mark's Church NYC, summer pastor 1940-42; Bennett Coll, instructor & assistant to pres 1940-43; Gammon Theological Seminary, dept head Christian educ & psychology 1943-48; Clark Coll, exchange teacher 1943-48; Natl Methodist Student Comm, adult counselor 1944-48; Central Jurisdiction Comm, dir corr school 1945-48; Central Christian Adv, editor 1948-56; Central Jurisdiction, bishop 1956, bishop Monrovia (Liberia) area 1956-64, NJ Area 1964-76. **ORGANIZATIONS:** Pres council bishops 1965-66; general bd mem Nat Council Churches 1966-69; chmn Commn Structure Methodism Overseas 1968-72; tst Drew Univ Madison, NJ; chmn com World Methodist Council 1971-76; chmn Div Chaplains & Related Ministries 1972-76; hon pres World Methodist Council comm 1976; Rotary Club; trustee many universities, colleges, hospitals, museums, seminaries. **HONORS/ACHIEVEMENTS:** Recipient St George's Award Medal for Distinguished Serv to Methodist Church 1964; Decorated Venerable Knighthood of Pioneers (Liberia); Rotarian; United Methodist Communicators Hall of Fame. **BUSINESS ADDRESS:** 193 Laurel Cir, Princeton, NJ 08540.

TAYLOR, QUINTARD, JR.
Educator. **PERSONAL:** Born Dec 11, 1948, Brownsville, TN; son of Quintard Taylor and Grace (Brown) Taylor; married Carolyn Elaine Fain, Aug 02, 1969; children: Quintard III, Jamila, William. **EDUCATION:** St Augustine's Coll, BA 1969;Univ of MN, MA 1971, PhD 1977. **CAREER:** Univ of MN, instructor 1969-71; Gustavus Adolphus Coll, instructor 1971; WA State U, asst prof 1971-75; CA Polytechnic State U, prof of history; Univ of Lagos, Akoka Nigeria, visiting Fulbright prof 1987-88. **ORGANIZATIONS:** Consult Great Plains Black Museum 1980-85; consult Afro-Am Cultural Arts Ctr 1977-78; reviewer Nat Endowment for the Humanities 1979-83; pres Martin Luther Fund 1983-85, mem 1979-; mem Endowment Comm "Journal of Negro History" 1983-; mem, California Black Faculty Staff Assn 1985-, Golden Key Natl Honor Society 1987-, Phi Beta Delta Society for International Scholars 1989-; bd of governors, Martin Luther King Vocational-Technical Coll, Owerri Nigeria 1989-, African-American Vocational Institute, Aba Nigeria 1989-. **HONORS/ACHIEVEMENTS:** Carter G Woodson Award ASALH 1980; Kent Fellowship The Danforth Found 1974-77; Bush Fellowship Univ of MN 1971-77; NEH Travel & Collections Grant, National Endowment for the Humanities 1988; The Emergence of Afro-American Communities in the Pacific Northwest 1865-1910; Carter G Woodson Award for best article published in the Journal of Negro History 1978-79. **BUSINESS ADDRESS:** Professor of History, California Polytechnic StateUniv, Faculty Office Bldg 27g, San Luis Obispo, CA 93407.

TAYLOR, REGINALD REDALL, JR.
Elected official. **PERSONAL:** Born Jun 30, 1939, Waycross, GA; married Laurine Williams; children: Robyn Michelle. **EDUCATION:** FL A&M Univ, BS 1961; Fort Valley State Coll, MS 1973. **CAREER:** Lee St HS, teacher & band dir 1961; Blackshear HS, teacher & counselor 1969; Pierce Co HS, counselor 1981; City of Blackshear, councilman 1979-. **ORGANIZATIONS:** Mem Composite Lodge #40 FA&M 1960; pres Pierce Co Teachers Assn 1964, 1973, 1984; pres Consolidated Mens Club Inc 1973; dir Pierce Co Chamber of Comm 1981. **HONORS/ACHIEVEMENTS:** Teacher of the Year Pierce Co Teachers Assn 1965; Father of the Yr Gaines Chapel AME Church 1980; Citizen of the Year Pierce Co Chamber of Commerce 1981. **HOME ADDRESS:** 913 Cherry St, Blackshear, GA 31516.

TAYLOR, RICHARD L.
Government official. **PERSONAL:** Born Jul 19, 1944, Richmond, VA; married Gloria Jean McLendon; children: Richard Marcus II. **EDUCATION:** Livingston Coll of Rutgers Univ, BA 1971; Rutgers Univ, MA City & Regional Planning 1974. **CAREER:** Grant Ave Community Center, pres/ceo 1976-; City of Plainfield, NJ, mayor 1984-. **ORGANIZATIONS:** Past chmn Plainfield Democratic City Comm 1975-76 (1st Black appointed); pres City Council of Plainfield 1979, 1982-83; ranking mem Natl League of Cities Comm & Econ Devel Steering Comm; natl bd mem Operation PUSH; mem Union Co Private Industry Cncl; mem Natl Black Caucus of Local Elected Officials; chmn Union Co Employment Educ & Training Adv Cncl 1979-82; mem Plainfield Bd of Schl Estimate 1980, 1982-84; mem Plainfield Area NAACP; mem Plainfield Model Cities Cncl 1970; mem Comm Ch of God; mem Rutgers Assn of Planning Students; pres Black Cultural Assn of Middlesex Co Coll 1968. **HONORS/ACHIEVEMENTS:** Plainfield Babe Rugh Award for Outstanding Serv 1985; Plainfield Clergy Assn Recogn Award for Outstanding Leadership 1979; Outstanding Young Man of Amer Award in Leadership and Exceptional Comm Serv 1980; Frederick Douglas Award for Civic Service Black Cultural & Historical Soc of Union 1983; Comm Church of God Award for Community Svc; Plainfield Science Center Award for Civic Svc; NJ Assn of Black Social Workers (Union Co Achievement Award); NJ Black United Fund Comm Serv Award 1984; panelist WNBC-TV "First Tuesday"; panelist WNDT-TV "Livingston College". **MILITARY SERVICE:** AUS 1966-68; Sgt E-5; Bronze Star for Valor; Purple Heart; Vietnam Combat Infantryman's Badge; Vietnam Serv Medal; All-Star Basketball and Football Post TeamsFort Dix, NJ and Fort Riley, KS. **BUSINESS ADDRESS:** Mayor, City of Plainfield, 403 W 7th St, Plainfield, NJ 07060.

TAYLOR, ROBERT, III
Family dentist. **PERSONAL:** Born Apr 12, 1946, Ashburn, GA; son of Robert Taylor, Jr. and Susie Bell Hudson Taylor; married JoAnne Davis; children: Robert IV, Quentin, Sonya, Bridget. **EDUCATION:** Albany State Coll, BS 1966; Atlanta Univ, MS 1970; Medical Coll of GA, DMD 1975; Post Grad US Navy, Certificate 1976. **CAREER:** Telfair Co GA, chemistry instructor 1966-69; Henry Co GA, biology instructor 1969-70; US Navy, asst sr dental officer 1975-78; Turner Job Corps GA, head dentist 1978-82; General Dentistry, self-employed. **ORGANIZATIONS:** Mem Amer Dental Assoc, Natl Dental Assoc, Amer Acad of General Dentists, Reserve Officers League, GA Acad of General Dentists, Phi Bet Sigma Frat Inc; chmn of bd NAACP; vice pres Congress of Black Organizations; mem Jack & Jill of Amer, Albany State Coll Foundation, Title Twenty Foundation, Prince HallMason

Lodge 360, Knights of Columbus 4th Degree 3607, Post 512 Amer Legion, VFW Post 7491; AL Ranken 142. **HONORS/ACHIEVEMENTS:** Certificates of Honor Medical Coll of GA, US Navy, NAACP; Outstanding Young Men of Amer 1980. **MILITARY SERVICE:** USN lt commander 16 yrs. **HOME ADDRESS:** 2120 Colquitt Ave, Albany, GA 31707. **BUSINESS ADDRESS:** Dir, Taylor's Dental Clinics, 512 S Monroe St, Albany, GA 31701.

TAYLOR, ROBERT EARLINGTON, JR.
General contractor. **PERSONAL:** Born Aug 20, 1937, Dayton, OH; married Beverly Jean Stark; children: Kevin, Robin Perkins. **EDUCATION:** Attended, Sinclair Comm Coll Dayton 1972-73. **CAREER:** Lake Pleasure Fishing Lakes, mgr 1970-75; Black Game Co of Dayton OH, founder/pres 1971-79; Delco Moraine General Motors Div, 1976-; World Toy Co of Amer, owner/pres 1979-; Taylor-Made Const & Remodelling Co Inc, pres & genl mgr 1980-. **ORGANIZATIONS:** Mem Natl Assoc of Black Mfg Distributors 1972-; breeder Koja Kennels 1973-80; mem bd of dirs Midas Landscaping Co Inc 1986-, Carefree Property Mgmt Co Inc 1986-. **HONORS/ACHIEVEMENTS:** Certificate Mgmt Training Church's Chicken Inc 1976; Merit Awd General Motors Inc 1983. **BUSINESS ADDRESS:** President, Taylor-Made Construction, 4538 St James Ave, Dayton, OH 45406.

TAYLOR, ROCKIE See OLOGBONI, TEJUMOLA F.

TAYLOR, RONALD A.
Reporter. **PERSONAL:** Born Aug 14, 1948, Washington, DC. **EDUCATION:** Morehouse Coll. **CAREER:** Washington Post, reporter 1971-; Atlanta Constitution, reporter 1970-71; Washington Daily News, reporter 1968-70; Greensboro NC Daily News, reporter intrn 1968.

TAYLOR, ROY MARCELLUS
Dentist. **PERSONAL:** Born Feb 12, 1925, Sumter, SC; son of Rev. and Mrs W M Taylor; married Virginia Marlene Beverly; children: Wayne M Taylor DDS, Sheryl Taylor Bailey, RDH; Anthony M. **EDUCATION:** Howard Univ, BS 1950; Meharry Med Coll, DDS 1950; Amer Univ of Oriental Studies, PhD 1984; Acupuncture Found of Sri Lanka, DSc 1984. **CAREER:** Aetna Life Ins Co, consult 1960-70; TV Dental School, asst prof of dentistry 1967-71; Temple Univ Comp Health Svcs, chf of dental serv 1967-70, centerdir 1970-72; Roy M Taylor Assoc, dentist/clinician 1954-. **ORGANIZATIONS:** Dir Wm H Feronce Co 1960-66; dir/treas Project IN 1966-69; memAcad of Stress and Chronic Diseases; mem Acad of Gen Dentistry; mem Acad of Endosseous Implants; mem Amer Acad for Funct Prosthodontics; mem Amer Dental Assn; mem Natl Dental Assn; mem Intl Assn for Orthodontics; mem Amer Endodontic Soc; mem Intl Coll of Oral Implantology; PA Dental Assn; mem Philadelphia Cnty Dental Soc; mem Philadelphia Soc of Periodontology; Northeast Gnathological Soc; mem Inst of Med and Dent Hypnosis; mem Amer Pub Health Assn; memNew Era Dental Soc; mem Chi Delta Mu Frat; mem Acupuncture Found. **HONORS/ACHIEVEMENTS:** Omicron Kappa Upsilon Natl Hon Soc 1954; Kappa Sigma Pi Honor Soc 1954; The Legion of Honor The Chapel of Four Chaplains Philadelphia in recognition of Outstanding Comm Serv 1969; Fellowship Acad of General Dentistry 1972; mem Intl Coll of Oral Implantology 1972; Recip President's Award for Outstanding Serv to Chi Delta Mu Frat 1973; Recip President's Award for Scientific Contrib Natl Dent Assn 1970-71; Who's Who Among Black Americans 1978; The NY Acad of Sciences 1979; The Intl Who's Who of Intellectuals Vol IV 1982; Recip President's Award Med Coll 1979; Listed "The First Five Hundred" Libr Edn; Publications including, "Dental Health Problems In the Ghetto"; "The Treatment of Occlusal Disturbances, The Study Cost" Quarterly of the Natl Dent Assn Vol 28 No 4 1970; "My Story of West Nicetown - Tioga Neighborhood Family Health Center" PA Dental Journal 1971; "Atlas of Complete Dentures" Lippincott 1970. **MILITARY SERVICE:** USMC Pvt 1st Class 1943-45; AUS Cpt 1954-56. **BUSINESS ADDRESS:** President, Roy M Taylor Associates, 5811 Cobbs Creek Parkway, Philadelphia, PA 19143.

TAYLOR, RUTH SLOAN
Educator. **PERSONAL:** Born Jun 08, 1918, Greenville, SC; widowed. **EDUCATION:** EdD 1962. **CAREER:** IN Univ Nw, asst chrmn div of ed 1969-; Summer HS Cairo, IL, engl teacher 1946-48; Roosevelt HS Gary, IN, eng 1948-66; Title I E SEA Gary, IN, sup 1966-68. **ORGANIZATIONS:** Coop Ed Res Lab Pgm Assc Northfield, IL 1967; asst prof IN-Univ Nw 1969; assc prof INUniv NW 1972; pres bd of trustee Gary Comm Sch; consult leec chmn Bi-Cen Comm INUniv Nw United Way Camp City Met Chmn 1974; mem Natl Soc Act Comm Delta Sigma Theta Sor 1973; asst chmn Div of Ed INUniv NW 1974-75; elected Natl Sec Delta Sigma Theta Sor Inc. **HONORS/ACHIEVEMENTS:** Auth of "Teaching in the Desegrated Classroom"; outst cit awrd for ed IU Dons Inc 1974; Who's Who Am Women; Who's Who in Midwest; ldrs in ed. **BUSINESS ADDRESS:** Indiana Univ NW, 3400 Broadway, Gary, IN 46408.

TAYLOR, SANDRA ELAINE
Psychologist. **PERSONAL:** Born Aug 08, 1946, New York, NY; daughter of Floyd L. Taylor and Berthenia Turner Taylor; married Alvin Green (divorced); children: Kwam Taylor Green. **EDUCATION:** Bronx Comm Coll of the City Univ of NY, AAS 1965, AA 1969; City Coll of NY, BA 1970; City Univ of NY, PhD 1976. **CAREER:** Bronx Psychiatric Ctr, head nurse 1965-73; Albert Einstein Clinical Internship Prog in Psychology, intern psychologist 1973-74; Bronx Psychiatric Ctr, staffpsychologist 1974-76; City College/Harlem Hosp Ctr Physician Asst Prog, educational coord 1977-80; Brooklyn Developmental Ctr, principal psychologist & exec Asst to the dir 1980-81; Bronx Develop Ctr, deputy dir treatment svcs. **ORGANIZATIONS:** Adjunct lecturer City Coll of the City Univ of NY 1974-75; adjunct asst prof St Joseph's Coll 1976-77; adjunct asst prof Marymount Coll 1976-77/1977-79; counseling psychologist Marymount Coll 1976-77; adjunct asst prof State Univ of NY Coll at Purchase 1977; adjunct counselor Brooklyn Coll of the City Univ of NY 1977-78; adjunct asst prof St Peter's Coll 1978-80; mem Natl Assn Female Executives 1983-; pres Kwam S.E.T. Publishing Co., Inc. 1989-. **HONORS/ACHIEVEMENTS:** Numerous honors, awards, special achievements, publications such as "The New York Urban League Presents," WBLS radio station guest speaker 1976; recipient of the First Pamela Galiber Memorial Scholarship Awd for Doctoral Dissertation Rsch in memory of NY State Senator Jos Galiber's late daughter The City Univ ofNY 1976; "The Meaning of Scholarship" New York Eastern Star Annual Scholarship Awd presentation principal speaker 1976; "Ethnic Self-Hatred in Black Psychotics, A Preliminary Report" Journal of the Bronx State Hosp Vol 1 No 2 Spring 1973; "Racism and Psychiatry" Bronx Psychiatric Ctr guest lecturer for visitingmedical residents 1973. **HOME ADDRESS:** 1000 Grand Concourse, Bronx, NY 10451. **BUSINESS ADDRESS:** Deputy Dir Treatment Serv, Bronx Developmental Center, 1200 Waters Place, Bronx, NY 10461.

TAYLOR, SCOTT MORRIS
Physician. **PERSONAL:** Born Oct 10, 1957, Berkeley, CA; son of Dr & Mrs Robert L Taylor. **EDUCATION:** Morehouse Coll, BS 1980; Meharry Medical School, MD 1984. **CAREER:** Highland Hospital, surgery resident 1984-86; Martin Luther King Hospital, orthopedic resident 1987-. **HOME ADDRESS:** 525 Mandana Blvd #311, Oakland, CA 94610.

TAYLOR, SINTHY E.
Company chief executive officer. **PERSONAL:** Born Aug 18, 1947, Dayton, OH; married Vivian Lorraine Lundy. **EDUCATION:** Union for Experimenting Colls & Univs Cincinnati, BS 1977. **CAREER:** Dayton Model Cities Planning Council, youth coord 1968-70; Dayton Youth Coalition, exec dir 1970-75; Dayton Voter Registration Educ Inst, adminis 1975-80; State of OH Dept of Administrative Svcs, job recruitment specialist 1980-83; Taylor-Made Construction Co Inc, vice pres of bd of dirs 1980-; Care-Free Property Mgmt Co Inc, consultant 1986-; Midas Landscaping & Develop Co Inc, pres and ecological planner 1986-; Dayton Democratic Progressive Club, pres; commissioned Notary Public 1980-. **ORGANIZATIONS:** Chmn of bd Wesley Comm Ctr 1975-76; mem Miami Consistory #26 1981-; mem Ancient Square 1981-, chaplin 1983; mem Royal Arch Masons 1982-, Boone Commandery of Knights Templar 1982-; Solomon Johnson Council #4 Royal & Select Masters 1982-; Knights of the Mystic Shrine 1982-; order of Easter Star 1983-, past worthypatron 1984; ; assoc pastor St Paul AME Zion Church Dayton 1983-; chmn ward & precinct Democratic Voters League 1985-86; chmn voter registration DemocraticVoters League 1986-87; mem Heroines of Jericho, Heroines of the Templars Crusade. **HONORS/ACHIEVEMENTS:** Letter of Commendation President of the United States 1976; Outstanding Young Man of Amer 1979; Elected Worthy Patron Deborah Chap #19 Order of the Eastern Star 1984; Evangelist of the Year Awd AME Zion Church Connection 1985. **HOME ADDRESS:** 4526 Alfred Drive, Dayton, OH 45417.

TAYLOR, STERLING R.
Life underwriter. **PERSONAL:** Born Jan 05, 1942, Philadelphia, PA; son of Willie Ray Taylor and Ellanora K. Bivens; married Sonia E Madden (divorced); children: Tiarzha M, Khara D. **CAREER:** Army & Air Force Exchange Svc, buyer 1964-70; Equitable Financial Companies, life underwriter, 1970-. **ORGANIZATIONS:** Pres So AK Life Underwriters 1974-75; past pres, AK State Assn Life Underwriters; life mem, exec comm, NAACP Anchorage Branch; founder, pres, AK Black Caucus; comm chmn, Alaska Black Leadership Conf; ambassador, Life Underwriters Political Action Comm; life mem, past pres, Alpha Phi Alpha, Nu Zeta Lambda Chapter; bd mem, Anchorage Community Health Center. **HONORS/ACHIEVEMENTS:** Natl Sales Achievement Awards; Natl Quality Awards; Life Mem, Million Dollar Round Table, 1986; Hall of Fame, Equitable Financial Companies, 1982. **BUSINESS ADDRESS:** Agent, Equitable Financial Companies, 3301 C St, Suite 500, Anchorage, AK 99503.

TAYLOR, STEVEN LLOYD
Social welfare. **PERSONAL:** Born Jun 08, 1948, New York, NY; married Dr Dolores Y Straker; children: Brian K Taylor. **EDUCATION:** Queens Coll (City Univ of NY), BA 1969; Fordham Univ, MSW 1971; Columbia Univ, DSW 1984. **CAREER:** Comm Serv Soc of NYC, research assoc 1971-73; Fordham Univ, adjunct prof 1972-83; New York City Human Resources Admin, rsch scientist 1975-76, dir of prog eval 1976-78, dir research 1978-83, deputy commr 1983-87; United Way of New York City, senior vice pres 1987-. **ORGANIZATIONS:** ACSW Natl Assn of Soc Workers 1973-; NY State Cert Soc Worker 1971-; mem Natl Assn of Soc Workers 1971-; mem Amer Statistical Assn 1975-. **HONORS/ACHIEVEMENTS:** Black Achievers Award, Harlem YMCA 1988. **BUSINESS ADDRESS:** Senior Vice President, United Way of New York City, 99 Park Ave, New York, NY 10016.

TAYLOR, STUART A.
Educator. **PERSONAL:** Born Jul 02, 1936, Providence, RI; married Ella Marie; children: Sandre, Stuart, Sabrina, Scott. **EDUCATION:** Oakwood Clg, BS Acct Bus 1960;Univ RI, MS Grad Sch Bus 1963; IN U, PhD Indsl Mgmt & Psych 1967. **CAREER:** Grad Sch of Bus Harvard U, assc prof; mgmt consult to various major corp. **ORGANIZATIONS:** Mem Acad of Mgmt; bd adv to Natl Uran Leagu; fdr RI Com for Advancement of Negro Ed; mem White House Fellows Pgm. **HONORS/ACHIEVEMENTS:** Enabled him to research US Dept of Urban Dev & Study Abroad; 1st Black to become Licensed Pblc Acctnt in RI & to Teach Full-time at Harvard Bus Sch.

TAYLOR, THAD, JR.
Dentist, educator. **PERSONAL:** Born May 06, 1937, Waxahachie, TX; married Emma L Choice; children: Thao IV, Tracye Lashon. **EDUCATION:** Prairie View A&M Coll, BS 1957; Howard Univ, DDS 1963. **CAREER:** Tulsa Jr Coll Bd of Regents, mem 1972-, chmn 1976-77, 1981-82; OK Coll of Osteopathic Med & Surgery, assoc prof oral pathology. **ORGANIZATIONS:** Life mem NAACP 1968-; pres OK Med Dental & Pharmaceutical Assoc 1982-84. **MILITARY SERVICE:** AUS Infantry capt 2 yrs. **BUSINESS ADDRESS:** Assoc Professor Oral Surgery, The Oklahoma College, Osteopathic Medicine & Surgery, PO Box 6428, Tulsa, OK 74106.

TAYLOR, THEODORE D.
Educational administrator. **PERSONAL:** Born Mar 29, 1930, Ocala, FL; married Daisy R Curry; children: Tiffany, Tamila, Cedric, Theodore N, Patricia. **EDUCATION:** FL A&M U, BS 1950, MS 1956; Atlanta U, MS 1962; Nova U, EdD 1972. **CAREER:** Marion Co Sch Dist, tchr 1954; Marion Co Sch Dist Ocala FL, admin 1958; Broward Co Sch Dist, cncl 1962; Broward Co Sch Dist Ft Lauderdale, admin 1963; Broward Comm Coll, dir of special serv 1970-85, dir of admissions/coll equity officer 1985-. **ORGANIZATIONS:** Desegregation cnclUniv of Miami 1972; mem Local Draft Bd 151 1973; basileus Omega Psi Phi Frat Zeta Chi Chap 1976-78; pres Kiwanis Clb of Cntrl Broward1978; exalted ruler Elks Clb 1978; chmn Equal Access/Equal Opprty Com for Broward Co Govtl Empl 1978-; mem Fac Task Force of Supt Commn on Pub Ed Broward Co Schs; mem Broward Co Detention Adv Bd, Broward Bar Special Comm for Children. **HONORS/ACHIEVEMENTS:** Omega man of yr 1956, 1965, 1976; ndea flw AtlantaUniv 1961; a study of attrition of a select grp of disadvantaged stdnt ERIC 1976. **MILITARY SERVICE:** USMC s/sgt 1950-53. **BUSINESS**

ADDRESS: Equity Officer, Broward Community College, 225 E Las Olas Blvd, Fort Lauderdale, FL 33301.

TAYLOR, THEODORE ROOSEVELT
Clergyman. **PERSONAL:** Born Oct 30, Arkansas; married Geraldine. **EDUCATION:** Eaden Sem Phillips Schl of Theo. **CAREER:** Chris Meth Ch, minister. **ORGANIZATIONS:** Grocery Store Bus 14 Yrs; past pres Danville NAACP 2 Yrs; pres Champaign NAACP 2 Yrs; pres Ministers Alliance in St Louis 1942-45; presiding elder Champaign Dist CME Ch 1962-65. **HONORS/ACHIEVEMENTS:** Recip awrd for serv rendered Weldon Spgs, MO 1942. **BUSINESS ADDRESS:** 7629 Natural Bridge Ave, St Louis, MO.

TAYLOR, THOMAS C.
Business executive. **PERSONAL:** Born Oct 12, 1926, New Haven, CT; divorced; children: Keith, Linda. **EDUCATION:** Howard U, BS Psych 1950, MSW 1952. **CAREER:** Children First Inc, pres 1979-; Natl Child Day Care Assc Inc, exec dir 1965-79. **ORGANIZATIONS:** Consult With Center For Human Sys Harbridge House VOLT & Control Sys Research Washington 1956-71; caseworker supr Child Welfare Div Dept of Pub Welfare DC 1952-62; welfare consult Hlth & Welfare Cncl of Natl Capital Area DC 1962-65; chmn Comm Coor Child Care Pgm DC; bd dir Pierce Warwick Adoption Serv; vice pres Comm Learn Ctr DC; exec com Met Washington Chap Natl Assc of Soc Workers; past pres HowardUniv Sch of Soc Work Alumni Assc; past Chmn Com on Inquiry Natl Assc of Soc Workers; past tres Natl Cncl for Black Child Dev; Local Arrange Com E Reg Conf Child Welfare League of Am; past presNatl Cncl for Black Child Dev; Leg & Com Natl Assc for Ed of Young Children; chmn Monitoring Com of the Child Abuse Proj; Natl Cncl for Blk ChildDev; mem Mayor's Com Interdept Interagy Com on Neglected & Abused Children; mem Viceroy Clb of Washington, DC; mem Natl Com on Inquiry; Natl Assc of Soc Workers. **HONORS/ACHIEVEMENTS:** Outst alumni awrd HowardUniv Sch of Soc Work 1961; distgshd serv awrd United Plng Orgn Washington, DC 1980. **MILITARY SERVICE:** AUS 1945-46.

TAYLOR, TIMOTHY MERRITT
Association executive. **PERSONAL:** Born Aug 08, 1931, New York, NY; married Nell Cochrane; children: Timothy Jr, Stuart, Blair, Scott, Marshall. **EDUCATION:** Yale U, BA 1953; NY U, LlB 1956. **CAREER:** Westchester Urban League, ofcr bd dir 1969-. **ORGANIZATIONS:** Mem Bd of Cnslr FordhamUniv 1969-; co-fdr Urban Ed Inc 1968; mem Harlem Lawyers Assc 1956; NY Co Lawyers Assc 1956; pres W Side Sch Comm Ctrs; exec com NY NAACP; v chmn bd trustee New Lincoln Shc; chmn New York City Confed of Local Sch Bds. **BUSINESS ADDRESS:** 277 Broadway, New York, NY 10007.

TAYLOR, TOMMIE W.
Public relations representative. **PERSONAL:** Born Mar 04, 1929, Blytheville, AR; married Aubrey Taylor Sr; children: Aubrey Jr, Darryl E, Roderic K, Cabot O. **EDUCATION:** Licensed cosmetologist 1948; Philander Smith Coll, BA 1955; Univ of AR at Little Rock, Graduate Study. **CAREER:** Johnson Publ Co, stringer 1954-65; Radio Station KOKY-AM, prog asst 1957-59; AR Baptist Coll, registrar psych instructor 1959-61; Teletype Corp, civil rel assoc 1962-75; AT&T Information Systems, public relations rep 1982-. **ORGANIZATIONS:** Pres Urban League of Greater Little Rock 1971-75; tammateous Sigma Gamma Rho Sor 1984-85, 2nd anti basileus 1985-86, 1st anti basileus 1986-87; dir of YoungPeoples Bapt Training Union Dept NH Zion Bapt Church. **HONORS/ACHIEVEMENTS:** Outstanding Serv Awd Urban League of Greater Little Rock 1973,75; Outstanding Volunteer Serv Awd Urban League 1975; Volunteer & Comm Serv Awd Urban League Guild 1975; Appreciation Awd for Service Rendered as Bd Mem Youth Home Inc 1979; Outstanding Serv Awd AR Bapt Coll Camera Club 1979; Appreciation Awd Natl Alumni Assoc of AR Bapt Coll 1984; Disting Serv Awd Philander Smith Coll United Negro Coll Fund 1987; Active Participant Awd Natl Alumni Assoc AR Bapt Coll 1987. **BUSINESS ADDRESS:** Public Relations Rep, AT&T Information Systems, 7600 Interstate #30, Little Rock, AR 72209.

TAYLOR, VERONICA C.
Speech therapist. **PERSONAL:** Born May 17, 1941, Pensacola; married Raymond. **EDUCATION:** TN State Univ, BS 1962; Trenton State Coll, MA 1970. **CAREER:** Booker T Wash HS, instr 1962-67; Trenton Publ School, speech therapist; Trenton State Coll, coadj faculty 1985-. **ORGANIZATIONS:** Pres Trenton Delta Sigma Theta 1973-75; pres TABS 1974-77; vice pres Trenton Ed Assoc; mem NJ Ed Assoc Pol Action Fund 1974-75; mem, bd of dir NJ Sickle Cell Soc 1972-74; pres, vice pres Trenton Inter Frat Council; bd of dir, chmn NJ EOF; pres Womans Steering Comm Shiloh Bapt Church, NAACP, Trenton Black Acad, Mercer Cty Cit Coalition, Ewing Twp Dem Club; mem Natl Scholarship Comm Delta Sigma Theta 1983-. **HONORS/ACHIEVEMENTS:** Most All Around, Most Outstanding Female Grad Wash HS; Winner many essay contests; toured USO; Outstanding Comm Serv Trenton Delta Sigma Theta Inc; listed in World's Who's Who, Outstanding & Dedicated; Outstanding Serv Awd NJ Dept Higher Ed 1982. **BUSINESS ADDRESS:** Coadjunct Faculty, Trenton State College, Clinton Ave, Trenton, NJ 08625.

TAYLOR, VIDA MAURICE JARMON
Educator. **PERSONAL:** Born Jul 17, 1901, Weimar, TX. **EDUCATION:** Samuel Huston Clg, BA 1932; Incarnate Word Clg, MA 1957; Trinity U, Further Study 1965. **CAREER:** SAISD San Antonio, TX, elem school teacher 1924-71. **ORGANIZATIONS:** Parlimentarian Dorie Miller Elem Sch PTA 1956-63; pres Woman's Soc of Christian Serv 1960-65; pres Alpha Phi Sigma Chpt; Sigma Gamma Rho Sorority Inc 1960-64; dist sec Missionary Ed 1960-62; conf sec Children's Work United Meth Ch 1964-66; tchr del San Antonio Tchr Cncl 1965-71; parlimentarian Huston-Tillotson Clg Alumni & Ex-Student Assoc 1971-74; proj dir Women in Comm Serv Inc 1972-. **HONORS/ACHIEVEMENTS:** Recipient Distngshd Serv Awrd Bd of Ed SAISD 1971; Cert of Appreciation for Ldrshp & Serv Rendered to Comm 1973; Cert of Appreciation for Ldrshp & Serv to Chap Alpha Phi Sigma Chap 1973; TX Star Awrd Radio Station KKYK 1973; many others.

TAYLOR, VIVIAN A.
Elected official. **PERSONAL:** Born Oct 27, 1924, Maryland; married Lula M; children: Lavon E, Myron A. **EDUCATION:** Stillman Coll, attended 1942-43; Fisk Univ, attended 1946-48; State Univ of NY, BA 1973; attended Coll of Fredonia. **CAREER:** Jamestown Parks Dept, parks commissioner 1976-85; Black Awareness Studies, dir 1984-85; TRW, bearings div; City of Jamestown, city councilman. **ORGANIZATIONS:** Bd of dirs Jamestown Better Living; former mem Environmental Council; original appointee Jamestown Human Rights Comm; bd of dirs Jamestown Family Svcs; former chmn bd of trustees Blackwell Chapel AME Zion Church; former Boy Scout Comm; chmn Jamestown Interacial Forum 1962-65; mem City Charter Adv Comm 1977; mem of governing bd Chautauqua Oppors Inc Anti-Poverty Agency 1977-79; bd of dirs Crystal Ballroom Sr Citizens Ctr 1981-84; mem United Auto Aerospace & Implement Workers of Amer 1985; committeeman Chautauqua Co Democratic Comm 1985; committeeman Jamestown City Democratic Comm 1985. **HONORS/ACHIEVEMENTS:** Cert of Honor AME Zion Church 1978; Martin Luther King Jr Peace Awd Southern Tier Peace Ctr 1982. **MILITARY SERVICE:** Engineers demolition specialist 3 yrs. **HOME ADDRESS:** 31 W 18th St, Jamestown, NY 14701. **BUSINESS ADDRESS:** City Councilman, City of Jamestown, Municipal Bldg, Jamestown, NY 14701.

TAYLOR, VIVIAN LORRAINE
Vocational educator. **PERSONAL:** Born Jun 28, 1948, Philadelphia, PA; married Sinthy Eugene Taylor. **EDUCATION:** Antioch College, BA 1970; Antioch Putney Graduate School, MA 1971. **CAREER:** Dayton Bd of Educ, English & history teacher, 1970-72; Natl Boys Clubs of Amer, dir of youth girls prog, 1970-72; Dayton Bd of Educ, counselor, 1970-79, teacher-coordinator of occupational work adjustment prog, 1972-; Midas Landscaping Development Co, co-owner and business mgr, 1986-; MacFarlane Intermediate School, business mgr, 1986-. **ORGANIZATIONS:** Mem, Natl Educ Assn, Ohio Educ Assn, Dayton Educ Assn, 1970-; recording sec, Democratic Progressive Club, 1976-; mem, Miami Assembly #22 Order of Golden Circle, 1982-; 3rd vice chmn, Montgomery County Republican Party, 1982-83; financial sec, Order of Eastern Star Chap PHA, 1983-85; mem, Burning Bush Court #3 Heroines of Jericho; mem, Amer Court #65 Daughters of Isis, 1984-; mem, Truth Guild #2 Heroines of the Templars Crusade, 1984-. **HONORS/ACHIEVEMENTS:** Outstanding Democrat of the Year, Democratic Progressive Club, 1977; Outstanding Young Woman of Amer, 1977; Academic Achievement Award, Dayton Bd of Educ, 1979; Kizzy Award, Kizzy Scholarship Fund, 1983; Vocational Teacher of the Year, Dayton Bd of Educ 1984. **HOME ADDRESS:** 4526 Alfred Dr, Dayton, OH 45417.

TAYLOR, WALTER SCOTT
Clergyman. **PERSONAL:** Born Dec 12, 1916, Jackson, MS; married Odella Wykle; children: Mary Overton, Susie England, Walter S, Jr. **EDUCATION:** Clark Clg Atlanta, AB 1943; Gammon Theol Sem, BD 1946. **CAREER:** Galilee Un Meth Ch Englewood, NJ, minister 1952-; Trinity Meth Ch Bronx, NY, assc minister 1945-52; Meth Chs Edwards, MS & Franklin, NC, pastor. **ORGANIZATIONS:** Spnsr Home State Bk Teaneck, NJ; chmn bd Christian Soc Concerns No NJ Conf UMC; mem bd Pensions No NJ Conf UMC; mayor Englewood, NJ 1972-75; mem NAACP; commr Urban Renewal 1953-61; commr Englewood Housing Auth; ldr Successful Intergrate Pub Schs; fdr past pres Gr Englewood Housing Corp 1968; mem Bergen Co Hlth & Wel Cncl; bd dir Bergen Co Philharmonic Soc; bd dir Peace Ctr Bergen Co Del; Dem Natl Conv 1973; Natl League Cities Task Force Study. **HONORS/ACHIEVEMENTS:** Mayor of yr awrd 1975; outst achvmnt human re Bergen Co Urban League; Natl Black Bus & Professional Women's Assc; Natl Conf Black Women; Bergen Co CnclChs. **BUSINESS ADDRESS:** Galilee United Methodist Churc, 325 Genesee Ave, Englewood, NJ.

TAYLOR, WELTON IVAN
Consulting microbiologist. **PERSONAL:** Born Nov 12, 1919, Birmingham, AL; son of Frederick Enslen Taylor and Cora Lee Brewer Taylor; married Jayne Rowena Kemp; children: Karyn, Shelley. **EDUCATION:** Univ of Illinois, AB 1941, MS 1947, PhD 1948. **CAREER:** Univ of Illinois, asst prof 1948-54; Swift & Co, micro 1954-59; Children's Memorial Hospital, micro-in-chief 1959-64; consultant, microbiologist 1963-; Micro-Palettes Inc, pres 1977-. **ORGANIZATIONS:** Founding chmn Chicago Chapter Episcopal Soc for Cultural & Racial Equality 1961; bd of Scientific Advisors 1970-82; bd dir Amer Bd Bioanalysis 1973-82; Amer Assn of Bioanalysts 1970-82; vice pres, pres Chicago Medical Mycological Soc 1967-69; Acad appointments, Assoc Dept Pathology NW Medical School 1961-67; asst prof Univ Illinois School of Medicine 1965-69; assoc prof Univ of Illinois School of Medicine 1969-86. **HONORS/ACHIEVEMENTS:** James M Yard Brotherhood Award, Natl Conf Christians & Jews 1961; Speciall Research Fellowship, Natl Inst Health 1961-62; Diplomate Amer Bd Med Microbiology 1968; Fellow Amer Acad Microbiology 1974; Educ Bds Applied Microbiology/Amer Soc Microbiology 1968-70; Lab Med Amer Soc Clinical Pathology 1971-77; Test of Month Amer Assn Bioanalysts 1971-82; Journal of Clinical Micro Amer Soc Microbiol 1975-84; new species of bacterium "Enterobacter taylorae" named for him 1985; Special Research Fellowship, NIAID: Pasteur Inst, Lillie, France, l96l; Central Public Health Laboratory, Colindale, London, England, l962; Intl Dissemination of Salmonellae by Import/Export Foods; authored more than 50 original scientific publications, book chapters and patents; formulated media/methods Salmonella/Shigella detection used by FDA an d Western Nations since l975. **MILITARY SERVICE:** AUS 1st Lieutenant 1941-46; Illinois Natl Guard major 1948-55. **BUSINESS ADDRESS:** President, Micro-Palettes, Inc, 7621 S Prairie AVe, Chicago, IL 60619.

TAYLOR, WILLIAM EDWARD
Jazz musician. **PERSONAL:** Born Jul 24, 1921, Greenville, NC; married Theodora Castion; children: Duane, Kim. **EDUCATION:** VA State, BS 1942; Univ of MA, EdD 1975. **CAREER:** Pianist, Composer, Recording Artist, Arranger/Conductor, Actor, Author, Teacher & Lecturer. **ORGANIZATIONS:** Mem Natl Cncl on the Arts; guest artist at White House; bd dir Am Soc of Composerrs & Authors & Publs; Creative Artist Pub Serv; Newport Jazz Festival; NY Jazz Reperatory Co; sec NY State Com Cultural Resources; vice pres Natl Assc of Rec Arts & Sci; fdr pres fdr Jazzmobile; consult adv mus schs Civic& Cultural Grps; mentor to Jazz Orgn; worked with Dizzy Gillespie, Roy Eldridge, Wilbur DeParis, Sid Catlett, Cozy Cole; featured pianist Slam Stewart Trio; soloist Don Redman Orch; featured soloist with groups as Charlie Parker, Dizzy Gillespie, Miles Davis, Kai Winding, Jo Jones, Lester Young, Oscar Pettiford; composer "I Wish I Knew How It Would Feel To Be Free"; selected by NY Times as One of The Great Songs of the Sixties; compositions Heard On Such Pgms As, Sesame Street, The Electric Co; written Spl Material for Ethel Smith, Charlie Parker & Many Other Top Entertainers; composed ragtime dance score for Anna Sokolow'sTV Spl; composed ballet music for "Your Arms Too Short To Box With God". **HONORS/ACHIEVEMENTS:** Written svrl Movie Scores "A Morning For Jimmy" Northside Ctr; freelance rec artist working With, David Frost, Ella Fitzgerald, Sarah Vaughn, Bing Crosby, Sammy Davis, Jr, & Many Others; muscl dir awrd winning "David Frost Show"; actor in hit "The Time of Your Life"; spokesman in Commercials for such products as, Cold Power, Schaefer, Budweiser, Schmidt's, Ballantine Bee, Pespi Cola, Peugeot, Campbell Soup, Coca Cola, Canada Dry & Many Others; author of 12 Books on Jazz & Jazz Plaing; articles

written for Cue, Downbeat, Saturday Rev, Tchr, CW Post Clg, Fellow At Yale; designer of Jazz Course For Manhattan Sch of Music;lectr 1st Intrntl Music Industry Conf, Berklee Clg of Music, Music Edctrs Natl Conf;Univ of PA, ColumbiaUniv & Many Others; cert of appreciation City ofNY; key to city Cleveland; numerou awrds from Jazz Comm; hon MusD VA State; FairfieldUniv & Clark Clg; Billy Taylor Collection of Original Manuscripts;Clg of Fine Arts Howard U; Billy Taylor Lect Series Howard U. **BUSINESS ADDRESS:** 119 W 57th St, New York, NY 10019.

TAYLOR, WILLIAM GLENN
Business executive. **PERSONAL:** Born Oct 17, 1942, Loma Linda, CA; son of Mr & Mrs William Taylor; married Gwendolyn A Mayeaux. **EDUCATION:** Riverside City College, 1963; Univ of San Francisco, BS 1979. **CAREER:** First Interstate Bank, business services super 1965-72; Union Bank of CA, admin officer 1972-76; Bank of CA, opers super 1976-77; Home Savings of America, branch mgr 1977-83; Saving Administration Specialists 1983- . **ORGANIZATIONS:** Member Pasadena Jr Chamber of Commerce 1965-67; member Oakland Chamber of Commerce 1977-82; member San Francisco Chamber of Commerce 1982-83; member Optimist Intl 1982-83. **BUSINESS ADDRESS:** Vice President, Home Savings of America, 6955 Sierra, Dublin, CA 94568.

TAYLOR, WILLIAM H.
Soil scientist. **PERSONAL:** Born Jan 29, 1948, Edison, GA; married Catherine. **EDUCATION:** FL A&M U, BS 1970. **CAREER:** Soil Cnsrvtn Svc, soil scintst. **ORGANIZATIONS:** Faith Tbrncl Bapt Ch; pres Men's Club; Yng Adult Choir; NAACP. **HONORS/ACHIEVEMENTS:** Local chap spl achiev awd Soil Cnsrvtn Serv 1972.

TAYLOR, WILLIAM HENRY, SR.
Labor leader. **PERSONAL:** Born Aug 28, 1931, Eathel, LA; married Thelma Watkins; children: Daryl, William Jr, Dawn, Diane. **EDUCATION:** Univ of IL Chicago, 1954-56; Roosevelt Univ, 1965-69. **CAREER:** Oil, Chem & Atomic Workers Union, Corn Council, pres 1973-; Inter-Union Wet Corn Milling US & Canada Council, chairperson 1979-; OCAW Comm on Minority Affairs, chairperson 1975-79, 1983; OCAWIU Local 7-507, pres 1971-. **ORGANIZATIONS:** Mem advisor council Amer Arbitration Assoc 1971-75, 1982-84; pres Bowen HS PTA 1973-75; instr Roosevelt Univ Labor Ed Prog 1975-; mem advisory council Comm Fund 1975-79; pres CEDA Southwest Devel Assoc 1977-80, 1983-; dir Cook County CEDA Bd of Dir 1978-81; exec comm Labor Coalition Publ Util 1981-. **HONORS/ACHIEVEMENTS:** Special Citation Crusade of Mercy 1977; Humanitarian Awd St Mathew AME Church 1974. **MILITARY SERVICE:** AUS sgt E-5 2 yrs; UN Ribon, Good Conduct 1952-54. **HOME ADDRESS:** 9608 S Yates St, Chicago, IL 60617. **BUSINESS ADDRESS:** President, OCAWIU Local 7-507, 6305 S Archer Rd, Argo, IL 60501.

TAYLOR, WILLIAM L.
Educator. **PERSONAL:** Born Oct 04, 1931, Brooklyn, NY; married Harriett Rosen; children: Lauren R, Deborah L, David S. **EDUCATION:** Brooklyn Coll, BA (cum laude) 1952; Yale Law Sch, LLB 1954. **CAREER:** NAACP Legal Def & Educ Fund, atty 1954-58; Ams for Dem Action, legis rep 1959-61; US Comm on Civil Rights, gen counsel 1963-65, staff dir 1965-68; Cath Univ Law Sch, adj prof; Natl Policy Review, dir 1970-86; Private Practice, law 1986-. **ORGANIZATIONS:** Mem exec comm Natl Bd of Ams for Dem Action 1971-; author "Hanging Together, Equality in an Urban Nation" 1971; bd Puerto Rican Legal Def Fund 1976-; Met Washington Planning & Housing Assn 1976-; mem Bars of NY, DC, US Supreme Ct; adjunct prof Georgetown Law School 1986-. **HONORS/ACHIEVEMENTS:** Sr Fellow Yale Law Sch 1969-70; Natl Endowment for Humanities Grant 1974. **MILITARY SERVICE:** AUS 1956-58. **BUSINESS ADDRESS:** Attorney-at-Law, William L Taylor, 1730 M St NW, Ste 600, Washington, DC 20036.

TAYLOR, WILLIE MARVIN
Materials and process engineer. **PERSONAL:** Born Apr 05, 1955, Milledgeville, GA; children: Donde R. **EDUCATION:** Fort Valley State, BS 1978; Atlanta Univ, MS 1980. **CAREER:** Dow Chemical, chemist 1980-82; Grumman Aircraft Systems, matls & process engr 1983-. **ORGANIZATIONS:** Assoc mem SAMPE 1983-; exec comm mem NAACP 1983-. **HONORS/ACHIEVEMENTS:** Mem Alpha Kappa Mu Honor Soc, Beta Kappa Chi Scientific Honor Soc; Outstanding Young Men of Amer 1981. **BUSINESS ADDRESS:** Matls & Process Engineer, Grumman Aircraft Systems, Highway 22 West, Milledgeville, GA 31061.

TEAGLE, TERRY EUGENE
Professional athlete. **PERSONAL:** Born Apr 10, 1960, Broaddus, TX. **EDUCATION:** Baylor Univ, BS Phys Ed 1982. **CAREER:** Houston Rockets, guard-forward 1982-. **HONORS/ACHIEVEMENTS:** 3-time All-SWC first team under Coach Jim Haller; 2nd team All-am as sr.

TEAGUE, GLADYS PETERS
City official, account executive. **PERSONAL:** Born Sep 14, 1921, Muskogee, OK; married LD Teague; children: Merron, Charles. **EDUCATION:** Draughon's Bus Coll, 1956-57; Correspondence Course for Postal Clerks, 1946. **CAREER:** Taft Post Office, postal clerk 1946-63; 1st Baptist Church, asst church clerk 1965-; Muskogee Cty, voter registrar 1984-; Town of Taft, city clerk 1984; Muskogee Cty Clerk, cty clerk deputy 1981-. **ORGANIZATIONS:** Mem Starlight Chap #11 OES 1949-; beautician Taft's Beauty Shop 1951-53; notary Muskogee Cty 1962-; mem school bd Dist I-17 Muskogee Cty 1972; hon aux mem Amer Legion Post #84 1973-; mem Muskogee Cty Fed Dem Women 1981-. **HONORS/ACHIEVEMENTS:** Superior Accomplishment Post Office Dept 1959. **BUSINESS ADDRESS:** County Clerk Deputy, Muskego County Clerk, PO Box F, Taft, OK 74463.

TEAGUE, ROBERT
Director. **PERSONAL:** Born Oct 26, 1929, Durant, MS; married Tresa Marie Smith. **EDUCATION:** Tougaloo Clg, BA 1955;Univ IL, MSW 1961, USC 1966. **CAREER:** Psychiatric Pgms S Bay Mental Htlh Ctr, dir 1974-; Whitney M Young, Jr Psychiatric Hosp, dir owner prof placement serv pres exec dir 1971-74; Harbor View House, dir part owner 1966-; CA Dept Mental Hygiene, pgm consult 1965-67, sr psychiatric soc worker 1964-65; Pvt Marital Cncl Clinic, assc dir 1962-64; Sepulveda VA Hosp, sr psychiatric soc worker 1961-64; Danville VA Neuropsychiatric Hosp, psychiatric team 1960-61; IL Pub Aid Comm 1959-60; Ed Oakley Training Sch, playground dir 1958-59. **ORGANIZATIONS:** Chmn Soc Work Res Com VA Hosp Sepulveda 1961-64; co-fdr Pvt Marital Guidance Clnc; bd dir W Reg Conf Mental Hlth Pgm Mgmt 1974-76; mem Ad HocCom Mntl Hlth Ctrs 1974; consult Westminister Neighbrhd Assc Mental Hlth Clnc 1964-65; Greater LA Mental Hlth Assc; bd dir Natl Assc Soc Workers; LA Welfare Plng Cncl; elder Westminister Presb Ch; pres Clg Alumni 1965-67; bd dir STEP Job Training Proj; bd dir S Cen Welfare Plng Cncl 1969-;mem Natl Assc Soc Workers; CA Registered Soc Workers; Am Psy Assc; CA Welfare Conf; Acad Certified Soc Workers; Clg of Nursing Home Admn. **HONORS/ACHIEVEMENTS:** LA men of tomorrow YMCA; comm serv awrd LA Sentinel 1972; author of Var articles & resolutions. **MILITARY SERVICE:** USAF crypot oper 1950-54.

TEAL, ELLA S. (ELLA J. SANDERS)
Association executive. **PERSONAL:** Born Sep 22, 1947, Georgia; married William Algenon; children: Tahirah Ain, Shakir Lateef. **EDUCATION:** Albany State Coll, BA 1965-69; Univ of CT Sch of Social Work Hartford, MSW 1971. **CAREER:** So New Eng Telephone Co, Stamford, CT, serv rep 1969; Morris Co Urban League Morristown, NJ, program dir 1971-79; Urban League of Union Co, pres 1979-. **ORGANIZATIONS:** Mem Alpha Kappa Alpha Sorrority 1967-; mem Nat Assn of Black Social Workers 1969-72; mem Nat Assn of Social Workers 1969-74. **HONORS/ACHIEVEMENTS:** Full acad scholarship Univ of CT Sch of Social Work Hartford, 1969-71. **BUSINESS ADDRESS:** President, Urban League of Union Co, 272 N Broad St, Elizabeth, NJ 07207.

TEAMER, CHARLES C.
Educational administrator. **PERSONAL:** Born May 20, 1933, Shelby, NC; married Mary Alice Dixon; children: Charles Carl, Roderic F, Cheryl R. **EDUCATION:** Clark Coll, BA 1954; Univ of Omaha, post grad 1962-63; Tulane Univ, post grad 1965-66. **CAREER:** SC State Coll Orangeburg, acct 1955-56; TN State Univ Nashville, asst bus mgr 1958-62; Wiley Coll Marshall, TX, bus mgr 1962-65; Dillard Univ New Orleans, vice pres fiscal affairs 1965-. **ORGANIZATIONS:** Dir New Orleans Pub Serv Co; bd dir Common Fund; vice pres United Way New Orleans; mem/past dir/pres Natl Assn Coll & Univ Bus Officers; vice pres bd dirnew Orleans Area Council; treas M & T Area Com Lafon Protestant Home; bd dir Ochner Med Found Children's Hosp; mem C of C New Orleans; mem Alpha PhiAlpha; life mem natl comptroller Methodist Clubs; Masons; Shriners. **HONORS/ACHIEVEMENTS:** Silver Beaver Award Boy Scouts of Amer 1968; 1 of 10 Outstanding Citizens of New Orleans 1979. **MILITARY SERVICE:** AUS 1956-58. **BUSINESS ADDRESS:** Vice President for Fiscal Aff, Dillard University, 2601 Gentilly Blvd, New Orleans, LA 70122.

TEARE, JOHN JAMES
Attorney. **PERSONAL:** Born May 18, 1924, Newark, NJ; married Robse Maybin; children: Cheryl, Siobhan. **EDUCATION:** Newark Clg Rutgers U, AB 1949; NY Law Sch, LlB 1961;Univ NV Natl Clg of State Judiciary 1973. **CAREER:** City Newark, 1st asst corp cncl; Motor Clb of Am Ins Co, stf atty; Essex Co Prosecutor, asst; E Orange, municipal ct judge. **ORGANIZATIONS:** Mem Essex Co Bar Assc; NJ Bar Assc; Am Bar Assc; founding mem Barristers Clb of NJ; Garden State Bar Assc; Natl Bar Assc; mem Judicial Cncl; Natl Bar Assc; Supreme Ct Com; Juvenile & Domestic Rel Cts; NAACP; Orange & Maplewood Chpt; Frontiers Intrntl; past pres Voters Info Cncl. **HONORS/ACHIEVEMENTS:** Awrds from various drug alchoholic rehab Pgms; Various In Mate Grps. **MILITARY SERVICE:** AUS 1943-45, 51-52.

TEARNEY, RUSSELL JAMES
Educator. **PERSONAL:** Born Aug 10, 1938, Syracuse, NY; married Katherine; children: Russell, William, Michele. **EDUCATION:** VA Union U, BS 1961; Howard U, MS 1969, PhD 1973. **CAREER:** Howard U, asst prof physiology & biophysics 1973-, grad stdnt 1965-72; US PO, clk 1961-65. **ORGANIZATIONS:** Mem Am Heart Assc Inc; Sigma XI; AAAS; Black Sci Am; Pub Hlth Serv 1966-69; Porter Flwshp 1969-72; Am Physiol Soc 1977; grad asst prof Grad Sch Arts & Sci 1977. **BUSINESS ADDRESS:** 520 W St NW, Washington, DC 20059.

TEASLEY, LARKIN
Business executive. **PERSONAL:** Born Sep 23, 1936, Cleveland, OH; married Violet M Williams; children: Lisa, Erica, Laura. **EDUCATION:** Fisk Univ, BA Magna Cum Laude 1957; Occidental Coll LA, grad work in Actuarial Sci 1957-58; Univ of CA, LA, Grad Sch of Bus Exec Prgm 1971-72. **CAREER:** Golden State Mutual Life Ins Co, LA, asst actuary 1958-63; NC Mutual Life Ins Co, Durham, NC, actuary 1963-69; Golden State Mutual Life Ins Co, president 1970-. **ORGANIZATIONS:** Dir Golden State Mut Life Ins Co 1971; dir Golden State Minority Found; dir Broadway Fed Sav & Loan Assn; dir LA Council Boy Scouts; dir NHS of Los Angeles; fellow Soc of Actuaries; former commr LA Co Econ & Efficiency Commn; mem LA world Affairs Council; mem Town Hall; mem Am Acad of Actuaries; mem Nat Assn of Bus Economists; mem Alpha Phi Alpha; Phi Beta Kappa; Beta Kappa Chi Scientific Honor Soc. **BUSINESS ADDRESS:** President, Golden State Mut Life Ins Co, 1999 W Adams Blvd, Los Angeles, CA 90018.

TEASLEY, MARIE R.
Editor. **PERSONAL:** Born in Hannibal, MO; daughter of George A Wright (deceased) and Rose Trott Wright (deceased); married Ronald; children: Ronald Jr, Timothy, Lydia. **EDUCATION:** Wayne State Univ; Univ of Detroit. **CAREER:** Writer for Black Publications, Aged 14; Fame Magazine writer; Pittsburgh Courier writer; WSU campus paper; Philip Morris Co; NW Papers; Food & Music Radio, host; Regular TV Show Guest; MI Chronicle, club & soc writer, 1966, women's editor. **ORGANIZATIONS:** mem, Women in Communications; advisory bd, WXYZ; advisory bd, Highland Park YWCA; Northwestern High School Alumni Assn; Detroit Chapter of Natl Assn of Media Women; Cancer Soc; numerous Civic Orgs; chmn, founder, Detroit Science Center Business Fund, 1983; pres, Madonna Women on Action; Coalition of 100 Black Women. **HONORS/ACHIEVEMENTS:** Named Natl Media Woman of Year, 1974-75; Bridal Book edited NAAPA Award, 1974; Woman of Year, Catholic Archidose of Detroit, 1974; SCLC Award, Top Communicator, 1973; Employee of the Year, MI Chronicle, 1972; Detroit Chapter of Negro Business & Professioanl Women Top Serv Award, 1974; Woman of Year, Detroit Chapter Media, 1974; NNAPA Best Women's Pages San Francisco 1975; profiles in black CORE NY Publication, 1977; Top Journalism Award, Business & Professional Women, Natl Negro B&P Detroit Chapter, 1977; Turner Broadcasting, Goodwill Ambassador to Moscow, 1986; Coalition of 100 Black Women; Outstanding Journalism & Reporting, 1987; Others, 1986-89. **BUSINESS ADDRESS:** Michigan Chronicle, 479 Ledyard, Detroit, MI 48201.

TEEKAH, GEORGE ANTHONY
Physician. **PERSONAL:** Born Mar 29, 1948; married Theresa Riley. **EDUCATION:** Howard Univ, BS (hon) 1971, MD 1975. **CAREER:** Greater SE Comm Hosp, med dir of icu, respiratory therapy 1980-83; Richmond Comm Hosp, med dir respiratory therapy 1984-. **HONORS/ACHIEVEMENTS:** Beta Kappa Chi Scientific Honor Soc 1972. **BUSINESS ADDRESS:** Medical Dir, 505 W Leigh St, Richmond, VA 23220.

TEELE, ARTHUR EARLE, JR.
Association executive, attorney. **PERSONAL:** Born May 14, 1946, Washington, DC; children: Arthur Patton. **EDUCATION:** FL A&M Univ, BA 1967; Army Ranger Sch, certificate 1970; Army Airborne School, certificate 1970; FL State Univ Coll of Law, JD 1972; Judge Advocate Gen School, certificate 1973. **CAREER:** US House of Reps, congressional intern 1966-67; US Army, sr aide-de-camp 1974-76; US Dept of Labor, expert consultant 1976-77; Private Practice, attorney atlaw 1976-81; US Dept of Trans, transition team leader 1980-81; Urban Mass Trans Admin, admin 1981-83; Anderson Hibey Nauheim & Blair, partner 1983-85; Sparber Shevin Shapo & Heinbronner, of counsel 1983-; Natl Bus League, pres & ceo. **ORGANIZATIONS:** Mem Amer, Natl, FL, Dist of Columbia Bar Assns; mem Supreme Court of the State of FL; mem US Court of Appeals for the Fifth Dist; mem US District Court for the Northern Dist of FL; mem Phi Alpha Delta Law Frat; mem Assn of the Army; bd of dir FL Voters League; mem Jefferson Island Club; mem Pi Gamma Mu Natl Honor Soc; life mem Natl Assn for the Advancement of Colored People; life mem Kappa Alpha Psi Frat; mem FL State Univ Gold Key Soc; mem AlumniAssns of FL A&M Univ and FL State Univ; pres S FL Business League of Miami; bd of dir Coalition for Black Colleges; 1980-; vice pres & gen counsel Assoc Indus of FL 1983-84; chmn of bd John G Riley Foundation 1983-; mem Jefferson Island Club 1983-; dir Silver Star Comm of FL 1983-; dir People's Natl Bank of Commerce 1983-; pres S FL Business League 1984-; pres Natl Business League 1984-; dir Rehom Corp 1984-; dir Booker T Washington Found 1984-; partner 1712 Assocs 1984-; chmn & ceo Mfg Tech Indus Inc 1984-; chmn & ceo Truxpacker Inc; 1984-. **HONORS/ACHIEVEMENTS:** Outstanding Young Man of Amer 1979; FL NAACP Gwendolyn Sawyer Cherry Awd 1981; Hon Doc of Aviation Mgmt Embry-Riddle Univ 1982; Frontiers Intl Achievement and Serv Awd 1985; FL Gold Key. **MILITARY SERVICE:** AUS capt 1967-76; Bronze Star for Valor; Bronze Star for Svs; Purple Heart; Combat Infantry Badge; Cross of Gallantry; Meritorious Svs Awd w/Cluster. **BUSINESS ADDRESS:** President/Chief Executive Ofcr, Natl Business League, 4324 Georgia Ave NW, Washington, DC 20011.

TEER, BARBARA ANN
Executive producer. **PERSONAL:** Born Jun 18, 1937, E St Louis; divorced; children: Omi, Folashade. **EDUCATION:** Univ of IL, BA. **CAREER:** Natl Black Theatre, founding dir, producer, writer, dir, actress, producer, educator. **ORGANIZATIONS:** Mem Theatre Com of Second World Black & African Festival of Arts & Culture Lagos, Nigeria 1975; mem Delta Sigma Theta Commn on Arts; mem Black Theatre Collective. **HONORS/ACHIEVEMENTS:** Cert of Participation FESTAC North Amer Region 1977; Cultural Arts Serv Awd Black Spectrum Theatre Co 1978; Universal Awareness Awd Toward A New AGe Inc1979; For Creative Excellence Harlem Week Blackafrica Promotions 1980; Comm Serv Awd Reality House Inc 1980; For Contribution to the Field of the Performing Arts Natl Assoc of Negro Business and Professional Women's Club Inc 1981; For Outstanding Contributions to the Performing and Visual Arts Natl Cncl for Cultureand Art 1983; Annual Positive Image of the Eighties Awd Rickey Productions Inc 1984; For Her Outstanding Contribution to Black Amer Theater The Natl Black Treasure Awd Hamilton Hill Arts Ctr 1984. **BUSINESS ADDRESS:** Founder/Chief Exec Officer, NBT, 2033 Fifth Ave, New York, NY 10035.

TEMPLE, DONALD MELVIN
Attorney. **PERSONAL:** Born May 27, 1953, Philadelphia, PA; married Vonterris Hagan. **EDUCATION:** Howard Univ, BA 1975; Univ of Santa Clara Law Sch, JD 1978; Georgetown Univ Law Ctr, LLM 1982. **CAREER:** US Dept of Housing, attorney advisor 1978-80; US House of Representatives, sr staff counsel 1980-. **ORGANIZATIONS:** Pres Student Bar Assoc Univ of Santa Clara School of Law 1977-78; mem Natl Bar Assoc 1980-87; pres Natl Conf Black Lawyers DC 1980-81; pres DC Chap Concerned Black Men Inc 1982-83; natl chmn 21st Century PAC 1983-87; mem WA Bar Assoc 1984-87; chairman Charles Hamilton Houston Legal Educ Inst 1984-87; mem Kappa Alpha Psi Frat 1985-; Prince Hall Masonic Lodge 1985-; chmn Adam Clayton Powell Soc 1987; mem Wash DC and PA Bars. **HONORS/ACHIEVEMENTS:** Role Model of Year in Legal Educ Natl Black Law Student Assoc 1985; Best of Washington Hall of Fame 1986; Harriet Tubman Awd Congressional Black Assoc 1987; Outstanding Black Professional Business Exchange Network 1987. **BUSINESS ADDRESS:** Senior Staff Counsel, US House of Representatives, 1310 Longworth HOB, Washington, DC 20515.

TEMPLE, HERBERT
Graphic artist. **PERSONAL:** Born Jul 06, 1919, Gary, IN; married Athelstan. **EDUCATION:** The Art Inst of Chgo, 1945-48. **CAREER:** "Ebony Ebony Jr" & "Black World" Mags, art dir; Supreme Beauty Prod Co, designs spl advertising & promotional material & packaging. **HONORS/ACHIEVEMENTS:** Illustrated a number of books including "The Ebony Cook Book", "Negro & Firsts in Sports", "The Legend of Africana"; Chmn Art Com Which Selected & Purchased$250,000 Worth of Paintings, Sculptures & Other Art Objects by Black Artists Around World for Perm Exhbn in Johnson Pub Co Bldg; judge for Numerous Art Shows. **BUSINESS ADDRESS:** Art Dir, Johnson Publishing Co, 820 South Michigan Ave, Chicago, IL 60605.

TEMPLE, ONEY D.
Automobile dealer. **CAREER:** Town & Country Lincoln-Mercury-Merkur Inc, Brunswick, OH, chief exec. **BUSINESS ADDRESS:** Town & Country Lincoln-Mercury-Merkur, 1700 Pearl Rd, Brunswick, OH 44212. *

TEMPLE, RONALD J.
Educator. **PERSONAL:** Born Sep 10, 1940, Chicago, IL; married Juanita Simpson; children: Ronald, Jr, Karyn A; Randall. **EDUCATION:** Eureka Coll, BA; Univ Cincinnati, MA; Univ MI, advanced study; Univ of Cincinnati, PhD History/Social Science. **CAREER:** Lyons Twp HS & Jr Coll, instructor 1965-67, asst dean men & instr history 1967, asst dean student groups & univ prog 1971, special asst to pres 1974; Univ of Cincinnati, dean univ coll & assoc prof of gen studies; Wayne County Comm Coll, pres 1985-. **ORGANIZATIONS:** Appointed bd Children Protective Serv 1969; appointed by Mayor Cincinnati

Human Relations Comm 1969-72; appointed b Natl Conf Christians & Jews 1970; elected Cincinnati Bd Educ 1971; appointed by gov to Natl Museum of Afro-Amer History & Culture Planning Council 1974-78; mem and 1982 pres Cincinnati Bd ofHealth 1979-82; bd trustees Cincinnati Historical Soc 1982-; consultant & moderator Progs sponsored by OH Humanities Council 1983-; consultant & evaluator of College & Univ Progs; co-chmn & co-founder "Conf of Major Univs which Offer Assoc Degree Progs on the Main Campus"; mem Amer Hist Assn, Amer AssnUniv Prof, Assn Study Negro Life & History. **HONORS/ACHIEVEMENTS:** Natl Conf Chief Order of Arrow Boy Scouts Amer 1961; elected Phi Alpha theta Natl Hon Scholarship History 1965; elected Omicron Delta Kappa Hon Scholarship & Leadership 1973; mem Alpha Phi Alpha and Sigma Pi Phi Fraternities. **BUSINESS ADDRESS:** President, Wayne County Community College, 801 W Fort St, Detroit, MI 48226.

TEMPLETON, GARRY LEWIS
Professional athlete. **PERSONAL:** Born Mar 24, 1956, Lockey, TX; married Glenda; children: Garry II, Gerome, Genae Nicole. **CAREER:** St Louis Cardinals, shortstop 1976-81; San Diego Padres, professional athlete 1982-. **HONORS/ACHIEVEMENTS:** Youngest shortstop in modern baseball history to reach the 200-hit plateau and only the 14th shortstop to ever reach the mark 1977; selected Baseball Digest and Topps Chewing Gum Rookie All Star Team 1977; 9 game stretch batted 400 12 for 30; finished 1st month of season hitting 338; matched his career high of 4 RBI; finished yr with a league leading 23 intentional walks; 1st season as Padre led Natl League shortstops in runs scored 76, RBI 64, game winning RBI 8; named to UPI & The Sporting News All-Star Teams; 1st Team selection to AP & The Sporting News All-Star Squads; 34 Stolen Bases; 148 games more than any other shortstop in Natl Legue 1984; MVP Awd 1985; mem All Star Team 1977 and 1985. **BUSINESS ADDRESS:** San Diego Padres, PO Box 2000, San Diego, CA 92102.

TENNANT, MELVIN, II
Convention sales manager. **PERSONAL:** Born Jul 02, 1959, Bryan, TX; children: Caroline, Brian, Matthew. **EDUCATION:** Rice Univ, BA 1982. **CAREER:** Hermann Hosp, asst to dir of nurse recruitment 1979-80; Houston Comm Coll, instructor-hotel 1985-; Houston Convention Cncl, assoc dir of sales 1980-. **ORGANIZATIONS:** Mem Houston Area Urban League 1984-, Natl Coalition of Black Meeting Planners 1985-, Amer Soc of Assoc Execs 1986-87; bd of dirs Hotel Sales/Mktg Assoc 1986-88; mem Amer Soc of Travel AGents 1987, People's Workshop for Performing & Visual Arts 1987; bd mem Hotel Sales/Marketing Assoc. **HONORS/ACHIEVEMENTS:** Certificate of Appreciation Natl Tour Assoc 1984; Monthly Sales Awds Houston Conv Cncl 1986/87; Appreciation Awd Women Admin Assoc 1987.

TERBORG-PENN, ROSALYN M.
Educator. **PERSONAL:** Born Oct 22, 1941, Brooklyn, NY; children: Jeanna. **EDUCATION:** Queens Coll CUNY, BA 1963; George Washington U, MA 1967; Howard U, PhD 1977. **CAREER:** The Assn of Black Women Historians, founder 1978; AHA Comm on Women Historians, mem 1978-81; Assn of Black Women Historians, natl dir 1978-82, natl treas1982-86; AHA Joan Kelly Prize Comm, judge 1984; Morgan State U, prof of history; Author, Afro-American Woman-Struggles and Images 1978, 1981, Women in Africa and the African Diaspora, 1987. **ORGANIZATIONS:** History editor Feminist Studies 1984-; commr Howard Cty MD Commn for Women 1980-82. **HONORS/ACHIEVEMENTS:** Grad History Essay Award Rayford Logan, HowardUniv 1973; Grad Fellowship in History HowardUniv 1973-74; "The Afro-Am Woman, Struggles and Images" Kennikat Press, NY 1978, 1981; Post Doct Fellowship for Minorities Ford Found 1980-81; Visiting Scholar Grant Smithsonian Inst 1982; Travel to Collections Grant Nat Endowment for the Humanities 1984. **BUSINESS ADDRESS:** Professor of History, Morgan State Univ, History Dept, Baltimore, MD 21239.

TERO, LAWRENCE (MR. T)
Actor. **PERSONAL:** Born 1952, Chicago, IL; children: Lesa. **EDUCATION:** Attended Prairie View A&M. **CAREER:** Muhammed Ali, Leon Spinks, Donna Summer, Diana Ross, Rev Jesse Jackson, Michael Jackson, bodyguard; DC Cab, Rocky III, The A-Team, actor. **ORGANIZATIONS:** Donated to churches & orgs to feed the hungry & clothe the naked. **HONORS/ACHIEVEMENTS:** Football Scholarship. **MILITARY SERVICE:** Military policeman. **BUSINESS ADDRESS:** Triad Artists, 10100 Santa Monica Blvd, 16th Floor, Los Angeles, CA 90067. *

TERRELL, ANGELA M. BROWN
Writer. **PERSONAL:** Born Feb 13, 1937, Brooklyn; married Frederick J; children: Brian, Jason, Jamal, Yahne. **EDUCATION:** Hunter Coll; Temple U; Columbia Univ Grad Sch of Journ; Michele Clark Fellowship Prgm 1969. **CAREER:** Philadelphia Evening Bulletin, reporter 1969-70; Washington Post, staff writer 1970-75; Shaw U, adj prof 1971-72; Encore Mag, correspondent 1972-; Spelman Coll, assoc dir of publs; Foxtrappe Mag, asst ed 1975-76; Synergy Mag, assoc ed. **ORGANIZATIONS:** Adv com YMCA Residential Intervention Ctr; guest journalist NET-TV, Nat Black Network Radio; mem Nat Council Negro Women; DC Black Writers Workshop; Black Women's Community Dev Found; fdr Columbia Black Writers Workshop. **HONORS/ACHIEVEMENTS:** Journalist of Yr, Caanan Bapt Ch 1972; Humanitarian Serv & Leadership, Shaw Univ 1972. **BUSINESS ADDRESS:** Assoc Dir of Publications, Spelman College, 350 Spelman Ln SW, Atlanta, GA 30314.

TERRELL, DOROTHY
Manufacturing manager. **PERSONAL:** Born Jun 12, 1945, Ft Lauderdale, MA; daughter of Charles W Terrell Sr and Pearl Weeks Terrell; married Albert H Brown; children: Dorian. **EDUCATION:** FL A&M Univ, BA 1966. **CAREER:** Digital Equip Corp, plant personnel mgr 1978-80, group personnel mgr 1980-84, plant mgr 1984-87, group mfg mgr 1987-. **ORGANIZATIONS:** Mem Delta Sigma Theta 1965-; adv comm OIC 1984-87; comm mem Boston C of C 1984-88; trustee Social Policy Rsch 1985-89; bd mem Boston YWCA 1985-89; bd mem Lera Park Comm Dev 1985-89; bd mem Boston Club 1986-89. **HONORS/ACHIEVEMENTS:** Achievement Awd Snowden Assoc 1984; Film "Choosing to Lead" AMA 1986; Achievement Awd YWCA 1986; Black Achievers YMCA 1987; Hecht-Shaw Award 1987; Museum of Afro-American History Award 1988; Leadership Pioneer Award 1988. **BUSINESS ADDRESS:** Manufacturing Manager, 10500 Ridgeview Ct, Cupertino, CA 95014.

TERRELL, ETHEL
State representative. **PERSONAL:** Born in Union Town, AL; widowed. **EDUCATION:** Perry Cty Training School, 1941; Highland Park Coll, attended; Art Ctr Music School, attended. **CAREER:** Highland Park Gen Hosp, chmn bd mgrs; Highland Park City Council, former pres; Highland Park Sec of State, mgr 15 yrs; City of Highland Park, former councilwoman; State of MI, representative dist 9. **ORGANIZATIONS:** Life mem NAACP, Natl Council of Negro Women; founder of natl group Women in Municipal Govt; mem Highland Park C of C; mem Guiding Light Chap # 50 Prince Hall Affil OES; mem State Central Comm Dem Party, Gamma Phi Delta, Alpha Eta Chapt. **HONORS/ACHIEVEMENTS:** Businesswoman Presentation Black Leadership Caucus; Fire Fighters Assoc of Highland Park MI; Disting Religious Org; Highland Park Caucus Club; Citizens for Good Govt Org; 1st black councilwoman in the State of MI.

TERRELL, FRANCIS
Educator. **PERSONAL:** Born Nov 25, 1944, Greensboro, GA; son of Emery Terrell and Carrie Terrell; married Sandra L; children: Ivanna Samal, Amani Shama, Elon Jadhal. **EDUCATION:** Wilmington Coll (OH), BS 1968; Univ of Pittsburgh, MS 1972; Univ of Pittsburgh, PhD 1975. **CAREER:** Univ of Pittsburgh, post-doctoral fellow 1975-76; TX Christian Univ, asst prof 1976-80; N TX State Univ, assoc prof & dir of clncl training. **ORGANIZATIONS:** Mem Am Psychol Assn 1976-80; mem Black Psychol Assn 1976-80; mem Sigma Xi 1976-80; rgnl mental health consultant US Labor Dept 1978-. **HONORS/ACHIEVEMENTS:** Pub "Self Concept of Jnvls Who Commit Black on Blacks Crimes" CORRECTIVE AND SOCIAL PSYCHIATRY 1980; pub "Effects of Race of Examiner & Type of Reinforcement on the Intelligence Test of Black Children" PSYCHOLOGY IN THE SCHS 1980; fellow Amer Psychological Assocn 1984; fellow Soc for Study of Personality 1984; Over 30 Jrnls Publshd. **MILITARY SERVICE:** USN 2nd class petty ofcr 1978-84. **BUSINESS ADDRESS:** Associate Professor & Dir, North Texas StateUniv, Psychology Dept, N Texas StateUniv, Fort Worth, TX 76203.

TERRELL, FRANCIS D'ARCY
Attorney. **PERSONAL:** Born May 13, 1940, Caledonia, NY; married Mary Jane Hawthorne; children: Derek M, Randall D. **EDUCATION:** Univ of Toledo, BS 1970; Columbia Law School, JD 1973. **CAREER:** Shearman & Sterling, assoc attorney 1973-75; Private Practice, attorney 1975-77; Jones & Terrell, partner 1977-82; Bronx Comm Coll, deputy chmn/prof 1982-. **ORGANIZATIONS:** Mem Amer Business Law Assocs 1984-. **HONORS/ACHIEVEMENTS:** Lt col 20 yrs; Bronze Star; Air Medal; Meritorious Serv Medal; Commendation Medal; Combat Infantry Badge. **HOME ADDRESS:** 788 Riverside Dr, Apt 3AA, New York, NY 10032. **BUSINESS ADDRESS:** Deputy Chairman, Bronx Comm College, Dept of Business, W 181st &Univ Ave, Bronx, NY 10453.

TERRELL, HENRY MATTHEW
Business executive. **PERSONAL:** Born Dec 06, 1940, Caroline Co, VA. **EDUCATION:** HowardUniv Sch Law, JD 1971; VA State Clg, BA 1963. **CAREER:** EGS Fin Mgmt Cons, pres 1971-; CT Hellmuth & Assc, mgr 1975-; Aetna Ins Co, brokerage mgr 1973-75; Am Security & Trust Co, estate & pension admn 1971-72; Prudential Life Ins Co, mktg & sls rep 1965-71. **ORGANIZATIONS:** Bd dir VA State Clg Alumni Assc; mem HowardUniv Sch Law Alumni Assc; Alpha Phi Alpha Frat; Delta Theta Phi Law Frat; pres VA State Clg Alumni Assc 1966-68; bd tst VA State Clg Found 1974; reg dir VA State Clg Alumni Assc 1974; bus mgr Nubian Enterprises; dir DC Chap Intrntl Assc Fin Plnrs; mem Natl Patent Assc. **MILITARY SERVICE:** AUS capt 1963-65. **BUSINESS ADDRESS:** 1025 Vermont Ave NW, Ste 407, Washington, DC 20005.

TERRELL, JOHN L.
Educational administrator. **PERSONAL:** Born May 19, 1930, Forest City, AR; married Betty R Phillips; children: Debra, Lanette, John, DeAnna. **EDUCATION:** Muskegon Business Coll, Business Admin 1956. **CAREER:** UAW Local 1243, sec-treasurer 1958; Howmet Employee Credit Union, pres 1962; Muskegon Heights School Bd, treasurer 1969-79, vice pres 1979-85. **MILITARY SERVICE:** AUS pfc 1952-54. **HOME ADDRESS:** 2336 Moffett St, Muskegon Heights, MI 49444.

TERRELL, MABLE JEAN
Association executive. **PERSONAL:** Born Aug 02, 1936, North Little Rock, AR; daughter of Rudolph C Webb and Mable Edwards Webb; married William B Terrell, Nov 04, 1956 (deceased); children: Venita Terrell-Chew, Vickie Terrell-Cox, Camelia Terrell-Cox. **EDUCATION:** Roosevelt Univ, Chicago IL, BA, 1970. **CAREER:** Honeywell, Inc, Chicago IL, senior rep, 1972-82; Walter E Hellen, Chicago IL, senior analyst, 1982-84; International Black Writers, pres and exec dir, 1984—. **ORGANIZATIONS:** Mem, NAACP; mem, Trans Africa; mem, Urban League; bd mem, Systems Programmers Soc; pres, Jones Alumni Assn. **HONORS/ACHIEVEMENTS:** Arkansas Travelers Award, 1984; Kool Achiever Award nominee, 1989. **BUSINESS ADDRESS:** President/Executive Director, International Black Writers Conference, Inc, PO Box 1030, Chicago, IL 60628.

TERRELL, MARY ANN
Lawyer. **PERSONAL:** Born Jun 03, 1944, Jacksonville, FL; married James Edward Terrell; children: Angela Rani, Mariessa Rebecca, James Stephen. **EDUCATION:** Howard Univ, BA 1966; Antioch Univ, MAT 1969; Georgetown Univ Law Ctr, JD 1981. **CAREER:** Peace Corps/India, volunteer 1966-68; Antioch Coll, dir of admin asst prof history 1969-73; Dix St Acad, dir/founder 1974-80; Mental Health Law Project, lawyer 1980-81; Dist of Columbia City Council, exec asst to council chmn 1981-82; DC Dept of Public Works, hearing examiner 1983-84; Antioch School ofLaw, adjunct prof 1987-; Office of US Attorney, asst US attorney. **ORGANIZATIONS:** Treasurer Natl Pol Congress Black Women 1985-; mem Natl Assoc of Black Women Attorneys 1985-, Women's Div of NBA 1986-; mem Women's Bar Assoc of DC 1987, Federal Bar Assoc 1987, The Washington Bar. **HONORS/ACHIEVEMENTS:** Outstanding Comm Serv Awd in Educ 1980; apptd Mayor's Intl Adv Council 1983-; selected DC State Adv Comm for Hands Across Amer 1986; apptd Legal Serv Bd Antioch School Law 1986-; selected vice chair Washington Lawyers Against Drugs Comm 1987. **BUSINESS ADDRESS:** Asst US Attorney for DC, Office of US Attorney, 555 4th St NW, Washington, DC 20001.

TERRELL, MELVIN C.
College administrator, educator. **PERSONAL:** Born Oct 05, 1949, Chicago, IL; son of Cleveland Terrell and Ethel Lee. **EDUCATION:** Chicago State Univ, BSEd 1971; Loyola Univ of Chicago, MEd 1973; Southern Illinois Univ at Carbondale, PhD 1978; Inst for Educ Mgmt Harvard Univ, Post-Doctoral Study/Mgmt Devel Program summer 1986; Univ of Virginia Annual Summer Professional Dept Workshop Educ Mgmt Strategies, 1988; Natl Assn of Student Personnel Admin, Richard F Stevens Inst, 1989. **CAREER:** Kennedy-King Coll Chicago, student devel specialist, counseling instructor 1973-75; Eastern New Mexico Univ, coordinator/counselor of black affairs & asst prof ethnic studies 1977-78; Univ of Arkansas at Monticello, dir learning devel center 1979-80; Univ of Wisconsin-Oshkosh, dir multicultural educ center 1981-85; Univ of Toledo, dir of minority affairs & adjunct asst prof 1985-. **ORGANIZATIONS:** Chmn Univ of Wisconsin 7 System Natl Conf on Multiculturalism 1981-85; educ bd Univ of Wisconsin System Amer Ethnic Studies Coord Comm/Urban Corridor Consortium Public Policy Series; exec bd mem Univ of Wisconsin Systems Amer Ethnic Studies Coord Comm 1982-83, Amer Assn of Higher Educ 1983; vice chmn of educ comm NAACP Toledo Branch 1985-; educ bd Natl Assoc of Student Personnel Admin Journal 1986-89 on Leadership Educ, 1986-; dir educ activities Alpha Phi Alpha 1987; Natl chmn, Ethnic Minority Network, Natl Assn of Student Personnel Assn, 1989; vice chmn, Amer Assn of Higher Educ, 1989; chmn, Amer Assn of Higher Educ, Black Caucus Exec; life mem, Alpha Phi Alphi Fraternity, Inc; evaluation team mem, Middle States Assn of Colls & Univs. **HONORS/ACHIEVEMENTS:** Illinois Teacher Academic Scholarship, Illinois State Govt 1968-71; Southern Illinois Univ Carbondale Scholarship 1978; Outstanding Admin, Univ of Toledo 1985, 1986; author, "From Isolation to Mainstream, An Institutional Committment" 1987; unpublished doctoral theses, "Identification & Comparison of the Perceptions of Selected Black & Selected White Students Toward the Student Affairs Area at Southern Illinois Univ at Carbondale" 1978; co-author, Model Field Based Program in Multicultural Educ for Non-Urban Univs" 1981, "Multicultural Educ Centers in Acad Marketplace" 1987. **BUSINESS ADDRESS:** Director, Adj Asst Professor, Univ of Toledo, 2801 W Bancroft St, Toledo, OH 43606.

TERRELL, RICHARD WARREN
Business manager. **PERSONAL:** Born Nov 16, 1946, Fort Riley, KS; son of Warren Terrell and Mary Terrell; married Phyllis Eileen Hargrove; children: Wesley, Rodney. **EDUCATION:** CA Poly SLO, BSEL 1968; San Jose State, MSEE 1974. **CAREER:** Prairie View A&M, adj prof 1976-77; IBM, engr, mgr lsi packaging 1968-. **ORGANIZATIONS:** Mem Alpha Phi Alpha, NAACP, Antioch Baptist Church. **HOME ADDRESS:** 4959 Massachusetts Dr, San Jose, CA 95136.

TERRELL, ROBERT E.
Educational admin. **PERSONAL:** Born Oct 04, 1943, Terry, MS; married Karen K; children: Kelley L Carson. **EDUCATION:** KS Univ, BS 1966, MPA 1975. **CAREER:** Turner House Inc, exec dir 1971-74; City of Ft Worth, budget analyst 1974-77; Ft Worth Econ Dev Corp, exec dir 1977-79; City of Ft Worth, asst to city mgr 1979-. **ORGANIZATIONS:** Past officer Kappa Alpha Psi Frat 1962-; mem NAACP 1977-; natl bd Conf of Minority Public Admin 1979-; mem Amer Soc of Public Admin 1979-; asst steering com Intl City Mgmt Assoc 1979-. **HONORS/ACHIEVEMENTS:** Fellowship NASPAA 1974-75. **BUSINESS ADDRESS:** Asst To City Manager, City of Fort Worth, 1000 Throckmorton, Fort Worth, TX 76102.

TERRELL, ROBERT L.
Educator, writer. **PERSONAL:** Born Jul 19, 1943. **EDUCATION:** Morehouse Coll Atlanta, BA 1969; Univ CA Berkeley, MA 1971; Univ of CA Berkeley, PhD 1970. **CAREER:** Publ poems short stories books 1967-; NY Post, reporter 1967-68; So Reg Council Atlanta, rsch writer 1968-69; Newsweek Mag, stringer 1968-69; Univ of CA,teaching asst 1969-70; Golden Gate Coll, instr 1969-71; San Francisco Crhonicle, copy ed 1970; CA Jrnl Teacher Ed, asst prof 1971-76, ed 1972-73; OffRsch & Plnng, coord 1974-75; St Mary's Coll Morage CA, office experimental progs 1975-76; Stanford Univ, asst prof 1976; Univ of MO, assoc prof jrnlsm 1976-; School of Jrnlsm Univ of CA Berkeley, vstg prof 1979; Beijing Review Mag Beijing China, copy ed 1981-82; NY Univ Dept of Jrnlsm & Mass Commun, vstg prof 1985-86;Univ Nairobi School of Jrnlsm, fulbright prof 1984-85. **ORGANIZATIONS:** Mem Amer Assoc Colls Teacher Ed, Amer Assoc Higher Ed, Amer Ed Rsch Assoc; bd dir CA Council Teacher Ed, Soc Coll & Univ; managing ed CA Jrnl Teacher Ed 1973; ed referee CA Jrnl Teacher Ed 1974-; adv screening comm commun Council for Intl Exchange of Scholars Fulbright Prog 1980-83. **HONORS/ACHIEVEMENTS:** Fellowship CA State 1969-72, Grad Minority 1969-72, Fund for Peace 1970-71, NDEA 1971-74; Deans Fellowship Univ of CA 1974-75. **BUSINESS ADDRESS:** Prof of News/Editing, 16 Walter Williams, Univ of MO, Columbia, MO 65211.

TERRELL, STANLEY E.
Reporter. **PERSONAL:** Born Feb 16, 1949, Newark, NJ; married Sallie F Sparks. **EDUCATION:** Hampton Inst, 1966-68; Essex Co Coll, 1969-70. **CAREER:** The Star-Ledger, gen assignment news reporter 1968-. **ORGANIZATIONS:** Contrib articles to numerous magazines; lectr, worked closely with NAACP; Urban League; Cong African People; Human Rights Commn; various tenant groups, juvenile programs, prison reform groups, drug rehab projects. **HONORS/ACHIEVEMENTS:** Merit Awd Newark Tenants Cncl 1974; Outst Achiev Awd Newark Hum Rights Commn 1974; Awd from Newark Title I ESEA Prog for Outst Serv to Newark Comm 1975; Star-Ledger Bonus 1971. **BUSINESS ADDRESS:** Star-Ledger, 1 Star Ledger Plaza, Newark, NJ 07102.

TERRILL, W.H. TYRONE, JR.
Government. **PERSONAL:** Born Aug 30, 1954, Kansas City, MO; married Suzanne E Fuller; children: Whitney Nicole. **EDUCATION:** Bemidji State Univ Bemidji MN, BS 1976. **CAREER:** MN Dept of Human Rights, compliance dir 1976-80; Minneapolis Dept of Civil Rights, dep dir 1980-. **ORGANIZATIONS:** Mem MN Afirmative Action Assoc 1978-; founder, mem Inter-Govt Compliance Inst 1978-; mem Minneapolis Urban League, Minneapolis Br NAACP 1984-; bd mem Hiawatha YMCA 1985-; chairperson Hennepin County NECAC 1986-. **HONORS/ACHIEVEMENTS:** Community Serv Minneapolis Urban League 1984. **BUSINESS ADDRESS:** Deputy Dir, Minneapolis Dept of Civil Rights, 239 - City Hall, Minneapolis, MN 55415.

TERRY, ADELINE HELEN
Attorney. **PERSONAL:** Born Apr 17, 1931, Wichita, KS; daughter of Clifford Johnson and Narcissus O'Grady Johnson; children: Catherine. **EDUCATION:** CA State Coll, BA Sociology 1960; Southwestern Univ of Law, LLB 1968. **CAREER:** LA Co Dist Attorney, investigator 1960-62; LA Co Superior Ct, domestic rel investigator 1962-65; LA Co Probation

Dept, 1965-69; LA Co Dist Atty, dep dist atty 1969-. **ORGANIZATIONS:** Mem Assn of Dep Dist Atty of LA; mem CA Dist Atty's Assn; Black Women's Lawyers of LA; Langston Law Club; Women Lawyers of LA; State Bar of CA. **BUSINESS ADDRESS:** Deputy District Attorney, Los Angeles Co Dist Atty, 210 W Temple St, Ste 17 1013, Los Angeles, CA 90012.

TERRY, ANGELA OWEN
University educator. **PERSONAL:** Born Feb 13, 1941, Memphis, TN; daughter of William Franklin Owen, Sr and Addie Griffin Owen; married Elbert A Terry (deceased); children: Angela Daphne, Warren Marshall. **EDUCATION:** The Univ of Vienna, Cert 1963; Spelman College, BA 1962; Fisk Univ, MA 1964; The Univ of CT, PhD 1973; Harvard Univ Cambridge Mass. Certificate July 1987 Management Development Program for College & University Administrators Institute for Educational Management. **CAREER:** Albany State Coll, asst prof psych 1964-69; Prospect Psycholog Serv Ctr, psychological serv worker 1969-71; CT State Dept of Educ, educ consul psych serv 1973-77; Univ of CT, asst dir dept of counseling serv 1978-83, asst to the vice pres for program evaluation & rsch 1983-. **ORGANIZATIONS:** Mem Amer Assoc for Counseling & Devel, Amer Coll Personnel Assoc, Assoc for Institutional Rsch, CT Assoc of Black Psychologists, NAACP Windham, YoungWomen's Christian Assoc, Delta Sigma Theta Sorority, Inc, Natl Assoc of Student Personnel Administrators; mem Amer Assoc for Higher Educ, The Black Caucus; Editorial Board NASPA Journal 1988-1991. **HONORS/ACHIEVEMENTS:** Scholarship Univ of Vienna 1963; Fellowship Harvard Univ 1969; Doctoral Fellowship The Univ of CT 1971-73; Pi Lambda Theta Natl Educ Honor Soc; Phi DeltaKappa; listed in Who's Who Among Human Services Profls, Who's Who of Amer Women, Two Thousand Women of Achievement, Natl Register of Prominent Amers, Personalities of the South, Outstanding Young Women of Amer. **HOME ADDRESS:** 36 Patriot Rd, Windham Center, CT 06280. **BUSINESS ADDRESS:** Asst to the Vice President, University of Connecticut, U-8, Storrs, CT 06268.

TERRY, BOB (NIGHTHAWK)
Business executive. **PERSONAL:** Born Jan 06, 1936, Franklin, KY; divorced; children: Donald, Mia. **EDUCATION:** NY Sch of Announcing & Speech, 1960. **CAREER:** WLIB NY, air personality; "Shade of Soul" Metromedia, Wash, DC, exec prod, host 1969-72; WRMA MT, AL, prog dir 1960-62; WTMP, Tampa, FL, prog mus dir 1962-63; WAME Miami, prog & mgr, oper mgr 1963-65; WOL, DC, Announcer, prog dir 1965-71; WHUR-FM, oper, mgr, air personality 1971-75. **ORGANIZATIONS:** Mem bd dir NATRA 1971-73; mem bd dir AFTRA 1971-73; bd mem Mayor's Proj Awareness Com 1968-70; bd mem Mayor's Youth Coun 1968-70; mem Mayor's Civ Def Commn 1968. **HONORS/ACHIEVEMENTS:** Best air personality of year, WOL-AM, 1966-70; best air personality of year, Ex-Consult Inc 1971; best comm of year, Eastman Kodak Co 1967; best comm of year,Natl Brewing Co 1966-; co-star of "Trouble Man" Universal Pictures 1972. **MILITARY SERVICE:** USN 1954-58. **BUSINESS ADDRESS:** 310 Lenox Ave, New York, NY 10027.

TERRY, CHARLES C.
General surgeon. **PERSONAL:** Born Jan 27, 1934, West Virginia; married Marthell; children: two. **EDUCATION:** Univ IL, BS 1955; Howard U, MD 1959. **CAREER:** MD Inc, gen surg 1966-; Pontiac Gen Hosp, intern 1959-60; pontiac Gen Hosp, surg res 1960-64. **ORGANIZATIONS:** LA Co Med Assn, CA Med Assn; AMA. **HONORS/ACHIEVEMENTS:** Alpha Omega Alpha hon Med Soc; Diplomate Am Bd of Surg; fellow Am Coll of Surg; fellow Intl Coll of Surg; fellow Am Soc of Abdominal Surg. **MILITARY SERVICE:** AUS Med Corp capt 1964-66. **BUSINESS ADDRESS:** 3756 Santa Rosalia Dr, #609, Los Angeles, CA 90008.

TERRY, CLARK
Business executive. **PERSONAL:** Born Dec 14, 1920, St Louis; married Pauline Reddon. **EDUCATION:** Private studies. **CAREER:** Pastel Music, pres; Etoile Music Prod Inc, pres; Clark Terry Big Bad Band; Itinerate Jazz, clinician & educator. **ORGANIZATIONS:** Exec dir Int Art of Jazz. **HONORS/ACHIEVEMENTS:** Rec numerous awards. **MILITARY SERVICE:** USN. **BUSINESS ADDRESS:** 756 7 Ave, New York, NY 10019.

TERRY, FRANK W.
Retired government official. **PERSONAL:** Born Jan 23, 1919, Los Angeles; son of Woodford H Terry and Jessie L Terry; married Valdoras Hancock; children: Charles Love, Susan Love; Mike. **EDUCATION:** Los Angeles City Coll, 1948-49; Army Officers Candidate School, 1942. **CAREER:** Freelance photographer repoter 1946-50; Joseph V Baker Assoc, west coast rep 1950-56; Douglas Aircraft Co, 1956-60; US Dept of Labor Office of Information, 1962-78; US Veterans Admin, 1978; Los Angeles Library, commr 1978-. **ORGANIZATIONS:** Chmn Los Angeles Fed Exec Bd 1975-76; bd mem CA Governor's Comm for Employment of Handicapped; bd mem Coll Fed Coun of Southern CA 1965-70; third vice pres LA Library Assn; bd mem Cultural Heritage Found; bd mem Fed of Black History & Arts; LA Urban League. **HONORS/ACHIEVEMENTS:** Various publications 1946-50; recipient Certificate of Merit, LA Fed Exec Bd 1967; Meritorious Achievement Award US Dept of Labor 1970; Lula Fields Exec Award Extraordinaire 1972; Aztec Award Mexican Amer Opportunities Found 1974. **MILITARY SERVICE:** AUS 1st lt 1941-46. **HOME ADDRESS:** 5350 Stillwater Dr, Los Angeles, CA 90008.

TERRY, GARLAND BENJAMIN
Dentist. **PERSONAL:** Born Mar 27, 1927, Norfolk, VA; married Marie Walker; children: Michael Quentin. **EDUCATION:** OH State Univ, BS 1953; Coll of Dentistry Howard Univ, DDS 1957. **CAREER:** AUS Dental Corps, 1957-60; Private practice, dentist 1960-. **ORGANIZATIONS:** Mem NJ Dental Assoc, Amer Dental Assoc, Omega Psi Phi, Capitol City Golf Club. **MILITARY SERVICE:** AUS 1946-49; Dental Corps 1957-60. **BUSINESS ADDRESS:** 701-703 Rutherford Ave, Trenton, NJ 08618.

TERRY, JOHN WILLIAM
Physician. **PERSONAL:** Born Apr 25, 1925, Indianapolis, IN; married Bertha Brame; children: Ingrid, Crystal. **EDUCATION:** Butler U, BS 1947; Meharry Med Coll, MD 1950. **CAREER:** Physician, gen prac 1951. **ORGANIZATIONS:** Mem Kappa Alpha Psi Frat; frontiers Club; Prince Hall Masonic Lodge. **MILITARY SERVICE:** AUS mc capt 1953-55. **BUSINESS ADDRESS:** 4383 N 27th St, Milwaukee, WI 53216.

TERRY, ROY D.
Business executive. **PERSONAL:** Born Dec 27, 1944, Dayton, OH; married Willo D Strickland; children: Corey Benjamin, Cotina. **EDUCATION:** Morehouse Coll, AB Bus Administration 1966; Atlanta Univ, post grad work 1967. **CAREER:** Hillcrest Corp; Terry Properties, officer & dir; Terry Mfg Co, sec treas 1963-71, pres 1971-. **ORGANIZATIONS:** Dir Natl Assn Black Mfgrs; Roanoke Area C of C; mem Am Apparel Mfrs Assn; Nat Bus League; sec of Minority Business Ent Legal Def & Educ Fund; charter mem Black Business Support Group of the NAACP; mem Minority Enterprise Brain Trust; mem bd of dirs Federal Reserve Bank of Atlanta-Birmingham Branch. **HONORS/ACHIEVEMENTS:** NAACP Black Enterprise Mag Achvmnt Award 1976; Nat Assn of Black Mfrs Achvmt Award 1977; first recipient of the AG Gaston Award by Alabama Democratic Conf 1980. **BUSINESS ADDRESS:** President, Terry Mfg Co, Inc, 924 South St, P O Box 648, Roanoke, AL 36274.

TERRY, SAUNDERS
Entertainer. **PERSONAL:** Born Oct 24, 1911, Greensboro, GA; married Emma Taylor. **CAREER:** Professional Entertainer, harmonica plyr & singer; Buck & The Preacher, mus sound tracks 1971; Cisco Pike, 1972; Book of Numbers, 1973; Leadbelly, 1976; Finnians Rainbow, mus featured 1946; Cat on A Hot Tin Roof, 1955. **ORGANIZATIONS:** Num radio & TV mus shows; recording artist since 1936; num records & albums on the market; tchr Harmonica Playing; films; mem Comm Civic Assn; mem Am Fedn of Musicians Local #802; mem AFTRA. **HONORS/ACHIEVEMENTS:** Certificate, Preservation & Advancement of the Harmonica 1963; autobiography published, The Harp Styles of Sonny Terry 1975.

TERRY, WALLACE HOUSTON, II
Journalist. **PERSONAL:** Born Apr 21, 1938, New York, NY; married Janice; children: Wallace III, Lisa, David. **EDUCATION:** Brown U, AB 1959; Chicago U, Classics & Religious Studies 1960; Harvard U, Nieman Fellow 1970. **CAREER:** Wash Post-Newsweek TV & Radio, commentator; Center for Natl Sec Studies, fellow 1975-; Howard Univ, prof 1974; Urban Jour Inst, dir 1975; J Walter Thompson Co, consult 1972-; Command-In-Chief USAF, special consultant 1972; Metro Applied Research Center, fellow 1971; Time Mag, corr 1963-71; The WA Post, reporter 1960-63; The Capital Press Club, pres 1962-65; Tuesday Mag, columnist 1965-67. **ORGANIZATIONS:** Nat Adv Bd Educ Devel Ctr; White House Corr Assn; Nat Press Club. **HONORS/ACHIEVEMENTS:** "The Bloods, The Black Soldier from Viet Nam to Am" ColumbiaUniv Press; "Guess Who's Coming Home" Motown Rec; Jour of the Yr Award Captial Press Club 1964; Image Award best documentary recording Hollywood Br NAACP 1972.

TESSEMA, TESFAYE
Artist. **PERSONAL:** Born May 05, 1951, Addis Ababa, Ethiopia. **EDUCATION:** Fine Arts School, Addia Ababa, Diploma, 1970; Howard Univ, MFA 1976. **CAREER:** Arts DC, Washington, DC, mural program coordinator, 1978-80; Museum of African Art Washington DC, designer/graphic artist 1977-78; City of Washington, muralist/program coordinator, 1976-77; muralist; sculptor; interior decorator; designer. **HONORS/ACHIEVEMENTS:** Arts competition Addis Ababa Ethiopia 1967; mural Howard Univ, Washington, DC 1975; graphics for film "The Harvest" Washington DC 1976; mural Museum of African Art, Washington DC 1978.

THACKER, SANDRA J.
Construction and engineering executive. **PERSONAL:** Married Floyd O. Thacker (died 1987). **CAREER:** The Thacker Organization, Decatur, GA, personnel director, then president and board chairperson. **BUSINESS ADDRESS:** The Thacker Organization Inc, 5400 Truman Dr, Decatur, GA 30035. *

THAMES, UVENA WOODRUFF
Educator. **PERSONAL:** Born Apr 15, 1944, Detroit, MI. **EDUCATION:** Wilberforce U, BS 1965; Wayne St U, MEd 1970. **CAREER:** Wayne Co Chldrn's, mntl hlth tchr 1976-; Detroit Pub Schs, pre-vo eval, lrnng dsblts spl 1975; Weldon Grp-Pub Rels, admin asst 1973-74; Atlanta & Area Tech, chld dev inst 1972; Emory U, dept of soc change 1972; Clark Coll, psychlgy instr 19970-72; Detroit Pub Schs, 1968-70; Highland Pk PubSchs,spl ed tchr 1965-68; Wayne St U, Proj Right to Read Dept HEW 1977-78; St Theresa-Visitation Sch, 1979-80; MI Inst of Child Dev, 1980-81; LewisColl of Busn, instr, psychometrist counselor 1981-82; Wayne State Univ, tutorial coord Project 350 1983-. **ORGANIZATIONS:** Mem Delta Sigma Theta Sor Inc 1965; Atlanta Mntl Hlth Assn 1970; exec bd Atlanta NAACP; adv Sigma Chap Delta Sigma Theta Sor; Nat Assn of Black Psychlgsts 1973; MI Assn of Lrng Dsblts; MI Assn of Emotionally Dstrbd Chdrn. **HONORS/ACHIEVEMENTS:** Schlrshp Nat Assn of Crippled Children 1967; fellow MI Dept of Ed 1968.

THANDEKA
Writer, producer, director. **PERSONAL:** Born Mar 25, 1946, Jersey City, NJ. **EDUCATION:** Univ of IL, BS Radio, TV, Films; Columbia Graduate School of Journalism, MA, 1968. **CAREER:** Children's TV Workshop, prodn asst Sesame St 1968; The Black Frontier hist film series, PBS Lincoln, NE, producer, dir 1969; KCET-TV, producer, reporter, writer 1970-73; KNBC-TV LA, producer "As Adam Early in the Morning" dramatic special 1972; CA State Univ Long Beach, assoc prof Dept Radio & TV 1973; KNBC-TV LA, author "Scripts for Hist" series 1973; KCET-TV LA, creative consult natl series 1974; KNBC-TV LA, writer, producer, dir "Compton, A Restless Dream" 1974; San Francisco State Univ, asst prof philosophy. **ORGANIZATIONS:** Mem Dir Guild of Am (first Black woman dir in guild); mem Delta Sigma Theta Sorority; Nat Assn of Media Women. **HONORS/ACHIEVEMENTS:** Recip Emmy as producer of "As Adam Early in the Morning" KNBC-TV; Emmy Citation contrb prod The LA Collective KCET-TV; Gold Medal & Grand Jury Award The Atlanta Intl Film Festival, co-producer "Soledad" KCET-TV; Best Documentary Assoc Press producer "Cleophus Adair, His Life, His World" KCET-TV; co-author "Cry At Birth" 1971; author articles for LA Times, LA Sentinel; co-author "Me" physiology book for elementary children. **HOME ADDRESS:** 2870 N Towne, #158, Pomona, CA 91767.

THATCHER, HAROLD W.
Physician. **PERSONAL:** Born Jul 07, 1908, KC, KS; married Marjorie. **EDUCATION:** Univ MN, BS 1929; MB 1931; MD 1932; Provident Hosp Chgo, interned. **CAREER:** Chicago, dermatolgst. **ORGANIZATIONS:** Mem staffUniv Hosp & Bellevue Hosp NY; chief of Med serv for regl & sta hosps Fort Huachucha WW II; mem bd trustees Cook Co Hosp Nrsng Sch; mem Chicago Met Dermatol Soc; consult Provident Hosp med staff; mem bd dir

Serv Fed Savs & Loan Assn Chgo; bd trustees YWCA Met Chgo. **HONORS/ACHIEVEMENTS:** DillardUniv recipient Legion of Merit for meritorious conduct US Dept of War. **BUSINESS ADDRESS:** 200 E 75 St, Chicago, IL 60619.

THAXTON, JUDY EVETTE
Electrical engineer. **PERSONAL:** Born May 28, 1961, Baltimore, MD. **EDUCATION:** Howard Univ, BSEE 1984. **CAREER:** Army Corps of Engrs, engrs aid 1982; Westinghouse, engrs aid summers of 1983,84; UTC Hamilton Standard, project engr 1985-86, analytical engr 1986-. **ORGANIZATIONS:** Mem Inst of Electronic & Electrical Engrs 1982; tutor Dunbar HS Washington DC; speaker ABC Program CT (A Better Chance) 1986, Windsor High School CT 1987. **HONORS/ACHIEVEMENTS:** Cover story US Black Engineer Magazine 1986; featured in Ebony Magazine 1987. **BUSINESS ADDRESS:** Analytical Systems Engineer, UTC Hamilton Standard, Hamilton Rd, Windsor Locks, CT 06096.

THAXTON, JUNE EVONNE
Electrical engineer. **PERSONAL:** Born May 28, 1961, Baltimore, MD. **EDUCATION:** Howard Univ, BSEE 1984. **CAREER:** Potomac Electric Power Co, engr electric system 1985-. **ORGANIZATIONS:** Mem IEEE 1986, NACE 1987. **HONORS/ACHIEVEMENTS:** Biographical article US Black Engineer Magazine 1986, Ebony Magazine 1987. **BUSINESS ADDRESS:** Engineer-Electric System, Potomac Electric Power Co, 1900 Pennsylvania Ave NW, Washington, DC 20068.

THEODORE, KEITH FELIX
Dentist. **PERSONAL:** Born Dec 28, 1948, Port-of-Spain, Trinidad and Tobago;married Deborah Ann Corbett; children: Tony, Jamal. **EDUCATION:** Howard Univ, BS 1974, DDS 1980. **CAREER:** Robert T Freeman Dental Soc, fin sec 1987-, chmn mem comm 1987-; Tooth-N-Nail Inc, pres 1985-. **HONORS/ACHIEVEMENTS:** Story published in Washington Post Newspaper 1987;TV documentary done on bus & profession. **HOME ADDRESS:** 7249 G St, Seat Pleasant, MD 20743. **BUSINESS ADDRESS:** President, Tooth-N-Nail Inc, 7845 Eastern Ave, Silver Spring, MD 20910.

THEODORE, YVONNE M. (NEE POWELL)
Personnel director. **PERSONAL:** Born Mar 16, 1939, Prince Georges Co, MD; divorced. **EDUCATION:** Mt St Agnes Coll, BA 1961; MakerereUniv Uganda E Africa, MA 1962; Johns Hopkins U, Cand M Lib Arts 1976; Fisk U, Spl Courses Race Rels 1964. **CAREER:** Johns Hopkins U, asst dir prsnl, affirm act ofcr 1971-; Provident Comp Nghbrhd Hlth Ctr, asst to dir; Baltimore City Comm Rels Commn, intrgrp rels spl 1965-68; Mt St Mary's Namagunga, Uganda E Africa, grad, std, flw tchr 1961-64. **ORGANIZATIONS:** Mem Nat Cncl of Negro Womn; Coll &Univ Pers Assn; Kampala Sngrs, Interracial, Interclt rl Classical Sngng Grp Uganda E Africa. **HONORS/ACHIEVEMENTS:** Recip Recog for Yth Motivation Nat Alliance of Busmn 1973-74; named Illustrious Wmn Baltimore Afro-Am Nwspr 1971; Acad Schlrshp HS, Music SchlrshpThe Cath HS of Baltimore; Acad Schlrshp Mt St Agnes Coll. **BUSINESS ADDRESS:** Johns Hopkins University, Garland Hall Room 276, 34th & Charles Sts, Baltimore, MD 21218.

THEUS, LUCIUS
Corporate executive, retired military of. **PERSONAL:** Born Oct 11, 1922, Near Bells, TN; married Gladys Marie. **EDUCATION:** Univ of MD, BS 1956; Geo Wash U, MBA 1957; Harvard Bus Sch, Grad Adv Mgmt Prgm 1969; Armed Forces Staff Coll, Disting Grad 1960; Air War Coll,1966; Indust Coll of Armed Forced (off campus), honor grad 1965. **CAREER:** The Bendix Corp South Field MI, asst corp controller; USAF, retired major gen; AF Acctng & Fin Ctr & HQ USAFF Dir of Acctg & Fin, comdr; USAF, p 1942. **ORGANIZATIONS:** Exec coun Harvard Bus Sch Assn; Harvard Club; vice-Pres & mem bd dir Harvard Bus Sch Club Wash DC 1972-74; bd dir mem Harvard Bus Sch Club Denver; mem Nat Assn of Acctnts; mem Nat Assn of Black Acctnst; mem Nat Black MBA Assn; Geo WashUniv Club; Assn for Comput Mach; AF Assn; chmn Mile High United Way 1976; dir & vice-chm Explorers Denver area couns BSA; mem dir AF Assn; mem Am Legion; mem Am Radio Relay Leag; mem & bd dir ARC Mile High Chrtr; pres Am Soc of Military Compt Wash Chptr 1973-74; pres Mile High Chptr 1975; mem Assn of Govt Accts; mem Denver C of C Military Aff Com; regl chmn Explorers BSA; mem & natl vice pres Tuskegee Airmen Inc; mem USO Denver Bd of Dir. **HONORS/ACHIEVEMENTS:** Decorated Disting Serv Medal with Oak Leaf Cluster; Legion of Merit Bronze Star Medal; AF Commend Medal with Oak Leaf Cluster; Denver Fed Exec Bd Dstng Fed Serv Awrd; Pitts Cour Top Hat Award; Who's Who in the World; Who's Who in Am; Who's Who in Govt; 1000 Successful Blacks. **MILITARY SERVICE:** USAF 3rd black to be prom to gen ofcr rank. **BUSINESS ADDRESS:** President, The US Associates, 4520 Stony River Dr, Birmingham, MI 48010.

THEUS, REGGIE
Professional athlete. **PERSONAL:** Born Oct 13, 1957, Ingelwood, CA. **EDUCATION:** Univ of Las Vegas NV, 1979. **CAREER:** Chicago Bulls, prof bsktbl plyr guard; Kansas City Kings, guard. **ORGANIZATIONS:** Involved various clubs Little City Prog, Athletes For Better Educ 1979, Natl Comm Against Child Abuse. **HONORS/ACHIEVEMENTS:** MVP, UNLV 1979; Coached All-Star Team IL HS; led Bulls in scoring (238), assists (59), steals (17) 1981-82,82-83; led the club 20 times with 6 double figure outings & a season high 13 vs Portland; had 23 doubled figure scoring nights, 7 of 20 or more points & a season-high 36 vs Los Angeles; Kings were 16-14 after he joined club; UNLV All-Amer selection; led the Rebels jr year in scoring with 190 ppg & scored in double figures in all 28 games; after jr campaign was named Rebel's MVP; in 3 seasons with Rebels UNLV posted a 78-13 mark.

THIBODEAUX, SYLVIA MARIE
Educator. **PERSONAL:** Born Nov 26, 1937, Breaux Bridge, LA; widowed. **EDUCATION:** BA 1967; MA 1973. **CAREER:** Tulsa, elem teacher 1960-62; Opelousa, teacher 1962-63; Tulsa, teacher 1963-65; Proj Commitment & Assn of Urban Sisters Boston 1968-69; Witness Prog Educ Component New Orleans, dir 1967-68; St Joseph Comm Sch Boston, principal 1970-74; mem Tchr Training Coll & Religious Formation Benin City Nigeria W Africa. **ORGANIZATIONS:** Bd mem, Campaign for Human Devel, Natl Office for Black Catholics; Natl Black Sisters Conf; DESIGN; Minority Evaluators Ginn & Co; bd trustees, Educ Devel Ctr; consul, AFRAM Assoc; mem, Planning Comm, Black Educ Conf. **HONORS/ACHIEVEMENTS:** NIA Awd Spec Achievement for Innovative Educ Prog; Outstanding Contrib to Black Comm Awd Roxbury Action Prog; SCLC Most Creative Educ Prog; Outstanding Educator of Amer Awd. **HOME ADDRESS:** Bishop's House, PO Box 35, Benin City, Nigeria.

THIGPEN, CALVIN HERRITAGE
Physician, attorney. **PERSONAL:** Born Jan 07, 1924, Greenville, NC; married Vera Belle Crawford; children: Calvin Jr, Karen. **EDUCATION:** VA State Coll, BS 1953; Univ VA, MD 1962, JD 1974. **CAREER:** Hopewell, VA, teacher 1953-58; Stuart Prod Co, cosmetics/chem plant mgr 1957-58; Med Coll VA, intern 1962-63; Petersburg General Hosp, staff mem 1963; private practice 1963; VA State Coll, assoc & physician 1964-71; Petersburg Gen Hosp, vice chief/general practice section 1969-70; Office Attorney General VA, intern 1972-73; Univ VA, rsrch asst legal adv 1973-74; Private Practice, attorney 1975-. **ORGANIZATIONS:** Mem, Sigma Pi Sigma Natl Physics Hon Soc; Beta Kappa Chi Natl Sci Hon Soc; Phi Delta Phi Legal Fraternity; Dem Com Hopewell 1965-75; bd dir Salvation Army; Hopewell Chamber of Commerce; Old Dominion Med Soc; exec com Old Dominion Med Soc 1965. **HONORS/ACHIEVEMENTS:** pres, Natl Guardsmen Inc 1967-70; Library Human Resources Amer Bicentennial Rsch Inst 1973; Fellow Amer Coll Legal Med 1976; Mem Bd of Visitors VA State Univ 1978-82; VA Delegate to the White House Conf on Library & Info Serv 1979; Chief of Staff Petersburg Gen Hosp 1980; Diplomate Amer Bd of Legal Med 1982. **MILITARY SERVICE:** AUS lst Lt 1944-49. **HOME ADDRESS:** 19801 Oakland Ave, Colonial Heights, VA 23834. **BUSINESS ADDRESS:** Physician Attorney, 734 South Sycamore St, Petersburg, VA 23803.

THIGPEN, EDMUND LEONARD
Musician. **PERSONAL:** Born Dec 28, 1930, Chicago, IL; widowed; children: Denise Mary, Michel Edmund. **EDUCATION:** Los Angeles City Coll, 1949; Manhattan Sch Mus, student 1955. **CAREER:** Performed with Cootie Williams 1951, Dinah Washington 1954, Johnny Hodges & Bud Powell 1955, Billy Taylor Trio 1956, 1959, Oscar Peterson Trio 1959; road tour with Ella Fitzgerald; free-lance musician in Los Angeles working with Johnny Mathis, Pat Boone, Andy Williams, Peggy Lee, Oliver Nelson, Gerald Wilson; re-joined Ella Fitzgerald as permanent mem of her trio until 1972; works from base in Copenhagen with Kenny Drew, Thad Jones, Ernie Wilkins, Clark Terry, Teddy Wilson; teaches jazz oriented percussion at Music Conserv in Malmo, Sweden; owner of percussion studio in Copenhagen. **ORGANIZATIONS:** Mem Percussion Arts Soc. **HONORS/ACHIEVEMENTS:** Author "Be Our Guest"; "Ed Thigpen Talking Drums"; with Ray Brown "Rhythm Analysis and Basic Co-ordination"; "The Sound of Brushes". **MILITARY SERVICE:** AUS 1952-54.

THOMAS, A. See SCOTT, PORTIA ADELE

THOMAS, ALICE WATERS
Retired educator. **PERSONAL:** Born Dec 15, 1912, Memphis, TN; married Joseph A Thomas; children: Jackie M, Alice (Mayhew). **EDUCATION:** TN State Univ, BS 1939; Fisk Univ, MA 1948; Univ of Chgo, Cert of Adv Study 1964. **CAREER:** Nashville Metro Public School System, retired teacher 1975. **ORGANIZATIONS:** Pres Nashville Sect Natl Council of Negro Women; mem chmn, chmn bd dir Nashville Teachers Assoc, Ed Council 1959-63, Met Nashville Ed Assoc 1964-71; chmn Vol Leadership Comm, Bd on Admin, Blue Triangle Br YWCA; mem Del Assembly, NEA, TEA, MTTA, MNEA, Amer Assoc of Univ Women, Phi Delta Kappa Peabody Chapt, Natl Sor Phi Delta Kappa, Alpha Beta Chapt; chmn Publ Rel; founder, past episloens Publ Affair Comm; pres Nashville Section of the Natl Council Negro Women; partic Gov Invitational Conf on Career Ed 1972; mem League of Women Voters Ed Comm 1977. **HONORS/ACHIEVEMENTS:** Honor Awd Metro Nashville Ed Assoc 1968,69,70; Natl Sor Phi Delta Kappa, Alpha Beta Chap Apprec Awd 1975; Serv to Nashville Teacher Assoc Metro Nashville Ed Assoc; Gold Serv Awd, Natl Council of Negro Women 1971; Dist Serv Awd, Natl Council of Negro Women, Rose of Sharon, Order of Eastern Star 1979; Cert of Appreciation, Natl Immunization Prog Natl Med Assoc, Natl Council Negro Women 1979.

THOMAS, ALVIN
Government official. **PERSONAL:** Born Apr 11, 1951, New Orleans, LA. **EDUCATION:** SoUniv A&M Coll, BA Pol Sci 1969-74; Union Bapt Theolog Sem, 1974; Univers Bible Inst. **CAREER:** Gov of LA, spec asst 1976; Iberville Parish Police Jury, police juror 1972-76; Bechtel Power Corp, ofc mgr 1975; LA House of Rep, page 1972; Indsl Plant Maint, supr 1972-74; US Pub Hlth Serv Hosp, clrk 1968-72; Jerusalem Bapt Ch St Gabriel, pastor 1973-74; Mt Zion Bapt Ch # 1, asst pastor 1967-69; Mt Bethel Bapt Ch, sec 1964-68; I. **ORGANIZATIONS:** Iberville Parish Hsng Auth 1972; LA Police Jury Assn 1972-76; Nat Assn of Co of Elect Ofcl 1972-76; Iberville Parish Person Com 1972-76; Iberville Parish Fin Com 1972-76; Iberville Parish Gas Com 1972-76; Iberville Parish Law Enforce Com 1972-76; E Iberville Recreation Ass 1972; Iberville Parish Indsl Voters Leag 1971; ward ldr Iberville Parish 1971-73; Iberville Parish Minis Counc 1972; mem 2nd Dist Bapt Assn 1972; mem 4th Dist Bapt Assn 1972; mem LA Bapt Convent 1972; mem Nat Bapt Convent USA Inc 1972; LA Hlth Assn Com 1972-76; fndr & pres E Iberville Vol Fire Dept 1972; vice pres E Iberville Imprv Assn 1971; mem Lemoyne Comm Action Fin Com 1968-70; dir Stud Govt Assn SoUniv 1970-71; mem Nat Foreign Miss Bd USA Inc 1972; youngest elect ofcl State of LA 1972; youngest Nat elect ofcl 1972; chmn 1st Nat Black Polit Convent 1972; deleg Nat Dem Convent 1972; vice pres Nat Assn of Black Counties Ofcls 1975-76; rep Natl Legislat Confer of NACO 1975; rep Iberville Parish Police Jury. **HONORS/ACHIEVEMENTS:** Outst Stdnt Govt Assn Wrkr SoUniv 1970-71. **BUSINESS ADDRESS:** Rt 1 Box 44 A St, Gabriel, LA 70776.

THOMAS, ARTHUR E.
University president. **CAREER:** Central State Univ, Wilberforce, OH, president. **BUSINESS ADDRESS:** President, Central State University, Wilberforce, OH 45384. *

THOMAS, AUDRIA ACTY
Physician, allergist, immunologist. **PERSONAL:** Born Jun 06, 1954, Washington, DC; married Harold Levy Thomas; children: Shaunta Lindsey. **EDUCATION:** Meharry Medical Coll, MD 1980. **CAREER:** Howard Univ Hosp, resident 1980-83; St Thomas/St John Medical Soc, chief allergy dept. **ORGANIZATIONS:** Soloist First Rock Baptist Church 1959-86; mem Natl Medical Assoc 1980-86; pediatric consultant 15-24 Free Clinic for Teenagers 1980-86; consultant Virgin Island Lung Assoc 1986-; singer Victory Christian Ctr 1986-. **HONORS/ACHIEVEMENTS:** Howard Univ Fellowship in Allergy Immunology 1983-86; published paper "Cystic Fibrosis in Black," Layman's Journal update in allergy 1985.

HOME ADDRESS: PO Box 60, Charlotte Amalie, St Thomas, Virgin Islands of the United States 00801. BUSINESS ADDRESS: Chief Allergy Dept, St Thomas/St John Med Soc, 4 Norre Gade, Charlotte Amalie, St Thomas, Virgin Islands of the United States 00801.

THOMAS, BENJAMIN
Publisher. **PERSONAL:** Born Sep 17, 1910, Pine Bluff, AR; widowed; children: Barry, Kevin. **EDUCATION:** Attended OH State Univ 1933. **CAREER:** St Louis Evening Whirl, founder/publisher/editor 1938-. **ORGANIZATIONS:** Mem NAACP, YMCA. **HONORS/ACHIEVEMENTS:** Citations many civic groups. **BUSINESS ADDRESS:** Publisher, St Louis Evening Whirl, P O Box 5088, Negal Station, St Louis, MO 63147.

THOMAS, BETTYE COLLIER
Educator. **PERSONAL:** Born in Macon, GA; married Charles John Thomas. **EDUCATION:** Allen U, BA (magna cum laude) 1963; Atlanta U, MA 1966; Geo Wash U, PhD 1974. **CAREER:** Univ of MD, lecturer History 1971-; William & Mary Coll, assoc prof 1969-70; Wash Tech Inst, asst prof 1969-71; Howard Univ Coll of Lib Arts, dir honors pgm 1969-71; Howard Univ, instr 1966-69; WA Perry Jr HS Columbia SC, instr 1963-65. **ORGANIZATIONS:** Mem Am Assn of Univ Profs; Nat Educ Assn; mem Assn for Study of Afro-Am Life & Hist; Alpha Kappa Alpha; Orgn of Am Histrns; Am Acad of Soc Sciences; Author of "The Baltimore Black Community 1965-1910"Univ of IL Press; author various articles. **HONORS/ACHIEVEMENTS:** Schlrshp Awrd Delta Sigma Theta 1960; Mark Schaefer History Awrd 1963; Nat Assn of Coll Women's Awrd 1963; Presdntl Schlrshp AtlantaUniv 1965-66; Ford Fndtn Flwshp So Flwshp Fund Grant & HowardUniv Rsrch Grant; listed Who's Who in Am Coll & Univ 1962-63.

THOMAS, BOOKER T.
Business executive. **PERSONAL:** Born Sep 18, 1936, McRoberts, KY; married Genevieve De La Cruz; children: James, Kim, Eurydice. **EDUCATION:** Wilberforce Univ, BS Math/Physics 1956; Pepperdine Univ, 1969-72; Univ of San Francisco, doctoral candidate 1981-. **CAREER:** Telco Industries, pres 1967-76; McDonnel Douglas, manager 1975-76; Stanford Research Inst, manager 1976-78; Phoenix Intl, pres 1978-. **ORGANIZATIONS:** Mem Alpha Phi Alpha 1954-; bd mem LA ICBO 1972-74; appoint mem State of CA Pvt Post Secondary Educ 1983; appointed by State Supt of Pub Instr Pvt Post Secondary Educ 1972. **HONORS/ACHIEVEMENTS:** Acad Achievement Award USAF 1959-60; Humanitarian Award Univ of CA San Diego 1982. **MILITARY SERVICE:** USAF Mathmetician (special assignment) served 3 1/2 years; Acad Achvmnt Award for Grad Study 1959; Letter of Techn Excellence 1960. **BUSINESS ADDRESS:** President, Phoenix International, 8703 La Tijera Blvd, Ste 205, Los Angeles, CA 90045.

THOMAS, C. EDWARD
Educator, executive. **PERSONAL:** Born Nov 19, 1935, Vineland, NJ. **EDUCATION:** Wheaton Coll; Am Conservatory of Music, M; StateUniv of Iowa City, DMA Cand. **CAREER:** Bethel Coll St Paul, MN, asso prof; KTCA-TV Channel 2 St Paul, MN, asst dir Creative Projs; concert artist for coll & Orgns; Totaltelemart, Inc, pres. **ORGANIZATIONS:** Mem MN Tchrs Assn; Music Tchrs Nat Assn; Music Educators Nat Conf; music dir 1st Bapt Ch Minneapolis; accompanist for Ethel Waters on concert & crusade appearances; fndr Afro-Am Music Opport Assn. **HONORS/ACHIEVEMENTS:** Recipient of numerous awrds for musical perfmncs; Corp for Pub Bdcstng Minority Grant for TV experience & devel 1975; Who's Who in Black Am 1976; Nat Assn of Negro Musicians awrd 1974; Ford Fnd Fellow 1969; Performer of 1st Pan-Am Festival 1967; Nat Fedn of Music Clubs Competition 1965; Artists Diploma Extraordinary 1962. **BUSINESS ADDRESS:** President, Totaltelemart, Inc, 2801 Wayzata Blvd, Minneapolis, MN 55405.

THOMAS, CALVIN LEWIS
Professional athlete. **PERSONAL:** Born Jan 07, 1960, St Louis, MO; married Bernadine; children: Nikkita. **EDUCATION:** IL, BA 1984. **CAREER:** Chicago Bears, running back 1984-. **ORGANIZATIONS:** Involved in Red Cloud Athletic Fund, Jr Variety Club, Big Brothers. **HONORS/ACHIEVEMENTS:** Played in final 13 games in 1983 after recovering from shoulder separation suffered in final pre-season game; primarily used on spcl teams in 1982 & 1983; had25 yds on 8 carries, 2 catches for 13 yds in 1983; 9 carries 59 yds, TD in 27-21 win over Raiders in 1983 preseason. **BUSINESS ADDRESS:** Running Back, Chicago Bears, Halas Hall, PO Box 500 Sta M Montreal, Lake Forest, IL 60045.

THOMAS, CARL ALAN
Educator, clergyman. **PERSONAL:** Born Mar 21, 1924, Jersey City, NJ; children: Edward, Algynan, Elaine, Stanley. **EDUCATION:** Rutgers U, BA 1946; Union Sem, BD 1949; NY U, MA 1950;Univ of KS, DD 1970. **CAREER:** Community Coll of Phila, dir/dean 1968-; Lincoln Univ of PA, dean 1968; Wilberforce Univ, dean 1964-66; FL A&M Univ, prof 1960-64; Exper In Intl Living, dir 1960; AME Zion Church, pastor; Lincoln Univ Oxford, prof of Black studies; Training Inst Lincoln Univ, teacher. **ORGANIZATIONS:** Mem Alpha Psi Omega Frat; mem Kappa Alpha Psi Frat Swords & Shields Wilberforce OH; Sons of Wilberforce OH. **HONORS/ACHIEVEMENTS:** Listed Who's who in Edn. **BUSINESS ADDRESS:** Community College of Philadelp, 34 S 11th St, Philadelphia, PA.

THOMAS, CARL D.
Coordinator. **PERSONAL:** Born May 13, 1950, Kansas City, MO; married Dana Morris. **EDUCATION:** Univ MA Amherst, BS 1973. **CAREER:** Office of Minority Business City of Boston, business develop specialist 1978-81; MA Dept of Commerce & Development, business educ training dir 1980-81; US Small Business Admin, ace counselor 1983-; Contractor's Assoc of Boston Inc, small business develop coord 1983-. **ORGANIZATIONS:** Mem Natl Assn of Minority Contractors 1984; mem Natl Business Admin 1984; steering comm Mass Minority Business Assistance 1985; mem NAACP Boston Chapt1984; mem ACE US Small Business Admin 1983. **HONORS/ACHIEVEMENTS:** Minority Advocate of Yr US Small Bus Admin 1985; Minority Advocate of Yr Commonwealth of MA 1985; Who's Who in American Univs of MA/Amherst 1971; Outstanding Young Men of Amer 1985. **BUSINESS ADDRESS:** Small Business Coordinator, Contractor's Assoc of Boston, 25 Center St, Roxbury, MA 02119.

THOMAS, CAROL M.
Federal government executive. **PERSONAL:** Born Dec 23, 1930, Washington, DC; married Laura Pedro; children: Kevin, Marla, Paul. **EDUCATION:** Yale U, BA 1953; John Hopkins U, MA 1961. **CAREER:** Navy Dept, management intern 1961; Navy Dept Washington, contract negotiator 1961-64; Office Econ Opportunity Wash, br 1964-65; Job Corps, project mgr 1965-67; Contracts Div Peace Corp Wash, dep dir 1967-69; Peace Corps Sierraie-one, dir 1969-71; Office Civil Rights & Urban Affairs US Environmental Protection Agy, dir 1972-74; Office Civil Rights US EPA Wash, 1974-77; Fed Trade Commn, sec 1977-; Am Acad Polit & Social Scis, 1973-; Am Soc Pub Adminstrs, 1972-; Manasas Educ Found. **ORGANIZATIONS:** Mem exec Com Bd Dir 1972-; Alpha Phi Alpha Frat; Federal City Club Wash 1972-; Reston Golf & Country Club 1971-. **HONORS/ACHIEVEMENTS:** Who's Who Am 1973-75; Who's Who Ecology 1973; Who's Who in Govt 1976-77. **MILITARY SERVICE:** USAF 1954-59. **BUSINESS ADDRESS:** 6th St & Penn Ave NW, Washington, DC 20580.

THOMAS, CHARLES COLUMBUS
Educator. **PERSONAL:** Born Sep 10, 1940, McAlester, OK. **EDUCATION:** Langston Univ, BA 1962; Brooklyn Coll, MFA 1972 City Univ NY, 1977. **CAREER:** Coll of Staten Island City Univ NY, asst prof; Afro-Amer Inst Richmond Coll, dir 1972-73; Univ Ghana, vis prof 1972; NY Comm Coll, asst prof 1971-74; Lefferst Jr HS, chmn 1966-69; Staten & Island Repertory Ensemble, dir; Mayor's Council on Youth & Physical Fitness, 1969; NY State Council on the Arts, 1968-70; OEO Proj, dir 1968; Egbe Omo Nago Folklorio Ensemble, dir 1967-69; Afro-Amer Folkloric Troupe, artistic dir 1963-70; African Heritage Studeis Assn; Big Bros; Epsilon Chap Omega Psi Phi; Natl Acad Rec Arts & Sciences; Natl Academy TV Arts & Sciences; Screen Actors Guild; Kappa. **HONORS/ACHIEVEMENTS:** Ebony Success Library, 1972; Research Award, CUNY faculty, 1972; Contributing author, We Speak as Liberators, 1971, Probes an introduction to & poetry 1973, Yarbird Reader 1977, Rinds for Revolution 1971. **BUSINESS ADDRESS:** 130 Stuyvesant Pl, Staten Island, NY 10301.

THOMAS, CHARLES RICHARD
Educator. **PERSONAL:** Born Jun 06, 1933, Evanston, IL; widowed; children: Charles Jr, Markham. **EDUCATION:** Univ of WI, BS 1957; NW U, MA 1966; NW Attended, Teachers Coll Columbia U, PhD 1978;Univ 1970. **CAREER:** N Chicago School Dist 64, supt 1973; IL Office of Educ, asst supt 1971-73; Evanston Public School, prin 1968-71; Evanston HS, asst prin 1964-67; Evanston HS, athletic coach 1957-68. **ORGANIZATIONS:** Mem IL Assn of Sch Admnstr; Am Assn of Sch Adminstr; Nat Alliance of Black Sch Educr; Lake Co Assn of Sch Adminstr; IL Assn of Sch Bd Assn; Am Assn of Sch Personnel Adminstr; Assn of Sup & Curriculum Devel; pres Phi Delta Kappa, N Chicago Rotary Club; N Chicago C of C; bd of dir LakeCo Urban Leg. **HONORS/ACHIEVEMENTS:** NAACP N Chicago Br Awd, Citz Participation in Sch Desegregation, IL Jour of Educ 1972; publ "Unique Problems Confronting the Black Sch Admnstr" , Eric Document Reprod Serv, 1972; "The Purpose & Value of HS Athletics",Univ of MI 1976; "Sch Desegregation what makes it work?" IL sch bd jour 1977. **MILITARY SERVICE:** AUSR capt 1957-65. **BUSINESS ADDRESS:** Superintendent, Board of Education, 2000 Lewis Ave N, Chicago, IL 60064.

THOMAS, CHARLES W.
Transportation company executive. **PERSONAL:** Born Mar 09, 1940, Boston, MA; son of Charles Edward Thomas and Pauline Delores Walker Thomas; married Ellen V Bell; children: Kevin Charles, Tracey Ann. **EDUCATION:** Northeastern Univ, Boston AS, 1963, BA, 1967; Univ of Redlands, Redlands CA, MA, 1983. **CAREER:** Raytheon Co, Bedford MA, draftsman, 1961-64, engineer mgr, 1967-70; RCA, Chelmsford MA, engineer, 1964-67; Regional Transit, Sacramento CA, asst gen mgr, 1970-78, gen mgr, 1978-81; SEPTA, Philadelphia PA, chief trans officer, 1981-85, deputy AGM operations, 1985-87. **BUSINESS ADDRESS:** Assistant General Manager-Operations, Southeastern Pennsylvania Transportation Authority, 200 West Wyoming Ave, Philadelphia, PA 19140.

THOMAS, CHARLES WILLIAM, II
Educator. **PERSONAL:** Born Apr 24, 1926, Davidsonville, MD; son of Charles and Estella; married Dr Shirley Wade; children: Charles III, Shawn. **EDUCATION:** Morgan State Univ, BS 1951; John Carroll Univ, AM 1955; Case Western Reserve Univ, PhD 1961. **CAREER:** John Carroll Univ, lecturer 1961-63; Univ of OR, asst prof rehab counseling 1963-66; Univ of S CA Sch of Med, assoc prof comm med 1966-69; CA State Univ, lecturer in social psych & black studies 1967-68; Ctr for the Study of Racial & Social Issues, dir 1969-71; Systems Devel Corp, prog devel consul 1968-71; CA State Coll Dominguez Hills, lecturer black studies & social psych 1970; AZ State Univ, vstg prof counseling psych 1970-71; Claremont Coll Black Studies Ctr, lecturer 1970-71; Howard Univ Inst for Urban Affairs, vstg scholar 1979-80; Urban Studies & Planning, coord 1977-82; Univ of CA-San Diego, prof urban studies & planning 1971-. **ORGANIZATIONS:** Secy treas Black Behavioral Scientists of CA 1966-69; WICHE Task Force 1969-70; adv bd LA Co Headstart Prog 1969-70; co-chair curriculum develop commCA Sch of Professional Psychology 1969; faculty affairs comm CA Sch of Professional Psychology 1970; bd of overseers CA Sch of Professional Psychology 1969-72; adv bd SoRegional Educ Assn; mem S CA Regional Plan Assn 1969-71; mem Amer Psychological Assn 1962-; fndg chmn Assn of Black Psychologists; chmn Task Force Amer Psychological Assn; mem Natl Acad of TV Arts & Scis 1968-71; adv bd Natl Council of Grad Educ in Psychology 1971-73; mem NAACP; mem CA State Bd of Educ Commn on Curriculum Materials & Instructional Develop 1975-79; bd dirs World Black Commns Congress 1980-83; bd dirs San Diego Comm Video Ctr 1979-82; fndr Annual Conf on Ethnicity & Mental Health 1978-; editorial bd Journal of Comm Psychology 1979-84; bd dirs Ctr for the Improvement of Child-Caring 1977-; Schlrshps Awds Comm Natl Cultural Found 1979-81; chair Educ & Rsch Comm CA Black Republican Council 1983-84. **HONORS/ACHIEVEMENTS:** Father of Black Psychology Awd 1971; Commendation NAACP 1977; Commendation State of OH 1979; Scholarship & Comm Serv Awd Prince Hall Masons 1975; Charles W Thomas Scholarship at Morgan State Univ 1976; Danforth Assoc; Educ Leadership Awd Omega Psi Phi Frat; Meritorious Awd Legal Aid Soc of San Diego 1979; Science Achievement Awd Action Enterprises Develop 1980; Outstanding Serv in Teaching & Educ Awd Council of Black Engrs 1982; Journalism Achievement Awd Action Enterprises Develop 1982; numerous visiting disting lectureships; book published "Boys No More, A Black Psychologist's View of the Community" Glencoe Press Publs 1971; numerous presentations & publications. **BUSINESS ADDRESS:** Prof Urban Studies, Univ CA San Diego, D009, La Jolla, CA 92093.

THOMAS, CLARENCE
Government official. **PERSONAL:** Born Jun 23, 1948, Savannah, GA; children: Jamal A. **EDUCATION:** Holy Cross Coll, BA 1971; Yale Law School, JD 1974. **CAREER:** State of MO Jefferson City, asst attny gen 1974-77; Monsanto Co St Louis, attny 1977-79; Sen John C Danforth Washington, legis asst; Dept Ed WA, asst sec for civil rights 1981-82; EEOC

Washington, chmn 1982-. **BUSINESS ADDRESS:** Chairman, Equal Emplmnt Opp Commission, 2401 E St NW, Washington, DC 20506.

THOMAS, CLAUDE RODERICK
Judge. **PERSONAL:** Born Mar 15, 1943, Clarksdale, MS; married Cindy Marie Hufnagel; children: Claude Roderick II, Jerry Jason, Patrick James, LaTonya Lizzie, Alexandra Nicole. **EDUCATION:** MI State Univ, BA 1972; Thomas M Cooley Law School, JD 1976. **CAREER:** Lansing Police Dept, police officer 1969-75; Ingham Cty Pros Office, asst prosecutor 1976-80; 54A Dist Court, district judge 1981-. **ORGANIZATIONS:** Mem State Bar Character & Fitness 1977-, Boys Club; bd dir Cooley Credit Union 1980-81. **HONORS/ACHIEVEMENTS:** Alumni of the Year Cooley Law School 1981. **MILITARY SERVICE:** USMC corpl 4 years; Good Conduct Medal 1964. **BUSINESS ADDRESS:** Judge District Court, 54A Judicial Dist, Lansing City Hall #6, 5th Floor, Lansing, MI 48933.

THOMAS, DEBI
Professional ice skater. **PERSONAL:** Born Mar 25, 1967, Poughkeepsie, NY; married Brian Vanden Hogen. **EDUCATION:** Attending, Stanford Univ. **CAREER:** World Class figure skater; performed in London for Live Aid; appeared at Celebration America on Ice in Indianapolis for 25th Anniversary of US Figure Skating Assoc Memorial Fund; special guest star Stars on Ice. **HONORS/ACHIEVEMENTS:** Winner 1985 Natl Sports Festival in Baton Rouge; two gold medal victories Skate America Intl Minneapolis and at St Ivel Intl Great Britain; United States Ladies Figure Skating Champion 1986; World Champions 1986; Olympic Bronze Medalist 1988.

THOMAS, DOUGLAS L.
Educator. **PERSONAL:** Born Feb 28, 1945, Jacksonville, FL; married Elaine. **EDUCATION:** City Coll NY, BA 1968; ColumbiaUniv Law Sch, JD 1971. **CAREER:** Harvard Law School, teaching fellow faculty; RCA Corp, atty 1973-74; Dewey Ballantine Busby Palmer & Wood, assoc 1971-73; Youth Serv Agy, coord 1971; Youth Serv & Agy, dir 1970; NYC Dept Prob, investigator 1969-71; Harlem Consumer's Union, law asst 1969; Jamaica Comm Corp, dir summer prog 1968; Morningside Comm Center, group leader 1967-68; Prima RE Corp, re salesman 1965-67. **ORGANIZATIONS:** Mem Assn Bar NYC; NY State Bar Assn Coun Concerned Black Execs; Emerging Black Profl; Intl Law Soc; Black Am Law Students Assn; Omega Psi Phi. **HONORS/ACHIEVEMENTS:** Outstanding achiev awards, goldman scholarship award City Coll Sch Social & Psychol Fndtns; Charles Evan Hughes Fellowship. **BUSINESS ADDRESS:** Harvard Law Sch, Cambridge, MA 02138.

THOMAS, EARLE FREDERICK
Business executive. **PERSONAL:** Born May 06, 1925, Preston, MD; married Bettie; children: Rodney, Sherri. **EDUCATION:** Morgan State Coll U, 1942; Hampton Inst; VA Bankers Sch, life underwriters. **CAREER:** VA Nat Bank, mgr 1975; loan exec 1975; asst mgr 1974-75; mktg ofcr 1974; Atlantic Nat Bank, pres, chf exec ofcr, dir sec 1972-74, vice pres dir sec 1971-72, org 1968-71; John Hancock Mutual Life Ins Co, underwriter 1966-68; Am Tobacco Co, state rep 1959-68; Newport New Shipyard, machinist 1951-59. **ORGANIZATIONS:** Mem bd visitors Norfolk State Coll 1977-; bd mem Retail Merchants Assn 1977-78; vice pres dir Tidewater Cncl Boy Scouts; bd mem Tidewater Red Cross; dir sec Tidewater Area Minority Contractors; bd mem Sickel Cell Anemia; mem adv cncl 4h Club; mem Sales Mktg & Exec Club; pres Club; Norfolk C of C; budget com United Fund; treas Norfolk State Coll Found Martin Luther King Comm. **HONORS/ACHIEVEMENTS:** Achvmt award 1975. **BUSINESS ADDRESS:** 3300 Princess Anne Rd, Norfolk, VA 23502.

THOMAS, EDWARD P.
Physician. **PERSONAL:** Born Jul 26, 1920, Mississippi; married Ruby; children: Paul A, Bradford E, Leeland M, Leah Ann. **EDUCATION:** Butler U, 1941; Meharry Med Coll, MD 1944. **CAREER:** Pvt Practice, physician practicing allergist, Indpls. **ORGANIZATIONS:** Mem AMA IN Med Assn; Nat Med Assn; Aesculapian Med Soc; mem staff Meth Hosp Winona Hosp St Vincent & Hosp Inspls; mem Medical Council MethHosp; mem Am Coll of Allergists; Am Acad of Allergy; Am Coll of Chest Physicians; Am Coll of Gastroenterology; mem Chi Delta Mu; Omega Psi Phi. **MILITARY SERVICE:** USN lt cmdr med corp 1954-56. **BUSINESS ADDRESS:** 3450 N Illinois St, Indianapolis, IN 46208.

THOMAS, ERMA LEE
Elected official, educator. **PERSONAL:** Born Jul 07, 1928, Rentiesville, OK; married Joe Elihue Thomas; children: Lee Wilbur, Dianna Kaye, Cheryl Lynn, Bonnie Sue, John Robert. **EDUCATION:** Langston Univ OK, BS 1951; Northeastern State Coll OK, ME. **CAREER:** St Thomas Primitive Bapt Church, treas 1974-80; Alpha Epsilon Omega Chap Alpha Kappa Alpha Sor Inc, basileus 1974-76; Local Langston Univ Alumni, sec 1977-85; Langston's Reg Midwestern Conf, sec 1980; State Dept OK, comm mem 1984-85; Muskogee School, lang arts teacher; City of Summit, mayor, trustee. **HOME ADDRESS:** Rt 4 Box 436C, Summit, OK 74401. **BUSINESS ADDRESS:** Mayor, Summit, 402 NS St, Muskogee, OK 74401.

THOMAS, EULA WILEY
Educator. **PERSONAL:** Born Apr 30, 1948, Arkadelphia, AR; married Herman L Thomas; children: Traci A, Tiffani A. **EDUCATION:** Ouachita Baptist Univ, BA Speech & Drama 1970; Henderson State Univ, MASAC Soc Agency Counseling 1976; Univ of CO Training Inst, attended 1980; Marquette Univ Training Inst for Spec Prog, attended 1981; Wichita State Training Inst, attended, 1984. **CAREER:** AR Human Dev Ctr, recreation leader 1970, speech pathologist 1971-76; Henderson State Univ, coord of handicapped serv 1984-, counselor/instructor 1976-. **ORGANIZATIONS:** Clerk, sec, deaconess Greater Pleasant Hill Baptist Church; co-sponsor Henderson State Univ Minority Students Org 1979-; pres Arkadelphia Women's Devel Council 1980-; bd of dir Arkadelphia Chamber of Commerce 1983; chairperson Arkadelphia Christmas Parade 1983, 1984; mem AR Counselor Assoc, AR Assoc for Student Assoc Programs, NAACP. **HONORS/ACHIEVEMENTS:** WP Sturgis Found Grant for Continuing Educ, 1966; AR Handicapped Award for Special Educ 1971. **HOME ADDRESS:** 1528 Walnut, Arkadelphia, AR 71923. **BUSINESS ADDRESS:** Counselor/Instructor, Henderson State Univ, H-7603, Arkadelphia, AR 71923.

THOMAS, EUNICE S.
Transportation officer, sorority leader. **CAREER:** Affiliated with US Dept of Transportation, Washington, DC. **ORGANIZATIONS:** Grand Basileus, Zeta Phi Beta Sorority Inc, Howard Univ, Washington DC. **BUSINESS ADDRESS:** US Department of Transportation, 201 Eye St SW, No 603, Washington, DC 20024. *

THOMAS, FRANCENA B.
Educator, consultant. **PERSONAL:** Born Mar 23, 1936, Belle Glade, FL; daughter of Andrew Bruton and Lovella Bingham Bruton (deceased); married Joseph Thomas, Nov 02, 1962; children: Nifretta, Joseph Nicholas, Nigel Edward. **EDUCATION:** FL A&M, BS 1959; Univ Miami, MEd 1971. **CAREER:** Dept Program Devel, teacher special assignment 1970-71; Little Rivere Elem, inservice coord curriculum specialist 1971-73; Olinda Center, summer school coordinator 1972; WSVN Weekly TV Show, hostess of Perspectives; WNWS Radio, host of weekly 3 hr talk show; "Degrees of Blackness", prod dir & appeared (a show based on contributions of Black poets); Miami Times, columnist 1972-; FL Intl Univ, dir div of univ relations 1973-87; Pres, Achievers Success Seminars, 1988-present. **ORGANIZATIONS:** Mem Dade Co Comm Relations Bd, FL Reg Manpower Planning Bd, FL Equal Educ Oppor Adv Council, Inner City Educ Found; Natl Org of Women "Her Story";Delta Sigma Theta; TV appearances; reading program instructor; literary workshops women prisoners Dade Co Jail; writer essays Black Lit 1971; Dade Co Comm Relations Bd; mem NOW; co-chairperson Greater United Miami 1984; vice chairperson, Greater Miami United Jri Ethnic Bd, 1981-present. **HONORS/ACHIEVEMENTS:** Best Columnist Award NNPA 1976; Second Best Columnist Award NNPA 1979; 1980 Headliner Award Women in Communications; 1982 Sara Weintraub Award of Excellence; Outstanding Journalist Concerned Black Women's Communications Award; Delta Sigma Theta Sorority Gold Key Award Intercollegiate Forensic Conf; Delta Sigma Theta Distinguished Minerva Award; Apptd by Pres Carter to be mem of Fed Judicial Screening Comm for 5th Circuit; Sigma Tau Mu Award Excellence in Debate; certificates from various comm org & school; one of 13 Miami "Young Success Stories" Miami Phoenix Newspaper; lead role play "The Man Nobody Saw"; also acted in several plays; Several others. **BUSINESS ADDRESS:** Special Projects Administrator, Metro-Dade Police Dept, 1320 NW 14th St, Suite 319A, Miami, FL 33125.

THOMAS, FRANKLIN A.
Attorney. **PERSONAL:** Born May 27, 1934, Brooklyn, NY; children: Keith, Hillary, Kerrie, Kyle. **EDUCATION:** Columbia Coll, BA 1956; Columbia Law School, LLB 1963. **CAREER:** So Dist of NY, asst us atty 1964-65; New York City Police Dept, dep police commissioner in charge of legal matters 1965-67; Bedford-Stuyvesant Restoration, pres, ceo 1967-77; Private Practice, atty 1977-79; The Ford Found, pres 1979-. **ORGANIZATIONS:** Dir Aluminum Co of Amer, CBS Inc, Cummins Engine Co Inc, Citicorp/Citibank NA; trustee The Ford Found; mem Sec of State's Adv Comm on South Africa 1985-87; bd of dirs, AT&T 1988-. **HONORS/ACHIEVEMENTS:** Hon LLD Yale Univ 1970, Fordham Univ 1972, Pratt Inst 1974, Pace Univ 1977, Columbia Univ 1979; Awd for Contribution to the Betterment of Urban Life Lyndon B Johnson Found 1974; Medal of Excellence Columbia Univ 1976; Alexander Hamilton Awd Columbia Coll 1983. **MILITARY SERVICE:** USAF SAC capt, navigator 1956-60. **BUSINESS ADDRESS:** President, The Ford Foundation, 320 East 43rd St, New York, NY 10017.

THOMAS, FRANKLIN WHITAKER
Personnel administrator, government official. **PERSONAL:** Born Nov 20, 1925, Winston-Salem, NC; son of Rev George J Thomas and Winnie C Thomas; married Erma Jean Sampson; children: Donald, Ronald, Franklin, Jr, Jean-Agnes, Peter. **EDUCATION:** Talladega Coll (AL), BA 1946; Chicago Theological Seminary, 1947; George Williams Coll, MS 1950. **CAREER:** Butler St YMCA-Atlanta, prog dir 1950-53; Tulsa & Denver YMCA's, exec dir 1953-65; Butler St YMCA-Atlanta, gen exec 1965-69; City of Atlanta, dir of personnel 1971-74; Nat'l Brd of YMCA'S-NYC, dir of personnel serv 1969-71 & 1974-76; Metro Atlanta Rapid Transit Authority, dir of personnel 1976-77; deputy commissioner, GA State Merit System 1977-. **ORGANIZATIONS:** Field work supvr Atlanta Univ Schl of Soc Work 1951-53 & 1966-69; natl alumni pres Talladega Coll 1971-75; chmn bd of dir's Cncl for Lay Life & Work-UCC 1974-76; moderator SE Conf-Natl Brd of YMCA'S-NYUnited Church of Christ 1975-77; guest lecturer Harvard Schl of Bus, summer 1977; adjunct profsr GA Inst of Technology 1978-; mem gvnrg brd Natl Cncl of Churches 1979-82; cnsultnt-trner Indstrl Mgmnt Inter 1979-; bd mem, United Church Bd for Homeland Ministries 1985-89; asst moderator, Central Cong'l UCC 1989-91; asst moderator, Gen Synod UCC 1989-91. **HONORS/ACHIEVEMENTS:** Dist serv awd Washington HS, Atlanta 1973; outstanding achvmnt award Omega Y's Men's Club, Atlanta 1983; Jazz Pianist, Organist, Dir of Male Choruses & Composer/Arranger. **BUSINESS ADDRESS:** Deputy Commissioner, State Merit System of GA, 200 Piedmont Ave SE, Atlanta, GA 30334.

THOMAS, GERALD EUSTIS
University lecturer. **PERSONAL:** Born Jun 23, 1929, Natick, MA; son of Walter W Thomas and Leila L (Jacobs) Thomas; married Rhoda Holmes Henderson, Oct 03, 1954; children: Dr Kenneth A, Steven E LLD, Lisa D Jacobs. **EDUCATION:** Harvard Univ, BA 1951; George Washington Univ, MS 1966; Yale Univ, PhD 1973. **CAREER:** US Navy, commanding officer USS Impervious, 1962-63; College Training Programs Bureau of Naval Personnel, head, 1963-65; US Navy, commanding officer USS Bausell, 1966-68; Prairie View A&M Coll Naval ROTC Unit, prof of naval science & commanding officer, 1968-70; US Navy, commander Destroyer Squadron Five, 1973-75, admiral, 1974-75; US Dept of Defense, acting deputy asst sec of defense for intl security affairs & dir of Near East, South Asia, & Africa Region, 1976-78, sr rear admiral US Pacific Fleet, 1978-81, retired, 1981; State Dept, US ambassador to Guyana 1981-83, US ambassador to Kenya 1983-86; Yale Univ, lecturer, currently. **ORGANIZATIONS:** Overseer, Bd of Overseers, Harvard Univ, 1981-88; bd of trustees, Univ of San Diego, 1981-86; life mem, Org of Amer Historians. **MILITARY SERVICE:** US Navy, rear admiral, 1951-81. **HOME ADDRESS:** 1980 Durham Rd, Guilford, CT 06437.

THOMAS, GLORIA V.
Educator. **PERSONAL:** Born Mar 23, Brenham, TX; divorced; children: Dino, Paul, Edwin. **EDUCATION:** Btx Southern U, BS 1953; TX Southern U, MS 1965; TX Southern U, Adm Cert 1968; Sorbonne, France, Cert in French; BaylorUniv & Univ So MS, Cert. **CAREER:** Phillis Wheatley HS Houston Indep School Dist, rgstr; Phyllis Wheatley Sr HS, chem teacher 1959-72. **ORGANIZATIONS:** Basileus Gamma Omega Zeta Zeta Phi Beta Sor 1971-72; mem Civil Rights Commn 1973-; ofcr Houston Tchrs Assn 1971-72; United Fund Budget Panel 1973-; Human Rel Commn & Sexism Commn Huston Ind Sch Dist; mem Houston Tchrs Assn; TX Statetchrs Assn; TX Clsrm Tchrs Assn; NEA; Nat'l Sci Tchrs Assn;MacGregor Park Civic Club; E Bethel Bapt Ch; TX Atomic Energy Commn; Black Caucus NEA; mem aux Big Bros of Houston 1965-; vol Multi Schlerosis 1972; sickle cell ane-

mia 1973-74; cancer fund 1970-74. **HONORS/ACHIEVEMENTS:** Scholarship Sorbonne 1954-56; res particip grant 1961; TX AECUniv TX; Dr IGE Outcomes Achvmnt 1974; outstanding ldrshp Award Zeta Phi Beta Sor 1971; 15 awards NSF 1961-74; Nat'l Educ Award 1968. **BUSINESS ADDRESS:** Income Tax Consultant, 4900 Market, Houston, TX 77020.

THOMAS, HARRY LEE
Physician. **PERSONAL:** Born Apr 05, 1919, Richmond, VA; married Betty; children: Harriet, Harry. **EDUCATION:** Lincoln Univ, AB 1939; Howard Univ, MD 1946. **CAREER:** Howard Univ, intern 1946-47, surg res 1947-52, instr 1952-53; USAF Hosp, chief surg 1953-56; VA Outpatient Facility, consult 1956-60; Mercy Douglass Hosp,sr attending surgeon; Med Coll of PA, clinical prof surgery. **ORGANIZATIONS:** Dir Cancer Detection Proj Mercy Douglass Hosp 1958-63; bd dir Amer Cancer Soc 1977. **MILITARY SERVICE:** USAF capt 1953-56. **BUSINESS ADDRESS:** Clinical Assoc Prof, Surgery, Med Coll of PA, 5555 Wissahickon Ave, Philadelphia, PA 19144.

THOMAS, HENRY H.
Business consultant. **PERSONAL:** Born Sep 13, 1946, Columbus, GA; married Hazel. **EDUCATION:** BS (marketing) 1973. **CAREER:** Min Asstnc Corpd exec dir 1975-; advert the columbus times, dir 1968-75; mrktg & mgmt meadows bus coll, instr 1974; gen elec credit Corp, asst supvr 1964-66. **ORGANIZATIONS:** Mem Columbus Jaycees; Delta Sigma Pi; Am Mrktg Assn; Alpha Phi Alpha; Fed Exec Assn; Columbus Civil Def Adv Bd. **HONORS/ACHIEVEMENTS:** Outst young men of Am US Jaycees 1977; Who's Who Among Black Am 1974-75; cert of Apprec Miss GA Pageant 1975. **MILITARY SERVICE:** AUS e-5 1966-68. **BUSINESS ADDRESS:** Ste 27 Cross Country Plaza, Columbus, GA 31907.

THOMAS, HERMAN EDWARD
Educator. **PERSONAL:** Born Dec 12, 1941, Bryson City, NC; married Mary Knox Thomas; children: Terence, Maurice, Katrina. **EDUCATION:** Hartford Sem Fdn, PhD 1978; Duke Univ Divinity Schl, ThM (honors) 1969; Duke Univ Divinity Schl, BD 1966; NCA&T State Univ, BS (cum laude)1963. **CAREER:** Berkley HS, Aberdeen, NC, HS teacher 1966-67; Student Affrs, Morris Coll, Sumter, SC, 1968-69; Religion & Phil, Springfield Col, Sprg, MA, instr 1969-74; Black Studies, Springfield Coll, Sprg, MA, coord 1971-74; Rel Stud, asst prof 1974-; AAA Studies UNCC, asst dir 1974-. **ORGANIZATIONS:** Mem Am Acdmy of Religion 1973-; chair steer commit NC Cncl of Black studies 1975-76; assoc Mnstr First Baptist Church-West 1975-; fdng mem Natl Cncl for Black Studies 1975-; chrmn brd of dir Afro-Amer Cultural Cntr 1979-84; mem Soc for the Study of Black Rel 1980-; brd mem Charl-Merk Arts & Science Cncl 1984-. **HONORS/ACHIEVEMENTS:** Mary Reynolds Babcock Schlrshp Duke Divinity Schl 1963-66; coord-Humanist Afro-Am Hist Project in Charlotte, NC Humanities Comm 1983-83; "Religion & Slavery in JWC Pennington Jrnl of ITC 1979; Author, Biographies (5) Encylopedia of Pel in the South 1984. **HOME ADDRESS:** 5913 Craftsbury Dr, Charlotte, NC 28215. **BUSINESS ADDRESS:** Asst Prof, Religious Studies, UNCC, 127 Garinger Bldg, UNCC Station, Charlotte, NC 28223.

THOMAS, ISAAC DANIEL, JR.
Business executive. **PERSONAL:** Born Jan 31, 1939, Birmingham, AL; married Mary E Ellison; children: Peter Neil, Isaac Daniel III. **EDUCATION:** Eastern MI Univ, attended; Wayne State Univ, BA 1960; LA City Coll, attended 1966; Pasadena City Coll, attended 1968. **CAREER:** Wayne Cty Boys Detention Home, boys group leader 1 1960; Allstate Ins Co, casualty claims suprv 1966, div personnel mgr 1969, western zone human resources mgr 1971, urban affairs dir 1976, asst vice pres employee relations. **ORGANIZATIONS:** Bd mem Oper Snowball Mental Health Assoc of Greater Chicago; bd of dir So Christian Leadership Council, DuSable Mus Chicago, SAFER Found Chicago; memKappa Alpha Psi. **HONORS/ACHIEVEMENTS:** Motivator of Youth Awd, YMCA of Met Chicago Black & Hispanic Achievers of Indust Recognition 1978. **MILITARY SERVICE:** AUS sp 4 1960-62. **BUSINESS ADDRESS:** Assistant Vice Pres Employee Rel, Allstate Insurance Co, Allstate Plaza, Northbrook, IL 60062.

THOMAS, ISIAH LORD
Professional athlete. **PERSONAL:** Born Apr 30, 1961, Chicago, IL. **EDUCATION:** IN Univ, attended. **CAREER:** Detroit Pistons NBA, basketball player 1981-. **HONORS/ACHIEVEMENTS:** Player NBA All-Star Game 1982-86; Most Valuable Player 1984,86. **BUSINESS ADDRESS:** Basketball Player, Detroit Pistons, 1200 Featherstone Rd, Pontiac, MI 48057.

THOMAS, JACQUELINE MARIE
Journalist. **PERSONAL:** Born Aug 31, 1952, Nashville, TN; daughter of John J. Thomas, Jr. and Dorothy Phillips Thomas. **EDUCATION:** Briarcliff Coll, AA 1970, BA (Cum Laude) 1972; Columbia Univ Sch of Intl Affairs, MA 1974. **CAREER:** Chicago Sun Times, reporter 1974-85; Courier Journal & Louisville Times, assoc editor 1985-86; Detroit Free Press, assoc editor. **ORGANIZATIONS:** Mem Natl Assoc of Black Journalists; mem American Society of Newspaper Editors; mem Natl Conf of Editorial Writers. **HONORS/ACHIEVEMENTS:** Nieman Fellow Harvard Univ 1983-84. **BUSINESS ADDRESS:** Associate Editor, Detroit Free Press, 321 W Lafayette, Detroit, MI 48231.

THOMAS, JAMES O., JR.
Government official. **PERSONAL:** Born Feb 12, 1930, Screven Co, GA; married Jacqueline Sewand; children: Toniae, James O III. **EDUCATION:** Savannah State Coll, BS Chemistry 1956; George Washington Law, 1957. **CAREER:** US Patent Office, primary examiner 1967; US Patent Office, supvr patent exr 1975; US Patent Office, group direction 1979. **ORGANIZATIONS:** Pres Assoc Investors Inc 1957; pres Savannah State Coll Alumni 1973; pres Far NE-SE Cncl 1974; chrmn brd Capitol View Development, Inc 1978; vice pres HELP, Inc 1981; chrmn Savannah State Fdn 1983; pres 3847 Corp Inc 1984. **HONORS/ACHIEVEMENTS:** President's Club Savannah State Coll 1973-81; Cynus Wiley Savannah State Coll 1979; NAFEO Distinguished Alumni Savannah State Coll 1981; Alumnus Of Year Savannah State Coll 1982; Gold Medal US Patent Off 1983; Medallion of Excellence Savannah Stte Coll 1986; EEO Supervisory Achievement Awd Patent and Trademark Office 1986. **MILITARY SERVICE:** AUS sgt, Korean Medal, Good Conduct, Defense Medal etc 1951. **HOME ADDRESS:** 4339 H St SE, Washington, DC 20019. **BUSINESS ADDRESS:** Director, Examining Group 150, US Patent Office, Commissioner of Patents, Washington, DC 20031.

THOMAS, JAMES SAMUEL
Clergyman. **PERSONAL:** Born Apr 08, 1919, Orangeburg, SC; married Ruth Naomi Wilson; children: Claudie Williamson, Gloria Jean, Margaret Yvonne, Patricia Elaine. **EDUCATION:** Clafin Coll Orangeburg, AB 1939; DD 1953; Gammon Theol Sem Atlanta, BD 1943; Drew U, MA 1944; Cornell U, PhD 1953; Bethune-Cookman Coll, LLD 1963; Simpson Coll, 1965; Morningside Coll, 1966; IA Wesleyan Coll Coe Coll, 1968; Cornell Coll, LHD 1965; OH Weslyan U, 1967. **CAREER:** Meth Ch, ordained to ministry 1942; Orangeburg Circuit, pastor 1942-43; York, SC, 1946-47; SC State Coll, chaplain 1944-46; Gammon Theol Sem, prof 1947-53; Meth Bd Edn, asso dir 1953-64; IA Area Meth Ch, bishop 1964-; Meth Bd Edn, chmn dept educ insts; Meth Commn Christian Vocations, vice-chmn; Negro Colls Danforth Found, consult 1957-60; Perkins Sch Theol So Meth U, vis prof 1958. **ORGANIZATIONS:** Tst Vbennett Simpson Claflin Clark Morningside Colls Gammon Theol Sem; mem Kappa Delta Pi; Phi Delta Kappa; Phi Kappa Phi. **BUSINESS ADDRESS:** 1019 Chestnut St, Des Moines, IA 50309.

THOMAS, JANICE MORRELL
Educator. **PERSONAL:** Born Oct 06, 1946, Elizabeth, NJ; married Aaron D. **EDUCATION:** Rutgers U, AB 1968, EdM 1975. **CAREER:** Rutgers Univ, sr admiss officer Newark Campus 1985, acting dir of admiss 1972-73, assoc dir of admiss 1971-72, asst dir of admiss 1970-71, Asst to dir of admiss 1969-70. **ORGANIZATIONS:** Mem Am Assn of Collegiate Registrars & Admiss Ofcrs; Middle Sts Assn of Collegiate Registrars & Admiss Ofcrs; Nat Assn of Coll Admiss Cnslrs; AmColl Prsnl Assn; Assn of Non-White Cncrns; RutgersUniv Black Org of Fclty; mem NJ Unit of Nat Assn of Negro Bus & Pro Wmns Clubs Inc; NAACP; UrbLeag Union Co; NJ Assn of Coll Admiss Cnslrs; NJ Assn of Black & Puerto Rican Admiss Cnslrs; Am Prsnl & Guidance Assn. **BUSINESS ADDRESS:** Rutgers StateUniv of NJ, Newark Campus, 249 University Ave, Newark, NJ 07102.

THOMAS, JANIS P.
Advertising executive. **PERSONAL:** Born Nov 23, 1954, Frankfurt, Federal Republic of Germany;married Edmond A Tapscott III. **EDUCATION:** Tufts Univ, BA English, BA French 1976; Howard Univ, MA Mass Commns 1978. **CAREER:** NBC/WRC-TV Washington DC, sales rsch coord 1980-82; Black Entertainment Television, dir of adv 1982-83, vice pres advertising 1983-. **BUSINESS ADDRESS:** Vice President Advertising, Black Entertainment TV, 1232 31st St NW, Washington, DC 20007.

THOMAS, JEWEL M.
Elected official, educator. **EDUCATION:** Miles Coll, BA 1960; Univ of AL, EdS 1976; CP Univ, EdD 1984. **CAREER:** Lawson State Comm Coll, grad adv, sophomore class adv 1980-; Kappa Delta Epsilon, pres 1981-84; Twentieth Century Club, pres 1982; Lawson Comm Coll, prof; City of Brighton, mayor. **ORGANIZATIONS:** Lecturer Natl Baptist Conv USA 1980; speaker AL Women's Natl Conv 1980; lecturer AL Jr Coll Assn 1980; pres AL Ed Assn 1984; 1st Lady Mayor of Brighton City of Brighton 1984. **HONORS/ACHIEVEMENTS:** Soror of the Year Alpha Kappa Alpha 1980; The Writing Lab Dir AL Jr Coll Jrnl 1982; Outstanding Ed UAB School of Ed 1984; KDE Pres Awd Univ Coll 1984. **HOME ADDRESS:** 4900 Letson St, Brighton, AL 35020. **BUSINESS ADDRESS:** Mayor, City of Brighton, 3700 Main St, Brighton, AL 35020.

THOMAS, JIM EUGENE
Professional athlete. **PERSONAL:** Born Oct 19, 1960, Ft Lauderdale, FL. **EDUCATION:** Indiana, 1983. **CAREER:** Indiana Pacers, guard 1983-. **ORGANIZATIONS:** Intern Marion Cnty Prosecutors Ofc; selected by Green Bay Packers of NFL & the Boston Breakers of USFL following career at IU. **HONORS/ACHIEVEMENTS:** Honorable ment All-Big Ten selection 1982-83; mem US World Chmpnshps Team; All-Final Four team; two year All-State selection in bsktbl. **BUSINESS ADDRESS:** Indiana Pacers, 300 E Market St Market Sq Arena, Indianapolis, IN 46204.

THOMAS, JOAN MCHENRY BATES
Elected official, business executive. **PERSONAL:** Born Jun 26, 1928, Atlanta, GA; daughter of Henry McHenry and Pearl McHenry; married Lee E Thomas (deceased); children: Edwin T Bates, Judith Z Stratton. **EDUCATION:** Dept US Ag, 1960; Temple Business School, 1963. **CAREER:** Catering Business, pres; Dept Human Resources, social worker retired after 31 yrs. **ORGANIZATIONS:** Chairperson US Military Widow 1980; pres Amer War Mothers 1984-87; chair person Adv Neighborhood Comm 1984; vice pres, treasurer Ward 4 Democrats; North West Boundary Civic Association, 1980-; District of Columbia Democratic Committee 1988-92. **HONORS/ACHIEVEMENTS:** Cert of Apprec from President Ronald Reagan 1980; Cert of Apprec from Mayor Marion Barry 1984; Outstanding Volunteer from American Red Cross 1974; Outstanding Community Volunteer 1984; Community Award, Rock Creek Church 1988. **HOME ADDRESS:** 715 Varnum St NW, Washington, DC 20011. **BUSINESS ADDRESS:** Advisory Neighborhood Commnr, 717 Kennedy St NW, Washington, DC 20011.

THOMAS, JOHN
Athlete. **PERSONAL:** Born Mar 03, 1941, Boston, MA. **EDUCATION:** Boston Univ, BS Phys & Psych Rehab 1963; Boston Conserv of Music, Ballet 1962-64; Boston School of Bus, Acctg 1969; Amer Red Cross, Basic Life Support Course in CPR. **CAREER:** Neighborhood Youth Corps, vocational counselor 1 1/2 yrs; Hawthorne House Neighborhood Ctr, dir 2 yrs; City of Boston, probation officer Roxbury Court 7 yrs; WCVB-TV Channel 5, acct exec 5 yrs; General Motors Truck Div, acct exec 3 yrs; New England Telephone, acct exec 3 yrs; AT&T Commun, acct exec 1 yr; Boston Univ, track coach part time 15 yrs. **ORGANIZATIONS:** Jr usher, bd Ebanzer Baptist Church; mem Cub Scouts, Boy Scouts, Eagle Rank, Silver Palms, Explorer Scouts-Apprentice Rank; chmn Explorer; bd mem Boys Clubs of Boston, Cooper Comm Ctr; bd mem Cambridge YMCA; mem Gov Council on Phys Fitness; mem pres Council on Physical Fitness; mem US Olympic Comm Spirit Team; intl dir Athlets United for Peace. **HONORS/ACHIEVEMENTS:** HS Capt Tennis Team, Capt Track Team, State Champ High Jump, State Champ Hurdles; Natl Champ High Jump; Natl & World Interscholastic Record Holder High Jump; New England Champ High Jump; New England Champ High Hurdles; All Amer Sr Yr High Jump US Natl Team High Jump; Boston Univ, 1st man to jump 7' indoors, Capt Track Team, Former School Record Holder Hurdles, Record Holder High Jump 7'3 3/4", IC4A Champ & Record Holder Indoors & Outdoors, NCAA, NAAU Champ & Record Holder High Jump Indoors & Outdoors, Former World Record Holder Running, High Jump Broken 13 Times 7'4", Bronze Medalist Rome Olympics, Co-Olympic Champ Tokyo Olumpics, Silver Medalist; Hall of Fame Inductee

Helms Found, Boston Univ, US Track & Field. **HOME ADDRESS:** Box 292, Roxbury Crossing, MA 02120.

THOMAS, JOHN
Boxing referee. **PERSONAL:** Born Sep 21, 1922, Meridian, LA; married Kathryn; children: Diane. **CAREER:** Open novice amateur champion 1938; AAU Feather Champ 1939; Pacific Coast Golden Gloves 1940; CA Lightweight Prof Champ 1943-47; CA Athletic Comm, boxing ref; Four Roses Distillers Co, sales suprv; Athletic Comm, 2nd black referee; Four Roses Co House Seagrams, public relations. **MILITARY SERVICE:** AUS pvt 1945. **BUSINESS ADDRESS:** Public Relations, Four Roses Co, 340 N Madison Ave, Los Angeles, CA 90004.

THOMAS, JOHN HENDERSON, III
Psychologist. **PERSONAL:** Born Sep 07, 1950, Washington, DC. **EDUCATION:** Univ of Detroit, AB 1972; Univ of Cincinnati, MA 1976, DEd 1982. **CAREER:** Mott Adults HS, consult 1972; Univ of Cincinnati, minority gp counseling ctr 1973; Mott Adult HS, instr psych, soc, engl 1973; Univ of Cincinnati Consult Svc, psychologist 1975; Univ of Cincinnati Walk-In-Clinic, psych; Ctr Devel Disorders, psych 1976; Ct Domestic Rel Ct Common Prac, psych 1976, cntrl clinic 1976; Inst of Psych Univ of Cincinnati, psych; Sonlight Lectures Inc, founder, pres. **ORGANIZATIONS:** Mem Urban League, NAACP, Black Student; grad student Psych Assoc, Kappa Alpha Psi. **HONORS/ACHIEVEMENTS:** Vocational Rehab Scholarship 1968-72; Avhievement Ed Awd Urban League 1968; Scholarship Grad Studies Univ of Cincinnati 1073-76; Miss Black Amer Leadership Awd 1973. **BUSINESS ADDRESS:** President, Sonlight Liectures Inc, PO Box 29842, Cincinnati, OH 45229.

THOMAS, JOHN HENRY
Corrections professional. **PERSONAL:** Born Apr 26, 1955, Salina, KS. **EDUCATION:** Bethany Coll, B Psych & Soc 1977. **CAREER:** KS Dept of Corrections, correctional officer 1977, correctional counselor 1977-78, 1984-87, psychologist 1978-84; Kansas Parole Bd, mem 1984-. **ORGANIZATIONS:** Mem Amer & Kansas Correctional Assocs, Amer Assoc of Paroling Authorities Intl, Natl Assoc of Blacks in Crim Justice, Big Brothers/Big Sisters, Amer Probation & Parole Assoc Inc, KS Council on Crime & Delinquency, Natl Rainbow Coalition. **BUSINESS ADDRESS:** Board Member, Kansas Parole Bd, 900 Jackson, Topeka, KS 66612.

THOMAS, JOHN WESLEY
Psychiatrist. **PERSONAL:** Born Feb 13, 1932, Birmingham, AL; son of Leila M. Hatcher; divorced; children: Courtland W, Stephen M. **EDUCATION:** TN State Univ, BA 1953; TN State U, Who's Who Among Stdnts 1953; Meharry Medical Coll, MD 1959; Rollman Inst of Psychiatry, Cincinnati, OH, Psychiatric Residency 1960-61; Western Psychiatric Inst Pgh, PA, Psychiatric Residency 1961-63. **CAREER:** Gen Psychiatry, Pittsburgh, PA, priv pract 1963-; various hosp & ints in Pgh Area, psychiatric cnsltnt & staff 1963-; Univ of Pittsburgh, Schl of Med, clinical instr in Psychiatry 1963-. **ORGANIZATIONS:** Brd of dir Amer Group Psychotherapy Assoc 1980-83; Natl Mdl Assn, Amer Group Psychotherapy Assn, Amer Psychiat Assn, Soc Keystone State Med Soc, PA Grp Psychotherapy Soc, Tri-State Grp Psychotherapy Soc, Pittsburgh Psychiatric Soc, Omicron Lambda Chapter, Alpha Phi Alpha, Pi Chapter, Chi Delta Mu. **HONORS/ACHIEVEMENTS:** George W Carver Award Natl Achvmnt Club, Inc 1980; fellow Amer Group Psychotherapy Assn 1985. **BUSINESS ADDRESS:** Psychiatrist, 3708 5th Ave, Pittsburgh, PA 15213.

THOMAS, JOHNNY B.
Elected official. **PERSONAL:** Born Nov 30, 1953, Glendora, MS; married Ella Rean Johnson; children: Leslie. **EDUCATION:** MS Valley State Univ, 1977,78. **CAREER:** Tallahatchie Cty, constable 1976-80; Town of Glendora, alderman 1981-82, mayor 1982-. **ORGANIZATIONS:** Chmn Anti Crime Commiss 1976-80, Voters League 1978-81; mem Criminal Justice Planning Commiss 1980-85, NAACP. **HONORS/ACHIEVEMENTS:** Mem Kirskey Foundation for Equity & Justice. **BUSINESS ADDRESS:** Mayor, Town of Glendora, PO Box 90, Glendora, MS 38928.

THOMAS, JOSEPH H.
Attorney. **PERSONAL:** Born May 16, 1933, Baltimore, MD; son of Dr & Mrs Joseph H Thomas; married Lois A Young MD (deceased) (deceased); children: Nina, Donna, Beth, Laura, Joseph III, Gordon. **EDUCATION:** Brown Univ, BA 1954; Univ of MD School of Law, LLB 1964. **CAREER:** Securities Inc, pres 1959-65; self employed attorney 1964-; Thomas & Welcome, 1988-. **ORGANIZATIONS:** Pres, Baltimore Alumni Kappa Alpha Psi 1964-65; pres Provident Hospital Found 1981-; pres Lafayette Square Comm Center 1982-84; Thomas letter 1983-. **MILITARY SERVICE:** USMCR capt 1954-58. **BUSINESS ADDRESS:** Attorney, 111 S Calvert St #1540, Baltimore, MD 21202.

THOMAS, JOSEPH W.
Attorney. **PERSONAL:** Born Aug 02, 1940, New Orleans, LA; son of Gerald H Thomas and Edith Winand Thomas; married Shawn Watkins; children: Jeffery, Anthony, Aisha, Adelle, Anne. **EDUCATION:** Loyola Univ of Chicago, BS; 1967; Loyola of New Orleans, JD 1973; Tulane Univ, MBA 1984. **CAREER:** New Orleans Legal Asst, staff attorney 1973; LA Dept of Justice, asst atty gen 1974-80; Law Office of Joseph O Thomas 1980-. **ORGANIZATIONS:** Mem Louis-Martinet Legal Soc; bd mem New Orleans Legal Asst Corp; mem DC Bar Assn; partner in firm Thomas & Davis; mem Amer, Louisiana Bar Assns; mem NAACP. **BUSINESS ADDRESS:** Law Offices of Joseph W Thomas, World Trade Center, 2 Canal Street, Suite 1905, New Orleans, LA 70130.

THOMAS, JOYCE CAROL
Author. **PERSONAL:** Born May 25, 1938, Ponca City, OK; daughter of Floyd Haynes and Leona Thompson; children: Monica Pecot, Gregory, Michael, Roy. **EDUCATION:** Stanford Univ, MA 1967; San Jose State Univ, BA (with honors) 1966. **CAREER:** Author of fiction books in the series about Abyssinia Jackson and her people, full-time writer 1981-84; Purdue Univ, visting professor of English 1984; author of fiction titles Marked by Fire, Avon 1982, Bright Shadow, Avon 1983, Water Girl Avon, 1986, The Golden Pasture, Scholastic, 1986, Journey, Scholastic, 1988. **HONORS/ACHIEVEMENTS:** Best Book, Young Adult Serv, Amer Library Assoc 1982; New York Times Outstanding Book of the Year 1983; The Amer Book Award (formerly Natl Book Award) NY 1983; awrd winning novels, Marked by Fire, Abon Books, NY, NY 1982, Bright Shadow, Avon Books, NY, NY 1983; Outstanding Woman of the Twentiteth Century Sigma Gamma Rho 1986. **BUSINESS ADDRESS:** Author, Mitch Douglas Intl Creat Mgmt, 40 West 57th Street, New York, NY 10019.

THOMAS, JUANITA WARE (JUANITA GLEE WARE)
Educator. **PERSONAL:** Born Oct 30, 1923, Little Rock, AR; married Morris E Thomas, Sr; children: Roumania T Wiggins, Morris, Jr, Veronica T Gray, Etelka, Pearl Thomas. **EDUCATION:** Philadners Smith & Dunbar Jr Coll, AA (elem ed) 1944; DC Tchrs Coll 1970; Howard Univ, 1974; N VA Comm Coll, 1984. **CAREER:** George W Carver Elementary School (No LR), elementary teacher 1944; War Dept (DC), typist 1945; Hibbler & Hibbler Attys at Law, law firm secy, notary 1946; US Navy Dept, congressional typist 1948; US Navy Dept, examiner 1949-51. **ORGANIZATIONS:** Elem sec Nalle Elem Schl (DC) 1956-63; elem sub tchr DC Public Schls 1963-; elem tchr Patterson Sch Admidon Schl 1974, 1980-81; tchr Headstart Pre-School-UPO 1982-; sec SE Civic Assoc 1963-65; chrmn SECA Beautification Progm 1965-68; pres PTA Buchanan Elem Sch 1957-65; advsry comm Adv Neghbrhd Comm 1975-85; prlmntrn W&V Womens Clubs-Natl Assoc C W Clubs 1985. **HONORS/ACHIEVEMENTS:** "Grass Roots Honoree" SE Civic Assocn 1965; "Woman of the Year" NE Federation Womens Clubs 1976; "Advisory Neighborhoods Comm Outstanding Serv" 1981-84; celebrating 10 yrs "Home Rule in DC" Since 1975; ANCS 1985. **HOME ADDRESS:** 1528 E St SE, Washington, DC 20003. **BUSINESS ADDRESS:** Teacher, United Planning Organization, 1288 Upshur St NW, Washington, DC 20011.

THOMAS, LATTA R., SR.
Educator, clergyman. **PERSONAL:** Born Oct 12, 1927, Union, SC; married Bessie Lowery; children: Latta, Jr, Ronald. **EDUCATION:** Friendship Jr Coll, AA 1949; Benedict Coll, AB 1951; Colgate Rochester Div Sch, BD 1955; STM 1966; Andover Newton Sem, DMin 1973. **CAREER:** Second Calvary Bapt Ch Columbia SC, pastor 1975-; acting dean stud affairs 1974-75; Benedict Coll Columbia SC, chaplain prof 1965-; Mt Olive Bapt Ch Newport, RI, pastor 1963-65; Monumental Bapt Ch Elmira NY, pastor 1952-63. **ORGANIZATIONS:** Mem SC Acad of Religion; SC Educ Assc; Natl Educ Assc; NAACP; Natl Assc of Univ & Clge Chaplains; Amer Assc of Univ Professors; Kappa Alpha Psi; pres Elmira Br NAACP 1957-62; faculty rep bd of trustees Benedict Coll 1973-75; mem bd trustees Babcock Ctr 1974-76; mem exec bd Friendship Ctr 1978-82; mem Richland-lexington Council on Aging 1980-84; mem Clinical Pastoral Educ Adv Cncl 1984-, Kiwanis, Greater Columbia Baptist Chamber of Ministers, Progressive Natl Baptist Convention, SC Democratic Party. **HONORS/ACHIEVEMENTS:** Cited for civic serv by Elmira Civic Improvement Club 1960; Elmira Neighborhood House 1961; Elmira Br NAACP 1972; listed in Comm Leaders & Noteworthy Amer 1973-74; Who's Who in Religion 1975-76; Directory of Amer Scholars 1978; Personalities of the South 1979; publication "Biblical Faith and The Black American," Judson Press 1976. **BUSINESS ADDRESS:** Chairman Division Humanities, Benedict College, Harden & Blanding Sts, Columbia, SC 29204.

THOMAS, LEROY, SR.
Business executive. **PERSONAL:** Born Dec 16, 1923, Evergreen, AL; married Minerva Washington. **EDUCATION:** Omaha Univ, BA 1951; Univ of NE; Tulsa Univ. **CAREER:** Amer State Bank, executive officer. **BUSINESS ADDRESS:** Executive Officer, American State Bank, 3816 North Peoria St, Tulsa, OK 74106.

THOMAS, LILLIE (MICKEY)
Special procedure radiology technologist. **PERSONAL:** Born Oct 20, 1950, St Louis, MO. **EDUCATION:** Forest Park Comm Coll, AAS 1970. **CAREER:** Peralta Hosp, spec procedure tech 1975-79; MO Baptist Hospital, rad tech 1970-74, spec procedure tech 1979-. **ORGANIZATIONS:** Mem Amer Registry Radiological Tech 1970-, Amer Soc Radiological Tech 1970-; mem Bd of Christian Educ 1982-; asst financial sec bd of trustees 1986-, youth dir New Sunny Mount Bapt Ch 1986-. **HOME ADDRESS:** 22 St Gabriel Ct, St Louis, MO 63114.

THOMAS, LLOYD A.
Pediatrician & educator. **PERSONAL:** Born Nov 03, 1922, New York, NY; son of Lionel Thomas and Ethel Thomas; married Mary Elaine Haley; children: Fern Leigh, Guy Roger, Tobi Thomas Nava. **EDUCATION:** City Coll of NY, BS 1943; Howard Univ Med Schl, MD 1946. **CAREER:** State Univ of NY, clinical asst 1955-; Downstate Medcl Cntr, clinical assistant professor of pediatrics 1955-; private practice, physician. **ORGANIZATIONS:** Consltnt Head Start 1960-65; pres Ped Sec Med Soc of Mc County of Kings 1974-75; aux brd Brooklyn Urban League 1954-57; brd chrmn W Hardgnow Mental Health Clinic 1960-70; brd Bedford Stuyvesant Comm MH Ctr. **HONORS/ACHIEVEMENTS:** KAPPA PI Hon Soc Howard Univ Med Schl 1945; Black Brooklynite The New Muse 1978. **MILITARY SERVICE:** AUS capt med corps 2 yrs; chief of Pec Camp Stoneman, CA 1951-53. **BUSINESS ADDRESS:** Physician, 825 Lincoln Pl, Brooklyn, NY 11216.

THOMAS, LOUPHENIA
Business exec. & educator. **PERSONAL:** Born Jan 19, 1918, Coaso Co, AL; widowed; children: Dr Juanita Q Whatley (dec). **EDUCATION:** Miles Coll Birmingham, AL, AB Soc Sci w/minor in Engl;Univ of AL in Birmingham, MA Voc Educ. **CAREER:** Beauty Salon & Restaurant, business owner 1950-76; Lawson Comm Coll, instructor 1970-80; LSCC, tech dir chairperson 1980-84 retired. **ORGANIZATIONS:** Mem Kappa Delta Pi; mem AL Educ Assn; mem Natl Educ Assn; mem Lawson State Educ Assn; mem AL Voc Assn; mem Bus & Prof Women Birmingham Chapt;mem Birmingham Urban League; mem NAACP; past coord Affairs of the AL Democratic Conf; pres emeritus Women Activities Comm of the Progressive Democratic Council of Jefferson Co; mem Amer Assoc of Univ Women; mem Nat'l Woman's Political Caucus. **HONORS/ACHIEVEMENTS:** Outstanding Achievement in Politics Omega Psi Phi Frat 1972; Woman of the Year Natl Bus & Prof Women 1973; Women of Distinction Iota Phi Lambda Sor 1976; Distinguished Serv Awd Delta Sigma Theta Sor 1976; Ms Democrat Loyalty & Dedication to the Democratic Party Jefferson Co Democratic Women Club 1976; Outstanding Achievement in Politics Awd Jefferson Co Progressive Democratic Council of Jefferson Co; Meritorious Serv Awd Metro Democratic Women's Club 1977; Hon Mem Gov's Staff State of AL 1976; Historic Achievement Awd in Recognition of Leadership & Representation of Black Women in Amer AL Black Mayors Conf 1978;first Black elected to the Natl Democratic Comm in the history of the Party from the State of AL; first Black Woman elected to the House of Representatives in the history of the State of AL Legislative Dist 39 Jefferson Co. **HOME ADDRESS:** 2736 Bush Blvd, Birmingham, AL 35208.

THOMAS, LUCIA THEODOSIA
Judge. **PERSONAL:** Born Mar 10, 1917, Cheyenne, WY. **EDUCATION:** Xavier Univ, BA 1936; Terrell Law Sch, LLB 1940; John Marshall Law Sch, LLM 1942, MPL 1943, JD 1970. **CAREER:** George A Parker, assoc atty 1940-41; Richard E Westbrooks, 1941-42; Prescott, Burroughs, Taylor & Corey, 1942-43; investigator atty 1943-47; Ben H Crockett, 1948-56; Soc Sec Admin, claims exam 1956-57; Cook Co, asst state's atty 1957-61,65-69; Juv Ct, asst to judge 1969-73; Appt Ct, law clerk 1973-74; City of Chicago, asst corp council 1974-77; Circuit Ct Cook County IL, judge 1977-87. **ORGANIZATIONS:** Mem, ABA, CBA, CCBA, FBA, WBAI, NBA, NAWL; IBA-FIDA; Cath Lawyers Guild; Amer Judicature Soc; life mem NAACP; Natl Bar Assc; Delta Sigma Thete Sor; mem Chicago Urban League; Field Mus; Art Inst of Chgo;DuSable Mus Beatrice Coffrey Yth Srv; King Comm Srv Ctr. **HONORS/ACHIEVEMENTS:** Richard Westbrooks Awd Cook Co Bar Assoc 1969; Silver Medal of Merit Natl Order of Knights & Ladies 1971; Merit Award Chicago Alumnae Chap Delta Sigma ThetaPres Citation Cook & City Bar Assc 1979; Extra Mile Award Delta Sigma Theta Sor 1980; Judicial Award We Can Found Inc 1980; John Marshall Alumni Awd 1982-84; Judicia Council Awd 1984; Gold Medal Knights & Ladies of Peter Claver 1984;Chicago Sr Citizens Hall of Fame; NBA Hall of Fame; Meritorious Serv Awd Knights & Ladies of Peter Claver; Meritorious Awd 4th Degree Odel Stadeker Chap KSPC Ladies Aux; Augustine Tolton Awd 1st Black Catholic Woman of the Year. **BUSINESS ADDRESS:** Judge, Circuit Court, Cook County, Daley Ctr Room 1407, Chicago, IL 60602.

THOMAS, LUCILLE COLE
Educational administration. **PERSONAL:** Born Oct 01, 1921, Dunn, NC; married George Browne (deceased); children: Ronald C, Beverly G Effatt. **EDUCATION:** Columbia Univ Schl of Lib Serv, MS 1957; NY Univ, MA 1955; Bennett Coll, BA 1941. **CAREER:** Bibb County Bd of Educ, teacher 1947-55; Brooklyn Public Library, librarian 1955-56; NY City Public School, librarian 1956-68; NY City Bd of Educ, supvr of Library 1968-77; NY City Bd of Educ, dir elementary school library 1978-83; Weston Woods Inst, consultant 1983-86; Graduate School of Library and Info Studies Queens Coll CUNY, prof 1987-. **ORGANIZATIONS:** Dir Amer Reading Cncl 1976-; mem NYS Regents Advsry Cncl on Lrng Technologies 1982-; exec brd Amer Libr Assn 1985- cncl amer lib assn 1980-; coordntr UNESCO/IASL Book Prog 1980-; pres NY (state) Libr Asssn 1977-78; pres NY Libr Club 1977-78; pres NY Black Librns Caucus 1974-75; pres Columbia Univ Schl of Libr Serv Alumni Assn 1980-81; sec Sch Libraries Sect of Intl Federation of Library Assoc 1985-; mem Schomburg Corp and Schomburg Commn for the Preservation of Black Culture; mem Centennial Comm for Columbia Univ Sch of Library Svcs. **HONORS/ACHIEVEMENTS:** Fndr Schl Libr Media Day in NY State 1974; fndr Annual City-Wide Storytelling Cont New York City Bd of Ed 1978; recp Medal of Excellence by NY State Brd of Regentss 1984; participant/cultural Exchg Prog (Guest of French Govt for 2 wks) 1982; Programs of Service Awd by Eta Omega Omega Chap Alpha Kappa AlphaSor. **HOME ADDRESS:** 1184 Union St, Brooklyn, NY 11225.

THOMAS, MABLE
State representative. **PERSONAL:** Born Nov 08, 1957, Atlanta, GA; daughter of Bernard Thomas and Madie Broughton Thomas. **EDUCATION:** GA State Univ, BS Public Admin 1982, working on Masters in Public Admin; Atlanta School of Real Estate, Atlanta GA, Salesperson License, 1987. **CAREER:** GA Dept of Natural Resources, personnel asst 1978-79; City of Atlanta Parks & Recreation, recreation super 1980-81; GA State Univ Educ Talent Srch, rsch asst 1981-82; City of Atlanta Comm Develop, worksite monitor 1983; Univ of Black Life & Culture Comm, chairperson GA State 1982-83; GA Gen Assembly, senate Intern 1984; Dist 31, state representative serves on house, educ, special judiciary & indust relations standing committees, served on State of GA housing needs study comm. **ORGANIZATIONS:** Vice pres GA State Univ Student Govt Assn 1983, 1984; consultant GA Democratic Party 1984; adv council Salvation Army Bellwood Boys & Girls Club 1984, 1985; bd of dirs GA Legislative Black Caucus 1985; membership chair Black Women's Health Project 1985; Hon mem chair NAACP Annual Membership Drive 1985; vol worker S Christian Leadership Conf 1981-; vol Martin Luther King Ctr for Nonviolent Social Change 1981-; vol United Way of Metro Atlanta 1982-; natl bd mem Natl Political Congr of Black Women 1985; bd mem West End Medical Ctr; bd of dirs Economic Opportunities Atlanta; bd mem, Georgia Housing Coalition, 1988-89. **HONORS/ACHIEVEMENTS:** GA State Univ Mortar Bd Leadership Awd 1982; Salvation Army Bellwood Girls Club Comm Serv Awd 1983; Outstanding Young Women of Amer 1983; GA State Univ Women of Excellence Awd 1983; Top Jesse Jackson Delegate to the Democratic Natl Convention 1984; City of Atlanta Cultural Affairs Bronze Jubilee Awd 1984; Royal Ark Worshipful Masters Legion of Honor Awd for Social Justice 1985; Ebony Magazine 30 Leaders of the Future 1985; Outstanding Serv Award Tony Garden Civic Assn 1985; NAACP Civic Award 1985; featured in Essence magazine August 1986 as Essence Women; Natl Assn of Black Social Workers Human Serv Awd 1986; Outstanding Freshman Legislator GA Legislative Black Caucus 1986; featured in December 1986 Washington Post "New Black Women-Mold Breakers in the Main Stream"; voted one of 20 Atlantans to Watch in 1987 by Atlanta Tribune newspaper; featured, Essence Magazine Profile, 1988; front page coverage Fast Forward Magazine, 1989; featured, India's national newspaper, India Times, 1988; Outstanding Georgia State University Alumni, GA State Univ, 1989. **BUSINESS ADDRESS:** Georgia State Representative, Georgia General Assembly, P O Box 573, Atlanta, GA 30301.

THOMAS, MARY A.
Nurse, educator. **PERSONAL:** Born Jul 22, 1933, Gary, IN. **EDUCATION:** Homer G Phillips Hosp Sch Nursing St Louis 1956; IN Univ, BS 1968; Valparaiso Univ, MLA Sociol; Univ IL Med Ctr, attd. **CAREER:** Cook Hospital Chicago, head nurse Obstetric 1957-63; Chicago Osteop Hospital Chicago, head nurse Med Unit 1963-64; Visiting Nurse Assoc E Chicago IN, staff nurse 1964-68; Gary IN, school nurse 1968-71; Gary Health Dept, asst dir nurses 1972-74; Gary Health Dept, dir nurses 1974-; Purdue Univ Calumet Hammond IN, asst prof nursing. **ORGANIZATIONS:** Consult Sr Cit Prog Gary IN 1972-; cnslr Sickle Anemia Proj 1975; schrlshp chmn Midtown Reg Nurses Club 1971-; alumni IN Univ & Valparaiso Univ; bd mem Fed Credit Union St Monica Ch 1973; parish council mem 1974. **BUSINESS ADDRESS:** Purdue Univ, 2233 171 St, Hammond, IN.

THOMAS, MAURICE MCKENZIE
Librarian. **PERSONAL:** Born May 01, 1943, St Croix, Virgin Islands of the United States;son of Maurice Thomas and Florence Bovell; married Monica Primas; children: Charles Randall, Onika Michelle. **EDUCATION:** Long Island Univ, BA History 1973; Atlanta Univ, 1982; Ball State Univ, MLS Libr & Info Sci 1983. **CAREER:** Abraham & Strauss NY, sales person 1969-73; Dept of Ed of The VI, social studies teacher 1973-82, librarian/information spec; coordinator of social studies Dept of Educ of the V.I. l987-. **ORGANIZATIONS:** Mem Courtyard Players Comm Theatre 1973-, Friends of Petersen Public Libr 1983-, School Libr Assoc 1983-, Amer Libr Assoc 1983-; bd mem Theatre DanceInc 1983-84; Phi Delta Kappa. **HONORS/ACHIEVEMENTS:** Libr Career Fellowship US Dept of Ed & Ball State 1982-83; Territorial Scholarship VI Govt 1982-83; joint author, Virgin Islands and Caribbean Communities. **MILITARY SERVICE:** AUS corpl sp4 1962-65. **HOME ADDRESS:** PO Box 7475 Sunny Isle, Christiansted, St Croix, Virgin Islands of the United States 00820. **BUSINESS ADDRESS:** Coordinator of Social Studies, Dept of Educ of the Virgin Islands, PO Box I, Christiansted, St Croix, Virgin Islands of the United States 00820.

THOMAS, MAXINE F.
Judge. **PERSONAL:** Born May 31, 1947, Los Angeles, CA; daughter of Mack Thomas and Freddie Thompson Thomas. **EDUCATION:** CA State Clge, BA 1968; Univ IA, JD 1971; Atlantic Richfield Co, legal div 1972-74. **CAREER:** Pacific Lighting Corp So CA Gas Co, legal div 1974-, coroprate litigation atttorney 1974-80; Atlantic Richfield Corp, corporate attorney 1972-74; Los Angeles Municipal Court, presiding judge 1986, judge 1980-89. **ORGANIZATIONS:** Mem Amer, CA, IA, Natl John M Langston; pres LA Bar Assc; LA Urban League; Black Lawyers of CA; mem Natl Bar Assc; bd dir Found for Small & Minority Bus Enterprises; LA Women Lawyers Assc; Natl Conf Black Lawyers; Phi Alpha Delta Law Frat; Second Bapt Ch; chmn bd dir Comm Legal Awareness Corp; treas bd dir Black Law Ctr; treas LA Br NAACP; pres, John M Langston Bar Assn, California Assn of Black Lawyers. **HONORS/ACHIEVEMENTS:** Woman of the Year, Los Angeles Sentinel 1986; Honoree, Natl Assn of Business & Professional Women 1986; Co-founder, Night Civil Court, LA Municipal Court 1984; Founder, Night Small Claims Court, LA Municipal Court 1982. **HOME ADDRESS:** 849 S Highland Ave, Los Angeles, CA 90036.

THOMAS, MAXINE SUZANNE
Educator. **PERSONAL:** Born Jan 23, 1948, Junction City, KS; daughter of Morris Daniels; married Larry Thomas; children: Lauryn, Noel. **EDUCATION:** Univ of WA, BA 1970, JD 1973. **CAREER:** Univ of OR Schl of Law, asst prof 1976-89; Univ of OR, asst dean 1976-79; WA, asst atty gen 1973-76; assoc dean and assoc prof Univ of Georgia l989-. **ORGANIZATIONS:** Mem Natl Assc of Clge & Univ Attys 1974-76; standing com on environmental law Amer Bar Assc 1979-; honorary mem Phi Delta Phi 1977-; mem OR Amer Counc on Educ Com to Promote Women to Higher Educ Admin 1978-. **HONORS/ACHIEVEMENTS:** Nominated OR Outst Young Women 1978, Kellogg Natl Fellow 1985-l988, Fulbright lecturer l988. **BUSINESS ADDRESS:** University of Georgia School of Law, Athens, GA 30602.

THOMAS, N. CHARLES
Clergyman, administrator. **PERSONAL:** Born Jun 24, 1929, Jonesboro, AR; married Mary Elizabeth. **EDUCATION:** MS Indsl Clge, BA 1951; Lincoln Univ Theol Sem, BD 1954; Lancaster Theol Sem, MDiv 1974. **CAREER:** CME Chs Waterford MS, pastor 1949-51; Roanoke VA, 1954; Wrightsville AR, 1954-57; Hot Springs AR, 1957-60; Little Rock AR, 1960-62; Memphis TN, 1966-67; CME Church, general secretary. **ORGANIZATIONS:** Dir of christian educ 1st Dist CME Ch 1958-74, admin asst to presiding bishop 1954-74; admin Ministerial Salary Supplement Prog CME Ch Gen Bd of Pensions CME Ch 1974-; sec Gen Conf CME Ch 1970-; presiding elder S Memphis Dist 1971-74; Mem Gen Bd of Christian Educ CME Ch 1958-; sec Gen Correctional Bd CME Ch 1971-; mem bd trustees Smith-Keys Housing Project Texarkana AR 1969-; bd dir Haygood-Neal Housing Project Eldorado AR 1970-; bd dir E Gate Vlge Union City TN 1970-; bd trustees Collins Chapel Hosp Memphis TN 1974-; bd dir Memphis OIC 1972-; mem CME Ministers Alliance Memphis; Interdenom Ministers Alliance Memphis; gen sec Gen Bd of Personnel Srv 1978. **HONORS/ACHIEVEMENTS:** Dr of Humanities TX Clge Tyler 1980. **BUSINESS ADDRESS:** General Secretary, CME Church, 531 S Parkway East, Memphis, TN 38101.

THOMAS, NATHANIEL
Film producer, director. **PERSONAL:** Born May 22, 1957, Warren, OH; son of Ace Thomas and Rose Thomas. **EDUCATION:** St Edward's Univ, BA Theatre Arts 1979; Univ of TX at Austin, grad study in film 1979-80; Univ of S CA, MFA Cinema Prod 1984. **CAREER:** Actor in TV commercials for Coca-Cola & New York Life Insurance, 1978; actor in stage productions of "The Petrified Forest" w/Greg Morris & "Room Service" w/Godfrey Cambridge, 1975; producer of award-winning PBS film "The Last of the One Night Stands," 1982-83; Walt Disney Productions/The Disney Channel, asst to production exec, 1984; dir/producer of "The Zone," anti-alcohol public service announcement geared for black women, 1987; dir/producer of "Under the Rainbow: Jesse Jackson '88 for President," 1988; dir/producer of featurette for Universal Picture's "Ghost Dad" starring Bill Cosby, 1989; dir/producer of various television commercials, music videos, etc, 1987-. **ORGANIZATIONS:** Mem NAACP 1972-; mem Screen Actors Guild 1979-; mem AFTRA 1979-. **HONORS/ACHIEVEMENTS:** Spec Youth Citation Urban League 1975; Scholarship Morning Star Grand Chap Order of Eastern Star 1976; Student Activities Awd of Excellence St Edward's Univ Austin TX 1978-79; Dean's List St Edwards Univ 1977-79; nominee Man of Yr St Edward's Univ 1979; pres Jr Class St Edward's Univ Austin 1977-78; The Natl Dean's List 1979; Scholarship USC Ebonics Support Group 1981; USC Cinema Fellowship from Warner Brothers 1982; USC Tommy Awd for Outstanding Achiev in Cinema TV 1984; Cine Golden Eagle & Honors at San Francisco Intl Film Festival for PBS film "The Last of the One Night Stands" 1984; Awd Black Amer Cinema Soc for PBS film "The Last of the One Night Stands". **BUSINESS ADDRESS:** Film Producer/Univ Instructor, Nate Thomas & Associates, 6546 Hollywood Blvd, Suite 201, Hollywood, CA 90028.

THOMAS, NATHANIEL
Educational administrator, manager. **PERSONAL:** Born Feb 26, 1936, Marks, MS; married Venus Youngbey. **EDUCATION:** Univ of So CA, BA honors 1960; Roosevelt Univ, BS honors 1973, MA 1977. **CAREER:** CIC & MPME, exec dir 1977-; IL Inst of Tech, dir admissions & financial aid 1975-77, asst dir coop/placement 1973-75, oper mgr Computer Ctr 1965-73, vice pres external affairs. **ORGANIZATIONS:** Mem Schlrshp Selection Comm USN 1974; chmn of bd Inroads Inc 1976-; adv bd mem Argonne Natl Labs 1977-; mem policy bd Comm on Minorities in Engr1977-; mem Assc of Prog Dirs for Minorities in Engr 1978-; mem adv council Conf Bd 1979. **HONORS/ACHIEVEMENTS:** Man of Week Award WBEE Radio 1974; Outst Black Achiever Award YMCA 1976; Outstanding Comm Srv Award Natl Tech Assc 1979; Srv to Youth Award Catalyst forYouth 1979. **MILITARY SERVICE:** USMC sgt e-4 1954-59; Good Conduct Medal 1958. **BUSINESS ADDRESS:** Assistant Vice Pres -External Affairs, Illinois Inst of Technology, 10 W 32nd St, Chicago, IL 60616.

THOMAS, NIDA E.
Assistant deputy commissioner. **PERSONAL:** Born Jun 19, 1914, Goldsboro, NC; widowed; children: Lutrica, Rosemary. **EDUCATION:** NY Univ Sch of Educ, BS 1942; Atlanta Univ Sch of Social Work, MSW 1944; Cntr for Human Relations Studies NY Univ, adv study. **CAREER:** EEO State of NJ Dept of Educ, asst deputy commr. **ORGANIZATIONS:** Chief Bur of Educ Integration NY State Dept of Educ; exec dir Urban League of Bergen Co Englewood NJ; comm org secr Union Co Urban League Elizabeth NJ; mem Natl Assc of Intergroup Rel Ofcls; Delta Kappa Gamma Soc; Alpha Kappa Alpha Sor; Mem bd dir YWCA Elizabeth NJ; bd of Theol Educ; mem at large Reformed Ch in Amer; Assc of Theol Schs US & Can; bd dir Occupational Ctr Union Co; Union Co Urban League; Union Co Urban League Guild; Natl Council of Negro Women. **HONORS/ACHIEVEMENTS:** Distg Srv Award Urban League Union Co 1979; recip The Arch Award Student Council of NY Univ; outst ldrshp serv in student activities; portrait includedin UN Disting Cits Gallery Garden State Plaza; Outst Cits in Bergen Co; citation Empire State Fed Women's Club Outst Contrib & Ldrshp in comm & state; cert of appreciation NE Region NY State Conf, NAACP; Earnest O Melby Award Human Rel NY Univ Sch of Educ Alumni Assc 1971; Outst Educator AwardAcad of Amer Educators 1973-74; others. **BUSINESS ADDRESS:** NJ Dept of Educ OEEO, 225 W State St, Trenton, NJ 08625.

THOMAS, NINA M.
Police officer. **PERSONAL:** Born Jul 29, 1957, Bridgeport, CT; daughter of Livingston Thomas and Eleanor McGarah Thomas. **EDUCATION:** Univ of Connecticut, Storrs CT, 1975-78; currently attending Univ of New Haven, New Haven CT. **CAREER:** Mechanics & Farmers Savings Bank, Bridgeport CT, mortgage rep, 1978-83; Bridgeport Police Dept, Bridgeport CT, police officer, 1983—. **ORGANIZATIONS:** Mem, National Black Police Assn; mem, Bridgeport Guardians Inc. **HOME ADDRESS:** 127 Judson Place, Bridgeport, CT 06610.

THOMAS, ORA P. (ORA P. WILLIAMS)
Accountant, historian, executive producer. **PERSONAL:** Born Dec 24, 1835, Montgomery, AL; daughter of Henry Pugh, Sr and Delia Webb Pugh; married Benjamin Thomas, Jun 10, 1987; children: Tanja Bernadette Williams, Chandra D W Brady. **EDUCATION:** Alabama State Univ, Montgomery AL, BA, 1985, MS, 1986, EdS, 1987. **CAREER:** Alabama State Univ, Montgomery AL, clerk/typist, 1964-65, data processor, 1965-77, accountant, 1977—; executive producer of BOT Productions (Ben,Ora Thomas), 1987—. **ORGANIZATIONS:** Mem, Amer Assn of Black Women Entrepreneurs, founder of Montgomery chapter; mem, National Assn of 100 Black Women. **HOME ADDRESS:** 2014 Grande Ave, Montgomery, AL 36116.

THOMAS, PAT CALVIN
Professional athlete. **PERSONAL:** Born Sep 01, 1954, Plano, TX; married Lenith; children: Patrick Jr; Tamara Nicole; Joshua Dominigue. **EDUCATION:** TX A & M, 1972-76. **CAREER:** Los Angeles Rams, defensive back 1976-83; Houston Gamblers, coach of def backs 1983-. **HONORS/ACHIEVEMENTS:** Voted All-Pro in 1979 & 1980; played coll ftbl where he was an All-Am 1975, his sr yr; competed in the Hula Bowl & the Japan Bowl.

THOMAS, PATRICIA O'FLYNN
Publisher. **PERSONAL:** Born Jul 28, 1940, East St Louis, IL; daughter of James Edward O'Flynn and Margaret W Matthews O'Flynn Burns; divorced; children: Terence N Thomas, Todd A Thomas. **EDUCATION:** Marquette Univ, Milwaukee WI, 1957-58; Southern Illinois Univ, Carbondale IL, BS, 1963; Univ of Wisconsin, Milwaukee WI, MA, 1973. **CAREER:** Milwaukee Public Schools, Milwaukee WI, teacher, 1963-68; Milwaukee Star Times, Milwaukee WI, sales mgr, 1970-73, co-publisher, 1973-76; Milwaukee Community Journal, Milwaukee WI, publisher, 1976—. **ORGANIZATIONS:** Pres, NNPA; mem bd dir, Milwaukee NAACP; mem bd dir, Milwaukee Operation Push; mem women's auxilliary, Milwaukee Urban League. **HONORS/ACHIEVEMENTS:** Mayoral Award, Milwaukee Commission on Community Relations, 1978; Publisher of Year Award, Chrysler Corp/NNPA, 1986; Gubernatorial Citation, 1987; Ida B Wells Barnett Award, National PUSH, 1988; named among 100 most influential black Americans, Ebony Magazine, 1988, 1989. **BUSINESS ADDRESS:** Milwaukee Community Journal, 3612 North M L King Jr Dr, Milwaukee, WI 53212.

THOMAS, PHILIP MICHAEL
Actor. **PERSONAL:** Born 1949. **EDUCATION:** Oakwood Coll Huntsville, AL; Univ of CA at Riverside; Univ CA Berkeley. **CAREER:** Actor in plays "Hair", "No Place to Be Somebody"; actor in movies "Sparkle", "Mr Ricco", "Book of Numbers"; actor inTV on Medical Center, Police Woman, Toma and Good Times; actor in "Society's Child"; actor on "Miami Vice". **HONORS/ACHIEVEMENTS:** Record album "Living The Book of My Life". **BUSINESS ADDRESS:** Miami Vice Production Office, 5225 Collins Ave, Miami, FL 33140.

THOMAS, PHILIP S.
Performing arts producer. **PERSONAL:** Born May 24, 1946, Accommac, VA; children: Terrance Seegers. **EDUCATION:** Montclair State Coll, BA Theater 1976. **CAREER:** Greater Paterson Arts Council, exec dir 1977-80; NJ State Council on the Arts, arts devel coor 1980-82; Newark Symphony Hall, dir of mktg 1982-84; Newark Bd of Educ, grants analyst 1984-85; Carter G Woodson Found, artistic dir 1985-. **ORGANIZATIONS:** Pres Carter G Woodson Found 1974-; evaluator Natl Endowment for the Arts 1981-; bd of dir NJ Black Issues Convention 1984-; mem bd of dirs Newark Arts Council; mem Minority Arts Panel Pennsylvania Council on the Arts; mem Natl Task Force on Presenting and Touring the Performing Arts. **HONORS/ACHIEVEMENTS:** Montclair State Coll Speech & Theater Alumni Award 1975; Fellowship Natl Endowment for the Arts 1976; Freedom Fund Award Paterson NJ NAACP 1984; Scholarship-Martin Luther King Jr Community Nonviolent Training Program 1982; Duke Ellington Award in the Arts Paterson NJ 1985. **MILITARY SERVICE:** AUS Spec 4 1965-67.

THOMAS, RALPH CHARLES, III
Attorney. **PERSONAL:** Born Apr 10, 1949, Roanoke, VA. **EDUCATION:** US Int'l Univ, AA; Univ of CA, BA 1975; Harvard Law School, JD 1978. **CAREER:** Bergson, Borkland, Margolis, & Alder, attorney assoc 1978-80; George Washington Univ Nat'l Law Center, clinical law inst 1982-83; Law Offices of Ralph C Thomas, III, chief counsel 1980-85; Nat'l Assoc of Minority Contractors, exec dir 1985-. **ORGANIZATIONS:** Veterans Benefits Clearinghouse, bd of dir 1977-; Jaycees, general counsel 1981-82; Metropolitan Police Boys & Girls Clubs, bd of dir 1982-83; Dist of ColuPublished "Davis-Bacon Act Hurts Minority Contractors" in MBE Mag 1986, "Organized Crime in the Construction Ind" - Crime & Delinquency 1977, "Student Parolembia Statehood Constitutional Convention, general counsel 1982-83; Jesse Jackson for Pres Nat'l Campaign Committee, general counsel 1983-84; Univ of MD-EastAides, Do They Really Help?" - Youth Authority Quarterly 1975; ern Shore Construction Ed Advisory Bd, mem 1986. **MILITARY SERVICE:** ASF, staff sergeant 1967-71; Commendation Medal 1970; Pres Unit Citation for Extraordinary Gallantry 1971. **BUSINESS ADDRESS:** Executive Dir, Nat'l Assoc Minortiy Cont, 806 15th St, NW #340, Washington, DC 20005.

THOMAS, ROBERT C.
Clergyman, educator. **PERSONAL:** Born Jul 02, 1922, Abbeville, LA; married Juanita; children: Ronita, Robert, Kelesha. **EDUCATION:** AB 1943; MRE 1968; Doctor Ministry 1973 grad study; Pacific Sc Rel Univ Denver; Southern Methodist Univ Dallas. **CAREER:** Church of All Faiths, minister; CA State Univ, retired prof. **ORGANIZATIONS:** Pres Natl Cncl of Comm Chs; adj prof San Francisco Theol Sem; tchr prin Louisiana; tchr pastor SF Oakland; pastor minden & s'port LA Civil Rights Activist; LA Comm Proj ; writer & organizer; mem Natl Black Educators; Alpha Phi Frat Inc; 32 Deg Prince Hall Mason; past bd mem cty YMCA; UBAC NewOakland Com; past pres Oakland Poverty Bd Lane Bryant award; Comm Srv 1968. **HONORS/ACHIEVEMENTS:** Black Man of Year Jack & Jill Inc Oakland Chpt. **MILITARY SERVICE:** AUS publ rel ofcr. **BUSINESS ADDRESS:** 2100 5th Ave, Oakland, CA.

THOMAS, ROBERT CHARLES
Musician, composer. **PERSONAL:** Born Nov 14, 1932, Newark, NJ; married Nicole; children: Lorna, Marc. **EDUCATION:** Juilliard Sch Music, BS 1961. **CAREER:** Billy Taylor Prods, musician & composer 1975-; perfomed with, Wes Montgomery, Herbie Mann, Carmen McRae, Burt Bacharach, Billy Taylor Orch (David Frost TV Show); ballet. **ORGANIZATIONS:** Consult E Harlem Tutorial Prog 1960-74; music coord "A Chorus Line" 1977; co-produced, composed music & lyrics "Sugar Boogie" 1976; wrote theme Black Jour for WNET 1975; mem NY Jazz Repertory Co; Jazz Mobile; wrkshps & seminars Univs & Clges. **HONORS/ACHIEVEMENTS:** Shakespeare Key to City Cleveland; mem of Billy Taylor Trio two command perf at White House 1973-75. **MILITARY SERVICE:** AUS corpl 1953-55.

THOMAS, ROBERT LEWIS
Educator. **PERSONAL:** Born Sep 25, 1944, Brewton, AL; son of Robert Lewis Thomas, Sr (deceased) and Earnestine Lane Thomas; married Wyvonnia Thompson, Jun 06, 1969; children: Michelle, Tiffani. **EDUCATION:** Stillman Coll, BA 1967; Troy State Univ, MS 1975. **CAREER:** Escambia County Bd of Educ, teacher 1967-83; Brewton Police Dept, patrolman 1969-; Faulkner State Jr Coll, teacher 1983-. **ORGANIZATIONS:** Mem Alabama Assn of Historians, NAACP; lifetime mem Kappa Alpha Psi Fraternity 1969-; delegate Conf on Black Amer Affairs 1984-86; vice pres AEA Faulkner State 1986-87; pres AEA Faulkner State 1987-88; delegate AEA Convention 1987-88; mem Alabama Peace Officers Assn, Alabama High School Athletic Assn; mem, bd of trustees Zion Fountain AME Church; NAACP, 1983-. **HONORS/ACHIEVEMENTS:** Achievement Award, Kappa Alpha Psi Fraternity 1972; Operation Crossroad African Alumni. **HOME ADDRESS:** 612 Liles Blvd, Brewton, AL 36426.

THOMAS, RONALD F.
Educator. **PERSONAL:** Born Jul 02, 1944, Wilmington, DE; married Marva Wyche, Dec 23, 1967; children: Ronald LeRoy, Olivia Necole. **EDUCATION:** Delaware State Coll, BS 1967; Central MI Univ, Master 1979, postgraduate studies, 1987. **CAREER:** 7th grad math teacher 1977; Capital School Dist Dover DE, math instructor 1970-74, reading & math ctr oper Title VII, Title I; Telegraph Road Learning Center, computer lab supvr; Red Clay School Dist, Wilmington DE, math/science teacher, 1988-. **ORGANIZATIONS:** Mem Groove Phi Groove Soc Fellowship 1963, VA 1967-; del State Educ Assoc 1970-; mem Natl Educ Assoc 1970-; mem Capital Educ Assoc 1970-; mem Church Laymens Assoc 1970-; mem Human Relations Conf Represent Capital School Dist 1972,73; mem Problems & Relations Comm 1971-73, 32nd Degree Mason & Shriner 1972-; mem lab del, assembly deliegate 1973, bldg rep 1972-74 State Educ Assn; negotiation team for schools 1974; chmn nom comm del State Educ Assembly 1974; pres DE State Minority Ed Assoc 1974-76; del Disadvantaged Found Inc 1974-; mem VFW 1974-, DOIC, GED, ABE Teacher 1963; advisory Coll Gospel Youth Group 1974; vice pres DeFrontier Intl Club; mem Omega Psi Phi. **HONORS/ACHIEVEMENTS:** State Civic Duty Award 1962; Outstanding Sr Choir & Band 1962; recorded "Love You So Bad Come Home Girl", "Your on Top Girl Slide On By"; 1st pl All Army Talent Show 1969; Outstanding Leaders In Elementary & Secondary Educ 1976; Citizen of the Year Award for Dover DE 1985; Thirty-Third Degree, United Supreme Council, 1988. **MILITARY SERVICE:** AUS sgt E-5 1967-70; DE NG captain.

THOMAS, ROY L.
Foreman. **PERSONAL:** Born Jul 27, 1938, Forest, MS; married Altemese Woods; children: Micheal, Sandra, Mark. **EDUCATION:** Univ MD. **CAREER:** Hercules Inc, Glen Falls, prod foreman; Minority Bus Oppor, enforcement offcr. **ORGANIZATIONS:** Bd chmn Local Housing Corp; Warren Co NY Sewer Dist 1; chmn NY St Conf NAACP, Prisons Affrs Com; ex dir Vol Housing Survey; bd & chmn Warren Hamilton Off Econ Oppo; bd mem E Adirondack Econ Devel Auth; bd mem, Warren Co Alcoholic Bev Con Bd; RE Salesman; pres Glen Falls Br NAACP; mem Warren Co Rep Comm; NYS Ancillary Mnpwr Plnng Bd; Senate Lodge 456 F&AM of Glens Falls. **MILITARY SERVICE:** USAF 4 Yrs. **BUSINESS ADDRESS:** 11 Darwin Ave, Glens Falls, NY 12801.

THOMAS, SHERRI BOOKER
Geologist. **PERSONAL:** Born in Richmond, VA; married Norman Thomas. **EDUCATION:** VA State Univ, BS 1980; Univ of SC, MS 1982. **CAREER:** Amoco, sr explor tech 1978-79; Natl Assoc of Black Geologists & Geophysicists, sec 1983-84; Conoco, geologist 1980-. **ORGANIZATIONS:** Mem Natl Assoc of Black Geol & Geophys 1982; sec Ella Bouldin Missionary Soc #5 1983-; mem Amer Assoc of Petroleum Geol 1984, Geol Soc of Amer 1985; mem Celestrial Choir Payne Chapel AME Church. **HONORS/ACHIEVEMENTS:** Article "Quartz Sand Province Changes" S Booker, R Ehrlich 1981. **BUSINESS ADDRESS:** Senior Geologist, Conoco, Inc, 600 N Dairy Ashford Rd, Ste 3064, Houston, TX 77079.

THOMAS, SIRR DANIEL
Construction manager. **PERSONAL:** Born Jul 21, 1933, Huntsville, AL; married Barbara Williams; children: S. **EDUCATION:** Tuskegee Inst, plumbing & mech drawing; Knoxville Coll, math; Howard Plumbing Co, Knoxville, journeyman plumber 1960-63; Elmer A Thomas Plumbing Co, foreman, plumber 1957-60, journeyman plumber 1953-55. **CAREER:** Thomas & Thomas Inc, gen contrctrs, Chattanooga, owner, mgr 1963-; Howard & Howard Plumbin Co, Knoxville, journeyman plumber 1960-63; Elmer A Thomas Plumbing Co, foreman, plumber 1957-60, journeyman plumber 1953-55. **ORGANIZATIONS:** Mem Nat Bus League; mem bd dir Eastern Seabord Plumbing & Heating Assn; mem bd dir Chattanooga Chap NAACP; mem bd dir Security Fed Sav & Loan Assn; mem bd dir Peoples Bank; chmn Chattanooga C of C Minority Bus Com; trained & tutored young black men in preparation for plumbing career. **MILITARY SERVICE:** AUS pfc 1955-56. **BUSINESS ADDRESS:** 617 Shallowford Rd, Chattanooga, TN 37411.

THOMAS, SPENCER
Physician. **PERSONAL:** Born in Gadsden, AL; married Lela; children: Spencer Jr. **EDUCATION:** Alabama State Univ, BS 1952; Howard Univ, MD 1959. **CAREER:** Mercy Douglas Hospital Philadelphia, intern/house physician 1959-61; Philadelphia General Hospital, urology special training 1972-76, asst attending physician 1976-77; Holy Name of Jesus Hospital & Baptist Memorial Hospital Gadsden, staff physician; private practice, Gadsden AL, physician. **ORGANIZATIONS:** Mem Indus Devel Bd Gadsden 1968-72 & 1978-; bd dir Gadsden Progress Council; sponsor Project Headstart 1964-72 & 1980-; pres Community League for Advancement of Social Socs Gadsden 1969; founder & mem of gov bd Colley Child Care Center Gadsden; medical dir Project Head Start 1968-72; pres Gadsden Alumni Assn of Alabama State Univ 1979-; NAACP; Alpha Phi Alpha Fraternity Inc, Alabama State Medical Assn, Natl Medical Assn, AMA, SCLC, Howard Univ Medical Alumni Assn, Sweethome United Methodist Church; chmn administrative bd, trustee Sweethome United Methodist Church 1979-81; church lay leader 1981-; mem Gadsden City Bd of Educ 1980-, vice pres 1984; mem bd trustees Alabama A&M Univ 1980-, chmn 1982-84; pres Gadsden-Etowah AL Branch of NAACP 1982-; pres AL State Alumni Assn Gadsden Chapter 1979-; mem Chamber of Commerce, Gadsden AL; mem bd dirs of Gadsden, AL Voters League (AL Democratic Conf); weekly columnist Gadsden Times Daily. **HONORS/ACHIEVEMENTS:** Recipient Serv Award, Gadsden Progress Council 1972. **MILITARY SERVICE:** AUS 1952-54. **BUSINESS ADDRESS:** PO Box 57, Gadsden, AL 35902.

THOMAS, STANLEY B., JR.
Business executive. **PERSONAL:** Born Apr 28, 1942, New York, NY. **EDUCATION:** Yale Univ, BA Political Sci & History 1964. **CAREER:** Time Inc, exec trainee, asst to vice pres 1964-66; Ofc of Comm & Field Svcs, dept asst, sec 1977-79; ITT, exec for marketing strategy planning 1977-79;Home Box Office, Inc, asst to chmn & chief exec ofcr 1979-80, vice pres Nat Account Group 1981, sr vice pres Natl Account Group 1983, sr vice pres Affiliate Operations 1984-. **ORGANIZATIONS:** Sec NY Anti-Poverty Operations Bd; mgr Personnel Rel Philip Morris Inc; trustee Horace Mann Sch. **HONORS/ACHIEVEMENTS:** Spl Citation Nominee YaleUniv Corp Sec's; Superior Serv Award HEW. **BUSINESS ADDRESS:** Sr Vice Pres Affiliate Operations, Home Box Office Inc, 1100 Avenue of Americas, New York, NY 10036.

THOMAS, WADDELL ROBERT
Business executive. **PERSONAL:** Born Jun 06, 1909, Washington, DC; married Irene. **EDUCATION:** Howard U, 1927-28; Robert H Terrell Law Sch, LlB 1941; Harvard U, Urban App I 1952; USC, Urban App Ii 1959. **CAREER:** Metropolis Real & Inv Co, 1946. **ORGANIZATIONS:** Past pres Bwa Real Est Brok Assn; past pres Nat Soc Real Est App; bd dir Dolphin & Evans Title Agy; Columbia Hosp; Ctrl City Prop Mgmt; mem Bdc Bd of Equal Rev; DC Condem Rev Bd; app panel Dist of Col Govt & Vet Adminstrn; mem NAACP; Urban Leag. **BUSINESS ADDRESS:** President, Metropolis Realty & Invest Co, 25 K Street, NW, Washington, DC 20011.

THOMAS, WADE HAMILTON, SR.
Consultant. **PERSONAL:** Born May 12, 1922, Jackson, MS; son of Harrison Spurgeon Thomas and Lealer Bandy Thomas; married Mary Katherine Scruggs; children: Wade Jr, Karl, Harrison, George, Kenneth, Korda, Ren'ee, Rex, Axel, Michelle. **EDUCATION:** TN State Univ, BS (with distincton) 1949; TN State Univ, Post Grad 1950; US Civil Serv Comm, Interne 1962; TX Central Univ, MBA 1962. **CAREER:** Southern Training Inst, instr 1947-49; Univ Life Ins Co, sp rep 1951-52; US Post Office Dept, gn clerk 1953-62; Drake & Thomas Pub Accts, co-ownr 1954-60; GSA, PBS, BMD (US Govt), fld mgr 1963-72; W H Thomas, Sr, Pub Acct, owner 1973-80; Confidential Assoc, Realtors, mgmnt, cnslt 1981-. **ORGANIZATIONS:** Mem NY Comm to Study Housintg 1981-83; mem Asheville Promo Comm 1984-; treas YMI Cultural Cntr 1984-; mem US Feed Exec Assoc 1967-72; basiceus Up Omc, Chapter Omega Psi Phi Frat 1970-71; mem Nat Soc Pub Acct 1973-; v chrmn Asheville Civil Serv Comm 1983-; chmn Asheville Brd of Adjstmnts 1988-; brd of dir Asheville Brd of Realtors 1984-; comm NC Housing Comm 1983-. **HONORS/ACHIEVEMENTS:** Sop Accomplishment Award-US Post Off Dept 1960; Spl Accomplishment Award Gen Serv Admin 1971; Outstanding Serv Award Omega Psi Phi Frat 1971 & 1983; Golden Anniv Award TN State Univ 1962. **MILITARY SERVICE:** USAAFR ofcr 1942-47, Reg Campaigns & Good Conduct 1945. **HOME ADDRESS:** 2 Mardell Circle, Asheville, NC 28806. **BUSINESS ADDRESS:** Management Consultant, Confidential Assoc, Realtors, 46 S Market St, Asheville, NC 28802.

THOMAS, WILBON
Farmer, station proprietor. **PERSONAL:** Born Mar 06, 1921, Midway, AL; married Mary E Warren; children: 3. **CAREER:** NAACP, vice pres 1954-56, pres 1964-; Midway Improvement Club, pres 1956-64; Bullock Cty Schools, bus driver 27 yrs; farmer, serv sta oper 1957-; Macon County Racing Commission. **ORGANIZATIONS:** Deacon, mem 1st Baptist Church Bullock Co ESPO; mem Jury Comm of Bullock Cty, Bullock Cty Dist Adv Council for Title I, BTU & Sunday School Teacher; state bd mem ESPO; supt of Sunday School; Pres of First Baptist Usher Board; Organized a Sunday School Program. **HONORS/ACHIEVEMENTS:** Bullock Cty PTA Awd; Serv Awd ASCAARV; AL NAACP; Youth Councils & Coll; 2 Leadership Awds AL Baptist State Conv; Cert Personal & Family Survival.

THOMAS, WILBUR C.
Educator. **PERSONAL:** Born Sep 23, 1916, Oberlin, OH; son of Phillip Norman Thomas and Beatrice Lillian Crawford Thomas; married Maria A Cambarare, Nov 04, 1942; children: Maria A Wakefield, Philip G, Diana R Hayward. **EDUCATION:** Kent State Univ, AB (cum laude) 1947. **CAREER:** Oberlin Conservatory of Music, instr 1938-39; Kent State Univ, instr & clinical psychologist 1947-49; Dane Co Mental Health Ctr, admin dir 1959-67; Warren Urban League, field sec 1950-58; WI Welfare Council, assoc dir 1958-59; Univ of WI Ext, chmn com dynamics inst, emeritus prof 1983; Univ of Wisconsin, Family Living Education, prof of Human Relations 1967-83. **ORGANIZATIONS:** Chmn Minority Employment Oppor Comm; exec comm Employee Relations Univ Ext Univ of WI; affirmative action officer Search & Screen Coms for Dean of Dept of Econ & Environ Devel; asso chancellor/prog coord Youth Devel/Asst to the Chancellor for Affirmative Action/Equal Employ Oppor; coord/mgr WI Ctr Fam Living Educ Child Splist; mem planning comm Univ of WI Ext, College Week for Women; mem Chancellor's Adv Human Relations Comm; chmn Chancellor's Employee Relations Min Com; mem Fellowship Adv Comm; mem Family Living Edn's Expanded Food & Nutrition Educ Adv Comm; mem Awds Comm; mem Dept of Comm Affairs Rank & Tenure Comm; mem Standards & Curriculum Com Juvenile Justice Personnel Devel Ctr; chmn Study Com for Devel of New Unit in Prog Area of Comm Devel; mem Comm Serv Activities; chmn Madison Metro Sch Dist Supt Human Relations Adv Comm; mem Mayors Sr Citizens Adv Comm; Dane Co Coord Council; chair Admin Council Calvary United Meth Ch; mem Friends of Foreign Students, WI Juvenile Jus Assn, Alpha Sigma Chap Epsilon Sigma Phi; mem, Madison Urban League, NAACP-Madison Branch, South Central District Superintendency Committee. **HONORS/ACHIEVEMENTS:** Hall of Respect Awd Madison Pub Schs; Outstanding Comm Serv Awd Madison Neighborhood Ctrs. **MILITARY SERVICE:** USAAF s/sgt 1942-46. **BUSINESS ADDRESS:** Emeritus Professor, Univ of WI Ext Lowell Hall, 610 Langdon St, Madison, WI 53706.

THOMAS, WILLIAM
Educational administrator. **PERSONAL:** Born Jan 01, 1935, Cairo, IL; son of William H Thomas and Claudia Mae Campbell Thomas; married Majoice Lewis; children: Joyce D, Sharon S, William E, Anjanette, Marcus K. **EDUCATION:** So IL Univ, BS 1967; Purdue Univ, MS 1969, PhD 1972. **CAREER:** City of Gary Schools, head teacher/teacher 1967-70; Purdue Univ, administ asst 1970-72; DePauw Univ, dir Black studies/asst prof 1972-73; Purdue Univ, dir special academic servcs/asst prof 1973-75; CIC Midwest Program for Minorities in Engrg, exec dir 1975-77; Thomas Distrib, vice pres 1977-79; Cairo School Dist #1, admin asst to supt 1979-83; Carbondale Elem School Dist #95, supt 1983-87; New Orleans Public Schools, New Orleans LA, assoc superintendent, 1987-. **ORGANIZATIONS:** Educ consultant, Joliet Area Schools 1973-74, Office of Educ Region V 1974-75, IN Dept Public Instructor 1975-77; corp dir Southern Med Center 1980-84; vp/sec/treas Kiwanis Club of Cairo 1979-83; mem Carbondale Rotary Club 1984-87; Western Reg chmn Egyptian Council Boy Scouts of Amer 1983-87; treasurer Egyptian Council Boy Scouts of Amer; mem, Partnership in Education Steering Committee, 1989. **HONORS/ACHIEVEMENTS:** Maintenance Man of the Month 13th Air Div (SAC) 1963; Martin Luther King Jr Fellowship Woodrow Wilson Found 1970-72; David Ross Fellow Purdue Univ 1972; President's Award Egyptian Council Boy Scouts of Amer 1985. **MILITARY SERVICE:** USAF Tech Sgt served 10 yrs; Natl Defense Serv Medal; Good Conduct Medal; Missileman's Badge. **BUSINESS ADDRESS:** Associate Superintendent Area II Schools, New Orleans Public Schools, 5931 Milne Blvd, New Orleans, LA 70124.

THOMAS, WILLIAM CHRISTOPHER
Administrator, management consultant. **PERSONAL:** Born Feb 04, 1939, Chicago, IL; married Joan Marie; children: Gene, Sean, Dawn, Theresa, Bill Jr. **EDUCATION:** Northeastern IL Univ, BE 1962; Harvard Grad Sch of Business, PMD 1972. **CAREER:** Sealy Mattress Co, personnel dir 1964-66, mfg supt 1966-67; Honeywell Inc, labor relations manager 1967-69, corporate training manager 1969-73; Univ of MN, assoc vice pres for finance, personnel and physical plant opers 1973-. **ORGANIZATIONS:** Pres Modern Mgmt Assoc Inc Consultants 1981-; pres MN State Affirm Action Assoc 1979-80; mem AMA Natl Adv Council 1979-82; mem Board Twin Cities Personnel Assoc 1978-79. **HONORS/ACHIEVEMENTS:** Bush Fellow Bush Foundation 1972. **HOME ADDRESS:** 2149 Scott Ave N, Golden Valley, MN 55422. **BUSINESS ADDRESS:** Assoc Vice Pres Personnel & Admn, Univ of Minnesota, 1919Univ Ave, St Paul, MN 55104.

THOMAS, WILLIAM L.
Business executive. **PERSONAL:** Born Apr 03, 1938, Cleveland; married Joyce; children: Menelik, Malaka. **EDUCATION:** OH U;Univ Madrid; Ghetto U;Univ MD; OH Drug Studies Inst, 1973-74. **CAREER:** City of Cleveland, engr inspector 1968-69; Black Unity House Inc, fdr, exec dir. **ORGANIZATIONS:** Mem exec com OH Black Polit Assembly 1974; Cleveland Black Polit Assembly 1974; trustee Community Action Against Addiction 1971-75; African Liberation Support Com 1969-75; Community Coalition on Construction 1971-75. **MILITARY SERVICE:** USAF a/2c 1960-65. **BUSINESS ADDRESS:** 1167 Hayden Ave, Cleveland, OH 44110.

THOMAS-BOWLDING, HAROLD CLIFTON
Social services executive. **PERSONAL:** Born Jul 24, 1941, Washington, DC; son of Benjiman and Helen; married Linda M; children: Harold Jr, William Staggs, Aneara, Emmatt, James Carter, Godtheson Benjamen. **EDUCATION:** Federal City Coll, 1970; UDC, 1974-75. **CAREER:** Anacostia Youth Environ Org Inc, pres 1971; DC Metro Youth Org & Enterprises Inc, pres 1976; Natl Love Comm Youth & Adult Org Inc, pres 1984-; pres Council of Peers, Inc. **ORGANIZATIONS:** Youth counselor SE Neighborhood House 1976; adv neighborhood comm 8B02 1979-84; AL Ave Rennisance Proj Dept of Housing/Comm Development 1982-83; adv neighborhood comm 8B01 1985-87; DC Comprehensive Plan DC Office of Planning 1983-84; Mayor's Ward 8 Adv Comm 1983-84; Mayor's Budget and Resource Adv Commappointee 1985. **HONORS/ACHIEVEMENTS:** Ward 8 Constituent Serv Cert Councilwoman Rolark 1982; Recognition of Leadership Frederick Douglass Dwellings Resident Council 1984; coord of Frederick Douglass' Recogn Day; Community Olympics 1985. **MILITARY SERVICE:** AUS sp/4 2 yrs; championship watch & jacket 2nd div football 1967. **HOME ADDRESS:** 1738 Stanton Terr SE, Washington, DC 20020.

THOMAS-CARTER, JEAN COOPER
Retired city official, educator. **PERSONAL:** Born Dec 16, 1924, Baltimore, MD; married Calvin Lavette Carter; children: Jacques S Maultsby. **EDUCATION:** Hampton Inst Hampton VA, BS 1946; Howard Univ School of Soc Work, MSW 1965; Univ of AL, Cert in Mgmt 1979. **CAREER:** Barrett School for Girls, teacher 1947-49; Baltimore City Dept of Soc Svcs, caseworker 1949-57, casework suprv 1957-66, dist suprv 1966-71; Logical Tech Serv Residential Drug Treatment Prog, deputy dir 1971-73; Baltimore City Dept of Soc Svcs, dist supvr group day care 1973-78, prog spec for day care 1978-79, chief/prog spec for serv to fami-

lies with children 1979-80, dist mgr 1980-83, asst dir of client serv oper 1983-84, bureau chief adult & family svcs. **ORGANIZATIONS:** Instr Comm Coll of Baltimore 1970-; exec comm Howard Univ School of Soc Work Alumni Assoc, Mayors Advisory Council on Drug Abuse; co-chairperson awds comm Conf on Women in State Svcs; past v chairperson of bd of dir Xcell Drug Treatment Center; past bd of dir Baltimore Assoc for Retarded Citizens; pasast MD Conf of Soc Concern; past budget allocations comm United Fund; dir Youth Ministry of Our Lady of Lourdes Parish, Baltimore MD 1985-; bd mem Campfire Council of the Chesapeake 1985-; volunteer panelist Administrative Review Bd for serv to families with children, Baltimore Dept of Social Services 1989-. **HONORS/ACHIEVEMENTS:** Awd of Recognition Chairperson for Annual Dr United Fund 1974; Publ "Does Existing Social Policy, Service Programs, & Support Systems Help the Children of Women Involved in the Criminal Justice System"? Natl Inst of Health 1979, "The Impact of PA Pmts & Social Policy on Family Functioning" Child Welfare League of Amer Eastern Reg Conf 1980. **HOME ADDRESS:** 2317 Monticello Road, Baltimore, MD 21216.

THOMAS-RICHARDS, JOS RODOLFO
Surgeon. **PERSONAL:** Born Jul 28, 1944; married Lynette; children: Jose, Raoul. **EDUCATION:** Andrews U, BA 1966; KS City Coll Osteo Med, DO 1970. **CAREER:** Orthopedic surgeon, self; Martin Luther King Hosp, dir emergcy med, chmn Dept Orthopedic & Hand Surgery, dir rehab med. **ORGANIZATIONS:** Med sec Central State Conf of Seventh Day Adventists; mem AMA 1975; !mo State Med Assn 1975; Jackson Co Med Soc 1975; KS City Med Soc 1973; SW Clinical Soc 1974; life mem NAACP 1975; nominee, bd dir Jackson Co Med Soc 1977; MO State Med Assn 1977; bd dir Martin Luther King Hosp; mem Nat Med Assn; life mem Golden Heritage NAACP; mem bd of trustees PUSH; fdr Excel-Health, a new prgm of PUSH; phys Wyandotte Co Jail & Dep Sheriff Kansas City, KS; Coll Emergency Med 1975; Surgery of the Hand 1977-78. **HONORS/ACHIEVEMENTS:** Mead-Johnson Award 1971. **BUSINESS ADDRESS:** Metro Medic Professional Bldg, Ste 100, Kansas City, MO 64130.

THOMAS-RICHARDSON, VALERIE JEAN
Allied health & social service consultant. **PERSONAL:** Born Apr 21, 1947, Akron, OH; daughter of Rev Charles Cooper Jr and Mary Carson Cooper. **EDUCATION:** Akron School of Pratical Nursing, LPN 1968-69; Thomas A Edison Coll, BA Soc Sci 1969-73; Univ of Pittsburgh, MSW 1974-76; Union Grad School, PhD 1976-78; Medina Hosp, Cardiopulmonary Tech Training Prog. **CAREER:** NEOCROSS, Inc, interim executive dir 1978-79; The Gilliam Family Service Center, exec dir 1979-82; Cleveland Adult Tutorial Services, exec dir 1983-86; Georgian Allied Health Educational Services, assoc dir 1986-. **ORGANIZATIONS:** Frst aid & personal safety instr, cpr instr Amer Red Cross 1975-87; former med newsletter editor "Heartbeat" Amer Heart Assoc Publ 1976; natl pres appointment exec comm Fed Council on Aging Wash DC 1978-; American Assoc for University Women 1984-86; Altrusa of Greater Cleveland 1985-86; Greater ClevelandBlood Pressure Coalition, board mem 1985-87; Ohio Entrepreneur Women's Directory 1986-87. **HONORS/ACHIEVEMENTS:** Zonta Club 1969; bd mem agency rep OH Legal Serv Commissions Consumer & Housing Task Force Comm Columbus OH 1977-78; many local, state natl and political proclamations commemorating "Women's Equality Day" and "Cardiopulmonary & Cardiovascular Technology Week" 1985-86; secured a natl special cardiovascular tech testing site in Northeastern OH for credentialing examination admin 1986; secured an "off-campus" site for Cuyahoga Community College's medical courses within the East Cleveland, OH community. **HOME ADDRESS:** 16000 Terrace Rd, East Cleveland, OH 44112.

THOMAS-WILLIAMS, GLORIA M.
Association executive. **PERSONAL:** Born Jul 05, 1938, NYC, NY; married Evrard Williams; children: Michelle. **EDUCATION:** Attended, NY Univ, Brooklyn Coll. **CAREER:** Gloria Thomas Modeling Sch, prop; Schaefer Brewing Co, mgr public relations; WCBS-TV, dir comm affairs. **ORGANIZATIONS:** Professional Commentator; Mistress of Ceremonies. **HONORS/ACHIEVEMENTS:** Outstanding Achiev Awd Bottle & Cork Sales 1970; Best Fashion Commentator Cabaret Prods 1971; Comm Serv Awd Mt Calvary Methodist Ch 1976; Awds in Black-Foundation for Educ in Sickle Cell 1973; Woman of the Yr 1972; Comm Serv Awd 1973; Awd of Merit WCBS-TV 1982; Police File Commendation 1974; Cert of Commendation Natl Assn for Visually Handicapped 1979; Mothers of Freedom Reward 1984; Outstanding Performance of Comm Serv Strivers Awd The Guardians Assn 1976; Alma John Comm Serv Awd 1984; Cert of Appreciation The Natl United Licensees Beverage Assns Inc 1972; Good Sportsmanship & Outstanding Serv WCBS-TV. **BUSINESS ADDRESS:** Dir of Community Affairs, WCBS-TV, 524 W 57th St, New York, NY 10019.

THOMPAS, GEORGE HENRY, JR.
Educator. **PERSONAL:** Born Jun 26, 1941, Philadelphia, PA; son of George and Olliebea; married Sharon Patton; children: George III, Orlando, Rhonda, Troy, Derek, Tanay, Jason, Brandi. **EDUCATION:** Federal Bureau of Law Enforcement Training Sch, Certificate 1969; Philadelphia Police Acad, police officer 1971; St Lukes and Children Medical Ctr, Certificate 1973; Community Coll of Philadelphia, A 1978; PA State Police Certification, Special Instructor; Municipal Police Officers Educ & Training Commn, Instructors Certification. **CAREER:** Reading Railroad (Conrail), railroad policeman 1968-71; City of Philadelphia, police officer 1971-85; Philadelphia Housing Authority, police officer 1986-; Watterson Sch of Bus and Tech, dir of security training 1985-. **ORGANIZATIONS:** Mem Variety Club for Handicapped Children 1968-, Guardian Civic League 1971-, Fraternal Order of Police 1971-, Missing Children Inc 1986; brethren, Mount Olive Lodge No 27 F&AM, 1988. **HONORS/ACHIEVEMENTS:** Public Service Safeway demonstrations for senior citizens groups and organizations 1978-. **MILITARY SERVICE:** AUS pfc 1963-66. **BUSINESS ADDRESS:** Dir of Security Training, Watterson Sch of Bus/Tech, 5800 N Marvine St, Philadelphia, PA 19141.

THOMPSON, ADELL, JR.
Educator. **PERSONAL:** Born Jun 17, 1932, Kansas City, KS; married Jacque D Nicholss; children: Adell III. **EDUCATION:** Univ of MO, PhD 1974; KS State Teach Coll of Pittsburg, MS 1958; Philander Ssmith Coll, BS 1954; NSF Inst attended 9, 1968. **CAREER:** Univ of MO, Kansas City, instr, 1969, asst prof 1974, assoc prof 1978, prof 1985. **ORGANIZATIONS:** Cir evaluator N Cent Assn of Sec schs & Coll 1979-; merit badge cncl Boys Scouts of Amer 1972-80; curr speclst Dept of Elem & Sec Educ (state) 1976-79; advsry brd Greater Kansas City Sci Fair 1980-; state dir MO Jr Acad of Sci 1981-84. **HONORS/ACHIEVEMENTS:** Biology Textbook Univ Press of Amer 1972-80; Outstanding Educator MO Acad of Sci 1984; Outstanding Alumni Philander Smith Coll 1982; Ford Found Educ Grant Univ of AK 1955. **MILITARY SERVICE:** AUS Medl Corp spclst III. **BUSINESS ADDRESS:** Prof of Biology & Sci Educ, Univ of MO Kansas City, 5100 Rockhill Rd, 5100 Rockhill Rd, Kansas City, MO 64110.

THOMPSON, ALBERT N.
Chief executive officer. **CAREER:** Consolidated Beverage Corp, New York, NY, chief exec. **BUSINESS ADDRESS:** Consolidated Beverage Corp, 235 West 154 St, New York, NY 10039. *

THOMPSON, ALBERT W., SR.
State official, attorney. **PERSONAL:** Born Jun 29, 1922, Ft Benning, GA; married Ozella N (deceased); children: Eloise, Charles III, Albert. **EDUCATION:** Savannah State Coll, BS 1942; Howard Univ Sch Law, JD 1950. **CAREER:** Atty Columbus, GA since 1951. **ORGANIZATIONS:** Elected 1-yr Term GA Gen Assembly 1965, re-elected seven 2-yr terms; apptd chmn Spl Judiciary Com 1975; mem State Crime Commn; mem State Bar GA; mem Columbus Lawyers Club; NAACP; YMCA; former mem Nat Council; dir Muscogee Co Red Cross; Social-Civic 25 Club; mem Dem Exec Com; apptd judge superior court Chattahoochee Judicial Circuit 1981-82. **HONORS/ACHIEVEMENTS:** State & Co Progressive Club's Man of Yr 1966. **MILITARY SERVICE:** AUS sgt 1943-46. **BUSINESS ADDRESS:** Administrative Law Judge, GA Bd of Workers Compensation, 17 10th St, Columbus, GA 31901.

THOMPSON, ALMOSE ALPHONSE, II
Educational administrator. **PERSONAL:** Born Feb 12, 1942, Shawnee, OK; son of Aimose Alphonse Thompson and Lucille Marshall Thompson; married Delma Jean Thompson; children: Almose A III, Jennie. **EDUCATION:** UCLA, BS 1962, Teaching Credential 1965, EdD 1972; Cal State Univ Long Beach, MA 1970; Vanderbilt Univ Law School, JD 1988. **CAREER:** LA Unified school Dist, secondary teacher 1965-68; CA State Univ, dir project upward bound & asst prof 1968-70; UCLA, part time instructor 1970-71; Holman &Thompson Inc, educ consul 1970-72; Univ of CA Santa Barbara, assoc dean of students; Portland State Univ, asst prof of curriculum & instruction 1972-74; Moorhead State Univ, asst prof of secondary educ 1974-75; CA State Univ, assoc prof & dir; Martin Luther King Jr Genl Hosp & Charles R Drew Post Grad Med School, educ eval specialist 1976-78; City of LA, prog dir 1978-79; Curatron Systems Inc, vice pres & Head of educ div 1978-79; Metropolitan Weekly, staff writer 1980-84; TN State Univ, prof of educ admin; syndicated columnist, Metropolitan Weekly, Nashville Tennessee is flagship newspaper. **ORGANIZATIONS:** Bd mem Walden Univ Bd of Rsch Advisors & Readers 1984-; rsch fellow selected 3 consecutive yrs Southern Educ Found 1980-83; mem ASPA, Natl Assn of Black, State of TN Pol Sci Assn; State's Media Corp; TN Prof Educational Admin Assn; Natl Assn of Social & Behavorial Scientists. **HONORS/ACHIEVEMENTS:** Awd for article "Blacks in America before Columbus" Negro History Bulletin 1975; 2 Grad Fellowships UCLA 1964 1970; Awd from The Black Caucus TN Genl Assembly 1982; Awd from the Mayor of Memphis 1982; numerous publications including, "Black Studies is Down to This" Black Times 1976; "Albina & Educational Reform" Portland Observer Special Issue Feb 15 1974; "The Student's Guide to Better Grades" NDS 1983; contributor "On Being Black, An In-Group Analysis" edited by David Pilgrim, published by Wyndham Hall Press 1986; passed written examination for Tennessee Bar, Tennessee Board of Bar Examiners, 1989. **MILITARY SERVICE:** USN E III 1963-65. **BUSINESS ADDRESS:** Professor, Educational Administration, Tennessee State University, 3500 John Merritt Blvd, Nashville, TN 37209-1561.

THOMPSON, ALVIN J.
Physician. **PERSONAL:** Born Feb 04, 1924, Washington, DC; married Faye; children: Michael, Donna, Kevin, Susan, Gail. **EDUCATION:** Howard Univ Coll of Liberal Arts, attended 1940-43, BS 1981; Howard Univ Med Sch, MD 1946; St Louis City Hosp, internship 1946-47; St Louis Hosp, residency 1947-51. **CAREER:** Providence Hosp, gastroenterology lab founder/dir 1963-77; Univ of Washington Sch of med, clinical prof; Providence Hosp, chief of medicine 1972-74; Veterans Adminstrn Hosp Univ Hosp, Harborview Med Ctr, attending physician; Providence Hosp, Swedish Hosp Med Ctr, attending staff; Veterans Administration Seattle, physician gastroenterologist 1953-59; Private Practice, physician gastroenterology internal medicine 1957-. **ORGANIZATIONS:** Certified Amer Bd of Internal Medicine 1953, recertified 1974; alternate delegate 1974-80 delegate 1980- Amer Medical Assn; gov Amer Coll of Physicians for WA & AK 1974-78; WA State Med Assn; WA State Soc of Internal Medicine; Puget Sound Health Planning Bd; Puget Sound Health Systems Agency; King Co Medical Soc; King Co Comprehensive Health Planning Council; King Co Blue Shield; Seattle Acad of Internal Medicine; Providence Hosp; Amer Coll of Physicians; Amer Med Assn; Amer Gastroenterologic Assn; Amer Soc for Gastrointestinal Endoscopy; N Pacific Soc of Internal Medicine; Amer Soc of Internal Medicine; Inst of Medicine Natl Acad of Scis; Natl Med Assn;President, WSSLU,med staff Providence Hospital, KSWS, WSWA, Seattle Academy of Med, State Assoc of Black Professionals in health care, delegate, AMA. **HONORS/ACHIEVEMENTS:** Kappa Cup for Superior Scholarship Howard Univ 1941; Robt H Williams Superior Leadership Awd Seattle Acad of Internal Medicine 1979; Inst of medicine Natl Acad of Scis 1978; Council for Cooporate Responsibility Seattle Chamber of Commerce 1983; Natl Assn of Medical Minority Educators for Outstanding Contrib in Health 1983; publs "Klebsiella Pneumoniae Meningitis" Archives of Intl Medicine 1952, "Mesenteric Valvular Insufficiency" Northwest Medicine 1962; numerous other editorials & articles. **MILITARY SERVICE:** Appointed US Naval Academy 1946; Major USAFCR.

THOMPSON, ANNE E.
Judge. **PERSONAL:** Born Jul 08, 1934, Philadelphia; married William H; children: William H Jr, Sharon A. **EDUCATION:** Howard Univ, BA 1955; Temple Univ, MA 1957; Howard Univ Law Sch, JD 1964. **CAREER:** Office of the Solicitor US Labor Dept Chicago, staff atty 1964-65; Legal Aid Soc of Mercer Co, staff atty 1966-67; Trenton, asst dep pub defender 1967-70; Twp of Lawrence NJ, prosecutor 1970-72; City of Trenton, munic ct judge 1972-75; Mercer Co Trenton NJ, prosecutor 1975-79; US Dist, judge. **ORGANIZATIONS:** Mem Amer Bar Assn; NJ Bar Assn; Mercer Co Bar Assn; life mem NAACP. **HONORS/ACHIEVEMENTS:** Recip award, Political Action Council of Mercer Co 1967; Achievement Week Award, Omega Psi Phi Frat 1973. **BUSINESS ADDRESS:** Judge, U S District Court, 402 E State St, Trenton, NJ 08605.

THOMPSON, BEATRICE R.
Psychologist. **PERSONAL:** Born May 05, 1934, Townville, SC; married Harry S; children: ; Nat, Family Counseling Bd; ElectedDaryl. **EDUCATION:** BA English; MA English; MA Guidance 1973; EdS Educ Psychology;Univ of GA, PhD 1978. **CAREER:** Anderson, SC, sch psychologist 1972-; Tri-Co Tech Coll, psychology instr 1972-74; Anderson, SC, HS guid couns 1967-71, HS Eng tchr 1954-65. **ORGANIZATIONS:** Mem Anderson United Way Bd; City Councilwoman, Anderson SC 1976-; mem SC Nat Bank Bd; mem Crippled Children Bd; mem Family Counseling Bd; elected SC Dem Nat Com Woman 1980; mem APGA; SCPGA; SC Pupil Pers Assn; SC Assn of Sch Psychologists; NEA; Nat Council for Excep Children; Nat Assn of Black Psychologists; sec Human Relations Council; den mother; vol Cancer Soc; chmn Sch Dist Five, Counslr Orgn; SC Pers & Guid Assn; pres Zonta Intl Bus & Professional Womens Club; mem Delta Sigma Theta Sor; Phi Kappa Phi Hon Soc; Phi Delta Kappa Hon Soc; sec-treas SC AMEG; sec-treas Anderson Family Counseling Ctr. **HONORS/ACHIEVEMENTS:** Listed in Who's Who in Am Coll & U; Outstanding Young Woman of Am 1974; NDEA Guid & Counseling Fellow; Gen Elec Guid Fellow.

THOMPSON, BENJAMIN FRANKLIN
Public administrator. **PERSONAL:** Born Aug 29, 1947, Philadelphia, PA; married JoAnne Snow; children: Kaif. **EDUCATION:** Boston State Coll, 1971-74; Antioch Univ, MEd 1979; Kennedy School Govt Harvard Univ, MPA 1982. **CAREER:** MA Halfway Houses Inc, prog dir 1975-78; MA Dept Corrections, dir of prog 1978-80; MA Dept Social Svcs, area dir 1980-82; Dept Social Svcs, consult 1983-84; Suffolk Cty Penal Dept, commiss 1984-; City of Boston, sr policy advisor on equal/humans rights, dep mayor 1984-. **ORGANIZATIONS:** Mem Intl Halfway Houses Inc 1976-84, Amer Correctional Assoc 1977-84; chmn Mayors Coord Council on Drug Abuse 1984-85; candidate Boston City Council 1984. **MILITARY SERVICE:** USAF sgt 4 yrs. **BUSINESS ADDRESS:** Senior Policy Advisor, Boston City Hall, Mayors Office, City Hall, Boston, MA 02201.

THOMPSON, BENNIE G.
Mayor. **PERSONAL:** Born Jan 28, 1948, Bolton, MS; married London Johnson. **EDUCATION:** Pol Sci, BA 1968; Educ Adminstrn, MSci 1972. **CAREER:** Town of Bolton, mayor 1973; Tri-Co Comm Cntr, proj dir 1970-74; Meadville MS, tchr 1968-70. **ORGANIZATIONS:** Asst dir Tchr Corps 1974-; chmn of bd Farish St YMCA; Mt Beulah Devel Found; vchmn of bd The Delta & Ministry; bd dir So Reg Cncl; Am Civil Lbrts Un. **HONORS/ACHIEVEMENTS:** Otstndng Yng Men of MS Awd NAACP; Otstndng Prsnlts of S 1971; Pltcn of Yr Jcksn St Coll 1973; Alumnus of Yr Awd Utica Jr Coll 1974. **BUSINESS ADDRESS:** PO Box 7, Bolton, MS 39041.

THOMPSON, BETTY E. TAYLOR
University associate professor. **PERSONAL:** Born Feb 06, 1943, Houston, TX; daughter of John Charles Taylor and Johnnie Mae Hart Brooks; married Oliver B Thompson Jr, Oct 20, 1985; children: Amnon James Ashe II, Ida Elizabeth Thompson. **EDUCATION:** Fisk Univ, Nashville TN, BA, 1963; Atlanta Univ, Atlanta GA, MLS, 1964; Howard Univ, Washington DC, MA, 1972, PhD, 1979. **CAREER:** Washington DC Public Library, technology librarian, 1969-72; Texas Southern Univ, Houston TX, instructor in English, 1974-75; Houston Independent Schools, Houston TX, English teacher/librarian, 1965-68, 1982-84; Texas Southern Univ, Houston TX, assoc prof of English, 1984—. **ORGANIZATIONS:** Mem, College Language Assn; mem, National Council of Teachers of English; mem, Southern Conf of Modern Language Assn, sec of Afro-Amer Section; mem, Southern Conf of Afro-Amer Studies. **BUSINESS ADDRESS:** Associate Professor of English, Texas Southern University, 3100 Cleburne Ave, King Center 208B, Houston, TX 77004.

THOMPSON, BETTY L.
Elected official & association executive. **PERSONAL:** Born Dec 03, 1939, Helm, MS; daughter of William S. Bolden and Lubirtha Lacy Bolden; married Jack Thompson, Apr 25, 1935; children: Anthony, Tyrone, Sonja, Kwame. **EDUCATION:** Harris Teachers Coll, 1959-62; Hubbard Bus Coll, 1963-65; Washington Univ 1972. **CAREER:** Daniel Boone PTO Univ City, past pres 1977-78; Women in Municipal Govt, past pres 1983-84; Assoc for Non-Violent Social Change for Amer, pres; KATZ RadioStation, host talk show 1963-; Human Develop Corp, area coordinator 1964-; 3rd Ward-University City, council woman; pres MLK MO Support Group. **ORGANIZATIONS:** Mem PUSH; mem NAACP; mem Natl League of Cities; past pres Black Women of Unity 1975-79; mem Camp Fire Girls 1982; mem Natl Assoc of Media Women 1980-. **HONORS/ACHIEVEMENTS:** Comm service Zeta Phi Beta Sor 1973; comm service George Washington Carver Awd 1977; Employee of the Year Human Development Corp 1978; comm service Martin Luther King Awd 1985; Best Speaker of the Year Award 1986; 1987 Women of Achievement May 1988; Two Speaking Albums, "Do Your Best But Don't Leave God Out," "Philosophy Called Anyway.". **HOME ADDRESS:** 8315 Seville, University City, MO 63132.

THOMPSON, BOBBY E.
Mayor. **PERSONAL:** Born Aug 15, 1937, Florence, AL; son of William Thompson and Althea Thompson Lovelace; married Vera L. Pride, Sep 03, 1960; children: Cheryl L., Karen E.. **CAREER:** Uptown Meat Market, Waukegan IL, owner, 1972-75; United Insurance Co, Chicago IL, agent, 1977-83; City of North Chicago, North Chicago IL, mayor, 1983—. **ORGANIZATIONS:** Lake County Economic Development Commission, Community Action Board. **HONORS/ACHIEVEMENTS:** Distinguished Service Award, We Do Care, 1981. **MILITARY SERVICE:** US Army, 1975-77.

THOMPSON, BRENDA SMITH
Educational administrator. **PERSONAL:** Born Jun 17, 1948, Richmond, VA; married Hugo Harrison Thompson; children: Rodney Harrison. **EDUCATION:** Virginia Union Univ, B 1970; Virginia Commonwealth Univ, M 1977; Virginia Polytechnic Inst & State Univ, D 1983. **CAREER:** Medical Coll of VA, lab specialist 1970-75; J Sargeant Reynolds Comm Coll, instructor 1977-80; State Council of Higher Educ for VA, asst coord 1984-85; Virginia Union Univ, dir enrollment mgmt 1985-. **ORGANIZATIONS:** Pres Natl Assoc of Univ Women Richmond Branch 1984-85; mem Richmond Professional Women's Network, VASFAA, SASFAA, NASFAA, VACRAO, SACRAO, NACDRAO; mem NAACP, Alpha Kappa Alpha Sor. **HONORS/ACHIEVEMENTS:** Doctoral Fellowship State Council of Higher Educ for Virginia 1980, 81; Disting Volunteer Parent for John B Gary Elem Sch 1981,83; Disting Alumni Awd Natl Assoc for Equal Oppor in Higher Educ 1986. **HOME ADDRESS:** 4004 Poplar Grove Rd, Midlothian, VA 23113. **BUSINESS ADDRESS:** Dir Enrollment Mgmt Serv, Virginia UnionUniv, 1500 North Lombardy St, Richmond, VA 23220.

THOMPSON, CARL EUGENE
Elected government official, insurance representative. **PERSONAL:** Born Aug 09, 1953, Siler City, NC; married Karen Mechelle McClain; children: Carla Michelle, Karen Nicole. **EDUCATION:** NC Central Univ, BA Phil 1976; Univ of MA at Amherst, Masters Reg Planning 1985. **CAREER:** Town of Pittsboro, patrolman 1976-78; Home Security Life Ins Co, sales rep 1978-80; North State Legal Svcs, legal asst 1980-83; liscensed realtor 1982-; Charlotte Liberty Mutual Ins Co, sales rep 1984-; Chatham Co, co commissioner; Monumental Life Insurance Co, sales rep 1986-. **ORGANIZATIONS:** Bd of dirs Capital Health Systems Agency 1978; bd of dirs Joint Orange Chatham Comm Action 1980; bd of dirs Council on Aging Chatham Co 1983; CEO Capital Development Inc 1982-; CEO NC Woodcutters Assn Inc 1984-; Rural Economic Develop consultant 1984-; consultant Social Security 1984-; Wesley Chapel United Church of Christ, assoc minister 1986-; Central Caroline Tech Coll, board of trustees 1986-. **HONORS/ACHIEVEMENTS:** Natl Rural Fellowship Nat Rural Fellows Inc NY 1983-84; Outstanding Young Men of America 1986. **HOME ADDRESS:** Rt 2 Box 263, Bear Creek, NC 27207. **BUSINESS ADDRESS:** County Commissioner, Chatham Co, Chatham Co Courthouse, Pittsboro, NC 27312.

THOMPSON, CAROL BELITA
Government official. **PERSONAL:** Born Aug 05, 1951, Washington, DC. **EDUCATION:** Smith Coll, BA 1973; NY Univ, MPA 1975. **CAREER:** Govt of the Dist of Columbia, spec asst housing 1979-81, act dir licenses, inv 1981-83, dir consumer & reg affairs 1983-86, mayor's chief of staff 1986-87, dep mayor econ dev 1987-. **ORGANIZATIONS:** Bd mem Natl Conf of Christians & Jews 1983-; bd mem Ronald McDonald House 1985-; bd pres Asbury Dwellings Home for Seniors 1985-; co-chairperson DC Downtown Partnership 1987-. **HONORS/ACHIEVEMENTS:** NASPFAA Urban Adm Fellow; Martin Luther King Jr Fellow; Outstanding Young Women in Amer 1982; Outstanding Prof Serv Awd Natl Assoc of Negro & Professional Women 1987; Outstanding Govt Serv Awd Natl Black MBA Assoc 1987. **BUSINESS ADDRESS:** Deputy Mayor - Econ Dev, District of Columbia, 1350 Pennsylvania Ave NW, Ste 401, Washington, DC 20004.

THOMPSON, CHARLES H.
Business owner. **PERSONAL:** Born May 24, 1945, Kimball, WV; son of Herbert Thompson and Ardella Richardson Thompson; married Harriet Jones Thompson, Jul 02, 1982; children: Charles Jr, Kellye, Eric, NaShawn. **EDUCATION:** Fisk U, BS 1967; TN St U, MA 1968; LA St U, PhD. **CAREER:** Southern Univ, swimming coach 1968-70; Dillard Univ, swimming coach 1970-74; Tuskegee Univ, assoc prof physical educ 1975; Charlie Tees Screen Printing, owner 1982-; Tuskegee Univ, head basketball coach 1975-88. **ORGANIZATIONS:** Aquatics dir YMCA; Am Swmng Coaches Assoc; Am Alliance Hlth Phy Ed & Rec ARC; aquatics adv New Orleans Rec Dept 1973-74; mem Natl Assoc of Basketball Coaches; pres SIAC Basketball Coaches Assoc; information dir SIAC 1981-85. **HONORS/ACHIEVEMENTS:** 1st Black Swmng Champ So AAU Coached 1973; SIAC Coach of the Year 1979; SIAC Championships 1979,80,82. **BUSINESS ADDRESS:** Owner, Charlie Tees, 108 S Main St, Tuskegee, AL 36083.

THOMPSON, CLARISSA J.
Educator. **PERSONAL:** Born Feb 24, 1930, Sugar Land, TX; divorced; children: Chanthini, Emmitt. **EDUCATION:** TX So U, BA 1951, MEd 1965. **CAREER:** Shrpstwn Jr High Hstn, emmitt asst prin 1971-; Hstn Independent School Dist, conselor 1965-71, english teacher 1955-65; Wdsn HS Nrmng, english math teacher 1952-55; Abrhm Schwrtz Firm Hstn, asst accountant 1951-52; Neighborhood Youth Corps, council 1970. **ORGANIZATIONS:** Mem Assn for Super & Curr Devel; TASCD; HASCD; TX Assn of Scndry Sch Prins; TX St Tchrs Assn; Hstn Prins Assn; Hstn Cncl of Edn; Phi DeltaKaapa Frat; cncl Delta Sigma Theta Sor One Am Proj 1970-72; mem Blue Bonnet Garden Club; Macgregor Civic Club; mem Strng Com Tri-U; Hrcrt Brace Invttnl Conf 1966; del TSTA Conv Dist IV 1974; mem HPA Exec Bd 1974-75; HPA Rep Consult Com for Mntn & Ops 1974-75. **BUSINESS ADDRESS:** Sharpstown Jr High St, 8330 Triola St, Houston, TX 77036.

THOMPSON, CLEON FRANKLYN, JR.
Educational administrator. **PERSONAL:** Born Nov 01, 1931, New York, NY; son of Cleon F Thompson Sr and Maggie Eady Thompson; divorced; children: Cleondra Thompson Jones. **EDUCATION:** NC Central Univ, BS 1954, MS 1956; Duke Univ, PhD 1977. **CAREER:** Shaw Univ, vice pres for academic affairs 1970, sr vice pres 1971-73; Univ of NC, acting vice pres 1975-76, vice pres student serv & special programs 1976-. **ORGANIZATIONS:** Mem advisory council NC Comm Coll Syst 1978-81; bd dir Shakespeare Festival 1978-81; pres Leadership Winston-Salem; mem, bd of dirs Winston-Salem Business. **HONORS/ACHIEVEMENTS:** Man of the Year Kappa Alpha Psi 1970; ACE Fellowship Acad Admin Amer Council on Educ 1970-71. **MILITARY SERVICE:** AUS 2nd lt 1953-55; Citation AUS Med Corps. **BUSINESS ADDRESS:** President, Winston-Salem University, Winston-Salem, NC 27110.

THOMPSON, DANIEL JOSEPH
Attorney. **EDUCATION:** Tskg Inst AL, 1948; Brown Univ (cum laude), BA 1970; Hrvrd Law Sch, JD 1973. **CAREER:** AT&T Co Wash DC, atty 1979-; S Cntrl Bell Tele Co, atty 1978-79; Lg Aldrdg Hnr Stvns & Smmr Atlnt GA, atty 1974-77; St of AL Mntgmry, asst atty gen 1973-74. **ORGANIZATIONS:** Vp AL Blk Lwyrs Assn 1974; mem Nat Bar Assn; Am Bar Assn 1975-80; exec com mem Gate City Bar Assn 1977; instr AbrnUniv Mntgmry 1974; bd of dir Atlnt Urban Leag 1975-77; mem Atlnt Jdcl Commn 1977. **BUSINESS ADDRESS:** American Telephone & Telegraph, 1120 20th St NW #1000, Washington, DC 20036.

THOMPSON, DAVID
Professional athlete. **PERSONAL:** Born Jul 13, 1954, Shelby, NC; son of Vellie Thompson and Ida Thompson; married Cathy; children: Erika, Brooke. **CAREER:** Denver Nuggets, guard 1975-82; Seattle Supersonics, guard 1982-85; director of Community Affairs, Charlotte Hornets, 1988-. **HONORS/ACHIEVEMENTS:** ABA Rookie of the Year 1975-76; All Star Game ABA 1976; All Star NBA 1977-79; 1 of only 2 players named MVP in both ABA & NBA All Star Game; All Star Game NBA 1979; Scored 10,000th point 1981; named All Atlantic Coast Conf Player of the Year 1973, 1974, 1975; named CO Athlete of the Year 1975;

Eastman Awd Collegiate Basketball Player of the Year 1974-75; Inducted into NC Sports Hall of Fame 1982; NBA All Star Starter, 1983. **BUSINESS ADDRESS:** Charlotte Hornets Dir of Community Affairs, 2 Firstunion Center, Charlotte, NC 28282.

THOMPSON, DEBORAH MARIA
Physician. **PERSONAL:** Born May 04, 1958, Philadelphia, PA; daughter of William C Thompson and Hazel Logan Thompson; married Omer Abadir, May 29, 1982. **EDUCATION:** Howard Univ, BS (Magna Cum Laude) 1980; Howard Univ Coll of Medicine, MD 1982; Univ of MD, Post Graduate 1982-85. **CAREER:** Dept of Family Medicine Univ of MD, chief resident 1984-85; Community Health Ctr, medical dir 1985-. **ORGANIZATIONS:** Mem Amer Acad of Family Physicians, LA Acad of Family Physicians. **HONORS/ACHIEVEMENTS:** Mem Alpha Omega Alpha Medical Honor Soc 1982-; Diplomate Amer Bd of Family Practice 1985-92. **BUSINESS ADDRESS:** Physician, Capital Area Permanente Medical Group, 4200 Wisconsin Ave, Suite 300, Washington, DC 20016.

THOMPSON, DEHAVEN LESLIE (DEE)
Reporter, journalist. **PERSONAL:** Born Aug 22, 1939, Philadelphia, PA; married Patricia Marlene Eberhardt; children: Shannon Leslie, Tara Neile. **EDUCATION:** Geneva Coll, BA 1968. **CAREER:** WIIC-TV Pittsburgh, news & sports rprtr 1975-; WTAE-TV Pittsburgh, prdcr, assgnmnt ed 1970-75; WTAE-TV & WTAE,RADIO AM Pittsburgh, 1st blk nws ed-rptr 1966-70; Beaver Falls News Trib, 1st blk asst sprts ed 1964-66, 1st blk sprts rptr 1959-64; Black Chronicle TV Show, crtr 1968. **ORGANIZATIONS:** Mem Pittsburgh Press Club; bd mem Pittsburgh Pastoral Inst; mem Sigma Delta Chi; mem Pittsburgh Yth Motivation Task Force; mem Bob Moose Meml Fund Com. **HONORS/ACHIEVEMENTS:** Recip PA Asso Press Award for Top Sports & News Story of Yr 1973; Golden Quill Award (Pittsburgh TV Emmy), Series on Hndcpd Athls 1977; Meritous Srv Award, Penn Hills NAACP 1977. **MILITARY SERVICE:** USNG 6 yrs. **BUSINESS ADDRESS:** WPXI-TV, 11 TV Hill, Pittsburgh, PA 15214.

THOMPSON, DONNELL
Professional football player. **PERSONAL:** Born Oct 27, 1958, Lumberton, NC. **EDUCATION:** Attended Univ of NC. **CAREER:** Baltimore, 1981-83; Indianapolis, defensive end 1984-. **BUSINESS ADDRESS:** Defensive End, Indianapolis Colts, PO Box 24100, Indianapolis, IN 46224.

THOMPSON, DONNIS HAZEL
Educator. **PERSONAL:** Born Apr 01, 1933, Chicago, IL; son of John and Katherine. **EDUCATION:** Geo Wms Coll, BS 1956, MS 1959;Univ of N CO, EdD 1967. **CAREER:** Sheil House CYO Youth Ctr, prog dir 1956-59; Hyde Park HS, dept chairperson 1956-60; USA Women's Track & Field Team, head coach 1962; Univ Women Athl, sel head coach 1975; HI State, supt of educ 1981-83, chair, Dr Martin Luther King Jr Goverors Interim Commission 1988-; Univ of HI, prof. **ORGANIZATIONS:** Am Assn of Hlth Phys Ed & Rec; Alpha Kappa Alpha Sor; Assn for Intrclgt Athl for Women; Polit Caucus; Intl Women's Yr. **HONORS/ACHIEVEMENTS:** Author "Women's Track & Fld", Allyn & Bacon 1969; "Modern Track & Fld for Girls & Women", Allyn & Bacon 1971; "Prentice-Hall Activities Hndbk", Prentice-Hall 1973; author of 20 articles in professional mags; Female Ed of Yr,Univ NC Alumni Assn 1976; Coaching Accmpl; 2 World Record Hldrs; 10 Natl AAU Champ; 6 Partic in Pan Am Games 1959, 1963; 6 Am Record Hldrs; 3 Natl AAU Team Champs; 1 Jr Natl AAU Team Champs; 9 Olympic Partic; Dist Srv Award, Hawaiian Athl Union 1962; feature article CA Phys Ed & Rec Jrnl 1974; recip Dist Srv Award, Hawaii St Am Assoc of Hlth Phys Ed & Rec 1974; pec resol HI St Legis CommendingUniv of Hawaii's Women's Athl Prog 1976; Univ of Hawaii Honor Award, Univ of Hawaii 1989; Outstanding Achievement Award, Hawaii Federation of Women's Clubs 1975-85; selected for Women of Vision Exhibit, YWCA 1987; selected for Women of Hawaii series on TV KCMB channel 9, Honoring Women Leaders 1988. **BUSINESS ADDRESS:** Professor, Univ of Hawaii, 1337 Lower Campus Rd, Honolulu, HI 96822.

THOMPSON, EDWIN A.
College president. **CAREER:** Atlanta Metropolitan College, GA, president. **BUSINESS ADDRESS:** President, Atlanta Metropolitan College, Atlanta, GA 30310. *

THOMPSON, EMMA M.
Educator. **PERSONAL:** Born Aug 21, 1920, Clinton, SC; married Benjamin L; children: Bennye Yolande, Herbert Godfrey, Peggy Cassandra, Vincent Edward, Andre Claudia. **EDUCATION:** Lander Coll, AA Erly Chldhd 1972; Allen U, BS Erly Chldhd 1974. **CAREER:** GLEAMS Comm Act Head Start, educ dir 1985; Newberry Co School Dist, teacher 1951; Spartanburg Co School Dist, teacher 1947; Tauber Mfg Co NY, machinist 1943-45; Marlboro School Dist, teacher 1942-43; SC St Funeral Dir Thompson's Mortuary, co-owner, family consultant 1949-75. **ORGANIZATIONS:** Asst sec SC Mortician Assn 1972-; OES 1951; bd, choir Friendship AME Ch; life mem NAACP. **BUSINESS ADDRESS:** 235 S Bell St, Clinton, SC 29325.

THOMPSON, ERA BELL
Editor. **PERSONAL:** Born in Des Moines, IA. **EDUCATION:** Morningside Coll, BA 1933, hon LLD 1965. **CAREER:** ISES, sr interviewer 1942-47; Johnson Pub, assoc editor 1947-51; Ebony, co-managing editor 1951-64; intl editor 1964-; Johnson Publ Co, editor. **ORGANIZATIONS:** Formerly Community Art Ctr 1942-44; bd mem Chicago Met YWCA 1944-47; author "American Daughters" 1946; author "Africa Land of My Fathers" 1954; mem Friends Chicago Pub Libr 1959-60; Nat Council of Christians & Jews 1960-69; Hull House 1960-64; dir Soc Midland Authors 1961-77; Chicago Press Club 1961-71; Zonta Int 1963-69; N Central Reg Manpower Adv Commn 1965-67; vol Cancer's Reach to Recovery 1972-78; spl pub com Amer Cancer Reach Com 1972; pub mem USIA Foreign Serv Selection Bd 1976; Intl Visitors Cntr 1976-78; Writing Chicago Prog Chicago Pub Libr 1976-79; life mem NAACP 1979. **HONORS/ACHIEVEMENTS:** Recipient Newberry Libr Fellowship 1945; Bread Loaf Writer's Conf fellow 1949; Capital Press Club citation 1961; Distinguished Alumni Award Morningside Coll1974; ND's Theodore Roosevelt Roughrider Award 1976; portrait hung in ND Hall of Fame 1977. **BUSINESS ADDRESS:** Johnson Publishing Co, 810 S Michigan Ave, Chicago, IL 60605.

THOMPSON, ERIC R.
Educator. **PERSONAL:** Born Mar 23, 1941, Warren, OH. **EDUCATION:** Hiram Coll, BA. **CAREER:** Hiram Coll, asst dir of admsn. **ORGANIZATIONS:** Reg rep Minority Ed Serv Assn. **HONORS/ACHIEVEMENTS:** Outstndng Coll Athl of Am 1970-71; listed in Who's Who Amoung Stds in AmUniv & Coll 1970-71; Outstndng Yuoung Men of Am 1974. **MILITARY SERVICE:** USMC. **BUSINESS ADDRESS:** Ofc of Admissions, Hiram Coll, Hiram, OH 44234.

THOMPSON, EUGENE EDWARD
Physician. **PERSONAL:** Born Sep 25, 1938, Brooklyn, NY; son of Eugene Thompson and Corrie Thompson; married Corine; children: Eugene, Carlton, Valerie. **EDUCATION:** Brooklyn Coll, BA 1960; Howard Univ Coll Med, MD 1968. **CAREER:** Dept Alchohol & Drug Abuse, med dir; NY City Fire Dept, med ofc; Mt Sinai Hosp, sr clinical asst; NIH, clinical asso 1969-71; Hempstead Pvt Prac,physician. **ORGANIZATIONS:** diplomate Nat Bd Med Exmrs; Am Bd Intrntl Med; mem Am Coll Physicians; Phi Beta Sigma. **HONORS/ACHIEVEMENTS:** Alpha Omega Alpha Hon Med Soc 1967; Josioh Macy Faculty Flw 1974-76. **MILITARY SERVICE:** USPHS lt comdr 1969-71. **BUSINESS ADDRESS:** 160 N Franklin St, Hempstead, NY 11550.

THOMPSON, FLOYD
Dental surgeon. **PERSONAL:** Born Aug 05, 1914, Houston, TX; married Nellie Crawford; children: 6 Children. **EDUCATION:** Wiley Coll, AB 1937; Howard, dds 1942; USC dntl sch, post grad 1964. **CAREER:** Dr of Dent Surg, self empl 1985. **ORGANIZATIONS:** Mem AZ S Dent Soc; Nat Dent Assn; Am Dent Assn; mem NAACP; trustee Mt Calvary Bapt Ch; mem Urban Leag. **HONORS/ACHIEVEMENTS:** Man of Yr Award, Tuscon Chptr NAACP 1961; Alumni Award for Outstndng Contri to Civic & Comm Act 1971. **MILITARY SERVICE:** US Military maj 1942-46. **BUSINESS ADDRESS:** 2600 W Ironwood Hills, #5122, Tucson, AZ 85745.

THOMPSON, FRANCES E.
Retired art educator. **PERSONAL:** Born Jul 11, 1902, Nashville, TN. **EDUCATION:** TN St A&I Normal, Acad Deg 1918; MA Coll of Art, Professional Coll Diploma 1923, BS 1936; Harvard U, MS 1945. **CAREER:** TN St Univ, head of dept 1969-(ret); TN St Univ A&I Normal, prof of art 1945-69, artist, teacher 1923-45; commissioned for numerous portraits 1934-. **ORGANIZATIONS:** Art illstrtr Bapt Sun Sch Bd 1925-35; past pres Tchrs Assn TSU; mem Fine Arts Club TSU Fisk & Meharry; mem Pub Lib Davidson Co; mem Cheekwood Botonical Gdn; mem Alpha Kappa Alpha Sor; mem Cresa Lenox Club 1st Bapt Ch Capitol Hill. **HONORS/ACHIEVEMENTS:** Recip Outstndng Portraits Award, Nat Bapt Pub Bd 1935; Fgn Studies Flwshp Prague Czechoslovakia 1937-80; commissioned all art work req by TSU in 5 bldgs & On Coll Seal 1922; two schlrshps named in hon of Frances E Thompson, MA Coll of Art 1975; two Copper Plate Award, RadcliffeUniv 1978-79; art gallery named in hon of Frances E Thompson, MA Coll of Art 1979. **BUSINESS ADDRESS:** TN State Univ, Nashville, TN 37203.

THOMPSON, FRANCESCA
Educator, nun. **PERSONAL:** Born Apr 29, 1932, Los Angeles, CA. **EDUCATION:** Marian Coll, BA 1960; Xavier Univ, MEd 1963; Univ of MI, PhD 1972. **CAREER:** Marian Coll Indianapolis IN, chairperson theatre dept 1966-82; Fordham Univ, asst dean assoc prof afro-amer studies 1982-. **ORGANIZATIONS:** Faculty Martin Luther King Fellows 1973-; Natl Office for Black Catholics; Natl Black Sisters Conf; Natl Conf for Christians & Jews; Amer Theatre Assn; Natl Black Theatre Prog; Mid-west Black Theatre Alliance; Armstead-Johnson Found for Theatre Rsch NY; Martin Luther King Jr Fellow; Natl Adv Bd to the Natl Caucus of Black Aged; Natl PUSH Adv Bd; Natl Adv Council for the Conference of American Bishops. **HONORS/ACHIEVEMENTS:** Sojourner Truth Awd Marian Coll; Key to the City Clarksdale MS; 1981 Brotherhood Awd Natl Conf of Christians & Jews; Jan 12 1981 declared by Mayor of Oakland CA to be Sister Francesca Thompson Day in appreciation for being "Scholar in Residence" for Oakland Public Sch System; Dr Martin Luther King Human RightsAwd Indianapolis Educ Assn; NY State English Council Awd for Tchr of Excellence in Drama; Disting Alumnus Awd Marian Coll; Outstanding Teacher of the Year Fordham Univ 1986. **BUSINESS ADDRESS:** Assistant Dean, FordhamUniv, Office of Dean, Ktng Hall 302, Bronx, NY 10458.

THOMPSON, FRANK
Educator. **PERSONAL:** Born Oct 01, 1927, West Helena, AR; married Deloise D; children: Frank Jr. **EDUCATION:** Crescent Sch of TV & Brdcstng, Grad 1952; CUNY Vo Tech Tchr Ed, grad 1968; Adams Coll, MAED 1975. **CAREER:** City of NY, jr HS tchr, bd of ed; TV Sales & Srv, ownr-optr; Armed Forces, elect tech; Shoe Shine Chain, ast mgr; NY Recorder, column. **ORGANIZATIONS:** Fdr, pres Better TV Dlrs Assoc; union del UFT; NYSUT; AFT; NEA; pres FACEJ Srv Corp; mem Black Trade Unionists Ldrshp Comm; mem Crispus Attucks Dem Club; worshipful mstr Essene Lodge AASRFM; command in chf Grand Consist of NY; patron Excel Chap 76 OES; patron, Matron & Patrons Cncl; OES. **HONORS/ACHIEVEMENTS:** Coronated "Soverign Grand Insp Gen", Supreme Cncl LA AASRFM; placque, letters of commendation Var Civ Grps. **MILITARY SERVICE:** GKCS cadet corp, col. **BUSINESS ADDRESS:** 131 Ave of Americas, New York, NY 10013.

THOMPSON, FRANK L.
Retired business executive. **PERSONAL:** Born Mar 28, 1903, New York, NY; son of Wilson Thompson and Laura Ann Johnson; married Marcie L Taylor, Dec 25, 1930; children: Dr Judy Hammer, Dr Carolyn Brown. **EDUCATION:** Cornell Univ, CE 1924; NY Univ, MBA 1929. **CAREER:** Design of New York City Projects Bridges-Water Supply, civil engr designer 1924-80; FL Thompson Assoc-Design of Homes, pres 1946-58; Slingerland Boosse Arch & Engr, assoc partner 1958-67; Allied Federal Savings & Loan, pres brd chrmn 1960-80; Money Management Service, pres, owner 1985-. **ORGANIZATIONS:** Trustee Long Island Jewish Hosp 1978-; brd of dir Greater Jamaica Chamber of Comm; brd of dir Jamaica Devel Corp 1975-85; mem Life, Am Soc Civil Engr 1948; mem NY Soc Municipal Engrs 1946; mem Nat Techl Assn, Alpha Phi Alpha Frat, Sigma Pi Phi Frat Cornell Univ Council 1976. **HOME ADDRESS:** 85-14 150th St, Jamaica, NY 11435.

THOMPSON, FRANK WILLIAM
Physician. **PERSONAL:** Born Jan 15, 1928, Georgetown, Guyana;married Nellie; children: Errington, Melissa, Michele, Frank II. **EDUCATION:** Morgan State Univ, BS 1955;

KS City Osteopathic Med Coll, DO 1961. **CAREER:** Dr Frank W Thompson & Assoc, pres. **ORGANIZATIONS:** Mem State Med Bd NY, OH, TX; diplomate Amer Ost Bd Gen Practice; flw Amer Coll Gen Practitioners; reg med consult Region V Job Corps 1976; adv bd TX Legislative Joint Sub-com on Pub Hlth 1974-75; mem TX Osteopathic Med Assn Govt Rels Com 1974-76; exec admissions com TX Osteo Med Coll 1974-76;hlth care com Comm Cncl Grtr Dallas 1975; mem Amer Coll Gen Prac Osteo Med & Surgery; Amer Osteo Assn; TX Osteo Med Assn; Amer Heart Assn; Natl Med Assn; Amer Public Health Assn; sec treas Alpha Phi Alpha Frat; bd mem Dallas Urban League; dir 2nd vice pres BSA; chmn W View Dist Health & Safety Comm; hon life mem US Lawn Tennis Assn; Amer Contract Bridge League. **BUSINESS ADDRESS:** President, Dr Frank W Thompson & Assocs, 2850 Singleton Blvd, Dallas, TX 75212.

THOMPSON, GARLAND LEE
Journalist. **PERSONAL:** Born May 02, 1943, Chester, PA; divorced; children: Consuella Alicia, Grace Lynn. **EDUCATION:** Temple Univ, BA Journalism 1975, JD 1983. **CAREER:** Bell Telephone of PA, switchman 1963-73; Philadelphia Inquirer, copy editor 1975-78, editorial writer 1978-81, reporter 1981-84; Philadelphia Tribune, exec editor. **ORGANIZATIONS:** Instr GED Prep Community Coll Philadelphia 1975-76; mem Joint Comm on Minority Editorialists of Broadcast Editorial Assoc 1979-81, Natl Assoc Black Jrnl, Natl Conf of Edit Writers; faculty editor Inst for Jrnl Ed-Editing Program for Minority Journalists 1980,81; mem PA Bar Assoc 1984-. **HONORS/ACHIEVEMENTS:** 1st Black Mem Inquirer Edit Bd 1978-81; Ed of Nation's oldest black newspaper Philadelphia Tribune; Put together largest single ed 100 pages in the Tribunes history 1984; Barristers' Awd Excellence in Trial Advocacy 1982. **MILITARY SERVICE:** USN electronics tech 2nd clas (commun) 1965-68; 2nd Honorman 1966. **BUSINESS ADDRESS:** Executive Editor, Philadelphia Tribune, 520-26 Tribune Walk, Philadelphia, PA 191469990.

THOMPSON, GERALDINE
Educator, nurse. **PERSONAL:** Born in Dunkirk, NY; married John W Thompson Sr; children: John Jr, T/Sgt Brian, Dennis. **EDUCATION:** Jamestown School of Practical Nursing, 1954; Jamestown Comm Coll, 1968. **CAREER:** Jamestown Gen Hosp, staff nurse 1954-75, psych nursing 1975-. **ORGANIZATIONS:** Bd of dir Elizabeth W Marvin Comm House 1957-59; 1st black Committeewoman City Dem Comm 1964-75; 1st black Jamestown Gen Hosp Womens Aux 1965-67; appt to Selective Serv Bd 1985-; mem Nurses Assoc of Jamestown Gen Hosp 1966-; treas Cty Dem Womens Club 1966-68; mem Chautauqua Cty Dem Womens Club 1968-72; 1st black Jamestown Soc Serv 1970-72; bd of dir YWCA 1972-75, 1985-; mem Family Serv Inc 1974-76, Chautauqua Cty Econ Devel Comm 1977-78, Amer Heart Assoc Southwestern 1976-81, Comm Serv Bd of Chautauqua Cty Mental Health Dept 1979-85; bd mem Striders Youth Org 1982-1985, Jamestown School Bd 1982-, Jamestown School of Practical Nursing 1983-1985; vice pres Jamestown Gen Hosp Nurses Assoc 1966-69; mem Nat'l Caucus of Blk Schl bd mem; chairperson, NY State School Board Assn Advisory Co mm on Minority Issues 1989-; 1st vice pres, YWCA 1986-; bd dir, NY State Small City School Assn 1987-, Chautauqua County School Boards Assn 1987-; honorary life mem, NY State PTA 1989. **HONORS/ACHIEVEMENTS:** 1st woman pres Jamestown School Bd 1983-; 1st black on Selective Serv Bd; Advisory Comm on Minority Issues of the NY ST Schl Bds Assoc 1987-. **HOME ADDRESS:** 95 Liberty St, Jamestown, NY 14701.

THOMPSON, GLORIA CRAWFORD
Public affairs manager lobbyist. **PERSONAL:** Born Aug 12, 1942, Philadelphia, PA; divorced. **EDUCATION:** Cheyney State Univ, PA, BS Ed1968; St Joseph Coll, PA, MBA candidate 1978; Temple Univ, PA, Pub Rel 1962; Univ of PA, PA, Real Estate 1973, Master, Government Administration 1990. **CAREER:** SmithKline Beckman Corp, adv & sales promo 1968-72, news relations assoc 1973-75; Opportunities Industrialization Center of Amer, edtr OIC Keynens 1970-72; Natl Alliance of Businessmen, dir, coll rel 1974-76; Smithkline Beckman Corp, adv & Sales promo 1968-72, news relations assoc 1973-75, public affairs assoc 1975-87, assoc mgr Penna govt 1987-; Ross Associates, Philadelphia PA, corporate relations consultant 1989-. **ORGANIZATIONS:** Frmr natl sec Natl Assoc of Mkt Dvlprs (NAMD); Philadelphia Chptr Pres (NAMD); mem Public Affrs Comm PA Chamber of Comm; mem State Govt Comm Philadelphia Chamber of Comm; bd of dir Art Matters, Inc; vice chmn bd of dirs Cheyney Univ Foundation, chmn 1988-; mem Mayor's Office of Comm Serv Adv Bd; mem Minority Retention TAsk Force, Hahnemann Hosp Univ. **HONORS/ACHIEVEMENTS:** Pres comdtn Pres Gerald Ford 1975; dist award Dr Charles Drew Awards Comm 1980; recogntn Natl Alliance of Businessmen 1975; mktr of the Yr Nat'l Assoc of Mkt Dvlprs 1974; hnry prfsn Prairie View State Univ 1975; Outstanding Young Women in Amer 1979-80. **HOME ADDRESS:** 2114 North 50th St, Philadelphia, PA 19131.

THOMPSON, HAROLD FONG
Architect. **PERSONAL:** Born Sep 01, 1943, Memphis, TN; married Delilah Dianne Smith; children: Alan Craig, Kimberly Jean, Roderie, Derrell. **EDUCATION:** Howard U, B Arch 1967. **CAREER:** Lyles Bissett Carlisle & Wolff, Wash, fallout shltr analyst, proj arch 1964-68; Walk Jones & Francis Mah, Memphis, proj arch 1968-69; job capt 1969-72; Clair Jones & Harold Thompson, Memphis, partner 1972-77; Thompson-Miller Arch, pres 1978-; Memphis Comm Design Ctr, vice pres 1972-74. **ORGANIZATIONS:** Mem Nat AIA; TN Soc Archs; Constrn Spcfctns Inst; mem Vollintine-Evergreen Comm Assn; natl trustee Hist Preservation; Ldrshp Memphis, Shelby FarmsPlng Bd 1979; mem Alpha Phi Alpha. **BUSINESS ADDRESS:** 1420 Union Ave, Memphis, TN 38104.

THOMPSON, HERMAN G.
Attorney. **PERSONAL:** Born in Cincinnati, OH; married Roberta Brown; children: Collette Hill, Janice Marwa. **EDUCATION:** Ludwig Coll of Music, BME 1952; Harris Teacher's Coll, BA 1957; Howard Univ Sch of Law, JD 1968. **CAREER:** Charlotte, NC, asst dist atty 1972; Private Practice, atty Wash, DC 1975-77; US House of Reps Post Office & Civil Serv Comm, atty 1977-80; Private Practice, atty Southern Pines, NC 1980-. **ORGANIZATIONS:** Atty Commerce Dept/Ofc of Minority Bus Enterprise Wash, DC 1972; pres Moore Cty Chap NAACP 1985-; chmn Minority Affairs/Moore Cty Republican Party 1985; NC State Bd of Transportation 1987-1989. **MILITARY SERVICE:** AUS Pfc. **HOME ADDRESS:** 105 Ft. Bragg Road, Southern Pines, NC 28387. **BUSINESS ADDRESS:** Attorney, 510 Broad Street N.W., Southern Pines, NC 28387.

THOMPSON, HILTON LOND
Educator. **PERSONAL:** Born Apr 29, 1927, Iota, LA; married Anne M Portlock; children: Ruth. **EDUCATION:** Tuskegee Inst, BS; Bradley Univ, MS; PA State Univ, Addl Study; Univ of SW LA, Cert. **CAREER:** Carpenter, architectural draftsman, estimator; Jackson Publ School Syst MS, teacher indust arts 1952-64; Acadia Parish School Bd, Lafayette Parish School Syt, Jeff Davis Parish School Syst, teacher indust arts & soc studies. **ORGANIZATIONS:** Mem NEA, LA Educ Assoc, Acadia Parish Teachers Assoc, LA Indust Arts Assoc, Amer Indust Arts Assoc, 7th Dist Ed Assoc,; past sec, treas 7th Reg Indust Arts Assoc; mem Reserve Officers Assoc, Omega Psi Phi, 32nd Degree Mason; evaluation comm So Assoc of Sec Schools & Colls; spec & consult IndustEd Sec Frontiers Intl Serv Club. **HONORS/ACHIEVEMENTS:** Designed buffing wheel jig; Publ 2 professional articles. **MILITARY SERVICE:** USAF capt 2 yrs.

THOMPSON, HOBSON, JR.
Librarian. **PERSONAL:** Born Sep 26, 1931, Tuscumbia, AL; son of Hobson Thompson Sr and Marie (Belue) Thompson (deceased); married Geneva S; children: Michael Stewart, Sharon M. **EDUCATION:** AL State Univ, BS in sec ed 1953; Atlanta Univ, MS in LS 1958. **CAREER:** Morris Coll, head librarian/Instr math 1954-62; elizabeth City State Univ, head librn/Ass't prof math 1962-74; Chicago Public Libr, branch head 1976-. **ORGANIZATIONS:** Mem Amer Libry Assoc 1953-; mem Amer Topical Assoc 1982-; mem Omega Psi Phi Frat 1951-; mem Beta Kappa Chi hnry sci soc 1952-; mem Ebony Society of Philatelic Events and Reflections 1989-. **HONORS/ACHIEVEMENTS:** Masters Thesis A Study Of The Communications Behavior Of The Residents Of Census Tract F-39, Atlanta GA. **MILITARY SERVICE:** USN rm/te 3rd class. **HOME ADDRESS:** 400 E 33rd St, Apt 212, Chicago, IL 60616. **BUSINESS ADDRESS:** Chicago Public Library, 115 S Pulaski Rd, Chicago, IL 60624.

THOMPSON, IKE
State representative. **PERSONAL:** Born Nov 08, 1915, Birmingham, AL; married Lodeamer; children: Arwilda Storey. **EDUCATION:** Attended, Fenn Coll, Cleveland State Univ. **CAREER:** Ohio House of Representatives, rep to the 14th dist. **ORGANIZATIONS:** Bd chmn 14th Dist Civic League 1971-; permanent mem Natl Conf of State Legislatures 1975-; exec vice pres Black Elected Democrats of OH 1975-; chmn Transportation and Urban Affairs Comm 1975-; mem Economic Develop/Small Business Comm 1985-; co-chair Cuyahoga Co Delegation 1985-; chmn Ohio Retirement Study Commn 1987-. **HONORS/ACHIEVEMENTS:** Man of the Year 13th Dist Civic League 1969; Outstanding Legislator House of Representatives 1973. **BUSINESS ADDRESS:** Representative of 14th Dist, Ohio House of Representatives, Statehouse, Columbus, OH 43215.

THOMPSON, IMOGENE A.
Educator. **PERSONAL:** Born Aug 13, 1927, Stonewall, MS; married Rev Marcellous C; children: Gail P. **EDUCATION:** Jackson St U, BS 1959; UW, MS 1967; MS S & MS St, Further Study. **CAREER:** Meridian Public School, teacher 32 Yrs. **ORGANIZATIONS:** Pres Bapt Ministers' Wives Alliance 1976-80; pres Assn of Meridian Educators 1979-81; mem Ed Com C of C 1979-81; mem Lay Adv Com St Dept of Ed 1977-81; mem St Bd of Mgrs Rprsntng MS Congress of Parents & Tchrs 1977-81. **HONORS/ACHIEVEMENTS:** Outstndng Ldrshp Award, St Tchrs Assn 1976; Hum Rels Award, St Tchrs Assn 1976; 11th Edition Prsnlts of the S, Am Biographical Inst 1980; MS Tchr of the Yr, St Dept of Ed 1980. **BUSINESS ADDRESS:** Meridian Public Schools, 4101 27th Avenue, Meridian, MS 39301.

THOMPSON, ISAIAH
Government official. **PERSONAL:** Born Nov 08, 1915, Birmington, AL; children: 1 daughter. **CAREER:** State of OH, rep Dist 14 1971-. **ORGANIZATIONS:** V chmn Cty Dem Party; founder 13th Dist Civic League. **BUSINESS ADDRESS:** Representative, State of Ohio, 899 E 128th St, Cleveland, OH 44108.

THOMPSON, JAMES W.
Dentist. **PERSONAL:** Born Jan 08, 1943, Birmingham; married Charlie Mae; children: Scott Frederick. **EDUCATION:** BS 1970; DDS 1974. **CAREER:** Jackson MI Pvt Prac, dent 1975-; Detroit Maternal & Infant Care Proj, dent 1974-75; Wayne Co Comm Coll, 1971-74; Difco Labs, 1967-71;Univ of TN 1965-67; Wayne St U, tissue culture tech 1961-65. **ORGANIZATIONS:** Mem Jackson Dist Dental Soc; Wolverine Dental Soc;Univ of Detroit Black Dental Alumni Assn; career prog Detroit Pub Schs; Detroit Head Start Proj, Dental Svcs; mem Detroit Jaycees; Children's Hosp Christmas Party Com; Omega Psi Phi Frat; chmn Soc Act Com. **HONORS/ACHIEVEMENTS:** Recip Nat Hlth Professional Schlrshp; Robt Tindal Schlrshp. **BUSINESS ADDRESS:** 123 N West Ave, Jackson, MI 49201.

THOMPSON, JEFFREY EARL
Certified public accountant. **PERSONAL:** Born Apr 13, 1955, Mandiville, Jamaica. **EDUCATION:** Univ of the District of Columbia, BBA 1980; Certified Public Accountant 1981. **CAREER:** Natl Rifle Assoc, asst comptroller 1978-80; Mitchell/Titus & Co, sr accountant 1980-81; Leeny Redcross & Co, mgr 1981-83; Thompson & Assocs PC, CPA's, pres 1983-. **ORGANIZATIONS:** Mem American Inst of Certified Public Accountants 1978-, Alumni Assoc Coll of Business & Public Admin Univ of DC 1980-, Natl Assoc of Black Accountants 1980-; chair tax issues subcommittee DC Chamber of Commerce 1985-. **HONORS/ACHIEVEMENTS:** Who's Who Among Colls & Univs 1979-80; Natl Deans List 1979-80; Most Outstanding Accounting Graduate Univ of DC 1980; Outstanding Young Men of America 1984; Most Outstanding Alumni Univ of DC 1986. **HOME ADDRESS:** 322 Peabody St NW, Washington, DC 20011. **BUSINESS ADDRESS:** President, Thompson & Associates PC, 1275 K St NW, Ste 500, Washington, DC 20005.

THOMPSON, JESSE
Automobile dealer, executive. **CAREER:** Duryea Ford Inc, Brockport, NY, chief executive. **BUSINESS ADDRESS:** Duryea Ford Inc, 4875 Lake Rd, Brockport, NY 14420. *

THOMPSON, JESSE M.
Government official & educator. **PERSONAL:** Born Nov 03, 1946, Oxford, MS; daughter of Jesse Thompson and Irma Thompson; children: Stacey L Thompson, Latoya S Taylor. **EDUCATION:** CS Mott Community Coll, AA 1968; Eastern Michigan Univ, BA 1970; Univ of Michigan, MA 1975; Central Michigan Univ, MS 1980. **CAREER:** Detroit College of Business, management instructor 1976-; Michigan State Univ School of Criminal Justice, staff specialist 1980-; CS Mott Community College,treasurer, board of trustees 1980-87; Intake, Assessment and Referral Center, executive director, 1973-88; City of Fling, dir of personnel

& labor relations, currently. **ORGANIZATIONS:** Chairman Genessee County Criminal Justice Staff Advisory 1981-84; member Flint Assn of Black Administrators 1981-84; Paul Harris fellow Rotary Internaional 1983-; Governor's Substance Abuse Advisory Commission 1989-. **HONORS/ACHIEVEMENTS:** Humanitarian of the Year Flint Inner-City Lions Club 1980; Social Worker of the Year Michigan Assn of Black Social Workers 1981. **HOME ADDRESS:** 1810 Montclair Avenue, Flint, MI 48503. **BUSINESS ADDRESS:** Director of Personnel and Labor Relations, City of Flint, 1101 S Saginaw Street, Flint, MI 48502.

THOMPSON, JOHN ANDREW
Clergyman. **PERSONAL:** Born Dec 24, 1907, McCool, MS; married Maudie Louise Lee; children: John Andrew, Karl Anthony. **EDUCATION:** Jackson Coll, Under-grad Study; Atlanta U, Grad Study;Univ of Chicago, Grad Study;Univ of Omaha, Grad Study; Howard U, Sch of Religion, Grad Study 1950;Ministerial & Ind Coll W Point MS, DD. **CAREER:** Choctaw Co Sch MS, prin; Charleston MS, tchr, prin; Oakland Jr HS, 1938-41; Coll Hill HS, Pontotoc MS, prin 1941-44; Holmes Co Tr Sch Durant MS, 1944-45; Lawrence Co Tr Sch Supt 1945-46; Louisville MS Ch, pastor; Pontotoc MS, pastor; Macon MS Ch, pastor; Tabernacl Bapt Ch, W Palm Bch FL, pastor 1950; Bethel Bapt, 1951-54; Douglas Co Yth Ctr, supr 1956-66; Juveniles for NE, parole ofcr 1966-72. **ORGANIZATIONS:** Org Corinth Meml Bapt Ch 1955; dir Western Bapt Bible Coll, Omaha Ctr; bd mem NAACP; pres New Era Bapt St Conv of NE; fndr, pres Nat Leag ofBrthrhd & Peace; mem Interdenom Ministerial Alliance; mem Bapt Ministers Conf; Bapt Pastors Interracial Union; fdr, dir Martin Luther King Jr & Cultural Arts Ctr; bd mem Nat Bapt Conv USA Inc. **HONORS/ACHIEVEMENTS:** Award Outstndng Contrib to the Comm of Omaha 1969. **BUSINESS ADDRESS:** 3938 Florence Blvd, Omaha, NE 68110.

THOMPSON, JOHN ROBERT, JR.
College basketball coach. **PERSONAL:** Born Sep 02, 1941, Washington, DC; son of Robert Thompson and Anna Thompson; children: John III, Ronald, Tiffany. **EDUCATION:** Providence Coll, BA Economics, 1964, MA Guidance and Counseling, UDC, 1971. **CAREER:** Boston Celtics, player, 1964-66; St Anthony's High School, Washington DC, head basketball coach, 1966-72; Georgetown Univ, Washington DC, head basketball coach, 1972-; US Olympic Basketball Team, asst basketball coach 1976, head basketball coach 1988. **ORGANIZATIONS:** Past pres, bd of dir, Nat'l Assoc of Basketball Coaches 1976-; trustee, Basketball Hall of Fame; mem, selection comm for several intl and natl competitions. **HONORS/ACHIEVEMENTS:** Mem of NIT Championship Team, 1963; inducted into Providence College Hall of Fame, 1974; recipient of President's Award, Patrick Healy Award, Georgetown Univ, 1982; LHD Hon, St Peter's Coll, 1982; HHD, Wheeling Coll, 1982; named US Basketball Writer's Assn Coach of the Year and The Sporting News, 1983-84, Natl Assn of Basketball Coaches, 1984-85, and twice by the Big East Conference, 1979-80, 1986-87; recipient of many other awards. **BUSINESS ADDRESS:** Head Basketball Coach, Georgetown University, 37th & O Sts NW, Washington, DC 20057.

THOMPSON, JOHN WESLEY
Physician, business executive. **PERSONAL:** Born Feb 14, 1939, Bude, MS. **EDUCATION:** Howard Univ, BS; Allen Univ, BS; grad Univ IA; KC Coll, med sch; Flint Gen Hosp, residency internship; Univ MI, post-grad. **CAREER:** J & J Mgmt Co, co-founder; Thompson Family Clinic, physician/founder. **ORGANIZATIONS:** Mem Detroit Med Soc, Intl Acad Prevention Med, Wayne Co Med Assn, MI Assn Osteopathic; chief athletic med exam State MI Boxing, mem Natl Med Assn Inc, Amer Prof Practice Assn, MI Diabetes, Smithsonian Inst, Alumni Assn KC, Coll Osteopathic Med; personal ringside physician former World ChampionJoe Frazier; mem Alpha Phi Alpha Frat; life mem NAACP, YMCA, NY Dept State Athletic Commn, Oak Grove African Meth Epis Church.

THOMPSON, JOHNNIE
Elected official. **PERSONAL:** Born Jan 10, 1930, Walterboro, SC; married Thelma; children: Anita P Fryar, Rochelle, Ronnie. **EDUCATION:** Palmer Coll, AS Public Serv Criminal Justice major 1976; attended Rice Bus Coll Charleston, SC. **CAREER:** Colleton Cty Political Action, pres & founder 1969; City of Walterboro, Teledyne Inc, production spvsr 1971-83; Big-O Chrysler, new car slsmn; City of Walteoro, city cnclmn. **ORGANIZATIONS:** 1st exalted ruler Colleton Cty Elk Lodge 1975; 32nd Degree Mason; mem NAACP, Amer Legion, AUS Retired Assoc; Piney Grove Baptist Church. **HONORS/ACHIEVEMENTS:** Noble of the Mystic Shrine Arabion Temple #139; Bronze Level of Professional Sales Chrysler 1984; Salesman of the Year Big-O Chrysler Plymouth Dodge 1984. **MILITARY SERVICE:** AUS Armor Tank Platoon Sgt; Army Commendation; CIB; Bronze Star; Korean Pres Citation; Retired after 20 yrs hon serv served 11 mo combat in Korean War. **HOME ADDRESS:** 502 Padgett Loop, Walterboro, SC 29488.

THOMPSON, JOSEPH ALLAN
Retired psychiatric social worker. **PERSONAL:** Born Nov 02, 1906, Atlantic City, NJ; son of William E Thompson and Fannie E Sims Thompson; married Tracy Harvey, Dec 28, 1936 (deceased). **EDUCATION:** Natl Training School for Boy Scout Exec Mendham NJ, 1936; Washburn Univ Topeka KS, AB 1948; Univ of Chicago School of Social Serv Admin, 1948-49. **CAREER:** Shawnee Cty Juvenile Cty Topeka, juvenile & adult probation officer 1932-40; Menninger Found Topeka, psychiatric aide 1950-51; US Disciplinary Barracks Ft Leavenworth, clinical social worker 1951-76; Dept of the Army, psychiatric social worker 1976-retired. **ORGANIZATIONS:** Deacon Grace Episcopal Cathedral Topeka 1956-; mem exec bd Jayhawk Area Council BSA, Amer Cancer Assoc KS; mem Governor's Advisory Council on Mental Health for KS; Topeka Housing Authority; Topeka Halfway House. **HONORS/ACHIEVEMENTS:** Silver Beaver Awd BSA 1962; Decorated for Meritorious Civilian Svc. **MILITARY SERVICE:** AUS sgt 1942-45, 1976. **BUSINESS ADDRESS:** Psychiatric Social Worker, Dept of the Army, US Disciplinary Barracks, Fort Leavenworth, KS 66027.

THOMPSON, JOSEPH E.
Interim college president. **CAREER:** Talladega College, Talladega, AL, interim president. **BUSINESS ADDRESS:** Talladega College, Talladega, AL 35160. *

THOMPSON, JOSEPH ISAAC
Postmaster. **PERSONAL:** Born Aug 21, 1922, Amelia County, VA; married Mabel K; children: Sina Joann. **EDUCATION:** VA Union U, 1942. **CAREER:** US Post Srv, postmaster; Postal Wrkr's Union WI, pres Madison WI, alderman 5 yrs. **ORGANIZATIONS:** Grand lect Prince Masonic Lodge; WI Dept of Hlth & Soc Srv Oral Exam Bd; pres City of Madison Water Commn 1970-75; Mem Nat Assn Pstmstrs US. **HONORS/ACHIEVEMENTS:** Sup Accomplish Award, Postal Srv 1968. **MILITARY SERVICE:** WW II vet. **BUSINESS ADDRESS:** Postmaster, US Postal Service, 300 Mill St, Beloit, WI 53511.

THOMPSON, KAREN ANN
Financial analyst. **PERSONAL:** Born Jun 12, 1955, Fairborn, OH; daughter of Jack Long Thompson and Marlien Vaughn Thompson. **EDUCATION:** Univ of Dayton, BS 1977; Indiana Univ, MBA 1984. **CAREER:** Coopers & Lybrand, auditor 1977-79; Cummins Engine Co, intl collections mgr 1979-82; Chrysler Corp, financial analyst 1984-. **ORGANIZATIONS:** Alumni bd of governors Univ of Dayton 1986-. **HONORS/ACHIEVEMENTS:** Certified Public Accountant State of IN 1980; Fellowship Consortium for Grad Study in Mgmt 1982-84. **HOME ADDRESS:** 4056 Three Oaks Blvd, Troy, MI 48098.

THOMPSON, LANCELOT C. A.
Educator. **PERSONAL:** Born Mar 03, 1925; married Naomi E; children: Lancelot Jr, Carol Lynn, Angela Maria. **EDUCATION:** BS 1952; PhD 1955. **CAREER:** Wolmers Boys School, teacher 1955-56; Penn St Univ, research fellow 1957; Univ Toledo, asst prof 1958, asst dean 1964, vice pres, prof 1966, vice pres student affairs 1985. **ORGANIZATIONS:** Chmn local sect Am Chemical Soc; mem NY Acad Sci; exec com Nat Std Prsnl Adminstrs 1972; editorial bd NASPA Jrnl 1972; mem Mayor's Com on Alcoholism; Toledo Dev Com; life mem NAACP; mem, Pres local grp Torch Intl 1974; Phi Kappa Phi 1963; Sigma Xi 1956; Blue Key 1964. **HONORS/ACHIEVEMENTS:** Key to Golden Door Award, Intl Inst 1973; Distngshd Bro Award, Mdwstrn Reg, Alpha Phi Alpha Frat 1973. **BUSINESS ADDRESS:** 2801 W Bancroft, Toledo, OH 43606.

THOMPSON, LARRY D.
Attorney. **PERSONAL:** Born Nov 15, 1945, Hannibal, MO; son of Ezra Thompson and Ruth Thompson; married Brenda Taggart;; children: Larry Jr, Gary. **EDUCATION:** Culver-Stockton Coll Canton MO, BA 1967; MI State Univ, MA 1969; Univ of MI Ann Arbor, JD 1974. **CAREER:** Monsanto Co St Louis MO; staff atty 1974-77; King & Spalding Atlanta GA, assoc 1977-82; US Dept of Justice, US attorney (Northern District of Georgia) 1982-86; King & Spalding Atlanta GA, partner 1986-. **ORGANIZATIONS:** Mem Amer Bar Assoc, Gate City Bar Assn, State Bar of GA, The MO Bar, Natl Bar Assoc, GA Comm on Bicentennial of US Constitution; bd of dir Atlanta Urban League; bd of dirs, King-Tisdale Cottage Foundation, Savannah GA; bd of dirs, Georgia Republican Foundation 1989; chmn, Georgia Lawyers for Bush 1988. **HONORS/ACHIEVEMENTS:** Dist Alumni Awd Culver-Stockton Coll Canton MO 1983; AT Walden Awd Gate City Bar Assn 1984. **BUSINESS ADDRESS:** Partner, King & Spalding, 2500 Trust Co Tower, Atlanta, GA 30311.

THOMPSON, LA SALLE LAVELLE
Professional athlete. **PERSONAL:** Born Jun 23, 1961, Cincinnati, OH. **CAREER:** Kansas City Kings, center. **HONORS/ACHIEVEMENTS:** Top Kings rebound (82) & shot blocker (147 total 21); had 38 double figure scoring games in 83-84 season; in college led NCAA Dev rebounding in 81-82 with 135 ave; set all TX rebounding records single game (21); most rebounds season (370 in 1980-81); led TX in scoring soph & jr years.

THOMPSON, LAURETTA PETERSON (LAURETTA NAYLOR)
Educator. **PERSONAL:** Born Sep 19, Chicago, IL; daughter of Arthur W Peterson and Ada Ferrell Peterson; married Gears H, Sep 22, 1973. **EDUCATION:** Wilson Jr Coll, 1942; Chicago Tchrs Coll, BA 1949, BE 1949; NWU, MA 1953; Vanderbilt Univ of George Peabody Coll, EdD 1983. **CAREER:** Wendell Smith, asst prin 1973-; McCosh Primary, asst prin 1960-69; Mntl Hlth Prog, coord dir 1969-73; rdng coord, adjstmnt cnslr 1954-60. **ORGANIZATIONS:** Elem Adjstmnt Tchrs Assn; Chicago Assn of Asst Elem Prins; former vice pres Woodlawn Mntl Hlth Ctr; former bd chmn Plano Child Dev Ctr; Alpha Kappa Alpha; Alpha Gamma Pi; NAACP; mem Kappa Delta Pi Hon Soc Educ; Natl Assn of Univ Wmn; vice pres Berean Ch Credit Union; 2nd vice pres Wendell Smith Hm & Sch Assn; Urban League; PUSH; gen supt Berean Baptist Church Sch; pres, Beatrice Caffrey Youth Service Inc. **HONORS/ACHIEVEMENTS:** Theta Omega Chap AKA; semi-finalist K Maremont Tchr of Yr; dedication awd AME Ch 1976; plywrtr, prod Credit Union Plays 1966-68, 1970, 1974, 1976; COSROW Award, Commission On the Status and Role of Women, South Shore United Methodist Church 1989. **BUSINESS ADDRESS:** Wendell Smith School, 744 E 103rd St, Chicago, IL 60628.

THOMPSON, LEONARD
Professional athlete. **PERSONAL:** Born Jul 28, 1952, Tucson, AZ; married Debbie; children: Christopher. **EDUCATION:** AZ Western Coll, attended; OK State, attended. **CAREER:** Detroit Lions, pro football wide receiver 1975-. **HONORS/ACHIEVEMENTS:** 82 Yd Recptn at New Engl, 3rd lngst in the NFL 1979; Man of the Year 1983. **BUSINESS ADDRESS:** Detroit Lions, 1200 Featherstone Rd, Box 4200, Pontiac, MI 48057.

THOMPSON, LEROY B.
Dentist. **PERSONAL:** Born Aug 13, 1921, New York, NY; son of William Thompson and Sarah Thompson; married Mary E McMichael. **EDUCATION:** St Augustine's Coll, BS (with Honors) 1947; Howard Univ Coll of Dentistry, DDS 1951. **CAREER:** VA, clerk 1943; US Immigration & Naturalization Serv NY Dist #3, clerk, typist 1947; Childrens Aid Soc Harlem, dentist 1953-54; Comm Serv Soc Harlem, dentist 1954-55; bur of Dentistry New York City Dept of Health, dentist 1955-81; private practice, dentist. **ORGANIZATIONS:** Mem Chi Delta Mu 1949; mem The Provident Clinical Soc of Brooklyn Inc 1959-79, Amer Dental Assn 1962-, Dental Soc of NY 1962-, 2nd Dist Dental Soc 1962-, Greater met NY Dental Soc 1972-, Natl Dental Assn 1975-. **HONORS/ACHIEVEMENTS:** Honorary mem, The Jamaica Dental Assn 1985. **MILITARY SERVICE:** AUS pvt 1942-43. **BUSINESS ADDRESS:** 805 Lincoln Pl, Brooklyn, NY 11216.

THOMPSON, LINDA JO
Association executive. **PERSONAL:** Born Aug 29, 1953, Oaklahoma City, OK; daughter of Moses E Paulden Jr and Emma Lucille Jones Paulden; married French F Thompson Jr, Aug 06, 1977; children: Emerald Michelle, French F III. **EDUCATION:** Lincoln Univ, Jefferson City MO, BA, 1975. **CAREER:** Mid-American Television, Jefferson City MO, office

mgr, 1978-84; Zeta Phi Beta Sorority, Inc, Washington DC, exec dir, 1984—. **ORGANIZATIONS:** Mem, Natl Coalition of Black Meeting Planners; bd mem, Natl Pan Hellenic Council; bd mem, Black Women's Political Action Forum. **HONORS/ACHIEVEMENTS:** Outstanding Young Women of America, 1985, 1986, 1988. **BUSINESS ADDRESS:** Executive Director, Zeta Phi Beta Sorority, Inc, 1734 New Hampshire Ave, NW, Washington, DC 20009.

THOMPSON, LITCHFIELD O'BRIEN
Educator, educational administrator. **PERSONAL:** Born Apr 15, 1937; married Bernadette Pearl Francis; children: Gennet, Hailu. **EDUCATION:** Enfield Coll of Tech LondonUniv Middlesex Eng, BS Sociology 1969;Univ of OR Eugene, MA Sociology 1972, PhD Sociology 1975. **CAREER:** WV St Coll, asst prof of sociology 1974-; Barbados Advocate Barbados WI, advertising layout spec 1959-61, advertising clk 1955-59. **ORGANIZATIONS:** Mem Am Sociological Assn; mem N Cent Sociological Assn. **HONORS/ACHIEVEMENTS:** Recip Radfen Medal Aden S Arabia, RAF 1966; flwshp Ford Found 1972-73; pub =Black Nationalism & the Garvey Movement toward an understanding", black Sociologist Vol 7 Nos 3/4 spring/sumer 1978. **MILITARY SERVICE:** RAF sr aircraftman 1961-66. **BUSINESS ADDRESS:** WV State Coll, Institute, WV 25112.

THOMPSON, LLOYD EARL
Physician. **PERSONAL:** Born Apr 10, 1934, Kingston, Jamaica;married Mercedee Ball; children: Damon, Arie. **EDUCATION:** Union Coll Lincoln NE, BA 1960; Howard Univ Washington DC, MD 1964. **CAREER:** Christian Welfare Hosp, chief of staff 1977-79; Homer G Phillips Hosp, supt; Washington Univ Med School, clinical instr; Private practice, physician. **ORGANIZATIONS:** Mem diplomate 1970, Fellow 1972, Amer Bd of Otolarynology 1970; pres St Clair Med Soc 1979; pres Comm Hosp Bd of Dir 1979; mem St Louis Ear Nose & Throat Club, Roman-Barnes Soc of Ophthalmology & Otolaryngology; bd mem So IL Med Utilization Review Org. **BUSINESS ADDRESS:** 4601 State St, Ste 375, East St Louis, IL 62205.

THOMPSON, LOWELL DENNIS
Artist. **PERSONAL:** Born Oct 08, 1947, Chicago, IL; children: Tanya Natasha. **EDUCATION:** Art Inst of Chicago, 1966. **CAREER:** Leo Burnett Co, art dir; J Walter Thompson Co, art dir, prod, creative grp head; Needham Harper & Steers Adv, art dir, prod 1972-74; Young & Rubicam Adv, art dir 1971-72; Greenwich Vlg NY, portrait art 1971; McLann Erickson Adv, art dir 1968-71; Am Assoc of Adv Agys, tchr 1974. **HONORS/ACHIEVEMENTS:** Two Awards Rep In Creativity 77 Show, Sponsored by Art Dir Magazine; Represented in Commun Arts Magazine, 1976; Honorable Mention Adv Club of NY 1971; 1st Prize Lk Meadows Art Fair 1966; scholarship Chicago Assn of Commerce & Indus Fire Prevention Poster Contest, 1966; Numerous Gold Keys & Scholarships in Scholastic Magazine Annual Art Competition. **BUSINESS ADDRESS:** Prudential Bldg, Chicago, IL 60601.

THOMPSON, M. T., JR.
Attorney and counselor. **PERSONAL:** Born Apr 15, 1951, Saginaw, MI; son of Rev. M. T. Thompson, Sr. and Pecola Matsen-Thompson; married Ivory C Triplet; children: Felicia L, Monica R. **EDUCATION:** Oakland Univ, BA 1973; Northeastern Univ Sch of Law, JD 1977. **CAREER:** Michigan Bell Telephone Co, mgr 1973-74; Natl Labor Relations Bd, attorney 1977-79; Lewis White & Clay PC, attorney 1979-83; MT Thompson Jr PC, attorney 1983-. **ORGANIZATIONS:** Admitted to practice MI Supreme Court 1977, US Sixth Circuit Court of Appeals 1980, US Supreme Court 1984. **HONORS/ACHIEVEMENTS:** Author "Institutional Employment Discrimination as a Legal Concept," 1981. **BUSINESS ADDRESS:** Attorney, MT Thompson Jr, PC, 330 South Washington Ave, Saginaw, MI 48607.

THOMPSON, MARCUS AURELIUS
Educator/musician. **PERSONAL:** Born May 04, 1946, Bronx, NY; son of Wilmore Thompson and H Louise Stewart Thompson. **EDUCATION:** Juilliard Sch Lincoln Ctr NYC, BM 1967, MS 1968, DMA 1970. **CAREER:** Juilliard School at Lincoln Center, viola faculty, 1969-70; Oakwood Coll, Alabama, asst prof of music, 1970-71; Wesleyan Univ, Middletown CT, viola faculty, 1971-73; Mt Holyoke Coll, S Hadley MA, lecturer, 1971-73; New England Conservatory, viola faculty, 1983-; Massachusetts Inst of Technology, prof of music, 1973-; viola soloist with Chicago Symphony, Natl Symphony, St Louis Symphony, Boston Pops, etc; recitalist, Carnegie Recital Hall, Kennedy Center Terrace Theatre, Orchestra Hall Minneapolis, Grace R Rodgers Auditorium NY, Hertz Hall Berkeley CA, Herbst Theater San Francisco, Teatro Nacional Dominican Republic, etc; chamber music appearances w/ Boston Chamber Music Soc, Chamber Music Soc of Lincoln Center, Concord, Vermeer, Manhattan, Muir String Quartets, Boston Musica Viva, etc; festival appearances at Aspen, Marlboro, Spoleto, Sitka, Newport, Seattle, Dubrovnik, Santa Fe, etc. **ORGANIZATIONS:** Mem Chamber Music & Solo Artist; PA Natl Endowment for Arts. **HONORS/ACHIEVEMENTS:** Recip First Prize, Hudson Vly Philharmonic Young Artists Comp 1967; winner Young Concert Artist Inc Auditions NY 1967; winner String Prize, Nat Black Colloquim Compet Kennedy Ctr for Performing Arts Wash DC 1980; NEA Solo Recitalist Fellowship; joint-recipient, NEA Commissioning Program. **BUSINESS ADDRESS:** Professor, Massachusetts Inst of Tech, 77 Massachusetts Ave, Cambridge, MA 02139.

THOMPSON, MARK RANDOLPH
Clergyman, psychologist. **PERSONAL:** Born Nov 14, 1955, Chicago, IL; married Jill Pilate; children: Ebonee Monique. **EDUCATION:** Bethel Coll, BA Psychology 1977; Univ of IL, MSW 1979; N Baptist Theological Sem, MA Theology Pastoral Care 1984. **CAREER:** Airwaves for Fellowship, pres 1980-85; Assn of Correctional Health Care, spokesman 1985; Cook Co Jail Dept of Psychiatry, super residential treatment unit. **ORGANIZATIONS:** Black Natl Religious Broadcasters, sec 1984-85; asst exec dir Broadcast Outreach Ministry; consul Psychiatric Treatment of Minority Inmates for Penal Institutions; mem Operation PUSH; mem NAACP. **HONORS/ACHIEVEMENTS:** Who's Who Among College Students 1978-79; dir & prod of the gospel prog "GOSPEL, Chicago Style". **BUSINESS ADDRESS:** Super Residential Treatment, Cook Co Jail Dept Psychiatry, 2800 S California Ave, Chicago, IL 60608.

THOMPSON, MARTTIE L.
Attorney. **PERSONAL:** Born Jul 05, 1930, Meridian, MS; daughter of Samuel L Thompson and Rosie L Young Thompson; married Cornelia Gaines. **EDUCATION:** Univ of Toledo, BS 1954; St Johns Univ School of Law, 1955-56; Columbia Univ Graduate School of Business Inst for Not for Profit Mgmt, 1977. **CAREER:** NL & JZ Goldstin Esq, tax certiorari, eminent domain 1958-62; Wolf Pepper Ross Wolf & Jones Esqs, surrogates practice 1963-65; Wm C Chance Jr, trial counselor 1965-66; Ft Green Comm Corp, house counselor, assoc dir for urban devel 1966-68; MFY legal Serv Inc, exec dir 1970-71, mng atty 1968-70; Comm Act for Legal Serv Inc, general counsel 1971-77; Seton Hall Univ School of Law, adjunct prof 1979; Legal Serv Corp, regional dir 1977-84; Private practice, atty 1984-. **ORGANIZATIONS:** Mem NY City Lawyers, NY State Bar, Panel for Indigent Defendants, Supreme Court Appeal Div, Natl Conf of Black Lawyers, ABA, Natl Bar Assoc, Bar of Washington DC 1980; former consultant Natl Conf on Law & Poverty, NW Univ Law School, Natl Legal Aid & Defense Assoc Chicago; mem New York County Lawyers Assoc; mem of housing advisory council Civil Court NY; mem East Orange Planning Bd; bd of dirs Citizens Union and Special Comm on Criminal Justice; mem Assoc of the Bar of the City of New York; vice chmn, New Jersey Chapter, Americans for Democratic Action; mem of the bd of dir, NY County Lawyers Assn; Amer Bar Assn (Labor Law Section) and a fellow of the Amer Bar Found; Natl Bar Assn; Assn of the Bar of the City of NY and Metropolitan Black Bar Assn. **HONORS/ACHIEVEMENTS:** Author, Social Activism in Legal Services, NY Law Journal Press, 1974. **MILITARY SERVICE:** USAF sgt 1946-49. **BUSINESS ADDRESS:** 335 Broadway Ste 1103, New York, NY 10013.

THOMPSON, MAVIS SARAH (MAVIS BLAIZE)
Physician. **PERSONAL:** Born Jun 22, 1927, Newark, NJ; married James Blaize; children: Clayton, Marcia Adele Callender, Sidney, Ronald, Kevin. **EDUCATION:** Hunter Coll, NYC, BA 1947; Howard Univ Medical School, MD 1953. **CAREER:** Kings County Hospital, internship 1953-54; Kings County Hospital, resident internal medicine 1954-57; Brooklyn, NY, private practice 1957-76; Lyndon B Johnson Health Complex Inc, medical dir 1970-71, 1974-76; New York City Bd of Educ, school medical instructor 1962-85; Medgor Evans Coll, teacher dept nursing 1975-76; Kingsboro Medical Group, family physician 1976-. **ORGANIZATIONS:** Mem bd of dir Camp Minisink New York City 1973-; mem advisory comm Gerontological Serv Ad New School for Soc Research 1983-; mem Amer Public Health Ass, Natl Medical Assn, Amer Gerontology Assn; den mother BSA; pres Black Caucus of Health Workers of the Amer Public Health Assoc 1976-77; lic lay St Georges Episcopal Church, Brooklyn. **HONORS/ACHIEVEMENTS:** Community Serv Award, St Mark's United Methodist Church 1973; past pres Award Black Caucus of Health Workers 1977; Alberta T Kline Serv Award Camp Minisink 1980; lecturer on med Care & Geriatrics 1984-. **BUSINESS ADDRESS:** Family Physician, Kingsboro Medical Group, 1000 Church Ave, Brooklyn, NY 11218.

THOMPSON, MYCHAL
Professional athlete. **PERSONAL:** Born Jan 30, 1955, Nassau, Bahamas. **EDUCATION:** MN, 1978. **CAREER:** Portland Trailblazers, professional basketbl forward/center. **HONORS/ACHIEVEMENTS:** All rookie team NBA 1978-79. **BUSINESS ADDRESS:** Portland Trailblazers, 700 NE Multnomah ST #380 L, Portland, OR 97232.

THOMPSON, PATRICIA MOULTRIE
Business executive. **PERSONAL:** Born Nov 28, 1942, Englewood, NJ; married Clifton Jerry Thompson Jr; children: Clifton III, James. **EDUCATION:** Bowling Green St U, BS 1964; Brooklyn Law Sch, JD 1969. **CAREER:** ABC, dir of bus affairs sestcoast 1985; NBC, cnsl acct 1966-67; Am Standard Inc, jr atty 1970-72. **ORGANIZATIONS:** Am Bar Assn; Delta Sigma Theta; Ozill Grand Chap Order of Estrn Star, ueen of Sheba Chap No 4; dau of IBPOEW. **HONORS/ACHIEVEMENTS:** Dau of Isis Dist Serv Awd Brooklyn Law Sch 1969; Who's Who Among Std in Am Coll &Univ 1969. **BUSINESS ADDRESS:** Dir Business Affairs, Capital Cities/ABC, Inc, 2040 Avenue of the Stars, 5th Floor, Century City, CA 90067.

THOMPSON, PORTIA WILSON
Government official. **PERSONAL:** Born Oct 23, 1944, Washington, DC; children: Lisa-Marie, Joseph M, Jared M. **EDUCATION:** Howard Univ, BA 1968. **CAREER:** Bd of Governors of Federal Reserve Syst, rsch asst 1968-71, programmer 1971-74, economic system analyst 1974-80, asst to EEO dir 1980-81, mgr, bd EEO programs, 1982-84, EEO programs officer 1984-. **ORGANIZATIONS:** Consultant, Soul Journey Enterprises 1979-; life mem, NAACP 1980-; mem, Amer Assn of Affirmative Action, 1980-; sec, Natl Black History Observance Comm 1982-83; treas Natl Black Heritage Observance Comm 1983-; mem Friends Bethune Museum Archives Inc 1984-; mem, Natl Assn of Banking Affirmative Action Dirs 1985-, Friends of Dusable Museum 1985-; sec, Washington Metro Amer Assn of Affirmative Action, 1985-; mem Friends of Armistad, 1986. **HONORS/ACHIEVEMENTS:** Outstanding Contributions HD Woodson Sch of Business & Finance 1984-85. **BUSINESS ADDRESS:** EEO Programs Officer, Bd of Governors, Federal Reserve System, 20th & C Sts NW, Washington, DC 20551.

THOMPSON, REGINA
Nurse, educator. **PERSONAL:** Born Dec 03, Beckley, WV; daughter of Elder L Thompson and Gracie M Allen Thompson. **EDUCATION:** Bluefield State Coll WV, BS; Lincoln Sch for Nurses NY, Dipolma; Columbia U, MA, Post Grad Work. **CAREER:** Sea View Hosp, Staten Isl NY, clin instr & acting asst educ dir 1955-57; Walter Reed Gen Hosp, Washington, staff nurse & acting head nurse; USPHS Hosp, NY, staff nurse 1960-61; Wagner Coll Sch of Nursing, NY, instr & asst prof of nursing 1961-64; ClemsonUniv Coll of Nursing, SC, asst prof of nursing. **ORGANIZATIONS:** Natl Assn of Black Nurses; NAACP; Natl League for Nursing; SC League for Nursing; Amer Nurses Assn SC Nurses Assn; Charter Mem, Gamma Mu Chapter Sigma Theta Intl Honor Soc for Nurses; Served as first vice pres, SC League for Nurses; mem, bd of dir, Oconee chapter, Amer Red Cross; sec, SC Council on Human Relations; Orzanizer of Oconee County Chapter of MADD; Past mem, SC Joint Practice Commn; Chair, Publicity and Public Relations Comm, Oconee Cancer Trust. **HONORS/ACHIEVEMENTS:** Awarded NY Regents Fellowship; Named Citizen of the Day by local Radio Station; Woman of Achievement, Lambda Chapter, Lambda Kappa Mu Sorority; Acting Dir, BS Degree Program, Clemson Univ Coll of Nursing; First advisor to student Nurse Assn, Clemson Univ; Nominated for the Jefferson Award; Certificate of Appreciation, Oconne County United Way Budget Review; Several articles published in the "Living Well" column, sponsored by the Coll of Nursing, Clemson Univ. **MILITARY SERVICE:** AUS

Nurse Corps 1st lt 1957-60; USAF Nurse Corps Res capt 1960-66. **BUSINESS ADDRESS:** 714 Strode Tower Box 72, Clemson Univ Coll of Nursing, Clemson, SC 29631.

THOMPSON, RICHARD ELLIS
Educator. **PERSONAL:** Born May 05, 1935, Gary, IN; son of Elija Thompson (deceased) and Roberta May Thompson (deceased); children: Kevin. **EDUCATION:** Beatty Mem Hosp Westville, IN, Psych-Aide Training Cert 1955; Indiana Univ Gary Center, AA 1956; Roosevelt Univ Chicago, BA 1963, MA 1966; DePaul Univ Chicago, EdM 1973. **CAREER:** Beatty Memorial Hospital, Westville IN psychiatric aide 1955-56, 1957-58; Lake County Children's Home, Gary IN, child care counselor 1958-63; Harlan HS (Chicago Bd of Edn), history teacher 1963-70; IL Dept Labor Chicago, employment counselor 1966 and 1967; City Colleges of Chicago, teacher/registrar/adm 1966-70 and 1973-79; Mayor's Summer Youth Program Chicago, training spec 1976 and 1977 & 1980-89; Harlan HS, asst prin 1970-; Lake County Children's Home, Gary IN, child care counselor 1958-63; Beatty Memorial Hospital, Westville IN, psychiatric aide 1955-56, 1957-58. **ORGANIZATIONS:** Corp mem/trustee Chicago Asst Prin Assn 1973-; consult Educ Adm Eval Comm Chicago State Univ 1984-; mem bd dir Headstart Program 1st Ch of Love & Faith Chicago, IL 1983-; trustee 1st Church of Love & Faith 1982-; mem Natl Assn of Secondary Prin 1975-; mem Phi Delta Kappa (Prof Frat in Educ Univ of Chicago Chap 1968-; notary public, Notaries Assn of Illinois 1979-; Natl Assn of Secondary School Principals 1973-; consultant, Curriculum Committee School of Education, Chicago State Univ 1984. **HONORS/ACHIEVEMENTS:** Kappa Delta Pi (Honor Soc in Edn) DePaul Chptr 1973-; Achievement Award Roosevelt HS Silver Assniv class of '53 1978; Eligible Bachelors Ebony Magazine 1975; Outstanding Educator of Amer 1975; Outstanding Sec Educ of Amer 1975; Certificate of Appreciation Chicago Asst Principal's Assoc 1978; Service Awd Div of Educ Governors State Univ Chicago 1982; 8 articles published in The Administrator, published by The Chicago Assistant Principals Assn 1973-83. **MILITARY SERVICE:** AUS Sgt E-5 (US 55-66 - 9790) 1959-62; Good Conduct Award 1961; Cert of Achievement 1962; Soldier of the Month Nov 1960. **HOME ADDRESS:** 500 E 33rd St #1601, Chicago, IL 60616. **BUSINESS ADDRESS:** Assistant Principal, Harlan High School, 9652 S Michigan Ave, Chicago, IL 60628.

THOMPSON, ROBERT DEWEY
Chief executive officer. **PERSONAL:** Born Jul 29, 1936, Cincinnati, OH; married Beverly; children: Anthony, Sonia. **EDUCATION:** Miami U, BS Math 1962; Wethersfield Essex, Eng, undergrad scholar 1958. **CAREER:** Community Elect Corp, pres bd chmn 1969-; Analysts Intl Corp, staff consult 1968-69; UNIVAC, prin computer prgmr 1966-68; RCA, sr computer prgmr 1964-66; Def Elect Supply Ctr, computer & prgmr 1958-64. **ORGANIZATIONS:** Bd dir United Way of Minneapolis 1970; Abbott NW Hosp 1971; North Gro Inc 1970-; hon bd mem TCOIC 1972-; MN commis St Athl comm 1973-. **HONORS/ACHIEVEMENTS:** Math Soc of Amer 1962; assn of Computing Machines 1966; publ =Fumdamental Definitions of Burroughs Computer Syst" UNIVAC 1967; "Polish Notation Made Comprehensible" Bits Bytes Twi City ACM Chptr pu 1966; "Virtual Memory Addressing Structures" UNIVAC 1968. **MILITARY SERVICE:** USAF 1954-58. **BUSINESS ADDRESS:** 2121 W River Rd, Minneapolis, MN 55411.

THOMPSON, ROBERT FARRIS
Educator. **PERSONAL:** Born Dec 30, 1932, El Paso, TX; married Nancy Gaylord; children: Alicia, Clark. **EDUCATION:** Yale U, BA 1955, MA 1961, PhD 1965. **CAREER:** African & Afro-Amer Art History Yale Univ, prof 1964-. **HONORS/ACHIEVEMENTS:** Authored "African Influence on the Art of the United States" 1969; "Black Gods & Kings" 1971; "African Art in Motion" 1974; "Four Moments of the Sun" 1981; "Flash of the Spirit" 1983. **BUSINESS ADDRESS:** Professor History of Art, Yale University, 63 Wall St, New Haven, CT 06510.

THOMPSON, ROSIE L.
Educator. **PERSONAL:** Born Aug 16, 1950, Macon, MS; daughter of Willie Lee Little Sr and Lula B Little; married Cornelius Thompson Sr; children: Cornelius Jr, Reginald Cornell. **EDUCATION:** Jackson State Univ, Jackson MS, BS, 1970, MS, 1976; Phillips Coll, Jackson MS, AS; Univ of Arkansas, Little Rock AR, MEd, 1985. **CAREER:** Canton Public Schools, Canton MS, science teacher, 1970-71; Tougaloo Coll, Tougaloo MS, data operator, 1971, teacher, 1983; South Central Bell, Jackson MS, data operator, 1972; Mississippi School for the Blind, Jackson MS, teacher, 1972-79, orientation & mobility specialist, 1985—. **ORGANIZATIONS:** Bd mem, Assn for Education on Blind; mem, Assn for Education and Rehabilitation of Blind and Visually Impaired; bd mem, Mississippi Assn for Education and Rehabilitation of Blind and Visually Impaired; mem, Black Women's Political Action Forum. **HONORS/ACHIEVEMENTS:** Outstanding Teacher's Award, Mississippi School for the Blind, 1988; Outstand Service Award, Black Women's Political Action Forum, 1988, 1989. **HOME ADDRESS:** 112 Needle Cove Dr, Jackson, MS 39206.

THOMPSON, SANDRA ANN
Municipal court judge. **PERSONAL:** Born in Hawkins, TX. **EDUCATION:** Univ of So CA, BA 1969; Univ of MI Law School, JD 1972. **CAREER:** Assembly Health Comm, State of California, legislative intern 1972-73; Assembly Judiciary Comm, State of California, analyst 1973-75; Dept of Consumer Affairs, State of California, legislative coord 1975-77; City Attorney's Office, City of Inglewood, CA, deputy city attorney 1977-81; Los Angeles County Dist Atty's Office, deputy district atty 1981-83; South Bay Judicial Dist, commnr 1983-84, judge 1984-86, presiding judge 1986-87, judge 1987-. **ORGANIZATIONS:** Mem CA Assoc of Black Lawyers, CA Court Commnrs Assoc, CA Judges Assoc; life mem CA Women Lawyers; mem Langston & Minority Bar Assocs; mem Municipal Court Judges Assoc, Natl Assoc of Women Judges, Natl Bar Assoc, Phi Alpha Delta Law Frat, Presiding Judges Assoc; mem South Bay Bar Assoc, South Bay Women Lawyers Assoc; mem Torrance League of Women Voters 1985-; mem Pacific Bell Consumer Adv Cncl IX on Plain Language 1986-87; mem bd of trustees Casa Colina Foundation of the South Bay 1987-; mem, Amer Assn of Univ Women, Torrance Branch, 1988-; mem, bd of dirs, Southern California Youth & Family Center, 1988-; mem Los Angeles Urban League, NAACP Los Angeles Chapt. **BUSINESS ADDRESS:** Municipal Court Judge, South Bay Judicial District, Los Angeles Municipal Court, 825 Maple Ave, Torrance, CA 90503.

THOMPSON, SARAH SUE
Attorney. **PERSONAL:** Born Nov 20, 1948, Eutaw, AL. **EDUCATION:** Univ of AL Stillman Coll, BA 1971; Univ of AL, JD 1974. **CAREER:** Legal Servs Corp of AL, mng atty 1978-; atty prvt prct 1974-78; AL Civil Liberties Union/Selma Proj, media specialist 1974. **ORGANIZATIONS:** Mem govrng bd AL Law Inst; mem Gov's Constitution Revision Com 1979-; bd of dirs Tuscaloosa Met YMCA 1976-78; sec Nat Bd of Dirs GSUSA; 1978-; mem Human Rel Counc Gadsden AL 1978-; bd of trust Stillman Coll 1980-; vice pres Natl Bd of Dir GSUSA 1981-84; mem bd AL Bar Examiners 1983-86; vchmn, bd trust Stillman Coll 1984-; founding mem AL New South Coalition 1986. **HONORS/ACHIEVEMENTS:** Rec pub serv awd Delta Sigma Theta Sorority Tuscaloosa Alumnae Chap 1975; outstndg serv awd Barnes Branch Tuscaloosa AL YMCA 1978; AL Vol Activist Pizitz/Germaine Monteil 1978; dist young woman Gadsden AL Jaycettes 1978. **BUSINESS ADDRESS:** Managing Attorney, Legal Services Corp of AL, 802 Chestnut St, Gadsden, AL 35901.

THOMPSON, SHERWOOD
Chief recreation therapist. **PERSONAL:** Born Aug 18, 1928, Poughkeepsie, NY; married Willie Bea Mclawhorn; children: Anthony Edmund, Kathy Ellen. **EDUCATION:** NC A&T State U, BS Phys Educ 1952; Tchrs Coll Columbia U, MA Spl Educ 1968. **CAREER:** Hudson River Psychiat Cnt Poughkeepsie, chief recreation thrpst 1964-; Mic-Hudson & Rehab Unit (narcotics) Beacon NY, cons/thrpst rec 1969; Mattewan St Hosp Beacon NY, consult thrpst recreation 1968; Dannemora St Hosp Dannemora NY, cons/thrpst receation 1966; Wassaic Dev Cnt Wassaic NY, sr institutional tchr 1962-64. **ORGANIZATIONS:** Pres NYS Mental Hygiene Rec Therapy Assn 1967-68; mem exec com Therapeutic Sect NYS Rec & Parks Assn 1974-77; chmn Mental Health Com NYS Rec & Parks Assn 1975-77; fndr/co-chmn/bd mem Hudson Valley Oppor Indsl Cnt 1968-; pres Catharine St Comm Cnt 1975-80; mem Poughkeepsie Rec Commn 1976-. **HONORS/ACHIEVEMENTS:** Who's Who in AmUniv & Coll NC A&T StateUniv 1951; rec Expert Infantryman's Badge AUS 1954-56; Sports Hall of Fame NC A&T StUniv Greensboro 1973-; dist serv awd NYS Rec & Parks Soc 1976. **MILITARY SERVICE:** AUS 1st lt 1954-56. **BUSINESS ADDRESS:** Hudson River Psychiat Cntr, Station B, Poughkeepsie, NY 12601.

THOMPSON, SYLVIA MOORE
Educator. **PERSONAL:** Born Nov 04, 1937, Cincinnati, OH; divorced; children: Yvette. **EDUCATION:** Univ of Cincinnati, BS Educ 1960; OH State Univ, MA Educ 1973; OH State Univ, post grad work. **CAREER:** Midwest Inst for Equal Educ Oppors, consul 1973; Office of Minority Affairs OH State Univ, consul 1974; Columbus City Schools, prog coord 1975-77; Otterbein Coll Reading Ctr, tutor 1979-84; Columbus City Schools, chap I reading instructor. **ORGANIZATIONS:** Consul Macedonia Bapt Ch Educational Facility; pres Youth Service Guild Inc 1983-85; pres Columbus Alumnae Chap Delta Sigma Theta Inc 1970-72; treas Bethune Serv Bd; bd of dirs The Learning Juncture. **HONORS/ACHIEVEMENTS:** Outstanding Leadership Awd Delta Sigma Theta Inc 1975-76; Meritorious Serv Awd United Negro Coll Fund 1985,86. **HOME ADDRESS:** 2589 Ipswick Cir, Columbus, OH 43224. **BUSINESS ADDRESS:** Chapter I Reading Instructor, Columbus City Schools, 3940 Karl Rd, Columbus, OH 43224.

THOMPSON, TAWANA SADIELA
Appointed govt. official. **PERSONAL:** Born May 24, 1957, Tallahassee, FL. **EDUCATION:** FL A&M Univ, BS Journalism/PR 1976. **CAREER:** FAMU Coll of Educ, editor The Educator 1976-78; Ocala Star Banner, staff reporter 1978-79; Capital Outlook Newspaper, editor in chief 1979; FL Occupational Info Coord Comm, clearinghouse coord 1979-80; Dade Co Partners for Youth, admin officer 1981-82; Metro Dade Co, public info officer. **ORGANIZATIONS:** Exec bd mem Dade Co Alumnae Delta Sigma Theta 1983-; mem Natl Forum for Black Public Admin 1984-85, 1987-88; consultant FL Inst of Education/Precollegiate Prog 1984-85; mem Urban League of Greater Miami 1984-; mem Coconut Grove Jaycees 1984-; deputy political dir Statewide Campaign 1986; exec bd mem Greater Miami Chap Natl Assoc of Media Women; consultant South Florida Business League. **BUSINESS ADDRESS:** Public Information Officer, Metro Dade County, 111 NW First St Ste 2510, Miami, FL 33128.

THOMPSON, TAYLOR
Business executive. **PERSONAL:** Born Nov 01, 1919, Forest, MS; married Rosie Hale; children: Taylor T, Bobby G, Betty J. **CAREER:** Thompson's Elec Supply Co Inc, pres. **ORGANIZATIONS:** Mem foll student consult proj u of pittsburgh; comdr vfw post no 46 1975-76; hampton inst alumni assn pittsburgh; past pres bus & prof Assn; Nat Bus League Pittsburgh 1964-74; past pres Nat Alliance TV & Elec Serv Assn; 1965-66; Kiwanis Internat; past potentate Sahara Temple No 2 AEAONMS; past imperial dep of Oasis of Pittsburgh AEAONMS 1972-74; past treas Pittsburgh Coord Counc Citation Bus & Prof Wmn's Assn 1969; past mstr Golden Star Lodge No 143 F&AM 1961-62; vice pres Nat Bus League Reg II 1980; chmn Nat Minority Purch Counc Min Input Com Pittsburgh Chap 1980; mem Nat Assn of Elect Dist; bd of dirs Brentwood-Whitehall C of C. **MILITARY SERVICE:** AUS 1941-45. **BUSINESS ADDRESS:** 4048 Saw Mill Run Blvd, Rt 51, Pittsburgh, PA 15227.

THOMPSON, THEODIS
Health services executive. **PERSONAL:** Born Aug 10, 1944, Palestine, AR; son of Percy Thompson (deceased) and Grozellia M Weaver Thompson (deceased); married Patricia Holley; children: Gwendolyn L Ware, Theodis E, III, Omari O Thompson. **EDUCATION:** Tuskegee Inst AL, BS 1968; Univ Michigan Ann Arbor, MPA 1969, PhD 1972; Harvard Univ, Cambridge MA, PHSM 1977. **CAREER:** Sr chem tech John T Stanley Co, New York NY, 1964-66; disc jockey/News reporter, Florence SC, Portsmouth VA, St Louis MO; research assoc Inst Soc Research Univ of Michigan, Ann Arbor MI 1969-71; asst prof, chmn Health Serv Admin Dept Howard Univ, Washington DC 1973-77; Howard Univ School of Business & Public Admin, acting asst dean 1977-78; Univ of Southern California Los Angeles, assoc prof 1978-79; Memphis Health Center Inc, Memphis TN, dir planning mktg research 1979-85, chief admin officer 1985-, pres/chief exec officer 1987-; Brooklyn Plaza Medical Center Inc, Brooklyn NY 1988. **ORGANIZATIONS:** Mem APHA 1970-, Alpha Phi Alpha Fraternity Inc 1962-; pres Metro Washington Public Health Assn 1970-72, Black Caucus Health Workers 1974-75; pres MGNAA Inc; mem Community Health Assn of New York State Inc 1989, Natl Assn of Community Health Centers, 1979-; mem, bd of dir Community Assoc Devel Corp 1989; co-owner The Medicine Shoppe Franchio, Memphis TN 1985. **HONORS/ACHIEVEMENTS:** Leadership Memphis 1982; Public Health Scholarship, Univ of Michigan School of Public Health 1970-72; Fellowship Natl Urban League 1968-69. **BUSINESS ADDRESS:** Exec Dir, Brooklyn Plaza Medical Center, Inc, 650 Fulton St, 2nd Fl, Brooklyn, NY 11217.

THOMPSON, WILLIAM B. D.
College president. **CAREER:** Roxbury Community College, Boston, MA, president. **BUSINESS ADDRESS:** Roxbury Community College, Boston, MA 02115. *

THOMPSON, WILLIAM COLERIDGE
Associate justice. **PERSONAL:** Born Oct 26, 1924, New York, NY; married Sybil Hart Kooper; children: William Jr, Gail. **EDUCATION:** Brooklyn Coll, BA 1948; Brooklyn Law Sch, LLB 1954. **CAREER:** City of New York, councilman 1969-73; New York State, senator 1965-68; Supreme Court of the State of New York, admin justice, assoc justice appellate div. **ORGANIZATIONS:** One of founders with late Sen R Kennedy of Restoration Corp; one of orig dir of Bed-Stuy Youth in Action; past reg dir NAACP; dir Bed-Stuy Restoration Corp; mem Amer Bar Assn, Kings Co Criminal Bar Assn, Bed-Stuyvesant Lawyers Assn; chmn St Leg Com on Child Care Needs; apptd to Appellate Term of Supreme Ct 2nd & 11th Dist 1977. **MILITARY SERVICE:** AUS plat sgt 1943-46; Purple Heart; Combat Infantry Badge; Three Battle Stars. **BUSINESS ADDRESS:** Associate Justice, Supreme Court Appellate Div, 45 Monroe Place, Brooklyn, NY 11201.

THOMPSON, WILLIAM HENRY
Dentist. **PERSONAL:** Born Dec 16, 1933, Trenton, NJ; son of John H Thompson and Fannie L Thomas Thompson; married Anne E Jenkins Thompson, Jun 19, 1965; children: William Jr, Sharon. **EDUCATION:** Lincoln Univ, BA 1956; Howard Univ Coll of Dentistry, 1963. **CAREER:** Private Practice, dentist. **ORGANIZATIONS:** Mem Omega Psi Phi Fraternity; life mem NAACP, ADA, New Jersey DA, Mer County Dental Assoc; dir, Sun Natl Bank, Trenton, New Jersey, 1989-; trustee, St Lawrence Hospital, 1986-. **MILITARY SERVICE:** AUS Honorable Discharge 1956-58. **BUSINESS ADDRESS:** 1302 W State St, Trenton, NJ 08618.

THOMPSON, WILLIE EDWARD
Educational administrator. **PERSONAL:** Born Sep 30, 1940, Turbeville, VA; married Mattie Smith; children: Eric, Jason. **EDUCATION:** Bay City Jr Coll, AA 1961; MI Univ, BSW 1964; Univ of MI, MA 1973. **CAREER:** City of Saginaw, asst youth ctr dir 1964-65, adult probation officer 1965-70; Delta Comm Coll, assoc dean of spec serv 1970-. **ORGANIZATIONS:** Bd of dir Capital Investment Inc; pres Saginaw Bd of Ed 1976-78; vice pres Saginaw Econ Devel Corp 1976-; mem of bd BOLD 1978-. **HONORS/ACHIEVEMENTS:** Liberty Bell Awd Saginaw Cty Bar Assoc 1970; Serv Awd Amer Assoc of Univ Professional 1972; Comm Serv Awd Negro Womens Professional Group 1975; Comm Serv Awd Black Nurses Assoc 1977. **BUSINESS ADDRESS:** Associate Dean of Spec Serv, Delta Community College, University Center, MI 48710.

THOMPSON, WILLIE EDWARD
Physician/orthopaedic surgeon. **PERSONAL:** Born Mar 27, 1947, Davisboro, GA; married Dorothy DeSequin; children: Margie, Heather Marie. **EDUCATION:** Jersey City State Coll, attended 1973-76; Howard Univ Coll of Medicine, MD 1980. **CAREER:** Univ of Medicine & Dentistry of NJ, surgical intern 1980-81; Howard Univ Hospital, orthopaedic surgical resident 1981-85, clinical instructor of orthopaedic surgery dept of surgery; George Washington Univ, Washington Hosp Ctr, Childrens Hosp, musculoskeletal oncology fellowship 1985086; Howard Univ Hospital, clinical instr orthopaedic surg, orthopaedic surgery. **ORGANIZATIONS:** Physician United States Amateur Boxing Federation 1984-; physician District of Columbia Boxing & Wrestling Commission 1985-; adv comm mem Upjohn Healthcare Serv 1987-; mem District of Columbia Medical Soc, Amer Medical Assoc. **HONORS/ACHIEVEMENTS:** Mem Alpha Omega Alpha Hon Med Soc Gamma Chap Howard Univ Medical School 1980; paper presentation "Surgical Staging of Musculoskeletal Sarcoma," Washington Metro Area Chap of Amer Coll of Surgeons 1984. **HOME ADDRESS:** 1802 Metzerott Rd, Adelphi, MD 20783. **BUSINESS ADDRESS:** Orthopaedic Surgeon, HowardUniv Hospital, 1603 Rhode Island Ave NE, Washington, DC 20018.

THOMPSON, WINSTON EDNA
Educational administrator, educator. **PERSONAL:** Born Apr 09, 1933, Newark, NJ; daughter of Dorsey Nelson West and Cora Edna West; divorced; children: Darren Eric Thompson. **EDUCATION:** Seton Hall Univ, BA 1965; Columbia Univ, Teachers College MS 1969; Rutgers Univ, EdD 1980. **CAREER:** Essex County Coll, dir of advising, counselor 1968-72; Rutgers Univ, Livingston College, assoc dean of students 1972-75; Tombrock Coll, dean of student dev 1975-76; Tombrock Coll, dean of student develop 1975-76; AT & T Bell Lab, consultant 1975-77; East Orange Board of Education, adult educator 1977-78; Salem State Coll, vice pres of student services 1978-88; Conneticut State Univ, assistant vice pres of academic affairs and research, 1988-. **ORGANIZATIONS:** American Council of Education, consultant 1981-86; AAA of New England, advisory bd mem 1986-88; Morgan Memorial Goodwill Industries, bd of trustee, mem 1986-88; HERS Wellesly Coll, advisory bd mem, faculty 1982; bd mem, LLS Enterprise 1979-; State Education Coordinator, Natl Coalition 100 Black Women 1988-89. **HONORS/ACHIEVEMENTS:** Salem State Coll, recipient women's awrd 1981; Univ of MA at Amherst, co-designer of non-traditional doctoral prog 1983; Northeastern Univ, Greater Boston Inter University Council report, minority student retention 1985; Distinguished Educator, Natl Coalition of 100 Black Women 1988; Meritorious Service Award, United Negro College Fund, Inc 1989; Black Women/Black Men lecture and writing 1989; Black Feminism, lecture and writing 1989. **BUSINESS ADDRESS:** Assistant Vice Pres/Academic Affairs & Research, Conneticut State University, 1615 Stanley St, Bernard Hall, PO Box 2008, New Britain, CT 06050.

THOMPSON-CLEMMONS, OLGA UNITA (OLGA UNITA JONES)
Social worker, case manager. **PERSONAL:** Born Jun 01, 1928, Philadelphia, PA; daughter of Ruppert Wilkes and Ruth Wilkes; married Earnest Thompson; children: Hennrietta, Henry, Charles, Jeffrey, Olga; married James Daniels Clemmons. **EDUCATION:** Hartford Coll for Women, Assn in Arts 1972; St Joseph Coll, BA (honors in sociology) 1974; Univ of CT Grad Sch of Social Work, MSW 1977. **CAREER:** Methadone Maintenance Prog, social worker 1974; Teenage Parents Prog, social worker 1975; Comm Renewal Team, social worker 1976; Migratory Children's Prog,social worker 1977; Albany Hosp, spec nurse aide trained to circulate in delivery room for gynecologists, infant care in reg & premature nursery's plus care of cardiac patients; Mt Olive Child Dev Ctr, social work coordinator; Department of Mental Retardation, case manager/SW 1987-. **ORGANIZATIONS:** Former councilwoman City of Hartford 1975-81; former chairwoman Hartford Non-Public Parent Adv Council; former vice chairwoman CT State-Wide Parent Adv Council; former fund raising chairwoman Prog Demo Woman's Club 1975; mem CT Fed of Dem Women's Club; Prog Dem Women's Club; Gr Hartford Black Dem Club; former mem Dem Town Com; former mem Natl Assn of Black Soc Workers Inc; former mem Univ of CT Org of Black Social Work Students; former mem Commsn on Inland Wet Lands Commsn for City of Hartford; former chmn non-pub school Parent Advis Coun 1974; former vice chmn city wide PAC 1974; former chmn Hartford's City Coun Housing Code Enforce & Hlth Com; president, Greater Hartford Progressive Democratic Women's Club, 1988-89; mem, St Michaels Choir, mem, Trellis Temple #663, State Director of Merit Dept; Local Director of Shoes for Kids Dept. **HONORS/ACHIEVEMENTS:** Recognition Service Natl Assn of Social Workers 1980; authored "Title One Evaluation Report" on Hartford's Elem & Secondary Sch Prog 1974; funded by the Title One Elem & Secondary Act of 1965 by the Fed Govt; Professional & Business Women's Schol 1974; Certificate Joint Ctr for Polit Studies 1976. **HOME ADDRESS:** 20 Clover Lane, Bloomfield, CT 06002.

THOMPSON-MOORE, ANN
Senior consultant education. **PERSONAL:** Born Oct 13, 1949, Edwards, MS; divorced; children: DeAnna. **EDUCATION:** Jackson State Univ, BA 1972, MSEduc 1974. **CAREER:** Jackson-Hinds County Youth Court, counselor 1972-74; MS Gulf Coast Jr Coll, dir special services prog 1974-82; Northern IL Univ, counselor 1983-84; MS Governor's Office Federal/State Prog, special project officer IV 1984-87; The Kelwynn Group, sr consultant 1987-. **ORGANIZATIONS:** Mem MS State Democratic Party 1980; mem Phi Delta Kappa Frat East MS Chap 1981; fundraising chair Hinds County Democratic Exec Comm 1984; pres United Black Fund of MS 1984; bd mem Hospice Friends Inc 1985; coord United Negro College Fund 1985-86, 1986-87; peer panelist MS Arts Commn 1986; mem Farish St Bapt Church; mem Delta Sigma Theta Sor Inc. **HONORS/ACHIEVEMENTS:** Outstanding Young Woman in Amer 1979; new articles The MS Press 1980, The Washington Star 1980, Black Enterprise 1981; participant A Presidential Classroom for Young Americans. **BUSINESS ADDRESS:** Senior Consultant, The Kelwynn Group, One Country Place, Jackson, MS 39208.

THOMSON, GERALD EDMUND
Physician, educator. **PERSONAL:** Born 1932, New York, NY; married Carolyn Webber; children: Gregory, Karen. **EDUCATION:** Howard U, MD 1959. **CAREER:** Harlem Hosp Center, pres 1976-; Columbia Univ, prof 1972-; Presb Hospital, atending physician 1970-; prec med 1963-; clin asst prof medicine 1968-70; Coney Island Hospital, assoc chief medicine 1967-70; State Univ NY Med Brooklyn Hospital, attending physician 1966-70; asst visiting physician 1963-70; Univ NY, instr 1963-68; clinical dir dialysis unit 1965-67; NY Heart Assn, fellow nephrology 1965-65; chief resident 1962-63; resident medicine 1960-62; State Univ NY Kings Co Hospital Center, intern 1959-60. **ORGANIZATIONS:** Pres Med Bd 1976-; asso prof med Columbia Coll Phys & Surg 1970-72; prof 1972-; mem Hlth Rsrch Cncl City of NY 1972-; hypertension adv com NY City Hlth Serv Adminstrn 1972-75; adv bd NY Kidney Found 1971-; mem Hlth Rsrch Cncl City of NY 1975-; mem NIH 1973-74; mem adv bd Nat Assn Patients on Hemodialysis & Transplantation 1973-; mem Com on Mild Hypertension Nat Heart & Lung Inst 1976; bd dir NY Heart Assn 1973-; chmn com high blood press 1976-; chmn com hypertension NY Met Regnl Med Prgm 1974-76; Diplomate Am Bd Internal Med Fellow ACP; mem AAAS 1973-74; Am Fedn Clin Rsrch Soc Urban Physicians 1972-73; Am Soc for Artificial Organs; NY Acad Med 1974-; Alpha Omega Alpha; mem adv bd Jour Urban Hlth 1974-. **BUSINESS ADDRESS:** Harlem Hosp Ctr, 135 S 7th & Lenox Ave, New York, NY 10037.

THORBURN, CAROLYN COLES
Educator. **PERSONAL:** Born Dec 20, 1941, Newark, NJ. **EDUCATION:** Douglass Coll, BA Spanish 1962; Rutgers Univ, MA Spanish 1964, PhD Spanish 1972. **CAREER:** Barringer HS, spanish teacher 1964-66; Rutgers Univ, teaching asst spanish 1966-67; Upsala Coll, assoc prof of spanish/coord of black studies 1967-. **ORGANIZATIONS:** Mem Modern Language Assoc, Natl Council of Black Studies, Amer Assoc of Univ Profs, Amer Assoc of the Teachers of Spanish & Portuguese. **HONORS/ACHIEVEMENTS:** Romance Language Honor Soc Phi Sigma Iota 1972. **BUSINESS ADDRESS:** Assoc Prof of Spanish, Upsala College, Prospect St, East Orange, NJ 07109.

THORNE, CECIL MICHAEL
Physician. **PERSONAL:** Born May 13, 1929, Georgetown, Guyana;married Sandra; children: Timothy, Christine, Christopher, Jonathan, Victor. **EDUCATION:** Queens Coll; Lincoln U, AB 1952; Mainz U, MD 1957. **CAREER:** Newark Pathologists Inc Licking Meml Hosp, pres 1967-; OH St Univ Patho, asst prof pathol 1964-65; W MA Hosp, demonstrator res 1962-63; Springfield Hosp, intern res 1958-62. **ORGANIZATIONS:** Flw Am Coll Patho; mem Am Soc Clinical Patho; clinical asso prof pathology OH StUniv 1980; pres elect OH Soc of Pathologists; past pres tst OH Assn Blood Banks; past pres Central OH Soc Patho; bd gov OH Soc Pathol; lab com OH St Med Assn; mem AMA; OSMA; Licking Co Med Soc; Am Assn Blood Banks; Acad Clinical Lab Physicians & Sci; past chmn bd dir Licking Co Chap Heart Assn; Licking Co ARG; past chmn Central OH Blood Prog Com; chmn Med Adv Com Central OH Blood Prgm; past dir Newark Area C of C; chmn Licking Co Metro Park Dist; Rotary Club. **BUSINESS ADDRESS:** 1320 W Main, Newark, OH 43055.

THORNELL, RICHARD PAUL
Educator. **PERSONAL:** Born Oct 19, 1936, New York, NY; married Carolyn O Atkinson; children: David Evan, Paul Nolan Diallo, Douglass Vashon. **EDUCATION:** Fisk Univ Nashville TN, (magna cum laude) 1952-56; Pomona Coll, Claremont CA, 1955; Woodrow Wilson Sch Princeton NJ, MPA 1956-58; Yale Law Sch New Haven CT, JD 1971. **CAREER:** Sch of Law Howard U, asso prof of Law; Rosenman Colin Freund Lewis & Cohen NYC, asso litigation dept 1975-76; US Comm Relations Serv Dept of Justice, chief fed progms staff 1965-66; Africa Reg Ofc US Peace Corps, chief program staff; US Dept of State Agency for Intl Develop, econ & intl rel ofcr 1958-61. **ORGANIZATIONS:** Mem Bars of NY/DC/Fed Cts/US Supreme Ct; bd of dir UMCA of Wash DC 1977-; bd of dir Africare 1977-; trustee Phelps Stoke Fund 1980-; lay mem bd of dir com Nat Bd of UMCA'S of USA; exec com mem & gen counsel FiskUniv Gen Alumni Assn 1977-; Phi Beta Kappa Delta Chap in FiskUniv 1956-; elected Council on Foreign Relations. **HONORS/ACHIEVEMENTS:** FiskUniv Serv Awd; FiskUniv Gen Alumni Assn 1978; Grad Fellowship Princeton U; Fellowship Grant Yale Law Sch; Intl Achievement Awd Willilam S Thompson Intl Law Soc dir com Nat Bd of UMCA'S of USA; exec com m1980. **MILITARY SERVICE:** AUS pfc 1959-61. **BUSINESS ADDRESS:** Howard University, 2400 Van Ness St NW, Washington, DC 20008.

THORNHILL, ADRINE VIRGINIA
Business administrator. **PERSONAL:** Born Feb 22, 1945, Birmingham, AL; divorced; children: Herschel III, Michelle Vertess, Adrienne Mychael. **EDUCATION:** Attended, Miles Coll 1963-65, Urbana Coll 1979. **CAREER:** Montgomery Co Human Svcs, administrative asst 1969-76; Dr Frederick Jackson DDS, office mgr 1976-78; Columbus Comm Action Org, administrator 1978-82;Care-Free Property Mgmt Co Inc, vice pres/genl mgr 1987-. **ORGANIZATIONS:** Bd of dirs Taylor-Made Construction Co Inc 1980-87; office mgr NAACP Dayton Branch 1985-87; bd of dirs Midas Landscaping Co Inc 1986,87, Care-Free Mgmt Co Inc 1986-87; 1st vice pres Democratic Progressive Club 1986-87; corresponding sec Democratic Voters League 1986-87. **HONORS/ACHIEVEMENTS:** Outstanding Democrat of the Year Awd Dem Progressive Club 1976.

THORNHILL, GEORGIA L. (NEE WHITFIELD)
Nurse. **PERSONAL:** Born Jul 27, 1925; married Clarence Thornhill; children: 8 Children. **EDUCATION:** Chicago Sch of Practical Nursing; St Louis U, BA. **CAREER:** St Louis Co Hosp, nurse Aide 1946, nurse 1946-68; Montgomery-hyde Park Hlth Clinic, hlth spl 1969-70, clinic dir 1970-. **ORGANIZATIONS:** Took part in orgn of Peoples Clinic, St Louis MO; mem Alliance for Regional Comm Hlth Inc; bd mem Optmetric Cntr Inc; mem Emergency Hlth Serv comm consult st louis comm med; bd mem tower village; mem nurses bd of first bapt ch webster groves mO. **BUSINESS ADDRESS:** 2820 N 25 St, St Louis, MO 63107.

THORNHILL, HERBERT LOUIS
Physician. **EDUCATION:** Univ Pittsburgh, BS 1951; HowardUniv Coll of Med Wash DC, MD 1955. **CAREER:** Div Rehab Med Montefiore Hosp & Med Cntr, asst attending 1963-66; Montefiore Hosp & Med Cntr, adjunct attending Div Rehab Med 1966-67; Albert Einstein Coll of Medicine, Yeshiva Univ, instructor, 1963-65, asst clinical prof of rehab medicine, 1965-67; Presbyterian Hospital, asst physician in rehab service 1968-84; Harlem Hospital Center, asst dir of rehab medicine, 1967-69, attending physician, 1969-, chief, amputee service, 1969-, assoc dir of rehab medicine, 1969-78, acting dir of rehab medicine, 1979-80, dir of rehab medicine, 1980-; Columbia Univ Coll of Physicians & Sugeons, asst clinical prof of rehab medicine, 1968-73, assoc prof of clinical rehab medicine, 1973-85, prof of clinical rehab medicine, 1985-. **ORGANIZATIONS:** Diplomate, Amer Bd Physical Med & Rehab 1964; mem Bronx Co Med Soc; mem Pub Comm 1970; mem Med Soc of St of NY; v chmn Sec on Phys Med & Rehab 1972; chmn Sec on Phys Med & Rehab 1973; mem NY Soc of Phys Med & Rehab Prog Chmn 1970-71, vice pres 1971-72, pres elect 1972, pres 1973; Fellow Am Coll of Phys 1972; mem Am Acad of Phys Med & Rehab; mem Con of Rehab Med; mem NY Acad of Med; Sec on Phys Med & Rehab; mem, Natl Planning Comm, President's Comm on Employment of the Handicapped, 1987-88; mem, Natl Advisory Comm, Howard Univ Research & Training Center for Access to Rehabilitation & Economic Opportunity, 1988-; surveyor, Commn on Accreditation of Rehabilitation Facilities, 1982-; mem, 1974-, chmn, 1981-, Medical Advisory Comm, Greater Harlem Nursing Home; mem, Advisory Comm on the Disabled, Borough of Manhattan, 1989-. **HONORS/ACHIEVEMENTS:** Author of 15 publications & 5 abstracts. **MILITARY SERVICE:** USN med officer 1957-59; USNR lt commander. **BUSINESS ADDRESS:** Dir, Dept of Rehabilitative Medicine, Columbia Univ, Harlem Hospital Center, 506 Lenox Ave, New York, NY 10037.

THORNS, ODAIL, JR.
Business executive. **PERSONAL:** Born Jan 03, 1943, Pine Bluff, AK; married Jo; children: Michelle, Camille, Octavia. **EDUCATION:** BS Chem 1964; KS State Univ, grad study 1964-65; Harvard Grad Sch of Business Admin, PMD 1984. **CAREER:** Delco-remy Div GMC, asst supt mfg; chemist, process engr, res engr mfg foreman, labor relations supr gnrl supr mfg, plant supt, plant mgr, mfg mgr, opers mgr. **ORGANIZATIONS:** Mem Industrial Mgmt Club; bd dir St Manpower Training Comm; bd dirs IN Forum & pres; IN St Conf of NAACP Br 1971-76; chmn Region III NAACP 1974-75; chmn bd United Way 1979; mem Natl Bd NAACP 1980-85; chmn bd Comm Hosp 1983-85; trustee Peerless Lodge F & AM; mem dir Madison Co Br NAACP; bd of dirs Anderson Leadership Acad; state advisor NAACP Women's Aux; pres emeritus IN State NAACP; chmn Martin Luther King Memorial Comm. **HONORS/ACHIEVEMENTS:** Finalist Jacees Outstanding Yhoung Man 1972; gM'S Top Ten in Community Svcs; Man of Yr Urban League of Madison Co 1972; B Harry Beckham Meml Awd NAACP 1975; Loren Henry Awd NAACP 1976; Disting Serv Awd United Way 1979; Outstanding Achievement in Business & Prof Leadership Develop Ctr 1983; Disting Honoree Urban League 1983; Disting Serv Awd Comm Hosp 1985; Professional Man of the Yr Peerless Lodge F&AM 1985; Life Membership Hall of Fame NAACP 1985. **BUSINESS ADDRESS:** Operations Manager, Delco Remy, GM, 2401 Columbus Ave, Anderson, IN 46018.

THORNTON, BRUCE
Professional athlete. **PERSONAL:** Married Gail Jones. **CAREER:** Cleveland Indians, professional baseball player. **HONORS/ACHIEVEMENTS:** Danny Thompson Meml Awd, Baseball Chapel.

THORNTON, BRUCE CALVIN
Professional athlete. **PERSONAL:** Born Feb 14, 1958, Detroit, MI. **EDUCATION:** Illinois. **CAREER:** Dallas Cowbows, defensive end 1979-; St Louis Cardinals, defensive end 1982-; Chicago Blitz, defensive end 1983-; Denver Gold, defensive end 1984-. **HONORS/ACHIEVEMENTS:** Played in NFC Championship Game; named to the All-Big Ten Acad Team in 1977.

THORNTON, CLIFFORD E.
Educator. **PERSONAL:** Born Sep 06, 1936, Philadelphia; widowed. **EDUCATION:** Juiliard, BM 1968; Manhattan Sch of Mus, MM 1971. **CAREER:** New York City Public School, teacher 1967; Black Arts Repertory Theatre School, 1965-66; NY School of Music 1966; Wesleyan Univ, asst prof of music 1969. **ORGANIZATIONS:** Founded & dir prog in Afro-am Mus; continuous activities as performer, composer & producer of concerts & recordings; mem Am Fedn of Mus jazz composersorch assn; pres third world records; pres third world mus; mem broadcast mus inc; mem kappa alpha psi. **HONORS/ACHIEVEMENTS:** Recipient Nat Endowment for the Arts; Jazz Composition Fellowships 1972 & 73; NY St Council on the Arts Performance Grant. **MILITARY SERVICE:** AUS 1st lt 1958-61. **BUSINESS ADDRESS:** Mus Dept, Wesleyan Univ, Middletown, CT 06457.

THORNTON, CLINTON L.
Farmer, elected official. **PERSONAL:** Born Aug 03, 1907, Bullock Co, AL; married Johnnie Woods; children: Morris, Eloise, Walter, Wilbert, Mose C. **EDUCATION:** Tuskegee Inst, BS 1955. **CAREER:** Bullock Cty Schools, mem bd of ed 1970-. **ORGANIZATIONS:** Pres Bullock Cty Improvement Org 1960-70; bd dir SE AL Self-Help Assoc 1967-, AL Assoc School Bd 1970, AL & Natl Retired Teachers Assoc 1970; mem NAACP.

THORNTON, DOZIER W.
Educator. **PERSONAL:** Born Jan 27, 1928, Aliquippa, PA; son of Dozier Thornton and Myrtle Ilga Wright Thornton; married Kazuko Otaki, Dec 28, 1976; children: Monica Thornton, Lisa Thornton, Hugh Heslep. **EDUCATION:** Univ Pittsburgh, PhD 1966. **CAREER:** MI St U, prof Dept Psychology, lectr 1964-65. **ORGANIZATIONS:** Mem Comm Mental Hlth & Educ Cons; psychtherapist; Cntr Rsrch Eval & Training Change Agents. **HONORS/ACHIEVEMENTS:** Phi Kappa Phi. **MILITARY SERVICE:** AUS 1951-53. **BUSINESS ADDRESS:** MI State Univ, Psychology Dept, East Lansing, MI 48824.

THORNTON, JACKIE C.
Marketing manager. **PERSONAL:** Born Apr 26, 1960, Pine Bluff, AR; son of Laudell Thornton and Beatrice Thornton. **EDUCATION:** Univ of AR Pine Bluff, BS 1981; Univ of WI Madison, MS 1983. **CAREER:** Phillips Petroleum, accountant 1981-82; IBM Corp, mktg sales asst 1983; NCR Corp, educ analyst 1984-1988; marketing manager Pitney Bowes 1988-. **ORGANIZATIONS:** Corres sec 1986, vice pres 1987 Dayton Chap Natl Black MBA Assoc; Amer Marketing Assn. **HOME ADDRESS:** 2055 E Whipp, Dayton, OH 45440.

THORNTON, JOHN C.
Behaviorist. **PERSONAL:** Born May 22, 1940, Louisville, KY; married Rochelle A Ray; children: Ardell N, Timothy. **EDUCATION:** KY State Univ, BS 1963; Northeastern Univ, MA 1975; Union Grad Sch, PhD 1977. **CAREER:** Chicago Bd of Educ, tchr 1963-66; City of Chicago, comm organizer, rsch analyst, criminal justice dir 1966-81; McDonald Franchise, owner. **ORGANIZATIONS:** Mem Nat'l Black McDonald's Owners' Assn 1981-. **HONORS/ACHIEVEMENTS:** Athletic Hall of Fame KY State Univ 1980; "Behavior Modification-The Road to Genocide" pub 1977. **HOME ADDRESS:** 10110 S Paxton, Chicago, IL 60617. **BUSINESS ADDRESS:** McDonald Franchise, 11201 S State St, Chicago, IL 60628.

THORNTON, MAURICE
University administrator. **PERSONAL:** Born Dec 31, 1930, Birmingham, AL; son of William Thornton and Alberta Thornton (deceased); married Elizabeth McDonald, Apr 15, 1961; children: Karen, Susan Thornton-Smith, Christopher. **EDUCATION:** Alabama State Univ, BS 1952; Cleveland State Univ, MEd 1973; Nova Univ, EdD 1981. **CAREER:** Cuyahoga Co welfare Dept Cleveland, investigative caseworker supervisor title V 1958-67, coord neighborhood youth corps asst dir personnel dept 1958-67; Cuyahoga Comm Coll Cleveland, eeo officer, minority recruiter dir equal oppor 1967-82; State Univ of NY Central Admin, dir affirmative action compliance, affirmative action officer 1982-. **ORGANIZATIONS:** Mem Capital District Black & Puerto Rican Caucus, Amer Assoc of Affirmative Action Officers, Colls & Univs Personnel Assoc; participant Loaned Exec Program, Leadership Develop Program; consultation training fund raising Cleveland Foundation; mem past chmn Lee/Harvard Branch NAACP, Urban League; fund raiser United Negro Coll Fund; mem Omega Psi Phi Frat Inc; past pres AL State Univ Alumni Assoc; rhetoricos Sigma Pi Phi Frat Beta Psi Chapt; treas 369th Veterans Assoc; deacon United Presbyterian Church; vice pres, pres-elect, Nova Univ Alumni Assn, New England, New York 1989-90; secretary of bd, Camp Opportunity, Albany NY 1989-90. **HONORS/ACHIEVEMENTS:** Academic Scholarships recipient in undergrad and grad schools; ERIC Univ of CA; published dissertation "An Analysis of Cuyahoga Community College's Progress at Equal Opportunity Compliance"; addressed the Ohio General Assembly in Columbus OH; addressed the Assoc of Bds of Trustees of the Community Colls of the State Univ of New York (64 campuses, 30 are community colls). **MILITARY SERVICE:** AUS corpl medical corpsman 2 yrs; Good Conduct Medal, Letters of Commendation. **HOME ADDRESS:** 7 Keith Rd, Delmar, NY 12054. **BUSINESS ADDRESS:** Dir Affirm Action Compliance, SUNY Central Administration, State University Plaza, Albany, NY 12246.

THORNTON, OSIE M.
Association executive. **PERSONAL:** Born Oct 06, 1939, Tuscaloosa, AL. **EDUCATION:** Wayne St U, BA 1961, MA 1963. **CAREER:** Wayne Co Bur Soc Welfare; soc worker; CA Dept Rehab Nat Rehab Assoc, voc rehab counselor; mem Am Personnel & Guidance Assoc; mem United High Blood Pressure Found; Nat Non-white Counseling Assoc & Crenshaw Center Optimist Club; Big Bro Greater Los Angeles; licensed Child Family Marriage Counselor. **ORGANIZATIONS:** Man of Yr Awd 1974, Optimist Club; citation for Comm Achvmnt LA Co Supv James Hayes. **BUSINESS ADDRESS:** 10925 S Central Ave, Los Angeles, CA 90059.

THORNTON, PEARL B.
Equal opportunity specialist & designer. **PERSONAL:** Born Jun 19, 1932, Houston, TX; divorced. **CAREER:** Deptof Defense, supr Job Opport Students. **ORGANIZATIONS:** Mem LA B Asin Equal Opportun Lealgue 5 yrs; mem Urban Lealgue Training Ctr Avdv Bd 1979-80; 2nd vice pres NAACP Beverly Hills Hollywood Br 1964-66; mem Adv Com 1964-75; 3rd vice pres NAACP Beverly Hills Hollywood Br 1967-68; co-/chrwmn NAACP Image Awds 1972; chrwmn Motion Picture Comm NAACP Image Awds 2 yrs; mem Crenshaw Christian Ctr. **HONORS/ACHIEVEMENTS:** "Outstanding Contributions Awd" Belles Sch for Retarded Children; "Recognition Awd" Urban League Training Ctr; Whos Who Among Black Am 1977-78. **BUSINESS ADDRESS:** Dept of Labor Offc of Fed Cont, 845 S Figuerda St Ste 550, Los Angeles, CA 90017.

THORNTON, WAYNE T.
Banker. **PERSONAL:** Born Aug 13, 1958, Harrisburg, PA. **EDUCATION:** Morgan State Univ, BS (Cum Laude) 1981. **CAREER:** Comptroller of the Currency, natl bank examiner 1979-85; Industrial Bank of Washington, asst vice president 1985-. **ORGANIZATIONS:** Realtor-assoc ERA Nyman Realty 1985-; bd of dirs Univ Legal Services 1986-. **HONORS/ACHIEVEMENTS:** Academic Merit Awd. **BUSINESS ADDRESS:** Assistant Vice President, Industrial Bank of Washington, 4812 Georgia Ave NW, Washington, DC 20011.

THORPE, HERBERT CLIFTON
Engineer. **PERSONAL:** Born Jan 09, 1923, New York, NY; married Jessie M Shorts; children: Jessica Davis, R Clifton. **EDUCATION:** NYU, BEE. **CAREER:** Rome Air Devel Ctr, elec engr. **ORGANIZATIONS:** Sec Rome Br NAACP; exec bd mem Mohawk Valley Frontiersmen; past pres Cosmopolitan Ctr. **MILITARY SERVICE:** Military Serv 2nd lt 1943-46. **BUSINESS ADDRESS:** Griffiss Air Force Base, New York, NY 13441.

THORPE, JOSEPHINE HORSLEY
Attorney. **PERSONAL:** Born Jun 03, 1943, Elizabeth, NJ. **EDUCATION:** Montclair St Coll, BA 1964; Seaton Hall Univ Sch of Law & Rutgers Sch of Law, jD 1969. **CAREER:** Newark Legal Serv Proj, staff atty 1969-70; Murphy Thorpe & Lewis NYC, law partner 1970-73; gen practice of law in Newark NJ 1973-74; Educ Law & Cntgr,atty 1974-75; Gen Attys Orgn Western Elec Co Inc NYC, atty 1975. **ORGANIZATIONS:** Mem Bar of NJ & NY; US Dist Ct for Dist of NJ; vice pres Educ Law Cntr Inc 1974-75; mem Garden St Bar Assn; Nat Bar Assn 100 Women for Integrity in Govt. **HONORS/ACHIEVEMENTS:** Recipient Regional Heber Smith Fellowship 1969; first place in oral presentation of Appellants brief in Rutgers Moot Ct Competition 1968. **BUSINESS ADDRESS:** 195 Broadway, New York, NY.

THORPE, OTIS L.
Appraiser. **PERSONAL:** Born Jun 21, 1953, Durham, NC; married Mildred W Walton; children: Johnny, Christine, Jerome, Michelle, Geoffery. **EDUCATION:** Morehouse Coll Atlanta, Bus Admn 1957; Atlanta U, econs 1958;Univ of Louisville KY, real estate 1960. **CAREER:** Joint City Co Bvd of Tax Assessors, chmn 1977-; Westside Realty Co, broker 1972-77; Metro Appraisal Sales Serv Inc, chief appraiser & pres 1969-77; Q V Williamson & Co, sales mgr 1962-69; Atlanta Empire Real Estate Bd, pres 1967-69; Nat Soc of Real Estate Appraisers, chmn educ com 1975; Nat Assn ofReal Estate Brokers, reg vice pres 1976. **ORGANIZATIONS:** Mem apptd by Pres of US, Adv Council Minority Enterprises 1972-74; mem bd of dirs Atlanta Urban League 1973; mem policy review bd Central Atlanta Progress 1976. **HONORS/ACHIEVEMENTS:** Cert of Merit NAACP 1975; Dist Achievement Awd Cincinnati OH Real Estate Brokers Assn Cincinnati 1976; Community Serv Awd, Nat Soc of Real Estate Appraisers 1977; Realist of Yr Awd, Empire Real Estate Bd 1977-78; Sharpshooter Awd AUS; Work & Performance. **MILITARY SERVICE:** AUS sp/4 1958-60. **BUSINESS ADDRESS:** 165 Central Ave SW, Rm 103, Atlanta, GA 30303.

THORPE, WESLEY LEE
Executive director. **PERSONAL:** Born Nov 20, 1926, Durham, NC; married Louise; children: Angela A, Wesley L Jr. **EDUCATION:** A&TUniv Greensboro NC, grad 1949. **CAREER:** Greaster New Haven Bus & Professional Mens Assn, exec dir; Delaney Cleaners Raleigh NC, asst mgr & tailor; Olin Matheson, scrap control mgr 1952-56; Siskorsky Aircraft, inspector 1956; Newhallville Cleaners, owner 1965. **ORGANIZATIONS:** Mem Widows Son Lodge # 1 PH Mason NH; trustee Immanuel Bapt Ch; sec Club 30 Inc; asst sec Widows Son Lodge 1955-56; bd dir Community Progress Inc; bd Dir BBB; bd Dir JC of New Haven. **MILITARY SERVICE:** USN 1945-46. **BUSINESS ADDRESS:** 261 Newhall St, New Haven, CT.

THRASH, ERNESTINE
Business mgmt. & educator. **PERSONAL:** Born Jul 30, 1942, Cleveland, TX. **EDUCATION:** Texas Southern Univ, Houston, TX, BS Business Ed 1964; Columbia Univ Teachers Coll, NY, NY, MA Industrial Psycology 1973. **CAREER:** McGraw-Hill Inc, asst training mgr 1967-69; Ford Found, asst admin officer 1969-74; Manhattan Comm Coll, adj lecturer 1969; LaGuardia Comm Coll, adj asst prof 1972-74; Avon Products Inc, mgr training 1974-77, eeo & selection 1977-78, personnel dir 1978-82; Bergen Comm Coll, adj asst prof 1984-86; Avon Products Inc, mgr mgmt devel & training 1982-. **ORGANIZATIONS:** Mem Delta Sigma Theta 1962-, Natl Comm on Arts & Letters 1974-76, Amer Soc for Training & Devel 1974-; vstg prof Natl Urban League 1975-; training consult United Methodist Church 1981; mem NY Personnel Assoc 1981-83, EDGES Group 1982-; nom comm YWCA of New York City 1985-87; mem council on ministers & admin bd Galilee United Methodist Church 1983-; pres Bergen Cty Alumnae Chap Delta Sigma Theta 1985-87.

THRASHER, WILLIAM EDWARD
Clergyman, government official. **PERSONAL:** Born Feb 28, 1950, Little Rock, AR; married Beverly Jean Broadnax; children: Tiffany Tarol, Willowry Elizabeth. **EDUCATION:** Jarvis Christian Coll Hawkins TX, 1968-69;Univ of AR Little Rock, BA 1973. **CAREER:** US Senastor David Pryor, adminstrv aide ; First Bapt Ch, pastor 1975-;Univ of AR Little Rock, dir of personnel 1977-80; Affirmative Action Section Officeof Gov, equal oppor splst 1975-77; AR Hwy Dept, personnel officer I 1974-75. **ORGANIZATIONS:** Bd mem Ouchita Counc Girl Scouts of Am 1978; bd mdm Urban League of Greater Little Rock 1979; coucil mem AR Merit Sys Coun 1979; elected convention del AR Constitutional Convention 1979-80. **HONORS/ACHIEVEMENTS:** Outstanding Yng Men of Am Nat Jr C of C 1978-79; Outstanding Personalities of S Am Biographical Inst 1979; elected v chmn Local Gov Com AR Constitutional Conv 1979-80. **BUSINESS ADDRESS:** Office of Univ S Sen David Pryor, 3030 Federal Bldg, Little Rock, AR 72201.

THREADGILL, WALTER LEONARD
Business executive. **PERSONAL:** Born Dec 20, 1945, New York, NY; married Jacqueline Cephas. **EDUCATION:** The City Coll of NY, BBA 1967; Long Island Univ, MBA 1976; Antioch Law Sch, MA Law. **CAREER:** Fiduciary Trust Co of NY, div vice pres 1970-77; United Natl Bank of Wash, sr vice pres 1977-79; Minority Broadcast Investment Corp, corp vice pres/chmn of bd 1979-. **ORGANIZATIONS:** Spl consult for tech Icelandic Govt 1973-77; lecturer Amer Mgmt Assn Howard Univ 1974-; dir Broad Jump Inc NY 1975-; trustee Boy Scouts of Amer exploring div 1976-; dir United Cerebral Palsy 1977-; pres The Compass Club Wash DC 1977-78; adv dir United Nat Bank of Wash 1978-; mem Natl Democratic Club,Natl Broadcasters Club, Urban Bankers, Amer Mgmt Assn Soc of Amer Value Engrs, Urban League. **HONORS/ACHIEVEMENTS:** Special Serv Awd Boy Scouts of Amer NY 1976; article Rev of Minority Institutional Assets Wash DC 1978; prod "Narrative of the Life of Frederick Douglass" Frederick Douglass Pageant Com Wash DC. **MILITARY SERVICE:** AUS res 1969-75.

THREATT, ROBERT
Educator. **PERSONAL:** Born Apr 04, 1928, Columbus, GA; married Helen Kilpatrick. **EDUCATION:** Morris Brown Coll, AB 1949; Atlanta U, MA 1958; Univ OK, edD 1963. **CAREER:** Morris Brown Coll, pres 1973-; Ft Valley St, chmn Dept Secondary Educ 1963-73; GA St Dept Educ, 1958-61; Marshall Jr High, GA, teacher 1953-58. **ORGANIZATIONS:** Mem NEA; Nat Assn Equal Opport Higher Edn; pres GA Assn Educators; bd mem Central Atlanta Progress; bd mem Citizens Trust Bank. **HONORS/ACHIEVEMENTS:** Tchr of Yr 1956; Alumnus of Yr Morris Brown Coll 1971; Alumnus of Yr AtlantaUniv 1971. **MILITARY SERVICE:** AUS corpl 1950-52. **BUSINESS ADDRESS:** 643 Hunter St NW, Atlanta, GA 30314.

THREATT, SEDALE EUGENE
Professional athlete. **PERSONAL:** Born Sep 10, 1961, Atlanta, GA. **EDUCATION:** West VA Tech, 1983. **CAREER:** Philadelphia 76er's, guard 1983-. **HONORS/ACHIEVEMENTS:** Was an NAIA first team All-am in his jr and sr years; was tabbed unofficially as the best "name" in the 1983 draft. **BUSINESS ADDRESS:** Philadelphia 76er's, Veterans Stadium, Ste 510, Philadelphia, PA 19141.

THROWER, CHARLES S.
Editor, publisher. **PERSONAL:** Born Sep 29, 1920, Philadelphia, PA; married Naomi Woo Yum; children: Charles Jr, Pamela, Teresa, Brian, Steven. **EDUCATION:** Univ Pa; UCLA. **CAREER:** Peninsula Bulletin, ed pub founder 1967-75; freelance writer; newscaster; radio & TV producer; bd Bay Area Urban League. **ORGANIZATIONS:** Life mem NAACP; BSA; Mid-peninsula Stanford Urban Coal; bd United Nations Assn; bd W Coast Black Publ Assn; Sigma Delta Chi Journalism Frat. **MILITARY SERVICE:** Army Vet. **BUSINESS ADDRESS:** 2332 University Ave E, Palo Alto, CA 94303.

THROWER, JULIUS A.
Clergyman. **PERSONAL:** Born Jul 31, 1917, Mobile, AL; married Omanda Harris; children: Yvonne, Julius, Randolph, Pearl, Leonard, Herbert, Saundra, Joseph, Orlando. **EDUCATION:** So State Acad, 1959; Cedar Grove Theol Sem; SelmaUniv Ext; Lutheran Theol Sem. **CAREER:** Mt Zion Missionary Bapt Ch; Lilly Bapt Ch; min; Fannie Bapt Ch, pastor; Bapt Training & Union Cong, inst. **ORGANIZATIONS:** Vol Youth Comm OH 1960-66; mem Ministeral All; vice pres Pastors Conf; Inst Dist Cong Christian Educ 1967-74; NAACP 1967-74; treas Human Right Fund for Jusitice 1973-74; vol Youth Comm OH 1966-74. **HONORS/ACHIEVEMENTS:** Bronze Zero Defects Award. **MILITARY SERVICE:** Air Force Logistics Comm 1967. **BUSINESS ADDRESS:** 1535 Dewey Ave, Columbus, OH 43219.

THROWER, JULIUS B.
Administrator. **PERSONAL:** Born Mar 26, 1938, Mobile, AL; married Louise Green; children: Julian, Jason. **EDUCATION:** SD Bishop State Jr Coll, AA; AL State Coll Mobile Ctr, 1962; AL State U, BS 1964; Auburn U, MEd 1971. **CAREER:** SD Bishop State Jr Coll, dir of admin 1977-, veterans coord; SD Bishop State Jr Coll, dir veterans affairs 1973-77; SD Bishop State Jr Coll, coord special serv & devel 1971-73; SD Bishop State Jr Coll, plant supr 1966-70; Mobile Co Public School, high school instructor 1964-66. **ORGANIZATIONS:** Mem VCIP adv bd US Dept HEW 1975-76; past v chmn (Amvpa) Am Assn of Minority Prog Admin 1977-78; commr Nat Commns from Employment Policy 1979; former sr warden F & AM Onyx Ldg #676 1975-76; asst recorder Shriner Palestine Temple 1975-76; bd of mgmt Metro YMCA Mobile Deaborn St Br; adv bd Mobile Consortium CETA; commr (presdl appointee) Nat Commns for Employment Policy 1979; Jr Coll Leadership Conf AuburnUniv 1969. **HONORS/ACHIEVEMENTS:** SGA Award student govt assn SD Biship State Jr Coll 1976; Good Conduct Medal. **MILITARY SERVICE:** USMC col 4 yrs. **BUSINESS ADDRESS:** Veterans Coordinator, SD Bishop State Jr Coll, 351 N Broad St, Mobile, AL 36603.

THURMAN, ALFONZO
Educator. **PERSONAL:** Born Oct 24, 1946, Mayfield, KY; son of Togo Thurman and Georgia May Jones Thurman; married Brazilian Burnette; children: Alfonzo II. **EDUCATION:** Univ of Wisconsin-LaCrosse, BS 1971, MA 1973, PhD 1979. **CAREER:** Univ of Wisconsin-Whitewater, coordinator minority affairs 1971-75; Univ of Wisconsin-Oshkosh, dir academic devel program 1975-80; Northern Illinois Univ, dir special projects 1980-84, asst to the provost 1984-87. **ORGANIZATIONS:** Pres Illinois Assn of Educ Opportunity Program 1983-84; chairman DeKalb Human Relations Comm 1983-86. **HONORS/ACHIEVEMENTS:** Outstanding Leadership Award ILAEOPP 1985; wrote "Establishing Special Services on Campus" (chapter) IN Handbook of Minority Student Services, and "Policy Making, Higher Education's Paradox" (article) in Thresholds 1986. **HOME ADDRESS:** 527 Ridge Rd, De Kalb, IL 60115. **BUSINESS ADDRESS:** Assoc Dean, Coll of Educ, Northern Illinois University, Graham Hall 321, De Kalb, IL 60115.

THURMAN, FRANCES ASHTON
Educator. **PERSONAL:** Born Mar 30, 1919, Washington, DC; married Henry L Thurman (deceased); children: Henry L Jr, Ashton W, Avis C Watts, Audrey E. **EDUCATION:** Howard Univ, AB 1935-39, MA 1939-41; Catholic Univ, Library Sci summer 1948; Howard, Ed summer 1962; Univ of CO Boulder, Anthropology summer 1963; Carnegie Inst of Tech, History summer 1965; Univ of Louisville, Black Studies summer 1971; Howard Univ, PhD 1974-78. **CAREER:** St Pauls Coll Lawrenceville, instr 1942-50; Cardoza evening School, teacher 1957-59; St Pauls Coll, assoc prof 1959-74, prof 1978-. **ORGANIZATIONS:** Mem VA Soc of History Teachers, Org of Amer Historians, Assn for the Study of Afro-Amer Life & History, Intl Toastmistress Clubs; sec Evette Club ITC, Delta Sigma Theta, Independent Rschr; mem Phi Alpha Theta Historical Soc, Afro-Amer Studies Inc, Southern Historical Assn. **HONORS/ACHIEVEMENTS:** Presented paper "The Public Response to Joe Lois" ASALH Convention in Chicago 1976; Guest Speaker Black History Month Local Public School Syst Lawrenceville 1984; "The History of St Pauls Co 1888-1959" dissertation topic; Ford T Johnson Cup of Teaching Excellence, St Paul's College 1988. **BUSINESS ADDRESS:** Professor of History, St Pauls College, 406 Windsor Ave, Lawrenceville, VA 23868.

THURMAN, MARJORIE ELLEN
Educator. **PERSONAL:** Born in Whiteville, NC. **EDUCATION:** Fayetteville State Univ, BS 1969; Seton Hall Univ, MA 1977. **CAREER:** Essex Coll of Business, instructor 1975-85; Sawyer Business School, evening dean 1979-80; Senator Wynona Lipman, part-time clerical 1985-; SCS Business & Tech Inst, part-time instructor 1986-; Newark Bd of Educ, teacher 1969-. **ORGANIZATIONS:** Mem YWCA 1972-83; Sunday school teacher St Paul's Church 1978-80; advisor Senior Class MX Shabazz 1985-87; mem Minority Business

Org 1985-; Natl Business Educ Assn/NJ Business Educ Assn; Newark Teacher's Union; Alpha Kappa Alpha Sorority. **HONORS/ACHIEVEMENTS:** Outstanding Teaching Plaque Essex Coll of Business 1983; Teacher of the Month-SCS Business & Technical Inst, 1987-88; created a successful program in Newark, NJ in 1981 called the "Newark Business Skills Olympics.". **BUSINESS ADDRESS:** Business Teacher, Malcolm X Shabazz HS, Newark, NJ 07108.

THURMOND, NATE (NATE THE GREAT)
Professional athlete. **PERSONAL:** Born Jul 25, 1941, Akron, OH. **EDUCATION:** BS 1963. **CAREER:** Golden State Warriors, center 1963-74; Chicago Bulls, center 1974; Cleveland Cavaliers, center 1974-76; The Beginning Restaurant San Francisco, owner; Gold State-Warriors, dir community rel. **ORGANIZATIONS:** Bd mem SCARE; promo appearances, youth clinics, speaking engagements throughout No CA. **HONORS/ACHIEVEMENTS:** Leagues 4th all-time leading rebounder with 14,464 career bds; honored for outstanding play with Golden State 1978; mem Basketball Hall of Fame. **BUSINESS ADDRESS:** Director, Community Relations, Golden State Warriors, Oakland Coliseum Arena, Oakland, CA.

THURSTON, CHARLES SPARKS
Dermatologist. **PERSONAL:** Born Mar 13, 1934, King & Queen, VA; married Marie; children: Renee, Cynthia, Patti, Carmen. **EDUCATION:** VA St Coll, BS 1953; Meharry Med Coll, MD 1958; Wm Beaumont Army Hosp, intern 1959;Univ MI Med Ctr, res 1965-66. **CAREER:** Self Empl, drmtlgst; Wilford Hall USAF Hosp, training dir, chf 1974-76; USAF Sur Gen, consult 1968-70, 1974-76; Weisbaden USAF Hosp, chf gen therapy srv 1972-74, chf dermat1970-74; Andrew AFB, 1966-68; Howard U, asst clinical prof 1968-70; G Wash U, 1968-70; Georgetown U, 1968-70;Univ TX, 1974-; Santa Rosa Hosp, chf dermat 1978. **ORGANIZATIONS:** Pres CA Whittier Med Soc 1977-78; vice pres Lone Star St Med Soc 1977; pres Assn Mltry Drmtlgy 1975; natl chmn dermat sect Nat Med Assn 1977-79; flw Am Acad Drmtlgy 1967-; mem AMA 1968-; Mat Med Assn 1968-; San Antonio Dermat Soc 1975-; Am Coll Phy 1975-; pres local chap Alpha Omego Alpha 1957-58. **HONORS/ACHIEVEMENTS:** R Braun Awd Most Outst Sr & Med Std Surg 1958; cert Achvmt Surg Gen 1970; V Marchbanks Awd Outst Air Force Phys 1974; Meritorious Srv Mdl USAF. **MILITARY SERVICE:** USAF chf, aviation med 1959-63, col 1956-76. **BUSINESS ADDRESS:** 343 W Houston St, Ste 909, San Antonio, TX 78205.

THURSTON, PAUL E.
Educator. **PERSONAL:** Born Jul 13, 1938, Williamsport, PA; son of Helen Louise Thurston. **EDUCATION:** Lafayette Coll, BS 1960; Cornell U, PhD 1964. **CAREER:** TX So U, asst prof 1966-73; TX So Univ asso prof 1973-; Texas Southern Univ Houston, TX prof, 1982-. **ORGANIZATIONS:** Mem Am Chem Soc; Am Assn of Univ Prof. **HONORS/ACHIEVEMENTS:** Recip Danforth Fellow & Woodrow Wilson Fellow; Phi Beta Kappa; Experimental Organic Chemistry, American Press 1987; General Chemistry: A Lab Manual, Vol I & 2, 1989. **MILITARY SERVICE:** AUS capt 1960-64. **BUSINESS ADDRESS:** Professor, Texas Southern University, c/o Dept. of Chemistry, 3100 Cleburne Street, Houston, TX 77004.

THURSTON, ROGER GRAVE
Physician. **PERSONAL:** Born Mar 09, 1912, Charlotte, NC; children: Roger III, Candace, Kathi. **EDUCATION:** Howard Univ Washington DC, BS, MD. **CAREER:** Private Practice, physician. **BUSINESS ADDRESS:** Medical Doctor, Roger G Thurston MD, 753 19th St NE, Washington, DC 20002.

THURSTON, WILLIAM A.
Minister, architect, human rights activist. **PERSONAL:** Born Jun 06, 1944, Chicago; married Silvia M Petty; children: William A, Peter O, Omyia N, Pauline A. **EDUCATION:** Univ of IL, bA 1967; Moody Bible Inst, 1979; Candler Sch of Theol, 1980; Graham Found Scholar, 1966. **CAREER:** Operation PUSH, natl dir; Seymour S Goldstein Asso Chicago, arch 1965-67; Dubin Dubin Black & Moutoussamy Chicago, arch 1967-69; Envrn Seven Ltd Chicago, pntr dir of planning 1969-74. **ORGANIZATIONS:** Asso minister Fellowship Missionary Bapt Ch; bd mem Comprehensive Research & Devel Chicago Arch Assis Cntr; mem Nat Assn of Housing Owners & Mgr. **BUSINESS ADDRESS:** 930 E 50 St, Chicago, IL 60615.

TIBBS, EDWARD A.
Elected official. **PERSONAL:** Born Apr 12, 1940, Pittsburgh, PA; son of Otis H. Tibbs and Mayme Yager Tibbs; married Sheila Christian Tibbs, May 10, 1988. **EDUCATION:** Allegheny Community College, associates 1976; Wilson College, certificate of instruction 1980; Univ Pittsburgh, evening studies; Wilson Coll, 1982-1989. **CAREER:** East Liberty-Garfield CAP, board member 1968-74; Allegheny County, democratic committeeman 1970-81, paymaster 1980-81; IBPOE of W Elks, asst to grand exalted ruler 1982-; Allegheny County, district magistrate. **ORGANIZATIONS:** Exec bd mem Local 2596 CWA 1973-80; chairman Allegheny County Black Political Assembly 1976-77; exalted ruler Greater Pgh Elks 1979-82; committee on ethicsCommunication Workers of Amer 1973-76; NAACP life mem Sixth Mount Zion Baptist Church. **HONORS/ACHIEVEMENTS:** Community Service Award Community Action Pgh 1975; Mr Elk IBPOE of W Pgh 1979; Meritorious Serv Awd PA Chaplains Dept IBPOE of W 1981; Disting Achievement Awd Steel City Council #8 IBPOE of W 1981; Leadership with Excellence Awd Faith Tabernacle Church 1986. **MILITARY SERVICE:** U.S. Army Specialist 4th Class 3 yrs; Missleman of the Month 1960. **HOME ADDRESS:** 7243 Somerset Street, Pittsburgh, PA 15235. **BUSINESS ADDRESS:** District Magistrate, Allegheny County, 1013 Lincoln Ave, Pittsburgh, PA 15206.

TIDWELL, ISAIAH
Banking executive. **PERSONAL:** Born Feb 13, 1945, Charlotte, NC; son of William Tidwell and Anna D Tidwell; married Hellena O Huntley; children: William DeVane, Damion Lamar. **EDUCATION:** NC Central Univ, BS 1967; Wake Forest Univ, MBA 1980. **CAREER:** Celanese Fibers Co Charlotte, accountant 1967-70; Celanese Fibers Co Rock Hill, cost acct 1970-71, supvr cost analysis 1971-72; Wachovia Bank & Trust Co, sr vp. **ORGANIZATIONS:** Pres, jr & sr class NC Central Univ 1965-67; pres Charlotte Chapter NC Central Univ Alumni Assoc 1967-76; various offices held Omega Psi Phi 1969-76; mem Charlotte Chamber of Commerce 1973-76; chmn of the bd Charlotte Business Devel Org 1974-76; bd mem Charlotte Business Resource Center 1975-76; mem bd of Deacons, bd of trustees, financial secretary First Baptist Church-E Winston; past pres PTA Moore Alt School; mem Comm on Finance, life mem NC Central Univ Alumni Assoc; Omega Psi Phi Fraternity Inc Baiseus, life mem; mem Statement Studies Comm Robert Morris Assoc; Mem Region IV Charlotte Advisory Council US Small Business Admin; mem bd of directors, chmn Business II Div 1982 Campaign United Way of Forsyth County; pres-bd of dir Winston-Salem Neighborhood Housing Serv; mem-exec bd, chmn communications comm BSA; mem-bd of dir, Finance comm YMCA-Metro Board; mem City/County Utility Commission of Winston-Salem & Forsyth County 1984, mem, W/S Chamber of Commerce, W/S Rotory. **HONORS/ACHIEVEMENTS:** 1st minority chmn Celriver Plant United Fund Campaign 1972. **BUSINESS ADDRESS:** Senior Vice President, Wachovia Bank & Trust Co, PO Box 3099, Winston-Salem, NC 27102.

TIDWELL, JOHN EDGAR
Educator. **PERSONAL:** Born Dec 13, 1945, Independence, KS; married Dorothy Webb; children: Levert, Trudy, Tuere. **EDUCATION:** Washburn U, AB 1968; Creighton U, AM 1972; MN U, postgrad. **CAREER:** St Olaf Coll Northfield, eng instr 1974-; Am Minority Studies, dir 1974-75; Black Studies Univ NE, acting chmn 1973-74. **ORGANIZATIONS:** Mem Nat Coun Eng Tchr. **HONORS/ACHIEVEMENTS:** Fac growth awd Am Lutheran Ch 1975; Annie B Sweet awd WashburnUniv 1965-67. **BUSINESS ADDRESS:** Afro Am Studies Dept, U of MN, Minneapolis, MN 55414.

TIEUEL, ROBERT C. D.
Business executive, clergyman. **PERSONAL:** Born Jun 26, 1914, Boley, OK; married Mary E Porter. **EDUCATION:** Lane Coll Jackson TN, AB & BD; TN St Coll; Langston U; TX Coll; Harvard Divinity School, spec study 1934-36. **CAREER:** Christ Call Mission Fund & News Serv, dir; Friendship Chapel CME Ch Pecos TX, pub rel consult journ churchman pastor; The Midland Reporter & Telegram andClovis Daily News Trib, staff col; NW TX Conf of CME Ch, circuit rider evang pastor; TX Coll Tyler, recruitment off. **ORGANIZATIONS:** Mem Hobbs NM C of C; Boley OK C of C; bd of Christ Edn; NW TX Conf CME Ch; Nat Retired Thcr Assn; chmn exec com Progressive Cit Leag Incof NM; mem Liano Estacado Hist Assn; sec treas United Clearing Syst Inc; mem Com of 100 to Make Boley OK a Nat Pk; ed Who's Who in the CME Ch 1962; religious editor of Southwest Digest Lubbock TX 1987; dir, public relations Christian Index. **HONORS/ACHIEVEMENTS:** First Black cand for NM stae rep 1958; cited by Pres Eisenhower for efforts in build christ interracial goodwill & rel as ed of The Christ Call; dir Mary P Tieuel's Scholarship fund for deserving minorities 1987-88. **BUSINESS ADDRESS:** Minister, Christian Meth Epis Church, 531 S Parkway East, Memphis, TN.

TILDON, CHARLES G., JR.
Government employee. **PERSONAL:** Born Sep 10, 1926, Baltimore, MD; married Louise Smith. **EDUCATION:** Morehouse Col; Morgan State Coll; Johns Hopkins U, BS 1954. **CAREER:** Dept Human Resources, asst sec community prog & admin 1980; Provident Hosp Inc, asso dir, coor, Neighborhood Hlth Cntr 1968-71; Biodynamics, consult off econ oppor 1968-70; Balt Pub Sch, tchr head science dept 1955-64; Balt City PO, postal clk 1951-55; Morgan St Coll, cnslr 1960-61. **ORGANIZATIONS:** Mem Adv Club Balt; mem Am Col Hosp Admin; mem Nat Assn Hlth Serv Executives (Charter mem & past vp) mem at Large, past chmn Archdiocesan Urban Comm; adv bd Advance Fed Savings & Loan, 1966; Am Cancer Soc; bd mem, mem exec comm, Citizens Planning & Housing Assn. **HONORS/ACHIEVEMENTS:** Achievement Awd Archdiocesan Council Cath men; Citizens Salute to Charles G Tildon, Jr 1969; Spec Serv Awd, Urban Comm, Archdiocese Balt 1972; Med Staff Awd, Provident Hosp 1967. **BUSINESS ADDRESS:** 1123 N Eutaw St, 605 Jackson Towers, Baltimore, MD 21201.

TILGHMAN, CYPRIAN O.
Union official. **PERSONAL:** Born May 19, 1913, Washington, DC; married Cecilia Cooke; children: 13 children. **CAREER:** Former UCF Bd; HWC delegate; vice pres MD State/DC AFL-CIO; Hotel & Restaurant Local #25, advisor/consultant. **ORGANIZATIONS:** Former mem MDTA; mem Skills Bank; Urban League; Old Dem Central Com; pres JEB. **BUSINESS ADDRESS:** Advisor/Consultant, Hotel & Rest Local #25, 1003 K St NW, Washington, DC 20001.

TILLES, GERALD EMERSON
Attorney & judge. **PERSONAL:** Born Jul 15, 1942, Detroit, MI; married Catherine Blakeley; children: Mikki, Jeffrey. **EDUCATION:** Wayne State U, BSED 1964, MA 1970, JD 1971. **CAREER:** Detroit Bd Educ, tchr 1964-70; prv prctc law 1972-75; Cty Wayne, asst corp cnsl 1975-84; Bureau Wrkrs Dsblty Comp State Of MI, admn law judge 1984-, funds administrator 1987, magistrate 1987. **ORGANIZATIONS:** Pstr/fndr Chapel Savior Ann Arbor, MI 1980-; wrtr MI Chronicle 1971-74; bd review chrmn Superior Twp 1984-; mem Wolverine Bar Assc, State Bar MI; minister United Methodist Church. **HONORS/ACHIEVEMENTS:** Robbins Awrd Wayne State Law Sch 1971. **BUSINESS ADDRESS:** Magistrate, State of MI, 1200 Sixth St, Detroit, MI 48226.

TILLETT, GEORGE EDWARD
Attorney. **PERSONAL:** Born Jun 09, 1923, Edenton, NC; married Martha D Gray; children: Joseph, Joyce. **EDUCATION:** Central U, JD 1953; A&T State U, BA 1948. **CAREER:** Pvt Prac, atty; State Hwy Commn, asst coord 1969-71; Eastern Dist of NC, asst US atty 1965-69. **ORGANIZATIONS:** Bd of dir Central Orphanage; mem Kappa Alph Apsi Frat; NC Acad of Trial Lawyers; Assn of Trial Lawyers of Am; NC Bar Assn; NC Assn of Black Lawyers. **MILITARY SERVICE:** USI corpl 1943-45. **BUSINESS ADDRESS:** 622 E Washington Dr, High Point, NC 27260.

TILLEY, FRANK N.
Physician. **PERSONAL:** Born Jul 17, 1933, New York, NY; married Frances A Payne. **EDUCATION:** Columbia Clge, BA 1955; State Univ of NY Sch of Medicine Downstate Med Ctr, MD 1959; Columbia Univ Sch of Pub Health & Admin Medicine, MPH 1964. **CAREER:** Dept of Family Prac State Univ of NY Downstate Med Ctr, clinical asst 1974-; Dept of Ambulatory Care Jewish Hosp & Med Ctr of Brooklyn Greenpoint Affil, chief 1973-; United Mutual Life Ins Co, med dir 1972-; United Mutual Life Ins Co, bd dir 1974-; Dept of Environmental Medicine & Comm Health State Univ of NY Downstate Med Ctr, lectr 1972-74; Jewish Hosp & Med Ctr of Brooklyn Greenpoint Affil, coord of Ambulatory Care 1971-73, asst dir EmerDept 1971, emer srv atndng physician 1965-7, 69-71. **ORGANIZATIONS:** Fellow Amer Clge of Preventive Medicine; Amer Clge of Emer Physicians; mem Med Soc

of State of NY; Med Soc of Co of Kings; Provident Clinical Soc;Amer Geriatrics Soc; Amer Pub Health Assc; New York City Pub Health Assc; Amer Soc of Tropical Medicine & Hygiene; New York City Soc of Topical Medicine; mem 100 Black Men. **HONORS/ACHIEVEMENTS:** Recipt Commendation Medal 1969; Certificate of Achievemnt AUS 1969. **MILITARY SERVICE:** AUS major 1967-69.

TILLIS, FREDERICK C.
Composer, performer, educator. **PERSONAL:** Born Jan 05, 1930, Galveston, TX; married E Louise; children: Patricia, Pamela. **EDUCATION:** Wiley Coll, BA 1949;Univ of IA, MA 1952;Univ of IA, PhD 1963. **CAREER:** Univ of MA, prof music theory & composition, dir Afro-Amer Music & Jazz Prog 1973; Univ of MA, assoc provost & prof music 1974; Univ of MA, spl asst to provost for the arts 1977, assoc vice chancellor 1989, director University Fine Arts Center, 1982; EMI Amer Federation of Musicians, composer, performer; P & P Publications, publisher. **ORGANIZATIONS:** Mus tchr, Natl Assn; natl chmn, Theory Composition Sect 1969-71; Danforth Asso, 1969); compostr, mem Amer Music Cntr; mem Amer Composers Alliance; composer mem Broadcast Music Industry; mem bd of dirs Concerts in Black & White Boston, 1979; Artists Foundation, Boston; bd of dir, WGBY, Channel 57, Springfield. **HONORS/ACHIEVEMENTS:** Composer of more than 85 compositions spanning both the European classical & jazz traditions; recip United Negro Coll Fund Fellowship 1961-63; recip Rockefeller Fund Grant for Devl Compstn 1978; recip Nat Endowment for the Arts, Composers Grant 1979; Chancellor's Lecturer, Univ of Massachusetts; author, In the Spirit and the Flesh, P & P Publications 1989. **MILITARY SERVICE:** US Air Force, 1952-56. **BUSINESS ADDRESS:** Professor and Assoc Vice-Chancellor, University of Massachusetts, Amherst, MA 01002.

TILLMAN, CHRISTINE L.
Elected official, social service. **PERSONAL:** Born Dec 14, 1952, Richmond, VA. **EDUCATION:** Radford Coll, BA 1975; VA Commonwealth Univ, 1976; J Seargeant Reynolds Comm Coll, 1981,84. **CAREER:** Richmond Oppty Indust Ctr, youth counselor 1975. **ORGANIZATIONS:** Basileus 1972-75, mem 1973-74 Alpha Kappa Alpha; mem bd of dir Dawn Progressive Assoc Inc 1978-; mem Caroline Co Rec Adv Comm 1984-, Caroline Co Ext Serv Adv Council, VA Politech Inst & State Univ 1984-, Caroline Co Bd of suprvs 1984-; v chmn Caroline Co Bd of Suprvs 1985, Caroline Co Local Welfare Bd 1985, NAACP Caroline Chapt; bd mem Tri-County Medical Corp 1985-; chmn Caroline Co Bd of Supervisors 1987. **HONORS/ACHIEVEMENTS:** 1st Black Female Mem Caroline Co Bd of Suprvs 1984-; Honoree Negro Achievers Awd Caroline Co Chap NAACP 1984. **HOME ADDRESS:** Rt 1 Box 101, Doswell, VA 23047.

TILLMAN, JOSEPH NATHANIEL
Executive. **PERSONAL:** Born Aug 01, 1926, Augusta, GA; son of Leroy Tillman and Canarie Tillman; married Areerat; children: Alice Tillman Jesse, Robert Bertram. **EDUCATION:** Paine Coll, BA (Magna Cum Laude) 1948; Northrop Univ, MS 1975, MBA 1976; Nova Univ, DBA 1988. **CAREER:** Rockwell Intl, dir 1958-84; Tillman Enterprises, president 1985-. **ORGANIZATIONS:** Guest lecturer UCLA 1980-85; pres NAACP San Gabrial Chap 1984; pres Soc of Logistics Engrs Orange Co Chap 1985; chmn organizational behavior Acad of Mgmt 1985; consultant Natl Univ 1986. **HONORS/ACHIEVEMENTS:** Listed in Who's Who in CA, Who's Who Historical Soc; Presidential Citation Natl Assoc for Equal Oppor in Higher Educ 1986; numerous publications including"Computer Algorithm for Optimizing Testability" 1976, "Testability Optimizing at all Levels of Maintenance" 1984; "An Evaluation of Middle Managers Coping Strategies in Aerospace Industries as a Predictor of their Success" 1986; "Job Stressors and Coping Strategies of Aerospace Managers: Their Influence on Healthy Life Styles and Job Performance" 1989. **MILITARY SERVICE:** USAF capt 9 yrs, navigator bombardier 1948-57. **HOME ADDRESS:** 1032 Sugarloaf Blvd, Big Bear City, CA 92314. **BUSINESS ADDRESS:** President, Tillman Enterprises, 4901 Green River Dr #5, Corona, CA 91720.

TILLMAN, LILLIAN G. (NEE GARLAND)
School principal. **PERSONAL:** Born Jan 27, 1934, Jamaica, NY; children: Kay Lynn, James Edward. **EDUCATION:** State Univ of New York, MS 1973-75; Roosevelt Univ, BA 1955; Russell Sage Coll, 1972-73; Hunter Coll, 1951-52, 1961; Queens Coll, 1960-61; Northwestern Univ, 1956; New York Univ, 1954. **CAREER:** St Acad of Albany NY, principal 1979; Arbor Hill School, Albany NY, resource teacher 1966-; Scudder Ave School, resource teacher 1962-66; Carousel Nursery School, teacher 1960-61; Albany, teacher 1956-57; Arbor Hill School, Albany NY, teacher 1956; Albany, teacher 1955-56. **ORGANIZATIONS:** Pres, Albany Interracial Council 1978-80; mem, City Club of Albany; mem, Phi Delta Kappa Frat; pres, vice pres, chairperson, Special Proj Comm, Albany Alumnae Chap, Delta Sigma Theta Sor Inc; first pres, Urban League Guild of Albany Area 1973-76; vice pres, chairperson, Personnel Comm, Albany Interracial Council; bd dir, Albany Co Div for Youth; chairperson, Twin Proj, Albany Dist PTA; hon life mem, PTA 1972; consultant, Natl PTA; bd dir, Albany Urban League; mem, Albany Public School Teachers Assn; NY State United Teachers; NEA; Urban League Guild; NAACP; participant in Inst for Study of Educ Problems Occasioned by Desegration State Univ NY 1967-68; Natl Staff Devel Ctr, Sem Open Classroom Denver 1971; Continuous Progress Learning Inst Albany 1972; Intl Conf & Symposium on Trans-Cultural Adaptation Port-au-Prince Haiti 1973; consultant Conf of Concern for Absenteeism in Schools Chicago 1974-75; co-hostess TV prog "Talking With the Tillmans" 1973-76. **HONORS/ACHIEVEMENTS:** Teacher Fellowship, NY State PTA 1975. **BUSINESS ADDRESS:** Arbor Hill Elem School, Lark Drive, Albany, NY 12210.

TILLMAN, PAULA SELLARS
Government official. **PERSONAL:** Born Jun 21, 1949, Chicago, IL; married James Tillman Sr; children: Lisa, James II:. **EDUCATION:** Loyola Univ Chicago, BA (Magna Cum Laude) 1974; DePaul Coll of Law, JD 1979; admitted to Illinois Bar 1979. **CAREER:** Chicago Police Dept, youth officer 1974-79, financial crimes investigation 1979-81, legal officer II 1981-, liaison mayor's commn on women 1984-, eeo officer1984-. **ORGANIZATIONS:** Mem Cook County Bar Assoc 1979-; commissioner IL Attorney Registration & Disciplinary Comm 1981-; chairperson personnel comm Chicago Coalition Against Abused Women 1984-85; sec Bd of Dirs Providence St Mel High School 1984-85; fellow Leadership Greater Chicago 1985-86; mem Campfire Inc 1986-; chairperson, personnel comm, mem Natl Hook-Up of Black Women Chicago Chap 1986-. **HONORS/ACHIEVEMENTS:** Natl Merit Scholar 1967. **BUSINESS ADDRESS:** Legal Officer II/EEO Officer, Chicago Police Dept, 1121 So State, Room 403, Chicago, IL 60605.

TILLMAN, TALMADGE CALVIN, JR.
Accountant, educator. **PERSONAL:** Born Nov 26, 1925, Brunswick, GA; married Leola Bennings; children: Timothy, Philip. **EDUCATION:** IN Univ, BS 1948; Syracuse Univ, MBA 1949; Univ of So CA, DBA 1967; CA, CPA 1965; Univ of MA, postdoctoral study 1972; Univ of CO, post doctoral study 1974. **CAREER:** CA State Univ Long Beach, prof of acct 1968-; Price Waterhouse, faculty & flwshp 1969; E Los Angeles Clge, assc prof of acct 1962-68; Sidney Spiegel CPA, auditor-acct; Joseph S Herbert & Co, acct; Gilbert Drummont CPA Dept, acct; TX So Univ, chmn of acct 1950-51. **ORGANIZATIONS:** Treas Syracuse Univ Alumni Assc of LA 1953; pres IN Univ Alumni Assc of LA 1978-79; basileus Omega Psi Phi, Lambda Omicron Chpt. **HONORS/ACHIEVEMENTS:** Van De Camp Award Best Article Written for Natl Assn of Acct LA Chap 1968; Natl Achievement Award in Acct Educ Natl Assn of Black Acct 1977; Citizen of Year 12th Dist Omega Psi Phi Frat; IN Alumni Assn Named Number One Chap in US during Presidency 1980. **MILITARY SERVICE:** USN storekeeper 2nd Class 1942-44. **BUSINESS ADDRESS:** Professor of Accounting, California State Univ at Long Beach, 1250 Bellflower Blvd, Long Beach, CA 90840.

TILMON, JAMES A.
Weatherman, pilot, business executive. **PERSONAL:** Born Jul 31, 1934, Guthrie, OK; divorced; children: John, Weatherman, WMAQ-TV, 1974-?; TV personality/host, pub. **EDUCATION:** Lincoln Univ, Music Educ grad 1955. **CAREER:** WMAQ-TV, weatherman 1974-, TV personality/Host pub affairs entertainment-discussion prog 1972-76; Amer Airlines, capt 1965-. **ORGANIZATIONS:** Pres chief exec ofcr Tilmon Enterprises Ltd 1975-; trustee Kendall Colge; bd trustees Ravinia Festival; claronist Lake Forest Symphony Orch; bd dir Comm Music Assc; bd dir Urban Gateways; mem IL Assc for Retarded Citizens Pub Educ Adv Comm; bd gov Chicago Heart Assc. **HONORS/ACHIEVEMENTS:** Recip Capt Chair Award Amer Airlines 1969; Humanitarian of Year Civil Libs League of IL 1970; Black Achievers Award YMCA; W Side Org #1 award 1974; Emmyaward Natl Acad TV Arts & Sci 1974; best dressed lift Fashion Guild of Amer Intl 1976; best dressed list Dress Horsemen Inc Chicago; permanent noncomp mem Dress Horsemen Inc Fashion Hall of Fame 1976. **MILITARY SERVICE:** AUS Corps of Engr capt. **BUSINESS ADDRESS:** c/o WMAQ-TV, Merchandise Mart, Chicago, IL 60654.

TIMBERLAKE, CHARLES E.
Chemist. **PERSONAL:** Children: 2 children. **EDUCATION:** Tuskegee Inst, MS 1960; A&T U, BS 1955; Syracuse U, 1974-75;Univ MO, 1961-64. **CAREER:** Gen Elec Co, organic chemist, process engineer 1964-;Univ KS Med Ctr, rsrch asso, organic chemist 1961-64; Onondaga Comm Coll, adj instr 1971-. **HONORS/ACHIEVEMENTS:** Bicentennial award for inventors Gen Elec 1976; patent award Gen Elec 1970; rsrch fellow George Washington Carver Found 1958-60; num publs. **MILITARY SERVICE:** USAF 1955-57. **BUSINESS ADDRESS:** Process Engineer, General Electric, PO Box 4840, Court St 5 - Room W2, Syracuse, NY 13221.

TIMBERLAKE, CONSTANCE HECTOR
Educator. **PERSONAL:** Born in St John, New Brunswick, Canada;married Charles Timberlake; children: Christian, Curtis. **EDUCATION:** Syracuse Univ, Doctorate in Educ Admin, 1979; MS; BA (cum laude); NYS, cert. **CAREER:** Syracuse Univ, assoc prof Col Human Develop; Syracuse Sch Dist, chief counselor & admin ABE prog; Neighborhood Ctr, exec dir; Syracuse Pub Sch Dist, commiss of educ; Adolescent Pregnancy Prevention Program, project dir, 1987-. **ORGANIZATIONS:** NY Sch Brds Assc; mem Prog Com; Central NY Sch Bd Inst mem planning com; AERA; AAUP; Syracuse Prof Women; HEW Task Force Social Justice Natl Literacy Volunteers Amer; Human Rights Comm of Syracuse & Onondaga Co; vice pres Syracuse NAACP; v chrprsn Coalition Quality Educ; v chrprsn Onondaga Urban League Guild; Natl Org Women; Adv Bd Onondaga Comm Clge; Neighborhood Health Ctr adv council; Metr Ch Bd Human Srv Com; Fair-Employ Review Bd Onondaga Co; PEACE Head Start Self-Evaluation & Performance Stand Improvement Plan; exec mem Black Political Caucus; numerous vol srvs; trust Pi Lambda Theta Inc; pres elect NYS Council Family Relations Council; mem SUNY at Oswego Adv Council Oswego NY; pres, New York State Council on Family Relations, 1988-89; honorary advisory bd mem, For Kids Sake, 1987-89; mem & program dir, Syracuse Boys Club of Syracuse; vice chair, Syracuse Univ Black & Latino Faculty Org, 1986-89. **HONORS/ACHIEVEMENTS:** Citations, Meritorious Srvs 1972, March Wash 1963, Ldrshp Agway 1974; Jefferson Award, WTVH-TV/Amer Inst for Public Service, 1989; author of 30 journal articles & reviews, 1974-; more than 20 media presentations & documentaries, 1980-. **BUSINESS ADDRESS:** Chair Child Family Comm Study, Syracuse University, 201 Slocum Hall CFCS Dept, Syracuse, NY 13244-5300.

TIMBERLAKE, JOHN PAUL
Business executive. **PERSONAL:** Born Nov 12, 1950, Fackler, AL. **EDUCATION:** NE State Jr Clge, AS engr 1969-72; AL A&M Univ, BS computer sci 1972-75. **CAREER:** Jackson Co NAACP, pres 1977-; Dept Ind Relation, programmer/Analyst 1977-; TN Valley Auth, engr asst 1976-77; Chattanooga Bd of Educ, sub tchr 1975-77. **ORGANIZATIONS:** Mem Jackson Co NAACP 1977-; mem Jackson Co Chamber of Comm 1980; mem & del Jackson Co Voter's League 1972-; mem & del AL Dem Conf 1975- sr wardenRed Rose Lodge No 352 1978-. **HONORS/ACHIEVEMENTS:** Received Outst Achievement Award Jackson Co NAACP 1979; Harvester Award for Membership Jackson Co NAACP 1979.

TIMES, BETTY J.
Appointed official. **PERSONAL:** Born Jan 16, 1939, Grambling, LA; daughter of George Coleman, Sr (deceased) and Alice May Coleman; married John H Times; children: Anthony, John H III, Brian K, Ida L, David L. **EDUCATION:** Hansell's Bus Coll, Certificate 1964; Coll of Marin, AS 1978; Univ of San Francisco, BS 1979. **CAREER:** Marin Co Library, head tech svcs, secty, typist 1964-77; Co of marin, dir citizens serv office. **ORGANIZATIONS:** Mem Natl Women's Political Caucus; trustee Saus Sch Dist 1972-; dir Marin Educ Foundation 1982-; pres CA Assn of Affirmative Action Officers 1983-85; 1st vice pres Natl Women's Political Caucus; mem Marin Co Democratic Cent Comm; chmn NWPC/Marin; mem California State Demo. Com. **HONORS/ACHIEVEMENTS:** Woman of the Year Awd Marin City Concerned Citizens 1981; Woman of the Yr Award Marin City Community Dev Corp 1982. **HOME ADDRESS:** 718 Drake Ave, Marin City, CA 94965. **BUSINESS ADDRESS:** Dir Citizens Serv Office, Co of Marin, Rm 423 Civic Ctr, San Rafael, CA 94903.

TIMMONS, JOAN BRUNER
Director performing arts. **PERSONAL:** Born Aug 07, 1943, Brooklyn, NY; divorced; children: Angela Joan, Yolanda Gail. **EDUCATION:** Morgan State Univ, BA 1966; Univ of Miami, MA 1977. **CAREER:** South FL Young Adults Program, coordinator, 1969-72; Model City Program, planner 1972-75; Model City Cultural Arts Center, dir, 1975-79; Miami-Dade Comm Coll, Dir, performing arts 1979-83; Caribbean Devel, consultant; Miami-Dade Comm Coll, Coordinator, creative focus 1979-. **ORGANIZATIONS:** Mem Alpha Kappa Alpha 1963-; vice pres Cultural Exec Council 1975-77; mem Cultural Arts Assoc 1975-, Urban Walls Comm 1976-79, Kwanza Steering Comm 1976-79, Phi Alpha Theta Natl Hist Hon Soc 1976, Players Conservatory Theatre 1977-79, Natl Council of Negro Women 1978-. **HONORS/ACHIEVEMENTS:** Outstanding Serv Black Achievers of S FL 1977; Outstanding Serv Dade County Comm Award 1977, 1979; Kwanza Award Outstanding Serv City of Miami 1978. **BUSINESS ADDRESS:** Coord Creative Focus, Miami-Dade Comm Coll, 11011 SW 104 St, Miami, FL 33176.

TIMPSON, CLARENCE B.
Clergyman. **PERSONAL:** Born Nov 07, 1933; married Delores Mason; children: 5 Children. **EDUCATION:** Georgetown Univ, attd; Univ of AK. **CAREER:** Youngstown Sheet & Tube, pipe tester 1948-53; FAA, gen mech 1965; US Army Civil Srv, parts expediter 1965-70; Lewis Temple CME Ch, part time pastor 1965. **ORGANIZATIONS:** Presiding elder AK Dist 1968-; pastor 1st CME Ch Anchorage 1970-; dir CME Walk-On Ctr; CME Halfway House for Indigents, Alcoholics; bd mem Anchorage OIC 1971-; exec bd NAACP; mem Jaycees. **HONORS/ACHIEVEMENTS:** NAACP Freedom Award 1972. **MILITARY SERVICE:** USAF sgt 1953-65. **BUSINESS ADDRESS:** 529 F St, Anchorage, AK 99501.

TINGLE, LAWRENCE MAY
Education administrator. **PERSONAL:** Born Jul 26, 1947, Canton, MS; son of Mamie Lee Smith; married Robert Earl Tingle; children: Aubrey F, Shella A, Robert L. **EDUCATION:** Alcorn State Univ, BS 1968; MS State Univ, Chisanbop Instructor 1979, MEd 1981; Jackson State Univ, KS State Univ, Law Enforcement Ed; Mississippi State University Meridian, MS, MEd (AA) 1987. **CAREER:** Newton Co Improvement Club, sec 1976-79; Newton Public Schools, classroom teacher 1972-82; NAACP, sec 1976-81; East Central Jr Coll, directress 1982-. **ORGANIZATIONS:** Mem Delta Sigma Theta; sec Newton Cty Heroines of Jericho; VBS instr Jerusalem MB Church 1982; deaconess Jerusalem MB Church 1973-; eval chair MS Assoc of Trio Prog for Colls 1982-; leader 4-H Club 1982-; sec 1985, vice pres, MS Assoc of Ed Oppty Progs 1985; vice pres Jerusalem MB Church Home Mission Soc 1984-; associate matron Order of Eastern Star; mem Calanthe; Friends of Children MS, Inc, Jackson, MS Programs Advisor/Task Force. **HONORS/ACHIEVEMENTS:** Sec Newton Cty NAACP 1975-79; Class Room Teacher MS Outstanding Educator 1976; lecturer & writer State of MS Dept of Mathematics 1980; sec Newton Democratic Exec Comm 1981-; Peer Tutor Speaker MAEOPP/AEOPP 1984; MS Assoc of Ed Oppty Prog Personnel Serv Awd 1985; Southeastern Assoc of Ed Oppty Prog Personnel Cert of Apprec 1985; 1st Black Female SS Directress East Central Jr Coll Decatur MS; Lifetime mem Delta Sigma Theta; mem Newton Political League. **BUSINESS ADDRESS:** Dir, East Central Jr College, Box 51, Decatur, MS 39327.

TINSLEY, FRED LELAND, JR.
Attorney. **PERSONAL:** Born Aug 30, 1944, Detroit, MI; married Ollie Brock. **EDUCATION:** So U, BA 1969; So U, JD 1972. **CAREER:** Champman Tinsley & Reese, prtnr present; Lone Star Gas Co, regulatory atty 1975-77; US Secur & Exchange Commn, trial atty 1973-75; LA Constl Conv, resrch asst 1973; Reginald Heber Smith Fellow Legal Serv 1972. **ORGANIZATIONS:** Bd of dir Mental Hlth Assn of Dallas 1976-78; mem adv coun TX Employ Commn 1977-79; bd of dir Dallas Legal Serv Found Inc 1979-; mem exec com Dallas Co Dem Party 1980-; bd of dir Jr Black Acad of Arts & Letters Inc 1980-; asso judge Dallas Muncpl Cts 1978-. **MILITARY SERVICE:** USMC corpl 1963-67. **BUSINESS ADDRESS:** Chapman Tinsley & Reese, One Brookriver Pl Ste 370, Dallas, TX 75247.

TINSLEY-WILLIAMS, ALBERTA
County commissioner. **PERSONAL:** Born Aug 14, 1954; daughter of Mary Louise Tinsley; divorced; children: Carla Louise Williams. **EDUCATION:** Eastern Michigan Univ, Ypsilanti MI, BS, 1976; Wayne State Univ, Detroit MI. **CAREER:** Detroit Police Dept, Detroit MI, rape counselor, 1976-78; United Auto Workers, Detroit MI, group worker, 1978-80; Comprehensive Youth Training & Community Involvement Program, Detroit MI, job development counselor, 1980-85; New Center Mental Health, Detroit MI, stress management instructor, 1985-87; Wayne County Commission, Detroit MI, county commissioner, 1987—. **ORGANIZATIONS:** Mem, Natl Organization of Black County Officials; mem, Natl Assn of Counties; mem, Women of NACO; mem, NAACP. **HONORS/ACHIEVEMENTS:** Outstanding Service Award, Govt Admin Assn, 1988; Shirley Chisholm Award, Natl Political Cong of Black Women, 1988; Spirit of Detroit Award, City of Detroit City Council, 1988. **BUSINESS ADDRESS:** County Commissioner, Wayne County Commission, 600 Randolph, 418 County Building, Detroit, MI 48226.

TIPPETT, ANDRE
Professional athlete. **PERSONAL:** Born Dec 27, 1959, Birmingham, AL; children: Janea Lynn. **EDUCATION:** Attended, Iowa. **CAREER:** New England Patriots, linebacker 1982-. **HONORS/ACHIEVEMENTS:** Played in Rose Bowl; AP, UPI, NEA, Football Writers and Football News 1st Team All-Amer selection 1981; named NFL Defensive Player of the Week by Pro FootballWeekly and ESPN 9/18/83; voted Best Linebacker/Defensive Back in AFC 1984; Patriots' MVP by 1776 QB Club 1984; selected AFC's Defensive Player of Week by Sports Illustrated and AFC's Defensive Player of Week by league office 11/3/85; took part in NBC's Superteams and Superstars competition 1985; selected to All-NFL team; The Sporting News All-Pro team; "101" AFC Defensive Player of the Year Awd; NY Daily News Defensive Player of the Yr Awd; Big Brothers/Big Sisters-Tums Neutralizer of the Year Awd; mem Pro Bowl teams 1986,87. **BUSINESS ADDRESS:** New England Patriots, Schaefer Stadium Route 1, Foxboro, MA 02035.

TIPTON, DALE LEO
Physician. **PERSONAL:** Born Jul 08, 1930, Parsons, KS; son of Dale Tipton and Ruby Tipton; married Aurora Anguay, Mar 26, 1988; children: Jill, Jan, Melanie Anguay, Desiree Anguay. **EDUCATION:** Univ of CA Berkeley, AB Physiology 1952; Univ of CA San Francisco, MS Pharmacology 1959; Univ of CA Sch of Medicine, MD 1959. **CAREER:** Kaiser Found Hosp, intern 1959-60; Univ of CA San Francisco, resident genl surgery 1960-62; Cancer Rsch Inst Univ of CA, natl inst health fellow 1962-63; Univ of CA San Francisco, resident otolaryngology 1963-66; Univ of CA Sch of Medicine Dept of Otolaryngology, assoc clinical prof 1976-; Private Practice, physician. **ORGANIZATIONS:** Delg to CA Med Assoc from San Francisco Medical Soc 1968-69; bd dirs San Francisco Med Soc 1972-75; med advisor CA Blue Shield 1977-; chmn Dept Ear Nose & Throat San Francisco Genl Hosp 1970-76; chmn Dept Ear Nose & Throat Franklin Hosp San Fran 1968-; bd dirs San Francisco Peer Review Oganization 1983-86; chief of medical staff Franklin Hosp San Francisco 1982-84. **HONORS/ACHIEVEMENTS:** Diplomat Amer Bd Otolaryngology 1966; fellow Amer Coll of Surgeons 1970; Amer Acad Otolaryngology Head & Neck Surgery 1967-; publs "Changes in Golgi Apparatus of Islets of Langerhans in the Rat following Glucose & Insulin Admins" Endocrinology 1959; "Effects of Chlorpromazine on Blood Level of Alcohol in Rabbits" Amer Journal of Physiology 1961; "Duration of Bronchial Squamous Metaplasia Produced by Dogs by Cigarette Smoke Condensate" Journal of the Natl Cancer Inst 1964; "The Experimental Effects of Cigarette Smoke Condensate on Laryngeal Mucosa" published in proceedings of Int Congress of Otolaryngology 1965; "Osteochondroma of the tongue" Arch Path 1970; "Physiologic Assessment of Black People" Journal of Black Health 1975. **MILITARY SERVICE:** USMC 1st lt 1953-55; USAR lt col 1984-. **HOME ADDRESS:** 458 Briarwood Drive, South San Francisco, CA 94080. **BUSINESS ADDRESS:** Associate Clinical Professor, University of CA Sch of Med, 45 Castro St, San Francisco, CA 94114.

TIPTON, ELIZABETH HOWSE
Educator, administrator. **PERSONAL:** Born Oct 17, 1925, Chattanooga, TN; married B Cortex; children: Cassandra Wilson, Bensonetta Lane, Eunice Taylor, Libbee. **EDUCATION:** Fisk Univ, BA 1945; Univ of Bridgeport, MS 1970; George Washington Univ, EdS 1974, EdD 1975. **CAREER:** Booker T Washington HS, teacher 1945-50; MDTA Ed Prog, dir 1965-70; Bowie State Coll, dean of students 1970-75; Bowie State Coll, vice pres student affairs 1975-. **ORGANIZATIONS:** Mem NAACP, NAFEO, AAHE, AAUP, AKA. **HONORS/ACHIEVEMENTS:** Outstanding Admin; Noteable Amer 1976-77. **BUSINESS ADDRESS:** Vice President Student Affairs, Bowie State College, Jericho Park Rd, Bowie, MD 20715.

TIPTON, THOMAS H.
Business executive. **PERSONAL:** Born Jun 15, 1933, Washington, DC; children: 3 daughters. **EDUCATION:** Morgan State Coll Baltimore, BS English. **CAREER:** Vanguard Advertising Agency Minneapolis, pres 1970-80; Twin Cities Opport Industrl Cntr Inc (TCOIC) Minneapolis, deputy dir 1968-70; Milton H Kronheim, Coor sales & pub rel 1962-68; Channel 5 WTTG Wash DC, TV personality 1958-62; WUST Wash DC, radio announ 1955-56. **ORGANIZATIONS:** Bd dir Midwest Fed Sav & Loan Assn; mem MN St Cable Commrn; pres Nat Assn Mkt Devel (NAMD) 1975-77; bd dir Guthrie Theatre; Pub Rel Soc of Am; Exchange Inc; Minneapolis Jaycees; Untd Nat Assn of Minneapolis; Butler Sch of Law; Fed Fin Mort Corp Atlanta; bd dir/treas Minneapolis Press Club; reg vice pres Nat Bus League; hon bd chmn TCOIC; bd dir Religious Heritage of Amer. **HONORS/ACHIEVEMENTS:** Proclamation declared Nov 23, 1975 Rom Tipton Day Gov/Mayor Minneapolis; hon doctorate Antioch Coll Minneapolis; varsity schol Basketball & Track Morgan St U; orig "Gospel Erupts"; wrtr/prod "Dat Feelin" Guthrie Theatre 1972; prod "Black Sounds of Our Time" WCCO TV; 1st black commr Cable TV MN; apprd Apptmnts Comn State jobs/brds/commns Gov MN; personal advr Pro-tem Sen Hubert H Humphrey; ldrshp awd AFL-CIO Pres Dave Roe. **MILITARY SERVICE:** AUS signal corp 1956-58. **BUSINESS ADDRESS:** President, Vangvard Associates, Inc, 1925 First Ave S, Minneapolis, MN 55403.

TISDALE, CELES
Educator. **PERSONAL:** Born Jul 31, 1941, Salters, SC; son of Norman and Rachel; divorced; children: Yvette, Colette, Eric. **EDUCATION:** State Univ Coll/Buffalo, BS 1963, MS 1969, PhD candidate. **CAREER:** PS 31 Buffalo, English teacher 1963-68; Woodlawn Jr High, English dept chmn 1968-69; WBEN TV, writer/producer 1969; WBFO-FM Radio, writer/announcer 1969-70; State Univ Coll Buffalo, English instructor 1969-72; WKBW TV, talk show host 1979-83; WKBW Radio, talk show host 1984-; Erie Community Coll/City, prof of English. **ORGANIZATIONS:** Assoc dir Buffalo Urban league 1966-; bd of dirs Artpark 1981-; dir Adolescent Vocational Exploration 1985-88; Young Audiences, Inc, 1975-. **HONORS/ACHIEVEMENTS:** NY State Univ Chancellors Award for Teaching Excellence 1975; Man of Year, Business & Professional Women 1977; Media Award Sickle Cell Assn 1978. **BUSINESS ADDRESS:** Professor of English, Erie Community College/City, 121 Ellicott St, Buffalo, NY 14203.

TISDALE, HENRY NEHEMIAH
Educator. **PERSONAL:** Born Jan 13, 1944, Kingstree, SC; married Alice Rose Carson; children: Danica, Brandon. **EDUCATION:** Clafin Coll, BS 1965; Temple Univ, EdM 1967; Dartmouth Coll, MA 1975, PhD 1978. **CAREER:** Philadelphia School Dist, math instructor, 1965-69; Univ of Delaware, special asst to the pres 1985-86; Delaware State Coll, instructor/summer engineering inst 1969-85, prof of math 1969-85, asst dir of inst rsch 1979-85, asst academic dean for admin & planning 1986-. **ORGANIZATIONS:** Bd mem Holy Cross School System 1985-; mem State of DE Task Force on High Technology 1986-87. **HONORS/ACHIEVEMENTS:** Southern Fellowship Fund Award 1976-78; Omega Psi Phi Man of the Year 1981. **HOME ADDRESS:** RD 3Box 19BW, Felton, DE 19943. **BUSINESS ADDRESS:** Asst Academic Dean, Delaware State College, 109 ETV, Dover, DE 19901.

TISDALE, HERBERT CLIFFORD
Business executive. **PERSONAL:** Born Nov 20, 1928, Green Cove Springs, FL; married Alberta Ryals. **EDUCATION:** Florida A & M, attnd 1949; US Quarter Master Sch US Non-Commd Officers Acad, various cert 1951-69; Real Estate Clover Park Educ Cntr, cert of completion 1971. **CAREER:** Tisdale Constrn Inc, pres 1971-80. **ORGANIZATIONS:** Mem Tacoma Rotary Club; mem & treas Minority Contr Assn; mem Assn Gen Contractors. **HONORS/ACHIEVEMENTS:** 1st Oak Leaf Cluster AUS 1962; 2nd Oak Leaf Cluster AUS 1967; AUS commendation medal AUS 1970; Outstndg Contrb & Serv to US Small Bus Adminstrn 1978; Prime Contractor of the Yr Nations need as Small Bus; cert of apprec Dept of the Army & Achiev Cert; cert of apprec (several) Dept of the Navy 1979. **MILITARY SERVICE:** AUS e-7 served 2 yrs. **BUSINESS ADDRESS:** 2502 South J St, Tacoma, WA 98405.

TITUS, LEROY ROBERT
Chief executive officer. **PERSONAL:** Born Dec 11, 1938, Pittsburgh, PA; married Anna

Mary Adams; children: Shelley Meredyth, Sherre Mishel, Shelbi Melany. **EDUCATION:** Lincoln Univ, AB 1960. **CAREER:** Natl Institutes of Health, microbiologist 1964-65; YMCA of Pittsburgh, program dir 1965-69; YMCA of Fort Wayne/Allen Co, exec dir 1969-72; YMCA of Metro LosAngeles, exec dir 1972-. **ORGANIZATIONS:** Dist vice pres Assoc of Professional Directors; pres Natl Black & Non White YMCA's; pres YMCA's Serving Disadvantaged Communities; pres PANDA Productions; mem Alpha Phi Alpha Frat; delegate Natl Council of YMCA's of the USA; master trainer YMCA of the USA 1981-. **HONORS/ACHIEVEMENTS:** APD Human Serv Awd Assoc of Prof Direct 1982; Outstanding Serv Awd CITIES Inc 1984; Dr Martin Luther King Human Dignity Awd LA Metro YMCA 1985; NAACP VPI Awd Los Angeles Chap 1987. **MILITARY SERVICE:** AUS E-5. **HOME ADDRESS:** 13282 Briarwood St, Cerritos, CA 90701. **BUSINESS ADDRESS:** Chief Executive Officer, Weingart Urban Centre, 9900 South Vermont, Los Angeles, CA 90044.

TITUS, MYER L.
College president. **CAREER:** State Board of Community Colleges and Occupational Education, Denver, CO, chief institutional officer; Philander Smith College, Little Rock, AR, president. **BUSINESS ADDRESS:** President, Philander Smith College, 812 West 13, Little Rock, AR 72202. *

TITUS-DILLON, PAULINE Y.
Physician. **PERSONAL:** Born Jan 01, 1938; married Owen Christopher; children: Denyse, Paul. **EDUCATION:** Howard U, BS 1960; HowardUniv Coll of Med, MD 1964. **CAREER:** Howard Univ Coll of Med, prof 1981-, assoc dean acad affairs 1980-;HowardUniv Med Serv DC Gen Hosp, chief 1977-; Howard U, asso prof med 1977-; Howard U, asst prof med 1971-77; GeorgetownUniv Hosp Wash DC, fellow endocrinology 1968-69; HowardUniv Hosp, post grad trainee internal medicine 1964-68; VA Hosp Outpatient Clinic Columbia SC, internist 1969-71. **ORGANIZATIONS:** Mem DC Med Soc; fellow Am Coll of Physicians; mem Program Dirs in Internal Med; mem Am Med Women's Assn Present; sec-treas Alpha Omega Alpha Honor Med Soc Gamma Chap Present; mem Natl Med Assoc, NY Acad of Sci, Amer med Assoc. **HONORS/ACHIEVEMENTS:** Daniel Hale Williams Award HowardUniv 1965 & 68; diplomate Am Bd of Intnl Med Philadelphia 1972; fellowship NIH Bethesda 1975-77; Inspirational Leadership Award Student Counc HowardUniv Coll of Med 1979.

TOBIAS, RANDOLF A.
Educator. **PERSONAL:** Born Jan 16, 1940, Bronx; children: Maurice, Tonya. **EDUCATION:** EdD 1975; MA 1968; BA 1961. **CAREER:** Black Stds Cert Prog Long Island Univ Brooklyn, dir 1972-74; Martin Luther King Jr Scholar Prog Long Island Univ, 1969-; Bedford Stuyvosant Talent Search, proj dir 1968-69; Mills Coll Educ, instr 1964-71; New York City Public Schools, teacher 1963-68; Teacher Educ Long Island Univ, asst prof. **ORGANIZATIONS:** Mem bd dir Willoughby House Settlement Brooklyn; bd dir Carlton Gardens Children's Cntr Flushing; VA UnionUniv Alumni Assn Alpha Phi Alpha Frat; Am AssnUniv Prof; African Heritage Studs Assn. **HONORS/ACHIEVEMENTS:** Nat Frat Student Musicians Awd 1956.

TOBIN, PATRICIA L.
Business executive. **PERSONAL:** Born Feb 28, 1943, White Plains, NY; divorced; children: Lauren. **EDUCATION:** Levitan Bus Sch, attended 1962; Charles Morris Price Sch of Advertising & Journalism, attended 1974-77; Regional Purchasing Council LA, cert of training 1978; Attended, CBS Mgmt Educ Seminar 1979. **CAREER:** Free lance model, 1967; Sun Oil Co, marketing rep 1974; KNXT-TV CBS LA, admin asst to mgr of press inform 1979; UCLA, guest instructor 1984; Tobin & Assocs, public relations consultant/pres/ceo; Communicon Cable TV,TV talk show host 1984; PT Enterprises, founder/pres. **ORGANIZATIONS:** Mem Philadelphia Club of Advertising Women 1976, The Poor Richard Club 1975, Philadelphia Public Rel Assn 1977, Natl Assn of Media Women 1977, natl Assn of Market Developers 1977; co-chrprsn of publicity for Philadelphia Tribune Charities 25th Anniversary Awds Banquet 1977; admin consult Screen Actors Guild of Amer Film Inst 1977;natl pub rels dir Spcl Markets for Sala & Assoc Ltd 1977; mem Black Women's Forum LA 1980; PIRATES (Pub Interest Radio & TV Educ Soc) 1978; mem steering com BEA-West (Black Employees Assn of CBS WCoast) 1979; pub rels consult Hal DeWindt Theatre Inc 1977; dir pub rel People United to Save Humanity;Urban Coalition Comm Task Force 1974; Triumph Bapt Ch; Opp Indsln Ctr Women's Aux 1977; comm serv broadcaster WDAS 1975-77; WIBF-FM 1977; host weekly forum The Speakeasy for media 1979; ABC-TV press info offcr to Summer Olympic Games; publicity coord for Black Journalists Assn of So CA; UCLA Instr Pub Relations 1983; Jessee Jackson for President Campaign 1984; co-founder Black Public Relations Soc 1983. **HONORS/ACHIEVEMENTS:** Reginald E Beauchamp Award 1977; PUSH Serv Award 1975; Miss Sun Torch United Fund Torch Drive 1969; Legion of Honor Chapel of 4 Chaplains 1972; Frandford Lions Club Cert 1975; NAACP Image Awards Nom as assoc prod of "One More Hurdle"; Outstanding Young Women of Amer 1982; WISE Tribute to the Black Woman 1981. **BUSINESS ADDRESS:** President, PT Enterprises, 3841 Mentone Ave, Ste 25, Culver City, CA 90230.

TOBY, WILLIAM
Goverment official. **PERSONAL:** Born Aug 12, 1934, Augusta, GA; son of William and Louise; married Diane Anderson; children: Michael, Kenneth. **EDUCATION:** WV State Clg, BA 1961; Adelphi U, MSW 1963; Harvard Univ John F Kennedy Sch of Govt, MPA 1986. **CAREER:** New York City Ofc Mayor, intr-gvntl rltns ofcr 1969-71; Hlth Ed Wlfrs Soc Rhbltn Serv, regnl cmsnr 1971-77; Hlth Care Fin Admn, regnl admn 1977-. **ORGANIZATIONS:** Bd mem Adelphi U; mem Natl Conf Soc Welfare. **HONORS/ACHIEVEMENTS:** John W Davis Meritorious Awrd WV State Clg 1984; apprctn awrd Intl Hlth Ec Mgmt Inst 1984; excptnl achvmnt Sec Hlth Human Serv 1982; gubernatorial Citation Gov of NY 1982. **MILITARY SERVICE:** USAF corpl 1951-55. **BUSINESS ADDRESS:** Regional Administrator, Hlth Care Fin Admn, 26 Federal Plaza Rm 3811, New York, NY 10278.

TODD, CHARLES O.
Educator. **PERSONAL:** Born Nov 12, 1915, Lawrence, KS; son of Mr and Mrs Hazel Todd; married Geraldine Mann; children: Chrystal Todd Johnson, Karen Todd Lang. **EDUCATION:** Emporia State Univ, BS 1940; Kansas Univ, MS 1948; Univ of So CA, MFA 1957; Univ of AZ, attended. **CAREER:** Mayview MO, Western Univ Quindaro, Kansas, teacher 1941-42; Dunban Elem School, Manhatten, Kansas, principal 1943; Dunbar Jr High School Tucson, teacher 1947; Manfield Jr HS, teacher 1951; Tucson HS, teacher 1967-retired. **ORGANIZATIONS:** Mem KS Teachers & Admin 1943, Phi Delta Kappa 1946, NEA, AEA, TEA 1947-82, Alpha Phi Alpha 1950; treas Tucson Fine Arts Assn 1950; pres NAACP Credit Union 1964; mem Tucson Civic Chorus 1966-67; pres, bd of dir, Tucson Big Brothers 1966-67; treas Tucson Br NAACP 1968-74; Mentor, APEX (Academic Preparation for Excellence) 1987-89; mem, Foster Care Review Board 1988-; pres, Eta Psi Lambda Chapter, Alpha Phi Alpha 1989-. **HONORS/ACHIEVEMENTS:** Service Awd Tucson Br NAACP 1975.

TODD, CYNTHIA JEAN
Newspaper reporter. **PERSONAL:** Born Jan 12, 1951, Peoria, IL; children: Wendy. **EDUCATION:** Northern Illinois Univ DeKalb, BA 1972. **CAREER:** Peoria Journal Star, reporter 1969-73; WMBD-AM-FM TV Peoria, reporter/anchor 1974-77; KSDK-TV St Louis, reporter/anchor 1977-79; Harris Stowe State Coll, dir publ; St Louis Post-Dispatch St Louis, reporter 1983-. **ORGANIZATIONS:** Mem Greater St Louis Black Journalist Assoc 1977-, AFTRA 1977, IL Newsbroadcasters Assoc 1975-77; mem adv comm Univ City HS, Univ City MO 1978; memAlpha Kappa Alpha Sor; bd dirs New City School St Louis 1980. **HONORS/ACHIEVEMENTS:** Broadcast History Awd McLean Cty IL Hist Soc 1976; Listed in Names & Faces Natl Publ 1978; Achiever in Industry Awd St Louis Metro Sentinel Newspaper 1978. **BUSINESS ADDRESS:** Reporter, St Lois Post-Dispatch, Harris Stowe State College, 3026 Laclede, St Louis, MO 63103.

TODD, DONALD
Educator. **EDUCATION:** Univ of Denver, BA 1948, MA 1951, further study 1952-59-60 1968-69; LA State Univ, attended 1964. **CAREER:** East Side Young Adult Center, drama dir 1967; Crusade for Justice, drama dir 1967; Univ of Denver, lecturer afro-amer literature and black music 1970; Comm Coll of Denver, inst afro-amer lit 1970; Univ of Denver, lecturer black religion 1971; Ft Carson Army Playhouse Colorado Springs, guest dir 1971; Metro State Coll, inst afro-amer lit 1972-73; Univ of CO, black studies 1976, inst black studies 1976; Denver Black Arts Company's School of Performing Arts, voice & diction instr 1979-80; freelance voice & theatre instructor 1979-84; Arvada Festival Playhouse, dir 1981; Adult Educ Tutorial Prog, tutor 1982; tap dance instr 1984-; Odyssey West Magazine, technical advisor 1986-. **ORGANIZATIONS:** Comm resource person Denver Public Schs 1978; consul Studio E Cultural & Performing Arts Ctr 1982; Region VIII Dir Assn Study of Afro-Amer Life & History; Amer Theatre Assn; Natl Assn of Speech & Dramatic Arts; Natl Historical Society; Natl Soc of Literature & Arts; Speech Communication Assn; Univ & Colls Theatre Assn; Theatre Consultant Justice Dept Comm Relations Serv 1972; mem adv comm for Colo Artists Arts Registry Colo Council Arts & Humanities 1972; columnist Rocky Mtn Kidney Ctr Express 1986-; treas of bd Denver Civic Theatre 1986-. **HONORS/ACHIEVEMENTS:** Best Dir Awd "Arvada" One Act Play Fest 1966; Larry Tajiri Mem Awd Outstanding Achievement in Performing Arts Denver Post 1969; CO Counc on Arts & Humanities Artist of the Yr 1972; Educ Ldrshp AwdUniv Negro Coll Fund 1976; Dir's Awd Eden Theatrical Workshop 1978; Judges Awd Arvada Festival Playhouse 1981; Donald Todd Theatre Studio E 1982.

TODD, MELVIN R.
Administrator. **PERSONAL:** Born Apr 24, 1933, Oklahoma City, OK; married Menzola Anderson; children: Sharon, Myra, David. **EDUCATION:** Langston U, BA History 1954; Univ of OK, MEd Secondary 1960; Univ of OK, EdD Soc Admin/Gen Adminstrn 1973. **CAREER:** OK State Regents for Higher Educ, vice chancellor for academic admin 1980-; OK State Regents for Higher Educ, special asst to chancellor & stud & officer 1975-80; OK City Public School, dir of cirriculum 1973-75; Consultative Center for Equal Educ Opport Univ of OK, field consultant 1971-73; NE H School OK City, prin 1969-71; NE H School OK City, asst prin 1967-69. **ORGANIZATIONS:** Mem bd of dir E&C Trades Ltd 1980; mem OK Educ Assn present; corp mem Am Coll Testing Prog Corp present; mem Phi Delta Kappa present; mem Urban League present; mem NAACP present. **HONORS/ACHIEVEMENTS:** Good conduct AUS 1954-56; outstndg edctr's awd OK Educ Assn 1975; distngd alumnus awd LangstonUniv 1976; presidential cit Nat Assn for Equal Educ Opport in Highter Educ 1980. **MILITARY SERVICE:** AUS spec 3rd 1954-56. **BUSINESS ADDRESS:** Oklahoma State Regents for Hig, 500 Educ Bldg State Capitol Com, Oklahoma City, OK 73105.

TODD, ORLANDO
Accountant. **PERSONAL:** Born Jan 21, 1958, Camden, AR; son of Mr and Mrs Oree Tood; married Glenda Faye; children: Anterryo, LaQuanta, Tiffaney. **EDUCATION:** Southern AR Univ, BBA 1980. **CAREER:** Price Waterhouse, staff accountant 1980-83; AR Power & Light Co, accountant 1983-1987; AR Power & Light Co, senior accountant. 1988-. **ORGANIZATIONS:** Mem Central AR Chap of CPA's 1982-, AR Soc of CPA's 1982-, Amer Inst of CPA's 1982-. **HONORS/ACHIEVEMENTS:** Outstanding Young Men of Amer 1982; Certified Public Accountant 1982. **HOME ADDRESS:** 10113 Woodbridge Dr, Little Rock, AR 72209.

TODD, THOMAS N.
Attorney. **PERSONAL:** Born Sep 24, 1938, Demopolis, AL; married Janis Roberts; children: Traci Neuborne, Tamarla Nicole. **EDUCATION:** Baton Rouge, BA 1959, JD 1963. **CAREER:** US Dept of Labor, office solicitor 1963-64; US Atty Chicago, officer 1967-70; Comm on Inquiery into Black Panthers & Law Enforcement NY, consult 1970-72; Chicago Capt So CLC, pres 1971; Oper PUSH, exec vice pres 1971-73; Midwest Task Force for Comm Report "Search & Destroy", dir; Northwestern Univ School of Law Chgo, asst prof of law, asst dir ctr for urban affairs; Private practice, attorney. **ORGANIZATIONS:** Mem Supreme Court of LA 1963, US Court of Mil Appeals 1965, Supreme Court of IL 1967, US Court of Appeals 7th Circuit 1968, US Dist Court, No Dist of IL, US Supreme Court 1971, Chicago Comm of United Negro Coll Fund; bd of dir Legal Oppty Scholarship Prog; adv bd of IL Black Legislative Clearing House Chgo; adv bd of Afro-Amer Patrolmans League Chgo. **HONORS/ACHIEVEMENTS:** Amer Jurisprudence Awd; Law Week Awd; JS Clark Mem Awd; Criminal Law Awd So Univ School of Law; 1 of 10 Outstanding Young Men in Chicago Jaycees 1970; Leadership Council for Met Open Comm 1970; Cert of Achievement Kappa Alpha Phi Northwestern Univ 1971; One of Best Dressed men, Dress Horsemen of Chicago 1971-73; Cert of Achievement Afro-Amer Policemens League 1971; Lawndale Peoples Planning & Action Comm 1971; SCLC Oper Breadbaskets Activist Awd 1971; IN Dem Org 1971; Achievement Awd Mens Fed So Univ 1972; Student Govt Awd So Univ 1972; Powr Inc Harambee Awd 1972; Listed One Thousand Success Stories 1973; Biog publ in Chicago Negro Almanac 1973; Outstanding Achievement Awd The Natl Consumer Info Ctr 1974; Black Excellence Awd for Comm Action PUSH Espo 1974;Natl Ed Awd Phi Beta Sigma 1975; Merito-

rious Serv Awd Natl Assoc of Black Polit Sci 1976; Apprec Awd Juneteenth Comm 1976; Apprec Awd Natl Consumer Info Ctr host Tom Todd Show WLS Radio Chgo; "Voice of Ebony" Radio Commercial Ebony Mag; Honorary Doctorate of Laws, Grambling State Univ 1987. **MILITARY SERVICE:** AUS; capt, judge advocate ofc 1964-67. **BUSINESS ADDRESS:** Attorney, 1 N La Salle, Chicago, IL 60602.

TODD, WILLIAM S.
Airline pilot. **PERSONAL:** Born Mar 10, 1940, Portsmouth, VA; divorced; children: David M, Kelly Yvette, William S IV. **EDUCATION:** VA Union Univ, BS 1962; CA State Univ, Master (Hon). **CAREER:** USAF Commander C-135 Aircraft, lt col; USAF Acad, liaison officer, dep commander; Western Airlines, airline pilot Boeing 727 1969-87, capt 1987-; Delta Airlines, Los Angeles, CA, boeing 737, captain, 1987-. **ORGANIZATIONS:** Mem Airline Pilots Assoc, Alpha Phi Alpha Fraternity, US Jaycees; advtsng ed, mgr US Jaycees Publ, Accident Investigator, Engrg & Air Safety Comm Airline Pilots Assoc; chmn Com to Select a City Slogan City of Cerritos CA; campaign mgr City Council Candidate 1974; mem Youth Motivation Task Force 1969-; mem Westside Fair Housing Council 1969-; owner Spectral Illuminations. **HONORS/ACHIEVEMENTS:** Scholarship VA State Coll 1958; Jaycee Sound Citation Award 1974; Awards, Youth Motivation Task Force 1970, 1972. **MILITARY SERVICE:** USAF captain 1963-68; Air Medal w/5 Clusters; Small Arms Expert Marksman; Viet Nam Expeditionary Medal 1965; USAF Meritorious Serv Medal 1984; US Air Force Achievement Medal 1985. **BUSINESS ADDRESS:** Airline Pilot, Delta Airlines, Hartsfield Atlanta Airport, Atlanta, GA.

TODMAN, JUREEN FRANCIS
Educational administrator. **PERSONAL:** Born Jun 30, 1935, St Thomas, Virgin Islands of the United States;divorced; children: Jens, Maurice, Monigue. **EDUCATION:** Philander Smith Coll, BA, BS 1959; NY Univ, graduate courses; Coll of Virgin Island, graduate courses. **CAREER:** St Thomas Fedn of Teachers, teacher sec 1976-78, 1st vice pres 1979-80, pres 1981, teacher, sec bd of election, 1st vice pres. **ORGANIZATIONS:** Mem Alpha Kappa Alpha; pres Women Aux Little League 1972; treasurer Central Labor Council 1978-80; sec Bd of Election 1982-; 1st vice pres St Thomas Fedn of Teachers 1982-; bd of dir chairperson fund raising St Thomas East Lioness Methodist Church Choir 1974-75 & 1984-85; sec AAA Baseball League; bd dir United Way; sec/1st vice pres, pres St Thomas Fedn of Teachers; trustee, Govt Employee's Retirement System of the Virgin Islands. **HONORS/ACHIEVEMENTS:** Athletic Scholarship VI Educ Dept 1954; Athletic Award Softball, Volleyball, Track; Poetry published in local daily news; Hugo Dennis Award Teachers Fedn 1983. **HOME ADDRESS:** Box 11898, St Thomas, Virgin Islands of the United States 00802. **BUSINESS ADDRESS:** Teacher, Sec, 1st Vice Pres, St Thomas Federation of Teachers, Department of Education, St Thomas, Virgin Islands of the United States 00801.

TODMAN, TERENCE A.
Ambassador. **PERSONAL:** Born May 13, 1926, St Thomas, Virgin Islands of the United States;son of Alphonse Todman and Rachel Callwood; married Doris Weston; children: Terence A, Patricia Rhymer, Kathryn Browne, Michael. **EDUCATION:** Poly Inst Puerto Rico, BA 1951; Syracuse Univ, MPA 1953; Amer Univ, Post Grad 1953-54; Colgate Univ, Hon Doctor's Degree 1981. **CAREER:** Dept of State, intl rel ofcr 1952-54, foreign affairs ofcr 1955; UN Intern Program, US nom 1955; UN Trusteeship Cncl Petit Com & Com Rural Econ Dev, US rep 1956-57; UN Gen Assembly, adv US del 1956-57; Amer Embassy New Delhi, India, polit ofcr 1957-59; Amer Embassy Tunis, polit ofcr 1961-64; Lome, Togo, DCM & charge d'affaires 1965-68; Bur of African Affairs Dept State, country dir for Kenya, Tanzania, Uganda & Seychelles 1968; US Ambassador to Chad 1969-72; US Ambassador to Guinea 1972-75; US Ambassador to Costa Rica 1975-77; Asst Sec State 1977-78; US Ambassador to Spain 1978-83; Dept of State Amer Embassy, US Ambassador; US Ambassador to Denmark 1983; US Ambassador to Argentina 1989. **ORGANIZATIONS:** Mem Amer Foreign Serv Assn; mem bd trustees Coll of the VI; Council on Foreign Relations; Assn of Black American Ambassadors. **HONORS/ACHIEVEMENTS:** Sup Honor Award Dept State 1966; Medal of Honor Govt of the VI 1977; mem Hall of Fame US Army Infantry Sch Ft Benning, GA; Grand Cross of the Highest Order of Isabela la Catolica by Spanish Govt 1983; Grand Cross of Order Dannebug by Govt of Denmark 1988; Disting Trustees Award Coll of the VI 1985; Presidential Distinguished Service Awd 1985; Honorary Doctorof Laws degree Syracuse Univ and honorary Doctor of Public Service degree Morgan StateUniv 1986; Natl Public Serv Awd 1987; Honorary Doctor of Laws Degree Boston Univ 1987; Honorary Doctor of Laws Degree Colgate Univ 1981. **MILITARY SERVICE:** AUS 1st Lt 1945-49. **BUSINESS ADDRESS:** US Ambassador, Dept of State American Embassy, Buenos Aires, Argentina, APO, Miami, FL 34034.

TOKLEY, JOANNA NUTTER
Social service administrator. **PERSONAL:** Born in Nanticoke, MD; daughter of Clifton Nutler and Iolia Williams; married E James Tokley; children: Tyrone, Charles, Michael. **EDUCATION:** Morgan State Univ, BS 1962; Univ of S FL, further study. **CAREER:** Hillsborough Cty Public Schools, teacher 1962-70, human relations spec 1970-74; Tampa Urban League Inc, dep dir, econ devel, employment dir 1974-82, pres. **ORGANIZATIONS:** Mem 1958-, pres 1966-69, 1975, Alpha Kappa Alpha; mem toastmasters Chap 1810 1980-, City of Tampa Private Ind Council 1981-; mem, bd of dir Community Housing Resource Bd 1983-, Community Housing Resource Bd 1983-; mem Governors Constituency Against Child Abuse 1984-, Bay Area Chamber of Commerce 1984-, Tampa Chamber of Commerce 1985. **HONORS/ACHIEVEMENTS:** South Atlantic Region Ruby J Gainer Human Relations Awd AKA 1975; Outstanding Comm Serv The Charmettes Inc Mt Calvary of Day Adventist Church 1979,85, Eddie Mitchell Mem Comm Serv Awd City of Tampa Office of Comm Relations 1980; Dist Dramatic Speech Toastmasters of FL 1981; Woman of the Year The Orchid Club 1983; Leadership Tampa, Greater Tampa Chamber of Commerce 1988. **BUSINESS ADDRESS:** President, Tampa Urban League, Inc, 1405 Tampa Park Plaza, Tampa, FL 33605.

TOLBERT, BRUCE EDWARD
Judge. **PERSONAL:** Born May 20, 1948, Tarrytown, NY; married Tanya Roberts; children: Justin, Bryce. **EDUCATION:** Fordham Univ Bronx, BA 1970; Columbia Univ Law Sch NY, JD 1973. **CAREER:** Pepsi Co Inc Purchase NY, law intern 1973; County of Westchester NY, contract coord 1974-76; Harlem Legal Serv Inc NY, staff atty 1976-80; City of Yonkers Law Dept, 1st deputy corp counsel 1980-85; City Court of Yonkers, judge 1985-. **ORGANIZATIONS:** Bd of dirs Westchester Legal Serv Inc, Yonkers Comm Action Program; mem Westchester Co Magistrate Assoc, Westchester Co Bar Assoc, Westchester Black Lawyers Assoc, Yonkers Lawyers Assoc, Natl Bar Assoc; mem bd of dirs Yonkers Comm Action Program Inc, Yonkers Comm Planning Cncl. **HONORS/ACHIEVEMENTS:** John Hay Whitney Fellowship 1970-72; Earl Warren Fellow 1971-73; Civic Awd Afro-Amer Civic Assoc 1984; Outstanding Young Man in Amer 1985; Joseph B GavrinMemorial Awd for Outstanding Achievement Westchester Comm Oppor Prog Inc 1985; Awd in recognition for outstanding contribution to the legal profession Assoc of Black Lawyers of Westchester Co Inc 1985. **HOME ADDRESS:** 1523 Central Park Ave, Yonkers, NY 10710. **BUSINESS ADDRESS:** Jude of the City Court, City of Yonkers, 87 Nepperhan Ave, Yonkers, NY 10701.

TOLBERT, EDWARD T.
Government official. **PERSONAL:** Born May 28, 1929, Toms River, NJ; married Thelma Neal; children: Karen Paden. **EDUCATION:** Toms River HS, HS Diploma, 1949. **CAREER:** Berkeley Township Housing Auth, chmn mem 1965-70; Ocean Co Mental Health Bd, vP 1967-73; Ocean Co Emer Police, deputy chief 1971-73; Berkeley Township, township committeeman 1973-79, mayor 1974-75, co-committeeman. **ORGANIZATIONS:** Deputy chf pres Manitou Pk Vol Fire Co 1958-78; trustee Scnd Bapt Church Toms River 1962-69; trustee Homes for All Inc 1986, Natl Council on Alcoholism Ocean County 1986. **MILITARY SERVICE:** AUS sgt 1950-53. **HOME ADDRESS:** 6 Fourth St, Toms River, NJ 08757.

TOLBERT, HERMAN ANDRE
Physician, psychiatrist. **PERSONAL:** Born May 29, 1948, Birmingham, AL; son of John Tolbert and Ruth Tolbert. **EDUCATION:** Stillman Coll, BS 1969; Univ CA San Diego, MD 1973. **CAREER:** OH State Univ, res 1973-77, child flw 1977-78, asst prof 1978-89; assoc prof 1989-. **ORGANIZATIONS:** Mntry flw Am Psychtr Assn 1977; edtr Spectrm Nwsltr APA/NIMH Flws 1981-83; mem Amer Psychtrc Assn 1978-, Amer Acad Child Pschtry 1979-, Assn Acad Psychty 1980-; secretary, Psychiatric Society of Central Ohio 1985-88; president-elect, Psychiatric Society of Central Ohio 1989-90. **HONORS/ACHIEVEMENTS:** Fellowship Amer Psychtrc Assn 1977; dipl Amer Bd Psychtry Neurology 1980-82; bk chptrs Behavioral Prblm Childhood & Adolescence; fellow, Amer Academy of Child & Adolescent Psych 1982; fellow, Amer Psychiatric Association 1989. **BUSINESS ADDRESS:** Assoc Prof, Ohio State Univ, 473 W Twelfth Ave, Columbus, OH 43210.

TOLBERT, JACQUELYN C.
Educational administrator. **PERSONAL:** Born Dec 20, 1947, Kilgore, TX; married Melvin Eugene Tolbert; children: Alexis N. **EDUCATION:** Kilgore Coll, AA (scholastic hnrs) 1968;Stephen F Austin St Univ, BA (Deans List) 1970, MA 1975, Mid-management administrators certificate 1980. **CAREER:** Longview Independent Sch Dist, teacher 1970-71; Kilgore Independent Sch Dist, teacher 1971-79, public info coord 1979-. **ORGANIZATIONS:** Mem bd of dirs Longview Fine Arts Assn; mem Public Relations Comm Jr Achievement of East TX; mem Delta Sigma Theta Sor Longview Alumnae Chap 1973-79; vice pres TX Sch PR Assn 1983-85; mem Natl Sch PR Assn Impact Comm 1984-85; mem Natl Sch PR Assn Journal Council 1984-85; mem TX Sch Admin Assn 1984-, Professional Journalists Inc 1985. **HONORS/ACHIEVEMENTS:** Rookie of the Yr 1981, Bright Idea Awd 1982, 1983 TX Sch Public Relations Assn; "How to Build a Sch Comm Prog" TX Educ Agency/TX Sch PR Assn 1984; Outstanding Woman Sigma Gamma Rho 1985. **HOME ADDRESS:** 2309 Pam St, Longview, TX 75602. **BUSINESS ADDRESS:** Public Information Coord, Kilgore Public Schools, 711 N Longview St, Kilgore, TX 75662.

TOLBERT, JOHN W., JR.
City official, caterer. **PERSONAL:** Born Jul 12, 1905, Charles Town, WV; married Virginia Gaskins; children: Thelma V Roberts, Carolyn L Ashton, Carol M Smith, John III. **EDUCATION:** Dunbar High School, 1924. **CAREER:** Maderia School, asst mgr & chef 13 yrs; Town of Leesburg, council mem at large. **ORGANIZATIONS:** Co-chmn March of Dimes 1940's; pres Londoun Cty Heart Assoc 1960's; mem of vestry St James E Church 1970's; mem NAACP, Masonic Lodge; dir chaplain RedCross; mem Kiwanis club; chmn Sr Citizens Volunteer Program, Community Div Incentive Prog; Leesburg Airport Commn; pres Keep Loundoun Co Beautiful; bddir Preservation Soc Loudoun Co; mem Natl Trust for Historic Preservation; mem Natl Geographic Soc; mem Smithsonian Assoc; vice pres Leesburg Kiwanis Club14 yrs. **HONORS/ACHIEVEMENTS:** Man of the Year Loudoun Co Chamber of Commerce 1981. **BUSINESS ADDRESS:** Vice-Mayor, 15 W Market St, PO Box 88, Leesburg, VA 22075.

TOLBERT, LAWRENCE J.
Business executive. **PERSONAL:** Born Feb 13, 1914, Villa Rica, GA; widowed. **EDUCATION:** OH State U, 1934-38. **CAREER:** B & T Metals Co, pres/treas 1966-, mgr/dev 1945-66, supr 1940-45, foreman 1936-40. **ORGANIZATIONS:** Trustee Nat Alliance of Bus 1971-80; dir Columbus C of C 1972-78; dir OH C of C 1975-80; trustee OH Dominican Coll 1973-78; trustee Grant Hospital (Columbus); pres Columbus Rotary Club 1979-80. **HONORS/ACHIEVEMENTS:** Manhattan Proj (Atom Bomb) Cit US Govt 1945. **BUSINESS ADDRESS:** 425 W Town St, Columbus, OH 43215.

TOLBERT, LOVE J., JR.
Professional athlete. **PERSONAL:** Born Mar 12, 1944, Fairfield, AL. **EDUCATION:** LincolnUniv Jeff City MO. **CAREER:** San Diego Chargers, prof football player 1965-72; Houston Oilers, 1972-73; St Louis, 1973-75; San Diego CA, custom tailor presently; land devel of shopping cntrs. **ORGANIZATIONS:** 32 Degree Mason; mem San Diego Urban League; San Diego NAACP. **MILITARY SERVICE:** AUSR 1968-71.

TOLBERT, ODIE HENDERSON, JR.
Educator, archivist. **PERSONAL:** Born Aug 21, 1939, Memphis, TN; son of Odie H. Tolbert, Sr. (deceased); married Maganolia Smith; children: Alisa, Carla, Odie III. **EDUCATION:** Owen Jr Coll, AA 1959; LeMoyne-Owen Coll, BA 1962; Northern IL Univ, MA 1969; Fisk Univ, Adv Cert Black Studies Librarianship 1973. **CAREER:** Memphis State Univ, catalog librarian 1969-. **ORGANIZATIONS:** Mem Memphis State Univ Library Assoc 1970-, TN Library Assoc 1973-, Amer Library Assoc & Black Caucus 1973-; archivist Historical Museum & Fine Arts CtrChurch of God in Christ 1986-; mem Disabled American Veterans (life mem) 1965-; assoc mem Center for Black Music Research 1988-; director of library service Pentecostal Temple COGIC (The Mother Church of the Denomination) 1984-. **HONORS/ACHIEVEMENTS:** Music Scholarship Owen Jr Coll 1957-59; Internship Black Studies Librarianship Fisk Univ US Dept of Educ 1973; A Bibliography of the Dr. Martin Luther King, Jr. Collection in the Mississippi Valley Collection, Memphis State University

Feb. 1983; The Church Library (in the Whole Truth newspaper, official paper of the Church of God in Christ (COGIC) April 1988. **MILITARY SERVICE:** AUS sp4 1963-65. **HOME ADDRESS:** 2146 Janis Dr, Memphis, TN 38116. **BUSINESS ADDRESS:** Catalog Librarian, Asst Prof, Memphis State University, Memphis StateUniv Library, Memphis, TN 38152.

TOLBERT, SHARON RENEE
Educator. **PERSONAL:** Born Feb 22, 1945, Chicago, IL. **EDUCATION:** Univ of N FL, MBA cand 1981; HarvardUniv for Educ Mgmt, attnd 1978; Stanford U, PhD 1975; Stanford U, MA 1975; StateUniv NY, MS 1970; Canisius Coll, AB 1968. **CAREER:** Edward Waters Coll, vice pres institutional plan & devel 1979-; Paine Coll, vice pres plan & devel 1977-79; Inst for Serv to Edn, sr prgm asso 1976-77; Nat Counc on Educ Rsch, asst to dir 1975-76; Presidential Commn on Longe-Range Plnng, rsch asso & coor 1974-75; Stanford Proj on Acad Governance, prin rsch asst 1972-74; DHEW-SSA, mgmt & educ spec 1970-72; Bethel Head Start Prgm, proj dir 1968-70. **ORGANIZATIONS:** Visiting sr fellow HowardUniv 1976-77; educ policy fellow Nat Inst of Educ 1975-76; visiting instr Foothill Coll 1974-75; lectr Golden GateUniv 1973-74; exec dir Nat Hook Up of Black Women 1976-77; natl co-chmn Rsch Com Nat Alliance of Black Sch Educ 1976-77; sec Metro-WA Chap Nat Alliance of Black Sch Educ 1976-77; Am Assn of Higher Adn 1972-; Women Equity Act League 1972-; mem Mayor's Adv Com on the Status of Women 1980. **HONORS/ACHIEVEMENTS:** WA Intern in Educ 1975-76; Di Gamma Alumni Awd 1972; HEW EEO Awd 1973; Educ Rsch in Am NIE Annl Rept 1975; lstd Diry of Significant 20th Century Am Minority Women 1977; Who's Who Among Black Am 1977; momntd Outst Yng Women of Am 1978. **BUSINESS ADDRESS:** c/o Edward Waters College, Jacksonville, FL 32209.

TOLENTINO, SHIRLEY A.
Judge. **PERSONAL:** Born Feb 02, 1943, Jersey City, NJ; daughter of Jack Hayes and Mattie Theresa Kelly Tart; married Dr. Ernesto A. Tolentino; children: Ana Ramonia, Candida. **EDUCATION:** Coll of St Elizabeth, AB 1965; Seton Hall Univ Sch of Law, JD 1971; New York Univ Graduate School of Law 1981 LLM. **CAREER:** Judge, Superior Court of New Jersey, 1984; Jersey City Mus Ct, judge 1976-1984; VA Newark, adjudicator 1971; Upward Bound Coll of St Elizabeth, asst proj dir 1966-68, 69-71; Henry Hudson Reg Sch Highland NJ, tchr latin & eng 1965-67; S HS Youngstown OH, tchr latin & eng 1968-69; State of NJ Div of Law, dep atty gen 1976. **ORGANIZATIONS:** Hudson Cty Bar Asson; Garden State Bar Assn; Mem Alumnae Bd of Coll of St Elizabeth; NJ Alumnae Chap Delta Sigma Theta; Jersey City NAACP; Hudson Cty Urban League; Natl Assn of Women Judges; bd of Regents St Peters College. **HONORS/ACHIEVEMENTS:** Rec Scholar to Coll of St Elizabeth; 1st full time female Mun Ct Judge in NJ; 1st black female judge in Jersey City & Hudson City; grad in top 20 rec hon in Philosophy; honorary doctorate of humane letters, College of St Elizabeth 1980; lst black female judge in Superior Court of NJ. **BUSINESS ADDRESS:** Judge, Superior Court of NJ Admin Bldg, 595 Newark Ave, Jersey City, NJ 07304.

TOLER, BURL ABRON
Educator. **PERSONAL:** Born May 09, 1928, Memphis, TN; married Melvia Woolfolk; children: Valerie D, Burl Jr, Susan A, Gregory L, Martin L, Jennifer L. **EDUCATION:** Univ San Fran, BS 1952;Univ San Fran, MA 1966. **CAREER:** SF Comm Coll Dist, dir personnel 1972-; Natl Football League, official 1965-; SF, prin 1965; SF Unified School Dist, asst prin counselor teacher 1955-74. **ORGANIZATIONS:** Mem AFT; CTA; CASSA; SFASA; ERA; ACCCA; commr San Francisco Police Dept 1978-; Kappa Alpha Psi; Life mem NAACP; African Am Hist Soc; Grand Jury 1961; Juvenile Just Com; bd dir Booker T Washington Comm Cen; adv bd YMCA; bd dir Mt Zion Hosp 1976; bd of govUniv of SF; bd of regents St Ignatius Coll Prep Sch; bd dir SF Entertainment Cen Corp 1976; Boys Cen 1977. **HONORS/ACHIEVEMENTS:** CA Senate Res Sen Eugene Mcateer; All Coast Football 1949-51; All Am Jr Coll 1948; All Am Hon Ment 1951; Coll All Star Game 1952; drafted Cleveland Browns 1952;Univ of SF Hall of Fame; Africa Am Hist Soc Hall of Fame 1977; Isaac Hayes achiev in sports awd Vanguard Club 1972. **BUSINESS ADDRESS:** Dir Personnel, S F Community College Dist, 33 Gough St, San Francisco, CA 94103.

TOLES, EDWARD BERNARD
Law and judiciary. **PERSONAL:** Born Sep 17, 1909, Columbus, GA; son of Alexander Toles and Virginia (Luke) Toles; married Evelyn Echols; children: Edward Bernard. **EDUCATION:** Univ Illinois, AB 1932, post-graduate 1932-34; Loyola Univ, JD 1936. **CAREER:** Private Practice Atty Chicago, 1936-39; US Housing Authority, asst atty 1939-40; Chicago Defender, asst gen counsel/war correspondence 1943-45; US Bankruptcy Court Chicago, judge 1969-86, retired. **ORGANIZATIONS:** Mem Amer Bar Assn; Natl Bar Assn; mem exec council Chicago Chapter Fed Bar Assn; former mem bd mgr Chicago Bar Assn 1969-70; former pres Cook County Bar Assn 1961-62; Amer Judicature Soc; Bar Assn of 7th Fed Circuit; World Peace Through Law Center; Natl Conf of Bankruptcy Judges; Alpha Phi Alpha; former trustee Church of Good Shipherd, United Church of Christ. **HONORS/ACHIEVEMENTS:** Author Albert B George First Black Chicago Judge 1924-30; Natl Bar Assn CF Stradford Award; Awarded by US War Dept; Natl Bar Assn Judicial Council Newsletter 1982; Gertrude E Rush Award Natl Bar Assn 1982; Chicago Bar Assn Hononrary 50 Year Mem Award 1986; Illinois State Bar Assn Sr Counsellor 50 Year Award 1986; Judicial Council Natl Bar Assn 50 Year Award 1986; Special Award Past Presiding Judge and Legal Historial Judicial Council 1986; Natl Bar Assn 1986-89.

TOLES, JAMES LAFAYETTE, JR.
Educator. **PERSONAL:** Born May 09, 1933, Monrovia, Liberia;married Barbara R Gallashaw; children: Patricia Ann, Cynthia Annette, James Lafayette III, Celia A, Jartu G. **EDUCATION:** Clark Coll, BS 1958; N TX State U, MBA 1962;Univ ND, PhD 1970. **CAREER:** Miles Coll Birmingham, asst prof 1958-59; Wiley Coll Marshall, asst prof 1960-62; Ft Valley State Coll, prof & accntg chmn div bus & econs 1962-75; Albany St Coll, prof of bus adminstr 1975-77; S Carolina State Coll, dean 1977; VA State Univ, dean School of Bus 1983-. **ORGANIZATIONS:** Consult in acad adminstrn Untd Bd for Coll Devel; mem Am Accntg Assn; Am Mgmt Assn; Nat Bus Tchr Educ Assn; Am Vocat Edn; Am Assn Collegiate Schs Bus; mem Com on Real Estate Law & Policy Devel GA Bd Regents; mem regl exec com BSA 1973-; mem Phi Omega Pi; Delta Pi Epsilon; Phi Beta Lambda Phi Delta Kappa; Alpha Phi Alpha; mem vestry bd Episcopalian Ch; Mason; contrib to professional publs. **HONORS/ACHIEVEMENTS:** Liberian Govt Scholar 1954-58; Ford Found & Fellow 1964; Republic Steel Fellow 1964; So Fellow Fund Grantee 1969-70; Outstanding Serv Awd GA Bus & Off Educ Assn 1973.

TOLIVER, WILLIAM HENRY, SR.
Company executive. **PERSONAL:** Born Sep 04, 1925, Stafford County, VA; children: William Jr, Paul A, Ingrid B, Anne F, Kim J. **EDUCATION:** Howard Univ, BS 1951, MS 1967; Univ of New Mexico, MA 1974; Union for Experimental Colls & Univs, PhD 1977. **CAREER:** US Naval Weapons Plant, analytical chemist 1953-70; Aenospara Medical Research Lab USAF, research chemist 1961-70, physical science admin 1970-79; Morgan State Univ, assoc prof 1979-86; Social Systems Mgmt Consultant Inc, pres. **ORGANIZATIONS:** Mgmt consultant Sandtown-Winchester Comm Org 1979-85; dir Haudi-Hut Enterprises Inc 1979-82; chmn finance comm bd dir Sojourner-Douglas Coll 1982-; mgmt consultant Minority Legal Defense & Educ Fund 1984-; vice pres/bd mem CHIPT Develop Corp 1984-86, New Horizons Develop Corp 1985-; mgmt consul Bethel AME Baltimore MD 1986-. **HONORS/ACHIEVEMENTS:** Mem Phi Alpha Alpha Honor Soc for Public Admin 1978; AMRL Commander's Awd for Excellence 1979; Fellowship Blacks in Mgmt Cleveland Elec Illuminating Co 1982; Teacher of the Yr in Business Sch Student Govt Morgan State Univ 1985. **MILITARY SERVICE:** USN pharmacist 1st class 3 yrs. **BUSINESS ADDRESS:** President, Social Sys Mgmt Consul Inc, PO Box 11325, Baltimore, MD 21239.

TOLLETT, CHARLES ALBERT
Physician. **PERSONAL:** Born in Muskogee, OK; married Katherine; children: Lynn, Charles Jr, Frank, Jeffery. **EDUCATION:** Howard Univ, BS 1950; Temple Univ Med School, MD 1952; Temple, intern 1953-56; Temple, surg resd 1956-57; jr instr surg 1956-57; sr surg resd 1957; Temple U, DSc (surgery) 1957. **CAREER:** Private practice, physician; Am Coll Surgeons, flwsp 1960; Am Bd Surgery, cert 1958. **ORGANIZATIONS:** Mem Phi Beta Kappa Med, AOA; Babcock Surg Soc; HowardUniv Alumni; Kappa Alpha Psi; Philadelphia Co Med Soc; AMA; OK State Med Dental & Pharm Assn; OK Co & State Med Soc; OK Surg Assn; Am Geriatrics Soc; Am Coll Surgeons; mem Outreach Com Cntrl Br YMCA; Cntrl Chap OK Howard Alumni Assn; bd dir M-D-P Invest Fund Inc; Med Ctr State Bank; pres OK Hlth Sci Ctr Faculty House 1974; mem Areawide Hlth Plng Orgn; assoc clinical prof surgUniv OK Hlth Sci Ctr; mem Natl Med Assoc, Pan Pacific Surgical Assoc; pres bd City County Health Dept. **HONORS/ACHIEVEMENTS:** Volunteer of the Year Awd in Recognition of Outstanding Serv to the Eastside Br YMCA 1984. **MILITARY SERVICE:** AUS m/sgt 1943-46. **BUSINESS ADDRESS:** Physician, 700 NE 37th, Oklahoma City, OK 73105.

TOLLIVER, JOEL
Pastor; administrator, educator. **PERSONAL:** Born Feb 26, 1946, Philadelphia, PA; married Sharon; children: Joel Jr, Paul. **EDUCATION:** Lincoln Univ, BA 1969; Yale Univ, MPH 1971; Colgate Bexler Crozer Theol Sem, MDiv 1985; SUNY at Buffalo, educ admin, PhD candidate. **CAREER:** Univ of Rochester, health educator 1971; Empire State Coll, asst prof 1973; Radio Sta WAXI, talk show host 1973-77; City of Rochester, asst to city mgr 1974-82; Monroe Comm Coll, chaplain & administrator; Brockport State Coll, chaplain, admin and inst 1987. **ORGANIZATIONS:** Consult Brockport State Coll 1974; consult Genessee Comm Coll 1974; bd mem United Ch Ministry Inc 1979; bd mem Bridge Vol Inc 1979; mem Urban League 1979; mem Alpha Phi Alpha Frat Inc; mem Alpha Phi Omega Nat Serv Frat; mem Benevolent Order of Elks; mem Nat'l Sickle Cell Org; mem Martin Luther King Health Center. **HONORS/ACHIEVEMENTS:** Young Man of Am Comm Serv US Jaycees 1977; Comm Serv to Black Ch & comm United Ch Ministry Inc 1978 & 79; Comm Serv NAACP Elmira State Prison 1980; Church & Comm Serv Award United Ch Ministry, Inc 1983; ed excel awd Black Student Union Monroe Comm Coll 1984; outstanding adult & student awd Rochester Area Coll 1985; leadership dev inst awd SUNY at Brockport 1986; Organization of Students of African Descent Awd for Service to Afro-American Students 1985-89; Nat'l Assoc of Negro Women Awd for Comm Service 1986; United Ch Ministry Awd for Service to Black Family & Community 1986,. **HOME ADDRESS:** 1 Old Forge Ln, Pittsford, NY 14534.

TOLLIVER, LENNIE-MARIE P.
Educator. **PERSONAL:** Born Dec 01, 1928, Cleveland, OH; married Alonzo H Tolliver. **EDUCATION:** Hampton U, BS 1950;Univ Chicago, AM 1952, Post Masters Cert 1961; Union Grad Sch, PhD 1979. **CAREER:** State NJ Mental Hygeine Clncs, psych soc wrkr 1952-55; DukeUniv Med Ctr, PSW inst actng 1956-58; Atlanta U, spvr field work instructor 1957-58; Johnston Training Rsrch Cntr NJ, spvr actg dir soc wrk 1959;Univ Chicago, fld instr 1961-64;Univ OK, prof 1964-; US Dept Hlth Human Svcs, US cmnsr aging 1981-84;Univ OK, prof soc work. **ORGANIZATIONS:** Acrdtn rvwr Cncl Soc Wrk Ed 1972-81; mem dir prof Stndrds Natl Assc Soc Wrkr 1967-70; east pres OK Hlth Wlfr Assc 1971-72; mem Fed Cncl Aging 1974-78; frmr vice pres OK City Urban League; past pres OK City Links Inc; past natl sec Delta Simga Theta Inc; mem advsry cncl Allied Corp Achvmnt Awrd Aging 1984; chair Commn on the Family and Primary Assocs, Natl Assoc of Social Workers Inc 1985-. **HONORS/ACHIEVEMENTS:** 20 yr alumni awrd HamptonUniv 1970; Who's Who Am Women 1970; Awrd Elvirita Lewis Fndtn 1982; Ellen B Winston Awrd Natl Cncl Aging 1984; equal Opprtny awrd US Dept Hlth & Human Serv 1984. **HOME ADDRESS:** 6001 Wildewood Dr, Oklahoma City, OK 73105. **BUSINESS ADDRESS:** Professor Social Work, U of OK, Rhyne Hall 1005 Jenkins, 1005 Jenkins, Norman, OK 73019.

TOLLIVER, NED, JR.
Educator, elected official. **PERSONAL:** Born May 02, 1943, Woodville, MS; son of Ned Tolliver, Sr and Charlotte Tolliver; married Dorothy Bickham; children: Tony L, Daphne A. **EDUCATION:** Mississippi Valley State Univ, BS 1967; Western Michigan Univ, Certificate 1969; Jackson State Univ, Certificate 1973; Delta State Univ, MA 1983. **CAREER:** Negro Civic Club, corresponding secretary 1973; East Side High School, team leader, Social Studies Dept 1973-; Summer Youth Program, coordinator 1973-; Cleveland Area Civic Club, vice pres 1978-; Selective Service Bd, member Bolivar Cty 1982-. **ORGANIZATIONS:** Mem Cleveland Assn of Educ 1967-, Mississippi Assn of Educators 1967-, Natl Educ Assn 1967-; sponsor Citizenship Club, East Side High 1968-; mem Democratic Party of Mississippi 1977-; notary public Bolivar County MS 1977-; mem Trustee Bd United Baptist Church 1980-, NAACP Cleveland Chapter 1982-; pres Cleveland Area Civic Club 1986. **HONORS/ACHIEVEMENTS:** Star Teacher, 1987-89. **HOME ADDRESS:** PO Box 814, Cleveland, MS 38732. **BUSINESS ADDRESS:** Teacher, Alderman, East Side High School, Wiggins St, Cleveland, MS 38732.

TOLLIVER, STANLEY EUGENE, SR.
Attorney. **PERSONAL:** Born Oct 29, 1925, Cleveland, OH; married Dorothy; children: Stephanie, Sherrie, Stanley Jr, Nathan. **EDUCATION:** Baldwin-Wallace, Pre-Law 1948; Cleveland Marshall Law School, LLB 1951, JD, LLD 1969. **CAREER:** Cleveland Assoc

of Realty Brokers, legal counsel 1954; Congress on Racial Equality, legal counsel 1960-66; Rev Dr Martin L King Southern Leaders Christian Conf, legal advisor 1965-68; CORE, atty 1966; prvt practice, atty. **ORGANIZATIONS:** Pres Natl Conf of Black Lawyers Cleveland Chap 1975; class rep Baldwin Wallace Coll 1980-82; reg dir Natl Conf of Black Lawyers 1980; natl co-chmn Natl Conf of Black Lawyers 1981; elected bd mem Cleveland School Bd 1981-; exec comm Dem Party Cuyahoga Cty 1981-; mem Cleveland Assoc of Black Ed 1981-, Natl Black School Bd 1984-; only elect publ official from OH to be elect as a delegate to the Natl Dem Conv for Rev Jesse Jackson for Pres of the US; mem bd managers Cleveland YMCA; marathon runner; elected pres Cleveland Bd of Educ 1987. **HONORS/ACHIEVEMENTS:** Hon Mention & Trophy Freedom Fighters 1964; Hall of Fame East Tech HS 1978; Frank D Reeves Awd Natl Conf of Black Lawyers 1981; Bus Awd WJMO Radio Cleveland 1983; Outstanding Alumnus Baldwin Wallace Coll 1978; baritone soloist. **MILITARY SERVICE:** AUS pfc army counter intelligence 1951-53; Passed OH Bar in the Army 1953. **BUSINESS ADDRESS:** Attorney, 1464 E 105th St, Ste 404, Cleveland, OH 44106.

TOLLIVER, THOMAS C., JR.
City official. **PERSONAL:** Born Oct 16, 1950, Woodville, MS; married Myrtis M McFarland; children: Tommie C. **EDUCATION:** Jackson State Univ, BS 1972, MS 1979; Univ of Southern MS, MS 1978. **CAREER:** Wilkinson Cty High School, teacher 1972-79; Wilkinson Cty, chancery clerk 1979-88. **ORGANIZATIONS:** Asst state dir Alpha Phi Alpha Frat 1970-75; bd of dir MS Chancery Clerk's Assoc 1979-85; bd of dir, chmn Chatwell Club Inc 1982-88; bd of dir Friends of Armisted 1984-; worshipful master F&AM Prince Hall Masons 1985. **HONORS/ACHIEVEMENTS:** Man of the Year Alpha Phi Alpha Frat 1972-73; Outstanding Young Man of Amer 1981-84; Personality of the South 1982. **HOME ADDRESS:** RFD 2, Box 1310, Woodville, MS 39669. **BUSINESS ADDRESS:** Clerk Chancery Court, Wilkinson Co, PO Box 516, Woodville, MS 39669.

TOMBS, LEROY CLEVELAND
Business executive. **PERSONAL:** Born Mar 13, 1921, Bonner Springs, KS; children: Wanda, Darlene, Leroy Jr, Phillip, Madlyn. **CAREER:** Tombs & Sons Inc, owner present. **ORGANIZATIONS:** Mem Banner Spring C of C; pres Nat Assn Serv Contractors; mem Statewide Hlth Coord Cncl; Life mem NAACP. **HONORS/ACHIEVEMENTS:** Small bus man of yr State of KS 1975. **MILITARY SERVICE:** USN cf petty ofcr 23 yrs. **BUSINESS ADDRESS:** 205 1/2 Oak, Bonner Springs, KS 66012.

TOMLIN, JOSEPHINE D.
Banker. **PERSONAL:** Born Jul 05, 1952, Pittsburgh, PA. **EDUCATION:** Allegheny Coll, BA 1974; Univ of Pgh, MEd 1975. **CAREER:** Univ of Pgh, prog counselor 1975-76; LaRoche Coll, upward bound dir 1976-81; Mellon Bank, corporate demand despoit mgr 1983-84, support serv sect mgr 1984-85, project consultant/asst vice pres. **ORGANIZATIONS:** Bd dir Women's Ctr of Pgh 1978-80; business & finance acad consultant Urban League 1985-86; career oppor comm advisor Allegheny Coll 1987; Perry Traditional Acad Partnership Tutor Mellon Bank/Bd of Educ 1987. **HONORS/ACHIEVEMENTS:** Premier Achievement Awd Mellon Bank 1985; Outstanding Trio Student MAEOPP 1986. **BUSINESS ADDRESS:** Project Consul/Asst Vice Pres, Mellon Bank, Three Mellon Bank Ctr, Pittsburgh, PA 15259.

TOMLINSON, MEL ALEXANDER
Dancer. **PERSONAL:** Born Jan 03, 1954, Raleigh, NC; son of Tommy W A Tomlinson and Marjorieline Henry Tomlinson. **EDUCATION:** North Carolina School of the Arts, Winston-Salem NC, BFA, 1974. **CAREER:** Heritage Dance Theatre, Winston-Salem NC, dancer, 1972-74; Dance Theatre of Harlem, New York NY, dancer, 1974-77, 1978-81; Alvin Ailey Dance Theatre, New York NY, dancer, 1977-78; New York City Ballet, New York NY, dancer, 1981-87; North Carolina Dance Theatre, Winston-Salem NC, dancer, 1988—, dir of educational services, 1988-89. **ORGANIZATIONS:** Mem, Intl Perform Assn; mem, AITRA; mem AFMA; mem, SEF; mem, Equity. **HONORS/ACHIEVEMENTS:** North Carolina Prize, New York Times, 1983; choreographed "No Right on Red," 1987, and "Carnival of the Animals," 1988. **HOME ADDRESS:** 5304 Quail Wood Dr, Apt I, Winston-Salem, NC 27104.

TOMLINSON, RANDOLPH R.
Editor, publisher. **PERSONAL:** Born Aug 28, 1920, Rebpulic of Panama; son of Myrtle C Tomlinson-Allen; married Eulalie; children: Randolph Jr, William, Marta, Edward, Levette. **EDUCATION:** Inst Nacional de Panama, 1940; Univ of Panama, 1950; NW Univ, Postgraduate Work 1958. **CAREER:** La Nacion Panama City, editorial page editor; The Star & Herald Panama City, reporter; The Panama Review, assoc editor; North Shore Examiner Newspaper, editor, publisher. **ORGANIZATIONS:** Mem Sigma Delta Chi Chicago Chapter, Chicago Headline Club, Black Business & Professional Assn; mem exec bd NE IL Cty BSA; sec, adv bd African-Amer Exchange Program NW Univ, Radio Stations WEAW/WOJO Evanston IL; mem exec bd Freedom of Residence Found, Emergency School Aid Act Project, ESAA, NW Univ; appointed mem Evanston Street Light Comm; mem Seniors Action Service Bd. **HONORS/ACHIEVEMENTS:** Outstanding Business Award; Outstanding Citizen Award for Public Serv Gamma Omicron Chapter Detla Sigma Theta Sorority; Candidate for Mayor of Evanston nominated by acclamation all black citizens of Evanston; served in a civilian capacity during WWII in the Canal Zone; mem Citizens Police Advisory Bd. **BUSINESS ADDRESS:** Editor &Publisher, North Shore Examiner Newspaper, 1901 Church St, Evanston, IL 60201.

TOMLINSON, ROBERT
Educator. **PERSONAL:** Born Jun 26, 1938, Brooklyn, NY. **EDUCATION:** Pratt Inst, Brooklyn, BFA 1961; Columbia Univ Teachers Coll NY, 1963; CUNY Graduate Center NY, PhD 1977. **CAREER:** Emory Univ Atlanta, assoc prof 1978-; Hunter Coll NY, adj asst prof 1972-78; HS of Art & Design NY, french instr 1968-72; Ministere de l'Education Nationale Paris, eng instr 1963-68; This Week Mag, asst art dir 1961-63. **ORGANIZATIONS:** Mem Am Soc for Eighteenth Cent Stud mem Mod Lang Assoc; chmn Emory Univ Commn on the Status of Minorities 1980-81, 1984-85. **HONORS/ACHIEVEMENTS:** Number 1 man exhibit of Painting Paris, London, NY, Washington 1968, 1971, 1979, 1984; rep in private coll; Advanced Study Fellow Ford Found, 1972-76; fellow, CUNY 1975-77; Amer Council of Learned Societies Grant 1979. **BUSINESS ADDRESS:** Associate Professor, Emory University, Modern Languages Dept, Atlanta, GA 30322.

TOMS-ROBINSON, DOLORES C.
Educator. **PERSONAL:** Born Dec 26, 1926, Washington, DC; married George L Robinson; children: Gigi, Greg. **EDUCATION:** Howard Univ, BS cum Laude 1947, MS 1948; Univ of MI, PhD 1957; Univ of IL Inst for Study of Mental Retardation, post doctoral study 1956-57. **CAREER:** Univ of UT, rsch child psychology, 1957-58; Jarvis Christian Coll, dir of psychol testing 1960-62; Jackson State Coll, dir fresh studies 1962-64; TX So Univ, prof of psychology 1964-70; Central MI Univ, chmn 1974-76, prof 1970-. **ORGANIZATIONS:** Mem Council for Exceptional Children; NEA; Phi Delta Kappa; Delta Kappa Gamma; Assn Childhood Edn. **BUSINESS ADDRESS:** Professor, Central Michigan Univ, 155 W Remus Road, Mount Pleasant, MI 48858.

TONEY, ANDREW
Professional athlete. **PERSONAL:** Born Nov 23, 1957, Brimingham, AL; married Priscillia; children: one daughter. **EDUCATION:** Univ of Southwest LA, attended. **CAREER:** Philadelphia 76ers, basketball player. **HONORS/ACHIEVEMENTS:** One of the best clutch performers in the game. **BUSINESS ADDRESS:** Philadelphia 76ers, Veteran Stadium, PO Box 25040, Philadelphia, PA 19147.

TONG, DALTON ARLINGTON
Financial administrator. **PERSONAL:** Born Apr 19, 1950, Guyana; married Linda V Smith; children: Sophia, Nicole. **EDUCATION:** Univ of Baltimore, BS Accntg 1973;Univ of Baltimore, MBA Corp Mgmt 1975; Harvard U, Cert in Fincl Mgmt & Strategy in Hlth 1976; State of MD cpa 1978. **CAREER:** S Baltimore Gen Hosp, fin contrl present, contrl 1976, asst contrl 1975, reimbursement spec 1974, gen accnt 1973; MD Farm Bur of Rec & Tax Servs, accntg intern 1970. **ORGANIZATIONS:** Evening fac Dundalk Commun Coll 1975; evening fac Howard Commun Coll present; mem Minority Recruitment & Equal Opport MD Ass of CPAs advanced; mem Hosp Finan Mgmt Assn present; mem Am Mgmt Assn present; advisory St Frances Charles Hall Sch 1979. **HONORS/ACHIEVEMENTS:** Who' Who Among Students in AmUniv and Colls 1972-73; Beta Alpha Nat Hon Soc; Magna (cum laude)Univ of Baltimore 1973. **BUSINESS ADDRESS:** 3001 S Hanover St, Baltimore, MD 21230.

TOOMER, KENNETH
Accountant. **PERSONAL:** Born Oct 24, 1943, St Louis, MO; married Ann M Wilson; children: Kara Ane, Kenneth Todd. **EDUCATION:** Univ of MO at St Louis, BS Bus Adminstrn 1968. **CAREER:** Toomer Mueller & Co CPA's, mng part 1972-; Ford Mrktg Corp, dlr rep 1972; Arthur Andersen & Co CPA's, auditor 1968-72. **ORGANIZATIONS:** Mem Am Inst of CPA's 1972-; mem MO Soc of CPA's 1972-; mem Nat Assn of Black Accnts 1973-74; sec Nat Assn for Min CPA Firms 1979-80; bd of trustees UMSL Sch of Bus Adminstrn 1973-75; adv coun acctng St Louis Jr Coll Dist 1973-75; bd of dir Cntrl Med Ctr Inc Hosp 1980.

TOOMER, VANN ALMA ROSALEE
Educator. **PERSONAL:** Born Oct 16, Franklin, VA; married J W; children: Dr Jethro W Jr. **EDUCATION:** Benedict Coll Columbia SC, BS; Hampton Inst Hampton VA, MA; TempleUniv PA, earned 30 hrs. **CAREER:** Broward Co Ft Lauderdale FL, ret school prin 11 yrs; Orange Co, oral dir one yr; SC, prin school 2 yrs; Orange Co, one yr; total yrs teacher & prin of schools 28 yrs. **ORGANIZATIONS:** Dept elem sch prin nationally; mem FL Educ Assn; Orange Co Tchrs Assn; Nat Educ Assn; Intl Reading Assn; pres Nat Counc Negro Women 1972-74; exec bd Christian serv ctr Orlando; exec bd mem Comprehensive Hlth Prog City Orlando; Ch Women Untd Orlando; orgnzd First Pres Bapt Ministers wives Alliance Broward Co; mem bd dir Girl Scout Counc Inc; Cradle Kindergarten & Nursery Broward Co. **HONORS/ACHIEVEMENTS:** FL Lives Who's Who 1966; Outstndg Personalities of the So 1967; Comm Leader Awd 1969 rec Past achiev & outstndg serv to comm & state.

TOON, AL
Professional athlete. **PERSONAL:** Born Apr 30, 1963, Newport News, VA; married Jane. **EDUCATION:** Attended, Univ of WI. **CAREER:** New York Jets, wide receiver 1985-. **HONORS/ACHIEVEMENTS:** Named 1st team All Big 10; voted Badges MVP 2 yrs in a row; MVP performance in Hula Bowl; NFL All-Rookie by Football Digest; mem NFL Pro Bowl team 1987. **BUSINESS ADDRESS:** New York Jets, 598 Madison Ave, New York, NY 10022.

TOOTE, GLORIA E. A.
Attorney. **PERSONAL:** Born Nov 08, 1931, New York, NY. **EDUCATION:** Howard Univ School Law, JD 1954; Columbia Univ Graduate School Law, LIM, 1956. **CAREER:** Natl Affairs Section Time Magazine, former mem; NYC, Praclaw 1954-71; Toote Town Publs Inc, pres; Action Agency Off Volunteer Action Liaison, asst dir 1971-73; Dept Housing & Urban Devel, asst sec 1973-75; author & lecturer; NYC, presently engaged in Practice of law; Treasurer, Estates & Enter Inc, pres. **ORGANIZATIONS:** Bd mem, Arbitrator Assn, Consumer Alert, Council of Economic Affairs for the Republic/Natl Black United Fund; cited by the following organizations, natl business league, Alpha Kappa Alpha Sorority, US Chamber of Commerce, Natl Newspaper Publication Assn. **HONORS/ACHIEVEMENTS:** Newsmakers awd Nat Assn of Black Women Atty NY Fed of Civil Serv Org Navajo Tribe Nat Assn of Real Estate Brokers Nat Citizens Participation Counc Nat Bar Assn; YMCA World Serv Awd Women's Nat Rep Club New York City Housing Auth Res Adv Counc MA-CT-NY-NJ Delta Sigma Theta Disting; Pol Ldrshp AwdNNPA Outstndg Serv Awd.

TOPPIN, EDGAR ALLAN
Educator. **PERSONAL:** Born Jan 22, 1928, New York, NY; married Antionette Lomax; children: Edgar Jr, Avis, Louise. **EDUCATION:** Howard Univ, AB cum laude 1949, MA 1950; Northwestern Univ, PhD 1955. **CAREER:** AL State Coll, instr 1954-55; Fayetteville State Coll, chmn Soc Sci Div 1955-59; Univ Akron, asst assc prof 1959-64; VA State Coll, full prof 1964-; NC Coll, vis prof 1959, 1963; Western Res Univ, 1962; Univ Cincinnati, 1964; San Francisco State Coll, 1969; IN Univ, 1971. **ORGANIZATIONS:** Natl Pres Assc study Afro-Amer life & history 1973-76; editorial bd Journal Negro History 1962-67; exec bd Orgn Amer Historians 1971-74; mem Natl Hist Pub Commn 1972- 1st black mem; adv bd Natl Parks Historic Sites Bldgs & Monuments 1st black mem; bd dir So Flwshps Fund 1966-; World Book Encyclopedia Socl Sci Adv Com 1968-; vice pres bd Akron Urban League 1961-64; bd dir Fayetteville United Fund 1957-59. **HONORS/ACHIEVEMENTS:** Author books, Pioneer Patriots 1954; Mark Well Made 1967; Unfinished March 1967; Blacks in Amer

1969; Biog History of Black in Amer 1971; Black Amer in US 1973; 30 lesson educ TV Course Amer from Africa; grad flwshps from Howard Univ 1949-50; Hearts Fnd 1950-51, 1952-53; John Hay Whitney Fnd opport Flwship History 1964; research grants from Amer Assc State Local History 1964; Old Dominion Fnd 1968; Ford Fnd 1970; Who's Who Amer 1972-73; Comtemporary Authors. **BUSINESS ADDRESS:** VA State Coll, Petersburg, VA 23803.

TORAIN, TONY WILLIAM
Clergyman, higher education administrator. **PERSONAL:** Born Jun 27, 1954, Mebane, NC; son of William Torain and Myrtle Juanita Woody Torain; married Celestine Best, May 25, 1985; children: Tony W. Torain, II (Nnamdi). **EDUCATION:** Univ of NC at Chapel Hill, BA 1975; Gordon-Conwell Theological Seminary, MATS 1979; Boston Univ, MA 1980; Univ of MD at Baltimore, MSW/JD 1984/85. **CAREER:** Boston State Coll, campus minister 1978-80; Twelfth Baptist Church, assoc minister 1978-80; Joint Orange-Chatham Comm Action, dir elderly serv 1980-81; Office of the Atty Gen MD, clerk 1982-83; Baltimore Assoc of Retarded Citizens, counselor 1983-85; Highway Church of Christ, assoc minister 1982-85; Highway Training Inst, dean 1984-85; US Dept of Health & Human Svcs, employee counseling serv asst 1984-85; Good Shepherd Church (COGIC) Baltimore Maryland pastor 1985-; Univ of Maryland School of Social Work, bd mem, 1986-. **HONORS/ACHIEVEMENTS:** North Carolina Governor's School 1971; Scholarship First Federal Scholar 1973; Scholarship Turrentine Scholar 1975; Awd Martin L King Jr Awd for Ministry 1979. **BUSINESS ADDRESS:** Director: African American Cultural Center, Towson State University, 8000 York Road, Towson, MD 21204.

TORAN, ANTHONY
Educational administrator. **PERSONAL:** Born Mar 13, 1939, New York, NY; married Marjorie Williamson; children: Anthony, Nicole. **EDUCATION:** Lehman Coll, BS Educ 1972; Queens Coll, dual Masters in Educ Admin & Urban Affairs 1975. **CAREER:** New York City Fire Dept, fire marshal 1966-73, educ coord 1973-85; Strategic Financial Services, pres; Bynes Electronics, exec vice pres 1985-. **ORGANIZATIONS:** Chairperson Minority Council Town of N Hempstead; bd of dirs Westbury Coalition 1974-79; bd of dirs Council of the Arts 1975-80; trustee Westbury Public Schools 1981-; pres Black Caucus of Sch Bd Mem Northeast Region 1984-. **HONORS/ACHIEVEMENTS:** Pres Birchwood Knolls Civic Assn 1976-81. **BUSINESS ADDRESS:** Executive Vice President, Bynes Electronics, 330 Motor Pkwy, Hauppauge, NY 11787.

TORAN, KAY DEAN
Government official, educator. **PERSONAL:** Born Nov 21, 1943, Birmingham, AL; married John Toran; children: Traci, John Dean. **EDUCATION:** Univ of Portland, BA 1964; Portland State Univ, MSW 1970. **CAREER:** Portland State Univ, asst prof counseling 1970-71; Portland State Univ Grad School of Soc Work, asst prof soc work; Adult & Family Serv Publ Welfare,asst mgr field oper 1976-79; Office of the Govt, dir affirm action 1979-. **ORGANIZATIONS:** Mem Delta Sigma Theta Soc Serv Sor 1964-; dir Girl Scouts Summer Camp 1968; prog consult Girl Scouts 1969-70; bd of dir Campfire Girls Inc 1975-77; bd of dirs Met Fam Serv 1976-82; bd of dirs Portland State Univ Found 1980-; bd of dir The Catlin Gable School 1980-84. **HONORS/ACHIEVEMENTS:** Rsch grant Curriculum Devel Western Interstate Comm for Higher Ed 1973; Publ "Curriculum Devel" 1974; Leader of the 80's Awd NW Conf of Black Publ Officials 1979; Outstanding Young Woman of Amer 1980; Woman of Excellence Delta Sigma Theta 1982. **BUSINESS ADDRESS:** Dir, Office of the Government, Affirmative Action, State Capitol Bldg, Salem, OR 97310.

TORIAN, EDWARD TORRENCE
City official. **PERSONAL:** Born Dec 20, 1933, New Rochelle, NY; married Pearl Cromartie; children: Curtis, Darlene. **EDUCATION:** Westchester Business Inst, Certificate in Accounting 1956; Iona Coll, BBA 1968, MBA Finance (50% complete). **CAREER:** Perkin-Elmer Corp, sr contract accountant 1966-; Hal-Tor Enterprises Co, partner & treasurer 1970-; Danbury Common Council, legislative leader 1983, councilman-at-large 1979-. **ORGANIZATIONS:** Mem Natl Assn of Accountants 1967-; mem Iona Coll Alumni Assn 1968-; mem NAACP 1980-; treasurer Black Democratic Assn of Danbury 1981-; sec Men's Council New Hope Baptist Church 1981-. **MILITARY SERVICE:** USN petty officer 3rd class 1951-54; Natl Defense Award. **HOME ADDRESS:** 18 Indian Head Road, Danbury, CT 06811.

TORRENCE, JACQUELYN SEALS (STORY LADY)
Professional story teller. **PERSONAL:** Born Feb 12, 1944, Chicago, IL; divorced. **EDUCATION:** Livingstone Coll Salisbury NC, att 1962-66; High Point Coll NC, BA 1977. **CAREER:** Nationwide, freelance storyteller, 1976-; High Point Public Library, NC, storyteller, 1973-76; Washington State Branch Library High Point, NC, branch librarian, 1970-72. **ORGANIZATIONS:** Consultant on creative storytelling NC Intl Reading Assn 1978-80; Long Island NY Suffolk Cooperative Library Syst, 1979-80; Oneonta Storytelling Org 1980; mem Natl Assn for Preservaton & Perpetuation of Storytelling 1976-80. **HONORS/ACHIEVEMENTS:** "Creative Story-Telling" workshops num sch & colls nationwide 1973-; concert performances colls & groups in num states; TV appearances TV 8 High Point NC, TV 2 Greensboro NC, TV 12 Winston Salem NC, num others; 1st performer to perform 3 conse yrs Jonesboro TN Nat Storytelling FestUniv Bridgeprot, Purdue U, Tuscolum Coll, Central Park NC 1976-78; recording "Jackie Torrence The Story Lady with Ghost Tales and Tall Tales for Young and Old".

TORREY, RUBYE PRIGMORE
Scientist consultant. **PERSONAL:** Born Feb 18, 1926, Sweetwater, TN; married Claude A; children: Claudia Olivia, Michael Angelo. **EDUCATION:** TN State U, BS 1946, MS 1948; SyracuseUniv NY, PhD 1968. **CAREER:** TN State Univ, asst, assoc prof chem 1948-63; Syracuse U, inst chem 1963-68; TN State U, prof chem 1969-70, radiation officer 1980-83; Natl Bureau Standards, res chem/cnsl 1983-84; private practice, consult plng & serv 1984-. **ORGANIZATIONS:** Cnslt Chem Inds 1981-82; flw Am Inst Chem 1976-; cmt mem Am Chem Soc 1976-82; collaborative sc Brookhaven Natl Lab 1970-74; advsry comm Mid-Cumberland Cncl Govt 1975-82; pgrm chrmn Am AsscUniv Women 1970-74; mem Amer Chem Soc, Amer Inst of Chemists, women chemists comm Amer Chem Soc 1976-86; health & safety comm Amer Chem Soc 1979. **HONORS/ACHIEVEMENTS:** Inst grant awrd Natl Sci Found 1980-83; res grant awrd Atomic Energy Comm Successors 1970-79; book in progress Analytical Chemistry; publ articles Profnl Jnrls; listed in Amer Men and Women of Sci, Outstanding Educators of Amer, Community Leaders of Amer, Who's Who in the South and Southwest, Personalities of the South, Intl Men of Achievement. **BUSINESS ADDRESS:** Consultant, P O Box 23044, Nashville, TN 37202.

TOSI, D'ASHNASH See CHASE-RIBOUD, BARBARA DEWAYNE

TOTTEN, BERNICE E.
Supervisor, elected official. **PERSONAL:** Born Sep 01, 1921, Mississippi; children: Othell, Adell, Bertrial, Mack C, Mildred Mitchell, Napolian Jr, Robert, Landon, Martha Jamison. **EDUCATION:** MS Ind Coll Holly Spring MS, Teacher License 1951; Tuskegee Inst AL, Early Childhood Ed 1968; Rust Coll, 1968-74. **CAREER:** Public School, teacher 1950-51; Head Start, teacher 1964-75; Marshall Cty MS, cty suprv 1974-88. **ORGANIZATIONS:** Mem NAACP 1965-85. **HONORS/ACHIEVEMENTS:** Shield MS Ind Coll Holly Spring MS 1975; Awd Inst Comm Serv 1979-80; Shield Mid South Comm Org Tenn 1980; Cert MS Head Start Assoc. **BUSINESS ADDRESS:** Supervisor, Marshall Cty Dist 4, Rt 3 PO Box 98, Holly Springs, MS 38635.

TOTTEN, HERMAN LAVON
Educator. **PERSONAL:** Born Apr 10, 1938, Van Alstyne, TX; son of Derrall Scott Totten and Dulvi Sims Totten. **EDUCATION:** Wiley Coll Marshall TX, BA 1961; Univ of OK, MLS 1964, PhD 1966. **CAREER:** Wiley Coll, librarian & dean 1966-71; Univ of KY, assoc dean 1971-74; Univ of OR, dean & prof 1974-77; N TX State Univ, prof 1977-. **HONORS/ACHIEVEMENTS:** SEF Fellow Southern Educ Found 1964-66; ACE Academic Internship Amer Council on Educ 1970-71; CLR Fellow Council on Library Resources 1977-78. **BUSINESS ADDRESS:** Prof Sch Library & Info, North TX StateUniv, PO Box 13796, Denton, TX 76203.

TOTTRESS, RICHARD EDWARD
Retired clergyman. **PERSONAL:** Born Nov 25, 1917, Newby Creek, OK; son of Reom M Totress (deceased) and Louisa Headspoth Totress (deceased); married Margarreau Fluorine Norton; children: 1 son (dec). **EDUCATION:** Pacific Union Coll, BA 1943; Oakwood Coll, BA 1969; Langston Univ; Home Study Inst; Ministerial Internship Evangelism, TX 1943-47; Univ of Beverly Hills, MA and PhD 1981. **CAREER:** Texaco Conf/Texas SDA, minister 1943-; SW Region Conf, pastor/evangelist 1947-52; So Atlanta Conf SDA, dist pastor/youth assoc 1952-63; Oakwood Acad & Coll, dean 1963-66, coll pastor/chaplain 1965-69 and 1972-73; Oakwood Coll Ch, co-pastor 1973-79; Your Bible Speaks radio show, producer/speaker 1953-. **ORGANIZATIONS:** Civilian chaplain 1944; dir Bibb County March of Dimes 1961; Fellow Intl Biog Assn 1970's & 1980's; coord Metro-Atlanta Area SDA Pastors 1982-84; dir Crusade for Voters Bibb County,GA 1959-60; mem Book of Honor Amer Biogr Inst 1979; broadcast programs WEUP Radio 1971-73. **HONORS/ACHIEVEMENTS:** Special Plaques Oakwood Coll Faculty & Student Ch Bld 1977; Special Plaques South Central SDA 1978; Plaque Notable Amer in the Bicentennial Era 1976; Certificate Outstanding Secondary Educator of Amer 1975; Poet and Author. **MILITARY SERVICE:** ASR Chaplain 1943-44. **BUSINESS ADDRESS:** Your Bible Speaks Inc, PO Box 310745, Atlanta, GA 30331.

TOUCHSTONE, JOHN E.
Appointed official. **PERSONAL:** Born Jul 27, 1939, New Kensington, PA; married Mary. **EDUCATION:** VA Union Univ, BA 1965; Howard Univ, MPA 1973. **CAREER:** Montgomery Co MD, admin asst 1971-72; Washington Metro COG, asst dir 1972-83; DC Dept of Public Works, dir 1983-. **ORGANIZATIONS:** Mem Eastland Garden Civic Assn 1977; mem DC Delphi Panel 1980; co-chair Washington Waterfront Action Grp 1981; mem 1973-85, exec bd, Intl City Mgmt Assn 1973-85; mem Coalition of Black Public Admins 1982-85; mem Intl Assn of Police; bd of dir, Natl Forum for Black Public Admin. **HONORS/ACHIEVEMENTS:** Scholarship Howard Univ 1970; Fellowship Intl City Mgmt Assn 1973. **BUSINESS ADDRESS:** Dir Public Works, District of Columbia, 2000 14th St NW 6th Fl, Washington, DC 20009.

TOUSSAINT, ROSE-MARIE
Physician. **PERSONAL:** Born Jun 15, 1956, Port-au-Prince, Haiti. **EDUCATION:** Loyola Univ, BS 1979; Howard Univ, MD 1983. **CAREER:** NIH, rsch assoc; Howard Univ Hosp, fourth year resident. **ORGANIZATIONS:** Mem Delta Sigma Theta Sor 1978; vice pres All African Physicians of North Amer 1984. **HONORS/ACHIEVEMENTS:** Best Surgical Resident DC General Hosp 1985-86. **BUSINESS ADDRESS:** Resident, Howard University Hosp, 2041 Georgia Ave, Washington, DC 20001.

TOWNES, CLARENCE L., SR.
Officer/corporate. **PERSONAL:** Born Jun 24, 1902, Richmond, VA; married Alice F Smith. **EDUCATION:** VA Unoin U, att 2 yrs; RPI Now VA Commonwealth U, att 1 yr. **CAREER:** VA Mutual Benefit Life Ins Co, vchmn 1933-; Jefferson Townhouse Corp Richmond, fndr pres 1964-80; Colsolidate Bank & Trust Co Richmond, dir chmn auditing com 1951-80; Nat Benefit Life Ins Co Washington, field supr dist mgr 1926-32; So Aid Society of VA, agent asst to gen mgr 1923-26. **ORGANIZATIONS:** Gen sec Nat Ins Assn Inc 1937-43; natl pres Nat Ins Assn 1954-55; natl treas Phi Beta Sigma Frat Inc Washington 1960-70; commr treas Richmond Reg Dist Planning Comm 1967-76; vchmn commr City of Richmond Comm on the Aging 1978-80. **HONORS/ACHIEVEMENTS:** Recip of num plaques awds & cit Nat Ins Assn, Phi Beta Sigma Frat, Richmond Reg Dist Planning Comn, VA Mutuel Benefit Life Ins Co, others. **BUSINESS ADDRESS:** 112 E Clay St, Richmond, VA 23219.

TOWNES, CLARENCE LEE, JR.
Business executive. **PERSONAL:** Born Jan 21, 1928, Richmond, VA; son of Clarence Townes, Sr. and Alice S. Townes; married Grace Elizabeth; children: Clarence III, Michael S, Lisa F, June E. **EDUCATION:** VA Union Univ, BS Commerce 1951. **CAREER:** Va Mutual Benefit Life Ins Co, dir of training 1948-66; Republican Natl Comm, asst to chmn/dir minority affairs 1966-70; Joint Ctr/Pol Studies, dir govtl affairs 1970-74; Metropolitan Coach Corp, pres & ceo 1974-l986; Richmond Renaissance Inc, deputy dir l982-. **ORGANIZATIONS:** Alternate delegate Republican Natl Convention 1964; comm Rich Redev & Housing Auth 1964-66; chmn Electoral Bd Richmond VA 1979-84; bd of dirs VA Mutual Benefit Life Ins Co 1985-88; mem Phi Beta Sigma Frat 1945-; pres/coo Jefferson Townhouse Corp 1964-; bd of dirs Consolidated Bank & Trust Co 1970-; bd of dirs Amer Bus Assn 1976-l982; pres Arts Council of Richmond l986-88. **HONORS/ACHIEVEMENTS:** Citizenship Awd Astoria Benefical Club Richmond 1968; Man of the Year Iota Sigma Chap Phi Beta Sigma 1969; Good Government Award Richmond First Club 1987; Brotherhood Citation Award, Richmond Chapter, Natl Conf of Christians and Jews, l987. **MILITARY SERVICE:** AUS 2nd lt 3 yrs. **HOME ADDRESS:** 3103 Hawthorne Ave, Richmond, VA 23222. **BUSINESS ADDRESS:** Deputy Dir, Richmond Renaissance Inc, 600 E Broad St #960, Richmond, VA 23219.

TOWNES, LINTON KEITH
Professional athlete. **PERSONAL:** Born Nov 30, 1959, Richmond, VA. **EDUCATION:** James Madison, 1982. **CAREER:** Los Angeles Clippers, forward 1983-; Portland Trail Blazers, forward 1982-83; Milwaukee Bucks, forward 1983. **BUSINESS ADDRESS:** Los Angeles Clippers, 3939 S Figueroa St, Ste 510, Los Angeles, CA 90037.

TOWNS, EDOLPHUS
Government official. **PERSONAL:** Born Jul 21, 1934, Chadbourn, NC; married Gwendolyn Forbes; children: Darryl, Deidra. **EDUCATION:** NC A&T State Univ Greensboro, MS 1956, PhD 1986; Adelphi Univ Garden City NY, MSW 1973. **CAREER:** Medgar Evers Coll Booklyn New York City Publi School, teacher, dep hosp admin 1967-71; Borough of Brooklyn, dep pres 1976-82; 98th Congress 11 Dist NY, congressman 1982-. **ORGANIZATIONS:** Mem adv council Boy Scouts Amer, Salvation Army, Phi Beta Sigma, Kiwanis. **MILITARY SERVICE:** AUS 1956-58. **BUSINESS ADDRESS:** Congressman, 98th Congress 11th Dist NY, Room 1726, Longworth House Office Bldg, Washington, DC 20515.

TOWNS, EVA ROSE
Child psychiatrist. **PERSONAL:** Born Feb 03, 1927, Ellwood City, PA; divorced; children: Ronald, James, Shaaron, Jennifer. **EDUCATION:** Univ of Pittsburgh, BS 1948; Howard Univ Coll of Med, MD 1953; Freedmen Hosp Washington DC, adult psych training; Johns Hopkins Hosp Balt MD, childpsych training. **CAREER:** North Community Mental Health Center Washington DC, medical officer; Private practice, child adolescent adult psychiatry. **ORGANIZATIONS:** Mem Amer Psychiatric Assoc, Natl Med Assoc, Med Chirurgical Soc of DC. **HONORS/ACHIEVEMENTS:** Prog Fellow Amer Psych Assoc 1973; Listed in Who's Who of Amer Women in Amer; Fellow Amer Acad of Child Psychiatry. **HOME ADDRESS:** 7739 16th St NW, Washington, DC 20012.

TOWNS, MAXINE YVONNE
Clergyman, educator. **PERSONAL:** Born Jan 12, 1941, Chester, PA. **EDUCATION:** Camden Co Comm Coll Blackwood NJ, AA 1975; Notre Dame Coll Manchester NH, BA 1978. **CAREER:** Notre Dame Coll Manchester NH, dean of students 1978-; Camden Co Jail NJ, chaplain 1972-77; Boston MA, rec dir 1970-72; Diocese of Fresno CA, religion educ tchr 1963-70; Wade Day Care Cntr Chester PA, day care asst 1960-61. **ORGANIZATIONS:** Sec of bd So NJ Prison Serv Comm 1973-75; sec Nat Balck Sisters' Conf 1975-77; treas NBSC 1980-; enterd Franciscan Sisters of the Atonement 1961; planning com Annuan NBSC Meeting 1977-79; planning com NH Person & Guidance Assn 1980; chprsn NH Diocesan Vocation Commn 1980-; pres NH Coll Person Assn 1980-81. **BUSINESS ADDRESS:** Notre Dame College, 2321 Elm St, Manchester, NH 03104.

TOWNS, MYRON B., JR.
Physician. **PERSONAL:** Born Dec 18, 1943, Greensboro, NC; son of Myron B Towns Sr and Miriam Gould Towns; married Barbara Taylor, Mar 20, 1978; children: Cindi, Amy, Sandra. **EDUCATION:** Fisk Univ, BA, foreign languages, 1970; Meharry Medical Coll, MD 1978. **CAREER:** The Tennesseean, copy editor, 1967-70; Waverly-Belmont Clinic Lab, co-organizer/founder 1972-74; Univ of GA Athens, electron microscopist div of genetics 1974-75; George W Hubbard Hospital Meharry Medical Coll, pathology resident 1978-83; Hebbronville Clinical Lab, dir co-owner pathologist 1984-86; Doctor's Clinic, associate 1986-87; Towns Clinic, primary and indigent care, owner, 1987-. **ORGANIZATIONS:** Jr mem Coll of Amer Pathologists 1980-83; mem Amer Soc Clinical Path & local medical socs 1980-; sole attending MD at indigent clinic Community Health Clinic TX 1984-86; consultant in clinical automation; associate, Sanford and Associates image processing; trustee, WILD rehabilitation center; certified foster parent for emergency cases of all ages. **HONORS/ACHIEVEMENTS:** Carter Woodson Award in journalism, 1969; honors in biochemistry, Meharry Medical College 1972; Clinical Pharmacology NSF Fellow Vanderbilt Univ Medical Ctr 1982; Commendation for Assisting in Student Research Meharry Medical College 1983. **BUSINESS ADDRESS:** Attending Physician/Owner, Towns Clinic, 113 South Fifth at West Ash, Blytheville, AR 72315.

TOWNS, ROSE MARY
Librarian. **PERSONAL:** Born Jan 07, 1934, Houston, TX; married George Elbert. **EDUCATION:** San Francisco State Coll, BA Soc Sci 1955;Univ of CA Berkeley, MLS 1956. **CAREER:** N Bay Cooperataive Libr Syst, syst prgm coor 1979-; Ref Referral Proj N Bay Coop Lib Sys, coord 1975-79; Richmond Pub Lib Richmond CA, city libr 1969-70; Richmond Pub Lib Richmond CA, asst city libr 1966-69; Oakland Pub Lib Oakland CA, sup libr 1962-66; Oakland Pub Lib Oakland CA, sr libr 1960-62; Oakland Pub Lib Oakland CA, jr libr 1956-60. **ORGANIZATIONS:** Mem Am Lib Assn; mem Am Lib Assn Black Caucus; mem CA Lib Assn; mem Intellectual Freedom Com CA Lib Assn 1966-69, 1980-; chpsn Intellectual Freedom Com CA Lib Assn 1967-68; Long Range Planning Com CA Lib Assn; sec CA Soc of Libr CA Lib Assn 1979; mem CA Libr Black Caucus N; sec CA Libr Black Caucus N 1972-73; mem Black Women Orgn for Polit Action. **HONORS/ACHIEVEMENTS:** Delegate CA Gov Conf on Lib & Infromation Serv 1979. **BUSINESS ADDRESS:** N Bay Cooperative Library Sys, 505 Santa Clara St, Vallejo, CA 94590.

TOWNS, SANNA NIMTZ
Educator. **PERSONAL:** Born Oct 12, 1943, Hawthorne, NV; children: Joseph IV, Jawad. **EDUCATION:** Southern Univ, BA 1964; Teachers Coll Columbia Univ, MA 1967; Univ of Southern MS, PhD 1985. **CAREER:** Amer Language Prog Columbia Univ, english lang instructor 1969-71; Office of Urban Affairs SUNY at Buffalo, prog coord 1973-75; Kuwait Univ, instructor & admin 1975-79; English Dept Univ of New Orleans, lang coord & instructor 1980-82, 1985-86; Delgado Comm Coll, asst prof & asst chair 1986-. **ORGANIZATIONS:** Mem Natl Council of Teachers of English 1980-, LA Assoc of Developmental Educ 1981-, Phi Delta Kappa 1984-, South Central Modern Language Assoc 1986-; speaker New Orleans Museum of Art Speakers Bureau 1987. **HONORS/ACHIEVEMENTS:** State of LA Bd of Regents Graduate Fellowship 1982-85; article "Integrating Reading & Writing Instruction" in ERIC 1984. **HOME ADDRESS:** 3883 Pauger St, New Orleans, LA 70122. **BUSINESS ADDRESS:** Asst Prof of English, Delgado Community College, 615 City Park Ave, New Orleans, LA 70119.

TOWNSEL, RONALD
State superintendent. **PERSONAL:** Born Nov 25, 1934, Chicago; children: 3 Children. **EDUCATION:** George Williams Coll, BS 1957; Governores State U, MA 1975. **CAREER:** IL Dept of Corrections, st supt of adult parole 1970-; IL Youth Commn, area parole supr juvenile parole agt 1960-70; Chicago Fed of Settlements, youthgang Worker 1958-60; Chicago Bd fo Edn, tchr 1957-58. **ORGANIZATIONS:** Mem ACA Compact of St Governors; NICO; IPPCA. **MILITARY SERVICE:** AUS 1953-54. **BUSINESS ADDRESS:** 160 N La Salle St, Chicago, IL.

TOWNSELL, JACKIE M.
Business executive. **PERSONAL:** Born Apr 07, 1936, Dallas, TX; married Jimmie; children: Aaron H. **CAREER:** Townsell Groc & Mkt, owner, mgr. **ORGANIZATIONS:** Served Dallas Cty Grand Jury 1971; adv comm mem Legis Dist Rep 1973; nominated 1st black appt to City Park Bd 1973; appt to serve Dallas Cty Mental Health Mental Retard Bd of Trustees; Dallas Cty Grand Jury Comm 1974; delegate City Council 1st black to seek publ office 1974; testified Environ Affairs Comm for creation of a state park 1975; elected Irving City Council 1977-; bd mem Helping Hand School for Retarded Children W Irving Improvement Assoc & Day Care Ctr; Irving Planning & Adv Comm; Irving Aid Inc; Dem for Responsible Govt; Dallas Cty Child Welfare; Liaison to Dallas Cty Foster Parent; nominated 1st black appt to City Housing Code Bd; appt Screening Sub-Comm charged with responsibility to fill a vacancy in Criminal Dist Ct #1; dep voter registrar; pres Young Womens Mission, Parent Leaders Org. **HONORS/ACHIEVEMENTS:** Worked with City Fathers to obtain park site & construct swimming pool; Worked with City Fathers to bring water lines through the comm; Suggested to City Officials the need to installment contract payments so people of Irving would have option of paying cash or installment to tie onto city water & sewer lines; This is Your Life Pen & Plaque 1965; Cit Awd Outstanding Young Women of the Year; Cert of Apprec Irving Parks & Rec Dept 1971; Serv & Outstanding Contrib to Citizens of Irving 1972; Accomplishment Awd Serv Rendered to Dallas Cty 1974; Cert of Apprec Merit Serv Outstanding Contrib Cty of Dallas 1974. **BUSINESS ADDRESS:** Manager, Townsell Grocery & Market, 3941 Carver St, Irving, TX 75061.

TOWNSEND, ARTHUR P.
Business executive. **PERSONAL:** Born Apr 30, 1921, Daytona Beach, FL; married Mary Ruth; children: Brian, Yolanda, Michael. **EDUCATION:** Bethune Cookman Coll, AA; UCLA, BS. **CAREER:** So CA, land devel; Real Estate, broker 1955-; Precinct Reporter Newspaper, publisher 1965-. **ORGANIZATIONS:** Co-fndr W Coast Black Pubs Assn; former br pres NAACP; past comdr Am Legion; former mem San Bernadino Co Dem Central Com9; former mem San Bernadino City Juvenile Comm; co-fndr CA Fend of Black Ldrshp; co-fndr Inland Empore Black Caucua; alt del to Dem Nat Conv 1960, 1964; former cand for mayorof San Barnardino. **HONORS/ACHIEVEMENTS:** Recip Urban Leag Awd for Outsnd Achvmnt; Operation Second Chance Cit for Outsnd Contrbn; cert of appr CA Dept of Employment; cert of execptional achmnt NAACP; spl awd for outstnd comm serv Mexican C of C of San Bernardino; Sheik Temple No 98 Awd for Outstnd Contrbn to Achmnt in Journ; cert fo appr San Bernadino W Side Comm Devel Corp; Publisher of the Year WCBPA 1985. **BUSINESS ADDRESS:** Publisher, Precinct Reporter, 1677 W Baseline St, San Bernardino, CA 92411.

TOWNSEND, MAMIE LEE HARRINGTON
Business executive. **PERSONAL:** Born Nov 20, 1920, Warwick, GA; married Calvin Louis Townsend; children: Roselyn Rochelle Greene Cole, Ervin Louis. **EDUCATION:** Purdue Univ, 1966; IN Univ 1966-68. **CAREER:** Finance Ctr AUS, branch mgr 1951-66; Faith United Christian Church, diaconate & bd 1981-; Auntie Mame's Child Devel Centers, founder/pres, 1969. **ORGANIZATIONS:** Pres IN Licensed Child Care Assn 1975; vice chmn IN Citizens Adv Comm 1977 & 79; central reg rep IN Assn for the Educ of Young Children 1978-79; bd of dirs Metro Bd of Zoning & Appeals 1979-82; Golden Heritage NAACP 1979-; steering comm Christian Churches of IN 1981-84; vol training Amer Cancer Soc 1982-85; steering comm mem United Negro Coll Fund Drive 1984; appty by Gov Bowen charter mem Title XX Bd, vice chmn 1975-79; mem Metropolitan Bd of License Review 1982-. **HONORS/ACHIEVEMENTS:** Proclamation of Mamie Townsend Day Mayor Wm Hudnut IN 1977-79; Indiana Jefferson Award Indianapolis Star Nwsp 1978; Woman of the Year Zeta Phi Beta Sor 1979; Distinguished Serv Indianapolis Chamber of Comm; Madame CJ Walker Center for Leadership Devel 1982; Outstanding Businesswoman Iota Phi Lambda Sor 1983; Sojourner Truth Award by Natl Assn of Negro Business & Professional Women's Clubs Inc 1985 for Meritorious Svcs; Human Rights Award for Outstanding Leadership in Educ; Hon Mem Zeta Phi Beta 1986. **BUSINESS ADDRESS:** President, Auntie Mame's Child Dev Ctrs, 3120 N Emerson Avenue, Indianapolis, IN 46218.

TOWNSEND, MURRAY LUKE, JR.
Retired government official. **PERSONAL:** Born Jul 06, 1919, Indianapolis, IN; son of Murray L Townsend Sr (deceased) and Novella Foster; married Evelyn; children: Cheryl, Murray III, Frederick. **EDUCATION:** Morehouse Coll, BA 1948; Boston U, LLB 1949. **CAREER:** PO, 1950-56; IRS, criminal investigator 1956-64; Boston and NY, dep equal employment policy ofcr 1963-66; Small Business Admin, sr compliance officer 1967-81 (retired); Consultant. **ORGANIZATIONS:** Mem Omega Psi Phi Frat 1939; deacon Union Bapt Ch 1955-62; mem Prince Hall Mason 1963-, mem Middleboro Lakeville Mental Health Comm Couns 1966; mem bd of dir, Central Baptist Church 1973-; mem NAACP; 336th Infantry Vet Assn; adv com bd of dir New Eng Village for Human Rights 1979; mem Afro Am Vet US 1980. **HONORS/ACHIEVEMENTS:** Citz Schrsp Found Middleboro 1968-70; Cits Schlrsp Found MA 1970-72; Paul Revere Bowl Citz Schlrsp Found Am 1976. **MILITARY SERVICE:** Infantry 1942-46; capt 1951-54; Bronze Star w/2 Oak Leaf Clusters, Silver Star Med 1951, Infantryman's Badge w/Star. **HOME ADDRESS:** 95 Thomas St, Middleboro, MA 02346.

TOWNSEND, P. A.
Retired attorney. **PERSONAL:** Born Nov 29, 1914, Poplar Bluff, MO; married Evelyn M; children: Prentice, Edward. **EDUCATION:** Univ of KS, AB 1934, LLB 1937. **CAREER:** Gen practice of law 1937-65; State of KS, spec asst to attny gen 1937-41; State Tax Comm, asst attny 1947-52; State Corp Comm, asst attny 1947-52; Missionary Bapt State Conv of KS, gen counsel 1948-62; Interstate Assoc of Church of God, gen counsel 1948-69; Prince Hall Grand Lodge of KS F&AM, grand attny 1956-77, past grand master 1979-81; KS Conf, AME Church, attny; State of KS, pardon attny 1965-67; State Corp Comm, asst gen counsel 1967-70; Dept of Housing & Urban Devel, attny, reg counsel 1970-82; Municipal Court of Topeka, judge pro-tem 1983-. **ORGANIZATIONS:** Del at large Rep Natl Conv 1960; del Gen Conf 1960,64,68,72,76,80,84; commiss Topeka Housing Auth 1963-70; exec bd Salvation Army 1965; adv comm Red Cross 1966; mem Gen Conf Comm 1964; pres Judicial Council 1968-; vchmn Rep State Comm two terms; vchmn Shawnee Cty Central Comm; 33 Degree Mason,. **HONORS/ACHIEVEMENTS:** Shriner, Alpha Phi Alpha, Washburn Univ Centennial

Fund Dr, Stormont-Vail Hosp Bond Dr; past comdr Jordan-Patterson Post #319, Amer Legion; former mem Legal Redress Comm, NAACP, St John, AME Church; bd of stewards, former mem, bd trustees Douglass Hosp. **MILITARY SERVICE:** Capt WWII.

TOWNSEND, ROBERT
Writer/producer/director/actor. **EDUCATION:** Attended, Illinois State Univ, Wm Paterson Coll NJ, Hunter Coll NY. **CAREER:** Actor, Cooley High, Ratboy, Streets of Fire, A Soldier's Story, American Flyers; actor/director/producer, Hollywood Shuffle; starring in Uptown Comedy Express on HBO; writer/actor/director/producer, Robert Townsend & His Partners in Crime I, II, III, IV for HBO, 1987-88. **BUSINESS ADDRESS:** c/o Leading Artists, Inc, 445 N Bedford, Penthouse, Beverly Hills, CA 90110.

TOWNSEND, RON
Vice president/general manager. **CAREER:** CBS-TV, dir of business affairs and programming 1964-69; Children's TV Workshop, dir of field services; WTOP-AM, business manager; WDVM-TV, station manager for 8 yrs; WUSA-TV, vice pres/general mgr.

TOWNSEND, WILLIAM HENRY
Elected official, optometrist. **PERSONAL:** Born Jul 30, 1914, West Point, MS; son of John Henry Townsend and Annie Harris Townsend; married Billye Gene McNeely, May 25, 1952; children: Yolanda Gene, Terezenha Ann, LaJuan Ursula. **EDUCATION:** Tuskegee Inst, BS 1941; Howard Univ, 1946; Northern Illinois Coll of Optometry, OD, 1950. **CAREER:** Optometrist, Little Rock, 1950-; Arkansas House of Representatives, Dist 63 Pulaski Co state rep, 1973-. **ORGANIZATIONS:** 15 organs including life member NAACP; mem Urban League; treas Prof Serv Inc; mem Alpha Phi Alpha; mem the Masonic; 1st vice pres AR Democratic Black Caucus; mem AR Comprehensive Health Bd; mem Uptown Toastmaster Club; former mem bd of dirs 1st Natl Bank & 1st Commercial Bank Little Rock. **HONORS/ACHIEVEMENTS:** First licensed black optometrist in Arkansas, 1950; Citizen of the Yr Awd Omega Psi Phi 1964; Imperial Club's Awd Outstanding Serv in Politics 1975; Serv Awd for Outstanding Serv 1975 Morris Booker Coll;Cert of Distinguished Serv as mem of the State Adv Comm for Special Needs Prog 1975; AR Council of Human Relation Life Serv Awd; Optometrist of the Year Awd 1981; The Jerome S Levey Awd 1981; Martin Luther King Jr Commemorative Award, 1986; Distinguished Legislative Achievement, Alpha Phi Alpha, 1989. **MILITARY SERVICE:** US Army Eng Unit, platoon sargeant, 1942-46. **BUSINESS ADDRESS:** State Representative, District 63 Pulaski County, 1304 Wright Ave, Little Rock, AR 72206.

TRADER, HARRIET PEAT
Social work, educator. **PERSONAL:** Born Jul 06, 1922, Baltimore, MD; married Herbert W Trader. **EDUCATION:** Morgan State Coll, AB 1944; Columbia Univ, MS 1946; Univ of PA, DSW 1962. **CAREER:** Bronx Hosp NY, med social worker 1952-53; Crownsville State Hosp MD, psychiatrist caseworker suprv 1953-62; Howard Univ School of Social Work, assoc prof 1963-65; Morgan State Coll, assoc prof 1965-68; Univ of MD School of Social Work, assoc prof 1968-84; Johns Hopkins Univ, assoc prof 1968-; Morgan State Univ; vice pres acad affairs 1980-85; Baltimore Urban League, consultant 1986-. **ORGANIZATIONS:** Past pres Social Work Vocational Bur 1973-; chairperson Natl Cabinet on Professional Standards; mem Natl Assoc of Soc Workers, Natl Assoc of Black Soc Workers, Urban League, NAACP, YWCA; bd mem, Commission on Community Relations, Family & Children's Service, Enoch Pratt Library. **HONORS/ACHIEVEMENTS:** Comm Contrib Awd Delta Sigma Theta 1969; Listed in Outstanding Ed in Amer 1971; Alumna of Year Awd Morgan State Coll 1972; 1st woman to be appt to bd trustees Enoch Pratt Library 1972; Honored as Living Maker of Negro History Delta Phi Lambda 1973.

TRAMIEL, KENNETH RAY, SR.
Educator. **PERSONAL:** Born May 31, 1946, Shreveport, LA; married Sandra Mackel; children: Kenneth Jr, Kendra, Kai. **EDUCATION:** Univ of CA, Berkeley, BA (Summa Cum Laude) 1973; CA State Univ, MS (Summa Cum Laude) 1976. **CAREER:** East Oakland Youth Devel, head counselor 1979-80; Federal Govt Vietnam Outreach program, asst team leader/counselor, 1980-82; Oakland Unified School Dist, head counselor/scholarship advisor 1982-87. **ORGANIZATIONS:** Pres bd of dirs Berkeley Youth Alternative 1981-82; pres 1984-85, mem Oakland Personnel & Guidance Assoc 1982-; mem CA Assoc for the Gifted 1984; consultant CA Assoc for the Gifted State Conf 1984-85; vice pres Oakland Public Sch Affirmative Action Comm 1985-86. **MILITARY SERVICE:** AUS personnel sp5 2 yrs; Outstanding Section Leader 1969. **HOME ADDRESS:** 2923 Jo Ann Dr, Richmond, CA 94806.

TRAMMELL, WILLIAM RIVERS
Educator. **PERSONAL:** Born Oct 19, 1926, Anniston, AL; son of Edward A Trammell Sr and Mattie Rivers Trammell; married Bertha Hicks. **EDUCATION:** Clark Coll Atlanta, AB 1948; Columbia Univ NY, MA 1961. **CAREER:** Calhoun County Schools, jr high principal 1948-65; Anniston Public Schools, elem principal 1965-75, interim sch supt 1978-79, asst supt and dir of finance 1975-85 (retired); Protective Industrial Insurance Company of Alabama, dir 1989-. **ORGANIZATIONS:** Dir of pilot state kindergarten prog Anniston City Schools 1973-77; sec Anniston Airport Commn 1980-86; mem Alabama Governor's Comm on Handicapped Employment 1985-; treas Calhoun Co Economic Develop Cncl 1986-; bd of dirs Alabama Easter Seal Soc 1986-. **HONORS/ACHIEVEMENTS:** Outstanding Serv Awd in Educ Alpha Kappa Alpha Sor 1984; Archon of the Year Sigma Pi Phi Frat Beta Kappa Boule 1986; Gold Awd Alabama Easter Seal Soc 1986. **HOME ADDRESS:** 2517 McKleroy Ave, Anniston, AL 36201.

TRAPP, DONALD W.
Financial administrator. **PERSONAL:** Born Sep 28, 1946, Hampton, VA; son of Chester A. Trapp and Ida Holt Trapp; married Shirley Ann Stokes; children: Rashaad, Brandon. **EDUCATION:** Virgina State U, BS Bus Admin 1968; IN U, MBA Finance 1973. **CAREER:** Cummins Engine Co Inc, dir pricing 1978-82; Cummings Engine Co, asst treas 1977-78; Cummins Engine Co Inc, finan spec 1976-77; Irwin Mngmt Co Inc, mgrtreas reporting 1973-76; Cummins Engine Co Inc, dir components strategy 1982-83, dir intl logistics 1983-84; Remote Equip Corp, pres 1985; vice pres and treasurer UNC Ventures, Inc. Boston, MA, 1988-. **ORGANIZATIONS:** Mem C of C 1975; mem Kappa Alpha Psi Frat Inc 1967-; bd of dir William R Laws Found 1975-84; bd of dir Columbus United Way of Am 1976-79; bd of directors Accent Hair Salons 1988-; bd of directors Xinix Corp 1989-. **HONORS/ACHIEVEMENTS:** Achmnt awd Wall St Jour 1968; distng serv cit United Negro Fund 1977; Outstnd Young Men of Am 1977; recip of commendation med AUS 1968. **MILITARY SERVICE:** AUS first lt 1968-70. **HOME ADDRESS:** 3241 Beechnut Ct, Columbus, IN 47203.

TRAPP, ELLEN SIMPSON
Educational administrator. **PERSONAL:** Born Dec 29, 1920, Chester, SC; married Vanis W Trapp; children: Karlus, Vanis, Ellan. **EDUCATION:** Benedict Coll Columbia, SC, BA 1943; NYU, pre-med. **CAREER:** Original Displays, owner/operator 1945-49; New York City Bd of Health, bacteriologist; School Bd, elected mem 1973-, chairperson 1983-. **ORGANIZATIONS:** Treas New York City School Bd Assn 1980-; bd mgr Soc Gifted Children 1976-; active mem LWV, served as Educ Task Force chairperson; active mem League for Better Govt; mem State Educ Adv Com 1975; Staten Island Better Govt Cncl 1961; Mayor's Comm on Inter-Group Relations 1976; Mothers March on Birth Defects/March of Dimes 1975; Staten Island Area Policy Bd 1983; Staten Isl Hunger Rights Comm 1984. **HONORS/ACHIEVEMENTS:** Rara Avis Mariners Harbor PS 44 1975; Woman of Achievement Staten Island 1979; Mills Skinner Award SI Urban League 1979; Except Childrens Club 1985; Martin Luther King Awd SI NY Richmond Occupational Training Center 1987; Maurice Wollin Educ of the Year Awd 1987; 1st Black person elected to public office on Staten Island elected to 5th term May 2, 1989. **BUSINESS ADDRESS:** Chairperson, Community School Board, 211 Daniel Low Terrace, Staten Island, NY 10301.

TRAPP-DUKES, ROSA LEE
Educator. **PERSONAL:** Born Dec 19, 1942, Bishopville, SC; married Ofield Dukes; children: Roxi. **EDUCATION:** Madonna Coll, BA 1965; Univ of MI, EdS 1970; E MI, MA 1969; Univ of MI, PhD 1973. **CAREER:** Univ of MI, teacher, training coord, lecturer 1970-71; Natl Inst Mental Health, dept of HEW fellow 1971-72; Dept of HEW, soc sci res analyst 1972-74; Howard Univ Center for Study of Handicapped Children & Youth, dir 1978-81; DC Parent Child Center, exec dir 1981-82; Howard Univ, assoc prof. **ORGANIZATIONS:** Mem bd dir Dist Hghts Youth Club 1975; mem Soc for Res in Child Dev 1976-77; mem adv bd Early & Periodic Screening Diag & Treatment Prog Natl Child Day Care Assn 1976-77; consult Natl Educ in res proposal & prgm devel; sr collaborator Inst for Child Devel & Family Life; vice pres for Health Aff HowardUniv; 3 year mem bd dir Day Care & Child Devel Coun of Amer; mem Soc for Res in Child Devel; Natl Assn for Educ of Young Children; Amer Ed Res Assn; Natl Coun for Black Child Devel. **HONORS/ACHIEVEMENTS:** Participant DHEW Fellowship Prgm 1971-72; Awarded $100,000 Title I Preschool Eval Contract DC Pub Sch 1975-76; elected Outstanding Young Women of AmerPrgm 1976; publ "Cognitive & Perceptual Devel in Low SES Minority Urban Children, Preschool Prgm Impact" Abstracts Soc for Res in Child Devel 1977; Awarded approx $300,000 by USDOE Office of Sp Ed for Interdisciplinary Model for Parent and Child Training Project IMPACT 1978-81. **BUSINESS ADDRESS:** HowardUniv Sch of Education, Washington, DC 20059.

TRAPPIER, ARTHUR SHIVES
Nuclear engineer. **PERSONAL:** Born Mar 22, 1937, Brooklyn, NY; children: Arthur S Jr, Jason M. **EDUCATION:** Lincoln U, BA physics 1960; Polytech Inst of Brooklyn, MS bioengr 1970; IN No U, DSc med engr 1973. **CAREER:** Dept Physic & Nuclear Med Mt Sinai Ch fo Med CityUniv of NY, research phys 198-0; Jewish Hosp Med Center of Brooklyn, radiol phys 1970-78; Downstate Med Center Kings Hwy Hosp, radio phys 1965-70; NYU Environ Med, research asst 1962-65; AUS Rockett Guided Missle Agency Red Stone Arsenal DC, physical sci 1961-62. **ORGANIZATIONS:** Prof of phsy Prat Inst 1978; consult phys Vet Adminstrn Med Center 1977-80; treas Grtr NY Hlth Physcis Soc 1978-79. **HONORS/ACHIEVEMENTS:** Pub "Rectum Bladdeer Dosimetry in the RX of Uterine Cancer" Radiology 1969; "Calibration of a Whole Body Counter for Clinical Investigation in a Psychiat Hosp" Physics in Med & Bioloiy 1971; pub "Postmortem Exam of an X-Ray Tube" Journ of the Nat Med Assn 1978. **MILITARY SERVICE:** AUS sp-4 1960-62. **BUSINESS ADDRESS:** 5th Ave & 100th St, New York, NY 10029.

TRAUGHBER, CHARLES M.
Government employee. **PERSONAL:** Born Feb 13, 1943. **EDUCATION:** TN State Univ, BS 1968, Grad School, 1970-71. **CAREER:** TN State Penitentiary, counselor I 1969, sr institutional counselor 1971; Adult Counseling Serv for Adult Inst State of TN, dir 1972; TN Bd of Paroles, mem 1972-. **ORGANIZATIONS:** Mem Amer Correctional Assoc, Natl Assoc for Advancement of Col People; enrolled MA Prog Criminal Justice TN State Univ; mem TN Correctional Assoc, Amer Paroling Assoc. **BUSINESS ADDRESS:** Tennessee Bd of Paroles, 3rd Floor, State Office Bldg, Nashville, TN 37237.

TRAVIS, ALEXANDER B.
Business executive. **PERSONAL:** Born Oct 19, 1930, Dallas; married Jo Ann Jones; children: Judy (erwin), Anthony, Paula. **EDUCATION:** Compton Jr Coll; SW Business Coll. **CAREER:** Bell Telephone Co, various jobs in co's plant dept comm mgr spec assign 1949-. **ORGANIZATIONS:** Bd mem of Park So YMCA; NAACP Area Chpter; Natl Alliance Businessmen & Venture Adv Inc; mem Dallas Urban League; mem Alliance of Business, Plans for Progress, US Dept of Labor & Career Guid Inst; Dallas Negro Chamber of Commerce; Moorland Branch YMCA; Natl All Market Devel; SCLC; Black Part Program; Maria Morgan Branch YWCA; sponsor Boy Scouts & Explorer Scout Troops of Amer; Betheleham Comm Center; Community Relations Comm; B & PW; Tele Poin Amer; Dallas All for Min Enterp; Amer Assn Min Consult Dallas Branch; New Bethel Baptist Church. **HONORS/ACHIEVEMENTS:** First black mgr of SW Bell Co; Presidential Citation for work with veterans & ex-offenders; Special Commendation Dallas Area former-Pres Jimmy Carter; 1st Black pres of Intl Lions Club. **BUSINESS ADDRESS:** Corp Secretary Youth Directory, Dallas Alliance of Business, 4501 Lemmon Ave, Dallas, TX 74219.

TRAVIS, BENJAMIN
Attorney. **PERSONAL:** Born in Brooklyn; married M; children: 3 Children. **EDUCATION:** Coll of Pugent Sound, 1951; San Francisco State Coll, 1954; Univ of CA Hastings Coll of Law, JD 1960. **CAREER:** Alameda Superior Court, judge; atty pvt prac 1961-66; Western Addition Law Ofc, opened first neighborhodd legal serv ofc in San Francisco as chief counsel 1966-72; Community Educ Proj & Neighborhood Lega Newspaper, founded 1968-; San Francisco State Coll, lecturing prof 1971. **ORGANIZATIONS:** Mem, bd dir Berkeley Neighborhood Legal Serv; mem, bd dir San Francisco Local Devel Corp; mem, bd dir Bay Area Social Planning Coun; past vp, bd dir San Francisco Neighborhood Legal Asst Found; mem, bd dir Bayview Hunter's Point Community Health Cntr; mem, bd dir Tassili Sch; mem,

bd dirNat Legal Aid & Defender's Assn; consult evaluator & technical asst Volt Inc Civil Defenders Com; mem, bd dir Nat Bar Assn; sec Charles Houston Law Club 1971; mem Task Force Com on Criminal Justice; mem, bd dir United Bay Area Crusade 1972; mem Judicare Experiment Prog 1973; pres Charles Houston Law Club 1973-. **MILITARY SERVICE:** USAF 1950-54. **BUSINESS ADDRESS:** Judge, Alameda Superior Court, 1225 Fallon St, Oakland, CA 94612.

TRAVIS, DEMPSEY J.
Business executive. **PERSONAL:** Born Feb 25, 1920, Chicago, IL; son of Louis Strickland and Mittie Strickland; married Moselynne. **EDUCATION:** Wilson Jr Coll, AA 1948; Roosevelt Univ, BA 1949; Northwestern Univ School Mortgage Banking, Certificate 1969; Olive Harvey Coll, Honorary Doctorate Economics 1975; Daniel Hale Williams Univ, Honorary Doctorate Business Admin 1976; Kennedy-King Coll Chicago, Honorary Doctorate of Humane Letters 1982. **CAREER:** Sivart Mortgage Corp, pres 1945-78; United Mortgage Bankers of Amer, founder & pres 1960-73; Dempsey J Travis Securities & Investment Co, pres 1960-76; Urban Research Press, pres 1969-; Travis Realty Co, founder & pres 1949-. **ORGANIZATIONS:** Mem trustee Northwestern Meml Hosp 1975-; bd trustees Garrett-Evang Seminar 1980-89; dir Uni Banc Trust 1976-87; trustee Chicago Historical Soc 1985-; dir Museum of Broadcast Communications 1985-; pres Soc of Midland Authors 1988-90. **HONORS/ACHIEVEMENTS:** Real Estate is the Gold in Your Future 1988; Harold: The People's Mayor 1989; The Soc of Midland Authors Award 1982; Author of, "An Autobiography of Black Chicago" 1981; "An Autobiography of Black Jazz" 1983; "Don't Stop Me Now"Children's Press 1970; "An Autobiography of Black Politics" 1987. **MILITARY SERVICE:** AUS Techn Sgt served 4 years. **BUSINESS ADDRESS:** President, Travis Realty Company, 840 E 87th St, Chicago, IL 60619.

TRAVIS, GERALDINE
Legislator. **PERSONAL:** Born Sep 03, 1931, Albany, GA; married William Alexander Sr; children: William, Michael, Ann, Gerald, Gwendolyn. **EDUCATION:** Xavier Univ, 1947-49. **CAREER:** Dem Natl Conv Miami, delegate 1972; Dem Mini-Conv KS, delegate 1974; Dem Natl Conv NY, delegate 1976; State of MT, legislator 1975-77. **ORGANIZATIONS:** Co-chmn Dem Party Minorities Comm 1972-74; mem Natl Steering Comm 1973-74; mem State Coord Comm of Intl Womens Year 1977; official observer Natl Womens Conf 1977; bd of dir YWCA Great Falls 1979; co-chmn Dem Women's Club; mem St Peter & Paul Cath Church, Natl Womens Polit Caucus, Natl Order of Women Legislators, YWCA, Natl Council of Negro Women, NAACP, natl Urban League, Amer Civil Liberties Union, Sierra Club, MT Womens Pol Caucus; MT Crime Control Bd, Human Resources Comm, Criminal Justice Info Comm; precinct comm Woman of Precinct #42 Cascade Cty; mem MT Adv Comm to US Comm on Civil Rights; chmn Cascade Cty Detoxification Adv Bd, Amer Indian Action Council; chmn sub-comm Admin of Justice. **HONORS/ACHIEVEMENTS:** Listed in Who's Who in Amer Politics, World's Who's Who of Women.

TRAWICK, LOUISE LAVERGNE
Retired educator. **PERSONAL:** Born Aug 26, 1917, Bainbridge, GA; married Lonnie H Trawick; children: LaVergne, Leon A Esq. **EDUCATION:** Savannah State Coll, AB 1935; Atlanta Univ, MEd 1945. **CAREER:** Decatur Co GA, teacher 1935; Tattnall Co GA, jeanes super 1942-45; DC Public Schools, teacher 1953-60; Reading Clinic Washington, reading specialist 1960-66; Howard Univ Reading Lab, supervisor 1961-64; Natl Teacher Corps Washington, team leader 1966-68; Right to Read Prog of DC Public Schools, acting supervising dir 1973-74. **ORGANIZATIONS:** Mem Trinity AME Zion Church; mem Natl Sor of Phi Delta Kappa 1955-; mem Intl Reading Assn 1967-76; mem Natl Retired Teachers Assn 1976-; adv neighborhood comm District of Columbia Govt 1980-84. **HONORS/ACHIEVEMENTS:** Meyer Fellowship DC Public Schools 1970; Excellence in Teaching & Reading Awd Cromwell Acad Washington 1984.

TRAYLOR, HORACE JEROME
Educator. **PERSONAL:** Born Mar 15, 1931, LaGrange, GA; married Theola Dennis; children: Sheryl Lynn, Linda Gail, Yohanna Faye, Chequeta Renee, Tonya Yvonne. **EDUCATION:** Zion Coll, AB 1953; Gammon Theolo Sem, BD 1958; Univ of TN Chattanooga, MEd 1965; Univ Miami, PhD 1978. **CAREER:** Chattanooga City Coll, pres 1964-69; Univ of TN, spec asst chancellor 1969-71; Miami-Dade Comm Coll, dean, Open Col 1971-74, pres develop 1974-79, vice pres develop 1979-. **ORGANIZATIONS:** Treas Leadership Inst Comm Develop Wash DC 1969-73; mem fndng bd dir United Bank of Chattanooga 1971-; adv bd United Bank of Chattanooga 1971; treas Counc on Black Am Affairs-Am Assn Com & Jr Coll 1974-; adv com Inst for the Study of Educ Policy Howard Univ 1967-. **HONORS/ACHIEVEMENTS:** Smith-Taylor Award for Excellence in Journalism 1958; Outstanding Young Man of Yr Award Natl Jaycees 1965; Ambassador Good Will Human Relations Counc Chattanooga 1969. **BUSINESS ADDRESS:** Vice President Development, Miami-Dade Comm College, Dist Adm, 300 NE 2nd Ave, Miami, FL 33132.

TRAYLOR, RUDOLPH A.
Retired business executive. **PERSONAL:** Born Aug 28, 1918, Providence, RI; son of Elijah and Julia; divorced; children: Tyrone Rene, Wayne Milan. **EDUCATION:** Philadelphia Acad of Music, BA 1941; NY Univ, Schillinger System of Music Composition Rudolf Schramm 1950. **CAREER:** CBS, staff TV & radio percussionist & arranger 1952-57; Roulette Records, A&R dir arranger conductor 1957-62; RKO Sound Studios, arranger conductor recording engr 1962-73; WOR-TV, engr asst supr tech dir 1973-86; Retired 1986. **ORGANIZATIONS:** Percussionist "Hazel Flagg" Broadway Show; mem Free & Accepted Masons Prince Hall NY. **HONORS/ACHIEVEMENTS:** First Black Engr employed by RKO General 1962. **MILITARY SERVICE:** AUS WW II sgt 1942-46. **HOME ADDRESS:** 816 New York Ave, 2nd Fl, Brooklyn, NY 11203-2721.

TREADWELL, DAVID MERRILL
Journalist. **PERSONAL:** Born Feb 21, 1940, Dayton, OH; son of Timothy D Treadwell (deceased) and Euretta Moore Boyce (deceased); divorced. **EDUCATION:** Ohio State Univ, BA English 1964, MA Journalism 1974. **CAREER:** US Bureau of Land Mgmt, public relations specialist 1969-70; Ohio State Univ, asst dir intl programs 1970-73; Associated Press, reporter 1974-80; Los Angeles Times, Washington correspondent 1980-85, Atlanta bureau chief, New York Bureau correspondent 1989-. **ORGANIZATIONS:** Mem Kappa Alpha Psi. **HONORS/ACHIEVEMENTS:** Sloan Found Fellowship in Economics Journalism Princeton Univ 1979-80. **MILITARY SERVICE:** USN lt 1964-69. **BUSINESS ADDRESS:** Correspondent, Los Angeles Times-New York Bureau, 780 3rd Ave, Suite 3801, New York, NY 10017.

TREADWELL, FAY RENE LAVERN
Music manager. **PERSONAL:** Born May 09, 1935, Okolona, AR; widowed; children: Tina. **EDUCATION:** AR Baptist Coll, AA; LA St Coll. **CAREER:** Drifters Inc, pres singing group which performs all over the world. **ORGANIZATIONS:** Life mem, NAACP; mem Personal Mgrs United Kingdom. **BUSINESS ADDRESS:** 161 W 54th St, New York, NY 10019.

TREES, CANDICE D.
Government official. **PERSONAL:** Born Jul 18, 1953, Springfield, IL; daughter of Clarence L Senor and Peggie D Neal Senor; married John F Trees; children: Peggi, Jessi, Johanna. **EDUCATION:** Sangamon State Univ, BA 1981. **CAREER:** Town & Country Bank, teller 1976-77; State of IL Office of Gov, exec correspondent 1977-79; City of Springfield, city clerk 1979-86; Circuit Court of Sangamon County, clerk 1986-. **ORGANIZATIONS:** Mem United Way of Sangamon County 1980-, Jr League of Springfield 1984-; program vice pres Springfield Area Arts Council 1984-; treas Municipal Clerks of IL 1984-86; vice pres Lincolnfest Inc 1984-; mem Springfield Area Labor Mgmt Comm 1984-; admin vice pres Springfield Area Arts Council 1985-; mem Jr League of Springfield 1985-; chmn of the bd HAT Construction 1986-; bd of dirs Kennerer Village Children's Home 1986; sec advisory bd Salvation Army 1987-; mem Greater Springfield Chamber of Commerce 1987-88; mem. IL Assn of Court Clerks 1986; bd mem, Mental Health Centers of Central Illinois, 1987; mem, Natl Assn of Court Managers, 1988; mem, Assn of Records Managers and Administration (ARMA) 1989. **HONORS/ACHIEVEMENTS:** Registered Municipal Clerk 1981; Plaque for Outstanding Serv Springfield Urban League 1985; Certified Municipal Clerk 1986; Certificate of Appreciation US Air Force 1986; State Co-chring 50th Anniversary, March of Dimes, Central Illinois Chapter 1988; Plaque for Service as President, Lincolnfest 1988. **BUSINESS ADDRESS:** Clerk of the Circuit Court, Sangamon County, County Bldg Room 412, Springfield, IL 62701.

TRENT, JAMES E.
Educational consultant. **PERSONAL:** Born Jan 14, 1936, Uniontown, PA; married Rosalie Mahaley; children: Jamie, Kelly, Jill. **EDUCATION:** Wayne State Univ, BS Bus Ad 1957; Univ Detroit, MBA 1965. **CAREER:** Chrysler Realty, vice pres comm opers 1970-79; City of Detroit Mayor's Office, exec asst productivity 1979-80; Chrysler Learning, vice pres govt training 1980-86; Chrysler Motors, educ consultant 1986-. **ORGANIZATIONS:** Polemarch Kappa Alpha Psi Detroit Alumni 1977-83; dir/secty Metro Detroit Youth Foundation 1978-; pres Detroit Assn of Black Organ 1985-; pres Detroit Black Inter-Greek Council 1985-; dir Univ of Detroit Black Alumni 1986-. **HONORS/ACHIEVEMENTS:** Roy Wilkins Awd Detroit Assn Black Organ 1985. **MILITARY SERVICE:** AUS sgt e-5 1959-60. **HOME ADDRESS:** 5366 Briarcliff Knoll, West Bloomfield, MI 48322. **BUSINESS ADDRESS:** Educ Consultant, UAW-Chrysler National Training Center, 2211 E Jefferson, Detroit, MI 48207.

TRENT, JAY LESTER
Manager. **PERSONAL:** Born Jan 27, 1940, Uniontown, PA; married Alma Dorothea Brown; children: Vincent S. **EDUCATION:** Electronic Computer Prgmng Inst, attnded 1966; Wayne St U, BS 1977; Univ of MI, public utilities exec progrm 1980; MI St Univ, MBA 1985. **CAREER:** MI Bell Telephone Co, analyst comp progmmng 1966-68, syst analyst comp progmmng 1968-70, sr syst analyst syst design 1970-74, staff supr person assessment 1974-76, dist data syst mgr 1976-. **ORGANIZATIONS:** Mem fund raiserUniv of Detroit Titan Club 1976-78;bud consult Jr Achvmnt 1978-; Governor's Exec Corps 1985-86; MSU advanced mngmnt program, MBT minority advisory panel, NAACP, Detroit Friends of Morehouse College. **MILITARY SERVICE:** AUS specialist 5th 1962-65. **BUSINESS ADDRESS:** District Manager, Michigan Bell Telephone Co, 23500 Northwestern Highway, Southfield, MI 48075.

TRENT, RICHARD DARRELL
Educational administrator. **PERSONAL:** Born Nov 23, 1925, Detroit, MI; married Cynthia Ganger; children: Giselle, Stephen, Bradley. **EDUCATION:** MI StUniv E Lansing, AB Psychology 1950; Tchrs Coll ColumbiaUniv NY, MA Devel Psychology 1951; Tchrs Coll ColumbiaUniv NY, EdD Social Psychololgy 1953;K. **CAREER:** Medgar Evers Coll of City Univ of NY, pres 1970-; Brooklyn Coll of City Univ of NY, assoc prof dept of educ 1965-69; Natl Inst of Health & Med Research Ghana Academy of Sci Accra Ghana, research off 1965-69; Puerto Rico Inst of Psychiatry Bayamon Puerto Rico, dir of research 1957-61; NY State Training School for Boys Warwick NY, staff psychologist 1954-57; City Coll of City Univ of NY, lect in educ psychology 1952-54; Youth House NY, boys supr 1950-52. **ORGANIZATIONS:** Bd of dir NY Urban Leag 1969-71; appointed educ chmn Brooklyn Bicentennial Commn 1974; bd of dir Brooklyn Rotary Club 1975; mem Nat Assn for Equal Opportunity in Higher Educ Wash DC 1976; mem exec com Coll Pub Agency Counc of US Civil Serv Commn 1977; mem Research Found Exec Com CityUniv of NY 1978; bd of dir Counc for Higher Educ Inst of NY 1978; mem Com on Research & Liaison of Am Assn fo St Coll &Univ 1979; appointed master Fed Ct for Educ Issues So Dist US Fed Ct 1969; mgr ed "Afro-Am Studies" 1969-74; asso Danforth Found Asso Prog 1969-70; external examiner in psychologyUniv of Lagos Lagos Nigeria 1973, 74, 80. **HONORS/ACHIEVEMENTS:** Mem blue key scholastic hon soc MI StUniv 1949; man of yr Brooklyn Club of Nat Assn of Bus & Professional Women's Club 1972; educ awd Intl Inc Brooklyn NY 1973; cit for outstnd educ & civic contrbns Pres of Borough of Brooklyn 1973; awd for outsnd conrbrns Nat Conf of Christ & Jews 1974; Who's Who in Am 1976; The Reciprocal Impacl of the Brown Decision of Higher Edn; The Plignt of the Urban Coll & Minority Students; A Study of Pictorial Porj AmongGhanians; A Study of Self-Concepts of Ghanian Children; The Sibling Rel in Group Psychotherapy for Puerto Rican Schizophrenics; Three Basic Themes in Mexican & Puerto Rican Family Values; The Expressed Values fo Inst Delinqueng Boys; The color of the Investigator as a Vriable in Exptl Research with Negro Subject; num others pubs. **MILITARY SERVICE:** AUS 1st lt 1944-47. **BUSINESS ADDRESS:** University of NY, 1150 Carroll St, Brooklyn, NY 11225.

TRENT, WILLIAM JOHNSON, JR.
Consultant. **PERSONAL:** Born Mar 08, 1910, Ashville, NC; son of William J Trent and Maggie Tate; married Viola Scales; children: Mrs Kay Holloway, Ms Judy Scales-Trent, Mrs Toni Parker. **EDUCATION:** Livingstone Clg, BA 1930; Wharton SchUniv PA, MBA

1932;Univ PA, Further Study 1937;Univ Chicago, Further Study Toward PhD. **CAREER:** Livingstone Clg, tchr 1932-34; Bennett Clg, tchr 1934-38; Dept of Interior, adv negro afrs 1936-39; Fed Works Agcy, rale rels ofcr 1939-44; United Negro Clg Fund, exec dir 1944-64; Time Inc, asst prsnl dir 1964-75; Bennett Clg, cnsltnt 1975-79. **ORGANIZATIONS:** Bd mem Buago St Lukes Hosp NY 1950-70; ofcr Natl Urban League 1965-75; mem Selections Bd Dept of State 1960; mem Bopro Whitney Young Found; mem bdNatl Found Imprvmnt Ed 1976-77. **HONORS/ACHIEVEMENTS:** Am delegate Indpdnc Celebration Upr Vulta Afrid; mem State Dept Evaluatn Tm Am Embassy Tokyo Japan; 5 honry doctorates. **BUSINESS ADDRESS:** Staff Consultant, Bennett Coll, Greensboro, NC 27420.

TRESCOTT, JACQUELINE ELAINE
Journalist. **PERSONAL:** Born Jan 02, 1947, Jersey City, NJ; married Edward M Darden; children: Douglass. **EDUCATION:** St Bonaventure Univ, BS 1968. **CAREER:** The Washington Star, reporter 1970-75; The Washington Post, reporter 1975-. **ORGANIZATIONS:** Mem Natl Assoc of Black Journalists; faculty Summer Program for Minority Journalists 1978-. **BUSINESS ADDRESS:** Reporter, Washington Post, 1150 15th St NW, Washington, DC 20071.

TRESVANT, JOHN BERNARD (TRES)
Professional athlete, communications consultant. **PERSONAL:** Born Nov 06, 1939, Washington, DC; married Ginny Ann Billington; children: Raquel, Sean Christopher, Kendra Ann. **EDUCATION:** Seattle U, BA 1965;Univ of Wash, MA. **CAREER:** Gen Tel & Electronics, sr communications 1977-; Shoreline Comm Coll, basketball coach 1977-78; Nat Basketball Assn, professional basketball player 1965-74. **ORGANIZATIONS:** Basketball coack Kirkland Boys & Girls Club 1978-80; basketball coack PAC Asian Basketball Leag Women 1980. **HONORS/ACHIEVEMENTS:** Names most valuable player basketball jr & sr SeattleUniv 1963-64; outstnd athlete pro basketball Epicureans Inc 1971; oustnd youth promotion Tri-State Assn of Elks 1971. **MILITARY SERVICE:** USAF airman 1st class 1958-60. **BUSINESS ADDRESS:** Gen Telephone & Electronics, 520 Bldg, Bellevue, WA 98004.

TRIBBLE, HUERTA CASSIUS
Government official. **PERSONAL:** Born Sep 15, 1939, Terre Haute, IN; children: Huerta Lee, Steven Harold, Kevin Eugene. **EDUCATION:** IN State U, AB 1961. **CAREER:** PR Mallory, pr ma eng 1966-69; Indpl Urban League Inc, proj dir asst dist 1969-81; US Small Bus Admn, dir 1983-. **ORGANIZATIONS:** Mem IN Mnrty Splr Dev Cncl 1983-85; trst Martin Cntr Clg 1984-85; crdntr IN Mnrty Bus Oprtnty Cncl 1983-85. **HOME ADDRESS:** 3710 N Meridian St #606, #606, Indianapolis, IN 46208.

TRICE, JESSIE COLLINS
Health care professional. **PERSONAL:** Born Dec 26, 1929, Baxley, GA; daughter of Herbert Collins and Hattie Eunice Peterkin Collins; widowed; children: Bradford, Valencia Batiste. **EDUCATION:** Grady Memorial Hosp, RN diploma 1950; Univ of MI, Certificate 1960, M Public Health Admin 1975; Univ of Miami, B Public Health Nursing 1965. **CAREER:** Dade Co Dept Public Health, public health nurse 1961-67; Dade Co Dept Public Health Children/Youth Project, asst county nursing dir 1967-70; Dade Co Dept Public Health, public health nurse supervisor II 1970-74, chief nursing serv 1975-80; Vstg Nurses Assoc Inc, exec dir 1975-78; Family Health Ctr Inc,chief exec officer 1980-. **ORGANIZATIONS:** Mem NAACP 1972-; chairperson FL Public Health Assoc 1978-79; pres FL Council Primary Care Ctrs 1984-85; pres Southeast Hlth Care Consortium 1985-86; chairperson FL State Bd of Nursing 1985-; bd of dirs Urban League of Greater Miami 1985-; mem Forum Minority Professional Assoc; mem/founder Black Nurses Assoc; sec Fla Assn of Community Health Centers, Inc. 1988-89; chairperson, screening committee Natl Association of Community Health Center, Inc. 1987-89. **HONORS/ACHIEVEMENTS:** Who's Who in Amer Women 1978; Florida Nurse of the Year FL Nurses Assoc 1984. **BUSINESS ADDRESS:** Chief Executive Officer, Family Health Center Inc, 5361 NW 22nd Ave, Miami, FL 33142.

TRICE, JUNIPER YATES
Educator, clergyman. **PERSONAL:** Born Aug 10, 1921, Verona, MS; married Detris Delois Scales; children: Juniper Olyen, Harriman Robert. **EDUCATION:** AB 1942; BTh 1950; DD 1958; MEd 1961; spl degree in adminstrn 1972. **CAREER:** Hall's Chapel New Albany MS, pastor City Rd Corinth MS; Naylor Chapel Pontotoc MS; Aberdeen Dist, presided; Jennings Temple Greenwood MS, Pastor; The Greenwood Dist, presided; Booneville Sch, prin; Carter HS Tishomingo MS; E HS Fulton MS; W Bolivar HS Rosedale MS; Rosedale MS Sch, asst supt; City of Rosedale, mayor. **ORGANIZATIONS:** Mem Selective Serv Bd Bolivar Co; mem City Coun; mem bd dir S Delta Plng & Devel Dist Inc; mem exec bd Delta Area Coun BSA; mem bd trst MS Indsl Coll; presiding elder Christ Meth Epis Ch; mem Hwy Com Delta Coun; mem MS Tchr Assn; Nat Educ Assn; 32 degree Mason; sec MS Educ FinCommin; mem So Regl Educ Bd; mem MS Adult Educ Assn; exec dir Bolivar Cncl on Aging; bd of dir First Ntl Bank of Rosedale; bd of trustees BolivarCty HOsp; mem MS Employment Security Cncl. **HONORS/ACHIEVEMENTS:** Listed in Outstnd Person of The S 1971; Leader of Am Sec Educ 1972; BSA awd for outstnd serv 1970; silv beaver awd Ousts Serv Yht of the Delta 1977. **HOME ADDRESS:** PO Box 819, Rosedale, MS 38769.

TRICE, LUTHER WILLIAM
Retired business executive. **PERSONAL:** Born Nov 05, 1910, Columbus, GA; son of Andrew J Trice and Martha Perice Trice; married Juanita Brooks, Sep 16, 1944; children: Jeanette, Jacqueline. **EDUCATION:** Wilberforce Univ, BE. **CAREER:** W Trice Inc; Painting Contractors Am, secr 1965-67; Painting Contractors of Am, pres 1967-73. **ORGANIZATIONS:** Warren City Plng Comm; trst Sec Bapt Ch Warren; asst dir Rep Sec Dist; active NAACP; Masons; bd mem, Warren Trumbull Community Service Agency, five years. **MILITARY SERVICE:** US Army Eng chaplin's asst 1943-44.

TRICE, WILLIAM B.
Dentist. **PERSONAL:** Born Jan 28, 1924, Newton, GA; married Mildred Moore; children: Sheila T Bell, Angela M. **EDUCATION:** Univ Pittsburgh, BS 1951; DMD 1953. **CAREER:** Private practice, dentist; Hamot Hospital, staff; Erie Univ Pittsburgh School of Dentistry, coord continuing educ; Univ of Pittsburgh School of Dental Med, lectr. **ORGANIZATIONS:** Mem Amer & Natl Dental Assns; Pierre Fauchard Acad; Federation Dentaire Internationale; Intl Assn for Dental Research; Amer Assn for Dental Research; Acad Gen Dentistry; Amer Acad Dental Electrosurgery; Alpha Phi Alpha; Rotary; pres Am Heart Assn; Knights Columbus; trustee Stoneleigh-Burnham School Fellow Amer Coll Dentists; Intl Dental Assn. **MILITARY SERVICE:** USN 1946. **BUSINESS ADDRESS:** 275 Professional Blvd, Erie, PA 16501.

TRIM, JOHN H.
Educator. **PERSONAL:** Born Apr 19, 1931, Ft Worth, TX; married Earnestine Trim. **EDUCATION:** Bishop Col, BA Social Sci; Prairie View A&M U, cert vocational indust ed. **CAREER:** US Air Force, 1953-57; Neiman Marcus, 1957-64; Franklin D Roosevelt HS Dallas TX, cvae coord instr mstr lvl 1964-. **ORGANIZATIONS:** Mem Prof Tchr Org; vice pres Assn Adv Artists & Writers; Human Interest Colum Post Tribune News 1970-; columinst Porters/Quall Ecumenical News 1975; mem deacon trst Morning Star Bapt Ch; Org orginal Dalworth Ldrshp Coun Grand Prairie TX; dir comm youth mural comm cntr. **HONORS/ACHIEVEMENTS:** Wrote book of poetry on life; fine arts shows; Airman of Mo 1954; cit of Mo KNOX 1954; Serv Awd 1969; Youth Awd 1973. **MILITARY SERVICE:** USAF 1953-57.

TRIMBLE, STEVE CALVIN
Professional athlete. **PERSONAL:** Born May 11, 1958, Cumberland, MD. **EDUCATION:** Maryland, Criminology Degree. **CAREER:** Denver Broncos, 1981-; Denver Gold, free safety 1983-. **ORGANIZATIONS:** Worked as a counselor with children in the off-season in Denver. **HONORS/ACHIEVEMENTS:** Competed in 1978 Sun Bowl & 1980 Tangerine Bowl.

TRIMIAR, J. SINCLAIR
Dentist, educator. **PERSONAL:** Born Dec 17, 1933, Lynchburg, VA; married Anna H; children: Stefanie, Jay. **EDUCATION:** Howard U, BS 1960; Howard U, DDS 1964; NY U, post grad oral surgery cerpt 1968. **CAREER:** Harlem Hosp Cntr, oral surgery intern 1964-65; Harlem Hosp Cntr, anethesia res 1965-67; Harlem Hosp Cntr, oral surgery res 1968-69; Harlem HospCntr Respiratory Therapy Serv, chief 1969; Ambulatory Anethesia Harlem Hosp Cntr, chf 1970; Infections Com Harlem Hosp Cntr, co-chmn 1971-74; Harlem Hosp Sch of Respiratory Therapy, dir 1974; Harlem Hosp Cntr Dept of Oral Surgery, asst vis att; Columbia Univ Coll of Physicians & Surgeons, asst prof of clinical anesthesiology. **ORGANIZATIONS:** Past pres Harlem Dental Soc of Grtr NY; past pres Harlem Hosp Soc of Oral Surgeons; mem Am Dental Assn; Nat Dental Assn; First Dist Dental Soc; NY St Soc of Oral Surgeons; Am Assn for Respiratory Therapy; Am Soc of Oral Surgeons; Am Soc of Dental Anesthesiology; 1st vice pres Black Caucus of Harlem Hlth Workers; One Hundred Black Men Inc; mem Omega Psi Phi Frat. **MILITARY SERVICE:** USAF 1952-56. **BUSINESS ADDRESS:** Asst Clinical Professor, Columbia University, 116th St & Broadway, New York, NY 10037.

TRIPP, LUKE SAMUEL
Educator. **PERSONAL:** Born Feb 06, 1941, Atoka, TN. **EDUCATION:** Wayne State Univ, BS 1966; Univ of MI, MA 1974, PhD 1980. **CAREER:** Community Skills Ctr, math/sci teacher 1972-73; Univ of MI, grad rsch dir 1977-80; Univ of IL, asst prof 1981-82; Southern IL Univ, asst prof 1982-. **ORGANIZATIONS:** Co-founder League of Revolutionary Black Workers 1969; dir political educ Natl Black Independent Political Party 1980-81; mem Natl Council for Black Studies 1983, IL Council for Black Studies 1983, Soc of Ethnic and Special Studies 1983; coord Southern IL Anti-Apartheid Alliance 1985-. **HONORS/ACHIEVEMENTS:** Faculty Service Awd Black Affairs Council 1983; Outstanding Contribution African Students Assn 1985; Outstanding Faculty Awd Black Affairs Council 1985; Outstanding Leadership Carbondale Black Coalition 1986; published article, Community Leadership and Black Former Student Activists of the 1960's, The Western Journal of Black Studies, 1986; published book, Black Student Activists, University Press of America, 1987; plaque, "In Appreciation for Continuing the Struggle for Excellence," African-American Student Assn 1989; plaque, Upliftment of the Human Spirit, The Muslim Community of Southern Illinois, 1989.

TRIVES, NATHANIEL
State commissioner, educator. **PERSONAL:** Born Dec 09, 1934, Birmingham, AL; married Ida. **EDUCATION:** Santa Monica State Coll, AA; CA State Univ at LA, BS; Univ of CA, MS. **CAREER:** San Fran Police Dept Consent Decree, No Dist Fed Ct, auditor monitor 1979-; CA Commn on Peace Ofcr Stndrds & Tng, chpn; Santa Monica CA, mayor 1975-77; Dept of Criminal Justice CA StUniv at LA, prof; N Dist Fed Ct Overseeing Integratn of San Fran Police Dept, working with; Santa Monica CA, mayor pro-tem 1971-73, councmn 1971-73; Dept of Adminstrn of Justice Santa Monica Coll, part-time faculty mem; Santa Monica Police Dept, sgt 1958-69. **ORGANIZATIONS:** Chmn Dept of Instrnl Affairs Com CA St U; affirmative action coordUniv of CA at LA 1973-75; chmn Hon Convoctn & Commencmnt Com 1973-; asso chmn Dept of Police Sci & Adminstrn 1972-73; mem Gen Adv Bd Santa Monica Coll; Pasadena Coll Crimnl Justice Adv Bd 1974; Santa Monica Coll Adminstrn of Justice Adv Bd; chmn Crimnl Justice Adv Transp Tech Task Force Com of SCAG; chmn Leag of CA Cities Crimnl Justice Adv Com; chmn LA Regional Criminal Justice Plng Bd Commn 1976; chmn of Crime Specific Subsyst LA Regnl Crmnl Justice Plng Bd 1975; hon pres Santa Monica Sisters City Assn 1975-77; mem Nat Black Caucas of Local Elected Ofcls; bd dir Santa Monica Chap ARC; bd dir Santa Monica Boys Club; pres trustees Crossroads Sch SantaMonica; chmn Human Serv Policies Commn of SCAG. **BUSINESS ADDRESS:** Santa Monica City Council, 1685 Main St, Santa Monica, CA 90401.

TROTMAN, RICHARD EDWARD
Educator. **PERSONAL:** Born Jun 22, 1942, East Orange, NJ; married Cordell Jones; children: Richard Jr, Raheem. **EDUCATION:** Shaw Univ, BA 1960-64; Kean Coll, MA 1970-71; Rutgers Univ, 1975-78. **CAREER:** NJ Dept of Educ, supervisor 1973-76; Kean Coll of NJ, assoc dir EOF 1976-79; Bergen Cmmty Coll, dir EOF 1979-82; Somerset Cnty Coll, dir, Spec Educ Services 1982-. **ORGANIZATIONS:** Passaic Cnty Manpwr Prog, Mayors Planning Council - Paterson, NJ 1971-73; mem NJ Assn of Black Educators 1984-86; mem, Advisory Board, Central New Jersey Colleges, LD programs, 1989; Reach Program Advisory Board, New Jersey Social Service, 1989. **HONORS/ACHIEVEMENTS:** Mem NAACP 1985-86, Natl Urban League 1985-86, NJ Educational Opportunity Funding Directors 1976-86; workshops relating to multi-cultural aspects of learning styles 1988-89. **BUSINESS ADDRESS:** Dir Special Ed Services, Somerset County College, PO Box 3300, Somerville, NJ 08876.

TROTTER, ANDREW LEON
Government. **PERSONAL:** Born Sep 07, 1949, San Antonio, TX. **EDUCATION:** New

Mexico State Univ, BA 1972. **CAREER:** Human Services Dept, caseworker 1972-79, supervisor 1979-. **ORGANIZATIONS:** Sec Mt Olive Bapt State Con Laymen Aux 1974-; christian educ dir BSBC 1983-; treas New Hope Bapt Dist Laymen's Assoc 1985-; treas Human ServicesConsortium; mem Amer Public Welfare Assoc; musician BSBC Mt Olive Baptist State Congress; mem El Paso Chap Gospel Music Workshop of Amer. **HONORS/ACHIEVEMENTS:** Certificate of Achievement State of New Mexico 1982; Advanced Certificate Natl Congress of Christ Educ NBC USA Inc 1983. **HOME ADDRESS:** 1440 North Paxton, Las Cruces, NM 88001. **BUSINESS ADDRESS:** Eligibility Worker Supv II, Human Services Department, PO Box 1959, Las Cruces, NM 88004.

TROTTER, DECATUR WAYNE
Senator. **PERSONAL:** Born Jan 08, 1932, Washington, DC; son of Decatur Trotter and Bernice Trotter; married LaGreta Trotter; children: Denise Glynn, Kathi Rieves. **EDUCATION:** VA State Univ, BS 1956. **CAREER:** Town of Glenarden, mayor 1970-74; MD House of Delegates, delegate 1975-79; Prince George's Co Orphan's Court, judge 1982-83; MD State Senate, senator 1983-. **ORGANIZATIONS:** Mem Kappa Alpha Psi Frat; residential prog super Bureau of Rehabilitation. **HONORS/ACHIEVEMENTS:** Outstand Comm Serv Awd Combined Comm in Action 1981; Legislator of the Year Prince George's Chap of the MD Municipal League 1983; Distinguished Serv Awd MD Municipal League 1983; Outstanding Govt Achievement Kappa Alpha Psi Frat 1984; Distinguished Alumnus National Association for Equal Opportunity in Higher Education (NAFEO) 1989. **BUSINESS ADDRESS:** Senator Dist 24, Maryland Senate, 313 James Senate Office Bldg, Annapolis, MD 21401.

TROTTMAN, ALPHONSO
Orthodontist. **PERSONAL:** Born Jun 15, 1936, St Louis, MO; married LeGrande; children: Yolanda, Gerald, Melanie. **EDUCATION:** IN U, 1954-57; INUniv Sch Dentistry, 1957-61; St Louis U, DDS 1966-68. **CAREER:** Orthodontist, pvt prac 1968-77; So ILUniv Sch, asst clncl prof ortho 1973-77; Yeatman Hlth Ctr, dental dir 1969-76; St LouisUniv Sch Dentstry, clncl instr 1967-70; Gen Prac, 1964-66. **ORGANIZATIONS:** Consult Human Devel Corp; Headstart Dental Prgm; St Louis Comprehnsv Hlth Ctr Dentl Dept; mem Am Dentl Assn 1961-74; Am Assn Orthod 1969-77; Mound City Dentl Soc 1969-77, treas 1970-72; bd dir Annie Malone Chldrns Home 1968-70; St Louis Family Plng Counc 1977-. **HONORS/ACHIEVEMENTS:** 1st black MS degree in Orthod St Louis U; 1st black Spec Bd & License Orthod MO; publ "Incidence of Malocclusion in Black Chldrn" MO Dentl Jour. **MILITARY SERVICE:** USAF capt 1961-64. **BUSINESS ADDRESS:** 7165 Delmar, St Louis, MO 63130.

TROTTMAN, CHARLES HENRY
Educator, historian, scientist. **PERSONAL:** Born Jul 29, 1934, Pine Bluff, AR; married Evelyn Marie Royal; children: Rodney, Jeniffer, Phyliss, Calliette, Charlette. **EDUCATION:** AR AM&N Coll, BS 1957; Syracuse U, MS 1961;Univ of WI, PhD 1972; Tuskegee Inst, 1959-61;Univ of NC, 1969. **CAREER:** Jackson St Univ, assoc prof chem 1972-; Coleman HS, instr 1957-59; So Univ, asst prof chem 1961-67; AR AM & N Coll, asso prof chem 1967-69; Univ of WI, research asst 1969-72. **ORGANIZATIONS:** Consult Argonne Nat Lab 1974-76; dir Nat Sci Found 1977-78; mem Sigma Xi; Am Chem Soc; MS Acad of Sci; Hist of Sci Soc; MS Assn of Edutrs; AmAssn for Adv of Sci; NAACP; AAUP; Omega Psi Phi Frat; Nat Orgn for Prof Adv of Black Chem & Chem Eng; mem Nat Inst of Sci. **HONORS/ACHIEVEMENTS:** Acad yr fllwshp Nat Sci Found 1960-61; Ford Found Fellow 1969-70; Sthrn Fllwshp Grant 1970-72; Nat Urban Leag Fellow 1974; Outst Edutrs of Am 1974; mem Fac Sen Jackson StUniv 1974-76; Outst Chem & Chem Eng 1976. **MILITARY SERVICE:** AUS 1953-55. **BUSINESS ADDRESS:** Dept of Chem, Jackson State Univ, Jackson, MS.

TROUP, ELLIOTT VANBRUGH
Ophthalmologist. **PERSONAL:** Born Feb 28, 1938, Brunswick, GA; married Linda; children: Elliott Jr, Traci, Patrick. **EDUCATION:** Fisk U, BA 1959; Meharry Med Coll, MD 1963;Univ MN, resd ophthal 1969. **CAREER:** Ophthalmlgst, pvt prac. **ORGANIZATIONS:** Mem Acad Ophthal & Otolaryn; pres St Paul Ophthal Soc 1977-78; mem Nat Med Assn; AMA; med & couns Med Prod Div 3m Co; mem Alpha Phi AlphaFrat. **HONORS/ACHIEVEMENTS:** Cert Am Bd Ophthal 1971. **MILITARY SERVICE:** USAF capt 1964-66. **BUSINESS ADDRESS:** 2233 Hamline Ave N, St Paul, MN 55113.

TROUPE, CHARLES QUINCY
Elected official. **PERSONAL:** Born May 12, 1936, St Louis, MO. **EDUCATION:** Attended, Washington Tech Sch, Hadley Tech Sch, Natl Inst of Electronics and Tech, Denver Univ. **CAREER:** Democratic First Ward St Louis, committeeman; Amalgamated Transit Union, vice pres; MO House of Representatives, state rep elected in 1978 re-elected in 1980,82,84,86. **ORGANIZATIONS:** Mem Prince Hall Mason Albert Holman Lodge 179, Eureka Consistory No 19 32 Degree, United Grand Commandery Knights Templar F and AM PHA, Medinah Temple No 39Shriner AEAONMS Inc; chmn Bi-State Comm on Racial Equality, 5th Senatorial Dist; mem League of Women Voters, Concerned Parents of North St Louis, Black Survival Inc, Minority Contractors Assoc, Coalition for the Environment; mem bd of dirs Broadcast Coalition, Early Child Care Corp, FREEDOM St Louis Inc,United Black Comm Fund, Citizens Comm to Save North St Louis; mem Action Against Apathy, CDA Housing Task Force; Democratic Committeeman First Ward; actively working with Black Survival Inc. **HONORS/ACHIEVEMENTS:** MO State Employes Awd for Exceptional Serv 1980; Optimists' Comm Serv Awd 1980; Comm Serv Awd Natl Alliance of Postal and Fed Employees 1981; Comm Serv Awd St Louis Ethical Police Assoc 1981; Child Care Awd Early Child Care Develop Corp 1981; Comm Serv Awd Sigma Gamma Rho Inc 1981; Humanitarian Awd Wellston Sch Dist 1982; Outstanding and Dedicated Serv Awd Wellston Sch Dist 1983; Outstanding Ded & Leadershp Black Leadership Assoc 1983; Outstanding Serv to the Comm Firefighters Inst of Racial Equality 1984; Comm Serv Awd Assoc Black Collegians 1984; Merit Awd Ded Comm Serv United Black CommFund 1984; Recognition of Housing Rehab First Ward Northside Pres Com Awds 1985; Comm Involvement Awd Natl Black Child Devel Inst St Louis Affiliate 1986; Outstanding Comm Leadership in the Interest of MO's Youth Primary care Cncl of Metro St Louis 1986; MO Perinatal Assoc Awd 1986; Special Serv Awd for Efforts in Reducing Teenage Pregnancy MO Family Plng Assoc 1986. **HOME ADDRESS:** 5338 Claxton, St Louis, MO 63120. **BUSINESS ADDRESS:** State Representative, MO House of Representatives, State Capitol Room 304B, Jefferson City, MO 65101.

TROUPE, MARILYN KAY
Curriculum development specialist. **PERSONAL:** Born Sep 30, 1945, Tulsa, OK; daughter of Ernest Robinson Troupe and Lucille Andre Troupe. **EDUCATION:** Langston Univ, BA 1967; Oklahoma State Univ, MA 1976. **CAREER:** Oklahoma State Univ, history instructor 1981-82; CETA City of Tulsa, summer youth counselor 1980-; Tulsa Public Schools, teacher 1969-81, cosmetology instructor 1982-87. **ORGANIZATIONS:** Treas Catholic Daughters of Amer Tulsa Court 1986-87; mem, Alpha Chi Omega Chap Alpha Kappa Alpha; mem Links Inc, Iota Lambda Sigma, Phi Delta Kappa, Theta Nu Sigma, Phi Alpha Theta, Langston Alumni, NAACP, Natl State Local Business and Professional Women's Club, Natl State Local Beauty Culturists League Inc, Amer and OK Vocational Assn, Voc & Industrial Clubs of Amer; mem, Stillwater Chamber of Commerce 1988-90; regional director, Natl Assn of Minority Political Women 1988-89; program chairperson, charter mem, State and Natl Assn for the Advancement of Black American Vocational Educators; bd mem, Greenwood Heritage Foundation, Tulsa OK. **HONORS/ACHIEVEMENTS:** Woman of the Year North Tulsa Chap Business & Professional Women 1979, Zeta Phi Beta Sor 1985; policy leadership program for the Oklahoma State Dept of Votech 1988-89. **HOME ADDRESS:** PO Box 27583, Tulsa, OK 74149.

TROUPE, QUINCY THOMAS, JR.
Poet and educator. **PERSONAL:** Born Jul 23, 1943, New York, NY; son of Quincy Troupe, Sr and Dorothy Marshall Smith Troupe; married Margaret Porter; children: Antoinette, Tymme, Quincy, Porter. **EDUCATION:** Grambling College (now Grambling State University), BA, 1963; Los Angeles City College, AA, 1967. **CAREER:** Watts Writers Movement, Los Angeles CA, creative writing teacher, 1966-68; Shrewd Magazine, Los Angeles, associate editor, beginning 1968; University of California, Los Angeles, instructor in creative writing and black literature, 1968; Ohio University, Athens, instructor in creative writing and third world literature, 1969-72; Richmond College, Staten Island NY, instructor in third world literature, beginning 1972; Columbia University, New York NY, member of faculty of Graduate Writing Program, 1985—; poet. **ORGANIZATIONS:** Poetry Society of America. **HONORS/ACHIEVEMENTS:** International Institute of Education grant for travel in Africa, 1972; National Endowment for the Arts award in poetry, 1978; grant from New York State Council of the Arts, 1979; American Book Award from Association of American Publishers, 1980, for Snake-back Solos: Selected Poems, 1969-1977, Reed Books, 1978; New York Foundation for the Arts fellowship in poetry, 1987. **HOME ADDRESS:** 1925 Seventh Ave, Apt 7L, New York, NY 10026. **BUSINESS ADDRESS:** Department of Performing and Creative Arts, City University of New York, 130 Stuyvesant Place, Staten Island, NY 10301. *

TROUPE-FRYE, BETTY JEAN
Elected official, nurse. **PERSONAL:** Born Mar 08, 1935, St Louis, MO; daughter of Phillip Jeffery Troupe and Ruth Townsend Troupe; divorced; children: Armont, Mona Long Roberts, Evette Boykins. **EDUCATION:** State Comm Coll, 1974; Tariko Coll, BS management 1988; Webter Univ, MA HRD 1988-91. **CAREER:** Wellston School Board, pres 1981-84; Wellston City Council, councilperson 1982-84. **ORGANIZATIONS:** Nurse Olsten Health Svcs; mem chmn ANSCA 1982-; mem Campaign For Human Dignity 1984; mem St Louis Chapter 46 OES Prince Hall Affiliate; ACORN. **HONORS/ACHIEVEMENTS:** Appreciation Noble 1982; Appreciation Women in Municipal Govt 1983; Appreciation St Louis Head Start 1983; Appreciation Enforcers Amateur Athletic Assn. **HOME ADDRESS:** 6431 Wellsmar, St Louis, MO 63133.

TROUT, NELSON W.
Clergyman, educator. **PERSONAL:** Born Sep 29, 1920, Columbus, OH; married Jennie Foster; children: Cassandra Ellis, Paula Crosby, Philip. **EDUCATION:** Capital U, AB 1948; Evang Theol Sem, 1952; Wartburg Coll, DD 1970. **CAREER:** Minority Minstry Stud Trinity Luth Sem, dir 1970-; Am Luth Ch, dir of urban evang 1968-70; Am Luth Ch, asso yth dir 1962-67; Eau Claire WI, pastor 1967-68; Los Angeles, pastor 1955-62; Montgomery, AL, pastor 1952-55. **ORGANIZATIONS:** Exec dir Luth Soc Serv Dayton OH 1970-75; pres Twin Cities Human Relat Assn 1962-67; vice pres Luth Human Relat Assn of Am 1969-70; pres Luth Human Relat 1971-72. **HONORS/ACHIEVEMENTS:** Citatn for outst work Commn on Evang ALC 1970; citatn for outst work Bd for World Missin & Inter-Ch Cooprtn ALC 1976; recip Purple Heart AUS. **MILITARY SERVICE:** AUS capt 21 yrs. **BUSINESS ADDRESS:** 2199 E Main St, Columbus, OH 43209.

TROUTMAN, PORTER LEE, JR.
Educator. **PERSONAL:** Born Apr 04, 1943, Newellton, LA; married Bobbie Jean Martin; children: Gregory, Portia. **EDUCATION:** Univ NV, Ed Spec Degree; N AZ 19, MA; SUniv Baton Rouge LA, BS; No AZ U, EdD 1977. **CAREER:** Rec Center, dir 1965-66; SELD Program Title I, curr spec 1968; Clark Co School Dist, teacher 1966-71; Clark Co Teacher Assn, staff rep 1970-71; Dis Office of Professional Studies Univ of NV Las Vegas, prof 1974; Teacher Corps Univ NV, lecturer, assoc dir 1971-74; Teacher Corps Univ NV, asst prof, dir 1974-75. **ORGANIZATIONS:** Mem CCSD Task Force; Acting Pring; mem Clark Co Tchr Assn; Clark Co Sch Dist Adv Facilities Com; chrm Jo Mackey Elem Sch Adv Brd; Clark Co Tchr Assn; mem Human Relations Com; Alternate Sen Jo Mackey Elem Sch; mem NV State Ed Resolution Com; Adv Student Nat Ed Assn UNLV; delegate Nat Ed Assn Detroit delegate First Nat Cong Black Prof Higher EdUniv TX; mem Nat Educ Assn; Knights Columbus; mem American Assn Sch Adm; American Assn Col Tchr Ed selected by AACTE Com on Perf Based Edn; one of twelve natl to receive training in C/PBE 1974; mem Kappa Delta Pi; Phi Delta Kappa Hon Soc in Edn. **MILITARY SERVICE:** ROTC Southern U. **BUSINESS ADDRESS:** Office of Professional Studies, Univ of Nevada at Las Vegas, 4505 S Maryland Parkway, Las Vegas, NV 89154.

TRUITTE, JAMES F.
Educator. **PERSONAL:** Born in Chicago. **EDUCATION:** Horton Sch, 1948. **CAREER:** Univ Cincnnt CCM Dance Div, asso prof of dance 1973-, lectr modern dance 1970-73; Yale U, fellow lectr 1972; Boston Coll Black Stud Prgm, 1969-70; Australia Counc on Arts, 1969; Brklyn Coll, 1968-70; NY Theatre Arts Prgm; Marjorie Mazia Sch of Dance; Mary Anthony Studio of Dance; New Dance Group; Clark Ctr, 1960; Alvin Ailey Am Dance Theatr, prin dancer, asso artistic dir 1960-68; Performed In, shows, motion pics, TV, nght clbs, concrts with companies;Choreography For, motion Pics, modern dance co, ballet co. **ORGANIZATIONS:** Recip John Hay Whitney Comm Fllwshp 1959; Warner Bros asked him to stage authentic African ritual num for film The Sins of Rachel Cade; work in Labanotation will be utilized in context with prep of a vol on Horton Techniques. **BUSINESS ADDRESS:** Dance Div Coll Conservatory of, U of Cincinnati, Cincinnati, OH 45221.

TRUMBO, GEORGE WILLIAM
Judge. **PERSONAL:** Born Sep 24, 1926, Newark, OH; son of George Frank Trumbo and Beatrice Trumbo; married Sara J Harper; children: Constance, James, Kimberlee, Karen, Adam. **EDUCATION:** OH State Univ, BS; Case Western Reserve Law School, LLB. **CAREER:** Court of Common Pleas, referee 1977-82; Cleveland Municipal Court, judge 1982-. **ORGANIZATIONS:** Mem Mt Olive Baptist Church; past sunday school teacher; past dir Jr Church of Mt Olive Baptist Church; mem Natl Bar Assn, Greater Cleveland Bar Assoc, OH Bar Assn, Cuyahoga Cty Bar Assn, Elks Lodge IBPOE of W, Kappa Alpha Psi, NAACP; bd of dir Jucicial Council of the Natl Bar Assn; pres Shaker Square Kiwanis Club; pres trustee bd Cleveland Public Library 1984; chmn Task Force on the House of Corrections; past pres Northern OH Municpal Judges Assn. **HONORS/ACHIEVEMENTS:** Cuyahoga Cty Criminal Court Bar Assn Awd 1973; Superior Judicial Service 1982,84,85. **MILITARY SERVICE:** USN 1944-46. **BUSINESS ADDRESS:** Judge, Cleveland Municipal Court, Justice Center, 1200 Ontario St, Cleveland, OH 44113.

TRYMAN, MFANYA DONALD
Educational administrator. **PERSONAL:** Born Jan 26, 1948, Montclair, NJ; married Maggie M McKinney; children: Cedric, Nyerere, Myesha. **EDUCATION:** Pasadena City Coll, AA Liberal Art 1969; CA State Polytechnic Univ, BS Political Science 1971; FL State Univ, MA 1972, MSPA 1974, PhD 1975. **CAREER:** TX Southern Univ, assoc prof 1975-81; Univ of Houston, prof 1981-82; Jackson State Univ, assoc prof 1981-85, dir MPPA program 1981-; Prairie View A&M Univ, assoc prof 1985-. **ORGANIZATIONS:** Mem conf of minority Public Admin 1976-; mem Natl conf of Black Political Scientists 1976-; natl campaign adv St Rep El Franco Lee 1978; bd mem advbd Congressman Mickey Leland 1978-80; voluntary boxing dir Hester House Comm Org 1979; vice pres Demographic Environs Rsch Inc 1980-85; project mgr Comm & Economic Develop Work Study Prog 1983-; dir Master of Public Policy & Admin Prog Jackson State Univ 1983-85; mem Natl Forum of Black Public Admins 1983-85, natl Conf of Black Studies 1985-87. **HONORS/ACHIEVEMENTS:** CA State Polytechnic Univ Magna Cum Laude 1971; Outstanding Black Sr Scholar Awd 1971; Outstanding Educator Legislative Black Caucus of TX Awd 1979; fellowDept of Labor & Howard Univ 1980; Scholar Spotlight on Scholars Awd 1983; Cert of Merit NASA Johnson Space Center 1986; publ of over 40 articles & two books on Black Politics Affirmative Action Public Policy and Econ Devel in professional journals & mags. **HOME ADDRESS:** 14543 Leacrest Dr, Houston, TX 77049. **BUSINESS ADDRESS:** Professor of Political Science, Benjamin Banneker Honors Coll, 14543 Leacrest Dr, Houston, TX 77049.

TUBBS, VINCENT TRENTON
Retired journalist, publicist, business executive. **PERSONAL:** Born Sep 25, 1915, Dallas, TX; divorced; children: Nantille H. **EDUCATION:** Morehouse Coll, AB 1938; Atlanta Univ, 1939; Blackstone Coll of Law, LLB 1949. **CAREER:** Macon Broadcast, ed & pub 1940-41; Norfolk Journal & Guide, news ed 1942-43; Baltimore Afro-Am, war correspondent 1943-47, editor 1947-54; Ebony Mag, assoc ed 1954-55; Jet Mag, managing ed 1955-59; Warner Bros, AIP, Columbia, CBS Cinema Center, Paramount, United Artists, sr publicist 1959-71; Warner Bros, dir comm rel 1971-80; retired journalist, publicist, business exec. **ORGANIZATIONS:** Founder & pres Delta Phi Delta Journalists Soc 1936; founder & pres Windy City Press Club 1956; mem Kappa Alpha Psi; Sigma Delta Chi; Overseas Press Club; Tokyo Corresp Club; Surf Writers of Hawaii; Academy of Motion Picture Arts & Sci; Hollywood Press Club; past pres & treas mem bd Publicists Guild of Am; Local 818 IATSE. **HONORS/ACHIEVEMENTS:** War Dept Citation 1947; Newsman's Newsman Award, Windy City Press Club 1957; Male Decision Maker in Comm Natl Assn of Media Women 1974; Oscar Micheaux Award Black Filmmakers Hall of Fame 1974; Bronze Jubilee Award WXET-TV Atlanta 1980; LA Giants in a Mold Award 1980; pres chmn of bd Black Filmmakers Hall of Fame 1980. **HOME ADDRESS:** 1359 S Masselin Ave, Los Angeles, CA 90019.

TUCKER, ANTHONY
Physician. **PERSONAL:** Born Aug 14, 1957, New York, NY; son of James W Tucker and Georgia O Tucker. **EDUCATION:** Harvard Univ Cambridge MA, AB 1980; Howard Univ Washington DC, MD 1985. **CAREER:** District of Columbia Hospital, physician 1985-86; Flushing Hospital & Medical Center, surgical resident 1986-89. **ORGANIZATIONS:** Mem US Chess Federation 1976-87; alumni interviewer Harvard Alumni Assn 1980-81; mem Student Natl Medical Assn 1980-85, Amer Medical Assn 1984-87, Harvard Club of NY 1980-82, Harvard Club of Washington DC 1983-85, Med Soc of the State of NY 1987-88, Queens County Med Soc 1987-88. **HONORS/ACHIEVEMENTS:** Polaroid Scholarship 1980; Natl Medical Fellowship 1980-81.

TUCKER, BILLY J.
Physician. **PERSONAL:** Born Feb 03, 1934, Magnolia, AR; married Cecelia; children: Karen, Kelly, Kimberly. **EDUCATION:** MI St U, 1953; Wayne St U, 1958;Univ MI Med Sch, 1962. **CAREER:** Norfolk Chesapeake, phys adminstr 1965-; Norfolk Drug Abuse Rehab Prgm, dir 1970-72. **ORGANIZATIONS:** Fdr & 1st pres Tidewater Area Bus Leag 1967-; fdr Atlantic Nat Bank 1968; fdr 1st pres Grtr Norfolk Devel Com 1967; mem Norfolk Med Soc; Old Dominian Med Soc; Nat Med Soc; Chesapeake Med Soc; Am Acad Fam Prac; Tidewater Acad Fam Prac; Cong Black Caucus Braintrust on Hlth; Tdwtr Area Bus& Contrctrs Assn; Norfolk Com for Imprvmnt Edn; Tdwtr Reg Polit Assn. **HONORS/ACHIEVEMENTS:** Serv award Tdwtr Area Bus Leag 1969; outst citz award Norfolk Chap Drifters Inc 1976; outst citz Chesapeake Chap Delicados Inc 1977; for vision & support Tdwtr Area Bus & Cont Assn 1977. **MILITARY SERVICE:** USAF 1953-57. **BUSINESS ADDRESS:** 490 Liberty St, Chesapeake, VA 23324.

TUCKER, C. DELORES
Government official. **PERSONAL:** Born Oct 04, 1927, Philadelphia, PA; daughter of Rev & Mrs Whitfield Nottage; married William. **EDUCATION:** Temple U; PA St U;Univ of PA; N Philadelphia Sch of Realty. **CAREER:** Secretary of State Pennsylvania 1971-77; Commonwealth of PA; Fed of Dem Women, natl pres 1977-; Dem Natl Comm Black Caucus, chmn 1984-; Philadelphia Tribune, vice pres 1989-. **ORGANIZATIONS:** Aff mem Exec Com Commonwlth PA 1971-; chprn Munic Empl Ret Bd 1971-; mem PA Bd of Fin & Rev; commr PA Athl Commn; mem PA Bd of Proprty;mem PA Commn on Interst Coop; mem PA Commn on Wmn 1971-; mem Gov Affirm Act Counc; mem Commnwlth Bd of Med Coll of PA; mem Bd of Martin Luther King Ctr for Soc Chng; natl sec Nat Bd of Dir PUSH; hon mem Bd Dir Hartranft Commun Corp; mem Links Inc; mem-at-large Dem Nat Com; mem PA Fed of Dem Wmn; vice pres Nat Assn of Sec of St; Nat Assn of Real Estate Brokers; Nat Assn of Mkt Devel; bd mem Natl Rainbow Coalition; mem Natl Org of Women; natl vice pres, NAACP Board of Trustees 1989; convening founder & vice chmn, National Political Congress of Black Women. **HONORS/ACHIEVEMENTS:** Named best qual to be Ambass to UN by Nat Women's Pol Caucus & Redbook Mag; recog one of the 100 most influential black Am Ebony Mag 1972-77; nom wmn of yr Ladies Home Jour 1975-76; nom wmn of yr Nat Assn of TV & Radio Artists 1972; commun serv award Quaker City Chap B'nai Birth 1974; Emma V Kelly achvmt award Nat Elks 1971; mkt serv & achvmnt award Nat Assn Real Estate Devel 1971; OIC Achvmnt Award; NAACP Freedom Fund Award 1961; Martin Luther King award Philadelphia Trade Unions Coun; recip of approx 175 Nat State 3 Local Awards; NAACP Thurgood Marshall Awd 1st recipient 1982; The White Noose, Home and Housing Journal; ABC's of Charitable Giving. **BUSINESS ADDRESS:** Chairperson, Dem Natl Comm Black Caucus, 6700 Lincoln Dr, Philadelphia, PA 19119.

TUCKER, CLARENCE T.
Chemical plant manager. **PERSONAL:** Born Feb 22, 1940, Elba, AL; son of Samuel T Tucker and Josephine Tucker; married Delores B Tucker, Nov 28, 1963; children: Reginald, Ryan. **EDUCATION:** Alabama A&M Univ, Huntsville AL, BS; Atlanta Univ, Atlanta GA, MS. **CAREER:** Chattanooga Public Schools, Chattanooga TN, teacher & dept chair, 1962-65, 1966-68; Clark Coll, Atlanta GA, laboratory instructor, 1968-69; Polaroid Corp, Waltam MA, process eng to production mgr, 1969—. **ORGANIZATIONS:** Exec bd chmn, NOBCCUE. **HONORS/ACHIEVEMENTS:** Outstanding Teacher Award, Chatanooga Science Fair Group, 1966; Outstanding Service Award, Atlanta Univ, 1984; Meritorious Service Award, NOBCCUE, 1985. **HOME ADDRESS:** 8 Longmeadow Rd, Westboro, MA 01581.

TUCKER, DONALD
Government official. **PERSONAL:** Born Mar 18, 1938, Newark, NJ; married Ms Cleopatra Gipson; children: Donna Marie, Kiburi. **EDUCATION:** Goddard Coll VT, BA 1973. **CAREER:** Congress Racial Equality, fld orgnzr 1961-63; Operation Ironbound UCC, dir 1965-70; City of Newark, cnclmn at large 1974-. **ORGANIZATIONS:** Vp Natl Blck Ldrshp Roundtable 1981-; chmn NJ Blck Issues Convention 1984-; mem Natl Blck Ldrshp Forum 1981-. **MILITARY SERVICE:** USAF airman frst cls 1955-59. **HOME ADDRESS:** 84 Hansbury Ave, Newark, NJ 07112. **BUSINESS ADDRESS:** Councilman at Large, City of Newark NJ, City Hall Rm 304, 920 Broad St, Newark, NJ 07102.

TUCKER, DOROTHY M.
Educator, psychologist. **PERSONAL:** Born Aug 22, 1942, Spartanburg, SC. **EDUCATION:** CA Sch of Professional Psychol, PhD 1976; OH State Univ, PhD 1972; Bowling Green U, BS; Univ Toledo, MEd. **CAREER:** Wright Inst Los Angeles, dir clncl Tng; (Ca St U, LA, asst prof 1968-69; OH St U, resrch asso 1969-71; Bureau of Drug Abuse, Columbus , consult psychologist 1971; Dept Defense, Spangdahlem, Germany, educator 1965-67; Brentwood Pub Sch & Ford Found, demnstrtn tchr & curriculom writer 1963-65. **ORGANIZATIONS:** Am Personnel & Guidance Assn; Western Psychol Assn; Am Psychol Assn; Assn Black Psychologists; So CA Assn Black Psychologists; Assn Cnslr Educ & Sprvsn; Assn Non-white Concerns; mem adv Cncl women concerns, FL Intl U; Assn of Soc & Behvrl Scientists; Assn Specs Group Work; FL Atlantic & FL IntlUniv Envrnmnt Rsrch Cncl; FL Intl Univ Steering Com for Interama Dade Co Psychol & Assn 1972; bd of dir, S Cntrl Hlth Plnng Cncl; Dade Co Mntl Health Assn, 1972-74; bd dir Cope S Dade Co Pub Schls, 1972-74; Black Educ Assn 1971-74; chrpsn StUniv Faculty Senate FL 1973-74; chrprsn FL Intl Univ Faculty Senate, 1972-74; chrprsn FL Intl Univ Black Concerns Cncl 1973-74; mem Clinical Child Psychology; mem Soc of Pediatric Psychology; mem Nat Inst for Behaviroal Science; mem Nat Women's Studies Assn; CA St Coordng Com for Intl Women's Yr; co-chmn Prog Com; mem exec bd 1977; chmn Conv Blk Women's Network, 1977. **HONORS/ACHIEVEMENTS:** NDEA Fellow, Univ Toledo, 1967-68; Pi Lambda Theta Educ Hon; Outstanding Young Women of Am 1970, 1972; Bowling Green St U, trustee, alumni bd, sec 1970-72; Sec FACES 1973-75; Who's Who in Child Devel 1975-76; ch 30th senatorial Task Force on Alcohol, 1976; ch Ask Force on Sex Role Issues in Agys, Div ofCouns Psychol 1976; Ch, Assn of Minor Schlrs in the Milit, 1976-77; Nat Women's Polit Caucus; mem, Nat Orgn Of women 1975; charter mem, Black's Women's Awd 1977; chmn exec com Forum 1979; commnr, CA Jud Nominees Evaluation Commn 1979; fld dir Cranston For Senate Com, 1980; chmn United Negro College Fund So CA Adv Bd 1980; cmmnr Inglewood Housing Commn 1980; nominee Sojourner Truth Awd 1974; NDEA Fellow,Univ Toledo, 1967-68; Ford Found Resrch Grant Recip 1964-65; Who's Who in the World of Women; who's Who of Am Women. **BUSINESS ADDRESS:** President, Crenshaw Consortium, 3636 S Bronson Ave, Los Angeles, CA 90018.

TUCKER, ERIC M.
Financial manager. **PERSONAL:** Born Dec 22, 1950, Kansas City, MO; son of Shirley A East. **EDUCATION:** Harvard Univ, BA Govt 1978; Northwestern Univ Kellogg Grad Sch of Mgmt, MM Fin 1980; DePaul Univ Grad Sch of Business, M Science Taxation 1990. **CAREER:** First Chicago, investment officer 1980-85; City of Washington DC, treasury expert 1986-87; The Univ of MD, mgr treasury operations. **ORGANIZATIONS:** Pres Professional Financial Mgmt 1981-; bd mem Travellers Aid Soc 1984-86; mem NAACP, Natl Assoc of Black MBA's, Natl Aquarium Soc, Natl Forum of Black Public Administrators. **HONORS/ACHIEVEMENTS:** Johnson & Johnson Leadership Awd; Harvard Club of Kansas City Scholarship; Outstanding Young Man of America. **HOME ADDRESS:** PO Box 60309, Washington, DC 20039-0309.

TUCKER, GERALDINE JENKINS
Director of human resources. **PERSONAL:** Born May 03, 1948, Newark, NJ; daughter of Richard Jenkins and Helen Jenkins; divorced; children: one child. **EDUCATION:** Fisk Univ, BA 1970; Howard Univ, MS 1972; Univ of TX, JD 1986. **CAREER:** Howard Univ WashDC, asst dir of admissions 1970-73; CA Sch of Professional Psych, dean for student affairs 1973-75; Hughes Aircraft Co LA, sr personnel rep 1975-77; ARA Food Servs LA, training mgr 15 states 1977-78; TX Rehab Commn Austin, civil rights specialist 1978-80; NuScope Cons, president 1980-85; Lower CO River Authority, mgr human resources 1986-. **ORGANIZATIONS:** Mem bd of trustees Fisk Univ Nashville 1970-74; columnist Village Newspaper Austin 1970-; western bd of adv United Negro Coll Fund 1975-77; bd of dir Austin Women's Center 1979-; mem Austin Area Urban League; mem Austin NAACP; mem Austin C of C; mem, Austin Children's Museum; pres, Howard Univ Alumni Assn 1989. **HONORS/ACHIEVEMENTS:** Ford Fellowship for Graduate Study Ford Found 1970; Alumni Leadership Award Fisk Univ 1970. **BUSINESS ADDRESS:** Manager, Lower Colorado River Authority, 3001 Lake Austin Blvd, Austin, TX 78704.

TUCKER, HERBERT E., JR.
Retired justice. **PERSONAL:** Born Aug 30, 1915, Boston, MA; son of Herbert E. Tucker, Sr and Ella Tucker; married Mary Hill; children: Gwendolyn, Gretchen. **EDUCATION:** Boston Latin Sch, Grad; Northeastern Sch of Law. **CAREER:** US Treas Dept IRS, dep clctr rvn agt 1943-52; Pvt Prac, 1952-; Cardozo & Tucker, former partner; Chf Finan Div Cmmnwlth MA, asst atty gen 1959-68; MA Dept Pub Utilties, commr 1969-72, chmn 1972-73; Muncpl Ct Dorchester Dist, spl justice 1973-74, prsdng jstc 1974-; Boston Coll, Boston U, Northeastern U, Wellesley Coll, Harvard U, lctr; Union Warren Savs Bank, corprtr 1969; presiding justice Edjartown District Court 1979-85; retired, 1985. **ORGANIZATIONS:** Grand basileus Omega Psi Phi Frat 1955-58; bd tst 1969-, chmn, exec comm, Simmons Coll 1969-; dir Nat Coun Northeastern U; TV Stn WGBH; Howard Benevolent Assn; mem num ofcs coms, num professional civ frat orgns. **HONORS/ACHIEVEMENTS:** Omega man of yr awd Nat 1958, Cleveland Chap 1966; alumnus of yr NortheasternUniv Sch of Law 1971. **HOME ADDRESS:** 66 Gorham Ave, Oak Bluffs, MA 02557.

TUCKER, JAMES F.
Business education. **PERSONAL:** Born Nov 02, 1924, Brooklyn, NY; married Caroline Hamblin; children: Kenneth, Lauren. **EDUCATION:** Howard U, AB 1947, MA1948;Univ of PA, PhD 1957. **CAREER:** Fed Res Bank of Richmond, vice pres 1974-; VA Polytechnic Inst & State U, prof econ dept 1970-74; VA St Coll, pres 1968-70; US Dept of Labor, dir ofoper 1965-68; NC Cntrl U, chmn dept of econs 1962-65; WV St Coll, chmn dept of bus 1956-62. **ORGANIZATIONS:** Pres bd of dir VA Counc for Econ Edn; mem VA St Adv Counc on Vocat Edn; mem liason bd Nat Consumer Econs Proj; mem bd of vis VA Polytechnic Inst & St U; mem bd of trustees Howard U; mem adv bd of dir Richmond Mem Hosp. **HONORS/ACHIEVEMENTS:** Auth Essentials of Econ Prentice-Hall Inc 1975; Current Econ Issues & Prblms Rand McNally 1976; Anathomy of High-Earning Minor Banks, Am Bankers Assn 1978; outst serv award VA Counc on Econ Educ 1978; various articles publ. **MILITARY SERVICE:** AUS pvt 1942-45. **BUSINESS ADDRESS:** 701 E Byrd St, Richmond, VA 23227.

TUCKER, KAREN
Legal editor. **PERSONAL:** Born Jul 18, 1952, Washington, DC; daughter of Willie Tucker Jr and Marie Roberson. **EDUCATION:** Trinity Coll Hartford, BA, 1974; Univ of Hartford, Grad Study Certificate, Business Admin 1979, Org Beh 1979; Antioch School of Law, MA, 1984. **CAREER:** CT General (CIGNA), supervisor of admin 1974-80; AT&T Long Lines, NJ opers supv 1980-81, NY cost support/admin mgr 1981-82; Pepper Hamilton & Scheetz, legal editor 1984-89. **ORGANIZATIONS:** Class agent Trinity Coll 1974-; panelist "Beyond the Degree" Trinity Coll 1980; speaker/facilitator Dow, Lohnes & Albertson Seminar, 1985-88; mem Trinity Club of Washington, Hobart Place Comm Block Club. **HONORS/ACHIEVEMENTS:** Class of 1916 Trophy, Trinity Coll, 1984; article "Organizing Basics," Washington Living 1985; article "Be Your Own Best Legal Editor," The Docket, 1986; "Getting the Word Out," The Docket, 1988. **HOME ADDRESS:** 749 Hobart Pl NW, Washington, DC 20001.

TUCKER, KELVIN TRENT
Professional athlete. **EDUCATION:** Univ of MN. **CAREER:** New York Nicks, bskbl player. **BUSINESS ADDRESS:** New York Nicks, Madison Sq Garden, 4 Pennsylvania Plaza, New York, NY 10001.

TUCKER, LEMUEL
Broadcast journalist. **PERSONAL:** Born May 26, 1938, Saginaw, MI. **EDUCATION:** Cntrl MI U, BA;Univ of MI & Cntrl U, Work on Master's Degree. **CAREER:** NBC News, copy boy, asst bureau chief in Vietnam 1965-72; ABC News NY City, reporter 1972-77; CBS News Washington DC, news corresp 1977-. **ORGANIZATIONS:** Mem Am Civ Librt Union; Rptrs Com for Freedom of the Press 1960; NY Civ Librt Union; Am Fedn TV & Radio Artists; mem AFTRA. **HONORS/ACHIEVEMENTS:** Recip Emmy Awd for series of news stories on hunger in Am 1968-69; Emmy Awd "The Dream in Still Deferred" 1983.

TUCKER, LEOTA MARIE
Business executive. **PERSONAL:** Born Aug 01, 1944, New Haven, CT; married Robert Clifton. **EDUCATION:** So CT St Coll, BA 1968;Univ of New Haven, MA 1975; Union Grad Sch, PhD Psych 1977. **CAREER:** Karonee Inc Ctr for Appld Behav Sci, pres 1980-; City of New Haven, dir of welfare 1978-80; Yale &Univ CT Mntl Hlth Ctr, dir preventn & commun educ proj 1975-78, mntl hlth adminstr 1973-75; Dixwell Crisis Prevntn Svc, proj dir 1973. **ORGANIZATIONS:** Bd dir United Way of Gr New Haven 1978-; bd dir ARC New Haven Chap 1979-; bd dir St Raphaels Hosp 1980. **HONORS/ACHIEVEMENTS:** Commun serv award Chi Omicron Chap Omega Psi Phi Frat 1978; Outst Yng Wmn Award 1978; commun serv award Mt Zion SDA Ch 1978; professional award New HavenChap of the Black Bus Professional Club 1979. **BUSINESS ADDRESS:** 280 Ray Rd, New Haven, CT 06515.

TUCKER, M. BELINDA
Social psychologist. **PERSONAL:** Born May 19, 1949, Washington, PA; married Russell L Stockard; children: Desmond, Daren. **EDUCATION:** Univ of Chicago, AB 1967-71; Univ of MI, MA, PhD 1971-75. **CAREER:** Univ of MI Inst for Social Rsch, study dir 1975-78; UCLA, psych & biobehavioral sci dept asst tsch psych 1983-, psych dept asst rsch psych 1987,asst dir Afro-Amer Studies 1978-. **ORGANIZATIONS:** Mem Drug Abuse Clinical Behavioral & Psych Rsch Review Comm Natl Inst on Drug Abuse 1978-81; ed bd Amer Jrnl of Drugs & Alcohol Abuse 1980-; consult editor Psych of Women Quarterly 1986-. **HONORS/ACHIEVEMENTS:** Rsch Scientist Devel Awd; "Social Support & Coping, Appl for the Study of Female Drug Abuse" Jrnl of Social Issues 1982; "Coping & Drug Use Behavior AmongHeroin Addicted Men & Women" Coping & Substance Use by W Shiffman & TA Wills 1985; "The Black Male Shortage in LA" Sociology & Social Rsch 1987. **BUSINESS ADDRESS:** Assistant Dir, UCLA Ctr Afro-Amer Studies, Univ of CA, Los Angeles, CA 90024.

TUCKER, MARCUS O., JR.
Judge attorney. **PERSONAL:** Born Nov 12, 1934, Santa Monica, CA; married Indira Hale; children: Angelique. **EDUCATION:** Univ Southern CA, BA 1952-; Howard Univ Sch Law, JD 1958-60. **CAREER:** Santa Monica, prv prctc law 1962-74, deputy city atty 1963-65; US Atty Ofc, asst us atty 1965-67; Cnty Los Angeles, spr ct cmsnr 1974-76; Long Beach Mncpl Ct, judge 1976-85; Los Angeles Superior Court, judge 1985-. **ORGANIZATIONS:** Pres John Langston Bar Assn 1972-73, Legal Aid Found LA 1977-78, Legal Aid Soc Santa Monica 1972-73; bd dir Boy Scouts Am Long Beach 1978-, Long Beach C Of C 1979-82; pres Comm Rhbltn Inds Found. **HONORS/ACHIEVEMENTS:** Judge of the Year Juvenile Dept of LA Superior Court 1986. **MILITARY SERVICE:** AUS spec e5 1960-66. **BUSINESS ADDRESS:** Judge, Los Angeles Superior Court, 210 W Temple St, Dept 233, Los Angeles, CA 90012.

TUCKER, NORMA JEAN
Educator. **PERSONAL:** Born Jan 28, 1932, Muskogee, OK; divorced. **EDUCATION:** LangstonUniv OK, bS 1953;Univ of OK, MEd 1966;Univ of CA Bereley; CA St U; Hayward. **CAREER:** Merritt Coll Oakland CA, dean of instr 1975-; N Peralta Coll, dean of coll 1974-75, dean of instr 1973, acting dean of instr 1972, coord of instr 1972; Merrit Coll, coll instr 1968-72; Oakland Tech HS, teacher 1962-68; Douglass HS, teacher 1953-56. **ORGANIZATIONS:** Sr vice pres bd of dirs United Way of the Bay Area; life mem Alpha Kappa Alpha Sor; past pres Alpha Nu Omega Chap Alpha Kappa Alpha Sor Inc; mem E Bay Area Club of Bus & Professional Wmn; mem Black Wmn's Orgn for Polit Action; mem Kappa Delta Pi; mem Counc on Black Am Affairs; former mem Christian EdnBd Park Blvd Presb Ch. **HONORS/ACHIEVEMENTS:** Reg Award Alpha Kappa Alpha Sor; Ida L Jackson Award Alpha Kappa Alpha Sor; Nat Nom Com Alpha Kappa Alpha Sor; selected as Outst Wmn of the E Bay, Allen Temple Bapt Ch; hon as an Outst Wmn in an Unusual Prof St Paul AME Ch; featured in February 1986 Ebony magazine Black Women College Presidents; 1986 Charter Day speaker for alma mater Langston Univ Langston, OK; several other hon & achvmnts. **BUSINESS ADDRESS:** President, Merritt College, 12500 Campus Dr, Oakland, CA 94619.

TUCKER, PAUL, JR.
Engineering consultant. **PERSONAL:** Born Jun 15, 1943, Detroit, MI; son of Paul Tucker Sr and Frances Jennet Sara Kinney Tucker; married Evelyn Virginia Reid; children: Kendrah, Kendall. **EDUCATION:** Detroit Inst of Technology, BSCE 1971; Eastern Michigan Univ, MBA 1975. **CAREER:** Ayres Lewis Norris & May Inc, consulting engr 1970-76; Giffels & Assoc Inc, sr engr 1976-78; Bechtel Power Corp, civil/site sr engr 1978-79; Camp Dresser & McKee, sr engr/mgr 1979-81; English Tucker & Assoc Inc, vice pres/chief engr 1981-84; Tucker Young Jackson Tull Inc, pres/ceo 1984-. **ORGANIZATIONS:** Bd of dirs Huron VAlley Land Develop Corp 1979-88, Detroit Chap MI Soc of Professional Engrs 1986-89; governing bd Tri City Renaissance 1987; mem Natl Soc of Professional Engrs, MI Water Pollution Control Federation, Amer Soc of Civil Engrs, Natl Black MBA's, Consulting Engrs Cncl of MI, Soc of Engrs & Applied Scientists; mem Soc of Amer Military Engrs. **HONORS/ACHIEVEMENTS:** Order of the Engineer Ann Arbor MSPE 1970; Certificate of Appreciation Tri-City Renaissance 1986. **MILITARY SERVICE:** AUS 1st lt 3 yrs. **BUSINESS ADDRESS:** President, Tucker Young Jackson Tull Inc, 1101 Washington Blvd Ste 410, Detroit, MI 48226.

TUCKER, ROBERT H., JR.
Business executive. **PERSONAL:** Born Jan 29, 1941, New Orleans, LA; married Janee Mercadel; children: Iam, David, Robert. **EDUCATION:** Clark Clg, BA 1963; Tulane U, MBA 1984. **CAREER:** City New Orleans, exec asst mayor 1970-78; Tucker & Assc Inc, pres ceo 1978-85. **ORGANIZATIONS:** Dir C Of C 1983-85; edtrl advsry bd Citibusiness Nwspr 1983-85; chrmprsn Pblc Fin Task Force 1983; dir Lee Cir YMCA 1984-85; trustee Childrens Hosp; life mem NAACP. **HONORS/ACHIEVEMENTS:** Otstndg yr New Orleans Jaycees 1977; otstndg comm serv Kiwanis Intrnt 1983; mem Blue Key Hon Soc 1977-85. **MILITARY SERVICE:** AUS sgt e6; Natl Defense Medal 1968. **HOME ADDRESS:** 3610 Carondelet St, New Orleans, LA 70115. **BUSINESS ADDRESS:** President/Chief Executive Ofcr, Tucker & Asso Inc, 904 FNBC Bldg, 210 Baronne St, New Orleans, LA 70112.

TUCKER, ROBERT L.
Attorney. **PERSONAL:** Born Feb 14, 1929, Chattanoga; married Shirley Cross; children: Terri E. **EDUCATION:** TN St U, BS 1951; NW Univ Sch of Law, JD 1955. **CAREER:** Tucker Watson Butler & Todd Attys Couns at Law Chgo, prtnr 1973-; NW Univ Sch of Law, mem of fclty; McCarty Watson & Tucker, prtnr 1971-73; Gen Couns, Metro Casualty Co Chgo, vice pres 1971-72; Equal Opport Chgo, asst reg asminstr 1968-71; Atty, pvt prac 1965-68; Metro Inter-Ins Exch, gen couns 1963-65; McCoy Min & Leighton Chgo, mem of firm 1963-65. **ORGANIZATIONS:** Spl couns St of IL Commn on Human Rel 1974-; gen couns & trustee MERIT Real Est Invest Trust 1972-; gen couns & mem bd People United to Save Hum1971-; mem Am Bar Assn; Chicago Bar Assn; Cook Co Bar Assn; Com on Cand Chicago Bar Assn; spl com on Civil Disorders; Phi Alpha Delta; Alpha Phi Alpha; Am Judicature Soc; PUSH; Chicago Urban Leag; NAACP; former mem Bd Dir IL Div Am Civil Liberties Union; Roger Baldwin Found; Nat Assn of Comm Leg Couns. **HONORS/ACHIEVEMENTS:** Citatn by Cook Co Bar Assn 1969; Richard E Westbrook Meml Award & Plaque Outst Contb to Legal Prfsn 1967; cited in 1000 Successful Blacks 1973. **BUSINESS ADDRESS:** One N La Salle St, #2525, Chicago, IL 60602.

TUCKER, SAMUEL JOSEPH
Psychologist, neuropsychologist. **PERSONAL:** Born Nov 05, 1930, Birmingham, AL; son of Daniel Tucker and Lucille McGhee Tucker; married Arlene Kelly, Jul 12, 1958; children: Samuel Jr, Sabrina, Sharon, Sterling. **EDUCATION:** Morehouse Coll Atlanta, BA 1952; Columbia Univ NYC, MA 1956; Atlanta Univ, PhD 1969, Harvard Univ, Post Doctoral 1973. **CAREER:** Morehouse Coll, dean of students 1963-71; Univ of FL Gainesville, asst prof 1971-73; Edward Waters Coll Jacksonville, pres 1973-76; AL State Univ Montgomery, dean & prof 1976-78; Langston Univ OK, pres 1978; Atlanta Human Devel Center, psychologist & pres 1978-. **ORGANIZATIONS:** Consult Stanford Research Inst Melo Park CA 1965-70; consult Princeton Univ 1965-70; consult Univ of MI Ann Arbor 1965-70; chap pres Alpha Phi Alpha Frat Inc 1971-73; mem Jacksonville Area Planning Bd 1973-76; bd of govs Jacksonville Area C of C 1973-76; member American Psychological Assn 1958-; member Natl Academy of Neuropsychologists 1988-. **HONORS/ACHIEVEMENTS:** Travel Grant Ford Found 1967; Research Grant Danforth Found 1968; Research Grant Univ of FL 1972; pub "Action Counseling" Journal of Non-White Concerns, 1973; 40 articles on mental health issues published. **MILITARY SERVICE:** AUS Spec Serv 1952-54. **HOME ADDRESS:** 735 Peyton Rd SW, Atlanta, GA 30310. **BUSINESS ADDRESS:** Clinical Psychologist and Neuropsychologist, 490 Peachtree Street N.E., Suite 358-B, Atlanta, GA 30308.

TUCKER, SAMUEL WILBERT
Lawyer. **PERSONAL:** Born Jun 18, 1913, Alexandria, VA; son of Samuel A Tucker, Jr (deceased) and Fannie L Williams Tucker (deceased); married Julia E Spaulding. **EDUCATION:** Howard Univ, AB 1933. **CAREER:** S W Tucker, Alexandria VA, lawyer 1934-36,

1938-41; S W Tucker, Emporia VA, lawyer 1946-61; Hill, Tucker & Marsh, partner 1961-. **ORGANIZATIONS:** Mem bd of dirs NAACP 1964-. **HONORS/ACHIEVEMENTS:** Wm Robert Ming Advocacy Award NAACP 1976; Peer Eminent Laureate of Virginia, Virginia Cultural Laureate Center 1978-79; Honorary LLD, St Paul's Coll, Lawrenceville VA 1980. **MILITARY SERVICE:** AUS lieutenant infantry 1936-38, lietenant, captain, major 1941-46. **BUSINESS ADDRESS:** Partner, Hill Tucker & Marsh, 509 North Third St, Richmond, VA 23219.

TUCKER, WILBUR CAREY
Physician. **PERSONAL:** Born Apr 03, 1943, Philadelphia, PA; married Faye; children: Maria, Caren. **EDUCATION:** Temple U, AB 1965, MD 1972; Howard U, MS 1968. **CAREER:** Temple U, clncl instr 1975-; Hosp Univ PA, asso 1975-; Temple Univ Hosp, resd ob-gyn 1972-75; Ofc Naval Res, physio 1968; NASA, biochem 1965-68. **ORGANIZATIONS:** Mem Phi Rho Sigma Med Frat; Omega Psiphi Frat. **HONORS/ACHIEVEMENTS:** Flw Am Coll OB-GYN; diplomate Am Bd OB-GYN. **BUSINESS ADDRESS:** 3400 Spruce St, Philadelphia, PA 19104.

TUCKETT, LEROY E.
Architect. **PERSONAL:** Born May 21, 1932, New York City; children: Amy, Lori, Lee, Lise. **EDUCATION:** Columbia Coll, 1954; Pratt Inst, 1960. **CAREER:** L E Tuckett Architects, PC, NY, NJ,CT, PA, MA, MD & Africa, pres. **ORGANIZATIONS:** Mem Am Inst of Architects; Nat Orgn of Minority Architects; NY Coalition of Black Architects; panelist with Am Arbitration Assn; archit adv panelist Bd of Higher Educ CityUniv of NY; mem several comm orgn. **MILITARY SERVICE:** Mil Korea 1952-54.

TUFFIN, PAUL JONATHAN
Attorney. **PERSONAL:** Born Sep 09, 1927, Charleston, WV; son of Gerald Tuffin and Nellie Carter Tuffin; married Virginia L Hamilton; children: Paula A, J Brian. **EDUCATION:** Bluefield State Coll, BS (Cum Laude) 1951; Cleveland-Marshall Law School, LLB 1956, JD 1968. **CAREER:** US Post Office, clerk 1952-55; Cleveland Bd of Educ, sub teacher 1952-54; IRS, revenue officer 1955-59; US Veterans Admin, adjudicator-section ch 1959-84;Cleveland Municipal Court, referee 1984-. **ORGANIZATIONS:** Asst supt of sunday sch & atty for trustee bd St John AME Ch 1957-; natl parliamentarian Bluefield State Coll Natl Alumni Bd 1986-87; mem Pi Omega Pi; mem NAACP, Kappa Alpha Psi. **HONORS/ACHIEVEMENTS:** Meritious & Conspicuous Serv Military Order of the Purple Heart 1984; Citation of Appreciation The Amer Legion 1984; Outstanding Serv Awd Disabled Amer Veterans 1984; Disting Serv Awd VFW-Cleveland 1984. **MILITARY SERVICE:** AUS corpl 1 1/2 yrs. **BUSINESS ADDRESS:** Referee, Cleveland Municipal Court, Justice Center, Cleveland, OH 44113.

TUGGLE, DOROTHY V.
Administrative assistant. **PERSONAL:** Born Mar 18, 1935, Mason, TN; married Rev Arthur; children: Alfonzo, Cynthia, Jerome, Vanessa, Tonya. **EDUCATION:** TN A&I St U, BS 1956; IN U. **CAREER:** Gary Income Mainten Exper G-X INUniv NW, asst dir of rsrch 1974-75; Reg Field Ofc Coord, Feb-Aug 1970; Day Care Dir, 1970-73; Day Care Splst 1973-74; Campbell Frndshp Hse, dir 1969-70; Comm Orgn Dept, head 1965-69; Presch, head tchr 1963-65; Headstart, tchr 1965. **ORGANIZATIONS:** Mem Nat Assn of Soc Work; AAUW; Gary Commn of Status of Wmn; NW Comp Hlth Plng Counc; 1st vice pres Gary Nghbrhd Svcs; NAACP; PTA; St John Amexion Ch. **HONORS/ACHIEVEMENTS:** Recip comm serv award Campbell Frndshp Hse. **BUSINESS ADDRESS:** 2400 Broadway, Gary, IN 46408.

TUGGLE, REGINALD
Clergyman, publication manager. **PERSONAL:** Born Apr 09, 1947, Denver, CO; son of Otis Tuggle and Mertis J Parker; married Marie R Peoples, Nov 13, 1976; children: Karleena Regina-Marie, Regine Perry. **EDUCATION:** Central Phillippine Univ, 1968; Bishop College, BA Philosophy/Psych 1969; Univ of Ghana, Certificate Economics 1971; Union Theological Seminary, MDiv 1972; Yale Univ, Master Corporate Ethics 1975; Commonwealth Univ, Hon DD 1985. **CAREER:** Urban League of Long Island NY, exec dir 1975-79; Town of Hempstead Presiding Super, exec asst 1979-81; Memorial Presbetary Church, pastor 1973-; Newsday Newspaper, community affairs mgr 1981-. **ORGANIZATIONS:** Chairperson Nassau County Health Systems Agency 1979; chairperson Nassau County Dept of Social Services 1980-81; vice pres Roosevelt Youth Bd 1983-. **HONORS/ACHIEVEMENTS:** Community Serv Award, Nassau County Press Club 1975; Reginald Tuggle Day Award, Suffolk Co 1979; Outstanding Prof Serv, Roosevelt Inter-Agency Council 1979; Community Serv Award, 100 Black Men of Nassau/Suffolk 1982; recepient of Nassau County Martin Luther King Jr Humanitarian Award, 1987; invited on fact finding visit to USSR by Soviet govt, 1988.

TUITT, JANE ELIZA
Educator. **PERSONAL:** Born Jan 08, 1908, St Croix, VI. **EDUCATION:** Hampton Inst VA, BS 1935; Tchrs Coll ColumbisUniv NY, MA 1951. **CAREER:** Coll of the VI, prof emeritus 1971-, asso dean & prof 1967-70; VI Dept of Educ, commr 1963-66, asst commr 1956-63, supr & dir elementary schools 1945-56, teacher 1935-44, 23-31. **ORGANIZATIONS:** Mem NEA 1935-50; mem Am Assn of Sch Adminstrs 1956-66; mem Counc of Chief St Sch Ofcrs 1963-66; mem St Thomas Bus & Professional Wmn 1963; adv counc Voc Educ & AVA 1967-77; mem Am Assn of Ret Prsns 1971. **HONORS/ACHIEVEMENTS:** Fllwshp Foresight Found NY 1950-51; Jane E Tuitt Sch Legisl of the VI 1958; wmn of yr St Thomas Bus & Professional Wmn 1963; centennial medallion HamptonInst VA 1968. **BUSINESS ADDRESS:** Coll of VI, St Thomas, Virgin Islands of the United States 00801.

TUNLEY, NAOMI LOUISE
Nurse. **PERSONAL:** Born Jan 10, 1936, Henryetta, OK. **EDUCATION:** Dillard U, BS Nurs Ed 1958;Univ of MO, KC, MA Sociology 1974;Univ Iowa 1966-67. **CAREER:** VA Hosp, staff nurse inservice Ed; Okla City VA Hosp, assoc chf nurs serv 1958-65; Iowa Luth Hosp, Des Moines, med & Surg instr 1965-66; Mercy Hosp Iowa City, IA, emerg rm chrg nurs 1966; VA Hosp, KC, assoc chf nurs serv, chrg Nurs, psychiatric unit, staff nurs, ins instr 1967-77, head nurs, patient care surgical coord 1977. **ORGANIZATIONS:** Natl Honor Soc of Nurs; Amer Red Cross; Amer Sociological Assn; Big Sisters Org Am; Iowa Nurs Assn Instr Home Nurs; Amer Red Cross; March Dimes; Muscular Dystrophy Assn; Mo Tchr Religious Ed, Faith Mission Ch. **HONORS/ACHIEVEMENTS:** KC, Mo Natl Honor Soc 1953-54; State Honor Soc, 1953-54; 4 yr Scholarship, EK Gaylor Philanthropist; First Black to hold position as Assoc Chief of Nurs Serv, Okla City First Black to hold position as Medi-surgi Instr, Des Moines; Notable Am, 1976-77. **BUSINESS ADDRESS:** Manager, KC VA Medical Center, Alcohol Depend Trmnt Center, 4801 Linwood Blvd, Kansas City, MO 64128.

TUNSTALL, JUNE REBECCA
Physician. **PERSONAL:** Born Jun 20, 1947, Baltimore, MD. **EDUCATION:** Bennett Coll, BS 1969; Meharry Coll, MD 1974. **CAREER:** Surry Co Fam Hlth Grp Inc VA, staff phys, med dir 1979-80; John Randolph Hosp Hopewell VA, staff phys 1979-; Med Coll of VA Dept Fam Prac Richmond, instr 1979-80; Surry Co HURA Proj, staff phys 1978; Univ of MA, fam phys & educ coord of fam prac dept 1977, resd 1975-77; Worchester City Hosp, intern 1974-75. **ORGANIZATIONS:** Chprn bd dir Surry Co Fam Hlth Grp Inc 1979-80; vice pres Surry Co Unit Am Heart Assn 1979-80; pres Surry Co Unit Am Heart Assn 1980-81; mem VA Acad Fam Phys; mem Med Soc Southside VA; bd dir So Chirstian Ldrshp Conf; mem Am Acad of Fam Phys; MA Acad of Fam Phys; New Eng Med Soc Bd; dir Fam plng serv of Gr Worcester; bd dir United Way of Cntrl MA. **BUSINESS ADDRESS:** Physician, PO Box 354, Surry, VA 23883.

TUNSTALL, LUCILLE HAWKINS
Educator. **PERSONAL:** Born in Thurber, TX; children: Ruth Tunstall Grant, Leslie Tunstall Dawkins. **EDUCATION:** Univ of CO Boulder, BS Med Tech 1943; Wayne State Univ, MS Biology 1959, PhD Biology 1963; Atlanta Law Sch, JD 1984. **CAREER:** Bishop Coll, chairperson dept of biology 1967-71; Natl Council of Churches, asst dir academic admin 1971-72; GA State Univ, clin prof physical therapy dept 1978-; Atlanta Univ, adj prof biology dept 1972-82; Clark Coll, prof of biology/chairperson allied health professions dept. **ORGANIZATIONS:** Consul United Bd for College Develop 1972-76; consul Moton Found 1971-78; consul Marc Prog Natl Inst of Genl Medical Sciences 1975-78; trustee Nulti-area Rape crisis Ctr Atlanta 1975-78; bd dirs Natl Soc of Health Professions 1983-; adv bd Atlanta Health Educ Consortium 1984-; pres GA Soc of AlliedHealth Professions 1978; chair biology sect GA Acad of Sciences 1976; regional vice pres Beta Kappa Chi Natl Honor Soc 1974-; treas Delta Theta Phi 1982-84; mem Sigma Xi 1958-. **HOME ADDRESS:** 620 Peachtree St NE Apt 1202, Atlanta, GA 30308. **BUSINESS ADDRESS:** Prof of Biology, Clark College, 240 James P Brawley St SW, Atlanta, GA 30314.

TUNSTALL-GRANT, RUTH NEAL
Artist, educator. **PERSONAL:** Born Jan 23, 1945, Denver, CO; married Duncan C Grant; children: Sheehan. **EDUCATION:** Delta Coll, AB 1965; Detroit Soc Arts & Crafts, attended 1965-67; Univ of Dallas, BS 1968, MFA 1971. **CAREER:** Delta Coll, artist 1965-67; OEO Summer Children's Prog, coord 1969; Dallas Pub Sch Dist, tchr 1970-71; Davis Art Ctr, tchr 1971-74; Self-employed, artist; San Jose Museum of Art, artist and dir Museum Art Sch. **ORGANIZATIONS:** Bd dirs YWCA 1980-83; mem CA Art Council Arts in Educ Panel 1987. **HONORS/ACHIEVEMENTS:** One Person Exhibitions, Siepps Gallery, Castelleja School Palo Alto 1983, San Jose Museum of Art San Jose CA 1981; Galleries, Oakland Museum Collectors GalleryCA, SFMOMA Rental Gallery Fort Mason San Francisco CA; Collections, IBM, Santa Teresa Lab, San Jose CA; 1st prize Saginaw Mus; scholarship Univ of Dallas 1968; Graphics Awd Atlanta Univ 1970; Exhibition, 8 Afro-Amer Art, Rath Museum Geneva Switzerland 1971; 4 moderns Brooklyn Museum NY 1972.

TURK, ALFRED J., II
Physician. **PERSONAL:** Born Jan 26, 1930, Atlanta, GA; married Charlotte Willis; children: Althea L MD, Alfred J Turk III Esq. **EDUCATION:** Clark Coll, BS 1951; Howard Univ, MD 1964. **CAREER:** Booker T Washington High School, teacher 1951-58; Private Practice, Newnan GA, physician 1964-69; Private Practice, Atlanta GA, family practice physician 1969-. **ORGANIZATIONS:** Life mem Alpha Phi Alpha Frat 1950-; trustee Beulah Baptist Church; mem Natl, GA State and Atlanta Medical Assocs; mem/supporter Clark Coll Alumni Assoc Inc, Howard Univ Alumni Assoc. **HONORS/ACHIEVEMENTS:** Silver Circle Awd Clark Coll; Loyalty Club Awd Clark Coll 1981,82,83; Southwest Comm Hosp Atlanta Awd 18 yrs serv 1984; Outstanding Serv Eta Lambda Chap Alpha Phi Alpha Frat Inc 1984. **HOME ADDRESS:** 3111 Eleanor Terrace NW, Atlanta, GA 30318. **BUSINESS ADDRESS:** 3455 Martin L King Jr Dr SW, Atlanta, GA 30331.

TURKSON, ALBERTINE BOWIE
Attorney. **PERSONAL:** Born in Houston, TX; married Eric Y B; children: Elizabeth, Eric Jr. **EDUCATION:** Palmer Meml Inst, 1950; VT Jr Coll, AA 1952; OH Wesleyan U, BA 1954; Univ of TX Law Sch, LLB 1957. **CAREER:** Prentice-hall Income Tax Rpt, atty 1960-62; Unempl & Comp Div, asst atty gen 1959; St of IL Welfare Commn, atty 1958; St of IL Welfare Dept, 1957. **ORGANIZATIONS:** Spec asst to chmn of Wmn Div, Rep Nat Com; mem Nat Pol Sci Assn; Bar-Appellant Ct St of IL; Ghana Wmn's Assn 1965-66; AfricanBrazilian Assn 1966-70; African Ambass Wives 1970-76; Princess Tenque Work Welfare Assn 1970-76; YWCA of Ethiopia 1970-76; Mus Soc of Ethipia 1970-76; Pol Rsrchr for author of African affairs & mag.

TURMAN, ROBERT L.
Educational administrator. **PERSONAL:** Born Sep 29, 1926, Gadsden, AL; son of Arthur Turman and Lillian Long Turman; married Maggie Dossie Turman, Jun 29, 1950 (died 1989); children: Daphne, Gregory, Robert II, Arthur, Oliver. **EDUCATION:** Tuskegee Inst, BS Ed 1949; NC A&T State Univ, MS Ed Admin 1962; Univ of Northern CO, Post-Grad 1975; Univ of CO, Post-Grad 1977. **CAREER:** US Army, lt col 1949-72; Carmel Jr HS, teacher 1972-74; John Adams Elementary School, asst principal 1974-75; Helen Hunt Elem School, principal 1975-77; Mark Twain Elem School, principal 1977-82; Will Rogers Elem School, principal 1982-84. **ORGANIZATIONS:** Mem Omega Psi Phi Frat 1949, Assoc of US Army 1955-, Phi Delta Kappa Ed Frat 1974-, Natl Assn Elem Principals 1975-, Amer Assn of School Admin 1975-, Natl Assn of School Bd 1979-, CO Black Caucus 1979-; pres Bd of Ed Harrison School Dist #2 1979-; mem NAACP 1981-. **HONORS/ACHIEVEMENTS:** Educator of the Year CO Springs Chap of Omega Psi Phi Frat 1981; Honor Roll CO Assn of School Bds 1984. **MILITARY SERVICE:** AUS lt col 1949-72; Army Commendation Medal, Purple Heart 1962, 1951; Joint Serv Commend Medal 1969; Legion of Merit, Bronze Star Medal 1971. **HOME ADDRESS:** 208 Chamberlin Ave, Colorado Springs, CO 80906.

TURNBULL, HORACE HOLLINS
Administrator. **PERSONAL:** Born Mar 26, 1949, Greenville, MS; married Eunice Carter; children: LaChandrea, Tamari, Courtney. **EDUCATION:** Tougaloo Coll, BS 1971; Columbia U, MA 1975; Long Island Univ, MBA 1978. **CAREER:** Abbott House Childrens Home, cons; Childrens Village, grp home parent; Leake & Watts Childrens Agency, soc worker 1971-72; Planned Parenthood of NYC, dir, coord 1974-76; St Peters Sch, coord; St Mary's in-the-Field, res dir; Lakeside School, exec dir 1983-86; The Equitable Financial Svcs, registered rep1986-. **ORGANIZATIONS:** Mem 100 Black Men; vice pres Harlem Boys Choir Bd of Dir; Interest Hlth & Human Serv Adminstn. **HONORS/ACHIEVEMENTS:** Listed Who's Who Amg Am Coll &Univ 1971; Acad & Athl Schlrshp 1967; hon mention Danforth Flwshp. **BUSINESS ADDRESS:** Registered Representative, Equitable Financial Serv, 2 Corporate Park Dr, White Plains, NY 10604.

TURNER, ALLEN H.
Engineer. **PERSONAL:** Born Oct 19, 1923, Detroit; married Beverly K; children: Linda K. **EDUCATION:** BS Elec Engr 1950. **CAREER:** Ford Motor Co, retired supr elec sys dept 1972-82, supr rsrch & devel ICPD Div 1965-72, rsrch engr sci lab 1952-65; Tuskegee Inst, rsrch asst 1950-52. **ORGANIZATIONS:** Mem Electron Microscope Soc of Am; Am Vacuum Soc; Soc of Am Engr Bd Dir Fam Svc. **MILITARY SERVICE:** USAF 2nd lt WW II. **BUSINESS ADDRESS:** Supervisor Elect Syst Dept, Ford Motor Co, Scientific Lab Ford Motor Co, Dearborn, MI.

TURNER, BAILEY W.
Salesman. **PERSONAL:** Born Dec 18, 1932, Sadlersville, TN; married Ruby McClure; children: Carolyn, Gayle. **EDUCATION:** TN State U, BS 1956; PA State U, MEd 1957; Union Grad Sch, PhD 1977. **CAREER:** Lincoln Heights Pub Schs, tchr 1960-61; Cincinnati Pub Schs, 1961-65; Comm Action Commn Cincinnati area, field rep comm organizer 1965-67; Metropolitan Life, sales rep 1967-72; Midland Nat Life, general agent;Univ Cincinnati, adj asst prof; RST Pub Relations & Consult firm, sr asso; Community Orgn, gen cons; Black-White Employee Relations, cons, mgmt tng. **ORGANIZATIONS:** Pres OH Black Political Assembly 1974-; chmn Coalition Concerned Black Citizens 1971-; United Black Community Orgns 1969-70; pres Avondale Commn Council 1967-69. **HONORS/ACHIEVEMENTS:** PUSH Black Excellence Award 1972; SCLC Cincinnati chap Distingshd Commn Serv Award 1969; Alumnus of Yr TN StateUniv 1965; Outstandng New Jaycee CincinnatiJaycees 1965. **MILITARY SERVICE:** USAF 1949-53.

TURNER, BILL (WILLIE T.)
Auto dealer. **CAREER:** Universal Ford, Inc, Richmond, VA, chief executive, 1983—. **BUSINESS ADDRESS:** Universal Ford, Inc, 1012 West Broad St, Richmond, VA 23220. *

TURNER, CARMEN ELIZABETH
Business executive. **PERSONAL:** Born in Teaneck, NJ; married Frederick B Turner, Jr; children: Frederick, Douglas. **EDUCATION:** Howard Univ, BA Political Sci; Amer Univ, MS Publ Admin. **CAREER:** Urban Mass Transp Admin Dept of Army, dep dir civil rights 1952-70; US Dept of Transp Wash DC, acctg dir civil rights 1976-77; Wash Metro Area Transit Auth, asst gen mgr admin 1977-83, gen mgr. **ORGANIZATIONS:** Bd mem Amer Publ Transit Assoc, Conf of Min Transit Officials, Women's Transp Seminar; past vestry St Georges Episcopal Church; chmn Advisory CouncilNatl Cap Negro Womens Assoc. **HONORS/ACHIEVEMENTS:** Women's Transp Seminar Achievement Awd 1983; Woman of the Year YWCA Wash DC 1985; Disting Alumni Howard Univ Wash DC. **BUSINESS ADDRESS:** General Manager, Washington Metro Area Transit, 600 5th St NW, Washington, DC 20001.

TURNER, CASTELLANO B.
Educator. **PERSONAL:** Born Jun 14, 1938, Chicago, IL; married Barbara; children: Adam, Shomari. **EDUCATION:** DePaul Univ, BA 1962, MA 1963; Univ of Chicago, PhD 1966. **CAREER:** Woodlawn-Hyde Park-Kenwood Prof, prog dir 1967-68; School of Social Serv Admin Univ of Chicago, sr rsch assoc; Collegiate Ed of Black Students Univ of MA, dir counseling & tutoring prog 1969-70; Univ of MA Amherst, prof of psych. **ORGANIZATIONS:** Mem Amer Psych Assoc, Assoc of Black Psych. **HONORS/ACHIEVEMENTS:** Listed in Amer Men & Women of Sci. **BUSINESS ADDRESS:** Professor of Psychology, Univ of Massachusetts, Tobin Hall, Amherst, MA 01003.

TURNER, CHARLES ROBERT (JACK)
Retired contractor. **PERSONAL:** Born Jun 29, 1910, Washington, DC; son of George G Turner and Dorothy Folks Turner; married Dorothy; children: Charles Jr, Wayne Micheal, Raymond E. **CAREER:** Contractor retired. **ORGANIZATIONS:** Mem Shiloh Bapt Ch; chmn, Deacon bd, mem, Odd Fellows Lodge; NAACP; Town Council; mem, bd of dir, Middle Commun Center, Marshall St Center. **HONORS/ACHIEVEMENTS:** Certif for 50 yr mem Shiloh Baptist Church. **MILITARY SERVICE:** USNR SP 2c, 1943-46.

TURNER, CLIFTON B.
Physician. **PERSONAL:** Born Aug 04, 1924, Cleveland; married Patricia Dalton; children: Clifton, Craig, Chris, Ivan, Philip, Rebecca. **EDUCATION:** John Carroll U, BS 1949; Western Reserve U, MD 1952. **CAREER:** Drs Ford Lewis & Turner Co, pediatrician, priv prac professional corp; E 35th St Clinic of Met Gen Hosp, med dir 1955-72; Univ Hosp Cleveland, first black res 1953-55. **ORGANIZATIONS:** Pres Med Staff Met Gen Hosp 1970-72; asst clinical prof of pediatrics Case-Western Reserve U; past sec-treas No OH Pediatric Soc; trustee Case-Western ReserveUniv Alumni Assn 1972-; sec Am Sickle Cell Anemia Soc 1973-; mem Nat Med Assn; Cleveland Academy of Med; OH State Med Assn; NAACP; diplomat Am Academy of Pediatrics. **MILITARY SERVICE:** USAAF 1943-45. **BUSINESS ADDRESS:** 14900 Kinsman Rd, Cleveland, OH 44120.

TURNER, DAIN CAMERON
Actor. **PERSONAL:** Born Mar 08, 1970, Dayton, OH. **CAREER:** Actor on TV: "The Little House on the Prairie," "Rafferty," "Police Story," "Harris & Co," "Wheels," "Most Wanted," NBC Movie of the Week "Love is Not Enough"; motion picture "Joni"; commercials. **HONORS/ACHIEVEMENTS:** 1st Child Grand Marshall Orange Co Parade CA 1980. **BUSINESS ADDRESS:** Dorothy Day Otis Agency, 6430 Sunset Blvd, Hollywood, CA 90028.

TURNER, DARWIN T.
Educator. **PERSONAL:** Born May 07, 1931, Cincinnati, OH; son of Darwin R and Laura K; married Maggie Jean Lewis; children: Pamela, Darwin K, Rachon. **EDUCATION:** Univ of Cin, BA Engl 1947, MA Engl 1949; Univ Chicago, PhD Engl, Engl & Amer Dramatic Lit 1956. **CAREER:** Clark Coll Atlanta, asst prof Engl 1949-51; Morgan St Coll Baltimore, asst prof eng 1952-57; FL A&M Univ prof & chrmn Dept Engl 1957-59; NC A&T Univ Greensboro, prof, chrmn Dept Engl 1959-66; NC A&T U, prof Engl Dean of Grad Sch 1966-70;Univ WI Madison, visit prof Engl 1969; Univ Mich Ann Arbor, prof Engl 1970-71;Univ Hawaii Honolulu, visit prof Engl, sum 1971; Univ Iowa, Iowa City, visit prof Engl 1971-72; Univ Iowa, prof Engl, chmn Afro-Amer stud 1972-; Univ of IA Found, disting prof 1980-. **ORGANIZATIONS:** Mem NAACP 1959-; mem Assn for Study of Afro-Amer Life & History 1965-; mem Educ Min Groups Modern Lang Assn 1957-; mem Coll Lang Assn 1957-; mem NCTE 1958-; trus NCTE Res Found 1970-73; mem Coll Engl Assn 1970-; mem Grad Rec Exam Bd 1970-73; trustee Natl Humanities Ctr 1977-; mem Coll Section Exec Comm NCTE 1977-80; mem Rockefeller Comm on Humanities 1978-80; chmn Ethnic Studies Div Mod Lang Assn 1978-80; authored & co-authored many publictns; mem bd of dir Blk Caucus of Coll Engl Tchrs; chmn IA Coll & U; consortium for teaching of Afro-Amer Culture; dir Comm on Lit NCTE 1983-85; chmn prog comm 1984-86, pres 1987-88 IA Humanities Bd; mem Exec Comm Black Amer Lit & Culture Div Mod Lang Assn 1984-; senator Phi Beta Kappa 1985-; mem, bd of directors, Federation of State Humanities Councils, 1988-; mem, board of advisors, Banneker Honors College, 1986-. **HONORS/ACHIEVEMENTS:** Phi Beta Kappa & Hon Soc; Post Doc Fellow in Univ NC-DUKE Univ Hum Prog 1965-66; Amer Coun Learned Soc Grant-in-Aid 1965; del African Regl Amer studies conf 1976; del 2nd World Festival of Black & African Cult 1977; Rockefeller Foun Res Grant 1971; Coll Lang Assn Creative Scholar Award 1970; Univ Chic Prof Achieve Award 1972; DLitt Univ Cincinnati 1983; Univ Cincinnati Distinguished Alumnus Awd 1982; Middle Atlantic Writers Assn Distinguished Writer Awd 1986; included in Five Black Scholars. **BUSINESS ADDRESS:** Professor of English, University of IA, 303 English Philosophy Bldg, Iowa City, IA 52242.

TURNER, DORIS (DORIS TURNER KEYS)
Association executive. **PERSONAL:** Born Jun 30, 1930, Pensacola, FL; married Willie D Keys. **CAREER:** Dist 1199 Nat Union of Hosp & Health Care Employees, exec vice pres 1961-. **ORGANIZATIONS:** Sec Nat Union of Hosp & Health Care Employees; union trustee Hosp League/Dist 1199 Training & Upgrading; union trustee Nat Benefit & Pension Fund for Hosp & Health Care Employees; mem Exec Com of Nat Benefit & Pension Funds; bd mem Am for Dem Action; bd mem Martin L King Cntr for Social Change; mem State of NY Comn on Health Educ & Illness Prevention; mem Coalition of Labor Union-Women; appntd mem NY State Hosp Review & Planning Cncl 1978-81. **HONORS/ACHIEVEMENTS:** Dist srvcs award New York City Central Labor Counc AFL-CIO 1969; award of merit The Black Trade Unionist Ldrshp Com of NY Central Labor Counc 1974; Hispanic Labor Com Award 1978; Eugene V Debs/Norman Thomas Award 1978. **BUSINESS ADDRESS:** President, 310 W 43rd St, New York, NY 10036.

TURNER, DORIS J.
Educator. **PERSONAL:** Born in St Louis, MO. **EDUCATION:** Stowe Coll St Louis, BA 1953; Universidade da Bahia Salvador Bahia Brazil, 1963; St Louis U, PhD 1967. **CAREER:** Kent State Univ, asso prof & coord Latin Amer studies Dept of Romance Lang & Lit 1967-. **ORGANIZATIONS:** Field reader US Ofc of Educ (HEW) 1976-77, 79; elected mem & past chmn Nat Ofc Steering & Com of Consortium of Latin Am Studies Prog 1973-76. **HONORS/ACHIEVEMENTS:** Fulbright Fellowship Brazil 1962-64; Research Grant to Brazil Kent StateUniv 1976; Danforth Asso 1976; NEH Summer Fellwshp BrownUniv 1979. **BUSINESS ADDRESS:** Kent State University, 101 Satterfield Hall, Kent, OH 44242.

TURNER, EDDIE WILLIAM
Crime prevention officer. **PERSONAL:** Born Apr 21, 1931, Toledo, OH; married Jacquelyn H; children: Edward, Kimberly. **EDUCATION:** Findlay Coll, 1954-56; Univ of Toledo, BS 1977. **CAREER:** Toledo Police Dept, crime prevntn offcr 1978-, comm relatns offcr 1968-78, detective 1962-68, patrol offcr 1959-62. **ORGANIZATIONS:** Mem Adv Bd Vol of Am; mem Adv Council E Toledo Helping Hand; mem Adv Bd E Mental Health Cntr; chaplin Omega Frat Xi Tau Chpt; mem City of Toledo Baseball & Softball Commn; pres Med-City Football Adv Bd. **HONORS/ACHIEVEMENTS:** 100 Membership Club NAACP Toledo Chap 1976; Shoplftg Study age 11 thru 14 toledo police dept 1978-79; crime prevntn offcr of yr asso for crime Prevntn 1979. **MILITARY SERVICE:** AUS corpl 1952-54. **BUSINESS ADDRESS:** Toledo Police Department, 525 N Erie St, Toledo, OH 43604.

TURNER, EDNA (NEE KOONTZ)
Editorial director. **PERSONAL:** Born in Shiner, TX; married Wilbert. **EDUCATION:** Tucker Bus Coll St Louis MO, 1953. **CAREER:** Good Publishing Co (magazines jive, bronze thrills, hip, soul confessions, sepia & soul teen) ft worth TX, editorial dir; circulation mgr, editor past 25 yrs. **ORGANIZATIONS:** Mem Baker Chapel AME Ch; mem NAACP; mem Ft Worth C of C. **HONORS/ACHIEVEMENTS:** Award Margaret Caskey Women in Commun Ft Worth Professional Chap of Women in Commun 1977. **BUSINESS ADDRESS:** 1220 Harding, Fort Worth, TX 76102.

TURNER, EDWARD L.
Councilman. **EDUCATION:** Univ GA, BA. **CAREER:** Com Preserving NE Athens, vice pres 1973; A Philip Randolph Inst, commun sec 1972-73; Clark Co Dem Club, 2nd vice pres 1972; Athens Central Labor Council, 2nd vice pres 1971; Voter Registration, chmn 1973-74. **ORGANIZATIONS:** Mem C of C; Jaycees; Optimist Brkfst Club; Black Professional Club; Black Bus League; mem Civic League; Generatn Gay Civic & Soc Orgn; Community Serv Club. **HONORS/ACHIEVEMENTS:** Man Yr NAACP 1973. **BUSINESS ADDRESS:** 393 3 St, Athens, GA 30601.

TURNER, ELMYRA G.
Educator. **PERSONAL:** Born Nov 27, 1928, Longview, TX; married James M Turner; children: 3 Children. **EDUCATION:** BS 1952; MEd 1959; MEd 1969; TX Ksouthern U, Admin Cert 1973. **CAREER:** Texas Southern Univ, sec 1952; Crawford Elementary School, 1953; Elmore HS, sec/teacher 1954; Langston Elementary School, teacher 1959; Lockett Jr High, 1964; Lincoln Jr-Sr High, 1968; Sam Houston Sr High, counselor 1970; Deady Jr High, asst prin 1970; all Houston TX. **ORGANIZATIONS:** Mem Nat Council Negro Women 1973; NAACP 1973-74; Houston Principals Assn 1970-; Houston Council of Educ 1972; supt com on Community Relatns for Area V 1972-74; Evaluatn Panel of Intervwrs-Area

V PTA Deady Jr HS; Lockhart Elem TX State Tchrs Assn vp; Top Ladiel of Distinctn Inc past pres; Beta Pi Chap Iota Phi Lambda Sor Inc past pres; organizer Houston Chap Nat Tots & Teens Inc; mem Houston League of Bus & prof Women; Home Improv & Protec Assn; chmn Youth Com; mem Delta Sigma Theta Sor Inc; mem AAUW; Univ Christian Ch publicatns "a study of Techniques for Improving Staff Morale" 1959, "The Etiology and Effect of Dialect Upon Behavior" 1969. **HONORS/ACHIEVEMENTS:** President's Award 1971 Iota Phi Lambda Sor Inc; Outstndg Woman Yr 1974-75 Iota Phi Lambda Sor Inc, Beta Pi Chap Houston TX; recv 1977 Human Rel EducAward for outst achvmt in human rel Houston Ind Sch Dist in coop with Anti-Defamation Leag of B'nai B'rith Houston Met Ministries & Nat Conf of Christians-Jews; Bicentennial Meml Edit of Comm Ldrs & Noteworthy Ams 1976-77; Notable Ams 1976-77; World Who's Who of Women 1977; Social Guide of TX (Who's Who of TX) 1977. **BUSINESS ADDRESS:** 2500 Broadway, Houston, TX 77012.

TURNER, ERVIN (PETER TURNER)
Business executive. **PERSONAL:** Born Mar 20, 1948, Monroe, LA; married Kathleen Lindsey; children: Christopher Earl, Roanita. **EDUCATION:** Northeast LA Univ, Associate 1972; Boys' Clubs of Amer, certification 1974. **CAREER:** Ouachita Parish Police Jury, police juror 1979-; EPT Enterprise AAA LTD, pres/owner 1982-; Tri-District Boys' Club, exec dir 1971-. **ORGANIZATIONS:** Mem NAACP; mem Northeast LA Sickle Cell Anemia; mem NLU Booster Club Business Action Assoc; mem Amer Entrepreneurs Assn; mem zoological Soc of LA Purchase Gardens and Zoo; bd mem Northeast LA Indus Dev Bd; bd mem Northeast LA Indus Bd; bd mem LA Minority Bus Develop Auth Bd; BCA Professional; coord Volunteer for Job Corps; sec Luminous Civic Club; bd mem Youth House of Quachita; bd mem Business Action Assn; bd mem Better Business Bureau; exec sec LA Area Council-BCA 1974; 2nd vice pres North Delta Regional Planning 1979-. **HONORS/ACHIEVEMENTS:** Man of the Year St Philip Baptist Church 1975; Man of the Year NAACP 1978; Monroe's Outstanding Young Man Monroe Jaycees 1982. **HOME ADDRESS:** 102 Roosevelt Circle, Monroe, LA 71202.

TURNER, EUGENE
Clergyman. **PERSONAL:** Born Apr 17, 1934, Macon, GA; married Sylvia Baskerville; children: Peter Eugene, Paul Eugene, Lennie Elis. **EDUCATION:** Knoxville Coll, BA; Pittsburgh Theological Sem, MDV; Harvard U, post grad work. **CAREER:** Pittsburgh, asst pastor; Patterson NJ, pastor; Philadelphia, organzng pastor; Presbeytery of Phila, assist for leadrshp devel, coord of Met Mission; Synod of the Golden Gate San Franc, asso exec; United Presby Ch Syracuse NY, exec of Synod of the Northeast. **ORGANIZATIONS:** Bd mem No CA Coun of Ch; bd mem Nat Planned Parenthd 1964-66; bd mem Coun of Black Clergy; bd mem Black Presby United; mem steering com Nat Black Conf 1968; bd mem Model Cities of Phila. **MILITARY SERVICE:** AUS 1957-59. **BUSINESS ADDRESS:** 3049 E Genesee St, Syracuse, NY.

TURNER, EVELYN EVON
College professor. **PERSONAL:** Born Sep 22, 1954, Buffalo, NY; daughter of Steven Turner and Mary Turner. **EDUCATION:** Bowie State Coll, BS 1978; Univ of Maryland at Baltimore, MSW 1980. **CAREER:** Homes for Black Children, social worker 1982-84; PG Dept of Social Services, social worker 1984-85; Bowie State Coll, instructor 1985-86, program coord 1986-. **ORGANIZATIONS:** Mem College Alumni Assoc 1978-; recording sec 1980-84, vice pres 1985-86 Natl Assoc of Black Social Workers; pres Sigma Gamma Nu Social Club 1981-84; sec Coalition of Black Child Welfare Advocates 1985-; mem Delta Sigma Theta Sor 1986-. **HONORS/ACHIEVEMENTS:** Outstanding Young Woman of Amer 1978,82; Certificate of Appreciation Natl Alliance of Business 1981; Certificate of Appreciation Natl Assoc of Black SocialWorkers 1981-85; Presidential Citation Natl Assoc on Equal Oppor in Higher Educ 1984. **HOME ADDRESS:** 3731 Halloway North, Upper Marlboro, MD 20772. **BUSINESS ADDRESS:** Coord of Social Work Program, Bowie State University, Bowie, MD 20715.

TURNER, FRANKLIN JAMES
Engineer. **PERSONAL:** Born Aug 16, 1960, Birmingham, AL. **EDUCATION:** Alabama A&M Univ, BS 1983. **CAREER:** Rockwell Intl, software engr 1984-86; Northrop, software quality engr 1986—. **HONORS/ACHIEVEMENTS:** Pride Awd Engrg Outstanding Achievement Rockwell Intl 1986. **HOME ADDRESS:** 19101 Pricetown Ave, Carson, CA 90746.

TURNER, GEORGE R.
Podiatrist. **PERSONAL:** Born Jun 14, 1944, Bryn Mawr, PA; married Betty; children: Gayle, Garrett, Avis. **EDUCATION:** Lincoln U, AB 1967; Temple U, EdM 1969; PA Coll of Podiatric Med, DPM 1976. **CAREER:** Lawndale Commun Hosp, podiatrist; PA Coll of Podiatric Med 1972-76; IBM, marktg rep 1969-72; Philadelphia Bd of Edn, tchr 1967-69. **ORGANIZATIONS:** Mem Amer Podiatry Assn; bd mem Natl Podiatry Assn; PA Podiatry Assn; Metrop Podiatry Assn; Philadelphia Co Podiatry Assn; consult Hardy's Orthopedic ApplInc; mem Omega Psi Phi Frat. **HONORS/ACHIEVEMENTS:** Outst Young Man in Amer 1976; Morris prize in bio 1967; Metrop Podiatry Assn achiev award 1976. **BUSINESS ADDRESS:** 1901-03-05 74 Ave, Philadelphia, PA 19138.

TURNER, GEORGE TIMOTHY
Auto dealer. **CAREER:** Plainfield Lincoln-Mercury-Merkur, Inc, Grand Rapids MI, chief executive, 1986—. **BUSINESS ADDRESS:** Plainfield Lincoln-Mercury-Merkur, Inc, 4140 Plainfield, NE, Grand Rapids, MI 49505. *

TURNER, ISIAH
Commissioner of state employment security department. **PERSONAL:** Born May 15, 1945, St Joseph, LA; son of Isiah Turner and Leona Johnson Turner; married Carmen Cayne, Jul 10, 1982; children: Damon Isiah, Terrie Lynn. **EDUCATION:** Evergreen State College, Olympia WA, 1986; Harvard Univ, 1987. **CAREER:** Seattle Opportunities Industrialization Center, Seattle WA, dir of education, 1971-79; Operation Improvement Foundation, Seattle WA, dir of industrial relations, 1980-83; Washington State Employment Security, Olympia WA, asst commissioner, 1983-85, commissioner, 1985—. **ORGANIZATIONS:** National Job Training Partnership, National Black Public Administrators Forum, Blacks in Government, Interstate Conference of Employment Security Agencies, Northwest Conference of Black Public Officials, Washington State Economic Development Board. **HONORS/ACHIEVEMENTS:** Administrator of the Year, National Job Service Employer Committee, 1986; Job Training Professional of the Year, National Alliance of Business, 1988; award of merit, International Association of Personnel in Employment Security, 1989. **BUSINESS ADDRESS:** Commissioner, Washington State Employment Security Department, 212 Maple Park, KG-11, Olympia, WA 98504.

TURNER, JOHN A., JR.
Attorney. **PERSONAL:** Born Sep 10, 1948, Washington, DC; married Cecelia Wirtz; children: John A III. **EDUCATION:** Howard Univ, BA 1970; Georgetown Univ Law Ctr, JD 1973; Georgetown Univ Law Ctr, LLM 1977. **CAREER:** Judge William C Pryor, law clerk 1974-75; Federal Privacy Protection Study Commiss, 1975-77; Turner & Carter, attorney 1977-. **ORGANIZATIONS:** Mem DC Circuit Judicial Conf 1983-87; pres WA Bar Assoc 1984-86; commiss DC Arts & Humanities Commiss 1984-; gen counsel Natl Bar Assoc 1985-86; vchair WA Urban League 1985-; cair of bd Shaw Coalition Redevel Corp 1987-; bd fo dir Bar Assoc of DC 1982-84. **HONORS/ACHIEVEMENTS:** Man of the Year Omega Psi Phi 1970; Service Awd DC United Way 1985, Natl Bar Assoc 1985; Service Awd Washington Bar Assoc 1986. **BUSINESS ADDRESS:** Attorney, Turner and Carter, 1420 N St NW, Washington, DC 20005.

TURNER, JOHN B.
Educator. **PERSONAL:** Born Feb 28, 1922, Ft Valley, GA; married Marian Floredia Wilson; children: Marian Elizabeth, Charles Brister. **EDUCATION:** Morehouse Coll, BA 1946; Case Western Resrv U, MSc 1948, DSW 1959. **CAREER:** Butler St YMCA, prog sec 1948-50; Atlanta Univ, instr 1950-52; Welfare Federation Field Serv Cleveland, dir 1959-61; Case Western Reserve Univ, chmn & community orgn sequence 1957-67; School Applied Social Scis, dean 1968-73; Univ NC, Kenan prof 1974-; Ency of Soc Work, editor 1977; Univ of NC School of Social Work, dean 1981-. **ORGANIZATIONS:** Consult Nat Urban League 1966-71; Intl Resrch Prog Cairo Egypt 1974; chmn Social Work Training Com Nat Inst Mental Hlth 1967-68; pres Nat Conf of Soc Welfare; mem Mayor's Com on Commun Resrcs Cleveland 1968-70; Cleveland Inst Art bd trustees 1970-74; city commnr E Cleveland 1967-69; sec, bd of trust Chapel Hill YMCA 1986; bd trust Council on Social Work Educ. **MILITARY SERVICE:** USAF 1st lt 1943-45. **BUSINESS ADDRESS:** Dean, University of North Carolina, School of Social Work, Chapel Hill, NC 27514.

TURNER, JOHN BARRIMORE
Educational administrator. **PERSONAL:** Born Feb 04, 1942, Sardis, MS; married Clevonne LaVerne Watkins; children: Stephanie, Robin, Bridget. **EDUCATION:** Fisk Univ, BA 1965; IN Univ Bloomington, MS Student Personnel Admin 1968, EdD 1972, Post-Doctorate Internship Admin 1973; Harvard Univ Inst for EdMgmt, 1979. **CAREER:** Fisk Univ, teaching asst math dept 1963-65; Westinghouse Elect Corp, mgmt trainee 1965-66; McNutt Quadrangle IN Univ, resident asst 1966-67; Foster Quadrangle IN Univ, asst head counselor 1967-68; Urban League Indianapolis, ed dir 1967; Upward Bound IN Univ, asst dean, div dir 1968-74; MIT, asst dean of grad school 1974-76, assoc dean of grad school, asst provost 1977-. **ORGANIZATIONS:** Mem Natl Assn of Grad School Deans, Amer Assoc for Higher Ed, Natl Assn of Student Personnel Admin, Phi Delta Kappa, Natl Black Alliance, Assn of Black Admin & Financial Aid Officers of the Ivy League & 7 Sister School; bd of dir Natl Consortium for Grad Degrees for Minorities in Engrg Inc; steeringcomm mem Ad Hoc Consortium on Minority Grad Ed Washington DC; pres Fisk Univ Alumni Assoc of Boston 1977-. **HONORS/ACHIEVEMENTS:** Outstanding Young Man of Amer Jaycees 1978; Martin Luther King Jr Awd for Disting Serv MIT Minority Comm 1978-79. **BUSINESS ADDRESS:** Associate Dean & Asst Provost, Massachusetts Inst of Tech, Grad School Office, Room 3-136, Cambridge, MA 02139.

TURNER, JOHN M.
Attorney. **PERSONAL:** Born Aug 24, 1948, Atlanta; married Carolyn. **EDUCATION:** Morris Brown Coll, BA 1969; Nat Law Ctr George Waslhingbton U, JD 1972. **CAREER:** Securities & Exchange Comm, atty adv Office of Gen Counsel 1972; Atlanta Reg Litigation Ctr EEOC, trial atty 1973; Northern Dist GA, asst US Dist Atty. **ORGANIZATIONS:** Mem DC Am Fed GA & Atlanta Bar Assns; Judicature Soc; Nat Assn Dist Attys; mem Resurgens Atlanta Club; Atlanta City Club. **HONORS/ACHIEVEMENTS:** Phi Beta Sigma Frat Awd, Morris Brown Coll Alumni Assn 1974; 1 of 10 Outstanding Young People of Atlanta 1975. **BUSINESS ADDRESS:** Rm 428, Old Post Office Bldg, Atlanta, GA 30301.

TURNER, JOHNNIE RODGERS
Educational administrator. **PERSONAL:** Born Jun 23, 1940, Hughes, AR; daughter of Clayton Rodgers and Charlie Mae Watson Rodgers; married Larry Turner; children: Larry R. **EDUCATION:** LeMoyne-Owen Coll, BS 1962; Memphis State Univ, MEd 1971. **CAREER:** Memphis City Schools, tchr 1965-, supr; dir, Staff Develmnt 1986-,. **ORGANIZATIONS:** Pres Memphis Br NAACP 1977-78; pres Memphis Alumnae Chap Delta Sigma Theta Sor 1978-; mem Leadership Memphis 1979-; ASCD 1980-; Natl Staff Dev Council 1980-; MABSE 1981-; Phi Delta Kappa 1982-; Natl Alliance of Black School Educators 1982-; bd mem, Health, Educational and Housing Facility Board of Shelby Cty, Tennessee, 1982-; pres, Memphis Alliance of Black School Educators (MABSE) 1988-90. **HONORS/ACHIEVEMENTS:** Merit Awd for Outstanding Serv Memphis Br NAACP 1975; co-editor "Why Doesn't An Igloo Melt Inside?" handbook for tchrs of the gifted 1978; Citizen of the Week Gilliam Comm Station WLOK 1978; Citizenship Awd Moolah Temple #54 Shriner 1979; Delta of the Year 1983; Golden Apple Award, Natl Alliance of Black School Educators (NABSE) 1988. **BUSINESS ADDRESS:** Dir, Memphis City Schools, 2597 Avery Ave, Memphis, TN 38112.

TURNER, JOSEPH ELLIS
Commercial airline pilot. **PERSONAL:** Born Sep 02, 1939, Charleston, WV; son of Joseph Turner and Annetta Frances Malone (deceased); married Norma Jean Sims, Apr 25, 1959; children: Alan, Brian, Joseph Jr. **EDUCATION:** WV State Clg, BS Math 1961;Univ Southern CA, Aviation Sfty 1968;Univ Utah, MS Human Rsrcs Mgmt; Command & Gen Staff Coll, grad; Indust Coll of Armed Forces, Air War Coll. **CAREER:** First Ofcr L1011 Delta Air Lines Atlanta, 1970-; Brigadier General USAR 1988-; deputy commander 335th signal command East Point GA; Master Army Aviator; U3a U6a 1963; CV2 1963; U8D, G, F, U21A 1968; U3A 1976; Fixed wing OH58 1975; UHIH 1975; rotary wing. **ORGANIZATIONS:** Mem Airline Pilots Assc 1970-, NAI 1969-, ROA 1970-, Am Soc Mltry Cmptrlrs 1984-; bd dir ORG Black Airline Pilots 1984; SARCA (Senior Army Reserve Commanders Assn 1988; AFCEA (Armed Forces Communications Electronics Assn) 1988; Signal Corp Regimential Assn 1988; The Black Military History Institute of America, Inc. 1989. **HONORS/**

ACHIEVEMENTS: Inducted into the WV State Coll ROTC Hall of Fame 1984; received the NAFEO 1989 Distinguished Alumni Citation of the Year Award 1989; WVA State College General Officer Hall of Fame (1988). **MILITARY SERVICE:** AUSR col 1961-; 2 Bronze Stars, 2 Meritorious Serv Medals, 3 Army Cmndtn Medals, 11 Air Medals Army Achmvmt Medal, Prsdntl Unit Citation, Army Rsrv Rbn;Vietnam Serv Medal w/8 Stars; Armed Forces Reserve Medal; Army Reserve Components Achievement Medal; Republic of Vietnam Campaign Ribbon; Master Army Aviator Badge; Republic Vietnam Gallantry Cross w/Palm; US Army Reserves Brigadier General March 1988-. **HOME ADDRESS:** 1630 Loch Lomond Trail SW, Atlanta, GA 30331. **BUSINESS ADDRESS:** Commercial Airline Pilot, Delta Airlines, Atlanta Hartsfield Intl Arpt, Atlanta, GA 30331.

TURNER, KEENA
Professional athlete. **PERSONAL:** Born Oct 22, 1958, Chicago, IL; married Therese Hopkins. **EDUCATION:** Purdue. **CAREER:** San Francisco 49ers, linebacker 1980-. **HONORS/ACHIEVEMENTS:** Second team all-pro (by-NEA) in 1982; two-time All-Amer & An All-big Ten pick as Purdue's MVP; recorded a team-high six total tackles in Super Bowl. **BUSINESS ADDRESS:** San Francisco 49ers, 711 Nevada St, Redwood City, CA 94061.

TURNER, KEITH
Physician. **PERSONAL:** Born Oct 13, 1943, Topeka, KS. **EDUCATION:** CreightonUniv Omahan NB, BS 1965; KansasUniv Med Sch, MD 1969; Metro Hosp NY Med Coll, psy res 1973. **CAREER:** Netro Hosp NY Med Coll, attending phy; Nastl Med Assn, clinical instr; Bronx Psychiat Ctr, sr psychiatrist; NY Med Coll Lincoln Hosp, attending psychiatrist. **ORGANIZATIONS:** Mem Black Psychiatrists of Am; Am Coll of Emergency Phys; Intl Forum of Phys. **BUSINESS ADDRESS:** Lincoln Hosp, Bronx, NY 10451.

TURNER, LONNIE CALVIN
Professional athlete. **PERSONAL:** Born Aug 31, 1959, Los Angeles, CA. **EDUCATION:** Cal-Poly Pomona. **CAREER:** Oklahoma Outlaws, 1984-; Denver Gold, wide receiver 1984-. **HONORS/ACHIEVEMENTS:** Teams 4th leading receiver.

TURNER, LOUIS EDOUARD
Administrator. **PERSONAL:** Born Jan 27, 1939, New Orleans, LA; married Iris Sorina; children: Gabrielle, Edward, Valerie. **EDUCATION:** LoyolaUniv of the S, BA 1974. **CAREER:** New Orleans Police Dept, present; num positions New Orleans Police Dept 1960-. **ORGANIZATIONS:** Mem Intl Assn of Chf of Pol; Nat Orgn of Black Law Enfcmtn Exec; LA Commn on Law Enfcmt 1973-; Criminal Justice Coord Com 1975-; Oral Review Bd, interviewer LA Civil Serv 1975-76; mem Org IL Club Inc; New Orleans Clean City Com. **MILITARY SERVICE:** USMC NCO 1957-60. **BUSINESS ADDRESS:** 715 S Broad St, New Orleans, LA 70119.

TURNER, MARK ANTHONY
Academic administrator/asst prof. **PERSONAL:** Born Feb 23, 1951, Lynch, KY; children: Andrea Kamille. **EDUCATION:** Univ of KY Southeast Comm Coll, AA 1972; Western KY Univ, BS 1974. **CAREER:** Arthur Young & Co, sr consultant-auditor 1980; Univ Coll Univ of Cincinnati, asst dean 1982-. **ORGANIZATIONS:** Treas NABA Cincinnati Chap 1980-84; founding mem Cincinnati Chap Natl Assoc of Black Accountants 1980; treas Bond Hill Comm Council 1980-84; consultant Sickle Cell Awareness Group of Greater Cincinnati 1982-84; company treas Cincinnatians for Yates for Council 1984-86. **HONORS/ACHIEVEMENTS:** Ford Foundation Scholarship 1973; Certificate of Appreciation Junior Achievement 1977-81; Certificate of Appreciation Cincinnati Chamber of Commerce Business Resource Ctr 1979-82; Certificate of Appreciation The Union of Experimenting Colleges 1986. **HOME ADDRESS:** 5411 Carrahen Ct, Cincinnati, OH 45237. **BUSINESS ADDRESS:** Asst Dean for Business Affairs, Univ of Cincinnati, Univ Coll ML #47, Cincinnati, OH 45221.

TURNER, MARVIN WENTZ
Staff supervisor. **PERSONAL:** Born Oct 17, 1959, Philadelphia, PA; son of Gilbert Turner and Frances Turner. **EDUCATION:** Howard Univ, BBA (Cum Laude) 1981, George Washington Univ, MBA. **CAREER:** Prudential Insurance, technical advisor 1982-84; Management Enterprise, business advisor 1984-86; CNA Group, tech analyst 1986-88; Bell Atlantic-Network Services Inc 1988-. **ORGANIZATIONS:** Mem Assoc of MBA Execs, Delta Sigma Pi Professional Business Frat, Assoc of Individual Investors; mem Howard Univ Sch of Business and Public Admin Alumni Assoc; mem Business and Economic Develop Comm Natl Black MBA Assoc 1986-; treasurer, Natl Black MBA Assn DC Chapter 1988-. **HONORS/ACHIEVEMENTS:** Vice pres Howard Univ Student Assoc Beta Gamma Sigma Business Honor Soc 1980-81; Outstanding Young Men of Amer 1986, 1988; Elizabeth B Adams Memorial Award 1988. **HOME ADDRESS:** 11367 Joyceton Dr, Upper Marlboro, MD 20772.

TURNER, MELVIN DUVAL
Administrator, director. **PERSONAL:** Born Jun 10, 1949, Detroit, MI; married Connie Jean Long; children: Melvin D. **EDUCATION:** Hartwick Coll, BA 1971; Universidad Ibero-americana, Mexico City;; attended. **CAREER:** CAPTURE, Citizens Crime Prevention Inc, exec dir 1974-; San Mateo Co;; adult probation officer 1972-74; OICW Job Training Ctr, bi-lingual vocational counselor 1971-72; Sickle Cell Anemia Research & Educ Found San Francisco, chmn of bd 1976-. **ORGANIZATIONS:** Mem Human Resource Comm City of San Mateo 1978-; mem CA Crime Prevention Officers Assn present; tech adv group mem CA Crime Resistancew Task Force, present. **HONORS/ACHIEVEMENTS:** Cert of Commendation Foster City Police Dept 1980; host weekly radio talk slhow "Crime the Courts & You" 1979-80; various publs 1977. **BUSINESS ADDRESS:** 2121 S El Camino Real, Ste 310, San Mateo, CA 94403.

TURNER, MIKOEL
Association executive. **PERSONAL:** Born Aug 22, 1950, New York, NY; son of Richard Turner and Enid Gordon; divorced; children: Mekell Mia. **EDUCATION:** Cobleskill A&T Coll, New York, AAS, 1971; Cornell Univ, Ithaca NY, BS, 1974. **CAREER:** Marriott Corp, dept mgr, 1975-81, gen mgr, 1981-84; Fletcher Consulting Service, partner, 1982—, Board of Ed, NJ, supervisor, 1984-88; Turner & Assoc, owner; Chelsea Catering, NJ, dept mgr, 1988—. **ORGANIZATIONS:** Bd mem, Union County Psych Clinic; bd mem, Plainfield Economic Development Corp. **BUSINESS ADDRESS:** President, National Association of Black Hospitality Professionals, PO Box 5443, Plainfield, NJ 07060.

TURNER, MOSES
Educator. **PERSONAL:** Born Mar 28, 1938, Athens, GA; married Joan; children: Shaul, Lisa, Chris. **EDUCATION:** Albany State Coll, BA 1962; Central Washington State Coll, MA 1969; Washington State Univ, PhD 1974; Harvard Univ Inst for Educ Mgmt 1982. **CAREER:** Columbia Basin Comm Coll, chair/dir music prog 1969-72; Washington State Univ, asst dean of students 1972-77; TX Tech Univ, dean/dir student life 1977-79; MI State Univ, vice pres student affairs 1979-. **ORGANIZATIONS:** Bd mem Opera Company of Mid-MI, Oakes Sports Program, Boy Scouts of Amer; mem Governor's Prayer Breakfast Commn; mem MI Black Caucus Foundation; bd memHiman Fdn for Awarding Scholarships to deserving high school students; spokesperson Youth Motivation in MI; bd mem Lansing Symphony Bd of Dirs; mem Subcomm on Fed Student Financial Assistance, Natl Assoc of State Univs and Land-Grant Colls; bd mem Golden Key Natl Honor Soc; Lansing Assn of Black Org; Lansing Chapter of Alpha Chi Boule; Editorial Bd of Natl Assn Student Personnel Administrators, Inc. **HONORS/ACHIEVEMENTS:** President's Awd Golden Key Natl Honor Soc 1986. **MILITARY SERVICE:** AUS sgt 1962-65. **BUSINESS ADDRESS:** Vice Pres for Student Affairs, MI State University, 153 Student Serv Bldg, East Lansing, MI 48824.

TURNER, PETER See TURNER, ERVIN

TURNER, RICARDO CORNELIUS, SR.
Elected official. **PERSONAL:** Born May 22, 1947, Baltimore, MD; children: Ricardo Cornelius Jr, Risheda Cheri. **EDUCATION:** Southern CT State Coll, Grad Course Alcohol Inst 1978; Comm Coll of Baltimore, Recreation & Leisure Ed Curriculum; New Hampshire Coll, Human Serv Classes. **CAREER:** MD Ctr for Public Broadcasting, project asst talent coord 1969-70; Alcoholic counselor, Dixwell Neighborhood Corp 1978; New Haven Aldermanic Minority Caucus, rsch asst 1977-80; City of New Haven Dept of Elderly Svcs, volunteer coord 1980-81; State of CT, exec asst to state treas 1981-82; New Haven CT Bd ofAlderman, alderman, pres pro-tempore. **ORGANIZATIONS:** Mem Congress of Racial Equality 1960-75, Natl Assn Ed Broadcaster 1970-72; sec, bd of dir Youth Org Under the Hill 1977-; v chmn Hill Devel Corp ofNew Haven 1978-; 3rd ward democratic chmn New Haven Democratic Party 1979-; volunteer Yale-New Haven Hospital Child Life Program 1979; justice of the peace State of CT 1981-; treas, bd of dir Community Action Agency of New Haven 1983-84; chmn Annual Giving Campaign New Haven YMCA Central Branch 1984-85; vchmn New Haven YMCA Central Br Bd of Mgrs; chmn Ed Comm Bd of Aldermen. **HONORS/ACHIEVEMENTS:** United Cerebral Palsy Humanitarian Serv & Outstanding Cooperation Citation 1963; 16 YMCA Serv Awds Baltimore YMCA 1966-77; Pres Cert of Merit Dept of Environment Protection 1972; Community Serv Awd Hill Devel Corp New Haven 1983; YMCA Serv Awds New Haven. **HOME ADDRESS:** 84 Sylvan AVe 1st Fl, New Haven, CT 06519.

TURNER, ROBERT LLOYD
Line dispatcher. **PERSONAL:** Born Sep 14, 1947, Columbus, MS; married Gloria; children: Robert, Roosevelt, Ryan. **EDUCATION:** Univ of Wisc. Parkside BS. **CAREER:** Self employed, real estate investor. **ORGANIZATIONS:** Mem NAACP, Urban League, Dem Party; mem issue comm Dem Party; Notory Public; mem Amer Legion, VFW, South Gate Lodge #6 Prince Hall, Intergovt PersonnelAct Adv Council; vice chmn License & Welfare Comm; pres Bd of Health; mem State Dem Affirm Action Comm; alderman City Council; state chmn Dem Black Pol Caucus; chmn Cable TV Comm; mem Northside Redevel Liaison Co; pres City Council, Bd of Dir Urban League of Racine & Kenosha WI; vice chmn City of Racine Exec Comm; chairman of Racine Personnel and Finance Committee; chairman of the State of Wisconsine Election Board; chairman Health and Sanitation Appeal Board; member Community Development Committee; chairman of Economic Development Committee City of Racine; member Board of Advisor's for Big Brothers and Big Sisters; chairman of Board of Direc tors Urban League of Racine and Kenosha; 2nd vice pres of NAACP; chairman of Racine County Drug Task Force; regent dir of Badger Boys Game of Wisc; R.A.M.A.C, Ambassador, mem Racine Raider Football board of Director; member of Racine County Youth Review and Evaluation Committee; member of Strategic Planning Committee for United School Dist of Racine. **HONORS/ACHIEVEMENTS:** Nominated Man of the Year Second Missionary Baptist Church. **MILITARY SERVICE:** USAF sgt 1967-71; Commendation Medal for Meritorious Service Vietnam. **BUSINESS ADDRESS:** Employment Coordinator, Private Industry Council, 440 Main St, Racine, WI 53403.

TURNER, SAMUEL A.
Circuit court judge. **PERSONAL:** Born Apr 06, 1926, Perry, GA; married Carmen A. Gazabon, Dec 12, 1964; children: Samuel A II, Jeffrey. **EDUCATION:** Morehouse Coll, Atlanta GA, BA, 1950; Wayne State Univ, Detroit MI, JD, 1955. **CAREER:** Detroit Welfare Dept, Detroit MI, supervisor/investigator; Samuel A Turner Law Offices, Detroit MI, attorney, 1958—; Wayne County Commissioners, Detroit MI, commissioner; Wayne County Corp Counsel, Detroit MI, corp counsel, through 1989; Third Judicial Circuit Court of Michigan, Detroit MI, currently judge. **ORGANIZATIONS:** Mem, National Bar Assn; mem, Wolverine Bar Assn; mem, Michigan Bar Assn; mem, Black Trade Unionists; chmn, Board of Commissioners; mem, NAACP.

TURNER, SHARON V.
Communication manager. **PERSONAL:** Born Jul 08, 1945, Kansas City, MO; daughter of O E Douglass and Eunice Weaver Douglass Shellner; divorced; children: Sheri Lynette Turner-Duff, Paul Eugene Jr. **EDUCATION:** Rockhurst Coll, Kansas City MO, 1980-81; Ottawa Univ, Kansas City MO, 1982-83, 1988. **CAREER:** Southwestern Bell Telephone, Kansas City MO, area manager, 1966-. **ORGANIZATIONS:** Trustee, Urban League, 1985-; trustee, Rehabilitation Loan Corp, 1987-; chair, scholarship comm, Southern Christian Leadership Conf, 1988-89; gen telethon chair, United Negro College Fund, 1989; vice pres, Black Achievers Society, 1989-; vice pres, Black Chamber of Commerce, 1989-. **HONORS/ACHIEVEMENTS:** Volunteer Service Award, YWCA, 1984; Kansas City's 100 Most Influential Black Women, Kansas City Globe Newspaper, 1984-; Outstanding Business Woman of the Year, Natl Assn of Negro Business and Professional Women, 1987; Presidents Award, Black Chamber of Commerce, 1988; Juneteenth Women of Year, Black Archives, 1989. **BUSINESS ADDRESS:** Area Manager, Southwestern Bell Telephone Company, 500 E 8th St, Rm 132, Kansas City, MO 64106.

TURNER, SHIRLEY
Educator. **PERSONAL:** Born Mar 22, 1936, South Bend, IN; divorced; children: Dawn, Kimberly, Steven. **EDUCATION:** WMU, BS 1972; WMU, MA 1977. **CAREER:** Fisk University, dean of students, dir of career planning & placement; WMU Placement Serv, asst dir; WMU Para School Learning Center. **ORGANIZATIONS:** Urban Leg of So Bend St Joseph Co Dir of Edn; Kalamazoo Pub Lib pub sch bd dir Planned Parenthood Assn; bd YMCA; YWCA Com Outreach Adv; Youth Serv Sys Adv Bd; Cont Educ for Young Women Adv Bd; consult Upward BounUniv of Notre Dame; Planned Parenthood Teen Clinics; Delta Sigma Theta Serv Sor; Dulcet Club of Kalamazoo; MI Assn of No White Concerns; Kalamazoo Personnel Assn; Midwest Cool Placement Assn. **HONORS/ACHIEVEMENTS:** Laubaugh Lit Inst Teach Awd; MI Nat All of Bus Career Guid Inst Awd; WMU Awds of Excel Sch of Soc Work Field Instr; Cert of Academic Apprec; Cert of Career Exploration Excel; produced, directed video tape, demo of prof interview tech. **BUSINESS ADDRESS:** Dean of StudentsFiskUniv, 17th Avenue North, Nashville, TN 37203.

TURNER, SHIRLEY K.
Educator. **PERSONAL:** Born Jul 03, 1941, Dover, NJ; married Donald R Turner; children: Jacqueline, Donald C. **EDUCATION:** Trenton St Coll, BS 1960-64; Rider Coll, MA Guidance & Coun 1971; Rutgers U, Doctoral Stud 1975-. **CAREER:** Rider Coll, dir Office of Career Devel 1975-, asst dir & couns of EOP Prog 1970-73; Trenton Bd of Ed, elem & secondary tchr 1966-70; Tri-kersey Inc;; pres & treas 1976-; Mercer Co Comm Action Prog, career educ consult 1977-; Mercer Co Improvement Authority;; commr 1979-. **ORGANIZATIONS:** Mem apptd by Gov NJ St Council on the Arts 1975-79; bd of dirs Urban League of Metro Trenton 1975-; chprsn of affirmative action Middle Atlantic Placement Assn 1977-78; mem zoning bd Lawrence Twsp 1979-. **HONORS/ACHIEVEMENTS:** Outstanding Young Woman of Am 1978; Hwos Who in the East 1979. **BUSINESS ADDRESS:** Dir Career Placement, Rider College, 2083 Lawrenceville Road, Lawrenceville, NJ 08648.

TURNER, TINA
Singer. **PERSONAL:** Born Nov 25, 1941, Nutbush, TN; children: Craig, Ronald Revelle. **CAREER:** Mad Max Beyond Thunderdome, co-star; singer. **HONORS/ACHIEVEMENTS:** 5 Grammy Awds incl "Better Be Good To Me" and best rock female for album Tina Live in Europe, 1989; 2 Amer Music Awds; Triple Platinum Album "Private Dancer"; Gold Single "Whats Love Got To Do With It?"; Silver Disk Awd "Lets Stay Together"; Honoree 1985 ABAA Music Award for achvmts as recording and performing artist, and for return to the forefront of music world with top-selling album, "Private Dancer"; honored with a star in the Hollywood Walk of Fame; book "I, Tina, My Life Story" 1986. *

TURNER, VIVIAN VANESSA
Accountant. **PERSONAL:** Born Feb 18, 1955, Kilmarnock, VA; daughter of John F Turner (deceased) and Vivian Alease Corbin Turner (deceased). **EDUCATION:** VA State Univ, BS Acctg Fin 1977; Univ of Hartford, MBA candidate 1990. **CAREER:** Texaco Inc, auditor 1977-78; The Traveler, accountant 1978-79; Aetna Life & Casualty, auditor 1979-80, sr admin corp human resources 1980-84, pension invest sales consult 1984-85, mgr accounting serv 1985-. **ORGANIZATIONS:** Dir Red Cross 1985-; dir YWCA 1985-; mem United Way 1985-; officer Alpha Kappa Alpha.

TURNER, W. BURGHARDT
Educator. **PERSONAL:** Born Jul 30, 1915, Jamaica, NY; son of Frank M Turner Sr and Frosty Duncan Turner; married Joyce Moore; children: Mitchell, Sylvia, Richard. **EDUCATION:** KY State Coll, AB, Columbia Univ, MA; Colunbia Univ & NY Univ, Post Grad. **CAREER:** NY City, Bay Shore, Patchogue, Long Island, teacher 15 yrs; Long Island Univ Southampton Coll, assoc prof history 1965-68; State Univ of NY Stony Brook, asst prof history 1968-79, prof emeritus 1979. **ORGANIZATIONS:** Mem, dir Natl Ed Assn Proj Civil Rights 1965; asst dir Inst School Integration Southampton Coll 1966; pres NAACP; chmn Suffolk Cty Human Rights Comm; vice pres United Fund; dir Legal Aid Soc Suffolk Cty; chmn Equal Oppty Employment Comm SUNY Stony Brook; chmn Curriculum Comm Continuing Ed; chmn bd dir Econ Oppty Council of Suffolk 1986-87. **HONORS/ACHIEVEMENTS:** Man of the Year Mens Club Temple Beth-El 1962; Man of the Year Eastern Long Island Assn Negro Bus & Professional Women 1963; Outstanding Serv Awd Natl Conf Christian & Jews 1972;co-author with Joyce Moore Turner, Richard B Moore: Caribbean Militant in Harlem (Univ of Indiana Press), Black American Writers, St Martins Press NY. **MILITARY SERVICE:** US Army 92nd Infantry Div 1942-45. **BUSINESS ADDRESS:** Assistant Professor History, StateUniv of NY, Stony Brook, NY 11794.

TURNER, WALLACE E.
Retired scientist. **PERSONAL:** Born Jan 02, 1923, Nashville, TN; son of Wallace Turner, Sr. and Imagene Johnson Turner; married Dr Jeannette M Simms; children: Reid, Lorraine, Paul, Geoffrey. **EDUCATION:** Knoxville Coll, BS 1944; NY Univ, MA 1947; Univ of NC Chapel Hill, MPH, Dr PH 1971. **CAREER:** VT Dept of Health Burlington, microbiologist 1953-68; PA Dept of Health Bur of Lab, dir of office of lab safety health & rsch 1971-80; retired l988. **ORGANIZATIONS:** Mem Amer Soc for Microbiologists 1970-80; former chmn for mem Amer Publ Health Assoc 1970-80; mem NAACP 1975-87, Knoxville Coll Club 1975-80. **HONORS/ACHIEVEMENTS:** Several articles on Microbiology Publ in Jrnl of Mycologiaetpathologica 1974, Annals of Internal Med 1978, Jrnl of Clinical Microbiology 1980. **MILITARY SERVICE:** USAF staff sgt 1944-46. **HOME ADDRESS:** 118 Petrie Ave, Rosemont, PA 19010.

TURNER, WILLIAM H.
Administrative director. **PERSONAL:** Born Aug 01, 1931, Miami, FL; married Shirley; children: 4 children. **EDUCATION:** Bethune Cookman Coll, BS 1956;Univ of Miami, MEd 1969. **CAREER:** City of Miami, policeman 1956-57; Dade Co Public School, teacher 1957-71. **ORGANIZATIONS:** Mem sch bd of Dade Co 1971; dir coll placement & comm rltns FL Memorial Coll 1971-75; vice chrmn Sch bd of Dade & Co 1972-74; bd of dir Coun of Great City Sch 1974-77; intergove liaison OTA; Edison Little Rvr Self Help Comm Cncl 1975-77, 1977-79; mem FL Schl Bd Assn 1971 ; Nat Sch Bd Assn 1971; bd mem City of Miami Comm Actn; bd mem Model Cities Prgrm Admnstr 1971; adv bd Miami Dade Comm Coll; mem Dade Co Assn for Retarded Chldrn; vice pres Black Grove; mem plnnng com Third Century; mem So Assn of Black Adminstr Persnnl 1974; dir of comm educ Charles R Drew Jr HS 1969-71; lgsltv Com FL Sch Bd Assn 1974; mem Ch of Incrntn (Episcopal); mem Dade Co Yng Dem; George Washington Carve R Br YMCA; adv bd Yth Indstrs; mem Dade Co Tax Adjustment Bd 1971; adv bd Edison Little Rvr 1971; adv bd Released Employment Placement Srv; exec com Elks Lodge; bd mgmt Carver YMCA; Dem Club of Miami Beach 1974. **HONORS/ACHIEVEMENTS:** Recip Cert Creative Writing, Bethune Cookman Coll; Sch Bell Awd Dade Co Dade Co Classroom Tchr Assn; Educ Srv Awd Miami Dade Comm Coll; Melvin Rolle Memrl Awd Liberty News Miami; Hi Beta Sigma, Tau Zeta Cit of Yr 1971; Nathan Collier Meritorious Srv Awd FL Memrl Coll 1971; Prsnlts S Outstanding & Distngshd 1971; Who's Who In FL 1973; Outstndng Civic Srv Awd Bethune Cookman Coll 1973; Certf Apprctn Nat Caucus Black Sch Bd Mem, Nat Sch Bd Assn 1974; Dictionary Intl Biography 1974; Certif Apprctn FL A&MUniv 1974; Plaque Miami Nrthwstrn Parent Adv Coun Dedicated Efforts Prvd Educ Opprtnts Yth Comm 1974; Cert Apprctn Dade Co Coun PTA 1974; Plaque for Otstnding & Meritorious Srv People Brothermen 1974; Educ of Yr Orchard Villa PTA 1974; Cert Merit Srv Big Brothers Miami 1974. **BUSINESS ADDRESS:** Sch Bd of Dade Co, 1410 NE 2 Ave, Miami, FL 33132.

TURNER, WILLIAM HOBERTT
Educator. **PERSONAL:** Born Jul 20, 1946, Lynch, KY; married Vivian Love; children: Kisha; William K; Hodari. **EDUCATION:** Univ of KY, BS 1968; Univ of Notre Dame, PhD 1974. **CAREER:** Howard Univ, sr rsch fellow 1977-79; Univ of KY, asst prof of sociology 1979-84; KY State Univ, dean of arts and sciences 1984-85; Winston Salem State Univ, chairman of social sciences 1985-. **ORGANIZATIONS:** Eastern KY Social/Heritage Soc, historian/archivist 1977-; USAID, consultant 1986; Comm on Religion in Appalachia, commissioner 1986-; EKSC, editor/publisher. **HONORS/ACHIEVEMENTS:** Nat'l Rsch Council, ford foundation fellow 1983; WSSU, favorite teacher 1986. **BUSINESS ADDRESS:** Social Sciences Chairman, Winston Salem StateUniv, Winston-Salem, NC 27110.

TURNER, WILLIE
Educator. **PERSONAL:** Born Feb 01, 1935; married Porter; children: Vincent, Austin, Nicole, Dina. **EDUCATION:** MD St Coll, BS 1957; OH St U, MSc 1959; PhD 1961. **CAREER:** MD State Coll, lab asst 1954-57; MD State Coll, rsch asst 1957; MD St Coll, grad asst 1957-59; Meharry Med Coll, instr of mcrblgy 1962-63; Meharry Med Coll, asst prof microbiology 1963-66; TN St A&I Univ, lecturer 1962; Bowie State Coll, 1969; Howard Univ, prof chmn microbiology Dept 1971; OH St Univ, NIH pre doctoral fellow 1959-61; Naval Med Rsch Inst, NIH postdoctoral fellow 1961-62; Nat Cancer Inst, NCI staff fellow 1966-69; Natl Cancer Inst, NCI sr staff fellow, 1969-70; head microbiology section 1970-71. **ORGANIZATIONS:** Mem, Sigma Xi; Am Soc for Microbiology; Am Assn Advancement Sci; NY Acad Sci; Amer Assn Cancer Rsch; Tissue Culture Assn; Soc Experimental Biology & Med; Amer Assn Immunologists; Am Assn Med School Chmn; Am Assn Dental School Chmn. **HONORS/ACHIEVEMENTS:** Recipient numerous NIH Rsch Grants; NCI Cancer Center Core Grant 1973; NIH ICC Exchange Fellow to Paris 1971. **BUSINESS ADDRESS:** 520 W St NW, Washington, DC 20059.

TURNER, WINSTON E.
Retired educator. **PERSONAL:** Born Aug 23, 1921, Washington, DC; son of Frederick F Turner and Mary Montague Turner; married Helen Smith Turner; children: Lisa, Valerie. **EDUCATION:** Miner Teachers Coll, BS 1947; NY Univ, MA 1949; St Coll Educ Plattsburgh NY; DC Tchrs Coll; Georgetown U; Univ Bridgeport Ct. **CAREER:** DC Pblc Schls, tchr 1947-54; Miner Tchrs Coll, monroe lab sch 1954-57; DC Tchrs Coll, asst prof educ truesdell lab sch 1957-59; HD Cooke Elem Sch Wash DC, prin 1959-69; River Terrace Elem Sch Wash DC, retired prin 1976. **ORGANIZATIONS:** Life mem Natl Educ Assn; Phi Delta Kappa; mem pres Natl Assn Elem Sch prins 1974-75; DC Elem Sch Prins Assn; Assn Study Negro Life History; pres vice pres treas prog ch Elem Sch Prins Assn Wash DC; ch non graded & Team Tchng Com Model Schs Div; mem exec com cncl offcrs DC Pub Schs; mem Examining Panels Prin Asst Prins DC Pub Schs; examining asst Day Elem Sch Prins NY City; mem bd dirs SE Neighbrhd Hse; mem Columbia Hghts Boys Clb; mem Queens Chapel Civic Assn; life mem NAACP; Omega Psi Phi Frat; Pigskin Clb Wash DC; Mt Jezreel Bapt Ch. **HONORS/ACHIEVEMENTS:** Guest lectr Howard Univ 1974; Outstndng Prin Awd DC Elem Sch Prin Assn 1974; Outstanding Ret Tr Award, Jr Citizens Corps 1978; Outstanding Public Service: Mayor Baltimore Md, Afro-American Newspaper, Central Summerfield United Meth Church, 1980; Man of the Year, New Bethel Baptist Church, 1981; publications, The Black Principal and the Bicentennial, Principal, 1976; Principals in the Pressure Cooker, Principal 1977; Expanding Our Horizons through Global Education, Principal 1980. **MILITARY SERVICE:** US Army 1st sgt 1942-46.

TURNER, YVONNE WILLIAMS
Housing counselor and community resources specialist. **PERSONAL:** Born Apr 05, 1927, Birmingham, AL; daughter of John H Williams and Leitha Williams; married James L Turner, Sr, Jun 09, 1945; children: Philandus C, Roderick G, Keith H, Leitha B, Stanley M. **EDUCATION:** Booker T Washington Junior College of Business, Birmingham, AL, diploma, 1950; Rosetta Reifer's School of Modeling, New York, NY, certificate, 1954; Anna Watson's School of Millinery Designing, 1958-68; Dale Carnegie School, Birmingham, AL, certificate, 1960. **CAREER:** Booker T Washington Insurance Company, Birmingham, AL, clerk, 1946-64; Clyde Kirby Insurance Agency, Birmingham, AL, secretary, 1965-66; Department of Housing and Urban Development, Birmingham, AL, clerk trypist, 1966-77, computer technician, 1977-82, community resources specialist, 1982-86, program assistant in single family division loan management, 1986-87; Birmingham Housing Authority, Birmingham, AL, housing counselor, 1987-. **ORGANIZATIONS:** Member, Alabama Christian Movement for Human Rights and Southern Christian Leadership Conference, 1956-; fund raiser, United Negro College Fund, 1965-; member, Birmingham Design Review Committee, Birmingham, AL, 1979-85; member, 1985-, secretary, 1989-, Birmingham Arts Commission, Birmingham, AL; member, Jefferson-Blount-St Clair Mental Health/Mental Retardation Authority Board, 1989-. **HONORS/ACHIEVEMENTS:** Certificate of recognition, Booker T Washington Junior College of Business Alumni Association, 1978; plaque for 25 years of outstanding service, National Southern Christian Leadership Conference, 1982; alumni merit award, Booker T Washington Junior College of Business, 1984; named in House of Representative Resolution 125, 1988; author of column "Socially Speaking," Birmingham Times, 1988-. **HOME ADDRESS:** 504-10th Court, West, Birmingham, AL 35204. **BUSINESS ADDRESS:** Housing Counselor for the Homeless, Birmingham Housing Authority, 2323-7th Ave, North, 2nd floor, Birmingham, AL 35203.

TURNER-GIVENS, ELLA MAE
Educator, liaison, pianist, organist. **PERSONAL:** Born Jun 05, 1927, Los Angeles, CA; daughter of Ezekiel Moore and Ruth Moore; married Walter Givens. **EDUCATION:** Univ of Southern California, BMusic 1957; State of California Dept of Educ, life diploma speciall secondary teaching credential in music 1965; Graduate School Univ of California, 1965, 1966,

1968; California Dept of Educ, life diploma standard secondary teaching credential; California Dept of Educ, life diploma standard & secondary teachng credential in Engish 1968. **CAREER:** Los Angeles Unified School Dist, teacher 1971-; Los Angeles High School, teacher 1967-71; Girls Social Adjustment School, teacher 1966-67; Markham Jr High School Summer Opportunity Center Program, teacher 1965; Manual Arts High School, teacher summer 1962; Markham Jr High School, teacher 1958-66; Foshay Jr High School, teacher 1957-58. **ORGANIZATIONS:** Chmn Natl Advisory Council Housing, Educ and Welfare; advisory council HUD; mem Textbook Adoption Comm Los Angeles City Church; adjudicator Southern California Vocal Assn; host, chmn Southern California Vocal Assn Choral Festivals; pres Secondary Music Teacher Assn; organizer First Boys Glee Club Foshay Jr High School; first piano classes Markham Jr High School; chmn, bd dir Do Re Me Child Devel Center; mem NEA; California Teacher Assn; Los Angeles Teacher Assn; Music Educ Natl Conf; Los Angeles County Music Educ Assn; Amer Choral Dir Assn; Southern California Vocal Assn; advisory health council State Dept of Health; Child Devel Advisory Bd; consultant California State Dept of Health; consultant UCLA; consultant State of California Personnel Bd; consultant W Interstate Commn on Higher Educ; consultant California Work Incentive Plan Program; consultant Neighborhood Adult Ptcptn Proj; Neumeyer Found mem Atty Gen Vol Advisory Council; representative State Control Comm; appointee California Gov Comm for Employment of the Handicapped; Statewide Planning Project Advisory Comm Vocational Rehabilitation; sec Advisory Comm Urban Affairs Inst; Dist Atty Advisory Council; Dist Atty Legis Council; consultant Delinquency Prevention Center. **HONORS/ACHIEVEMENTS:** Recipient 10th Dist PTA 4 year scholarship; Delta Sigma Theta Sor Scholarship; Order of the E Star Scholarship awarded twice; Women's Political Study Club Scholarship; first black woman in US history to chair a Natl Advisory Council. **HOME ADDRESS:** 2158 W 82nd St, Los Angeles, CA 90047.

TURNIPSEED, CARL WENDELL
Business executive. **PERSONAL:** Born Dec 21, 1947, Baltimore, MD; son of Willis Turniseed and Alice P. Turniseed; married Joyce Hill; children: Danielle. **EDUCATION:** Morgan State Coll, BS 1969; NY Univ Grad Sch of Business, MBA 1974. **CAREER:** Fed Reserve Bank of NY, over 18 yrs of mgmt experience in various areas incl acctng, govt bonds, check proc, elect funds trnsfers, personnel, foreign relations, asst vp. **ORGANIZATIONS:** Urban Bankers Coalition internal vice pres; Keeper of the Exchequer Brooklyn Long Island Alumni Kappa Alpha Psi Fraternity 1988-; mem Union Baptist Church 1980-; mem NAACP 1982-; mem Assoc of MBA Executives 1982-; mem Urban Bankers Assn 1983-; mem Black MBA Assn 1983-; mem MBA Executives; member 16th South East Asia, New Zealand & Australia Central Banking Program 1986; vstg prof Natl Urban League BEEP. **HONORS/ACHIEVEMENTS:** Martin Luther King Jr Alumni Assoc of NY Univ Awd for Achievements in Commerce 1978; President's Award for Excellence Federal Reserve Bank of N.Y. 1987. **MILITARY SERVICE:** AUS 1st lt 2 yrs; Honorable Discharge. **BUSINESS ADDRESS:** Assistant Vice President, Federal Reserve Bank of NY, 33 Liberty St, New York, NY 10045.

TURNLEY, RICHARD, JR.
Government official. **PERSONAL:** Born Nov 15, 1933, Plaquemine, LA; married Joyce; children: Tamera, Sharon, Richard. **EDUCATION:** So U, BS; SoUniv Law Sch, JD. **CAREER:** So Tchr & Parents Credit Union, treas mgr; Legis Budget Com, mem; Criminal Justice Appropriation Com, admin; Air Port Dist, vp; State of LA, state rep dist 63 1972-. **ORGANIZATIONS:** Mem PBS Pinceback Elks Lodge; bd mem Com Cncl Drug Prevention & Treatment; mem Credit Union Nat AssnUniv WI; Comprehensive Hlth & Rehab Bd; pres-Scotlandville Area Adv Cncl; mem Prince Hall Mason 32nd Deg; Cncl Mem Meth Ch. **MILITARY SERVICE:** AUS 1955-57.

TURPIN, MEL KEITH
Professional athlete. **PERSONAL:** Born Dec 28, 1960, Lexington, KY. **EDUCATION:** Kentucky, 1979-84. **CAREER:** Cleveland Cavalier, center 1984. **HONORS/ACHIEVEMENTS:** Finished career at KY with 1509 points to rank 9th on the schools all-time scoring list. **BUSINESS ADDRESS:** Cleveland Cavaliers, The Colesium, Ste 510, Richfield, OH 44286.

TUTMAN, WILLIAM L.
Business executive. **PERSONAL:** Born Oct 26, 1931, Baltimore, MD. **EDUCATION:** Morgan State Coll, BS 1957; Amer Univ, MS 1961; Union Grad Sch, PhD 1973; Hubbard Guidance Ctr Acad DSci 1982. **CAREER:** US Peace Corps Tanzania, dir 1969; Univ of MA, prof 1973; Exec Mgmt Inst, owner 1973-84; Phoenix Inst of Peace Tech, pres. **ORGANIZATIONS:** Mem Natl & Local Chap Assn Black Psychologists; mem bd Reg Learning Ctr Baltimore. **MILITARY SERVICE:** AUS 1950-52. **BUSINESS ADDRESS:** President, Phoenix Inst of Peace Tech, 3609 Silver Park Dr, Suitland, MD 20748.

TUTT, LIA S.
Financial planner. **PERSONAL:** Born May 04, 1960, Washington, DC; daughter of Dr Walter C Tutt and Julia Smith Tutt; divorced; children: Fiana T Brown. **EDUCATION:** Howard Univ, BS 1982; Attending, George Washington Univ. **CAREER:** ICA Financial Planning Ctr, registered rep and financial planner; T Natl Financial, Washington, DC, certified financial planner. **ORGANIZATIONS:** Mem various comm serv organizations 1972-85; sec Jack & Jill of Amer Assn 1972-78; mem Natl Black MBA Assoc 1986-; lecturer on financial mgmt and wealth accumulation. **HONORS/ACHIEVEMENTS:** Certificate and Trophy Outstanding Participation & Congeniality Howard Univ 1979, 1980; Certificate Tribute to Ideal Black Womanhood Ebony Magazine 1980; certificate: Outstanding Performance on the bd of dir to Biomedical Research Engineering JTF, 1988. **BUSINESS ADDRESS:** Certified Financial Planner/Investment Consultant, PO Box 6366, Washington, DC 20707.

TUTT, WALTER CORNELIUS
Dental surgeon. **PERSONAL:** Born Jan 29, 1918, Birmingham, AL; son of Rev. Walter Andrew Tutt and Corinne Flood Tutt; married Julia Smith (deceased); children: Lia. **EDUCATION:** Livingstone Coll, BS 1939; Howard Univ, Grad School 1942-43, DDS 1957; Univ of Florence 1945. **CAREER:** NC Publ School, teacher 1941-42; VA Publ School, teacher 1947-48; Private practice, dental surgeon 31 yrs. **ORGANIZATIONS:** Mem Robert T Freeman Dental Soc, Natl Dental Assoc, Amer Dental Assoc; formerly utilization rev subcomm Home Care prog DC Gen Hosp; past pres Prince Williams Cty Teacher Assn 1948; mem, past pres WA Grad Chap Chi Delta Mu Natl Med Frat; grand exec comm Grand Chap Chi Delta Mu; mem Kappa Alpha Psi; past mem adv comm WA Alumni Chap Kappa Alpha Psi; bd of dir WA Alumni Chap Kappa Alpha Psi; mem Rock Creek E Neighborhood League, Pigskin Club WA, Howard Univ Gen & Dental Alumni Assoc; treas Hellians Inc. **HONORS/ACHIEVEMENTS:** Conspicious Serv Awd Chi Delta Mu; Citation Disting Alumni of Historically Black Coll Natl Assoc for Equal Oppty in Higher Ed. **MILITARY SERVICE:** AUS 1944-45; Combat Infantry Badge, Three Battle Stars, Two Campaign Ribbons, Good Conduct Medal. **BUSINESS ADDRESS:** Dental Surgeon, 4122 16th St NW, Washington, DC 20011.

TWEED, ANDRE R.
Physician. **PERSONAL:** Born Apr 16, 1914, New York City, NY; married Ruth; children: Phyllis, Roland, Wayne, Andrea. **EDUCATION:** Brooklyn Coll, BA 1936; Howard U, MD 1942. **CAREER:** Columbia Univ Montefiore Hospital, 1949; Loma Linda Univ Med esmnr Superior Ct LA Co, asso clinical prof psychiatry 1950-74; psychologist in private practice, 1950-; Kedren Community Mental Health Center, chief of children in patient, chief of adult day care. **ORGANIZATIONS:** Mem, life fellow Amer Psychiatric Assn; Black Psychiatrist of Southern CA; Black Psychiatrists Amer Hon LlD, Forensic Psychiatry CA Coll Law, 1973; diplomate, Amer Bd of Psychiatry & Neurology, 1949; AAAS; fellow, Amer Assn for the Advancement of Psychotherapy. **HONORS/ACHIEVEMENTS:** Hon JD, CA College of Law; established private museum of Ethiopian religious artifacts. **MILITARY SERVICE:** AUS capt 1943-46, 50-51. **BUSINESS ADDRESS:** 3750 W 54th St, Los Angeles, CA 90043.

TWIGG, LEWIS HAROLD
Physician. **PERSONAL:** Born Oct 05, 1937, Muskogee, OK; married Myrna; children: Lewis III, Karen. **EDUCATION:** Morehouse Coll, BS 1958; Atlanta Univ, MS 1960; Meharry Med Coll, MD 1967. **CAREER:** MI State Coll, assoc clinical prof dept ob-gyn & reproductive biology of human med; Hurley Med Ctr, vice chmn dept ob-gyn 1978-81; Private Practice, physician. **ORGANIZATIONS:** Mem Flint Acad Surgery; mem Alpha Phi Alpha Frat; diplomate Amer Bd Ob-Gyn; Fellow Coll Ob-Gyn. **BUSINESS ADDRESS:** 4250 N Saginaw St, Flint, MI 48505.

TWINE, EDGAR HUGH
Attorney. **PERSONAL:** Born Oct 09, 1935, Chicago, IL; married Lillian; children: Deborah Jeleen, Edgar H. **EDUCATION:** Univ of IL, BS 1956; Univ of IL Coll of Law, LlB 1958, MIT, MS 1973. **CAREER:** Atlantic Richfield Co, assoc gen couns 1973-; US Dept of Justice, atty 1958-69. **ORGANIZATIONS:** Mem bd of Contract Appeals US Dept of Transport 1969-70; gen atty Atlantic Richfield Co 1971-72; sr atty Atlantic Richfield Co 1970; admitt to pract IL Sup Ct; US Ct of Claims; US Sup Ct; CA Sup Ct; DC Ct of Appeals; US Ct of Milit Appeals; bd of dir Econ Resour Corp 1974-; mem bd of visitUniv of OR Sch of Law; Com on the envior; CA State Bar Assoc; lect Black Exec Exchan Prog; mem Amer Bar Assoc; CA State Bar Assoc; lect BlackExec Exchan Prog; mem Amer Bar Assoc; CA Bar Assoc; DC Bar; Langston Bar Assoc; Los Angel Co Bar Assoc; Natl Bar Asso; Alpha Phi Alpha Frat JohnHay Whitney Flwshp 1957-59. **HONORS/ACHIEVEMENTS:** Merit Serv Awd Dept of Justice 1965; Bd of Stud EditrsUniv of IL Law Forum 1956-58; Order of the CoifUniv of IL Coll of Law 1958; Sloan Fellow MIT Sloan Sch of Mang 1972-73; Outstdng Alum Achiev AwdUniv of IL Coll of Law 1976. **MILITARY SERVICE:** USAR capt 1958-67. **BUSINESS ADDRESS:** Associate General Counsel, ARCO, 515 S Flower St, AP-4535, Los Angeles, CA 90071.

TWYMAN, LUSKA J.
Former mayor. **PERSONAL:** Born May 19, 1914, Hiseville, KY; married Gladys Woodson. **EDUCATION:** KY State U, AB; IN U, MS; Simmons U, LlD. **CAREER:** Glasgow, KY, mayor 1969-; Ralph Bunche Sch, prin, tchr coach 2 yrs.

TYLER, GERALD DEFOREST
Educational administrator. **PERSONAL:** Born Feb 28, 1946, Louisa Co, VA; son of John Tyler and Annie Tyler; married Pamela Celeste Preston; children: Michael Jerome. **EDUCATION:** Norfolk State Univ, BS (honors) 1977, MA (highest honors) 1983; Old Dominion Univ, pursuing PhD 1983. **CAREER:** Dalmo Sales Co, salesman 1964-66; US Marine Corps, admiral's orderly 1966-69; Tidewater Regional Transit System, bus oper 1969-77; Elizabeth City State Univ, spec asst to chancellor 1977-84; Norfolk State Univ, dir of univ relations, 1984-. **ORGANIZATIONS:** Mem, NAACP, 1979-; Adv ECSU Student Chap NAACP 1980-84; mem NC State Employees Assn Inc 1980-84; pres Prof Business Assn 1980-81; alternate delegate 35th Annual NCSEA Convention Comm 1980-81; mem S Humanities Conf 1980-82; chmn NC State Employees Assoc Inc 1981-82; mem Greater Bibleway Temple 120 Club 1981; 1st vice pres Pasquotank Co Branch NAACP 1981-84; mem NCSEA Inc Area 24 Exec Bd 1981-84; adv ECSU Sr Class 1981-84; 1st vice chmn Pasquotank Co Voting Precinct 3B 1981-82; mem NCSEA Inc Bd of Governors 1981-82; chmn NCSEA Inc Area 24 1981-82; bd mem Gov's FOTC Assn 1982-84; bd mem Albemarle Develop Auth 1982-84; head adv ECSU Sr Class 1982-84; mem NCSEA Inc State Organ Study Comm 1982-83; mem Pasquotank Co Voting Precinct 3B 1983-84; mem Pasquotank Co Improvement Assn 1983-84; mem New Towne Civic League 1984-86; mem Tidewater Media Prof Assn 1984-; bd mem New Towne Civic League 1984-; mem VA Social Sci Assn 1984-; mem Virginia Assn of Printing, Publications & Public Relations, 1986; bd of dirs & advisors, Pepper Bird Found, 1988. **HONORS/ACHIEVEMENTS:** Safe Driving Awd for operating 32 passenger bus free of accidents while employed at TRT 1969-77; Outstanding Young Men of America Awd 1979; Certificate of Appreciation UNCF New York 1979; Outstanding Boxer Awd USMC; First AwdCert as Asst Head Coach for ECSU's Lady Vikings Softball Team 1980-81; NCSEA Inc Employee of the Year Awd 1981-82; Awd for Outstanding Leadership Unselfish and Dedicated Serv rendered as Sr Class Advisor 1982-84. **MILITARY SERVICE:** USMC E-6/staff sgt 6 yrs; recipient of the Presidential Unit Citation; USN Commendation; Good Conduct Medal; Natl Def Medal. **BUSINESS ADDRESS:** Dir of University Relations, Norfolk StateUniv, Wilson Hall, Suite 340, 2401 Corprew Ave, Norfolk, VA 23504.

TYLER, HUBERT
Educator. **PERSONAL:** Born May 23, 1934, Ridgeland, SC; married Jessie Wright; children: Dr Yasmin Tyler-Hill, Mrs Kahn Tyler-Smith, Khandra Y. **EDUCATION:** Savannah State Coll; BS 1959; Armstrong-Savannah State Grad Sch, MS 1976. **CAREER:** Robert Smalls Jr HS, math & science teacher 1959-. **ORGANIZATIONS:** Mem BCEA, SCEA, NEA 1959-; leader St John Ame Church 1965-; sr warden Shiloh Lodge #92 1976-; mem Live Oak Hosp Bd 1976-86; mem Jasper Co Bd of Educ 1976-89; vice pres Ridgeland Chap of NAACP 1984-; mem Beaufort Jasper Career Ctr 1985-89. **HONORS/**

ACHIEVEMENTS: Family of Year Jasper Co 1980; Serv Awd Ridgeland High Athletic Dept 1980, 1983; Serv Awd Jasper Co School Dist 1983; Serv Aws Cystic Fibrosis FoundSC Chap 1983; listed in Who's Who in American Politics 1983-84. **MILITARY SERVICE:** AUS sgt 1951-54; Combat Inf Badge; Korean Serv Medal; 2 Bronze Stars; UN Serv Medal; Good Conduct Medal; Natl Defense Serv Medal. **HOME ADDRESS:** Route 3 Box 472, Ridgeland, SC 29936.

TYLER, JOHN LEWIS
Retired social work executive. **PERSONAL:** Born Jan 25, 1914, Clifton Forge, VA; married Elizabeth Moultrie; children: Ingrid Elizabeth, Johnetta Louise. **EDUCATION:** VA State Coll, BA, 1939; Loyola Univ School of Social Work, MA, 1951; St John's Univ, NY, studied law. **CAREER:** VA Lakeside Hospital, social work serv, 1967-; Hines Hospital, prog supvr social work serv, 1965-67, supvr, social work serv, 1955-63; Cook County, program dir, juvenile home, 1951-54, social worker, 1949-51; Farmville, VA, school teacher, 1940; Maywood, IL, social work consultant, child home, 1960-65. **ORGANIZATIONS:** Natl Assn of Social Work; mem, Amer Police Center Museum, 1975; Federal Exec Bd, EEOC, 1975. **HONORS/ACHIEVEMENTS:** Acad of Certified Social Workers; Certified Social Worker, State of IL, chmn, Chiefs Social Work Serv Comm, VA Med Dist No 18, 1974; Bronze Star AUS. **MILITARY SERVICE:** AUS 1943-46. **BUSINESS ADDRESS:** 333 E Huron St, Chicago, IL 60611.

TYLER, LEE MALCOLM
Educator. **PERSONAL:** Born Mar 24, 1917, Norway-orangeburg; married Mary M Ferguson; children: Benard Lee, Malcaretta Hudson, Joyce Jones, Marthella Odoms, Gwendolyn McClam, Lee Mathis. **EDUCATION:** SC State Coll, MEd 1960; Universal Bible Inst, DD 1977. **CAREER:** Newberry Coll, coor minority affairs 1976-; Cedar Br SS Conv Aiken Co, pres organ 1966-73; Orangeburg Orthodox SS Conv, pres 1954-64; Norfield Sch & Norway Orangeburg Co, prin 1941-73; Prince Ele Sch Orangeburg Co, prin 1938-41. **ORGANIZATIONS:** Mem adv bd Connil Maxwell Home Greenwood 1974-; mem adv bd Newberrry Co Counc on Aging 1979-; moderator Beaver Creek Bapt Assn 1958-73; pres GreaterNewberry Ministers Assn 1978-79; pres Mid-carolina Ministers 1979-; pres Newberry Ministerial Alliance 1979-. **HONORS/ACHIEVEMENTS:** Awd of Appreciation Secondary Sch Prin Conv 1969; Awd of Appreciation Morris Coll Sumter, SC 1976; Outstdg Serv Field of Educ Bushy David Bapt Ch Norway 1979. **BUSINESS ADDRESS:** New Berry College, 2100 College St, Newberry, SC 29108.

TYLER, ROBERT JAMES, SR.
Elected govt. official. **PERSONAL:** Born Dec 14, 1935, Darby, PA; son of Joseph Tyler and Katharine Tyler; married Phyllis E Jones-Tyler, Aug 30, 1958; children: Mary E, Robert J Jr. **EDUCATION:** Univ of PA, ABA in Business 1978. **CAREER:** Philadelphia Svg Fund Soc, mortgage loan solicitor 1967; Hope Develop Corp, mgmt 1971; First PA Bank NA, appraisal dept 1973; Tyler Realty Co, owner 1978. **ORGANIZATIONS:** Co-chair Equal Oppor & Govtl Agencies PA State Realtor 1983-84; pres Darby-Lansdowne Rotary 1984-85; treas Delaware Co Bd of Realtors 1985; Equal Opportunity co-chair Bd of Realtors 1985; mem Darby Salvation Army Adv Council 1985; mem Wm Penn Sch Authority 1983-; trustee First Baptist Church of Darby 1960-; director, Delaware County Red Cross 1985-88; president, 1988, dir, 1989-92, Delaware County Board of Realtor, Equal Opportunity chmn, Pennsylvania Assn of Realtor 1989. **HONORS/ACHIEVEMENTS:** Civic Awd The Chapel of Four Chaplains 1970; Civic Awd Penguin Club of Darby 1972; Civic Awd First Baptist Church of Darby 1980; Community Service, The Penguins of Darby 1988. **MILITARY SERVICE:** USMC corpl, E-4, 12 yrs. **BUSINESS ADDRESS:** Realtor, Self Tyler Realty Co, 850 Main St, PO Box 121, Darby, PA 19023.

TYLER, SHIRLEY NEIZER
Educational administrator. **PERSONAL:** Born in Philadelphia, PA; daughter of Raymond F Neizer and Frances W Neizer; divorced; children: Richard J Jr, Kathryn T. **EDUCATION:** Simmons Clg, BS 1950; u VA. **CAREER:** Natl Schlrshp Serv Fund Negro Stdnt, assc cnslng pr, Arlington Cty Pblc Sch VA, edctr, Gilchrist Co Boston VA, prsnl admn, US Natl Stdnt Assc Madison, WI, exec sec, Grace Episcopal Sch, dir. **ORGANIZATIONS:** Bddir Mid Atlantic Episcopal Sch Assc 1984-87; mem Govnr Ed Block Grant Cmt 1982-, Natl Assc Elem Sch Prncpl, Natl Assc Ed Yng Chldrn; chmn/v chmn Alexandria City Sch Bd 1973-82; former bd dir vchrmn Alexandria Comm Hlth Clnc; mem Alexandria Hosp Corp;former bd dir Northern VA Fmly Svc, NAACP, VA Urban League. **HONORS/ACHIEVEMENTS:** Distngshd serv Citizens Alexandria, VA 1982; otstndtg serv ed Washington Urban League N Virginia 1982; otstndg comm serv NAACP Alexandria Brch 1980; communit activist etc Hopkins House Assc 1982. **HOME ADDRESS:** 3703 Edison St, Alexandria, VA 22305.

TYLER, WALDO H.
Government employee, pharmacist. **PERSONAL:** Children: 2 daughters. **EDUCATION:** Muskingum Coll New Concord OH, 1953-56; OH State Univ, BS 1960; OSU, 1971. **CAREER:** Chicago Urban League, dep exec dir; Tyler Drugs Columbus OH, owner, pharmacist 1960-70; Urban Resources Columbus OH, vice pres 1970-72; East Central Citizens Org, dir 1972; Office of Minority Bus Enterprise, mgr 1972-73, bureau chief econ & comm dev 1973-76; Isabelle Ridgeway Nursing Ctr, cons, pharmacist 1984. **ORGANIZATIONS:** Former mem, exec comm St Anthony Hosp Adv Bd; founder Martin Luther King Branch Libr Council; past pres bd dir Isabelle Ridgway the Aged Comm Indust Devel Corp of CMA-CAO; chmn Stock Sales Comm; bd of dir Beneficial Acceptance Corp; fellow Amer Soc Consult Pharmacists. **HONORS/ACHIEVEMENTS:** Citizen-Jrnl Outstanding Man of the Year Awd 1964; Columbus Metro Area Comm Action Org Leadership Awd in Ed 1969.

TYLER-SLAUGHTER, CECIL LORD
Social services consultant. **PERSONAL:** Born Oct 15, 1958, Peoria, IL; son of Willie Albert Scott and Verline Tyler-Scott. **EDUCATION:** Illinois State Univ, cultural anthropology & micro-economics 1974-78. **CAREER:** Florida Job Serv, interim super to private sector 1979; Learning Tree Prep Sch, publicity dir & after school coord program 1980-84; Central IL/Eastern IA Salvation Army Headquarters, housing relocation specialist 1984; Peoria Assn Retarded Citizens, residential counselor-consultant 1985-. **ORGANIZATIONS:** Club leader Peoria County 4-H 1976-83; black history research reporter Traveler Newspaper 1980-84; mem Peoria Historical Soc 1982-; mem Peoria Lake View Museum for Arts Sci 1982-; media rsch consultant NAACP 1983-84; minority prog rsch journalist GE cable radio CCI 1984-. **HONORS/ACHIEVEMENTS:** Outstanding Young Man in Amer US Jaycees 1980; 4-H Bronze Leadership Peoria Co 4-H/Peoria 1982; nominated White House Fellowship US Chamber of Commerce 1982; Special Merit Citation Save the Children Fund Mayor's Office 1983. **BUSINESS ADDRESS:** Residential Counsel-Consultant, Peoria Assn Retarded Citizens, P O Box 5942, Peoria, IL 61602.

TYNER, CHARLES R.
Clergyman, educator. **PERSONAL:** Born Jun 23, 1950, Murfreesboro, NC. **EDUCATION:** ShawUniv Raleigh, NC, 1972; Southeastern Bapt Sem Wake Forest, NC. **CAREER:** Mt Moriah Bapt Church, pastor 1969-; White Oak Bapt Church, 1972-; Tarboro City Schools, admin asst supt 1972-. **ORGANIZATIONS:** Mem W Roanoke Bapt Assn, exec com; Shaw Theological Alumni Assn; pres Hertford Co Min Alliance; NC Assn Educ mem NAACP; Prince Hall Grand Lodge F& A Masons of NC; vice pres New Hope Bapt Assn. **HONORS/ACHIEVEMENTS:** Merit Outstdg Leadership ShawUniv 1969, 70, 71, 72; merit Great Ldrshp in Comm Murfreesboro, NC 1973; merit Outstdg Work General Bapt Conv NC 1971, 72, 73.

TYNER, MCCOY
Jazz musician. **PERSONAL:** Born Dec 11, 1938, Philadelphia, PA; married Aisha. **EDUCATION:** Studied at West Philadelphia Music School and at the Granoff Music School. **CAREER:** John Coltrane's Group, pianist 1960's; Cal Massey, trumpeter; McCoy Tyner, composer/arranger/bandleader. **HONORS/ACHIEVEMENTS:** Album "Looking Out" (Columbia Records); wrote music and lyrics to "In Search of My Heart.". **BUSINESS ADDRESS:** Abby Hoffer Enterprises, 223 1/2 E 48th St, New York, NY 10017.

TYNER, REGINA LISA
Company executive. **PERSONAL:** Born Jul 05, 1945, New York, NY; daughter of William H Kearney (deceased) and Edith H Williams (deceased); married Berson J Tyner Sr, Nov 12, 1983; children: Jane Marie Glenn, Bonita Jo Glenn. **EDUCATION:** Univ of Puget Sound, BS Bus Admin 1969, MA Bus Admin 1971; Harvard Univ, State & Local Exec Prog, 1980. **CAREER:** City of Tacoma, minority empl spec civil serv coord 1971-72; City of Tacoma Tech Transfer Ctr, dir 1972-77; Office of Intergovt Affairs City of Tacoma, dir 1977; WA State Dept of Retirement Systems, dep dir 1977-79; City of Seattle, dir dept of licenses & consumer affairs, 1979-86; Continental Telephone of NW, dir public affairs, 1986-88; Amer Communications Enterprises Inc, pres, 1988-. **ORGANIZATIONS:** Mem, Alpha Kappa Alpha Sorority Inc, 1975-; Vice chair found comm Intl City Mgmt Assoc 1975; rep City of Seattle Public Tech Inc 1982; mem Amer Soc of Prof Admins 1982; bd of dir United Way of King Cty 1980-86, Leadership Tomorrow 1983-87; instr South Seattle Comm Coll 1985; mem, Ladies Auxiliary of Veterans of Foreign Wars, Post 2289, Seattle, WA, 1985-; bd of dir, Washington Leadership Inst, 1988-, Municipal League of King County, 1988-, Medina Children Services, 1988-. **HONORS/ACHIEVEMENTS:** Award of Excellence, Amer Soc Public Admin, 1986. **BUSINESS ADDRESS:** Pres, Owner, American Communications Enterprises Inc, 1800 112th Ave NE, Suite 360E, Bellevue, WA 98004.

TYNES, RICHARD H.
Engineer. **PERSONAL:** Born Apr 28, 1942, Washington, DC; married Charlene L Bracken. **EDUCATION:** Lake MI Coll, AA Indsl Engr 1962; Western MI U, BS Engineering 1965; MI St U, MBA 1969; Gen Motor Dealer Devel Academy, grad 1975. **CAREER:** Tynes Chev Cadillac Inc, pres 1976; Whirlpool Corp 1965-73; indsl & engr 1965-68; spl assingments with inner city bus 1970; budget mgr 1971-73; Notre Dame U, Engineering Dept, instr 1969-71; Lake MI Coll, instr 1968. **ORGANIZATIONS:** Bd mem, pres, treas, vp, So Bend Chap Am Inst of Indsl Engrs 1966-71; bd mem Mercy Hosp Benton Harbor MI 1969-76; Berrien Co Canvassars, 1970-75; bd mem, "Y" uncle, YMCA 1969-71; bd of dirs Grady Hosp Delaware OH; pres Benton Harbor Alumni Chap Kappa Alpha Psi; chmn NAACP Freedom Fund Banquet 1972. **BUSINESS ADDRESS:** 680 Sunbury Rd, Delaware, OH 43015.

TYRANCE, HERMAN J.
Educator. **PERSONAL:** Born Feb 03, 1911, Attleboro, MA; married Marian Taylor; children: Carol, Dianne, Linda. **EDUCATION:** VA State Coll, BS 1938; Boston U, MEd 1947; PA State U, PhD 1954. **CAREER:** Dept of Physical Educ & Recreation, chmn 1949-; FL A&M Univ, visiting prof 1969; Jackson State Coll, 1955-60; Wash Action of Youth WAY Workshop for DC Public School Teacher, group leader 1964; Howard Univ, dir of Intramurals; DC Dept of Recreaton's Prog, dir 1968; City of Wash's Summer Enrichment Prog, dir 1967; Operation Champ, dir 1966; Summer Adven for Youth SAY, dir 1965; Labor Dept Project CAUSE, prog coor eval 1964; Howard Univ, dir two Peace Corps Prog summer 1952 & fall 1953; Lincoln HS MD, dir health & phsysical educ coach 1939-42. **ORGANIZATIONS:** Mem Affiliation for Hlth Physical Educ & Recreation; DC Assn for Hlth Physical Educ & Recreation; Nat Intramural Assn; Nat Coll Physical Educ Assn; Phi Epsilon Kappa; Phi Delta Kappa kappa alpha psi; intl assn of approved basketball officials; big bros inc; YMCA; am coll of sports med; Neighbors Inc; nominating com of Eastern Dist AAHPER; Pres's Com on review criteria for Journal of AAHPER; consult summer prog Brookings Inst 1967; spl ocns DC dept of Recreation until 1968; consult Mr Gordon Shea NERA Columbia Inc. **HONORS/ACHIEVEMENTS:** Author of num pub vestryman of St Luke's Epis Ch; panelist of examiners of State Merit Sys of HEW 1959-65; parliamentarian & historia of Nat Intramural Assn 1956-65; vP Physical Educ DC AHPER 1967-68; pres DC AHPER 1968-70; steering com Nat Dairy Coun 1969; sports editor Kappa Alpha Psi Journal 1954; pres Progressive Club Guild of St Luke's Episcopal Ch; Tri-state Meeting at Annapolis 1965; Boy Scout Master; mem bd of scouting at St Luke's Episcopal Ch invited to part Wash Urban League's Leadership Training Prog 1961; listed in Who's Who in Am Educ 1955-58; cert of merit Wash Alumni Chap of Kappa Alpha Psi 1964; Nat Intramural Assn apl serv awd 1965; bd dir Jr Cit Corps Wash DC; Distgshd Serv Awd for 10 yrs as adv Kappa Alpha Psi Frat 1958. **BUSINESS ADDRESS:** Howard Univ, 2400 6 St NW, Washington, DC 20059.

TYREE, PATRICIA GREY
Business executive. **PERSONAL:** Born Nov 08, 1942; married Winston E. **EDUCATION:** Carlow Coll, BS 1966; Antioch Coll, MA 1973;Univ Pittsburgh, PhD 1974. **CAREER:** Holy Family Sch, tchr 1966-67; St Mary's Sch, 1967-68; Carlow Coll, moderator couns Project Upward Bound Mt Mercy 1968; Diocesan Office Econ & Oportunity, asso dir Compensatory Educ Prog 1968-69; Nat Black Sisters' Conf, dir 1969-72; Antioch Putnam Grad Sch Educ & Carlow Coll, design training lab 1972-73; Design Progs Inc, 1972-74; Tyree Corp, corp vice pres 1974-, bd dirs; Black Women's Comm Dev Found; Design Prog Inc; num previous offices, coms proflorgan; publs in field. **HONORS/ACHIEVEMENTS:** Religion

in Action Awd Delta Sigma Theta. **BUSINESS ADDRESS:** 318 Leader Bldg, Cleveland, OH 44114.

TYRRELL, JAMES A.
Business executive. **PERSONAL:** Born Dec 15, 1931, NYC, NY; married Ruby Belk; children: Milton, Cheryl, Joi Nandra. **EDUCATION:** CBS Sch of Mgmt, certificate; BS Industrial Educ. **CAREER:** Record producer, professional musician, 1954-69; Intl Tape Cartridge Corp, vice pres 1965-70; Epic & Columbia Custom Labels, vice pres marketing & Sales 1973-74;Epic/Portrait & all CBS Assoc Labels, vice pres marketing 1974-79; T-Electric Records Co, pres chmn bd 1979-; T-Associates, owner; JTRT Corporation, owner 1980-. **ORGANIZATIONS:** Pres & founder NY Chap Frat of Recording Exec 1970-; bd dir Black Music Assn; mem finance com exec com Black Music Assn; ombudsman Black Record Retailers Assist Pilot Prog through BMA; bd dirs Metro Liquid Assets Inc, Melbaba Management Co, Lopat Industries Inc; advisor/lectr Inst of New Cinema Artists; advisor Youth Activists NOW Orgn; trustee vice prs gov Natl Academy Recording Arts & Scis; mem bd advisrs Natl Assn Recording Merchandisers. **HONORS/ACHIEVEMENTS:** First Black vice pres CBS with appt as vice pres sales 1973; established a scholarship & career guidance awd for New York City HS students called PACE Awd; listedin Who's Who in Finance & Industry; Entertainment Indus Publ Poll recognized him among 100 Most Influential Execs of the Decade 1978; Citations for Leadership, Boro President of Manhattan, MA State Legislature, New Communicators Organs, Natl Youth Movement, Youth Activists NOW, NY Media Assocs. **BUSINESS ADDRESS:** Owner, JTRT Corporation, 828 East 222 St, New York, NY 10467.

TYSON, BERTRAND OLIVER
Physician. **PERSONAL:** Born Apr 03, 1931, Baton Rouge, LA; married Maureen; children: Lisa, Celeste, Bertrand Jr, Michelle, Kevin, Melissa, Amber. **EDUCATION:** Howard U, BS 1950; Meharry Med Coll, MD 1959. **CAREER:** Physician; Crown City Ob Gyn Med Grp Inc, pres; Bar-Tram Ranch. **ORGANIZATIONS:** Mem Alpha Phi Alpha Social Frat 1947-; del Dem Nat Conv State LA 1968; ldr Civil Rights Demon 1963; fr Flw Am Coll Ob-Gyn; flw Intl Coll Surgeons; mem Am Fertility Soc. **MILITARY SERVICE:** AUS corpl 1952-54. **BUSINESS ADDRESS:** 2657 E Washington Blvd, Pasadena, CA 91107.

TYSON, CICELY
Actress. **PERSONAL:** Born in New York, NY; married Miles Davis. **EDUCATION:** Attended New York Univ, Actors Studio. **CAREER:** The Blacks, Off-Broadway, Moon on a Rainbow Show, Tiger, Burning Bright, stage actress; E Side W Side 1963, Miss Jane Pittman 1974, King 1977, Roots 1977, Sounder 1972, Bluebird 1976,TV actress; Twelve Angry Men 1967, Odds Against Tomorrow 1959, The Last Angry Man 1959, A Man Called Adam 1966, The Comedians 1967, The Heart is a Lonely Hunter 1968, The Blue Bird 1976, The River Niger 1976, A Hero Ain't Nothin' But a Sandwich 1978, The Concorde-Airport 79 1979, The Marva Collins Story 1981, Benny's Place 1982, film actress; A Woman Called Moses 1978, specTV play. **ORGANIZATIONS:** Co-founder Dance Theater of Harlem; bd dir Urban Gateways; trustee Human Family Inst, Amer Film Inst. **HONORS/ACHIEVEMENTS:** NAACP Awd; Awd Natl Council Negro Women; Awd Capital Press; Vernon Rice Awd 1962; Named Best Actress for Sounder Atlanta Film Fest 1972; Nom Best Actress Sounder Acad Awds 1972.

TYSON, CLEVELAND ALLEN
Attorney. **PERSONAL:** Born Jan 07, 1946, Chicago, IL; married Patricia D Mcdowell; children: Cleveland A. **EDUCATION:** LoyolaUniv of Chicago Sch of Law, JD 1976. **CAREER:** IL Hosp & Hlth Serv Inc, dir legal serv; Washington Nat Ins Co, asst couns 1976-80; Chicago Bd of Edn, security insp 1971-76; Chicago Police Dept, patrolman evidence tech 1967-71. **ORGANIZATIONS:** Mem Am Bar Assn IL; mem Winnebago County Bar Assn mem State Bar Assn; mem Chicago Bar Assn. **HONORS/ACHIEVEMENTS:** Recip Vietnam Service Medal Bronze Star w/Combat V Navy Unit Commendation USMC. **MILITARY SERVICE:** USMC sgt 1964-67.

TYSON, JOHN C.
Eduator. **PERSONAL:** Born Aug 04, 1951, Richlands, VA; son of Isaac McKnight Tyson, Jr. and Catherine Rutledge Tyson; married Rogenia Laverne Motley, Nov 22, 1974; children: James Louis Townsend, Natasha Nicole. **EDUCATION:** Concord College, Athens WV, 1969-72; Univ of Illinois at Urbana, Urbana-Champaign IL, MLS, 1976; West Virginia Univ, Morgantown WV, MPA, 1979; Simmons College, Boston MA, DALA, 1988. **CAREER:** Fairview Jr High School, Bluefield WV, teacher of Spanish, 1972-73; Concord College, Athens WV, circulation supervisor, 1973-75; West Virginia Univ, Morgantown WV, reference librarian, 1976-77; Univ of Wisconsin-Parkside, Kenosha WI, public services librarian, 1977-79; Northern Illinois Univ, DeKalb IL, asst dir for planning, administration & development, 1979-86; University of Richmond, Richmond VA, university librarian, 1986—. **ORGANIZATIONS:** Black Caucus of the American Library Association. **HONORS/ACHIEVEMENTS:** Outstanding Young Man of America Award, JAYCEES, 1979. **BUSINESS ADDRESS:** University Librarian, University of Richmond, Boatwright Memorial Library, Richmond, VA 23173.

TYSON, LORENA E.
Educator. **PERSONAL:** Born Dec 01, 1933, Montclair, NJ; widowed. **EDUCATION:** Coll of St Elizabeth Convent Station, BS Chemistry 1956; Catholic Univ of Amer Washington DC, MS Chemistry 1965; Seton Hall Univ, Orange NJ, Certificate 1966-67; Rutgers Univ; NJ Inst of Technology. **CAREER:** Sacred Heart Acad, Hoboken NJ, teacher chemistry & math 1956-59; St Joseph High School, teacher chemistry & math 1959-62; St Peter & Paul High St, Thomas VI, teacher chemistry & math 1962-71; Essex County Coll, Newark NJ, adj math 1971-78; Kean Coll of NJ, adj math 1971-83; Montclair Bd of Ed, teacher chemistry 1971-. **ORGANIZATIONS:** Mem Natl Educ Assn 1971-, New Jersey Educ Assn 1971-; mem rep council, exec bd treasurer Montclair Educ Assn 1971-; mem, rep council, exec bd, sec Essex County Educ Assn 1972-82; mem ACS Lackawanna Div 1974-, League of Women Voters Montclair 1974-, New Jersey Science Teachers 1975-, NJEA Exceptional Child Comm 1975-, EOF Adv Bd Coll of St Elizabeth 1976-83, Natl Council of Negro Women 1978-82; consultant, editor Educ Unlimited Magazine 1978-82; mem New Jersey Math Teachers 1979-83; treasurer MEA 1981-; mem Phi Delta Kappa 1981-; treasurer Phi Delta Kappa Montclair State Coll 1987-. **HONORS/ACHIEVEMENTS:** NSF Fellowship Chem NSF Catholic Univ of Amer 1962-64; NSF Fellowship Math, NSF Seton Hall 1966-67; Human Relations Award, Essex County Educ Assn, W Orange NJ 1980; Contribution to Educ Award, Montclair Educ Assn, Montclair NJ 1980; Resolution of Commendation, Montclair Bd of Educ, Montclair NJ 1980; NJ Governor's Teachers Recognition Program 1987; Montclair Teacher of the Year, Montclair Bd of Educ 1989; Eve Marchiony Outstanding Teacher Grant, Montclair Bd of Educ 1989. **BUSINESS ADDRESS:** Chemistry Teacher, Montclair Board of Education, 22 Valley Rd, Montclair, NJ 07042.

TYSON, MIKE
Professional boxer. **PERSONAL:** Born Jun 30, 1946, Brooklyn, NY. **CAREER:** World Heavyweight Boxing Champion. **HONORS/ACHIEVEMENTS:** Youngest Heavyweight Champion in Boxing History; voted Boxer of the Year WBC Quantas, US Boxing Writers and other organizations; featured in Guinness Bookof World Records. **BUSINESS ADDRESS:** World Heavyweight Champion, c/o Jim Jacobs/Bill Cayton, The Big Fights Inc, 9 East 40th St, New York, NY 10016.

TYUS, WYOMIA
Athlete, public relations. **PERSONAL:** Born Aug 29, 1945, Griffin, GA; children: Simone, Tyus. **EDUCATION:** TN State Univ, BS 1968. **CAREER:** Afro-Amer Cntr UCLA, research asst 1969-70; Bret Harte Jr HS Los Angeles, phys ed tchr 1970-72; Beverly Hills HS, trach coach 1972-73; Intl Track Assn, pub rel staff 1973-76; ABC coverage of Olympic Games in Montreal, commentator 1976; Councilman David Cunningham, community liason 1978; US Dept Labor sponsored Sports and Career Dev, instructor 1979-81; Coca-Cola USA, public relations 1981-84. **ORGANIZATIONS:** Competed in amateur and prof track & field 1963-75; for past 15 years instructed at dozens of sports clinics in US and abroad; particip in numerous panels and lectured on role of sports in culture; TV appearances include talk shows throughout US ie The Merv Griffin Show, ABC Superstars, Challenge of the Sexes. **HONORS/ACHIEVEMENTS:** Publications and film appearances, "Inside Jogging for Women" pub by Contemporary Books Chicago 1978; "Olympic Let Down" Women's Sports Mag 1976; "Women in Sports" filmed by the Women's Sports Found 1979; "Women Gold Medal Winners" filmed by Bud Greenspan; TN Sports Hall of Fame Nashville 1972; US Track and FieldHall of Fame Angola, IN 1976; Black Athletes Hall of Fame New York 1978; Natl Track and Field Hall of Fame Charleston, WV 1980; Olympic Flag Carrier in the XXIIIrd Olympic Games Los Angeles 1984; Ten times AAU Natl Champ and All-Amer Athlete in both indoors and outdoors competition; Five times world record holder in 50/60/70 and 100-yard dashes and 100 meters sprint; Represented the US in more than twenty international competitions winning most; Gold Medal winner in 200 meter dash in the 1967 Pan Amer Games; Winner of three Olympic Gold Medals and one Silver Medal - The only person in the hist of the modern Olympic Games among men and women to ever win a Gold Medal in 100 meter dash in two consecutive Olympics (1964 and 1968).

TZOMES, CHANCELLOR ALFONSO (PETE)
Director. **PERSONAL:** Born Dec 30, 1944, Williamsport, PA; son of James Tzomes and Charlotte Tzomes; married Martu Hall; children: Chancellor II. **EDUCATION:** US Naval Academy, BS 1967. **CAREER:** USS Will Rogers (SSBN659), electrical officer main propulsion asst 1970-71; USS Pinzado (SSN672), damage control asst 1971-73; USS Drum (SSN677), engr officer 1973-76; USS Pacific Fleet, nuclear propulsion examining bd 1976-79; USS Cavalla (SSN684), exec officer 1979-82; USS Houston, commanding officer 1983-86; Submarine Force US Pacific Fleet, force operations officer 1986-88; Naval Military Command. **ORGANIZATIONS:** Mem Natl Naval Officers Assoc 1976-, NAACP 1989. **MILITARY SERVICE:** USN capt 22 yrs; Navy Commendation Medal with 2 gold stars; Meritorious Service Medal with 3 gold stars, various Unit Commendations and Campaign Ribbons. **BUSINESS ADDRESS:** Military Personnel Command, NMPC-61, Washington, DC 20370.

U

UGGAMS, LESLIE
Entertainer. **PERSONAL:** Born May 25, 1943, New York, NY; married Grahame Pratt. **EDUCATION:** Juillard School of Music, 1963. **CAREER:** Beulah TV Show, TV appearance 1949; Sing Along With Mitch, featured performer 1961-64; Broadway's "Hallelujah Baby", appeared on 1967; film "Skyjacked", 1972; nightclubs mus variety shows on TV; appeared on ABC "Roots" 1977,TV mini-series Backstairs at the White House 1979; star Broadway musical Blues in the Night 1982; co-host The Book of Lists 1982. **HONORS/ACHIEVEMENTS:** Critics Awd Best Supporting Actress "Roots"; author "The Leslie Uggams Beaut Book" 1966; recip Drama Critics Awd 1968; Tony Awd 1968; chosen Best Singer onTV 1962-63. **BUSINESS ADDRESS:** c/o William Morris Agency, 151 El Camino, Beverly Hills, CA 90212.

UKU, EUSTACE ORIS, SR.
Attorney, business consultant. **PERSONAL:** Born Jun 01, 1947, Ibadan, Oyo, Nigeria;son of Augustine Uku and Mabel Uku; married Jul 01, 1976 (divorced); children: Eustace Jr, Austin. **EDUCATION:** University of Lagos, Lagos Nigeria, LLB, 1970; Nigerian Law School, Lagos Nigeria, BL, 1971; Long Island University, Brooklyn NY, MBA, 1974; Duquesne University, Pittsburgh PA, Cert in Law, 1981. **CAREER:** Lawrence & Co, Lagos Nigeria, attorney, 1971; Garrick & Co, Benin Nigeria, attorney, 1976-79; Delstacy Mgmt Serv, Benin Nigeria, managing dir, 1976-79; Greater Pittsburgh Business Development Corp, Pittsburgh PA, financial analyst, 1980-81; Equibank, Pittsburgh PA, asst vice pres, 1981-85; Exico Inc, Pittsburgh PA, pres, 1985—. **ORGANIZATIONS:** Mem, Pennsylvania Bar Assn; dir, Functional Literacy Ministry. **BUSINESS ADDRESS:** Attorney/President, Exico, Inc, 1040 Fifth Ave, Pittsburgh, PA 15219.

UMBREIT, LEBERTHA
Education administration. **PERSONAL:** Born Aug 10, 1952, Decatur, IL; married D Scott Umbreit; children: Tracie, Jason. **EDUCATION:** Richland Comm Coll, AA 1976; Sangamon State Univ, BA 1980. **CAREER:** Neighborhood Youth Corps, youth worker 1971; Torrence Park Citizen Comm, vista volunteer 1974-75; Indo-Chinese Refugee Prog, english tutor 1979-80; Macon CoCETA Prog, employment counselor 1980-82; Sangamon Co Comm Action Agency, dir JTPA 1984; Lincoln Land Comm Coll, dir JTPA Progs 1984-. **ORGANIZATIONS:** Mem IL Management Assn 1980-82; mem IL Employment Training Assn 1983-; mem Amer Assn Univ Women 1983-; mem Dislocated Dirs Assn 1984-; mem Urban League Women Guild 1984-. **HONORS/ACHIEVEMENTS:** Governor's Internship Prog

State of IL Family Serv 1979. **BUSINESS ADDRESS:** Dir JTPA Programs, Lincoln Land Comm College, Shepherd Rd, Springfield, IL 62708.

UMOLU, MARY HARDEN
Educator. **PERSONAL:** Born Nov 24, 1927, Newsoms, VA. **EDUCATION:** NY U; Brooklyn Coll, MA 1951, BA 1949. **CAREER:** Medgar Evers Coll City Univ NY, prof dir comm art & science; Eastern Nigera Broadcasting, orgr producer artist 1960-67. **ORGANIZATIONS:** Bd dir Nat Assn Educ Brdcst; chmn Minoirites in Telecomm NAEB; mem Joint com on Pub Brdcstg; mem Action for Children's TV bd mem Kings Co Hosp Ctr; bd dir Comprehensive Hlth Sys NYC; mem Zeta Phi Beta Sor; Nat Sor Phi Delta Kappa. **HONORS/ACHIEVEMENTS:** Brdcst Preceptor's Awd; San Francisco StateUniv Tch Excellence Awd; Media Woman Yr CityUniv NY; Outsdng Tchr Awd CityUniv NY. **BUSINESS ADDRESS:** 1150 Carroll St, Brooklyn, NY 11225.

UNDERWOOD, FRANKYE HARPER
Educator, labor union official. **PERSONAL:** Born Nov 19, 1953, Coal Valley, AL; daughter of Will Harper and Sarah Harper; married Harold Underwood, Dec 17, 1957; children: Angela, Harold Jr. **EDUCATION:** Alabama State Univ, Montgomery AL, BS, 1957; Univ of Alabama, Tuscaloosa AL, MA, 1968. **CAREER:** Anniston City Schools, Anniston AL, teacher, 1957-62; Walker County Board of Education, Jasper AL, teacher, 1963-67; Alabama Education Assn, Montgomery AL, vice pres, 1987-88, pres, 1988-89; Jasper City Schools, Jasper AL, teacher, 1967—. **ORGANIZATIONS:** Mem, NEA; mem bd of dir, Alabama Education Assn; mem, Alabama Committee for Educational Excellence; trustee, Alabama State Univ. **HONORS/ACHIEVEMENTS:** Teacher of Year Award, Jasper City Board of Education, 1985. **HOME ADDRESS:** PO Box 2144, Jasper, AL 35501.

UNDERWOOD, MAUDE ESTHER
Broadcasting executive. **PERSONAL:** Born Jul 07, 1930, Cotton Valley, LA; married David C Underwood; children: Marcus, Sharon, Yvonne Holmes, James. **EDUCATION:** Ruth Beauty Sch, diploma 1958; Springhill HS, GED 1979; Northwest LA Vo-Tech School, diploma 1982. **CAREER:** State of LA, LSU Ext Agent 1976; City of Cullen, alderman 1982,87; Black Comm Broadcast (KBSF), producer 1983-. **ORGANIZATIONS:** Organizer treas Springhill-Cullen Improvement Assn 1962; organizer treas Cullen Ladies Club; chmn Cystic Fibrosis; mem Order of Eastern Star; orator Clantha Pride of LA. **HONORS/ACHIEVEMENTS:** Outstanding Serv Awd Webster Parish Comm Action 1978; Black Pride Awd-Black Pride Comm 1983; Bible Teachers Awd 13th North Calvary Dist 1981. **HOME ADDRESS:** PO Box 336, Cullen, LA 71021. **BUSINESS ADDRESS:** Broadcasting Executive, Radio Station KBSF, 226 North Main, Springhill, LA 71075.

UNGER, GEORGE D.
Educator. **PERSONAL:** Born Apr 27, 1924, Las Cruces, NM. **EDUCATION:** Prairie View Coll, BS 1941, MS 1956; N TX State U, ABD 1960. **CAREER:** San Fran State Coll, asso prof 1970-72; USAID/LIBERIA, consult 1968-70; Tuskegee Inst USAID/LIBERIA, asst prof 1965-68; Dallas Ind School Dist, teacher, supv of stud teaching, asst prin 1941-65; State of NY; coor of affirmative act. **ORGANIZATIONS:** Frmr dir StateUniv of NY Educ Oppor Cntr 1972 Governing bd dir Buffalo Found Inc; SUNYAB Coor Intl Women's Yr; com for Charter Revision Buffalo Common Counc; mem Am Assn of Univ Women; Nat Educ Assn; Civic; SUNYAB Minority Faculty Assn mem United Way Fund; Urban League; Alpha Kappa Alpha. **HONORS/ACHIEVEMENTS:** Outstdg Women in Educ Awd Buffalo Urban League Inc 1975. **BUSINESS ADDRESS:** 465 Washington St, Buffalo, NY 14203.

UNSELD, WES
Athlete. **PERSONAL:** Born Mar 14, 1946, Louisville, KY; married Connie; children: Kimberly, Westley. **EDUCATION:** Univ of Louisville. **CAREER:** Washington Bullets, professional basketball player 1968-81, vice-president 1981-. **ORGANIZATIONS:** Head of Capital Centre Charities; volunteer at Kernan Hosp; bd trustees Mt St Mary's College. **HONORS/ACHIEVEMENTS:** All-American honors at Univ of Louisville; Rookie-of-the Year; League's Most Valuable Player; selected to play in NBA All-Star Game (1st of 5 appearances); Most Valuable Player of the 1978 NBA Championship series that brought Washington 8ts first sports title in 36 years; Bullets all-time leader in games played, rebounds, minutes played and assists; 1st Recip of Walter Kennedy Citizenship Award. **BUSINESS ADDRESS:** Vice President, Washington Bullets, Capital Center, 1 Harry S Truman Drive, Landover, MD 20786.

UPSHAW, GENE
Executive director. **PERSONAL:** Born Aug 15, 1945, Robstown, TX; married Theresa; children: Eugene Upshaw III. **EDUCATION:** TX A&I Univ, BS 1968; CA State Univ, 1968; Golden Gate Univ, 1980. **CAREER:** NFL Players Assn, player rep/alternate 1970-76, exec comm 1976-80, pres 1980-82, exec dir 1982-. **ORGANIZATIONS:** Partner Gene Upshaw & Assoc (Mgmt Consult Firm Oakland) 1970-78; pres Fedn of Professional Athletes AFL-CIO 1984-; CA Governor's Cncl on Wellness & Physical Fitness; CA Bd of Governors for 104 Community Colleges; former planning commr for Alameda County; coord Voter Regis/Fundraising in Alameda County. **HONORS/ACHIEVEMENTS:** Byron (Whizzer) White Humanitarian Awrd NFL Players 1980; A Philip Randolph Award A Philip Randolph Inst 1982; Inducted into Hall of Fame (Football) 1987. **MILITARY SERVICE:** AUS Spc 4th Class 1967-73 Ft Jackson, SC. **BUSINESS ADDRESS:** Executive Dir, NFL Players Associaton, 2021 L St NW, 6th Floor, Washington, DC 20036.

UPSHAW, WILLIE CLAY
Professional athlete. **PERSONAL:** Born May 27, 1957, Blanco, TX; married Cindy; children: Brock Anthony, Courtney, Chad. **CAREER:** Toronto Blue Jays, outfielder/1st baseman. **HONORS/ACHIEVEMENTS:** Labatt's Blue Player of Month for June 1982, & May/Sept/Oct 1983; co-winner Labatt's Blue Player of the Yr 1983.

UPTON, E. H.
Elected government official. **PERSONAL:** Born Jan 04, 1924, Sweetwater, TN; married Edna M Roberts. **EDUCATION:** Dale Carnegie Course, grad. **CAREER:** Union Carbide Corp, matls dispatching & handling, indust engrg div retired after 26 yrs. **ORGANIZATIONS:** Mem Commiss of the City of Oak Ridge 1974, Oak Ridge City Council 1975-; hon mem Constitutional Convention TN 1977; mem NBC/LEO Nominating Committee 1982;Oak Ridge Masonic Lodge 345, TML Human Resources Comm, Oak Ridge Chamber of Commerce; mem bd of dir HOPE of Oak Ridge Inc, Melton Hill Reg Indust DevelAssoc; campaign chmn Jesse Jackson Committee for Pres in Oak Ridge. **HONORS/ACHIEVEMENTS:** Recipient of Union Carbide Corp Comm Serv Awd, Hon Sgt at Arms of House of Rep State of TN; Hon Mem of Staff of Senator Anna Belle Clement O'Brien, Black Caucus of the TN Gen Assembly. **BUSINESS ADDRESS:** Councilmember, City of Oak Ridge, 134 Houston Ave, Oak Ridge, TN 37830.

URDY, CHARLES E.
Educator. **PERSONAL:** Born Dec 27, 1933, Georgetown, TX; son of William Braxton Urdy and Pearl Roberta Jackson Urdy; married Margaret Bright, Apr 07, 1962; children: Steven Eugene Urdy. **EDUCATION:** Huston-Tillotson Coll, BS Chem 1954; Univ of TX at Austin, PhD Chem 1962. **CAREER:** Huston-Tillotson Coll, prof of chem 1972-; Prairie View A&M Univ, prof of chem 1963-72; NC Central Univ, prof of Chem 1962-63; Huston-Tillotson Coll, prof of chem 1961-62; Univ of TX at Austin, post-doc Fellow 1962-63; Dow Chem Co Freeport TX, summer employee 1970; MIT Lincoln Lab Boston, natl urban league fellow 1972. **ORGANIZATIONS:** Mem Alpha Phi Alpha Frat; Am Chem Soc; Am Crystallographic Assn; Sigma Xi; Fellow in Am Inst of Chemists; mem numerous local civic organ & com; campaign mgr first Black Wilhelmina Delco elected to TX Legis from Travis Co 1974; state sec-treas TX Assn of Coll Tchrs 1970; elected chmn First Prairie View A&M Fac Council 1969; mem Hon Soc Phi Lambda Upsion Alpha Kappa Mu; Nat Sci Found Fellow 1959;Univ of TX Fellow 1960; Proctor & Gamble Fellow 1960; mem Beta Kappa Chi Hon Sci Soc; mem Cty of Austin Charter Revision Com; chmn Black Voters Action Proj Pol Com; elected council mem Austin City Council 1981-. **HONORS/ACHIEVEMENTS:** Recipient Prairie View Alumni Award for Leadership 1967; Huston Tillotson Alumni Award for Acad Achievement 1967 Alpha Phi Alpha Frat Community Serv & Leadership Award 1974; NAACP commun serv award 1975; City of Austin community serv award 1976. **MILITARY SERVICE:** AUS sp-3 1954-57. **BUSINESS ADDRESS:** Professor of Chemistry, Huston-Tillotson College, 1820 East 8th St, Austin, TX 78702.

URQUHART, JAMES MCCARTHA
Business executive. **PERSONAL:** Born Jul 31, 1953, Wakefield, VA; married Linda Diane Ricks (divorced); children: Torrey. **EDUCATION:** Paul D Camp Coll, 1975-77; Richard Bland Coll, Bus Mgmt Cert 1979; John Tyler Coll, Acct Cert 1983. **CAREER:** Horton Furn Co, asst mgr 1981-83; Gen Electric, serv tech 1973-81; Horton Furn Co, pres. **ORGANIZATIONS:** Mgr, coach Wakefield Eagles Men League 1979,80,81; councilman Wakefield Town Council 1983,84,85,86; mem NAACP 1983-85, SCLC 1983-85, Union Love Lodge 153; young adult teacher 1st Baptist Church; comm chmn Wakefield Improvement Assoc; past club master Wakefield Pack 75. **BUSINESS ADDRESS:** President, Horton Furn Co, PO Box 698, Main St, Wakefield, VA 23888.

USRY, JAMES LEROY
Mayor. **PERSONAL:** Born Feb 02, 1922, Macon, GA; son of Leroy Usry and Louise Usry; married LaVerne Stephens, Mar 31, 1984. **EDUCATION:** Lincoln Univ, Lincoln University PA, BA, 1946; Glassboro State Univ, Glassboro NJ, MA, 1971; Temple Univ, Philadelphia PA. **CAREER:** Harlem Globetrotters and New York Rens Basketball Team, New York NY, basketball player, 1946-51; Atlantic City Board of Education, Atlantic City NJ, teacher, principal, asst superintendent, 1952-84; City of Atlantic City, Atlantic City NJ, mayor, 1984—. **ORGANIZATIONS:** Pres, Natl Conf of Black Mayors; commissioner, Natl Council on Educational Research and Improvements; mem of bd of governors, Rutgers State Univ and Lincoln Univ; dir, New Jersey Casino Reinvestment Authority; mem of bd of dir, MidLantic National Bank South; mem exec bd, Atlantic City NAACP; mem, Congress of Community Organizations; mem bd of dir, YMCA; mem, Martin L King Jr Commission of New Jersey; mem bd of overseers, Governors School of New Jersey. **HONORS/ACHIEVEMENTS:** Elected to Bob Douglas Hall of Fame, 1984; Man of Year Award, Omega Psi Phi, 1986; Community Service Award, 101 Women Plus, 1986; Richard Hatcher Distinguished Black Mayor Award, 1987; elected to Lincoln University Hall of Fame, 1988. **MILITARY SERVICE:** US Army. **BUSINESS ADDRESS:** Mayor, City of Atlantic City, 1301 Bachrach Blvd, Suite 706, Atlantic City, NJ 08401.

UTLEY, RICHARD HENRY
Public relations marketing consultant. **PERSONAL:** Born Jan 02, 1949, Pittsburgh, PA; married Audrey L Ross. **EDUCATION:** Univ of Pittsburgh, BA 1972, Law School 1972-73. **CAREER:** PA Legal Svcs, dir of prog devel 1980-82; City of Harrisburg Dept of Public Safety, tech asst 1982-83; Auditor Gen PA, asst dir; Utley Assoc, pres; Public Affairs Consultants Inc, vp. **ORGANIZATIONS:** Pres Utley Assoc; vice chair Dauphin Cty Demo Comm, NAACP; Big Brothers of Amer; vice chair Harrisburg Housing Authority; sec of bd Directors of Uptown Sr Citizens Center; bd dir River Rescue Inc. **HOME ADDRESS:** 122 Locust Street, Harrisburg, PA 17104.

UTTERBACK, EVERETT EMORY
Retired attorney. **PERSONAL:** Born Mar 02, 1906, Mayfield, KY; son of Edlridge Utterback and Monima Utterback; married Bernice Brown, Jun 22, 1935; children: Everett E Utterback, Jr. **EDUCATION:** Univ Pitts, 1932; Duquesne Univ, JD 1947. **CAREER:** Private Practice, atty 1969-; Utterback Brown & Harper, partner 1955-69; Pittsburgh Housing Authority, mgr exec asst to admin dir mgmt general counsel dep admin 1940-71; Kay Boys' Club, dir 1936-40; Juvenile Ct Pittsburgh, probation officer 1933-36; Kay Boys' Club, phy dir 1931-32. **ORGANIZATIONS:** Admitted practice US Supreme Ct, 1955; past bd mem Pitts Housing Assn; mem Pittsburgh NAACP; Center Ave YMCA; chmn Legal Redress Com Pittsburgh NAACP; mem Gov Study Com State's role promoting home constrn Slum Clearance & Redevel 1956; mem Legal Com Nat Assn Housing & Redevel Authority 1968-71; mem Biography & Hist Com Alleghny Co Bar Assn; admitted practice local state federal & PA Ct & Supreme Ct PA; bd trustee Univ Pittsburgh 1966-74; emeritus trustee 1974 Presb Univ Hosp; mem Omega Psi Phi; Sigma Pi Phi Frat Capt Univ Pittsburgh Track & Field Team 1931. **HONORS/ACHIEVEMENTS:** Letter man distinction Univ Pittsburgh 1964; Western PA Sports Hall Fame 1976. **BUSINESS ADDRESS:** Consultant, Byrd R Brown Assoc, 515 Grant St, Pittsburgh, PA 15219.

UZOIGWE, GODFREY N.
Educator. **PERSONAL:** Born Sep 25, 1938; married Patricia Maria Cahill; children: Emeka, Amaechi, Jaja. **EDUCATION:** Univ Coll Dublin, BA 1963; Trinity Coll, Higher Diploma in Educ 1964; Hist Christ Ch Oxford U, DPhil 1967. **CAREER:** Univ of MI, prof of history 1976-; Univ of MI, asso prof of history 1972-76; Univ of MI, asst prof 1970-72;

Makerere Univ Kampala Uganda, lecturer 1967-70. **ORGANIZATIONS:** Fellow African Studies Assn USA; Am Hist Assn Fellow; Ryoal African Soc; Uganda Soc; Uganda Acad; Hist Soc of Ghana Nigeria; Kenya & Tanzania; lifefellow Oxford Union Soc; hon chief Umunoha Town Nigeria with title of Ezeugoma 1976. **HONORS/ACHIEVEMENTS:** Num publ include "Britain & the Conquest of Africa" "The Age of Salisbury"Univ of M Press 1974; "Revolution & Revolt in Bunyoro Kitara" Longsmans 1970. **BUSINESS ADDRESS:** Dept of History, U of MI, Ann Arbor, MI 48109.

V

VALDES, LAURA
Attorney. **PERSONAL:** Born Oct 19, Havana, Cuba. **EDUCATION:** NY Univ, BS 1943; NY Law School, JD 1960. **CAREER:** NY State Dept of Labor, es supt 1936-73; Private Practice, law 1973-. **ORGANIZATIONS:** Pres Co-op City Br NAACP 1973-; pres Bronx Municipal Hosp Adv Bd 1976-80; mem Bronx Co Bar Assn; pres Williamsbridge Sr Citizens Assn 1974-; mem NY State Bar Assn; delegate mem comm on Character & Fitness Appellate Court NY State Supreme Court. **HONORS/ACHIEVEMENTS:** Human Rights Awd NY State Div Human Rights 1970; Woman of Yr B'nai Brith 1973; Comm Recognition Awd Butler United Methodist Ch 1969; numerous others. **BUSINESS ADDRESS:** Attorney, 3820 Paulding Ave, Bronx, NY 10469.

VALDES, PEDRO H.
Business executive. **PERSONAL:** Born Jan 20, 1945, Havana, Cuba;son of Pedro H. and Hesma; married Maria A Bermudez; children: Hesma, Pedro III, Xiomara. **EDUCATION:** City Coll of NY, BA 1969; NY Univ, attended 1974-75; Middlebury Coll, MA 1971; SUNY at Stony Brook, attended 1972-73. **CAREER:** SEEK Prog, tutor 1963-65; NY Philantropic League, rehabilitation counselor 1966-69; Alcur Tours Inc, tour guide & planner 1968-72; Wm H Taft HS, Spanish Language tchr 1969-72; State Univ of NY Stony Brook, teaching asst dept of hispanic languages & lit 1972-73; NY Coll of Podiatric Medicine, asst dean for student affairs 1973-75, vice pres for student affairs 1975-77, exec vice pres 1977-80; Premo Pharmaceutical Labs Inc, export sales mgr 1980-81, exclusive export sales agent 1981-82; International; pres Protecom, Inc. **ORGANIZATIONS:** Mem United Federation of Teachers 1969-80; mem Amer Assn of Univ Professors 1972-80; mem Amer Assn of Colls of Podiatric Medicine 1973-80; mem Amer Public Health Assn 1973-; mem Natl League of Nursing Policies & Procedures Comm 1977-; mem Natl Health Council Inc 1980-; mem Natl Ctr's Advisory Council for Rsch in Vocational Educ 1981-84. **HONORS/ACHIEVEMENTS:** Outstanding Educator of Amer Awd 1974; Tching Assistantship State Univ of NY Stony Brook 1972-73. **BUSINESS ADDRESS:** President, Protecom, Inc., 262 Griggs Ave, Teaneck, NJ 07666.

VALENTINE, ANTHONY JAMES
Engineer. **PERSONAL:** Born Nov 01, 1941, New York, NY; married Olivia Jonette Harris; children: Omari Malik. **EDUCATION:** NY Inst of Tech, BEE 1963; Natl Aero & Space Admin, Cert 1964; Columbia Univ, MBA 1973. **CAREER:** Lewis Turner Partnership, engr consult; Pacific Missile Range Dept of Defense, engr cons; Grumman Aerospace Corp Apollo Spacecraft, test dir; LST DesignCollabor, partner, treas. **ORGANIZATIONS:** Mem Omega Psi Phi, Natl Assoc of Black MBA's. **HONORS/ACHIEVEMENTS:** Grumman Aerospace Mang Fellowship 1971-73; Cogme Mang Fellowship 1971-73.

VALENTINE, DARNELL
Professional athlete. **PERSONAL:** Born Feb 03, 1959, Chicago, IL. **EDUCATION:** Univ of KS, BS Pol Sci 1981. **CAREER:** Portland Trail Blazer, guard 1981. **HONORS/ACHIEVEMENTS:** One of the most honored players in Big Eight Conf history Univ of KS; All Conf all 4 seasons; Led the Big Eight in steals all 4 seasons & was 1st in assistsin 3 of 4 years. **BUSINESS ADDRESS:** Portland Trail Blazers, 700 NE Multnomah St, Portland, OR 97232.

VALENTINE, DEBORAH MARIE
Environmental protection specialist. **PERSONAL:** Born Feb 18, 1951, Boston, MA; daughter of Roger Valentine and Virginia Alleyne Valentine. **EDUCATION:** Howard Univ, BS 1972; Howard Univ Law Sch, JD 1972-75; certificate in catering training L'Academie de Cuisine Bethesda, MD July 1988.. **CAREER:** Minority Counsel Senate Select Subcomm Small Business, legal intern 1974-75; US Securities & Exchange Comm 1975-76; Fed Energy Admn Dept Energy, regulatory analyst 1977-80; ERA Housing Ctr Inc, group sales leader 1982-84; Assoc Legal Title Co, Inc, settlement officer 1986-87; US Dept Energy, environmental protection specialist; owner Valentine's Catering Upper Marlboro, MD Nov. 1988-. **ORGANIZATIONS:** Notary public State MD 1979-86; realtor assc ERA Nyman Realty; mem Natl Assc Realtors 1981-86, MD Assoc Realtors 1981-86, Prince Georges Cty Bd Realtors 1981-86, Phi Alpha Delta Legal Frat 1973-81; vp, bd of dir Prince Place III at Northampton; chairperson of social & cultural committee Howard Univ Law Alumni Assoc 1988-89; senior tutor Prince Georges Literacy Council 1987-. **HONORS/ACHIEVEMENTS:** Final eis cnvrsn coal brandon shores Dept Energy 1984; Outstanding Work Performance Award Dept Energy 1980; scholarship Howard Univ 1973; scholarship Alpha Kappa Alpha 1968; chairperson Environmental Reg Compliance Working Group 1986-88; Outstanding Work Performance, Dept of Energy 1989. **BUSINESS ADDRESS:** Environmntl Protectn Spclst, US Dept of Energy, 1000 Independence Ave, SW, Washington, DC 20585.

VALENTINE, HERMAN E.
Business executive. **PERSONAL:** Born Jun 26, 1937, Norfolk, VA; son of Frank and Alice; married Dorothy Jones; children: Herman Edward Jr, Bryce Thomas. **EDUCATION:** Norfolk State Coll, BS 1967; Amer Univ, 1968; Coll of William & Mary, 1972. **CAREER:** Grad School Dept of Agriculture, exec officer, 1967-68; Systems Management American Corp, chmn and pres, 1970-; Norfolk State Coll, Norfolk, VA, business mgr, 1968-70. **ORGANIZATIONS:** Founder/chmn Tidewater Regional Political Assoc; mem Amer Mgmt Assoc, Armed Forces Communications and Electronics Assoc; bd of dirs Cooperating Hampton Roads Org for Minorities in Engrg; bd of dirs and exec comm Greater Norfolk Corp; adv comm VA Chapter of St Jude Children's Rsch Hosp; adv council The Virginia Stage Co; Air Traffic Control Assn (ATCA); Tidewater Regional Minority Purchasing Council (TRMPC); Soc of Logistics Engineers (SOLE); bd of dir, Operation Smile; bd of dir, PUSH Intl Trade Bureau, Inc. **HONORS/ACHIEVEMENTS:** Distinguished Serv Awd United Way 1981; Presidedntial Citation Natl Assoc for Equal Oppor in Higher Educ 1981; named to President's Council of the Amer Inst of Mgmt; Resolution of Appreciation Bd of Visitors Old Dominion Univ 1981; Meritorious Serv Awd United Negro Coll Fund 1982; Outstanding Serv Awd Links Inc 1983; Presidential Citation Entrepreneur of the Year Dept of Commerce Minority Business Develop Agency 1984; Certificate of merit for Natl Leadership & Citizenship City of Chicago 1985; Distinguished Serv Awd VA State Conf NAACP 1985; Delicados Inc Awd for Entrepreneurship in Blazing New Horizons 1986; named to the President's Council of the Amer Inst of Mgmt; Citizen of the Yr Awd for Outstanding Leadership & Serv to the Comm 1986; Regional Minority Mfg of Year Award, MBDA, 1988; one of Top 10 minor city owned federal govt contractor, Govt Computer New, 1988; Certificate of Recognition, lieutenant governor, Commonwealth of VA, 1987; Outstanding Org for large financial contributions and employment of minorities, NAACP Area II, 1988; Outstanding Businessperson of Year, State of VA Award, black pres Roundtable Assn, 1987; Class III Supplier of the Year Award, Natl Minority Supplier Devel Council, 1987; Ambassador of the City of Norfolk, CA, 1986. **BUSINESS ADDRESS:** Chairman and President, Systems Mgmt American Corp, 254 Monticello Ave, Norfolk, VA 23510.

VALENTINE, J. T.
Retired attorney. **PERSONAL:** Born Sep 21, 1918, Suffolk, VA; son of Miles E. Valentine and Annie Valentine; married Rosetta M Cason. **EDUCATION:** Howard U, BS 1948; Howard U, LLB 1951. **CAREER:** Washington Contracts Office Fed Aviation Adminstrn 1970, chief contract servcs 1970; Fed Aviatio Adminstrn, suprv contracts specialist 1970; FAA, superv procurement officer 1966-; Small Business WA FAA, officer 1971. **ORGANIZATIONS:** Pres E Coast Chapter Tuskegee Airmen; mem Israel Baptist Church; mem NAACP; mem Natl Camping & Hiking Assn. **MILITARY SERVICE:** AUS black airman 1943-46 (Tuskegee Airman). **HOME ADDRESS:** 3608 Carpenter St SE, Washington, DC 20020.

VALIEN, PRESTON
Retired government official. **PERSONAL:** Born Feb 19, 1914, Beaumont, TX; married Bonita Harrison. **EDUCATION:** Prairie View State Coll TX, BA; Univ of WI, PhM & PhD; Univ of PA, postdoctoral study. **CAREER:** American Embassy Nigeria, cultural attache 1960-62; Brooklyn Coll NY, assoc prof sociology & anthropology 1962-65; HEW Washington, dir prog analysis br 1965, chief grad acad progs 1965-66, dir div grad progs 1966-67, assoc commr higher educ 1967-73, dir coll & univ unit 1973-82; retired federal govt executive. **ORGANIZATIONS:** Fellow, Amer Sociological Assn, African Studies Assn; DC Scoiol Soc (pres, 1970-71). **HONORS/ACHIEVEMENTS:** Superior Serv Award Educ 1970; Hon LLD Rio Grande Coll OH 1971; Hon D Hum Rust Coll, MS 1974. **MILITARY SERVICE:** AUS S/Sgt 1943-46. **HOME ADDRESS:** 8020 W Beach Dr NW, Washington, DC 20012.

VALLEY, THOMAS JAMES
Account executive. **PERSONAL:** Born Feb 08, 1945, Galveston, TX; divorced; children: Rico Todd, Tiffany Danielle, Torrian Dominique. **EDUCATION:** FiskUniv Nashville, 164-66; TX SoUniv Houston, BA 1975. **CAREER:** Priv Indust Counc Mrktng Asso Affil of St Louis Regional Commerce & Growth Assn, dir 1978-; Dial-Am Mrktng Co Houston, asst br mgr 1976-78; Procter & Gambel Cincinnati, sales mrktng rep 1975-76; Kaiser Aluminum Houston, qual control splst 1970-75; Continental Airlines Houston, sales reservationist 1968-70; Shell Oil Co Houston, lead computer operator 1966-68. **ORGANIZATIONS:** Bd of dirs Human Devel Corp St Louis 1980; tech adv staff mem OIC St Louis 1980; adv counc mem Proj 70-001 St Louis 1980; adv counc mem Youth Employment Coalition St Louis 1980. **HONORS/ACHIEVEMENTS:** Recipt professional serv commen Coord of Pvt Indust Counc CETA Sales Training Sem St Louis 1980; professional serv commen St Louis Agency on Training & Employment's Youth Career Day 1980; pub serv aw cert Nat Seminar for Youth Proj 70-001 St Louis 1980. **BUSINESS ADDRESS:** St Louis Regional Commerce & G, 10 Broadway, St Louis, MO 63102.

VAN, VESTER L., JR.
Attorney. **PERSONAL:** Born Aug 05, 1941, Chicago, IL; married Saundra L Upshaw; children: Darian, Derek. **EDUCATION:** Chadron State, BA 1967; Howard Univ, JD 1971. **CAREER:** Reginald Heber Smith, attorney 1971-72; HUD, atty advsr 1973-74; US Dept of Commerce, bus spec 1974-76; Cook Co Public Defender, atty 1976-82; Private Practice, atty 1982-84; City of Chicago, sr staff atty 1984-, asst corp council 1986-; private practice 1986-. **ORGANIZATIONS:** Mem Amer Bar Assn 1971-, Natl Bar Assn 1973, Chicago Bar 1971-, Cook Cty Bar, IL Bar 1976-, DC Bar 1979-; bd dir Cook Cty Bar 1986-87. **HONORS/ACHIEVEMENTS:** Certificate of Appreciation participating & contributions HEW 1970; bd mem Cook Cnty Bar Assoc 1986-87.

VANALLEN, MORTON CURTIS
Clergyman. **PERSONAL:** Born Mar 10, 1950, New York, NY; children: Richard. **EDUCATION:** City Coll of NY, AA 1970; Antioch Coll, BA 1972; Harvard Grad Schl of Bus, MBA 1978. **CAREER:** Ordained minister 1969; Youth Services Agency City of NY, asst to commissioner 1970-71; Urban Crisis Task Force, founder & chief exec officer 1971-80; servedas dir of United Black Fund of Tri State (NY, NJ & CT) 1978-80; Willing Workers Baptist Church, pastor 1976; Public Utility Review Bd NY City Cncl, chrmn 1980; presently employed as a consultant. **HONORS/ACHIEVEMENTS:** Black Better Business Bureau, man of the yr awd 1984; rec'd commendation from Pres James Carter; former sec'y HUD Pat Harris; Mayors Beame & Koch citationof merit from Bronx Borough president and NY Housing Auth Police Dept all for comm work in the south Bronx and Harlem area of NYC. **BUSINESS ADDRESS:** Consultant, 80 Wall St, New York, NY 10005.

VAN AMSON, GEORGE LOUIS
Investment banking executive. **PERSONAL:** Born Jan 30, 1952, New York, NY; married Wendy Alicia Tempro. **EDUCATION:** Columbia Coll, AB 1974; Harvard Business School, MBA (honors) 1982. **CAREER:** Revlon Inc, financial analyst 1974-76; Citibank NA, asst controller 1976-77; Goldman Sachs & Co, senior financial analyst 1977-80, vice pres 1982-. **ORGANIZATIONS:** Dir Urban Leadership Forum 1983-, 21st Century PAC of NY 1984-, Minisink Townhouse Inc 1985-; mem economic develop comm 100 Black Men 1985-; pres HBS Black Alumni Assoc 1985-87; mem intl comm Securities Traders Assoc of NY 1987-. **HONORS/ACHIEVEMENTS:** Curtis Gold Medal Columbia Coll 1974; Leadership Awd Harvard Business School 1982. **HOME ADDRESS:** 230 West 76th St #9D, New York,

NY 10023. **BUSINESS ADDRESS:** Vice President, Goldman Sachs & Co, 85 Broad St 29th Floor, New York, NY 10004.

VANCE, IRVIN E.
Educator. **PERSONAL:** Born Apr 08, 1928, Mexico, MO; married Ann M Vance; children: Barbara Lecesnes, Velesha, Katrina Humphrey. **EDUCATION:** Wayne State Univ, BS 1957; Washington Univ, MA 1959; Univ of MI, EdD Math 1967. **CAREER:** Northeastern HS, math instr 1957-59; Southeastern HS, math instr 1959-62; Univ of MI, teachiing fellow math dept 1962-64, instr in math 1964-66; MI State Univ, asst prof of math 1966-69, assoc prof of math 1969-71; Educ Develop Ctr, dir of sch comm outreach for project one 1973-75; NM State Univ, dir of black progs 1971-72, assoc prof of math 1971-82, prof of math 1982-. **ORGANIZATIONS:** Consultant to numerous schools & univs; NM State Univ, chmn mem Math Educ Comm, planning grant comm, advisory comm, promotion to assoc & tenure comm, master comm, doctoral comm, comm on evalutation of ethnic progs; external affairs comm Natl Cncl of Teachers of Math; chmn bd dirs Development of Rsch & Human Resources; mem Natl Council for Accreditation of Teacher Educ; bd of dirs NAACP; reader of advance placement exam in math Educational Testing Serv 1979-84; judge at Black History Knowledge Bowl; review panel for the Minority Institution Science Improvement Program Natl Science Found; vice pres for univs NM Council of Teachers of Math 1978-81; pres NM Council of Teachers of Math 1984-85; prog chmn Annual Conf NM Council of Tchrs of Math 1984 1985; lecturer in math Boston Univ 1975, Lesley Coll 1974; dir of worksh op for Coll Teachers of Math Spelman Coll 1975; fndr dir NM State Univ Elem Teachers Math Project 1977-80; Math Inst for In-Serv Teachers at MI State Univ 1968 1971; assoc dir Grand Rapids MI Middle Sch Math Lab Project 1967-68. **HONORS/ACHIEVEMENTS:** Recd grants from NSF, NMSU; numerous works & papers published & presented. **MILITARY SERVICE:** AUS 1950-52. **BUSINESS ADDRESS:** Dean of Math, MI State Univ,, East Lansing, MI 48824.

VANCE, LAWRENCE N.
Communications journalist. **PERSONAL:** Born Dec 20, 1949, Chicago, IL; children: 2 children. **EDUCATION:** Roosevelt Univ, BS 1973; Chicago Kent Law School, JD 1977. **CAREER:** Cook County Public Defender, investigator 1973-79, atty 1977-79; Private Practice, attorney. **ORGANIZATIONS:** Mem Natl, Cook Cty, IL and Chicago Bar Assocs 1977-87. **BUSINESS ADDRESS:** Attorney, 201 North Wells, Chicago, IL 60602.

VANCE, TOMMIE ROWAN
Manager. **PERSONAL:** Born Apr 13, 1929, Frederick, OK; divorced; children: Michael, Nathan, Noretha. **EDUCATION:** Golden Gate Univ, attending 1979-. **CAREER:** Gray's Grocery, cashier 1955-59; Nevada Bell Telephone Co, mgr 1960-78; Pacific Telephone Co, mgr 1978-. **ORGANIZATIONS:** Sec Dem Ctr Comm 1974-; mem NV State Dem Affirmative Action Comm 1975-76; coor State of NV 1975-76; mem Intl Women's Yr Conf; chrpsn Reno Comm onthe Status of Women 1972-74; mem Washoe Cnty Demo Women's Club 1968-72. **HONORS/ACHIEVEMENTS:** Speech winner Pipe & Wire Toastmistress 1968; winner Council Level 1968; Boss of the Yr Amer Bus Women of Sparks 1971; Commendation United Fund. **BUSINESS ADDRESS:** Manager, Pacific Telephone Co, 530 E 14th St, San Leandro, CA 94577.

VANCE, VERA R.
Educator. **PERSONAL:** Born Jul 11, 1908, Waskom, TX; children: James R. **EDUCATION:** BA 1939; MEd 1962; Grad Stud 1971. **CAREER:** Notre Dame HS, consultant 1973-; JS Clarke Jr HS, teacher & counselor 1961-72 Central Jr HS, teacher 1959-61; Mooretown Elementary Shreveport, teacher 1951-56; Dixie Elementary, prin teacher 1948-81; Beaver Pond Elementary, prin teacher 1945-47; Gainsville Elementary, prin teacher 1931-45; Galilee Elementary Gilliam LA, teacher 1929-31; Velie Elem, teacher 1924. **ORGANIZATIONS:** Past sec Inter Scholastic League; TX & LA SS & BTU Congress 1932-50; sec Dist I SS Inst 1932-47; basileus of Sigma Gamma Rho; sec of chap 1974; mem YWCA; YMCA; Caddo Ed; ASS; Tchrs Assn Am Personnel-Guidance; LA Guidance Assn; Breezy Hill Comm Club; treas Trinity Bapt Ch. **HONORS/ACHIEVEMENTS:** Award Sigma Gamma Rho 1962; award for 20 yrs contin serv Sigma Gamma Rho 1974; award in bus Sigma Gamma Rho 1974; Who's Who of Professional Women of Am 1974.

VANCE, WILLIAM J., SR.
Clergyman. **PERSONAL:** Born Jan 14, 1923, Des Arc, AR; son of Ignatius D Vance and Esther Butler Vance; married Jacqueline G; children: Rene J, William Jr Jr. **EDUCATION:** Roosevelt Univ, 1946-54; Moody Bible Inst, 1961; Gov State Univ, BA 1974, MA 1975; "Parish Context Training" Pastoral Psysho-Therapy Institute 1983-84. **CAREER:** Chicago Post Office, 1948-69; Older Boys & Girls Conf, bible teacher, couns, summer camp 1958-74; Berean Baptist Church, pastor 1969-. **ORGANIZATIONS:** Chmn bd of dir Douglas Tubman Christian Ctr 1976-78; bd mem 1974-, ed 1969-75, Berean News. **HONORS/ACHIEVEMENTS:** Great Guy of Day WVON 1970; E Chicago Heights Comm Ctr Awd 1975; Great Amer Awd 1976. **MILITARY SERVICE:** USAF 1943-46. **BUSINESS ADDRESS:** Pastor, Berean Baptist Church, 5147 S Dearborn, Chicago, IL 60609.

VANDERPOOL, EUSTACE ARTHUR
Educator. **PERSONAL:** Born Dec 11, 1934, Nassau, Bahamas;married Andrea Taylor; children: Sheely, Scot-Erik. **EDUCATION:** Howard U, BS 1964; Howard U, MS 1967; Howard U, Doctorate 1971. **CAREER:** Howard Univ Coll of Med, asso prof 1973-; Dept Microbiology Howard Univ Coll of Med, virologist 1973; Microbiology Assoc MD, electron microscopist- Virology 1969; Naval Med Res Inst, guest scientist 1974. **ORGANIZATIONS:** Mem Am Soc of Microbiology 1964; mem Tissue Culture Assn 1967; mem Nat Inst of Sci 1978. **HONORS/ACHIEVEMENTS:** Res grant Am Cancer Soc Institutional Res Grant #1n-132; appt asso prof grad sch of Arts & Sci HowardUniv 1979; latest pub Proc of Soc Exp Bio Med 160389-395 1979. **BUSINESS ADDRESS:** 520 W St NW, Washington, DC 20059.

VANDROSS, LUTHER R.
Singer/songwriter/producer. **PERSONAL:** Born Apr 20, 1951, New York, NY. **EDUCATION:** Attended Western Michigan Univ. **CAREER:** Wrote song "Everybody Rejoice" featured in Broadway show The Wiz 1972; toured with David Bowie 1974; sang on albums with Bette Midler, Carly Simon, Chaka Khan,Average White Band; first Epic Solo album "Never Too Much" 1981 sold more than 1,000,000 copies; second solo album "Forever, For Always, For Love" 1982; wrote and recorded third solo album "Busy Body" 1983; fourth solo album "The Night I Fell in Love"; produced albums for Dionne Warwick "How Many Times Can We Say Goodbye and Aretha Franklin Jump To It, Get It Right 1983; sang backup and arranged vocals for three tracks on Diana Ross' "Silk"; Solo Album, "Any Love", 1989. **ORGANIZATIONS:** Mem ASCAP, SAG, AFTRA. **HONORS/ACHIEVEMENTS:** Platinum LP's "Never Too Much", "Forever For Always", "Busy Body", "The Night I Fell in Love" 1981-86; dubbed by People magazine "The Pavarotti of Pop". **BUSINESS ADDRESS:** Alive Enterprises, 1775 Broadway, New York, NY 10019.

VAN DYKE, HENRY
Author. **PERSONAL:** Born Oct 03, 1928, Allegan, MI. **EDUCATION:** Univ MI, BA 1953, MA 1955. **CAREER:** Basic Books, edtr 1958-66; Kent State U, writer-in-residence 1969-. **HONORS/ACHIEVEMENTS:** Guggenheim 1971; literary award Acad Arts & Letters 1973; Published, Ladies of the Rachmaninoff Eyes 1965, Blood of Strawberrs 1969, Dead Piano 1971, Lunacy and Caprice 1987. **MILITARY SERVICE:** AUS corpl 1947-50. **HOME ADDRESS:** 40 Waterside Plz, New York, NY 10010. **BUSINESS ADDRESS:** Kent State Univ, Kent, OH 44242.

VAN HOOK, WARREN KENNETH
Educator. **PERSONAL:** Born Jun 26, 1920, Elverton, WV; married Cora; children: Sharyl, Warren Jr, Fay. **EDUCATION:** WV Coll, 1941-42, 1945-47; Howard U, BS 1951. **CAREER:** Howard Univ, dir minority business 1976-; Inst Minority Business Educ School Business Public Admin Howard Univ, dir 1973-; Small Business Guidance & Devel Center Howard Univ, assoc dir 1968-73; Van-Park Drugs, owner 1954-68; Div Drugs Inc, mgr pharm 1951-54; United Comm Natl Bank WA, founding dir vice pres 1964-68; Antioch School Law, adv dir 1970-73; Minority Business & Orgn, mgmt consultant 1974-; DC Commn Against Drug Abuse, commr 1976-77; United Natl Bank WA, dir 1976-. **ORGANIZATIONS:** Cofoundr vice pres treas memsp Neighbors Inc 1958-68; mem Alpha Phi Alpha Frat; Nat Bus League; Am Soc Training & Devel; Am Pharm Assn; Nat Pharm Assn; NAACP; Urban League. **HONORS/ACHIEVEMENTS:** Outsdng serv Aw Ministerial Alliance NE WA 1964; key to cty Savannah GA 1977; pbul "Crime & Small Bus" Black Enter 1971; "Combating Crime in the Small Bus Arena" Jour Small Busm Mgmt 1971; "Tech & Asst & the Busmn" DC Dealer 1971; bronze star aw. **MILITARY SERVICE:** AUS capt 1942-45. **BUSINESS ADDRESS:** 2361 Sherman Ave NW, Washington, DC 20059.

VAN LIER, NORM
Athlete, radio sportscaster. **PERSONAL:** Born Apr 01, 1947, E Liverpool, OH. **EDUCATION:** St Francis, 1969. **CAREER:** Bulls WVON Chicago, radio sprtscstr; Chicago Bulls, player 1971-78. **ORGANIZATIONS:** Mem Bulls Starting Line-up 5 out of 7 yrs. **HONORS/ACHIEVEMENTS:** All star team 1974, 76-77; one of top ten all-time NBA Ldrs in assists; team 4th all-time in num of Games played field goal attempts field goals made free throws made & pts scored; all-time team 3rd in min played; all-time Team 8th in rebounds; 1st in assts & 1st in steals.

VAN LIEROP, ROBERT F.
Attorney. **PERSONAL:** Born Mar 17, 1939, New York, NY; son of Edward and Sylvia; married Toy. **EDUCATION:** Hofstra Univ, BA Econ 1964; NY Univ Sch of Law, LLB (JD) 1967. **CAREER:** Asst counsel NAACP 1967-68; assoc Fleisher, Dornbush, Mensch, Mandelstam 1968-71; Atty; Self-employed, film prod photojournalist 1971-; "Like It Is" WABC/TV, co-prod 1977-78; Privte Practice, atty 1968-71; NY City Community Bd #9 Manhattan, hmn 1985-87; Republic of Vanuatu, Ambassador to the United Nations 1981-. **ORGANIZATIONS:** Bd of dir Black Economic Research Center; past mem exec comm Amer Comm on Africa; founding mem Natl Conf of Black Lawyers; former bd mem Harlem Children's Theatre; past mem natl exec bd Natl Lawyers Guild; past bd mem Bny Civil Liberties Union; mem, bd of directors, Manhattan Borough Development Corp 1988-. **MILITARY SERVICE:** USAF 1956-60. **BUSINESS ADDRESS:** H.E. Republic of Vanuatu, 416 Convent Ave, New York, NY 10031-4217.

VAN LIEW, DONALD H.
Educator. **PERSONAL:** Born Oct 04, 1929, Somerville, NJ; married Ruth E Kauffmann; children: Ingrid E, Hans P, Nil C. **EDUCATION:** Univ of New Mexico, BFA 1956; Columbia Teachers Coll, MA 1979. **CAREER:** Univ of MI, asst counselor intl center 1960-64; Inst of Intl Educ NYC, program specialist 1964-65; NSSFNS, assoc 1965-66, sr assoc 1966, assoc dir 1966, dir 1967-69; Columbia Univ, asst to dean of student affairs 1969-71; Marymount Coll, dir comm leadership program 1971-, dir HEOP, asst dean 1985-. **ORGANIZATIONS:** Mem Planning Comm NACAC 1968; pres Croton Comm Nursery School 1968; mem NY State Educ Dept Head Task Force on Consortia 1973; chairperson Cross-cultural program com Marymount Coll 1973; mem ex-officer Com on Academic Standing & Retention Marymount Coll 1971-79; sec NY State Higher educ Opportunity Program Professional Org 1975; mem Academic Dean Search Comm Marymount Coll 1977; mem Bd of Trustees Common Marketing Marymount Coll 1978; mem Commn on Independent Coll & Univ Higher Educ Oppor Program 1979; Westchester Regional Rep NY State Higher Educ Opportunity Program Professional Org 1979; mem Taks Force on Admissions Marymount Coll 1972-74; chairperson Fact Finding Comm to the Presidential Search Com 1974; mem NY State Task Force on HEOP Guidelines 1974; mem Affirmative Action Task Force Marymount Coll 1975; chmn Calendar Comm 1985-; mem national assoc of academic affairs administrators 1988; mem committee for bridging academic and student affairs 1986; mem committee on the troubled student 1986; mem committee on racial and cultural diversity 1989. **HONORS/ACHIEVEMENTS:** Ford Found Grant to participate in program for educ leadership Teacher Coll Columbia Univ 1970-71. **MILITARY SERVICE:** Served 1951-53. **HOME ADDRESS:** RD #1, Box 155 Wooddale Ave, Croton-on-Hudson, NY 10520.

VANN, ALBERT
Assemblyman. **PERSONAL:** Born Nov 19, 1934, Brooklyn, NY; married Mildred E; children: Scott, Fola, Binta. **EDUCATION:** Univ of Toledo, BBA; MS; LIU; Yesiva U, MA. **CAREER:** Tchr; couns; adminstr; educ cons. **ORGANIZATIONS:** Dir Talent Serach Prog Dept HEW; mem NY State Assem; pres African-Am Tchr Assn; bd dir Bedford-Stuyvesant Restoration Corp; pres Bannguard Civic Assn; chmn NY State Blk & Puerto Rican Legis Caucus 1977; bd mem NAACP; mem Blk Educs; Medgar Evers Coll Comm Coun; mem Alpha Phi Alpha Frat. **HONORS/ACHIEVEMENTS:** Recipt polit achvmt aw IDEA Inc; comm serv aw Bus & Professional Negro Women Inc; outstdng educ aw Bro & Sister

Afro-Am Unity. **MILITARY SERVICE:** USMC sgt 1952-55. **BUSINESS ADDRESS:** State Capitol, Albany, NY 12225.

VANN, GREGORY ALVIN
Consultant. **PERSONAL:** Born Apr 17, 1954, Washington, DC; married Joan A Simpson. **EDUCATION:** Howard Univ, BArch 1977; Univ of FL, MConst Mgt 1978; Drexel Univ, MBA 1985. **CAREER:** Bryant & Bryant Architects, designer 1976-77; Whiting Turner Contracting Co, project engr 1977; Catalytic Inc, sr planning engr 1978-81; Burns & Roe Inc,sr planning engr 1981-84; The Vann Org, pres 1984-. **ORGANIZATIONS:** Mem Amer Assoc of Cost Engrs 1980-; mem Amer Inst of Architects 1986-87; mem Philadelphia Chap Natl Black MBA Assoc 1986-, Cherry Hill Minority Civic Assoc 1986-. **BUSINESS ADDRESS:** President, The Vann Organization, 3026 W Chapel Ave, Cherry Hill, NJ 08002.

VAN NESS, STANLEY C.
Attorney & business executive. **PERSONAL:** Born Feb 28, 1934, Somerville, NJ; children: David. **EDUCATION:** Rutgers Univ, BS (cum laude) 1955; Rutgers Univ Law Sch, LLB (cum laude) 1963; Rider Univ, Dr of Laws (Hon) 1977; Stockton Coll, Dr of Laws (Hon) 1980; Rutgers Univ, Dr of Laws (Hon) 1983. **CAREER:** Hon S Goldmann, law sec 1963; US Atty, asst 1963-64; Gov State NJ, counsel 1964-69; State NJ, public defender 1969-82, public advocate 1974-82; Seton Hall Law Sch, distinguished prof law 1982-84; Jamieson Moore Peskin & Spicer, atty, partner. **ORGANIZATIONS:** Dir Jersey Cntrl Pwr & Light 1982-, Delaware Vly United Way 1983-, v chrmn State Law Enforcement Cmsn 1969-82; v chrmn Cts Task Force Pres Cmsn 1974; chrmn Trenton Human Rltns Cncl 1972. **HONORS/ACHIEVEMENTS:** Reginald Heber Smith Awrd; Brotherhood Awd Christian & Jews; Disting Alumnus Awd Rutgers U; Gene Carte Criminal Justice Awd Trenton St Coll; Thurgood Marshall Awd Seton Hall Law School. **MILITARY SERVICE:** USAF capt; Instr Navigator MATS 1955-60. **BUSINESS ADDRESS:** Attorney, Partner, Jamieson Moore Peskin & Spicer, 300 Alexander Pk, Princeton, NJ 08540.

VAN PEEBLES, MARIO
Actor. **PERSONAL:** Born in Mexico City, Mexico. **EDUCATION:** Columbia Univ, BA Economics 1980. **CAREER:** Appeared in Heartbreak Ridge with Clint Eastwood, Sweet Sweetback's Baadass Song (a movie written directed and produced by his father), Exterminator II, Cotton Club, presently working on Jaws, The Revenge; regular on TV series "LA Law"; appeared in Off-Broadway comedy A Thousand Clowns, Broadway comedy Waltz of the Stork, TV specials "Sophisticated Gents" and "Children of the Night"; starred in NBC series "Sonny Spoon"; co-staring NBC/Disney series "Orleans" with Alfre Woodward; directed "21 Jump Street" episode called "High High.". **HONORS/ACHIEVEMENTS:** Bronze Halo Award for performance in Children of the Night; Pioneers of Excellence Award, World Institute of Black Communications.

VAN PEEBLES, MELVIN
Writer, actor, composer, film director. **PERSONAL:** Born Aug 21, 1932, S Chicago, IL; divorced; children: Mario, Meggan, Melvin. **EDUCATION:** Graduated from Ohio Wesleyan Coll. **CAREER:** American Stock Exchange, floor trader; Mabon, Nugent & Co, consultant; worked as an actor; made first feature film, "The Story of a Three-Day Pass," in France; directed motion pictures for Columbia Studios, including "Watermelon Man," 1969; wrote, directed, and financed film "Sweet Sweetback's BaadAsssss Song"; wrote and produced two Broadway plays "Ain't Supposed to Die A Natural Death" and "Don't Play Us Cheap"; directed a music video of the group Whodini's song "Funky Beat"; composer for recordings. **ORGANIZATIONS:** mem, Directors Guild of Amer; mem, French Directors Guild. **HONORS/ACHIEVEMENTS:** First Prize from Belgian Festival for "Don't Play Us Cheap"; author of Bold Money, A New Way to Play the Options Market, Warner Books, 1986, and Bold Money: How to Get Rich in the Options Market, Warner Books, 1987. **MILITARY SERVICE:** US Air Force; served as navigator-bombardier. *

VAN TRECE, JACKSON C.
Educator. **PERSONAL:** Born Aug 31, 1928, Edwardsville, IL; married Dolores Wilson. **EDUCATION:** KS State Tchr Coll, BS 1952; KS State Coll Pgh, MS 1960; UMKC & KS State Tchrs Coll Emporis KS. **CAREER:** NE Jr HS, teacher 1952-56; NE Jr HS, counselor 1965-66; Sumner HS Kansas City KS, 1966-70; Univ of MO KC, asst vice chanchellor student affairs 1980-. **ORGANIZATIONS:** Admin & dir Black Motivation Training Cntr KC 1970; life mem NEA; pres Region VII Trio Proj Dir Orgn; dir Trio ProgsUMKC; Boy Scouts Am Troop Ldr 1952-58; devel Turner House KC; Kappa Alpha Psi Frat; dir Area Youth Groups; YMCA exec bd KC MO 1973. **HONORS/ACHIEVEMENTS:** NamedUniv MO first Black Acad Deanf. **MILITARY SERVICE:** AUS 1946-48. **BUSINESS ADDRESS:** 5100 Rockhill Rd, Kansas City, MO 64110.

VARGUS, IONE D.
Education administration. **PERSONAL:** Born Jul 19, 1930, Medford, MA; daughter of Edward Dugger and Madeline Kelley-Dugger; married William H Adams; children: Suzanne Vargus Holloman; William D. **EDUCATION:** Tufts U, AB 1952;Univ Chicago, MA 1954; Brandeis Univ, PhD 1971. **CAREER:** Several Yrs Social Work Practice Family Servcs, Child Welfare Public Housing Home Mgmt Informal Educ 1954-71; Brandeis Univ Wharton MA, asst prof 1969-71; Univ IL Urbana, asst prof 1971-74; Temple Univ, dean sch social admin. **ORGANIZATIONS:** Chmn bd mgr Philadelphia Found 1983-; trustee Tufts Univ 1981-, Helen Spalding Found 1977-; cmsr Mayors Commssion Women 1984-; bd of directors PA Institute on Public Policy 6-1989. **HONORS/ACHIEVEMENTS:** Significant first achievement award Crisis Intervention Network 1984. **HOME ADDRESS:** 429 East Durham St, Philadelphia, PA 19119. **BUSINESS ADDRESS:** Dean, School of Social Admin, Temple University, Ritter Hall Annex Rm 555-556, Philadelphia, PA 19122.

VARNADO, ARTHUR
Business executive. **PERSONAL:** Born Oct 19, 1932, Buffalo, NY; married Theresa E; children: Debra, Karen, Arthur. **EDUCATION:** Cameron Coll, 1971; Dowling Coll, BS 1973; FAA Exec Sch, 1974;Univ Louisville, MS 1975; Air War Coll, Prof Diploma 1976; Auburn U, MPA 1976. **CAREER:** FAA, spl asst to dir 1976-; Air Traffic Control Tower, chief 1973-75; Air Traffic Control Tower JFK Tower, chief 1972-73; Newark Tower, dep chief 1971-72; radar controller 1968-71; Newark Tower, radar controller 1963-68. **ORGANIZATIONS:** Kappa Alpha Psi 1977; Black Controllers Coalition 1968-72; Fed Exec Assn 1973; Louisville Urban League 1973-76; Louisville Eastern Area Counc 1974-76; NAACP 1963-68; White Oaks Civic Assn 1969-73. **HONORS/ACHIEVEMENTS:** Grad dean's honor awd 1976; outst rating awd FAA 1975; disting citizens awd Louisville 1975; hon Bky Col Louisville 1974; we point with pride awd FAA1966. **MILITARY SERVICE:** USAF s/sgt 1952-56. **BUSINESS ADDRESS:** 800 Independence Ave SW, Washington, DC 20591.

VARNER, HAROLD HOSEA, JR.
Physician. **PERSONAL:** Born Mar 16, 1952, Alabama. **EDUCATION:** Univ of Notre Dame, BS 1974; Howard Univ, MD 1976. **CAREER:** Howard Univ, biochem tutor 1974-75; Howard Univ Health Serv, chief extern 1975-76; Los Angeles County, postgrad phsyician psychiatry 1976. **ORGANIZATIONS:** Mem AAAS 1987-. **HOME ADDRESS:** 24-20th Avenue South, Birmingham, AL 35205.

VARNER, JAMES
Business executive. **PERSONAL:** Born Nov 02, 1934, Jersey City, NJ; son of Charles Varner and Mamie Dickerson Varner; married Florence Johnson; children: 4 Children. **EDUCATION:** Univ of ME, BS 1957; Rutgers Univ, MS 1970, M City & Regional Planning 1972. **CAREER:** Mt Siani Hosp, chemist 1957-58; Trenton NJ & Plainfield NJ Public School, high school teacher 1960-66; Plainfield Comm Action, assoc dir 1966; Morris Co Human Resources Agency, exec dir 1966-82; Drew Univ, counselor & lectr part time 1972-82; Black Enterprise Magazine, acct exec 1982-85; Fallis Communications Inc, vice pres, 1985-86; vice pres, Informatoin Mgmt Resources, Inc, 1986-; host and producer, radio program, "Community Update" WMTR radio, Norristown, NJ, 1970-. **ORGANIZATIONS:** Mem Amer Inst of Planners; Amer Soc of Planning Officials; Natl Assn of Planners; Amer Found for Negro Affairs; Congress of African Peoples; Natl Assn for Comm Devel; mem Rotary Club of Morristown NJ; bd mem Plainfield NJ Area YMCA; bd mem Morris Co NAACP; named chmn emeritus of Natl Assn of Planners 1972; bd mem Natl Assn of Comm Devel; past bd mem Amer Soc of Planning Officials. **HONORS/ACHIEVEMENTS:** First place in NJ Jaycees Area Speak Up Finals 1967; Community Service Award, The Morris County Urban League, Inc, 1989. **MILITARY SERVICE:** US Sig Corps Res capt. **HOME ADDRESS:** 301 Kings Rd, Madison, NJ 07940.

VARNER, JEWELL C.
Association director. **PERSONAL:** Born Apr 12, 1918, Tatums, OK; daughter of Joseph Carter and Jannie Carter; married Jimmy Lee (deceased); children: Jimmie Mae, Rose Marie. **EDUCATION:** Langston Univ, BS; KS State Teachers Coll Emporia, MS; OK State Univ, Post Graduate Studies. **CAREER:** Big Five Devel Found Head Start HEW, dir; Jewell's Ceramics & Gifts, owner 1975-; Tatums OK Public Schools, teacher 28 yrs; Golden Acre Enterprizes, owner, dir. **ORGANIZATIONS:** Mem Eastern Star; Delta Sigma Theta; vice pres OK Assn Children Under Six; OK Educ Assn; life mem NAACP; mem NTU, NAMPU, Natl Set Inc, OK Chapter Langston Alumnus Assoc; Links Inc Oklahoma City Chapter. **HONORS/ACHIEVEMENTS:** Black Voise Better Business Award 1973; best dressed woman OK State Soul Bazaar 1973; Outstanding Civic Serv Fed Club Women; Tatums Comm Action Agency Chmn War on Poverty Gov's Advisory Group; Inducted into OK Afro-Amer Hall of Fame 1984. **HOME ADDRESS:** 3405 E Maxwell Drive, Oklahoma City, OK 73121.

VARNER, NELLIE M.
Educator, real estate investment broker. **PERSONAL:** Born Aug 27, 1935, Lake Cormorant, MS; daughter of Tommie Varner and Essie Davis Varner (deceased); divorced; children: Janniss LaTronia Varner. **EDUCATION:** Wayne State Univ, BS 1958; Wayne State Univ, MA 1959; Univ of MI, PhD 1968. **CAREER:** Detroit Public School, teacher 1959-64; Coll of Literature Sci & Arts Univ of MI, spl asst to dean 1968-70; Ctr for Russian & European Studies Univ of MI, faculty assoc 1968-69; Univ of MI, asst prof political science 1968-69; Harvard Univ, rsch fellow 1970-71, rsch assoc 1970-71; Affirmative Action Progs Univ of MI; dir 1972-75; Rackham School of Grad Studies Univ of MI, assoc dean 1976-79; Strather & Varner Inc Real Estate Invest Brokers, vice pres 1979-; Primco Foods, Inc, Southfield, MI, pres, 1988-. **ORGANIZATIONS:** Mem Amer Council on Educ Comm on Women in Higher Educ 1976-; mem Natl Sci Found Adv Com for Minority Progs in Sci Educ 1977-; chair Real Estate Adv Bd State of MI 1978-79; del White House Conf on Small Business 1980-; bd of regents Univ of MI 1980-; bd dir Highland Park YMCA 1980-83; exec bd Detroit Chapter NAACP 1985-86; mem bd dir Amer Inst for Business 1986-; mem Southern Oakland County Bd of Realtors, Detroit Bd of Realtors; chair Equal Opportunity Com Natl Assn of State Univ & Land Grant Coll; mem Econ Action Com New Detroit Inc; mem MI Bd of Realtors & Natl Bd of Realtors; mem Equal Opportunity Task Force Amer Council on Educ, Acad Affairs Faculty Analysis Proj Adv Com Univ of MI, Senate Assem Adv Com on State Real Univ of MI; exec bd Wayne State Univ, Univ of MI; mem Inst of Gerontology; exec com Ctr for Afro-Amer African Studies Univ of MI; HEW Title I State Adv Council to Bd of Educ Stateof MI; consult Natl Sci Found Panel on Awds to Minority Coll & Univ, Proj for Acad Affirm Action Training Intl Assoc of Official Human Rights Agency, Dept of HUD US Govt, Pi Sigma Alpha, Phi Kappa Phi, Delta Sigma Theta; trustee, New Detroit, Inc, 1987-; dir, Inst of Amer Business, 1986-. **HONORS/ACHIEVEMENTS:** Florence Sweeney Scholarship 1958; Detroit Women Principals Club Scholarship 1959; teaching fellowship 1964; NDFL Fellowship 1966-76; congressional internship US Congress 1966; CIC grant for Field Study in USSR 1968; Wilton Park Fellowship for Amer participation in Wilton Park Conf Steyning Sussex England 1969; social Sci Rsch Council Rsch Training Fellowship 1970-71; rsch grant Univ of MI 1970-71; recip rsch travel grant to study Black Political Elites in Africa US & the Caribbean Carnegie Endowment for Intl Peace 1970-; Distinguished Community Leadership Award Natl Assoc of Women Business Owners 1984. **BUSINESS ADDRESS:** Vice President, Strather & Varner, Inc, 3000 Town Center, Ste 2460, Southfield, MI 48075.

VARNER, ROBERT LEE
Manager. **PERSONAL:** Born May 03, 1932, Birmingham, AL; married Annie C; children: Venetia, Dwayne, Robert II. **EDUCATION:** Nat U, BB 1976; Nat U, MBA 1978. **CAREER:** Bank of Am, commercial loan ofcr 1979-; Pacific Coast Bk San Diego, vice pres 1976-79; NAACP San Diego, exec sec 1975-76. **ORGANIZATIONS:** Adv bd mem Nat Conf of Christians & Jews Inc; mem San Diego Regional Emply Training Consortium; vice pres Mt View Tennis Club; exec sec San Diego NAACP; memSan Diego USO; bd chmn Comm Rel Bd; adv bd mem Proj YES; adv counc mem San Diego Co Human Resources; dir San Diego Boy Scouts; reg coord San Diego United Way; adv counc mem San Diego YMCA; pres emeritus CA Fedn of Black Ldrshp; mem San Diego Coalition; mem San Diego Nghbrhd House; mem San Diego Urban League; mem Councmn Leon William's Adv Counc; mem Trinity Bapt Ch; third degree mason Prince Hall; del White House Conf on Small Bus; dir Brookins Bus Inst. **HONORS/ACHIEVEMENTS:** Nat Def Serv Medal (2); Korean Serv

Medal (3); United Nations Serv Medal; Korean Presidential Unit Citation; Vietnamese Serv Medal (3); Vietnamese Combat Medal (2); Good Conduct Medal; San Diego Co Human Rel Aw for Comm Involvement; Am Tennis Assn for outstanding serv. **MILITARY SERVICE:** USMC capt 1950-75. **BUSINESS ADDRESS:** Bank of Am, 801 W 7th St, Los Angeles, CA 90017.

VASSALL, SIDNEY AUSTIN
Director. **PERSONAL:** Born Mar 27, 1934, Brooklyn, NY; divorced. **EDUCATION:** Columbia U, BA 1955. **CAREER:** Nat Broadcasting Co, dir 1956-; Taledega Coll, lect 1975. **ORGANIZATIONS:** Mem exec comm Friends of Medger Evens Coll Inc 1977; mem exec comm Willoughby Walk Corp 1977. **HONORS/ACHIEVEMENTS:** Emmy Asso Dir 1970; emmy Asso Dir 1971. **MILITARY SERVICE:** AUS sgt 1957-59. **BUSINESS ADDRESS:** Natl Broadcasting Co, 30 Rockefeller Plaza, New York, NY 10020.

VAUGHAN, GERALD R.
Certified financial planner. **PERSONAL:** Born Sep 09, 1957, Bronx, NY; son of Raymond Vaughan and Juanita B Smith-Vaughan; married Ramona D Girtman. **EDUCATION:** NC A&T St Univ, BS (Magna Cum Laude) 1980; Atlanta Univ, MBA (Magna Cum Laude) 1983; Adelphi Univ, CFP 1985. **CAREER:** Liberty Mutual Insurance Co, personal risk underwriter/industry regulator/tech analyst 1976-80; Citizens & Southern GA Corp, strategic planner/invest analyst 1982-83; Entrepreneur, certified financial planner 1985-; Grumman Corp, sr financial analyst 1983-89. **ORGANIZATIONS:** Mem Assoc of MBA Executives 1982-, Natl Black MBA Assoc 1982-; keeper of finance Omega Psi Phi Frat Inc 1985-89. **HONORS/ACHIEVEMENTS:** Fellowship Grants NC A&T St Univ/Atlanta Univ 1975-83; Outstanding Young Americans Intl Biographical Inst 1978-80. **HOME ADDRESS:** 3666 Cherry Ridge Blvd, Decatur, GA 30034.

VAUGHAN, JAMES EDWARD
Broadcast minister. **PERSONAL:** Born Mar 07, 1943, Herdford County, NC; married Della M; children: Alvin, Patrinia, Meimii. **EDUCATION:** NC Central Univ, BA Art/English 1969. **CAREER:** NY Courier Newspaper, managing editor 1969; Capital Cities Comms Inc, promotions mgr 1971-74; WYAH-TV, mgr promotion/producer 1977-81; T-TAC TV Inc, founder/chmn/pres 1980-; Small Bus Broadcasting Serv Co, founder/chmn/pres 1982-; WJCB TV Tidewater Christian, founder/chmn/pres 1983-. **ORGANIZATIONS:** Bd of dirs The STOP Org; mem Amer Mgmt Assoc, Interdenominational Ministers Forum, AEHRO Broadcast Frat; vice pres Southern Christian Leadership ConfVA; chmn media Tidewater for Jesus Assoc; chmn black broadcast ownership Natl Relig Broadcasters. **HONORS/ACHIEVEMENTS:** Ex Umbra Radio/TV Broadcasts and weekly column 1977-; Citation of Merit Natl Multiple Sclerosis Soc 1984; Certificate of Service VA State Adv Comm US Commn on Civil Rights 1985; Oliver J Allen Awd WRAP Radio Gospel Music Awds 1986. **BUSINESS ADDRESS:** Founder/Chairman, Tidewater Christian Comm Corp, WJCB-TV Plume Ctr West, 100 W Plume St Ste 514, Norfolk, VA 23510.

VAUGHAN, SARAH LOIS
Singer. **PERSONAL:** Born Mar 27, 1924, Newark, NJ; married Waymon Reed; children: Deborah. **CAREER:** Singer with orchestras led by, Earl Hines 1943-44, Billy Eckstein 1944-45, John Kirby 1945-46; solo performer and rec artist 1945-. **HONORS/ACHIEVEMENTS:** Numerous albums Mercury Records, Natl Mus Craft, Columbia, Em Arcy Records, Roulette Records; "Lover Man"; "Alfie"; "A Lover's Concerto"; "Foggy Day in Londontown"; winner Apollo Amateur Contest 1942; recip Annual Vocalist Award Downbeat Mag 1946-52; Grammy Award 1983; Downbeat Hall of Fame 1985; special Grammy award, 1989; Jazz Master Fellowship, 1989. *

VAUGHN, ALVIN
Educator. **PERSONAL:** Born Aug 30, 1939, Philadelphia, PA; son of Rogert Vaughn and Martha Vaughn; married Eloise Stephens; children: Lois Jonneen. **EDUCATION:** Temple Univ, BS 1963, MS 1964; Intl Grad School, EdD 1984. **CAREER:** School Dist of Philadelphia, teacher 1963-70, acting super 1970-71, dept head 1971-74, vice principal 1974-; evening school principal 1976-. **ORGANIZATIONS:** Bd of dirs Drew Comm Mental Health Ctr 1975-85; counselor/admin Negro Trade Union Leadership Council 1978-84; bd of sch dirs Cheltenham Township PA 1978-87; bd of dirs Philadelphia PUSH 1982-87, Cheltenham Art Ctr 1982-86. **HOME ADDRESS:** 1108 Curtis Dr, Wyncote, PA 19095. **BUSINESS ADDRESS:** Educational Administrator, School District of Philadelphia, George Washington High School, Philadelphia, PA 19116.

VAUGHN, CLARENCE B.
Clinical scientist. **PERSONAL:** Born Dec 14, 1928, Philadelphia, PA; son of Albert Vaughn and Aretha Johnson Vaughn; married Sarah Campbell Vaughn, Sep 14, 1953; children: Steven, Annette, Carl, Ronald. **EDUCATION:** Benedict Coll, BS 1947- 1951; Howard Univ, MS, 1951-1953/1955, MD 1953-1957; MD 1957; DC Gen Hosp, Intern 1957-58; Freedmans Hosp, Residency 1958-59; Wayne State Univ, PhD 1965. **CAREER:** Rsch Physician 1964-70; Milton A Darling mem Ctr, clin dir 1970-72; SW Oncology Study Group, principle investigator 1978-; Wayne State Univ, assoc clinical prof 1978-; Providence Hospital, dir oncology 1973-1988; 1988 Southfield Oncology Institute, Inc; Clinical Prof Oakland Univ. **ORGANIZATIONS:** Bd of dir Amer Coll Physicians, Amer Assoc Univ Prof, AMA; natl chmn Aerospace & Military Sect of NMA, mem Amer Soc Clin Oncology, Natl Med Assn, Wayne Cty Med Soc, Oakland Cty med Assn, Reserve Officers Assn, US Assn Military Surgeons, USAF Assn, Detroit Cancer Club, Detroit Physiological Soc; pres Amer Cancer Soc MI Div 1986-; chmn adv comm minority involvement field serv comm Amer Cancer Soc; educ review comm Natl Cancer Inst; mem Natl Surgeon of Reserve Officers Assoc; mem Metropolitan Detroit Steering Comm for The Cancer Prevention Awareness; medical dir, Oncology, Samaritan Health Center 1986-; clinical prof, School of Medicine, Wayne State Univ 1988-. **HONORS/ACHIEVEMENTS:** Outstanding Reserve Aerospace Med Physician Awd 1974; AFRES Command Flight Surgeon of the Year 1974; Humanitarian of the Year 1988. **MILITARY SERVICE:** USAF col 1978; US Air Force Col; 1959-1961 Active 1961-1988 Reserve. **BUSINESS ADDRESS:** Dir Oncology, Southfield Oncology Institute, Inc., 27211 Lahser Road, Southfield, MI 48034.

VAUGHN, EUGENIA MARCHELLE WASHINGTON
Social worker. **PERSONAL:** Born Oct 31, 1957, Columbus, OH; daughter of Eugene G. Washington and Lula Augusta Edward Washington; married Tannis Eugene Vaughn, Jun 09, 1984; children: Shannon Eugene, Ieasha Michelle. **EDUCATION:** Columbus Tech Inst, A 1977; OH Dominican Coll, BA 1982; OH State Univ, MSW 1985. **CAREER:** Franklin Co Children Svcs, caseworker I 1977-83, child welfare caseworker II 1984; Columbus Area Mental Health Ctr, contract worker 1985; Franklin Co Children Svcs, child welfare caseworker II, III Foster Care 1985-87, social worker III 1987-; treatment manager Franklin Co Children Svcs, Cols, Ohio 2/1989-. **ORGANIZATIONS:** Speakers bureau mem Choices for Victims of Domestic Violence 1985-; mem Natl Assoc of Social Workers, Natl Assoc of Black Social Workers; rec'd LSW Status Natl Assoc of Social Workers 1986; Sunday school tchr, ABYPU officer Rehoboth Temple Church; mem Rehoboth Scholarship Fund Comm; initiator Scholarship Alumni Assoc. **HONORS/ACHIEVEMENTS:** Minority Fellowship 1983-84, Child Welfare Traineeship 1984-85 OSU; mem Delta Epsilon Sigma Hon Soc, Alpha Delta Mu Social Work Honor Soc. **HOME ADDRESS:** 65 S Algonquin Ave, Columbus, OH 43204. **BUSINESS ADDRESS:** Social Worker III, Franklin Co Children Serv, 1951 Gantz Rd, Grove City, OH 43123.

VAUGHN, JACKIE, III
Legislator. **PERSONAL:** Born Nov 17, 1930, Birmingham, AL. **EDUCATION:** Hillsdale Coll, BA; Oberlin Coll, MA; Oxford U, Fulbright Scholar & Fellow Oxon BLitt Social Sci. **CAREER:** Former MI State Rep; Dist 5, state senator; Univ of Detroit, instructor, Wayne State Univ, instructor. **HONORS/ACHIEVEMENTS:** First black pres Young Dem of MI; author of 18-year-old Voting Rights Bill in MI; Statewide Chmn, Michigan Dr Martin Luther King Jr Holiday Commn; Top vote-getter of any state legislator in MI; Selected "Outstanding and Model Legislator", Michigan Chronicle; Distinguished Senator and Man of Peace Award, D'etre Univ in Detroit; Elected to Omicron Delta Kappa Honor Leadership Soc; Grand Marshal of the Homecoming Celebration, Olivet Coll; Grand Marshal of the Cotillion Club Debutante Ball; Alumni Achievement Award, Hillsdale Coll; Named Legislator or Senator of the Year, by various organizations; Honorary mem, the Most Worshipful King David Grand Logde, AM & FM; Mem, The Rosa L Gragg Educational & Civic Club (first male ever to receive this high honor); Human Touch Award, Kappa Rho Zeta Chapter; Serv Award for Outstanding Community Serv & Dedicated Leadership, Women's Asn of Metro Baptist Church; Youth Leader Serv Award, Rotary Intl; Legislator of the Year Award, Jaycees. **BUSINESS ADDRESS:** Assoc Pres Pro Tempore, The Michigan Senate, State Capitol, P O Box 30036, Lansing, MI 48909.

VAUGHN, JACQUELINE BARBARA (JACQUI ROBINSON)
Union official. **PERSONAL:** Born Jul 27, 1935, St Louis, MO; married Robert H; children: Karl T Wright; Roderick Vaughn, Wendy Vaughn, Sharmen Lett. **EDUCATION:** BE primary educ 1956; ME spec educ EMH 1965; Harvard Univ, Language Arts 1966. **CAREER:** Classroom teacher grades Kg-3 1956-67; IL Federation of Teachers, vice pres 1969-; Chicago Teachers Union, reading coordinator, language arts cons, recording sec; Urban Reading Program Ginn Publ Co, cons; apptd to IL Adv Bd of Future Business Leaders of Amer (FLBA) 1973; apptd to Cook County Special Educ Adv Bd 1974; Amer Federation of teachers, vice pres 1974-; apptd to Teacher Center Adv Group of Amer Fed of Teachers 1977; apptd to City Wide Adv Com for devel Student Equal Educ Oppor for Children of Chicago 1977; Chicago Teachers Union, vice pres 1972-84, pres 1984-. **ORGANIZATIONS:** Mem Dleta Kappa Gamma Soc Inc 1978; mem Alpha Kappa Alpha; Nat Council of Negro Women; IKA Women's Auxiliary Pilgrim Bapt Ch; Coalition Labor Union Women Urban League; Labor Humanities Flwshp CityUniv NY 1977; mem Alpha Gamma Pi Windy City Chapt, Links. **HONORS/ACHIEVEMENTS:** Black Labor Leader Award 15 Outstnd Women; NACW Distinctive Impring Award; PUSH Salute to 100 Outstnd Women in Field of Educ & Labor 1975; Top Ladies of Distinction Nat Award 1976; Distinguished Serv Award Cook Co Educ Serv Region 1976; author article Educ Leadership Jour of the Assn for Suprvn & Curriculum Devel (ASCD) 1976; The Expanding Role of Tchrs in Negotiation Curriculum; participant in 11th World Congress of Intl Fed of Free Tchrs Union (IFFTU) Florence Italy 1975; Woman of the Year Zeta Tau Chap of Zeta Phi Beta Sorority 1979; represented Am Fedn of Tchrs by conducting tn seminar in Lusaka Zambia Africa 1979; elected vice pres IL State Fedn of Labor 4 yr term 1980. **BUSINESS ADDRESS:** President, Chicago Teachers Union, 201 North Wells Ste 900, Chicago, IL 60606.

VAUGHN, NORA BELLE
Artistic director. **PERSONAL:** Born Sep 20, 1914, Crystal Springs, MS; married Birel Vaughn (dec) (deceased); children: Wilma Jones, Dr Mona Scott, Birel Vaughn Jr. **EDUCATION:** Jackson State Univ, BA General Educ 1934; LaSalle School of Drama, 1936-38; Univ of CA Berkeley, 1968-69; State of CA, Teaching Certificate 1972. **CAREER:** Oak Unified School Dist, volunteer drama specialist 1948-63; Downs Mem Methodist Church, drama specialist 1948-78; Berk Unified School Dist; workshop instructor 1966-69; UC Berkeley, lecturer 1971-72; Black Repertory Group Inc, founder exec dir 1964-. **ORGANIZATIONS:** Volunteer drama spec Oakland Unified School Dist PTA 1948-63; drama specialist Downs Mem Methodist Church 1948-78; founded, exec dir Black Repertory Group 1964-; conducted workshops Berkeley Unified School Dist 1966-69; guest lecturer Univ of CA Berkeley 1971-72; mem Phyllis Wheatley Club 1979-. **HONORS/ACHIEVEMENTS:** Published "Black Theatre Finds It's Place in the Community" 1971; contrib to Youth Through Involvement with Comm Awd North Oakland Baptist Church Conf on Excellence 1973; Founder of 1st Black Theatre Conf 1974; Devoted Serv to the Community Award Beta Phi Sigma Inc 1980; Outstanding Comm Serv Award Natl Council for Black Studies 1983; The Paine Knickerbocker Award Bay Area Theatre Critics Circle 1983; Pre-KWANZAA Award Assoc of Africans & African-Amer 1983; The Fannie Lou Hammer Award presented by the Univ of CA Black Studies Dept for Contributions to Community in Black Theater Arts. **BUSINESS ADDRESS:** Executive Dir, Black Repertory Group Inc, 3201 Adeline St, Berkeley, CA 94703.

VAUGHN, PERCY JOSEPH, JR.
Educational administrator. **PERSONAL:** Born Jan 11, 1932, New Orleans, LA; married Doris C; children: Percy Darrell, Rene, Denise, Tracy. **EDUCATION:** Morris Brown Coll, BS 1957; Atlanta U, MBA 1959; TX Tech U, DBA 1975; Harvard U, Post Grad Study 1978. **CAREER:** Coll of Business Admin AL State Univ, dean 1975-; TX Tech Univ, instructor 1972; Southern Univ, asst prof 1968; Jackson Brewing Co, sales & pub relations rep 1960. **ORGANIZATIONS:** Proj dir Small Bus Inst of the US Small Bus Adminstrn 1978; chmn of bd AL Consortium of Deans of Coll of Bus Adminstrn for the estab of ASBCD 1978; pres AL Council of Deans of the AL Assn for Higher Educ in Bus 1979; faculty coord Nat Urban Leagues' Black Exec Exchange Prog 1976; mem natl advcounc Fasculty Coord Career Awareness Prog 1976; mem Active Corp of Execs of the Nat SCORE/ACE Counc 1978. **HONORS/ACHIEVEMENTS:** Co-author "Managing New Enterpises" 1976; article Free Enter-

prise in Focus 1978; article The Approaching Eighties New Management Challenges 1979; co-author "An Investigation of Small Bus Inven Policy" 1979. **MILITARY SERVICE:** AUS 1948-52. **BUSINESS ADDRESS:** AL State University, 915 S Jackson St, Montgomery, AL 36195.

VAUGHN, WILLIAM SAMUEL, III
Physician. **PERSONAL:** Born Jul 11, 1955, Detroit, MI; children: William S. Vaughn IV. **EDUCATION:** Rensselaer Polytechnic Inst, BS 1977; Howard Univ Coll of Medicine, MD 1982. **CAREER:** Howard Univ Hospital, attending physician emergency room; clinic physician Kaiser Permanente Washington D.C. 2-23-87; emergency Room physician Capital Hill Hosp Washington D.C. 1988-. **ORGANIZATIONS:** Pres Student Natl Medical Assoc Howard Univ Chap 1980-82; assoc AMA 1982-, Amer Acad of Pediatrics 1982-, Amer College of Physicians 1982-; vice pres 1984-85, pres 1985-86 Howard Hospital House Staff Assoc. **HONORS/ACHIEVEMENTS:** Resident Dir Academic Opportunity Consortium 1978-80; Resident of the Year HU College of Med Student Council 1985. **HOME ADDRESS:** 9914 Grayson Ave, Silver Spring, MD 20910. **BUSINESS ADDRESS:** Kaiser Permanente, 1011 North Capital Street N.E., Washington, DC 20002.

VAUGHN, WILLIAM SMITH
Government official. **PERSONAL:** Born Feb 19, 1930, St Louis, MO; widowed; children: La Vonna J, Lisa M, William S Jr, Michael E. **EDUCATION:** Univ of MO, BS 1973; Webster Univ, MA 1975; Southern IL Univ, MBA 1976. **CAREER:** St Louis Cty Police Dept, commander 1955-81; US Dept of Justice, marshal 1981-. **ORGANIZATIONS:** Mem FBI Natl Acad Assoc 1977-, Intl Assoc of Chiefs of Police 1978-, NOBLE 1978-, St Louis Crusdade Against Crime 1979-, MO Peace Officers 1979-. **HONORS/ACHIEVEMENTS:** Pres St Louis NOBLE 1980. **MILITARY SERVICE:** USA corpl 1951-53; Good Conduct Medal 1953. **BUSINESS ADDRESS:** US Marshal, US Dept of Justice, 1114 Market St, St Louis, MO 63101.

VAUGHNS, FRED L.
Dentist. **PERSONAL:** Born Apr 29, 1923, Monroe, NC; son of Mrs M L Vaughns; married Frances Branson; children: William Maurice, Lisa Gayle, Dana Gareth. **EDUCATION:** Johnson C Smith Univ, BS 1944; Howard Univ Coll of Dentistry, DDS 1949; Am Inst of Hypnosis, Certificate 1966; Post Grad Course Efficient Endodontics for Every Day Practice 1974. **CAREER:** Private Practice, dentist 1949-; Longshoreman, 1945-46; Curtiss Public Co, dispatcher 1944-45; Davidson HS, teacher 1944; Assoc Trasport, freight caller 1943. **ORGANIZATIONS:** Pierre Fauchard Intl Dental Academy; life Amer Dental Assn; PA Dental Assn; Odontological Soc W PA; past pres Fayette Co Dental Soc; past pres W PA Soc of Dentistry for Child; Assn to Advance Ethical Hypnosis; Acad of General Dentistry; Am Endodontic Soc; charter mem Brownsville-Uniontown Branch NAACP; mem past vice pres PA State Con of Branch NAACP; past pres PA State Conf of NAACP Br 1970-73; mem Hosp Assn of PA; med staff Uniontown Hosp Assn; trustee bd Uniontown Hosp Assn; bd of trustee Nursing Com Hosp; past vice pres bd dirs Fayette Co Mental Health Assn; mem Fayette Co Planning & Zoning Comm 1976; past pres PA State Conf Branch of NAACP; assoc mem Dental practice; exec bd mem Westmoreland-Fayetteville Council Boy Scouts Amer; mem Pvt Industry Council of Westmoreland/Fayette County; mem bd of dir Uniontown Chamber of Commerce; Uniontown Indus Fund; Ed Council of Chamber of Commerce Advisory, bd Fayette Campus of Penn State Univ; bd of dir Fayette City Devel Council, Ambassadors Club, Chamber of Commerce Univ. **HONORS/ACHIEVEMENTS:** Recip Outstanding City for 1974; Natl Register 1973; nominated outstanding prof in human serv Educ Bd Am Acad of Human Serv 1974; man of yr award Harriett Beecher Class Mt Zion Church 1964; award of merit judge in PA Jr Acad of Sci 1973; testimonial dinner Brownsville, Uniontown NAACP 1973; certificate of appreciation Affirmative Action Com 1970; most outstanding negro newspaper carrier Charlotte Observer Newspaper 1943; Dr F L Vaugns Scholarship Comm.. **BUSINESS ADDRESS:** 333 Coolspring, Uniontown, PA 15401.

VAUGHNS, JOHN CLAUDE
Retired research chemist. **PERSONAL:** Born Jul 10, 1914, Baton Rouge, LA; married Evelyn M; children: Eileen Wells, Claudine Phillips, Dr Christopher. **EDUCATION:** Southern Univ, BS (Cum Laude) 1936; Northwestern Univ, MS 1949. **CAREER:** General Motors, research chemist (retired). **ORGANIZATIONS:** Mem Arts and Humanities of Baton Rouge 1978-; bd of dirs Greater Baton Rouge Safety Cncl 1982-85; bd of dirs Amer Red Cross 1985-; pres Bananza Social Club 1986-; gramateus Alpha Xi Boule Sigma Phi Pi 1987-. **HONORS/ACHIEVEMENTS:** John C Vaughns Scholarship Fund founded 1963-; Black Achievers of Industry Awd YMCA of Metro Chicago 1974; General Motors Awd for Excellence in Comm Activities 1975. **HOME ADDRESS:** 2504 Gilford Dr, Baton Rouge, LA 70808.

VAUGHNS, SYLVESTER J., SR.
Administrator. **PERSONAL:** Born Sep 06, 1935, Charlotte, NC; married Doris Robinson. **EDUCATION:** Johnson C Smith U. **CAREER:** Prince George's Co, admn asst dept lic & permit ; Prince George Co, zoning enforc off; Prince Georges Co MD, admn asst chief off; Model Cities Cit Bd, exec sec 1970-74; Marriott Corp, unit mgr 1963-70. **ORGANIZATIONS:** Mem Fairmont Lodge #92 Free & Accepted Masons Prince Hall; past pres NAACP; former mem Prince Georges Co Central Rep Com; Black Rep Club. **HONORS/ACHIEVEMENTS:** Achvmt awd NAACP 1969; outstnd cit awd Blck Voice Newspaper 1973. **BUSINESS ADDRESS:** Prince George's Co, Serv Bldg, Hyattsville, MD 20783.

VEAL, HERMAN KEITH
Professional athlete. **PERSONAL:** Born Mar 16, 1961, Jackson, MS. **EDUCATION:** Maryland, 1980-84. **CAREER:** Phoenix Suns, forward 1984-. **HONORS/ACHIEVEMENTS:** Voted the Terrapins Best Defensive player as jr; twice won the Competitive Spirit & Most Unselfish Contribution Award. **BUSINESS ADDRESS:** Phoenix Suns, P O Box 1369, Ste 510, Phoenix, AZ 85001.

VEAL, HOWARD RICHARD
Business executive. **PERSONAL:** Born Oct 24, 1942, Jackson, MS; married Elizabeth; children: Howard Jr, Jason. **EDUCATION:** Alcorn A&M Coll, BS 1966; Utcc Jr Coll, 1964; IN U, 1969; Sngmn St U, 1975. **CAREER:** Spfld Urban Leag, exec dir 1972-; Elkhrt Urban Leag, 1971-72, act exec dir 1970-71, dir hsng comm serv 1968-70. **ORGANIZATIONS:** Pres IL Cncl Urban Leags 1975-; sec Urban Leag Cncl; Cntrl Reg Civic Serv; mem chmn prgm rev subcom Gov Adv Cncl Emp & Training 1974; mem Bd Hghr Educ Plng Com 1975; mem adv plan com White Hs Conf of Lbrrs 1977; mem City Spfld Citz Adv Com 1974; Omega Psi Phi Frat; co-chmn Fed Jdgt JW Ackrmns Mont Commn for Spfld Sch Dsgrgtn 1976-77; 1st bd Zion Bapt Ch. **HONORS/ACHIEVEMENTS:** Recpt Outsdng Citz Awd NAACP 1970, 1975; outsdng serv Spfld Urban Leag Bd Dir 1976. **BUSINESS ADDRESS:** 2500 S Grand Ave E, Springfield, IL 62708.

VEAL, YVONNECRIS SMITH
Physician. **PERSONAL:** Born Dec 24, Ahoskie, NC; married Henry Veal Jr; children: Michael. **EDUCATION:** Hampton Inst, BS 1957; Med Coll VA, MD 1962. **CAREER:** Downstate Med Ctr, asst instr 1965-66; Kings Co Hosp, clinical asst 1966-68; Windham Child Care, 1967-72; Private Practice, pediatrician 1967-71; Sickle Cell Clinic, atdg 1967-76; Carter Comm Hlth Ctr, pediatrician 1968-84; Private Practice, pediatrician 1984-. **ORGANIZATIONS:** Delta Sigma Theta Sor 1955-; pres Gamma Iota 1956-57; mem queens Clinical Soc 1967-, sec 1967-71, treas 1971-73, vice pres 1979-81; bd dir com Early Childhood Devel 1971-; mem AMA 1969-; mem Natl Med Assn 1973-; vice pres Queens Alumnae 1973-76, pres 1980-84; Susan S McKinney Steward Med Soc 1974-; YMCA-YWCA Day Care Inc 1975-, vice pres 1976-79, 1982-; chairperson Eastern Reg Nominating Comm 1978-82; mem NAACP, YWCA; chairperson Region I 1982-, treas Region I 1980-82 Queens Clinical Soc; bd of dirs Comm Family Planning Council 1981-, vice chairperson 1982-. **HONORS/ACHIEVEMENTS:** Who's Who Among Students Amer Colls & Univs 1955-56 1956-57; Salute to Black Women Awd Jamaica Club Natl Assn Negro Bus & Prof Women's Club Inc 1972; Comm Serv Awd St Albans Presby Church 1980; Comm Serv & Leadership Awd St Albans Cong Church 1984; Beta Kappa Chi Sci Hon Soc; Alpha Kappa Mu Hon Soc; Gold Awd Social Action Commns Delta Sigma Theta. **BUSINESS ADDRESS:** 130-20 Farmers Blvd, Jamaica, NY 11434.

VENABLE, ABRAHAM S.
Business executive. **PERSONAL:** Born Apr 10, 1930, Washington, DC; married Anna Graham; children: Karen, Douglas, Stephen. **EDUCATION:** Howard U, BA 1951; Grand Vlly St Coll; Howard, MA; Woodrow Wilson School of Public & Intl Affairs Princeton Univ, fellow; MIT, sr exec prog. **CAREER:** Gen Motors Corp, exec dir urban affrs 1971-, staff coord chmn corp intrstf minrty affrs comm; US Dept Commc, dir mnrty bus entrprs 1969-71,dir affirm actn prog 1966-68; Motor Entrprs Inc, vice pres 1975-; New Cntr Devel Prtnrshp, vice pres 1975-. **ORGANIZATIONS:** Mem bd dirs Nat Corp Hsng Prtnrshps Wash; chmn BPRC; commr Urban Affrs Com US C of C; v chmn bd dir Nat Bus Leag; bus adv Com Congrssl Blk Caucus; Nat Advis Cncl SBA Govt; chmn Inst for Amer Bus; vice pres Motor Enterprises Inc; vchmn Greater Detroit Foreign Trade Zone; bd of dir Detroit Br NAACP. **HONORS/ACHIEVEMENTS:** Man of Yr Nat Bus Leag; author Bldng Blk Bus an Anlys & a Plan; procds from bk used to estblsh Abrhm S Vnbl Stdnt Loan Fund at Sch of Bus & Pub Admin Hwrd U. **BUSINESS ADDRESS:** Exec Dir Urban Affairs, General Motors Corp, 3044 W Grand Blvd, 6-252 GMB, Detroit, MI 48202.

VENABLE, ANDREW ALEXANDER, JR.
Library administrator. **PERSONAL:** Born Nov 11, 1944, Staunton, VA; married Maxine Cockrell; children: Angela, Andrew III. **EDUCATION:** Virginia State Univ Petersburg, BS Bus Admin, 1967; Case Western Res Univ Cleveland, MSLS 1978. **CAREER:** Cleveland Pub Library, head comm serv 1978-, clerk treas 1976-78, dep clerk treas 1975-76, dir finance admin serv 1972-78, asst dir personnel serv 1970-71; Standard Oil Co Marketing Dept Ohio, capital budget planning controls analyst 1968-70. **ORGANIZATIONS:** Pres, Pub Library Employees Credit Union, 1978-; library tech adv comm, Cuyahoga Comm Coll, 1978-; mem, Ohio Library Assn; mem, Amer Library Assn, 1978-; trustee, Urban Leage of Greater Cleveland Inc, 1979-82; trustee, Consumer Protection Assn, 1979-; mem, Cleveland City Club; trustee, Harvard Community Serv Ctr; allocations pnl United Way Serv, 1979-81; mem, Beta Phi Mu Intl Library Sci Hon Soc, 1979. **HONORS/ACHIEVEMENTS:** Andrew A Venable Scholar, Virginia State Univ Almumni Assn 1973; serv appreciation award, Alpha Phi Alpha Frat Inc, Cleveland Grad Chap, 1977; Outstanding Young Men of Amer, 1978; Outstanding Greek of the Year, Greater Cleveland Pan Hellenic Council, 1979. **BUSINESS ADDRESS:** Library Dir, Gary Public Library, 220 W Fifth Ave, Gary, IN 46402.

VENABLE, HOWARD PHILLIP (PHIL DRAWOH)
Retired physician. **PERSONAL:** Born Jan 27, 1913, Windsor, Ontario, Canada;married Katie Waters Venable. **EDUCATION:** Wayne State Univ, BS, BM, MD 1935-39. **CAREER:** Ethel Waters, Don Redman, Duke Ellington Orchestras, professional musician; Homer G Phillips Hosp, dir eye dept; Amer Bd Ophthalmology, assoc examiner 1959-. **ORGANIZATIONS:** Life mem Amer Acad of Ophthalmology 1941-; Royal Vaugabonds, Inc 1941-; mem Intl Congress Ophthalmology 1944-; diplomate Am Bd Oph 1944-; life mem Amer Coll of Surgeons 1952-; mem Mound City Med Forum; St Louis Med Soc; flw Amer Acad Ophth; mem Yr Diocese of MO 1967; Adminstr Elect Serv Commn Pres Roosevelt; bd of dir ARC 1979-; life mem, Oxford Academy of Ophthalmology, 1984; mem, Metropolitan Aids Commn, St Louis, St Louis County. **HONORS/ACHIEVEMENTS:** Ecumenical Citation Metro Church Federation 1961-62; Distinguished Merit Award Homer G Phillips Hosp Internes Alumni Assn 1967-77; Tchr Yr St Louis Univ 1963; publ"Glaucoma in the Negro" 1944, 1952, 1958; "Pseudo-Tumor-Cerebri Benigh Intraeranial Hypertention & Otitic Hydrocephalus, Are They Synonymous?", 1971, 1973, 1974; "Empty Sella Syndrome" 1977; "Sudden Blindness From Blunt Trivial Trauma" 1979; Honored by Washington Univ Med Sch for 25 years of dedicated serv to students, faculty and community 1983.

VENABLE, MAX
Professional athlete. **PERSONAL:** Born Jun 06, 1957, Phoenix, AZ; married Molly; children: William Dion. **EDUCATION:** Cordova HS Sacramento, grad 1976. **CAREER:** San Francisco Giants, outfielder 1982-83; Montreal Expos, outfielder 1984-. **HONORS/ACHIEVEMENTS:** Hit the Expos only pinch-hit homer in 1984 on August 16 at Candlestick Park; compiled a 993 defensive percentage second among outfielders in the NL with 100 or more chances.

VENABLE, ROBERT CHARLES
Clergyman. **PERSONAL:** Born Jan 26, 1950, Camden, NJ; married Cherly A Pitts; children: Tisa L, Lovell V, Marc R. **EDUCATION:** Shaw Univ Coll of the Bible. **CAREER:** New Wesley AME Zion Church, assoc pastor 1975-82; Harris Temple AME Zion, pastor 1982-. **ORGANIZATIONS:** Camden City Bd of Educ 1982-85; dir of educ Camden Ministerial Alliance; chairperson Affirmative Action; chairperson BSIP; chairperson Finance for

the Bd of Educ; chairperson Legislature; chairperson Salary; mem Camden Ministerial Alliance; mem PA Ministerial Alliance; mem Camden Dist Ministerial Alliance of the AME Zion Church; mem NAACP; mem S Christian League Conf; mem Urban League; mem Assn of Sch Business Officials of the US and Canada; mem NJ Sch Bds Assn; mem PTA; mem Boy Scouts of America; mem Natl Black Caucus of State Legislators; mem Natl Caucus of Black Sch Bd Members; mem Joint Ctr for Political Studies; mem Natl Black Elected Officials; mem NJ Pan Methodist Comm Liaison; mem PA Pan Methodist Celebration Finance; mem Camden CoDemocratic Comm; mem Natl Parks and Conservation Assn Wash, DC; mem Natl Trust for Historic Preservation; mem Oriental Lodge No 1 F&AM-PHA. **BUSINESS ADDRESS:** Pastor, Harris Temple AME Zion Church, 926 Florence St, Camden, NJ 08104.

VENEY, HERBERT LEE
Physician. **PERSONAL:** Born Jun 24, 1953, Baltimore, MD; son of Vinson Randolp Veney and Alice Brown Veney. **EDUCATION:** Howard Univ, Coll of Liberal Arts BS (Cum Laude) 1974, Coll of Medicine MD 1978; Johns Hopkins Sch of Hygiene & Public Health, MPH 1982. **CAREER:** Alexandria VA YWCA, youth counselor 1973; US Dept of Housing & Urban Develop, program asst 1974; Howard Univ Hospital, resident physician 1978-81; East Baltimore Drug Abuse Ctr, staff physician 1979-81; Warsaw Health Care Ctr, medical director/owner 1982-84; Warsaw Medical Ctr, owner 1981-. **ORGANIZATIONS:** Fellow Amer Acad of Family Physicians 1978; mem Natl & Amer Medical Assocs 1978-; diplomate Amer Bd of Family Practice 1981; dir Richmond Community Serv Assoc 1982-; chairperson Black Business & Professional Coalition of NN VA 1985-; dir Family Focus of Richmond Co Inc 1986; trustee St Paul's Coll Lawrenceville, VA 1988-91. **HONORS/ACHIEVEMENTS:** Special Achievement Awd US Dept of Housing & Urban Develop 1974; Natl Phi Beta Kappa, Natl Beta Kappa Chi Howard Univ 1978. **HOME ADDRESS:** 202 Washington Ave, Warsaw, VA 22572. **BUSINESS ADDRESS:** Warsaw Medical Center, 404 Main St, Warsaw, VA 22572.

VENSON, JEANINE
Corporate relations manager. **PERSONAL:** Born Aug 02, 1962, Racine, WI. **EDUCATION:** Univ of WI-Madison, BA Comm 1984. **CAREER:** Univ WI-Madison Publications, general clerk 1981-84; Carthage Coll, admissions rep 1985-. **ORGANIZATIONS:** Mem IL Assoc of College Admissions 1985-, Natl Assoc of College Admissions 1985-, Lutheran Council in the USA 1985-, WI Educ Assoc 1985-; admin adv Black Student Union 1985-, Affirmative Action Task Force-Carthage 1985-. **HONORS/ACHIEVEMENTS:** Big Ten Cheerleader for Univ WI-Madison 1980-83; Eta Phi Beta Scholarship 1980; 1st runner up Miss Racine 1984; 4th runner up Miss Black America of WI 1984. **HOME ADDRESS:** 1932 1/2 Mead St, Racine, WI 53403.

VENSON, JOHN E.
Manager. **PERSONAL:** Born May 16, 1922, Augusta, GA; children: Andre Wright, Paula Wright. **EDUCATION:** Paine Coll Agst GA, AB 1947; NY U; BstnUniv Sch of Edn, 1948; BstnUniv Sch of Commu, MS 1952. **CAREER:** Gillette Co, mgr corp comm affrs 1976-; Gillette N Am, com rel rep 1968-76; Gillette Sfty Rzr Co, asst to dir of adv & pr 1966-68; Urban Leag of Grtr bstn inc, dir ecnmc devel 1961-66; New Engl Untd Negro Coll Fund Inc, reg dir 1953-61; Paine Coll Agst GA, asst to pres 1948-51. **ORGANIZATIONS:** Pres Bstn Chap Nat Assn of Mrkt Devel 1972-76, mem of bd 1973-76; chmn of bd Nat Cnsrtm for Blk Professional Devel 1979-; mem Adv Cncl S End Boys Club 1973-; bd mem Paine Coll Nat Almn Assn 1974-; adv bd mem Grtr Bstn Slvtn Army 1974-. **HONORS/ACHIEVEMENTS:** Otstndng com serv awd Bstn Urban Leag Gld 1972; com serv awd Bstn Negro Bus & Professional Wmns Clubs 1975; This Is Your Life Awd Union Bapt Ch Cmbrdg MA 1978; almns of the yr Paine Coll Agst GA 1979. **MILITARY SERVICE:** USAAF corp 1943-46. **BUSINESS ADDRESS:** Manager, Community Affairs, The Gillette Company, Prudential Tower Bldg, Boston, MA 02199.

VERA, NDORO VINCENT
Educator. **PERSONAL:** Born Oct 03, 1933, Harare, Zimbabwe;children: Vincent Joy Jr, Helen. **EDUCATION:** St Augustine's Coll Zimbabwe, teachers dipolma 1956; Claremont Teachers Coll Western Australia, art teaching 1963; Lincoln Univ, BA 1968; Georgetown UnivMA(ABT) 1971; Union Graduate School, PhD 1974. **CAREER:** St Matthias Primary School Zimbabwe, teacher 1957-60; Hezemv Govt School Zimbabwe, teacher 1960-62; Pingley High School W Australia, teacher 1963; Bowie St Coll, prof 1976; Antioch College DC Branch, prof 1971-76; Univ of DC, assoc prof Political Science. **ORGANIZATIONS:** Board mem RAP Inc 1975-80. **HONORS/ACHIEVEMENTS:** Volunteer educator RAP inc Drug Treatment Prog 1974-; mem Natl Conf of Black Politacal Scientists 1972; 1st Place Awd Lincoln Univ 1968; Swedish Agency educ awd Swedish Govt 1965; Faculty Award Antioch College 1976; appreciation Inst for Serv to Educ 1976; cmmty serv Volunteers of Amer 1986. **HOME ADDRESS:** 1673 Columbia Rd NW #300, Washington, DC 20009.

VERBAL, CLAUDE A.
Engineer, business executive. **PERSONAL:** Born Nov 12, 1942, Durham, NC; son of Sidney Verbal, Sr. and Mary Gladys Verbal; married Dorothy Simmons. **EDUCATION:** NC St Univ, BSME 1964. **CAREER:** Buick Motor Div GMC, engr rsch devel 1964-66, experimental lab test engr 1966-69, chassis design engr 1969-73, staff proj engr supv experimental engr 1974-75, asst supt quality control 1976-77, supt quality control 1977; Milford Proving Ground, engr supv 1973-74; BOC Powertrain GMC, supt mfg 1985-87; Serv Parts Operation GM, plant mgr 1987-. **ORGANIZATIONS:** Pres Flint Econ Devel Corp; 1st vice pres Flint Inner City Lion's Club; Mid-Mi Govng Bd Soc of Auto Engr 1970-; mem Soc of Mech Engr; Natl Soc of Professional Engr Registered 1971; Bsls Omcrn Rho Chap Omega Psi Phi Frat Inc 1971-; mem Leadership Flint; FAM Mstr Mason Erk Lodge 32 Degree; Flnt Urban League Hrt in City Adv Bd; bd dir Hurley med Ctr 1984-; natl bd of dir BAE Soc of Automotive Engrs 1988, pres of bd dir Hurley Med Ctr 1989. **HONORS/ACHIEVEMENTS:** Young engr of the yr Flint Chap Professional Engr 1974; Omega Man of Yr Omicron Rho Chap Omega Psi Phi 1974; Natl Media Women Award 1977. **BUSINESS ADDRESS:** Plant Manager, Serv Parts Operation GM, 5260 Williams Lake Rd, Drayton Plains, MI 48020.

VEREEN, BEN AUGUSTUS
Entertainer. **PERSONAL:** Born Oct 10, 1946, Miami, FL; married Nancy; children: Benjamin, Malaika, Naia, Kabara, Karon. **EDUCATION:** Emerson Coll, DHL (Hon) 1977. **CAREER:** The Prodigal Son, Sweet Charity, Golden Boy, Hair, Jesus Christ Superstar, Pippin, Cabaret, stage actor 1965-; Sweet Charity, Funny Lady, Louis Armstrong-ChgoStyle, movie actor 1970-; Roots, "Chicken George" actor 1977; Ben Vereen His Roots TV Spec, performer 1978; Tenspeed & Brown Shoe, Webster, actor. **ORGANIZATIONS:** Chmn, Amer Lung Assn, 1977. **HONORS/ACHIEVEMENTS:** Theatre World Award, Jesus Christ Superstar 1972; Tony Award; Drama Desk Award; CLIO Pippin Humanitarian Award Israel 1975; George M Cohen Award Agva; Best Song & Dance Star; Best Rising Star; Entertainer of the Year 1976; TV Critics Award, Roots 1977; Image Awd Roots NAACP 1977, 1978; Cultural Award Roots Israel 1978. **BUSINESS ADDRESS:** c/o Lee Solomon, William Morris Agnecy, 1350 Avenue of the Americas, New York, NY 10019.

VEREEN, NATHANIEL
Mayor. **PERSONAL:** Born Mar 03, 1924, Forest City, FL; married Rosetta G; children: Mark, Roslyn, Nathaniel Jr, Gloria Ann, Valerie. **EDUCATION:** Svnnh St Coll, BS 1949; Brdly U, MA 1952. **CAREER:** Etnvll FL, mayor 1973-, prt time mayor 1963-72, cnclman 1958; Etnvll Dvrsfd Inc, owner pres; Vrn Cnstrctn Co, owner pres. **ORGANIZATIONS:** Mem Orng Co Cncl Lcl Gvt; Orng Co Dem Exec Com; adv bd Vlnc Comm & Smnl Comm Colls; Tri-Co Gvt Cities; sec FL Constrn Lcns Bd; New Prvdnc Bapt Ch. **MILITARY SERVICE:** AUS. **BUSINESS ADDRESS:** PO Box 2185, Eatonville, FL 32751.

VEREEN-GORDON, MARY ALICE
Educator. **PERSONAL:** Born Jul 09, 1950, Cerro Gordo, NC; married James Leon Gordon. **EDUCATION:** NC A&T State Univ, BS 1972; Atlanta Univ, MA 1975; Univ of WI-Madison, PhD 1983. **CAREER:** Winston-Salem State Univ, english instructor 1975-76; Nakina High School, english/french teacher 1976-77; KY State Univ, english instructor 1977-80; Morris Coll, academic dean 1984-. **ORGANIZATIONS:** Mem Phi Delta Kappa 1981-; mem Amer Educ Rsch Assoc 1981-; mem NAACP, Alpha Kappa Mu Natl Honor Soc. **HONORS/ACHIEVEMENTS:** Advanced Oppor Fellowship Adv Oppor Program 1980-82; Pre-Doctoral Scholarship for merit WI Ctr for Educ Rsch 1982-83; Tribute to Women and Industry YWCA 1983. **BUSINESS ADDRESS:** Academic Dean, Morris College, N Main St, Sumter, SC 29150.

VERNON, FRANCINE M. (NEE JOHNSON)
Educator. **PERSONAL:** Born Nov 14, 1939, New York, NY; married Bernard R; children: Richard, Carolyn-Michelle, Michael. **EDUCATION:** Hwrd U, BS 1961; Hntr Coll, MS 1973; Frdhm U, Prof Dip 1976. **CAREER:** New York City Bd of Educ, dir adult basic educ program num pos 1968-; Hunter Coll, instructor 1973-75; Dept of HEW, claims rep 1962-67. **ORGANIZATIONS:** NY Assn for Cntng Comm Edn; Nat Assn for Pub Cntng Adlt Edn; Kappa Delta Pi; NY St Engl as 2nd Lang & Blngl Educ Assn; Nat Assn Tchrs of Engl to Spkrs of other Langs; pres Ossng NAACP; trst Afro-Am Cltrl Found of Wstchstr Co; past pres trst Ossng Bd of Edn; bd mem Ossng Comm Actn Prgm; bd mem Ossng Coll Cltn to Fght Unemploy Agnst Infltn. **HONORS/ACHIEVEMENTS:** Achvmt awd Nat Assn for Pub Contng Adlt Educ 1975; recog awd Commrs Nat Conf on Career Educ 1976; apprec awd Ossng Jycs 1977. **BUSINESS ADDRESS:** 347 Baltic St, Brooklyn, NY 11201.

VERRETT, JOYCE M.
Educator. **PERSONAL:** Born May 26, 1932, New Orleans, LA; married Wilbert; children: Lester McKee, Jeannine, Stanley, Rory. **EDUCATION:** Dillard U, BA 1957; NY U, MS 1963; Tulane U, PhD 1971. **CAREER:** Orleans Parsih LA, hs teacher 1958-63; Dillard Univ Div of Ntrl Sci, instr prof chmn. **ORGANIZATIONS:** Ent Soc Am; Nat Inst Sci; Beta Beta Beta Bial & Hon Soc; Beta Kappa Chi Sci Hon Soc Cncr Assn Grtr ND 1974; LA Hrt Assn 1973-; NAACP 1960-; Reg 9 Sci Fair 1958-. **HONORS/ACHIEVEMENTS:** HS Vldctn 1948; Who's Who Amng Coll Stdnts 1956; Alpha Kappa Mu Nat Hon Soc 1956; Beta Kappa Chi Nat Sci Hon Soc 1956; Grad Summa Cum Laude DillardUniv 1957; NSF Fllwshp for Adv Study 1960-62; 1st blk wmn to recv PhD in Bio from TulaneUniv 1971; Otstndng Educ of Am 1972. **BUSINESS ADDRESS:** Dillard Univ, 2601 Gentilly Blvd, New Orleans, LA 70122.

VERRETT, SHIRLEY
Opera & concert artist. **PERSONAL:** Born May 03, 1933, New Orleans, LA; married Louis La Monacao; children: Francesca. **EDUCATION:** Ventura Coll, AA 1951; Juilliard School of Music, 1961. **CAREER:** Bolshoi Opera, singer 1963; NY City Opera, singer 1963; Royal Opera, Covent Gardens, singer 1966; Teatro Communale Florence, singer 1967; Met Opera, singer 1968; La Scala, singer 1970; Vienna State Opera, singer 1970; Dallas Civic Opera, singer 1971; Teatro Liceo, Barcelona, singer 1971; Paris Opera, singer 1972; SanFrancisco Opera, singer 1972; Opera Co of Boston, singer 1975; Norma, Les Troyens, The Siege of Corinth, Philharmonic Orch, London Symph, Paris Symph, RAI,opera singer; RCA, Columbia Angel Records, Deutsche Grammophon, ABC Audio Treasury, operatic, recital & concert rec. **ORGANIZATIONS:** Mem Mu Phi Epsilon. **HONORS/ACHIEVEMENTS:** Chevalier de L'Ordre des Arts et do Lettres 1970; Marian Anderson Awd 1955; Woman of the Year Los Angeles Times 1969; Natl Fed of Music Clubs Awd; Martha Baird Rockefeller Aid to Music Fund Fellowship; Ford Found Fellowship; Albert Einstein Achievement Awd.

VERTREACE, WALTER CHARLES
Attorney & personnel administrator. **PERSONAL:** Born Sep 17, 1947, Washington, DC; son of Walter C. Vertreace and Modena K. Vertreace; married Peggy A; children: Bryan, Kelly, Erin. **EDUCATION:** Howard Univ, BA 1968, MS 1970; Temple University School of Law, JD 1982. **CAREER:** USAF Human Resources Lab, research psychologist 1970-72; Information Science, Inc, human resources consultant 1972-75; The Hertz Corp, mgr EEO programs 1975-76; INA Corporation, mgr EEO operations 1976-80; Amerada Hess Corp, mgr corporate EEO 1980-. **ORGANIZATIONS:** Member board of dir Equal Employment Adv Council 1982-85; first vice president, United Way of Central Jersey; mem Amer and Ntl Bar Assns; member New Jersey State Bar Assn; vice chairman Manhattan Affiliate NY Urban League, Philadelphia Urban League; vice pres The EDGES Group, Inc; mem Omega Psi Phi; mem bd of dir New York State Advisory Council on Employment Law. **HONORS/ACHIEVEMENTS:** NIMH Fellow; Howard Univ Fellow; Beta Kappa Chi Natl Scientific Honor Soc; Psi Chi Natl Honor Society in Psychology. **MILITARY SERVICE:** USAF First Lieutenant; Systems Command Cert of Merit 1972. **BUSINESS ADDRESS:** Mgr Corp EEO, Amerada Hess Corp, 1 Hess Plaza, Woodbridge, NJ 07095.

VESSUP, AARON ANTHONY
Educator. **PERSONAL:** Born Mar 28, 1947, Los Angeles, CA. **EDUCATION:** NE Wesleyan Univ, BS 1970; IL State Univ, MA Sci 1972; Univ of Pgh, PhD 1978; Univ of Edinburgh

Scotland, media studies 1984. **CAREER:** IL State Univ, comm instr 1971-72; City of Bloomington, human relations coord 1972-75; Univ of Pittsburgh, teaching fellow 1975-78; Rockwell Intl, communications intern 1977-78; TX Southern Univ, asst prof of communications 1978-; Intercultural Communications, cons; Elgin Comm Coll, dir of forensics. **ORGANIZATIONS:** Mem Soc for Intl Educ Assn; mem TX Speech Comm Assn; mem US Tennis Assn; mem Intl Comm Assn; mem Amer Mgmt Assn; mem Speech Communication Assn; edited Interracial Comm Bloomington Press 1977; pub in textbook Urban Comm Winthrop Press 1977. **HONORS/ACHIEVEMENTS:** Co-author of Conflict Mgmt Acad of Mgmt Review 1979; dir of Grant Proj TX Comm for Humanities 1979-80; author Symbolic Communication, Understanding Racial Stereotypes Brethren Press 1983. **BUSINESS ADDRESS:** Dir of Forensics, Elgin Community College, 50 Slade Ave, Elgin, IL 60120.

VEST, DONALD SEYMOUR, SR.
Business manager. **PERSONAL:** Born Apr 05, 1930, Ypsilanti, MI; son of Eugene L Vest and Vida Carter Vest; married Hilda Freeman Vest, Jul 12, 1953; children: Karen Vest, Donald Vest, Jr, Carl Vest. **EDUCATION:** Michigan State Univ, East Lansing, MI, BA, Social Serv, 1952. **CAREER:** US Army, lieutenant, 1952-54; Detroit Mutual Insurance, Detroit, MI, agent, 1954-55; City of Detroit, MI, playleader, 1955-56; State of Michigan, Detroit, MI, interviewer, 1956-57; City of Detroit, MI, recreation instructor, 1957-60; Boy Scouts of Amer, Detroit, MI, dist exec, 1960-62; Ford Motor Co, Dearborn, MI, mgr, 1962-87, personnel mgr, 1987; Broadside Press, Detroit, MI, business mgr. **ORGANIZATIONS:** Pres bd of trustees, 1986-87, chair collections comm, 1987-88, Museum of African-Amer History; pres bd of dir, Brazeal Dennard Chorale, 1989. **HONORS/ACHIEVEMENTS:** Community Serv Award, Ford Motor Co, 1968, 1969; Special Serv Award, Detroit Bd of Educ, 1977; San Kofa Award, Museum of African-Amer History, 1988. **MILITARY SERVICE:** AUS, first lieutenant, 1952-54. **BUSINESS ADDRESS:** Business Mgr, Broadside Press, PO Box 04257, Detroit, MI 48204.

VEST, HILDA FREEMAN
Publisher. **PERSONAL:** Born Jun 05, 1933, Griffin, GA; daughter of Dr Pharr Cyral Freeman and Blanche Heard Freeman; married Donald Vest, Jul 12, 1953; children: Karen Vest, Donald Vest, Jr, Carl Vest. **EDUCATION:** Wayne State Univ, Detroit, MI, BS, Educ, 1958. **CAREER:** Detroit Bd of Educ, Detroit, MI, teacher, 1959-1988; Broadside Press, Detroit, MI, publisher, editor, 1985-. **HONORS/ACHIEVEMENTS:** Southeastern Michigan Regional Scholastic Award, Detroit News, 1950; author, Lyrics I, self-published poetry, 1981; Writing Award for Poetry, Detroit Women Writers, 1982; featured in Broadside Poets' Theater, 1982; featured in Detroit Sings Series, Broadside Press, 1982; scholarship to Cranbrook Writers' Conf, 1984. **BUSINESS ADDRESS:** Publisher, Editor, Broadside Press, PO Box 04257, Detroit, MI 48204.

VESTER, TERRY Y.
Physician. **PERSONAL:** Born Sep 09, 1955, Houston, TX; daughter of Willie T. Busby; married Dr Alphonza Vester; children: Jennifer, Alexandria, Geoffrey. **EDUCATION:** Univ of San Francisco, BS 1978; Howard Coll of Medicine, MD 1982. **CAREER:** Montgomery Residency Program, family practice 1982-85. **ORGANIZATIONS:** Mem Amer Acad of Family Physicians 1982-87, Natl Medical Assoc 1986-87, Southern Medical Assoc 1986-87, Medical Assoc of the State of AL 1986-87, Chambers Co Medical Assoc 1986-87. **BUSINESS ADDRESS:** 404-B 9th St SW, Lafayette, AL 36862.

VICK, HARVEY OSCAR, III
Scientist. **PERSONAL:** Born Jan 06, 1957, Fulton, KY; married Valeria Gail Collier. **EDUCATION:** TN Technological Univ, BS Geology 1980. **CAREER:** Cities Service Oil and Gas Corp, geologist 1980-. **ORGANIZATIONS:** Mem Oklahoma City Geological Soc 1981-, Amer Assoc of Blacks in Energy 1983-85, Amer Assoc of Petroleum Geologists 1984-; mem NAACP 1987. **HONORS/ACHIEVEMENTS:** Minority Scholarship Amer Geological Inst 1979-80; Outstanding Young Men of Amer 1982; Certificate of Appreciation Oklahoma City Geological Soc 1984; AmerAssoc of Petroleum Geologists; author and co-author of Poster Presentation 1987 Mid-Continent Sect Meeting. **HOME ADDRESS:** 8389 Michael Dr, Boynton Beach, FL 33437. **BUSINESS ADDRESS:** Staff Geologist, Cities Service Oil & Gas Corp, 3545 NW 58th St, Oklahoma City, OK 73112.

VICK, MARIAN
Professor of reading. **PERSONAL:** Born in Newton Grove, NC; daughter of Reverend and Mrs Milford E Lee; children: Linda Vick Davis, Charles Alphonso. **EDUCATION:** Fayetteville State Univ, BS 1948; Univ of MI, MA 1954; Syracuse Univ, CAGS 1961; Duke Univ, EdD 1968. **CAREER:** NC Public Schools, elementary teacher 1948-60; Bennett Coll, dir of reading center 1961-62; Winston-Salem State Univ, asst prof of reading 1962-66; Dept of Elementary Educ, acting chairperson 1977-80, chairperson 1980-83; NC A&T State Univ, assoc prof of Reading Educ 1968-70, prof of Reading Educ 1970-77, 1984-. **ORGANIZATIONS:** Life mem NAACP 1979-; mem Alpha Kappa Alpha Sor Beta Iota Omega Chapter; mem Kappa Delta Pi, Phi Delta Kappa, NEA-NCAE, Intl Reading Assoc, St James Presbyterian Church. **HONORS/ACHIEVEMENTS:** NAFEO's 1985 Distinguished Alumni Award 1985; author of nine published articles. **HOME ADDRESS:** 1601 S Benbow Rd, Greensboro, NC 27406. **BUSINESS ADDRESS:** Professor of Reading, NC A&T State University, 1601 E Market St, Greensboro, NC 27411.

VICKERS, MILTON DAVID
Appointed official. **PERSONAL:** Born Nov 09, 1949, Miami, FL; children: Kelli Nicole. **EDUCATION:** Pacific Western Univ, BA Public Admin, MPA Public Admin 1981. **CAREER:** Natl Training & Devel Svc, consult 1978; Intl Cty Mgrs Assoc, consult 1978; Metro Dade Cty Affirm Action Div, dir 1976-82, dir off min bus dev. **ORGANIZATIONS:** Mem Amer Soc for Public Admin 1974-, Conf of Minority Public Admin 1980-, Forum for Black Public Admin 1983-, Judicial Nominating Comm State of FL 1983-87, Governor Council on Minority Bus 1984-85; chmn Dade Cty Grand Jury 1984; pres FL Black Caucus 1985. **HONORS/ACHIEVEMENTS:** Black Leaders of Miami-Miami News 1980; Outstanding Serv Egelloc Civic Club of Miami 1980; Outstanding Young Men of Amer OYM 1982; Man of the Year Egelloc Civic Club of Miami 1984.

VINCENT, DANIEL PAUL
Business executive. **PERSONAL:** Born Jun 19, 1939, New Orleans, LA; son of Howard Vincent and Josephine Vincent; married Leatha; children: Dannette, Robin, Daryl. **EDUCATION:** Southern University, BS Loyola Univ, MBA; Univ of No CO, MA; UECU, PhD Cand; Shrtr Coll, Hon PhD. **CAREER:** Total Community Action Inc, exec dir 1969-; Equity Funding Corp of Amer, reg rep 1968-70; Chrysler Corp, engr 1966-68; Mayor of New Orleans, spec adv vice chmn mayor's charter rev com 1970-. **ORGANIZATIONS:** Pres chmn EDU Inc 1975-; consultant lecturer LSUNO; Cppn State Coll; lectr Tln U; lectr Xavier Univ; Univ of WI; adv bd NO Area Boy Scouts; chmn LA Housing Asstance Corp; pres TCA Fed Credit Union; exec bd Natl Assn for Comm Devel; pres LA Assn of Comm Action Agencies; fdr NO Human Serv Inst; mem Natl Assn of Housing & Redevelopment; vice chmn NO Manpower Adv Planning Council; bd of dir NO Chap Intrcl Council for Business Opportunity; bd dir NO Area Health Planning Council; NY Stock Exchange; Attitional Study of Orlns Prsh Sch Syst. **HONORS/ACHIEVEMENTS:** Beta Gamma Sigma Hon Soc; Army Commd Medal John H Whitney & Fellowship; officials publications Patterns of Poverty in NO; manpower training needs for the City of NO; Governance of New Comm; hist of other world stock exchanges. **MILITARY SERVICE:** UAS capt 1960-66. **BUSINESS ADDRESS:** Broker, Vincent Insurance Agency, P.O. Box 13115, 3238 South Carrollton Avenue, New Orleans, LA 70185.

VINCENT, IRVING H.
Producer, director, actor, tchr. **PERSONAL:** Born Nov 28, 1934, StLouis, MO; married Delora Sherleen Sinclair; children: Dr Terrel Lynn French, Mark, Paul, Samantha. **EDUCATION:** St Louis Univ, BS Speech 1957; Brooklyn Coll, 26 MFA credits 1974; HB Studios Lee Strasberg professional acting, attended 1961-70; Third World Cinema, attended 1976-77. **CAREER:** Broadway, Off-Broadway, stage mgr 1961-69, stage dir 1966-; Downstate Medical Ctr, personnel dir 1966-69; Brooklyn Coll, tchr 1969-74; freelance video artist 1977-81; ABC-TV, unit mgr. **ORGANIZATIONS:** Bd of dir Media for the Other Arts 1981-; pres The Seminole Group 1979-81. **HOME ADDRESS:** 155 Bank St, New York, NY 10014.

VINCENT, JAY FLETCHER
Professional athlete. **PERSONAL:** Born Jun 10, 1959, Kalamazoo, MI; married Doris; children: Jayson. **EDUCATION:** MI State Univ, 1981. **CAREER:** Jay Vincent's Records & Tapes, owner 2 stores; Dallas Mavericks, professional athlete. **HONORS/ACHIEVEMENTS:** 1st Maverick ever to win a player-of-the week awd; Unanimous choice on the all-rookie team; 3rd behind Buck Williams & Kelly Tripucka for Rookie of the Year; voted MVP; career-high 41 point 1981; won Big Ten scoring title jr & sr seasons MI State. **BUSINESS ADDRESS:** Dallas Mavericks, Reunion Arena, 777 Sports St, Dallas, TX 75207.

VINES, BENJAMIN GLENN
Physician. **PERSONAL:** Born Jan 20, 1930, Little Rock, AR; married Verma; children: Sharon, Dara. **EDUCATION:** Tougaloo Coll, BS 1948; Howard Univ Coll Med, MD 1954; Ancker Hosp, Intern 1955. **CAREER:** Univ of MN Hosp, physician 1955-57; Univ CO Hosp, residency 1957-58; physician internal med 1958-. **ORGANIZATIONS:** Mem Natl Med Assn, AMA, San Antonio Comm Hosp, Doctors Hosp, Alpha Phi Alpha, Kappa Phi Hon Med Soc. **MILITARY SERVICE:** USAF 1948-50. **HOME ADDRESS:** PO Box 2221, Montclair, CA 91763.

VINSON, JULIUS CEASAR
Insurance salesman. **PERSONAL:** Born Feb 16, 1926, Macon, GA; married Sara Rogers; children: Saralyn, Walter. **EDUCATION:** CA Plytchnc at San Luis Obsp CA;Univ of GA, Cert In Mncpl Gvt. **CAREER:** Professional Ins Corp, life ins; Macon GA, cty cnclmn; All Star Life Ins, slsmn mnl 1974. **ORGANIZATIONS:** Mem GABEO; mem NAACP; mem Pres Club Ins Slsmn; GA Mncpl Assn; tst St Paul AME Ch; mem Mddl GA Area Plng & Devel Commn. **HONORS/ACHIEVEMENTS:** 32nd Dgr Mason Prc Hall Affil; awd Cncrnd Ctzn Club Civil Rghts 1976; ldng slsmn Hlth Life Ins Professional Ins Co 1975; awd Mlln Dllr Rndtbl Club 1975; 1st blk city cnclmn in Macon GA. **BUSINESS ADDRESS:** PO Box 4402, Macon, GA 31208.

VIRDURE, BERNEL B.
Clergyman. **PERSONAL:** Born Jul 12, 1923, Baton Rouge, LA; married Clintonia French; children: Phillip, Michael, Dennis, Andrew, Stephen. **EDUCATION:** Attended, TX SW Coll, Sacramento City Coll. **CAREER:** US Civil Svcs, past instr; Virdure Prod Co San Jose CA & Virdure's Guest Home E Palo Alto, owner; free lance writer; newspaper colmnst; real estate invstr; Intl Divine Temple Inc, pres/founder. **ORGANIZATIONS:** BSA Neighborhood Commn; 32nd Degree Scottish Rite Mason; mem Eagle Scouts; Optimist Club; Toastmasters Intl; Honor Cert Ldrshp Fund Raising & Orgn. **HONORS/ACHIEVEMENTS:** Private collection of 1000 rare & special books; 20 yrs NAACP Ldrshp Awd. **MILITARY SERVICE:** AUS 1941-44. **BUSINESS ADDRESS:** President, Intl Divine Temple Inc, Box 62078, Sunnyvale, CA 94088.

VIVIAN, CORDY TINDELL
Clergyman. **PERSONAL:** Born Jul 30, 1924, Howard County, MO; married W Octavia Geans; children: Jo Anna, Denise, Cordy Jr, Kira, Mark, Charisse, Albert. **EDUCATION:** Western IL Univ, BA 1948; Amer Baptist Theol Sem, BD 1958; New School for Social Rsch, Doctorate 1984; Western IL Univ, Doctorate 1987. **CAREER:** Natl Bapt Conv USA Inc, natl dir 1955-61; 1st Comm Church, pastor 1956-61; Cosmo Comm Church, pastor 1961-63; SCLC, natl dir 1962-67; Shaw Univ, minister 1972-73, natl dir sem without walls 1974-; Black Action Strategies & Info Center Inc (BASIC), bd chmn. **ORGANIZATIONS:** Chmn Natl Anti-Klan Network; mem Natl Black Leadership Roundtable; chmn Southern Organizing Comm Educ Fund; bd mem Inst of the Black World; bd mem Intl United Black Fund; co-dir Southern Reg Twentieth Anniversary March on Washington For Jobs Peace & Freedom; bd mem Southern Christian Leadership Conf, Souther Organizing Comm, Natl Council of Black Churchmen, The African Inst for the Study of Human Values; mem Racial Justice Working Group Natl Council Churches; vstg prof Wartburg Theol Sem; intl lecture & consult tours Africa, Tokyo, Isreal, Holland, Manila, Japan. **HONORS/ACHIEVEMENTS:** Author Black Power & The Amer Myth, Amer Joseph, Date & Fact Book of Black Amer; editor the Baptist, Layman Mag for Baptist Men; listed in Who's Who in Amer Bicentennial Ed, 1000 Successful Blacks, The Ebony Success Library, Odyssey, A Journey Through Black Amer, From Montgomery to Memphis, Clergy in Action Training, Unearthing Seeds of Fire, The Idea of Highlander, The Trouble I've Seen. **BUSINESS ADDRESS:** Chairman, BASIC, 595 Parsons St, Atlanta, GA 30314.

VIVIANS, NATHANIEL ROOSEVELT
Engineer & educator. **PERSONAL:** Born Feb 06, 1937, Mobile, AL; married Dorothy C

Willis; children: Venita Natalie, Mark Anthony. **EDUCATION:** Tuskegee Inst, BSEE 1961; Univ Dayton, MS Eng 1973, MS Mgmt Sci 1977. **CAREER:** Air Defense Command, radar officer, 1961-64; Aeronautical Systs Div, Elec Eng, 1964-71, program mgr 1971-80, tech advisor 1980-. **ORGANIZATIONS:** Asst prof, Univ of Wilberforce 1980-; ltc/air force officer AF Reserve 1967-; basileus Omega Psi Phi Fraternity 1957-; trustee Holy Trinity Amer Church 1975-; chptr pres Natl Soc Professional Eng 1970-; EEO counselor Aeronautical Systs Div 1969-; pres WCPOVA 1974-80. **HONORS/ACHIEVEMENTS:** Outstanding Serv NSPE Greene Xenia, OH 1975; commendation ASD/AE WPAFB, OH 1978; man yr Omega Psi Phi Fraternity 1980; outstanding performance Aeronautical System Div 1983. **MILITARY SERVICE:** USAF capt; USAF Reserves lt col; Commendation 1967. **HOME ADDRESS:** 967 Stover Dr Box 194, Wilberforce, OH 45384. **BUSINESS ADDRESS:** Technical Advisor, USAF/AFSC/ASD/AXA, ASD/AXA, Wright Patterson AFB, Dayton, OH 45433.

VOGEL, ROBERTA BURRAGE
Psychologist, educator. **PERSONAL:** Born Jun 13, 1938, Georgetown, SC; daughter of Demosthenes Edwin Burrage, Sr and Vivian Helen Bessellieu Burrage; divorced; children: Duane Stephen Vogel, Shoshana Lynn Vogel. **EDUCATION:** Temple Univ, Philadelphia, PA, BA 1960, MA 1962; Michigan State Univ, E Lansing, MI, PhD 1967; Ackerman Inst of Family Therapy, New York, NY, Post-Doctoral Certificate 1981. **CAREER:** Michigan State Univ, E Lansing, MI, instructor 1966-67, asst prof 1967-68; Center for Change, New York, NY, co-leader and staff mem 1970-72; N Richmond Comm Mental Health, Staten Island, NY, staff psychologist 1971-72; Staten Island Comm Coll (now College of Staten Island), NY, asst prof and counselor 1972-74, assoc prof 1974-78, director of SEEK Program 1978-; consultant and eval researcher for RH Clark Associates, 1978-83, and CUNY Office of Special Prog, 1981-88; consultant and psychologist for Steinway Family & Child Devel Center, 1984-88, and Harlem-Dowling Child & Family Services, 1989-. **ORGANIZATIONS:** Dir of clinical serv, Black Psych Inst of NY Assn of Black Psychologists, 1978-81; advisory board mem, NY Urban League, Staten Island Branch, 1980-; pres, NY Assn of Black Psychologists, 1982-83; mem, Staten Island Human Rights Advisory Comm, 1986-; board mem, Staten Island Mental Health Society, 1987-; mem, Staten Island Task Force on AIDS, 1988-; commissioner, NY Black Leadership Commn on AIDS, 1988. **HONORS/ACHIEVEMENTS:** Research fellow, Natl Insts of Health, 1964. **BUSINESS ADDRESS:** Assoc Prof, Director/Chair, SEEK Program, College of Staten Island, City Univ of New York, 715 Ocean Terrace, Room H-11, Staten Island, NY 10301.

VOORHEES, JOHN HENRY
Air force chief executive. **PERSONAL:** Born Aug 12, 1936, New Brunswick, NJ; married Jeanine Carter; children: Melanie Shemyne, John Carter. **EDUCATION:** Rutgers Univ, BS Chemistry 1958; Univ of Southern CA, MS Mgmt 1967; Harvard Univ, Senior Exec Fellow 1981. **CAREER:** Oklahoma City Air Logistics Ctr, chief B-52 and missile div syst 1979-81; Sacramento Air Logistics Ctr CA, dir matl mgt 1981-82; Defense Contract Admin Serv Region LA, commander 1982-84; Headquarters European Command Germany, deputy dir logistics 1984-86; Defense Personnel Support Ctr, commander. **ORGANIZATIONS:** Mem Air Force Assoc 1960-, Tuskegee Airman Inc 1981-, Federal Exec Bd LA 1982-84, Federal Exec Bd Philadelphia 1986-; mem Greater Philadelphia Chamber of Commerce 1987; mem exec bd United Way of SE PA 1987; chmn Combined Federal Campaign 1988. **HONORS/ACHIEVEMENTS:** Senior Executive Fellow Harvard, JFK School of Govt 1981. **MILITARY SERVICE:** USAF major general 29 yrs; Defense Superior Svc, Legion of Merit, Distinguished Flying Cross, Defense Meritorious Svc, Air Medal 1958-. **HOME ADDRESS:** Quarters "L", US Naval Base, Philadelphia, PA 19112.

W

WADDELL, CHARLES M.
Educator, psychologist. **PERSONAL:** Born Nov 26, 1938, Duquesne, PA; married Cheryl W Coleman; children: Marcus Garvey, Karimu Laini, Sekou Kahari. **EDUCATION:** VA State Univ, BS 1957-62; Howard Univ, MS 1964-66; MI State Univ, PhD 1968-71. **CAREER:** Leo Burnett Co Inc, res psychologist 1966-68; So Univ Baton Rouge, prof & chairperson dept of psych 1971-73; Univ of Cincinnati, adj assoc prof psych 1972-73; Central Comm Mental Health Ctr, assoc exec dir, dir of res eval 1972-73; The Peoples Clinic Santa Ana CA, dir of clinical serv 1973-74; Central City Comm Mental Health Ctr coord of clinical serv 1974-76; Los Angeles CA, private practice & consult 1974-; Loyola Marymount Univ, clinical psychologist, assoc prof psych 1974-. **ORGANIZATIONS:** Mem Psi Chi Natl Honor Soc Psych 1965, Hon Soc Phi Kappa Phi 1971, So Reg Coord, Natl Assoc of Black Psychologist 1972-73, APA's CEOP 1973-74; co-chairperson So CA Assoc of Black Psych 1975-76; consult Exceptional Children's Found 1975-; chairperson Amer Psychol Assoc Comm on Equality of Oppty in Psychol 1976-78; consult Dept of Family Med Martin L King Hosp LA 1978. **HONORS/ACHIEVEMENTS:** Several articles & presentations in various areas of psychology 1966-; NIMH Traineeship MSU E Lansing MI 1968-71; Invited respondent to Dr William Shockley Nobel Laureate NBC's Speak-up Amer 1980. **MILITARY SERVICE:** AUS 1st lt 1962-64. **BUSINESS ADDRESS:** Clinical Psych, Assoc Prof, Loyola MarymountUniv, Loyola Blvd at W 80th, Los Angeles, CA 90045.

WADDELL, THEODORE R.
Electronics engineer. **PERSONAL:** Born Mar 03, 1934, Wilmington, NC. **EDUCATION:** NC A & T, BS 1962; Bthn Ckmn Coll, 1954; Grg Wash U, 1970. **CAREER:** Fed Commu Comm, chf dmstc mcrwv rd br 1980-, rep oncmps rcrtmnt of gradtng stdnts at prdmntly blkUniv 1965-; Engineer, various other postns; Common Carrier Bur, 1962-80. **HONORS/ACHIEVEMENTS:** Recip cert of aw for hgh qlty prfrmnc Fed Commu Commn 1965, 1973, 1974. **MILITARY SERVICE:** AUS splst 5 1955-58. **BUSINESS ADDRESS:** 1919 M St NW, Washington, DC 20554.

WADDLES, CHARLESZETTA LINA
Mission director. **PERSONAL:** Born Oct 07, 1912, St Louis, MO; married Payton Jr (deceased); children: Beatrice, Lathet L, Latheda, Annette, Lorraine, Andrea, Roosevelt, Charles, Dennis, Theresa. **CAREER:** Waddles Perpetual Mission Inc, founder (1956), national director, pastor; Emergency Service Program maintains kitchens on fringes of Skid-Row, serves 7500 meals each month for 35 cents per meal or free, provides clothing, shelter, medicine, transportation & anything required by the needy. **ORGANIZATIONS:** Life mem NAACP; Mayor's Task Force Committee; City's Bicentennial Committee. **HONORS/ACHIEVEMENTS:** Honorary chairman, Women's Conference of Concern; received nearly 80 awards among which are Ford Motor Co Bell Ringer, Lane Bryant Citizens Award, Sojourner Truth Award, Religious Heritage Award, State of Michigan Special Tributes, State of Michigan Legislative Body, Humanitarian Award presented by President Richard Nixon, Volunteer Leadership Award presented by Governor William Milliken, Humanitarian Award presented by Mayor Roman S Gribbs of Detroit; described by Bishop Emrich as "One Husky St Joan of Arc"; "A One Woman War On Poverty," Life Magazine; "Detroit's Resident Who Really Proves Her Concern by Doing for Her Fellow Man" Detroit editorial column; included in Black Woman Oral History Project, Schlesinger Library, Radcliffe College; included in Black Woman of Courage Traveling Exhibit, Smithsonian Institution; Woman of Courage Exhibit, Walter P Reuther Library, Archive of Labor & Urban Affairs, Black History Month; A Philip Randolph Institute Special Award; Honorary Doctor of Humanities Degree; Mission & School, Kumast, Ghana, West Africa; Humanitarian Award, Urban League, 1988. **BUSINESS ADDRESS:** Founder, Director, Pastor, Perpetual Mission Inc, 12479 Grand River, Detroit, MI 48204.

WADDLES, GEORGE WESLEY, SR.
Clergyman, psychologist. **PERSONAL:** Born Jul 19, 1948, Wichita, KS; married Karen Lavern Winn; children: George Jr, Nicholas, Nathanael, Genesis Maian. **EDUCATION:** Bethel Coll N Nwtn KS, BA Soc Wk 1974; KSUniv Lwrnc, MSW 1976. **CAREER:** Vncnns Univ, pastor psch conselor 1977-; 2nd Bapt Church, pastor 1977-; Ottawa Univ, prof 1976-77; KS Univ, adm asst to dean 1976-77; Mt Olive St Cngrs of Christian Educ, dean 1977-; WVUT, TV host blkns is 1977-. **ORGANIZATIONS:** Staff mem Nat Bapt Cngrs of Chrstn Educ 1978-; pres Grtr Vncnns Mnstrl Alli 1978-79; bd mem Knox Co Chld Protctn Team 1978-; coor hndcppd VncnnsUniv Stdnt Serv 1979-. **HONORS/ACHIEVEMENTS:** Grad Sch Schol Nat Inst of Mtl Hlth 1974; Otstndng Yng Men of Am US Jr C of C 1977. **BUSINESS ADDRESS:** Vincennes University, Vincennes, IN 47591.

WADDY, ARTHUR ROBERT
Attorney. **PERSONAL:** Born Jul 17, 1943, Evansville, IN; children: April, Arthur. **EDUCATION:** Loyola Univ, BA 1965, JD 1969. **CAREER:** Private Practice, attorney; Sheriff's Merit Bd, vice chmn. **ORGANIZATIONS:** Mem Chicago & Natl Bar Assocs, Amer Arbitration Assoc; bd of dirs Brass Foundation; mem 100 Club. **BUSINESS ADDRESS:** Vice Chairman, Sheriff's Merit Board, 188 W Randolph # 1825, Chicago, IL 60601.

WADDY, WALTER JAMES
Administrator. **PERSONAL:** Born Dec 31, 1929, Irvington, VA; married Clorie M Byrd; children: Waltia Suzanne. **EDUCATION:** George Meany Labor Studies Center, labor courses 1973; Goucher Coll, labor courses 1975. **CAREER:** Amer Fedn of Labor & Cong of Industrial Organizations, Region III covering 7 states & DC, dir 1973-; AFL-CIO, Region IV covering 3 states & DC, dir 1971; AFL-CIO Region IV, field rep 1961; United Papermakers & Paperworkers AFL-CIO, field rep 1959; Local #632 United Papermakers AFL-CIO, pres 1956. **ORGANIZATIONS:** Exec bd mem VA St AFL-CIO 1956; coord Coord Div of MD & DC Coop Orgn 1964; sec/tras Baltimore Chap APRI Orgn Cmpgn 1968; bd mem Nat APRI 1973-80; prog dir Cedar-Morris Hill Improv Assn 1974; mem Ancient Egyptian AONMS; mem Jerusalem Tmpl No 4 AEAONMS; mem 32 degree Mason Hiram Consistory No 2; mem Landmark Lodge #40 F&AM. **HONORS/ACHIEVEMENTS:** Trd unionist of the yr Met Baltimore Counc AFL-CIO 1975; govr's awd for Contrib to Labor Movement MD 1975; mayor's awd for Contrib to Labor Movement Baltimore City 1975; A Philip Randolph Awd Negro Labor Union Counc 1976. **BUSINESS ADDRESS:** 2701 W Patapsco Ave, Baltimore, MD 21230.

WADE, ACHILLE MELVIN
Educator. **PERSONAL:** Born Nov 05, 1943, Clarksville, TN; children: Chaka L. **EDUCATION:** OK State Univ, BA 1966, MA 1969. **CAREER:** Black Studies Center, Univ of CA Santa Barbara, acting dir 1969-70; Black Studies Univ of Omaha NB, dir 1970-71; Black Studies Vassar Coll, dir 1971-73; Black Studies Univ of Austin TX, lecturer 1973-86; Moorhead State Univ MN, Minority Student Affairs, coordinator 1988-89; Yale Univ, asst dean of students, dir Afro-Amer Cultural Center 1989-. **ORGANIZATIONS:** Arts commission City of Austin 1981-; bd mem Laguna Gloria Art Museum 1982-84; pres TX Assn for the Study of Afro-Amer Life and History Inc 1985-88. **HOME ADDRESS:** PO Box 6336, Yale Station, New Haven, CT 06520.

WADE, BRUCE L.
Musician. **PERSONAL:** Born Jul 17, 1951, Chicago, IL. **CAREER:** Baltimore Symphony Orchestra, violinist 1977-; Mil Symphony, 1972-73; Grant Park Symphony of Chicago 1971-; Civic Orchestra of Chicago, 1968-72. **ORGANIZATIONS:** Mem Pro Musica Rara. **HONORS/ACHIEVEMENTS:** $50000 Award Louis Sudler 1971. **BUSINESS ADDRESS:** Violinist, Baltimore Symphony, 1212 Cathedral St, Baltimore, MD 21201.

WADE, EUGENE HENRY-PETER
Physician. **PERSONAL:** Born Nov 20, 1954, Washington, DC; son of Samuel Wade and Dorothy Wade; married Portia Battle; children: Kim M, Eugene HP II. **EDUCATION:** Brown Univ, AB, ScB, 1978; Howard Univ, Coll of Medicine, MD, 1981; Univ of Alamaba, Postgrad training. **CAREER:** Private Practice, family physician. **ORGANIZATIONS:** Co-chairman, North Carolina Acad of Family Physicians, Minority Affair Comm; mem, Indigent Care Task Force of North Carolina Medical Soc, North Carolina Gen Assembly Indigent Health Care Study Commr. **HONORS/ACHIEVEMENTS:** Diplomate, Acad of Family Physicians. **BUSINESS ADDRESS:** 723 Edith St, Burlington, NC 27215.

WADE, JACQUELINE E.
Educator. **PERSONAL:** Born Sep 07, 1940, Murfreesboro, TN; children: Sharon Elizabeth Rose. **EDUCATION:** Fisk Univ, BA 1962; Univ of PA, MSW 1972, PhD 1983. **CAREER:** Univ of PA, dir Penn Children's Ctr 1973-80, assoc dir of student life 1980-84, faculty school of social work 1973-, dir afro-amer studies prog 1984-. **ORGANIZATIONS:** Consultant Trenton State Coll AFAMS Dept 1984-, Philadelphia Sch Dist Desegregation Office 1985-, Benj Bannekar Honors Coll Prairie View A&M 1985-, Conrad Hilton Foundation 1985-. **BUSINESS ADDRESS:** Dir Afro-Amer Studies, University of Pennsylvania, Afro-American Studies Prog, 204 Bennett Hall, 3340 Walnut, Philadelphia, PA 19104.

WADE, JAMES NATHANIEL
Business executive. **PERSONAL:** Born Oct 02, 1933, Patterson, NJ; children: Valarie, JaJa, Atiba. **EDUCATION:** Voorhees Coll, AA 1982-54; St Augustines Coll, BA 1954-56; Howard Univ, MSW 1965-67; Univ of Pittsburgh, post grad 1973-75. **CAREER:** Erie Community Action Committee, deputy of operations 1967-69; Erie Urban Coalition, exec dir 1969-71; Dept of Community Affairs/Commonwealth, deputy sec 1971-73, gov special asst 1973-75, sec of admin 1975-79; Wade Communications, Inc, chairman of the bd. **ORGANIZATIONS:** First and Second Philadelphia United Negro Coll Fund, chairman; THe Basan Development, v p; Crisis Intervention Network, exec committee, mem; PhiladelphiaDance Co, bd mem; Congreso De Latinos Unidos, Inc, bd mem; NAACP, life mem; Kappa Alpha Psi, life mem; Nat'l Black MBA Association, mem; Bay City Masonic Lodge, mem. **HONORS/ACHIEVEMENTS:** NAACP, presidential award 1975, humanitarian award 1976; United Negro Coll Fund, award of distinction 1976; St Augustines Coll, achievement & meritorium award; Chapel of Four Chaplains, legion of honor award; Ame Union Church, christian businessman of the year award; Nat'l Assoc for Equal Opp in Higher Ed, pres citation distinguished alumni award; Omega Psi Psi, citizen of the year award. **MILITARY SERVICE:** AUS, sp 4 1956-58; Leadership Training Award, 1957.

WADE, JOSEPH DOWNEY
Educational administrator. **PERSONAL:** Born Jan 16, 1938, Beaumont, TX; son of Rufus and Lorene; married Judith Allen; children: Stacy, Joseph Jr. **EDUCATION:** Oregon State Univ, BS, 1959, MEduc, 1961; Univ of Oregon, PhD, 1982. **CAREER:** Compton Coll, head football coach, 1969-71; Univ of Oregon, asst football coach, 1972-75, assoc dir of admissions, 1975-76, assoc dir academic adv & student serv, 1976-84, dir academic adv & student serv, 1985-. **ORGANIZATIONS:** Commr, Oregon Commn on Black Affairs; univ senate, Faculty Advisory Council. **BUSINESS ADDRESS:** Dir, Acad Adv & Student Serv, Univ of Oregon, 164 Oregon Hall, Eugene, OR 97403.

WADE, JOYCE K.
Banker. **PERSONAL:** Born May 02, 1949, Chicago, IL; daughter of Ernest S Wade, Sr and Martha L Davis Wade. **EDUCATION:** Northwestern Univ, Evanston IL, BS educ, 1970; Univ of Chicago IL, MBA, 1977. **CAREER:** US Dept of Housing & Urban Development, Chicago IL housing rep, 1970-78; IL Housing Devel Authority, Chicago development office rep, 1978-79; Community Bank of Lawndale, Chicago loan office rep 1979-87, office CEO 1987-, mem Bd of Dir 1988-. **ORGANIZATIONS:** Dir, treas, Carole Robertson Center for Learning, 1980-; mem of Bd of Control, treas & chair of Loan Comm, Neighborhood Network & Housing Services, Marshall Sq & Douglas Park, 1984-; mem, Urban Renewal Bd of City of Chicago, 1987-; mem, treas, Natl Assn of Negro Business & Professional Women, 1987-; dir, Amer Civil Liberties Union of IL, 1988-; mem, Urban Bankers Forum of Chicago, 1988-. **HONORS/ACHIEVEMENTS:** Marilyn V Singleton Award, US Dept HUD, 1975; Bank Operation Outstanding Student Award, Assn of Bank Oper Mgmt, 1980; Top 100 Business & Professional Women, Dollars & Sense Magazine, 1988; Positive Self Image Award, Westside Center for Truth, 1988; Outstanding Service Award, Carole Robertson Center, 1989.

WADE, KIM MACHE
Beauty industry. **PERSONAL:** Born Sep 25, 1957, Manhattan, NY; daughter of Curtis Wade and Jean Wade; children: Rossi Jewel, Courtney Semaj. **EDUCATION:** Attended, A&T State Univ 1972-73, UNC Greensboro 1973-74, Shaw Univ 1976-78; Sandhills Comm Coll, license cosmetology 1986. **CAREER:** Moore County Arts Council, playwright/producer 1984; Innervision Theater Co, producer/playwright/director 1984-; Hometown News Magazine, assoc editor 1984-; Mache Beauty Station, owner. **ORGANIZATIONS:** Mem NAACP Moore Co Chap 1975-; am clerk and newsletter reporter UPS 1981-; summer youth counselor Southern Pines Recreation Dept 1984-85; missionary Harrington Chapel Young Adult Missionary 1986-; activity coord Ebonette Cultural Club 1986-. **HONORS/ACHIEVEMENTS:** Young Black Achiever Awd Black History Month Observation 1986; columnist Hometown News Magazine "WORD" 1986-; productions performed "Innervisions," "Go Tell it on the Mountain," "Black Folk Got Dey'Selves T'Gather," "Can I Get a Witness," 1989. **HOME ADDRESS:** 240 S Stephens St, Southern Pines, NC 28387.

WADE, LAWRENCE S.
Administrator. **PERSONAL:** Born Apr 11, 1926, Memphis, TN; children: 2 Children. **EDUCATION:** Univ TN, 1961-62; Lemoyne-Owen Coll, BA 1946-50. **CAREER:** State of TN, special asst to Gov present; Metro Shopping Plaza, devel 1967-71; VA, fee appraiser 1968; Mutual Fed Savings & Loan Assn, mgr pres 1964-66; Shelby Co Assessors Office, staff appraiser 1961; Arnold & Asso, vice pres 1959; Johnson Pub Co, vice pres; Ebony Fashion Fair, coordinator; Memphis Star Times Newspaper TN Assn of Assessing Officials, editor. **ORGANIZATIONS:** Past Pres, Memphis Chapter Natl Business League; past pres Omnibus 100 Serv Club; Lemoyne-Owen Alumni Assn; St of TN Small Business Admin Advisory Council; past mem, Shelby Co Bd of Equal; bd dir regional vice pres, Natl Business League; past chmn bd Memphis Business Resource Center; mem, Natl Conf of Christians & Jews; past pres Comm Day Care & Comprehensive Soc Serv Agency; bd mem Shelby Co Neighbors; exec community United Way of Greater Memphis; bd mem Better Bus Bur; Goodwill Homes; Fam Serv of Memphis; bd mem Dixie Homes Goodwill Boys Club; Goodfellows; Memphis Area Chamber of Commerce; Mid-S Med Center Council. **HONORS/ACHIEVEMENTS:** Bus & indus award Memphis StUniv 1969; Goodwill Boys Club Fdrs Club Awd 1968; Intl Council of Shopping Centers 1970; Ward Chapel Churchm Awd 1971; man of year award Bluff City Jaycees 1971; Shelby Untd Nghbrs 1971-72; MS Blvd Christian Church Men's Fellow Award 1971; Award for Achievement in Minority Economic Devel 1972; TN StateUniv No 1 Comm 1974; 100% Right Comm, Fisk Univ 1974. **MILITARY SERVICE:** AUS 1944-56.

WADE, LYNDON ANTHONY
Social worker. **PERSONAL:** Born Jun 30, 1934, Atlanta, GA; married Shirley M; children: Lisa, Nora, Jennifer, Stuart. **EDUCATION:** Morehouse Coll, AB 1956; Atlanta Univ, MSW 1958; Menninger Found Topeka KS, adv cert psy soc wk 1963. **CAREER:** Emory Univ, asst prof 1963-68; The Atlanta Urban League Inc, pres, ceo 1968-. **ORGANIZATIONS:** Mem Acad of Cert Soc Workers, C&S Affirm Action Prog, Atlanta Action Forum. **HONORS/ACHIEVEMENTS:** Disting Comm Serv Atl Morehouse Alumni Club 1965; Disting Serv Fulton Cty Medical Soc 1971; Social Worker of the Year North GA Chap of NASW 1971; 10 Years Outstanding Serv Atlanta Urban Leag 1978. **MILITARY SERVICE:** USA Med Serv Corp, 1st lt 1958-62. **BUSINESS ADDRESS:** President, CEO, Atlanta Urban League, Inc, Citizens Trust Bank, 75 Piedmont Ave NE Ste 310, Atlanta, GA 30303.

WADE, MILDRED MONCRIEF
Assistant director, educator. **PERSONAL:** Born Feb 05, 1926, Pittsburgh, PA; daughter of Lawrence Moncrief and Fannie Primus Moncrief; divorced; children: Judith L Johnson. **EDUCATION:** Univ of Pittsburgh, BA 1947; Tuskegee Inst, EdM 1951. **CAREER:** Selma AL Public Schools, teacher 1947-50; Tuskegee Inst, instr 1951-52; YWCA, prog dir 1953-55; Youth Devel Ctr, teacher 1955-59; Home for the Aged, 1959-60; Dom Rltns Ct, counselor 1960-65; Pittsburgh Publ School, teacher 1965-67; Louise Child Care Ctr, asst exec dir. **ORGANIZATIONS:** Mem bd of dirs PA Assoc of Child Care Agencies, Natl Conf of Christians & Jews, Sickle Cell Soc of Pittsburgh, Kingsley Assoc; mem Urban League Guild of Pittsburgh, Natl Council of Negro Women Pittsburgh section, Delta Sigma Theta Inc Pittsburgh Alumnae chapter; life mem NAACP; mem Wesley Ctr AME Zion Church, Pittsburgh, PA; mem African Heritage Room Comm, University of Pittsburgh, Pittsburgh, PA; mem Day Care Comm, Mayor's Task Force for Women; Who's Who in America, Who's Who among Black Americans since 1979; Martin Luther King, Jr, Outstanding Citizen's Award, Hand in Hand Inc, 1986. **BUSINESS ADDRESS:** Asst Exec Dir, Louise Child Care Center, 336 S Aiken Ave, Pittsburgh, PA 15206.

WADE, NORMA ADAMS
Newspaper staff writer. **PERSONAL:** Born May 15, 1944, Dallas, TX. **EDUCATION:** Univ of Texas at Austin, BJ 1966. **CAREER:** Dallas Morning News TX, staff writer 1974-; Post Tribune Dallas TX, staff writer/asst to editor 1972-74; Bloom Advertising Agency Dallas, advertising copywriter production asst 1968-72; Collins Radio Co Dallas, editor/proofer of tech equipment manuals 1966-68. **ORGANIZATIONS:** Mem Blacks in the Mass Media Local journalism group; bd mem 1970 & 1975, mem 1966-, Dallas Civic Chorus; People United for Justice for Prisoners 1975; "Friend of Southwest Research Center Museum for Afro-Amer Life & Culture 1975. **HONORS/ACHIEVEMENTS:** Comm serv plaque Black Knights Youth Found 1975. **BUSINESS ADDRESS:** Dallas Morning News, Communication Center, Dallas, TX 75222.

WADE, WILLIAM C., JR. See JAMALUDEEN, ABDUL HAMID

WADE-GAYLES, GLORIA JEAN
Educator. **PERSONAL:** Born in Memphis, TN; daughter of Robert Wade and Bertha Reese Willett; married Joseph Nathan Gayles, Aug 24, 1967; children: Jonathan Gayles, Monica Gayles. **EDUCATION:** LeMoyne Coll, AB (Magna Cum Laude with Distinction) 1959; Boston Univ Woodrow Wilson Fellow, AM 1962; George Washington Univ, doctoral work 1966-67; Emory Univ NEH Fellow, 1975; Emory Univ, PhD 1981. **CAREER:** Spelman Coll, instructor of English 1963-64; Howard Univ, instr of English 1965-67; Morehouse Coll, asst prof 1970-75; Emory Univ, graduate teaching fellow 1975-77; Talladega Coll, asst prof 1977-78; Spelman Coll, asst prof 1984-. **ORGANIZATIONS:** Teacher COFO Freedom School/Valley View MS 1964; mem bd dir WETV 30 - WABE-FM 1976-77; sec Guardians for Quality Educ 1976-78; mem editorial bd of Callaloo 1977-80; exec bd Coll Language Assn 1977-80; mem NAACP, ASNLC, CORE; mem Alpha Kappa Alpha Sorority Inc; partner in Jon-Mon Consultants Inc; speech writer. **HONORS/ACHIEVEMENTS:** Woodrow Wilson Fellowship 1959-62; Merrill Travel Grant to Europe The Charles Merril Found 1973; Danforth Fellow 1974; Faculty Award of the Year Morehouse Coll 1975; mem Alpha Kappa Mu Natl Honor Soc; editor CLANOTES 1975-; poems published in, Essence, Black World, The Black Scholar, First World; articles published in, Callaloo, Liberator, The Atlantic Monthly; wrote the preface to " Sturdy Black Bridges" Doubleday 1979; author of "No Crystal Stair, Visions of Race and Sec in Black Women's Fiction 1946-1976" Pilgrim Press 1984 (won 1983 manuscript award); UNCF Mellon Rsch Grant 1987-88, Liaison with Natl Humanities Faculty. **BUSINESS ADDRESS:** Associate Professor, Spelman College, Atlanta, GA 30314.

WAGNER, DAVID H.
Attorney. **PERSONAL:** Born Jul 23, 1926, Davidson Co, NC; married Mollie Craig; children: Brenda C, Davida S. **EDUCATION:** A&T U, BS 1948; A&T State U, MS 1957; Wake Forest U, JD 1968. **CAREER:** Atty, pvt practice 1969-; Wachovia Bank, closing atty & housing spec 1968-69; Lexington NC, instr principal 1958-66; Pender Co, instr principal 1954-58. **ORGANIZATIONS:** Gen couns Winston Mut Life Ins 1969-; pres Urban Housing Inc 1970-; pres Assoc Furniture Inc 1970-; mem NBA; NC Black Bar Assn; Forsyth Co Bar Assn; NC Bar treas Goler Met AME Zion Ch; vice pres life mem NAACP; bd mem & stockhldr Vanguard Invest Co; Forsyth Econ Devel Corp; life mem Alpha Phi Alpha; life mem NEA. **HONORS/ACHIEVEMENTS:** Listed in Who's Who in NC 1973-74; Who's Who in Black Amer 1973-74. **MILITARY SERVICE:** AUS 1st lt 1948-53. **BUSINESS ADDRESS:** PO Box 998, Winston-Salem, NC 27102.

WAGNER, VALLERIE DENISE
Engineer. **PERSONAL:** Born Apr 10, 1959, San Antonio, TX. **EDUCATION:** Southern Univ, BSME 1981; Tuskegee Inst, MSEE 1983. **CAREER:** Detroit Diesel Ausion/GM, test engr 1979; Jet Propulsion Lab, engr I 1981-82, mem tech staff engr III 1983-. **ORGANIZATIONS:** Boule mem Alpha Kappa Alpha Sor Inc 1979-; mem Eta Kappa Nu Honorary Frat 1982-. **HONORS/ACHIEVEMENTS:** GM Scholar General Motors 1979; GEM Fellowship 1981-83; First female to receive MS degree in engineering Tuskegee Inst 1983; Outstanding Young Women of America 1986. **HOME ADDRESS:** 2345 Merton Ave, Los Angeles, CA 90041. **BUSINESS ADDRESS:** Voyager SAS System Engr, Jet Propulsion Laboratory, 4800 Oak Grove Dr, Pasadena, CA 91109.

WAHLS, MYRON HASTINGS (MIKE)
Judge. **PERSONAL:** Born Dec 11, 1931, Chicago, IL; son of Frederica B. Wahls; married Shirleyan Chennault; children: Myron Jr, Julie K. **EDUCATION:** Univ of MI, BA; Northwestern Univ Sch of Law, JD; Univ of Virginia Law School Charlottesville Master of Laws in Judicial Process 1980-88. **CAREER:** Keith Conyers Anderson Brown & Wahls, atty 1964-75; Wayne Co Circuit Court, judge 1975-82; MI Court of Appeals, judge 1982-; chief judge pro tem Mich Court of Appeals 1988-91. **ORGANIZATIONS:** Mem MI Judicial Inst; bd mem Fund for Equal Justice; chmn MI Court Reporting/Recording Bd of Review; guest lecturer Univ of Florence Italy, Univ of Pisa Italy & Univ of Clermont Ferrand Law Sch; adjunct prof Cooley Law Sch & Amer Inst for Paralegal Studies; bd dirs Natl Cncl on Alcoholism, MUSIC, Gamma Lambda Chap Alpha Phi Alpha Frat Inc, Ashland Theol Seminary, Save Orchestra Hall Inc, Jazz Development Workshop Inc, Kenneth Jewell Chorale, Fund for Equal Justice; Univ of MI Alumni Assn, Northwestern Univ Alumni Assn, Wayne State Univ Ctr for Black Studies, Jimmy Wilkins Cultural Found Inc, Sigma Pi Phi Frat Inc Iota

Boule, Tabernacle Missionary Bapt Ch; life mem NAACP; NARCO; bd of directors Harmonie Park Playhouse; bd of directors Detroit Symphony Orchestral Hall; bd of directors Detroit Science Center. **HONORS/ACHIEVEMENTS:** Outstanding Jurist Awd 1975; Dr Martin Luther King Awd First Annual MI Elks 1976, Disting Serv Awd Courville PTA 1977; Outstanding Serv Awd Webber MiddleSch 1981; Outstanding Jurist Awd Wall St 1981; D Augustus Straker Outstanding Jurist Awd Wolverine Bar Assn 1982; H H Humphrey Humanitarian Awd Alpha Tau Chap Alpha Phi Alpha Frat Inc 1982; Disting Serv Awd Assn of Black Judges of MI; Disting Serv Awd Wayne Co Circuit Court 1982; Outstanding Serv Achievement Awd Markley Minors Affairs Cncl Univ of MI 1983; Disting Serv Awd Epsilon Chap Alpha Phi Alpha Frat Inc 1983; Appreciation Awd MI Chap Natl Mgmt Assn 1984; Cert of Recognition Tabernacle Missionary Bapt Ch 1984; Listed in Detroit Jazz Who's Who 1984; Distinguished Citizen of the Year - Rush County NAACP 1987; Outstanding Community Service United Citizens for Detroit 1988; Bridge Builder Award New Calvary Baptist Church 1988; Guest Jazz Pianist with Lionel Hampton Orchestra Tour of Europe 1988. **BUSINESS ADDRESS:** Judge, Michigan Court of Appeals, 900 First Federal Bldg, Detroit, MI 48226.

WAIGUCHU, MURUKU
Educator. **PERSONAL:** Born Nov 29, 1937, Kenya; divorced; children: 2 children. **EDUCATION:** Central Coll, BA 1965; Queens Coll, MA 1967; Temple Univ, PhD 1970. **CAREER:** African Studies Ctr St John's Univ, instr 1968-69; Urban Univ, Rutgers Univ, asst prof 1969-70; Office of Minority Student Ed Univ of MD Coll Park, dir 1978-80; William Paterson Coll of NJ, assoc prof, chairperson 1973-78, full prof publ admin 1980, prof sch of mgt. **ORGANIZATIONS:** Mem AHSA, ASA, NCBPS, ABSW, NJABE, INCCA. **HONORS/ACHIEVEMENTS:** Recipient UN Fellow 1967-68. **BUSINESS ADDRESS:** Professor, William Paterson College, School of Management, Wayne, NJ 07470.

WAINWRIGHT, GLORIA BESSIE
Elected official. **PERSONAL:** Born Jul 13, 1950, Cleveland, OH; married Roy Wainwright; children: Roy Jr, Jason. **EDUCATION:** Case Western Reserve Univ, 120 hr Cert 1971; Jane Addams School of Practical Nursing, Diploma 1975; Cuyahoga Comm Coll, 3 credits 1980. **CAREER:** Ward 5 Block Club, pres 1980; New Bethel AME Church, steward bd 1984-85; Bathsheba Order of Eastern Star, chaplain 1983; Oakwood Village City Council, councilmem 1984-. **HOME ADDRESS:** 7226 Wright Ave, Oakwood Village, OH 44146. **BUSINESS ADDRESS:** Councilmember, Oakwood Village City Council, 24800 Broadway Ave, Oakwood Village, OH 44146.

WAINWRIGHT, OLIVER O'CONNELL
Business executive. **PERSONAL:** Born May 06, 1936, Nanticoke, MD; married Dolores Moorman; children: Oliver Jr, Stephen C, Eric C. **EDUCATION:** Hampton Inst, BS 1959; William Paterson Coll, MA Commun 1972; Central MI Univ, MA Indust Mgmt 1974; US Army Command & Gen Staff Coll, 1975; Nova Univ, MPA 1980, DPA 1981. **CAREER:** AUS, various positions to lt col, 1959-79; SCM Corp, mgr corp security 1979-. **ORGANIZATIONS:** Mem Kappa Alpha Psi; mayoral appt Human Resources Council Piscataway 1980; trustee North Stelton AME Church 1980-81; mem Assoc of Political Risk Analysts 1982; mem cert bd Acad of Security Ed & Trainers 1983-85; mem disting lecturer series Dept of Mgmt & Criminal Justice 1985; bd of dir Acad for Security Ed & Trainers 1982-85; standing comm mem Amer Soc for Indust Security Intl; assoc mem Intl Assoc of Chiefs; bd of dir Amer Soc for Indust Sec 1985-87, Amer Soc for Indust Security 1985-87. **HONORS/ACHIEVEMENTS:** Natl Training Awd Defense Intelligence School Natl Training Officers Conf 1977; Political Risk Assessment Article Risk Planning Group 1980; Cert Protection Professional Amer Soc of Indust Sec Intl 1981; Cert Security Trainer Acad Security for Security Ed & Trainers 1981; Black Achievers in Indust Awd Harlem YMCA 1982; Mgmt of the Future Article Security Mgmt Mag 1984. **MILITARY SERVICE:** AUS Military Intelligence lt col 1959-79; Bronze Star w/1 OLC; Air Medal w/2 OLC; Pres Unit Citation, Natl Defense Ser Medal, Defense Meritorious Svc. **BUSINESS ADDRESS:** Manager of Corporate Security, SCM Corp, 299 Park Ave, New York, NY 10171.

WAITE, NORMA LILLIA
Physician. **PERSONAL:** Born Oct 14, 1950, Kingston, Jamaica;married Ainsley Blair; children: Craig, Duane, Andre Blair. **EDUCATION:** Howard Univ, BS 1972; Howard Univ Medical School, MD 1977. **CAREER:** Brookdale Hospital, ob resident program 1977-81; Private Practice, physician. **ORGANIZATIONS:** Mem Orange Co Medical Soc 1982-; attending physician Orlando Regional Hosp, FL Hospital, Humana Hospital Lucerne; fellow Amer Bd of Ob/Gyn. **BUSINESS ADDRESS:** 5750 Major Blvd, Ste 220, Orlando, FL 32819.

WAITERS, GAIL ELENORIA
Government administrator. **PERSONAL:** Born May 15, 1954, Kansas City, MO; daughter of Lloyd Winfred Waiters and Lenora Sampson Waiters. **EDUCATION:** California State Univ, Hayward, BA 1981, MPA 1989. **CAREER:** California State Univ, Hayward, administrative services coordinator, 1974-82; Univ of California, Berkeley, administrative analyst, 1982-85; City of Sunnyvale, CA, administrative assistant, 1985-. **ORGANIZATIONS:** Bd dir, Berkeley YWCA 1983-85, Leadership Sunnyvale 1985-86, Natl Forum for Black Public Administrators, Oakland-San Francisco Chapter 1986-; mem, Intl City Management Assn 1987-, Org Development Network 1987-, Intl Assn of Business Communicators 1987-. **BUSINESS ADDRESS:** Administrative Assistant, City of Sunnyvale, Office of the City Manager, 456 West Olive Ave, Sunnyvale, CA 94086.

WAITERS, GRANVILLE KEITH
Professional athlete. **PERSONAL:** Born Jan 08, 1961, Columbus, OH. **EDUCATION:** Ohio State, 1983. **CAREER:** Indiana Pacers, center 1984; Portland Trailblazers. **HONORS/ACHIEVEMENTS:** Ohio Class AAA State Championship; won All-Ohio honors as well as Honorable Mentn All-Am honors 1979. **BUSINESS ADDRESS:** Indiana Pacers, 300 E Market St Market Sq Arena, Indianapolis, IN 46204.

WAITES, SHIRLEY JEAN
Public relations consultant. **PERSONAL:** Born Dec 29, 1948, Philadelphia, PA; children: Demarcus Reginald. **EDUCATION:** The Pennsylvania State Univ, BA Psychology 1971; Bryn Mawr The grad Sch of Social Work, MSS 1977. **CAREER:** Mental Health Consortium Inc, specialist/social worker therapist; West Philadelphia Community, consultation & educ 1971-77; LaSalle Univ, instructor social work dept 1980-83; WDAS-AM Talk Show, program asst 1982-84; Women's Network Consultants, public relations consultant 1974-. **ORGANIZATIONS:** Clinical dir Baptist Children's Serv 1978-80; instructor Villanova Univ 1980-85; psychiatric social worker Haverford State Hosp 1983-85; instructor LincolnUniv 1984; coord Prison Project; advisor/team mem Triple Jeoparty Third World Women's Referral Org; mem Natl Assoc of Black Psychologists, Natl Assoc of Black Social Workers, Natl Assoc of Social Workers. **HONORS/ACHIEVEMENTS:** Outstanding Young Women of Amer 1981; Achievement Awd Black Students of LaSalle Univ 1983. **HOME ADDRESS:** 1708 No 55th St, Philadelphia, PA 19131.

WAITH, ELDRIDGE
Security consultant. **PERSONAL:** Born Jan 13, 1918, NYC; married Elsie Torres; children: Mariann, Linda. **EDUCATION:** John Jay Coll of Criminal Justice CityUniv of NY, BS 1966. **CAREER:** UBA Security Serv Inc, security cons, pres 1974-; NJ Civil Serv Commn on Police Promotns, consult; Police-Comm Relations for Nat Conf of Chris & Jews; New York City Bd of edn, chief adminstr, Sch Safety 1972-74; Coll of Virgin Islands, instr Police Sci 1971; New York City Police Dept, served every rank up to & including asst chief inspector. **ORGANIZATIONS:** Life mem NAACP; bd mem Urban League Gr NY; bd mem 100 Black Men; mem Uptown Rotary Club; Inter Assn of Chiefs of Police; Acad of Police Sci; Captains Endowment Assn NYCPD; Nat Assn of Sch Sec Dirs; Interracial Colloquy NYC; Nat Conf of Chris & Jews; bd mem Guardians Assn Found of NYCPD. **HONORS/ACHIEVEMENTS:** Recip 17 Departmental awards for outstanding police work; numerous comm awards.

WAKEFIELD, JAMES ALVIN
Business executive. **PERSONAL:** Born Jul 25, 1938, New York, NY; children: Shawna Michelle, Adam Malik. **EDUCATION:** NY Univ, BA Eng Lit 1957-60; Pace Grad Schl of Bus, MBA 1970-72. **CAREER:** Worldwide Avon Prod Inc, mgr empl rel 1973-74, dir oper 1974-76, gen mgr-home off 1976, vice pres prsnl 1977-80, vice pres admn 1980-81; Korn/Ferry Internatl, prtnr v pres 1981-83; Wakefield Ent Inc Wil-Evn Inc, chrmn/pres-CEO 1984-. **ORGANIZATIONS:** Mgr Recruitment exec recrtmnt coll rel Singer Co 1970-72; supv empy rel comensation asst Celanese Co 1968-70; emplye rel supr empl rel asst Mobil Oil Corp 1966-68; chrmn Cncl of Concerned Blk Execs 1970-73; brd mem NY Urban League 1980-83. **HONORS/ACHIEVEMENTS:** Acdmc schlrshp Syracuse Univ 1957; outstanding achvmnt awd Black Retail Action Group 1979. **MILITARY SERVICE:** USAF cpt 1961-66; spot capt 1963-66.

WALAKAFRA-WILLS, DELPANEAUX V.
Psychologist/educator. **PERSONAL:** Born May 23, 1952, Los Angeles, CA; married Eyamide Ella Smith-Wills; children: Delpaneaux Adetunjie, Adeyemie. **EDUCATION:** Univ of NE at Omaha, BA (w/Honors) 1976; Penn State Univ, MS 1979; Univ of England at Oxford, PhD 1982. **CAREER:** Penn State Univ, faculty 1978-79; Sacramento Sheriff's Dept, dir of rec & ed serv 1982-85; CA Inst, dean for academic afrs/continuing educ 1985-86; Advanced Educational Mgmt Sys, pres 1985-. **ORGANIZATIONS:** Pres Friends of Sierra Leone 1980-; vice pres Natl Recreation Correctional Assoc 1982-86; vice pres African Amer Chamber of Commerce 1987; mem The AmerFamily and Adolescent Inst 1987; professor at large Univ of Training College, Los Angeles; chief consultant to the president California Career Inst/CRI; staff psychologist AFSA Long Beach; chief consultant Tech Hlth Careers School Los Angeles. **HONORS/ACHIEVEMENTS:** Literary Awd Natl Recreational Correctional Assoc 1984; Honorary Counsul for the Republic of Sierra Leone in CA 1985-. **HOME ADDRESS:** PO Box 675, Long Beach, CA 90801. **BUSINESS ADDRESS:** President, Advanced Educational Mgt Sys, 211 East Ocean Blvd, Ste 247, Long Beach, CA 90802.

WALBEY, THEODOSIA EMMA DRAHER
Artist. **PERSONAL:** Born Apr 13, 1950, Bangor, ME; married Daniel A Draher; children: Timothy W Wright, Stephen S Wright, Daniel A Draher, Jr. **EDUCATION:** Univ of MD; Univ of CO; Kinman Bus Univ. **CAREER:** Music writer & co-wrote songs on latest Ritchie Family Album "Give Me A Break"; appeared before King & Prince of Morrocco & Princess Caroline's engagement party; 2 movies "La Borbichette" & "Can't Stop the Music"; TV performances, Dinah Shore, Merv Griffin, Rock Concert, Midnight Special, Soul Train, Amer Bandstand, Mike Douglas, Dance Fever, Soap Factory, numerous countries around the world; group called "The Ritchie Family", singer 1975-; Can't Stop Productions, singer, dancer, actress. **HONORS/ACHIEVEMENTS:** Gold & Platinum Records from around the world 1976-77; Featured "Ebony Magazine" 1980; Featured "Black Stars Magazine"; Featured "Blacktress Magazine". **BUSINESS ADDRESS:** Can't Stop Productions, 65 E 55th St, Ste 302, New York, NY 10022.

WALBURG, JUDITH ANN
Fund raiser. **PERSONAL:** Born Feb 19, 1948, New York, NY; daughter of Charles A Walburg and Florence Perry Walburg. **EDUCATION:** Fisk Univ, Nashville TN, BA 1969. **CAREER:** Olivetti Corp of Amer, NYC, customer relations rep 1970-72; United Negro College Fund, NYC, asst dir of educational services 1972-75, dir of alumni natl org 1975-. **ORGANIZATIONS:** Mem, New York Fisk Alumni Assn 1975-79, Natl Urban Affairs Council 1984-89, Corporate Women's Network 1986-89; bd mem, Council on the Environment 1987-89. **HONORS/ACHIEVEMENTS:** Outstanding Young Woman of America, 1976 & 1978. **HOME ADDRESS:** 284 Convent Ave, New York, NY 10031. **BUSINESS ADDRESS:** Director, Alumni Groups, National Organizations, United Negro College Fund, 500 East 62 St, New York, NY 10021.

WALCOTT, JERSEY JOE **See CREAM, ARNOLD**

WALDEN, BARBARA
Company executive/president. **PERSONAL:** Born Sep 03, 1936, Camden, NJ. **EDUCATION:** Attended, Vogue Finishing School, Eccles Business Coll. **CAREER:** Film and TV Actress, The Ten Commandments w/Charlton Heston, What A Way to Go w/Paul Newman, Global Affair w/Bob Hope, Satin's Seven Sinners w/Mickey Rooney, Freaky Friday w/Jodi Foster;TV appearances include Hour Magazine, The CBS Morning News, The Morning Show, Newsnight, The Tom Snyder Show, AM Los Angeles plus many more; Barbara Walden Cosmetics, founder/president. **ORGANIZATIONS:** Bd mem ACLU 1985-, United Way 1986-; bd mem May Co So CA Women's Adv Council 1986-; mem Committee of 200, Coalition of 100 Black Women; co-sponsor Self-Image workshop seminars; lectures at colleges, univs, for women's groups, orgs, caucuses and for the Los Angeles Unified School Dist yearly

"Career Day"; keynote speaker New York's Dept of States' Comm Economic Develop Prog Syracuse NY; guest lecturer UCLA's Women in Management, Southern CA Business Women's Caucus. **HONORS/ACHIEVEMENTS:** Women in Business Awd; YWCA's Silver Achievement Awd; Watts Summer Pageant Awd; Special Merit Awd from LA Mayor Tom Bradley; The Baptist Business Women'sAssoc Awd; The Women's Network Conf Achievement Awd; The Crenshaw LaTierra Business Women's Assoc Awd; cited the disting Congressional Record from the House of Reps in Washington DC; indepth interview in Entrepreneur Magazine entitled "Advice from some of the Nation's Most Powerful Businesswomen". **BUSINESS ADDRESS:** Founder/President, Barbara Walden Cosmetics Co, 5824 Uplander Way, Culver City, CA 90230.

WALDEN, EMERSON COLEMAN
Physician. **PERSONAL:** Born Oct 07, 1923, Cambridge, MD; son of Charles E and Lillian E; married Celonia; children: Emerson C Jr, Thomas E, Celonia. **EDUCATION:** Howard Univ, MD 1947. **CAREER:** USAF Hosp Mitchell AFB, chief of surg serv 1951-53; Provident Hosp Baltimore, chief surgery 1964-68; Luther, Johns Hopkins, Provident, S Baltimore Gen Hosps, attending surg; Baltimore City Health Dept, part time school physician; Private practice, physician. **ORGANIZATIONS:** Past pres Natl Med Assn, pres MD Med Assn; vice pres Monumental City Med Soc; bd regents Univ of MD; mem Baltimore City Med Soc; chmn bd trustees Natl Med Assn; dir health serv Providence Comprehensive Neighborhood Health Ctr. **HONORS/ACHIEVEMENTS:** One of physicians who toured People's Rep of China 1972. **BUSINESS ADDRESS:** 4200 Edmondson Ave, Baltimore, MD 21229.

WALDEN, NARADA MICHAEL
Musical entertainer, producer. **PERSONAL:** Born Apr 23, 1952, Kalamazoo, MI; married Anukampa Lisa Coles. **EDUCATION:** W MI Univ, attended 1970-72. **CAREER:** Warner Bros Records, rec artist, writer, record producer; songwriter Gratitude Sky 1976-; drummer various groups; pianist various rec artists albums; Perfection Light Productions, pres 1976-. **HONORS/ACHIEVEMENTS:** Hon Citizen Awd Atlanta 1979; Hon Shelby Co Commr Shelby Co TN 1980; Hon Citizen New Orleans 1980; Outstanding Black Contemporary Artist Awd Bay Area Music Awds San Francisco 1982; numerous albums Atlantic Records; 1986 Grammy Awd Best R&B Song "Freeway of Love" Aretha Franklin; 1986 Producer of the Year Billboard Magazine; spokesperson for "The Peace Run" 1987 (27,000 mile intl relay run for peace). **BUSINESS ADDRESS:** 1925-G Francisco Blvd, San Rafael, CA 94801.

WALDEN, ROBERT EDISON
Educator psychiatrist. **PERSONAL:** Born Apr 05, 1920, Boston, MA; son of Charles W Walden and Mary E James Walden; married Ethel Lee Bazar, Jun 24, 1953; children: Kenneth E, Roberta E Miller, Robert E Jr, Mark E, Mary E. **EDUCATION:** Lincoln Univ Chester Cty, PA, AB 1942; Meharry Medical Coll, MD 1945. **CAREER:** Lakin St Hosp Lakin, WV, supt 1962-65; Oakland County CMHS Bd, psych dir 1965-68; Medical Coll of OH, assoc prof psych 1968-88; Medical Coll of OH, prof clinical psych 1988-. **ORGANIZATIONS:** Med dir Cordelia Martin Health Cntr Toledo, OH 1969-72, Comm Hlth & Educ & Screen Prog 1972-76; psych dir Adult Psych Hosp MCOH 1977-88; med dir Taft State Hosp Taft, OK 1950-53; bd mem Comm Plann Cncl NWO 1969-72; sec, treas & prog chmn mem of cncl OH Psychiatric Assn 1969-; private practice (inpatient & outpatient). **HONORS/ACHIEVEMENTS:** Diplomate Amer Bd Psychiatry & Neurology 1962-; life fellow Amer Psychiatric Assoc; honoree Dist Serv Award OH Psychiatric Assoc 1964-. **MILITARY SERVICE:** AUS, USAFR, USAR, Colonel; Army Achievement; Good Conduct; Victory. **BUSINESS ADDRESS:** Professor Clinical Psychiatry, Medical College of OH, 3000 Arlington Ave, Toledo, OH 43699.

WALDO, CAROL DUNN
Financial administrator. **PERSONAL:** Born Mar 30, Springfield, TN; married Steiner L Waldo; children: Sean, Candice. **EDUCATION:** TN State Univ, BS 1970; Atlanta Univ, MBA 1973. **CAREER:** Exxon Co USA, economic analyst 1973-76; RJ Reynolds Aminoil USA, sr financial analyst 1976-79; SC State Health & Human Serv Commn, dir of budgeting 1979-. **ORGANIZATIONS:** Instructor Univ of SC 1980; mem ed comm League of Women Voters 1982-85; bd mem Columbia Urban League 1983-; mem chmn Natl Black Child Develop Inst 1983-; mem Les Amis Des Enfants (affiliated w/children unlimited adoption svcs) 1985-. **HONORS/ACHIEVEMENTS:** Scholastic Recognition Delta Mu Delta Honor Soc 1972; Outstanding Young Women of Amer, Outstanding Young Women of Amer Bd 1984; listed in Who's Who of Amer Women, Marquis Who's Who. **HOME ADDRESS:** 2125 Beaver Lane, West Columbia, SC 29169. **BUSINESS ADDRESS:** Dir of Budgeting, Hlth & Human Serv Finan Comm, PO Box 8206, Columbia, SC 29202.

WALDON, ALTON RONALD, JR.
Assemblyman. **PERSONAL:** Born Dec 21, 1936, Lakeland, FL; son of Alton R Waldon, Sr and Rupert Juanita Wallace; married Barbara, Jun 03, 1961; children: Alton III, Dana, Ian. **EDUCATION:** John Jay Coll, BS 1968; NY Law Sch, JD 1973. **CAREER:** New York City Housing Auth Police Dept, capt 1962-75; NY State Div of Human Rights, dep commr 1975-78; New York State Assembly, assemblyman 33rd dist. 1983-86; County Service Grp NYS OMRDD, counsel 1981-; US House of Representatives, congressman 1986-87; NY State Investigation Commn, commissioner 1987-. **ORGANIZATIONS:** Mem United Black Men of Queens, K of C, Amer Bar Assn, NAACP, Alumni Assn NY Law Sch, Macon B Allen Bar Assoc; bd of dirs USO Greater NY; bd USO of Greater Metropolitan NY; NYS Nurses Assoc; American Leadership Conf. **HONORS/ACHIEVEMENTS:** Golden Quill Awd John Jay Coll 1968; NY Law Sch; Thurgood Marshall Fellowship. **MILITARY SERVICE:** US Army, specialist 4th Class, 1956-59. **HOME ADDRESS:** 115-103 222nd St, Cambria Heights, NY 11411.

WALKER, A. MACEO, SR.
Insurance executive. **PERSONAL:** Born Jun 07, 1909, Indianola, MS; married Harriette; children: Patricia Walker Shaw (dec), Antonio M, Harriette Lucile. **EDUCATION:** Fisk Univ, BA 1930; New York Univ, MA 1932; Univ of MI, MA Actuarial Sci 1935. **CAREER:** Memphis Mortgage Guaranty Co, pres; Tri State Bank of Memphis, bd chairman; Universal Life Insurance Co, bd chmn pres. **ORGANIZATIONS:** Represented US Govt at the Amer Exhibition in Mali Africa 1964; selected by Pres Johnson as mem Natl Citizens Comm 1965; chmn trustee bd Mississippi Blvd Christian Church; mem bd of dirs Abe Scharff Branch YMCA, Memphis C of C; vice pres exec sect, bd mem, first vice pres and pres Natl Insurance Assoc; bd mem Shelby United Neighbors; elected mem Natl Conf of Christians and Jews; bd of dirs United Negro College Fund; mem Memphis Rotary Club 1975-, Future Memphis Inc 1976-. **HONORS/ACHIEVEMENTS:** St named in honor of A Maceo Walker Sept 30, 1976; Hon DL degree Fisk Univ 1978; appointed to White House Conf on Small Business Commn by Pres Carter 1979; LeMoyne-Owen Coll named the Computer and Information Mgmt Serv Ctr "Walker-Hyde" Sept 26, 1979; article Exclusive Profile, A Maceo Walker featured in March 1980 issue Memphis magazine; Brotherhood Medallion and Scroll The Natl Conf of Christians and Jews 1981; Special President's Awd Operation PUSH 1982; rec'd Plaque as one of the two living founders of Mississippi Boulevard Christian Church (1921-83) 1983; Laurel Wreath (highest honor) Kappa Alpha Psi Frat 1983; Master of Free Enterprise Jr Achievement of Memphis 1984. **BUSINESS ADDRESS:** Board Chairman, Universal Insurance Co, 480 Linden Ave, Memphis, TN 38126.

WALKER, ALBERT L.
Educational administrator. **PERSONAL:** Born Aug 10, 1945, Memphis, TN; son of Mr & Mrs Roosevelt Walker; married Mary Tipler; children: Brian K, Albert Jr, Kimberly Lynn. **EDUCATION:** Lincoln Univ, Jefferson City, MO, Bs, Educ, 1967; Bradley Univ, Peoria, IL, 3-MA, 1970, 1972, 1976; Inidana Univ, Bloomington, EdD, 1974. **CAREER:** Peoria Public Schools, Elementary teacher, 1967-70, dir, 1970-71, elementary school principal, 1971-76; Lincoln Univ, Jefferson City, assoc prof of educ, 1976-79; Missouri State Dept of Elementary & Second Educ Jefferson City, asst commn of educ, 1979-84; North Carolina A&T State Univ, School of Educ, dean, 1984-. **ORGANIZATIONS:** Mem, Phi Delta Kappa, 1970; Mem, Alpha Phi Alpha; Sec, Jefferson City Personnel Bd. **HONORS/ACHIEVEMENTS:** Noteworthy Amer & Comm Leaders Award. **MILITARY SERVICE:** AUS NG Capt 1979-87. **BUSINESS ADDRESS:** Dean, NC A&T State University, School of Education, Greensboro, NC 27411.

WALKER, ALBERTINA
Gospel singer. **PERSONAL:** Born Aug 28, 1929, Chicago, IL; daughter of Ruben Walker and Camilla Colemon Walker; married Lesley Reynolds, Aug 20, 1967 (divorced). **ORGANIZATIONS:** Bd mem, Operation Push, 1971-79; bd mem, Gospel Music Workshop of Amer, 1975-; mem, Governing Bd of Recording Arts and Sciences, Chicago chapter, 1985-; hon mem, Eta Phi Beta, 1986-; life mem, Natl Council of Negro Women. **HONORS/ACHIEVEMENTS:** Has recorded over 40 albums, including 4 gold records; founder of World Famous Caravans singers, 1952; Intl Woman of the Year Award, PUSH, 1975; performed in MGM film "Save the Children," 1976; Black History Month tribute, Univ of Mississippi, 1981; 7 Grammy Award nominations, 1981-87; Albertina Walker Scholarship founded at Central State Univ, Wilberforce OH, 1983; appeared on 26th annual Grammy Award Show, 1986; Albertina Walker Day proclaimed by Chicago IL mayor Harold Washington, Aug 29, 1986; Lifetime Achievement Award, Black Gospel Awards, London, England, 1986; special articles in Black Family magazine, spring, 1986. **HOME ADDRESS:** 7740 S Essex Ave, Chicago, IL 60649.

WALKER, ALICE MALSENIOR
Writer. **PERSONAL:** Born Feb 09, 1944, Eatonton, GA; daughter of Willie Lee Walker and Minnie Tallulah Grant Walker; married Melvyn Rosenman Leventhal, Mar 17, 1967 (divorced 1976); children: Rebecca Grant. **EDUCATION:** Attended Spelman Coll, 1961-63; Sarah Lawrence Coll, BA 1965. **CAREER:** Voter registration worker, GA; Head Start, MS, staff mem; NYC welfare dept, staff mem; writer-in-res & teacher of blk studies, Jackson State Coll 1968-69, Tougaloo Coll 1970-71; Wellesley Coll & Univ of MS-Boston, lecturer in lit, 1972-73; Univ of CA-Berkeley, distinguished writer in Afro-Amer studies, 1982; Brandeis Univ, Fannie Hurst Prof of Lit, 1982; Wild Trees Press, Navarro CA, co-founder & publisher, 1984-; writer; author of poetry volumes Revolutionary Petunias, Harcourt 1973, Horses Make a Landscape Look More Beautiful, Harcourt 1984; author of fiction You Can't Keep a Good Woman Down, Harcourt 1981, The Color Purple, Harcourt 1982, To Hell With Dying, Harcourt 1988; author of nonfiction In Search of Our Mothers' Gardens, Harcourt 1983, Living by the Word, Harcourt 1988. **ORGANIZATIONS:** Consultant on blk history, Friends of the Children of Mississippi, 1967; bd of trustees, Sarah Lawrence Coll, 1971-73. **HONORS/ACHIEVEMENTS:** Merrill writing fellowship, 1966; McDowell Colony fellowship, 1967 & 1977-78; Natl Endowment for the Arts grant, 1969 & 1977; Radcliffe Inst fellowship, 1971-73; PhD from Russell Sage College, 1972; Lillian Smith Awd, Southern Regional Council, 1973; Natl Book Awd nomination, 1973; Rosenthal Foundatn Awd, Amer Acad & Inst Arts & Letters, 1974; Guggenheim Awd, 1977-78; Natl Endowment for Arts fellowship, 1979; Natl Book Critics Circle Awd nomination, 1982; Amer Book Awd, 1983; Pulitzer Prize, 1983; O Henry Awd, 1986. **BUSINESS ADDRESS:** Wild Trees Press, PO Box 378, Navarro, CA 95463. *

WALKER, ALLENE MARSHA
Health services administrator. **PERSONAL:** Born Mar 02, 1953, Chicago, IL; daughter of Major Walker and Mabel H Thompson Walker. **EDUCATION:** Univ of IL-Chicago, BS 1974; Michael Reese Hosp Sch of Med Tech, MT 1973; Roosevelt Univ, MS 1983. **CAREER:** Damon Clinical Labs, lab supervisor 1974-85; Med Care HMO, provider rep 1985-. **ORGANIZATIONS:** Exec sec Operation PUSH Inc 1972-; sec treas Personalities Intl Inc 1984-. **HONORS/ACHIEVEMENTS:** Bd Certification Amer Soc of Clinical Pathologists 1975. **HOME ADDRESS:** 1417 W 73rd Pl, Chicago, IL 60636.

WALKER, ANN B.
Appointed government official, manager. **PERSONAL:** Born Nov 01, 1923, Columbus, OH; married Linwood Philip; children: Phillip, Julialyn, Amelia, Keith. **EDUCATION:** Prairie View Coll, 1942; Northwestern Coll, post-grad 1944; Geo Wms Coll, BS 1944. **CAREER:** Comm Serv Adminstrn Wash DC, dir media/pub liason; WCMH-TV Outlet & Broadcasting Columbus OH, dir/producer 1976-80; WLWC-TV Avco Broadcasting ColumbusOH, dir community servs 1968-76; WVKO Radio Skyway Broadcasting Columbus, asst news dir 1963-67; OH Sentienel Columbus, womans editor 1959-63; Chicago SPark YWCA Chicago, girl reserve sec 1944. **ORGANIZATIONS:** Reg vice pres Women in Communications 1968-; natl bd of dir Women in Communications 1974-76; reg dir Nat Assn Black Journalists 1976-78; pres Columbus Leadership Prog 1976-79; mem Columbus Consumer Affairs Commn; mem OH Bur Employ Servs Adv Council 1971-. **HONORS/ACHIEVEMENTS:** Career Woman of Yr Columbus OH 1971; Talaria Award Am Women in Radio/TV 1975; Emmy Nat Acad Radio-TV Artists 1976; Gov's Award State of OH 1976; Myrtle Wreath/Comm Serv Hadassah 1977; OH Women's Hall of Fame 1978. **BUSINESS ADDRESS:** Community Services Adminstrn, 1200 19th St NW, Washington, DC 20015.

WALKER, ANNIE MAE
Educator. **PERSONAL:** Born Jan 07, 1913, Daytona Beach, FL; married William H Walker; children: Garland James. **EDUCATION:** Bethune-Cookman Coll, BS Elem Educ 1944; Bank St Coll of Edn, MS (equiv) 1946; Edn/Soc Adelphi Univ, MA 1965; East Coast Univ, PhD Anthropology 1970; Yale U, Danforth Fellow 1971. **CAREER:** State Univ of NY Stony Brook, prof of educ 1946-; New York City Plainedge & Plainview Public Schools, taught in elementary schools; dir pre-school progs; Amityville NY, founded & dir "After School Tutorial Prgm"; "in Service courses in Black Studies for Teachers in LI school dist", conducted; Afri-Amer & Native Amer Ind History, spec; Afri Hist & Culture & Seminole Hist, prof lecturer; conduct classes in Black Comm called "Heightened Black Awareness" for youths 8 to 13. **HONORS/ACHIEVEMENTS:** Outstndg ldrshp award 1973; outstndg comm serv Martin L King Award 1970; Danforth Found post-Doc res Black Studies Award 1970; Human Relations Award Natl Conf Chris & Jews 1969; Nat Sojourner Truth Award for serv in comm 1964; most promising tchr Bethune Cookman Coll Award 1944. **BUSINESS ADDRESS:** StateUniv of NY, Stony Brook, NY 11794.

WALKER, ARTHUR B. C.
Attorney. **PERSONAL:** Born Dec 01, 1901; married Hilda G Forte; children: Dr Arthur BC Jr. **EDUCATION:** City Coll of NY, attended; Cleveland Coll, attended; John Marshall Law School, LLB 1936. **CAREER:** Van-Bert Realty Corp, pres 1950-65; Hil-Art Holding Corp, 1975-; City of NY, asst corp counselor 1954-. **ORGANIZATIONS:** Mem Draft Bd Cleveland; pres Truman Dem Club NYC; mem Comm on Canons Episcopal Diocese of NY; mem Vestry Trinity Episcopal Church. **BUSINESS ADDRESS:** Asst Corp Counselor, City of New York, 271 W 125 St, New York, NY 10027.

WALKER, BETTY STEVENS
Attorney. **PERSONAL:** Born Feb 03, 1944, New York, NY; daughter of Anne Wood; married Paul T Walker, Jun 17, 1965; children: Camarf, Tarik, Kumi. **EDUCATION:** Spelman Coll Atlanta, BA 1964; Harvard Law School, JD 1967. **CAREER:** Harvard Business School, research asst 1966; Wake Opportunities Inc Raleigh, coordinator of youth program 1968; Shaw Univ, curriculum consultant 1968, asst prof political science 1968-70; So Railway Co Washington, DC, atty 1974-77; Farmers Home Admin US Dept of Agr, asst to the admin 1977-; attorney (present). **ORGANIZATIONS:** Mem DC Court of Appeals; US Dist Court for DC; US Court of Appeals for DC District; DC Bar Assn; Washington Bar Assn; Natl Bar Assn; Spelman Coll & Harvard Law Alumni Assns; mem Bethel AME Church, Baltimore; steward, Bethel AME Church, 1989. **HONORS/ACHIEVEMENTS:** John Hay Whitney (2) 1964; Aaron Norman Fellowships 1964; Harvard Law School 1964; 1st Black woman to Ames Competition 2 consecutive semesters at Harvard Law. **BUSINESS ADDRESS:** Attorney, 1100 6th St, N W, Washington, DC 20001.

WALKER, CARL, JR.
Attorney. **PERSONAL:** Born May 13, 1924, Marlin, TX; married Janice Martin. **EDUCATION:** TX St U, BA 1950, MA 1952, LLB 1955. **CAREER:** US Dept of Justice, exec asst US atty 1968; So Dist TX, asst US Atty 1961; Dent King Walker & Wickliff, atty 1956-61. **ORGANIZATIONS:** Mem Houston Lawyers Assn; Houston Bar Assn; TX Bar Assn; NBA; Fed Bar Assn; ABA; Kappa Alpha Psi; past Pres Houston Bus & Professional Men's Clb 1971; past chmn bd Harris Comm Action Assn; chmn bd of mgrs YMCA S Cen Br Houston; pres chmn bd TX SoUniv Ex Student's Assn 1970; mem bd dir USO, ARC. **HONORS/ACHIEVEMENTS:** Recip US Selective Serv System Srvc Awd with Bronze Medl 1974; cert of Merit Kappa Alpha Psi 1962; many local serv Awd. **MILITARY SERVICE:** AAF sgt 1943-46. **BUSINESS ADDRESS:** PO Box 61129, Houston, TX 77061.

WALKER, CAROLYN
State representative. **PERSONAL:** Born in Yuma, AZ. **CAREER:** Arizona House of Representatives, Phoenix AZ, state representative, 1983-86; state senator, district 23, 1986-. **BUSINESS ADDRESS:** House of Representatives, State House, Phoenix, AZ 85007. *

WALKER, CHARLES
Educator, actor. **PERSONAL:** Born Jan 21, 1945, Chicago, IL; son of Charles Walker and Robbie Edith Hutchinson Walker; married Lillian Beatrice Lusk Walker, Feb 07, 1976; children: Leah Cher Walker, Chasen Lloyd Walker. **EDUCATION:** Career Academy School of Broadcasting, Milwaukee, WI, broadcasting degree, 1967; Wilson City College, Chicago, IL, 1967; California State Univ, Los Angeles, CA, BA, 1980, MA, 1982. **CAREER:** WVOL-Radio, Nashville, TN, radio news reporter, WXYZ-TV, Detroit, MI, television news reporter, 1967-68; professional actor in Los Angeles, CA, working in television, film and commercials, 1968—; Los Angeles Unified School District, Los Angeles, CA, substitute teacher for day and evening classes, 1980—; California State University, Los Angeles, CA, instructor in speech communication, 1980-81; City of Los Angeles, Los Angeles, CA, lecturer for work experience program, 1981-83; Hollywood High School, Los Angeles, CA, teacher, 1984; Los Angeles Southwest College, Los Angeles, CA, instructor in public speaking, 1984—; California State University, Dominguez Hills, CA, instructor in fundamentals of speech, acting, and intercultural communication, 1984—. **ORGANIZATIONS:** NAACP; Screen Actor's Guild; American Federation of Television and Radio Artists; Mt Zion Missionary Baptist Church. **BUSINESS ADDRESS:** California State University—Dominguez Hills, Speech/Theatre Department, 1000 East Victoria St, Carson, CA 90747.

WALKER, CHARLES A.
University president/chancellor. **CAREER:** University of Arkansas, Pine Bluff AR, president/chancellor. **BUSINESS ADDRESS:** University of Arkansas, Pine Bluff, Pine Bluff, AR 71801. *

WALKER, CHARLES DOUGLAS
Attorney. **PERSONAL:** Born Jan 10, 1915, Cleveland, OH; son of Charles D. Walker and Lydia Ruth Coleman Walker; widowed. **EDUCATION:** Ball State, AB 1936, MA 1945; IN Univ, JD 1953; Attended, George Washington Univ 1955, OH State Univ 1956. **CAREER:** Crispus Attucks HS, teacher dept head 1936-73; IN State Dept of Public Instruction, dir adult educ 1973-77; Marion Co Municipal Courts, public defender 1981-; private practice, atty. **ORGANIZATIONS:** Adv council IN Vocational Ed 1965-83; bd dir All Souls Unitarian Church 1986-; nom comm OH Valley Unitarian Univ Assn. **HONORS/ACHIEVEMENTS:** Pi Gamma Mu Natl Soc Sci Hon; Phi Delta Phi Law Hon. **MILITARY SERVICE:** AUSAC, 2nd lieutenant, 38 months. **HOME ADDRESS:** 5215 Will Scarlet Ln, Indianapolis, IN 46208.

WALKER, CHARLES E.
Clergyman. **PERSONAL:** Born Jun 28, 1935, Chicago; married Sylvia Saunders; children: Pierre, Jason. **EDUCATION:** DePaul U, BM 1957, MM 1959; Colgate Rochester Div Sch, BD 1970. **CAREER:** 19th St Bapt Ch, pastor; Requiem for Brother Martin, composer Jazz Mass & Dr Watts; Charles Walker Chorale, dir. **ORGANIZATIONS:** Mem Am AssnUniv Profs; Am Symphony Orchestra League; Liberian Symph Orchest 1977; Federation Musicians; Theol Commn Nat Bapt Conv schlrshp commn; exec bd Hampton Inst Ministers Conf; Foreign Mission Bd Nat Bapt Conv; natl vice pres E Reg OPERATION PUSH pres Philadelphia br. **BUSINESS ADDRESS:** 1253 S 19 St, Philadelphia, PA 19146.

WALKER, CHARLES H.
Attorney. **PERSONAL:** Born Nov 11, 1951, Columbus, OH; son of Watson H Walker and Juanita Webb Walker; married Amanda T Herndon; children: Katrina Della, Allison Lyles, Carlton Wesley. **EDUCATION:** Tufts Univ, BA (magna cum laude), 1969-73; Emory Univ School of Law, JD, 1973-76. **CAREER:** Bricker & Eickler, assoc, 1976-81, partner, 1982-. **ORGANIZATIONS:** Bd of dir, Salesian Boys Club, 1983-; Planned Parenthood of Central, OH, 1984; past pres & mem, The Columbus Acad Alumni Assn, 1979-83; mem, The Columbus Acad Alumni Assn, 1982-83; chmn, Tufts Univ Alumni Admissions Program, Central, OH, 1986-; bd mem, Battelle Youth Scholars Program, 1988-; mem, City of Columbus Sports Arena Commn, 1989, Ohio State Bar Assn, Professional and Legal Ethics Comm, 1988. **BUSINESS ADDRESS:** Attorney, Bricker & Eckler, 100 S Third St, Columbus, OH 43215.

WALKER, CINDY LEE
Program director. **PERSONAL:** Born Jul 24, 1952, Alexandria, VA; divorced; children: Tracey J, Mark A. **EDUCATION:** N VA Comm Coll, assoc Bus Admin 1974; BA. **CAREER:** WYTV Inc ABC Affiliate, prgm dir & exec producer 1979-; WRC-TV, exec producer Knowledge series 1978-79; NBC WRC-TV, mgr prgm adminstrn 1976-79, prgm &sched coordntr/prodn asst 1974-76, prgm asst/prodn asst 1973-74; WRC radio AM-FM, continuity coordntr 1972-73. **ORGANIZATIONS:** Mem Nat Acad TV Arts & Scis 1974-; mem Nat Assn of TV Program Execs 1979-; mem Nat Assn Media Women 1980-; exec bd mem NAACP 1970-; mem NatAssn Negro Women 1977-. **HONORS/ACHIEVEMENTS:** First black female in prgm mgmt NBC 1976; first black female prog dir commercial TV station 1979. **BUSINESS ADDRESS:** 3800 Shady Run Rd, Youngstown, OH 44502.

WALKER, CLAUDE
Educational administrator, clergyman. **PERSONAL:** Born Jan 13, 1934, Martinsville, VA; married Zola Mason; children: Obie, Sharron, Michele. **EDUCATION:** Jarvis Christian Coll Hawkins TX, BA 1956; Lexington Theol Sem Lexington KY, BD 1959; TX ChristianUniv Brite Div Sch Ft Worth TX, DMin 1977. **CAREER:** Right Alternatives for People, exec dir; Bonnie View Christian Church Dallas tX, pastor; Jarvis Christian Coll, dir religious life 1968-71,78-86; BakerUniv Baldwin City KS, dir of student serv & counselor minority students 1974-78; Central Christian Ch KC MO, pastor 1972-76; E 6th St Christian Ch Okla City, pastor 1964-68; Gay-Lea Christian Ch Nashville, pastor 1960-63; Mt Beulah Christian Cntr, prog dir 1959-60. **ORGANIZATIONS:** Mem Gen Bd Christian Church 1969-78; pres Natl Convocation of Christian Church 1972-74; bd mem Disciples of Christ Historical Soc 1972-82; mem Com onMinistry of Christian Church in the SW; pres Hawkins Ministerial Alliance 1980-81; trust Lexington Theol Sem Lexington KY 1980-86. **BUSINESS ADDRESS:** Executive Dir, Right Alternatives for People, PO Box 8693, Dallas, TX 75216.

WALKER, CORA T.
Attorney. **PERSONAL:** Born Jun 20, 1926, Charlotte, NC; divorced; children: Lawrence R Jr, Dr Bruce E. **EDUCATION:** St John's U, BS 1945, JD 1946. **CAREER:** Atty, Priv Pract 1947-54; Doles Sandifer & Walker, 1954-58; Doles & Walker, 1958-60; priv pract 1960-; Walker & Bailey, partner 1975-. **ORGANIZATIONS:** Mem numerous offcs, coms, numerous professional civic political orgns; NY State Beauty Culturists Assn 1969; Bermuda Benevolent Assn 1968; Mid-Eastern Coop Inc 1969; "21" Brands Inc 1968; bd of gov Natl Bar Assoc 1977-. **HONORS/ACHIEVEMENTS:** Award Women for Achievement Inc; citation Mayor's Vol Lawyers Adv Com 1957; Hall of Fame Alumni Award James Monroe HS 1967; comm leader Congressman Adam Clayton Powell; award Nat Beauty Culturists' League Inc 1969; award Negro Women Inc; NY Club Professnl Award 1969; achvmnt award IBPOE & W Grand Temple 1967; awards Hood Memorial AME Ch 1969; Actors' Fund 1968; Woman of Yr Delta Mu Zeta Chap Zeta Phi Beta Sor Inc 1971; Malcolm X Award 1969; Only Black Mother & Son Law Firm, Walker & Bailey; founder Harlem River & Consumers Coop Inc; Recipient of Natl Bar Assoc Gertrude Rush 1986; Recipient of Judicial Friends Jane M Bolin Awd 1986. **BUSINESS ADDRESS:** Partner, Walker & Bailey, 270 Lenox Ave, New York, NY 10027.

WALKER, CRAIG J.
Investment banker. **PERSONAL:** Born Aug 16, 1962, Chicago, IL; son of Phillip R Walker and Joanne Bell Walker; married Nancy Ann Rybak, Aug 23, 1986; children: Craig J Walker II. **EDUCATION:** Univ of IL, Chicago, BS Econ, 1986. **CAREER:** Shatkin Securities, Chicago Options Exchange, IL, floor runner, broker's asst, 1986; Daniels & Bell Inc, Chicago, IL, vice pres, 1986-89; WR Lazard & Co, Kansas City, MO, vice pres, 1989-. **HONORS/ACHIEVEMENTS:** Featured in Black Enterprise, May 1988, and Wall Street Journal, Feb 1989. **BUSINESS ADDRESS:** Vice President, W R Lazard & Co, 106 West 11th St, Suite 1133, Kansas City, MO 64105.

WALKER, CYNTHIA BUSH
Educator. **PERSONAL:** Born Dec 08, 1956, Ft Benning, GA; daughter of Rev & Mrs Otis Bush; married Robert B Walker Jr, Jul 03, 87; children: Christina S Walker. **EDUCATION:** Morehead State Univ, BA 1977, MHE 1978. **CAREER:** KY Metroversity, counselor 1978-80; Jefferson Comm Coll, counselor, assoc prof 1980-. **ORGANIZATIONS:** Mem KY Assn of Coll Admissions Counselors 1981-; vice chairperson Southwest Campus Faculty 1982-83; mem KY Assn of Counseling & Devel; chairperson Educ Opportunity Center Adv Bd 1983-; treasurer Assn of Black in Higher Educ; mem JCC Faculty Council. **BUSINESS ADDRESS:** Associate Prof of Counseling, Jefferson CommunityColl/SW Campus, 1000 Community College Dr, Louisville, KY 40272.

WALKER, DARRELL TRENT
Professional athlete. **EDUCATION:** AR Univ;Cks, bskbl player. **CAREER:** New York Nicks, bskbl player. **HONORS/ACHIEVEMENTS:** NBA's All-Rookie team. **BUSI-**

NESS ADDRESS: New York Nicks, Madison Sq Garden, 4 Pennsylvania Plaza, New York, NY 10001.

WALKER, DOUGLAS F.
Editor. **PERSONAL:** Born Dec 28, 1937, Detroit, MI; married Mattie Ruth. **EDUCATION:** LaSalle, BA; Wayne State U. **CAREER:** The Transition Newspaper, editor Model Neighborhood Health Prog; Library of Cong, Braille transcriber; Sound Off Newspaper, editor; author numerous articles for various publications. **ORGANIZATIONS:** Mem New Bethel Bapt Ch; mem Mayor's Com for Human Resources. **HONORS/ACHIEVEMENTS:** Recip Outstndg Newsp Publ of Year 1973; achievmnt award Lion's 1970; Citizen of Year Medal 1971.

WALKER, ERNEST L.
Electrical engineer. **PERSONAL:** Born Feb 12, 1941, Montrose, MS; married Vivian Huey. **EDUCATION:** Ind Inst of Technology, BSEE 1967; Syracuse Univ, MSEE 1973; NC State Univ, PhD 1982. **CAREER:** IBM Corp, sr assoc eng 1969-72, staff engr 1973-82; NC Central Univ, lecturer 1985-; IBM Corp, adv eng 1985-. **ORGANIZATIONS:** Sr mem IEEE; mem SIAM, OSA, AAAS. **HONORS/ACHIEVEMENTS:** 5 issued patents IBM Corp 1969-80; published papers; mem NY Acad of Sci 1984. **MILITARY SERVICE:** AUS e-4. **BUSINESS ADDRESS:** Advisory Engineer, IBM Corp, G37/002, Research Triangle Park, NC 27601.

WALKER, ERNESTEIN
Educator. **PERSONAL:** Born May 26, 1926, McDonough, GA; married Solomon. **EDUCATION:** Spelman Coll, AB 1949; Atlanta U, MA 1953;Univ Edinburgh, 1958; Western Res U, PhD 1964. **CAREER:** Morgan State U, prof hist 1965-; SC State Coll, instr prof 1956-65; Fort Valley State Coll, instr 1955-56; KY State U, 1954-55. **ORGANIZATIONS:** Mem Am Hist Assn; Assn Study Afro Life & Hist; So Hist Assn; medieval acad pres Baltimore Chap Nat Alumnae Assn, Spelman Coll Publ, "Disestablishment of the Ch of Ireland", Jour Social Sci 1960; "Age of Metternick a study in nonmenclature" exploration educ 1962; "the influence of Lord Liverpool 1815-1827" Jour Higher Educ 1967; "The Struggle for Parliamentary Reform" 1977; "The Black Woman" The Black Am Ref Book 1976. **BUSINESS ADDRESS:** Morgan StateUniv, Baltimore, MD 21239.

WALKER, ETHEL PITTS
Business administrator, educator. **PERSONAL:** Born Feb 04, 1943, Tulsa, OK; daughter of Opie Donnell Pitts; married Phillip E Walker, Aug 06, 1977; children: Travis Donnell. **EDUCATION:** Lincoln Univ MO, BS Ed 1964; Univ of CO, MA Speech & Drama 1965; Univ of MO Columbia, PhD Theatre 1975. **CAREER:** Southern Univ Baton Rouge LA, instr 1965-68; Lincoln Univ Jefferson City MO, asst prof 1968-77; Univ of IL Urbana, asst prof 1977-79; Laney Coll Oakland CA, instr 1979-80; African Amer Drama Co San Francisco, exec dir 1980-; Univ of CA Berkeley, asst prof 1988; Wayne State Univ, visiting asst prof 1988-89. **ORGANIZATIONS:** Mem 1984-85, chmn 1985- Amer Theatre Assoc, Natl Assoc of Dramatic & Speech Arts, Theta Alpha Phi Dramatic Frat, Speech Commun of Amer, Zeta Phi Beta; Third Baptist Church (San Fransisco), parents alliance, public relations dir; Children's Performance Center, pres of advisory council; Black Theatre Network, past pres 1985-88. **HONORS/ACHIEVEMENTS:** Ira Aldridge Scholarship 1963; Outstanding Ed 1974; Outstanding Instr Sr Class Lincoln Univ 1977; Best Actress Awd Lincoln Univ Stagecrafters 1963, Mother of the Year, Representative Teola Hunter of Michigan, 1989; "The Amer Negro Theatre" Black Amers in the Theatre; study, toured with Phelps/Stokes West African Heritage Seminar 1975; article "The Diction in Ed Bullins" In new Eng Winter, Encore 1977; Krigwa Players: A Theatre For, By, and About Black People in Theatre Journal 1989; directed, When the Jumbie Bird Calls at Bonstelle Theatre, Detroit MI 1989. **BUSINESS ADDRESS:** Executive Dir, African American Drama Co, 394 Fifth Ave, San Francisco, CA 94118.

WALKER, EUGENE HENRY
Physician. **PERSONAL:** Born Sep 29, 1925, Morristown, TN; son of Eugene Walker and Mabel Walker; married Dorothy Ransburg; children: Eugene C, Paula J, Erica J. **EDUCATION:** UCLA, BA 1950; Howard Univ Coll of Med, MD 1954; Univ of MN, Med Fellow 1955-58. **CAREER:** Private Practice, physician. **ORGANIZATIONS:** Diplomat Amer Bd Intl Med; fellow Amer Coll Chest Physicians; assoc fellow Amer Coll Physicians; mem Natl Medical Assn, Kappa Alpha Psi Fraternity. **MILITARY SERVICE:** USAF sgt 1943-46. **BUSINESS ADDRESS:** Physician, 231 W Vernon, Los Angeles, CA 90037.

WALKER, FRANCES
Educator. **PERSONAL:** Born Mar 06, 1924, Washington, DC; married H Chester Slocum (deceased); children: George Jeffrey Slocum. **EDUCATION:** Oberlin Conservatory, BMus 1945; Curtis Inst, 1945-46; Columbia Univ Teachers Coll, MA 1952, Professional diploma 1971. **CAREER:** Barber Scotia, 1948-49; Tougaloo Coll, 1949-50; Rutgers Univ, 1968-72; Univ of DE, 1968-79; Oberlin Conservatory, prof of pianoforte 1976-. **ORGANIZATIONS:** Pres Pi Kappa Lambda Theta Chap 1983-85. **HONORS/ACHIEVEMENTS:** Achievement Awd Natl Assoc of Negro Musicians 1979, 1985; Lorain Co Women of Achievement Award 1984. **BUSINESS ADDRESS:** Professor of Pianoforte, Oberlin Coll Conserv of Music, Oberlin, OH 44074.

WALKER, FRANK
Schedule clerk, dispatcher, expediter. **PERSONAL:** Born 1934; children: 4 Children. **EDUCATION:** Berkshire Comm Coll, 1969. **CAREER:** GE Co Pittsfield MA, schedule clk, dispatcher, expediter, stockkeeper 1942-. **ORGANIZATIONS:** Dir Greater Pittsfield Urban Coalition; dir Rev Samuel Harrison Non-Profit Housing Corp; dir Berkshire Council MA Commn Against Discrimination; dir Black Ecumenical Commn; chmn Social Relations Com of First Meth Ch; mem Pittsfield Area Council of Chs; pres Berkshire Co Br NAACP; pres New Eng Regnl Conf NAACP; mem Mayors Bi-Racial Com Pittsfield; chmn exec bd New Eng Regional NAACP; pres Berkshire Ebony Club Inc. **HONORS/ACHIEVEMENTS:** Recip citation in Bettering Comm & Racial Relatns in New Eng Region Berkshire Ebony Club; citation New Eng Regional NAACP; citation Berkshire Co NAACP; originator Black is Beautiful contest & Miss Black Teenager contest Berkshire Co Black Festival. **MILITARY SERVICE:** AUS 1943-46.

WALKER, G. EDWARD
Physician. **PERSONAL:** Born Apr 22, 1942, Waynesville, NC; married Patricia; children: Gregory, Michael. **EDUCATION:** BC Central U, BS 1964; Meharry Med Coll, MD 1968. **CAREER:** Physician, Self-emplyd; SW Comm Hosp; Crawford W Long Hosp; GA Bapt Hosp; Meharry Med Coll, chf res 1971-72. **ORGANIZATIONS:** Mem adv panel Clark Coll Sch Med Tech; Nat Med Assn; GA State Med Assn; Atlanta Med Assn; Med Assn GA; mem Atlanta City Club. **HONORS/ACHIEVEMENTS:** Distgsd serv medal USAF 1974. **MILITARY SERVICE:** USAF MC maj 1972-74. **BUSINESS ADDRESS:** 401 Peachtree 707, Atlanta, GA 30308.

WALKER, GARY S.
Attorney, appointed government official. **PERSONAL:** Born May 14, 1947, Atlanta, GA; married Carolyn Smith. **EDUCATION:** Morehouse Coll, BA History (with Honors) 1968; Howard Univ School of Law Washington DC, JD (with Honors) 1973; Univ of GA Atlanta, Cert Systematic Counseling Skills 1975; Natl Coll of Criminal Defense Lawyers & Public Defenders, Cert Trial Prep & Presentation 1976. **CAREER:** Dept of HUD, investigation & prep asst 1972-73; Child Advocate Fulton Cty Juvenile Court, represented juveniles or indigent parents on matters coming underthe jurisdiction of the court 1975-76; Fulton Cty Public Defender's Office, represented indigent defendants charged with violations of state criminal laws 1976-77; City of Atlanta Public Defenders Office, 1st asst public defencer 1977; City of Atlanta GA, purchasing task force 1982, records mgmt admin bd 1983-; Office of City Attny, asst city attny. **ORGANIZATIONS:** Mem Natl Assoc for the Advancement of Colored People 1968-, Delta Theta Phi Law Frat 1972-, Gate City Bar Assoc, 1975-, Atlanta Bar Assoc 1975-, Amer Bar Assoc 1975-, State Bar of GA 1975-, Warren United Meth Church Bd of Admin 1976-80, Neighborhood Planning Unit S 1977-82, Local Govt Sect State Bar of GA1977-, Urban Govt Sect Amer Bar Assoc 1977-, Natl Bar Assoc, 1980-, Neighborhood Planning UnitUniv 1982-, Heritage Valley Neighborhood Assoc 1982-, Natl Forum for Black Public Admin 1984-; vice chmn Comm Affairs Comm Gate City Bar Assoc 1984-85; coach Cascade Youth Assoc Little League 1984; chmn Law Day Comm Gate City Bar Assoc 1985. **HONORS/ACHIEVEMENTS:** Cert of Merit Howard Univ School of Law 1972; Plaque Acknowledgement of Participation Howard Univ School of Law Moot Court Team 1973; 1st Black Child Advocate Fulton Cty, Juvenile Court 1976; Cert of Appreciation Gate City Bar Assoc 1982; 1st Place Student Photography Exhibit Southeastern Ctr for the Photographic Arts 1983; Speaker City County Attnys Inst 1983, Natl United Affiliated Beverage Assoc 1984; Seminar Panelist Natl Forum for Black Public Admin 1984; Cert of Appreciation Cascade Youth Assoc 1984. **BUSINESS ADDRESS:** Assistant City Attorney, City of Atlanta, 1100 S Omni Intl, Atlanta, GA 30335.

WALKER, GEORGE EDWARD
Art director. **PERSONAL:** Born May 16, 1940, Memphis, TN; married Delores Prince; children: Genen Delise, Darren George Edward, Devin George Edward. **EDUCATION:** Memphis State Univ, BFA, MA. **CAREER:** Freelance designer & artist 1969-71; NAACP (Memphis Branch) art dir, 1977-; Graphic Arts Memphis, owner/artist 1978-; Shelby State Comm Coll, art dir. **ORGANIZATIONS:** Mem Alpha Phi Alpha 1977. **HONORS/ACHIEVEMENTS:** Designer & Publ "Our Precious Baby" (1st complete black baby book) 1971; Pyramid Award Advertising Fedn Memphis 1972 & 1977; Editirial Distinct (design) SD Warren Co 1978. **MILITARY SERVICE:** AUS 1958-61. **BUSINESS ADDRESS:** Dir Graphic Arts, Shelby State College, PO Box 40568, Memphis, TN 38106.

WALKER, GEORGE RAYMOND
Educator. **PERSONAL:** Born Oct 13, 1936, Little Rock, AR. **EDUCATION:** San Franc State U, BA 1959;Univ of So CA, MS 1967;Univ of So CA, EdD 1972. **CAREER:** CA State Univ Dominguez Hills, dean School of Educ 1976-; CA State Univ Pomona, prof of educ 1972-76; US Dependent Schools Spain, dir of curriculum 1967-69; US Dependent Schools Germany, teacher 1962-67; San Francisco City Schools, teacher 1959-62; Compton Coll Compton CA, instr 1970; CA Commn for Teacher Prep & Licensing, consultant 1971-72. **ORGANIZATIONS:** Pres CSUDH Chap Phi Delta Kappa 1977-78; mem profs of secondary educ Nat Assn of Secondary Sch Prin 1979-80; mem Alpha Phi Alpha Frat. **HONORS/ACHIEVEMENTS:** Rosenwald Award 1960; Ambassador's Award German-Am Serv 1964; Am Studies Hon AwardUniv of Notre Dame 1968; cert of apprec Research Utilization Bd State of CA 1977. **BUSINESS ADDRESS:** 1000 E Victoria St, Carson, CA 90747.

WALKER, GEORGE T.
Composer, pianist, eduator. **PERSONAL:** Born Jun 22, 1922, Washington, DC; son of Dr George T Walker and Rosa K Walker; divorced; children: Gregory, Ian. **EDUCATION:** Oberlin Coll, Mus B, 1941; Curtis Inst of Music, Artist Diploma, 1945; Univ of Rochester, DMA, 1957; Lafayette Coll, Hon Dr Fine Arts, 1982; Oberlin Coll, Hon Dr Music, 1983. **CAREER:** Smith Coll, prof, 1961; Univ of Colorado, prof, 1968; Univ of Delaware, prof, 1975; Peabody Inst of Johns Hopkins Univ, 1975-78; Rutgers Univ, 1969-. **ORGANIZATIONS:** New York City; mem ASCAP, Amer Symphony League. **HONORS/ACHIEVEMENTS:** Fulbright Fellow, 1957; John Hay Whitney Fellow, 1958; Rockefeller Fellow, 1972, 1975; Guggenheim Fellow, 1969; Amer Acad & Inst of Arts & Letters Award, 1981; Koussevitsky Prize, 1988; Guggenheim Fellow 1988. **BUSINESS ADDRESS:** Distinguished Professor, Rutgers Univ, Music Dept, Newark, NJ 07102.

WALKER, GROVER P.
Attorney, financial planner. **PERSONAL:** Born Jan 14, 1941, Chicago, IL; divorced; children: Faye Jasmine. **EDUCATION:** Univ MO, AB (summa cum laude) 1963; UCLA, JD Victor Wilson Scholar 1967; Harvard Bus Sch, MBA 1971. **CAREER:** CA State Atty Gen, deputy atty gen 1968-69; Rand Corp, consult 1969; McKinsey & Co, internatl consult 1970; Exxon Corp, corp atty 1971-73; Johnson Prod Co, gen corp counsel 1973-75; LA State Univ, asst prof law & bus admin 1973; Chicago State Univ, 1974; Private Practice, financial planning 1975-. **ORGANIZATIONS:** Mem IL Bar Assoc 1974; mem FL Bar Assn 1976; mem City of Miami FL Zoning Bd 1977-79; mem of bd New Wash Hghts Comm Devel Corp 1976-77; Total Care Home Health Agency FL 1976-77; mem Amer, Natl, CA, IL, Cook Co & Chicago Bar Assns; Harvard Bus Sch Century Club; Harvard Club Chicago; PAD Legal Frat; bd mem Afro-Amer Family Comm Serv; elected co-chmn Afro-Amer Student Union Harvard Bus Sch 1969; exec dir Black Agenda 1982-84. **HONORS/ACHIEVEMENTS:** Harvard Leadership Awd 1970; Intl Men of Achievement 1977; Outstanding Young Men of Amer 1971; Leaders Black Amer 1973; Who's Who in CA 1981. **BUSINESS ADDRESS:** Attorney/Financial Planner, 4154 W Washington Blvd, Los Angeles, CA 90018.

WALKER, HERSCHEL
Professional athlete. **PERSONAL:** Born 1962, Wrightsville, GA; married Cindy De An-

gelis. **EDUCATION:** Univ of GA, attended. **CAREER:** Univ of GA, football player; NJ Generals, professional football player; Diversified Builders Inc Athens GA, owner; Dallas Cowboys, professional football player. **HONORS/ACHIEVEMENTS:** Heisman Trophy 1982; 3 times All Amer; USFL Outstanding Running Back 1983; League leading rusher 1983, 85; voted MVP 1985.

WALKER, HORACE L.
Business executive. **PERSONAL:** Born Apr 07, 1938, Augusta, GA; married Mercedes; children: Lisa, Tod, Jana. **EDUCATION:** MI State Univ, BA, MA 1963; Harvard Univ, Prgm Mgmt Devel 1973. **CAREER:** Ford Motor Co, labor rel rep/coll recruit/salary admin 1965-69; Cummins Engine Co, dir empl/personnel sys devel/mgr human resources 1971-75; Crocker Natl Bank, vice pres staffing/orgn planning 1975, vice pres urban affairs 1976-, vice pres business devel. **ORGANIZATIONS:** Pres Urban Bankers 1978; Tri Valley Spec Olympics 1976-; Connecting Links 1985-; John Rossi Youth Foundation 1983-; CA Bankers Assn; Natl Business League; NEA; Urban Devel Com Amer Bankers Assn; Interracial Cncl for Bus Opportunity; LA Regional Purch Cncl; Recruitment Training Prgm; Black BusinessmenAssn of LA; Regional Purchasing Cncl Recruit Training Prgm; Black Businessmen Assn of LA; The Brotherhood Crusade Amer Heart Assn; life mem NAACP;Giant Step; bd dir LA Urban League; Black Exec Exchng Prgm; MI State Univ Varsity Alumni Club; bd dir Tri Valley Balck Families Museum Proj; MI State Univ Coll of Edn; MI State Univ Devel Cncl; bd dir LA Cncl for Peace & Equality in Edn; consult Watts Comm Orchestra & Olympic Com; United Negro Coll Fund; Big Ten; Councl for Econ Priority Booker T Washington Com Serv Cntr; Natl Assn for Sickle Cell Disease; Help Line; Pasadena Urban Coalition; Harvard Bus Sch Black Alumni Assn; CA St Univ (Long Beach) Pilot Prgm Organ for Bus Educ & Community Advancement; Young Exec Club of San Francisco. **HONORS/ACHIEVEMENTS:** All Star Basketball Team Russia & Europe 1961; S Amer 1960; All Amer & JS Basketball 1954-56; All Big Ten MSU 1960; AAU All Amer 1961; Midwest Basketball League All Stars 1964/1966; AAU Coach of the Year 1965; Amer Splst Prgm Chile 1967; Splst Prgm Belgium 1968. **BUSINESS ADDRESS:** Vice Pres Business Development, Crocker Nat'l Bank, 333 S Grand Ave, Los Angeles, CA 90071.

WALKER, HOWARD KENT
Ambassador/director. **PERSONAL:** Born Dec 03, 1935, Newport News, VA; son of William Walker and Jean Walker; married Terry B Taylor; children: Gregory, Wendy. **EDUCATION:** Univ of MI, AB (High Honors) 1957, MA 1958; Boston Univ, PhD 1968. **CAREER:** George Washington Univ, assoc prof 1968-70; American Consulate Kaduna, consul 1970-73; Dept of State, desk officer 1973-75; American Embassy Amman, political counselor 1975-77; American Embassy Dai es Salaam, dep chief of mission 1977-79; American Embassy Pretoria, deputy chief of mission 1979-82; American Embassy Lome, ambassador to Togo 1982-84; Foreign Affairs Fellow, 1984-85; Dept of State, dir, Office of West Africa, 1985-87; sr inspector, Office of Inspector General, Dept of State, 1987-89. **HONORS/ACHIEVEMENTS:** African Studies Fellow Boston Univ 1958-60; Foreign Affairs Fellow Center for the Study of Foreign Affairs Foreign Serv Inst 1984-85. **MILITARY SERVICE:** USAF 1st Lt 2 1/2 years. **BUSINESS ADDRESS:** Ambassador/Dir, State Dept/Office of W Africa, Dept of State (AF1W), Washington, DC 20520.

WALKER, J. WILBUR
Retired educational administrator. **PERSONAL:** Born Jun 23, 1912, Troy, AL; married Ollie Elizabeth Bridges. **EDUCATION:** Paine Coll Augusta GA, AB 1938; Atlanta Univ, MEd 1947. **CAREER:** Elementary Schools, asst principal/teacher 1939; Gower Elementary School, Oscar Elementary School, Union Elementary School, supvr principal 1939-60; Washington High of Emen School, principalship 1960-70; Gower Neighborhood Assn Inc, community volunteer/chairperson. **ORGANIZATIONS:** Advisor to Mayor & City Officials of Greenville SC 1939-; mem Natl Ed Assn 1939-72, Palmetto Ed Assn 1939-69, Natl Dept of Elementary School Principals 195-72, Natl Assn of Secondary School Principals 1960-; bd of dir St Anthony's Catholic Church 1967-70; mem SC Ed Assn 1970-79; bd of dir Gower Neighborhood Assoc Inc 1972-, Western Carolina Clients Council 1979-; mem City of Greenville Comm Devel Advisory Comm 1980-; bd of dir Legal Serv of Western Carolina 1981-, The Human Endeavor Inc 1981-, Greenville Comm Housing Resource Bd Inc 1982-, ACLU 1983-; life mem Natl Assn for the Advancement of Colored People; mem Alpha Phi Alpha Fraternity Inc, Gamma Gamma Lambda Chapt; life mem Young Laymen Christian Methodist Church, Natl Congress of Parents & Teachers Assn. **HONORS/ACHIEVEMENTS:** Organized 1st Parent Teacher Assn for Public Schools in Greenville County 1939, State-wide Elementary School Principals Assn in SC 1950; Organized Operation New Broom Clean Sweep Program 1979, Operation New Broom Clean Sweep Camera 1979; Received Most Prestigious Comm Person Award presented by Sunbelt Human Advancement Resources Inc 1980; Nominated for the Jefferson Award by the City of Greenville to persons contributing distinguished community serv; I Care Award SC Gov Volunteer Award Hon Richard W Riley Gov; The Lou Rawls 1986 Met Award; The Human Relations Commission's R Cooper White, Mayor Award, 1988; Mayor's Achievement Award, 1989; Gower Neighborhood Assn Award, 1988; Phillis Wheatley Community Center Post Fellows Assn Scholarship; A Community Profile: J Wilbur Walker Involvement in Race Relations Video Presentation, 1989. **HOME ADDRESS:** 214 N Leach St, Greenville, SC 29601.

WALKER, JAMES
Business executive, former elected official. **PERSONAL:** Born Jan 24, 1926, Greenville, SC; son of James Booker Walker and Della Palmore; married Matilda Roumania Peters; children: James G, Frances D. **EDUCATION:** Univ of Illinois, AB, 1954, MS, 1955; Univ of Maryland, further study; Johns Hopkins Univ, further study. **CAREER:** Univ of Illinois, grad asst, 1954-55; Tuskegee Inst, Morgan State, Hampton Jr Coll, math instructor, 1955-60; District of Columbia, Government-DC Public Schools, research & statistics, 1960-77; The Chelsea School, sub teacher, teacher, 1978-83. **ORGANIZATIONS:** Vice chmn, ANC Comm 4A, 1985-; treasurer, Walker Pharmacy Inc, 1983-; dir, Walker Pharmacy Inc, 1983-; commr, 4A-03, 1977; chmn, ANC Comm 4A, 1980; treasurer, ANC Comm 4A, 1982; sec, ANC Comm 4A, 1984. **HONORS/ACHIEVEMENTS:** Fellowship James Fund-Tuskegee Inst 1955. **MILITARY SERVICE:** USN & USAF; Good Conduct Medal; Asiatic Pacific Medal; Victory Medal. **HOME ADDRESS:** 1412 Whittier Place NW, Washington, DC 20012. **BUSINESS ADDRESS:** Treasurer, Walker Pharmacy Inc, 7849 Eastern Ave, Silver Spring, MD 20910.

WALKER, JAMES C.
Actor, comedian. **PERSONAL:** Born Jun 25, 1947, Bronx, NY. **CAREER:** Professionally known as Jimmy Walker; commenced career age 18 stand-up comic, disc jockey/engr; motion pictures, Let's Do It Again, Concorde-Airport '79, Airplane, Water, Deadly Serious, My African Adventure; television, Good Times, At Ease, Bustin' Loose, The Greatest Thing That Almost Happened, Murder Can Hurt You;variety shows, Bob Hope, Dean Martin, Mac Davis, Donny & Marie, Gladys Knight & The Pips, Cher, John Davidson; talk shows, The Tonight Show, Merv Griffin, JohnDavidson, Dinah, Mike Douglas; recordings, Dyn-o-mite (Buddah Records); frequent guest on game shows, Hollywood Squares, Celebrity Sweepstakes, Match Game; personal appearances at comedy clubs, colls and theatres. **HONORS/ACHIEVEMENTS:** Most Popular TV Performer Family Circle Mag 1975; Hon Chmn LA Free Clinic 1977; Time Mag Comedian of the Decade; various awds from civic groups in regard to role as JJ Evans. **BUSINESS ADDRESS:** Genl Management Corp, 9000 Sunset Blvd Ste 400, Los Angeles, CA 90069.

WALKER, JAMES ZELL, II
Editor, business executive. **PERSONAL:** Born Mar 23, 1932, Birmingham; married Jeanette Adams; children: Jimmy Zelbulg, Debra Leartine, Ronnetta Marie, Freda Michetta, James, III. **EDUCATION:** Jr San Francisco Coll, 1953-55. **CAREER:** Clarion Defender Newspaper, editor; Knockout Indstrs Inc, pres; KGAR Radio, weekend disk jockey 1968-76; KNEY Radio, talk show host 1977; Organic & Bio Degradable Cleanser, mfr. **ORGANIZATIONS:** Voting mem Portland Local 8 & ILWU 1980; past trustee chmn Billy Webb IBPOE of W 1962-70; spnsr Campfire Bonnie Blue Birds; pres Jefferson PTA 1974-75, 1977-78; Portland City Club 1970; C of C 69 Fed Title 1 Mem 1973; co-chmn Pub Sch Career Educ 3 Yrs; bd mem Portland Br NAACP 1967; Jefferson Cluster Study Com; adv bd Beach Sch; adv com Jefferson High Portland Pub Sch; co-fndr Miss Tan Am Pageant 1965; spnsrd OR & WA, Blk Am Contest 1970-75; adv on 4 bds Portland YMCA 1959; n br Portland YMCA; Freedom Bnk of Fin 1968; fndr Jimmy Bang Bang Yth Found 1969; mem OR Black Caucus 1972; mason Odd Fellws Pact Inc 1972; Am Cancer Soc Neighborhood Chap 1978-80; mem Nat Busns Leg 1968; Nat Black Mfg 1977; chrtr Mem Albina Lions Club 1970; Cold Card Mem Billy Webb Elks Ldg; FiskUniv Boosters Club 1979; Jesuit HS Parents' Grp. **HONORS/ACHIEVEMENTS:** First Black nom maj Polit Party in OR GOP 1970; electd Precinct Ldr 4 dists; 1974 Delegate OR Dem Conv; Sponsor 4 Prize Winning Floats Portland RoseFestvl Parade 1968, 69, 70, 71; Spl Portland PMSC Awd 1973; Albina Women Leg Achvmt Awd 1972; 3 Time 100% UGN Portland Area Chmn 1970-73; Who's Who in Am 1975-80; Who's Who in the W & MW 1975-80; Who's Who in W Cst & Mfg 1976; Personalities of hte W & MW 1978-80; Men of Achvmt 1977; Golden Gloves 1953-54; Diamond Belt 1950; AAU Western Boxing Champ 1954; San Francisco Pacif NW Pro Boxing Champ 1958-63. **MILITARY SERVICE:** AUS s sgt 1950-53; 3 Purple Hearts Bronze Star; 5 Battle Awds. **BUSINESS ADDRESS:** PO Box 11095, Portland, OR 97211.

WALKER, JERRY EUCLID
Educational administrator. **PERSONAL:** Born Sep 15, 1932, Statesbury, WV; married Patricia A; children: Faye L, Jonathan L, Sue L. **EDUCATION:** Univ of MD ES, BA 1958; Case-Western Res U, MSSA 1962. **CAREER:** Los Rios Comm Coll Dist, v chancellor-personnel 1974-; Sears Roebuck & Co, corporate emplymnt speclst 1966-74; Sears Roebuck & Co Cleveland OH, dir urban affairs; Lorain Co OH, exec dir econ devel; Family Serv Assn Mansfield OH, acting dir; OH State Reformatory Mansfield, dir soc serv 1958. **ORGANIZATIONS:** Bd of dirs Council on Blacks in Am Affairs 1979; mem NAACP; mem Urban League bd of dirs Cuyahoga Co Red Cross 1967; bd of dirs Half-way House for Boys 1968. **MILITARY SERVICE:** USAF a-1c 1949-52. **BUSINESS ADDRESS:** Los Rios Comm Coll, Dist 1919 Spanos, Sacramento, CA 95825.

WALKER, JIMMIE
Director. **PERSONAL:** Born Nov 04, 1945, Mendenhall, MS; married Virginia Finley; children: Baron, Lorria, Erica. **EDUCATION:** Prentiss Jr Coll Prentiss MS, AA 1967; LA Bapt Coll, BA 1969. **CAREER:** Farish St Br YMCA Jackson MS, exec dir 1977-; Valley N Family Br YMCA Jackson, exec dir 1978-; Farish St YMCA, prog dir 1974-77; Voice of Calvary Mendenhall MS, rec dir/pub rel Dir 1973-74; Campus Crusade for Christ, natl Cocoord Black campus ministry 1969-73. **ORGANIZATIONS:** Sec Assn Professional Dir Cluster 1974; bd mem Farish St Historic Dist Revitalizatn Assn 1980; mem Noon Optimist Club of Jackson 1980; bd mem Youth for Christ 1975-; bd mem S Cntrl Rural Health Assn 1979-; bd mem Voice of Calvary Ministeries 1980. **HONORS/ACHIEVEMENTS:** Outstndg basketball plyr Sports Writers Assn So CA 1969; Sports Ambassador S Pacific 1970; inductee Los Angeles Bapt Coll Hall of Fame 1971. **BUSINESS ADDRESS:** Farish St Br YMCA, 806 N Farish St, Jackson, MS 39202.

WALKER, JOE
Journalist. **PERSONAL:** Born Mar 11, 1934, Buffalo, NY; son of Luther Walker and Emma Parker Walker; married Isabel Castro; children: Joseph. **EDUCATION:** Champlain Coll, 1952-53; Adelphi Coll, 1953-55. **CAREER:** Local 144 Hotel Hospital Nursing Home & Allied Serv Union SEIU AFL-CIO, editor pub relations dir; Workers Defense League, researcher, 1978-79; New York Bur Bililian News, chief journalist, 1968-77; Third World Comm Vanguard, producer, 1973-77; WBAI Radio; Drug & Hospital Union New York City, editor of pubs, 1963-68; Muhammad Speaks, staff correspondent, 1962-63; Empire Star Weekly Buffalo, ed-in-chief, 1961-62, reporter feature writer, columnist, 1957-61. **ORGANIZATIONS:** Pres, US Chapter Inter Org of Journalists, 1971-73; mem, IOJ Harlem Writers Guild; producer moderator Buffalo Roundtable radio WUFO Buffalo, 1961-62; past vice pres, exec bd mem, Afro-Amer Labor Council, 1964-73; pub inf dir, Tri-Partisan Masten Dist Com for Rep Govt, 1957-62; public relations dir, Civil Rights Party, 1960; mem, Harlem Anti-Colonial Comm, 1962-63; Julius Fucik Med Intl & Org of Journalist, 1976; pres, USA Chapter, Intl Org of Journalists, 1989-; chmn, bd of advisors, Natl Alliance of Third World Journalists, 1989-. **MILITARY SERVICE:** AUS pfc 1955-57. **HOME ADDRESS:** 334 E 108 St, # 18 F, New York, NY 10029. **BUSINESS ADDRESS:** Exec Asst to Pres, SEIU Local 114, Hotel, Hospital, Nursing Home Union, 233 W 49th St, New York, NY 10019.

WALKER, JOHN LESLIE
Banking executive. **PERSONAL:** Born May 04, 1933, York, SC; son of Walter Walker and Neely Walker; married Mary Alberta Carlton; children: John L. **EDUCATION:** Wilberforce Univ OH, BS 1956; Stonier Graduate School of Banking Rutgers Univ, 1972; Harvard Exec Seminar, 1978. **CAREER:** Cairo Chemical Bank, vice pres 1980-83; Paris Chemical Bank, vice pres 1978-80; Republic Natl Bank of New York, natl private banking officer of Middle East and Africa 1989-. **ORGANIZATIONS:** Mem Natl Bankers Assn 1973-78; fi-

nance sec United Black Men of Queens Co NY 1976-78; treasurer Urban Bankers Coalition 1977-78; mem Kappa Alpha Psi Fraternity; mem Prince Hall Masons; mem NAACP; mem Urban League; bd of trustees Wilberforce Univ; bd mem Jamaica Serv Program for Older Adults. **HONORS/ACHIEVEMENTS:** Good Conduct Medal AUS 1958; Serv Award United Black Men of Queens Co 1978. **MILITARY SERVICE:** AUS sgt 1956-58. **BUSINESS ADDRESS:** First Vice-President, Republic Natl Bank of New York, 452 Fifth Ave, 6th Fl, New York, NY 10018.

WALKER, JOHN T.
Clergyman. **PERSONAL:** Born Jul 27, 1925, Barnesville, GA; son of Joseph Walker and Mattie Wyche Walker; married Rosa Maria Flores; children: Thomas, Ana Maria, Charles. **EDUCATION:** Wayne State Univ, BA 1951; VA-Theological Seminary, M Div 1954; Interdenominational Theological Center, DD 1975; VA Theological Seminary, D Humane Letters 1978; Georgetown Univ, D Laws 1978; Wayne State Univ, DHumane Letters 1981; Univ of MD, D Humane Letters 1986; Washington Coll, D Humane Letters 1987, Princeton Univ, D.D., 1989. **CAREER:** St Mary's Church Detroit, rector 1954-57; St Paul's School NH, teacher 1957-64; WA Cathedral, canon 1966-71; Diocese of WA, suffragan bishop 1974-76, bishop coadjutor 1976-77; Bishop of Washington, 1977-; dean Washington Cathedral, 1978-. **ORGANIZATIONS:** First chmn Interfaith Conf of Met DC Urban Bishops Coalition 1976; bd mem VA Theological Seminary; chmn bd mem St Paul's School Concord NH, Black Student Fund; chmn bd Africare 1977-, Eisenhower Foundation 1985-; mem Standing Commn on Peace 1986-. **HONORS/ACHIEVEMENTS:** Serv award Natl Conf of Christians & Jews 1978; Washingtonian of the Year Washingtonia Magazine 1981; Distinguished Serv Award Africare 1981. **BUSINESS ADDRESS:** Dean of Washington Cathedral, & Episcopal Bishop of Wash, Episcopal Church House, Mt St Alban, Washington, DC 20016.

WALKER, JOSEPH
General construction contractor. **CAREER:** Original Construction Co, Inc, Detroit MI, chief executive, 1969—. **BUSINESS ADDRESS:** Original Construction Co, Inc, 16501 Wyoming, Detroit, MI 48221. *

WALKER, JOSEPH A.
Playwright. **PERSONAL:** Born Feb 23, 1935, Washington, DC; son of Joseph Walker and Florine Walker; married Barbara Brown (divorced 1965); married Dorothy A Dinroe, 1970. **EDUCATION:** Howard University, BA, 1956; Catholic University of America, MFA, 1970; New York University, PhD. **CAREER:** Educator, actor, director, playwright, choreographer, producer; worked as taxi driver, salesman, postal clerk; English teacher at junior high and high schools in Washington, DC, and New York City; actor, set designer, and playwright in New York City, beginning 1967; Negro Ensemble Co, New York City, playwright, director, and choreographer, beginning 1969; Yale University, New Haven CT, playwright-in-residence, 1970-71; City College of City University of New York, New York City, currently instructor; Howard University, Washington DC, currently instructor of advanced acting and playwriting. **HONORS/ACHIEVEMENTS:** Obie Award, 1971, Antoinette Perry (Tony) Award, 1973, Elizabeth Hull-Kate Award from Dramatists Guild, First Annual Audelco Award, John Gassner Award from Outer Circle, Drama Desk Award, Black Rose Award, all for the play "The River Niger"; Rockefeller Foundation grant, 1979. **MILITARY SERVICE:** US Air Force; became second lieutenant. **BUSINESS ADDRESS:** Department of Speech and Theatre, City College of the City University of New York, New York, NY 10031. *

WALKER, KENNETH R.
Reporter. **PERSONAL:** Born Aug 17, 1951, Washington, DC; divorced. **EDUCATION:** Catholic Univ of Amer. **CAREER:** Washington Star Newspaper, natl affairs journalist/staff reporter 1969-; WJZ-TV Baltimore MD, prog moderator/asst producer 1978-79. **ORGANIZATIONS:** Exec vice pres Nat Media Sys Inc 1970-74; mem bd of dir Townsend Reading Ctr Inc 1976. **HONORS/ACHIEVEMENTS:** Recip Wash StarUniv Schlrshp 1969; first pl Wash-Baltimore Newsppr Guild Award 1977. **BUSINESS ADDRESS:** 225 Virginia Ave SE, Washington, DC.

WALKER, KENNETH R.
Educator. **PERSONAL:** Born Dec 19, 1930, East Providence, RI; son of Frank and Lillian; married Gail Beverly Smith; children: Kenneth Jr, Michele, Leanne. **EDUCATION:** Providence Coll, AB 1957; Rhode Island Coll, MEd, 1962; Boston Univ, EdD, 1976; Providence Coll, Hon SocD, 1983. **CAREER:** East Providence Rhode Island School Dept, teacher, 1957-68, asst principal, 1968-70; Rhode Island Coll, assoc prof, 1970-, dir, Early Enrollment Program. **ORGANIZATIONS:** Consult HEW Title IV; mem Guidance & Personnel Assn; Intl Assn of Approved Basketball Officials; Collegiate Basketball Officials Assn; Assn Curriculum Devel Specialist; Amer Fedn Teachers; Rhode Island State Parole Bd; consult, Rhode Island State Dept Educ; Omega Psi Phi Fraternity; mem, Governor's Task Force, 1991 Report on Education Rhode Island. **HONORS/ACHIEVEMENTS:** Exemplary Citizenship Award, 1974; IBA Man of Year Award, 1967; Recip Afro-Am Award EPHS, 1971; Serv to Youth Award No Kingston Jr HS 1969; RI Big Brother of Yr Award, 1963; Educ Award NAACP, 1980; East Providence High School Hall of Fame, 1987. **MILITARY SERVICE:** AUS Sgt 1951-53. **HOME ADDRESS:** 399 Brown St, East Providence, RI 02914. **BUSINESS ADDRESS:** Dir Early Enrollment Program, Rhode Island College, 600 Mt Pleasant Ave, Providence, RI 02908.

WALKER, LARRY
Construction executive. **CAREER:** Pyramid Industries Inc, Riverdale IL, chief executive, 1979—. **BUSINESS ADDRESS:** Pyramid Industries Inc., 14225 S Halstead, Riverdale, IL 60627. *

WALKER, LARRY M.
Artist, educator. **PERSONAL:** Born Oct 22, 1935, Franklin, GA; son of W B Walker and Cassandra Walker; married Gwendolyn Elaine Howell; children: Dana, Larry, Kara. **EDUCATION:** BS 1958; Wayne State Univ, MA 1963. **CAREER:** Coll of Pacific, Univ of Pacific, prof chmn dept of art; Detroit Public School System, art instructor 1958-64; Oakland Museum's Collectors Gallery, practicing affiliated artist; 28 one-man exhibitions; 58 group exhibitions; GA State Univ Dept of Art, prof, chmn 1983-85; GA State Univ School of Art & Design, prof, dir 1985-. **ORGANIZATIONS:** Mem 1976-77, chmn 1978-80 Stockton Arts Comm; bd dir 1976-80, chmn 1978-79 Natl Council of Art Admins; mem Natl Assoc of Schools of Art & Design 1983-, Marta Arts Council 1983-; mem, bd dir, sec 1985, chmn 1986, 1987 Natl Council of Art Admins; bd dir Atlanta Arts Festival 1986-; advisory council Binney & Smith Co 1986-; Dekalb Council for the Arts, 1987, pres, 1989. **HONORS/ACHIEVEMENTS:** Recipient Pacific Family Award 1968; Distinguished Faculty Award 1975; over 80 awards from 100 juried art exhibits; listed in The Black Artist on Art, The Afro-Amer Slide Coll, Black Professional in Predominently White Educ Inst, Community Leaders & Noteworthy Amer 1975-76; Black Arts Quarterly Summer 1978; public collections; Univ of the Pacific & Oakland Art Museum CA State Univ Stanislaus City of Stockton; Pioneer Museum & Haggin Gallery; publications, "Univ Art Classes for Children" School Arts Magazine, "Pioneer, Promote & Prosper, A View on the Visual Arts in Higher Educ" The Visual Arts in the Ninth Decade NCAA 1980; article "Site Sculpture" Atlanta Arts Festival; "The State of the Arts in San Joaquin County" 1981, "San Joaquin County Arts Council" reports by L Walker & C Watanabe 1982; Award for Leadership & Appreciation of Serv to the Stockton Arts Commn Annual Recognition Awards Program, 1981; Plaque for Serv to the Arts Community Stockton City Council, 1981; Certificate of Appreciation for Serv to the Community Involvement Program Univ of the Pacific, 1982; Founders Wall Plaque La Guardia HS of the Arts NYC; Certificate of Appreciation, Natl Council of Art Admin, 1988. **BUSINESS ADDRESS:** Director, Professor, Georgia State University, School of Art & Design, University Plaza, Atlanta, GA 30303.

WALKER, LARRY VAUGHN
Educational administrator. **PERSONAL:** Born Aug 08, 1939, Meridian, MS; children: Derrick B, Terri L. **EDUCATION:** Jackson State Coll, MS Sci 1960; Fisk Univ, MA Sci 1964; Roosevelt Univ, MST Chem 1974; Northern IL Univ, EdD Ed Adm 1983. **CAREER:** Wayne Cty Schools, teacher 1961-65; Proviso Twp HS, teacher 1965-74; Proviso Twp HS, dean, asst principal 1974-82; Oak Park & River Forest HS, assoc principal 1982-. **ORGANIZATIONS:** Bd mem Family Serv & Mental Health Oak Park 1982-; presenter Natl Assoc of Secondary School Principals 1985; bd mem Oak Park YMCA 1985-. **HONORS/ACHIEVEMENTS:** NSF Summer Inst Dillard Univ 1963; NSF Acad Year Inst Fisk Univ 1963-64. **BUSINESS ADDRESS:** Assoc Principal Pupil Service, Oak Park-River Forest High Sch, 201 N Scoville, Oak Park, IL 60302.

WALKER, LEE H.
Business executive. **PERSONAL:** Born Oct 06, 1938, Troy, AL; married Audrey Davis. **EDUCATION:** AL State; Fordham U, BA 1975. **CAREER:** Sears Roebuck & Co Chicago IL, grp dist mgr 1970-; Winston-Muss Corp NY, dir employee relation 1961-70; Am Prog of NYC, ins 1960-61. **ORGANIZATIONS:** Mem Sears Roebuck & Co contrib com; Am Mgmt Assn; mem bd AIM; Urban Problems Com 1968-69; mem Nat Urban League Guild NYC; Westchester Co blk rep; NAACP past vice pres Brooklyn Br; AIM bd dirs 1970, chmn 1970-72; past pres political club Rep; past mem Local Draft Bd 1969-72. **HONORS/ACHIEVEMENTS:** Recip Black Achievers in Industry Award Harlem Br YMCA 1972; distin serv award New Rochelle Br NAACP 1967. **BUSINESS ADDRESS:** Sears Tower, Chicago, IL.

WALKER, LEROY TASHREAU
University chancellor, coach. **PERSONAL:** Born Jun 14, 1918, Atlanta, GA; widowed; children: LeRoy, Carolyn. **EDUCATION:** Benedict Coll, BS 1940; Columbia Univ, MA 1941; NY Univ, PhD 1957. **CAREER:** Benedict Coll Columbia SC, chmn phys educ, coach basketball, football, track & field 1941-42; Bishop Coll Marshall TX, chmn phys dept, coach basketball, football, track & field 1942-43; Prairie View State Univ, 1943-45; NC Central Univ Durham, chmn phys dept, coach basketball, football, track & field 1945-73, vchancellor for univ relations 1974-83, chancellor 1983-. **ORGANIZATIONS:** Educ spec Cultural Exchange Prog Dept State 1959,60,62; dir prog plnng Peace Corps Africa 1966-68; coach Ethipoian & Israeli teams Olympic Games Rome 1960; adviser track & field teams throughout world; mem US Collegiate Sports Council 1972; chmn Coll Commrs Assn 1971-74; chmn track & field com Athletic Union USA 1973-75; head coach US Track & Field Team Olympic Games Montreal 1976; bd dirs US Olympic Com author Manual of Adapted Physical Educ 1960;, Physical Educ for the Exceptional Student 1964, Championship Tech in Track & Field 1969; bd dirs USA China Relations Com; mem AAHPERD 1972, NEA, US Track Coaches Assn, Intl Assn Athletic Fedns, Sigma Delta Psi, Alpha Phi Omega, Omega Psi Phi. **HONORS/ACHIEVEMENTS:** Recipient James E Shepard Outstanding Teacher Awd Hamilton Watch Co 1964; Achievement Awd Central Intercollegiate Athletic Assn 1967; Disting Alumnus Awd Benedict Coll 1968; Disting Serv Awd Kiwanis Intl 1971, City of Durham 1971, Durham C of C 1973; Gov's Ambassador of Goodwill Awd 1974; O Max Gardner Awd 1976; Named to HC Hall of Fame 1975; SC Hall of Fame 1977; Natl Assn sport & Phys Educ Hall of Fame 1977. **BUSINESS ADDRESS:** Chancellor, North Carolina CentralUniv, PO Box 19617, Durham, NC 27707.

WALKER, LEWIS
Educator. **PERSONAL:** Born Oct 22, 1936, Selma, AL; son of Joseph Walker and Thelma Freeman; married Georgia Doles. **EDUCATION:** BA, 1959; MA, 1961; PhD, 1964. **CAREER:** Wilberforce Univ, student instructor, 1958-59; Ohio Higher Educ Asst Commn, admin specialist, 1962; Ohio State Univ, lecturer, 1964; Ohio Hospital Assn, research specialist, 1964; W Michigan Univ, asst professor, 1964-67, assoc professor, 1967-71, professor, 1971-; chmn, sociology, 1989-. **ORGANIZATIONS:** Mem, Douglass Comm Assn, 1965-69; Senior Citizens Inc, 1967; founder & dir, Kalamazoo Resources Devel Council, 1967-68; consultant & program devel, Ford Motor Co, 1968-69, Police-Comm Relations Programs, 1968-70; ARC Bd, 1969-70; adv bd, Learning Village, 1970; Amer Soc Assn, 1974-; Michigan Soc Assn, 1974-; Miami Valley Soc Assn, 1974-; numerous in-service & human relations programs; mem, Kalamazoo Co Crime Commn, 1984-; bd, Goodwill Indus, 1986-, Differential Flow Systems Inc, 1986-; pres, Walker-Taylor Thermies Inc, 1984-, Spare Time Pursuits Inc 1986-. **HONORS/ACHIEVEMENTS:** Recipient, Distinguished Serv Award Jaycees, 1967; One of Five Outstanding Young Men of Michigan Jaycees, 1967; Award for Teaching Excellence W Michigan Univ Alumni Assn, 1971; inventor, US patent on low pressure boiler heating system, 1984; invention, US patent on furnace system ,1986; three US copyrights, registrations, on three separate game boards and texts. **BUSINESS ADDRESS:** Professor, W Michigan University, Dept of Sociology, Kalamazoo, MI 49001.

WALKER, LUCIUS
University dean. **CAREER:** Howard University, School of Engineering, Washington, DC, dean. **BUSINESS ADDRESS:** Howard University, School of Engineering, 1016 Downing Hall, 2300 6th St, NW, Washington, DC 20059. *

WALKER, LUCIUS, JR.
Clergyman. **PERSONAL:** Born Aug 03, 1930, Roselle, NJ; married Mary; children: Lucius, Donna, Gail, Richard, Edythe. **EDUCATION:** Shaw Univ, AB; Andover Newton Theol Sem, MDiv; Univ of Wisconsin, MA 1963; Malcolm X College (Chicago), Hon LHD; Shaw Univ, Raleigh NC, LHD. **CAREER:** Interreligious Found for Comm Orgn NY, exec dir 1967-73; Natl Coun of the Churches of Christ NY, assoc gen sec 1973. **ORGANIZATIONS:** Mem bd trustees Shaw Univ; mem bd trustees Andover Newton Theol School; mem Black Foundation Executives. **BUSINESS ADDRESS:** 475 Riverside Dr, Rm 577, New York, NY 10027.

WALKER, LULA AQUILLIA
Elected official. **PERSONAL:** Born Mar 01, 1955, Derby, CT; children: William Zimmerman Jr, Tyron, Garrett. **EDUCATION:** Shaw Coll Detroit, Med Asst Cert 1974; US Acad of Health & Sci, Med Spec Cert 1977. **CAREER:** Olson Dr Tenants Assoc, pres 1979; Housing Authority City of Ansonia, asst treas (1st tenant to be appointed to Housing Auth Bd) 1980; City of Ansonia, co-chmn printing & signs 1982, chmn claims comm 1984; Ansonia Bd of Alderman, fourth ward alderman (1st Black female to be elected to Bd of Alderman); State of CT, mental health worker II. **ORGANIZATIONS:** Advisory bd Valley legal Asst 1980; asst recording sec A Philip Randolph Lower Naaugatuck Valley Chap 1982; mem of bd Lower Naugatuck Valley Chap ofNAACP 1983; sgt of arms Lower Naugatuck Valley Chap of Black Democratics 1983; vice dgt ruler Lily of the Valley Temple H406 IBPOE of the World 1984-; chmn Claims Comm 1986; serve on Police Comm of bd of aldermen. **HONORS/ACHIEVEMENTS:** Woman of the Month Women's Center of Ansonia 1979; 3 Awds for Dedicated Serv in the Community Friends of Lulu of Ansonia 1984; Dedicated Serv Plaque in the Comm Magicians AC 1984. **MILITARY SERVICE:** Army NG sgt 11 yrs; Army Natl Guard Achievement Medal 1982. **HOME ADDRESS:** 15 Olson Dr, Ansonia, CT 06401.

WALKER, LYNN JONES
Attorney. **PERSONAL:** Born in Fort Lee, VA; daughter of Lawrence N Jones and Mary Ellen Jones. **EDUCATION:** Attended Fisk Univ 1963-65; Barnard Coll, AB Sociology 1967; Columbia Univ School of Law, JD 1970. **CAREER:** Bernard Baruch Coll, teaching asst 1969-70; Judge Motley US Dist Ct NY, law clerk 1970-71; NAACP Legal Defense & Educ Fund Inc, asst counsel 1971-73; New York City Comm on Human Rights, general counsel 1973-75; NAACP Legal Defense Fund Inc, asst counsel 1975-78; Civil Rights Div US Dept of Justice, chief special litigation section 1978-81; Civil Rights Div US Dept of Justice, deputy asst atty general 1981-82; The Ford Foundation, program officer 1982-87; deputy director in charge human rights and social justice program 1987-. **ORGANIZATIONS:** Mem Natl Bar Assn; admitted to Bar for US Dist Ct for So Dist of NY; US States Ct of Appeals for 2nd & 5th circuits; mem NY State Bar; former chair Fed Women's Program Advisory Comm at US Dept of Justice; former mem Black Affairs Program Advisory Comm; former mem bd of dirs Sheltering Arms Children's Svc; mem NAACP; former columnist Essence Magazine; former mem NY State Sentencing Guidelines Comm; former sec Black Amer Law Students Assn; former mem Columbia Law Review; bd mem The Legal Aid Soc; mem, NYS Govenors Advisory Committee on Black Affairs; bd mem Assoc of Black Foundation Execs. **HONORS/ACHIEVEMENTS:** First Black Woman on Columbia Law Review; Speciall Commendation Award at the US Dept of Justice; Sr Exec Serv Outstanding Performance Award & bonus at the US Dept of Justice; Outstanding Performance rating at the Ford Found. **BUSINESS ADDRESS:** Deputy Director, Human Rights and Social Justice Program, The Ford Foundation, 320 E 43rd St, New York, NY 10017.

WALKER, M. LUCIUS, JR.
Educator. **PERSONAL:** Born Dec 16, 1936, Washington, DC; married Oswaldene E Cocking; children: Mark, Monique. **EDUCATION:** Morehouse Coll, 1952-54; Howard Univ, BSME 1957; Carnegie Inst of Tech, MSME, PhD 1957-63. **CAREER:** Howard Univ, School of Eng, Asst Dean, 1965-66, Acting Chmn, dept of Mechanical Engineering, 1968-73, chmn dept of mech engrg 1968-73, assoc dean 1973-74, acting dean 1977-78, dean 1978-. **ORGANIZATIONS:** Consultant Biomedical Cardiovascular Renal Rsch Team 1966-, consultant Ford Motor Co 1971-; mem Engr Manpower Comm of Engrs Council Prof Devel 1972-; mem Amer Soc for Engrg Ed, Amer Soc of Mech Engrs, Tau Beta Pi; mem bd of trustees Carnegie Mellon Univ; biotech resources review comm Natl Inst of Health 1980-84; Amer Soc of Mech Engrs Ad Hoc Visitor for Accreditation Bd for Engrg & Tech; mem, past pres Howard Univ Chap Sigma Xi. **HONORS/ACHIEVEMENTS:** Nominee NYAS; Fellowship Ford Found Carnegie Inst of Tech. **BUSINESS ADDRESS:** Dean, HowardUniv School of Engrg, 2300 6th St NW, Washington, DC 20059.

WALKER, MAGGIE L.
Retired physician. **PERSONAL:** Born Feb 16, 1918, Richmond, VA; married Dr John W Lewis; children: John Jr, Harriett. **EDUCATION:** VA Union Univ, BS 1937; Univ of MI, LM 1941. **CAREER:** Provident Hosp, pediatric resident training 1941-43; Mid-S Med Ctr VSPHS Birmingham FL, dir 1943-46; Provident Hosp, attending ped 1946-retired; Childrens Meml Hosp, ped resident training 1951-52; Children's Meml Hosp, attending ped 1952-retirement. **ORGANIZATIONS:** Diplomate Amer Bd of Pediatrics, Amer Acad Pediatrics; mem AMA, Amer Heart Assoc, Pan-Amer Med Assoc, Natl Med Assoc Dir Chicago Council to End Racial & Religious Discrimination 1952, Assoc Family Living 1957, Chicago Urban League 1948-51.

WALKER, MANUEL LORENZO
Physician. **PERSONAL:** Born Mar 22, 1930, Battle Creek, MI; son of Dr & Mrs Charles S. Walker; married Joan Lucille Carter Parks; children: Linda Lee Walker McIntyre, Lorenzo Giles, Gregory Tracy Parks. **EDUCATION:** Howard Univ Coll of LA, BS 1951; Howard Univ Coll of Med, MD 1955; Philadelphia Gen Hosp, Intern 1955-56. **CAREER:** Mercy-Douglass Hosp, staff mem 1958-73; Private Practice Since 1958; Mercy Catholic Med Cntr, staff mem 1968-; Lakenau Hosp, staff mem 1979-; St Joseph's Hosp, staff mem 1987-; St Ignatius Nursing Home, med dir 1972-. **ORGANIZATIONS:** Mem Natl Medcl Assoc PA Med Soc & Philadelphia Cnty Med Soc; v pres HowardUniv Med Alumni Assoc 1970-75; pres Philadelphia Acadmy of Fam Phys 1982-84; Keystone State Medcl Soc 1971-73; Med Soc of Eastern PA 1968-70,;Yeadon (PA) Bd of Schl Dir 1968-71; alumni pres Class of 1955-HowardUniv Med Assoc; hnr soc Kappa Pi Medical, Alpha Omega Alpha Medical. **HONORS/ACHIEVEMENTS:** Practitioner of year Philadelphia Cnty Med Soc 1979; alumni pres Class of 1955 HowardUniv Med Schl 1955-; legion of Honor Chapel of Four Chaplains 1978-; med honor soc Kappa Pi & Alpha Omega Alpha; Practitioner of the Year Natl Medical Assoc 1986. **MILITARY SERVICE:** USNR lt cmdr 1956-66. **HOME ADDRESS:** 425 Jamaica Dr, Cherry Hill, NJ 08002. **BUSINESS ADDRESS:** Family Physician/Medical Dir, St Ignatius Nursing Home, 5740 W Girard Ave, Philadelphia, PA 19131.

WALKER, MARGARET See ALEXANDER, MARGARET WALKER

WALKER, MARIA LATANYA
Physician. **PERSONAL:** Born Jul 03, 1957, Greenwood, SC; daughter of H W Walker Jr and Leola Grant Walker. **EDUCATION:** Furman Univ, Greenville, SC, BS, 1978; Harvard Medical School, Boston, MD, MD, 1982. **CAREER:** Emory Univ School of Medicine, faculty, clinic physician, 1983-. **ORGANIZATIONS:** Mem, Delta Sigma Theta, 1976, Medical Assn of Georgia, Peabody Acad Soc/Harvard Medical School, Amer Medical Assn. **HONORS/ACHIEVEMENTS:** Phi Beta Kappa Beta Chapter, Furman Univ, 1978. **HOME ADDRESS:** 817 Tuxworth Cir, Decatur, GA 30033.

WALKER, MARK LAMONT
Surgeon/teacher. **PERSONAL:** Born Jan 05, 1952, Brooklyn, NY; son of Philip David Walker and Ann (Boston) Walker; married Alicia Watson; children: Kweli, Akilah, Olabisi, Rashanna, Sharufa, Rahsaan. **EDUCATION:** City Coll of New York, BS 1973; Meharry Medical Coll, MD 1977. **CAREER:** Howard Univ Hosp, instructor dept of surgery 1983-85; Morehouse Sch of Medicine, asst prof of surgery 1985-. **ORGANIZATIONS:** Fellow Intl Coll of Surgeons 1984; mem Assoc of Academic Surgery 1984, Atlanta Medical Assoc 1985, Natl Medical Assoc 1986, Cert Surgical Critical Care 1987; Fellow American Coll of Surgeons 1988. **HONORS/ACHIEVEMENTS:** Mem Alpha Omega Alpha Honor Medical Soc 1976-; Daniel Hale Williams Awd for Residency Howard Univ 1982; Awd of Merit Dept of Surgery Howard Univ 1985; Annual Awardee Science Skills Ctr Brooklyn NY 1986. **BUSINESS ADDRESS:** Asst Prof of Surgery, Morehouse Sch of Medicine, 35 Butler St, Atlanta, GA 30355.

WALKER, MARY ALICE
Educator. **PERSONAL:** Born Feb 05, 1941, Warrenton, GA; married James. **EDUCATION:** Brockport State U, BS 1963; Nazareth Coll, MEd 1975. **CAREER:** Rochester NY OIC, bd chmn 1980-; Rochester City School Dist, reading teacher 1963-. **ORGANIZATIONS:** Dir of Christian educ NY Dist 1973-75; rec Rochester Tchrs Assn 1976-77; mem Rochester Reading Assn 1979-80; mem NY State Tchrs Assn; mem Urban League 1978-80; chmn trustee bd New Bethel CME Ch 1970-80; mem Dem Party Com Monroe Co 1979-80. **BUSINESS ADDRESS:** Rochester OIC, 287 N Union St, Rochester, NY 14605.

WALKER, MAURICE EDWARD
Educator. **PERSONAL:** Born Oct 31, 1937, Rochester, NY; married Rosie Lee Williford; children: Christina, Juliana, Gwendolyn, Maurice Jr, Lawrence. **EDUCATION:** LA Tech Univ, BA Speech 1968-70; Univ of So CA, MS Ed 1977. **CAREER:** USAF March AFB CA, airborne controller 1963-66; USAF Osan AB Korea, Lockbourne OH, Barksdale AFB LA, command post controller 1967-70; 49 Supp Sq Holloman AFBNM, sq sect comdr 1971-73; 610 Mass Yokota AB Japan, sq sect comdr 1973-77; 2052 Comm Keesler AFB MS, sq sect comdr 1977-79; USAF Acad CO The Colorado Springs School, athletic dir and eng teacher. **ORGANIZATIONS:** Mem 2nd deg black belt Kodokan Judo Inst Tokyo Japan 1962-; military affiliate radio oper AUS 1968-; amateur radio oper FCC licensed 1968-; life mem Amer Radio Relay League 1970-; retired Multi-WSAF, USAFA. **MILITARY SERVICE:** USAF capt 27 yrs retired; AF Commendation Medal w/1st Oak Leaf Cluster 1970,79. **BUSINESS ADDRESS:** Athletic Dir, Colorado Springs School, Colorado Springs, CO 80906.

WALKER, MELFORD WHITFIELD, JR.
Lawyer. **PERSONAL:** Born Jun 15, 1958, Winchester, VA; son of Rev and Mrs M W Walker, Sr. **EDUCATION:** Hampton Inst, BS Acct (Summa Cum Laude) 1980; Harvard Law School, JD 1986; Harvard Graduate School of Business Admin, MBA 1987. **CAREER:** Arthur Andersen & Co, staff accountant 1980-81; Watson Rice & Co, consultant 1983-84; Walker Rental Co Inc, asst to the pres 1984; Long Aldridge & Norman, assoc 1987-. **ORGANIZATIONS:** Consultant Volunteer Consulting Org at Harvard Business School 1983; Black Law Students Assn; Harvard Law School; Afro-Amer Student Union, Harvard Business School; mem, Amer Bar Assn; State Bar of GA; mem, Atlanta Bar Assn, 1987-. **HONORS/ACHIEVEMENTS:** Chapter pres and natl student rep to the exec comm Alpha Kappa Mu Honor Soc 1979-80; Fellowship, Council on Graduate Mgmt Educ 1982; co-author of Best Brief and Oral Argument Semi-Fanialist, 1982 Jessup Moot Court Competition, Harvard Law School. **HOME ADDRESS:** 1175 La Vista Rd, NE,, Apt 215, Atlanta, GA 30324.

WALKER, MELVIN E., JR.
Educational administrator. **PERSONAL:** Born Oct 23, 1946, Shivers, MS; son of Melvin E Walker and Rosie Walker; married Jeraldine Wooden Walker; children: Daphne Melinda, Melvin Earl III, Melanie Latrice. **EDUCATION:** Alcorn A&M College, Lorman, MS, BS 1969; Univ of Illinois, Urbana-Champaign, MS, MS 1971, PhD 1973. **CAREER:** Fort Valley State College, Fort Valley, GA, asst prof 1973-77, coordinator of rural development research 1977-78, dean of school of agriculture 1978-, acting president 1988-. **ORGANIZATIONS:** Chair, Assn of Research Directors, 1982-86; chair, Assn of 1890 Agricultural Administrators, 1984-85; treas, Assn of Research Directors, 1986-; vice-pres, Camp John Hope NFA Alumni Assn, 1986-; member of Am Agricultural Economics Assn, Camp John Hope NFA Assn, Optimist Club. **HONORS/ACHIEVEMENTS:** Outstanding Service Awards from USDA Honors Program 1982, US Dept of Commerce Census Advisory Bureau 1983, and FVSC Agriculture Alumni Assn 1984; Honorary State Farmers Award from FFA, 1984; author of "Custom and Rental Rates Used on Illinois Farms," University of IL, 1973, of "Poverty and Alienation: A Case Study," in Journal of Social and Behavioral Sciences, 1978, of "Effects of the Changing Structure of Agriculture on Nonwhite Farming in the US, the South, and Gerogia," in Sociological Spectrum, 1984. **HOME ADDRESS:** 102 Duncan St, Fort Valley, GA 31030. **BUSINESS ADDRESS:** Acting President, Fort Valley State College, 1005 State College Drive, Fort Valley, GA 31020-3298.

WALKER, MOSES ANDRE
Hospital administrator. **PERSONAL:** Born Oct 03, 1929, Savannah, GA; son of Moses Walker and Annie Mae Kelsey Walker (deceased); married Ann Bryant, Aug 03, 1958 (divorced). **EDUCATION:** Morehouse Coll, BS Biology 1951; Columbia Univ Sch of Public

Health, MS Hosp Admin 1957. **CAREER:** Middlesex Hosp NJ, dir of patient serv & asst deputy dir 1958-59; St John Episcopal Hosp NY, adminstrative asst 1959-60; Kingsbrook Jewish Medical Ctr NY, asst dir 1960-61; NY Medical Coll Flower & Fifth Ave Hosp, admin asst 1961-62; NY City Health & Hospitals Corp; Lincoln Hospital Bronx, asst administrator 1962-64, deputy asst commnr 1969-71; Bellevue Psychiatric Hosp, administrator 1964-65; Lincoln Hosp, deputy asst commnr 1969-71; Lincoln Medical Ctr, assoc exec 1971-80; Harlem Hospital Ctr, assoc dir 1980-87. **ORGANIZATIONS:** Mem Alpha Phi Alpha Frat 1949-; mem/founder Natl Assoc of Health Serv Execs 1965-; guest lectr Columbia Univ Sch of Dentistry 1971-72; bd mem Sickle Cell Disease Found of Greater NY 1973-75; bd mem New York City Managerial Employees Assn 1983-; mem Metro Health Adminstrs Assn 1983-; mem Amer Hosp Assn 1983-; mem St Philips Episcopal Ch, NAACP; mem Schomburg Corp serving The Schomburg Ctr for Rsch in Black Culture NY. **HONORS/ACHIEVEMENTS:** Professional Achievement Chi Eta Phi Sor Omicron Chap 1983; Civic Awd Comm Serv Abyssinian Bapt Ch 1965; Leadership Awd Comm of Friends of Lincoln Hosp 1972; Comm Serv Awd New Mt Zion Bapt Ch 1977; Man of the Yr Awd South Bronx NAACP 1974. **MILITARY SERVICE:** AUS spl agent, Counterintelligence Corps (l08th Detachment) 1951-53. **BUSINESS ADDRESS:** Pres, Hospital Initiatives, Inc, 788 Columbus Ave, Suite l6K, New York, NY 10025.

WALKER, MOSES L.
Social agency executive. **PERSONAL:** Born Oct 21, 1940, Kalamazoo; married Ruthie; children: Tari, Mark, Stacy. **EDUCATION:** Western MI U, BS 1966; Wayne State U, MSW 1968. **CAREER:** Douglass Comm Assn, outreach worker 1966; Kalamazoo County Comm Action Prog, team capt 1966; Comm Serv Council, adminstr asst 1966; Archdiocese Detroit, comm affairs dept 1967; Douglass Comm Assn, dir, asso dir 1968. **ORGANIZATIONS:** Mem Rotary Club; city commr mem Northside Assn; Educ Advancement Scholarship Com chmn 1973; Nat Assn Social Workers; United Negro Coll Fund chmn 1973; Nat Asso Black Social Workers steering com. **HONORS/ACHIEVEMENTS:** Outstanding Young Men of MI MI Jaycees 1969; Outstanding Serv Award Northside Assn Educ Advancement 1972; Distinguished Serv Award Kalamazoo Jaycees 1969;Comm Serv Award NASW 1974. **MILITARY SERVICE:** AUS 1961-64. **BUSINESS ADDRESS:** 231 E Ransom St, Kalamazoo, MI 49007.

WALKER, RONALD PLEZZ
Educational administrator. **PERSONAL:** Born Oct 16, 1953, Boley, OK; married Glenda Gay; children: Terrance Scott. **EDUCATION:** Langston Univ, BS 1974; Central State Univ, MEd 1978; OK State Univ. **CAREER:** OK City Schools, sci teacher 1973-76, biomedical prog dir 1976-77, sci/eng ctr dir 1977-80; Boley Public Schools, supt 1980-. **ORGANIZATIONS:** Pres Natl Young Adult Council CME Church; vice pres Langston Univ Alumni Assn; vice pres Organization of Rural OK Schools; pub relations dir Zeta GammaLambda Chap Alpha Phi Alpha. **HONORS/ACHIEVEMENTS:** Outstanding Young Man Natl Jaycees 1980; Outstanding Serv Awd Adams Day Care Ctr 1983; Outstanding Serv Awd OK City Dist Young Adults 1983; Outstanding Young Man Natl Jaycees 1984. **BUSINESS ADDRESS:** Superintendent, Boley Public Schools, PO Box 248 St, Boley, OK 74829.

WALKER, SHEILA SUZANNE
Educator, anthropologist. **PERSONAL:** Born Nov 05, 1944, Jersey City, NJ; daughter of Dr James O Walker and Susan Robinson Walker; divorced. **EDUCATION:** Bryn Mawr Coll, BA (cum laude) 1966; Sorbonne & Institut d'Etudes Politiques Paris, Jr Yr Abroad 1964-65; Univ of Chicago, MA/PhD 1969/1976. **CAREER:** Operation Crossroads Africa, escort-interpreter 1966-74; Divinity School Harvard Univ, rsch asst 1972-73; Schomberg Ctr for Rsch in Black Culture, scholar-in-residence 1987; Univ of CA Berkeley, asst/assoc prof 1973-; Coll of William and Mary, Williamsburg VA, visiting prof of anthropology 1989-90. **ORGANIZATIONS:** Social Science Analyst Center for Rsch in Economic Devel & Agency for Intl Devel 1978; lecturer toured francophone Africa Intl Comm Agency 1979; editor Assn of Black Anthropologists 1979-81; educ comm Black Film Makers Hall of Fame 1980-84; sr social science consultant Africare Washington DC 1984-85; foreign travelAfrica Central &S America Europe Asia 1964-; team leader United Nations Develop Program project design team West Africa 1986; intl jury Pan-African Film Festival of Ouagadoujou Burkina Faso 1987. **HONORS/ACHIEVEMENTS:** African Amer Scholars Council Rsch Grant 1976; Soc Science Rsch Council Rsch Grant 1979; Spencer Found Rsch Grant 1984; Sr Post-Doctoral Fellow Natl Rsch Council Washington 1984-85; publications, Ceremonial Spirit Possession in Africa and Afro-America 1972, African Christianity, Patterns of Religious Continuity 1979, The Religious Revolution in the Ivory Coast, The Prophet Harris and the Harrist Church 1983; editor, Anthropology & Educ Quarterly 1978, Notes from the ABA 1978-82, The Black Scholar Two-Volume Special Issue Black Anthropology 1980 co-edited; many articles including, Witchcraft and Healing in an African Christian Church 1980, Reflections on Becoming a Black Anthropologist 1983; 18 anthropological journals including, Master Didi Black Art, An Intl Quarterly 1983, Candomble, A Spiritual Microcosm of Africa Black Art, An Intl Quarterly 1983, The Bahian Carnival Black Art, An Intl Quarterly 1983; invited lectures & presentations include, Spirit Possession in the Religious Life of Black Peoples in the Americas Black History Month Conf Rutgers Univ Newark NJ 1984; media presentations, Women in Afro-Brazilian Religion, Bay Area Black Psychologists 1983, Trenton State Coll Trenton NJ 1984, Seton Hall Univ S Orange NJ 1984. **BUSINESS ADDRESS:** Visiting Professorr, Dept of Anthropology, College of William and Mary, Williamsburg, VA 23185.

WALKER, SIDNEY HARRIS
Dentist. **PERSONAL:** Born Aug 14, 1925, Christanburg, VA; married Annie. **EDUCATION:** Hampton Inst, BS 1950; Howard U, DDS 1958. **CAREER:** Guggenheim Dntl Clin NYC, intern 1958-59; pri pract dental surg 1959-. **ORGANIZATIONS:** Mem Robt T Freeman Dntl Soc; Ntnl Dntl Soc; Omega Psi Phi; mem Amer Leg Jones Mem Meth Ch; Kiwanis Intnl Club; various lodgs; NAACP; Urban Lgue; YMCA; Chillum-ray Citzn Assn; Chpl Oaks Civ Assn; DC Boys Club. **MILITARY SERVICE:** USMC. **BUSINESS ADDRESS:** 601 Eastern Ave NE, Ste 104, Washington, DC 20019.

WALKER, SOLOMON W., II
Insurance executive. **CAREER:** Pilgrim Health & Life Insurance Co, Augusta GA, chief executive. **BUSINESS ADDRESS:** Pilgrim Health & Life Ins Co, 1143 Laney Walker Blvd, Augusta, GA 30901. *

WALKER, SONIA (NEE LOUDEN)
Community relations director. **PERSONAL:** Born Apr 10, 1937, Columbus, OH; married Walter; children: 3 Children. **EDUCATION:** Wilbur Force U, undergrad 1954-56; Bennett Coll, BA 1958; HowardUniv Sch of Soc Work, MSW 1963. **CAREER:** WHBQ-TV RKO-GEN, dir commn rel 1975-;soc work in priv & pub agenc 1963-74;Univ of Chicago Housing Staff, 1970-74; elem tchr 1958-61. **ORGANIZATIONS:** Mem Memphis Assn of Black Comm; bd of dir Memphis Orch Soc Memphis Urban Leag Nat Conf of Christ & Jews Beale St Reprtory Co Memphis Art & Sci Comm; prog coord TN Womens Mtg; supt adv coun Memphis Pub Sch; mem PUSH; NAACP.

WALKER, STANLEY M.
Attorney/educator. **PERSONAL:** Born Jul 15, 1942, Chicago, IL; son of Alfred Walker and Georgia Walker; married Elizabeth Mary Pearson; children: Darryl, Edana. **EDUCATION:** Harvard Coll, AB 1964; Yale Univ Law School, JD, 1967. **CAREER:** Judge A Leon Higginbotham Univ S Dist Ct, law clerk, 1967-69; Dechert Price & Rhoads, assoc, 1969-71; Pepper, Hamilton & Scheetz, Assoc, 1970-71; Pennsylvania St Bd of Law Exam's, examiner, 1971-74; Comm Legal Services, staff & Mng Atty, 1971-72; Greater Philadelphia Comm Devel Corp, exec vice pres, 1972-73; The Rouse Co, sr atty, 1973-79; Univ of Texas School of Law, assoc prof, 1979-89; Exxon Co, USA, counsel, 1989-. **ORGANIZATIONS:** mem, Amer Bar Assn & Natl Bar Assn; mem, of Bars of US Supreme Court, District of Columbia, Pennsylvania, Maryland, & Texas; mem, Austin Econ Devel Comm, 1985-89; alt mem, City of Austin Bd of Adjustment 1985-86; mem, Action for Metropolitan Govt Comm, 1988-. **BUSINESS ADDRESS:** Associate Professor of Law, Univ of TX Sch of Law, 727 E 26th St, Austin, TX 78705.

WALKER, STERLING WILSON
Attorney. **PERSONAL:** Born Dec 25, 1912, Wakefield, VA; married Marion B. **EDUCATION:** VA Union Univ, BS 1938; NC Central Univ, LLB 1958. **CAREER:** High School, teacher 1938-42; postal employee 1944-55; Private practice, attorney 1959-. **ORGANIZATIONS:** Appt by Gov Linwood Holton to serve on Council of Criminal Justice of Commonwealth of VA 1971-76; mem Amer Bar Assoc, Natl Bar Assoc, The Amer Trial Lawyers Assoc, VA Trial Lawyers Assoc, Tidewater Trial Lawyers Assoc, Old Dominion Bar Assoc, Twin City Bar Assoc. **HONORS/ACHIEVEMENTS:** Honored by Tidwater Aluminae Assoc NC Univ; Plaque for work in criminal law. **MILITARY SERVICE:** AUS 1942-44. **BUSINESS ADDRESS:** Attorney, 2840 Mapleton Ave, Norfolk, VA 23504.

WALKER, TANYA ROSETTA
Legal assistant, office administrator. **PERSONAL:** Born Apr 02, 1953, Philadelphia, PA; daughter of James and Lucille; divorced; children: Al Qadir R. **EDUCATION:** Stenotype Inst of New York , Certified 1970; Rutgers State Univ, BA 1974; Essex Coll of Business, Certified Legal/Admin Asst 1977. **CAREER:** Lofton & Lester Esqs, paralegal 1979-83; Former Gov Brendan T Byrne, exec asst 1983-85; Althear A Lester Esq, legal asst 1985-. **ORGANIZATIONS:** Mem Natl & Essex Cos Legal Secretaries & Paralegals Assoc 1979-89; mem Notary Public of NJ 1982-92; volunteer Big Brothers & Big Sisters of Amer 1983-88; bd mem Boy Scouts of Amer 1983-; bd of dirs & vice pres Make-AWish Foundation of NJ 1983-86; mem Union County C of C 1986-87; pres (1st black and 1st woman) Make-A-Wish of NJ 1986-89. **HONORS/ACHIEVEMENTS:** Awd of Excellence Aunt Millie's Childrens Learning Ctr 1984,85; Achievement Awd Tri-City Sr Citizens Group 1986; Black Heritage Awd for Achievement Teachers' Union 1986; Recognition Awd Shearson Lehman Bros Inc 1986. **BUSINESS ADDRESS:** President, Make-A-Wish Foundation of NJ, 326 Morris Avenue, Elizabeth, NJ 07208.

WALKER, THOMAS L.
Clergyman. **PERSONAL:** Born Jul 30, 1948, Rocky Mount, NC; married Joyce Norwood; children: Timothy, Teresa. **EDUCATION:** ShawUniv Sch of Religion;Univ of Miami; Mgmt Training Sch, Phila. **CAREER:** Rocky Mount Opps Indstrlztn Cntr Mnpwr Training, cnslr; Drug Amnesty Inc Rocky Mnt, dir; Yth Crusade Assn Rocky Mnt, dir; Thornes Chpl Bapt Ch Rocky Mnt, asst pastor; Minrty Entrprs Inc Rocky Mnt, cnslt. **ORGANIZATIONS:** Pres Nash Co Sunday Sch BTU Conv; pres The Rocky Mnt Mnstrl Conf; chmn Yth Actn Com NAACP; chmn ESEA Title I Adv Bd; mem adv bd Nash AdvncmntRhbltn Cntr; mem bd dirs Rocky Mnt OIC Chld Devl; pres PTA Bulluck Sch. **BUSINESS ADDRESS:** Ebenezer Bapt Ch, 652 Raleigh Rd, Rocky Mount, NC.

WALKER, WALTER LORENZO
Education executive. **PERSONAL:** Born Sep 04, 1935, Chicago; married Sonia L Louden; children: Walter Noland, Aaron Jordan, Marcus Elliot. **EDUCATION:** Brandeis U, PhD 1969; Bryn Mawr Coll, MSS 1962;Univ of Chicago, AB 1955. **CAREER:** LeMoyne Owen Coll, pres 1974; Univ Chicago, vice pres 1969-74; Howard Univ, staff assoc 1963-66; Philadelphia Redevelopment Assn, comm relations rep 1962-63; Fed Resrv Bank St Louis, dir 1978-80; Cmmrcl Appl, clmnst 1979. **ORGANIZATIONS:** Mem Nat Assn Social Wrkrs; CORE; NACP; Urbn Leg; Am Dem Actn; Cncl Scl Wrk Edn; bd Dir 1st TN Nat Bnk 1980; mem bd Amrcn Cncr Soc; mem bd vice pres Memphis Untd Way 1976; dir Memphis Area C of Co 1977-79; mem Memphis Rotary Clb; mem bd Chicago Chld Care Soc. **HONORS/ACHIEVEMENTS:** Recip Golden Gavel, Chicago Caucus 1974; Educator of Yr Gr Memphis State 1977; 100 Top Yng Edctrs Change Magazine 1978; 10 Top Citizens in Memphis, Comm Appeal 1980; Edctr of Yr Memphis, Phi Beta Sigma Tau Iota Sigma Chap 1980. **MILITARY SERVICE:** USAF 1st lt 1955-60. **BUSINESS ADDRESS:** 807 Walker Ave, Memphis, TN 38126.

WALKER, WATSON HERCHAEL
Physician. **PERSONAL:** Born Apr 07, 1918, Senoia, GA; married Terri Springer; children: Watson Jr, Charles, James, Wilheminia. **EDUCATION:** Fisk U, BS 1939; Meharry Med Coll, MD 1944. **CAREER:** Physician, private pract 1948; Lockbourne Air Force Base Hosp, dir 1948; Riverside Meth Hosp, surg tchr; OH St Univ Coll, inst. **ORGANIZATIONS:** Chrmn Riverside Meth Hosp; Am Coll of Surg; Intl Coll of Surg; Am Geriatric Soc; Nat Med Assoc; diplmt Am Bd of Surg; pres Columbus of Educ1964-65, 69-70; mem Metro Bd YMCA; bd Slvtn Army; bd St Joseph's Coll; mem Mt Olivet Bapt Ch; mem Lambda Boule; mem Sigma Pi Phi Hon Frat. **HONORS/ACHIEVEMENTS:** Outstndng Man, Columbus Jr C of C 1953; dist srv,Univ Appls 1966. **MILITARY SERVICE:** AUS cpt 1954-56. **BUSINESS ADDRESS:** 254 Woodland Ave, Columbus, OH 43203.

WALKER, WENDELL P.
Director. **PERSONAL:** Born Jun 06, 1930, Painesville, OH; son of Robert M Walker and

Evelyn Wieker Walker; married Doris Thomas Walker; children: Kevin, Andrea, Brian. **EDUCATION:** John Carroll Univ, 1948-49; Defiance Coll, BS, 1949-51; Univ of KS, 1969-71; Western Reserv Univ, 1955-56; Lake Erie Coll, teaching Certificate, 1972. **CAREER:** Northwestern OH General Hosp; OH State Soc Am Med Technologists, pres 1972; Lake Co Health & Welfare Council, 1973-74; Lake Co Metro Housing Authority Med Technologists; Painesville Night School, social sci instructor. **ORGANIZATIONS:** Bd United Way of Lake Co 1974; central branch YMCA Bd; Metro YMCA; mem, pres Free Clinic, 1975; cub pack chmn, Boy Scouts of Amer; Bd Pres, Catholic Serv Bureau of Lake County, 1979-89; Bd Pres, Lifeline to Economically Disadvantaged Consumers; Bd mem, Lake Metro Housing NAACP of Lake County; Painesville City Councilman, 1986-89; Metropolitan Health Planning Corp of Cleveland; Bd of Zoning Appeals mem. **HONORS/ACHIEVEMENTS:** Rec OSSAMT Journal Award, 1973; Technologist of the Year, 1974; Natl Pres Award, 1974; Natl Pres, Letter of Recognition, 1973; Layman of the Year, Lake Co YMCA, 1972. **MILITARY SERVICE:** Srvd AUS s sgt 1952-55. **HOME ADDRESS:** 26 Orchard Grove, Painesville, OH.

WALKER, WESLEY
Professional athlete. **PERSONAL:** Born May 26, 1955, San Bernardino, CA; married Judy; children: John, Taylor. **EDUCATION:** CA, majored in economics. **CAREER:** NY Jets, wide receiver 1977-. **HONORS/ACHIEVEMENTS:** NFL All Rookie Team 1977; NCAA Record Aver Gain per Recpt in a Career; Jets MVP and NFL Leader in Rec Yds 1978. **BUSINESS ADDRESS:** New York Jets, 1000 Fulton Ave, Hempstead, NY 11550.

WALKER, WILBUR P.
Educator. **PERSONAL:** Born May 06, 1936, Okmulgee, OK; son of Hugh Walker and Mae Ella Hill Walker; married Tomycine Lewis, Aug 30, 1958; children: Wilbur Jr, Natalie. **EDUCATION:** Langston Univ, BA 1958; Central State Univ, MT 1968; Univ of OK, EdD 1974. **CAREER:** OK City Public Schools, teacher 1967-69; Urban League of OK City, dir comm org 1969; Univ of OK, special asst to pres 1970-73; OK Univ, dir special student program 1973-75; Benedict Coll, dean acad affairs 1975-78; OK State Regents for Higher Educ, dean acad affairs Benedict Coll 1975-78, asst vice chancellor student affairs. **ORGANIZATIONS:** Mem Phi Delta Kappa; bd of dir OK Business Devel Center; mem Urban League of OK City, Black Inc; Natl Assn of Student Personnel Admin; Oklahoma Coll Personnel Assn. **HONORS/ACHIEVEMENTS:** Amer Council on Educ Inst Fellow 1978; Outstanding Citizen of the Year 1984. **HOME ADDRESS:** 2200 NW 118th Terrace, Oklahoma City, OK 73120.

WALKER, WILLIAM HAROLD
Retired educator. **PERSONAL:** Born Jun 06, 1915, Carbondale, IL; married Viola Alba Crim; children: William Harold Jr. **EDUCATION:** S IL Univ Carbondale, BA Educ 1937, MS Educ 1948. **CAREER:** Rural School Perks IL, principal/teacher 1937-38; Douglas Grade Sch, principal 1938-41; Corporal Army Engineer Training Battalion, clerk 1941; Officer Training School, army engineer 1942; Corporal Air Corps, cadet pilot training 1942-43; 99th Fighter Squadron, pilot 1943-45; Tuskegee Army Air Base, base operations 1945-46; K thru 8 Elementary Centralia, principal 1948-75. **ORGANIZATIONS:** Teacher sunday sch supt deacon Second Baptist Church 1949-; life mem Natl Educ Assn 1953-; life mem IL Principals 1954; mem & chmn of comm Rotary Intl 1963; tchr high school and coll Sunday School classes, financial sec Second Baptist Church. **HONORS/ACHIEVEMENTS:** Outstanding Citizen Awd Centralia Jaycees 1976; Certificate of Merit Educ Council of 100 and Educ Dept of Southern IL Univ at Carbondale 1977. **MILITARY SERVICE:** USAC capt 6 yrs. **HOME ADDRESS:** Rte 6 Box 82 Airport Rd, Centralia, IL 62801.

WALKER, WILLIAM HENRY
Attorney. **PERSONAL:** Born Aug 09, 1914, El Dorado, AR; married Dorothy; children: William Jr, Sidney, Sybil. **EDUCATION:** Prairie View Coll; Wilberforce U; IN U; DePaul Univ Law Sch, JD 1947. **CAREER:** E Chgo, city atty 1974, asst City Atty 1953; dep pros atty 1947-48, juvenile prbtn offcr 1938-47. **ORGANIZATIONS:** Mem Am Bar Assn; IN Bar Assn; Am Judicature Soc; Am Trl Lawyer's Assn; Nat Bar Assn; E Chicago Bar Assn; Chicago Bar Assn; dir 1st Nat Bk of E Chgo; DePaulUniv Law Cncl. **HONORS/ACHIEVEMENTS:** Guest, num White House fnctns; num civic awds & Citations. **BUSINESS ADDRESS:** 2208 Broadway, East Chicago, IN 46312.

WALKER, WILLIAM PAUL, JR.
Business executive. **PERSONAL:** Born Jul 25, 1940, Denmark, SC; married Mamie Odena; children: Daryl Lamar. **EDUCATION:** Howard U, BS 1963; Howard U, MD 1967. **CAREER:** DC Gen Hosp, chf dept rdtn thrpy; Georgetown U, asst prof; Howard U, asst prof; Radiological Assocs, dept chmn. **ORGANIZATIONS:** Mem DC Med Soc; Am Coll Radiology; Med Chi DC; Mid Atlantic Soc Radctn Onclgst; mem Natl Medical Assoc, Amer Cancer Soc, Southern Medical Assoc; mem Randall Memorial United Methodist Church. **HONORS/ACHIEVEMENTS:** Upjohn Awd for Rsch 1967; 1985 Alumni Awd Voorhees Coll. **BUSINESS ADDRESS:** Department Chairman, Radiological Associates, 2024 Georgia Ave NW, Washington, DC 20001.

WALKER, WILLIAM SONNY
Federal executive. **PERSONAL:** Born Dec 13, 1933, Pine Bluff, AR; son of James Walker and Mary Coleman Bell Walker; children: Cheryl, James II, William Jr, Lesli Patricia. **EDUCATION:** Univ of AR Pine Bluff, BA 1955; AZ State Univ, certification 1962; Univ of Oklahoma, certfication 1968; Fed Exec Inst, certification 1979. **CAREER:** State of AR/Gov Winthrop Rockefeller, agency dir/asst to gov 1969-71; US Dept of Housing & Urban Devel, div dir 1971-72; US Office of Economic Opportunity, regional dir 1972-75; US Comm Serv Admin, regional dir 1975-81; Natl Alliance of Business, vice pres, 1981. **ORGANIZATIONS:** Bd of dirs United Way of Metro Atlanta 1977-87; bd of dirs Martin Luther King Jr Center, for Nonviolent Social Change 1979-87; bd of dirs Southern Christian Leadership Conf 1980-87; bd of dirs Metro Atlanta Comm Design Ctr 1981-87; bd of dirs Metro Atlanta Black/Jewish Coalition 1981-87; vice chair GA Assn of Black Elected Officials/Corporate Roundtable 1982-87; bd of trustees Metro Atlanta YWCA 1982-87; Resurgens Atlanta 1984-87; chmn Economic Develop Task Force of Natl Conf of Black Mayors 1983-87; vice chair bd of trustees Metro Atlanta Crime Commn 1983-87; chmn Collections of Life & Heritage 1984-87; bd of dirs Public Broadcasting Assoc of Atlanta 1984-87; bd of dirs Consumer Credit Counseling Assoc 1984-87; life mem Kappa Alpha Psi Frat, NAACP; bd of trustees Bennett College North Carolina 1987; principal Center for Excellence in Government 1988. **HONORS/ACHIEVEMENTS:** State of GA House & Senate Resolutions Outstanding Public Serv 1979; Achievement Kappa Alpha Psi Frat 1980; Comm Serv Atlanta Business League 1984; Dr of Laws, Shorter Coll, Allen Univ, Edward Waters Coll, Morris Booker Coll; Atlanta Urban League Distinguished Serv Awd 1986; Roy Wilkins Awd Georgia NAACP 1986; President's Awd Natl Conf of Black Mayors Economic Devel Task Force 1986; Leadership Award Metro-Atlanta United Way 1987; President's Award National Alliance of Business 1988. **BUSINESS ADDRESS:** Vice President, Natl Alliance of Business, 100 Edgewood Ave Ste 1800, Atlanta, GA 30303.

WALKER, WILLIE F.
Organization executive. **PERSONAL:** Born Feb 06, 1942, Vernon, AL; son of Willie B. Walker and Naomi Ford Walker; married Frizal Glasper, May 22, 1971; children: Shannon, Willie Jr., A;lex, Teresa. **EDUCATION:** Southern Illinois University, BS, 1965; University of Wisconsin, Milwaukee, WI, MS, 1971. **CAREER:** Venice School System, East St Louis, IL, teacher, 1965-69; Venice-Lincoln Educational Center, Venice, IL, director of placement, 1971-73; Madison/St Clair County, Alton, IL, director of manpower, 1973-76; National Urban League Regional Office, Chicago, IL, regional coordinator, 1976-77; Madison County Urban League, Alton, IL, executive director, 1977-85; Dayton Urban League, Dayton, OH, president and chief executive officer, 1985—. **ORGANIZATIONS:** Co-chair, Black Leadership Development, 1986—; board treasurer, Dayton Free Clinic, 1987—; co-chair, Ohio Black Family Coalition, 1987—; board member, Ohio Elected Public Officials, 1987—; board secretary, Ohio Council of Urban League, 1987—; member, Black Managers Association, 1987—; president, United Way Agency of Executives, 1989; member of steering committee, Black Agenda for the Year 2000, 1989; account chair, United Way Campaign, 1989. **HONORS/ACHIEVEMENTS:** Honorary member, National Business League, 1985; Gold Award, United Way of Greater Dayton, 1985-89; community service award, Dayton Jobs Corps Center, 1987; Century Club award, YMCA, 1987; honorary recognition, Black Leadership Development, 1989. **BUSINESS ADDRESS:** Dayton Urban League, 184 Salem Ave, United Way Building, Suite 240, Dayton, OH 45406.

WALKER, WILLIE M.
Engineer. **PERSONAL:** Born Aug 18, 1929, Bessemer, AL; son of John Walker and Annie M Thompson Walker; married Mae R; children: Patricia, Mark, Karen M Brown. **EDUCATION:** Marquette Univ, BEE 1958; Univ Of WI, MSEE 1965. **CAREER:** AC Spark Plug Div GMC, devel tech 1953-56, proj engr 1956-60, engr supvr 1960-65; AC Electronics Div GMC, sr devel eng 1965-71. **ORGANIZATIONS:** Mem IEEE since 1955, NSPE WI Soc of Prof Engrs 1981; reg prof Engr State of WI 1963; mem Computer Sci Adv Bd Milwaukee Area Techncl Coll since 1982; pres Potawatomi Area Cncl BSA 1982-84; mem Natl Council Boy Scouts of Amer; mem usher St Mary Catholic Church Men Falls, WI; chief camp inspector Area 1 East Central Region BSA; vice pres program Area One East Central Regoin BSA 1987-; chairman Computer Science Advisory Board Milwaukee Area Tech Coll 1988-89; sr mem Institute of Industrial Engineers 1988-; sr mem CASA Society of Manufacturing Engineers 1989-. **HONORS/ACHIEVEMENTS:** GM Awd for Excellence Comm Act Delco Electronics 1980; Man of the Year Rotary Club Menomonee Falls WI 1983; Black Achiever Bus/Ind YMCA Milwaukee WI 1984; Silver Antelope Awd East Central Region Boy Scouts of Amer 1987. **MILITARY SERVICE:** USAF sgt 1949-53. **BUSINESS ADDRESS:** Senior Production Engineer, Delco Electronics Div GMC, 7929 S Howell Ave, Oak Creek, WI 53154.

WALKER, WOODSON DUBOIS
Attorney. **PERSONAL:** Born Apr 06, 1950, Springfield, AR; married Hope Labarriteau King; children: Yedea H, Ajamu K. **EDUCATION:** AM&N Coll; Univ of AR Bine Bluff, BA History & Phil 1971; Univ of MN Sch of Law, JD 1974. **CAREER:** City of Allport AR, legal consult 1980; Cinula & Walker PA, Ltl Rock, partner 1978; City of Menifee AR, city & atty 1977; Walker Kaplan & Mays PA Little Rock, asso Atty 1976-77; Cntrl MN Legl Srv Corp Minneapolis, asso atty 1974-76. **ORGANIZATIONS:** Mem AR MN Am & Nat Bar Assn 1974; sec Ebony Plz Corp (Rtl Clthng Store) Little Rock AR 1976; mem Little Rock Wastewtr Utlty Com 1979; mem AR St Bd of Crrctns 1980. **HONORS/ACHIEVEMENTS:** Who's Who Amng Stdnts in AmUniv Coll 1970-71; Outstndng Stdnt Ldr Zeta Phi Beta SortyUniv of AR Pine Bluff 1971; Hghr Achvmnts Awd Phi Beta Omega Frat Inc Chi Psi Rho Chap Pine Bluff AR 1971; cum laude grad,Univ of AR Pine Bluff 1971. **BUSINESS ADDRESS:** Ste 1850 Union Nat Bank Bldg, Little Rock, AR 72201.

WALKER, WYATT TEE
Clergyman. **PERSONAL:** Born Aug 16, 1929, Brockton, MA; married Theresa Edwards; children: Ann Patrice, Wyatt Tee, Robert Charles, Earl Maurice. **EDUCATION:** VA Union Univ, BS (magna cum laude) 1950, MDiv (summa cum laude) 1953, LHD 1967; Colgate-Rochester Div School, PhD 1975; Gettysburg Coll, DD, 1989. **CAREER:** Historic Gillfield Baptist Church, Petersburg VA, minister, 1953-60; Dr Martin Luther King Jr, chief of staff; SCLC, Atlanta, vice pres, bd exec dir, 1960-64; Abyssinian Baptist Church, NYC, pulpit minister, 1965-66; Governor NYC, special asst on urban affairs; Cannan Baptist Church of Christ NYC, minister, CEO, 1967-. **ORGANIZATIONS:** mem, World Peace Council, 1971-;. **HONORS/ACHIEVEMENTS:** Author, Black Church Looks at the Bicentennial, Somebody's Calling My Name, Soul of Black Worship, Road to Damascus, Del World Conf on Religion and Peace, Japan; Received numerous human rights awards including the Elks Human Rights Award, 1963; Natl Alpha Awards in Civil Rights, 1965; Shriners Natl Civil Rights Award, 1974; Civil Rights Award, ADA, 1975. **BUSINESS ADDRESS:** Minister, CEO, Canaan Baptist Church, 132 West 116th St, New York, NY 10026.

WALKER-JOHNSON, GENEVA MARIE
Educator. **PERSONAL:** Born Dec 13, 1944, Philadelphia, PA; married Sidney Johnson; children: Ja-Neene Danielle, Sydnei Daniel. **EDUCATION:** Loretta Heights Coll, BA 1975; Univ of Northern CO, MA 1983. **CAREER:** Metropolitan State Coll, activities advisor 1972-74, student activities dir 1974-75, program dir 1975-77, dir student activities 1977-84; Illinois State Univ, asst dir residential life 1984-. **ORGANIZATIONS:** Exec bd CO Coll Personnel Guidance Assoc; mem Assoc of College Unions Intl Region XIII; mem Mountain Plain's Dean Conference; consultant Point O'Pines Corporation; mem Assoc of Coll and Univ Housing Officers; mem Friends of Higher Educ. **HONORS/ACHIEVEMENTS:** Listed in Outstanding Young Women of Amer; Kappa Delta Pi; Pi Lambda Theta; authored concept paper "The Departmental Community, A Program Concept for Urban Commuter Institutions,"; article "What Is A Program? A Student Leader Guide to Successful Programming for Students". **BUSINESS ADDRESS:** Assistant Dir, Illinois State University, Office of Residential Life, Normal, IL 61761.

WALKER-SHAW, PATRICIA
Business executive. **PERSONAL:** Born Jul 26, 1939, Little Rock, AR; married Harold R Shaw Sr; children: Harold R Jr. **EDUCATION:** Fisk Univ, BA (cum laude) 1961; TN State Univ, Teacher Cert 1962; Univ of TN Graduate School, social work 1966. **CAREER:** Tri-State Bank of Memphis, accounting trainee 1958-59; Universal Life Ins Co, underwriting clerk 1961; IL State Dept of Public Aid, caseworker 1961-62; TN State Dept Public Welfare, caseworker children 1963-66; Universal Life Ins Co, keypunch oper exec vice pres 1966-82, pres chief exec officer 1983-. **ORGANIZATIONS:** Pres Natl Ins Assn; bd of trustees Stillman Coll; bd of comm Memphis Light Gas & Water 1973-; bd of dirs Memphis Branch Fed Reserve Bank of St Louis 1981-. **HONORS/ACHIEVEMENTS:** Outstanding Leadership Awd Coca-Cola & Dr Pepper Bottling Co of Memphis; Amer Black Achievement Awd Ebony Mag; Par Excellence Awd PUSH; Ten Outstanding Bus & Prof Dollars & Sense Mag 1983; JE Walker Minority Bus Person of the Year Memphis NBL 1983. **BUSINESS ADDRESS:** President, Universal Life Ins Co, 480 Linden Ave, Memphis, TN 38101.

WALKER-TAYLOR, YVONNE
University president. **PERSONAL:** Born Apr 17, New Bedford, MA; married Robert H Taylor (deceased). **EDUCATION:** Wilberforce Univ, BS 1936; Boston Univ, MA 1938; Univ of KS, Educ Spec 1964. **CAREER:** Wilberforce Univ, asst acad dean 1967-68, vice pres academic dean 1973-83, provost 1983-84, president 1984-. **ORGANIZATIONS:** Bd dirs Natl Commn on Coop Educ 1977-72, 1983-; sec Greene Oaks Health Ctr 1983-; chmn Culture Planning Council Natl Mus Afro-Amer History 1983-; bd mem Dayton Art Inst 1984-; bd dirs United Way Xenia OH 1985; mem Links, Alpha Kappa Alpha. **HONORS/ACHIEVEMENTS:** Woman of the Year Met Civic Women's Assoc Dayton 1984; one of Top Ten Women Dayton Newspapers Women's Coalition 1984; Outstanding Woman of Yr Iota Phi Lambda 1985; Drum Major for Justice Awd SCLC 1986. **BUSINESS ADDRESS:** President, WilberforceUniv, Brush Row Rd, Wilberforce, OH 45384.

WALKER-WILLIAMS, HOPE DENISE
Educational administrator. **PERSONAL:** Born Dec 24, 1952, Chicago, IL; daughter of Welmon Walker and Maryann Walker; children: Albert Lee, Ebony Emani Denise. **EDUCATION:** Harvard Univ Graduate School of Design, Certificate 1981; St Ambrose Univ Davenport IA, BA Psychology 1985; St Ambrose Univ, MBA prog; Marycrest Coll Masters in Educ Program, 1989. **CAREER:** African Amer Drama Co, midwest regional coord 1982-83; Dramatic Mktg Assoc, opers mgr 1983-84; Scott County Davenport IA, admin intern 1985-86; Marycrest Coll Davenport, campus counselor 1986-87, asst to the dean 1987-. **ORGANIZATIONS:** Treas Quad Cities Career Womens Network 1983; student senator MBA Senate St Ambrose Coll 1985; mem Natl Assoc of Black MBAs 1986; bd mem HELP Legal Aid 1986; mem panel United Way Allocations 1987; bd mem, NACADA, 1988-. **HONORS/ACHIEVEMENTS:** Certificate of Appreciation Conf of Black Families 1979/82; Certificate of Recognition Church Women United 1983; Yellow Belt Tae Kwon Do Karate 1984; Recognition for Personal Dedication Jr Achievement, 1989-89. **HOME ADDRESS:** 1217 Ripley, Davenport, IA 52804. **BUSINESS ADDRESS:** Campus Counselor, Marycrest College, 1607 West 12th St, Davenport, IA 52804.

WALLACE, ARNOLD D., SR.
Educational administrator. **PERSONAL:** Born Feb 01, 1932, Salisbury, MD; son of G Linwood Wallace and Margaret Townsend-Wallace; married Theresa, Sep 27, 1950; children: Deborah, Terry, Arnold Jr, Michael, Stephen, Stephanie. **EDUCATION:** Rutgers Univ, AS 1974, BS 1977, MBA 1977; Howard Univ, MA 1986. **CAREER:** RCA Camden, engr tech 1957-61; Univac Philadelphia PA, engr tech 1961-68; WCAU-TV, engr tech 1963-72; WCAU-TV, dir of comm affairs 1972-79; Rutgers Univ, co-adj prof admin studies 1978-79; Howard Univ, dir univ relations 1979-80; New Breed Media Group, pres; WHMM-TV Howard Univ, gen mgr 1980-. **ORGANIZATIONS:** Pres Pennsauken NJ Bd of Ed 1975-76; mem Capitol Press Club, Natl Press Club, NAACP, Legal Defense Fund Steering Comm, Friends of the Kennedy Ctr, Oriental Lodge 1 FAM Camden NJ, Zamora Temple AEONMS Camden; mem Omega Psi Phi, Kiwanis Intl, FAA Commercial Pilot Multi-Engine-Land, Aircraft Owners & Pilots Assoc, Negro Airmen Intl, NJ State Bds of Ed fin Comm; bd of dir Dist of Columbia C of C, Intl United Black Fund, Metro YMCA; sec central education network bd of dir 1983-85; Nat'l Assoc of Public TV Stations, sec 1986-; DC Youth Orchestra, bd of dir 1986-; pres New Breed Media Group, Inc. 1975-. **HONORS/ACHIEVEMENTS:** Prod Negro Airmen Intl documentary film "Journey to Paradise-Nassau" 1972; article "Ebon Eagles" Flying Mag 1972; prod, wrote & filmed Negro Airmen Intl documentary "Journey to Paradise-Barbados" 1973; article "Integrated Cockpit" Aero Mag 1974; prod half-hour CBS training film "Careers in Broadcasting" 1974; Kappa Alpha Psi Frat Media Awd Media Accompl Exec Prod "Year 2000 & Beyond" Amer Found for Negro Affairs 1976; article "The Sharecropper" Rutgers Univ Lit Mag 1977; prod, dir film "Reaching Out" Camden Cty United Way 1979; the four chaplains awd 1979; exec prod Profiles In Creativeness" series 1983-; Awd for Film "Prime Minister Phillip "Barrow; prod, host "Turn to Ten" CBS-TV Philadelphia; Nat'l Assoc of Minority Contractors public service awd 1985; DC Chamber of Commerce media awd 1986; Private Sector Initiatives, pres of US Ronald Regan 1987; Silver Circle Natl Academy of TV Arts & Sciences 1988; Broadcasting Decision Making in the Area of Children's TV (dissertation) 1986; Delaney's Business Report (US Govt Contracts Newsletters) 1989. **BUSINESS ADDRESS:** General Manager, Howard Univ/WHMM-TV, 2222 4th St NW, Washington, DC 20059.

WALLACE, C. EVERETT
Attorney, appointed government official. **PERSONAL:** Born Aug 16, 1951, Chicago, IL. **EDUCATION:** Northwestern U, BA 1969-73; Northwestern U, JD 1973-76. **CAREER:** US Senate Budget Comm, sr analysis & energy couns 1980; Sen Howard Baker US Sen, legal asst 1977-80; Memphis Light Gas & Water Div Memphis, staff atty 1976-77; Clausen Miller & Gorman Caffery & Witous Law Firm, rsch assoc 1975-76; Shelby Co Black Rep Council, legal counsel & co-founder 1977; Progressive Assembly Reps, gen counsel & co-founder 1979. **ORGANIZATIONS:** Vice chmn & cofounder Black Rep Cong Staffer's Assn 1979; counsel sec of 1980 Republican Natl Conv; mem Natl Bar Assn; mem Amer Bar Assn; pres Alpha Mu Chap; Alpha Phi Alpha Frat Inc. **HONORS/ACHIEVEMENTS:** Northwestern Univ Top Ten Debator, Illinois State Contest; Natl Achievement Scholar, Thornton Township High School, Harvey IL; Natl Merit Scholar; Illinois State Scholar; Honors Grad, Northwestern Univ School of Law; admitted to Bar of Tennessee, 1977. **BUSINESS ADDRESS:** US Senate, Washington, DC.

WALLACE, C. EVERETT
Chief executive of beer distributorship. **CAREER:** City & Suburban Distributors, Inc, Chicago IL, chief executive, 1985—. **BUSINESS ADDRESS:** City & Suburban Distributors Inc, 1501 W Pershing Rd, Chicago, IL 60609. *

WALLACE, CHARLES LESLIE
Business executive. **PERSONAL:** Born Dec 26, 1945, Monmouth, IL; son of Leslie Wallace and Harriet Wallace; married Marie Elizabeth Lancaster; children: Allison, Bryan. **EDUCATION:** Northern IL Univ, BS Accounting 1967; Univ of Chicago, MBA Finance 1973; CPA 1973. **CAREER:** Arthur Andersen & Co, auditor 1967-74; Jos Schultz Brewing Co, financial analyst 1974-76; Univ Foods Corp, treasurer 1976-81; Pabst Brewing Co, treasurer 1981-85; Norrell Corp, treasurer 1985-87; North Milwaukee State Bank, pres 1987-89; Ameritech Mobile Communications Inc, vice president/chief financial officer 1989-. **ORGANIZATIONS:** Bd of dirs Medical Coll of Wisconsin; mem Finance Execs Inst Chicago Chapter; Amer Inst of CPA's, Kappa Alpha Psi. **MILITARY SERVICE:** USMC 1st lt 1967-72. **BUSINESS ADDRESS:** Vice President/Chief Financial Officer, Ameritech Mobile Communications Inc, 1515 Woodfield Rd, Schaumburg, IL 60173.

WALLACE, CLAUDETTE J. (NEE DELGADO)
Educator. **PERSONAL:** Married Elmo; children: Elmo Jr, Renee, Andre. **EDUCATION:** FL A&M U, BS; NY U, MS;Univ of Hartford, 6th yr prof cert; Springfield Coll, Triniy Coll,Univ of CT, Cntrl CT St Tchr Coll, grad Studies. **CAREER:** Barber Scotia Coll, past dir physical educ, FL Meml & Indstrl Inst, past dir girls physical educ. **ORGANIZATIONS:** Pres Black Bus & Professional Women Clb; area rep NYUniv Alumni Clb; mem Life Nat Educ Assn; mem Life Nat Hlth Phy Educ & Rcrtn Assn; exec sec New Britain Chap FL A&MUniv Alumni Assn; mem Coll Club; mem Am Assn of Univ Women; mem Life NAACP; mem Grtr New Britain Comm Cncl; den mother 1960-65; st pres of educ CT Diocese of the Ch of God in Christ; bd chrprsn Black Resrch Informtn Cntr 1970; dir New Britain Tutrl Schl 1969; chrtr mem Women's Aux of Salvation Army; mem New Britain Gen Hosp Vol Aux Assn; mem New Britain HS Music Club & Parents Booster's Athltc Assn; past vice pres Little Leg Basebll & Midget & Football Clubs. **HONORS/ACHIEVEMENTS:** Recip Testmnl Dinner 1972. **BUSINESS ADDRESS:** Head Dept of Physical Educ, Slade School, 183 Steel St, New Britain, CT 06052.

WALLACE, DERRICK D.
Business executive. **PERSONAL:** Born Nov 04, 1953, Orlando, FL; son of Theressa Williams Wallace; divorced; children: Daunte, Deja. **EDUCATION:** FL A&M Univ, BS Accounting 1975. **CAREER:** Price Waterhouse & Co CPA, staff accountant 1975-77; Tuttle/White Constructors, Inc, chief accountant 1977-79; Construc Two, Inc. owner/pres 1979-. **ORGANIZATIONS:** Bd mem Central State Assn of Min Contr; mem Greater Orlando Chamber of Commerce 1984; bd mem Greater Orlando Chamber of Commerce 1989 3 yr term; chairman Private Industry Council of Central Florida, past 2 years; commr Mayor's Commission on the Arts; subcommittee chair Mayor's Youth Comm (business involvement); class mem Leadership Orlando 1988; mem Greater Florida Minority Purchasing Council; partner Partners in Education - Washington Shores Elementary; partner Partners in Education - Rock Lake Elementary; sponsored minority (Black) Role Model Project for Orange County Schools as the Private Industry Council Chairman, gathered over 120 Black professionals to speak to children in school about what their life experiences had been and the importance of educ ation. **HONORS/ACHIEVEMENTS:** Construction Firm of the Year, US Dept of Commerce Minority Business Devel Agency 1984; Outstanding Achievement as Minority Business Entrepreneur, Central Florida Minority Development Council, Inc., 1988; named Outstanding Young Man of America in 1986; Entrepreneur of the year GFMPL; Up and Comer Award 1989 Orlando Business Journal and Price Waterhouse. **BUSINESS ADDRESS:** General Contractor, Construct Two, Inc., 4409 Old Winter Garden Rd, Orlando, FL 32811.

WALLACE, HARDEN WILSON
Business executive. **PERSONAL:** Born Sep 10, 1922, Natchez, MS; married Bernice Williams; children: Josephine Cottingham, LaVern Little, Harden Jr, Tom L, Ruth Diane Harris, Darlene Price, Keith. **EDUCATION:** Alcorn State Univ, BS 1965; Univ of Southern MS, Business Ed. **CAREER:** Armstrong Tires, super 1965-84; Family Fashions, pres 1985-. **ORGANIZATIONS:** Mem NAACP 1960-85; pres Natchez Bus & Civic League 1967-85; supt MS Conf Sunday School 1976-85; mem Architectural Review Bd City of Natchez 1979-85; bdmem Natchez Chamber of Commerce. **HOME ADDRESS:** 712 N Pine, Natchez, MS 39120. **BUSINESS ADDRESS:** President, Family Fashion, 600 Franklin St, Natchez, MS 39120.

WALLACE, HAROLD GENE
Educational administrator. **PERSONAL:** Born Aug 13, 1945, Gaffney, SC; son of Charles T Wallace Sr and Melinda Goudelock Wallace; married Carrie Lucinda Littlejohn, Jul 13, 1963; children: Toya Bonita, Shonda Lee, Harold Gene Jr, Charles Marion. **EDUCATION:** Claflin College Orangeburg SC, BS summa cum laude 1967; Duke Univ Div School Durham NC, MDiv 1971. **CAREER:** Bethesda Presbyterian Church, Gaffney, SC, pastor and youth counsellor, 1968; Durham Community House, Inc, counsellor, 1968-69; Duke Univ, Summer Transitional Program, assistant director, 1969, associate director, 1970, co-director, 1971, director, 1972, assistant to dean of undergraduate education, student advisor, 1969-72, assistant provost, dean of black student affairs, interim director of community and field work for Afro-American majors, seminar instructor for Afro-American studies, 1972-73; Univ of NC, Chapel Hill, associate dean of student affairs, director of department of special programs, 1973-79, assistant vice chancellor for student affairs, 1979-80, vice chancellor for student affairs, 1980—. **ORGANIZATIONS:** Group moderator So Regional Educ Bd Conf on Black Students & Univ 1971; mem Nat Commn of United Ministers in Higher Educ 1971-75; consult Minority Student Progs Univ SC Furman & Wake Forest 1971-78; sec treas Black Faculty Staff Caucus Univ NC Chapel Hill 1974-80; bd dir Wesley Found Campus Ministry Univ NC 1976-80; mem Inst Desegregation NC Cen Univ Durham NC 1977-80; pres Alpha Kappa Mu Nat & Honor Soc Claflin Coll 1966-67. **HONORS/ACHIEVEMENTS:** Rockefeller Fellow, Duke Univ 1967; publ "Studies in Black" 1969; "Three Years of the Duke Summer Transitional Program" 1973; Faculty awards for outstanding achievements, Black Student Movement, Univ NC Chapel Hill, 1981, Univ NC Black Alumni Association, 1982. **BUSINESS ADDRESS:** U of NC Chapel Hill, CB 9100, 103 South Bldg, Chapel Hill, NC 27599.

WALLACE, HELEN WINFREE-PEYTON
Educational administrator. **PERSONAL:** Born Dec 19, 1927, New York, NY; daughter

of Hugh Winfree and Agnes Winfree; married Mr Charles (divorced); children: Walter S Peyton IV. **EDUCATION:** VA Union Univ, BA 1949; NW Univ, MA 1955; VA Union Univ, BA 1959; Univ of CA, VA State Univ, Petersburg, VCU, Richmond, Univ of Caltolica, Di Milano Italy, 1960-68. **CAREER:** Richmond Public Schools, tchr 1949-69, lang arts consultant 1969-71, diagnostic & prescriptive reading, coord 1971-75; Richmond Public Schools chptr I reading coordinator 1975. **ORGANIZATIONS:** Consltnt Comm Groups 1975-83; pres Elem Tchrs Assoc 1967; v pres Assoc Classroom Tchrs 1973; slsmn Real Estate 1968; mem Natl Ed Assoc 1950; v pres Richmond Ed Assoc 1950; mem Crusade for Voters 1949; exec Brd of NAACP IRA-RARC-VSRA. **HONORS/ACHIEVEMENTS:** Tchr First Black to integrate Westhampton Sch 1965-69; execl serv Chapter I Reading Teacher 1982; achievements Alliance for Black Social Welfare 1983; co-sponsored Book Bowl. **HOME ADDRESS:** 1710 Hungary Rd, Richmond, VA 23228.

WALLACE, HOMER L.
Business executive. **PERSONAL:** Born Jan 18, 1941, Effingham Co; married Mary C; children: Sandra R, Cynthia L. **CAREER:** Coastal State Life Ins, debit mgr. **ORGANIZATIONS:** Srvd supt Sunday 15 Yrs 1960-75; chmn Deacon Bd; pres ESAA; Effingham Co Sch Sys. **HONORS/ACHIEVEMENTS:** Built first washeteria, Guyton GA for Blacks 1968; first car wash Guyton GA 1968; orgnzd frst NAACP br Springfield GA 1968; elctd frst vice pres 1968, presNAACP 1974; Expert Rifleman AUS 1968; awd Top Agnt Ins Sls 4 yrs Row 1968-72. **MILITARY SERVICE:** AUS 1963-65 e4. **BUSINESS ADDRESS:** PO Box 349, Springfield, GA 31329.

WALLACE, JAMES ALFONSO
Chief executive officer. **PERSONAL:** Born Oct 11, 1948, Clearwater, FL; children: Dwanetta Peoples; Nicole Chandler, Kenneth H Williams II. **EDUCATION:** Bethune-Cookman Coll, BS Business 1970; Southern Methodist Univ, MBA Acctng 1971. **CAREER:** OICS of Amer Inc, fiscl mgt spec 1971-72, sr field spec 1972-74, proj offcr 1974-76. **ORGANIZATIONS:** Advsry dir Med Ctr State Bank 1984; treas OICs of Am Exec Dir Assnc 1978-80 1984; corp dir OK City NE, Inc 1977-; v pres Last Frontier Cncl-BoyScouts of Amer 1984; allocations review United Way of OK City 1978-; mem Alpha Phi Alpha Frat, Inc 1968. **HONORS/ACHIEVEMENTS:** Flwshp General Foods 1970; schlrshp Theodore Luce-Putnam 1966-70. **HOME ADDRESS:** 1101 NE 14th St, Oklahoma City, OK 73117. **BUSINESS ADDRESS:** Executive Dir, Opportunities Indstrlztn Cntr, 400 N Walnut, Oklahoma City, OK 73104.

WALLACE, JEFFREY J.
Educational administrator. **PERSONAL:** Born Apr 07, 1946, Mobile, AL; married Patricia A Henderson; children: Jeffrey, Jennifer, Justin, Jawaan. **EDUCATION:** State Univ College at Fredonia, BA History 1964-68; State Univ of NY at Buffalo, MEd Counseling 1973, PhD History & Philosophy of Educ 1980. **CAREER:** SUNY Fredonia, admin asst for adm & records 1969-72, dir EOP 1972-81, asst vice pres for academic affairs 1977-81; State Univ College at Buffalo, dir EOP 1981-86, asst vice pres acad affairs 1986-. **ORGANIZATIONS:** SUNY Chancellors' Taskforce on Minority Graduate Oppor 1983; Natl Assn of Academic Advisors 1984; bd chairperson of the Buffalo Post-Secondary Consortium of Special Progs 1985; pres Special Prog Personnel Assn 1984-; evaluator/ ed consultant PNJ Consultling. **HONORS/ACHIEVEMENTS:** Polotics & Precusors The EOP/SEEK at SUCB Urban Educ vol 18 no 4 pgs 503-519 Jan 1984; Special Services for Disadvantaged Students Grant SUNY 1979; SpecialServices for Disadvantaged Students Grant SUCB 1984. **BUSINESS ADDRESS:** Asst Vice Pres Academic Affairs, StateUniv Coll at Buffalo, 1300 Elmwood Ave CA 306, Buffalo, NY 14222.

WALLACE, JOHN E., JR.
Superior Court Judge. **PERSONAL:** Born Mar 13, 1942, Pitman, NJ; married Barbara A Coles; children: John III, Andrea Lynn, Kimberly Denise, Michele Eileen, Michael Ernest. **EDUCATION:** Univ of DE, BA 1964; Harvard Law Sch, LlB 1967. **CAREER:** Atkinson Myers Archie & Wallace, atty-ptnr; Washington Township, municipal ct judge 1977-; Trustees of PA Central Transp, atty 1971-75; Montgomery McCracken Walker & Rhoads Co, asso 1970-71. **ORGANIZATIONS:** Sec Gloucester Co Municipal Ct Judges Assn 1974-; bd of trustees, treas Gloucester Co Coll; mem Am Bar Assn; mem NJ Bar Assn; mem Barrister's Club; baseball & basketball coach Washington Township 1970-; mem Comm Activities Commn, Washington Township 1971; mem Kappa Alpha Psi 1978-. **HONORS/ACHIEVEMENTS:** Cert of Achvmnt, AUS 1969; Outstanding Serv Award, NJ State Fedn of Colored Women's Clubs 1976. **MILITARY SERVICE:** AUS capt 1968-69. **BUSINESS ADDRESS:** State of New Jersey, Woodbury, NJ 08096.

WALLACE, JOHN HOWARD
Educator. **PERSONAL:** Born Mar 08, 1925, Cincinnati, OH; married Kathryn; children: John, Jean. **EDUCATION:** Howard U, BS 1947; OH St U, MS 1949; OH St U, PhD 1953. **CAREER:** Morehouse Coll School Med, assoc dean academic affrs, prof & chmn dept microbiology & immnlgy; Univ of Louisville, prof 1971-79; OH St Univ, 1970-71; Tulane Univ, 1966-70; Meharry Med Coll, 1961-66; Meharry Med Coll, asst prof 1959-61; Harvard Med School, research assoc 1955-59; NIH Natl Inst on Drug Abuse, consult 1977. **ORGANIZATIONS:** Mem NIH Task Force on Immunization 1977; NIH Nat Cancer Inst Rsrch Manpower Rev Com 1977; consult Inst on Heart & Lung Disease 1977; chmn NIH Nat Inston Allrgy & Infctn Disease Bd of Sci Cnslrs 1975-76; mem Nat Inst on Allrgy & Infct Dis Bd of Sci Cnslrs 1972-76; commr KY Commn of Human Rghts1976; chmn Educ Com NAACP 1972; bd dir Louisville NAACP 1972; Leukemia Soc of Am 1975; bd grad adv Meharry Med Coll 1972. **HONORS/ACHIEVEMENTS:** NIH Rsrch Career Dvl Awd 1961-66; NIH Postdoctoral Flwsp 1954-55, 59-61; mem Sigma Xi Hon Soc; Distgsd Alumnus Cit OH StUniv 1977. **BUSINESS ADDRESS:** Professor/Chairman, Univ of Louisville, Dept of Microbiol/Immunology, Louisville, KY 40292.

WALLACE, JOSEPH FLETCHER, JR.
Dean of education. **PERSONAL:** Born Aug 03, 1921, Ethelsville, AL; married Ethel Theresa Ward; children: Patrick, Katherine T Wallace Casey. **EDUCATION:** West Coast Univ, BA 1953; Amer Baptist Theol Seminary, Certificate 1975, Diploma 1977; Union Univ, DTh 1982. **CAREER:** US Government, clerk 1949-54; General Motors Corp, sr inspector 1955-82; Thomas & Sons Building Inc, consultant 1982-; The Religious Council of Amer, dean of educ. **ORGANIZATIONS:** Nobles of the Mystic Shrine 32 Degree Mason 1979; mem LA Police Clergy Council 1985-, NAACP. **HONORS/ACHIEVEMENTS:** Awd of Merit for Outstanding Achievement USC 1975. **MILITARY SERVICE:** AUS s/sgt 6 yrs; Good Conduct Medal, Combat Infantry, Bronze Star. **BUSINESS ADDRESS:** Dean of Education, The Religious Council of Amer, PO Box 82004, Los Angeles, CA 90082.

WALLACE, KAREN SMYLEY
Educator. **PERSONAL:** Born Dec 11, 1943, New Orleans, LA; married Perry E Wallace. **EDUCATION:** Hunter Coll NY, BA 1965; Middlebury Grad Sch, MA 1967; City Univ of NY, PhD 1977. **CAREER:** SUNY Stony Brook, instructor 1967-71; Univ of MD, instructor 1972-75; Howard Univ Washington, assoc prof 1975-. **ORGANIZATIONS:** Chair of educ comm Mayor's Intl Advisory Council 1980-. **HONORS/ACHIEVEMENTS:** Fulbright Hayes Study Abroad 1965-67; Ford Found Dissertation Grant 1971; Phelps Stokes Teacher Exchange 1979; AW Mellon Rsch Grant 1984. **BUSINESS ADDRESS:** Associate Professor, HowardUniv, HowardUniv, Washington, DC 20059.

WALLACE, LEWIS S., JR.
Military educator. **PERSONAL:** Born Nov 14, 1944, Washington, DC; married Annie Ruth Elson; children: Steven, Marten, Karen Torrey. **EDUCATION:** Syracuse Univ NY, AB Soviet Area Studies (summa cum laude) 1972; OH State Columbus, OH, MA Slavic Langs & Lit 1977; pushkin Russian Lang Inst Moscow USSR, cert in Russian 1977; GeorgetownUniv Wash DC;; Ph D cand 1981. **CAREER:** Dept of State, diplomatic pouch clerk 1962-65; Russian USAF Acad, course dir of basic & intermd 1977-78; USAF Academy, asst prof Russian 1978-80; DefenseIntelligence Agency, soviet area spclst 1980-83; Hampton Univ, lecturer in Russsian 1983-84; HQ TAC IG Langley AFB, VA, chief intelligence inspctr 1984-85. **ORGANIZATIONS:** Mem Am Assn of Tchrs of Slavic Langs 1977-85; Am Cncl of Tchrs of Russian 1978-85; Natl Mltry Intlgnce Assoc 1980-85; proj ofcr DC Spcl Olympics 1980-83; City of Colorado Spgs Intercultural Festvl 1978-80; mem USAF Acad Spkrs Bureau 1977-80. **HONORS/ACHIEVEMENTS:** Outstanding Young Men of Am US Jaycees AL 1980; dist grad Defense Lang Inst Syracuse, NY 1966, AF Inst of Technology 1977; achvmnt awd DC Olympic DC 1983. **MILITARY SERVICE:** USAF mjr 20 yrs, Defense Meritorious Serv Medal; Air Medal (8); ASFCM (2); AF Achvmnt Medal 1966-84.

WALLACE, MILTON DE'NARD
Principal. **PERSONAL:** Born Jul 07, 1957, Tyler, TX; son of John Wallace and Thelma Jackson Wallace; married Gwen Wheeler Wallace, Apr 08, 1989. **EDUCATION:** East TX State Univ, BS 1978, MEd 1979; Univ of North Texas, Denton, TX 1988. **CAREER:** Commerce ISD, teacher 1978-83, asst principal 1983-84; Union Hill ISD, principal 1984-; Denton Independent School Dist, Denton, TX asst principal, 1987-. **ORGANIZATIONS:** Pres RAWSCO Inc 1983; vice pres Professional Men's Serv Club 1983-84; mem TX Assoc of Elementary School Principal 1983, TX Assoc of Secondary School Principals 1984, TX Assoc of Secondary School Principals 1986; owner M & L Educational Scholarship Service; mem Texas Assn of Black School Educators 1989-. **HONORS/ACHIEVEMENTS:** Director of Summer Workshop - Texas Assn of Student Councils 1989. **HOME ADDRESS:** PO Box 2843, Denton, TX 76202.

WALLACE, PAUL STARETT, JR.
Attorney. **PERSONAL:** Born Jan 22, 1941, Wilmington, NC; married Priscilla H Harris; children: Shaunia Patrese. **EDUCATION:** North Carolina Central Univ, BS, in Comm 1962, JD, 1966. **CAREER:** US Copyright Office Library of Congress, copyright examiner, 1966-71; Congressional Research Serv, Library of Congress, former senior legislative atty, head of the congress section, amer law div, Washington, DC, 1984-86. **ORGANIZATIONS:** Advisory bd, Comm Action for Human Serv Inc, 1983-; Fed Bar Assn News & Jrnl, 1980-81; sec, Cncl of Crct; vice pres, Fed Bar Assn, 1981-82; pres, Capitol Hill Chapter Fed Bar Assn, 1979-80; natl vice pres, District of Columbia Circuit Fed Bar Assn, 1981-82; chairperson, Section on the Admin of Justice, 1984-86; bd of trustees, Peoples Congregational Church, Washington, DC, 1984-89; mem, Dist of Columbia Bar Assn, US Supreme Court; continuing educ bd, Fed Bar Assn, 1985-; vice-chairperson, Library of Congress US Savings Bond Campaign, 1985; mem, Omega Psi Phi, US Dist Ct for District of Columbia; mem, US Court of Appeals for the DC Circuit; special editor Fed Bar Assn News & Journal, 1984, 1986; mem US Dist Court for the 8th Circuit, Phi Alpha Delta Law Fraternity Intl; mem, Natl & Amer Bar Ass oc; 33 Degree Mason; chairperson continuing educ bd, Fed Bar Assn, 1987-; trustee, Peoples Congragational Church, Washington, DC, 1984-89. **HONORS/ACHIEVEMENTS:** Mem, Pi Gamma Mu Natl Science Honor Soc; Commendation Award Outstanding Qualities of Leadership & Decicated Serv, 1980; Distinguished Serv Award, 1984; Fed Bar Assn Longstanding and Dedicated Serv Award, 1986. **HOME ADDRESS:** 3271 Van Hazen St NW, Washington, DC 20015.

WALLACE, PERRY EUGENE
Attorney. **PERSONAL:** Born Feb 19, 1948, Nashville, TN. **EDUCATION:** Vanderbilt U, BE 1966-70; Columbia Univ Law Sch, 1973. **CAREER:** US Justice Dept, atty 1980; George Washington U, adj instr & asst dir 1977-80; Mayor's Ofc Washington DC, lgsltv anlyst. **ORGANIZATIONS:** Mem DC Bar; mem World Bnk Intnl Mntry Fnd 1979; mem Chrl Soc; mem Intnl Am Chmbr Sngrs 1979. **HONORS/ACHIEVEMENTS:** First Black Vrsty Athlete, SE Conf VndrbltUniv 1966-70; B of Ugliness 1970; SEC Sprtsmnshp Awd, SE Conf 1970; Faculty Awd Outstndng Srvc 1970; Charles Evans Hughes Fellow ColumbiaUniv Law Sch 1973. **MILITARY SERVICE:** Army ng. **BUSINESS ADDRESS:** Main Justice Bldg, Pennslyvania Ave, Washington, DC.

WALLACE, PHYLLIS A.
Educator. **PERSONAL:** Born in Baltimore, MD; daughter of John Wallace and Stevella Parker Wallace. **EDUCATION:** NY Univ, BA 1943; Yale Univ, MA 1944, PhD 1948. **CAREER:** Natl Bur Econ Rsch, economist 1948-52; CCNY, lecturer 1948-51; Atlanta Univ, assoc prof 1953-57; US Govt, econ analyst 1957-65; US EEOC, chief tech studies 1966-69; New York City Met Applied Rsch Ctr, vice pres rsch 1969-72; MIT Sloan School of Mgmt, vstg prof 1973-75, prof 1975-. **ORGANIZATIONS:** Dir State Bank & Trust Co Boston; trustee Brookings Inst Washington; trustee Teacher Ins & Annuity Assoc NY, mem Pres Pay Adv Comm; pres, Industrial Relations Research Assn, 1988; overseer, Boston Museum of Fine Arts. **HONORS/ACHIEVEMENTS:** Hon degree Valparaiso Univ 1977; Wilbur Cross Medal Yale Univ 1980; Hon deg Mount Holyoke Coll 1983; Hon deg Brown Univ 1986; Northeastern Univ, 1987; Distinguished Service Award, Harvard Business School, 1988; published 6 books. **BUSINESS ADDRESS:** Professor, Massachusetts Inst of Technology, Sloan School of Management, 50 Memorial Dr, Cambridge, MA 02139.

WALLACE, RENEE C.
Psychologist. **PERSONAL:** Born in New Britain, CT. **EDUCATION:** Central CT State Univ, BA 1974; Univ of IA, MA 1975, PhD 1977. **CAREER:** Univ of IA, admin asst 1974-77; Morgan State Univ, admin/asst prof 1977-79; Clayton Univ, adjunct faculty 1979-; James Madison Univ, counseling psychologist 1980-84; Wallace & Wallace Assocs, dir 1980-; SUNY Potsdam, dir of counseling 1984; Dept of Corrections, administrator 1986-. **ORGANIZATIONS:** Sec Phi Delta Kappa 1979; consultant Southern Assoc of Colls & Schools 1981, 84; educ consultant Black Educational Res & Inf Ctr 1984; bd dirs NatlComm of Educating Youth on Energy. **HONORS/ACHIEVEMENTS:** Publications "Prospective Teachers' Responses on an Adjective Checklist to Descriptions of 3 Students in 3 Different Socioeconomic Classes," US Govt 1978; "Black Administrators & Career Stress," proceedings of the 8th Natl Conf on Blacks in Higher Educ 1983. **HOME ADDRESS:** 153 South Mountain Drive, New Britain, CT 06052.

WALLACE, RICHARD WARNER
Engineer, government executive. **PERSONAL:** Born Nov 06, 1929, Gary, IN; married Lillian Mozel. **EDUCATION:** Purdue U, BS 1951; George Washington U, AmUniv Wash DC, post grad studies; Def Weapon Systms Mgmt Cntr, slctd spcl stdys 1971. **CAREER:** USN Naval Sea Systems Command, e dsgnr dvl & tstng elec, elctrnc systms on ships & submarines 1951, rspnsbl mngmnt tech & lgstcs support navy's deepsubmergence vehicle prgrms, & nuclear pwrd submarine NR 1, rgstrd Prfl Engr Wash DC 1958-85 retired; TRW Inc, sr staff engr systems div systems & engrg dept. **ORGANIZATIONS:** Mem Nat Soc Professional Engrs; Am Soc Navl Engrs; Nat Oceanographic Fnd; Marine Tech Soc Amateur Radio Astrnmy Photography; life mem Alpha Phi Alpha; chartr mem Iota Upsilon Lambda Chpt, Montgomery Cnty MD; mem The Guardsmen, Wash DC Chpt; The Pigskin Clb Washington DC; Bachelor Benedict Club. **HONORS/ACHIEVEMENTS:** Navy Meritorious Civilian Srv Awd 1974; Navy Grp Achvmnt Awd 1972; Dept of the Navy Superior Civilian Serv Awd 1985. **MILITARY SERVICE:** AUS sgnl corp 1955-57. **BUSINESS ADDRESS:** Senior Staff Engineer, TRW, Inc, 7600 Colshire Dr, McLean, VA 22102.

WALLACE, RONALD WILFRED
Business executive. **PERSONAL:** Born Nov 14, 1941, Aliquippa, PA; married Kay Francis; children: Duane, Ronald Jr, DuBoise, Elaine, LaRanna. **EDUCATION:** Aliquippa HS, graduate 1956-60. **CAREER:** Natl Life Ins Co, agent 1966-69; LTV Steel Co, security services 1969-; Bd of Educ; secretary; Commonwealth of Pennsylvania, auditor. **ORGANIZATIONS:** Church in the Round bd of ministers 1979-, bd of trustees 1982-; exec bd NAACP 1983-; rep Legislative Action Comm 1984-. **MILITARY SERVICE:** AUS security agency staff sgt 3 yrs; Good Conduct, Natl Defense, Oversea Medal; Vietnam Service NCO Leadership; Japan Svs Medal; Far East Svs Medal. **HOME ADDRESS:** 131 Orchard St, Aliquippa, PA 15001.

WALLACE, RUBY ANN See DEE, RUBY

WALLACE, SAMUEL
President/advertising. **PERSONAL:** Born Jul 24, 1949, New York, NY. **EDUCATION:** Howard Univ, BA 1971; Columbia Univ, MBA 1973. **CAREER:** Procter & Gamble, brand asst 1973-76; The Best Foods Co, assoc brand mgr 1976-77; Clorox Co, acquisitions mgr 1977-80; Xodex Enterprises Ltd, 1980-87; Williams Wallace Mgmt Consultants 1987-. **ORGANIZATIONS:** Chairperson NAACP Corporate Task Force, East Bay Black Chamber; vice pres US Chamber of Commerce; co-chairperson White House Conf on Small Business; mem Natl Black Republicans, Natl Federation of Independent Business; chairperson, Blacks for Bush. **HONORS/ACHIEVEMENTS:** Comm Serv Awd Alpha Kappa Psi; Business Awd Sickle Cell Anemia Assoc; Natl Business League Chap Leadership Awd.

WALLACE, THEODORE RICHMOND
Government official. **PERSONAL:** Born Nov 12, 1949, Fitzgerald, GA; children: Kim, Rychod, Terrance, Todd. **EDUCATION:** South GA Coll, AA 1972; Ft Valley State Coll, BA 1974; Ben Hill/Irwin Tech 1979. **CAREER:** South GA Area Planning & Devel, mem 1980; City Government, alderman-at-large. **ORGANIZATIONS:** Mem south GA Area Planning & Devel 1980-85, Fitzgerald City Council 1980-85, GA HS Officials Assoc 1981-85. **HONORS/ACHIEVEMENTS:** Awd for Excellence Gen Motors 1980; Awd for Excellence Gen Motors 1984. **MILITARY SERVICE:** AUS boiler tech 3rd class 4 yrs. **BUSINESS ADDRESS:** Alderman-at-Large, City Government, Perry House Rd, Fitzgerald, GA 31750.

WALLACE, WILLIAM JAMES LORD
College president. **PERSONAL:** Born Jan 13, 1908, Salisbury, NC; son of Thomas Wallace and Lauretta Wallace; married Louise Eleanor Taylor; children: Louise Eleanor. **EDUCATION:** Univ of Pittsburgh, BS 1927; Columbia Univ, AM 1931; Cornell Univ, PhD 1937; Teachers Coll, attended 1947; Livingstone Coll, LLD 1959; Concord Coll, LHD 1970; Alderson-Broaddus Coll, DSc 1971; West Virginia State Coll, Doctor of Letters 1981; Marshall Univ, Doctor of Pedagogy 1983. **CAREER:** Livingstone Coll, instructor science 1927, chemistry 1928-32; Lincoln Univ, Jefferson City MO, prof chemistry 1932-33; West Virginia State Coll, instructor chemistry 1933-34, asst prof 1934-37, assoc prof 1937-43, prof 1943-, acting admin asst to pres 1944-45, admin asst 1945-50, acting pres 1952-53, pres 1953-73 retired; West Virginia State Coll, bd of advisors 1982-89. **ORGANIZATIONS:** Trustee 1939-, presiding elder 1964-, AME Zion Church West Virginia Dist 1964-; trustee Herbert H Thomas Memorial Hospital Assn 1970-78; comm Kanawha Parks & Recreation Comm 1973-79; non-lawyer mem of Legal Ethics Comm of West Virginia State Bar 1980-86; chmn Kanawha County Library Bd 1958-; chmn advisory comm to pres 1982-84,86-88, vice chmn 1984-86 West Virginia State Coll. **HONORS/ACHIEVEMENTS:** Distinguished West Virginia Gov John D Rockefeller IV 1979; awarded third Washington-Carver Award for Outstanding Serv to the Citizens of West Virginia, West Virginia Dept of Culture & History 1986; Certificate & Plaque by West Virginia State Bar in recognition of Outstanding & Superb Contribution & Serv to the legal system & to justice 1986; presented Martin Luther King Jr"Living the Dream" Award for Scholarship 1987; Citations from Univ of Pittsburgh and West Virginia Univ. **BUSINESS ADDRESS:** Board of Advisor West Virginia State College, PO Box 417, Institute, WV 25112.

WALLER, CALVIN A.H.
Military officer. **PERSONAL:** Born Dec 17, 1937, Baton Rouge, LA; married Marion L Estes; children: Michael, Mark. **EDUCATION:** Prairie View A&M Univ, BS 1959; Shippensburg State Univ, MS 1978. **CAREER:** 24th Infantry Div, chief of staff 1983; XVIII Airborne Corps, chief of staff 1984; 82d Airborne Div, asst div comm operations; I Corps & Fort Lewis, dep commanding gen. **ORGANIZATIONS:** Mem Assn US Army 1970-85; mem Rocks Inc 1980-85. **MILITARY SERVICE:** AUS major gen 27 yrs; Defense Superior Serv Medal; Bronze Star w/Oak Leaf Cluster; Meritorious Serv Medal w/3 Oak Leaf Clusters. **BUSINESS ADDRESS:** Deputy CG, I Corps, I Corps & Ft Lenis, Fort Lewis, WA 98433.

WALLER, EUNICE MCLEAN
Educator. **PERSONAL:** Born Jun 29, 1921, Lillington, NC; daughter of Absalom McLean and Mary Tucker McLean; married Dr William DeHomer Waller, Aug 09, 1958; children: Deborah, Kenneth. **EDUCATION:** Fayetteville State Univ, BS, highest honors, 1942; Univ of Pennsylvania, MEd, 1953; North Carolina Central Univ, further study in psych, 1953-54; Wayne State Univ; Univ of Vermont, further study in math, 1963. **CAREER:** Harnett HS, teacher, 1942-46; Shawtown HS, teacher, 1947-55; Fayetteville Univ, teacher, 1955-56; Sarah Nance Elementary School, teacher, 1956-58; Eiton Elementary School, teacher, 1958-60; Connecticut Coll, instructor, 1965-71; Clark Lane Jr High, teacher, 1961-89. **ORGANIZATIONS:** Mem, AAUW; Delta Kappa Gamma; trustee Waterford Country School; pres Waterford Educ Assn, 1965-66; treasurer, Waterford Educ Assn, 1969-75; pres, Dr Martin Luther King Trust Fund ,1969-84; pres bd of dirs, Child Guidance Clinic, 1976-78; dir, Connecticut Educ Assn, 1979-82; corporator, Lawrence Memorial Hospitals, 1975-89; trustee, Mitchell Coll, 1975-; trustee, Connecticut Coll, 1988-89; mayor, City of New London, 1988-89; city councilor, City of New London, 1987-89. **HONORS/ACHIEVEMENTS:** EE Smith Memorial Award, Fayetteville Univ, 1942; Natl Science Fellowship, Univ of Vermont, 1963; Connecticut Educ Assn Human Relations Award, 1980; OIC Comm Service Award, New London, 1982; NAACP McNair Award for Political Involvement, 1984. **HOME ADDRESS:** 337 Vauxhall St, New London, CT 06320. **BUSINESS ADDRESS:** Mayor, 181 Captain's Walk, New London, CT 06320.

WALLER, JUANITA ANN
Marketing research analyst. **PERSONAL:** Born Feb 20, 1958, Gretna, VA. **EDUCATION:** Drexel Univ, BS Marketing 1981. **CAREER:** Drexel Univ, student admissions counselor 1979-80; Clover Div of Strawbridge and Clothier, customer service mgr 1981-82; Drexel Univ, asst dean of admissions 1982-86; First Pennsylvania Bank, marketing research consultant 1986-. **ORGANIZATIONS:** Mem Urban Bankers Assoc of Delaware Valley 1986-, Natl Black MBA Assoc 1986-; mem The Natl Assoc of Negro Business and Professional Womens Clubs Inc 1986-. **HOME ADDRESS:** 10825 E Keswick Rd, Apt #260, Philadelphia, PA 19154.

WALLER, LARRY
Entrepreneur, contractor. **PERSONAL:** Born Jun 09, 1947, Chicago, IL; son of Willis Waller and Hulena Hubbard; married Ruby L. Waller, Dec 24, 1969; children: Kelly D. Waller. **EDUCATION:** Malcolm X College, Chicago, IL, AA 1974; Governors State Univ, Park Forest South, IL, BS 1978, MBA 1979. **CAREER:** Associated with Fullerton Mechanical Contractors, Elk Grove Village, IL, 1969-76; Dyd Construction, Phoenix, IL, superintendant, 1977-79; Pyramid Industries Inc, Riverdale, IL, president, 1979-. **ORGANIZATIONS:** Dir, Black Contractors United 1979-; mem, Natl Assn of Independent Business 1979-, Assn of Energy Engineers 1984-, Builders Assn of Chicago 1984-; founder & dir, Black Mechanical Contractors Assn 1983-; mem, original founding comm, Ben Wilson Foundation 1985-; comm mem, Black Musicians Hall of Fame 1986-87, Little Ciy Foundation 1986-. **HONORS/ACHIEVEMENTS:** Became first black company to install elevators in the US, 1987; copyright on seminar material, "Wisdom," 1989. **MILITARY SERVICE:** US Air Force, E-4, 1965-69, honorable discharge. **BUSINESS ADDRESS:** President/CEO, Pyramid Industries, Inc, 14225 S Halsted St, Riverdale, IL 60627.

WALLER, LOUIS E.
Business executive. **PERSONAL:** Born Sep 10, 1928, Washington, PA; married Shirley James; children: Phyllis, Lorraine, Louis. **EDUCATION:** W PA Tech Inst, Associate 1949; Univ of Pittsburgh, 1960-65. **CAREER:** Plaster Products Corp, mgr of estimating 1963; McAnallen Corp, pres. **ORGANIZATIONS:** Pres Kiwanis Club of Washington PA 1970, United Way of Washington Cty 1975; dir 1st Fed Savings & Loan; pres Interstate Contractors Supply; vice pres PA State Contractors; pres Master Builders Assoc. **HONORS/ACHIEVEMENTS:** Man of the Year Jaycees 1969; Honorary Degree Waynesburg College, Waynesburg, PA 1985. **BUSINESS ADDRESS:** President, Louis E Waller Co, Inc, PO Box 757, Washington, PA 15301.

WALLER, ROBERT LEE
Educator. **PERSONAL:** Born Apr 23, 1924, Memphia, TN. **EDUCATION:** Howard Univ, AB 1949, MA 1956; Memphis State Univ, MA 1970; W CO Univ, EdD 1974. **CAREER:** Memphis City Schools, teacher/consultant/curriculum coord 1951-82; LeMoyne-Owen Coll, assoc prof of history 1982-. **ORGANIZATIONS:** Mem Memphis Educ Assn 1960-; mem Natl Council for the Social Stud 1960-; mem Phi Delta Kappa 1972-; mem Assn of Amer Hist 1974-; mem Shelby Co Historical Com 1975-; mem Memphis Black Writers Project 1979-. **HONORS/ACHIEVEMENTS:** RJ Reynolds Fellow in Econ Univ of NC 1961; Fulbright Fellow in Brazil Univ of Brazil 1963; NDEA Fellow in History Univ of Chicago 1966; Fulbright Fellowin W Africa 1984. **MILITARY SERVICE:** USN petty off 1st class 1942-46; Asiatic Pacific Ribbon; Amer Theater Ribbon; Victory Medal; Good Conduct Medal. **HOME ADDRESS:** 3352 Alta Rd, Memphis, TN 38109. **BUSINESS ADDRESS:** Asst Prof History, LeMoyne-Owen College, 807 Walker Ave, Memphis, TN 38126.

WALLETTE, ALONZO VANDOLPH
Executive. **PERSONAL:** Born Aug 02, 1940, Shreveport, LA; married Teresa Robinson; children: Brett Vandolph. **EDUCATION:** Howard Univ, BS, 1962; Univ of Maryland, Grad Business studies, 1969; New York Inst of Finance, NASD Securities license, 1971. **CAREER:** Western Electric Co, supvr industrial relations, 1965-68; Omni Spectra Inc, mgr employment & training, 1968-69; Control Data Corp, dir personnel & admin, 1969-70; Electronic Data Systems, dir employee relations, 1970-71; DuPont, vice pres admin div, 1972-74; Carnation Co, dir of eeo, 1974-78; AVW Electronic SystemsInc, chmn of bd/ceo/pres. **ORGANIZATIONS:** Mem, Alpha Phi Alpha, 1960; charter mem, Fraternity of Friends of the Dorothy Chandler Music Center, 1980; mem, Electronics Assn of California, 1982-, Natl Assn of Manufacturers, 1983-, Armed Forces Communications & Electronics Assn, 1983-, 100 Black Men of Los Angeles, 1983-; dir, Merchant Bank of California, 1986-. **HONORS/ACHIEVEMENTS:** California's Black Business Hall of Fame, The Observer Newspaper, 1981; Outstanding Small Business in High Tech, Hon Mention, Governor's Award, State of

California, 1986; Black Business of the Year, Los Angeles Black Business Assn, 1987. **MILITARY SERVICE:** AUS capt 3 yrs. **BUSINESS ADDRESS:** Chmn of Bd/CEO/ President, AVW Electronic Systems Inc, 2233 E Grand Ave, El Segundo, CA 90245.

WALLICK, ERNEST HERRON
Government executive. **PERSONAL:** Born Jan 15, 1928, Huntingdon, TN; married Jean Ellen Allen; children: Claudia Marie Barkley, John Herron. **EDUCATION:** TN A&I State Univ, BS 1950; Michigan State Univ, MS 1955. **CAREER:** Carroll Co Bd of Educ, high school voc educ instr 1950-51; MI Wayne Co Dept of Soc Svcs, public welfare worker 1955-58, special investigator 1958-64,asst supv of personnel 1964-65, supv of office mgmt 1965-66, supv of mgmt planning 1966-67; MI Dept of Civil Svcs, dir of special progs 1967-72, dirspecial and regional serv div 1972-75, dir bureau of selection 1975-82, chief deputy dir 1982-. **ORGANIZATIONS:** Mem Lansing Comm Coll Social Work Curriculum Adv Comm 1970-75, State Voc Rehab Adv Cncl 1973-80, Governor's MI Equal Empl Oppor Cncl 1975-82; mem Trinity AME Bd of Trustees 1978-; mem & treas Alpha Chi Boule Sigma Pi Phi Frat 1982-; mem MI Correctional Officer's Training Cncl 1982-, Governor's MI Equal Employ and Business Oppor Cncl 1983-; mem bd of trustees Alpha Phi Alpha Frat 1985-; pres Natl Inst for Employment Equity 1985-; mem Natl Urban League, NAACP. **HONORS/ACHIEVEMENTS:** Mem Phi Beta Kappa Honor Soc; Outstanding Public Serv & Achievements in EEO area and redesign of MI Civil Service Selection System MI Senate Concurrent Resolution 1979; Mayor's Proclamation for Outstanding Public Serv in EEO and Personnel Admin Detroit MI 1979. **MILITARY SERVICE:** AUS staff sgt 1951-53. **HOME ADDRESS:** 1400 Wellington Rd, Lansing, MI 48910. **BUSINESS ADDRESS:** Chief Deputy Dir, MI Dept of Civil Service, 320 So Walnut St, Lansing, MI 48909.

WALLS, CRAIG CALVIN
Professional athlete. **PERSONAL:** Born Dec 24, 1958, Pittsburgh, PA. **EDUCATION:** Indiana. **CAREER:** Pittsburgh Maulers, linebacker 1983; Memphis Showboats, linebacker 1984-; Denver Gold, linebacker 1985-. **HONORS/ACHIEVEMENTS:** Named UPI's Midwest Player of the Week; second team All-Big Ten selection.

WALLS, EVERSON
Professional athlete. **PERSONAL:** Born Dec 28, 1959, Dallas, TX; married Shreill; children: Charis. **EDUCATION:** Grambling, Accounting degree. **CAREER:** Dallas Cowboys, cornerback 1981-. **ORGANIZATIONS:** Supporter Big Brothers of Arlington TX, Amer Heart Assoc, Foster Parents Program. **HONORS/ACHIEVEMENTS:** Named to Pro Bowl in 3 seasons; All-Pro Bowl; Pro-Bowl career record of 4 interceptions; All-Rookie choice 1981; NFL Defensive Back of the Yr 1982; All-Pro 1983; only Player to lead the NFL in interceptions in 2 seasons; Only Cowboys player ever to lead the League in interceptions 2 times; Team Record & League Leading 11 interceptions; mem 1986 NFL Pro Bowl team.

WALLS, FREDRIC T.
Clergyman. **PERSONAL:** Born Oct 28, 1935, Denver, CO; married Delorez Louise; children: Fredric T, II, Agu Odinga Ivan, Malaika Annina Emma Delorez Lo. **EDUCATION:** LA City Coll, AA 1957; Knoxville Coll, BA 1963; Princeton Theol Sem, MDiv 1963; Union Grad Sch, PhD 1979; Urban Training Inst, Chicago, cert Univ of TN. **CAREER:** Houston Urban U, pastor 1969-;Univ of Houston, chmn dept religious activities 1974-;Univ Presb Ch, minister 1968-69; Knoxville Coll, dir Upward Bound 1967-68, asso dean of students 1965-68; Bel-Vue Presb Ch, LA, supply asst pastor 1964-65; Good Shepherd-Faith, Broadway & Sound View Presb Ch, stud asst pastor 1960-63; Westminister Neighborhood Assn, orgnr 1960. **ORGANIZATIONS:** Bd dir, vice pres Houston Met Ministries 1971-74, pres 1975-76; bd dir Ministries to Blacks in Higher Edn; mem Presb Housing Commn 1969-74; Houston JailChaplaincy Exec Com 1973-75; SW Steering Com, United Presb HEW 1971-74; Nat Communications Com, United Ministries in Higher Educ 1972-75; Gulf Coast Presb Com 1969-; exec com TX United Campus Christian Life Com 1973-75; policy bd United Ministries in Higher Edn; bd dir Cit for Good Sch 1969; Human Relations Training of Houston Police Cadets 1970-72; Bi-Racial Com HISD 1973-75; pres sr class, JCFremont Sr HS 1953-54; pres sr class, KnoxvilleColl 1959-60; treas sr class, Princeton Theological Sem 1962-63; exec dir Fund for the Self-Devel of People United Presb Ch USA NY. **HONORS/ACHIEVEMENTS:** Outstanding Young Men of Am 1966; Danforth-Underwood Fellow 1976-77. **BUSINESS ADDRESS:** Univ of Houston, 208 A D Bruce Religion & Cente, Houston, TX 77004.

WALLS, MELVIN
Educator, city official. **PERSONAL:** Born Nov 09, 1948, St Louis, MO; married Veronica Estella Robinson; children: FarRell L, Delvin L. **EDUCATION:** Florissant Valley Comm, AA 1973; Harris Teachers, BA 1976. **CAREER:** St Louis City School, wrestling coach 1977-83, tennis coach 1979-80, baseball coach 1981, football coach, pe teacher; City of Northwoods, city collector. **ORGANIZATIONS:** Treas Boy Scouts of Amer 1981-; coord Normandy Baseball 1981-. **HONORS/ACHIEVEMENTS:** St Louis City School All Conf Player 1965-67; St Louis City School All Star Player 1965-67; Project MEE Awd 1983; NMC Human Serv Awd 1987. **BUSINESS ADDRESS:** City Collector, City of Northwoods, 4600 Oakridge Blvd, Northwoods, MO 63121.

WALSH, DELANO B.
Engineer. **PERSONAL:** Born Apr 16, 1945, New York, NY. **EDUCATION:** Power Mem Acad, Diploma 1963; NY Univ, BEEE 1967; Bernard Baruch Coll, MBA 1972. **CAREER:** Consol Edison of NY, assoc engr 1967-69, proj engr 1969-76, proj equip engr 1976-79; Pepsi Cola Co of NY, proj mgr 1979-. **ORGANIZATIONS:** Mem IEEE; vol math instr Malcom-King Harlem Coll Ext. **HONORS/ACHIEVEMENTS:** Cert of Appreciation Natl Urban League 1976. **BUSINESS ADDRESS:** Project Manager, Pepsi Cola Co, Anderson Hill Rd, Purchase, NY 10577.

WALSH, EVERALD J.
Mental health administrator. **PERSONAL:** Born May 06, 1938, New York, NY; children: Evette Michelle, Eric Michael. **EDUCATION:** City Coll of NY, BA 1963; Adelphi U, MSW 1970, CSW 1980. **CAREER:** Colony S Brooklyn Houses, dir mental retardation staff training prgm 1978-; Brooklyn Devel Ctr; Manhattan Childrens Psychiatric Ctr, team ldr 1974-77; Fed of Addiction Agy, exec dir 1971-74; Little Flower Children Svc, grp Hm Supr, Soc Worker 1966-71; Catholic Youth Orgn, grp Worker 1963-66. **ORGANIZATIONS:** Nat Fedn of Concerned Drug Abuse Workers 1972. **BUSINESS ADDRESS:** 888 Fountain Ave, New York, NY.

WALSTON, WOODROW WILLIAM
Assistant director. **PERSONAL:** Born Jul 12, 1918, Edgecombe County, NC; married Hazel Howell. **EDUCATION:** NC Central U, BS 1946; Congress of the Am Coll of Hosp Adminstrs, yrly Sem 1954-. **CAREER:** Richmond Comm Hosp Inc, adminstr 1973-80; Provident Hosp, Baltimore, asst adminstr, asst dir, asso dir for adm, dir of adm 1969-73; Richmond Comm Hosp Inc, adminstr 1958-69; Comm Hosp Martinsville, VA, 1952-58; Kate Bitting Reynolds Meml Hosp, ofc mgr 1946-52. **ORGANIZATIONS:** Mem Am Coll of Hosp Adminstrs 1970-; mem VA Hosp Assn & Roanoke Area Hosp Counc 1958-69; mem VA, MD, DE, DC Hosp Assn 1969-; mem Nat Assn of Hlth Serv Exec Inc 1969-; treas, bd mem MD Chap Hosp Fin Mgmt Assn; mem Am Hosp Assn 1954-; adv mem Hosp Fin Mgmt Assn 1958-; mem Cntrl VA Hosp Counc 1973-; VA Hosp Assn 1973-; mem VA Hosp Fin Mgmt Assn 1973-; Alpha Kappa 1946; bd mem Crusade for Voters; fin sec Spring Lk GolfClub; pres NC Coll CntrlUniv Alumni Assn; bd mem, life mem Kappa Alpha Psi Frat Inc; mem Ku Wat Temple #126 Imperial Counc, Ancient Egyptian ArabicOrder Nobles of the Mystic Shrine; pres Nat Assn of Hlth Svc; exec, bd mem Eastern Province Coun; treas Spartans Soc & Civic Club Inc; bd mem YMCA; bd mem NAACP; treas, deacon All Souls Presb Ch; dist commr BSA; bd mem, exec com Big Bros of Am; bd mem, treas Colonial Golf Club Inc; treas Pan Hellenic Counc of Richmond; mem, treas Club 533 Inc. **HONORS/ACHIEVEMENTS:** Cert of Apprec, Blue Ridge Counc BSA; Outst Svcs, Pan Hellenic Counc of Richmond 1969; Cert of Apprec, Walston Group, Baltimore 1973; Cert of Apprec, Kappa Alpha Psi Frat Inc 1974; Cert of Commend, Nat Assn of Hlth Serv Exec NY 1976; recog award, Richmond Alumni Chap Kappa Alpha Psi Frat Inc 1976; Cert of Achvmt, Chap Bro of the Yr Award, VA Chap Kappa Alpha Psi Frat Inc 1977. **MILITARY SERVICE:** AUS msgt 1942-46. **BUSINESS ADDRESS:** 1500 N 28th St, Richmond, VA 23223.

WALTER, JOHN C.
Educator. **PERSONAL:** Born May 05, 1933. **EDUCATION:** AR AM&N Coll, BS (Cum Laude) Mech Engrg, History; Univ of Bridgeport, MA Amer History; Univ of ME at Orono, PhD Afro-Amer & US History. **CAREER:** Purdue Univ, instr history 1970-72, asst prof history 1972-73; IN Univ at Kokomo, vstg asst prof black politics 1971-73; John Jay Coll of Criminal Justice CUNY, assoc prof history, chmn black studies 1973-76; Bowdoin Coll, dir, asst prof history Afro-Amer Studies Prog 1976-80; Smith Coll, assoc prof Afro-Amer Studies 1980-. **ORGANIZATIONS:** Dir Afro-Amer Studies Prog Bowdoin Coll 1976-80; org, 1st chmn 1976-80, exec bd mem 1978- New England Conf of the Natl Council for Black Studies; exec comm Five Coll Black Studies 1982-; bridge comm & instr Smith Coll 1980-; devel & org Bridges to Pluralism 1983-; contrib ed Jrnl of Afro-Amer inNY Life & History State Univ Coll NY 1976-, UMOJA A Scholarly Jrnl of Afro-Amer Affairs Univ of CO 1976-, Review of Afro-Amer Issues & Culture Syracuse Univ 1976-, New England Jrnl of Black Studies Hampshire Coll 1981-; mem Amer Historical Assoc, Assoc of Caribbean Historians, Assoc for the Study of African-Amer Life & History, Caribbean Studies Assoc, Coll Lang Assoc, New England Historical Assoc, Natl Assoc of Interdisciplinary Ethnic Studies, Org ofAmer Historians, So Historical Assoc; consult Denison Univ 1979, Wesleyan Univ 1978; reader Natl Endowment for the Humanities, Univ Press of Amer. **HONORS/ACHIEVEMENTS:** Num rsch, book reviews & publ incl, A Passion for Equality 1977, Politics & Africanity in West Indian Soc Brown Univ 1983, The Black Immigrant & PoliticalRadicalism in the Harlem Renaissance 61st Annual Conf of the Assoc for the Study of Afro-Amer Life & History 1976, Franklin D Roosevelt & the Arms Limitation 1932-41 Hofstra Univ Conf 1982, Politics & Africanity in West Indian Soc Brown Univ 1983, The Transformation of Afro-Amer Politics, The Contribs of theWest Indian Immigrant Colby Coll 1983, Women & Identity in the Caribbean Smith Coll Women's Studies Cluster Comm Sem 1983, Enterprise Zones, Conservative Ideology or Free-Floating Political Fantasy? Simon's Rock of Bard Coll Bulletin 1984. **BUSINESS ADDRESS:** Associate Professor, Smith College, Dept Afro-American Studies, Northampton, MA 01063.

WALTERS, ARTHUR M.
Social service administrator. **PERSONAL:** Born Nov 06, 1918, Magnolia, KY; married NoraLee Bryant; children: Reginald G, Artye M, Michele B. **EDUCATION:** CO Coll, BA;Univ of Louisville, MEd; The Engr Sch, Asso Adv Engrng. **CAREER:** Louisville Urban League, soc serv adminstr, exec dir; past dir Econ Devel & Employ, Educ & Youth Incentives. **ORGANIZATIONS:** Mem Alpha Phi Alpha Frat; bd dir Boys Haven; bd dir KY Educ TV; bd dir Louisville C of C/Bus Resource Ctr; mem Louisville & Jefferson Co Human Rltns Commn Employ Com; Louisville Labor Mgmt Com; NAACP; Retired Ofcrs Assn; Soc of Am Mil Engrs; Downtown Rotary Club; adv counc KY Min Bus Enterprise; mem Pres Com on Employ of the Handicapped. **HONORS/ACHIEVEMENTS:** AFL-CIO Gr Louisville Cntrl Labor Counc Comm Serv Award 1970; cited by Bd of Edn, Louisville Pub Sch 1971; Merit Comm Serv Medallion, Louisville & Jefferson Co Human Rltns Commn 1972; listed in 1,000 Successful Blacks, Ebony Success Library 1973; Outst Kentuckian, Intl Assn of Personnel In Employ Security 1974; cit, State of KY 1975; Merit Award, AKA Sor 1975; listed in Who's Who Among Black Am 1975; Whitney M Young Jr Award, Lincoln Found 1976; appearance on KY Educ TV, "Bicent Profile of Outst Kentuckians" 1976; Disting Serv Cit, United Negro Coll Fund; Young Gifted & Blk Hon Roll, Plymouth Settlement House; cert of achvmnt, Nat Urban League Exec Devel Prgm; hon alumnus UNCF; Good Neighbor Award, LOU; Ambassador of Goodwill, City of Louisville; Black Students Award,Univ of Louisville; AUS decorations commend medal for merit svc; bronze star for heroism; Soldiers Medal for Bravery; Am Campaign Medal; European-african-middle Eastern Campaign Medal W/4 bronze serv stars; WW II Victory Medal; Army of Occupation Medal; Nat Defense Serv Medal; Korea Serv Medal w/1 silver serv star; Armed Forces Reserve Medal. **MILITARY SERVICE:** AUS lt col ret 1962.

WALTERS, CURLA SYBIL
Educator. **PERSONAL:** Born Jun 03, 1929. **EDUCATION:** Andrews U, BA 1961; Howard U, MS 1964; Georgetown U, PhD 1969; Karolinska Inst, Post Doc 1969-70. **CAREER:** HowardUniv Dept Med, med asso prof 1975-; CO U, instr asst prof 1971-74; Howard U, rsrch asso 1964-65. **ORGANIZATIONS:** Mem Am Assn Emmunologist 1972-. **HONORS/ACHIEVEMENTS:** AAS Parker Flwsp Aw 1963; flwsp Am AssnUniv Women 1969; NIH grant Aw 1974-77; biomed rsrch support grant 1975-76; natl inst ageing grant 1977; publ "Infection & Immun Proc Soc Exp Bio & Med & Fedn Proc. **BUSINESS ADDRESS:** 2041 Georgia Ave, Washington, DC 20060.

WALTERS, HUBERT EVERETT
Music educator. **PERSONAL:** Born Apr 27, 1933, Greenville, NC; married Regina P Thomas; children: Sonya Yvette, Hubert Sharif. **EDUCATION:** NC Central Univ, BA 1951-55; vA State Univ, 1959; E Carolina Univ, MM 1963-65; Boston Univ, DMA (pending)

1969-. **CAREER:** TX Coll Tyler, TX, chrmn dept of Music 1965-66; Shaw Univ Raleigh, NC, asst prof Music 1966-69; Harvard Univ, lctr on Black Music 1970-74; Goddard Coll VT, lecturer on Black Music 1971-73; Boston State Coll, asst proj of Music 1971-82; Boston Coll, lecturer on Black Music 1982-; Univ of MA-Boston, asst prof of Music 1982-. **ORGANIZATIONS:** V pres NC State Music Teachers 1963; mem Music Educators Natl Conf; mem Amer Choral Dir Assoc; Omega Psi Phi Frat; deacon Emmanuel Bapt Church. **HONORS/ACHIEVEMENTS:** LO Kelly Award Excell in Music NC Central Univ 1955; mem Pi Kappa Lambda; Natl Music Honor Soc; Martin Luther King, Jr flwshp Award from Woodrow Wilson Fdn 1969. **MILITARY SERVICE:** AUS sp 3. **BUSINESS ADDRESS:** Assistant Professor of Music, Univ of MA, Harbor Campus Columbia Pt, Harbor Campus, Boston, MA 02125.

WALTERS, MARY DAWSON
Librarian. **PERSONAL:** Born Oct 06, 1923, Mitchell Cnty, GA; married William Lamar Gantt; children: Marjorie M Smith, MD, Robert H McCoy. **EDUCATION:** Savannah State Coll Savannah, GA, BS; Atlanta Univ Atlanta, GA, MSLS 1957; OH State Univ Cols, OH, Russian Courses 1963; OH Historical Soc Cols, OH, Oral History Cert 1966; Miami Univ of OH, Lib Mgmt Cert 1973. **CAREER:** GA Public Schls, public schl tchr 1943-52; Carver Jr HS, schl librn 1952-56; Albany State Coll, libry dir 1956-61; OH State Univ Cols, OH, G&E lbrn 1961-63, head, procsng Div 1963-71, head, acqstns dept 1974-74, collection development officer 1978-84, mgr of collection development prog 1984-, asstuniv librarian. **ORGANIZATIONS:** Head, acqustns CA State Univ LA 1974-78; coll dev ofcr CA State Univ, LA 1978-80; asst univ lbrn CA State Univ, LA 1980-; cnclr at large Am Lbry Assoc 1982-86; comm status women librnshp 1984-86; mem Black Caucus of AL 1974-. **HONORS/ACHIEVEMENTS:** Director's Citation of Merit OH State Univ Cols, OH 1963; They Did so Can You Greyhound Bus Corp 1973; 1,001 Successful Blacks Ebony Success Libry 1973; Who's Who in Amer 1975 to Date (Marquis) 1975-; "Black Literature, Works by Afro-Amer Writers in the United States" a bibliography of the Black History Month Exhibit in the John F Kennedy memorial Library Cal State LA 1984; "Approval Program Timing Study, Baker & Taylor vs Blackwell North Amer" Collection Bldg 1985. **BUSINESS ADDRESS:** Assistant University Librarian, CA State Univ, LA, 5151 State University Dr, 5171 StateUniv Dr, Los Angeles, CA 90032.

WALTERS, RONALD
Educator. **PERSONAL:** Born Jul 20, 1938, Wichita, KS; married Patricia Ann. **EDUCATION:** Fisk Univ, BA History 1963; Amer Univ, MA 1966, PhD 1971. **CAREER:** Georgetown & Syracuse Univ, instr; Brandeis Univ African & Afro-Amer Studies, chmn 1969-71; Howard Univ, chmn pol sci 1971-74, prof of pol sci. **ORGANIZATIONS:** Past pres African Heritage Studies Assoc; mem bd Natl Black Election Study, Inst of Social Rsch, Univ of MI; mem adv bd Southern Christian Leadership Conf; founder Natl Black Independent Political Party; secty/founding mem Natl Black Leadership Roundtable; founder/past mem Bd of TransAfrica; consultant United Nations Special Comm Against Apartheid of the Security Cncl. **HONORS/ACHIEVEMENTS:** Speaks & writes on US Foreign Policies toward Africa & Black Amer Politics; over 70 articles in several scholarly jrnls; three books in press; Disting CommServ Awd Howard Univ 1982; Disting Scholar/Activists Awd The Black Scholar Magazine 1984; The Ida B Wells Barnett Awd Natl Alliance of Black School Educators 1985; Rockefeller Foundation Rsch Grant 1985; The Congressional Black Associates Awd 1986. **BUSINESS ADDRESS:** Professor, Howard University, Washington, DC 20001.

WALTERS, WARREN W.
Dentist. **PERSONAL:** Born Nov 20, 1932, NYC; married Joan Husbands; children: Pennye, Pamela, Warren Wayne. **EDUCATION:** Columbia Coll, BA 1953; ColumbiaUniv Sch of Bus, MBA 1955; HowardUniv Sch of Dentistry, DDS 1960. **CAREER:** Priv Prac, dent 1962-; Rotating Intrnshp Prog Harlem Hosp, coord; Intrnshp Harlem Hosp, oral surg 1960-61; NYS Unempl Ins, auditor 1955-56. **ORGANIZATIONS:** Vp Midtown Dental Soc; vice pres Greater Metro Dental Soc; bd of dir First Distr Dental Soc; pres progressive Com Real Estate Corp; mem Sigma Pi Phi Boule; past pres Harlem Hosp Dental Soc 1966, 74; mem ADA; NDA; Acad Gen Dentistry; dir Prog Comml Real Estate Inc; pres HowardUniv Studnt Coll of Dent 1959-60; mem Reveille Club; Omega Psi Phi. **BUSINESS ADDRESS:** 200 W 145 St, New York, NY 10039.

WALTON, CEDAR ANTHONY
Agricultural agent. **PERSONAL:** Born Dec 23, 1901, Wilcox, TX; married Ruth Sylvia Grimstead. **EDUCATION:** Prairie View Agr & Mech Coll, BS 1926. **CAREER:** Liberian Govt Monrovia Liberia W Africa, agr agt & adv 1951-59; Dallas Co TX A&M Civi Serv, co agr agt 1927-51. **ORGANIZATIONS:** Exec sec Moorland Br YMCA 1960; exec sec Dallas Black C of C 1962067; couns SCORE Sm Bus Adminstrn 1969-75. **HONORS/ACHIEVEMENTS:** Award for Noteworthy Agr Achvmnts Testimonial Citizens of Dallas & Dallas Co 1951; meritorious serv in Human Rel Phi Beta Sigma Frat 1964; testimonial of ldrshp ability & Vision Dallas Black C of C 1970.

WALTON, DEWITT T., JR.
Dentist. **PERSONAL:** Born May 25, 1937, Macon, GA; married Joan G Robinson; children: Jimmie Alisa, Gwen Noel, Gayle Nicole, Joy Alexia. **EDUCATION:** Howard Univ, BS 1960, DDS 1961. **CAREER:** Private Practice, dentist. **ORGANIZATIONS:** Life membership President's Club Howard Univ; mem Amer Dental Assn; Natl Dental Assn, Acad of Gen Dentistry; Amer Soc of Dentistry for Children; GA Dental Soc; AAAS; Natl Rehab Assn; life mem Fedn Dentaire Internationale; sustaining mem BSA; life mem NAACP; life mem Omega Psi Phi Frat; mem Washington Ave Presby Ch; Prince Hall Mason Local #12; mem GA Dental Assoc, Amer Endodontic Soc, Acad of Dentistry Intl, Amer Coll of Dentists, Intl Coll of Dentists; sustaining mem The Southern Poverty Law Ctr; mem Amer Fund for Dental Health-Century Club II, Amer Analgesic Soc, Acad of Continuing Educ. **HONORS/ACHIEVEMENTS:** NAACP Community Serv Awd; Five Dental Fellowships; Outstanding Young Men in Amer 1970; Lambda Phi Chap Omega Man of Yr 1969; Lambda Phi Chap Omega Citof Yr 1971; listed in Who's Who in the S & SW 1971-72; Personalities of the South 1972; Who's Who in GA 1973; Dictionary of Intl Biography 1975; North GA Dental Soc Dentist of the Year 1979; GA Dental Soc Citizenship Awd 1979-80; GA Dental Soc Humanitarian Awd 1981-82; Boy Scouts of Amer Silver Beaver Awd 1981; Alpha Kappa Alpha Sor Comm Serv Awd 1982; The United Negro Coll Fund Meritorious Serv Awd 1983; Outstanding Serv Awd The Southern Poverty Law Ctr 1984; Whitney M Young Jr Serv Awd 1985; Outstanding Alumni Awd Coll of dentistry Howard Univ 1985; Boy Scouts of Amer Diamond Jubilee Awd for Serv to Youth 1985. **MILITARY SERVICE:** AUS Dental Corps capt 1961-63. **BUSINESS ADDRESS:** 591 Cotton Ave, Macon, GA 31201.

WALTON, ELBERT ARTHUR, JR.
Attorney & elected official. **PERSONAL:** Born Feb 21, 1942, St Louis, MO; son of Elbert A. Walton, Sr. and Luretta B. Ray Walton; married Juanita Alberta Head (divorced); children: Rochelle, Rhonda, Angela, Elbert,III, Johnathan. **EDUCATION:** Harris Junior College, AA 1963; Univ of Missouri St Louis, BA Business 1968; Washington Univ, MBA 1970; St Louis Univ, JD 1974. **CAREER:** Continental Oil Corp, financial analyst 1969; Univ of Missouri St Louis, instructor of business law & accounting 1971-78; St Louis Municipal Court, judge 1977-78; attorney at law 1974-; Missouri House of Representatives, state representative 61st district 1979-90. **ORGANIZATIONS:** Beta Alpha Psi Hon Acct Fraternity 1971; Phi Delta Phi Intl Legal Frat 1973; natl vice pres Natl Assn of Black Accountants 1976-77; parliamentarian Mound City Bar Assn 1979; parliamentarian MO Legislative Black Caucus 1979-85; grand counselor Omega Psi Phi Frat 1980-83. **HONORS/ACHIEVEMENTS:** Omega Man of the Year Omega Psi Phi Fraternity, St Louis, MO 1964; Outstanding Young Man of America 1974; Outstanding Achievement Award Natl Assn of Black Accountants 1976; Citizen of the Year Omega Psi Phi Fraternity St Louis, MO 1978. **MILITARY SERVICE:** USNR E-4 1959-61; Honorable Discharge. **BUSINESS ADDRESS:** State Representative 61st Dist, Missouri House of Reps, 8776 N Broadway, St Louis, MO 63147.

WALTON, FLAVIA BATTEAU
Association executive. **PERSONAL:** Born Apr 18, 1947, Tucson, AZ; daughter of Matthew Batteau and Elgie Batteau; married Col William Howard Walton; children: Nissa Mike, William Howard III. **EDUCATION:** Mills College, BA 1967; Univ of AZ, MS 1968, PhD 1977. **CAREER:** Troy State University at Montgomery, adjunct professor 1976-77; Bexar Cty Mental Health Mental Retardation, unit coordinator 1977-80; Our Lady of the Lake University, lecturer in social work 1981; Natl Institute of Drug Abuse, special consultant 1984-1987; White House Conf for a Drug Free Amer, consultant, 1987-88; Project Lead: High Expectations, The Links Found, Inc, project dir. **ORGANIZATIONS:** Chapter pres vice pres comm chairs Alpha Kappa Alpha 1965-; mem Natl Rehabilitation Assn 1967-; mem natl Rehabilitation Counselors Assn 1967-; natl dir serv to youth The Links Inc 1968-; mem Personnel & Guidance Assn 1975-; chapter pres comm chairperson Jack & Jill of Amer Inc 1977-; chmn Natl Black Advisory Comm on Drug & Alcohol Abuse Policy 1984-85. **HONORS/ACHIEVEMENTS:** Pi Lambda Theta Educ Honorary Univ of AZ 1968. **BUSINESS ADDRESS:** Project Lead: High Expectations,, The Links Found, Inc, 1200 Massachusetts Ave NW, Washington, DC 20005.

WALTON, HARRIET J.
Educator. **PERSONAL:** Born Sep 19, 1933, Claxton, GA; daughter of Ester and Mable Junior; children: Renee Yvonne, Anthony Alex, Jennifer Denise, Cyrus Bernard. **EDUCATION:** Clark Coll, AB (Cum Laude) 1952; Howard Univ, MS 1954; Syracuse Univ, MA 1957; GA State Univ, PhD 1979; Atlanta Univ, MS 1989. **CAREER:** Hampton Inst, instr of Math 1954-55, asst prof of Math 1957-58; Morehouse Coll, instr of Math, asst prof of Math, assoc prof of Math, prof of Math 1958-. **ORGANIZATIONS:** Clerk Providence Baptist Church 1968-84; sec/treas Natl Assn of Math 1982-; treas Phi Delta Kappa 1984-85; deacon Providence Baptist Church 1984-; mem of advisory bd Benjamin E Mays Acad, MAA, AAUP, NCTM, GCTM, Pi Mu Epsilon, Beta Kappa Chi; treas/pres Delta Sigma Theta; mem YWCA, NAACP, ACLU; consult Atlanta Publ Schls. **HONORS/ACHIEVEMENTS:** UNCF Faculty Fellow 1964-65, 1975-77; NSF Sci Faculty 1965-66; Teaching Asst, Rsch Asst Howard Univ 1952-54; Proj Dir Contr for Math Educ 1981-84; Proj Dir Math for Middle Sch Tchrs 1981-82; Bronze Woman of the Yr Iota Phi Lambda Sor 1984; Phi Beta Kappa Delta of GA Morehouse Coll 1984. **HOME ADDRESS:** 860 Venetta PL NW, Atlanta, GA 30318. **BUSINESS ADDRESS:** Prof of Mathematics, Morehouse College, 830 Westview Dr SW, Atlanta, GA 30314.

WALTON, JAMES DONALD
Sales and marketing executive. **PERSONAL:** Born Jan 31, 1952; son of Allen Walton and Zymord Louise Burrell Walton; married Jun 20, 1980 (widowed); children: Darius James. **EDUCATION:** Univ of Vermont, BS 1975. **CAREER:** Xerox Corp, sales rep 1976-79; Abbott Laboratories, chemistry systems specialist 1979-82, natl account mgr 1982-83, district mgr 1984-87; regional marketing mgr 1987-. **HONORS/ACHIEVEMENTS:** Presidents Club 1980, 1981, 1986, Senior Salesman 1980, 1st Black District Mgr 1983, 100% Club 1984, 1985, all from Abbott Laboratories. **HOME ADDRESS:** 14447 White Pine Ridge Lane, Chesterfield, MO 63017.

WALTON, JAMES EDWARD
Educator. **PERSONAL:** Born Sep 13, 1944, Bessemer, AL; married Doris Dell Harrington; children: Leonard, Tiffany. **EDUCATION:** Andrews Univ, 1962-64; Kent State Univ, BS 1964-66; University of Akron, MA 1970-73, PhD 1973-78. **CAREER:** Canton McKinley HS, english teacher 1967-70; Mount Union College, assoc prof of english 1970-. **ORGANIZATIONS:** Dir Freedom House Project 1975; member Jaycees 1975; yearbook advisor Mount Union College 1975-83; board member Stark County Fair Housing Comm 1978-; board member Assoc for Better Community Development 1984-; member Alliance City Planning Commission 1984-. **HONORS/ACHIEVEMENTS:** Poetry, essays Black Arts Society, Ohio State Univ 1971; essay English Language Arts Bulletin 1980; article Natl Council of Teachers of English 1980; essayModern Language Association 1985. **BUSINESS ADDRESS:** Associate Professor of English, Mount Union College, 1972 Clark Ave, Alliance, OH 44601.

WALTON, JAMES MADISON
Lawyer, retired judge. **PERSONAL:** Born Aug 17, 1926, Norfolk, VA; son of Willie J Walton and Willie Ann Smallwood; married Jean Onie Barnes; children: James Jr, Janet Marie Dukes, Joan Denise Collaso, Julian Mark. **EDUCATION:** VA Union Univ, AB (Cum Laude) 1952; De Paul Univ Coll of Law, JD 1958; Roosevelt Univ, MA 1982. **CAREER:** Cook Cty Dept of Public Aid, caseworker 1953-60; Cook Cty State's Atty, asst state's atty 1961-63; Cook Cty Public Defender, asst public defender 1964-65; Circuit Court Cook Cty, magistrate 1966, assoc judge 1970, appointed judge 1979; Circuit Ct of Cook County, elected judge 1980. **ORGANIZATIONS:** Trustee Bethany-Garfield Comm Hosp 1966, St Stephen African Methodist Church 15 years; mem Cook Co Bar Assn; Chicago Bar Assn; Natl Bar Assn; past pres IL Cncl of Juvenile Ct Judges; mem Natl Cncl of Juvenile and Fam Ct Judges;

mem The Original Forty Club of Chicago. **MILITARY SERVICE:** USAAF T/5 22 months; Good Conduct, Marksman, Phillipine Independence 1945-46. **HOME ADDRESS:** 405 Fernwood Farms Road, Chesapeake, VA 23320.

WALTON, LLUDLOO CHARLES
Insurance company executive. **PERSONAL:** Born Nov 24, 1950; son of William B Walton and Muriel A Walton; married Rosemerrie, Jun 18, 1975; children: Sheree Rosemerrie, Carlene Nicole. **EDUCATION:** Attended Mico Training Coll of the Univ of the West Indies. **CAREER:** Mutual of Omaha, Livingston NJ, sales agent 1979-82, sales mgr 1982-84; Mutual of Omaha, Rutherford NJ, gen mgr 1984-. **HONORS/ACHIEVEMENTS:** NASD License, Federal License, 1982; Mgr of Year, Mutual of Omaha, 1982 & 1983. **HOME ADDRESS:** 30 Manchester Rd, West Orange, NJ 07052. **BUSINESS ADDRESS:** General Manager, Mutual of Omaha, 201 Rt 17 North, Suite 501, Rutherford, NJ 07070.

WALTON, MILDRED LEE
Educational administrator. **PERSONAL:** Born Dec 08, 1926, Atlanta, GA; daughter of James Forrest Collier and Pauline Dickerson; married Borah W; children: Berle Burse, Denise Mickelbury, Charna Turner. **EDUCATION:** Spelman Coll, BA 1947; Atlanta Univ, MA 1962; Nova Univ, EdD 1976; Harvard Univ, Summer Fellow 1984. **CAREER:** DeKalb Co School System, teacher 1947-56; Turner HS, teacher 1956-69; Harwell Elem Sch, principal 1969-73; Atlanta Univ, asst prof 1970; Miles Elementary School, principal 1973-. **ORGANIZATIONS:** SE zone dir Natl Assoc of Elementary School Principal 1980-83; adv bd Rockefellar Fund for Art Educ 1981-85; foundation bd Amer Assoc of Univ Women 1982-85, Phi Delta Kappa 1984-85; St Paul's Vestry St Paul's Episcopal Church 1984-87; pres Natl Assoc of Elementary School Principals 1985-86; mem Delta Kappa Gamma Hon Soc 1986-; pres, Natl Alumnae Assn of Spelman College. **HONORS/ACHIEVEMENTS:** Boss of the Year Natl Business Women's Assoc 1983; Bronze Woman in Educ Black Heritage Assoc 1984; Georgia Educ of Excellence State Bd of Educ 1984; Natl Distinguished Principal US Dept of Educ 1986. **BUSINESS ADDRESS:** Executive Director, Georgia Association Of Elementary School Principals, 1176 Oakcrest Drive, Atlanta, GA 30311.

WALTON, ORTIZ MONTAIGNE
Sociologist, musician. **PERSONAL:** Born in Chicago, IL; married Carol Dozier, PhD; children: Omar Kwame. **EDUCATION:** Univ of CA, Berkeley, BS 1966, MA 1970, PhD 1973. **CAREER:** A Sample Survey of Alchol & Drug Use Among Adolescents & Young Adults, Funded b Y Natl Inst on Alchol Abuse & Alcoholism, princpl investigator 1978-81; contrabass soloist, author & composer; The Multi-Ethnic Inst for Resch & Ed, pres 1978-. **ORGANIZATIONS:** Prof sociology Univ of CA Berkeley 1969-74, Univ of CA Santa Cruz 1975, The Wright Inst of Berkeley 1974-75; double bassist The Boston Symphony Orchestra 1957-63; presented NY Debut Recital at Mekin Concert Hall NYC; recorded solo contrabass works of WA Mozart & recorded premiere of The Walton Statement by Arthur Cunningham 1986; composed Night Letter for unaccompanied contrabass dedicated to Edward Kennedy Ellington 1968. **HONORS/ACHIEVEMENTS:** Author of work on the sociology of Amer music "Music, Black White & Blue" publ by William Morrow. **HOME ADDRESS:** 242 West 123rd St, New York, NY 10027.

WALTON, REGGIE BARNETT
Judge. **PERSONAL:** Born Feb 08, 1949, Donora, PA. **EDUCATION:** WV State Coll, BA 1971; Amer Univ, JD 1974. **CAREER:** Defender Assn of PA, staff atty 1974-76; US Atty's Office DC, asst US atty 1976-80, exec asst 1980-81; Superior Ct of DC, assoc judge 1981-. **ORGANIZATIONS:** Mem Bar of the Supreme Ct of PA admitted 1974; US Dist Ct for the Eastern Dist of PA admitted 1975; DC Ct of Appeals admitted 1976; US Ct of Appeals for the DC Circuit admitted 1977; taught classes on trial tactics and in charge of atty training US Atty's Office 1980-81; instr Trial of a Homicide Case DC Bar Assn Crim Pract Inst 1980; Supreme Ct of the US admitted 1980; US Dist Ct for the Dist of DC admitted 1981; instr ABA Traf Ct seminar 1984, Natl Inst for Trial Advocacy 1984; mem DC Bar, Amer Bar Assn, Wash Bar Assn, Black Assist US Attorneys Assn, Judicial Conf for DC 1980-; mem DC Criminal Just Supvr Bd; Natl Academy of Scis Panel on Rsch on Criminal Careers 1983-; Criminal Jury Instr Comm 1984-; DC Bar Assn Criminal Instr Comm 1984-; Amer Bar Assn Lawyer Competency Comm 1984-; mem Joint Comm for DC Courts 1985-; consultant (peer reviewer) Natl Inst of Justice Office of Justice Prog 1986-; delegate Natl Conf of State Trial Judges Amer Bar Assoc 1986-; mem Natl Adv Comm Natl Inst for Citizen Educ in the Law1987-90. **HONORS/ACHIEVEMENTS:** Who's Who Among Students in Amer Univ & Coll 1970-71; Who's Who Among Greek Fraternities and Sororities in Amer 1970-71; Achievement Award from 11th Dist of OEO - PHA 1975; The Attorney General Cert Award 1980; Exec Office for the US Attys - Dir Award for Superior Perf as an Assist US Atty Dept of Justice 1980; Who's Who Among Black Americans 1980-81; Outstanding Young Men of Amer US Jaycees 1984; Black Eagle Alumni Award Amer Univ Black Alumni Assn 1984; Who's Who in Amer Law 1985; Who's Who in Society 1986; Men of Achievement Intl Biographical Ctr Cambridge England 1987. **BUSINESS ADDRESS:** Associate Judge, Superior Ct of the Dist Columb, 500 Indiana Ave NW, Washington, DC 20001.

WALTON, ROLAND J.
Auto dealer. **CAREER:** Walton Buick-Volkswagen, Inc, Medford MA, chief executive, 1977—. **BUSINESS ADDRESS:** Walton Buick-Volkswagen, Inc, 4100 Mystic Valley Parkway, Medford, MA 02155. *

WALTON, SIDNEY F., JR.
Educator. **PERSONAL:** Born Jun 02, 1934, Chicago, IL; children: Lynn, Kevin. **EDUCATION:** San Fran Coll, BA 1959, MA Guidance & Counseling 1964; Univ of CA Berkeley, MA 1972; Boalt Hall Sch of Law. **CAREER:** Positions in administration, counseling, education; CA State Univ at Fresno, former asst prof; Univ of CA Berkeley, lecturer; Real Estate Sales & Investments. **ORGANIZATIONS:** Mem Amer Soc of Planning Ofcl; Assn of Pacific Coast Geographers; Black Law Students Assn; CA Assn of Marriage & Family Counselors; Natl Alliance for Family Life Inc; Natl Council for Geographic Edn. **HONORS/ACHIEVEMENTS:** Editor of "Encyclopedia of Self-Publishing, The Complete Reference for Self-Publishing Writers"; Author of two books; contributing & adv editor, "Black Scholar", Journal of Black Studies & Research. **MILITARY SERVICE:** AUS Fire Dept; Fire Chief 1953-55. **HOME ADDRESS:** PO Box I, Alameda, CA 94501.

WALTON, TRACY MATTHEW, JR.
Radiologist. **PERSONAL:** Born Nov 12, 1930, Columbia, SC; married Mae; children: Adrienne, Tracy III, Terri, Brien. **EDUCATION:** Morgan State Coll, BS 1953; Howard Univ Coll Med, graduated 1961. **CAREER:** Freedman's Hosp, asst radiology 1965-66; Howard Univ, asst radiology 1965-66; Georgetown Univ Sch of Med, clinical instr 1968; DC General Hosp, med ofcr 1967-71, acting chf med ofcr 1971, chf med ofcr 1971-80. **ORGANIZATIONS:** Rgnl radiotherapy com of Met WA Regnl Med Prog 1968-; mem Cancer Aid Plan Com DC Chap ACS 1968-81; chmn Amer Cancer Soc 1968-; adv bd United Nat Bank of WA 1974-; licensure SC Bd of Med Examiners 1981; vice pres DC Div Amer Cancer Soc 1983-; Speaker House of Delegates Natl Medical Assn 1983-; natl chmn Radiology Sect Natl Med Assn 1983-; Med Soc of DC; Natl Med Assn; Amer Coll of Radiology; So Med Assn; licensure MD Bd of Med Exam; DC Bd of Med Exam. **HONORS/ACHIEVEMENTS:** Dictionary of Intl Biography London 1968; pres Medico-Chirurgical Soc of DC 1975-78. **BUSINESS ADDRESS:** Retired Chief Med Officer, DC General Hospital, 4645 Nannie Helen Burroughs NE, Washington, DC 20019.

WALTRIP, ROBERT See SHORT, BOBBY

WAMBLE, AMOS SYLVESTER, SR.
Retired minister. **PERSONAL:** Born Aug 16, 1916, Warren, AR; married Earlene E; children: E Don, Brenda Honoday, John W, Amos Jr, Marcus L, Minnie W, Carl D, Theresa Kindle, Phillip K, Angel Mason, Eunice. **EDUCATION:** Philander Smith Coll, AA 1949, Bth 1951, BS 1953, Hon Doc 1970; Philander Smith Coll-Western Sem Rockhurst Coll; Lincoln Univ MO; Garrett Sem 1978. **CAREER:** US Post Office, KC MO, US mail clerk 1945-46; United Methodist Church, minister 1945, dist supt 1970-72, assoc dir 1972-78; United Methodist Church, clergyman. **ORGANIZATIONS:** Ins agent Triple A-OKC 1967-70; retired Civil Serv 28 Yrs; msgnr Vet Adm KC MO 1947-48; grain shipping clerk Comm Credit-KC MO 1948-; trfc shpg clkFAA (Civil Serv) 1966-78; supply Tech FAA OKC 1970-77; book The History of the Negro & Methodism 1938-72. **HONORS/ACHIEVEMENTS:** Book Who's Who Among B/A 1975-76 & 1977-78; Men of Achvmnt 1977; Notable Americans 1976-77; mem NAACP; Urban League, Interdenom Ministers; Soc SW Con F; Organized Church KS MO. **MILITARY SERVICE:** AUS personel s/mjr 1940-45. **HOME ADDRESS:** 3004 N Creston Dr, Oklahoma City, OK 73111.

WANAMBWA, SARA LOUISE
Mayor. **PERSONAL:** Born May 26, 1945, Chicago, IL; married James Wanambwa (deceased); children: Edward, Lillian. **EDUCATION:** Roosevelt Univ, BS 1966. **CAREER:** US Peace Corps, volunteer 1966-68; East African Freshwater Fisheries, librarian/sub-editor 1972-77; Legal Serv Corp, comm educ coord 1982-84. **ORGANIZATIONS:** Mem Intl Inst of Municipal Clerks; mem Toastmasters Intl; mem Coalition of 100 Black Women. **HONORS/ACHIEVEMENTS:** Various speech contests Toastmasters Intl Econchati Chap Montgomery AL; Role Model Coalition of 100 Black Women 1985. **BUSINESS ADDRESS:** Mayor, Town of Shorter, PO Box 117, Shorter, AL 36075.

WANSEL, DEXTER GILMAN
Director. **PERSONAL:** Born Aug 22, 1950, Bryn Mawr, PA; married Lorna Millicent Hall. **CAREER:** Philadelphia Intl Records, dir of artist & repertoire 1980; Philadelphia Intl Records, musician & recording artist 1980; Wansel Interprises, indep record producer 1973-75; Various Record Companies, musician, arranger, orchestral dir, synthesizer & programmer 1973-75. **ORGANIZATIONS:** Mem Wissahickan Civic Assn 1978. **HONORS/ACHIEVEMENTS:** 17 Gold & Platinum Records 1976-80; Grammy Award Amer Assn of Recording Artists 1978. **MILITARY SERVICE:** AUS e-5 3 yrs serv. **BUSINESS ADDRESS:** Philadelphia International Rec, 309 S Broad St, Philadelphia, PA 19107.

WANTON, EVA C.
Educator. **PERSONAL:** Born 1935, Tunderbolt, GA; married Albert E Wanton; children: Jacquelyne G Maxey, Debra P Mitchell, Michelle V Jones, Dwanna Di Shon. **EDUCATION:** Savannah State Univ, BS 1961; Interamerican Univ, MA 1964, PhD 1970; FL State Univ, PhD 1980. **CAREER:** FL A&M Univ, dir summer session 1971-75, asst to dean 1975-79, dir gen educ 1977-79, dean 1982-. **ORGANIZATIONS:** Mem The Chamettes Inc 1971-; bd mem Jack & Jill Found 1986-. **HONORS/ACHIEVEMENTS:** Dean of the Year FL A&M Univ 1986. **HOME ADDRESS:** 3736 Sulton Court, Tallahassee, FL 32312. **BUSINESS ADDRESS:** Dean, Florida A&MUniv, Martin Luther King Blvd, Tallahassee, FL 32307.

WARD, ALBERT A.
Retired educator. **PERSONAL:** Born Sep 20, 1929, Detroit, MI; son of Abe and Mattie Smith; married Doris; children: Cheryl, David, Donald. **EDUCATION:** Wayne State Univ, BA, 1949; Wayne State Univ, MEd, 1962; Univ Michigan, EdD, 1971. **CAREER:** Elliot Elementary, Wayne-Westland Comm School, principal; Inkster Public Schools, supt; Jackson Public Schools, principal, 1966-71; Michigan Bell Telephone Co, act commercial mgr, 1965-66; Detroit Public Schools, teacher, 1958-63; Detroit Housing Commn, public housing aide, 1955-57, 1950-53; retired, 1988. **ORGANIZATIONS:** Mem, Phi Delta Kappa, Amer Assn School Admin, Michigan Assn School Admin, Natl Assn Elementary School Principals, Metro Detroit Soc Black Educ Admin, Natl Alliance Black School Educ, elementary rep Michigan State Com for N Central Coll & Schools Steward, Grace CME Church, Toastmasters: chmn, Westland Library Bd; mem, professional vstr, AASA Natl Acad School Exec, 1969, Horace Rackham Predoctoral Fellowship, 1969, 33rd Annual Supt Work Conf Teacher Coll, Columbia Univ, 1974. **MILITARY SERVICE:** AUS, 2nd lt, 1953-55; AUSR, capt, 1955-65.

WARD, ALBERT M.
City official. **PERSONAL:** Born Aug 05, 1929, Baltimore. **EDUCATION:** Hampton Inst, BA 1972. **CAREER:** Electrl Bd Cty of Hampton, 1st black chmn; Hampton Comm Fed Credit Union, vp; Diversified Serv & Commod Limited, corp Ofcr mem bd dir; Hampton Funeral Home; Hampton Roads Devel Corp, bd mem exec vp; HEW, corr clk 1949-58; Customs Woods Inc, interior designer 1958-60; King Merritt Baltimore, registred rep; Baltimore Post Ofc, distrib clk 1961-62; Bassette Real Estate, real estate & ins agt ofc mgr 1963-67. **ORGANIZATIONS:** Mem VA Electoral Bd Assn Exec Bd Hampton Br NAACP 1964-; exec bd Hampton Chap Nat Hampton Alumni Assn; steering com & co-founder Comm Progress Com; steering com Pirate Boosters; adv com Comm Devel & Housing Funds; chmn W Hampton Target Area Sub Com; former v-chmn Rep Party 1st Congressnl Dist; mem VA Crusade of Voters; Esquire Inc; Hampton Cty Com Rep Party; 1st black Electoral Bd Hampton 1971-;

parliamentarian & mem exec bd GROUP; mem Peninsula Heart Fund; Peninsula Cerebral Palsy; Am Red Cross; March of Dimes; Multi Sclerosis Soc; W Hampton Civic Assn; Hampton Sch Dist Supt Equal & Inequal Comm; sub-comm chmn Stud Conduct & Respons; bd dir mem Hampton Heritage Trust Inc; organizer Doctrus Sentry Soc. **HONORS/ ACHIEVEMENTS:** Recip merit serv award for Voter Regis & Voter Educ NAACP; merit serv award for Labor & Indust NAACP; cert of Apprec for Valuable serv Hampton Inst 1973 & 1975; listed Comm Ldr & Noteworthy Am; trhee commendation Awards AUS; competitive all expense schlrshp to Hampton Inst 1946. **MILITARY SERVICE:** AUS e-4 1951-53. **BUSINESS ADDRESS:** PO Box 544, Hampton, VA 23669.

WARD, ANNA ELIZABETH
City official, consultant. **PERSONAL:** Born Dec 20, 1952, Miami, FL; married Sterling Andrew Ward; children: Johnathan Travis, Rochelle Marie. **EDUCATION:** Miami Dade Com Coll, AA 1976-78; FL Intl Univ, BS Criminal Justice 1978-80, M Public Admin 1979-80. **CAREER:** FL Intl Univ, 1971-80; Sangamon State Univ, circulation dept admin 1980-81; City of Dallas, asst to asst city mgr 1981-83; Dallas Cty Com Coll District, asst internal auditor 1984-85; City of Emporia, VA, asst to city mngr. **ORGANIZATIONS:** Pres North Central TX COMPA 1982-83; teen counselor Women in Community Serv 1983; co-chairperson program com Urban Mgmt Asst of North TX 1983; mediator Dispute Mediation of Dallas Inc 1982-85, Better Business Bureau of Dallas 1982-85; bd mem North Central TX ASPA 1983-85. **HONORS/ACHIEVEMENTS:** Nominee Outstanding Young Amer 1981; program moderator Intl City Mgmt Assoc 1982; author Public Mgmt ICMA 1982-84; serv awd North TX Conf of Minority Public Admin 1983. **MILITARY SERVICE:** AUS Pvt 7 mo's; Defense Awd, Cert of Achievement, 1974-75. **HOME ADDRESS:** 5737 Valley Mills Drive, Garland, TX 75043. **BUSINESS ADDRESS:** Assistant to City Manager, City of Emporia, City Hall PO Box 511, Emporia, VA 23847.

WARD, ARNETTE S.
Educational administrator. **PERSONAL:** Born Dec 02, 1937, Jacksonville, FL; daughter of Isiah Scott and Albertha E Scott; married John W Ward; children: Elra Douglas. **EDUCATION:** Edward Jr Coll, AA; Florida A&M Univ, BS, 1962; Arizonia State Univ, MA, 1972. **CAREER:** Lincoln High School, teacher, 1963; Florida A&M Univ, asst prof, 1964; Fall Recreation Dept, dir of rec, 1964; Roosevelt School Dist, elementary school teacher, 1968; Mesa Comm Coll, counselor, 1971; dean of student sevr, 1979; Chandler-Gilbert Educ Center, provost, 1985-. **ORGANIZATIONS:** mem, Commn on Trail Court Appt, 1985; nominating comm, Arizonia Cactus Pine Girl Scout; mem, Black Women in High Educ, 1986; mem, Amer Assoc of Comm & Jr Co, 1986; mem, Natl Council of Black Amer; mem, Affairs Council of AACJS; mem, Amer Assoc of Women in Jr Coll, 1986; pres, Delta Sigma Theta, 1986. **HONORS/ACHIEVEMENTS:** Music Scholarship, Edward Water Jr Coll, 1957; honorable mention as singer, Alex Haley "Author of Roots," 1974; Outstanding Participation, Tempe School Dist, Black Culture Week, 1976; Women of the Year, Mesa Soroptomist/ Delta Sigma Theta, 1977 & 1984; Merit Award, Black Youth Recognition Conf, 1982. **BUSINESS ADDRESS:** Provost, Maricopa Comm Coll District, 40th Street & Washington, Phoenix, AZ 85234.

WARD, BENJAMIN
Commissioner. **PERSONAL:** Born Aug 10, 1926, Brooklyn, NY; son of Edward Ward and Loretta Ward; married Olivia; children: Benjamin, Jacquelyn Ward-Shepherd, Gregory, Margie Lewis, Mary I. **EDUCATION:** Brooklyn Coll, BA 1960, AAS 1957; Brooklyn Law Sch, LLB 1965, cnvrtd to JD 1967. **CAREER:** NYS Dept of Crctnl Svcs, commr 1975-78; New York City Hsng Authority, police chf 1979; New York City Dept of Crctn, commr 1979-83; New York City Police Dept, commr 1984-. **ORGANIZATIONS:** Mem bd dir Police Athltc League 1972-85; mem Crime Cntrl Plng Bd 1980, 1984-85; mem bd dir Natl Inst of Policing 1984-85; mem bd of trustees StJosephs Coll 1984; mem bd of dir NY Convntn & Vstrs Bureau 1984; mem bd dir Natl Conf of Chrstns & Jews. **HONORS/ACHIEVEMENTS:** August Volmer Awrd Wnr Am Soc of Crmnlgy 1984. **MILITARY SERVICE:** AUS stf sgt 1945-46. **BUSINESS ADDRESS:** Commissioner, New York City Police Dept, 1 Police Plaza, 14th Floor, New York, NY 10038.

WARD, C. DOUGLAS
Military officer. **PERSONAL:** Born Mar 16, 1930, Montgomery, TX; married Mary Ruth DuPont; children: Michael, Rosemary. **EDUCATION:** Univ CO, 1949-50; Century Coll, 1950-51; TX So U, LLB 1959. **CAREER:** Aero Med Div, staff judge adv 1976-; US Forces U-Tapao Royal Thai Naval Air Base Thailand, staff judge adv 1975-76; Gen Law Br Ofc of the Judge Adv Gen, chief 1971-75; Hq USAF Mi Personnel Security Com, mem 1972-75; Hq USAF Drug & Alcohol Abuse Prevention Com, 1973-75; 14th Strategic Aero Div, staffjudge Adv 1969-71; Fourth Air Force, asst staff judge adv 1967-69; US Forces Instanbul Turkey, staff judge adv 1965-67; Pvt Law Practice, 1959-61; mil judge 1969. **ORGANIZATIONS:** Mem TX Bar Assn; Fed Bar Assn; former mem Am Bar Assn & Nat Bar Assn; USAF Trial Observer for Overseas Forces. **HONORS/ACHIEVEMENTS:** Merit serv medal with 3 oak leaf clusters USAF; Air Force commend medal; works written "Critical Issues Affecting US Sec Energy Unemployment & The Sovite Mil Buildup"; "Strategy for Limited War in Europe" 1977; "Arms Limitation Agreements & US Security" Nat DefenseUniv Washington, DC 1979. **MILITARY SERVICE:** USAF lt col. **BUSINESS ADDRESS:** Executive Secretary, USAF, Office of the Secretary of the, Air Force/SAF/Minc, Washington, DC 20330.

WARD, CAROLE GENEVA
Educator. **PERSONAL:** Born Jan 14, 1943, Phoenix City, AL. **EDUCATION:** CA StateUniv at San Jose, BA 1965; MA 1973;Univ of CA, Grad Studies 1970; Intl Comm Coll, PhD;Univ of Ile-lfe Nigeria, 1970;Univ of Sci & Tech, 1970; Kumasi Ghana Forah Bay Coll Sierra Leone, 1970; Sorbonne, 1963. **CAREER:** Ethnic Studies Laney Coll, chrwmn; Goddard Coll, mentor consult teacher for masters degree stud 1973-74; Laney Coll, 1970-; CA Coll of Arts Cabrillo Coll, 1970; Andrew Hill HS, 1965-69; airline stewardess, 1966-68. **ORGANIZATIONS:** Mem Bay Area Black Artists 1972-; Nat Conf of Artists 1973-74. **HONORS/ACHIEVEMENTS:** Recip purchase award 27th Annual SF Art Festival 1973; alpha phi alphaaward outstanding black woman for achvmnt & serv 1974; selec com chmn for Black Filmmakers Hall of Fame Paramount Theatre of the Arts; publ Images of Awareness Pan Africanist Mag 1973; Afro-Am Artists Bio- biographical Dir Theres Dickason 1973; black artist on Art Vol 2 by Samella Lewis Ruth Waddy 1970. **BUSINESS ADDRESS:** Laney Coll, 900 Fallon St, Oakland, CA 94607.

WARD, CLARKE G.
Attorney. **PERSONAL:** Born Mar 16, 1930, Montgomery Co, TX; married Dorothie Callie Smith. **EDUCATION:** State Coll of Wash, 1948-49; USAF Sch of Electronics; Univ of ME; Lincoln U, AB 1955; Grad Sch TX So U, 1955; Sch of Law Univ of MO, 1955-56; TX So Univ Sch of Law, JC 1959. **CAREER:** NW Houston Water Suply Corp, dir 1971-; Priv Prac, 1970-; US Bd of Vet Appeals, staff counsel; Houston Legal Found, mng atty 1967-70; Harris Co TX, asst dist atty 1965-66; Law Firm Muldrow Jordan & Ward, 1963-66; Bankruptcy Sect US Dist Ct Chicago, dep clk 1963. **ORGANIZATIONS:** Mem TX Bar Assn; Fed Bar Assn; Bar of US Customs Ct; Bar of Tax Ct of US; Am Bar Assn; Houston Lawyers Assn; Spl Counsel; The Auerbach Corp ; staff legal adv Bd of Appeals; mem bd dir Epis Soc for Cultural & Racial Unity; gen counsel dir Greater Anacostia Peoples Corp; exec vice pres dir & gen counsel No Highlands Mohawk Co; dir NW Houston Water Supply Corp; mem Ad Hoc Com of Housing Crisis in DC; World Peace through Law Cntr; Ctnr for Study of Dem Inst. **HONORS/ACHIEVEMENTS:** Feature article Ebony Mag 1966; editorial mention Time Mag Oct 1966; Who's Who in Commerce & Industry. **BUSINESS ADDRESS:** Ste 1410, 1 Allen Cn Tr, Houston, TX 77002.

WARD, DANIEL
Educational administrator. **PERSONAL:** Born Mar 15, 1934, Memphis, TN; son of Mr and Mrs Gus Ward; married Margie Marie Brittmon; children: Muriel Dawn, Maria Diane, Marcus Daniel. **EDUCATION:** TN State Univ, BS Music Educ 1956; USAF Multi-Engine Pilot Training Sch, Cert 1957; USAF Radar Controller Tng, Cert 1958; USAF Air Force Instr Course, Cert 1960; TN State Univ, MS Secondary Sch Instr 1960; USAF Air Command & Staff Sch, Cert 1976; Drug & Alcohol Abuse Workshop, Cert 1975; 36 post-grad hours. **CAREER:** USAF, pilot and radar contr 1956-59; Douglass HS, program coord 1962-65; Hyde Park Elem Sch, asst prin 1965-67; Grant Elem Sch, principal 1967-68; Porter Jr HS, principal 1968-70; Douglass HS, tchr vocal music 1969-72; Vance Jr HS, principal 1970-81; Fairley HS, principal 1981-83; Memphis City Schools, dist IV supt 1983-; asst supt, secondary dept, l987-. **ORGANIZATIONS:** Assn of Supervision and Curriculum Dev; Omega Psi Phi Frat Inc; AASA; TN State Univ Alumni Assn; Natl Guard Assns of TN; mem bd trustees Metropolitan Baptist Ch; Memphis-Shelby County Airport Authority 1967-; mem NAACP; minister of music Metropolitan Bapt Church. **HONORS/ACHIEVEMENTS:** Four-year scholarships to, TN State Univ, AR State Univ, Howard Univ, LeMoyne Coll, Stillman Coll; Omega man of the Year Epsilon Phi Chptr 1976 nominated1980; Awarded Meritorious Serv Medal 1981 by Pres of the US; 1st Oak Leaf Cluster 1984; Minute-man Award for Outstanding Serv to the TN Air Natl Guard; Danforth Admin Fellow 1983-84. **MILITARY SERVICE:** USAF Lt Col served 28 years. **BUSINESS ADDRESS:** District Superintendent, Memphis Cty Schools South Area, 2300 Hernando Rd, Memphis, TN 38106.

WARD, DORIS MARGARET
Educator. **PERSONAL:** Born Jan 27, 1932, Chicago, IL. **EDUCATION:** Univ CA, PhD; San Francisco State U, MA 1974; IN U, MS 1964; IN U, BA 1953. **CAREER:** San Mateo Co Office Educ, coord; San Francisco State Univ, adj lectr 1969-70, 72; IN State Teacher Corps, team leader 1967-68; Indianapolis Public School, teacher 1959-67. **ORGANIZATIONS:** Betty J Olive Meml Found; Commn Instr CA Comm & Jr Coll Assn; vice pres San Francisco Black Ldrsp Forum; mem Black Women Orgn Action; consult Waterloo IA Sch; Sioux City; Milwaukee; MN; Dayton Police Dept on Conflict & Violence; vice pres bd Sanfracisco Comm Coll Dist Bd Tst 1972-; tst Minority Affairs Assem Assn Comm Coll; mat exec cncl Assn Study Afro-Am Life & Hist; natl bd western reg bd Cncl Black Am Affairs Assn Am Comm & Jr Coll; mem NAACP; SF Div Nat Women's Polit Caucus; Alpha Kappa Alpha. **HONORS/ACHIEVEMENTS:** NDEA grant IN StateUniv 1966; lilly found grant IN StateUniv 1967; NDEAUniv CA 1968; rockefeller found grant 1974; gov hon Pi Sigma Alpha; educ hon Pi Lambda Theta; spl merit award Sup Reporter 1973; living legend award Black Women Orgn Action 1975; distgsd woman award Girls' Club of Med-Peninsula & Lockheed Missilies & Space Co Inc 1975; recog comm serv Kappa Alpha Psi 1975; bicentennial award Trinity Bapt Ch 1976f recog exemplary comm ldrsp Black Student Psychol Assn 1976; publ "Indianapolis Comm Ctr Proj" 1968-69. **BUSINESS ADDRESS:** San Franciso City-County, 440 Davis Ct #1409, San Francisco, CA 94111.

WARD, DOUGLAS TURNER
Playwright, actor. **PERSONAL:** Born May 05, 1930, Burnside, LA; married Diana Hoyt Powell; children: 2 children. **EDUCATION:** Attended, Univ MI, Wilberforce Univ, Paul Mann Actors Workshop NYC. **CAREER:** Broadway debut in A Raisin in the Sun 1959; appeared in plays One Flew Over the Cukoo's Nest, The Iceman Cometh, The Blacks, Pullman Car Hiawatha, Bloodknow, Happy Ending, Day of Absence, Kongi's Harvest, Ceremonies in Dark Old Men; dir A Soilder's Play, Mark Taper Forum LA 1982-83, Goodman Theatre Chicago 1983; Negro Ensemble Company, artistic director/co-founder with Gerald Krone and Robert Hooks. **BUSINESS ADDRESS:** Artistic Dir, The Negro Ensemble Company, 424 W 55th St, New York, NY 10019.

WARD, GARY LAMELL
Professional athlete. **PERSONAL:** Born Dec 06, 1953, Los Angeles, CA. **CAREER:** Minnesota Twins, outfielder 1981-84; Texas Rangers, outfielder 1985-. **HONORS/ ACHIEVEMENTS:** Selected Twins Player of the Yr & Most Improved Player 1982; named AL Rookie of the Yr Baseball Digest 1979-81; selected to Major League All-Rookie Team 1981.

WARD, HASKELL G.
Business executive. **PERSONAL:** Born Mar 13, 1940, Griffin, GA; married Kathryn Lecube; children: Alexandra, Michelle. **EDUCATION:** Clark Coll, BA 1963; UCLA, MA 1967. **CAREER:** Cmnty Dvlpmnt Agncy, commr; State Dept, Africa adv/policy plng stf; City of New York, dpty mayor 1979; Hlth & Hsptls Corp City of New York, chmn of bd 1979, pres. **ORGANIZATIONS:** Rep Ford Fndtn, Lagos, Nigeria; pgm ofcr Ford Fndtn, New York; bd dir Am Cncl on Germany; mem Mid-Atlantic Clb. **HONORS/ACHIEVEMENTS:** Woodrow Wilson Hnry Flw; John Hay Whitney Flw. **BUSINESS ADDRESS:** President, Health & Hospital Corp, 444 E 57th St, New York, NY 10022.

WARD, JAMES DALE
Educator. **PERSONAL:** Born Feb 03, 1959, Nettleton, MS; son of Alice Harper Marion. **EDUCATION:** Univ of MS, BA Journalism/Sociology 1980; Univ of Cincinnati, M Public Affairs 1983, PhD Political Science 1988. **CAREER:** Knoxville News-Sentinel, staff writer 1980; WCBI-TV Columbus, TV reporter 1981; Univ of Cincinnati, instructor, 1986-76; Winona State Univ, Winona, MN, asst prof, 1989; Univ of AL, Tuscaloosa, AL, instructor, 1987-88.

ORGANIZATIONS: Mem Amer Soc for Public Admin; mem Natl Forum for Black Public Admins; mem Amer Political Science Assn. **HONORS/ACHIEVEMENTS:** Contracting out a local political culture presentation, Amer Soc for Public Admin, 1989 convention; contracting out a regional comparison presentation Midwest Political Science Assn, 1988 conf. **BUSINESS ADDRESS:** Asst Prof, Dept of Political Science, Winona State Univ, Winona, MN 55987.

WARD, LORENE HOWELTON
Personnel administrator. **PERSONAL:** Born Sep 08, 1927, Menifee, AR. **EDUCATION:** AR Bapt Coll, BA 1964;Univ of OK, 1964; Wayne U, 1965; Harding Coll, 1966;Univ of AR, 1969. **CAREER:** EOA, personnel adminstr 1976-; EOA, dir asst 1974-76; EOA, coord 1972-74; Nghbrhd Multi-Purpose Ctrs, dir 1968-72; Soc Serv Wrkrs, supr 1967-68;Philander & Smith Coll, asst dean 1964-67. **ORGANIZATIONS:** Consult Relig Comm Outreach of Archview Bapt Ch 1977; consult Volt Tech Corp 1972; mem Panel of Am Women 1976-77; bus mgr Sunday Sch Class-Grtr Archview Bapt Ch 1977; AR Food & Mut Counc 1976-; pres Sr Choir Grtr Archview Bapt Ch 1975-76; mem Area Agency on Aging 1975-; pres Nat Assn for Comm Devel Region VI affiliate 1975-77; 1st anti-basileus Sigma Gamma Rho Sor Inc 1975-; Black Female Action Inc 1974-; Fairfield Bay Comm Club 1973-; sec Ldrshp Roundtable of AR 1973-75f AR Black Citz Orgn 1972-74. **HONORS/ACHIEVEMENTS:** Cert of merit Nat Inst of Sr Citz 1975-76; Betty Bumpers Immunz Prgm for Prevention of Childhood Dis 1974; achvmt Award Pro-Plan Intl Ltd Inc 1974; outst comm serv & Human Devel Shorter Coll Alumni Assn 1973; award of achvmt SE Mgmt & Tech Inst 1972; cert of merit Volt- tech Corp 1970;award of Aprec Laubach Literary Assn 1968; Nat Assn for Comm Devel Serv Award 1975, 77. **BUSINESS ADDRESS:** 2501 State, Little Rock, AR 72206.

WARD, MELVIN FITZGERALD, SR.
Representative. **PERSONAL:** Born Jul 02, 1918, New Bern, NC; married Lessie Pratt; children: Frances, Dorothy, Nancy, Melvin Jr. **EDUCATION:** Nat Bible Inst, DD 1944; Lawson Bible Inst, BTh 1945; Teamers Bible Inst, DD 1972; Union Christian Bible Inst, DD 1974. **CAREER:** Tobacco Wrks Intl Union, rep 1977; African Meth Epis Zion Ch, minister 1943-; TWIU, pres 1950-68. **ORGANIZATIONS:** Bd mem AME Zion Ch; bd tst Christian Bible Ins; mem Home Mission Bd AME Zion Ch; dir Pub Rel for the Virgin Islands & South AM Conf; mem Human Rel Comm 1960-65. **HONORS/ACHIEVEMENTS:** Award Pres of Local 256 TWIU 25 yrs; Who's Who in Labor 1976. **BUSINESS ADDRESS:** PO Box 1634, Wilson, NC 27893.

WARD, NOLAN F.
Attorney. **PERSONAL:** Born Jan 14, 1945, Columbus, OH; son of Clifforn Loudin Ward and Ethel Shaffer Ward (deceased); married Hazel Williams Ward, Sep 06, 1966; children: Penelope Kaye Ward. **EDUCATION:** Prairie View A&M U, BA MA 1968;Univ of NE, 1967; So U, 1969; Univ of TX, JD 1973. **CAREER:** State of TX, chmn exec dir Texas Employment Commn; Gov Dolph Briscoe, legal staff 1976-; Private Practice, 1975; Co Judge Bill Elliott, clerk 1975; St Rep Anthony Hall, admin aid 1973-74; EEOC, case analyst 1970-73; Waller ISD, instr 1967-69; Job Corps, advr 1966-67; attorney general, Austin, TX, 1983-. **ORGANIZATIONS:** Mem NAACP; TX Bar Assn; Omega Psi Phi; Omicron Kappa Delta; Delta Theta Phi; Thurgood Marshall Legislative Sec; District & County Attorney's Assn, Urban League. **BUSINESS ADDRESS:** Attorney General's Office, Supreme Court Bldg, Austin, TX 78711-2518.

WARD, PERRY W.
College president/chancellor. **CAREER:** Lawson State Community College, Birmingham AL, president/chancellor. **BUSINESS ADDRESS:** Lawson State Community College, Birmingham, AL 35221. *

WARD, VAL GRAY
Theatre director. **PERSONAL:** Born 1933, Mt Bayou, MS. **CAREER:** Kuumba Wrksp, fndr dir; Howard U, vis lectr 1971; Western IL U, 1972. **ORGANIZATIONS:** Culture chprsn League of Black Women; mem Who's Who Hon Soc. **HONORS/ACHIEVEMENTS:** Amer receipt dr of the streets degree, Black Students, Univ MI 1969.

WARD, WALTER L., JR.
State representative. **PERSONAL:** Born Oct 28, 1943, Camp Forest, TN; divorced; children: Dionne, Walter L III. **EDUCATION:** Univ of WI, BS 1969fUniv of WI Law Sch; Milwaukee Area Tech Coll; Marquette U, Grad Work. **CAREER:** District 17, state rep 1972-. **ORGANIZATIONS:** Couns work; chmn OIC Industrial Adv Bd; Martin Luther King Orgn Bd mem. **BUSINESS ADDRESS:** 325 W Capitol, Madison, WI 53702.

WARD, ZANA ROGERS
Association executive. **PERSONAL:** Born Oct 18, 1915, Miller, MS; widowed. **EDUCATION:** TN State Univ, Cert; LeMoyne-Owen Coll, BS 1955; Brooklyn Coll of NY Univ, 1966; Memphis State Univ, MEd 1971. **CAREER:** Pres Memphis Chap Fed of Colored Womens Clubs, pres 1966-; Memphis Sect Natl Council of Negro Women Inc, pres 1972-. **ORGANIZATIONS:** Mem Zeta Phi Beta 1959-, Memphis Pan-Hellenic Council 1960-, Lambda Gamma Chap of Kappa Delta Pi 1971-; fin sec SE Reg Assoc of Colored Womens Clubs 1971-73; proj dir Memphis Unit of Women in Comm Serv Inc 1972-; mem Corp of Natl Women in Comm Serv Inc 1972-74; bd of dir Comp Youth Serv 1973-; 1stvp TN State Fed of Colored Womens Clubs 1974-; bd dir Memphis Shelby Cty Unit of Amer Cancer Soc 1974-; mem YWCA; pres Council Mt Pisgah CME Church;bd mem Chris Ed; vice pres Stewardess Bd #4; pres BR Danner Club; treas Sr Choir. **HONORS/ACHIEVEMENTS:** Disting Club Womans Aws Natl Assoc of Colored Womens Clubs Inc 1963; Memphis Intl Fellowship 1968; Plaque SE Region of Assoc of Colored Womens Clubs 1971; Zeta Phi Beta Sor 1973; Memphis Sec Natl Council Negro Women 1974.

WARD-BROOKS, JOYCE RENEE
Systems analyst. **PERSONAL:** Born Sep 09, 1952, Kansas City, MO; married John L Brooks; children: Carmen, Leah. **EDUCATION:** Washington Univ, BS Bus Admin 1974. **CAREER:** Mobil Oil Corp, programmer/analyst 1972-73; Southwestern Bell Tele Co, acctg office supv 1974-78, acctg mgr 1978-80, asst staff mgr 1980-85, systems analyst 1985-. **HOME ADDRESS:** 12844 Stoneridge, Florissant, MO 63033. **BUSINESS ADDRESS:** Systems Analyst, Southwestern Bell Tele Co, One Bell Ctr, 23 D-1, St Louis, MO 63101.

WARDER, JOHN MORGAN
Bank administrator. **PERSONAL:** Born Jan 07, 1927, Ellsworth, KS; married Margie; children: Linda, Kent, David. **EDUCATION:** Univ KS ba 1952. **CAREER:** Plymouth Natl Bank, pres 1969-82; First Plymouth Natl Bank, cob 1982-84; First Bank Minneapolis, vice pres urban devel 1984-86; First Bank System Inc, vice pres urban devel 1987-. **ORGANIZATIONS:** Trust Macalester Coll 1970-81; bd mem Minneapolis Found 1972-; Helen Harrington Trust 1972-; Bush Found Panel Judge 1973-; treas Minneapolis UNCF Campaign 1975-; mem Alpha Phi Alpha Frat; co-chmn Alpha Phi Alpha 1978; Nat Conf Com; Minneapolis Club; Prince Hall Masons; Dunkers Club; vchmn 1980-85, bd mem 1985- Nat Med Flwsps Inc; treas Delta Dental of MN 1984; trustee Univ of MN Med Found 1985-; bd mem MN News Council; treas W Harry Davis Found 1986-;bd mem MN Bus League 1985-; mem NAACP, Minneapolis Urban League, Zion Bapt Ch Cty of Mpls. **HONORS/ACHIEVEMENTS:** Disting Serv Awd 1964; Outstanding Serv Awd Afro-Am Educator's Assn 1968; Bmn Fedn of Tchrs Pennel Awd for life time serv to children 1973; Gtr MplsC of C Awd 1973; Miss Black MN Outstanding Achievement Awd 1975; Minneapolis Urban League's Cecil E Newman Humantarian Aw 1976; Man of the Year Awd Insight Publ 1977; Outstanding Serv Awd Alpha Phi Alpha 1978; Man of the Year Awd Alpha Phi Alpha 1979; Outstanding Serv Awd MN Black Chemical Abuse 1982; MN Urban League Volunteer Serv Awd 1986. **MILITARY SERVICE:** AUS 1946-47; USAF corpl 1947-48. **HOME ADDRESS:** 5133 Garfield Ave S, Minneapolis, MN 55419.

WARDLAW, ALVIA JEAN
Art historian. **PERSONAL:** Born Nov 05, 1947, Atlanta, GA. **EDUCATION:** Wellesley Coll MA, AB 1969; NYU. **CAREER:** Dept of Art TX Southern Univ, art hist 1977-; Gallery of Traditional African Art TX Southern Univ, curator 1978-; Barbara Jordan Archives TX Southern Univ, curator 1978-; Museum of Fine Arts Houston, assoc curator of primitive art and educ 1974-77. **ORGANIZATIONS:** Commr Municipal Arts Commn Houston 1975; mem TX Conf of Art Historians 1977-; exec bd mem So Coll of Afro-Am Writers Houston Chapter 1978-; exec bd mem Third Ward Preservation Assn 1976-; mem Natl Conf of Artists Houston Chapter 1977f mem Am Assn of Museums, 1980. **HONORS/ACHIEVEMENTS:** Published over 10 articles for Mus of Fine Arts, Houston Bulletin, Callaloo, Studio Museum in Harlem, Pelham von Stoffler Gallery 1972-80; curated over 20 Exhibitions Houston Museum of Fine Arts 1974-77; one of Houston's 20 Most Prominent Black Women Houston Focus Magazine, 1978 guest curator Laguna Gloria Art Mus Austin TX 1980. **BUSINESS ADDRESS:** 3201 Wheeler Ave, Houston, TX 77004.

WARDLAW, ALVIN HOLMES
Educator. **PERSONAL:** Born Jan 03, 1925, Atlanta; married Virginia Cage; children: Alyia W Shore, Joy Elaine. **EDUCATION:** Morehouse Coll, BS 1948; Atlanta U, MS 1950;Univ MI, Further Study 1951-54, 1959-60;Univ WI, 1965-66. **CAREER:** TSU, asst prof 1950-65; TX Southern Univ Coop Center of MN Math and Sci Teaching Proj, dir 1963-64; Upward Bound Proj, dir 1970-73; TSU, acting dept head 1969-72; EPDA Inst TSU, assoc dir 1970-73; TX Southern Univ, asst vice pres academic affairs. **ORGANIZATIONS:** Consult Adminstr Conf Houston Indep Sch Dist 1960; Nat Sic Inst So U; faculty rep Athletics TSU 1969-72; Athletic Adv Counc 1974-75; mem NAIA Dist #8 eligibility com 1971-73; pres TX Assn Stud Assist Progs 1973; Rockefeller Found Fellow 1952-54; NSF Faculty Fellow 1959-60; Carnegie Found Fellow 1965-66. **MILITARY SERVICE:** AUS 1944-46. **BUSINESS ADDRESS:** 3200 Cleburne St, Houston, TX 77004.

WARDLAW, MCKINLEY, JR.
Educational administrator. **PERSONAL:** Born Jul 24, 1927, Columbus, GA; married Thelma Sears; children: Pamela Lynch, Vanessa, Marcus. **EDUCATION:** Tuskegee Inst, BS Chem 1951; PA State Coll, BS Meteorology 1952; Westfield State Coll, MEd 1969; Univ of DE, MEd 1973; Temple Univ, EdD 1983. **CAREER:** Kent Cty Vo-Tech, dir of guidance 1970-79; Dept of Public Instruction, state supv 1979-. **ORGANIZATIONS:** Mem Kappa Alpha Psi Frat 1949-; professional mem AMS 1960-; mem DASA 1979-, DSBA 1982-, ROA 1982-; vice pres Capitol School Dist School Bd 1982; commercial pilot. **HONORS/ACHIEVEMENTS:** Kappa Man of the Year Dover Alumni Chap 1983. **MILITARY SERVICE:** USAF major 20 years. **HOME ADDRESS:** 617 Buckson Dr, Dover, DE 19901.

WARE, CARL
City councilman. **PERSONAL:** Born Sep 30, 1943, Newman, GA; married Mary Alice; children: Timothy Alexander. **EDUCATION:** Clark Coll, BA 1965; Carnegie Mellon Univ, postgrad 1965-66; Univ of Pittsburgh, MPA 1968. **CAREER:** Atlanta Housing Authority, dir 1970-73; City of Atlanta, pres city cncl 1974-79; The Coca-Cola Co Atlanta, vice pres 1974-. **ORGANIZATIONS:** Mem Policy Com of Nat League of Cities; GA Muni Assn; Comm Devel Com; bd dirs Metro Atlanta Council on Alcohol & Drugs; elected to Atlanta City Council 1973; bd of dirs US Civil Rights Commn 1983, Natl Cncl Black Agencies 1983-, United Way of Metro Atlanta 1983-; trustee Clark Coll; mem GAmmon Theol Sem, GA State Univ Found, Sigma Pi Phi. **HONORS/ACHIEVEMENTS:** Recip Jessie Smith Noyes Fellowship Award 1966; numerous Civic Award. **BUSINESS ADDRESS:** 310 North Ave NW, Atlanta, GA 30301.

WARE, CHARLES JEROME
Attorney. **PERSONAL:** Born Apr 22, 1948, Anniston, AL; son of John Ware and Marie Ware; married Lucinda Frances Hubbard; children: Lucinda Marie. **EDUCATION:** Univ of FL Gainesville, fellow in med & sci 1969 & 1971; Univ of AL School of Medicine, attended 1970-71; Talladega Coll AL, BA 1970; Howard Univ Law Sch, JD 1975; Boston Univ Sch of Bus MA, MBA fellowship 1976. **CAREER:** Inst for the Study of Educ Policy, legal legislative & econ asst 1974-75; Boston Coll Law Sch, atty writer & consult 1975-76; Boston Univ Martin Luther King Ctr, atty 1976; Middlesex Co MA Dist Attys Ofc, asst dist atty 1976-77; Arent Fox Kintner Plotkin & Kahn, anti-trust atty 1977; Criminal Div US Dept of Justice, trial atty appellate atty 1977-79; US Dept of Justice, anti-trust atty 1979-82; US Immigration, judge 1980-81; US Fed Trade Comm, first asst to the dir bureau of competition 1982-83, spcl counsel to the chmn 1983-86; St Paul's College Lawrenceville VA, exec vice pres and genl counsel 1986-87; private practice of law, Ware and Assoc, P.A., Columbia, MD 1988-. **ORGANIZATIONS:** Life Mem NAACP 1966-, SCLC 1966-; mem dir & editor Amer Bar Assn, DC Bar Assn, PA Bar Assn 1975-, MD Bar Assoc, VA Bar Assoc; founder & pres The William Monroe Trotter Polit Rsch Inst 1978-; principal partner Charles J Ware & Assocs Law Firm 1986-; natl legal advisor Natl Tots and Teens Inc 1986-; General Counsel, Maryland State Conf of the NAACP. **HONORS/ACHIEVEMENTS:** Who's Who in Amer Colls & Univs 1970; finalist White House Fellowship Prog 1978; Outstanding Young Columbian Co-

lumbia MD Jaycees 1979; Who's Who in Amer Law Marquis 1979; Outstanding Young Man of Amer Amer Jaycees Montgomery AL 1980; Who's Who in Maryland. **HOME ADDRESS:** 7468 Weather Worn Way, Columbia, MD 21046.

WARE, DYAHANNE
Lawyer. **PERSONAL:** Born Jul 26, 1958, Chicago, IL. **EDUCATION:** Univ of IL, AB 1980; The John Marshall Law School, JD 1984; Univ of Chicago, graduate School of Business, Candidate l990 MBA. **CAREER:** Encyclopedia Britannica USA, atty ftc compliance audit staff 1984-85, staff atty 1985-86, atty general counsel/dir legal compliance staff 1986-/special foreign asst, Guadeloupe, FWI. **ORGANIZATIONS:** Mem Chicago Bar Assn 1985-; America Bar Assn; Chicago Volunteer Legal Services, Natl Bd of Realtors, Natl Black MBA Assn., Urban League, Natl Conference of Black Lawyers. **HONORS/ACHIEVEMENTS:** Honoree YWCA Leadership Award 1985; Honoree YMCA Black & Hispanic Leaders of Industry 1987. **HOME ADDRESS:** 4100 North Marine Dr, Apt 4H, Chicago, IL 60613. **BUSINESS ADDRESS:** Asst Genl Cnsl/Dir Legal Staff, Encyclopaedia Britannica USA, 310 South Michigan Ave, Chicago, IL 60604.

WARE, GILBERT
Educator. **PERSONAL:** Born Jul 21, 1933, Elkton, VA; divorced. **EDUCATION:** Morgan State Univ, BA 1955; Princeton Univ, MD, PhD 1962. **CAREER:** State of MD, program exec 1967-68; Washington Tech Inst, exec asst to pres 1968-69; The Urban Inst, sr rsch staff mem 1969-70; Drexel Univ, assoc prof/prof political science 1970-. **ORGANIZATIONS:** Life mem NAACP; exec dir Judicial Council of the Natl Bar Assoc 1971-81; bd of dirs Historical Soc of the US District Court for Eastern PA 1986-. **HONORS/ACHIEVEMENTS:** Fellowships, Ford Foundation, Amer Council of Learned Societies, Amer Philosophical Soc, Metropolitan Applied Rsch Ctr; Natl Bar Assoc Presidential Awd1977; publications "From the Black Bar, Voices for Equal Justice," Putnam 1976; "William Hastie, Grace Under Pressure," Oxford Univ Press 1984. **MILITARY SERVICE:** AUS 1st lt 4 yrs. **BUSINESS ADDRESS:** Professor Political Science, Drexel University, 32nd & Chestnut Sts, Philadelphia, PA 19104.

WARE, IRENE JOHNSON
Business executive. **PERSONAL:** Born Apr 24, 1935, Blacksher, AL; married Fred E; children: Darryl, Ronald. **EDUCATION:** Allen Inst 1953; Besteda's Sch of Cosmetology 1961. **CAREER:** Gospel Serv ABC/Dunhill Records, dir; WGOK Radio, announcer/gen mgr 1962-; Record World Mag NYC, gospel editor 1967-. **ORGANIZATIONS:** Mem NATRA; BAMA; GMWA; exec dir Nat Assn Gospel Announcers & Affiliates; gospel editor Black Radio Exclusive Magazine; vice pres bd of dir Gospel Music Assn1980; bd dir OIC Mobile Area; mem Operation PUSH Chgo. **HONORS/ACHIEVEMENTS:** Named 1 of Top 10 Gospel Announcers Open Mike Mag 1965; Humanitarian Award NATRA 1971; Woman of the Yr Black Radio Conf 1977; Gospel Announcer of Yr GospelMusic Workshop of Am 1979; Black Gospel Announcer of Yr Award SESAC 1978; Outstanding Citizen of the Yr Stewart Meml CME Ch 1980; Jack Walker Award for Excellence in Broadcasting NATRA 1973; Excellence in Broadcasting by Utterbach Concert Choir Carnegie Hall 1969. **BUSINESS ADDRESS:** PO Box 2261, Mobile, AL 36601.

WARE, J. LOWELL
Publisher. **PERSONAL:** Born Jun 16, 1928, Wetumpka, AL; married Alyce Martin; children: Rhonda Dunn, Janis. **EDUCATION:** A&M U, AB 1951. **CAREER:** Atlanta Voice Newspaper, publ editor 1985; Atlanta Daily World, linotype setter; Morris Brown Coll, mgr 1953; Atlanta Inquirer, founder 1960; Atlanta Pub Schs, tchr 1955. **ORGANIZATIONS:** Dir Journalism Summer Prgm; Alpha Phi Alpha. **HONORS/ACHIEVEMENTS:** NAACP Plaque Voice News Network; Plaque Class of 1951 Outst Class Grad; Plaques for Disting Serv Media Women. **MILITARY SERVICE:** AUS sgt 1950-52. **BUSINESS ADDRESS:** Editor/Publisher, The Atlanta Voice Newspaper, 633 Pryor St SW, Atlanta, GA 30312.

WARE, JUANITA GLEE See THOMAS, JUANITA WARE

WARE, OMEGO JOHN CLINTON, JR.
Consultant, executive. **PERSONAL:** Born Mar 13, 1928, Washington, DC; son of Omego J C Ware, Sr and Bertha S Ware; married Elinor Gwen Smith; children: Karl R, Keith R, Karlene R. **EDUCATION:** Georgetown Univ, BS Foreign Commerce 1960; USA War College, graduate 1969. **CAREER:** Central Intelligence Agency, intelligence specialist-office director, mem Exec Committee, dir Center for study of Intelligence 1955-82; UC Lawrence Livermore Natl Lab, administrator/operations specialist 1982; consultant-advisor, US Dept of Energy, Washington, DC. **HONORS/ACHIEVEMENTS:** CIA Awards, charter mem, Senior Intelligence Service,. **MILITARY SERVICE:** AUS military intelligence 1946-55. **HOME ADDRESS:** 3244 Pope St SE, Washington, DC 20020. **BUSINESS ADDRESS:** Univ of CA,, Lawrence Livermore Natl Laboratory, PO Box 808, Livermore, CA 94550.

WARE, WILLIAM L.
Educator. **PERSONAL:** Born May 15, 1934, Greenwood, MS; son of Leslie Ware (deceased) and Katherine Bowden; married Lottie Herger, Apr 18, 1958; children: Felicia Joyner, Trevor Wore, Melvinia Abdullah. **EDUCATION:** Mississippi Valley State Univ, ITTA Bena, MS, BS, 1957; California State Univ, Los Angeles, CA, MA, 1969; Univ of Southern California, Los Angeles, CA, PhD, 1978. **CAREER:** Greenwood Public School, health educ/coach, 1957-63; Bellflower Public School, physical educ/coach, 1963-72; California State Univ, Northridge, CA, asst prof, 1964-78; Mississippi State Univ, Mississippi State, MS, assoc professor,1979-. **ORGANIZATIONS:** Dir, United Way of Oktibbeha City, 1982-85; Boy Scouts of Amer, Pushmatha Council, 1983-85; Volunteers for Youth, 1985; pres, Kiwanis Club, Starkville, 1986-87. **HONORS/ACHIEVEMENTS:** Leadership Starkville Starkville Chamber of Comm 1985; Serv Awd CA Congress of Parents & Teachers Inc 1969; Kiwanian of the Year 1985; Distinguished Educ Award, IDEA, 1987; Outstanding Serv Award, Phi Delta Kappa, 1989; Pres Citation; Natl Assn for Equal Opportunity in Higher Educ, 1989. **HOME ADDRESS:** 75 ChoctawRd, Starkville, MS 39759. **BUSINESS ADDRESS:** Assoc, Professor, Mississippi State Univ, PO Box, 2987, Mississippi State, MS 39762.

WAREHAM, ALTON L.
Dentist. **PERSONAL:** Born Jul 01, 1920, New York, NY; married Helene; children: Roger, Lynn Howell. **EDUCATION:** Lincoln Univ, PA, AB 1938-42; HowardUniv Coll of Dntstry, DDS 1944-48. **CAREER:** Medicaid Comm of NYC, chmn & mem 1968; Dntl Care Serv of 125th St, asst dir 1968-69; Headstrt Pgm of NYC, chmn & mem 1970-72; Grtr Harlem Nrsng Home, dntl cnsltnt 1977-; attending Dentist Harlem Hospital staff. **ORGANIZATIONS:** Cnsltnt Blue Shld Blue Crs Dntl Care Pgm of New York City 1972; life mem NAACP, PA L Urban League; mem 1st Dist Dntl Soc Atndng Stf Dntst Harlem Hosp Oral Srgry Dept; life mem ADA. **HONORS/ACHIEVEMENTS:** Fellow Acad of Gen Dnststry 1982; Apprctn Awrd Dedicated Serv to Harlem Hosp & Oral Srgry Clnc 1984. **MILITARY SERVICE:** AUS CAPT 1952-54; Bronz Star; Unit Awrd; Combat Medic Badge 1953. **HOME ADDRESS:** 2235 5th Ave, New York, NY 10037.

WARFIELD, MARCIA
Actress, comedienne. **PERSONAL:** Born in Chicago, IL; divorced. **CAREER:** Began as standup comic in Chicago IL; film and television actress; comedienne. **HONORS/ACHIEVEMENTS:** Regular appearances on The Richard Pryor Show; actress in movies, including Marva Collins, DC Cab, Gidget Goes To Harlem, and Mask; semi-regular appearance s on Riptide; plays bailiff Roz Russell on Night Court; won San Francisco Intl Stand-up Comedy Competition, 1979. **BUSINESS ADDRESS:** 6310 San Vicente Blvd # 407, Los Angeles, CA 90048. *

WARFIELD, PAUL D.
Professional athlete. **PERSONAL:** Born Nov 28, 1942, Warren, OH; married Beverly A Keys; children: Sonja La Shawn, Malcolm Joseph. **EDUCATION:** OH State U, BS 1964; Kent State U, MA 1975. **CAREER:** Cleveland Browns, professional football player 1964-69; Miami Dolphins, player 1970-74; Memphis Southmen (WFL), player 1975; Cleveland Browns 1976-77; NBC-TV, sports announcer 1977; Cleveland Browns, asst dir of propersonnel 1985-. **ORGANIZATIONS:** Mem NFL Players Assn 1964-75; Aftra 1970-75; lifetime mem Phyllis Whestley Assn; sr life mem NAACP Youth Motivation Task Force; mem OH StateUniv Alumni Assn; Speaker for Numerous Youth Group. **HONORS/ACHIEVEMENTS:** Recipient Golden Helmet Award 1969-72; Miami Dolphins Best Receiver 1972 1973; mem Pro Football Hall of Fame Official All-Pro Team 1969; mem Hall of Fame OHAssn of Track Coaches; Voted All-Pro 1964 1968-74; Miami Dolphins Most Valuable Player 1970; Nat Guard Discharged 1973. **BUSINESS ADDRESS:** Dir of Player Relations, Cleveland Browns, Tower B Cleveland Statium, Cleveland, OH 44114.

WARFIELD, WILLIAM C.
Educator. **PERSONAL:** Born Jan 22, 1920, West Helena, AR; son of Robert Warfield and Bertha McCamey Warfield; divorced. **EDUCATION:** Eastman Sch of Music, BM 1942; Univ of AR, D Laws 1972; Univ of Boston, DMusic 1981; Milliken Univ, D Music 1984. **CAREER:** Univ of IL, chmn voice div. **ORGANIZATIONS:** Pres Natl Assn of Negro Mscns 1984; bd mem Opera Ebony 1983-85; music panal Natl Assn for Advncmnt in the Arts 1981-87. **HONORS/ACHIEVEMENTS:** Handel Medallion New York City 1974; Govs Awrd State of IL 1979; Grammy Award NARAS l984. **MILITARY SERVICE:** AUS sgt 4 yrs. **BUSINESS ADDRESS:** Chairman, Voice Division, Univ of IL, 1114 W Nevada, Urbana, IL 61801.

WARFIELD-COPPOCK, NSENGA PATRICIA
Psychologist. **PERSONAL:** Born Oct 28, 1949, Minneapolis, MN; daughter of Walter Warfield and Grace Warfield; married Bertram Atiba, PhD, Jan 17, l970; children: Khary Coppock, Akua Coppock, Safiya Warfield. **EDUCATION:** The Am Univ, BA Psych 1971, Med Spcl Ed 1972; The Fielding Inst, PhD 1986. **CAREER:** Assn of Black Psych, natl adm 1971-81, organizational psych. **ORGANIZATIONS:** Consultant The Gray Panthers 1980-; consultant AMTRAK 1982; teacher Watoto Sch 1985; hist bd dir Assoc of Black Psych 1982-87; mem Assn of Black Psych 1971-; mem Various Chld, Aging & Women's Orgs. **HONORS/ACHIEVEMENTS:** Fellow HEW Washington, DC 1972; Fellow Natl Science Fndtn 1979-82; artcl "Liberation & Struggle" in Reflctns in Blk Psych 1977; num papers, presentations & wrkshps; " Teen Pregnacy Prevention: A Rites of Passage Resource Manual" l989; "Transformation: A Rites of Passage Manual for African American Girls" l988. **BUSINESS ADDRESS:** President/Organizational Psychologist, Baobab Associates, Inc./PMS Resource Center, 7614 16th Street N.W., Washington, DC 20012.

WARLICK, ROBERT L.
Business executive. **PERSONAL:** Born Mar 20, 1941, Hickory, NC. **EDUCATION:** Pueblo Jr Coll CO, AA 1961; PepperdineUniv Los Angeles, BS 1963; Denver U, Attended. **CAREER:** Purex Industries, vice pres civic & govt relations 1974-; Purex Corp, spl asst to pres 1972-74; So COUniv Pueblo, instr 1971-72; NBA San Francisco Phoenix, professional basketball palyer 1965-71; Interchange Program The White House, exec 1977-78; Under Sec ESA US Dept Labor, spl asst. **ORGANIZATIONS:** Mem Phi Beta Sigma; All Am Player of Year Nat Jr Coll of Am 1960-61; All W Coast Player of Year PepperdineUniv 1961-63; All Am PepperdineUniv 1961-63.

WARMLY, LEON
Reporter. **PERSONAL:** Born Apr 28, 1941, Shreveport. **EDUCATION:** San Diego City Coll, AA 1973; Bill Wade Sch Modern Radio, Certificate 1966; San Diego State U, Attending. **CAREER:** KFMB Radio, radio news reporter 1967-. **ORGANIZATIONS:** Mem Toastmasters Intl Dist 5; San Diego Club Bi-Centennial 2675 1969-74. **HONORS/ACHIEVEMENTS:** 5FMB Radio News Scholarship 1974. **MILITARY SERVICE:** USMC 1966. **BUSINESS ADDRESS:** 1405 5 St, San Diego, CA.

WARNER, EDWARD L.
Rector. **PERSONAL:** Born Oct 20, 1939, Franklin Twnshp, NJ. **EDUCATION:** Rutgers U, AB 1961; MDiv 1964. **CAREER:** St Augustine's Episcopal Ch, rector 1968-; St Albans, vicar 1964-67. **ORGANIZATIONS:** Mem Diocesan Council & Steering Com of Council; Standing Com; chmn Mayor's Commn on Hum Rights New Brunswick NJ; past pres Interdenominational Ministerial Alliance; mem bd of educ & chmn Comm Rel Com Presby. **HONORS/ACHIEVEMENTS:** Interracial Award 1969; Omega Si Phi Citizenship Award 1973; Citizenship Award Kansas City C Of C 1974. **BUSINESS ADDRESS:** St Augustine's Episcopal Ct, 2732 Benton Blvd, Kansas City, MO.

WARNER, ISAIAH H.
Clergyman. **PERSONAL:** Born May 17, 1916, Erwinville, LA; married Elvira; children: Gloria M, Mary A, Alton Ray, Carlyn Ann. **EDUCATION:** Leland Coll, AB 1959. **CA-**

REER: Mt Bethel Alsin LA, pastor; Christ Bapt Ch; King David Bapt Ch; Union Bapt Ch 2 yrs; Colonial Funeral Home Inc Port Allen LA, part-owner. **ORGANIZATIONS:** Bd mem 4th Dist Missionary Bapt; asso pres WBR Ministers Conf; mem Sheriff's Planning Commn of WBR Affiliated LA Bapt State Convention; Nat Bapt Convention Inc; Nat Bapt BTU Convention; mem West Baton Rouge Parish Bicentennial Commn; mem Stone Square Lodge #8. **HONORS/ACHIEVEMENTS:** Recipient Certificate of Appreciation King David Bapt Ch Baton Rouge; Certificate of Appreciation Young Adults of Shiloh Bapt Ch Port Allen LA.

WARNER, IVAN
Attorney, judge. **PERSONAL:** Born Feb 18, 1919, New York, NY; married Augustine; children: Sylvester. **EDUCATION:** Amer Univ, attended; CCNY, attended; NY Law School, LLB 1955. **CAREER:** NY State, assemblyman 1958-60; NY State Senate, senator 1961-68; chmn ed comm 1965; NY Supreme Court Justice, judge 1969-82, 1982-. **ORGANIZATIONS:** Mem 100 Black Men Inc; tester Cathedral St John Devine; mem Harlem Bronx & NY State Bar Assoc; dir Supreme Ct Justices Assoc NYC; pres Bronx Council BSA; life mem NAACP; vestryman Trinity Episcopal Church; dir NY Law School Alumni Assoc; trustee Metro Museum of Art NY; trustee Union Hospital Bronx NY. **HONORS/ACHIEVEMENTS:** Comm Serv Awd Bronx Urban League 1963; Disting Merit Cit Natl Conf Christians & Jews 1964; Special Achievement Awd Natl Council Negro Women 1969; Comm Achievement Awd Negro Business & Professional Womens Club 1969; Citizens Achievement Awd Joppa Lodge 1969; Leadership Awd Soc Afro-Amer Transit Empl 1969; Life Mem Chmn Awd NAACP 1969; Outstanding Achievement & Serv to Comm Awd Alumni Assoc Lincoln School Nurses 1969; Ecumenical Awd Council Chs 1970; Silver Beaver Awd BSA 1974; Serv Beyond Call of Duty to God & Humanity Mt Carmel Baptist Church 1974; Honored by Criminal Court Bar Assoc Bronx NY 1986, Black Bar Assoc Bronx NY 1986. **BUSINESS ADDRESS:** Judge, Supreme Court Justice, 851 Grand Concourse, New York, NY 10462.

WARNER, MALCOLM-JAMAL
Actor. **PERSONAL:** Son of Pamela Warner. **CAREER:** Actor. **HONORS/ACHIEVEMENTS:** Actor in film The Father Clements Story, 1987; host of Friday Night Videos; plays Theo Huxtable on The Cosby Show; author of Theo and Me, Growing Up Okay, Dutton, 1988. **BUSINESS ADDRESS:** c/o The Cosby Show, NBC-TV, 30 Rockefeller Plaza, New York, NY 10020. *

WARNER, WILMOT MELVILLE
Orthodontist. **PERSONAL:** Born May 31, 1933, Charlestown, St. Kitts and Nevis;married Gloria J Williams; children: Janeen, Andrew, Christopher. **EDUCATION:** Howard Univ Coll of Liberal Arts, BS 1955; Howard Univ Coll of Dentistry, DDS 1959; Racham Sch of Grad Studies Univ of MI, MS Orthodontics 1969. **CAREER:** Howard Univ Coll of Dentistry, instructor 1959-61; Ministry of Health Jamaica, dental officer 1962-63; Private Practice Jamaica, dentist 1962-67, 1969-79; Spanish Town Hospital Jamaica, dental officer 1963-67; Private Practice Anchorage AK, orthodontist 1979-. **ORGANIZATIONS:** Secty-treas 1982, pres 1984 AK State Soc of Orthodontists. **HONORS/ACHIEVEMENTS:** Mem Omicron Kappa Upsilon Honorary Dental Soc; First Rsch Awd of Special Merit Amer Assoc of Orthodontists 1970. **BUSINESS ADDRESS:** 4200 Lake Otis Pkwy Ste 204, Anchorage, AK 99508.

WARREN, FRED FRANKLIN
Business executive. **PERSONAL:** Born May 22, 1922, Stokesdale, NC; married Della; children: Larry, Brenda, Bonnie, Judy, Vanessa, Gladys. **EDUCATION:** A&T U. **CAREER:** Warren Carpet Serv Inc, pres 1959-; Warren Woodcraft Co 1969-72; My Ladies Sportswear 1972. **ORGANIZATIONS:** Bd mem Employment Training Commn; Alamance Comm Action Prgm; Alamance Co Civic Affairs; chmn Deacon Bd Glen Raven First Bapt Ch; mem Am Cancer Soc; BSA.

WARREN, HENRY L.
Electric utility company executive. **PERSONAL:** Born Aug 27, 1940, Pine Bluff, AR; son of Henry Warren and Rissie Combs Warren; married Jean Henderson, Aug 21, 1960; children: Jacque, Gregory, Sandra. **EDUCATION:** Univ of Arkansas, Pine Bluff, BS bio & chem, 1968; Univ of Arkansas, Fayetteville, MS oper mgt, 1978. **CAREER:** Arkansas Power & Light, Pine Bluff, design asst 1968-70, methods analyst 1970-74; AR Power & Light, Little Rock, office mgr 1974-77, equal employment mgr 1977-78; AR Power & Light, Conway, district mgr 1978-80; AR Power & Light, Little Rock, dir of internal auditing 1980-85, vice pres & asst to pres 1985-86, vice pres of admin services 1986-88, vice pres of planning & control 1988-. **ORGANIZATIONS:** Vice pres, Natl Soc to Prevent Blindness, AR Division, 1987-89; pres, Business Volunteer Council, 1988-89; vice pres, Leadership Roundtable, 1988-91; vice pres, Community Affairs, Greater Little Rock Chamber of Commerce, 1989-90; vice chair, United Way Volunteer Services, 1989-90; bd mem, Arkansas Opera Theatre, 1989-90; mem, Edison Electric Inst Strategic Planning Comm, 1989-90. **HONORS/ACHIEVEMENTS:** Career for Youth award, Chicago Public School System, 1989. **BUSINESS ADDRESS:** Vice President, Planning & Control, Arkansas Power & Light, PO Box 551, Little Rock, AR 72203.

WARREN, HERMAN LECIL
Educator, professor. **PERSONAL:** Born Nov 13, 1933, Tyler, TX; son of Cicero Warren and Leola Mosley Warren; married Mary K Warren, Dec 10, 1963; children: Michael J, Christopher L, Mark H. **EDUCATION:** Prairie View A&M, BS 1953; Michigan State Univ, MS 1962; Univ of Minnesota, PhD 1969. **CAREER:** Olin Chem Corp New Haven CT, research scientist 1962-67; US Dept of Agriculture Beltsville MD, plant pathologist 1969-71; USDA Purdue Univ W Lafayette IN, prof & plant Pathologist 1971-88; Virginia Technic Institute and State Univ, Blacksburg, VA, professor. **ORGANIZATIONS:** Professor, Virginia Polytechnic Inst & State Univ 1989-. **HONORS/ACHIEVEMENTS:** Military Serv 1953-56. **MILITARY SERVICE:** Military Serv 1st lt 1953-56. **BUSINESS ADDRESS:** Doctor, Virginia Polytechnic Institute & State University, Plant Pathology, Physiology and Weed Science Department, Blacksburg, VA 24061.

WARREN, JOSEPH DAVID
University administrator. **PERSONAL:** Born 1939, New York, NY; son of Harold H Warren, Sr and Geraldine McDaniel Warren; married Elpidia Lopez Warren; children: Makeda, Setti, Kara. **EDUCATION:** North Carolina A&T Univ, Greensboro NC, BS 1969; Brandeis Univ, Waltham MA, MA 1973, PhD 1983. **CAREER:** United Planning Org, Washington DC, dir of comm organization, 1965-67; Policy Management System, New York NY, natl VISTA training coordinator, 1967-69; Brandeis Univ, Waltham MA, exec dir of Upward Bound, 1970-74; Commonwealth of Massachusetts, Boston MA, asst sec of educational affairs, 1975-79; Northeastern Univ, Boston MA, urban asst to president 1979-82, dir of community affairs 1982-. **ORGANIZATIONS:** Pres, Devel & Training Associates; chair, Industrial Sites Devel Assn, Boston Mayor's Minority Business Advisory Council, MA Human Resource Center; mem, United Way of Greater Boston, Roxbury Multi-Service Center; trustee, Emmanual Coll. **HONORS/ACHIEVEMENTS:** MA Black Achievers Awards, Phi Kappa Phi Society award, First Annual MA Affirmative Action Award, award for minority business from Gov of MA, award for youth service from Mayor of Boston; created & directed univ-based academy for pre-high schools; created & directed special highter educ opportunity for public housing residents; chaired Blue Ribbon Panel on Racial Incident, Newton MA; lead devel of MA business set-aside program. **MILITARY SERVICE:** US Air Force & US Naval Reserve, commander, 1956-85. **BUSINESS ADDRESS:** Director, Office of Community Affairs, Northeastern University, 334 Massachusetts Ave, Boston, MA 02115.

WARREN, JOSEPH W.
Educator, businessman. **PERSONAL:** Born Jul 02, 1949, Rocky Mount, NC; son of James W Waren Jr and Marjorie Johnson Warren; married Cynthia Taylor, Jul 02, 1972; children: Camille, Joseph II, Jerrick. **EDUCATION:** Oakwood Coll, BA (summa cum laude), 1971; Ohio State Univ, MA, 1973, PhD, 1982. **CAREER:** Ohio State Univ, grad asst, 1973-76; Lake Michigan Coll, adjunct professor, 1978-80; Andrews Univ, assoc professor of English, 1976-. **ORGANIZATIONS:** Pres, Exec Enterprises, 1973-76, founder, Mid-Amer Network Marketing, Inc, 1984-; pres, Brentwood Assocs, 1984-85, Inst for Christian Educ and Youth Devel, 1985-; co-founder, Scholastic Study Lab, Andrews Univ, 1984; founder, owner, Mid-Amer Premiere Brokerage, 1986-. **HONORS/ACHIEVEMENTS:** United Negro Coll Fund Fellowship, 1971; PhD, Fellowship, Ohio State Univ, 1971; Research Grant, Andrews Univ, 1984. **HOME ADDRESS:** 508 N Bluff, Berrien Springs, MI 49103. **BUSINESS ADDRESS:** Associate Professor of English, Andrews University, Berrien Springs, MI 49103.

WARREN, LEE ALDEN (TICO)
Media consultant/representative. **PERSONAL:** Born Sep 17, 1954, Crestline, OH. **EDUCATION:** Ohio Univ Athens OH, BS Journalism (Cum Laude) 1976. **CAREER:** Central State Univ Wilberforce OH, admissions counselor 1977-78; Xerox Corp Columbus OH, marketing exec 1978-83; Amer Hospital Supply Corp OH, product specialist/territory mgr 1983-86; KSBW-TV, NBC Salinas-Monterey CA, acct exec 1986-87; KLRS New Age Radio San Jose CA, account mgr 1987-. **ORGANIZATIONS:** Past vice pres & treas Xerox Mid Ohio Corporate Few 1978-83; mem Ohio Univ Alumni Assoc 1980-, South Bay Area Urban Bankers 1986-, San Jose Advertising Club 1986-, San Jose Women in Advertising 1986-, San Jose Jazz Soc 1986-, TV Bureau of Advertising 1986-; mem Broad Net Inc (Black Broadcasters in Northern CA) 1987-; on air commercial announcer/radio. **HONORS/ACHIEVEMENTS:** Account Rep of Month Xerox Corp 1979,80; President's Club 1979-80, Par Club 1979-80 Xerox Corp; Columbus Branch winner Xerox Sales Presentation contest 1981. **HOME ADDRESS:** 4361 Marshall Rd, Kettering, OH 45429. **BUSINESS ADDRESS:** Account Manager, KLRS, 3031 Tisch Way Ste 200, San Jose, CA 95128.

WARREN, MARK EDWARD
Producer, director. **PERSONAL:** Born Sep 24, 1938, Harrodsburg, KY; married Barbara A Rudy; children: Andre Mark, Brian Rudy, Christopher. **EDUCATION:** Lincoln Inst, 1951-55. **CAREER:** CTV Network Ottawa, Can, stage mgr/performer 1957-61; CBC Toronto, Can, stage mgr 1961-62; Producer/director TV & film, Beverly Sills & Co, Baby I'm Back,Big City Comedy, Wolfman Jack Show, Tribute to Count Basie, Rowan & Martin's Laugh In, new Bill Cosby Show Series, Burns & Schreiber Comedy Hour, Get Christie Love, Sanford & Sons series, Funny Side of Sports Special Diahann Carroll Spl, Cher series, Sammy & Co special series, soul special w/Diana Ross/Supremes/Temptations; Black Achievement Awards special, What' Happening series, Fish series, Barney Miller series, Tribute to Martin L King special. **ORGANIZATIONS:** Mem LA Film Devel Councl; mem Directors Guild Amer; Natl Acad TV Arts & Scis; Amer Acad Humor. **HONORS/ACHIEVEMENTS:** Feature films includes, The Legends of Isaac Murphy, Come Back Charleston Blue, Crunch, My Secret Romance, Tulips; Emmy Award Best Dir Variety/Music 1970-71; NAACP Image Award Best Dir 1973; Sickle Cell Research Special Award 1972. **MILITARY SERVICE:** USAF Col.

WARREN, MICHAEL
Actor/producer. **PERSONAL:** Born Mar 05, 1946, South Bend, IN; married Susie W (divorced); children: Koa, Cash. **EDUCATION:** UCLA, BA Theatre Arts. **CAREER:** Appeared in TV series Hill St Blues (Emmy nomination); appeared in motion pictures Fast Break 1979, Norman Is That You, Drive He Said; guest appearances numerousTV series; MTM Studio City, CA, TV Pilot "Home Free", actor/producer, 1988. **HONORS/ACHIEVEMENTS:** All American Basketball Player UCLA; Academic All American NCAA 1966. **BUSINESS ADDRESS:** c/o Sandy Bresler & Associates, 15760 Ventura Blvd, Ste 1730, Encino, CA 91436.

WARREN, MORRISON FULBRIGHT
Educator. **PERSONAL:** Born Dec 06, 1923, Marlin, TX; married Margaret Mosley; children: Morrison, Carolyn Pitts, Dwight, Wayne, Howard, Marilyn Shumate, Kevin. **EDUCATION:** AZ State Univ, BA 1948; AZ State Univ, MA 1951, EdD 1959. **CAREER:** Phoenix Elem School Dist 1, teacher 1948-53, principal 1953-68; AZ State Univ Explt Progs Coll Ed, dir 1968-84, prof emeritus of education 1984-. **ORGANIZATIONS:** Mem 1966-70, v mayor 1969 Phoenix City Council; pres Fiesta Bowl 1981-; life mem NEA; dir 1st Interstate Bank of AZ NA 1986; bd of dir Samaritan Health Svc, AZ Publ Svc. **HONORS/ACHIEVEMENTS:** Named one of four Outstanding Young Men of Phoenix Jr C of C 1958. **MILITARY SERVICE:** AUS 1943-46. **BUSINESS ADDRESS:** Prof Emeritus of Education, Arizona State University, Tempe, AZ 85287.

WARREN, NAGUEYALTI
Educator, administrator. **PERSONAL:** Born Oct 01, 1947, Atlanta, GA; married Rueben C Warren; children: Alkamessa, Asha, Ali. **EDUCATION:** Fisk Univ, BA 1972; Simmons Coll, MA 1974; Boston Univ, MA 1974; Univ of Mississippi, PhD 1984. **CAREER:** Northeastern Univ, instructor 1977-78; Univ of Calabar, lecturer 1979; Fisk Univ, asst prof, and

chairperson, Dept of English 1984-88; asst dean & assoc prof, Emory Univ, 1988-. **ORGANIZATIONS:** Mem College Language Assoc, Modern Language Assoc, Natl Council of Teachers of English, Southern Conf on Afro-Amer Studies. **HONORS/ACHIEVEMENTS:** Awd for Contribution to Black History Month Meharry Medical Coll 1984; Golden Poet Awd World Poetry Assoc 1985; poetry published in the following The American Poetry Anthology, Mississippi Earthworks, Janus, Riders of the Rainbow, Earthshine. **HOME ADDRESS:** 7469 Asbury Drive, Lithonia, GA 30058. **BUSINESS ADDRESS:** Assistant Dean, Emory College Office, 215 White Hall, Emory University, Atlanta, GA 30322.

WARREN, RUEBEN CLIFTON
Health services administrator. **PERSONAL:** Born Aug 16, 1945, San Antonio, TX; son of Bobbi Owens; married Nagueyalti Wright Warren, Feb 00, 1982; children: Alkamessa Dalton, Asha Warren, Ali Warren. **EDUCATION:** San Francisco State Univ, BA 1968; Meharry Med Coll, DDS 1968-72; Harvard Sch of Dental Med, residency in dental publ health 1973-75; Harvard Sch of Public Health, MPH 1973, Dr PH 1973-75. **CAREER:** Harvard Sch of Dental Medicine, instructor 1976-77; Univ of CT Hlth Ctr, asst prof 1977-80; State of MS, dental dir 1981-83; Univ of MS Med Cntr, clin assoc prof 1982-83; Meharry Med Coll, assoc prof & dean 1983-; Centers for Disease Control, Atlanta GA, Asst Dir for Minority Health 1988-. **ORGANIZATIONS:** Mem Amer Dental Assn, Meharry Alumni Assn, Natl Dental Assn, CT Black Caucus of Dentists, Operation PUSH, NAACP, Amer Public Hlth Assn, Meharry Specialty Group, Nigerian Dental Assn, Natl Black Child Develop Inst, Natl Urban League, Amer Assn of Public Health Dentists; chairperson Natl Dental Assn Delegation Conf 1982. **HONORS/ACHIEVEMENTS:** Dental School Student of the Yr Meharry Med Coll 1970; 2nd Place Awd Table Clinics 1971; Omega Man of the Yr Delta Chap 1971-72; Intermediate-UndergradOmega Man of the Yr 5th Dist 1971-72; Awd for Outstanding Achievement in 4 yrs of Dental Coll Intl Coll of Dentists 1972; Comm Serv Awd Roxbury Med Tech Inst 1973; Outstanding Young Man of Amer 1974; Pres's Awd Natl Dental Assn 1978; Robert Wood Johnson Health Policy Fellowship Finalist 1979; ScholarProg Veteran's Admin Fellowship Finalist 1980; 21 publications including "Implementing School-Based Dental Svcs, The Mississippi Model" 1984; 24 presentations including "A Natl Mgmt Model to Facilitate Health Serv for Head Start Children" presented at Natl Head Start Assn 9th Annual Training Conf 1982. **BUSINESS ADDRESS:** Assistant Director for Minority Health, Centers for Disease Control, 1600 Clifton Road, NE, Building 1, Room 2122, Atlanta, GA 37208.

WARREN, STANLEY
Educator. **PERSONAL:** Born Dec 18, 1932, Indianapolis, IN. **EDUCATION:** Indiana Central Coll, BS 1959; Indiana Univ, MAT 1964; Indiana Univ, EdS; Indiana Univ, EdD 1973. **CAREER:** DePauw Univ, dir black studies prof educ; Indianapolis Publ Sch, tchr admin; Indiana-Purdue Univ; Indiana Univ; Indiana Commn for Humanities, assoc; DePauw Univ, assoc dean. **ORGANIZATIONS:** Fellowship & Grant, Carnegie; Wingspread; Eli Lilly; NSF; Natl Def Educ Act; John Hay; NEH; State Ethnic Studies Advisory Council; bd mem, Indiana Historical Society. **MILITARY SERVICE:** AUS. **BUSINESS ADDRESS:** Professor, De Pauw University, Asbury Hall, Greencastle, IN 46135.

WARRICK, ALAN EVERETT
Judge. **PERSONAL:** Born Jun 18, 1953, Hampton, VA; son of John H. Warrick and Geri Warrick-Crisman; children: Alan Everett II, Whitney Blair. **EDUCATION:** Howard Univ, BA (Magna Cum Laude) 1975; IN Univ Sch of Law Indianapolis, Dr of Jurisprudence 1978. **CAREER:** Joint Ctr for Political Studies, rsch asst 1972-74; IN Civil Rights Comm, civil rights specialist 1975; US Senator R Vance Hartke, campaign aide 1976; Marion Co Prosecutors Office, intern 1977-78; attorney, Branton & Mendelsohn, Inc. 1978-1982; City of San Antonio, Judge, municipal court 1982-. **ORGANIZATIONS:** Bd of dir Ella Austin Comm Ctr 1979-80; Leadership San Antonio partic leadership prog sponsored by C of C 1979-80; area adv council Small Bus Assn 1980-81; bd of dirs San Antonio Symphony 1980-83; exec comm United Negro Coll Fund 1980-81; 3rd vice pres San Antonio Br NAACP 1980-81; State Bar of TX Municipal Judges Sect sec treas 1982-83; vchmn 1983-84; chmn 1984-85; exec comm & bd of dirs San Antonio Festival Inc 1982-; pres Dignowitty Hill AreaNeighborhood Assn 1982-83; bd of dir Eastside San Antonio Economic Develop Council 1982-83; adv bd Mediation Ctr of Bexar Co 1983-89; selection panel Golden Rule Awd JC Penney 1984; exec bd of govs United Way of San Antonio 1985-; Amer Bar Assn; Natl Bar Assn; Assn of Trial Lawyers of Amer; TX Young Lawyers Assn; TX Trial Lawye rs Assn; San Antonio Bar Assn; San Antonio Young Lawyers Assn; bd of dirs San Antonio Trial Lawyers Assn 1981-82; sec 1979-80, vice pres 1980-81 San Antonio Black Lawyers Assoc; Ancient Free & Accepted Masons l982-; Omega Psi Phi Fraternity NY l973-; Van Courtland Social Club l982-. **HONORS/ACHIEVEMENTS:** Assoc editor Indiana Law Review 1977-78; first place awd winner Amer Bar Assn Regional Moot Court Competition 1978; Scroll of Honor for Outstanding Achievin Field of Law Psi Alpha Chap Omega Psi Phi Frat 1982; Achievements Recognition Van Courtlandt Social Club 1982; Man of the Year Elks Mission Lodge #499; Citizen of the Year Psi Alpha Chap Omega Psi Phi Frat 1982; Appreciation Awd Alamo Branch YMCA 1983; Outstanding Leadership Awd Alpha Tau Omega Chap Alpha Kappa Alpha Sor 1984; Recognition Awd Smart Set Social Club 1984; Phi Beta Kappa Howard Univ; Pi Sigma Alpha Political Science Honor Soc; Iota Phi Lambda Honoree Law Enforcement 1985; Outstanding Service Award Judicial Council, Natl Bar Assn l989. **HOME ADDRESS:** 7914 Ray Bon #804, San Antonio, TX 78218. **BUSINESS ADDRESS:** Judge, Municipal Court, City of San Antonio, 214 West Nueva St, San Antonio, TX 78207.

WARRICK, BRYAN KEITH
Professional athlete. **PERSONAL:** Born Jul 22, 1960, Moses Lake, WA. **EDUCATION:** St Josephs, 1982. **CAREER:** Washington Bullets, 1982-84; Los Angeles Clippers, guard 1985-. **HONORS/ACHIEVEMENTS:** Was named an Honorable Mentn All-Am by AP and The Sporting News. **BUSINESS ADDRESS:** Los Angeles Clippers, 3939 S Figueroa St, Ste 510, Los Angeles, CA 90037.

WARRICK-CRISMAN, JERI EVERETT
Appointed official. **PERSONAL:** Born May 22, Gary, IN; married Bruce Louis Crisman; children: Judge Alan E Warrick, Ingrid-Joy. **EDUCATION:** Hampton Univ, AB (High Honors) 1952; Univ of Chicago, BA (Magna Cum Laude) 1956. **CAREER:** Froebel High, guidance counselor, 1956-64; WMAQ-TV, producer, broadcast stds supvr, 1964-72; WNBC-TV, sr editor, broadcast stds, 1972-73; Natl Broadcasting Co, dir, natl comm, 1973-81; WNJR Radio, pres, gen mgr, owner, 1981-84; State of New Jersey, asst state treas, 1984-87; Port Authority of New York and New Jersey, mgr regional communications educ and govt analysis. **ORGANIZATIONS:** Mem, Alpha Kappa Alpha Sorority, 1950-85; mem, The Doll League, 1977-85; mem of bd, Union County Urban League, 1981-85; natl pres, Amer Women in Radio & TV, 1983-84; mem, Natl Women's Coalition, Republican Natl Comm, 1984; mem of bd, Essex County Planned Parenthood, 1985; mem, Links Inc, 1987; chair, Carter G Woodson Foundation Adv Bd. **HONORS/ACHIEVEMENTS:** Benjamin Hooks Award, NAACP, Gary IN, 1979; Kappa Tau Alpha Award, Hampton Univ Communications Dept, 1983; asst sec, Republican Natl Convention, Dallas TX, 1984.

WARWICK, DIONNE
Vocalist. **PERSONAL:** Born Dec 12, 1941, East Orange, NJ; married Bill Elliott (divorced); children: 2 children. **EDUCATION:** Attended, Ed Hartt Coll Music Hartford CT. **CAREER:** As a teen-ager formed gospelaires, then sang background for recording studio 1966; Philharmonic Hall NY Lincoln Ctr, debut 1966; appearances include London Palladium, Olympia, Paris, Lincoln Ctr Performing Arts NY; records include I'll Never Love This Way Again, That's What Friends are For; albums include Valley of the Dolls 1968, Promises Promises 1975, Dionne 1979, Then Came You, Friends 1986; screen debut The Slaves 1969, No Night, So Long; co-host TV show Solid Gold; host TV show A Gift of Music 1981; star TV show Dionne Warwick. **ORGANIZATIONS:** Formed own chairty group BRAVO (Blood Revolves Around Victorious Optimism); spokeswoman Amer Sudden Infant Death Syndrome Inst; participant USA for Africa song "We Are the World" and performed at Live Aid Concert; proceeds from sale of album "Friends" to the Amer Foundation for AIDS Rsch. **HONORS/ACHIEVEMENTS:** Recipient Grammy Awds 1969,70,80; Whitney M Young Jr Awd Los Angeles Urban League; honored with a star on Hollywood Walk of Fame 1985; Entertainer of the Year 1987.

WASH, GLENN EDWARD
Business executive. **PERSONAL:** Born Feb 26, 1931, Grand Rapids, MI; children: Glennda Marie. **EDUCATION:** Highland Park Coll; Univ of Detroit; The Builders Exchange (CAM). **CAREER:** Practical Homes Builders Oak Pk, MI, const supt 1961-65; HL Vokes Co Cleveland, OH, construction supt 1965-67; GE Washington Construction Inc, pres 1967-77; Glenn E Washington & Assocs Inc, pres 1977-. **ORGANIZATIONS:** Construction supt, AJ Etkin Construction Co Oak Park, MI 1957-61; construction supt Leonard Jarosz Const Co Oak Pk, MI 1954-57; mem Assoc Gen Contracts of Am Det Chptr 1977-85; mem, Better Business Bureau 1979-85; mem Eng Soc of Detroit 1977-85; mem bd trustees New Detroit Inc 1980-85; sec/chmn MI Minority Business Devel Council, 1979-85; mem Minority Input Comm Wayne State Univ 1984-85; mem Com on Soc Econ Policy Am Concrete Inst 1984-85. **MILITARY SERVICE:** USN builder 2nd Class 2 yrs; Far East Construction Btln. **BUSINESS ADDRESS:** President, Glenn E Wash & Assoc Inc, 14541 Schaefer, Detroit, MI 48227.

WASHINGTON, ARNA D.
Consultant. **PERSONAL:** Born Oct 05, 1927, Trawick, TX; married Marcellus J; children: Derek M(dec), Deirdra M. **EDUCATION:** Houston Tillotson Coll Austin TX, Grad; Master's TX So U. **CAREER:** Houston Tchrs Assn, sec 1968-70; HTA, vice pres 1971-72; Sch Chmn 1970 1972; Legislative, assemblyperson; NEA TSTA TCTA HTA Conv & Conf, del 1966-80; Classroom Reading Instr 20 yrs; Houston Comm Coll, reading instr 2 Yrs; Houston Tchrs Assn Houston Ind Sch Dist Houston Tchrs, pres; Magnet Sch, Coord1 yr; HISD Title 1, consult 1985; Houston Independent Sch Dist, cons; Houston Ind Sch Dist, reading lab instr 1985-87. **ORGANIZATIONS:** TX State Tchrns Assn; TX Classroom Tchrs Assn; Nat Educ Assn; TX Assn of Intl Reading Dist Officer United Meth Women of SW; rep TX Conf at World Devel Seminar for United Meth Ch; Outstanding Meth Woman in United Meth Women; mem Delta Sigma Theta Sor Houston; mem NEA Minority Caucus & NCATE. **HONORS/ACHIEVEMENTS:** Tchr of Yr Reynolds Elem Sch for 2 yrs; 1974 Nominee for Outstanding Secondary Educator; Delta Sigma Theta Spl Achievement Awards; Many Spl Recog Awards; NEA Sp Serv TCTA Plaque for Bd Mem; UMW Awd for Svc. **BUSINESS ADDRESS:** Reading Lab Instructor, Houston Ind Sch District, 3830 Richmond, Houston, TX 77027.

WASHINGTON, ARNIC J.
City official. **PERSONAL:** Born Nov 19, 1934, Ladson, SC; married Rosalee Williams; children: Myra, Raymond. **EDUCATION:** Nielson Computer Coll Charleston SC. **CAREER:** Lincolnville Sc, vice mayor 1967-. **ORGANIZATIONS:** Chmn St Dept; mem Health Dept; Pub Bldg Dept; mem SC Municipal Assn SC; Small Towns Assn SC; Black Mayors Assn; So E Conf Black Elected Officials; So E Regional Council Inc Nat League of Cities; Berkeley Co Chap NAACP; W Master Saxon Lodge #249 FAM Midland Park SC; mem Wesley Meth ChLadson SC Chmn Trustee Bd; pres Willing Workers; Admin Bd; Council Ministries; Adult Class Tchr; vice pres Carnation Gospel Singers. **HONORS/ACHIEVEMENTS:** Certificate of Recognition SC Legislature House of Rep Outstanding Contbns in Field of Comm & Pub Affairs; For Civic & Polit Leadership & Accomplishmentsin Country Charleston; Outstanding Performance as Councilman Historic Town of Lincolnville SC. **MILITARY SERVICE:** USAF airman first class 1954-57. **BUSINESS ADDRESS:** PO Box 536, Summerville, SC 29483.

WASHINGTON, ARTHUR, JR.
Retired business executive. **PERSONAL:** Born Oct 22, 1922, StLouis, MO; son of Arthur Washington Sr (deceased) and Frankey Riley Washington (deceased); married Toni; children: Steven Elliott, Marjory Anita, Tiffany Elizabeth, Nancy Wooten. **EDUCATION:** Univ of Louisville, BA; Kent School of Social Work Univ of Louisville, MSW. **CAREER:** IL Dept soc Svcs, caseworker 1954-55; Fam Serv Ctr Kalamazoo, marriage counselor 1955-65; Kalamazoo Dept of Social Services, child welfare supvr 1956; Kalamazoo City, commission 1959-67; Kalamazoo Coll Social Work, instructor 1963-65; Calhoun County Dept Social Services, deputy dir 1965-72; MI Dept of Social Services, dir admin, asst payments 1972-76; Bureau of Field Op, admin consultant, asst payments; Kalamazoo City Dept of Social Services, deputy dir. **ORGANIZATIONS:** Pres Kalamazoo Chapter NAACP 1957-60; mem County Bd Commiss 1959-65; mem, chmn Kalamazoo Recreation Comm 1959-65; bd mem Kalamazoo Human Relations Commission 1959-60; org leader Kalamazoo Bombardiers Drum & Bugle Corp 1960-71; mem Al Zabir Tpl Shriners 1966-67, 1980-; mem advisory comm Kalamazoo Valley Jr Coll. **HONORS/ACHIEVEMENTS:** Outstanding Masonic Award, Plaque Outstanding Achievement Northside Assoc; Cert & Plaque Outstanding Citizenship NAACP; other civic awards; Irvins Gilmore Lifetime Achievement Award 1989; Community Service Award, Kalamazoo NAACP 1989. **MILITARY SERVICE:** AUS corpl 1943-46; reserves 1946-48. **HOME ADDRESS:** 719 Staples Ave, Kalamazoo, MI 49007.

WASHINGTON, ARTHUR CLOVER
Educator. **PERSONAL:** Born Aug 19, 1939, Tallulah, LA; married Almrta Hargest; children: Arthur, Angela, Anthony. **EDUCATION:** TX Coll, BS 1961; Tuskegee Inst, MS 1963; IL Inst of Tech, PhD 1971. **CAREER:** Talladega Coll, instructor 1965-67; City Coll of Chicago, assoc prof 1967-71; Langston Univ, prof 1972-74; Prairie View A&M Univ, dean graduate school & prof 1974-87. **ORGANIZATIONS:** Extramural assoc Natl Inst of Health 1979; pres Woodedge Civic Assoc 1981; natl exec sec Natl Inst of Sci 1983-. **HONORS/ACHIEVEMENTS:** American Men and Women of Science 1982; several scientific articles published 1974-87. **HOME ADDRESS:** 10303 Green Creek, Houston, TX 77070. **BUSINESS ADDRESS:** Dean of Grad School, Prairie View A&MUniv, Box 2784, Prairie View, TX 77446.

WASHINGTON, AVA F.
Human resources manager. **PERSONAL:** Born Aug 09, 1949, New York, NY; daughter of Robert W Francis and Ivy B Philp; married Donald L Washington Jr, Apr 05, 1980; children: Damien, Darin, Ashley. **EDUCATION:** Univ of Wisconsin, Madison WI, BA 1971; Univ of Illinois, Champaign IL, MS 1973. **CAREER:** Farleigh Dickinson Univ, Rutherford NY, asst dir of affirmative action, 1975-77; Exxon Corp, New York NY, mgr of headquarters employee relations office, 1977-. **ORGANIZATIONS:** Mem, Alpha Kappa Alpha 1968-, NAACP 1974-, St Catherine's AME Zion Church 1984-, Corporate Women's Network 1985-, exec bd of Jack & Jill of Westchester County 1986-, Edges 1987-, Amer Society fo r Personnel Admin 1989-; volunteer, Junior Achievement of NYC, 1988. **BUSINESS ADDRESS:** Manager, Headquarters Employee Relations Office, Exxon Corporation, 1251 Ave of Americas, Room 5060, New York, NY 10020-1198.

WASHINGTON, BENNETTA B.
Consultant, advisor. **PERSONAL:** Born May 01, 1918, Winston-Salem, NC; daughter of Rec George O Bullock and Rebecca Burgess Bullock; married Walter Edward Washington; children: Bennetta. **EDUCATION:** Howard Univ, AB 1937, MA 1939; Catholic Univ, PhD 1951. **CAREER:** Baltimore Public Sch System, counselor 1941-45; DC Public Sch System, tchr counselor principal 1946-64; New York Univ, visiting prof counseling & guidance 1952-63; Cardozo Project in Urban Teaching, dir 1962-64; Natl Women's Job Corps Washington, dir 1964-70; New York Univ Inst for teachers & counselors VI 1967; Washington Sch Psychiatry, prof 1968; Rutgers Univ, Martin Luther King Scholar in Residence 1969; Women's Progs & Educ Job Corps, asso dir 1970-73; US Dept of Labor, spec asst to asst sec for Manpower 1974-80, independent rsch & consultation, cons/expert adv 1980-. **ORGANIZATIONS:** Pres's Comm on Juvenile Delinquency 1962-64; mem Mayor Lindsay's Panel for Decentralization of New York City Schools 1966-67; White House Conf on Food Nutrition & Hunger 1969; White House Conf on Children 1970; White House Conf on Youth 1971; bd of dir Amer Univ, Mt Vernon Coll, Henry Strong Found, Meridian House Intl, Wash Opera Soc, Wash Symphony; mem pres com Employment of Handicapped; mem Alpha Kappa Alpha Sor; author various articles for professional publications,"Background Factor & Adjustment", "Youth in Conflict", "Counseling the Disadvantaged Girl", "Colored by Prejudice". **HONORS/ACHIEVEMENTS:** Howard Univ Achievement Alumni Awd to Distinguished Post Grad 1969; Distinguished Serv Awd Natl Council of Negro Women 1971; Presidential Citation Amer Univ 1974; Hon mem Soroptomist Intl of WA 1975; Hon mem Altrusa Intl Inc 1975; Distinguished Vol Leadership Awd Fight Against Birth Defects 1975; Lucy Slowe Awd Howard Univ Women's Club 1975; Mother of Yr Awd Amer Mothers 1978; Hon Degrees, LLD Wilson Coll, DHL Smith Coll, DHL Trinity Coll, DHL Rider Coll, DHL Dunbarton Coll, DHL Mt Vernon Coll; Outstanding Alumnus Catholic Univ; Scouter of the Yr Awd (first woman). **BUSINESS ADDRESS:** Cons/Expert Adv, 410 T Street, Washington, DC 20001.

WASHINGTON, BETTY LOIS
Business executive. **PERSONAL:** Born Apr 16, 1948, New Orleans, LA. **EDUCATION:** So Univ New Orleans, BA 1970; MI State U, MA 1971; Tulane Univ Sch of Law, Attending. **CAREER:** Mgmt Asso New Orleans, pres 1985; Ward Design Team, team chief 1985; Teach A Brother, exec dir 1979-80; Desire Area Comm Council, exec dir 1975-79; NO Urban League, program dir 1973-75; So Univ in New Orleans, counselor 1972-73; Images Corp, sec 1985; Mgmt Assoc, pres; So Univ System, bd of supr 1978-80. **ORGANIZATIONS:** Mem Phi Alpha Theta Hist Honor Soc 1969-; mem Zeta Phi Beta Sor 1968-; credit com SoUniv Alumni Assn 1977-. **HONORS/ACHIEVEMENTS:** Who's Who in Am Coll &Univ 1969; EPDA Fellowship MI StateUniv 1970; Outstanding Volunteer Award Lansing MI Juvenile Court System 1971; Outstanding Women in Am Nat Affiliation 1978. **BUSINESS ADDRESS:** Management Assoc, 8500 Fordham Ct, New Orleans, LA 70127.

WASHINGTON, C. CLIFFORD
EDUCATION: Cheyney State Normal Sch, Grad 1921; Temple Univ, Elem Educ 1923; Cheyney State Coll, BS Educ 1960; Virginia Union Univ, Post Grad 1965. **CAREER:** School District of Phila, teacher elem educ, special educ, coord work training and job placement prog for retarded educables 1926-69; Model Cities Sr Wheels West, dir. **ORGANIZATIONS:** Mem St John's Settlement House Bd of Dirs 1934-; vice pres PA State BYPU Convention 15 yrs; 1st vice pres New England Missionary Bapt Training Union Convention 1948-; chmn Martha Washington Sch Adv Cncl 1970-; mem Cheyney State Coll Past Presidents Cncl, PA Dept of Welfare Southeastern Region Adv Comm; Pennsylvania delegate White House Conf on Aging 1971; mem Bd of the Natl Caucus on the Black Aged 1972-; chmn Philadelphia Urban Coalition Sr Citizens Task Force 1976-; one of eight non-agency persons on the newly formed Affirmative Action Task Force of the State Adv Comm on Aging for the State of Pennsylvania 1976-78; chmn Coalition of Advocates for the Rights of the Infirm Elderly 1977-. **HONORS/ACHIEVEMENTS:** Outstanding Educators Awd Black Educ Forum; Elder Watson Diggs Awd Kappa Alpha Psi; Dr Charles Drew Community Serv Awd.

WASHINGTON, CARL DOUGLAS
Business executive. **PERSONAL:** Born Aug 11, 1943, Tuscaloosa, AL; son of Sam Washington and Estella Washington; married Charlene; children: Carl, Micheal, Chimiere, Jason. **EDUCATION:** Long Beach State Univ, BA Pol Sci, Speech 1967. **CAREER:** Washington Bros Distr Co, pres; Freedom Inv Corp, pres 1977; Teleport Oil Co, pres; Kong TV Inc, pres chairman. **ORGANIZATIONS:** Bd Brown Boys Home; mem Big Brother Prog 1966; org mem SF Private Industry Council; mem Comm Improvement League 1965; comm mem Optimist Club 1966; Kappa Alpha Psi; Hunter Point Boys Club; Soc of 100 Men; S F Police Athletic League; bd S F Black Chamber of Commerce. **HONORS/ACHIEVEMENTS:** Coll Dean's List; Athlete of Year Long Beach Poly HS; listed in Who's Who in Amer in bus & Fin; Outstanding Black Bus, SF Black Chamber, Top 100 BlackBusinesses in American 1982-86. **HOME ADDRESS:** 1037 Longridge Rd, Oakland, CA 94610.

WASHINGTON, CHESTER LLOYD
Publisher. **PERSONAL:** Born Apr 13, 1902, Pittsburgh, PA; married Alma; children: Chester, Douglas. **EDUCATION:** VA Union Univ, BA. **CAREER:** Pittsburgh Courier, reporter, city editor; Courier, chief w coast bur 1949; Los Angeles Times, 1st black full-time reporter ed staff 1955-60; Mirror News, ed staff 1955; Los Angeles Sentinel, reporter 1960-61, editor 1961-65, editor-in-chief; KWOL, news commentator; Joe Lewis' book My Life Story, ghost writer; Central News-Wave Publs, publisher, owner 1966-. **ORGANIZATIONS:** Past mem Amer Delegation Isreal; vchmn LA Cty Parks & Rec Comm; mem CA State Bicentennial Comm; suprv Kenneth Hahn; mem LA City Council, Brotherhood Crusade, Crenshaw YMCA, So Are Boys Club, Women for Good Govt, LA Cty, LA Dist Attny, Crenshaw C of C, Women at Work, Central C of C, Natl Assoc Media Women; pres Sigma Delta Chi. **HONORS/ACHIEVEMENTS:** Merit Awd Amer Legion; Best Editorial Awd Gr LA Press Club 1976; Robert S Abbot Best Editorials Awd Natl Newspaper Publ Assoc; Western Golf Course in LA was renamed the Chester L Washington Golf Course 1982. **BUSINESS ADDRESS:** Publisher, Central News-Wave Publs, 2621 W 54 St, Los Angeles, CA 90043.

WASHINGTON, CLAUDELL
Professional athlete. **PERSONAL:** Born Aug 31, 1954, Los Angeles, CA; married Cynthia; children: Camille, Caludell III, Crystal. **CAREER:** Cincinnati Reds, outfielder; Atlanta Braves, outfielder 1980-. **HONORS/ACHIEVEMENTS:** Amer League All Star 1976; hit 3 home runs in 1 game 1979; NL All Star Squad 1984. **BUSINESS ADDRESS:** Atlanta Braves, PO Box 4064, Atlanta, GA 30302.

WASHINGTON, CONSUELA M.
Attorney. **PERSONAL:** Born Sep 30, 1948, Chgo. **EDUCATION:** Harvard Law Sch, JD 1973; Upper IA U, BA Cum Laude 1970. **CAREER:** Com on Interstate & Foreign Commerce, prof staff mem 1985; Ofc of Chief Coun Div of Corp Fin Securities & Exchange Com, spl counsel/atty adviser 1976-79; Allis-Chalmers Corp Corp Law Dept, atty 1975-76; Kirkland & Ellis Chgo, asso 1973-74. **ORGANIZATIONS:** Mem ABA IL Bar Assn; Washington Bar Assn; Harvard Law Sch Assn; mem SEC; Atty Recruiting & Hiring Subcom; investment adv com DC Tchrs Retirement & Annuity Fund 1978; bd of trustees Upper IAUniv 1978; Secretary Inroads Inc 1975; Various Others. **HONORS/ACHIEVEMENTS:** SEC Lump Sum Merit Award for Spl Act or Service 1976; Dean's List 1967-70; Scholastic Honor Soc, Hon Leadership Soc 1968-70; Bradley Invit Speech Tourn Award of Excellence 1969; 4th Listed World Who's Who of Women 1977 & 78; Who's Who Among Students in AmUniv & Coll 1968-70; Notable Am 1978-79; Intl Who'sWho of Intellectuals 1978-79; Who's Who Among Black Am 1975-78; Equal Employment Opportunity Award SEC 1978; Alumni Achievement Award Upper IAUniv 1977; Variours Others; Who Among Studnets in Am Univs & Colls. **BUSINESS ADDRESS:** US House of Rep Comm on Inters, Room 2125 RayburnH O B, Washington, DC 20515.

WASHINGTON, CRAIG A.
State senator, attorney. **PERSONAL:** Born Oct 12, 1941, Longview, TX; married Dorothy M Campley; children: Craig A II, Chival A. **EDUCATION:** Prairie View A&M Univ, BS 1966; TX So Univ, JD Cum Laude. **CAREER:** TSU Law School, asst dean 1969-70; self-employed attorney 1970-; TX House of Rep, 1973-82; TX Senate, senator 1983-. **HONORS/ACHIEVEMENTS:** Listed Who's Who Among Stud in Am Coll & Univ 1969. **HOME ADDRESS:** 2323 Caroline, Houston, TX 77004.

WASHINGTON, DAVID WARREN
Director. **PERSONAL:** Born Jan 13, 1949, Mound Bayou, MS; married Clotee Woodruff; children: Rynetta Rochelle, Vernekia Bradley, Monique Caldwell, Rodney Brown, Vietta Leflore. **EDUCATION:** Coahoma Jr Coll, AA, 1970; Delta State Univ, BS, 1972, addtional graduate study in guidance and counseling, 1972-74; Ford Found Leadership Devel Program, Leadership Degree, 1975. **CAREER:** Ford Found Leadership Devel Program, 1974-75; Bolivar County Community Action Agency, equal opportunity officer, 1977-79; serving 3rd term as vice-mayor of Town of Pace, MS; Bolivar County Headstart Personnel/Training, dir. **ORGANIZATIONS:** Dir, Bolivar County Summer Food Serv Program; former pres, Pace Voters League; former mem, Bolivar County Democratic exec comm, 1984-86; school bd chmn, Bolivar County School Dist I; election commr, Bolivar County Dist I, 1984-88; mem, Spangle Banner MB Church; chmn, Bolivar County Election Commr, 1988-92; chmn of by-laws comm, Bolivar County Assn of Black Officials, 1989-92. **HONORS/ACHIEVEMENTS:** In Appreciation for Outstanding Serv As Equal Opportunity Officer Bolivar County Community Action Agency Bd Dir, 1980; Outstanding Serv Rendered to the Town of Pace, Mississippi Pace Community Assn, 1980; Concern and Dedication Shown The Staff of the Bolivar County Headstart Training Center, 1982; Appreciation for Faithful Serv As Guest Speaker St James Missionary Baptist Church, 1983; Most Outstanding Citizen Award Pace Community Assn, 1983; Dedicated Serv Award, The Parents of the Bolivar County Headstart Training Center, 1984. **BUSINESS ADDRESS:** Dir of Personnel/Training, Bolivar County Headstart, PO Drawer, 1329, Cleveland, MS 38732.

WASHINGTON, EARL MELVIN
Educator. **PERSONAL:** Born Jun 22, 1939, Chicago, IL; married Dianne Elizabeth Taylor; children: Jason Todd, Tiffany Anne. **EDUCATION:** Western MI Univ, BA 1963, MA 1968;Univ of MI, 1971; Western MI Univ EdD. **CAREER:** Cleveland Public Schools, teacher 1963-68; Kalamazoo Valley CC, instructor 1968-70; Western MI Univ, asst prof communications 1975-82, assoc prof communications, dir black faculty devel prog 1982-, asst dean 1984-. **ORGANIZATIONS:** Knappen Voight Co, consultant 1977; Kalamazoo Valley Int Schl Dist, consultant 1979; WMU, dir blk college prog 1984. **HONORS/ACHIEVEMENTS:** 2nd vice pres Kalamazoo PTA; various articles publ in communication, educ and communication quartery and black issues in higher education 1980-; press/publ dir Kalamazoo Metro Branch NAACP 1984-84; vice pres 100 men of Kalamazoo 1983-85; papers presented including at Natl Assn for Equal Oppty. **BUSINESS ADDRESS:** Asst Dean Coll of Arts/Sci, Western Michigan University, 2020 Friedmann Hall, Kalamazoo, MI 49008.

WASHINGTON, EDITH MAY FAULKNER
Educator. **PERSONAL:** Born Jul 28, 1933, Queens, NY; daughter of Henry Ozman Faulkner and Edalia Magadalene O'neal Faulkner; married George Clarence Washington; children: Desiree Elaine Brown, James Henry, Edalia Magdalene Woods. **EDUCATION:** New York State Univ Coll, Buffalo, BS, H, Ec, Ed, 1968, MS, H, Ec, Ed, 1971; Indiana No Univ, Gas City, IN, DHR, Human Relations Psych, 1973; Elmira Coll, MS, Ed, Behavior Sci, 1981. **CAREER:** SEEK Disadvantaged Students, coord, 1969-71; NY State Univ Coll, at Buffalo, instructor, Afro-Amer studies, 1969-71; PEACE Inc, consultant, 1971; NY State Office of Drug Abuse Serv Masten Park Community Rehabilitation Center, inst teacher, 1971-76; NY State Office of Drug Abuse Serv Manhattan Rehabilitation Center, inst teacher, 1976-77; Church of God in Christ Area Central Amer West Indies, masonry worker/teacher, 1980-; NY State Dept of Correction Serv, acad classification analyst, correction counselor. **ORGANIZATIONS:** State pres, Business & Professional Women, Church of God in Christ; bd mem, Church of God in Christ Dept of Missions; mem & workshop leader, Corr Educ Assn, 1971; prod/dir, Benefits for Missions Church of God in Chrst Inc, Missions Benifit Breakfast; exec dir, Anegada House Cultural Inst; co-founder, Afro-Amer Cultural Center Buffalo, NY, 1960; bd mem, NAACP Elmira Corning Center, 1977; bd mem, Adv Council Citizens Advisory Council to the Commr of Soc Serv, 1978, Southern Tier Regional Planning Bd, 1976; Chemung Co Planning Bd, 1976, Applied Christianity Church of God in Christ, 1980-; ordained Evangelist of the Independent Holiness Assembly Church Inc, 1986; volunteer nutritionist/coord, Applied Christianity Inc, Food Pantry; admin, Applied Christianity Church of God In Christ. **HONORS/ACHIEVEMENTS:** Ford Co Town Crier Award, Ford Motor Co, Outstanding Community Serv, 1969; Outstanding Community Serv Award, ACCEP Buffalo, NY, Frontier Citizens & Agng Comm, Cultural Educ Program Center, 1970; Outstanding Acad Achievement Award Pentecostal Temple Church of God in Christ, 1971; Outstanding Community Serv, Chemung Co (exec), 1979; Humanitarian Award from Natl Assn of Blacks in Criminal Justice, 1985; Mt Nebo Ministries MLK Drum Major for Freedom Award, co-recipient w/spouse, Rev G C Washington, 1986; Sigma Gamma Rho, Hon Mem, 1988; named among the Outstanding women of the twentieth century. **BUSINESS ADDRESS:** Academic Classification Analyst, NY State Dept Corr Serv, Elmira Corr & Reception Ctr, Elmira, NY 14902.

WASHINGTON, EDWARD
Business executive. **PERSONAL:** Born May 02, 1936, Pittsburgh, PA; married Paula G; children: Felicia D, Teresa S, Jacquelyn R, Nicolas E. **EDUCATION:** VA State Univ Petersburg VA, BS Psych 1963; Univ of Southern CA, MBA 1973. **CAREER:** Coca-Cola USA, acct exec 1964-75; Uniworld Advertising, acct suprv 1975-79; Del Monto Corp, eastern div sales mgr 1979-82; Mid-Atlantic Coca-Cola Bottling, gen mgr 1982-83. **ORGANIZATIONS:** Mem Natl Assoc of Mktg Devel 1978-85; bd of dir Jr Achievement 1982-85, Bowie St Coll 1983-85, Boys & Girls Club 1983-85, WHMM Radio 1983-85; mem Prince George Chamber of Commerce 1983-85, Natl Business League 1985. **HONORS/ACHIEVEMENTS:** Achievement Spec Olympics 1983,84; Achivement Greater Wash Korean Assoc 1984; Outstanding Citizen DC Dept of Recognition 1984; PUSH Achievement Operation PUSH 1984. **MILITARY SERVICE:** USAF airman 2/c 3 1/2 yrs. **BUSINESS ADDRESS:** VP OF Market Development, Md-Atlantic Coco-Cola Bottling, 1710 Elton Rd, Silver Spring, MD 20903.

WASHINGTON, EDWARD, JR.
Foreman. **PERSONAL:** Born Nov 25, 1931, Logan Co, KY; married Ruth Shorton; children: James, Phillip, Terry, Bobby, Francine Wynn, Cherri, Nancy. **CAREER:** Auburn Hosiery Mill, foreman; fireman; emer worker; ambulance svc. **ORGANIZATIONS:** Mem Barroh River Health System; Adairville City Council; S Hogan Cham of Comm; Mason. **BUSINESS ADDRESS:** Gallatin, Adairville, KY 42202.

WASHINGTON, ELMER L.
Educator. **PERSONAL:** Born Oct 18, 1935; married Anna Ross; children: Lisa, Lee. **EDUCATION:** TX So U, BS 1957 TX So U, MS 1958; IL Inst of Tech, PhD 1965. **CAREER:** Univ of Chicago, research asst 1958-61; Pratt & Whitney Div of United Aircraftd asst project engr & research assoc 1965-69; chicago state univ, dean of naturalsci & math 1972-74; Chicago State Univ, former dean of coll of arts & sci; Research & Devel Chicago State Univ Consult Health Career Opportunites Program of HEW, vice pres 1975. **ORGANIZATIONS:** Mem Am Chem Soc; Electrochem Soc; Am Assn for Advancement of Sci; Am Assn of Univ Prof; Am Assn of Univ Adminstr Alpha Kappa Mu Honor Soc 1956. **HONORS/ACHIEVEMENTS:** Welch Found Scholarship 1957; Voted Most Likely to Suceed in Class 1957; Petroleum Research Fellowship 1961-65; Phi Lambda Upsilon Scientific Honor Soc 1964. **BUSINESS ADDRESS:** 95 King Dr, Chicago, IL 60628.

WASHINGTON, GENE ALDEN
Athlete. **PERSONAL:** Born Jan 14, 1947, Tuscaloosa, AL. **EDUCATION:** Stanford U. **CAREER:** Detroit Lions, retired professional football player 1978-79; San Francisco 49ers, wide receiver 1969-77; NFC Championship Game 1970-71. **ORGANIZATIONS:** Led League in Pass Receiving Yd 1,100 & Avg Yd Per Catch 208 1970; Sporting News NFL Western Conf All-Star Team 1969; Sporting News NFC All-Star Team 197071 72; Pro Bowl 1969-72. **BUSINESS ADDRESS:** San Francisco 49ers, 1255 Post St Ste 300, San Francisco, CA 94109.

WASHINGTON, GLADYS J. (GLADYS J. CURRY)
Educator. **PERSONAL:** Born Mar 04, 1931, Houston, TX; daughter of Eddie Joseph and Anita Joseph. **EDUCATION:** BA 1952; MA 1955; Univ of So CA & Tulane Univ, addl study. **CAREER:** So Univ Baton Rouge, Eng instr; So Univ New Orleans, assoc prof of Eng; TX So Univ, assoc prof of English. **ORGANIZATIONS:** Mem Coll Language Assn, S Central Modern Languages Assn, Natl Council of Teachers of English, TX Assn of Coll Teachers, Women in Action; Church Women United; sec, South Central Language Assn (Women of Color Section), 1988-89; mem, Modern Language Assn & Southern Conf on Afro-Amer Studies l988-; pres, Churches Interested in Premature Parentage l989; artistic director, Cyrenian Productions (Drama Group) l985-. **HONORS/ACHIEVEMENTS:** Alpha Kappa Mu Natl Honor Soc; Lambda Iota Tau Literary Honor Soc; has done extensive work with school & little theatre groups in New Orleans & Houston; pub "Viewpoints From Black Amer" 1970; editor "Cultural Arts Review"; "A World Made Cunningly, A Closer Look at the Petry's Short Fiction, CLA Journal 1986; Teacher of the Year, Texas Southern Univ l988; author, A Core Curriculum Approach to College Writing, Littleton, MA, Copley Publishing Group, 1987. **BUSINESS ADDRESS:** Assoc Prof of English, TX SoUniv, 3201 Wheeler Ave, Houston, TX 77004.

WASHINGTON, HENRY L.
Clergyman. **PERSONAL:** Born Nov 15, 1922, Earlington, KY; married Azlea; children: Argene, Lamar, Henry, Clyone. **EDUCATION:** Ashland Theol Sem, OT-NT 1976; Dyke Coll, Cert Realtor 1978. **CAREER:** Metro Ins Co, sales rep 1969-76; Alpha & Omega COGIC, pastor 1970-85; City of Mansfield OH, councilman 1983. **ORGANIZATIONS:** Pres Concerned Black Citizens 1976-78; mem Real Estate Mgrs Assn 1978-85; comm chmn NAACP 1982-84; councilman City of Mansfield 1983-85; mem Richland Transit Bd 1983-84, Affirmative Scholarship DSU 1984-85. **HONORS/ACHIEVEMENTS:** House of Rep State of OH 1979; Mayors Awd City of Mansfield OH 1982. **MILITARY SERVICE:** AUS pfc 1 1/2 yrs; Purple Heart, European Theater Ribbons 1943-44. **HOME ADDRESS:** 312 Second Ave, Mansfield, OH 44905. **BUSINESS ADDRESS:** Pastor, Alpha & Omega COGIC, 530 Pearl St, Mansfield, OH 44905.

WASHINGTON, ISAIAH EDWARD
Educator. **PERSONAL:** Born Oct 19, 1908, Augusta, GA; married Dr Justine E Wilkinson. **EDUCATION:** Paine Coll Augusta, AB 1937; Temple Univ Phila, MS 1948; Allen Univ Columbia SC, LittD 1959. **CAREER:** Richmond County Bd of Educ, principal 1938-75; Albany State Coll, summer school instructor 1955-64; City of Augusta, councilman 1975-88. **ORGANIZATIONS:** Pres GA Teachers Educ Assoc 1943-45; regional dir American Teachers Assoc 1945-52. **HONORS/ACHIEVEMENTS:** Silver Beaver Awd Boy Scouts of Amer. **HOME ADDRESS:** 1228 Kent St, Augusta, GA 30901.

WASHINGTON, J. BARRY
Executive administrator. **PERSONAL:** Born Aug 23, 1947, Newark, NJ. **EDUCATION:** Catholic Univ, BChE 1969; Washington Univ, MBA 1971. **CAREER:** Exxon Chemical, chem engr 1969; Prudential Ins Co, sr investment analyst 1971; City of Newark, program mgmt officer 1976; Connection Commun, pres & ceo1979-. **ORGANIZATIONS:** Mem Black MBA Assoc 1972-; reg rep NY Stock Exchange 1973-79; mem Assoc MBA Exec 1976, Natl Cable TV Assoc 1982; exec bd NAACP 1982-; dir NJ Cable TV Assoc 1983-; v chmn Natl Assoc of Minorities in Cable TV 1983. **HONORS/ACHIEVEMENTS:** Fellowship Consortium for Minorities in Mgmt 1969; Spec Awd Natl Cable TV Assoc 1984. **BUSINESS ADDRESS:** President, Connection Communications Corp, 360 Central Ave, Newark, NJ 07013.

WASHINGTON, JACQUELIN EDWARDS
Business executive. **PERSONAL:** Born May 20, 1931, St Augustine, FL; married Kenneth B; children: Saundra, Byron, Kristin. **EDUCATION:** Fisk U, BA 1951; Wayne State U, MSW 1965. **CAREER:** New Options Personnel Inc, pres 1975-; Detroit Pub Sch, sch soc worker 1965-75; Detroit Dept of Pub Welfare, case worker & supr 1957-63. **ORGANIZATIONS:** Mem Nat Assn of Soc Workers 1965-; mem State of MI Employ Agency Council 1978-; trustee Detroit Inst of Arts 1975-; pres Detroit Club Nat Assn Negro Bus & Professional Women 1978-; 1st vice pres Girl Scouts of Metro Detroit 1979-80; mem NOW Legal Defense & Educ Fund 1979-. **HONORS/ACHIEVEMENTS:** Spirit of Detroit Award Detroit Common Council 1978; Female Pioneer Award Women Lawyers' Assn 1978; Feminist of the Yr Award Detroit Chap Nat Orgn for Women 1978. **BUSINESS ADDRESS:** New Options Personnel, 2908 Book Bldg, Detroit, MI 48226.

WASHINGTON, JACQUELYN M.
Sales manager, hotel/motel industry. **PERSONAL:** Born Apr 25, 1965, Philadelphia, PA; daughter of Edward Washington Jr and Arlene Berry Calerdale. **EDUCATION:** Univ of Massachusetts, degree in hotel/rest/travel admin, 1987. **CAREER:** Philadelphia Convention & Visitors Bureau, PA, sales rep, 1987-89; Adams Mark Hotel, Philadelphia PA, sales manager, 1989-. **ORGANIZATIONS:** Membership chair & body rep, local Alpha Kappa Alpha; young professional mem, Philadelphia Urban League. **HOME ADDRESS:** 4909 Parkside Ave, Philadelphia, PA 19131.

WASHINGTON, JAMES A.
Publisher. **PERSONAL:** Born Apr 26, 1950, Chicago, IL; son of Frank S. Washington and Cecelia Burns Jones; married Victoria Meek, May 09, 1980 (deceased); children: Patrick James, Elena Cecele. **EDUCATION:** Southern University, Baton Rouge, LA, BA, 1971; University of Wisconsin, Madison, WI, MA, 1973. **CAREER:** Tennessee State University, Nashville, TN, worked in Development Office; American Heart Association, public relations specialist; Dallas Ballet, public relations manager; Focus Communications Group, Dallas, TX, founder and president; Ad-Mast Publishing Co, Dallas, TX, chairman. **ORGANIZATIONS:** Member of board of directors, Cotton Bowl, I Have a Dream Foundation, Science Place, Dallas Zoological Society, Family Guidance Center; member, advisory council of small business and agriculture, Federal Reserve Bank of Dallas; chairman, minority business advisory committee, Dallas Independent School District; member, Dallas Together; member of executive committee and board, Dallas Chamber of Commerce, American Heart Association, Greater Dallas Planning Council, Junior Achievement; member of admissions committee, United Way, 1983; chairman of public relations committee, National Newspaper Publishers Association. **HONORS/ACHIEVEMENTS:** Danforth Fellow, University of Wisconsin—Madison; Woodrow Wilson Fellow. **BUSINESS ADDRESS:** Ad-Mast Publishing, Dallas Weekly, 3101 Martin Luther King, Dallas, TX 75215.

WASHINGTON, JAMES EDWARD
Optometrist. **PERSONAL:** Born Jun 19, 1927, Beaufort, NC; son of John C Washington and Nancy Parker Sandlin; married Ethelyn Marie Irby Pigott, Jun 12, 1984; children: Jeffrey, Shelly, John. **EDUCATION:** Fayetteville State Univ, attended; NY Univ Washington Square Coll, attended; No IL Coll of Optometry, BS 1953; No IL Coll of Optometry, OD 1954; Rutgers Univ Grad School Newark, MPA 1983. **CAREER:** Nation Optometric Assn reg dir 1972-79; Essex Cty Optometric Soc, pres 1974; Natl Optometric Assoc, pres 1974-75; Diversified Vision Svcs, exec dir; Private practice, solo practitioner; private practice, optometrist. **ORGANIZATIONS:** Chmn, bd of dir NOA 1975-76; preceptor PA Coll of Optometry; fellow Coll of Optometrists in Vision Devel; vstg lecturer New England Coll of Optometry; mem Amer Optometric Assoc, Natl Optometri Found, New Jersey Optom Assoc, Essex Cty Optom Soc, Optom Extension Program Found, Natl Optometric Asoc, NJ Eye Care Council; health adv bd East Orange Head Start; adv bd Montclair State Coll Health Careers. **HONORS/ACHIEVEMENTS:** Optometrists of the Year Essex Cty Optom Assoc 1972; Optometrist of the Year Natl Optom Assoc 1973; mem Tomb & Key Honor Optom Frat; Black Heritage Awd City of East Orange 1987; Distinquished Service Award, New Jersey Optomet-

ric Assn 1987. **MILITARY SERVICE:** AUS 1946-49. **BUSINESS ADDRESS:** Optometrist, 104 S Munn Ave, East Orange, NJ 07018.

WASHINGTON, JAMES LEE
Mayor. **PERSONAL:** Born Jun 14, 1948, Glendora, MS; married Zenolia; children: James Jr, Jessica. **EDUCATION:** Coahoma Jr Coll, AA, MS; Delta State MS, BS; attended Camelville Coll. **CAREER:** Coahoma Agricultural HS, head basketball coach; Coahoma Jr Coll, head men's basketball coach; Friars Point NC, mayor. **ORGANIZATIONS:** Mem Natl Conf Black Mayors, Natl Conf Black Coaches. **HONORS/ACHIEVEMENTS:** Outstanding Serv Awd N Atlantic Conf Boys Track 1976; Class A State Championship Coahoma Agricultural HS (basketball) 1984. **BUSINESS ADDRESS:** Mayor, Friars Point, PO Box 185, Friars Point, MS 38631.

WASHINGTON, JAMES MELVIN
Clergyman, educator. **PERSONAL:** Born Apr 24, 1948, Knoxville, TN; son of James W. Washington (deceased) and Annie B. Washington; married Patricia Anne Alexander; children: Ayanna Nicole. **EDUCATION:** Univ of TN Knoxville, BA 1970; Harvard Divinity School, MTS 1970-72; Yale Univ, MPhil 1972-75, PhD 1975-79. **CAREER:** Yale Divinity School, instr 1974-76; Union Theol Sem, assoc prof 1976-86; Haverford Coll, vstg assoc prof 1983-84; Columbia Univ, vstg assoc prof 1984-85; Oberlin Coll, vstg assoc prof 1985-86; Union Theol Sem, prof of Modern & American Church History 1986; visiting lecturer Princeton Theological Seminary Princeton, NJ l989-90; visiting prof Princeton Univ Princeton, NJ l989-90. **ORGANIZATIONS:** Bd mem Amer Baptist Churches USA 1982-85, Natl Council of Churches 1985-87, Amer Baptist Historical Soc 1977-82; mem, exec comm Faith & Order Commissof the Natl Council of Churches 1985-87; consult Religious Affairs Dept, NAACP; Publications, A Testament of Hope, The Essential Writing of Martin Luther King,Jr (Harper & Row 1986); Frustrated Fellowship, The Black Baptist Quest for Social Power (Mercer Univ Press 1986); assoc editor American Natl Biography l989-. **HONORS/ACHIEVEMENTS:** Fellow Woodrow Wilson Found 1970-71; Protestant Fellow Fund for Theol Ed 1971-72; Rockefeller Doctoral Fellow Fund for Theol Ed 1972-74; Teaching Fellow Harvard Univ 1971-72; book Frustrated Fellowship 1985; Christopher Award for editing A Testament of Hope, The Essential Writings of Martin Luther King, Jr 1987. **HOME ADDRESS:** 99 Claremont Ave, New York, NY 10027. **BUSINESS ADDRESS:** Professor Church Hist, Union Theological Seminary, 3041 Broadway, New York, NY 10027.

WASHINGTON, JAMES W., JR.
Painter, sculptor and print maker. **PERSONAL:** Born Nov 10, Gloster, MS; son of Rev James W Washington and Lizzie Howard; married Janie R Miller. **EDUCATION:** Natl Landscape Design & Gardening Inst Los Angeles CA, attended 1947; Mark Tobey, studied painting 1947-50; Hon Doctor of Fine Arts Degree, Theological Union Center of Black Urban Studies, Berkeley CA 1975;. **CAREER:** Camp Joseph T Robinson, Little Rock AR, orthopedic mechanic-in-charge, 1941-43; Puget Sound Naval Shipyard, Bremerton WA, journeyman electrician, 1943-50; Studio Fine Arts, painter & sculptor. **ORGANIZATIONS:** Pres Seattle Chap Artists Equity Assn 1960-61; mem Gov's State Arts Commn 1962-; NAACP; 33rd Degree Mason; exhibition Feingarten Gallery San Francisco 1958; one-man exhibitions, Haydon Calhoun Galleries Dallas 1960; Woodside Gallery Seattle 1962-65; Foster/White Gallery Seattle 1968-76; exhibition Squibb Gallery Princeton NJ 1982; represented w/ writings, lectures on tape & sculpture Natl Museum of Amer Art Washington 1984. **HONORS/ACHIEVEMENTS:** Author of "The Arts Are Color Blind," "Christianity and the Arts," and "Northwest Today," Seattle Pl, Seattle WA 1965-66; Hon Degree AFD, Theological Union Center of Black Urban Studies, 1975; 2nd prize sculpture Seattle World's Fair 1962; purchase prize sculpture San Francisco Museum Art 1956; Gov's Awd Cultural Contrib State Heritage Group Exhibition Huntsville Museum of Art 1979; Lawrence H Bloedel Collection Whitney Museum of Amer Art NY 1976; elected mem of Professional Artists by the Redevelop Authority of Philadelphia PA 1975; Kings Co Arts Comm Arts Serv Awd 1984; Certificate of Recognition WA State Gov John Spellman 1984; Washington State Centennial Hall of Honor Tacoma Washington 1984; sculpture commissions, "Phoenix and Esoteric Symbols of Nature" Sheraton Hotel Seattle WA 1982, "Life Surrounding the Astral Altar, in Matrix" law firm of Smith Rosenblume & Assoc Seattle WA 1987; "The Oracle of Truth," Mt Zion Baptist Church, Seattle WA 1988; sculpture "Young Queen of Ethiopa" accepted in the Smithsonian Inst Natl Museum of Amer Art, Washington DC 1984; retrospective exhibit, Bellevue Art Museum, Seattle WA 1989. **MILITARY SERVICE:** 2nd World War, exempted from service to work in the Puget Sound Naval shipyard Bremerton WA. **HOME ADDRESS:** 1816 26th Ave, Seattle, WA 98122.

WASHINGTON, JOE
Professional athlete. **PERSONAL:** Born Sep 24, 1953. **EDUCATION:** Oklahoma. **CAREER:** San Diego Chargers, 1976-78; Baltimore Colts, 1978-81; Washington Redskins, running back 1981. **ORGANIZATIONS:** Works with Bob Hope-Hughen Sch facility handicapped US Bum Phillips Celebrity Golf Trnmt; chrmn Anne Arundel Cnty Assc Retarded Citizens; active MD Spec Olympics; spkmn OK Soc Prevent Blindness; advsry bd Wednesday's Child; serves Sports Cncl Natl Found Lietis & Colitis; worked with No Greater Love Christmas Celbration Children of Fathers Killed in Service; filmed pblc serv anncmnt with Joe Theismann to make the pblc aware of need Vital Organ Donors Specifically Livers; spoken to Boys Clb Grps, Washington Bd Trade, Fight Against Drug Abuse; appeared with Mrs Reagan Local Ele m Sch Spoke Against Drug Abuse; offseason oversees Oil Equipment Lsng Co OK; radio Pgm WMAL AM. **HONORS/ACHIEVEMENTS:** Selected Pro Bowl 1979; man of yr for off-the-field conriburtions to soc Washington Redskins 1983; chosen redskin mvp by Teammates 1981.

WASHINGTON, JOHN CALVIN, III
Elected official. **PERSONAL:** Born Dec 12, 1950, Coatesville, PA; son of John II and Mildred; children: Nathaniel, John IV, Tamara. **EDUCATION:** Coatesville Sr HS, diploma 1968; Coll Prep. **CAREER:** City of So Coatesville, councilmem. **ORGANIZATIONS:** Elk Mt Vernon Lodge #151 1975; mem NAACP 1975; volunteer VA Med Ctr 1978; mem Chester Co Recreation Council 1981; master mason Lily of the Valley #59 1981; dir S Coatesville Recreation 1981; mem FOP 1981; mem Hypertension Ctr 1981; chmn Grievance Comm for the Handicapped of S Coatesville 1984; chmn Property Comm 1984. **HOME ADDRESS:** 34 1/2 Penn Ave, South Coatesville, PA 19320. **BUSINESS ADDRESS:** Borough Councilman, Modena Rd, South Coatesville, PA 19320.

WASHINGTON, JOHN WILLIAM
Retired physician. **PERSONAL:** Born Oct 03, 1921, Boston, MA; son of Lawrence M Washington, Sr and Marion Louise Underwood; married Glynn Nell Lott; children: John III, Byron Lott. **EDUCATION:** Northeastern, 1939; West VA State Coll, 1943; Yale Univ, 1944; Meharry Med Coll, MD 1948. **CAREER:** Ob-Gyn St Elizabeth Med Ctr, past chief; St Elizabeths Hosp, staff mem; Miami Valley Hosp, staff mem, emeritus staff Unity State Bank Dayton OH, dir; Private practice, physician; Wright State School of Med, asst clinical prof ob-gyn. **ORGANIZATIONS:** Vol faculty Wright State Med School; mem Alpha Phi Alpha, Natl Med Assoc, AMA; life mem NAACP; mem Dayton Ob-Gyn Soc; diplomate Amer Bd Ob-Gyn; fellow Amer Coll Ob-Gyn; life mem Wright State Univ Acad of Medicine. **MILITARY SERVICE:** AUS corpl 1942-45; AUS MC capt 1952-54; Battle Stars & Ribbons. **HOME ADDRESS:** 849 Olympian Cir, Dayton, OH 45427.

WASHINGTON, JOHNNIE M.
Clergyman. **PERSONAL:** Born Sep 23, 1936, Paris, TX; married Naaman C; children: Mary M Jones, Leontyne. **EDUCATION:** So Evang Assn, LVN 1970, DD 1974; Roosevelt U, BS 1979. **CAREER:** Full Gospel Temple, rev 1985; Hotel Dieu Hosp, endoscopy supr 1970-; McGraw Concern Munich Germay, sec & financial 1964-68; Nat Gastroenterology Tech, certified gi techn 1973-80; NYUniv Albany, ungrad nurse 1977-80. **ORGANIZATIONS:** Sec El Paso Black Caucus 1977-79; pres El Paso Br NAACP 1979-; corr sec El Paso Black Caucus 1979-. **HONORS/ACHIEVEMENTS:** Certificate of Appreciation Black History Week 1975; Outstanding Black Citizen White Sands Missile Range 1978; Certificate of Appreciation YMCA El Paso 1979; Outstanding Civil Rights Award NAACP 6 Region Conf 1980. **BUSINESS ADDRESS:** 4631 Atlas, El Paso, TX 79904.

WASHINGTON, JOSEPH R., JR.
Educator. **PERSONAL:** Born Oct 30, 1930, Iowa City; married Sophia Holland; children: Bryan Reed, David Eugene. **EDUCATION:** Iron Cross Univ of WI, BA 1952; Andover Newton Theol Sch, BD 1957; Boston Univ, ThD 1961. **CAREER:** Univ of CA Riverside, prof Religious Studies chmn Black Studies 1975-; Univ of VA, prof Religious Studies chmn Afro-Amer Studies 1970-75; Beloit Coll, dean of chapel prof religion 1969-70; Albion Coll, dean of chapel assoc prof of religion 1966-69; Dickinson Coll, chaplain asst prof religion 1963-66; Dillard Univ, dean of chapel asst prof philosophy religion 1961-63. **ORGANIZATIONS:** Mem Amer Soc of Chris Etheics; Amer Acad of Religion. **HONORS/ACHIEVEMENTS:** Books publ, Black Religion 1964; Politics of God 1967; Black & White Power Subreption 1969; Marriage in Black & White 1970; Black Sects & Cults 1972. **MILITARY SERVICE:** AUS lt military police 1952-54.

WASHINGTON, JOSIE B.
Educator. **PERSONAL:** Born Mar 13, 1943, Leona, TX; married Rev Eugene J Washington; children: Eugenia J, Giovonna J. **EDUCATION:** AA, BA, MS. **CAREER:** San Juan Sch Dist 1968; Sacramento Co Welfare Dept Bur of Investigation 1972; State Dept of Rehab 1974; Sacramento City Unified Sch Dist; Sacramento Urban League, site adminis. **ORGANIZATIONS:** Mem Sacramento Urban League; mem Youth Devel Delinq Proj Bd; mem Neighborhood Council; advr Youth Outreach; mem Vista Neuva Adv Com; mem N Area Citizen for Better Govt; mem Natl Rehab Assn; CA Sch Bd Assn; San Juan Unified Sch Dist; adv com Bus Skills Handicapped; trustee Grant HS Dist Bd of Educ; mem Sacramento Area Regional Adult & Vocational Educ; council rep Sacramento Co Sch Bd; clerk Grant HS Bd of Educ; Sacramento Co Central Democratic Comm; mem Sen SI Hayakawa CA Constituency Council; mem Comm to elect Mayor Tom Bradley for Gov of CA; Comm to elect vice pres Mondale for Pres; Comm to elect Pres Jimmy Carter; mem White House invite by Pres Jimmy Carter & wife 1980; mem NAACP. **HONORS/ACHIEVEMENTS:** Written contributions Resource Directory of Black Bus Sacramento area; 1st Black & Woman elected to Grant Bd of Educ. **BUSINESS ADDRESS:** Site Administrator, Sacramento Urban League, 3515 Broadway, Sacramento, CA 95817.

WASHINGTON, KENNETH S.
Education administrator. **PERSONAL:** Born Oct 19, 1922, Chicago, IL; married Henriella Dunn; children: Lordice Hopkins, Marcella Kingi, Henry Kingi, Corine DeBlane, Kim Wilkins, Kent. **EDUCATION:** RooseveltUniv Chicago, BA 1948; CA StateUniv Los Angeles, MA 1954;Univ of So CA, PhD 1970. **CAREER:** City Coll of San Francisco, pres 1985; State of CA, asst supt for pub instr 1971-75; CA State Univ & Coll, asst dean for educ oppor 1968-71; UCLA, asst to chancellor 1966-68; Centennial High Compton CA, bd couns 1960-66; Centennial High, teacher Math & Sci 1951-60. **ORGANIZATIONS:** Pres CA Council for Educ Oppor 1964-69; dir Baskin Found 1956-66; dir KQED Pub Broadcasting Sta 1976-80; dir San Francisco Devel Fund 1976-; electedtrustee LA Comm Coll Dist 1969-75; mem "Black BRAINTRUST" of Rep Shirley Chisholm; vice pres Ocean Ave Merchants' Assn 1975-80; bd of dir SF Mus Soc 1979-80. **MILITARY SERVICE:** AUS s/sgt 1940-45. **BUSINESS ADDRESS:** 50 Phelan Ave, San Francisco, CA 94112.

WASHINGTON, KERMIT
Athlete. **PERSONAL:** Born Sep 17, 1951, Washington, DC. **EDUCATION:** Amer Univ, attd 1973. **CAREER:** Portland Trailblazers, prof bsktbl plyr 1979-; San Diego Clippers, prof bsktbl plyr 1978-79; Boston Celtics, prof bsktbl plyr 1978-; LA Lakers, prof bsktbl plyr 1973-78. **HONORS/ACHIEVEMENTS:** All-Star Def Team NBA 1979; NBA All-Star Game 1979; led Trailblazers in rebounds (842); ranked 9th in NBA W/106 Aver 1979; set All-Time New Trailblazer Record Shooting from Field (553); ranked 8th NBA 1979; led Team in Blocked Shots (131) 1979. **BUSINESS ADDRESS:** Portland Trailblazers, Ste 380, Lloyd Bldg, Portland, OR 97232.

WASHINGTON, LEROY
Educator. **PERSONAL:** Born May 01, 1925, Greenville, FL; married Edith; children: 3 Children. **EDUCATION:** FL A&M Univ, BA 1950; Univ of Miami, MA 1972. **CAREER:** Charlotte Jr Coll, drama coach; Dade Public School of Miami, drama coach; Booker T Washington HS; Miami Sr HS; Miami Jackson Sr HS, drama coach & teacher; SW Miami Sr HS; sabbatical; Miami Northwestern Sr HS, teacher. **ORGANIZATIONS:** Past pres NC HS Drama Assc; FL State Interscholastic Speech & Drama Assc; Dade Co Speech Tchr Assc; mem UTD Prof Sect; mem Screen Actors Guild; Natl TV & Radio Broadcasters Union; Youth Emphasis Club Sponsor; NW Br YMCA; block ldr Model Cities; dir/Vice Pres CL Williams Meml Schlrshp Fnd Inc; sponsor Creative Dance & Interpretative Reading Training Classes; Comm Sch Vol Work; several TV appearances; acted various prof plays Dade Co & several other states; host & prod of weekly TV show "Amazing Grace"; managed & dir several shows for TV; mem Congregational Ch of Open Door. **HONORS/ACHIEVEMENTS:**

Man of Year 1975; Zeta Phi Beta Sorority Inc; Miami Chpt; Outst Cit & Civic Ldr Charles L Williams Meml Schlrshp Fnd; TV Personality of the Month BTW Alumni Assc; coached drama grp Booker T Washington HS; invited as one of top eight drama grps throughout cty to perform at Univ of IN; 2nd place Rowe Peterson's annual drama photo contest; 2nd place Natl Thespian Soc annual printed prog contest. **MILITARY SERVICE:** USAF corpl WWII; 1st lt Korena Conflict. **BUSINESS ADDRESS:** Miami Northwestern Sr HS, 7007 NW 12 Ave, Miami, FL 33150.

WASHINGTON, LINDA PHAIRE
Scientist. **PERSONAL:** Born Aug 11, 1948, New York, NY; married Joey Washington; children: Kamau, Imani. **EDUCATION:** Boston Univ, BS Biology 1970; Mt Sinai Med Ctr CUNY, PhD 1975; Rockefeller Univ, Post Doctoral Res Fellow 1977; Ctr for Adv Training in Cell and Molecular Biol, adv rsch training 1983. **CAREER:** Laguardia Coll, lecturer 1973-75; Rockefeller Univ, post doctoral rsch fellow 1975-77; City Univ, asst prof 1976-77; Howard Univ Coll of Med, asst prof 1977-79; Tuskegee Inst, Dept of Biology prof 1981-; Cell Culture Science Ctr dir 1981-, prof of immunol/cell biol, Natl Sci Rsch Div dir 1984-. **ORGANIZATIONS:** Consultant Intl Progs Tuskegee Inst Liberia Linkage 1982-83; mem gen rsch support review comm Natl Inst of Health DRR 1983-87; proposal reviewer Nat'l Science Foundation 1985; panel reviewer Nat'l Inst of Health DRR 1986-87. **HONORS/ACHIEVEMENTS:** Murray J Steele Awd for scientific rsch NY Heart Assn 1975; nominee recognition awd for young scholars Amer Assoc of Univ Women Educ Prog 1980; outstanding faculty awd in rsch Tuskegee Inst 1981; UNCF distinguished scholars awd United Negro Coll Fund 1984-85; mem GRSRC Subcommittee Natl Inst of Health DRR 1983-87; Who's Who in Science and Technology 1986. **BUSINESS ADDRESS:** Dir Natural Sciences Rsch, Tuskgee University, Carver Research Foundation, Tuskegee, AL 36088.

WASHINGTON, LOISE
Health service manager. **PERSONAL:** Born Nov 01, 1944, Ft Lauderdale, FL; divorced; children: Keith, Renee. **EDUCATION:** CCNY, BS 1978, MS 1980. **CAREER:** G&S Rsch Analyst, statistician 1981-82; Childrens Circle Daycare Ctr, spec ed coord 1982-84; MLK Health Ctr, mgr/MIS analyst. **ORGANIZATIONS:** Consult Hospital Billing Systems; dir Bronx Youth in Action 1985-. **HONORS/ACHIEVEMENTS:** Outstanding Comm School Bd Mem Bronx Democratic Club 1985. **HOME ADDRESS:** 540 East 169th St, Bronx, NY 10456.

WASHINGTON, LUISA
Business executive. **PERSONAL:** Born Sep 07, 1946, Detroit. **EDUCATION:** Univ of MI Ann Arbor, BA 1972; NY Univ, post grad courses. **CAREER:** MEC/REP/CO Inc Intl, dir pub rel N Africa. **ORGANIZATIONS:** Past sec Intl Afro-Amer Museum 1972. **HONORS/ACHIEVEMENTS:** Teaching Fellow Univ of MI Ann Arbor 1971. **BUSINESS ADDRESS:** 1200 6 Ave Suites M180 190, Detroit, MI 48226.

WASHINGTON, MARY HELEN
Professor. **PERSONAL:** Born Jan 21, 1941, Cleveland, OH; daughter of David C Washington and Mary Catherine Dalton Washington. **EDUCATION:** Notre Dame College, BA, 1962; University of Detroit, MA, 1966, PhD, 1976. **CAREER:** High school teacher of English in Cleveland OH public schools, 1962-64; St. John College, Cleveland, instructor in English, 1966-68; University of Detroit, Detroit MI, assistant professor of English, 1972-75, director of Center for Black Studies, beginning 1975; currently associate professor of English, Boston Harbor College, University of Massachusetts, Boston. **ORGANIZATIONS:** National Council of Teachers of English, College Language Association, Michigan Black Studies Association. **HONORS/ACHIEVEMENTS:** Richard Wright Award for Literary Criticism from Black World, 1974. **BUSINESS ADDRESS:** Department of English, Boston Harbor College, University of Massachusetts, Boston, MA 02125. *

WASHINGTON, MARY PARKS
Artist, educator. **PERSONAL:** Born in Atlanta, GA; children: Eric, Jan. **EDUCATION:** Spelman Coll, AB 1946; Univ of Mexico 1947; Fourah Bay Coll Sierra Leon WA; Univ of Illeffe Nigeria; Univ of Science & Tech Ghana; San Jose State Univ, painting graduate; San Jose State Univ San Jose CA, MA Fine Arts 1978. **CAREER:** Union School Dist, teacher; Dartmouth Jr HS, teacher, 1961-80; Howard, 1948-51. **ORGANIZATIONS:** Mem CA Teachers Assn; Natl Congress of Artists; Natl Art Assc; counc mem CA Art Educ Assc; council dir Tutoring Program for Minority Stud; bd mem NAACP; chmn NAACP 1958-; charter mem San Jose Chapter AKA Sorority; San Jose Chapter Jack & Jill; Human Relations chmn Union School Dist Teachers Assn, 1968-72; San Jose Art League 1960, 1977; Collector's Choice chmn fund raising for San Jose Art League; vol Amer Cancer Soc; bd mem Info Referral of Santa Clara Co 1974-75; Rosenwood Scholarship Black Mt Coll, 1947. **HONORS/ACHIEVEMENTS:** Artist of Year Links Inc; publ Black Artist on Art Vol 1; A Soul A Mirror by Sarah Webster Fabia; The Spelman Story; Black Soul, Ebony Mag; num one woman shows; Johnson Publ Art Coll.

WASHINGTON, MICHAEL HARLAN
Educator. **PERSONAL:** Born Sep 25, 1950, Cincinnati, OH; married Sandra Lavonne; children: Michael Jr, Milo Robeson. **EDUCATION:** Raymond Walters Coll, AA 1971; Univ of Cincinnati, BS 1973, MEd 1974, EdD 1984. **CAREER:** Univ of Cincinnati, learning skills specialist 1974-79; Northern KY Univ, learning skills specialist 1979-80, dir of Afro-Amer Studies program 1986-, assoc prof, History 1980-. **ORGANIZATIONS:** Consultations Office of In-Service Educ No KY Univ 1980, United Christian Ministeries and Black Campus Ministries Univ of Cincinnati 1980-81, Univ of Cincinnati Medical Ctr 1980, No KY Univ Div of Continuing Educ 1980-81, Inservice Tchr Training at Southwestern Business Coll 1982, Diocesan Secondary SocialStudies Tchr Thomas Moore Coll 1982; mem KY Assoc of Teachers of History 1981-, Black History Archives Comm 1985-, Phi Alpha Theta 1985-. **HONORS/ACHIEVEMENTS:** Staff Develop grant KY Council on Higher Educ 1979, 80; founder of the Minority Student Retention Scholarship No KY Univ 1986; founder of the Afro-Amer Studies Prog at No KY Univ 1986; author of poem "On Time," publ in Amer Poetry Anthology 1986; author of book "Academic Success & the College Minority Student," 1986. **BUSINESS ADDRESS:** Dir Afro American Studies Prog, Northern Kentucky University, 440 Landrum, Highland Heights, KY 41076.

WASHINGTON, MICHAEL LEE
Professional athlete. **PERSONAL:** Born Jul 01, 1953, Montgomery, AL; married Veronic; children: Michelle Lee, Chavon. **EDUCATION:** AL, BA Educ. **CAREER:** Baltimore Colts, prof ftbl def back 1975. **HONORS/ACHIEVEMENTS:** All-NFC Newark Star-Ledger Team 1979. **BUSINESS ADDRESS:** Buccaneers, One Buccaneer Pl, Tampa, FL 33607.

WASHINGTON, NANCY ANN
Certified public accountant. **PERSONAL:** Born Nov 30, 1938, Kansas City, KS; daughter of E B Owens and Essie Mae Williams Owens; married Charles Washington, Mar 26, 1964 (deceased); children: Georgetta Grigsby, Bertram Grigsby, Charles Washington III. **EDUCATION:** KCK Comm Coll, Kansas City KS, AA 1977; St Mary Coll, BSBA 1979; Univ of Missouri, Kansas City KS, MBA 1989. **CAREER:** Internal Revenue Service, Kansas City MO, agent, 1979-80; Washington Accounting Service, Kansas City KS, owner, 1980-83; Kansas Corp Commn, Topeka KS, senior utility regulatory auditor, 1983-88; Bd of Public Utilities, Kansas City KS, internal auditor, 1988-. **ORGANIZATIONS:** Mem, League of Women Voters 1985-, AICPA 1987-, KS Certified Public Accountants Soc 1988-, Inst of Internal Auditors 1988-; asst treas, Freeman Ave Church of God 1987-. **HONORS/ACHIEVEMENTS:** Candlelight Service Award, KCK Comm Coll, 1976. **BUSINESS ADDRESS:** Internal Auditor, Board of Public Utilities, 700 Minnesota Ave, Kansas City, KS 66101.

WASHINGTON, OSCAR D.
Educator. **PERSONAL:** Born Feb 18, 1912, Tulsa; married Doretha Lumbard; children: Cynthia, Alisa. **EDUCATION:** Creighton Univ, BS 1935; Univ of MI, MS 1948; St Louis Univ, PhD 1973. **CAREER:** St Louis Bd of Educ, teacher; poet; writer; musician; scientist; Soli Music Publishers Ballad Record Co, pres & Organizer; songwriter; US Govt, chemist 1943; St Louis Argus, newspaper columnist 1974. **ORGANIZATIONS:** Mem Broadcast Music Inc; organizer prof tchrs orgn Bristow OK 1945; Bristow Civic Impro Orgn; mem Bristow Cham of Comm 1946. **HONORS/ACHIEVEMENTS:** Recipt Quiz Kids Best Tchr Winner 1948; Star Award Winner Natl Sci Tchr Assc; 1956. **MILITARY SERVICE:** Srv as govt chemist WWII.

WASHINGTON, PAUL M.
Clergyman. **PERSONAL:** Born May 26, 1921, Charleston, SC; married Christine Jackson; children: Marc, Kemah, Michael, Donyor. **EDUCATION:** Lincoln Univ, attd 1943; Philadelphia Div Sch 1946. **CAREER:** Ch of the Advocate, rector 1962-; St Cyprians Ch, vicar 1954-62; Cuttington Clge Liberia W Africa, tchr 1948-54. **ORGANIZATIONS:** Mem Philadelphia Commn on Human Rel 1964-71; host Black Power Conv 1968; host Black Panter Conv 1970; host The Philadelphia Ordinations of 11 Women to Priesthood 1974; chmn Black Polit Conv 1969; delegate 5 Gen Conv of Epis Ch; mem exec council Epis Ch; Gov Bd Natl Council of Chs Delegate to Conference on US Intervention in Iran 1980. **BUSINESS ADDRESS:** 18 Diamond, Philadelphia, PA 19121.

WASHINGTON, PHILEMON (PHIL)
Educator. **PERSONAL:** Born Sep 19, 1934, Chester, SC; married Geraldine Jacobs. **EDUCATION:** SC State Coll, BS 1957; Seton Hall Univ, MA 1964; Univ of MN, PhD 1974; grad courses NYU, Jersey City State Coll. **CAREER:** Dickinson HS Jersey City, teacher biol sci 1959-69; Essex Co Coll Newark, teacher biol 1968-70; Snyder HS Jersey City, principal 1969-78; Adult Even Sch, principal 1971-74; Snyder HS Jersey, admin 1978-. **ORGANIZATIONS:** Omega Psi Phi Frat 1955-; pres Jersey City Fedn of Teachers 1960-65; coord Sci & Math Dept 1961-69; vice pres NJ Fed of Teachers 1963-65; exec bd Admin & Suprv Assn of NJ 1969; pres NJ SC State Coll Alumni 1972-; mem Natl Assn of Secondary Sch Prin 1973; mem NJ Assn of Black Educs 1975; exec bd NJ Assn of Secondary Sch Principals 1976-; Natl Adv Bd NASSP; test devel com NJ Dept of Educ; Operation PUSH; min test review comm NY Dept of Educ; mem Phi Delta Kappa; mem NAACP; bd of examiners Jersey City Bd of Educ. **MILITARY SERVICE:** AUS 1st lt 1957-59; USAR 1960-65; Commandant of the Radio Co Commander. **BUSINESS ADDRESS:** Administrator, Snyder HS, 239 Bergen Ave, Jersey City, NJ 07305.

WASHINGTON, RICHARD
Professional athlete. **PERSONAL:** Born Jul 15, 1955, Portland, OR. **EDUCATION:** UCLA, attd 1977. **CAREER:** Cleveland Cavaliers, bsktbl plyr 1980-; Dallas Mavericks, plyr 1980; Milwaukee Bucks, plyr 1979-80; Kansas City Kings, plyr 1976-79. **ORGANIZATIONS:** Active in Soulville Federation Los Angeles CA Summer Jobs for Youth. **HONORS/ACHIEVEMENTS:** Participated in playoffs 1979-80.

WASHINGTON, ROBERT BENJAMIN, JR.
Attorney. **PERSONAL:** Born Oct 11, 1942, Blakeley, GA; married Nola Wallette, Dec 27, 1969; children: Todd, Kyle W. **EDUCATION:** St Peters Coll, BS; Howard Law School, JD 1970; Harvard Law School, LLM 1972. **CAREER:** Harvard Law School, teaching fellow, 1970-72; US Senate Comm on the District of Columbia, attorney, 1971-72; Howard Univ Law School, assoc prof of law, 1972-73; US House of Representatives Comm on the District of Columbia, attorney, 1973-75; George Washington Univ Law Center, assoc professorial lecturer, 1975, assoc prof of law, 1978; Danzansky, Dickey, Tydings, Quint & Gordon, sr partner, 1975-81; Finley, Kumble, Wagner, sr partner & mem of the natl mgmt comm, 1981-88, managing partner, Washington office, 1986-88; Finley, Kumble, Wagner, Heine, Underberg, Manly, Myerson & Casey, co-managing partner, 1986-88; Laxalt, Washington, Perito, & Dubuc, managing partner, 1988-. **ORGANIZATIONS:** Mem: State of New York First Judicial Dept Bar, District of Columbia Bar, Amer Bar Assn, Natl Bar Assn, Washington Bar Assn, Federal Bar Assn, Amer Judicature Soc, Supreme Court Historical Soc, Phi Alpha Delta Legal Fraternity; Mem, bd of dirs: Washington Bancorp, Natl Bank of Washington, Medlantic Healthcare Group, Healthcare Partners Inc, Metropolitan Washington Bd of Trade, Natl Symphony Orchestra Assn; mem, Metro AME Church; mem, President's Export Council; former Assoc of Dem State Chairs; former mem Dem Party's Comm on Presidential Nom & Party Structure; chmn, former mem Task Force on Pre-Del Selection of Dem Party Commiss on Presidential Nom & Party Structure; ed bd & bus mgr Howard Law Review. **HONORS/ACHIEVEMENTS:** Cobb Fellowship Howard Law School 1969; Harvard Law School Teaching Fellowships 1970-72. **BUSINESS ADDRESS:** Managing Partner, Laxalt, Washington, Perito & Dubuc, 1120 Connecticut Ave, NW, 10th Fl, Washington, DC 20036.

WASHINGTON, ROBERT E.
Administrator. **PERSONAL:** Born Jan 07, 1936, Phoenix, AZ. **EDUCATION:** Univ of

CA, BS 1958; Pepperdine Univ, MPA 1973-74. **CAREER:** Corp for Pub Broadcasting, asst to pres for human resources dev; Libr of Congress Research Srv HUD, fed govt 1974-79; Wells Fargo Bank, comm relations 1964-70. **ORGANIZATIONS:** Mem Amer Mgmt Assc; mem Intl City Mgmt Assc; mem Reserved Ofcrs Assc. **HONORS/ACHIEVEMENTS:** Service Award USAR. **MILITARY SERVICE:** AUS & USAR lt col 1959-. **BUSINESS ADDRESS:** Corporation for Public Broadcast, 1111 16th St NW, Washington, DC 20036.

WASHINGTON, RONALD
Professional athlete. **PERSONAL:** Born Apr 29, 1952, New Orleans, LA. **CAREER:** MN Twins, infldr 1981-84. **BUSINESS ADDRESS:** Minnesota Twins, 501 Chicago Ave S, Minneapolis, MN 55415.

WASHINGTON, ROOSEVELT, JR.
Educator. **PERSONAL:** Born Feb 08, 1932, Swan Lake, MS; children: LuWanna, Ronald, Kenneth, Pamela. **EDUCATION:** Roosevelt Univ, BA 1960, MA 1962; Marquette Univ Chicago State Univ DePaul Univ, adv study; No IL Univ, EdD. **CAREER:** Univ of North Texas, Denton Texas prof 1974-; Harambee Indpt Comm Sch Inc, chief admin 1973-74; Marquette Univ, asst prof 1971-74; No IL Univ 1969-71; McDade Elem Sch, asst prin 1968-69; Manley Upper Grade Ctr, tchr/Dept chmn 1961-68; Center St Sch & Fulton Jr HS, tchr/Cnslr 1960-61. **ORGANIZATIONS:** Mem Natl Assc of Secondary Sch Prins; Amer Educ Research Assc; Assc for Supervision & Curriculum Devel; Phi Delta Kappa; Amer Assc of Sch Admin; Natl Organ on Legal Problems in Education. **HONORS/ACHIEVEMENTS:** Author numerous publ for professional journals. **MILITARY SERVICE:** US Navy, HM3, 1950-54. **HOME ADDRESS:** 2125 Woodbrook, Denton, TX 76205.

WASHINGTON, RUTH V.
Attorney. **PERSONAL:** Born in Buffalo, NY; daughter of James and Alice. **EDUCATION:** Hunter, BA 1944; NY Univ Law Sch, LLB 1947, JD 1968. **CAREER:** Private practice of Law, 1987-; SDNY, US Magistrate 1979-87; US Courthouse Foley Square New York City 1979-87. **ORGANIZATIONS:** Pres Ruth V Washington Assoc Labor Relations Consulting Firm 1977-79; chairperson Benefits Review Bd US Dept of Labor 1974-77; commr, NY State Workmen's Comp Bd commr 1968-74; referee NY State Workmen's Comp Bd 1963-68; assc counsel NY State Commn for Human Rights 1961-63; private law practice New York City 1957-61; atty adv Solicitor's Office US Dept of Labor Washington DC 1954-57; probation officer & parole officer NY Ct General Sessions Magistrates Ct NY State Parole 1945-54; Public Representative Fed Adv Council on Unemployment Insurance; mem of advisory council on Economic Role of Women; mem Natl Adv Council on Economic Opportunity; Westchester Bar Assn; Amer Bar Assn; NY State Bar Assn; mem bd St Christopher's School Dobbs Ferry NY; Girl Scouts, bd mem United Way, Westchester Region Natl Conf Christains & Jews. **HONORS/ACHIEVEMENTS:** Recipient Greenburgh/White Plains Branch NAACP Community Award Lecturer; Martin Luther King "Drum Beater for Justice Award," 1985; Award Outstanding Woman, Westchester Women's Political Caucus, 1983; Hunter Coll, Hall of Fame. **BUSINESS ADDRESS:** Attorney, 26 Broadway, 17th Fl, New York, NY 10004.

WASHINGTON, SAMUEL T.
Educator. **PERSONAL:** Born May 22, 1901, Washington, DC; married Madge E Hughes. **EDUCATION:** Lincoln Univ PA, AB cum laude 1923; Atlanta Univ, AM 1935; Wharton Sch Univ of PA mba 1951. **CAREER:** Lincoln Univ PA, prof actng 1946-72; FL A&M Coll, ret acct 1945-46; Avery Inst, dir 1944-45; GA, bookkeeper cashier 1941-42; GA Normal Coll, registrar 1938-39; Cits Trust Co Atlanta, bank employee 1934-38; Memphis Louisville Wilmington DE, teacher hs math 1924-33. **ORGANIZATIONS:** Mem Alpha Phi Alpha Frat; Master Mason; Beta Kappa Chi Sci Soc 1923; fac adv Soc for Adv of Mgmt Lincoln Univ PA 1967. **HONORS/ACHIEVEMENTS:** Recipt Chrisitan R & Mary F Lindback Fnd Award for Distinguished Tchng Lincoln Univ PA 1965; recipt Economics in Action Flwshp Prog Case Inst Cleveland 1962; Urban League Corp Bus Flwshp Corn Prod Co 1963. **MILITARY SERVICE:** AUS 1942-43.

WASHINGTON, SANDRA BEATRICE
Educator. **PERSONAL:** Born Mar 01, 1946, Nashville, TN; daughter of Henry F Tucker and Sadie Lewis Tucker; married LaMont Washington, Apr 23, 1971; children: Howard LaMont. **EDUCATION:** Loyola Univ, BA, 1968; Univ of Nebraska, MS, 1977; attended, Vanderbilt Univ. **CAREER:** Sacred Heart Grade School, teacher, 1968-71; Omaha OIC, instructor, 1972-73; Greater Omaha Comm Action, counselor/supvr, 1972-75; PCC/Head Start, pi/soc serv coord, 1976-78; Metro-Tech Comm Coll, counselor/career devel, 1978-81; Computer Inst for Youth, educ coord, 1984-85; Nashville Public Schools, counselor, 1986-. **ORGANIZATIONS:** Career consultant Girl's Club of Omaha, 1978-81; counselor-on-call Planned Parenthood of Nashville, 1985-. **HONORS/ACHIEVEMENTS:** Outstanding Young Women of Amer, 1978-79. **BUSINESS ADDRESS:** Guidance Counselor, ML King Jr Magnet High School, 613 17th Ave North, Nashville, TN 37203.

WASHINGTON, SARAH M.
Educator. **PERSONAL:** Born Aug 10, 1942, Holly Hill, SC; daughter of Harry D McCord and Sarah Harmon McCord; married Jun 04, 1967 (divorced); children: Walter Dawit Washington. **EDUCATION:** Tuskegee Inst, Tuskegee AL, BS 1964; Univ of Illinois, Urbana IL, BS 1970, PhD 1980. **CAREER:** Spartanburg District, Inman SC, Eng teacher, 1964-65; Anderson Public Schools, Anderson SC, Eng teacher, 1965-67; Sumter Schools, Sumter SC, social studies teacher, 1967-68; AL State Univ, Montgomery AL, Eng instructor, 1971-74; Univ of IL, Urbana IL, teaching asst, 1974-80; SC State Coll, Orangeburg SC, Eng prof, 1979-89. **ORGANIZATIONS:** Pres, Orangeburg Branch, Assn of the Study of Afro-Amer Life & History, 1980-85; chaplain, Phi Delta Kappa, 1982-89; mem, SC State Dept Writing Advisory Bd, 1983-89; mem, Amer Assn of Univ Women, 1987-89; reader, Natl Teachers Examination, 1989. **HONORS/ACHIEVEMENTS:** Sigma Tau Delta Natl Eng Honor Soc, 1981; author of literary biog of Frank Horne, 1985; field coordinator, Assessment Performance in Teaching, 1988-90. **BUSINESS ADDRESS:** South Carolina State College, PO Box 2034, Orangeburg, SC 29117.

WASHINGTON, THOMAS
Educator. **PERSONAL:** Born Dec 08, 1937, Rock Island, IL. **EDUCATION:** Univ of IL, BA 1961, MA 1964; Univ of MN, PhD 1982. **CAREER:** Champaign Centennial HS, teacher English, Spanish 1968-70; Hamline Univ MN, instructor Spanish 1970-73; Univ of MN, instructor Spanish 1974-78, 1980-81; Womens Self Defense Empowering Women, lecturer, instructor 1972-87. **ORGANIZATIONS:** Lecturer Women's Self Defense seminars & workshops 1982-87, The Nodarse Language Learning Method 1978-87. **HONORS/ACHIEVEMENTS:** Phi Kappa Phi Natl Hon Soc Univ of MN 1977; Fulbright Scholarship Year's Study in Guatemala 1962; YMCA SCholarship Study/Travel in USSR Hungary Poland 1961; Sigma Delta Pi Spanish Hon Soc Univ of IL 1961. **BUSINESS ADDRESS:** Director, Lecturer, Instructor, Women's Self Defense, P O Box 10119, Minneapolis, MN 55458.

WASHINGTON, THOMAS KIGHT, SR.
Business executive. **PERSONAL:** Born Feb 23, 1937, Dayton, OH; married Shirley Ann. **EDUCATION:** Miami Dade Jr Clge & FL Meml Clge, attd; Pepperdine Univ, attd. **CAREER:** WRBO FM Radio Sta, talk master; Tom Washington Dry Cleaners & Laundry, fnd/Owner/Pres; WMBM Radio, talk master; Tom Washington Comm Theaters Inc, owner. **ORGANIZATIONS:** Bd dir BBB of Dade Co; bd dir Econ Devel Ctr; Cntrl Boys Club; Comm Rally Against Crimes; dist commr BSA S FL Council; Adv bd mem Dade Co Pub Sch of Voc Tng; FL Meml Clge Upward Bound Prog; Dade Co Planning Bd; mem Intl Rotary; Frontiers of Amer; Elks; S FL Zoning Council; Ministers Layman Voters Registration Com of Dade Co; Big Bros of Amer; chmn ML King Blvd Bus Assc; trustee Friendship MB Ch. **HONORS/ACHIEVEMENTS:** Recipt Cert of Appreciation Natl Urban League for spec serv on behalf of Black Execs Exchange Prog 1974-75; Cert of Appreciation Model City Admin Bd 1975; Distng Serv Award Amer Soc of Pub Admin 1974; Cert of Appreciation United Black Students Univ of Miami 1974; USAADC 1st Region 1968; Outst Comm Serv Orchard Villa Sch 1971; "E" Cert in Recog of Achievements Miami Edison Sr High 1974; Bus Ldr Nathan W Collier Meritorious Serv Award FL Meml Clge 1971; Cert of Appreciation Bd of Co Commr Dade Co FL; Orchard Villa Sch 1972; Primary Sch "C" Honor 1972-73; Recog of Bigger & Better Bus Phi Beta Sigma Frat Rho Sigma Chap 1970; Hnry mbrshp FOOTE 1970; Youth Motivation Task Force Prog; Natl Alliance of Businessmen. **MILITARY SERVICE:** AOS sp5 1958-64. **BUSINESS ADDRESS:** 1342 NW 62 St, Miami, FL 33147.

WASHINGTON, U. L.
Professional athlete. **PERSONAL:** Born Oct 27, 1953, Stringtown, OK; married Sandra; children: Shawnte Richelle, Christopher. **EDUCATION:** Murray State Univ. **CAREER:** Kansas City Royals, infielder 1977-84; Montreal Expos, infielder 1985-. **HONORS/ACHIEVEMENTS:** Played in two League Championship Series (1980-84) and one World Series (1980); was Royals' top utility player at second base and shortstop; Appalachian League's All-Star shortstop in 1973; selected Omaha's Most Popular Player by fans in 1977.

WASHINGTON, VALDEMAR LUTHER
Circuit court judge. **PERSONAL:** Born Jun 21, 1952, Baltimore, MD; son of G Luther Washington and Vivian E Washington; married Ada C Miller, Aug 11, 1984; children: Valdemar L, II, Christopher James. **EDUCATION:** Baltimore Polytechnic Inst, B 1970; MI State Univ, BA 1974; Univ of MI Law School, JD 1976. **CAREER:** Baker Law Firm Bay City, assoc lawyer 1/77-12/77; Acct Aid Soc of Flint, dir 1978; Private Practice, attorney 1978-81, 1981-86; Robinson Washington Smith & Stanfield, partner 1981; Circuit Court Judge Genesee Co, judge 1986-. **ORGANIZATIONS:** Mem MI State Bar Assoc 1977-; mem Big Sisters Bd of Dirs 1981-82; pres McCree Theatre Adv Bd 1982-83; mem NAACP Legal Redress Comm 1984-86; mem Amer Judges Assoc 1986-; judicial mem MI Trial Lawyers Assoc 1986-, Amer Trial Lawyers Assoc 1986-. **HONORS/ACHIEVEMENTS:** University Rhodes Scholarship nom MI State Univ 1974; The Argus Award, The Genesee County Consortium on Child Abuse and Neglect, 1989. **BUSINESS ADDRESS:** Circuit Court Judge, Genesee County Circuit Court, Room 107 Genesee Cty Courthse, Flint, MI 48502.

WASHINGTON, WALTER
College president. **PERSONAL:** Born Jul 13, 1923, Hazlehurst, MS; son of Kemp Washington (deceased) and Mable Washington (deceased); married Carolyn Carter. **EDUCATION:** Tougaloo Coll, BA 1948; IN Univ, MS 1952; Yale Univ, Cert of Alcoholic Studies 1953; George Peabody Coll, Educ Spec 1958; Univ So MS, PhD 1969; Tougaloo Coll, Hon Doctor Laws 1972; IN Univ, Hon Doctor Laws 1983; certificate, Harvard Inst for Ed Management. **CAREER:** Crystal Springs, MS, tchr 1948-49; Parrish HS, asst prin/tchr 1949-52; Utica Jr Coll, dean 1952-55; Sumner Hill HS, principal 1955-57; Utica Jr Coll, pres 1957-69; Alcorn State Univ, pres 1969-. **ORGANIZATIONS:** Dir Middle So Utilities 1977-; dir Miss Power & Light 1977-; dir Blue Cross/Blue Shield of MS 1977-; gen pres Alpha Phi Alpha Frat 1972-76; mem pres com Natl Collegiate Athletic Assn 1984-1989; pres & life mem MS Teachers Assn 1964-65; pres MS Assn Colleges 1983-84; pres of NAC United Negro Coll Fund 1959-60. **HONORS/ACHIEVEMENTS:** State & Natl 4-H Alumnus Recogn Award Coop Ext Serv 1975 & 1977; Silver Beaver Award Boy Scouts of Amer 1975; Man-of-Year in Educ total Living for Fifty Plus 1981; Disting Alumni Award Peabody Coll 1972; Alumnus of Year Tougaloo Coll 1959. **BUSINESS ADDRESS:** President, Alcorn State University, Box 359, Lorman, MS 39096.

WASHINGTON, WALTER E.
Attorney. **PERSONAL:** Born Apr 15, 1915, Dawson, GA; married Bennetta Bullock; children: Dr B Jules Rosette Hayward. **EDUCATION:** Howard Univ, AB 1938, LLD 1948; Amer Univ, grad courses 1939-43; Hon LLD Degrees, Fisk Univ, Georgetown Univ, Catholic Univ, Boston Univ, George Washington Univ, Princeton Univ, Gonzaga Coll, Washington Coll, Indiana Coll, Boston Coll, Carnegie-Mellon Univ, Howard Univ, Trinity Coll, Colgate Univ, Univ of the Dist of Columbia, Lincoln Univ. **CAREER:** Natl Capital Housing Authority DC, Housing mgr, 1941-45, various exec positions 1945-61, exec dir 1961-66; NY Housing Authority NYC, chmn 1966-67; District of Columbia, appointed mayor 1967-74, elected mayor, 1974-79. **ORGANIZATIONS:** vice chmn Human Resources Devel Comm Natl League of Cities; mem Adv Bd US Conf of Mayors; mem Club Cosmos Fed City Wash, Natl Lawyers NYC; mem Amer Bar Assn; bd dir Big Bros Inc; trustee John F Kennedy Ctr for the Performing Arts; mem Natl Adv Bd BSA; Ctr for Internatl Scholars. **HONORS/ACHIEVEMENTS:** Honorary LLD & DHL degrees from various colls & Univs; Disting Serv Awd Howard Univ Law Alumni Assn 1974; Capital Press Club 1974; Silver Beaver Awd BSA 1973; Natl Jewish Hosp Awd for Outstanding Serv 1973; Human Relations Awd DC Br NAACP 1969; a number of other honors. **BUSINESS ADDRESS:** Mayor, 1025 15th St NW, Washington, DC 20005.

WASHINGTON, WILLIAM MONTELL
Corporate officer. **PERSONAL:** Born Apr 02, 1939, Columbia, MO; married Beverly Wells. **EDUCATION:** Lincoln Univ MO, BS Educ/Math 1962; Univ of MO at Kansas City, MA Educ 1970. **CAREER:** United Telephone Syst Inc, affirmative action officer, 1971-; Urban League of Kansas City, assoc dir econ devel, 1967-71; KC MO Sch Dist, high school teacher & coach 1963-67. **ORGANIZATIONS:** mem, Personnel Mgmt Assn, 1971; chmn of bd, Urban League Kansas City 1978; Natl bd mem Natl Urban Affairs Council 1979; mem Omega Psi Phi 1959; bd dir, Metro YMCA 1973; adv bd United Negro Coll Fund 1976. **HONORS/ACHIEVEMENTS:** Outstanding Leadership Award, Minority Business Awareness Prog, Black Econ Union, 1977. **BUSINESS ADDRESS:** United Telecom, Inc, Box 11315, Kansas City, MO 64112.

WASSWAS, EDGAR S.
Educator. **PERSONAL:** Born May 17, 1939, Kampala, Uganda;married Elizabeth Naziwa; children: Makubuya, Nanteza, Rhoda. **EDUCATION:** Halki Theol Sem Instanbul, BD 1965; Yale Univ Div School, STM 1966; Columbia Univ, MA, PhD 1980; Rhode Island Coll, MSW 1982. **CAREER:** SUNY Stony Brook, asst prof 1960-78; Adelphi Univ Garden City, adj asst prof 1974-78; Univ of New Haven CT, asst prof 1969-70; Brown Univ Long Term Care Geront, admin assoc 1980-82. **ORGANIZATIONS:** Founder Masanafu-Amer Friendship School Kampala Uganda East Africa 1980; mem, cantor Church of the Annunciation Greed Orthodox Parish of Gr Providence RI 1979-; assoc mem Intl Assoc School of soc Work 1979-; mem African Orthodox Youth Assoc Amer 1981-; bd of reg of soc workers DSRS State of RI 1981-. **HONORS/ACHIEVEMENTS:** DSRS Fellowship State of Rhode Island 1979-80; The World Council Scholarship Awd Ecumenical Patrriachate Istanbul 1961-65; Faculty Awd Rhode Island Coll 1981. **BUSINESS ADDRESS:** Marketing Dir, Baglab Ltd, PO Box 88, Providence, RI 02901.

WATERMAN, HOMER D.
Business executive. **PERSONAL:** Born Mar 17, 1915, Nashville, TN; married Marie Kenyon; children: Homer Elton Jr, William O. **EDUCATION:** Wayne State Univ, 1935. **CAREER:** Waterman & Sons Printing, pres. **ORGANIZATIONS:** Pres Booker T Washington Busn Assn 1969-71, 1973-75; bd mem Southwest Detroit Hosp 1970; bd mem Detroit Urban League 1969; bd mem BTWBA; past bd mem Met Fund; past bd mem United Comm SVc past bd mem Econ Edn; past bd mem Met Detroit Cit Devel Authority; past bd mem Brewster Old Timers. **HONORS/ACHIEVEMENTS:** Recipient Pres Award BTWBA 1970 & 1975; Wolverine State Rep Citation 1969; Certs of Award Detroit Housewives League Detroit Area Dad's Club; Detroit Fire Dept Fire Prev Kick-off Parade 1974; Outstanding Achievement in Business World Award Wright Mutual Ins Co 1973; Cert of Excellence Award MI Office of Minority Business Enterprise 1974. **BUSINESS ADDRESS:** President, Waterman & Sons Printing, 17134 Wyoming Ave, Detroit, MI 48221.

WATERMAN, THELMA M.
Educator. **PERSONAL:** Born Jun 10, 1937, Hartford, CT; married Donal Meikle; children: Steven, Kevin. **EDUCATION:** Hartford Coll for Women, Hartford CT, AA 1969; Trinity Coll, Hartford CT, BA 1971; Yale Univ Divinity School, MDiv 1978. **CAREER:** Proof oper bank 1956-57; dept store salesgirl 1959-61; Headstart Prog, teacher aide 1964-67; Trinity Coll, resident counselor of grad & undergrad students; City Hartford, teacher 1971; coll admin 1971-; Office of Community Affairs, Connecticut Coll, dir; New Haven Boys and Girls Club, New Haven CT, admin, 1984-85; United Way of Southeastern Connecticut, Gales Ferry CT, assoc exec dir, 1985-. **ORGANIZATIONS:** Conducted leadership training sessions, community leaders devel manpower prog, workshops, seminars, conf prog evaluation; co-organizer of 1st public housing proj pre-school ctr 1963; group counselor, Parker Memorial Ctr Hartford 1967-68; counselor, Drop Outs Anonymous Hartford 1967-69; comm rep, Hartford Bd of Educ 1970; vice pres, Dwight School PTA Hartford 1970-71; pres, POWER Hartford 1970-71; bd mem, OIC 1972; United Way 1972; Connecticut Talent Asst Coop 1973-76; Southeastern Connecticut Youth Serv 1973-74; Info & Referral Agency 1974-77; vice pres, Black Seminarians 1974-75; Yale Univ Divinity School Comp Youth Serv 1972-75; Catholic Charities 1971-74; Educ Task Force Model City 1972-75; Minority Navy Wives Scholarship Comm 1972-74. **HONORS/ACHIEVEMENTS:** Delta Sigma Theta Sorority Award, 1965; citationist, Lane Bryant Annual Awards Competition, 1965; Rudolph Haffner Award for Community Service, Hartford Coll for Women, 1971; Samuel S Fishzoln Award, Trinity Coll, 1971; Community Service Recognition, Norwich Branch NAACP, Norwich CT, 1980; Martin Luther King Jr Community Service Award, Club Cosmos, New London CT, 1980. **BUSINESS ADDRESS:** United Way of Southeastern Connecticut, PO Box 375, Gales Ferry, CT 06335.

WATERS, BRENDA JOYCE
Reporter, journalist. **PERSONAL:** Born Jan 29, 1950, Goldsboro, NC. **EDUCATION:** Univ of MD, BS 1973; Amer Univ, MS 1975. **CAREER:** WTVR-TV-6, reporter/anchor 1975-76; WLOS-TV-13, reporter/anchor 1977-79; WPXI-TV-11, reporter 1979-85; KDKA-TV-2 1985-. **ORGANIZATIONS:** Mem NAACP 1981-; bd mem Hill House Assn 1984-86; bd mem Program to Aid Citizen Enterprise 1984-86. **HONORS/ACHIEVEMENTS:** Cert of Recognition Jimmy Carter Fed Disaster Assist Admin 1977; First Place Assoc Press Awd 1982 and 1984. **HOME ADDRESS:** 508 Cedar Avenue, Pittsburgh, PA 15212. **BUSINESS ADDRESS:** TV Reporter, KDKA-TV-2, One Gateway Center, Pittsburgh, PA 15222.

WATERS, HENRIETTA E.
Educator. **PERSONAL:** Born Jul 04, 1927, Augusta, AR; married Robert H Waters Sr. **EDUCATION:** Central State Clge, BS 1949; Loyola Univ, 1950; Univ of KS, MSW 1961. **CAREER:** Barry Coll School of Social Work, assc Prof 1972-; Univ of KS School Social Welfare, asst prof 1966-72; KS Dept Social Welfare, dist off supv/Child welfare consultant 1958-66; Chicago Welfare Div, child welfare supv 1953-58; IL Child Welfare Div, child welfare worker 1950-52; Dade Co Comm Action Agency, consultant 1975-. **ORGANIZATIONS:** Trustee Bd of Pub Health Trust 1978-; house of Del counc on Social Work Educ 1979-80; mem Natl Assc Soc Wrks; mem Acad Cert Soc Wkrs; mem NatlAssc Black Soc Wkrs; former vice pres Greater Miami YWCA 1976-78; vice pres Greater Miami Urban League 1979-; exec com Children's Psychiatric Ctr 1979-. **HONORS/ACHIEVEMENTS:** Srv Award Barry Clge Chap Natl Assc of Black Soc Work Students 1975, 1979; Barry Clge Prof Achievement Barry Clge 1979. **BUSINESS ADDRESS:** 11300 NE 2nd Ave, Miami, FL 33161.

WATERS, JOHN W.
Educator, minister, financial management executive. **PERSONAL:** Born Feb 05, 1936, Atlanta, GA; son of Henry Waters and Mary A. Waters. **EDUCATION:** Atlanta Univ Summer School, 1955-58; Fisk Univ, BA 1957; Univ of Geneva Switzerland, Cert 1962; GA State Univ, 1964,84; Boston Univ, STB 1967, PhD1970; Univ of Detroit, 1974-75. **CAREER:** Army Ed Ctr Ulm W Germany, admin 1960-63; Atlanta Bd of Ed, instr 1967-60,63-64; Myrtle Baptist Church W Newton MA, minister 1969; Ctr for Black Studies Univ of Detroit, dir, assoc prof 1970-76; Interdenom Theol Ctr, prof 1976-86; The Gr Solid Rock Baptist Church Atlanta, minister 1984-; AL Williams, reg vice pres 1984-. **ORGANIZATIONS:** Mem bd dir Habitat for Humanity in Atlanta 1983; sales rep AL Williams 1984-; mem bd of trustees Interdenom Theol Ctr 1980-84; treas Coll Park Ministers Fellowship; chair South Atlanta Joint Urban Ministry 1984-; Prison Ministries with Women, 1988-. **HONORS/ACHIEVEMENTS:** The Natl Fellowship Fund Fellowship in Religion 1968-70; Fellowship The Rockefeller Doctoral Fellowship in Religion 1969-70; Disting Lecturer Inst for Christian Thought John Courtney Murray Newman Ctr MI 1975; first faculty lecturer, Interdenominational Theological Center, 1979. **MILITARY SERVICE:** US Army, sp 1960-63. **HOME ADDRESS:** 1516 Niskey Lake Trail SW, Atlanta, GA 30331. **BUSINESS ADDRESS:** Regional Vice President, AL Williams, 3485 N. Desert Drive, Suite 120, East Point, GA 30034.

WATERS, MARTIN VINCENT
Attorney. **PERSONAL:** Born Nov 05, 1917, Maryland; married Gloria Wood; children: Rita, Marcia, Martin. **EDUCATION:** Lincoln Univ, BA cum laude 1939; Fordham Univ, JD 1942; NY Univ, LLM 1956. **CAREER:** Lawyer pvt prac 1964; Amer Title Ins Co, vice pres chief cnslr 1962-64; Guaranteed Title & Mortgage Co, vice pres mgr 1959-60; Home Title Guaranty Co, coun 1953-59; Amer Arbitration Assc, arbitrator; Ministry of Housing Ghana, consult 1956; Mauritania to UN, consult to Permanant Mission. **ORGANIZATIONS:** Mem various prof org; mem Interracial Council for Bus Opport NY, dir 1965, pres 1969-72; trustee Arthur C Logan Mem Hosp 1975-; pres Lincoln UnivAlumni 1955-58; Law Comm NY Bd of Title Underwriters 1959-64. **HONORS/ACHIEVEMENTS:** Recipt Economic Mainstream Award 1964; LU Alumni Award; Interracial Council Award; Amer Arbitration Assc Plaque; listed Who's Who in East; Opport for Negros in Law; Assc of Amer Law Schs; Bronze Star Medal. **MILITARY SERVICE:** AUS 1942-46. **BUSINESS ADDRESS:** 29 W 57 St, New York, NY 10019.

WATERS, MAXINE
Government official. **PERSONAL:** Married Sidney Williams; children: Edward, Karen. **EDUCATION:** CA State Univ LA, Sociology. **CAREER:** Head Start, asst teacher; State of CA, assemblywoman. **ORGANIZATIONS:** Mem Dem natl Comm; del, alternate Dem Convs; mem Commiss on the Status of Women, Natl Women's Political Caucus Adv Comm; comm Black PACS; natl bd dir Trans Africa; former chief dep LA City Councilman David Cunningham. **HONORS/ACHIEVEMENTS:** 1st woman to be ranked #4 on the leadership team; 1st black female mem of Rules Comm; 1st nonlawyer on the Judiciary Comm; one of the outstanding leaders atthe Intl Women's Year Conf in Houston; among her bills that have become law are those concerning tenant protection, small bus protection, a much-publicized bill to limit police authority to strip & search people arrested for minor crimes. **BUSINESS ADDRESS:** Assemblywoman, California Legislature, 7900 S Central Ave, Los Angeles, CA 90001.

WATERS, NEVILLE R., III
Radio program director. **PERSONAL:** Born Feb 22, 1957, Washington, DC. **EDUCATION:** Springfield Coll, BS (Magna Cum Laude) 1978, MEd 1980. **CAREER:** WMAS Radio, announcer 1980-81; A&M Records, promotion/merchandising 1982-83; WQXQ Radio, traffic dir/music dir 1983; WOL Radio, prog dir 1985-. **BUSINESS ADDRESS:** Program Dir, WOL Radio, 400 H St NE, Washington, DC 20002.

WATERS, SYLVIA ANN
Journalist. **PERSONAL:** Born Sep 29, 1949, Corsicana, TX. **EDUCATION:** East Texas State Univ, BA 1971. **CAREER:** Corsicana Daily Sun Newspaper, reporter 1972-. **ORGANIZATIONS:** Publicity chairwoman Navarro Co United Fund 1975-; mem Natl Federation of Press Women, TX Press Women 1982-; pres Jackson Ex-Students Assoc Inc 1983-; mem NAACP 1986, Natl Assoc of Black Journalists 1986-, Amer Business Women Assoc Golden Horizons Chap 1986-; chairwoman Navarro Co Coalition Black Democrats 1986-. **HONORS/ACHIEVEMENTS:** James Collins Scholarship 1968; TX Press Women third place awd in photography 1987. **HOME ADDRESS:** 601 E 14th Ave, Corsicana, TX 75110. **BUSINESS ADDRESS:** Corsicana Daily Sun Newspaper, 405 East Collin, Corsicana, TX 75110.

WATERS, WILLIAM DAVID
Government executive. **PERSONAL:** Born Sep 14, 1924, Camden, NJ; son of William A Waters and Rebecca Jones Waters; married Viva Edwards. **EDUCATION:** Temple Univ Philadelphia, BS Acctng 1947, MBA Acctng 1948. **CAREER:** IRS, Mid-Atlantic Region Philadelphia fiscal mgmt & officer 1964-66; asst Dist Dir Albany 1966-67; asst dist dir Baltimore 1970-73; dist dir Baltimore 1973-74; reg commr Mid-Atlantic Region 1974-85; NJ Casino Control Commission, commissioner 1986-. **ORGANIZATIONS:** Vp, dir YMCA of Camden Cnty 1980-; mem St John's United Meth Ch Columbia; mem Housing Task Force Columbia, MD. **MILITARY SERVICE:** AUS 1st Lt (USAR) 1943-52. **HOME ADDRESS:** 1011 Rymill Run, Cherry Hill, NJ 08003.

WATERS, WILLIAM L.
Business executive. **PERSONAL:** Born Sep 23, 1941, Philadelphia. **EDUCATION:** BS 1966. **CAREER:** Consolidated Edison of NY, design engr 1966-68, cost engr 1968-71; proj construction engr 1971-73; William L Waters Inc, pres. **ORGANIZATIONS:** Mem Mech Contractors Assc of Amer; Natl Assc of Minority Contractors; Council of Construction & Prof NY; Mem 100 Black Men NY. **HONORS/ACHIEVEMENTS:** Recipt Black Achievers Award 1972. **BUSINESS ADDRESS:** 211 E 43 St, New York, NY 10017.

WATERS, WIMBLEY, JR.
Business executive. **PERSONAL:** Born Oct 03, 1943, Leesburg, GA; married Andrea Lois Hannans; children: Nina, Princey, Tia, Dana, Elissa. **EDUCATION:** Monroe Area Voc Tech Albany GA, attd 1963; Daytona Beach Comm Clge Daytona Beach FL, attd 1968. **CAREER:** Daytona Typographical Union No 892, pres 1973-; News-Jour Corp, printer 1963-; Equifax Srv, ins investigator 1974-78. **ORGANIZATIONS:** Pres FL GA Typo-

graphical Conf 1980-; secr/Treas Union Label Srv Trades Council Cntrl Labor Union Volusia Flagler FL 1980-. **BUSINESS ADDRESS:** Daytona Typographical Union No, PO Box 771, Daytona Beach, FL 32015.

WATIKER, ALBERT DAVID, JR.
Construction company executive. **PERSONAL:** Born May 16, 1938, Zanesville, OH; son of Albert David Watiker and Lora Bell Robinson Morgan; married Rachel Almeda Carnes; children: Leslie, Leisha, Lionel, Lori, Lynn, Lachelle. **EDUCATION:** Ohio Univ, Athens OH, accounting degree, 1958; Bliss Coll, Columbus OH, senior accounting degree, 1961; attended Muskingum Tech, Zanesville OH, 1973-75; attended Ohio State, Columbus OH, 1976. **CAREER:** Simmons Co, Pittsburgh PA, office mgr, 1961-65; United Technologies, Zanesville OH, foreman, 1965-72; City of Zanesville OH, compliance officer, 1970-72; State of Ohio, Columbus OH, deputy dir, 1973-81; Watiker & Son Inc, Zanesville OH, pres, 1981-. **ORGANIZATIONS:** Mem, Greater Apostolic Church 1970-, NAACP 1979-. **HONORS/ACHIEVEMENTS:** Outstanding Co award, Small Business Assn, 1987; Top 50 Black Companies in USA, Black Enterprise, 1987; Top 100 Black Companies in USA, Black Enterprise, 1988; Outstanding Performance, City of Columbus, 1988; Outstanding Performance Award in Region V, SBA, 1989. **HOME ADDRESS:** 3290 Bowers Ln, Zanesville, OH 43701.

WATKINS, ARETHA LA ANNA
Print journalist. **PERSONAL:** Born Aug 23, 1930, Blairsville, PA; daughter of Clifford Fox, Sr. and Carrie Thompson Fox; married Angelo Watkins, Sr., Apr 14, 1967; children: Angelo Watkins, Jr.. **EDUCATION:** Wayne St U, 1950; WSU Coll of Lifelong Learning; Marygrove Coll. **CAREER:** Detroit Courier, staff writer 1963-64, asst to editor 1964-66; MI Chronical, staff wirter, columnist 1966; MI Chronicle Publ Co, asst managing editor 1968-1981; managing editor 1981-. **ORGANIZATIONS:** Sigma Delta Chi Professional Journ Soc adv bd mem, Prog Comm Assn 1968; NAACP. **HONORS/ACHIEVEMENTS:** Best Editorial Awd, Nat Newspapers Publ Assn 1972; Black Communicator Awd MI SCLC 1972; Dist Comm Serv Awd Lafayette Allen Sr 1974; Community Serv Awd Aopha Theta Chap GAmma Phi Delta 1981; Corp Serv Awd African Amer Museum of Detroit 1984; Sojourner Truth Awd Bus Woman of the Year Detroit Chap Natl Assoc of Negro Bus & Professional Women's Clubs Inc 1984; MI SCLC Martin Luther King Jr Awd for Journalists Achievement 1986. **BUSINESS ADDRESS:** Managing Editor, Michigan Chronicle, 479 Ledyard, Detroit, MI 48201.

WATKINS, BENJAMIN WILSTON
Physician. **PERSONAL:** Born Jan 14, 1922. **EDUCATION:** NY Coll of Pod Med, dPM 1962; SE U, MA 1977; CCNY, BS 1951. **CAREER:** New York City Dept of Hlth, dir of Podiatry Prog 1971-; MJ Lewi Coll of Pod, act chf adminstr 1973; NY City Dept Soc Svcs, dir of nurs home prog 1966-71; Am Pod Coun vice pres 1962; Nat Bd of Pod, diplomate 1962. **ORGANIZATIONS:** Am Pub Hlth Assn 1962; Am Assn of Hosp Pod 1964; Pd Clinic, Harlem Hosp 1964; mem NY City Pub Hlth; YNS Pub Hlth; Am Pub Hlth Assn Gov Coun; Am Pub Hlth Assn Accred & StandA Com; PSRO NY Med Soc/RmMp/CHP/HSA; bd mem Carver Fed Svgs & Ln Assn; chmn bd Marcus Garvey Nrsg Home; vchmn Innercity Brdcstg Corp; vchmn Amistad Dot Venture Captl Corp Nat Security Sem, US Def 1977; Civ Aide to Sec of Army for New York City 1972-. **HONORS/ACHIEVEMENTS:** Hon by New York City Mayor, NY St Gov & Manhattan Boro Pres. **BUSINESS ADDRESS:** 470 Lenox Ave, New York, NY 10037.

WATKINS, CHARLES B.
Educator. **PERSONAL:** Born Nov 20, 1942, Petersburg, VA; son of Charles B Watkins, Sr and Haseltine Thurston Clements; married Judith Leslie Griffin; children: Michael, Stephen. **EDUCATION:** Howard Univ, BSME 1964; Univ of New Mexico, MS 1966, PhD 1970. **CAREER:** Sandia Natl Labs, staff mem 1964-71; Howard Univ, asst prof 1971-73, dept chmn 1973-86; Natl Governor's Assoc, sr fellow 1984-85; City Coll of New York, dean sch of engrg. **ORGANIZATIONS:** Consultant US Navy 1975-82, Natl Science Foundation 1976-78, US Army 1979, Firestone Tire & Rubber Co 1981-86; natl chair dept heads comm 1986-87, mem bd on engrg educ 1986-88, vice chair engrg & public policy dir 1987-88 Amer Soc for Engrg Educ. **HONORS/ACHIEVEMENTS:** Elected Tau Beta Pi 1963, elected Sigma Xi 1978; Ralph R Teetor Awd Soc of Automotive Engrs 1980. **BUSINESS ADDRESS:** Dean, City College of New York, School of Engineering, Convent Ave at 140th St, New York, NY 10031.

WATKINS, CHARLES BOOKER
Retired educator. **PERSONAL:** Born Oct 28, 1913, Richmond, VA; son of Freeland Watkins and Nannie Watkins; married Haseltine Thurston (divorced); children: Dr Charles Jr, Richard, George. **EDUCATION:** VA State Coll, BS 1936; Univ of Pgh, MA 1947. **CAREER:** VA Pub Schls, teacher 1936; Pgh Public Schls, teacher 1947; Univ of Pgh Teacher Corps, coord 1969; Pgh Bd of Educ, coord 1971, 1973-79 (retired). **ORGANIZATIONS:** Mem VA State Coll track & football teams 1932-35; rec dir Summer Prog Pgh PA 1947; coach City Champ Track Teams 1949-56; deputy dist rep Omega Psi PhiFrat 1951-58; dist marshal Omega Psi Phi 1955, 1963; mem Pgh Sch Nutrition Prog Comm 1964-67; founder Youth Character Club 1964; exec comm Fed of Teachers 1967; mem More Effec Schls Comm 1967-68; mem Human Relations Comm 1967; mem Proj REAL Temple Univ 1969; mem Boy Scout Comm; mem Pgh Council of Men; mem F&AM Prince Hall Masons; mem NAACP; past basileus iota Phi Omega Psi Phi; mem ESEA Comm 1972-73; mem Natl Science Found. **HONORS/ACHIEVEMENTS:** HC Frick Scholarship PA State Univ 1963; Council of Men Awd for Outstanding Serv rendered the Comm of Pgh 1984; Omega Man of the Year Pittsburgh 1985. **MILITARY SERVICE:** USMC siapan 1944. **BUSINESS ADDRESS:** Bd of Educ, 635 Ridge Ave, Pittsburgh, PA 15212.

WATKINS, GLORIA ELIZABETH
Business executive. **PERSONAL:** Born Nov 28, 1950, Kankakee, IL; married Darryl Louis Watkins; children: Tia Monet, Valerie Viola. **EDUCATION:** Loyola Univ of Chicago, BA, 1977. **CAREER:** The First Natl Bank of Chicago, commerical loan rep, 1972-81; Drexel Natl Bank, vice pres, 1981-, sr vice pres, exec vice pres, 1989. **ORGANIZATIONS:** Mem, Natl Assn of Bank Women; bd of dir, Urban Bankers Forum, Kenwood-Oakland Com Org, Cosmopolitan Chamber of Commerce, 1982-, Mercy Hosp Women's Bd, ETA, Abraham Lincoln Center, Kuumba Workshop Theatre; pres, Chicago Chapter; vice pres, Illinois State Council, Natl Assn of Bank Women, 1989-90. **HONORS/ACHIEVEMENTS:** "Chicago's Up and Coming Black Business and Professional Women" Dollars & Sense Magazine, 1985; Ten Outstanding Young Citizens, Chicago Jr Assn of Commerce and Industry, 1986; "Amer Top 100 Black Business & Professional Women," Dollars & Sense Magazine, 1986. **BUSINESS ADDRESS:** Exec Vice Pres, Drexel Natl Bank, 3401 S. King Dr, Chicago, IL 60616.

WATKINS, HANNAH BOWMAN
Health educator. **PERSONAL:** Born Dec 23, 1924, Chicago, IL; widowed; children: Robert A, Melinda Geddes, Melanie E. **EDUCATION:** FiskUniv Nashville TN, BA 1947;Univ of Chgo, attended 1948-49; Jane Addams Sch of Soc Work, grad courses 1966-69; IL Dept of Pub Hlth st cert Audiometrist 1978. **CAREER:** Univ of Chicago, clinical rsch assoc 1947-60; IL Dept Public Aid, med soc worker 1960-73; Clinic in Altgeld Chicago, consultant 1975-; IL Dept of PublicHealth, publ health training cons/supr 1973-, grants mgmt consultant. **ORGANIZATIONS:** Exec com mem Chicago Hearing Conservation Com 1975-; sec alumni commn Fisk Univ 1976-; mem Natl Assoc Univ Women 1978-; vice pres midwest region Fisk Univ Genl Alumni Assoc 1979-81; mem Hlth Systems Agency Council City of Chicago Hlth Systems Agencies 1980-; exec council mem IL Pub Hlth Assn 1980-82;mem Lincoln Congregational United Ch of Christ; bd of trustees Hull House Assoc; bd of dirs Parkway Comm House; mem Black Caucus Public Health Workers,Amer Public Health Assoc; mem comm IL Public Health Assoc. **HONORS/ACHIEVEMENTS:** Special Commendation Hlth Coord Patricia Hunt Chief Family Health IDPH 1977-80; Special Commendation Walter J Leonard Pres Fisk Univ 1979; publications "Effect ACTH on Rheumatoid Arthritis" Journal Amer Chem Soc, "Lipoprotein & Phospholipoid in Animals" Journal Amer Chem Soc, "Early Identification of Pregnant Adolescents and Delivery of WIC Services," Amer Journal of Public Health 1985. **BUSINESS ADDRESS:** Grants Mgmt Consultant, IL Dept of Public Health, 100 W Randolph 6-652, Chicago, IL 60601.

WATKINS, HAROLD D., SR.
Fire department chief. **PERSONAL:** Born Feb 19, 1933, Detroit, MI; son of Jesse Watkins and Clara B McClenic; married Edna Jean Ridgeley, Dec 22, 1954; children: Harold D Jr, Kevin Duane, Keith Arnette. **EDUCATION:** Macomb Community Coll, Mt Clemens MI, AA, 1976. **CAREER:** City of Detroit MI, fire fighter 1955-76, sergeant 1976-78, lieutenant 1978-84, captain 1984-88, battalion chief 1988, chief of fire operations 1988-. **ORGANIZATIONS:** Mem, 47-4900 Spokane Block Club, 1959-; pres, Lay Ministers, CME Church, 1965-; bd of dir, Manhood Organization, 1986-; pres, Manhood Org, 1988-. **MILITARY SERVICE:** US Air Force, sgt, 1950-1954; honorable discharge. **BUSINESS ADDRESS:** Chief of Fire Operations, Detroit Fire Department, 250 West Larned, Third Floor, Detroit, MI 48226.

WATKINS, HERBERT NATHANIEL
Educator. **PERSONAL:** Born Aug 29, 1940, El Dorado, AR; married Beverly Ann; children: Donna, Herbert Jr. **EDUCATION:** KY State Univ, BS (High Distinction) 1965; Univ of WI, MBA 1967; Univ of WI, PhD 1970. **CAREER:** NC A&T State Univ, chmn acct 1970-71, dean, school of business, acting chair, prof acct 1971-72; Univ of Louisville, asst prof acct 1972-75; CA State Univ, assoc prof acct 1975-76; Howard Univ, asst dean graduate prog, assoc prof of acct 1976-77; Central Univ, dean coll of business admin, prof acct, acting chair business admin 1977-78; TX Southern Univ, dean school of business, prof acct 1980-83; Prairie View A&M Univ, exec vice pres admin 1983-. **ORGANIZATIONS:** Former mem bd of dir Continental Natl Bank of KY 1973-75; minority recruitment, equal oppt comm Amer Inst of CPA 1983-86; coop Ed Inst 1984-85; CPA KY, WI; mem TX Soc CPA, Beta Alpha Psi, Beta Gamma Sigma, Alpha Kappa Mu, Houston Natl Bus League, Amer Acctg Assoc, Rotary Club of SE Houston, Knightsof Peter Claver, Alpha Phi Alpha, Sigma Pi Phi. **HONORS/ACHIEVEMENTS:** All Around Sr Awd 1964-65; Outstanding Grad KSU Alumni Assoc Award 1965; Mayor of Frankfort Citizenship Awd 1964; The Wall St Jrnl Student Achievement Awd 1965; Listed in Who's Who Among Amer Coll & Univ Students 1964-65; Univ of WI Fellowship 1965-66, Vilas Fellowship 1967-69; US Govt Title IV Fellowship1969-70; Publ "Another Look at Advertising by Acctg Practitioners" The Natl Public Accountant 1976. **MILITARY SERVICE:** USAF with serv in Japan and the Philippine Islands; hon discharged.

WATKINS, IZEAR CARL
Government official. **PERSONAL:** Born Aug 19, 1926, Denver, CO; married Rose Anna Maxine Miles; children: Sheila A Delaney, Carol A Mitchell, Pamela I Elmore, Grace D Paulson, Lynda N. **EDUCATION:** Denver Oppor School of Business & Trades 1945-47. **CAREER:** US Govt, vice pres mobilization of econs resources 1968-74; DFL, state affirmative action commr 1974-77; Minneapolis City Govt, city chtr commr 1977-. **ORGANIZATIONS:** One of founders of Legal Rights Ctr Inc 1970; bd of dir Legal Rights Ctr 1970-; bd of dir U-Meet Sr Citizens 1972-80; bd of dir Minneapolis Assn forRetarded Children 1973-80; bd mem Natl Comm Devel; del Natl Conv Washington DC 1972; bd mem and pres bd of dirs Legal Rights Ctr Inc. **HONORS/ACHIEVEMENTS:** Commendation Awd & Plaque City of Minneapolis Elected Officials 1972. **BUSINESS ADDRESS:** City Charter Commr, Minneapolis City Govt, 301 City Hall, Minneapolis, MN 55415.

WATKINS, JAMES DARNELL
Dentist. **PERSONAL:** Born Aug 29, 1949, Reidsville, NC; son of James Granderson Watkins and Sadie Lamberth Watkins; married Hardenia; children: Daryl Granderson, Deveda Camille. **EDUCATION:** VA Polytechnic Inst StUniv Blacksburg VA, BS Biology 1967-71; Med Coll of VA Sch of Dentistry Richmond, DDS 1971-75. **CAREER:** Private Practice, dentist 1977-; USN Dental Corp Norfolk VA, 1975-77. **ORGANIZATIONS:** Mem Am Dental Asso & Acad of Gen Dentistry 1975-; sec Old Dominion Dental Soc 1978-; vice pres Century Investment Club 1979-; mem NAACP; mem Grad Chap ofGroove Phi Groove Soc Fellowship Inc; mem Beau Brummels Social & Civic Club; fellow Acad of Gen Dentistry; pres, bd dir Citizens Boys Club of Hampton VA; mem Penninsula Dental Soc, VA Dental Assoc. **HONORS/ACHIEVEMENTS:** President's Awd Old Dominion Dental Soc 1986; Dentist of the Year for Old Dominion Dental Society, 1987. **MILITARY SERVICE:** USN lt 1975-77. **BUSINESS ADDRESS:** Dentist, 1425 Kecoughtan Rd, Hampton, VA 23661.

WATKINS, JAY B.
Business executive. **PERSONAL:** Born Jul 22, 1948, Plaquemine, LA; married Muriel Thompson; children: Jillian C. **EDUCATION:** Brandeis University, BA 1971; Harvard University, MPA 1979. **CAREER:** Univ of MA at Boston, instructor in english 1972-74; freelance writer and filmmaker 1975-77; ICF, Inc, associate 1979-81; Executive Office of the Mayor, Washington, DC, special assistant to the director, office of planning 1981-83; ICF, Inc, sr associate 1984-. **ORGANIZATIONS:** Consultant Institute of Contemporary Art-Boston 1978. **HONORS/ACHIEVEMENTS:** Independent study & travel in Europe & the

Caribbean, Thomas J Watson Fellow, Thomas J Watson Foundation, Providence, RI 1971-72; screenwriter of the film A Minor Altercation 1976. **HOME ADDRESS:** 5339 Nevada Ave NW, Washington, DC 20015.

WATKINS, JERRY D.
Automobile dealer. **PERSONAL:** Born Mar 26, 1939, Guilford County, NC; son of Charles L Watkins and Rosa Gorrell Watkins; married Elizabeth Harris Watkins, Jun 20, 1960; children: Jerry D Watkins Jr, Carl B Watkins. **EDUCATION:** Univ of Detroit MI, degree in automotive mgmt, 1979. **CAREER:** Jerry Watkins Catillac-GMC Truck Inc, Winston-Salem NC, currently pres; Watkins Cadillac Oldsmobile Inc, currently pres; Tot's Haven Nursery Inc, currently vice pres. **ORGANIZATIONS:** Past mem, Bd of Dir, Chamber of Commerce; mem, Kiwanis Club. **BUSINESS ADDRESS:** President, Jerry Watkins Cadillac-GMC Truck Inc, 7726 North Point Blvd, Winston-Salem, NC 27106.

WATKINS, JOSEPH PHILIP
Journalist. **PERSONAL:** Born Aug 24, 1953, New York, NY; married Stephanie Taylor; children: Tiffany Ann, Courtney Andrea. **EDUCATION:** Univ of PA, BA History 1975; Princeton Theological Sem, MA Christian Educ 1979. **CAREER:** Talladega Coll, chaplain religion instructor 1978-79; IN Purdue Univ at Ft Wayne, campus minister 1979-8l; US Sen Dan Quayle, asst state dir 1981-84; US Congress, Republican nominee for 10th dist 1984; Merchants Natl Bank, commercial accts rep 1984; Saturday Evening Post, vice pres & dir of missions 1984-. **ORGANIZATIONS:** Bd of dir Big Brothers of Greater Indianapolis; bd of dir Arthritis Found of Indianapolis; bd of dir Poison Control Ctr of IN; Natl Assn for the Advancement of Colored People, bd of dir Salvation Army of Indianapolis; bd of dir Penrod Soc; bd of dir Children's Bureau; adv bd Training Inc; bd of dir Humane Soc; bd of dir Jameson Camp; life member NAACP. **HONORS/ACHIEVEMENTS:** Selected as one of the Outstanding Young Men of Amer 1983; selected as one of 50 Young Leaders of the Future by Ebony Magazine 1983; winner of the IN Jaycees Speak-Up Competition 1983; winner of the US Jaycees Speak-Up Competition 1983; selected as one of the 10 Outstanding Young Hoosiers by the IN Jaycees 1984. **BUSINESS ADDRESS:** Vice Pres & Dir of Missions, Saturday Evening Post, 1100 Waterway Blvd, Indianapolis, IN 46202.

WATKINS, JUANITA
Representative. **PERSONAL:** Born May 11, 1939, Chicago, IL; children: Karen D, Thaddeus C, Tammara L, Margie. **EDUCATION:** Great Lakes Med Inst, medical tech course 1965-67; Wayne State Univ, 1975. **CAREER:** Pontiac Osteopathic Hosp, med tech 1967-70; Ins Co of N Amer, underwriting asst 1970-73; Ford Motor Co, inventory spec 1973-79; MI House of Reps, state rep 1979-86. **ORGANIZATIONS:** Mem NAACP UAW-Local 600; mem NOW Gamma Phi Delta Sor; mem Natl Caucus Black State Legislators; treas MI Legislative Black Caucus 1983-86; vice pres Nat'l Org of Black Elected Legislative/Women; advisory bd Labor Studies Cntr Oakland Univ; chairwmn Labor Comm MI House of Reps. **HONORS/ACHIEVEMENTS:** Disting Legis Awd Univ of MI 1982; Pathfinders Awd Oakland Univ 1983; HAP/PAC Salute BCBSM/Employees MI 1984; Awd of Distinction Reg Minority Womens Empl Conf 1981-84; Univ of MI, Distinguished Legislator awd. **BUSINESS ADDRESS:** Representative Dist 16, MI House of Representatives, State Capitol, Lansing, MI 48909.

WATKINS, LENICE J.
Mayor, business executive. **PERSONAL:** Born Dec 17, 1933, Palestine, TX; married Ethel L Sims; children: Geraldine, Deborah, Ricky, Sabrina, Lenice. **EDUCATION:** Univ of Denver, BA 1960. **CAREER:** Town of Sunset, mayor; Sunset Grocery, co-owner; Jet Mag, copy ed 1963-73; Cleveland Call & Post, gen assignment rptr 1961-63; Afro Am Newspaper Wash DC, gen assignment rptr 1960-61. **ORGANIZATIONS:** Freelance writer fiction & nonfiction; manuscript, nonfiction, writing for The Black Press; novel "Where From Here". **BUSINESS ADDRESS:** Sunset Grocery, Hwy 77 at Gannt St, Marion, AR 72364.

WATKINS, LEVI
Educator. **PERSONAL:** Born Jan 15, 1911, Montgomery, KY; married Lillian Bernice Varnado. **EDUCATION:** TN St U, BS 1933; Northwestern U, MA 1940; AR Bapt Coll, LLD 1958; AL St U, LLD 1974. **CAREER:** Burt HS, asst prin 1935-40; Parsons Jr Coll, Douglass Schools, asst dean supv prin 1940-53; AL St Univ, admissions & vet officer & adminstr asst topres 1948-53. **ORGANIZATIONS:** Founder, pres Owen Coll 1953-59; pres AL StUniv 1959-; vice pres council of pres, AL Commn on Higher Edn; pres AL Assn Coll Adminstrs; st dir Am Assn St Colls & Univ; mem AL Educ Seminar; AL Postsecondary 1202 Commn; bd mem AL Adv Com Am Coll Testing Prog; Phi Delta Kappa; 33 deg Mason; bd mem AL Citizens for Transp; Consumer Credit Counseling Serv; sec Navys Adv Bd on Educ & Gng; YMCA Inner City; Childrens Ctr of Montgomery Inc; AL St Safety Coor Com; Alpha Kappa Mu; Kappa Delta Pi; Kappa Kappa Psi Band & Frat. **HONORS/ACHIEVEMENTS:** Mayors Keys, Memphis TN; Birmingham AL; Boss of Yr Tuskegee Chap Nat Sec Assn Internat.

WATKINS, LEVI, JR.
Educator, surgeon. **PERSONAL:** Born Jun 13, 1944, Montgomery, AL; son of Dr Levi Watkins. **EDUCATION:** Tennessee State Univ, BS, 1966; Vanderbilt Univ, School of Med, MD, 1970. **CAREER:** Cardiac Surgeon, Johns Hopkins Hospital, 1978-present. **ORGANIZATIONS:** NYAS; Soc of Thoracic Surgeons; Soc of Black Acad Surgeons; Assn for Thoracic Surgery; Amer Coll of Chest Physicians; SE Surgical Congress; North Amer Soc of Pacing & Electrophysiology; Assn of Acad Minority Physicians; Physicians for Human Rights; Baltimore City Med Soc; Soc of Univ Surgeons; Fellowship, Amer Coll of Surgeons; Assn for Acad Surgery; Hypertension Task Force, Health Systems Agency of Maryland; Bd of Dir, Amer Heart Assn of Maryland; Diplomate, Natl Bd of Med Examiners. **HONORS/ACHIEVEMENTS:** Highest Honors, Pres, Student Body, Student of the Year, Tennessee State Univ, 1965-66; Natl Vice Pres, Alpha Kappa Mu Honor Soc, 1965; Natl Med Fellowship Awardee, 1966-70; Alpha Omega Alpha; Doctor of Humane Letters, Sojourner-Douglass Coll, 1988, Meharry Med Coll, 1989. **BUSINESS ADDRESS:** Assoc Prof, Cardiac Surgery, Johns Hopkins Univ, 600 North Wolfe St, Baltimore, MD 21205.

WATKINS, LOTTIE HEYWOOD
Business executive. **PERSONAL:** Born in Atlanta, GA; widowed; children: Joyce Bacote, Judy Yvonne Barnett. **CAREER:** Alexander-Calloway Realty Co Atlanta, sec 1945-54; Mutual Fed S&L Assn, teller-clerk 1954-60; Lottie Watkins Enterprises, president 1960-. **ORGANIZATIONS:** Sec So Christian Leadership Conf 1967; vice chmn Fulton Co Dem Party 1968; Fulton Co Jury Commr 1972-; Gov's Comm on Voluntarism 1972; Fulton Co Bd of Registration & Elections 1973-; Citizens Exchange with Brazil 1973; participant White House Conf on Civil Rights; GA Residential Finance Auth 1974; chmnAmer Cancer Soc; chmn Comm Chest; mem exec comm bd dir NAACP; mem League of Women Voters, Atlanta Women's C of C; active mem of innumerable civic & prof organs. **HONORS/ACHIEVEMENTS:** Recipient of various leadership citations including citations from Pres John F Kennedy, Pres LB Johnson, vice pres Hubert Humphrey and many others; listed in many biographical publications; GA House of Reps 34th Dist; 10 Leading Ladies of Atlanta Channel 11 Comm Serv Awd. **BUSINESS ADDRESS:** President, Lottie Watkins Enterprises, 1065 Gordon St SW, Atlanta, GA 30310.

WATKINS, MARY FRANCES
Administrator. **PERSONAL:** Born Sep 09, 1925, Towson, MD; divorced; children: Martin, Betty Merrill, John, Ralph, 9 foster children. **EDUCATION:** Maorgan St U, 1955; Southampton Coll NY; StUniv of NY, 1967; StUniv of NY Stony Brook, MSW 1979. **CAREER:** Smith Haven Ministries, proj dir emerg food 1973-; EOC Suffolk Cty, dir emerg food & med prog 1970-73; Comm Act Agency Suffolk, youth & proj dir 1969; Econ Oppty Coun Suffolk, comm orgn spec. **ORGANIZATIONS:** Founder & adminstr Smithtown Comm Serv Sch 1964; dir Suffolk Cty Black Youth in Action, present; chprsn Suffolk Ho Servs Pers Com, present; bd memLong Island Sickle Cell Proj, present; vice pres Smithtown NAACP present; bd mem Nat Assn of Black Social Wrkrs, present. **HONORS/ACHIEVEMENTS:** Foster Mother of Yr, Foster Mother Assn NY 1967; Comm Serv Awd, Central Islip Comm Act 1968; Woman of Yr, Nat Coun of Negro Women 1970; Humanitarian Awd, Suffolk Cnty Human Rights Commn 1979; conducted Minority Women of 50 Wrksp, Minority Women Hlth Conf StUniv Stony Brook, 1979. **BUSINESS ADDRESS:** Program Dir, Urban League of Long Island, 535 Broad Hollow Rd, Melville, NY 11747.

WATKINS, MOSE
Director. **PERSONAL:** Born Jul 09, 1940, Eudora, AR; married Tommie Orlett White; children: Dwayne Andre, Nikole Michelle. **EDUCATION:** Weber State Coll, BS Soc Phys Ed 1958-70; Univ of UT Salt Lake City, MSW 1972, PhD Ed Admin 1973. **CAREER:** Union Pacific RR, cook 1956-60; Swifts Packing Co & ZP Smith Constr Co, gen laborer; Athletic Dept Weber State Coll Ogden UT, publ relations asst 1966-67; Calgary Stampeders Canadian Football League, defensive end & offensive tackle 1967; Natl Job Corps Ctr Dir Comm, comm mem; Grad School of Soc Work Univ of UT, clinical instr; Thiokol Corp Clearfield Job Corps Ctr Clearfield UT, ctr dir, dirof group life/supr residential living/couns 1967-. **ORGANIZATIONS:** Jr pres Ogden Br NAACP 1959; mem Natl Soc Workers Org; vice pres NAACP; mem Clearfield & Salt Lake City C of C, Kiwanis, New Zion Bapt Church, Masonic Temple. **HONORS/ACHIEVEMENTS:** Outstanding Honors as Lineman All Army Football Team 1964; Licensed Cert Soc Worker State of UT 1973; Outstanding Young Men of Amer 1977; Meritorious Serv Awd NAACP 1977; Man of the Year Clearfield Job Corps Ctr Student Govt 1979; Outstanding Serv Awd US DOL/ETA Reg 8 Job Corps 1979; Light Heavyweight & Heavyweight Championship AAU & Golden Gloves. **MILITARY SERVICE:** AUS pfc 1963-65. **BUSINESS ADDRESS:** Center Dir, Clearfield Job Corps Ctr, Management & Training Corp, PO Box 1388, Clearfield, UT 84016.

WATKINS, MOZELLE ELLIS
City official. **PERSONAL:** Born May 18, 1924, Crockett, TX; daughter of Leroy Ellis (deceased) and Sallie Elizabeth Fleeks Ellis (deceased); married Charles Philip Watkins (deceased); children: Phyllis Caselia Duff, Eunice Juaquina Cothran. **EDUCATION:** Hughes Bus Coll, diploma 1944-45; Extension Sch of Law, 1960; Famous Writers Sch Hartford, certificate 1970; Catholic Univ, certificate public speaking 1970; Georgetown Univ, St Law 1976-77; Montgomery Coll, spanish certificate 1978; Equal Employment Comm Federal, State, Local, human rights law 1976-. **CAREER:** Federal Government, statistical clerk & sec 1945-69; Anacostia Citizens & Merchants Assn, admin asst 1969-70; Montgomery Co Govt Human Relations Comm,investigator 1971-. **ORGANIZATIONS:** mem TASSL Block Club; mem Upper Northeast Family Day Comm;mem Citizens Adv Comm to the District of Columbia Bar; mem Chinese-Amer Lion Club; mem 19th St Baptist Church; comm ANC-5A Single Member District 14 1976-; mem Brookland Comm Corp 1978-, deaconess 1987; mem 12th St Neighborhood Corps 1979-; pres 19th St Baptist Church Jarvis Mem Club 1983-; bd of dirs christian ed 19th St Baptist Church; chairperson ANC 5A 1978,79,85; elected delegate to 1986 DC Democratic State Convention; mem Mayor Marion S Barry Jr Comm Adv Comm; vice chairperson, DC Advisory Neighborhood Commn 5A 1989; mem Ward V Unity in the Community Comm 1988. **HONORS/ACHIEVEMENTS:** Author "Two Zodiac Calendars" 1975 & 1977; author proposal entitled "Resolution for the Conservation of a Section of the Nation's Capital as a tribute to AfroAmericans" published in the DC Register; certificates of appreciation from Amer Red Cross, DC Cahpt Howard Univ, Moorland-Spingarn Rsch Ctr, Anacostia Citizens & Merchants Assn, Dept of Defense, Bureau of Supplies and Accounts, District of Columbia Council, mayor Marion S Barry Jr of the District of Columbia;DC Ward V Council mem William R Spaulding the Northeast News Publishers 1986; Outstanding Service & Dedication, Advisory Neighborhood Commn 5A 1989. **HOME ADDRESS:** 3225 Walnut Street, N E, Washington, DC 20018.

WATKINS, ROBERT CHARLES
Construction. **PERSONAL:** Born Apr 06, 1927, Detroit, MI; married Cleo. **EDUCATION:** Corning Free Acad, 1948; NY St, 1955. **CAREER:** Corning Glass Works; machine bldr rsrch & devel, 28 yrs. **ORGANIZATIONS:** Mem Finger Lakes St Prk & Rec Commn 1975-77; chmn Town of Corning Dem Com 1975-77; commn Steuben Co Dem Com 1974-77; exec Bd Stgeuben Co Dem Com 1975-77; chmn Steuben Co Manpower Planning Cncl 1975-77; dir NY St NAACP 1966-77; So Tier Legal Serv 1973-77; dir chtr mem Tier Empl Cncl 1970-77; life mem NAACP Fndr; Crystal City Social Club 1955-77; Corning Bi-racial Club 1967-69. **MILITARY SERVICE:** AUS corpl 1947-50. **BUSINESS ADDRESS:** Rsrch & Devel DV 1, Corning, NY 14830.

WATKINS, SYLVESTRE C., SR.
Business executive. **PERSONAL:** Born Oct 08, 1911, Chicago, IL; son of Charles and Ada; married Mabel Fleming; children: Adrienne M, Sylvestre C Jr (dec). **EDUCATION:** Northwestern Univ School of Business, attended. **CAREER:** Near South Post, editor, publisher 1959-60; Chicago Daily Defender, natl circ dir 1960-61; US Savings Bonds Div US Treas, dir 1961-68; Metro Washington, DC, dir, 1968-76; Negro/Black Heritage Magazine, editor, publisher 1961-82; Warner Cable TV, TV host, producer The Syl Watkins Show 1978-88; publisher/editor, The Syl Watkins' Drum, 1986-. **ORGANIZATIONS:** Pres, bd of

trustees Abraham Lincoln Ctr 1956-68; mem bd of trustees Joint Negro Appeal 1961-63. **HONORS/ACHIEVEMENTS:** Distinguished Serv Century of Negro Progress Exposition 1963; Mem of 150 IL Sesquicentennial Commn 1967; Freedom Eagle Awd, 2 Special Achievement Awds, Superior Performance Awd, Silver Platter Awd 1968-70, 1974, 1976; Appreciation Awd Warner Amex Cable Commn Inc 1980. **BUSINESS ADDRESS:** 5720 P G A Blvd, #513, Orlando, FL 32809.

WATKINS, TED
Corporation executive. **PERSONAL:** Born Sep 03, 1923, Meridian, MS; married Bernice Stollmach; children: Ted Jr, Tamlin, Timothy, Tom, Teryl, Lyssa. **EDUCATION:** Watts Labor Comm Action Com, Adminstr 1966-; UAW, intl rep 1966-. **CAREER:** Watts Labor Comm Actioon Com 1966-; UAW, intl rep 1966-. **ORGANIZATIONS:** Mem Mayors Bicentennial Com; Jr Achievement Exec Bd; vice pres Martin Luther King Gen Hosp Auth Commn; mem United Civil Rights Cong; Watts-willowbrook -Compton Improvement Assn; STEP; LA Citizens Adv Com; Watts Citizens Adv Com; Watts Station Com; Police Adv Council; adv com Upward Bound,Univ CA; Watts Comm Dev; LA County Delinquency & Crime Commn; Watts-willowbrook Dist Hosp Med Prog; mem Citizens Resource Com, Bd Edn; LA Urban Coalition; SE Coll Adv Com; Black Heritage Subcommittee. **HONORS/ACHIEVEMENTS:** Awards, Baha'i Human Rights 1970; City LA Human Relations Commn 1971; Urban League 1971; Council Comm Clubs 1973; County LA 1972; Assn Elem Sch Administrs 1968; DA County LA 1973; Interracial Council for Bus Opportunity 1971; Benedict Canyon Assn 1969; Cath Labor Inst 1968; Am Soc Pub Adminstrs 1972; Outstanding Com Serv Awd Watts NAACP 1977; Outstanding Com Serv Awd; Help Pub Serv Found 1978; Participation in Black Econ Devel Awd, Black Blusinessmens Assn of LA 1978; Recog & Apprec for Outstanding Contbns to Com, Oscar Joel Bryant Assn 1978; Outstanding Serv Awd, Training & Research Found Head Start & Pre/Sch 1979; Awd The Senate-cA Legislature 1980; Outstanding Contbns & Devotion, City of Compton 1980; Recog of Humanitarian Concepts, Black Caucus of CA Dem Party 1980; Awd, Assemblywoman Maxine Waters 1980; Cert of Spl Congressional Recog 1980; Honor Awd, Service Employees Joint Counc SEIU AFL-CIO 1980; Recog of Contbns WLCAC Exec Bd & Proj Dir 1980; Grateful Apprec Awd So CA CAP Council 1980; Awd as Founder of WLCAC & dedicated efforts, Mayor Tom Bradley of LA, 1980; Dedicated Serv Awd, Consolidated Realty & Bd 1980. **MILITARY SERVICE:** AUS 1942-44. **BUSINESS ADDRESS:** 11401 S Central Ave, Los Angeles, CA.

WATKINS, WALTER C., JR.
Corporate officer. **PERSONAL:** Born Aug 08, 1946, Nashville, TN; married Harriett Drake; children: Che, Celeste. **EDUCATION:** FiskUniv Nashville, BA 1968; Wayne StUniv Detroit, MBA 1977. **CAREER:** Nat Bank of Detroit, second vice pres 1974-, credit analyst 1972, branch mgr 1972. **ORGANIZATIONS:** Bd mem Black Family Devel Inc Rehab & Inst 1979-; participant, Leadership Detroit 1979-80; pres Urban Bankers Forum 1980. **HONORS/ACHIEVEMENTS:** Black Banker of Yr, Black Bankers Assn Detroit 1978. **BUSINESS ADDRESS:** 611 Woodward, Detroit, MI 48226.

WATKINS, WILLIAM, JR.
Business executive. **PERSONAL:** Born Aug 12, 1932, Jersey City, NJ; son of William Ree and Willie Ree; married Sylvia I Mulzac; children: Cheryl, Rene M, Linda M. **EDUCATION:** Pace Univ, BBA 1954; NY Univ, MBA 1962. **CAREER:** Consol Edison Co NY Inc, staff asst 1957-65; Volkswagen of Amer Inc, syst mgr 1965-71; Volkswagen NE Wilmington MA, exec 1971-72; New England Elect Sys Westborough MA, exec 1972-82; Narragansett Electric, vice pres 1982-86; New England Power Service Co 1986-; brd of dirs Rhode Island Hospital Trust Natl Bank 1987-; bd of dir Peerless Precision Corp 1982-. **ORGANIZATIONS:** Chmn RI Council on Econ Educ 1984-86; dir OIC Econ Devel Corp 1982-; chmn RI Urban Proj 1985. **HONORS/ACHIEVEMENTS:** Human Relations Awd Urban League of Bergen Cty 1963; listed in Who's Who in Fin & Indust in Amer 1975-; Urban League of RI Community Srv Awd 1986; John Hope Settlement House Award 1987. **MILITARY SERVICE:** AUS sp4 1955-57. **BUSINESS ADDRESS:** Vice President, New England Power Service Co, 25 Research Drive, Westboro, MA 01581.

WATKINS, WILLIE S., III
Business executive, educator. **PERSONAL:** Born Mar 24, 1941, Richmond, VA; married Dianne Nelson; children: Karen L, Willie S IV. **EDUCATION:** Howard U, BS 1964; Am U, Sci Cert Merit 1968; John Tyler Comm Coll, AAS (cum laude) 1971; Med Coll VA, Post-mortem Eye Enucleation 1973. **CAREER:** WS Watkins & Son Funeral Home, Richmond, VA, mgr 1972-; John Tyler Commun Coll;; instr path 1972; Proj Upward Bound, coord Sci Curr Dev 1970-72; Clark Coll, asst prof biol 1967-70; Howard U, instr biol 1964-67. **ORGANIZATIONS:** Vp Richmond Funeral Dirs Assn 1974; ex bd VA Morticians Assn 1974; mem Nat Funeral Dirs & Morticians Asnns; Am Assn Advancement Sci; mem Richmond City Strategy Tm 1972-; commun ldr Dev Approach Commun Change 1974-; pres Richmond Fun Dir Assn 1975-76; editor VA Morticians Assn Bulletin 1976-;pres Richmond Comm Sr Ctr 1977; mem N Richmond Br UMCA 1976-; mem & bd of adm 1974-77; exec sec UK Corp 1975-; mem Metrop Lbus League & Nat Bus League; mem Pi Sigma Eta Nat Morticians Frat; mem exec bd Richmond Comm Sr Ctr 1974-; mem Omega Psi Phi NSF asst 1964; fellow, 1965; Merit Seminar sesignate, Biol Pathways & Complete Cell 1966; study various Invertebrate Groups, 1967. **BUSINESS ADDRESS:** 2700 North Ave, Richmond, VA 23222.

WATLEY, MARGARET ANN
Educator. **PERSONAL:** Born Oct 19, 1925, Nashville; widowed. **EDUCATION:** TN A&I St U, BS 61947; Columbia U, MA 1965. **CAREER:** Jasper County GA, teacher 1950-53; HM Nailor, Cleveland, MS, 1954-57; Winchester Comm School, 1958. **ORGANIZATIONS:** Life mem NEA; life mem NANB & PW Inc; pres New Haven Club of Nat Assn Negro Business Prof Womens Clubs Inc 1971-72; New Haven Educ Assn 1972-76;mem CT Educ Assn, CT Del NEA Rep Assembly 1972; NE Dist Orgn Nat Assn of Negro Bus & Prof Womens Clubs Inc 1976; founded & organized The Elm City Sr Club & Elm City Youth Club 1976; founded & organized The Elm City Yng Adult Club 1977; reappointed organizer NE Dist Gov of NANBPW Inc 1979; pres Elm City Sr Club of New Haven & Vicinity 1977-79 & 79-81; Christian Tabernacle Bapt Ch; League of Women Voters, New Haven. **HONORS/ACHIEVEMENTS:** Outstanding Elem Tchrs Am 1972; Outstdng Participation Awd NANB & PW Clubs, Inc 1976, 77; "The Innavators" 1976, 77; Silver Tray 1976; Ldrshp Devel Awd CT Educ Assn; Nat Sojourner Truth Meritorius Serv Awd, Elm City Sr Club, 1978; Crystal & Silver Bud Vase for Work with Orgn Nat Assn Conv Pittsburg 1979. **BUSINESS ADDRESS:** 209 Dixwell Ave, New Haven, CT 06511.

WATLINGTON, JANET BERECIA
Appointed government official. **PERSONAL:** Born Dec 21, 1938, St Thomas, Virgin Islands of the United States;married Michael F MacLeod; children: Gregory, Kafi. **EDUCATION:** PaceUniv NY, 1957; Geo WashUniv Wash DC, 1977. **CAREER:** ACTION Wash DC, asst dir cong affairs 1979-; Hon Ron deLugo US House of Reps Wash DC, adminstrv asst 1968-78; Legislalture VI St Thomas, exec sec 1965-68. **ORGANIZATIONS:** Co-chmn Dem Nat Conv Rules Com 1976; appointee Dem Party Commn Presidential Nomination & Party Struc 1976; dem nominee congress VI 1978; vchprsn Dem Nat Com Eastern Region, 1972; steering com Dem Nat Com Black Caucus, 1974; exec com Dem Party Chtr Commn 1974; Congressional Black Caucus, 1974; chtr mem Sr Exec Serv Fed Govt 1979. **BUSINESS ADDRESS:** 806 Connecticut Ave NW, Washington, DC 20525.

WATLINGTON, MARIO A.
Educational administrator, elected official. **PERSONAL:** Born Nov 09, 1917, Charlotte Amalie, VI; married Lysia Audain; children: Roy, Audrey Wood. **EDUCATION:** Baruch School of Bus Admin, BBA 1960; Exec Mgmt Inst, Diploma 1962; NY Univ, MA 1966. **CAREER:** Coll of Virgin Islands, dir of admiss, registrar & admiss officer; Govt of Virgin Islands, dep commiss of ed 1962-67; chmn bd of ed, mem bd of trustees, director. **ORGANIZATIONS:** Pres St Thomas Music Assoc 1960's; prof Continuing Ed Div Coll of the VI 1963-84; charter mem 1967, pres 1967-, St Thomas Lions Club; chmn SCORE US Small Bus Admin 1984; trustee Coll of VI 1984-; dir St Thomas Racquet Club 1985-; mem nominating comm Natl School Bd Assoc 1986-87; St Thomas Raquet Club awd for promoting tennis in VI 1986. **HONORS/ACHIEVEMENTS:** Sesguicentennial Awd Plate NY Univ 1981; Testimonial Coll of VI 1982; Cited in Book of Outstanding VI; Project Introspection Dept of Ed St Thomas 1984-86. **MILITARY SERVICE:** VI home guard WW II.

WATSON, ANNE
Financial administrator. **PERSONAL:** Born Feb 19, 1945, Belzoni, MS; married John. **EDUCATION:** Western MI U, BA 1970;Univ of MI, attended 1976-78. **CAREER:** Univ of Detroit, financial aid dir; Wayne St Univ, financial aid counselor 1974-75; Shaw Coll Detroit, financial aid dir 1971-76; Western MI Univ, tutor counselor & asst dorm dir 1967-70; Dept of HEW, consult 1976, discussion leader 1977-; MI Financial Aid Assn, presentor/panelist 1980. **ORGANIZATIONS:** Mem Nat Assn for Fin Aid Adminstr 1975-80; chprsn Com for the Physically/Mentally Handicap 1978-79; bd of dir Black United Fund 1979-80. **HONORS/ACHIEVEMENTS:** Certificate (Proposal Writing), Moton Consortium Dept HEW 1974-75; Certificate (Professional Devel & Operational Procedures) Moton Consortium, Dept HEW 1975. **BUSINESS ADDRESS:** 4001 W McNichols, Detroit, MI 48221.

WATSON, BARBARA M.
Assistant secretary of state. **PERSONAL:** Born Nov 05, 1918, New York. **EDUCATION:** Barnard Coll, BA; NY Law Sch, LLB;Univ of MD, hon LLD; Mt St Mary Coll, hon D Humane Letters. **CAREER:** Hampton VA Inst, foreign student adv 1958-59; Bd Statutory Consolidation City NY, atty 1961-63; City of NY, asst corp counsel 1963-64; New York City Commn to United Nations, exec dir 1964-66; Bureau Security & Consular Affairs, Dept State, adminstr 1966; Consular Affairs, asst sec of state 1977-80. **ORGANIZATIONS:** US Amb to Malaysia 1980; mem Am Bar Assn; Wolf Trap Found for Performing Arts. **HONORS/ACHIEVEMENTS:** Hadassah Myrtle Wreath Achvmnt Awd 1968; Am Caribbean Schlrshp Fund Inc Awd 1969; Womens Div United Hias Serv Awd 1970; United Seamens Serv Awd 1970; Intl Aviation Club of Wash Awd of Merit 1971; Black Womens Dist Serv Awd, Nat Council Negro Women Inc 1971; Women of Yr Awd, Deliverance Evangelistic Ctr Inc 1971; Wash Urban League Cert Recognition 1971; Intl Consular Acad Fellow 1971; Rev Hirsch Masliansky Awd 1972; Am Immigration & Citizenship Conf Awd 1972; Jr Citizens Corps Inc Achievement Awd 1972; St Beauty Culturist Assn Inc Woman of Yr 1973; decoration Nat Orver Ivory Coast Republic 1973; Woman of Yr Awd Utility Club Inc of NY 1979. **BUSINESS ADDRESS:** Dept State, Washington, DC 20520.

WATSON, BERNARD C.
Educator. **PERSONAL:** Born Mar 04, 1928, Gary, IN; son of Homer Bismarck Watson and Fannie Mae Brown; married Lois Lathan; children: Barbra Diane, Bernard Charles. **EDUCATION:** IN Univ, BS 1951; Univ of IL, MEd 1955; Univ of Chicago, PhD 1967; additional study Harvard Univ 1968. **CAREER:** Gary Public Schools Gary, IN, teacher/counselor/prin 1955-65; Philadelphia Sch Dist, dept supt 1968-70; Temple Univ, chmn dept urban educ 1970-76, vice pres acadadm 1976-81; William Penn Foundation, pres & chief exec officer 1982-. **ORGANIZATIONS:** Exec Comm, Nat'l Urban Coalition, 1972-81;chrmn Natl Adv Council on Educ Professions Devel 1967-70 (appointed by Pres Lyndon B Johnson); mem Natl Counc on Educational Rsch 1980-82 (appointed by Pres Jimmy Carter); mem bd of Overseers Sch of Educ Harvard Univ 1981-; mem bd of trustees and exec com 1981 sr v chmn Natl Urban League 1983-; mem Fed Judicial Nominating Commn of PA 1981-; mem Philadelphia City Planning Commn; Mayor's Commn for the 21st Century; Fidelcor and Fidelity Bank; Comcast Inc; Comcast Cablevision of Phila, Inc; Vice Chrmn, Penn Convention Ctr Authority; Vice Chmn Penn Cncl on the Arts; Comm, William T Grant Found Comm on Work, Family & Citzenship; sec, bd of dirs, New Jersey Aquarium, Camden, NJ, 1989-; mem, bd of dirs, The Philadelphia Contributorship, 1989-. **HONORS/ACHIEVEMENTS:** Honorary Doctor of Humanities, Wilberforce Univ; Honorary Doctor of Laws degrees: Lincoln Univ, Florida Memorial Coll, Temple Univ, Medical Coll of Philadelphia; Honorary Doctor of Humane Letters degrees: Allen Univ, LaSalle Univ, 1987, Spring Garden Coll, 1988, Elizabethtown Coll, 1988, Beaver Coll, 1988, Harris-Stowe State Coll, 1989, Morris Brown Coll, 1989; author, In Spite of the System: The Individual & Educ Reform, Ballinger Publishing Co 1974; author, Plain Talk About Educ: Conversations with Myself, Natl Urban Coalition, 1987; author, Tomorrow's Teachers: Who Will They Be, What Will They Know?, published in The State of Black Amer, 1988, Natl Urban League, 1988; 12 monographs; chapters in 14 books; 100 career folios by Harcourt, Brace Jovanovich; 35 articles in professional journals; Dr Bernard C Watson Graduate Sem; Awd presented for best social science dissertation in Coll of Educ Bernard C Watson Awd for undergraduate student admitted through Russell Conwell Ctr who earns highest grade point average. **MILITARY SERVICE:** USAF 1st Lt 1951-54. **BUSINESS ADDRESS:** President/Chief Executive Ofcr, William Penn Foundation, 1630 Locust St, Philadelphia, PA 19103.

WATSON, BETTY COLLIER
Educator. **PERSONAL:** Born Aug 26, 1946, Thomasville, GA; married William Watson; children: Letoynia, Maxie, Mar-yoi, Lemoya, Zaittrarrio, Shartriya, Kirk, Keith. **EDUCATION:** Fisk Univ Nashville TN, BA History, English 1967; Cornell Univ Ithaca, MA Equivalent 1968; Howard Univ Washington DC, 1968-69; Amer Univ Washington DC, PhD Econ

1984. **CAREER:** Cost of Living Council, labor economist 1972-73; Morgan State Univ, instr history 1969-71; Howard Univ, lecturer 1971-73; Univ of DC, asst prof of econ 1973-80; Econ Impact Rsch & Info Staff Dept of Energy, Office of Minority, consult 1980-81; Sonoma State Univ, asst prof mgmt studies 1981-84; Howard Comm Coll, asst prof bus 1983-84; Trinity Coll, asst prof econ 1984-; College of Notre Dame Baltimore MD, assoc prof. **ORGANIZATIONS:** Instr history Morgan State Univ 1969-71; lecturer econ Howard Univ 1971-73; Affirm Action Comm 1975-76; The Grievance Comm 1975-76; The Faculty Senate 1979-80; Grants Comm, The Sonoma Enterprises Bd of Dir, Grad Screening Comm; faculty consult San Francisco State Univ 1981-82; econ/statistician Howard Univ 1982-84; principal investigator An Analysis of the Displacement Process in the District of Columbia; bd of dir Bldg Comm ARB 1980-; ed bd Univ Renaissance Jrnl 1982-. **HONORS/ACHIEVEMENTS:** Woodrow Wilson Fellow 1967-68; Publ "On Love & Death" 1977, "Keeping Washington Beautiful" 1978; Paper "Economic Status of Women in the US, 1983; Published, "Differential Economic Status of Black Men & Women, Perception Versus Reality", 1984, "Math Bus & Textbook Constraint" 1985. **HOME ADDRESS:** 6012 Jamina Downs, Columbia, MD 21045. **BUSINESS ADDRESS:** Associate Professor, College of Notre Dame, Dept of Economics, Baltimore, MD 21210.

WATSON, CAROLE M.
Chief executive officer. **PERSONAL:** Born Aug 03, 1944, New Orleans, LA; children: Dionne. **EDUCATION:** Western MI Univ, BS 1965; Wayne State Univ, MSW 1970. **CAREER:** Milwaukee Area Tech Coll, instr 1972-73; TN State Univ Dept of Social Welfare, instr, curriculum coord 1973-77; Univ of TN School of Social Work, asstprof 1977-79; WZTV Channel 17 Black Pulse, hostess 1981-; Nashville Urban League, exec dir 1979-. **ORGANIZATIONS:** Mem Delta Sigma Theta Nashville Alumnae 1963-; mem Acad of Certified Social Workers 1975-; adv coun Bd of Cert for Master Soc Workers 1980-81; dir TN Chap of Natl Assoc of Social Workers 1980; 1st vice pres natl council of execs Natl Urban League; consumer adv comm South Central Bell; bd of dirs Nashville Class of 1981 Alumni 1982-83; bd of dir TN Oppor Prog Legal Serv of Middle TN, NAACP, Bay Area Assoc of Black Social Workers 1986-87. **HONORS/ACHIEVEMENTS:** Outstanding Young Woman of Amer 1971,77,79; listed in Personalities of the South Bicentennial Ed 1975; Appreciation Awd Alpha Delta Mu Natl Soc Worker Hon Soc Iota Chap TN State Univ 1978; Citizen of the Year Riverside Seventh Day Adventist Church; Congressional Record Awd presented by Bill Booner 5th Congresional Dist State of TN 1985; Wall of Distinction Western MI Univ 1986. **BUSINESS ADDRESS:** Executive Dir, Nashville Urban League, 244 20th St Ste 211, Oakland, CA 94612.

WATSON, CLARENCE
Business executive. **PERSONAL:** Born May 12, 1916, Fernwood, MS; married Maxine; children: Delores Lemons, Clarence Jr. **EDUCATION:** Jackson St, BA 1939. **CAREER:** Cleveland Herald, sports editor 1942. **ORGANIZATIONS:** Pres Dry Cleaning 4 plants, grocery store, custom tailoring store 1946-. **HONORS/ACHIEVEMENTS:** Jackson St Football Hall of Fame 1976; mem NAACP; Urban League; Ludlow Comm Assn; pres 6 City Golf Club; ch supt, deacon, Friendship Bapt Ch. **MILITARY SERVICE:** USAF 1943-46. **BUSINESS ADDRESS:** 867 E 93rd, Cleveland, OH 44108.

WATSON, CLIFFORD D.
Educational administrator, editor. **PERSONAL:** Born Jan 30, 1946, Akron, OH; married Brenda Chapman; children: Angera, Amina. **EDUCATION:** Ashland Coll, BS 1964; Wayne St, MEd 1970, PhD 1973. **CAREER:** Detroit Bd of Educ, staff coordinator, present, dean of students 1979, multi-ethnic studies coordinator 1974; writer educ serv 1972; contrib editor, McGraw Hill Book Co, 1979. **ORGANIZATIONS:** Pres United Black Educ Assn 1978-; pres/commn Nat Alliance of Black Sch Educ 1979; Author Pride Educ Serv Inc 1972. **HONORS/ACHIEVEMENTS:** Urban League Comm Serv Awd, Urban League, 1975; contr ed for Sci Reading Series, Magraw Hill, 1979; article "Black Gifted", MI Chronicle 1979. **BUSINESS ADDRESS:** 5057 Woodward, Detroit, MI.

WATSON, CLYNIECE LOIS
Physician. **PERSONAL:** Born Jan 27, 1948, Chicago, IL; married Sloan Timothy Letman III; children: Sloan Timothy Letman IV. **EDUCATION:** LoyolaUniv Chicago, BS 1969; Meharry Med Coll, MD 1973;Univ IL, MPH 1977. **CAREER:** Cook Co Hosp Dept Pediatrics, resident 1973-75; Provident Hosp, assoc med dir 1977; Private Practice, pediatrician. **ORGANIZATIONS:** Mem Am Med Womens Assn; Am Pub Hlth Assn; Black Caucus Hlth Wrkrs; mem Am Coll Prvntv Med/AMA/IL St Med Soc/Chicago Med Soc/IL Pub Hlth Assn/Am AssnUniv Women/Nat Med Assn; bd of dir Komed Hlth Ctr; mem Phi Delta Kappa Hon Educ Frat Mem, Womens Flwsp Congregation Ch, Park Manor;bd Religions Edn, Congregational Ch, Park Manor; Meharry Alumni Assn;Univ IL Alumni Assn; Martin Luther King Jr Flwsp; mem Asso Physicians of Cook Co 1971-73; mem Alpha Kappa Alpha Sor Inc Lambda Alpha Omega Chapt. **HONORS/ACHIEVEMENTS:** Merit Awd, Womens Flwsp Congregational Ch, Park Manor; Outst Yng Citzn Chicago Jaycees 1980. **BUSINESS ADDRESS:** 1750 East 87th St, Chicago, IL 60617.

WATSON, CONSTANCE A.
Public relations consultant. **PERSONAL:** Born Aug 17, 1951, Nashville, TN; children: Shannon. **EDUCATION:** TN State Univ, MSSW 1978. **CAREER:** Dede Wallace Mental Health Ctr, psychiatric social worker 1973-82; Neuville Industries, dir ocean pacific div 1982-86; W/W & Associates Public Relations, president/founder 1985-. **ORGANIZATIONS:** Chairperson Natl Hook-Up of Black Women 1980-82; exec comm 1984-86, 2nd vice pres 1986-, Beverly Hills/Hollywood NAACP; bd dir Found for Educ 1984-. **HONORS/ACHIEVEMENTS:** Achievement Awd Golden West Magazine 1987; Public relations consultant for major Hollywood and Los Angeles celebrities and events, ie 19th NAACP Image Awdstelevised on NBC. **BUSINESS ADDRESS:** President, W/W & Associates, 1539 West 56th St, Los Angeles, CA 90062.

WATSON, D'JARIS H.
Administrator. **PERSONAL:** Born Nov 02, 1928, Houston, TX; married Judge James L Watson; children: Norman, Karen, Kris. **EDUCATION:** Talladega Coll, BA 1948; Atlanta Univ School of Social Work, MSW 1953; Univ of PA School of Soc Work, Postgrad. **CAREER:** Butler St YMCA, soc group worker 1949; Mayor JS Clark Jr Philadelphia, publ info spec 1952-53; Wharton Settlement House, girls group worker 1952-54; Nicetown Club for Boys & Girls, girls prog dir, asst dir 1954-56; New York City Anti-Proverty prog, prog dir, asst dir, 1964-67; Cit Comm for Children of New York City Inc, ocns, rsch assoc 1967-68; Mayor K Gibson NJ, cons; CUNY, spec asst to vchancellor for urban affairs 1968-70; Automation House, vp, bd of mediationfor comm disputes 1970-71; CUNY, dep to vchancellor for urban affairs, asst to dean for urban policy & progs 1971-. **ORGANIZATIONS:** Bd mem Northside Ctr for Child Devel/ adv comm Fordham Univ School of Soc Work; former mem Pres Comm on Equal Employment Oppty appt by JF Kennedy; vice pres NY Urban league; bd mem Cit Comm for Children, Amer Arbitration Assoc. **BUSINESS ADDRESS:** Deputy to Vice Chancellor, CityUniv of New York, 33 W 42 St, New York, NY 10036.

WATSON, DANIEL
Owner. **PERSONAL:** Born Apr 11, 1938, Hallettsville, TX; married Susan Smallwood; children: Pamela, Bradley, Stanley, Jodney, Narlan. **EDUCATION:** Univ of Wash, BS 1959, MS 1965. **CAREER:** Washington Natl Ins Co, agent 1966-68, mgr 1968-71, gen agent 1971-. **ORGANIZATIONS:** Article published Psychological Reports 1965; mem Seattle Planning of Redevel Council 1967-71; mem Natl Gen Agents & Mgrs Assn 1971-; mem Wash Natl Gen Mgts Assn 1971-; mem Chicago Assn of Life Underwriters 1979-. **HONORS/ACHIEVEMENTS:** Agency Builder Awd Wash Nat 1970-75, 1977; Top 10 Agencies Wash Nat 1976-78. **BUSINESS ADDRESS:** Agent, Washington Natl Ins Co, 2603 W 22nd St Ste 18, Oak Brook, IL 60521.

WATSON, DENNIS RAHIIM
Lecturer, author, entertainer. **PERSONAL:** Born May 14, 1953, Hamilton, Bermuda;son of Eula Watson-Stewart. **EDUCATION:** Fordham Univ Bronx NY, 1974-76; Pace Univ, 1976-78; New York Univ, 1980-. **CAREER:** Theatre of Everyday Life, Exec Dir 1980-83; New York City Council, Exec Asst 1983-84; NBYLC, Exec Dir 1984-. **ORGANIZATIONS:** UNCF, 1980-86; New York Urban League, 1980-86; volunteer Bayview Correctional Facility for Women NY 1980-86; Natl Alliance Black School Educators 1984-86; Council Concerned Black Execs 1980-86; NAACP, 1984-86; Black Leadership Roundtable 1984-86. **HONORS/ACHIEVEMENTS:** Outstanding Young Man of Amer 1982, 86; Sigma Gamma Rho Inc, Performing Arts Award 1984; Natl Black Leadership Roundtable Awd 1984; US Dept of Justice Drug Enforcement Admin Volunteer Awd 1984; Mayors Ethnic New Yorker Awd 1985; Presidential White House Citation 1985; Private Sector Initiative Awd 1986; Bayview Correctional Facility for Women Male Performer of the Year 1986; Americas Best & Brightest Young Business & Professional Man, 1987; OIC Appreciation Award, 1988; Leadership Appreciation Award, UCLA, 1989; The Black Women Task Force Award, 1989. **BUSINESS ADDRESS:** Executive Dir, Natl Black Youth Leadership Council, 250 W 54th St, Suite 800, New York, NY 10019.

WATSON, DIANE EDITH
Government official, educational adminis. **PERSONAL:** Born Nov 12, 1933, Los Angeles, CA. **EDUCATION:** Los Angeles City Coll, AA; Univ of CA Los Angeles, BA 1956; CA State Los Angeles, MS 1967; CA State Sch of Psychology, PhD 1976. **CAREER:** LAUSD, teacher 1956-60, asst prin & teacher 1963-68; AUS Okinawa & France, teacher 1960-63; Linguistic Approach to Reading, teacher 1967-68; LAUSD Child Welfare & Attendance, asst supr 1968-69; Dept of Guidance LAUSD, school psychologist 1969-70; Cal State LA Dept of Guidance, assoc prof 1969-70; UCLA Secondary Schools Allied Health Proj, dep dir 1969-71; Health Occupation LAUSD, specialist 1971-73; LAUSD, school psychologist 1973-75; Bd of Educ, mem 1975-; State of CA, senator 1978-. **ORGANIZATIONS:** Mem CA Elected Women's Assn for Educ & Rsch; Natl Adv Panel mem UCLA Ctr for Study of Evaluation; bd of trustees Blue Shield; mem Med Policy Comm; author & adv com mem McGraw Hill/Gregg Div; consult CA Commn on the Status of Women; participant Career Orientation Manual; mem Los Angeles City Coll Pres's Adv Council; mem Natl Sch Bds Assn; mem CA Sch Bds Assn; mem CA Assn of Sch Psychologists & Psychometrists; mem LA Elem Counseling & GuidanceAssn; mem United Teachers of LA; mem CA Tchrs Assn; Hon Life mem PTA; mem exec bd Council of Great Cities Schs; bd mem Urban League; bd mem Stevens House; mem Friends of Golden State Minority Found; mem Natl Black Womens Polit Caucus; mem Council of Black Admins; mem CA Dem Central Com Educ Comm; mem NAACP; mem Media Women Inc; mem Alpha Kappa Alpha Natl Sor. **HONORS/ACHIEVEMENTS:** 1980 CA State Univ of LA Alumnus of the Yr Awd; 1980 LA Comm Coll Alumnus of the Yr Awd; 1981 Outstanding Rep Awd from the Sacramento Assn of Black Attorneys; 1982 UCLA Alumnus of the Yr Awd; 1982 Senator of the Yr Awd from the CA Trial Lawyers Assn; 1983 Comm Coll Senator of the Yr Awd; CA State Psychological Assn Humanitarian Awd; Bank of Amer Awd; Outstanding Comm Serv Awd YWCA; Mary Ch Terrell Awd; listed in Who's Who in Black Amer, Who'sWho in Amer Politics, Personalities of America, Who's Who of Amer Women, Dictionary of Intl Biography; published numerous books on Health Occupations. **BUSINESS ADDRESS:** Senator, State of CA, 4401 Crenshaw, Los Angeles, CA 90043.

WATSON, EUGENIA B. (NEE BASKERVILLE)
Retired educator. **PERSONAL:** Born Oct 01, 1919, Bridgeport, CT; married J Mervyn; children: James Jr, Donald, Charles. **EDUCATION:** A&T Coll, BS 1941; Bridgewater St Coll; MEd 1964. **CAREER:** War Dept, Washington, secretary 1942; Army Ordinance Dept, Detroit, sec 1942-43; stat clk, homemaker, grad student to 1963; Brockton Sch Dept, Brockton, 1963-68; Bridgewater St Coll, asst prof educ 1968; Brockton Business Coll, 1964-66; student underUniv CT, traveled W Africa 1970; student under Howard Univ Washignton, DC, East Africa 1971; student under NAACP, traveled W Africa 1974. **ORGANIZATIONS:** Lecturer African History & Culture; mem Natl Teachers Assn, MA Teachers Assn, Urban League of Eastern MA, Brockton Mayors Adv Comm for Cable TV; life mem NAACP; 2nd vice pres local br NAACP; black history instr Summer School Inst; mem Lincoln Congregational Church, Amer Mothers Assn 1969, MA State Merit Mother1969, Natl Black All Grad Level Educ, Educators to Africa & African Amer Inst, NY Delta Kappa Gamma Intl Hon Soc, Women Educators, Alpha Kappa Chap Alpha Upsilon St Orgn, Professional Womens Club Boston, Natl Jack & Jill Amer Inc; bd trustees Brockton Library System 1971-; bd dir Brockton Vstg Nurse Assn 1972-75; pres 1977-79, membership chmn 1987-Links Inc Middlesex County Chapt; exec bd Parliamentarian Link Chap 1980-; adv bd Brockton Art Museum 1980-; professor emeritus Bridgewater State Coll 1985; vstg lecturer Bridgewater State Coll; supv of student teachers Early Childhood and Elementary 1985-. **HONORS/ACHIEVEMENTS:** Distinguished Serv Awd MA Teachers Assoc 1985; Outstanding Serv Awd Bridgewater State Coll Alumni Assoc 1985; Awd of Recognition Brockton Chap NAACP 1985.

WATSON, FRED D.
Contractor. **PERSONAL:** Born Jul 03, 1919, Loris, SC; married Ilean; children: Martin. **EDUCATION:** Small Engine Repair 1980. **CAREER:** Paint Store, owner, contractor.

ORGANIZATIONS: Council mem 16 yrs; deacon of church; mason for 20 yrs. **HONORS/ACHIEVEMENTS:** Cert of Achievement; Outstanding Work in Loris Community. **MILITARY SERVICE:** Staff sgt 4 1/2 yrs; Good Conduct Medal. **BUSINESS ADDRESS:** Contractor, 3824 Church St, Loris, SC 29569.

WATSON, GEORGETTE
President/co-founder. **PERSONAL:** Born Dec 09, 1943, Philadelphia, PA. **EDUCATION:** Univ of Massachusetts, Boston, Legal degree, 1979, BA, 1980; Antioch Univ, M Educ, 1981. **CAREER:** Massachusetts Commn Against Discrimination, investigator; Roxbury Multi-Ser Anti-Crime, assoc mem, 1984-; FIRST Inc, assoc mem, 1985-; Parent's Discussion Support, founder, 1987-; Mother's Against Drugs, co-founder, 1987-; Drop A Dime Intelligence Data Inc, pres, co-founder, 1983-; Dorchester Comm News, writer. **ORGANIZATIONS:** Mem, NAACP, 1987-; assoc mem, United Front Against Crime Area B, 1987-; bd mem, Boston Gr Legal Comm Liaison Program; mediator Boston Urban Court Program. **HONORS/ACHIEVEMENTS:** Massachusetts Assn of Afro-Amer Police Inc Award, 1984; Shamnim Soc of Massachusetts In Appreciation to Georgette Watson, 1985; Comm Serv Award Boston Branch of NAACP, 1985; Martin Luther King Award Union Methodist Church, 1985; Disting Serv Award Eastern Region of Alpha Phi Alpha Fraternity, Inc, 1986; A Woman Meeting the Challenges of Time Award Boston Chapter Girlfriends Inc, 1986; Tribute to Women Award Cambridge YWCA, 1986; Citizen of the Year Award, Kiwanis Club of Roxbury, 1986; Comm Serv Award Action for Boston Comm Devel, 1986; 100 Heroes Newsweek, 1986; 1987 Black Outstanding Women, Essence Magazine, 1987; Sojourner Truth, Natl Assn of Negro Business & Professional Women's Club, 1989; President's Citation Volunteer Program, 1989. **BUSINESS ADDRESS:** President/Co-founder, Drop-A-Dime Intelligence Data, PO Box 644, Dorchester, MA 02125.

WATSON, HERMAN DOC
Security specialist. **PERSONAL:** Born Nov 10, 1931, Jersey City, NJ; married Shirley Moss, Apr 30, 1955; children: Phillip, Alan, Tracey, Elliott. **EDUCATION:** Hofstra Univ, Criminal Justice course 1974; Georgetown Univ, Criminal Justice course 1977. **CAREER:** US Customs Svcs, criminal investigator 1952-82; Jersey City Bd of Educ, security guard 1982-. **ORGANIZATIONS:** Pres Jersey City Vikings Inc 1982-; vice chief antler Passexalted Ruler Council #17 IBPOE of W; scholarship and archives comm Most Worshipful Oriental Grand-Lodge AF&AM Masons; co-chairperson Hudson County United Negro Coll Fund Telethon. **HONORS/ACHIEVEMENTS:** Outstanding Serv Awd Sentinel Soc Inc 1978; Certificate of Appreciation Concern Comm Women Inc 1981; Comm Achievement Awd Martin Luther King Jr Assoc1987; Andrew Young Black Male Achievement Awd Tau Gamma Delta Sor Inc Lambda Omega Chap 1987. **MILITARY SERVICE:** NJNG sfc 10 yrs. **HOME ADDRESS:** 232 Union St, Jersey City, NJ 07304.

WATSON, J. WARREN
Judge. **PERSONAL:** Born Feb 20, 1923, Pittsburgh, PA; son of James Watson and Eula Watson; married Carole A Whedbee; children: James Guy, Meredith Gay Young, Wrenna Leigh, Robert Craig, Sheila Tyler, Kevin McDowell. **EDUCATION:** Duquesne Univ, BA Political Sci, Econ 1949, LLB 1953. **CAREER:** Private practice, atty 1960-66; City of Pittsburgh, city solicitor 1962-66; Commonwealth of PA, judge 1966-. **ORGANIZATIONS:** Bd mem Judicial Inquiry & Review Bd 1981-85; chmn Media Rel Comm Bd of Judges 1984; bd mem Estate Planning Comm State Trial Judges Conf 1984; pres council Carlow Coll; bd of dir Comm Action Pittsburgh; trustee Comm Serv of PA. **HONORS/ACHIEVEMENTS:** Man of the Year Disabled Amer Veterans 1969; Hon Mem Chiefs of Police; Certificate of Merit Natl Assoc of Negro Business Professional Civic & Cultural & Political Endeavor 1972. **MILITARY SERVICE:** USN 3 yrs. **HOME ADDRESS:** 4305 Dakota St, Pittsburgh, PA 15213.

WATSON, JAMES L.
Judge. **PERSONAL:** Born May 21, 1922, New York, NY; son of James S. Watson and Violet M. Lopez; married D'Jaris Hinton; children: Karen, Kris. **EDUCATION:** NY Univ, BA 1947; Brooklyn Law School, JDS 1951. **CAREER:** 21st Senate Dist NY State Senate, senator 1954-63; City of NY, judge civil ct 1963-66. **ORGANIZATIONS:** Bd of dir 100 Black men. **MILITARY SERVICE:** AUS 92nd Inf Div Comat Inf 1942-45; Purple Heart. **BUSINESS ADDRESS:** Judge, Court of Intl Trade, 1 Federal Plaza, New York, NY 10007.

WATSON, JOANN NICHOLS
Civil rights executive. **PERSONAL:** Born Apr 19, 1951, Detroit, MI; daughter of Jefferson Nichols Sr and Lestine Kent Nichols; married Fred B Watson, Aug 08, 1970; children: Damon Gerard, Celeste Nicole, Stephen Bernard, Maya Kristi. **EDUCATION:** Univ of Mich, Ann Arbor MI, BA 1972; attended Mich State Univ, E Lansing MI, 1975-76; attended New York Univ Inst for Educational Leadership's Educational Policy Fellowship Program, 1987-88. **CAREER:** Community Parents Child-Care Center, Benton Harbor MI, exec dir, 1973-75; Lake Mich Coll, Benton Harbor MI, instructor in racism & sexism, 1975-76; Coalition for Peaceful Integration, Detroit MI, editor & social worker, 1976-77; Focus Hope, Detroit MI, resource coordinator, 1978; YWCA of Metropolitan Detroit, MI, branch exec dir, 1979-87; YWCA of the USA, New York NY, asst exec dir, 1987-. **ORGANIZATIONS:** Mem, Natl Council of Negro Women 1979-, MI Women's Hall of Fame Review Panel 1982-, Affirmative Action Top 10 1987, Racial Justice Working Group of Natl Council of Churches 1987-, Assn of Black Women in Higher Educ 1987-, Black Child Devel Inst 1987-; vice pres, Mich NAACP 1982-87, City of Detroit Human Rights Commission 1984-87; exec board mem, Natl Project Equality of EEO 1988-; pres, New York Alumni of NYU Inst for Educ Leadership 1988-, Natl Interreligious Civil Rights Commission 1988-. **HONORS/ACHIEVEMENTS:** NAACP Thalheimer Awards, Newsletter Editor, Mich Mobilizer, 1978-88; NAACP Thalheimer Award, Newspaper Editor, Detroit Reporter, 1986; State of Mich Governor & Legislator Proclamation, 1987; City of Detroit "Spirit of Detroit" Award, 1987; Life Achievement Award, Womens Equality Day, City of Detroit, 1987; Hall of Fame Award, YWCA of Detroit, 1987-88; organizer & co-sponsor, Women in Civil Rights Movement Conference, 1988; organizer & co-sponsor, Martin Luther King 1st Annual Youth Conference, 1988; vice chair, 25th Commemorative March in Washington, 1988; listed in Dollars & Sense Magazine's Salute to 100 Outstanding African-Amer Business Women, 1989. **BUSINESS ADDRESS:** Assistant Executive Director, Office of Racial Justice, YWCA of the USA, 726 Broadway, 5th Floor, New York, NY 10003.

WATSON, JOHNNY (JOHNNY GUITAR WATSON)
Musician. **PERSONAL:** Born 1935, Houston, TX. **ORGANIZATIONS:** Rec Gangster of Love; Lonely, Lonely Nights; Motorhead Baby; Lonely Nights; Space Guitar, 1951; The Blues Soul of Johnny Guitar Watson; Misty; I Cry For You; Reconsider; Listen; I Don't Want To Be Alone, Stranger; I Don't Want To Be Alone, Ranger; Ain't That A Bitch; Since I Met You Baby; I Want To Ta Ta You Baby; Superman Lover; I Need It.

WATSON, JOSEPH W.
Educator. **PERSONAL:** Born Apr 16, 1940, New York, NY; married Mary Slater; children: Ruth, Jerome, Jennifer, Elizabeth. **EDUCATION:** City Coll of NY, BS 1961; UCLA, PhD 1966, postdoctoral 1966. **CAREER:** UCSD, asst prof 1970-; Third Coll UCSD, provost 1970 UCSD, asst prof 1966. **ORGANIZATIONS:** Mem Am Chem Soc; Nat Orgn for Professional & Advancement of Black Chems & Chem Engrs; CA Black Coll Faculty & Staff Assn Inc. **HONORS/ACHIEVEMENTS:** Anniversary Medal, City Coll of NY 1973; Outst Young Man, San Diego 1975. **BUSINESS ADDRESS:** D-009, U of California San Diego, La Jolla, CA 92093.

WATSON, JUANITA
Councilwoman. **PERSONAL:** Born Apr 26, 1923, Bessemer, AL; married Joe. **EDUCATION:** Miles Coll. **CAREER:** Brownville; councilwoman 1972. **ORGANIZATIONS:** Mem Civic League of Brownville; Bessemer Voter League; comm mem Dem Exec Com Jefferson Co; vice pres Les Amies; vice pres Matrons, Sunday Sch Tchr & mem of Sr Choir New Bethel Bapt Ch.

WATSON, LEONARD WAYNE
Business executive. **PERSONAL:** Born May 25, 1923, Parkersburg, WV; married Julia Irene Lawson; children: Sharon, Leonard, Leon. **EDUCATION:** St Barber Coll, Grad 1947. **CAREER:** Your Fathers Mustache Hair Styling Cntr, vice pres 1972-; W & W Contracting, partner 1976-78; Patricia Gray Realty, real estate salesman 1975-77; Watsons Hair Styling Serv, owner 1946-72. **ORGANIZATIONS:** Mem Journeyman Barbers & Beauticians 1947-79; chmn WV St Bd Barbers & Buticians 1956-79; examiner Nat St Barber Bd 1960-79; mem Am Letion Post #104 1950-80; mem NAACP 1956-80; adv Small Bus Adminstrn 1976-78; mem Zion Bapt Ch Parkersburg WV. **MILITARY SERVICE:** USN mm 2/c 1944-46. **BUSINESS ADDRESS:** Your Fathers Mustache, Family Hair Styling Center, Monroeville, PA 15146.

WATSON, LEONIDAS
Educator. **PERSONAL:** Born Sep 12, 1910, Fodice, TX; married Lelia Landry. **EDUCATION:** Prairie View U, bS 1936, MS 1952;Univ of TX, grad study; Ok St U. **CAREER:** San Antonio Union Jr Coll Dist, dean Evening Div; St Philips Coll, instr 1954; Ext Serv Grime Co, TX, 1943-54; Houston Co, instr 1936-43; independent real estate broker. **ORGANIZATIONS:** Charter mem Eastside Optimist Club; Basileus, Psi Alpha Chap Omega Psi Phi; v chmn trustee bd, St Paul Meth Ch; Charter mem bd Dir Comm Housing Assn; Century Mem UMCA; mem Epsilon Pi Tau Internat; mem City Pub Serv Bd Contracts Gas Distbr, San Antonio 1974; Phi Delta Kappa 1974; mem Jr Coll Tchrs Assn; mem Jr Coll Adminstrs. **HONORS/ACHIEVEMENTS:** Recipient Spl Citation from TX Leg for Contrib to Educ 1973; Comm Awd for Contrib to Educ 1957; listed Whos Who in TX 1968; Citastion KUKA Radio 1974; Citizen for Day WOAI Radio 1974. **BUSINESS ADDRESS:** 2111 Nevada St, San Antonio, TX 78203.

WATSON, MILDRED L.
Attorney. **PERSONAL:** Born May 25, 1923, Kansas City, MO; daughter of Stewart B Watson (deceased) and Arnicholas North Watson (deceased). **EDUCATION:** Lincoln Univ MO, BS 1942; Univ Chicago, MA 1954; Univ MO Kansas City, JD 1974. **CAREER:** USN Dept Washington, mathematician 1943-45; Chicago Welfare Dept & Amer Red Cross Chicago, social worker 1946-52; Bureau Family Serv Chicago, child welfare supvr 1953-57; Univ KS Med Center, chief social worker 1957-62; Univ KS, assoc prof 1963-76; North Colbert Fields Law Firm, assoc 1976-81; North Watson & Bryant Law Firm, 1981-84; Jackson Co Circuit Court, comm juvenile div 1984-. **ORGANIZATIONS:** MO Bar Assn; mem Jackson Co Bar Assn; mem Kansas City Bar Assn; life mem NAACP; past pres Beta Omega Chapter Alpha Kappa Alpha; mem Twin Citians Club of Greater Kansas City. **HONORS/ACHIEVEMENTS:** Community Serv, Natl Assn, Business & Professional Women, 1984; key woman, Urban League Guild, 1985; Educ & Social Serv, Essence Magazine, 1985; public serv, Univ of MO, Kansas City Law Found, 1989. **BUSINESS ADDRESS:** Commissioner, Juvenile Div, 16th Circuit Ct, Kansas City, Jackson County, MO, 625 E 26th St, Kansas City, MO 64108.

WATSON, MILTON H.
Business executive. **PERSONAL:** Born Mar 12, 1927, Detroit, MI; married Mary Kathryn; children: Milton P, Kathryn M. **EDUCATION:** Univ of MI, MSW 1962; Wayne State Univ, BA 1949. **CAREER:** MI Health Maintenance Org, vice pres/admin; Health Council Inc, exec dir; Millar Agency Equitable Life Assurance Soc, asst agency mgr; State of MI, suprv childrens div dept of soc svc; Harvard Univ JF Kennedy School of Govt, lecturer 1971; Univ of MI School of Publ Health, lecturer 1971; CottillionClub, fin sec 1971-84. **ORGANIZATIONS:** Mem Amer Publ Health Assoc, Natl Assoc of Social Workers. **MILITARY SERVICE:** USMC. **BUSINESS ADDRESS:** Financial Secretary, 7650 Second Ave, 2200 Walker Cisler Bldg, Detroit, MI 48202.

WATSON, NORMA (NEE MIMS)
Attorney. **PERSONAL:** Born Apr 30, 1939, Houston, TX; married Robert Harvey. **EDUCATION:** TX So U, BS 1967; Thurgood Marshall Sch Law, JD 1971. **CAREER:** Law Office of Norma Mims Watson, owner 1985; Thurgood Marshall School of Law TS Univ, prof of law 1972-76; Gulf Coast Legal Found, staff atty 1972; Act Prog VISTA, atty 1971-72. **ORGANIZATIONS:** St Bar of TX; US Dist Ct; So Dist TX; US Ct of Appeals; 5th Circuit Nat Bar Assn; Am Bar Assn; Houston Bar Assn; Houston Lwyrs Assn; Nat Assn of Women Lwyrs; Phi Alpha Delta; TX Assn of Coll Tchrs; Black Women Lwyrs Assn; Hiram Clarke Civic Club; Grant Cncl on Legal Ed for Professional Responsibility 1974; Am Women in Law 1973. **HONORS/ACHIEVEMENTS:** Serv Award ABA Std Div 1970-71; Am Jurisprudence Awrd Legal Ethics 1971. **BUSINESS ADDRESS:** 609 Fannin, Ste 104, Houston, TX 77002.

WATSON, ODEST JEFFERSON, SR.
Educator, researcher, sociologist. **PERSONAL:** Born Sep 27, 1924, Milledgeville, GA; divorced; children: Odest Jr, Thelma, Aurora. **EDUCATION:** Savannah St Coll, BS; Wayne St U, BS 1962, MS 1964, EdD 1971; N TX State Univ, Cert in Gerontology 1981. **CAREER:** Bethune-Cookman Coll, chmn soc sci; Detroit Bd of Ed, consult Wayne Co Comm Coll, instr. **ORGANIZATIONS:** Mem Omega Psi Phi Frat 1947; Pigskin & Peepers Ftbl Grp 1957; Continentals Inc 1972; adv bd Comm Dev; bd mem, tst Rose Marie Bryon Childrens' Ctr. **HONORS/ACHIEVEMENTS:** Omega Psi Phi Award Omicrop-Epsilon 1977; Outstndng Edcr of Am 1974-75; Apprct of Srv to FL 1970-72. **MILITARY SERVICE:** AUS sgt 1945-46. **BUSINESS ADDRESS:** Division Chairman, Bethune Cookman College, 640 2nd Ave, Daytona Beach, FL 32014.

WATSON, ROBERT C.
Educator. **PERSONAL:** Born Mar 02, 1947, Hazelhurst, MS; married Aisya JK; children: Tarik Emilio. **EDUCATION:** Tougaloo Coll, BS 1965; Washington Univ, MA 1973. **CAREER:** Anderson Bank Nichols & Levanthal MS, rsch asst 1969; Manpower Inst St Louis, consult 1974; Lever Bros Co, quality control tech; Vaughn Cultural Ctr/Urban League of Metropolitan St Louis, director. **ORGANIZATIONS:** Counselor YMCA Camp Becket MA 1966; memUniv City MO Comm on Human Rel; mem Big Bros of Amer Inc; mem Amer Chem Soc 1968-69; mem of experiment in Intl Living Expidition to Ghana W Africa; Operation Crossroads Africa Kenya 1984; mem Alpha Phi Alpha Frat Inc; spec achievement researched blk Historical College. **HONORS/ACHIEVEMENTS:** Author "History of Black Protest vs Official Lies" 1975. **BUSINESS ADDRESS:** Dir, Vaughn Cultural Ctr/ Urban Leag, 1408 N Kingshighway, St Louis, MO 63113.

WATSON, ROBERT JOSE
Coach. **PERSONAL:** Born Apr 10, 1946, Los Angeles, CA; married Carol; children: Keith, Kelley. **EDUCATION:** Attended, LA Harbor Coll. **CAREER:** NY Yankees, professional baseball player 1979-; Boston Red Sox, baseball player 1979; Houston Astros, outfielder; Oakland A's, full-time batting coach. **HONORS/ACHIEVEMENTS:** Nat Leag All Star 1973-79; Led FL St Leag Catchers in Double Plays (14) 1966; plyd in All Star Games 1973 & 1975; established Major Leag Record by Hitting for the Cycle in both Leags 1977 & 1979; tied Major Leag Record Fewest Times Caught Stealing 1 Season (0) 1977. **BUSINESS ADDRESS:** Batting Coach, Oakland Athletics, Oakland Coliseum, Oakland, CA 94621.

WATSON, SOLOMON B., IV
Lawyer. **PERSONAL:** Born Apr 14, 1944, Salein, NJ; son of S Brown Watson and Denise Jones Watson; married Brenda J Hendricks Watson, Apr 28, 1984; children: Katitti M, Kira P. **CAREER:** New York Times Co, New York NY, general counsel, currently. **BUSINESS ADDRESS:** General Counsel, New York Times Company, 229 West 43rd, New York, NY 10035.

WATSON, THERESA LAWHORN
Business executive, attorney. **PERSONAL:** Born Jun 15, 1945, Washington, DC. **EDUCATION:** HowardUniv Wash DC, BA (cum laude) 1969; Geo WashUniv Nat Law Cen DC, JD 1973. **CAREER:** Am Savs & Loan Leag Inc, exec vice pres 1980-; Dechert Price & Rhoads, aso atty 1979-80; Senate Subcom on Housing & Urban Affairs, asst minority cnsl 1977-79; Office of Gen cnsl HUD, atty-adv 1973-77. **ORGANIZATIONS:** Mem DC Bar 1973; mem US Dist Ct 1974; mem US Supreme Ct 1976; treas Women's Bar Assn of DC 1979-80; mem Bd of Appeals & Review DC 1979-80; mem Women in Hosing & Fin; mem Am Nat Fed Bar Assn 1973-; treas MA Black Lwyrs Assn 1976-77; mem exec com Black Senate Lgsltv Staffers 1977-78; bd of dirs Nat Low Income Housing Coalition 1979-80; bd of Dir DC Housing Fin Agency 1980-83; bd of dir Women in Housing & Fin 1980. **BUSINESS ADDRESS:** 1435 G St NW, Ste 1019, Washington, DC 20005.

WATSON, THOMAS S., JR.
Executive. **PERSONAL:** Born in Cleveland, OH; son of Thomas S. Watson and Geraldine Wray Watson; children: Kimberly, Timothy, Andrew. **EDUCATION:** Cleveland State University, Cleveland, OH, BBA, 1970, MBA, 1976; Case Western Reserve University, Cleveland, OH, 1973-74; Harvard Business School, Boston, MA, 1979-83. **CAREER:** General Motors, Inc, Cleveland, OH, accountant, 1968-69; Ernst & Whinney, Cleveland, OH, accountant, 1969-70; Tonche Rass, Cleveland, OH, accountant, 1970; Watson, Rice & Co, Washington, DC, chairman, 1970—. **ORGANIZATIONS:** Member, Federal Government Executive Committee, Post Baccalaureate Education Committee, International Practice Committee, AICPA; member, Small Business Advisory Council, Republican National Committee; member, National Advisory Council, Administrator of Small Business Admistration; chairman, Industry Sector Advisory Committee on Small and Minority Business for Trade Policy. **HONORS/ACHIEVEMENTS:** Award of Leadership/Appreciation, staff of White House Conference on Small Business; Small Business Advocate of the Year, US Small Business Administration. **BUSINESS ADDRESS:** Watson Rice & Co, 1220 L St NW, Ste 650, Washington, DC 20005.

WATSON, VERNALINE
Educator. **PERSONAL:** Born Jul 05, 1942, Hobgood, NC. **EDUCATION:** NC Ctrl U, BA 1964, MA 1968; OH St U, PhD 1972. **CAREER:** Thomas Shields School Hobgood NC, 8th grade teacher 1966-67; Dept of Research Planning & Program Devel NC Fund Durham NC, historical writer 1968; St Augustine's Coll Raleigh NC, instr dept of sociology 1968-69; Div Disability Research OSU, research asst dept of physical med 1970; Mershon Center OH St Univ, research assoc 1971-72; Fisk Univ, asst prof sociology 1972-76; Center for Health Care Research Meharry Medical Coll Nashville, research assoc 1985. **ORGANIZATIONS:** Mem Am Soc Assn; Assn of Soc & Beh Scientists; Caucus of Black Sociologists; Acad of Polit Sci; Am Pub Hlth Assn; rsrch activities Structure of Hlth Care Serv for Poor; Soc Psychol Studies in Afro-Am Womanhood; mem NAACP; YMCA; Am Civil Liberties Union. **HONORS/ACHIEVEMENTS:** So Poverty Law Ctr Fulbright Flwshp 1965-66; Vo Rehab Flwshp 1969-71; listed World's Who's Who of Women 1977; Who's Who of Women 1977; who's Who in HlthCare 1977; who's Who Among Stds in Am Coll &Univ 1964. **BUSINESS ADDRESS:** Ctr for Hlth Care Rsrch, Meharry Med Coll, Nashville, TN 37208.

WATSON, WILBUR H.
Educator, medical sociologist, author. **PERSONAL:** Born Apr 14, 1938, Cleveland; married Shirley Washington; children: Stephen, Sheryl Lynn. **EDUCATION:** Kent St U, BA 1964, MA 1966;Univ of PA, PhD 1972. **CAREER:** Temple Univ Phila, asst prof of Soc 1973-; Rutgers Coll, asst prof of Soc 1970-74; Cheyney St Coll, asst prof of soc 1969-70; Kent St Univ, instr 1966-68; Lincoln Univ, instr 1966-68. **ORGANIZATIONS:** Mem Am Soclgcl Assn; Soc for Study of Soc Problems; Assn of Black Soclgsts; Assn for Study of African Am Life & Hist; Assn of Soc & Behvrl Scientests; mem bd govs Ctr for Rsrch on Acts of ManUniv of PA 1969-70; chmn steering com Proj-Learn;Exprmntl Elem Sch 1970-71; steering com Nat Black Alliance for Grad Level Ed 1972-74; cnsltng rsrch soclgst Stephen Smith Geriatric Ctr Philadelphia 1972-; founding ed The Black Soclgst 1975-. **HONORS/ACHIEVEMENTS:** Recip of Numerous Flwshps & Awards; listed in Outstndng Profls in Hum Srrv 1974-75; Who's Who in the East 1977; author of "Hum Aging & Dying" (with RJ Maxwell) 1977; "Stress & Old Age" 1980; other Publications. **BUSINESS ADDRESS:** Dept Sociology, Temple Univ, Philadelphia, PA 19122.

WATT, GARLAND WEDDERICK
Judge. **PERSONAL:** Born Feb 10, 1932, Elizabeth City, NC; married Gwendolyn LaNita Canada. **EDUCATION:** Lab Sch, Prep Ed; Elizabeth City St U; NC Ctrl U, AB 1952; (Magna cum laude); Harvard U, DePaul U, JD 1961. **CAREER:** Circuit Ct of Cook Co, judge 1975-; Gen Prac, atty 1961-75; DePaul Law Rev, asso ed 1960-61. **ORGANIZATIONS:** Past bd mem Independence Bk of Chgo; adv bd Supreme Life Ins Co of Am; mem Union Leag Club of Chgo; Econ Club of Chgo; bd mem Am Red Cross 1973; Chicago NAACP; v chmn, chmn Leagal Redress Com 1964-70; bd mem Joint Negro Appeal; Chicago Hearing Soc 1972-74; City Club of Chicago 1971-73. **HONORS/ACHIEVEMENTS:** Recpt Richard E Westbrooks Award Cook Co Bar Assn 1972; Judical Award Cook Co Bar Assn 1975; PUSH Found Award 1977. **BUSINESS ADDRESS:** 1340 S Michigan Ave, Chicago, IL 60605.

WATTERS, LINDA A.
Automotive executive. **PERSONAL:** Born Aug 07, 1953, Dayton, OH; married Ronald Edd Watters. **EDUCATION:** Bowling Green State Univ, BA 1975; Univ of Dayton, MBA 1979. **CAREER:** General Motors Corp, staff auditor 1978-80, financial analyst 1980-82, supervisor accts receivables 1982-84, sr market analyst 1984-. **ORGANIZATIONS:** Mem Detroit Chap Natl Black MBA Assoc 5 yrs; solicitor Boy Scouts of Amer 1985; bd mem Natl Black MBA Assoc 1986-88; mem Delta Sigma Theta Sor. **HONORS/ACHIEVEMENTS:** Outstanding Young Women in Amer 1985; Top 100 Black Business & Professional Women Dollars & Sense magazine 1986. **HOME ADDRESS:** 1332 Balfour Rd, Grosse Pointe Park, MI 48230. **BUSINESS ADDRESS:** Senior Market Analyst, General Motors Corp, 485 W Milwaukee Argo A-690, Detroit, MI 48202.

WATTERSON, RICHARD HARVEY
City official, business executive. **PERSONAL:** Born May 19, 1926, Kingsport, TN; divorced; children: Richard, Jr, Ronald, Gail, Elaine, Gregory, Richard Jeffery. **EDUCATION:** Livingstone Coll, BA 1952. **CAREER:** ANC Commission 8d01, 1976; Kingsport TN, city alderman; Red Lion Pkg Store, mgr 1970-76. **ORGANIZATIONS:** Pres Esquire Club; Merry Makers Club; apptd by DC City Cncl to DC Nghbhd Reinvestment 1976; bd dir Kingsport Boys Club; mem Adv Bd for Gov of TN mem St Bd Law Enforcement; bd dir Kingsport Yth Hm for Juv Del; chmn Ways & Means Com Bethel AME Zion Ch; mem Phi Beta Sigma; past comdr Am LegionBurdine Post 123; past sec Elks Clinch Mtn Lodge; mem Kiwanis; Optimists. **HONORS/ACHIEVEMENTS:** Recip Man of Yr Award Bethal AME Zion Ch 1975; Esquire Award for Outstndng Achiev 1965; Man & Boy Award Kingsport Boys Club 1968; Men of Achiev 1977. **MILITARY SERVICE:** USN 1943-46. **BUSINESS ADDRESS:** Red Lion Pkg Store, 904 E Ctr St, Kingsport, TN 37660.

WATTLETON, ALYCE FAYE (FAYE WATTLETON)
Association executive. **PERSONAL:** Born Jul 08, 1943, St Louis, MO; married Franklin Gordon. **EDUCATION:** Ohio State Univ, BS (nursing), 1964; Columbia Univ, MS (nursing), 1967. **CAREER:** Miami Valley School of Nursing, Dayton, OH, instructor, 1964-66; Dayton Public Health Nursing Assn, asst dir of nursing, 1967-70; Planned Parenthood Assn of Miami Valley, Dayton, OH, exec dir, 1970-78; Planned Parenthood Federation of Amer Inc, pres, 1978—. **ORGANIZATIONS:** Bd mem, Natl Urban League, 1979; bd mem, Ind Sector, 1980; mem, Amer Public Health Assn; mem, Amer Coll of Nurse-Midwives; bd mem, Ohio State Alumni Assn, 1980. **HONORS/ACHIEVEMENTS:** Citations for Outstanding Achievememt from State of Ohio House Rep, 1978; selected by Ms Magazine, Citation for Outstanding Achievement Ohio State Univ, 1979. **BUSINESS ADDRESS:** President, Planned Parenthood Federation of Amer, 810 7th Ave, New York, NY 10019. *

WATTLETON, FAYE See WATTLETON, ALYCE FAYE

WATTLEY, THOMAS JEFFERSON
Entrepreneur. **PERSONAL:** Born Aug 28, 1953, Dallas, TX; son of Thomas Jefferson and Johnnie Scott Wattle; married Cheryl Elizabeth Brown; children: Marissa, Scott, Elizabeth, Andrew. **EDUCATION:** Amherst Coll, BA, 1975; Yale School of Org and Mgmt, MPPM, 1980. **CAREER:** The LTV Corp, coporate planner, 1980-82; Grant Thornton, sr mgmt project dir, 1982-86; Stewart-Wattley Material Handling Equipment Co, pres/CEO, 1987-. **ORGANIZATIONS:** Chmn bd of dirs, Creative Learning Center, 1981-; mem bd of trustees, Dallas Ballet Assoc, 1981-86; mem bd of dir, Dallas Black C of C, 1983-; mem, Dallas Assembly 1984-, Mayor's Task Force on Housing and Economic Devel in Southern Dallas, 1985; mem bd of dirs, Child Care Partnership, Inc, 1986-; mem, Chief Exec Round Table, 1988. **HONORS/ACHIEVEMENTS:** Amherst Memorial Fellowship in Business, 1975; Quest for Success, Miller Brewing, Dallas Morning News, Black Chamber of Commerce, 1989. **HOME ADDRESS:** 1620 Kent St, Dallas, TX 75203. **BUSINESS ADDRESS:** President/ CEO, Stewart-Wattley Matl Handling, Equipment Company, 2512 Summitt Ste 306, Plano, TX 75074.

WATTS, ALEXANDER ALFRED
Clergyman. **PERSONAL:** Born May 04, 1904, Portsmouth, VA; married Edythe E Harper. **EDUCATION:** Drew U, BD 1928, MA 1930, ThD 1933,; CA Grad Sch Theol, PhD 1974; Harvard U, Grad Diploma 1942; Chicago Coll Chiropody & Pedic Surg, DPM 1955. **CAREER:** HS Richmond, supply tchr; Coll Marshall, vis tchr; VA, NJ Chicago LA, pastor of Chs 1926-; 30th St Christian Ch Disciples Christ LA, pastor 1985; Chicago Pract, podiatry 1955-70; Chicago Bapt Inst, instr; Bishop Coll Marshall, vis prof. **ORGANIZATIONS:** Civic spkr Radio, TV, Chicago WGN, Faith of Our Fathers, Time to Reflect. **MILITARY SERVICE:** AUS capt chpln 1942-45.

WATTS, ANDRE
Concert pianist. **PERSONAL:** Born Jun 20, 1946, Nuremberg, Federal Republic of Germany. **EDUCATION:** Peabody Conservatory Baltimore, grad. **CAREER:** Philadelphia Orchestra Children's Concert, debut age 9; NY Philharmonic Orchestra, debut 1963, annual appearances; Los Angeles Philharmonic, annual appearances, toured Europe as soloist for US State Dept, 1967; Philadelphia Orchestra, annual appearances; Chicago Symphony, annual appearances; Boston Symphony, annual appearances; Cleveland Orchestra, annual appearances; other major orchestras, annual appearances; London Symphony, European debut 1966; toured Europe with leading orchestras, annually; toured Japan, 1969, biennially thereafter; toured South Amer, 1972. **ORGANIZATIONS:** Soloist for US State Dept; toured Soviet Union with San Francisco Symphony, 1973; narrated Copland's "A Lincoln Portrait" at Ford's Theatre, 1975; ten years on series "Great Performers," Lincoln Ctr; first live recital soloist ever to be nationally telecast, Avery Fisher Hall, Lincoln Ctr, 1976; Order of the Zaire Congo, 1970. **HONORS/ACHIEVEMENTS:** Hon Doctor of Music, Yale Univ, 1973; Lincoln Ctr Medallion, 1974; hon Doctor of Humanities, Albright Coll, 1975; recording artist, CBS Records. **BUSINESS ADDRESS:** Concert Pianist, c/o Columbia Artists Mgmt, 165 W 57th St, New York, NY 10019.

WATTS, CHARLES DEWITT
Physician, surgeon. **PERSONAL:** Born Sep 21, 1917, Atlanta, GA; son of Lewis Gould Watts and Ida N Hawes; married Constance Merrick, Jan 05, 1945; children: C Eileen Welch, Deborah C Hill, Charles D Jr, Winifred Hemphill. **EDUCATION:** Morehouse Coll, BS 1938; Howard Univ Coll of Med, MD 1943; Freedmen's Hosp Wash DC, intern & residency. **CAREER:** Durham City Gen Hospital, attending surgeon; Howard Univ, instr of surgery; Cancer Clinic Freedmen's Hospital; NC Mutual Life Ins Co, sr vice pres, medical dir 1960-88; Private practice, surgeon; bd of dirs NC Mutual Life Ins Co 1965-89. **ORGANIZATIONS:** Past dir Student Health Serv NC Central Univ; bd dir Health Systems Agency Reg IV; chmn Ed Comm Staff of Durham Cty Gen Hosp; mem NC Health Ins Adv Bd, Inst of Med, Natl Acad of Sci; clinical instr Duke Med Ctr; past pres Durham-Orange Cty Med Soc; founder, dir Lincoln Comm Health Ctr, mem bd Durham C of C; past chmn bd Oper Breakthrough; mem Durham Human Relations Comm; mem Council of Inst of Med; bd dir Comm Plnng Bd; bd dirDurham United Fund; bd trustees Howard Univ; mem St Josephs AME Church; bd of dirs, Howard Univ 1975-89. **HONORS/ACHIEVEMENTS:** Dr of the Year Awd Old No State Med Soc; Doctor Humane Letters, St Pauls Coll, Honorary; Diplomate American bd of surgery; Fellow of Amer Coll of Surgeons. **HOME ADDRESS:** 829 Lawson St, Durham, NC 27701.

WATTS, FREDERICK, JR.
Attorney. **PERSONAL:** Born Feb 09, 1929, New York, NY; married Janice A Cordes; children: Karen Rene, Frederick John. **EDUCATION:** Brooklyn Law Sch, JD 1956; Coll of City of NY, BSS 1951. **CAREER:** New York City Police Dept, 1955-76; 6th Area Det Homicide Squad Cen Harlem, supr 1973-76; Det Squad Cen Harlem, supr 1971-73; 25th Det Squad Cen Harlem, supr 1967-71; Police Commr Confidential Investigation Unit, sgt 1965-67; New York City Police Legal Dept Leagal Div, atty 1957-65; Atty, 1976-. **ORGANIZATIONS:** Mem NAACP; 100 Black Men Inc. **HONORS/ACHIEVEMENTS:** Hon atty Patrolmens Benevolent Assn New York City Police Dept 1977-; five commend Meritorious Police Duty; three commend Excellent Police Duty. **MILITARY SERVICE:** AUS 1951-53. **BUSINESS ADDRESS:** 30 Broad St, New York, NY 10004.

WATTS, JOHN E.
Dentist. **PERSONAL:** Born Feb 24, 1896, Columbia, SC; widowed. **EDUCATION:** HowardUniv Dental Sch, DDS 1918. **CAREER:** Winston Salem Tchrs Coll, tchr 1923-24; Pub Schs Columbia, tchr 1924-30; Scotia Coll NC, tchr. **ORGANIZATIONS:** Mem Nat Dent Assn; mem Commonwealth Dent Soc; mem Newark Dent Club; consult NJ St Med; mem Amega Psi Phi; elder Elmwood United Presby Ch E Orange NJ; bd v chmn, asst treas Union Pub Library; mem Sickle Cell Found of the Oranges; mem NAACP. **MILITARY SERVICE:** AUS dental corp pvt 1918-19. **BUSINESS ADDRESS:** 2180 Springfield Ave, Vauxhall, NJ 07088.

WATTS, JOHN E.
Executive director. **PERSONAL:** Born Oct 19, 1936, Atlanta. **EDUCATION:** AL St U, BS 1958; Intrdnmntnl Theol Ctr, MDiv 1961; Pepperdine U, MA 1972. **CAREER:** 3 Chs, pastor, adminstr 1959-69; prog coord, writer 1966-68; City of Vallejo, asst to city mgr for com reltns 1968-70; Intrgvrnmntl Mgmt, prog mgr,lt gov ofc 1970-73; Model Cities Agency, exec dor ofc of the mayor 1973-. **ORGANIZATIONS:** Mem Omega Psi Phi; NAHRO; Am Soc of Urban Planners; life mem Nat Hum Rights Dir; mem Interntl Hum Rights Org. **HONORS/ACHIEVEMENTS:** 1st Black City Adminstr for City of Vallejo; named Most Outstndng Young Clergyman by AME Zion Ch. **BUSINESS ADDRESS:** 814 Mission St, San Francisco, CA 94103.

WATTS, LUCILE (NEE ALEXANDER)
Judge. **PERSONAL:** Born in Alliance, OH; married James. **EDUCATION:** Detroit Coll of Law, LLB; Detroit Coll of Law, JD 1962. **CAREER:** Twp of Royal Oak, former gen council; House Labor Comm, former legal council; Lucile A Watts PC, pres; City of Detroit Common Pleas Court, judge. **ORGANIZATIONS:** Mem Amer Bar Assoc, MI Bar Assoc, Detroit Bar Assoc, Women Lawyers of MI, Wolverine Bar Assoc; past pres Womens Div of Natl Bar Assoc; past pres Metro Soc for Crippled Child & Adults; chmn bd of dir Focus Hope; mem YWCA, Detroit Golf Course Prop Own Assoc, Delta Sigma Theta, Cath Inter-Racial Council, Womens Econ Club; life mem NAACP; past pres Assoc of Black Judges of MI; reg dir Women Judges Assoc. **BUSINESS ADDRESS:** Judge, Common Pleas Court Detroit Cty, 1907 City County Bldg, Detroit, MI 48226.

WATTS, RICKEY
Professional athlete. **PERSONAL:** Born May 16, 1957, Longview, TX. **EDUCATION:** Tulsa, BAPE. **CAREER:** Chicago Bears, professional ftbl plyr wide rcvr 1979-. **HONORS/ACHIEVEMENTS:** Led Hurricane Rushers with 234 carries 1,166 yds (50 average) 14 TD'S 1976-77; Tullsa MVP 1977-78; recip Tulsa Pres Award. **BUSINESS ADDRESS:** Chicago Bears Halas Hall, 240 W Washington PO Box 204, Lake Forest, IL 60045.

WATTS, ROBERT B.
Retired judge. **PERSONAL:** Born Mar 04, 1922, Baltimore, MD; married Jacquelyn Johnson; children: Robert, Jr, Rodney M, Jacquelyn, Gennelle, Bobette. **EDUCATION:** Morgan State Coll, BS, 1943; Univ of Maryland School of Law, LLB, 1949; Morgan State Coll, Hon Doctor Law, 1974; Towson State Univ, Hon Doctor Human Letters 1976. **CAREER:** Office of Price Stabilizalin, asst chief enforcment attny, 1955-56; Municipal Court, assoc judge, 1961-68; Circuit Court of Baltimore, assoc judge, 1968-. **ORGANIZATIONS:** Mem State Bd of Coll Trustees,1967-71; pres of bd, N Charles Gen Hospital, 1984-; bd mem, Harriott Lane Johns Hopkins Hospital, 1968-, Legal Aid Bd, 1971-, Family & Children Serv, 1974-, Glenwood Drug Program, Dismass Hospital, War Memorial Comm. **HONORS/ACHIEVEMENTS:** Man of the Year NAACP, 1962; Man of the Year B'nai B'rith, 1962; Disting Serv Award, VA Union Alumni, 1983; Natl Council Christian & Jews Disting Serv, 1969. **MILITARY SERVICE:** AUS sgt 1943-46. **BUSINESS ADDRESS:** Piper & Marbury, 36 So Charles St, Baltimore, MD 21201.

WATTS, ROBERTA OGLETREE
Educational administrator. **PERSONAL:** Born May 12, 1939, Lawrenceville, GA; married Roger William Watts Sr; children: Roger Jr, Roderick Dewayne. **EDUCATION:** Tuskegee Inst, BSN 1961; Emory Univ, MN 1969; Univ of AL, EdD 1982. **CAREER:** VA Hosp, staff nurse 1961-62; Etowah Cty Health Dept, staff nurse 1969; Jacksonville State Univ, asst prof 1969-; Jacksonville State Univ, dean, prof 1982-. **ORGANIZATIONS:** Chrpsn Etowah Quality of Life Inc 1978-85, Colley Child Care Ctr Inc 1970-, Deans of Bacc & Higher Degree Prog 1984, Human Rel Council; various positions Alpha Kappa Alpha 1975, Wisteria Club 1964; Kappa Delta Pi. **HONORS/ACHIEVEMENTS:** Achievement Awd NAACP 1982; Serv Awd Alpha Kappa Alpha 1983, Amer Assoc Univ Women 1982, Etowah Quality of Life. **BUSINESS ADDRESS:** Dean, Professor, Jacksonville StateUniv, LB Wallace Coll of Nrsg, Jacksonville, AL 36265.

WATTS, WILSONIA
Educator. **PERSONAL:** Born in Campbellsville, KY; married Rudolph Watts; children: Endraetta. **EDUCATION:** KY School of Mortuary Science; Western Univ, Rank I; Kentucky State Univ, AB; Western Univ, MA. **CAREER:** EB Terry Elem, math teacher; Campbellsville City Elem School, elem teacher; Taylor County Elem School, teacher; Glasgow Indep Schools, teacher grades 1-3. **ORGANIZATIONS:** President, vp, sec, treasurer Kay Bledsoe BPW; chairman Local Glasgow Jr Miss Pageant; sec treasures Glasgow URBAN Remewal; city council rep (4 years); chairman Red Cross; co-chair Muscular Dystrophy; captain Easter Seals. **HONORS/ACHIEVEMENTS:** Rotary Award Campbellsville Rotary Club; (Ch) Music Award KY BPW Organization; (Ch) Business and Profess Women's Week (KY BPW Organization); Woman of Achievement Glasgow Kiwanis; Woman of Achievement Kay Bledsoe BPW. **BUSINESS ADDRESS:** Teacher, Glasgow Indep Schools, 506 S Lewis St, Glasgow, KY 42141.

WAUGH, JUDITH RITCHIE
Broadcaster. **PERSONAL:** Born Jun 05, 1939, Indianapolis, IN. **EDUCATION:** Indiana Univ, BA 1961, MA 1969; Attended, Purdue Univ NDEA Grant 1966. **CAREER:** Indianapolis Public Schools, teacher of english and humanities 1961-73; McGraw Hill Broadcasting WRTV 6, dir of public affairs 1973-. **ORGANIZATIONS:** Life mem NAACP; bd of dir Indianapolis Arts Council; pres Indpls Chapter of Links 1989-1991; bd of dir Indpls Urban League 1973-; vice pres bd of dir of Mme. Walker Urban Life Center & Chr of Capital Campaign; mem Marion County Literacy Task Group; bd of dir Big Sisters of Indpls. **HONORS/ACHIEVEMENTS:** Full Year John Hay Fellowship Northwestern Univ 1964-65. **BUSINESS ADDRESS:** Dir of Public Affairs WRTV, Mc Graw-Hill Broadcasting Co, 1330 No Meridian St, Indianapolis, IN 46202.

WAULS, INEZ LA MAR (NEE FULLEN)
Commissioner. **PERSONAL:** Born Feb 11, 1924, Williamson, WV; divorced; children: Agatha Kenner, Rita, Luther J Jr, Ronald. **EDUCATION:** Howard Univ Wash DC, BA 1951. **CAREER:** Natl Commiss for Women, natl dir 1978-80; Bel Vue UN Presbyterian Church, presiding elder 1977-80, 1980-81; Howard Univ Alumni Assoc, west reg rep; LA Cty Symphony League, 1st black pres 1977-79; Allpha Kappa Alpha Sor Theta Alpha Omega Chapt, gramma 1976-; Foster Care Serv LA Cty Dept of Soc Svc, soc work consult 1955-; Compton Comm on the Stat of Women, commiss. **ORGANIZATIONS:** Minority womens task force CA State Comm on the Stat of Women 1984-; re-elected to far west reg rep Howard Univ 1984-86. **HONORS/ACHIEVEMENTS:** Consistent Serv Howard Univ Alumni Assoc So CA 1962; Jill of the Year Jack & Jill of Amer Inc So LA 1976; Sor of the Year Alpha Kappa Alpha, Theta Alpha Omega 1979; Exemplary Citizenship & 20 yrs of Civic & Cultural Serv Mayor & City Council Compton CA 1979. **BUSINESS ADDRESS:** Commissioner, Compton Comm/Stat of Women, 205 S Willowbrook Ave, Compton, CA 90220.

WAY, CURTIS J.
Business executive. **PERSONAL:** Born Jun 19, 1935, Columbia, SC. **EDUCATION:** Benedict Coll, BA 1962; NU Univ, MPA 1970; Fordham Univ, New School of Soc Rsch, Grad Stud; Nova Univ, DPA 1977. **CAREER:** Philadelphia Cty Juvenile Cty, prob off; Newark Title V Proj, dir training & job devel; Newark City Neighborhood Youth Corps, dep dir, summer exec dir 1965-67; NAACP & Multi-Purpose Ctr, dir, chmn of bd; Newark Inst of Urban Prog, chief exec officer. **ORGANIZATIONS:** Consult Natl Alliance of Bus; dir City of Passiac NJ; proj housing packagor & consult Neighborhood Youth Corp 1967-69; planner & prog devel Early Childhood Ed; planner & prog devel NJUP Theater for Arts Newark NJ, Sickle Cell Anemia Proj; fundraiser & alumni org Amer Inst Planners; mem Amer Soc Planning Official; mem Amer Soc Publ Admin, Amer Acad Pol & Soc Sci; past trustee Benedict Coll; past mem Reg Health Planning Council, Newark Urban Coaltion, Minority Econ Devel Corp; past pres NJ Chap Benedict Alumni; life mem NAACP; founder Hillcreek Commun Ctr Philadelphia, NAACP Multi-Purpose Ctr & Cultural Ctr; panelist Amer Arbitration Assoc; mem 32 Degree Mason. **HONORS/ACHIEVEMENTS:** Oustanding Serv Awd Benedict Coll 1970; Outstanding Young men in Amer 1970; Outstanding Serv Awd Dept HUD 1971; Excellent Cit Serv Awd L Miller Civic Assoc 1972; Better Comm newark Br NAACP 1973; Outstanding Comm Serv Newark 1973,79; Outstanding Leadership Awd NAACP MPC 1974. **MILITARY SERVICE:** AUS E-5 1953-57; Appreciation Awd US Navy 1971; Outstanding Serv Awd USN Recruiting 1972. **BUSINESS ADDRESS:** Chief Executive Officer, Newark Inst of Urban Programs, PO Box 8221, Newark, NJ 07108.

WAY, GARY DARRYL
Attorney. **PERSONAL:** Born Feb 25, 1958, Newark, NJ; son of Robert Way and Pearl Rosser Childs; married Jill Green, Nov 28, 1987. **EDUCATION:** Rutgers Coll, New Brunswick, NJ, BA 1980; New York Univ School of Law, New York City, JD 1983. **CAREER:**

Haight, Gardner, Poor & Havens, New York City, associate, 1983-86; National Basketball Assn, New York City, staff attorney, 1986-88; NBA Properties Inc, New York City, asst general counsel, 1988-. **HONORS/ACHIEVEMENTS:** Author of "Japanese Employers and Title VII," 1983. **MILITARY SERVICE:** US Army, captain, 1980-; Distinguished Military Graduate, Rutgers Army ROTC, 1980; Army Achievement Award with Oak Leaf Cluster. **BUSINESS ADDRESS:** Assistant General Counsel, NBA Properties Inc, 645 Fifth Ave, Olympic Tower, New York, NY 10022.

WAYMER, RICHARD TURNER
Retired educator. **PERSONAL:** Born Mar 13, 1911, Elloree, SC; married Sara. **EDUCATION:** SC St Coll, BS 1935; Tchrs Coll Columbia U, MA 1939;Univ LA, EdD (honorarius) 1975; Appalacian St U, Prof Media Specialist Diploma 1967. **CAREER:** Audiovisual Aids Center SC St Coll, asso prof educ, dir 18 yrs; Agr & Educ DE St Coll, asst prof 8 yrs; Agr Educ Ft Valley St Coll, asst prof 1 yr; Agr Educ FL A&M Univ, asst prof 2 yrs; Agr Educ TN A&I St Univ, acting chmn dept agri, instr 1 yr. **ORGANIZATIONS:** Mem, past vice pres AECT SC; mem, exec bd Nat Schlrshp Com 1985; mem, past pres AAUP Orangeburg; rep Nat Assn Conv 3 yrs; mem Nat Ed Assn SC StColl; Nat Alumni Assn 1985; mem, exec cncl bd dirs, pres Alumni Hse Orangeburg Co; mem Kappa Alpha Psi Frat Orangeburg Alumni; mem NAACP; mem, exec cncl, chmn Legal Redress Com Orangeburg. **HONORS/ACHIEVEMENTS:** Publ, rsrchd the relation of institutional aspect of ec to the assumptions of ec theroy 1947; the plight of dE st coll 1947; career steps of dirs of Divs of Ed in 100 Colls & U, by previous positions held 1955-56; audiovisual mats, prod of instr tapes, slide-sound, TV-VIDEO Progs for classroom instr SC St Coll AV Libry; recip Achiev Award Outstndng AV Educator, Sthestrn Bus Assn 1972.

WAYNE, GEORGE HOWARD, SR.
Educational administrator. **PERSONAL:** Born Mar 10, 1938, Meridian, MS; married Juanita R Robinson; children: Lisa Monet, George Howard Jr, Kimberly Ann. **EDUCATION:** Univ of NE, MA 1967; Univ of CO, MPA 1971; Univ of Denver, MA, EdD 1979. **CAREER:** Asst prof hist 1972-76, intelligence ofcr 1967-71;Univ of CO, asst prof 1974; USAF Acad, asst prof, cnslr 1976-, Dean 1986. **ORGANIZATIONS:** Pres Kappa Alpha Psi Frat 1978; bd of dirs Kappa Alpha Psi Frat 1980; pres Aspen Educational Consulting. **HONORS/ACHIEVEMENTS:** Outstndng Kappa Alpha Psi Frat 1979; Minority Alcoholism, Aspen, Publishing 1985; Black Migration to CO Jrnl of the W 1976; Race Relations a time for phase III Air Univ Rev 1972; Industrial Use of Disadvantaged Ams, Air Univ Rev 1974; ed Who's Who in Black CO 1976; Bronze Star; Meritorious Srv Medal; Commendation Medal. **MILITARY SERVICE:** USAF. **BUSINESS ADDRESS:** Dean, Student Academic Servs, Univ of CO, 1100 14th St, Denver, CO 80919.

WAYNES, KATHLEEN YANES
Social worker. **PERSONAL:** Born Aug 12, 1920, New York, NY; daughter of Pedro Yanes and May Stewart; married William D Waynes; children: Consuelo, Regina Joseph, Victoria Clement, Christina. **EDUCATION:** Attended, Catholic Univ, Washington, DC, 1940; Coll of St Benedict, St Joseph, MN, BS, 1942; Columbia Univ, Training for Natl Cath Comm Serv, USO Div, 1944. **CAREER:** Friendship House of Harlem, asst dir, 1942-44; Natl Catholic Social Serv, USO asst dir, 1944-46; New Jersey Commission for the Blind, social worker, 1966-82 (retired); War Assets Admin, inspector, 1946-. **ORGANIZATIONS:** Mem, Assoc of Workers for the Blind, 1970-82; various positions permanent membership, US Coast Guard Aux, 1970-; mem, Black Social Workers of New Jersey, 1980-82; mem, NAACP, Aux Amer Legion, Aux Knights of Columbus, AARF; leader, Girl Scouts of Amer; artistic dir, Negro Womens Club. **HONORS/ACHIEVEMENTS:** Information officer, Flotilla 13-06 Award, US Coast Guard Aux, 1984-86; liturgical chairperson, Golden Agers OLGC Church, 1985; The Zeta Amicae of Zeta Delta Zeta Chapter, Mother of the Year Award, Moorestown, NJ. **HOME ADDRESS:** 337 Farmdale Rd, Moorestown, NJ 08057.

WAYNEWOOD, FREEMAN LEE
Dentist. **PERSONAL:** Born Jun 30, 1942, Anson, TX; married Beverly; children: Tertia, Dorian. **EDUCATION:** Univ of TX, attended; Univ of WA, BAED 1970, DDS 1974. **CAREER:** Real Estate, salesman 1968-71; Weyhauser, 1970-71; Richardson's Assoc, constr rsch 1971-73; Private practice, dentist; FL Waynewood and Associates, PA; pres. **ORGANIZATIONS:** Mem Amer Dental Assoc, MN Dental Assoc, St Paul Dist Dental Soc, Amer Soc Preventive Dentistry, Amer Soc Dentistry for Children; staff mem United Hosp St Paul; bd mem Model Cities Hallie Q Brown Comm Ctr; mem Alpha Phi Alpha, Flight Unltd; bd mem Webster School; mem St Paul Opera Workshop. **MILITARY SERVICE:** Navy cmdr 20 yrs; Vietnam Campaign Ribbon Natl Def 1964-68. **HOME ADDRESS:** 2028 Upper St Dennis Rd, St Paul, MN 55116. **BUSINESS ADDRESS:** President, Waynewood and Associates PA, 588 University Ave, St Paul, MN 55103.

WEAD, RODNEY SAM
Administrator. **PERSONAL:** Born Jun 28, 1935, Omaha, NE; son of Sampson Lester Wead and Daisy Shanks Wead; divorced; children: Denise Michelle Wead Rawles, Owen Eugene, Ann Lineve Wead Kimbrough, Melissa Cheryl Wead Rivas. **EDUCATION:** Dana Coll, Blair NE, BS Educ 1957; Roosevelt Univ, Chicago IL, MA Urban Studies 1976; The Union Inst, Cincinnati OH, PhD Sociology 1981. **CAREER:** Prof, Creighton Univ, 1986-; United Methodist Community Centers Inc, Omaha NE, exec dir 1983-; Community Renewal Society, Chicago IL, assoc exec dir 1973-83. **ORGANIZATIONS:** Life mem Kappa Alpha Psi Fraternity Inc 1955-; mem Clair United Methodist Church, Omaha NE, 1955-; life mem NAACP 1967-; mem Natl Assn of Black Social Workers 1981-; commr Metropolitan Area Transit, Omaha NE, 1985-; mem bd of dirs North Side Villa, Omaha NE, 1986-. **HONORS/ACHIEVEMENTS:** Economic Democracy in Low Income Neighborhoods, research publication 1982; Outstanding Volunteer, Urban League of Nebraska-Omaha 1987; Dr Rodney S Wead Scholarship, Dana Coll, Blair NE, 1989; The African-Amer Family in Nebraska, research publication 1989. **BUSINESS ADDRESS:** Executive Director, United Methodist Community Centers Inc, 2001 N 35th St, Omaha, NE 68111.

WEARY, DOLPHUS
Business executive. **PERSONAL:** Born Aug 07, 1946, Sandy Hook, MS; married Rosie Marie Camper; children: Danita R, Reginald, Ryan D. **EDUCATION:** Piney Woods Jr Coll, AA 1967; Los Angeles Baptist Coll, BA 1969; LA Bapt Theol Sem, M Rel Ed 1971; Univ of So MS, MEd 1978. **CAREER:** Voice of Calvary Ministries, dir summer leadership 1968-71; LA Baptist Coll, coach freshmen team 1969-71; Voice of Calvary Ministries, dir 1971-75; PineyWoods School, coord of christian ed 1975-84; Mendenhall Ministries Inc, president. **ORGANIZATIONS:** Bd of dir Voice of Calvary Health Ctr, So Central MS Rural Health Assoc, Koinonia Farms Americus GA, Voice of Hope Dallas TX; mem Natl Alumni Assoc Piney Woods School, Mendenhall Ministries bd, Nat'l Black Evangelical Assoc bd; Faith at Work, nat'l bd; bd of dir mem Mississippi Religious Leadership Conference (MRLC); bd of dir mem Mississippi Children's Home Society (MCHS). **HONORS/ACHIEVEMENTS:** Basketball Hall of Fame LA Baptist Coll 1969; listed in Who's Who in Amer Coll 1969; Outstanding Athlete Outstanding Coll Athlete in Amer 1969; Outstanding Citizen Civic Circle Club; Alumnus of the Year LA Baptist Coll 1979. **BUSINESS ADDRESS:** President, Mendenhall Ministries Inc, 309 Center St, PO Box 368, Mendenhall, MS 39114.

WEATHER, LEONARD, JR.
Gynecologist, laser surgeon. **PERSONAL:** Born Jul 06, 1944, Albany, GA; married Bettye Jean Roberts; children: Marcus, Kirstin. **EDUCATION:** Howard Univ, Coll of Pharmacy, BS 1967; Rush Medical Coll, MD 1974. **CAREER:** Johns Hopkins Univ, intern, resident 1978; Tulane Univ, instructor 1978-86; Xavier Univ, assoc prof 1984-; Omni Fertility Inst, dir 1985-. **ORGANIZATIONS:** Radio host medical talk show WBOK 1980-84; dir and vice pres Bayou Federal Svgs & Loan 1983-; dir YMCA 1984-; host radio talk show Doctor's Corner WYLD AM 940 1985-; mem Omega Psi Phi Frat 1985; pres Black Leadership Awareness Council 1985; natl pres Chi Delta Mu Medical Frat 1986. **HONORS/ACHIEVEMENTS:** Book "Why We Can't Have a Baby," 1985; article "Carbon Dioxide Laser Myomectomy" Journal Natl Medical Assoc 1986; "CO2 Laser Laproscopy-Treatment of Disorders of Pelvic Pain and Infertility" 1986. **MILITARY SERVICE:** USAR major 19 yrs. **HOME ADDRESS:** 6831 Lake Willow Dr, New Orleans, LA 70126. **BUSINESS ADDRESS:** Dir, Chef Women Clinic/Omni Fert, 7820 Chef Menteur Hwy, New Orleans, LA 70126.

WEATHERLY, TOM
Poet. **PERSONAL:** Born Nov 03, 1942, Scottsboro, AR; son of Thomas Elias Weatherly and Lucy Belle Golson Weatherly; divorced; children: Regina, Thomas Elias III. **EDUCATION:** Morehouse College, 1958-61; Alabama Agricultural and Mechanical College (now University), 1961. **CAREER:** Rutgers University, Newark NJ, adjunct instructor in art, 1969-70, instructor in creative writing, summer, 1970; Bishop College, Dallas TX, poet-in-residence, 1970-71; Morgan State College, Baltimore MD, poet-in-residence, 1971-72; E. S. Webb School, Westchester NY, teacher of poetry, 1972; St. Mark's Church, New York NY, teacher of creative writing, beginning 1972. **ORGANIZATIONS:** Governor-general of poetry association of Guild of Order, 1988-89. **HONORS/ACHIEVEMENTS:** Three grants from National Endowment for the Arts to support poetry workshops. **HOME ADDRESS:** 286 E Second Ave, Apt A, New York, NY 10009. *

WEATHERS, ALICE ANN
Corporate director. **PERSONAL:** Born Apr 21, 1944, St Louis, MO; children: Avril. **EDUCATION:** Lincoln Univ Jefferson City, BS 1975. **CAREER:** Dept of Revenue, asst personnel officer 1975-77; MO Council on Criminal Justice, chief juvenile section 1977-79; State Econ Oppty Office, dir 1979-. **ORGANIZATIONS:** Treas Natl Assoc State Community Serv 1981-84; bd mem Reg VII Headstart Adv Comm. **HONORS/ACHIEVEMENTS:** Outstanding Serv MO Community Action Assoc. **BUSINESS ADDRESS:** Dir, State Office of Economic Oppty, 308 E High St, Jefferson City, MO 65101.

WEATHERS, J. LEROY
Clergyman. **PERSONAL:** Born May 21, 1936, Georgetown Co. **EDUCATION:** Allen U, AB 1964; Dickerson Theol Sem SC, BD 1965; Urban Training Ctr for Christian Mission Chicago IL, attend 1970;Univ of Miami Drug Ed, 1973; Air Force Chaplain Sch, 1974. **CAREER:** Young Chapel AME Ch Irmo SC, pastor 1960; Mt Olive AME Ch Myrtle Bch SC, pastor 1961-; Myrtle Bch AFB SC, civilian aux chaplain 1975. **ORGANIZATIONS:** Del Gen Conf AME Ch 1968; civilian adv Religious Adv Com Myrtle AFB SC 1969; pres Myrtle Bch Ministerial Assn 1973-74, sec 1975-76; Mil Chaplains Asn; SC Com on Pastoral Care in Alcohol & Drug Abuse 1975-76; mem Masonic Lodge 423; life mem NAACP; fdr, pres Myrtle Bch NAACP; chmn Mayor's Bi-racial Com 1964; Horry-Georgetown Ec Opport Bd 1965-; trustee Allen U; asst treas SC NAACP 1969-73; Myrtle Bch C of C 1970; v-chmn Dem Party Myrtle Bch 1970-72; chaplain Myrtle Bch Jaycees 1970-74, dir 1971-72; Horry Co Ambulance Serv Commn; Fed Prog Adv Cncl, Horry Co Dept of Ed 1971; sec Kiwanis Club of Myrtle Bch 1971; numerous others com. **HONORS/ACHIEVEMENTS:** Recip Outstndng Ldrshp Award, Mt Olive AME Ch 1967; cert of Merit SC NAACP 1967; cert of Appreciation Ec Opport Comm Act 1971; US Jaycees Spkr-of-the-Month Award 1971-72; Jaycee-of-the-Month Myrtle Bch Jaycees 1972; Key Man Award Myrtle Bch Jaycees 1972; Kiwanian-of-theYr 1972; Outstndng Young Man Award Jaycees 1972; Outstndng Young Man With Distinguished Serv Award SC Jaycees 1972; ed bldg at Mt Olive AME Ch named the JL Weathers Religious Ed Bldg1973; Hm Coming Award Singleton AME Ch SC 1973; Cit of Yr Beta Tau Chap of Omega Psi Phi Frat; listed in Outstndng Young Men of Am; Personalities of the S; recip Distinguished Unit Pres/Unit Citation; AF Outstndng Unit Award; Army Good Conduct Medal; Nat Def Serv Medal. **MILITARY SERVICE:** AUS 1953-55. **BUSINESS ADDRESS:** Route 1, Box 138, McClellanville, SC 29458.

WEATHERS, MARGARET A.
Association executive. **PERSONAL:** Born Feb 09, 1922, Forest City, AR; daughter of Oscar Allman and Lillie Allman; married Ernest A Weathers; children: Margaret Kathryn. **EDUCATION:** Lincoln Univ; Western Reserve Univ; MS Indus Coll; Tulane Univ, Certificate, Inner City Training Program 1971; Capital Univ, BA. **CAREER:** MO, teacher 1940-50; GM Chevrolet Plant Cleveland, worker 1951-55; Child Welfare Dept Cleveland, operated nursery 1955-60; Head Start Comm Act for Youth & Council of Churches, teacher 1964-66; Cleveland Div Rec, 1966-70; Weathers Unique Cleaners, co-mgr; EA Weathers Realty; Weathers Travel Agcy; Mags Kustard, co-owner; Multi-Serv Center, past pres corp bd Lk Erie Girl Scout Council, field dir 1985-. **ORGANIZATIONS:** Mem, Health Planning & Devel Comm, Welfare Fed; past bd mem Hough Area Devel Corp & Council. **HONORS/ACHIEVEMENTS:** Plaques Hough Multi-Serv Center Bd 1973; Parkwood CME Church, 1973; Certificate of Merit, Hough Comm Council 1973; plaque To One Who Served with Dedication, The Hough Multi-Serv Center Bd of Trustees; Congressional Achievement Award; City of Cleveland Congratulatory Award 1977. **BUSINESS ADDRESS:** Membership Specialist, Lake Erie Girl Scout Council, 19201 Villaview Rd, Cleveland, OH 44119.

WEATHERS, ROBERT
Professional athlete. **PERSONAL:** Born Sep 13, 1960, Westfield, NY; married Denise; chil-

dren: Michael. **EDUCATION:** AZ St; Northeastern Center for the Study of Sports & Society degree completion prgm. **CAREER:** New England Patriots, running back 1982-. **ORGANIZATIONS:** Charitable Spkng Engagements at New England Area Schls & VA Hosps; Adams & Russell Cable Co (MA), sports talk show host 1987. **HONORS/ACHIEVEMENTS:** All American & MVP; AZ St Glen Hawkins sportsman awd 1980; Bud Light tennis tournament, 2nd place 1983; Frito Lay, community serv awd for Muscular Dist 1984; Boys Clubs of America, cert of appreciation 1985; Patriots "Lite" man of the yr awd 1985; MA Special Olympics (JFK Found), cert of appreciation 1986; given the key to the city of Ft Pierce, FL 1986. **BUSINESS ADDRESS:** New England Patriots, 11 Shannon Lane, Mansfield, MA 02035.

WEATHERSPOON, J. B.
Business executive. **PERSONAL:** Born Jul 04, 1936, Cairo, GA; married Ann R; children: Jamel, Daryl, Lawrence. **EDUCATION:** Ft Valley State Coll, BS 1957; KS State Univ, MS 1959; MI State Univ, PhD 1970. **CAREER:** Amer Husbandry, tech 1959, instr 1959-60, utility worker 1960-61; W Nigeria Africa, reg beef officer 1961-66, meat tech 1966-68; Peter Eckrich & Sons, vice pres R&D 1970-. **ORGANIZATIONS:** Mem Sigma Xi Sci, Intl Union Food Tech. **HONORS/ACHIEVEMENTS:** 1st black to receive PhD in food sci.

WEATHERSPOON, JIMMY LEE
Elected official. **PERSONAL:** Born Mar 10, 1947, Ft Lauderdale, FL; married Marian Wilson; children: Joy LaWest, Kendra LaVett. **EDUCATION:** Automation School, Cert 1968; FL Atlantic Univ,. **CAREER:** Carver Cmmty Middle Schl PTA, mem advisory bd 1981-82, vice pres 1982-83; Delray Beach Voters League, vice pres 1982-84; IBM, Asst Systems Analyst 1980-. **ORGANIZATIONS:** Chrmn Commty Primitive Bapt Church Trustees 1982-; rep Dist 69 Palm Beach Cty Democratic Exec Comm 1984; mem Delray Beach Democratic Club 1984; mem TheNaciremas Club, Inc 1984. **HONORS/ACHIEVEMENTS:** Vice mayor polled highest vote in 1984 Delray Beach - first black so honored. **BUSINESS ADDRESS:** Associate Systems Analyst, IBM, PO Box 1328, Boca Raton, FL 33432.

WEATHERSPOON, KEITH EARL
Investment banker. **PERSONAL:** Born Dec 13, 1949, New Orleans, LA; married Marie L Slade, Aug 07, 1981; children: Ashley M Weatherspoon. **EDUCATION:** Xavier Univ, BS 1970; Northeast LA Univ, MBA 1973. **CAREER:** McNeal Labs, medical representative, 1973-78; EF Hutton, stock broker, 1978-82; Small Business Admin, exec asst to admin, 1982-84; Donaldson, Lufkin & Jenrette, investment banker, 1984-. **ORGANIZATIONS:** Dir bd, LA Small Business Equity Corp, 1981-83, Bd of City Trust of City of New Orleans, 1981-, Dashiki Project Theatre, 1985-, Dryades St YMCA, 1986-; mem, Kappa Alpha Psi, Zulu Mardi Gras Club; chmn of bd, Dashiki Project Theatre. **HOME ADDRESS:** 6810 Glengary Rd, New Orleans, LA 70126. **BUSINESS ADDRESS:** Vice President, Donaldson, Lufkin & Jenrette, 2237 So Acadian Hwy, Baton Rouge, LA 70808.

WEAVER, AUDREY TURNER
Retired business executive. **PERSONAL:** Born Jul 11, 1913, Racine, WI; daughter of Thaddeus S. Turner and Esker Trabue Turner; married Albert L. Weaver, Sep 27, 1942 (deceased). **EDUCATION:** Univ WI, 1943. **CAREER:** Chicago Defender, mng ed, city ed, time rptr 1955-; Jet Mag, asso ed 1953-54; Layout Afro-am Nwspr, rptr, copy ed 1943-53. **ORGANIZATIONS:** Mem, bd dir Black United Fund 1976; Chicago Press Club; Headline Club; Sigma Delta Chi CNDA; Nat Assn Media Women; NAACP; Chicago Urban Leag; Harris YWCA;Univ WI Alumni. **HONORS/ACHIEVEMENTS:** Recip Recog Award Prospair Ladies 1975; Freedom Fighters Award 1963; Woman Yr Media Women 1970; Black Achiev Award 1974; Distinctive Imprint Award Nat AssnUniv Women 1977; Midwest Comm Cncl Citation. **HOME ADDRESS:** 534 E 89th Pl, Chicago, IL 60619.

WEAVER, FRANK CORNELL
Director of marketing. **PERSONAL:** Born Nov 15, 1951, Tarboro, NC; son of Dr Frank B Weaver and Queen Lewis Weaver; married Kathryn Ann Hammond; children: Christina. **EDUCATION:** Howard Univ, BS Elect Engr 1972; Univ NC Chapel Hill, MBA Mktg 1976. **CAREER:** Westinghouse, asst sales engr 1972-73; NC Central Univ, asst prof 1975; Mellon Bank, credit analyst 1976-77; RCA Astro-Space Div, mgr commun satellites 1977-88; General Dynamics Comm Launch Servs, dir, Washington office 1988-. **ORGANIZATIONS:** Bd dir Direct Broadcast Satellite Assoc 1983-86; vstg prof Natl Urban League BEEP 1978-; panelist Congressional Black Caucus Comm Braintrust 1983; mem NAACP, RCA Minorities in Engrg Prog; Washington Space Business Roundtable, Society of Satellite Professionals; National Space Club, Tau Beta Pi Engr Honor Society. **HONORS/ACHIEVEMENTS:** "D-Sign Graphics", "UDI Supermkt" Case Studies Minority Venture Mgt 1975; "Intro to Commun Satellites" RCA Engr 1983; "RCA's Series 4000 Commun Satellites" Satellite Comm 1984; "DBS Satellite Tech" IEEE Electro 1985; Disting Author RCA 1984,85; Harlem YMCA Black Achiever in Industry 1986; "Atlas Family of Launch Vehicles", 1991 McGraw Hill Yearbook of Science and Technology. **BUSINESS ADDRESS:** Director, Washington Office, General Dynamics Commercial Launch Services, 1745 Jefferson Davis Hwy Suite 1000, Arlington, VA 22202.

WEAVER, GARLAND RAPHEAL, JR.
Dentist. **PERSONAL:** Born Jun 08, 1932, Baltimore, MD; married Barbara C Gee; children: Garland III, Edward. **EDUCATION:** Howard Univ, BS 1958; Howard Univ, DDS 1966. **CAREER:** Self Employed, dentist. **ORGANIZATIONS:** Past pres, MD Dental Soc; mem Kappa Alpha Psi Fraternity. **BUSINESS ADDRESS:** 5441 Park Heights Ave, Baltimore, MD 21215.

WEAVER, GARRETT F.
Lecturer. **PERSONAL:** Born Jun 17, 1948, Durham, NC. **EDUCATION:** NC Cntrl, Attend;Univ of NC, PhD 1987. **CAREER:** Univ of NC, lectr Afro-Amer studies 1985; Univ of WI, 1973-74; St Augustine Coll, 1972-73; NC St Univ, 1972-73; Rio Grande Coll; Marshall Univ; WV Univ, 1968-72; Afro-Amer & African Studies, 1985; Jackson State Univ, asst prof of history 1975-88. **ORGANIZATIONS:** Mem Am Historical Assn; Assn for Study of Afro-Am & Life & History; Nat Geo Soc; pres NAACP Charleston; mem Kanawha Co Div Comm Wlfr Bd; NASALH Biecennial Com; Phi Beta Sigma Frat; Afro-Am Studies Cons; Black Geneological Rsrchr; dir Public & Applied History Prop; dir of history English Link Proj Jackson State Univ. **BUSINESS ADDRESS:** Assistant Professor of History, Jackson StateUniv, 301 Peabody, UNC Chapel Hill, Chapel Hill, NC 27514.

WEAVER, GARY W.
Chief executive officer. **PERSONAL:** Born Sep 03, 1952, Washington, DC; married BV Goodrich. **EDUCATION:** VA Commonwealth U, BS Bus Adm 1974. **CAREER:** Trifam Sys Inc, pres 1977-; VA Hsg Dev Auth Richmond, proj mgr 1975-77; City of Richmond, zoning ofcr insp dept 1974-75; Assn of Fed Appraisers, appraiser 1978-; Soc of Real Est Appraisers, asso 1978-; N VA Bd of Rltrs, rltr 1978-. **ORGANIZATIONS:** Exec com Neighbors for a Better Comm 1979-; mem McLean Task Force (Planning) 1985. **BUSINESS ADDRESS:** 1401 Spring Hill Rd, McLean, VA 22102.

WEAVER, GEORGE LEON-PAUL
Consultant. **PERSONAL:** Born Jun 18, 1912, Pittsburgh, PA; married Mary. **EDUCATION:** Roosevelt Univ, 1940-42; Howard Univ Law School, 1942-43; Howard Univ, 1962. **CAREER:** World ORT Union, consultant, 1975; Intl Labor Org Geneva Switzerland, special asst to dir general, 1969-retirement. **ORGANIZATIONS:** Mem, CIO War & Relief Comm 1941-42; asst to sec treas CIO 1942-55; exec sec AFL-CIO 1955-58; spec asst to Sec of Labor 1961; asst sec of Labor Intl Affairs 1969; mem bd United Negro Coll Fund; vice chmn Atlanta Univ Ctr.

WEAVER, HERBERT C.
Civil engineer. **PERSONAL:** Born in Pittsburgh, PA; son of Joseph G Weaver and Lucy Gardener; married Rayma Heywood; children: Carol, Jonathan. **EDUCATION:** Univ of Pittsburgh, BS 1961. **CAREER:** Commonwealth of PA, bridge designer, hydraulic engr; Rust Engr Co, civil engr; Pullman Swindell Co, proj engr, civil engr; Allegheny County Dept of Engrg & Construction, prof & mgr; Herbert C Weaver Assoc Inc, pres, founder. **ORGANIZATIONS:** Mem ASCE, PSPE, NSPE; appt to panel arbitrators of Amer Arbitration Assoc 1970; reg professional engr; reg land surveyor; trustee Grace Presbyterian Church 1963-69; vice pres Booster Club of Wilkinsburg Christian School 1971-72; mem E Hills Pitt Club 1974-; asst track coach Churchill Area Track Club 1980-; certified official, The Athletics Congress, 1980. **MILITARY SERVICE:** AUS.

WEAVER, JOHN ARTHUR
Physician. **PERSONAL:** Born Nov 23, 1940, Hemingway, SC; son of Arthur C Weaver and Winnie Mae Williams; married Yvonne Jackson; children: Jennifer, Jessica. **EDUCATION:** Virginia Union Univ, BS, 1964; Howard Univ, MS, 1968, PhD, 1970, MD, 1978. **CAREER:** North Carolina State Univ, assoc professor of chemistry, Greensboro, NC, 1970-74, summer, 1975; Howard Univ, intern, 1978-79, resident, 1979-81; The Johns Hopkins Institutions, fellow in nuclear medicine, 1981-83; Weaver Medical Assocs, PC, pres, 1983-. **ORGANIZATIONS:** Mem, AMA, NMA, RSNA, SNM. **HONORS/ACHIEVEMENTS:** NSF grantee 1972; NIH grantee 1972; Piedmont grantee 1973. **BUSINESS ADDRESS:** Pres, Weaver Medical Assoc, PC, 505 West Leigh St, Suite 102, Richmond, VA 23220.

WEAVER, JOSEPH D.
Physician. **PERSONAL:** Born Sep 11, 1912, Winton, NC; married Rossie P Clay; children: Jesse R, Claudia P. **EDUCATION:** Howard Univ, BS 1934; Howard Univ Med School, MD 1938. **CAREER:** Roanoke Chowan Hosp, staff 1972-74; ECU Med School, asst prof med family practice; Hertford Cty NC, med examiner 1971-. **ORGANIZATIONS:** Mem Beta Kappa Chi Honor Soc 1935-; vice pres 1st Dist Medical Soc 1973-; treas Eastern NC Med, Dental & Pharm Soc; mem Hertford Cty Med Soc, NC Med Soc, Amer Med Assoc, Natl Med Assoc, Amer Publ Health Assoc, Amer Geriatrics Soc, Natl Rehab Assoc, Amer Acad Fam Physicians; mem Elks, 32 Deg Mason, Airplane Owners & Pilots Assoc; chmn bd Roanoke Chowan Med Ctr; grand medical dir IBPOE of W. **HONORS/ACHIEVEMENTS:** Amer Negro Commemorative Soc Achievement Awd Kappa Alpha Psi 1964; Scroll of Hon Omega Psi Phi 1963; Dr of the Year Awd No State Med Soc 1962-63; Cert of Merit & Sel Serv Medal from Congress of US 1945; Cert of Merit, Scottish Rite, Masons. **MILITARY SERVICE:** AUS 1st lt 1942-44. **BUSINESS ADDRESS:** Medical Examiner, Hertford County NC, 111 No Maple St, Ahoskie, NC 27910.

WEAVER, REGINALD LEE
Educator, association executive. **PERSONAL:** Born Aug 13, 1939, Danville, IL; married Betty Jo Moppin; children: Reginald Von, Rowan Anton. **EDUCATION:** IL St U, BA 1961; Roosevelt U, MA 1973. **CAREER:** IL Ed Assn, vice pres 1977-81, president; School Dist 152, teacher 1961-; Budget Com IL Ed Assn, chmn 1977-81; IPACE Com IL Educ Assn, vice chmn 1977-81; Staff & Retirement Com IL Ed Assn, chmn 1979-81. **ORGANIZATIONS:** Mem Tchr Certification Bd IL Ofc of Ed 1972-83; mem Intrntl Reltns Com NEA 1975-81; del WCOTP Wash DC Lagos Nigeria Brasilia Brazil 1976-80; mem Masons 1965-; pres Harvey Ed Assn 1967-68; vice pres Negotiating Team Harvey Ed Assn 1970. **HONORS/ACHIEVEMENTS:** Listed Outstndng Young Men of Am 1972; Hum Rels Award IL Ed Assn 1974; numerous Spkng Engagements 1977-. **BUSINESS ADDRESS:** President, Illinois Education Association, 100 E Edwards, Springfield, IL 62704.

WEAVER, ROBERT C.
Retired government adminstrator and educator. **PERSONAL:** Born Dec 29, 1907, Washington, DC; son of Mortimer G Weaver and Florence Freeman Weaver; married Ella V Haith; children: Robert C (dec). **EDUCATION:** Harvard Coll, BS (Cum Laude) 1929; Harvard Univ, MA 1931, PhD 1934. **CAREER:** Dept Int Consult Housing Div, adv neg affrs 1933-38; US Housing Auth, spec asst 1938-40; Nat'l Def Adv Comm, admin asst 1940-42; Labor Div Office of Prod Mgmt & War Bond Bd 1942-43; War Manpower Comm 1943-44; Chicago Mayor's Comm on Race Relations, dir 1944-45; Am Council on Race Relations, dircomm services 1945-48; UNRRA Mission to the Ukraine kiev, reports officer and acting chief 1946; John Hay Whitney Found, dir Oper Fellowship 1949-54; Fulbright Fellowships, selection committee for 2 European areas 1952-54; NY Dept of Comm Housing 1954; NY State Rent Admin 1955-59; Ford Found, consult 1959-60; New York City Hsng & Redev Bd, vchmn 1960-61; US Housing & Fin Agency, admin 1961-66; US Dept of Housing & Urban Devel, sec 1966-68; Baruch Coll, pres 1969-70; Hunter Coll NY, dist prof 1971- 78 retired. **ORGANIZATIONS:** Bd of dir Metro Life Ins Co 1969-78, Municipal Asst Corp 1975-; bd of trustees Bowery Savings Bank 1969-80, Mt Sinai Hosp & Med School 1970-; Lincoln Inst of Land Policy board; mem Const Panel US Controller General 1973-; New York City Concilliation & Appeals Bd for rent stabilization 1973-84; Harvard Univ Sch of Design, visiting com 1978-83; exec comm of bd of NAACP Legal Defense Fund 1978-; Am Acad of Arts & Sciences 1985; Publications, Negro Labor, A Natl Problem 1946,The Negro Ghetto 1948, The Urban Complex 1964, Dilemmas of Urban America 1985; 175 articles; chmn of Task Force on the Democratic Developments of New Towns Twentieth Century Fund, 1971-72; mem of Bd of Dir and

Research Policy Comm, Economic Devel Comm for the 1970's; chmn of Bd of Dir, NAACP, 1960-61; pres, Natl Comm Again st Discrimination in Housing, 1973-87. **HONORS/ ACHIEVEMENTS:** Spingarn Medal NAACP 1962; Russworm Award 1963; delivered The Annual Godkin Lectures at Harvard, 1965; Albert Einstein Commemorative Award 1968; Merrick Moore Spaulding Achievement Award 1968; Award for Public Serv US Gen Acctg Office 1973; New York City Urban League Frederick Douglass Award 1977; Schomburg Collection Award 1978; Elected to Hall of Fame Nat'l Assoc of Home Builders 1982; M Justin Herman Award of the Nat'l Assoc of Hsng & Redevelopment Officials 1986; Equal Opportunity Day Award of Natl Urban League, 1987; recipient of some 30 honorary degrees from Amherst, Boston Coll, Columbia, Elmira Coll, Howard, Harvard, Morehouse, Rutgers, Univ of Illinois, Univ of Michigan, Univ of Pennsylvania and others; Award for Innovations in Buildings, Amer Buildings Magazine, 1965. **HOME ADDRESS:** 215 E 68th St, New York, NY 10021.

WEBB, ALLAN
Director. **PERSONAL:** Born Jan 22, 1931, Washington, DC; son of Allen Webb and Catherine Webb; married Olga; children: Lisa, Marc. **EDUCATION:** Attended, Univ of Bridgeport, CT, (formerly Arnold Coll), 1953. **CAREER:** New York Giants, starting safety, 1962-63, scout, 1972, offensive backfield coach, 1974; Cleveland Browns, dir of pro personnel; San Francisco 49er's, dir of pro personnel. **HONORS/ACHIEVEMENTS:** Inducted into Coll Hall of Fame, 1984; inducted into High School Hall of Fame 1986. **MILITARY SERVICE:** USN 2 yrs.

WEBB, HAROLD H.
Retired government employee, educator. **PERSONAL:** Born Apr 30, 1925, Greensboro, NC; son of Haywood Eugene Webb, Sr and Vina Wadlington Webb; married Lucille Holcomb, Jan 15, 1949; children: Kaye. **EDUCATION:** A&T StateUniv Greensboro NC, BS 1949; MS 1952. **CAREER:** Hillsborough, tchr 1948-54; princ 1954-62; State Sci Consult Raleigh 1962-66; Nat Def Educ Act, asst dir 1966-69; Hum Rel, asst dir 1969-70; Tit I ESEA, dir 1970-73; Comp Edn, dep asst supt 1973-77; Ofc of State Personnel NC, state personnel dir. **ORGANIZATIONS:** Mem NEA; NSTA; vchmn NC Assn Adminstr Comp Edn; Nat Comp Educ Mgmt Proj; trust Wake Tech Inst; bd dir Raleigh Little Theatre; bd dir New Bern Ave Day Care Cent; bd dir Raleigh Cncl for Aging; exec com Raleigh Ctzns Assn; past mem Orng Co Bd Pub Wlfr Outstg Adminstr Orng Co Schs 1960; del Nat Conf on Educ of Poor Chicago 1973; chmn, Wake County North Carolina Planning Bd, 1988-; mem, Univ of North Carolina Bd of Governors, 1989-. **HONORS/ACHIEVEMENTS:** Honorary Degree Doctor of Humanities, North Carolina A&T State Univ, 1978; Tarheel of the week, Raleigh News and Observer, 1980. **MILITARY SERVICE:** USAC 1943-46. **HOME ADDRESS:** 1509 Tierney Circle, Raleigh, NC 27610.

WEBB, HARVEY, JR.
Business executive. **PERSONAL:** Born Jul 31, 1929, Washington, DC; married Z Ozella; children: Tomai, Harvey III, Hoyt. **EDUCATION:** Howard Univ, BS 1956, DDS 1960; St Elizabeth's Hosp, intern 1960; Howard Univ, MS 1962; Johns Hopkins Univ, MPH 1967. **CAREER:** Howard Univ, fellow 1960-62; Grp Health Assn Am, grp pract 1962-63; Howard Univ, instr 1962-63; Univ MD, school of nursing 1976-77; dentist pvt pract 1960-77; Johns Hopkins Univ, 1969-71; Constant Care Comm Hlth Ctr, exec dir 1971-87. **ORGANIZATIONS:** Guest lectr Howard Univ Coll Dent 1962-65; dental ofcr Bur DC Dept Pub Health 1963-66; flw Johns Hopkins Univ 1966-67; asst prof Howard Univ 1968-69; asst clinical prof Univ MD 1969-; dent coord Provident Hosp 1968-69; staff mem Provident Hosp 1968-; Children's Hosp 1970-; Johns Hopkins Hosp 1969-71; bd mem MD Heart Assn 1969-74; trustee Howard Co Genl Hosp 1978-85; pres Health Resources Inc 1978-80; bd mem Howard Cnty Gen Hosp 1979-82; mem Central MD Hlth Sys Agen 1980-81; constructed Constant Care Hlth Cntr Balt 1980; mem Alpha Phi Alpha; Am Dent Assn; Nat Dent Assn; Robert T Freeman Dent Soc; AAAS; Intl Assn Dent Rsch; DC Dent Soc; Maimonides Dent Soc; DC Pub Hlth Assn; DC Hlth & Welfare Cncl; Am Pub Hlth Assn; Polit Action Com RT Freeman Dent Soc; Am Assn Pub Hlth Dentists; MD State Pub Hlth Assn; coord Comm Vol Dent Svc; Dent Coord Provident Hosp; mem Balt City Dent Soc; life mem NAACP; mem Howard Univ Alumni; Neighbors Inc; Brightwood Civic Assn; WA Urban League; bd dir WA, DC Home Rule Comm. **HONORS/ACHIEVEMENTS:** Outstanding Men of Decade 1979; Com Serv Award Pi Eta Chi 1979; NM Carroll Meth Home Award 1980; numerous publs & presentations. **MILITARY SERVICE:** AUS 2nd Lt 1948-52; AUSR Maj 1953-70 (retired). **BUSINESS ADDRESS:** 100 Meto Plz, Baltimore, MD 21215.

WEBB, JAMES EUGENE
Business executive. **PERSONAL:** Born Aug 03, 1956, Cleveland, OH; children: Brian James, Richard Anthony. **EDUCATION:** Attended, Cleveland Institute of Banking 1976, Cuyahoga Comm Coll 1978. **CAREER:** Warrensville Ctr for Mentally Retarded, caseworker 1975-78; Republic Steel, mill wright 1978-82; Webb Mfg/Webb World Inc, president 1982-. **ORGANIZATIONS:** Consultant Career Programs Cleveland Public Schools 1985; vice pres Cleveland Business League 1985-86; speaker for several groups; parent advisory comm Canterbury School. **HONORS/ACHIEVEMENTS:** Business of the Year for City of Cleveland (Webb Mfg) 1984; Entrepreneur of the Year City of Cleveland 1984; Man of the Year Cleveland Senior Council 1985. **HOME ADDRESS:** 2404 Rinard Rd, Cleveland Heights, OH 44118.

WEBB, JAMES O.
Business executive. **PERSONAL:** Born Nov 25, 1931, Cleveland, OH; son of James O Sr and Bessie R; married Frankie L Lowe; children: Lisa S, Paula R Webb Dixon. **EDUCATION:** Morehouse Coll, BA 1953; Univ of Michigan, MBA 1957. **CAREER:** Mutual of NY, actuarial asst 1957-62; Supreme Life Ins co, vice pres actuary 1962-66; Blue Cross-Blue Shield of IL, sr vice pres 1966-84; Dental Network of Amer, pres & CEO 1984-. **ORGANIZATIONS:** Dir South Shore Bank 1975-; dir treasurer exec comm Amer Acad of Actuaries 1975-78; mem Planning Exec Inst, Midwest Planning Assoc; founder & convenor Business Devel Inst Blue Cross-Blue Shield 1983-; pres Glencoe School Bd 1971-77; exec comm, vice pres No Cook Cty Private Industrial Council 1983-86; chmn, dir Home Investments Fund 1968; Chicago Metro Housing & Planning Council 1980-85; gov comm Health Asst Prog 1979-83; pres & ceo, Effective Data Processing, Inc 1984-; pres Managed Dental Care of Canada 1986-. **HONORS/ACHIEVEMENTS:** Outstanding Businessmen's Awd Young Blacks in Politics 1984;. **MILITARY SERVICE:** AUS corpl E-4 1953-55. **BUSINESS ADDRESS:** President, Dental Network of Amer, 1220 Kensington Rd, Oak Brook, IL 60521.

WEBB, JOE
Elected official. **PERSONAL:** Born Aug 18, 1935, San Antonio, TX; married Frances; children: Joe Jr, Linda Ray, Vincent, Daniel. **EDUCATION:** San Antonio Coll, Associates; St Marys Univ, Pre-Law Courses; HEB Mgmt School, Cert, Guadalupe Theol Seminary, Assoc Minister. **CAREER:** YMCA, public relations dir 1957-69; HEB Supermarket, store dir 1969-80; Neighborhood Grocery Store, independent grocer 1980-; Webb Way Supermarket, pres/owner 1983-; City of San Antonio, city councilman. **ORGANIZATIONS:** Mem Black Congressional Caucus 1977-; city councilmem City of San Antonio 1977-; state grand sr warden Masonic Lodge 1981-; assoc minister Zion Star Baptist Church 1982-; steering comm mem Natl League of Cities 1983-85; SA TX chmn Jesse Jackson Campaign 1984; chmn bd dir AAOMMS of North and South America Imperial Grand Council NBC/LEO Reg Dir XVII; mem Alamo City C of C. **HONORS/ACHIEVEMENTS:** Father of the Year 20th Century Club; Man of the Year Elks; Patterson Awd United Negro Coll Fund. **BUSINESS ADDRESS:** City Councilman, City of San Antonio, PO Box 9066, San Antonio, TX 78228.

WEBB, JOSEPH G.
Police officer. **PERSONAL:** Born Dec 03, 1950, Chicago, IL; son of Wellington M Webb and Mardina G Williams; married Marilyn L Bell, Oct 23, 1978; children: Alishea R, Ami R, Ciara M. **EDUCATION:** Attended Univ of Colorado, Boulder CO, 1969-71; attended Metropolitan State Coll, Denver CO, 1982-86, received AAs & BA; attending Univ of Denver Coll of Law, Denver CO, 1988-. **CAREER:** Denver General Hospital, mental health worker, 1972-77; Denver Police Dept, sergeant, 1977-. **ORGANIZATIONS:** Mem, Natl Black Police Assn 1983-, Colorado Business League 1985-86, Colorado Black Roundtable 1985-; consultant, Oasis Project 1986-87, NE Denver Task Force on Drug Abuse 1988-89. **HONORS/ACHIEVEMENTS:** Citizens Appreciate Police Award; SCAT Appreciation Award; Peer Support Recognition Award; Black Officer of the Year; Officer of the Month; Optimist Intl Law Enforcement Recognition; Intelligence Bureau Appreciation Award; Natl Black Police Assn Leadership Award.

WEBB, LUCIOUS MOSES
Labor liaison. **PERSONAL:** Born Sep 19, 1928, Canfield, AR; married Dewene Jeanette Hale; children: Ronnette, Richard, Steven. **EDUCATION:** Creighton U, Attended 1953-54;Univ of Omaha, Attended 1955-56; Commercial Bus Sch, Attended; George Washington U, Attended 1969-70. **CAREER:** Labor Participation ARC, regional dir 1985. **ORGANIZATIONS:** Mem United Packing House Workers Local #8 Armour & Co 19 Years; chmn of COPE Met Packing House Workers 10 Years; del Intl Union Conv; mem NE State& Douglas Co Dem Central Com; mem Mayor of Omaha Citizen Com & Omaha EEOC; ex-ocl YMCA; master mason Nathaniel Hunter AM & FM Lodge #12; mem Ch of Jesus Christ of Latter Day Saints. **MILITARY SERVICE:** AUS corpl 2 Years. **BUSINESS ADDRESS:** Dir, American Natl Red Cross, Labor Participation, 615 N St Asaph St, Alexandria, VA 22814.

WEBB, MELVIN RICHARD
Educator. **PERSONAL:** Born Feb 09, 1940, Cuthbert, GA; married Brenda Janet Burton. **EDUCATION:** Albany State Col, BS 1992; Atlanta U, MS 1968; OH State U, PhD 1977. **CAREER:** Clark Coll, prof biol & science educ 1972-; Resource Center for Science & Engineering Atlanta Univ, asst dir, 1978-; Atlanta Bd of Educ, biology teacher 1967-69; Dougherty Co Bd of Educ, biology and chemistry 1963-66; Lee Co Bd of Educ, science teacher 1962-63. **ORGANIZATIONS:** Mem Nat Sci Tchrs Assn; mem GA Sci Tchrs Assn; mem Phi Delta Kappa; mem NAACP; mem So Christian Leadership Conf. **HONORS/ ACHIEVEMENTS:** Who's Who Among Students in Am Us & Colls 1961-62; Sci Dept Citation Albany State 1962; STAR Tchr, GA State C of C 1969; Acad Year Grants to AtlantaUniv and OH State U; Nat Sci Found 1966-67 1969-70. **BUSINESS ADDRESS:** 240 Chestnut St SW, Atlanta, GA 30314.

WEBB, SCHUYLER CLEVELAND
US navy officer. **PERSONAL:** Born Jun 28, 1951, Springfield, MA; son of Cleveland Webb and bettye Wright Webb; children: Kayla Monique. **EDUCATION:** Morehouse Coll, BA (Cum Laude) 1974; Amer Inst for Foreign Study, Certificate 1975; Univ of MA, MS 1978; Natl Univ, MBA 1986. **CAREER:** Univ of Massachusetts, asst trainer & alcoholism counselor 1974-77; Inst for Studying Educ Policy Howard Univ, rsch asst 1978; Lawrence Johnson & Assoc Inc, tech staff/consultant 1978-81; US Navy Medical Serv Corps, rsch psychologist & hospital corpsman 1981-; Howard Univ Center for Sickle Cell Disease, Washington, DC, editorial comm mem/consultant 1979-81; Higher Horizons Day Care Center, Crossroads, VA, consultant 1980-81. **ORGANIZATIONS:** Mem Assoc of Military Surgeons, Human Factors Soc, Sleep Rsch Soc, Assoc of Black Psychologists, Amer Psychological Assoc; public relations & scholarship comm Natl Naval Officer Assoc San Diego Chap 1983-; co-chair Cultural Heritage & Black History Comm San Diego USN 1984-86; advanced open water diver Professional Assoc of Diving Instructors 1986-; mem NAACP, Alpha Phi Alpha, Urban League, Morehouse Alumni Assoc, Equal Opportunity Officer, Combined Federal Campaign Officer; vice pres of membership, natl Naval officers Assn 1988-89; mem Second Harvest Food Bank 1987-. **HONORS/ACHIEVEMENTS:** Certificate of Achievement in Comm and Counseling Psychology 1974; Horace Barr Fellowship 1974-77; Collegiate Comm for the Educ of Black Students Fellowship1974-75; Our Crowd Scholarship; Springfield Teachers Club Scholarship; Springfield Coll Comm Serv Awd; Academic Scholarship (4 year tuition scholarship), Morehouse College 1970-74; Psychology Department honors, Morehouse College, 1974; Natl Univ leadership Scholarship, Natl Univ, 1984; "Jet Lag in Military Operations", Naval Health Research Center, San Diego, CA 1986; publication "Comparative Analysis of Decompression Sickness", Journal of Hyperbaric Medicine, 2:55-62, 1987. **MILITARY SERVICE:** USN lt 6 yrs; Leadership Awd, Pistol Sharpshooter, Physical Fitness Awd, Commendation Letter; Rifle Expert 1988. **BUSINESS ADDRESS:** Medical Serv Corps Officer, US Navy, Naval Biodynamics Lab, PO Box 29407, New Orleans, LA 70189.

WEBB, WELLINGTON E.
Health official. **PERSONAL:** Born Feb 17, 1941, Chicago, IL; married Wilma J; children: Keith, Tony, Allen, Stephanie. **EDUCATION:** CO State Coll, BA 1964;Univ No CO, MA 1972. **CAREER:** CO State Univ Manpower Lab, dir 1969-74; State Rep 1973-77; CO Carter/Mondale Campaign, 1976; US Dept Health & Human Serv, principal reg offical 1977-; City of Denver, auditor. **ORGANIZATIONS:** Chmn Dem Caucus CO House of Rep 1975-; chmn Health Welfare & Inst Com 1975-76; del Dem Nat Conv 1976; trustee bd Denver Childrens Hosp 1975-; bd dir Denver Operation PUSH 1975-; bd dir Denver Urban Coalition 1975; chmn United Negro Coll Fund 1973-75. **HONORS/ACHIEVEMENTS:** Barney Ford Award for Political Action 1976; Leadership of Yr Award Thomas Jefferson HS 1976.

BUSINESS ADDRESS: Executive Dir, State of CO, Dept of Regulatory Agencies, 1525 Sherman St Rm 110, Denver, CO 80203.

WEBB, ZADIE OZELLA
Physician, administrator. **PERSONAL:** Born Aug 22, 1932, Washington, DC; daughter of John V Thompson and Zadie O Sizemore Thompson; married Harvey Webb Jr, DDS,MPH; children: Tomai Adana, Harvey III, Hoyt Kelan. **EDUCATION:** Howard Univ Coll of Liberal Arts, BS 1954; Howard Univ Coll of Med, MD 1958; Johns Hopkins School of Hygiene & Public Health, MPH 1974. **CAREER:** DC Schools, school health physician 1963-64; Dept of Public health, med officer pediatrics 1963-68; Howard Univ Coll of Med, pediatric consultant 1964-68; Childrenin Foster Care, dir health serv 1968-73; Head Start Program Washington DC & Cambridge MD, pediatric consult 1969-76; Washington DC Govt, chief med asst div 1973-76; Washington DC Govt Health Admin, chief maternal & child health 1976-80. **ORGANIZATIONS:** Mem Links, NAACP, Urban League, Capezios, Carats, Parents and Alumni Univ PA, Howard Univ Medical Alumni Assn, Montague Cobb Med Soc, Natl Medical Assn. **HONORS/ACHIEVEMENTS:** Fellowships NIH, Natl Inst Mental Health 1956-59; published numerous med articles 1970-75; Physicians Recognition Award AMA 1971; Certificate of Appreciation Natl Dental Assoc.

WEBBER, JESSIE LOUIS
Businessman. **PERSONAL:** Born Apr 16, 1947; married Nancy Thomas; children: Dione, Mary, Jesse Jr, Rita, Renee, Samual. **EDUCATION:** Grambling Coll, 1966; Central Trade School, 1969. **CAREER:** Sunbeam Elect Appl, electrician 1970; Webbers Elect Svcs, self employed 1981-; Red River Parish School Bd, bd mem 1973-85. **ORGANIZATIONS:** Pres PTO 1974; mem fin, comm mem, Building & Grounds 1976; vice pres personnel, bd comm mem PTO 1984.

WEBBER, PAUL R., III
Judge. **PERSONAL:** Born Jan 24, 1934, Gadsden, SC; married Fay DeShields; children: Paul IV, Stephen, Nikki. **EDUCATION:** BA, 1955; South Carolina State Coll, JD, 1957. **CAREER:** Neighborhood Legislative Serv Program, District of Columbia, mng atty, 1967-69; Antritrst Div US Dept Just, trial atty, 1964-67; Golden State Mutual Life Insurance Co LA, assoc counsel, 1960-64; UCLA, asst law lib, 1959-60; Allen Univ, Columbia, SC, private practice & lecturerr, 1958-59; Dolphin Branton Stafford & Webber, atty, 1969-77; Howard Univ, lectr; Geoorge Washington Univ Law School, visiting prof, Summer, 1973; District of Columbia Superior Court, judge. **ORGANIZATIONS:** mem, Amer Natl District of Columbia, California & South Carolina Bar Assn; Alpha Phi Alpha; Sigma Pi Phi; The Guardsmen; past chmn Civil Practive & Family Law; Sec Natl Bar Assn. **HONORS/ACHIEVEMENTS:** Trial Judge of the Year, 1985-86 by unanimous vote of the Trial Lawyers Assn of Metro Washington, DC. **MILITARY SERVICE:** UAS Artillery 2nd lt 1957. **BUSINESS ADDRESS:** Judge, DC Superior Court, 500 Indiana Ave, NW, Washington, DC 20001.

WEBBER, WILLIAM STUART
Elected official. **PERSONAL:** Born Oct 17, 1942, Hartshorne, OK; married Betty I; children: Natalie Jewell, Stuart Franklin. **EDUCATION:** Eastern OK A&M, 1960-62. **CAREER:** Rancher Santa Gertudis Breeder, 1958-85; electronic tech Rockwell Intl 1964-83; county comm Pittsburgh County 1983-. **ORGANIZATIONS:** Mason AF&M Pittsburgh County Cattlemans Assoc 1967-; real estate developer; professional coon hunter Professional Coon Hunters Assoc 1981-85; inducted mem Amer Cattle Breeder Hall of Fame; mem Church of God in Christ. **MILITARY SERVICE:** OK NG E5 8 years. **HOME ADDRESS:** Rt 1, Box 240, Hartshorne, OK 74547.

WEBER, DANIEL
Attorney. **PERSONAL:** Born Sep 25, 1942, New Orlean, LA; married Shirley Ann Nash; children: Akilah F, Akil K. **EDUCATION:** Los Angeles City Coll, history 1961-63; CA State Coll LA, BA History, Sciology 1968; UCLA School of Law, JD 1971. **CAREER:** Los Angeles City Attny Office, law clerk 1972-73; CA State Attny Gen, grad legal asst 1973-74; Legal Aid Soc of San Diego, attny 1975; Grossmont Coll, teacher 1974-75; Employment Devel Dept State of CA, legal counsel 1975; Private Practice of Law, self employed 1975-76; Mira Mesa Jr Coll, teacher bus law 1979-82; Soc Sec Admin Office, govt lawyer 1976-83; Private Practice of Law, self employed 1983-; Earl B Gilliam Bar Assoc, president. **ORGANIZATIONS:** Mem 1973-, bd of dir 1979-80, NAACP; mem 1976-80, chmn 1976-80, treas 1978-79, court comm pres 1981-82 & 1984-85 Earl B Gilliam Bar Assoc; San Diego Mncpl Ct Appt Attny List 1976; bd of gov 1977, chmn 1977-80, judicial sel pres-elect 1979-80, pres 1980-81 CA Assoc of Blk Lawyers; San Diego bd of zoning Appeals 1978-82; bd of dir State Fed & Appellate Defenders Inc 1979-80;Indigents Defense Bd 1979-80; Aequus Dist Comm BSA 1980-; bd of dir 1981-, chmn 1981-, BAPAC; bd of gov San Diego Bar Assoc, Amer Bar Assoc, Natl Bar Assoc 1981-82; Phi Alpha Delta; rep, mem bar relations comm Student Bar Assoc; rep, student rep acad senate sub-comm on equal oppty, comm of housing, Grad Student Assoc; org mem Black Law Students Assoc; chmn BLSA Defense Comm, co-chmn BLSA Recruitment Comm' org mem UCLA Black Law Jrnl; courts adm to practice before, CA State Courts, NJ State Courts, US Dist Courts in NJ, Supreme Ct of US, US Cts of Appeals-9th, 5th & DC, US Tax Court, US Customs Court. **HONORS/ACHIEVEMENTS:** Cert of Appreciation 1979,80, Outstanding Pres Awd 1980-81, CA Assoc of Black Lawyers; Outstanding Pres Awd 1981-82 Earl B Gilliam Bar Assoc of San Diego Cty; Cert of Appreciation for Serv on Bd of Zoning Appeals City of San Diego; Spec Commendation 1983 City Council of San Diego; Resolution for Outstanding Service to Legal Profession CA State Assemblyman Pete Chacon 79th Assembly Dist; Cert of Appreciation for Outstanding Contribs to the Delivery of VoluntaryLegal Service in CA 1983 The State Bar of CA Bd of Governors; Outstanding Serv Awd 1985 San Diego Volunteer Prog. **BUSINESS ADDRESS:** President, Earl B Gilliam Bar Assn, 443 West C St Ste 111, San Diego, CA 92101.

WEBER, SHIRLEY NASH
Education admin. **PERSONAL:** Born Sep 20, 1948, Hope, AR; married Daniel Weber; children: Akilah Faizah; Akil Khalfani. **EDUCATION:** Univ of CA LA, BA 1966-70, MA 1970-71, PhD 1971-75. **CAREER:** Episcopal City Mission Soc LA, caseworker 1969-72; CA State Coll LA, instructor 1972; San Diego State Univ, prof 1972-. **ORGANIZATIONS:** Bd mem CA Black Faculty & Staff 1976-80; pres Black Caucus Speech Comm Assoc 1980-82; pres Natl Comm Assn 1983-85; regional editor Western Journal of Speech 1979-; adv bd Battered Women's Serv YWCA 1981-; Council of 21 Southwestern Christian Coll 1983-; 1st vice pres Natl Sor of Phi Delta Kappa Delta Upsilon Chapt; trustee Bd of Educ San Diego Unified School District 1988-92. **HONORS/ACHIEVEMENTS:** Fellow Woodrow Wilson Fellowship 1970; Outstanding Young Women in America 1976, 1980; Notable Americans 1978; Black Achievement Action Interprise Develop 1981; Women of Distinction Women Inc 1984; Natl Citation Award, Natl Sorority of Phi Delta Kappa, Inc. July 1989. **BUSINESS ADDRESS:** Professor & Chairperson, San Diego State Univrsity, Afro-American Studies, San Diego, CA 92182.

WEBSTER, CECIL RAY
Military officer/educator. **PERSONAL:** Born Mar 29, 1954, Franklin, TX; married Marsha E Burnett; children: Cecil Jr. **EDUCATION:** Prairie View A&M Univ, BS 1976; Texas A&M Univ, MS 1984. **CAREER:** US Army Engr School, instructor 1981-82; Grad School, 1982-84; US Military Acad, asst prof 1984-87. **ORGANIZATIONS:** Mem Assoc of United States Army 1976-; sec Soc of Amer Military Engrs 1984-. **MILITARY SERVICE:** AUS major 10 yrs; Army Commendation Medal, Airborne Badge, Air Assault. **BUSINESS ADDRESS:** Assistant Professor, US Military Academy, Dept of Mechanics, West Point, NY 10996.

WEBSTER, CHARLES
Dentist. **PERSONAL:** Born Dec 15, 1936, LeCompte, LA. **EDUCATION:** Southern Univ, BS 1959; Howard Univ, MS 1971, Coll of Dentistry DDS 1977. **CAREER:** GA Ave Kiwanis Club, business mgr 1984-85; Private Practice, dentist; Dept Human Svcs, dental officer. **ORGANIZATIONS:** Mem Kappa Alpha Psi 1957-; dental intern St Elizabeth Hosp Washington DC 1977-78; dental dir Montgomery Co Detention Ctr 1978; mem Amer Soc of Dentistry for Children 1978; mem Amer Dental Soc 1981, Assoc of Military Surgeons 1981, Anethesiology Training Uniform Serv Medical Sch 1982-84. **HONORS/ACHIEVEMENTS:** Mem Eta Chi Sigma Hon Biological Soc, Beta Beta Beta Hon Biol Soc; Certificate Amer Cancer Soc 1977. **MILITARY SERVICE:** AUS major Army Natl Guard 1981-. **HOME ADDRESS:** 6713 14th St NW, Washington, DC 20012. **BUSINESS ADDRESS:** Dental Officer, Dept Human Services, 7723 Alaska Ave NW, Washington, DC 20012.

WEBSTER, DEWITT T., JR.
Dentist. **PERSONAL:** Born Dec 24, 1932, Hattiesburg, MS; married Carol Daniels. **EDUCATION:** Toucaloo Coll, BS 1956; HowardUniv Coll of Dentistry, DDS 1965. **CAREER:** Dentist, pvt prac 1985. **ORGANIZATIONS:** Mem Nat Dental Assn; Am Dental Assn; Academy of Gen Dentistry; Am Endodontic Soc; Met Dental Assn; MD Dental Soc; mem Kappa Alpha Psi Gamma Rho Chap Polemarch 1949; Washington DC Chap Kappa Alpha Psi; Lambda Chpt; Chi Delta Mu; Silver Spring Chap Kappa Alpha Psi. **MILITARY SERVICE:** USN 1950-54.

WEBSTER, ISABEL GATES
Judge. **PERSONAL:** Born Apr 16, 1931, Henderson, NC; daughter of C. Jerry Gates and Rowena Gregory Gates; married Donald George Webster; children: Donald E, Jerry G, Karen E, Michael G. **EDUCATION:** NC Coll at Durham, attended 1948-49; Boston Univ, BS 1953, JD 1955; Harvard Law School, Program of Instruction for Lawyers, Cambridge, MA June 1985 certificate. **CAREER:** Self-employed, attorney; Jackson Patterson Parks & Franklin, attorney 1972-74; City of Atlanta, asst city atty, first asst city atty 1978-86; City Court of Atlanta, assoc judge 1986-. **ORGANIZATIONS:** Mem Commission on Continuing Legal Education 1983-88; mem Fed Bar Council NO GA 1983-86 State Bar of GA, Gate City Bar Assn, GA Assn Black Women Attys; pres Atlanta Urban League 1974-76; mem Gate City Day Nursery Assn; mem Atlanta Links, Chataugua 1981-; vice chmn GA State Personel Bd 1978-84; trustee, Bd of Trustees, Stillman Coll 1987-; mem, Georgia Assn of Black Women Attorneys (GABWA); Steering Committee, Atlanta Chapter Links, Inc. Project LEAD (Links Erase Alcohol and Drug Abuse) 1988-89. **HONORS/ACHIEVEMENTS:** Comm Serv Awds Atlanta Branch NAACP; Adjunct Prof Litigation Emory Univ 1974-80; Iota Phi Lambda; Bronzewoman of the Year 1986; 1989 Academy of Women Achievers, Greater Atlanta YWCA, 1989; panelist "A Better Answer" Title VII Training Film 1973; Attorney-Client Privilege Conflicts of Interest in Municipal Litigation City-County Attys Institute 1984. **BUSINESS ADDRESS:** Associate Judge, City Court of Atlanta, 104 Trinity Avenue SW, Atlanta, GA 30335.

WEBSTER, LESLEY DOUGLASS
Attorney. **PERSONAL:** Born Jun 09, 1949, New York City, NY; married Jules A Webster; children: Jules S Webster. **EDUCATION:** Northeastern Univ Boston, BA 1972; Georgetown Univ Law Ctr, JD 1972-75. **CAREER:** Cambridge Redevel Authority MA, comm org 1970-72; Criminal Justice Clinic, Georgetown Univ Law Center, prosecution coord 1974-75; US Dept of Energy Region II NY, atty, adv 1975-77; Coll of Staten Island NY, adjunct prof 1977-78; US Dept of Energy Reg II NY, deputy regional counsel 1977-79; Northville Ind Corp, compliance counsel 1979-84; NY Dept of Commerce, deputy commiss, counsel. **ORGANIZATIONS:** Chairwoman of bd Assoc of Energy Profls Inc 1980-84. **HONORS/ACHIEVEMENTS:** Superior Serv Awd US Dept of Energy 1976. **BUSINESS ADDRESS:** Deputy Commissioner, Counsel, NY Dept of Commerce, 1 Commerce Plaza, Albany, NY 12245.

WEBSTER, LONNIE
City official. **PERSONAL:** Born Sep 03, 1922, Tillar, AR; married Modest Bishop; children: Earlene, Annette. **CAREER:** Reed AR, mayor; Webster Affiliated Food Store; Delta Fish Company; New Bethel Missionary Bapt Ch, pastor; Farm Worker. **ORGANIZATIONS:** Recipient Bookers Memorial College Banquet Award 1975.

WEBSTER, MARVIN NATHANIEL
Professional athlete. **PERSONAL:** Married Maderia; children: Marvin Nathaniel II. **EDUCATION:** Maorgan State. **CAREER:** Denver Nuggets, bskbl plyr; Seattle Supersonics, bskbl plyr; New York Nicks, bskbl plyr. **ORGANIZATIONS:** Founder Gaililee Baptist Ch Baltimore. **HONORS/ACHIEVEMENTS:** Set NY record for shot blocks iwth 131 in one season in 1982-83; led Morgan Stae to the NCAA's Div II title in 1975; Player of the Year for a 2nd tiem. **BUSINESS ADDRESS:** New York Nicks, Madison Sq Garden, 4 Pennsylvania Plaza, New York, NY 10001.

WEBSTER, NIAMBI DYANNE
Educational administrator. **PERSONAL:** Children: K Tyronne Colemon. **EDUCATION:** Drake Univ, BA English/Drama 1973; Mankato State Coll, MS Curriculum & Instr

1975; Doctoral Candidate Curriculum & Instruction, Univ of Iowa 1988-89. **CAREER:** Des Moines Public Schools, instructor 1975-78; Univ of IA, coord minority progs 1978-83, grad asst instructor 1980-83; IA Arts Council, touring music/theatre folk artist 1978-; Coe Coll, instr dir special servs; Dir Multicultural & International Student Affairs, Skidmore College 1989-. **ORGANIZATIONS:** Outreach counselor YMCA Des Moines 1974-78; instr Gateway Oppor Pageant 1975-78; press & publicity chair NAACP Des Moines Chap 1976-78; free lance writer & assoc editor Iowa Bystander 1976-80; founder/dir Langston Hughes Co of Players 1976-82; co-chair Polk Co Rape/Sexual Assault Bd 1977-80; artist-in-the schools IA Arts Council 1978-; mem 6th Judicial Dist Correctional Serv CSP & News Editor Volunteer 1984-; chairperson Mid-Amer Assoc of Ed Oppty Prog Personnel Cultural Enrichment Comm 1984-; mem Delta Sigma Theta Sor, Iowa City/Cedar Rapids Alumnae; Iowa City Comm Schools Equity Comm mem 1985-87. **HONORS/ACHIEVEMENTS:** Comm Service in the Fine Arts NAACP Presidential 1978; Black Leadership Awd Univ of IA 1979; Social Action Awd Phi Beta Sigma Frat 1980; Outstanding Young Woman in the Arts NAACP Natl Women Cong 1981; Women Equality & Dedication Comm on the Status of Women 1981; Trio Achievers Awd Natl Cncl of Educ Oppor Assoc 1985; Outstanding Woman of the Year Awd Linn Co Comm 1986. **HOME ADDRESS:** Saratoga Springs, NY. **BUSINESS ADDRESS:** Skidmore College, Saratoga Springs, NY 12866.

WEBSTER, THEODORE
Chief executive of demolition & excavation business. **CAREER:** Webster Engineering Co, Inc, Dorchester MA, chief executive, 1977—. **BUSINESS ADDRESS:** Webster Engineering Co, Inc, 50 Ceylon, Dorchester, MA 02121. *

WEBSTER, WILLIAM H.
Attorney. **PERSONAL:** Born Oct 26, 1946, New York City, NY; son of Eugene B Webster and Verna M Bailey Webster; married Joan Leslie; children: Sydney. **EDUCATION:** New York Univ, BA (cum laude), 1972; Univ of California, Berkeley, School of Law, JD, 1975. **CAREER:** Black Law Journal, UCLA & Univ of California at Berkeley, research assoc, 1973; Natl Economic Devel & Law Project, post-grad, 1974-76; Natl Economic Devel & Law Center, Berkeley, CA, atty, 1976-82; Hunter & Anderson, partner, 1983-. **ORGANIZATIONS:** Past mem bd of dirs, Natl Training Inst for Comm Economic Devel, Artisans Cooperative Inc; past mem, Mayor's Housing Task Force Berkeley; mem, State Bar of California, US Dist Ct No Dist of California, US Tax Ct, Natl Assoc of Bond Lawyers, Natl Bar Assoc, Charles Houston Bar Assn; past mem, City of Berkeley Citizens Comm on Responsible Investments; Kappa Alpha Psi. **HONORS/ACHIEVEMENTS:** Martin Luther King Fellowship; New York State Regents Incentive Awards; Howard Memorial Fund Scholarship; Alpha Phi Alpha Scholarship; pub, "Tax Savings through Intercorporate Billing," Economic Devel Law Center Report, 1980; pub, "Housing, Structuring a Housing Development," Economic Devel Law Center Report, 1978; various other publications. **BUSINESS ADDRESS:** Attorney, Hunter & Anderson Law Office, 1305 Franklin St Ste 500, Oakland, CA 94612.

WEBSTER, WINSTON ROOSEVELT
Attorney. **PERSONAL:** Born Apr 22, 1943, Nashville, TN. **EDUCATION:** Fisk U, AB 1965; Harvard U, LLB 1968. **CAREER:** Practicing Atty 1971-; TX So U, mem bd of regents 1979-; TX So U, law prof 1974-77; Cable TV Info Ctr, regional dir 1972-74; Office of Legal SvcsWA, supervisory gen atty 1970-72; Urban Inst, think tank rsrchr 1969-70; Nghbrhd Legal Serv Prgm, staff atty 1968-69. **ORGANIZATIONS:** US Dist Ct DC & TC; Superior Ct DC; Supreme Ct TX; DC Bar Assn; TX Bar Assn; Am Assn of Trial Lawyers; Nat Conf of Black Lawyers; bd dir Nat Paralegal Inst 1972-75; legal adv com TX Assn of Coll Tchrs 1976-77; bd gov WA Athletic Club 1974. **HONORS/ACHIEVEMENTS:** Prof of Year Thurgood Marshall Sch of Law 1976-77; Outst Young Men of Am 1977; KY Col 1973; Duke of Paducah 1972; Hon Citizen New Orleans 1971; Num Articles.

WEDDINGTON, RACHEL THOMAS
Educator. **PERSONAL:** Born Mar 09, 1917, Atlantic City, NJ. **EDUCATION:** Howard Univ, Washington DC, AB 1938, AM 1940; Univ of Chicago, PhD 1958. **CAREER:** Rosenwald Foundation, fellow 1946-48; Atlantic City NJ, bd of educ 1941-45; Howard Univ, instructor 1948-57; Merrill-Palmer Inst Detroit, research assoc 1957-61; Queens Coll NY, asst, assoc prof 1961-75; CUNY, univ dean for teacher educ 1975-79, prof 1975-85, prof emerita. **ORGANIZATIONS:** Mem Pi Lambda Theta Univ of Chicago 1947; mem Kappa Delta Pi Howard Univ 1954.

WEDDINGTON, WAYNE
Otolaryngologist. **PERSONAL:** Born 1936, McGee, AR. **EDUCATION:** University of Arkansas Agricultural, Mechanical and Normal College, BS, 1963; Howard University College of Medicine, Wasshington, DC, MD, 1967; Andrews Air Force Base, Camp Springs, MD, intern. **CAREER:** Temple University Health and Science Center, Philadelphia, PA, resident; Germantown Hospital and Medical Center, Department of Otolaryngology, Philadelphia, PA, chairman, 1974-; St Mary's Hospital, Philadelphia, PA, staff physician; St Christopher's Hospital, staff physician. **BUSINESS ADDRESS:** Germantown Hosptial and Medical Center, Department of Otolaryngology, One Penn Blvd, Philadelphia, PA 19144. *

WEDGEWORTH, ROBERT, JR.
Administrator. **PERSONAL:** Born Jul 31, 1937, Ennis, TX; married Chung Kyun. **EDUCATION:** Wabash Coll, BA; Univ of IL, MS Library Sci; Park Coll, DLitt 1975; Wabash Coll, DLitt 1980. **CAREER:** KC Publ Library, cataloger 1961-62; Seattle Worlds Fair Library 21, staff mem 1962; Park Coll, asst librarian 1962-63, acting head librarian 1963-64; Meramec Comm Coll Kirkwood, head librarian 1964-66; Brown Univ Library, asst chief order librarian 1966-69; Library Resources & Tech Serv ofcl ALA Jrnl, ed; Rutgers Univ, asst prof; Univ of Chicago, lecturer; Amer Library Assoc Chgo, exec dir. **ORGANIZATIONS:** Mem NAACP, Publ Serv Satellite Consortium Bd; ed AL Yearbook, AL World Encyc of Library & Info Svcs; mem trustees Newberry Library; mem adv comm USABk & Library; vice pres Wabash Coll Alumni Bd; mem adv council WBEZ Chgo; mem Amer Antiquarian Soc. **BUSINESS ADDRESS:** Executive Dir, Amer Library Assoc, 50 E Huron St, Chicago, IL 60611.

WEEDEN, ALICE LATIMER See LATIMER, ALLIE B.

WEEKES, MARTIN E.
Attorney. **PERSONAL:** Born Jun 06, 1933, New York, NY; children: Shelli, Dawn, Nicole. **EDUCATION:** Manhattan Coll NY, BS 1954; Univ of So CA, JD 1961. **CAREER:** Douglas Aircraft Santa Monica CA, engr draftsman 1956-60; Charles Meram Co Los Angeles, engr 1960-62; Deputy District Atty 1962-63; Div Chief; Co Counsel 1963-. **ORGANIZATIONS:** First pres Frederick Douglass Child Devel Cntr 1963; mem bd dir Rose Brooks Sch of Performing Arts 1974-; mem Reserve Faculty EPA; Lectured on Enviromental Law; guest lecturer USC; Twenty Publications Library of Congress; contrib author CA Adminstr Agency Practice CEB. **HONORS/ACHIEVEMENTS:** Rector's Award Episcopal Ch of the Advent 1967; Finished Second in All-Army Talent Contest 1956. **MILITARY SERVICE:** AUS 1954-56. **BUSINESS ADDRESS:** Asst County Counsel, County Counsel, LA County, 648 Hall of Administration, Los Angeles, CA 90012.

WEEKS, RENEE (NEE JONES)
Assistant general counsel. **PERSONAL:** Born Dec 28, 1948, Washington, DC; married Timothy. **EDUCATION:** Rugers Law Sch, JD 1973; Ursuline Coll, BA 1970. **CAREER:** Prudential Ins Co of Am 1985; State of NJ, dep atty gen 1973-75. **ORGANIZATIONS:** Past pres Women's Div Nat Bar Assn; mem Am Bar Assn; past pres Assn of Black Women Lawyers of NJ; past asst treas Nat Assn of Black Women Attys; Alpha Kappa Alpha Sor; mem Minority Interchange; bd of gov NJ State Opera; vice pres Nat Bar Assn; trustee Essex Co Bar Assn; past-sec Garden State Bar Assn. **HONORS/ACHIEVEMENTS:** Who's Who in Am Colls &Univ 1970. **BUSINESS ADDRESS:** Prudential Ins, 745 Broad St, Newark, NJ 07101.

WEEMS, LUTHER B. See AKBAR, NA'IM

WEEMS, VERNON EUGENE, JR.
Attorney-at-law. **PERSONAL:** Born Apr 27, 1948, Waterloo, IA; son of Eugene Weems and Anna Marie Hickey Weems. **EDUCATION:** Univ of IA, BA 1970; Univ of Miami Sch of Law, JD 1974. **CAREER:** US Small Business Admin, atty/advisor 1977-78, 1979-81; A Nation United Inc, pres/ceo/chmn bd 1982-85; Weems Law Office, attorney 1978-; Weems Productions and Enterprises, ceo/consultant 1987-. **ORGANIZATIONS:** Mem Amer Bar Assoc 1977-82, IA State Bar Assoc 1977-82, St Johns Lodge Prince Hall Affil 1977-86, Federal Bar Assoc 1979-82; mem bd of dirs Black Hawk County Iowa Branch NAACP. **HONORS/ACHIEVEMENTS:** Publication "Tax Amnesty Blueprint for Economic Development," 1981; Leadership Awd OIC/Iowa 1982; Service Appreciation Awd Job Service of Iowa 1985; article "Chapter 11 Tax Subsidies," 1986; Recognition of Excellence 1986. **BUSINESS ADDRESS:** Attorney at Law, Weems Productions/Enterprises, PO Box 72, Waterloo, IA 50704-0072.

WEIL, ROBERT L.
Educator. **PERSONAL:** Born Apr 22, 1932, Alexandria, LA; married Judith Adams; children: Pam, Martha, Sarah, Mathew. **EDUCATION:** Wayne State U, MA 1963; John Hay Whitney Fellow 1960-61; Cntr for Asian Studies Proj for Intl Communications to Make Film in Japan, award grant 1970. **CAREER:** Head Sculpture Dept MI State Univ, asso prof 1985; Sculptor Painter Film Maker 1985; Detroit Bd Educ, art instr 1958-60; Robt O'Boyal Assoc on Lansing MI Waterfront Park, designer 1975-76; Play Structure in Edgwood Village E Lansing MI, design installed 1973-74. **ORGANIZATIONS:** Co-chprsn E Lansing Fine Arts & Cultural Heratage Com. **HONORS/ACHIEVEMENTS:** Recip Albert Kahn Prize for Archit Sculpture. **MILITARY SERVICE:** Served USN 1949-53. **BUSINESS ADDRESS:** Professor, Michigan State University, Kresge Art Center, East Lansing, MI 48823.

WEISS, ED, JR.
Automobile dealer. **CAREER:** Allegan Ford-Mercury Sales, Inc, Allegan MI, chief executive, 1984—. **BUSINESS ADDRESS:** Allegan Ford-Mercury Sales, Inc, Allegan, MI 49010. *

WEISS, JOYCE LACEY
Educator. **PERSONAL:** Born Jun 08, 1941, Chicago, IL; daughter of Lois Lacey Carter; divorced. **EDUCATION:** Bennett Coll, BA 1963; Troy State Univ, MS 1971; Univ of Michigan, EdD, 1988. **CAREER:** Coweta County GA, elementary class teacher, 1963-64; Montgomery AL, elementary class teacher, 1964-69; Montgomery AL, elementary school principal 1969-75; Troy State Univ, instructor/supvr student teachers 1975-, asst prof/dept chmn, elementary educ, 1988-. **ORGANIZATIONS:** Mem Delta Sigma Theta; mem Montgomery AL Chap NAACP; mem Links Inc; mem Natl Educ Assn 1963-; mem Zeta Gamma Chapter of Kappa Delta Pi 1973-; mem Assn of Teacher Educators 1975-; mem Troy Univ Chap of Phi Delta Kappa 1980-; Intl Reading Assn; Alabama Reading Assn; Amer Educational Research Assn; Alabama Educ Assn. **HONORS/ACHIEVEMENTS:** Natl Merit Scholarship Bennett College 1959; School of Educ Fellowship Univ of MI 1984-85; Rackham Grad Fellowship 1985; MI Minority Fellowship 1985-87; School of Educ, Dean's Merit Fellowship, 1988; Rackham School of Graduate Studies, dissertation/thesis grant, Univ of Michigan, 1987; Michigan Minority Merit Fellowship, 1985-87, School of Educ Fellowship, 1985-86, Univ of Michigan. **HOME ADDRESS:** 4947 Park Towne Way #46, Montgomery, AL 36116. **BUSINESS ADDRESS:** Assistant Professor, Troy State University, Troy, AL 36082.

WELBURN, EDWARD THOMAS, JR.
Business executive. **PERSONAL:** Born Dec 14, 1950, West Chester, PA; married Rhonda Doby; children: Adrienne, Brian. **EDUCATION:** Howard Univ, BFA 1972. **CAREER:** GM Design Staff, creative designer 1972-75, sr creative designer 1976-81, asst chief designer 1981-. **ORGANIZATIONS:** Mem Founders Soc of the Detroit Inst of Art; pres IDEA a recently formed assoc of Black Auto Designers; mem of The Cabinet 1983-. **HONORS/ACHIEVEMENTS:** Contribute to the design of Oldsmobile's product line 1976 to date. **BUSINESS ADDRESS:** Assistant Chief Designer, General Motors Design Staff, GM Technical Center, Warren, MI 48090.

WELBURN, RONALD GARFIELD
Writer. **PERSONAL:** Born Apr 30, 1944, Berwyn, PA; son of Howard Watson and Jessie W Watson; married Eileen D Millett, Aug 21, 1971. **EDUCATION:** Lincoln University, Lincoln University PA, BA, 1968; University of Arizona, MA, 1970; New York University, PhD, 1983. **CAREER:** File clerk in New York NY, and Philadelphia PA, 1962-64; Lincoln

University, Lincoln University PA, instructor in humanities, summer, 1968; Syracuse University, Syracuse NY, assistant professor of Afro-American studies, 1970-75; Rutgers University, New Brunswick NJ, formerly affiliated with Institute for Jazz Studies, assistant professor of English, fall, 1983; writer. **HONORS/ACHIEVEMENTS:** Silvera Award for poetry, Lincoln University, 1967 and 1968; author of Peripheries: Selected Poems, 1966-1968, Greenfield Review Press, 1972; fellow, Smithsonian Institute and Music Critics Association, 1975; author of Heartland: Selected Poems, Lotus Press, 1981; Langston Hughes Legacy Certificate, Lincoln University, 1981. **HOME ADDRESS:** Box 692, Guilderland, NY 12084. **BUSINESS ADDRESS:** Poets & Writers, New York, NY. *

WELCH, EDWARD L.
Attorney. **PERSONAL:** Born Mar 10, 1928, Helena, AR; son of Arthur and Leola; married Susan L Welch; children: David, Karen, Joseph, Christopher. **EDUCATION:** St Louis Univ, BS, Commerce, 1957; Washington Univ, St Louis, MO, JD, Order of Coif, 1960. **CAREER:** Stockham Roth Buder & Martin, assoc atty; Univ of Wisconsin, Milwaukee, lecturer; Allis-Chalmers Mfg Co, Milwaukee, WI, & Springfield, IL, labor law atty, 1961-67; Natl Labor Relations Bd 14th Region; staff atty, 1967-69; atty. **ORGANIZATIONS:** Gen counsel, Natl Alliance of Postal & Fed Employees, Washington, DC, 1971-; adj prof, Southern Illinois Univ, Carbondale, 1974-; school bd atty, East St Louis School Dist, 189, 1978-; mem, Amer Bar Assn, Illinois State Bar Assn, Madison City Bar Assn; life mem, NAACP. **MILITARY SERVICE:** USN, radioman, 3rd class, 1946-47. **BUSINESS ADDRESS:** Attorney, 216 N Main St, Edwardsville, IL 62025.

WELCH, HARVEY, JR.
Education administration. **PERSONAL:** Born Jun 05, 1932, Centralia, IL; married Patricia Kay; children: Harvey, Gordon, Karen, Brian. **EDUCATION:** SIU-C, BS 1955; SIU-C, MS 1958. **CAREER:** Southern IL Univ, dean for student life 1985; Southern IL Univ Amer Assn for Counseling & Development Assn, former dean of students; Natl Assn of Student Personal Admin; Natl Assn of Student Financial Aid Admin; Natl Assn of Women Deans. **ORGANIZATIONS:** Mem NAACP; Cdale Planning Commn 1976-78; IL Guid & Personel Assn; adv bd IL State Scholarship Com; Mid-west Equal Educ Oppty. **HONORS/ACHIEVEMENTS:** Assn Hon Sco HS Fellowship SIU-C 1958; Distgn Mil Student 1954; Hon Mention Little All Am Basketball 1954; Met Serv Med 1975; Joint Serv Com 1973. **MILITARY SERVICE:** USAF Col 1955-75. **BUSINESS ADDRESS:** Dean of Student Life, Southern Ill University, Bldg T-40, Carbondale, IL 62901.

WELCH, JESSE ROY
Educator. **PERSONAL:** Born May 29, 1949, Jonesville, LA; married Vickie Ragsdale (divorced); children: Symia. **EDUCATION:** Washington State Univ, BA 1971, ED Candidate 1977. **CAREER:** Big Brother-Big Sister Program Benicia CA, dir, head counselor 1967-68; Pullman YMCA, program adv 1968-70; Washington State Univ, fin aid counselor 1970-71, assoc dir of admissions 1971-. **ORGANIZATIONS:** Participant Johnson Found Wingspread Conf on Minority Groups in Coll Student-Personnel Programs 1971; mem Amer Assoc of Coll Registrars & Admissions Officers 1971-, WA State Univ Affirmative Action Council 1972-74; comm min affairs WA Council of HS Coll Rel 1973-; consultant Spokane Nursing School Minority Affairs Comm Spokane 1973-74, WICHE Faculty Devel to Meet Minority Group Needs 1973-74; advisory bd 1974-, co-chmn 1974-76 YMCA Pullman WA. **HONORS/ACHIEVEMENTS:** Numerous publications & papers.

WELCH, JOHN L.
Business administration. **PERSONAL:** Born Apr 27, 1929, Newark, NJ; married Delorian; children: Elizabeth, Anthony, Michael. **EDUCATION:** Steton Hall Univ, 1970-72; Rampo Coll NJ, BA 1975. **CAREER:** US Post Office, clerk 1962-67; Bergen Cty Dept of Health Svcs, sanitary inspector 1967-78; Roman Catholic Archdiocese Newark NJ, youth minister 1976-78; Jersey Youth Drill Team Judges, chief 1977-83; Borough of Bergenfield, health admin 1978-. **ORGANIZATIONS:** Scout leader 1960-82; camping chmn Essex Cty Council Boy Scouts of Amer; pres bd of ed Queen of Angels Parochial School Newark NJ; track coach Queen of Angels Parochial School Newark NJ 1958-80; mem Essex Cty Park Commiss 1974-77, Boy Scout Troop 155, Queen of Angels 1960-82, Track Official Newark YMCA 1979-83; trustee Queen of Angels Church Newark NJ; pres Queen of Angels Choir 1968-75; mem Robert Treat Council BSA; olympics coord, vice pres Newark Central Ward Athletic Assoc 1968-; vice pres Frontiers Intl Newark Club 1982-84; life mem NAACP Newark Br; mem NJ Health Officers Assoc, Bergen Cty Health Officers Assoc, NJ Assoc of Public Health Admins. **HONORS/ACHIEVEMENTS:** Outstanding Achievement Awds, Silver Beaver BSA 1972; Newark Central Ward Athletic Assoc 1975; Frontiers Intl 1982,83,84. **MILITARY SERVICE:** USMC 1951-53. **BUSINESS ADDRESS:** Health Administrator, Bergenfield Health Department, 198 N Washington Avenue, Bergenfield, NJ 07621.

WELCH, JOSEPH NATHANIEL
Plumber, engineer, photographer. **PERSONAL:** Born Feb 10, 1882, Georgetown, French Guiana;married Bessie Sims; children: Irene Francina, James Albert, Pearl E, Josephine, Cathrine, Lillian. **EDUCATION:** HowardUniv Sch of Dentistry, Attended 1914-15. **CAREER:** Br Guiana, gold miner 2 yrs; Chicken & Pig Farming 1921-25; New Bruals Br NAACP, pres. **ORGANIZATIONS:** Mem True Reformers of Richmond VA; Elks of New Brunswick; Pythian Notary of Pub; ND Justice of Peace 1936-42. **HONORS/ACHIEVEMENTS:** Recipient Ford Howard Scholarship 1914. **MILITARY SERVICE:** Spl Award 1971 For Serv From 1910-.

WELCH, ODELLA T.
Director. **PERSONAL:** Born Jun 06, 1934, Eckman, WV; children: Denise McKnight, Melanie Mitchell, Sheri Lynn, Lori. **EDUCATION:** OH State Univ, attended. **CAREER:** Office of Rsch & Publ Info State of OH Auditors Office, dir; OH State Univ, asst to dir of budget 1970-71; OH State Univ, asst off-campus scheduling 1970-73; Community Relations City of Columbus, dir 1973; Dept of Comm Serv City of Columbus, dir 1973-83; Private Indus Council of Columbus OH, dir 1983-84. **ORGANIZATIONS:** Former mem 1st black female Natl Council of YMCA 1969; mem US Civil Rights Comm SAC 1970-80; mem Amer Soc for Publ Admin 1973-80; cabinet of exec Met Human Serv Comm 1975-80; mem CETA dir Work Group 1977-80; vice pres Employment & Training Council US Conf of Mayors 1979. **HONORS/ACHIEVEMENTS:** Outstanding Leadership, Mayor's Proclamation, City of Columbus OH, 1974; Outstanding Community Serv Award, Ohio House of Rep 1974, 1977, The Ohio Senate 1974, Columbus Urban League 1976.

WELCH, OLGA MICHELE
Education administrator. **PERSONAL:** Born Dec 30, 1948, Salisbury, NC; married George E Welch; children: Taja Michele, Stephani Amber. **EDUCATION:** Howard Univ, BA History/English/Educ (Salutatorian) 1971; Univ of TN, MS Deaf Educ 1972, EdD Educ Admin & Super 1977. **CAREER:** The Model Secondary Sch for the Deaf, instructor 1972-73; The TN Sch for the Deaf, instructor 1973-75; TN Sch for the Deaf, supervising principal 1977-78; Univ of TN Dept of Spec Educ & Rehab, assoc prof & dir 1978-, dir deaf educ prog. **ORGANIZATIONS:** Mem Council of Exceptional Children; mem Alexander Graham Bell Assn; mem Convention of Amer Instructors of the Deaf; mem Natl Educ Assn; mem Assn for Supervision & Curriculum Develop; Project HELP tutorial prog for disadvantaged students 1983; vice pres Knoxville Chap Natl Black Women's Hook-Up 1980-81; Girl Scout neighborhood chmn "NighHawks" Neighborhood 1977-; mem Interdenominational Concert Choir 1975-. **HONORS/ACHIEVEMENTS:** Phi Beta Kappa; Phi Delta Kappa; Phi Kappa Phi; Phi Alpha Theta; Dept Awd "Most Creative Dissertation Topic" Univ TN; named one of the Outstanding Young Women of Amer 1980; appointment to the Natl Educ Adv Bd 1983. **HOME ADDRESS:** Rt 3 Whittaker Rd, New Market, TN 37820. **BUSINESS ADDRESS:** Dir Deaf Education Prog, Univ of TN, Claxton Addition Rm 129, Knoxville, TN 37996.

WELCH, WINFRED BRUCE
Psychologist, educator. **PERSONAL:** Born Jun 25, 1918, Atlanta; married Rizpah Louise Jones. **EDUCATION:** Livingtone Coll, AB 1939; IN U, EdD 1952; Sch Psychology Am Bd of Professional Psychologists, diplomate 1970; VA OH, cert licensed psychologist. **CAREER:** Univ of Cincinnati, prof educ psychology 1969-75; Elementary Secondary School Teacher Admin; Coll Univ Prof Admin; USOM/Iran Asia, educ specialist 1954-56; USOE Specialist, disadvantaged & handicapped; Counseling Bureau of Indian Affairs Dept of Interior, chief; Rosenwald Found Scholarship; Gen Educ Bd Fellow; OH State Univ, advanced study; Columbia Univ, psychologist privt practice; Learning Personal Adjustment; School of Educ Psychology VA Union Univ, dir prof 1975-. **ORGANIZATIONS:** Mem VA Pastorial Care Bd; past mem Richmond Urban League Bd; Educ Therapy Cntr Bd; Richmond Mental Health Bd. **BUSINESS ADDRESS:** VA Union Univ, Richmond, VA 23220.

WELCOME, VERDA F.
State senator. **PERSONAL:** Married Dr Henry C Welcome; children: Mary Sue Mercer. **EDUCATION:** Morgan State Coll, BS; NY Univ, MA; Howard Univ, Hon DDL; Univ of MD, Hon DSS. **CAREER:** Former teacher; House of Delegates, mem 1959; State of MD, senator 1963-. **ORGANIZATIONS:** Mem Natl Order of Women Legislators; Legislative Council; Amer Assn of Univ Women; Task Force to Study Campaign Financing; Com to Study Rape & Related Crimes; Com to Study Juvenile Crime; mem 4th Dist Democratic Organ of Baltimore City Inc; Valient Women's Democratic Club; Citizens Planning & Housing Assn; Intl League of Peace & Freedom. **HONORS/ACHIEVEMENTS:** Achievement Awd Office of Minority Affairs Towson State Univ; Women of the Yr Awd Women's Aux Natl Med Assn 1962; Achievement Awd Afro-Amer Newspapers; Achievement Awd Natl Council of Negro Women; Alumnus of the Yr Awd Morgan State Univ; Howard Univ Alumni Assn Awd; Outstanding Woman Dem Awd Leagueof Women Voters; Central Nassau Club Serv Awd; Outstanding Serv Awd Tau Gamma Delta. **BUSINESS ADDRESS:** Senator, State of MD, 3423 Holmes Ave, Baltimore, MD 21217.

WELDON, DEBORAH (NEE MORGAN)
Performer. **PERSONAL:** Born Sep 20, 1951, Dunn, NC; married Charles Jauverni. **EDUCATION:** Manhattan Community Coll, AA 1972; Herbert H Lehman Coll, Attended. **CAREER:** Warner Bros TV "Roots The Next Generations", performed in 1978; ABC TV "The Love Boat", guest star 1978; Broadway "What Wine Sellers Buy", actress 1975; TV Film "Love Savage Fury", co-star; Guest Star in Many Dramatic TV Series. **ORGANIZATIONS:** Maj Artistic Accomplishments Protraying Aunt Liz in Alex Haley's "Roots the Next Generation" Aging From 18-83.

WELDON, ONAH CONWAY
Civil service commissioner. **PERSONAL:** Born Jun 22, 1926, Philadelphia, PA; married Thomas A (deceased); children: Thomas Anthony. **EDUCATION:** Fisk U, BA 1949; Temple U, Grad Courses. **CAREER:** Philadelphia Pub Sch, tchr 1954; PA Fed Conv, del; Nat AFT Conv; State AFL-CIO Conv; PA Federation of Tchrs, vp; Public School Employees Credit Union, pres; Philadelphia Federation of Teachers, union rep 1985. **ORGANIZATIONS:** Bd mem Afro-Amer Hist & Cultural Museum; mem Educ Comm of the Black Music Assn; coordinator PFT United Negro Coll Fund Dr; bd of dir Mid-City YWCA; bd of dir Philadelphia Citizens for Children & Youth Serv Community Planning Council; chair Philadelphia Congress of the Natl Political Congress of Black Women; bd of dirs Amer Women's Heritage Soc; dir, Mayor's Office of Consumer Services; pres, Credit Union, Grace Baptist Church of Germantown, 1984-85. **HONORS/ACHIEVEMENTS:** Distinguished Serv Citation United Negro Coll Fund; Hobart C Jackson Memorial Award Philadelphia Inter-Alumni Council; E Roosevelt Humanities Award State of Israel Bond; Outstanding Serv Award Black Women's Educ Alliance; C. Delores Tucker Tribute, Natl Political Congress of Black Women, 1986.

WELDON, RAMON N.
Law enforcement. **PERSONAL:** Born Jul 26, 1932, Keokuk, IA; married Betty Jean Watkins; children: Ramon N Jr. **EDUCATION:** Keokuk Senior High School, diploma 1938-51. **CAREER:** Keokuk Police Department, patrolman 1962-74, detective 1974-80; captain 1980-82; chief of police 1982-. **ORGANIZATIONS:** Member Lee County Juvenile Restitution Bd 1982; member Keokuk Humane Society 1982; trustee Keokuk Library Board in 2nd six year term; active member Iowa Chief's Assoc Natl Chief's Assn Intl Chief's Assn 1982-. **MILITARY SERVICE:** AUS Corporal 2 yrs; Soilder of the Month 1953. **HOME ADDRESS:** 2510 Decatur St, Keokuk, IA 52632. **BUSINESS ADDRESS:** Police Chief, Keokuk Police Dept, 1222 Johnson St, Keokuk, IA 52632.

WELLS, BILLY GENE
Mayor, printing company entrepreneur. **PERSONAL:** Born Mar 30, Bluff City, TN; son of Harley Boyd Wells and Grace Isbella Black; married Irene Elizabeth Coleman, Dec 31, 1962; children: Cynthia Anita Wells, Rebecca Jean Wells. **CAREER:** TN Eastman Co, Kingsport, TN, printer, 1964-; B&I Offset Printing, Bluff City, TN, owner, 1971-; City of Bluff City, TN, mayor, 1985-. **ORGANIZATIONS:** Board member, Senior Citizens, United Way, and Teen World, all 1985-; comm member, Martin Luther King Jr State Holiday

Comm, 1986-. **HONORS/ACHIEVEMENTS:** First black mayor elected in Tennessee; first mayor elected 3 times in a row in Bluff City. **HOME ADDRESS:** 198 Holston Dr, Bluff City, TN 37618.

WELLS, ELMER EUGENE
Educational administrator. **PERSONAL:** Born Oct 06, 1939, Mt Pleasant, IA; married Georgia Lee Gehringer; children: Monte, Debra, Christian, Kori. **EDUCATION:** Univ of AK, MA 1970;Univ of NM, PhD 1974. **CAREER:** Intl Student Serv Univ of So CO, dir 1978-; USC Teacher Corps Cycle 9 & 11 Pueblo, educ spec 1974-78; Albuquerque Public School, teacher 1973-74; Bureau of Indian Affairs Pt Barrow AK, teacher/asst prin/prin 1966-71; Office of Econ Opportunity, teen post dir 1965-66; Mobil Oil Co Santa Fe Springs CA, explorationworker 1964-65; Low Mt Boarding School Bureau of Indian Affairs AZ 1962-64. **ORGANIZATIONS:** Pres/founder Albuquerque Ethnic Communities Inc 1973-74; pres/founder CO Ethnic Communities Inc 1975-80; exec bd Pueblo Chap NAACP 1979-80; "Destroyinga Racial Myth" The Social Studies Vol 69 No 5 1978; pub "The Mythical Negative Black Self Concept" R & E Research Assn 1978; TV Debate Grand Wizard KKK CO-Springs Involvement Program Channel 11 1979. **HONORS/ACHIEVEMENTS:** Speaker Annual Freedom Fund Banquet CO Springs Chap NAACP 1980. **BUSINESS ADDRESS:** 2200 Bonforte Blvd, Pueblo, CO 81001.

WELLS, IRA J. K., JR.
Attorney. **PERSONAL:** Born Oct 26, 1934, New York, NY; children: Joseph, Anita, JoAnne. **EDUCATION:** Lincoln U, BA 1957; Temple Law Sch, LLD. **CAREER:** US Ct App 3rd Circ Phila, law clk/ct crier 1964-66; US Dist Ct Estn Dist PA, law clk 1966-68; US Dept Hsg & Urban Dev Phila, atty 1968. **ORGANIZATIONS:** Mem/bd dir Zion Invstmt Assn Inc, Zion Non-Profit Char Trst, Opport Ind Cent Inc; OIC Intl Inc 1968-; Ejay Trav Inc 1970; mem Nat/Am PA & Philadelphia Bar Assn; treas Philadelphia Intl Prog 1974-75; mem Barristers Club of Phila; mem Lawyers Club of Phila; bd dir Mental Hlth Assn PA; treas/bd dir Mntl Hlth Assn 1977-78; leg cnsl EMAN Grp Homes Inc; E Mt Airy Neighborhood Inc. **MILITARY SERVICE:** AUS sp/4 1957-59. **BUSINESS ADDRESS:** Ste 700 Robinson Bldg, 42 S 15th St, Philadelphia, PA 19102.

WELLS, JAMES A.
Business executive. **PERSONAL:** Born Aug 13, 1933, Atlanta, GA; married Mary E; children: James A, Jr, John F. **EDUCATION:** BSEE 1965; MSAT 1976. **CAREER:** Systems Test Mgr IBM-Owego, project engr 1974-; Aerospace & Avionic Computer Sys Final Test IBM-Owego 1967-74; Process Equipment Design IBM-Endicott, engineering 1965-67. **ORGANIZATIONS:** Assoc mem IEEE Assn; past vice pres Jaycees; den leader WEBELOS; mem Amvets; AOPA. **MILITARY SERVICE:** USAF t/sgt 1952-57. **BUSINESS ADDRESS:** IBM-FSD 001 A310 Bodle Hill Rd, Owego, NY 13827.

WELLS, JAMES LESESNE
Educator. **PERSONAL:** Born Nov 02, 1902, Atlanta; married Ophelia Davidson; children: James Lesesne, Jr. **EDUCATION:** Nat Acad of Design 1918-19; LincolnUniv 1921-22; ColumbiaUniv 1923-27; Columbia U, BS MS 1938; Atelier "17" 1948-49. **CAREER:** Howard Univ, retired educator; Howard Univ, educ art Dept 1929-68; Delphic Gallery of Art & Brooklyn Museum, painter with numerous one-man two-man & group man Exhibitions 1965; Spellman Coll Rochkefeller Jr Fine Arts Bldg 1966; Smith-Mason Gallery 1971; Carl Van Vechtan Gallery of Art 1973; The Gallery of Art 1977; Numerous Natl & Intl Exhibitions. **ORGANIZATIONS:** Mem Alpha Phi; Am Fedn of Arts; NAACP; Urban League; Assn for Study of Afro-Amer Life & History. **HONORS/ACHIEVEMENTS:** Awarded Harmon Gol Medal Harmon Fdn 1931; 1st Prize Washington DC Religious Art Exhibition Smithsonian 1958; Spl Exhbt Prints of Two Worlds Philadelphia Mus of Art 1967; El Museo Arte Moderno 1967; Afro-Am Art FiskUniv 1975; Two Centuries of Am Art LA Co Mus 1976; Recpt Van Der Zee Award Afro-am Hist & Cultural Mus 1977.

WELLS, JOSEPH L.
Government official. **PERSONAL:** Born Aug 08, 1936, St Louis, MO; married Naomi. **EDUCATION:** Hubbards Bus Coll 3 Yrs; St Louis Univ 1 Yr. **CAREER:** PO 14 yrs; Gen Motors; Restaurant Owner. **ORGANIZATIONS:** Mem YMCA; NAACP; Sch Bd Ferguson Flor Dist. **MILITARY SERVICE:** USAF 4 yrs.

WELLS, LAWRENCE LEON
Educator. **PERSONAL:** Born Feb 28, 1933, Vicksburg, MS; married Dorothy Jean House; children: Victoria, Lawrence Jr, Christopher. **EDUCATION:** Univ of the Pacific, BA 1955; San Francisco State Univ, MA 1960; Univ of CA, EdD cand. **CAREER:** Franklin Elementary School, teacher 1957-61, vice prin 1961-65; Lincoln Elem School, prin 1965-59; San Francisco State Coll, asst prof 1969-70; Berkeley Unified School Dist, asst dir 1970-71, dir of expmtl schools 1971-73, asst supt 1973-76; Sonoma Co Office of Educ, asst supt. **ORGANIZATIONS:** Consult Natl Consortium on Educ Alternatives 1971-74; chmn bd of dirs Berkeley Youth Alternatives 1972-75; consultUniv of CA 1972; chmn Educ Planning & GradeConfiguration 1973-75; chmn Excellence for Youth Awds Com Bank of Amer 1973-75; Alternative Appr to Educ Today 1973; Options in Public Educ 1973; consult CASE Study 1974; spkr Amer Assn of Sch Admins Conf 1974; consult Midwest Ctr for Equal Educ Oppor 1974; mem Amer Educ Rsch Assn, Natl Assn of BlackEducs, Natl Educ Assn, CA Tchrs Assn, CA Assn of Sch Admins, Assn for Supervision & Curriculum Devel, CA Assn of Comp?ensatory Educ, Sonoma Co Sch Admin Assn, Black Educ Forum; life mem NAACP; Consorts Soc Club; First Black Youth Gov of CA. **HONORS/ACHIEVEMENTS:** YMCA Scholastic Schlrsp 1951; life memshp PTA; Who's Who in Amer Colls & Univs 1955. **MILITARY SERVICE:** USN. **BUSINESS ADDRESS:** Assistant Superintendent, Sonoma Co Office of Educ, 2555 Mendocino Ave, Room 111 E, Santa Rosa, CA 95401.

WELLS, LINDA IVY
Administrator. **PERSONAL:** Born Jun 18, 1948, McKeesport, PA. **EDUCATION:** Allegheny County Comm Coll, AA Humanities 1968; Seton Hill Coll, BA History Sociology 1970; Howard Univ, Masters Stud Personnel 1971-72. **CAREER:** Seton Hall Coll, asst dir special servs, 1970-71; Bowie State Coll, grad coun Opportunity Unlimited Program, 1972; Howard Univ, admin asst stud per program 1972; Catholic Univ, dir minority student affairs, 1972-75; Stanford Univ, financial aid advisor, 1978-83. **ORGANIZATIONS:** NAMEPA mem Reg E Natl Assoc MN Eng Admin; mem Amer Personnel & Guidance Assoc; Amer Assoc for Higher Educ; CA Assoc of Student Financial Aid Adminstrs; Amer Indian Science and Eng Soc. **HONORS/ACHIEVEMENTS:** Ford Foundation Fellowship Grant 1971-72; Thomas Lynch Scholarship 1968-70; Negro Educ Emer Drive Scholarship 1966-70; Senior Century Scholarship 1966; NatlHonor Soc 1966; Staff Appreciation Award 1983. **HOME ADDRESS:** PO Box 3805, Stanford, CA 94305. **BUSINESS ADDRESS:** Asst Dean, School of English, StanfordUniv, Room 208 Terman Eng Center, Stanford, CA 94305.

WELLS, LLOYD C. A.
Professional football scout. **PERSONAL:** Born Mar 02, 1924, Houston, TX. **EDUCATION:** Texas Southern Univ, BS 1950; Univ of Hawaii. **CAREER:** Informer Chain of Newspapers, former sports editor/exec dir 10 years; Texas High School All Star Games, founder/dir; World Heavy Weight Boxing Champion Muhammad Ali, asst mgr. **ORGANIZATIONS:** Mem Natl Assn Press Photographers; Professional Photographers of Amer; former coach/owner of Houston Olympians AAU Basketball Team; 100 Percent Wrong Club Atlanta GA 1962. **HONORS/ACHIEVEMENTS:** 1st full time black scout in history of professional football 1963-; Sports Editor of the Year; Professional Football Scout of the Year 1970; Pittsburgh Courier RC Cola Black Coll All Amer Awards Dinner. **MILITARY SERVICE:** USMC 1943-46, 1950-53.

WELLS, PATRICK ROLAND
Educator. **PERSONAL:** Born Apr 01, 1931, Liberty, TX; son of Luther T. Wells, Sr (deceased) and Stella Wickliff Wells (deceased). **EDUCATION:** TX Southern Univ, BS 1957; Univ of NE-Lincoln, MS 1959, PhD 1961. **CAREER:** Fordham Univ, asst prof pharmacology 1961-63; Univ of NE, asst prof of pharmacology 1963-65, assoc prof & dept chmn 1965-70; College of Pharmacy TX Southern Univ, dean & prof 1970-. **ORGANIZATIONS:** Grant regent Kappa Psi Pharmaceutical 1983-87; mem TX Pharmaceutical Assn, Amer Pharmaceutical Assn, natl Pharmaceutical Assn, Sigma Xi Science Hon, Rho Chi Pharmacy Hon; mem St Philip Neri Parish; mem, St Philip Neri Council #222 Knights of Peter Claver; lay oblate Order of St Benedict; Permanent Deacons Diocese of Galveston-Houston; Assn of Minority Health Professions Schools; Amer Assn of Colleges of Pharmacy; editor, Journal of the National Pharmeaceutical Assn; host, Radio Show "Lifeline" KTSU-FM. **MILITARY SERVICE:** USAF s/sgt 1951-55. **BUSINESS ADDRESS:** Dean & Professor, TX SouthernUniv, 3100 Cleburne, Houston, TX 77004.

WELLS, PAYTON R.
Business executive. **PERSONAL:** Born Jun 24, 1933, Indianapolis, IN. **EDUCATION:** Butler Univ Indianapolis IN, 1955-57. **CAREER:** Payton Wells Ford Inc, pres; GM & Ford Motor Co Automotive Sch; Preston Hwy Chrysler Plymouth, pres; Payton Wells Chevrolet, pres. **ORGANIZATIONS:** Bd mem Jr Achievement; mem NAACP; mem Urban League; vice pres Flanner House Inc; bd mem Three Sisters Nursing Home. **MILITARY SERVICE:** AUS pfc 1953-55. **BUSINESS ADDRESS:** President, Payton Wells Chevrolet, 1510 N Meridian St, Indianapolis, IN 46202.

WELLS, ROBERT BENJAMIN, JR.
Executive administration. **PERSONAL:** Born May 21, 1947, Cleveland, OH; married Phillis Sharlette McCray; children: Michelle Renne', Bryan Jamison. **EDUCATION:** Miami Dade Comm Coll, AA 1974; FL A&M Univ, BS 1976; 1st Yr NC Central Univ, Law Student 1985. **CAREER:** General Telephone of the Southeast, serv cost admin 19878-80, gen acct suprv 1980-81, gen tax suprv 1981-. **ORGANIZATIONS:** Consult Youth Motivation Task Force 1979-82; pres Employees Club 1980-81; dept rep United Way Campaign 1982-84; chair econ devel comm NC Assoc of Black Lawyers Land Loss Prevention Proj; vice pres mem & mktg Natl Assoc of Accountants; chairperson Natl Alliance of Business Youth Motivation Task Force 1982-; presDurham Area Chap Natl Assoc of Accountants 1986-87, 1987-88; GTE Loaned Exec United Way Campaign 1986; chairperson Greater Durham United Way Loaned Exec Alumni Comm 1987. **HONORS/ACHIEVEMENTS:** Disting Serv Awd Miles Coll Birmingham AL 1982; Disting Serv Plaque Edward Waters Coll Jacksonville FL 1984; Disting Serv Plaque Florida A&M Univ Tallahassee 1986. **MILITARY SERVICE:** USAF sgt 4 yrs; Disting Serv Medal, Bronze Medal 1966,68. **HOME ADDRESS:** 1313 Clinton Rd, Durham, NC 27703. **BUSINESS ADDRESS:** General Tax Supervisor, General Telephone of the South, 3632 Roxboro Rd, PO Box 1412, Durham, NC 27702.

WELLS-DAVIS, MARGIE ELAINE
Food product development, manager, social psychologist. **PERSONAL:** Born Apr 27, 1944, Marshalltown, IA; daughter of Gladstone Wells and Ida Wells; married Allan C; children: Allana. **EDUCATION:** Simpson Coll, AB 1966; Syracuse Univ, MA 1968; Univ of Cincinnati, PhD 1979. **CAREER:** Procter & Gamble, affirmative action coordinator 1977-; Cincinnati Health Dept, dir of staff & org devel 1974-77; US Public Health Service DHEW, sociologist 1973; Central Comm Health Bd, coordinator consulting educ 1972; Syracuse Univ, acting dir 1971; Univ of Cincinnati, asst dean of students 1968-70; St Louis Syracuse NY, teacher 1966-68; Procter & Gamble, human resources mgr. **ORGANIZATIONS:** Mem Am Soc for Training & Devel 1977-80; mem Original Devel Network 1978-80; bd mem New Life for Girls 1977-80; treasurer bd mem Cincinnati Human Relations Commn 1978-80; bd mem Cincinnati Womens City Club 1979-80; consultant E Harlem Ext Serv Jewish Hosp 1973-76; bd mem General Protestant Orphan Home. **HONORS/ACHIEVEMENTS:** Resolution for Outstanding Serv City of Cincinnati Bd of Health 1976; Hon Soc Epsilon Sigma, Gold Key Hon Soc 1966. **BUSINESS ADDRESS:** Human Resources Mgr, Proctor & Gamble, Food Product Devel, PO Box 599, Cincinnati, OH 45201.

WELSING, FRANCES CRESS
Psychiatrist. **PERSONAL:** Born Mar 18, 1935, Chicago, IL. **EDUCATION:** Antioch Coll, BS 1957; HowardUniv Sch of Med, MD 1962. **CAREER:** Cook Co Hosp, internsp 1962-63; St Elizabeth Hosp, res gen psychiatry 1963-66; Children's Hosp, flwshp child psychiatry 1966-68; HowardUniv Coll of Med, asst prof of pediatrics 1968-75; Hillcrest Children's Ctr, clinical dir 1975-76; Private Pract. **ORGANIZATIONS:** Mem Nat Med Assn; Am Med Assn; Am Psychiatric Assn. **HONORS/ACHIEVEMENTS:** Author, "The Cress Theory of Color Confrontation & Racism". **BUSINESS ADDRESS:** 7603 Georgia Ave NW, Washington, DC.

WELTON, EVELYN R.
Coordinator. **PERSONAL:** Born Oct 04, 1928, Madison, AR. **EDUCATION:** Univ KS, BA 1949;Univ MO, grad study; Webster Coll, M Pub Admin 1975. **CAREER:** Univ NE Coll Med Microbiology/Serol, 1954-59; HEW, microbiolohy 1959-71; Health Planning &

Health Ed, adm 1971-73; Univ MO & W MO Area Health Educ Center, coord consumer health educ 1973-75; Acad of Health Professions Univ of MO Med School, consumer health educ spclst. **ORGANIZATIONS:** Bd mem Visiting Nurse Assn; mem MO women's CC; bd mem Self Devel People Pgm; mem League Women Voters 1974-76; pres KC Chap Links Inc; past pres Local Chap Alpha Kappa Alpha; past pres Presbyterian Interracial Cncl; bd mem KC Chap Opportunities Industrialization Ctr; bd mem Kaw Valley Med Careers Prog Turner Comm Ctr; mem Presb & Synod Com of Presb Ch; PM Interlude Social Club; Nat Cncl of Negro Women; Nat Soc of Patient Reps chrprsn OEO Bd; bd mem Local OEO Comm Action Pgm; co-chrpsn KS Hlth Planning Cncl gov appointed 1969-77; served on Human Relations Comm appointedby mayor 1968-73; appointed by Nat Pres Alpha Kappa Alpha to Pub Rel Comm 1974-76; Nat Pres Ladies Aux Nat Dental Assn Inc 1972-73. **HONORS/ACHIEVEMENTS:** Humanitarian Award from Presbyterian Interracial Cncl 1969.

WENG, PETER A.
Business executive. **PERSONAL:** Born Jul 14, 1939, Brooklyn; married Marilyn; children: Robin, Christopher. **EDUCATION:** Coll of Emporia, KS, 1962;Univ of CA;Univ of IA. **CAREER:** US Peace Corp, vol 1963-65; Pall Corp, export sales mgr 1965-69; Marine Midland Bank, operations officer 1969-; Berkeley Federal, vice pres. **ORGANIZATIONS:** Bd dir Glen Cove Housing Auth 1965-70; former mem Bd of Govs Long Island World Trade Club 1968-69; mem EDGES Bus Group 1970-; mem Greenlawn Lions Club1970-73; Glen Cove Boys Club 1974-. **HONORS/ACHIEVEMENTS:** Recipient Spl Award for Peace Corp Serv Kiwanis Club 1965; Spl Serv Award City of Glen Cove NY 1971; Spl Serv Award Glen Cove Housing Auth 1971. **BUSINESS ADDRESS:** Vice President, Berkeley Federal, 21 Bleeker St, Millburn, NJ 07041.

WERTZ, ANDREW WALTER, SR.
Retired educational administrator. **PERSONAL:** Born Dec 18, 1928, Hamlet, NC; son of Andrew J Wertz and Johnnie B Wertz; married Bernice Spires; children: Alonzo W, Janis M, Brian L, Andy Jr, Ray J. **EDUCATION:** Lincoln Univ PA, BA 1949; USAF Command & Staff Coll, 1965; Syracuse Univ, MS, 1980. **CAREER:** Penn Fruit Co Inc, 1st African American Cashier, 1949; Detective Serv Inc, Private Investigator 1950; USAF, navigator/admin 1950-70; Hamilton Coll, dir Bristol Campus Center & dir student activities 1970-88; Retired, Freelance Consultant/Admin. **ORGANIZATIONS:** Bd mem OIC Utica, 1972-74; bd mem ARC Utica Chapter, 1973-79; bd mem Council of Churches, Mohawk Valley Area, 1974-78; pres, Mohawk Valley Club Frontiers Intl, 1975-77; mem Natl Conf Assn of Coll Unions Intl 1976; bd mem A Better Chance Inc Clinton NY 1977-80; host dir Region 2 conf Assn of Coll Unions Intl 1978; coord of minority progs Assn of Coll Unions Intl 1979; mem bd of dirs Frontiers Intl 1982-; mem NAACP; mem Kappa Alpha Psi; Pres, A Better Chance Inc, 1988-. **HONORS/ACHIEVEMENTS:** Distinguished Serv Award, USAF 1968; Internal Serv Awd, Frontiers Intl, 1978. **MILITARY SERVICE:** USAF lt col 1950-70 (retired).

WESLEY, BARBARA ANN
Educational administrator. **PERSONAL:** Born Jun 07, 1930, Wichita, KS; widowed; children: Ronald Frank, John Edgar. **EDUCATION:** Univ of Puget Sound, BA 1963; Univ of Puget Sound Tacoma, MEd 1972; Univ of MA, EdD 1977. **CAREER:** Clover Park School Dist, elem teacher 1960-64; Tacoma Public School, classroom teacher 1964-74; Westfield St Coll, proj dir/cons 1974-75; Alternative Prog Tacoma Public School, educ specialist 1975-78; Foss HS Tacoma Public Sch, high sch admin 1978-79; Wilson HS Tacoma Public School, hs admin 1979-82; Magnet Prog, dist admin 1982-. **ORGANIZATIONS:** Inst for Elem Tchrs Denver Univ 1969; Adult Educ Inst Univ of WI/NY State Univ of Albany 1972-73; Natl Sci Found Western MI Univ Santa Clara Univ 1972-73; bd of trustees Tacoma Comm Coll 1977-82; mem Delta Sigma Theta; bd of dirs YWCA Tacoma 1977-78; bd of dirs Campfire Tacoma 1979-83; State Vocational Council on Voc Educ 1982-; Wash Women Employ & Educ Bd of Dirs 1982-; mem Phi Delta Kappa, Delta Kappa Gamma. **HONORS/ACHIEVEMENTS:** Delta Kappa Gamma Post-doctoral AZ State Univ 1978; Harvard Univ Mgmt Inst summer 1981; Baylor Univ Leadership/Development Seminar summer 1982. **BUSINESS ADDRESS:** District Administrator, Magnet Prog Tacoma Public Sch, Central Admin Bldg, PO Box 1357, Tacoma, WA 98401.

WESLEY, CLARENCE E.
Business executive. **PERSONAL:** Born Sep 24, 1940, Coffeyville, KS; married Peggy L; children: Keira, Marquel. **EDUCATION:** Pittsburgh State U, BS 1962; Wichita State U, MA 1968. **CAREER:** Wichita Area C of C, mgr comm devel 1970-; Upward Bound Wichita State, asst dir 1969-70; Wichita State, KS State, Sterling Coll, lectr 1968-75; Wichita Pub Sch Sys, tchr/adminstrv asst 1962-70. **ORGANIZATIONS:** Pres Wes/Berry Intl; pres Central Sys Devel Corp; bd dir KS Ofc of Minority Bus; mem Nat Adv Cncl Small Bus Admin; pres Wichita Urban League;chmn trustee cncl Black Heritage Park of KS; trustee/dir Wichita Cncl of Ch; CETA Manpower Bd; bd dir Vet Adv Cncl. **HONORS/ACHIEVEMENTS:** Recipient Outstand Young Man of KS 1973-; KS Outstand Cit 1974; KS Pub Cit of Yr 1975; NCCJ State Brotherhood Award 1975; Wichita's Disting Serv Award 1973; Cert of Merit Nat Alliance of Businessmen & Wichita Pub Sch Sys 1972. **BUSINESS ADDRESS:** 350 W Douglas, Wichita, KS 67202.

WESLEY, CLEMON HERBERT, JR.
President of informations systems company. **PERSONAL:** Born Feb 24, 1936, Daingerfield, TX; son of Clemon Herbert Wesley and Zannie Benson Wesley; married Modestine Delores Truvillion Wesley, Sep 27, 1958; children: Yolanda Wesley, Deborah Hall, Eric Wesley. **EDUCATION:** Prairie View A & M University, BS, 1957; attended Army War College and Armed Forces Staff College; Shippensburg State College, MS, 1970; LaSalle University, LLB, 1972. **CAREER:** Texcom, Inc, Landover, MD, founder and president, 1981—. **ORGANIZATIONS:** President, National Business League of Southern Maryland; board member, Coalition of Concerned Black Christian Men, Phi Beta Sigma Education Foundation; member, National Urban League Black Executive Exchange Program, Prince George's County Chamber of Commerce, Minority Business Enterprise Legal Defense and Education Fund, St Paul United Methodist Church, Prairie View A & M Alumni Association, US Army War College Alumni Association. **HONORS/ACHIEVEMENTS:** Business achievement award, National Business League of Southern Maryland, 1986; Service Industry Award, US Department of Commerce, 1987; National Minority Small Business Person of the Year, and Minotiry Small Business Firm of the Year for region III, US Small Business Administration, 1988. **MILITARY SERVICE:** US Army, Signal Corps, 2nd lieutenant, 1957, retired as colonel, 1981; served on Department of Army Headquarters, 1975-79; received Vietnam Service Medal, Bronze Star, and Legion of Merit. **BUSINESS ADDRESS:** TEXCOM, Inc, 4200 Forbes Boulevard, Lanham, MD 20706.

WESLEY, GLORIA WALKER
Social worker. **PERSONAL:** Born May 21, 1928, Rochester, NY; married Cleo; children: Eric, Lia. **EDUCATION:** Fisk U, BA 1950; Loyola U, MSW 1959. **CAREER:** Income Maint Experiment IN U, coord social svc/day care 1970-74; City of Gary Sch, 1960-70, 1974; Lake Co Dept of Pub Welfare Gary, 1953-60; Lake CoChildren's Home Gary, 1952-53; Developmentally Disabled Sch City of Gary, social worker. **ORGANIZATIONS:** Mem Nat Assn of Social Workers 1959-; pres NW IN Cncl of Professional Sch Social Workers & Attendance Cncl 1975-79; mem IN State Cncl of Professional Sch Social Workers & Attendance Cnlsrs 1976-77; Intl Assn of Pupil Personnel Workers 1960-70; Tri-State Assn of Pupil Personnel Workers 1963-70; IN State Conf onSocial Welfare 1953-; bd dir/treas Gary Comm Mntl Hlth 1975; Urban League 1973-, adv bd 1971-73; 2nd vice pres Urban League NW IN 1979-80; dir YMCA 1973-; Campbell Friendship House 1969-74; Cerebral Palsy of NW IN 1964-65; Gary Neighborhood House 1963-65; Lake Co Assn for Retarded Children 1963-65; adv bd Hidden Talent 1971-76; INUniv NW Spl Serv 1973-75; Green's Geriatric Hlth Ctr 1965-; mem Gary Comm Mntl Hlth Planning Com 1974; NW IN Comprehensive Hlth Planning Council's Sub-Com on Alcoholism/Drug Addiction & Mntl Hlth 1970-74; chmn subcom Developmntl Disabilities 1974-; co-chairlady Project "Keep Sears in Gary" 1974; mem Gary Neighborhood Serv 1971-75; vol cnslr IN State Parole 1969. **HONORS/ACHIEVEMENTS:** Listed in Who's Who of Am Women 1973; Who's Who in the Midwest 1974. **BUSINESS ADDRESS:** 620 E 10 Place, Gary, IN.

WESLEY, NATHANIEL, JR.
Administrator. **PERSONAL:** Born Jan 13, 1943, Jacksonville, FL; married Ruby L Williams; children: Nataniel Wesley III. **EDUCATION:** FL A&M U, BS 1965;Univ of MI, MHA 1971. **CAREER:** DC Hosp Assn, asst exec dir 1979-; Meharry Med Coll, asst prof 1977-79; Sidney A Sumby Meml Hosp, exec dir 1975-76; SW Comm Hosp, dept dir 1973-75; New York City Hlth & Hosp Corp, spl asst to vice pres 1972-73; Albert Einstein Coll of Med, adminstr/cons 1971-72. **ORGANIZATIONS:** Sec/exec Nat Assn of Hlth Serv 1974-78; pres Detroit & Nashville Chpts NAASE 1975-79; pres NRW Asso Inc; mem BCHW of Alpha; mem Am Pub HlthAssn. **HONORS/ACHIEVEMENTS:** Nominee Am Coll of Hosp Adminstrs; WK Kellogg Fellow ACEHSA Wash, DC; Serv Award BSOUniv of MI Ann Arbor 1977; Comm Serv Award Peoples Comm Serv Detroit 1978; Tchr of the Yr Meharry Med Coll 1979-. **BUSINESS ADDRESS:** DC Hosp Assn, 1725 Eye St NW Ste 301, Washington, DC 20006.

WESLEY, RICHARD ERROL
Playwright. **PERSONAL:** Born Jul 11, 1945, Newark, NJ; son of George R Wesley and Gertrude Thomas Wesley; married Valerie Wilson; children: 2 Children. **EDUCATION:** Howard University, Washington, DC, BFA, 1967. **CAREER:** Wesleyan University, African Cultural Institute, Middletown, CT, adjunct professor, 1974; Manhattanville College, Purchase, NY, adjunct professor, 1974; Borough of Manhattan Community College, New York, NY, instructor in Black Theatre, 1980-81, 1982-83; Rutgers University, Newark, NJ, instructor in Black Theatre, 1989; Elegba Productions, president; Black Theatre Magazine, past editor. **ORGANIZATIONS:** Bd of dirs, Frank Silvera Writers Workshop, 1976-84; bd of dirs, Theatre of Universal Images, Newark, NJ; mem of selection comm, Newark NJ Black Film Festival. **HONORS/ACHIEVEMENTS:** Playwright "The Black Terror," Public Theatre, New York, NY, 1971, "Goin' Thru Changes," Billie Holiday Theatre, New York, NY, 1974, "The Sirens," Manhattan Theatre Club, New York, NY, 1974, "The Last Street Play," Manhattan Theatre Club, New York, NY, 1974, "The Mighty Gents," B'way Prod, 1978-, "On the Road to Babylon," Milwaukee Rep, Milwaukee, WI, 1980, "The Dream Team," Goodspeed Opera House, 1984, "The Talented Tenth," Manhattan Theatre Club, New York, NY, 1989; Drama Desk award, 1972; Rockefeller Grant, 1973; Audelco Award, 1974, 1977; author of screenplays "Uptown Saturday Night," Warner Bros, 1974, "Let's Do It Again," Warner Bros, 1975, "Fast Forward," Columbia Pictures, 1985, "Native Son," Cinecom Pictures, 1986; author of TV screenplay "The House of Dies Dear," PBS, 1984. **BUSINESS ADDRESS:** President, Elegba Productions, PO Box 43091, Upper Montclair, NJ 07043.

WESLEY, RUTH BAILEY
Government employee. **PERSONAL:** Born May 21, 1945, Baton Rouge, LA; married Lee T Sr; children: Lee, Jr, Dana Aeneid. **EDUCATION:** So U, BA 1968; Wash Journalism Ctr, Cert 1971. **CAREER:** Bur of Pub Info, asst dir; State of LA Gov Edwards, press sec; Pub Affairs Res Cncl of LA, researcher/writer 1971-72, asst press sec 1973; Alumni Fedn So U, sec 1968; Comm Advancement Inc, tchr manpower training pgm 1969-71. **ORGANIZATIONS:** Mem Delta Sigma Theta; Baranco-Clark YMCA; bd dir YWCA; Baton Rouge Press Club; adv com Pelican Bowl Classic; Alpha Kappa Alpha 1974. **HONORS/ACHIEVEMENTS:** Outstand Comm Worker OES & Masons 1973; Disting Serv Citation LA Educ Assn 1973; Polit Achievement in State Gov Delta Sigma Theta 1973; Alumnae of Yr Capitol Sr HS 1974; Outstand Contrib & Achievement Award Clerical Cncl of New Orleans 1974.

WESSON, CLEO
Councilman. **PERSONAL:** Born Aug 27, 1924, Ozan, AR; married Julia (deceased); children: Helayne. **EDUCATION:** Gary Coll. **ORGANIZATIONS:** Mem John Will Anderson Boys Club; Lake City Lodge #182; King Solomon Lodge #57; Magic City Consistory #62; Mohomet Temple #134; Rebecca Chap #39; Sallie Wyatt Stewart Guild; Urban League of NW IN Inc; life mem NAACP; mem Israel CME Ch; bd dir March of Dimes. **HONORS/ACHIEVEMENTS:** Recipient Cert of Merit Gary Br NAACP 1965; Serv Award 3rd Episcopal Dist CME Ch 1965; J Claude Allen Presiding Bishop Seepa 1967; Disting Serv & Outstand Leadership as pres of Common Cncl City of Gary 1966. **MILITARY SERVICE:** USAAF WW II 1943-45.

WESSON, KENNETH ALAN
Business executive. **PERSONAL:** Born Aug 05, 1948, Oakland, CA. **EDUCATION:** Coll of San Mateo, AA;Univ of CA at Berkeley, AB 1970; CA StateUniv San Jose, MA 1972; UC Berkeley, grad work EdD 1970-72. **CAREER:** Laidlaw Bros Pub Co, 1975-; Nartrans Mfg Corp Canoga Park, CA, Canoga Park, CA, indsl psychol & exec asst to chmn of bd 1974-75; San Jose State U; San Jose Cty Coll; Foothill Coll Los Altos, instr 1972-74; Santa Clara Vall Med Ctr, prof of psy/social/mntl hlth/afro-am studies 1972-74; Stanford Research Inst,

educ consult 1970; Am Consult Asso, cons; CE Bump & Asso Glendale, CA, consult 1974-75; Berkeley HS, tchr; Triskiellion Growth Ctr in SoCA, psychologist. **ORGANIZATIONS:** Mem Santa Clara Co Mntl Hlth Adv Bd; bd of dir Cncl of the Arts; mem CA Tchrs Assn; mem Assn for Supervision & Curric Devel; mem CA Alumni Assn; mem CA Sch Hlth Assn; mem San Jose Real Estate Bd; bd of dir San Jose Jaycees; mem Western Psychol Assn; Assn of Black Psychols; Faculty Assn of CA Comm Coll; United Professors of CA.

WEST, CHARLES FREMONT
Physician. **PERSONAL:** Born Jan 25, 1899, Washington, PA; married LaVerne Gregory; children: Charles Nathaniel, Linda Nickens. **EDUCATION:** Wash & Jefferson Coll, BS 1924; HowardUniv Med Sch, MD 1928. **CAREER:** Private Pract, Physician 1929-; TB Assn of Alexandria Hlth Dept, clinician 1940-79; Employee Recreation Dept DC, 1934; Howard U, coach football/track 1925-30; HU Hosp (Freedmans) Alexandria Hosp, staff mem. **ORGANIZATIONS:** Mem Pigskin Club 1930-; mem Alexandria Urban League 1970-; life mem Alpha Phi Alpha Frat. **HONORS/ACHIEVEMENTS:** Winner Penn Relays 1922-23; quarterback Rose Bowl Team 1922; qualified Olympic Team 1924; Appreciation Award for promoting growth of E Skeet & Trap Assn Metro Club 1964; Citation for Community Serv Alexandria Urban League 1976; Disting Serv Award Gen Alumni Assn of Wash & Jefferson Coll 1978; Med Almuni Award HowardUniv Med Alumni Inc 1978; Plaque & Citation Western PA & PA State Sports Hall of Fame 1979. **BUSINESS ADDRESS:** 1006 Cameron St, Alexandria, VA 22314.

WEST, CHRISTOPHER O.
Dentist. **PERSONAL:** Born May 20, 1915, Lexington, MS; married Bertha Drungole; children: Angela, Chrystal, John, Jean (Harper). **EDUCATION:** Alcorn A&M Coll, BS;Univ of IL, BS, DDS; Air Force U. **CAREER:** Private Pract, dentist. **ORGANIZATIONS:** Chmn Sci Com Chicago Dental Soc; pres Kenwood-Hyde Park Br Chicago Dental Soc; mem various dental soc; life mem NAACP; Urban League; YMCA;Univ of IL Alumni Assn; organizer/1st dir Rehab Clinic. **MILITARY SERVICE:** USAF & AUS 12 yrs. **BUSINESS ADDRESS:** 7257 S Jeffery Ave, Chicago, IL 60649.

WEST, EARL M.
Business executive. **PERSONAL:** Born Feb 15, 1912, Arkansas City, KS; married Erma Ratliff. **EDUCATION:** Univ of KS, BA 1939; KS State Teachers Coll Emporia, attended; Univ of MD, Grad Ed Study; Amer Savings & Loan Inst, Grad Diploma 1961; Amer Univ, attended; Union Theol Sem, attended; Univ of Denver, attended. **CAREER:** CCC, ed adv 1940-42; USO, dir 1942-46; UNRRA European Opers, ins broker, contractor real estate broker 1946-48; Equity Fed Savings Bank, pres. **ORGANIZATIONS:** Mem Denver Bd of Realtors, Denver C of C; sr warden Vestry-Episcopal Church; mem Bd of Health & Hosps for City & Cty of Denver 1965-77; chmn E Denver YMCA 1975-77, Alpha Phi Alpha, Sigma Pi Phi. **HONORS/ACHIEVEMENTS:** Outstanding & Dedicated Serv Awd Alpha Chi Pi Omega; Awd for Continuing Support of Comm Effort Sigma Gamma Phi; 50 Plus Years Membership Honor YMCA. **BUSINESS ADDRESS:** President, Equity Federal Savings Bank, Denver Federal Center, Box 25385, Denver, CO 80225.

WEST, GEORGE FERDINAND, JR.
Attorney. **PERSONAL:** Born Oct 25, 1940, Adams Co, MS; son of George Ferdinand West, Sr and Artimese M West; married Billie Guy; children: George III, Heath. **EDUCATION:** Tougaloo Coll, BA 1962; SoUniv Sch of Law, JD 1966;Univ MS, JD 1968. **CAREER:** Natchez Adams Co Sch Bd, appt/co-atty 1967; State Adv Bd for Voc Edn, appt 1968; Natchez-Adams Co C of C, appt/dir 1974; Jeff Co Sch Sys, atty 1974; MS Sch Bd Assn, dir/atty; Radio Pgm "FACT-FINDING", modrtr; Copiah-Lincoln Jr Coll Natchez Br, bus law prof; Natchez News Leader, mg edtr;Private Practice Natchez, MS,. **ORGANIZATIONS:** Mem MS Bar Assn 1968; rsrchr/procter MS StateUniv 1973; NAACP; Natchez Bus & Civ Lgue; vice pres Gov Com Hire the Hndcp; trust/sunday sch tchr Zion Chap AME Ch; contributing editor, Bluff City Post, 1978-; chmn, Natchez-Adams School Bd, 1988-. **HONORS/ACHIEVEMENTS:** Outstand Yng Men in Am 1967-; Comm Ldr of Am 1972; Lifetime Rosco Pound Fellow 1972; Most Distinguished Black Attorney Travelers Coalition, 1988; Doctor of Humane Letters, Natchez Coll, 1989. **BUSINESS ADDRESS:** Attorney, George F West, PO Box 1202, Natchez, MS 39120.

WEST, GERALD I.
Psychologist. **PERSONAL:** Born Jun 03, 1937, St Louis; married Blondel B McKinnie, Aug 20, 1960; children: Gerald I West, Jr.. **EDUCATION:** U Univ of Denver, BA, 1958; So IL Univ, MS 1963; Purdue Univ, PhD 1967. **CAREER:** San Francisco State Univ, prof of counseling; Westside Comm Mental Health, comm psychologist; Diagnostic & Evaluation Center Contra Costa Co Hosp, dir; STEP-UP San Francisco State Univ, psychologist & dir; California State Univ, admin fellow, 1986-87, chmn, Dept of Counseling, presently. **ORGANIZATIONS:** mem, Assn of Black Psychologists; APA; Natl Council on Measurement in Educ; Amer Personnel & Guid Assn; consult Bureau of Indian Affairs Dept of Interior; consultant, CA Youth Authority; San Francisco & Berkeley Public School; CA State Dept of Mental Hygiene; EOC San Francisco; Partner & Bd of Dir, Psychological & Human Resources Consultants Inc, 1969-present; Assoc Dir, Psychologist, STEPII Educ/Vocational Center, 1983-present; Amer Psychological Assn, Amer Assn of Counseling & Devlopment, Sigma Pi Phi, Kappa Alpha Psi. **HONORS/ACHIEVEMENTS:** Lead case in Larry P vs State of CA (Bay Area Assn of Black Psychologists) to stop IQ testing of Black Youth Fed Moritorium granted Dec 18, 1974; Recipient of Bay Area Black Student Psychology Assn Award, 1974; Danforth Associateship 1969; elected 1st Human Rights Commr of CA Personnel & Guid Assn 1973; Certificate of Honor, City County of San Francisco, 1983; Professional Devel Award, Amer Assn of Counseling & Develop, Multicultural Counseling, 1985; Annual Mem Award, Assn of Black Psychologist, 1980; Award of Merit, San Francisco State Univ, 1985; Admin Fellow, California State Univ, 1987; Annual Award, Public Advocates, 1983; Lead case of Larry P vs State of California, first successfully litigated case disproving the theory of racial genetic intellectual inferiority according to IQ tests, which led to federal law prohibiting the use of IQ tests on African American children in CA. **MILITARY SERVICE:** AUS Med Servs Corps, lt 1966; Biochemist, 374th General Hospital. **BUSINESS ADDRESS:** Clinical Psychologist, Prof, San Francisco State Univ, 1600 Holloway, San Francisco, CA 94132.

WEST, HAROLD DADFORD
Educator. **PERSONAL:** Born Jul 16, 1904, Flemington, NJ; married Jesse Juanita Penn; children: Edna, Harold Dadford. **EDUCATION:** Univ of I, BA 1925; Julius Rosenwald Fund Fellow, MS 1930; Rockefeller Found Fellow, PhD 1937. **CAREER:** Morris Brown Coll Atlanta, prof chem/head dept sci 1925-27; Meharry Med Coll, asso prof/physical chem 1927-, asso prof biochem 1927-38, prof biochem/chmn dept 1938-52, acting chmn/div basic sci 1947; mem interim com 1950, vice chmn 1951, coll pres 1952-66, prof biochem 1966-73; trustee, presently retired. **ORGANIZATIONS:** Mem Am Soc Biol Chemists; Soc Exptl Bio & Med; mem Sigma Xi; Kappa Delta Pi; Sigma Pi Phi; Alpha Phi Alpha; Kappa Pi; Alpha Omega Alpha; Omicron KappaUpsilon. **HONORS/ACHIEVEMENTS:** Received Hon LLD Morris Brown Coll 1955; Hon DSc Meharry Med Coll 1970.

WEST, HERBERT LEE, JR.
Educator. **PERSONAL:** Born May 04, 1947, Warrenton, NC; married Mary Bentley; children: Tamekah Denise, Marcus Delaney-Bentley. **EDUCATION:** NC Central Univ, BA 1969; Univ of MN, MA 1972, PhD 1974. **CAREER:** Teacher asst, Univ of Minnesota, 1972; asst prof, Univ of Maryland Baltimore County, 1974-1980; asst prof, Howard University, 1980-1985; faculty intern, House Urban Devel, 1980; advisor, Summer Work Program-Prince Georges County, Maryland; educator/admin, Howard County Bd of Education, 1985-; adjunct faculty Univ of Maryland Baltimore County, 1986-. **ORGANIZATIONS:** Mem NAACP, Triangle Geographers, Natl Council of Black Studies, Assoc for the Study of Afro-Amer Life; Black Student Achievement Program, Howard County, Maryland. **HONORS/ACHIEVEMENTS:** Ford Found Fellow 1971; NEH Fellow Atlanta Univ 1978; Outstanding Teacher Univ of MD Baltimore Cty 1978,79; Smithsonian Fellow Smithsonian Inst 1985; NEH Fellow Univ of NC 1983; Summer Fellow UMTA/Atlanta Univ 1984; Univ of Indiana guest lecturer 1988; NEH Fellow Columbia Univ 1989; Comga Graduate Fellowship Univ of Minnesota 1969. **HOME ADDRESS:** 9461 Riverark Road, Columbia, MD 21045.

WEST, JOHN ANDREW
Attorney. **PERSONAL:** Born Sep 15, 1942, Cincinnati, OH; married Miriam Evonne Kennedy; children: Melissa Evonne. **EDUCATION:** Univ of Cincinnati, BA, BS 1966; Salmon P Chase Law Sch, JD 1971. **CAREER:** Pitzer West Cutcher & Gilday, atty; GE Co Large Jet Engine Div, buyer & contract admin 1968-71. **ORGANIZATIONS:** Mem Nat/Am & OH Bar Assn 1972-; chmn Hamilton Co Pub Defender Commn 1976. **BUSINESS ADDRESS:** Pitzer West Cutcher & Gilday, 3886 Reading Rd, Cincinnati, OH 45229.

WEST, JOHN RAYMOND
Administrator. **PERSONAL:** Born Apr 09, 1931, Birmingham, AL; son of John H. West and Milnonette Mason; married Suzanne Marie Lancaster; children: Ronald, John Jr, Gerald, Reginald, Teresa, Semara, Tia, Joshua. **EDUCATION:** CA State Univ Fullerton, BA Anthro 1969, MA Anthro 1970; Nova Univ FL, EdD Admin 1975. **CAREER:** USMC, avionics admin 1950-61; So Counties Gas Co, sr scheduler 1961-69; State of CA, employment serv officer 1969-70; Santa Ana Coll, anthro, sociol, prof 1970-73; Nova Univ, cluster coord 1976-; Saddleback Coll Mission Viejo, instr 1976-; Afro Ethnic Studies CA State Univ Fullerton, lecturer; Santa Ana Coll, dean student serv 1970-. **ORGANIZATIONS:** Founding pres Orange Cty Chap Sickle Cell Disease Rsch Found 1972; bd of dirs, vice pres Legislative Affairs Western Region Council on Black Amer Affairs; bd of dir Assoc of CA Comm Coll Admin 1972; bd of dir CA Comm Coll Extended Oppty Prog & Serv 1977-79. **HONORS/ACHIEVEMENTS:** 5 publ Clearinghouse Clearing UCLA 1974-75. **MILITARY SERVICE:** USMC gunnery sgt 1950-61; presidential Unit Citation/United Nations Serv 1950. **BUSINESS ADDRESS:** Dean of Student Services, Santa Ana College, 1530 W 17th St, Santa Ana, CA 92706.

WEST, JOSEPH KING
County court judge. **PERSONAL:** Born Sep 11, 1929, Yonkers, NY; son of Ralph West and Nellie Brown West; married Shriley Arvene Gray; children: Rebecca, Joseph Jr. **EDUCATION:** Howard Univ, BS 1952; Brooklyn Law School, JD 1961. **CAREER:** City of Yonkers, asst corp counsel 1964-65, city court judge 1983-84; County of Westchester, deputy dist atty 1965-82; State of New York, Westchester Co court judge 1985-. **ORGANIZATIONS:** Mem Alpha Phi Alpha Frat 1948-; bd of dirs Yonkers Big Brother-Big Sisters 1982-, St Joseph's Hosp 1983-, Westchester Comm Oppor Prog 1983-. **HONORS/ACHIEVEMENTS:** Achievement Awd Assoc of Black Lawyers of Westchester Co 1981; Comm Serv Westchester Rockland Guardians Assoc 1984; Comm Serv Awd Yonkers Cncl of Churches 1985; Civic Awd Frederick D Patterson Alpha Phi Alpha 1987. **MILITARY SERVICE:** AUS 1st lt 1952-56. **BUSINESS ADDRESS:** County Ct Judge Westchester, New York State, 111 Grove St, White Plains, NY 10601.

WEST, MARCELLA POLITE
Educator. **PERSONAL:** Born in Savannah; daughter of James H Polite (deceased) and Mary Smith-Polite (deceased); divorced; children: Maralyn C West-Craddock, Rodney Cecil West. **EDUCATION:** Montclair State Coll, MA 1973; St Philip School of Nursing Med Coll of VA, 1946-48; Upsala Coll, 1969; Newark State Coll, 1970-71. **CAREER:** Cornelius E Gallagher 13th Congressional Dist NJ, congressional staff 1957-66; NJ Comm Action & Training Inst Trenton, NJ, training officer 1966-67; Bergen Co Comm Action Program Hackensack, NY, training dir 1967-69; Montclair State Coll, admin to vice provost 1969-71; Urban Educ Corps Montclair State Coll, dir 1971-73; Montclair State Coll Div Student Personnel Svc, educ adv counselor 1973-; Rutger's Univ Intern Program, 1966-67; Inner City Broadcasting Corp WLIB, bd dir; WLIB/WBLS AM/FM, exec com 1972-; Human Devel Consulting Serv Inc, consultant/facilitator 1975-. **ORGANIZATIONS:** Mem Am Mgmt Assn 1967-71; mem Am Soc for Training & Devel 1967-73; mem/officer Local/State/Regional & Natl Participation of NAACP 1956-67; mem Delta Sigma Theta Sorority; mem Phi Delta Kappa Educ Fraternity; Hudson Co Dem & Com Woman 1959, 1964, 1975; del Nat Dem Women 1963-64; del Pres Nat Com on Civil Rights 1962-; del Educ Conf Harvard Univ Black Congressional Caucus 1972; guest journalist Jersey Journal covering civil rights/events, including 1962 March on Washington; Natl Youth Advisory Bd 1961; NJ State Conf NAACP Branch 1963; Spanish Teacher Corps 1970; corp sec, Inner City Broadcasting Corp, bd of dir, New York, NY, 1978-; bd of trustees, Sr Care & Activities Center, Montclair, NJ, 1989. **HONORS/ACHIEVEMENTS:** Recipient NAACP Serv Award Jersey City Branch 1965; Am Mgmt Assn Sup Certificate 1966; Serv, Govt of NJ Affirmative Action Awareness Program, 1986-87; Certificate of Appreciation, State of NJ, Dept of Civil Serv: The Next Phase, 1987; Merit Award Program, Montclair State Coll, Upper Montclair, NJ, 1989. **BUSINESS ADDRESS:** Teacher Certification Coord/Advisor, Post B, Montclair State Coll, Normal Ave, School of Professional Studies, Chapin Hall, Rm 102, Upper Montclair, NJ 07043.

WEST, MARCELLUS
Mayor. **PERSONAL:** Born Oct 16, 1913, Jackson, MS; married Fannie; children: Eddie,

Doris, Fannie. **CAREER:** Brooklyn, IL, mayor; Restaurant Bus; Lovejoy Sch, supr/maint/truant ofcr 10 yrs; Armour Packing House. **ORGANIZATIONS:** Chmn Lovejoy Adv Bd; 3rd v chmn EOC. **HONORS/ACHIEVEMENTS:** EOC Bd Award Willing Wrkrs Assn Comm Work; Award for Serv Rendered EOC Bd; Outstand Job & as Mayor 1975.

WEST, MARK KEITH
Professional athlete. **PERSONAL:** Born Nov 05, 1960, Ft Campbell, KY. **EDUCATION:** Old Dominion, BS 1979-83. **CAREER:** Dallas Mavericks, center 1983-. **HONORS/ACHIEVEMENTS:** 1984 Summer League Capsule, started at center & avgd 113 ppg, 87 rebounds & shot 490 as the Cavs went 10-2 and won league chmpnshp; 1983-84 Capsule, Coach Motta's project for 1983-84, West played just 202 minutes in 34 games; Big Games, biggest contrbtns came at Chicago on 12/17/83 when he had 6 pts and 6 rebounds in 12 min and at Portland On 2/7 when he had 2 pts And 6 rebounds in a season-high 24 min. **BUSINESS ADDRESS:** Dallas Mavericks, Reunion Arena, Ste 510, Dallas, TX 75207.

WEST, PHEORIS
Artist, educator. **PERSONAL:** Born Aug 17, 1950, Albany, NY; son of James West and Mary Wilson McDowell; married Michele Barbette Hoff, May 05, 1979; children: Jahlani, Adwin, Pheannah, Adji West. **EDUCATION:** State Univ of NY Coll at Brockport, 1968-70; PA Acad of Fine Arts, 4 yr Professional Cert 1970-74; Yale U, MFA Painting 1974-76. **CAREER:** OH State U, asst prof to assoc prof of art 1976-; Hillhouse HS New Haven, Ct, artist-in-residence 1976; Educ Ctr for the Arts, dir/artist-in-residence 1976. **ORGANIZATIONS:** mem Natl Confernce of Artists 1970; mem Artist Equity 1978-; bd mem CMACAO Cultural Arts Ctr 1979-; mem Bahia Bridge 1988-; bd mem Columbus Art League 1988-. **HONORS/ACHIEVEMENTS:** James A Porter Grand Prize $1000 Nat Exhibit of Black Artists 1971; Cresson Award Travelling Flwshp to Europe PA Acad of Fine Arts 1973, J Scheidt Award Travelling Flwshp to Ghana 1974; Commn Mural 8' X 12' Lower Washington Hgts New York City Commn on Arts 1975; special recognition OH House of Representatives 1988; Individual Artists Grant OH Arts Council 1988. **HOME ADDRESS:** 756 Seymour Ave, Columbus, OH 43205.

WEST, ROY See DARLING, LEROY

WEST, TOGO DENNIS, JR.
Attorney. **PERSONAL:** Born Jun 21, 1942, Winston-Salem, NC; son of Togo Dennis and Evelyn Carter West; married Gail Estelle Berry; children: Tiffany Berry, Hilary Carter. **EDUCATION:** Howard Univ, BSEE 1965, JD (cum laude) 1968. **CAREER:** Duquesne Light & Power Co, elec engr 1965; Sughrue Rothwell Mion Zinn & McPeak, patent reseacher 1966-67; US Equal Employment Opportunity Comm, legal intern 1967; Covington & Burling, law clerk 1967-68, summer assoc 1968, assoc 1973-75, 1976-77; Hon Harold R Tyler Judge US Dist Court for the Southern Dist of NY, law clerk 1968-69; Dept of Justice, associate deputy atty general 1975-76; Dept of Navy, gen counsel 1977-79; Dept of Defense, special asst to sec & deputy sec 1979-80, general counsel 1980-81; Patterson Belknap Webb & Tyler, partner 1981-. **ORGANIZATIONS:** District of Columbia Bar 1968; New York Bar 1969; US Ct Mil Appeals 1969, US Supreme Ct 1978; managing editor Howard Law Journal 1968; mem Amer Bar Assn; mem Natl Bar Assn; dir Washington Council of Lawyers 1973-75; US Court of Claims 1981; mem Eagle Scout with Bronze Palm; trustee The Aerospace Corp 1983-; mem 1984, treasurer 1987-, Natl Council of the Friends of the Kennedy Center; commissioner 1982-89, chmn 1985-89, District of Columbia Law Revision Commission; trustee, Institute for Defense Anaylses, 1989-; trustee, Center for Strategic and International Studies, 1987-; chairman, Legislative Bureau, Greater Washington Board of Trade, mem, Board of Directors, 1987-; bd of dir, DC Law Students in Court Program 1986-; mem DC Committee on Public Education, 1989-; mem Vestry, St Jo hn's Church at Lafayette Square; mem Alpha Phi Omega Fraternity; mem Sigma Pi Phi Fraternity; mem Omega Psi Phi Fraternity. **HONORS/ACHIEVEMENTS:** Distinguished Public Service Medal Dept of Defense 1981. **MILITARY SERVICE:** AUS served to capt judge adv gen corps AUS 1969-73; decorated Legion of Merit. **BUSINESS ADDRESS:** Attorney, Patterson Belknap Webb & Tyler, 1730 Pennsylvania Ave NW, Washington, DC 20006.

WEST, WILLIAM LIONEL
Educator. **PERSONAL:** Born Nov 30, 1923, Charlotte, NC; married Edythe; children: William II, Edythe P. **EDUCATION:** Johnson C Smith U, BS 1947; StateUniv IA, PhD 1955. **CAREER:** Howard U, prof/chmn dept pharmacology 1972-, prof dept radiology 1971-; Coll Med Howard U, prof dept pharm 1969-72; Dept Pharm Coll Med & Howard, asso prof/asst prof/instr 1956-69; Radiation Rsrch Dept Coll Med StateUniv IA, rsrch asso 1954-56; Zoology Dept StateUniv IA, rsrch asst 1949-54. **ORGANIZATIONS:** Mem Am Soc Pharmacology & Experimental Therapeutics; Intl Soc Biochem; Am Nuclear Soc; Am Assn Clinical Chem; Am Soc Zoologist; Soc for Experimental Biology & Med; Am Physiol Soc; Am Inst Chemist; Mem Am Assn Cancer Rsrch; flw Am Inst Chem; Intl Acad of Law & Sci; Sigma Xi Sci Soc; NYAcad Sci; flw AAAS Num Publ.

WESTBROOK, ELOUISE
Supportive service coordinator. **PERSONAL:** Born Apr 20, Gatesville, TX; children: Evelyn Snelgro, Odie Lee Criner. **EDUCATION:** Tillson Clg, MA. **CAREER:** Housing Dev Corp CA, supportive serv coordinator; Bayview Hunters Point Med Assc, coordinator; Econ Opportunity Cncl, trainer; Econ Opportunity Cncl CA, intake & referral wrkr; Youth Opportunity Cncl Bayview Hunters Point of San Francisco, pres; Welfare Rights Orgn, organizer; Tchr Assistance Pgm, orgnzr 1970. **ORGANIZATIONS:** Past pres San Francisco Med Ctr Outpatient Improvement Pgm Inc; chmwmn Bayview Hunters Joint Housing Com; mem bd of regents Lone Mountain Clg; GoldenGate Transp Adv Com; mem Consumer Action Com; Assc of Neighborhood Hlth Ctrs Inc; pres Natl Assc of Neighborhood Hlth Ctrs; pgm planning com Natl Assc of Neighborhood Hlth Ctrs; Mayor's Com for Comm Devel. **HONORS/ACHIEVEMENTS:** Recip first comm serv awrd 1965; women of yr awrd Sun Reporter 1968; ridgepoint sr cit awrd 1968; 1969 awrd Zelta Zeta Omega Chap Alpha Kappa Sorority; silver spur awrd 1969; Awrd of Dev Positive Black Females Images living legend awrd 1974; Black Women Organized for Action; christian welfare soc awrd 1974; merit awrd for outst performance 1971; cert of appreciation Bayview Hunters Point Comm. **BUSINESS ADDRESS:** 1715 Yosemite Ave, San Francisco, CA 94124.

WESTBROOK, FRANKLIN SOLOMON
Automobile industry engineer. **PERSONAL:** Born May 04, 1958, Buffalo, NY; son of Solomon C Westbrook Jr and Daisy M Pursley Westbrook; married Helen Juanita Goble, Mar 28, 1980; children: Anthony F, Reyhan M, William C, Gregory R. **EDUCATION:** General Motors Inst, Flint, MI, BEE, 1981; Purdue Univ, West Lafayette, IN, MSIA, 1988. **CAREER:** CPC Tonawanda Engine GMC, co-op student, 1976-81, assoc engineer, 1981-83, plant engineer, 1983-86, sr engineer, 1986-; General Motors Corp, Tonawanda, NY, sr plant engineer, 1986-87, sr mfg engineer, 1988-. **ORGANIZATIONS:** Pres, 1986-87, vice pres, 1982-83, mem, Rho Lambda-Alpha Phi Alpha Fraternity, 1978-; part-time instructor, Erie Community Coll, 1983-85; mem, Urban League, Coalition for the Redevelop of Unified Community Involvement and Leadership, NAACP; exec comm, United Negro Coll Fund, Buffalo, NY, 1989-. **HONORS/ACHIEVEMENTS:** Serv Award, Delta Sigma Theta Sor, Mu Phi Chapter; publication "A Proprietary Monitoring System". **HOME ADDRESS:** 549 Dartmouth Ave, Buffalo, NY 14215.

WESTBROOK, GILSON HOWARD
Business executive. **PERSONAL:** Born Oct 15, 1947, Jefferson, TX; married Darlene Renfro; children: Nicholas, Darrell, Dedera. **EDUCATION:** Stephen F Austin Univ, BA 1971; Syracuse Univ, 1982. **CAREER:** Community devel coord 1972-74; comm devel admin 1974-80; comm devel grant coord & planning 1980-85; Westbrook & Assoc Plan & Mgt Co, pres. **ORGANIZATIONS:** Inst rep Boy Scout Troup 1975-83; pres Civic & Betterment Soc 1980-85; bd mem Chamber of Comm 1982-84; mem US Chamber ofComm 1984-85; mem Rotary Club. **HONORS/ACHIEVEMENTS:** Citizen of the Year Thetha Sigma 1980; Man of the Year Simpson United Methodist Church 1983; Henderson County Black Achievement Award 1987. **MILITARY SERVICE:** AUS pfc 1967. **BUSINESS ADDRESS:** President, Westbrook & Assoc Grant Mgt, PO Box 2087, Malakoff, TX 75148.

WESTBROOK, JOSEPH W., III
Retired educator. **PERSONAL:** Born Jul 13, 1919, Shelby Co, TN; son of Joseph W. Westbrook, II and Clara Nelson Westbrook; married Dorothy Greene, Jul 13, 1919; children: (1 dec). **EDUCATION:** B 1943; M 1961; D 1970. **CAREER:** Dev of Plan of Decentralization, dir; Supvr Scndry Instr 8 Yrs; Sr HS, asst prin 3 Yrs; Clsrm Tchr Athletic Coach 15 Yrs; area superintendant Memphis City Schools, Memphis, TN 1971-81. **ORGANIZATIONS:** Mem Natl Ed Assc; Assc for Supvsn & Curr Dev; Phi Delta Kappa Ed Frat; Natl Sci Supvrs Assc; past pres TN Ed Assc; mem Memphis Ed Assc; Natl Sci Tchrs Assc; Am Assc of Sch Admntrs; Natl Assc of Scndry Sch Prins; Exec Com Natl Cncl on Tchrs Retirement; mem bd dirs Memphis UrbanLeague; bd dirs Dixie Homes Goodwill Boys Clb; Glenview YMCA; Frontiers Clb Intrntl; Memphis Reg Sickle Cell Cncl; past pres Alpha Phi Alpha Frat; Local Chpt; mem Exec Com of Un Way of Memphis; Exec Com of LeBonheur Hosp; bd of dir Natl Urban League 1978-82; bd of dir Natl Assn of Sickle Cell Disease 1979-83; bd of dir Natl Educ Assn 1984-90; pres Natl Educ Assn 1984-90. **HONORS/ACHIEVEMENTS:** Recip acad professional devel award Natl Acad for Sch Execs; Outstanding Alumnus LeMogne-Owen Coll 1973; Greek of Year Alpha Phi Alpha Fraternity Memphis Chapter 1973.

WESTBROOK, SCOTT C., III
Educational administrator. **PERSONAL:** Born Feb 27, 1939, Houston, TX; son of Scott C Westbrook Jr and Kathryn Robinson Westbrook; married Ruth Devereaux; children: Scott IV, Reseda. **EDUCATION:** Prairie View A&M Univ, BA 1960; TX Southern Univ, MEd 1962; Wayne State Univ, EdD 1980. **CAREER:** Houston Ind Schools, teacher 1960-68; Joske's, TX, dept mgr, assoc buyer, div mgr 1968-70; Yankee Dept Store Detroit, asst mgr 1970-71; Project Growth Pontiac, MI, vocational counselor 1971-72; Oakland Co OEO, personal mgr 1972-73; Project Growth Pontiac, MI, dir 1973-75; Vocational Specialist Needs Pontiac School Dist, supr. **ORGANIZATIONS:** Pres Detroit Prairie View Alumni Club 1972-74; Relocation Asst Adv & Grievance Com Pontiac MI 1972; bd mem Pontiac Area Urban League 1972-; sec Kappa Alpha Psi Detroit Alumni Chapter 1973-76; mem Voc Educ Task Force Oakland Co 1974; chmn Oakland Co Youth Asst Employment Com 1977-88; council on ministries chmn Fellowship United Methodist Church; growth chmn Pontiac Dist BSA; pres MI Occupational Special Needs Assn 1977-78; bd mem MI Occupational Educ Assn 1978-79; com mem Natl Assoc for Advancement of Black Amer in Voc Educ 1978-; exec bd mem MI Occupational Educ Assn 1979-83; vice pres Natl Assoc of Voc Specialist Needs Personnel 1979-; mem Pontiac YMCA 1979; trustee Natl Urban League 1984-86; exec bd mem Oakland Co Cultural Council 1987; bd chairperson Oakland County OIC 1988-. **HONORS/ACHIEVEMENTS:** Outstanding male graduate HS 1956; One of Ten Outstanding Graduate of Prairie View 1960; Journalism Award Prairie View 1958; SW Reg Student YMCA Award 1960; Houston Alumni Kappa Alpha Psi Serv Award 1969; Detroit Prairie View Alumni Club Serv Award 1974; Pace Setters Award Natl Prarie View Alumni Assn 1978; Outstanding Achievement Award No Province Kappa Alpha Psi 1979; numerous other awards. **BUSINESS ADDRESS:** Dir of Vocational Education, Pontiac School Dist, 300 W Huron St, Pontiac, MI 48053.

WESTBROOKS, LOGAN H.
Business executive. **PERSONAL:** Born Aug 28, 1937, Memphis, TN; married Geraldine Douthet; children: Babette. **EDUCATION:** Lincoln Univ, 1957-61; Lemoyne Coll, 1955-57. **CAREER:** Source Record Co Inc, founder/pres 1977-; CA State Univ LA PAS Dept, part-time prof 1977-; Intrntl Markets CBS Records, vice pres 1977; Special Markets CBS Records Intl, dir 1971-76; Special Markets Coll Records US, dir 1970-71; R&B Mercury Rec, dir natl promotion, 1970; Mkt Capitol Records Inc, admin asst to vice pres 1969-70; R&B Capitol Rec, mid-west prom mgr 1965-67; RCA Vic Dist Corp, mgmt trn asst to market mgr. **ORGANIZATIONS:** Co-founder, Cont Inst of Tech 1971; mem Omega Psi Phi; PUSH Chicago; FORE NY; bd trust Merit Rl Est Invst Trust Chicago 1973; consultant, Natl Med Assn 1971. **HONORS/ACHIEVEMENTS:** Recognition Comm cert LA City Council 1970; Certificate of Merit LA Urban League 1970; Merit citation proj 1975; Boston 1973; special pres Mrs Martin Luther King Atlanta 1974. **MILITARY SERVICE:** Military 1961-63. **BUSINESS ADDRESS:** Source Record Co Inc, 1902 5th Ave, Los Angeles, CA 90018.

WESTERFIELD, LOUIS
Educator. **PERSONAL:** Born Jul 31, 1949, Dekalb, MS; son of Louis Westerfield and Helen Clayborne Westerfield; married Gelounder Brumfield; children: Anthony, Anika, Anson. **EDUCATION:** Southern Univ New Orleans, BA 1971; Loyola Univ Law School, JD 1974; Columbia Univ Law School, LLM 1980. **CAREER:** New Orleans, LA, asst district attorney 1974-75; Southern Univ Law School, asst prof 1975-77; Loyola Law School, professor 1978-83; Univ of Mississippi, prof 1983-86; NC Central Univ School of Law, dean and

professor 1986-. **ORGANIZATIONS:** Mem Expedited Arbitration Panel US Steelworkers 1975-83; mem bd dirs LA Civil Liberties Union 1982-83; chairman Mississippi Adv Comm US Comm on Civil Rights 1985-86; Governor's Constitutional Study Comm for State of Mississippi 1986. **HONORS/ACHIEVEMENTS:** Outstanding Young Man in America US Jaycees 1977; Outstanding Jaycee Capital Area Chapter 1977; Distinguished Alumni of the Year NAFEO 1981 & 1986; Faculty Awd Most Outstanding Grad of Southern Univ 1986. **BUSINESS ADDRESS:** Dean, North Carolina CentralUniv, School of Law, Durham, NC 27707.

WESTMORELAND, SAMUEL DOUGLAS
Educator. **PERSONAL:** Born May 29, 1944, W Chester, PA; son of Nip T Sr and Ella D Westmoreland; married Mary E Hampton; children: Lesia A, Samara E, Diana Haskins. **EDUCATION:** Kutztown State Coll, BS 1966, MEd 1971; Lehigh Univ, MA. **CAREER:** Reading PA, detached worker prog 1966-67; YMCA, detached worker (gang worker); 9th Grade World Cultures, teacher 1967-71; Kutztown Univ, assoc prof of sociology 1971-. **ORGANIZATIONS:** Consult Black Cultural Org Kutztown State Coll 1970-71; mem Eastern Sociol Soc; Assn of Social & Behavioral Sciences; Black Conf on Higher Educ 1972-74; PA Sociological Soc; Black Conf on Basic Educ 1972-73; Lehigh Valley Black Adminstr; mem NAACP; lectr Apr 1972 "Educ & The Black Child" Downington Br NAACP;TV appearances guest spot Nov 1972; mem Natl Conf on the Black Family 1976-87; chairperson and presented paper on "The Myth of the Black Matriarchy" 1977, 1979-83; guest lectr Black Hist Week Easton PA 1977; "Objectives of Black History Week" Coatesville PA 1981-83, Pine Forge PA 1984; NAACP panel discussion Feb 1972; chrpsn PA Sociological Assn Conf 1983 & 1984; elected to the exec bd Assn of Science & Behavioral Scis 1984-87; presentation "Sports & The Black Youth" Sertoma Club Reading PA 1983; presentation "Black History Past, Present, Future" and "Future Prospects for Blacks" 1986; elected chairperson The Anthropology/Sociology Dept 1987-90. **BUSINESS ADDRESS:** Associate Professor, KutztownUniv, Kutztown, PA 19530.

WESTON, LARRY CARLTON
Attorney. **PERSONAL:** Born Jul 06, 1948, Sumter, SC. **EDUCATION:** SC State Clg, BA 1970; Univ of SC, JD 1975. **CAREER:** Gray & Weston Attys at Law, atty 1976-; BF Goodrich Footwear Co, asst persnl mgr 1970-72. **ORGANIZATIONS:** Dist cnsl SC Conf of Br NAACP 1978-; bd of dir, v chmn Sumter Co Pub Defender Corp 1979-; adv bd YWCA 1977-78; mem Sumter Co Commn on Higher Ed 1979-; mem Sumter Co Election Commn 1980-. **BUSINESS ADDRESS:** 110 S Sumter St, Sumter, SC 29150.

WESTON, M. MORAN, II
President. **PERSONAL:** Born Sep 10, 1910, Tarboru, NC; married Miriam Drake; children: Karann Christine, P Gregory M. **EDUCATION:** Columbia Univ, BA 1930; Union Theol Seminary, MDiv 1934; Columbia Univ, PhD 1954. **CAREER:** Career Federal Svgs Bank, founding dir chmn of bd 1948-; St Philip's Epis Church, rector/pastor 1957-72; Comm Serv Council, pres/chair 1957-85; StateUniv of NY Albany Ctr, prof social hist 1969-77, prof emeritus 1977-; Douglass Circle Develop Corp, pres 1982-; Natl Assoc for Affordable Housing, co-developer w/Glicis Construction Corp of condo apts 1980-, pres. **ORGANIZATIONS:** Trustee Legal Defense Fund NAACP 1964-; trustee Columbia Univ 1969-82; founder/pres Upper Manhattan Day Care and Child Develop Ctr 1970-85; trustee Mt Sinai Medical Sch & Hosp 1971-; trustee/former chmn St Augustine's Coll 1971-; trustee emeritus 1982-, pres Greater Harlem Nursing Home 1975-; pres Sr House Co SPOH Housing Corp 1975-; mem Grievance Comm NY Bar Assoc 1976-80; bd of dirs NY Chap of Amer Red Cross 1978-82; pres Housing for People Corp 1980-; governor Foreign Policy Assoc 1982-; sire archon Sigma Pi Phi Zeta Boule 1985,86; pres non-profit housing corp which constructed 1000 housing units in Harlem. **HONORS/ACHIEVEMENTS:** Virginia Theol Seminary DD honoris causa; Columbia Univ STD honoris causa 1969; research travel to Africa 1972,74,77, Peoples Republic of China, Japan, Hong Kong 1984, to Caribbean 1963,72,74,75,84,86 to Guatemala 1986; vstg prof social history Univ of Ife, Ile Ife Ogun State Nigeria; vstg theologian guest Archbishop of Ethiopian Orthodox Church 1973-74; Honorary Canon The Cathedral Church of St John the Divine New York City 1980-; St Augustine's Cross "In Appreciation" Archbishop of Canterbury 1981; Humanitarian Awd Harlem Commonwelath Council 1982; Man of the Year NY Urban League 1982; Excellence Awd Columbia Univ Grad Fac 1982; Comm Serv Awd Manufacturers Hanover Bank NY 1984. **HOME ADDRESS:** 253 Boulevard East, New Rochelle, NY 10801. **BUSINESS ADDRESS:** President, Natl Assoc Affordable Housing, 123 W 135th St, New York, NY 10030.

WESTON, SHARON
Communications consultant. **PERSONAL:** Born Oct 01, 1956, Chicago, IL. **EDUCATION:** Univ of WI LaCrosse, BA 1978; CBN Univ Va Beach, MA 1984. **CAREER:** Arts & Humanities Cncl of Greater Baton Rouge, regional develop officer 1985; Discover Magazine, sales manager 1985; Baton Rouge Opera, mktg and promotions asst 1986; The Nathan Group, dir of communications 1987-; public affairs dir, WKG TV, Channel 98, co host "IMPACT" Baton Rouge, 1987; councilwoman Metropolitan District 7, City of Baton Rouge 1989. **ORGANIZATIONS:** Vice pres Love Outreach Ministries 1980-82; advisor Love Outreach Faith Fellowship 1985-; treas Finesse & Assocs 1985-; mem of the Capital Improvements Comm, 1989; exec bd, Samaritan House Project (A Home for Run-aways), 1989; bd of dirs Real Life Educ Found, 1989; East Baton Rouge Housing Authority Task Force, 1989; comm mem Louisiana Elected Women Officials. **HONORS/ACHIEVEMENTS:** Certified Human Resource Consultant Performax Systems Intl 1985; Certificate of Appreciation South Baton Rouge Kiwanis Club 1985; Certificate of Appreciation Zeta Phi Beta Sorority Workshop Consultant, 1989; Achievement Award for Accomplishments, Greens Chapel AME Church 1989. **HOME ADDRESS:** 3352 Osceola St, Baton Rouge, LA 70805.

WESTRAY, KENNETH MAURICE
Roman Catholic priest. **PERSONAL:** Born Jun 15, 1952, Washington, DC; son of Kenneth Maurice Westray, Sr and Jean Virginia Hughes Westray. **EDUCATION:** US Merchant Marine Acad, Kings Point, NY, BS 1974; attended Mount St Mary's Seminary, Emmitsburg, MD, 1976-78; St Patrick's Seminary, Menlo Park, CA, MDiv 1979, MDiv 1981; attended Graduate Theological Union, Berkeley, CA, 1986. **CAREER:** Amer Export Isbrandsten Lines, New York, NY, third mate, 1974-76; Nativity Grammar School, Washington, DC, teacher, 1979; Sacred Heart Parish, San Francisco, CA, deacon/seminarian, 1980-83; Saint Elizabeth Parish, San Francisco, associate pastor, 1983-85; Sacred Heart Parish, San Francisco, pastor, 1983-. **ORGANIZATIONS:** Bd mem & past pres, Archdiocese of San Francisco Black Catholic (Apostolate) Affairs, 1979-; mem & former bd mem, Natl Black Catholic Clergy Caucus, 1980-; councilor, Archdiocese of San Francisco Priests Council, 1985-88; regent, Saint Ignatius High School, 1986-89; bd mem, Natl Federation of Priests Council, 1988-; bd mem, Catholic Charities of San Francisco, 1988-. **HONORS/ACHIEVEMENTS:** Rep to Intl Federation of Priests Council, Ghana, 1988. **MILITARY SERVICE:** Naval Reserves, lieutenant, 1974-.

WHALEY, JOSEPH S.
Physician. **PERSONAL:** Born Nov 29, 1933, Yuma, AZ; married Doris Naomi Pettie; children: Craig, Tyler, Dawna, Teresa. **EDUCATION:** Univ Of AZ, BA 1954; Hahnemann Med Clg, MD 1958. **CAREER:** USAF, physician flight surg 1959-63; Private Practice Tucson, AZ 1963-. **ORGANIZATIONS:** St pres AZ Chptr Am Acad of Fam Physicians 1972; del Am Med Assn 1980-; bd of dir AZ Physicians IPA 1983-; Masonic Lodge; Archon Sigma Pi Phi Boule Frat; Kappa Alpha Psi. **HONORS/ACHIEVEMENTS:** Phi Beta KappaUniv of AZ 1954; Dist Military GradUniv of AZ 1954; High Hnr GradUniv of AZ 1954. **MILITARY SERVICE:** Air Force Capt 1959-63. **BUSINESS ADDRESS:** Physician, Self Employed, 368 E Grant Rd, Tucson, AZ 85705.

WHALEY, MARY H.
Educational administrator. **PERSONAL:** Born in Clarksville, TN; children: Brian Cedric, Kevin Allen. **EDUCATION:** Fisk Univ, AB 1959; Univ of TN Sch of Soc Wrk, MSW 1968, doctoral student 1978-, EdD candidate 1986. **CAREER:** TN Dept of Human Svcs, caseworker 1961-63, casework super 1966-72; Knoxville Coll, vis instr 1971-73; TN Dept of Human Svcs, staff consult E TN 1972-74;Knoxville Coll, asso dean students 1974-78; Univ of TN, professional asst 1978-. **ORGANIZATIONS:** Chmn various com Natl Assn of Soc Wrks 1968; chmn various com Assn of Black Soc Wrks 1972; bd of dir Phyllis Wheatley 1972-74; Comm Imprvmt Found Bd1972-74; bd of dirs Planned Parenthood 1973-77; UTSSW com Minority Admission & Retention 1974-76; mem League of Women Voters 1976; bd of dir Helen Ross McNabb 1977; edited What Next? Child Welfare Serv for the 80's 1982; proj dir and co-author Parmanency Planning, The Black Experience 1983; contributed "Ethnic Competent Family Centered Svcs" Basic Family Centered Curriculum for Family Serv Workers & Parent Aides; bd of dir TN NASW Chapter 1985; Friends of Black Children St Adv committee and the local affiliate; Soc Serv Panel TN Black Legislators Caucus; adv committee Child & Family Serv; bd mem Natl Resource Cntron Family Based ServUniv of Iowa; Bijou Limelighters; nominating comm Girl Scout Council; RAM House Board. **HONORS/ACHIEVEMENTS:** Outstanding Young Woman of Amer 1971; Dict of Intl biography of Women 1978; Amer Biog Inst 1979; Who's Who Among Human Service Proffessionals. **BUSINESS ADDRESS:** Prof Asst, Univ of TN, 1838 Terrace Ave, Knoxville, TN 37916.

WHALEY, WAYNE EDWARD
Educator. **PERSONAL:** Born Oct 23, 1949, Lincoln, DE; married Janice Evans; children: Sean, Dane. **EDUCATION:** Delaware State Coll, BS 1971; Univ of Delaware, MA 1977. **CAREER:** Red Clay School Dist, asst principal 1978-86; Smyrna School Dist, teacher 1971-75, asst principal 1978-86, teacher 1986-. **ORGANIZATIONS:** Volunteer YMCA and Delaware Special Olympics 1975-; mem Delaware Exceptional Childrens Council 1985; bd pres Centennial United Methodist Church 1985; mem Natl Assoc for Equal Oppor in Higher Educ 1986; bd mem Wilmington Lions Club 1986; mem Natl Sch Curriculum Assoc 1986. **HONORS/ACHIEVEMENTS:** Special Mbr Governor's Task Force on Educ 1976; Man of the Year Epsilon Chap of Omega Psi Phi 1982. **HOME ADDRESS:** 12 Fieldstone Cir, Hockessin, DE 19707.

WHALUM, KENNETH TWIGG
Minister. **PERSONAL:** Born Mar 23, 1934, Memphis, TN; son of Hudie David Whalum and Thelma Miller Twigg Whalum; children: Kenneth Twigg Jr, Kirk Wendell, Kevin Henry. **EDUCATION:** LeMoyne Coll, attended, 1951-57; Tennessee Baptist School of Religion, DD, 1975; Mgmt Programs, Univ of Michigan, Univ of Texas-Austin, Memphis State Univ, Harvard Univ, 1975-81. **CAREER:** US Postal Serv, mem, dir of personnel, 1968-71, mid-south asst dist mgr, e&lr, 1971-77, south reg gen mgr employee relations div, 1977-79, dist mgr, Michigan dist, 1979-81; Olivet Baptist Church, senior pastor. **ORGANIZATIONS:** Vice pres-at-large, 1977-81, pres, 1981-85, Tennessee Baptist M&E Convention; vice pres, 1981-85, mem bd of dirs, 1981-, Natl Baptist Convention USA Inc; bd of dirs Morehouse School of Religion, 1981-; bd of trustees, LeMoyne-Owen Coll, 1983-; vice chmn bd of trustees, LeMoyne-Owen Coll, 1985-86; bd of dirs, Goals for Memphis, 1986-; chmn labor industry comm, NAACP, 1987-; city councilman, Dist 4, City of Memphis, 1988. **HONORS/ACHIEVEMENTS:** Jerry D Williams Award, Community Serv Agency, 1977; Man of the Year Award, ACT of Memphis, 1979; CW Washburn Achievement Award, Booker T Washington High School, 1982; Man of the Year Award, Shelby Co Dist Assn, 1985; Life & Golden Heritage NAACP, 1985; Golden Gallery Distinguished Alumni Award by Lemoyne-Owen Coll, Memphis, TN, 1987. **MILITARY SERVICE:** USN personnel man 2nd class 1951-55; Natl Defense Medal, Korean Serv Medal, Good Conduct Medal 1951-55. **BUSINESS ADDRESS:** Senior Pastor, Olivet Baptist Church, 3084 Southern Ave, Memphis, TN 38111.

WHARTON, A. C., JR.
Educator, attorney. **PERSONAL:** Born Aug 17, 1944, Lebanon, TN; married Ruby; children: A C III, Andre Courtney, Alexander Conrad. **EDUCATION:** TSU, BA 1966; Univ MS, JD 1971. **CAREER:** EEOC, decision drafter 1967-68; trial attorney, 1971-73; Lawyers Com for Civil Rights Under Law, proj dir 1973; Univ MS, adj prof; Shelby Co TN, pub defender 1980; Private Practice, Wharton & Wharton. **ORGANIZATIONS:** Past exec dir Memphis Area Leagl Serv Inc; mem Amer Bar Assn; Natl Legal Aid & Defender Assn; Natl Bar Assn; TN Bar Assn; NAACP; pres Leadership Memphis Alumni Assn 1979; Operation PUSH; Urban League. **HONORS/ACHIEVEMENTS:** US Atty Gen Honor Law Grad Prog 1971. **BUSINESS ADDRESS:** Attorney, 161 Jefferson Ave, Ste 402, Memphis, TN 38103.

WHARTON, CLIFTON R., JR.
Educator. **PERSONAL:** Born Sep 13, 1926, Boston, MA; married Dolores Duncan; children: Clifton III, Bruce. **EDUCATION:** Harvard Univ, BA (cum laude) 1947; Johns Hopkins Univ, MA 1948; Univ Chicago, MA 1956; Univ Chicago, PhD 1958. **CAREER:** MI State Univ, economist educ frgn policy expert 1970-78; State Univ of NY, chancellor 1978-; Teachers Insurance Annuity Assoc & Coll Retirement EquitiesFund, chairman/ceo. **ORGANIZATIONS:** Dir Ford Motor Co; Burroughs Corp; Equit Life; Rockefeller Found; Carnegie Found; Asia Soc; Agr Devel Coun; Overseas Devel Coun Vis ProfUniv Malaya 1958-64; Stanford Univ 1964-65; ch bd Intl Food & Agr Devel AID Dept St 1976-; Amer Acad Arts & Sci; Amer Agr Econs Assn; Amer Consult Assn; Econ Club Detroit; NAACP; Natl Urban

League; Univ Club of NY. **HONORS/ACHIEVEMENTS:** Numerous publs & monographs; 12 Hon Degrees; Man of Yr Boston Latin Sch 1970; Amistad Awd Amer Missionary Assn 1970; Alumni Professional Achievement Awd 1971; Joseph E Wilson Awd 1977; named first Black chancellor of the State Univ of New York; first Black chairman Rockefeller Foundation; first Black admitted Johns Hopkins Univ Sch Adv Intl Studies. **BUSINESS ADDRESS:** Chairman/CEO, TIAA-CREF, 730 Third Ave, New York, NY 10017.

WHARTON, DOLORES D.
Association executive. **PERSONAL:** Born Jul 03, 1927, New York, NY; married Clifton R Wharton Jr; children: Clifton III, Bruce. **EDUCATION:** Chicago State Univ, BA. **CAREER:** Contemp Art of Malaysia Mem, author; Fund for Corporate Initiatives Inc, pres. **ORGANIZATIONS:** Sec Malaysia Cncl of the Asia Soc 1965-67; dir Phillips Petroleum Co, Kellogg Co, MI Bell Telephone Co, Gannett Co, MI Natl Bank, Mus of Modern Art, China Med Bd, Detroit Symphony Orchestra, Detroit Inst of Art Hon Deg 1965-67; mem Natl Comm for Bicent Era 1971-75; mem MI Cncl for the Arts 1972-76; vice chmn MI Bicentennial Commn 1972-76; bd of visitors Tulane Univ. **HONORS/ACHIEVEMENTS:** DHL Central MI Univ 1973. **BUSINESS ADDRESS:** President, Fund for Corp Intiatives Inc, 866 United Nations Plaza, Ste 4052, New York, NY 10017.

WHARTON, FERDINAND D., JR.
Business manager. **PERSONAL:** Born in Henderson, NC; son of F. D. Wharton and Annie Harris Wharton; children: F. D. III, Tam Eric, Clifford Alan, Marc David. **EDUCATION:** A&T Coll of NC, BS Agr Educ 1939; Univ of CT, MS Poultry Nutrition 1948; Monsanto Intl Div Key Mgmt Trng, adv mgmt course 1966. **CAREER:** Vocational Agriculture, instr 1940-42; Princess Anne Coll, head poultry dept 1942-43; Triumph Explosives, asst dir race relations 1943-44; Avon Training Sch, head poultry dept 1944-46; Univ of CT, rsch asst 1946-48; Dawes Lab Inc, asst dir nutrition rsch 1948-60; USAID Ghana, adv animal nutrition 1960-64; Monsanto Co, sr project mgr 1964-67, develop mgr 1967-72; Monsanto Commercial Prods Co, mgr environmental affairs 1972-77; Continental Diversified Indus, dir public affairs plastic beverage bottle div 1977-79, dir of public affairs 1979-82; Continental Can Company, dir of public affairs, 1982-84; Continental Group Inc, dir of public affairs, 1984-85. **ORGANIZATIONS:** Mem Soc of the Plastics Industry Inc; mem Soc of the Sigma Xi; mem Amer Inst of Nutrition; mem Amer Assn for the Advancement of Science; charter mem UN food and agricultural org/industry adv comm, 1965-66; mem oilseed program planning comm, US Dept of Agriculture, 1966-70; mem food industry adv comm, Nutrition Foundation, 1967-71; bd dirs, 1966-73, treas, 1968, pres, 1969-71, St Louis Comm on Africa, St Louis, MO; bd dirs, 1969-73, treas, 1972, St Louis Comm for Environmental Information, St Louis, MO; bd dirs, 1969-73, 1975-77, treas, 1970, vice pres, 1971, pres, 1973, Grace Hill Settlement House; mem White House Conference on Food, Nutrition, and Hunger, 1969; bd dirs Lakeside Ctr for Boys of St Louis Co, 1971-77, 2nd vice pres, 1974-; bd dirs Mark Twain Summer Inst, 1973-77; fellow Scientist Inst for Public Info, 1971-; bd dirs Univ City Home Rental Trust, 1971-77; bd dirs St Louis Council on World Affairs, 1971-77; mem Citizens Adv Council Hogan St Regional Youth Ctr, 1975-77; bd dirs Keep Brown Univ Beautiful, 1983-84; charter mem Hartford Chap Omega Psi Phi Frat; consult Natl Exec Serv Corps, 1985-; exec recruiter Intl Exec Serv Corps, 1986-. **HONORS/ACHIEVEMENTS:** Career Achievement Award, Urban League, St Louis, MO, 1976; Black Achievement in Industry Award, YMCA, Harlem, CA, 1980; National Urban League Visiting Professor, Black Exchange Program, 1982-84; author or co-author of 45 published technical & scientific papers and 30 reports presented at scientific meetings; US Patent #3,655,869 "Treatment of Diarrhea Employing Certain Basic Polyelectrolyte Polymers"; editor "Proceedings of the Symposium Envirronmental Impact of Nitrile Barrier Containers, Lopac: A Case Study.". **HOME ADDRESS:** 19 Ledgebrook Dr, Norwalk, CT 06854.

WHARTON, MILTON S.
Judge. **PERSONAL:** Born Sep 20, 1946, St Louis, MO. **EDUCATION:** SIU Edwardsville, BS 1969; DePaul Univ School Of Law, JD 1974. **CAREER:** St Clair Co Pub Defender, atty; IL Judiciary, judge 1976. **ORGANIZATIONS:** V chm IL St Bar Asso Standing Comm on Juvenile Justice; v chm St Louis Bi-state Chptr Am Red Cross; bd mem YMCA of So IL; bd mem St Marys Hosp of E St Louis; bd mem Higher Ed Ctr of St Louis. **HONORS/ACHIEVEMENTS:** Alumnus of the Yr SIU at Edwardsville 1977; Dist Serv Awd Belleville Jaycees 1983; Man of Yr Nat Cncl of Negro Women-E St Louis 1982; Man Of Yr So Dist IL Asso of Club Women 1982; Civic Serv Phi Beta Sigma-zeta Ph I Beta 1985. **HOME ADDRESS:** 23 Hilltop Pl, East St Louis, IL 62203.

WHARTON-BOYD, LINDA F.
Educator, government official. **PERSONAL:** Born Apr 21, 1951, Baltimore, MD; daughter of Frank Wharton and Thelma L Kirby Wharton; divorced; children: Duke Boyd. **EDUCATION:** Univ of Pgh, BA 1972, MA 1975, PhD 1979. **CAREER:** Howard Univ, asst prof 1979-83; Washinton DC office of the Mayor, communications specialist 1984-86; dir of public affiars 1986-88. **ORGANIZATIONS:** Mem Delta Sigma Theta Sor 1971-; exec treas Natl Speech Comm Assn Black Caucus 1975-; publ "Black Dance, It's Origin & Continuity" Minority Voices 1977; hon bd mem Pgh Black Theatre Dance Ensemble 1978-; bd mem Natl Arts Prog Natl Council of Negro Women 1979-; consult NAACP Labor & Indus Sub-com on Comm; adv "Stuff" childrens prog NBC Washington DC; chairperson, Joint Chapter Event, Natl Coalition of 100 Black Women Inc. **HONORS/ACHIEVEMENTS:** Outstanding Black Women's Awd Communication Arts Creative Enterprises 1974; Doctoral Honor's Seminar Prog Howard Univ Speech Comm 1977; Bethune Legacy Award, Natl Council of Negro Women 1986; Natl Public Radio Documentary Award 1985.

WHATLEY, BOOKER TILLMAN
Educator. **PERSONAL:** Born Nov 05, 1915, Anniston, AL; married Lottie Cillie. **EDUCATION:** AL A&M U, BS 1941; Ruthgers U, PhD 1957. **CAREER:** Univ of AR, lecturer; Univ of MD; Univ of FL; Cornell Univ, adj prof 1972-; USDA/ARS, colbtr 1970; Tuskegee Inst, prof 1969-; Peace Corp, consult 1962-66; US/AID, adv 1960-62; So Univ, prof 1957-69; Cobb High & Vet School, prin 1958-50; US Postal Serv, carrier 1947-48; Butler Co, co ext agt 1946-47. **ORGANIZATIONS:** Mem Am Soc for Hortl Sci; Assc of So Agr Sci; Assc for Tropical Bio; Am Soc of Plant Psysiologist; Intrntl Plant Propagators Soc; Soc of Ec Botany; Soc of Sigma Xi Sweet Potato Collaborators Grp. **HONORS/ACHIEVEMENTS:** Listed Personalities of The S 1970; outst alumni awrd AL A&MUniv 1971; faculty achvmt awrd Tuskegee Inst 1972; omega man of the yr Iota Omega & Lambda Epsilon 1974; serv to agr awrd AL Farm Bur Fed 1974; elected Fellow of Am Soc for Hortl Sci 1974; mem Sec Earl Butts' USDA Hon Award Com 1975; outst sci awrd RD Morrison & FE Evans 1976; chmn Annual & Meeting Am Soc of Hortl Sci 1976; cit State of AL House of Reps 1977; Apr 15 Booker T Whatley Day Hometown Anniston & Calhoun Co; outst sci awrd Natl Consortium for Black Professional Dev 1977; num publs. **MILITARY SERVICE:** AUS maj 1975. **BUSINESS ADDRESS:** Tuskegee Institute, Tuskegee Institute, AL 36088.

WHATLEY, ENNIS KEITH
Professional athlete. **PERSONAL:** Born Aug 11, 1962, Birmingham, AL. **EDUCATION:** Univ of AL, 1979-83. **CAREER:** Chicago Bulls, guard 1983-. **HONORS/ACHIEVEMENTS:** Led Bulls in assists (83) & steals (15); led club in assists 57 games including 28 of last 30 contests; CBS Sports named him among their 5 All-Stars as he won MVP honors in televised games against UCLA, Tennessee, & Georgia. **BUSINESS ADDRESS:** Chicago Bulls, 333 N Michigan Ave, Ste 510, Chicago, IL 60601.

WHEADON, A. WENDEL
Attorney. **PERSONAL:** Born Dec 07, 1938, St Louis, MO; married Rosetta; children: Michael. **EDUCATION:** Univ IA, BS CE 1962; St Louis U, JD 1968. **CAREER:** Met E Sanitary Dist, exec dir; Metro Housing Corp St Louis, atty, pvt prac, law, engr, pvt prac, exec dir; E St Louis Housing Dev Corp, dep dir; Monsanto Co, engr; City of E St Louis Urban Renewal Dept, il hwy dept cons; Model City Agy. **ORGANIZATIONS:** Chmn bd tst State Comm Clg E St Louis 1969; mem ASCE; IL Bar Assc; St Clair Co Bar Assc; Met E Bar Assc; Natl Bar Assc; Alpha Phi Alpha Frat; grand atty Prince Hall Grand Lodge IL Registered Professional Engrl IL & MO; registered real estate broker IL; land surveyor-in-tng IL; atty IL. **MILITARY SERVICE:** AUS 1st lt 1962-64.

WHEADON, ROSETTA FAY (NEE DAWKINS)
Educator. **PERSONAL:** Born Dec 27, 1934, East St Louis, IL; divorced; children: Michael. **EDUCATION:** IL State Univ, BS 1956; Univ of IL, MS 1960; St Louis Univ, PhD 1968; Attended, Univ of Heidelberg Sprachzeugnis. **CAREER:** KS City KS, teacher 1956-59; St Louis MO, teacher 1959-68; State Comm Coll of E St Louis, interim pres dean 1969-77, former pres 1977-84; Buena Vista PublicSchool Dist, teacher. **ORGANIZATIONS:** Consultant for education; past mem Amer Assn of Comm & Jr Coll; Mayor's Adv Cncl; mem Alpha Kappa Alpha Sor; E St Louis Women's Club; Wesley BethelUnited Methodist Ch; mem Bethel AME Church Saginaw MI. **HONORS/ACHIEVEMENTS:** Cert of Achievement Mayor of E St Louis Lovejoy IL & Centerville IL; 1984 Disting Alumni Awd IL State Univ.

WHEAT, ALAN
Government official, economist. **PERSONAL:** Born Oct 16, 1951, San Antonio, TX. **EDUCATION:** Grinnell Coll, BA 1972. **CAREER:** HUD Kansas City MO, economist 1972-73; Mid-Amer Reg Council Kansas City, econ 1973-75; Cty Exec Office KC, aide 1975-76; MO House of Reps Jefferson City, rep 1977-82; 98th Congress 5th Dist WA, congressman 1983-. **ORGANIZATIONS:** Mem Rules Comm, Select Comm on Children Youth & Families 1983-; mem NAACP; exec comm Dem Study Group; mem Dem Caucus Com on Party Effectiveness, Congl Woman's Caucus, Environ & Energy Study Conf; vice pres Dem New Member Caucus; mem Fed Govt Serv Task Force, Congressional Human Rights Caucus; vchmn Congressional Black Caucus; chmn Subcomm on Govt Operations & Metro Affairs of the Comm on Dist of Columbia. **HONORS/ACHIEVEMENTS:** Third freshman Congressman in history to be appointed to the Rules Committee; Best Freshman Legislator St Louisan Mag 1977-78; 1 of 10 Best Legislators Jefferson City News Tribune 1979-80; MO Times Newspaper 1979-80. **BUSINESS ADDRESS:** Congressman, 98th Congress 5th Dist WA, US House of Reps, 1204 Longworth House Off Bldg, Washington, DC 20515.

WHEATON, JANICE C.
Educator. **PERSONAL:** Born Jan 14, 1943, Cherryvale, KS. **EDUCATION:** Univ of KS-Lawrence, BA 1964; Univ of WI-Madison, MS 1985. **CAREER:** WI State Lab of Hygiene, bacteriologist 1964-66; Univ of WI-Madison, lecturer dept of bacteriology 1967-80, office of academic student affairs dir student services 1980-. **ORGANIZATIONS:** Mem City of Madison Affirmative Action Comm 1982-; mem and former advisor Alpha Zeta Hon Agric Frat 1983-; mem Gamma Sigma Delta Hon Agric Frat 1984-. **BUSINESS ADDRESS:** Dir of Student Services, University of WI Madison, Rm 116 Agriculture Hall, 1450 Linden Dr, Madison, WI 53706.

WHEATON, THELMA KIRKPATRICK
Retired educator. **PERSONAL:** Born Jul 29, 1907, Hadley, IL; daughter of Arthur McWorter and Ophelia Walker; married Allen J Kirkpatrick I; children: Allen J Kirkpatrick II, Dr David A Kirkpatrick, Dr Juliet E K Walker, Marye A K Taylor; married William M Wheaton. **EDUCATION:** Fisk Univ, BA 1929; Case Western Reserve Univ, MS 1931; Univ of Chicago, Graduate courses. **CAREER:** Cleveland Phyllis Wheatley Assoc, social worker 1929-31; St Louis MO Family Welfare AGency, social worker 1931; Chicago YWCA, comm social worker 1931-38; Chicago Bd of Educ, educator 1947-72. **ORGANIZATIONS:** Anti-Basileus, Theta Omega Chapter, chairperson, Theta Omega Seniors, Alpha Kappa Alpha Sor; pres IL Housewives Assoc; faculty rep Natl Educ Assoc, IL Natl Educ Assoc; pres, Wesleyan Service Guild; chairperson, program resources, United Methodist Women of Gorham Church; historian Natl Assoc Univ Women, Chicago Branch; chairperson, exhibit comm & archives, African Amer Geneological Soc of Chicago; life mem & bd mem, S Side Community Art Center; life mem, Du Sable Musuem of African Amer History; chairperson, Annual Heritage Jubilee Book Festival; life mem, Natl Assn of Colored Women; life mem, Natl Council of Negro Women. **HONORS/ACHIEVEMENTS:** Volunteer Serv Awd Comprehensive Com Serv of Metro Chicago Inc 1981; Outstanding Service Assoc for Study of Afro-Amer Life and History 1984; Teacher of the Year, Doolittle Parent Teacher Assn; Mother of the Year, Gorham United Methodist Church; Mother of the Year, Illinois Mothers of the Amer Mothers Inc; Retired Sr Volunteer Program Annual Award; Intl Travelers Assn Award. **HOME ADDRESS:** 7931 St Lawrence, Chicago, IL 60619.

WHEELAN, BELLE LOUISE
Educational administrator. **PERSONAL:** Born Oct 10, 1951, Chicago, IL; divorced; children: Reginald. **EDUCATION:** Trinity Univ, BA 1972; Louisiana State Univ, MA 1974; Univ of TX, PhD 1984. **CAREER:** San Antonio Coll, assoc prof of psychology 1974-84, dir of devel educ 1984-86, dir of acad support serv 1986-87; Thomas Nelson Community Coll, dean of student serv, 1987-89; Tidewater Community Coll, Portsmouth Campus, provost, 1989. **ORGANIZATIONS:** Mem Alpha Kappa Alpha Sor Inc 1969-; mem Amer Assoc of Women in Comm & Jr Colls, 1983-; corr sec of San Antonio chapter, 1985-87, pres-elect San Antonio chapter, 1987-89 The Link's Inc; pres Texas Assoc of Developmental Educators

1987. **BUSINESS ADDRESS:** Provost, Tidewater Community Coll, Portsmouth Campus, State Rte 135, Portsmouth, VA 23703.

WHEELER, ALBERT HAROLD
Mayor. **PERSONAL:** Born Dec 11, 1915; married Emma Monteith; children: Mary McDade, Alma Smith, Nancy Francis. **EDUCATION:** LincolnUniv PA, BA; IA State Clg, MS;Univ of MI, MSPH PhD . **CAREER:** HowardUniv Med Sch, 1938-40;Univ of MIUniv Hosp Serology Lab, rsrch assc 1944-52;Univ of MI, asst prof; first full-time black mem of regular permanent faculty 1952-59; Dept of Microbiology & Immunology, assc & prof 1959-; Ann Arbor, MI, mayor 1975-78. **ORGANIZATIONS:** Dir Dept of Christian Serv; mem Archdiocesan Pgm Review Com; Cath Archdiocese of Detroit; mem Com to Study Racial Imbalance in Ann Arbor Sch 1965; vice-chmn chmn Cit Plng Com; Ann Arbor Model Cities Cit Bd; MI Adv Com to US Civil Rights Commn 1967-75; first pres Natl Com for Campaign for Human Dev 1970-74; del Natl Dem Conv Chicago 1968; mem Steering Com of MI Dem Black Caucus 1968-71; mem Commn to Study Pblms of the Aging; MI Adv Com to Study Financing of Pub Schs; Commn to Study Problems of Youth. **HONORS/ACHIEVEMENTS:** First Black Mayor of Ann Arbor, MI.

WHEELER, BETTY MCNEAL
Educator. **PERSONAL:** Born Oct 10, 1932, St Louis; married Samuel; children: Gayle. **EDUCATION:** St Louis U, BS 1953;Univ of MO St Louis, MEd 1970. **CAREER:** Metro St Louis Public HS, prin 1971-, work study coord 1969-71, instrl coord 1967-69, reading specialist 1966-67, elec teacher 1963-66; St Louis YWCA, young adult pgm dir 1956-61. **ORGANIZATIONS:** Mem Natl Assc of Scndry Sch Prins; Assc for Supvsn & Curr Dev; St Louis White Hse Conf on Ed; Urban League Ed Com; mm bd dirs Urban League 1973-; bd dirs Metro YMCA; NAACP Alpha Kappa Alpha Sor; installed mem Delta Kappa Gamma Soc; Hon Soc for Women Educators 1975; mem Danforth Found Scndry Sch Admnstr Fwlshp Pgm. **BUSINESS ADDRESS:** Principal, Metro High School, 5017 Washington Ave, St Louis, MO 63108.

WHEELER, HAROLD
Conductor, composer, arranger, performer. **PERSONAL:** Born 1943, St Louis, MO. **EDUCATION:** Howard Univ. **CAREER:** Music Arranger. **ORGANIZATIONS:** Mus arranger "Promises Promises", "Two Gentlemen of Verona", "Ain't Supposed to Die a Natural Death", "The Wiz" for Singers Aretha Franklin, Roberta Flack, Lena Horne, Billy Taylor, Nina Simone, Numerous Others; writer arranger TV Commercial Pan-Am Airlines. **BUSINESS ADDRESS:** C/O RCA Records, 1133 Ave of Ams, New York, NY 10036.

WHEELER, JOHN HERVEY
Attorney. **PERSONAL:** Born Jan 01, 1908, Kittrell, NC; married Selena Warren; children: Julia, Warren. **EDUCATION:** Morehouse Clg, AB 1929; NC Central U, LlB 1967; Shaw U, LlD 1954; Johnson C Smith U, 1963; Morehouse Clg, LHD 1967; Duke U, 1970; NC Ctrl U1971. **CAREER:** Mechanics & Farmers Bank, pres 1952-. **ORGANIZATIONS:** Mem Sec Invst Com; NC Mutual Life & Ins Co 1933-; bd of dir NC Mutaul Life Ins Co; Mechs & Farmers Bank; Mutual Real Estate Investment Trust; Mutual Savings & Loan Assc; Natl Corp for Housing Ptnrsp; mem AtlantaUniv Ctr; bd of tst AtlantaUniv Morehouse Clg; chmn tst of Lincoln Hosp; tres St Joseph's AME Ch; v chmn of bd Durham City Co Library; chmn Durham Com on Negro Affairs 1957-; pres So Reg Cncl 1963-68; tres John Avery Boy's Clb; tst Com for Econ Dev; pres NC Low Income Housing Dev Corp 1967-; mem Minbanc Capital Corp; mem Beta Phi; chmn Redevel Commn of City of Durham. **BUSINESS ADDRESS:** PO Box 1932, Durham, NC 27702.

WHEELER, LLOYD G.
Executive. **PERSONAL:** Born Aug 26, 1907, St Joseph, MO; married Margaret. **EDUCATION:** Univ IL, BS 1932; John Marshall Law Sch, Studied; Northwestern U. **CAREER:** Supreme Life Ins Co of Am Chgo, pres & chief operating ofcr, mem of bd dirs & exec com been with co since 1923-. **ORGANIZATIONS:** Former vice pres Natl Ins Assc; former bd mem Chicago Chap ARC; mem Kappa Alpha Psi Frat; Juvenile Inst of Chgo. **HONORS/ACHIEVEMENTS:** Named man of yr Supreme Life Colleagues. **BUSINESS ADDRESS:** Supreme Life Insurance Co, 3501 S Dr Martin Luther King J, Chicago, IL 60616.

WHEELER, PATRICIA A.
Advertising manager. **PERSONAL:** Born Dec 29, 1950, Washington, DC. **EDUCATION:** Univ of MD, BS 1973; Columbia Univ, MBA 1981. **CAREER:** WRVA Radio, reporter 1973-74; KOAP-TV, producer/dir 1974-76; WBAL-TV, asst comm serv dir 1976-79; Time Life Books, asst dir of mktg 1981-84; Howard Univ, lecturer 1983-; Gannett Outdoor, dir of advtg & public relations. **ORGANIZATIONS:** Mem bd of dirs Maryland Media 1977-82; prc comm chair 1984-86, 1985 conf pr chair Natl Black MBA Assoc 1981-; vice chair WDCU Comm Adv Bd 1985-86; mem Amer Mktg Assoc 1986-, NAACP; corresponding sec NY Chap Natl Black MBA Assoc 1987-. **HONORS/ACHIEVEMENTS:** Journalism Fellow Natl Endowment for the Humanities 1978; Philip L Graham Grant COGME/Columbia Univ 1979; NW Ayer Grant Columbia Univ 1980. **BUSINESS ADDRESS:** Dir Advtg & Public Relations, Gannett Outdoor, 535 Madison Ave, New York, NY 10022.

WHEELER, PRIMUS, JR.
Educational administrator. **PERSONAL:** Born Mar 03, 1950, Webb, MS; married Earlene Jordan; children: Primus III, Niki. **EDUCATION:** Tougaloo Coll, BS Biology 1972; Hinds Jr Coll, AD Applied Sci 1977; Jackson State Univ, MST Educ 1982; Univ of MS. **CAREER:** Univ of MS Med Ctr, respiratory therapy tech 1975-77, respiratory therapist 1977-78, instructor of respiratory therapy 1978-80, instructor/clinical coord respiratory therapy 1980-81, chmn asst prof respir therapy 1981-. **ORGANIZATIONS:** Mem MS Soc for Respiratory Therapists 1978-; mem Amer Assn for Respir Therapy 1978-; adv UMC Med Explorers Post #306 1983-; mem Natl Soc for Allied Health 1984-; mem bd of dirs Northwest Jackson YMCA 1984-. **HONORS/ACHIEVEMENTS:** Scholastic Honor Phi Kappa Phi Natl Honor Soc JSU 1982; One of 30 Outstanding Mississippians; 1985 Leadership MS Delegate 1985. **MILITARY SERVICE:** USAF ei Honorable Discharge 1973. **HOME ADDRESS:** 132 Azalea Circle, Jackson, MS 39206. **BUSINESS ADDRESS:** Chmn Asst Prof Respir Therap, Univ of MS Medical Center, 2500 N State St, Jackson, MS 39216.

WHEELER, RONALD C.
Physician. **PERSONAL:** Born Jul 09, 1957, Chicago, IL; married Ann M Payne; children: Lauren Patrice. **EDUCATION:** Howard Univ, BA 1979; Howard Univ Coll of Medicine, MD 1983. **CAREER:** Howard Univ Ctr for Sickle Cell, rsch asst 1980; Natl Institutes of Health, rsch asst 1981; IL Masonic Medical Ctr, resident physician 1983-86; Methodist Hosp of Chicago, emergency room physician 1985-; Weiss Medical Complex, physician; Dixie Medical & Surgical Assoc Ltd, assoc physician internal med 1987-. **ORGANIZATIONS:** Mem Chicago Medical Soc 1986-, Amer Medical Assoc 1986-, Assoc Amer Coll of Physicians. **HONORS/ACHIEVEMENTS:** Upjohn Achievement Awd Outstanding Proficiency 1983. **BUSINESS ADDRESS:** Associate Physician, Weiss Medical Complex, 15643 Lincoln Ave, Harvey, IL 60426.

WHEELER, SHIRLEY Y.
Nurse, educator. **PERSONAL:** Born Feb 14, 1935, Pittsburgh, PA; married Bennie, Jr; children: Teresa Marie, Bryan Joseph. **EDUCATION:** Univ of Pittsburgh, BSN 1957, MNEd 1965, Post Master's Ed 1967-68. **CAREER:** Magee Woman's Hospital Pittsburgh, staff nurse 1957-58; Montefiore Hospital Pittsburgh, staff nurse 1958-59; Lillian S Kaufmann School of Nursing, instr & maternity nursing 1959-60; Univ of Pittsburgh School of Nursing, instr maternity nursing 1963-67, asst prof maternity nursing 1967-72; Duquesne Univ School of Nursing, assc prof 1972-. **ORGANIZATIONS:** Adv Basic Stdnt Nrs Assc; cnslr Eta Chap Sigma Theta Tau Hon Nurses Soc 1967-68; recruitment com Dist 6 PA Nurses Assc 1973; comm on Nrsg Dist 6PA Nurses Assc 1973; adv Pittsburgh Orgn Childbirth Ed 1967-; test writer for Maternity Nurse Certification Exam; Am Nurses Assc 1975; mem PA Nurses Assc; Am Nurses Assc; lectr Ed Med Sch for Unwed Mothers 1967-68; Master's Degree Rep Nrsg Alumnae Assc;Univ of Pittsburgh; moderator for Nurses Assc of Am Clg of Obstetricians & Gynecologists Conf 1974; Clinical Speclst in Maternity & Infant Care 1963-; mem Sigma Theta Tau Professional Nurses Hon Soc; curriculum devUniv of Pittsburgh Sch of Nrsg 1967-70; admsns comUniv of Pittsburgh Sch of Nrsg; coordUniv of Pittsburgh Sch of Nrsg Dept of Maternity Nrsg; adv Black Stdnt NursesUniv of Pittsburgh; 1st vpUniv of Pittsburgh Nurses Alumni Assc 1976, pres 1977; mem Resolutions Com PA Nurses Assc; com mem Minority RecruitmentUniv of Pittsburgh Sch of Nrsg; nurse Am Yth Chorus European Tour 1977. **BUSINESS ADDRESS:** Duquesne Univ, Pittsburgh, PA 15219.

WHEELER, SUSIE WEEMS
Retired educator. **PERSONAL:** Born Feb 24, 1917, Bartow County, GA; daughter of Percy Weems and Cora Smith Weems Canty; married Daniel Webster Wheeler Sr; children: Daniel Jr. **EDUCATION:** Ft Valley State Coll, BS 1945; Atlanta Univ, MEd 1947; Univ of KY, Sixth Year Certificate, 1960, EdD 1977; Univ of GA, Educ Specialist, 1976. **CAREER:** Bartow County & Cartersville, classroom teacher 1938-46; Bartow Cartersville Calhoun Systems, jeanes supvr, 1947-63; Atlanta Univ, teacher 1962,63,64; Bartow Cty School System, curriculum dir 1963-79; mem of GA Student Finance Commn, 1985-89; columnist, The Daily Tribune News 1978-83. **ORGANIZATIONS:** State rep Assoc for Supv & Curriculum 1962-64; pres GA Jeanes Assoc 1968-70; pres GA Assn Suprv & Curriculum 1970-72; vice pres Bartow Cartersville Chamber of Commerce 1980-82; ed rep Amer Assn Univ Women 1980-82; natl nominating comm Delta Sigma Theta 1985; chair for restoration of Rosenwald Schl as Noble Hill-Wheeler Mem Heritage Ctr 1985; world traveler with Friendship Force 1980-86;mem of Helen A Whiting Society; share travelogues with schls, civic and social groups; Intl Relations Chair, Amer Assn of Univ Women, 1987-89; Natl Planning & Devel Comm, Delta Sigma Theta Sorority, 1989-92; Georgia Student Finance Commn, State of GA, 1985-89, 1989-93. **HONORS/ACHIEVEMENTS:** Travel Study Award to West Africa, GA Dept of Educ, 1972; Johnnye V Cox Distinguished Award, GA Assn Supvr & Cur, 1975; Mem, Writing Comm Jeanes Supvr in GA Schools 1975; Bartow County Woman of the Year Professional & Business Women, 1977; mem, Writing Comm, The Jeanes Story, 1979. **HOME ADDRESS:** 105 Fite St, Cartersville, GA 30120.

WHEELER, THEODORE STANLEY
Athletic coach. **PERSONAL:** Born Jan 30, 1931, Chattanooga, TN; divorced; children: Theodore, Mary Frances, James. **EDUCATION:** BS, 1956. **CAREER:** Amer Cyanamid, sales 1959-69; Presb St Lukes Hosp, admin dir 1969-72; Univ of IA, head men's track coach, head men's cross country coach. **HONORS/ACHIEVEMENTS:** All Amer Cross Country 1951; All Amer Track 1952; All Serv 800 Champ 1955; US Olympic Team 1500 M 1956; Melbourne Australia Drake Hall of Fame 1962; Track Scholarship in name. **MILITARY SERVICE:** AUS 1953-55. **BUSINESS ADDRESS:** Head Men's Track Coach, Univ of Iowa, Rm 235 Carver-Hawkeye Arena, Iowa City, IA 52242.

WHEELER, WARREN HERVEY
Business executive, pilot. **PERSONAL:** Born Oct 01, 1943, Durham, NC. **EDUCATION:** A&T State U; Am Flyers Flight Sch. **CAREER:** Piedmont Airlines, capt 1966-; Wheeler Flying Serv Inc, pres 1969-. **ORGANIZATIONS:** Mem Gov Commission on Transp NC 1979-; mem Gov Com on Travel & Tourism NC 1980-. **HONORS/ACHIEVEMENTS:** Plaque for outst achvmnt Durham Bus & Professional Chain 1975; plaque for outst achvmt Black Pilot Assc 1977. **BUSINESS ADDRESS:** PO Box 12034, Research Triangle Park, NC 27709.

WHIPPER, LUCILLE SIMMONS
Educational administrator. **PERSONAL:** Born Jun 06, 1928, Charleston, SC; married Rev Benjamin J Whipper Sr; children: Benjamin J Jr, Ogretta W Hawkins, Rosmond W Black, J Seth, Stanford Edley (dec), Cheryl D, D'Jaris Whipper-Lewis. **EDUCATION:** Talladega Coll, AB Economics Soc 1948; Univ of Chicago, MA Pol Sci 1955; SC State Coll, counseling cert 1961. **CAREER:** Charleston Co Sch, tchr & counselor 1949-65; Burke HS, counselor/chmn of dept 1965-73; Charleston Co Office of Econ Oppor, admin/prog dir 1966-68; Charleston Co Sch, dir proj ESAA 1975-77; Coll of Charleston, asst to the pres/dir of human relations 1973-75, 1977-81 (retired); South Carolina House District 109, representative. **ORGANIZATIONS:** Panelist & discussion leader "Financial Aid to Minority Poverty Students", "Coll Access for Minority Students" 1967-70; bd of dir Family Serv to CharlestonCo 1967-72, 1975-79; mem Charleston Area Comm Relations Comm 1968-74; mental health comm State of SC 1969-71; mem Budget Bd United Way 1975-77; mem SC Adv Council on Vocational & Tech Educ 1979-; mem Charleston Constituent Bd Twenty 1980-84; mem Coll Entrance Exam Bd. **HONORS/ACHIEVEMENTS:** Fellowship grant for grad study Univ of Chicago 1954-55; Comm Serv Awd Charleston Chap Omega Psi Phi 1968; Mental Health Comm 1969-71; Mayor's Adv Comm on Human Relations 1971; Comm on Minimal Competency SC Gen Assembly 1977-78; SC Adv Tech Educ 1979-. **BUSINESS ADDRESS:** Representative, SC General Assembly, 328-A Blatt Bldg, Columbia, SC 29211.

WHIPPS, MARY N.
Assoc. executive. **PERSONAL:** Born Mar 23, 1945, Bolton, MS; divorced; children: Edgar Whipps Jr. **EDUCATION:** Utica Jr Coll, attended 1964; Campbell Jr Coll, attended 1965. **CAREER:** IBEW Local Union 2262, negotiating comm 1970-, financial sec 1971-78; Hammond Jr HS PTA, 1st vice pres; A Philips Randolph Conf, resource person & workshop instructor. **ORGANIZATIONS:** Corresp sec MS A Philip Randolph Inst 1973-76; sec, treas Jackson Central Labor Union AFL-CIO COPE Dir 1974-78; labor sect chrpsn United Way Kick-Off Fund Dr; sec Indust Employee Credit Union Bd of Dirs; mem Labors' Panel on Easter Seal Telethon; vp, pres Ramsey Rec Ctr Alexandria 1984-86; steering comm Natl A Philip Randolph Inst 1984; mem IBEW Minority Caucus 1974-78. **HONORS/ACHIEVEMENTS:** Among first Black females at Presto Mfg Co; delegate to many Union activities including MS AFL-CIO Convention, Jackson Central Labor Union, MS Electrical Workers Assn, Natl Conference of A Philip Randolph; crowned Miss Mississippi A Philip Randolph; 2 Outstanding Serv Awds MS A Philip Randolph Inst; Serv Awds IBEW Local 2262, IBEW Syst Council EM-6; 1st black female Intl Rep of Intl Brotherhood of Elect Workers AFL-CIO (IBEW); Labor's Ad Hoc Committee of Nat'l Council of Negro Women. **BUSINESS ADDRESS:** International Representative, Interntl Brotherhood Elec Wkrs, 1125 15th St NW, Washington, DC 20005.

WHISENTON, ANDRE C.
Librarian. **PERSONAL:** Born Feb 04, 1944, Durham, NC; son of Andrew and Margret; married Vera Norman; children: Andre Christopher, Courtney Yvonne. **EDUCATION:** Morehouse Coll, BPS 1965; Atlanta Univ, MLS 1966. **CAREER:** Naval Sea Sys Command, lib dir 1973-76; US Dept of Labor, exec devpgm 1979, lib dir 1980-82, dir eeo. **ORGANIZATIONS:** Bd mem Natl Asso of Blacks Within Govt 1985; mem NAACP 1988; Alpha Phi Alpha 1988; Montgomery Co MLK Jr Commem Comm 1988-89. **HONORS/ACHIEVEMENTS:** DOL ECO Awd 1978; Fed Womens Impact Awd 1979; Sec of Labor Rec Awd 1982. **BUSINESS ADDRESS:** Chief, EEO, US Dept of Labor, 200 Constitution Ave NW, Washington, DC 20210.

WHISENTON, JOFFRE T.
Educational administrator. **PERSONAL:** Born in Hattiesburg, MS; married Zadie E Bedford; children: Joffre Conrad. **EDUCATION:** Tougaloo Clg MS; Sprngfld Clg MA;Univ of AL, PhD 1968. **CAREER:** So Assoc of Coll's & Schools, assoc exec dir 1977-; HEW, spec asst to sec for educ policy 1975-77; Stillman Coll, prof/chmn/various posts 1956-69; Univ of AL, pgm assoc. **ORGANIZATIONS:** Mem Am Psychol Assc; mem APGA; mem AAHPER; mem Am Assc ofUniv Profs; life mem NAACP; mem Phi Delta Kappa; mem Urban League; mem Omega Psi Phi Frat.

WHITAKER, ARTHUR L.
Clergyman, psychologist. **PERSONAL:** Born Jul 23, 1921, Malden, MA; son of Robert W Whitaker (deceased) and Elizabeth Hinton Whitaker (deceased); married Virginia Carter; children: Ronald, Paul, Mark, Keith. **EDUCATION:** Gordon Coll, AB 1949; Harvard University Divinity School, STB 1952; Andover Newton Theological School, STM 1954, DMin 1973. **CAREER:** Amer Baptist Churches of MA, assoc exec minister 1970-78; Pilgrim Baptist Church, St Paul MN, pastor 1967-70; Mt Olivet Baptist Church, Rochester NY, pastor 1956-67; Amer Baptist Home Missionary Soc New York, field rep 1955-56; Calvary Baptist Church, student pastor 1950-55; Univ of Rochester, asst prof of sociology 1958-66; Gordon Coll, visiting prof Afro-Amer history 1972; Amer Baptist Churches USA, ordained minister 1951; Commonweatlh of MA Bd of Reg of Psychologists, licensed psychologist; Amer Baptist Churches of NYS, exec minister 1978-83; Vet Admin Medical Center Syracuse NY, protestant chaplain 1984-86; private practice, pastoral, counseling, psychologist 1986-. **ORGANIZATIONS:** Mem Amer Sociological Assn; mem Amer Psychological Assn; Editor & Author 1958-; mem Rotary Club of Boston 1970-; trustee Gordon Coll 1973-81; corporator Suffolk-Franklin Savings Bank Boston 1974-78; diplomate Prof Counseling Intl Acad of Professional Counseling Psychotherapy Inc; trust Keuka Coll 1978-83; Colgate Rochester Divinity School 1978-83; bd dir NY State Council of Churches 1978-83; mem Rotary Club of Syracuse 1978-83; Hiscock Legal Aid Soc 1983-86; mem, Harvard Divinity School Alumni Council, 1989-; mem, The New York Academy of Sciences, 1989-. **HONORS/ACHIEVEMENTS:** Cited as one of outstanding Negro alumni at work The Andover Newton Theological School 1965; author of The New Morality in Contemporary History, God's Doing Man's Undoing, 1967; author of The Urban Church in Urban Community, 1974; numerous editoral citations & other distinguished serv awards. **MILITARY SERVICE:** 9th US Cavalry Band t/sgt; ETO, N Africa, Naples-Foggia, Central Europe & Rhineland; 4 Battle Stars 1943-46. **BUSINESS ADDRESS:** Psychologist Pastoral, 9 James Tighe Rd, Randolph, MA 02368.

WHITAKER, LOUIS RODMAN
Professional athlete. **PERSONAL:** Born May 12, 1957, New York, NY; married Crystal McCreary; children: Asia, Sarah. **CAREER:** Detroit Tigers, infielder 1977-. **HONORS/ACHIEVEMENTS:** MVP of FL State League 1976; Won AL Rookie of Year Award 1978; named second baseman on The Sporting News Amer League All-Star Team 1983,1984; named second baseman on The Sporting News Amer League Silver Slugger team 1983-85; mem All Star Team 1983-86. **BUSINESS ADDRESS:** Detroit Tigers, 2121 Trumbull Ave, Detroit, MI 48216.

WHITAKER, MICAL ROZIER
Theatrical director, college instructor. **PERSONAL:** Born Feb 10, 1941, Metter, GA; son of Ellis Whitaker and Alma Whitaker; married Georgenia; children: Mical Anthony. **EDUCATION:** Attended, Howard Univ 1958-61, Amer Acad of Dramatic Arts New York City 1961-62, Circle-in-the-Square New York City 1966; North Carolina A & T State Univ BFA, Greenboro, N.C. 1988-1989. **CAREER:** East River Players, founder/artistic dir 1964-76; Union Settlement's Dept of Perf Arts, founder/dir 1972-76; Ossie Davis & Ruby Dee Story Hour, producer/dir 1977-78; Richard Allen Ctr for Culture & Art, artistic dir 1978-81; Georgia Southern Coll, theatre dir. **ORGANIZATIONS:** Co-founder/coord Lincoln Ctr St Theatre Fest 1970-81; dir Black Theatre Festival USA Lincoln Ctr 1979; dir Intl Black Theatre Festival Lincoln Ctr 1980. **HONORS/ACHIEVEMENTS:** CEBA for radio station production "The Beauty of Things Black" 1978; AUDELCO Awd Dir of Musical 1979; Emmy Production and Set Design "Cellar George" Seattle Chap 1979; Paul Robeson Theatre Award North Carolina A&T State Univ 1989. **HOME ADDRESS:** 515 Washington St, Metter, GA 30439. **BUSINESS ADDRESS:** Instructor in Theatre, Georgia Southern College, Landrum Box 8091, Statesboro, GA 30460.

WHITAKER, WILLARD H.
Mayor. **PERSONAL:** Born Feb 13, 1912, St Francis, AR; son of Joe Whitaker and Polly Moore Whitaker; married Erma Pitts (deceased); children: Gwendolyn Starlard, Vhaness Chambers. **EDUCATION:** LeMoyne College, Memphis, TN, attended two years. **CAREER:** Fun Dir Exch Madison AR, foreman; ASCS, asst state dir; Headstart, dir; City of Madison, mayor 1970-. **ORGANIZATIONS:** Mem Sel Serv Bd St Francis Cty, St Francis Cty Non-Part Voters League; mem of exec bd Natl Conference of Black Mayors; pres Self Help Housing; mem Selective Service; mem Chamber of Commerce. **HONORS/ACHIEVEMENTS:** Outstanding Contractor Award, AMCA, Little Rock, AR, 1975; 4th Annual Man of the Year, Delta Sigma Lambda Chapter, 1976; Outstanding Superintendent of Forest City Public Schools, Forest City, AR, 1976. **BUSINESS ADDRESS:** Mayor, City of Madison AR, PO Box 109, Washington St, Madison, AR 72359.

WHITE, ALPHONZA F.
Educational administrator. **PERSONAL:** Born Apr 01, 1935, Cartwright, OK; married Erma Jean McGee; children: B Randall, Stacy N, Alfreda Jean. **EDUCATION:** Carnation Farms Artificial Insemination & Cattle Mgmt Sch, Cert Pgm 1970; Southeastern OK State U, BS 1977, MBS 1978. **CAREER:** Southeastern OK State Univ, counselor talent search 1978-, dir asst of coll & high school relations 1976-78; Johns-mansville Products Corp, utility handler 1960-70; AL'MARS Farms Registered Cattle Operation, owner-mgr 1963-; Texoma Artificial Insemination & Consulting Center, owner-mgr 1970-; Livestock Breeders Interntl Inc, breeding Consult 1971-74. **ORGANIZATIONS:** Bd of dir Bryan Co Community Action Found 1966-; chrtr mem dir Am Gelbvieh Assc 1972-; vice pres OK Gelvieh Assc 1973-74; mem OK Div of Stdnt Asst Pgm 1978-; spnsr & Mem Delta Sigma Alpha 1975-. **HONORS/ACHIEVEMENTS:** First Black in US to Own Artificial Insemination & Breeding Consult Serv Co; Texoma Artificial Insemination Ctr Calera OK, 1971-; first black & mem of a Three Man Team to Perform World's First Live Embryo Transplant in Cattle Cardsdon Alberta Canada 1971. **MILITARY SERVICE:** AUS stf sgt e-6 1957-62. **BUSINESS ADDRESS:** Texoma Talent Search, Station A, Box 4112, Durant, OK 74701.

WHITE, ANTHONY CHARLES GUNN See KAMAU, MOSI

WHITE, ARTHUR W., JR.
Business executive. **PERSONAL:** Born Oct 25, 1943, St Louis, MO; married Virginia A Green; children: Arthur W III. **EDUCATION:** Lincoln Univ, BS 1965; USAF Officers Training School, (Distinguished Military Grad) 1967; USAF Management Analysis School, cert of grad 1967. **CAREER:** Equitable Life Assurance, admin trainee 1965-66; Society of the US, group sales rep 1971-74, div group sales mgr 1974-76, dir of sales 1976-77, vice pres 1977; United Mutual Life Insurance, pres & chief exec officer 1985. **ORGANIZATIONS:** Vp NAACP 1961-62; mem Alpha Phi Alpha 1962; chmn social performance comm Equitable Life Assurance Soc 1984; adv bd Bronx Lebanon Hosp 1986; adv bd Rory Sparrow Foundation 1986; mem adv bd The Salvation Army of Greater NY 1986. **HONORS/ACHIEVEMENTS:** Outstanding Performance Awd Equitable Life Assurance Soc Grp Oper 1969; Man of the Year Awd Alpha Phi Alpha; Outstanding Achiever Econ Devel New Era Demo Club 1985; TOR Special Inspiration Awd Theatre of Renewal 1986; cited in Who's Who in Amer Colls and Univ, Outstanding Young Men of Amer, Men of Achievement, Comm Leaders and Noteworthy Amers, Notable Americans. **MILITARY SERVICE:** USAF, captin 1966-71. **HOME ADDRESS:** 5 Sylvan Way, Short Hills, NJ 07078. **BUSINESS ADDRESS:** Pres & Chief Exec Officer, United Mutual Life Insurance, 310 Lenox Avenue, New York, NY 10027.

WHITE, ARTIS ANDRE
Dentist. **PERSONAL:** Born Sep 13, 1926, Middletown, OH. **EDUCATION:** Morehouse Coll, BS 1951; Howard Univ, DDS 1955; UCLA, Post Doctoral Cert 1970. **CAREER:** UCLA, lecturer 1969-72; Drew Postgrad Med School LA, lecturer; Maxillofacial Prosthetic Div Martin Luther King Hosp LA, dir 1972-; Univ Guadalajara Mexico, lecturer 1975-; Private practice, dentist, maxillofacial prosthetics 1972-. **ORGANIZATIONS:** Fellow Royal Soc of Health Engr; fellow Acad of Dentistry Intl; mem Amer Prosthdontic Soc, Amer Cleft Palate Assoc, Amer Dental Assoc, Natl Dental Assoc; fellow Acad of Dentistry for the Handicapped, Amer Assoc of Hosp Dentists. **BUSINESS ADDRESS:** 333 E Nutwood St, Inglewood, CA 90307.

WHITE, AUGUSTUS A., III
Orthopaedic surgeon, educator. **PERSONAL:** Born Jun 04, 1936, Memphis, TN; son of Augustus White and Vivian Dandridge White; married Anita Ottemo; children: Alissa Alexandra, Atina Andrea, Annica Akila. **EDUCATION:** Brown Univ, BA (Cum Laude) 1957; Stanford Univ, MD 1961; Karolinska Inst Sweden, Dr Medical Science 1969; Univ Hospital, rotating intern 1961-62; Presbetary Medical Center, asst residential surgeon 1962-63; Yale-New Haven Hospital, asst residential orthopedic surgeon 1963-65; Newington Children's Hospital, resident 1964-65; Yale-New Haven Hospital, chief resident 1965; VA Hospital New Haven, CT, chief resident 1966; Natl Inst Health, orthopedic trainee 1968-69; Harvard Business School, Advanced Mgmt Program 1984. **CAREER:** VA Hospital West Haven, CT, consulting orthopaedic surgeon 1969-78; Hill Health Center, consulting orthopaedic surgeon 1969-78; Yale Univ School of Medicine, assoc prof orthopaedic surgery 1972-76; CT Health Care Plan, chief of orthopaedics 1976-78; Yale Univ School of Medicine, prof orthopaedic surgery 1977-78; Harvard Univ School of Medicine, prof orthopaedic surgery 1978-; Massachusetts General Hospital, visiting orthopaedic surgeon 1979-; Children's Hospital Medical Center, sr assoc in orthopaedic surgery 1979-; Peter Bent Brigham Hospital, assoc in orthopaedic surgery 1979-80; Sidney Farber Cancer Inst, consulting div surgeon 1980-; Brigham & Woman's Hospital; Beth Israel Hospital Boston, orthopaedic surgeon in chief 1978-; Univ of Maryland at Baltimore, pres-designate, 1990-. **ORGANIZATIONS:** Numerous memberships and organizations including, consultant/participant NIH Workshop on Bioengineering Approaches to Problems of the Spine 1970; Fellow Bradford Coll Yale Univ 1971-78; mem Resident Selection Comm Dept or Orthopaedic Surgeons Yale Univ School of Medicine 1972-73; mem Brown Univ Comm on Medical Educ 1973-; mem Medical Conf Comm Beth Israel Hospital 1978-; mem Faculty Council Comm Harvard Medical School 1978-; Area Concent Adv Musculoskeletal Harvard-MIT Div of Health Science and Technology 1981-; mem Sub-Comm of Prof Harvard Medical School 1982; mem Editorial Bd of SPINE published by Harper & Row 1976-; mem Editorial Bd Annals of Sports Medicine 1983; advisory bd Med-Techn Manpower Devel Program Roxbury, MA 1969-71; mem Allocation Comm United Way of Greater New Haven 1972-75; bd dir Quinnipiac Council Boy Scouts of Amer 1973; New Haven Chapter NAACP; Sigma Pi Phi Fraternity 1979; visitng prof at over 11 colleges & univs ; mem visiting comm to evaluate minority Life and Educ Brown Univ 1985,86; pres-elect Cervical Spine Research Soc. **HONORS/ACHIEVEMENTS:** Pres Delta Upsilon Fraternity Brown Chapter 1956; Sigma Xi Soc; Ten Outstanding Young Men Award US Jaycees 1969; Martin Luther King Jr Award Medical Achievement Award 1972; Amer Orthopaedic Assn ABC Exchange Fellow 1975; Capdelta Award for Outstanding Research in Orthopaedic Surgery 1976; Natl Award for Outstanding Orthopaedic Research Kappa Delta; Honoree Ebony Magazine Black Achievement Awards in the Professions 1980; Eastern Orthopaedic Assn Award for Spine Research 1980; Bd of Fellows Brown Univ 1981-1992; Exceptional Black Scientist Ciba-Geigy Corp Poster Series 1982; Distinguished Serv Award Northfield Mt Hermon Alumni Assn 1983; Honorary Mem Liverpool Orthopaedic Soc; Honorary Citizen of New Orlean s; Dir of the Partnership 1984-; William Rogers Award Assoc Alumni Brown Univ & Delta Upsilon Fraternity 1984; Delta Upsilon Frat Award for Outstanding Achievement 1986; Honorary DHL Univ of New Haven 1987. **MILITARY SERVICE:** AUS Captain Med Corps 139th Med Detachment KB Vietnam 1966-68; Bronze Star 1967. **BUSINESS ADDRESS:** Chief Dept Orthopaedic Surgery, Beth Israel Hospital, 330 Brookline Ave, Boston, MA 02215.

WHITE, BARBARA WILLIAMS
Educator. **PERSONAL:** Born Feb 26, 1943, Macon, GA; daughter of Ernestine Austin; married Julian E White; children: Tonja, Phaedra. **EDUCATION:** Florida A&M Univ, BS, 1964; Florida State Univ, BS, 1974, MSW, 1975, PhD, 1986. **CAREER:** Lake County Public Schools, teacher, 1964-65; Duval County Public Schools, teacher, 1965-73; Leon County 4-C Council, dir, 1975-77; Florida A&M Univ, asst professor, 1977-79; Florida State Univ, assoc dean, 1979-. **ORGANIZATIONS:** Mem, Acad of Certified Social Workers, 1978-; natl 1st vice pres, Natl Assn of Social Workers, 1983-85; commissioner/on accreditation, Council on Social Work Educ, 1984-87; mem, Links Inc, Tallahassee Chapter, Alpha Kappa Alpha Sor; vice pres, for Planning, United Way of Leon County, 1988-90. **HONORS/ACHIEVEMENTS:** Social Worker of the Year, NASW Florida Chapter, 1982; Florida Bd of Regents Grant for Grad Study, 1982-83, 1983-84; editor of book "Color in a White Society," published by NASW, 1985; Teacher of the Year Florida State Univ, 1986; Professor of the Year, School of Social Work, Florida State Univ, 1988-89; published author in professional journals & books-gen theme, Black Amer. **BUSINESS ADDRESS:** Assoc Dean, Florida State Univ, School of Social Work, Tallahassee, FL 32306.

WHITE, BARRY
Singer, composer. **PERSONAL:** Born Sep 12, 1944, Galveston, TX; married Glodean; children: 4 children. **CAREER:** Together Unlimited, pres; Soul Unlimited, pres; Love Unlimited, producer; singer, composer, record producer. **HONORS/ACHIEVEMENTS:** Wrote "Walkin In The Rain With The One I Love", "Can't Get Enough of Your Love Babe, You're The First, My Last, My Everything", "I Belong to You"; more than 60 gold records; 15 platinum records; composed music for several motion pictures.

WHITE, BILLY RAY
Elected government official. **PERSONAL:** Born Jun 29, 1936, Center, TX; married Zerlene Victor; children: Elbert Ray, William Douglas, Jeanetta Marie, Johnetta Marie, Charles Vernon, Billy Ester. **EDUCATION:** Prairie View A&M Univ TX, attended 1955-57. **CAREER:** Meth Hosp Lubbock TX, clerk 1957-64; Varian Assoc CA, mechanic 1964-77; Ray Chem Corp CA, buyer 1977-. **ORGANIZATIONS:** Mem consult gr Menlo-Atherton Bd of Raltors; mem plan bd State CA for E Palo Alto 1971-72; chmn plan comm City of Menlo Park 1974-78; chmn HCD bd Coof San Mateo 1978-; Center for Independence of the Disabled, Inc, bd of dir. **HONORS/ACHIEVEMENTS:** First Black elected to Council of City of Menlo Park; Tulip L Jones Women's Club Inc 1978; Man of Yr Belle Haven Home Assn 1980. **BUSINESS ADDRESS:** Buyer, Ray Chemical Corp, 300 Constitution Drive, Menlo Park, CA 94025.

WHITE, BOOKER TALIAFERRO
Educator. **PERSONAL:** Born Sep 03, 1907, Tryon, NC; married Lucynda Stewart. **EDUCATION:** WV State Clg, BS 1929; OH State U, MS 1937, PhD 1945. **CAREER:** AL A&M Univ, prof of chem 1968-; A&T Coll, prof dir of research 1953-61, chmn dept of chem 1947-53; AL A&M Coll, 1945-47; Morristown Coll, prin instr 1940-41; Halifax Co Training School, instr 1938-40; Brewer Jr Coll, 1937-38; Coxe HS, prin instr 1932-36; Kittroll Coll, instr 1930-32. **ORGANIZATIONS:** Mem Am Chem Soc; Am Dairy Sci Assc; Am Assc for Advancement of Sci; NC Acad of Sci; Beta Kappa Chi Sci Soc; Natl Institutional of Sci Author of Articles for Professional Journals.

WHITE, CHARLES R.
Civil engineer. **PERSONAL:** Born Nov 25, 1937, NYC, NY; son of Clarence R White and Elise White; married Dolores; children: Darryl, Sherryl. **EDUCATION:** Howard Univ, BS 1959; Univ So CA, MS 1963. **CAREER:** Civil engr planner registered prof engr CA 1965; State CA LA Dept of Water Resources Southern Dist, prog mgr geothermal resources 1959-, chief planning branch. **ORGANIZATIONS:** Mem Omega Psi Phi Frat 1956; Amer Soc Civil Engrs 1957; Tau Beta Pi Town Hall of CA 1970; Toastmasters Intl 1970. **HONORS/ACHIEVEMENTS:** Principal author Planned Utilization of Ground Water Basins San Gabriel Valley 1969; Meeting Water Demands Chino-Riverside Area 1971; Meeting Water Demands SanJuan Area 1972; co-author Water & Power from Geothermal Resources in CA-An Overview 1974; publ paper on Lake Eisinore Flood Disaster of March 1980 Natl AcadPress 1982; author San Bernardino-San Gorgonio Water Resources Mgmt Investigation 1986. **BUSINESS ADDRESS:** Chief Planning Branch, State CA Dept Water Res, 849 S Broadway, Los Angeles, CA 90014.

WHITE, CLARENCE DEAN
Financial administrator, artist. **PERSONAL:** Born Nov 27, 1946, Ellaville, GA; son of Charlie G. White and Tymy Hartage White. **EDUCATION:** Univ of Paris, attended 1967-68; Morehouse Coll, BA (cum laude) 1969; Northwestern Univ, MBA 1972. **CAREER:** First Natl Bank of Chicago, trust officer 1969-82; Artist & Art Critic, free lance basis; Clarence White Contemporary Art, art dealer 1974-; The Film Symposium, dir 1976-. **ORGANIZATIONS:** Mem Men's Council Museum of Contemporary Art Chicago.

WHITE, CLAUDE ESLEY
Attorney. **PERSONAL:** Born Jan 02, 1949, Bridgeton, NJ; son of John White (deceased) and Viola White; married J Denise Rice; children: Claude Jr, Stephanie, Christopher. **EDUCATION:** Rutgers Coll, BA 1971; Rutgers Law Sch, JD 1974. **CAREER:** Pitney Hardin & Kipp, assoc atty 1974-76; Grand Met USA, atty 1976-85; Quality Care Inc, vice pres and general counsel 1985-87; Staff Builders Inc, vice pres/Gen Counsel 1988-. **ORGANIZATIONS:** Chmn Rutgers Coll Econ Oppor Prog Adv Com; Natl Study Register 1971; bd dir Inmate-Self Help Com Inc 1974-76; bd trustees treas St Paul Bapt Ch; mem Amer, NJ Bar Assns; adv Sigma Delta; chairman Home Health & Staffing Serv Assoc 1987-88; mem, bd of dir Natl Assoc of Home Care 1986-89. **HONORS/ACHIEVEMENTS:** Listed in Who's Who in American Law 1987. **BUSINESS ADDRESS:** Vice Pres & General Mgr, Staff Builders Inc, 1981 Marcus Ave, Lake Success, NY 11042.

WHITE, CLAYTON CECIL
Educator. **PERSONAL:** Born Nov 04, 1942, New York, NY; married Le Tretta Jones; children: Shannon. **EDUCATION:** TempleUniv Clg of Music, MusB 1964, MusM 1969. **CAREER:** Comm Coll of Phila, assoc prof music dept 1970-; School Dist of Phila, music teacher dept head 1964-69; Natl Opera Ebony, chorus master & conductor 1976-; Clayton White Singers, music & dir/founder 1978-. **ORGANIZATIONS:** Minister of music Canaan Bapt Ch 1980; dir Cultural & Ed Ctr Heritage House 1962-69. **BUSINESS ADDRESS:** 34 S 11th St, Philadelphia, PA 19107.

WHITE, CLOVIS LELAND
Educator. **PERSONAL:** Born Mar 09, 1953, Rochester, NY; son of Edward A. White and Alberta Morris White; married Denise Andre White; children: Vanessa M. White. **EDUCATION:** Southeastern MA Univ, BA 1975; State Univ of NY/Albany, MA 1977; Indiana Univ, MA, PhD 1984. **CAREER:** Charles Settlement House; youth worker 1977-78; Indiana Univ, instructor 1981-84; Univ of WI, asst prof of afro-amer studies 1984-88; asst prof of Sociology, Oberlin Coll. **ORGANIZATIONS:** Mem Amer Sociological Assoc 1981-, Assoc of Black Sociologists 1983-, Southern Sociological Soc 1984-. **HONORS/ACHIEVEMENTS:** Minority Fellow CIC Minority Fellowship Program 1978-84, Amer Sociological Assoc 1983-84; Nord Faculty Fellow Oberlin Coll 1988-90. **BUSINESS ADDRESS:** Asst Professor of Sociology, Oberlin College, King Hall, Rm 305, Oberlin, OH 44074.

WHITE, COHEN W.
Real estate broker. **PERSONAL:** Born Oct 06, 1887, Blackshear, GA; married Maude Stafford; children: Zenobia Myles, Cohen Milton, Harold Lewis. **EDUCATION:** Spl Course in Real Estate Appraisal. **CAREER:** CW White Real Estate Instrumental in Orgn of Real Estate Brokers Assc in Detroit, owner 1931. **ORGANIZATIONS:** Pres Real Estate Broker Assc Detroit; bd dir Natl Assc of Real Estate Brokers; prsntly hon mem bd dir Natl Assc of Real Estate Brokers; past pres Booker T Washington Trade Assc; helped organize Superior Life Ins Soc 1934; sec Superior Life Ins Soc 1934-57; v chmn bd dir Mammoth Life & Accident Ins Co; past treas Detroit Chap NAACP; founded & pres GA Clb 1938; mem Adv Com Fed Housing Admn 1954; mem Mayor's Com for Neighborhood Conservation& Improved Housing 1953; mem trustee Scott Meth Ch. **HONORS/ACHIEVEMENTS:** Recipient merit awrd Commr of MI Corp & Securities Commn 1954; past-presidents achievement awrd Booker T Washington Bus Assc 1965; distinguished serv& awrd Booker T Washington Bus Assc Past Pres & Founder 1974. **BUSINESS ADDRESS:** 6337 14 St, Detroit, MI 48208.

WHITE, D. RICHARD
Attorney at law. **PERSONAL:** Born Aug 05, 1947, Richmond, VA; children: Maleeka Renee. **EDUCATION:** NY City Comm Coll, AAS 1968; Bernard Baruch Coll, BBA 1974; Kansas Univ, JD 1983. **CAREER:** Reliance Ins Co, claims adj; Liberty Mutual Ins Co, claims exam 1972-83; Nationwide Inter-Co Arbitration, arbitrator 1977. **ORGANIZATIONS:** Mem Omega Psi Phi, Dem Club of NY; fndr Coop Adventure 1977; mem Natl Free Lance Photographers Assn 1977; Com for a Better New York. **HONORS/ACHIEVEMENTS:** Bedford-Stuyvesant Civ Awd 1974; Achievement Scroll Omega Psi Phi 1974; Bernard Baruch Act Collgn Awd 1974; Recog of Achvmt Reliance Ins Co 1976. **BUSINESS ADDRESS:** Attorney, 901 Tennessee Ste 3, Lawrence, KS 66044.

WHITE, DAMON L.
Affirmative action director. **PERSONAL:** Born May 19, 1934, Nyack, NY; married Sheila D; children: Damon, Ramon, Patricia, Dana, Kevin. **EDUCATION:** Univ of Detroit, PhB 1957; Wayne State Univ, MA 1966. **CAREER:** Western MI Univ, dir affirmative action.

ORGANIZATIONS: Mem Phi Delta Kappa; Area V Coord Amer Assoc Affirmative Action; mem Public Safety Comm City of Kalamazoo; Pres Affirmative Action Computerized ResourceSystem; mem Alpha Phi Alpha; elected three 4 yr terms to City Council Highland Park MI; mem Council for Exceptional Children. **HONORS/ACHIEVEMENTS:** PTA Natl Disting Serv Awd; Howardite of the Yr Howard Univ Alumni Assoc. **MILITARY SERVICE:** AUS staff sgt 2 yrs; Combat Infantry Badge; Korean Service Medal; 2 Bronze Stars. **BUSINESS ADDRESS:** Dir Affirmative Action, Western Michigan University, 3020 Administration Bldg, Kalamazoo, MI 49008.

WHITE, DAVID D.
Attorney. **PERSONAL:** Born Jan 31, 1901, Winston-Salem, NC; married Frances Anderson. **EDUCATION:** BS JD 1928-32. **CAREER:** Bell, White & Saunders Attys, atty; Atty Gen Ofc OH, spl asst atty. **ORGANIZATIONS:** Past mem Civil Rights Commn OH 1968-73; referee Campus Disorder StateUniv 1970-; aptd by OH Bd of Regents; mem Bd Of Govs Columbus Bar Assc; delegate 7th Dist OH State Bar Assc; mem Black Lawyers OH; Am Bar Assc; OH State Bar; Columbus Bar; RB Elliott Law Clb; Natl Bar Assc; NAACP; Kappa Alpha Psi; Urban League; Various City Civic Orgn; past pres Franklin Co Chap MS Soc. **HONORS/ACHIEVEMENTS:** Recip hope chest awrd Natl Multiple Sclerosis Soc 1975. **BUSINESS ADDRESS:** 21 E State St, Columbus, OH 43215.

WHITE, DEZRA
Physician. **PERSONAL:** Born Dec 11, 1941, Beaumont, TX; married Geraldine; children: Dezra Jr, Nicole, Darren. **EDUCATION:** Morehouse Coll, BS 1963; Univ of TX, MD 1968. **CAREER:** Houston Med Forum, asst secty; Univ of TX Med Sch, clinical assoc; Dept OB/GYN St Elizabeth Hosp, chmn 1980-84, 1984-85; Hollins & Lord Assocs, physician. **ORGANIZATIONS:** Mem Amer Assn of GYN LSP, Harris Co Med Soc; mem Houston GYN & OB Soc, Natl Med Assn; pres Houston Morehouse Alumni Assn; mem Alpha Phi Alpha, Tots & Teens; fellow Amer Coll of OB & GYN; certified Amer Bd of OB & GYN. **BUSINESS ADDRESS:** Hollins & Lord Assoc, 4315 Lockwood Dr, Houston, TX 77026.

WHITE, DON LEE
Educator. **PERSONAL:** Born Oct 25, Los Angeles, CA; son of Kenneth White and Willie Rose (Benson) Brown. **EDUCATION:** Los Angeles City Coll, AA 1949; CA State Coll, AB 1952; Univ of S CA, MM 1959; Stanford Univ, study toward Dr of Musical Arts 1968-69; Univ of So CA, study toward Dr of Musical Arts 1970-72; Hon D Law Monrovia Coll 1984. **CAREER:** Prairie View A&M Coll, organist 1955-61; Los Angeles City Coll, instructor music 1961-62; Jefferson High Adult School, instructor 1961-63; Trade Tech Coll, instructor 1962-63; CA State Coll LA, lecturer 1962-64; CA State Univ LA, assoc prof 1964, prof of music 1983-. **ORGANIZATIONS:** Dir Music So CA Conf AME Church; dir Music Fifth Dist AME Church (14 states); 2nd vice pres Natl Assn of Negro Musicians 1980-84; western regional dir Natl Assn of Negro Musicians 1984-87. **HONORS/ACHIEVEMENTS:** Resolution City of Los Angeles Tribute Tenth Dist Councilman Thomas Bradley 1967; Los Angeles Philharmonic Orchestra 1974; lecture, "The Black Experience in Art, Aestetic meaning of Black Religious Music" presented at CA State Polytechnic Univ 1983; conductor for the Third annual Choral Festival for the Ecumenical Center for Black Church Studies 1983; elected First Vice Pres of the Natl Assn of Negro Musicians Inc 1983; an Annotated Biography of Negro Composers State LA Found Grant; The Afro-Amer Hymnal 1978; Organs in Historic Black Churches; choral arrangements, Blessed are the Meek, When Shall I (we) Meet Him?, O for a Thousand Tongues (all published by Marvel Press), Rejoice the Lord is King, How Great the Wisdom, Glorious Things of Thee, The AME Hymn, Ye Are Baptised, Introit and Amen; organ compositions, Christmas Fantasy, Jesus Keep Me Near The Cross, Thanksgiving Prelude, Chorale Prelude on Fairest Lord Jesus, By the Waters of Babylon, Magnificat for organ; cantata "Jesus Said from the Cross"; A Musical Masque SATB Children Choir, Adult, Dancing and educ instruments; Dance Elegy for Bass solo instructor and piano; anthem Blessed are the Meek. **MILITARY SERVICE:** USN 1945-47. **BUSINESS ADDRESS:** Prof of Music, Cal StateUniv Los Angeles, 5151 State University Dr, Los Angeles, CA 90032.

WHITE, DONALD EDWARD
Musician, educator. **PERSONAL:** Born Jul 09, 1925, Richmond, IN; married Dolores; children: Darrow, Diana. **EDUCATION:** Roosevelt Univ, B 1953; Hartford Univ, M 1957. **CAREER:** Cleveland Orchestra, cellist; Hartford Symphony Orchestra, past asst principal cellist; Cleveland Music School Settlement, Teacher; Wooster Coll, adjunct prof of music. **ORGANIZATIONS:** Advisory bd Urban League Cleveland Heights; bd trust mem Karamu House; community project bd Cleveland Orchestra. **MILITARY SERVICE:** USN.

WHITE, DONALD F.
Architect/engineer. **PERSONAL:** Born May 28, 1908, Cicero, IL; married Sue. **EDUCATION:** Univ of MI Coll of Archt, BS Archt 1932; Rackam Sch of Grad Stud, MS Archt 1934. **CAREER:** White & Griffin Detroit, 1946-58; Giffels & Vallet Detroit, design archt 1950-53; Off of Gen Serv St of NY, proj chief off 1964-68; Prairie View -ICA Liberia Cont Liberia W Africa, proj archt 1954-67; Nathan Johnson & Assocs Inc, architect/engineer. **ORGANIZATIONS:** Am Inst of Archt 1944; pres Nat Tech Assn 1949-51; Nat Soc of Prof Eng 1951; Eng Soc of Detroit 1950; Econo Club of Detroit; BT Wash Bus Assn Detroit; Detroit Bd of Commrc 1958; bd mem Albany Inter-racial Counc 1962-66; bd mem Model Nghbrhd Devel Corp; mem AIA Urban Plng & Dsgn Com;NAACP Albany Chpt; Urban Leag Albany Chpt; 5th Ave AME Zion Ch; Omega Psi Phi Frat; bd mem BT Wash Inst Kakata Liberia W Africa 1955-57. **HONORS/ACHIEVEMENTS:** 1st black reg Archt St of AL 1935, St of MI 1938; 1st black reg as Reg Archt & reg Professional Eng; est 1st Off in MI 1938 which hired black archt eng & drftsmn; 1st black design archt; 1st black to hold off in chpts of AIA. **BUSINESS ADDRESS:** Architect/Engineer, Nathan Johnson & Assocs Inc, 2512 West Grand Blvd, Detroit, MI 48208.

WHITE, DWIGHT LYNN
Athlete. **PERSONAL:** Born Jul 30, 1949, Hampton, VA. **EDUCATION:** E TX St U. **CAREER:** Pitts Steelers, professional ftbll plyr 1976; US Dept of Comm OMBE, prgm spec 1975. **ORGANIZATIONS:** Bd dir SW Min Corp; pres Pro Calenders Inc. **HONORS/ACHIEVEMENTS:** Coll All Am (Ftbll); All AFC-nFL 1972-73; All Pro NFL 1972-73.

WHITE, EARL HENRY
Telephone services manager. **PERSONAL:** Born Jun 05, 1959, Los Angeles, CA. **EDUCATION:** LA Southwest Coll, AA. **CAREER:** Imperial Bank, bank teller 1979-; St Earn's Hosp, adminstrv intern 1979; Hawthorne Hosp, pscy tech 1979; View Hgts Convelscnt, pscy tech 1977-79. **ORGANIZATIONS:** Pres & fdr Beta's Men Club LASW; mem at large ABA of So CA; pres NAACP LA SW Chap 1979; mem at large Mayors Yth Counc 1979; mem ASB Chap LA SW 1979; mem Dem Com LA Chap 1979. **BUSINESS ADDRESS:** Telephone Employees Crdt Union, 639 S New Hampshire Ave, Los Angeles, CA 90005.

WHITE, ED PEARSON
Retired elected official. **PERSONAL:** Born Mar 16, 1911, Woofruff County, AR; son of Link Pearson and Peraline Simpson Pearson; married Dorothy Mae Hill, Oct 14, 1962; children: Robert. **EDUCATION:** Eudora High School 1923. **CAREER:** American Synimite Bauxite Co, laborer 1939-46; Minnesota Mine, tank cleaner 1947-60; White's Grocery, owner 1960-83; White's Recreation Center, owner; City of Wrightsville, mayor 1983-86. **ORGANIZATIONS:** Member Wrightsville Chamber of Commerce; member NAACP; deacon Zion Hill Baptist Church; member Black Mayor's Assn; chmn Wrightsville Citizens In Action. **HONORS/ACHIEVEMENTS:** Martin Luther King Award-Black Community Devel Program of Hoover UMC for struggle to incorporate the township of Wrightsville; Outstanding Leadership, The Univ of Arkansas at Pine Bluff 1986; Outstanding Leadership & Dedicated Serv, City of Wrightsville 1986.

WHITE, EDWARD CLARENCE, JR.
Leveraged buyout fund manager. **PERSONAL:** Born Oct 09, 1956, Newark, NJ; son of Edward C White, Sr. and Viola L (Williams) White; married Yolanda Simmons. **EDUCATION:** Princeton Univ, BA Economics 1977; New York Univ, MS Quantitative Analysis 1981. **CAREER:** Merrill Lynch Pierce Fenner & Smith, industry analyst 1977-79; LF Rothschild Unterberg Towbin, vice pres 1979-83; E F Hutton & Co vice pres 1983-86, first vice pres 1986-l987; managing general partner Technology LBO Partners, L.P. New York, N.Y. l988-; Tucker Anthony (John Hancock Financial Serv), New York, N.Y. first vice pres l988. **ORGANIZATIONS:** Mem NY Soc of Securities Analysts 1978-; mem Semiconductor Equipment and Materials Inst 1980-. **HONORS/ACHIEVEMENTS:** CFA Designation Inst of Chartered Financial Analysts 1984; Ranked among top analysts worldwide in Euro Money Mag Global Rsch Survey 1985; ranked as runner up in Inst Investor Mag Analyst Survey 1986. **BUSINESS ADDRESS:** Managing General Partner, Technology LBO Partners, L.P., 43 Broad Street, Suite 419, New York, NY 10004.

WHITE, ELLA FLOWERS
Educator. **PERSONAL:** Born Apr 26, 1941, Blakely, GA; married Joseph Earl White; children: Derek, Dineen. **EDUCATION:** Morris Brown Coll, attended 1959-61; Kean Coll Union NJ, BA 1970; Seton Hall Univ, MEd 1977. **CAREER:** Newark Bd of Educ, teacher 1970-87. **ORGANIZATIONS:** Mem NJ Educ Assoc, Newark Teachers Assoc 1970-, 13th Ave School PTA 1971-; co-chair Black History Comm 1983-; chairperson Delta Comm Awds Brunch 1983; co-chairperson Natl Jr Honor Soc 1984-; parliamentarian Delta Sigma Theta Sor Inc 1985-87. **HONORS/ACHIEVEMENTS:** Appreciation Awd, Teacher of the Month 13th Ave Sch PTA 1982. **HOME ADDRESS:** 1230 E 7th, Plainfield, NJ 07062. **BUSINESS ADDRESS:** Basic Skills Instructor, Newark Board of Education, Thirteenth Ave School, Newark, NJ 07062.

WHITE, ERNEST G.
Businessman. **PERSONAL:** Born Dec 12, 1946, Dayton, OH; married Mae Charlotte Lampkins; children: Yvette M White Ransan, Letika, Charika. **EDUCATION:** Central State Univ, BS 1968; Gen Motors Dealer Devel Acad Univ of Detroit, 1973-75. **CAREER:** George White Oldsmobile, vp/gen mgr 1974-80; Ernest White Ford-Lincoln-Mercury, chief exec. **ORGANIZATIONS:** Mem Minority Dealer Operation; mem Kiwanis Delaware, OH Chpt; Frontier Intl; Operation PUSH; C of C; bd dir Black Ford-Lincoln-Mercury; natl bd dir Black Ford-Lincoln & Mercury Dealer Assn Great Lake Region. **HONORS/ACHIEVEMENTS:** Outstanding New and Used Car Minority Operation 1980; Recogn from Governor for 3rd highest volume in sales minority in state of OH 1980-85; Truck Leadership Award for Ford in zone 1982; Outstanding Business Award for Delaward Comm 1983; Dealer with Direction Award from Ford Motor Co (Dealer Dev) 1984; Black Consumer Goods of the Year 1984; Lincoln and Mercury Cent Reg Linchpin Award (Breakthrough Soc 8%) 1984; Top 100 Businessmen in Nation (Black Enterprise Mag) 1984; First and only second generation Black new car dealer in America. **BUSINESS ADDRESS:** Chief Executive Officer, Ernest White Ford Lincoln, 1599 Columbus Pike, Delaware, OH 43015.

WHITE, FRANK, JR.
Athlete. **PERSONAL:** Born Sep 04, 1950, Greenville, MS; married Gladys; children: Frank III, Terrance, Adrianne, Courtney. **CAREER:** KS City Royals, infielder 1973-. **HONORS/ACHIEVEMENTS:** Played in AL Championship Series 1976-78; received 7 Gold Glove Awds; named 2nd Baseman Sporting News AL All Star Fielding Team 1977-79; named 2nd BasemanSporting News AL All Star Team 1978; Played in 5 All Star Games; Championship Series 1976,77,78,80,81,84, World Series 1980; AL Record for Second Baseman; 4 Time All Star; received a Special Awd at the 11th Annual Kansas City Baseball Awds Dinner to recognize achievements in career with Royals 1981; Royals Player of the Year 1983,86; Casey Stengal League was renamed the "Frank White League" in 1985; selected to All Star Team that toured Japan 1986; named to the Sporting News AL Silver Slugger team 1986. **BUSINESS ADDRESS:** Kansas City Royals, PO Box 1969, Kansas City, MO 64141.

WHITE, FRANKIE WALTON
Attorney. **PERSONAL:** Born Sep 08, 1945, Yazoo City, MS; children: Carlyle Creswell. **EDUCATION:** Tougaloo Coll, BA (Magna Cum Laude) 1966; Univ of CA at Los Angeles, MA 1967; Univ of MS, JD 1975. **CAREER:** Fisk Univ, instructor of english 1967-69; Wellesley Coll, lecturer in english 1969-70; Tougaloo Coll, asst prof of english 1970-71; Syracuse Univ, asst dir of financial aid 1971-72; Central MS Legal Svcs, staff atty 1975-77; State of MS, spec asst atty general 1977; TX Southern Univ, student legal counselor 1977-79; State of MS, asst atty general 1979-. **ORGANIZATIONS:** Mem Alpha Kappa Alpha Sor Inc 1964-; mem Magnolia, Mississippi Bar Assocs 1975-; mem The Links Inc 1977-; mem Commission of Colleges Southern Assoc ofColls & Schools 1982-. **HONORS/ACHIEVEMENTS:** Woodrow Wilson Fellow; Reginald Heber Smith Comm Lawyer Fellow; First Black Woman to be apptd Special Asst Attorney General 1977 and Asst Attorney Gen-

eral 1986; Women of Achievement Awd in Law & Govt Women for Progress of Mississippi Inc 1981; Distinguished Alumni Citation NAFEO 1986. **BUSINESS ADDRESS:** Asst Attorney General, State of Mississippi, P O Box 220, Jackson, MS 39205.

WHITE, FREDERIC PAUL, JR.
Educator. **PERSONAL:** Born Feb 12, 1948, Cleveland, OH; son of Frederic and Ella; married Dierdre Cheryl Gainey; children: Alfred Davis, Michael Lewis. **EDUCATION:** Columbia Coll New York, BA, 1970; Columbia Law School New York, JD, 1973. **CAREER:** Squire Sanders & Dempsey, assoc attny, 1973-78; Cleveland State Univ, asst professor, 1978-81, assoc prof, 1981-86, prof, 1986. **ORGANIZATIONS:** Mem, bd of trustees, Cleveland Legal Aid Soc, 1981-84, Trinity Cathedral Comm Devel Fund, 1981-; pres, Norman S Minor Bar Assn, 1984; acting judge & referee, Shaker Heights Municipal Court, 1984-; mem, Omega Psi Phi Fraternity Inc, Zeta Omega Chapter; host, CSU City Focus radio show, 1981-85; bd of advisors, African-Amer Museum, 1986-. **HONORS/ACHIEVEMENTS:** Book, "Ohio Landlord Tenant Law," Banks-Baldwin Law Publ Co, 1984; 2 law review articles, "Cleveland Housing Ct," "Ohio Open Meeting Law"; Contrib Author Antieau's Local Govt Law; co-author chapts "Criminal Procedure Rules for Cleveland Housing Ct"; Frequent guest on local TV/radio landlord-tenant law subjects; contributing editor, Powell on Real Property. **BUSINESS ADDRESS:** Professor of Law, Cleveland State University, 1801 Euclid Ave, Cleveland, OH 44115.

WHITE, GARLAND ANTHONY
Physician. **PERSONAL:** Born Dec 09, 1932, Alexandria, LA. **EDUCATION:** Fisk Univ 1950-55; Meharry Med Coll, 1955-59; intern Geo Hubbard Hosp 1959-60; resd Kaiser Hosp 1963-65. **CAREER:** Permanente Med Group, physician 1965-. **ORGANIZATIONS:** Fisk Jubilee Singers 1952-54; life mem NAACP; Golden State Med Soc; Alpha Phi Alpha. **HONORS/ACHIEVEMENTS:** Who's Who Among Students in Amer Univs & Colls 1953-54; AMA Physicians Recog Awd 1975; Cert of Achievement 1962. **MILITARY SERVICE:** AUS mc capt 1960-62. **BUSINESS ADDRESS:** Permanente Med Group, 1515 Newell Ave, Walnut Creek, CA 94596.

WHITE, GARY LEON
Company chief executive. **PERSONAL:** Born Dec 17, 1932, Windsor, Ontario, Canada;son of George White and Louella White; married Inge Topper; children: Karen, Janet, Gary, Christopher, Steffanie. **EDUCATION:** Univ of MD; Wayne State Univ; Carnegie Mellen Univ, Pittsburgh Grad School of Indus Administration, 1980. **CAREER:** Cobo Hall, convention, 1960-64; The Jam Handy Org, assoc prod 1964-65; Tom Thomas Orgn, exec vice pres & general mgr, 1965-70; The White Assoc Inc, pres 1970-75; Ford Motor Co, mgr; City of Detroit, dir public info, 1975-77; Jones Transfer Co, chmn, CEO. **ORGANIZATIONS:** mem, bd of dir, Natl Minority Business Campaign, Metro Affairs Corp, United Way, Monroe MI, Monroe High School Scholarship Fund, Natl Minority Enterprise Legal Defense Fund, Greater Detroit Interfaith Round Table of the Natl Conf of Christians & Jews, Boysville of Michigan, Nation Assn of Black Automotive Suppliers; NAACP; mem, advisory bd, Liberty Mutual Ins Co, African Devel Found; mem, regional advisory council, Small Business Admin; mem, bd of govs, Michigan Trucking Assn; mem, Jobs & Economic Devel Task Force, Detroit Strategic Planning Project, mem, Minority Economic Devel Comm, Communications Comm, Amer Trucking Assn. **HONORS/ACHIEVEMENTS:** Testimonial resolution, Detroit City Council; State of MI (Governor) State Senate, State House Resolutions; Outstanding Serv, Corp Coordinator, NMSDC; Concurrent Resolution, Michigan Legislature, 1987; Certificate of Special Tribute, Governor, State of Michigan, 1987; Letter of Commendation, Pres Ronald Reagan, 1987; Black Enterprise Magazine Top 100, 1988. **MILITARY SERVICE:** USAF nco 1952-57. **BUSINESS ADDRESS:** Chairman, Trans Jones Inc, 300 Jones Ave, Monroe, MI 48161.

WHITE, GEORGE
Dentist. **PERSONAL:** Born May 19, 1934, Houston Co, GA; son of Robert White Sr and Lula Woolfork White; married Delores Foster; children: Terrilynn, George Jr, Miriam L. **EDUCATION:** Florida A&M Univ, BA 1956; Meharry Med Coll, DDS 1963. **CAREER:** Private Practice, dentist Bell Glade FL. **ORGANIZATIONS:** Mem Amer Dental Assn, Natl Dental Assn, FL Dental Assn, Atlantic Coast Dist Soc, T Leroy Jefferson Med Soc, FL Med Dental Pharm Assn; mem Bell Glade C of C; Deacon St John 1st Baptist. **HONORS/ACHIEVEMENTS:** Oral Surgery Honor Student; mem Soc of Upper Tenth of Meharry Med Coll; Cert of Honor Comm Serv FL A&M Univ Alumni Chap Palm Beach. **MILITARY SERVICE:** AUS 1st lt 1956-58.

WHITE, GEORGE W.
Federal judge. **PERSONAL:** Born 1931. **EDUCATION:** Baldwin-Wallace Coll, attended 1948-51; Cleveland-Marshall Coll of Law, JD 1955. **CAREER:** Cleveland pvt practice, 1956-68; Ct Common Please OH, judge 1968-80; US Dist Court OH, judge 1980-. **ORGANIZATIONS:** Mem ABA, Fed Bar Assn. **BUSINESS ADDRESS:** Federal Judge, Ohio Northern District, U S Courthouse, Cleveland, OH 44114.

WHITE, GLORIA WATERS
Personnel administrator. **PERSONAL:** Born May 16, 1934, St Louis, MO; daughter of James Thomas Waters and Thelma Brown Wrice; married Dr W Glenn, Jan 01, 1955; children: Terry Anita White. **EDUCATION:** Harris-Stowe Teachers Coll, BA 1956; Washington Univ, MA 1963, M of Juridical Studies 1980. **CAREER:** St Louis Pub Sch Sys, elem tchr 1956-63; St Louis Pub Sch Sys, secondary counselor 1963-67; Upward Bound Washington, DC, assoc dir 1967-68; Washington Univ, dir ofc spcl program projs 1968-74, asst v chancellor-personnel & affirm action 1974-80, assoc v chancellor-personnel & affirm action 1980-87; vice chancellor for Personnel and Affirmative Action Officer Washington Univ St. Louis, MO 1988-. **ORGANIZATIONS:** Vol comm fund drives, Arts & Educ, United Way, Heart Fund, Leukemia Dr 1969-87; bd dir Amer Assn for Affirm Action 1975-77; faculty/staff relation cncl Coll & Univ Personnel Assn 1978-80; vice pres Rsch & Publ Coll & Univ Personnel Assn 1980-84; desegration & monitoring comm Eastern Dist of MO 1981; Blue Cross Corporate Assemb 1984-87; bd dir St Louis Scholarship Found booster Urban League Scholarship Fund; pres elect Coll & Univ Personnel Assoc 1985-86; bd of trust Blue Cross & Blue Shield of MO 1985-90; pres Coll & Univ Personnel Assoc 1986-87; vice pres Delta Sigma Theta St. Louis Alumnae Chapter 1989; Advisory Bd Mem Teachers Insurance Annuity Assn 1988-90; Blue Cross-Blue Shield Bd of Trustees 1988-90. **HONORS/ACHIEVEMENTS:** Publ Affirm Action in Small Insts ERIC Microfiche Collect Rsch in Educ 1974; Outstanding Serv Awd Amer Assn for Affirm Action 1977; "White Bibliography of Human Resource Lit" compiled & edited for Coll & Univ Personnel Assn 1979; Creativity Awd CUPA 1981; "Bridge Over Troubled Waters, An Approach to Early Retirement" The Journal of the College & Univ Personnel Assn Vol 32 1981; "Personnel Program Appraisal Workbook" College & Univ Personnel Assn 1982; Who's Who Among Women 1983-84; Disting Serv Awd CUPA 1983; The World Who's Who of Women 1984,86; Who's Who Among Women 1985-86; Donald E. Dickason Coll and Univ Personnel Assn 1988. **BUSINESS ADDRESS:** Washington University, One Brookings Drive - Room 126, Box 1184, St Louis, MO 63130.

WHITE, GORDON E.
Attorney, law enforcement. **PERSONAL:** Born Feb 13, 1935, Guthrie, OK; married La Phern Harmon; children: Gordon M, Christopher D. **EDUCATION:** St Benedicts Coll, BS Biol 1955; Univ of Houston Law Ctr 1975-78. **CAREER:** Federal Law Enforcement Officer, asst spec agent in charge 1960-. **ORGANIZATIONS:** Mem NAACP 1965-, Natl Assoc of Black Narcotic Agents 1978-, TX State Bar 1978-, Amer Bar Assoc 1978-. **MILITARY SERVICE:** USAF 1st lt 1958-60. **HOME ADDRESS:** 218 Tumblebrook, Slidell, LA 70463. **BUSINESS ADDRESS:** Asst Special Agent in Charge, Drug Enforcement Admin, 1661 Canal St #220, New Orleans, LA 70112.

WHITE, GRANVILLE C.
Business executive. **PERSONAL:** Born Apr 16, 1927, Tyronza, AR; married Daisy Pugh; children: Granvernet, Leeta, Maurice, Eugene, Kawanda, Vernard. **EDUCATION:** Coll 1 yr. **CAREER:** CBS Records, asso dir, art Rel & promo 28 yrs. **ORGANIZATIONS:** PUSH; Urban Leag; NATRA & various record orgn. **HONORS/ACHIEVEMENTS:** Billboard Pub Record Exec of Yr 1973; CBS Reg Pro Mgr of Yr 1972. **MILITARY SERVICE:** 1945-46. **BUSINESS ADDRESS:** CBS Records, The Tower Ste 301, Rolling Meadows, IL.

WHITE, GREGORY DURR
Retired educator. **PERSONAL:** Born Oct 13, 1908, Birmingham, AL; widowed; children: Eugene A, Roger A. **EDUCATION:** Fisk Univ, BA 1930; Northwestern Univ MusB 1940, MusM 1948. **CAREER:** Miles Coll, teacher 1930-47; Ullman High School, teacher 1947-70; Ramsay High School, teacher 1970-72; 6th Ave Baptist Ch, piano teacher, accompanist, choirdir 1955-84; Birmingham Public Schools, retired teacher. **ORGANIZATIONS:** Advisory Bd, YWCA, 1976-80; Natl Assn of Negro Musicians 1976; trustee AL Symphony Orchestra, 1977-80; Adv Bd, Positive maturity, 1977-82; AAUW, 1978, NAACP, Urban League. **HONORS/ACHIEVEMENTS:** Mem Alpha Kappa Alpha 1930-; Mother of the Year UNCF 1977; Golden Sor 1980; Outstanding Artist Awd Zeta Phi Beta 1975; Alpha Pi Chi Music & Religion Awd 1977; Cited by City of Birmingham & AL Sen for serv to the people of the gr Birmingham area through contribs to the cultural life of the community 1977; Serv Awd St Mark Christian Meth Episcopal Ch 1977; Hon Mem 6th Ave Baptist Church for dedicated serv as organist & choir dir 1977; Omega Psi Phi Serv Awd 1983; inducted as a mem AL Voter Hall of FAme 1986.

WHITE, H. MELTON
Dentist. **PERSONAL:** Born Oct 02, 1924, Chester, SC; son of Robert E White and Sarah S White; married Berthenia Stephens; children: 2. **EDUCATION:** St Augustine's Clge, BS 1949; Meharry Med Clge, DDS 1956. **CAREER:** Private Practice, dentist. **ORGANIZATIONS:** Mem Amer Dental Assc; mem Natl Dental Assc; mem Phi Beta Sigma Frat; 1st Black amitted FL Dental Assc Dade Co FL. **MILITARY SERVICE:** AUS capt; USAR col retired. **BUSINESS ADDRESS:** 4800 NW 7th Ave, Miami, FL 33127.

WHITE, HAROLD CLARK MITCHELLE
Military educator. **PERSONAL:** Born Feb 24, 1948, Temple, TX; married Lonnetta E Wade; children: Mitch II. **EDUCATION:** St Mary's Univ San Antonio, BA 1974; Peabody Coll of Vanderbilt Univ, MEd 1981. **CAREER:** USAF, various positions in counseling law enforcement and administration 1969-81; Rome Air Develop Ctr, chief security police 1981-83; USAF Acad, instructorfreshman eng 1983-84; USAF Acad Prep School, dir counseling & student develop 1984-87; USAF Systems Cannal Inspector, chief security 1987-. **ORGANIZATIONS:** Mem Air Force Assoc 1977-, Assoc of Black Psychologists 1985-, Amer Assoc of Counseling & Develop 1986, Rocky Mountain Assoc of Coll Admissions Counselors 1986, Alpha Phi Alpha Frat Inc 1986-. **HONORS/ACHIEVEMENTS:** USAF Acad Prep Co Grade Officer of the Year 1986. **MILITARY SERVICE:** USAF capt 17 yrs; 2 Meritorious Serv Awds, 2 Commendation Medals, Achievement Medal. **BUSINESS ADDRESS:** Dir Counseling/Student Develop, USAF Acad Preparatory School, USAF Academy/PLC, Colorado Springs, CO 80840.

WHITE, HAROLD ROGERS
Retired educator. **PERSONAL:** Born Jun 03, 1923, Durham, NC; son of Dr John L and Nora B; married Estelle Marie Brown; children: Darryl M, Constance A, John W. **EDUCATION:** Johnson C Smith Univ, BS 1942; Univ of Buffalo, Grad Certificate 1951 & MSS 1953; Univ of Pittsburgh, attended 1965, doctoral studies. **CAREER:** Travelers Aid Soc of Buffalo, caseworker 1951-57; Buffalo Urban League, dir group work dept 1953-56; USO/Travelers Aid, exec dir 1953; Buffalo Youth Bd, youth proj coord 1956-61; Hollidaysburg State Hosp, dir social serv dept 1961-64; Grad School of Social Work Univ of Pittsburgh, field asst prof 1964-69; WV Univ Sch of Social Work, assoc prof of social work 1969-89. Now Emeritus Status. **ORGANIZATIONS:** Mem bd of contributing editors Child Welfare League of Amer 1980-83; mem bd of dirs Natl Conf on Social Welfare 1979-82; mem West Virginia Univ Comm on Alcohol 1983-; sec bd dirs West Virginia Univ Employees Credit Union 1983-89; chair elected 1986 Behavioral Health Adv Cncl West Virginia Dept of Health 1981-88; bd mem & pres Monongalia Co Assoc for Mental Health 1982-86; bd mem Scotts Run Settlement House 1979-83; mem Comm on Self-Develop Help for People 1984-89; bd mem West Virginia State Mental Health Assoc; faculty advisor Undergrad of Alpha Phi Alpha; mem West Virginia Univ Affirmative Action Comm; faculty advisory council West Virginia Univ Black Cultural Center; bd mem Fraternal Order of Police Associates; life mem Assoc Ed to the Sphinx; charter mem Acad of Certified Soc Workers and Natl Assoc of Soc Workers, Council on Soc Work Educ; mem session, First Presbyterian Church; mem Minority Scholarship Comm of Synod of The Trinity, Pennsylvania, West Virginia. **HONORS/ACHIEVEMENTS:** Meritorious Serv Pittsburgh Pan Hellenic Assn 1969; Outstanding Teacher WV Univ 1975-76; Humanitarian Awd Dale Carnegie Assoc Altoona PA 1963; Sabbatical Leave Grant Sun Petroleum Prods Corp 1978; comm service awards 1986, 1987, 1989 Fraternal Order of Police; published article in Arete, Vol 13 Winter 1988 Number 2 of Journal College of Social Work,

Univ of South Carolina Titled: "Pros And Cons of Student Placements with Employers". **MILITARY SERVICE:** AUS pvt 7 1/2 months medical discharge 1945.

WHITE, IDA MARGARET (IDA KILPATRICK JONES)
Government official. **PERSONAL:** Born Aug 01, 1924, Atlanta, GA; married Luther Randolph (dec) (deceased); children: Victor A Jones, Russell C Jones. **EDUCATION:** Spelman Coll Atlanta, AB (Summa Cum Laude) 1945; Atlanta Univ, MA Sociology 1946; Fed Exec Inst, attended 1973; Brookings Inst, attended 1979. **CAREER:** New York City Dept Welfare, case work supr 1958-61; Dept HUD NY Regional Office, dir relocation 1966-70; Dept HUD NY Area Office, dir housing mgmt 1970-74; Cleveland Dept Community Devel, dep dir 1974-77; Cleveland City Council, exec asst to pres 1977-78; Dept HUD Richmond Office, mgr; HUD Washington DC, mgr. **ORGANIZATIONS:** Guest lectr Practicing Law Inst 1970; lectr NYU 1971; lectr Cleveland State Univ 1976; lectr Case Western Reserve & Kent State Univ 1977; lectr Builders Inst at VPI; mem Amer Soc Pub Adminstrn; past mem bd Eliza Bryant Home for the Aged Kathryn Tyler Neighborhood Center; Real Property Inventory; Neighborhood Housing Svcs. **HONORS/ACHIEVEMENTS:** 1st Black Woman NY Area Office Dept HUD 1970-74; Award Salute to Black Clevelanders The Greater Cleveland Interchurch Cncl & Cleveland Call & Post 1979. **BUSINESS ADDRESS:** Manager, Dept Housing Urban Dev, 451 7th St SW, Washington Field Office, Washington, DC 20410.

WHITE, J. ARTHUR
Clergyman. **PERSONAL:** Born Oct 20, 1903, Clover, SC; married Sara Williams McClain; children: Patrick Gordon, Dennis Gregory, Marshall Brady. **EDUCATION:** Friendship Jr Clge, AA, BTh, DD; Johnson C Smith Univ, AB; Teamers Sch qof Religion, BD SE Sem, further study. **CAREER:** Shiloh Inst Bapt Ch, pastor 1953-; Mt Calvary Bapt Ch 1941-53; prin & elem Sch 1929-45. **ORGANIZATIONS:** Pres Mt Peace SS & Bapt Training Union Cong; moderator Mt Peace Missionary Bapt Assc; mem Amer & Natl Bapt Conv; exec bd mem Bapt SS Congress; Lott Caret Foreign Missionary Conv; past pres Minister's Conf; bd mem Natl Conf Christians & Jews; family Srv; YMCA; NAACP; mem Cham of Comm; Young Dem Club; Johnson C Smith Univ Alumni Assc; Council of Churches. **HONORS/ACHIEVEMENTS:** Recipt numerous awards & citations; listed in Personalities of the South Men of Achievement.

WHITE, JAMES LOUIS, JR.
Telephone company executive. **PERSONAL:** Born Jul 14, 1949, Charlottesville, VA; son of James Louis White and Myrtle Virginia Garland White; married Cynthia Phina Austin, Jun 29, 1973; children: James Louis III, Charles Marquas, Matthew David. **EDUCATION:** St Paul's Coll, Lawrenceville VA, BS 1973; Univ of Kansas, Lawrence KS, certificate 1982; Univ of Pennsylvania, Philadelphia PA, certificate 1982; attending Florida State Univ, Tallahassee FL. **CAREER:** Centel Telephone, div & dist eng in Charlottesville VA, 1973-74, dist mgr & personnel mgr in Des Plaines IL, 1974-75, asst staff mgr in Chicago IL, 1975-77, asst customer service mgr at Florida state operation, 1977-79, gen customer staff mgr in Chicago, 1979-84, gen customer service mgr at Florida state operation, 1984-88; Centel Cellular, FL, regional vice pres, 1988-. **ORGANIZATIONS:** Mem, Chamber of Commerce & Economic Club, 1985-89; pres, Big Ben Independent Telephone Pioneer Assn, 1988; mem of bd of dir, Dick Howser Center for Cerebral Palsy & Florida Special Olympics, 1989. **HONORS/ACHIEVEMENTS:** Author of article "Centel Puts Prewiring Costs Where They Belong," Team magazine, August 15, 1980. **BUSINESS ADDRESS:** Regional Vice President, Centel Cellular Company, 1801 N Meridian, Suite B, Tallahassee, FL 32303.

WHITE, JAMES S.
Attorney. **PERSONAL:** Born Jan 08, 1930, Beaumont, TX; married Dolores; children: James, Jr. **EDUCATION:** JD 1966. **CAREER:** Atty pvt prac. **ORGANIZATIONS:** Past pres Charles Houston Law Club; pres Lawyers Club of Alameda Co; bd dir Alameda Co Bar Assc; chmn State Bar Subcom; bar Examiner Hearings; past chmn bd dir Men of Tomorrow & Minority Adoption Com Childrens Home Soc; past pres Commnr Oakland Civil Srv Commn 1969-73. **MILITARY SERVICE:** USN 1948-51. **BUSINESS ADDRESS:** 4705 Grove St, Oakland, CA 94608.

WHITE, JAVIER A.
Attorney. **PERSONAL:** Born May 02, 1945, Limon, Costa Rica;married Rene M; children: Naomi N, Javier R. **EDUCATION:** Columbia Univ Law Sch, attd 1971; Princeton Univ 1967. **CAREER:** h. **ORGANIZATIONS:** Mem NY Co Lawyers Assc; NY State Bar Assc; mem Assc of Black Princeton Alumni; bd mem Washington Heights Inwood Devel Corp; Sch Com of Princeton Univ. **BUSINESS ADDRESS:** Attorney at Law, Sterns, Hinds & White, PC, 209 West 125th St, New York, NY 10027.

WHITE, JERIS
Professional athlete. **PERSONAL:** Born Sep 03, 1952, Ft Worth, TX. **EDUCATION:** Hawaii, BA Bus Adminstrn. **CAREER:** Wash Redskins, crnrbck 1980-; Miami Dolphins; Tampa Bay Buccaneers. **ORGANIZATIONS:** Licensed Securities Dealer; Licensed Real Estate Agent. **BUSINESS ADDRESS:** NFL Players Association, 1300 Connecticut Ave NW, Ste 407, Washington, DC 20036.

WHITE, JESSE C., JR.
State representative. **PERSONAL:** Born Jun 23, 1934, Alton, IL. **EDUCATION:** Alabama State Coll, BS 1957; North Texas State Univ, graduate work 1966. **CAREER:** Isham Memorial YMCA, physical ed dir 1955-74; Jenner School, teacher 1959-63; Schiller Elem School, teacher 1963-; Illinois General Assembly, state representative 1975-77 and 1979-; consultant, Chicago Bd of Educ, 1989-. **ORGANIZATIONS:** Coach Jesse White Tumbling Team, 1959; scoutmaster Boy Scouts of America 1967; consultant Northside Service Center 1975-; member Elem & Secondary Ed Comm Assembly 1975-; chairman Human Serv Comm, Il General Assembly 1983-; member Public Utilities 1985-; mem, Personnel & Pensions Comm; mem, Select Comm on aging; mem, Select Comm on Children. **HONORS/ACHIEVEMENTS:** Most Dedicated Teacher Citizen's School Committee 1969; Excellence in Education Superintendent of Public Instruction 1974; Outstanding Legislator of the Year Illinois Hospital Assn 1984; Partner in Building Better Communities Gov James R Thompson 1985; Legislator of the Year Child Care Assn Cycle, Comm Service Award, 1987; Excellence in Public Service, Illinois Hospital Assn, 1987. **MILITARY SERVICE:** AUS 101st Airborne 1957-59. **HOME ADDRESS:** 300 W Hill #714, Chicago, IL 60610. **BUSINESS ADDRESS:** Representative Dist 8, Illinois Gen Assembly, Room 2105 Stratton Bldg, Springfield, IL 62706.

WHITE, JIMMIE L.
Educator & scientist. **PERSONAL:** Born Dec 13, 1920, Texarkana, AR; married Vanilla Ruth Potter; children: Jimmie L, Robert M, Clarice G White Wiggins, Mary Ann White Phifer, Paul H. **EDUCATION:** Arkansas AM&N College, BS 1943; Michigan State Univ, MS 1947. **CAREER:** Southern Univ, instructor & head of dairy 1947-48; Langston Univ, professor of Animal Science 1949-. **ORGANIZATIONS:** Member and clerk Langston Board of Ed 1956-68; executive dir Town of Langston Housing Authority 1971-76; member Logan County Planning Comm 1973-78; exec dir Langston Senior Citizen Organ 1973-80; member board of dir Langston Univ Dev Found; treasurer Town of Langston; member and sec of credit committee Langston Federal Credit Union. **HONORS/ACHIEVEMENTS:** Life Mem Alpha Phi Alpha Frat Inc; Life Mem AR AM&N (UAPB) Natl Alumni Assn. **MILITARY SERVICE:** AUS Pfc 1943-46; Good Conduct Medal.

WHITE, JO JO
Athlete. **PERSONAL:** Born Nov 16, 1946, St Louis, MO. **EDUCATION:** KS 1969. **CAREER:** Boston Celtics, player 1969-79; Golden State, player 1979. **HONORS/ACHIEVEMENTS:** Player All Star Team 1970-77; US Gold Medal Olympic Bsktbl Team 1968; 2 NBA World Champ Teams; MVP Playoffs 1976; 13th All-Time NBA Scorer (13546 pts) selected by Dallas Cowboys NFL. **BUSINESS ADDRESS:** c/o Golden State Warriors, Oakland, CA 94621.

WHITE, JOHN CLINTON
Journalist. **PERSONAL:** Born May 05, 1942, Baltimore, MD; married Elaine B; children: Anthony C, David E. **EDUCATION:** Morgan State Univ, BS 1970. **CAREER:** The WA Star, staff writer 1972-; The Evening Sun, reptr 1969-72; The Balt Afro-Amer, reptr 1969; WJZ-TV, news prdcr/Wrtr 1968-69. **ORGANIZATIONS:** Treas Assc of Blk Media Wkrs 1975-77; mng ed The Spokesman Morgan State Univ 1969-70. **HONORS/ACHIEVEMENTS:** Grp W Award completion of Westinghouse Broadcasting Int prog 1968. **MILITARY SERVICE:** USAF 1961-64. **BUSINESS ADDRESS:** 225 Virginia Ave SE, Washington, DC 20061.

WHITE, JOHN F.
Design developer. **PERSONAL:** Born Jun 09, 1924, Berlin, MD; married Sylvia; children: John, Jr, Michael. **EDUCATION:** Bowie State, BS 1943; Univ of PA Fel Inst of Govt, atnd 1970. **CAREER:** Co Store Product Co, new design devel; Rice-Bayersdorfer Co, gen supt pub rel ofcr. **ORGANIZATIONS:** Pres Philadelphia Co Bd of Pub Asst 1970-; mem & Pres Men of Encounter 1968-; pres Black Polit Forum 1968-; NAACP. **HONORS/ACHIEVEMENTS:** Recept Man of Year YMCA 1975; Acad of Human Serv Award 1975; Comm Serv Award 1974. **BUSINESS ADDRESS:** 200 Park Ave, Warminster, PA 18974.

WHITE, JOHN LEE
Educational administrator. **PERSONAL:** Born Jul 23, 1962, Charleston, SC; married Carmen Montgomery. **EDUCATION:** Washington & Lee Univ, BA 1974; Radford Univ, MS 1976; Washington & Lee School of Law, JD 1985. **CAREER:** Radford Univ, admissions counselor 1974-75; Charleston Cty Public Schools, counselor 1975-76; Trident Tech Coll, devel coord 1976-84; Washington & Lee Univ, dir minority affairs 1979-85; Knoxville Coll, asst to pres 1985-86; Allen Univ, dir of admissions 1987-. **ORGANIZATIONS:** Consult Creative Vibrations Norfolk VA 1980; appt comm computerized career ed Gov of SC 1976; consult Chas YWCA 1978; Black Students at Wash & Lee, Wash & Lee Ofc of Publ 1979; special consultant KC Alumni Counsel 1985; bd of dirs Wilkinson & Perry Philadelphia PA 1985. **HONORS/ACHIEVEMENTS:** Special Appreciation Awd Knoxville Optimist Club 1985. **HOME ADDRESS:** 2705 Ashley Ferry, Charleston, SC 29407.

WHITE, JUNE JOYCE
Retired correctional officer. **PERSONAL:** Born Feb 25, 1949, Flushing, NY; daughter of Marion Luther Hampton and Jean Dolores DeVega Hampton; married James R White, Dec 01, 1984; children: Wenty Morris III, Ellie Morris, Mario St John, Lena White, James White. **EDUCATION:** Attended Queens Coll, Flushing NY, 1969-71; NYC Health & Hosp, New York NY, respiratory therapy certificate, 1973; New Mexico Corrections Academy, Santa Fe NM, certified officer, 1983; received numerous law enforcement educational conference certificates, 1985-. **CAREER:** New York City Hospital Police, New York NY, police officer, 1973-74; Jamaica Hospital, Jamaica NY, respiratory therapist, 1975-76; Brunswick Hospital, Amityville NY, respiratory therapist, 1978-83; New Mexico State Corrections, Central NM Corrections Facility, Los Lunas NM, officer until 1983, lieutenant 1984-88. **ORGANIZATIONS:** Mem, NAACP, 1969-; mem, NM Correctional Workers Assn, 1983-88; consultant, NM Multi Investors, 1983-; pres, Black Officers Assn of NM, 1983-; mem, NM Special Needs Children, 1984-; NM delegate, Natl Black Police Assn, 1985-; pres, Rio Rancho Human Rights Commission, 1988-; chair, NAACP Educ Comm, 1988; chair, Natl Black Police Southern Region Conference, 1988; mem, Comm in Defense of Human Rights in the Workplace, 1988-; mem, Amer Correctional Assn. **HONORS/ACHIEVEMENTS:** Editor, NM Law Enforcement Journal, 1983-; panelist, "Women Officers, Rewards & Regrets," Natl Black Police, 1986; founder, Outstanding Service Black Officers of NM, 1986; Joseph "Tree Top" Turner Achievement Award, Natl Black Police Assn, 1987; Guardian of the Treasury, Governors Office, 1988; TV special "Blacks in Law Enforcement: Racism & Sexism," 1988; 4th culture TV special "History of Black Officers Assn NM," 1988; Award of Excellence, Black Officers Assn of NM, 1989. **HOME ADDRESS:** 2379 Lema Rd, Rio Rancho, NM 87124.

WHITE, KATIE KINNARD
Educator. **PERSONAL:** Born Feb 28, 1932, Franklin, TN; daughter of Arthur Kinnard and Era Smith Kinnard; married Joseph White, Jun 29, 1963; children: Joletta, Angela. **EDUCATION:** Tennessee State Univ, Nashville, BS 1952, MS 1959; attended Eastern Michigan Univ, Ypsilanti, 1961; attended George Peabody Coll, Nashville TN, 1965; Walden Univ, Naples FL, PhD 1976. **CAREER:** Bedford County Schools, Shelbyville TN, teacher 1952-53; Shelbyville City Schools, Shelbyville TN, teacher 1953-59; Nashville City Schools, Nashville TN, teacher 1959-62; Tennessee State Univ, Nashville TN, prof of sci educ 1962-70, prof of biophysical science and coordinator of teacher educ for biology, 1970-. **ORGANIZATIONS:** Mem, Imperial Club 1962-, Carondelet Civic Assn 1972-, Natl Assn of Biology

Teachers 1972-, Natl Council of Negro Women 1980-, NAACP 1980-; life mem, Alumni Assn of Tenn State Univ 1968-, Tenn Acad of Science 1970-; honorary advisory board mem, Amer Biographical Inst 1982-89; public educ co-chair, Assault on Illiteracy Program 1988; natl pres (Grand Basileus), Sigma Gamma Rho 1988-. **HONORS/ACHIEVEMENTS:** Outstanding Service Award, Sigma Gamma Rho, 1964 & 1976; citation, Outstanding Young Women of Amer, 1965; Teacher of the Year, Tenn State Univ, 1975; listed in "Salute to Business & Professional Women," Dollars & Sense, 1989; listed among 100 Most Influential Blacks, Ebony, 1989; author of articles "The Maturation of Biology as a Science" 1965, and "The Place of Biology in Family of Human Knowledge" 1971, both in Tenn State Univ Faculty Journal; co-author of books Learning About Living Things for the Elementary School, and Learning About Our Physical World for the Elementary School, both 1966, and A Laboratory Manual for the Biophysical Sciences, 1981. **HOME ADDRESS:** 9007 Oden Ct, Brentwood, TN 37027.

WHITE, KERMIT EARLE
Dentist. **PERSONAL:** Born Jul 15, 1917, New York City, NY; married Loretta Bagwell; children: Kermit Eston. **EDUCATION:** Shaw Univ Raleigh NC, BS 1937; Meharry Med Clge Nashville TN, DDS 1950. **CAREER:** Elizabeth City NC, dentist pvt prac 1952; Craven Co Bd of Educ, h s sci tchr 1940-41; Beaufort Count Bd of Educ, hs sci & math tchr 1937-40. **ORGANIZATIONS:** Secr/Treas Old N State Dental Soc 19757-75; secr Eastern NC Med Dental & Pharm Soc 1957-; pres Old N State Dental Soc 1976-77; mem Omega Psi Phi Frat Inc 1935; pres Elizabeth City Civic Improvement Assc 1960-67; mem Elizabeth City State Univ Bd of Trustees 1967-; chmn Corner Stone Missionary BaptCh Trustee Bd 1968-79; mem 1st black Elizabeth City Pasquotank Bd of Educ 1973-; mem past chmn Elizabeth City State Univ Bd of Trustees 1976-; chmn Elizabeth Pasquotank Bd of Educ 1976-79; life mem Omega Psi Phi Frat Inc 1978. **HONORS/ACHIEVEMENTS:** Pres Unit Citation 3 Bronze Stars Pacific Campaign 1942-46; European Theater Medal 1949-52; Kappa Sigma Pi Hnry Soc Meharry Med Clge 1949; Omicron Kappa Upsilon Hnry Natl Dental Soc 1950; Meritorious Srv Award NC Joint Council on Health & Citizenship 1960; Dentist of Year Old North State Dental Soc 1970; Citizen of Year Omega Psi Phi Frat Delta Iota Chap 1973. **MILITARY SERVICE:** AUS 1st sgt 1942-46; Dental Corps capt 1949-52. **BUSINESS ADDRESS:** 504 Shepard St, Elizabeth City, NC 27909.

WHITE, LUTHER D.
Business executive. **PERSONAL:** Born Mar 09, 1937, Minden, LA; married Betty Jean Haynes; children: 8 Children. **CAREER:** D&H Tire Co, D&H Auto Mart, D&H Realty, owner & pres 1965-. **ORGANIZATIONS:** Life mem NAACP; mem Salem Bapt Church; chmn Deacon Bd; pres KS State Laymen's Movement; KC Chap Jr Achievement. **HONORS/ACHIEVEMENTS:** Recipt Outst Enterprising Businessmen Award 1972; Award Cham of Comm 1973; Seller of Year Award 1974; Black Enterprise Mag Top 100; World Christian Assc 1973. **BUSINESS ADDRESS:** President, D & H Tire Company, 919 Troup, Kansas City, KS 66104.

WHITE, LUTHER J.
Chief executive automotive dealership. **PERSONAL:** Born in Gary, IN; married Archousa Bobbie; children: Keith, Keddi, Eric, Alan, Scott. **EDUCATION:** Drake University. **CAREER:** Westfield Ford Inc, Westfield MA, owner & chief executive, 1989; Spencer Ford Co, Northfield MA, owner. **BUSINESS ADDRESS:** Westfield Ford Inc, 234 East Main St, Westfield, MA 01085. *

WHITE, MABLE
Real estate broker. **PERSONAL:** Born in Bastrop Co; married William E White. **EDUCATION:** Bus Clge. **CAREER:** RE Broker Wm E White's RE Co. **ORGANIZATIONS:** Pres Good St Missionary Soc; fin sec Dallas Assc RE Brokers; treas Zeta Amicae of Kappa Zeta Chap of Zeta Phi Beta; pest pres of Bus & Prof Women's Club; chmn Pub Educ of Amer Cancer Soc; mem bd dir Day Care Assc of Metro Dallas; Skyline Voc Sch fin secr LK Williams Inst Bishop Clge; life mem YWCA; Natl Council Negro Woman; Natl Assc Negro Bus & Prof Women; mem Woman's Aux Natl Bapt Convention; NAACP; Intergrated Citizens Grp. **HONORS/ACHIEVEMENTS:** Woman of Year 1965; Christian Srv Award Good St Bapt Ch; Natl Sojourner Truth Award; Bishop Clge Inst Award; Amer Cancer Award; other hnrs & awards. **BUSINESS ADDRESS:** 4211 S Oakland Ave, Dallas, TX 75215.

WHITE, MAJOR C.
Clergyman. **PERSONAL:** Born May 13, 1926, Muskogee, OK; married Rue Pearl Haynes; children: Major A, Marvin E, Maurice N. **EDUCATION:** Pacific Un Coll, BA 1948; Univ of Pacific, MA 1966. **CAREER:** Pastorates in Tucson 1948-51, Richmond CA 1951-61, Stockton CA 1961-68, Los Angeles 1968-70; San Jose, ch deptl dir 1970-71; Pacific Union Conf 7th Day Adventists, sec 1971-78; Glendale CA, exec sec 1979, church admin 1971-. **ORGANIZATIONS:** Contra Costa co No CA Easter Seal Soc 1954-61; chmn Contra Costa Co sheltered workshop 1956-57. **HONORS/ACHIEVEMENTS:** Who's Who Among Students in Amer Colls & Univs Pacific Union Coll 1948; Who's Who in Rel 1974. **BUSINESS ADDRESS:** Church Administrator, Pacific Union Conf of Seventh, Day Adventists, 2686 Townsgate Rd, Westlake Village, CA 91361.

WHITE, MARGARETTE PAULYNE MORGAN
Association executive. **PERSONAL:** Born Sep 11, 1934, Tattnall Co, GA; married Frank White; children: Lairalaine. **EDUCATION:** Reids Business Coll, diploma 1952; Morris Brown Coll, BA 1957; Univ of Toledo; Univ of TN. **CAREER:** Teacher, 1957-66; communications specialist, 1967-69; Morris Brown Coll, dir Public Relations; The Atlanta Enquirer, youth educ. **ORGANIZATIONS:** Natl PR dir Business & Professional Women's Assn, 1973; PR chmn Delta Sigma Theta; Guys & Dolls Inc; Amer Business Women; Atlanta Club Business & Professional Women; founder/pres Sparklers Inc; founder, Atlanta Jr Club; pres Gay G Club; Atlanta League of Women Voters. **HONORS/ACHIEVEMENTS:** Newspaper Fund Fellow; Wall St Journal Fellow; Leading Lady of Atlanta Assoc Editor The Atlanta Inquirer 1977; life mem, Award Journal Educ Assn; natl treas Natl Assc of Media Women; Delta Women Breaking New Ground Award; Appreciation Award Journalism Educ Assc; Best Youth Page Award NRPA.

WHITE, MARILYN MILDRED
Educator. **PERSONAL:** Born Jun 01, 1947, Newark, NJ. **EDUCATION:** Hampton Inst, BA Engl 1969; IN Univ, MA Folklore 1971; Univ of TX, attd 1973. **CAREER:** Western KY Univ, dir Afro-Amer studies & inst of folk studies 1977-; Central WA State Clge, instr of engl 1971-73. **ORGANIZATIONS:** Mem Amer Folklore Soc 1971-; mem Amer Anthrop Assc 1975-; mem exec bd Assc of African & African-Amer Folklorists 1975-; mem/Chap adv WKU Delta Sigma Theta Sorority 1969-; mem/Vice Pres AWARE Bowling Green KY 1977-; mem NAACP 1979-. **HONORS/ACHIEVEMENTS:** Recipt Flwshps So Flwshps Fund 1974-77; Research Grants Univ of TX 1975-76; elected to Mbrshp Phi Kappa Phi Natl Hon Soc 1977; pub "On Linguistic Sociocultural Legitimacy of Black Engl"; "WKU Faculty Research Bulletin" 1978. **BUSINESS ADDRESS:** Western Kentucky Univ, Bowling Green, KY 42101.

WHITE, MAURICE
Singer, songwriter. **PERSONAL:** Born Dec 19, 1941, Memphis, TN. **EDUCATION:** Chicago Conservatory Coll, Music. **CAREER:** Booker T & the MG's, drummer; Chess Records, musician; Chuck Berry, Jackie Wilson, Curtis Mayfield, The Dells, musician; Salty Peppers renmaed Earth Wind & Fire, formed the group; singer, songwriter. **HONORS/ACHIEVEMENTS:** #1 album "That's the Way of the World" featuring "Shining Star" 1975; 1 of top rhythm & blues bands in the country; 6 double platinum albums; 12 gold, 6 grammyrecords.

WHITE, MELVYN LEE
Business executive. **PERSONAL:** Born Sep 15, 1941, Winston-Salem, NC. **EDUCATION:** Rutgers Univ, 1976. **CAREER:** Century Natl Bank, pres chf exec ofcr 1976-; Natl Bank of Westchester, asst vice pres bd mgr 1964-76. **ORGANIZATIONS:** Mem Amer Bankers Assc; Natl Bankers Assc; FL Bankers Assc; Bank Admin Inst; Amer Inst of Banking; bd mem Golf Brook Day Ctr; bd mem & treas Valhalla NY Rotary Club 1968-69; Eastchester NY Rotary Club 1974-75; treas/Exec com mem Westchester Div of Amer Cancer Soc 1973-76; bd memUniv N FL Found; WJCT TV; Jacksonville Urban League; Cham of Comm; Amer Cancer Soc Natl Mental Hlth Assc; Comm Investment Coop; chmn Comm Econ Devel Cncl; mem Mayor's Overall Econ Devel Plan for Duval Co; Frontiers Intl; bd mem treas Hillcrest Ctr for Children 1969-70; bd dir New Rochelle JC's 1966-67; treas ML King Breakfast Com 1972-75; fin chmn Rep Campaign Com 1974. **MILITARY SERVICE:** AUS e5 1960-63. **BUSINESS ADDRESS:** 5859 Moncrief Rd, PO Box 2215, Jacksonville, FL 32209.

WHITE, MICHAEL REED
Elected official. **PERSONAL:** Born Aug 13, 1951, Cleveland, OH. **EDUCATION:** Ohio State, BA Educ 1973, M Public Admin 1974. **CAREER:** City of Cleveland, councilman 1977-84; Burks Elec Co, salesmanager 1982-85; Beehive & Doan Partnership, partner 1983-84; Burks Develop Corp, assoc 1984-85; OH Senate, senator 21st Dist OH. **ORGANIZATIONS:** Bd mem Cleveland Scholarship Prog 1981-85; bd mem Glenville Housing Found 1978-; bd mem Glenville Develop Corp 1978-; mem Glenville Festival Found,United Black Fund, Greater Cleveland Dome Corp, Royal Ridge-Pierce Found, Waterfront Devel Corp, Amers for Constitution Freedom-Univ Circle Inc. **HONORS/ACHIEVEMENTS:** Outstanding Man of Amer Who's Who in Amer 1979; Outstanding Young Leader Cleveland Jaycees 1979; Service Awd East Side Jaycees 1979; The Natl Assoc of Black Vet Cleveland Chap Outstanding Serv Awd 1985; Community Serv Awd of the East Side Jaycees.

WHITE, MIKE
Professional athlete. **PERSONAL:** Born Aug 11, 1957. **EDUCATION:** Albany State GA, attd. **CAREER:** Cincinnati Bengals, prof ftbl def lineman 1979-. **HONORS/ACHIEVEMENTS:** Clge Div All-Amer; Black All-Amer Pittsburgh Courier.

WHITE, NAN E.
Independent consultant. **PERSONAL:** Born Mar 15, 1931, Jacksonville, IL; daughter of Grace Cook; married Wilmer M White; children: Michael, Laforest, Livia. **EDUCATION:** Bradley Univ, BS, 1951; Wahington Univ, St Louis, MSW, 1955; attended, Chicago Univ School of Continuing Educ, 1964. **CAREER:** Family Children & Individual Serv Agencies, 1955-67; Childrens Serv of Greater St Louis, caseworker III and student supvr, 1967-68; Lincoln HS, East St Louis, school social worker, 1968-70; Annie Malone Children's Home, social work dir, therapist, 1970-78, exec dir, (retired 1978); Child Welfare, consultant, 1979-. **ORGANIZATIONS:** Mem, United Way Allocations Panel, 1978-88, Permanency Planning Review teams, St Louis Div of Family Serv, 1982-85; various voluntary serv for Amer Cancer Soc and St Louis Public School System including counseling pregnant teenagers, 1985-; mem, United Way Admissions Comm, 1989-. **HONORS/ACHIEVEMENTS:** Distinguished Serv Award 1976. **BUSINESS ADDRESS:** Child Welfare Consultant, Contract Serv Child Welfare Ag, 8412 Old Bonhomme Rd, University City, MO 63132.

WHITE, NATHANIEL B.
Retired companyexecutive. **PERSONAL:** Born Sep 14, 1914, Hertford, NC; son of George White and Annie Wood White; married Jean Briscoe; children: Nathaniel B Jr, Joseph M. **EDUCATION:** Hampton Inst, BS 1937. **CAREER:** Serv Printing Co Inc, pres/general mgr 1939-82; The Carolina Tribune, prod mgr 1937-39. **ORGANIZATIONS:** Past pres mem Exec Com Durham Business & Professional Chain; mem Natl Bus League; mem Durham Cham of Comm; mem exec com Durham Com of Affairs of Black People; chmn trustees White Rock Baptist Church; Scoutmaster 1942-68; mem bd trustees Durham Tech Inst 1965-; chmn Citizen Advisory Comm Workable Prog for Comm Improvement 1969-71. **HONORS/ACHIEVEMENTS:** Durham Housewives League Man of Year 1953; Silver Beaver Award BSA 1953; NC Hamptonian of Year 1956; City of Durham Recreation Award 1958; Civic Award Durham Com on Affairs of Black People 1971; Ann Serv Award Durham Branch NAACP 1978; Nathaniel B White Building at Dunham Technical Community Coll. **HOME ADDRESS:** 1501 S Alston Ave, Durham, NC 27707.

WHITE, O. C.
Director, manager. **PERSONAL:** Born Aug 26, 1932, Greenwood, MS. **EDUCATION:** Milwaukee Area Tech Clge, BS 1975; Univ of WI, M 1976. **CAREER:** Construction foreman 1952-62; WAWA-WLUM Radio Milwaukee, WAWA KACE Radio Los Angeles, KYOK-Houston, KQIN Seattle, corp vp; OC White Soul Club, dir fnd 1968-. **ORGANIZATIONS:** Bd dir BSA; exec bd Summerfest; mem NAACP St Matthew CME; chmn Milwaukee Metro Sewerage Dist. **HONORS/ACHIEVEMENTS:** Natra & Citation Award for Merit 1972; Man of Year of Milwaukee NAACP; Medgar Evers Award; Disc Jockey of Year 1964; Frontiers Man of Year 1974; Wilber Halyard Civic Award 1974; Hon Fire Chief 1974; Helped w/the conviction of over 500, Community Against Drug Pushers Program 1987.

BUSINESS ADDRESS: O C White Inc, 2212 N Dr Martin Luther King, Milwaukee, WI 53208.

WHITE, QUITMAN, JR.
Certified quality auditor. **PERSONAL:** Born Jun 27, 1945, Newellton, LA; son of Quitman White and Florida Lamay White; married Eula M Wiley, Aug 14, 1987; children: Alphonse White, Quitman White III, Heath Kyle Davis, Lenia Wiley, Eric J Wiley, Eric D Wiley. **EDUCATION:** Attended various colleges. **CAREER:** Chief inspector, machine operator, & set-up in plastics & metal industry, 1963-72; MoMac Div, Brearley Co, Rockford IL, QC mgr & safety dir, 1972-75; Anthony Co, Streator IL, QA mgr, 1975-76; Mardon Mfg, Ladd IL, QA mgr & safety dir, 1976; Babcock & Wilcox, WF & John Barnes Co, Rockford IL, audit coordinator QC, 1976-80; UNC Inc, UNC Naval Products, Uncasville CT, div audit coordinator & QCE, 1980-. **ORGANIZATIONS:** Mem, Natl Tech Program Comm of Amer Soc for QC 1980-, Customer Supplier Tech Comm 1980-, Quality Audit Tech Comm 1981-; exec comm mem, Tech Program, ASQC, 1986-89; IBPOE of W, exalted ruler 1986, aide to grand loyal knight 1986-, state pres 1987, grand exalted ruler 1988; IBPOE, special asst to state pres 1986-, special asst of Grand Lodge Security 1988-, exalted ruler 1988-; pres, UNC Mgmt Club, 1988-; local officer, ASQC; parliamentarian, New London Federation of Black Democratic Clubs. **HONORS/ACHIEVEMENTS:** Author of several articles for ASQC, Prentice Hall, etc, 1980-; certified quality auditor, first black certified by ASQC, 1988; first ASQC certified quality auditor in Naval Reactor Program, 1988; Volunteer of the Month award, ASQC, June 1989; cited in "Speaking of People," Ebony, 1989. **BUSINESS ADDRESS:** Division Audit Coordinator, Quality Control Engineering, UNC Inc, UNC Naval Products, 67 Sandy Desert Rd, Uncasville, CT 06382.

WHITE, RALPH L.
City official. **PERSONAL:** Born Feb 14, 1943, Dallas; children: Rhonda, Sophia, Connie, Rachael, Rodney. **CAREER:** City councilman; Ralph White Bail Bonds, owner; Exec Supper Club, owner; Ralphs Sq 24 Hr Mini Mkt, owner. **ORGANIZATIONS:** Past v mayor Stockton CA; mem bd dir Natl Black Caucus of Local Elected Officials; Mayor 1972-73; pres Ebony Young Men of Action 1968-. **MILITARY SERVICE:** AUS sgt 1960-62. **BUSINESS ADDRESS:** 2230 S Airportway, Stockton, CA 95406.

WHITE, RALPH L.
Telephone company executive. **PERSONAL:** Born Mar 13, 1930, Decatur, AL; son of Edmond White and Bertha M Smith Rogers; married Chrysanthemum Robinson White, May 06, 1955; children: Rodney M, Lorrie C, Kimberly L. **EDUCATION:** Alabama A&M Coll, Huntsville, BS, 1951; Texas Christian Univ, Fort Worth, MS, 1965; Webster Univ, St Louis MO, MBA, 1983. **CAREER:** Herf Industries Inc, Little Rock AR, president-founder, 1972-75; Southwestern Bell Telephone Co, AR, worked in engineering planning, switching systems engineering, outside plant construction, & as district personnel mgr, currently regional manager of external relations, 1975-. **ORGANIZATIONS:** Consultant, AR Business Council, 1988; trustee, Hendrix Coll, 1988-; mem, Governor's Task Force on School Dropouts 1988-89, Little Rock Chamber of Commerce Education Comm 1988-, AR Private Industry Council Bd of Dir 1988-, AR Advocates for Children and Families 1989, Legislative Planning Group for Children. **HONORS/ACHIEVEMENTS:** Graduated cum laude, Alabama A&M Coll, 1951; mem, Natl Biological Honor Society, 1964; author of "Effect of Capacitor Discharge on Microorganisms," 1965. **MILITARY SERVICE:** US Air Force, lt colonel, 1952-72; Air Force Inst of Tech honor grad, 1958; commander of best electronics squadron in 2nd Air Force, 1967-68; Air Force Commendation Medal, 1971; Air Force Meritorious Service Award. **HOME ADDRESS:** 913 South Hughes, Little Rock, AR 72204.

WHITE, RANDOLPH LOUIS
Publisher. **PERSONAL:** Born Oct 12, 1897, Bridgewater, VA; son of John White and Sarah White; divorced; children: Sherman R. **EDUCATION:** Sohio Business & Vocational School, machinist 1916-19; US Army Clerical School Manila PI, 1922; George Washington Univ, inhalation respiratory therapy 1948-49; Hartford General Hospital, 1948-49; MA General Hospital, 1949. **CAREER:** Neil House, 1915-18; Jeffrey Mfg Co, mach helper 1918-19; Cooper-Bessemer, mach shop 1928-31; Univ of VA Hosp, supv 1931-49; Univ of VA Hosp, chf tech 1949-65; Charlottesville-Albermarle Tribune, editor 1954-. **ORGANIZATIONS:** Mem NAACP 1939-; org Local 550 CIO 1944-53; past mem Amer Inhalation Therapy Assn 1950-65; chmn Legal Redress Comm 1956-62; rep Univ VA Hosp Inhalation Therapy Dept; past mem Charlottesville-Albermarle Chamber of Commerce. **HONORS/ACHIEVEMENTS:** Outstanding Serv & Cont to Comm Award City of Charlottesville 1966; Outstanding Public Serv Award, US Dept HEW 1970; Outstanding Young Man of the Year Judge Award Jr C of C 1974; Outstanding Serv Award, VA State Conf NAACP 1974; Honored by the Univ of VA Health Science Center, 1989, portrait placed wall of new $240 Million Hosp. **MILITARY SERVICE:** US Cav corporal, 1919-22, staff sgt, 1922-28. **BUSINESS ADDRESS:** Editor, Charlottesvl-Albermarle Trib, P O Box 3428, Charlottesville, VA 22903.

WHITE, RAYMOND RODNEY, SR.
County official. **PERSONAL:** Born Feb 15, 1953, Newark, NJ; son of Henry W White, Sr and Lucille M Jackson-White Sr (deceased); married Linnie B Adams; children: Raymond Rodney Jr. **EDUCATION:** Rutgers Univ, BA 1971-75; GA Inst of Tech, Master of Planning 1975-77. **CAREER:** Fulton Co Planning Dept, planner II; City of Plainfield, sr planner 1977-78; Williams Russell & Johnson Inc, sr planner 1981-82; Harrington George & Dunn PC, sr planner 1982; Oglethorpe Power Corp, land use analyst 1982-83; DeKalb Co Planning Dept, economic develop mgr principal planner 1983-; White & White Inc, [res/CEO, 1989-. **ORGANIZATIONS:** Vice pres Grad Planning Soc GA Inst of Tech 1976-77; mem Affirmative Action Comm Sch of Arch 1977; mem Amer Planning Assn 1979-, awds comm chmn 1986-87, scholarship comm mem 1987-88; planning task force chmn College Park Neighborhood Voters League 1980-; mem DeKalb Co Chamber of Comm 1983-; bd mem Foxhead Develop Corp 1983-; volunteer Habitat for Humanity in Atlanta 1984-; pres Develop Alliance Unlimited Inc 1984-; mem GA Indus Developers Assn 1984-; mem Natl Forum for Black Public Admins 1984-; action volunteer Univ Year in Action Prog Plainfield NJ 1973; bd chairman Oakhurst Commun Health Ctr 1989; mem DeKalb County General Vocational Tech Adv Comm 1985-88; mem Georgia Dept of Labor, Wagner Peyser 7A Employment Task Force 1987; mem Metro Atlanta Chamber of Commerce, Corporate Mktg Task Force, Sou th Side Develop Task Force; Local Exhibits Committee Chairman, Amer Planning Assn 1988-89; Leadership DeKalb, Alumni Assn 1989. **HONORS/ACHIEVEMENTS:** Departmental Distinction Academic Excellence Rutgers Univ 1975; Thesis Option Paper "Urban Homesteading Its use as a Residential Revitalization Tool" GA Inst of Tech 1977; Cert of Awd Distinguished Comm Serv College Park Civic and Educ Club 1984; Georgia Planning Assoc Certificate of Appreciation 1986; United Negro College Fund Meritorious Serv Awd 1986; Leadership DeKalb Palque 1988, DeKalb County Chamber of Commerce, GA 1988; Youth Leadership DeKalb Program Org Plaque YLD Progrm DeKalb County GA 1989. **HOME ADDRESS:** 3972 Cheru Dr, Decatur, GA 30034. **BUSINESS ADDRESS:** Pres/CEO, White & White Inc, PO Box 372393, Ste 308, Decatur, GA 30037.

WHITE, REGGIE
Professional athlete, minister. **PERSONAL:** Born Dec 19, 1961, Chattanooga, TN; son of Charles White and Thelma Collier; married Sara Copeland White, Jan 05, 1985; children: Jeremy, Jecolia. **EDUCATION:** Univ of TN, BA Human Svcs. **CAREER:** Licensed minister; Memphis Showboats USFL, defensive end 1984-85; Philadelphia Eagles, defensive tackle 1985-. **ORGANIZATIONS:** Mem Fellowship of Christian Athletes, Children's Hospital of Chattanooga TN blood drives, Highway House; active in Young Life, Eagles Fly For Leukemia, The Ram House Ministry. **HONORS/ACHIEVEMENTS:** Named Southeastern Conference Player of the Year in coll; made USFL all-rookie team 1984; named first team All-USFL 1985; NFC Defensive Rookie of the Year 1985; first team NFL all rookie Football digest 1985; mem, Pro Bowl team 1987, 1988, 1989; Most Valuable Player Pro-Bowl 1987; USFL Def Player of Year 1985; USFL Man of the Year 1985; co-founder w/ wife Sara of Alpha & Omega Ministry. **BUSINESS ADDRESS:** Philadelphia Eagles, Veterans Stadium, Broad St & Pattison Ave, Philadelphia, PA 19148.

WHITE, RICHARD C.
Artist manager. **PERSONAL:** Born Feb 22, 1941, New York City, NY. **EDUCATION:** NYU, BS 1962; Howard Univ, JD 1967. **CAREER:** Boston Symphony Orch, asst to mgr; pvt consult & artist mgr. **ORGANIZATIONS:** Mem NAACP; ACLU; Phi Alpha Delta Legal Frat. **HONORS/ACHIEVEMENTS:** Ford Found fello 1967. **BUSINESS ADDRESS:** Symphony Hall, Boston, MA 02115.

WHITE, ROBERT L.
Association executive. **PERSONAL:** Born Mar 22, 1916, Jackson, MS; married Helen Harper; children: Helen Oladipo, Roberta Battle, Robert H, Ramon, William, Elizabeth, Dorothy, Mark, Mary, Stephen, Christopher. **EDUCATION:** Howard Univ, 3 yrs. **CAREER:** US Post Office, employee 1943-. **ORGANIZATIONS:** Natl pres Natl Alliance Postal Fed Employees 1970-; pres WA Local 1953-70; past bd dir NAACP; past mem, bd dir WA Urban League; past bd mem Christ Child Settlement House; assoc mem Dem Natl Com. **HONORS/ACHIEVEMENTS:** One of the 100 Most Influential Black Amers Ebony Mag 1971-74; Civil Rights Awd DC Civic Assoc 1972; Natl Urban Coalition's Disting Natl Leadership Awd 1984; Hon DL Howard Univ 1984. **BUSINESS ADDRESS:** US Post Office, NAPFE, 1628 11th St NW, Washington, DC 20001.

WHITE, RORY KEITH
Professional athlete. **PERSONAL:** Born Aug 16, 1959, Tuskegee, AL; married Ruth. **EDUCATION:** South AL, Phys Ed 1982. **CAREER:** Los Angeles Clipper, forward 1983-; Phoenix Suns, 1983; Milwaukee Bucks, 1983. **HONORS/ACHIEVEMENTS:** While a soph at South AL was voted Sun Belt Player of Year; First Team All-Conf honors his jr & sr years. **BUSINESS ADDRESS:** Los Angeles Clippers, 3939 S Figueroa St, Ste 510, Los Angeles, CA 90037.

WHITE, SANDRA LAVELLE
Immunobiologist, medical educator. **PERSONAL:** Born Aug 30, 1941, Columbia, SC; daughter of Christopher O. White and Rosena E. Benson; married Dr Kenneth Olden; children: Heather Alexis. **EDUCATION:** Hampton Inst, BA Biol 1963; Univ MI, MS Microbiology 1971, PhD Microbiology 1974. **CAREER:** Sloan Kettering Inst for Cancer Res, res asst 1963-69; AT&T, res asst 1969; Univ MI Dept Microb, tchng asst 1969-71; Med Sch, asst lectr microb1970; Univ MI, guest lectr in immunology 1973; Howard Univ Coll of Med, asst prof of Microbiology 1973-76; Natl Inst of Health, staff fellow 1976-79; Howard Univ Coll of Med assoc prof microbiol & oncology, member Cancer Center. **ORGANIZATIONS:** Mem Amer Soc of Microbiologists, Amer Assn for Women in Sci, Amer Assn Coll Profs; Delta Sigma Theta Sor; Volun of the Shelters Inc; Bus & ProflWomen's League; Sigma Delta Epsilon Grad Women in Sci; Natl Science Found Traineeship 1970-71; mem Amer Soc of Cell Biology; The Reticuloendothelial Soc. **HONORS/ACHIEVEMENTS:** Ford Found Fellowship 1970-74; Kaiser Permanente Awd for Excellence in Teaching 1982; mem Pathology B Study Section Natl Insts of Health 1980-84; Bd of Scientific Counselors, Div Cancer Biology & Diagnosis, Natl Cancer Inst, N/H 1985-89; mem Natl Board of Medical Examiners, Microbiology Test Committee 1989-93. **BUSINESS ADDRESS:** Associate Professor, Howard Univ Medical School, Dept of Mircobiology, Oncology, 2041 Georgia Ave, NW, Washington, DC 20060.

WHITE, SCOTT A., SR.
Clergyman. **PERSONAL:** Born Aug 06, 1909, Wilmington, VA; married Mary Elizabeth (deceased); children: 15 children; 59 grandchildren; 18 great grandchildren. **EDUCATION:** Lincoln Univ, Cert in Religious Studies 1952; Accelerated Christian Educ Inst, Cert in Religious Admin 1982; New Jersey Bible Inst, in current studies 1984-. **CAREER:** First Zion Primitive Baptist Church, pastor 1950-68; 2nd Natl Ketoctan Primitive Baptist Assoc, vice-moderator 1977-84, moderator 1984-; New Hope Primitive Baptist Church, pastor 1968-. **ORGANIZATIONS:** Baccalaureate speaker Steelton-Highspire HS 1962; co-hostTV program "Maranatha" 1970-74; delegate White House Conference of Natl Religious Leaders 1980; mem Interdenominational Ministers Conf 1970-; hon mem Elks, Eastern Star & Masons 1972-; chmn of bd Ministers Alliance of the 2nd Natl Ketoctan Assoc 1984-. **HONORS/ACHIEVEMENTS:** Citation by House of Reps State of PA 1980 & 1984; Commendation from the Governor of the State of PA 1983; Commendation May of City of Harrisburg PA 1983. **HOME ADDRESS:** 215 N Harrisburg St, Oberlin, PA 17113. **BUSINESS ADDRESS:** New Hope Baptist Church, 2nd & Elm Sts, Steelton, PA 17113.

WHITE, SHERMAN EUGENE
Professional athlete. **PERSONAL:** Born Oct 06, 1948, Manchester, NH; children: Naomi. **EDUCATION:** Univ of CA Berkeley, social sci deg 1972. **CAREER:** Cincinnati Bengals, professional football player 1972-76; Buffalo Bills, def end 1976-. **ORGANIZATIONS:** Works with disadv yth San Francisco Bay "Pros of Oakland". **HONORS/ACHIEVEMENTS:** Recip All Pacific 8 Conf; All W Coast; consensus All Am 2nd player

chosen in 1st round of coll draft 1972; All Rookie Team; team capt & MVP at CA 1976; Hula Bowl & E-w Shrine Game; led Bills in Quarterback Tackles 1977 & 79.

WHITE, SYLVIA KAY
Fashion consultant. **PERSONAL:** Born Dec 05, 1955, Washington, DC; daughter of George D White Sr (deceased) and James Odessa White. **EDUCATION:** Fashion Institute of Tech, AA 1975; State Univ of NY, Degree in Fashion Buying. **CAREER:** Alexander Inc, buyer/mens 1975-83; Montgomery Ward Inc, buyer/boys 1983-87; Nordstroms, McClean, Virginia, sales men's merchandise, 1988-. **ORGANIZATIONS:** Trustee 1985-, chairperson budget & finance comm First Union Baptist 1986-88. **HONORS/ACHIEVEMENTS:** Outstanding Young Women of Amer 1985. **HOME ADDRESS:** 7912 Grant Dr, Lanham, MD 20706.

WHITE, TOMMIE LEE
License clinical psychologist and university professor. **PERSONAL:** Born May 20, 1944, Dublin, GA; son of Mack F White, Sr. **EDUCATION:** Yankton, BA 1966; Univ SD, MA 1967; California State Univ, MA 1978; Univ Southern Calfornia, PhD 1974; Univ of Southern California, PhD 1982;. **CAREER:** CA St Univ Northridge, prof of kinesiology and sport psychology; Horace Mann Jr H LA, tchr history phys educ 1967-70;Univ SD, grad asst 1966-67; Univ SC, asst research dir 1967; LA City Schools, recreation dir youth serv 1968. **ORGANIZATIONS:** The Amer Psychological Assn; NAACP; Assn Black Psychologist; United Prof CA; Am Assn Health Phys Educ & Rec; Am Federation Tchrs; Athletic Congress, Yankton Coll; Clinical Sport Psychologist, US Olympic Comm. **HONORS/ACHIEVEMENTS:** Alumni of yr 1976; All-Amer Track Hon 1965; SD Athlete of Yr Awd 1965; Howard Wood Hall of Fame 1978; dean's list hon student Yankton Coll 1965-66; SD Coll Track Athlete of Decade 1960-69; Nat Amateur Athlete Rep to AAU 1975-; Track & Field News All-Amer Awd 1971; Broke world's record 60 meter high hurdles 74 sec Moscow 1972; pr high hurdles 133 Sec 1973; publs "the relationship between physical educ admin values & their attitudes toward education" 1974, "innovations Innovations" 1974, "A Social Aspect of Individual Aging", "Recreation & Its Effect on Individual Aging" 1969, " The Relationship Between Cognitive & Internal-External Locus of Reinforcement" 1978, "Essentials of Hurdling" Athletic Journ 1980, "Hurdling-Running Between The Hurdles" Athletic Journal 1980; Publication, "Reparenting Schizophrenic Youth in a Hospital Setting" 1985.

WHITE, ULYSSES
Business executive. **PERSONAL:** Born Jul 06, 1939, Madison, GA. **EDUCATION:** FL A&M U, BA 1962. **CAREER:** Royal Crown Cola Co Columbus GA, dir spl markets & conv serv 1974-; Dade Co Bd Pub Instruction, art instr 1962-70; Royal Crown Cola Co, advn pos since 1970. **ORGANIZATIONS:** Mem Nat Assn of Market Devel; Am Marketing Assn; mem Boy Scouts; YMCA. **BUSINESS ADDRESS:** 1000 10 Ave, Columbus, GA 31902.

WHITE, VAN FREEMAN
Government official. **PERSONAL:** Born Aug 02, 1924, Minneapolis, MN; married Javanese Verona Ewing; children: Perri Merle, Javoni Verona. **EDUCATION:** Henry HS, graduate 1943; Univ of MN, college courses. **CAREER:** Dept of Public Works City of Mpls, construction 1956-68; Dept of Economic Security, interviewer/counselor 1968-79; City of Minneapolis, council member 5th Ward. **ORGANIZATIONS:** Chairperson Govt Operations Comm; mem Comm on Youth Employment; mem Comm Develop Comm; mem Public Health & Safety Comm; co-author First Source Agreement Economic Develop Linked with Job Oppor for Disadvantaged & Unemployed Minneapolis Residents; chmn Viking Council Hiawatha Dist Comm Task Force Boy Scouts of Amer; founder & past chairperson Willard-Homewood Organ; 1st coord City Crime Prevention Prog; established Women/Minority Business Enterprise Set-AsideProg Minority Women's Economic Task Force; mem Licenses & Consumer Services Comm. **HONORS/ACHIEVEMENTS:** Political Achievement Awd NAACP 1980; Outstanding Civic Serv Awd Minneapolis Urban League 1981; article published in Essence magazine "Pornography & Pride" 1984; Outstanding Serv to Comm Phyllis Wheatley Comm Ctr 1984; Cert of Recognition USAF Acad Outstanding Contribution through USAF Academy & AFROTC CommissioningProgs; Outstanding Awareness Awd Minneapolis City Adv Comm on People with Disabilities; awd Natl Alliance of Business Jobs; Leader for Excellence Award - Natl Assn of Minority Contractors 1988; Outstanding Leadership Award from Twin Cities O.I.C. 1988. **HOME ADDRESS:** 800 Washburn Ave N, Minneapolis, MN 55411. **BUSINESS ADDRESS:** Councilmember, City of Minneapolis, 307 City Hall, Minneapolis, MN 55415.

WHITE, VINCENT CALVIN
Professional athlete. **PERSONAL:** Born Aug 26, 1961, Kansas City, MO. **EDUCATION:** Stanford University, Sociology Major. **CAREER:** Oakland Invaders, slot back 1983-; Denver Gold, slot back 1984-. **ORGANIZATIONS:** Cardinal asst coach 1983. **HONORS/ACHIEVEMENTS:** Gold single-game record holder for most yards rushing (159); holds Gold record for best avg yds per carry for one season; honorable mention All-Am, All-PAC 10 & All-West Coast by UPI following his sr year.

WHITE, WENDELL F.
Business executive. **PERSONAL:** Born Aug 20, 1939, Atlanta, GA. **EDUCATION:** Morehouse Coll, BA 1962; Atlanta Univ, MBA 1967; UCLA, post grad study. **CAREER:** Williamson & Co Real Estate, 1961-65; Johnson Publishing Co; General Motors Corp, 1965; Coca-Cola Co, marketing exec 1965-70; US Dept Commerce, dir office of minority bus enterprise 1970-74; Empire Investment Enterprises Inc, exec vice pres; Empire Realty, pres. **ORGANIZATIONS:** 1st vice pres Empire Real Estate Bd; mem Atlanta Bus League; mem Citizens Trust Bank Adv Bd; mem Natl Assn of Market Developers; mem bd of dirs Travelers Aid Soc; mem SCLC; mem NAACP, Urban League, Butler St YMCA. **HONORS/ACHIEVEMENTS:** Outstanding Young Man of Amer 1973; Who's Who Among Black Amers 1975-76; Leadership Awd Butler St YMCA; Letter of Commendation from Pres of US; Cert ofMerit NAACP. **MILITARY SERVICE:** AUS 1963-65. **BUSINESS ADDRESS:** President, Empire Realty, 569 Ashby St SW, Atlanta, GA 30310.

WHITE, WILLIAM
Chairman/general manager. **PERSONAL:** Born Jun 28, 1934, St Louis, MO; son of Ephriam White and Laura White; married Virginia M McDade; children: Diana, William Jr, Arnold. **EDUCATION:** Attended, Lincoln Univ. **CAREER:** Kansas City Monarch, Memphis Red Sox, Kansas City AThletics Org Chicago White Sox, professional baseball player; Kirby Company, franchise factory distributor; WETU of Montgomery, owner; KIRL Radio, chairman/genl mgr. **ORGANIZATIONS:** Mem, deacon Newstead Ave Bapt Church; business mgr O'Neal Twins and Interfaith Choir; bd mem Natl Gospel Workshop of Amer, Natl Gospel Evangelist Musicians and Choral Org; mem NAACP; apptd Manpower Planning and Training Council for St Louis County by Supervisor Gene McNary, States Comm of Citizens Adv Commn on Mal-Practice by Atty Genl John Ashcroft; mem Women Self Help Bd, Salvation Army Bd, Pace Bd, St Charles County Bd of Realtors, Employers Support of Natl Guard and Reserve. **HONORS/ACHIEVEMENTS:** Business Man of the Year Elks Lodge. **MILITARY SERVICE:** Armed Forces President's Personal Honor Guard; Honorable Discharge. **BUSINESS ADDRESS:** Chairman/General Manager, KIRL-AM, 3713 Hwy 94 North, St Charles, MO 63301.

WHITE, WILLIAM H.
Educator. **PERSONAL:** Born Feb 16, 1932; married Dolores; children: Michele, Michael, Sharon. **EDUCATION:** Morgan St Coll, BS 1961; Am Coll Law, LLB 1965. **CAREER:** Health Dept NYC, chemist; Kings Co Research Labs, clinical lab mgr; Physicins Assoc prog Long Island Univ, clinical lab instr & coor; United Bapt Church, asst pastor 1963-74; New Revival Community Church, pastor 1974-. **ORGANIZATIONS:** Mem NAACP; Concerned Citz; Black Assn; Assoc Royal Soc Pub Hlthl. **MILITARY SERVICE:** Paratroopers sgt 1953-56. **BUSINESS ADDRESS:** 4037 Laconia Ave, Bronx, NY 10466.

WHITE, WILLIAM J.
Electrical engineer. **PERSONAL:** Born Aug 06, 1926, Philadelphia, PA; married Althea de Freitas; children: Karen, William Jr. **EDUCATION:** A&T Clg, 1943; Syracuse U, 1950; NY City U, BS 1960; Army Command & Gen Staff Clg, 1966. **CAREER:** Andrea Radio & TV, tech wrtr 1955; NY Transit Auth, elec engr 1958; US Navy Appl Sci Lab, elec engr 1959; Fed Aviation Adm elec engr 1961-, mgr Systems & Equipment Branch. **ORGANIZATIONS:** Pres Local 2791 Am Fed of Govt Empl 1972-80; pres/mem Hempstead Bd of Ed 1973-78; pres SE Civic Asso 1972-; chm bd Trustee United Cong Ch 1970-72; pub rel Hempstead Little League 1970-78; mem Authors Guild 1974-, Natl Writers Club 1975-, Hempstead Planning Board; Hempstead editor "The Prospective" a monthly newspaper; editor, Hempstead Little League monthly newsletter. **HONORS/ACHIEVEMENTS:** Man of Yr Hempstead Little League 1972; Bk "Airships for the Future Publ 1976 by Sterling Pub; Free Lance Writer, Frequent Flyer, Newsday/Natl Rifleman Christian Herald; Listed in, Community Leaders & Noteworthy Americans, Contemporary Authors vols 97-100, Men of Achievement. **MILITARY SERVICE:** AUS mjr 1945-46, 1950-53; CIB; Purple Heart 2; Bronze Star; Assorted Minor Awds; USAR major, retired. **BUSINESS ADDRESS:** Manager, Systems Branch FAA, NY Aircraft Cert Office, 181 S Franklin Ave, Fed Bldg, Valley Stream, NY 11581.

WHITE, WILLIAM J.
Superintendent. **PERSONAL:** Born Mar 03, 1935, Bouard, PA; married Idella M Hatter; children: Sheryl, Karen, Sandra. **EDUCATION:** Westminster Coll, BA 1957f Alex Hamilton Bus Inst, atnd; Youngstown St Ud mgmt training prog metallurica courses. **CAREER:** Sharon Steel Corp, supt trans labor & material control; supt material control 1969; gen foreman degassing 1968-69; sr melter 1965-68; heat balance cal 1962-65; stock foreman 1960-62; quality control analyst 1960; pit foreman 1958-60; trainee 1957-59; cert scndry educ hist social students. **ORGANIZATIONS:** Mem Jr Chamber 1959; Shenango Valley United Fund 1969-72; Y's Men 1962; Shenango Valle Urban Leag 1968-75; pres Kiwanis 1979; pres Westminster Coll Alumni Assn 1974; adv bd McDowell Nat Bank; dir George Jr Rep; dir NAACP; dir Boy Scouts of Am 1974. **HONORS/ACHIEVEMENTS:** Recip Little All Am Football AP 1955-56; first black foreman gen foreman supt Sharon Steel Corp hist. **MILITARY SERVICE:** AUS sgt 1957-63. **BUSINESS ADDRESS:** Box 270, Farrell, PA.

WHITE, WILLIAM T., III
Business executive. **PERSONAL:** Born Nov 12, 1947, Jacksonville, FL; married Patricia E; children: William Thomas IV. **EDUCATION:** Bethune-Cookman Coll, 1965-66; TN State Univ, BS Pol Sci 1969; Emory Univ, MA Metropolitan Govt 1970-72. **CAREER:** Office of the Mayor, Model Cities Atlanta GA, rsch eval spec 1973-75; Inst for School Rsch, rsch assoc 1975-78; Grassroots Inc, exec dir 1978-80; DeKalb Cty Planning Dept, human serv facilities coord 1980-. **ORGANIZATIONS:** Worshipful Master Royal Ark Masonic Lodge F&AA York Rite Masons 1978; past Grand Jr Warden Smooth Ashlar Grand Masonic Lodge 1978-82; mem of bd Community Relation Comm DeKalb Cty 1979-82; CEO Kirkwood/Edgewood Eastlake Econ Devel Corp 1982; mem Natl Forum for Black Public Admin 1983; mem SE Atlanta Intown Businessmen Assn 1985; mem DeKalb-Atlanta Voter's Cncl 1982; bd mem SE Atlanta YMCA. **HONORS/ACHIEVEMENTS:** Grad Fellowship Emory Univ 1970; Illus Inspector Gen Natl Supreme Council Scottish-Rite 33rd degree Mason 1978; Outstanding Young men of Amer 1979; Lt Col Aid-de-Camp Office of the Govt State of GA 1983; Special Deputy Sheriff DeKalb Cty; Worshipful Master of the Year Masons 1980-81. **HOME ADDRESS:** 3316 Toney Dr, Decatur, GA 30032. **BUSINESS ADDRESS:** Coord, Human Serv Facil, Dekalb County Plng Dept, 30 Warren St, Atlanta, GA 30317.

WHITE, WINIFRED VIARIA
Television executive. **PERSONAL:** Born Mar 23, 1953, Indianapolis, IN; daughter of Walter H White and Winifred Parlean White. **EDUCATION:** Harvard Radcliffe Coll, AB, 1974; Lesley Coll, MA, Educ. **CAREER:** NBC, mgr, project peacock, 1981-82, children's programs, 1982-84, dir, children's programs, 1984-85, vice pres, family programs, 1985-89, dir, motion pictures for television, 1989-. **ORGANIZATIONS:** Bd of dirs, Harvard-Radcliffe Club, 1983-; bd of governors, TV Acad, 1986-; bd of dirs, Planned Parenthood, 1986-. **BUSINESS ADDRESS:** Dir, Motion Pictures for Television, NBC, 3000 L. Alameda, Rm 247, Burbank, CA 90064.

WHITE-WARE, GRACE E.
Educator. **PERSONAL:** Born Oct 05, 1921, St Louis, MO; daughter of James Eathel White, Sr MD and Madree Penn White; married Aug 17, 1947 (divorced); children: Oloye Adeyemon (James Otis Ware III). **EDUCATION:** Harriett Beecher Stowe Teacher's Coll, BA 1943; attended Columbia Univ NY 1944-45, Scott Foresman Inst summer 1951, Wayne State Univ 1966, St John Coll John Carroll Univ 1974-75, Kent State Univ 1976, Ohio Univ 1978. **CAREER:** St Louis, Chicago, Cleveland, teacher 1946-61; Cleveland Public Sch, teacher elem & adult educ 1954-82; Delta Sigma Theta Sor Inc Tutoring & Nutrition Proj, prog admin 1983-88. **ORGANIZATIONS:** Mem Greater Cleveland Neighborhood Centers

Assn; Food First Prog; Black Econ Union; Youth Understanding Teenage Prog; Cleveland Council Human Relations; Cong Racial Equality; Tots & Teens; Jr Women's Civic League; Afro-Amer Cultural/Hist Soc; Talbert Clinic & Day Care Ctr; Langston Hughes Library; Women's Allied Arts Assn; mem NAACP Phyllis Wheatley Assn; Natl Council Negro Women; Natl Sor Phi Delta Kappa; Delta Sigma Theta; Top Ladies of Distinction Inc; Eta Phi Beta; Phi Delta Kappa Frat; Smithsonian Inst; natl treas Eta Phi Beta Sor Inc 1984-88; mem Delta Kappa Gamma Soc Intl, The Natl Museum of Women in Arts; mem Kiwanis International 1987. **HONORS/ACHIEVEMENTS:** Most Outstanding Volunteer of the Year, New York 1949; Outstanding Teacher Awd 1973; Certificate of Appreciation Cleveland 1973; Master Teacher Award-Martha Jennings 1973; Pan-Hellenic Outstanding Greek Awd 1979, 1984; Educational Serv Awd Urban League of Greater Cleveland 1986; Humanitarian Awd Top Ladies of Distinction Inc 1986. **HOME ADDRESS:** 14701 Milverton Rd, Cleveland, OH 44120-4227.

WHITEHEAD, EDDIE L.
Business executive. **PERSONAL:** Born Jul 07, 1944, Clarksdale, MS; son of Mr & Mrs Jodie Whitehead; married Lynn Demarest; children: Pax, Maya, Luke. **EDUCATION:** Univ of Louisville, Kentucky, BS, 1967; Univ of California, Berkeley, MSW, 1974, MS, 1977. **CAREER:** Honeywell Info Systems, account exec, 1971-73; Rubicon Programs Inc, dir, 1974-78; Colonial Realty, sales, 1978-80; Whitehead & Co, owner, broker, 1980-84; Whitco Broadcasters Inc, pres, gen mgr; Silver King Broadcasting of Hollywood Inc, vice pres, gen mgr; Channel 66 of Vallejo Inc, pres, gen mgr; Whitehead Communications Inc, pres. **ORGANIZATIONS:** Dir, human relations council Lajes Azores Portugal, 1969; pres, bd of dir, J-Pax Broadcasters Inc, 1981-; pres, gen mgr, Whitco Broadcasters Inc, 1984-; mem, Natl Assn of Broadcasters, 1984-87; pres, Channel 69 of Hollywood Florida Inc; mem, Natl Assn of Black Owned Broadcasters, Broward County Civilian Review Bd. **HONORS/ACHIEVEMENTS:** US Olympic Basketball Training Camp, 1970; Head of Delegation, Counseil Intl du Sports Militaire, Tehran, Iran, 1970. **MILITARY SERVICE:** USAF, capt, 1967-71. **BUSINESS ADDRESS:** Vice President, Gen Manager, Silver King Broadcasting of Hollywood Inc, 3600 S State Rd 7, Suite 251, Miramar, FL 33023.

WHITEHEAD, JAMES T., JR.
Pilot, flight engineer. **PERSONAL:** Born Dec 10, 1934, Jersey City, NJ; divorced; children: Brent, Janet, Kenneth, Joel, Marie. **EDUCATION:** Univ of IL, BS 1957. **CAREER:** USAF Univ of IL, commd 2nd lt 1957-AFROTC; USAF, pilot training 1958; KC-135, co-pilot 1959-63; KC-135, aircraft comdr 1963-65; Vietnam combat, 1965; U-2 Reconnaissance, aircraft comdr 1966-67; TWA, flight eng 1967, first officer Boeing 707 1968, flt engineer/instr/flt engr/check airman B-747. **ORGANIZATIONS:** Mem Airlines Pilot Assn 1967; ALPA activities; TWA co-chmn Hazardous Materials Com 1974-; TWA Master Exec Cncl Flt Security Com 1975; pres Kiwanis Madison Township NJ 1968; Jaycees Madison Township 1973-; served as squadron commander 103rd Tactical Air Support Squardon 1977-83; appointed as Hdqtrs PA Air Natl Guard dir of operations 1983-; promoted to Colonel 1983; Kappa Alpha Psi Frat; chmn 111th Tactical Air Support Group Minority Recruit com 1972-74. **HONORS/ACHIEVEMENTS:** First and only Black U-2 Pilot until recently; Outstanding Assn Mem Madison Township Jaycees 1974; Pres Old Bridge Township Bd Educ elected 3 years 1975. **MILITARY SERVICE:** USAF 1957-67 Colonel. **BUSINESS ADDRESS:** Flight Engineer, TWA Building 95, JFK Airport, Jamaica, NY.

WHITEHEAD, JOHN L., JR.
Retired government employee. **PERSONAL:** Born May 14, 1924, Lawrenceville, VA; son of John L Whitehead and Jasper U Whitehead; married Colleen J, Jan 28, 1960; children: Lisa Colleen. **EDUCATION:** Tuskegee Inst, pilot training 1943-44; WV St Coll, BS ind engr 1948; USAF Test Pilot Sch Edwards AFB, grad 1958; American River Coll, Sacramento, CA, AA electronics, 1984. **CAREER:** USAF Northrop Aircraft Corp, prod test pilot, 1953-56; Ogden Air Material Depot USAF, chief quality analysis sec, 1959; USAF Europe, chief flight test air material forces, 1959-63; McCellan AFB CA, chief of Flight test, 1964-67; Quality Control Sec 56 Special Operations Wing Thailand, chief, 1967-68; Standardization & Evaluation Sec USAF Flight Test Ctr Edwards AFB, chief, 1968-70; Edwards AFB, cmdr field maintenance sq, 1970-71; Maintenance & Supply Group Edwards AFB, dept group cmdr, 1971-72; City of Sacramento, assoc mgmt analyst, 1972-82; American River Coll, Sacramento, CA, instructor in electronics, 1984-89. **ORGANIZATIONS:** Mem Nat Security Agency 1979-89; mem NAACP 1978-89; bd dir Tuskegee Airman Inc 1978-89; mem Reserve Off Assn 1979-89; mem Military Order of World Wars, 1980-89; mem California State Park and Recreation Comm, 1984-; pres Tuskegee Airman, Inc, 1987-89; mem Veterans of Foreign Wars, 1988-89. **HONORS/ACHIEVEMENTS:** Military Med air med w/7 oak leak clusters USAF 1952; army commendation med UAF 1953; DFC w/3 oak leaf clusters USAF 1953; dist unit citation cluster USAF 1963; military order of world wars USAF 1979; European ribbon w/3 battle stars USAF; Vietnam ribbon w/3 battle stars USAF. **MILITARY SERVICE:** USAF lt col served 29 yrs. **HOME ADDRESS:** 4217 American River Dr, Sacramento, CA 95864. **BUSINESS ADDRESS:** American River College, College Oak, Sacramento, CA.

WHITEHEAD, TIMOTHY DWIGHT
Elected official. **PERSONAL:** Born Sep 03, 1934, Marion, AL; married Kaye Cromer; children: Steven, Christopher. **EDUCATION:** Carthage Coll, 1974-75. **CAREER:** US Navy ESO, dir civilian personnel 1971-74; US Army Ft Sheridan, dir wage & position mgmt 1974-77; Foss Park Dist, pres bd of commiss 1979-85; US NavyCCPO, dir employee devel 1977-. **ORGANIZATIONS:** Mem Lake Cty Urban League 1971-73; chmn originator North Chicago Classic Annual City Days 1981-83; pres Timac Counselling Serv 1981-85; personnel adv Mayor City of North Chicago 1983-85; mem Shiloh Bapt Church choir; chmn One Church One Child" Adoption Referral Svc. **HONORS/ACHIEVEMENTS:** 3 Civilian Outstanding Performance Awd 1971-81; Publ "How Many Roads" 1963, "Blackness of Man" 1973; Meritorious Civilian Serv Awd USN ESO 1974; Instrumental in naming new school for Dr Martin Luther King; Instrumental in naming several parks in the city for some of its black citizens; Worked with mayor to communwith "Gangs" created job situations & recreational outlets to quell the problems summers 1983,84. **MILITARY SERVICE:** AUS pvt 6 mo; Leadership Trainee of the Cycle 1967. **BUSINESS ADDRESS:** Director, Empl Development, Federal Govt/Civilian Persnl, CCPO Building 1-H, Great Lakes, IL 60088.

WHITEHURST, CHARLES BERNARD, SR.
City official. **PERSONAL:** Born Jun 04, 1938, Portsmouth, VA; son of John E Whitehurst, Sr (deceased) and Bernice N Whitehurst; married Vandelyn Smith Whitehurst; children: Miriam Simmons, Lisa Lucas, Lisa, Charles Jr. **EDUCATION:** Norfolk State Univ, BS (Magna Cum Laude) 1978; Univ of CO-Boulder, Grad Degree Bank Marketing 1982. **CAREER:** United States Marine Corps, retired major 1955-76; Central Fidelity Bank, asst vice pres & loan officer 1977-85; City of Portsmouth, treasurer 1986-. **ORGANIZATIONS:** Mem Portsmouth Sch Bd 1977-81; pres Portsmouth Chamber of Commerce 1982; chmn Portsmouth Seawall Festival 1984,85; mem Kiwanis Club 1984-; bd of dirs Old Dominion Univ 1984-, Maryview Hosp 1985-; life mem NAACP; pres Downtown Portsmouth Assoc; pres Retired Officers Assoc (Portsmouth Area Chap) 1989. **HONORS/ACHIEVEMENTS:** Alpha Kappa Mu Honor Soc Norfolk State Univ 1978; Disting Alumni NAFEO Washington DC 1984; Eurekan of the Year Eureka Club Portsmouth 1984; Citizen of the Year Omega Psi Phi Frat 1985; "The Other Side of a Gemina" book of poetry 1986. **MILITARY SERVICE:** USM major 21 yrs; Good Conduct, three stars; Navy Achievements, Navy Commendation w/Combat V, Staff Serv Honor Medal, Republic of South Viet Nam.

WHITEMAN, HERBERT WELLS, JR.
Bank vice president. **PERSONAL:** Born Sep 11, 1936, New York, NY; son of Herbert W Whiteman, Sr. and Catherine Caton; married Nola Lancsater; children: Cheryl Alyse Whiteman Brooks. **EDUCATION:** Columbia Univ, BS Engrg 1964; NY Univ, MS Civil Engrg 1973; Harvard Univ Grad Bus Admin, Adv Mgmt Prog 1985. **CAREER:** IBM Corp, system engr 1965-70, mktg rep 1970-73, industry mktg rep 1973-74, sys engrg mgr 1974-75, intl mktg mgr 1975-77; Fed Reserve Bank, vice pres 1977-84, group vice pres 1984-. **ORGANIZATIONS:** Grammateus Sigma Pi Phi Boule' 1982-; vice pres Colony South Brooklyn Settlement 1985-, Urban Bankers Coalition 1987-. **HONORS/ACHIEVEMENTS:** Banker of the Year Urban Bankers Coaliton 1980; Golden Circle IBM; Systems Symposium IBM; Presidents Awd Fed Reserve Bank 1983. **BUSINESS ADDRESS:** VP Security & Control Gp, Federal Reserve Bank of NY, 33 Liberty St, New York, NY 10045.

WHITESIDE, ERNESTYNE E.
Educator. **PERSONAL:** Born Mar 04, Pine Bluff, AR. **EDUCATION:** Mech & Normal Coll Pine Bluff, BA agri; NY U, MA; Europe, post grad; OuachitaUniv Arkadelphia; HI; OK U; Univ AR. **CAREER:** Dollarway Public School Dist, english instr. **ORGANIZATIONS:** Mem pres Jeferson Co Reading Coun; AR Educ Assn; bd AR Educ Assn; Assn Classrooms Tchrs; Nat AR Coun Tchrs English; Nat Reading Coun; Nat Assn Univ Women; Gov's Coun Aerospace Edn; St Orgn Minority Evolvement; Nat Alumni Assn A M & N Coll; Eastern Star; Delta Sigma Theta; Am Woodman Assn. **HONORS/ACHIEVEMENTS:** Cert oustnd serv yth Jack & Jill 1974; hon cit Negro Yth Ogn; outsng tchr of mo Townsend Park HS; natl TV signing doc mergin st PTA with ACPT 1970; cit of day Radio St KCAT; judge Miss Black Am So Central AR Gamma Phi Delta 1972; listed in Dict of Intl Biog Vol 12.

WHITESIDE, LARRY W.
Journalist. **PERSONAL:** Born Sep 19, 1937, Chicago, IL; married Elaine Fain; children: Anthony. **EDUCATION:** Wilson Jr Coll, AA 1955-57; Drake Univ, BA 1957-59; Stanford Univ, John Knight Fellow 1987-88. **CAREER:** Johnson Publishing Co, researcher, 1958-59; Kansas City, sports reporter, asst editor, 1959-63; Milwaukee Journal, sports reporter, 1963-73; Milwaukee Sporting News, correspondent, 1970-74; Boston Sporting News, correspondent, 1974-78; The Boston Globe, sports reporter columnist, 1973-. **ORGANIZATIONS:** Mem, Kappa Alpha Psi, 1957-; mem, US Basketball Writers, 1960-80; mem, NAACP, 1970-; chmn ticket comm, Boston Baseball Writers, 1973-; mem, NBA Basketball Writers, 1975-; bd of dir, Baseball Writers Assn of Amer, 1980; delegate, Natl Assn of Black Journalists, 1982-. **HONORS/ACHIEVEMENTS:** Wisconsin Sports Writer of the Year, Milwaukee Press Club, 1973; Investigative Reporting (2nd & 4th), Assoc Press Sports Editor, 1980, 1985; John S Knight Fellow, Stanford Univ, 1987. **HOME ADDRESS:** 64 Kirkstall Rd, Newtonville, MA 02160. **BUSINESS ADDRESS:** Sports Reporter, Columnist, The Boston Globe, 135 Morrissey Blvd, Boston, MA 02107.

WHITEST, BEVERLY JOYCE
Government official, human relations consultant. **PERSONAL:** Born Aug 28, 1951, Tarboro, NC; daughter of Barbara Pittman; divorced; children: Malik, Jelani. **EDUCATION:** Univ of WI LaCrosse, exchange student 1973; NC A&T State Univ, BS Political Science 1974; Atlanta Univ, MPA (Carnegie Fellow) 1976; Nova Univ, 1988-. **CAREER:** City of Atlanta, urban planner 1977-78; Dept of Trans Nashville, trans planner 1978-80; Rsch & Policy Assn Jackson, planning consultant 1980-82; Div of Public Health, dir planning & evaluation 1982-86; Public Health, dir office of organizational develop, 1986-. **ORGANIZATIONS:** Conf on Minority Public Admin 1975-84; pres Black Prof Network 1984-85; Master trainer Southwest Serv Area Girls Scouts 1984-; exec sec Atlanta Health Prof Assn 1983-85; GA Public Health Assn 1984-; consultant Assoc of Creative Change 1984-; volunteer United Way; trainer Northwest Georgia Girls Scouts; mem Delta Sigma Theta Sorority Inc; bd of dir, Counsil on Battered Women and the West End Medical Center; mem, Coalition of 100 Black Women. **HONORS/ACHIEVEMENTS:** Fellowship Public Admin Dept Atlanta Univ 1975-76; Serv Award Adamsville Area Girl Scouts 1984-85. **HOME ADDRESS:** 6615 Cedar Hurst Trail, College Park, GA 30349. **BUSINESS ADDRESS:** Dir Office of Organizational Dev, Div of Public Health, 878 Peachtree St, Atlanta, GA 30309.

WHITFIELD, TERRY BERTLAND
Professional athlete. **PERSONAL:** Born Jan 12, 1953, Blythe, CA; children: Charles. **CAREER:** San Francisco Giants, outfldr 1977-80; Seibu Lions (Japan), outfldr 1981-83 los angeles dodges, outfldr 1984-. **HONORS/ACHIEVEMENTS:** Seibu Lions selected All Star tm second time 1983; led Pacific Leag total bases; twice Int'l League All Star tm 1973; League MVP; Appalachian Leag hme run RBI; titles prof season Plyr of the Yr H Schl All-Am & CA State H Schl Plyr Yr. **BUSINESS ADDRESS:** Los Angeles Dodgers, 1000 Elysian Park Ave, Los Angeles, CA 90012.

WHITFIELD, VANTILE E.
Association executive. **PERSONAL:** Born Sep 08, 1930, Washington, DC; married Lynn C Smith; children: Elizabeth, Lance, Bellina. **EDUCATION:** Howard U, BA 1957;Univ CA, MA 1960. **CAREER:** Nat Endowment for the Arts, prog dir expansion arts; Howard U, instr 1957-58; Ad Graphics of Hollywood, prod mgr, art dir 1960-61; Theatre of Being, co-fdr, gen mgr 1963-64; LA Sch Dist, instr 1965-66; Universal City Studios, set designer 1966-67; KTTV LA "From the Inside Out", creator, prod-dir 1968-69; Performing Arts Soc of LA, fdr, dir 1966-71; KNXT LA "Anatomy of Change, creator-prod 1970; DC Black Repertory Co Wash DC, guest artistic dir1971-. **ORGANIZATIONS:** Mem Directors' Guild of Am 1968-; SAG 1964-; AFTRA 1965-; Set Design & Model Makers Guild 1966-; mem Banneker City Club Wash DC 1974-. **HONORS/ACHIEVEMENTS:** Recip Commenda-

tion of Merit LA Co 1967; Commendation of Merit City of LA 1968; Image Award Hollywood-Beverly Hills NAACP 1969; Nat Assn of Media Women 1970; LA Critics' Cir Award 1970. **MILITARY SERVICE:** USAF a/1c 1950-51. **BUSINESS ADDRESS:** Nat Endowment for Arts, Washington, DC 20506.

WHITING, ALBERT NATHANIEL
Educational administrator. **PERSONAL:** Born Jul 03, 1917, Jersey City, NJ; son of Hezekiah O. Whiting and Hilda Whiting; married Lottie Luck; children: Brooke E Whiting. **EDUCATION:** Amherst Coll, AB 1935; Fisk Univ, MA 1941; The Amer Univ, PhD 1948 1952. **CAREER:** Bennett Coll, instructor sociology 1941-43 1946-47; Atlanta Univ, asst prof sociology 1948-53; Morris Brown Coll, dean of college 1953-57; Morgan State Coll, Dean of College 1957-67; NC Central Univ, pres chancellor 1967-83, chancellor emeritus. **ORGANIZATIONS:** MD Commn for New York World's Fair; mem commn on academic affairs Amer Council on Educ 1968-70; mem bd dirs Amer Council on Educ 1970-73 1974-75; membd trustees Educ Testing Serv 1968-72; mem policies & purposes comm bd dirs pres Amer Assn of State Colleges & Univs; mem Coll Entrance Examination Bd; mem bd dirs Natl League for Nursing Inc 1970-71; vice pres 1971-74,1975-78 treas 1978-84 Intl Assn of Univ Presidents; mem bd dirs NC Memorial Hospital 1974-77; mem Joint Panel on the Grad Record Examinations Bd and the Council of Graduate School in the US, former mem; bd govs exec comm of bd Rsch Triangle Inst Rsch Triange Park NC; mem bd dirs Greater Durham Chamber of Commerce; mem US Civil Serv Commn Southern Region; mem bd dirs General Telephone Co of the Southeast; mem bd dirs Rose's Stores Inc 1981-. **HONORS/ACHIEVEMENTS:** Natl Urban League Fellowship Univ of Pittsburgh; Teaching & Rsch Fellow Fisk Univ; Alpha Kappa Delta Hon Sociological Fraternity; numerous books reviews & contributions to professional journals; Six Hon Degrees LLD's & LHD's. **MILITARY SERVICE:** AUS 1st lt 1943-46.

WHITING, BARBARA E. (NEE WRIGHT)
Attorney. **PERSONAL:** Born Jul 28, 1936, Tabb, VA; widowed. **EDUCATION:** Hampton Inst Hampton VA, BS 1963; Howard Univ Sch Law, JD 1963. **CAREER:** US Customs Srv Wash, customs law spec 1964-; Howard Univ Dept Med, med sec 1957-63; Howard U, lib 1964. **ORGANIZATIONS:** Mem, treas Howard Law Alumni Assn Geo Wash Nat 1968-; Bar Assn; vol, rehab juv girls Operation Sue 1974. **HONORS/ACHIEVEMENTS:** 1st Black female appointed Customs Law Spec US Customs Srv. **BUSINESS ADDRESS:** Customs Law Specialist, US Customs Service, 1301 Constitution Ave, Washington, DC 20229.

WHITING, EMANUEL
Accountant. **PERSONAL:** Born in Philadelphia, PA; married Estelle; children: Denise, Kevin. **EDUCATION:** Temple U; Peirce Sch Bus Admin. **CAREER:** Emanuel Whiting & Co, cpa; IRS. **ORGANIZATIONS:** Mem Am Inst CPA's; PA Inst CPA's; treas Philadelphia Chap PA Inst CPA's; mem Philadelphia City Controller's Adv Commn; adv com Bus Subject of Sch Dist Phila; mem Am Acctg Assn; Nat Assn Minority CPA Firms; Nat Assn Black Accnts; bd mem Germantown Dispensary & Hosp; vchmn Philadelphia Commn Srv to Aging; mem Philadelphia Chap PA Inst of CPA's; United Way; treas, bd dir Philadelphia Tribune Charities Inc; mem, bd mgrs YMCA Germantown; bd dir Allens Ln Art Ctr; mem, fund com Am Red Cross; bd tst Pop Warner Little Schlrs Inc; mem NAACP; Frontiers Intrntl Flwsp Commn; Urban Leag Phila; Interested Negroes; Nat Bus Leag; Tuscan Morning Star Lodge 48, Free & Accepted Masons; DeMolay Consistroy, Ancient & Accepted Scottish Rite Free Masons. **MILITARY SERVICE:** AUS 1947. **BUSINESS ADDRESS:** 844 Suburban Sta Bldg, 1617 John F Kennedy Blvd, Philadelphia, PA 19103.

WHITING, LEROY
Government official. **PERSONAL:** Born May 17, 1938, Rodney, MS; son of Johnnie Whiting and Gertrude Jackson Whiting; married Annette Mattie Watkins, Aug 08, 1959; children: Oran. **EDUCATION:** Alcorn A&M Coll, BS, 1959; Mich State Univ, MAT, 1965; Univ of IL, Chicago, 1975-80. **CAREER:** Meridian Board of Educ, MS, science teacher 1959-60; Chicago Board of Educ, IL, science teacher 1960-68; City of Chicago, IL, executive 1968-, dir of external affairs. **ORGANIZATIONS:** Member, Alpha Phi Alpha 1957-, Francis Parker School Bd of Trustees 1968-75, GAP Community Org 1983-, Natl Forum of Black Pub Admins 1986-89, Dental Assisting Natl Board 1988-, Alpha Kappa Mu Honorary Society; chair, User Requirement Pub Tech Inc 1980. **MILITARY SERVICE:** US Army Reserves, spec 2, 1958-61. **HOME ADDRESS:** 3344 South Calumet Ave, Chicago, IL 60616.

WHITING, MAYBELLE STEVENS
Senior clerk. **PERSONAL:** Born Aug 25, 1925, Flushing, NY; children: Leonard D Usher. **EDUCATION:** Manhattan Trade Sch, attended 2 yrs; Bordentown Indsl Sch, attended 2 yrs; Attended, Fred Waring Workshop for conductors. **CAREER:** Macedonia AME Ch, organist 1944-49; So Baptist Ch, organist 1958-66; Springfield Gardens Meth Ch, organist 1966-69; St Marks AME Ch, organist 1970-71; N Queens Sect of Natl Council of Negro Women Inc, pres 1970-74; Peoples United Meth Ch, choir dir 1976-79; New York City Dept of Social Serv , sr clerk, dir choristers. **ORGANIZATIONS:** Mem Mus Masters NY 1956-62; former mem Brooklyn NY Philharmonic Choral Soc; mem Opera Ebony 1979; life mem Natl Council of Negro Women Inc; mem NAACP;appeared in "Talent 59" "Dark of the Moon" Equity Library Theatre NY; mem David I Martin Branch Natl Assn of Negro Musicians. **HONORS/ACHIEVEMENTS:** Achievement Awd N Queens Sect NCNW 1974; Bicentennial Achvmt Awd & Cert of Recog Natl Coun of Negro Women Inc 1976; Cert of Appreciation Dept of Social Serv NYC.

WHITING, OLLIE BETH
Microwave oven company executive. **PERSONAL:** Born Jun 18, 1953, Oakland, MS; married John H Whiting; children: Dedrick Shaunn, LaKeisha Elizabeth. **EDUCATION:** Northwest Mississippi Jr College, attended 1971-72; Univ of Mississippi, BBA 1974; Univ of Arkansas, MBA 1986. **CAREER:** Dobbs-Life Savers Inc, general acctg clerk 1975-77, inventory accountant 1977-79; Kimberly Clark Corp, inventory control 1979-83, cost specialist 1983-86; Litton Microwave Cooking Products, cost analyst. **ORGANIZATIONS:** Sec Toastmasters Kimberly Clark Corp 1986; mem Natl Assoc of Female Executives, Phi Gamma Nu Business Sor; sunday school teacher, unit dir girl scoutsMiddle Baptist Church; reading comm Gardenview Elem School; tutor Adopt-A-School Program Memphis City Schools. **HONORS/ACHIEVEMENTS:** Career Day Representative LeMoyne Owen College 1986. **BUSINESS ADDRESS:** Cost Analyst, Litton Microwave Cooking Prod, 4450 Mendenhall Rd, Memphis, TN 38101.

WHITING, THOMAS J.
Government employee. **PERSONAL:** Born Oct 01, 1923, Haverhill, MA; married Florence Brock. **EDUCATION:** Howard Univ, BA 1947; Univ of Michigan, MBA 1948; Cleveland-Marshall Law School, LLB 1956. **CAREER:** Nairobi, Kenya, area auditor gen, 1974-; Intl Audit AID/WASHINGTON, dep dir, , 1971-74; S Asia New Delhi, dep area auditor gen, 1970-71; AID/NEW DELHI, chief auditor, 1967-70; AID/WASHINGTON, auditor, 1965-67; IRS Cleveland, appellate adv, 1949-65. **ORGANIZATIONS:** Mem OH Bar Assn 1956; CPA OH 1957. **HONORS/ACHIEVEMENTS:** Award OH CPA Soc 1957; Sam Silbert Award 1956. **MILITARY SERVICE:** AUS 1943-46. **BUSINESS ADDRESS:** PO Box 30261, Nairobi, Kenya.

WHITING, WILLIE
Judge. **PERSONAL:** Born in Chicago, IL; son of James Whiting and Elise Jones Whiting Harkness; divorced. **EDUCATION:** Fisk Univ, attend; Roosevelt Univ; John Marshall Law School, LLB, JD, 1950. **CAREER:** Cook Co, circuit judge, 1978, asso judge, circuit court, 1970-78, asst state Atty, 1961-65; asst US atty, 1965-66; Circuit Court, previous magistrate; G J Harkness Law Firm, law clerk, atty, 1950-55; Cook Co Dept of Public Welfare, caseworker, resource consultant, 1955-56; Chicago NAACP, exec sec, 1957-59; City of Chicago, asst corp counsel, 1959-61. **ORGANIZATIONS:** Admitted to Illinois Bar, 1951; mem, Amer Assn of Univ Women; hon mem, Delta Kappa Gamma Educ Soc; mem, Natl Bar Assn; Amer Bar Assn; admitted to prac, US Dist Court & US Supreme Court, 1964-; mem, Advisory Counsel Cook County Temp Juv Detention Center, Hm Ec Related Occup; mem, Cook Coounty Natl Women's Bar Assns; adv bd, Midwest Comm Council; Amer Vets Comm; mem bd, Chicago NAACP; past pres, Professional Women's Club; res agt Zeta Phi Beta; mem advisory counsel, Urban Health Comm, Univ of Illinois, Chicago, 1984-89. **HONORS/ACHIEVEMENTS:** Young Lawyers Section, Chicago Bar Assn, Certificate of Appreciation Award, 1985-88. **MILITARY SERVICE:** AUS, pfc, 1944-46. **BUSINESS ADDRESS:** Circuit Court of Cook County, Daley Center Room 1806, Chicago, IL 60602.

WHITLEY, FRANK JAMES
Educator, clergyman. **PERSONAL:** Born Mar 21, 1894, Norwood, MO; widowed; children: Helen G Bardwell, Geneva Carple, Irene Marcus. **EDUCATION:** Amer Life Sci Found Univ, DD 1968. **CAREER:** Universal Negro Improvement Assn LA CA, 1922-30; Rising Sun Realty Co CA, real estate broker 1922-77; NAACP LA CA, ret 1923-79. **ORGANIZATIONS:** Pres LA Forum 1938-39; pres Golden West Realty Bd LA 1938-43. **HONORS/ACHIEVEMENTS:** Hon Cert of merit Drury Coll Springfield MO 1977; apptd Gov Adv Comm Jeff City MO.

WHITLEY, R. JOYCE
City planner. **PERSONAL:** Born Mar 20, 1930, Monroe, NC. **EDUCATION:** Fisk U, BA Engl (cum laude) 1950; Wstrn Rsrv U, MA Socl 1953; Univ Chi, MA City & Reg Plann 1956. **CAREER:** Whitley-Whitley Inc, archs, plnrs; City Planner, vp; US Dept Hsg & Urban Dev, chief plnr, adv model cities Adm 1967-68; Ctr for Urban Studies & Univ Chgo, rsrch asso 1965-68. **ORGANIZATIONS:** Mem Var Pub & Pvt Plnng Staffs in Chicago Wash Baltimore; bd gov 1970-73; exec com Am Inst of Plnrs 1970-71; Nat Assn Hsg & Redev Ofcls; Am Soc of Plnrs; dir Nat Org of Minority Archt; mem vis com HarvardUniv Grad Sch of Design 1973-75; pres commn HowardUniv Sch of Archt & Plnng; adv commn on Housing & Urban Growth; Am Bar Assn 1974-75; bd trust Karamu House Cleveland 1973-75; vice pres Opers Div United Torch Cleveland 1974-75. **HONORS/ACHIEVEMENTS:** Dr Mary McLoed Bethune Award of Merit Nat Cncl Negro Women Chicago 1972; S Shore Commun Plng Assn Award 1972; Prog Archt Design Award 1972. **BUSINESS ADDRESS:** 20600 Chagrin Blvd, Shaker Heights, OH.

WHITLEY, WILLIAM N.
Business executive, architect. **PERSONAL:** Born Apr 29, 1934, Rochester; married Kaysonia Forney; children: Kyle, Kym, Scott. **EDUCATION:** Kent St U, BS 1957. **CAREER:** Whitley-Whitley Inc, vice pres arch; Registered in OH, IL, IN. **ORGANIZATIONS:** Am Inst Archs; Archs Soc OH; Cleveland Eng Soc; Soc Arch Design 1974; OH Prestressed Concert Assoc Design 1973; Womn's Allied Arts Assoc 1974. **HONORS/ACHIEVEMENTS:** United Torch Progressive Arch Design Award 1972; AIA Am Soc Arch 1st Hon Design 1969. **MILITARY SERVICE:** USAF capt 1958-60. **BUSINESS ADDRESS:** 20600 Chagrin Blvd, Shaker Heights, OH.

WHITLOCK, FRED HENRY
Mathematician. **PERSONAL:** Born Jun 17, 1936, Winston-Salem, NC; married Barbara Hill; children: Carlton Fred, Kenneth Henry, Jacquelyn Ewaugh. **EDUCATION:** NC A&T State U, BS 1959. **CAREER:** NASA Goodard Space Flight Cntr Greenbelt, MD, mathematician, sci programmer 1962-. **ORGANIZATIONS:** Mem Math Assn; Am Assn for Computing Machinery. **HONORS/ACHIEVEMENTS:** Author "Orbit Prediction Accuracy Theory" 1963; "Interplanetary Trajectory Encke Method Prog anual 1" 1967, Manual 2 1967; manual for IBM OS/360 1970; also articles in field. **BUSINESS ADDRESS:** Code 642 Bldg 1, Goodard Space Flight Center, Greenbelt, MD 20771.

WHITLOW, WOODROW, JR.
Aerospace researcher. **PERSONAL:** Born Dec 13, 1952, Inkster, MI; son of Woodrow Whitlow and Willie Mae O'Neal Whitlow; married Michele C. Wimberly, Jan 06, 1971; children: Mary Annessa, Natalie Michele. **EDUCATION:** Massachusetts Institute of Technology, Cambridge, MA, SB, 1974, SM, 1975, PhD, 1979. **CAREER:** NASA Langley Research Center, Hampton, VA, research scientist, 1979-86, research scientist/group leader, 1986-88, senior research scientist, 1988—; adjunct professor, Old Dominion University, 1987—; lecturer, Cario University Aeronautics Seminar Series, 1988. **ORGANIZATIONS:** American Institute of Aeronautics and Astronautics; coach, Phillips Athletic Association Girls Softball, 1981-84; president, Hampton University Laboratory School Advisory Board, 1982-83; member, MIT Aeronautics and Astronautics Visiting Committee, 1987—; member, MIT Educational Council, 1987—. **HONORS/ACHIEVEMENTS:** First place, Student Research Competition, AAIA New England Section, 1974; James Means Memorial Prize, MIT Aeronautics and Astronautics, 1974; special achievement awards, NASA Langley Research Center, 1982, 1986, 1989; Black Engineer of the Year in Government, Career Communications Group, 1989. **BUSINESS ADDRESS:** National Aeronautics and Space Administration, Langley Research Center, Mail Stop 173, Hampton, VA 23665.

WHITMAL, NATHANIEL
Certified public accountant. **PERSONAL:** Born Jul 28, 1937, Memphis, TN; son of Na-

thaniel Johnson and Eunice Johnson; married Yolanda Frances Pleasant; children: Nathaniel A, Angela M. **EDUCATION:** Chicago City Coll Wilson Br, AA 1957; Loyola Univ Chicago, BSC 1961, post graduate studies. **CAREER:** Internal Revenue Serv Chicago, agent 1962-69; Booz, Allen & Hamilton Inc, tax mgr 1969-71; Mayfair Coll (Chicago City Colleges), faculty mem 1971-72; Private Practice, CPA 1971-77; Zenith Electronics Corp, manager corp tax 1977-87; Whitmal Oil Services; CEO l987-; concurrent public accounting practice. **ORGANIZATIONS:** Mem Tax Executives Inst 1977-87; mem Amer Inst of CPA's 1968-; mem IL CPA Soc 1971-; mem Commr of Internal Revenue Sm Bus Adv Comm 1975-76; mem Chicago Urban League; mem NAACP; alt mem Chicago Bd of Educ Citywide Adv Comm 1977-78. **HONORS/ACHIEVEMENTS:** CPA Univ of IL 1968. **MILITARY SERVICE:** IL Natl Guard/AUS Reserves Sp 4 1961-67. **BUSINESS ADDRESS:** CEO Whitmal Oil Services, Inc., 11328 S. Halsted Street, Chicago, IL 60639.

WHITMORE, ARNOLD PAUL
Business executive. **PERSONAL:** Born Jul 26, 1940, Amarillo, TX; married Sunsiray Smith; children: Nicole, Justin. **EDUCATION:** Los Angeles City Coll, AA 1958-60; Los Angeles State Coll, BBA 1960-62. **CAREER:** Arnold Whitmore & Assoc, pres 1962-79; Church's Fried Chicken Inc, dir of oper. **ORGANIZATIONS:** Advisory bd Pacesetter Div Boy Scouts of Amer 1982; bd of dir Shorter Coll 1984, Northwest Optimist Club 1984; mem Urban League, Operation PUSH, NAACP. **HONORS/ACHIEVEMENTS:** Volunteer Serv Award, United Negro Coll Fund, 1982 March of Dimes, 1984; included in Congressional Records, 1983; Received proclamations from E. Cleveland, OH, Cleveland, 1982-84; Entrepreneur of the Year Award, US Dept of Commerce & Minority Business Devel Agency 1986; Key to the City of Cleveland 1985, 1986.

WHITNEY, W. MONTY
Educator, executive administrator. **PERSONAL:** Born Sep 07, 1945, Philadelphia, PA; son of Wilbur M Whitney and Bessie M Whitney; married Vance Saunders; children: Erica, Michelle. **EDUCATION:** Lycoming Coll, BA, 1967; Howard Univ, MS, Psych, 1969; Michigan State Univ, PhD, Psych, 1974. **CAREER:** Southern Univ, instr, 1969-71; Univ of Cincinnati, asst professor, 1974-76; Seven Hills Neighborhood Houses Inc, assoc dir. **ORGANIZATIONS:** Pres, Social Tech Systems, 1978-; natl pres, Assn of Black Psych, 1084-85; mem, TransAfrica, NAACP. **HOME ADDRESS:** 393 Terrace Ave, Cincinnati, OH 45220. **BUSINESS ADDRESS:** Exec Dir, Eincinnati Human Relations Commn, 901 Plum St, Rm110 City Hall, Cincinnati, OH 45202.

WHITNEY, YENWITH KELLY
Educator, advisor African affairs. **PERSONAL:** Born Dec 22, 1924, New York, NY; married Lorenza Neighbors; children: Saundra Curry, Earl Tucker, Karen. **EDUCATION:** MA Inst of Tech, SB 1949; Columbia U, MA 1962, EdD 1977. **CAREER:** Prog Agency United Presb Church, Africa desk 1980; Boggs Acad, pres 1978-80; Program Agency United Presby Church USA, assoc educ serv 1975-78; Commn Ecumenical Miss & Relations UPC USA, sec for Planning & Research 1970-75; Cameroon W Africa Bd for Miss UP CUSA, asst prin (missionary) 1958-66; Republic Aircraft Edo Corp, aeronautical engr 1950-56. **ORGANIZATIONS:** Mem Inst of Aeronautical Sci 1949-56; mem African Studies Assn 1966-78; mem NEA 1978-; mem Alpha Phi Alpha Frat 1950-; pres Teaneck (NJ) Afro Am Civic Assn 1976-78; mem Tuskegee Airmen 1976-. **HONORS/ACHIEVEMENTS:** Book review NATIONAL Urban League" Weiss Pub Migration Today Geneva 1976; bio sketch "Black Presbyterians in Mission" F Wilson NYD 1979; article "Black Eagles" Augusta News & Reveiw Waynesboro True Citizen Augusta & Waynesboro, GA 1980. **MILITARY SERVICE:** USAF 1st lt 1943-45. **HOME ADDRESS:** Boggs Acadmey, Keysville, GA 30816.

WHITSY, CHARLES H., JR.
Business executive. **PERSONAL:** Born Oct 01, 1945, Memphis, TN; married Dorothy Jean; children: Javana, Derrick. **EDUCATION:** Univ NM, BA 1968. **CAREER:** Delta Sales Corp, gen mgr 1971-; Delta Found Inc, chf fin officer 1971; Goodyear Tire & Rubber Co, credit sales mgr 1969-71; Mainstream Computer Svc,dir of sys 1969; Kroger Food Co, mgr trainee 1968-69. **BUSINESS ADDRESS:** Rt 1 Box AB 40, Greenville, MS 38701.

WHITT, DWIGHT REGINALD
Friar, priest. **PERSONAL:** Born Jul 17, 1949, Baltimore, MD. **EDUCATION:** Loyola Coll, AB 1970; Pontifical Fac of Immaculate Conception, STB 1974, STL candidate. **CAREER:** Order of Friars Preachers, mem Friar; Dominicans; ordained Roman Cath priest, 1976; Spalding Coll, chaplain. **ORGANIZATIONS:** Mem Nat Black Cath Clergy Caucus. **HONORS/ACHIEVEMENTS:** Listed in Who's Who Among Am Coll &Univ Students 1970.

WHITTAKER, TERRY MCKINLEY
College administrator. **PERSONAL:** Born Mar 14, 1950, Newport News, VA; son of Julius Whittaker and Blanche Sutton-Whittaker; divorced. **EDUCATION:** Univ of Wisconsin-Madison, BA 1972; Univ of Minnesota MA 1974. **CAREER:** Youth Counsel Bureau Brooklyn NY, juvenile delinquent officer 1973; Univ of Minnesota, pre-major advisor 1974-76, business sch coord student affairs 1976-79; INROADS, dir 1979-83; Univ of Delaware, dir minority engrg program 1983-85, dir undergrad advisement 1985-. **ORGANIZATIONS:** Mem Kappa Alpha Psi 1969-; mem Amer Soc of Training and Develop 1980-; bd dirs Forum to Advance Minorities in Engrg 1983-; mem Brandywine Professional Assoc 1984-; Natl Academic Advising Assoc 1985-; chmn Region A Natl Assoc of Minority Engrg Program Administrators 1986-; mem DE Soc of Professional Engrs Natl Engrs Week Festivities Comm 1986; mem Natl Assoc of Academic Affairs Administrators 1986. **HONORS/ACHIEVEMENTS:** Ivan Williamson Award, Univ of Wisconsin 1972; Twin City Student Assembly Outstanding Contribution Award Univ of Minnesota 1979; Comm Serv Award Kappa Alpha Psi 1982; MN Guidance Assoc Award 1983; Black Alumni Achievement Award Univ of Minnesota 1983; Educ of the Year INROADS/Philadelphia Inc 1985; Outstanding Young man of Amer 1979. **BUSINESS ADDRESS:** Dir Undergraduate Advisement, University of Delaware, College of Engrg, 135 du Pont Hall, Newark, DE 19716.

WHITTED, ANDREW EUGENE
Clergyman. **PERSONAL:** Born Aug 29, 1924, Delco, NC; married Annette Estella Williams. **EDUCATION:** Livingstone Coll Salisbury, NC, AB 1956; Hood Theol Sem Salisbury, BD MDiv DD 1972. **CAREER:** St Luke AME Zion Ch Western NY Conf, pastor 1972-; St Catherine AME Zion Ch, pastor 1960-72; Park St AME Zion Ch, pastor 1959-60; Doggett Grove Circuit AME Zion Ch, pastor 1958-59; Rhoney's Circut AME Zion Ch, pastor 1956-58; Providence AME Zion Ch, pastor 1954-56. **ORGANIZATIONS:** Founder pres Carrington Arms Apt Corp 1964-72; mem cntrl com World Council of Chs 1968-75; pres H Ood Theol Sem Alumni Assn 1972-; pres Comm OrgnProg 1966-70; pres New Rochelle NAACP 1967-71; pres BUILD Inc Buffalo, NY 1975-77. **HONORS/ACHIEVEMENTS:** Omeaga Man of th Eyr Omicron Iota Ch Pt Omega Psi Phi 1968; Man of the Yr The New Rochelle Chap of the Nat Assn of Negro Bus & Professional Women Inc 1971; Merit Serv Awd Livingstone Coll Gen Alumni Assn 1972; Comm Sev Awd New Rochelle NAACP 1972. **BUSINESS ADDRESS:** Price Memorial AME Zion Church, 920 Dryden Ave, Youngstown, OH 44505.

WHITTED, EARL, JR.
Attorney. **PERSONAL:** Born Mar 26, 1931, Goldsboro, NC; married Ruby Weaver; children: Lynn, Stephen, Kenneth. **EDUCATION:** NC Central U, BA LlB JD 1955. **CAREER:** Pvt Prac, atty 1970-; Criminal Law Legal Consult Fed Housing Prog, atty. **ORGANIZATIONS:** Mem Goldsboro Bd Aldermen 1964-; NAACP; Alpha Phi Alpha. **HONORS/ACHIEVEMENTS:** Recip Alpha Phi Alpha Man of the Yr awd 1970. **MILITARY SERVICE:** AUS 1956-58. **BUSINESS ADDRESS:** 105 S John St, Goldsboro, NC 27530.

WHITTEN, BENJAMIN C.
Educator. **PERSONAL:** Born Jul 25, 1923, Wilmington, DE; married Lucretia Bibbins; children: Benjamin, Jr. **EDUCATION:** BS indl edn; PA State Coll, MS indl arts educ 1948; PA State U, EdD indl educ 1961; Rutgers U;Univ of MD. **CAREER:** Baltimore City Public School, asst supr Voc Educ 1968-; Cherry Hill Jr HS Balitmore, prin 1966-68; Granville Woods Gen Voc School, prin 1964-66; Edmondson HS, asst prin 1963-64; Carver Voc Tech HS, asst prin 1958-63, industriall arts teacher 1958; VA, training specialist 1946-67. **ORGANIZATIONS:** Bd dir MD Voc Assn chmn Voc Educ Com Counc of Great Cities Sch; chmn Am Voc Assn Task Force on Voc Educ in Urban Area 1972-; pres Nat Assn of Large City Dir of Voc Educ 1974-; mem Gov Manpower Adv Com Nat Adv Com Nat Cntr for Voc Tech Educ OH State U; Kappa Phi Kappa; Iota Lambda Sigma; Phi Delta Kappa; Pi Omega Chap of Oemga Psi Phi. **MILITARY SERVICE:** AUS m/sgt 1943-46. **BUSINESS ADDRESS:** Dept of Educ, Annex 23 Calvert Sts, Baltimore, MD 21218.

WHITTEN, CHARLES F.
Educator, educational administrator. **PERSONAL:** Born Feb 02, 1922, Wilmington, DE; son of Tobias and Emma; married Eloise; children: Lisa, Wanda. **EDUCATION:** Univ of PA, AB 1942; Meharry Med Coll, MD 1945; Univ of PA Graduate School 1954; Buffalo Children's Hospital, resd 1955, fellow 1956; Pediatric Hematology, Children's Hospital of Michigan, fellow 1957. **CAREER:** Wayne State Univ, assoc dean curr affairs prof of pediatrics 1976-, dir comp Sickle Cell Center 1973-, dir clincal rsch center 1962-73; Detroit Receiving Hospital, dir pediatrics 1956-62; Wayne State Univ, instructor prof ped 1962-70. **ORGANIZATIONS:** Mem Amer Acad Pediatrics; Amer Fed Clinical Rsch; Amer Pediatric Soc; Amer Soc Clinical Nutrition; Amer Soc Hematology Mid-west Soc for Pediatric Rsch; Soc Pediatric Rsch; bd dir Gerber Prod Co 1972-; com nutritional info Natl Acad Science; pres Natl Assn for Sickle Cell Disease Inc; vice pres Amer Blood Commn; chmn Task Force Personal Health Serv Workshop MI Public Health Statute Revision Project; mem vice chmn Public Health Advisory Council State MI; advisory com Blood & Blood Pressure Resources Natl Heart Lung & Blood Inst; mem Ad Hoc Com S Hemoglobinpathies Natl Acad Science Mem Alpha Omega Alpha; Xigma Xi; Physician Yr Detroit Med Soc 1964 & 75; chmn Genetics Disease Advisory Comm State Health Dept; bd of dir Natl Bank of Detroit Bancorp 1988-. **HONORS/ACHIEVEMENTS:** Distinguished Achievement Award Detroit NAACP 1972; Franklin Lecturer in Human Relations Wayne State Univ 1972; Kennedy Lecturer Georgetown Univ Medical School 1973; Detroit Science Center Hall of Fame 1987; Distinguished Serv Award Wayne State Univ School of Medicine 1987. **MILITARY SERVICE:** AUS Med Corp captain 1951-53; Served in Japan & Korea. **BUSINESS ADDRESS:** Prof Pediatrics-Assoc Dean, Wayne State University, School of Medicine, 540 E Canfield, Detroit, MI 48201.

WHITTEN, ELOISE CULMER
Banking executive. **PERSONAL:** Born Apr 23, 1929, Philadelphia, PA; married Charles F Whitten MD; children: Lisa A PhD, Wanda J Whitten-Shurney MD. **EDUCATION:** Temple Univ, BA Political Science 1950; Univ of PA, MA Political Science, Public Admin 1951; Wayne State Univ, Univ of MI, Post-Masters Degree. **CAREER:** 1st Independence Bank, bd of dir. **ORGANIZATIONS:** Mem Planned Parenthood League of Detroit 1959-; mem 1973-, vice-chmn 1980-Detroit-Wayne County Community Mental Health Bd; bd mem Wayne County Social Serv 1977-; mem Pi Gamma Mu, Amer Public Welfare Assn, Natl Conf on Social Welfare, MI Assoc of Black Social Workers; bd dir Center for Humanistic Studies 1981-; Human serv task force New Detroit Inc 1983-; bd dir Natl Council of Community Mental Health Centers 1984-; mem Natl Task Force on Governance 1985-. **HONORS/ACHIEVEMENTS:** Efforts in Behalf of Individuals and Families in Need Aed Federation for Aid to Dependent Children 1967; Humanitarian Award for Leadership in Natl Advocacy Family Serv Assoc of Amer 1974; Public Citizen of the Year MI Captain Natl Assoc of Social Workers 1978; Sojourner Truth Award for serv in the freedom fighter's tradition Detroit Chapter Natl Org of Black Business & Professional Women 1980. **BUSINESS ADDRESS:** Board of Directors, 1st Independence Natl Bank, 234 State St, Detroit, MI 48226.

WHITTEN, THOMAS P.
Social work administrator. **PERSONAL:** Born Sep 26, 1937, Anderson, SC; son of Benjamin J Whitten and Hattie Brown Whitten; married Ruthann DeAtley, Jul 26, 1964; children: Karen, Alexander, Bryan. **EDUCATION:** Lincoln Univ, Jefferson City, MO, BA, 1963; Case Western Reserve Univ, Cleveland, OH, 1963-64. **CAREER:** Chicago Renewal Soc, camp dir 1963; League Park Center, Cleveland, OH, dir of special interest groups 1963-65; Intl House of RI, exec dir, 1965-67; Harriet Tubman House, Boston, MA, 1967-70; Providence Human Relations Commission, exec dir, 1970-73; Hall Neighborhood House, Bridgeport, CT, assoc exec dir, 1973-77; John Hope Settlement House, exec dir. **ORGANIZATIONS:** Bd of dirs Decisions Inc, New Haven, CT, Lippitt Hill Tutorial, Wiggin Village, Providence Branch NAACP, West End Community Center, Mount Hope Neighborhood Assoc; exec dir Assoc Comm, United Neighborhood Centers of America, Washington, DC; mem adv comm Central High School, Hope High School, WPRI-TV; City of Providence Affirmitive Actions Comm, State of RI, Minority Adv Commission, Minority Advisory Comm, Congresswoman Claudine Schneider; Corporation mem Citizens bank, Volunteers in Action, Deputy Registrar State of RI, First Unitarian Church of Providence, RI. **HONORS/**

ACHIEVEMENTS: Math Awd; Scholarship Awd Valedictorian Riverside HS 1966; Deans List Lincoln Univ, Jefferson City, MO, 1960-61. **MILITARY SERVICE:** AUS sp3, 2nd lt 1956-63. **HOME ADDRESS:** 132 Colonial Rd, Providence, RI 02906. **BUSINESS ADDRESS:** Executive Dir, John Hope Settlement House, 7 Burgess St, Providence, RI 02903.

WHITTINGTON, HARRISON DEWAYNE
Association executive. **PERSONAL:** Born Jun 09, 1931, Crisfield, MD; married Louise Holden. **EDUCATION:** Morgan State Coll, BS, 1952; Pennsylvania State Univ, MEd, 1961; Nova Univ, EdD, 1980. **CAREER:** CG Woodson School Crisfield, teacher, 1954-62, principal, 1962-68; Somerset Co Bd Educ, coord, 1968-70, dir fed programs, 1968-70; Maryland State Dept Educ, coord human relations, 1974-81, asst superintendent 1981-, superintendent, 1981-. **ORGANIZATIONS:** Mem, NEA (state delegate 1968-70); chmn, Natl Hard Crab Derby Parade, 1971-73; mem, Teacher's Assn, Somerset Co; mem, Maryland State Teacher's Assn; mem, Maryland Assn Supvr & Curric Devel; mem, Maryland Council Adms Compensatory Educ; Assn School Business Officials; Phi Delta Kappa; Amer Assn Supvr & Admin; Maryland Assn Publicly Supported Con Educ; Somerset Co Admins Assn; Omega Psi Phi; mem, Maryland Adv Council; mem, Comm Coord Child Care; Maryland County Family Relations, Mason (32 deg); bd dir, Somerset Co Head Start; past chmn, bd dir, Somerset Co Soc Servs Agcy; bd dir, ARC; McCready Memorial Hospital; mem, Somerset Co Heart Assn; mem, Rec Commn; mem, C of C; pres, Intl Assn Basketball Officials; mem, Physical Fitness Comm; Comm Org for Progress. **HONORS/ACHIEVEMENTS:** Rep Comm Leader of Amer Award, 1969; Omega City of Year, 1971; Outstanding Educ in Amer, 1973-74; Outstanding Black Comm Leader, 1974, 1976; Chancellors Award UNES, 1978; Omega Man of the Year, 1978; Afro-Amer of the Year, 1982; Outstanding Citizen; Comm Achievement Award, 1985. **MILITARY SERVICE:** US Infantry capt 1952-54. **BUSINESS ADDRESS:** Superintendent, Somerset Co Public Schools, Prince Wm St, Princess Anne, MD 21853.

WHITWORTH, CLAUDIA ALEXANDER
Editor, publisher. **PERSONAL:** Born Nov 07, 1927, Fayetteville, WV; married Clifton B Whitworth Jr (deceased); children: Robyn A Hale, Stanley R Hale, Eva J Crump, B Clifton Whitworth. **EDUCATION:** Bluefield State Coll, attended; Natl Business Coll, attended. **CAREER:** Roanoke Tribune, linotype operator 1945; New York City, Cleveland, Columbus, Fayetteville Newspapers, linotype oper; Roanoke Tribune, owner 1971-. **ORGANIZATIONS:** Bd mem WBRA-TV; mem Amer Red Cross, Roanoke Fine Arts Museum, Mill Mtn Playhouse; bd of dir Roanoke Vocational Ed Found for Roanoke Public Schools; adv bd Salvation Army; comm Roanoke Coll Constance J Hamlar Mem Fund Comm, League of Older Amers, Meals on Wheels; mem Baha'i Faith, Spiritual Assembly, life mem NAACP, YWCA. **HONORS/ACHIEVEMENTS:** Outstanding Serv in News Media, 1 of 20 Civic Leaders selected from throughout the State of VA to accompany Gov Linwood Holton to Strategic Air Comm Hdq Offutt NE Roanoke Valley Bus League & Ladies Aux VFW #1444; Selected Leaders Pictorial Review Yesterday & Today 1976; Woman of the Year Omega Zeta Chap Zeta Phi Beta 1982. **BUSINESS ADDRESS:** Editor & Publisher, Roanoke Tribune, 2318 Melrose Ave NW, Roanoke, VA 24017.

WHITWORTH, E. LEO, JR.
Dentist. **PERSONAL:** Born in Kingston, Jamaica;married Jennifer Ann Brown; children: Bianca, Lennox Valencia. **EDUCATION:** Northeastern Univ, BA 1971; Howard Univ, DDS 1976. **CAREER:** St Anns Bay Hosp, dental surgeon 1976-77; Comprehensive Clinic Kingston Jamaica, dental surgeon 1976-77; Private Practice, dentist 1977-; Mattapan Health Clinic, dental dir 1977-79; Harvard Univ, clinical instructor operative dentistry 1981-. **ORGANIZATIONS:** Mem Amer & Natl Dental Assocs 1977-, Metropolitan District Dental Soc 1977-, MA Dental Soc 1977-; pres William B Price Unit of the Amer Cancer Soc 1978-80; mem Commonwealth Study Club 1979-, Acad of General Dentistry 1979-; chairperson MA Div Amer Societies Conf "Meeting the Challenge of Cancer in BlackAmericans" 1980-81; mem and completed post grad course Mid-Amer Orthodontic Soc 1983; mem Intl Orthodontic Org 1986; mem bd of dirs William B Price Unit Amer Cancer Soc; mem Congressional Adv Bd; life mem NAACP. **BUSINESS ADDRESS:** Clin Instr for Oper Dentistry, Harvard University, 1519 Blue Hill Ave, Mattapan, MA 02126.

WHYTE, GARRETT
Artist, educator. **PERSONAL:** Born Sep 05, 1915, Mt Sterling, KY; married Horrezelle E. **EDUCATION:** NC A&T State Univ, BS Art Ed 1939; School of the Art Inst Chicago IL, Grad Study 1950-51. **CAREER:** Chicago Defender, artist 1947-51; Chicago Agency, art dir 1951-56; Chicago Dunbar Voc HS, art teacher 1956-72; Chicago City Coll System, art prof 1972-80 retired. **ORGANIZATIONS:** Bd mem Southside Comm Art Ctr 1962-85, Natl Conf of Artists, DuSable Mus of Afri-Amer Hist. **HONORS/ACHIEVEMENTS:** Creator of cartoon comic "Mr Jim Crow" Chicago Defender, one of the 1st civil rights graphic satires 1946-51; 2 pg color reprod of painting Midwest Mag ChgoSun-Times 1965; art work reprod Chicago Sun-Times Mag "Mid-West", "Glory Forever 1974; cover story Chicago Defender Mag "Accent" 1974; slides & lecture on paintings at Art Inst of Chicago "The Art of Garrett Whyte" 1975; Amer Fed of Teachers Mag Chang Ed "Children of the Ghetto" 1967; art gallery mag work reprod 1968; Black Dimension in Contemp Amer Art 1971; Black Power in the Arts 1970; art exhibit Felician Coll 1975; painting Wolfson Collection NY Life Ins 1974; winner of Grand Awd for Art Teacher IL Reg Vocational Exhibit 1970-72. **MILITARY SERVICE:** AUS sgt 1942-45. **HOME ADDRESS:** 8648 Kenwood, Chicago, IL 60619.

WHYTE, HARTZELL J.
Attorney. **PERSONAL:** Born Jul 20, 1927, Kansas City, KS; married Ola Mae; children: 3. **EDUCATION:** KS St U, BS 1952; Univ MO, JD 1956. **CAREER:** Asst Gen Counsel, st KS corp commn 1957-59, KS st sec comm 1959-61; Wyandotte, KS, asst co couns 1963-ABA; Nat Bar Assoc; Wyandotte Bar Assoc KS St Bar Assoc; KS Bar Assoc, pres KC. **ORGANIZATIONS:** Pres Fellowship House 1969-70; NAACP; trustee Un Meth Ch bd dir Spofford House; KS Lung Assn; Kappa Alpha Psi Phi Delta Phi. **HONORS/ACHIEVEMENTS:** Fellowship House dist srv awd 1976; Legal Aid Clinic Awd 1956. **MILITARY SERVICE:** AUS sgt 1945-47f. **BUSINESS ADDRESS:** 2038 N 42nd, Kansas City, KS 66104.

WHYTE, JAMES W., JR.
Business executive. **PERSONAL:** Born May 20, 1921, Philadelphia, PA; married Dorothy E Woodson; children: Keith, Stephen. **EDUCATION:** Howard U, BS 1948. **CAREER:** US Naval Resrch Lab Washington, mech engr 1948-54; Boeing Commercial Airplane Co, mngr 747 noise tech staff. **ORGANIZATIONS:** Mem Acoustical Soc of Am mem NAACP; BSA; Eagle Scout Review Bd; Tuskegee Airmen Assn. **MILITARY SERVICE:** USAAF 1st lt 1942-45. **BUSINESS ADDRESS:** Boeing Commercial Airplane Co, PO Box 3707, Seattle, WA 98124.

WICKER, HENRY SINDOS
Physician. **PERSONAL:** Born Aug 08, 1928, New Orleans, LA; married Geralyn; children: Henry ?, Jr, Stephen. **EDUCATION:** Xavier U, BS 1948; Howard U, MD 1953. **CAREER:** St Elizabeth's Hosp, chf dept of ophthalgy; Am Bd of Ophthalgy, dipl; Am Acad of Ophthalgy, fellow; Howard U, asst prof; George Washington U, asst prof. **ORGANIZATIONS:** Mem Medico-chirurgical Soc; mem Med Soc of DC; mem Nat Med Assn bd dir Nat Conf of Christians & Jews 1971-75; bd of regents Ascension Acad 1970-74; bd dir Mater Dei Sch 1970-74; mem Common Cause; Alpha Phi Alpha frat. **MILITARY SERVICE:** USAF capt 1957-60; USAFR maj 1960-75.

WICKER, ISABELLE
Educator. **PERSONAL:** Born May 11, 1944, Goldston, NC. **EDUCATION:** Fayetteville State Univ, BS 1966; E Carolina Univ, MA Educ. **CAREER:** H B Sugg School, teacher 1966-68; Sam D Bundy School Farmville NC, teacher 1968-. **ORGANIZATIONS:** Pres Pitt Co Assn of Classroom Teachers 1971-72; mem NC Assn of Educ Com Human Relations 1972-73; chmn Finance Com Assn of Classroom Teachers grade chmn 1973-74; mem NC Assn of Educators; Natl Educ Assn; mem Alpha Kappa Alpha Sor; mem NAACP; mem Thompson Chaptel AME Zion Church, Sunday School Teacher, mem Farmville PTA. **HONORS/ACHIEVEMENTS:** Salutatorian 1962; French Awd 1962; Teacher of the Yr Pitt Co 1980.

WICKHAM, DEWAYNE
Journalist. **PERSONAL:** Born Jul 22, 1946, Baltimore, MD; son of John T Wickham and DeSylvia Chase Wickham; married Wanda Nadine Persons, Jun 1987; children: Vanessa Baker, Zenita Wickham. **EDUCATION:** Community Coll of Baltimore, 1970-72; Univ of MD, BS Journ 1974, Certificate in Afro-Amer Studies 1974; Univ of Baltimore, Masters of Pub Admin, 1982. **CAREER:** Baltimore Evening Sun, MD, reporter intern 1972-73; Richmond Times-Dispatch, VA, copy editing intern 1973; US News & World Report, Washington DC, Capitol Hill corresp 1974-75; Baltimore Sun, MD, reporter 1975-78; WBAL-TV, Baltimore, MD, talk show host 1976-; Gannett News Service, Arlington, VA, columnist 1985-. **ORGANIZATIONS:** Life mem, NAACP; mem, Advisory Bd, Multicultural Management Prog of Univ of MO Journ School 1986-; pres, Natl Assn of Black Journalists 1987-89; mem, Alumni Assn Board of Univ of Baltimore 1989-. **MILITARY SERVICE:** US Air Force, sgt, 1964-68; Vietnam Service Medal, Good Conduct Medal. **BUSINESS ADDRESS:** Columnist, Gannett News Service/USA Today, 1000 Wilson Blvd, 10th Floor, Arlington, VA 22209.

WICKHAM, MURIEL JEANNETTE
Assoc. executive. **PERSONAL:** Born Jan 21, 1957, Corpus Christi, TX; married Kevin W Wickham; children: Ashleigh Janelle. **EDUCATION:** Texas A&I Univ, BS 1980. **CAREER:** Texas A & I, sports reporter 1976-80; Leadership Kingsville, member 1983-84; Kleberg Mem Hosp Home Health Adv Committee, board member 1984; Kleberg County Camp Fire, Inc, executive director. **ORGANIZATIONS:** Pres, membership, sec treasurer, graduate advisor Alpha Kappa Alpha Sorority 1976-85; pres Grad Chap Delta Gamma Omega Alpha Kappa Alpha Sor 1987-87; member NAACP, PTA, Eastern Stars. **HONORS/ACHIEVEMENTS:** Daughters of American Revolution 1975; one of six srs selected to Hall of Honor W B Ray 1975. **HOME ADDRESS:** PO Box 140852, Austin, TX 78714-0852. **BUSINESS ADDRESS:** Executive Dir, Kleberg County Camp Fire, Inc, 609 W Yoakum, Kingsville, TX 78363.

WICKLIFF, ALOYSIUS M., SR.
Attorney. **PERSONAL:** Born Oct 11, 1921, Liberty, TX; married Mary E Prilliman; children: 4 Children. **EDUCATION:** Am U, BS; The Cath Univ of Am, LIB 1949. **CAREER:** Pvt Pract, atty; TX So U, asso prof 1955-58. **ORGANIZATIONS:** Mem Knights of Peter Claver; Eliza Johnson Home for Aged Negros; TX So Finance Corp; TX Finance & Invest Co; Comm Chapel Funeral Home; Comm Chapel Funeral Benefit Assn; MESBIC pres Harris Co Cncl of Orgn 1975, 76; Bus & Professional Men's Club 1973. **HONORS/ACHIEVEMENTS:** Comm Serv Awd 1967; campaign mgr Barbara Jordan for US Congress. **MILITARY SERVICE:** AUS 372nd infantry WW Ii. **BUSINESS ADDRESS:** 4720 Dowling, Houston, TX 77004.

WICKS, SIDNEY
Professional basketball player. **PERSONAL:** Born Sep 19, 1949, California; married Andra K Johnson; children: Sibahn K. **EDUCATION:** Santa Monica Jr Coll, 1967-68; UCLA, BA 1971. **CAREER:** San Diego Clippers, professional basketball player 1978-; Boston Celtics, professional basketball player 1977-78; Portland Trail Blazers, professional baketball player 1971-78. **HONORS/ACHIEVEMENTS:** NBA Rookie of the Yr 1971-72; Outstdg Coll Athletes 1970-71; TV Guide All Am Basketball Team Assn Writers 1970-71; received 1st Jose Lidchick Awd 1970-71; Player of the Yr Basketball News 1970-71; Most Valuable Player UCLA 1971. **BUSINESS ADDRESS:** San Diego Clippers, 3500 Sports Arena Blvd, San Diego, CA 92110.

WIDEMAN, JOHN E.
Novelist. **PERSONAL:** Born Jun 14, 1941, Washington, DC; married Judith Goldman; children: Daniel, Jacob, Jamila Ann. **EDUCATION:** Univ of PA, BA 1963; Oxford Univ, Rhodes Scholar, BPhil 1966; attended writers workshop, Univ of IA. **CAREER:** Howard Univ, instr 1965; Univ of PA, instr 1966, prof 1974, dir afro-amer studies prog 1971-73, asst basketball coach 1968-72; Univ of WY, prof of english. **ORGANIZATIONS:** State Dept Lecture Tour-Europe Near East 1976; Phi Beta Kappa Assoc Lectr 1976; novelist visiting writer/lecturer at various campuses across country; mem bd dir Amer Assn of Rhodes Scholars; state & natl selection comm Rhodes Competition; Natl Humanities Faculty; consult secondary schs across country 1968-. **HONORS/ACHIEVEMENTS:** Author of 3 publs novels, "A Glance Away" "Hurry Home" "The Lynchers"; short sotries reviews & essays in various natl publs Ben Franklin Scholar Univ of PA; Phi Beta Kappa Univ of PA 1959-63; Rhodes Scholar Oxford England 1963-66; Thouron Fellow Oxford 1963-66; Kent Fellow Univ of IA 1966; Philadelphia Big Five Basketball Hall of Fame 1974; Natl Endowment for

the Humanities; Young Humanist Fellowship 1975-. **BUSINESS ADDRESS:** Prof of English, Univ of Wyoming, Box 3434, University Station, Laramie, WY 82071.

WIDENER, WARREN HAMILTON
Government official. **PERSONAL:** Born Mar 25, 1938, Oroville, CA; married Mary Lee Thomas; children: Warren Jr, Michael, Stephen. **EDUCATION:** Univ of California Berkeley, AB 1960; Bolt Hall, Univ of California, JSD 1967. **CAREER:** Real Estate Safeway Stores, atty 1968-70; Berkeley, CA, cnclman 1969-71; Housing & Econ Devel Law Proj Univ of CA, atty 1970-72; Berkeley, CA, mayor; CA NHS Found, pres 1977-; Urban Housing Inst, pres 1979-. **ORGANIZATIONS:** Bd of dir Golden West Fin Corp 1980-; bd of dir World Svngs & Loan Assn 1980-; pres Natl Black Caucus of Local Elected Officials 1975; bd of dir, The Col Prep School 1984; bd of dir Berkeley Repertory Theatre 1984; bd dir E Oakland Youth Dev Ctr 1984; Alameda County, supvr 1989. **HONORS/ACHIEVEMENTS:** Chm Mayors Del to Hungary 1978; Dist Citizen Bay Area Urban League 1975. **MILITARY SERVICE:** USAF capt 4 yrs.

WIEGAND-MOSS, RICHARD CLIFTON
Cable television company executive. **PERSONAL:** Born Jul 17, 1947, Cleveland, OH; son of Richard Clifton Moss, Sr and Ethel Carey Moss; married Sara Wiegand-Moss; children: Chandra, Jason, Nicole, Adam Elliott, Jordan Sinclair. **EDUCATION:** Borromeo Seminary Coll, BA 1970; Cleveland State Univ, Teaching Certificate 1973; John Carroll Univ, MA currently; AMA, Understanding the Computer 1985; Wright State Univ, Fundamentals of Mktg 1985; Business Week Seminar, Writing a Winning Business Plan 1985, Pricing for Profit 1986. **CAREER:** Medina County Youth Svcs, exec dir 1977-79; Dept of Justice, legislative lobbyist 1979-82; Continental Cablevision, vice pres & dist mgr 1982-. **ORGANIZATIONS:** OH Cable TV Assoc; regional grassroot organizer Natl Cable TV Assn; bd of trustee mem OH Youth Advocacy Program Inc. **MILITARY SERVICE:** AUS E-4 1970-77; Graduated 4th Highest in Class 1970.

WIGFALL, SAMUEL E.
Financial administrator. **PERSONAL:** Born May 04, 1946, Jacksonville, NC; married Mildred Z Jones; children: Tara, Darian. **EDUCATION:** NC A&T State Univ, BS Accounting 1969; Univ of Louisville, Cost Acctg Sys 1973; Governor's State Univ IL, MBA work 1978; NY Univ, Capital Inv Acq Sem 1982. **CAREER:** Brown & Williamson Tobacco Co, financial accountant 1969-73; Johnson & Johnson Corp, sr cost accountant 1973-77; Brunswick Corp, sr financial analy 1977-79; Sherwood Medical Co, Div Fin Plng & Budget Mgr 1979-83, natl dealer comm mgr 1983-. **ORGANIZATIONS:** Scout master Broadway Temple Scout Troop 1971-72; dir B&W Employee's Credit Union 1972; advisor Jr Achievement KY 1972; pres sr choir Broadway Temple AME Zion Church 1972, 1973; vice pres Richmond Park IL Jaycees 1975; dir Brunswick Employees Credit Union 1976. **HONORS/ACHIEVEMENTS:** Varsity football scholarship NC A&T State Univ 1965-69; parts control proc manual Johnson & Johnson Corp 1972; youth motivation prog Chicago Assn of Commerce & Ind 1973-74; pub annual budget manual Brunswick Corp 1978; Speaking of People Ebony Magazine 1984. **HOME ADDRESS:** 1446 Chandellay Dr, Creve Coeur, MO 63146. **BUSINESS ADDRESS:** Natl Dealer Comm Manager, Sherwood Medical Co, 1831 Olive St, St Louis, MO 63103.

WIGGINS, ALAN
Professional athlete. **PERSONAL:** Born Feb 17, 1958, Los Angeles, CA; married Angie; children: Cassandra. **CAREER:** San Diego Padres, 2nd bsemn 1980-. **ORGANIZATIONS:** San Diego Police Dept assoc with drup/crime prev prog h schl aged youths. **HONORS/ACHIEVEMENTS:** Used outstdng spd best leadoff men in Nat'l Leag; finished yr club records stolen bases (70) runs scored (106); stolen base eclipsed club mark set 1983; 106 runs broke Dave Winfield's prev recd 104 in 1977; streaks 19 consec steal not caught; 17 times more than SB. **BUSINESS ADDRESS:** San Diego Padres, P O Box 2000, San Diego, CA 92102.

WIGGINS, CHARLES A.
Physician. **PERSONAL:** Born Aug 17, 1943, Pennington Gap, VA. **EDUCATION:** Morristown Coll, AA 1963; Fisk Univ, BA 1965; Meharry Medical Coll, MD 1969. **CAREER:** Charles A Wiggins MD, med dir; Crestview Nursing Home, med dir; Nashville Manor, med dir; Meharry/Hubbard Hosp Skilled Nursing Facility, med dir. **ORGANIZATIONS:** Mem Natl Medical Assoc, RF Boyd Medical Scis, Southern Medical Assoc, NY Acad of Sci, Amer Geriatrics Soc, TN Long Term Physician Soc. **HONORS/ACHIEVEMENTS:** Listed in Who's Who in South Health Aid, Intl Men of Distinction 1976, Outstanding Young Men of Amer. **MILITARY SERVICE:** AUS Medical Corp major 2 yrs. **BUSINESS ADDRESS:** Medical Dir, Meharry Hubbard Hosp, 1205 8th Ave So, Nashville, TN 37204.

WIGGINS, CLIFTON ALLEN, SR.
Educator. **PERSONAL:** Born Jun 21, 1912, Savannah, GA; married Alma Hayes; children: Drusilla Deanna Rucker, Ima Wilhelmina Burney, Cliftena Allette Kirkling, Clifton Allen Jr. **EDUCATION:** Savannah State Coll, BS Soc Studies/Biology 1947; Atlanta Univ, MA Admin & Supervision 1955; Tuskegee Inst, further study 1955. **CAREER:** Rosenwald Indus School, asst principal 1937-41; Clyo HS, principal, 1949-56; Central HS, principal, 1956-66; Riceboro Elementary School, principal, 1966-70; Liberty Co Schools, asst supt compensatory educ, 1970-80 (retired). **ORGANIZATIONS:** mem, Chatham Co Retired Teachers Assn 1980-; mem, GA Retired Teachrs Assn, 1980-; mem, Natl Retired Teachers Assn 1980; deacon & financial secretary, Skidaway Baptist Church, 1940-; pres, 42nd St Comm Civic Club, 1980-; mason Pastmaster Clyo Lodge #262 F&AM 1948-73; chairperson Homemaker Serv Prog Chatham Co Dept of Family & Children Serv 1982; chairperson Retired Sr Citizens Volunteer Prog Adv Cncl 1982-; mem Savannah Art Commn 1983-; appointed to special comm Chatham Co Admin Search Comm 1985; chairperson Adult Serv Advisory Council-Chatham Co Dept of Family & Children Serv 1986; mem NAACP Task Force Black on Black Crime, 1985; mem Savannah Coalition on Aging 1986. **HONORS/ACHIEVEMENTS:** Plaque Outstanding Contribution Toward the Devel of Central HS Springfield Effingham Co GA 1966; selected for Inclusion in Library of Human Resources of the Amer Bicentennial Rsch Inst in Recognition of His Professional & Civic Attainments within the Comm of Amer Men; plaque from Chatham Co Commnr Appreciation for Voluntary Serv in Selection of a Co Admin, 1985; Liberty County Assn of Educators for Dedicated Serv to Educ, 1980; Title I Staff for Outstanding Serv to Educ in Liberty County Schols, 1979-80; Riceboro Comunity in Appreciation for Years of Serv Rendered as Principal, 1980; retired sr voluntary & chairperson RSVP, 1983-85; Certificate of Appreciation, GA Dept of Educ, Liberty Co Schools; Commissioned Lieutenant Colonel, Aide, DeCamp Governor's Staff, by Governor, Joe Frank Harris, GA, 1989. **HOME ADDRESS:** 1112 W 42 St, Savannah, GA 31401.

WIGGINS, DAPHNE CORDELIA
Clergywoman. **PERSONAL:** Born Oct 21, 1960, Newark, NJ; daughter of Arthur Lee Wiggins, Sr. and Thelma G. Wiggins. **EDUCATION:** Eastern Coll, BA 1982; Eastern Baptist Theological Seminary, MDiv 1985; Ph.D. program Boston Univ 1987-. **CAREER:** Eastern Coll, resident asst 1981-82; Second Baptist Church Wayne PA, assoc minister 1981-84; Yeadon Presbyterian Church, pastoral asst 1983; Saints Memorial Baptist Church Bryn Mawr PA, dir of youth ministries 1984-85; Union Baptist Church Pawtucket RI, assoc minister 1985-; Brown Univ, assoc chaplain 1985-; interim pastor Union Baptist Church 1989-. **ORGANIZATIONS:** Natl Assoc of Campus and Univ Chaplains 1985-; univ rep Soc Organized Against Racism 1985-; bd mem Dorcas Place 1986-88; bd of advisors One Church One Child Adoption Program 1987-; vice pres Society Organized Against Racism in New England 1989-; vice pres Ministers Alliance of RI 1987-88. **HONORS/ACHIEVEMENTS:** Preaching license Calvary Baptist Church East Orange NJ 1980; ordination Second Baptist Church Wayne PA 1983; Recognition of Ordination American Baptist Churches of R.I. 1987. **HOME ADDRESS:** 212 Cottage St, Apt 1, Pawtucket, RI 02860. **BUSINESS ADDRESS:** Associate Chaplain, Brown University, Box 1931, Providence, RI 02912.

WIGGINS, EDITH MAYFIELD
Educational administrator. **PERSONAL:** Born Mar 18, 1942, Greensboro, NC; children: Balaam, David. **EDUCATION:** Univ of NC Greensboro, BA 1962, MSW 1962-64. **CAREER:** NC Memorial Hospital, pediatric clinical social worker 1964-67; Dept of Defense Middle School, Clark Air Force Base Phillipines, guidance counselor 1970-71; Inter Ch Council for Social Serv, social worker 1971-72; YMCA, YWCA, Univ of NC, dir campus 1972-; Univ of NC, asst vice chancellor and assoc dean of student affairs 1981-. **ORGANIZATIONS:** Mem Natl Assn Social Workers; past mem Chapel Hill Human Relation Comm Order of the Valkyries Univ of NC 1976; Order of the Golden Fleece Univ of NC 1976; Acad of Cert Social Workers Natl Assn Social Workers 1977-; bd of educ mem Chapel Hill-Carrboro 1979-. **BUSINESS ADDRESS:** Asst V Chanc & Associate Dean, Univ of NC, Chapel Hill, NC 27514.

WIGGINS, JOSEPH L.
Educator. **PERSONAL:** Born Feb 13, 1944, Norfolk, VA. **EDUCATION:** State Coll, BA 1966; Old Dominion U, MS 1970, pursuing cert of adv study educ leadership serv & rsrch;Univ of NC, further study 1967. **CAREER:** Shelton Park Elem School VA Beach, prin 1974-; VA Beach, admin aide to supt admin coordinator of standards of quality & prog 1972-74, asst elem school prin; Norfolk City Public Schools, teacher; Norfolk State Coll, asst instr govt. **ORGANIZATIONS:** Mem Sigma Rho Sigma; life mem Kappa Alpha Psi Frat Inc; life mem Nat Educ Assn; VA Assn of Sch Execs; VA Educ Assn; VA Bch Educ Assn; trustee St Thomas AME Zion Ch Norfolk. **HONORS/ACHIEVEMENTS:** Recip Academic Achvmt Awd Epsilon Zeta Chap Kappa Alpha Psi 1965; Active Chap Achvmt Awd Estrn Province Counc Kappa Alpha Psi 1965; Alumni Serv to theFrat Awd Estrn Province Counc Kappa Alpha Psi 1969; ldrs of Am Elem Educ Citation 1971; Achvmt in Educ Awd Estrn Province Counc Kappa Alpha Psi 1973; Outstng Young Men of Am 1974, 75; Achvmt Awd for Frat Serv Norfolk Alumni Chap Kappa Alpha Psi 1974. **BUSINESS ADDRESS:** Staff Assistant, Virginia Bch City Sch Board, 2512 George Mason Dr, Virginia Beach, VA 23456.

WIGGINS, LESLIE
Business executive. **PERSONAL:** Born Aug 18, 1936, Enfield, NC; married Pauline Faulkner. **EDUCATION:** Lincoln U. **CAREER:** Delaware Trust Co, asst vice pres 1971-, various adv pos since 1955. **ORGANIZATIONS:** Mem bd Children's Home; Acct Rep United Way; treas bd mem Peoples Settelment Assn; vice pres Wilmington Housing Corp; Urban Coalition of Gr Wilmington; bd mem Assn Gr Wilmington Neighborhood Ctrs; mem Union Bapt Ch. **HONORS/ACHIEVEMENTS:** Recip Minority Achiever of Wilmington Awd YMCA 1974. **BUSINESS ADDRESS:** Delaware Trust Co, 900 Market St, Wilmington, DE 19899.

WIGGINS, LILLIAN COOPER
Journalist. **PERSONAL:** Born Jun 26, 1932, Cincinnati, OH; divorced; children: Karen, Michael. **EDUCATION:** Attended Cortex Peters Business Sch, 1953; attended Howard Univ, Berlitz Sch of Language Foreign Serv Inst & Inservice Training Sch, USMC, Univ of Puerto Rico 1957. **CAREER:** USMC, property & supply office 1950; Washington DC, Ghana Embassy 1960-65; Ghana Govt, press & info officer; Washington Afro-Amer Newspaper, journalist pasteditor; Lil & Face Place, co-owner. **ORGANIZATIONS:** Past pres DC Tots & Teens; pub relations dir Natl Tots & Teens; talk show hostess "From the Desk of Lil" sta WHUR; former membership chmn Capitol Press Club; former mem State Dept Corres Assn; mem Women in Journalism; Media Women; appt DC Commn on Status of Women; roving chair Orgn of Black Activist Women; vice pres Cornelius Wiggins Intl Black Owned Bus; appt polit action chairperson DC Br NAACP; founder DC Survival Conf; mem Eagles, Black Entrepeneurs; bd mem United Black Fund; Sigma Delta Chi; vice chair DC Charitable Games Control Bd. **HONORS/ACHIEVEMENTS:** Journalist of the Yr 1965; 1st Prize Natl Publishers Convention 1974. **MILITARY SERVICE:** USMCR 1957. **BUSINESS ADDRESS:** Journalist/Consultant, Wash Inf, 3117 Mlk Ave SE, Washington, DC 20032.

WIGGINS, MITCHELL KEITH
Professional athlete. **PERSONAL:** Born Sep 28, 1959, Lenoir County, NC. **EDUCATION:** Clemson Univ; FL State Univ. **CAREER:** Chicago Bulls, guard 1983-; Houston Rockets, guard 1984-. **ORGANIZATIONS:** US team in 1982 World Games in Columbia. **HONORS/ACHIEVEMENTS:** 2nd among NBA rookies; led Chicago in steals 25 times; second team All-Junior Coll honors at Truett-McConnell in GA. **BUSINESS ADDRESS:** Houston Rockets, The Summit, Ste 510, Houston, TX 77046.

WIGGINS, WILLIAM H., JR.
Educator. **PERSONAL:** Born May 30, 1934, Port Allen, LA; married Janice Louise Slaughter; children: Wesley Howard, Mary Ellyn. **EDUCATION:** OH Wesleyan U, BA 1956; Phillips' Sch of Theol, BD 1961; Louisville Prebyn Theol Sem, MTh 1965; IN U, PhD 1974. **CAREER:** IN Univ, asso prof 1980-, asst prof 1974-79, grad teaching asst & lecturer

1969-73; TX Coll, dir rel life 1965-69; Freeman Chapel CME Church, pastor 1962-65; Lane Coll, prof 1961-62. **ORGANIZATIONS:** Fellow of the Folklore Inst IN U; founder dir Afro-Am Folk Archive IN U; so reg dir IN Chap Assn for the Study of Afro-Am Life & History; mem Smithsonian Inst African Diaspora Adv Gr Com; exec bd Hoosier Folklore Soc; ed bd The Jour of the Folklore Inst; prestr Am Folklife Fest 1975-76; field wk Smithsonian Inst 1975-76; pres Assn of African -Am Folklorists Minister Christian Meth Epis Ch; mem Am Folklore Soc; Nat Cncl for Blk Studies; Assn for the Study of Afro-Am Life & History; Assn of African & African-Am Folklorists; Hoosier Folklore Soc; Pop Cult Assn;Num Grants. **HONORS/ACHIEVEMENTS:** Num grants & flwhps; num publ; doc film "In the Rapture" anthologized wks appear in num publ & jour. **BUSINESS ADDRESS:** IN Univ Mem Hall E M26, Bloomington, IN 47401.

WILBER, MARGIE ROBINSON
Government official. **PERSONAL:** Born in Florence, SC. **EDUCATION:** SC State, AB 1942; Am U, grad stdt 1955; George Wash U, 1958; Dept of Agr Grad Sch, 1966. **CAREER:** Washington, state dept 1945-, editor publ div 1962-; Neighbd Adv Comm, elec commr 1976; Marion, SC, tchr 1942-44; The Crime Stoppers Club Inc, fdrexec dir. **ORGANIZATIONS:** Mem bd of dirs DC Women's Commn for Crime Prevention; mem Woman's Nat Dem Club; WA Urban League; NAACP; DC Fedn of Bus Professional Women's Club; Delta Sigma Theta Sor. **HONORS/ACHIEVEMENTS:** Comm Serv Awd Boy's Club of Gr WA 1968; Comm Serv Awd Sigma Gamma Rho Sor 1971; Action Fed Employee Disting Vol 1973; Comm Sev Awd Iota Chi Lambda1973; Comm Serv Awd United Nation's day (Human Rights) 1973; Outst Citizen Capitol Hill Restoration Soc 1974; Wash Vol Act Awd 1977; composer DC-TRIBUTE to Nation's Capital 1971; Future Am; Safe for the Children 1972. **BUSINESS ADDRESS:** 21st Virginia Ave NW, Washington, DC 20520.

WILBON, JOAN MARIE
Attorney. **PERSONAL:** Born Aug 21, 1949, Washington, DC; daughter of Addison Wilbon and Louise Wilbon. **EDUCATION:** Adelphi Univ Garden City NY, attended; New York Univ, BA (honors) 1971; George Washington Univ Law School Washington DC, JD 1974. **CAREER:** Dept of Labor Office of Solicitor, law clerk 1974; Equal Employment Oppor Comm, trial atty 1974-76; Howard Univ Sch of Law, supervising atty 1976; Natl Bar Assn EEO Div, dep dir 1976-78; Dept of Justice, trial attorney 1978-82; Joan M Wilbon & Assocs, attorney 1982-. **ORGANIZATIONS:** Mem Amer, DC, Women's, Washington Bar Assns; mem PA Bar Assn; mem bd of dirs Intergenerational Theater Co. **HONORS/ACHIEVEMENTS:** Presidential Scholar Adelphi Univ 1967; Martin Luther King Scholar NY Univ 1969-71; Fed Employee Litigation Natl Bar Law Journal 1978. **BUSINESS ADDRESS:** Attorney at Law, Joan M Wilbon & Assocs, 1511 K Street, NW, Ste 405, Washington, DC 20005.

WILBORN, LETTA GRACE SMITH
Educator. **PERSONAL:** Born May 12, 1936, Magnolia, AR; daughter of Henry Smith and Bulah Wilson Smith; married Leonard B Wilborn; children: Leonardo, Leilani. **EDUCATION:** Univ of AR Pine Bluff, BA (Cum Laude) 1958; CA State Univ Los Angeles, MA 1969. **CAREER:** Simmons High School, teacher 1958-59; Rowland Unified School District, teacher 1963-. **ORGANIZATIONS:** Pres Ward AME Community Music School 1975-; mem Assoc for the Study of Afro-Amer Life and History 1984-; sec Blair Hills Neighborhood Assoc 1986-; chairperson Oratorical Contest/OASC Los Angeles Branch; mem Rowland Educ Assoc, CA Teachers Assoc, Natl Educ Assoc; mem Sigma Gamma Rho Sor Inc, Ward AME Church, Summit Climbers Intl Training in Communications, NAACP. **HONORS/ACHIEVEMENTS:** Service Awd Our Authors Study Club/ASALH 1986; Quality of Life Awd Sigma Sigma Chap Sigma Gamma Rho Sor 1986. **HOME ADDRESS:** 5934 Blairstone Dr, Culver City, CA 90232.

WILBUN, SHEPPERSON A.
Judge. **PERSONAL:** Born Oct 14, 1924, Helena, AR; married Rubye L Knowles; children: Shepperson Jr, Gary R. **EDUCATION:** Philander Smith Coll, 1941-44; New York Univ, 1944-45; Howard Univ School of Law, LLB 1945-48. **CAREER:** Sam Houston Coll, instructor 1948-50; AR & TN Law Practice, private practice 1950-64; City Atty Memphis TN, asst to city atty 1964-73; Memphis TN, Memphis mun judge 1974-78; State of TN, judge circuit court-first black to serve in post. **ORGANIZATIONS:** Attended Amer Acad Judicial Educ Boulder CO 1974 & 1975; attended Natl Judicial Coll Reno NV 1978 & 1981; mem Amer Bar Assn TN Bar Assn; Memphis & Shelby Co Bar Assn BF Jones Chap NBA; mason & mem Moolah Temple Shrine; trustee & mem MT Olive Christian Methodist Episcopal Church. **BUSINESS ADDRESS:** Circuit Court Div 5, 15th Jud Cir Shelby Co, 140 Adams St, Memphis, TN 38103.

WILBURN, ISAAC EARPHETTE
Educational administrator. **PERSONAL:** Born Sep 11, 1932, Forrest City, AR; married Birdie Mae; children: Isaac E III, Berlinda, Michael E, Benjamin D, Loretta M, Darrell. **EDUCATION:** Dunbar Jr Coll, 1953; Philander Smith Coll, BS 1955; TN State Univ Nashville, MEd 1969. **CAREER:** Dist 5 Admin Assn, sec/treas 1965-70; Crowley Ridge Fed Credit Union, treas 1978-83; Forrest City Fed Housing, vice chmn 1978-85; East AR Comm Coll, chmn of trustee bd. **ORGANIZATIONS:** Chmn/trustee Beth Salem MB Church 1980-85; finan sec Beth Salem MB Church 1965-85. **HOME ADDRESS:** 822 East Garland Ave, Forrest City, AR 72335.

WILBURN, VICTOR H.
Architect. **PERSONAL:** Born Jan 23, 1931, Omaha, NE; married Sally; children: Victor, Jeff, Josh, Kim, Diane, Susan, Leslie. **EDUCATION:** Univ Chicago, 1954; Harvard Univ, MArch 1959. **CAREER:** Victor Wilburn Assoc Architects & Managers, owner 1962-; Urban Devel Group Inc, pres 1970-. **ORGANIZATIONS:** Mem Am Inst Architect; dir Easter Seal Soc; prof Drexel & Howard Univ. **HONORS/ACHIEVEMENTS:** Professor of Architecture at Univ of Penn, Univ of VA, and Howard Univ. **BUSINESS ADDRESS:** Victor Wilburn Assoc, 4301 Conn Ave, Washington, DC 20008.

WILCOX, JANICE HORDE
Educational administrator. **PERSONAL:** Born Nov 02, 1940, Baltimore, MD; daughter of Robert Harrison Horde and Gertrude Baker Horde; married Marvin Marlowe Wilcox, Oct 14, 1972 (divorced); children: Kia Miguel Smith. **EDUCATION:** Coppin State Univ, Baltimore, MD, BS 1965; Pepperdine Univ, Los Angeles, CA, MS 1976. **CAREER:** Los Angeles City Schools, CA, teacher 1968-73, reading coordinator 1973-75, early childhood educ coordinator 1975-77; CA Commn on Teacher Prep & Licensing, Sacramento, consultant 1977-78; US Dept of Educ, Washington DC, program analyst 1978-81, educ program specialist 1983-88, special asst for higher education program services, 1988-. **ORGANIZATIONS:** Member, Natl Council of Negro Women 1965-, Natl Urban League 1970-, Alpha Kappa Alpha 1974-, League of Women Voters 1978-, Black Women's Agenda 1988-, Natl Coalition of 100 Black Women 1988-. **HONORS/ACHIEVEMENTS:** Outstanding Fundraiser, Wilshire Heritage Group, 1973; Woman of the Year, CA Women's Assn, 1974; Distinguished Citizen, Jefferson Coalition, 1976; Outstanding Achievement awards, US Dept of Educ, 1984, 1985, 1986, 1989. **HOME ADDRESS:** 14000 Castle Blvd, No 1109, Silver Spring, MD 20904.

WILCOX, PRESTON
Association executive. **PERSONAL:** Born Dec 27, 1923, Youngstown, OH; divorced; children: Gwynne, David, Susan, Liana. **EDUCATION:** Attended, Youngstown Coll, Morehouse Coll, CUNY, NY Univ, Columbia Univ. **CAREER:** Parent Implementation in Educ, co-fndr; New Approach Method, an educ model primary cons; JERE Media Features "Big Red" & "Black Am", syndiacated columnist; Medgar Evers Coll La Guardia Com Coll, archivist/soc analyst/prof; VISTA & Peace Corps, tchr comm orgn trained; Bedford Stuyvesant D & S Corp, staff;Princeton Univ, soc rsrchrs; AFRAM Assoc Inc, exec dir. **ORGANIZATIONS:** Consult World Wide; mem Black Comm; Black Adv Task Force; Harlem Commonwealth Cncl; convenor Aframovement; Natl Black Political Assembly; United Black Assc; cncl adv edtr Afrika Must Unite; Black Schlr; Black Journalism Review; chmn bd dir Harlem Commonwealth Cncl Found Inc; edit bd Black Schlr; mem J Raymond Jones Democratic Club, The Harlem Comm for Intl Visitors, Harlem Reclamation Project, Harlem Solidarity Comm, Schomburg Library Adv Comm; mem Council for the Economic Develop of Black Americans, The Black United Fund of NY; founding bd chairperson East Harlem Youth Employment Serv Inc, Coll for Human Svcs; mem Prince Hall Masons. **HONORS/ACHIEVEMENTS:** Developed a copyrighted and tested educ model Parent Implementation in Educ and served as primary consultnat to The New Approach Method Reading Program; 40 Yr Plaque Psi Chap Omega Psi Phi Frat. **BUSINESS ADDRESS:** President, Afram Alternative Information, 68-72 East 131 St, New York, NY 10037.

WILDER, CORA WHITE
Educator. **PERSONAL:** Born Jul 31, 1936, Columbia, SC; married Kenneth Wilder; children: Michelle, Maxine, Marilynn, Marlene. **EDUCATION:** Howard Univ, grad 1956; Howard Univ School of Social Work, 1958. **CAREER:** Dept Pub Welfare, Washington DC, child welfare worker 1958-61; VA Clinic, Brooklyn, clinical social worker 1961-63; VA Neuro-Psychiatric Hospital, Montrose, NY, 1963-64; Rockland & Co Mental Health Clinic, Monsey, NY, psychiatric social worker 1964-67; St Agatha Home for Children, supr; Fordham Univ, field work instr 1967-69; Rockland Community Coll Human Serv Dept, asst prof & coord of field instr 1969-; Rockland Comm Coll, assoc prof social sci dept 1984-. **ORGANIZATIONS:** Sec Amer Fed of Teachers 1973-; dir Comp Child Welfare Sem Scandinavia; mem Delta Sigma Theta Sorority; life mem NAACP; Rockland Negro Scholarship Fund; Day Care & Child Devel Coun of Rockland Co; co-hosted radio prog 1972-75; Rockland Co Cit adv comm, affirmative action comm; mem United Way 1972-74, bd dir 1974-; mem Rockland Co Bicentennial Comm 1975; comm person Rockland Co Dem Comm; gov's appointee to bd of visitors, Letchworth Vlg Devel Ctr; co-partner Kenco Art Assoc Art Dist & Cons; consultant, Staff Devel & Programming in Day Care & Child Welfare; mem Natl Conf on Artists; bd dir Assn of Community-Based Artists of Westchester. **HONORS/ACHIEVEMENTS:** Outstanding Leadership Award, Spring Valley NAACP 1972. **BUSINESS ADDRESS:** Assoc Prof, Social Sci Dept, Rockland Community College, 145 College Rd, Suffern, NY 10901.

WILDER, LAWRENCE DOUGLAS
Government official. **PERSONAL:** Born Jan 17, 1931, Richmond, VA; children: Lynn, Loren, Lawrence Jr. **EDUCATION:** VA Union U, BS 1951; Howard Univ Sch of Law, JD 1959. **CAREER:** Attorney; state senator; lt governor. **ORGANIZATIONS:** Mem VA State Senate; Am Bar Assc; Am Trial Lawyers Assc; VA Bar Assc; Am Judicature Soc; Old Dominion Bar Assc; Richmond Trial Lawyers Assc; Richmond C of C; Richmond & Urban League; Red Shield Boys Clb; mem Privileges & Elections Com; Soc Serv & Rehab Com; chmn Transportation Com; Gen Laws Com; chmn VA Adv Legislative Cncl; VA Hsng Stdy Commn; chmn Serv to Youthful Offenders Commn; Profns & Occupations Study Commn; Pari-Mutuel Betting Study Commn; Welfare Study Commn; mem Crusade for Voters; NAACP; vice pres VA Human Relations Cncl; Mason; Shriner; Guardsman; v chmn Un Negro Clg Fund; Natl Conference of Lt Governors. **HONORS/ACHIEVEMENTS:** Recip bronze star medal Heroism in Ground Combat Korean War 1952; cert of merit VA State Clg 1974; hon doctor of laws VA UnionUniv 1979; dist alumni 1979; man of yr awrd Omega Psi Phi; astoria benefit assc awrd Delver Womens Clb; citizenship awrd 4th Afrcn Bapt Ch; alumnus of yr HowardUniv Law Sch 1970;cert of merit HowardUniv Law Sch 1974; civic awrd Omega Psi Phi Third Dist; civitan awrd Red Shields Boys Clb. **MILITARY SERVICE:** AUS. **BUSINESS ADDRESS:** Lieutenant Governor, State of Virginia, 101 N 8th St, Supreme Court Bldg, Richmond, VA 23219.

WILDERSON, FRANK B., JR.
Psychologist. **PERSONAL:** Born Jan 17, 1931, Lutcher, LA; married Ida Lorraine; children: Frank III, Fawn, Amy, Wayne. **EDUCATION:** Xavier U, BA 1953;Univ of MI, MS 1957, PhD 1962. **CAREER:** Student Affairs Univ of MN, vice pres 1975-; Univ of MN, asst prof to prof asst dean 1962-74; Univ of MI School of Educ, lecturer 1960-62; OutPatient Educ Pgm, dir 1961-62; Reading Clinic Univ of MI, dir 1958-61; Univ of MI Child Psychiatric Hospital School, teacher 1957-58; Orleans Parish Public Schools, teacher 1953-57. **ORGANIZATIONS:** Mem MN Psychol Assc; Am Psychol Assc; Cncl for Execeptional Children; Cncl for Children with Behavior Disorders; natl adv com Handicapped Children;adv com US Pub Hlth Serv; natl adv com Handicapped Childrens Early Ed; chmn HEW/BEH Panel; MN Assc for Group Psychotherapy; MN Assc for Brain-Damaged Children; Assc of Black Psychologist; publ com Cncl for Exceptional Children; dir Bush Found; trustee Breck Clg Prep Sch; mem Phi Delta Kappa; mem Black Coalition; mem num task forces & spec coms; MN Bd of Ed; chmnUniv Com on devel BA Pgm in the Area of Afro-am Studies Publ; Classroom Mgmt of Withdrawn Children 1963; A Concept of an Ideal Tchrl-Pupil Relationship in Classes for Emotionally Disturbed Chldrn 1967; An Exploratory Study of ReadingSkill Deficiencies & Psychiatric Symptoms in Emotionally Disturbed Children 1967. **BUSINESS ADDRESS:** Vice Pres of Student Affairs, Univeristy of Minnesota, 100 Church Street, SE, 1100 Morrill Hall, Minneapolis, MN 55455.

WILDERSON, THAD
Educational administrator. **PERSONAL:** Born Nov 13, 1935, New Orelans, LA; married Beverly; children: Troy, Dina, Lori, Marc. **EDUCATION:** Southern Univ, BS 1960, MA 1968; Tulane Univ, addl psychology courses; Univ of MN, Doctoral candidate. **CAREER:** Tulane Univ, interviewer/analyst 1959-69; St James Parish Sch, teacher 1960-65; Orleans Parish Sch, teacher/counselor 1965-69; Juvenile Diagnostic Ctr, counselor 1966; Upward Bound, counselor 1968; psychologist private practice 1970-; MN State Dept of Educ, consultant 1973-; Carleton Coll, counselor/consultant1971-75; Macalester Coll, assoc dean of students/dir of Minority Prog Psychologist 1969-. **ORGANIZATIONS:** Mem Amer Personnel & Guidance Assn; mem MN Personnel & Guidance Assn; mem Amer Psychological Assn; mem Midwest Psychological Assn; mem MN Psychological Assn. **HONORS/ACHIEVEMENTS:** "Housing Discrimination in New Orleans" published in 1970 Tulane Univ; "Impact of Model City Educ Progs upon the Model City Area" 1973; "Techniques for Assessing Minority Students" 1974; "Guidance Under the Knife A Case Study" 1974; "Factors Assoc with Drop Outs of Negro HS Students in Orleans" 1974; OutstandingComm Serv Awd from Minneapolis Urban League. **BUSINESS ADDRESS:** Assoc Dean of Stdts/Dir Min, Macalester College, 1600 Grand Ave, St Paul, MN 55105.

WILDS, CONSTANCE T.
Educator. **PERSONAL:** Born Jul 22, 1941, Stamford, CT; married Willie E; children: William Ernst. **EDUCATION:** Fairfield U, MA 1972; Wilberforce U, BA 1969. **CAREER:** Western CT State Coll, counselor comm coord 1971-73; Neighborhood Youth Corps, dir manpower CTE Inc, acting dir; CTE Inc, admn asst. **ORGANIZATIONS:** Mem CT Sch Cnslr Assc; APGA; Am Personnel & Guidance Assc; Assc Black Persnl Higher Ed; vice pres Minority Higher Ed; Master Plan Higher Ed; mem Urban League; Mental Hlth Assc; Afro-Am Dem Clb. **HONORS/ACHIEVEMENTS:** Cert Am Forum Internatl Study. **BUSINESS ADDRESS:** 181 White St, Danbury, CT.

WILDS, JETIE BOSTON, JR.
Government official. **PERSONAL:** Born Jan 10, 1940, Tampa, FL; married Ozepher Virginia Harris; children: Jemelle, Jeria. **EDUCATION:** Morehouse Coll, BA Math 1962; Portland State Univ, MS Adm 1972. **CAREER:** USDA Forest Service, job corps official 1966-70, personnel mgmt specialist 1970-75, dir civil rights 1975-86, dir mgmt planning 1986-1989, US Office of Personnel Management, Quality Executive 1989-. **ORGANIZATIONS:** Mem Amer Mgmt Assoc, Amer Forestry Assoc, Amer Soc of Public Admin, NAACP, Omega Psi Phi Frat; Natl Forum for Black Public Administrators. **HONORS/ACHIEVEMENTS:** Disting Alumni Awd Natl Assoc for Equal Oppor in Higher Educ 1986; Outstanding Employee of the Year; Jaycees Man of the Year; Amer Business Women Boss of Yr; articles published in Natl Assoc of Personnel Workers, Washington State Ed Journal. **HOME ADDRESS:** 9477 Old Deep Ct, Columbia, MD 21045.

WILES, JOSEPH ST. CLAIR
Pharmacologist. **PERSONAL:** Born Jul 27, 1914, Brooklyn, NY; married Esther Louise Ogburn; children: Carmen Christiana Artis; Carole Lucille Gibson. **EDUCATION:** Brooklyn Coll, attended 1932-38; Morris Brown Coll, AB Biology 1941; Atlanta Univ Grad Sch, attended 1941-42; Columbia Univ, 1950; Univ of MD Grad Sch, attended 1960-63. **CAREER:** Corps of Engrs Water Lab Fort Benning GA, bacteriologist 1942-43; Medical Rsch Lab Edgewood Arsenal MD, biologist 1946-52; Rsch Div Chem Systems Labs APG MD, pharmacologist (toxicology) 1953-80; Natl Academy of Scis, consultant. **ORGANIZATIONS:** Pres Zeta Sigma Chap Phi Beta Sigma Frat Inc 1976-79; vice dir 1977-79 dir 1979-81 Brotherhood of St Andrew St James Episcopal Church. **HONORS/ACHIEVEMENTS:** Wm A Fountain Status Achievement Awd Morris Brown Coll Atlanta 1970; Academic Scholarship Awd Atlanta Univ Grad Sch 1941; US Edgewood Arsenal Patent Awd Edgewood Arsenal MD 1971; Dept of Army Spec Act Awd Edgewood Arsenal Science Conf 1967. **MILITARY SERVICE:** AUS s/sgt 1943-46 1950-51; American Campaign Medal; european African Middle Eastern Campaign Medal; Asiatic Pacific Campaign Medal; Good Conduct Medal. **HOME ADDRESS:** 3004 N Ridge Rd, Apt 504, Ellicott City, MD 21043.

WILES, LEON E.
Educator. **PERSONAL:** Born May 28, 0947, Cincinnati, OH; married Maliaka Johnson; children: Tanzania, Saleda. **EDUCATION:** Baldwin-Wallace Coll, certificate; Harvard U, certificate; Yale U, certificate; Philander Smith Coll, BA (Cum Laude) 1970;Univ of Pittsburg, MEd 1972. **CAREER:** Silppery Rock St Coll, chairperson 1974-78; PA State Univ, dir of fresham studies 1978-82; Univ of SC, dean of students 1982-. **ORGANIZATIONS:** Human relations counsultant Alleghney Comm Coll 1970-72; minority affairs consultant Carnegre Mellan Univ 1970-72; exec educational comm Model Cities 1970-74; pre-medica advisor Univ of Pittsburgh 1972-74; sec Jaycees 1974-78; sec Sertoma 1985. **HONORS/ACHIEVEMENTS:** Outstanding admin PA State 1976, 1978; communication awrd Jaycees 1974; certificate Leadership Spartanburg 1984; Outstanding Young Man of America 1986. **BUSINESS ADDRESS:** Dean of Students, University of SC-Spartanburg, 206 Hodge Center, Spartanburg, SC 29303.

WILES, SPENCER H.
Educator. **PERSONAL:** Born Apr 13, 1944, NYC, NY; married Jean Ford. **EDUCATION:** Lincoln Univ, BA 1965; NY Univ, MA 1969. **CAREER:** NY City Coll, lecturer; Manhasset Public School, asst prin 1970-72, elem principal 1972-80; WNBC-TV New York, mgr comm relations 1980-83; WRC-TV Washington, acct executive 1984-. **ORGANIZATIONS:** Mem AASA, NAESP, NASCD, NAACP; mem Town of Hempstead adv com on Cable TV 1976-77. **HONORS/ACHIEVEMENTS:** Youngest prin history Manhasset; first black prin Manhasset. **BUSINESS ADDRESS:** Account Executive, WRC-TV, 4001 Nebraska Avenue NW, Washington, DC 20016.

WILEY, FLETCHER HOUSTON
Attorney. **PERSONAL:** Born Nov 29, 1942, Chicago, IL; son of Fletcher Wiley and Mildred Wiley; married Benaree Drew Pratt; children: Pratt Norton, Benaree Mildred. **EDUCATION:** USAF Acad, BS, 1965; Univ of Paris (Fulbright), 1966; Georgetown Univ, 1968; Harvard Law School, JD, 1974; JFK School of Govt, MPP, 1974. **CAREER:** ABT Assoc Inc, consultant, 1972-75; Fine & Ambrogne, atty, 1975-78; Budd, Wiley & Richlin, PC, atty/mng partner, 1979-89; Wiley & Richlin, PC, atty/pres, 1989-. **ORGANIZATIONS:** Assoc comm, Massachusetts Alcoholic Beverage Control Commn, 1977-81, 83-84; consvtr, Unity Bank & Trust Co, 1982; bd mem, Boston Chamber of commerce, 1980-; bd mem, Econ Devel & Indus Corp, 1981-; bd mem, Dana-farber Cancer Inst, 1978-86; bd mem, New England Aquarium, 1982-86; chmn, Govt commr on Minority Business Devel, 1985-; natl pres, Black Entertainment & Sports Lawyers Assn, 1986-. **HONORS/ACHIEVEMENTS:** Flw US Fulbright Comm (Paris), 1965-66; flw Joint Center for Political Studies, 1970-71; flw Massachusets Intl Fellowship Program (London), 1984; Ten Otstndng Young Leaders Boston Jaycees, 1978. **MILITARY SERVICE:** USAF, captain, 4 years. **HOME ADDRESS:** 29 Fort Ave, Roxbury, MA 02119. **BUSINESS ADDRESS:** Pres, Wiley & Richlin, PC, 75 Arlington St, Boston, MA 02116.

WILEY, FORREST PARKS
Business executive. **PERSONAL:** Born Nov 01, 1937, Weldon, NC; married Gloria; children: Joseph, John, Linda. **EDUCATION:** Tuskegee Isnt, BS 1966. **CAREER:** Harris Corp Dilitho Systems, mgr sls mgr serv mgr 1975-; Letterflex Systems WR Grace, reg mgr 1973-75, system engr 1970-73; New Ventures Inc, dir rsrch 1970-73; WR Grace, rsrch asst bio chem 1967-70. **ORGANIZATIONS:** Pres Tuskegee Alumni Housing Found 1977-; bd dir WA Tuskegee Housing Found; mem Natl Geog Soc; Botanical Soc Am Am Soc Plant Physiologists; Am Inst Biol Sci; Tuskegee Alumni Assc; pres Wa-tuskegee Clb; mem Interntl Platform Assc. **BUSINESS ADDRESS:** Mechanic St, Westerly, RI 02891.

WILEY, GERALD EDWARD
Human resource/industrial relations executive. **PERSONAL:** Born Jun 20, 1948, Belleville, IL; son of Mr & Mrs George Wiley; married Marquita Trenier; children: Raymond, Johanna. **EDUCATION:** St Louis Univ, BS, Sociology, 1970, MA, Urban Affairs, 1974. **CAREER:** Container Corp of Amer, personnel mgr, 1974-75; Gen Dynamics, employee relations dir, 1975-78; Wiley, Ette & Assoc, vice pres, 1978-80; Monsanto Co, professional employment dir, 1980-. **ORGANIZATIONS:** Bd of dirs, St Louis Univ, Tip Off Club, 1980-, pres, 1983-84; atheletic advisory council, St Louis Univ, 1989; Social & Labor Legislative Council of Missouri. **HONORS/ACHIEVEMENTS:** Inducted into the Illinois Basketball Hall of Fame, 1977; assembly mem, Midwest Coll Placement Assoc, 1986-88. **HOME ADDRESS:** 13 Town Hall Estates, Belleville, IL 62223. **BUSINESS ADDRESS:** Dir Professional Recruiting, Monsanto Co, 800 N Lindberg Blvd, St Louis, MO 63167.

WILEY, HERLEY WESLEY
Clergyman. **PERSONAL:** Born Dec 16, 1914, Caswell County, NC; married Doris White; children: Howard Wesley, Dennis Wayne. **EDUCATION:** BS 1944. **CAREER:** 1st Bapt Ch, pastor 1943-47; Friendship Bapt Ch, 1947-53; Forsyth County, mission dir 1953-55; Zion Bapt Ch, 1955, 1964-68. **ORGANIZATIONS:** Dir Coop Ministries Co Bapt Home Mission Bd, So Bapt Conv 1968-; pastor Covenant Bapt Ch; Budget Com Progressive Nat Bapt Conv; exec bd Lott Carey Foreign Missionary Conv; Council Chs Greater Wash; mem Inter-Faith Com. **BUSINESS ADDRESS:** 3845 S Capt St, Washington, DC 20032.

WILEY, JOHN D., JR.
Educator. **PERSONAL:** Born Sep 24, 1938, Fodice, TX; married Clara. **EDUCATION:** BS 1959; MS 1960;Univ Houston, advncd stdy. **CAREER:** Dillard Univ, instructor 1960-63; Inst Serv to Educ, consultant 1967-68; TX So Univ, acting head math dept 1972, asst prof. **ORGANIZATIONS:** Mem Math Assn Am; Nat Math Assn. **BUSINESS ADDRESS:** Dept of Mathematics TX Sou, 3201 Wheeler St, Houston, TX 77004.

WILEY, KENNETH LEMOYNE
Physician. **PERSONAL:** Born Jan 10, 1947, San Antonio, TX; son of Elmer Wiley (deceased) and Dolores Shields Wiley (deceased); married Linda Diane Nixon; children: Kenneth Jr, Brian. **EDUCATION:** Trinity Univ, BS 1968; OK State Univ, MS 1970; Meharry Medical Coll, MD 1977. **CAREER:** Private Practice, internal medicine 1980-. **ORGANIZATIONS:** Mem Alpha Phi Alpha, Alpha Omega Alpha, Society of Sigma Xi. **HONORS/ACHIEVEMENTS:** Cedar Tree Award Lebanon Chamber of Commerce 1989. **MILITARY SERVICE:** AUS capt 3 yrs; Bronze Star, Technical Service Medal. **HOME ADDRESS:** Rt 1 Davis Corner Rd, Mount Juliet, TN 37087. **BUSINESS ADDRESS:** Wiley Professional Center, 501 Park Avenue, Suite 8, Lebanon, TN 37087.

WILEY, LEROY SHERMAN
Government official. **PERSONAL:** Born Oct 30, 1936, Sparta, GA. **EDUCATION:** Ft Valley State Coll, BS 1960; Clark Coll, 1968; Univ of GA, 1966-69; GA Coll, MS 1975-77. **CAREER:** Ft Valley State Coll, suprv maintenance dept 1958-60; Hancock Central HS, instr dept chmn 1960-61; Boddie HS, instr 1963-64; Hancock Central HS, instr, chmn of sci dept 1964-70; Upward Bound Study Ctr, dir 1973; Learning Ctr, couns asst field rep 1975; Hancock Cty Emergency Mgmt Agency, dir, coord 1984; Hancock Cty, clerk of superior ct 1970-. **ORGANIZATIONS:** Mem Kappa Alpha Psi, CB Radio Club Inc, Masonic Orders, Hancock Cty Dem Club, Hancock Cty Br NAACP, GA Assoc of Black Elected Officials, Veterans Assoc of GA Coll of Milledgeville, GA Ed Assoc, GA Farm Bur Assoc, Natl Assoc of Retarded Children, Cty Officials Assoc of GA; comm chmn BSA; post comdr Amer Legion #530 1984-85; mem, trustee bd St Mark AME Church. **HONORS/ACHIEVEMENTS:** 1st black since reconstr & only black serving as clerk of Superior Court; Outstanding Contrib in Civil Rights Movement in Hancock Cty 1982. **MILITARY SERVICE:** Army GA Natl Guard 2yrs. **BUSINESS ADDRESS:** Clerk of Superior Court, Hancock County, PO Box 451, Sparta, GA 31087.

WILEY, LUCISH D.
Engineer. **PERSONAL:** Born Jul 06, 1950, Houston; married Patricia. **EDUCATION:** TX A&M U, BSCHE 1972. **CAREER:** EI DuPont Chem Co, chem engr; Minority Manpower Resources Proj, partcpnt; Coop Educ TX A&M EI DuPont; Affiliated with Minority Manpower Res Proj,adv rep DuPont Co. **ORGANIZATIONS:** Bible Tchr First Hon Student Elem & Jr HS; Nat Honor Soc & vp; Salutatorian HS; Achvmnt Award 1967; Hon Mention Most Outstndg Boy HS. **HONORS/ACHIEVEMENTS:** Bible Tchr First Hon Student Elem & Jr High; Natl Honor Soc & vp; Salutatorian HS; Achvmnt Award 1967; Hon Mention Most Outst Boy HS. **BUSINESS ADDRESS:** PO Box 347, La Porte, TX 77571.

WILEY, MARGARET Z. RICHARDSON
Business executive. **PERSONAL:** Born Jun 27, 1934, Jackson, NC; married Sampson; children: Brian, Judith. **EDUCATION:** City Coll of NY, 1955-56; Scott's Coll of Cosmetology, 1963-65; IN U, 1967-69. **CAREER:** Nat Minority Supplier Devel Council, exec dir/chf oper ofcr 1978-; Devco Local Devel Corp, pres 1973-78; Natl Devel Council, exec dir 1972-78; Summit Labs Indpls, educ & mrktng dir 1965-72; Americana Salon, owner 1974-. **ORGA-**

NIZATIONS: Adv bd Enterprising Women 1978-; mem Revenue Plng Bd of Montclair NJ 1978; mem NAACP 1980. **HONORS/ACHIEVEMENTS:** Recipient Outst Sales & Outst Mgmt/Sales Awrds Summit Labs Indianapolis 1969-70; Distng Achvmnt/Serv Awrd The Links Inc Seattle 1976; Mayor Citation City of Baltimore 1979; recipient Woman's Outst Award in Bus NAACP NY 1980; recipient Woman of the Year Awrd Serv/Devel of Minority Bus Natl Assn of Black Manufactrs Wash DC 1980. **BUSINESS ADDRESS:** Broker, J H Rudd Real Estate Agency, 312 Orange Rd, Montclair, NJ 07042.

WILEY, MAURICE
Administrative assistant. **PERSONAL:** Born Jan 13, 1941, Pine Bluff, AR; son of Mr and Mrs Hosie Wiley. **EDUCATION:** Univ of AR-Pine Bluff, BS 1963; CA State Univ Los Angeles, MA 1972. **CAREER:** Pasadena Unified School Dist, math teacher 1966-69; Inglewood Unified School Dist, math teacher 1969-72, guidance counselor 1972-82, coordinated coll prep programs 1982-88; admin asst to the supt, 1989. **ORGANIZATIONS:** Consultant College Preparatory Programs & H S Counseling; mem Inglewood Chamber of Commerce Educ Comm; mem Phi Delta Kappa Educ Frat 1974-; pres Inglewood Counseling & Psychology Assoc 1986; participant NAFEO Conf Nations Black Colls 1986; participant UCLA Counselors Inst Univ of CA 1986; mem Inglewood Mgmt Assoc, Inglewood/Centinela Valley Youth Counseling Adv Comm. **HONORS/ACHIEVEMENTS:** Outstanding Young Men in Amer Pasadena Chamber of Commerce 1970; Most Eligible Bachelor Ebony Magazine 1971; Counselor/Teacher of the Yr Inglewood High School 1980; Awd of Excellence Inglewood Sch Dist 1984; Comm Unity Commendation City of Inglewood CA 1986. **MILITARY SERVICE:** AUS staff sgt 1963-65; Outstanding Achievement Awd 1965. **BUSINESS ADDRESS:** Coord of College Prep Programs, Inglewood Unified Schl Dist, 401 S Inglewood Ave, Inglewood, CA 90301.

WILEY, RENA DELORIS
Social service. **PERSONAL:** Born Jul 29, 1953, Effingham County, GA; daughter of Rev J B Canady and Rena Elizabeth Canady; married Willie Frank Wiley Jr, Sep 14, 1974; children: Hawa Shahlette, Sherri Latrice, Elizabeth Renae. **EDUCATION:** GA Southwestern Coll, BS Psych 1976; Augusta Coll, MS Clinical Psych 1977. **CAREER:** Sumter Cty Taylor Cty Mental Retard Ctr, behavior spec 1977-78; Taylor Cty Mental Retard Ctr, acting dir 1978; Americus Area Mental Health, equal employment oppty rep 1978-, part time employment with area PhD Psychologist; behavior spec child & adolescent prog 1978-. **ORGANIZATIONS:** Mem Delta Sigma Theta 1973-; school bd mem Amer City Bd of Ed 1980-; area workshop panel Child Sexual Abuse/Child Abuse 1982-; sec Early Bird Civitan Club 1983-84; jr hs group facilitator Taylor Cty Pregnancy Prevention Prog 1984-; pres Sumter Cty Mental Health Assoc 1984-85; bd of dir GA Mental Health Assoc 1984-85; group facilitator Arrive Alive GA 1985; pres elect Early Bird Civitan Club 1985, pres 1986-; District 8 Infant Mortality Task Force 1986-; Sumter 2000 Committee; consultant to area agencies and schools; vice chairman, Americus City Board of Ed 1980-. **HONORS/ACHIEVEMENTS:** Blue Key Natl Honor Frat GA Southwestern Coll 1981; Outstanding Serv Awd Sumter Cty Mental Health Assoc 1982. **HOME ADDRESS:** 212 Barnum Dr, Americus, GA 31709. **BUSINESS ADDRESS:** Behavior Specialist, Sr., Americus Area Mental Health, 415 W Forsyth, Americus, GA 31709.

WILEY, WILLIAM R.
Director (corporate). **PERSONAL:** Born Sep 03, 1931, Oxford, MS; married Myrtle Louise Smith; children: Johari. **EDUCATION:** Tougaloo Coll, BS Chemistry 1954; Univ of IL, MS Microbiology 1960; Washington State Univ, PhD Bacteriology 1965. **CAREER:** Battelle Pacific NW Labs, rsch scientist 1965-69, mgr cellular & molecular biology sect 1969-72, coord life sci prog 1972-74, mgr biology dept 1974-79;dir of rsch 1979-84; Washington State Univ Pullman WA, adj assoc prof of bacteriology 1969-; Battelle Meml Inst Pacific NW Div, vp, dir 1984-. **ORGANIZATIONS:** Mem Amer Soc of Biological Chemists, Amer Soc of Microbiology, Amer Assoc for the Advancement of Sci, Soc for Experimental Biol & Med; lecturer Black Exec Exchange Prog 1969-; adj assoc prof microbiol WA State Univ 1968-; mem WA Tech Ctr Sci Adv Panel 1984-; mem bd dir WA MESA Prog Univ of WA Seattle 1984-, WA Tech Ctr 1984-, United Way of Benton & Franklin Counties 1984-, Tri-City Indust Devel Council 1984-, Econ Devel Partnership for WA 1984-; mem WA Council for Tech Advancement 1984-85; mem bd dir The Northwest Coll & Univ Assoc for Sci 1985-; mem Tri-City Univ Center Citizens Adv Council 1985-; mem Gov Gardner's Higher Educ Coord Bd 1986-; mem bd trust Carver Tsch Found of Tuskegee Univ 1986-; mem bd trustees WA State Univ Found 1986-. **HONORS/ACHIEVEMENTS:** Listed in Who's Who in Amer, Amer men and Women in Sci; author and co-author of 22 journal publs, co-author of one book. **MILITARY SERVICE:** AUS corpl 1954-56. **BUSINESS ADDRESS:** Dir, Battelle Memorial Inst, Pacific NW Div, PO Box 999, Richland, WA 99352.

WILEY-PICKETT, GLORIA
Government official. **PERSONAL:** Born Jul 05, 1937, Detroit, MI; daughter of Elmer Wiley and Fannie (Wiley) Smith; divorced; children: Michele Joy Pickett-Wells. **EDUCATION:** Attended, Detroit Inst of Tech 1954-56, Wayne State Univ 1980-82. **CAREER:** US Dept of Defense, accounting tech, federal womens prog coord 1971-73, supervisory procurement asst 1973-75; US Dept of Labor/ESA/OFCCP, equal opportunity specialist 1975-81, supervisory equal opportunity specialist, asst district dir, currently. **ORGANIZATIONS:** Mem Courtesy Comm March of Dimes Fashion Extravaganza 1971-, Natl Assoc of Human Rights Workers 1981-, Natl Assoc of Female Execs Inc 1983-; treasurer DGL Inc 1984-86; chairperson Prog Comm Amer Business Women's Assoc Spirit of Detroit Chap 1985-; mem, Founder's Soc, Detroit Inst of Arts; mem, Natl Assn of Human Rights Workers; mem, Natl Assn of Female Executives Inc; mem, NAACP. **HONORS/ACHIEVEMENTS:** Letter of Commendation for Performance DOD DLA DCASR; Special Achievement Awd for Outstanding Contributions to the EEO Prog Dept of Defense DLA DCASR. **BUSINESS ADDRESS:** Asst District Dir, US Dept of Labor/ESA/Office of Federal Contract Compliance, Patrick V McNamara Bldg, 477 Michigan Ave, Rm 1065, Detroit, MI 48226.

WILFONG, HENRY T., JR.
Accountant. **PERSONAL:** Born Feb 22, 1933, Ingals, AR; married Aline Jane Guidry; children: Bernetta, Brian. **EDUCATION:** UCLA, BA 1958, MBA 1960. **CAREER:** Wilfong & Co, sr prtnr; Nat Assn Minority CPA Firms, pres 1971. **ORGANIZATIONS:** Elected city councilman 1973; apptd CA Council Criminal Justice 1974; bd dir Nat Bus League & Ca Soc CPA'S. **HONORS/ACHIEVEMENTS:** Fred D Patterson Awrd 1974; 10 Top Minority Bus Yr Awrd 1972. **MILITARY SERVICE:** AUS sgt 1954-56. **BUSINESS ADDRESS:** Associate Administrator, Minority Small Business Admin, Small Business Administration, Washington, DC 20416.

WILFORD, HAROLD C.
Editor. **PERSONAL:** Born Sep 18, 1924, St Louis, MO; married Dorothy; children: Jacquelyn. **CAREER:** Studebaker Auto Mfg, machinist 1946; Smart Cleaners, owner 1947; US Post Office, clerk 1951; East St Louis Nightclub, owner 1953-60; Grace Durocher Dress Design, clk 1962; Slays Restaurant, chef 1966; Argus Newspaper, ad mgr 1967, entertainment editor 1967; Entertainment Artists, personnel business mgr. **ORGANIZATIONS:** Mem Amvets; pres & dir Jazzville USA 1970-72; press agent Regal Sports Promotions Inc; Ebony Fashion Fair; consult Sonic Soul Enterprises 1973; hon judge pr Miss Black Am Pagent MO 1970-73; PR Congressman Wm Clay 1968-74; mem Police Youth Corp; Ardell Film Intl Prod Co; pr dir United Black Comm Fund; St Louis Expo; Black Packing House Workers Pres. **HONORS/ACHIEVEMENTS:** Citation Armed Svcs; Good Conduct Medal; Distinguished Serv Awrd Amvets 1972; Certificate Serv 1969. **MILITARY SERVICE:** AUS corpl 1943-46. **BUSINESS ADDRESS:** 4595 Martin Luther King Dr, St Louis, MO 63113.

WILFORK, ANDREW LOUIS
Appointed official. **PERSONAL:** Born Apr 27, 1947, Quitman, GA; married Viola Irene Godwin; children: Jermaine. **EDUCATION:** FL Intl Univ, BS Soc Work 1974. **CAREER:** Metro-Dade County Waste Dept, service rep 1971-72, enforcement officer to coordinator 1972-74, area supr 1974-78; Metro-Dade Cty Public Works Dept, transfer station 1978-80, supr transfer station admin 1980-86; superintendent 1986-, acting dir dept of solid waste collection; deputy dir. **ORGANIZATIONS:** Mem Governmental Refuse Collection & Disposal Assn, Natl Black Public Admin, Amer Public Works Assn, Human Resource Systems Professionals. **HONORS/ACHIEVEMENTS:** Certificate of Recognition Peabody Solid Waste Management 1979; Certificate of Completion of Media Relations Class; Certificate from Gov Bob Graham (FL) for Valuable and Distinguished Serv to the State of FL. **MILITARY SERVICE:** AUS sergeant 3 yrs. **HOME ADDRESS:** 1520 NW 203rd St, Miami, FL 33169.

WILHOIT, CARL H.
Registered professional engineer. **PERSONAL:** Born Aug 15, 1935, Vandalia, MO; married Daisy Glascoe; children: Raquel, Marcus. **EDUCATION:** Lincoln U, 1958-60; Howard U, BS 1962; Catholic U, M 1973. **CAREER:** New Town Devel DC Dept of Housing & Comm Devel, engrng coord; DC Dept of Hwys & Traffic, civil engr 1962-67; Dept of Civil Engrng Fed City & Coll Washington DC, lctr 1975-76. **ORGANIZATIONS:** Mem ASCE; Nat Assn of Housing & Redevelopment Officials 1971; mem Nat Soc of Professional Engrs (NSPE) 1977. **MILITARY SERVICE:** USAF a/1c 1955-58. **BUSINESS ADDRESS:** 1325 G St NW, Washington, DC 20005.

WILKENS, LEONARD R.
Professional basketball coach. **PERSONAL:** Born Oct 28, 1937, Brooklyn, NY; son of Henrietta Cross Wilkens; married Marilyn J. Reed, Jul 28, 1962; children: Leesha, Randy, Jamee. **EDUCATION:** Providence College, BA, 1960. **CAREER:** St Louis Hawks, St Louis, MO, player, 1960-68; Seattle Super Sonics, Seattle, WA, player-coach, 1968-72; Cleveland Cavaliers, Cleveland, OH, player, 1972-74; Portland Trail Blazers, Portland, OR, player-coach, 1974-75, coach, 1975-76; Seattle Super Sonics, head coach, 1977-85, general manager, 1985-86; Cleveland Cavaliers, Cleveland, OH, head coach, 1986—. **ORGANIZATIONS:** Honorary chairman, Marymount-Cavs RP Golf Classic, 1987—; chair, Make-a-Wish Golf Tournament, 1988; Boys and Girls Clubs of Greater Cleveland; Catholic Diocese of Cleveland; Rainbow babies; Children's Hospital; Kidney Foundation. **HONORS/ACHIEVEMENTS:** National Invitation Tournament, Most Valuable Player, 1960; Rhode Island Heritage Hall of Fame, 1961; NBA All-Star Game, Most Valuable Player, 1971, representative, 1973; coached Seattle Super Sonics to NBA Championship, 1979; City of Hope Sportsman of the Year, Congressional Black Caucus Coach of te Year, CBS Coach of the Year, Black Publisher of America Coach of the Year, 1979; honorary doctor of humanities, Providence College, 1980; Urban League-Witney Young Outstanding Citizen Award, 1980; Golden Shoe Award, Shoes for Kids, 1988; Digital NBA Coach of the Month, December, 1988; elected to Naismith Memorial Basketball Hall of Fame, 1989. **MILITARY SERVICE:** US Army, Quartermaster Corps, 2nd Lieutenant, 1961-62. **BUSINESS ADDRESS:** Cleveland Cavaliers Management Corp, Richfield Coliseum, PO Box 355, Richfield, OH 44286.

WILKERSON, DOUG
Professional athlete. **PERSONAL:** Born Mar 27, 1947, Fayetteville, NC; children: Melanie, Gia. **EDUCATION:** NC Central U. **CAREER:** Mesa Distributors, sales rep; San Diego Chargers, guard 1970-. **ORGANIZATIONS:** Dir Membership Devel for San Diego Chamber of Commerce; March of Dimes; Kidney Found. **HONORS/ACHIEVEMENTS:** Voted starter in Pro Bowl by AFC Peers prior to 1983; named Chargers Lineman of the Yr by teammates 6 times in career; named All-AFC by UPI 1981; Players Assn Whizzer White Award 1981.

WILKERSON, HENRY C.
Attorney. **PERSONAL:** Born May 24, 1922, Clinton, MS. **EDUCATION:** Tougaloo Coll, AB 1948; Howard U, JD 1952. **CAREER:** Self-Employed, atty. **ORGANIZATIONS:** Mem Am Bar Assn; Judicature Soc; Langston Law Assn; YMCA; NAACP. **MILITARY SERVICE:** AUS.

WILKERSON, MARGARET BUFORD
Educator. **PERSONAL:** Born Apr 03, 1938, Los Angeles, CA; daughter of George Buford and Gladys Buford; married Stanley; children: Darren, Cullen, Gladys-mari. **EDUCATION:** Univ of Redlands, BA History (magna cum laude) 1959; UCLA, Teachers Cred960-61;Univ Of CA Berkeley, MA Dramatic Art 1967, PhD Dramatic Art 1972. **CAREER:** YWCA Youngstown OH, adlt pgm dir 1959-60; YWCA Los Angeles, adlt gm dir 1960-62; Jordan HS LA CA, drama/engl tchr 1962-66; English Dept Dramatic Art Dept, lctr 1968-74; Dept Afro-Am Studies UC Berkeley, lctr 1976-83; Ctr for Study Ed & Adv of Women, dir 1975-83;Univ of CA Berkeley Afro-Am Studies Dept, prof and chair, 1988-. **ORGANIZATIONS:** V pres/adm Am Theatre Asso 1983-85; chair Black Theatre Prog/Am Theatre Asso 1979-83; adv bd Bus & Prof Womens Fndtn 1983-; consult Am Cncl on Ed Natl Identification Prog for Womdn Adms 1980-; panelist Natl Rsrch Cncl/Lhumanitgies Doct Comm 1983-; consult CA Arts Cncl 1984-; mem Natl Cncl of Negro Women; memUniv of CA Berkeley Black Alumni Club; mem NAACP; founder/dir Kumoja Players 1971-75; bd of trustees, San Francisco Theological Seminary, 1987-. **HONORS/ACHIEVEMENTS:** Hon dr/Humane LettersUniv of Redlands 1980; humanities flwshp Rockefeller Fndtn 1982-83; sr postdoctoral

flwshp Natl Rsrch Cncl/Ford Found 1983-84; Ford Flwshp/Dissertation Ford Fndtn 1970; otstndng black alumnaUniv of CA Berkeley Black Alumni Club 1976; Kellogg Lecturer Am Cncl on Ed 1980; co-editor Black Scholar theatre issue & other publs; author of "9 Plays by Black Women" New Amer Library 1986; Honoree, Equal Rights Advocates, 1989. **BUSINESS ADDRESS:** Professor and Chair, U of CA Berkeley, 3335 Dwinelle Hall, Berkeley, CA 94720.

WILKES, JAMAAL
Professional athlete. **PERSONAL:** Born Apr 02, 1953, Berkeley, CA. **EDUCATION:** Univ of CA, 1974. **CAREER:** Golden State Warriors NBA San Francisco, forward 1974-77; Los Angeles Lakers, basketball player. **HONORS/ACHIEVEMENTS:** All Star Team 1976. **BUSINESS ADDRESS:** Los Angeles Lakers, PO Box 10, Inglewood, CA 90306.

WILKES, REGGIE WAYMAN
Professional football player. **PERSONAL:** Born May 27, 1956, Pine Bluff, AR. **EDUCATION:** GA Tech, BS Biology 1978; attending Morehouse School of Med, Univ of PA Med School exchange prog. **CAREER:** Philadelphia, 1978-85; Atlanta Falcons, linebacker 1986-. **HONORS/ACHIEVEMENTS:** Played in NFC Championship Game following 1980 season; played in NFL Championship Game following 1980 season. **BUSINESS ADDRESS:** Linebacker, Philadelphia Eagles, Philadelphia Veterans Stadium, Broad St & Pattison Ave, Philadelphia, PA 19148.

WILKES, SHELBY R.
Ophthalmologist. **PERSONAL:** Born Jun 30, 1950, Crystal Springs, MS; married Jettie M Burnett MD; children: Martin. **EDUCATION:** Alcorn State Univ, BS (Summa Cum Laude) 1971; Johns Hopkins Univ Sch of Medicine, MD 1975. **CAREER:** Univ of Rochester Sch of med Dept of Surgery, intern-resident 1975-76; Mayo Clinic, resident 1977-79; MA Eye & Ear Infirmary, fellow retina serv 1980-81; Univ of IL Eye & Ear Infirmary, rsch fellow 1976; Harvard Univ Sch of Medicine, clinical asst in ophthalmology 1982-83; Emory Univ Sch of Medicine, asst prof of ophthalmology; Morehouse School of Med Atlanta GA, asst clinical prof dept of surgery; vitreoretinal surgion, ophthalmologist; Atlanta Eye Consultants, pres. **ORGANIZATIONS:** Mem Alpha Phi Alpha, NAACP, Atlanta Med Assoc, GA State Med Assoc, Assoc for Rsch in Vision & Ophthalmology 1978-, Amer Med Assoc 1978-; fellow AmerAcad of Ophthalmology 1981-; mem Natl Medical Assn 1981-; mem bd of dir Amer Diabetes Assoc GA Affiliate Inc 1985. **HONORS/ACHIEVEMENTS:** Who's Who in Amer Colleges & Univs 1970-71; Honors Soc Alcorn State Univ 1970-71; Ophthalmic Alumni Awd Mayo Clinic 1980; Disting Alumni Citation selected by natl Assoc for Equal Oppor in Higher Educ 1985; papers, SRWilkes & ESGragoudas "Regression patterns of uveal melanomas after proton beam irradiation" Ophthalmology 1982 89,7 p840; SRWilkes MBeard DMRobertson & LKurland "Incidence of retinal detachment" Rochester MN Amer Journal of Ophthalmology 1982. **BUSINESS ADDRESS:** President, Atlanta Eye Consultants, 615 Peachtree St NE, Ste 815, Atlanta, GA 30308.

WILKES, WILLIAM R.
Clergyman. **PERSONAL:** Born Apr 10, 1902, Eatonton, GA; married Nettie Julia; children: William, Alfred. **EDUCATION:** Morris Brown Coll, AB; Garret Theol Sem; Northwestern U; Morris Brown, hon DD; other hon DD & LLD. **CAREER:** 13th Episcopal Dist (KY & TN) of AME Ch, bishop 1972-; 3rd Dist, bishop; also presided over 16th, 12th & 6th dist. **BUSINESS ADDRESS:** 1002 Kirkwood Ave, Nashville, TN 37204.

WILKIE, EARL A.
Educator, artist. **PERSONAL:** Born Mar 15, 1930, Philadelphia; married Nancy Kirby. **EDUCATION:** BS 1961. **CAREER:** Special educ school teacher 1961-62; dir vocational training 1962-65; dir adult educ 1965-69; dir secondary educ program 1968-; Elwyn Inst Consultant Upward Bound Program, 1967-68; Lancaster School Dist, 1969; Mantua Drug Rehabilitation Program, 1969-70; SE Comm Health Center, 1973-74; Philadelphia School Dist, 1973-74. **ORGANIZATIONS:** Many published related to educ; lecturer many coll & inst; mem Art League Philadelphia 1971-72; many art exhibitions Philadelphia. **MILITARY SERVICE:** USAF 1951-55. **BUSINESS ADDRESS:** Elwyn Inst, Elwyn, PA.

WILKINS, ALLEN HENRY
Educator. **PERSONAL:** Born May 23, 1934, Elberton, GA; married Jean E; children: Linton, Deniz. **EDUCATION:** Tuskegee Inst, BS 1957; Catholic Univ, MS 1973. **CAREER:** Washington DC Govt, Dept of Highways, horticulture inspector 1961-69; Navy Facilities Engineers, landscape architect, general engineer 1969-73; Univ District of Columbia, prof of horticulture/landscape design. **ORGANIZATIONS:** Licensed landscape architect State of MD 1973-86; mem Amer Soc Landscape Architects 1973-86; vice pres Washington DC NEA 1982-84; mem Amer Horticulture Scientists 1986; mem Alpha Psi Alpha; deacon choir mem Washington DC Congregational Church. **HONORS/ACHIEVEMENTS:** First Black horticultural inspector for Washington DC Govt; Public Service Award, Washington DC Govt 1960; Citation for Public Service, Mayor City of Greenbelt MD 1985; Devel of master plans for several Dept of Defense projects; Landscape-urban design plans for several parks, two schools. **BUSINESS ADDRESS:** Prof Horticulture/Landscaping, Univ District of Columbia, 4200 Conn Ave NW, B644 Rm 2036, Washington, DC 20008.

WILKINS, BETTY
Founder/journalist. **PERSONAL:** Born Mar 31, 1922, Braddock, PA; children: Gloria, Raymond, Robert Jr, Donald, Margaret, Patricia. **EDUCATION:** Denver Opportunity Sch Journalism, Grad 1957. **CAREER:** KFML Radio, 2 hr gospel show; KC Call, Denver editor; KDKO Radio, soc columnist with Honey Bee's show; Denver Weekly News, editor. **ORGANIZATIONS:** Pres Sophisticates & Soc & Civ Club; vice pres Astro Jets; sec Pond Lily; mem Jane Jefferson Dem Club; Mayors council human relations; mem Bronze Dau Am; State Assn Colored Wmns Clubs; Council Negro Wmn; CO Spress Wmns Club; black del for Geo McGovern from Denver to Miami 1972; committeewoman in E Denverfor 20 yrs; res Delta Mothers Club; Zion Circle Seven; The Denver Beauty Guild; life mem & pub rel chmn NAACP. **HONORS/ACHIEVEMENTS:** Syl Morgan Smith Comm Aw Trophy 1976; Publ Relat Aw Astro Jets 1977; Originator of "Ten Best Dressed Blk Women" Denver; Miss Bronze Dau Awrd 1958; Robert L Vaden Aw 1972; Harriet Tubman Dist Serv Aw 1973; Wmn Yr 1972; Com Awrd Metro Club 1979; Hall of Fame Aw May D & F 1980.

WILKINS, DOMINIQUE
Professional athlete. **PERSONAL:** Born Jan 12, 1960, Sorbonne, France. **EDUCATION:** Attended, Georgia 1983. **CAREER:** Utah Jazz, player; Atlanta Hawks, forward. **HONORS/ACHIEVEMENTS:** MVP 1981 SEC Tournament; NBA All-Rookie team 1982-83; NBA Player of the Week Awds in each of last two seasons; NBA Scoring title 1985-86; winner NBA Slam Dunktitle 1985, runner up 1986; NBA Player of the Month January 1986; has led Hawks in scoring in 136 of last 159 games; mem NBA All Star team 1986. **BUSINESS ADDRESS:** Atlanta Hawks, 100 Techwood Dr NW, Atlanta, GA 30303.

WILKINS, ERVIN W.
Attorney. **PERSONAL:** Born Mar 29, 1919, Asheville, NC; son of Cornelius Wilkins and Ruth Wilkins; married Eppsyline Tucker; children: Sharee, Ervin Jr, La Verne. **EDUCATION:** Livingstone Coll, AB, 1940; Northwestern Univ, Grad Work, History, 1941; Howard Univ, AM, 1946; Ohio State Univ, Law, 1947-50; Western Reserve Univ, Law, 1959-60; Cleveland Marshall Law School, JD, 1960, Grad Law, 1965; Western Reserve Univ, Grad School Law, Law Medicine, 1967. **CAREER:** Post Office, postal clerk, acting foreman 14 yrs; Cleveland School System, hs teacher, 11 yrs; real estate salesman, 6 years; gen practice, 1960-66, 1969-72; State Ohio, spl counsel atty-gen, 1970-72; US Atty, VA, atty, 1972-82; private practice, atty. **ORGANIZATIONS:** Ohio Bar Assn; Natl Bar Assn; Civic League Greater Cleveland; NAACP; elected trustee, Livingstone Coll, North Carolina, 1976; mem, trustee, co-chmn, Men's Plng Comm, St Paul AME Zion Church, Cleveland; dist trustee, Ohio, Ann Conf AME Zion Church; trust Srs of Ohio, 1978-82; mem, Screening Comm Civic League of Greater Cleveland, 1982-85; successor to Congressman Louis Stokes as atty for St Paul AME Zion Church. **HONORS/ACHIEVEMENTS:** Magna Cum Laude; salutatorian, class 1940; Livingstone Coll; mem, Zeta Sigma Pi; completed 4 year coll course in 3 1/2 years A average, grad school, history, Howard Univ; winner treatises, Lawyers Co-operative Pub Co, highest average law sales law damages Cleveland Marshall Law School; scored 3245 state bar exam; awarded meritorious achievement award, Cleveland Bar Assn; Fed Outstanding Comm Serv Award, 1976; outstanding legal serv, Cleveland, 1971; citation, Alumni Meritorious Serv Award, Livingston Coll, 1975.

WILKINS, HENRY, III
Government official, educator. **PERSONAL:** Born Jan 04, 1930, Pine Bluff, AR; son of Henry Wilkins Jr and Minnie B Jones-Wilkins; married Josetta Edwards, Oct 30, 1954; children: Henry IV, Felecia, Mark, Angela. **EDUCATION:** Univ of Arkansas at Pine Bluff (AM&N) BA 1957; Atlanta Univ, MA 1963. **CAREER:** AR Dist 54; state rep; Univ of AR at Pine Bluff, assoc prof History & Political Sci 1959-89. **ORGANIZATIONS:** Mem AR Delegation Dem Natl Conv 1972; mem Am Assn Coll & Univ Prof; Am Political Sci Assn; So Political Sci Assn; Am Alumni Council; mem Elks Lodge; American Political Science Assn, Arkansas Political Science Assn; Interested Citizens for Voter Education and Registration; Chamber of Commerce. **HONORS/ACHIEVEMENTS:** NAACP Political Achvmnt Award Negro Youth Org 1960; AR State Dem Party Exec Committe; Merrill Fellows grant; Korean Commendations Medals; Some Aspects of the Cold War 1945-1950, Brown Book Company 1963. **MILITARY SERVICE:** AUS sgt 1954. **HOME ADDRESS:** 303 N Maple St, Pine Bluff, AR 71601. **BUSINESS ADDRESS:** AR State Representative & Prof of Political Science, Univ of Arkansas at Pine Bluff, University Drive—Childres Hall Rm #122, Pine Bluff, AR 71601.

WILKINS, HERBERT PRIESTLY
Business executive. **PERSONAL:** Born Jan 09, 1942, Boston, MA; son of William Wilkins and Katherine Wilkins; married Sheran R Morris; children: Herbert Jr, Monique, Michelle. **EDUCATION:** Boston Univ, BS 1965; Harvard Univ Grad School of Business Admin, MBA 1970. **CAREER:** Lucas, Tucker & Co, principal 1969-73; Urban Natl Corp, senior vice pres 1973-75; Wilkins & Co, consultant 1975-77; Syndicated Communication Inc (Syncom), president 1977-. **ORGANIZATIONS:** Mem bd of overseers Harvard Comm Health Plan Boston 1973-; former chmn of bd Amer Assoc of Minority SBC's 1979-; pres Stellar Comm Corp 1981-; dir Natl Assoc of Minorities in Cable TV 1983-; pres OFC, Inc 1984-; dir, Freedom Natl Bank, 1987; dir, Black Entertainment Television, 1984-; dir, Chicago Cable Television, 1985; dir, Minorities in Cable, 1984; mem, mgmt, Comm District Cablevision, L.P., 1983. **HONORS/ACHIEVEMENTS:** Service Awds Natl Cable TV Assoc 1983, Federal Communications Comm Adv Committee on Minority Ownership 1984; Natl Assn of Investment Co Natl Cable Television Assn. **BUSINESS ADDRESS:** President, Syncom, 1030 15th St NW, Washington, DC 20005.

WILKINS, JESSE THEODORE
Attorney. **PERSONAL:** Born Aug 12, 1947, Washington, DC; divorced; children: 2 Children. **EDUCATION:** Duke U, BSE 1969; Wayne State U, MBA Finance 1978; Vanderbilt Univ, JD 1986. **CAREER:** Westinghouse Elect Corp, sales engr 1969-73; NE Power Coord Council, staff engr 1973-74; The Detroit Edison Co, prin cost analyst 1974, supv cost of syvc div 1974-; LeBoeuf Lamb Lieby & MacRae, atty public utilites. **ORGANIZATIONS:** Engineering Soc of Detroit. **HONORS/ACHIEVEMENTS:** Who's Who in the East 1975-76; Westinghouse 120 Sales Club 1972; Prtcptd in Mgmt Sci Prog Japan-Am Inst of Mgmt Sic Honolulu HI 1975-76. **BUSINESS ADDRESS:** Attorney, LeBoeuf Lamb Lieby & MacRae, 520 Madison Ave, New York, NY 10022.

WILKINS, KENNETH C.
County government official. **PERSONAL:** Born Sep 20, 1952, New York, NY; son of James A Wilkins and June I (Whitehead) Wilkins. **EDUCATION:** Shaw Univ, Raleigh NC, BA 1974; Bowling Green State Univ, Bowling Green OH, MA 1975; Univ of Kentucky, Lexington, JD 1978; NC Inst of Politics, fellow, 1989. **CAREER:** NC Dept of Correction, Raleigh, legal staff, 1978-79; Shaw Univ, Raleigh NC, asst to exec vice pres, 1979-83; County of Wake, Raleigh NC, register of deeds, 1983-. **ORGANIZATIONS:** Bd mem, Mediation Services of Wake County, 1982-; exec comm, NC Leadership Forum, 1985-; bd mem, Haven House, 1986-; bd mem, Garner Road Family YMCA, 1986-; chair, United Negro Coll Fund Campaign, Raleigh, 1988-; Natl Assn of Counties; NC Assn of Registers of Deeds. **HONORS/ACHIEVEMENTS:** Distinguished Alumni Public Service Award, Shaw Univ, 1984; Heart & Soul Award, WAUG-AM, 1988; plaque, Garner Road YMCA, 1988; fellow, NC Inst of Politics, 1989. **BUSINESS ADDRESS:** Register of Deeds, County of Wake, PO Box 1897, Wake County Courthouse, Room 814, Raleigh, NC 27602.

WILKINS, LEONA B.
Educator. **PERSONAL:** Born Feb 09, 1922, Winston-Salem, NC. **EDUCATION:** NC Central Univ, BA 1941; Univ MI, MMus 1944, PhD 1971; Sarbonne Univ Paris, cert 1968.

CAREER: Raleigh NC, teacher 1942-44; St Louis, teacher 1952-55; Detroit, teacher 1955-64; Bluefield State, 1944-45; Hampton Inst, 1945-48; TN State Univ, 1948-52; E MI Univ 1964-68; Temple Univ, 1968-72; Northwestern Univ, assoc prof 1972-. **ORGANIZATIONS:** Mem Music Educ Conf; Intl Soc of Music Educators; Amer Assn of Univ Profs, Am Orff-Schulwerk Assn; Coll Music Soc; Alpha Kappa Alpha; mem Bicentennial Commn for MENC 1974-76; Comn for Revision of Natl Tchrs Exam for Music Educ 1974-75; consult IL State Arts Plan; Comn for Revision of Music Objectives for Natl Assessment of Educ Progress Task Force; Role of the Arts Comm USOE; MENC; consult Evanston Public School Dist 65. **HONORS/ACHIEVEMENTS:** Consult Silver Burdett Music Series 1970-71. **BUSINESS ADDRESS:** Associate Professor, NorthwesternUniv, Sch of Music, Evanston, IL 60201.

WILKINS, PATRICIA CHALMERS
Educational administrator. **PERSONAL:** Born in Sanford, NC; married James E. **EDUCATION:** NC A&T StateUniv Greensboro, BS 1970, MS 1974;Univ of SC Columbia SC, Grad Study. **CAREER:** Voorhees Coll, AIDP coordinator/fed relations officers 1978-, dir special programs 1975-78, counselor/instructor 1973-75; US Atomic Energy Commn, docket specialist 1970-72. **ORGANIZATIONS:** Sec SC Council of Spl Progs 1974-77; sec/sch tchr Mt Moriah Bapt Ch 1970-74; mem APGA/AMEG/ACPA/SCPAG 1973. **HONORS/ACHIEVEMENTS:** Listed Who's Who in the S & SW The Marquis Who's Who 1978-79; recipient Membrshp Awrd Am Soc 1979; Outst Young Women of Am Awrd for Outst Ability Accmplsmnts & Serv 1979. **BUSINESS ADDRESS:** Voorhees Coll, Denmark, SC 29042.

WILKINS, RILLASTINE ROBERTA
Systems analyst. **PERSONAL:** Born Jul 24, 1932, Taft, OK; married Clarence E Wilkins; children: Nathlyn Barksdale, Clarence Henry. **EDUCATION:** Muskegon Comm Coll; Muskegon Business Coll; Tech Instr Inst; Univ of WI Eau Claire. **CAREER:** General Telephone Co of MI, telephone oper 1957-62, serv rep 1962-67, div comm instr 1967-71, contact records suprv of bus accts 1973-79, phone mart mgr 1979-81, customer serv mgr 1981-83, analyst customer relations 1983-. **ORGANIZATIONS:** Co-chairperson, Human Resources Commn, Muskegon Couty; chairperson, Comm Devel Commn, bd mem, Econ Devel Commn, City of Muskegon Heights; bd mem, Muskegon Area Transcript Syst, Muskegon County; chairperson, Zoning Bd of Appeals City of Muskegon Heights; chairperson, Community Serv Commn, Muskegon County; Reg Convenor Natl Urban League; past pres Urban League Bd of dir; life mem NAACP; past pres Every Woman's Place; past pres Tri-City Woman's Club; past pres Urban League Guild of Greater Muskegon; bd mem Heritage Hosp; bd mem Greater Muskegon Chamber of Comm; bd mem Black Women's Political Caucus of Greater Muskegon; St Bd Podiatric Med; pres pres Women in Municipal Govt State of MI 1979; co-chairperson, Allocations & Review Comm United Way 1980-81; bd mem, sec Greater Musk Seaway Fest 1980-82; vice pres Mondale Task Force on Youth Employment 1980; vice-chmn, Reg Planning Comm, Muskegon County, 1981; Chairperson, Community Emer Clrghs, 1983; Vice pres, Natl Black Caucus of local elected officials, 1984; reg convenor, Natl Urban League, 1983-84; Reg Dir for MI, OH, WI, IL; Natl Black Caucus of Local Elected Officials, 1976-; Jr Achievement Advisor, 1972. **HONORS/ACHIEVEMENTS:** Jr Achievement Advisor 1972; 1st Woman Post Advisor for Explorers Career Devel 1973; Speakers Bureau Gen Telephone of MI 1973; Citizens Awd from Residents of Muskegon & Muskegon Hts 1974; Women's Ed Resource Comm 1979; Cert of Commendation Muskegon Comm Coll 1979; Boss of the Day WZZR Grand Rapids MI 1980; Cert of Merit St Josephs Christian Comm Ctr 1980; Pace Awd Muskegon Comm Coll, 1980; Plaque of Congratulations Black Women's Political Caucus 1980; Chosen Woman of the Year by the Black Women's Political Caucus, 1983; served 3 consecutive terms as mayor pro-tem of the City of Muskegon Heights, MI (a first for male/female). **BUSINESS ADDRESS:** Analyst, General Telephone, 455 E Ellis Rd, Muskegon, MI 49441.

WILKINS, ROGER L.
Scientist. **PERSONAL:** Born Dec 14, 1928, Newport News, VA; married Nasira Ledbetter; children: Yvonne Diane, Roger (dec'd). **EDUCATION:** Hampton Inst, BS 1951; Howard Univ, MS 1952; Univ So CA, PhD 1967. **CAREER:** Lewis Flight Propulsion Lab, aeronautical rsch scientist 1952-55; Rocketdyne, sr tech spl 1955-60; Aerospace Corp, sr staff scientist 1960-. **ORGANIZATIONS:** Mem Combustion Inst; Amer Inst Aeronautics & Astronautics; Gen Alumni Assn Univ So CA; pres 1972-74, 1979-81 So CA Natl Hampton Alumni Assn treas 1974-75. **HONORS/ACHIEVEMENTS:** Urban League Vocation Awd 1965; Serv Awd Natl Sor Phi Delta Kappa Betta 1969; Aerospace Corp Advanced Study Grant 1965-66; Men Science; Who's Who Amer; Hon Chemical Soc. **BUSINESS ADDRESS:** Senior Staff Scientist, Aerospace Corp, 2400 El Segundo Blvd, El Segundo, CA 90245.

WILKINS, ROGER W.
Columnist. **PERSONAL:** Born Mar 25, 1932, Kansas City, MO; divorced; children: Amy T, David E. **EDUCATION:** Univ MI, AB 1953, LLB 1956. **CAREER:** NY Times, urban affairs columnist, editorial bd; Washington Post, editorial page staff 1972-74; Ford Found, prog dir 1969-72; Gen Dept Justice DC, asst Atty 1966-69; Foreign Aid Dir State Dept, special asst 1962-66; NYC, atty 1956-62. **ORGANIZATIONS:** Mem NAACP legal defense fund; bd dir atty com Civil Rights Order Law; past chmn com pub justice past mem bd trustees Legal Defender Svc; mem NAACP;Urban League; Council Fgn Rels; Am Dem Action; bd of visitorsUniv MI Law Sch. **HONORS/ACHIEVEMENTS:** Hon LLD cntrl MIUniv 1974; cited ColumbiaUniv in Awrd of 1972 Pulitzer Prize Wash Post as Watergate edtrl writer. **BUSINESS ADDRESS:** 229 W 43 St, New York, NY 10036.

WILKINS, ROGER WOOD
Educator. **PERSONAL:** Born Mar 25, 1932, Kansas City, MO; son of Earl W Wilkins and Helen Jackson Clayton; married Patricia A King, Feb 21, 1981; children: Amy T, David E, Elizabeth W C. **EDUCATION:** Univ of Michigan, Ann Arbor MI, AB 1953, LLB 1956. **CAREER:** US Dept of Justice, Washington DC, asst attorney general of US, 1966-69; Ford Foundation, New York NY, program dir & asst to pres, 1969-72; Washington Post, Washington DC, mem of editorial bd, 1972-74; New York Times, New York NY, mem of editorial bd & columnist, 1974-79; Washington Star, Washington DC, assoc ed, 1980-81; Inst for Policy Studies, Washington DC, senior fellow, 1982-; George Mason Univ, Fairfax VA, Clarence J Robinson Prof of History & Amer Culture, 1987-. **ORGANIZATIONS:** Bd mem, NAACP Legislative Defense Fund 1970-, Pulitzer Prize Bd 1980-89, Fund for Investigative Journ 1980-, Villers Foundation 1987-, Natl Constitution Center 1988-, PEN/Faulkner Foundation 1989-, Univ of District of Columbia 1989-; vice chair of bd, African-Amer Inst, 1982-; mem of Comm for Racial Justice Policy, Joint Center for Pol Studies, 1982-; mem of comm of overseers, Harvard Univ Afro-Amer Studies, 1984-; mem of steering comm, Free South Africa Movement, 1984-; chair of bd, Pulitzer Prize Bd, 1987-88. **HONORS/ACHIEVEMENTS:** Shared Pulitzer Prize for reports on Watergate, 1973; hon LLD from Central MI Univ 1975, Wilberforce Univ 1984, Union of Experimenting Universities 1986; author of A Man's Life, Simon & Schuster, 1982; regents lecturer, Univ of Calif, Santa Cruz, 1985; Woodrow Wilson School lecturer, Princeton Univ, 1987; Roger Baldwin Civil Liberties Award, New York Civil Liberties Union, 1987. **BUSINESS ADDRESS:** Clarence J Robinson Professor of History and American Culture, Robinson Professors, 207 East Bldg, George Mason University, Fairfax, VA 22030-4444.

WILKINS, THOMAS A.
Government executive. **PERSONAL:** Born Feb 01, 1930, Lawrenceville, VA; married A Delores Bohannon; children: Lisa Delores, Thomas Alan, Mark Anderson. **EDUCATION:** NO VA Univ dpa 1976, mpa 1975; fed exec inst 1971; NYU, ma 1957; st pauls coll, bs 1951. **CAREER:** DC Dept of Manpower, dir 1972-; US Dept of Labor, Manpower admin 1965-72; Voc Rehab Serv Glenn Dale Hosp DC Dept Pub Hlth, chief 1959-65; Voc Serv Dept of Corr NYC, asst dir 1957-59; Dept of Corr NYC, prin instr 1955-57. **ORGANIZATIONS:** Mem Am Soc of Pub Admin; bd dir Interstate Conf of Emplymnt Sec Agency Inc; Fed Bus Assn; Am Personnel & Guid Assn; Nat Voc Guid Assn; charter mem Natl Rehab Counselisng Assn; Nat Rehab Assn; Mayor's Cabinet DC; Mayor's Adv Com on Narcotics Addiction DC; mem Metro Washington DC Bd Trade (Businessman's Adv Com); DC Bicentennial Commn; Fed Adv Bd DC Sch System; Fed Review Team, Coord Comm Child Care DC; layman Episcopal Ch; Omega Psi Phi; DAV & mem Reston Homeowners Assn; Hunters Woods Village Council, Reston VA; mem bd trustees St Paul's Coll; past mem bd exec comm ACLU; past bd mem Fair Housing Inc; mem Mayor's Overall Econ Devel Com; mem Mayor's Com on hndcpd; bd trustees Davis Meml Goodwill Industries. **HONORS/ACHIEVEMENTS:** Recipient Sustained Superior Perf Awrd US Dept Labor 1974; Who's Who in the Black World 1973; So Historcl Preservations of Am 1976-77; Intl Men of Achvmnt 1976-; Who's Who in Govt 1975-76; Who's Who Among Black Am 1974-75; Distng Trustee Awrd St Pauls Coll 1972; Outst Perf Awrd Manpower Admin 1969; Vocational Rehab Admin Intern & Flwshp 1960. **BUSINESS ADDRESS:** DC Dept of Manpower, 500 C St NW, Washington, DC 20001.

WILKINS, THOMAS ALPHONSO
Educator/orchestra conductor. **PERSONAL:** Born Sep 10, 1956, Norfolk, VA; son of Wallace Y Wilkins, Sr.; married Sheri-Lee, Jun 14, 1985. **EDUCATION:** Shenandoah Conserva of Music, BME 1978; New England Conserva of Music, MM 1982. **CAREER:** Shenandoah Conservatory Symphony, asst conductor 1976-78; Busch Entertainment Corp, music dir 1971-82; New England Conservatory Repetory Orches, asst conductor 1981-82; North Park Coll Orchestra, music dir; director orchestral studies Univ of Tennessee, Chattanooga. 1987-89. **ORGANIZATIONS:** Active mem Phi Mu Alpha Frat 1976-; conductor Northwest IN Youth Orchestra 1983-; asst conductor Northwest IN Symphony Orchestra 1983-. **BUSINESS ADDRESS:** Assistant Conductor, Richmond Symphony Orchestra, 1801 E Broad Street, Richmond, VA 23227.

WILKINS, VINCENT, JR.
Attorney. **PERSONAL:** Born Oct 02, 1942, Crowley, LA; married Helene Green; children: Randalan Fernel, Alesia Yvetta, Vincent III. **EDUCATION:** So U, BA 1967; So Univ Law, JD 1970; Nat Coll Crim Defense Lawyers & Pub Defenders, 1973. **CAREER:** Law Students Civil Rights Rsrch Cncl, intern 1968; US Dept Justice Civil Rights Div, 1969; Baton Rouge Legal Aid Soc, 1969-70; US Dept Trans, 1970-71; E Baton Rouge Office Pub Defender, 1972; Wilinks & Carnes, atty 1972-. **ORGANIZATIONS:** Mem Am Nat LA Baton Rouge Bar Assn; LA Martinent Legal Soc 1970; mem Legal Aid Soc; E Baton Rouge Comm Action Team; vice pres Baton Rouge Imprvmnt Assn. **HONORS/ACHIEVEMENTS:** Award SoUniv Student Bar Assn 1973. **MILITARY SERVICE:** AUS e-4 1964-66. **BUSINESS ADDRESS:** 1822 N Acadian Thruway W, Baton Rouge, LA 70802.

WILKINS, WILLIE T.
Dentist. **PERSONAL:** Born Dec 10, 1929, Durham, NC; married Burma Whitted; children: Willie T III. **EDUCATION:** NC A&T State Univ, BS; Howard Univ, DDS; postgrad oral surgery. **CAREER:** Private Practice, dentist. **ORGANIZATIONS:** Mem Amer & Natl Dental Assns, Amer Dental Soc Anesthesiology, Amer Soc Geriatric Dentistry; fellow Acad Gen Dentistry; Royal Soc Health; Am Sch Health Assn Intercont Biog Assn; mem Bethel AME Church, YMCA, Triad Sickle Cell Anemia Found; Greensboro Med Soc; Guilford Co Dental Soc. **HONORS/ACHIEVEMENTS:** Who's Who in the S & SW; Personalities of the S; Comm Ldrs S; IBA Yearbook; Dictionary Intl Biog; Blue Book; Ldrs Amer Sci; Val Contrib Awd DC Dental Soc 1961; Wisdom Honor Awd Wisdom Soc 1972; pubs & clin presentations. **BUSINESS ADDRESS:** 1607 Asheboro St, Greensboro, NC 27406.

WILKINSON, BRENDA
Poet and writer for children. **PERSONAL:** Born Jan 01, 1946, Moultrie, GA; daughter of Malcolm Scott and Ethel Anderson Scott; children: Kim, Lori. **EDUCATION:** Hunter College of the City University of New York. **CAREER:** Poet and author of books for children. **ORGANIZATIONS:** Mem, Authors Guild; mem, Authors League of America. **HONORS/ACHIEVEMENTS:** National Book Award nomination, 1976, for Ludell; Ludell and Willie was named one of the outstanding children's books of the year by New York Times and a best book for young adults by American Library Assn, both 1977. **BUSINESS ADDRESS:** Board of Global Ministries, 475 Riverside Dr, New York, NY. *

WILKINSON, CHARLES BROCK
Physician. **PERSONAL:** Born Jan 16, 1922, Richmond, VA; son of Charles Summer and Willa Brock Wilkinson; married Ethel Virginia Herriford; children: Steven. **EDUCATION:** Virginia Union Univ, BS 1941; Howard Univ, MD 1944; Univ of CO Medical Ctr, MS 1950. **CAREER:** Howard Univ Coll of Med Div of Neuropsychiatry, instructor 1950-54; Howard Univ Coll of Medicine, asst prof 1954-55; Sch of Medicine Univ MO, assoc prof 1959-65, prof 1965-71; Sch of Med Univ MO Kansas City, asst dean 1970-77, prof 1971-, assoc dean 1977; Greater Kansas City Mental Health Foundation, dir of adult outpatient serv 1959-65, dir of training 1960-69, assoc dir 1960-69, exec dir 1969-. **ORGANIZATIONS:** Bd of trustees 1971-74, bd treas 1976-80 Amer Psychiatric Assoc; treas Group for Advancement of Psychiatry 1983-. **HONORS/ACHIEVEMENTS:** 4 NIMH Rsch Grants; 1 book published; 9 book chapters; 40 articles in scientific journals. **MILITARY SERVICE:** AUS Medical Corps major 4 1/2 yrs. **BUSINESS ADDRESS:** Executive Director, Greater Kansas City Mental Health Foundation, 2055 Holmes, Kansas City, MO 64108.

WILKINSON, DONALD CHARLES
Educator. **PERSONAL:** Born Feb 12, 1936, Madison, FL; divorced; children: Donald Clark. **EDUCATION:** Wilbur Wright Tech, 1960-64; Detroit Inst of Tech, 1964-65;Univ of MI, BA 1969; Sonoma State Coll, MA 1972. **CAREER:** Sonoma State Coll, asst prof & counselor of Physiology 1971-; Educ Devel Center Newton MA, 1970-71; WJ Maxey Boys Training School, boys supr 1965-69; Detroit Courier, staff wsrither repoter 1961-62; Detroit Water Dept, engr 1956-61; sculptr in wood 1970. **ORGANIZATIONS:** Mem, Alpha Phi Alpha; mem Freelance Civil Rights Activist 1960-68; conslt Blk Tutorial Project 1965; advisor, Morgan Comm School, 1970-71; Ford Found Grant in Early Childhood Educ; rsch & teaching British Infant School Syst, Sherard Infant School Engineering. **BUSINESS ADDRESS:** 1801 Cotati Ave, Rohnert Park, CA 94928.

WILKINSON, DORIS Y.
Educator. **PERSONAL:** Born in Lexington, KY; daughter of Howard T Wilkinson (deceased) and Regia L Wilkinson. **EDUCATION:** Univ of Kentucky, BA, 1958; Case Western Univ, MA, 1960, PhD, 1968; Johns Hopkins Univ, MPH, 1985. **CAREER:** Macalester Coll, assoc/full, professor 1970-77; Amer Soc Assn, exec assn, 1977-80; Howard Univ, professor, 1980-84; Univ of Virginia, visiting professor, 1984-85; Univ of Kentucky, Lexington, KY, professor, 1985-. **ORGANIZATIONS:** Vice pres, Soc for Study of Social Problems, 1984-85, Eastern Sociological Soc, 1983-84; pres, District of Columbia Sociological Soc, 1982-83; bd of overseers, Case Western Reserve Univ, 1982-; public educ, Comm Amer Cancer Soc, 1982-85; exec office budget comm, American Sociological Assn, 1985-; pres, Soc for the Study of Social Problems, 1987-88. **HONORS/ACHIEVEMENTS:** Articles & books published, 1968-; fellowships & grants received; NIH Fellow, 1963-66; Woodrow Wilson Fellow, 1959-61; NIE Grant, 1978-80; NCI, research contract, 1985-; Dubois-Johnson-Frazier Award, Amer Sociological Assn, 1988; Omicron Delta Kappa Natl Leadership Hon, 1987; Grant from the Kentucky Humanities Commr for a project on Afro-Amer physicians, 1988-89. **BUSINESS ADDRESS:** Professor, University of KY, Department of Sociology, Lexington, KY 40506.

WILKINSON, FREDERICK D., JR.
Business executive. **PERSONAL:** Born Jan 25, 1921, Washington, DC; son of Mr & Mrs F D Wilkinson; married Jeane; children: Sharon, Dayna, Frederick III. **EDUCATION:** Howard Univ, AB 1942; Army Univ Center of Oahu, Certificate, Business Law, Accounting, 1946; Harvard Univ, MBA, 1947. **CAREER:** Macy's, jr asst buyer, 1949-50, sr asst buyer 1950-52, store buyer 1952-68, vice pres 1968-74; New York City Transit Auth, exec officer passenger serv 1974-76; Exec Officer, Surface Transit, exec officer 1976-77; American Express Co, vice pres travel 1977-79, vice pres travel related serv 1979-85, Sr Vice Pres 1985-present. **ORGANIZATIONS:** Natl Urban League (Natl Treasurer), Empire Blue Cross/Blue Shield, Cornell Univ Med Coll & Graduate School of Medical Sciences, UNC Ventures, MTA Inspector General Advisory Bd, Brookdale Center of Hunter Coll (Co-Chair), Westchester Clubmen Found (Pres). **HONORS/ACHIEVEMENTS:** Good Scout of the Yr BSA; Alumni Achievement Awd Howard Univ; Wm H Moss Brotherhood. **MILITARY SERVICE:** AUS infantry capt 4 yrs. **BUSINESS ADDRESS:** Sr Vice Pres, American Express Co, World Financial Center, 200 Vesey St, New York, NY 10285-4720.

WILKINSON, JAMES WELLINGTON
Physician. **PERSONAL:** Born Dec 08, 1935, Hampton, VA; married Cormay; children: Yolanda. **EDUCATION:** Wesleyan Univ Hampton Inst, BA 1962; Hampton Inst, MA 1965; Med Coll of VA, MD 1970. **CAREER:** Hampton Publ School, teacher 1962-65; Hampton Inst, teacher 1965-69; Private practice, physician, family med 1971-. **ORGANIZATIONS:** Chmn Med Records Comm Whittaker Mem Hosp; mem PSRU, Peninsular Med Soc, Old Dominion Med Soc, Natl Med Assoc; bd of dir YWCA; mem Wesleyan UnivAlumni Assoc, Hampton Inst Alumni Assoc, Med Coll VA Alumni Assoc. **HONORS/ACHIEVEMENTS:** Cert Adv Study AMA, VA Med Soc; Fellow Amer Acad of Family Physicians 1982, The Amer Soc of Contemporary Med & Surgery 1983, The Acad of Psychosomatic Med 1984. **BUSINESS ADDRESS:** 100 Bridge St, Hampton, VA 23669.

WILKINSON, MARIE L.
Owner. **PERSONAL:** Born May 06, 1910, New Orleans, LA; married Charles; children: Donald, Sheila Scott. **EDUCATION:** New Orleans U, Bus 1921; Straight Coll (now known as Dillard U). **CAREER:** P & W Truck Parts Equip Inc, pres; Aura Human Rels Commn, pres 20 yrs Marie Wilkinson Child Devel Ctr, pres 10 yrs; Aurora Feed the Hungry Inc, pres 10 yrs. **HONORS/ACHIEVEMENTS:** Cath Woman of Year Diocese of Rockford 1956; Beautiful People Awrd Chicago Urban League 1970; Citizenshp Citation Awrd No IL Dist Optmist 1968; fndng pres emeritus Aurora Urban League 1978. **BUSINESS ADDRESS:** 648 N View St, Aurora, IL 60506.

WILKINSON, RAYMOND M., JR.
Automobile dealer. **PERSONAL:** Born Oct 28, 1943, St Louis, MO; son of Raymond M Wilkinson and Elizabeth Wilkinson; married Betty J Taylor, Nov 06, 1965; children: William, Ray III, Heather. **EDUCATION:** General Motors Inst, Flint MI, dealer-operator degree, 1981. **CAREER:** US Postal Service, St Louis MO, carrier, 1961-75; Don Darr Pontiac, St Louis MO, salesperson 1975-80, manager 1981-83; Ray Wilkinson Buick-Cadillac Inc, currently pres & gen mgr. **ORGANIZATIONS:** Mem, NAACP-Racine 1984-, UNCF-Racine 1985-; bd mem, Racine Wed Optimists 1984-, West Racine Businessmen 1985-, Racine Sickle Cell 1986-. **HONORS/ACHIEVEMENTS:** Best Buick Dealer in Class, Buick Motor, 1986, 1987, & 1988. **BUSINESS ADDRESS:** President & General Manager, Ray Wilkinson Buick-Cadillac Inc, 6001 Washington Ave, Racine, WI 53406.

WILKINSON, ROBERT SHAW, JR.
Physician. **PERSONAL:** Born Jul 11, 1928, Brooklyn, NY; son of Robert S Wilkinson (deceased) and Melissa Ruth Royster Wilkinson (deceased); married Carolyn; children: Amy, Karin, Robert. **EDUCATION:** Dartmouth Coll, BA 1950; NY Univ, MD 1955. **CAREER:** George Washington Univ, assoc clinical prof med; Amer Bd Intl Medicine, diplomate; Group Health Assn Inc, staff physician 1962-68; George Washington Univ Hosp, attending phys 1962-; Private Practice, physician 1968-; medical advisor, Inter-Amer Devel Bank 1976-. **ORGANIZATIONS:** Mem Med Soc DC, AMA, NMA, Amer Heart Assn, Natl Capital Affiliate; fellow Amer Coll of Physicians; mem Acad Medicine DC. **HONORS/ACHIEVEMENTS:** The Dartmouth Alumni Award, Darmouth Coll, 1987. **MILITARY SERVICE:** AUS MC capt 1956-58. **BUSINESS ADDRESS:** 2141 K St NW, Ste 401, Washington, DC 20037.

WILKINSON, ROBERT STEVEN
Computer marketing executive. **PERSONAL:** Born Jun 23, 1955, Nashville, TN; married Juliana Nita Cornish. **EDUCATION:** Indiana Univ, BS Finance 1978; Harvard Univ, MBA 1982. **CAREER:** Xerox Corp, sr sales rep 1979-80, asst product mgr 1981-82, sales mgr 1982-83; Smith Barney Harris Upham, acct exec 1983-84; IBM, mktg rep 1984-. **ORGANIZATIONS:** Pres bd of dirs Oakland Ensemble Theatre 1985-; co-chair political action comm Black MBA's 1986-; life mem Kappa Alpha Psi. **HONORS/ACHIEVEMENTS:** Outstanding Young Man of Amer 1984; Who's Who in CA 1986,87.

WILKINSON, SHEPPARD FIELD
Business executive. **PERSONAL:** Born in Jefferson, TX; son of Rev. John Seaborn Wilkinson (deceased) and Millie Elizabeth Wilkinson. **EDUCATION:** Butler Jr Coll, Grad; Prairie View A&M U; Tyler Jr Coll. **CAREER:** Tyler Leader, owner fndr; Dallas Star Post, advertising mgr; Tyler Tribune, advertising mgr; Port Arthur Edition Houston Informer, editor advertising mgr; Prairie View A&M U, pub rels publicity ofcr; Jarvis Christina Coll; Wiley Coll. **ORGANIZATIONS:** Mem Tyler Orgn Men; Tyler, Smith Co Voters League; NAACP; Bethlehem Bapt Ch. **HONORS/ACHIEVEMENTS:** Recpt Best Publ Awrd TX Coll; recg Outsdng Serv USN; Cert Awrd Delta Sigma Theta Sor; spl awrd for Serv BSA; N Tyler Br YMCA. **BUSINESS ADDRESS:** 407 W. 24th Street, Tyler, TX 75702.

WILKS, CARL S.
Educator. **PERSONAL:** Born Apr 30, 1940, Springfield, MO; married Jacqueline Elaine Sanders; children: Carl Jr, Eric, Jennifer. **EDUCATION:** Southwest MO State Univ, BS Ed 1962; St Louis Univ, MSW 1966, PhD 1974. **CAREER:** St Louis Univ Child Devel Center, chief social worker 1969-77; Southern IL Univ, adjunct prof 1970-77; St Louis Univ, adjunct prof 1974-75; Wash Univ, adjunct prof 1974-76; Univ of TN, assc prof of Social Work. **ORGANIZATIONS:** Mem Natl Comm of Inquiry Natl Assc of Social Wrkrs 1973-79; bd dir Lambuth Clge 1984-; chrprsn Whitney Young Schlrshp Comm NASW 1979-, Ethnic Minority Local Church Comm Memphis Conf 1979-. **HONORS/ACHIEVEMENTS:** Child Mental Health Fac Dev Grant NIMH 1983-84; manuel on Sex Educ Publ 1980; "Past Conflicts & Current Stress" Publ 1980; Factors in the Abuse of The Elderly. **MILITARY SERVICE:** AUS Corp of Engr 1st lt 1962-64. **BUSINESS ADDRESS:** Assc Prof of Social Work, Univ of TN, 847 Monroe, 1246 Union Ave &, Memphis, TN 38163.

WILKS, GERTRUDE (NEE DYER)
Educational administrator. **PERSONAL:** Born Mar 09, 1927, Lisbon, LA; married Otis; children: Otis Jr, Danny, Patricia. **CAREER:** Mothers for Equal Educ, dir 1965; Nairobi Day & High School, dir 1966; Orignator for "Sneak-Out Prgm" 1965. **ORGANIZATIONS:** Fndr MEE 195; fndr Recherch Corp 1965; fndr Sat Tutorial Day Sch 1966; org Annette Latorre Nursery & Sch 1967; fndr Mothers Homemkng Ind 1968; org black & white conf; org MEE Educ Day Care 1970; org MEE Extended Day Care 1976; org one parent fam grp; consult HEW; consult Ravenswood Elem Dist; consult Stanford Tchr Trng; consult San Jose Sch Dist; consult Palo Alto Sch Dist; consult Coll of San Mateo; consult Foothill Coll; consult Wright Inst Coun; mem EPA Munic coun; mayor 1976; mem United Way Plng; chmn bd of trustees Great Friendship Bapt Ch; commr & vchm Redevel E Palo Alto; chrtr mem Nairobi Coll Bd1963-72; comm coun Ravenswood Elem Dist; bd dir EPA Neigh Hlth Ctr; commr San Mateo Co Econ Oppty Commin; ex-of mem Comm Action Councs; pres Missionary Bapt Soc. **HONORS/ACHIEVEMENTS:** Outst comm serv OICW 1966; St Sen Rules Resol 1973; Black Child Devel Inst Awrd 1973; Phoebe Hearst Awd 1974; Resol of Commend EPA Muni Coun 1974; citizen awd Kiwanis Club 1976; commend CA Lt Gov 1976; bicen awd Trinity Bapt Ch 1976; proclam Palo Alto & EPA Muni Coun 1976; serv to mankind awd Los Altos Sertoma Club 1977; "Black Strength & Black Survival" 1968; "What is the Problem" 1969; "Nairobi Sch Syst" 1969. **BUSINESS ADDRESS:** 2358 University Ave, East Palo Alto, CA 94303.

WILLACY, HAZEL M.
Attorney. **PERSONAL:** Born Apr 20, 1946, Mississippi; daughter of Julious Martin and Willie Barnes Martin; married Aubrey B; children: Austin Keith, Louis Samuel. **EDUCATION:** Smith Clg, BA 1967; Case Western Reserve U, JD 1976. **CAREER:** Bureau of Labor Stats, lbr ecnmst 1967-72; Baker Hostetter, atty 1976-80; Sherwin Williams, labor rel atty 1980-82, asst dir labor relations, 1983-87, dir Labor Relations, 1987-. **ORGANIZATIONS:** Mem ABA OH St Bar Asso 1976-; Case Western Reserve Univ Visiting Comm for Student Affairs, mem 1985-; trustee, Federation for Community Planning 1987-; mem, Bd of Directors, Northeast Chapter, Industrial Relations Research Assn 1988-; mem, Bd of Directors, Meridia Institute and Health Ventures 1989-; mem, Bd of Directors, Cleveland Music School Settlement 1988-. **HONORS/ACHIEVEMENTS:** Order of Coif 1976; articles publ 1970, 76, 80. **HOME ADDRESS:** 3145 Laurel Rd, Cleveland, OH 44120. **BUSINESS ADDRESS:** Dir, Labor Relations, Sherwin Williams Company, 12 Midland Bldg, 101 Prospect Ave, Cleveland, OH 44115.

WILLARD, LU
Jewelry designer. **CAREER:** Lu Willard Enterprises, jewelry designer. **ORGANIZATIONS:** Active with Leake Watts School, Abbott House; bd dir United Neighborhood Cts of Amer; supporter Harlem Dowling Adoption Ctr, The YMCA, The Dance Theatre of Harlem. **HONORS/ACHIEVEMENTS:** Women's Hall of Fame in Chgo; Amer Heritage & Freedom Awd; Mary McLeod Bethune Awd.

WILLIAM, THOMPSON E.
City government official. **PERSONAL:** Born Dec 26, 1924, Nyc, NY; married Elaine Allen; children: 2 Children. **EDUCATION:** Brooklyn Coll, BA; LLB. **CAREER:** NY State Senate, mem 1964-66; New York City Council, mem. **ORGANIZATIONS:** Mem Am Bar Assn; Bedford Stuyvesant Lawyers Assn; mem exec bd regional dir chmn legal redress com Brooklyn Br. **HONORS/ACHIEVEMENTS:** Dem Recipient Purple Heart Combat Infantrymen's Badge. **MILITARY SERVICE:** AUS WW II. **BUSINESS ADDRESS:** 768 Putnam Ave, Brooklyn, NY.

WILLIAMS, A. CECIL
Clergyman. **PERSONAL:** Born Sep 22, 1929, San Angelo, TX; married Evelyn Robinson; children: Kim, Albert. **EDUCATION:** Houston-Tillotson Coll, BA 1952; Perkins School of Tehol, BD 1955; Pacific School Religon, Grad Work. **CAREER:** St Pual Meth Church, asst minister 1954; Meth Church, minister 1955; Houston-Tillotson Coll, chaplain & teacher 1956-59; St James Meth Church, minister 1961-64; Glide Mem United Meth Church, minister

1964-. **ORGANIZATIONS:** Instr Ch Soc Crisis; bd mem Martin Luther King Ctr Soc Change; host KPIX-TV Vibrations for a New People; interviewed Angela Davis in prison, Sammy Davis Jr, Coretta Scott King. **HONORS/ACHIEVEMENTS:** Have been publ in many mags; created Glide Celebrations; Emmy Awd San Francisco Natl Acad TV Arts & Sci 1972; Man of the Year Sun Reporter 1967. **BUSINESS ADDRESS:** Minister, Glide Memorial United Meth Ch, 330 Ellis St, San Francisco, CA 94102.

WILLIAMS, ADA L.
Guidance counselor. **PERSONAL:** Born Aug 22, 1933, Waxahachie, TX; daughter of Henry Lee Gipson and Lulada Gregory Gipson Lewis; married Clyde L Williams, Jun 08, 1957; children: Adrian Dwight Williams. **EDUCATION:** Houston-Tillotson Coll, BA, 1955; North TX Sate Univ, MA, 1968. **CAREER:** Dallas Independent School Dist, specialist, counselor, employee relations, 1955-present. **ORGANIZATIONS:** Life mem, NEA; TEA evaluation team, 1975; NE Univ Eval Team 1975; mem TX Assn of Parlimentarians, Natl Assn of Parlimentarians; pres Classroom Tchrs of Dallas 1975-79; mem coord bd Natl Council of Accreditation for Teacher Educ; mem St Paul AME Church; mem NAACP; appointed by Governor to 6 yr term as one of the commrs on the Credit Union Commn for the State; mem Dallas Teachers Credit Union Bd 1979-; mem Delta Sigma Theta Sor Inc; mem Delta Kappa Gamma Soc Inc; mem Oak Cliff B & PW Club Inc; mem Natl Cncl of Accreditation for Teacher Educ; visiting team Univ of North Florida , Eastern New Mexico Univ, and OK Christian Univ; parliamentarian for TX PTA 1984-86; mem Appeals Bd NEA/NCATE 1985-. **HONORS/ACHIEVEMENTS:** Teacher of the Year, 1969-71; nominee 1984 TX's Gov's Women Hall of Fame; 1984 Obudswoman Awd South Dallas B&PW Club; Outstanding Educator TX Legislation 1983-85; Honored by Delta Kappa Gamma Soc Inc 1984, 1986, 1987; Achievement Awd Natl Women of Achievement Orgs 1987; Honored w/the TX Honorary Life Membership, 1987; Achievement Award Delta Kappa Gamma Soc, 1981-89; Trailblazer Award, South Dallas B&PW Club Inc, 1976, TV presentation on Parlimentary Procedures, 1989; Have written many parliamentary opinions; many educational, civic, religious, and club awards. **BUSINESS ADDRESS:** Specialist Employee Relations, Dallas Independent Sch Dist, 3700 Ross Avenue, Dallas, TX 75204.

WILLIAMS, ADDIE GATEWOOD
Dentist. **PERSONAL:** Born Oct 18, 1899, Richmond, VA; widowed. **EDUCATION:** VA Coll, BA 1915; Columbia U, MA 1917; Howard U, DDS 1921. **CAREER:** Murry & Leonie Guggenheim Clinic, dentist 1967-72; NY City Hlth Dept 1934-54; Richmond Pub Sch, tchr 1915-16. **ORGANIZATIONS:** Mem St Philip's Ch; Episcopal Ch Women; Bus & Professional Women's Grp St Philip's Ch; Order of The Daughters of the King Inc; Nat Cncl Inc; pres Providence 2 D of K; vice pres Hope Day Nursery Bd Inc; bd mem corr sec Am Mothers Com Inc 1977. **BUSINESS ADDRESS:** 1809 7th Ave, New York, NY 10026.

WILLIAMS, ALBERT P.
Judge. **PERSONAL:** Born in Savannah, GA; son of Albert P Williams Jr and Marion Elizabeth Williams; married Julia Noble (deceased). **EDUCATION:** Lincoln Univ, AB, 1940; Brooklyn Law School, JD, 1952. **CAREER:** Queens Co Civil Ct Torts Div, chief trial atty, 1962-69; City of New York, asst corp counsel; Civil Ct New York, NY, judge, 1970-77; New York State Supreme Ct, 1st Dist, supreme court justice, 1978-. **ORGANIZATIONS:** Mem, Harlem Lawyers Assn, bd dir, Brooklyn Law School Alumni Assn; mem, St Martin's Episcopal Church, New York, NY; past jr warden vestry, St Martin's Epis Church, New York, NY; 369 Vet's Assn, New York, NY; mem, NAACP, Kappa Alpha Psi. **HONORS/ACHIEVEMENTS:** Distinguished Alumni Award, Brooklyn Law School Class, 1952 1972; Outstanding Achievement Award, New York, Alumni Chapter, 1979. **BUSINESS ADDRESS:** Justice, NY State Supreme Court, 100 Centre St Rm 1727, New York, NY 10013.

WILLIAMS, ALPHONZA
Justice of the peace. **PERSONAL:** Born Sep 10, 1933, Marshall, TX; divorced; children: Anthony Kirk. **EDUCATION:** Wiley Coll Marshall TX, BS 1961; Prairie View Coll, 18 sem hrs 1961,73; Elba School of Ins Denver CO, Cert 1968; East TX Police Acad, Police Ct 1968; Kilgore Coll TX, 90 hrs Real Estate 1971-72; TSU School of Law Houston, JD 1976 96 hrs; Southwest TX State Univ St Marcus, 1983. **CAREER:** Marshall, TX, police officer 1958-73; Dallas ISD Dallas, TX, tchr 1962-63; GC Stephens Real Estate, salesman 1969-73; Milburn Real Estate, Salesman 1974-76;Ave C Apts, mgr 1975-76; Oleus Williams Real Estate, salesman 1977; Williams Asphalt, pres; William & Hicks Constr Co, co-owner; Rosehill Garden, vp/asst treas/corp mgr; Marshall-Harrison Cty, justice of the peace 1983-. **ORGANIZATIONS:** Plnng & zoning bd City of Marshall 1978-80; bd mem Jobs Training Serv 1978-79; bd mem North East TX Econ Devel Dist 1983; bd of dir, 1st vice chmn East TX Human Devel Corp 1983; bd mem Douglas Memorial Hosp 1984; mem Kiwanis Club Intl, Phi Alpha Delta, Phi Beta Sigma, Criminal Defense Lawyers Assn,TX Assoc of Realtors, Longview Bd of Realtors, Justice of the Peace Assoc, Intl Assoc of Personnel in Employment Sec; Phi Alpha Delta Law Frat Intl; bd mem The First Senatorial Dist TX Minority Affairs Cncl appointment by Sen Ed Howard. **HONORS/ACHIEVEMENTS:** Phi Beta Sigma Bus Awd 1971; Cert of Achievement Galilee Sr Matrons 1983; Disting Citizenship Awd Alpha Kappa Alpha 1984; Cert of Honor The Links Intl 1984; Prof License to Practice Law Enforcement; 1st black police officer & sgt in Marshall TX; 1st black Appeal Referee in Eastern TX; 1st black Justice of the Peace in Eastern TX. **MILITARY SERVICE:** USAF a/1c 4 yrs; USAF Reserves 2 yrs. **HOME ADDRESS:** 2207 South St, Marshall, TX 75670.

WILLIAMS, ALTHEA BULLS
Deputy curator, educator. **PERSONAL:** Born Oct 25, Tuskegee, AL; married Emmett R; children: Leslie Katherine, Terrance Allison. **EDUCATION:** Univ of IA, BFA 1943;Univ of OR, MS 1970;Univ of OR, PhD 1972. **CAREER:** Oakland Music, dept curator of Educ 1980-; Univ of DE Newark, art educ prof 1974-79; OR State Univ Corvallis, art & art educ prof 1973-74; Univ of OR Eugene, art educ (visting prof) 1973-74; Lane Community Coll, art & art educ; SW OR Community Coll 1972-74; Public School, community agent 1966-70; YMCA Teenage Dept, dir 1964-66; Portland OR, co welfare social work 1954-62; Tuskegee Inst Tuskegee Inst AL, asst dean of women 1950-53; Minority Concerns Rep Natl Art Educ Assn 1978-80; Moore Coll of Art Philadelphia, pres parent assn 1979-80. **ORGANIZATIONS:** Mem Alpha Kappa Alpha Sorority; mem Nat Assn ofUniv Women; bd mem Urban League 1964-70; mem OR State Scholarship Commn 1965-74; 900 Task Force Arts & Humanities 1967-68; chairperson OR State Scholarship Commn 1972-73; mem DE State Art Educ Advisory Council 1976-77; mem Commn Status of WomenUniv of DE 1976-77; Distinguished Pub Serv Pub Educ Portland Pub Sch 1968; Cross Cultural Relations Am Assn ofUniv Women Portland 1968; Ford Found. **HONORS/ACHIEVEMENTS:** Fellowship Ford Found 1971-72; Bay Area Image Award Coll Bounders Scholarship Orgn 1979; Teaching Effectiveness GrantUniv of DE Newark 1980-81.

WILLIAMS, ANDREW
Clergyman. **PERSONAL:** Born Jun 27, 1889, Washington, DC; married Grace Fletcher; children: 5 Children. **EDUCATION:** HowardUniv Washington, Diploma 1926; BTh 1970. **CAREER:** Comm Inst Ch, pastor founder 1975-; Comm Institutional Corp, pres; Real Estate Agt; Nat Council Sr Citizens, club leader & pres. **MILITARY SERVICE:** Vet WW I.

WILLIAMS, ANGIE BASS
Business executive/owner. **PERSONAL:** Born Oct 25, 1939, Halifax County, NC; married Rivers L; children: Kelvin Barth, Bertram Don. **EDUCATION:** Geroge W Carver H S Val, 1954-57; Eastern Mennonite Clg, 1972-73, 81-83. **CAREER:** US Continental Army Command Ft Monroe, VA, sec steno 1958-63; The Pentagon Wash DC, sec steno 1963-66; Smithsonian Inst Wash DC, exec sec 1968-71; Eastern Mennonite Clg, adm asso 1971-76; Choice Books Media Mnstrs, adm 1976-82; Specialty Office Svcs, owner/operator 1982-. **ORGANIZATIONS:** V pres Womens Missionary and Serv Comm 1973-81; chm Choice Books Title Selection Comm 1979-82; pub dir Clyde Dupin Reachout Crusade 1982; pub dir Worldwide Pictures Film "Prodigal" 1983; bd of dir Greenbelt Citizens for Fair Housing 1968-71; bd of dir & chm ways & means comm Harrisonburg/Rockingham CoChild Care Ctrs Inc 1979-81; bd of dir Mennonite Renewal Serv 1981-84; bd of elders New Covenant Mennonite Flwshp 1982-. **HONORS/ACHIEVEMENTS:** Author "I Will Hear What God the Lord Will Speak" 1979; editor/ghost writer various religious booklets 1982-; supervised writing 2 devotional bklts annually 1973-81; retreat ldr/public speaker US and Canada 1973-; articles "Festival Quarterly", "Voice", "Gospel Hearld" & "Beautiful Feet" 1973-; editor "The Edge" 1978-82. **HOME ADDRESS:** 30 Grandview Dr, Harrisonburg, VA 22801. **BUSINESS ADDRESS:** Specialty Office Services, 30 Grandview Dr, Harrisonburg, VA 22801.

WILLIAMS, ANITA SPENCER
Educator. **PERSONAL:** Born in Philadelphia, PA; daughter of Thomas Spencer and Julia Walker Spencer; married Willie G Williams, Jun 07, 1958; children: Diane, Stephen, Karen. **EDUCATION:** Cheyney Univ, Cheyney PA, BS (cum laude), 1967; Temple Univ, Philadelphia PA, EdM 1971, EdD 1988. **CAREER:** School District of Philadelphia PA, grade teacher 1967-71, reading specialist 1971-85, auxiliary vice principal 1985-86, teacher trainer 1986-87, administrative asst 1987-. **ORGANIZATIONS:** Mem, Alpha Phi Sigma Natl Honor Soc, 1966-; mem, Intl Reading Assn, 1972-; consultant, Progress Educational Program, 1977-80; mem, Black Women's Educational Alliance, 1980-82; educational dir, Waters Community Center, 1980-88; mem, Phi Delta Kappa Educational Fraternity, 1985-. **HONORS/ACHIEVEMENTS:** First Scholar of the Year, Cheyney Univ, 1966.

WILLIAMS, ANN CLAIRE
Judge. **PERSONAL:** Born Aug 16, 1949, Detroit, MI; daughter of Joshua M Williams and Dorothy E Garrett Williams; married David J Stewart, Aug 25, 1979; children: one son and one daughter. **EDUCATION:** Wayne State Univ, Detroit MI, BA, Education, 1970; Univ of Michigan, Ann Arbor MI, MA, Guidance/Counseling, 1972; Univ of Notre Dame Law School, Notre Dame IN, JD, 1975. **CAREER:** Judge Robert A Sprecher, Chicago IL, law clerk, 1975-76; United States Attorney, Chicago IL, assistant, 1976-83; Naional Institute for Trial Advocacy, faculty mem, 1979-; Organized Crime Drug Enforcement Task Force for North Central Region, US Atty, , Chicago IL, chief, 1983-85; Northwestern Univ, adjunct prof; US Dist Ct, Chicago IL, judge. **ORGANIZATIONS:** Mem, Univ of Chicago Laboratory School Bd of Trustees, 1988-, Univ of Notre Dame Bd of Trustees 1988-. **HONORS/ACHIEVEMENTS:** Edith S Sampson Memorial Award, Illinois Judicial Council, 1986; Thurgood Marshall Award, Chicago Kent College of Law, 1986; Headliner Award, Women of Wayne State Univ Alumni, 1987; Honorary JD, Lake Forest College, 1987. **BUSINESS ADDRESS:** United States District Court, 219 South Dearborn St, Room 1956, Chicago, IL 60604.

WILLIAMS, ANN E. A. (NEE ANDERSON)
Educator. **PERSONAL:** Born Sep 21, 1946, Jacksonville, FL; divorced. **EDUCATION:** FL A&M U, BS 1968. **CAREER:** Duval Co Bd of Public Instruction, instr; Duval Co Juvenile Court, coun 1969; A Philliph Randoph Inst, exec counc; FL Jr Coll Jax FL Adult Educ, instructor; Minority Affairs Com of Duval Teachers United. **ORGANIZATIONS:** Jacksonville Jaycees; Ebenezer United Meth Cub Scout Den Ldr; pres Dem Women's of FL Inc; Dem Exec Com; Nat Coun of Negro Women Inc; exec com NAACP Leag of Women Voters; Coun of Soc Studies; vice pres Duval Tchrs United; memshp com YWCA; United Meth Women. **BUSINESS ADDRESS:** Assistant Principal, Duval Co Bd of Public Instruct, 1840 W 9th St, Jacksonville, FL 32208.

WILLIAMS, ANNALISA J. STUBBS
Employee relations officer & attorney. **PERSONAL:** Born Sep 23, 1956, Youngstown, OH; daughter of Julius Saffold Stubbs and Eula Grace Harris Stubbs; married Michael D Williams, Sep 07, 1985; children: Michael James (dec), Alexandria Katherine-Grace Williams. **EDUCATION:** Kent State Univ, BA 1977; Univ of Akron, MA 1979; Univ of Akron Law Sch, JD 1984. **CAREER:** Kent State Univ, pre-law adv 1976-77, orientation instr 1976-77, resident staff adv 1976-77; OH Civil Rights Comm, investigator/intake spec 1977-79; Metro Regional Transit Auth, personnel equal employment minor bus dir 1979-84, employee relations officer 1984-85; City of Akron, asst law dir 1985-88; Roadway Services Inc Akron OH, manager, 1988-. **ORGANIZATIONS:** Adv council Upward Bound Kent State 1979-; mem Delta Sigma Theta 1980-; mem Assn of Minorities in Public Transit 1980; mem EEO Officers in Summit Co 1981; mem Urban League's Minority Bus Enterprise Counsel for the State of OH; mem NAACP; bd of trustees YWCA Akron Urban Leagues Youth Committee; bd of dirs Information Line; bd of trustees, Prep Ohio; mem Delta Sigma Theta Sor Inc; mem Akron Barristers Club; mem Akron Bar Association; mem Akron Urban League; mem West Side Neighbors; treas Comm to Re-elect Councilman Michael D Williams. **HONORS/ACHIEVEMENTS:** Superior Scholarship Alpha Lambda Delta Kent State 1977; Disting Scholarship Pi Sigma Alpha Kent State 1977; Outstanding Black Student Black United Students Kent State 1977; Outstanding Young Woman in Amer 1982; 1st place Akron Law Sch Client Counseling Competition 1983. **HOME ADDRESS:** 584 Avalon Ave, Akron, OH 44320.

WILLIAMS, ANNIE M.
Educator. **PERSONAL:** Born Oct 21, 1937, Limestone Co; married Nathaniel; children:

Angelia Nicole. **EDUCATION:** Prairie View A&M U, BS 1960; TX Women's Univ, MA 1968. **CAREER:** Bishop Coll, asst prof of health physical educ 1968-; Richardson Ind School Dist, inst 1963-68; Dallas Ind School Dist, instr 1960-63. **ORGANIZATIONS:** Mem present sw reg dir The Nat Sorority of Phi Delta Kappa (past Basileus Dallas Chpt); pres Bishop Chap Am Assn of Univ Women; adv S Dallas Child Devel Center; owner/dir S Dallas Sch of Ballet; mem St James Cath Ch; Maria Morgan YWCA; bd dir Dallas Dance Council; TX Assn of Health Phy Educ Recreation. **HONORS/ACHIEVEMENTS:** Recipient Outstanding Tchr in HPER 1969; Outstanding Serv to Sorority 1973-74; Listed Outstanding Educators of Am 1973. **BUSINESS ADDRESS:** 3837 Simpson Stuart Rd, Dallas, TX 75241.

WILLIAMS, ARMSTRONG
Director. **PERSONAL:** Born Feb 05, 1960, Marion, SC. **EDUCATION:** SC State Coll, BS (Honors) 1981. **CAREER:** Senator Strom Thurmand, legislative aide 1980; Congressmen Carroll Campbell, legislative aide 1981; Congressmen Floyd Spence, legislative aide 1981; US Dept of Ag, legislative analyst 1981-83; US Equal Employment Opport Comm, confidential asst to chmn. **ORGANIZATIONS:** Bd advisors Dupree Constr 1981-; bd of dir Comptex Assoc 1982-; advisory bd Child-Help USA 1982-; consult marketer Smooth as Silk Enterprises James Wilkes Pres 1984-; chmn bd of dir Travis Winkey Fashion Mag 1982-. **HONORS/ACHIEVEMENTS:** Bicentennial Public Speaking Award 1976; ROTC Sojourner Awd 1978; Who's Who in Amer Coll & Univ 1981; Who's Who in Amer 1983; Youth of the Year Congressional Black Caucus 1982-83; Falcons Public Serv The Falcons 1983-84; Public Serv Phi Beta Sigma 1982-83; Liberal Arts Howard Univ School of Liberal Arts 1983-84;One of 30 most influential young Blacks in Amer under 30 March, 1985 Ebony Mag; appeared on Phil Donahue Show Feb 25 "America's Top Black Conservatives". **HOME ADDRESS:** 201 Masschusetts Ave NE, #217-A, Washington, DC 20002.

WILLIAMS, ARNETTE L.
Educator. **PERSONAL:** Born Sep 03, Logan, WV; married Clarence L Williams; children: Cheryl, Reginald. **EDUCATION:** BS 1943. **CAREER:** Marion Co WV, former teacher. **ORGANIZATIONS:** Former vol work Girl Scouts Boy Scouts Little League PTA Grey Lady ARC Military Hosps Overseas; chairwoman of bd co-founder Reston Sect Nat'l Council Negro Women 1973; mem Reston Planned Parenthood Comm Established Community Clinic 1974; aptd mem Planned Parenthood Council No VA; mem Wolf Trap Asso forPerforming Arts; FISH; United Fund; Int'l Womens Org 1975; mem Social Club "Sagarities" Serv Oriented; Lions Aux Maternal Grandmother Grandfather Were Among First Black Tchrs in Henry Co VA.

WILLIAMS, ART S.
Administrative assistant. **PERSONAL:** Born Sep 25, 1912, Dubach, LA; married Della Gray; children: Sammye Hitchye, Art S. **EDUCATION:** WilberforceUniv OH, BS 1938; Tulsa U, MEd; AR U, postgrad;Univ of OK, OK State U; Cntrl MO; AZ State U; KS State U. **CAREER:** Comm Affairs Tulsa Public Schools, admin asst 1971-; Athletic Coach 1942-68; Dean Boys 1968-71. **ORGANIZATIONS:** Mem Nat Prin Assn; OK Educ Assn; Nat HS Athl Assn; OK Collegiate Athl Assn; Grtr Tulsa Ofcl Assn; SW Coaches Ofcl Assn; Mid West Coaches Ofcl Assn; commr Am Leag TJAA; mem YMCA; Esquire Men's Club; Kappa Alpha Psi Frat; Optimist Club; seacon Morning Star Bapt Ch; NAACP Cert Bravery ARC. **HONORS/ACHIEVEMENTS:** 30 yr Award Coaching & Tchng; Football All-Am WilberforceUniv 2 Yrs. **MILITARY SERVICE:** AUS 1941. **BUSINESS ADDRESS:** 3027 S New Haven, Tulsa, OK.

WILLIAMS, ARTHUR G., JR.
Judge. **PERSONAL:** Born Feb 11, 1919, New Haven, CT; married Carolyn Downs; children: Arthur G. **EDUCATION:** Howard U, AB 1943; Columbia Law Sch, LLB 1948. **CAREER:** Ct of Common Pleas St of CT, ret judge 1965-76; Ct of Common Pleas CT, judge 1966-76; Circ Ct CT 1961-75; Madison CT, corp couns 1953-60. **ORGANIZATIONS:** Dir Union Tr Co. **BUSINESS ADDRESS:** P O Box 351, Madison, CT 06443.

WILLIAMS, ARTHUR K.
Business executive. **PERSONAL:** Born Sep 25, 1945, Albany, GA. **EDUCATION:** Monroe Area Voc-Tech School, Cert 1965; Albany Jr Coll, 1975; Albany Area Voc Tech School, Continuing Ed 1979-; Nationwide Ins Training School, Independent Agent 1979. **CAREER:** Al Rankim Shriners, bookkeeper 1973; Albany State Coll, accountant 1965-79; City of Albany Ward 3, commiss 1982-86; Arthur Williams Ins Agency, agent 1979-. **ORGANIZATIONS:** Corp mem Boys Club of Albany 1979-85; treas NAACP 1980-85; mem GA Municipal Assoc 1982-85; reg coord Rainbow Coalition 1984; mem Nationwide Ins Independent Cont Assoc 1984. **MILITARY SERVICE:** AUS Reserve sfc E-7 16 yrs; US Commendation, Viet Service 1969. **HOME ADDRESS:** 518 Holloway Ave, Albany, GA 31701. **BUSINESS ADDRESS:** Agent, Arthur Williams Ins Agency, 600-A S Jefferson St, Albany, GA 31701.

WILLIAMS, ARTHUR LOVE
Physician. **PERSONAL:** Born Jun 04, 1940, Priscilla, MS; married Patricia; children: Terri, Toni, Tara. **EDUCATION:** Jackson State Coll, BS 1962; Meharry Med Coll, MD 1966; Hubbard Hosp, Intern 1966-67; Hubbard Hosp, Resd 1970-73. **CAREER:** Pvt Prac, physician 1974; Med Prgm Baylor Coll Med, tchr comm 1974-; Hubbard Hosp Dept Internal Med, instr asst prof chf resd 1972-74;Univ TX Med Educ Prgm, tchg staff 1976-; St Elizabeth Hosp, chf staff pres med 1977-. **ORGANIZATIONS:** Mem Houston Med Forum; Harris Co Med Soc; Nat Med Assn; AMA; bd mem CCEMS 1976-77; sec Houston Med Forum 1977; chmn Educ Com 1975-77; ann GPA-Forde Meml Lectr & Banq 1975-77; bd cert Internal Med 1973. **HONORS/ACHIEVEMENTS:** Air Medal Commendation 1969-70; Flight Surgeon 1967-70. **MILITARY SERVICE:** USAF capt 1966-70. **BUSINESS ADDRESS:** Mullins & Williams, 4315 Lockwood, Houston, TX 77026.

WILLIAMS, ATHER, JR.
Business executive. **PERSONAL:** Born Nov 21, 1943, Chicago, IL; married Sandra; children: Michele, Christopher. **EDUCATION:** Loyola U, BS 1968;Univ Chicago, grad student 1974-75. **CAREER:** Johnson & Johnson Baby Products Co, production supr 1966-68; Special Proj Mgr 1968; Dept Mgr 1968-71; Prod Control & Inv Mgr 1972; Production & Dist Supt 1972-74; Mgr Admn & Production Supt 1974; Prod Mgr 1975; Nat'l Assoc Market Developers 1972-74; Nat'l Council Physical Distribution, mgmnt 1973-74. **ORGANIZATIONS:** Mem Yth Motivation Prog 1972-74; Operation PUSH 1970-74; Urban League 1970-74; sch bd Holy Name of Mary 1973. **HONORS/ACHIEVEMENTS:** Geo F Smith Awd Mgr Yr 1970; WGRT Radio Great Guy Awd 1971. **BUSINESS ADDRESS:** 2645 Johnson Rd, Park Forest South, IL 60466.

WILLIAMS, AVON NYANZA, JR.
Attorney. **PERSONAL:** Born Dec 22, 1921, Knoxville, TN; married Joan Marie Bontemps; children: Avon Nyanza III, Wendy Janette. **EDUCATION:** Johnson C Smith U, AB 1940; Boston U, LLB LLM 1947-48. **CAREER:** MA, admitted bar 1948; TN 1948; US Ct Appeals 1953; Military Appeals 1956; Sup Ct US 1963; Hon ZA Looby, atty 1953; ABA, priv prac 1969; 19th Dist of TN, senator 1968-; Williams & Dinkins, attorney. **ORGANIZATIONS:** Mem Amer Judicature Soc, Davidson Co Trail Lawyers Assoc, NAACP 1953-; elder St Andrews Presbyterian Church 1956-; Davidson Co Independent Political Cncl 1962-; general chmn TN Voters Cncl 1966-85; So Regional Cncl 1968-; mem Omega Psi Phi Frat, Sigma Pi Phi Frat. **HONORS/ACHIEVEMENTS:** Davidson Co Independent Political Cncl Outstanding Serv in Civil Rights 1977; Disting Achievement Awd for Legal Leadership TN State Univ 1977; Legislatorof the Yr Humanitarian Awd TN Black Caucus 1978; Disting Serv & Outstanding Person in Civil Rights NAACP 1978; TN State Univ Awd for Comm Serv Continuing Educ and Public Educ Recognition Day 1978; Davidson Co Independent Political Cncl Awd for Outstanding Serv to Higher Educ 1979; MG Ferguson Disting Comm Serv Awd 1979; Outstanding & Dedicated Serv Pearl HS 1981; 10th Annual Legislative Retreat Awd of Excellence TN Black Caucus of State Legislators 1984; Resolution Honoring Outstanding Career The Cncl of Metro Govt of Nashville & Davidson Co 1985; Citation for Outstanding Serv to the Improvement of Judicial System and the Promotion of C ivil Justice TN Trial Lawyers Assoc 1986. **MILITARY SERVICE:** USAR lt col. **BUSINESS ADDRESS:** Attorney at Law, Williams and Dinkins, 203 Second Ave North, Nashville, TN 37201.

WILLIAMS, BENJAMIN VERNON
Journalist. **PERSONAL:** Born Jan 25, 1927, StLouis, MO; married Vivian Hickman; children: Benjamin Jr, Gregory, Alan. **EDUCATION:** San Francisco State Univ, BA 1961. **CAREER:** San Francisco Sun-Reporter, news reporter 1963-66; San Francisco Examiner, newspaper reporter 1963-66; San Francisco State Univ, lecturer 1968-; KPIX-TV Ch 5, news reporter 1966-. **ORGANIZATIONS:** Mem Oakland Athletic Club 1975-; bd of dir Oakland Boys Club 1975-; bd of dir Oakland YMCA 1977-; bd of dirs Amer Red Cross Oakland Branch; mem Amer Heart Assoc Alameda Chapt. **HONORS/ACHIEVEMENTS:** Jane Harrah Awd in Journalism San Francisco Lawyers Club 1965; San Francisco Press Club Awd (2) San Francisco Press Club (tv & radio news) 1966 & 1971; McQuade Awd Disting Programming Assn of Catholic Newsmen 1974; Broadcast Media Awd for Single Accomplishment & Highest Standards in TV-News San Francisco State Univ 1976; Emmy Awd for TV News No CA Emmy 1976. **MILITARY SERVICE:** AUS sgt 1945-47. **BUSINESS ADDRESS:** News Reporter, KPIX-TV, 855 Battery St, San Francisco, CA 94111.

WILLIAMS, BERNICE
Government director. **EDUCATION:** Miles Coll, BA 1973; Johns Hopkins Univ, MIntl Publ Policy candidate 1985; Miles Coll, Hon PhD 1984. **CAREER:** Birmingham Urban League, stat researcher/intern 1972-73; Republic Personnel, personnel specialist 1974-75; Westinghouse Elec Corp, staff assoc 1975-76; Johnson Products Co, sales exec 1976-78; Neiceon Enterprises Inc, CEO 1978-81; Park Lane Limousine Inc, chmn of bd 1985-; US Dept Housing Urban Dev, dir small & disadvantaged business utilization 1981-. **ORGANIZATIONS:** Bd mem Junior Achievement Metro Wash 1978-81; chmn Fed Stategic Pplanning Comm for Sm & disad Bus 1984-85; mem President Reagan Interagency Comm for Women's Bus Enterprises. **HONORS/ACHIEVEMENTS:** Presidential Citation Natl Assn for Equal Oppt in Higher Edn; mem President Reagan's transition team 1980; Public Issues Educ Award The Greyhound Corp 1983; Who's Who in the World of Women 1984-85. **BUSINESS ADDRESS:** Dir, Small/Disadvantaged Business Utilization, Dept of Housing & Urban Devel, 451 7th St SW, Room 10226, Washington, DC 20410.

WILLIAMS, BERTHA MAE
Educator, psychologist. **PERSONAL:** Born Jul 10, 1927, Brighton, TN; divorced; children: Kenneth M. **EDUCATION:** AZ State U, BA 1964; AZ State U, MA 1966; AZ State U, PhD 1973. **CAREER:** Univ of CA Los Angeles, counseling psychologist 1976-; Univ of TN Knoxville, asst prof/psychologist 1973-76; AZ State Univ Tempe, couns 1971-73; Luke Elem School Luke AFB, couns 1967-71; Luke Elem School Luke AFB, teacher 1963-67. **ORGANIZATIONS:** Bd of dirs Desert Sch Fed Credit Union 1968-71; Sch Bd Louisville KY, consult 1975; bd of mgmt YWCA 1977-80; vice pres bd of mgmt YWCA 1980-. **HONORS/ACHIEVEMENTS:** Outstanding Achievement in EducUniv of TN 1974; "Trust & Self-Disclosure Among Black Coll Students" Journal of Counseling Psychology 1974; "Black Women, Assertiveness vs Agressiveness" Journal of Afro-Am Issues 1974; "Assertion Traing" The Orientation Review 1978. **BUSINESS ADDRESS:** UCLA, 4223 Math Science, Los Angeles, CA 90024.

WILLIAMS, BERYL E. W. (NEE WARNER)
Education administrator. **PERSONAL:** Born May 23, 1913, Bangor, ME; daughter of James H Warner and Elizabeth Jackson Warner; married Roger K; children: Scott Warner. **EDUCATION:** Univ of ME, AB 1935; Univ of ME, MA 1940; Univ of ME, DPed 1972; courses & workshops at, Univ of Chicago, MI State Univ, Johns Hopkins Univ, Univ of MD. **CAREER:** Gilbert Acad, teacher 1936-37; Claflin Coll, teacher 1937-40; A&T Coll, teacher 1946-48; Morgan State Univ, teacher 1948-63; Ctr for Continuing Educ Morgan State Univ, dean 1963-81, dean Emeritus Continuing Studies, 1981-. **ORGANIZATIONS:** Pres MD League of Women's Clubs 1957-59; comm orgnzr troop ldr Central MD Girl Scout Council 1959-63; trust US Assn of Evening Students 1966-; bd Greater Baltimore YWCA 1967-70; vice pres Baltimore City Bd of School Commissioners 1974-84; lay speaker United Methodist Church 1975-; bd mem Advance Fed Savings & Loan Assoc 1978-; chmn adv bd MEOC 1981-; dir Baltimore Women's Fair 1982,83; vice pres bd mem Park Heights St Acad 1982-; bd mem Women's Civic League ofBaltimore 1985-; golden life mem NAACP; life mem Coll Language Assn; mem N Amer Assn of Summer Sessions; chmn Intl Div, NCNW of Greater Baltimore, historian, Morgan State Univ Women, Natl Caucus on Black Aged (Morgan Chapter.). **HONORS/ACHIEVEMENTS:** Woman of the Year; Vol of The Yr; Conselling Adults; Pubs "How to Take Tests"; listed in "Twenty Black Women" F Beckles; Community Serv Award; Sojourner Truth Award, Natl Assoc of Negro Business & Professional Women's Clubs; Humanitarian Award Howard Cornish Alumni Assoc Morgan State; Mother's Day Peace Award.

WILLIAMS, BETTY SMITH
Nurse, educator. **PERSONAL:** Born Jul 22, 1929, South Bend, IN; daughter of John W Smith and Nellie Lindsay Smith; married Harold Louis Williams, Jul 10, 1954. **EDUCATION:** Howard Univ, BS; Western Reserve Univ, MN; School of Nursing, UCLA, MS; School of Public Health UCLA, Dr PH. **CAREER:** Visiting Nurse Assn Cleveland, staff nurse 1954-55; LA City Health Dept, staff nurse 1955-66; Mt St Mary's Coll LA, asst prof 1956-69; Charles Drew Post Graduate Medical School LA, public health nurse consultant 1970-71; UCLA School of Nursing, asst prof 1969-, asst dean student affairs 1974-75; asst dean acad affairs 1975-76; School of Nursing Univ of CO Health Science Center Denver, dean & prof 1979-84; Kaiser Permanente, consultant; Delta Sigma Theta Center for Life Develop, exec dir; prof, California State Univ Long Beach, 1988-. **ORGANIZATIONS:** Founder 1968, pres 1969-74 Council of Black Nurses Inc LA; mem Natl Caucus of Black Health Workers APHA; bd dirs exec comm Natl Black Nurses Assn Inc; affirmative action task force Amer Nurses Assn; mem CA Nurses Assn; bd dir Blue Cross of Southern CA 1976-84; pres DST Telecomm Inc 1975-79, natl treasurer 1971-75; Delta Sigma Theta Inc Public Serv Org; Op Womanpower Inc; Watts Towers Art Center; Com for Simon Rodia's Towers In Watts; Charles Drew Post-Graduate Med School Continuing Educ for Nurses' Task Force; LA Alumnae Chapter Delta Sigma Theta Inc; mem NAACP; dir Blue Cross of California 1986-. **HONORS/ACHIEVEMENTS:** Nurse Traineeship Grant Graduate Study US Public Health Serv 1965-66; Fellow Amer Public Health Assn 1969; Natl Sojourner Truth Award Natl Business & Professional Womens Clubs Inc 1972; Fellow Amer Acad of Nursing; Hon mem Chi Eta Phi. **BUSINESS ADDRESS:** Professor, Dept of Nursing, California State Univ Long Beach, 1250 Bellflower Rd, Long Beach, CA 90840.

WILLIAMS, BILLY DEE
Actor. **PERSONAL:** Born Apr 06, 1937, New York, NY; married Teruko Nakagami Williams; children: Corey, Miyako, Hanako. **EDUCATION:** Natl Acad Fine Arts & Design, Hallgarten Scholar. **CAREER:** The Cool World, A Taste of Honey, Halleliyah Baby, Firebrand of Florence, Brian's Song, Lady Sings the Blues, Mahogoney & Scott Joplin, The Last Angry Man, 1959, I Have a Dream, 1976, Star Wars, The Empire Strikes Back, The Return of the Jedi, Night Hawks, Marvin & Tige, Fear City, Deadly Illusions, 1989, actor; TV films Carter's Army, Brian's Song, The Glass House, The Hostage Tower, Children of Divorce, Shooting Stars, Chiefs, Time Bomb; guest appearances TV series The Jeffersons, The Interns, The FBI, Mission Impossible, Mod Squad, Police Woman, Dynasty; appeared in TV movie Scott Joplin, King of Ragtime 1978. **ORGANIZATIONS:** Mem Actors Workshop in Harlem. **HONORS/ACHIEVEMENTS:** Emmy nom Brian's Song; 1 of the Most Promising Young Men of Manhattan by Cosmopolitan Mag. *

WILLIAMS, BILLY LEO
Professional baseball coach. **PERSONAL:** Born Jun 15, 1938, Whister, AL; married Shirley Williams; children: Valarie, Nina, Julia, Sandra. **CAREER:** Began in minor league 1956; Chicago Cubs, player 1961-74; Oakland A's, player 1974-76; Chicago Cubs, coach 1976-82; Oakland A's, hitting instr; Chicago Cubs, hitting instructor; Oakland A's, coach. **HONORS/ACHIEVEMENTS:** Rookie of the Yr Natl League 1961; Player of the Yr Natl League 1972; Major League Player of the Yr 1972; Played in the All Star Game six times; Holds theNatl League Record for Most Consecutive Games Played 1,117; Tied major league records most home runs 2 consec games (5) 1968; 3 home runs 1 game 1968; led NL total bases 1968-70-72; tied major league record most consec doubles in 1 game (4) 1969; NL record most consec yrs 600 or more at bats 1970; led NL inslugging (606) 1972; inducted into Chicago Sports Hall of Fame 1982; elected to Baseball Hall of Fame 1987. **BUSINESS ADDRESS:** Baseball Coach, Chicago Cubs, 1060 W Addison St, Chicago, IL 60613.

WILLIAMS, BILLY MYLES
Research manager. **PERSONAL:** Born Sep 06, 1950, Kings Mountain, NC; son of Willis F. Williams and Mattie Ashley Williams; married Rosemarie Delores Wesson. **EDUCATION:** Univ of NC Chapel Hill, BS 1972; Central MI Univ, MS 1980. **CAREER:** Martin Marietta Chemicals, rsch chemist 1972-74; Dow Chemical Co, 1974-. **ORGANIZATIONS:** Mem Sigma Xi 1982-, Sigma Iota Epsilon 1984-, AAAS 1985-, Big Brothers; chmn Midland Sect Amer Chemical Soc 1988-89. **HOME ADDRESS:** 605 Nakoma Drive, Midland, MI 48640.

WILLIAMS, BISMARCK
Educator. **PERSONAL:** Born Sep 08, 1928, Mobile, AL; married Avery W; children: Bismarck Jr, Rhonda. **EDUCATION:** Morehouse Coll, AB 1947; Atlant U, MBA 1950. **CAREER:** Roosevelt Univ, asso dean; Walter E Heller Coll, dir; Advanced Mgmt Rsch, lectr 1967-; Roosevelt Univ, prof 1957; Roosevelt Univ, lectr 1955-57; AM&N Coll, purch agent/instr 1952-54. **ORGANIZATIONS:** Mem Fin Mgmt Assn; mem Midwest Fin Assn Trustee Chicago Coll of Osteo Med & Hosp; bd of dir Kenny Ryan Monigal Inc; dir Chicago Econ Dev Corp; dir Chicago Fin Dev Corp. **BUSINESS ADDRESS:** 430 S Michigan Ave, Chicago, IL 60605.

WILLIAMS, BOOKER T.
Business executive. **PERSONAL:** Born Apr 28, 1920, Corapeake, NC; married Jeanne LeBlanc; children: 9. **EDUCATION:** Univ of Michigan Law School, LLB 1955. **CAREER:** MI Indep Press Inc, business mgr 1976-; Pherc Inc Elec Installation Co, business mgr 1970-76; Washtenaw Co MI, asst prosecuting atty 1964-70; private practice 1956-64; Willow Run Branch NAACP, legal counsel 1957-68; Washtenaw Co Black Economic Devel League, legal counsel 1970-73. **ORGANIZATIONS:** Mem Alpha Phi Alpha and several other civic organizations. **HONORS/ACHIEVEMENTS:** Certificate of Merit, Natl Police Officers Assn of Amer, 1970; Certificate of Appreciation, Washtenaw Co Sheriff Dept Jr Deps, 1968; Freedom Award Certificate, NAACP. **MILITARY SERVICE:** AUS 1st lt 1942-47. **BUSINESS ADDRESS:** 124 E Washington St, Ann Arbor, MI 48104.

WILLIAMS, BRENDA PAULETTE
Business owner/broadcaster. **PERSONAL:** Born Jul 07, 1946, St Louis, MO; daughter of Herman Williams and Hattie Williams. **EDUCATION:** OH Univ Athens, BJ 1969; Univ MO Columbia, Postgrad. **CAREER:** KATZ St Louis, newscaster 1969-70; KPLR-TV St Louis, talk show producer/host 1973-74, KSD-TV & Radio St Louis, talk show producer/host news and reporter 1974-77; KMBC-TV Kansas City MO, weekend anchor-reporter 1977-81, weekday anchor-reporter 1981-85; Kansas City Skywave Inc, pres 1986-; H Pearl Investments Inc, pres 1986-; financial consultant, Merrill Lynch, 1987-. **ORGANIZATIONS:** Mem Alpha Kappa Alpha, Sigma Delta Chi. **HONORS/ACHIEVEMENTS:** Woman of Involvement Awd Alpha Kappa Alpha 1974; Cert of Appreciation St Louis Urban League-St Louis Sentinel 1975; Human Relations Awd Natl Assn Colored Women's Clubs 1975; Documentary Reporting Awd MO Radio & TV Assn 1979; Consumer Reporting Awd MO Dept Consumer Affairs 1979; Outstanding Achievement in Journalism Awd MO Black Leadership Assn 1981; Headliner Awd Outstanding TV Reporting 1982; selected for Amer Journalists Tour of Israel, Israeli Journalist Assn 1980; Black Achiever Awd SCLC 1981. **BUSINESS ADDRESS:** President, H Pearl Investments Inc, 4423 N Taylor, St Louis, MO 63115.

WILLIAMS, BRIAN CALVIN
Professional athlete. **PERSONAL:** Born Oct 14, 1957, New Orleans, LA; married Debra. **EDUCATION:** Southern U. **CAREER:** Oakland Invaders, tight end 1984. **HONORS/ACHIEVEMENTS:** Named All-Southwest Athletic Conf as a jr and sr.

WILLIAMS, BRUCE E.
Business executive. **PERSONAL:** Born Sep 02, 1931, St Paul, MN; married Wilma Allen; children: Deborah Lynn, Lisa Marie. **EDUCATION:** Mankato State Coll, BS 1956; MS 1970; Union Grad Sch, PhD 1977. **CAREER:** Rockefeller Found, asst director; 1972-; Minneapolis Schs, asst supt 1971-72; Minneapolis Schs, prin 1968-71; Minneapolis Schs, tchr 1962-68; Summer Staff Devel Prog Minneapolis Pub Schs, dir 1966; Juv Detention Group, supvr 1960-61; Registered Basketball & Football, official. **ORGANIZATIONS:** Mem Am Assn Sch Adminstr; Assn Supervision & Curriculum Dev Nat Alliance Black Sch Educators; Mankato State Coll Alumni Assn; YMCA; vice pres Afro-Am Educators Assn (Mpls); Who's Who Am Colls & Univs 1956; Hall of Fame Mankato State U; Rockefeller Found Fellow; trustee Macalester Coll St Paul; pres gen educ bd NY School Bd System; mem NY State Human Rights Advisory Council; mem Educ Adv Comm Natl Urban League;; mem NY Gov's Adv Comm of Black Affairs. **MILITARY SERVICE:** AUS sp 4th class 1957-59. **BUSINESS ADDRESS:** Associate Dir, Rockefeller Foundation, 1133 Avenue of the Americas, New York, NY 10036.

WILLIAMS, BUCK
Professional athlete. **PERSONAL:** Born Mar 08, 1960, Rocky Mount, NC. **EDUCATION:** Univ of MD College Park MD, attended. **CAREER:** NJ Nets, basketball player 1981-. **HONORS/ACHIEVEMENTS:** Mem US Olympic Team 1980; NBA All-Rookie Team 1982; NBA Rookie of the Year 1982; Named to All-NBA Second Team 1983. **BUSINESS ADDRESS:** Basketball Player, New Jersey Nets, Byrne Meadowlands Arena, East Rutherford, NJ 07073.

WILLIAMS, BUSTER See WILLIAMS, CHARLES A.

WILLIAMS, CAMILLA
Operatic soprano. **PERSONAL:** Born Oct 18, Danville, VA; married Charles T Beavers. **EDUCATION:** VA State Univ, BS 1941. **CAREER:** Created role of Madame Butterfly as 1st black contract singer at New York City Ctr 1946; created 1st Aida at New York City Ctr 1948; 1st NY perf of Mozart's "Idomeneo" w/Little Orch Soc 1950; 1st tour of Alaska 1950; 1st European tour 1954; 1st Viennese perf of Menotti's "Saint of Bleecker St" 1955; Amer Fest in Belgium 1955; 1st African tour for US State Dept 1958-59; 1st tour of Israel 1959; guest of Pres Eisenhower-concert for Crown Prince of Japan 1960; tours in Europe, Asia & Australia 1962; NY perf of Handel's "Orlando"; 1st tour of Poland 1974; Bronx Coll, prof of voice 1970; Brooklyn Coll, prof of voice 1970-73; Queens Coll, prof of voice 1974-; IN Univ, 1st black prof of voice 1977-. **ORGANIZATIONS:** Mem Natl Soc of Arts & Letters 1981. **HONORS/ACHIEVEMENTS:** Listed in first edition of Who's Who in the World 1971; Honored by the Gov of VA Linwood Holton as Distinguished Virginian 1971; listed in Danville VA Museum of Fine Arts & History Hall of Fame 1974; Camilla Williams Park designatd in Danville VA 1974; listed in first edition of World Who's Who of Women 1974; honoredby IN Univ Sch of Music Black Music Students Orgn for Outstanding Achievements in the field of music 1979; honored by Gov Julian M Carroll of KY as a "Kentucky Colonel" 1979; Hon mem Sigma Alpha Iota 1980; Nat'l Soc of Arts & Letters, mem 1981; honored guest of the NY Philharmonic 10,000th Concert Celebration1982; honored by Philadelphia Pro Arte Soc 1982; first black prof of voice to teach at Central Conservatory of Music Beijing People's Republic of China 1983; Disting Awd of Ctr for Leadership & Develop 1983; included in first ed of Most Important Women of the Twentieth Century; included in new ed of Grove's Dictionary of Music & Musicians 1984; Taylor-Williams student residence hall is named at VA State Univ in honor of Billy Taylor & Camilla Williams; VA St Univ at Petersburg, rec'd honorary doctor of music degree 1985; listed in Foremost Women of the 20th Century, 1988; Arts and Humanities Award, Virginia State University, 1989. **HOME ADDRESS:** 2610 E 2nd St, Bloomington, IN 47401. **BUSINESS ADDRESS:** Professor of Voice, INUniv, School of Music, Bloomington, IN 47401.

WILLIAMS, CARLETTA CELESTE
Nurse. **PERSONAL:** Born Mar 05, 1956, Steubenville, OH; married Calvin C Williams Jr; children: Charles, PJ, Cecilia. **EDUCATION:** WV Northern Comm Coll, AD of Nursing 1977; West Liberty State Coll, BS Nursing 1986. **CAREER:** OH Valley Hosp, dietary aide 1972-77; Weirton Medical Ctr, registered nurse 1977-79; Johns-Hopkins Hosp, registered nurse CCU 1979-80; Weirton Medical Ctr registered nurse ccu 1980-. **ORGANIZATIONS:** Mem AACN 1986, BPW 1986; church nurse Second Baptist Church 1987. **HONORS/ACHIEVEMENTS:** Who's Who in Nursing 1986; Who's Who Among Human Service Profls 1987. **HOME ADDRESS:** 522 Maxwell Ave, Steubenville, OH 43952. **BUSINESS ADDRESS:** Head Nurse CCU, Weirton Medical Center, 601 Colliers Way, Weirton, WV 26062.

WILLIAMS, CARLTON RAY, JR.
Educational administrator. **PERSONAL:** Born Sep 06, 1957, New York City, NY; married Deborah Whitten. **EDUCATION:** Radford Univ, BS General Psych 1979, MS Industrial/Organ Psych 1984. **CAREER:** Radford Univ, residential life dir 1980-82, asst dir of admissions 1982-84; Roanoke Coll, asst dean of admissions 1984-. **ORGANIZATIONS:** Co-founder Radford Univ Chap of Amer Soc of Personnel Admin 1980; mem VA Assn of Student Personnel Admins 1982-; mem VA Assoc of Collegiate Registrars & Admiss Counselors 1982-; co-founder parliamentarian VA Admissions Council on Black Concerns 1983-; mem Amer Soc of Personnel Adminis 1984-; mem Personnel Assoc of Roanoke Valley 1985-. **HONORS/ACHIEVEMENTS:** Co-authored grant Summer Transition Program for Minority Students Peer Counseling Network Prog for Minority Students 1983; panelist/presenter

VA Assoc of Coll Registrars Conf 1983, 1984; mem State Accessibility Task Force for Blacks in Higher Educ VA Admiss Coun on Black Concerns & VA State Council on Higher Educ 1984. **BUSINESS ADDRESS:** Assistant Dean of Admissions, Roanoke College, Salem, VA 24153.

WILLIAMS, CAROLYN CHANDLER
Educator. **PERSONAL:** Born Jan 13, 1947, Maben, MS; married LT Williams; children: Lori Tysandra, Letonya. **EDUCATION:** MS Valley State Univ, BA 1968; MS State Univ, MEd 1973, PhD 1975. **CAREER:** Aberdeen Pub Schs, eng teach 1968-70; Oktibbeha Co Schs, eng teach 1970-71; Mary Holmes Coll, inst 1971-73; MS State Univ, inst 1974-75, asst prof 1975-78; assoc prof 1978-82; prof 1982-. **ORGANIZATIONS:** Vice pres Amer Assn of Univ Women 1982-84; educ chair Amer assn of Univ Women 1982-84; bd of dirs Mid South Educ Rsch Assn 1982-. **HONORS/ACHIEVEMENTS:** Outstanding Univ Prof Assn of Univ Prof 1977; Outstanding Young Woman State Jaycees MS 1981; Outstanding Young Woman Starkville Jaycees local 1981; Outstanding Young Educator Phi Delta Kappa local 1982. **HOME ADDRESS:** P O Box 1940, Mississippi State, MS 39762. **BUSINESS ADDRESS:** Prof of Instruction, MS StUniv, P O Box 5365, Mississippi State, MS 39762.

WILLIAMS, CAROLYN RUTH ARMSTRONG
Educator, educational administrator. **PERSONAL:** Born Feb 17, 1944, Birmingham, AL; daughter of Lonnie Armstrong and Lois Adel America Merriweather; married James Alvin Williams Jr, Mar 16, 1968. **EDUCATION:** TN State Univ, BS 1966; HI Univ, Cert in Asian Studies 1970; Northwestern Univ, MA 1972; Cornell Univ, MA 1978, PhD 1978; Fellow Harvard Univ, postdoctorate 1981-83; Exeter Univ England, selected to particip in course seminar "Educational Admin, The Management of Change" 1985. **CAREER:** Barringer HS, history tchr 1967-69; Thomas Jefferson HS, history teacher 1969-70; Union Coll, instr dept of history 1970-73; Tompkins Cty Comm Coll,adj prof 1973-76; SUNY Cortland, lecturer dept history 1973-76; Cornell Univ Career Ctr, assoc dir 1976-82; Harvard Univ, head proctor 1983; US Senator Paul Tsongas, spec proj asst 1983; NC Central Univ, asst to the vice chancellor for univ relations 1983-87; Vanderbilt Univ, asst dean for Minority Affairs & Women Engineering Programs & assoc prof 1987-. **ORGANIZATIONS:** Exec bd mem admin counselors NAWDAC 1980-82; mem Comm Blacks in Higher Ed & Black Coll & Univ 1980-81; ed consult LeMoyne Coll Higher Ed Preparation Prog 1981-; ed consult & co-founder Youth Data Inc 1981-; exec bd mem Phi Delta Kappa, Natl Assoc for Women Deans; mem Delta Sigma Theta Inc; appointed to Natl Assoc for Women Admin, counselors journal board 1986-88; proposal reader for US Dept of Educ 1989; executive regional bd Natl Society of Black Engineers 1987-; Rotary Intl; Technical Coordinator for Natl Society of Women Engineers 1989. **HONORS/ACHIEVEMENTS:** Woodrow Wilson Admin Fellow 1983-86; Thycydidean Honor Soc Awd YWCA Women of Achievement Awd; Phi Delta Kappa, Sigma Rho Sigma Honor Soc Awd Phi Alpha The Awd; Doctoral Dissertation Funded by Rockefeller Found, Fellowship/Scholarship Cornell Univ, Northwestern Univ; YNCA Women of Achievement Awd 1984-85 & 86-87; Burton Lecturer for Harvard Univ Ed School Colloquiam Bd 1983; Natl Soceity of Black Engineers Community Leadership Award, 1987; 1st women's dean in engineering school. **HOME ADDRESS:** 36 Morningside Dr, Cortland, NY 13045. **BUSINESS ADDRESS:** Vanderbilt Univ, School of Engineering, PO Box 6006, Station B, Nashville, TN 37235.

WILLIAMS, CARROLL BURNS, JR.
Scientist/educator. **PERSONAL:** Born Sep 24, 1929, St Louis, MO; son of Carroll B Williams and Maxine Henderson Williams; married Mizuko Morinoto, Jun 24, 1982; children: Robyn Claire, Margaret "Maya", Carroll Blake. **EDUCATION:** Univ MI, BS 1955, MS 1957, PhD 1963. **CAREER:** US Forest Service, rsch forester 1961-65, rsch entomologist 1965-68, proj leader 1968-72; Yale Sch of Forestry, lectr 1969-72; US Forest Svc, forest insect ecologist 1972-75, pioneer sci 1975-84; proj leader 1984-88; adjunct prof Univ CA, Berkeley 1988-. **ORGANIZATIONS:** Consult Ecology & Ecosystems NSF 1971-74; tech consult USFS Insecticide Field Tests 1973-; registered professional forester CA; Entomol Soc of Amer; Soc of Amer Foresters; dir Berkeley Sch Bd Berkeley Unified Sch Dist 1977-84; vis prof Black Exchange Prog Natl Urban League 1975-; youth counselor NAACP; Yale Minority Recruitment Prog 1969-72; Congress of African Peoples 1972; Unitarian Universalist Black Affairs Council 1973-75. **MILITARY SERVICE:** USMC staff sgt 1951-53. **BUSINESS ADDRESS:** Adjunct Professor, Dept Forestry & Resource Mgmt, Univ of California, Berkeley, 145 Mulford Hall, Berkeley, CA 94720.

WILLIAMS, CASSANDRA FAYE
Exploration palaeontologist. **PERSONAL:** Born Aug 16, 1948, Sherrill, AR; daughter of Lewis Williams and Millye L. Dickerson-Beatty; children: Kyra Erica. **EDUCATION:** Northeastern Illinois State University, 1966-67; University of Arkansas, Pine Bluff, AR, BS, 1970; Kent State University, South Dakota School of Mines, 1978; Tulane University, New Orleans, LA, MS, 1979. **CAREER:** University of Chicago Hospitals and Clinics, Chicago, IL, clinical biochemist, 1970-71; Orleans Parish School Board, New Orleans, LA, biology teacher, 1971-72; Chevron USA, New Orleans, LA, exploration palaeontologist, 1972—. **ORGANIZATIONS:** American Association of Stratigraphic Palynologists; Gulf Coast section, Society of Economic Palaeontologists and Mineralogists; International Commission for Palynology; American Association of Blacks in Energy; Tau Iota Mu; national convention delegate, 1984-88, president, New Orleans club, 1985-86, national convention co-chair, 1986, National Association of Negro Business and Professional Women's Clubs; Delta Sigma Theta. **HONORS/ACHIEVEMENTS:** Voluntary service awards, NAACP, 1984, Chevron USA, 1984; outstanding achievement awards, National Association of Negro Business and Professional Women's Clubs, 1984, 1986; outstanding service award, New Orleans chapter, National Business League, 1987; World Service Award, and Volunteer Service Award, Girl Scouts of America, 1988. **HOME ADDRESS:** 7601 Briarwood Dr, New Orleans, LA 70128.

WILLIAMS, CATHERINE G.
Appointed government official. **PERSONAL:** Born Nov 21, 1914, Des Moines, IA; married Richard Jr. **EDUCATION:** Cortez Bus Coll, grad 1948; Soc WorkUniv of IA MA 1965; Drake U, grad soc/psy. **CAREER:** IA Dept of Social Serv, dep commr 1975-; Div of Comm Serv IA Dept of SS, dir 1973-75; Bureau of Family & Adult Serv IA Dept of Asso, dir; Bureau of Family & Adult Serv ID of SS, assoc Dir; IA Dept of Social Serv, child welfare staff dev; Polk Co IA Dept of Social Serv Com, child welfare supr. **ORGANIZATIONS:** Mem NAACP Scholarship; commr Planning & Zoning Commn Des Moines 1980-; bd mem Willkie Hosue Inc. **HONORS/ACHIEVEMENTS:** Social Worker of the Year NASW IA Chap 1980; IA Hall of Fame for Women Women's Hall of Fame 1980; Black Women of Achievement Cultural Devel Com 1980; MarkHall LectrUniv of IA Sch of Social Work 1980. **BUSINESS ADDRESS:** Iowa Dept of Social Services, 5th Floor Hoover Bldg, Des Moines, IA 50319.

WILLIAMS, CHARLENE J.
News reporter. **PERSONAL:** Born Jul 13, 1949, Atlantic City, NJ. **EDUCATION:** Columbia U, MS 1972; Cum Laude Boston U, BS 1967-71. **CAREER:** WTOP Radio Post Newsweek Stas Inc Wash DC, radio news editor 1972-; Westinghouse Broadcasting Co NY, part-time rewriter; Columbia U, adminstr asst 1971-72; WBUR BostonUniv FM Radio Sta, disc-jockey editorl writer prod dir; BostonUniv Year Book Hub, gen assignment editor; WCRB Waltham Am Fed TV & Radio Artists. **ORGANIZATIONS:** Communications Assn Inc; Sigma Delta Chi; writer for Columbian Comm Newsletter; Adams Morgan Orgn; vol Heart Fund; ARC; DC Black Repetory; CRI Inst; pres Student Body BostonUniv 1970-71; pres Student Body ColumbiaUniv 1971-72. **HONORS/ACHIEVEMENTS:** Scarlet Key Honor Soc BostonUniv 1971; Nat Honor Soc Atlantic City HS 1967. **BUSINESS ADDRESS:** 4646 40th St NW, Washington, DC 20016.

WILLIAMS, CHARLES A. (BUSTER WILLIAMS)
Musician. **PERSONAL:** Born Apr 17, 1942, Camden, NJ; married Veronica Williams; children: Verdiana Tayamisha, Toku. **EDUCATION:** Gene Ammons Sonny Stitt, worked with 1960; Dakota Staton 1961-62; Sarah Vaughn 1963; Betty Carter, Lee Morgan, Jimmy Heath, Nancy Wilson 1964-68; Herbie Hancock 1969-73; Miles Davis, Jazz Crusaders, Herbie Mann, Art Blakey, Sonny Rollins, Mary Lou Williams, McCoy Tyner, Stan Getz 1973-; Ron Carter 1985; Jazz Mobile Prog, taught bass 1975-76; Dexter Gordon, IL Jacquet, Joe Farrell, Norman Connors, Bennie Maupin, Carlos Garnett, Eric Kloss, Harold Land, Eddie Henderson, Woody Shaw, recordings with all the above plus these; Combs Coll of Music Philadelphia PA, Composition, Harmony, Theory. **CAREER:** Nichiren Shoshu Acad 1972; mem ASCAP; formed Tayamisha Mus Co 1975; Recorded 1st Album Under own name 1975; Second Album 1977; Recorded Third Album "Heartbeat" 1979; Recorded Fourth Album "Dreams Come True" 1980; Formed co-operative group called "Sphere" 1982; recorded "Four In One" 1982, "Flight Path" 1984, "On Tour" 1985, "Live At Umbria Jazz" 1986, "Four For All" 1987; toured with Herbie Hancock 1986-87; performed on Grammy Awds 1987. **HONORS/ACHIEVEMENTS:** Nominated for Grammy Awd for Best Instrumental Performcance Group for "Love for Sale-The great Jazz Trio" Album with Hank Jones and Tony Williams 1980; Recieved Min-On Awd 1986; Soka Gakkai Culture Awd 1986; Citation from Mayor of New Orleans & Gov of LA 1987; Citation from Mayor of Camden NJ 1987; Citation from Camden Bd of Educ 1987. **HOME ADDRESS:** 372 Central Park West, Apt 17K, New York, NY 10025.

WILLIAMS, CHARLES C.
Real estate developer. **PERSONAL:** Born Oct 10, 1939, Pontiac, MI; children: Charles C III, Cassandra, Veronica. **EDUCATION:** FL A&M Univ, Po Sci 1958-62; NC Central Univ Law School, 1962-63. **CAREER:** Atlanta Reg Commission, dir of commun 1974-78; GA Power Co, manpower resources coord 1978-80; Amertelco Inc, exec vice pres 1980-84; Air Atlanta, spec consto chair of bd 1984-; Fulton Cty Bd of Commiss, commissioner. **ORGANIZATIONS:** Bd mem West End Med Center 1980-83; bd of managers, mem Assn of Cty Commiss of GA 1978-; vice pres Natl Assn of Counties 1985-88; exec comm mem Natl Dem Cty Officials 1985-; district mem at large Boy Scouts of Amer 1985-86; bd mem Neighborhood Justice Ctr 1985-86; Mem Coalition of 100 Black Men; GABEO; NAACP; Kappa Alpha Phi; Natl Assn of Black Cnty Officials; West End Neighborhood Developemnt, Inc. **HONORS/ACHIEVEMENTS:** Plaque YMCA Butler St Century Club 1973-; Atlanta Southside Comm Hlth Center Comm Serv Awd; West End Med Center Cert of Appreciation; plaque from Atlanta Medical Assn 1980-; Atlanta Business League Torch Bearer Awd 1985; plaque Concerned Citizens of Atlanta; plaque Jomandi Prod 1986-; Mem United Negro Coll und; mem Neighborhood Arts Center; Metro Atlanta SCLC Comm Serv Awd; Hearts and Hands Fdn for Hanicapped, Inc. **BUSINESS ADDRESS:** Commissioner, Fulton Cty Commissioners, 165 Central Ave, Atlanta, GA 30303.

WILLIAMS, CHARLES E., III
Attorney. **PERSONAL:** Born May 10, 1946, New York City, NY. **EDUCATION:** Franklin & Marshall Coll, AB 1966; Columbia Univ School of Law, JD 1969. **CAREER:** Marshall Bratter Greene Allison & Tucker NYC, assoc 1970-72; NAACP Legal Defense & Ed Fund Inc, asst counsel; Bureau of Labor Serv City of NY, dir 1978-79; Dep Sec of State NY State Dept, gen counsel 1979-82; State of NY, acting sec of state 1982; New York City Housing Authority, gen counsel 1983-. **ORGANIZATIONS:** Mem New York City Bar Assoc, NBA, Natl Conf Black Lawyers. **MILITARY SERVICE:** USAR spl 4/c 1969-. **BUSINESS ADDRESS:** General Counsel, New York City Housing Auth, 250 Broadway, Room 620, New York, NY 10007.

WILLIAMS, CHARLES FREDERICK
Business executive. **PERSONAL:** Born Nov 27, 1924, Kalamazoo; married Jean Goins; children: Rebecca, Eric, Kim, Kevin. **EDUCATION:** Western MI Univ, BS 1952; MA Inst of Tech 1960. **CAREER:** Mattel Toys, vice pres, 1972-; Mattel Toys, quality control mgr dir quality assurance 1962-72; Brunswick Corp, chief chem 1959-62; Shakespeare Co, asst tech dir 1952-59; Black Exec Exch Prgrm, visiting prof 1975-76; Intl Electrotech Commn, chief delegate, 1972-76. **ORGANIZATIONS:** Mem, AAAS, ASTM, ASQC, Amer Public Health Assn; Amer Statistical Assn; Toy Mfr of Amer; Natl Safety Council; Federation of Amer Science; Indus Advisory Council Underwriters Lab; Inst for the Advancement of Engineering; Math Assn of Amer; Prof Designer's Workshop; NBS CPSC; Soc for Indus & Applied Math; Soc of Plastics Engrs; Syst Safety Soc; Standing Com Vol Prod Stds PS 72-76 US Dept of Commerce; NAACP; Urban League; Sigma Pi Phi XI Boule; Amer Museum of Natural Hist; Conf of Consumer Org; Natl Consumers Congress; Natl Museum of Science & Indus; Drafted 1st Comprehensive Toy Safety Standards US; Drafted 1st Intl Safety Standards for Electrical Toys; contributed Safety in the Marketplace; Featured in Cover Story of Dec 1969 Issue of Quality Program; Dubbed Father of Toy Safety US Bureau of Product Safety 1972. **HONORS/ACHIEVEMENTS:** Distinguished Alumnus Award Western MI Univ, 1975; Outstanding Merit Award, Inst for Advancement of Engineering 1976. **MILITARY SERVICE:** USAAF 1943-46. **BUSINESS ADDRESS:** 5150 Rosecrans, Hawthorne, CA 90250.

WILLIAMS, CHARLES J., SR.
Institutional clergyman. **PERSONAL:** Born Apr 01, 1942, Wayne Co, NC; married Linda Oates; children: Valerie, Charles, Jr, Antraun. **EDUCATION:** Christian Inst 1966; Shaw U, AB 1973; M Div, 1975; Ibis, DMin 1975. **CAREER:** Cherry Hosp, Clinical I Chaplain,

mental health tech 1960-74; Western Assembly Disciples of Christ Churches, bishop. **ORGANIZATIONS:** Chmn Western Disciples Chs of Christ Council Bd 1969-72; pastor White Oak Disciples Ch 1968-; chmn of Evangelism Com of Wester Assy NC Assn of Chplns1972-74; mem Disciples Chs of Christ Council; bd mem Afro-ministers Alliance; Masons Founder Western Assembly Disciples of Christ Ushers Conv 1970; Bishop1977. **BUSINESS ADDRESS:** Bishop, Western Assembly Disciples of, Christ Churches, PO Box 133, Goldsboro, NC 27530.

WILLIAMS, CHARLES RICHARD
Black exposition executive. **PERSONAL:** Born Jan 11, 1948, Indianapolis, IN; divorced; children: Maisha, Charles Jr, Robert, Ramone. **EDUCATION:** Black Hawk Coll. **CAREER:** Comm Serv Div Indianapolis, asst to dir 1974-76; Gov Comm Serv Studeis 1974; NAACP Nat Conv, exec coord 1972-73; Alaska Barge & Transport, purchasing agt 1968-72; City of Indianapolis, special asst to the Mayor 1976-83; pres, Indiana Black Expo, Inc. 1983-. **ORGANIZATIONS:** V ward chmn Center Township Wards; precinct com Pike Township; v chmn Rep Nghbrhd Fin Com; mem Screening Com 11th Dist; chmn So Dist IN State Black Rep Cncl; exec mem Marion Co Rep Club; mem Pike Township Rep Club; Marion Co Young Rep Club; personnel chmn Inspls Pre-schl; mem Market Pl; vice pres IN Black Expo; mem Big Bros; NAACP; rep Mayor on Bd Goodwill Ind; bd Heritage Place Sr Citizens; bd Indianapolis Clean City Com; bd Fallcreek YMCA; mem Afro-care. **HONORS/ACHIEVEMENTS:** Achvmt award Rep Central Com; outsdng serv award Rep Nghbrhd Fin Com; comm serv award Butler Tarkington; jefferson award Indianapolis Star IN 1979; freedom award IN Prince Hail Masons 1978; serv & award Tech 300 Prgm; cert recog outsdng ldrshp; award; Office of Human Resources City Indlps; The Educ Assoc Human Rights Awd. **MILITARY SERVICE:** USN 1965-68. **BUSINESS ADDRESS:** President, Indiana Black Expo Inc, 3130 Sutherland Ave, Indianapolis, IN 46205.

WILLIAMS, CHARLES THOMAS
Company executive. **PERSONAL:** Born May 04, 1941, Charleston, MO; married Janet E McLaughlin; children: Robin, Tracey, Justin, Drew, Douglass. **EDUCATION:** Lake Michigan Coll, AA 1962; Western MI Univ, BS 1965; Univ of MI, MA 1970, PhD 1971. **CAREER:** Detroit Schools, teacher 1965-69; MI Educ Assn, educ consult 1971-73, educ adminstr, assoc exec dir 1973-84; Nat Educ Assn, dir human & civil rights 1984-. **ORGANIZATIONS:** Mem Natl Alliance of Black Sch Educators, Amer Soc for Curriculum Develop, Phi Delta Kappa, Black Roundtable, Martin Luther King Jr Ctr for Nonviolent Social Change; bd mem Center for Democratic Renewal. **BUSINESS ADDRESS:** Dir Human & Civil Rights, Natl Educ Assn, 1201 Sixteenth St NW, Washington, DC 20036.

WILLIAMS, CHARLES THOMAS
Business executive. **PERSONAL:** Born Jan 25, 1916, Nogales, AZ; son of James Williams and Zellee Williams; married Brenda Smith; children: Dr Charles Williams II, Kirk G, Rhoda J Alexander. **EDUCATION:** Attended, Los Angeles City Coll, Univ of Southern California. **CAREER:** Schenley Industries Inc, sales representative 1947-51; Schenley Distillers Co, natl brands devel mgr 1951-53, asst natl sales mgr 1953-58, asst div mgr 1959-61, vice pres 1961-76; Schenley Affiliated Brands Corp, corporate vice pres 1977-. **ORGANIZATIONS:** Trustee Inter-Racial Counsel for Business Opportunity 1966; Long Island Fund; pres Booker T Washington Found; pres Natl Found of Neighborhood Center of Amer; Natl Nassau Co; chmn Economic Opportunity Commn 1963-68; vice chmn Roslyn Non-Profit Corp 1966-70; bd mem Nassau Co Health & Welfare Counsel 1968-72; chmn Natl Business League 1966. **HONORS/ACHIEVEMENTS:** Honorary Doctorate in Humane Letters, King Memorial Coll; Indus Award, 1956, 1958, 1959; Honorary Doctor of Laws, Bishop Coll. **MILITARY SERVICE:** USAF 1st lieutenant 1943-46. **BUSINESS ADDRESS:** Corp Vice President, Schenley Affil Brands Corp, 888 7th Ave, New York, NY 10019.

WILLIAMS, CHARLOTTE LEOLA
Health service asst. **PERSONAL:** Born May 28, 1928, Flint, MI; married Charles Clifford Williams, Sr; children: Charlita Walker, Charles C Williams Jr, Cathryn Sanders. **EDUCATION:** Flint Sch of Practical Nursing, Cert/License 1961. **CAREER:** St Joseph Hosp Flint, rcvry rm nrs 1961-65; Flint Bd of Ed, hm-sh cnslr 1965-68; Genesee Co Govt, elected ofcl 1965-84; Flint Osteo Hosp, asst to the pres 1980-83; Beecher Ballenger Hlth Sys, asst to the pres 1983-. **ORGANIZATIONS:** Pres Natl Assn of Counties 1st Black Female 1979-80; co comm Genesee Co Bd of Comm 1st Female Elected 1965-80; chair Genesee Co Bd of Hlth Genesee Co Hlth Dept 1968-85; officer/Mem Quinn Chapel AME Ch Lifetime; aging comm MI Office of Services to the Aging 1983-; bd mem YWCA of Greater Flint 1980-; bd mem United Way of Genesee & Lapeer Counties 1985. **HONORS/ACHIEVEMENTS:** Downtown merchants awd Flint Downtown Merchants 1976; pol achvmnt Negro Bus & Prof Womens Club 1975; AME Church Missionary Awd African Meth Episcopal Ch Missionary Women 1983; law day awd '84 Genesee Co Bar Asso 1984; pub serv awd Natl Assn of Counties 1980. **HOME ADDRESS:** 2030 Barks St, Flint, MI 48503. **BUSINESS ADDRESS:** Assistant to the President, Beecher Ballenger Health Sys, 3921 Beecher Rd, Flint, MI 48502.

WILLIAMS, CHESTER ARTHUR
Clergyman. **PERSONAL:** Born in Valls Creek, WV. **EDUCATION:** Moody Bible Inst Chicago, gen bible 1964; Greenville Coll IL, BA 1966; New Sch for Soc Research NYC, MA 1968; RutgersUniv New Brunswick NJ, PhD 1977. **CAREER:** New Brunswick Comm Church NJ, minister; Douglass Coll Rutgers State Univ New Brunswick, asst prof 1973-; Family Day & Care Brooklyn, dir 1970; Comm Progress Ctr Brooklyn, health & welfare specialist 1969; Brooklyn Coll, lectr 1968; Comm Action Council Akron, soc worker 1966; Afro-spanish Consumer Coop Brooklyn, dir 1970; Save the Youth/Children Orgn Brooklyn, founder & dir 1973. **ORGANIZATIONS:** Founder & bd chmn Parents Coop Nursery Sch 1974; chief organizer & consult Nat Black Quadra-centennial 1976; Alpha Kappa Sigma Greenville Coll 1966; Comm Serv Family Day Care Careers Program 1970. **HONORS/ACHIEVEMENTS:** Founde & directed "St olympics" Brooklyn & New Brunswick 1974; black & puerto rican faculty & staff award Douglass Coll Rutgers 1978; comm serv award Martin Luther King Jr Players; new brunswick & high sch model students; neighborhood girls' club 1978-80; first am black to receive PhD in sociology RutgersUniv New Brunswick NJ 1977. **BUSINESS ADDRESS:** Douglass Coll, Rutgers State Univ, New Brunswick, NJ 08901.

WILLIAMS, CHESTER LEE
Educator, businessman. **PERSONAL:** Born Jul 24, 1944, Durham, NC; married Lauren B Sapp; children: Corey T, Christopher J, Cheston J. **EDUCATION:** North Carolina Central Univ, Durham, NC, BA 1967; Univ of Michigan, Ann Arbor, MI, MFA 1971. **CAREER:** Wright Re-Educ Sch, instr 1964-68; Fiberglass Unltd Co, fiberglass techn 1965-69; St Thomas Moore's Sch, instr 1966; Sch of Design, instr creative woodwork & furn design 1968; Duke Univ Women's Club, instr water color techn 1968-69; Natl Air Pollution Contr Cntr, illustrator 1969; Voorhees Coll, asst prof of art apprec & arts & crafts 1971-74; FL A&M Univ, assoc prof of art, sculpture; NC Central Univ, assoc prof of sculpture dept art; Williams Foundry, Durham, NC, pres. **ORGANIZATIONS:** Mem Coll Art Assn; Natl Conf of Artists; So Assn of Sculptors Inc; mem Faculty Senatre FL A&M Univ 1980; pres cabinet FL A&M Univ 1984; dir FAMU Art Gallery FL A&M Univ 1974-78 & 1983-84; adv to Esquire Soc Club Voorhees Coll 1971-74; parliamentarian comm on faculty Voorhees Coll 1973-74; Fine Arts Council of FL Div of Cultural Affairs; mem Visual Arts Adv Panel 1977 & 1983; Tallahassee City Comm app to Arts Selection Comm 1977-79; bd mem LeMoyne Art Found Tallahassee, FL 1979-84; visiting artist, Duke Univ Women's Club 1969; Univ of TX at Odessa 1973; Alppalachian State Univ 1975; Leon Dist Schools &the Tallahassee Arts Cncl 1976-78; Broward Comm Coll Pompano Beach, FL 1977; Elizabeth City State Univ 1984. **HONORS/ACHIEVEMENTS:** Recipient Sculpture Award 17th Ann Major FL Artists Show 1980; Grant Fine Arts Council of FL 1977-78; Pres Disting Serv Award Voorhees Coll 1973-74; particip in many art shows & exhibitions incl NC Mus of Art, Downtown Art Gallery, numerous others; researching a bibliography of materials by and about the Blacks of the Fine Arts; writing basic textbook on the fundamentals of beginning sculpture; writing and illust a book on the Black protest art of the 1960's; numerous other articles and reviews including, Joy McLlwain "Sculptor with a Message of Hope" Tallahassee 1984 p 15; A L Nyerges "The Black Artist as Artist" EPOCH Feb 1983 p 14-16. **BUSINESS ADDRESS:** President, Williams Foundry, PO Box 25169, 610-C Ramseur Street, Durham, NC 27702.

WILLIAMS, CLARA BELLE
Educator. **PERSONAL:** Born Oct 29, 1885, LaGrange, TX; married Jasper B Williams (deceased); children: Jasper F (deceased), James B, Charles L. **EDUCATION:** Prairie View State College, Grad (valedictorian) 1905; NM State Coll, BA 1937 (1st Black grad); NM State Univ, Hon LLD 1980. **CAREER:** Cameron TX City Sch, tchr 1905-06; Austin TX City Sch, tchr 1906-09; Prairie View State Coll TX, tchr 1909-17; Las Cruces Pub Schs NM, tchr 1924-51; Williams Clinic/Parkway Lab, receptionist 27 yrs. **HONORS/ACHIEVEMENTS:** Disting Alumni Awd 1961; Outstanding Mother The Fine Arts Guild Order Eastern Star Chicago 1966; Educ Assn Hall of Fame State & Natl.

WILLIAMS, CLARENCE (BIG CAT)
Athlete, real estate broker. **PERSONAL:** Born Sep 03, 1946, Brazoria, TX; married Icy Lee Eatmon; children: Clarence, Jr, Cary Leon, Marla Rachelle. **EDUCATION:** Prairie View A&M Coll, BS 1977. **CAREER:** Green Bay Packers, football player; real estate broker 1980. **ORGANIZATIONS:** Player rep NFLPA 3 yrs.

WILLIAMS, CLARENCE
Association administrator. **PERSONAL:** Born Oct 01, 1945, Shreveport, LA; son of Rev and Mrs Leonard Williams; children: Kevin M, Makala O. **EDUCATION:** Southern Univ; Seattle Comm Coll. **CAREER:** Seattle Black Fire Fighter Assoc, pres 1970; Intl Assoc of Black Professional Fire Fighters, nw reg dir 1975, exec vice pres & a/a officer 1980; Seattle Fire Dept, lt 1981; Barden Cablevision of Seattle, dir of oper 1982; IABPFF, pres 1984-88. **ORGANIZATIONS:** Pres Bd of Dir for CACC 1975; bd mem NW Conf Black Public Officials 1980; co chmn Sea Urban League Scholarship Fund Raising 1981; trustee Mt Zion Baptist Church 1981; chmn of publicity Girls Club of Puget Sound 1984; bd mem Seattle Urban League; rep Nat'l Black Leadership Roundtable; mem WA State MLKJr Commission; Alumni Leadership Tomorrow Prog/Seattle Chamber of Comm; mem Southern Univ Alumni of Seattle WA. **HONORS/ACHIEVEMENTS:** Hon fire fighter Shreveport LA Fire Dept 1976; Most Outstanding Young Man of Amer The US JayCees 1978, 1981; Furthering the Cause of Human Rights United Nations Assn 1979; Affirmative Action Awd Seattle Urban League 1982; Comm Serv Black Law Enforcement Officers Assoc 1984. **MILITARY SERVICE:** WA State NG spec 4th class 6 years. **BUSINESS ADDRESS:** Past President, Intl Assn Black Professional Firefighters, PO Box 22005, Seattle, WA 98122.

WILLIAMS, CLARENCE EARL, JR.
Clergyman. **PERSONAL:** Born May 10, 1950, Tuscaloosa, AL. **EDUCATION:** St Joseph Coll Rensselaer IN, BA Sociology & French 1973; Cath Theol Union Chicago, MDiv & MA 1974-80. **CAREER:** Natl Black Seminarians Assn, bd chmn 1970; Acad of the Afro-World Comm, founder & pres 1977; St Anthony RC Ch, pastor 1978; The Black Catholic Televangelization Network, pres 1986; Soc of the Precious Blood, clergyman 1978-. **ORGANIZATIONS:** Exec dir of This Far by Faith, The Black Catholic Chapel of the Air a natl radio evangel prog; created in 1983 the "Come and Go" evangelization training prog of cassettes & filmstrips; participant intl "Mass for Shut-Ins"TV prog from Detroit 1982-; producer of documentary series onTV "Search for a Black Christian Heritage"; producer and host of syndicatedTV series "Black and Catholic" 1986. **HONORS/ACHIEVEMENTS:** 1st producer & dir of Black vocations filmstrips 1978; 1st black priest ordained in Diocese of Cleveland 1978; author of numerous articles and pamphlets on the Black Catholic experience; Natl Black Catholic Seminarians Assn named its annual achievement awd "The Fr Clarence Williams Awd" 1984. **BUSINESS ADDRESS:** Pastor, Soc of the Precious Blood, 5247 Sheridan, Detroit, MI 48213.

WILLIAMS, CLARENCE G.
Educator. **PERSONAL:** Born Dec 23, 1938, Goldsboro, NC; married Mildred Cogdell; children: Clarence Jr, Alton. **EDUCATION:** NC Central, BS 1961; Hampton Univ, MS 1967; Univ of CT, PhD 1972; Cornell Univ, graduate study 1965; Harvard Univ, postdoctoral study 1975. **CAREER:** Williamsburg Public Schools VA, teacher 1961-64; Hampton Univ, asst dean of men, instructor, 1964-68; Univ of CT, professional counselor 1968-72; MIT, asst dean of graduate school 1972-74, asst to pres 1974-. **ORGANIZATIONS:** mem, Org Devel Network Amer Assn Higher Educ; Amer Personnel & Guidance Ass n; Assn of Non-White Concerns; Coll Student Personnel Assn; Phi Delta Kappan; mem Oak Hill Elementary School Com, Black Citizens of Newton, NAACP, NC CU Alumni Assn, Hampton Inst Alumni Assn, Univ of CT Alumni Assn, Alpha Phi Alpha, Amer Mgmt Assn; bd dir 1978-, pres 1986- MA Pre-Engineering Program; founder, co-chmn Black Admin Conf on Issues Facing Black Admin at Predominantly White Inst 1982-84; consultant, founder Greater Boston Interuniversity Council 1984-; bd dir Buckingham Browne & Nichols School 1985-; bd dir Freedom House 1986-; consultant, Bank of New England 1986-. **HONORS/ACHIEVEMENTS:** Recipient Hampton Inst Summer Study Fellowship; certificate, Harvard Univ Inst for Educ Mgmt 1975; Ford Found Fellowship for Admin; YMCA Black Achievers 1979; publication,

"Proceedings First Natl Conf on Issues Facing Black Admin at Predominantly White Colleges & Univs", "Black Students on White Campuses During a Period of Retrenchment". **BUSINESS ADDRESS:** Assistant to the President, Massachusetts Inst of Tech, 77 Mass Ave, 3-221, Cambridge, MA 02139.

WILLIAMS, CLARICE LEONA
District school superintendent. **PERSONAL:** Born Dec 26, 1936, Los Angeles, CA; married Jarrod B Williams; children: Jarrod Barrett II, Courtni Clarice. **EDUCATION:** CA State Univ Los Angeles, BA 1966; CA State Polytechnic Univ, MA 1974; Univ of NE-Lincoln, PhD 1978. **CAREER:** Los Angeles Unified School Dist, teacher 1965-66; Ontario-Montclair School Dist Ontario CA, teacher 1966-72; Fr Flanagan's Boys Town School System NE, reading specialist, reading coord, asst principal, curriculum coord 1972-79; Riverside Unified School Dist, principal Monroe Elem, principal Central Middle School, dist dir of special educ 1979-82; Lucerne Valley Union School Dist CA, dist superintendent 1982-. **ORGANIZATIONS:** Mem Phi Delta Kappa, Assoc of CA Sch Administrators, Assoc for Supervision and Curriculum Develop, Lucerne Valley Chamber of Commerce. **HONORS/ACHIEVEMENTS:** US Congressional Awd 1984; Honors Masters Program. **BUSINESS ADDRESS:** School District Superintendent, Lucerne Valley Union Sch Dist, LVSR Box 900, Lucerne Valley, CA 92356.

WILLIAMS, CLAYTON RICHARD
Associate judge. **PERSONAL:** Born Dec 02, 1920, StLouis, MO; married Virginia Tyler; children: Shari. **EDUCATION:** Attended Shurtleff Coll 1946-48; Lincoln Univ Sch of Law, LLB 1954. **CAREER:** Private Practice, attorney 1955-65; Madison Co IL, asst public defender 1966-67; Madison Co Legal Serv Soc, dir 1967-71; Madison Co IL, asst states atty 1972-73; Third Judicial Circuit Edwardsville IL, assoc judge. **ORGANIZATIONS:** Vice pres & pres Alton Wood River Bar Assn 1968-70; pres Alton Br NAACP. **HONORS/ACHIEVEMENTS:** Whitney Young Awd Madison St Clair City Urgan League 1975; Outstanding Black Judge Cook Co Bar Assn 1975; Brotherhood Awd Campbell Chapel AME Church 1976. **MILITARY SERVICE:** AUS t/5 1942-45. **BUSINESS ADDRESS:** Third Judiciary Circuit, Madison Co Courthouse, Edwardsville, IL 62025.

WILLIAMS, CLYDE
Attorney. **PERSONAL:** Born Feb 23, 1939, South Carolina; children: 2 Children. **EDUCATION:** JD, BA 1960-65. **CAREER:** Williams, DeLaney & Simkin, former atty. **ORGANIZATIONS:** Mem Gen Counsel Ofc Staff of Fed Hsng Adminstrn DC; mem Wayne Twp Board Richmond; elected pub ofcl mem Rep Party of IN; vice pres Hoosier State Bar Assn; ABA Assn; Nat Bar Assn. **BUSINESS ADDRESS:** 48 S 7 St, Richmond, IN 47374.

WILLIAMS, CYNTHIA MARIE
Attorney. **PERSONAL:** Born Dec 06, 1954, Philadelphia, PA. **EDUCATION:** PA State Univ, BA 1975; Univ of PA Law School, JD 1979. **CAREER:** Philadelphia Bd of Educ, substitute teacher 1976; Comm Legal Svcs, law clerk 1977,78; PA Dept of State, asst general counsel 1980-84; PA Human Relations Commn, asst counsel 1984-. **ORGANIZATIONS:** Mem Amer 1976-, PA 1979-, Natl 1983- Bar Assocs; chairperson Greater Philadelphia Health Action 1984-; mem bd of dirs Univ of PA Black Alumni 1986-; pres bd of dir TSB Church Com Outreach Corp 1986-. **HONORS/ACHIEVEMENTS:** Chapel of Four Chaplains Awd 1967,81; Outstanding Young Women of Amer Awd 1980. **BUSINESS ADDRESS:** Assistant Counsel, PA Human Relations Commn, 711 State Office Bldg, Broad & Spring Garden Sts, Philadelphia, PA 19130.

WILLIAMS, DANIEL EDWIN
Clinical psychologist. **PERSONAL:** Born Nov 24, 1933, Mobile, AL; son of Robert Williams and Demaris Lewis; married Mildred E Olney, Jun 15, 1957; children: Denise, Michele, Melanie. **EDUCATION:** Seton Hall US, Orange, NJ, BA, 1962; St Johns Univ, New York, MS, 1963, PhD, 1968. **CAREER:** Mt Carmel Guild, Newark, NJ, psych, 1963-65; East Orange, NJ, Public Schools, school psych, 1965-68; Daniel E Williams, PhD, PA, clinical psychologist, 1974-; Montclair State Coll, assoc professor of psych. **ORGANIZATIONS:** Pres, Natl Assn of Black Psychologists, 1980-81; pres, New Jersey chapter Assn of Black Psychologists, 1973-75 & 1981-83; bd mem, Psychological Examiners, State of New Jersey, 1973-75; mem, bd of educ, Plaingfield, NJ, 1972-74. **HONORS/ACHIEVEMENTS:** ABPP diplomate in clinical psychology, Amer Bd of Prof Psych, Amer Psychological Assn, 1977. **MILITARY SERVICE:** USAF, staff/sargent, 1951-55. **BUSINESS ADDRESS:** Assoc Professor of Psych, Montclair State Coll, Montclair, NJ 07043.

WILLIAMS, DANIEL LOUIS
Contractor. **PERSONAL:** Born Aug 15, 1926, Hardeeville, SC; son of Adbell Williams Sr and Mattie Freeman Williams; married Pauline Cave; children: Sharon, Daniel Jr, Brenda, Derrick, Devon, Dewitt. **EDUCATION:** Savannah State Coll, 1946-48. **CAREER:** Masons (Prince Hall), sr warden, 1950; Shriners, Illinois potentate, 1968-70; St Phillips Baptist Church, decon, 1968; Beaufort-Jasper Career Educ Center, vice-chmn, 1974; Career Educ Center, chmn, 1986; Jasper County; school bd mem. **MILITARY SERVICE:** USN, stm 1st class, Victory award, 1944-45. **HOME ADDRESS:** PO Box 417, Hardeeville, SC 29927.

WILLIAMS, DANIEL SALU
Educator. **PERSONAL:** Born Feb 14, 1942, Brooklyn, NY; son of David D Williams and Loriene H Williams; married Sheila; children: Peter, Megan. **EDUCATION:** Brooklyn Coll, BA Art 1965; Univ of OR, MA Jrnlsm 1969. **CAREER:** Ohio Univ, assoc prof of Art 1969-88, chmn Photography 1980-81, special asst provost 1987-, chmn of Photography 1989-, full prof of Art 1988-. **ORGANIZATIONS:** Mem Natl Conf of Artists 1972-; mem Soc for Photographic Ed 1970-; advisory bd mem, Images Gallery, Cincinnati, OH 1989-. **HONORS/ACHIEVEMENTS:** Ind artists flwshp OH Arts Council 1984-85; OHUniv Rsrch Grant 1984-; ind artists flwshp OH Arts Cncl 1983-84; OHUniv Rsrch Grant 1982; tchng asstUniv of OR 1967-69; Langston Hughes Visiting Professor of African and African American Studies, Univ of Kansas, 1991; Individual Artist Fellowship, Ohio Arts Council 1988; The Natl African American Museum & Cultural Center, Wilberforce, OH, commission: Photo-Montage Wall Murals 12 Panels, 22'H x 25'W each & three simultaneous slide show projections depicting Afro American life in the 1950's era, overall title, African American Life From WW II to the Civil Rights Act of 1965, completed 1988. **HOME ADDRESS:** 42 Sunnyside Dr, Athens, OH 45701. **BUSINESS ADDRESS:** Asst Provost, Prof of Art & Chmn of Photography, Ohio University, 311 Cutler Hall, Athens, OH 45701.

WILLIAMS, DAVE
Professional athlete. **PERSONAL:** Born Mar 10, 1954, Minden, LA. **EDUCATION:** Finance CO, BA. **CAREER:** Chicago Bears, professional football running back/Kickoff return 1979-. **HONORS/ACHIEVEMENTS:** CO MVP Option Quarterback sr yr; twice named Big-8 All Academic Team; finished 8th in NFC KORs 1978. **BUSINESS ADDRESS:** Chicago Bears, PO Box 204, Lake Forest, IL 60045.

WILLIAMS, DAVID GEORGE
Physician. **PERSONAL:** Born Jan 05, 1939, Chicago, IL; married Judith; children: Sheryl, John, Jacqueline. **EDUCATION:** Provident Hosp Chicago, RN 1961; Trenton State Coll, BA 1972; Hahne Mannmedical Coll Philadelphia, MD 1976. **CAREER:** Physician, private practice, cons, prison furlough bd. **ORGANIZATIONS:** Pres Bell-Williams & Med Assn PA 1979-; dir med NJ Prison System 1977; residentUniv of PA 1976-79; mem AMA; vice pres Medical Class 1972. **HONORS/ACHIEVEMENTS:** Nat Defense Serv Medal; Vietnam Serv Medal 1965; Republic of Vietnam Campaign Medal w/Device; hon soc Trenton State Coll 1972. **MILITARY SERVICE:** AUS 1960; AUS Capt 1963-68. **BUSINESS ADDRESS:** Trenton State Prison, 3rd & Fed Sts, Trenton, NJ 08625.

WILLIAMS, DAVID S., JR.
City manager. **PERSONAL:** Born Jan 29, 1945, Virgin Islands; children: Kathryn, David III, Douglas. **EDUCATION:** Lincoln Univ PA, BA 1965; Temple U, MA 1967; Wayne State U, MCP 1970. **CAREER:** Trenton NJ, business administrator 1979-; City Inkster MI, city mgr 1973-79; City of Inkster, plng dir 1971-73; SW MI Council Govt's, regional planner; Detroit & Philadelphia Sch Sys, tchr. **ORGANIZATIONS:** Mem Intl City Mgmt Assn 1973; Am Inst Planners 1971; Precinct Del 1972; Nat Task Force on Plng & Mgt. **HONORS/ACHIEVEMENTS:** Outstanding Young Men Am 1972; Inkster Unification Com Award 1973. **BUSINESS ADDRESS:** Essex County, 465 Martin L King Blvd, Newark, NJ 07102.

WILLIAMS, DAVID W.
Judge. **PERSONAL:** Born Mar 20, 1910, Atlanta, GA; married Ouida M White; children: David Jr, Vaughn Charles. **EDUCATION:** AB 1934; LLB, 1937. **CAREER:** Law Practice, 1937-55; Municipal Ct, judge, 1956-62; Superior Court, judge 1963-69; US Dist, judge, 1969-. **ORGANIZATIONS:** Amer Bar Assn; Amer Law Inst; LA Bar Assn; Langston Law Club; NAACP; bd of councilors, USC Law School. **HONORS/ACHIEVEMENTS:** Professional Achievement Award, UCLA Alumni, 1966; Professional Achievement Award, USC Alumni, 1973. **BUSINESS ADDRESS:** 312 N Spring Street, Room 324, Los Angeles, CA 90012.

WILLIAMS, DEBORAH ANN
Association executive. **PERSONAL:** Born Nov 28, 1951, Washington, DC; daughter of Harold Williams and Marguerite Stewart Hamilton. **EDUCATION:** Ripon College, BA 1973. **CAREER:** Overlook Elem/Prince George's MD, teacher 1973; C&P Telephone Co, service rep 1973-77; Natl Inst of Educ, corres coord 1977-80, admin officer 1980-86;Dept of Education/Office of Rsch, staff asst 1986-; program analyst US Dept of Educ Washington D.C. 1989-. **ORGANIZATIONS:** Sec Ever Ready Chorus & Club Corinthian Baptist Church 1972-; mem Stereophonic Chorale of Washington DC 1980-. **HONORS/ACHIEVEMENTS:** Dir's Superior Serv Awd Natl Inst of Education 1979. **BUSINESS ADDRESS:** Staff Assistant, US Dept of Education, 555 New Jersey Ave NW, Washington, DC 20208.

WILLIAMS, DENISE RENEE
Consultant. **PERSONAL:** Born Jun 03, 1958, Cleveland, OH. **EDUCATION:** Wittenberg Univ, BA 1980. **CAREER:** Sears Roebuck & Co, dept mgr 1979-82; United Resources, sales mgr 1983-84; Bennington-York Ltd, vice pres 1984-. **ORGANIZATIONS:** Mem Amer Mktg Assoc, Natl Black MBA Association, Operation PUSH, NAACP; sponsor Save the Children.

WILLIAMS, DENNIS
Military officer. **PERSONAL:** Born Nov 12, 1957, Los Angeles, CA; son of Joseph Williams (deceased) and Earnestine Wright Williams; married Roberta M Clair, Mar 08, 1980 (deceased); children: Nikolas D. **EDUCATION:** Univ of Southern CA, BA 1980; USAF Lowry AFB, Munitions Maintenance School, attended 1980-81; Webster Univ, MA 1982. **CAREER:** USAF McConnell AFB, munitions maintenance officer 1981-84; Univ of Akron, asst prof aerospace studies 1984-87; Kadena AB, aircraft maintenance officer 1987-. **ORGANIZATIONS:** Mem Univ of Akron Black Alumni Assoc 1984-86; advisor Univ of Akron Arnold Air Soc 1984-87, Univ of Akron Angel Flight 1984-87; Natl Soc of Black Engineers 1986-87. **HONORS/ACHIEVEMENTS:** Mem Omicron Delta Kappa 1985-87. **MILITARY SERVICE:** USAF capt 8 yrs; Air Force Commendation Medal, Outstanding Unit Awd, Longevity, Training, Marksmanship Ribbons 1980-87. **HOME ADDRESS:** PSC #2 Box ll084, APO, APO San Francisco, CA 96367.

WILLIAMS, DONALD EUGENE
Business executive, clergyman. **PERSONAL:** Born Jan 04, 1929, DeLand, FL; son of John Kenner-Williams and Willie Kenner-Williams; married Leah Keturah Pollard-Williams, Sep 11, 1955; children: Donald, Jr, Celeste, Michele A Williams. **EDUCATION:** Kane Bus School, 1951-52; Shelton Coll, 1952-54; Wayne Coll, 1970-72. **CAREER:** Church of God, pastor 1962-76; Church of God World Svc, dir minority min 1976-81; Church of God Missionary Bd, assoc exec sec 1981-. **ORGANIZATIONS:** Pres Ministerial Assoc 1964-69; vice pres Literacy Council 1964-69; cty jail chaplain Wayne Cty MI 1972-76; dir Rotary Intl 1983-; police chaplain Detroit Police Dept 1972-76; mem Commiss on Human Rights 1983-. **HONORS/ACHIEVEMENTS:** Dedicated Serv Girls Clubs of Amer 1969, Boys Clubs of Metro Detroit 1975, Detroit Police Dept 1976. **BUSINESS ADDRESS:** Associate Executive Secretary, Church of God Missionary Bd, 1303 E 5th St, Anderson, IN 46018.

WILLIAMS, DONALD H.
Educator. **PERSONAL:** Born Oct 29, 1936, Chicago, IL; son of Herbert G. Williams and Theresa P. Williams; married Sharon Rebecca Hobbs, PhD, Jun 18, 1983; children: David, Jonathan, Rebecca. **EDUCATION:** Univ of IL, BA 1957, MD 1962; Univ of IL Rsch & Educ Hosp, internship 1962-63, residency 1964-67. **CAREER:** Connect Mental Health Cntr, chief inpatient serv 1971-73; Yale Univ, asst prof 1971-77; Connect Mental Health Cntr,

head Med Eval Unit 1973-78, chiefComm Supp Serv 1973-79; Yale Univ, assoc prof of psych 1977-84; Connect Mental Health Center, asst chief for clin aff 1979-84; MI State Univ, prof/chairperson of Psychiatry 1984-. **ORGANIZATIONS:** Amer Publ Health Assn 1968; Amer Orthopsychiatric Assn 1968; consult Natl Inst of Mental Health 1971-81; consult West Haven Veterans Admin Hosp 1971-80; Fellow Amer Psychiatric Assn 1974; treas Black Psychiatrists of Amer 1978-80. **HONORS/ACHIEVEMENTS:** IL Psychiatric Soc Resch Award Referee 1968; Archieves of Gen Psychiatry; Amer Journl of Psychiatry; Social Psychiatry; 17 articles and numerous professional presentations. **MILITARY SERVICE:** AUS Reserves Psychiatrist 801 Gen Hosp 1968-69; Cpt Medical Corps 1963-68. **BUSINESS ADDRESS:** Prof/Chairperson of Psychiatry, Michigan State University, Room 223A East Fee Hall, East Lansing, MI 48824.

WILLIAMS, DOROTHY DANIEL
Educator. **PERSONAL:** Born Aug 22, 1938, Kinston, NC; daughter of Mr & Mrs Fonic & Willie M Daniels; divorced; children: William Daniel. **EDUCATION:** Hampton Inst, BSN, 1960; New York Univ, Grad Courses, 1965; Baltimore Community Coll, 1973; East Carolina Univ, MS, HEC, 1977, MSN, 1980. **CAREER:** New York City & Los Angeles, CA, staff nurse, 1960-66; Einstein Hospital, Bronx, NY, head nurse, 1966-69; Baltimore City Schools, Vocational Div, teacher, 1969-73; Lenoir Mem Hospital, School of Nursing, instructor, 1973-74; East Carolina Univ, School of Nursing, asst professor of maternal-child nursing, 1974-. **ORGANIZATIONS:** By law comm mem, North Carolina Nurse Assn, 1983-85; sec convention delegate Dist 32, NCNA, 1983-85; vice pres, Delta Rho Zeta Chapter, Zeta Phi Beta Sor Inc, 1983-85; lecturer, State Bd of Nursing Review Courses, AHEC; mem, 1980-, chmn, 1981-82, 85, School of Nursing Curriculum Comm; developer, Leadership Seminar; panelist, consultant, developer, Adolescent Pregnancy/Parenting Seminar; by laws comm, Assn of Black Nursing Faculty in Higher Educ, 1986-. **HONORS/ACHIEVEMENTS:** Natl Nurse Honor Soc, Beta Chapter, Sigma Theta Tau, 1978; ECU Lambda Mu Chap Zeta Phi Beta, advisor, 1983-; Selected to participate in the minority health leadership workshop, Chapel Hill, NC, 1985; ECU Greek Affairs Advisor Comm, appointed, 1984; HERA, for Outstanding Sorority Advisor, Panhellenic Council of ECU, 1986; appointment to Research Bd of Advisors, Amer Biographical Inst, Inc, 1987. **BUSINESS ADDRESS:** East Carolina Univ Asst Professor, Nursing, Nursing Bldg, Greenville, NC 27834.

WILLIAMS, DOROTHY P.
Educator, librarian. **PERSONAL:** Born Nov 24, 1938, Tallahassee, FL; divorced; children: Gerald Herbert, Debra Michelle. **EDUCATION:** FL A&M Univ, BS 1960; Syracuse Univ, MSLS 1967; Univ of North FL, 1974-75. **CAREER:** Lincoln Memorial HS, librarian 1960-61; JW Johnson Jr HS, head librarian 1962-68; Raines HS, head librarian 1968-71; Univ of North FL, asst dir libs 1971-82; FL A&M Univ, dir of publications 1983-. **ORGANIZATIONS:** EEO/AA coord Univ of North FL 1976-82; staff coord State Bd of Educ Adv Comm on the Educ of Blacks in FL 1984-; bd mem Jacksonville Comm Economic DevCouncil 1981-83; past pres Jacksonville Natl Council of Negro Women 1978-81; pres Jacksonville Chapter of Links Inc 1985-; pres Friends of FAMU Black Archives 1985-. **HONORS/ACHIEVEMENTS:** Teacher of the Year James Weldon Johnson Jr HS 1966; Service Award Alpha Kappa Alpha Sorority 1978; Community Serv Award Grant Meml AME Church 1979. **HOME ADDRESS:** 9403 Sibbald Rd, Jacksonville, FL 32208. **BUSINESS ADDRESS:** Dir of Publications, FL A&MUniv, 410 Administration Center, Tallahassee, FL 32307.

WILLIAMS, DOUGLAS LEE
Professional athlete. **PERSONAL:** Born Aug 09, 1955, Zachary, LA. **CAREER:** Grambling Univ, professional football player; Buccaneers, football player; AZ Outlaws, football player. **HONORS/ACHIEVEMENTS:** Offensive Rookie of the Year New Pittsburgh.

WILLIAMS, E. FAYE
Association executive, attorney. **PERSONAL:** Born Dec 20, 1941, Melrose, LA; daughter of Vernon Williams and Frances Lacour Williams. **EDUCATION:** Grambling State Univ, BS 1962; Univ of Southern CA, MA Public Admin 1971; George Washington Univ DC, Educ Policy Fellow 1981; Howard Univ School of Law JD (Cum Laude) 1985. **CAREER:** Los Angeles City Schools, teacher/dept chairperson 1964-71; Natl Ed Assoc, dir atlanta assoc of ed 1971-73, dir overseas ed assoc 1973-75; MI Ed Assoc/NEA, dir org & public relations 1975-81; MI Ed Assoc/NEA, dir prof devel & human rights 1981-82; Dist of Columbia Committee, congress fellow judiciary & ed; Office of General Counsel of Natl Football League Players Assoc in Sports Law, intern; MI Ed Assoc, dir professional devel & human rights; Larvadain & Scott Law Offices, atty-at-law, prof of law, Southern Univ Law Center, Baton Rouge, Louisiana. **ORGANIZATIONS:** Mem Alpha Kappa Mu Natl Hon Soc 1959-; life mem Delta Sigma Theta 1959-; natl pres Grambling State Univ Alumni Assoc 1981-; bd of dir Grambling State Univ Found 1981-; chairperson Law Week Howard Univ School of Law 1985; bd dir Grambling Univ Athletic Found; candidate for US Comgress won 49.3% of vote after winning the Dem Nom. **HONORS/ACHIEVEMENTS:** Magna Cum Laude Grambling State Univ of LA 1962; Outstanding Alumnus of Historically Black Coll NAFEO 1981; mem Women in Law Howard Univ School of Law 1983-; mem law jrnl staff Howard Univ School of Law 1983-; Joan of Arc Awd LA Women in Politics; mem Hall of Fame of Black Women Attorneys 1986; Martin Luther King, Jr Commemorative Award, 1988. **HOME ADDRESS:** 4206 Third St, Alexandria, LA 71302.

WILLIAMS, E. THOMAS, JR.
Private investor/banker. **PERSONAL:** Born Oct 14, 1937, New York, NY; son of Edgar T Williams and Elnora Bing Williams; married Auldlyn; children: Brooke Higgins Bing Williams; Eden Bradford Bing Williams. **EDUCATION:** Brooklyn College, BAEcon 1960. **CAREER:** Chase Manhattan Bank, Vice Pres & Sr Loan Officer for Int'l Private Banking 1972-83; Fordham Hill Owners Corp, President 1983-. **ORGANIZATIONS:** Trustee Boys Harbor Inc; trustee Central Park Conservancy Bd; trustee Atlanta Univ Ctr; bd mem NAACP Legal Defense Fund; mem Sigma Pi Phi, 100 Black Men, Inc, Thomas Franklin Bing Trust, Nehemiah Housing Trust, Berkeley Divinity Schl at Yale; trustee Vestry of Trinity Church Wall St; trustee Cathedral Church St John the Divine Treasurer; The Schomberg Ctr for Rsch in Black Culture; chmn Schomberg Soc. **HONORS/ACHIEVEMENTS:** Black Enterprise cover story April 1986 issue; New York Magazine covery story January 19, 1987 issue. **MILITARY SERVICE:** Peace Corps, Ethiopia I 1962-63. **HOME ADDRESS:** 130 East 67th St, New York, NY 10021. **BUSINESS ADDRESS:** President, Fordham Hill Owners Corp, 1 Fordham Hill Oval, Bronx, NY 10468.

WILLIAMS, EARL
Musician. **PERSONAL:** Born Oct 08, 1938, Detroit, MI; son of Paul Williams and Evelyn Williams; married Ronda G Snowden MD; children: Earl Jr, Kevin, Damon. **EDUCATION:** Detroit Conserv of Music, attended 1949-51; Detroit Inst of Musical Arts, attended 1951-53; Borough of Manhattan Comm Coll, attended 1973-75; Empire State Coll, New York, NY BA 1986-88. **CAREER:** Paul "Hucklebuck" Williams Orchestra, musician (drummer) 1957-59; Eddie Heywood Trio, musician 1959-61; Recording/TV/Radio, studio drummer 1961-73; Sam "The Man" Taylor Japan Tour, drummer 1964-65 & 1972; Music Matrix Publ Co, musician/pres. **ORGANIZATIONS:** Mem NARAS (Natl Acad of Recording Artists Arts and Scis) 1979; lectures/demonstrations/concerts in various univs and cultural inst 1968-85; mem Broadcast Music Inc BMI, 1960. **HONORS/ACHIEVEMENTS:** Drummer with, Diahann Carroll-Cannes Film Festival 1965; WNET-TV "Soul Show" 1968-69; NBC-TV "Someone New Show" 1969-72; ABC-TV "Jack Parr Show" 1973-74; Lena Horne 1973-74; A Chorus Line (Broadway) 1975-79; Alvin Ailey Dance Co 1979; Jean-Pierre Rampal 1980-81. **BUSINESS ADDRESS:** President, Music Matrix Publishing Co, 184 Evergreen Dr, Westbury, NY 11590.

WILLIAMS, EARL WEST
Government official. **PERSONAL:** Born Jul 20, 1928, Montgomery, AL; married Frances Jenkins; children: Earl Jr, Reginald, Eric. **EDUCATION:** Morehouse Coll, attended 1947; Alabama State Univ, BS 1950; Cleveland State Univ, attended 1973. **CAREER:** Cleveland Bd of Educ, teacher 1953-55; Beneficial Finance Co, asst mgr 1956-62; City of Cleveland Comm Devel, citizen participation adv 1962-64, project dir 1964-70; Community Relations Bd, executive dir. **ORGANIZATIONS:** Pres elect 1986-87, mem Natl Assoc of Human Rights Workers; trustee Greater Cleveland Interchurch Cncl, Office of School Monitoring and Comm Relations, St James AME Church; mem Leadership Cleveland, Omega Psi Phi Frat Inc, Beta Rho Boule-Sigma Psi Phi Frat. **HONORS/ACHIEVEMENTS:** US Congressional Certificate of Achievement US Congress 1982; Disting Awd Cleveland Comm Relations Bd 1986; Outstanding Citizen Omega Psi Phi Frat 1986; President's Certificate of Appreciation Natl Assoc of Human Rights Workers 1986. **MILITARY SERVICE:** AUS t/sgt 2 yrs. **BUSINESS ADDRESS:** Consultant, 18219 Van Aken Blvd, Shaker Heights, OH 44122.

WILLIAMS, EDDIE, SR.
Construction executive. **CAREER:** Williams & Richardson Co, Inc, Detroit MI, chief executive, 1980—. **BUSINESS ADDRESS:** Williams & Richardson Co, Inc, 10611 W McNichols, Detroit, MI 48221. *

WILLIAMS, EDDIE NATHAN
Research institution executive. **PERSONAL:** Born Aug 18, 1932, Memphis, TN; son of Ed Williams and Georgia Lee Barr (Williams); married Jearline F Reddick, Jul 18, 1981; children: Traci Lynne, Edward Lawrence. **EDUCATION:** Univ of Illinois, Urbana, BS, 1954; Atlanta Univ, Atlanta GA, postgraduate degree, 1957; Howard Univ, Washington DC, postgraduate degree, 1958. **CAREER:** Atlanta Daily Newspaper, Atlanta GA, reporter, 1957-58; US Senate Comm on Foreign Relations, Washington DC, staff asst, 1959-60; US Dept of State, Washington DC, foreign service res officer, 1961-68; Univ of Chicago IL, vice pres, 1968-72; Joint Center for Political Studies, Washington DC, pres, 1972-. **ORGANIZATIONS:** Chair, Natl Coalition on Black Voter Participation; exec comm, WETA Television; bd of dir, Children's Defense Fund, The Foundation Center, Inst for Educational Leadership; Carnegie Council on Ethics and Intl Affairs, The Maxima Corp; Natl Endowment for Democracy; Markle Foundation Commn on Media & Political Education; Black Leadership Forum; Kettering Foundation; Kappa Tau Alpha Journalism Honor Society; Omega Psi Phi; Sigma Pi Phi. **HONORS/ACHIEVEMENTS:** Hon LLD, Univ of the District of Columbia; hon DHL, Bowie State Univ, 1980; Congressional Black Caucus Adam Clayton Powell Award, 1981; Keynote Address Award, Natl Conf of Black Political Scientists, 1988; Achievement Award, Black Alumni Assn, Univ of IL, 1988; MacArthur Foundation Fellows Award, MacArthur Foundation, 1988; author of numerous newspaper, magazine, journal, and book articles, 1963-. **MILITARY SERVICE:** US Army, first lieutenant, 1955-57. **BUSINESS ADDRESS:** President, Joint Center for Political Studies, 1301 Pennsylvania Ave NW, Suite 400, Washington, DC 20004.

WILLIAMS, EDNA C.
Educator, musician. **PERSONAL:** Born Oct 22, 1933, Chicago, IL. **EDUCATION:** Roosevelt Univ, Mus B 1957, Mus M 1959. **CAREER:** Joliet Conservatory of Mus, instr 1962-64; Northern IL Univ, assoc prof. **ORGANIZATIONS:** Mem IL Assn for Supvsn and Curriculum Devel 1974; mem Natl Assn of Tchr of Singing Inc 1965; bd mem Natl Assn of Negro Musicians 1976. **HONORS/ACHIEVEMENTS:** Sue Cowan Hintz Voice Award 1955; Oliver Ditson Voice Scholarship 1956; John Hay Whitney Fellowhsip 1959; Kenwood Male Chorus Award 1959. **BUSINESS ADDRESS:** Associate Professor, Northern Illinois University, Dept of Music, De Kalb, IL 60115.

WILLIAMS, EDWARD ELLIS
Business executive. **PERSONAL:** Born Jun 23, 1938, Hazelhurst, MS; married Sarah Robertson; children: Karen, Edward Jr. **EDUCATION:** Univ of IL Coll of Pharmacy, B 1963. **CAREER:** Walgreen, pharmacist 1964, store mgr 1965, dist mgr 1967, dist mgr 1979, dist mgr 1979-. **ORGANIZATIONS:** Mem Chicago South End Jaycees 1966; mem Chicago Pharmacist Assn 1967; dir of events MS State Traveling Club 1976. **HONORS/ACHIEVEMENTS:** Outstanding Young Man of the Yr Chicago S End Jaycees 1966; Spl Achiever Chicago YMCA 1978; Humanitarian Awd MS State Traveling Club 1979. **BUSINESS ADDRESS:** District Manager, Walgreen Co, 200 Wilmot Rd, Deerfield, IL 60015.

WILLIAMS, EDWARD JOSEPH
Chief executive officer. **PERSONAL:** Born May 05, 1942, Chicago, IL; married Johnnita E Daniel; children: Elaine, Paul. **EDUCATION:** Roosevelt Univ, BBA, 1973. **CAREER:** Mut Home Delivery, Chicago, owner, 1961-63; Harris Trust & Savings Bank, Chicago, sr vice pres, 1964-. **ORGANIZATIONS:** Trust Adler Planetarium, 1982; mem, Consumer Adv Council, Washington, 1986-; chmn, Provident Medical Center, 1986; mem, Natl Bankers Assn, Urban Bankers Forum, Methodist Clubs, Metro Union League, The Economic Club of Chicago. **HONORS/ACHIEVEMENTS:** Distinguished Alumni Award, Clark Coll, Atlanta, 1985; Pioneer Award, Urban Bankers Forum, 1986. **BUSINESS ADDRESS:** Senior Vice President, Harris Bank, 111 W Monroe, Chicago, IL 60690.

WILLIAMS, EDWARD M.
Oral surgeon. **PERSONAL:** Born Dec 10, 1933, Augusta, GA; married Davide Bradley; children: Brent, Kurt, Scott. **EDUCATION:** Morehouse Coll, BS 1954; Atlanta Univ, MS 1963; Howard Univ, DDS 1968, cert oral surgy 1971. **CAREER:** Atlanta Pub Sch Sys, tchr 1958-63; Priv Prac, oral surgeon. **ORGANIZATIONS:** Mem Am Dent Assn GA Dent Assn; Am Soc Oral Surg; GA Soc Oral Surg; Internal Assn Oral Surg; Fellow Am Dent Soc of Anethesiology; mem NAACP; Am Cancer Soc; YMCA; Alpha Phi Alpha; Beta Kappa Chi. **HONORS/ACHIEVEMENTS:** Award in Anesthesiology Howard Univ 1968; Award in Periodontics Howard Univ 1968. **MILITARY SERVICE:** AUS 1956-58. **BUSINESS ADDRESS:** 75 Piedmont Ave NE, Ste 440, Atlanta, GA 30303.

WILLIAMS, ELLIS
Clergyman, law enforcement. **PERSONAL:** Born Oct 27, 1931, Raymond, MS; son of Curry Williams and Elise Morrison McDowell; married Priscilla Norman, Jan 09, 1954; children: Debra Lucas, Rita Singleton, Claude, Lathan, Glenn, Zelia. **EDUCATION:** Loyola Univ, BA, 1972, MEd, 1974, MCJ, 1981. **CAREER:** New Orleans Police Dept, police officer, 1965, fingerprint tech, 1968, polygraphist, 1974; Jefferson Vocational & Tech School, lecturer, 1981-; New Orleans Police Dept, police commander; Historic Second Baptist Church, New Orleans, LA, assoc minister. **ORGANIZATIONS:** Historian Kappa Delta Pi, 1973-74; vice chmn, Louisiana Polygraph Bd, 1981-82; mem, Louisiana & Amer Polygraph Assn, Louisiana & Intl Assn of Ident, Freedmens Missionary Baptist Assoc of Louisiana, Natl Baptist Training Union, Sunday School Congress; mem, Police Management Assn, Natl Org of Black Law Enforcement Exec. **HOME ADDRESS:** 3108 Metropolitan St, New Orleans, LA 70126. **BUSINESS ADDRESS:** Police Commander, New Orleans Police Dept, 715 S Broad St, New Orleans, LA 70119.

WILLIAMS, ELYNOR A.
Business executive/public relations. **PERSONAL:** Born Oct 27, 1948, Baton Rouge, LA; daughter of Albert Berry Williams and Naomi Douglas Williams. **EDUCATION:** Spelman Coll, BS Home Economics 1966; Cornell Univ, MPS Communication Arts 1973. **CAREER:** Eugene Butler Jr-Sr HS, home economics teacher 1966-68; Genl Foods Corp, publicist package editor copy editor 1968-71; Cornell Univ, COSEP tutor 1972-73; NC Agricultural Extension Svc, comm specialist 1973-77; Western Elec, sr public relations specialist 1977-83; Hanes Group, dir corporate affairs; Sara Lee Corp, dir public affairs. **ORGANIZATIONS:** Bd of dirs Univ of NC at Greensboro 1981-89; bd of dirs YWCA 1984-86; adv bd NC Women's Network 1985; mem Natl Tech Adv Comm OICs of Amer Inc 1985-89; mem Exec Comm Natl Women's Economic Alliance 1985; vice pres public affairs & comm bd of dirs Gr Winston-Salem Chamber of Commerce 1985-86; mem Business Policy Review Council, 1988-; mem Women's Institute, 1988-; bd of dirs Cosmopolitan Chamber of Commerce, Chicago, IL, 1988-; mem National Hispanic Corporate Council; natl corporate adv bd Natl Org for Women; corporate adv bd Natl Women's Political Caucus; mem League of Women Voters; mem Intl Assn of Business Comm; mem Public Relations Society of Amer; mem Natl Assn of Female Execs; bd of dirs Exec Leadership Council. **HONORS/ACHIEVEMENTS:** Dist Alumnae of the Yr Natl Assn for Equal Oppor in Higher Educ 1983; Bus & Entrepreneurship Awd Natl Alumnae Assn of Spelman Coll 1984; Hon Doc of Humane Letters Clincon Jr Coll SC 1984; Acad of Achievers YWCA NY 1984; Boss of the Yr Winston-Salem Chap Prof Secretaries Intl 1984-85; Outstanding Contribution in Business Winston-Salem Chap Natl Council of Negro Women 1985; Kizzy Award, Black Women's Hall of Fame, 1987; Outstanding Service Award, National Council of Negro Women, Midwest chapter, 1988; Black & Hispanic Achievers Industry Award, YMCA, 1988; Vanguard Award, Women in Communications Inc, 1988; Spectra Award of Excellence, Intl Assoc of Business Communicators, Chicago, IL, 1988; Racial Justice Award, YWCA, 1988; Trio award, University of Illinois, 1989. **HOME ADDRESS:** 2335 North Commonwealth, Chicago, IL 60614. **BUSINESS ADDRESS:** Director of Public Affairs, Sara Lee Corporation, 3 First National Plaza, Chicago, IL 60602.

WILLIAMS, ENOCH H.
City official. **PERSONAL:** Born Jun 21, 1927, Wilmington, NC; son of Howell Williams and Pauline Williams; married Elizabeth Peterson; children: Dr Kamau Kokoyi, Charrise Williams Adamson. **EDUCATION:** Long Island Univ, BS, Business Admin, 1967; attended New York Univ, Real Estate Inst. **CAREER:** The Stuyvord Action Council, founder & former vice pres, 1964-66; School Dist No 11, Bronx, admin officer, 1967; Youth-in-Action Inc, comm org specialist, 1967-69; Brooklyn Local Economic Devel Corp, pres, 1967-73; Enoch Williams & Assocs Inc, pres, 1967-77; Commerce Labor Indus corp of Kings, vice chmn, bd of dirs, 1968-77; Housing Devel Corp Council of Churches, exec dir, 1969-78; Columbia Univ, Fed Annual Housing Specialist Program, lecturer, 1970-72; Housing Devel & Mgmt Training Seminars, dir, coord & lecturer, 1970-76; New York City Council, city councilman. **ORGANIZATIONS:** Vice pres, Unity Democratic Club, 1961-73; chmn, Businessmen Advisory Bd, 1966-67; mem, Urban League, NAACP, Interfaith Housing Strategy Comm of New York, NY, Citizens Housing & Planning Council; duty training officer New York City Selective Serv; brigadier gen colonel, New York Army Natl Guard; youth serv comm chmn New York City Council; committeeman, New York State 55th AD; state dir, New York City Selective Serv. **HONORS/ACHIEVEMENTS:** Delegate Natl Democratic Convention, 1968 & 1972. **MILITARY SERVICE:** AUS brigadier general. **BUSINESS ADDRESS:** City Councilman, New York City Council, 1670 Fulton St, Brooklyn, NY 11213.

WILLIAMS, ERNEST DONALD, JR.
Clergyman. **PERSONAL:** Born Aug 27, 1949, Baltimore, MD. **EDUCATION:** Benedict Coll Columbia SC, BA 1972; Interdenominational Theol Ctr Atlanta, MDiv 1976. **CAREER:** Friendship Coll Rock Hill SC, instr/dir ch relations 1978-79; Geneva H Clark Home for Aged, owner 1979-; Shiloh Baptist Ch, minister 1970-. **ORGANIZATIONS:** Mem Natl Council of Tchr of English 1972; mem Marlboro Co Betterment League; past pres Gordon-Jenkins Theol Assn 1971-72; pres Marlboro Co Ministerial Alliance 1975-80; pres Marlboro Co NAACP 1976-80; mem Marlboro Co Multidisciplinary Council 1980; mem Delta Kappa Lamba Chap APA Frat Inc 1980. **HONORS/ACHIEVEMENTS:** Son of the Amer Revolution Awd Daus of the Amer Revolution 1968; Outstanding Young man of Amer US Jaycees 1976; Living the Legacy Honoree Natl Council ofNegro Women. **BUSINESS ADDRESS:** Minister, P O Box 470681, Box 875, Brooklyn, NY 11247.

WILLIAMS, ERNEST Y.
Educator, physician. **PERSONAL:** Born Feb 24, 1900, Nevis, WI; married Matilda; children: Ernest Y, Shirley Y, Joan C. **EDUCATION:** HowardUniv Med Sch, BSMD. **CAREER:** Howard Univ Med School, Prof Emeritus dept neurology & psychiatry, head of NP serv 32 yrs. **ORGANIZATIONS:** Chmn 13 yrs, past consult Crownsville State Hosp; VA Hosp; NIMH Consult St ElizHosp; MS Soc of DC; co-founder DC Orgn for Alcoholsim; Child Psychiatric Clinic. **HONORS/ACHIEVEMENTS:** Recipient plaque from NMA for Med Leadership; plaque in Recgntn 30 yrs serv NMA; Outstanding Tchr HowardUniv 1948. **BUSINESS ADDRESS:** Howard Univ Hosp, Ga Ave & W Sts NW, Washington, DC.

WILLIAMS, ETHEL LANGLEY
Retired librarian. **PERSONAL:** Born in Baltimore, MD; daughter of William H. and Carrie A.; married Louis J Williams (deceased); children: Carole J Jones. **EDUCATION:** Howard Univ, AB 1930; Columbia Univ NYC, BS 1933; Howard Univ, MA 1947-50. **CAREER:** Bd of Public Welfare Wash DC, caseworker 1933-35; Library of Congress, process filer & order searcher 1936-40; Moorland Springarn Collection, supr project 271 & 328, works progress adminstrn 1939; Howard U, reference librarian cataloger 1941-47; HowardUniv Sch of Religion Library, retired librarian 1946-75; Writings, A Catalogue of Books in the Moorland Found 1939, Afro-Am Newspaper 1945-46, Negro History Bulletin 110-16 1945, Journal of Negro Educ 1945-46, Handbook of Instr in the Use of the Sch of Rel Library 1955, Revised 1968; Editor, Biographical Dir of Negro Ministers 1965, 1970, 1975. **ORGANIZATIONS:** Co-editor, Afro-Am Rel Studies A Comprehensive Bibliography with Locations in Am Libraries 1970, HowardUniv Bibliography & African & Afro-Am Relig Studies 1977.

WILLIAMS, EVERETT BELVIN
Business executive. **PERSONAL:** Born Oct 26, 1932, Hennessey, OK; married Marianne Hansson; children: Karin Cecelia, Barbro Susanne. **EDUCATION:** Denver Univ, BA 1955; Columbia Univ, MA 1957, PhD 1962, MS 1970. **CAREER:** Various NY & NJ VA Hosps, trainee 1957-60; Hunter Coll, lectr councelor 1960-62; Columbia Univ, research assoc teachers coll 1961-62; Barnard Coll, lectr 1962-63; Columbia Coll, counselor 1963-64; Columbia Univ Computer Center, dir 1964-71; Columbia Univ, assoc prof 1970-71, assoc dean 1970-71, adj prof 1971-75, vice pres operations 1972-75, vice pres coll bd prog 1975-77; Educ Testing Serv, sr vice pres prog areas 1982; Williams & Weisbrodt, partner/private consultant. **ORGANIZATIONS:** Certified Psychologist NY 1964; mem Amer Psychol Assn, Amer Assn for the Advancement of Sci, NY State Psychol Assn, Philosophy of Sci Assn, Amer Acad for Polit & Soc Sci, Assn for Educ Data Sys, Assn for Computing Machinery, Assn for Symbolic Logic, Phi Delta Kappa, Kappa Delta Pi; bd dir Lisle Fellowship 1964-67; adv com Response of NYSPA to Social issues; Inst of Elec & Electronic Engrs; mem NY State Com for Children 1971-74; bd trustees Dalton Schs 1967-74; Harvard Bd of Overseers 1973-74; dir Index Fund of Amer Inc 1974; sr consul Belmar Computer Serv Inc; chmn Assn of Black Psychol; field assessment officer field selection officer Peace Corps; field selection officer Tchrs Corps; consult psychol SEEK Prog; consult Metro Mental Health Clinic; consult Fresh Air Fund; consult Natl Urban League; chmn Review Com on Testing of Minorities; mem Intercoll Knights; mem Natl Sci Found; mem Omicron Delta Kappa, Psi Chi, Phi Beta Kappa, Danforth Fellowship, Danforth Teaching; fellow Sigma Xi; rsch fellow Conf on Learning & Educ Process 1965. **HONORS/ACHIEVEMENTS:** Publ Deductive Reasoning in Schizophrenia 1964, Intro to Psychology 1963, Assn Between Smoking & Accidents 1966, Driving & Connotative Meanings 1970.

WILLIAMS, FALBA W.
Business executive. **PERSONAL:** Born Mar 05, 1935, Rayville, LA; married Oscar K; children: Elizabeth LeMoyne, Eric Lydell. **EDUCATION:** Gambling State U, BS 1958. **CAREER:** Simms & Gundy, funeral dir 1961-; Purple Shield Life Ins Co, vice pres 1974-; Peoples Progressive Burial Co, vice pres 1963-74; NE LA Funeral Dirs & Morticians Assn, Tchr 1962-, mem sec 1958-61; Assn of Funeral Dirs & Embalmers of LA, asst exec sec, sec. **ORGANIZATIONS:** Nat Assn of Funeral Dirs & Embalmers; co-dir Nat Educ Commn 1974; Monroe Alumnae Chpt; Delta Sigma Theta Sor; past pres Gayelite Civic & Social Club pres1974-; mem bd dirs Monroe Utilities Commn; bd dirs LA Assn of Mental Health; treas Local Chap NE LA Health Council; bd mem LA Demo Voters League; Am Legion Ladies Aux. **HONORS/ACHIEVEMENTS:** Recip Women of Yr Nat Funeral Dirs & Morticians 1974. **BUSINESS ADDRESS:** President, Funeral Co Inc, 1407 Washington St, Monroe, LA 71201.

WILLIAMS, FELTON CARL
Educational administrator. **PERSONAL:** Born Mar 30, 1946, Los Angeles, CA; son of Abraham Williams; married Maryetta Baldwin; children: Sonia Yvette, Felton Jr. **EDUCATION:** Los Angeles Harbor Community Coll, AA, 1970; California State Univ, Long Beach, BA, 1972, MBA, 1975; Claremont Grad School, PhD, 1985. **CAREER:** CSU, Long Beach, junior staff analyst, 1972-73, admin asst, 1972-73, supvr, 1974-79; CSU, Dominguez Hills, affirmative action officer, 1985-86, dir learning assistance center. **ORGANIZATIONS:** Pres, San Pedtro-Wilmington NAACP 1976-, Region I NAACP 1979-80; bd mem, Selective Serv System, Region IV, 1981, Employee Readiness Support Center, 1986-87. **HONORS/ACHIEVEMENTS:** Resolution Outstanding Community Contr California Legislature, 1980; Certificate of Appreciation Chamber of Commerce/Community Devel, 1980. **MILITARY SERVICE:** AUS, specialist, 5 E-5, 2 years. **HOME ADDRESS:** 2126 Daisy Ave, Long Beach, CA 90806. **BUSINESS ADDRESS:** Dir Learning Assistance Ctr, California StateUniv, 1000 E Victoria St, Dominguez Hills, Carson, CA 90747.

WILLIAMS, FORREST WESLEY
Engineering manager. **PERSONAL:** Born May 29, 1937, Geiger, AL; married Dorothy M Lee; children: Forrest Wesley Jr, Carol Lee. **EDUCATION:** IN Inst of Tech, BSEE 1962; LA State Univ, MSEE 1968; Univ of Santa Clara, DEEE. **CAREER:** Boeing Co, elec engr 1962-65; Gen Elec Co, elec engr 1965-69; Intl Business Machines, sr eng mgr 1969-. **ORGANIZATIONS:** Trustee First African Methodist E Zion 1969-; bd member Oak Grove Sch Dist 1975-; bd of directors San Jose Alumni Chapter-Kappa Alpha Psi Frat 1980-; bdof directors CA School Bds Assn 1981-. **HONORS/ACHIEVEMENTS:** Awd of Excellence Martin Luther King Committee 1979; President's Awd IBM-GPD San Jose 1980; Businessmen Awd San Jose Black Businessmen 1981. **MILITARY SERVICE:** AUS spec-4 4 yrs.

WILLIAMS, FRANK, JR.
Chief executive of bank. **CAREER:** Security National Bank, Shreveport LA, chief executive, 1982—. **BUSINESS ADDRESS:** Security National Bank, 2800 N Hearne Ave, Shreveport, LA 71107. *

WILLIAMS, FRANK CHRISTOPHER, JR.
Educational administrator, consultant. **PERSONAL:** Born Mar 29, 1950, Newark, NJ.

EDUCATION: Montclair State Coll, BA 1971; Kean Coll, MA 1975; Boston Coll, PhD 1981-. **CAREER:** Kean Coll, asst dir of admissions 1972-75; Montclair State Coll, coord fresh admiss 1975-78; Coll Bd, reg prog mgr 1978-85. **ORGANIZATIONS:** Bd mem Montclair Comm Devel Corp 1977; professional mem Assoc of Ed Rschrs 1981-85, Natl Council on Meas in Ed 1981-85; trustee Pond St Baptist Church 1983. **HONORS/ACHIEVEMENTS:** "Admissions Criteria & the Min Student" NACAC Rschrs Jrnl 1982; Award Outstanding Young Men in Amer 1983. **BUSINESS ADDRESS:** Regional Program Manager, College Board, 470 Totten Pond Rd, Waltham, MA 02154.

WILLIAMS, FRANK COPELAND
Educational administrator. **PERSONAL:** Born May 28, 1935, Tifton, GA; married Mary Elizabeth Friday; children: Jan, Cedric, Tiffany. **EDUCATION:** Univ of NE, BS 1970, MS 1973. **CAREER:** Salisbury State Coll, asst dir of admissions & financial aid/dir of vet affairs; Los Angeles Community Coll Overseas, instr 1976-78; Univ of HI, instr 1976-78; Univ of MD-japan, instr 1975-78; USAF Okinawa Japan, dir of educ 1975-78; USAF Rehabilitation Group Denver CO, dir of criminal justice 1974. **ORGANIZATIONS:** Mem Am Personnel & Guidance Assn; mem MD Personnel & Guidance Assn; mem Adlerian Soc; mem Alpha Phi Alpha Frat; written article Time Mag; article Uof MD Overseas Newsletter. **HONORS/ACHIEVEMENTS:** "Island Personality" award pub in "This Week on Okinawa" Mag. **BUSINESS ADDRESS:** Salisbury State Coll, Camden Ave, Salisbury, MD 21801.

WILLIAMS, FRANK J.
Real estate broker. **PERSONAL:** Born Aug 29, 1938, Arkansas; son of Seldon Williams and Ada (Frye) Jones; married Joanne; children: Michael, Craig, Renee, Jannie. **EDUCATION:** Attended Bogan Jr Coll; Kennedy-King Coll; Real Est Inst at Central YMCA Comm Coll. **CAREER:** US Post Ofc, mail carrier 1961-66; Midwest Realty, salesman 1966-68, sales mgr 1968-70; EW Realty Co, prof 1970-71; Licensed Real Estate Broker 1969-; F J Williams Realty Co, founder/pres 1971-. **ORGANIZATIONS:** Mem Councl of Local Bd; pres Natl Assn of Real Estate Brokers; mem Licensed Real Estate/License Law Officials Liaison Com; mem natl Assn of Realtors-Area Prop; Mgmt Broker for VA Admin; instr Real Est Sales & Brokerage Real Est Inst of Cent YMCA Comm Coll; instr Real Est Trans Course Chicago Real Est Bd/Hall Inst Univ of Chicago; chmn NAACP Housing Com; asst chmn adv com Utilization of Subsidies to Increase Black Adoptions; past chmn SE Section Luth Athletic Assn; mem Urban Homestead Coalition; mem Chicago Real Est Bd Admis Com; mem Timothy Luth Ch; mem Community Devel Adv Committee (appointed by Mayor Harold Washington); pres NAACP Chicago Southside Branch 1978-85; chmn Chicago Real Est Bd's Equal Opportunity Comm; chmn New Horizons Task Force appted by Gov James R Thompson; mem Recreational Task Force apptd by Gov James R Thompson; adv bd mem Black on Black Love; bd mem Black Historic Checagou Dusable Fort Dearborn Historical Commn Inc; mem Cancer Prevention Soc; sec Chicago Bd of Realtors 1987; bd mem Ada S. McKinley Service 1989; bd mem Neighborhood Housing Service 1989; pres elect Chicago Bd of Realtor 1989; bd mem Community Investment Corp 1988. **HONORS/ACHIEVEMENTS:** Recipient of Educ Devel Award Dearborn Real Estate Bd; Educ Cert of Appreciation Phi Beta Lambda; Award of Achievement CA Assn of Real Estate Brokers Inc; Black Businessman of the Month Award Chicago South End Jaycees; Award of Recogn Chicago Real Est Bd 1973; Elmore Baker Award from Dearborn Real Est Bd; Appreciation Awd Realtors Real Estate School; Outstanding Service Awd Natl Caucus and Ctr for the Black Aged Inc. **BUSINESS ADDRESS:** Real Estate Broker-Appraiser, F J Williams Realty, 7825 South Western Ave, Chicago, IL 60620.

WILLIAMS, FRANKLIN H.
Association executive. **PERSONAL:** Born Oct 22, 1917, Flushing, NY; married Shirley Broyard; children: Franklin Jr, Paul Anatole. **EDUCATION:** Lincoln Univ, AB 1941; Fordham Univ, JD 1945. **CAREER:** Natl Office NAACP, asst spec counsel 1945-50; NAACP, west coast dir 1950-59; State of CA, asst attny gen 1959-61; US Peace Corps, African reg dir 1961-63; UN Econ & Soc Council, rep 1963-65; Ghana, ambassador 1965-68; The Urban Ctr Columbia Univ, dir 1968-69; Phelps-Stokes Fund, pres. **ORGANIZATIONS:** Vchmn Jackie Robinson Found; trustee Lincoln Univ; dir New York City Opera Co, Resources for the Future, URS Inc CA; dir Borden Inc, Chem Bank, Consolidated Edison NY; trustee Spencer Found Chgo; pres The African Student Aid Fund; life mem NAACP; mem NY CA & US Supreme Ct Bars, The Century Assoc; Assoc of Black Ambassadors, chmn; Council of American Ambassadors, V Chmn. **BUSINESS ADDRESS:** President, Phelps-Stokes Fund, 10 E 87 St, New York, NY 10128.

WILLIAMS, FREDDYE HARPER
State official. **PERSONAL:** Born Jan 09, 1917, Bay Springs, MS; daughter of Fredrick Harper and Mittie Harper; married Calvin Williams, Feb 02, 1933 (deceased); children: John Frederick, James Altrice, Candy Calvina. **EDUCATION:** OU Extension School; USAF Inst of Tech,. **CAREER:** Tinker AFB, management analyst 1943-73; OK City Bd of Education, pres-member 1973-79; State of OK, state representative 1980-. **ORGANIZATIONS:** Bd mem Urban League, YWCA; mem League of Women Voters; mem Zeta Phi Beta Sorority; Natl Black Caucus of State Legislators; Natl Conf State Legislators; Federation of Colored Women's Clubs. **HONORS/ACHIEVEMENTS:** Finer Womanhood Award Zeta Phi Beta Sorority; Black History Award Langston Univ 1984-85; 1985 Citizen of the Year Omega Psi Phi Fraternity 1985; Outstanding Humanitarian Award 1985; YWCA Leadership Award 1989; YMCA Special Achievement Award 1989. **BUSINESS ADDRESS:** State Representative, State of OK, State Capitol Bldg-Rm 435A, Oklahoma City, OK 73105.

WILLIAMS, FREDERICK DANIEL CRAWFORD
Elected government official, pharmaceuticals salesman. **PERSONAL:** Born Dec 13, 1943, Marysville, OH; married Vivian Roe Andrews; children: Sharonne, Tawanna, Duane. **EDUCATION:** Villanova Univ, AB Humanities w/Sci Conc 1969, 36 graduate hours Social & Political Philosophy 1972. **CAREER:** Hosp of the Univ of Penna, medical lab technologist 1968-75; American Red Cross, medical lab technologist 1975-77; The Upjohn Co, pharmaceutical sales rep 1977-81; Warner-Lambert Techn AO Scientific Instruments Div, sales rep 1981-82; MDS Health Grp Inc, acct rep 1982-84; Borough of Lawnside, vice pres of council. **ORGANIZATIONS:** Member New Jersey Black Issues Convention; member Natl Assoc of Local Elected Officials; member Natl Black Leadership Roundtable; chaplain Omega Psi Phi - Muchap 1969-71; mem Natl Rifle Assoc. **MILITARY SERVICE:** AUS E-3 hon discharge 1961-64. **HOME ADDRESS:** 526 Pacific Ave, Apt 1007, Atlantic City, NJ 08401. **BUSINESS ADDRESS:** Vice President of Council, Borough of Lawnside, 4 E Douglas Avenue, Lawnside, NJ 08045.

WILLIAMS, GEORGE ARTHUR
Dentist. **PERSONAL:** Born Feb 09, 1925, Huntsville, AL; son of Alexander Samuel Williams (deceased) and Ola Grace Hicks Williams (deceased); married Mary Ann Brown; children: George A Jr, Chappelle Miles, Valeria Tomme, Gina Ann Reid, Michael Alexander (dec), Grayson Andrew, George Ransom Reid Jr. **EDUCATION:** Attended, Gary Jr Coll, Clark Coll, Meharry Med Coll Sch of Dentistry 1948. **CAREER:** Private Practice, dentist 1948-. **ORGANIZATIONS:** Pres Ewell Neil Dent Hon Soc Meharry Med Coll 1946; mem Implant Denture Acad 1953; mem Bd Dirs United Fund 1959; mem TrusteeBd Allen Univ 1960; pres Inter-co Med Dental & Pharm Assn 1961; served Florence Comm Relations Comm 1962-65; mem SC Del to White House Conf on Youth and Children Wash DC 1960; mem Gen Conf Los Angeles 1960; mem Aiken Found Rehab Com 1962; mem Genl Conf Cincinnati 1964; personal dedication chmn bd of dirs Boys Club of Florence 1965-; mem Genl Conf Philadelphia 1968; pres NC SC Area Council Boys Clubs Amer 1968-70; mem Chicago Dental Soc 1968-73; mem bd of Gr Florence Cof C 1970; mem bd of dirs Citizens of So Nat Bank 1977-; mem NAACP; mem Local State and Natl Dental Orgns; chmn bd of dirs Mt Zion AME Housing Projects; apptd by Gov John C West as commr Florence Darling Tech Educ 1971-84; general chrm United Negro Coll Fund, Fl Area 1984. **HONORS/ACHIEVEMENTS:** Doctor of the Yr Inter-Co Med Dental and Pharm Assn 1961; Who's Who in the S and SE 1963; Outstanding Serv Awd Boys Club of Florence 1966; Man and Boy Awd Boys Club of Florence 1968, 1977; Outstanding Comm Serv Zeta Phi Beta Sor Inc 1972-73; Citizen of the Yr Sta WYNN 1977; Professional and Humanitarian Awd Alpha Phi Alpha Frat 1978; 25 Yrs of Serv to Mankind Meharry Med Coll 1948-73; Fellow Roval Soc of Health London Eng 1973-; "This is Your Life" in recognition of 35 years of Dental Service 1983; elected chrm bd of dir C & S Bank 1985; chrm bd of dir Florence-Darlington Tech Coll 1985; honorary chrm "Florence Salute to Harry Carson" 1987; Boy's Club of America-Bronze Keystone & Serv Bar for 21 years of devoted serv 1985. **MILITARY SERVICE:** AUS Army Denatl Corp. **BUSINESS ADDRESS:** 350 N Dargan St, Florence, SC 29501.

WILLIAMS, GEORGE L., SR.
Educational administrator. **PERSONAL:** Born Aug 06, 1929, Florence, SC; married Jean McKiever; children: Sandra, George Jr, Karen, Charles. **EDUCATION:** SC State Coll, AB Pre-Law Major 1953, Masters Educ & Public Sch Admin 1961; Catholic Univ. **CAREER:** Pilgrim Ins, dist mgr 1953-55; Chestnut High School, govt/econ teacher, 1956; Whittemore High School, govt/econ teacher, 1960; Conway High School, history/geography teacher, 1968, asst principal, 1969; Coastal Carolina Coll, evening prof 1969-74; McKievers Funeral Home, gen mgr; North Myrtle Beach High School, principal 1974-86 (retired). **ORGANIZATIONS:** Mem, Natl Assn of Secondary School Principals; mem, State Assn of Secondary School Principals; mem, Horry County Assn of School Admin, Omega Fraternity Inc; adv delegate, Natl Student Council Convention, 1965; pres, Horry County Assn of School Admin, 1974; delegate, Natl Educ Convention, 1974 & 1975; pres, Horry County Educ Assn, 1975; chmn, Conway Housing Authority, 1979; discussion chmn, Natl Assn of Secondary School Principals, 1982; appointed by Pres Ronald Reagan to Local Selective Serv Bd. **HONORS/ACHIEVEMENTS:** Omega Man of the Year, Beta Tau Chap, 1975; chmn bd of trustees, Horry Georgetown Technical Coll, 1977-84. **BUSINESS ADDRESS:** Retired Principal, North Myrtle Beach High School, Route 1 Box 27, North Myrtle Beach, SC 29582.

WILLIAMS, GEORGE W., III
Educator. **PERSONAL:** Born Dec 27, 1946, Chattanooga, TN; married A Virginia Davis; children: Darius. **EDUCATION:** Lane Coll Jackson TN, BS 1968. **CAREER:** WI Educ Assn Council, organizer 1973-; Beloit Mem High School Beloit WI, math teacher 1968-73; Vice Pres 1971; Beloit Educ Assn, pres 1973; Rock Valley United Teachers, bd dirs 1972-73. **ORGANIZATIONS:** Mem WI Council Math Tchrs 1968-73; WI Educ Assn 1968-74; Official Black Caucus 1971-73; Greater Beloit Kiwanis Club; Alpha Phi Alpha; bd dirs Black Resource Personnel; del to rep assembly WI Educ Assn 1969-73; del Nat'l Educ Assn Conv 1971-73; del & chmn Resolutions Com 1971-73; bd dirs Beloit Teen Cntr 1971-73; chmn Martin Luther King Scholarship Fund. **HONORS/ACHIEVEMENTS:** Beloit Corp Scholarship Awd 1972; Outstanding Tchr of Beloit 1972. **BUSINESS ADDRESS:** WI Educ Assn, 10201 W Lincoln Ave, Milwaukee, WI.

WILLIAMS, GEORGIANNA M.
Educator. **PERSONAL:** Born Sep 23, 1938, Kansas City, KS; married Wilbert B Williams, Sr; children: Candace R Cheatem, W Ben Williams, II. **EDUCATION:** Univ of MO in Kansas City, BA 1972; UMKC, MPA 1973; Ford Fellowship Program, MPA 1973; Drake Univ, Ed Adm 1986. **CAREER:** Kansas City, MO School Dist, language dev specialist 1972-77; DM School Dist, 20th century rdg lab specialist 1977-81, reading teacher 1981-86, gifted/talented consultant 1986-. **ORGANIZATIONS:** Recording sec Central Iowa Reading Assoc 1979-; exec bd mem Iowa Future Prob Solving 1982; exec bd Iota Zeta Omega 1983; mem Alpha Kappa Alpha; bd of dirs Young Women's Resource Ctr 1985-; mem Intl Reading Assoc; s 1985-; mem Drake Univ Grad Adv Cncl; mem Assoc of Supervision & Curriculum Develop, Iowa Women in Educ Leadership, Natl Assoc of Gifted Children, Iowa Talented & Gifted Assoc, Des Moines Talented & Gifted Cncl, Des Moines Public Schools Staff Devel Adv Cncl, Professional Growth Adv Commn, Natl Alliance of Black School Educators. **HONORS/ACHIEVEMENTS:** Ford Fellowship grant 1973; Connie Belin Fellowship Univ of IA Gifted Educ 1982; Thatcher Awd Nat'l Daughters of the American Revolution 1986; mem Pi Lambda Theta Hon Frat, Phi Theta Kappa Honor Frat. **HOME ADDRESS:** 4515 63rd St, Urbandale, IA 50322. **BUSINESS ADDRESS:** Gifted/Talented Consultant, Des Moines Indep School Dist, 1800 Grand Ave, Des Moines, IA 50307.

WILLIAMS, GRADY CARTER
Educational administration. **PERSONAL:** Born Mar 01, 1939, Norfolk, VA; children: Candice R, Grady C Jr. **EDUCATION:** Norfolk State Univ, BA 1968; Columbia Univ, 1967; Yale Univ, 1968; Princeton Univ, MPA 1970. **CAREER:** DC Dept of Human Resources, program analysis officer 1974-76, pmts & collection officer 1976-81, chief office of inspection & comp 1981-83, chief office of admin 1983-. **ORGANIZATIONS:** Mem Amer Soc of Public Admin, Natl Acad of Political Sci, Conf of Minority Public Admin, Natl Forum of Black Public Admin. **HONORS/ACHIEVEMENTS:** Natl Honor Soc Secondary Schools 1957; Alpha Kappa Mu Hon Soc Norfolk State Univ 1966; Intensive Summer Studies Program Yale-Harvard-Columbia 1967-68; Fellowship Woodrow Wilson School 1968-70. **MILITARY SERVICE:** USMC corpl 3 yrs; Good Conduct Medal. **BUSINESS ADDRESS:** Chief Administrative Officer, Dept of Human Services, 801 N Capitol St NE, Washington, DC 20002.

WILLIAMS, GREGORY HOWARD
Educator. **PERSONAL:** Born Nov 12, 1943, Muncie, IN; son of James A Williams; mar-

ried Sara C; children: Natalia, Zachary. **EDUCATION:** Ball St U, BA 1966; Univ of MD, MA 1969; George Washington U, JD 1971, MPhil 1977, PhD 1982. **CAREER:** Delaware Co, IN, deputy sheriff 1963-66; US Senate, legal aide 1971-73; GW Washington Project Washington DC, coord 1973-77; Univ of IA, assoc dean law prof 1977-87. **ORGANIZATIONS:** Consultant Foreign Lawyer Training Prog Wash DC 1975-77; consultant Natl Inst (Minority Mental Health Prog) 1975; mem IA Adv Comm US Civil Rights Commn 1978-88; mem IA Law Enforcement Academy Council 1979-85. **HONORS/ACHIEVEMENTS:** Book, Law and Politics of Police Discretion 1984; article "Police Rulemaking Revisited" Journal Laws & Cont Problems 1984; article "Police Discretion" IA Law Review 1983; book The Iowa Guide to Search & Seizure 1986. **BUSINESS ADDRESS:** Prof of Law & Assoc Dean, University of Iowa, College of Law, Univ of IA, Iowa City, IA 52240.

WILLIAMS, GREGORY M.
Chief executive automotive dealership. **CAREER:** Sentry Buick Inc, Omaha NB, chief executive, 1988; Executive Pontiac-GMC Truck Inc, Tustin CA, chief executive, 1989. **BUSINESS ADDRESS:** Executive Pontiac-GMC Truck Inc, 16 Auto Center Dr, Tustin, CA 92680. *

WILLIAMS, GUS
Professional athlete. **PERSONAL:** Born Oct 10, 1953, Mt Vernon, NY. **EDUCATION:** Southern CA, Deg Commun 1975. **CAREER:** Golden State Warrior, guard 1975; Seattle Supersonics, guard 1977; Washington Bullets, guard 1984. **HONORS/ACHIEVEMENTS:** Made 2 All-Star Game appearances; 2nd team All-NBA performer following the 1980 season & chosen to 1st team in 1982; League's Comeback Player of the Year 1982;NBA All-Rookie team in 1976; All-PAC-8 selection jr & sr yrs So CA; All-Amer Honors following sr season. **BUSINESS ADDRESS:** Washington Bullets, One Harry S Truman Dr, Landover, MD 20785.

WILLIAMS, GUTHRIE J.
Clergyman. **PERSONAL:** Born Feb 05, 1914, Rochelle, LA; married Tee L Penister; children: Harold Earl, Guthrie John Jr, Timothy James. **EDUCATION:** Dunbar Jr Coll, Attended 1941; Green's Sch of Religion 1935-38; Contra Costa Jr Coll 1953;Univ of Eastern FL, DD 1970. **CAREER:** Stelle's Meml Bapt Ch, asst pastor 1937-39; Moore's Dry Dock & Co, joiner; Hopeman Brothers Const Co, joiner; Valmor Product Co, saleman; Mt Carmel Bapt Ch, presently pastor. **ORGANIZATIONS:** Organized MtCarmel Missionary Bapt Ch 1944; organized Queenly Drives 1945; co-founder Mt Calvary Educ Missionary Bapt Assn 1946-48; Concerned Allied Units for Social Elevation, human rights worker, founder, organizer, pres; CAUSE 1973-; co-founder & pres New Salem Bapt Congress "Exploratory Black-Theology" 1980; vice pres CA State Sunday Sch & Bapt Training Union Congress 1946-47; pres Interdenominational Ministerial Alliance of Richmond & Bay Cities 1951-52; chmn Bd of Christian Edn; dean Seminar of Richmond Missionary Bapt Ministers Union 1969-72; natl Treas United Negros of Am1944-45; charter mem NAACP; founder organizer Universal Non-Partisan League 1949, pres 18 yrs; instr Advanced Carpentry Parks Job Corps Ctr Pleasanton CA 1968-69; del Dist Council of Carpenters of No CA 1969. **BUSINESS ADDRESS:** 539 S 15th St, Richmond, CA 94804.

WILLIAMS, GUY KEITH
Professional athlete. **PERSONAL:** Born Jul 01, 1960, Los Angeles, CA. **EDUCATION:** Washington State, BA 1982. **CAREER:** Washington Bullets, forward-guard 1983. **HONORS/ACHIEVEMENTS:** Named the Northern CA Freshman of Year & MVP of NCAA'S Western Rgnl 1978-79. **BUSINESS ADDRESS:** Washington Bullets, One Harry S Truman Dr, Ste 510, Landover, MD 20785.

WILLIAMS, HAL
Actor. **PERSONAL:** Born Dec 14, Columbus, OH; son of Kenneth M Hairston; divorced; children: Halroy, Mark, Teri. **EDUCATION:** Attended acting classes at Theatre 40, Theatre West, and Ralph Nichols workshops. **CAREER:** TV Actor, On the Rocks, Sanford & Son, The Waltons, Harry O, Roots II-The Next Generation, Knots Landing, The White Shadow, Nobody's Perfect, Off the Wall, The Jeffersons, Caribe, SWAT, Gunsmoke, Kung-Fu, Good Times, Policewoman, The Magician, Cannon, 227, numerous others; TV movies, The 10 Commandments, Police Story, Skin Game; Film Actor, Private Benjamin, Hard Core, Nickel St, Cool Breeze; Stage Comedy, "Art Jensen," "227"; Halmarter Enterprises, Inc, Los Angeles, CA, owner. **ORGANIZATIONS:** Bd mem LA Actors Theatre 1976-; involved w/Watts Health Foundation, Natl Brotherhood of Skiers Western Region Orgn; mem Natl Brotherhood of Skiers, United States Ski Assn, Four Seasons West. **HONORS/ACHIEVEMENTS:** Keys to City of San Bernardino for participation as Grand Marshal in Annual Black History Parade 1980, 1981; Drum Major Award, Southern Christian Leadership Conference, 1986; Image Award, NAACP, 1987; awards for participation & other activities from San Bernadino, CA, & Riverside, CA. **BUSINESS ADDRESS:** Halmarter Enterprises Inc, 3870 Crenshaw Blvd, Ste 217, Los Angeles, CA 90008.

WILLIAMS, HARDY
Legislator. **PERSONAL:** Born Apr 04, 1931, Philadelphia, PA; married Carole; children: Lisa, Anthony, Kelly. **EDUCATION:** PA State U, grad; Univ of PA, LLB. **ORGANIZATIONS:** Mem PA Legislature 1970-; practicing Atty bd mem Comm Legal Svc; lawyers Com for Civil Rights; Philadelphia Council for Comm Advancement; bd of dir Children Servs; Omega Psi Phi. **BUSINESS ADDRESS:** 5939 Cobbscreek Pkwy, Philadelphia, PA 19143.

WILLIAMS, HAROLD CLEOPHAS
Government official. **PERSONAL:** Born Mar 18, 1943, Texarkana, AR; married Cal Robertson; children: Natasha, Harold II. **EDUCATION:** Multnomah Jr Coll, AS 1965; Univ of CA, cert 1967; Portland State U, BS 1969;Univ of Zagreb, cert 1972; Portland State U, MS 1972. **CAREER:** Labor Relations Div State of OR, labor relations mgr; State of OR, affirm action & dir, dir 1973-75; OR State Univ, prof 1975; Linfield Coll 1973-74; Linn-Benton Comm Coll 1973-74; Portland State Univ, dir 1969-73; Timber Lake Job Corps, supr 1966-68; Concilators Inc, consult 1970-73; KGW-TV, host. **ORGANIZATIONS:** Mem Portland StateUniv Fac Senate; bd Mem Portland Metro Steering Com; HEW Metro Goals Com; bd mem Career Oppr Prgm; chmn Model Cities Educ Com; bd mem Boise Environmental Educ Proj; mem Portland C of C; mem Portland City Club; bd mem Urban League of Grtr Portland; bd mem NAACP; bd mem OR Cncl of Christians & Jews. **HONORS/ACHIEVEMENTS:** Human Right award OR Educ Assn 1970; Outst work in educ award OR Educ Assn 1971; fed & TTT intl grant 1972; Man of the Yr Portland Jaycee 1973-; Outsdng Yng Man of Am 1974; Jet Mag 1974; nom White House Fellow 1975. **BUSINESS ADDRESS:** 155 Cottage St N E, Salem, OR 97310.

WILLIAMS, HAROLD EDWARD
Elected official. **PERSONAL:** Born Oct 12, 1949, Starkville, MS; married Ozzie Ann Hill; children: Tonya, Tracey. **EDUCATION:** MS State Univ. **CAREER:** Brookville Garden Apts, aptmt mngr 1978-; City of Starkville, alderman 1977-. **ORGANIZATIONS:** Mem NAACP 1969-; mem MS Mncpl Assoc 1977-; vice chrmn of board Prairie Oppty Inc 1979-; mem Rising Star Lodge #31 1979-; scoutmaster BSA 1980-; accred resident mngr Inst of Real Estate Mgt 1984. **HONORS/ACHIEVEMENTS:** Outstanding Young Men of Amer 1979 & 1981; Wood Badge Pushmataha Area Cncl 1985. **HOME ADDRESS:** 14 Eutaw St, Starkville, MS 39759. **BUSINESS ADDRESS:** Alderman Ward 6, City of Starkville, PO Box 629, Starkville, MS 39759.

WILLIAMS, HAROLD LOUIS
Architect. **PERSONAL:** Born Aug 04, 1924, Cincinnati, OH; married Betty L Smith. **EDUCATION:** Wilberforce Univ Acad, graduate 1943; Talladega Coll 1946-47; Miami Univ OH BArch 1952; Univ of Southern CA 1976. **CAREER:** Harold L Williams Assoc Archt & Urban Planners, owner 1960-; Paul R Williams FAIA, proj arch 1955-60; Fulton Krinsky & DelaMonte, arch draftsman, 1952-55. **ORGANIZATIONS:** Mem, AIA; founding mem, Natl Org of Minority Arch; vice pres, NOMA, 1976-77; mem, Soc of Am Registered Arch; mem Constr Specs Inst; fdg mem 1st pres Minority Arch & Planners; mem, Univ of So CA Arch Guild; LA C of C; LA Gen Plan Task Force, 1977; mem, LA Town Hall Forum; chmn, Comm for Simon Rodia's Towers in Watts 1966-70; vice pres bd of dir Avalon Carver Comm Ctr 1964; mem Western Reg Urban League; mem NAACP. **HONORS/ACHIEVEMENTS:** Rec'd achvmt award Comm Simon Rodia's Towers in Watts 1970; award for Design Excell Compton City Hall; award Design Excel LA Child Dev Cntr; Society Am Reg Arch 1973; Onyx Award NOMA 1975. **MILITARY SERVICE:** USNR radioman 1st class 1943-46. **BUSINESS ADDRESS:** 1930 Wilshire Blvd, Ste 800, Los Angeles, CA 90057.

WILLIAMS, HARRIETTE F.
Educator. **PERSONAL:** Born Jul 18, 1930, Los Angeles, CA; daughter of Orlando Flowers; married Irvin F Williams; children: Lorin, Lori. **EDUCATION:** UCLA, BA 1952; CA State Univ at LA, M Secondary Admin 1956, Genl Pupil Personnel Serv Credentials; UCLA, Genl Administration Credential, Comm Coll Adminstrn Credentials, Genl Elem Tchng Credential 1973, Doctorate Urban Educ Policy & Planning 1973. **CAREER:** Ramona HS, head counselor & acting prin 1960-63; Drew Jr HS, head counselor 1963-66; Div of Secondary Educ, proj coord & asst admin coord 1966-68;Hollenbeck Jr HS, vice prin 1968; Bethune Jr HS, vice prin 1968-70; UCLA, fellow & asst dir 1970-73; Pepperdine Univ, asst prof 1975-80; PalisadesHS, asst principal 1973-76; Foshay Jr HS, principal 1976-80; Manual Arts HS Principal 1980-82; Sr HS Div, dir of instruction 1982-85, admin opers 1985-. **ORGANIZATIONS:** Mem Natl Assn of Second Sch Principals; adv bd Honor Societies; Jr High Vice Principals Exec Comm; Sr High Asst Principals Exec Comm; Women in Educ Leadership; Statewide Assn of CA Sch Adminstrs Urban Affairs for Region 16; Council of Black Administrators; pres, ACSA Region XVI 1989; resource person Liaison Citizen Prog; chairperson Accreditation Teams for Western Assn of Schs & Colls; citywide chmn Girls' Week; sponsor for Student Week 1984-86; sponsor for Girls' Week 1981-84; exec bd mem UCLA Doctoral Alumni Assn; vice pres Cncl of Black Adminstrs 1982-83; mem Ralph Bunche Scholarship Comm, UCLA AlumniAssoc; bd of dirs mem UCLA Gold Shield, UCLA Educ Assoc, CA State Univ LA Educ Support Group; treasurer Inglewood Pacific Chapter, Links, Inc. 1987-89; pres Lullaby Guild, CHS 1987-8 9; mem Wilgandel Club 1970-. **HONORS/ACHIEVEMENTS:** Pi Lambda Theta 1952; Kappa Delta Pi 1972; Delta Kappa Gamma 1977; LA Mayor's Golden Apple Awd for Excellence in Educ Spring 1980; PTA Hon Life Membership 1975 & 1981; Sojourner Truth Awd LA Chap of the Natl Assn of Business & professional Women's Clubs; Minerva Awd; Delta Sigma Theta Inc; Sentinel Comm Awd; Affiliated Tchrs of LA Serv Awd; listed in Comm Ldrs of Amer, Comm Leaders & Noteworthy Americans, Personalities of the West & Midwest, The World Who's Who of Women, Who's Who Among Black Amers, Notable Amers, Who's Who of American Women, Who's Who in the West; Who's Who Among World Intellectuals. **BUSINESS ADDRESS:** Administrator of Operations, Los Angeles Unified Schl Dist, 644 W 17th St, Los Angeles, CA 90015.

WILLIAMS, HARVEY
Psychologist, educator. **PERSONAL:** Born in Arkansas; divorced; children: 3 Children. **EDUCATION:** BS Psychology; MS Counseling & Guidance; PhD Psychology. **CAREER:** Peoples Clinic Santa Ana, family cons; US Dept of Justice Fed Prison System, psychology instr; Williams & Assocs, dir 1959-; Orange Co Grant Jury, sgt-at-arms 1973; Long Beach Sch for Adults, faculty mem; Univ of CA Irvine, asst dean of students, psychologist. **ORGANIZATIONS:** Mem Assn of Black Psychol, Natl Assn of Adult Educ; coord Health Careers Univ of CA Irvine & Orange Co Med Ctr; mem Orange Co Commn on Criminal Justice; Orange Co Commn on Health Planning; chancellor Adv Com on Status of Women; Amer Assn of Mgmt; youth adv Pres John F Kennedy; pre-med adv UCI Coll of Med; consult Sickle Cell Anemia, Death & Dying, Teacher Training for Head Start, Human Sexuality, Health Delivery Systems; speclst Affirmative Action Guidelines, Adult Educ Curr Design; lectr Human Behavior UCI Coll of Med; mem Natl Assn for Pub Continuing & Adult Educ; mem Statutory Comm Extended Oppor Progs & Serv for the CA Comm Colls, CA Personnel & Guidance Assn, The World Congress of Professional Hypnotist, Alpha Epsilon Delta; mem Orange County GrandJury Assoc; intl lecturer Human Behavior. **HONORS/ACHIEVEMENTS:** Hon DD 1965 ACLU; Man of Yr 1968; Comm Improvement League Man of Yr 1969; Ten Gentlemen "Man of Yr" Milwaukee WI 1953; Select as Notable Amer 1976-77;Univ of CA Irvine Alumni Awd; author chap in "Attitudes on Death & Dying"; "Wisdom for Today" "Study Skill Handbook"; listed The Intl Who's Who of Intellectuals; Fellow American Biographical Inst. **BUSINESS ADDRESS:** Psychologist, University of CA, College of Medicine, Irvine, CA 92717.

WILLIAMS, HARVEY DEAN
Commanding general. **PERSONAL:** Born Jul 30, 1930, Whiteville, NC. **EDUCATION:** WV State Coll, BA polit sci; George Wash U, MS intl relations; Artillery Sch; Armed Forces Staff Coll; US Naval War Coll. **CAREER:** Vii Corps Artillery AUS Europe, comdg gen 1978-; AUS Mil Dist of Wash, DC, dep comdg gen 1977-78; AUS Mil Dist of Wash Ft Lesley

J Mcnair Wash, DC, chf of staff 1977; AUS Garrison Ft Myer, VA, comdr 1975-77; Spl Review Bd Ofc Dep Chif of Staff for Personnel AUS Wash, DC, mem 1975; 75th Field Artillery Group Iii Corps Artillery Ft Sill, OK, comdg ofcr 1973-74; AUS Control & Disarmament Agency Wash, DC, mil adv 1972-73; Naval War Coll Newport, RI, student 1971-72; Chief of Staff for Intell AUS Wash, DC, chf sec div ofc asst 1970-71. **HONORS/ACHIEVEMENTS:** Recip Legion of Merit, Bronze Star Medal with Oak Leaf Cluster, Merit Serv Medal with Oak Leaf Cluster, Air Medals, Army Comm Med with 3 Oak Leaf Clusters.

WILLIAMS, HARVEY JOSEPH
Orthodontist. **PERSONAL:** Born Sep 04, 1941, Houston, TX; married Beverly; children: Nichole, Natasha, Nitalya. **EDUCATION:** San Fernando Valley State Coll, BA 1964; UCLA, 1964-65; Howard Univ Coll Dentistry, DDS 1969; Howard Univ Coll Dentistry, Cert Ortho 1969-71. **CAREER:** General practice, 1969-71; Natl Med Assn, asst regional dir, proj 75 1971-74; Univ of California, clinical prof 1972-; Martin Luther King Jr County Hospital, staff orthodontist 1972-; private practice, orthodontist 1972-. **ORGANIZATIONS:** Mem Western Dental Soc, Natl Dental Soc, Amer Assn Ortho, Pacific Coast Soc Ortho, Amer Dental Assn, Angel City Dental Soc, Channels; mayor City of LA; comm Ind & Commerce San Fernando Valley; comm econ devel NE San Fernando Valley; bd of trustees Western Dental Soc; adv bd LA Mission Coll. **HONORS/ACHIEVEMENTS:** Certificate of Appreciation Pacific Coast Soc Ortho. **BUSINESS ADDRESS:** 8615 Crenshaw Blvd, Inglewood, CA 90305.

WILLIAMS, HAYWARD J.
Dentist. **PERSONAL:** Born Jun 27, 1944, Port Arthur, TX; married Haslett J; children: Hoyt, Jason. **EDUCATION:** LA Southwest Coll, predental major 1967;Univ of So CA, DDS 1976. **CAREER:** Dublin GA, dentist private practice 1976-; Bibb Co Health, dentist 1976. **ORGANIZATIONS:** Bd of dir NAACP 1980; vice pres Optimist Club Laurens Dublin 1980. **HONORS/ACHIEVEMENTS:** AFDH Scholarship 1976; Most Inspiring Minority StudentUniv of So CA 1976. **BUSINESS ADDRESS:** 112 C Rowe St, Dublin, GA 31021.

WILLIAMS, HAZEL BROWNE
Educator. **PERSONAL:** Born in Kansas City, MO; widowed. **EDUCATION:** Univ of KS, AB 1927; Univ of KS, MA 1929; Columbia Univ, MA 1943; Pi Lambda Theta; NY Univ, PhD 1953; Univ of Berlin, Kappa Delta Pi foreign study 1930; Alpha Kappa Alpha Foreign fellowship. **CAREER:** Univ of MO KC, prof emeritus english educ; Southern Univ, visiting lectr 1967; Atlanta Univ, 1946-47; Vienna Austria, fulbright exchange teacher 1956-57; TN A&I State Univ, prof 1953-56; NY Univ, instr 1948-51; Louisville Muni Coll, asst prof 1932-42; KC MO Public Schools, english teacher 1927-32. **ORGANIZATIONS:** Life mem NCTE; Internatl Soc of Gen Semantics; inst for Gen Semantics; MLA, AAUP; Phi Beat Kappa; Gr Assn of Chappers; MO State Tchrs Assn Golden Heritage; mem NAACP; mem KC NAACP Exec Bd; YWCA; life memUniv of MO KC Friends of the Library;Univ of KS Alumni Assn. **BUSINESS ADDRESS:** U of MO KC, 5100 Rockhill Rd, Kansas City, MO 64130.

WILLIAMS, HELEN B.
Educator. **PERSONAL:** Born Mar 29, 1916, Dewmoine, IL; widowed. **EDUCATION:** So IL U, BEd 1942; NC Coll, MSPH 1952; SIU Carbondale, MA 1962. **CAREER:** Purdue Univ, asst prof & counselor 1968-; Tougallo Coll, asst prof 1964-67; Benedict Coll Columbia SC, asst prof french 1957-62. **ORGANIZATIONS:** Mem IN Interreligious Commn Human Resources; Am AssnUniv Women; NAACP OEO. **HONORS/ACHIEVEMENTS:** Award Urban Serv 1968; Dist Educator Award Alpha Phi Alpha 1973; Lane Bryant Vol Citation 1968; Harambee Black Student Award 1975; Purdue Leather Medal Award1972; Purdue Helen Schleiman Award 1975. **BUSINESS ADDRESS:** HSSE PURDUE Univ, West Lafayette, IN 47906.

WILLIAMS, HELEN ELIZABETH
Educator. **PERSONAL:** Born Dec 13, 1933, Timmonsville, SC; children: Broderick Kevin, Terrence Meredith. **EDUCATION:** Morris College, BA 1954; Phoenix College, Certificate 1959; Atlanta Univ, MSLS 1960; Queens College, Certificate 1966; Univ of IL-Urbana, CAS 1969; Univ of WI-Madison, PhD 1983. **CAREER:** Percy Julian Elem Sch, librarian 1959-60; Brooklyn Public Library, librarian 1960-62; Mt Vernon Public Library, librarian 1963-64; Jenkins Hill High School,librarian/teacher 1964-66; Westchester Co Library System, librarian 1966; White Plains City Public Schools, librarian 1966-68, 1969-73; Bro-Dart Inc, library-consultant 1976-81; Univ of MD, lecturer 1981-83, professor 1983-. **ORGANIZATIONS:** Mem Library Adminis and Managerial Assoc 1977-80; mem Black Caucus of the Amer Library Assoc 1977-; mem MD Educ Media Organization 1981-; mem Amer Library Assoc 1977-; mem Amer Assoc of School Librarians; mem Young Adults Serv Div; mem Assoc of Library Services to Children. **HONORS/ACHIEVEMENTS:** Beta Phi Mu Intl Library Sci Honor Frat 1960-; Fellow Higher Education Act 1966; Fellow Natl Defense Educ Act 1967-68; Fellow Comm on Institutional Cooperation 1973-76; Book Reviewer School Library Journal 1981-; Disting Alumnus Awd Morris Coll 1985; Disting Alumni of the Year Citation Natl Assoc for Equal Oppor in Higher Educ 1986; listings Who's Who in Library and Information Svcs, Personalities of the South, Dir of Distinguished Americans, 1985 Networking Directory of NCTE; editor "The High/Low Consensus," Bro-Dart Publishing Co 1980; editor "Independent Reading, K-3" Bro-Dart Publishing Co 1980. **HOME ADDRESS:** 8404 Cathedral Ave, New Carrollton, MD 20784. **BUSINESS ADDRESS:** Professor of Librarianship, Univ of Maryland, College of Library & Info, Hornbake Bldg Rm 4105, College Park, MD 20742.

WILLIAMS, HENRY
Mason. **PERSONAL:** Born Nov 07, 1923, St Louis, MO; son of Aljay Williams, Sr; married Nellie S Williams; children: Soammes F. **EDUCATION:** Attended Iowa Univ, Iowa City IA; Lincoln Univ, Jefferson City MO; Heidelberg Univ, Heidelberg, Germany; and American Univ, Ft Benning GA. **CAREER:** Hanknell Construction Co, proprietor. **ORGANIZATIONS:** Supreme Grand Master of Modern Free & Accepted Masons of the World, Inc. **MILITARY SERVICE:** US Army, sergeant major. **BUSINESS ADDRESS:** Supreme Grand Master, Modern Free & Accepted Masons of the World, Inc, PO Box 1072, Columbus, GA 31901.

WILLIAMS, HENRY CALVIN
Professional athlete. **PERSONAL:** Born Dec 02, 1956, Greensboro, AL. **EDUCATION:** San Diego State. **CAREER:** Oakland Invaders, cornerback 1984-. **HONORS/ACHIEVEMENTS:** Named All-WAC and All-Am as a sr; played in Blue-Gray Game, East-West Shrine Game & Senior Bowl.

WILLIAMS, HENRY R.
Oral surgeon. **PERSONAL:** Born Nov 03, 1937, Birmingham; married Juanita; children: Leslie Alison, Mark, Matthew. **EDUCATION:** Univ Cincinnati, BS 1959; Meharry Med Coll, DDS 1967;Univ MD, resident oral surg 1970. **CAREER:** Albert B Sabin, research asst 1959-61; Leon H Schmidt, research asst 1961-63; Christ Hosp, inst med rearch 1963-67; Provident Hosp, intern 1968-70. **ORGANIZATIONS:** Mem Natl Dental Assoc; MC Dental Soc treas; bd Oral Surg; Middle Atlantic Soc & Baltimore Soc Oral Surgs; 1st Black Oral Surg ResidentUniv MD. **HONORS/ACHIEVEMENTS:** Winner Natl Elks oratorical contest 1954. **BUSINESS ADDRESS:** 2523 Liberty Hgts, Baltimore, MD 21215.

WILLIAMS, HENRY S.
Physician. **PERSONAL:** Born Aug 26, 1929, New York City, NY; son of Hiram and Margaret; married Frances S; children: Mark, Paul, Bart. **EDUCATION:** NY City Coll, BS 1950; Howard Univ, MD 1955; Brooke Army Hosp, intern 1956; Letterman Army Hosp, resd 1957-60. **CAREER:** LA Co Sheriff's Dept, radiologist; Charles R Drew Med Sch LA, clinical assoc prof of radiology; Private Practice, radiologist. **ORGANIZATIONS:** Mem CA Bd of Med Quality Assurance; diplomate Natl Bd of Med Examiners; diplomate Amer Bd of Radiology; fellow Amer Coll of Radiology; fellow Amer Coll of Angiology; mem LA Radiological Soc; mem CA Radiological Soc; mem Natl Med Assn, Golden State Med Assn; mem Charles R Drew Medical Soc; mem Amer Medical Assn; mem CA Med Assn; mem LA Co Medical Assn; past mem CA Physicians Service; past mem The Harvard Sch; past mem Joint Commn Accreditation of Hosps; past chmn Urban Health Comm CA Med Assn; past counselor CA Med Assn. **MILITARY SERVICE:** AUS Med Corps maj. **BUSINESS ADDRESS:** Radiologist, 3756 Santa Rosalia, Ste #203, Los Angeles, CA 90008.

WILLIAMS, HERB KEITH
Professional athlete. **PERSONAL:** Born Feb 16, 1959, Columbus, OH. **EDUCATION:** Ohio State, 1981. **CAREER:** Indiana Pacers, forward/center 1981-. **ORGANIZATIONS:** Holds bsktbl camp each summer in hometown. **HONORS/ACHIEVEMENTS:** Twice has rejected nine shots in a single game most by a Pacer in an NBA game; 3 time honorable mentn All-Am selection; fnshd career as Ohio State's all-time leading scorer (2011); named Ohio's Class AAA Player of Year. **BUSINESS ADDRESS:** Indiana Pacers, Two West Washington St, Ste 510, Indianapolis, IN 46204.

WILLIAMS, HERBERT C.
Agency director. **PERSONAL:** Born Jan 17, 1930, Redbird, OK; married Ruthie M; children: 5 Children. **CAREER:** Am Woodmens Life Ins Co, agency dir 19620. **ORGANIZATIONS:** Mem Nat Assn of Life Underwriters; vP Millionaires Club Nat Inst Assn; bd mem Underwriters Assn; life mem NAACP 1972-; Elks Lodge 1959; Ch Educ Com Elks 1974; mem New Breed Repub Club 1964 Pres 1974; adv bd mem KWKI Radio 1972; YMCA; Friendship Bapt Ch. **HONORS/ACHIEVEMENTS:** Awared Certificate Science of Personal Achievement 1963; Life Ins Agency Mngmt Assn 1972; Nat Ins Assn Certificate of Achievmens 1964. **BUSINESS ADDRESS:** 845 Minnesota Ave, Kansas City, KS 66101.

WILLIAMS, HERBERT LEE
Physician. **PERSONAL:** Born Dec 23, 1932, Citronelle, AL; divorced; children: Lezli, Candace. **EDUCATION:** Talladega Coll, BA 1952; Atlanta U, MS 1954; Meharry Med Coll, MD 1958. **CAREER:** Surgeon pvt prac 1965-. **ORGANIZATIONS:** Pres Herbert Williams MD Inc; mem Alpha Omega Alpha Hon Med Soc; diplomate Am Bd Surgery; flw Am Coll Surgeons; Intl Coll Surgeons; Am SocAbdominal Surgeons Chf sug serv Williams AFB Hosp 1963-65. **MILITARY SERVICE:** USAF maj. **BUSINESS ADDRESS:** 575 E Hardy St, Inglewood, CA 90301.

WILLIAMS, HERMAN
Elected official. **PERSONAL:** Born Dec 07, 1943, Washington; children: Herman III, Daniel, James. **EDUCATION:** Academy of Health Sciences, 1973; Baylor Univ, 1975; Montgomery College, 1980. **CAREER:** Upper Maple Ave Citizens Assn, liaison 1980; Commission on Landlord Tenant Affairs, commissioner 1980-82; Metropolitan Washington Planning & Housing Assn, bd member 1980-82; Metropolitan Council of Governments, committee member 1983-. **ORGANIZATIONS:** Bd of directors United Planning Assn 1964-65; founder Winchester Tenants Assn 1978; vice pres Parkview Towers Tenant Assn 1980; city-county liaison Upper Maple Ave Citizens Assn 1981; organizer Takoma Parks Ceremony in honor of Martin Luther King, Jr 1982-; instrumental in redistricting Takoma Park voting policy 1982; establishing Dept of Housing 1983; organized Takoma Park Youth Day. **HONORS/ACHIEVEMENTS:** Elizabeth Skou Achievement Awd Winchester Tenants Assn 1978; 2nd Black elected official in Takoma Park, MD since 1890; only Black elected official in Montgomery County, MD; selected for Honorary Dinner Committee NAACP 1984-85. **MILITARY SERVICE:** AUS specialist 5 1974-77; Letter of Commendation Good Conduct Natl Defense 1974-77; Expert Field Medical Badge 1976. **HOME ADDRESS:** 7600 Maple Ave Apt 1711, Takoma Park, MD 20912. **BUSINESS ADDRESS:** City Councilman, City of Takoma Park, 7500 Maple Ave, Takoma Park, MD 20912.

WILLIAMS, HILDA YVONNE
Administrator. **PERSONAL:** Born Aug 17, 1946, Washington, NC. **EDUCATION:** Hunter Coll, 1978-. **CAREER:** Teachers Coll, exec sec 1964-67; Bus Careers, exec 1967-69; Esquire Mag, admin asst 1969-73; RCA Corp, admin asst 1973-75, reg promotion mgr 1975-87; Polygram Records, reg promo dir 1987-. **ORGANIZATIONS:** Mem Frat of Rec Exec 1976-; mem Black Music Assn 1973-; mem NAACP 1976; co-producer 5th Annual Superstar Celebrity Games 1980. **BUSINESS ADDRESS:** Dir, Polygram Records, 810 7th Ave, New York, NY 10019.

WILLIAMS, HOMER LAVAUGHAN
Physician. **PERSONAL:** Born Dec 10, 1925, Kalamazoo, MI; married Ruth; children: Aaron, Valerie, Andre. **EDUCATION:** OH Coll Chiropody, DSC 1954; Western MI U, BS 1962; HowardUniv Sch Med, MD 1966; Adron Gen Hosp, Dr ortho surg 1971. **CAREER:** Orthopaedist, self. **ORGANIZATIONS:** Mem Charles Drew Soc; LA Co Med

Assn; AMA; Nat Med Assn Chmn orthopaedic & bd Morningside Hosp. **HONORS/ACHIEVEMENTS:** W Adams Hosp Pub "Intraosseous Vertebral Venography in Comparison with Myelograph in Diagnosing Disc Disease" 1969. **MILITARY SERVICE:** AUS cp 1944-46. **BUSINESS ADDRESS:** 336 E Hillcrest Blvd, Inglewood, CA 90301.

WILLIAMS, HOSEA L.
State representative. **PERSONAL:** Born Jan 05, 1926, Attapulgus, GA; married Juanita Terry; children: Barbara Jean, Elizabeth LaCenia, Hosea Lorenzo II, Andre Jerome, Yolanda Felicia. **EDUCATION:** Morris Brown Coll, BA Chemistry; Atlanta Univ, MS. **CAREER:** Crusader Newspaper, publisher 1961-; SCLC, natl prog dir 1967-69, natl exec dir 1969-71, reg vice pres 1970-71, organizer & pres Metro Atlanta 1972-; Poor Peoples Union of Amer; organizer & pres 1973-; Martin Luther King Jr People's Church of Love Inc, pastor 1972-; GA State Rep 54th House Dist, rep 1974-; Kingwell Chem Corp, pres 1975-76; SE Chem Mfg & Distrib Corp, fndr ceo 1976-; So Christian Leadership Conf, natl exec dir 1977-79; Pres RW Reagan, advisor 1980-; Peoples Crusader newspaper 1981; Voice of the Crusader TV Show 1982; Black Promoters Survival Council 1983; Afro-Amer Japanese Intl Econ Inst Inc 1984; City of Atlanta GA, city councilman. **ORGANIZATIONS:** Mem Phi Beta Sigma Inc, Natl Order of Elks & Free & Accepted Masons, Southern Christian Leadership Conf, NAACP, Disabled Amer Veterans, Veterans of Foreign Wars, Amer Legion, Natural Sci Soc, Black Image Theatre, Metro Summit, GA's Voter League, Amer Chem Soc, Natl Black Leaders for Pres Reagan, Natl Black Coalition, Natl Comm of Black Churchmen, Natl Democratic Party. **HONORS/ACHIEVEMENTS:** Comm Serv Awd Delta Sigma Theta Sor Inc 1963; Cause of Freedom in the Tradition of True Democracy GA State 1963; Unselfish Public Serv in the Field of Race Relations Awd Coastal Empire Emancipation Assn 1962; Ten Yrs of Satisfactory Serv Awd US Dept of Agriculture 1961; Civic Achievement Awd US Dept of Agriculture Marketing Serv 1956; Chapter of the Yr Awd Atlanta Chap SCLC 1973; Afro-Amer Patrolmen's League Comm Serv Awd 1975; Civic Achievement Awd Comm & Race Relations Natl Alumni Assn of Morris Brown Coll; Citizen of the Yr Awd Eta Omega Frat Inc 1975; Business of the Yr Awd Bronner Bros 1975; Civil Rights Leader of the Yr Awd Black Media Inc Black Publishers of Amer 1975; Most Courageous Leadership in the Freedom Movement Awd NAACP 1960-61; SCLC Natl Affiliate of the Yr Awd Natl Southern Christian Leadership Conf 1963; Comm Action Agency Awd Tuskegee AL 1976; Antler Guard Awd IBPOE of W of the Grand Exalter Ruler of the Elks 1954; Civil Rights Demonstrator of the Decade (arrested 124 times). **MILITARY SERVICE:** AUS staff sgt 1944-46. **BUSINESS ADDRESS:** City Councilman, City of Atlanta, 1959 Boulevard Dr SE, Atlanta, GA 30317.

WILLIAMS, HOWARD COPELAND
Supervisory agricultural economist. **PERSONAL:** Born May 29, 1921, Quitman, GA; married Blanche; children: Stephanie, Howard. **EDUCATION:** BS, MS, PhD 1953. **CAREER:** A&T State Univ, assoc prof 1947-51; OH State Univ, assoc prof 1953-61; Nommensen Univ Medan Indonesia, visiting prof 1961-63; Africa Regional Study by the Big Ten Univ's to evaluate AID Univ Contracts Worldwide, home campus liaison 1965-67; OH State Univ, prof 1964-71; Office of Specl Trade Rep Exec Office of the Pres, sr agr advisor 1973-75; ASCS Office of Admin, dir analysis staff 1976-81; ASCS, dir commodity analysis div 1981-. **HONORS/ACHIEVEMENTS:** Social Sci Res Council Post-Doc Fellowship NC State Univ 1956; Soc Sci Council Travel Grant to attend Intl Conf of Agr Economists 1964; Mershon Natl-Security Prog Grant for Study of European Economic Comm. **MILITARY SERVICE:** AUS pfc 1942-46. **BUSINESS ADDRESS:** Director/Analysis Staff, ASCS, Rm 234 W, 14th & Independence Ave SW, Washington, DC 20250.

WILLIAMS, HUBERT
Police director. **PERSONAL:** Born Aug 19, 1939, Savannah, GA; married Annette; children: Alexis, Susan, Hubert Carl. **EDUCATION:** Elec Engr Tech, Cert 1962; John Jay Coll of Criminal Justice, AS 1968, BS 1970; Harvard Law Sch, Fellow 1970-71; RutgersUniv Sch of Law, jD 1974; FBI Acad Nat Exec Inst, 1977. **CAREER:** City of Newark Police Dept, police dir 1974-; Newark High-impact Anti-crime Prgm, exec dir 1973-74; Newark Police Dept, police offcr 1962-73; Rutgers Sch of Criminal Justice, adjunct prof. **ORGANIZATIONS:** Intl Assn of Chiefs of Police; Am Soc of Criminology; adv com Nat Inst; pres Nat Orgn of Black Law Enforcement Offcrs; adv bd Police Found Exec Training Sem 1976; selection com mem City of Stanford CT Pol Ice Chief 1977; FBI Acad Nat Exec Inst 1977; New Scotland Yard Eng 1977; selection com mem City of LA Police Chief 1978; pres Nat Assn of Police Com Relations Ofcrs 1971-73; Mayors Educ Task Force 1971-76; bd of of dir Nat Assn of Urban Criminal Justice Planners 1972-74; Intl Assn of Chiefs of Police 1973-; turstee Tw Hundred Club 1973-; bd of dir Police Exec & Research Forum 1975-; camp mgmt com UMCA 1975-78; Am Bar Assn 1976-; fdng pres Nat Orgn of Black Law Enforcement Exec 1976-79; NJ Bar Assn 1976-; Fed Bar Assn 1977-; St & Com Educ Task Force 1977-; adv bd Esex Co Coll Crim Justice Prgm 1978-; consult to pub safety com Nat League of Cities 1978-; edit adv bd mem John Jay Coll Jour of Am Acad of Professional Law Enforcement 1978-; mem 74th Dist Rotary Intl. **HONORS/ACHIEVEMENTS:** Research Fellow Harvard Law Sch for Criminal Justice; Bronze Shields & Merit Awds 1965; honored Com for Incentive for Human Achvmt 1967; Humanitarian Awd Newark Businessmens Assn 1968; Appcrt Awd S Ward Little League 1970; ldrshp Awd Nat Assn of Police Comm Relations Ofcr 1973; achvmt Awd Police AcadAssn 1974; Man of Yr Awd 4H 1974; Apprct Awd Spcl Police Assn 1975; Achvmt Awd Bronze Shields Orgn 1975; Comm Serv Awd Speedy Olympics 1975; Recog of Excel Awd Dr King Comm Ctr 1976; spcl Crime Recog Awd NJ Voice Newspaper 1977; spcl Narcotic Enforcement Awd Drug Enforcement Adminstrn 1977; Whos Who in East 1978; Whos Who Among Black Am 1977-78; Whos Who in Govt 1977; Apprct Awd Newark Intl Airports 50th Anniv 1978; publ articles various magazines 1978-79. **BUSINESS ADDRESS:** 22 Franklin St, Newark, NJ 07102.

WILLIAMS, HUGH HERMES
Physician, educator. **PERSONAL:** Born Nov 11, 1945, Port of Spain, Trinidad and Tobago;son of Hugh L Williams and Norma D Williams; married Leandra M, Jul 08, 1977; children: Kelly Victoria, Janelle Victoria. **EDUCATION:** Attended Univ of West Indies, Kingston, Jamaica 1965-72, Howard Univ, Washington DC 1974-76, McMaster Univ, Hamilton, Ontario, Canada 1976-78, Cleveland Clinic Foundation, Cleveland, OH 1978-80; received BSC and MD. **CAREER:** Univ of Tennessee, Memphis, instructor 1980-81, asst prof of medicine 1981-. **ORGANIZATIONS:** Member of Amer Society of Nephrology, Natl Kidney Foundation, Intl Society of Nephrology, Amer Society of Internal Medicine, Amer Heart Assn; fellow of Amer College of Physicians. **HONORS/ACHIEVEMENTS:** Author of "Reversible Nephrotic Range Proteinuria and Renal Failure in Athero Embolic Renal Disease," 1989, and "Altered Sensitivity of Osmotically Stimulated Vasopressin Release in Quadriplegic Subjects," 1989. **HOME ADDRESS:** 2926 Meadow Wood Cove, Germantown, TN 38138.

WILLIAMS, IOLA (NEE CRAFT)
City council member. **PERSONAL:** Born Feb 02, 1936, Hattiesburg, MS; married George E Williams; children: Jennifer G, Audrey Lynn, Beverly E, George III, Vincent J, Ila N, Kevin L. **EDUCATION:** Attended, Jackson State Coll; Yuba Coll Nrsg Prog, grad 1962. **CAREER:** Various nursing positions 1962-72; Yerba Buena HS, dir health off 1972-73; home sch cons, 1973-79; Crisis Intervent Ctr for Adoles Eastside Sch Dist, coord 1975-79; City of San Jose, mem city council 1979-. **ORGANIZATIONS:** Consult sch dist on Comm Involve Crisis Interr Bd of Educ Franklin McKinley Elem Dist; mem bd of dir Natl Caucus of Black Sch Bd Mems 1974-; membd of dir CA Coal Black Sch Bd Mem 1975-; mem bd dir CA Elected Women 1975-; mem CA Sch Bd Assn Student Needs Min Educ Comm 1975-; chmn Stud Needs Min Educ Comm; pres Franklin McKinley Sch Bd 1976-; City of San Jose Proj '75 Commr 1975; mem City Genl Plan Comm 1975-76; City Chart Comm 1976-; mem Measure B Fed Rev Task Force 1977. **HONORS/ACHIEVEMENTS:** Employee of the Yr Santa Clara Co CA 1975; Outstanding Vol Cert Santa Clara Co CA 1976. **BUSINESS ADDRESS:** City Councilwoman, City of San Jose, 801 N First St, Room 600, San Jose, CA 95110.

WILLIAMS, IRA JOSEPH
Minister. **PERSONAL:** Born Aug 05, 1926, Elizabeth City, NC; married Elsie Moore; children: Pamela, Anthony, Angela. **EDUCATION:** Store Coll; Kingsley Sch of Rel, BTh 1952, BD 1954; Am Bible Coll, DD; Union Chris Bible Inst, AB 1972; Howard U; Shaw U, Cert in Social Studies & Bapt Doctrine;Univ of NC; Pacific Coll, M 1974. **CAREER:** Antioch Bapt Ch Norfolk VA, minister. **ORGANIZATIONS:** Pres & found Peoples Pleasing Prod Ltd; organizer & 1st pres Washington Br NAACP; served on NC Com of young cits for Humphrey-muskie; organized quarterly meeting unino in Washington NC; served as pres for 9 yrs; moderated Washington Areas Ministers Alliance; served as Exec Sec NC Bapt Dist Conv; memCivil Rights Coord Team Nashville mem exc bd old eastern bapt assn of nC; past mem beaufort co mental hlth Assn; Nat Pres United Chris Front for Brotherhood; moderator Old Dominion Missionary Bapt Assn; former vice chmn Berkeley Neighborhood Avd Bd; exec bd of VA Bapt St Conv; Mayors Adv Com; Atlantic Nat Bank Adv Bd; past exec sec United Chris Front for Brotherhood; former sec Tidewater Metro Bapt Ministers Conf; former Chancellor Union Chris Bible Inst; exec bd Norfolk Com for Improvement of Edn; life mem NAACP; former pres Norfolk Chap NAACP; mem AOA Fvrat Inc; mem bd dir Organist Guild, Hampton Ministers Conf; Evangelical Bd of Nat Bapt Conv. **HONORS/ACHIEVEMENTS:** Recip awd United Eastern Bapt Dist Conv of NC, ldrshp roll in Chris Educ 1963; awd of honor in Washington NC otstndng Rec Dir 1967; plaque Greenville NC Educ Forum, Cits Adv Com otstndng serv in Human Relations & Social Rehab 1968; proclamation City of Norfolk Humanitarian Work styled as Soc Amb for Goodwill; Citation of Honor, Womens Aux of Norfolk Comm Hosp; comm Leaders & Noteworthy Am 1976-77; Humanitarian Plaque, SE Tidewater Oppor Proj; Manof Yr WRAP Radio Station Tidewater VA 1979; Mason 32 Deg; author of several pamphlets. **MILITARY SERVICE:** USN WWII, Korean War. **BUSINESS ADDRESS:** President, People Pleasing Products Inc, Box 476, Norfolk, VA 23501.

WILLIAMS, IRA LEE
Union official. **PERSONAL:** Born Jul 30, 1930, Benson, NC; son of Sam Williams and Carrie Williams; children: Sharon. **EDUCATION:** North Carolina Central Univ, BA, 1961; North Carolina Central Law School, JD, 1964. **CAREER:** New York, NY, Bd of Educ, teacher, 1964-68; Marion Gaines Hill, PC, clerk, 1970-72; New York, NY, legal staff, 1972-79; Bronze Amer Sports Network, Inc, chmn of the bd, 1973-86; SSEU Local 371, vice pres, 1983-86; video tape productions, entertainment agent, producer, sports promoter, 1983-86. **ORGANIZATIONS:** Pres, United Neighbors Civic Assn, 1964-68; personnel dir, Baisley Park Coalition, 1970-78; mem, Natl Bar Assn, 1970-86; natl pres, Natl Orgn for Athletic Devel, Inc. **MILITARY SERVICE:** AUS, corpl, 1948-53. **HOME ADDRESS:** 140-17-160 St, Jamaica, NY 11434. **BUSINESS ADDRESS:** Vice Pres, SSEU Local 371, 817 Broadway, New York, NY 10003.

WILLIAMS, J. BEDELL
Business executive. **PERSONAL:** Born Mar 03, 1923, Woodville, MS; married Archanna Porter. **EDUCATION:** SD St U, UCSD. **CAREER:** Bedell Williams Mens Wear, owner. **ORGANIZATIONS:** Pres Assn of Bus; Worshipful Master of Masons; Elks; NAACP; BRC Mayors Com adv bd. **HONORS/ACHIEVEMENTS:** Recipient San Diego Bus Achivement Awd. **MILITARY SERVICE:** AUS 1944-46. **BUSINESS ADDRESS:** 5055 Fed blvd, San Diego, CA.

WILLIAMS, JAMES ARTHUR
Educator. **PERSONAL:** Born May 09, 1939, Columbia, SC; children: Angela, Melody, James II. **EDUCATION:** Allen U, BAMusic Ed 1960; Univ IL, MS 1964. **CAREER:** Stillman Coll, chmn Dept of Music choral dir; CA Johnson HS SC, educator 1960-69; Morris Coll, 1965 & 68; Univ IL, Allen Univ, Columbia, SC Public School; Sidney Pk CME Church SC, choir dir; Bethlehem Baptist Church SC. **ORGANIZATIONS:** Guest cond All City HS Chorus SC; Columbia SC All City HS Chorus; Univ AL Tuscaloosa AL; Tuscaloosa Comm Singers AL; adjudicator Univ AL 1972; Tuscaloosa Co Jr Miss Pageant 1972; past pres Palmetto St Music Tchrs Assn; mem Am Choral Dir Assn; Music Educators Nat Conf; Alpha Phi Alpha Frat Inc; bd dir Columbia SC Choral Soc 1967-69; steering com Mus Arts Dr; bd dir Tuscaloosa Comm Singers; Music Com Tuscaloosa Arts & Humanities Council.

WILLIAMS, JAMES DEBOIS
Communications director. **PERSONAL:** Born Nov 05, 1926, Baltimore, MD. **EDUCATION:** Temple Univ, BA 1948. **CAREER:** Philadelphia Tribune, reporter 1950-51; The Carolinian, city editor 1951-53; Afro-Am, city editor 1953-57; Baltimore Afro-Amer, mng editor 1959-64; Morgan St Coll, visiting prof 1961-63; Washington Afro-Am, editor-mgr 1964-67; Office of Econ Oppor, dir pub affairs for comm act prog 1967-68, deputy dir 1968-69; US Comm on Civ Rights, dir off of info & publ 1970-72; Natl Urban League, commun dir 1972-. **ORGANIZATIONS:** Mem Howard Univ, PA Newspaper Publ Assn, Towson St Tchr Coll; MD-DE Press Assn; mem Natl Newspaper Publ Assn; DC Police Dept; consult Census Bur& Pres Comm on Rural Pov; mem US Inter-Agcy Task Force on Inner-City Comm; mem Exec Comm Natl Commun Coun of Health & Welfare Agcy; v chpsn AdvCounc of Nat Org to Corp for Pub Broad; mem Pub Rel Soc of Amer; mem Adv Bd REBOP TV Prog. **HON-**

ORS/ACHIEVEMENTS: Merit Awd Balt Branch NAACP 1961; Best Feature story of the yr MD-DE Press Assn 1963; Best Editorial of the Yr MD-DE Press Assn 1964; 2nd Prize Best Edit of the Yr Publ Assn 1965; Best Feature Story of the yr Natl Newspaper Publ Assn 1965; Newsman of the Yr Capital Press Club; Awd for Serv Off of Econ Oppor 1968; Excell in Commun Howard Univ 1973; author "The Black Press & The First Amendment"; editor "The State of Black America". **BUSINESS ADDRESS:** Communications Dir, Natl Urban League, 500 E 62nd St, New York, NY 10021.

WILLIAMS, JAMES E., JR.
Army officer. **PERSONAL:** Born Aug 28, 1936, Philadelphia, PA; married Lois Collins; children: Karl, Robert, Renee. **EDUCATION:** West Chester PA Univ, BS 1959; Siena Coll, MS 1968. **CAREER:** Montgomery Ward & Co Inc, field personnel mgr 1984-86, hq personnel mgr 1986-; Dept of Military Sci Howard U, chmn/prof 1976-79; Honolulu Dist Recruiting Command Honolulu, comdg officer 1974-76; Armed Forces Examining Entrance Station Honolulu, commanding ofcr 1973; CORDS Adv Team MACV Vietnam, operation adviser 1972; 3d Bn 26 Artillery, exec ofcr 1970-71; 101st Airborne Div Vietnam, insp gen 1969; Mil Sci Siena Coll, asst prof 1965-68; Btry A 2d Bn 73d Arty Germany, commanding ofcr 1964; Btry A 2d Rocket/Howitzer Bn 73 Artillery Germany, commanding ofcr 1963. **ORGANIZATIONS:** Mem Siena Coll Alumni Assn; mem HowardUniv Alumni Assn; life mem Alpha Phi Alpha; mem Assn of US Army; life mem NAACP; West Chester State Alumni Assn;Alpha Phi Alpha; mem The Retired Officers Assoc, Aircraft Owners & Pilots Assoc. **HONORS/ACHIEVEMENTS:** Listed in Who's Who Among Students in Amer Univs & Colls 1958-59; Anne Hines Allen Human Rights Awd The Mainline Branch NAACP 1979; Disting Alumni Awd West Chester Univ Alumni Assoc 1978. **MILITARY SERVICE:** 5th Training Battalion Ft Sill OK commanding ofcr 1979-81; AUS Field Artillery Training Ctr Ft Sill OK exec ffcr 1981, dep commander 1982; HQ US Army Depot System Command Chambersburg PA, dir security plans & operations 1983-84 retired col 1984. **BUSINESS ADDRESS:** Personnel Manager, Montgomery Ward & Co Inc, 1 Montgomery Ward Plaza, Chicago, IL 60671.

WILLIAMS, JAMES EDWARD
Attorney. **PERSONAL:** Born Jan 02, 1955, Alexandria, LA; married Sharon Valencia; children: Tenisha Nicole. **EDUCATION:** New Mexico State Univ, BA 1976, MA 1977; Georgetown Univ Law Ctr JD 1980; Columbia Univ Law Sch/Parker Sch of Foreign & Comparative Law, attended 1986. **CAREER:** Honeywell Inc, contract mgmt 1980-81, corporate atty 1981-. **ORGANIZATIONS:** Mem Delta Theta Phi Law Frat 1979; mem EEO Adv Council Honeywell 1980; mem United Way Solicitation Comm 1980-81; mem Amer Bar Assn 1981; mem MN Bar Assn 1981; mem MN Minority Lawyers Assn 1981; vice pres FOCUS 1981; adv United Way Allocations Comm 1981-82; advisor Junior Achievement 1981-83; bd mem African American Cultural Ctr 1981-84; mem City of Golden Valley Human Rights Comm 1982-; prog chmn West Suburban Black History Month Comm 1982-; prog chmn Rotary Intl 1984-; mem Govs Art's Task Force 1985. **HONORS/ACHIEVEMENTS:** Who's Who in Amer Colls & Univs; Omega Psi Phi Dist Scholar; Natl Soc of Sons of the Amer Revolution Medal, Ribbon of Excellence, Academic Cluster, Arnold Air Soc; Phi Kappa Phi; Rhodes Scholar Nominee 1976; Outstanding Young Men of America 1981, 1984. **BUSINESS ADDRESS:** Senior Counsel, Honeywell Inc, Honeywell Plaza, Minneapolis, MN 55408.

WILLIAMS, JAMES H., JR.
Educator. **PERSONAL:** Born Apr 04, 1941, Newport News, VA; son of James H. Williams and Margaret L. Mitchell; children: James H III, Sky M M. **EDUCATION:** MA Inst Tech, SB 1967, SM 1968; Trinity Coll, Cambridge Univ PhD 1970. **CAREER:** Newport News Shipbuilding & Dry Dock Co, apprentice-sr design engr 1960-70; Intl Consultant, 1970-87; MIT, asst prof, asst prof of mech engrg 1970-87. **ORGANIZATIONS:** Mem NTA 1975-87, ASME 1978-87, ASNT 1978-87; fellow I Diag Eng 1983-87; advisor Natl Science Foundation 1985-87. **HONORS/ACHIEVEMENTS:** Charles F Bailey Bronze Silver & Gold Medals 1961-63; Ferguson Scholar MIT 1963-67; So Fellowship Fund Fellow Cambridge Univ 1968-70; Ralph Teetor Awd SAE 1974; Everett Moore Baker Awd, Outstanding Undergrad Tech MIT 1973; Grant NSF Faculty Partic 1974; duPont professorship; Edgerton professorship; Den Hartog Disting Ed Awd 1981. **BUSINESS ADDRESS:** Prof of Mechanical Engrg, MA Inst of Technology, 77 Massachusetts Ave Rm 3-360, Cambridge, MA 02139.

WILLIAMS, JAMES HIAWATHA
Educational administration. **PERSONAL:** Born Sep 10, 1945, Montgomery, AL; son of James Hiawatha Williams and Johnnie Mae Robinson-Strother; married Odessa Elaine Godley, Mar 19, 1983; children: James M, John V (deceased), Kasha G, Jameelah I. **EDUCATION:** Los Angeles City Coll, Los Angeles CA, AA, 1967; California State Univ, Los Angeles CA, BA, 1973; Pepperdine Univ, Los Angeles Ca, MS, 1974; Washington State Univ, Pullman WA, PhD, 1983. **CAREER:** California State Polytechnic Univ, Pomona CA, asst prof 1977-81, assoc dean & assoc prof 1980-85, dean of Coll of Arts & full prof 1988-. **ORGANIZATIONS:** Mem, Phi Delta Kappa, 1977-; mem, Urban Affairs Assn, 1980-; pres, Pomona Valley NAACP, 1984-86; mem, Phi Beta Delta, 1988-; exec bd, Natl Assn for Ethnic Studies, 1988-. **HONORS/ACHIEVEMENTS:** Prism of Excellence Award, Jerry Voorhis Claremont Democratic Club, 1986; Martin Luther King Jr Humanitarian Award, Pomona Valley NAACP, 1987; Services to Youth, Claremont Area Chapter Links Inc, 1988. **BUSINESS ADDRESS:** Dean, College of Arts, California State Polytechnic University, 3801 West Temple Ave, 5-158, Pomona, CA 91768.

WILLIAMS, JAMES R.
Attorney, judge. **PERSONAL:** Born Sep 16, 1933, Lowndes Co, MS; married Catherine; children: Michael, Jacqueline. **EDUCATION:** Univ of Akron, BA, JD 1965. **CAREER:** Northern Dist of OH, US Atty 1978-; Parms Purnell, Stubbs & Williams, former partner 1969-78; City of Akron, former councilman-at-large 1970-78. **ORGANIZATIONS:** Former treas Akron Bar Assn; former pres Summit Co Legal Aid Soc; natl pres Alpha Phi Alpha Frat Inc. **HONORS/ACHIEVEMENTS:** Outstanding Achievement Awd Alpha Phi Alpha 1973; Liberian Humane Order of African Redemption Citation, Dr William R Tolbert Jr, Pres of Rep of Liberian 1973; TopHat Awd, Pittsburgh Courier 1977; Ebony's 100 Most Influential Black Americans 1980. **MILITARY SERVICE:** AUS 1953-55. **HOME ADDRESS:** 1733 Brookwood Dr, Akron, OH 44313.

WILLIAMS, JAMES THOMAS
Physician, educator. **PERSONAL:** Born Nov 10, 1933, Martinsville, VA; son of Harry Williams and Ruth Williams; married Jacqueline; children: Lawrence, Laurie. **EDUCATION:** Howard Univ, BS 1954, MD 1958. **CAREER:** Philadelphia Gen Hosp, intern 1958-59; DC Gen & Freedmens Hosp, resd 1959-62, 1964-65; Howard Univ Coll Med, fellow endocrinology 1965-67; DC Gen Hosp, physician 1967-; Howard Univ Hosp, physician 1967-; Howard Univ Coll of Med, asst prof 1967-74; Assoc Prof 1974-85; Professor 1985. **ORGANIZATIONS:** Mem Amer Bd Internal Med 1967,74, Amer Diabetes Assoc Cert 1967, Med Officer Home Care Prog Dept Human Resources 1968-, Amer Bd Endocrinology & Metabolism 1972, Medico-Chirurgical Soc, Natl Med Assoc, Med Soc DC, Endocrine Soc; fellow Amer Coll Physicians; re-cert by Amer Bd of Internal Med 1980;certified,Am Brd of Internal Med 1967; Am Brd Endocrinology & Metobolism 1972;Re-certified, Am Brd Internal Med 1974-80. **MILITARY SERVICE:** AUS MC capt 1962-64. **BUSINESS ADDRESS:** Professor of Medicine, HowardUniv Coll of Med, 2041 Georgia Ave NW, Washington, DC 20060.

WILLIAMS, JAMYE COLEMAN
Educator. **PERSONAL:** Born Dec 15, 1918, Louisville, KY; married McDonald; children: Donna W Selby. **EDUCATION:** Wilberforce Univ, BA 1938; Fisk Univ, MA 1939; Ohio State Univ, PhD 1959. **CAREER:** Edward Waters Coll, Jacksonville FL, educator 1939-40; Shorter Coll Little Rock, 1940-42; Wilberforce Univ OH, 1942-56; Morris Brown Coll, 1956-58; Tennessee State Univ, dept head of communications; 1959. **ORGANIZATIONS:** Exec comm Nashville Branch NAACP 1960-; sec Tennessee Voters Council 1969-; sec bd dir comm Equity & Economic Devel Corp 1973-; mem bd of governors Natl Council of Ch 1976-82; mem Speech Comm Assn, Amer Assn Univ Prof, Amer Women Radio & TV, Theta Alpha Phi, Pi Kappa Delta, Kappa Delta Pi; chmn bd dir John W Work III Found; mem Links Inc, Delta Sigma Theta. **HONORS/ACHIEVEMENTS:** Outstanding Teacher Award 1976; Teacher of the Year, TN State Univ 1968; Woman of the Year, Nashville Davidson & Co Business & Professional Women's Club 1978; Citizen of the Year, Nashville Alumnae Chapter Delta Sigma Theta 1979; co-editor "The Negro Speaks the Rhetoric of Contemporary Black Leaders"; editor AME Review. **BUSINESS ADDRESS:** Dept Head of Communications, Tennessee State University, 3500 John Merritt Blvd, Nashville, TN 37203.

WILLIAMS, JANICE L.
Manager. **PERSONAL:** Born Aug 23, 1938, Allentown, PA; daughter of William E Merritt and Cora L Merritt; married Robert Smith; children: Lisa, Jerome. **EDUCATION:** Muhlenberg Coll, BA, 1970; Lehigh Univ, MEd, 1974. **CAREER:** Muhlenberg Coll, asst dir admissions, 1970-74; Pennsylvania Power & Light Co, various positions to mgr placement & EEO programs, 1974-. **ORGANIZATIONS:** Mem, Muhlenberg Coll, Council for Continuing Educ, 1976; bd mem, YWCA, 1975-77; pres, Negro Cultural Center, 1975-77; bd mem, Head Start of Lehigh Valley, 1975-77; educ comm, Pennsylvania Chamber of Commerce, 1976-77; bd mem, Allentown Police Civil Serv, 1979-, United Way of Leghigh Cty, 1981-; bd, friends comm, Muhlenberg Coll Corp, 1987-; mem, Muhlenberg Coll Bd of Assocs, 1987-; pres, Lehigh Valley Personnel Assoc, 1989-; dir, Allentown School Bd of Educ, 1987-. **HONORS/ACHIEVEMENTS:** Woman of the Year, Allentown NAACP, 1987. **BUSINESS ADDRESS:** Mgr of Placement & EEO Prog, Pennsylvania Power & Light Co, Two North Ninth St, Allentown, PA 18101.

WILLIAMS, JEAN CAROLYN
Educator. **PERSONAL:** Born Aug 30, 1956, Mullins, SC; daughter of Fred Gause, Jr and Remel Verlaska Graves Gause; married Vaugn McDonald Williams, Jr, Jul 21, 1979. **EDUCATION:** Spelman Coll, Atlanta, GA, BA 1978; Universidad Iberoamericana, Mexico City, Mexico, certificate 1983; University of Georgia, Athens, certificate 1987; Georgia State University, Atlanta, MAT, 1983. **CAREER:** Douglas County Schools, Douglasville, GA, Spanish teacher 1978-, teacher of English as a second language 1982-86; ambassador, speaker, consultant for Georgia Dept of Education, 1988. **ORGANIZATIONS:** Mem of Steering Comm, Academic Alliances, 1986-; mem of Staff Devel Council, Douglas County Schools, 1986-; head of Instructional & Professional Devel Comm, Douglas County Assn of Educators, 1987-88 & 1989-90; chair of Challenge, Douglas County High School, 1989-92; member of Foreign Language Assn of Georgia, GA Athletic Coaches Assn, Advisory Bd of the Southern Conf on Language Teaching, Amer Assn of GA, Phi Delta Kappa, Alpha Kappa Alpha, Delta Kappa Gamma, National Educators Assn's Congressional Contact Team, Professional Negotiation Task Force. **HONORS/ACHIEVEMENTS:** Editor of Albricias!, Spanish Today, and The Beacon, 1980-89; grant to attend seminar on Afro-Hispanic literature, GA Endowment for the Humanities, 1984; assoc editor of Afro Hispanic Review; Douglas County Teacher of the Year (Christa McAuliffe Award), Douglas County Schools, 1987-88; AATSP-GA Teacher of the Year, GA chapter of Amer Assn of Teachers of Spanish and Portuguese, 1987-88; GA Teacher of the Year award from Encyclopaedia Brittanica, Good Housekeeping, and Council of Chief State School Officers, 1987-88; Certificate of Excellence, Foreign Lang Assn of GA, 1988; Excellence in Education award from NASSP, Burger King, and CCSSO, 1988. **HOME ADDRESS:** 630 Whisper Ct, 303B, Austell, GA 30001. **BUSINESS ADDRESS:** Head of Department of Arts and Languages, Douglas County Comprehensive High School, Douglas County Schools, 8705 Campbellton St, Douglasville, GA 30134.

WILLIAMS, JEANETTE MARIE
Educational administrator,assistant dean. **PERSONAL:** Born Jul 11, 1942, Shaw, MS; married Howard S Williams Sr (divorced); children: Renee L Burwell, Howard S Jr, Karen A, Sharon A Gober, Willie James Harrington. **EDUCATION:** Wilson Jr Coll, 1968; Chicago State Univ, BS, Biology, 1969; Chicago State Univ, MS, Biology, 1977. **CAREER:** Haven Middle School, teacher, 1971-72; Chicago Public Schools, teacher, 1972-74; Malcolm X Coll, curriculum spec, 1974-77; Kennedy-King Coll, asst prof of biology, 1977-, Title III, dir, 1983-86. **ORGANIZATIONS:** Mem, Natl Assn of Biology Teachers, 1978-, Assn for Supvr & Curriculum Devel, 1980, Assn for the Study of Afro-Amer Life & History, 1982-; consultant, Educ Mgmt Assn, 1982-83; sponsor, Phi Theta Kappa, 1982-; bd dir, Black Women's Hall of Fame, 1983-; vice pres, Black Woman Hall of Fame Found Teachers Guild; mem, Pinkie Jackson # 1, Order of the Eastern Star of the Adoptive Rite of USA; bd of dir, Kennedy-King Coll, Natl Youth Sports Program, 1987-. **HONORS/ACHIEVEMENTS:** Scholarship Chicago Chemical Co, 1971; Sponsor's Hall of Honor Illinois, Phi Theta Kappa, 1984; Distinguished Teacher Award Local 1600, Kennedy King Chapter, 1984; Sponsor's Hall of Honor IL Phi Theta Kappa 1985; IL Phi Theta Kappa Most Disting Sponsor 1985; Outstanding Illinois Advisor, Phi Theta Kappa, 1989; Illinois Advisors Hall of Honor, Phi Theta Kappa, 1989. **BUSINESS ADDRESS:** Asst Dean Student Serv, Chicago City Coll,(Kennedy-King Coll), 6800 South Wentworth Ave 1132 W, Chicago, IL 60621.

WILLIAMS, JESSE
Elected official. **PERSONAL:** Born Jul 18, 1922, Sylvania, GA; son of Evenezer Williams and Ethel Prescott Williams; married Edna Williams, Oct 27, 1967; children: Ethel M Cooper,

Jesse Jr, Walter A, Pamerla J Ellis, Josie P, Thmas H, Pancia Oliver, Mary A, Keith L, Tami L Singleton, Danny R, Janice R Prescott; children: Alda M Burgest, Angela F Bassett. **CAREER:** Lovell Hill Baptist Church, chmn of bd 1948; Frank Cooper Baptist Assn, treas 1970-89; Frank Cooper Sunday School Convention, supt 1972-89; City of Hilltonia, city council. **ORGANIZATIONS:** Mem Mason Lodge No 433; mem Lemar Carter Conser of 32nd. **HOME ADDRESS:** Rte 1 Box 203, Sylvania, GA 30467.

WILLIAMS, JESSE J., JR.
Business executive. **PERSONAL:** Born Aug 05, 1940, Gleenville, GA; married Charlotte; children: Jesse J. **EDUCATION:** SC St Coll, BS 1963. **CAREER:** IBM Corp, chemist 1963; Douglas Aircraft; United Aircraft Corp; Tele Dynamics Inc; JWM, formed corp 1969-. **ORGANIZATIONS:** Mem Amer Mgmt Assoc; Hon Societies. **BUSINESS ADDRESS:** 13540 Philmont Ave, Philadelphia, PA 18950.

WILLIAMS, JESTER C.
Educator, clergyman. **PERSONAL:** Born Oct 27, 1924, Greenwood, MS; son of Rev J W Williams and Maggie Ellington Williams; children: Jester C Jr, India Ruth, James Carter. **EDUCATION:** Alcorn A&M Univ, 1950; MS Valley State Univ, Delta State Univ, MS State Univ, Gammon Theol Sem, attended; Laural School of Medical & Dental Assistants, graduated, 1988. **CAREER:** Oak Park HS Laurel MS, 1949-50; Brooks HS Drew MS, principal 1951-56; Walnut Grove, Pleasant Valley United Church, 1960-61; Belzoni-Inverness Charges, 1961-63; Greenville, Revels United MC, 1963-64; Providence Buford Chapel United Meth Church, Epworth United Meth Church 1964-66; Decel United Meth Church 1967-68; Hopson Bayou Elementary, principal, 1968; Marshall HS, N Carrollton MS, 1968-72; Rasberry Univ Meth Ch 1969; Revels United Meth Ch 1970-71; Vaiden Circuit MS 1971-72; Greenwood City School, sub teacher 1973-77, 1985; Corinth, 1974; St Paul United Meth Ch, Lindsey Chapel, Jones Chapel West Point MS 1975-77; Pickens Circuit Union mem United Meth Ch, Franklin United Meth Ch, 1977-80. **MILITARY SERVICE:** USAF sgt 1943-46.

WILLIAMS, JEWEL L.
Elected official. **PERSONAL:** Born Feb 11, 1937, Canton, MS; married Frank Williams (divorced); children: Anthony, Frank, Kerry, Debra Whitehead, Darcy Donaldson. **EDUCATION:** Mary Holmes Jr Coll, Bus; Jackson State Univ, Soc 1969-71. **CAREER:** Head Start, comm organizer 1966-73; Canton Public Schools, social worker 1974-84; Universal Life Ins Co, sales rep 1984-; City of Canton, alderman 1979-. **ORGANIZATIONS:** Vp NCNW Canton Chapler 1969-; sec, bd of dir MYL Family Health Ctr 1973-79; bd mem Central Miss Legal Serv 1976-83; bd mem NAACP 1979-; pres MadisonCty Women for Progress 1980-82; exec comm MS Democratic Party. **HONORS/ACHIEVEMENTS:** Outstanding Service Project Unity Inc 1979; Outstanding in Community Women for Progress 1983; Outstanding Sales Service Universal Life Ins Co 1985. **HOME ADDRESS:** 513 Cauthen St, Canton, MS 39046.

WILLIAMS, JOE
Entertainer. **PERSONAL:** Born 1918, Cordele, GA. **CAREER:** Count Basie Orchestra, singer 1954-61, soloist 1961-. **HONORS/ACHIEVEMENTS:** Recording "Everyday I Have The Blues", "All Right , Okay, You Win", "Smack Dab In The Middle", "Teach Me Tonight". **BUSINESS ADDRESS:** Abby Hoffer Enterprieses, 223 1/2 E 48th St, New York, NY 10017.

WILLIAMS, JOE H.
Elected official. **PERSONAL:** Born Oct 07, 1937, Tuskegee, AL; married Marilyn Bryant Hainesworth; children: Melani, Mario. **EDUCATION:** Republic Indus Educ Inst, Elect Maint 1970-78. **CAREER:** General Motors Corp, electrician 1965-; Williams Electric Co, owner 1973-; Seventh Ward Warren OH, councilman 1977-; Precinct D Warren OH, precinct comm head 1984-; Warren 7th Ward, councilman. **ORGANIZATIONS:** Bd mem NAACP 1968-; pres West Warren Improvement Council 1968-; bd mem Warren Electrician Bd 1980-. **HONORS/ACHIEVEMENTS:** Honorary Mayor of Tuskegee AL 1977; Gen Motors Awd for Excellence General Motors Lordstown 1984; Outstanding Community Serv NAACP 1984; Award from Natl Assn of Negro Business & Professional Women's Club for Distinguished Serv as a Black Elected Official for the City of Warren, OH 1985; Joe H Williams Day April 14, 1985 for Outstanding Comm Serv from Mayor Daniel J Sferra Warren, OH; Governor's Special Recognition from richard Celeste 1985; Hon Auditor of State from Thomas E Ferguson 1985. **HOME ADDRESS:** 2855 Peerless SW, Warren, OH 44485. **BUSINESS ADDRESS:** Councilman, Warren 7th Ward, 2855 Peerless SW, Warren, OH 44485.

WILLIAMS, JOHN
Athlete, dentist. **PERSONAL:** Born Oct 27, 1945, Jackson, MS; married Colleen. **EDUCATION:** Univ MN BS 1969;Univ MD & Morgan St Coll, Pre-dental Progs;Univ MD, DDS 1978. **CAREER:** Los Angeles Rams, retired professional football player 1972-79; Baltimore Colts, professional football player 1968-71. **ORGANIZATIONS:** AFC Championship Games 1970-71; NFC Championship Games 1974-75-76-78; NFL Championship Games 1968-70; AFL-NFL Championship Games 1968. **BUSINESS ADDRESS:** Los Angeles Rams, 10271 W Pico, Los Angeles, CA.

WILLIAMS, JOHN ALFRED
Author, educator. **PERSONAL:** Born Dec 05, 1925, Jackson, MS; son of John H. Williams and Ola M. Williams; married Lorrain Isaac; children: Gregory, Dennis, Adam. **EDUCATION:** Syracuse Univ, BA 1950; SE MA Univ, DLitt 1978. **CAREER:** Coll of the Virgin Islands, lecturer black lit 1968; CUNY, lecturer creative writing 1968-69; Sarah Lawrence Coll, guest writer 1972-73; Univ of CA Santa Barbara, regents lecturer 1973; CUNY LaGuardia Comm Coll, disting prof 1973-78; Univ of HI, vstg prof 1974; Boston Univ, vstg prof 1978-79; Rutgers Univ, prof of engl 1979-; Exxon vstg prf New York Univ 1986-87. **ORGANIZATIONS:** Columnist, stringer, spec assignment, staff The Natl Leader, Progressive Herald, Assoc Negro Press, The Age, The Defender, Post-Standard, The Tribune, The Courier; Holiday Magazine Europe 1965-66; corresp Newsweek Africa 1964-65; spec events WOV NY 1959; dir of info Amer Comm on Africa 1958; corresp Ebony-Jet Spain 1958-59; writer, narrator on location Nigeria, Spain; bd of dir Coord Council Literary Mags 1983-85; bd of dir Jrnl of African Civilizations 1980-;contrib ed Politicks 1977, Amer Jnrl 1972-74; ed bd Audience Mag 1970-72; contrib ed Herald-Tribune Book Week 1963-65; asst to publ Abelard Schuman 1957-58; editor & publ Negro Mkt Newsletter 1956-57. **HONORS/ACHIEVEMENTS:** Num novels incl, "The Berhama Account Horizon" press 1985, "Mothersill and the Foxes" Doubleday 1975, "The Man Who Cried I Am" Brown Little 1967; non-fictionbooks incl, "Minorities in the City" Harper & Row 1975, "Africa, Her History, Lands & People" Cooper Sq 1963; anthologies incl, "Intro to Lit McGraw-Hill 1984, "Beyond the Angry Black" Cooper Sq 1967, "Literature, An Intro to Fiction Poetry & Drama" Brown Little 1983, "Giant Talk" Random House 1974, "Harlem, Community in Transition" Citadel Press 1964; introductions "Artists Abroad, Middleton" Studio Museum in Harlem 1982; articles/essays "Race War & Politics" Negro Digest: !Click Song 1982 novel; Junior Bachelor Soc 1976; "Jacob's Ladder" 1987 novel. **MILITARY SERVICE:** USN WWII 1943-46. **BUSINESS ADDRESS:** Professor of English, RutgersUniv, 360 Martin Luther King Blvd, Newark, NJ 07102.

WILLIAMS, JOHN EARL
Mortician, elected official. **PERSONAL:** Born Aug 07, 1948, Raleigh, NC; son of Thaddeus Williams and Lucy Johnson Williams; married Karen A Brown-Williams, Apr 17, 1987. **EDUCATION:** NC Central Univ, BS Commerce 1967; Fayetteville Tech Inst, AAS Funeral Serv Ed 1977. **CAREER:** Scarborough & Hargett Funeral Home Inc, staff mem, admin asst 1967-72; Durham Cty Hosp Corp, dir, admin asst 1972-73; Beaunit Corp Rsch Triangle Park, vice pres of fin 1973-74; Scarborough & Hargett Funeral Home Inc, bus mgr 1977-78; Haywood Funeral Home Inc, mortician 1978-79; NC Dept of Commerce, Natural Resources & Commun Devel, auditor 1979-86; owner and operator, Weaver & Williams Funeral Service, Inc, 1986-. **ORGANIZATIONS:** Mem Durham City Cncl 1983; Hayti Development Corp; bd dir Durham C of C; Highways and Streets Comm; NC & Natl Funeral Directors & Morticians Assns; NC Museum of Life and Science; bd dir Triangle "J" Cncl of Govt; mem Advisory Cncl on Employment NAACP Durham Chapter; Durham Comm on Affairs of Black People; Durham Alumni Chapter of Kappa Alpha Psi Fraternity. **HOME ADDRESS:** 3315 Waterbury Drive, Durham, NC 27707. **BUSINESS ADDRESS:** Bynum Weaver - Williams Funeral Service, Inc., 110 N. Merritt Mill Road, Chapel Hill, NC 27516.

WILLIAMS, JOHN F.
Educator. **PERSONAL:** Born Oct 05, 1928, Winston-Salem, NC; divorced; children: Kenneth, Vanessa, Reginald, Sidney. **EDUCATION:** TN State Univ, BA 1953; NY Univ, MA 1957. **CAREER:** PA Dept of Public Welfare, social caseworker 1956-59; San Diego Co, supervising social worker 1959-64; San Diego, comm educ proj coord 1964-66; San Diego City Sch, adult educ specialist 1966-68; YMCA Youth Involvement Prog, dir proj contact 1968; Minority Relations consul 1968-69; San Diego Model Cities Prog, dir 1969-72; Employment Placement Agency, consult owner 1972-75; San Diego Co Human Relations Comm, proj dir regional affirmative action clearinghouse 1975-76; San Diego Comm Coll, instructor 1973-. **ORGANIZATIONS:** Past mem CA Adv Council on Vocational Educ; former mem San Diego C of C; past pres Big Brothers of San Diego Co; founder SE Art Assn; past dir SEComm Theater; mem Omega Psi Phi Frat. **HONORS/ACHIEVEMENTS:** Successfully demonstrated against Gary Player in 1970 which partially led to Lee Elder being invited to S Africa in 1971. **MILITARY SERVICE:** USAAF 1946-49.

WILLIAMS, JOHN H.
Elected official. **PERSONAL:** Born Jun 02, 1934, Coahoma, MS; children: Sandra, Lester, Shelia, Ronald, Eddie, Latesia. **EDUCATION:** Bishop Coll, BA 1976; Harvard Univ, MPA anticip 1986. **CAREER:** Kaiser Steel Corp, first black foreman 1968; Life Investors Corp, stock broker 1971; City of Muskegon, first elected Black commissioner. **ORGANIZATIONS:** Mem Goals for Dallas 1974; bd of dirs OIC of Amer 1981; past vice pres Muskegon Shoreline Regional Develop Comm 1984; pres Muskegon Ministers Fellowship 1984; life mem NAACP; pastor John Wesley AME Zion Church; mem MI Municipal League, Legislative/Urban Affairs Comm; mem Muskegon Chamber of Comm; mem MI Seaway Festival 1983. **HONORS/ACHIEVEMENTS:** Deans List Bishop Coll 1975; Cert of Appreciation Black Cultural Expo West MI Seaway Festival 1983. **MILITARY SERVICE:** USN E-5 6 yrs; Honorable Discharge; Natl Defense Medal. **BUSINESS ADDRESS:** Commissioner Ward 2, City of Muskegon, 933 Terrace, Muskegon, MI 49443.

WILLIAMS, JOHN HENRY
Clergyman. **PERSONAL:** Born Feb 24, 1948, Venice, IL; married Emma Jean Johnson; children: Reginold, Dean, John Jr, Shelonda, Nicole, Milton. **EDUCATION:** Southern IL Univ Edwardville, 1976-78; State Comm Coll E St Louis, 1981. **CAREER:** Venice Independent Baseball League, pres 1970-81; Madison Branch of NAACP, pres 1976-80; Venice Citizen Comm Devel, chmn 1977-78; People Org to Benefit Children in Venice, pres 1981-83; Venice Local Utilities Bd, vice chmn 1983-; Venice Neighborhood Crime Watch Prog, mem 1984; New Salem MB Church, pastor 1982-. **ORGANIZATIONS:** Mem Intl Union of Operating Engrs 1971-, Free & Accepted Ancient York Rite Mason 1972-; former pres Venice Park Bd of Commiss 1982-83; mem Venice Park Bd of Commiss 1987. **HONORS/ACHIEVEMENTS:** Million Dollar Club Madallion 71st Annual NAACP Convention 1980; Two Local Awards Madison Branch NAACP 1980; Citation for Community Serv Tri-Cities Area UnitedWay 1982; Pastor of the Year Awd Spot Light Review 1983; Comm Serv Madison Progressive Women Org 1984. **HOME ADDRESS:** 619 Washington, Venice, IL 62090. **BUSINESS ADDRESS:** Pastor, New Salem MB Church, 1349 klein St, Venice, IL 62090.

WILLIAMS, JOHN JOSEPH
Retired administrator. **PERSONAL:** Born Mar 02, 1906, Monmouth, IL; widowed; children: Joanne E Spriggs. **EDUCATION:** Milwaukee Teachers Coll, BE 1931; Univ of WI Platteville, MS 1976. **CAREER:** WI, OK, MO, school teacher 1931-37; US PO Milwaukee, employment officer 1942-67; Milwaukee Globe, editor 1947-49; Milwaukee Urban League, dir of manpower 1968-70; Higher Educ Bd State of WI, dir of talent search 1970-72; Milwaukee Urban League, dir of manpower 1972-75; Univ of WI Plateville, special asst to the vice chancellor retired 1982; career counselor-private. **ORGANIZATIONS:** Pres, Natl Alliance of Postal Workers Milwaukee 1959-61; life mem NAACP; Amer Soc for Training & Devel WI Chapter 1975-; 32 Degree Mason Widow's Son Lodge 1929; polemarch Kappa Alpha Psi Milwaukee 1976-78; dir Multi-Cultural Educ Center Univ of WI-Platteville 1976-; Mayor of Bronzville Milwaukee WI 1938. **HONORS/ACHIEVEMENTS:** Man of the Year Milwaukee Urban League 1947; Serv Award US PO 1965; Serv Award 50 Years Milwaukee Urban League 1974.

WILLIAMS, JOHN L.
Clergyman. **PERSONAL:** Born Dec 31, 1937, Lubbock, TX; married Annie L Emmanuel; children: LeCretria, Stephanie, John Jr, John Mark, Mandilyn, LaShenda, Samuel John. **EDUCATION:** TX Southern U, BChem 1960; Howard Dental Sch, DDS 1965. **CAREER:**

Charles H George Dental Soc, 1965; Houston Dist Dental Soc; Am Dental Asso; TX Dental Asso; Academy of Gen Dentistry; Faith Tabernacle COSIC, gen prctnr/pastor. **ORGANIZATIONS:** Am Chem Soc; supt So Houston Dist 1983. **HONORS/ACHIEVEMENTS:** Alpha Phi Alpha Frat 1960; sal Dunbar Sr Hi Lubbock, TX 1956. **HOME ADDRESS:** 4436 S Mcgregor Way, Houston, TX 70021. **BUSINESS ADDRESS:** Pastor, Faith Tabernacle COGIC, 7811 Cullen Blvd, Houston, TX 77051.

WILLIAMS, JOHN R.
Optometrist. **PERSONAL:** Born Mar 14, 1937, Richmond; married Sandra; children: 3 Sons. **EDUCATION:** Virginia Union U, BS 1959; IL Coll Optometry, OD 1963. **CAREER:** Optometrist, self emp mem VA. **ORGANIZATIONS:** Am Optometric Assn 1960-; Nat Optometric Assn 1968-; Metro Dev Corp 1972-; Asso Investors 1972-73; Mem Capitala Reg Park Auth 1968-71; bd mem Salvation Army Boys Club 1965-74; bd mem Friends Assn; bd mem Big Bro Am Inc 1968-74; bd mem v chmn Church Hill Multi-serv Ctr Inc; v chmn Richmond, IN Auth 1973-74. **BUSINESS ADDRESS:** 1122 N 25 St, Ste D, Richmond, VA 23223.

WILLIAMS, JOHN WALDO
Clergyman. **PERSONAL:** Born Mar 15, 1911, Como, TX; married Susie Marguerite Green; children: Clara L Woods, Nona R Fisher, Anita J Gates. **EDUCATION:** Butler Coll, BA, 1935, DD 1939. **CAREER:** Cypress Baptist Assoc, moderator 1960-85; BM&E Convention of TX, vice pres 1961-85; Natl Bapt Con USA Inc, bd of dir 1982-85. **ORGANIZATIONS:** Pastor Ebenezer Baptist Church 1941-85. **HONORS/ACHIEVEMENTS:** 30 Yrs Loyal Serv Ebenezer Bapt Church Youth 1941-71; Invaluable Serv Cypress Baptist Assn 1961-71; Meritorious Serv Cypress Congress of Christian Ed 1943-81. **HOME ADDRESS:** PO Box 253, Como, TX 75431.

WILLIAMS, JOHNS CALVIN
Professional athlete. **PERSONAL:** Born Oct 26, 1960, Muskegon, MI; married Victoria Ann; children: John Alan II. **EDUCATION:** Wisconsin, Agr Econ. **CAREER:** Michigan, 1983-84; Oakland Invaders, halfback 1984. **HONORS/ACHIEVEMENTS:** Names USFL Lite Beer Player of Week for his Perf against Chgo; was voted Most Inspirational Player as sr; named honorable mention All-Big 10 as a jr; played in Garden State Bowl & Independence Bowl.

WILLIAMS, JOSEPH B.
Judge. **PERSONAL:** Born Jul 12, 1921, Annapolis; married Eva; children: Joseph Jr, John. **EDUCATION:** New York Univ, LlB, LlM 1949-52; Hampton Inst, BS 1942; US Merchant Marine Acad 1944. **CAREER:** Law Offices, 1949-66; NY, judge 1966-70; New York City Model Cities Administr, 1970-73; Family Ct, judge 1973-; New York City Admin Judge Family Div, dep 1974 senate of NY, justice sup ct 1977. **ORGANIZATIONS:** Former chmn bd trustees Cornerstone Bapt Ch; former chmn bd Bedrford Styvesant Rest Corp; trustee Nat Counc of Juv & Fam Ct Judges; trustee New Sch for Soc Rsrch; mem Brooklyn Museum; mem Brooklyn Inst Arts & Sc; past v chmn Hampton Inst Bd Trustees; NY Co Lawyers Assn; Am Bar Assn; Kings Co Criminal Bar Assn; Vera Inst Justice; Wiltwyck Sch Boys. **MILITARY SERVICE:** UNS 1944-46 lt 1950-52. **BUSINESS ADDRESS:** Supreme Court of Kings County, 360 Adams St, Brooklyn, NY 11201.

WILLIAMS, JOSEPH B.
Chief executive insurance firm. **CAREER:** Central Life Ins of Florida, Tampa FL, chief executive, 1989. **BUSINESS ADDRESS:** Central Life Insurance of Florida, 1400 N Blvd, Tampa, FL 33607. *

WILLIAMS, JOSEPH HENRY
Physician. **PERSONAL:** Born Jun 15, 1931, Columbia, SC; married C Patricia; children: Joseph Jr. **EDUCATION:** Howard U, BS 1950, MD 1954; NY U, diploma 1960. **CAREER:** Park City Hosp, attdng surgeon 1962-. **ORGANIZATIONS:** Am Bd Surgery 1967; mem Fairfield Co Med Soc; CT St Med Soc. **HONORS/ACHIEVEMENTS:** Flw Am Soc Abdominal Surgeons 1963; Fellow American Coll of Surgeons, 1982. **MILITARY SERVICE:** AUS 1956-58. **BUSINESS ADDRESS:** 2045 Park Ave, Bridgeport, CT 06304.

WILLIAMS, JOSEPH LEE
Business executive elected official. **PERSONAL:** Born Mar 25, 1945, Madison, WV; son of Joseph Lee Williams and Loretta Lawson Williams; married Shirley Ann Johnson; children: Yvette, Yvonne, Mary, Joseph. **EDUCATION:** Marshall Univ, BBA Finance 1978; Mayors' Leadership Inst 1984. **CAREER:** Ebony Golf Classic, founder/dir 1971-87; City of Huntington, mem city council 1981, asst mayor 1983-84, , mayor 1984-85; Basic Supply Co, pres/gen mgr 1977-. **ORGANIZATIONS:** Comm Huntington Urban Renewal Authority 1983-85; mem Huntington Rotary Club 1983-; bd of dirs Huntington Area Chamber of Commerce 1984-85; bd of trustees Cabell-Huntington Hosp 1984-85; bd of dirs United Way of the River Cities 1984-; mem City of Huntington Interim Loan Comm 1985; life mem NAACP; Huntington Area Chamber of Commerce, West Virginia Partnership for Progress Council, 1989-. **HONORS/ACHIEVEMENTS:** Outstanding Black Alumni Marshall Univ 1984; Outstanding Citizen Awd Huntington WV Negro Business & Professional Women's Clubs 1985; Subcontractor of The Year, West Virginia SBA, 1987; Minority Business Person of the Year, West Virginia SBA, 1988; featured in Union-Carbide Corp's Natl Newsmagazine, 1989; featured in E I DuPont DeNemours & Co's TEMPO Natl Newsletter, 1989. **BUSINESS ADDRESS:** Pres/General Manager, Basic Supply Co, 1341 10th Ave, P O Box 936, Huntington, WV 25717.

WILLIAMS, JOSEPH R.
Clergyman. **PERSONAL:** Born Oct 22, 1918, St Joseph, LA; son of Abram Williams, Sr and Ellen Brown Williams; married Georgia Lee Van; children: Josephine W White, Robert C Williams, Linda W McLemore,Ronald J Williams, Yvonne W Shropshire, Kevin R Williams. **EDUCATION:** Leland Coll, AB 1954; UASFI, AM 1963; CCRI, DD 1983. **CAREER:** Pastor at Following Churches little zion 1943-47; evergreen 1944-50, 1952-64; straight life 1957-59; mt olivet 1946-48; mt pilgrim 1956-59; pastor Elm Grove Baptist Church 1952-; pastor New Sunlight Baptist Church 1958-; Semi Extn Dean 1958; Org EPIC; Aff HMB Southern Baptist Convention; Bible Exp; mem advisory bd Comm Advancement Inc (CAI); vice pres E Baton Rouge Min. **HONORS/ACHIEVEMENTS:** Honarary Mayor, Baton Rouge, LA, 1977; Adjutant General, State of LA, 1978; Honorary Colonel State of LA, 1985; Honorary DA, EBR Parish, 1983; 25yrs Pastors Award, Elm Grove Baptist Church, 1977; 25yrs Pin Award Home Mission Bd Southern Baptist, 1983; Minister of the Year, Baton Rouge, Laymen, 1987; Deaconiate Instruction Award, 1987; 50yrs Gospel Preacher Award, State of LA Dept of Chr Educ, 1986. **MILITARY SERVICE:** AUS 1948-51; Fourregre (fr.) 1949; SEATO; Asiatic Combat Ribbon, Good Conduct Ribbon, 1951.

WILLIAMS, JUNIUS W.
Attorney. **PERSONAL:** Born Dec 23, 1943, Suffolk, VA; married Ollie Ruth Malveaux; children: Camille, Junea. **EDUCATION:** Amherst Coll, BA 1965; Yale Law Sch, JD 1968; Inst of Pol Kennedy Sch of Gov Harvard Univ, fellow 1980. **CAREER:** Newark Comm Devel Admin & Model Cities Prog, dir 1970-73; Essex Newark Legal Svcs, exec dir 1983-85; City of Newark, candidate for mayor 1982; Private Practice, attorney 1973-83, 1985-. **ORGANIZATIONS:** 3rd vice pres Natl Bar Assn; 2nd vice pres 1976; pres Natl Bar Assn 1978-79; mem bd of dirs Agricultural Missions Inc; mem Natl, Amer, NJ, Essex Co Bar Assn; mem Critical Minorities Problems Comm; Natl Assn Housing & Redevel Officials; mem Equal Oppor Fund Bd 1980; Essex Co Ethics Comm 1980; fndr & dir Newark Area Planning Assn 1967-70; co-chmn Comm Negotiating Team NJ Coll Med & Dentistry Controversey 1967; guest spkr/lecturer Yale Univ, Harvard Law Sch, Rutgers Univ, Cornell Univ, Univ NC; pres Yale Law Sch Assoc of NJ 1981-82; fndr/pres Leadership Development Group 1980-; consultant Council of Higher Educ in Newark; sec bd of trustees Essex Co Coll 1980-; mem & former sec Newark Collaboration Group; founder/first chmn Ad Hoc Comm of Univ Heights 1984-86. **HONORS/ACHIEVEMENTS:** Listed in Ebony Magazine "100 Most Influential Blacks in America"; Disting Service Awd Newark Jaycees 1974; Concerned Citizens Awd Bd of Concerned CitizensColl of Med & Dentistry of NJ; Fellow MARC 1967-68, 1973. **HOME ADDRESS:** 120 Vassar Ave, Newark, NJ 07112. **BUSINESS ADDRESS:** Attorney, 972 Broad St, Newark, NJ 07102.

WILLIAMS, KAREN HASTIE
Attorney. **PERSONAL:** Born Sep 30, 1944, Washington, DC; daughter of William H Hastie and Beryl Lockhart Hastie; married Wesley S Williams Jr Esq; children: Amanda Pedersen, Wesley Hastie, Bailey Lockhart. **EDUCATION:** Univ of Neuchatel Switzerland, Cert 1965; Bates Coll, BA 1966; Fletcher School of Law & Diplomacy Tufts Univ, MA 1967; Columbus Law School Catholic Univ of Amer, JD 1973. **CAREER:** Fried Frank Harris Shriver & Kampelman, assoc atty 1975-77; US Senate Comm on Budget, chief counsel 1977-80; Office of Fed Procurement Policy Office of Mgmt & Budget, admin 1980-81; Crowell & Moring, of counsel 1982, sr partner. **ORGANIZATIONS:** Chmn, legislative liaison comm Amer Bar Assoc Publ Contract Law Sect; bd of dir NS&T Bank Washington DC, Lawyers Comm for Civil Rights Under Law; mem Bd on Professional Responsibility DC Court of Appeals; trustee Black Student fund; bd of dir exec comm DC Chap Amer Red Cross; vp, bd of dir Greater Washington Rsch Ctr; bd of dir NAACP Legal Defense Fund; mem Trilateral Commission; vice chair, bd of trustees Natl Cathedral Sch. **BUSINESS ADDRESS:** Senior Partner/Attorney, Crowell and Moring, 1001 Pennsylvania Ave, NW, Washington, DC 20004.

WILLIAMS, KAREN RENEE
Pediatrician. **PERSONAL:** Born Jan 27, 1954, Baton Rouge, LA; married Cornelius A Lewis; children: Geoffrey Lewis. **EDUCATION:** Xavier Univ, BS 1975; Howard Univ Coll of Medicine, MD 1978; Tulane Univ, Pediatric Residency Program 1978-81. **CAREER:** LA State Univ Sch of Medicine/Earl K Long Hosp, instructor/dir pediatric emergency room 1981-87. **ORGANIZATIONS:** Mem East Baton Rouge Parish Medical Assoc 1981-87, East Baton Rouge Parish medical Soc 1985-87; chairperson of programs Parents Anonymous of LA 1984-85. **HONORS/ACHIEVEMENTS:** Alpha Omega Alpha Medical Honor Soc. **BUSINESS ADDRESS:** Instructor/Dir Pediatric ER, LA StateUniv Sch of Medicine, Earl K Long Hospital, 5825 Airline Highway, Baton Rouge, LA 70805.

WILLIAMS, KATHERINE
Government official. **PERSONAL:** Born Sep 07, 1941; daughter of Hugh L. Williams and Norma D. Baird Williams; divorced; children: Garvin J. **EDUCATION:** Harvard Univ, MEduc 1984, EdD 1987. **CAREER:** Workers Bank of Trinidad & Tobago, operations officer/acting chief accountant 1971-75; Matouk Intl, import officer 1976; Caribbean segment of Festival of Amer Folklife Smithsonian Inst, coord 1979-80; Festivals Mag, editor/publisher 1979-83; Smithsonian Inst, consul rsch inst on immigration & ethnic studies 1979-83; Dept of State Washington DC, consultant writer and software evaluator 1985-86;New York State Dept of Social Serv, project dir, currently. **ORGANIZATIONS:** Mem Phi Delta Kappa. **HONORS/ACHIEVEMENTS:** Author, "Computers, Our Road to the Future" used as text Washington DC Public Sch System 1982-; author "Where Else But America?"; named Women of Achievement in Montgomery Co 1977; Fellowship grant DC Comm on the Arts & Humanities 1981; photographic exhibit Museum of Modern Art of Latin America OAS Washington DC 1981.

WILLIAMS, KENNETH HERBERT
Attorny & elected official. **PERSONAL:** Born Feb 15, 1945, Orange, NJ; married Susan Marie Griffin; children: Kenneth H, Meryl E. **EDUCATION:** Howard Univ Liberal Arts, BA 1967; Howard Univ School of Law, JD 1970. **CAREER:** US Capitol Police, patrolman 1969-70; Newark Urban Coalition, asst to dir 1970; City of East Orange, judge municipal 1977-82, asst city counsel 1972-75; Ermst & Ermst CPA Firm, tax attorney 1970-71; City of East Orange, city councilman 1984-85. **ORGANIZATIONS:** Mem NAACP 1970-, Amer Bar Assn 1971; counsel East Orange Jaycees 1972; chmn City of East Orange Juvenile Conf Com 1973-75; mem Natl Bar Assn; Judicial Comm 1977-82, Amer Judges Assn 1978. **HONORS/ACHIEVEMENTS:** Outstanding Black Attorney Black Women Lawyers of NJ 1979; White House Fellow Nomination 1981; Outstanding Citizenship NJ Fed of Colored Women's Clubs Inc 1984; Cert of Appreciation Seton Hall Univ 1985. **MILITARY SERVICE:** ROTC 1963-65. **BUSINESS ADDRESS:** City Councilman, City of East Orange, 44 City Hall Plaza, East Orange, NJ 07019.

WILLIAMS, KENNETH RAYNOR
Retired chancellor. **PERSONAL:** Born Aug 16, 1912, Norfolk, VA; married Edythe; children: Kenneth, Ronald, Norman. **EDUCATION:** Morehouse Coll, AB 1933; MA 1936; STB 1952; PhD 1962. **CAREER:** Jour Tchr Educ, 1963-66; Assn Orgns Teacher Educ, 1966-69; Natl Council Tchr Accreditation Bd, 1969; NC Naturalization Comm, 1971-73; Winston-Salem State Univ, retired chancellor 1975-77; Faculty-Winston-Salem ST Univ 1936-1961; Alderman-Cty of Winston-Salem, 1947-1951; Pres-Winston-Salem ST Univ, 1961-

1972; Chancellor-Winston-Salem ST Univ, 1972-1977; retired, 1977. **ORGANIZATIONS:** Mem Rotary. **HONORS/ACHIEVEMENTS:** Freedom Found Awd 1952; Hon Degrees LLD Wake Forest Univ 1961; LLD So IL Univ 1972; DHL Morehouse Coll 1973. **MILITARY SERVICE:** AUS chaplain 1942-46; rank-Major. **BUSINESS ADDRESS:** Winston-Salem StateUniv, Winston-Salem, NC 27102.

WILLIAMS, KEVIN CALVIN
Professional athlete. **PERSONAL:** Born Jan 07, 1958, Los Angeles, CA. **EDUCATION:** Univ of Southern CA. **CAREER:** New Orleans Saints, wide receiver 1981-; Baltimore Colts, wide receiver 1981-; Los Angeles Express, wide receiver 1982-; Denver Gold, wide receiver 1983-. **HONORS/ACHIEVEMENTS:** Gold record holder for most yards receiving in one game; Gold leader in most consecutive games catching a pass; Gold's leader in best avg per catch over one season; 1st team All-PAC 10 selection; voted honorable memtion All-Am by Sporting News; Parade Mag All-Am.

WILLIAMS, KNEELY
Clergyman. **PERSONAL:** Married Dorothy M. **EDUCATION:** Central Baptist Seminar, 1948; Bethel Baptist Coll, 1979. **CAREER:** New Hope Baptist Church, pastor. **ORGANIZATIONS:** Pastor New Hope Baptist Church 1985; bd mem NAACP 1985, St Paul OIC 1985, Urban League 1985. **HONORS/ACHIEVEMENTS:** Serv MN State Human Rights 1970, St Paul Human Rights 1975, MN State Council of Churches 1977, MN State Bapt Convention 1980. **BUSINESS ADDRESS:** Pastor, New Hope Baptist Church, 1115 Dayton Ave, St Paul, MN 55104.

WILLIAMS, L. COLENE
Clergyman. **PERSONAL:** Born Jul 04, 1921, Laurens, SC; married Anthony; children: Garnita M, Gloria J, Reginald. **EDUCATION:** Moody Bible Inst, Philadelphia Coll Bible, Am Bible Coll, thB 1957, Rn 1955. **CAREER:** Holy Temple Ch Living God, pastor 1953-. **ORGANIZATIONS:** Natl Frgn Missions Bd Ch, Natl Pres 1960-; Anti-poverty prog bd mem United Fund; past sec Interdenominational Union . **HONORS/ACHIEVEMENTS:** Hon deg MillerUniv 1962; Jameson Bible Coll 1972. **BUSINESS ADDRESS:** Willis & Cumberland St, Penns Grove, NJ 08069.

WILLIAMS, LAFAYETTE W.
Dentist. **PERSONAL:** Born Dec 17, 1937. **EDUCATION:** Morehouse Coll, BS 1960; Meharry Med Coll, DDS 1968. **CAREER:** Central St Hosp Milledgeville GA, mem staff 1968-69; Pvt Practice Valdosta, dentistry 1969-; Valdosta Nursing Home Intl Nursing Care Center, mem staff. **ORGANIZATIONS:** Mem Valdosta Black Comm Action Group; Beta Kappa Chi; Alpha Phi Alpha; Mason Shriner, 32 Deg; Elk mem; Fedn Dentaire Internatiolnale; trustee Lowndes Co Prog Voters League; mem Nat Assn of Realtors; Am Profnl Practice Assn; Puritan Intl Dental Soc; Am Soc for Preventive Dentirstry; Chicago Soc; Acadeny of Gen Dentistry; Nat Dental Assn; Am Dental Assn; GA; SW Ldist Dental Socs; owner Reasonable Rentals Valdosta-lowndes Co; C of C; NAACP. **HONORS/ACHIEVEMENTS:** Listed Whos Who in Am In S & SE 1975. **BUSINESS ADDRESS:** 415 S Ashley St, Valdosta, GA 31601.

WILLIAMS, LARRY C.
Attorney. **PERSONAL:** Born May 17, 1931, Seneca, SC; married Theresa; children: Margo, Larry Jr, Edward, John, Lauren, Joseph, David. **EDUCATION:** Howard U, BA 1954, LIB 1959. **CAREER:** Corp Cnsl Office DC, asst Corp cnsl; Houston,, Waddy, Bryant & Gardner Regional Cnsl US & Brewers Assn, asso atty; N. **ORGANIZATIONS:** Former gen cnsl Nat Bus League; Nat Funeral Dir & Morticians Assn; United Way of Nat Capitol Area; mem past pres DC C of C; Metro WA Bd Trade; bd Metro UMCA; former bd mem Nat Cncl Christians & Jews; life mem Alpha Phi Alpha Frat Inc; mem 32nd Deg Mason; Shriner; Mecca Temple #10; Mem Transition Commn to Devel Orgn of First City Cncl under Home Rule. **BUSINESS ADDRESS:** 1430 K St NW, Washington, DC 20005.

WILLIAMS, LASHINA BRIGETTE
Product planner. **PERSONAL:** Born Oct 22, 1957, Houston, TX; daughter of Chauncey K Morrew Jr and Myrtle Morrow; married Michael Williams. **EDUCATION:** Prairie View A&M Univ, BS, Mechanical Engineering, 1980; Atlanta Univ, MBA, 1984; IBM, Gaithersburg, MO, financial analyst, 1985-87, product planner, 1987-. **CAREER:** Phillips Petroleum, mechanical engineer, 1980-82; Digital Equipment, financial analyst, intern, 1983; IBM, financial analyst, 1985-. **ORGANIZATIONS:** Mem, Natl Black MBA Assn, 1983-, Delta Sigma Theta Sor. **HONORS/ACHIEVEMENTS:** Appreciation Award, MBA, Forum Speaker, Natl Black MBA Assn, 1986. **HOME ADDRESS:** 11122 Cedar Bluff Ln, Germantown, MD 20874.

WILLIAMS, LEA E.
Educator. **PERSONAL:** Born Dec 21, 1947, Paducah, KY; daughter of Nathanial H Williams and Mae Frances Terrell Williams. **EDUCATION:** Kentucky State Coll, Frankfort KY, BA, 1969; Univ of Wisconsin, Milwaukee WI, MS, 1973, Teachers Coll, Columbia Univ, New York NY, MA 1977, EdD 1978. **CAREER:** Milwaukee Public Schools, WI, sixth grade teacher, 1969-73; Milwaukee Area Tech Coll, WI, ABE instructor, 1973-74; United Negro College Fund, New York NY, program evaluator 1978-80, proposal writer 1980-81, CAI research dir 1981-82, asst dir of Educ Services 1982-86, dir of Educ Services 1982-86, vice pres of Educ Services 1988-. **ORGANIZATIONS:** Editorial board, Thrust employment journal, 1980-85; panelist, Natl Endowment for the Humanities, 1983-85; Natl Leadership Forum, Amer Council on Educ, 1986; mem, Amer Educ Research Assn, 1986-; consulting editor, NY State Governor's Advisory Comm on Black Affairs, 1987-88; pres, Assn of Black Women in Higher Educ, 1987-89; advisory comm, Assn of Amer Colleges, 1988; commissioner, Natl Assn of Independent Colleges and Univs, 1988-91; exec bd, Amer Assn of Higher Educ, 1989-91; division chair, Natl Assn of Women Deans, Administrator, & Counselors, 1989-91. **HONORS/ACHIEVEMENTS:** Graduated with distinction & departmental honors, Kentucky State Univ, 1969; Alpha Kappa Mu Honor Society, 1969; Phi Delta Kappa, 1975; author of "The United Negro College Fund in Retrospect" 1980, "The Plight of Junior Faculty at Black Private Colleges" 1985, "Missing, Presumed Lost: Minority Teachers in the Nation's Classroom" 1989. **BUSINESS ADDRESS:** Vice President, Department of Educational Services, United Negro College Fund, Inc, 500 East 62nd St, New York, NY 10021.

WILLIAMS, LEAFORD CLEMETSON
Business executive. **PERSONAL:** Born Oct 03, 1924, Mulgrave, Jamaica;married Bertha Mae Bussey; children: Valerie Ann Williams, Brenda Joyce Minor, Kharl Anthony Williams. **EDUCATION:** Am U, BA 1961, MA 1972; Sch of Fgn Svc, Georgetown U; Sch of Intl Svc, Am U. **CAREER:** Trans World Marketing Asso Inc, pres & chief exec ofcr; Dept of Transp 1968-80; Urban League 1967-68; Consult Intl Marketing, fcgn serv officer 1961-67; serve black Am Businessmen in Caribbean Bus Investments; available for consult serv on Far East, S Asia & Caribean areas; coord Minority Bus Enterprise Prgm FFA; chief adv White House Conf on Small Bus Candidate for City Council in 1st election under Home Rule in WA. **ORGANIZATIONS:** Chmn UN Assn for DC; mem US China Rels Com; mem bd dir Fgn Students Serv Council; written a number of articles on govt & politics in Far E. **HONORS/ACHIEVEMENTS:** Whos Who in Govt. **MILITARY SERVICE:** USAF tech sgt 1948-60.

WILLIAMS, LEE R.
Writer. **PERSONAL:** Born Jun 15, 1936, Houston; children: Leslie, Lorelei, Leone. **EDUCATION:** Long Beach St; Harbor Coll. **CAREER:** LA Pol Dept 1960-63; KIIX TV, newscopy writer 1964; Universal City Studios 1964; foundr Inner City Writers Workshop 1970. **ORGANIZATIONS:** Charter mem Studio W 1963; Jr Mgmt Universal Studios Tours 1964-66; Inner City Cultural Ctr 1967-69; asst bus rep Local 776 1972; post prod coord Unite Artists 1972-74; past mem Ch Council St Thomas Aspostolic Ch LA; Writers Guild Am W; Motion Picture Editors Guild; bd dir Motion Picture Editors Guild; 7th Army NCO Acad Munich 1956. **HONORS/ACHIEVEMENTS:** 7th Army Engr Sch Expert Infantrymans Badge, Germany 1956; commendation Training Officer 1957; Civilian Citation LAPD Police Chief 1972. **MILITARY SERVICE:** AUS 1954-57. **BUSINESS ADDRESS:** Chasman & Landau Assn, 6725 Sunset Blvd #506, Hollywood, CA 90028.

WILLIAMS, LEON LAWSON
Elected official. **PERSONAL:** Born Jul 21, 1922, Weeletka, OK; children: Karen E, Leon L Jr, Susan P Rogers, Penny, Jeffery, Alisa O. **EDUCATION:** San Diego State Univ, BA 1950; Univ of San Diego School of Law, 1961; Natl Univ, Doctorate 1985. **CAREER:** San Diego County Sheriff Dept, admin officer 1957-66; Neighborhood Youth Corps, dir 1966-70; San Diego Urban League, exec dir 1968; City of San Diego, councilman 1969-82; County of San Diego, supervisor; chairman County of San Diego Board of Supervisors. **ORGANIZATIONS:** Consultant Fed Mart Corp 1972-76; dir San Diego Coll of Retailing 1986; life mem NAACP; dir Metro Transit Develop Bd, Natl Assoc of Counties; mem exec comm County Supervisor Assoc of CA; dir SD Region Water Reclamation Bd; chmn Service Authority for Freeway Emergencies. **HONORS/ACHIEVEMENTS:** Distinguished Serv to Community Black Federation of San Diego County, Greater San Diego Business Assoc, Metro Transit Develop Bd, Natl Cultural Foundation; Outstanding Contribution 1978, Distinguished Serv Awd 1985 NAACP; Black Achievement Awd 1981, Freedom Awd 1981 Action Enterprises; Recognition for being First Black Chairman of the Bd of Supervisors County of San Diego Black Leadership Council 1985. **BUSINESS ADDRESS:** County Supervisor, County of San Diego, 1600 Pacific Highway (A500), San Diego, CA 92101.

WILLIAMS, LEONARD, SR.
Educator. **PERSONAL:** Born Sep 07, 1945, Youngstown, OH; son of Arvella Church; married Maxine Graves, Jun 16, 1979; children: Leonard Jr, Lucy Arvella, McKenzie Michael. **EDUCATION:** Youngstown State Univ, Youngstown OH, AAS 1973, BS 1975, MS 1979. **CAREER:** Commercial Shearing, Youngstown OH, draftsman, 1969-70; Youngstown Police Dept, OH, patrolman 1970-77, sergeant 1977-81, lieutenant 1981-85; Youngstown Bd of Education, part-time security officer, 1973-85; Eastern Ohio Forensic Lab, part-time polygraph examiner, 1976-78; Tri-State Lab, part-time polygraph examiner, 1978-85; consultant, East Cleveland OH Civil Service Commn; Cuyahoga County Jail, Cleveland OH, administrator, 1985-87; Univ of Akron OH, prof, 1987-. **ORGANIZATIONS:** Bd mem, Natl Black Police Assn, 1981-; co-founder & bd mem, Advisory Council, United Humanitarian Fund, 1982-; chair, Eastern Region NBPA, 1983-87; chair, Natl Black Police Assn, 1986-88; mem, Ohio Court of Claims Public Awareness Advisory Council, 1988-. **HONORS/ACHIEVEMENTS:** Police Officer of the Year, Bd of Realtors, 1970; Mem of Year, Black Knight Police Assn, 1976; Man of Year, Natl Assn of Negro Bus & Prof Women, 1983; Mem of Year, Eastern Region NBPA, 1984; Renault Robinson Award, NBPA, 1987; author of "Peace Keeping and the Community: A Minority Perspective," 1988, and "Use of Excessive Force in the Minority Community," 1989. **MILITARY SERVICE:** US Air Force, E-3, 1963-67.

WILLIAMS, LEROY JOSEPH
Auditor. **PERSONAL:** Born Apr 13, 1937, New Orleans, LA; married Verna M Lewis; children: Linda M Thomes, Gregory C Lewis, Sandra Lewis. **EDUCATION:** Olympic Coll, AA 1969;Univ WA, BA 1972;Univ Puget Sound, grad work 1973-74. **CAREER:** City of Seattle, City Council Legislative Auditor; Seattle Model City Prgm, fiscal consult 1972-73; The Boeing Co, cost accounting 1972-73, material controller1961-72; USN Exchange Bremerton, buyer 1960-61. **ORGANIZATIONS:** Mem Bremerton Sch Bd 1971-77; mem WA St Educ TV Commn 1974-77; mem WA St Ferry Adv Com 1973-77; Williams Pvt Tax Consult 1972-; legislative rep WA St Sch Dir 1974-; mem Hamma Hamma #35 Masonic Lodge Prince Hall Grand Lodge WA Jurisdiction 1965-; mem Cascadian Consistory PHA AASR 1970-; mem Supreme Counsel 33 Deg Mason 1977; mem Sinclair Bapt Ch 1960-; ch sch Supt 1965-70; mem trustee bd 1965-; chtr mem Cr Union Audit Com 1972-73; Worshipful Master Hamma Hamma Lodge #35; mem Olympic Coll Assn of Higher Educ 1973-; mem Aldephil Inst 1975-. **MILITARY SERVICE:** USN 3rd class yoeman 1955-59. **BUSINESS ADDRESS:** Municipal Bldg, 600 4th Ave, Seattle, WA.

WILLIAMS, LESLIE J.
Health service administrator. **PERSONAL:** Born Aug 18, 1947, New Orleans, LA; children: Kimberly, Kevin. **EDUCATION:** Southern Univ BR, BS Pre-Med 1967; Southern Univ NO, BS Bus Admin 1975, AA Real Estate 1978. **CAREER:** VD/Tuberculosis Clinic NO Health Dept, adm dir 1979-83; City Health Dept, deputy dir. **ORGANIZATIONS:** Mem Urban League of Greater NO; mem Natl Assn of Real Estate Brokers; mem Amer Public Health Assn; 32 Degree Mason Ancient & Accepted Scotch Rite of Free Masonry 1980-85; instructor Southern Univ NO 1983-85. **HONORS/ACHIEVEMENTS:** Licensed Real Estate Salesperson LA; Licensed Sanitarian State of LA; Cert of Participation Amer Med Assn 1981; comparison of minocycline & penicillin in the treatment of male with gonorrhea AMA. **MILITARY SERVICE:** AUS commissioned warrant officer 2-11 yrs; Army Achievement Medal; Natl Defense Ribbon. **BUSINESS ADDRESS:** Deputy Dir, City Health Department, 1300 Perdido St Rm 8E73, New Orleans, LA 70112.

WILLIAMS, LILLIAN C.
Educator. **PERSONAL:** Born Dec 16, 1924, Athens, GA; daughter of Will Henry Cheney and Mattie L Cheney; widowed; children: George B, Jerome, Lanette, Gregory, Ronald. **EDUCATION:** Morris Brown Coll, AB 1945; Atlanta Univ, MA 1982. **CAREER:** Atlanta Public School System, teacher 1962-. **ORGANIZATIONS:** Mem Wheat St Baptist Church 1953-, Alpha Kappa Alpha, Natl Council for the Soc Sci; adv student govt Parks Jr HS 1966-70; chair Soc Studies Dept Parks Jr HS 1969-70; coord Close Up 1975, 1979, 1981, 1983, 1985-89; team coach WGN Chicago IL Natl TV "Know Your Heritage" 1984; chair Top Ten Percent Hon Students Bass HS 1977-86; guest teacher "Teen Talk" TV Atlanta GA 1986. **HONORS/ACHIEVEMENTS:** Completed the IGA Workshop 1978; produced & dir "Take a Look At Yourself" a black history play 1980; Dedication of Yearbook Bass HS 1984; Fellowship Grant The Humanities 1985; participant C-Span TV Close Up Washington DC 1985; asst chair, Social Studies Dept Southside Comprehensive HS 1986-87; Social Sci Semi-Finalist for Area II "Academic Incentive Prog" Atlanta bd of educ 1987. **HOME ADDRESS:** 711 Lynhurst Dr SW, Atlanta, GA 30311. **BUSINESS ADDRESS:** Classroom Teacher, Atlanta Public School System, 801 Glenwood Ave SE, Atlanta, GA 30312.

WILLIAMS, LLOYD A.
Executive officer. **PERSONAL:** Born Jan 16; married Wynora McCants; children: Lateef Ade. **EDUCATION:** Syracuse U, BA; Fordham U, MBA; Eastern Real Estate Inst, grad. **CAREER:** Uptown C of C, exec ofcr 1975-. **ORGANIZATIONS:** Pres LM Resouces Inc Marketing Research/Public Rel Firm 1971-; chmn Blackfrica Promotions Inc Third World Speakers Artists Bur 1968-; vice pres Rutherford Asso (PR Marketing) 1970-71; natl pub rel dir Congress of Racial Equality 1968-69; dir Manhattanville Youth Centre 1967-68; mem White House Commn on SmBus Devel; mem Nat Assn of Market Devel; bd of dir Harlem Commonwealth Council Inc; chmn Harlem Week Com 1976-; bd of dir City Coll of NY; bd of dir Private Investment Council; exec vice pres LLL Food Corp Restauranteurs 1979-. **HONORS/ACHIEVEMENTS:** Father Of Yr NY Day Care Assn 1974; Dist Serv Awd Blackfrica Promotions Inc 1977; Otstndng Comm Serv Awd NY Urban Coalition 1978; pres awd Malcolm-king Coll 1979. **BUSINESS ADDRESS:** President, Uptown Chamber of Commerce, 310 Lenox Ave, New York, NY 10027.

WILLIAMS, LLOYD L.
Legislator. **PERSONAL:** Born Jul 26, 1944, St Thomas, Virgin Islands of the United States;married Irene Creque; children: Lisa Marie, Taya Ayanna. **EDUCATION:** Polit Sci Maravian Coll PA, BA 1966; NY U, mA Cert Orthodics & Presthetics; VA Commonwealth U, MA Cert; Polit Sci AmUniv Wash DC. **CAREER:** VI Legislature, senator; VI Legislature 10th & 11th & 12th Legis VI, majority ldr 1976-78; VI Legislalture, spl asst to legis 1972; Dept of Social Welfare, vocational rehab counselor; Wayhne Aspinall JHS, tchr; Youth Club In Action Inc, adv tutu. **ORGANIZATIONS:** Mem Task Force Criminal Code Rev Proj; mem Board Tri-island Eco Devel Council; mem Bd VI Montessori Sch Delegate to Constl Conv. **BUSINESS ADDRESS:** Legislature Veterans Drive, Box 477 Charlotte Amalie, St Thomas, Virgin Islands of the United States 00801.

WILLIAMS, LONDELL
Government official. **PERSONAL:** Born Apr 23, 1939, Texarkana, AR; married Mary. **EDUCATION:** Los Angeles St Coll, BA 1958; Los Angeles Bible Inst, dD 1960;Univ AR 1953-55. **CAREER:** Ave Bapt Ch, pastor 1969-; Dept HEW Soc Security Admn, claims Develr 1969-; AUS, personnel specl 1964-68; US Treas Dept Bur Customs, acctg tech 1958-59; AUS Corps Engr, contract specl 1955-58. **ORGANIZATIONS:** City Bd Dir Texarkana AR 1977-; mem Texarkana AR & Texarkana TX C of C 1976-; jury commr Miller, Hempstead, Lafayette, Howard 1975-76; bd mem Texarkana Human Devel Ctr 1977; grand mastger Master Mason AF & AM Bronzeville Lodge 83 1974-77; Texarkana Ministerial Alliance 1971-77. **HONORS/ACHIEVEMENTS:** Bert Lambert Awd 1974-75; Otsdng Integrity & Character Displayed in City 1973; high quality Increase Awd HEW 1976; Sharp Shooter Awd; Good Conduct Medal . **MILITARY SERVICE:** AUS Lambert Awd 1974-75; Otsdng Integrity & Character Displayed in City 1959-61. **BUSINESS ADDRESS:** Po BOX 1214, State Line, Texarkana, AR 75501.

WILLIAMS, LONNIE RAY
Educational administrator. **PERSONAL:** Born Jan 21, 1954, Stephens, AR; son of Lonnie Williams and Rosie M Williams; married Mary Woods, Apr 10, 1987 (divorced); children: Landra, Kevin, Keaton. **EDUCATION:** Univ of AR, Fayetteville, BSBA, 1977, MEd, 1983. **CAREER:** Univ of Arizona-Fayetteville, police patrolman, 1976-78, night mgr, student union, 1978-84, dir minority engineering, 1983-86, asst dean of students, 1986-. **ORGANIZATIONS:** Mem, NAACP; Region V, adv bd mem, Natl Soc of Black Engineers, 1984-87; Region B, chairperson elect, NAMEPA 1985-86; chairperson, Arizona Assn for Multicultural Counselling, 1986-87; mem, Arizonia Assn for Counseling Guidance & Devel, 1986-; mem, Omega Psi Phi Fraternity; bd mem, Washington County Equal Opportunity Agency, 1988-91. **HONORS/ACHIEVEMENTS:** Outstanding Serv, Univ of Arizona Chapter, NSBE, 1983-86; Co-Outstanding Adv Bd Mem, Region V Adv Bd, NSBE, 1985; Outstanding Faculty/Staff Mem Black Student Assoc, 1985. **HOME ADDRESS:** 151 E Mountain, Fayetteville, AR 72701. **BUSINESS ADDRESS:** Asst Dean of Students, University of Arkansas, Arkansas Union M407A, Fayetteville, AR 72701.

WILLIAMS, LORECE P.
Educator. **PERSONAL:** Born Jan 22, 1927, Luling, TX; married Nathan H; children: Nicholas, Natalie. **EDUCATION:** Huston Tillotson Coll, BS 1947; Our Lady Lake Coll, MSW 1962; TulaneUniv New Orleans, further study. **CAREER:** ARC Brooke Army Med Ctr, dir 1969-; Our Lady Lake Coll, prof social work 1965-69; Incarnate Word Coll San Antonio, diagnostician 1969, lectr, cons, group ldr - San Antonio Jr League at incarnate word coll, trinity u, texas u, church groups, social work agencies, schs, natl assn Social Workers; Council Social Work Edn. **ORGANIZATIONS:** Faculty Welfare Council; Admissions & Schlrshp; Alpha Kappa Alpha Sorority; Race & Rel Commn; Sex & Religion; Status Women; Governors Commn Crime & Prevention; Cath Family & Child bd dir; Child Serv Bureau bd dir. **HONORS/ACHIEVEMENTS:** Excellence in Writing Awds; Theta Sigma Phi, Growing Up - Texas, pub 1972; co-author Bientennial Book, Folklore Texas Cultures. **BUSINESS ADDRESS:** 411 SW 24 St, San Antonio, TX 78285.

WILLIAMS, LOTTIE MAE
Government official. **PERSONAL:** Born Sep 02, 1931, Kinloch, MO; daughter of John B Hughes and Ora Pearl Townsend Cherry; married Ronald D Williams, Jun 25, 1977; children: Oranda Celastine Burns, Lenora Goolsby. **EDUCATION:** Florissant Valley Junion Coll, St Louis MO, degree in accounting, 1972; St Louis Univ, St Louis MO, liberal arts degree 1980, urban affairs degree 1982. **CAREER:** General Amer Insurance, St Louis MO, claims examiner, 1966-67; Bozada Drayage, St Louis MO, office mgr, 1967-71; City of St Louis MO, asst accountant, 1971-73; State Arts Council, St Louis MO, fiscal/budget officer, 1973-76; City of St Louis MO, Child Nutrition Dept, food monitor/budget officer, 1977-80; City of Velda Village MO, mayor, 1981-83 & 1987-. **ORGANIZATIONS:** Mem 1969-, deaconess 1982-, Christ Pilgrim Rest MB Church; project dir, Cultural & Recreation Center, 1976-78; mem 1978-, bd of dir 1979-87, Lupus Foundation of MO; mem, League of Women Voters, 1979-; sec 1981-83, mem 1987-, treas 1988-, MO Chapter of Black Mayors; mem, St Louis County Municipal League, 1981-83 & 1987-; mem 1981-83, city rep 1987-, MO Municipal League; co-chair, Citizens for County Progress, 1985-; chair, Task Force to Monitor the Metropolitan Sewer District, 1986-; bd of dir, Health Care Is a Human Right, 1986-; bd of dir, Coalition for the Environment, 1986-; bd of dir, Municipal Radio Systems, 1987-; co-host, radio talk show on KIRL, 1987-; mem, Task Force Comm for County Reorganization, St Louis County Municipal League, 1988; mem, Natl Conf of Black Mayors, 1988-; vice chair, Black Elected Officials for Balanced Govt, 1989. **HONORS/ACHIEVEMENTS:** Women in Management award, Univ of Kansas, 1974; Governmental Acct award, US Civil Service Commn, 1976; Electronic Data Processing award, MO State In-Service Training, 1976; Back to School award, MO Natl Educ Assn, 1981; first black female mayor elected in MO, 1981; Certificate of Appreciation, Amer Cablevision, 1982; Certificate of Appreciation, MO House of Reps, 1982; Certificate of Appreciation, Natl League of Cities' Women in Municipal Govt, 1983; Certificate of Recognition, Campaign for Human Dignity, 1985; Certificate of Appreciation, Bethel African Methodist Episcopal Church, 1987; Certificate of Appreciation, St Louis County Municipal League, 1988. **HOME ADDRESS:** 7100 Lexington, Velda Village, MO 63121.

WILLIAMS, LOUISE BERNICE
City official. **PERSONAL:** Born May 30, 1937, Abinton, PA; daughter of Richard S. Duncan and Mary Grasty Duncan; divorced; children: Cynthia Whitfield, Robert Whetts, Brian Whetts, Kimberly Williams. **EDUCATION:** Lancaster School of Business, exec sec 1964; Lincoln Univ attended; Shippenburg State Coll, Cert for Dist Justices 1973. **CAREER:** Dist Justice Office, admin clerk 1970-73; City of Lancaster 3rd & 7th Ward, dist justice 1973-85; Consolidated Dist Justice Offices City of Lancaster, admin dist justice 1983-85. **ORGANIZATIONS:** Mem Planned Parenthood of Lancaster 1978-81, Urban League of Lancaster 1979-84; pres Girls Serv of Lancaster Inc 1975-81, NAACP 1980-82; mem Lancaster County District Justice Assn; bd mem Planned Parenthood of Lancaster County 1988-; mem Commn of Cultural Diversity Millersville Univ. **HONORS/ACHIEVEMENTS:** Boss of the Year Amer Business Women's Assoc 1976; Outstanding Citizen City of Lancaster 1981; Past Pres Awd Girls Serv of Lancaster Inc 1981. **HOME ADDRESS:** 331 S Franklin St, Lancaster, PA 17602. **BUSINESS ADDRESS:** Administrative Dist Justice, Lancaster Consol Justice Off, 225 W King St, Lancaster, PA 17603.

WILLIAMS, LUCIUS LEE, JR.
Educational administrator. **PERSONAL:** Born Jun 18, 1927, Starkville, MS; married Willa Mae Harris; children: Darlene Maria, Lucius Daryl, John Patric. **EDUCATION:** Jackson StateUniv MS, BS 1951; Boston U, EdM 1957; AdelphiUniv Garden City NY, MA 1965; Tchrs Coll/Columbia U, PhD 1972. **CAREER:** Univ of MS, asst vice chancellor 1976-80; Central Elem School Roosevelt Public Schools NY, prin 1972-76; Hempstead Public Schools NY, math teacher/supr 1960-72; Haverhill HS MA, math teacher 1957-60; Sharkey Co Rolling Fork MS, math teacher 1951-54; Jackson State Univ, guest lectr 1967; Hempstead NY, acting hs prin 1970; Tate Co Senatobia MS, math consult 1979; Rust Coll Holly Springs MS, curriculum consult 1979-80. **ORGANIZATIONS:** Pres Roosevelt Mental Health Bd NY 1973-75; sec Oxford Housing Bd City of Oxford MS 1977-80; Pres Phi Delta KappaUniv MS Chap 1978-79; charter mem Jackson State Chap Omega Psi Phi Frat. **HONORS/ACHIEVEMENTS:** Letters of Commendations AUS 1955-56; Experienced Tchr Fellow Tchrs Coll ColumbiaUniv 1968-69; Omega Psi Phi Service Award Ole MS Chap of Omega Psi Phi 1980; YMCA Serv Award Haverhill MA YMCA. **MILITARY SERVICE:** AUS spec/3 1954-56. **BUSINESS ADDRESS:** University of Mississippi, Box 126, University, MS 38677.

WILLIAMS, LUCRETIA MURPHY
Educational administrator. **PERSONAL:** Born Aug 16, 1941, Springfield, OH; daughter of Lenore Dorsey Smith; married Robert H Williams; children: David Walter Bentley, Robin Lenore. **EDUCATION:** Central State Univ, BS, Elementary Educ, 1965, MEd, Guidance & Counseling, 1969; Ohio State Dept of Educ, gen aptitude test battery training, vocational guidance training certification, 1974; Xavier University, admin certification elementary & secondary, 1976. **CAREER:** Onondago Co Welfare, social worker, 1966-67; AT&T Technologies, personnel counselo, summer, 1970; Columbus Public Schools, guidance counselor, 1969-77, asst principal, 1977-78; Neptune Township Public Schools, principal, 1978-79; Columbus Public Schools, admin, 1979-. **ORGANIZATIONS:** Life mem, Natl Alliance of Black School Employees; mem, Natl Assn of Secondary School Principals, Ohio Alliance of Black School Educ, Columbus Alliance of Black School Educ, Columbus Admin Assn, Columbus Central Office Admin Assn; Delta Sigma Theta; mem, Circle-Lets, Inc; bd dirs, Center Stage Theatre, Columbus, OH, 1985; mem, Mayor's Council on Youth. **HONORS/ACHIEVEMENTS:** A Comparative Study of Faculty Knowledge of Guidance Serv in the High Schools of Springfield, OH, Master Thesis, Central State Univ, 1969. **BUSINESS ADDRESS:** Dir, Pupil Personnel, Columbus Public Schools, North Educ Center, 270 East State St, Columbus, OH 43215.

WILLIAMS, LUTHER STEWARD
Educational administrator. **PERSONAL:** Born Aug 19, 1940, Sawyerville, AL; married Constance Marion; children: Mark S; Monique M. **EDUCATION:** Miles Coll, BA 1961; Atlanta Univ, MS 1963; Purdue Univ, PhD 1968; St Univ of NY at Stoney Brook, postdoctoral 1968-69. **CAREER:** Atlanta Univ, asst prof 1969-70; Prudue Univ, asst prof 1970-73; MA Inst of Tech, assoc prof 1973-74; Prudue Univ, assoc & full prof 1974-80, asstprovost 1976-80; Washington Univ, dean of grad sch 1980-83; Univ of CO, vice pres of acad affairs 1983-84; Atlanta Univ, pres 1984-. **ORGANIZATIONS:** Atlanta United Way, bd of dir, mem 1976-; DNA Nat Advisory Council, mem 1979-81; Nat'l Inst of Hlth, council mem 1980-85; Miles Coll, bd of trustees 1985-. **HONORS/ACHIEVEMENTS:** Nat Inst of Hlth, predoctoral fellowship 1966-68, postdoctoral 1968, career development awrd 1972-75; Scientific Publications, 1969-86; 81 publications. **BUSINESS ADDRESS:** President, Atlanta University, 223 Brawley Drive, Atlanta, GA 30314.

WILLIAMS, MACEO MERTON
Educational administrator. **PERSONAL:** Born Oct 27, 1939, Baltimore, MD; married Margaret D Moon. **EDUCATION:** Morgan State Univ, AB 1959-63; Univ of Baltimore, MPA 1975-76; CA Western Univ, MA 1976-77; Wesley Theological Seminary, M Div Prog 1985; Howard Univ, MDiv 1986; Howard Univ Divinity Sch, DMin 1987. **CAREER:** State of MD, probation agent 1965-66; Dept of Housing, area coord 1966-71; Concentrated Employ Program US Dept Labor, coord 1971-74; MD Parole Comm, parole comm appointed by Gov Harry Hughes 1983-88; Bay Coll of MD, dean of students 1974-79; Centreville-Cordova Charge United Methodist Church, pastor 1986-. **ORGANIZATIONS:** Mem NAACP 1962-; bd mem Dept of Housing & Comm Devel United Meth Ch 1970-; pres Five in Five Dem Club 1974; Charter Revision Commn 1974-76; bd of trustees Keswick Nursing Home 1973-76; mem Prince Hall Grand Lodge F&AM of MD Zion Lodge #4; mem Natl Assn of Student Svcs; mem Natl Assn of Coll Couns. **HONORS/ACHIEVEMENTS:** Outstanding Young Man of Amer 1974. **BUSINESS ADDRESS:** Pastor, Centerville-Cordova UM Church, 530 N Howard St, Baltimore, MD 21201.

WILLIAMS, MALCOLM DEMOSTHENES
Retired university dean. **PERSONAL:** Born Sep 26, 1909, Warsaw, NC; son of Holly Williams and Martha Eliza Williams; married Rosa Lee Kittrell, Jun 30, 1930 (deceased); children: Frances Eliza. **EDUCATION:** Fayetteville State Tchrs Coll, diploma (w/honors) 1934; Hampton Inst, BS (w/honors) 1938; Columbia Tchrs Coll, MA 1944, EdD 1951; diploma (with honors) Fayette State University, Fayetteville, N.C. 1928-1934; BS (with honors) Hampton Univ, Hampton, VA 1934-38. **CAREER:** NC, tchr prin supr pub sch 1928-52; Columbia Univ Teachers Coll, asst to the prof 1947; teacher Hampton Inst summer 1949; Shaw Univ, prof/dir Audio-visual aids 1952-55; TX So Univ, teacher summer school 1954-55; TN State Univ Nashville, faculty 1955-75. **ORGANIZATIONS:** Life mem NEA; mem Religious Heritage of Amer; past pres Frontiers Intl Inc; Phi Delta Kappa; Kappa Delta Pi UNA/USA; mem Omega Psi Phi Frat, Natl Soc for the Study of Educ. **HONORS/ACHIEVEMENTS:** Silver Beaver Awd BSA; Disting Educator Religious Heritage of Amer; Nashville Urban League's Equal Oppor Day Awd. **HOME ADDRESS:** 630 Nocturne Dr, Nashville, TN 37207.

WILLIAMS, MALVIN A.
Educator. **PERSONAL:** Born Apr 20, 1942, Mayersville, MS; son of Oscar and Catherine; married Delores G; children: Angela, Katrina, Tiffany, Malvin Jr. **EDUCATION:** Alcorn State Univ, BS 1962; AZ State Univ, MNS 1966; Univ of Southwestern LA, PhD 1971-75. **CAREER:** Greenville Public Schools, instructor 1962-65; Alcorn State Univ, instructor 1966-71, registrar & asst dean 1975-76, dean of academic affairs 1976-. **ORGANIZATIONS:** Bd dirs Watson Chapel AME Church 1975-; mem planning/steering comm Mgmt Info System Jackson MS 1979-; bd dirs Claiborne Co Chamber of Comm 1982-; chmn Council of Chief Academic Officers 1984-86. **HONORS/ACHIEVEMENTS:** Sci Faculty Fellowship Awd NSF 1971-72; ASU Ed Office Personnel Assoc Boss of the Year 1982. **BUSINESS ADDRESS:** Dean of Academic Affairs, Alcorn StateUniv, PO Box 869 ASU, Lorman, MS 39096.

WILLIAMS, MARCUS DOYLE
Judge, university lecturer. **PERSONAL:** Born Oct 24, 1952, Nashville, TN; son of John F Williams and Pansy D Williams; married Carmen Myrie Williams, MD; children: Aaron Doyle, Adam Myrie. **EDUCATION:** Fisk Univ, BA, 1973 (university honors); Catholic Univ of Amer, School of Law, JD, 1977. **CAREER:** Office of the Commonwealth Atty, asst commonwealth atty, 1978-80; George Mason Univ, lecturer in business legal studies, 1980-; Office of the County Atty, asst county atty, 1980-87; Gen Dist Court, judge, 1987. **ORGANIZATIONS:** Bd mem, Fairfax-Falls Church, Criminal Justice Adv Bd, 1980-81; freelance writer and reviewer, 1981-; mem, Amer Business Law Assn, 1984-; bd of assocs, St Paul's Coll, 1986-87; vice chmn, Continuing Legal Educ Comm, Fairfax Bar Assn, 1986-87. **HONORS/ACHIEVEMENTS:** Omega Psi Phi Fraternity, 1971; Beta Kappa Chi, Scientific Honor Soc, Fisk Univ Chapter, 1973; Distinguished Youth Award, Office of the Army, Judge Advocate Gen, 1976; Thomas J Watson Fellow, 1977-78; Fairfax County Bd of Supvr, Serv Commendation, 1987; Serv Appreciation Award, Burke-Fairfax Jack & Jill, 1989; articles: "Arbitration of Intl Commercial Contracts: Securities and Autitrust Claims," Virginia Lawyer, 1989, "European Artitrust Law and its Application to Amer Corp," Whittier Law Review, 1987. **BUSINESS ADDRESS:** Judge Marcus D. Williams, Gen Dist Court, 4110 Chain Bridge Rd, Fairfax, VA 22030.

WILLIAMS, MARGO E.
Journalist. **PERSONAL:** Born Dec 30, 1947, St Louis, MS; daughter of James Williams and Bertha Williams. **EDUCATION:** Harris Teachers Coll, BA, 1970; St Louis Univ, MA, 1972; Southern Illinois Univ, BA, 1975; St Louis Univ, Post Grad. **CAREER:** St Louis Bd of Educ, teacher/counselor, 1970-75; KMOX-TV, CBS, St Louis, TV teacher, 1973-75; Southern Illinois Univ, acad advisor, 1975-76; WMAR-TV, Baltimore, MD, host/producer, 1976-77; WKBN-TV, CBS, Youngstown, OH, minority affairs dir, 1977-82, TV & radio producer/host; WKBD-TV, Detroit, MI, producer/host "For The Record," Black History Segments Week, news reporter, 1982-88; WKBD TV, Detroit, MI, media consultant, public relations specialist, 1989-; Freelance, writer, 1989. **ORGANIZATIONS:** Mem, Alpha Kappa Alpha, NAACP, Urban League, Soc of Professional Journalists; vice pres, Amer Business Women's Assoc, 1983-87; chmn, Ways & Means Comm, 1984, Altrusa Club Intl; media-workshop coord, Natl Assn of Black Journalist, 1983-84; coord, Women's Career Workshops; vice pres, Natl Assn of Black Journalists, Jim Dandy Ski Club; hosted, United Negro Coll Telethon, ABC, Youngstown, OH; co-coord, Afro-Amer Festival, Youngstown, OH; pres, Consumer Credit Advisory Bd, Youngstown, OH; pres, Natl Assn of Black Journalists; Your Heritage House Writers. **HONORS/ACHIEVEMENTS:** Received 15 Community Serv Awards, 1977-84; Outstanding Black Woman in the Media; Ohio Media Award, Honored for Community Serv with a special resolution & plaque from Youngstown City Council; Appeared in Glamour Magazine Career Section; Woman of the Year Award, 1982; appeared in Ebony Magazine, Broadcasting Magazine, Millimeter Magazine & RCA Today Magazine; Guest Speaker, Special Programs, Black History Month, Youngstown State Univ;Motivational Speaker, Women's Conf of Concerns, Detroit, MI, 1989. **HOME ADDRESS:** 25660 Southfield Rd, 102, Southfield, MI 48075.

WILLIAMS, MARTHA S.
Educator. **PERSONAL:** Born Nov 30, 1921, Philadelphia, PA; divorced. **EDUCATION:** State Coll, BS 1949; Wayne St U, MSLS 1971. **CAREER:** Foch School, arts teacher 1974-; Detroit Schools, librarian 1964-74; teacher, owner of nursery school 1949-64; Phil Tribune, newspaper exper 1942-44; Gary Neigh House, dir of nursery prog; Bristol England, exchange teacher 1977. **ORGANIZATIONS:** Mem Am Lib Assn; Asso Sch Libr; Mich Assn Media Edn; Active in Rep Party 1952-; prec del Gary IN 1952-; v chmn Gary City Rep Comm; del StateConv 1954-; del Rep Nat Conv 1976; Mich Rep State Comm Nat Black Rep Counc; mem 5th Pct Police Comm Coun; mem Grtr Christ Bapt Ch; mem Sch Comm Coun Apptd by Pres Ford to Adv Comm to Nat Comm on Lib & Inform Serv 1977; mem Delta Sigma Theta Sor. **BUSINESS ADDRESS:** 2962 Fairview, Detroit, MI 48214.

WILLIAMS, MARY D.
Executive secretary. **PERSONAL:** Born Jul 22, 1922, Littleton, NC. **EDUCATION:** A&T State U, BA 1944; Famous Artists Comm Art Course, 1955. **CAREER:** Tgri-State NAACP, sec; PPC News Mag, prod ed 1963-66; Philadelphia Psychiatric Ctr, sec to admn 1957-60, med sec 1951-54; Williams Spaulding Tucker & Watson, sec/bkkpr 1948-51; Philadelphia NAACP, sec/off mgr 1945-47; Family Bus, partner 1945-49. **ORGANIZATIONS:** Co-fdr Creative Bus Cncl 1967; Vol Consult in Orgnl Planning; life mem NAACP; A&T StateUniv Alumni Assc. **HONORS/ACHIEVEMENTS:** Author Negro Heritage Handbooks 1966-67; nominated 3 times for community serv awrds Ch of Four Chaplains Phila. **BUSINESS ADDRESS:** 1 N 13 St Rm 900, Philadelphia, PA 19107.

WILLIAMS, MARY HALEY
Educational administrator. **PERSONAL:** Born May 20, 1936, Edwards, MS; children: Phoebe Johnette, Mark Leonard, Kerry Janee. **EDUCATION:** S IL Univ, BS 1964; Univ of IL, Masters 1968, Doctorate Admin 1977. **CAREER:** Champaign Unit Four Schools, elem teacher 1964-72, guidance counselor 1973-77, coord fed progs 1978-81, dir comp educ 1981-. **ORGANIZATIONS:** Life mem Univ of IL Alumni Assoc; mem Urban League 1973-75; vice-pres Champaign Educ Assn 1974-75; dir christ educ Mt Olive Baptist Church 1976; sec YWCA Exec Bd 1976-78; IEA bd of directors IL Educ Assn 1976-79; prog chair Educ Adm Alumni Assn 1973-; mem IL Women's Admin 1981-; chair of salary Champaign Admins Ed Assoc 1982-. **HONORS/ACHIEVEMENTS:** Discipline rsch Champaign Unit Four Schools 1969; Black Women-20 Top Freewill Baptist 1980; Top Educator Awd Greater Holy Temple; 20-Service Awd Champaign Unit Four Schools 1984; Resource Person Champaign Comm Resource 1968-; bd of dir ALO-Parkland Comm Coll 1984-; Mary H Williams Ed Acad Mt Olive Baptist Church 1985-.

WILLIAMS, MARY ANN SHERIDAN
Educator. **PERSONAL:** Born Aug 06, 1945, Columbus, OH; married Kojo Kamau (Robert Jones Jr). **EDUCATION:** Wilmington Coll, BA 1968; Kettering Fellowship Study Abroad Basel Switzerland 1966-67; OH State Univ, MA 1972; The Union Grad Sch for Experimenting Colls & Univs, PhD 1977. **CAREER:** Valley View Schs, tchr of mass comm 1969-70; Centerville Schs, tchr of creative writing 1970-71; OH State Univ, teaching assoc div of comparature lit 1971-72, asst prof of comparative lit div black studies dept 1972-74, asst prof of theatre black studies dept 1975-77, acting chairperson black studies dept, assoc prof of black studies 1977-. **ORGANIZATIONS:** Guest lecturer & dir Coll of Wooster OH 1972; exec prod & moderator "Black Studies Broadcast Jour" WOSU radio 1972-80; hostess & exec prod "Afromotion" WOSUTV 1973-79; visiting artist & consult Wilmington Coll 1975-76; mem natl adv bd "Options in Educ" Natl Pub Radio 1977-80; mem adv panel OH Arts Council 1977-80; chmn theatre adv panel OH Arts Council 1979-80; pres Columbus Area Leadership Prog 1984-85. **HONORS/ACHIEVEMENTS:** Resolution for Outstanding Achievement for First Annual Wilmington Coll Trustees Awd for Young Alumni OH House of Reps 1975; Letter of Commendation Fed Comm Commr Benjamin Hooks 1975; Nomination for Emmy Awd Regional Chapts of Natl Acad of TV Arts & Scis 1976; 1 of 32 Natl Finalists White House Fellowship Prog 1978-79. **BUSINESS ADDRESS:** Associate Prof Black Studies, Ohio StateUniv, 486Univ Hall 230 N Oval, Columbus, OH 43210.

WILLIAMS, MATTHEW ALBERT
Physician. **PERSONAL:** Born Jun 24, 1929, Atlanta, GA; son of Charles R Williams and Alberta Hendricks Williams; married Vira E Kennedy; children: Linda M Lucas, Nanci J Newell, Pamela L. **EDUCATION:** Morehouse Clg Atlanta, Ga, BS 1950; HowardUniv Washington DC, MD 1955; Harbor Gen Hosp Torrance, CA, Int Med 1961. **CAREER:** Paradise Vly Med Staff, pres 1975-77; Matthew A Williams MD Med Corp, pres. **ORGANIZATIONS:** Mem Am Clg of Physicians; Am Soc of Int Med; Alpha Pi Boule; Alpha Omega Alpha; Hnr Med Soc; mem bd of dir, Paradise Valley Hosp; past mem cncl San Diego Med Soc 1977; past mem cncl San Diego Soc of Int Med 1977; mem Bd of OverseersUniv of CA at San Diego 1984; mem Alpha Phi Alpha Frat. **HONORS/ACHIEVEMENTS:** Elder Untd Pres Ch. **MILITARY SERVICE:** USN lt comm med 1955-58. **HOME ADDRESS:** 5740 Daffodil Ln, San Diego, CA 92120. **BUSINESS ADDRESS:** President, Matthew A Williams MD, 502 Euclid Ave, Ste 201, National City, CA 92050.

WILLIAMS, MAXINE BROYLES
Social worker. **PERSONAL:** Born Aug 06, Pittsburgh, PA; widowed. **EDUCATION:** Wilberforce U, BS;Univ of M, Adv Social Admn; WSU, Ldrshp Training & Pub; WCSW, In-Training Pgm Cert Ed Soc Serv. **CAREER:** Wayne Co Mental & Estates Div 1966-73; Wayne Co Dept Soc Welfare 1949-66; Wane Co Probate Ct Med Div 1940-45. **ORGANIZATIONS:** Dir Publicity & Pub Rel Communication Commn; St Matthew's & St Joseph's Epis Ch; exec bd mem African Art Gallery Com, vestry-woman St Matthew's & St Joseph's Epis Ch; pub relat chrwmn AAGC; fdrs Soc Detroit Inst of Arts; consult Santa Rosa Comm Grp; mem Women's ComUnited Negro Clg Fund; Cathedral Ch of St Paul Chpt; coord Cncl on Human Relat; Ch Women United; League of Women Voters; Detroit Assc of Women's Clbs; Detroit Hist Soc; Intrntl Inst; Metro YWCA; NW Voters Regis Grp; Alpha Kappa Alpha Sor; Alpha Rho Omega Detroit; NAACP; Detroit Friends of Pub Libr Inc; Detroit Urban League; Soc Wrkrs Clb of Detroit; fdrs Soc Detroit Inst of Art; exec bd mem Women's Council United Negro Coll fund; chmn Annual Banquet UNGF; exec bd Amer Assoc Univ Women; pres Parish Council St Matthew's & St Joseph Episcopal Church. **HONORS/ACHIEVEMENTS:** Humanitarian Awd Wo-He-Lo Literary Soc; 15 yr Serv Pin Detroit Urban League 1953-68; 30 Yr Serv Medallion Alpha Kappa Alpha Sor 1946-77; num awrds for Vol Work & Comm Partic; Spirit of Detroit Awd in Recognition of Exceptional Achievement Outstanding Leadership and Dedication to Improving the Quality of Life; Awd of Merit of many years of serv to Friends of African Art Founders Soc Detroit Inst of Arts; Community Awd Volunteer Work Detroit Receiving Hosp; Nation-Wide Net Work Participant Boston MA Convention, Amer Assn Univ of Women; Citation Detroit Church Woman United; Induction Prestigious Quarter Century Club Natl Urban league; Annual meeting Los Angeles CA Detroit Citation AAUW 25 Yr Serv Pin Detroit Urban League; Gen Chairperson & Coord Anniv Celebrations St Mattew's St Jospeh's Episcopal Church; 1941-86.

WILLIAMS, MCDONALD
Educator. **PERSONAL:** Born Nov 13, 1917, Pittsburgh; married Jamye H Coleman; children: Donna Selby. **EDUCATION:** Univ Pittsburgh, BA 1939, LittM 1942; OH State Univ, PhD 1954. **CAREER:** Wilberforce Univ OH, educator 1942-56; Tuskegee Inst, visiting prof, Eng, 1955; Morris Brown Coll GA, educator 1956-58; Atlanta Univ, 1957; TN State Univ, educator, honors program dir 1958-. **ORGANIZATIONS:** Modern Language Assn; Natl Council Eng Teachers; Conf Coll Comp & Communication; Am Assn of Univ Profs; pres Minority Ec Dev Corp 1970-; exec com Nashville Chap ARC 1973-; exec com Nashville Vista Pgm; mem NW Nashville Civitan Club; exec com Bordeaux YMCA Center; exec com Nashville Br NAACP 1968-; TN Voters Council; asst treasurer, Amer Red Cross. **HONORS/ACHIEVEMENTS:** Teacher of the Year, TN State Univ 1979; Corp sec NW Nashville Civitan Clb; co-editor "The Negro Speaks, The Rhetoric of Contempory Black Leaders". **BUSINESS ADDRESS:** Honors Program Dir, Tennessee State University, 3500 John Merritt Blvd, Nashville, TN 37203.

WILLIAMS, MELVIN
University administrator. **PERSONAL:** Born Jun 17, 1944, Kansas City, MO; son of Naomi Long; married Beate Charlotte Farran; children: Amy, Micah, Jonah, Naomi Long. **EDUCATION:** Pittsburg State Univ, BS Ind Tech 1967, MS Sociology 1973. **CAREER:** Peace Corps, volunteer 1967-69; Southeast KS Comm Act Program, dir social serv 1970-76; City of Parsons, dir affirmative action 1976-78; Univ of KS Medical Ctr, dir affirmative action/health careers pathways prog 1978-. **ORGANIZATIONS:** Pres SDOP Mid-America Synod 1971-; pres Greater KC Affirmative Action 1980-82; mem Civic Leadership Training Council 1985-; councilman City of Mission KS 1985-. **HONORS/ACHIEVEMENTS:** Grant Health Careers Pathways Program Div of Disadvantaged Assistance 1986-89; Black Achiever Kansas City MO SCLC 1986. **BUSINESS ADDRESS:** Dir, Univ of KS Medical Center, 39th & Rainbow Blvd, Kansas City, KS 66103.

WILLIAMS, MELVIN D.
Educational administrator. **PERSONAL:** Born Feb 03, 1933, Pittsburgh, PA; son of Aaron and Gladys; married Faye W Strawder; children: Aaron E, Steven R, Craig H. **EDUCATION:** Univ of Pittsburgh, AB Econ (Honors), 1955; Univ of Pittsburgh, MA Anthropology, 1969, PhD Anthropology, 1973; Carlow Coll, Natl Certificate in Secondary Educ, 1973. **CAREER:** Wholesale periodical Distr Co, owner-oper, 1955-66; Johnson Publishing Co, field representive, 1958-61; NDEA Title IV, fellow anthropology, 1966-69; Carlow Coll, faculty instr, asst prof, dept of sociology & anthropology, 1969-75; Colgate Univ, Olive B O'Connor, chair, 1976-77; Univ of Pittsburgh, faculty, assoc prof, anthropology, 1976-79; Intl Journal of Cultural & Social Anthropology, assoc educ of ethnology, 1976-79; Univ of Pittsburgh, adj research prof, anthropology, 1979-82; Purdue Univ, faculty, prof of anthropology, dept of sociology & anthropology, 1979-83; Univ of Maryland Coll Park, affil prof, urban studies, 1984-, faculty prof of anthropology, 1983-88; Univ of Michigan, faculty, prof of anthropology, dir, Comprehensive Studies Program, 1988. **ORGANIZATIONS:** 24 acad committees including chmn minority affairs comm, Colgate Univ, affirm action comm, Colgate Univ; deans grad review bd, Faculty of Arts & Sci, Univ of Pittsburgh, rep faculty assembly Univ of Pittsburgh; Univ senate, Purdue Univ; chancellors commiss on ethnic minority issues Univ of Maryland, campus senate to represent anthropology & Afro-Amer studies, Univ of Maryland, pres, Black Faculty Staff assoc, Univ of Maryland; 24 mem incl fellow vstg lecturer Amer Anthropological Assoc, Amer Assoc of Univ Prof, Anthropological Soc of Washington, Phi Delta Kappa, pres, org NAACP, Sigma XI, Soc of Ethnic & Special Studies, NYAS, fellow Soc of Applied Anthropology, Deans Council, Univ of Michigan. **HONORS/ACHIEVEMENTS:** 53 publications incl "Observations in Pittsburgh Ghetto Schools" Anthrop Educ Quarterly 1981; "On the St Where I Lived" Holt Rinehart & Winston 1981; "Notes from a Black Ghetto in Pittsburgh" Critical Perspective of Third World Amer Race Class Culture in Amer 1983; "Community in a Black Pentecostal Church"; 51 honors & awards incl Black Achiever Award by Talk Mag, Hon Reception in Recognition of Scholarly Achievements by Dept of Anthrop Univ of Pittsburgh 1975; MC, The Presidents Dinner for Graduating Seniors, Carlow Coll 1975; Bishops Serv Award, Catholic Diocese of Pittsburgh 1975; Hadley Cantril Memorial Award 1976; received highest teaching evaluations in the history of the univ 1976; keynote speaker, Afro-Amer Family Conf, Purdue Univ; invited speaker, Martin Luther King Program, 1983. **MILITARY SERVICE:** AUS, PA Natl Guard. **BUSINESS ADDRESS:** Prof, Dept of Anthropology, Univ of Michigan, 1054 LS&A Bldg, Ann Arbor, MI 48109.

WILLIAMS, MELVIN THOMAS, JR.
Business executive. **PERSONAL:** Born Nov 24, 1942, New York, NY; married Diane Cephas; children: Keith, Todd. **EDUCATION:** Central St U, BS 1964; ColumbiaUniv Grad Sch of Bus, MS 1976. **CAREER:** Intl Basic Economy Corp, exec vice pres plnd nghbrhd div 1970-73, mgr oper div 1973-75; Patient Care Publ Inc Med Publs, vice pres & dir 1975-80; Patient Care Intl Inc Intl Med Pblshng, pres 1980-82; Delphi Cnsltng Grp Inc, pres. **ORGANIZATIONS:** Bd of dir Johnston Intl Publ Corp 1982-; mem Intl Exec Asso 1978-; chm Intl Publ Comm 1979-80; mem One Hundred Black Men Inc 1984-; chm Invstmnt Comm NY Chap of Minorities in Cable 1984-; mem Omega Psi Phi Frat 1963-; mem The Columbia Club of NY 1980-. **HONORS/ACHIEVEMENTS:** Otstndng prof achvmnt Central StUniv Clg of Bus Adm 1983-84; otstndng young man, Otstndng Young Men of am US Jaycees 1977. **MILITARY SERVICE:** AUS Armor 1st lt 1964-66. **BUSINESS ADDRESS:** President, Delphi Consulting Group Inc, 16 Thorndal Cir, Darien, CT 06820.

WILLIAMS, MELVIN WALKER
Physician. **PERSONAL:** Born Jan 28, 1939, New York, NY; married Marilyann Thomas; children: Jennifer, Martin. **EDUCATION:** Fordham Univ, BS 1960; Howard Univ, MD 1967. **CAREER:** US Public Health Serv Hosp, internship 1967-68; US Public Health Serv, commd ofcr 1967-77; St Elizabeth's Hosp, 1968-70; MA Gen Hosp Boston, residency 1970-73; NIMH-Staff Coll, assoc dir 1973-77; Job Corp Hlth Office US Dept of Labor, consult 1973-; NIMH, teacher 1973-; Howard Univ, tchr dept of psychiatry 1974-75; Amer Bd of Psychiatry & Neurology, certified 1976; Amer Bd of Psychiatry & Neurology, examiner 1977-; Private Practice, psychiatry. **ORGANIZATIONS:** Mem Black Psychiatrists of Amer, Natl Med Assn, Alliance for Psychiatric Prog, Amer Psychiatric Assn, Amer Med Assn, Commd Ofcrs Assn of US Pub Hlth Serv; WA Psychiatric Soc Chi Delta Mu Frat; Kappa Alpha Psi Frat; assoc NIMH Mental Hlth Career Devel Prog 1970-75; fellow Harvard Med Sch Deptof Psychiatry 1970-73; co-author Black Parent's Handbook 1975; US Pub Hlth Serv 1967-77. **BUSINESS ADDRESS:** 1800 R St NW, Washington, DC 20009.

WILLIAMS, MICHAEL PATRICK
Minister. **PERSONAL:** Born Dec 18, 1951, StLouis, MO; married Donna J Morton. **EDUCATION:** Westminster Coll Fulton MO, BA 1973; Yale Univ, MDiv 1976. **CAREER:** Compensatory Ed/Action for Bridgeport Comm Devel, dir 1977-78; E End Bapt Tabernacle, pastor 1974-84; Antioch Baptist Ch of Christ Houston, sr pastor 1984-. **ORGANIZATIONS:** Mem bd dirs Natl Baptist Convention USA 1982-; mem Governing Bd Natl Council of Churches 1983; founder Abundant Life Ministries; chmn acad affairs/planning comm/mem exec comm CT Bd of Higher Educ 1977-81; Com on Youth Ministry Bapt World Alli 1979-81; pres bd dir Greater Bridgeport Regional Narcotics 1979-; editorial staff Publishing Bd Natl Bapt Conv USA 1977; mem Alpha Phi Alpha Frat; pres Greater Bridgeport NAACP 1980-82. **HONORS/ACHIEVEMENTS:** Protestant Fellowship Rockefeller Found 1974-76; Doctoral Study Fellowship Rockefeller Found 1976-77; publ The Black Evang Ministry in the Ante-Bellum Border States Found 1978; Outstanding Young Man of Amer US Jaycees 1979; publs "The Bible, What's In It and How to Use It" 1985; publ The Black Evang Ministry in the Ante-Bellum Border States Foundations 1978; Hon Doctorate VA Baptist Seminary S CT Theol Seminary. **BUSINESS ADDRESS:** Senior Pastor, Antioch Baptist Ch of Christ, 500 Clay St, Houston, TX 77002.

WILLIAMS, MILTON See EL-KATI, MAHHMOUD

WILLIAMS, MORRIS O.
Business executive. **PERSONAL:** Born Oct 20, Texarkana, AR; married Geraldine Copeland; children: Sr M Shawn Copeland, OP. **EDUCATION:** Wayne State Univ, BS BA 1940; Univ of Detroit, grad studies. **CAREER:** Detroit Housing Commission, jr acct 1941-47; Morris O Williams & Co, owner 1946-. **ORGANIZATIONS:** Enrolled agent US Treasury Dept; mem Nat'l Society Public Accts; mem (past state treasurer) Ind Accts Assoc Mich; brd of dirs YMCA, Fisher Branch; mem Omega Psi Phi Fraternity; mem African Methodist Episcopal Church; mem NAACP; mem Detroit Idlewilders, Inc. **MILITARY SERVICE:** Infantry Volunteer Officer Candidate 1943. **BUSINESS ADDRESS:** President, Morris O Williams & Co, 2101 W Grand Blvd, Detroit, MI 48208.

WILLIAMS, MOSES, SR.
Policeman. **PERSONAL:** Born Aug 15, 1932, Franklin Parish; married Matra; children: Rhonda, Matra, Lula, Otha, Brenda, James, Jessie, Moses, Jr, Robert, Allen, Betty. **CAREER:** Tallulah Police Dept, lieutenant. **ORGANIZATIONS:** Pres Steering Comm 1967-77; vice pres Madison Vote League Inc 1964-84; pres Delta Comm Action Colo Gov Treen Staff 1979-83; bd of dir Devel Block Grant Washington DC; elected to state HH Way from the 5th Regional 1980-; pres vice pres bd dirs Delta Comm Action 1965-76; pres Madison Parish Bd of Econ Devel Loan Bd 1971-77; vice pres Madison Parish Police Jury 1972-77; HEW Police Jury Assn; Municipal Police Off Assn; 5th Dist Black Caucus Comm; commr Madison Parish Port; adv coun bd Title IV Sch Bd; NAACP; RDA Rural Devel Assn; Magnolia St Peace Off Assn; BSA; McCall Sr High PTA; MarquisWho's Who Publ Bd 1976-77; 5th Dist LA Educ Assn 1972; Evening Star Lodge No 113 1972. **HONORS/ACHIEVEMENTS:** Notable Amer in Bicentennial 1976; Personalities of So 1975-76; Colone Gov Staff 1973, 1979-83; Reg VII Drug Training & Resource Ctr.

WILLIAMS, NANCY WEBB
Government official. **PERSONAL:** Born Aug 01, Quincy, IL; daughter of Charles Webb and Garnet Davis Webb; married Jesse B Williams (deceased), Apr 11, 1959 (deceased); children: Cynthia, Troy, Peter, Wendy. **EDUCATION:** Quincy Coll, BA 1957; Tennessee A&I Univ, 1961; Univ of Nevada, MPA 1977. **CAREER:** Shelby Cty Training School, teacher 1957-61; State of Nevada, sr dep prob ofcr 1961-74; Clark Co NV, dir probation serv 1974-80; exec dir Cultural Alliance Found, publishing firm 1985-; freelance writer, Las Vegas, NV 1985-;. **ORGANIZATIONS:** Mem NV Crime Commn 1970-; NV So Reg Dist Allocation Comm 1970-; adv bd NV Juv Delinquency 1974; mem NV Peace Officers Standards Comm 1975-; chmn Juv Task Force So NV 1974-; Task Force Corrections So NV 1970-74; field faculty Intl Coll 1977; dir Child Haven 1981-84; bd mem Univ of Humanistic Studies Las Vegas NV, Faculty of UHS 1984. **HONORS/ACHIEVEMENTS:** Doctor of Humane Leters, Univ of Humanistic Studies 1986; Distinguished Woman Award, Soroptomist Intl 1986; When We Were Colored, publication/poetry volume 1986; Dinah's Pain and other poems of The Black Life Experience 1988. **BUSINESS ADDRESS:** Director Child Protective Services, Clark Co, 3401 E Bonanza Rd, Las Vegas, NV 89101.

WILLIAMS, NAOMI B.
Educator. **PERSONAL:** Born Dec 04, 1942, New Smyrna, FL; married Mac James Williams, Sr; children: Pam, Mac Jr, Essie, Brenda Yolanda, Roderick, Wendell. **EDUCATION:** Bethune-Cookman Coll, BS 1963; Florida A&M Univ, MEd 1973; Stetson Univ, Certificate Counseling 1974; Rollins Coll, Specialist in Educ 1976; Nova Univ, EdD 1980. **CAREER:** Volusia Co Public Schools, teacher 1963-67, dean of girls/counselor 1967-73, asst high school principal 1973-74; Daytona Beach Jr Coll, dir of admissions/recruiting 1974-78; St Petersburg Jr Coll, dir of admissions/registrar 1978-; 1986 coll registar/campus registar/dir of admissions, St Petersburg Junior Coll. **ORGANIZATIONS:** Mem Amer Assoc of Collegiate Registrars and Admission Officers, FL Assoc of Collegiate Registrars and Admission Officers, FL Assoc of Comm Colls, Southern Assoc of Collegiate Registrars and Admissions Officers; bd of dirs United Way; mem Bethune-Cookman Coll Alumni Assoc; bd of dirs "Spirit"; pres Youth Dept Church of God by Faith; sunday school teacher Church of God by Faith; mem Grad Chap Kappa Delta Pi, Grad Chap Delta Sigma Theta Sor, Urgan League; adult advisor Clearwater Youth Council NAACP; dir of adult sunday sch dept Mt Carmel Baptist Church. **HONORS/ACHIEVEMENTS:** First Black Female Asst Principal in a Sr High School Volusia Co Schs Daytona Beach FL; First Black Dir of Admissions Daytona Beach Comm Coll Daytona Beach FL; First Black Registrar St Petersburg Jr Coll; graduation speaker Trinity Arts and Technical Acad The Philippines; Teacher of the Year Awd Campbell Sr High School Daytona Beach; Mother of the Year from Ben and Mary's Kindergarten Daytona Beach; founders day speaker Delta Sigma Theta Sor Clearwter Branch. **HOME ADDRESS:** 1300 Ridge Avenue, Clearwater, FL 34615. **BUSINESS ADDRESS:** Dr. Naomi B Williams, Registar, St. Petersburg Junior College, 2465 Drew Street, Clearwater, FL 34625.

WILLIAMS, NAOMI FISHER (MRS. C. DELMAR WILLIAMS)
Educator. **PERSONAL:** Born May 20, 1913, Arlington, AL; married Charles Delmar. **EDUCATION:** Knoxville Coll, Knoxville, TN, BA, 1930; Coll of the City of NY, BS, 1941; Columbia Univ NYC, MA 1944. **CAREER:** Bd of Educ Brooklyn, teacher, special educ 1944; Bd of Educ, teacher adult educ 1945-76; United Negro Coll Fund, teacher. **ORGANI-**

ZATIONS: Bd dir, United Negro Coll Fund, 1960; vice pres, Knoxville Coll, Natl Alumni Assn, 1965-69; life mem NAACP 1966-; bd of trustees Knoxville Coll, TN 1969-77; exec bd NY Inter-Alumni Council 1976-; mem Zeta Phi Beta Sorority. **HONORS/ACHIEVEMENTS:** Individual Performance Award, Natl Alumni Cncl UNCF 1966; Dedication Serv Fund Raising Award Greater NY Inter-Alumni Council, 1975; Alumni Recognition Dedication Knoxville Coll Natl Alumni Assn 1975; Dedication & Support Award, Girl Scout Cncl of Greater NY 1976; UNCF Distinguished Leadership Award 1981; Knoxville Coll Medallion, 1985. **BUSINESS ADDRESS:** United Negro Coll Fund Inc, 500 East 62nd St, New York, NY 10021.

WILLIAMS, NAPOLEON
Business executive, elected official. **PERSONAL:** Born Nov 24, 1900, Vienna, GA; married Joyce Henry; children: Gail L, Sonya. **EDUCATION:** Ft Valley State Coll, BS Soc Studies, Natural Sci; Atlanta Univ, MA Admin; Atlanta School of Mortuary Sci. **CAREER:** Vienna High & Indus School, principal 1952-70; Vienna HS, principal 1970-76; GA Southwestern Coll, instructor, 1977-78; JW Williams Funeral Home, pres. **ORGANIZATIONS:** Mem Dooly Cty Bi-Racial Comm, 32 Degree Mason, Noble of the Mystic Shrine of Amer; chmn Dooly Cty Bd of Health; mem NAACP; mem bd of dir West Central GA Comm Action Council; pres GMA 3rd Dist 1984-85. **HONORS/ACHIEVEMENTS:** Hon Doctor of Law Degrees; Co-author Dooly Cty School Bldg named in honor of N Williams Health & Phys Ed Bldg; Gtea for Meritorious Serv to the Cause of Ed; Intl Personnel Rsch Creativity Awd Creative & Successful Personalities 1972; Distinguished Serv Awd Recipient Ft Valley State Coll 1981; Distinguished Serv Awd Recipient City of Vienna 1976. **MILITARY SERVICE:** WWII Vet; Awarded, WWII Vict Medal, Amer Serv Medal, European/African/Middle East Serv Medal, Good Cond Medal AR 600-68 Philippine Liber Serv Ribbon. **BUSINESS ADDRESS:** President, JW Williams Funeral Home, 407 17th Ave West, Cordele, GA 31015.

WILLIAMS, NORRIS GERALD
Educational administrator, journalist. **PERSONAL:** Born May 12, 1948, Oklahoma City, OK; son of Norris Williams and Mattye Williams; married Carolyn Ann Moch, Aug 28, 1970; children: Diarra Koro, Ayanna Kai, Jawanza Jamaal; Norris Emanuel. **EDUCATION:** Wiley Coll TX, BS (Honor Student) 1970; Central State Univ OK, MS 1977. **CAREER:** Douglass HS, OK City, all conf pitcher 1966; Images KFGL & KAEZ, radio talk show host 1977-78; R&B Prod, Jam Prod, Feyline Prod, C&F Prod, promotional consultant, 1979-82; OK City Publ Schools, coach 1970-75, teacher 1970-77; Park & Rec Dept OK City, mgr 1970-82; Black Dispatch Publ Co, sports ed 1979-82; Univ of OK Black Student Servcs, coord 1977-. **ORGANIZATIONS:** Sec, treas Kappa Alpha Psi 1968-70; pres KAZI Comm Serv 1972-73; pres Images Comm Serv 1976-78; pres Assoc of Black Personnel Univ of OK 1979-80; Pres Assoc of Black personnel 1982-83; mem OKABSE 1984-85; commiss OK Black Historical Soc 1984-85; mem Alpha Chi Chap Kappa Alpha Psi; polemarch Norman Alumni Chapter, Kappa Alpha Psi 1986-88. **HONORS/ACHIEVEMENTS:** Outstanding Student Kappa Alpha Psi Alpha Chi Wiley Coll 1969; Baseball Coach of the Year Capitol Conf OK City 1975; Staff Person of the Year Black Peoples Union Univ of OK 1977-79; Comm Serv Awd 1983; Univ of OK Outstanding Achievement Awd 1984; Commissioner Higher Educ for OK Assoc of Black School Educators 1985. **BUSINESS ADDRESS:** Coordinator, Univ of Oklahoma, Black Student Services, 731 Elm Room 219, Norman, OK 73019.

WILLIAMS, NOVELLA STEWART
Business executive. **PERSONAL:** Born Jul 13, 1927, Johnston Co, NC; married Thomas; children: Thomas, Kim, Michelle, Pamela, Willis, Frank, Charles. **EDUCATION:** Rutgers U, 1971;Univ of PA, 1976. **CAREER:** Citizens for Prog,, fndr pres 1974-. **ORGANIZATIONS:** Chmn bd dir W Philadelphia Comm Free Sch 1969-; dir Philadelphia Anti Poverty Commin 1970-; rep Citizens for Prog & Non-govtl Org 1968-; pres Peoples Hlth Serv 1973-; prtnr & consult Ed Mgmt Assc 1973-; sec bd dir Hlth Sys Agcy of SE PA 1976-; consult US Consumer Prod Safety Commin 1975-76; v chmn YMCA 1970; bd dir RCHPC; bd dir SE PA Am Red Cross 1976; bd dir Philadelphia Urban Coalitition 1977; mem By Laws; person & consumer aff Com Philadelphia Hlth Mgmt Corp 1976-; del Dem Natl Conv 1976; mem dem Crdntl Com 1976; mem Dem Rules Com 1976; Dem Del Whip 1976; coord 513 Women's Com Carter-Mondale Camp; White House Conf on Hunger 1970; Red Book 1970; prin Natl Ed Assc 1972; Seven Sch 1971; Harcourt-Brace-World-Measurement & Conf 1969; House Foreign Aff Sub-comCongrssnl Rec 1970. **HONORS/ACHIEVEMENTS:** Black Interprise Mag; Philly Talk; Jet Mag; Time Mag; Afro Am; NY Times; Wall St Jour. **BUSINESS ADDRESS:** President, Citizens for Progress, Inc, 5308 Spruce St, Philadelphia, PA 19139.

WILLIAMS, ORA
Educator. **PERSONAL:** Born Feb 18, 1926, Lakewood, NJ; daughter of Charles Williams and Ida Rolles Roach Williams. **EDUCATION:** Virginia Union University, Richmond, VA, AB, 1950; Howard University, Washington, DC, MA, 1953; University of California, Irvine, CA, PhD, 1974. **CAREER:** Southern University, Baton Rouge, LA, instructor, 1953-55; Tuskegee Institute, Tuskegee, AL, instructor, 1955-57; Morgan State University, Baltimore, MD, instructor, 1957-65; Camp Fire Girls, Inc, New York, NY, program advisor, 1965-68; California State University, Long Beach, CA, assistant professor, professor, 1968-88, professor emerita, 1988—. **ORGANIZATIONS:** College Language Association; National Council of Teachers of English; Modern Language Association; board of directors, BEEM Foundation for the Advancement of Music, 1982; NAACP; member, Afro-American Youth Association, 1984. **HONORS/ACHIEVEMENTS:** Author of article "Johnny Doesn't/Didn't Hear," Journal of Negro History, spring, 1964; author, American Black Women in the Arts and Social Sciences: A Bibliographical Survey, Scarecrow Press, 1973; Second Annual Achievement Award in humanities and performing arts research, Virginia Union University Alumni Association of Southern California, 1983; Pillar of the Community Award, Long Beach Community Improvement League, 1988; Outstanding Service Award, Mayor of Long Beach, 1988. **BUSINESS ADDRESS:** Department of English, California State University, 1250 Bellflower Boulevard, Humanities Office Building, Long Beach, CA 90840.

WILLIAMS, ORA P. See THOMAS, ORA P.

WILLIAMS, OTIS P.
Business executive. **PERSONAL:** Married Lillian C Black; children: Gia, Sheryl. **EDUCATION:** Bethune-Cookman Clg, BS 1959;Univ of MI;Univ of NY. **CAREER:** Marshall HS Plant City, FL, tchr coach 1960-66; Prudential Ins Agt 1966-67; Laughner Kelly Dev Corp, sls mgr 1968-70. **ORGANIZATIONS:** Ins gen agt Otis P Williams Assc 1967-; mem New Mt Zion Bapt Ch; Most Worshipul Prince Hall AF&AM of FL St James Lodge No 18; pres Lakeland Br NAACP 1967-73; state pres FL NAACP 1972-74; chmn of pgm Comm Action Migrant Pgm. **HONORS/ACHIEVEMENTS:** Pi iota man of yr Omega Psi Phi Prat 1967; appointed by gov askew to Bd Dir FL Legal Serv Inc 1973-; sold $1,000,000 worth of life ins within 15 Wks first in history of co. **BUSINESS ADDRESS:** 521 W Meml Blvd, Lakeland, FL.

WILLIAMS, PATRICIA ANNE
Attorney. **PERSONAL:** Born Dec 16, 1943, NYC; daughter of David Charles Williams, Jr and Kathleen Valerie Carrington Williams. **EDUCATION:** Cornell U, BA 1965; Cert of African Inst Columbia U, MA 1967; Yale Univ Law Sch, JD 1972. **CAREER:** SDNY, asst us atty 1977-86; Willkie Farr & Gallagher, assc atty 1972-76; New Haven Legal Asst Assc, legal clk 1971-72; New York City Crim Justice Coord Council, law clerk 1970; Phelps-Stokes Fund NYC, sec admin asst 1967-69. **ORGANIZATIONS:** Assn of the Bar of the City of New York; Federal Bar Council. **HONORS/ACHIEVEMENTS:** Scroll of Achievement North Shore Chapter of Natl Assn of Negro Business and Professional Women's Clubs Inc 1985.

WILLIAMS, PATRICIA HILL
Educational administrator. **PERSONAL:** Born May 03, 1939, Richmond, VA; daughter of Marshall Hill and Virginia Hill; divorced; children: Tory Therese. **EDUCATION:** State Univ of New York, BA, 1976; New York Inst of Tech, MA, Communications Art, 1981. **CAREER:** Babylon Beacon Newspaper, assoc editor, 1971-79; New York Amsterdam News, columnist, 1972-84; Amer Cancer Soc, public information officer, 1972-80; State Univ of New York at Farmingdale, asst to the pres for devel. **ORGANIZATIONS:** Pres Partners of the Americas, Long Island/St Vincent; mem, Alpha Kappa Alpha Theta Iota Omega, Business Advisory Council Suffolk Co; trustee, bd mem, 100 Black Women of Long Island, 1978-; bd mem, State Univ Confederation of Alumni Assoc, 1983-, State Univ of New York, Council for Univ Advancement, 1985; commr, Babylon Historic Comm; presidential appointee, Natl Advisory Council on Women's Educ Programs, 1987-90; northeast region chairperson Natl Black Republic Council; mem, New England Alumni Trust Fund; LI center for Business & Professional Women, NAACP, NCNW. **HONORS/ACHIEVEMENTS:** Woman of the Year Media Award, Bethel AME Church, 1980; PR Award of Excellence, LI Flower Show, 1983; Comm Serv in Public Relations & Comm 100 Black Men of LI, 1983; Fellow Intl Devel WK Kellogg Found, 1984-86; Woman of the Year, New York State Council of Black Republicans, 1986; Outstanding Alumna of the Year, Suny/Coll of Old Westbury, 1988. **BUSINESS ADDRESS:** Asst to the Pres for Devel, State Univ of New York-Farmingdale, Admin Bldg, Farmingdale, NY 11735.

WILLIAMS, PATRICIA R.
Educator. **PERSONAL:** Born Oct 04, 1943, Detroit. **EDUCATION:** BS 1968; MS 1974; MI State U, Grad Study;Univ of Chgo. **CAREER:** Farrand School Detroit Public School System, teacher consult educator; Wayne State Univ, supv teacher 1972-. **ORGANIZATIONS:** Project Read Tchr 1969-73; sch librairan 1969-71; fdr adv Trowbridge Girls Clb 1971-; bd Govs Wayne StateUniv Alumni Assc 1974; mem Cncl for Exceptional Children; mem Metro Reading Cncl; mem Mich Assc for Emotionally Disturbed Children Natl; 3rd vice pres Natl Assc of Negro Bus & Prof Women's Clbs Inc;past Natl Youth Ldr; past Dist Youth Ldr; mem Women's Conf of Concerns; mem Natl Cncl of Women in US. **HONORS/ACHIEVEMENTS:** Recipient outst elem tchrs of am awrd 1972; outst ldrshp & serv awrd Bus & Prof Women 1971; del White House Conf on Youth 1969; comm serv awrd1967; bus & prof wommen's serv awrd 1970; united found torch drive awrd. **BUSINESS ADDRESS:** 5057 Woodward Ave, Room 602, Detroit, MI 48202.

WILLIAMS, PATRICK NEHEMIAH
Construction company executive, board of education member. **PERSONAL:** Born Sep 28, 1928, St Croix, Virgin Islands of the United States;son of Norman P. A. Williams and Ingerborg Cassimeer; married Inez Byron, Dec 21, 1951; children: Glenice, Sharon, Lindel, Wayne, Patrice, Denise, Donna, Patrick M, Raymond, Aisha. **EDUCATION:** Pace Univ, BPS 1976. **CAREER:** Dist of St Croix, senator 1963-65; Legislature of VI, consult 1965-70, exec dir 1970-81; The Chase Manhattan Bank, asst mgr 1981-82; VI Dept of Ag, commiss. **ORGANIZATIONS:** State chmn Dem Party of the VI 1964-72; sec, treas NASBE 1976-78; chmn VI Bd of Ed 1978-80; trustee VI Bd of Trustees 1978-; commiss VI Dept of Agriculture 1983-87. **HONORS/ACHIEVEMENTS:** Listed in Intl Who's Who of Intellectuals 1976; Author "Virgin Islands 1917-Present" Pace Univ 1976; Legislative Resolution 1988. **MILITARY SERVICE:** USMS lance corp 8 yrs. **BUSINESS ADDRESS:** Assistant to President, Zenon Construction Corp, PO Box 5440, Sunny Isle, St Croix, Virgin Islands of the United States 00823-5440.

WILLIAMS, PAUL
Government executive. **PERSONAL:** Born Aug 06, 1929, Jacksonville, IL; son of Russell Williams; married Ora Mosby; children: Reva. **EDUCATION:** Jacksonville IL, BA 1956; Fed Exec Inst, attended 1971; Brookings Inst, attended 1975; Harvard Univ Kennedy School of Govt, attended 1980; Pacific Inst, Seattle WA, Certificate, Facilitator Investment in Excellent, 1988; Amer Univ, Washington DC, Certificate, Exec Devel Seminar 1984. **CAREER:** UPO Washington DC, assoc dir fin & admin 1956-63; Dept of State, internatl admin officer 1963-68; HUD, 1965-68; Office of Management Housing FHA Commr, dir1968-; City of Chicago, Chicago IL, dir of finance 1956-63; State Dept, Washington DC, foreign serv officer, 1963-68; UPO, Washington, DC, assoc dir of Finance 1964; HUD, Washington, DC, dir office of management 1968-. **ORGANIZATIONS:** Dir of finance City of Chicago; bd dir MD Sch for Performing Arts; mem Natl Assn Housing & Redevel Officials; Amer Soc for Public Admins; past pres Bel-pre PTA; past pres Strathmore, bel Pre Civic Assoc treas 1986-87; sr exec assoc HUD Chapt. **HONORS/ACHIEVEMENTS:** Certificate of Merit HUD 1974; HUD Superior Serv Awd 1975; Nom Pres Awd for Outstanding Civilian Serv HUD 1973; Outstanding Serv Awds 1968-69; Citation from US Sec of State; Commendation US Commn Pacific 1967; Distinguished Citizens Awd IL Coll 1976; Hon Litt D IL Coll 1979; Outstanding Performance Rating 1982, 1983; Sr Executive Serv Performance Awd 1983; Certificate of Special Achievement Comm on Fraud Waste & Mismanagement 1984; Certificate of Special Achievement Hud 1984. **MILITARY SERVICE:** AUS 1948-52. **BUSINESS ADDRESS:** Dir, Office of Mgmt Housing, Rm 9114 HUD Bldg, 451-7 St SW, Washington, DC 20410.

WILLIAMS, PEYTON, JR.
Educator. **PERSONAL:** Born Apr 10, 1942, Cochran, GA; married Sandra E Pryor; chil-

dren: Rachelle Lenore, Tara Alyce. **EDUCATION:** Ft Valley State Coll, BS; Tuskegee Inst, MA;Univ GA, EDS. **CAREER:** State Schools & Special Activities GA Dept of Educ, asso state supt 1977-; Cen Middle School, prin 1970-77; Cen Elementary School, prin 1967-70; Cen HS, prin vice-prin 1964-67. **ORGANIZATIONS:** Chmn First Dist Professional Devel Commn; mem GA Tchr Educ Council 1974-77; mem GA Assn of Educators Gov Task Force; sec GA Middle Sch Prins Assn 1973; mem Adv Com Gov Conf on Educ 1977; mem bd dir Screen-Jenkins Regional Library 1973-77; bd dir Screven Co Dept of Family & Children Svcs; mem Citizens Adv Coun Area 24 Mental Health/Mental Retardation; bd dir CSRA Office of Econ Opportunity 1971-77; mem Bd dir Screven Co C of C 1974; mem Screven-Sylvania Arts Coun; mem adv bd Screven Co Assn for Retarded Children; mem Omega Psi Phi Frat; mem Selective Serv Local Bd #128; mem Policy Com CSRA OEO; scoutmaster Boy Scout Troop 348; organist choir dir St Paul Bapt Ch. **HONORS/ACHIEVEMENTS:** Educator of the Year Screven-Sylvania Optimist Club 1976; Distinguished Serv Award Screven Co Bd of Edn; Most Valuable Mem Trophy GA Council of Deliberation 32 Degree Masons PHA; Outstanding Serv Award Screven Co Chap NAACP; Plaque of Appreciation Screven Co Chap Am Cancer Soc; Meritorious Serv Award St Paul Bapt Ch; Adminstr of Yr Award Phi Delt Kappa 1980. **BUSINESS ADDRESS:** Ste 231, State Office Bldg, Atlanta, GA 30334.

WILLIAMS, PHILIP B.
Attorney. **PERSONAL:** Born Dec 30, 1922, Gonzales, TX; married Frances A. **EDUCATION:** Roosevelt U, BSC 1952; DePaul U, LlB 1963, JD 1969. **CAREER:** Self Employed Atty, 1966-; Chgo, po clk 1947-52; IRS, collection ofcr & revenue agent 1952-64; Serv Fed Savings & Loan Assc, mgr 1964-66. **ORGANIZATIONS:** Bd mem cncl Park Grove Real Est Inc 1967-; bd mem cncl Crestway Maint Corp 1970-; mem Cook Cty IL State & Am Bar Assc; mem Tech Asst Adv Bd; United Bldrs Assc of Chgo; mem Comm Adv Cncl; chgo Bapt Isnt. **MILITARY SERVICE:** AUS sgt 1943-45. **BUSINESS ADDRESS:** 8032 S Cottage Grove Ave, Chicago, IL.

WILLIAMS, PRESTON N.
Theology educator. **PERSONAL:** Born May 23, 1926, Alcolu, SC; son of Anderson James Williams and Bertha Bell McRae Williams; married Constance Marie Willard; children: Mark Gordon, David Bruce. **EDUCATION:** Washington & Jefferson Coll, AB 1947, MA 1948; Johnson C Smith Univ, BD 1950; Yale Univ, STM 1954; Harvard Univ, PhD 1967. **CAREER:** Boston Univ School Theol, Martin Luther King Jr prof social ethics 1970-71; Harvard Div School, acting dean 1974-75, Houghton prof theol & contemporary change 1971-. **ORGANIZATIONS:** Acting dir WEB DuBois Inst 1975-77; editor-at-large Christian Century 1972-; mem, pres Amer Acad Religion 1975-; dir, pres Amer Soc Christian Ethics 1974-75; mem Phi Beta Kappa. **HONORS/ACHIEVEMENTS:** Contrib articles to professional jrnls; ordained to ministry Presb Church 1950. **BUSINESS ADDRESS:** Theology Professor, Harvard Divinity Schl, 45 Francis Ave, Cambridge, MA 02138.

WILLIAMS, RALEIGH R.
Real estate broker, tax service. **PERSONAL:** Married Vernell Johnson; children: Rudolph, Karen, Kevin, Kenneth. **EDUCATION:** EconomisUniv Omaha, Bge. **CAREER:** Retired Serviceman; Raleigh A Williams Realty Construction & Income Tax Serv, re broker, income tax cons, gen contractor & mgmt cons. **ORGANIZATIONS:** Pres Dulleton Ct NAACP; Boy Scout Master; mgr Little League Baseball; coach Little League Football; mem Am Inst Industrial Eng; pres Young Men Bus Assc; tres OEO; NCO of Qtr; Perrin AFB 1967. **HONORS/ACHIEVEMENTS:** Baseball Champion Colorado Springs 1965; spec recognition for political work NAACP Chpt. **MILITARY SERVICE:** USAF 1952-72. **BUSINESS ADDRESS:** 611 A Padgett Loop, Walterboro, SC 29488.

WILLIAMS, RANDOLPH
Attorney. **PERSONAL:** Born Mar 29, 1944, Montgomery, AL; children: Randall. **EDUCATION:** Bowie State Coll, BA 1969; Georgetown Univ Law School, JD 1973. **CAREER:** District Attorney's Office, chief asst dist attny. **ORGANIZATIONS:** Mem Natl Conf of Black Laywers, Natl Bar Assoc, Amer Bar Assoc, Natl Dist Attny Assoc. **MILITARY SERVICE:** USAF airman 1st class 1962-65. **BUSINESS ADDRESS:** Chief Asst District Atty, District Attorney's Office, 1300 Chestnut St, Philadelphia, PA 19107.

WILLIAMS, RAY H.
Attorney, educator. **PERSONAL:** Born Jul 16, 1931, Brooklyn; married Gwendolyn Stringer; children: Gayle, Tonirae, Adrienne, Robert. **EDUCATION:** CityUniv of NY (Baruch Sch), BBA 1957; Brooklyn Law Sch, JD 1961. **CAREER:** John Jay Coll of Criminal Justice CUNY, assc prof law & crim justice 1979-; Crim Div New York City Legal Aid Soc, asst atty 1977-79; Admn of Justice Pgm Inst for Urban Affairs & Research Howard Univ, faculty/dir 1975-77; Crim Justice Forest Park Comm Coll St Louis, assc prof 1971-; St Louis, asst circ atty 1970-71; Leg Aid Soc St Louis, assc dir 1970; Bedford-Stuyvesant Leg Serv Corp, exec dir 1968-69; B-S Youth in Action Comm Corp, legal counsel 1966-68; private practice 1963-66; NY Co, asst dist atty 1961-63; New York City Police Dept, police officer & atty 1955-61. **ORGANIZATIONS:** Mem NY Bar 1961; mem Mo Bar 1970; mem Fed Bars of NY & MO. **HONORS/ACHIEVEMENTS:** Recip 3 Medals of valor as Police Ofcr; comm ldrshp awrd YMCA; 2 Awrds for Pub Serv NY Recorder Nwspr; comm serv awrd Brooklyn NAACP 1964; edtrl commendation NY Post & NY Times Nwspr; edtr commendation Natl Catholic Reporter; commendation US Congressional Record 1968. **BUSINESS ADDRESS:** John Jay Coll of Criminal Jstc, 444 W 56th St, New York, NY 10019.

WILLIAMS, REGGIE
Professional athlete. **PERSONAL:** Born Sep 19, 1954, Flint, MI; married Marianna; children: Julian, Jarren. **EDUCATION:** Dartmouth U. **CAREER:** Cincinnati Bengals, linebacker 1976-; Orchem Inc, vp/genl mgr. **ORGANIZATIONS:** Mem bd of trustees Cincinnati Nat Assn of Speech & Hearing (NASHA); Cincinnatians to Support Edn; spokesperson Big Brothers & Big Sisters of Greater Cincinnati; Cincinnati Playhouse in the Park; chmn Greater Cincinnati Chamber of Commerce Sports Cncl; Kentucky Diabetes Found; co-chairperson Cincinnati CerebralPalsy Telethon 1983; United Way; Ricky King Fund; Dartmouth Club of Cincinnati. **HONORS/ACHIEVEMENTS:** All-Ivy League 3 seasons; Am Football Coaches All-Am; Voted by fans Bengals' Man of the Yr 1982-83. **BUSINESS ADDRESS:** Cincinnati Bengals, 200 Riverfront Stadium, Cincinnati, OH 54202.

WILLIAMS, REGINA VLOYN-KINCHEN
Appointed city official. **PERSONAL:** Born Nov 15, 1947, Detroit, MI; daughter of Mr and Mrs Nathaniel Kinchen; married Drew B Williams; children: Traci A, Kristin L, Drew Michael. **EDUCATION:** Eastern MI Univ, BS 1971; Virginia Commonwealth Univ, MPA 1987. **CAREER:** City of Ypsilanti, dir of personnel & labor relations 1972-79; City of Richmond, dir of personnel 1979-82; Commonwealth of VA, state dir of personnel & training 1982-84; J Sergeant Reynolds Comm Coll, adjunct prof 1982-; City of Richmond, VA 1988-; adjunct faculty, Natl Fire Training Adademy, 1989-. **ORGANIZATIONS:** Mem bd of dirs Natl Forum for Black Public Administrators; vice pres, Intl City Managers Assoc, Amer Soc for Public Administrators; co-founder past pres Richmond Chap Conf of Minority Public Administrators; workshop leader, guest lecturer at natl professional conferences; adjunct faculty mem J Sargent Reynolds Comm Coll; mem Alpha Kappa Alpha Sor Inc. **HONORS/ACHIEVEMENTS:** Outstanding Young Women of Amer 12th edition; contributor to Virginia Govt textbook "By the Good People of Virginia, "by C Fleming, Serwa Award, Virginia Chapter, Natl Coalition of 100 Black Women, 1989. **BUSINESS ADDRESS:** Deputy City Manager, City of Richmond, 900 E Broad St Rm 301, Richmond, VA 23219.

WILLIAMS, REGINALD CLARK
Government administrator. **PERSONAL:** Born Aug 22, 1950, DeLand, FL; married Ella Mae Ashford; children: Deirdre LaFay, Andre Terrell. **EDUCATION:** Seminole Jr Coll, AA Gen Studies 1975-77; Univ of Central FL, BS Bus Admin 1977-80. **CAREER:** East Central FL Reg Planning Co, rsch analyst 1971-77; Cty of Volusia Planning Dept, program coord 1977-80, comm devel admin asst 1980-81, acting caadir 1985-, comm devel dir 1981-. **ORGANIZATIONS:** Coach West Volusia Pop Warner Football Assoc 1976-; mem Natl Assoc of Hsg & Redevel Off 1977-; sponsor Electrifying Gents 1982-84; bd mem FL Comm Devel Assoc 1983-, Comm Hsg Res Bd 1984-. **HONORS/ACHIEVEMENTS:** Cert of Recogn West Volusia YMCA 1981; Cert of Apprec Youth of St Annis Prim Baptist Church 1982; Cert of Apprec Electra Lytes Charity Club 1983; Coachof Year West Volusia Pop Warner Parents Assoc 1983; Cert of Recogn Electra Lyles Charity Club 1985. **BUSINESS ADDRESS:** Dir Community Development, County of Volusia, 250 N Beach St, Daytona Beach, FL 32014.

WILLIAMS, REGINALD T.
Executive director. **PERSONAL:** Born May 14, 1945, Newark, NJ; married Gisela; children: Robbie, Robin, Shawn. **EDUCATION:** Essex Cty Coll, AAS 1970; Rutgers Univ New Brunswick NJ, BA 1972; Temple Univ Philadelphia, MA 1975. **CAREER:** Essex Cty Urban League, dir of econ devel & employment 1969-72; City of Newark NJ, dir of consumer affairs 1970-72; Bucks Cty Comm Action Agency, asst exec dir 1973-74; Various Corps & US Govt, consult minority affairs, various corps 1973-; United Way of Central MD, dir of affirmative action 1976-79; UrbanLeague of Lancaster Cty PA, exec dir. **ORGANIZATIONS:** Sec Eastern Reg Council of Urban League; dept host Evening Mag WJZ-TV Baltimore. **HONORS/ACHIEVEMENTS:** "Guide to Minority Bus in Newark" Barton Press 1970; Consumer Protection Awd US Fed Trade Comm 1971; Howard Cty Human Relations Awd Howard Cty MD 1976; Outstanding Young Columbian Awd Columbia Jaycees 1979; "A Buyers Guide to Doing Business with Minority vendors," TPC Printing Ctr HRMC Publisher 1985.

WILLIAMS, RICHARD, JR.
Elected official. **PERSONAL:** Born Feb 10, 1933, Alcoa, TN; son of Richard Williams and Gertrude Williams; married Evelyn Robinson; children: Vivien Williams. **EDUCATION:** Ft Gordon Military Acad of Leadership, Certificate 1953; US DOE Courier Training Serv Albuquerque NM, 1973. **CAREER:** Greyhound Bus Lines, baggage & matl handler 1963-73; US DOE Courier Serv Oak Ridge TN, courier 1973-79; Sears Roebuck & Co, catalog sales; Blount County Dist 1, commissioner. **ORGANIZATIONS:** Past worshipful master Granite Lodge #289 1977; commiss Blount Cty TN 1984-; mem Blount Cty Exec Comm of the Republican Party 1984-; serves as Minority-at-Large Rep of 16-County East Tennessee Devel Dist; 33rd Degree Mason; illustrious potentate Almas Temple #71; deacon & Sunday School tchr St John Baptist Church Alcoa, TN; mem Committee on Committees, Cable Authority Comm, Highway Comm, Airport Hazard Comm, Community Action Comm; alt delegate to 1984 Natl Republican Conv; past commander-in-chief of Alcoa Consistory No 175; mem Homecoming '86 Comm; mem Martin Luther King State Holiday Comm; commander in chief Alcoa Consistory #175; past pontentate Almas Temple #71; sheriff comm Blount County Beer Bd. **HONORS/ACHIEVEMENTS:** Mason of the Year East Tennessee Chap 1977; Shriners Outstanding Leadership Awd Alcoa TN 1979; Devoted Serv Awd Shriners East TN; Colonel Aide De Camp presented by Governor Lamar Alexander 1984; 3 Performance Awards for Professionalism from US Dept Energy; numerous church awards for Christian Leadership. **MILITARY SERVICE:** AUS, US Corp of Military Police corpl 1953-55; Grad with top honors from Ft Gordon Military Acad Ft Gordon GA. **HOME ADDRESS:** 167 McMillan St, Alcoa, TN 37701.

WILLIAMS, RICHARD LENWOOD
Dentist. **PERSONAL:** Born Mar 11, 1931, Schenectady, NY; married Martha E; children: Brian Lenwood, Kevin Allyn, Darren Wayne, Lori Elaine. **EDUCATION:** Fisk U, BA 1953; Howard U, DDS 1957. **CAREER:** Queens Gen Hosp 1958-73; Self Employed Dent 1977. **ORGANIZATIONS:** Mem Dent Assc Queens Clinc Soc; fin sec Queens Clin Soc; record & sec Queens Clin Soc 1977; mem Alpha Phi Alpha Frat; chmn Les Amis of Queens 1970; tres Les Amis of Queens 1977. **BUSINESS ADDRESS:** 120-27 New York Blvd, Jamaica, NY 11434.

WILLIAMS, ROBERT B.
Attorney. **PERSONAL:** Born Aug 10, 1943, Washington, DC. **EDUCATION:** Univ of MD, BA 1966;Univ of MD Sch of Law, JD 1972. **CAREER:** Howard Cty MD, pvt prac. **ORGANIZATIONS:** Mem Howard Cty Bar Assc; Am Bar Assc; Vol Fire Co Clarksville, MD; mem Sigma Phi Epsilon Chesapeake Rubgy Ftbl Clb. **HONORS/ACHIEVEMENTS:** Recipient dean's ListUniv of MD. **MILITARY SERVICE:** AUS sp/4 1967-69; Army Commendation Medal. **BUSINESS ADDRESS:** 8370 Court Ave, Ellicott City, MD.

WILLIAMS, ROBERT D.
Educator. **PERSONAL:** Born Jun 04, 1931, Newport News, VA; married Jackie Murray. **EDUCATION:** Howard U, BS 1957, MS 1960;Univ of MN, PhD 1975. **CAREER:** Shaw Univ, div chmn/human resources 1979-; State Univ of NY, assc prof 1975-79; Franklin-Marshall Coll, asst prof 1974-75; Norfolk State Univ, asst prof 1964-70; Natl & Inst of Mental

Health, res psychologist 1959-60 & 1962-63; Howard Univ, instr 1960-61 & 1962-64; SE Tidewater Opportunities Proj, psychologist 1966-68. **ORGANIZATIONS:** Cncl LEAA Norfolk, VA 1967-68; mem Natl Assc of Black Psychologists 1974; mem Assc of Afrcn Peoples Westbury NY 1979; flwshp Psychometrick Rsrch Educ Testing Serv 1971. **HONORS/ACHIEVEMENTS:** Hon soc in psychology Psi Chi HowardUniv 1957; pub "A Measure of Competence in Clg Stdnts" 1975; pub "Criteria for Competence Psychological Reports" 1979; recipient of Good conduct medal USAF. **MILITARY SERVICE:** USAF stf sgt 1947-52. **BUSINESS ADDRESS:** 118 South St, Raleigh, NC 27611.

WILLIAMS, ROBERT D., SR.
Educator. **PERSONAL:** Born Sep 13, 1916, Frankfort, KY; son of Sylvester L. Williams (deceased); married Anna, Feb 05, 1942; children: Robert Jr, Valarie, Marsha, Rachelle. **EDUCATION:** KY Stae Univ, AB 1941; IN Univ, MS 1955; IN Univ, adv study 1965-66. **CAREER:** KY Publ School System, coach 1946-53, head tennis coach 1955-57, head baseball coach 1955-71, asst football coach 1955-65, head basketball coach 1966-67, assoc prof dept of health & pe 1953-82. **ORGANIZATIONS:** Mem Natl Intramural Assoc; mem 1950, exchecquer 1977 KAY 1950; charter mem Alpha Phi Omega 1967; city commiss Frankfort City Recreation Bd 1968-; bd trustees YMCA 1971-75; pres Esquire Club 1973-75; vice pres Esquire Club 1975-77; mem bd of dirs Big Brothers & Big Sisters 1984-86; trustee 1st Bapt Church; memKAAPER, AAHPER, AAUP, Natl Basketball Coaches Assoc, 32nd Deg Mason, Retired Officers Assoc, KY Teachers Retired Assoc, Natl Assoc of Retired Teachers; life mem Reserve Officers Assoc; VFW 4075. **MILITARY SERVICE:** AUS retired maj 1941-76; 1st black tactical officer Ft Benning GA. **HOME ADDRESS:** 108 Deepwood Rd, Frankfort, KY 40601.

WILLIAMS, ROBERT H.
Physician, educator. **PERSONAL:** Born Dec 01, 1938, Washington, DC; married Judy R Williams. **EDUCATION:** Howard U, BS 1959, MS 1960; HowardUniv Clg of Med, MD 1964. **CAREER:** Family Practice Howard Univ Coll of Med, asst prof; Comm Group Health Found Inc, med dir; Walter Reed Army Hosp & Med Officer, intern 1965-67; DeWitt Army & Hospital, chief med clinics 1968-69 15th inf div vietnam, med officer 1967-68; Howard Univ Coll of med, fellow 1970-71. **ORGANIZATIONS:** Mem Natl Med Assc; mem Med Soc of DC; chmn Fmly Prac Scientific Pgm; Natl Med Assc 1971. **HONORS/ACHIEVEMENTS:** Recipient Milton K Francis Schlrshp Awrd 1961; bronze star Army Commendation Medal 1968; combat medic badge 1968. **MILITARY SERVICE:** AUSMC capt/mjr 1964-69. **BUSINESS ADDRESS:** Howard Univ Coll of Med, 2400 Sixth St NW, Washington, DC 20059.

WILLIAMS, ROBERT JERRY
Professional athlete. **PERSONAL:** Born Sep 01, 1954, Yazoo City, MS; married Linda; children: Rodrick, Aisha. **EDUCATION:** Univ of MS, attended. **CAREER:** Buffalo Bills, professional football player. **HONORS/ACHIEVEMENTS:** Earned a berth on the AFC squad in the 1983 Pro Bowl following the 1982 season; a second team All-AFC choice in 1979 by UPI; one of the defensive ends on the Bills' Silver Anniv All-Time team; 4 letters & a tri-capt as a sr Univ of MS; All-Southeastern Conf honors on both UPI & AP clubs; 1st team honors as a sophomore & jr of the UPI team; played in the Senior Bowl, East-West Shrine game, All-Amer Bowl; AP Natl Lineman-of-the Week as a sophomore Univ of MS.

WILLIAMS, ROBERT L.
Educator. **PERSONAL:** Born Feb 20, 1930, Biscoe, AR; married Ava L; children: Robbie, Julius, Yvonne, Larry, Reva, Dorothy, Robert A Michael. **EDUCATION:** Philadner Smith Coll, BA 1953; Wayne St Univ, MEd 1955; Washington Univ, PhD 1961. **CAREER:** AR St Hosp, asst psychologist 1955-57; VA Hosp, psychology trainee 1957-61, St Louis asst chief psychology serv 1961-66; Spokane WA, exec dir hospital improvement 1966-68; NIMH, 9th region mental health consultant psychology 1968-69; VA Hosp, chief psychology serv 1969-70; Washington Univ, assoc prof psychology 1969-70, prof of psychology dir black studies prog 1970-74; Robert L Williams Assoc Inc, founder/pres 1973-; Washington Univ, prof psychology 1970-. **ORGANIZATIONS:** Bds & comms NIMH 1970-72; past natl chmn Assoc Black Psychologists; Amer Personel & Guidance Assoc; chmn bd of dir Inst of Black STudies Inc Cognitive Styles of Black People, Identity Issues, Personality Development Tsts Black People; dir Comprehensive Trtmt Unit & Psychological Consult at Lindell Hospital St Louis MO; many articles published. **HONORS/ACHIEVEMENTS:** Citizen of the Yr 8th Dist Meeting KC MO 1983; Yes I Can Awd 1984. **BUSINESS ADDRESS:** Prof of Psychology, WashingtonUniv, Box 1109, St Louis, MO 63130.

WILLIAMS, ROBERT LEE
Educational executive. **PERSONAL:** Born Jul 19, 1933, Lorman, MS; married Wilma McGee; children: Schelia, Robert, Philvester, Dennis, Meshell. **EDUCATION:** Bd Ed Alcorn State U, pres. **HONORS/ACHIEVEMENTS:** Naacp awrd 1969; hon citizen Kenner, LA 1969; ms state conv NAACP 1969.

WILLIAMS, ROBERT LEE
Dentist, educational administrator. **PERSONAL:** Born Jun 03, 1936, Shreveport, LA; married Dorothy Young; children: Janis, Jennifer, Ginetta, Tara. **EDUCATION:** Grambling State Univ, BS 1959; Xavier Univ, Further Study 1960; LA Tech Ruston, Further Study 1970; Southern Univ Baton Rouge, MEd 1970. **CAREER:** Southern Univ at Shreveport, dr upward bound 1978, chmn speech dept 1979-85, dir of evening div. **ORGANIZATIONS:** Owner Private Employment Agency 1964, Product Co 1968, Dixie Janitorial Serv 1970-85, Restaurant 1972; bd mem Caddo Par School Bd 1975-84; mem bd of dir Caddo Comm Action Agency 1975-84; supt sunday school Mt Corinth Baptist Church. **HONORS/ACHIEVEMENTS:** Grant in cont ed Southern Univ New Orleans 1972; Received approx 50 awards. **HOME ADDRESS:** 1538 Martha Ave, Shreveport, LA 71101. **BUSINESS ADDRESS:** Dir of Evening Division, SouthernUniv, 3050 Dr Martin L King Dr, Shreveport, LA 71107.

WILLIAMS, ROBERT LEE, JR.
Physician. **PERSONAL:** Born May 16, 1955, Dayton, OH; son of Robert Lee Williams and Loretta Delores Thomas Williams; married Dawn Manning, Jul 11, 1987; children: Camille Monique. **EDUCATION:** Morgan State Univ, BS, 1977; Meharry Medical Coll, MD, 1986; Hahnemann Univ Hospital, 1986-. **CAREER:** US Army Chemical Corps, military instructor, 1977-79; Third Armored Div Europe, chem staff officer, 1979-82; Meharry Medical Coll, medical student, 1982-86; Hahnemann Univ Hospital, ob/gyn resident, 1986-. **ORGANIZATIONS:** Life mem, Kappa Alpha Psi Fraternity, 1976-; mem, Amer Medical Assn, 1982-; Natl Alumni Assn of Morgan State Univ, 1984-; Natl Alumni Assoc of Meharry Medical Coll, 1986-; mem, NAACP, 1986-; junior fellow, Amer Coll of Ob/Gyn, 1986-; mem, Natl Assn of Doctors, 1987-; mem Natl Medical Assn, 1986-. **HONORS/ACHIEVEMENTS:** Upjohn Achievement Award in Obstetrics and Gynecology, 1986; Promethean Kappa Tau Honor Society, MSU, 1974; Beta Kappa Chi, Science Org, MSU, 1975-77; author, "A Retrospective Study of Pregnancy Complicated with Infection by Treponema Pallidum," Hahnemann Hospital, 1988, "Cocaine Use in a High-Risk Obstetrical Population: How Serious Is the Problem," Hahnemann Hospital, 1989. **MILITARY SERVICE:** AUS capt 5 yrs; Army Achievement Medal 1982. **BUSINESS ADDRESS:** Resident Physician, Hahnemann University Hospital, Ob/Gyn Dept, Philadelphia, PA 19102.

WILLIAMS, ROBERT W.
Business executive. **PERSONAL:** Born Sep 21, 1922, Ottumwa, IA; son of Henry H. Williams and Bertha E. Williams; married Joan R Moore; children: Angela, Robin, Robert W II. **EDUCATION:** Temple Univ, attended; UCLA, attended. **CAREER:** Bohemian Dist Co, salesman 1952-55; Falstaff Brewing Co, mgr 1957-65; Somerset Importers Ltd, mgr; Hunt Wesson, retired pres; True Image Prod, pres. **ORGANIZATIONS:** Mem LA African Sister City Comm, Natl Assoc Market Devel, Screen Actors Guild, Amer Fed TV Artists, Urban Coalition, Amer Friends Serv Comm, Brookside Mens Golf Club, NAACP, PTA; pres Devel Bd CA State Univ LA; mem Black Bus Assoc, Tuskegee Airmen Inc; commr, Utility Commn of Pasadena; President's Advisory Bd, California State Univ, Los Angeles; mem, Found Bd, California State Univ, Los Angeles. **HONORS/ACHIEVEMENTS:** "The Ottumwa Kid", creat, prod & hosted human relatTV shows; 1st natl to host black talk show 1962; author "Redtails at Ramitelli". **MILITARY SERVICE:** USAF capt 1942-47; Disting Flying Cross; Air Medal w/6 OLC; Pres Unit Cit. **BUSINESS ADDRESS:** President, True Image Prod, 1220 N. Arroyo Blvd, Pasadena, CA 91103.

WILLIAMS, RODNEY ELLIOTT
Retired chief of police. **PERSONAL:** Born Nov 14, 1928, San Francisco, CA; son of Nelson Williams and Ruby Williams; married Joyce Gray; children: Rodney II, Brian, Vivian. **EDUCATION:** San Francisco City Coll, AA 1956; San Francisco State Univ, BA 1972; Golden Gate Univ, MA 1973. **CAREER:** San Francisco Police Dept, dir 1969-77; City & Cnty of San Francisco, insp of police retired July 1983; Peralta Comm College Dist, chief of police 1983-88. **ORGANIZATIONS:** Bd of dir Westside Mental Health 1971-75; Reality House W 1972-76; bd of dir Comm Streetwork Ctr 1972-76; guest lecturer Golden Gate Univ 1973; Life tchng credential State of CA Comm Coll Dist in Pub Adm. **HONORS/ACHIEVEMENTS:** Commendation State of CA Assembly 1968, 1977; Cert of Hon Bd of Supr 1968; Liberty Bell Award SF Bar Assn 1974; commendation, CA State Asembly 1983; commendation, CA State Senate 1983. **MILITARY SERVICE:** AUS 1951-53.

WILLIAMS, ROGER
Education administrator. **EDUCATION:** Morehead Clg, BA 1965; Atlanta U, MA 1972. **CAREER:** Paine Coll, asst to dean 1977-; French Paine Coll, dir instr 1976-77; Wonder World Child Devel Center Inc 1971-74; Twilight Sewing Plant, bookkeeper 1968; W Side High School, French instructor 1966-68. **ORGANIZATIONS:** Mem Assn Overseas Educators; NAACP; sec Twilight Improvement Assn, financial officer Amer Legion Post 597; Fulbright Assistantship 1965-66; French Govt. **HONORS/ACHIEVEMENTS:** Fellowship Lycee Marcel Pagnol, Marseilles France, 1965-66. **MILITARY SERVICE:** Military Serv 1968-70. **BUSINESS ADDRESS:** Rt 2 Box 230 D, Lincolnton, GA 30817.

WILLIAMS, ROGER KENTON
Educator. **PERSONAL:** Born Feb 18, 1914, Harrisburg, PA; married Beryl Elisabeth Warner; children: Scott Warner PhD. **EDUCATION:** Claflin Coll, BA 1936; PA State Coll, MS 1940, DPhil 1946. **CAREER:** Claflin Coll, asst dean/personnel 1936-38; AT&T Coll, asst prof psych 1940-41, prof of psych 1946-48; Morgan State Coll, prof of psych 1948-74, vice pres acad affairs 1972-75, vice pres planning/op analy 1975-77, retired prof of psych 1977-83. **ORGANIZATIONS:** Pres Ed Computing in Minority 1973-76, Wilson Park Improvement Assn, 1980-. **HONORS/ACHIEVEMENTS:** Omega Psi Phi Fraternity, 1936; lifetime mem, NAACP 1975; Student Govt Award Distinguished Teacher of the Year, Morgan 1966-67; acting dean, Grad School Morgan State Coll 1967-68. **MILITARY SERVICE:** USCG chief yeoman 1942-45. **HOME ADDRESS:** 4905 The Alameda, Baltimore, MD 21239.

WILLIAMS, RON ROBERT
Assistant basketball coach. **PERSONAL:** Born Sep 24, 1944, Weirton, WV; son of Raymond and Blanche; married Faye; children: Eric, Raynia. **EDUCATION:** West Virginia Univ, BS 1968. **CAREER:** San Francisco Warriors, professional basketball player 1968-73; NBA Milwaukee Bucks Retired Sphix, professional basketball plyr 1968; Univ of California, Berkeley CA, assistant basketball coach 1981-84; Iona Coll, New Rochelle, NY assistant basketball coach 1984-. **ORGANIZATIONS:** First basketball player to Play So Conf All-Amer 1967-68; All Conf So & Conf 1965-68. **HONORS/ACHIEVEMENTS:** Athlete of year 1968; All Dist All-Amer NBA Team; Upper Ohio Valley Hall of Fame 1985; West Virginia Sport Hall of Fame 1987.

WILLIAMS, RONALD CHARLES
Attorney. **PERSONAL:** Born Jun 19, 1948, Corsicana, TX; divorced; children: Steven, Anita. **EDUCATION:** CO Sch of Mines, BS 1971; Univ of Utah, MBA 1978; Univ of CO, JD 1979. **CAREER:** US Dept of the Interior, patent counsel 1979-82; Storage Tech Corp, corp & patent counsel 1982-85; private practice, attorney-at-law. **ORGANIZATIONS:** Pres Tapestry Films Inc; bd of dirs Cadric Drug Rehab Org. **MILITARY SERVICE:** AUS capt 4 1/2 yrs. **BUSINESS ADDRESS:** Attorney-at-Law, 2413 Washington #250, Denver, CO 80205.

WILLIAMS, RONALD LEE
Elected official. **PERSONAL:** Born Aug 31, 1949, Washington, DC; married Fern M; children: Ron Williams II, Nateshia, Natiia M. **EDUCATION:** Univ of the Dist of Columbia, Soc 1977. **CAREER:** Shaw UM Food & Clothing Bank, vice chmn 1981-; SE Vicarate Cluster of Churches, chmn of the bd 1984-85; Advisory Neighborhood Commiss, chairperson 1984-; Camp Simms Citizen Adv Task Force, chmn 1984-; Christian Social Concerns, dir.

ORGANIZATIONS: Mil personnel tech Sec of the Army/Army Discharge Review Bds 1973-; bd mem Concerned Citizens on Alcohol/Drug Abuse 1982-, Comm Action Involvement 1983-; Unied Way 1983; UBF 1983-. **HONORS/ACHIEVEMENTS:** Letters Appreciation/Commendations and Plaques from Community Org, Mayor, City Council 1980-. **MILITARY SERVICE:** AUS 124th Signal Battalion 3 yrs. **BUSINESS ADDRESS:** Dir, Church & Soc Christians for, Social Concerns, 2525 12th Pl SE, Washington, DC 20020.

WILLIAMS, RONALD WESLEY
Transportation manager. **PERSONAL:** Born Nov 16, 1946, Chicago, IL; son of Richard G Williams and Odessa Shelton Williams; married Doris; children: Donna, Michele. **EDUCATION:** Chapman Coll, BA, 1974. **CAREER:** United Airlines, asst to vice pres, 1976-79, passenger serv mgr, 1979-80, city mgr, 1980-83, customer serv mgr, 1983-84, general mgr customer serv. **ORGANIZATIONS:** Treasurer North Merced California Rotary Club, 1974; vice pres, Lions Club, 1979; mem, Toledo Sales & Mktg, 1980; bd mem, WGTE TV Comm Adv Bd, 1980; comm mem, Bowling Green Univ, Aerotech Advisory Comm, 1980; volunteer, United Way Corp Rep, 1981; mem, Skal Club, 1976; mem, Madison, WI, Public Safety Review Bd, 1989-; bd of dir, Wexford Village Home Owners Assn, 1989-. **HONORS/ACHIEVEMENTS:** Award of Merit, United Airlines, 1988; Private Pilot, 1976-. **MILITARY SERVICE:** IL Army Natl Guard 1966-67. **BUSINESS ADDRESS:** Gen Manager, Customer Serv, United Airlines, 4000 International Lane, Madison, WI 53704.

WILLIAMS, ROOSEVELT
Manager. **PERSONAL:** Born Jan 30, 1944, Clewiston, FL; married Mary L Flemming; children: Tanana R, Menkara R. **EDUCATION:** Tuskegge Inst, 1962-63; FL A&MUniv Tallahasee, BS Pol Sci 1966; SyracuseUniv Grad Sch, 1966-67; Computer Systems Analysis/Proj Mgmt/ALC/COBOL/OS Syst Cntrl for Pgmrs, cert. **CAREER:** MI Bell Telephone Comptrollers, dist data processing mgr 1979-; Am Tele Co, prsnl reltns supr 1976-78; MI Bell Tele Co, data processing mgr1972-75,pub reltns supr 1971-72, cmptr oper mgr 1970-71, systm analyst 1970; NY Tele Co, acctg mgr 1967-70; Rainbow Children's Ctr, co-owner. **ORGANIZATIONS:** Pres Hubbard-King Comm Cncl 1974-76; visiting prof Black Exec Exchange Prog Urban League; steward Baber Meml AME Ch; intern US Info Agency 1965. **HONORS/ACHIEVEMENTS:** (magna cum laude) FL A&MUniv 1966; fgn afrs schlr Ford Found Syracuse U, 1966-67. **BUSINESS ADDRESS:** MI Bell Telephone Co, 23500 Northwestern, Southfield, MI.

WILLIAMS, ROSA B.
Public relations manager. **PERSONAL:** Born Sep 29, 1933, Starke, FL. **EDUCATION:** Santa Fe Comm Coll, AA 1976. **CAREER:** Comm Action Agency, super of Outreach workers 1965-70; Bell Nursery, supervising cook 1965-70; Comm Action Agency, super 1971-72; Alachua Co Coord Child Care, eligibility worker 1972; Sunland Ctr Dept of HRS, activities coord 1983-. **ORGANIZATIONS:** Mem of the following organs Elk 33 Degree; chmn Concerned Citizen for Juvenile Justice; League of Women Voters; chmn Alachua Co Democratic Club; Alachua Co Democratic Exec Comm; chmn Debonaire Social Club; bd of dirs Shands Hosp; chmn bd of dirs United Gainesville Comm Develop Corp; Comm on the Status of Women; Sickle Cell Organ of Alachua Co; Alachua Co Girls Club of Amer; NW 5th Ave Neighborhood Crime Prevention Prog; adv council Displaced Homemaker Prog; 1st vice chmn Alachua Co NAACP; dir United Way; Alachua Co Coord Child Care; Alachua Co Economic Develop; Comm Policy Adv Comm; chairperson, Black on Black Task Force. **HONORS/ACHIEVEMENTS:** Recognition of Contribution Cultural Arts Coalition; Gainesville Sun's 6th Most Influential Citizen Recognition; Comm Serv Awd NAACP 1968; Very Important Citizen Recognition City of Gainesville 1974; Leadership & Achievement Awd Alpha Phi Alpha Frat 1974; dir United Way 1968-71, 1975-80; Outstanding Serv to Comm Awd Gainesville Review of Issues & Trends 1978; Comm Serv Awd Alpha Phi Alpha 1979; Disting Serv to the Comm in Field of Educ Lodge 1218 IBPOE Elks 1983; Disting Serv Awd Alachua Co Educ Assn 1983; Citizen Against Criminal Environment Gainesville Police Dept 1984; Springhill Baptist Church contribution to Black Comm 1984. **BUSINESS ADDRESS:** Public Relations Manager, Sunland Training Ctr, PO Box 1150, Gainesville, FL 32602.

WILLIAMS, RUBY MAI (NEE MCKNIGHT)
Association executive. **PERSONAL:** Born Aug 30, 1904, Topeka, KS; married Melvin Williams. **EDUCATION:** KS State Tchrs Clge, tchng credential 1931. **CAREER:** Pasadena NAACP 1966-; real estate sales; natl Youth Work Com 1962-69; Golden State Life Ins Co, cashier & clk 1936-43; CA State Employment, cnslng & Placement 1932-36. **ORGANIZATIONS:** Pres Pasadena Dem Womens Club 1967-68; pres Interracial Womens Club 1969-70; org & pres NW Citizens of Pasadena 1978; chmn Pasadena Recreation Commn 1971-72; adv Com Citizens Urban Renewal Pasadena 1977; mayors com City of Pasadena 1979-; adv com Kid Space-Mus for Children 1979-. **HONORS/ACHIEVEMENTS:** Citizen of Year Pasadena Human Relations 1975; listed in Pasadena 100 Yrs of History 1975; Woman of Year Knights of Pythians LA CA 1976; Citizens Award PTA 1977; YWCA Woman of Year Pasadena YWCA 1977; Youth Work Award Natl Youth Work Com NY 1977; 1st Black Kindergarten Tchr Topeka.

WILLIAMS, RUDY V.
Educational administrator. **PERSONAL:** Born in Waxahachie, TX; married Ora Ruth Pitts; children: Keith W, Derwin B, Cedric L, Risha V. **EDUCATION:** Huston-Tillotson Clge Austin TX, bS Bus Admin; Univ of AZ Tucson, MEd 1964; FL Atlantic Univ Boca Raton FL, edS 1975. **CAREER:** Miami-Dade Comm Coll, assc dean 1970-, admin asst 1969-70; Comm Action Agency EOPI Miami FL, prog admin 1966-69; Sears Roebuck & Co, salesman 1967-69; Tucson Public School, teacher 1963-66; Bureau of Indian Affairs, prin teacher 1956-63; Southern Assn of Coll & School, consult 1972-; FL Intl Univ Miami, adj prof 1975-. **ORGANIZATIONS:** Mem Phi Beta Sigma Frat 1952-; vice pres St Albans Day Nursery 1970-; mem Phi Delta Kappa 1972-. **HONORS/ACHIEVEMENTS:** "Unemployment Waste Away" FL Voc Jour 1978; "FL Comm Clge Occupational Deans & Dir Competencies" unpub 1979; "Viable Guidance for the Minority Student"Minority Educ 1979. **MILITARY SERVICE:** AUS sgt 1954-56. **BUSINESS ADDRESS:** Miami-Dade Comm Coll, 1101 SW 104 St, Miami, FL 33176.

WILLIAMS, RUNETTE FLOWERS See FLOWERS, RUNETTE

WILLIAMS, RUTHANN EVEGE
Business executive. **PERSONAL:** Born May 13, 1945, Buffalo, NY; divorced; children: Nichole Suzanne. **EDUCATION:** SUNY Buffalo, BS Secondary Ed 1962-66, MS History Ed 1971, PhD Higher Ed Admin 1981. **CAREER:** Buffalo Pulbic Schools, teacher 1966-71; Erie Comm Coll, asst to prof 1971-75; SUNY Buffalo, dir of urban planning 1975-76; Northern VA Comm Coll, asstto pres 1976-77; Burroughs Corp, dir public affairs 1982-86; Equitable Life Assurance Soc of the US, dir of corporate support 1986-, exec asst to the chairman. **ORGANIZATIONS:** Bd of dir Children's Hosp, Detroit Historical Soc; mem bd of control Lake Superior Coll; mem, bd of dir Gifts in Kind Natl United Way; mem Public Relations Soc of Amer, Detroit Chap of Links Inc; bd of dir Health Watch. **HONORS/ACHIEVEMENTS:** Article CASE Currents 1981; Women in Educational Fundraising. **HOME ADDRESS:** 200 E 71st St Apt 15G, New York, NY 10021. **BUSINESS ADDRESS:** Exec Asst to Chrmn of Board, Equitable Life Assurance Soc, of the US, 787 7th Avenue, New York, NY 10019.

WILLIAMS, SAMM-ART (SAMUEL ART WILLIAMS)
Director. **PERSONAL:** Born Jan 20, 1946, Philadelphia, PA; son of Samuel Williams and Valdosia. **EDUCATION:** Morgan State Coll, BA, Political Science, Psychology, 1968. **CAREER:** Freedom Theater, Philadelphia, PA, actor, 1968-73; Negro Ensemble Co, actor and mem of Playwrights Workshop, 1973-78; independent playwright, New York, NY, and Los Angeles, CA, beginning in 1974; actor in stage, television, and film productions, 1974—. **ORGANIZATIONS:** Mem, Omega Psi Phi Frat, 1967—; mem, Screen Actors Guild; mem, Writers Guild of Amer; mem, Dramatist Guild. **HONORS/ACHIEVEMENTS:** Playwright for stage productions, including "Home," produced on Broadway, 1980, "The Sixteenth Round," produced Off-Broadway, 1980, and "Friends," produced in New York, NY, 1983; co-author of teleplay "Solomon Northrup's Odyssey," PBS, 1985, and author of teleplay "Charlotte Forten's Mission: Experiment in Freedom," PBS, 1985; contributing writer to musical stage productions, including "Sophisticated Ladies," Philadelphia, PA, 1980; Tony Award Nomination for play "Home," 1980; Outer Critics Award for play "Home," 1980; Guggenheim Fellowship for playwriting, 1981; North Carolina Governor's Award, 1981; Natl Endowment Fellowship for playwriting, 1984. *

WILLIAMS, SAMUEL ART See WILLIAMS, SAMM-ART

WILLIAMS, SANDRA K. (SANDRA W. GORHAM)
Attorney. **PERSONAL:** Born Mar 17, 1954, Houston, TX; daughter of Joe Williams and Claretha Bradley Williams; divorced; children: Katherine A. **EDUCATION:** Smith Coll, Northampton MA, AB, 1975; Univ of Michigan, Ann Arbor MI, JD, 1978. **CAREER:** Natl Labor Relations Bd, Washington DC, staff atty, 1978-81, Los Angeles CA, field atty, 1981-82; CBS Inc, Los Angeles CA, labor atty, 1982-. **ORGANIZATIONS:** Mem, State Bars of Texas, Washington DC & California, 1978-, LA County Bar Assn, 1983-, Assn of Black Women Lawyers of Los Angeles, 1985-; bd of advisors, Magalink, 1985-; mem, California Assn of Black Lawyers, 1986-; volunteer atty, Harriett Buhai Center for Family Law, 1989. **BUSINESS ADDRESS:** Labor/Broadcast Counsel, CBS Inc, 7800 Beverly Blvd, Los Angeles, CA 90036.

WILLIAMS, SANDRA ROBERTS
Educator. **PERSONAL:** Born Nov 02, 1940, Houston, TX; daughter of Brownie Roberts and Thelma Roberts; children: David, Michele. **EDUCATION:** Texas Southern Univ-Houston, BM, Educ, 1961; Univ of New Mexico-Albuquerque, MA, 1980. **CAREER:** Houston Independent School, music & classroom teacher, 1962-64; Albuquerque Public Schools, classroom teacher, 1964-70; Univ of New Mexico, academic advisor/counselor, 1973-81; Univ of Texas, Medical Branch, program coord, 1982-. **ORGANIZATIONS:** Consultant, analytical reading, test taking skills, note taking skills, time management skills; admin, Saturday Biomedical Sciences Forum, 1983-; mem, Natl Assn of Medical Minority Educ, Science Inc, School Health Programs, Advisory Comm, Delta Sigma Theta Inc, Galveston Alumni, Natl Tech Assn. **HONORS/ACHIEVEMENTS:** Publications, "Medical School Familiarization Program, Health Careers Network," Vol III, No 2, November, 1983; "Academic Support Services presents, Learning Strategies Workshop, Featuring Test Taking and Reading Skills," w/JE Spurlin, UTMB Publication, March, 1983. **HOME ADDRESS:** 10201 Schaper Dr, Galveston, TX 77551. **BUSINESS ADDRESS:** Program Coord, Univ of Texas Medical Branch, G210 Ashbel Smith, Galveston, TX 77550.

WILLIAMS, SCOTT W.
Educator. **PERSONAL:** Born Apr 22, 1943, Staten Island, NY. **EDUCATION:** Morgan State Clge, BS 1964; Lehigh Univ, MS 1967, PhD 1969. **CAREER:** PA State Univ Allentown Center, instr 1968-69; Morgan State Coll, instr 1969; PA State Univ Univ Park, reseach assc 1969-71; State Univ of NY at Buffalo, asst prof 1971-; SUNY, assc prof math 1977-; Rochester Folk Art Guild, instr 1975-; Amer Math Soc Notices, editor 1975-. **ORGANIZATIONS:** Mem Amer Math Soc; mem Rochester Folk Art Guild 1972-; chmn Balck Uhuru Soc 1967-69.

WILLIAMS, SELASE See WILLIAMS, WAYNE RICHARD

WILLIAMS, SHAHRON G.
Executive administrator. **PERSONAL:** Born May 05, 1949, New York, NY. **EDUCATION:** City Coll of NY, BA 1968; Amer Univ of Beirut, MA 1970; City Univ NY/Graduate Ctr, PhD 1980. **CAREER:** Savin Bus Machines NY, systems support rep 1971-73; Queens Coll NY, grad fellow 1973-76; Grey Adv NY, rsch exec 1978-80; Doyle Dane Bernbach, Inc, sr rsch super 1980-84. **ORGANIZATIONS:** Exec mem Amer Marketing Assn 1984-. **HONORS/ACHIEVEMENTS:** Black Achievers in Industry YWCA Harlem Branch 1981.

WILLIAMS, SHAWNELL
Systems analyst. **PERSONAL:** Born Nov 02, 1962, Springfield, OH. **EDUCATION:** Central State Univ, BS 1985; General Electric's Information Systems, Management Program 1987. **CAREER:** Armco Steel Inc, insutrial engr/co-op 1983-85; General Electric Space Craft Opers, programmer/analyst 1985-86; General Electric Aerospace Business Group, electronic data interchange project leader 1986-. **ORGANIZATIONS:** Mem Central STates Computer Science Club 1981-85, Central States Co-op Club 1983-85; mem Kappa Alpha Psi Frat Delta Zeta Chapt. **HONORS/ACHIEVEMENTS:** Listed in Who's Who Among Amer Colls and Univs 1984-85.

WILLIAMS, SHERLEY ANNE
Educator, author. **PERSONAL:** Born Aug 25, 1944, Bakersfield, CA; daughter of Jessee Winson Williams and Lelia Maria (Siler) Williams; children: John Malcolm. **EDUCATION:** Fresno State Coll (now California State Univ, Fresno), BA, 1966; Howard Univ, graduate study, 1966-67; Brown Univ, MA, 1972. **CAREER:** Fresno State Coll (now California State Univ, Fresno), co-dir of tutorial program, 1965-66, lecturer in ethnic studies, 1969-70; Miles Coll, Atlanta, GA, admin internal asst to pres, 1967-68; affiliated with Systems Devel Corp, Santa Monica, CA, 1968-69; Federal City Coll, Washington, DC, consultant in curriculum devel and community educator, 1970-72; California State Univ, Fresno, assoc prof of English, 1972-73; Univ of California, San Diego, La Jolla, asst prof, 1973-76, assoc prof, 1976-82, prof of Afro-Amer literature, 1982—, dept chrpsn, 1976-82. **ORGANIZATIONS:** Mem, Poetry Soc of Amer; mem, Modern Language Assoc. **HONORS/ACHIEVEMENTS:** Author of Give Birth To Brightness: A Thematic Study in Neo-Black Literature, Dial, 1972, The Peacock Poems, Wesleyan Univ Press, 1975, Some One Sweet Angel Chile (poems), Morrow, 1982, and Dessa Rose, Morrow, 1986; Natl Book Award nomination, 1976, for The Peacock Poems; Fulbright lecturer, Univ of Ghana, 1984; Dessa Rose was named a notable book in 1986 by the New York Times. *

WILLIAMS, SHIRLEY STENNIS
Educational admin. **EDUCATION:** Loyola & Chicago Teachers College; Jackson State Univ, Valedictorian BS 1958; Peabody Coll of Vanderbilt Univ, MA 1964, EdD 1972. **CAREER:** Jackson State Lab School, teacher 1958-59; Chicago Public Schools, teacher 1959-64; Peabody Coll of Vanderbilt Univ, teaching assistant 1964-66; Univ of WI Oshkosh, 1st Black asst prof 1966-72, 1st Black coord of field experience 1975-83, 1st Black assoc prof 1972-83, professor 1982-, asst vice chancellor. **ORGANIZATIONS:** State delegate Founding Conv Natl Women's Studies Conf 1980; board of directors Wisc Council of Teachers of Engl 1981-83; district dir Wisc Council of Teachers of Engl 1981-83; founding president Wisc State Human Relations Assn 1982-83; board of directors Midwest Human Relations Assn 1982-83. **HONORS/ACHIEVEMENTS:** Natl Defense Education Act Doctoral Fellowship 1963-66; Dissertation - "Student Teaching in the Chicago Public Schools 1856-1964" 1972. **BUSINESS ADDRESS:** Asst Vice Chancellor, University of Wis Oshkosh, 800 Algoma Blvd, Dempsey Hall Room 131, Oshkosh, WI 54901.

WILLIAMS, SHIRLEY YVONNE
Physician. **PERSONAL:** Born in Washington, DC. **EDUCATION:** Howard Univ, 1955, 1959; NY Med Ctr, resd 1962. **CAREER:** Outpatient Ambulatory Svc, dir. **ORGANIZATIONS:** Mem State Bd of Mental Health; State Cncl of Alcohol & Drugs; chmn Assc of CT Outpatient Clinics; Assc of Nervous & Mental Disease; Amer Psych Assc; Amer Acad of Sci; Natl Med Assc; AMA; Fairfield Co Assc; life mem NAACP; chmn Keystone House; mem bd Carver Fnd Father Looney 1977. **HONORS/ACHIEVEMENTS:** Fellow Amer Psychiat Assc. **BUSINESS ADDRESS:** 24 Stevens St, Norwalk, CT 06856.

WILLIAMS, SIDNEY B., JR.
Patent attorney. **PERSONAL:** Born Dec 31, 1935, Little Rock, AR; married Carolyn. **EDUCATION:** Univ WI, BS 1961; George WashingtonUniv Law Sch, JD 1967. **CAREER:** Upjohn Co, patent atty; US Patent Office, patent exmr; Gen Am Transp Corp, rsrch devel engr; Montreal Alouettes, professional ftbl player. **ORGANIZATIONS:** Mem MI DC Bar Assn; Kalamazoo Co MI Am Nat Patent Law Assn Bd; tsts Borgess Hosp bd dir Douglas Comm Assn All Am Ftbl Team Chem & Engring; News 1957-58; mem Iron Cross Hon Soc 1958. **MILITARY SERVICE:** USMCR. **BUSINESS ADDRESS:** 301 Henrietta, Kalamazoo, MI 49081.

WILLIAMS, SNOWDEN J.
Account marketing representative. **PERSONAL:** Born Jul 19, 1959, Detroit, MI. **EDUCATION:** Guilford Coll, BS 1981; IESA Caracas Venezuela, MBA 1982; Univ NC-Chapel Hill, MBA 1983. **CAREER:** IBM, public sector consultant 1983-85, acct mktg rep 1986-. **ORGANIZATIONS:** Consultant NBMBA Assoc 1986-. **HONORS/ACHIEVEMENTS:** Consortium Fellowship for Grad Study in Mgmt 1981-83. **BUSINESS ADDRESS:** Account Mktg Representative, IBM, 9200 Corporate Blvd, Rockville, MD 20850.

WILLIAMS, SONYA DENISE
Doctoral student. **PERSONAL:** Born May 31, 1963, Birmingham, AL; daughter of Sam Williams and Carolyn Williams. **EDUCATION:** Brown Univ, BA (honors) 1984; The Univ of MI Business School, MBA (honors) 1986. **CAREER:** Irving Trust Co, account rep 1986-88; doctoral student, Univ of MI, 1988-. **ORGANIZATIONS:** Pres Brown Univ Chapter Alpha Kappa Alpha 1982-83; mem Natl Black MBA Assoc, Financial Mgmt Assoc 1985-. **HONORS/ACHIEVEMENTS:** Fellowship Consortium for Graduate Study in Mgmt 1984-86; Scholarship Natl Black MBA Assoc 1985; Honor Soc Financial Mgmt Assoc 1985-. **HOME ADDRESS:** 3381 Burbank Dr, Ann Arbor, MI 48105.

WILLIAMS, STANLEY KING
Government official. **PERSONAL:** Born Jan 25, 1948, Columbus, GA; son of Robert Williams and Lucille Williams. **EDUCATION:** Shaw Univ, BA 1970. **CAREER:** Supvr, Employment Serv/DC Dept of Employment Serv 1986-; veterans Employment DC Dept of Labor/VA Regional Office, supvr/coordinator 1976-; Dept of Manpower, job devel specialist 1972; AUS Germany, neuropsychiatric tech/drug counseling 1970-72; Shaw Univ, student counselor 1967-70; COPE Newark, youth job devel specialist 1968-69; DC Dept of Employment Serv, Washington, DC, supvr, Employment & Serv, 1986-. **ORGANIZATIONS:** Chmn Mt Pleasant Advisory Neighborhood Commn 1976-80; coordinator Father's Program Gales Maternity Clinic 1972-74; NC Dept of Corrections, classification specialist 1970; Dept of Human Resources, consultant sex educ program 1973; DC Govt establishment of ANC Citizens Neighborhood Council Coordinating Comr, advisor 1975; pres King Enterprises Inc; mem Amer Legion WA Alliance for Neighborhood Govts; chmn Mt Pleasant Advisory Neighborood Comm; del DC Black Assembly; mem Shaw Univ Alumni Assn; mem Bancroft PTA; student of Economics & Political Trends; com S African Self-determination; Smithsonian Fellow Smithsonian Inst; asst in estab 1% St Army drug program in Germany 1971; coordinator & supvr Veterans Employment Center VA Regional Office 1976; pres, King Enterprises, 1976; assoc dean, Shiloh Baptist Church/Washington, DC, 1981. **HONORS/ACHIEVEMENTS:** Appreciation Award ANC 70 1977; Congressional Appreciation Award Congressional Fountroy 1978; Outstanding Srv Award Mt Pleasant Advisory Neighborhood Commn 1978; Meritorious & Distinguished Serv Award VFW 1978; Commend Award Vietnam Veteran Civic Council 1978; Comm Serv Award Natl Black Veteran Org 1979; drafted adopted signed the org Neighborhood Bill of Responsibilities & Rights Independence Square Philadelphia 1976; promoter/sponsor, promoted largest gospel convention given in Washington, DC, 1983. **MILITARY SERVICE:** AUS sergeant E-5 1970-72. **HOME ADDRESS:** 1806 Lawrence St, NE, Washington, DC 20018.

WILLIAMS, STARKS J.
Physician. **PERSONAL:** Born Feb 16, 1921, Orangeburg, SC; divorced; children: Michael, Sara, Mary. **EDUCATION:** SC State Clge Orangeburg, BS 1942; Meharry Med Clge Nashville, MD 1945. **CAREER:** Doctors Clinic, sec/assc 1954-; Richard Cabot Clinic Prog City Proj Mercy Hospital KC MO, chief pediatrician 1965-70. **ORGANIZATIONS:** Reg VII med consult Head Start Consultation Proj HEW 1977-; med consult State of MO Sickle Cell Prog 1974-; bd mem Visiting Nurse Assc KC MO 1972-78; com mem Site-Selection & Establishment Met Jr Clge KC MO 1969; med dir Niles Home for Children 1965-; bd mem/treas Comm Dev Corp; pres bd dir Lincoln Redevelopment Corp; bd mem/treas Alpha Plastic Corp; chmn bd dir Third World Trading Corp; pres TNW Intl; mem Natl Med; assc mem KCMed Soc; mem Jackson Co Med Soc; mem Mid Westerners Club; mem Omega Psi Phi Frat; diplomate Amer Bd of Pediatrics 1951; fellow Amer Acad of Pediatrics; clinical assc prof Univ of MO Sch of Med. **MILITARY SERVICE:** AUS capt med corp & reserve 1952-54. **BUSINESS ADDRESS:** 2701 E 31st St, Kansas City, MO 64128.

WILLIAMS, STERLING B., JR.
Physician. **PERSONAL:** Born Apr 03, 1941, Little Rock, AR; divorced; children: Angela, Spencer, Sterling III. **EDUCATION:** Univ of IL, BS 1963; Northern IL Univ, MS 1966; Univ of AR Med Center, MD 1973; Univ AR Med Center, PhD. **CAREER:** IL Inst of Tech Rsch Inst, rsch asst 1963; School of Nursing Univ AR Med Center, instr 1971; Private practice, physician 1976-; Univ of KS Med Ctr, assoc prof 1979-; Columbia Univ Coll of Physicians & Surgeons, prof 1987-; Harlem Hospital Center ; dir of dept of Ob/Gyn, 1987-. **ORGANIZATIONS:** Mem, Natl Coalition on Health; general council, KC Union Presbyterian; coord Minority Student Admissions Adv Comm; mem Univ KS Med Center, KC Civic Chorus, Alpha Phi Alpha Soc Frat, Sigma Xi Rsch Hon soc, NIH Predoctoral Fellow Univ of AR 1966-69; solo singing pref KC Symphony Orchestra; vice chmn Presbyterian Council on Theology & Culture; mem Kaw Valley Med Soc, Sigma Pi Phi Frat. **HONORS/ACHIEVEMENTS:** Phi Eta Sigma Scholastic Honorary. **BUSINESS ADDRESS:** Professor, Columbia Univ/Harlem Hosp, 506 Lenox Ave, Dept of Ob & Gyn, New York, NY 10037.

WILLIAMS, SYLVIA J.
Educator. **PERSONAL:** Born Jul 11, 1939, Washington, DC; daughter of Wallace Burnett and Mary Burnett; married Edward, Feb 04, 1966; children: Deborah, Rodney. **EDUCATION:** Bowie State Coll, BS 1964, MA, 1970; attended Univ Maryland. **CAREER:** Prince Georges Co Bd of Educ, teacher 19 yrs. **ORGANIZATIONS:** Mem NAACP; chmn Educ Com Local Branch; past sec King George Citizens Assn 1973-74; past counseling & testing coord Sickle Cell Assn; sec Vikingettes Social Club; mem Dial a Ride; coord Local Rainbow Coalition, Wilder for Lt Governor, Host and Hostesses for Mayor Marion Barry's Inagural Reception; mem NAACP; coord Health and Social Serv of Natl Capitol Baptist Convention; bd mem Rappohonack Assoc; Citizens Advisory Comm to the District of Columbia, mem of exec bd; DC Branch NAACP, mem of exec bd. **HONORS/ACHIEVEMENTS:** Charlotte B Hunter Citizenship Awd 1962; Mayors Youth Council Awd 1963; listed in Who's Who in Amer Colleges 1963; Citizen of the Yr Omega Psi Phi 1974; Sickle Cell Assn Awd 1971-83; American Citizenery Awd 1983; Instructor of the Year Mt Bethel Bapt Assoc 1983; Outstanding Serv Awd by Life Membership Divof Natl Office NAACP 1983; Rainbow Coalition Awd of Merit 1984; American Humanitarian Awd 1984; Volunteer of the Year AT&T; Unsung Heroine Awd NAACP. **HOME ADDRESS:** Rt 4 Box 112C, Fredericksburg, VA 22405.

WILLIAMS, TERRI L.
Educational administrator. **PERSONAL:** Born May 18, 1958, Bridgeton, NJ. **EDUCATION:** Howard Univ, BS 1981, MEd 1984. **CAREER:** The Wash Alcohol Counseling Ctr, admin asst 1980-82; Howard Student Special Svcs, educ specialist 1984-85; Howard Upward Bound, sr counselor 1985-86; St Lawrence Univ, asst dir of admissions 1986-. **ORGANIZATIONS:** Mem Delta Sigma Theta Inc 1978-; public relations coord BOF Howard Univ Alumnae 1983-; volunteer DC Mayor's Re-election Comm 1986; exhibitors coord Mid-Eastern Assoc of Educ Oppor Prog Personnel 1986. **HONORS/ACHIEVEMENTS:** Outstanding Young Women of Amer 1982,85; MEAEOPP Conf Serv Awd 1986; Mayor's Summer Youth Emp Program Contribution Awd. **HOME ADDRESS:** RD 2 Russell Rd, Box 166, Canton, NY 13617. **BUSINESS ADDRESS:** Asst Dir of Admissions, St Lawrence University, Admissions Office, Canton, NY 13617.

WILLIAMS, TERRIE MICHELLE
Corporate public relations consultant. **PERSONAL:** Born May 12, 1954, Mt Vernon, NY; daughter of Charles and Marie. **EDUCATION:** Brandeis Univ, BA (Cum Laude) 1975; Columbia Univ NY, MA 1977. **CAREER:** New York Hosp, medical social worker 1977-80; The Black Filmmaker Foundation, prog admin 1980-81; The Black Owned Comm Alliance, exec dir 1981-82; The World Inst of Black Communications, exec dir 1982; Essence Communications Inc, vp/dir of corporate communication 1982-87; pres the Terrie Williams Agency 1988-. **ORGANIZATIONS:** Mem-at-large Brandeis Univ Alumni Assoc; mem Natl Corporate Adv Bd; mem communications comm Amer Heart Assoc; mem Women in Communications. **HONORS/ACHIEVEMENTS:** DParke Gibson Awd for PR Public Relations Soc of Amer 1981; Who's Who of Amer Women 1983; Outstanding Young Woman of Amer 1983; Building Brick Awd New York Urban League 1987. **BUSINESS ADDRESS:** The Terrie Willams Agency, 1841 Broadway #914, New York, NY 10036.

WILLIAMS, THEARTRICE
Consultant. **PERSONAL:** Born May 16, 1934, Indianolia, MS; son of Fred Mack Williams and Ollie Gray Williams; married Mary Louise Sales, May 19, 1962; children: Christopher, Jeffrey, Laurie. **EDUCATION:** Univ of IL ba 1956; u of pA, msw 1962; northwestern u, 1971. **CAREER:** Phyllis Wheatley Comm Ctr Mpls, Mn, exec dir 1965-72; State of MN, ombudsman for corrections 1972-83; Minneapolis Comm Dev Agcy, dir public hsng 1983-85;Survival Skills Inst, prvt cnsltnt bus & comm rel, hum ser, hum res; Humphrey Inst of Public Affairs Univ of MN, senior fellow. **ORGANIZATIONS:** Dir Lutheran Soc Serv MN 1981-; trustee Minneapolis Fndtn 1974-83; 1st vice pres Natl Assn of Social Wrkrs 1981-83; consult US Dept Justice, Comm Rel Serv 1980-; dir The Citizens League 1980-83; chm Minority Schlrshp & Grants Prog Am Luth Ch 1970-; co-chm MN Friends for Publ Ed 1984-; Oper-

ation De Novo; mem bd of dir Courage Center of Minnesota 1989-; commr Minnesota Sentencing Guidelines Commn 1986-. **HONORS/ACHIEVEMENTS:** Ldrshp flw Bush Fndtn Mpls, Mn 1970; dist Serv NASW Mn Chptr 1977, Natl Chptr 1983; otstandng achvmnt Natl Assn Blacks in Criminal Justice 1978; Polemarch, St. Paul-Minneapolis Alumni Chapter, Kappa Alpha Psi Fraternity 1988-; Achievement Award North Central Province, Kappa Alpha Psi Fraternity; Venture Capital and Job Development Strategies for The Black Community, Special Report; Humphrey Inst of Public Affairs, 1987. **MILITARY SERVICE:** AUS sp4 1958-60. **BUSINESS ADDRESS:** Senior Fellow, Univ of Minnesota Humphrey Institute, 134 Humphrey Ctr, Minneapolis, MN 55455.

WILLIAMS, THEODORE EDWARD
Corporate director. **PERSONAL:** Born Nov 13, 1943, Kansas City, KS; married Patricia Ann; children: Bryce, Shawnna. **EDUCATION:** AZ State Univ, BS 1979. **CAREER:** AZ Dept of Health Srv, dept dir 1976-; Gov Office of Gov Phoenix, spec asst 1975-76; Intl Bus Machines Phoenix, systems eng 1969-75. **ORGANIZATIONS:** Bd dir AZ Council of Blind Soc Srv & Rehab Inc 1977-78; bd dir State Advisory Com to Fed Civil Rights Comn 1974-; bd dir State Manpower Srv AdvCounc AZ Acad 1978-; bd dir Deferred Compensation Com 1976-. **HONORS/ACHIEVEMENTS:** Comm Srv Award IBM Corp 1974. **BUSINESS ADDRESS:** 1740 W Adams St, Phoenix, AZ 85007.

WILLIAMS, THEODORE M.
Administrative judge. **PERSONAL:** Born Aug 17, 1905, Cleveland, OH; married Irene (deceased); children: Theodore Jr, Charles, Ann, Jane, Florence. **EDUCATION:** Univ of MI; Cleveland-Marshall Law School, JD, LLB. **CAREER:** City of Cleveland, asst police prosecutor 1941-47; Cuyahoga Cty, asst cty prosecutor 1948-52; Cleveland City Council, mem 1952-60; Cleveland Municipal Ct, judge 1960-, admin judge 1975; Cuyahoga Comm Coll, part time lecturer 1970-; Cleveland Municipal Court, vstg judge 1976-. **BUSINESS ADDRESS:** Visiting Judge, Cleveland Municipal Court, Justice Center, Cleveland, OH 44113.

WILLIAMS, THEODORE R.
Educator. **PERSONAL:** Born Jan 17, 1931, Palestine, TX; married Louise M Pogue; children: Wayne R, Darrell R, Brian K, Marica L, Thea Elaine. **EDUCATION:** TX Southern Univ, BS 1948, MS 1954; Attended, OR State Univ, St Lawrence Univ, Univ of Washington, AZ State Univ; Univ of IA, PhD 1972. **CAREER:** St Philip's College, chmn biology dept 1954-75, asst/assoc dean 1972-82, acting pres 1982, vice pres of acad affairs emeritus 1983-. **ORGANIZATIONS:** Mem Phi Beta Sigma Frat 1951; mem bd trustees San Antonio Museum Assoc 1973-82; adv bd mem United Colls of San Antonio 1973-; dir Bexar Co Anemia Assoc 1978-80; appraisal review bd mem Bexar Appraisal Dist 1985-; dir Guardianship Adv Bd 1985-. **HONORS/ACHIEVEMENTS:** Natl Medical Fellowship Grant 1959-60; Summer Grant Natl Sci Foundation 1963, 67; Fellowship Southern Fellowship Found 1969-71; mem Beta Kappa Chi Scientific Hon Soc; Vice Pres Academic Affairs Emeritus St Philip's Coll 1986. **MILITARY SERVICE:** AUS pfc 2 yrs. **HOME ADDRESS:** 1315 Virginia Blvd, San Antonio, TX 78203.

WILLIAMS, THEOPOLIS CHARLES
Physician. **PERSONAL:** Born Apr 06, 1956, Phoenix, AZ; married Diana Marie Taylor; children: Erin Aisha. **EDUCATION:** Whitman Coll, BA 1979; Howard Univ Coll of Medicine, MD 1983. **CAREER:** Howard Univ Hosp, surgery intern 1983-84; San Jose Hosp, family practice resident 1984-87. **ORGANIZATIONS:** Mem Alpha Omega Alpha 1983-87, Amer Acad of Family Physicians 1984-87. **HONORS/ACHIEVEMENTS:** All Amer Wrestling NAIA 1976,78. **BUSINESS ADDRESS:** Physician, San Jose Hospital, 25 N 14th St, San Jose, CA 95112.

WILLIAMS, THOMAS ALLEN
Government official. **PERSONAL:** Born Mar 23, 1959, New York, NY; son of Jessie Williams and Minnie Johnson Williams. **CAREER:** Matt's Handi Mart, Buena Vista GA, mgr; ET's Arcade, Buena Vista GA, owner; T-N-T Restaurant, Buena Vista GA, owner; City of Buena Vista GA, mayor, currently. **ORGANIZATIONS:** Vice pres, GA Conf of Mayors; chair, 3rd District Gabeo; mem, Area Planning & Development, Marion County Bd of Health, Advisory Bd of Community Service, Sen Citizens Meals on Wheels Program. **HONORS/ACHIEVEMENTS:** Black Business Award, Columbus Times Newspaper; Mayor's Motorcade, West Central Regional Hosp, 1986, 1987 & 1988; 30 Leaders of the Future, Ebony magazine, 1988.

WILLIAMS, THOMAS PEDWORTH
Government official. **PERSONAL:** Born Oct 17, 1910, Brunswick, GA; married Birdie Palmer. **EDUCATION:** Clark Clge Atlanta GA, BA 1933; NY Univ NYC, MA 1956. **CAREER:** City of Brunswick GA, mayor pro tem 1978-80; McIntosh Co Acad Darien GA, asst prin 1970-79; Eulonia Elem Sch Eulonia GA, prin 1954-70; Folkston HS Folkston GA, asst prin 1951-54. **ORGANIZATIONS:** Elected to city commn S Ward Brunswick GA 1976; bd dir Chamber of Comm City of Brunswick 1978-80; mem Chamber of Comm Tourist & Conv Council 1978-80; adv council mem Job Corp Glynco GA 1978-80; mem Brunswick-St Simons Causeway Com 1978-80; bd dir CAPDC Coastal Area Planning & Devel Commn 1978-80. **HONORS/ACHIEVEMENTS:** Hnr mem GA Peace Officers Assc Brunswick GA 1977-81; Manifold Contrib to Mankind Prince Hall Grand Lodge 1979; serv rendered to Admin Fac Staff & Students Darien 1979; distg serv to Tourism Chamber of Comm Brunswick GA 1980; Travel Rep City of Brunswick to Taiwan China (Sisters City Prog) 1978; & Olinda Brazil (GA's Partners Prog) 1980. **BUSINESS ADDRESS:** City of Brunswick, Gloucester St PO Box550, Brunswick, GA 31520.

WILLIAMS, TOMMYE JOYCE
Educator. **PERSONAL:** Born Jan 24, 1930, Muskogee Co; married Paul Williams Jr; children: Cheryl Elizabeth Jackson, Jacquelyn Elaine. **EDUCATION:** Wichita State Univ, BA 1965, EdM 1974. **CAREER:** Bd of Educ USD 259, teacher 1965-. **ORGANIZATIONS:** Trainer Local Bldg Dir Ldrshp Acad K NEA 1975-76; New York City Couns Bd of Educ 1971; co-org Ethnic Minority Caucus NEA Wichita 1975-76; chmn Pub Affairs TV Prog NEA Wichita 1975; elected mem PR&R Com NEA Wichita 1979; delegate Local State Natl Rep Assemblies NEA 1974, 75, 79, 80; adv 1980, historian pub rel 1976-78 Sigma Gamma Rho Sorority; life mem NAACP; Political Action Com 1979; mem Holy Savior Cath Ch Wichita. **HONORS/ACHIEVEMENTS:** Wichita's Tchr of Year 1975; recipt mini-grant Prog, Teaching with Interest Centers 1975; Chair Small Grp Session KS Conf on Language Arts Studies 1978; article to editor Wichita Eagle-beacon 1979. **BUSINESS ADDRESS:** Natl Education Assn, 906 George Washington Dr, Wichita, KS 67211.

WILLIAMS, ULYSSES JEAN
Educator. **PERSONAL:** Born Sep 15, 1947, Memphis, TN; daughter of Ulysses Warren and Ann Moton Warren; married Foster Williams, Sr; children: Tasha A, Foster, LaQuentin D, AnQuentin T. **EDUCATION:** Philander Smith College, 1964-67; Univ of Central Ark, BSE 1969, MSE 1973; Ark State Univ, Cert Behavior Disorders 1980, Gifted and Talented Certification 1985; AR State Univ, Elementary Principalship Certification 1987. **CAREER:** Cotton Plant Elem School, secretary 1969-70; Helena-West Helena Public Schools, 1970-78; East Ark Regional Mental Health Center, educational specialist 1978-81; Lucilia Wood Elem School, educator 1982-. **ORGANIZATIONS:** Mem Ark Ed Assn 1970-; member Natl Ed Assn 1970-; member Parent Teacher Assn 1970-; pres Theta Gamma Zeta; organized the Archonette (teenaged girls organiz); advisor to Amicae; regional & state coord South Central Region; chairman of Operation Big Vote; member NAACP; member Second Baptist Church; chairman Christian Board of Ed; secretary Matrons; dir church choir; organized Young Adult Choir and church scholarship fund; organized Theta Gamma Zeta of Zeta Phi Beta Sorority Inc and served as first pres for four yrs; adv comm Gifted and Talented; mem Helena-West Helena Bd of Educ 1980-; state dir AR Zeta Phi Beta Sor Inc 1987-; mem Elaine Six Year Plan Comm; devel state-wide pledge program to be used by Zeta Phi Beta Inc; comm mem Governor's Rural Devel Action Program 1987-88; tutor Laubach Board Member 1988-. **HONORS/ACHIEVEMENTS:** Outstanding Elem Teacher of Amer 1975; developed the Educational Component of the Adolescent Residential Facility 1978-81; Outstanding Serv as Ed Specialist 1980; Dedicated Serv as Therapeutic Foster Parents 1981-84; Zeta of the Year 1982; Outstanding Serv in the Community and Church 1983; designed a report card and daily independent work sheet for emotionally disturbed youth; AR Zeta of the Yr Award 1985; Outstanding Serv to South Central Region of Zeta Phi Beta Sor Inc. **HOME ADDRESS:** 239 Desota Street, West Helena, AR 72390.

WILLIAMS, VANESSA
Actress, singer. **PERSONAL:** Married Ramon Hervey; children: Melanie Lynne. **CAREER:** Former Miss America; movie debut in The Pick Up Artist, appeared in movie Under the Gun; recorded album The Right Stuff, 1988; hit singles The Right Stuff, He's Got The Look, and Dreamin; hostess of NBC's Showtime At The Apollo; appearances on Soul Train, Live!, Dick Clark Presents, Club MTV, BET'S Video Soul, and Live at the Improv. *

WILLIAMS, VERNICE LOUISE
Telephone company manager. **PERSONAL:** Born Aug 13, 1934, Indianapolis, IN; daughter of Herman S Whitelaw Sr and Laura Chubbs Guthrie; married Andrew I Williams, Aug 26, 1950; children: Crystal B Thomas, Andrea J, Marlon I, Sherman A, Dewayne M, Karen R. **EDUCATION:** Attended Indiana Univ-Purdue Univ at Indianapolis, 1970-72. **CAREER:** Army Finance C&R, Ft Benjamin, Harrison IN, auditor, 1952-67; Indiana Bell, Indianapolis IN, manager, 1974-. **ORGANIZATIONS:** Bd mem & vice chair, Indiana Black Expo, 1974-; mem of steering comm, United Negro Coll Fund, 1982-; bd mem, Dialogue Today, 1985-; bd mem, Police Chief Advisory Council, 1987-; chair, IBE Youth Corp, 1988-. **HONORS/ACHIEVEMENTS:** Minorities Engineering, Indiana Bell, 1984; Leadership Award, Chamber of Commerce, 1986; Outstanding Volunteerism, United Way, 1988; Mt Summitt award, Indiana Bell, 1989; Presidents Club award, Indiana Bell, 1989. **HOME ADDRESS:** 6136 N Meridian W Dr, Indianapolis, IN 46208.

WILLIAMS, VIRGINIA WALKER
Journalist. **PERSONAL:** Born in Alabama; divorced; children: Mamie W. **EDUCATION:** AL State Univ, BS; Marquette Univ, Masters Journalism. **CAREER:** Milwaukee Publ Schools, reading specialist; Milwaukee Publ Schools, journalist editor; Milwaukee Fire & Police Comm, journalist. **ORGANIZATIONS:** Mem Soc of Prof Journalist, Women in Communication, Pi Lambda Theta, Phi Delta Kappa NAACP; asst journalist Zonta Club of Milw; edit staff West Side News; publ Echo Magazine; freelance writer published in five anthologies. **HONORS/ACHIEVEMENTS:** Headliner Award Women in Communications; Good Citizens City of Milw; ach Black Women's Network; srv award Milwaukee Public Schl; Women Against the Odds WI Humanities Soc; listed in Who's Who in Professional and Executive Women 1987; Poet Honored by Zonta Club of Milwaukee for poetry published in Zonta newsletter monthly. **HOME ADDRESS:** PO Box 2107, Milwaukee, WI 53201.

WILLIAMS, W. BILL, JR.
Salesman. **PERSONAL:** Born Aug 19, 1939, Chicago, IL; married Sylester; children: Kevin, Keyth. **EDUCATION:** Olive Harvey Coll Chicago State Univ, attended; Inst of Intl Transp, BA Bus Admin Mktg BOAC. **CAREER:** Butler Aviation, oper suprv 1964-72; Sullair Corp Air Copressor Co, mgr, transp 1972-74; Sullair Corp, sales engr 1974-75; Chicago Conv & Tourism Bur McCormick Place, dir of sales. **ORGANIZATIONS:** Mem Hotel Sales Mgrs Assoc, Amer Soc of Assoc Execs, Prince Hall Masonic Frat, Ancient Egyptian Arabic Order Nobles of Mystic Shrine N&SA, Improved Benevolent Prot Order of Elks of World; bus adv counc Chicago State Univ; vchmn, bd of dir Chicago OIC; mem Natl Conv Mgrs Sem, Norman LaHarry Scholarship Found, Natl United Ch Ushers Assoc, NAACP, Urban League, Montford Point Marine Assoc, Mt Calvary Bapt Church; dir Morgan Park Roots Band; bd of dir Amer Mktg Assoc, Natl Assoc of Mkt Devel Chicago Chapt, Rat Pack Chgo; bd of dirs Mt Calvary Bapt Church; bd of dirs Urban Programs West YMCA; bd of dirs Natl Coalition of Black Meeting Planners. **MILITARY SERVICE:** USMC corpl 1957-60. **BUSINESS ADDRESS:** Dir of Sales, McCormick Place on the Lake, Chicago Conv & Visitors Bureau, Chicago, IL 60616.

WILLIAMS, W. CLYDE
Educational administrator. **PERSONAL:** Born in Cordele, GA; married Elaine; children: Joyce, Clyde, John, Gregory. **EDUCATION:** Holsey Cobb Inst 1951; Paine Clge, AB 1955; Howard Univ, BD 1959; Interdenom Theol Ctr, MRE 1961; Atlanta Univ, MA 1969; Paine Clge, DD 1972;Univ of AL, Hon PhD 1976. **CAREER:** Miles Coll, pres 1971-; Consult on Church & Union, assc gen sec 1969-71; Assc for Christ Train & Svc, staff assc 1969-; Interdenom Theol Ctr, regist & dir of admin 1967-69, dir 1963-67; Christ Meth Epis Church, dir of youth work & adult educ 1960-63; Howard Univ, asst dir of stud act 1959-; NY St Coun of Church, chaplain 1957-58. **ORGANIZATIONS:** Dir boys work Bethlehem Ctr 1954-56; adv com US Dept of St; stud fin aid coun US Dept of HEW; res adv panel US Ofc of Educ Sch Monitor & Consum Prot Proj; Sickle Cell Dis adv com NIH; co-chmn Comm Aff Com of Oper New Birmingham; v chmn AL Comm for Human & Pub Policy; bd dir UnitNegro

Clge Fund; bd dir Birmingham Cable Comm; bd dir Birmingham Urban Leag; bd dir Natl Com of Black Chmen; bd dir Amer Natl Red Cross; bd trustee Birmingham Symphony Assc; exec bd BSA; exec com Jefferson Co Child Dev Counc; Cit Adv Counc Jefferson Co; Birmingham Manpower Area Plan Coun; Lay Adv Coun St Vincent's Hosp; AL Assc for Adv of Private Clge ch commn on scout; NAACP; YMCA; Alpha Phi Alpha Frat Educ Hon Soc Kappa DeltaPi 1975. **HONORS/ACHIEVEMENTS:** Man of Year Omega Psi Phi Frat; Alumni Achiev Award Paine Clge 1971; Outst Educ So Beauty Cong 1972; Outst Educ Fed of So Coop 1975; Cit Award Lawson St Comm Clge 1974; City of Birmingham Mayor's Cit 1974; Outst Achiev in Spt of Police Athlet Birmingham Police Athlet Team 1975. **BUSINESS ADDRESS:** Miles Coll, P O Box 3800, Birmingham, AL 35208.

WILLIAMS, W. DONALD
Physician. **PERSONAL:** Born Mar 05, 1936, Winter Park, FL; son of Eldridge L Williams, Sr and Emma Austin Williams; divorced; children: Susan A, Jordan H. **EDUCATION:** San Francisco State Coll, AB 1967; Stanford Univ School of Med, MD 1974. **CAREER:** NYC, rsch chem 1958-59; San Francisco, med tech 1964-69; Dept of Lab Med, chief res 1975-77; Univ CA San Francisco, MD 1974-; Univ of Chicago, asst prof pathology; LAC-USC Med Ctr, chief clinical hematology, pediatrics. **ORGANIZATIONS:** Org mem Black Students Union San Francisco State Coll 1966; Beta Nu Chapter Alpha Phi Alpha 1954; co-founder Black Man's Free Clinic San Francisco 1968; founder dir Mid-Peninsula Sickle Cell Anemia Fnd 1971; mem UCSF Med School Admissions Comm 1976-77; CA State Advisory Commn for Sickle Cell Anemia 1972-75; mem Sci Adv Commn Natl Assn for Sickle Cell Disease 1972-75; mem Amer Soc Hematology; fellow Amer Soc Clinical Pathology; fellow, Amer Academy Pediatrics. **MILITARY SERVICE:** AUS sgt 1959-65; AUS maj 1978-79; USAR ltc 1982-. **BUSINESS ADDRESS:** Chief Clinical Hematology, LAC-USC Medical Center, Dept of Pediatrics, Los Angeles, CA 90033.

WILLIAMS, WALKER RICHARD, JR.
EEO officer. **PERSONAL:** Born Jul 11, 1928, Dayton, OH; married Emma Jean Griffin; children: Yvette, Timothy, Walker III. **EDUCATION:** Attended, Univ of Dayton. **CAREER:** Supervisor-supply cataloger 1961-66; USAF 2750 ABW, WPAFB, personnel mgmt spec 1966-69, employee relations specialist 1969-70, equal employment oppor officer 1971-, chief eeo & affirm action prog. **ORGANIZATIONS:** Bd mem & past pres Jefferson Township Bd of Educ; mem Dayton Bd of Educ Guidance Adv Comm for Project VEET, City Wide Vocational Educ Adv Comm; bd of dirs Dayton Opportunities Industrialization Ctr; bd of dirs Domestic Action Programs of Wright-Patterson AFB Inc; mem Governor's Commn to Preserve the Statue of Liberty; mem OH Bureau of Employment Serv Job Serv Employees Commn; mem Greene Vocational Sch Business Adv Comm; mem and past pres Dayton Selectmen; bd of dirs and 3 times past pres Wright-Patterson Quarter Century Club; mem Urban League, Blacks in Govt; mem business adv comm United Negro Coll Fund; mem Natl Black Caucus of Local Elected Officials, Natl Black Caucus of Black School Bd Members; historian and past chmn Dayton Intergovt Equal Employment Oppor Cncl; mem NAACP, Miami Valley Personnel Assoc, Intl Personnel Mgmt Assoc, Air Force Assoc. **HONORS/ACHIEVEMENTS:** James W Cisco Awd Dayton Intergovt EEO Cncl; EEO Employee of the Year Awds Dayton Chamber of Commerce, Dayton Intl Personnel Mgmt Assoc; Special Awd Dayton Chap Jack & Jill Inc; President's Awd Blacks in Govt; Certificate of Recognition Accomplishment in Humanities St Margaret's Episcopal Church; Certificate of Recognition for Outstanding Service and Dedication to Humanity Dayton NAACP; Certificate of Awd for Outstanding Accomplishments in Comm Serv Dayton Urban League; Certificate for Outstanding Serv to Youth Girl Scouts of Amer; Walker Williams Day in Dayton February 15, 1987 by Mayor R Clay Dixon; Special Awd United Negro Coll Fund; numerous Air Force Awds for Performance, including Air Force Civilian Serv Awd. **MILITARY SERVICE:** AUS Natl Guard capt 20 yrs. **HOME ADDRESS:** 5050 Fortman Drive, Dayton, OH 45418.

WILLIAMS, WALLACE C.
Business executive. **PERSONAL:** Born in North Carolina; divorced; children: Wallace Jr, Joyce. **EDUCATION:** Boro-Hall Acad NY 1946; Pace Clge NY 1948; Columbia Univ 1950; Detroit Inst of Tech 1958; Wayne State Univ 1970; Univ of Detroit. **CAREER:** CCAC-ICBIF, dir 1979; MI Dept of Commerce, econ dev exec 1969-; Employment Sec Exec MI Employment Sec Commn 1965-69; MI Employ Sec Commn, interviewer 1958-65; Correctional Aid Prison Fiscal Ofcr US Bur of Prisons 1953-58; NY State Employ Svc, interviewer 1947-53. **ORGANIZATIONS:** Trustee mem Exec Coun Trade Union Ldrshp Council; mem bd dir Booker T Washington Bus Assc; mem exec bd Inner City Bus Improvement Forum; chmn Minority Bus Oppor Com; ed & Publ Minority Bus Newsletter; deacon Cen Woodward Christian Ch; bd mem HOPE Inc; mem New Detroit Minority Adv Com; Wayne Co Bd of Commr Minority Adv Co; Serv Ofcr VFW TF Burns Post 5793; bd mem Lewis Bus Clge; mem bd dir People's Comm Civic League; mem Bus Adv Com Detroit Chamber of Comm; mem Tr Bd Orchestra Hall Fnd; life mem NAACP; coord Christian Prison Flwshp Prog; asst reg vice pres Natl Bus League; v chmn Highland Park YMCA; mem Adv Planning Council Wayne Co. **HONORS/ACHIEVEMENTS:** Layman of Year Award; United Christian Ch; Outst Perf Award IAPES MI Chpt; Outst & Dedicated Serv Award, Contacts Inc; Valuable Serv to Bus Comm City of Detroit; various other awards. **MILITARY SERVICE:** AUS sgt 1942-46.

WILLIAMS, WALTER
Attorney. **PERSONAL:** Born Jun 13, 1939, Yazoo City, MS; son of Walter Williams, Sr; married Helen M Hudson, Jul 04, 1964; children: Toni Marshea. **EDUCATION:** Univ of WI, Cert 1961; John Marshall Law Sch, JSD 1970; Jackson State Univ Jackson MS 1958-62. **CAREER:** Williams, Slaughter & Williams, partner; Malcolm X Coll, tchr. **ORGANIZATIONS:** Amer Bar Assc; Chicago Bar Assc; pres Cook Co Bar Assc; IL St Bar Assc; Natl Bar Assc; Alpha Phi Alpha Frat; Jackson St Univ Alumni; John Marshall Law Sch Alumni; IL Judicial Council; IL Judges Assn; American Judges Assn. **HONORS/ACHIEVEMENTS:** Cook County Bar Assn Leadership Award 1964; Jr Coun Award Cook Co Bar Assc 1975; Outstanding Yazoo Citizen Award 1975; Outstanding Achievement Award Yazoo Brothers Club 1987. **MILITARY SERVICE:** DOS spec e-5 1966. **HOME ADDRESS:** 5555 S Everett, Chicago, IL 60637.

WILLIAMS, WAYNE RICHARD (SELASE WILLIAMS)
Educator. **PERSONAL:** Born Jan 18, 1945, Waukegan, IL; married Elaine Amewusika Gail Chaney; children: Elizabeth, Bibi Miller. **EDUCATION:** Univ of WI Madison, BA Linguistics 1968, MA Afr Lang/Lit 1970; IN Univ, MA Linguistics 1971, PhD Ling/Afr Studies 1976. **CAREER:** Western Washington Univ, adj faculty 1979; Portland State Univ, vstg lecturer 1983; Univ of Washington, dir afro-amer studies 1975-. **ORGANIZATIONS:** Screening com SSRC-Africa Prog 1977-78; afr lang consult Pan-Afr Studies Dept Kent St 1979; linguistic consult Natl Labor Rel Bd 1980; pres Natl Council for Black St-Reg X 1981-85; exec bd Natl Council for Black Studies 1981-; ed comm Seattle Urban League 1983-; mayors' task force Afr Amer Heritage Museum 1985-. **HONORS/ACHIEVEMENTS:** Adv Study Fellowship Ford Found 1972-73; For Area Fellowship Soc Sci Rsch Counc 1973-75; Rsch Grant Inst for Ethnic Studies in US 1982; NEH Postdoct Fellow Summer Seminar Atlanta Univ, 1984. **BUSINESS ADDRESS:** Dir of Afro-Amer Studies, Univ of Washington, Afro-American Studies, Mail Stop GN-07, Seattle, WA 98195.

WILLIAMS, WESLEY S., JR.
Attorney. **PERSONAL:** Born Nov 13, 1942, Philadelphia; married Karen Roberta Hastie; children: Amanda, Wesley, Bailey. **EDUCATION:** Harvard U, Magna Cum Laude 1963; Woodrow Wilosn Fellow Fletcher Sch of Law & Dipl, MA 1964; Harvard U, JD 1967; Columbia U, LLM 1969. **CAREER:** Covington & Burling, partner 1975-, asso 1970-75; Georgetown U, adj prof law 1971-73; US Sen Com on DC, couns 1969-70; Columbia U, assoc-in-law 1968-69; DC City Cncl, couns 1967-69. **ORGANIZATIONS:** Mem US Circuit Judge Nominating Comm 1977-; mem Com on Legislation Bar 1973-; mem Exec Ecom Wash Lawyers' Com for Civil Rights Under Law 1972-; mem Circuit Judicial Conf 1971-; pres Bd Trustees Family & Child Serv Wash 1974-; mem Bd Dir Nat Symphony Orch Assn 1972-; pres bd trustees Nat Child Rsrch Ctr 1980-; life mem Wash Urban League. **BUSINESS ADDRESS:** Covington & Burling, 1201 Pennsylvania Ave NW, Washington, DC 20044.

WILLIAMS, WILBERT
Labor official. **PERSONAL:** Born Mar 30, 1924, Crockett, TX; married Theresa; children: Gentry, Raschelle, Keola, Lewis, Kimberly. **EDUCATION:** Phillis Wheatley HS, diploma 1942; TX Southern Univ, BS 1947-52. **CAREER:** Intl Assn Machinist #2007, pres 1957-61; AFL-CIO, field rep 1964-74; AFL-CIO Dept of Org & Field Svcs, asst to dir 1974-83; AFL-CIO Region IV, admin 1983-86, dir, 1987-. **ORGANIZATIONS:** Pres AME Church TX Conf Laymen 1972-73; life subscriber NAACP 1974-; Natl Bd A Philip Randolph Institute 1974-. **HONORS/ACHIEVEMENTS:** Outstanding Laymen TX Conf Laymen 1983; William E Pollard TX State A Philip Randolph Inst 1985. **MILITARY SERVICE:** USN BM 2/C 1943-45. **BUSINESS ADDRESS:** Regional Dir, AFL-CIO, 55 North 1-H 35 #100, Austin, TX 78702.

WILLIAMS, WILBERT EDD
Software engineer. **PERSONAL:** Born Sep 13, 1948, Fayetteville, NC; married Yolanda Faye DeBerry; children: Danica Michelle, Donata Merie. **EDUCATION:** Fayetteville State Univ, BS (Summa Cum Laude) 1977; Univ of MI-Ann Arbor, MS 1978; Duke Univ, MBA 1986. **CAREER:** US Navy, digital display tech 1967-74; Bell Labs, mem of tech staff 1977-79; Westinghouse Electric Corp, systems & software engr 1979-86, mgr product software 1986-. **ORGANIZATIONS:** Mem Amer Soc of Naval Engrs 1978-, Jack & Jill of Amer 1982-; corporate minority spokesperson Westinghouse 1983-; comm ambassador Westinghouse Electric 1983-; mem St Matthew Budget & Finance Comm 1984-; vice pres St Matthew Scholarship Comm 1986-87. **HONORS/ACHIEVEMENTS:** Fellowship to Univ of MI Bell Laboratories 1977-78; Distinguished Corporate Alumni NAFEO 1983; Tuition Support for Duke MBA Westinghouse Electric 1984-86. **MILITARY SERVICE:** USNR lt commander 19 yrs; Armed Forces Reserve Medal 1986.

WILLIAMS, WILBERT LEE
Clergyman, educator. **PERSONAL:** Born Aug 25, 1938, Corsicana, TX; son of Calvin Williams, Sr; married Catherine L Lemons, Dec 30, l961; children: Sheila, Stuart, Cynthia. **EDUCATION:** Prairie View A&M Coll, BS 1960; Howard Univ School of Law, JD 1971; Inst for New Govt Attys 1971; Howard Univ School of Divinity, 1987-. **CAREER:** US Dept of Agr, farm mgmt supr 1965-68; United Planning Org Wash DC, exec ofcr 1968-71; US Dept of Agr Office of Gen Counsel Wash DC, atty 1971-73; US Dept of Agr, equal opportunity officer; pastor, The First New Horizon Baptist Church. **ORGANIZATIONS:** Past vice pres & founding mem CHAS Inc; former mem DC Neighborhood Reinvestment Commission; past mem bd dir Neighborhood Legal Serv Program Washington DC; past mem bd trustee United Planning Org Washington DC. **HONORS/ACHIEVEMENTS:** Recip 1st Annual Achievement Award OEO Natl Advisory Comm for Legal Serv Program 1968. **MILITARY SERVICE:** AUS 1961-64. **BUSINESS ADDRESS:** Pastor, The First New Horizon Baptist Church, PO Box l76, Clinton, MD 20735.

WILLIAMS, WILLIAM J.
Educator, public administrator. **PERSONAL:** Born Dec 25, 1935, Montgomery, AL; son of Eugene W Phillips and Celestine Reynolds Phillips; children: Morgan Lynn, Paige Whitney. **EDUCATION:** Morehouse Coll, B 1952; NY Univ, M 1954; Univ of So CA, PhD 1966. **CAREER:** NY State Com/Govtl Operations NY City, admin adv 1959-60; Bldg Serv Union, rsch dir joint council #8 1960-61; CA State Legislature, consult 1961-62; USCongressman Augustus F Hawkins, congressional field dir 1962-66; US Equal Employment Oppor Comm, dep staff dir 1966-67; US Commn on Civil Rights, dir western progs 1967-68; LA Co/LA City, employee relations bd mediator 1974; Univ So CA, prof. **ORGANIZATIONS:** Exec dir Negro Polit Action Assn CA 1964-66; dem candidate Sec of State of CA 1966; pres, USC Chapter, Amer Assn Univ Profs, 1974-75; Pres, Inst for Applied Epistemics; Dir, Educ Consulting & Counseling Serv; Pres, Diversified Servs. **HONORS/ACHIEVEMENTS:** Teaching Excellence Award, School of Public Admin, USC, 1978; Man of the Year, Alpha Phi Omega; several publications; Distinguished Prof Award, USC graduate Student Assn. **MILITARY SERVICE:** USAF sgt 1952-54. **BUSINESS ADDRESS:** Professor, Univ So CA, University Park, Los Angeles, CA 90007.

WILLIAMS, WILLIAM THOMAS
Educator. **PERSONAL:** Born Jul 17, 1942, Cross Creek, NC; son of William T Williams and Hazel Davis Williams; married Patricia A DeWeese; children: Nila, Aaron. **EDUCATION:** City Univ of NY/New York City Comm Coll, AAS 1962; Pratt Inst, BFA 1966; Skowhegan Schl of Painting and Sculpture, 1965; Yale Univ, MFA 1968. **CAREER:** Pratt Inst, painting fac 1970; Schl of Visual Arts, painting fac 1970; CUNY Brooklyn Coll, prof of art 1971-; Skowhegan Schl of Painting & Sculpture, res painting fac 1971, 1974, 1978; VA Commonwealth Univ, distinguished visiting commonwealth prof of art 1984; bd of trustees Grace Church School 1984-87. **ORGANIZATIONS:** Govenor Skowhegan Schl of Painting & Sculpture 1972-; artistic bd Cinque Gallery 1978-; bd trustees Grace Church Schl 1984-.

HONORS/ACHIEVEMENTS: Individual Artist Award Painting Natl Endowment for the Arts and Humanities 1965, 1970; painting Creative Arts Public Serv Grant 1975, 1981; Faculty Research Award City Univ of NY 1973, 1984, 1987; John Simon Guggenheim Fellowship/ John Simon Guggenheim Memorial Foundation 1987. **HOME ADDRESS:** 654 Broadway, New York, NY 10012. **BUSINESS ADDRESS:** Professor of Art, CUNY, Brooklyn Coll, Brooklyn, NY 11210.

WILLIAMS, WILLIE
Educator. **PERSONAL:** Born Mar 24, 1947, Independence, LA; son of Willie Williams Sr and Leanner Booker Williams; married Leona I Lathers (divorced). **EDUCATION:** Southern Univ, BS, 1970; IA State Univ, MS, 1972, PhD, 1974. **CAREER:** Lincoln Univ, asst prof, Physics 1974-77, chmn, Science div, 1976-80, assoc prof, Physics 1977-84; Dept of Defense, physical scientist 1980-82; Lincoln Univ, chmn Science Math div 1984-, prof & chmn of Physics. **ORGANIZATIONS:** Consultant, Mobil Oil Co 1976; physical scientist, Natl Bureau of Standards, 1976-77; NASA Fellow NASA 1978; ONR Fellow Naval Research Lab 1980; chrmn Cheyney Lincoln Temple Cluster 1978-80; mem PRIME Bd of Dir 1977-, AAPT NY Acad Of Sciences, Sigma Xi; Dir, Lincoln Advance Science & Engineering Reinforcement Program, 1982-; mem, Oxford Rotary, 1986-. **HONORS/ACHIEVEMENTS:** Lindback Award, Lincoln Univ, 1976; CLT Award, Cheyney Lincoln Temple Cluster, 1980; Excellence in Science & Technology; White House Initiative on HBCU's, 1989. **BUSINESS ADDRESS:** Chmn, Physics, Lincoln Univ, Physics Dept, Lincoln University, PA 19352.

WILLIAMS, WILLIE, JR.
Business executive. **PERSONAL:** Married Nellie Redmond. **EDUCATION:** Benedict Coll, BA; Rutgers U, grad study; MI State U; SC State Coll;Univ of SC. **CAREER:** Willie Williams Real Estate Inc, pres & Founder; Richland Co, inst pub schs; Upward BoundUniv of SC, couns; Midland Tech Ctr; Benedict Coll, placement dir; SC Chap NAREB, pres; chmn bd Palmetto Home Counseling Inc & Success Investment Co. **ORGANIZATIONS:** Mem Columbia Bd of Realtors; State Mfgrs Housing Commn; Richland Co Planning Commn Bd Dir Columbia Urban League; adv bd Columbia Opportunities Industrialization Ctr of SC; bd trustees Benedict Coll; Friendship Jr Coll; life mem NAACP; Omicron Phi Chap of Omega Psi Phi; city chmn 1974 UNCF Campaign. **BUSINESS ADDRESS:** Willie Williams Real Est Inc, 6023 Two Notch Rd, Columbia, SC.

WILLIAMS, WILLIE ELBERT
Educator, mathematician. **PERSONAL:** Born Jun 06, 1927, Jacksonville, TX; married Doris Lee Matlock; children: Lois E, Willys E, Donald A, Linda W, Dorwyl L. **EDUCATION:** Huston Tillotson Clge Austin TX, BS Math cum laude 1952; TX So Univ Houston, MS Math 1953; MI State Univ, PhD Math 1972. **CAREER:** Lufkin Independent School Dist, teacher 1953-59; Cleveland Bd of Educ, chmn of dept math 1960-73; Case-Western Reserve Univ, adj prof of math 1964-68; Deep Accellerated Math Prog, dir 1973-78; Florida Intl Univ, assoc prof. **ORGANIZATIONS:** Consult Natl Follow Through Prog 1974-75; deacon 2nd Bapt Ch 1975-80; state rep Omega Psi Phi Frat State of FL 1979-80; pres Concerned Black Educ in Higher Educ in FL 1980-81; evaluator of College Title III Programs; vice pres, chair anticrime comm PULSE; pres Black Faculty FL Intl Univ; lecturer ABAM; recruiter Black Faculty and Black Students. **HONORS/ACHIEVEMENTS:** Outstanding Teacher Awd Univ of CO 1954; Master Tchr Award Martha Holden Jennings Fnd 1973. **MILITARY SERVICE:** AUS corpl 1945-49; Occupation Good Conduct Medal. **BUSINESS ADDRESS:** Associate Professor, Florida InternationalUniv, Miami, FL 33199.

WILLIAMS, WILLIE J.
Educator. **PERSONAL:** Born Jan 08, 1949, Chester Co, SC; married Louvenia Brooks. **EDUCATION:** Voorhees Clge, BS. **CAREER:** Industrial Educ Devel Corp Proj Dir Jobs 70 Prog 1970-73; Atlanta GA Custom Packagers & Processors Inc, personnel dir 1973-74; Colquitt Co Bd of Educ Moultries GA, teacher 1974-. **ORGANIZATIONS:** Mem Amateur Softball Assc Umpires 1975-; mem Free Accepted Masons 1973-; Omega Psi Phi Frat 1968-; Natl State & Local Educ Assc 1974-75; Steering Com Quarter Sys for Colquitt Co Sch 1974-75; mem Colquitt Co Civil Defense Rescue Team 1973-; registered Emer Med Tech State of GA; mem State of GA Dept of Defense Rescue Workers; Honor Soc Finley Sr High Sch 1964-66. **HONORS/ACHIEVEMENTS:** Dale Carnegie Cert of Appreciation for Grad Asst 1973. **BUSINESS ADDRESS:** Norman Pk High Sch, Norman Park, GA.

WILLIAMS, WILLIE LAVERN
Educator. **PERSONAL:** Born Dec 24, 1940, Little Rock, AR; married Margaret Jean Lee; children: Gregory, Kristy, Karen, Stephen. **EDUCATION:** San Jose State Clge, BA 1962; CA State Univ Long Beach, Tchng Cert 1963; Univ of AZ, MEd 1977. **CAREER:** Univ of AZ, adj assc prof & coach 1969-; Compton HS, educ & coach 1964-69; CA State Univ Long Beach, coach 1963-64. **ORGANIZATIONS:** Mem intl competition com The Athletics Congress 1977-; chmn US Olympic Com 1977-; mem coaches com Track & Field/USA 1979-; mem NAACP 1969-; mem Natl Urban League 1972-; regl chmn The Athletics Congress 1974-; reg VII rep US Track Coaches Assc 1976-80; regl dir Track & Field USA 1978-. **HONORS/ACHIEVEMENTS:** CA Interscholastic Federation Coach of Year CIF 1969; NCAA Region VII Coach of Year NCAA 1972; NCAA Region VII Coach of Year NCAA 1973-; Assist US Olympic Team Coach US Olympic Com 1980. **BUSINESS ADDRESS:** The Univ of AZ, McKale Cntr #238, Tucson, AZ 85721.

WILLIAMS, WILLIE S.
Psychologist. **PERSONAL:** Born May 08, 1932, Prattville, AL; married Marva R Flowers; children: Kevin, Keith, Karla. **EDUCATION:** Wichita State Univ, AB, Chem & Math, 1958; Xavier OH, MEd, Admin & Personnel Serv 1960; MI State Univ, PhD Counseling Psychology 1970. **CAREER:** Case Western Reserve Univ School of Med, assoc dean for student affairs; NIMH Min Ctr, asst chief for Psychology Rsch & Training Program; Univ of Cincinnati, sr counselor & asst prof of psychology, Cincinnati Police Dept, psychology conselor; Willie S Williams PhD Inc, pres. **ORGANIZATIONS:** Pres, Phi Delta Kappa ANWC; Amer Personnel & Guild Assn; treasurer, Assn, Black Psychologists; Amer Psychology Assn; Kappa Alpha Psi. **MILITARY SERVICE:** AUS 1953-55. **BUSINESS ADDRESS:** President, Willie S Williams PhD Inc, 20310 Chagrin Blvd, Shaker Heights, OH 44122.

WILLIAMS, WINSTON
Reporter. **PERSONAL:** Born in Norfolk, VA. **EDUCATION:** Columbia Univ, BA 1973, MS 1974. **CAREER:** Business Week Magazine Pittsburgh, bureau chief 1974-77; New York Times, reporter 1978-. **BUSINESS ADDRESS:** New York Times, 229 West 43rd St, New York, NY 10036.

WILLIAMS, WYATT CLIFFORD
Federal employee organizer. **PERSONAL:** Born May 29, 1921, Pittsburgh, PA; married Dorothy Mae Jones; children: Angelica Angell, Valeria, Marva. **EDUCATION:** Attended, Duquesne Univ 1939, Univ of Pgh 1952-54, Penn State Univ, American Univ. **CAREER:** Natl Alliance of Postal & Federal Employees, pres local 510 Pgh 1959-65, natl 1st vice pres 1965-70, presidential aide 1970-71, natl 2nd vice pres 1979-. **ORGANIZATIONS:** Mem Amvets, Klan Watch-NOW, Common Cause, NAACP, League of Women Voters. **MILITARY SERVICE:** AUS acting platoon staff sgt 1943-46. **BUSINESS ADDRESS:** 2nd Natl Vice President, NAPFE, 1628 11th St NW, Washington, DC 20001.

WILLIAMS, YARBOROGH, JR.
Elected official. **PERSONAL:** Born Mar 24, 1950, Warrenton, NC; married Carolyn M; children: Consherto V, Yarbro8ugh, Juroid C. **EDUCATION:** NC State Univ, voc; Vance Granvillco Coll, drafting. **CAREER:** Franklinton City Schools, teacher 17 yrs; Warren Co Pub Sch Dist, sch bd mem. **ORGANIZATIONS:** Mem NAACP; pres Warren Co Political Action Council; pres Boys Club; mem School Bd; Warren Co Bd of Election; Warren Co Democratic Party; mem NCSBA; mem NCEA. **HONORS/ACHIEVEMENTS:** Teacher of the Year Assoc of General Contractors of Amer 1986. **HOME ADDRESS:** Rt 2 Box 75, Warrenton, NC 27589. **BUSINESS ADDRESS:** School Board Member, Warren Co Pub Sch Dist, P O Box 397, Franklinton, NC 27525.

WILLIAMS, YARBOROUGH BURWELL, JR.
Community & government relations. **PERSONAL:** Born Mar 04, 1928, Raleigh, NC; married Shirley; children: Dennis, Craig, Yarvette. **EDUCATION:** VA Union U, BA 1954;Univ of VA, MEd 1966. **CAREER:** Comm Affairs Newport News Shipbuilding A Tenneco Co, vice pres 1985; Newport News Shipbuilding, pres staff 1970-73; John Marshall HS, asst prin; HS of Richmond Lynchburg VA, soc studies tchr. **ORGANIZATIONS:** Mem City Council 1973-74; pres Richmond Educ Assn 1967-69; mem State Bd Comm Colls 1969-; bd mem Peninsula Un Way; bd of trustees VA Union U; Nat Urban Affairs Council; Peninsula Drug Abuse Council; Peninsula Human Resources Council. **HONORS/ACHIEVEMENTS:** Recip Pres Citation Peninsula Family Serv 1975; Distin Serv Awards City of Hampton 1974; Comm Serv Honor Metro Mag Tidewater VA 1974. **MILITARY SERVICE:** AUS 1950-52. **BUSINESS ADDRESS:** 4101 Washington Ave, Newport News, VA 23607.

WILLIAMS, YVONNE CARTER
Educator. **PERSONAL:** Born Feb 12, 1932, Philadelphia, PA; daughter of Patterson H. Carter (deceased) and Evelyn Lightner Carter (deceased); married Dr Theodore Williams, Jul 03, 1954; children: Lynora A, Alison P, Meredith J, Lesley Y. **EDUCATION:** PA State Univ, BA (cum laude) 1953; Harvard Law Sch, 1953-54; Univ of CT, MA (honors) 1955; Case Western Reserve Univ, PhD 1981. **CAREER:** Dept of Educ Univ of CT, admin Asst; Ashland Wayne Comm Action Comm, dir of rsch 1964-66; Wayne Co Headstart, social worker 1967-68; Wooster Public Schools, visiting teacher 1968-69; OH State Univ, lecturer 1971-72; College of Wooster, asst to the dean, asst prof of pol sci; dir of black studies 1973-74, assoc prof of pol sci/black studies, dir of black studies 1983-89, dean of faculty 1989-; consultant/evaluator, Lilly Foundation, Kent State Univ, Wayne County Career Center. **ORGANIZATIONS:** Alpha Kappa Alpha Sor 1953; Wayne Co Bd of Mental Health & Retardation 1969-76; Wooster City Charter Comm 1971-72; League of Women Voters delegate to NatlConvention 1972; Head Start Parents' Adv Council 1970-73; Mayor's Alternate to NEFCO 1974-75; bd of dirs College Hills Retirement Village 1973-; Wooster City Charter Review Comm 1980; City of Wooster Human Relations Council 1978-; bd of governors Wooster Comm Hosp 1981-; bd of trustess Health Trustee Inst 1986-1988; Advisory Bd, Wayne County Adult Basic Educ, 1987-. **HONORS/ACHIEVEMENTS:** John Hay Whitney Fellowship 1954; AHS Fellowship Case Western Reserve Univ 1976-77; Alumni Fellowship Case Western Reserve Univ 1977-78; Jessie Smith Noyes Found Scholarship; Faculty Develop Grant 1980-81; Morris Fund Grant Coll of Wooster 1981, 1983. **HOME ADDRESS:** 659 College Ave, Wooster, OH 44691. **BUSINESS ADDRESS:** Dean of Faculty, College of Wooster, Wooster, OH 44691.

WILLIAMS, YVONNE LAVERNE
Attorney, higher education executive. **PERSONAL:** Born Jan 07, 1938, Washington, DC; daughter of Smallwood E Williams and Verna L (Rapley) Williams. **EDUCATION:** Barnard Coll, BA, 1959; Boston Univ, MA, 1961; Georgetown Univ, JD, 1977. **CAREER:** US Info Agency, foreign serv officer, 1961-65; African-Amer Inst New York, dir womens Africa comm, 1966-68; Benedict Coll, Columbia, SC, assc prof African studies, 1968-70; US Congress Washington, DC, press sec Hon Walter Fauntroy, 1970-72; African-Amer Scholars Council Washington, DC, dir 1972-73; Leva Hawes Symington Martin, Washington, DC, assoc atty, 1977-79; Brimmer & Co Washington, DC, asst vice pres, 1980-82; Tuskegee Inst, vice pres for Fed & Intl Rel & Legal Counsel 1983-. **ORGANIZATIONS:** Mem Oper Crossroads Africa, 1960-, Barnard-in-Washington, 1960-; mem Amer Bar Assoc, 1980-, Natl Bar Assoc, 1980-, Dist of Columbia Bar, 1980-; mem, Natl Assoc of Coll & Univ Atty, 1983-; mem, legislative comm Natl Assoc State Univ & Land Grant Coll, 1983-; alumnae trustee, Barnard Coll, New York, NY, 1988-; mem, Overseas Devel Council, Washington, DC, 1988-; bd of dir, Golden Rule Apartments, Inc, Washington, DC, 1986-. **HONORS/ACHIEVEMENTS:** Fellowship African Research & Studies Program, Boston Univ, 1959-60; author, "William Monroe Trotter, (1872-1934)"; Reid "The Black Prism," New York, 1969. **BUSINESS ADDRESS:** Vice Pres Fed & Intl Rel & Legal Counsel, Tuskegee University, Washington Office, 11 Dupont Circl, NW, Suite 220, Washington, DC 20036.

WILLIAMS-DAVIS, EDITH G.
Geophysicist. **PERSONAL:** Born Apr 08, 1958, Passaic, NJ; married Warren C Davis Jr, May 25, 1984. **EDUCATION:** Univ of Miami, BS Geology 1981, geological expedition Guatemala C Amer 1978; Stanford Univ, MS Geophysics 1982, geophysical field expedition Nevada 1982; Univ of TX, Austin, MBA, 1989. **CAREER:** Oxygen Isotopic Lab, coord 1977, asst to Dr Cesare Emiliani 1977-78; US Geological Survey, geological field asst 1980; Marathon Oil Co, geophysical asst 1981; US Geological Survey, exploration geophysicist 1981-82; Mobil Oil Inc, exploration geophysicist 1983-86; Continental Airlines, Houston, TX, general sales reservation, 1987; Univ TX Grad School of Business Dean office, Austin, minority student affairs coordinator, 1987-89; 3M Headquarters, St Paul, MN, marketing intern,

1988. **ORGANIZATIONS:** Mem Miami Geological Soc 1976-78; pres United Black Students Organ 1978-79; sci coord Upward Bound Prog 1979; mem Delta Sigma Theta Sor 1979; mem AGU 1981-82; mem AAPG 1982-84; mem Amer Assn of Exploration Geophysics 1982-84. **HONORS/ACHIEVEMENTS:** Dean's List 1977-78; John F Kennedy/Martin Luther King Scholarship Grant 1977-80; President's List 1978; United Black Students President's Awd 1978; Univ ofMiami Honors Scholarship 1978; Shell Oil Scholarship Grant 1978-80; Amer Geologic Union Awd 1981-82; US Geologic Survey Fellowship 1981-82; Amer Geological Inst Fellowship 1981-82; featured in Ebony mag 1984; featured in Mobil World Newspaper 1984; recipient, National Black MBA Fellowship, 1987; recipient, Consortium for Graduate Study in Management Fellowship, 1988.

WILLIAMS-GREEN, JOYCE F.
Educational administrator. **PERSONAL:** Born Sep 06, 1948, Sanford, NC; daughter of Joseph A Williams; married Edward W Green, Sep 01, 1984. **EDUCATION:** North Carolina Central Univ, BS, 1970; Herbert H Lehman Coll, MS, 1976; Virginia Polytechnic Inst & State Univ, EdD, 1984. **CAREER:** New York City Public School, teacher, 1971-76; Livingstone Coll, dir of learning center, 1976-80; Virginia Polytechnic Inst and State Univ, asst to the provost, 1984-. **ORGANIZATIONS:** Consultant, Janus Learning Center, 1986, North Carolina A&T, 1986; citizen representative, Blacksburg in the 80's, 1984-86; mem, co-chair, Phi Kappa Phi, 1986-87; mem research comm, NACADA, 1986; bd mem, Warren Health Found, New River Community Sentencing Inc. **HONORS/ACHIEVEMENTS:** Cunningham Research Fellowship, Virginia Tech, 1983; "The Effect of the Computer on Natl Educ," Computing Conf proceedings, 1983; Natl Certificate of Merit, NACADA, 1986. **BUSINESS ADDRESS:** Asst Provost, Virginia Polytechnic Inst and State Univ, 201 Burruss Hall, Blacksburg, VA 24061.

WILLIAMS-HARRIS, DIANE BEATRICE
Educational administrator. **PERSONAL:** Born Feb 01, 1949, Newark, NJ; married Karl Anthony Harris; children: Karl. **EDUCATION:** Boston Univ, BA 1971; Rutgers Univ Grad Sch of Educ, MEd 1977. **CAREER:** Prudential Ins Co, pension administrator 1971-73; Rutgers Univ Office of Undergrad Admissions, asst to the dir 1973-76, asst dir 1976-78, dir douglassc 1978-82, assoc dir 1982-. **ORGANIZATIONS:** Mem Natl Assoc of College Admissions Counselors, Delta Sigma Theta, 100 Black Women. **HONORS/ACHIEVEMENTS:** Sponsored participant in Women in Higher Educ 1977; Rutgers Univ Merit Awd 1986. **BUSINESS ADDRESS:** Assoc Dir/Undergrad Admissions, Rutgers University, PO Box 2101, New Brunswick, NJ 08903.

WILLIAMSON, CARL VANCE
Government/private agency. **PERSONAL:** Born Oct 03, 1955, Portsmouth, VA; son of Shelton Williamson and Carolyn Williamson. **EDUCATION:** Virginia Commonwealth Univ, BS 1977; Univ of South FL, MBA 1984. **CAREER:** Group W Cable Inc, financial analyst 1983-85; MCI Telecommunications, sup-acctg & analysis 1985-86; Hampton Redevelopment/Housing Auth, housing mgmt sup 1986-. **ORGANIZATIONS:** Mem Omega Psi Phi Frat Inc 1974-, Amer Assoc of MBA Exec 1984-, Natl Black MBA Assoc 1985-; mem NAACP. **HOME ADDRESS:** 1229 Darren Dr, Portsmouth, VA 23701. **BUSINESS ADDRESS:** Housing Mgmt Supervisor, Hampton Redevel/Hsg Authority, PO Box 280, Hampton, VA 23669.

WILLIAMSON, CARLTON
Professional athlete. **PERSONAL:** Born Jun 12, 1958, Atlanta, GA; married Donna; children: Kevin Carlton. **EDUCATION:** Pitt Univ, Urban Science degree 1981. **CAREER:** San Francisco 49ers, safety 1981-. **HONORS/ACHIEVEMENTS:** All Rookie 1981; named Coll and Pro Football Weekly second team all-pro and AP honorable mention all pro 1985; mem Pro Bowl teams 1985,86. **BUSINESS ADDRESS:** San Francisco 49ers, 711 Nevada Ave, Redwood City, CA 94061.

WILLIAMSON, COY COLBERT, JR.
Nursing home owner/manager. **PERSONAL:** Born Mar 27, 1936, Commerce, GA; married Betty Brown; children: Coylitia, Bettrena. **EDUCATION:** Stillman Coll, BA Business 1962. **CAREER:** Atlanta Life Insurance Co, debit mgr 1963-64; Teachers Agency of GA, claims mgr 1964-66; ACTION Inc, fiscal officer 1966-70; Atlanta Mortgage Co, asst vice pres 1970; Univ of GA, asst mgr of loans and receivables 1970-71; Athens Model Cities, fiscal coord 1972-73; State of GA, fiscal mgmt spclst 1973-74; Grandview Care Ctr Inc, mgr 1974-83; We Care Enterprises Inc, mgmt specialist/consultant, owner 1983-. **ORGANIZATIONS:** Founder Athens Business and Professional Org 1978-82; mem Classic City Toastmasters 1980-81; sec & mem at large GA Health Care Assoc 1980-; fellow Amer Coll of Long-Term Administrators 1982-; mem Metro Atlanta Cncl of Nursing Home Adminis; life mem and polemarch Kappa Alpha Psi Frat; deacon and sunday sch supt Hill First Bapt Church; mem Athens Area Chamber of Commerce. **HONORS/ACHIEVEMENTS:** Achievement & Leadership Awd Kappa Alpha Psi Frat; President's Golden/Dist List Stillman Coll 1983-; First black apptd by Gov to serve on GA Public Safety Bd 1984-. **MILITARY SERVICE:** USAF a/1c 1954-58; US Peace Corps 1962-63. **HOME ADDRESS:** 1125 Whit Davis Rd, Athens, GA 30605. **BUSINESS ADDRESS:** Owner/Manager, We Care Enterprises Inc, PO Box 146, Athens, GA 30603.

WILLIAMSON, GEORGE H., JR.
Business executive. **PERSONAL:** Born Aug 24, 1929, LakeCity, FL; married Beatrice Roslyn Taylor; children: La Vera Renee, Bernard, Trudy, Solomon. **EDUCATION:** Labor School, Cert 1947; Welding School, 1957. **CAREER:** Ferry Retail Liquor, propr; Bethlehem Steel Co, bricklayer; Waldem Mem Fun Home, pres 1978-. **ORGANIZATIONS:** Life mem NAACP, 32 Degree Mason, St John Lodge #16, Bison Consistory #49, Hadji Shriners Temple #61; chmn USW Dist Civil Rights Comm; chief steward Bricklayer Dept 21 yrs. **HONORS/ACHIEVEMENTS:** Comm Leaders & Noteworthy Amer Awd; Black Ed Awd for Disting Accompl; Recog for Successful Bus Canisus Coll; Disting Serv in Labor Movement Awd Mary Wheatly; Outstanding Achievement from St John Lodge 1984. **BUSINESS ADDRESS:** President, Waldem Memorial Fun Home, 219 E Ferry St, Buffalo, NY 14208.

WILLIAMSON, HANDY, JR.
Higher education administrator. **PERSONAL:** Born Oct 24, 1945, Louin, MS; son of Handy Williamson Sr and Lilla Nobles Williamson; married Barbara Jean Herndon, Dec 28, 1968; children: Lilla-Marie Juliana Williamson. **EDUCATION:** Pineywood Jr Coll, Pineywood MS, AA, 1965; Alcorn State Univ, Lorman MS, BS, 1967; Tennessee State Univ, Nashville TN, MS, 1969; Univ of Missouri, Columbia MO, MS 1971, PhD 1974. **CAREER:** Tennessee State Univ, Nashville TN, res asst, 1967-69; Univ of Missouri, Columbia MO, grad res asst, 1969-74; Tuskegee Univ, Tuskegee AL, assoc dir of res, 1974-77; Tennessee State Univ, Nashville TN, res dir, 1977-85; USAID, Washington DC, director/AD-15, 1985-88; Univ of Tennessee, Knoxville TN, dept head & prof, 1988-. **ORGANIZATIONS:** Pres, Phi Beta Sigma, Tuskegee chapter, 1975-77; charter mem, Optimist Club of Tuskegee, 1975-77; consultant, Tennessee Valley Authority, 1979-80; consultant, Bd for Intl Food & Agric Devel, 1981-85; mem, legislative subcomm, ESCOP, 1981-84; mem, Paster Parish Comm, Clark UMC Church, 1981-85; mem, US Joint Council on Food & Agric, 1982-83; bd mem, Assn of Intl Prog Dirs, 1984-88; White House Comm liaison, USAID, 1985-88; dir, Virginia Business Devel Center, 1987-. **HONORS/ACHIEVEMENTS:** Gamma Sigma Delta, Univ of MO, 1971; Outstanding Young Man of America, Univ of MO, 1973; spearheaded establishment of Optimist Club of Tuskegee, 1975; internatl devel consultant, 1975-; author of articles on Black universities, 1977-89; testimony before US House & Senate subcomms, 1981-85; co-author of book on small farms in Tennessee, 1985; Presidential Plaques, TN State Univ, 1985 & 1987; Oustanding Service, USAID/Washington DC, 1986; Distinguished Alumni, Alcorn State Univ, 1987; mem of Pres Club, Univ of TN, 1988. **HOME ADDRESS:** 12108 East Ashton Ct, Knoxville, TN 37922.

WILLIAMSON, JOHN
Athlete. **PERSONAL:** Born Nov 10, 1952, New Haven, CT; married Bertha; children: Raushanah, John. **EDUCATION:** NM State 1974. **CAREER:** Washington Bullets, guard 1979; NJ Nets/IN Pacers, basketball Player 1976-77; NY, basketball player 1973-76. **ORGANIZATIONS:** Mem ABA Championship Team 1973-74; Was NJ Nets All-Time Leading Scorer. **BUSINESS ADDRESS:** c/o Washington Bullets, 1 Harry S Truman Dr, Landover, MD 20786.

WILLIAMSON, KAREN ELIZABETH
Administrator. **PERSONAL:** Born Dec 20, 1947, St Louis, MO; daughter of Irving and Elizabeth; divorced; children: Stephanie Elizabeth. **EDUCATION:** Wellesley Coll MA, BA 1965-69;Univ of Chicago Grad Schl Bus, MBA 1969-71. **CAREER:** Philip Morris Inc NYC, asst brand mgr 1971-73; Avon Prod Inc NYC, prod couns 1973-76; Asst Sec Dept of HUD Wash, spl asst 1977-78; The White House, dep spl asst 1978-81; Satellite Business Systems, acct rep 1981-86; MCI, sr mgr natl accts 1986; Intl Ctr for Information Tech Washington, dir external relations 1987-88; MCI, sr mgr natl accounts, 1988-. **ORGANIZATIONS:** Bd of dir Nat Black MBA Assn 1972-75; mem Natl Black MBA Assoc 1986-, Coalition of 100 Black Women of DC, Washington Wellesley Club, Univ of Chicago Women's Business Group; Leadership Washington. **HONORS/ACHIEVEMENTS:** Black Achievers Awd Harlem YMCA 1975. **HOME ADDRESS:** 528 Brummel Ct NW, Washington, DC 20012. **BUSINESS ADDRESS:** Sr Manager, Nal Accounts, MCI, 1133 19th St, NW, Washington, DC 20036.

WILLIAMSON, SAMUEL R.
Attorney. **PERSONAL:** Born Nov 22, 1943, Ellaville, GA; son of Joseph Williamson and Mizzie Williamson; married Barbara Ann Elliott; children: Patricia, Michael. **EDUCATION:** Hampton Inst, BS 1965; Seton Hall Univ, JD 1975; Attended, Command & General Staff Coll 1982. **CAREER:** AT&T Bell Lab, elec engr 1968-75, patent atty 1976-. **ORGANIZATIONS:** Mem Assoc of Black Lab Employees 1970-85, Garden State Bar Assoc 1976-89, Natl Bar Assoc 1976-89, New York Urban League Inc 1982-89; bd mem pres Natl Patent Law Assoc 1988-89; mem New Jersey Wing Civil Air Patrol 1983-89; BEEP lecturer; mem NAI Inc, The Alliance Inc, AUSA, Amer Legion, YMCA, Phi Alpha Delta, Scabbard & Blade, Explorers. **HONORS/ACHIEVEMENTS:** Electronics Assoc Honor Awd for Military Leadership; Awd for Unselfish Devotion to ABLE Inc. **MILITARY SERVICE:** AUSR lt col 1965-87; Armed Forces Commendation. **BUSINESS ADDRESS:** Attorney, AT&T Bell Laboratories, Crawfords Corner Rd, Holmdel, NJ 07733.

WILLIAMSON-IGE, DOROTHY KAY
Educator. **PERSONAL:** Born Apr 18, 1950, Parma, MO; daughter of Rufus A Williamson and Florida B Madden Williamson; married Adewole A Ige; children: Olufolajimi Wm. **EDUCATION:** Southeast Missouri State Univ, BS, Speech, 1971; Central Missouri State Univ, MA, Speech Comm, 1973; Ohio State Univ, PhD, Speech, 1980. **CAREER:** Webster Grove Schools, speech & drama teacher, 1971-77; DOD Dependents Schools, drama teacher, 1977-78; Bowling Green State Univ, faculty & field exper coord, 1980-84; Indiana Univ NW, faculty, 1985-. **ORGANIZATIONS:** Public adv bd, Bowling Green State Univ, 1980-83; assoc, Ohio State Univ Black Alumni, 1980-; Phi Delta Kappa, 1980-; speech comm, assoc black caucus pres, legislative council, Black Oppor Task Force, 1981-87; State of Ohio Bd Redesign of Educ Programs, 1982; pres, Women Investing Together & program chairperson, Human Relations Comm, Bowling Green State Univ, 1984; TV radio newspaper interviews, keynote speeches, papers & consultantships in Midwest USA, Africa, Caribbean & Europe. **HONORS/ACHIEVEMENTS:** Academic Scholarship Certificate Southeast Missouri State Univ, 1970; (Civilian) Intl Talent Search Judge, US Military, Ramstein, Germany, Air Force Base, 1978; TV, radio, newspaper interviews and keynote speeches, papers, consultantships in Midwest US, Africa, Caribbean & Europe, 1978-; published over 15 articles & book chapters on minority, handicapped and women's communication 1981-87; Third World Peoples Award, Bowling Green State Univ, 1984. **BUSINESS ADDRESS:** Univ Teacher-Speech Comm, IndianaUniv NW, Communications Dept, 3400 Broadway, Gary, IN 46408.

WILLIE, CHARLES VERT
Educator. **PERSONAL:** Born Oct 08, 1927, Dallas, TX; son of Louis J Willie and Carrie S Willie; married Mary Sue Conklin; children: Sarah S, Martin C James T. **EDUCATION:** Morehouse Coll, BA 1948; Atlanta Univ, MA 1949; Syracuse Univ, PhD 1957; Berkeley Divinity School at Yale, DHL (Hon) 1972; Episcopal General Seminar of NY, DD (Hon) 1974; Harvard Univ, MA (Hon) 1974; Morehouse Coll, DHL (Hon) 1983. **CAREER:** Syracuse Univ, inst, asst prof, asso prof, prof of sociology 1952-74; Upstate Med Center Syracuse, NY Dept Preventive med, instructor 1955-60; Pres Comm on Delinquency Wash DC Project, research dir 1962-64; Dept of Psychiatry Harvard Med School, visiting lecturer 1966-67; Dept of Sociology Syracuse Univ, chm 1967-71; Syracuse Univ, vice pres 1972-74; Harvard Univ, prof educ & urban studies. **ORGANIZATIONS:** Mem Tech Adv Comm Falk Fund 1968-; ind mem United Negro Coll Fund 1983-86; court appointed master expert witness/consultant school desegration cases in Boston, Denver, Dallas, Houston, Little Rock, St Louis, Kansas City MO, Seattle, North Carolina San Jose, Milwaukee, St Lucie, FL 1974-; pres Eastern Sociological Soc 1974-75; council mem Amer Sociological Assn 1979-82; bd mem Soc Sci Rsch

Council 1969-76; trustee Episcopal Div School 1969-88; former vice pres General Convention of Episcopal Church in USA 1970-74; sr warden Christ Episcopal Church, Cambridge 1984-; chmn of bd, Dana McLean Greeley Found for Peace and Justice, 1989-; former mem, President's Commn on Mental Health, (USA,) 1978. **HONORS/ACHIEVEMENTS:** Mem Phi Beta Kappa (Morehouse Coll) 1972; male hero Ms Magazine (10th anniversary issue) 1982; Distiguished Alumnus Awrd Syracuse Univ 1974, Natl Assn for Equal Opportunity in Higher Ed 1979; recent books, The Ivory and Ebony Towers 1981, A New Look at Black Families 1981, Race, Ethnicity and Socio-economic Status 1983, School Desegration Plans that Work 1984, Black and White Families 1985, Five Black Scholars 1986, Effective Education 1987; social goals and educational reform, 1988, The Caste and Class Controversy on Race and Poverty; publication summary, 20 books, 100 articles or chapters in books. **BUSINESS ADDRESS:** Prof Education & Urban Study, Harvard University, Graduate School of Education, Harvard, Cambridge, MA 02138.

WILLIE, LOUIS J.
Business executive. **PERSONAL:** Born Aug 22, 1923, Fort Worth; son of Louis J Sr and Carrie Sykes; married Yvonne Kirkpatrick; children: Louis J III. **EDUCATION:** Wiley Coll, BA 1943; Univ Michigan, MBA 1947; Amer Coll Lf Underwr, CLU. **CAREER:** Tennessee State Univ, instr 1947; McKisack Bro Nashville; office manager 1950; Booker T Washington Ins Co B'Ham, exec vice pres 1952-; Citzens Fed Saving & Loan, vice pres sec treas 1956-; Booker T Washington Ins Co, pres. **ORGANIZATIONS:** Former dir Birmingham Branch Fed Reserve Bank of Atlanta; bd dir Assn of Life Ins Cos; Natl Ins Assn; chrt Life Undrwrtrs; adv bd Salvation Army; bd dir A G Gaston Boys Club; mem City Bd Amer South Bank NA; dir Alabama Power Co; mem Newcomen Soc North America; vice pres/treas United Way Central Alabama; mem NAACP; Univ of Michigan Alumni Club; president's council Univ of Alabama in Birmingham; mem Natl Black MBA Assoc; bd of dirs Birmingham Area Chamber of Commerce; bd of trustees Alabama Trust Fund; bd of dirs Meyer Found; bd of dirs Alabama Management Improvement Assn. **HONORS/ACHIEVEMENTS:** Outstanding Ctzns Award Miles Coll 1972; Distinguished Ser Award; Comm Ser Council 1972-73; 1985 Brotherhood Awd Natl Conference of Christians and Jews; inducted into AL Acad of Honor 1986. **MILITARY SERVICE:** WW II veteran. **BUSINESS ADDRESS:** President, Booker T Washington Ins Co, PO Box 697, Birmingham, AL 35201.

WILLIFORD, CYNTHIA W.
Retired educator. **PERSONAL:** Born Mar 14, 1917, Seneca, SC; married Preston. **EDUCATION:** SC St Clg, BHE 1939; MI St U, MHE 1963. **CAREER:** HS Home Economics, teacher 1939-44; Clemson Coop Ext Serv, home economist 194474. **ORGANIZATIONS:** Sch bd mem Anderson Dist #5 1980-; v chm Anderson Dist #5 Sch Bd 1985-. **HOME ADDRESS:** 222 Hillcrest Circle, Anderson, SC 29624.

WILLIFORD, STANLEY O.
Copy editor, freelance writer. **PERSONAL:** Born Jan 03, 1942, Little Rock, AR; son of Claude Williford and Mary Williford; married Corliss M; children: Steven D Woods, Nicole O Woods, Brian M, Brandon A. **EDUCATION:** CA State Univ, B 1968. **CAREER:** Newsweek mag Detroit, trainee summer 1968; LA Times, reporter 1969-72; LA Sentinel, reporter 1972-74; LA Herald Examiner, copy editor 1975-76; Travel & Art Mag, co-publ 1977-78; Ichthus Records/Productions; LA Times, copy editor 1976-. **ORGANIZATIONS:** Mem Sigma Delta Chi, 1968. **HONORS/ACHIEVEMENTS:** Fellowship to Washington Jrnl Ctr 1968; writer freelance articles in num nationally know mags in US; Natl Assoc of Media Women Awd 1974; Michele Clark Found Awd for General Excellence in Reporting Columbia Univ 1974; 1st black to edit CA State Univ newspaper 1967. **MILITARY SERVICE:** AUS e-4 1964-66. **BUSINESS ADDRESS:** Copy Editor, LA Times, Times Mirror Square, Los Angeles, CA 90053.

WILLINGHAM, VONCILE
Government manager. **PERSONAL:** Born Nov 09, 1935, Opp, AL; daughter of L K Lee and Ida Lee Liggins Lee; married Anderson Willingham, Jr; children: Donna Marie, Doretta Monique. **EDUCATION:** AL State Univ, BS Educ 1957; Univ of District of Columbia, MS Bus Educ 1977; The Amer Univ, MS Personnel and Human Resources Mgmt 1987. **CAREER:** Greene Co Bd of Educ, business educ instr 1957-58; UA Agency for Intl Develop, exec asst 1961-69, employee dev specialist 1970-77, equal employ mgr 1978-. **ORGANIZATIONS:** Mem Delta Sigma Theta Sor 1955-; mem Sargent Memorial Presbyter Chancel Choir 1975-; mem Southern MD Choral Soc 1983-; mem bd dirs Foreign Affairs Recreation Assoc 1985-; mem bd dirs Univ District of Columbia Sch of Business Educ; mem US AID Administrator's Adv Comm on Women; mem interagency commMartin Luther King Federal Holiday Comm 1986. **HONORS/ACHIEVEMENTS:** Fellowship Beta Eta Chap Delta Sigma Theta 1957; Equal Employment Oppor Awd US AGency for Intl Dev 1977; Certificates for Community Outreach to DC Public Schools 1979-84; Superior Honor Awd US Agency for Intl Dev 1981. **BUSINESS ADDRESS:** EEO Manager, US Agency for Intl Develop, 21st St & Va Avenue NW, Washington, DC 20523.

WILLIS, ANDREW
Executive director. **PERSONAL:** Born Oct 05, 1938, Jamesville, NC; married Shirley; children: LaShirl, Anqileena. **EDUCATION:** NC A&T State U, BS 1964; Kent State U, MA 1967;Univ of NY at Buffalo, Atnd. **CAREER:** Urban League of Onondaga Co, exec dir 1973-; Erie Comm Coll, asst prof 1972-73; Buffalo Urban League Feb-Aug, acting exec dir 1972; Buffalo Urban League, dep dir 1968-72; StateUniv Coll at Buffalo, pt instr 1969-72; Health & Welfare Buffalo Urban League, asso dir 1967-68; StateUniv of NY at Buffalo, tchng asst 1964-67; Kent State U, grad asst 1964-67; Pub Welfare Dept Norfolk VA, caseworker Summer 1964. **ORGANIZATIONS:** Mem bd dirs PEACE Inc; mem NY State Health Planning Adv Council; bd dirs Intl Cntr of Syracuse; adv Council on Equal Opp; Manpower Adv Planning Council; EOP Com Educ Opp Cntr; exec Councils Nat Eastern Regional State; mem Com to Reactivate Local NAACP Chpt. **HONORS/ACHIEVEMENTS:** USAF a1/c 1956-60. **BUSINESS ADDRESS:** 100 New St, Syracuse, NY 13202.

WILLIS, CECIL B.
Chief executive automotive dealership. **CAREER:** Peninsula Pontiac, Inc, Torrance CA, chief executive, 1988. **BUSINESS ADDRESS:** Peninsula Pontiac, Inc, 2909 Pacific Coast Highway, Torrance, CA 90505. *

WILLIS, CHARLES L.
Judge. **PERSONAL:** Born Sep 11, 1926, New York, NY; married Judith Lounsbury; children: Lisa Willis, Michael Elliott, Susan Elliott, Chrisophe Willis, John Elliott. **EDUCATION:** NY Univ, 1947-51; CCNY, 1950-51; St John Univ School of Law, LLB 1955. **CAREER:** Monroe County District Attorney Office, asst district attorney, 1967-68; Monroe County, public defender, 1968-70; City of Rochester, corp counsel 1970-71, city court judge 1971-72; McKay Comm, 1st dep counsel 1972; State of NY Family Court, supervising judge 1980-. **ORGANIZATIONS:** Trustee, Monroe County Bar Assn, 1970-72; Advisor, 4th Judicial Dept, NY Advisory common Law Guardians; mem, Assn of Family Court Judges; dir, Urban League, Rochester Children's Convalescent Hospital, 1980-83, SPCC 1981-83, Center for Govt Rsch 1981-84. **MILITARY SERVICE:** USN seaman 1st class 2 yrs. **BUSINESS ADDRESS:** Justice, NY State Supreme Court-7th Judicial Dist, Hall of Justice Exchange St, Rochester, NY 14614.

WILLIS, FRANK B.
Elected govt. official, publisher. **PERSONAL:** Born Mar 13, 1947, Cleveland, MS; married Bobbie M Henderson; children: Oji-Camara Khari. **EDUCATION:** Rochester Bus Inst, AA 1968; Dyke Coll, BS 1971. **CAREER:** City Urban Renewal Dept, family relocation aide 1972-74; Okang Commun Corp, pres 1973-; Cty Dept of Soc Svcs, eligibility examiner 1974; Communicade Newspaper, publisher/editor 1981-; Rochester City School Dist, commiss. **ORGANIZATIONS:** Legislative intern Rapic Comm network Judicial Process Commiss 1977-78; mem Coalition of Chap I Parents 1978-; editor/writer Horambee Parents Newsletter Chap I Program 1979-80; mem Natl Alliance of Black School Educators 1980-, Caucus of Black School Bd Mems 1983-. **HONORS/ACHIEVEMENTS:** Outstanding Personality Afro-Amer Soc Dyke Coll 1971; Serv Awd Greater Rochester Tougaloo Coll Alumni Assoc Inc 1983; Outstanding Serv Rochester City Schools Dist Advisory Council to Chap I 1983; Serv Urban League of Rochester 1984. **HOME ADDRESS:** 67 Elba St, Rochester, NY 14608.

WILLIS, FRED DOUGLAS
Business executive. **PERSONAL:** Born Apr 15, 1918, Winston-Salem, NC; married Mildred E Cureton; children: Mildred Gill. **EDUCATION:** CAO-Drug Abuse Rsrch & Treatment Ctr, exec dir 1985; Youth Devel Prgm CAO, dir 1968-71; VISTA-CAO, coord 1966-68; CAO Erie Co, comm 1966; Buffalo Psychiat Ctr 1975-. **CAREER:** Bd dir Buffalo Gen Hosp 1970-; Bflo Children's Psychiat Clinic 1971-; Black Devel Found; mem Drug Directorate Erie Co Dept of Mental Health 1971-; Task Force Drug Prgm Design 1968-71; Nat Assn Comm Developers 1968-71; Erie Co Mental Health Assn; Emmanuel Temple Chorale 1958-; Lloyds Meml United Ch of Christ Choir 1971-72; bus mgr Royal Serenaders Male Glee Club 1965-70; Cert A&T Coll 1943; cert Chicago 1973. **HONORS/ACHIEVEMENTS:** USAAF WW II 1944-45. **MILITARY SERVICE:** USAAF WW II. **BUSINESS ADDRESS:** 80 Goodrich St, Buffalo, NY 14203.

WILLIS, FREDERIC L.
District attorney, community affairs representative. **PERSONAL:** Born May 14, 1937, Handley, WV; divorced. **EDUCATION:** LA Cty Coll, AA 1961; CA State U, BS 1970; UCLA, grad study 1971; PepperdineUniv 1973. **CAREER:** Comm Aff Rep, LA dist atty; LA Dist Atty, investigator, 1967-71; LA Sheriff, deputy sheriff 1964-67, communications expert 1960-64; W LA Coll Admin of Justice, instructor, 1972-; SW LA Coll Admin of Justice Dept, coordinator, 1973-. **ORGANIZATIONS:** Chmn LA Brotherhood Crusade Campaign 1971; chmn Sons of Watts OR Prog Adv Coun 1972; mem Men of Tomorrow; NAACP; New Frontier Dem Club. **MILITARY SERVICE:** USAF airman 1st class 1956-59. **BUSINESS ADDRESS:** 210 West Temple St, Los Angeles, CA 90012.

WILLIS, GLADYS JANUARY
Educator. **PERSONAL:** Born Feb 29, 1944, Jackson, MS; daughter of Emily January; married Rev A H Willis, Jr; children: Juliet Christina, Michael Lamont. **EDUCATION:** Jackson State Univ, BA 1965; Bryn Mawr Coll, Independent Study 1966; Michigan State Univ, MA 1967; Princeton Univ, PhD 1973; Lutheran Theological Seminary, Philadelphia PA, MDiv candidate. **CAREER:** Cheyney State Univ, instructor, engineer 1967-68; Rider Coll, instructor, engineer 1968-70; City of New York, asst prof, engineer 1976-76; Pennsylvania Human Relations Commn, educ representative 1976-77; Lincoln Univ, assoc prof, chair 1977-84, prof, dept chair 1977-. **ORGANIZATIONS:** Founder, dir Coll Preparatory Tutorial 1974; mem, bd of dir Philadelphia Christian Academy 1977-, Natl Council of Teachers of English; reviewer Middle States Assn. **HONORS/ACHIEVEMENTS:** Woodrow Wilson Natl Fellowship, Woodrow Wilson Natl Fellowship Found 1966-67; Princeton Univ Fellow, Princeton Univ 1970-73; The Penalty of Eve, John Milton and Divorce New York, Peter Lang 1984; Ordained Chaplain 1988. **HOME ADDRESS:** 4722 Larchwood Ave, Philadelphia, PA 19143. **BUSINESS ADDRESS:** Professor of English/Dept Chair, Lincoln University, English Dept, Lincoln University, PA 19352.

WILLIS, HENRY STOKES, JR.
Director (corporate). **PERSONAL:** Born Jun 07, 1947, Washington, DC; married Betty Lou Morton. **EDUCATION:** Howard U, BA 1970;Univ of Chicago Grad Sch of Bus, MBA 1973. **CAREER:** Pace Univ Grad School, marketing lectr 1980; Fordham Univ Grad School of Business, marketing lectr 1979-; Revlon Inc, marketing dir 1977-; The Gillette Co, sr product mgr 1974-77; Foote Cone & Belding Inc, vice pres & account supr 1972-74; Morton Stokes Willis & Assoc, managing partner 1977-78. **ORGANIZATIONS:** Mem 100 Black Men Inc 1978-; mem Council of Concerned Black Exec 1978-; mem Nat Black MBA Assn 1978-. **HONORS/ACHIEVEMENTS:** Fellowship and StipendUniv of C Grad Sch of Bus 1971-73; Fellowship SuffolkUniv Law Sch 1976; Outstanding Young Men of Am 1979; Who's Who in the East 1980. **BUSINESS ADDRESS:** 767 Fifth Ave, New York, NY 10022.

WILLIS, ISAAC
Educator. **PERSONAL:** Born Jul 13, 1940, Albany, GA; children: 2 children. **EDUCATION:** Morehouse Coll, BS 1961; Howard Univ Coll of Med, MD 1965; Philadelphia Gen Hosp, Internship 1965-66; Howard Univ, Sepc Training Derm Resident, Post-Doctoral Rsch Fellow 1966-67; Univ of PA, Derm Resident, Post-Doctoral Rsch Fellow 1967-69. **CAREER:** Univ of PA, assoc of dermatology 1969-70; Univ of CA Med Ctr, attending physician 1970-72; Johns Hopkins Univ School of Med, asst prof of med dermatology 1972-73; Johns Hopkins Hosp, Baltimore City Hosps, Good Samaritan Hosp, attending physician 1972-73; Howard Univ Coll of Med, consult asst prof dermatology 1972-75; Emory Univ School of Med, asst prof of med 1973-75, assoc prof of med 1975-82; VA Hosp Atlanta GA, chief of dermatology 1973-80, acting chief of dermatology 1980-81; Morehouse School of Med, prof

dept of med 1982-. **ORGANIZATIONS:** Mem Amer Dermatological Assoc, Soc for Investigative Dermatology, Amer Soc for Photobiology, Amer Acad of Dermatology, Dermatology Found, PhiladelphiaDermatological Soc, Natl Med Assoc, Amer Med Assoc, Natl Prog for Derm, Amer Fed for Clinical Rsch, Intl Soc of Tropical Derm, So Med Assoc,Atlanta Derm Assoc, GA Med Assoc; bd of med dir Atlanta Lupus Erythematosus Found; bd of spec GA Dept of Human Resources Vocational Rehba; mem Dermatology Found Med & Scientific Comm, comm Dermatological med Devices of the Council on Govt Liaison of the Amer Acad of Dermatology; photobiology task force Natl Prog for Dermatology; mem Amer Dermatological Assoc; self assessment comm Continuing Med Ed Amer Acad of Derm; mem Skin Cancer found; student affairs adv Office of Predoctoral Prog of the Johns Hopkins Univ School of Med 1972-73; affirm action comm Johns Hopkins Med Inst 1972-73; promo comm Johns Hopkins Univ School of Med 1972-73; mem comm Rsch & Investigation Involving Human Subjects Univ of PA 1969-70. **HONORS/ACHIEVEMENTS:** Carter L Marshall Awd in Med Howard Univ Coll of Med 1963-65; Avalon Found Awd in Med; Dome Chem Co Awd Natl Med Assoc Dermatology Sect 1967; Derm Found Awd for Rsch Univ of PA 1970; Derm of the Year Awd Natl Med Assoc 1973; Amer Derm Assoc 1979; Morehouse Coll Alumni Achievement Awd 1983; Frontiers Intl Med Annual Awd 1983; listed in Who's Who in the South & Southwest 1971-84, Who's Who in Frontier Sci & Tech 1984-85, Who's Who in the World 1984-85; several grants incl NIH, Hoescht Pharm, VA Projects, US EPA; guest prof, vstg prof, guest lecturer speaker at several coll & confs; 69 publs,books & abstracts incl Diagnosis of Photosensitazion Reaction by the Scotch Tape Provacative Tech 1968, Evaluating Sweat Gland Activity with Imprint Techs 1972, The Effects of Long Ultraviolet Light on Skin Photoprotective or Photoaugmentative? 1972, Treatment of Resistant Psoriasis, A Combined Methaxsalen-Anthralen Regimen 1973, Effects of Varying Doses of UV Radiation of Mammalian Skin, Simulation of Decreasing Stratospheric Ozone 1983, Photoaugmentation of UBV Effects by UVA 1984, Photochem, A New Promising Chem Dirivative 1982, Ultraviolet Light & Skin Cancer 1983, Polymorphous Light Eruptions 1985. **MILITARY SERVICE:** Letterman Army Inst of Rsch, maj1970-82; 3297th USA Hosp col 1982-. **BUSINESS ADDRESS:** Professor of Dermatology, Morehouse School of Medicine, 720 Westview Dr SW, Atlanta, GA 30310.

WILLIS, JILL MICHELLE
Social worker. **PERSONAL:** Born Jan 04, 1952, Atlanta, GA. **EDUCATION:** Wellesley Coll, BA 1973; Columbia Univ Sch of Social Work, MS 1975; Rsch Scholar Natl Women's Educ Centre Saitama Japan 1979-80; Univ of Chicago LawSch, JD 1984. **CAREER:** United Charities of Chicago Family Serv Bureau, caseworker III 1975-79; Chapman & Cutler, assoc 1984-86; Allstate Insurance Co, senior attorney 1986-. **ORGANIZATIONS:** Adv bd Thresholds S 1977-78; mem bd of dirs Howe Developmental Ctr 1984-86. **HONORS/ACHIEVEMENTS:** Waddell Fellowship Wellesley Coll Study E Africa 1972; Henry R Luce Scholar Asia Internship 1979-80.

WILLIS, KATHI GRANT
Corporate attorney. **PERSONAL:** Born Dec 02, 1959, Knoxville, TN; daughter of Lorenzo D Grant and Henrietta Arnold Grant; married Henry W Willis, Oct 19, 1985; children: Elizabeth Danielle. **EDUCATION:** Univ of VA, BA 1981; Univ of TN Coll of Law, (mem TN Law Review) JD 1984. **CAREER:** Black American Law Students Assn, treasurer 1981-83; Chattanooga Chapter NAACP Legal Redress Comm. **ORGANIZATIONS:** Phi Delta Phi; Alpha Kappa Alpha Inc; sec Chattonooga Chapter of Links Inc 1987-. **HONORS/ACHIEVEMENTS:** Recipient of Graduate Prof Opportunities Program Fellowship 1981-84. **HOME ADDRESS:** 4719 Rocky River Rd, Chattanooga, TN 37416. **BUSINESS ADDRESS:** Law Department, Provident Life & Accident Ins, Fountain Square, Chattanooga, TN 37402.

WILLIS, LAWRENCE LATTIMER
Business executive. **PERSONAL:** Born Jun 10, 1947, Columbus, OH; married O Joyce Carr; children: Monice A, Danielle N. **EDUCATION:** Coll of Wooster, BA; OH State U, MA. **CAREER:** Standard Oil Co, sr recruiter 1974-; Ofc of Minority Affairs OH State U;; coord for recruitment 1971-74; CONSOC Homeownership Program, project dir commorganizer, 1970-71. **ORGANIZATIONS:** Bd chmn The Exec Card Co; adv com Ofc of Minority Affairs OH State U; Alpha Phi Alpha Frat; sgt of arms Delta Alpha Lambda Chpt; mem Am PersonnelGuidance Assn; mem Am Coll Personnel Assn; co-founder 1st Chmn Black Caucus of OH Admissions Counselors & Officers Coll of Wooster W Assn OSU Alumni Assn 1972-73. **HONORS/ACHIEVEMENTS:** Outstanding Young Man in Am 1973.

WILLIS, LEVY E
Chief executive of bank. **CAREER:** Atlantic National Bank, Norfolk VA, chief executive, 1988. **BUSINESS ADDRESS:** Atlantic National Bank, 415 St, Norfolk, VA 23510. *

WILLIS, RAYMOND EARL
Psychologist. **PERSONAL:** Born Oct 16, 1953, Los Angeles, CA. **EDUCATION:** OR State Univ, George Fox Coll, BA Journalism, Psych 1976; Portland State Univ, MA Clinical Psych 1978; Univ of Washington, PhD in progress. **CAREER:** Good Samaritan Hosp, psych 1980-84; Parent Educ Training Program Tacoma Pierce Cty, coord 1982; Seattle Medium Newspaper, journalist 1983; Washington Dept of Social & Health Serv, psychologist (on leave) 1981-84. **ORGANIZATIONS:** Mem NAACP 1971; youth affairs coord Portland Urban League 1978-79; cons/psych Natl Drug Adv Council 1979; program consult Region 10 Minority Consortium 1980-; mem Blacks in Politics 1982-; cons/psych Parents in Charge Inc 1982-; psych Natl Black Child Devel Inst 1982-. **HONORS/ACHIEVEMENTS:** Draft Choice 8th Round Protland Trailblazers Natl Backetball Assoc 1975; Minority Fellowship Grant OR State Urban Educ Prog 1976; Community Serv Awd Fellowship Carnation Found Portland 1977, Seattle 1983; Humanitarian Serv Awd Portland State Univ 1978,79; Article "Drug Abuse with Black Adolescents in Inner Cities" Black Amer Jrnl 1980. **HOME ADDRESS:** 14655 NE 31st #B, Bellevue, WA 98133.

WILLIS, ROSE W.
Cosmetologist and photographer. **PERSONAL:** Born Jan 02, 1939, Columbus, GA; daughter of Leonard Wright and Christine Wright; divorced; children: Gwendolyn D Hunt, Sherry Gorcrum. **EDUCATION:** Natl Inst of Cosmetology, BA 1971, MA 1974, PhD 1978. **CAREER:** Lovely Lady Beauty Salon, Hollywood, FL, manager, owner, 1967-; Orange Blossom Cosmetologists Assoc, local pres unit 24 1969-78, parade state chmn 1970-80, state photographer 1980; Natl Beauty Culturists League, chmn of finance and registrar 1984-. **ORGANIZATIONS:** Pres, 1978-, chairman of finance, 1984-, National Beauty Culturists' League, North Miami beach, FL; member, National Council of Negro Women, 1979-; treasurer, Theta Nu Sigma, Mu chapter, 1983-; financial secretary, South Florida Business Assoc, 1988-; member, Dade County School Board of Cosmetology, 1988-. **HONORS/ACHIEVEMENTS:** Woman of the Year Theta Nu Sigma Sor 1984; Outstanding Service Award, Bahamian Cosmetologists Association, 1989. **HOME ADDRESS:** 20820 NE 14th Ave, North Miami Beach, FL 33179. **BUSINESS ADDRESS:** Lovely Lady Beauty Salon, 5424 Pembroke Road, Hollywood, FL 33023.

WILLOCK, MARCELLE MONICA
Physician. **PERSONAL:** Born Mar 30, 1938, Georgetown, Guyana. **EDUCATION:** College of New Rochelle, BA 1958; Howard Univ, MD 1962; Columbia Univ, MA 1982. **CAREER:** NY Univ Sch of Medicine, asst prof 1965-74; Columbia Univ Coll of Physicians and Surgeons, asst prof 1978-82; Boston Univ Medical Ctr, chief of anesthesiology 1982-; Boston Univ Sch of Medicine, professor and chairman 1982-. **ORGANIZATIONS:** Pres Louis & Marthe Deveaux Foundation 1965-; pres Amer Medical Womens Assoc 1985-86; vice pres MA Soc of Anesthesiologists 1986-87; delegate Amer Soc of Anesthesiologists 1986-; mem Assoc of Univ Anesthetists. **HONORS/ACHIEVEMENTS:** Commencement Speaker Howard Univ Sch of Medicine 1982. **BUSINESS ADDRESS:** Professor and Chairman, BostonUniv Sch of Medicine, Dept of Anesthesiology, 75 E Newton St, Boston, MA 02118.

WILLOUGHBY, CLARICE E.
Business executive. **PERSONAL:** Born Aug 06, 1934, Aliquippa, PA; married Paul. **EDUCATION:** Central State U, BS 1958;Univ of Pittsburgh, MEd 1968; PA StateUniv & MI St U, certificate for mgmt devel program 1973. **CAREER:** Marketing Researc H J Heinz Co, sr research asso, 1985;Univ of Pittsburgh, research asst 1964-68; Singer Lab Allegheny Gen Hosp Pittsburgh, research asst 1958-64. **ORGANIZATIONS:** Mem Am Marketing Asso Pittsburgh & NY Chpts; former student Affiliate of Am Chem Soc; matron Ermae Chap OES; treas Greater Pittsburgh Chap Central State Alumni Assn; past recording sec adv to Mu Chap atUniv of Pittsburgh; vice pres pres Pittsburgh Alumni Chap Delta Sigma Theta Inc; mem Youth Motivation Task Force. **BUSINESS ADDRESS:** PO Box 57, Pittsburgh, PA 15230.

WILLOUGHBY, SUSAN MELITA
Educational administrator. **PERSONAL:** Born Nov 25, 1925; married Ralph M McNaughton; children: Gerald M, Juliette M. **EDUCATION:** Atlantic Union Coll So Lancaster MA, BA Chemistry 1956; ClarkUniv Worcester MA, MA Educ 1969; HarvardUniv Cambridge, EdD Admin 1972; Boston Univ Sch of Social Work, MA, MSW 1984; Boston Univ Sch of Medicine, MPH 1985. **CAREER:** Worcester Found for Experimental Biol, sr rsch chemist 1961-68; Center for Urban Studies Harvard Univ, dir counseling serv 1970-72; MA Consumer Council, gubernatorial appointee 1973-75; MA Public Health Council (Gov Dukakis), gubernatorial appointee 1975-79; Atlantic Union Coll, prof educ & behavioral sci 1972-, tenured prof & chmn dept of sociology and social work 1983-. **ORGANIZATIONS:** Mem Phi Delta Kappa/Pi Lambda Theta/AAUP 1972-; chmn Health Task Force MA State Consumer Council 1974-75; chmn Centennial Commn Atlantic Union Coll S Lancaster MA 1978-82; mem bd of trustees Atlantic Union Coll 1986-. **HONORS/ACHIEVEMENTS:** Scholar Clark Univ, Harvard Univ 1968,71; several articles published Atlantic Union Gleaner (local) 1974-78, Atlantic Union Coll Accent Nat 1976-, Journal of Review & Herald (Intl) 1978; author "The Go-Getter" Pacific Press Publishing Assoc Boise ID 1985. **BUSINESS ADDRESS:** Chairman, Sociology Dept, Atlantic Union College, Main St, South Lancaster, MA 01561.

WILLOUGHBY, WINSTON CHURCHILL
Dentist. **PERSONAL:** Born Jul 21, 1907, Port-of-Spain, Trinidad and Tobago;married Anselee Ellen Daniels; children: Ann Michelle, Gina Marie. **EDUCATION:** HowardUniv Dntl Coll, 1933. **CAREER:** DC Hlth Dept Sch Clinic, staff 1938-44; Sci Session, chaired 4 sprks 1967-75; Table Clinics, svcd as judge. **ORGANIZATIONS:** Chmn Ticket Com; co-chmn Lunch & Learn; Pblcty Com; chmn Chldrns Com; chmn Tellers Com; chmn Necrology Com; chmn Attendance Com; spec asst genchmn Spring Postgrad Mtg 1976; chmn Pub Rels; chmn Dinner-Dance; mem DC Dntl Soc; Am Dntl Assn; Intl Assn of Anestheologists; intl Acad of Orthodontists; Fed Dentaire Intl; Chi Lambda Kappa Honor Dntl Soc; St Georges Episcopal Ch; Alpha Phi Alpha; Intl Platform Assn; The Smithsonian Inst Hearst Sch PTA; Am Assn for Advncmnt of Sci; WA Performing Arts Soc; Kiwanis Intl NW Club; adv bd Ward 3 Educ Fnd; Journalist Club in Sydney Australia; S Freemantle Pro Ftbl Club; bd mem WETA; mem bd govs Natl GradUniv Fellow Intl Coll of Dntsts; fellow Royal Soc of Hlth London, England; Comm Leader of Am 1968. **HONORS/ACHIEVEMENTS:** Outst Personal Assistance to Dev Nations of the World, Dict of Intl Biography 1968; cert for rendering Salk Vaccine Oper Sugar Cube; Dentist of Year NEW 1975; num letters of appreciation comendations certs of appreciation; Who's Who in SW Am; The Royal Blue Book of London; Comm Leaders of Am; Personalities of the S; 2000 Men of Achvmt; The Green Book Social Register; Nat Soc Directory; Intl Personnel Rsrch; The Blue Book; Intl Who's Who in Comm Svc; Who's Who in the E 1977; Notable Ams in Bicentennial Era. **BUSINESS ADDRESS:** 1616 18th St NW, Washington, DC 20009.

WILLRICH, EMZY JAMES
Advertising sales consultant. **PERSONAL:** Born Sep 16, 1959, Dallas, TX; son of Rev Theodis Willrich, Sr. and Margie Crew Willrich. **EDUCATION:** Univ of Texas at Arlington, BBA-Marketing 1983. **CAREER:** Consolidated Freightways, account mgr. **ORGANIZATIONS:** Mem Amer Marketing Assoc 1982-87; charter mem Metroplex Egyptian History Soc; mem World Future Soc 1985-86; UTA Alumni Assoc Phonathon 1985; Hands Across America 1986; Black Enterprise Professional Network Exchange 1987; Grand Prairie NAACP, 1989; Dallas Urban League, 1989; UTA Alumni Assn, 1989; African-American Men an Endangered Species, Inc. **HONORS/ACHIEVEMENTS:** UTA Academic Achievement Awd 1981, 1982; UTA Alumni Leadership Scholarship for Academic Excellence and Campus Involvement 1982; Jesse Jackson Delegate to State Convention, 1988. **HOME ADDRESS:** 705 Manning Road, Grand Prairie, TX 75051.

WILLS, JAMES WILLARD
Physician. **PERSONAL:** Born Jan 23, 1933, Aquasco, MD; son of Rossie H. Wills and Clara Wright Wills; married Waltine; children: Phyllis, John, Cecil. **EDUCATION:** Morgan State Coll, BS 1954; Howard Univ, MD 1961. **CAREER:** Glenn Dale Hosp, exec dir 1973-77; Glenn Dale Hosp, chief, med svc; Private practice, physician 1975-; chief medical officer, Area "C" Chest Clinic (Washington D.C.) 1981-. **ORGANIZATIONS:** Mem Alpha

Phi Alpha, Medico-Chirurgical Soc DC, Natl Med Assoc. **HONORS/ACHIEVEMENTS:** AUS 1st lt 1954-56. **BUSINESS ADDRESS:** 14310 Old Marlboro Pike, Upper Marlboro, MD 20772.

WILMORE, GAYRAUD STEPHEN
Educator. **PERSONAL:** Born Jan 20, 1921, Philadelphia, PA; married Lee Wilson; children: Stephen, Jacques, Roberta Wilmore Hurley, David. **EDUCATION:** Lincoln Univ, BA 1947; Lincoln Univ Theol Sem, BD 1950; Temple Univ School of Religion, stm 1952; Drew Theol Sem, doctoral studies 1960-62. **CAREER:** 2nd Presbyterian Church West Chester, pastor 1950-53; Mid-Atlantic Student Christian Movement, reg sec 1953-56; Pittsburgh Theol Sem, prof of soc ethics 1960-63; United Presbyterian Council on Church & Race, exec dir 1963-72; Boston Univ School of Theol, prof soc ethics 1972-74; Colgate Rochester Div School, ML King Jr prof 1974-; Interdenominational Theological Center, disting vstg scholar 1986-87;New York Theol Sem, dean of mdiv prog, prof of afro-amer religious studies 1983-. **ORGANIZATIONS:** Mem Amer Soc of Christian Ethics 1961-78; bd mem Faith & Order Commiss World Council of Church 1973-; bd of dirs Black Theol Proj 1974-; prof Black Church Studies Colgate Rochester Div School 1974-83; mem Ecum Assoc of Third World Theol 1976-; bd dir Black Theology Project Inc 1977-; consult Eli LillyEndowment 1979-; pres Soc for the Study of Black Religion 1979-80; contrib ed Christianity and Crisis 1986-. **HONORS/ACHIEVEMENTS:** Hon DD Lincoln Coll & Tusculum Coll 1965,72; Bruce Klunder Awd Presbyterian Interracial Council 1968; Hon LHD Lincoln Univ 1972; Payne Theological Seminary 1986. **MILITARY SERVICE:** AUS sgt 1943-46. **BUSINESS ADDRESS:** Dean, Professor, New York Theological Seminary, S W 29th St, New York, NY 10001.

WILMOT, DAVID WINSTON
Attorney, educator. **PERSONAL:** Born Apr 26, 1944, Panama; son of David Wilmot and Bertha Wi;mot; married Mary Elizabeth Mercer; children: Michele, Kristy. **EDUCATION:** Univ of AR, BA 1970; Georgetown Univ Law Ctr, JD 1973. **CAREER:** Little Rock, asst city mgr 1968-70; Dolphin Branton Stafford & Webber, legal asst 1970-72; Georgetown Univ Law Ctr, rsch asst; OEO Legal Svcs, intern; DC Proj on Comm Legal Asst, dep dir 1972-73; DC Convention Ctr Bd of Dirs, general counsel; Hotel Assoc Washington DC, general counsel; Georgetown Univ, asst dean, dir 1973-. **ORGANIZATIONS:** Pres Stud for Equality 1967-68; vice pres GULC Legal Aid Soc 1972-73; pres Black Amer Law Stud Assoc 1972-73; adv bd DC Bds & Comms Adv Bd Georgetown Today 1973-76; mem DC Bar, PA Bar;, US Ct of Appeals, DC Ct of Appeals, Supreme Ct of PA, Assoc of Amer Law Schools, Law School Admin Council, Amer Bar Assoc, Trial Lawyers Assoc, Natl Bar Assoc, Natl Conf of Black Lawyers, Alpha Kappa Psi, Lawyers Study Group, Potomac Fiscal Soc; public employees relations bd Wash DC; mem Firemens & Policement Retirement Bd; mem bd of dirs Federal City Natl Bank, Washington Waterfront Restaurant Corp; mem bd of governors Georgetown Univ Alumni Assoc; mem bd of dirs District Cablevision Inc. **HONORS/ACHIEVEMENTS:** Dean's List 1967-70; Dean's Counselor Awd Univ of AR 1969; Outstanding Serv Awd Georgetown Univ Stud Bar Assoc 1971; Cert of Merit DC Citz for Better Ed 1972; Jeffrey Crandall Awd 1972; WA Law Reptr Prize 1973; Robert D L'Heureux Scholorship. **MILITARY SERVICE:** USAF E/5 1963-67. **BUSINESS ADDRESS:** Assistant Dean, Dir, GeorgetownUniv, 600 New Jersey Ave NW, Ste 464, Washington, DC 20001.

WILRIDGE, CLARENCE
Attorney. **PERSONAL:** Born Mar 22, 1936, Rayne, LA; married Eva; children: Reginaly Tracy, Clarence, Tami. **EDUCATION:** So Univ Baton Rouge, AB 1957; Hastings Coll of Law, LLB 1963. **CAREER:** Self-Employed, atty; Postmaster San Francisco, admin asst 1966-68; SF Neighborhood Legal Asst Fdn, 1968-69; Bancroft & Wilridge, partner 1969-70. **ORGANIZATIONS:** Mem Am Bar Assn; Nat Bar Assn; SF Lawyers Club; SF Lawyers Guild; CA Trial Lawyers Assn; Charles Houston Law Club. **MILITARY SERVICE:** AUS 1st lt 1957-59. **BUSINESS ADDRESS:** 3047 Fillmore St, San Francisco, CA 94123.

WILSON, ALICIA SANTANA
Designer/retail jewelry. **PERSONAL:** Born Dec 17, 1948, Baltimore, MD; married Thomas Howell Wilson; children: Lolita Christina, Ramona Monique. **EDUCATION:** Edmondson High School, diploma Business Educ 1966; Coppin State Coll, attended 1975-77. **CAREER:** Alicia's Unique Jewelry, owner. **ORGANIZATIONS:** Mem Baltimore Marketing Assoc 1976; chmn Loudoun Commission on Women 1983-85; chair Educ Comm NAACP 1984-86; co-chair Domestic Violence Conference Common Women 1984; vice pres Loudoun Chap NAACP 1984-; bd dirs, exec comm, personnel comm American Red Cross 1985-; bd dir Amer Cancer Society 1986-. **HONORS/ACHIEVEMENTS:** Outstanding Citizens Awd NAACP Fairfax 1983. **HOME ADDRESS:** 812 Wilkison Dr NE, Leesburg, VA 22075.

WILSON, ALVA L.
Clergyman. **PERSONAL:** Born Nov 21, 1922, Lake City, SC; married Carrie Williams; children: Allesia Muldrow, Charles K, Benita F. **EDUCATION:** Allen Univ, AB 1949; Gammon Theological Seminary, attended 1961. **CAREER:** Owner/Farmer 1950; Freelance Horticulturist/Landscaper 1979-; UMSC Conf, clergyman. **ORGANIZATIONS:** Barber Shaw AFB 1949-75; sec Trustee Bd mem of the Sch Bd 1970-; vice chmn Health Education & Welfare Minister 1972-78. **HONORS/ACHIEVEMENTS:** Leadership Training Inst Awd SC Sch Bd Assoc 1975. **MILITARY SERVICE:** AUS pfc 3 yrs. **HOME ADDRESS:** 330 West Thomas St, Lake City, SC 29560.

WILSON, AUGUST
Playwright. **PERSONAL:** Born in Pittsburgh, PA. **CAREER:** Playwright, Ma Rainey's Black Bottom, Fences, Joe Turner's Come and Gone. **ORGANIZATIONS:** Co-founder Pittsburgh's Black Horizons Theatre. **HONORS/ACHIEVEMENTS:** New York Drama Critic's Circle Awd; Tony nomination for Best Drama of the Season for Ma Rainey's Black Bottom; Pulitzer Prize for "Fences"; Tony Awd 1987 for "Fences".

WILSON, BARBARA JEAN
Business executive. **PERSONAL:** Born Jun 05, 1940, Dallas, TX; married Porterfield; children: Porterfield Christopher. **EDUCATION:** Prairie View A&M Coll, BS 1960-64; Gen Motors Inst Flint MI, 1975; Hadley Dealer Accounting School Royal Oak MI, 1975; Reynolds & Reynolds Computer SchoolDayton OH, 1980. **CAREER:** TC Hassell School Dallas TX, exec sec 1964-73; Chrysler Corp Mound Rd Engine Detroit, bookkeeper 1965-73; Porterfield Wilson Pontiac GMC Truck Mazda-Honda, exec sec 1973-79; Mazda Honda, pres oper 1979-84; Ferndale Honda, pres 1984-. **ORGANIZATIONS:** Past pres Carats Inc Detroit Chap Natl Club 1969-; mem women's Econ Club 1975-; life mem NAACP 1975; mem Palmer Woods Assoc 1976, Amer Imported AutoDealers 1979-, Detroit Auto Dealers Assoc 1979-, Negro Bus & prof Women 1979; mem Coalition of 100 Black Women of Detroit 1980. **HONORS/ACHIEVEMENTS:** Spec Recog Awd Carats Inc Detroit Chap 1979. **BUSINESS ADDRESS:** President, Ferndale Honda, 21350 Woodward Ave, Ferndale, MI 48220.

WILSON, BLENDA J.
Educator. **PERSONAL:** Born Jan 28, 1941, Woodbridge, NJ; daughter of Horace and Margaret; married Dr Louis Fair, Jr. **EDUCATION:** Cedar Crest Coll, AB 1962; Seton Hall Univ, AM 1965; Boston Coll, PhD 1979. **CAREER:** Rutgers Univ, exec asst to pres 1969-72; Harvard Univ Grad Sch, assoc dean for admin 1972-75, sr assoc dean 1975-82; Independent Sector, vice pres effective 1982-84; CO Commn on Higher Educ, exec dir 1982-88; The Univ of MI, Dearborn, Chancellor. **ORGANIZATIONS:** Sec Navy's Adv Bd of Educ & Training 1980-83; bd of dirs The Adult Learning Ctr 1986-87; adv comm Intl Foundation for Educ & Self-Help 1986-; bd of trustees Boston Coll, Children's TV Workshop; bd of dirs The Foundation Ctr, The Commonwealth Fund, Henry Ford Hospital Corp, Metropolitan Center for High Technology; exec bd Detroit Area Boy Scouts of Amer; Detroit Chapter Natl Coalition of 100 Black Women; Michigan Women's Forum; Dearborn Rotary; Advisory Council of Presidents; Assn of Governing Boards. **HONORS/ACHIEVEMENTS:** One of 100 Emerging Leaders in Amer Higher Educ Change magazine 1978; Hon DHL Cedar Crest Coll, Loretto Heights Coll, Univ of Detroit, Rutgers Univ. **BUSINESS ADDRESS:** Chancellor, Univ of Michigan-Dearborn, 4901 Evergreen, Dearborn, MI 48128.

WILSON, BOBBY L.
Educator. **PERSONAL:** Born Sep 30, 1942, Columbus, MS; son of Johnnie B Wilson and Lillie Coleman Wilson; married Mary, Dec 22, 1966; children: Anthony, Melanie, Malissa, Melinda. **EDUCATION:** Alabama State Univ, BS 1966; Southern Univ, MS 1972; MI State Univ, PhD 1976. **CAREER:** Booker T Washington HS, instructor 1966-70; Jefferson Davis HS, instructor 1970-71; Michigan State Univ, grad asst 1971-76; TX Southern Univ, asst prof 1976-80, assoc prof, 1980-82; Exxon Rsch & Engineering, visiting prof 1982-83; TX Southern Univ, assoc prof 1983-85, prof 1985-86; Coll of Arts & Sciences, prof & assoc dean 1986-; TX Southern Univ, Prof, Head, Chem, 1987. **ORGANIZATIONS:** mem, ACS, Beta Kappa Chi Honor Soc, Kappa Alpha Psi Frat, NAACP, Natl Geographic Soc, Natl Org for the Advancement of Black Chemists & Chemical Engrs, Natl Urban League, Smithsonian Inst, TX Acad of Sci, TX Assn of Coll Teachers, Tri-County Civic Assn, TX Faculty Assn, The Forum Club of Houston, Sigma Xi, TX Inst of Chemists, Student Awards Comm, 1988, Scientific Rsch Soc, 1988, Bylaws Comm, 1988; Pres, Childrn Against Drugs & Drinking Inc. **HONORS/ACHIEVEMENTS:** TSU Program Council's Showcase of Black Talent Award, 1989; The Briargate community Audrey Logan Citizenship Award, 1988; White House Initiative Faculty Award for Excellence in Sci & Tech, 1988; Kappa Alpha Psi Southwest Province Graduate Brother of the Year Award, 1988; Kappa Alpha Psi Service Award, 1988; TX Southern Univ Researcher of the Year, 1988; Fellow, The Amer Inst of Chemists, 1988; Albert Einstein World Award of Science Diploma, 1987; ROTC Gold Citation, 1967; Briargate Comm Citizen of the Year Award, 1980; Alpha Kappa Alpha Sorority Community Serv Award, 1983; Natl Org of Black Chemists & Chemical Engrs Appreciation Award, 1984; Houston Alumni Chapter of Kappa Alpha Psi Fraternity Spotlight Award, 1984; numerous publications, patent. **BUSINESS ADDRESS:** Prof Dept of Chem, Texas Southern University, 3100 Cleburne, Houston, TX 77004.

WILSON, CALVIN T.
Judge. **PERSONAL:** Born Feb 25, 1928, Philadelphia, PA; son of Ernest Wilson and Beatrice Culbreath Wilson; married Yvonne Garnett; children: Captain Calvin T. Wilson, II, M.D.. **EDUCATION:** Lincoln U, BA 1949; Howard U, Juris LLD 1952. **CAREER:** Sec Bd of Judges, asst atty gen 1961; PA Mun Court, court admin 1971; Court of Common Pleas, judge 1971-. **ORGANIZATIONS:** Mem Bd of City Trusts; mem Bd of Taxes & Rev; mem Comm of Mun Crt; mem Barristers Club of Philadelphia Bar Assn; mem The Pres Comm for Civ Rights UnderLaw; mem Met Hosp bd of dir 1976; mem trustee Mt Zion Bapt Ch; mem Boy Scouts of Am; Boystown; Stenton Neighbors Comm; PA Guardsmen Inc; pres Southeastern Pa. Area Chptr. of Muscular Dystrophy Assn l989; a national vice pres Muscular Dystrophy Assn l989. **HONORS/ACHIEVEMENTS:** Chapel of the Four Chaplains Awrd 1977; NAACP Awrd; Awrd of the Puerto Rican Cit Comm; Black Pol Beauty Pagent Awrd; various comm awrds; Cert of Achvmnt Philadelphia Bar Assn 1968; Judge of the Year Natl Assn of Black Lawyers 1981; Sec Bd of Judges of Phila. **BUSINESS ADDRESS:** Judge, Commonwealth of PA, Court of Common Pleas, 1st Judicial Dist, Philadelphia, PA 19107.

WILSON, CARL L.
Architect. **PERSONAL:** Born Dec 24, 1921, Warren, OH; son of Michael Robert Wilson, Sr and Georgia Russell Crawford Wilson; married Doris Hazel Bass; children: 1 son. **EDUCATION:** OH State Univ, BS 1951. **CAREER:** Wright-Patterson Area Ofc Dayton, proj engr 1951-62; US Corps of Engrs, architect; USACE Asmara, Ethiopia, asst rsch eng 1962-66; Munsan-ni Korea 2nd Inf Div, install plng officer 1966-67; US Fed Bldg Canton, rsch eng 1968-69; IRS Add Covington KY, 1969-70; Baltimore Post Office, 1970-72; Cincinnati Bulk Mail Ctr, suprvsng staff of seventeen 1972-75; OH Area Office Dayton, asst area engr 1975-80; Montgomery Cty OH Bldg Reg Dept, dir 1980-83; Mt Olive Baptist Church, Dayton, Ohio, assoc minister, 1987-. **ORGANIZATIONS:** Reg arch State of OH 1958-; imp officer AEA Order Nobles Mystic Shrine 1968-86; past master progress Lodge 85; past commander in chief LD Easton Consistory 21; companion Johnson Chap 3 Columbus OH; past patron Lily of the Valley 55 Middletown OH; companion Solomon Johnson Council 4; sir knight Boone Commandery 27; mem US Supreme Council AASR North Jurisdiction; former natl dir Student Aid for Boys of Prince Hall Shriners; mem NAACP, Dayton Urban League; sec genl USC AASR (PHA) NJ 1975-83; imp potentate AEAONMS 1984-86; archon, Sigma Bowle, Sigma Pi Phi Fraternity, l986-; coordinator, Minority Contractors Assistance Program, Dayton, Ohio l989-. **HONORS/ACHIEVEMENTS:** Only black grad OSU School of Architecture l919-1951; highest rank black fld official US Corps of Engrs; resident contracting officer on over 90 million dollarsof US Gov Constrn Contracts; US Council's Gold Medal Achievement Awd for Meritorious Svc, Sovereign Grand Commanders Awd for Excellence; first black to serve as deputy dir Dept of Public Works State of OH 1983-84; cited in Ebony Magazine as one of 100 Most Influential Blacks in Amer 1985-86. **MILITARY SERVICE:** AUS Sig Corps & Army Air Corps, WWII 1942-46. **BUSINESS ADDRESS:** Box 382, Mid City Station, Dayton, OH 45402.

WILSON, CARROLL LLOYD
Educator. **PERSONAL:** Born Jul 09, 1937, Jamaica; married Barbara Ellen Jones; children: Mark Lloyd, Eric Theodore, Ellen Clarice. **EDUCATION:** Univ of ME at Orono, BA 1962; Kean Clge NJ, MA 1969; Rutgers Univ, Grad Studies. **CAREER:** Publ Health Educ State of ME, asst to dir 1962-63; Plainfield Publ Schl Plainfeild NJ, tchr & asst track coach 1963-69; Job Corps at Camp Kilmer NJ, recr spec 1966-67; Somerset Co Clge & Annandale Youth Corr Inst Annandale NJ, coord sp prog 1973-74. **ORGANIZATIONS:** Mem NJ Assc of Dev Educ 1980-; Cub Master Pack 1776 Boy Scouts of Amer 1982-85; mem Natl Council on Black Amer Affairs 1983-; bd dir Somerset Co Mental Health Assc 1978-81; bd trustees Corr Inst for Women Clinton NJ 1978-82; coach Hillsborough NJ Recreation Soccer 1981-; evulator, Middle States Assn of Colleges & Universities, 1986-. **HONORS/ACHIEVEMENTS:** Special Faculty Srv Award Somerset Co Coll 1975, Special Faculty Serv & Admin Award 1976, Black Student Union Adv Serv Award 1975-76. **BUSINESS ADDRESS:** Professor of English, Raritan Valley Community Coll, PO Box 3300, Somerville, NJ 08876.

WILSON, CHARLES F.
Business executive. **PERSONAL:** Born Mar 22, 1925, Apalachicola, FL; married Jean Cyrus; children: Charles, Valerie, Michael. **EDUCATION:** FL A&M U, BS 1948; Howard U, LLB 1951. **CAREER:** Jim Walter Corp, vp; US EOE Commn, conciliator asso gen counsel 1966-73; FL, asst atty gen 1965-66; atty 1951-65. **ORGANIZATIONS:** Mem FL Bar Assn; Nat Bar Assn; Omega Psi Phi; chmn FL State Bd of Indep Colls & U'S; mem Gov Mgmt & Efficiency Commn 1973. **HONORS/ACHIEVEMENTS:** Career Serv Awrd Natl Civil Serv League 1972. **BUSINESS ADDRESS:** 1500 Dale Mabry Hwy, Tampa, FL 33607.

WILSON, CHARLES STANLEY, JR.
President. **PERSONAL:** Born Aug 08, 1952, St Louis, MO. **EDUCATION:** Boston U, BS 1974; Forest Park Sch of Mortuary Sci, 1976. **CAREER:** A L Beal Funeral Homes Inc, pres; McDonnell Douglas Corp, rep 1979-80; Maritz Travel, travel dir 1976-79. **ORGANIZATIONS:** Mem Kappa Alpha Psi 1970-87; mem Caution Lodge No 23 Masons 1975-87; mem Urban League of St Louis 1976-80; mem Danforth Found Leadership Program 1979-80;mem Camp Wyman Bd of Dir 1979-80; trustee bd Central Bapt Ch 1975-87; mem Black United Fund of St Louis 1974-80; pub rel chmn St Louis Undertakers Assn 1979-80; mem MO State Bd of Embalmers & Funderal Dirs 1985-90; appointed by MO Govt Ashcroft 2nd vp, bd of dir Annie Malone Children's Home 1985-87; mem MO Funeral Dirs Assoc, St Louis Gateway Funeral Dirs Assn, Natl Funeral Dirs & Morticians Assn, Natl Funderal Dirs Assn 1985-87. **HONORS/ACHIEVEMENTS:** Trustee Schlrshp Awd Sch of Educ BostonUniv 1972-73; Undergrad Achvmnt Awd; Northeastern Province Kappa Alpha Psi 1973-74. **BUSINESS ADDRESS:** President, AL Beal Funeral Homes Inc, 1150 N Kings Highway, St Louis, MO 63113.

WILSON, CHARLES Z., JR.
Educator. **PERSONAL:** Born Apr 21, 1929, Greenville, MS; widowed; children: Charles Zachary, III, Joyce Lynne, Joanne Catherine, Gary Thomas. **EDUCATION:** Univ Of IL, BS 1952, PhD 1956; Carnegie Mellon U, post grad work 1959-61. **CAREER:** UCLA, vice chancellor Academic Prog , Prof Educ 1970-; Educ Planning Programs, special asst to adminstrv vice chancellor 1968-70; St Univ of NY, asso prof economics 1959-67; DePaul Univ, asst prof economics 1957-59. **ORGANIZATIONS:** Mem nominating com Am Assn for Advancement of Sci; bd trustees Tchrs Ins & Annuity Assn Coll Retirement Equities Fund 1971-; pres adv council on Minority Bus Enterprise 1972-76; UNA Panel for Advancement of US Japan Relations 1972-; consult Nat Inst of Educ Dept of HEW 1973- mem Adv Bd on Educ &Human Resources, The Rand Corp 1972-; chmn Bd Trustees The Joint Cntgr for Comm Studies 19702; mem bd dirs LA Co Museum of Art 1971-; bd dirs Black Economic Res Cntr New York City 1970-; mem Am Educ Res Assn; Inst of Mgmt Sci; Am Economics Assn; Am Assn ofUniv Profs. **HONORS/ACHIEVEMENTS:** Am Men of Sci Recip, Am Council on Educ Fellow 1967-68; Visiting Res Asso, Carnegie-mellonUniv 1961-62; Jr C of C Outstanding Young Man of Yr 1965, Binghamton NY; author "Orgnl Decision-making" 1967. **BUSINESS ADDRESS:** UCLA 2127 Murphy Hall, 405 Hilgard Ave, Los Angeles, CA 90024.

WILSON, CLARENCE NORTHON
Dentist. **PERSONAL:** Born Jun 06, 1920, Pittsburgh, PA; married Dorothy; children: Michelle, Candace. **EDUCATION:** VA State Coll, BS 1942; Howard Univ Dental Sch, 1947. **CAREER:** Jersey City Med Ctr, intern 1949; Dental Health Clinic, dir 1974-; Self-employed, dentist. **ORGANIZATIONS:** Pres Essex Co Dental Soc 1973-77; treas Commonwealth Dental Soc. **BUSINESS ADDRESS:** 576 Central Ave, East Orange, NJ 07019.

WILSON, CLEO FRANCINE
Foundation director. **PERSONAL:** Born May 07, 1943, Chicago, IL; daughter of Cleo Chancey and Frances Page Watson; children: David Patrice Silbar, SuLyn Silbar. **EDUCATION:** Univ of IL-Chicago, BA 1976. **CAREER:** Playboy Enterprises Inc, supervisor 1980-82, dir, Public Affairs, 1989; grants mgr 1982-84, exec dir 1984-. **ORGANIZATIONS:** Vp Donors Forum of Chicago 1986; sec Chicago Women in Philanthrophy 1986, task force IL Interdisciplinary AIDS Adv Council 1986; pres Emergency Loan Fund 1987; chmn, Chicago Funders Concerned with AIDS, 1989; Advisory Council, Chicago Dept of Cultural Affairs, 1988,89. **HONORS/ACHIEVEMENTS:** Distinction in English, Univ of Illinois, 1976; Kizzy Image Awd Black Woman Hall of Fame 1984; Chicago's Up & Coming (Black Business & Professional Women) Dollars & Sense Magazine 1985. **HOME ADDRESS:** 6571 N Glenwood, Chicago, IL 60626. **BUSINESS ADDRESS:** Dir, Playboy Enterprises Inc, 919 North Michigan Avenue, Chicago, IL 60611.

WILSON, CLEROW **See WILSON, FLIP**

WILSON, CONNIE DRAKE
Educational administrator. **PERSONAL:** Born May 05, 1953, Franklin, VA; married Lowell Van Wilson; children: Rodney Theron, Benton Lowell. **EDUCATION:** St Pauls Coll, BS 1975; Univ of VA, MA 1978. **CAREER:** Greensville Cty Public Schools, teacher 1976-77; Univ of VA Afro-Amer Affairs, dir 1978; St Pauls Coll, instr 1979-, dir instr 1983-. **ORGANIZATIONS:** Organist Mt Calvary Baptist Church 1963-; past mem Greensville Cty School Bd 1981-83; consult St Pauls Coll 1983, Southampton Correctional Ctr 1983; speccorrespondent Richmond Times-Dispatch Newspaper 1984-. **HONORS/ACHIEVEMENTS:** Randall-McIver Fellow Univ of VA 1977; Governors Fellow Univ of VA 1978; Outstanding Young Woman of Amer 1984; Nom UNCF Disting Scholars Prog 1985.

WILSON, DEMOND
Evangelist. **PERSONAL:** Born in Valdosta, GA. **EDUCATION:** Hunter Coll, attended. **CAREER:** Sanford & Son, actor 1972-77; Demond Wilson Ministries, evangelist. **BUSINESS ADDRESS:** Demond Wilson Ministries, Ste C-322, PO Box 30730, Laguna Hills, CA 92654.

WILSON, DONALD P.
Association executive. **CAREER:** International Benevolent Protective Order of Elks of the World, grand exalted ruler. **BUSINESS ADDRESS:** Grand Exalted Ruler, International Benevolent Protective Order of Elks of the World, PO Box 159, Winton, NC 27986. *

WILSON, DONELLA JOYCE
Educator. **PERSONAL:** Born Jul 28, 1951, Milwaukee, WI; daughter of Paul Lawrence Wilson and Emily Frenchie Bailey-Wilson. **EDUCATION:** Johnston Coll Redlands Univ, BA 1973; TX Southern Univ, MS 1977; Purdue Univ, MS 1979, PhD 1981. **CAREER:** Washington Univ, rsch assoc 1981; Harvard Sch Dental Medicine, assoc of oral pathology 1981-83; Whitehead Inst & MIT, Radcliffe Coll Bunding fellow 1983-85; Meharry Medical Coll, asst prof 1985-. **ORGANIZATIONS:** Mem Amer Assoc Adv Sci 1982-; vstg prof Univ of MA Boston 1983-84; mem Harvard Health Professions Admissions Comm 1985; FASEB vstg scientist Fed Amer Soc Biol 1986-; mem NSF Grant Review Panel Cell and Mol Biol 1987; St Henry's Choir; mem Beta Kappa Chi, Beta Beta Beta. **HONORS/ACHIEVEMENTS:** Outstanding Young Amer Women 1982; recipient NSF and NIH First Awd 1986,87; Woman of the Year Compton CA 1987; "Future Makers," Ebony Magazine, Aug l985; Outstanding Women of the World, l989. **HOME ADDRESS:** 300 Cross Timbers Dr, Nashville, TN 37221. **BUSINESS ADDRESS:** Assistant Professor, Meharry Medical College, Div Biomedical Sciences, 1005 DB Todd Blvd, Nashville, TN 37208.

WILSON, EARL, JR.
Manager. **PERSONAL:** Born Oct 09, 1932, St Louis, MO; married Marjorie Black; children: Denise, Stacey, Kimberly,Richard. **EDUCATION:** Lincoln Univ, BS 1957, PhD 1981. **CAREER:** IBM Corporation, sales rep 1968, mgr office products 1968-70, asst branch mgr Clayton Branch 1970, branch sales mgr Washington 1973, baseline products mgr for GBG/I 1975, opers mgr of office products 1978, dealer market support mgr 1981, mgr of information products marketing support IBM World Trade 1983, dealer operations mgr northeast area 1985, branch mgr. **ORGANIZATIONS:** Chmn of bldg & ground comm Lincoln Univ Bd of Curators 1966-69; General chmn United Negro College Fund 1971-73; pres Lincoln Univ Natl Alumni Assoc 1972-81; mem Lincoln Univ Natl Alumni Assoc; life mem NAACP; United States Foreign Services Selection Bd Dept of State 1985; Dept of State Task Force on Minority Recruitment for the Foreign Serv under Sec Ronald I Spiers 1985; State of Dept Conference for Natl Minority and Women Orgs 1985. **HONORS/ACHIEVEMENTS:** Lincoln Univ Natl Alumni Achievement Awd 1978; Honorary Doctorates Lincoln Univ Jefferson City 1981; St Louis Sentinel Newspaper Outstanding Citizen Awd 1984; Lincoln Univ Bd of Curators Emeritus Awd 1985; Natl Assoc for Equal Oppor in Higher Educ Disting Alumni Citation Awd 1986; Natl Distribution Div Mgr of the Year for 1985 IBM; 100 % Club and Golden Circle IBM 1986; Leadership Awd IBM 1986; Summer Series Grand Slam Awd IBM 1986. **MILITARY SERVICE:** AUS Corps of Engrs capt 5 1/2 yrs; Fifth Army Certificate of Achievement US Army Parachute Badge 1959; USAEUR Certificate of Achievement Awd 1963. **BUSINESS ADDRESS:** Branch Manager, IBM Corporation NDD, 201 Merritt 7, Third Fl, Norwalk, CT 06852.

WILSON, EARL LAWRENCE
Administrator. **PERSONAL:** Born Jul 16, 1923, Philadelphia, PA; son of James R and Helen J. **EDUCATION:** Villanova Univ Criminal Justice Courses, attended 1969-73; PA State Univ, certificate 1970; St Joseph Univ, attended seminars labour relations; Amer Arbitration Assn, certificate; PA Dept of Corrections, certificate. **CAREER:** Philadelphia Prison System, warden prison security coord capt lt sgt correction officer 1951-78, prison warden 1979-. **ORGANIZATIONS:** Examiner PA Civil Serv Commn 1974-; mem PA Warden's Assn 1978-; mem Amer Correctional Assn 1978-; consultant/adviser Criminal Justice System; mem Amer Correctional Assn; PA Prison Wardens Assn. **HONORS/ACHIEVEMENTS:** Article on crime published in Ebony Magazine 1979. **MILITARY SERVICE:** USAF s/sgt 1944-46; Good Conduct Medal; Asiatic Pacific Ribbon. **BUSINESS ADDRESS:** Consultant/Corrections, 547 W Roosevelt Blvd, Philadelphia, PA 19120.

WILSON, ED
Sculptor, educator. **PERSONAL:** Born Mar 28, 1925, Baltimore, MD; son of Edward N Wilson Sr and Alice W Wilson; divorced; children: Craig, Julie. **EDUCATION:** U Univ of IowA, BA, MA, 1951; Univ of NC, 1961. **CAREER:** Sculpture commissions, Dr Mamie P Clark Bronze Northside Center for Child Dev New York City 1982-83, Jazz Musicians 12'L Bronze Relief City of Balto MD 1984, Dr Mamie P Clark Bronze for Dr Kenneth BClark Hasting NY 1984, Whitney M Young Jr Whitney M Young Jr Memorial Found New York City Bronze 1985-86; exhibitions, Studio Faculty Univ Art Gallery 1982-86, Unbroken Circle, Afro-Amer Artists of 30's & 40's Kenkeleba Gallery New York City 1986; Dept of Art NC Coll, chmn 1953-64; SUNY, chmn 1964-66, 1968-71, 1982-85 vice chmn 1974-78, prof of art 1986-, sculpture. **ORGANIZATIONS:** Sculpture commn accepted Oklahoma Co Libraries Oklahoma City Ralph Ellison Library 1974; sculpture commn accepted New Boy's High Brooklyn NY New York City Fine Arts Commn 1973; sculpture commn accepted Harlem Commonwealth Council Harlem NY 1972; ref, Christian Science Monitor, Art & Rebuttal 1971; appointed bd of dirs Coll Art Assn of Am 1970; accepted Sculpture Commn from City of Baltimore, 1970; accptd sculpture commn SUNY at Binghamton Sr Class 1970. **HONORS/ACHIEVEMENTS:** Appointed Natl Screening Comm; Sculpture Fulbright Hayes Program Inst of Internal Educ, New York City 7 Bronze Reliefs; 7 Seals of Silence; Macquettes for the JFK meml San Francisco Museum of Art; participant, Sculpture 2nd World & Blk Festiv of Fine Arts & Cult Lagos Nigeria sponsored by US State Dept 1977; Lecturer,Univ of Western Ontario, London Ontario/Howard U/U of IL; sculpture commn accptd Bronze Trophy BC Open PGA Golf Tour Endicott NY 1977; sculpture commn accptd Schomburg Collctn ofBlack Lit New York City 1979; sculpture comptn invtn acptd Frederick Douglass US Dept of Int 1979; Mellon & Scholar/artist in Res Tougaloo Coll MS 1980. **MILITARY SERVICE:** AUS 1943-46. **BUSINESS ADDRESS:** Professor, Sculptor, SUNY, Dept of Art & Art History, Binghamton, NY 13901.

WILSON, EDITH HUNDLEY
Singer. **PERSONAL:** Born Sep 02, Louisville, KY; married Millard. **CAREER:** Just returned from Paris doing a show for French TV audience; appeared for WA Post on Harrambee with Eubie Blake on TV; featured at Carnegie Hall; Pasadena Playhouse; motion pictures; recorded "Bradfords Nervous Blues", with Johnny Dunns Jazz Hounds; Edith & Florence Mills opened in Dover St to Dixie, London Pavillion; starred in "Leslies's Blackbirds"; appeared in "Hot Chocolates Revue"; sang with Duke Ellington Orch Cotton Club; appeared at London Colisuem 1934; appeared as Aunt Jemima on TV & pancake festivals 18 yrs.

WILSON, EDITH N.
Educator. **PERSONAL:** Born Apr 20, 1938, Columbia, SC; daughter of John Friday and Ruth Sulton Friday; married James E Wilson, Jan 03, 1980 (deceased); children: Michael J Harrison. **EDUCATION:** Benedict Coll, BA 1961; Univ of OR, MA 1971. **CAREER:** Roosevelt HS, principal 1976; Univ of OR, coord Dir Asst Dir, 1970-76; Tongue Point Job Corp, teacher corp dir 1968-69; Portland Public Schools, art tchr 1968-70; Albina Art Center, cons; Stanford Ctr for Rsch & Devel; Western Tchr Corp Recruitment Ctr; Univ of NE Urban Educ Ctr; Natl Tchr Corp; CMTI, assoc Dir; Natl League of Cities, rep; State Dept Disadvantaged & Handicapped Commr Metro Arts Commn, cons; Gov Commn on Youth; principal, Tulsman Middle School 1979-80; dir of instruction 1982-. **ORGANIZATIONS:** Mem Natl Alliance of Black School Educators; Natl Cncl of Admin Women; Delta Sigma Theta Sor; ASCD Art Intrnshp Grant Univ of OR 1967; devel Afro-Amer Art Curriculum; Portland Public School; 1969; Course Goals for State Art Program 1970; exh Maryhurst Coll 1968-69; Devel Minority Career Educ Prgm; Career Educ Assessmnt Model 1973; bd of dir Childrens Museum 1987-88; Portland City Club 1987-. **HOME ADDRESS:** 19818 S W Statford Rd, West Linn, OR 97068.

WILSON, ERNEST
Government official. **PERSONAL:** Born Feb 24, 1925, Baton Rouge, LA; married Merry; children: Diane, Stephen. **EDUCATION:** Univ IL, BS 1949; Princeton Univ, med-career fellow 1975-76. **CAREER:** US Aid Mission, asst dir, 1977; US Agency for Intl Devel Mission, controller 1976-77, asst dir, controller, chief auditor, financial controller, 1967-75. **ORGANIZATIONS:** Asst contr YMCA Met Chicago 1967; auditor US Dept HEW 1966; US Agency Intl Devel 1963-65; chief acct Housing Authority Cook Co 1957-63; supr acct Ind Mun Corp Chicago Housing Authority 1949-57; mem Amer Accounting Assn; Amer Foreign Serv Assn; Fed Govt Acct Assn. **HONORS/ACHIEVEMENTS:** Superior Performance Award USAID Ghana 1975. **MILITARY SERVICE:** USAF 1943-46. **BUSINESS ADDRESS:** NAIROBI/State Department, Washington, DC 20520.

WILSON, ERNEST
Manager. **PERSONAL:** Born Nov 04, 1936, New York, NY; children: Ernest Jr, Steven, Patricia. **EDUCATION:** New York Univ, BA. **CAREER:** Freight Liner Corp, personnel mgr 1966-71; MBM Corp, personnel dir 1971-72; TRW Corp, personnel admin 1972-74; Commutronx Corp, personnel dir 1974-75; City of San Bernardino, dir affirmative act and comm affairs 1975-85, dir of safety, comm affairs 1985-. **ORGANIZATIONS:** Vol leg adv to assemblyman 67th Dist State of CA 1979-80; mem Kiwanis Intl, Mexican/Amer Personnel Assn, Urban League, NAACP, Amer Soc for Training &Develop; mem Kiwanis Club San Bernardino; bd mem Black History Found. **HONORS/ACHIEVEMENTS:** Outstanding Achievement OSC Comm Orgn 1975; Outstanding Achievement Just X Club 1976; Cert of Outstanding Participation & Contributions CA Poly Univ 1979; Cert of Outstanding Achievement Mexican/Amer Mgmt Assn 1978; Cert of Appreciation Dr Martin Luther King Meml & Scholarship Fund Inc 1980; Citation for Comm Serv San Bernardino Light House of the Blind 1982; Scroll of Honor Omega Psi Phi Frat 1983; Cert of Achievement San Bernardino Black History 1983; Good Will Ambassador City of San Bernardino 1982; We Serve Awd Highland Dist Lions Club; Resolution by Mayor and Council City of San Bernadino Commending Leadership of the Affirmative Action Prog; Commendation Dept of Fair Employment & Housing State of CA; Cert of Achievement Equal Employment Oppty Comm. **MILITARY SERVICE:** AUS staff sgt 1954-57. **BUSINESS ADDRESS:** Dir Safety/Comm Affairs, City of San Bernardino, 300 North D St, San Bernardino, CA 92418.

WILSON, F. LEON
Social-political writer. **PERSONAL:** Born Sep 20, 1953, Akron, OH. **EDUCATION:** Ohio State Univ, BS 1975, MBA 1983. **CAREER:** Central Control Systems, publisher/principal writer; The Black Agenda, Regional coordinator, 1983-. **ORGANIZATIONS:** Chmn Americans Against Apartheid 1985-87. **HONORS/ACHIEVEMENTS:** Publications The Black Agenda, Educating Blacks for Social, Political and Economic Development, Dorran Press 1983; Black Unity, Definition and Direction, CCS Press 1985; The Black Woman, Center of the Black Economy, CCS Press 1986; Emancipatory Psychology CCS Press 1990. **BUSINESS ADDRESS:** Regional Coordinator, The Black Agenda, PO Box 24187, Columbus, OH 43224.

WILSON, FLIP (CLEROW WILSON)
Entertainer. **PERSONAL:** Born Dec 08, 1933, Jersey City, NJ; children: 4. **CAREER:** World famous comedian & star of own weekly TV show, "The Flip Wilson Show"; started career as night club comic Manor Plaza Hotel, San Francisco 1954; appeared on numerous TV shows including Johnny Carson, Ed Sullivan, Mike Douglas, Merv Griffin & Today; appeared in film "Uptown Saturday Night" 1974; recorded several comedy albums; TV show "Charlie & Company", starring role 1985-86. **HONORS/ACHIEVEMENTS:** Recipient of numerous awards including Grammy award for Best Comedy Record 1971. **MILITARY SERVICE:** USAF 1950-54.

WILSON, FLORABELLE W.
Retired. **PERSONAL:** Born Jan 12, 1927, Indianapolis, IN; married John A. **EDUCATION:** IN CentralUniv Indpls, BS Educ 1949; INUniv Bloomington, MA Lib Sci 1961. **CAREER:** Krannert Meml Lib IN Cntrl U, head librarian (1st & only black head librarian of an acad library in IN) 1971-; IN Central U, asst librarian 1957-71; Indianapolis Pub Sch, elem tchr 1949-57. **ORGANIZATIONS:** Mem/vp/pres elect coll &Univ div IN Library Assn 1949; mem Am Library Assn 1980; mem IN Hist Soc Library Bd 1980-; bd of dirs Cntrl Area IN Library Serv Auth 1979; bd of dir Zonta Intl Indianapolis Womens Serv (1st black mem in Indianapolis Chap 1976) 1979; life mem NAACP 1979-.

WILSON, FLOYD EDWARD, JR.
Councilman. **PERSONAL:** Born Nov 22, 1935, Lake Charles, LA; son of Floyd Edward Wilson Sr and Leada R Wilson; married Dorothy Lyons, Apr 09, 1988; children: J Keith, Tanya R Derryck M. **EDUCATION:** Dillard Univ, BA 1959. **CAREER:** Eastern HS, tchr 1962-72; Hallmark Acad Children Ctr, owner admin 1968-78; Glenarden MD, councilman vice mayor 1969-74; Prince George's County Council, councilman 1974-. **ORGANIZATIONS:** Mem PG Bd Dir Social Srvs 1976-; vice chrmn NACO Criminal Justice Comm 1983-; chrmn COG Air Quality Comm 1984; First Black Elected to PG Cty Council 1974-; mem Alpha Phi Alpha Frat; Life Mem NAACP. **BUSINESS ADDRESS:** County Councilman, Prince George's County Govt, County Admin Bldg, Upper Marlboro, MD 20772.

WILSON, FRANK FREDRICK, III
Physician. **PERSONAL:** Born Jun 14, 1936, Oklahoma City, OK; married Jacquelyn; children: Frank IV, Nathan, Yolanda, Coreen. **EDUCATION:** Fisk Univ, BA 1956; attended Univ OK; Howard Univ Sch Med, BA 1961; Univ MO, intern spec educ Gen Hosp & Med Ctr 1961-65. **CAREER:** Physician Ob-Gyn. **ORGANIZATIONS:** Dir Bd Park Commr 1971-74; Eastside YMCA 1972-73; Collins Garden Housing Corp 1972-74; OK City Ob-Gyn Soc sec treas 1973-74, exec bd 1974-77, pres 1975-76, vice pres 1976-77, pres 1977-; Touchstone Montesosori Sch 1973-74; mem OK Co Med Soc, OK State Med Assn, AMA, Natl Med Assn; diplomateNatl Bd Med Exmnrs; Amer Fertility Soc; Amer Bd Ob-Gyn; fellow Amer Coll Ob-Gyn; Central Assn Ob-Gyn; clincial asst prof Univ OK Med Ctr. **MILITARY SERVICE:** AUS MC capt 1965-67. **BUSINESS ADDRESS:** 700 NE 37th St, Oklahoma City, OK 73105.

WILSON, FREDERICK A.
Business executive. **PERSONAL:** Born Aug 06, 1946, Brooklyn, NY; married Patricia B Bridges; children: Jacqueline, Deidre. **EDUCATION:** Johnson C Smith U, BA Psych 1969. **CAREER:** NY Life Ins Co, asst sales mgr; Bay Ridge Gen Office, asst mgr 1974, field underwriter 1971-74. **ORGANIZATIONS:** Mem Nat Assn of Securities Dealers; mem 100 Black Men; mem Omega Psi Phi; mem NY Jaycees; US Jaycees. **HONORS/ACHIEVEMENTS:** Black Achievers in Indstry Awd YMCA NY 1977. **BUSINESS ADDRESS:** 9512 Third Ave, Brooklyn, NY 11209R.

WILSON, GEORGE G.
Physician. **PERSONAL:** Born Sep 14, 1929, Summitt, NJ; married Margie Kellam; children: Bruce T, Judy Wilson Gomez. **EDUCATION:** Howard Univ, attended 1956-59; Upsala College, BS 1960; Meharry Medical Coll, MD 1964. **CAREER:** Lyons VA Hosp, staff position neurology 1968-71; Orange NJ, city physician 1971-73; East Orange NJ, police surgeon 1972-74; Record Ambulance, president 1975-76; Private Practice, physician. **ORGANIZATIONS:** Mem NAACP; life mem Alpha Phi Alpha Fraternity; pres Orange Mountain Medical Soc 1984-85. **MILITARY SERVICE:** AUS sgt 1946-49. **BUSINESS ADDRESS:** 84 Sanford St, East Orange, NJ 07018.

WILSON, GERALD STANLEY
Composer, arranger, trumpeter. **PERSONAL:** Born Sep 04, 1918, Shelby, MS; married Josefina Villasenor; children: Geraldine, Lillian, Nancy Jo. **CAREER:** Composer, Royal Ste 1948, Josefina 1950, Blues for Yna Yna 1962, Viva Tirado 1963, Pace 1964, El Viti 1965, Carlos 1966, Teotihuacan Ste 1966, Collage 1968, Debut, Los Angeles Philharmonic Orch; trumpeter, arranger, composer for orchs Jimmie Lunceford 1939-42, Count Basie 1947-49, Duke Ellington 1947-66 ; mus performed at Carnegie Hall 1948, 1966, Mus Ctr Los Angeles 1968, Hollywood Bowl 1967; San Fernando Valley State Coll, mus dept 1969; CA State Univ Northridge. **ORGANIZATIONS:** Condr own orch; participant Kongsberg Jazz Festival Norway 1973; arranged & orchestrated for Nancy Wilson/Ray Charles/Al Hibbler/Bobby Darin/Julie London/Al Hirt; music dir many TV shows; contributed orchestrations to Library of Ella Fitzgerald; faculty Music Dept San Fernando Valley State Coll 1969. **HONORS/ACHIEVEMENTS:** Recipient awards Downbeat Mag 1963-64; nominations Nat Acad Rec Arts & Scis 1963-64.

WILSON, GREER DAWSON
College administrator. **PERSONAL:** Born Jan 05, 1943, Richmond, VA; divorced; children: Sarita M, Samia J. **EDUCATION:** Indiana Univ, BME 1964; Hampton Inst, MA Counseling 1976; College of William & Mary, EdD 1984. **CAREER:** ACU-I, chmn comm on minority progs 1979-81, educ commn mem 1984-87, intl conf chairperson 1987; State Bd Mental Health & Mental Retardation, vice chmn 1985-; Hampton Univ, coord student activities & dir of student union. **ORGANIZATIONS:** Bd mem Peninsula Family Serv Travelers Aid 1984-; bd mem Alternatives Substance Abuse Prog 1985-; mem Assoc for Counseling & Develop; organist Bethel AME Church; mem Delta Sigma Theta Sor, Hampton HS Guidance Comm. **HONORS/ACHIEVEMENTS:** Mem Kappa Delta Phi Honor Soc, Tau Beta Sigma Music Honor Soc; concert pianist; consultant on Leadership Develop & Racism for ACU-I. **BUSINESS ADDRESS:** Coord Student Activities, Hampton University, Box 6224, Hampton, VA 23368.

WILSON, HARRISON B.
Educator. **PERSONAL:** Born Apr 21, 1928, Amstead, NY; married Lucy; children: Benjamin, Harrison, John, Richard, Jennifer, Marquarite. **EDUCATION:** KY State U, BS IN U, MS, DHS. **CAREER:** Norfolk State Coll, pres 1975-; Fisk Univ, exec asst pres; TN State Univ, dir coop educ; Jackson State Coll, chmn dept health physical educ 1960-67, head basketball coach 1951-60. **ORGANIZATIONS:** Mem bd dir VA Nat Bank; mem lay adv bd DePaul Hosp; mem VA State Adv Cncl on Vocational Edn; mem bd dir Hlth Welfare Rec Plng Cncl; Alpha Kappa Mu. **BUSINESS ADDRESS:** President, Norfolk State University, 2401 Corprew Ave, Norfolk, VA 23504.

WILSON, HELEN TOLSON
Retired business executive. **PERSONAL:** Born Feb 22, New Franklin, MO; daughter of Rev A A Tolson; married Jesse Wilson (deceased). **EDUCATION:** Kansas City Conservatory of Music, attended 4 yrs; Dale Carnegie Inst of Charm & Voice, grad med tech; Attended Wayne State Univ, Tacome Warren, MI Univ; Wayne State Univ, BA Humanities 1957; Urban Bible Coll, DH Detroit MI 1984. **CAREER:** KC Young Matrons, pres founder 1939; Detroit Soc Charm Sch, dir 1973-; US Govt, accounting tech retired 26 yrs; DSACE Coords Council for the Arts, founder/pres. **ORGANIZATIONS:** Founder ZONTA Bus & Professional Women's Club 1944; mem, presidency elder, ME Medical Conference, Kansas City district, Kansas City, MO, 1954-; chmn Cinerama in Fashions Ford's Auditorium, 1957; gen

chrmn dir organizer Alpha Theta Chap, 1960; gen chrmn Detroit Urban League 4th Annual Gala Dinner Ball, 1968; chrmn Natl Founders Day Gamma Phi Delta Sor 1969-; founder, pres, dance coordinator Council for the Arts, 1972-85; pres, founder Youth Assembly of Detroit Urban League, 1973-78; bd trustees Gamma Phi Delta Sor; gen chrmn & dir Gamma Phi Delta Sor's Exec Staff; gen chrmn dir of publicity N Region Gamma Phi Delta Sr Inc; natl boule chmn Gamma Phi Delta Sor Inc; mem Wheatley Provident Hosp Aux; dir Civic Fashion Show; supr KC MO HS Press; founder Youth Assembly of the Detroit Urban League. **HONORS/ACHIEVEMENTS:** Rose Pin Awd Gamma Phi Delta Sor Inc 1971; The Gov Awd (2) token 27 yrs; 25 yr pin Detroit Urban League Guild; Highest Awd The Detroit Zonta Club 1939-46; DHL, Wayne State Univ Detroit MI 1983; Picture Honor Roll Natl Urban League Inc 1986; Honored at 1986 Urban League & Guild Annual Gala.

WILSON, HENRY, JR.
Business exec. **PERSONAL:** Born Nov 10, 1938, Taylor, TX; married Carrie L Twyman; children: Peggy Annette, Pamela Ann. **EDUCATION:** Univ of Cincinnati, AS Engr 1968. **CAREER:** Cincinnati Water Work, engr tech 1957-64; Kaizer Engrs, engr 1964-68; Turner Constr Co, engr 1968-71; Wilson & Assc Arch & Engrs, pres 1971-. **ORGANIZATIONS:** Mem Natl Soc of Professional Engrs 1968-; dir Hamilton County State Bank 1980-; trustee Univ Cincinnati Fnd 1981- secr zoning bd appeals silverton oH 1980-; pastor cornerstone missionary Baptist Church 1984-; instr Cornerstone Bible Inst 1985; trustee Greater Cincinnati C of C 1985-88. **HONORS/ACHIEVEMENTS:** Min Small Bus; Person of the Year US Small Bus Admin 1984. **HOME ADDRESS:** 6737 Elwynne Dr, Cincinnati, OH 45236. **BUSINESS ADDRESS:** President, Wilson & Assc Inc, 4439 Reading Rd, Cincinnati, OH 45229.

WILSON, HUGH A.
Educator. **PERSONAL:** Born Jun 20, 1940, Kingston, Jamaica. **EDUCATION:** Howard U, BA 1963; FordhamUniv Sch of Social Svc, MSW 1967. **CAREER:** Adelphi Univ NY, asst prof; Inst for Suburban Studies, dir. **ORGANIZATIONS:** Dir Welfare Tenants Coord Com Mineola NY 1968-70; comm organizer Comm Coord Coun Long Beach, NY 1966-67; consult Westchester Urban League 1973; Yonkers Comm Action Prgrm 1971-72; Addiction Serv Agency of NY 1973; co-fndr & sec Alliance of Minority Group Ldrs in Nassau-Suffolk 1970. **HONORS/ACHIEVEMENTS:** Awarded $45,000 by N Shore Unitarian Ch to set up Inst for Suburban Studies At AdelphiUniv 1973. **BUSINESS ADDRESS:** Inst for Suburban Studies Leve, 300 Adelphi Univ, Garden City, NY 11530.

WILSON, HUGHLYNE PERKINS
Educator. **PERSONAL:** Born Jul 12, 1931, Louisville, KY; married Charles A Wilson; children: Stuart K. **EDUCATION:** Howard Univ, BA 1951; Univ Louisville, MEd 1964. **CAREER:** Louisville Public Schools, teacher 1956-68; Univ KY, coord 1968-70; Louisville Public Schools, asst dir div certificated personnel 1970-72, dir 1972-74; KY School Dist, asst supr dept empl personnel serv. **ORGANIZATIONS:** Mem NEA, KY Assn Sch Admin, Amer Assn Sch Personnel, Amer KY Louisville Assns Childhood Educ; mem Urban League, Delta Sigma Theta Sor; mem Phi Delta Kappa; mem KY Assn of Sch Supts; mem bd of regents Western KY Univ Bowling Green. **HONORS/ACHIEVEMENTS:** First woman asst supt Louisville Pub Schs; Who's Who in Am Colls & Univs. **BUSINESS ADDRESS:** Asst Supr Dept Emp Personnel, KY Sch Dist, 3332 Newburg Rd, Louisville, KY 40218.

WILSON, JACQUELINE PROPHET
Director. **PERSONAL:** Born Jun 08, 1949, Washington, DC. **EDUCATION:** Univ of Tennessee, BS 1974. **CAREER:** WIVK Radio Knoxville TN, news reporter 1973-74; WBIR-TV Knoxville TN, producer & program host 1974-77; TN Educ Assoc, public relations/media specialist 1977-82; Meharry Medical Coll, public relations dir 1982-. **ORGANIZATIONS:** Mem Intl Assoc of Business Communicators 1984-86, Public Relations Society of America 1984-85; bd dirs Nashville Urban League 1983-86. **HONORS/ACHIEVEMENTS:** Certificate of Recognition Black College Fund-United Methodist Church 1985; Gold Medal Awd (for public relations) Council for the Advancement and Support of Educ 1986. **BUSINESS ADDRESS:** Dir, Meherry Medical College, 1005 DB Todd Blvd, Nashville, TN 37208.

WILSON, JAMES, JR.
Attorney. **PERSONAL:** Born Aug 21, 1919, Mound City, IL; married Ethel Pearson. **EDUCATION:** St Louis U, BA, LlB, JD 1957. **CAREER:** Workmens Comp Com. **ORGANIZATIONS:** Past pres Pulaski Co; NAACP IL; Bus Instr Hubbards Bus Coll; atty Bell Wilson Attys; Mound City Bar Assn; MO Bar; Am Bar St of MO; RE Broker St MO; Land Surveyor; Notary Public; St MO Mason 32nd Deg. **MILITARY SERVICE:** USAF pilot. **BUSINESS ADDRESS:** 1023 N Grand, St Louis, MO 63106.

WILSON, JAMES DAVIS
Business executive. **PERSONAL:** Born Jun 30, 1937, Kingstree, SC; married Lorraine Louise Poret; children: Angele, Tanya, Arianne. **EDUCATION:** Morehouse Coll; XavierUniv Coll of Pharmacy New Orleans; TX So U, BS 1963. **CAREER:** Wilson's Surgical Supplies, pres; Walgreens Drug Store, phrmcst & mgr 1963-69. **ORGANIZATIONS:** New Orleans Prog Phrmcsts Assn; LA Pharm Assn; mem bd dir Natl Pharm Assn; Am Pharm Assn; LA State bd of Phrmcy; Nat Assn of Retail Druggists; Pharm Reference Agent; NAACP; Urban League of Grtr New Orleans; presUniv Meth Men Assn; 3rd degree Mason; Chi Delta Mu Med Frat; Kappa Alpha Psi; bd mem YMCA; consult State C A P Agys; rep High Blood Pressure Symposium 1975; fndr & Co-Dir Boys City Res Camp 1964-67; mem bd dir Multi Media Ctr; consHeadstart Prog. **HONORS/ACHIEVEMENTS:** Perceptor for Pharm Interns Awrd 1st black owner of surgical supplies co; ICBO Distinguished Achvmnt Awrd 1974; 1st black appt LA Bd of Pharm 1976. **BUSINESS ADDRESS:** 2019 Louisiana Ave, New Orleans, LA 70115.

WILSON, JAMES PARIS
Clergyman. **PERSONAL:** Born Nov 07, 1907, Memphis, TN; married Marthel. **EDUCATION:** MST, BA BD 1954. **CAREER:** Mt Olive Bapt Ch, mnstr. **ORGANIZATIONS:** Moderator Saginaw Valley Dist Assn 1959; pres Wolverine Bapt State Conv 1964; co commnr Saginaw Co 1964-68; mem Bd of Co Hlth Dept 1968-71. **BUSINESS ADDRESS:** 1114 N 6 St, Saginaw, MI 48601.

WILSON, JOHN
Artist, educator. **PERSONAL:** Born Apr 14, 1922, Boston, MA; married Julia Kowitch; children: Rebecca, Roy, Erica. **EDUCATION:** Museum Fine Arts School, grad 1944; Tufts Univ, BS 1947; Fernand Leger's Sch Paris 1949; Inst Politecnico Esmeralda School Art Mexico City 1952; Escuela de lasArtes del Libro Mexico City 1954-55. **CAREER:** NY Bd of Educ, 1959-64; Boston Univ, prof art 1964-86, prof emeritus. **ORGANIZATIONS:** Mem bd Elma Lewis Sch Fine Arts Boston 1970-75. **HONORS/ACHIEVEMENTS:** Prizes natl exhibits 1951-69; purchase prize Hunterdon Art Ctr Annual Print Exhibit NJ 1958; num awds & citations; exhibits colls, univs, galleries, NY Metro Mus Art, France; illustrations in books, art pubns; created Dr Martin Luther King Jr Monument Buffalo NY 1983; created Dr Martin Luther King Jr Commemorative Statue US Capitol Washington DC. **BUSINESS ADDRESS:** Professor Emeritus, Boston Univ Sch Visual Arts, 855 Commonwealth Ave, Boston, MA 02159.

WILSON, JOHN A.
Politician. **PERSONAL:** Born Sep 29, 1943, Baltimore, MD; married Bonita A Biro. **EDUCATION:** MD State Coll, 1962-65; Attended, John F Kennedy Sch of Govt Harvard Univ 1985. **CAREER:** Ward 2 Council of DC, councilmember 1974-, re-elected in 1974, 1976, 1980, 1984, 1988. **ORGANIZATIONS:** Dep natl chmn Student Non-Violent Coord Comm 1961-67; co-chmn Natl Mobilization to End the War in Vietnam 1966-69; natl chmn Natl Black Anit-War/Anti-Draft Union 1966-69; visting fellow Inst for Policy Studies 1969-70; legislative dir Nat Sharecroppers Fund 1968-77; mem & vice chmn DC Dem Party 1970-74; natl dir Com to Save the Office of Econ Devel 1972-74; host bi-weekly talk show on Georgetown Univ radio sta WGTB 1972-74; mem Nat Urban League; mem NAACP; mem Human Serv Comm, Housing and Economic Development, Consumer and Regulators Affairs; chmn Finance & Review. **HONORS/ACHIEVEMENTS:** Vstg Fellow Inst for Policy Studies Washington 1971; Outstndg Serv Nghbrhd Plng Council #17 1973; assistance & Contrib Pub Affairs Inst-Frostburg State Coll 1977; Outstndng Serv to commnty United Planning Org 1977; Leadership Natl Student Bus League 1979; Fellow Inst for Politics John F Kennedy Sch of Govt Harvard Univ 1985; Hon Doctorate Univ of MD Eastern Shore 1986. **BUSINESS ADDRESS:** City Council Member Ward 2, City of Washington DC, 1350 Penn Ave NW, Washington, DC 20004.

WILSON, JOHN E.
Business executive, accountant. **PERSONAL:** Born Dec 09, 1932, Chicago, IL; son of Leroy Wilson and Carrie Wilson; married Velma J Brown; children: Ginger, Kelly. **EDUCATION:** BS 1954; CPA 1965. **CAREER:** Arthur J Wilson CPA, acct 1957-63; IL Commerce Comm, auditor 1963; Bowey's Inc, general acct 1964; Capitol Food Industries Inc, treasurer 1969-; Bates Packaging Co, controller 1969; John E Wilson Ltd, pres; Public Building Commission, Chicago IL, asst treasurer. **ORGANIZATIONS:** Mem Amer Inst of CPA's; IL Soc of CPA's; Natl Assn of Minority CPA's; mem Kappa Alpha Psi; Sigma Pi Phi. **MILITARY SERVICE:** USN 1955-57. **BUSINESS ADDRESS:** President, John E Wilson, Ltd, 53 West Jackson Blvd, Chicago, IL 60604.

WILSON, JOHN LOUIS
Architect. **PERSONAL:** Born Jan 24, 1899, Meridian, MS; married Hazel Thomas; children: Judith Ann. **EDUCATION:** Dillard Univ, AB 1920; Columbia Univ, BA 1928. **CAREER:** Philander Smith Coll, instr 1920-21; Harlem River Houses, co-architect 1939; self-employed architect. **ORGANIZATIONS:** Reg architect NY State 1930; chmn Council for Advancement of Negro in Architecture 1957-64; chmn NY AIA's Equal Oppor Comm; mem Coll of Fellows Amer Inst of Architects; chmn bd trustees St Mark's United Methodist Ch NYC; mem NAACP, Urban League, Alpha Phi Frat. **BUSINESS ADDRESS:** Architect, 209 W 125 St, New York, NY 10027.

WILSON, JOHN T., JR.
Educator of occupational & environmental medicine, educational administrator. **PERSONAL:** Born Jun 02, 1924, Birmingham, AL; son of John T Wilson and Rosalie Rush Wilson; married Artee F Young, Jun 21, 1980. **EDUCATION:** Howard Univ, (cum laude) BS 1946; Columbia Univ, MD 1950; Univ of Cincinnati, ScD 1956. **CAREER:** Univ of Washington, chmn & prof Dept of Environmental Health 1974-; Howard Univ, prof & chmn Dept of Comm Health Practice 1971-74; Stanford Univ, asst prof Dept of Comm & Prevent Med 1969-71; Lockheed A/C Corp CA, life scis adv 1961-69; Bur of Occupational Health Santa Clara Co Health Dept CA, chief 1957-61. **ORGANIZATIONS:** Mem Armed Forces Epidemiology Bd 1977-; dir NW Occupational Safety & Health Endl Resource Center 1977-; dir Amer Acad of Occupational Med 1979-; spec inoccupatonal med; Amer Bd of Preventive Med 1960; mem Washington Assn of Black Health Care Providers; life mem NAACP; dir Emerald City Bank, Seattle 1988-. **HONORS/ACHIEVEMENTS:** Natl Scholarship Awd Howard Univ Alumni Assn 1965. **BUSINESS ADDRESS:** Prof, Dept of Environmental Health, Univ of Washington, Seattle, WA 98195.

WILSON, JOHN W.
Administrator, educator. **PERSONAL:** Born Jun 10, 1928, St Marys, GA; son of Albert and Ora; divorced; children: John Jr, Larry, Dwaughn. **EDUCATION:** Albany St Coll, BS, Elementary Educ, 1951; Univ of Akron, MA, Educ Admin, 1970, EdD, 1983. **CAREER:** Albany State Coll, employee,1951; USAF, educ specialist, 1951-55; Cleveland Public Schools, elementary teacher, 1957-69; Univ of Akron, dir, Black Cultural Center & Afro-Amer Studies. **ORGANIZATIONS:** Pres, Natl Black Alliance Grad Educ, 1972-; overseas ext teacher, Univ of Wisconsin, (English), Korea, 1952; Higher Educ Comm, Natl Alliance of Black School Educ, 1984-; mem, Phi Delta Kappa, 1970-; NAACP, Omega Psi Phi, 1947-. **HONORS/ACHIEVEMENTS:** Certificate & plaque, Martha Holden Jennings Scholar, 1966-67; certificate, Regional Council of Intl Educ, 1970-71, Ivory Coast and Lome, West Africa Workshop & Tour of Lagos, Dakar, Benin, 1980. **MILITARY SERVICE:** USAF, Educ Spec, 1951-55. **HOME ADDRESS:** 11511 Martin Luther King Jr Dr, Cleveland, OH 44105. **BUSINESS ADDRESS:** Director, Black Cultural Cntr, University of Akron, East Hall #202, Akron, OH 44325.

WILSON, JON
Account executive. **PERSONAL:** Born Sep 29, 1955, Canton, OH. **EDUCATION:** OH Sch of Broadcast Technique Cleveland 1974. **CAREER:** WKNT Radio Kent OH, asst news dir 1974; WHBC Radio, combo announcer/engr 1974-76; United Companies Life Ins Baton Rouge, regional dir 1976-77; WHBC Radio,production specl 1976-77, Black music dir 1977-84; WHBC AM & FM, account exec 1984-; WHBC AM & FM, research dir/ co-op coord. **ORGANIZATIONS:** Mem Soc of Broadcast Engrs 1975; mem Black Music Assn 1979; mem

bd of dir Canton Black United Fund Pub Relations Div 1979; mem bd of dirs Stark Co NAACP 1980, 1983; bd mem Metropoliatian Office Canton; youth committee YMCA; dir Presenters Bureau Commerce Div for The United Way; youth coach YMCA. **HONORS/ACHIEVEMENTS:** Outstanding Teenagers of Amer Inc 1973; spec comm Stark Co NAACP 1979; Serv Awd E Central OH Easter Seals 1979; Outstanding Young Man of Amer Awd US Jaycees 1980; Spec Commendation Stark Co NAACP 1982; Spec Serv Awd Canton Area Big Bros/Big Sisters 1984-85; Ford Motor Marketing Inst Certification "Satisfying Customer Needs". **BUSINESS ADDRESS:** Account Executive, WHBC AM & FM, 550 Market Ave South, Canton, OH 44701.

WILSON, JOY JOHNSON
Health policy commission staff member. **PERSONAL:** Born Jul 12, 1954, Charleston, SC; married Ronald E Wilson; children: Devon. **EDUCATION:** Keene State College NH, BS 1976; Univ of NC at Chapel Hill, MRP 1978. **CAREER:** Natl Conf of State Leg, rsch assoc 1978-79, staff assoc 1979-82, sr staff assoc 1982-83, staff dir 1983-. **ORGANIZATIONS:** Adv Neighborhood Commission 1981-84, treas of commission 1982-83; treas Women and Health Roundtable 1986,87; mem Women's Govt Relations; mem American League of Lobbyists. **HOME ADDRESS:** 6413 Hollins Dr, Bethesda, MD 20817.

WILSON, KIM ALESIA
Educational administrator. **PERSONAL:** Born Sep 14, 1959, Long Branch, NJ. **EDUCATION:** Smith Coll, BA 1981. **CAREER:** IBM, stockholder info spec; Natl Multiple Sclerosis Soc, prog cons. **ORGANIZATIONS:** Sec 1982-83, co-chmn 1984-85, Assoc of Black Admission & Financial Aid Officers in Ivy League & Sister Schools; treas New England Minority Women Admin Inc; bd of dir Sojourn Inc 1983-85; bd dir 1985-, candidates comm chair 1985- Smith Coll Club of New York City. **HONORS/ACHIEVEMENTS:** Cigna Corp Grant for Minority Rec Cigna Corp 1983-85; Otelia Cromwell Awd Black Students Alliance Smith Coll 1984. **BUSINESS ADDRESS:** Program Consultant, Natl Multiple Sclerosis Soc, 205 E 42nd St, New York, NY 10017.

WILSON, LANCE HENRY
Attorney, investment banker. **PERSONAL:** Born Jul 05, 1948, New York City, NY; son of William H. Wilson and Ruth Thomas Wilson; married Deirdre Jean Jenkins; children: Jennifer Lee. **EDUCATION:** Hunter College, AB 1969; Univ of PA Law Sch, JD 1972. **CAREER:** Mudge Rose Guthrie & Alexander, attorney 1972-77; Equitable Life Assurance Soc of the US, assoc counsel 1977-81; US Dept of Housing & Urban Develop, exec asst to the sec 1981-84; New York City Housing Develop Corp, pres 1984-86; first vice pres Paine Webber Inc. 1986-. **ORGANIZATIONS:** Mem NY State Bar Assn; vice pres NY Co Republican Comm; public mem Admin Conf of the US 1984-; dir Visiting Nurse Service of NY 1984-; trustee St Luke's/Roosevelt Hosp Center 1984-; Dir Nat'l Housing Conf 1986-; mem Federal Natl Mortgage Assn Advisory Council 1986-88. **HONORS/ACHIEVEMENTS:** Legal Writing Teaching Fellowship Univ of PA Law School 1971; Outstanding Leadership Awd IL Council of Black Republicans 1982; Outstanding Leadership Awd NYState Council of Black Republicans 1982; Secty's Awd for Excellence US Dept of Housing & Urban Develop 1984; Outstanding Public Serv Awd Natl Assoc of Home Builders 1984; Exemplary Leadership Awd Natl Black Republican Council 1984; Outstanding Young Men of America Awd 1984;Housing Man of the Year, Nat'l & NYHousing Conf 1985; Humanitarian Awd, Southern Brooklyn Comm Org 1985; Private Sector Initiative Commendation, The White House 1986. **MILITARY SERVICE:** US Army capt 3 months duty 6 yrs reserves. **BUSINESS ADDRESS:** First Vice President, Paine Webber Inc, 1285 Ave of the Americas, New York, NY 10019.

WILSON, LAVAL S.
Educational administrator. **PERSONAL:** Born Nov 15, 1935, Jackson, TN; married Constance Ann; children: Laval Jr, Holly, Shawn, Nicole. **EDUCATION:** Chicago Teachers Coll, BEd 1958; Univ of Chicago, MA 1962; Northwestern Univ, PhD 1967. **CAREER:** Chicago Schools, teacher/counselor 1958-64; Northwestern Univ Inst, asst dir 1965 & 1966; Evanston, IL, asst prin 1966-67, dir integration inst & follow-up prog 1967-70; Central School Evanston, IL, prin 1967-70; Philadelphia & Detroit Schools, supt's intern prog 1970-71; Hempstead, NY, asst supt curric & instr 1971-72 & 1973-74, acting supt of schools 1972-73; Berkeley, CA, supt of schools 1974-80; Rochester, NY, supt of schools 1980-85; Boston, MA, supt of schools 1985-. **ORGANIZATIONS:** Mem Amer Assn of Schl Adminis, Assn for Supvsn and Curric Develop, Kappa Alpha Psi Frat, NAACP, Phi Delta Kappa, New York Cncl of Schl Dist Admin, League of Women Voters; mem Adv Bd of Girl Scouts of Genesee Valley 1984-; mem bd dirs Rochester Area Found 1984-; mem bd dirs Center for GovtRsch Inc 1984-; mem bd dirs Buffalo Br of Fed Reserve Bank of NY 1984-; mem bd dirs Junior Achieve of Rochester 1983-; mem Otetiana Cncl Exec BdBoy Scouts of Amer 1981-; mem bd trustees Rochester Museum & Sci Center 1981-; mem Rochester Rotary 1981-; mem Metro Adv Bd Lincoln First Bank 1981-83; mem Berkeley Rotary 1977-80; mem bd dirs Berkeley Red Cross 1975-79; editorial consult to Phi Delta Kappan publn of Phi Delta Kappa 1974-78; mem HempsteadKiwanis 1973-74; consultant to NY Univ, Common of PA Act 101 Western Reg, Amer Assn of Schl Admin, Race Deseg Inst Univ of Pittsburgh, Natl Inst ofEdn, Natl Schl Boards Assn, Office of Edn, Far West Lab, Los Angeles Co Schl Dist, San Francisco State Univ, Wyandanch, NY Sch Dist, New York City Sch Dist 12, Encyclopedia Brittanica. **HONORS/ACHIEVEMENTS:** Cert of Recogn for contribns to Rochester community by United Church Ministry 1985; Leadership Award by Rochester Chapter of Phi Delta Kappa 1985; Top Executive Educator Award Executive Educator 1984; Cert of Apprec by Mason Eureka Lodge No 36 1984; Commitment Plaque by Hospitality Charity Club 1984; Apprec Award by Grad Sch of Educ and Human Dev Univ of Rochester 1984; Community Serv Award by Rochester Assn of Black Communicators 1983; Special Serv Award by Rochester WEB DuBois Acad 1983; Apprec Plaque by Dist Adv Council to Chap 1 1982; Community Serv Plaque by Rochester Alumni Chap of Kappa Alpha Psi 1982; Apprec Plaque by Natl Conf on Parent Involvement 1981; City Proclamation of Apprec by Mayor "Gus" Newport and City Council members of Berkeley 1980; Congressional Award by Congr Ronald Dellums 1980; Legislative Resolution of Spec Publ Recogn and Commend by CA Assemblyman Tom Bates, Assemblyman Eluhu Harris &Sen Nicholas Petris 1980; Resolution of Apprec by Berkeley Bd of Educ 1980; Recogn Plaque by the Berkeley Black principals 1980; Apprec Plaque by Phi Delta Kappa 1978. **BUSINESS ADDRESS:** Superintendent, Boston Public Schools, 26 Court St, Boston, MA 02108.

WILSON, LAWRENCE C.
Business executive. **PERSONAL:** Born May 16, 1932, Kansas City, KS; son of John R and Alfretta; divorced; children: Stacey Marie. **EDUCATION:** LA Coll; KC Metro Jr Coll. **CAREER:** Neighborhood Serv Syst KC MO, dir 1971-72; Greater KC Council on Religion & Race, proj dir 1969-71; Human Resources Corp KC MO, area coordinator 1963-69; gen machinist 1955-68; Shawnee Co Comm Assistance & Action, In Topeka, exec dir. **ORGANIZATIONS:** Mem Topeka Opt Club; Natl Assn Comm Develop; Lawrence C Wilson Assoc; chmn KS Comm on Civil Rights; advr KS Sec of Social Rehabilitation Series; Topeka-Shawnee Co Metro Plng Comm; League of KS Municipalities Human Resources Comm; NAACP; Black Econ Union; KS Assn of Comm Action; dir OEO. **HONORS/ACHIEVEMENTS:** Urban Serv Award; Alliance of Businessmen Jobs Award; Appreciation Award Black Economic Union. **MILITARY SERVICE:** USN 1949-53. **BUSINESS ADDRESS:** Deputy Dir, City of Topeka Housing Authority, 1312 Polk, Topeka, KS 66612.

WILSON, LAWRENCE E., III
Marketing manager. **PERSONAL:** Born Feb 13, 1951, New London, CT. **EDUCATION:** Drew Univ, BA 1973; Univ of PA Wharton Grad Div, MBA 1975. **CAREER:** Philip Morris Inc, corp affairs rep 1975-77; Drew Univ, adg instr part time 1976; Philip Morris Inc, publ relations mgr 1977-78; Marlboro, asst brand mgr 1978-79; Fairleigh Dickinson Univ, instr part time 1979; Norwalk Comm Coll, adj instr part time 1980-83; Virginia Slims, brand mgr 1980-82; Benson & Hedges, brand mgr 1982-. **ORGANIZATIONS:** Mem Amer Mgmt Assoc, Publ Rel Soc of Amer 1976; bd of dir Natl Assoc of Tobacco Distrib Young Exec Div 1983-84; pres Drew Univ Alumni Assoc 1982-84; mem Wharton Bus School Club of NY 1976-, Dem Town & City Comm 1982-. **HONORS/ACHIEVEMENTS:** 1st Ed Awd Martin Luther King Found New London CT 1969; Spec Honors in Econ & Music Drew Univ 1973; Fellowship Sperry & Hutchinson 1974; Outstanding Young Men of Amer 1980; Finalist White House Fellowship Prog 1984; bd of dir NAACP Norwalk CT Chap 1983-. **BUSINESS ADDRESS:** Branch Manager, Benson & Hedges, Philip Morris USA, 120 Park Ave, New York, NY 10017.

WILSON, LEON A.
Manager. **PERSONAL:** Born Nov 10, 1930, Pittsburgh, PA; married Margaret Dorothy. **EDUCATION:** Tuskegee Inst, BA 1952. **CAREER:** Dow Jones & Co Inc, asst prod mgr 1965-69, prod mgr 1969-71; Washington Post, asst prod mgr 1974, publ mgr 1974-76, night asst prod mgr. **ORGANIZATIONS:** Mem Alpha Phi Alpha, NAACP, ACLU. **MILITARY SERVICE:** USAF lt 1952-54. **BUSINESS ADDRESS:** Asst Prod Mgr, The Washington Post, 1150 15th St NW, Washington, DC 20071.

WILSON, LEONARD D.
State program officer. **PERSONAL:** Born Dec 06, 1933, Raleigh, NC; married Cynthia T; children: Edwin G, Anita V. **EDUCATION:** BS 1970. **CAREER:** Raleigh-Wake Co Civil Def Agy, supr prsnl acctng distrib & inspection of Geiger Counters 1966; Am Optical Co Raleigh, NC, messenger 1966-67; Wake CoOpport Inc Raleigh, 1969-71; Manpower, dir; Chavis Heights Comm Action Ctr, dir; NC Council of Ch Migrant Project, 1971-72; Emergency Food & Med Serv Guidlines, tech asst; Durham Co Hosp Inc, Lincoln Hosp, Durham, NC, employment coord 1975-73; Action Domestic Program, state prgm ofcr; US Govt Additional Traning, Mid-Level Mgmt Trng, Bettsy Jeff Penn 4-H Cntr Winston-Salem 1969, Mid-Level Mgmt Follow-up Training 1970. **ORGANIZATIONS:** Pub prsnl mgmt disadvantaged trainingUniv of NC 1969; Low Income Housing Devel Tng, Low Income Housing Devel Corp, Durham NC 1969; Manpower Training Conf, Coastal Plains Regnl CommnUniv of GA Ctr for Continuing Educ Athens GA 1970; Audio-Visual Tng, Bettsy Jeff Penn 4-H Ctr 1970; Audio-Visual Training NC Cntrl Univ 1969; Auto Mech Tng, Ligon HS; Underwriter for NC Mutual Ins Co Raliegh 1964; Survival Training USN San Diego 1963; commissioned notary public 1970-75. **HONORS/ACHIEVEMENTS:** Comm Orgns letter of appreciation Wayne Action Group for Econ Solvency Goldsboro, NC; Certificate of Membership NC Hosp Personnel Assn; US Naval Air Facility China Lake CA. **MILITARY SERVICE:** AUS paratrooper 1953-56; USN 1960-64; USNR 3 yrs active. **BUSINESS ADDRESS:** Action Domestic Programs, Federal Bldg Plaza, Louisville, KY 40201.

WILSON, LEROY, III
Educational administrator. **PERSONAL:** Born Oct 11, 1951, Clearwater, FL; married Alpha Marie Allen; children: Jobyna Nadirah; Sisina Eudora. **EDUCATION:** East Side High School Newark NJ, HS Diploma 1969; Seton Hall Univ, South Orange NJ, (Political Science) BA 1973, (Asian Studies) MA 1977, (Public Admin) MPA 1988. **CAREER:** Newark Star, Leger, newsreporter 1969-73; NY Stock Exchange, stock investigator 1973-75; Seton Hall Univ, Upward Bound, assoc dir, 1975-79, dir 1979-. **ORGANIZATIONS:** Assn for Equality & Excellence in Educ, chmn, bd of dirs 1977-; East Orange NJ Branch-Kiwanis Intl, vice pres 1981; East Orange, NJ YMCA, vice chmn, bd of mgmt 1981; Eta Pi Chapter-Omega Psi Phi Fraternity, basileus 1987-88; Abyssinia Temple No 1, potentate, 1986-87; Amer Mgmt Assn, 1985-; Amer Soc for Public Admin, 1985-. **HONORS/ACHIEVEMENTS:** Mayor's Medal for Outstanding Student Leadership-City of Newark, NJ 1969; Omega Man of the Year-Kappa Eta Chapter-Omega Psi Phi Fraternity 1982; Distinquished Alumnus-New Jersey Educational Opportunity Fund 1986. **BUSINESS ADDRESS:** Dir, Seton Hall University, 400 South Orange Ave, South Orange, NJ 07079.

WILSON, LEROY, JR.
Attorney. **PERSONAL:** Born Jun 16, 1939, Savannah, GA; son of Leroy Wilson, Sr and Mary Louise (Frazier) Wilson; married Helen Odum (divorced); children: Andrea; married Jane Marie Beaver; children: Jason, Christopher. **EDUCATION:** Univ of Vienna Austria, 1959-60; Morehouse Coll, BS 1962; Univ of CA Berkeley, MS, JD 1965, 1968. **CAREER:** IBM, attny 1968-72; Covington Grant Howard, attny 1972; IBM, attny 1972-74; Private practice, attny 1974; Union Carbide Corp, attny 1974-82; Private practice, attny 1982-. **ORGANIZATIONS:** Dir The Assoc of Black Laywers of Westchester Co Inc 1978-; gov mem exec comm Natl Bar Assoc 1979-1980; mem, Amer Bar Assoc; vice pres Natl Bar Assoc; public mem NY State Banking Bd 1983-; chmn Assoc of Black Lawyers of Westchester Co Inc 1987-; public mem New York State Banking Bd 1984-1988. **HONORS/ACHIEVEMENTS:** Hon Woodrow Wilson Fellow 1962; Thayer Awd Civil Counsel to Sickle Cell Anemia Benefit US Mil Acad; Personal Counsel to His Excellency Godfrey Lukongwa Binaisa Fifth Pres of the Republic of Uganda. **BUSINESS ADDRESS:** Attorney, 149 Grand St, White Plains, NY 10601.

WILSON, LIONEL J.
Government official. **PERSONAL:** Born Mar 14, 1915, New Orleans, LA; married Dorothy P; children: Lionel B, Robin, Steven. **EDUCATION:** Univ of CA Berkeley, BA 1939; Hastings Coll of Law, JD 1949. **CAREER:** Private practice, attny 1950-60; Oakland Pied-

mont, municipal court judge 1960-64; Alameda Cty, superior ct judge 1964-76; Criminal Div Alameda Superior Court, presiding judge; Appellate Dept of Alameda Cty Superior Court, presiding judge; City of Oakland, mayor 1977-. **ORGANIZATIONS:** Chmn Presiding Judges of CA & Superior Courts; mem CETA; past pres, founding mem, bd of dir New Oakland Comm; adv com Alameda Cty Council on Alcoholism, Alameda Cty Mental Health Assoc; consult Far West School; chmn, pres Oakland Econ Devel Council Inc, Oakland Men of Tomorrow, Charles Houston Law Club; bd dir Oakland & Berkeley Br NAACP; chmn Oakland Anti-Pvoerty Bd; former chmn Legal Redress Com of Alameda Cty & Berkeley Br NAACP. **HONORS/ACHIEVEMENTS:** 1st black judge in Alameda Cty; West Coast Reg Merit Awd NAACP; Awd for Outstanding Professional Serv No CA Med Dental & Pharmaceutical Assoc; The Oak Ctr Inc Awd "A Judge for All Seasons"; Man of the Year Oakland Lodge 252 B'Nai Brith 1977-78; 1st black mayor of Oakland CA 1977; Leadership Awd Chinese Amer Citizens Alliance 1979; Marcus-Foster Inst Awd; Outstanding Alumnus of the Oakland Publ School for Law & Govt 1979; appointed State Comprehensive Employment Training Act Bd Gov Edmund G Brown Jr; appointed by Pres Jimmy Carter to US Com on Selection of Fed Judicial Officers for US Court of Patents & Appeals. **MILITARY SERVICE:** AUS 1st sgt 1941-45. **BUSINESS ADDRESS:** Mayor, City of Oakland, 1421 Washington St, Oakland, CA 94612.

WILSON, LUCY R.
Educational administrator. **PERSONAL:** Born Sep 23, 1930, Hartsville, SC; married Harrison; children: April, Jennifer, Richard, John, Harrison, Benjamin. **EDUCATION:** SC St Coll Orangeburg, (cum laude), BS 1951; INUniv Bloomington, MS Guidance & Counseling 1954, EdD Guidance & Counseling 1960. **CAREER:** Darden School of Educ Old Dominion Univ, assoc dean 1975-; TN Mental Health Dept Nashville, dir adult serv 1967-75; Southern Univ Baton Rouge, prof psychology 1964-67; Educ Testing Serv Princeton, asst prog dir guidance serv 1962-67; Claflin Coll Orangeburg, dean of students 1956-62; Albany St Coll GA, dean of women 1954-56; Educ Testing Serv Princeton, consult 1971; HEW, consult 1974-78; Portsmouth Public School VA, consult 1974-80. **ORGANIZATIONS:** Area fol dir Nat March of Dimes 1975-77; chprsn Human Sexuality Task Force 1978-; bd of dir Planning Council of Tidewater 1978-. **HONORS/ACHIEVEMENTS:** Scholar, Danforth Found 1958-59; Whos Who Am Women 1971; 12 publs juried jours. **BUSINESS ADDRESS:** Hampton Blvd, Norfolk, VA 23508.

WILSON, MANNIE L.
Clergyman. **PERSONAL:** Born in O'Brien, FL; married Bettie; children: Ruth C. **EDUCATION:** Roger Williams U; Am Bapt Theol Sem; Benedict Coll, (Hon DD). **CAREER:** Covent Ave Bapt Ch NYC, pastor. **ORGANIZATIONS:** Chmn of bd of council of Chs of City of NY; mem gbd trustees Union Theol Sem; pres bd tlrustees Knickerbocker Hosp; mem esec com So Christian Leadership Conf; preached sermon at White House at request of Pres Richard M Nixon Feb 1, 1970. **HONORS/ACHIEVEMENTS:** Recipient of many honors including Silver Beaver Awd of BSA; Man of Yr Harlem Br YMCA. **BUSINESS ADDRESS:** 420 W 145 St, New York, NY 10031.

WILSON, MARGARET BUSH
Attorney. **PERSONAL:** Born Jan 30, 1919, St Louis, MO; daughter of James T Bush Sr and M Berenice Casey Bush; divorced; children: Robert Edmund III. **EDUCATION:** Talladega Coll, (cum laude) BA 1940; Lincoln Univ Sch of Law, LLB 1943. **CAREER:** St Louis Lawyers for Housing, asst dir 1969-72; Acting Dir St Louis, Model City Prog, dep dir 1968-69; MO Comm Serv & Continuing Educ adminstr 1967-68, Legal Sv Cs Spl MO 1965-67; Asst Atty Gen MO, 1961-62; Pvt Practice St Louis, 1947-65; Rural Electrification Admin Dept Agr St Louis, legal atty 1943-45; Council on Legal Educ Oppor Inst St Louis Univ Sch of Law, instr Civil Procedure 1973; Wilson & Associates, sr partner. **ORGANIZATIONS:** V chmn Land Reutilization Aluth St Louis 1975-77; mem MO Council on Criminal Justice 1972-77; treas NAACP Nat Housing Corp; mem Arts & Educ Council, St Louis; Lawyers Assn; ABA; NBA; MO Bar Assn; Mound City Bar Assn; St Louis Bar Assn; Alpha Kappa Alpha; former dir Monsanto Co; trust Mutual Life Ins Co of NY; chmn natl Bd NAACP 1975-85; chmn bd trust St Augustine's Coll 1986-88; chmn bd dir The Intergroup Corp 1986-87; chmn bd of trustees, Talladega Coll 1988-. **HONORS/ACHIEVEMENTS:** Recipient Bishops Awd Episcopal Diocese MO 1963; Juliette Derricotte Fellow 1939-40; Honorary Degrees: Boston Univ, Washington Univ, Alabama State Univ, St Paul's College, Kenyon College, Smith College, Talladega College. **BUSINESS ADDRESS:** Senior Partner, Wilson & Associates, 4054 Lindell Blvd Ste 100, St Louis, MO 63108.

WILSON, MARGARET F.
Librarian. **PERSONAL:** Born Aug 08, 1932, Monroeville, AL; daughter of Leo Fountain and Carrie Fountain; married Willie C Wilson; children: Monica R Shular, Veronica E McCarthy, Danita Y Wooten, Constance K Harris, Willie C II. **EDUCATION:** AL State Coll, BS 1953; FL A&M Univ, MEd 1969; FL State Univ, MSLS 1972, AMD 1979. **CAREER:** Rosenwald High School, secretary/teacher 1953-55; FL A&M Univ, librarian 1963-. **ORGANIZATIONS:** Mem FL Library Assn 1972-, Special Libraries Assn 1972-, Heroines, Eastern Stars, 1979-, NAACP 1980-, Beta Phi Mu 1980-, Urban League 1980-, Amer Library Assoc 1983-, Amer Coll & Research Library 1983. **HONORS/ACHIEVEMENTS:** Article "Zora Neale Hurston, Author & Folklorist," Negro History Bulletin 1982; "School Media Specialist Undergraduate Library Science Program," Journal Educ Media & Library Science 1986; "Selected Speeches of Florida A&M Univ, pres, 1987," unpublished. **BUSINESS ADDRESS:** University Librarian, Florida A&M University, Box 164, BB Tech Center, Tallahassee, FL 32307.

WILSON, MARKLY
Administrator. **PERSONAL:** Born Mar 30, 1947, Bridgetown, Barbados;married Gonul Mehmet; children: 2 children. **EDUCATION:** St Clair Coll Onterio Canada, attended; Adelphi Univ NY, attended. **CAREER:** Barbados Bd of Tourism, recept/clerk 1967-74; Skinner Sec School, bus englissh teacher 1967-74; Ministry of Civil Aviation, clerical officer 1967; BarbadosBd of Tourism, publ rel officer 1974, slaes rep 1974-78, mgr 1978-. **ORGANIZATIONS:** Mem Photographic Soc Lindfield School 1959-62; pres Christ Church HS Debating Soc 1963; sec Christ Church HS Old Scholars Assoc 1967; mem Toastmasters Intl Bridgetown Chap 1968; mem Graybar Toastmasters Club 1974-; mem bd of dir CTA 1981-82; chmn Assembly of Natl Tourist Office Rep NY 1982,83 memNY Skal Club; dir Travel & Tourism Rsch Assoc; mem bd of adv Tourism Dept New School for Social Rsch. **HONORS/ACHIEVEMENTS:** Awarded Cup for Most Outstanding Athlete of the Year Lindfield School; Victor Ludorum in Athletics Christ Church HS; Tourism Dir of the Year NY Based World Tourism Comm 1984; Awarded Tourist Dir of the Year by the World Travel Awd Comm 1984. **BUSINESS ADDRESS:** US Manager, Barbados Board of Tourism, 800 Second Ave, New York, NY 10017.

WILSON, MARVIN H.
Physician. **PERSONAL:** Born Jul 02, 1938, Ottawa, KS; married Dixie M Carruthers. **EDUCATION:** OttawaUniv KS, BS 1960; HowardUniv Coll of Med Wash DC, MD 1964. **CAREER:** Private Practice, physician 1971-; Stormont-Vale Hosp Med Ctr Topeka, staff; Sabetha Comm Hosp, staff; Topeka St Hosp, cons; Ransom Mel Hosp Ottawa, courtesy staff; USAF Anchorage, physician 1969-71; Tuscon Hosp; resident 1965-69; St Francis Hosp Wichita, intern 1964-65. **ORGANIZATIONS:** Pres Shawnee Brdcstng Co 1974-; partner Vascular Diagnostic Ctr of Topeka 1978-; vice pres Capitol City Credit Union Topeka 1978-; dir Smokey Hill Brdcstng Co 1979-; bd mem UMCA 1972-77; exec com sec St Francis Hosp Topeka 1973; bd of alumni OttawaUniv KS 1975-78; adms comUniv of KS Med Sch 1975-79 & 79;mem governor apptd Employment Sec Adv Council 1975-80; coach flag football 1977-78; mem Black Economic Council 1978-; bd of trustees OttawaUniv KS 1979-;bd mem The Topeka Club 1980; mem Physicians Utilization Review Bd. **HONORS/ACHIEVEMENTS:** Otstndng Stdnt Psychiatry HowardUniv 1964; Otstndng Men of Am 1970. **MILITARY SERVICE:** USAF; maj; 1969-71. **BUSINESS ADDRESS:** Shawnee Broadcasting Inc, KTPK-FM, Topeka, KS 66603.

WILSON, MARY
Singer. **PERSONAL:** Born Mar 06, 1944, Greenville, MS; married Pedro Antonio Ferrer (divorced); children: Turkessa, Pedro, Rafael, Willie. **CAREER:** Supremes singing group, mem 1959-77; intl fame through records on Motown record label & through personal appearances; singer. **HONORS/ACHIEVEMENTS:** Records include, "Inside Out", "Green River", "Save Me", "Love Talk", "You Dance My Heart Around the Stars"; PBS film "Brown Sugar"; musical documentary "The Girl Groups"; author "Dreamgirl, My Life as a Supreme". **BUSINESS ADDRESS:** President, Mary Wilson Enterprises Inc, PO Box 6423, Glendale, CA 91205.

WILSON, MICHAEL
Business executive. **PERSONAL:** Born Sep 19, 1942, Chicago, IL; married Stephanie Pettus; children: Mark Michael. **EDUCATION:** Univ of SD, BS 1966; Bowling Green State Univ, Prof Develop Certification 1966; St Francis Coll, MS 1972; AMA Management Prog, 1982. **CAREER:** Magnavox, indus relations trainee 1969-70, college recruiter 1970-71, compensation analyst 1971-72, prof recruiter 1972-73; TX Instruments, sr tech recruiter 1973-74, personnel admin 1974-75; Western Co of N Amer, group dir employment 1975-77, group dir employee relations 1977-79, corporate dir employment 1979-80, corp dir prof staffing 1980; Armco Natl Prods Systems, mgr personnel & indus relations 1980-83, div human resources mgr 1983; Armco Corporate Human Resources, mgr special projects 1983-, corporate mgr of recruiting & outplacement; Armco Rsch and Tech Ctr, mgr human resources and staff serv 1986-. **ORGANIZATIONS:** Amer Soc of Personnel Admin 1971-79; Employment Mgrs Assn 1976-85; Amer Mgmt Assn 1977-82; College Placement Council 1980-82; Amer Compensation Assn 1981-82; Amer Soc for Training & Develop 1981-82; mem I-75 Group 1985-, Employment Mgrs Assoc 1986-, Black Mgmt Assoc 1986-; lecturer and consultant on employment and outplacement issues. **HONORS/ACHIEVEMENTS:** Former mem MENSA; TV show host "Opportunity Line" 1968-69; Who's Who in Black America 1980; MVP Univ of SD 1966. **MILITARY SERVICE:** AUS pvt E2 6 months; AUSR 1960-68. **BUSINESS ADDRESS:** Corp Mgr of Recruit & Outplac, Armco Inc, 703 Curtis, Middletown, OH 45043.

WILSON, MICHAEL
Physician/podiatrist. **PERSONAL:** Born Jan 26, 1953, Brooklyn, NY; married Valeria Dyer; children: Monica Louise, April Marie, Michelle Alyse. **EDUCATION:** Delaware State Coll, BS 1975; Tuskegee Inst, MS 1979; NY Coll of Podiatric Medicine, DPM 1986. **CAREER:** St Albans NY VA Hosp Extended Care Ctr, resident in podiatric medicine & surgery; Family Health Ctrs Inc Orangeburg SC, podiatrist. **ORGANIZATIONS:** Mem Alpha Phi Alpha Frat Inc 1972-; natl pres Student Natl Podiatric Medical Assoc 1984-85; affiliate mem Amer Soc of Podiatric Medicine 1986-; assoc mem Amer Soc of Podiatric Dermatology 1986-; mem Natl Podiatric Med Assoc. **HONORS/ACHIEVEMENTS:** Published rsch "Dyshidrotic Eczema" Journal of Amer Podiatric Medical Assoc 1985; winner scientific paper competition Amer Soc of Podiatric Medicine NatlConvention Miami Beach FL 1986; publ rsch, "The Two Foot-One Hand Syndrome" Jrnl of the Amer Podiatric Med Assoc. **BUSINESS ADDRESS:** Podiatrist, VAECC, 179th & Linden Blvd, St Albans, NY 11425.

WILSON, MILTON
Educational administrator. **PERSONAL:** Born Jul 20, 1915, Paducah, KY; son of Jess Wilson and Shea Ray Wilson; married Zelda Summers; children: Zelda C Jefferson, Milton James Jr, Rhea Ann Farley. **EDUCATION:** West Virginia State Coll, BS, Business, 1937; Indiana Univ, MCS, Business, 1945, DBA, Business, 1951; Univ of Chicago, attended, 1959-60. **CAREER:** St Phillips Jr Coll, head of business dept, business mgr, 1940-41; Samuel Plato Genl Contractor, chief accountant, 1941-43; Office For Emergency Mgmt, chief cost accountant, 1943-44; Hampton Inst, head of dept of acct, 1944-46; Dillard Univ, head of business dept, 1946-49; Texas Southern Univ, dean school of business, 1949-70; Harvard Univ, visiting professor of business, 1957-58; Private Practice, Houston, cpa, 1952-56; Wilson & Cooke, consultant in field, 1952-, sr partner, 1957-; Gen Acct Office, consultant, 1971-; Howard Univ, dean school of business & public admin, 1970-. **ORGANIZATIONS:** Consultant, City of Houston, TX, 1952-; mem, Dist of Columbia Inst of CPA; mem bd dirs, Amer Assembly of Collegiate Schools of Business; mem, Govt Relations Comm AACSB; chmn, advisor bd of dirs, United Natl Bank; mem, Comm on Minorities of the Amer Acct Assn; consult, Gen Acct, 1971-; mem, Dean's Advisory Council, Indiana Univ, 1979-; pres, Intl Assn of Black Business Educ, 1980; chmn, Deans Comm on Faculty Eval; mem, univ wide advisory comm on Student Recruitment & Articulation; mem steering comm, Center for the Study of Handicapped Children & Youth; mem minority recruitment & equal opportunity comm, Amer Inst of CPA's; memm Beta Gamma Sigma, Minority Doctoral Fellows Comm AICPA; mem bd of dirs, Inst for Amer Business, Howard Health Plan Inc; mem consult panel, Proctor & Gamble Business, Curriculum Devel Program United Negro Coll Fund Inc; mem, The Campaign for Indiana, Indiana Univ Found, 1985; sec/treas, Beta Gamma Sigma, 1984; mem, Commn on Educ for the Business Profession; mem bd of dir, Howard Health Plan Inc, Great Western Financial Corp, Great Western Savings & Loan Assn; advisor to Select Comm on small business; mem, Initial Accreditation Comm; mem, deans's advidory council, Indiana Univ. **HONORS/ACHIEVEMENTS:** Mem, Mu Chap Delta Mu Delta Natl Honor Soc in Business, Theta

Chap Beta Gamma Sigma Hon Business Fraternity, Beta Alpha Psi Hon Acct Fraternity; Achievement Award Natl Assn of Black Accountants Inc, 1974; mem, Acad of Alumni Fellows School of Business Alumni Assn, Indiana Univ, 1978; Dow Jones Award AACSB, 1979; Award from Deans and Dirs Academic Affairs Area Howard Univ, 1980; Medal of Excellence Golden State Minority Found, 1981; recipient of medal of Excellence by the Golden State Minority Found, 1981; The undergrad baccalaureate programs of the School of Business & Public Admin at Howard Univ were accredited 1976 by the AACSB; The grad programs were accredited 1980 by AACSB. **HOME ADDRESS:** 14124 Northgate Dr, Silver Spring, MD 20906. **BUSINESS ADDRESS:** Dean, Howard University, 2600 Sixth St NW Ste 571, Washington, DC 20059.

WILSON, NANCY
Singer, performer. **PERSONAL:** Born Feb 20, 1937, Chillicothe, OH; married Rev Wiley Burton (divorced); children: Samanthia, Sheryl, Kenneth C. **EDUCATION:** Central State Univ, Hon Doct Music. **CAREER:** Began career as singer with local groups then joined Rusty Bryant Band, singer 1956; Midwest & Canada, singing tour 1958; singing independently 1959-; Capitol Records, EMI Records Japan, Nippon Columbia Japan, Interface Japan, Epic Sony/CBS, recording artist; I'll Be A Song, Just To Keep You Satisfied, Forbidden Lover, singer; US, Japan, Europe, Indonea, intl concert tours; Police Story, Hawaii Five-O, FBI, Room 222, performer; TV series Nancy Wilson Show, hostess 1974-75; The Big Score, performed. **ORGANIZATIONS:** Mem Proj Equality, Black Caucus, Pres Council for Min Bus Enterprises, NAACP, SCLC; chmn Oper PUSH, United Negro Coll fund; mem Comm for the KennedyCtr of Performing Arts; contrib performances to many fund raising projs. **HONORS/ACHIEVEMENTS:** Recorded over 50 record albums some of which brought her Grammy Awds; Paul Robeson Awd Urban League; Ruby Ring Awd Johnson & Johnson Co; 2 Emmy Awds; Black Book Awd; Best Female Vocalist Awd Playboy, Downbeat Jazz Polls; Grammy for Best Rhythm & Blues Recording 1964; Emmy for The Nancy Wilson Show. **HOME ADDRESS:** PO Box 128, Pioneer Town, CA 92268.

WILSON, NATARSHA JULIET
Sales representative. **PERSONAL:** Born Oct 22, 1961, Atlanta, GA. **EDUCATION:** Berry Coll, BS 1982. **CAREER:** Continental Distributors, sales consultant; Soft Sheen Products Inc, territorial sales merchandiser; Redken Laboratories Inc, district sales mgr. **HOME ADDRESS:** 2795 Dodson Lee Dr, East Point, GA 30344.

WILSON, NEVIA ANEICE
Physician. **PERSONAL:** Born Feb 02, 1946, New York, NY; divorced; children: Selwya C. **EDUCATION:** Howard Univ, 1963-65; Temple Univ, 1966; Cheyney State Coll, BS 1968; Meharry Med Coll, MD 1973. **CAREER:** School Dist Philadelphia, sub teacher 1968; Univ of Chgo, intern 1973-74; Chicago Lying-In Hosp Univ Chgo, resd, ob/gyn 1974-76; Univ of TN Ctr for the Health Sci Memphis, resd, ob/gyn 1978-79; Private practice, physician; Mercer Univ School of Med Macon, physician, instr, cons, ob/gyn dir min affairs; private practice, ob/gyn 1983-; OH State Univ School of Med, clinical asst prof ob/gyn 1983-. **ORGANIZATIONS:** Mem Delta Sigma Theta Inc; foreign rep Tourist Bur Liberia 1973-74; mem Natl Assoc Rsch & Interns; mem Jr Fellow Amer Coll of Ob & Gyn; mem Natl Assoc of Med Minority Ed; mem Alpha Phi Sigma Natl Scholastic Frat; bd mem Macon-Bibb Cty GA Amer Cancer Soc 1980-83, GA Div Amer Cancer Soc 1981-83; mem adv bd Amer Cancer Soc Columbus OH 1985-; mem advisory council Women Infants & Children 1986-; mem Continental Societies Inc 1986-. **HONORS/ACHIEVEMENTS:** Health professions Scholarship 1970-71; Natl Med Fellowship Scholarship 1971-72 Davidson-Foreman Found Scholarship 1971-72; Med Assoc Prog Inc Readers Digest Intl Fellowship to Liberia; Maternal Child Health Family Planning Fellowship Meharry Med Coll 1973; exec bd mem OH Hunger Task Force 1985-; bd memGrant Medical Center Grant Ob/Gyn Assoc 1986-. **BUSINESS ADDRESS:** Clinical Assistant Professor, Ohio StateUniv Sch of Med, 393 E Town St, Ste 201, Columbus, OH 43215.

WILSON, NORMA JUNE See DAVIS, N. JUNE

WILSON, OLLY W.
Composer, educator. **PERSONAL:** Born Sep 07, 1937, St Louis; married Elouise D; children: Dawn, Kent. **EDUCATION:** Washington U, BM 1959;Univ of IL, MM (Honors) 1960;Univ of IA, PhD 1964. **CAREER:** Univ of CA Berkeley, prof of music; musician with local jazz groups in St Louis; played bass violin with St Louis Philharmonic Orch, St Louis Summer Chambers Players & Cedar Rapids Symphony Orch; educator FL A&M U; educator Oberlin Conservatory of Music Univ of CA Berkeley; author of compositions including chamber works, orchestral works & works for electronic media; conducted num concerts of contemporary music; orchestral compositions performed by major orchestras include Boston, Cleveland, San Francisco, St Louis, Houston, Oakland, Detroit Symphony Orchestras; Univ of CA Berkeley, prof of music, asst chancellor intl affairs. **ORGANIZATIONS:** Consult Natl Endowment for the Arts, Natl Endowment for the Humanities; bd dir Meet the Composer; mem Univ of CA Bekreley Young Musicians Prog; bd of overseers vstg comm Harvard Dept of Music; mem ASCAP, NAACP, Natl Urban League, Alpha Phi Alpha, Sigma Pi Phi. **HONORS/ACHIEVEMENTS:** Recipient Dartmouth Arts Council Prize 1968; awarded Commission, Boston Symphony, Orchestra & Fromm Foundation 1970; awarded Guggenheim Flwslhp 1972-77; commission Oakland Symphony Orch 1973; award Otstandng Achvmnt in Music Composition Am Acad of Arts & Letters & Nat Inst of Arts & Letters 1974; natl Assoc of negro Musicians Awd 1974; Vstg Artist at Amer Acad in Rome 1978; Natl Endowment for Arts Commissions for Composition 1976; Koussevitsky Found Commission 1984; Houston Symphony Fanfare Commission 1986. **BUSINESS ADDRESS:** Professor, Asst Chancellor, Univ of CA Berkeley, 126 California Hall, Berkeley, CA 94701.

WILSON, ORA BROWN
Federal liaison. **PERSONAL:** Born Jul 13, 1937, Austin, TX; children: Evelyn J Jones. **EDUCATION:** Huston-Tillotson Coll, BA 1960; Prairie View A&M Univ, MEd 1979. **CAREER:** Public Schools, teacher 1964-67; Austin Comm Coll, part-time instructor 1977-79; Huston-Tillotson Coll, teacher/adm asst 1967-79, title III coord 1979-. **ORGANIZATIONS:** Mem Austin-Travis Co MH-MR Adv Comm 1981-86; licensed Professional Counselor State of TX 1983; volunteer Austin Hospice 1983-; mem bd dirs Family EldeCare Inc 1986; mem Alpha Kappa Alpha Sor. **HONORS/ACHIEVEMENTS:** Professional Proposal Developer Huston-Tillotson Coll 1979-; Special Service Awd Huston-Tillotson Coll 1981. **HOME ADDRESS:** 1801 Loreto Dr, Austin, TX 78721. **BUSINESS ADDRESS:** Title III Coordinator, Huston-Tillotson College, 1820 East Eighth St, Austin, TX 78702.

WILSON, OTIS CALVIN
Professional athlete. **PERSONAL:** Born Sep 15, 1957, New York, NY; married Melinee Simon; children: Quincy, Chyla. **EDUCATION:** Attended, Louisville. **CAREER:** Chicago Bears, linebacker 1980-. **ORGANIZATIONS:** Involved in Red Cloud Athletic fund & Lake Forest C of C. **HONORS/ACHIEVEMENTS:** Defensive MVP in 1977 Independence Bowl; teams 2nd leading tackler in 1981; 3rd leading tackler in 1983; made 1st pro start in finale of rookie season vs Tampa Bay in place of injured Jerry Muckensturm; NEA Sporting News all-Am at Louisville; defensive MVP in 1977 Independence Bowl; mem 1986 NFL Pro Bowl team. **BUSINESS ADDRESS:** Chicago Bears, Halas Hall, P O Box 500 Sta M Montreal, Lake Forest, IL 60045.

WILSON, PATRICIA A.
Educator. **PERSONAL:** Born Feb 01, 1948, Conway, SC. **EDUCATION:** Univ of MI BA, MA, PhDd candidate. **CAREER:** Univ of MI, asst dir of undergraduate addmissions. **ORGANIZATIONS:** Mem Black Faculty & StaffUniv of MI. **BUSINESS ADDRESS:** 1220 SAB Univ of MI, Ann Arbor, MI 48104.

WILSON, PATRICIA JERVIS
Administrator. **PERSONAL:** Born Apr 18, 1951, Miami, FL; children: Lennard, Patrice. **EDUCATION:** Miami-Dade Community Coll, AA, 1981; Barry Univ, BS, 1983. **CAREER:** Dade Cty Circuit Court, court calendar clerk, 1974-77; Dade Cty Dept of Human Resources, admin officer, 1977-83; Thomas & Doyle Real Estate, Inc, assoc realtor, 1979-; ERA Empress Realty Inc, assoc realtor, 1985-; DHR Directline Newsletter, asst editor, 1983-87; Dade County Dept of Human Resources, dir, admin serv unit, 1987-; Coldwell Bankers, referral agent, 1986-. **ORGANIZATIONS:** Mem, Natl Forum of Black Public Admin, Iota Phi Lambda Sor, SCLC, NAACP; trustee, bd chair, Valley Grove MB Church; Assn of Records Mgr and Admin; Barry Univ, Alumni Assn; Florida Real Estate Council; Natl Assn of Female Exec. **HONORS/ACHIEVEMENTS:** Employee of the Year Dept of Human Resources Office of Admin, 1985; Honored for Outstanding Business Achievement, 1989. **HOME ADDRESS:** 2045 NW 206th Street,, Miami, FL 33055.

WILSON, PRINCE E.
Educator. **PERSONAL:** Born in Asheville, NC; married Veola Kittles; children: Kristal, Sherrill. **EDUCATION:** Talladega Coll, AB 1939;Univ Chicago, AM 1942, PhD 1954. **CAREER:** Bennett Coll, prof hist 1942-45; Morris Brown Coll, prof hist 1945-57; Morris Brown Coll, acad dean 1957-62; Central St Univ, grad dean 1962-66; Atlanta U & Center, exec sec 1966-73; Atlanta Univ, vice pres Academic Affairs 1974-; US Civil Rights Comm, res cons; Amer Lib Assoc OH Emancipation Proclamation Centennial Comm, cons; Miles Coll prog for cirriculum revision, Orgn of Cluster Coll in CT, Clustering Black Colleges AL. **ORGANIZATIONS:** Consortium Devel Tuskegee Inst, Consortium Higher Edn, Tactics, sponsor Govt Affairs Inst Am Assn Higher Edn; Am Historical Assn; Alpha Phi Alpha Frat; Assoc Sltudy Afro-am Life & History, exec comm; Comm Humanikties in GA chmn elect 1975-; Nat Endowment Humanities; NAACP; Central Atlanta Progress Comm bd trustees; Interuniv Urban Coop; United Bd Coll Devel trustee; Fund Appeals Review Bd Atla; Educ Plans & Policies Adv Com, So Regional Educ Bd. **HONORS/ACHIEVEMENTS:** Conference So Grad Sch Coll Sclholar, History, Talladege 1938-39; gen educ bd fellow History, Luniv Chgo; Alpha Kappa Mu Honor Soc; Delta Tau Kappa, Atla Univ Center; Nat Alliance Businessmens Cluster. **BUSINESS ADDRESS:** Atlanta Unvi, 223 Chestnut St SW, Atlanta, GA 30314.

WILSON, RALPH L.
Clergyman, accountant. **PERSONAL:** Born Mar 30, 1934, Tallahassee; son of Perman Wilson and Mamie Roberts Wilson; married Joyce Ann Wright; children: Louis James Arnold, Sonja Libre, Kimberly Lefay, Ralph Larry II. **EDUCATION:** FL A&M Univ, BS 1971; Univ of IL, graduate study; FL A&M, graduate study; FL Conf School Religion Tallahassee, certificate 1969. **CAREER:** FAUM, asst prof acct; N FL Jr Coll, instructor religion; Vocational Tech Inst III FAMU, 1966-69; Lincoln High School, business mgr 1965-66; FAMU, messenger 1955-65; AME Church, conf sec 1965-78; FAMU Religious Activities, pastor 1973-77; AME Church Dist, presiding elder; FL Conf School of Religion, dean. **ORGANIZATIONS:** Mem Mason; mem 4-H leadership 1952; FL Conf Bd of Examiners; Co-advisor NAACP FAMU Chapter 1967-70; dir Methodist Student Union FAMU 1971-; mem United Methodist Church work area on Campus Ministry 1971-78; dir FAMU religous activities 1973-77; Organizer & Chmn Chan Supervisory Com 1976-79; treasurer FL Conf AME Churches Fed Cred Union; mem Ministers Blacks Higher Educ; mem United Campus Ministry; vice-pres NU Eta Lambda. **HONORS/ACHIEVEMENTS:** Outstanding Young Minister FAMU 1970; Outstanding Religious Leader FAMU 1973.

WILSON, RAY F.
Educator. **PERSONAL:** Born Feb 20, 1926, Giddings, TX; married Deanovoy; children: Ray, Jr, Freddie Roy, Mercedes. **EDUCATION:** Huston Tillotson, BS 1950; TX So U, MS 1951;Univ TX, bS 1953; TX So U, JD Law 1973. **CAREER:** Univ TX Austin, res scientist II 1951-53; TX Southern Univ, prof chem 1972-; Houston Comm Coll, part time instr chem 1972-; TX Southern Univ, grad & res adv presently. **ORGANIZATIONS:** Dir SE TX Sect Am Chem Soc L1967-68, 1969-70; counselor SE TX Section Am Soc 1968-69; Phi Alpha Delta Law Frat; Phi Beta Sigma Frat; vice pres 1955 SW Regional Meeting Am Chem Soc; Legislative Couns to US Congresswoman; slupt Pilgram Congregational Ch present; Comm Consult & Adv underprivilege on real estate; hs lect; chmn & Master of Ceremonies 1974 install banquet for Rev Dr Prestis M Moore. **HONORS/ACHIEVEMENTS:** Awd Hustontillotson Coll acad achievement 1953; Beta Kappa Chi Achievement Awds TSU 1965; Faculty Forum Achievement Awd 1969; Faculty Forum Post DoctoralCert of Achievement TSU 1970; 2000 men of achievement 1971; Huston-tillotson Alumni Asso Sci Achievement 1971; Whos Who In The S & SW 1974; Comm Leadersof Am 1973; Human Resource of the US 1974. **MILITARY SERVICE:** USN; petty officer 1944-46.

WILSON, REGINALD
Educator. **PERSONAL:** Born Feb 24, 1927, Detroit, MI; married Dolores Stewart; children: Adam, Kafi. **EDUCATION:** BS 1950; MA 1958; PhD 1971. **CAREER:** Detroit Public School, teacher & psychologist 1950-65, chief psychologist 1960-65; Oakland Univ, asso dir Project Upward Bound 1965-67; Oakland Comm Coll, dean of testing 1967-70; Univ of Detroit, dir of Black Studies & prof of Psychology 1970-71; Wayne Co Comm Coll, pres 1971-; Univ of MI, adj instr psychology 1974-; Research & Educ Serv Inst, chan 1965-70. **ORGANIZATIONS:** Chmn bd Your Heritage House Detroit 1975-; pres MI Assn of Black

Psychologists 1971-; mem MI Psychological Assn 1958-; exec bd mem Am Civil Liberties Union 1973-74; bd mdm New Detroit Inc 1972-; v chmn United Negro Coll Fund Detroit Campaign 1975-; chmn Career Educ Com Nat Urban Coalition 1973-; pres bd dir Detroit Educ TV Sta TWVS 1973-. **HONORS/ACHIEVEMENTS:** Dist Alumnus & Coll of Educ Wayne StUniv 1974 & 1979; Man of Yr Prince Hall Masons 1974; rcgntn Awd City Coun of Detroit 1975; Dist Serv Awd City of Detroit 1976-77; Otstndng Citizen Detroit PTA 1971; Recognition MI Legislature 1971; Phi Delta Kappa; past pres instr Jim Dandy Ski Club. **MILITARY SERVICE:** USAF. **BUSINESS ADDRESS:** 4612 Woodward Ave, Detroit, MI 48201.

WILSON, ROBERT H.
Association executive. **PERSONAL:** Born in Columbia, SC; son of Ellot Wilson and Marrian Wilson; married Elizabeth Wilson. **EDUCATION:** Benedict Co. **CAREER:** Butchers Union of Greater New York & New Jersey Local 174, pres. **ORGANIZATIONS:** Bd trustees Benedict Coll; exec bd Coalition of Black Trade Unionist 1972; adv bd Voc Ed New York City 1969; chmn Politics, Civil Politics & Civil Rights Comm Tst, Calvary Baptist Church; NAACP; Fexec & cncl A Philip Benedict Coll Alumni Assn NAACP; exec cncl A Philip Randolph Ldrs of Tomorrow Schlshp Fund Inc; adv council Benedict Coll Alum Assn Inc No Jersey Chpt; ex bd New York St Coalition of Black Trade Unionist; bd of educ New York City Youth Empl & Training Program; bd of trustees Myopia Intl Rsrch Found Inc; life mem NAACP; commissioner of Plainfield Housing Authority New Jersey; chmn bd of trustees UFCW Local 174 Health and Pension Funds; chmn bd of trustees Commercial Health and Pension Funds; chmn bd of Trustees Local 174 Retail Health and Pension Funds. **HONORS/ACHIEVEMENTS:** Deborah Hosp Found Award 1978; Easter Seal Soc Awd 1981; State of Israel Bonds Awd 1984; ACRMD Humanitarian Awd 1985. **BUSINESS ADDRESS:** President, UFCW Local 174, 120 E 16th St, New York, NY 10003.

WILSON, ROBERT L.
Architect. **PERSONAL:** Born Oct 17, 1934, Tampa, FL; married Mary; children: Kevin, Brian, Bret. **EDUCATION:** Columbia U, BArch 1963, MArch 1969, M Urban Design 1971. **CAREER:** Private Practice, architect 1966-; Charles Luckman Asso Arch, proj arch 1963-66; Emery Roth & Sons, Arch, proj arch 1959-63; Voorhees, Walker, Smith & Haynes, arch designer 1957-59; Robt J Reilly, Arch, arch draftsman 1956-57. **ORGANIZATIONS:** Mem Amer Inst of Arch 1966-; pres CT Soc of Arch 1975; co-founder, dir Natl Organ of Minority Arch 1971-; dir Am Inst of Arch 1975; natl vice pres Am Inst of Arch 1976-77; consult Natl Acad of Scis; consult Natl Endowment for the Arts; lectr Yale U/Hampton Inst/Tuskegee Inst/ Southern U/U of KS/U of TX; Dir City of Stamford Family & Children Serv 1974-75. **HONORS/ACHIEVEMENTS:** Recip Design Awd CT Soc of Arch 1973. **BUSINESS ADDRESS:** The Wilson Group, Inc, 231 E 51st Street, New York, NY 10022.

WILSON, ROBERT LEE MILES
Personnel administrator. **PERSONAL:** Born Mar 29, 1930, Jackson, AL; married Autrey Dickerson; children: Dianne Rhodes, Dan P. **EDUCATION:** Our Lady of the LakeUniv San Antonio TX, BA Pol Sci 1971, MEd 1975; NovaUniv Ft Lauderdale FL, candidate for EdD. **CAREER:** UA Columbia Cablevision of TX Inc, dir personnel & comm relations 1979-; St Philips Coll San Antonio TX, dir student activities 1977-79, instr bus mgmt 1975-77; Manpower Programs City of San Antonio, asst dir 1971-75; AUS Intelligence Command Baltimore MD, counter intelligence officer 1957-70. **ORGANIZATIONS:** Dir adult bus prog Nat Alliance of Bus San Antonio 1979-; mem com San Antonio Personnel & Mgmt Assn 1979-; bd of dirs Jr Coll Student Personnel Assn of TX 1979-; pres United Meth Men St Paul Ch 1960-65; life mem Delta Rho Lambda Chap Alpha Phi Alpha Frat 1976-; pres St Philips Col Chap Am Asn ofUniv Profs 1977-79; pres San Antonio Chap Nat Pan Hellenic Council 1978-. **HONORS/ACHIEVEMENTS:** Recipient of Meritorious Serv Meda AUS 1970; Man of Yr St Paul United Meth Ch 1977-78. **MILITARY SERVICE:** AUS; chief warrant officer; 1947-70. **BUSINESS ADDRESS:** UA Columbia Cablevision of TX, 415 N Main Ave, San Antonio, TX 78205.

WILSON, ROBERT STANLEY
Physician. **PERSONAL:** Born Dec 16, 1923, Bessemer, AL; son of Derry Wilson and Katie Wilson; married Velma Jones. **EDUCATION:** Howard Univ, BS (cum laude) 1950; Howard Univ Coll of Medicine, MD 1955; Fed Interagency Inst, Cert Adv Hosp 1967; Cornell Univ, Develop Prog HADP Hosp Admin/Health Admin 1968. **CAREER:** Wilkes Barre Gen Hosp, intern-gen rotating 1955-56; Vet Admin Hosp, resident internal med 1956-57; Vet Admin Rsch Hosp Chicago, resident rehab med 1958-61; Vet Admin Hosp, chief rehab med 1961-64; VA Central Office Washington DC, chief policy & prog develop 1965; Vet Admin Hosp Tuskegee, chief of staff 1965-69; Vet Admin Hosp, hosp dir 1969-72; Baylor Coll of Med, asso prof 1969-75; WAB Birmingham, clinic asso prof rehab med 1976-; Private Practice, physician 1969-. **ORGANIZATIONS:** Bd certified Natl Bd Med Examiners 1958; bd certified Amer Bd Phys Med Rehab 1963; Cert Hosp Admin VA Inter Agency Inst 1967; bd dirs exec com Birmingham Regional Health Systems Agency 1978-; mem AMA-NMA Jefferson Co Med Soc. **MILITARY SERVICE:** AUS pfc 1943-46; Combat Infantry Badge 1945. **BUSINESS ADDRESS:** 2930 9th Ave, Bessemer, AL 35020.

WILSON, RONALD M.
Economic development policy analyst. **PERSONAL:** Born Feb 19, 1949, Norfolk, VA; son of Guy Wilson and Wilhelmena Luster Wilson; married Katherine Stewart, Aug 30, 1986. **EDUCATION:** Evergreen State Coll, Olympia WA, BA 1984; Baruch College of City Univ of NY, MPA 1985. **CAREER:** Metro Devel Council, Tacoma WA, program mgr, 1975-81; House of Reps, Olympia WA, legislative asst, 1981-84; Natl League of Cities, Washington DC, special asst to exec dir, 1984-85; Commonwealth of Pennsylvania, Harrisburg PA, exec policy specialist, 1985-. **ORGANIZATIONS:** Past local pres, Omega Psi Phi 1969-; mem, Natl Forum for Black Public Administrators 1984-, Intl City Mgmt Assn 1985-88, Amer Soc for Public Admn 1986-88. **HONORS/ACHIEVEMENTS:** Future Leader Award, NW Conf of Black Public Officials, 1982; masters fellowship, Natl Urban Fellows, 1984; author of poetry collection Reflections of Spring, 1987; author of monthly column "Status Quotes," 1989. **MILITARY SERVICE:** US Army, E-6, 1970-75; highest ranking leadership graduate. **BUSINESS ADDRESS:** Executive Policy Specialist, Governor's Policy Office, 506 Finance Bldg, Harrisburg, PA 17120.

WILSON, RONALD RAY
Lawyer. **PERSONAL:** Born Sep 24, 1953, Galveston, TX; children: Erik. **EDUCATION:** Univ TX Plan II Prog, BS 1977; Univ TX Law Sch, JD 1988. **CAREER:** Comm on State Pension Sys, vice chmn; Subcomm on Energy Resources, chmn; Calendars Energy Resources & Finance Inst, com 1976; House of Rep 65th Session, state rep 1976-77, 66th session 1978-80, 67th session 1980-81; chmn Liquor Regulation 70th & 71st Sessions; Fisher Gallagher Perrin & Lewis. **ORGANIZATIONS:** Mem Harris Co Council of Organ 1976-80; liaison com Commissioning of Battleship USS TX 1976; chmn Select Comm on Jr Coll Funding 1980. **HONORS/ACHIEVEMENTS:** The Prairie View A&M Univ Centennial Distinguished Pub Serv Awd Prairie View Business Indus Cluster Grp 1978; Cert of Appreciation Jerusalem Youth & Young Adults 1978; One of Ebony Mag's "50 Future Leaders of Amer.". **BUSINESS ADDRESS:** State Representative, House of Representatives, PO Box 2910, Austin, TX 78769.

WILSON, RUDOLPH GEORGE
Educator. **PERSONAL:** Born Jun 17, 1935, River Rouge, MI; married Sandra Lavernn; children: Trent Duron, James Aaron, Dana Nicole, Amy Lynette. **EDUCATION:** Los Angeles City Coll, AA, BA 1962, MA 1964; Washington Univ, PhD Candidate. **CAREER:** Southern Illinois Univ, assoc prof 1975-; Second Educ, lecturer 1969-72; Claremaont High School, English teacher dept chmn 1964-69, master English teacher 1967-69; Juv Hall Couns 1961-63; Consult Affect Educ Drug Use & Abuse, Moral Educ, Val Educ, Ald Psychology, Methods of Teaching, Adult Educ, Flex Schedule, Humanistic Educ, Motiv of Reluctant Learner, English Educ, Supvr of Student Teachers, Teaching Learn Ctrs, Disc in the Sec Schools, Parent Effect Train, Transact Analy, Devel Teacher Compet; Southern IL Univ, dept chairperson curriculum instructor/prof. **ORGANIZATIONS:** Mem Kappa Alpha Psi; funder, pres Southern IL Adoptive Parents Assn; bd mem Sr Citizens Inc; bd mem SW IL Area Agency on Aging; mem Edwardsville Dist 7 Bd of Educ 1972-; past pres Natl Assn for African Educ 1970-71; pres Faculty Sen, Southern IL Univ 1975-76; elected mem Pres Search Com, SIUE; vice pres Business Affairs Search Com; chmn Search Com for vice pres for student affairs. **HONORS/ACHIEVEMENTS:** Teaching Excellence Award 1971; art pub Harcourt-Brace 1971; "Inner City Teaching Training Program" Office of Educ Journal 1972; Great Teacher Award 1974; Danforth Leadership Award; Danforth Fellow. **MILITARY SERVICE:** USNA, ASA spec four 1957-60. **BUSINESS ADDRESS:** Professor, Southern Ill University, Box 1122, Edwardsville, IL 62026.

WILSON, SANDRA E.
Educator. **PERSONAL:** Born Jun 13, 1944, Abington, PA; daughter of Mr & Mrs James O Walton; married John H Wilson Jr; children: John III, Shawn. **EDUCATION:** Cheyney Univ, BS Educ 1962-66; Montclair State Coll, MS Soc Science 1971; Beaver Coll, MA Humanities w/a concentration in Fine Arts 1984. **CAREER:** Abington School Dist, teacher, 1966-67, 1969-80; teacher, mentally gifted program, 1981-86; Endicott School Dist, teacher 1967-68; Abinton School Dist, teacher, 1986-. **ORGANIZATIONS:** Mem Cheyney Alumni, NAACP, Exec Council for Abington Educ Assn, Natl Conf of Artists, Alpha Kappa Alpha, Amer Assn for Univ Women; program dir Comm Oppor Council 1982-84; region rep PSEA Minority Affairs Comm 1984; state rep PSEA NEA Natl Rep Assembly; pres, Montgomery County Chapter, Black Women's Educ Alliance 1981-85; PA Assn for Gifted Children; state rep Psea NEA Natl Rep Assembly 1986; vice pres Natl Chapter, Black Women's Educ Alliance, 1986; Coordinator youth council NAACP; sec Amer Assoc for Univ Women; teacher testing comm PSEA/Educ Testing Serv 1987; Pres-elect, Natl Chapter, Black Women's Educ Alliance, 1988-; YOuth Consel coordinator of the NAACP, willow Grove Branch; Bethlehem Baptist Church. **HONORS/ACHIEVEMENTS:** Phi Delta Scholarship 1962; Richard Humphrey's Scholarship 1962-66; Student Teacher of the Year Cheyney Univ 1966; Art Award Jenkintown Festival of the Arts 1980; vol serv NAACP Youth Job Conf 1983; Outstanding Serv Dedication Awd Citizen for Progress 1983; Distinctive Serv Award Black Women's Educ Alliance 1985; Black Women's Educ Alliance Leadership, 1986; NAACP Serv to Youth Award, 1988; Optomist of Amer Youth Serv Award, 1989. Poem published in voices of Amer, 1990. **HOME ADDRESS:** 3106 Ori Place, Dresher, PA 19025.

WILSON, SHERMAN ARTHUR
Educator. **PERSONAL:** Born Nov 02, 1931, Crowley, LA; married Cozette Givens; children: Sherman Jr, Sherod Andrew. **EDUCATION:** Leland Clge, BS 1952; Tuskegee Inst, MSEd 1964; Univ of Southwestern LA, Masters30 1966. **CAREER:** Veteran Night School, teacher 1955-57; Carver HS, teacher 1956-65; Ross HS, princ 1965-70; Acadia Parish School Bd, supr sec educ 1970-84, admin of fed prog 1984-. **ORGANIZATIONS:** Pres St Martin Parish Educ Assc 1960-61, LIALO Dist III 1969-70, LA Assc of Supr & Consult 1976-79, Acadia Admin Assc 1980-81; chmn Acadia Parish Computer Steering Comm 1983-; treas PA Fed Credit Union 1970-; alderman City of Crowley Ward 3 Div B 1982. **HONORS/ACHIEVEMENTS:** 32nd Degree Mason CF Ladd Lodge 48 1982; hnry Farmer of Year Crowley High Future Farmers 1974. **MILITARY SERVICE:** AUS pvt 1st class 1952-54. **HOME ADDRESS:** 515 Ross Ave, Crowley, LA 70526. **BUSINESS ADDRESS:** Admin of Federal Programs, Acadia Parish Schl Bd, PO Drawer 309, PO Drawer 309, Crowley, LA 70527.

WILSON, SODONIA MAE
Educator. **PERSONAL:** Born Feb 25, Galveston, TX; daughter of Rev. Jasper Moore and Willie M. (Reed) Moore; married Dr James Wilson, Jr, Mar 24, 1957; children: Demetrius D. **EDUCATION:** French Hosp Sch of Nrsng, RN 1957; San Francisco City Clge, AS 1961; San Francisco State U, BA 1963, MA 1965; CA Schl of Prof Psycholgy, PhD 1973. **CAREER:** French Hosp SF CA, rn 1956-57; Ft Miley VA Hosp SF CA, rn 1957-60; SF Youth Guidance Ctr, cnslr 1966, probation ofc 1967; Office of Economic Opport, head start analyst 1968; SF Redvlpmnt Agcy, soc srv rep 1969; Sequoia Union HS Dist, cnslng coord 1969-72; Contra Costa Clge San Pablo CA, cnslr 1972-73, dir spec prog 1973-83, dir spec prog & serv fin aid officer 1983-85, mgr of instr & tech support serv 1985-86, dir spec progs & serv 1986-. **ORGANIZATIONS:** Mem Assc of CA Comm Clge Admin 1975-; pres CA Comm Clge Extended Opport Prog & Srvs Assc 1977-78; mem SF Unified Schl Dist 1982-; Commsr CA Student Aid Comm 1982-1985; vice pres SF Bd of Educ 1982-; mem Natl Women's Pol Caucus 1981-86, Black Women of Pol Action 1979-, Bay Area Black Women United 1982-84, SF Business & Prof Women's Club 1978-, Women in Higher Educ Assc 1980-84; pres SF Bd of Educ 1986-88; student aid commn l982-85; vice pres S.F. Bd of Educ l982-84. **HONORS/ACHIEVEMENTS:** Evaluation of Coll Counseling Prog publ in ERIC 1972-; Merit of Honor Ernest Kay Hnr General Editor of Intl Biography 1973-; Schlrshp upon grad from HS; Resolution for Disting Serv to Student Aid Commiss 1985; Cert of Merit form CA Community Colls EOPS Assoc 1985; Cert of Apprec for Outstanding Dedicated Serv 1985; Cert of Awd from Marina Middle Schools 1985; Cert of Apprec for Support of Mathematics Engrg & Sci Acheivement 1986; Educational Acad Achievement Awd 1987; Cert of Commendation for natl Assoc Negro Bus & Professional Women's Clubs Inc 1987; Certificate of Award for Ex-

ceptional Achievement 1989; Woman of the Year Award 1989; Education Award for Development of Community Based Education Centers 1989. **HOME ADDRESS:** 540 Darien Way, San Francisco, CA 94127.

WILSON, STANLEY CHARLES
Educator. **PERSONAL:** Born Feb 02, 1947, Los Angeles, CA; son of Ernest Charles Wilson and Eleanol Reid Wilson; married Jacquelyn Patricia Bellard; children: Jendayi Asabi. **EDUCATION:** Chouinard Art School, 1965; California State Polytechnic Univ, Pomona, 1966; California State Univ, Los Angeles, CA, 1967; Otis Art Inst, Los Angeles, CA, BFA 1969, MFA, 1971;. **CAREER:** Jr Art Center, Los Angeles, CA, instructor, 1969-72; Southwestern Coll, Chula Vista, CA, asst professor, 1972-73; Otis Art Inst, Parsons Watts Towers, instructor, 1981; California State Polytechnic Univ, Pomona, CA, prof Visual Art, 1984-, Univ Art Gallery, dir, 1988-. **ORGANIZATIONS:** Gallery curator dir, California State Polytechnic Univ, Pomona, CA, 1975-85; planning & dir, Los Angeles Weave, Los Angeles Olympic Exhibit, 1984 planning bd west coast black artist Exhib, 1976; Brand Art Center, Glendale, CA; bd advisors, Watts Towers Art Center, Los Angeles, CA, 1977-79; bd artists, Brockman Gallery Productions, Los Angeles, CA, 1980-85; bd advisors, Africa Quarter, California State Polytechnic Univ, 1984-85; awards panelist, New Genre Fellowships, Gal Arts Council, Sacaramento, CA, 1989; bd of advisors, Latin Amer Quarter, California Polytechnic Univ, Pomona, CA, 1989. **HONORS/ACHIEVEMENTS:** Works published in Black Artist on Art, Vol #2, Lewis & Waddy 1971, Afro-Amer Artist, Boston Public Library 1973; Nominated Fulbright Fellowship West & East Africa, 1984-85; Intl Reg of Profiles, Cambridge, England, 1981; visiting artist in residence Aberdeen, SD, 1975; Art works in permanent collection of Atlanta Life Insurance Co & Prairie Coll, Texas A&M & Univ Union, California Polytechnic Univ, 1984, 1981, 1977; awarded artist fellowship; Natl Endowment of Art; artist in residence studio museum in Harlem, NY, 1986-87; awarded meritorious & professional promise award by California Polytechnic Univ, Pomona, CA, 1986; catalog, 6 African Amer Artist, California State Univ, Dominquez Hills, CA, 1989; California Art Review, 2nd edition, Chicago, Il, 1989. **HOME ADDRESS:** 3407 Verdugo Rd, Los Angeles, CA 90065.

WILSON, STEPHANIE Y.
Economist. **PERSONAL:** Born Feb 16, 1952, Pittsburgh, PA. **EDUCATION:** Goddard Coll, BA 1973; State Univ of New York at Stonybrook, MA 1975, PhD 1978. **CAREER:** Abt Associates, Washington DC, vice pres & area mgr 1985-86, managing vice pres 1987-. **ORGANIZATIONS:** Pres Natl Economic Assn 1989; mem American Economic Assn; bd of economists Black Enterprise Magazine; big sister Youth At Risk Program, Washington DC. **BUSINESS ADDRESS:** Managing Vice President, Abt Associates Inc, 4250 Connecticut Ave, NW Suite 500, Washington, DC 20008.

WILSON, WADE
Educator. **PERSONAL:** Born Jul 29, 1914, Birmingham, AL; married Naomi; children: Glenn Alan. **EDUCATION:** Cheyney St Coll, BS 1936; PA St U, MS 1937; NY U, DEd 1954. **CAREER:** Cheyney St Coll, pres emeritus 1968-81, dir 1967-68, chmn & prof 1957-67, assoc prof 1952-57, instr 1947-52; Air Corp Tech School, instr 1942-43; TN A&I St Univ, chmn 1940-42; Savannah St Coll, chmn 1939-40; MD St Coll assoc prof 1937-39, 1946-47. **ORGANIZATIONS:** Mem Am Fnd for Negro Aff; bd vstrsUniv of Pittsbugh; bd dir Res for Better Sch; bd trustees Hahnemann Med Coll & Hosp; Liaison NEA Exec Com to Human Rights Coun; bd dir Afro-am Hist & Cultural Museum; bd dir Life of PA Finan Corp; chmn adv coun Urban Ctr Carees Educ Prog; vice pres ConcordvilleRotary Club; chmn DE County Authority 1982-. **HONORS/ACHIEVEMENTS:** Num awards for civic serv; Honoris Causa, Hahnemann Univ, LLD 1969, Lincoln Univ, LLD 1981, Villanova Univ, DPS 1983, City Univ of Los Angeles, Doctor of Letters. **BUSINESS ADDRESS:** President Emeritus, Cheyney University of Penn, Cheyney, PA 19319.

WILSON, WAYNE
Professional athlete. **PERSONAL:** Born Sep 04, 1957, Montgomery, MD. **EDUCATION:** Shepherd, Deg Recreation. **CAREER:** Houston Oilers, football player 1979; New Orleans Saints, halfback 1979-. **HONORS/ACHIEVEMENTS:** Hon Mention All-Amer 1978; led Shepherd to 2 div titles in WV Conf.

WILSON, WESLEY CAMPBELL
Management consultant. **PERSONAL:** Born Nov 29, 1931, Philadelphia, PA; son of Wesley Wilson and Emily Wilson; married Elaine Epps; children: Carl B, Wayne K, Michael K, Eric W. **EDUCATION:** Morgan St U, BS 1954; The Coll of Wm & Mary, MEd 1974, adv cert educ 1978; Ed.D 1986. **CAREER:** The Coll of Wm & Mary in VA, asst to the pres 1976-; C & W & Asso Inc Mgmt Cons, vice pres 1976; The Coll of Wm & Mary, asst to the pres 1974-76; US Arny Aviation, army officer 1954-74. **ORGANIZATIONS:** Chmn Gov's commn Adv Gov of VA on EEO 1975-79; chmn sch bd Newport News VA Pub Sch 1977-; bd of trustees Peninsula United Way 1979-; mem Newport News Dem Com 1974-; exec bd 1st Dist Black Caucus 1975-; pres Alpha Alpha Chap Omega Psi Phi 1975-76. **HONORS/ACHIEVEMENTS:** Recipient Legion of Merit/Vietnamise Cross/Bronze Star/Dist Flying Cross AUS 1964-65; Citizen of Yr, Omega Psi Phi Newport News VA 1977 & 78; Man of Yr, Peninsula Negro Bus & Prof Women 1979; Educ & Politics Strange Bedfellows, Reading in VA 1979. **MILITARY SERVICE:** AUS lt col 1954-74. **BUSINESS ADDRESS:** C & W Associates Inc, 14749 Warwick Blvd, Newport News, VA 23602.

WILSON, WILLIAM E.
Dentist, educator. **PERSONAL:** Born Apr 12, 1937, Lebanon, OH; son of Mary Joseph Fredrick; married Doris Ashworth PhD; children: William, Edwina, Edward II, Chester. **EDUCATION:** TN St Univ, BS 1951; Meharry Dental Coll, DDS 1955. **CAREER:** Miami College, educator; Sociol Inst Malone Coll, educator; Ohio Mobile Dental, dentist/pres. **ORGANIZATIONS:** Pres Canton Health Admin Comm, 1962-63; Canton City School Steering Comm, 1968-69; vice pres, Canton Dental Soc; SCDS; ASPDC; Charter Commr, City of Canton 1967; pres, Canton Black Coalition; US Civil Rights Comm of OH, 1969-80; Canton Welfare Fed Exc Com; mem NAACP; Kiwanian; United Fund Budget Comm, 1960-75; vice pres, Tri Co March of Dimes 1979-80; pres Buckey St Dental Soc 1977-80; chmn Canton United Negro Coll Fund; chmn Campaign for Canton Black United Fund 1978-79; pres Urban League; bd Red Cross; tst Nat Dental Assn; tst OH Dental Assn; pres Children Dental Assn; Amer Dental; Assn Educator of Am Kiwanis; pres Tri Co March of Dimes 1976-77, 1977-; co-chmn, US Gov Urban Project; chmn, Educ Com of US CRC for OH Comm Planning Com City Of Canton Human Relations; Alpha Phi Alpha Fraternity. **HONORS/ACHIEVEMENTS:** Citizen of the Year, 1968; JC of the Year, 1963. **MILITARY SERVICE:** AUS Captain dental corp, 1955-57. **BUSINESS ADDRESS:** Dentist/President, Ohio Mobile Dental, 602-4 Cherry, NE, Canton, OH 44702.

WILSON, WILLIAM HAYWARD
Professional athlete. **PERSONAL:** Born Feb 09, 1956, Bamberg, SC. **EDUCATION:** Univ SC, Bus Adm; Spartanburg Jr Coll. **CAREER:** NY Mets, outfldr 1980-. **HONORS/ACHIEVEMENTS:** Led Mets steals 4th straight yr 1984; set club recd 10 triples; lifetine steal 189, num one all time Met list; All Rookies club 1981; Led Mets 7 offensive categ 1982; Led Nat'l Leag with 638 at bats 1983; named leag All-Starr tm, Rookie Of The Yr, chosen Tidewater's Most Valuable Plyr by tmmts and local fans 1979; All-Star centerfldr 2nd straight yr, picked first tm Nat'l Assoc Class AAA All-Star tm 1980; Good Guy Awd. **BUSINESS ADDRESS:** New York Mets, Shea Stadium, Flushing, NY 11368.

WILSON, WILLIAM JULIUS
Sociologist. **PERSONAL:** Born Dec 20, 1935, Derry Township, PA; son of Esco Wilson (deceased) and Pauline Bracy Wilson; married Beverly Huebner; children: Colleen, Lisa, Carter, Paula. **EDUCATION:** Wilberforce Univ, BA 1958; Bowling Green State Univ, MA 1961; Washington State Univ, PhD 1966. **CAREER:** Univ of MA, asst prof os sociology 1965-69, assoc prof of sociology 1969-71; Univ of Chicago, asso prof of sociology 1972-75, prof of sociology 1975, chmn sociology dept 1981-84, Lucy Flower disting serv prof of sociology 1984-, chmn dept of sociology 1985-87. **ORGANIZATIONS:** Soc sci rsch review com Natl Inst of Mental Health 1972-75; exec com Ethnic Race & Minority Relations Com Intl Sociol Assn 1974-; bd of univ publ Univ Chicago Press 1975-79; sociol visiting com Harvard Coll Bd of Overseers 1975-; chmn rsch adv com Chicago Urban League; bd of dirs Social Sci Rsch Counc 1979-; natl bd A Philip Randolph Inst 1981-; bd of dirs Chicago Urban League 1983-; comm on youth employment progs Natl Rsch Council 1983-; rsch adv comm Proj on the Future of the Welfare State Ford Found 1984-; natl bd Inst for Rsch on Poverty; rsch adv comm Joint Ctr for Political Studies; "Power Racism & Privilege NY" Free Press 1973; "Through Different Eyes" NY Oxford Press 1973; "The Declining Significance of Race" Univ of Chicago Press 1978; bd of dirs Spencer Foundation, George M Pullman Found; mem Carnegie Council on Adolescent Devel, William T Grant Foundation's Commn on Youth and America's Future; pres American Sociological Assn 1989-90; bd of dirs, Center for the Advanced Study of the Behavioral Sciences 1989-95; bd of dirs, Russell Sage Found 1989-94; bd of trustees, Spelman College 1989-95; bd of dirs, Center for Natl Policy 1989-. **HONORS/ACHIEVEMENTS:** Sidney M Spivack Awd Amer Sociol Assn 1977; Dr of Humane Letters Honoris Causa Univ of MA 1982; A Philip Randolph Awd; "The Truly Disadvantaged" Univof Chicago Press 1986; MacArthur Prize Fellow, The John D and Catherine T MacArthur Found 1988; Fellow Amer Acad of Arts and Sciences, 1988; Fellow Amer Assn for the Advancement of Science 1988; The Godkin Lecturer, Harvard Univ 1988; author, The Truly Disadvantaged, Univ of Chicago Press, 1987; Dr of Humane Letters Honoris Causa, Depaul Univ, 1989, Santa Clara Univ, 1988, Long Island Univ, 1986, Loyola Coll of Maryland, 1988, Columbia Coll in Chicago, 1988; Dr of Laws honoris Causa, Mt Holyoke Coll, 1989, Marquette Univ, 1989; Distinguished Alumnus Award, Washington State Univ, 1988; C Wright Mills Award, Society for the Study of Social Problems, 1988; North Central Sociological Assns Scholary Achievement Award, 1988; Washington Monthly's Annual Book Award, 1988. **MILITARY SERVICE:** AUS spec 4 class 1958-60; Meritorious Serv Awd 1960. **BUSINESS ADDRESS:** Distinguished Serv Prof of Soc, Univ of Chicago, 1126 E 59th St, Chicago, IL 60637.

WILSON, WILLIE MAE (NEE CAREY)
Executive director. **PERSONAL:** Born Mar 18, 1942, Birmingham, AL; married William L; children: Bertrand Russell, Pelina. **EDUCATION:** Univ of MN, BA, MA. **CAREER:** St Paul Urban Leag, exec dir 1974-, chief exec offcr 1972-74, adminstr dep; Twin Cities Met Counc, 1971; St Paul Urban Coal, housing & coord 1969-74; Urban Leag, housing dir 1967-69; Econ Dev & Employ St Paul Urban Leag, acting dir 1967; Urban Leag Comm, organizer proj 1966-67; St Paul Bpu Lib, asst librar 1965-66; MN St Comm against Discrim, research clerk 1964. **ORGANIZATIONS:** Chpsn bd of comm St Paul Housing & Redev Auth & Comm 1972-76; chpsn Unit Way Counc of Agcy Dir; vice pres St Paul Ramsey Counc of Agcy Dir; mem bd of dir 1st Nat Bank of St Paul; mem Cit Leag; mem bd of dir Comm Dev Corp; mem Oper 85 Planning Comm; MN Met Org for Displaced Women; mem Counc qof Exec Dir Nat Urban Leag Tri-chmn, St Paul Publ Sch Sec Educ Adv Comm on Desegrat; mem Delta Sigma Theta Sor; Iota Phi Lambda Bus & Prof Womens Sor; Am Soc of Planning Off; Am Soc for Pub Administrn; St Paul Urban Leag; NAACP; vice pres Urban N Non-prof Housing Corp 1973; del St Paul Dem Farm Labor 1974; co-chmn SummitUniv Coalition apptd Joint Planning & Coord Act for Ramsey Co by St Paul Mayor Lawrence Cohen 1973. **HONORS/ACHIEVEMENTS:** Apptd City Planning Comm St Paul Malyor George Latimer 1976; schlrshp Cup, Birmingham Exch Club 1960; Samuel Ullman Schlrshp Awd 1960; Whos Who in Am Coll &Univ 1962-64; Deans List Knoxville Coll 1960-64; Woodrow Wilson Enrichment Schlrshp ColUniv 1964; US Dept Housing & Urban Dev Urban Studies; Flwshp for Grad wkUniv of MN; grad 1st out of 116 stud Ullman HS 1960; grad 5th out of 95 stud Knoxville 1964. **BUSINESS ADDRESS:** 401 Selby V, St Paul, MN 55102.

WILSON, WILSON W.
Retired military officer. **PERSONAL:** Born May 31, 1942, Quachita Parish, LA; son of Phillip Wilson and Christel Jones Wilson; married Georgia Crawford Wilson, Mar 1963; children: Suzzon Nivins Wilson, Ellen M Wilson, Warren M Wilson, Gladys C Wilson. **EDUCATION:** Southern Univ, BA 1964; McNeese State Univ, Roosevelt Univ, Univ KY, graduate study; Western KY Univ, M Public Admin 1975; further studies completed at Northeast State Univ. **CAREER:** AUS, min army off procurement; rep of Vietnam joint US staff for military assistance 1969-70, supply part officer 2nd infantry div Fort Polk LA 1978, 5th AUS headquarters staff off deputy chief of staff for ROTC, equal opportunity officer 5th infantry div Ft Polk LA, deputy comm commander Wertheim Military comm Wertheim Germany. **ORGANIZATIONS:** Office holder Hardin Co KY Branch NAACP 1973-75; Assn of AUS 1965-73; Minority Business Assn Alpha Phi Alpha Fraternity 1963; YMCA 1963; Prince Hall Masonic 1967. **HONORS/ACHIEVEMENTS:** Numerous military decor; rec'd numerous commend for part in educ seminars MW U's; part in lecture series at these same MW Univs; numerous TV appearances disc the role of Black soilder in AUS & Black Military Hist; Legion of Merit Award, US Army, 1989. **MILITARY SERVICE:** AUS lt col 1964-89; numerous military awards.

WILSON-FELDER, CYNTHIA ANN
Music therapist. **PERSONAL:** Born Feb 15, 1951, New Orleans, LA; married Rev Luther B Felder II; children: Chiantia Aniell, Llewon Bene. **EDUCATION:** Dillard Univ, BA

(Magna Cum Laude) 1973; Wayne State Univ, 1978-79; Southern Methodist Univ, MSM 1986. **CAREER:** Rochester City Sch Dist, elem music teacher 1973-75; City of Detroit, dir of music 1976-79; instructor Gospel Music Workshop Amer 1978-87; Grace United Meth Church, dir of music 1985-86; Mid-Cities Montessori Sch, choir dir 1985-; Prof Youth Conserv, instructor 1986-87; Polytechnic United Meth Church, minister of music; Natl Advisory Task Force Songs of Zion; Psychiatric Liason Consultation Services, PA, music therapist/prog dir. **ORGANIZATIONS:** Mem Delta Sigma Theta Inc, NAACP; mem-at-large Perkins Alumni Council SMU. **HONORS/ACHIEVEMENTS:** Outstanding Young Women of Amer 1980; Crusade Scholarship Prog Bd Global Min UMC 1985-86; Who's Who in American Colleges & Univ 1969. **HOME ADDRESS:** 1305 Lovell St, Arlington, TX 76012.

WILSON-SMITH, WILLIE ARRIE
Retired educator. **PERSONAL:** Born Jan 12, 1929, Charlotte, NC; daughter of Booker T Wilson (deceased) and Katie A Wilson Vance; married Jack, Aug 27, 1949. **EDUCATION:** Johnson C Smith Univ, BA 1956; Western Reserve Univ, MEd 1962. **CAREER:** Charlotte Medklenburg School System, tchr 1957-80 retired; JB Iveys Millinery Shoe Repairing, 1951-54; Belks Shoe Repairing, 1954-57. **ORGANIZATIONS:** Mem NEA; life mem NCAE; life mem NCACT; mem Charlotte & Mecklenburg Unit of Assn of Classroom Tchrs; mem Alpha Kappa Alpha Sor Inc; Charlotte Mecklenburg Unit of NCAC; Medklenburg County Dem Womens Club; deputy dir 9th Dist Dem Women 1977-79; democratic candidate Charlotte City Council Dist 1; NC Dem Exec Comm; Womens Forum of NC; Charlotte BPC; Charlotte CRC 1974-82; life mem New Emmanuel Congregational Christian Ch; mem Charlotte Mecklenburg NCCJ; PTA; Girl Scout Adv; Appt Study Comm on Relation Between Professional Employee Assn & Schl Bd 1973-75; apptd NC Adv Comm On Tchr Educ 1974-76; soror of yr AKA 1965; only black elected Mecklenburg Co Dem of Yr 1977; bd of trustees Central Piedmont Comm Coll 1979-87; volunteer office helper Charlotte Business League 1986, 1987; treasurer New Emmanuel Cong UC Chr ist 1989. **HONORS/ACHIEVEMENTS:** Grad Adv Award 1967; Oper Cir 1966; Apprec Award Gamma Delta 1965-74; Apprec Award Alpha Lambda Omega 1965-74; Service/Plaque New Emmanuel Congressional UCC 1987; Service/Plaque Central Piedmount Community Coll 1987. **HOME ADDRESS:** 1822 Grier Ave, Charlotte, NC 28216-5043.

WILTZ, CHARLES J.
Dentist. **PERSONAL:** Born Oct 18, 1934, New Orleans, LA; married Vivianne Carey; children: Charles Jr, Cary E. **EDUCATION:** Xavier Univ, BS 1956; Howard Univ Sch of Dentistry, DDS 1967. **CAREER:** MA Genl Hosp, asst hematlgst 1959-61; Amer Polymer & Chem Corp, jr orgnc chmst 1962-63; Westside VA Hosp, staff dent 1968-69; Mile Sq Hlth Ctr, Chicago staff dentist 1970-71; Private Practice, dentist 1970-. **ORGANIZATIONS:** Consult IL Dental Serv; mem Academy Gen Dentistry, Chicago Dental Soc, IL State Dental Soc, Amer Dental Assn, Natl Dental Assn; Chi Delta Mu; bus mgr 1973 memshp chmn 1974 Lincoln Dental Soc; bd mem Billiken Wrld of Arts & Scis; mem Alpha Phi Alpha. **HONORS/ACHIEVEMENTS:** Awds city & state hs basketball LA 1952; Outstanding Merit of Achvmt VA Hosp 1968; Ten Best Dressed Blk Men 1974-75-76 Chicago. **MILITARY SERVICE:** AUS sp 4 1957-59 1961-62. **BUSINESS ADDRESS:** 8701 S Racine Ave, Chicago, IL 60620.

WILTZ, PHILIP G., JR.
Physician. **PERSONAL:** Born Jun 05, 1930, New Orleans, LA; married Barbara Allen; children: Teresa, Phyllis, Yvette. **EDUCATION:** Savannah State Coll, BS 1952; NY Univ, MA 1956; Howard Univ, MD 1968. **CAREER:** NY Public Schs, teacher 1957-60; Washington DC Public Schs, teacher 1961-64; US Public Health Svcs, internship 1968-69, resident orthopedic surgery 1969-73; Private Practice, physician orthopedic surgery. **ORGANIZATIONS:** Mem Alpha Phi Alpha Frat. **HONORS/ACHIEVEMENTS:** Phi Delta Kappa Hon Soc NY Univ 1957. **MILITARY SERVICE:** AUS corpl 1952-54; USPHS lt comdr 1968-73. **BUSINESS ADDRESS:** 75 Piedmont Ave N E, 504, Atlanta, GA 30303.

WIMBERLY, ANNE STREATY
Educator/musician. **PERSONAL:** Born Jun 10, 1936, Anderson, IN; married Edward Powell Wimberly; children: Michael Haynie. **EDUCATION:** OH State Univ, BS 1957; Boston Univ School of Fine Arts, MMus 1965; GA State Univ, Graduate Certificate, Gerontology 1980; GA State Univ, PhD 1981; School of Theology at Claremont CA, Postdoctoral 1982. **CAREER:** Harwood Girls School, dir of music, 1957-58; Detroit Public Schools, specialist, 1958-64; Boston Univ School of Arts, doctoral teaching fellow 1964-66; Newton Public Schools, music consultant/demo teacher 1967-68; Worcester Public Schools, music consultant/demo teacher 1968-73; Western St Coll, asst prof, music educ, 1973-75; Atlanta Jr Coll, assoc prof, music, 1975-83; School of Theology ORU, assoc prof, Christian Educ. **ORGANIZATIONS:** Advisory comm mem Bethlehem Sr Ctr Atlanta 1978-83; admin asst Summer Series on Aging GA State 1980; bd of dirs, DeKalb Co Council GA 1981-84; mem World Methodist Family Life Comm 1981-85; chairperson Title III Task Force in Improving Instruction Atlanta Jr Coll; coordinator Performing Arts Series & Arts Outreach Program to Elderly; Atlanta coordinator Campus Ministry Program for Faculty and Admins Atlanta Jr Coll. **HONORS/ACHIEVEMENTS:** Elected to Pi Kappa Lambda Music Honoor Soc 1965; Teacher of the Year May St and Upsala St Schools 1973; Elected to Kappa Delta Pi Honor Soc in Educ 1980; Men & Women of Distinction 1980. **HOME ADDRESS:** 537 Michigan Ave Apt B-1, Evanston, IL 60202.

WIMBERLY, EDWARD P.
Educator, clergyman. **PERSONAL:** Born Oct 22, 1943, Philadelphia, PA; son of Edgar V Wimberly and Evelyn P Wimberly; married Anne Streaty, Jun 04, 1966; children: Michael Haynie. **EDUCATION:** Univ of Arizona, BA, 1965; Boston Univ, School of Theology, STB, 1968, STM, 1971; Boston Univ Graduate School, PhD, 1976. **CAREER:** Emmanuel Church, pastor, 1966-68; St Andrews United Methodist Church, pastor, 1968-74; Worcester Council of Churches, urban minister, 1969-72; Solomon Carter Fuller Mental Health Center, pastoral consultant, 1973-75; Interdenominational Theological Center, Atlanta, assoc professor, 1975-83; Oral Roberts Univ, School of Theology, Tulsa, assoc professor, assoc dean, doctoral studies, 1983-85; Garrett Evangelical Theological Seminary, Evanston, IL, assoc professor, pastoral care, 1985-. **ORGANIZATIONS:** Bd of dirs, United Methodist Children's Home, 1977-83, Interdenominational Theological Center, 1982-83; mem, Amer Assn of Pastoral Counselors, 1976-, Amer Assn of Marriage & Family Therapists, 1976-, Friends of Wesley Comm Center, 1983-; mem & bd of dirs, Destination Discovery, 1983-. **HONORS/ACHIEVEMENTS:** Serv award, United Methodist Children's Home, 1983; published, "Pastoral Counseling and Spiritual Values," 1982; co-author with Anne Wimberly, "Liberation and Human Wholeness," 1986; co-author with wife, "One House One Hope," 1989. **BUSINESS ADDRESS:** Assoc Prof, Pastoral Counseling/Psych, 2121 Sheridan Rd Garrett Evangel Theological Seminary, Evanston, IL 60201.

WIMBERLY, JAMES HUDSON
Educator. **PERSONAL:** Born Oct 30, 1935, Macon, GA; married Margie R Simmons; children: James Jr, Marcus, Nathaniel. **EDUCATION:** Paine Clge, BA 1957; Atlanta Univ, MA 1964, AS-5 1969, AS-6 1972. **CAREER:** Federal Prog Macon, evaluator 1965-67; Dudley Hughes Sr High Macon cnslr 1967-69; Dudley Hughes Jr High Macon, princ 1969-72; Bibb cty publ schl, curriculum dir 1972-. **ORGANIZATIONS:** Cnslr William James HS Statesboro 1962-65; tchr cnslr Carver High Dawson 1958-60; pres GA Council for Soc Studies 1983-85; state dir Afro-Am Life & History 1976-; consult Econ Educ 1978-; bd of dirs Broadway Arts Alliance 1980-; delegate at large NCSS 1985-88; supreme recorder/treas Supreme Cncl of Knights of Pythagoras 1985-; adv bd Middle GA Area Plng Commn 1986. **HONORS/ACHIEVEMENTS:** Ldrshp Award Middle GA Historic Soc 1976; Srv Award SCLC 1981, GA Assc of Educ 1984; coord Ethnic Heritage Proj 1983; Social Studies Educator of the Yr 1986; Chairman's Awd State Comm on Life & History of Black Georgians 1986. **MILITARY SERVICE:** AUS sp-4 1959-61; Ldrshp Award 1961. **HOME ADDRESS:** 100 Arlethia Dr, Macon, GA 31211.

WIMBISH, C. BETTE
Assistant secretary. **PERSONAL:** Born in Perry, FL; children: Barbara, Ralph, Terence. **EDUCATION:** FL Agr & Mech U, BS 1944, JD 1967. **CAREER:** FL Dept of Commerce, dep sec 1973-; City of St Petersburg, vice-Mayor 1971-73, city cncl 1969-71; St Petersburg, gen law prac 1968-73; Pub Sch Sys, Hillsborough Co, instr, 1947-52; FL Mem Coll, instr 1945-46. **ORGANIZATIONS:** Mem Leag of Women Voters; mem Am Arbitration Assn; pres Caribe Export Mgmt Co; legal adv Delta Sigma Theta Sor; Nat Cncl of Negro Women; bd dirs Am Civil Libs Union; NAACP; bd mem S Reg Cncl, Task Forces on Sthrn Rural Dev & Ec Dev; FL Bar Assn; FL Gov Bar Assn; vice pres selec com Dem NatCom; consult CRS, Support Serv for US Dept of Justice & Ofc of Contract Compliance Support Serv of US Dept of Labor; guest lectrUniv of S FL; ABA; NBA; past mem Factory-Built Hsng, Adv Cncl; mem Commn on Ed Outreach & Svc; FL Dept of Commerce & Employer-employee Rels Adv Cncl; bd trustees The S Ctr for Intrntl Studies; comiitteewmn at large Dem Nat Com; FL A&M Univ Cncl of Advs. **HONORS/ACHIEVEMENTS:** Recip Outstndng Women of FL, Gov Commn on Status of Women 1975; Outstndng Woman in Gov Award, Orlando FL, Chap of Delta Sigma Theta Sor 1975; FL Women of Dist 1974. **BUSINESS ADDRESS:** 51/ Collins Bldg, Tallahassee, FL 32304.

WIMBUSH, F. BLAIR
Attorney. **PERSONAL:** Born Jul 24, 1955, Halifax County, VA; son of Freddie B. Wimbush and Sue Carol (Lovelace) Wimbush; married Jane (Seay) Wimbush, Aug l981. **EDUCATION:** Univ of Rochester, BA 1977; Univ of Virginia, JD 1980. **CAREER:** Norfolk & Western Railway Co, attorney 1980-83; Norfolk Southern Corp, solicitor 1983-85, asst general solicitor 1985-89, general attorney l989-. **ORGANIZATIONS:** Mem Amer, Natl, VA, Old Dominion and Norfolk-Portsmouth Bar Assocs; mem Assoc of Transportation Practitioners, VA State Bar; mem Roanoke Museum of Fine Arts 1981-,secty 1982-84, vice pres 1984-86, pres 1986-87; mem Legal Aid Soc of Roanoke Valley 1982-86; mem United Way Special Study of Agencies 1983; mem Roanoke Co Transportation Safety Commn 1984-85; mem Roanoke City Arts Commn 1984-87; mem VA Commn for the Arts Area III Adv Panel 1985-87, Area VI Adv. Panel l988-; mem natl bd dirs Big Brothers/Big Sisters of Amer 1986-; mem Western VA Foundation for the Arts and Sciences 1986-87. **HONORS/ACHIEVEMENTS:** Roanoke Valley Chamber of Commerce Leadership Roanoke Valley 1984-85; listed in Outstanding Young Men in Amer 1985; Who's Who in Railroading and Rail Transit 1985. **BUSINESS ADDRESS:** General Attorney, Norfolk Southern Corporation, 3 Commercial Place, Norfolk, VA 23510-2191.

WIMBUSH, GARY LYNN
College administrator. **PERSONAL:** Born Oct 13, 1953, Warren, OH; married Aundra Diana Lewis; children: Brennan Jevon, Kyle Jameson. **EDUCATION:** Oakwood Coll, BA 1975; Andrews Univ, MDiv 1977; Western State Univ Sch of Law, JD 1984. **CAREER:** Allegheny West Conference of SDA, sr clergymen 1975-80; Southeastern CA Conf of SDA, sr Clergyman 1980-84; Oakwood College, dir of admissions & recruitment1984-. **ORGANIZATIONS:** Chaplain (volunteer) Orange County Hospital System 1982-84; business mgr Viewpoint, A Theological Journal 1983-85. **HONORS/ACHIEVEMENTS:** Pastor of the Year Awd Allegheny West Conference of SDA 1979; Outstanding Young Men of Amer 1986. **HOME ADDRESS:** 6001 Matter Place, Huntsville, AL 35810. **BUSINESS ADDRESS:** Dir of Admissions/Recruitment, Oakwood College, Oakwood Road, Huntsville, AL 35896.

WIMP, EDWARD LAWSON
Owner. **PERSONAL:** Born Feb 12, 1942, Chicago, IL. **EDUCATION:** Roosevelt U, BS, BA 1966. **CAREER:** King Terco McDonald's Franchises, owner-operator 1969-; DEW Rlty, vp, broker 1961-69. **ORGANIZATIONS:** Pres Black McDonald's Operator's Assn 1985; bd mem Chicagoland McDonald's Operators Assn 1985; exec bd mem Nat Black McDonald's Operators Assn; bd, chmn Wabash YMCA 1985; bd of Mgrs Met YMCA'S 1985; mem Sigma Pi Phi Frat 1985. **HONORS/ACHIEVEMENTS:** Nat Champion & World Speed Record Hldr, Am Hot Rod Assn 1963; Philanthropic World Community of Islam 1978; Outstndng Young Am US 1979; James H Tilehman Award, YMCA 1979. **MILITARY SERVICE:** USNG Res 1965-71. **BUSINESS ADDRESS:** 449 E 31st St, Chicago, IL 60616.

WINBURN, B. J.
Elected official. **PERSONAL:** Born Oct 12, 1918, Richmond, IN; married Aldene A Guest. **EDUCATION:** Wayne State Univ, mortuary sci 1948; Un Puerto Rico, 1962; Davenport Inst, 1957; Army Adm, 1944. **CAREER:** Peace Corps, adm aide Peru 1962-64, adm off Tehran 1965-67; Defense Dept, prop con Viet Nam 1967-68; Cond C Diggs, congressional aide 1968-71; Lake Co,dr comm dev 1975-77; Yates Twp, mayor-Idlewild 1980-84; Winburn Mem Chapel, dir owner. **ORGANIZATIONS:** Elector 5th Dist MI 1960; mem Natl Conf of Black Mayors 1983-85; mem World Conf of Mayors 1984-85; jury bd Lake Co 1984-85; Region #8 Planning Comm dir econ dev 1976-, dir econ dev corp 1984-. **HONORS/ACHIEVEMENTS:** Dev 1st mortuary lab in S America 1962; book "Mort Practices Overseas" Peace Corps 1967. **MILITARY SERVICE:** AUS t/sgt 27 mths. **BUSINESS ADDRESS:** Dir, Winburn Mem Chapel, 5431 Paradise Path, PO Box 321, Idlewild, MI 49642.

WINBUSH, LEROY
Graphic designer. **PERSONAL:** Born Dec 07, 1915, Memphis, TN; married Frances A Robinson. **CAREER:** Winbush Design & Design Consultant, owner 1985; Goldblatt Bros Dept Stores, art dir 1938-45; Johnson Publs, art dir 1945-55; Ebony Magazine, 1945-54; Winbush Assocs Inc, pres; Art Inst of Chicago, asst prof of visual communications. **ORGANIZATIONS:** Mem Chicago Defender Round Table of Comm; Nat Soc of Communicating Arts; Chicago Artists Guild; exhibit chmn Intl Design Conf; pres Twenty Fathom Skin & Skuba Divers Club; vice pres Our World Underwater; bd of trustees Good Will Indus. **HONORS/ACHIEVEMENTS:** Received Awards form Chicago Soc of Communicating Arts, Soc of Typographic Arts, Interntl; display World Mag Chicago Com of One Hundred.

WINDER, ALFRED M.
Business executive. **EDUCATION:** Allan Hancock Jr Coll, AA 1966; Rockhurst Coll, BS Indust Rel 1969. **CAREER:** KS City Area Transp Authority, mgr equal employment/minority bus enterprise 1978-80; Saudi Public Transit Co, mgr admin/personnel 1980-83; Bi-State Devel Agency, dep gen mgr admin 1983-84; Suburban Bus/West Towns, gen mgr; Gary Public Transp Corp, pres, gen mgr. **ORGANIZATIONS:** Mem COMTO 1983-85; exec bd IN Transp Assoc; policy comm mem Northern IN Reg Plng Commiss; mem Gary IN C of C; exec, v,o, COMTO Natl 1986-; Anderson Boys Club bd mem 1986-. **HONORS/ACHIEVEMENTS:** AAU All Amer Basketball San Francisco CA 1962-63; Jr Coll All Amer Basketball Allan Hancock Coll CA 1975-66; Natl Assoc Intercollegiate Athletics All Amer Basketball MO 1968-69; Outstanding Citizen's Awd Black United Appeal MO 1978; Contractor of the Year Awd MO-KS Contractors Assoc 1978; Volunteer of the Year Boys Clubs of Greater Kansas City 1977-79; Volunteer of the Year Awardee St Louis MO School Dist 1984; Prestigous Presidents Awd 1986. **MILITARY SERVICE:** AUS Canine Corp pfc 1962-64; Presidio of San Francisco. **BUSINESS ADDRESS:** President, General Manager, Gary Public Transporation Corp, 100 West 4th Avenue, Gary, IN 46402.

WINDHAM, REVISH
Counselor. **PERSONAL:** Born May 31, 1940, Panola, AL; son of Ike Windham, Sr and Lillie Green; married Janice Bowman, Sep 22, 1985. **EDUCATION:** Morris Brown Coll, BA 1958-66; Old Dominion Coll, 1967; New York City Coll, 1963; GROW NYC; New York Univ, New York, NY, MPA, 1989. **CAREER:** New York City Dept Soc Srv, caseworker 1968-70; NYS Div for Youth, youth counselor 1970-83; Black Forum Magazine, editor in chief 1978-80; NYS Div for Youth, youth empl voc spec 1984-. **ORGANIZATIONS:** Poetry editor Black Forum Magazine 1975-77; bd mem Black Caucus of DFY Employees Inc 1974-; pres Morris Brown Coll Alumni 1978-82; charter mem MLK, Jr Ctr for Soc Change NY 1978-, Support Grp Minorities in Criminal Justice 1978; Amer Correctional Assn, Natl Criminal Justice Assn, 369th Veteran's Assn, Inc., Phi Beta Sigma Fratenity, Inc. **HONORS/ACHIEVEMENTS:** Poet of Year J Marks Press 1972; Comm Ldr of Amer 1979-80; award of Appreciation Black Caucus of DFY Empl Inc 1984, 1987, Morris Brown Coll Alumni Assn of NY, 1981, Phi Beta Sigma Fraternity, 1987, Natl Library of Poetry, Editor's Choice Award, 1989. **MILITARY SERVICE:** USN petty ofc 3rd class 1964-68. **BUSINESS ADDRESS:** Youth Employment Prog Spec, NYS Div for Youth, 163 W 125th St 14th Fl, New York, NY 10027.

WINEGLASS, HENRY
Pharmacist. **PERSONAL:** Born Sep 11, 1938, Georgetown, SC; son of Johnnie Wineglass and Alberta Drayton Wineglass; married Josephine Arkwright, May 28, 1965; children: Vincent Antonio, Sheri LaDonna. **EDUCATION:** Howard Univ, Washington DC, BS, 1962. **CAREER:** Fantle's Drugstore (formerly Dart Drug Corp), Landover MD, pharmacist, 1965-. **ORGANIZATIONS:** Mem, Amer Pharmaceutical Assn, 1965-; mem, Natl Pharmaceutical Assn, 1965-; mem, DC Pharmaceutical Assn, 1965-; sec, Lambda Chapter, Chi Delta Mu, 1976-; sec/meeting planner, Chi Delta Mu Inc Grand Chapter, 1981-; mem, Maryland Pharmacist Assn, 1982-; mem, Natl Coalition of Black Meeting Planners, 1986-; sergeant-at-arms, Howard Univ Alumni Club, 1988-89. **HONORS/ACHIEVEMENTS:** Certif of Appreciation, Lambda Chapter, Chi Delta Mu, 1973 & 1985; Citation of Appreciation, Dart Drug Prof Services Dept, 1980; Certif of Appreciation, Langdon School PTA, 1981; doctor of pharmacy, Maryland Pharmaceutical Assn, 1982; Man of the Year, Lambda Chapter, Chi Delta Mu, 1986; Certif of Appreciation, Howard Univ Coll of Pharmacy & Pharmacal Sciences, 1987; Grand President's Award, Chi Delta Mu Grand Chapter, 1988; Man of the Year, Plymouth Congregational UCC Men's Club, 1988. **MILITARY SERVICE:** US Army, SP-5, 1961-64; honorable discharge, 1967. **HOME ADDRESS:** 1509 Evarts St, NE, Washington, DC 20018-2017.

WINFIELD, ARNOLD F.
Business executive. **PERSONAL:** Born Sep 29, 1926, Chicago, IL; married Florence Frye MD; children: Michael A, Donna Winfield-Terry. **EDUCATION:** Howard Univ, BS 1949; Wayne State Univ, Grad Study Biochem 1949-51. **CAREER:** Abbott Labs, reg prod mgr 1953-71; Ordinance Corp, chemist 1952-59, biochemist 1969-71; 2nd Ward Evanston, alderman 1963-; Abbott Labs, mgr reg affairs, admin consumer div 1971-83; Winfield & Assoc, consult 1983-; Colfield Foods Inc, corp sec 1983-. **ORGANIZATIONS:** Mem NAACP, Urban League, ACS, Reg Affairs Prof Soc, ASQC, Alpha Phi Alpha, Evanston Neighbors at Work; alderman, City of Evanston, 2nd Ward, 1963-77; bd mem, Victory Gardens Theater, 1979-. **HONORS/ACHIEVEMENTS:** Recip Youth Alliance Scholarship 1943; Jr Chamber of Commerce Man of the Year 1964; Serv Award Ebenezer Church 1966. **MILITARY SERVICE:** AUS pfc 1945-46; WWII Victory Medal. **BUSINESS ADDRESS:** Corporate Secretary, Colfield Foods Inc, 2233 Northwestern Unit H, Waukegan, IL 60085.

WINFIELD, DAVID M.
Professional baseball player. **PERSONAL:** Born Oct 03, 1951, St Paul, MN; married Winfield Found. **EDUCATION:** Univ of MN, Pol Sci. **CAREER:** Vikings, baseball player; ABA Utah Stars, baseball player; Atlanta Hawks, baseball player; San Diego Padre, baseball player; NY Yankees, baseball player. **ORGANIZATIONS:** Sponsor, founder Daivd M Winfield Found to Aid Underpriveleged Youth in Var Comm; mem Oxford Rec Ctr. **HONORS/ACHIEVEMENTS:** Outstanding Coll Athlete Attucks Brooks Amer Legion 1972; Williams Scholarship Univ of MN 1970-71; David Winfield Day Mayor St Paul 1972; Outstanding CommServ Amer Legion; Led NFL in runs (118) 1979; Amer All Star Team 1981-85; 3 Golden Glove Awds.

WINFIELD, ELAYNE HUNT
Counselor. **PERSONAL:** Born Feb 09, 1925, Waco, TX; married Walter Lee; children: Daryl Lynn, Kevin Ren. **EDUCATION:** Paul Quinn Coll, BS 1954;Univ of TX, MA 1975; Cert in Educ Adm 1977. **CAREER:** Ector Co Public Schools, elementary counselor 1977; Special Educ Dept, Odessa TX, elementary counselor; Odessa TX, L/LD res teacher, teacher; Big Springs TX, teacher 1957-58; Midland TX, teacher 1955-56. **ORGANIZATIONS:** Mem, bd of dir NEA 1976-79; TX St Tchr Assn, Hum Rel Com 1974-78; TX Ed Agency Eval Team 1976; adj instrUniv of TX Permian Basin 1975; mem Alpha Kappa Alpha Sor; Am Assn ofUniv Women; Delta Kappa Gamma Soc; 1st vice pres Qepa Kappa Chap 1976-79; Phi Delta Kappa Frat. **HONORS/ACHIEVEMENTS:** Outst Elem Tchrs of Am 1973; Odessa Clsrm Tchrs HR Award 1974; TSTA Hum Rel Award 1974; Who's Who in Am, Child Dev Profl. **BUSINESS ADDRESS:** PO Box 3912, Odessa, TX 79762.

WINFIELD, FLORENCE F.
Physician. **PERSONAL:** Born Sep 21, 1926, Danville, KY; daughter of John G Frye and Margaret Allen Frye; married Arnold F Winfield; children: Michael A, Donna E Terry. **EDUCATION:** Univ of WI, BA 1948; Woman's Medical Coll of PA, MD 1952. **CAREER:** Near North Children's Center, asst med dir 1969-71, med dir 1971-82; Winfield-Moody Health Clinic, acting med dir 1987. **ORGANIZATIONS:** Admissions Comm Northwestern Med School 1970-76; Med Consultant Evanston HS 1972-80; school bd Dist 65; bd Shore Schooll 1974-80, Family Focus 1978-; Mental Health Bd of Evanston 1989. **HONORS/ACHIEVEMENTS:** Appreciation Award North Shore Assn for Retarded 1980; Appreciation Award Family Focus 1985. **HOME ADDRESS:** 862 Forest Ave, Evanston, IL 60202. **BUSINESS ADDRESS:** Pediatrician, Winfield-Moody Health Clinic, 1276 N Clyboum, Chicago, IL 60610.

WINFIELD, GEORGE LEE
Government official. **PERSONAL:** Born Jul 06, 1943, Petersburg, VA; son of Robert Lee Winfield and Bessie Mae Jones Winfield; married Ruby Rosenia Judd Winfield, Aug 26, 1967; children: G. Talawn, Tamory Beck, Takirra Amber. **EDUCATION:** Howard University, Washington, DC, BSCE, 1972, MS, 1975. **CAREER:** Department of Public Works, Baltimore, MD, public works engineer, 1973-84, chief, 1984-86, acting bureau head, 1986-87, bureau head, 1987-88, deputy director, 1988—. **ORGANIZATIONS:** American Public Works Association; Governmental Refuse Collection and Disposal Association; board member, Managerial and Professional Society; American National Standards Committee; US Representative, International Solid Waste Association; American Planning Association; Board of Estimates; Planning Commission; Consultants Evaluation Board; chairman, Change Order Review Committee; EPA Peer Review Task Group; Risk Insurance Committee; president, Lida Lee Tall PTA, 1983-84; board member, Lida Lee Tall Governing Board, 1983-84. **HONORS/ACHIEVEMENTS:** Black Engineer of Year, Career Communications/Mobile, 1989; Afro-American Pacesetter, African-American Heritage Society, 1989. **MILITARY SERVICE:** US Air Force, 1964-68. **BUSINESS ADDRESS:** Baltimore City Department of Public Works, 600 Abel Wolman Municipal Building, Baltimore, MD 21202.

WINFIELD, JAMES EROS
Attorney. **PERSONAL:** Born Mar 20, 1944, Port Gibson, MS; son of Elias Winfield Jr and Gertrude Moran Green; married Linda H Evans, Jun 09, 1968; children: James Jr, Paul, Michael. **EDUCATION:** Morris Brown Coll, BA, 1967; Univ of Mississippi, JD, 1972. **CAREER:** Vicksburg, MS, city prosecutor, 1977-81; Vicksburg-Warren School Dist, atty, 1986-; Winfield & Moran, atty. **ORGANIZATIONS:** Mem, Mississippi State Bar Assn, 1972-; bd mem, WCB & P Credit Union, 1975-85; pres, Morris Brown Coll Natl Alumni Assn, 1977-84; trustee, Morris Brown Coll, 1977-84; sec, treasurer, Warren County Park Commn, 1984-; bd of Governors, Mississippi Trial Lawyers Assn, 1988-; chmn, Vicksburg-Warren Community Health Center, 1987-. **HONORS/ACHIEVEMENTS:** Alumnus of the Year, Morris Brown Coll, 1977. **HOME ADDRESS:** 2043 Sky Farm Ave, Vicksburg, MS 39180. **BUSINESS ADDRESS:** Attorney, 1116 Main St, Vicksburg, MS 39180.

WINFIELD, LINDA FITZGERALD
Educational psychologist. **PERSONAL:** Born Dec 09, 1948, Wilmington, DE; daughter of William L Fitzgerald and Bertha M Fitzgerald; married Kenneth W Winfield; children: Kenneth Jr, David. **EDUCATION:** Univ of DE, BA (with Honors) 1975, MA 1981, PhD 1982. **CAREER:** New Castle County School Dist Consortium, supervisor rsch 1982-85; Educ Testing Servs, NAEP visiting scholar 1985-86; Temple Univ, asst prof of educ 1986-; Temple & Johns Hopkins Univs, Baltimore MD, Center for Study of Effective Schooling for Disadvantaged Students 1986-89. **ORGANIZATIONS:** Mem Amer Educ Rsch Assoc 1977-, Amer Evaluation Assn 1985-, Intl Reading Assn 1986-, Phi Delta Kappa; chmn planning comm Brandywine Professional Assocs 1986-; Amer Psychological Assn. **HONORS/ACHIEVEMENTS:** Woman of the Year in Rsch, Natl Assn of Univ Women 1984; Distinguished Alumni Gallery, Univ of Delaware 1984; "Teachers' Beliefs Towards At-Risk Students in Inner Urban Schools," The Urban Review 1987; "Teachers' Estimates of Content Covered and First Grade Reading Achievement," Elementary School Journal 1987; Rockefeller Foundation Minority Research Fellowship 1987. **BUSINESS ADDRESS:** Principal Research Scientist, Johns Hopkins Univ, 3505 N Charles St, Baltimore, MD 21218.

WINFIELD, SINETTE JOHNSON
Personnel administrator. **PERSONAL:** Born Jul 09, 1940, Buffalo, NY; children: George A. **EDUCATION:** WV St Coll, BA Sociology 1962; Rensselaer Polytechnic Inst, Troy NY, MS Urban Planning 1977. **CAREER:** St Univ of NY Buffalo, prsnl admin 1978-; New York City Dept of Motor Vehicles, sr prsnl admin 1977-78; New York City Div of Budget, budget examiner 1977; New York City Civil Srv, sr fld rep 1973-77; Child & Family Srv, supr soc wrkr 1971-73; ARC Wash DC, family casewrkr 1969-71. **ORGANIZATIONS:** Mem bd of dir Buffalo Urban Leag 1973-74; mem The Girl Friends Inc; mem NAACP; mem Delta Sigma Theta Sor. **BUSINESS ADDRESS:** 106 Crofts Hall, Amherst Campus, Amherst, NY 14260.

WINFIELD, SUSAN REBECCA HOLMES
Judicial officer. **PERSONAL:** Born Jun 13, 1948, East Orange, NJ; children: Jessica L. **EDUCATION:** Univ of Pennsylvania, BA, Math 1970; Boston Coll Law School, JD, 1976. **CAREER:** Law Office of Salim R Shakur, assoc atty 1976-78; Dept of Justice Criminal Div, staff atty 1978-79; Office of the US Attorney, asst US atty 1979-84; District of Columbia Superior Court, assoc judge 1984-. **ORGANIZATIONS:** mem, Asst US Attorney's Assn, 1979-, Shiloh Bapt Church, 1982-, The Barker Found, 1982-, Natl Assn of Women Judges, 1984-,

Amer Judges Assn, 1984-, Women's Bar Assn of DC, 1984-, Black Adoptive Parents, Barker Found, 1983-present; DC Bar, 1978, Massachusetts Bar, 1976. **HONORS/ACHIEVEMENTS:** Special Achievement Award, Office of US Attorney 1983-84. **BUSINESS ADDRESS:** Associate Judge, District of Columbia Courts, 500 Indiana Ave NW, Room 1000, Washington, DC 20001.

WINFIELD, THALIA BEATRICE
Business executive. **PERSONAL:** Born Oct 17, 1924, Surry, VA. **EDUCATION:** VA State Univ, BS 1947. **CAREER:** Storer Coll Harpers Ferry, sec to pres 1947-49; Morehouse Coll Atlanta, sec to bursar 1949-54; Columbia Svgs & Loan Assn, pres 1954-. **ORGANIZATIONS:** Dir Carter Child Devel Ctr 1976-; trustee Citizens for Govtl Rsch Bur 1977-; Christ Presb Church elder 1978-, treas 1984; trustee Presbytery of Milwaukee 1984. **BUSINESS ADDRESS:** President, Columbia Savings & Loan Assn, 2000 W Fond du Lac Ave, Milwaukee, WI 53205.

WINFIELD, WILLIAM T.
Manager. **PERSONAL:** Born Oct 24, 1944, Baton Rouge; married Rita Gurney; children: William Gurney, Darlene Teresa. **EDUCATION:** SU LA St U, Attend. **CAREER:** Homestead Maint & Supplies, gen mgr 1985. **ORGANIZATIONS:** Mem Eden Pk Act Com; exec bd First Ward Voters Leag; Mason. **HONORS/ACHIEVEMENTS:** Hon Dist Atty 1973; listed in Who's Who in Govt 1975-76. **BUSINESS ADDRESS:** 1331 N 39 St, Baton Rouge, LA 70802.

WINFREE, MURRELL H.
Educator. **PERSONAL:** Born Jul 24, 1910, Richmond, VA; married Vivian Thompson. **EDUCATION:** VA St Coll, BA 1937; Columbia U, MA 1947. **CAREER:** Richmond Public School, instr, prin 1940-75. **ORGANIZATIONS:** Mem 1st Bapt Ch 1922-; rep 24th Dem Precinct 1969; past master Hobson Lodge 23 AF&M 1951-52; mem Alpha Phi Alpha 1953-; chmn Organ & Expansion Com BSA 1954; mem exec bd Richmond Area Assn for Retarded Children; 33 deg Mason. **HONORS/ACHIEVEMENTS:** Author "A Curriculum Guide for Teachers of Secondary Spl Ed" 1963; first recip of Bicentennial Medal Awarded by Prince Hall in Free Masonry for Outstndng Serv in Ed in the Comm 1975; recip, plaque Faculty of Randolph Sch 1973; Srv Award, Drill Team 1974. **BUSINESS ADDRESS:** Chandler Sch, 201 E Brookland Pk Blvd, Richmond, VA 23222.

WINFREY, AUDREY THERESA
Nurse specialist - hospital base home care. **PERSONAL:** Born May 21, Houston, TX; children: Jennifer Holland. **EDUCATION:** Grant Hosp, Diploma 1962; DePaul Univ, BSN 1969, MSN 1973; Univ of IL School of PH, MPH 1976. **CAREER:** Michael Reese Med Ctr School of Nursing, instr 1970-73; Univ of IL Coll of Nursing, instr 1973-74; Chicago City Coll, asst prof 1974-77; VA Westside Med Ctr, coord adm amb care nursing 1977-; Veterans Admin Chicago, IL nurse specialist hospital base home care 1987-;. **ORGANIZATIONS:** Public health nurse I Mile Square Health Center 1968-70; nurse adv USAID Vietnam Bureau 1966-68; public health nurse I Chicago Health Dept 1963-66; mem Zeta Phi Beta, Amer Nursing Assoc, Natl League for Nurs, Amer Publ health Assoc, DePaul Univ, Univ of IL Alumni Assoc; Women of Achievement membership committee 1987-; Planned Child Development Center bd member, VIP 1978-; Planning Board of VIA at St. James Catholic Church 1986-. **HONORS/ACHIEVEMENTS:** Civilian Govt Awd; Medal of Achievement; Recog Awd; Volunteer Service Award Plano Child Development Center 1983; CAHMCP Recognition Award Illinois Inst of Technology 1982; published article: "Maximum Amount of Medication: How Much is too Much Injected into One Site" Nursing, July 1985. **MILITARY SERVICE:** US Army Nurse Corp, Reserve, leiutenant colonel, 1973-. **BUSINESS ADDRESS:** Nurse Specialist, Hospital Base Home Care, VA Westside Medical Center, 820 S. Damen, # 1, Chicago, IL 60612.

WINFREY, CHARLES EVERETT
Clergyman, educator. **PERSONAL:** Born Mar 06, 1935, Brighton, TN; married Ernestine. **EDUCATION:** Lane Coll, BA 1961; Vanderbilt U, MDiv 1964;Univ of TN, MS 1974. **CAREER:** Metro Public School Nashville, english teacher 1966-; CME Church Nashville, minister Capers Mem 1965-; Phillips Chapel CME Church Nashville, minister 1964-65; W Jackson Circuit CME, 1961-64; Graham Chapel CME Church Savannah, 1958-61. **ORGANIZATIONS:** Mem Ad Hoc Com; Kappa Alpha Psi; life mem NEA; mem Met Act Commn; TE MNEA; dean of ldrshp training Nashville-Clarksville Dist CME Ch. **HONORS/ACHIEVEMENTS:** Rel Man of Yr, Kappa Alpha Psi 1971; Good Conduct Award, USMC 1954; chaplain St Sen 1973; Hon Sgt-at-Arms, St Leg 1974. **MILITARY SERVICE:** USMC sgt 1950-54. **BUSINESS ADDRESS:** 319 15 Ave N, Nashville, TN.

WINFREY, OPRAH
Talk show hostess/actress/producer. **PERSONAL:** Born 1954, Kosciusko, MS; daughter of Vernon Winfrey and Vernita Lee. **EDUCATION:** TN State Univ, BA Speech & Drama. **CAREER:** WVOL Radio Station, reporter; WTVF-TV Nashville, reporter, news anchorperson; WJZ-TV, news anchorperson 1976-77, host of morning talk show "People Are Talking" 1977-83; appeared in feature films "The Color Purple" 1985, "Native Son" 1986; AM Chgo, talk show hostess "AM Chicago" 1984-85, renamed "The Oprah Winfrey Show" 1985, syndicated 1986-; star and co-executive producer ABC mini-series "The Women of Brewster Place," 1989. **HONORS/ACHIEVEMENTS:** Miss Black Tennessee 1971; Academy Award Nomination & Golden Globe 1986 for "The Color Purple"; Woman of Achievement Award Natl Organization for Women 1986; selected one of Playgirl Magazine's Ten Most Admired Women of 1986; Outstanding Talk/Service Host Awd 1987; Outstanding Talk/Service Program The Oprah Winfrey Show 1987, 1988; Broadcaster of the Year Award, Intl Radio and Television Society, 1988; formed own movie and television production company, Harpo Productions, Inc. in 1986; Harpo Productions assumed ownerhship and all production responsibilities for "The Oprah Winfrey Show" October 1988; bought 88,000 square foot movie and television production studio, renamed Harpo Studios, Nov. 1988. **BUSINESS ADDRESS:** PO Box 909715, Chicago, IL 60690.

WINGATE, LIVINGSTON L.
Judge. **PERSONAL:** Born Sep 02, 1915, Timmonsville, SC; married Mamie Watson; children: Linda E. **EDUCATION:** St John's Univ, 1940-42, 1945-46; St John's Univ Law Sch, LLB 1949. **CAREER:** Criminal Ct NYC, judge 1985; NY Urban Leag, exec dir 1968-74; Citizen's Crusade Against Poverty, asso dir 1966-68; Haryou-Act, exec dir 1965-66; Asso-Comm Teams, exec dir 1963-64; Ed & Labor Commn House of Rep US Congress & Chmn Adam Powell, spl asst, asso chief cnsl 1961-63; Weaver Evans Wingate & Wright, partner 1955-61. **ORGANIZATIONS:** Mem Cooper Ostrin & Devarco 1953-55; sp cnsl Local 1814 ILA 290 & 202 UTSE 1951-61; past mem, pres Assn Am Mgmt Assn 1970-73; pres Estrn Reg Cncl Nat Urban Leag; charter mem One Hundred Black Men; created United Fed of Black Comm Orgns 1970-. **BUSINESS ADDRESS:** New York City Criminal Court, 125-01 Queens Blvd, Kew Gardens, NY 10037.

WINGATE, ROSALEE MARTIN
Educator. **PERSONAL:** Born Mar 10, 1944, New York, NY; daughter of Lucille Martin; children: Deshon, Tishana, Yvette. **EDUCATION:** Univ of TX El Paso, BA 1967; Univ of TX Austin, MSSW, 1970, PhD 1979. **CAREER:** Meridell Achievement Ctr, social worker/administrator 1969-73; Mental Health-Mental Retardation, caseworker 1981-88; Huston-Tillotson Coll, head social sci div 1973-; Outreach Director for Project Reach (AIDS Project,) 1988-; private therapist, 1987-. **ORGANIZATIONS:** Social work certification State of TX 1983-; licensed professional counselor TX Bd of Examiner 1983-; vice pres Black Arts Alliance 1985-; mem, Natl Sorority of Phi Delta Kappa; teacher, Vocation Bible School in Belize, Central Amer, 1985, 1986, 1988-89,. **HONORS/ACHIEVEMENTS:** Leadership Austin Chamber of Commerce 1981; Black Author's Award, 1984, Rishon Lodge #1 Community Serv Award, 1988; H-TC President's Faculty Achievement Award, 1989; John Seabrook Professorship in Social Science, 1989-; author of book "I Like Myself" (children's book,) 1977; article, "Feeling Secure in A Single Parent Home," 1986; article, "Empowering Black Youths: AIDS Prevention," 1989. **HOME ADDRESS:** 2105 Teakwood Dr, Austin, TX 78758. **BUSINESS ADDRESS:** Head Social Science Div, Houston-Tillotson Clg, 1820 E 8th St, Austin, TX 78702.

WINGFIELD, HAROLD LLOYD
Educator. **PERSONAL:** Born Sep 22, 1942, Danville, VA. **EDUCATION:** Fisk Univ, BA, 1970; Univ of Oregon, MA, 1973, PhD, 1982. **CAREER:** Sonoma State Coll, visiting asst professor, 1976-77; Tennessee State Univ, visiting asst professor, 1977-78; Arizona State Univ, visiting instructor, 1979-80; Univ of Rhode Island, visiting asst professor, 1980-84; Kennesaw State Coll, asst professor, 1985-. **ORGANIZATIONS:** Mem, Amer Political Sciecne Assn, Western Political Science Assn, Southern Political Science Assn, Natl Conf of Black Political Scientists, Amer Judicature Soc, NAACP, Amer Civil Liberties Union, Common Cause, People for the Amer Way; exec bd, Georgia Political Science Assn. **HONORS/ACHIEVEMENTS:** "Black Ministers, Roles, Behavior, and Congregation Expectations," (with W Jones, Jr and A Nelson) in Western Journal of Black Studies 1979; "The Historical and Changing Role of the Black Church: The Social and Political Implication," Western Journal of Black Studies, 1988. **MILITARY SERVICE:** AUS, 1967-69. **BUSINESS ADDRESS:** Asst Professsor Political Science, Kennesaw Coll, PO Box 444, Marietta, GA 30061.

WINGO, A. GEORGE
Government administrator. **PERSONAL:** Born Dec 24, 1929, Detroit, MI; married Helen B Glassco; children: Alicia, Scott Andre. **EDUCATION:** OH State Univ, 1954-57; Oakland Univ, 1970-71; Dept of Defense Schools. **CAREER:** Tank Automotive MI, systems analyst 1966-74; Wright Patterson AFB OH, country mgr 1974-75; Eglin AFB OH, foreign military sales mgr 1976; USAF, program mgr. **ORGANIZATIONS:** Announcer Mid OH Assn; mem Citizens Council 1968-72. **HONORS/ACHIEVEMENTS:** Father of the Year New Haven Schools 1973. **MILITARY SERVICE:** AUS corpl 1951-54. **BUSINESS ADDRESS:** Program Manager, Wright-Patterson AFB, ALXS, Dayton, OH 45433.

WINN, JOAN T.
Attorney/real estate broker. **PERSONAL:** Born Apr 11, 1942, Dallas; divorced; children: Elbert Ikoyi. **EDUCATION:** Dillard U, BA 1962; S Meth U, JD 1968. **CAREER:** Durham & Winn Dallas, atty 1968-70; US Dept of Labor & Off of Solicitor Dallas, trial atty 1970-73; Fed Appeals Auth US Civil Srv Commn, asst appeals ofcr 1973-75; Danas Co Ct at Law No 2, judge 1975-78; 191st St Judicial Dist Ct, judge 1978-80; Honeymill & Gunn Realty Co Inc, pres. **ORGANIZATIONS:** Mem St Bar of TX, Am Bar Assn, Dallas Bar Assn, JL Turner Leg Soc, Delta Sigma Theta, The Links Inc Dallas Chapt. **HONORS/ACHIEVEMENTS:** Woman of the Year Zeta Phi Beta 1978; Women Helping Women Awd 1980; Women in Business Iota Phi Lambda 1986. **HOME ADDRESS:** 3912 Weeburn Dr, Dallas, TX 75229.

WINNINGHAM, HERMAN S., JR.
Professional athlete. **PERSONAL:** Born Dec 01, 1961, Orangeburg, SC; son of Rev Herman S Winningham, Sr and Lucille Briz Winningham. **EDUCATION:** South Comm College. **CAREER:** NY Mets, outfielder 1984; Montreal Expos, outfielder 1984-88; Cincinnati Reds, 1988-. **HONORS/ACHIEVEMENTS:** Collected first big-league hit in second game of double-header against Padres with an RBI double against Eric Show; finished the 1984 season going 5 for 10 500 in a three-game series vs the Expos at Olympic Stadium; voted Jr Coll Player of the Yr at DeKalb (GA) South Comm Coll. **HOME ADDRESS:** 1542 Belleville Rd, Orangeburg, SC 29115.

WINSLOW, ALFRED A.
Retired regional director. **PERSONAL:** Born Jun 16, 1923, Gary, IN; married Maude E Franklin. **EDUCATION:** Northwestern Univ, BA 1969; Wilson Jr Coll, AA 1964; Univ of Chicago, 1957-60. **CAREER:** Manpower Devel, various positions 1947-66, Chicago Reg Office, dir personnel div 1966-71, Central Reg, mgr 1971-73; US Postal Serv Office of Employee Relations, reg dir 1973-83 retired; Univ Park Condominium Assn, vice pres bd of dirs. **ORGANIZATIONS:** mem, Indus Relations Assn of Chicago; past chmn Post Ofc Bd of US Civic Serv Examiners in IL & MI; mem Field Museum of Natural Hist, Art Inst of Chgo,Chicago Ed TV Assn; past pres Cheryl Condominium, Evans-Langley Neighborhood Club; former capt, mem drive comm, exec bd, life mem NAACP; mem Amer Legion; life mem Northwestern Alumni Assoc; mem Soc of Personnel Admin. **HONORS/ACHIEVEMENTS:** Pres Citation Pres Comm on Employment of Handicapped 1966; Outstanding Achievement Awd Chicago Assoc of Comm & Indust 1968-70; WGRT Great Guy Awd Comm Activities 1969; Delta Mu Delta Hon Soc; 1st Black Officer. **MILITARY SERVICE:** USCGAF 1943-46.

WINSLOW, CLETA MERIS
Government official. **PERSONAL:** Born Jul 18, 1952, Rockford, IL. **EDUCATION:** TN State Univ, BS Social Work (w/Honors) 1973; Atlanta Univ Sch of Social Work, M 1975. **CAREER:** Vanderbilt Univ Rsch Ctr, psychotherapist social worker's aide 1972-73; Atlanta Univ Sch of Social Work, rsch asst 1974; Morehouse Coll Public Relations, sec 1975-76; Carrie Steele Pitts Children's Home, chief social worker 1976-79; Fulton County Bd of Commissioners, admin asst. **ORGANIZATIONS:** Chair/mem West End Neighborhood Dev Inc 1977-; mem 1979-, natl treas 1985-, Natl Assoc of Neighborhoods; bd mem Christian Council of Church 1983-, West End Parents in Action Youth Anti-Drug 1985-, Joel Chandler Harris Assoc 1986-; mem Brown HS PTSA Magnet Prog and Voc Adv Cncl 1986-; Black Women's Coalition 1987-; Delta Sigma Theta; bd mem Boatrock Family Serv Center; bd Mental Hlth/ Mental Retardation 1985. **HONORS/ACHIEVEMENTS:** Outstanding Young Women of Amer 1981,83; Citywide Neighborhood Serv Awd Urban Life Assoc 1983; Movers and Shakers of Atlanta The Atlanta Constitution Newspaper 1984; APPLE Corps Honor for Outstanding Volunteer Serv in Educ; Awd for Volunteer Serv with Brown HS PTSA 1986; Cert of Appreciation from Fulton Cnty Employees Assn. **HOME ADDRESS:** 1123 Oglethorpe Ave, SW, Atlanta, GA 30310. **BUSINESS ADDRESS:** Administrative Assistant, Fulton Co Bd Off Commsnrs, 165 Central Ave, SW, Atlanta, GA 30303.

WINSLOW, EUGENE
Business executive. **PERSONAL:** Born Nov 17, 1919, Dayton, OH; son of Harry and Lenora; married Bernice Vital; children: Kenneth, Michele Goree, Elesa Commerse. **EDUCATION:** Dillard Univ, BA (cum laude) 1943; Art Inst of Chicago, Post Grad 1946; Inst of Design (IIT), Post Grad 1950. **CAREER:** Impac Inc, creative dir 1959-67; Barickman & Selders, art dir 1967-68; E Winslow & Assc, owner consult 1968-; Afro-Am Publ Co Inc, pres. **ORGANIZATIONS:** Mem DuSable Museum, Southside Comm Art Ctr, Assc for the Study of Afro-Amer Life & History. **HONORS/ACHIEVEMENTS:** Author illustrator "Afro-Americans "76" 1975, Study Prints and other Educ Materials 1964-84; illustrator designer "Great Negroes Past and Present" 1964. **MILITARY SERVICE:** USAAF 1st lt 1943-45. **BUSINESS ADDRESS:** President, Afro-Am Publ Co Inc, 819 S Wabash Ave, Ste 610, Chicago, IL 60605.

WINSLOW, KELLEN BOSWELL
Professional athlete. **PERSONAL:** Born Nov 05, 1957, St Louis, MO; married Katrina McKnight. **EDUCATION:** Attended, Univ MO. **CAREER:** San Diego Chargers, tight end 1979-. **ORGANIZATIONS:** Commissioner Kellen Winslow Flag Football League 1982; mem San Diego Police Dept reserve prog. **HONORS/ACHIEVEMENTS:** Led NFL in receptions 1980-81; AFC Pro Bowl squad fourth yr; earned consensus first team all-Pro honors following 1980, 81 & 82 seasons; off player of game honors in Pro Bowl 1981; most catches by NFL rec since 1981; set Chargers record for most points in game with 30 1981; earned consensus all-Pro & All AFC honors, starting tight end for AFC Pro Bowl squad 1980; consensus All-Amer & played in Liberty Bowl, East-West Shrine game & Senior Bowl 1979; selected on Walter Camp Fdn All-Amer squad 1979.

WINSLOW, REYNOLDS BAKER
Engineering college administrator. **PERSONAL:** Born Jul 25, 1933, Auburn, NY; son of George M. Winslow and Mary Baker Winslow; married Ovetra Russ; children: Reynolds, Danielle Winslow Stamey, Christopher, Ericka. **EDUCATION:** Syracuse Univ, BID 1961. **CAREER:** Thomas L Faul Assoc, Skaneateles NY, industrial designer, 1962-63; Crouse Hinds Co, industrial designer 1963-69; General Elec Co, industrial designer 1969-75; Syracuse Univ, minority engrg program coord 1976-83; Univ MA Coll of Engrg, dir Minority Engineering Program 1983-. **ORGANIZATIONS:** Allocation panel United Way of Central NY 1980-82; bd dirs Univ MA Comm for Collegiate Educ of Blacks & Minorities 1983-; bd dirs MA Pre-Engrg Program 1984-; regional chair Natl Assoc of Minority Engrg Prog Administrators 1985-86; natl treas Natl Assoc of Minority Engrg Program Admin 1986-89. **HONORS/ACHIEVEMENTS:** Achievement Recognition Awd United Way of Central NY 1980; Silver Beaver Awd Boy Scouts of Amer 1980; Serv to Youth Awd YMCA 1980; Syracuse Univ AdvocacyAwd Office of Minority Affairs 1981; Dean's Award 1987. **MILITARY SERVICE:** AUS Artillery sgt 2 yrs; Natl Defense Medal. **BUSINESS ADDRESS:** Dir, Minority Engineering Program, Coll of Engineering, University of Massachusetts, Amherst, MA 01003.

WINSTEAD, VERNON A., SR.
Business exec., attorney, social worker. **PERSONAL:** Born Sep 15, 1937, Roxboro, NC; married Dr Claudette McFarland; children: Vernon Jr, Claudette. **EDUCATION:** NC Central Univ, BS & BA Sociology & Health Educ, LLB 1962; attended John Marshall Law Sch; Univ of IL, MSW 1969, AM 1971, PhD 1972. **CAREER:** NC Dept of Public Aid, social worker 1962-63; NC Redevelopment Comm, relocation & contract spec 1963-65; US Labor Dept of Manpower Admins, manpower devel specialist 1965; serves as consul to various business and labor groups; VAW Indus Inc, labor rel specialist. **ORGANIZATIONS:** Consultant; arbitrator; interdenominationa minister; pres So East Area Kiwanis Intl 1982-84; mem NAACP, Natl Educ Assn, Natl Conf Black Lawyers, NatlBar Assn, Cook Co Bar Assn, SE Kiwanis Businessmen's Orgn; exec bd S Shore Commn; life mem Alpha Phi Alpha Frat; exec bd Joint Negro Appeal; leaderBoy Scout Troop #576; chmn St Philip Neri Parish Sch Bd; rep Region V of Cath Order of Foresters; mem S Shore Ministerial Assn; life mem Male Affiliate Natl Council of Negro Women Inc; cons/servs contractor Intl Corps, Zayre Dept Store, Jewel Food Stores; co-pastor/co-founder Holy Family United in GodFirst Church & Soc Inc; exec co-dir/founder A Connecting Link; exec co-dir/founder McFarland-Winstead Conf Ctr; mem Culver Military Acad Fathers Club; co-owner Winstead Rest & Convalescent Homes Inc Durham NC; mem Bravo Chap Chicago Lyric Opera; ordained Christian Life Interdenominational Minister Univ Life Church; mem Univ Chicago Parents Assn; mem Connecting Link, Morehouse Coll Parents Assoc. **HONORS/ACHIEVEMENTS:** Outstanding Leadership Awd Danforth Found. **BUSINESS ADDRESS:** Labor Relations Specialist, VAW Industries Inc, 7426 So Constance, Chicago, IL 60605.

WINSTON, BONNIE VERONICA
Journalist. **PERSONAL:** Born Mar 13, 1957, Richmond, VA. **EDUCATION:** Northwestern Univ, BSJ 1978. **CAREER:** The Southern Illinoisan, reporting intern 1976; The Richmond VA Times-Dispatch, reporting intern 1977; The Huntington WV Advertiser, reporting intern 1978; TheRichmond VA Times-Dispatch, reporter 1979-86; The Boston MA Globe, state house bureau reporter 1986-. **ORGANIZATIONS:** Minority journalist-in-residence Tougaloo Coll Amer Soc of Newspaper Editors 1980; bd of dir VA Press Women of the Natl Fed of Press Women 1982-86; stringer The NY Times, 1983-86; bd of dir Richmond Chap Sigma Delta Chi, Soc of Professional Journalists 1983-86; plnng comm, staff mem Urban Journalism Workshop 1984-85; mem Natl Assoc of Black Journalists 1985-; free-lance writer Black Engr Mag 1986-. **HONORS/ACHIEVEMENTS:** Natl Achievement Awd Northwestern Univ 1974; Alpha Lambda Delta Hon Soc Northwestern Univ 1975; Outstanding Young Women in Amer Awd 1982; Achievement Awd Miles W Conner Chap VA Union Univ Alumni Assoc 1982; 1st Place VA Press Assoc Writing Contest VPA 1983; United Press Intl Best Writing Awd UPI Virginia 1983. **BUSINESS ADDRESS:** State House Bureau Reporter, The Boston Globe, 135 Morrissey Blvd, Boston, MA 02107.

WINSTON, DENNIS RAY
Educator. **PERSONAL:** Born Feb 28, 1946, Hanover County, VA; son of James L. Winston and Evelyn C. Winston; married Karen D Douglas; children: Kendra, Dennis. **EDUCATION:** Norfolk State Coll, BA (Magna Cum Laude) 1969; Univ of Richmond, M 1979; Virginia Commonwealth Univ 1975-1979. **CAREER:** East End Middle School, art teacher 1971-75; Professional Artist, 1975-; Henderson Middle School, art teacher 1975-86; Richmond Public Schools Humanities Ctr, arts resource teacher 1986-; Studio Faculty Virginia Museum of Fine Arts 1988-. **ORGANIZATIONS:** Mem Smithsonian Assocs, VA Museum of Fine Arts, NAACP, Norfolk State Univ Alumni Assoc, Natl Conference of Artists, Xi Delta Lambda Chap Alpha Phi AlphaFrat Inc; treas Central Region VA Art Educ Assoc 1985-87; mem political action comm Richmond Educ Assoc 1985; mem Phi Delta Kappa; bd of dirs Hand Workshop Crafts Museum; bd of dirs Printmaking Workshop - Richmond, VA; Natl Art Education Assn. **HONORS/ACHIEVEMENTS:** Teacher of the Yr Richmond Public Schools 1984-85; Teacher of the Yr Henderson Middle School 1984-85; Middle School Art Teacher of the Yr 1985, Secondary Art Teacher of the Yr 1985 VA Art Educ Assoc; Purchase Awd African-Amer Museum Dallas 1985; Fitz Turner Comm Awd for Human Rights VA Educ Assoc 1985; Disting Alumni Citation of the Yr Awd Norfolk State Univ 1985; Recognition of Outstanding Achievements in Art Museum of Sci and Industry Chicago 1986; Disting Alumni Citation Natl Assoc for Equal Oppor in Higher Educ 1986; Man of the Yr 1986 VA Chapts of Alpha Phi Alpha Frat Inc, Eastern Region Alpha Phi Alpha Frat Inc; 1986 7th Annual Natl Art Exhibition & Competition Atlanta Life Insurance Co; Award of Honor, Ghent Arts Festival, Norfolk, VA 1987; Educator of the Year, Phi Delta Kappa (VCU Chapter) 1988; Citation of Service, Wilberforce Univ Nat Alumni Assn 1987; selected Virginia Museum's Artists in Education Program 1988; Educator of Year Virginia Commonwelth Univ Phi Delta Kappa 1988. **MILITARY SERVICE:** AUS CW2 officer (USAR) 1969-; Honorable Discharge; Letter of Commendation US Army Europe 1971; Letter of Commendation USAR 1985; Natl Defense Service Medal. **HOME ADDRESS:** 417 Whitaker Dr, Richmond, VA 23235. **BUSINESS ADDRESS:** Arts Resource Teacher, Richmond Public Schools, Arts & Humanities Center, 1000 N Lombardy St, Richmond, VA 23220.

WINSTON, HATTIE
Actress, vocalist. **PERSONAL:** Born 1945, Mississippi. **EDUCATION:** Howard Univ, Graduate. **CAREER:** "Two Gentlemen of Verona", actress; "Scapino", actress. **ORGANIZATIONS:** Mem, The Electric Co.

WINSTON, HENRY
Administrator. **PERSONAL:** Born Apr 02, 1911, Hattisburg, MS; married Mary Fern Pierce. **EDUCATION:** Honoris Causa Acad of Science of the USSR, 1976. **CAREER:** Unemployed Councils Natl, organizer 1931-33; S Negro Youth Congress, fnd & Org 1937-42; Young Communist League, natl admin sec 1938-42; Communist PartyUSA, natl org secr 1947-56, natl vice chrmn 1962-66, natl chrmn 1966-. **ORGANIZATIONS:** Mem Natl Council Amer Soviet Friendship 1970-, Natl Alliance Against Racist & Pol Repression 1972-, Natl Anti-Imperialist Movement in Solidarity with African Liberation 1973-. **HONORS/ACHIEVEMENTS:** Medal Order of the October Revolution USSR 1976, Order of Seku-Bator Mongolia 1981, Order Frndshp of the Peoples USSR 1981, Order of Karl Marx German Democratic Rep 1982; title George Dimitrov Laureate Bulgaria 1982; "Strategy For A Black Agenda" Intl Publ Co Inc 1973; "Class, Race and Blk Lbrtn" Intl Publ Co Inc 1977. **MILITARY SERVICE:** AUS sp-5 1942-45; Cert of Merit AUS 1944. **BUSINESS ADDRESS:** Natl Chairman, Communist Party USA, 235 W 23rd St, New York, NY 10029.

WINSTON, HUBERT
Chemical engineer. **PERSONAL:** Born May 29, 1948, Washington, DC; son of Hubert Winston and Helen Simmons Vincent. **EDUCATION:** NC State Univ, BS 1970, MS 1973, PhD Chem Engineering 1975. **CAREER:** NC State Univ, asst prof dept of chem engrg 1975-77; Exxon Prod Rsch Co, rsch spec 1977-83; NC State Univ, assoc prof, undergrad admin dept ofchem engrg 1983-86; NC State Univ, dir of acad affairs school of engrg 1986-. **ORGANIZATIONS:** Mem Amer Inst of Chem Engrs, Natl Org for the Professional Advancement of Black Chemists & Chem Engrs, Instrument Soc of Amer, Engineer-in-Training with State of NC; mem Amer Assoc for the Advancement of Science. **MILITARY SERVICE:** USAR captain, fin 1974. **BUSINESS ADDRESS:** Dir of Academic Affairs, North Carolina StateUniv, School of Engineering, Raleigh, NC 27695.

WINSTON, JANET E.
Commissioner. **PERSONAL:** Born Feb 07, 1937, Morristown, NJ; married Shurney Winston II; children: Shurney III. **CAREER:** Ernestine Mcclendon Agency NY, professional model 1960-65; Belafonte Enterprises NY, sec/recpt 1960-61; Music Corp of Amer NY, sec to vice pres 1961-62; Johnson Publ Co, Ebony fashion fair model 1963-64; Janet Winston Sch of Charm NJ, owner-dir 1966-70; Winston's Taxi Serv NJ, owner 1970-72; Winston's Family Tree Bar Club, owner 1972-; Morristown Housing Auth, Commr. **ORGANIZATIONS:** Pres Morris Co Urban League Guild NJ 1967-68; bd of dir Morristown Neighborhood House NJ 1972-; vol Morristown Meml Hosp 1975-76. **BUSINESS ADDRESS:** Commissioner, Morristown Housing Authority, 31 Early St, Morristown, NJ 07960.

WINSTON, JEANNE WORLEY
Educator. **PERSONAL:** Born May 27, 1941, Washington, DC; daughter of Gordon Worley Sr and Rosetta Curry Worley; married Reuben Benjamin Winston; children: Kimberly L, Kandace J, Kia L, Reuben B II. **EDUCATION:** District of Columbia Teachers College, BS, in elementary educ, 1963; George Washington Univ, MA, in elementary admin, 1967; Univ of Washington, DC, and Maryland Univ, admin post masters, 1967-78. **CAREER:** District of Columbia Alliance of Black School Educ, research comm mem, 1984-; Dist of Columbia Assn for Supervision and Curriculum Devel, mem, 1986-; District of Columbia Public Schools, teacher, 1963-67, grade chairperson, 1965-67 & 1968-, supervising instructor, 1967-

69, teacher, 1969-76, acting asst principal, 1976-77, staff devel coord, 1977-86, competence based curriculum comm chairperson, 1977-, teacher, 1977-, teacher's convention building coord, 1984-, AIMS coord, 1985-, residential supervisory support program, 1985-, math, science and minorities program, 1985-, mentors program, 1986-; District of Columbia Public Schools, Brightwood Elementary, Washington, DC, asst principal, 1988-. **ORGANIZATIONS:** Delta Sigma Theta, 1960-; PTA, 1963-; mem, Gethsemane Baptist Church, 1966-; NAACP, 1969-; Geo Washington Alumni Assoc, 1970-; Washington Teachers Union, 1970-; Urban League, 1975-; volunteer, Annual Toy Drive at Brookland School, 1980-; Natl Council of Negro Women, 1980; mem, Dist of Columbia Assn for Retarded Citizens, 1980-; District of Columbia Govt Employees Recreation Assn, 1985-; congributor and walk-a-thon participant, March of Dimes, 1985-; volunteer, Dist of Columbia Village, 1986-, District of Columbia Homeless Shelters, 1986-. **HONORS/ACHIEVEMENTS:** Outstanding Teacher, Truesdell Elementary School, 1975; Outstanding Teacher, Research Club of Washington, DC, 1975. **HOME ADDRESS:** 1930 Kearney St NE, Washington, DC 20018.

WINSTON, JOHN H., JR.
Physician. **PERSONAL:** Born Aug 07, 1928, Montgomery, AL; married Bertha Moore; children: Georgette, Dr Joni Winston Canty, Diva Dotson, Terri. **EDUCATION:** AL State Univ, BS 1949; Columbia Univ, MA 1951; Meharry Medical Coll, MD 1956. **ORGANIZATIONS:** Mem Amer Coll of Surgeons, AMA, NMA; bd mem YMCA, Montgomery Co Bd of Education, Red Cross. **MILITARY SERVICE:** USAF 1 yr. **HOME ADDRESS:** 1521 Robert Hatch Dr, Montgomery, AL 36106. **BUSINESS ADDRESS:** 1156 Oak St, Montgomery, AL 36108.

WINSTON, LILLIE CAROLYN
Retired educator. **PERSONAL:** Born Sep 26, 1906, Goodman, MS; daughter of John Morgan and Mattie Morgan; married Julises Winston; children: Lillie Howard, Sandra L Young, Juilses, Johnny Walker. **EDUCATION:** Rust Coll, BS 1958; Univ of KY, Training Program 1966. **CAREER:** Bd of Ed, teacher, retired 1935-71; Bd of Ed, vp; principal Tallahassee Charleston, MS. **ORGANIZATIONS:** Teacher Headstart Program 1966, Art 1968; sub teacher Goodman Elem 1972; coord Holmes Cty Dem Party 1984; pres PTA, Cemetary Club, Goodman Missionary Baptist Church; Retired Teacher's Assn; mem Bd of Education 1980-. **HONORS/ACHIEVEMENTS:** Council of Aging MS Virtute Armis 1980; Outstanding Grandparent Goodman Elem 1981. **HOME ADDRESS:** PO Box 224, Goodman, MS 39079.

WINSTON, MICHAEL R.
Educator. **PERSONAL:** Born May 26, 1941, NYC, NY; married Judith Marianno; children: Lisa M, Cynthia A. **EDUCATION:** Howard Univ, BA 1962; Univ CA, MA 1964, PhD 1974. **CAREER:** Howard Univ, instr 1964-66; Inst Serv Edn, exec asst & assoc dir 1965-66; Educ Asso Inc, educ consult 1966-68; Langston Univ, devel consult 1966-68; Howard Univ, asst dean liberal arts 1968-69, dir res hist dept 1972-73; Moorland-Spingarn Res Ctr, dir 1973-83; Howard Univ, vice pres academic affairs 1983-. **ORGANIZATIONS:** Mem Amer Historical Assn, Assn Study Afro-Amer Life & Hist; co-author "Negro in the US"; co-editor "Dict Amer Negro Biography". **HONORS/ACHIEVEMENTS:** Fellow Woodrow Wilson Intl Ctr for Scholars-Smithsonian Inst 1979-80. **BUSINESS ADDRESS:** Vice Pres Academic Affairs, HowardUniv, Admin Bldg Room 300, Washington, DC 20059.

WINSTON, SHERRY E.
Musician, international negotiator, broker. **PERSONAL:** Born Feb 15, 1947, New York, NY. **EDUCATION:** Howard Univ, BMus 1968. **CAREER:** Flutist with own jazz band, performed at Black Expo with Quincy Jones 1976; performed at Carnegie Hall with flutist Hubert Laws 1977 & 1978; performed at Women's Jazz Festival Lincoln Ctr 1980; The Black News, Channel 5 News, NBC News, 1980; Sherry Winston Enterprises; Club Med Guadeloupe Haiti 1983; The Metropolitan Museum of Art 100 Black Women; recorded as executive producer album "Do It For Love," album was #1 on black radio exclusive chart, #2 on radio & records jazz chart performed at Orlando Jazz Festival 1987 on same bill with Ramsey Lewis Trio; corporate performances, Pepsi Cola, Coca Cola, Equitable Life, Amer Express, Xerox; Sherry Winston Enterprises, owner. **HONORS/ACHIEVEMENTS:** Howard Univ Alumni Awd 1984.

WINTER, DARIA PORTRAY
English instructor. **PERSONAL:** Born Sep 07, 1949, Washington, DC; daughter of Reginald C Winter and Michael Alan Winter; married Reginald C Winter, Oct 06, 1973; children: Michael Alan Winter. **EDUCATION:** Hampton Inst, Hampton, Virginia, B.S., English educ, 1967-72; Univ of Virginia, Charlottesville, Virginia, M.A. English, 1973. **CAREER:** DC Office of Bicentennial Programs, asst to exec dir 1975-76; UDC Coop Extension Program, education specialist 1976-77; Univ of the District of Columbia, instructor of English 1977-. **ORGANIZATIONS:** Alternate Natl Committee woman DC Dem State Comm 1980-87; mem NEA Standing Comm on Higher Educ 1981-87; vice chair DC Democratic State Comm 1984-88; mem Democratic Natl Comm 1984-88; delegate to Democratic Convention 1984, 1988; Modern Language Assn, Coll Language Assn; NCTE; editor, Newsletter Natl Educ Assn Black Caucus 1987-89; mem, Public Defender Service Bd of Trustees, 1988-; mem, District Statehood Commn 1987-. **HONORS/ACHIEVEMENTS:** NEA Delegate to Natl Union of Teachers of England Annual Meeting 1984; Grant to Shakespeare for Gifted and Talented Brent Elementary 1984; Fellowship for Ph.D. Program The George Washington Univ, 1988-; Hester Prynne and Sula Peace Paper delivered CLA, 1988; Review of Afro-Amer Poetics by Houston Baker UDC. **HOME ADDRESS:** 1107 "K" St NE, Washington, DC 20002.

WINTERS, JACQUELINE F.
Government official, business executive. **PERSONAL:** Born Apr 15, 1936, Topeka, KS; daughter of Forrest V. Jackson and Catherine L. Green Jackson; married Marc P; children: Anthony, Marlon, William, Brian Mc Clain. **CAREER:** St of OR, asst to gov 1979-, prog exec 1971-79, field mgr 1969-70; Pacific NW Bell, srv adv 1968-69; Portland Model Cities, vol coord 1967-68. **ORGANIZATIONS:** Bd of dir OR Coll of Ed Found Bd of Trustees; mem st exec srv dir Marion-Polk United Way 1975; vp, pres Salem Br NAACP 1975-78; vice pres Salem HumRights Commn 1975. **HONORS/ACHIEVEMENTS:** Distinguished Srv, City of Salem 1976-77; Presidential Award, Salem NAACP 1977; Outstndng Comm Srv, United Way 1979; Outstndng Ldrshp, OR Woman of Color1979. **BUSINESS ADDRESS:** President, Jackie's Ribs Inc., 3404 Commercial S.E., Salem, OR 97302.

WINTERS, JAMES ROBERT
Elected government official. **PERSONAL:** Born Aug 26, 1937, Pittsburgh, PA; married Diane Herndon; children: Angela, Richard, Lisa. **EDUCATION:** Fayetteville State Univ, BS 1965; Univ of Pgh, grad work sch of social work 1972. **CAREER:** YMCA Prog Ctr Pgh, caseworker 1966-67, prog dir 1967-70, exec dir 1970-72; Old Fort & Kiwanis YMCA Fort Wayne IN, urban dir 1972-78; Wayne Township Trustee's Office, trustee 1978-. **ORGANIZATIONS:** Adv comm Univ Pgh Learn Leisure Prog 1967-70; organized Grambling-Morgan State Football Game (proceeds for Pgh YMCA) 1970; organized Pgh Pirate BaseballWives Benefit for Pgh YMCA Capital Campaign Fund Dr 1971; bd mem IN Criminal Justice Planning 1980; bd mem IN State Black Assembly 1980. **HONORS/ACHIEVEMENTS:** Cert of Commendation Mayor's Office 1979; Hon Commander of the Garrison 1979. **MILITARY SERVICE:** USN radarman 2nd class 1956-60; Good Conduct Medal. **BUSINESS ADDRESS:** Trustee, Wayne Township Trustee's Ofc, 425 S Calhoun St, Fort Wayne, IN 46802.

WINTERS, KENNETH E.
Investment portfolio manager. **PERSONAL:** Born Oct 22, 1959, Gonzales, TX; married Wendy C Gordon. **EDUCATION:** St Mary's Univ, BBA 1985. **CAREER:** United Serv Automobile Assoc, financial reporting analyst 1979-83; USAA Real Estate Co, real estate analyst 1983; real estate asset manager 1983-87; Real Estate Acquisitions 1987-. **ORGANIZATIONS:** Mem Natl Assoc of Business Economists, Amer Finance Assoc; tutor English/Reading San Antonio Literacy Council. **HOME ADDRESS:** 14803 River Vista N, San Antonio, TX 78216. **BUSINESS ADDRESS:** Real Estate Acquisition Rep, USAA Real Estate Company, USAA Bldg, San Antonio, TX 78288.

WINTERS, WENDY GLASGOW
Educational executive. **EDUCATION:** Central CT State Coll, BS (Hon) Elem Ed 1952; Columbia Univ, MS Psych Social Work 1954; Yale Univ, PhD Sociology 1975. **CAREER:** Herrick House Bartlett IL, dir girls unit 1954; Comm Serv Soc NY, family caseworker, intake admin 1954-65; Norwalk Bd of Ed, social worker 1965-68; Univof CT School of Social Work, field instr 1967-80; Atlanta Univ School of Social Work, field instr 1970-71; Yale Univ Child Study Ctr, chief soc worker 1968-75, instr 1968-71, asst prof social work 1971, rsch assoc 1975-82; Univ of CT School of Social Work, assoc prof, asst dean for acad affairs 1975-78; Smith Coll Northampton, adj assoc prof social work, assoc prof sociology & anthropology, dean 1979-84. **ORGANIZATIONS:** Mem Amer Assoc of Univ Women, Amer Orthopsychiatric Assoc, Amer Sociological Assoc, Black Analysis Inc, Natl Assoc of Social Workers, New England Deans Assoc, New England Minority Women Admins; bd of corps Northampton Inst For Savings 1979-; bd dir 1977-80, exec comm 1977-79 Amer Orthopsychiatric Assoc; reg adv council 1975-78; chmn eval sub-comm 1977-78; CT State Dept of Children & Youth Svcs; sub-comm on commun serv grants of adv comm Commiss for Higher Ed 1976-77; bd of dir Leila Day Nurseries 1975-78, Gr New Haven Urban League 1969-71, Norwalk-Wilton Ed Proj 1967-68; juv justice adv comm CT Justice Commiss 1977; ed cultural adv comm Yale Office for Comm Affairs Devel 1974-75; adv comm Norwalk Comm Coll Ed Vocational Resource Ctr 1967-68; adv bd Project Upward Bound Cherry Lawn School 1966-68. **HONORS/ACHIEVEMENTS:** Univ Fellowship Yale Univ 1971-72,73-74; Ethel B Morgan Fellowship 1972-73; Commun Serv Soc Fellowship 1952-54; Univ of CT Rsch Found Grant 1976-78; New England Learning Resource System Fed Reg Resource Ctr Grant 1975-76; CT State Dept of Ed Grant BB103 1972-74; num guest lecturers & consult incl, NY, CT,GA, MA, ME, DC, VA, New Orleand, Toronto; LA State Bd of Ed & Natl Assoc of Social Workers "The Practice of Social Work in Schools" workshop Baton Rouge 1984; taped film on "Excellence" for Gen Elect Corp 1983; Bryn Mawr/Haverford Coll Evaluating team regarding diversity 1983. **BUSINESS ADDRESS:** Dean, Smith College, College Hall 21, Northampton, MA 01063.

WISDOM, DAVID WATTS
Dentist. **PERSONAL:** Born Oct 19, 1929, Bristol, TN; married Blanche C. **EDUCATION:** Howard U, BS 1951; Meharry Med Coll, DDS 1957. **CAREER:** Priv Prac, dental surg. **ORGANIZATIONS:** Mem Kappa Slpha Psi Frat 1949; pres HowardUniv Alumni Assn of Detroit 1968; sec, sgt at arms Wolverine Dental Soc 1969-70. **BUSINESS ADDRESS:** 1440 E Forest Ave, Detroit, MI 48207.

WISE, C. ROGERS
Physician. **PERSONAL:** Born Apr 08, 1930, Ft Worth, TX; married Margaret. **EDUCATION:** Fisk U, BA ;Univ de Lausanne, MD, PhD. **CAREER:** Self-Employed, physician 1985; Meml Hosp, chf, dept anesth 1972-74; DePaul Hosp, 1971-75. **ORGANIZATIONS:** Mem Intrntl Anesth Rsrch Soc; Am Soc Anthes; mem, bd tst Laramie Co Comm Coll 1968; chmn, bd1974; v chmn 1973-77. **BUSINESS ADDRESS:** PO Box 1144, Cheyenne, WY.

WISE, FRANK P.
City manager. **PERSONAL:** Born Oct 28, 1942, Norfolk, VA; divorced; children: Terri Lynn, Dawne Shenette. **EDUCATION:** BBA 1965; MUA 1972. **CAREER:** US Nat Std Assn, resrchst 1966-67; E Airlines, airline coord 1967-68; Prince Geo Co, admin asst 1970-72; City of Cincinnati, mgmt analyst 1972; asst to the city mgr 1973-74; City of Svannah, asst city mgr 1975-78. **ORGANIZATIONS:** Mem Intrntl City Mgmt Assn; chmn Minority Coalition 1972-73; mem Fin Com, Conf Planning Com 1973, 1975; vP at-large 1975-76; vice pres at-large Am Socfor Pub Admin, Conf of Minority Pub Adminstrs Sect on Hum Res Admin 1978-79; Nat Dev Dir Assn. **HONORS/ACHIEVEMENTS:** Citations YMCA 1973; Mayoral Proclamation 1974; ICMA Urban Fellow 1970; publ article "What Role for Minority Asst? the Second Dilemma", Pub Mgmt Mag 1972;"The Art of Srvng Two Masters", Pub Mgmt Mag 1975; "Toward Equity of Results Achieved one approach", pub mgmt mag 1976; award of merit, oH Pks & Rec Assn; Vietnamese, Cross Gallantry 1970; Bronze Star 1970; Staff Medal 1970; Commendation Medal 1969. **MILITARY SERVICE:** AUS capt 1968-72. **BUSINESS ADDRESS:** Assist Dir-Fin/Admin, City of Dallas, 1500 Marilla St #6FN, Dallas, TX 75201.

WISE, HENRY A., JR.
Physician. **PERSONAL:** Born May 26, 1920, Cheriton, VA; married Roberta Morse; children: Henry II, Keith Evan. **EDUCATION:** VA Union Coll, BS; Howard Univ, MS 1949, MD 1954. **CAREER:** Howard Univ, prof 1949-50; Bowie State Tchr Coll, coll physician 1957-; Private Practice, physician. **ORGANIZATIONS:** Trustee Prince George Comm Coll MD 1963-65; bd dir Dr's Hosp MD; mem Comprehensive Health Planning Adv Council Dr's Hosp; mem Alpha Phi Alpha Frat,Natl Med Assn, Assn former Interns & Residents

Howard Univ, Howard Univ Med Alumni Assn, Amer Professional Practice Assn, Amer Acad of Family Practice; Med Chi-of-State of MD; mem Prince George's Co Med Assn; Peer Review Comm Prince George's Genl Hosp sponsor MD Debutantes; mem Glenwood Park Civic Assn;mem Plymouth Congregational Church. **HONORS/ACHIEVEMENTS:** Outstanding Medical Serv to the Communities MD Debutantes; recipient awds from various civic groups for work with the MD Debutantes. **MILITARY SERVICE:** USAF 1st lt WWII. **BUSINESS ADDRESS:** 8901 George Palmer Hwy, Lanham, MD 20801.

WISE, HERBERT ASHBY
Manager. **PERSONAL:** Born Feb 05, 1918, Philadelphia, PA. **EDUCATION:** FranklinUniv Philadelphia, B of Bus Mgmt 1977; NJ Coll of Commerce, bus Admin, Acct 1949. **CAREER:** Housing Auth & Urban Redev Agy; pub housing mgr; Housing Auth & Urban Redev Agy, control clrk, sr acct clrk, mgmt aide, asst housing mgr, sr housing mgr,; Conf Wide Young Adult Flwshp Conf, Methodist Ch, pres Salem United Methodist Ch, asst pastor; tchr, ch sch, HS, jr HS, 40 Yrs. **ORGANIZATIONS:** 1st black chaplain Dept of NJ VFW; cmdr 16th Dist VFW; cmdr Atlantic-Cumberland Co Cncl VFW; adjutant-qtrmstr Dist Co VFW; past post Cmndr, adjutant-qtrmstr Bruce Gibson Post 6594; intrntl treas Frontiers Intrntl; exec sec Atlantic City Frontiers Intrntl. **HONORS/ACHIEVEMENTS:** Medal of Merit NJNG; Two Medals for Faithful Srv NGNG; Medal of Armed Forces Res NJNG; Medal of Asiatic Pacific Campaign; Medal Am Campaign; Medal WW II; Good Conduct Medal; Bronze Stars; plaque Outstndng Military Person NJNG 1962; Outstndng Qrtrmstr Award, 16th Dist 1955-76; Outstndng Adjutant Award 16th Dist 1955-76; citation Mbrshp Dr, Srvs Rendered as St Historian & St Guard in the Dept of NJ VFW 1943-46. **MILITARY SERVICE:** Nat Gd sgt major 1953-72. **BUSINESS ADDRESS:** 2311 Fairmount Ave, Atlantic City, NJ 08401.

WISE, WARREN C.
Chief executive general construction firm. **CAREER:** Wise Construction Co Inc, Dayton OH, chief executive, 1983—. **BUSINESS ADDRESS:** Wise Construction Co Inc, 9 North Edwin C Moses Blvd, Dayton, OH 45407. *

WISE, WILLIE M.
Retired professional athlete. **PERSONAL:** Born Mar 03, 1947, San Francisco; children: Anitra D. **EDUCATION:** Drake U, BS 1969. **CAREER:** Seattle Supersonics, pro bsktbl plyr 1976; Denver Nuggets; Los Angeles Lakers. **ORGANIZATIONS:** ABA Schlrshp Selctn Com. **HONORS/ACHIEVEMENTS:** All Pro 2 Yrs; All Star 3 Yrs; All Def Team 4 of 5 Yrs; most votes All Rookie; most votes All Def Team 1973-74.

WISHAM, CLAYBRON O.
Personnel administrator. **PERSONAL:** Born Dec 28, 1932, Newport, AR; son of Charlie Wisham and Willie Wisham; married Evelyn Bailey, Sep 04, 1964; children: Deshay Appling, Lorna, Karen. **EDUCATION:** Philander Smith Coll, BA, 1954; Univ of AR, MEd, 1963. **CAREER:** Cleveland Elec Illuminating Co, General Mgr, Operations, 1983-present, Personnel Admin, 1974-83, personal admin 1965-70; Cleveland State Univ, affirmative action officer, 1972-74; Union Commerce Bank, asst, vice pres personnel, 1970-72; E End Boy's Club, exec dir 1957-59; AR Bapt Coll, dir of athletics, 1956-59. **ORGANIZATIONS:** Alpha Phi Alpha, 1952-present; Urban League of Cleveland, Blacks in Mgmt, 1970-present (secretary), NAACP, Greater Cleveland Growth Assn, Amer Assn of Blacks in Energy (charter mem); Sr arbitrator, Cleveland Better Business Bureau; Trustee Bd, Center for Rehabilitation Servs, Miles Ahead Inc. **HONORS/ACHIEVEMENTS:** 1st Black Personnel Recruiter in Corp Position, City of Cleveland, OH, 1965-; 1st Black Asst VP, Union Commerce Bank Personnel Dept, 1970; 1st Black Conf Chmn of EEO, Natl Sem for Edison Elec Inst, 1979; 1st Black Operations Mgr at Cleveland Elec Illuminating Co. **MILITARY SERVICE:** AUS pfc 1954-56. **BUSINESS ADDRESS:** General Mgr, Cleveland Electric Illuminating Co, #55 Public Sq, Cleveland, OH 44101.

WITHERSPOON, ANNIE C.
Educator. **PERSONAL:** Born Oct 29, 1928, Bessemer, AL; married Willie George; children: Carole Lejuene, Yvas Lenese. **EDUCATION:** WV St Coll, AB Ed 1951;Univ of AL, MA Elem Ed 1968. **CAREER:** Jefferson County School System Birmingham, teacher social studies 1985; guidance counselor 1956-70; Tuscaloosa, teacher 1952-56. **ORGANIZATIONS:** Mem AL Ed Assn; Nat Ed Assn; Jefferson Co Ed Assn; NEA Minority Involvement Prog; coord Dist VI, Jefferson Co Area Wrkshp for Tchrs; ofcr Jefferson Co Voice of Tchrs for Ed; vp, bd dir New Pilgrim Bapt Ch Day Care Ctr. **HONORS/ACHIEVEMENTS:** Tchr of Yr 1968; AL Soc Studies Fair Dist & St Tchr Recog Awards 1972-74; first black pres of Jefferson Co Assn of Classroom Tchrs. **BUSINESS ADDRESS:** 3200 Old Columbiana Rd, Birmingham, AL 35226.

WITHERSPOON, AUDREY GOODWIN
Educational administrator. **PERSONAL:** Born Aug 19, 1949, Greenwood, SC; daughter of Hudson Goodwin and Essie Goodwin; married Rev Lavern Witherspoon; children: Jacintha Dyan, Andre LaVern. **EDUCATION:** Lander Coll, BA Sociol 1971; Clemson Univ, MEd Admin & Suprv 1977; Vanderbilt Univ, Grad Study Educ Leadership 1982-83. **CAREER:** McCormick Co Sch Dist, teacher 1971-72; GLEAAMS Head Start Program, social worker parent coord 1972-74, educ dir 1974-75; GLEAAMS Human Resource Comm, child develop founder/dir 1975-. **ORGANIZATIONS:** Lander Coll Class Agent 1988-89; Reg vice chairperson Gov Task Force 1979-82; vchairperson bd trustees Greenwood Sch Dist 50 1977-89; Natl Assoc for Ed of Young Children 1975-89; treas Greenwood-96 Br NAACP 1979-89; chart mem, pres 1987 SC Child Develop Providers, Inc 1978-89; Negro Business & Professional Womens Club 1981-87; proj coord for reg V SC Voices for Children 1984-85; mem Gov Riley's Ed Transition Team 1983-84; planning comm Effective Schools SC 1985; mem Mt Moriah Baptist Church; State Advisory Comm on Day Care Regulations, 1987-89. **HONORS/ACHIEVEMENTS:** Female Citizen of the Year 1982; various community awards 1982-89; Distinguished Alumni Award 1989, Lander Coll. **HOME ADDRESS:** 131 Valley Rd, Greenwood, SC 29646.

WITHERSPOON, FREDDA
Educator. **PERSONAL:** Born in Houston, TX; daughter of Fred and Vanita; married Robert L; children: Vanita, Robert, Jr. **EDUCATION:** Bishop Coll, AB; Hughes Business Coll, Grad; Washington Univ, MSW, MAEd; St Louis Univ, MS, PhD. **CAREER:** Social worker; social work supr; HS English teacher; HS guidance counselor; Job Corps Ctr Wmn, guidance cons; Hum Rels & Guidance St Louis Univ & Lincoln Univ, Washington Univ staff mem; Forest Pk Community Coll, prof, ed, guidance cnslr. **ORGANIZATIONS:** Mem Am Assn Univ Prof; AM Assn for Coun Devel; Am Coll Prsnl Assn; Am Assn Jr Coll; MO Assn Jr Coll; Am Assn Univ Wmn; Kappa Delta Pi Hon Frat; mem St Louis Conservatory School for the Arts; mem St Louis Ambassadors; life mem, natl bd NCNW; organizer, 1st pres St Louis Barristers Wives & Natl Barristers Wives; mem Jack & Jill; natl vice pres Top Organizor Ladies Distinction; youth dir W Side Baptist Ch 1959-73; MO st pres NAACP; v chmn Urban League; Heart Assn; Commn Crime & Law Enforcement 1970-76; Mayor's Council on Yth 1970-76; chmn UNCF 1978; chmn UNCF Telethon 1980; gov commn on Pub Safety 1976-77; natl pres Iota Phi & Lambda Sor 1977-81; St Louis City Manpower Commin; Childrens Srvs; Girl Scouts; organizer Continental Societies St Louis, UNCF Inter-Alumni Council; pres & organizer Coalition of 100 B lack Women Metro St Louis; Mo NEA Pi Lambda Theta, Phi Delta kappa; bd mem Adult Educ Adv Bd; The Links, Inc, Charter Parliamentarian 1986-88; Presiding vice chmn Natl NAACP Life Mem Comm; sec, Amer Heart Assn bd of dirs 1986-; Junior League Comm Advisory Bd. **HONORS/ACHIEVEMENTS:** First Black Pres, Met YWCA 1977-78; Awards from WIL Radio 1970; Mayor 1970; Heart Assn; St Louis Argus & Greyhound Bus Corp; Iota Phi Lambda Nat Woman of Yr 1970; St Louis Globe Dem 1971; NAACP Outstanding Educ Am 1971; Afro-Amer Hist Week 1971; Serv to Youth Award 1973; Outstanding Cnsl Award 1975; Urban Leag Serv Award 1972, 1975-76, 1979, 89; NAACP Awards 1976-79; Natl Barristers Wives Award 1976,77,79,86; St Louis City Children's Serv Award 1977; Mayor's Award for Comm Serv 1977; Sentinel's Signal Hon Award for Comm Serv 1977; NAACP Reg Award 1977; Som Serv Award, Masjid Muhammed No 28 1979; Civil Rights Award Coalition of Black Trade Unionists 1979; USCF Serv Award 1979; Pres Award, Metro YMCA 1979; Com Serv Award, St Louis Bd of Police Commr 1980; plus numerous additional awards; Natl Outstanding "Top Lady" Top Ladies of Distinction 1974; Natl NAACP Youth Advisor of the Year NAACP 1977.

WITHERSPOON, JAMES (JIMMIE)
Singer. **PERSONAL:** Born Aug 08, 1923, Gordon, AR. **CAREER:** Jay McShaun, singer 1940's; rhythm & blues singer 1950's; toured US, Europe 1960's; appearances incl Monterey Jazz Festival 1959. **HONORS/ACHIEVEMENTS:** Recordings include, "Evolution of the Blues Song", "At the Renaissance" 1960, "Baby, Baby, Baby" 1964, "Best Blue Soon" 1965, "Blues Around Clock" 1964, "Bluesfor Easy Livers" 1967, "Blues Singer", "Evening Blues", "How", "Song of My Best Friends" 1965, "Spoon in London" 1966; Recipient New Star Award Critic's Poll Downbeat Mag 1961. **BUSINESS ADDRESS:** c/o Abby Hoffer Enterprises, 223 1/2 E 48th St, New York, NY 10017.

WITHERSPOON, R. CAROLYN
Corporate executive. **PERSONAL:** Born Oct 02, Detroit, MI; married William C Witherspoon; children: W Roger, L Courtney, David J. **EDUCATION:** City Coll NY, BS 1951, MS 1956. **CAREER:** Town Hall NY, accountant 1945-48; Foreign Relations Library, treas; Council of Foreign Rel Inc, asst treas/comptroller 1952-87, retired. **ORGANIZATIONS:** Natl financial sec Natl Assn of Negro Business & Professional Women's Clubs Inc; mem Comm Rel Bd; adjustment com Teaneck; mem Kappa Delta Pi, Beta Alpha Psi.

WITHERSPOON, WILLIAM ROGER
Journalist. **PERSONAL:** Born Mar 03, 1949, New York, NY; son of William C. Witherspoon and Ruth C. Witherspoon; married Cynthia O Bedford; children: Kir, Brie. **EDUCATION:** Univ of MI Ann Arbor, 1966-67; Rider Coll Trenton NJ, 1973; Rutgers Univ, Livingstone Coll, New Brunswick NJ, 1975; Fairleigh-Dickinson Univ (Edward Williams Coll) Hackensack NJ, Liberal Arts 1976. **CAREER:** Star-Ledger Newark NJ, investment reporter, columnist, op-ed page, st house corr, columnist senate, assembly, banking, transportation & agriculture, general; assignment reporter 1970-75; NY Daily News, Sunday assignment editor NJ, health & environmental reporter Pasaic Cty reporter, New York City editor gen assignment reporter 1975-79; The Atlanta Constitution, columnist, health & science writer 1979-82; Time Magazine, SE Bur, Cable News Network, writer/producer; Black Enterprise Magazine, Newsweek, GQ Magazine, Fortune, Essence Magazine, Natl Leader, freelance writer 1982-85; Dallas Times Herald, editorial bd 1985-. **ORGANIZATIONS:** Mem, Atlanta African Film Soc, Natl Assn Black Journalists, Black Perspective 1970-73; contributing editor Essence Magazine; editorial advisory bd NAACP Crisis Magazine 1979-80; Dallas-Fort Worth Assn of Black Communicators. **HONORS/ACHIEVEMENTS:** Special Citation, Reporting Awards Ed Writers Assn, 1982; 1st place Reg 5 Natl Assoc of Black Journalists 1982; Natl Headliners Club Award for Consistently Outstanding Special/Feature Column Writing 1981; Journalism Acolade Award GA Conf on Social Welfare 1981; 1st place energy series Media Award for Economic Understanding Series Amos Tuck School of Business Admin Dartmouth Coll 1980; 1st place outstanding news feature Atlanta Assn of Black Journalists 1980; UPI GA Newspaper Awds, 2nd place column writing, 3rd place spot news coverage of Three Mile Island 1979; author "Martin Luther King Jr To The Mountaintop" Doubleday & Co1985; Katie Award Best Editorial Press Club of Dallas 1986; First Place Editorial Writing TX Assoc Press Managing Editors 1987. **BUSINESS ADDRESS:** Editorial Writer, Dallas Times Herald, 1101 Pacific Ave, Dallas, TX 75202.

WITT, BURKETT L.
City official, business executive. **PERSONAL:** Born May 26, 1926, Athens, TN; married Mildred Scott; children: Harold, Gwendolyn. **CAREER:** City of Athens, TN, mayor; Burkett's Bar B Q, owner; Former City Councmn at Large. **ORGANIZATIONS:** Sec treas Big Orange Jantrl Svcs; 1 of 18 People on mission team C Am Boaz Masonic Lodge; Athens Reg Plng Com Bd Zoning Appeal; bd dir Athens C of C; Local Draft Bd; chmn bd trustees St Mark AME Zion Ch. **HONORS/ACHIEVEMENTS:** Annl yr book dedicated in my hon TN Wesleyan Coll Athens 1962. **MILITARY SERVICE:** USN 1-C steward WW II 1944-47. **BUSINESS ADDRESS:** Burkett's Bar B-Q, 117 E Madison Ave, Athens, TN 37303.

WOFFORD, ALPHONSO
Information systems manager. **PERSONAL:** Born May 21, 1958, Spartanburg, SC. **EDUCATION:** Univ of SC, BA Acctg 1980; Golden Gate Univ, MBA Mgmt 1984. **CAREER:** Univ of SC, computer programmer 1978-80; US Air Force, systems engr 1980-86; Sinclair Comm Coll, comp science instructor 1986-; RCF Information Syst Inc, general mgr 1986-. **ORGANIZATIONS:** Mem Omega Psi Phi Frat Inc 1978-, Assoc for Individual Investors 1980-, NAACP 1982-, Air Force Communications & Electronics Assoc 1984-, Assoc for Computing Machinery 1984-, Natl Black MBA Assoc 1985-. **MILITARY SERVICE:** USAF capt 6 1/2 yrs; Air Force Commendation Medal 1983. **BUSINESS ADDRESS:** General Manager, RCF Information Services, 333 West First St Ste 224, Dayton, OH 45402.

WOLFE, DEBORAH CANNON (NEE PARTRIDGE)
Educator, clergywoman. **PERSONAL:** Born Dec 22, Cranford, NJ; daughter of Rev Dr David W Cannon and Mrs M Gertrude Moody Cannon Morris; divorced; children: H Roy Jr. **EDUCATION:** Columbia Univ, EdD, MA; Jersey City State Coll, BS; Hon Degree, Seton Hall Univ, Morris Brown Coll, New Rochelle Coll; Postdoctoral Study, Vassar Coll, Union Theological Seminary, Jewish Theological Seminary of Amer. **CAREER:** Tuskegee Univ, prof & dir grad work 1938-50; vstg prof, NY Univ 1951-54, Univ of MI 1952, Fordham Univ 1952-53, Columbia Univ 1953-54, TX Coll 1955,Univ of IL 1956-57, Wayne State Univ 1961, Grambling Univ; US House of Reps, ed chief comm on ed & labor 1962-65; McMillan Publ Co, ed consult 1964; NSF, consult 1967-70; City Univ Ctr for African & Afro-Amer Studies, dir 1968-77; Natl Leadership Training Inst US Ofc of Ed, cons, vocational & tech ed 1968-71; First Baptist Church Cranford NJ, assoc minister; Queens Coll, prof ed 1950-. **ORGANIZATIONS:** Consultant Encyclopedia Britannica; chmn All Non-Govt Reps to UN NGO, DPI, UN; pres Clergy Council Cranford NJ, NJ Womens Div Conv of Progressive Baptists; chmn Intl Fellowship Comm Pi Delta Kappa Hon Soc; grand basileus Zeta Phi Beta 1954-65; chair NJ State Bd of Higher Educ 1968-; mem ed comm NYC; bd dir AAUW 1969-75; del IFUW Conf 1971; chmn admiss comm Queens Coll CUNY, UN Rep for Ch Women United 1971-; chmn AAUW Legis Prog Comm 1973-; mem Commn on Fed Rel Amer Council on Ed 1972-; vice pres Natl Alliance for Safer Cities 1972,73-74; chmn Review Council Assoc for Supervision & Curriculum Devel 1973-75; chmn membership comm Assoc of Prof of Curriculum 1973-75; pres Natl Alliance of Black School Educators 1975-77; mem trustee bd science serv AAAS; mem trustee bd Seton Hall Univ; affirm action officer Queens Coll of CUNY 1975-76; advisory com Bd of Educ Cranford NJ; chair Zeta Phi Beta Educ Found; sec Kappa Delta Pi Educ Foundation; vice pres Natl Council of Negro Women; bd dirs Home Mission Council, Progressive Natl Baptist Convention; mem, Natl Alliance of Black Educators Educational Foundation; resolutions comm, Natl Assn of State Boards of Education; mem, NJ State Board of Education. **HONORS/ACHIEVEMENTS:** Cited Natl Baptist Convention for Outstanding Contributions to Religious & Civic Welfare of Amer 1952; Achievement Award Atlantic Reg of Zeta Phi Beta 1957; one of NY's Outstanding 10 Women Personal Products & Pittsburgh Courier 1958; Natl Achievement Award Natl Assoc of Negro Business & Professional Womens Clubs 1958; Woman of the Year Women of Morgan State Coll 1959; Today's Makers of History Award The Assoc for the Study of Negro Life & History 1959; News Honoree Amsterdam 1959; Jr-Sr HS named in honor of Deborah Wolfe Macon County AL 1962; Bldg named in honor of Deborah Wolfe tenton State Coll 1970; Award Hon Mem Natl Soc for Prevention of Juvenile Delinquency for Contributions in Field; Women of Courage Radcliffe Coll; Special Honors Natl Alliance of Black School Educators, Northeastern Region Natl Assoc of Colored Women's Clubs, Sh rewsbury AME Zion Church; Citizen of the Year B'nai B'rith 1986; Citation Serv Omega Psi Phi Fraternity Sojourner Truth Award Natl Assn of Business & Professional Women; Top Ladies of Distinction Hon Mem 1986; Medal for Comm Serv Queens Coll of CUNY 1986; Distinguished Service Award, Univ of Medicine & Dentistry of New Jersey and Seton Hall Univ; Hon Doctorate Stockton State Coll, Kean Coll of NJ, Jersey City State Coll Monmouth Coll, Centenary Coll, Bloomfield Coll, William Paterson Coll, Drew Univ, Glassboro State Coll. **BUSINESS ADDRESS:** Chair,, NJ State Board of Higher Education, 20 W State St, Trenton, NJ 08625.

WOLFE, ESTEMORE A.
Educator, business executive. **PERSONAL:** Born Dec 29, 1919, Crystal Springs, MS; divorced. **EDUCATION:** Jackson State Univ, BS 1947; Wayne State Univ, MEd; NY Univ, DFA; Boston Univ, D Ed. **CAREER:** Ins exec 30 yrs; writer lecturer teacher 39 yrs; Wright Mutual Ins Co, vice pres sec 1968-. **ORGANIZATIONS:** Couns consult tech organizer fdr pres Detroit Chap Friends of AMISTAD; mem Amer Fed Teachers, Detroit Fed Teachers, Acad Soc & Polit Sci, Amer Reading Assn; mem NAACP, Amer Assn Higher Educ, Natl Assn Intergroup Relat Officials; 1977 Centennial Plng Comm Jackson State Univ; Smithsonian Inst Assn; Cntrl United Methodist Ch; life mem Amer Museum Natl History; natl pres Friends of AMISTAD & bd chmn Brooklyn; natl chmn Urban Planning Comm; Natl Ins Assn; trustee Jackson State Devel Found Jackson MS, Boston Univ, Alumni of MI; past bd chmn Detroit Met Symphony Orch; notary pub with seal 32 yrs; organized voter registration & gathered more than 500 witnesses to US Senate Hearing of late Sen Theo G Bilbo Jackson MS proving intimidation of Negroes & other min causing the Senator to lose his Senate Seat in WA 1946-47; educ soc Wayne StUniv & Purdue U. **HONORS/ACHIEVEMENTS:** 2000 Men of Achvmt Awd 1973; Who's Who in Amer 1972-80-84; Who's Who in the World 1973-77-80; Who's Who in the Midwest 1975-76-77-84; Men of Achievement of World Awd 1975; Outstand Black Am 1976; Who's Who in Fin & Ind 1976-77-80; Who's Who in Bicent Amer 1976; Who's Who in Educ 1977; Who's Who Among Child Devel Professional 1976-78; Who's Who in the South 1978; Centennial Medallion & cit Jackson State U; Kiwanis Intl Brass Ruby-Studded Pin, Bronze Plaque, Test Banquet 1976; Estemore A Wolfe Day plaque & cit BostonUniv Alumni Assn; Bronze Plaque Wharton Sch Univ of PA 1977; Col on Gov Cliff Finch's Staff MS 1977; Bronze Pla/Citation Estemore A Wolfe Day Detroit 1978; Case II Awd Coun for the Adv & Support to Higher Ed 1979; Century Aw & Sch Dev Fnd of Jackson StU 1979; Pres Citation NAFEO Awd Wash DC Pres Carter as guest spkr 1979; 1st Century Pres Plaque 1980; Who's Who in the Intl Biog Rec 1980; Spirit of Detroit Plaque City Council & Mayor Coleman A Young 1980; Disting Leadership Awd State Senate of MI 1983; Gold "J" w/diamonds President's Club Jackson State Univ 1984; Hon LLD Syracuse Univ; Hon LHD Wilberforce Univ. **MILITARY SERVICE:** AUS t/sgt 1942-46. **BUSINESS ADDRESS:** Division Vice Pres, Wright Mutual Ins, 2995 E Grand Blvd, Detroit, MI 48202.

WOLFE, JOHN THOMAS
Educational administrator. **PERSONAL:** Born Feb 22, 1942, Jackson, MS; son of John Wolfe and Jeanette Wolfe; children: Wyatt, John T, David A. **EDUCATION:** Chicago State Univ, BEd 1964; Purdue Univ, MS 1972, PhD 1976. **CAREER:** Purdue Univ, mgr employee relations 1975-77; Fayetteville State Univ, english dept chair 1977-79, div head humanities & fine arts 1979-83, academic dean 1983-85; Bowie State Univ, provost and vice pres for academic affairs 1985-. **ORGANIZATIONS:** Pres Black Caucus Natl Council Teacher of English 1982-88; bd of dirs Bowie New Town Ctr Minority Adv Bd 1985-; steering comm Prince George's Co MD Univ High School 1985-87; standing comm of teacher preparation Natl Council of Teachers of English 1984-87; chair, advisory bd Prince George's County, MD Entrepreneurial Develop Program. **HONORS/ACHIEVEMENTS:** Kappa Delta Pi Educ Honor Soc 1972; Hon Mem Alpha Kappa Mu Honor Soc 1983; Fellowship Amer Council on Educ 1982-83. **BUSINESS ADDRESS:** Provost & Vice Pres Academic Affairs, Bowie State University, Office of Provost, Bowie, MD 20715.

WOLFE, WILLIAM K.
Company executive. **PERSONAL:** Born Feb 09, 1926; son of Carl L Wolfe and Margaret Langston Wolfe Burrell; married Virginia King Wolfe, Jun 16, 1956 (divorced); children: Jane, Betty, Jonathan Wolfe. **EDUCATION:** Springfield Coll, 1951; Adelphi U, MS 1960. **CAREER:** YMCA Dayton OH, sec 1951-53; Stuyvesant Residence Club, children's supr 1953-54; New York City Housing Auth, housing coord 1954-58; Stuyvesant Comm Ctr, exec dir 1959-63; Urban League of Westchester Co Inc, exec dir; United Comm Corp, exec dir 1966-67; Ft Greene Comm Corp, exec dir 1968-69; Hunter Coll School of Soc Work, lecturer 1970-; Urban League of Gr Cleveland, exec; CEOGC, dep exec dir 1985-87, interim exec dir 1987-; Urban League, Whitesplain, NY, CEO, 1963-67, Cleveland, OH, CEO, 1972-85. **ORGANIZATIONS:** Vol pres OH Wilberforce Conf 1978-; mem Natl Assn of Soc Workers; Natl Assn of Inter-Grp Relations Officers; mem Alpha Phi Alpha Fraternity; Rotary Club; Area Councils Assn; Businessmen Interracial Com; Cleveland Area Manpower Council; NAACP; City Club; bd trustees Metro Cleveland Jobs Council; Afro-Amer Cultural & Historical Soc; Natl Assn of Soc Welfare; instructor, Hunter School, SW New York, 1967-72; CEO, Urban League of Bridgeport, 1989; pres & bd mem, Ohio Welfare Coucil, 1979-84; bd mem, N.A.B.SW., 1968. **HONORS/ACHIEVEMENTS:** Co-author "Reaching Out a Puerto Rican dialogue"; author, ed of many articles & papers; Founder Award, BPA, 1987, Award of Appreciation, Operation of Big Vote, 1981; Column Call-Post, 1982; Publication for urban League, 1978-84. **MILITARY SERVICE:** Army Air Force, Master Sergeant, 1944-46.

WOLFMAN, BRUNETTA REID
Educational administrator. **PERSONAL:** Born Sep 04, Clarksdale, MS; married Burton I Wolfman; children: Andrea C, Jeffrey Allen. **EDUCATION:** Univ of CA Berkeley, BA 1957, MA 1968, PhD 1971; Boston Univ, DHL 1983; Northeastern Univ, DPed 1983; Regis College, DLaws 1984; Suffolk Univ, DHL 1985, Stonehill College 1985. **CAREER:** Univ of CA Berkeley, teaching fellow 1969-71; Dartmouth Coll, CA coord 1971-72, asst dean of faculty/asst prof 1972-74; Univ of MA, asst vice pres 1974-76; Wheelock Coll Boston, academic dean 1976-78; MA Dept of Educ, exec planner 1978-82; Roxbury Comm Coll, president 1983-. **ORGANIZATIONS:** Program dir YWCA Oakland & Berkeley CA 1959-63; exec dir Camp Fire Girls Berkeley 1963-67; consult Arthur D Little Inc 1977-78; pres New England Minority Women Admins 1977-78; bd dir Natl Ctr for Higher Educ Mgmt Systems 1978-; bd dir Boston Fenway Prog1979-; two articles in black separtism & social reality Pergamon Press 1977; overseer Boston Symphony Orchestra 1984; Museum of Fine Arts 1984; overseer Stone Ctr Wellesley Coll; bd Natl Conf of Christians &Jews; bd United States Trust Bank; bd Boston Private Indus Council; bd Amer Council on Education; councilor Council on Education for Public Health; urban commission AACJC. **HONORS/ACHIEVEMENTS:** Paper presented & pub OECD Paris 1978; Natl Inst of Educ grant Superwomen Study 1978-79; papers presented annual meeting Amer Educ Rsch Assn 1980; "Roles" Westminster Press 1983. **BUSINESS ADDRESS:** President, Roxbury Community College, 625 Huntington Avenue, Boston, MA 02215.

WOMACK, ANDREW A.
Clergyman. **PERSONAL:** Born Nov 11, 1904, Prospect, VA; married Helen Womack. **EDUCATION:** AB 1941; BD 1944; VA Coll & Sem, DD 1949. **CAREER:** Mercy Seat Bapt Ch, Hampden Sidney VA, stu pastor 1936-40; Main St Bapt Ch, Clifton Forge VA, pastor 1944-57; Mt Haven Bapt Ch, Cleve, pastor 1957-; VA Hosp, Cleveland, chaplain 1972-. **ORGANIZATIONS:** Chmn Exec Com Conf 1956; chmn fgn miss Bapt Conv, Cleve 1972-74; life mem, Bd Dirs 1973-74; pres NAACP; 33 Deg Mason; pres Cong Chris Ed, NDist Asso OH 1972-73; bd VA Sem & Coll. **BUSINESS ADDRESS:** 3484 E Blvd, Cleveland, OH 44104.

WOMACK, BOBBY DWAYNE
Recording artist. **PERSONAL:** Born Mar 04, 1944, Cleveland, OH; son of Friendly Womack and Naomi Womack; married Regina K B Banks, Dec 31, 1975; children: Vincent, Bobby Truth, GinaRee. **CAREER:** Truth Records Inc recording artist. **HONORS/ACHIEVEMENTS:** Provided schlrshp fund Harry Womack Scholarship Fund; Youth Inspirational Awd 1975; Appreciation Awd Walter Reed Army Med Ctr; several gold records. **HOME ADDRESS:** 2841 Firenze Pl, Hollywood, CA 90046.

WOMACK, HENRY CORNELIUS
Educator. **PERSONAL:** Born Feb 18, 1938, Grapeland, MS. **EDUCATION:** Alcorn St U, BS (#Summa cum laude) 1961; Wayne St U, MS 1965, PhD 1974. **CAREER:** Ball St Univ, asst prof pysiology & health 1969-; Harper School of Nrrsing Detroit, dir basic science 1965-69. **ORGANIZATIONS:** Mem Fed of Am Scientists 1974-80; mem IN Acad of Sci 1974-80; mem Hum Biology Cncl 1974-80; mem ACLU 1974-80; mem AAAS 1974-80; mem AAUP 1974-80. **HONORS/ACHIEVEMENTS:** Listed Who's Who Among Stds in Am Coll &Univ 1960-61; Scholar of Yr, Omega Psi Phi Frat Inc 1961; fellow NDEA 1970-74. **MILITARY SERVICE:** USAF au/c 1954-58. **BUSINESS ADDRESS:** Ball State Univ Dept of Psyslgy &, Muncie, IN 47306.

WOMACK, JOHN H.
Chief executive janitorial service & supply firm. **CAREER:** JJS Services Inc, Peabody MA, chief executive, 1989. **BUSINESS ADDRESS:** JJS Services Inc, 197 Washington St, Peabody, MA 01960. *

WOMACK, ORLANDO
Public utility employee, school board member & president. **PERSONAL:** Born Nov 14, 1939, Riceville, VA; married Darlyne Mae Baughn; children: Aileen McCollum, Michelle Guinn, Valerie Anderson, Orlena. **EDUCATION:** Ridley Twp HS, Grad 1958. **CAREER:** Reynolds Aluminum, suprv elect cable 1962-77, mgr serv ctr 1977-79, gen suprv cable dept 1979-82; AR Power & Light, stores clerk 1983-84. **ORGANIZATIONS:** Dir, 1974-77, pres 1975 Hot Spring Cty Ctr Exceptional Ctr; 1st black pres Malvern Jaycee Chap 1975-76; dir Malvern Civitan Club 1979-82; suprv Reynolds Aluminum 1984-85; store clerk AR Power & Light 1985; usher, brotherhood, pres transportation mgr 1st Baptist Church. **HONORS/ACHIEVEMENTS:** Distinguished Serv Awd Malvern AR 1974; 1st black elected school bd mem 1982, pres 1985 Malvern AR. **MILITARY SERVICE:** AUS spec 4 1959-62; Honor Guard, 2 Soldier of the Month Awds, Good Conduct Medal. **HOME ADDRESS:** 1717 N Babcock Rd, Malvern, AR 72104-2417.

WOMACK, ROBERT W., SR.
Columnist, professional musician. **PERSONAL:** Born Jul 10, 1916, Jackson, TN; married Mary L Moore; children: Bobby. **EDUCATION:** Univ of IL, attended 1930's; McArthur & Jordan Consult of Music 1940's. **CAREER:** Indianapolis Recorder Newspaper, assoc the-

atrical editorial columnist; BobCats TV All-Stars, bandleader 1939-67; Ferguson Bros Theatrical Agency, founder/prof of music 1940-50; Recorder Newspaper, assoc theatrical editor. **ORGANIZATIONS:** Began first interracial large band 1943; helped pass State Record Piracy Ban Bill in state leg 1974; mem Indianapolis NAACP; pol rep Elks Lodge 709; pres Womack Enterprises; mem Marion Co Sheriff's & Police Press Clubs 10 yrs, recorder 20 yrs; prof musician incl sideman 30 yrs; plays part-time drummer; one of first blacks of AFM Loc 3. **HONORS/ACHIEVEMENTS:** Started Musi-Entertainers' Club 1970; Writer of Yr by loc mus 1974. **BUSINESS ADDRESS:** Assoc Theatrical Ed, Recorder Newspaper, 2901 N Tacoma Ave, Indianapolis, IN 46218.

WOMACK, STANLEY H.
Architect. **PERSONAL:** Born Jul 08, 1930, Pittsburgh, PA; married Winona; children: S Mathew, Deborah, Scott. **EDUCATION:** Howard Univ, BArch 1954. **CAREER:** Bellante & Clauss Arch & Engrs St Thomas VI, asst office mgr 1964-66; Edmund G Good & Partners Arch, job capt 1964-66; Lawrie & Green Arch, arch 1966-72; Murray/Womack Arch, partner 1972-76; Bender Royal Ebaugh Womack Inc Arch Engrs, principal 1976-78; Stanley H Womack Assoc Arch, owner. **ORGANIZATIONS:** Mem Amer Ins of Arch, PA Soc of Arch; life mem Omega Psi Phi; basileus Kappa Omega Chap Harrisburg PA; bd of dir Tri-Cty OIC; bd dir Police Athletic League; life mem NAACP; mem Urban league, St Paul Bapt Church; past comm chmn Cub Pack 21; bd dir Tri Cty Area YMCA; bd dir Tri-Cty United Way; track & cross country team Howard Univ; mem Harrisburg Tennis Team, Riverside Optimist Club, Harrisburg Rotary, Jaycees; bd dir Natl Jr Tennis League; pres Harrisburg Frontiers; mem Omega Psi Phi, Kappa Omega. **HONORS/ACHIEVEMENTS:** 1975 Omega Man of the Year; Comm Leaders of Amer Awd; Achievement Awd Jaycees Intl; Sports Achievement Awd Pittsburgh Centennial. **MILITARY SERVICE:** USAF 1st lt. **BUSINESS ADDRESS:** Stanley H Womack Assoc Arch, Payne-Shoemaker Ste 301, Harrisburg, PA 17101.

WOMACK, WALTER ANDERSON
Educational administrator. **PERSONAL:** Born May 10, Chester, PA; married Jean Richberg; children: Cheryl Ann, Chad. **EDUCATION:** Cheyney State Coll, BA 1953; Antioch Grad School of Ed, MEd 1971; Rutgers Univ, EdD 1979. **CAREER:** Philadelphia Bd of Educ, teacher 1953-68; Prog Mgmt Econ Devel OIC, natl dir spec prog 1968-70; Antioch Grad School, dir elem educ 1971-72; Antioch Grad School, dir grad studies 1972-73; Drexel Univ, assoc dean of students 1973-80; Temple Univ, dir spec recruit & admiss prog 1980-85; Cheltenham School District, educator 1986-. **ORGANIZATIONS:** Leader Neighborhood Youth Corp Proj 1966; dir Wister Council Summer Proj 1968; coord Human Relations Dist #6 Philadelphia Bd of Ed 1965; aux principalPhiladelphia Bd of Ed 1967; admin asst Rhoades School 1970-71; mem Alpha Phi Alpha; team mem Championship State Coll Mile Relay Team Penn Relays 1953; exhibit oil & watercolor; soloist HS & Coll Semi-Professional & Profl. **HONORS/ACHIEVEMENTS:** State Champion Awd 100 & 220 Yard Dashes 1949-53; Team Capt Football Track Basketball Cheyney 1950-53; Pres Awd Cheyney State Coll 1953. **BUSINESS ADDRESS:** Educator, Cheltenham School District, Washington Lane & Ashbourne Rd, Wyncote, PA 19095.

WOMACK, WILLIAM MARTIN
Physician. **PERSONAL:** Born Jun 14, 1936, Lynchburg, VA; married Mariette. **EDUCATION:** Lincoln U, bA 1957;Univ of VA, MD 1961. **CAREER:** Univ WA School of Med, head div child psychiatry 1980-, head div com 1979-, asso prof; Harborview Comm Mental Health Ctr, exec dir 1974-79, assoc dir 1970-74; Univ of WA, assoc prof 1975-, instr 1969-71. **ORGANIZATIONS:** Fellow Am Psychiat Assn; mem Am Med Assn; sec Am Psychiatry Assn 1973-75; mem Task Force on Transcultural Psychiatry 1970-73; consult Baranof Ctr forHum Groth 1975; consult Job Corps 1970; mem gov adv cncl on Mntl Hlth & Mntl Retard 1970-72; mem NIMH Rev Com Psychiatry Ed Training Br 1977-; mem WWA Cncl of Mntl Hlth Prog 1974; bd dir Cncl for Prev of Child Abuse & Neglect 1975. **HONORS/ACHIEVEMENTS:** Alpha Phi Alpha Schlrshp 1954-57; Sci Award, Rohm & Haas, Nat Med Flwshp 1957-61; Outstndng Yng Man of Am Award 1967-68; NIMH Fellow, Kinsey Inst for Sex Rsch 1975. **MILITARY SERVICE:** USNR lcdr 1966-69. **BUSINESS ADDRESS:** 326 9th Ave, Seattle, WA 98104.

WONDER, STEVIE
Entertainer, songwriter. **PERSONAL:** Born May 13, 1950, Saginaw, MI; children: Aisha, Keita Sawandi, Mumtaz Ekow. **EDUCATION:** MI School for Blind, grad 1968. **CAREER:** Performed in Eng, Cont Europe, Japan, Okinawa, Nigeria; appeared in motion pictures; guest appearances on TV including, Ed Sullivan, Mike Douglas, Tom Jones,Amer Bandstand, Dinah Shore, 1975 Grammy Awds, Amer Music Awds, One-to-One Telethon, Sat Night Live; rec 18 Gold Records & num others including, I Wish,, For Once in My Life, My Cherie Amour, Superstition, I Call It Pretty Music, Fingertips; recorded 5 Gold Albums, 5 Platinum Records including, Songs in the Key of Life, his 1976 triple record set was number one album over 15 weeks; performed at FESTAC '77 2nd world black & african cultural fest in Lagos Nigeria, he also brdcst by satellite a perf w/ 15 Amer mus to the Grammy Awds TV Show. **HONORS/ACHIEVEMENTS:** Won 14 Grammy Awards including Album of the Year 1973, 1974, 1976; Amer Music Award 1978; received num honors including Show Bus Inspiration Award; Distinguished Serv Award; Bnai Brith Man of the Year Award; Annual Human Kindness Day Spl Honoree; Amer Video Award for Best Rhythm and Blues Video for Ebony & Ivory 1982; inducted Songwriters Hall of Fame 1982; Academy Award Best Original Song "I Just Called to Say I Love You" from The Lady in Red, 1984. **BUSINESS ADDRESS:** Singer, c/o Theresa Cropper, Esq, 4616 Magnolia Blvd, Burbank, CA 91505.

WOOD, ANDREW W.
Clergyman, convention executive. **PERSONAL:** Born Oct 13, 1919, Clinton, SC; married Gertrude M Burton; children: Verna M Adams, Jesse. **CAREER:** Kilrny Temple Baptist Church, pastor 1947-54; Plgrm Rest Bapt Church, 1947-51; Mt Zion Baptist Church, 1951-60; First Bapt Church 1954-60; Missionary to Kenya EA 1981; Bethany Baptist Church 1960-. **ORGANIZATIONS:** Pres Windng Gulf Dist Sun Sch Conv 1949-51; Nr Nth Side Fellowship of Chs sec 1962, pres 1964; cor sec Cong Christian Ed 1962-71; spksman Civ Rights Org of Columbus 1966-69; exec sec OH Baptist Gen Conv; sec WV Bd Evnglsm; sec Coal River Dist Assn; mem exec bd WV Baptist St Conv; pres Baptist Pstrs Conf Columbus; asst dean Estn Union Dist Assn; judctry Metro Area Ch Bd of Columbus; mem Bapt Minstrl All of Columbus; mem Inter-denom Minstrl All; Nat Bapt Conv USA Inc; mem NAACP, CLASP, Inst 1st Dist Women;s Conv; bursar EU Bible School; coord Columbus Baptist Simultaneous Revival. **HONORS/ACHIEVEMENTS:** OH Leadership Conf Plaque; OH Bapt Gen Conv for Outstanding Leadership & Achievements; Spec Recog & Hons because of work done in Bush country of Kenya in 135 Baptist Churches. **BUSINESS ADDRESS:** 959 Bulen Ave, Columbus. OH 43206.

WOOD, ANTON VERNON
Business executive. **PERSONAL:** Born Jun 07, 1949, Washington, DC. **EDUCATION:** Shepherd Clge, BS 1971; Montgomery Clge, AA 1969. **CAREER:** DC Office of Consumer Prot, comm educ spec, serv area mgr; DC Power Inc, pub affairs dir; Wash Ecology Cen, prog dir; Wash Area Military & Draft Law Panel, couns. **ORGANIZATIONS:** Consult numerous elections in Wash; chmn Neighborhood Commn 6a 1975-; publ mem DC Nghbrhd Reinvestment Commn; chair com on Employment prac 1976-; bd dir Metro Wash Planning & Housing Assc; past chmn DC Statehood Party. **HONORS/ACHIEVEMENTS:** Who's Who in Amer Jr Clge 1969. **BUSINESS ADDRESS:** 509 C St NE, Washington, DC 20002.

WOOD, CURTIS A.
Attorney. **PERSONAL:** Born Jul 31, 1942, Memphis, TN; married Claire O. **EDUCATION:** Columbia Clge, BA 1964; Columbia Law Sch, LLB 1967. **CAREER:** Bedford Stuyvesant Restoration Corp, pres 1977-82, gen counsel 1972-77; Wood, Willias, Rafalsky & Harris, managing partner 1982-. **ORGANIZATIONS:** Mem NY Bar Assc; IL Bar Assc. **BUSINESS ADDRESS:** Managing Partner, Wood, Williams,, Rafalsky & Harris, 11 Hanover Square, New York, NY 10005.

WOOD, DONNA JEAN
Educator. **PERSONAL:** Born Nov 21, 1954, New York City, NY. **EDUCATION:** Julienne High School. **CAREER:** Dayton Contemporary Dance Co, dancer 1961-67; Dayton Ballet Co, dancer 1967-72; Hamburg Opera W Germany, guest soloist 1979; Dance Dance Alberta Canada, guest soloist 1980; Alvin Ailey Amer Dance Theater, professional dancer 1972-; performer guest soloist; CA Inst of the Arts, prof of dance 1986-. **ORGANIZATIONS:** Guest soloist Vienna State Opera Dancing Joseph's Legende, 1979,81,82,83,84, Leonard Bernstein's Mass 1980, Royal Danish Ballet 1981. **HONORS/ACHIEVEMENTS:** Outstanding Young Women of Amer Awd 1984; Hon Degree Wheaton Coll 1985.

WOOD, GARLAND E.
Investment banker. **PERSONAL:** Born Dec 29, 1943, New York, NY; children: Michelle, Cynthia, Scott. **EDUCATION:** Columbia Coll, AB 1965; Columbia Business School, MBA 1972. **CAREER:** Goldman Sachs & Co, partner 1972-. **BUSINESS ADDRESS:** Partner, Goldman, Sachs & Co, 85 Broad St, New York, NY 10004.

WOOD, HAROLD LEROY
Judge. **PERSONAL:** Born Dec 06, 1919, Bridgeport, CT; married Thelma Anne Cheatham; children: Gregory Lance, Laverne Jill Wertz. **EDUCATION:** Lincoln Univ, AB 1942; Cornell Univ Law Sch, JD 1948; New York Univ Law Sch, LLM 1952. **CAREER:** Westchester Co Bd of Supers, super 1957-67; NY State Senate Albany, leg asst 1964; Mt Vernon City Common Council, alderman 1968-69; Westchester Co, family court judge 1969-71; Westchester Co, co court judge 1971-74; Supreme Court NY, justice of the supreme court 1974-. **ORGANIZATIONS:** Local pres NAACP Mt Vernon NY; bd of dirs Mt Vernon Hosp; bd of dirs Urban League White Plains NY. **MILITARY SERVICE:** USAF 2d lieut 1942-46. **BUSINESS ADDRESS:** Justice, Supreme Court NY, Westchester County Courthouse, 111 Grove St, White Plains, NY 10601.

WOOD, JEROME H., JR.
Educator. **PERSONAL:** Born Mar 22, 1941, Washington, DC; son of Jerome H Wood, Sr and Aramenta Alston Wood. **EDUCATION:** Howard Univ, BA (summa cum laude) 1962; Brown Univ, PhD 1969. **CAREER:** Temple Univ, instructor history 1966-69, asst prof history 1969-70; Haverford Coll, visiting asst prof history 1969-70; Swarthmore Coll, prof history, 1970-; Asst Provost, 1986-89. **ORGANIZATIONS:** Assoc dir Afro-Amer Historical & Cultural Museum Philadelphia 1975-76; bd mem Media Fellowship Hse PA 1975-81; mem Historical Soc of PA, PA Abolition Soc, Amer Historical Assn, Latin Amer Studies Assn; several publications including "The Negro in Early PA" Eugene Genovese "Plantation Town & Co" 1974; "Conestoga Crossroads Lancaster PA 1730-1790" Harrisburg 1979; mem Phi Beta Kappa, Phi Alpha Theta; bd mem of Historian, Lansdowne (PC) Symphony Orchestra. **HONORS/ACHIEVEMENTS:** Fulbright Research Scholar (Uruguay, Brazil, Venezuela) 1980; Fulbright Lecturer in US History Nankai Univ People's Republic of China 1983-84; Woodrow Wilson Dissertation Fellow, 1965-66; Honorary Woodrow Wilson Fellow, 1962-63; fluent in Spanish, Portuguese Languages. **BUSINESS ADDRESS:** Prof Dept of History, Swarthmore College, Swarthmore, PA 19081.

WOOD, JUANITA WALLACE
Director. **PERSONAL:** Born Jun 30, 1928, Waycross, GA; divorced. **EDUCATION:** Cntrl State Univ, BA; Northeastern IL Univ, MA Inner City Studies; John Marshall Sch of Law, atnd; Loyola Grad Schl Soc Work. **CAREER:** Dept of Human Resources Div Corrections on Youth Svcs, comm unit dir corrections soc work 1969-; counseling youths & families involved in Correctional Sys; neighborhood worker commn on youth welfare; caseworker childrens div 1958-64; Cook Co Juvenile Ct, probation ofcr 1953-58; Cook Co Pub Aid, caseworker 1952-53. **ORGANIZATIONS:** Mem NASW Law Sor 1958-61; Sensitivity Training Sessions & Seminars; mngrl training with present agcy US Civil Serv Commn; Cook Co Com on Crim Justice. **HONORS/ACHIEVEMENTS:** Recip Award from Devel Grp Progs to deal with Youths & Families involved in Juvenile Justice Sys. **BUSINESS ADDRESS:** Control Office, 640 N La Salle St, Chicago, IL.

WOOD, LAWRENCE ALVIN
Ophthalmologist. **PERSONAL:** Born Jan 05, 1949, New York, NY; son of Lawrence Wood and Lillian Wood; married Yvette Marie Binns. **EDUCATION:** Hunter Coll, BS 1972; Meharry Medical Coll, MD 1979. **CAREER:** Harlem Hosp, physical therapist 1972-75; Howard Univ Hosp, intern 1979-80; Public Health Svcs, general practitioner 1980-82; US Navy, flight surgeon 1982-85; dept head, ophthalmology, Millington Naval Hospital. **ORGANIZATIONS:** Mem Acad of Ophthalmology 1985, Amer Medical Assoc 1986, Dramatist's Guild 1986. **HONORS/ACHIEVEMENTS:** Flight Surgeon of the Year 1984; production of play "No Marks, Just Memories" 1986. **MILITARY SERVICE:** USN lt cmdr 7 yrs; Navy Commendation Medal, Combat Action Ribbon, Navy Expedition Ribbon, Fleet

Marine Force Ribbon 1984. **BUSINESS ADDRESS:** Millington Naval Hospital, Millington, TN 38054-5201.

WOOD, MARGARET BEATRICE
Treasurer. **PERSONAL:** Born in Charleston, WV; daughter of John D Morris and Ivory B Morris; married Alvin B Wood; children: Alvin B Jr, Irene B, Llewellyn. **EDUCATION:** Howard Univ, BA (Cum Laude) 1934; Central Connecticut State Univ, Elemementary Educ30 hrs 1949; Univ of Hartford, MEd30 hrs 1964; Bank State Coll NY, NDEA Inst 1969. **CAREER:** Hartford Public Schools, teacher 1948-60, reading consultant 1960-66, asst supvr reading & dir of IRIT 1966-75, coord of reading & communiction Arts 1975-80. **ORGANIZATIONS:** Dir Summer School 1974; devel of Language Arts Generalist 1972; pres Comm Assoc of Reading Research 1976; adjunct prof Univ of Hartford Seminar St Croix & St Thomas 1978; councilman Town of Bloomfield CT 1969-75, deputy mayor 1974-75; Democratic Town Comm of Bloomfield 1970-. **HONORS/ACHIEVEMENTS:** Sojourner Truth Award, Natl Council of Negro Women 1972; Distinguished Serv Award, Hartford Chapter Delta Sigma Theta 1981. **HOME ADDRESS:** 131 Wadhams Rd, Bloomfield, CT 06002.

WOOD, MICHAEL H.
Medical doctor/general surgery. **PERSONAL:** Born Mar 28, 1942, Dayton, OH; married Florentina Serquina; children: Mark, Anthony, Michael Jr. **EDUCATION:** IN Inst Tech, BS 1968; Meharry Medical Coll, MD 1972. **CAREER:** Westland Medical Ctr, chief dept surgery 1984-; WSO Sch of Medicine Dept Surgery, instructor 1977-78, clinical asst prof 1978-. **ORGANIZATIONS:** Chmn of bd Detroit Medical Group 1985-86. **HONORS/ACHIEVEMENTS:** Biomedical Rsch Grant 1979-80, Rsch Awd Program 1980-81, Biomedical Rsch Support Grant 1981-82 Wayne State Univ; sponsor Frederick Coller Awd Amer Collof Surgeons MI Chap 1980. **MILITARY SERVICE:** USAF A2/c 4 yrs. **BUSINESS ADDRESS:** Clinical Asst Professor, Wayne StateUniv Sch of Med, 4160 John R Ste-805, Detroit, MI 48201.

WOOD, WILLIAM L., JR.
Attorney. **PERSONAL:** Born Dec 04, 1940, Cleveland, OH; married Patricia Mixon; children: Robin, Melissa. **EDUCATION:** Brown U, BA 1962; Yale Law Sch, JD 1965. **CAREER:** Untd Ch of Christ, 1964; Mandell & Wright Houston TX, assoc 1965-68; Intl Nickel Co N Y & Pfizer Inc NY atty 1968-71; Union Carbide Corp NY atty 1971-74; City of N Y, gen cnsl & controller 1974-79; NY S Atty Gen, chief ed bureau 1979-81; NY St Office of Prof Disc, exec dir 1981-85; Wood & Scher, Attys, partner 1985-. **ORGANIZATIONS:** Contributing edtr to "Dicipline" natl jrnl covering prof dicipline 1982-83-84; "Information Please Almanac" 1981 edit, 1982 edit; "NY St Dental Journal"what every dentist should know about prof misconduct, June/July 1982 (vol 48 no 6 pp 378-380); "NY St Dental Journal" an interview On prof dicipline Oct 1982 (vol 48 no 8 p 538); "NY St Pharmacist" recent changes in prof dicipline" (vol 57 no 1, Fall 1982, p v); "NY St Dental Journal" record retentiona professional responsibility even after the patient has gone, feb 1984 (vol 50, no 2, p 98); "nY St Pharmacist" to the new suprv pharmacist congratulations & a word of warning, summer 1983, vol 57, no 4; "nY st pharmacist" the violations comm vol 58, no 3, Spring 1984; "Veterinary News" legal remedies for unpaid fees, May 1984; admtd to TX Bar 1965, NY Bar 1969; mem NY St Bar Asso, Am Arbitration Asso, One Hundred Black Men Inc, Am Pub Hlth Asso, Natl Clearinghouse on Licensure, Enfrcmnt & Regulation. **HONORS/ACHIEVEMENTS:** Black Achvrs in Industry Awd 1974 (Nom by Union Carbind Corp); listed in Whos Who Among Black Americans 1975-76 & subsequent editions. **HOME ADDRESS:** 39 Sunset Dr, Croton-on-Hudson, NY 10520. **BUSINESS ADDRESS:** Attorney, Wood & Scher Attys at Law, One Chase Rd, Scarsdale, NY 10583.

WOOD, WILLIAM S.
Attorney, judge. **PERSONAL:** Born Dec 03, 1926, Chicago, IL; children: William Jr, Eugene T. **EDUCATION:** Univ of Iowa, BA, 1947, LLD, 1950. **CAREER:** State Atty Office, asst atty, 1956-60; Private practice, 1960-83; Cook County Courts, assoc judge. **ORGANIZATIONS:** Mem, Def Lawyer Assn, Cook County Bar, Chicago Bar. **MILITARY SERVICE:** USA 1950-53. **BUSINESS ADDRESS:** Associate Judge, Cook County Court, Richard J Daley Center, Chicago, IL 60602.

WOOD, WILLIE VERNELL, SR.
President. **PERSONAL:** Born Dec 23, 1936, Washington, DC; married Sheila Peters; children: LaJuane, Andre, William Jr. **EDUCATION:** Coalinga Jr Coll, 1956; Univ of So CA, BS 1957-60. **CAREER:** Philadelphia Bell WFL, head coach 1976-77; Toronto Argonauts Football Team, asst coach 1979-80, head coach 1980-82; Willie Wood Mech Sys Inc, pres 1983-. **ORGANIZATIONS:** Free safety Green Bay Packers NFL 1960-71; bd of dir Police Police Boys & Girls Club 1984-87. **HONORS/ACHIEVEMENTS:** All-Pro 6 Yrs NFL 1960-71; Pro-Bowl 8 yrs NFL 1960-71; 5 World Championship Team Greenbay Packers 1961,62,65,66,67; 1st two Superbowl Championship Teams 1966-67; All 25 yrs Team NFL 1982. **HOME ADDRESS:** 7941-16th St NW, Washington, DC 20012. **BUSINESS ADDRESS:** Owner, President, Willie Wood Mechanical Systems, 1335-11th Street, NW, Washington, DC 20001.

WOODALL, ELLIS O., SR.
Educational administrator. **PERSONAL:** Born Aug 18, 1927, Lithonia, GA; married Annie L; children: Diana A, Ellis Jr, Cynthia F, Melanie K. **EDUCATION:** Morris Brown Coll, AB, BS; Atlanta Univ & Univ GA, grad work. **CAREER:** HS teacher 20 yrs; Pub Housing Comm; Rural Health Comm State of GA, past mem; City of Lithonia, city councilman; DeKalb Co, training officer. **ORGANIZATIONS:** Master Boy Scouts; past pres Lithonia Civic Club; mem Credit Union Fdrs Club; vice pres Lithonia Fed Credit Union; deacon clk Union Baptist Church; chmn City Finan. **HONORS/ACHIEVEMENTS:** Com Tchr of Yr; Citizen of Yr Awd Lithonia Civic Club; Area Boy Scout Master Awd of Yr. **MILITARY SERVICE:** WW II Victory Medal; Occupation of Japan Awd; PTO Metal Citation for Serv on War Crimes Trials.

WOODALL, JOHN WESLEY
Physician. **PERSONAL:** Born May 24, 1941, Cedartown, GA; son of Japheus and Esther; married Janet Carol Nunn; children: John Wesley Jr, Japheus Clay, Janita Carol. **EDUCATION:** Ball State Univ, BS Med Tech 1959-64; St Johns Med Ctr, Internship Med Tech 1964-65; IN Univ School of Med, MD 1965-69; Whishard Memorial Hospital, Rotating Internship 1969-70. **CAREER:** St Johns Hosp, chief Ob-Gyn 1974, chief family practice 1977; Bridges-Campbell-Woodall Med Corp, physician, owner. **ORGANIZATIONS:** Mem, diplomate Amer Acad of Family Practice; mem Fellow of Amer Acad of Family Practice, Aesculapian Med Soc, Amer Med Dir Assn, The Amer Geriatric Soc, Natl Med Assn, Urban League, Friendship Baptist Church; life mem NAACP. **MILITARY SERVICE:** USAF capt 1970-72. **BUSINESS ADDRESS:** Bridges Campbell Woodall Med, 1302 Madison Ave, Anderson, IN 46016.

WOODARD, A. NEWTON
Physician. **PERSONAL:** Born Aug 03, 1936, Selma, AL; married Bettye Davillier. **EDUCATION:** Xavier Univ New Orleans, BS 1956; Meharry Med Clge Nashville, MD 1960. **CAREER:** Central Med Ctr Los Angeles, co-owner & co-dir 1970-; Kate Bitting Reynolds Mem Hosp Winston-Salem, intern 1960-61; Charlotte Comm Hosp, resident 1961-62; Kate Bitting Reynolds Mem Hosp, 1962-66; Portsmouth Naval Hosp, 1966-68; Dr Bassett Brown, ptnrshp 1968-. **MILITARY SERVICE:** USN lt com 1966-68. **BUSINESS ADDRESS:** 2707 S Central Ave, Los Angeles, CA 90011.

WOODARD, ALFRE
Actress. **PERSONAL:** Born in Tulsa, OK; married Roderick Spencer. **EDUCATION:** Boston Univ, BFA (cum laude). **CAREER:** Films, Extremities, Mandela, Cross Creek, Health, Remember My Name; Television, St Elsewhere, Unnatural Causes, Sara, Words by Heart, Fairie Tale Theatre, ForLove of a Soldier, Go Tell it on the Mountain, The Killing Floor, Ambush murders, Colored Girls, Sophisticated, Freedom Rd, Trail of the Moke, Games Before WeForget, The Good Witch of Laurel Canyon, Hill St Blues, Palmerstown, Enos, White Shadow, Two by South; Theatre, Split Second, For Colored Girls, Bugs Guns,Leander Stillwell, Me and Bessie, Horatio, Vlast, A Christmas Carol, Map of the World. **HONORS/ACHIEVEMENTS:** Miss KAY Chi Chap Boston Univ 1974; Acad Awd Nominee Best Supporting Actress 1984; Emmy Awd Winner Best Supporting Actress 1984; Golden Apple Awd Best newcomer 1984; NAACP Image Awd Best Actress 1984; Emmy Nominee 1985,86.

WOODARD, ALLEN C., III
Real estate broker. **PERSONAL:** Born Sep 09, 1911, Houston; married Clothilde Curry. **EDUCATION:** Univ CA Los Angeles; Southwestern Law Sch; Univ So CA, cert govt; Los Angeles Clge Law, LLB 1938. **CAREER:** Real estate broker 1940-. **ORGANIZATIONS:** Chmn bd dirs Golden West Real Est Bd; mem bd dirs Broadway Fed Sav & Loan Assc, mem exec com 1930's; mem exec com USO; mem Omega Psi Phi; charter mem Lambda Omicron Chapt; Basileus chapt; grand marshall Omega conclave LA 1955; dist keeper of records & seal; mem Natl Reclamation Com 1973, chmn 12th dist 1973-74; mem Natl Com Artifacts & Memorabilia 1974; mem exec com LA Br NAACP; mem bd 28th St Branch YMCA; pres West View Hosp Org; joined class-action suit against LA Fire Dept discrim hiring policy; mem Far-Western Reg Com Natl Urban League; mem & pres bd dir Pacific Town Club;mem St Philip's Epis Ch. **HONORS/ACHIEVEMENTS:** Led fight against discrim in housing 1940's & 50's; advertised would pay legal fees of clients in defense of right to occupy property they owned; Omega Man ofYear 1955; citation YMCA; rector's citation St Philip's Epis Ch; Citizen of Year 1972. **BUSINESS ADDRESS:** 4800 W Venice Blvd, Los Angeles, CA 90019.

WOODARD, CHARLES JAMES
Education administration. **PERSONAL:** Born Jun 09, 1945, Laurel, MS; married Jean Eileen Wiant; children: Andrea, Craig, Ashley. **EDUCATION:** Edinboro Univ of PA, BS 1968; Wayne State Univ, MA 1972; Univ of MI, PhD 1975. **CAREER:** Univ of MI Flint, asst/asst dean for special proj 1973-75; Allegheny Coll, assoc dean of students 1975-82; Coppin State Coll, dean of student services 1982-85; IN Univ Northwest, dean for student services 1985-. **ORGANIZATIONS:** Natl Assoc Financial Aids for Minority Students, mem 1972-75; Amer Personnel & Guidance Assoc, mem 1975-; Non-White Concerns in Guidance, mem 1975-; Unity Inst for Human Devel, board mem 1976-80; Boy Scouts of America, board mem 1977-82; PA State Educ Assoc, race relations consultant 1978-81; American Higher Educ Assoc, mem 1985-; Salvation Army, board mem 1986. **HONORS/ACHIEVEMENTS:** Who's Who in American Colleges and Univ 1967-68; Kappa Delta Pi 1968; Publication, "The Challenge of Your Life - A guide to help prepare students to get screened into higher education" 1974; Outstanding Young Men of America 1977; co-authored paper, "A Comparative Study on Some Variables Related to Academic Success asPerceived By Both Black and White Students" 1977; co-authored paper, "Enhancing the College Adjustment of Young Culturally Different Gifted Students" 1986. **BUSINESS ADDRESS:** Dean, Student Services, Indiania University Northwest, 3400 Broadway, Gary, IN 46408.

WOODARD, LOIS MARIE
Systems analyst. **PERSONAL:** Born in Porter, TX; married Laverne; children: Alesia Brewer, Erica Brewer, Cheryl Brewer. **EDUCATION:** Los Angeles Trade Tech Coll, AA 1970; Cal Poly State Univ San Luis Obispo, BS 1975. **CAREER:** Cal Poly San Luis Obispo CA, data processor 1972-76; Burroughs Corp, programmer 1976-77; Long Beach Coll of Business, instructor 1977-80; Natl Auto & Casualty Ins, system analyst 1980-. **ORGANIZATIONS:** Business woman Esquire Cleaners 1979-87; pres Stewardess Bd #2 1st AME Ch 1980-82; natl auto co coord Youth Motivation Task Force 1984-87; conductress Order of Eastern Stars 1985-86; corresponding sec Zeta Phi Beta Sor 1986; mem NAACP 1986-87. **HONORS/ACHIEVEMENTS:** Appreciation Awd 1st AME Church Pasedena CA 1981. **HOME ADDRESS:** 804 W Figueroa Dr, Altadena, CA 91001.

WOODARD, SAMUEL L.
Educator. **PERSONAL:** Born May 26, 1930, Fairmont, WV; married Ethel Banks; children: Mary Ellen, Charlene, Gail. **EDUCATION:** Mansfield State, BS 1953; Canisius Clge, MS 1959; State Univ of NY Buffalo, EdD. **CAREER:** Howard Univ, prof of educ admin; IL State Univ, assc prof of educ admin 1970-73; Philadelphia School Dist, dir prog impl 1968-70; Temple Univ, asst prof of educ 1967-68; Genesee-Humboldt Jr High Buffalo, vice prin 1966-67; Buffalo & LA, teacher 1954-66. **ORGANIZATIONS:** Intl Assc Appl Soc Scient; Intl Transactional Analysis Assc; Phi Delta Kappa; Natl All of Black Sch Educ; life mem NAACP; life mem Alpha Phi Alpha. **HONORS/ACHIEVEMENTS:** 1st Black to rec Phoenician Trophy as outst Schlr-Athlete HS 1948; 1st Black to rec Doc in Educ Admin at State Univ of NY Buffalo 1966; 1st Black toteach on Educ TV in NY State Buffalo WNED-TV 1961-62. **BUSINESS ADDRESS:** Sch of Educ HowardUniv, Washington, DC 20059.

WOODBECK, FRANK RAYMOND
Executive. **PERSONAL:** Born Feb 02, 1947, Buffalo, NY; son of George Woodbeck and Avil Woodbeck; married Virginia Ann Carter; children: Harrison, Terry, Frank Raymond II. **EDUCATION:** State Univ of NY at Buffalo, BS 1973. **CAREER:** Capital Cities Comm WKBW Radio, gen sales mgr 1977-80, pres and gen mgr 1980-84; Capital Cities Cable Inc, vice pres advertising 1985-86; Post-Newsweek CableInc, vice pres advertising 1986-. **ORGANIZATIONS:** Mem Omega Psi Phi Frat 1976-; ticket chmn Dunlop Pro Am Awds Dinner 1979-84; vice chmn/chairman Humboldt Branch YMCA 1979-84; mem Sigma Pi Phi Frat 1983-; treas ABC Radio Dir Affil Bd 1983-84; pres Buffalo Radio Assoc 1983-84. **MILITARY SERVICE:** USAF staff sgt 1964-68; Air Force Commendation Medal, Natl Defense Medal, Vietnam Service Medal. **HOME ADDRESS:** 8319 E Wethersfield, Scottsdale, AZ 85260. **BUSINESS ADDRESS:** Vice President Advertising, Post-Newsweek Cable, 2621 E Camelback Rd, Phoenix, AZ 85016.

WOODBURY, ARLINE ELIZABETH
Business executive. **PERSONAL:** Born Mar 06, 1953, Asheville, NC. **EDUCATION:** Drew Univ, BA 1975; Univ of MI Medical Sch, MD 1980; Rutgers Univ/ICBO Mgmt Trng, Business Courses 1987. **CAREER:** Sinai Hosp of Detroit, intern/resident 1980-84; Natl Health Serv Corp, medical assignee 1984-87; State of NJ Medical Consultant, medical specialty consultant 1985-; Private Practice, physician 1987-; ArGera Inc, pres 1986-. **ORGANIZATIONS:** Mem Natl Medical Assoc 1979-, Alpha Kappa Alpha Sor Inc 1979-, Black Psychiatrists of Amer 1982-, North Jersey Medical Soc 1985-; assoc mem Travel Charter Agency 1983-85; conf moderator Transcultural Conf in Nairobi Kenya 1986; conf participant Natl Black MBA Assoc Inc 1986; franchise Everything Yogurt Inc/Bananas Kiosk 1987-. **HONORS/ACHIEVEMENTS:** Mem Tri-Beta Zoology Honors Soc Drew Univ Chap 1973-75; US Public Health Service Scholarship 1977-78, 1978-80; Outstanding Young Women of Amer Awd 1982. **HOME ADDRESS:** 156 Lincoln St, Montclair, NJ 07042.

WOODBURY, DAVID HENRY
Scientist. **PERSONAL:** Born Mar 29, 1930, Camden, SC; son of David and Arline; married Margaret Jane Claytor; children: Arline E, Brenda L, Laura R, Kathryn L, Larry D, David H. **EDUCATION:** Johnson C Smith Univ, BS (cum laude) 1951; VA State Coll, MS (With Disc) 1952; Univ of MI, MD 1961. **CAREER:** Atomic Energy Comm, biologist 1955-57; Westland Med Center, dir nuclear med 1968-; Univ of MI, asst prof internal med 1968-; USPHS, dir Nuclear med 1967-68; Westland Med Center dir nuclear medicine. **ORGANIZATIONS:** Consultant FDA Radiopharmaceuticals Advisor 1978-82, NRC Advisory Comm 1979-; bd regents Amer Coll of Nuclear Physicians 1980-; chief med staff Wayne County Hosp 1974-75; vice pres Johnson C Smith Alumni Assn 1978; pres club Johnson C Smith Univ 1984; pres American Coll of Nuclear Physicians 1987. **HONORS/ACHIEVEMENTS:** Robert C Word Scholar Johnson C Smith Univ 1950; fellow Amer Clge Nuclear Physicians 1982. **MILITARY SERVICE:** AUS cpl; USPHS lt col 1961-68. **BUSINESS ADDRESS:** Dir Nuclear Medicine, Westland Medical Ctr, Michigan At Merriman Rd, Westland, MI 48185.

WOODBURY, MARGARET CLAYTON
Physician. **PERSONAL:** Born Oct 30, 1937, Roanoke, VA; daughter of John Bunyan Claytor Sr (deceased) and Roberta Morris Woodfin Claytor (deceased); married David Henry Woodbury, Jr MD; children: Laura Ruth Young, Lawrence DeWitt Young Jr, David Henry Woodbury III. **EDUCATION:** Mount Holyoke Coll, AB Cum Laude 1958; Albany Medical Coll, Trustee Bio-Chem Award 1960; Meharry Med Coll, MD Pediatric Prize 1962. **CAREER:** US Pub Health Serv Hosp, Staten Island NY, asst chief med/endo 1967-68; US Pub Health Serv Hosp, Detroit MI, chief outpatient clinic 1968-69; US Pub Health Serv Outpatient Clinic, Detroit MI, med officer in charge 1969-71; Univ of Michigan Med School, instr med endo 1969-80, asst prof 1980-, HCOP proj dir 1984-, asst dean student & minority affairs 1983-. **ORGANIZATIONS:** Admissions comm, Univ of Michigan Med Sch, 1978-83; mem chmn, ACAAP Univ of Michigan Med School, 1983-; chair steering comm MLKCHC Series, 1984-85; nominating comm, bd alumnae 1981-85, trustee 1985-90, Mount Holyoke College; co-chair precinct, Ann Arbor Democratic Party, 1972-73; parent rep, Engrg Indust Support Program, 1978-82; founding mem, Ann Arbor Alliance of Achievement, 1981-; volunteer various health related committees. **HONORS/ACHIEVEMENTS:** Elected to membership, Alpha Omega Alpha Honor Medical Soc, Meharry Med Coll, 1962; Alumnae Medal of Honor, Mount Holyoke Coll, 1983; diplomate, Amer Bd of Internal Med, 1969; Dean's List, Albany & Meharry Med Coll 1959-62; 1st Biochemistry Award, Albany Med Coll, 1959; Pediatric Prize, Meharry Med Coll, 1961; cited as Outstanding Young Woman of Amer, 1967; elected Hon Mem, Sigma Gamma Rho Sor Inc, Outstanding Woman for the 21st Century, 1986; has published numerous articles in field of endocrinology, including "Quantitative Determination of Cysteine in Salivary Amylase," Mt Holyoke Coll, 1958; "Hypopituitarism in Current Therapy," WB Saunders Co, 1967; "Cushing's Syndrome in Infancy, A Case Complicated by Monilial Endocarditis," Am J Dis Child, 1971; "Three Generations of Familial Turner's Syndrome," Annals of Int Med 1978; "Virilizing Syndrome Associated With Adrenocortical Adenoma Secreting Predominantly Testosterone," Am J Med 1979; "Hormones in Your Life From Childbearing (Or Not) to Menopause," Mt Holyoke Alumnae Quarterly 1980; "Scintigraphic Localization of Ovarian Dysfunction," J Nuc Med, 1988. **MILITARY SERVICE:** US Public Health Serv Senior Surgeon 1961-71. **BUSINESS ADDRESS:** Asst Dean, Student/Minority Affairs, Univ of Michigan Medical School, Box 025 Furstenberg, Ann Arbor, MI 48109.

WOODEN, RALPH L.
Educator. **PERSONAL:** Born Mar 29, 1915, Columbus, OH; son of Isaiah Wooden and Lozanie Wooden; married Rosalie McLeod; children: Mari, Ralph L, Jr. **EDUCATION:** North Carolina A&T State Univ, BS, 1938; Ohio State Univ, MA, 1946; Ohio State Univ, PhD, 1956; Virginia State Coll, Post-Doctoral Study; Michigan State Univ, Post-Doctoral Study. **CAREER:** North Carolina A&T State Univ, professor of educ, dir educ, media center; No State High School, Hagerstown, ME, teacher, 1938-39; Univ North Carolina, Greensboro, NC, tech, 1939-40; Dudley High School, teacher, 1940-41; USAF, grade school instructor, 1941-45; Univ of Wisconsin, Madison, WI, visiting professor in audiovisual educ, 1971. **ORGANIZATIONS:** Mem, Sigma Chapter, Phi Delta Kappa, 1950, Edit advisory bd, Audiovisual Ins Assn for Educ Comm & tech, 1974; mem, Natl Assn for Educ Comm & Tech; past pres & chmn bd dir North Carolina Assn for Educ Comm & Tech, 1973; mem, Natl Conv Plan Comm Assn for Educ Comm & Educ Tech Detroit, 1970, Minneapolis 1972; off delegate, Assnc for Educ Comm & Tech Las Vegas, 1973; delegate, Univ North Carolina, Fac Assmbl, 1972-77; Leadership Conf, Lake Okoboj, IA, 1974; past chmn, Grad School Public Comm; mem Fac Ath Comm, adv grad stu in educ & media fac rep, Grad County, NC, A&T State Univ; advisory & consult to num schools in North Carolina; Gamma Tau Chapter, Alpha Kappa Mu Natl Hon Soc, 1936; Beta Chap Beta Kappa Chi Natl Science Hon Soc, 1947; Alpha Chapter, Epsilon Pi Tau Intl Hon Soc in Educ, 1950; Theta Chap Kappa Delta Pi Int Hon Soc, 1961. **HONORS/ACHIEVEMENTS:** Merrick Medal for Excellence in Tech Science, North Carolina A&T State Univ, 1938; Citizen of Year; Greensboro Citizens' Assn, 1965; North Carolina Outstanding Audio-Visual Educ, SE Businessmen's Assn, Minneapolis, 1972; Outstanding Alum in School of Educ, Natl Alum Assn of North Carolina A&T State Univ, 1973; Student, NEA, North Carolina A&T State Univ, Outstanding Achievement Award, 1973. **MILITARY SERVICE:** USAF. **BUSINESS ADDRESS:** NC A&T StateUniv, Greensboro, NC 27411.

WOODFOLK, JOSEPH O.
Educator. **PERSONAL:** Born Mar 04, 1933, St Thomas, Virgin Islands of the United States;divorced. **EDUCATION:** Morgan State Coll, AB; NM Highlands Univ, ME 1955; Morgan State Coll, MA; Indian Culture Univ Mysore India, cert grad studies 1973. **CAREER:** Baltimore Co Bd Educ, chmn Social studies dept 1969-; Baltimore Co Public Schools, teacher 1955-; State Univ NJ, teacher "Blacks in Amer Soc", "The Black Family"; NJ; DE; Johns Hopkins Univ. **ORGANIZATIONS:** Dev curriculum K-12 soc stud prog Balti Co 1969-; dir Fulbright Alumni India summer stud prog; mem Tchr Assc Balt Co; MD State Tchr Assc; Natl Educ Assc; Phi Alpha Theta; Gamma Theta Upsilon; Amer Hist Soc; MD Hist Soc; Org Amer Historians; Soc Hist Educ; NAACP; Friends of Kenya; Assc Foreign Students; Alumni Assc; NM Highlands Univ; mem Phi Delta Kappa John Hopkins Univ; Eastern reg dir of publ Phi Beta Sigma Frat; mem Amer Heart Assc Minority Comm Affairs; Phi Beta Sigma. **HONORS/ACHIEVEMENTS:** Fulbright Flwshp 1973; spec recog award Eta Omega chap Phi Alpha Theta. **BUSINESS ADDRESS:** Woodlawn Sr High Sch, 1801 Woodlawn Dr, Baltimore, MD 21207.

WOODFORD, HACKLEY ELBRIDGE
Physician. **PERSONAL:** Born Jul 02, 1914, Kalamazoo, MI; son of Thomas Elbridge Woodford and Bessie Agnes Hackley Woodford; married Mary Imogene Steele Woodford, Jun 07, 1940; children: Peggy Ann Forbes, John Niles Woodforr, Joan Mary Abu Bakib, Barbara Ellen Tolbert. **EDUCATION:** Western Michigan Univ, AB, 1936; Mary S Woodford, Howard Univ, BA; Univ of Chicago, MA; Howard Medical School, MD, 1940; Attended Post Grad School; Chicago, New York Univ, Tufts, Northwestern Univ, Harvard, Allegemeines, Krakenhaus Vienna Austria; Univ of Michigan Medical School. **CAREER:** Provident Hospital, intern, 1940-41, resident, 1941-42; Private Practice, 1945-70; Memorial Hospital, St Joseph, Michigan, medical chief of staff, 1964-69; Southern California Permanente Medical Group, physician. **ORGANIZATIONS:** Certified Amer Bd Family Practice, 1970, 76, 82; mem, AMA, NMA; fellow Amer Acad Family Practice; Intl Soc Internal Medicine; fellow Amer Geriatric Soc; mem, N Shore School Bd; life mem, NAACP; bd dir, Pasadena Foothill Urban League, Alpha Phi Alpha Fraternity, Alpha Pi Boule Sigma Pi Phi; scholarship donor, Howard Univ Medical School; contributing editor, US Black Business Recognition Award, AMA; life mem, Amer Medical Soc of Vienna Austria, Amer Acad of Family Practice. **HONORS/ACHIEVEMENTS:** Listed Dir of Med Specialists.

WOODFORD, JOHN NILES
Journalist. **PERSONAL:** Born Sep 24, 1941, Chicago, IL; married Elizabeth Duffy; children: Duffy, Maize, Will. **EDUCATION:** Harvard Univ, BA (High Honors) 1964, MA 1968. **CAREER:** Ebony Magazine, asst editor 1967-68; Muhammed Speaks Newspaper, editor in chief 1968-72; Chicago Sun Times, copy editor 1972-74; New York Times, copy editor natl desk 1974-77; Ford Motor Co, sr editor Ford Times 1977-80; Univ of MI, exec editor 1981-. **ORGANIZATIONS:** Journal editor Natl Alliance Third World Journalists; exec bd mem Black Press Inst; mem Intl Org of Journalists; US correspondent Rauhan Puolesta Journal of the Peace Comm of Finland; bd mem Ann Arbor Civic Theater, Univ of MI Assoc of Black Profls and Admins, Univ of MI Council on Minority Affairs. **HONORS/ACHIEVEMENTS:** 3 Gold Medals and other Awds Council for Advancement and Support of Educ 1984-86; "A Journey to Afghanistan," article Freedomways 1985; numerous other articles with special interest in intl affairs. **HOME ADDRESS:** 1922 Lorraine Pl, Ann Arbor, MI 48104. **BUSINESS ADDRESS:** Executive Editor, Univ of Michigan, 412 Maynard, Ann Arbor, MI 48109.

WOODFORK, CAROLYN AMELIA
Pediatric resident. **PERSONAL:** Born Feb 15, 1957, Washington, DC. **EDUCATION:** Howard Univ, BS 1979; Meharry Medical Coll, MD 1984. **CAREER:** Howard Univ, student lab instructor comp anat 1978-79; Howard Univ and Affl'd Hospitals, 3rd year resident in pediatrics. **ORGANIZATIONS:** Alto St Augustine RCC Gospel Choir 1978-; junior fellow Amer Acad of Pediatrics 1987. **HONORS/ACHIEVEMENTS:** Phi Beta Kappa Washington DC 1979; Outstanding Pediatric Resident 1986-87.

WOODHOUSE, ENOCH O'DELL, II
Attorney. **PERSONAL:** Born Jan 14, 1927, Boston. **EDUCATION:** Yale Univ, atnd 1952; Univ of Paris France, jr yr 1951; Yale Law Sch; Boston Univ Law Sch, LLB 1955; Acad of Intl Law Peace Palace Hague Netherlands, 1960. **CAREER:** Pvt prac atty; US State Dept, diplomatic courier; City of Boston, asst corp coun; Intl French & German, pvt prac law; trial couns corp law. **ORGANIZATIONS:** Intl Bar Assc; mem Boston Bar Assc; Mass Trial Lawyers Assc exec com; Yale Club of Boston; Reserve Ofcrs Assc; amer Trial Lawyers Assc elected bd of Govs Yale 1975; aptd Liaison Ofcr for AF Acad; Judge Adv Gen. **MILITARY SERVICE:** Srvd WW II, lt col AF Res. **BUSINESS ADDRESS:** US Trust Bldg, 40 Court St, Boston, MA 02108.

WOODHOUSE, JOHNNY BOYD
Clergyman. **PERSONAL:** Born Nov 09, 1945, Elizabeth City, NC; married Darlyn Blakeney; children: Yolanda, Johnny Jr, Fletcher, Touray. **EDUCATION:** Elizabeth City State, BS 1967; Shaw Divinity, MD 1973; Virginia Seminary, DD 1983. **CAREER:** PW Moore HS, teacher 1970; NC Dept of Corrections, instr 1977; Johnston Tech Coll, instr 1978; St John Bapt Red Oak NC, sr minister 1979; Johnston Tech Coll, dir of human resources develop. **ORGANIZATIONS:** Mem NAACP; mem MIZPAH Temple #66 Goldsboro NC; instructor Women Correctional Cntr Raleigh NC; Master Mason Prince Hall; Natl Bapt Conv Inc; treas Smithfield Ministerial Conf; chmn bd NC Child & Day Care Ctr; vice pres Smithfield Minister's Conf 1975; vice moderator Tar River Missionary Bapt Assn 1980-. **HONORS/ACHIEVEMENTS:** NAACP Awd 1970; Pastor of Yr 1972; Who's Who Among Black Ministers 1973. **HOME ADDRESS:** PO Box 2103, Smithfield, NC 27577.

WOODHOUSE, ROSSALIND YVONNE
Appointed government official, education. **PERSONAL:** Born Jun 07, 1940, Detroit, MI; married Donald; children: Joycelyn, Justin. **EDUCATION:** Univ of WA, BA sociology 1963; Univ of WA, MSW 1970; Univ of WA, doctoral candidate. **CAREER:** WA State Dept of Licensing Olympia, dir 1977-; Edmonds Comm Coll Lynnwood, instr coord 1973-77; Cntrl Area Motiv Prgm Seattle, exec dir 1971-73; Seattle Hsg Auth, comm orgn splst 1969-70; New Careers Proj Seattle, prog coord guid consult 1968. **ORGANIZATIONS:** State designee US Consumer Prod Sfty Commn 1978-; pres NW Conf of Black Pub Ofcls 1979-; pres Am Asso of Motor Vehicle Adminstrs Western Region 1980; pres Seattle Women's Commn 1971-72, 1975-76; mem Counc on Black Am Affairs; mem Alpha Kappa Alpha Sor Nat Fellow the Nat Fellow Fund 1976-77. **HONORS/ACHIEVEMENTS:** Outstndg yng woman of Am Outstndg Ams Bd Atlanta 1977-78; first female Motor Vehicle Dir in US or Canada; first black woman to direct a Cabinet & Level Agency in WA State. **BUSINESS ADDRESS:** Seattle Urban League, 105 14th Ave, Seattle, WA 98122.

WOODIE, HENRY L.
Engineer. **PERSONAL:** Born Oct 24, 1940, Tallahassee, FL; married Ruth. **EDUCATION:** FL A&M Univ, BS 1963; Stetson Univ, BBA 1974; Rollins College, MSM 1979. **CAREER:** Brevard County Sch Sys FL, tchr; RCA Patrick AFB FL, mathematician; Auditor Gen Office FL, auditor; Daytona Beach Comm Coll, internal auditor; Southern Bell Telephone Co, engr mgr. **ORGANIZATIONS:** Mem Omega Psi Phi. **BUSINESS ADDRESS:** Engineer/Manager, Southern Bell, 301 W Bay St, Jacksonville, FL 32201.

WOODING, DAVID JOSHUA
Physician. **PERSONAL:** Born Apr 10, 1959, Cleveland, OH; married Karen Aline Rogers; children: Joshua David. **EDUCATION:** Oakwood Coll, BA 1981; Meharry Medical Coll, MD 1986. **BUSINESS ADDRESS:** 11549 Honey Hollow, Moreno Valley, CA 92387.

WOODING, SAMUEL DAVID
Musician, composer, arranger, executive. **PERSONAL:** Born Jun 17, 1895, Philadelphia, PA; married Rae Harrison. **EDUCATION:** Univ of PA, BA 1944; Univ of PA School of Educ, MS. **CAREER:** Pan-Jebel Inc, pres & founder. **ORGANIZATIONS:** Orchestra leader, composer, arranger 1918-; 1st Jazz Orchestra Leader in Europe 1925; toured Russia 1926; toured S Amer 1927; performed 1st Jazz Concert Copenhagen 1931; guest Prince Carl of Sweden, Duke of Windsor, King Alphonse & Queen Victoria of Spain; Pres Nixon 1973, Pres Carter 1979. **MILITARY SERVICE:** AUS military band 1918. **BUSINESS ADDRESS:** PO Box 713 Radio City Station, New York, NY 10019.

WOODLAND, CALVIN EMMANUEL
Educator. **PERSONAL:** Born Nov 03, 1943, LaPlata, MD; son of Philip H. Woodland (deceased) and Mildred Woodland (deceased). **EDUCATION:** Morgan State Univ, BS 1965; Howard Univ, MA 1970; Rutgers Univ, EdD 1975. **CAREER:** MD Dept of Health & Mental Hygiene, music & rehab therapist 1966-70; Essex Co Coll, counselor/dir of educ advisement 1970-74; Morgan State Univ Sch of Educ, dir of teacher corps, assoc prof of educ asst dean 1974-81; Coppin State Coll, dir of spec svcs, acting dean of students 1981-82; Charles County Comm Coll, dean 1982-86; Northern Virginia Comm Coll, dean 1986-. **ORGANIZATIONS:** Evaluator Middle States Assoc of Colleges & Schools 1979-; chmn Southern MD Educ Enrichment Fund 1984-; mem Amer Educ Research Assoc, Amer Psychological Assoc, Amer Assoc for Counseling Dev, Amer Assoc of Rehab Therapists, Southern MD Private Industry Council. **HONORS/ACHIEVEMENTS:** HEW Fellow US Dept of Health, Educ Welfare 1976; ERIC Publications on Data Base as a Tool for Recruitment of Minority Students 1979, 85; Innovations in Counseling Psychology Book Review Journal of Contemporary Psychology 1979; Outstanding Achievement and Comm Serv Southern MD Chain Chap of Links 1986. **HOME ADDRESS:** 2425 E. Rosecraft Village Circle, Oxon Hill, MD 20745.

WOODRIDGE, WILSON JACK, JR.
Architect. **PERSONAL:** Born Aug 29, 1950, East Orange, NJ; divorced. **EDUCATION:** Essex Cty Coll, AAS 1970; Cornell Univ Coll or Arch, BA 1975. **CAREER:** Bernard Johnson Inc, designer 1976-77; Skidmore Owings & Merrill, designer 1977-80; Welton Becket Assoc, project designer 1981; The Grad Partnership, project architect 1981-85; Essex County College, dir of Architecture Programs 1983-; Woodridge & Ray Architects 1985-. **ORGANIZATIONS:** Official interviewer Cornell Univ Alumni Secondary Comm 1975; chmn proj comm Houston Comm Design Ctr 1978-80; chmn fin comm Essex Cty Coll Alumni Assoc 1982-84; sec exec comm Houston Urban Bunch 1979-80. **HONORS/ACHIEVEMENTS:** Outstanding Alumni Awd Essex Cty Coll 1984; East Orange Merchants Awd 1987. **HOME ADDRESS:** 305 South Burnet St, East Orange, NJ 07018. **BUSINESS ADDRESS:** Dir of Architecture Prog, Essex County College, 303 University Ave, Newark, NJ 07102.

WOODRUFF, CONSTANCE ONEIDA
Director, community relations. **PERSONAL:** Born Oct 24, 1921, Rochelle, NY; married William Woodruff. **EDUCATION:** Cornell Univ, AA Labor Stud 1971; Empire State Clge, BA Lab Stud 1974; Rutgers Univ, MA Lab Stud 1975. **CAREER:** Intl Garment Wkrs Union AFL-CIO, dir comm rel East Reg; NJ Hearld News, cty ed; pol columnist for sev mag; legal secr; bus rep & ed dir; Essex Co Clge Newark, adj prof Lab Studies, dir public relations/development. **ORGANIZATIONS:** 1st Black to head spec dept in ILGWU; del to '72 Dem Conv; sec NJ Dem St Comm 1974; ex-off mem state del Dem Mini Conv KC MO 1974. **HONORS/ACHIEVEMENTS:** Num awards, Newark Sr Cit for prom welf of Old Amer; The Leaguers for 25 yrs srv in high educ opp for Black Youths; A Phillip Randolph Award for ach in Lab Rel; Radio Stn WWRL for outst comm srv; Thelma McFall Fnd for srv to handic child. **BUSINESS ADDRESS:** Dir Public Relations/Devlop, Essex County College, 303 University Avenue, Newark, NJ 07102.

WOODRUFF, HALE A.
Artist, educator. **PERSONAL:** Born Aug 26, 1900, Cairo, IL; married Theresa. **EDUCATION:** John Herron Art Inst; Fogg Art Mus; Harvard Univ; Amademie Scandinave; Academie Moderne Paris. **CAREER:** NYU, prof emeritus, artist, teacher. **ORGANIZATIONS:** Exhibited numerous pl, NY World's Fair, Art Ctr of NY, Chicago Art Inst; important works, The Amistad Mutiny & Founding of Talladega, Talladega Clge & Histof CA, The Art of the Negro & Red Landscape at Johnson Pub Co; collections, Metro Mus of Art NYC, IBM, The High Museum of Art, Atlanta, Newark Museum, NJ Library of Congress, Atlanta Univ, Spelman Coll, Atlanta, NYU, Joseph Davis; Assoc past mem NJ Soc of Artists; Soc of Mural Painters; Com on Art Educ of Museum of Modern Art; past mem NY State Coun on Arts, appointed by Gov Nelson Rockefeller; New York City Art Commn; appointed by Mayor John Lindsay; lecture tour W Africa US Dept of State Hon Dr Morgan State Coll, 1968; hon LHD, Atlanta Univ 1972. **BUSINESS ADDRESS:** 22-26 E 8 St, New York, NY 10003.

WOODRUFF, JAMES W.
Chief executive automotive dealership. **CAREER:** Woodruff Oldsmobile Inc, Detroit MI, chief executive, 1988. **BUSINESS ADDRESS:** Woodruff Oldsmobile, Inc, 15000 West Seven Mile Rd, Detroit, MI 48235. *

WOODRUFF, JEFFREY ROBERT
Director. **PERSONAL:** Born Jul 13, 1943, Pittsburgh, PA; married Vickie; children: Jennifer. **EDUCATION:** Springfield Coll, BS 1966; New York Inst of Tech, MBA 1978. **CAREER:** KQV Radio Inc, dir rsch & devel 1968-70; WLS Radio Inc, dir rsch 1970-72; ABC AM Radio Stas, dir rsch & devel 1972-77, dir sales & rsch 1977-79; WDAI Radio, natl sales mgr 1979-80; IL Bell Telephone Co, acct exec indus consul 1980-83, mgr promos marketing staff 1983-. **ORGANIZATIONS:** Mem Radio TV Rsch Cncl; Amer Marketing Assn; Delta Mu Delta; Radio Advertising Bur; GOALS Com; mem Black Exec Exchange Prog; Natl Urban League Inc; YouthMotivation Task Force; adjunct faculty New York Inst of Technology; adjunct faculty N Central Coll; consult Network Programming Concepts Inc; industry advisor Arbitron Adv Council Mensa Ltd. **HONORS/ACHIEVEMENTS:** Natl Alliance of Bus Innovator Awd Amer Rsch Bur 1972; Black Achievers in Ind Awd Harlem YMCA 1972; vis prof Sem Prog Knoxville Coll. **MILITARY SERVICE:** USMC corpl 1966-68. **BUSINESS ADDRESS:** Manager of Promotions, IL Bell Telephone Co, 225 W Washington, Chicago, IL 60606.

WOODS, ALLIE, JR.
Actor, stage director, educator, writer, lecturer. **PERSONAL:** Born Sep 28, Houston, TX; son of Allie Woods Sr and Georgia Woods; married Beverly; children: Allyson Beverly, Stewart Jordan. **EDUCATION:** TX Southern Univ, BA; TN State Univ, MS; New School, producing for television; NY Univ, film production/writing for film/television; Ctr for the Media Arts,TV production. **CAREER:** TX So Univ, 1961-63, artist-in-resd 1983; Alley Theatre Co, actor 1963,66; Houston Pub Sch, tchr 1964-66; Day of Absence, actor 1967; Chelsea Theatre Ctr Brooklyn Acad of Music, actor/dir 1968-69; A Black Quartet, co-dir 1969; Intl Theatre Fest London, actor 1969; Brooklyn & John Jay Coll CUNY, tchr 1970-75; LaMama Experimental Theatre Club NYC, 1971-73; Intl Theatre Fest Venice Milan, 1972; John Jay Coll Rutgers Univ, Univ of MO, Univ of Ibadan, Univ of Wash, Brooklyn Coll, dir Sunday Series NY Shakesphere Fest Pub Theatre 1972; New Fed Theatre NYC, dir 1981,82; State Univ of NY Old Westbury, asst prof 1982-83; Coll of New Rochelle, lecturer speech comm; Bergen Comm Coll, Paramus, NJ, lecturer comm/theatre 1988-89; New York Shakespeare Festival/New York City, actor, 1989. **ORGANIZATIONS:** Staging consultant Tony Brown's Journals "Malcolm and Elijah" (drama segment) PBS-TV 1981; vstg dir Michigan State Univ 1983; artist-in-residence Texas Southern Univ 1983; producer/director/commentary writer "Divestment" video sponsored by Ctr for the Media Arts 1985; lecturer speech comm Hudson Co Comm Coll; mem Actors Equity Assn; Screen Actors Guild; mem Black Filmmaker Foundation; Playwrights-Directors Unit/The Actors Studio; mem The Dramatists Guild 1987-; mem Writers Workshop/The Negro Ensemble Co 1989. **HONORS/ACHIEVEMENTS:** Theatre Production Grant OEO Houston 1967; Fellowship Grant Ford Found 1973; Ford Found Grant Univ of Ibadan Nigeria 1973; Plays performed or directed: In White America 1965, Song of the Lusitanian Bogey 1968, The Gentleman Caller 1969, Ceremonies in Dark Old Men 1971, No Place to be Somebody 1973, One Flew Over the Cuckoo's Nest 1973, A Conflict of Interest 1973, Tiger at the Gates 1974, The Black Terror 1975, Cotillion 1975, When the Chickens Came Home to Roost 1981, Dreams Deferred 1982, No Place to be Somebody 1983; directed readings/workshop productions, Open Admissions 1983, Scenes from God's Trombones and Short Eyes 1983,Cage Bird 1985, Alias, Othello 1986/87; Best Dir Drama AUDELCO Awds Comm 1981; Filmmaker Grant Amer Film Inst 1978; "Mrs Evers' Boys", actor 1989; "The Brownsvil le Raid", dir 1988; "The Forbidden City", actor 1989; "Zora and Langston", dir 1989; "Lady Bugs", unpublished novel, writer 1988.

WOODS, ALMITA (NEE ROBINSON)
Administrator. **PERSONAL:** Born Jul 06, 1914, Eastover, SC; married Willie Michael; children: Robert, Leonard Michael. **EDUCATION:** Benedict Coll, BA 1937; AtlantaUniv Sch of Work, 1938-40;Univ TX, 1950&54; AtlantaUniv Sch of Soc Work, MSW 1960. **CAREER:** Sickle Cell Syndrome Prgm NC Dept of Human Resources, Cons; Comm & Svcs, comm 1973; adoptions spec 1970-73; Tri-city Comm Action Prgm, dir 1969-70; psychiatric consult 1968-69; Nat OEO, consult 1967-70; Comm Serv Agency, 1960-66. **ORGANIZATIONS:** Pr Dir Jarvis Christian Coll 1957-60; dir Quaker's Merit Employment 1951-56; dir YMCA Br Austin 1950-51; mgr Robinson Const Co 1944-49; exec sec Negro Welfare Council 1941-44; interim dir Atlanta Urban League 1940-41; tchr 1935-38; fdr Ft Worth Urban League 1943; Woodlawn Comm Serv Council 1961; orgnrOnslow Co Sickle Cell Anemia Assn 1971; Nat Ladies Aux & Camp Lejeune Chpt; Montford Point Marine Assn 1974; NC Black Womens Polit Caucus 1977; columnist weekly nespapers; columnist Atlanta & Jour; initaited prgm weekly commentator The Negro Hour; mem adv com Chicago Human Relation Commn; adv com Woodlanw Urban Prog Ctr; mem Mayor's Com for Urban Renewal; chmn Onslow Co Sickle Cell Anemia Assn; past pres Ladies Aux Montford Point Marine Assn; MemMidville Bapt Ch; Nat Assn of Soc Works; Acad of Cert Soc Workers; Sigma Gamma Rho Sor; Alpha Gamma Pi Sor; Staff NCO Wives Club; NAACP; Nat Assn of Black Soc Workers; various local orgns. **HONORS/ACHIEVEMENTS:** Spec commendation MINUTE Am Friends Serv Com; 1 of 12 most outstanding women in chicago; Alpha Gamma Pi Sor 1964; outstanding serv to woodlawn comm American Friendship Club 1966; spl letter of commendation Mayor & Richard J Dailey 1966; marine wife of the yr Tri-command Camp Lejeune NC; finalist mil wife ofthe yr; appointed gov holshouser Gov Hunt States Council on Sickle Cel Syndrome; natl register of prominent ams. **BUSINESS ADDRESS:** 404 St Andrews St, Greenville, NC 27834.

WOODS, ARLEIGH MADDOX
Judge. **PERSONAL:** Born Aug 31, 1929, Los Angeles, CA; son of Benjamine Maddox and Ida Maddox; married William T. **EDUCATION:** Chapman Coll, BS 1949; Southwestern Univ, LLB 1952; Univ of VA, LLM 1983; Univ of West Los Angeles, DDL 1984. **CAREER:** Levy Koszdin & Woods, atty 18 yrs, vice pres; CA Court of Appeal, presiding justice. **ORGANIZATIONS:** vice pres Constitutional Rights Foundation 1980-; bd of dir Cancer Research Foundation 1983-; Trustee, Southwestern Univ Schl of Law 1986. **HONORS/**

ACHIEVEMENTS: Justice of the Year (CA) 1983; Woman of the Year Business & Professional Women 1982, YWCA 1984; Judicial Officer of the Year Southwestern Univ 1987. **BUSINESS ADDRESS:** Presiding Justice, CA Court of Appeal, 3580 Wilshire Blvd, Los Angeles, CA 90010.

WOODS, BARBARA MCALPIN
Educational administrator. **PERSONAL:** Born Dec 09, 1945, Nashville, TN; daughter of Dr Neal McAlpin Sr and Ruth DuVall McAlpin; married James F Woods; children: Trieste, Travis, Tamara. **EDUCATION:** Univ of Kansas, BS 1967; St Louis Univ, MA 1982. **CAREER:** St Louis City Schools, teacher secondary English 1967-70; St Louis Univ, asst dir special academic programs 1972-77, acting dir Afro-American studies 1977-80, dir Afro-Amer stud/center-interdis studies 1980-. **ORGANIZATIONS:** Moderator/producer "Black Issues Forum" KADI radio-FM 1978-86; vice pres 84-85 & bd of dir Conference on Educ 1979-85; educ committee Urban League of Metro St Louis 1980-; charter member & chair Missouri Council for Black Studies 1982-84; bd of dirs Girl Scout Council 1981-85; task force Educ Prof Missouri, comm chair & steering comm 1984-87; bd of dir Kiwanis Camp Wyman St Louis 1984-87; moderator/producer "Postscript" KETC-TV; mem President's Advisory Council of Greater St Louis Girl Scout Council; natl advisory bd HERstory in Silhouette Project of the St Louis Public Schools; founder/convener Cross Cultural Conf on Women (biannual conf); founder, chair, bd of dirs, Youth Leadership St Louis Inc 1987-88; mem, bd of dirs, YWCA of Metropolitan St Louis 1988-90; mem, bd of trustees, St Louis Art Museum 1989-91. **HONORS/ACHIEVEMENTS:** Fellowship Multicultural Women's Inst, Univ of Illinois Chicago 1983; Top Ladies of Distinction Award, St Louis Chapter Top Ladies of Distinction 1984; Fellow, Leadership St Louis, Leadership St Louis Inc 1987-88; established/coordinated devel of Youth Leadership St Louis initially as a class project for the Ledership St Louis Fellows 1987-88, this high school leadership project is now an institionalized program. **BUSINESS ADDRESS:** Dir, St Louis University, Afro-American Studies & Center, 221 N Grand Blvd, St Louis, MO 63103.

WOODS, BERNICE
Nurse, elected official. **PERSONAL:** Born Sep 27, 1924, Port Arthur, TX; married Melvin J Woods; children: Melvin J Jr, Mary Jane, Jule Norman, Pernilla, Lewis, Kenneth Dale, Paulette, Dwight Clayton, Muriel Gale, Gregory Wayne. **EDUCATION:** Attended East Los Angeles Jr Coll; CA School & Nursing, BS 1948; Univ of CA Los Angeles, BS Behavioral Sci 1965; CA State Univ Long Beach, MEd 1968. **CAREER:** Los Angeles Cty Gen Hosp, nurse retired after 28 yrs service; Compton Unified School Dist, bd of trustees mem. **ORGANIZATIONS:** Mem Queen of Sheba Grand Chap OES 1964; representation Delegate Assembly CA School Bd Assoc 1975-83; mem bd of trustees Compton Unified School Dist 1975-; mem Union Baptist Church, Democratic Club of Compton; pres Ladies Aux POP Warner Football; grand pres of Matron's Council OES; pres of Compton Union Council; PTA Parent Teacher Assn; mem Willowbrook State Park; pres/1st vp/2nd vice pres Natl Council of Negro Women; juvenile protect chmn 33rd Dist PTA; mem Southeast Mental Health Liaison Comm; mem NAACP Compton Chpt. **HONORS/ACHIEVEMENTS:** Numerous awards incl, life mem Natl Council Negro Women 1974; Co-author Book "I Am a Black Woman Who" 1976; Helping All Children Natl School Bd Assoc 1978; 50 Year Serv Awd Parent Teacher Assoc 1978; Natl PTA Award 1984; Woman of the Year 1970 & 1975; mem Task Force to Secure Funds for Compton Unified Sch Dist 1974-75; Alternate Del to Dem Natl Conv NY 1976; Inner City Challange; Natl Council of Negro Women Achievers Award (4 times); Youth Athletic Assn Award; Comm Award Block Clubs; Fraternal Award Order of the Eastern Star; Help All Agencies Dedicated Serv Award; Bethune Outstand Achieve Award; OutstandingChurch Serv Award; Outstanding Serv Award Lt Gov Mervyn Dymally; Bronze Medal Award Achievers Wash, DC; C of C Christmas Award. **HOME ADDRESS:** 1515 W 166th St, Compton, CA 90220. **BUSINESS ADDRESS:** Board of Trustees, Compton Unified Sch Dist, 604 S Tamarind Ave, Compton, CA 90220.

WOODS, CHARLOTTE ANN
Elected official. **PERSONAL:** Born Jan 07, 1932, Ft Wayne, IN; divorced; children: Beauford K, Brenda K McDonald, Parnell L Jr, Jeffry C. **EDUCATION:** Central HS Ft Wayne, 1946-50. **CAREER:** Peg Leg Bates Country Club, ba mgr 1976, asst mgr 1980-86 off mgr 1987. **ORGANIZATIONS:** Bd mem Bd of Ethics Kerhonkson 1969-73, Ulster Cty Mental Health Assn 1970-76; chmn Tower of Rochester Dem Club 1970-; Prevention Connection Comm Drug & Alcohol Abuse.

WOODS, DELBERT LEON
Association executive. **PERSONAL:** Born Mar 08, 1913, Lorain, OH; married Thelma Ruth Hamilton; children: Delbert L. **EDUCATION:** E Tech Inst Cleveland, diploma 1929; Western Res, atnd 1930; Provost Marshall Gen Sch, cert 1943. **CAREER:** Charleston Br NAACP, pres; Charleston Naval Shipyard, painter & personnel rep 1947-; Port of Embarkation Charleston SC, gen foreman 1946-47; Lorain Co Sheriff's Dept, dept sheriff 1933. **ORGANIZATIONS:** Natl rep Natl Assc Govt Employees 1972-; comdr Fed Employees Vets Assc 1956-59; state labor chmn/2nd vice pres SC State Conf NAACP 1960-70. **HONORS/ACHIEVEMENTS:** Recip Marksmanship & Expert Rifel Badge AUS 1942-45; citation aptmnt bd of rev Charleston Naval Shipyard 1948-55; Cert of Merit Natl Office NAACP State Conf NAACP 1959-63; adv council Study of SC Ethnic Hist 1975; cert of Achievement Alpha Phi Alpha Frat Inc 1977; Citation Kappa Alpha Psi Frat 1980. **MILITARY SERVICE:** AUS corpl 1942-45.

WOODS, GENEVA HALLOWAY
Registered nurse anesthetist. **PERSONAL:** Born Sep 16, 1930, Saluda, SC; daughter of Lonnie Halloway and Mattie Dozier Halloway; married Sylvania Webb Sr; children: Sylvania Jr, Sebrena. **EDUCATION:** Grady Hosp Sch of Nursing Atlanta, diploma 1949; DillardUniv Sch of Anesthesia New Orleans LA, cert 1957; Real Estate Certificate - P.G. Comm. Coll Largo, MD 1983. **CAREER:** DC Gen Hosp Wash DC, staff nurse anesthetist 1979-; St Elizabeth Hosp Wash DC, chief nurse anesthetist 1976-79; Providence Hosp Wash DC, chief nurse anesthetist 1971-76; DC Gen, staff nurse anesthetist 1960-70; Freedmen Hosp HowardUniv Wash DC, staff nurse 1955-57; Grady Meml Hosp Atlanta, asst head nurse 1952-54; Grady Meml Hosp Atlanta, prvt duty polio nurse 1950-52; DC ANaA, pres 1968-70; DC Lawyers Wives, parliamentarian 1974-76; PG Co Lawyers Wives, parliamentarian; certified real estate salesperson; registered nurse Providence Hosp. D.C. Substance Abuse. **ORGANIZATIONS:** Mem Upper Room Bapt Ch Wash DC 1961-; parliamentarian & charter mem Jack & Jills of PG Co Chap 1973-75; chmn Glenarden Inaugural Ball 1979; Chairman Saluda Rosen Wald/Riverside School Alumni Assn/Grady Nurses Alumni Assn D.C. Md. Va. Chapter. mem, bd of ethics, PG Co. **HONORS/ACHIEVEMENTS:** Recipient mother of the yr award BSA Troop 1017 1966; cert parliamentarian parliamentarian Parliamentary Procecures Chicago IL 1970; continued professional excellence award Am Assn Nurse Chicago 1975&78; outstanding performance award St Elizabeth Hosp Wash DC 1978. **HOME ADDRESS:** 7816 Fiske Ave, Glenarden, MD 20801.

WOODS, GEORGE WASHINGTON
Chief executive officer. **PERSONAL:** Born Mar 18, 1916, Colt, AR; married Ophelia Henry; children: Dr George W, Michael F. **EDUCATION:** AM&N Coll Pine Bluff AR, BA 1946; So IL U, attended 1968. **CAREER:** State Equal Oppor Office, dir; insurance estimator several insurance cos 1945-80; Office of Neighborhood Devel & Improvement, comm relations adv 1968-; City of Omaha NE, dir rehab 1968-71; Mechanic Drafting OIC Inc, instr 1970-; Woods Gen Home Improvement Co, owner 1951-68; OIC, drafting G instr 1971-; City of Omaha, land appraiser 1972-80; Woods Timber and Ranch Inc, operator; Woods Gen Home Improvement Co, owner 1951-68, dir. **ORGANIZATIONS:** Mem NACP 1935-80; Urban League 1950-56; minority rep Dem Party & Gov 1970-80; mem Omega Psi Phi Frat Inc, NAACP Inc; mem Allen Chapel AME Ch; mem Nat SEOO Exec Com; mem Kellom Comm Council; mem State System Com oranized United Contractor Assn of NE/COMM Serv Agt/Infant Devel EncouragementProgram; chmn 11th Legislative Dist of Democratic Party 1987; chmn Urban League Legislative Comm; mem Catfish Farmers of Amer, Kellom Library Bd, South Omaha Neighborhood Assoc. **HONORS/ACHIEVEMENTS:** Man Of The Year Kellom Community Council 1973; Leadership Award Kellom Community Council 1974; Service Awd Comm Action Assoc of NE 1985; Harry S Truman Awd 1986; numerous other awards. **BUSINESS ADDRESS:** Dir, Woods General Home, 3327 Ruggles St, Omaha, NE 68111.

WOODS, GERALDINE PITTMAN
Special consultant. **PERSONAL:** Born in W Palm Beach, FL; married Dr Robert I Woods Sr; children: D Jan, Jerri S Robert I Jr. **EDUCATION:** Talladega Clg, 1968-40; Howard U, BS 1942; Radcliffe & Harvard U, MS 1943, PhD 1945; Benedict Clg, DSc 1977; Talladega Clg, DSc 1980. **CAREER:** NIH, spec consult 1969; placed ground work & asstd dvlpmnt of Minority Access to Rsrch Careers & Minority Biomedical Rsrch Support. **ORGANIZATIONS:** Chm Bd of Trustees Howard Univ 1975-; mem Natl Bd Girl Scts of USA 1975-78; mem chr of Ed Policy Comm Atlanta U; 1974-; mem Inst of Med Natl Academy of Sciences 1974-; mem bd of dir Natl Comm for Cert of Phys Assts 1974-81; mem bd of dir Robert Wood Johnson Hlth Pol Flwshp IOM NAS 1973-78; mem vice pres CA Post Secondary Ed Comm 1974-78; mem bd of trustees CA Museum Fndtn of CA Museum of Sci & Ind 1971-79; chm Defense Adv Comm on Women inServices 1968; natl pres Delta Sigma Theta Sor 1963-67; life Mem of NAACP NCNW & mem of Urban League; mem AAAS; Federation of Am Scientists, Natl Inst of Sci; pres Delta Rsrch of Edctnl Fndtn; pres Howard Univ Fndtn. **HONORS/ACHIEVEMENTS:** Mbr Phi Beta Kappa; listed in Whos Who of Women of the World; recipient of many awds & citation by org & govt; recd "Scroll of Merit" from NMA, highest awd of LA Alumnae Chapter of Delta Sigma Theta; Merit Awd, highest awd of the Natl Org; Mary Chutch Terrell Awd; many awds from Howard U; selected as one of 20 famous am black scientists; one of "Black Women Achieving Against the Odds", an exhibit by the Smithsonian Inst. **HOME ADDRESS:** 12065 Rose Marie Ln, Los Angeles, CA 90049.

WOODS, HORTENSE E.
Librarian. **PERSONAL:** Born Mar 17, 1926, Malvern, AR; married Walter F; children: Marcia Laureen. **EDUCATION:** AR AM & N Coll Pine Bluff, bA 1950; CathUniv Washington, lS; UCLA & pepperdine U, study;Univ of Southern CA, grad. **CAREER:** Vernon Br Sr Lib, pub lib; Pine Bluff Pub Lib Bran Lib, 1954-59; Wilmington Br LA Pub Lib 1st Black Lib, 1961-65; Enterprise Sch Dist LA Co, org lib 1966-69; Lincoln HS Camden AR Sch Lib, 1950-51. **ORGANIZATIONS:** Dir All Cty Emp Asn LA 1973-; sec Cent C of C LA 1973-; mem Am Film Inst; bd mem Cntr for Women Dvel Long Beach CA; editorial consult Saturday Mag 1979; mem Staff Assn LA Pub Lib 1970-; mem Grant AME Ch Women's Day Nat Coun Negro Women. **HONORS/ACHIEVEMENTS:** Edtr "Fav Delta Recipes" pub by Bev-ron Publ 1974; mem natl hon soc. **BUSINESS ADDRESS:** Branch Librarian, Vernon Branch Library, 4504 S Central Ave, Los Angeles, CA 90011.

WOODS, JACQUELINE EDWARDS
Educator. **PERSONAL:** Born Oct 10, 1947, Detroit, MI; children: John E Kemp. **EDUCATION:** MI State Univ, BA 1969; Wayne State Univ, MEd 1970. **CAREER:** Various Educ Assocs/Colls, speech path/prof 1971-74; Long Beach Comm Coll District, dean resource develop energy prog dir 1975-79; Amer Assoc of Comm/Jr Colls, dir prog develop 1979-83; Amer Coll Testing Program, dir Washington DC office 1983-. **ORGANIZATIONS:** Teaching asst consultant/trainer Jr Community College Inst 1979-; mem bd dirs United Way/United Black Fund Mgmt Serv 1982-84; mem DC bd dirs MI State Univ Black Alumni 1983-; chmn steering comm Women Administrators in Higher Educ 1984-; mem adv bd Natl Consortium for Educ Access 1985-; mem bd dirs Amer Assoc Higher Educ Black Caucus 1986-; convocation speaker Livingstone Coll 1986. **HONORS/ACHIEVEMENTS:** Woman of the Yr Amer Business Women's Assoc Port City Chap 1973; Outstanding Young Women of Amer 1975; Appreciation Awd Natl Council Resource Dev (AACJC) 1983; Appreciation Awd League of United Lation Amer Citizens 1986; Outstanding Serv Awd AAHE Black Caucus (Nat) 1986. **BUSINESS ADDRESS:** Dir, The Amer Coll Testing Program, One DuPont Circle NW, Ste 340, Washington, DC 20036.

WOODS, JANE GAMBLE
Publisher. **PERSONAL:** Born Aug 26, 1928, St Louis, MO; widowed; children: JoAnn Austin, Judy W Williams, Patricia W May, Gail W McDuffie. **EDUCATION:** Attended, Stowe Jr Coll, Lincoln Univ Jefferson City MO. **CAREER:** St Louis Sentinel Newspaper, publisher. **ORGANIZATIONS:** Past bd mem Natl Assn of Media Women; past bd mem St Louis Chap United Nations of Amer; past bd mem St Louis Chap ICBO; bd mem Natl Newspaper Pub Assn; bd mem Amalgamated Pub Inc; bd mem OIC St Louis Ch; pst bd mem KETC Ch 9 St Louis Regional Ed & Pub TV; pst trustee Deaconess Hosp;past bd mem Northside YMCA; mem adv bd Salvation Army; past mem adv bd Small Bus Adminstrn; past bd mem Com on Adminstrn Phyllis Wheatley YWCA; bd mem Jr Kindergarten; past bd mem MO Assn for Social Welfare; commr MO Housing Development Comm; bd mem Urban League of Metro St Louis; 2nd vice pres Natl Newspaper Publishers Assn. **BUSINESS ADDRESS:** Publisher, St Louis Sentinel Newspaper, 3338 Olive St Ste 206, St Louis, MO 63103.

WOODS, JESSIE A.
Executive director. **PERSONAL:** Born Apr 08, 1914, Chicago, IL; married James H (deceased); children: Victoria W Burgoyne, James A. **EDUCATION:** Univ of Chicago, attended 1931-32; Univ of IL, attended 1932-33; Univ of Chicago, attended 1937-38; Harvard Univ, fellowship & certificate Arts Admin 1972. **CAREER:** Graham Artist Bureau, agent 1935-37; Univ of Chicago, research asst 1937-39; Woods Brothers Inc, office mgr 1941-53; Task Force/Alt Educ Natl Endowment for the Arts, consultant/co-chmn 1976; Urban Gateways, exec dir 1965-81; Reading Is Fundamental In Chicago, exec dir 1985-. **ORGANIZATIONS:** Mem Alpha Gamma Pi 1975-; mem exec com Chicago Council on Fine Arts, Natl Council on Fine Arts, Dept of Cultural Affairs 1976-; mem Dusable Museum of African-Amer Histoty; Presidential appointment Natl Council on the Arts, 1978-84; appointed chmn advisory board, Chicago Dept of Cultural Affairs, 1985-; mem Bd of Overseers for Campus Life, Illinois Inst of Technology; visiting comm, School of Social Serv Admin, Univ of Chicago 1985-. **HONORS/ACHIEVEMENTS:** Governor's Award/Contribution to Arts State of IL 1978; Chicago Comm on Human Relations Award Chicago 1978; Honorary Doctorate of Humane Letters Columbia Coll Chicago 1979; Honorary Doctor Fine Arts, Univ of IL. **HOME ADDRESS:** 5530 S Shore Dr, Chicago, IL 60637.

WOODS, JOE
Vice president. **EDUCATION:** Michigan State Univ, BA Advertising. **CAREER:** Image Packaging Co, co-owner and dir of sales and mktg; Burrell Adv, account exec; Vince Cullers Adv Inc, vice pres/account supervisor.

WOODS, LAWRENCE CHARLES
Business executive. **PERSONAL:** Born Jun 25, 1916, Hot Springs Nat Pk, AR; married Florence Byrd; children: Mabel Ann Cole, Ronald D. **EDUCATION:** Univ So CA, BA; Bonds Bus Coll;Univ WA. **CAREER:** CCI CCCMI & Fortune Carpet Ind, pres bd chmn; Congressman William L Dawson, 1st Congressiona Dist Chgo, top adminstrv aide; Com on Govt Operations Which Monitores All Fed Spending, chmn; Dem Party, natl v-chmn; Cook Co Regular Dem Orgn, v-chmn 1960-68. **ORGANIZATIONS:** Trustee Quinn Chapel AME Ch; mem NAACP; Urban League; Operations PUSH. **HONORS/ACHIEVEMENTS:** Breadbasket commercial assn chgo gazette article, hailed as Carpet King; pioneer in carpet mfging Black Enterprise Mag 1977; 1st black mfr carpeting to receive contract from natl concern Congressman Parren Mitchell; recd three-fourth million dollar carpet contract Chicago's Dearborn Park; del White House Conf for Small Bus 1979; prs Black Contr United Div of Urban League 1979. **MILITARY SERVICE:** USN 1941.

WOODS, MANUEL T.
Educator. **PERSONAL:** Born May 10, 1939, Kansas City, KS; married Gloria Smith; children: Susan, Daniel. **EDUCATION:** Univ of MN, AA 1968, BA 1970, PhD 1978; Univ of Hartford, MEd 1973. **CAREER:** Univ of MN, new careers prog counselor 1967-70, office of admissions/reg asst dir 1970-85, office of student affairs asst to vice pres 1985-86, educ student affairs office dir 1986-. **ORGANIZATIONS:** Pres MN Counselors & Dirs of Minority Programs Assoc; pres Univ Assoc of Black Employees; program chairperson Upper Midwest Assoc of Collegiate Registrars and Admissions Officers; program convenor MN Counselors and Directors of Minority Programs, Counseling the Disadvantaged Student; comm mem Minneapolis Comm Coll Adv Bd. **HONORS/ACHIEVEMENTS:** Bush Fellowship Awd Bush Foundation 1973; Outstanding Alumnus Minneapolis Comm Coll 1986. **BUSINESS ADDRESS:** Dir Student Affairs, University of Minnesota, College of Educ, 1425 University Ave SE, Minneapolis, MN 55414.

WOODS, MELVIN LEROY
Business executive. **PERSONAL:** Born May 10, 1938, Lexington, KY; married Elnora; children: Gregory, Alyssa. **EDUCATION:** Jackson State U, BS 1962; VA Hosp, cert 1962;Univ IL, mS 1967; IUPUI, 1973-75. **CAREER:** Eli Lilly & Co, comm rel asso; Lilly Endowment Inc, prgm ofcr, 1973-77; Marion Co Asn Retarded Citz, dior adult serv 1970-73; So WI Colony & Union Cp Training Sch, supr therapist 1966-70; WI Parks & Recreation &3Univ WI consult 1967; St Lukes Hosp, 1969-70; So IN Retardation Serv 972-73. **ORGANIZATIONS:** Mem WI Parks & Rec Assn 1966-73; IN Assn Rehab Facilities; bd mem Intl Assn Rehab Facilities 1972-73; Nat Assn Retarded Citz 1970-75; Am Assn Mental Deficiency 1973-77; mem Kappa Alpha Psi; Alpha Kappa Mu 1962. **HONORS/ACHIEVEMENTS:** Listed Who's Who Among Students in Am U'S & Coll's 1962; distd hoosier citation IN Gov Office 1972; flwsp grantUniv I 1965; publ "The Devel of a Pay for Recreation Procedure in a Token Economy System; Mental Retardation 1971. **MILITARY SERVICE:** AUS sp 4 1962-65. **BUSINESS ADDRESS:** 307 E Mc Carty St, Indianapolis, IN 46206.

WOODS, PHILIP WELLS
Alto saxophonist, clarinetist, composer. **PERSONAL:** Born Nov 02, 1931, Springfield, MA; married Jill Goodwin; children: Kim Parker, Baird Parker, Garth, Aimee, Allisen Trotter. **EDUCATION:** Saxophone w/Harvey LaRose; Attended, Julliard Conservatory 1948-52. **CAREER:** Played with Dizzy Gillespie Band US Overseas 1965; played with Quincy Jones Band on European tours 1959-61; played with Benny Goodman Band touring USSR 1962 & Monterey Jazz Festival 1962; rec artist; Phil Wood Quintet, pvt tchr leader; European Rhythm Machine based in Paris, 1968-73. **ORGANIZATIONS:** Composer "Rights of Swing" 1960; Sonata for Alto & Piano; Three Improvisions; I Remember. **HONORS/ACHIEVEMENTS:** Winner on Alto Saxophone Down Beat Critics' & Readers' Polls 1975-86; Grammy Awds "Best Instrumental Jazz Performance Group" 1977 1982 1983. **BUSINESS ADDRESS:** Box 278, Delaware Water Gap, PA 18327.

WOODS, ROBERT LOUIS
Public health dentist. **PERSONAL:** Born Oct 24, 1947, Charlotte, NC; son of Clifton Woods, Jr. and Effie E. Woods; married Cynthia Dianne Hawkins; children: Sonja Nicole, Cheryl Lynnette. **EDUCATION:** NC Central Univ, BS Biol 1964, MS Biol 1971; Univ of NC School of Dentistry, DDS 1977. **CAREER:** Duke Univ Med Ctr, rsch tech 1969; NC Agricultural & Tech Univ, instr of biol 1971-73; pvt practice, 1977-; Univ of NC School of Dentistry, clinicalinstr 1979-81; Orange Chatham Comprehensive Health Svcs, lead staff dentist 1982-89. **ORGANIZATIONS:** Mem Amer Dental Assoc 1977-, NC Dental Soc 1977-, Old North State Dental Soc 1977-; bd dir fin comm chair Person Family Med Ctr 1979-81; bd dir facility comm chair Person Family Med Ctr 1979-81; mem, bd dir Parents for the Adv of Gifted Educ 1982-83. **BUSINESS ADDRESS:** 214 N. Madison Blvd, Roxboro, NC 27573-5399.

WOODS, ROOSEVELT, JR.
Educator. **PERSONAL:** Born Aug 15, 1933, Idabel, OK; son of Roosevelt Woods, Sr. and Nannie Wharry Woods; married Wanda; children: Dwynette, Senina. **EDUCATION:** AZ State Univ, BS, MAE 1958. **CAREER:** AZ State Univ, prof; CO Clge Fine Art, assc prof 1968; Phoenix Dist HS, tchr 1958; artist painter/Printmaker. **ORGANIZATIONS:** One man & group shows 1955; works rep pvt & Pub collections throughout country; ptcpnt FESTAC 1977.

WOODS, SYLVANIA WEBB, JR.
Legislator. **PERSONAL:** Born Jan 26, 1954, Atlanta, GA; son of Sylvania Woods, Sr and Geneva H Woods. **EDUCATION:** Attended The Am Univ 1972-74; attended Univ of MD 1974-76. **CAREER:** State of MD, del state rep. **ORGANIZATIONS:** Mem Region III Citizens Union; past chmn Dem Precinct; past mem Citizen's Adv Com on Block Grant; past mem Glenarden Housing Auth; past councilman Glenarden MD 1975-79; past vice chmn Glenarden Town Council 1976-77; past chmn Glenarden Town Council 1977-79; past acting mayor Glenarden MD; bd of dirs Young Dems of MD; mem Young Dems of Prince George's Co MD; mem 24th Dist Dem Club; past mem 18th Dist Dem Club; mem MD House of Dels; mem Natl Conf of State Legislators; mem Natl Conf Black State Legislators; mem Natl Eagle Scout Assn; mem NAACP of Prince George's Co MD; past mem Recreation Council Glenarden MD; mem Order of the Arrow; past mem trustee bd Upper Room Bapt Church Wash DC; mem Prince George's Co Jaycees; mem SCLC of Prince George's Co MD; mem bd of dirs Student Assistance Proj; chmn membership drive BSA Prince George Co; regional chmn, Natl Black Caucus of State Legislators; chmn Prince George's County House Delegation. **HONORS/ACHIEVEMENTS:** Outstanding Young Man of Amer 1978-86; Legislator of the Year, Maryland Muncipal League, 1982-85; Citizen of the Year 1985 Omega Psi Phi; Legislator of the Year 1987 Alpha Kappa Alpha Sorority. **BUSINESS ADDRESS:** MD State Representative, House of Representatives, 5611 Landover Rd, Landover, MD 20784.

WOODS, SYLVANIA WEBB, SR.
Judge. **PERSONAL:** Born Aug 04, 1927, Fort Gaines, GA; married Geneva Holloway; children: Sylania Jr, Sebrena. **EDUCATION:** Morris Brwn Coll Atl, BA 1949; Atl Univ GA, 1951; Wash Coll of Law Wash DC, LLB 1960. **CAREER:** Dist Ct of MD, judge 1976-; Priv Prac, atty 1960-76; US Pstl Aerv Wash DC, clerk 1955-60; Wash DC Plc Dept, plc ofcr 1954-55. **ORGANIZATIONS:** Mem Wash DC Bar Assn 1961; mem Nat Bar Assn; mem MD Bar Assn 1969; mem Am Bar Assn mEM PRINCE GRGS CO MD BAR ASSN; mEM WASH DC Unfd Bar Assn; mem Am Legn; pst st judge adv Am Legn Dept of MD; pst v chmn Dem Cntrl Com PG Co MD; past mem 18th Dist Dem Club; mem YMCA; mem NAACP; past asst Sctmstr Boy Sct Trp 1037 Glnrdn MD; past mem AMVETS; mem dcn bd Upper Rm Bapt Ch Wash DC; past mem VFW; past mem 25th Dist Dem Club; mem Flx Ldg No 3 Free & Accptd Masons; past mem tst bd Upper Rm Bapt Ch; mem J Davis Cnsstry 32nd Dgr Masons; past mem Dem Plghmn & Fshrmn of PG Co. **HONORS/ACHIEVEMENTS:** Prpl Hrt Erpn & Pcfc Thtrs USN 1943-45. **MILITARY SERVICE:** USN stewart's mate 1st cls 1943-45. **BUSINESS ADDRESS:** District Court of MD, Upper Marlboro, MD.

WOODS, TIMOTHY L.
Auto dealer. **CAREER:** Chino Hills Ford, Inc, Chino CA, chief executive, 1988. **BUSINESS ADDRESS:** Chino Hills Ford, Inc, 13101 Central Ave, Chino, CA 91710. *

WOODS, WILLIE G.
Education administrator. **PERSONAL:** Born Nov 03, Yazoo City, MS; daughter of Rev. John Wesley Woods and Jessie Turner Woods. **EDUCATION:** Shaw Univ Raleigh NC, BA Ed 1965; Duke Univ Durham NC, MEd 1968; Temple Univ PA, PA State Univ, NY Univ, attended; Indiana University of Pennsylvania, Indiana, PA, presently attending PhD program. **CAREER:** Berry O'Kelly School, language arts teacher 1965-67; Preston School, 5th grade teacher 1967-69, adult ed teacher 1968-69; Harrisburg Area Comm Coll, prof english/ed 1969-, dir acad found prog, 1983-87, asst dean of Academic Foundations and Basic Education Division, 1987-89, asst dean of Social Science, Public Services, and Basic Education Division, 1989-. **ORGANIZATIONS:** Bd of mgrs Camp Curtin Branch of Harrisburg YMCA 1971-79; rep council 1972-, sec 1977-79, assoc ed 1981-, PA Black Conf on Higher Ed; exec bd 1978-, council chairperson 1981-82, Western Reg Act 101 Dir Council; bd of dir Alternative Rehab Comm Inc 1978-; bd of dir 1979-, charter mem sec 1981-82, treas 1982-83, PA Assoc of Devel Ed; bd of dir 1981-, sec 1984-85, Dauphin Residences Inc; bd of advisors 1981-, chairperson, acting chairperson, bd sec Youth Urban Serv Harrisburg YMCA; inst rep Natl Council on Black Amer Affairs of the Amer Assoc of Comm & Jr Coll 1983-. **HONORS/ACHIEVEMENTS:** Listed in Who's Who Among Students in Amer Coll & Univ 1964-65; Cert of Merit for Community Serv Harrisburg 1971; Meritorious Faculty Contrib Harrisburg 1977; Outstanding Serv Awd PA Black Conf on Higher Ed 1980; Who's Who in the East 1981-82, 1983-84; Central Reg Awd for Serv PA Black Conf on Higher Ed 1982; Personalities of Amer 1982; Two Thousand Notable Amer 1982; Dir of Dist Amers 1982-83; Comm Leaders of Amer 1982; The Book of Honor 1982; Alpha Kappa Alpha Sor Outstanding Comm Serv Awd Harrisburg 1983; YMCA Youth Urban Serv Volunteer of the Year Awd 1983; Alpha Kappa Alpha Sor Basileus' Awd for Excellence as Committee Chair 1985; Administrative Staff Merit Award, Harrisburg Area Comm College, 1986; Outstanding Service Award, Black Student Union at Harrisburg Area Comm College, 1989; tribute for outstanding contributions to Harrisburg Area Comm College and to comm-at-large, HACC Minority Caucus, 1989; Alpha Kappa Mu Natl Hon Soc; Brooks Dickens Mem Award in Education. **HOME ADDRESS:** 226 Brian Drive, Enola, PA 17025. **BUSINESS ADDRESS:** Assistant Dean, Social Science, Public Serv, & Basic Educ Div, Harrisburg Area Community College, 3300 Cameron Street Road, Whitaker Hall, Office 111, Harrisburg, PA 17110-2999.

WOODSON, BERNARD ROBERT, JR.
Educational administrator. **PERSONAL:** Born Oct 13, 1923, Richmond, VA; married Drosi W Walker; children: Bernard III, Wayne, Gerald, Gregory. **EDUCATION:** VA State Coll, BS 1945; Howard Univ, MS 1948; MI State Univ, PhD 1958. **CAREER:** VA State Coll, prof of biology and res 1960-78, dir of acad year inst 1967-72; EPA Washington DC, environ specialist 1977-78; Lincoln Univ PA, exec vice pres provost 1978-. **ORGANIZATIONS:** Minority sch bio-med rsch NIH 1971-76; sci prog in devel Moton Coll Serv Bur 1972-73; sci adv bd Environ Protection Agency 1974-78; bd of dir Youth Advocates of Petersburg VA 1975-76; bd of dir Cultural Laureate Soc of VA 1976-78; bd of trustees Children's Home of VA. **HONORS/ACHIEVEMENTS:** Fellow Harbison Awd Finalist as Outstanding Teacher 1970; Amer Men of Sci; Who's Who in the S & SW; Dictionary of Intl Biography; Personalites of the S; The Two Thousand Men of Achievement; Comm Leaders of Amer; natl

Register of Prominent Ams & Intl Notables; listed in Who's Who in the East. **MILITARY SERVICE:** AUS sgt 1949-52. **HOME ADDRESS:** Lincoln Rd, Lincoln University, PA 19352.

WOODSON, CHARLES R.
Health services officer. **PERSONAL:** Born Feb 22, 1942, Louisville, KY. **EDUCATION:** Univ of Lsvl, MSSW 1969; LincolnUniv MO, BS 1963. **CAREER:** DHHS Pub Hlth Svc, proj ofcr 1979-; Assn of Colls of Ostpthc Med, dir ofc of spl opp 1974-79;Univ of Lsvll, dir ofc of blk afrs 1971-74; ActnCommn, dir nghbrhd orgn comm 1970-71; Sthflds Trtmnt Ctr, supt 1969-70. **ORGANIZATIONS:** Mem Am Prsnnl & Guid Assn 1972-; mem Am Pub Hlth Assn 1974-; mem Am Assn for Hghr Educ 1973-; mem Nat Assn of Blk Soc Wrkrs 1972-; mem bd dir Met Untd Way 1972-74; mem bd dir Falls Rgn Hlth Plng Cncl 1973-74; mem Kappa Alpha Psi. **BUSINESS ADDRESS:** 5600 Fishers Ln, Rockville, MD 20857.

WOODSON, CLEVELAND COLEMAN, III
Manufacturing executive. **PERSONAL:** Born Sep 05, 1946, Richmond, VA; son of Cleveland C Woodson, Jr and Naomi Wilder Woodson; married Jannifer Eileen Vaughan; children: Cleveland C IV, Camille C. **EDUCATION:** VA Union Univ, BS Acct 1970; Case Western Reserve Univ, MBA. **CAREER:** Ernst & Whinney, sr auditor 1970-76; Marathon Oil Co, advanced auditor 1976-78, task force mem 1978, advanced acct analyst 1979, sr acct analyst 1979-80, supvr 1980-83; marathon Petroleum Co, mgr 1983-86. **ORGANIZATIONS:** Bd of dir Natl Assn of Black Accts 1971-73; mem Amer Inst of CPA's 1973-; chairperson acct personnel comm Cleveland Chapter OH Soc of CPA's 1975; treas/auditor Cleveland Jaycees 1975-76; Children Services Advisory Board, 1975-76; treasurer Wilson Vance Parent Teacher Org 1981-83, Central JH Parent Teacher Org 1983-84; mem Amer Assn of Blacks in Energy 1983-; treasurer, Findlay High Citizens Advisory Comm, 1984-; mem, Hampton Univ Industry Advisory Cluster, 1982-. **HONORS/ACHIEVEMENTS:** CPA State of OH 1973. **HOME ADDRESS:** 516 Bright Rd, Findlay, OH 45840. **BUSINESS ADDRESS:** Manager, Marathon Oil Co, Oil Revenue Accounting, 539 S Main, Findlay, OH 45840.

WOODSON, JEFFREY ANTHONY
Senior budget and management analyst. **PERSONAL:** Born May 21, 1955, Baltimore, MD; son of Alfred C Woodson and Evelyn Trent Woodson; married Paula Mason; children: Jeffrey Jr, Devon. **EDUCATION:** Virginia State Univ, BA, 1976; Virginia Commonwealth Univ, MPA, 1983. **CAREER:** Southside Virginia Training Center, social worker, 1976-78, asst program mgr, 1978-83; City of Richmond, budget & mgmt analyst. **ORGANIZATIONS:** Mem, Omega Psi Phi, 1973; chmn, membership comm, Amer Soc for Public Admin, 1983-; mem, Conf of Minority Public Admin, 1983-; Natl Forum for Black Public Admin, 1983-; chapter council, Amer Soc for Public Admin, 1985-87. **HONORS/ACHIEVEMENTS:** Natl Jr Honor Soc, 1968; Outstanding Aced Frmn Award,Virginia State Univ, 1972; Outstanding Young Man of Amer, Jaycees, 1983; Productivity Analysis, Virginia Town & City Magazine (VA Municipal League), 1984. **HOME ADDRESS:** 10211 Duryea Dr, Richmond, VA 23235. **BUSINESS ADDRESS:** Budget & Management Analyst, City of Richmond, 900 E Broad St Rm 311, Richmond, VA 23219.

WOODSON, MIKE LAVELLE
Professional athlete. **PERSONAL:** Born Mar 24, 1958, Indianapolis, IN; married Terri Waters. **EDUCATION:** IN Univ, 1980. **CAREER:** Kansas City Kings, guard. **ORGANIZATIONS:** Kings hon capt of Spec Olym team. **HONORS/ACHIEVEMENTS:** Scored in double figures 52 times with 16 games of 120 or more points; 2 of 30 or more and a season-high 33 points against Cleveland 3/18; Kings leading scorer12 games; season-high 8 rebounds 11/25 against Dallas & 9 assists vs San Diego 12/30; co-captain of US team which won a gold medal in 1979 Pan Amer Games; was named MVP in 79 IN Classic; won all-tourney honors 3 straight years; also won all-tourney honors in the Far West Classic and the Gator Bowl.

WOODSON, ROBERT L.
Business executive. **PERSONAL:** Born Apr 08, 1937, Philadelphia, PA; married Ellen Hylton Woodson; children: Robert L Jr, Ralph L, Jamal J. **EDUCATION:** Cheyney State Coll, BS 1962; Univ of PA, MSW 1965; Univ of MA, doctoral prog. **CAREER:** Natl Urban League, dir; AEI Neighborhood Revitalization Proj, dir, resd fellow; Amer Enterprise Inst for Public Policy Rsch, adj fellow; Council for aBlack Economic Agenda, chmn; Natl Ctr for Neighborhood Enterprise, pres. **ORGANIZATIONS:** Consult US House of Rep Subcom on Crime-Judiciary Com 1978-79; dir Admin of Justice Div Natl Urban League 1972-78; mem Pres Commun on Mental Health 1978; fellow Natl Endowment for the Humanities 1977; bd dir Natl Ctr on Insts & Alternatives; bd of dir Ctr for Commun Change; bd dir Corp for Enterprise Devel; adv Natl Black Police Assoc, The Grassroots Network; pres adv council Private Sector Initiatives; lecturer at colls & univs in US & Europe; appeared on numTV & radio talk shows. **HONORS/ACHIEVEMENTS:** Commun Serv Awd Martin Luther King Comm Ctr Houston 1976; Disting Serv Awd Natl Black Police Assoc 1980; publs incl, "Day Care" 1984, "Youth Crime Policies" 1983, "Investing in People, A Strategy to Combat, Not Preserve Poverty" 1983, "Helping the Poor Help Themselves" 1982, "The Importance of Neighborhood Organizations in Meeting Human Needs", "Youth Crime Prevention, An Alternative Approach", "Child Welfare Policy" 1982, "A Summons to Life, Mediating Structures &the Prevention of Youth Crime 1981; editor "Youth Crime & Urban Policy, A View From the Inner City" 1981, "Mediating Structures Can Control Youth Crime" 1980, "The Justice Depts Fight Against Youth Crime, A Review of the Office of Juvenile Justice & Delinquency Prevention of LEAA" 1978, "Predatory Crime & Black Youth" 1978; articles in Washington Post, Washington Star, NY times; editor Black Perspectives on Crime & the Criminal Justice System 1976. **BUSINESS ADDRESS:** President, Ntl Cntr for Neighborhood Ent, 1367 Connecticut Avenue, NW, Washington, DC 20036.

WOODSON, RODERIC L.
Attorney. **PERSONAL:** Born Aug 23, 1947, Philadelphia, PA; married Karen Smith; children: Roderic L. **EDUCATION:** PA St U, BA 1969; Hwrd U, JD 1973. **CAREER:** Wdsn & Wdsn Attys & Cnsl at Law, prtnr; SEC, spl cnslr frdm of info ofcr 1976-79, atty advr corp fin 1973-75. **ORGANIZATIONS:** Mem PA Bar Assn 1973; mem St Bar Assn of GA 1974; mem DC Bar Assn 1979; mem Nat Bar Assn; mem Am Bar Assn; mem Fed Bar Assn; wash Bar Assn; mem Philadelphia Brstr's Assn; mem Gate City Bar Assn; corr sec Wash Bar Assn 1977-79, rec sec 1979-, bd of dir 1977-; Delta Theta Phi Lgl Frat; Kappa Alpha Psi Frat; Skull & Bns Soc. **HONORS/ACHIEVEMENTS:** Am Jrsprdnc Awd 1972; outst almn awd Hayes Snt Delta Theta Phi Lgl Frat 1974; Outst Yng of Am 1980. **BUSINESS ADDRESS:** Ste 220 806 15th St NW, Washington, DC 20005.

WOODSON, S. HOWARD, JR.
Government official, clergyman. **PERSONAL:** Born May 08, 1916, Phila, PA. **EDUCATION:** Cheyney St Coll PA; Mrhs Coll Atl. **CAREER:** State Leg, frmr gov ofcl 1963-76; Trenton, cnclmn at lrg 1962-65; Shiloh Bapt Ch Trntn NJ, pastor; Elctd Gen Assem, 1964; Elctd Min Ldr Lwr Hs, 1967; NJ, srvd as actng gov; Civil Serv Comm, pres 1976-. **HONORS/ACHIEVEMENTS:** 1st blk Assoc Ldr Lwr Hs; 1st blk spkr of the House 2 trms; recip of over 100 awds & 4 doctrts. **BUSINESS ADDRESS:** 215 E State St, Trenton, NJ 08625.

WOODSON, SHIRLEY A.
Educator, artist. **PERSONAL:** Born Mar 03, 1936, Pulaski, TN; married Edsel Reid; children: Khari, Senghor. **EDUCATION:** Wayne State Univ, BFA 1958; Art Inst of Chicago, grad study 1960; Wayne State Univ, MA 1965. **CAREER:** Highland Park Comm Coll, instr, cons; Exhibitions, Childe Hassam Found NY 1968, Gallery Seven Detroit 1969-70, Arts Exended Gallery Detroit 1969, Gallery Seven Detroit 1970, J Walter Thompson Advertising Agency 1971, Chico State Coll 1972, McGregor Library 2nd World Festival MI Region 1974, McGregor Library Highland Park MI 1973, 2nd World Festival of African Culture Lagos Nigeria 1977, Howard Univ 1975; Broadside Press, illustrator; Forever Free Art by African Amer Women 1961-1980; Joslyn Museum Omaha NE 1981; natl Conf of Artists Dakar Senegal 1985; Your Heritage House Museum Detroit Feigenson Gallery Detroit 1986. **ORGANIZATIONS:** Arts extended group 1958-72; Natl Conf of Artists 1975-; Natl Art Educ Assn. **HONORS/ACHIEVEMENTS:** MacDowell Colony Felowship 1966; Artist-in-Residence Your Heritage House Museum 1984; First Prize Visual Arts Toledo Art Commiss Toledo OH 1984; Artist-in-Reisdency Chene Park Installation Detroit 1986. **BUSINESS ADDRESS:** Artist, 214 David Whitney Bldg, 1553 Woodward, Detroit, MI 48226.

WOODSON, THELMA L.
Retired educator. **PERSONAL:** Born Sep 01, 1920, Rutherford County, TN; daughter of Evans E Pate Sr and Della Mae Jackson Pate; married Theodore B Woodson, Nov 12, 1955 (deceased); children: Kevan B Woodson. **EDUCATION:** Wayne State Univ, Detroit MI, BS Ed 1955, MEd 1960; educational specialist at University of Michigan, Ann Arbor MI, Michigan State Univ, Lansing MI, & Wayne State Univ, Detroit MI. **CAREER:** City of Nashville TN, recreation leader, 1941-43; Federal Govt, Detroit MI, statistical clerk, 1943-44; City of Detroit MI, recreation leader, 1944-55; Board of Educ, Detroit MI, teacher 1955-66, administrative intern 1966-68, asst principal 1968-72, principal 1972-86; T&T Industries Inc, corp dir 1964-74, corp pres 1974-79. **ORGANIZATIONS:** Mem, pres, Rho Sigma Chapter, Sigma Gamma Rho, 1954-; mem, Wayne Univ Alumni, 1955-; mem, bd chair, pres, Amer Bridge Assn, 1966-; mem, Amer Assn of Univ Women, 1968-86; mem, Natl Assn of Elementary School Principals, 1972-; mem, Urban Program in Health, 1977-81; mem, bd chair, Kirwood Mental Health Center, 1979-. **HONORS/ACHIEVEMENTS:** Citations from Detroit Bd of Educ 1963, National Education 1984, State of MI 1985, City of Detroit 1985, City of Nashville 1989. **HOME ADDRESS:** 2016 Glynn Ct, Detroit, MI 48206.

WOODSON, TRACY TODD
Engineer/project engineer. **PERSONAL:** Born Mar 15, 1960, Newark, NJ; married Deanna Washington; children: Vernon Anthony. **EDUCATION:** NJ Inst of Tech, BS 1984. **CAREER:** US Military Sealift Comm, internal auditor; Wilmington Finishing Co, asst proj engr; ITT Defense Communications, prog admin 1984-86; General Elec RSO, engr 1986-. **MILITARY SERVICE:** AUS E-3 1 yr. **HOME ADDRESS:** 3205 N Madison St, Wilmington, DE 19802. **BUSINESS ADDRESS:** Project Engineer, General Electric, 3198 Chestnut St, Philadelphia, PA 19101.

WOODSON, WILLIAM D.
Attorney. **PERSONAL:** Born Sep 09, 1929, Baltimore. **EDUCATION:** BA 1952; JD 1958. **CAREER:** Staff Coll, command gen 1965; Asso Lgstcs Exec Devel, 1972; Nat Scrty Mgt, 1971; Dept Treas Nat Ofc IRS, tax law spl. **ORGANIZATIONS:** NBA; ACLU; NAACP; NON; NHR; MCHR; AUSCS; UNICEF; ACDS; USAR; LTC. **BUSINESS ADDRESS:** 1111 Constitution Ave NW, Washington, DC 20224.

WOODWARD, AARON ALPHONSO, III
Executive. **PERSONAL:** Married Joan J; children: Aaron A IV, Allen A. **CAREER:** Various Insurance Cos, licensed insurance broker 1975-83; Count Basie Enterprises, business mgr 1983-84, secretary/treas 1983-84, mgr Count Basie Orchestra1983-, co-trustee Diane Basie Trust 1983-, chief executive officer & co-executor. **ORGANIZATIONS:** Chmn trustee bd Christ Baptist Church Coram NY; life mem NAACP; past pres Central State Univ Metro Alumni Chapt; mem Omega Psi Phi Frat Nu Omicron Chapt; mem Local 802 Musicians Union; mem Natl Alliance of Business Youth Motivation Task Force; consultant & chairperson Amer Mgmt Assoc. **HONORS/ACHIEVEMENTS:** Harlem YMCA Black Achiever in Industry; US Presidential Commendation for Service to Others; various Sales Achievement Awds for Insurance Sales; Natl Allianceof Business Youth Motivation Task Force Chairperson Awds; 1984 Grammy for "88 Basie Street" Natl TV; Presidential Medal of Freedom from President Reagan; Basie Awd Gov Kane of NJ; various other awds worldwide. **BUSINESS ADDRESS:** Chief Executive Officer, Count Basie Enterprises, Inc, PO Box 262, Selden, NY 11784.

WOODWARD, ISAIAH ALFONSO
Physician. **PERSONAL:** Born Mar 06, 1912, Washington, DC; married Louise. **EDUCATION:** Blfld Tchr Coll, BS 1936; Atl U, MA 1936; WV U, PhD 1969. **CAREER:** Morgan St U, asst prof prof chmn 1947-; Wash DC Census Dept, supr 1940-43. **ORGANIZATIONS:** Mem Phi Alpha Theta Hon Soc; Pi Gamma Mu Nat Soc; Sci Hon Soc; MD Bcntnnl Commn. **MILITARY SERVICE:** USN 1943-47. **BUSINESS ADDRESS:** 105 Morgan State Univ, Cold Spring Ln, Baltimore, MD 21239.

WOOLCOCK, OZEIL FRYER
Editor & journalist. **PERSONAL:** Born in Atlanta, GA. **EDUCATION:** Clark Coll, AB; Atlanta Univ, Graduate Studies. **CAREER:** Atlanta Daily World Newspaper, Women's Interest editor/columnist 1985; Atlanta Public Schools, teacher (retired). **ORGANIZATIONS:** Mem Natl Assoc Media Women; Delta Sigma Theta Sor; Amer Busn Women, Soc of Professional Jrnlsts; Clark Coll Alumni Assoc. **HONORS/ACHIEVEMENTS:** Tchr

of Yr Atlanta Publ Schl 1966-6; serv award Delta Sigma Theta Inc 1969; excel in journ Sigma Gomma Pho Inc (nat) 1970; Comm Serv, C&S- comm 1972; excellency in Journ, Clark Coll Alumni Assn 1975; Media Women of Yrar Natl Assn of Media 1980; comm serv High Museum of Art 1984; Natl Cncl of BlackMayors 1984. **HOME ADDRESS:** 175 Florida Ave SW, Atlanta, GA 30310. **BUSINESS ADDRESS:** Womens Interest Editor, Atlanta Daily World, 145 Auburn Ave, Atlanta, GA 30303.

WOOLDRIDGE, DAVID
Business executive. **PERSONAL:** Born Dec 06, 1931, Chicago, IL; married Juana Natalie Hampton; children: David Juan, Samuel William, Gregg Wayne. **EDUCATION:** RsvltUniv Chgo, BS Physics 1961; MA Inst of Tech, MS Mgmt Sci 1973. **CAREER:** Motorola Inc, vice pres st & lcl sls commun & elctrncs 1978-, prod mgr 1976-78, prog mgr 1974-76; Hughes Arcrft Co, prog mgr 1973-74, mgr GED prog 1968-72, design engr 1961-68; LA City Coll, instr 1968-74. **ORGANIZATIONS:** Mem com to Mtvt Min Stud to Prs Engrng & Sci Crrs City Coll of NY 1980. **HONORS/ACHIEVEMENTS:** Otstndng cntrbtn Yth Mtvtn Task Frc 1969; comm serv awd Alpha Kappa Alpha Sor 1971; otstndng serv & cntrbtn Prairie View A&M Coll 1971; Alfred P Sloan Fellow Hughes Arcrft Co. **MILITARY SERVICE:** USAF a/1c 1949-52. **BUSINESS ADDRESS:** 1303 E Algonquin Rd, Schaumburg, IL 60196.

WOOLFOLK, E. OSCAR
Retired educator. **PERSONAL:** Born Mar 09, 1912, Tupelo, MS; son of Rev. & Mrs E. O. Woolfolk; married Norma B; children: David, Dennis. **EDUCATION:** Talladega Coll, BA 1934; OH State Univ, MS 1939; Univ of Pgh, PhD 1949. **CAREER:** Claflin Coll, chem 1940-42; Scioto Ordnance Plant War Dept, chem 1942-43; US Bureau of Mines Pgh, rs chem 1943-49; Central States Univ, prof & chmnchem dept 1949-68; Central State Univ, dir div of natu sci & math 1955-57, dean coll arts & sci 1967-68, vice pres academic affairs 1968-71; Urbana Coll, visiting lecturer 1967-68; Fisk Univ, retired dean of univ 1973-78. **ORGANIZATIONS:** Exec sec Beta Kappa Chi 1954-62; pres Beta Kappa Chi 1963-64; fellow Amer Chem Soc; fellow 1966-67 Amer Assn for Adv of Sci; fellow/pres OH Acad ofSci; fellow Amer Inst of Chem; mem Amer Assn of Univ Prof, Natl Educ Assn, Amer Assn for Higher Educ, Phi Lambda Upsilon, Sigma Xi.

WOOLFOLK, GEORGE RUBLE
Educator. **PERSONAL:** Born Feb 22, 1915, Louisville, KY; son of Lucien Woolfolk and Theodosia Woolfolk; married Douglass G; children: George Jr. **EDUCATION:** Louis Municipal Coll Univ of Louisville, AB 1937; OH State Univ Columbus, MA 1938; Univ of WI Madison, PhD 1947. **CAREER:** Prairie View A&M Univ, head & prof, Dept of History, 1943-; emeritus prof, History, chmn, Div of Social Sciences, 1984. **ORGANIZATIONS:** Waller County Historical Commn, Assn for the Study of Afro-Amer Life & History, Amer Assn of Univ Profs, TX State Teachers Assn, TX State Historical Assn, Southern Historical Assn, Organization of Amer Historians, Amer Historical AssnAlpha Phi Alpha. **HONORS/ACHIEVEMENTS:** Minnie Stevens Piper Prof 1973; elected Fellow, TX State Historical Assn (Texas oldest Learned Soc, 1897) the first Black to be chosen 1986. **BUSINESS ADDRESS:** Emeritus Prof of History, Prairie View A&MUniv, Prairie View, TX 77446.

WOOLRIDGE, OROLANDO KEITH
Professional athlete. **PERSONAL:** Born Dec 16, 1959, Mansfield, LA. **EDUCATION:** Notre Dame, 1977-81. **CAREER:** Chicago Bulls, forward 1981-. **HONORS/ACHIEVEMENTS:** Led Bulls in scoring avgng 193 pts per game; ranked 2nd in fld goal percentage hitting on 525 from field; mem of NBA Slam Dunk Team; was Bulls number onepick in 1981 coming out of Notre Dame. **BUSINESS ADDRESS:** Chicago Bulls, 333 N Michigan Ave, 777 Sports St, Chicago, IL 60601.

WOOLRIDGE, THOMAS JERRY
Physician. **PERSONAL:** Born Dec 07, 1943, Baltimore, MD; married Karen Elaine; children: Courtney, Jay, Chrissie, Blair, Daniel. **EDUCATION:** Morgan State Univ, BS 1974; Meharry Medical Coll, MD 1978. **CAREER:** Howard Univ Hosp, psychiatric resident 1978-80; TN Valley Authority, med dir Hartsville nuclear plant 1980-81; Wayne State Univ, family practice residency 1981-84; Detroit Medical Ctr, private practice 1984-85; Fisk Univ/Meharry Med Coll, dir student health 1985-; Meharry/Hubbard Hospital, dir employee health 1985-; Meharry Alcohol & Drug Abuse Prog, med dir 1986-; Meharry Medical Coll, asst dir family practice residency 1985-86. **ORGANIZATIONS:** Mem Amer Acad of Family Physicians 1984-; chmn and pi Meharry AIDS Group 1985-; mem RF Boyd Med Soc 1985-; mem Physician's Adv Bd to Amer Red Cross 1985-. **HONORS/ACHIEVEMENTS:** Numerous organizationalTV and radio public service presentations on AIDS 1985-. **MILITARY SERVICE:** USAF e-4 6 yrs. **BUSINESS ADDRESS:** Dir Family Practice Res, Meharry Medical College, 1005 DB Todd Blvd, Nashville, TN 37208.

WOOTEN, CARL KENNETH
Advertising sales manager. **PERSONAL:** Born Oct 14, 1947, Chester, PA; son of Adam D Wooten and Hortense Wooten; married Barbra J Daniely; children: Tracy, Darryl. **EDUCATION:** Univ of Pittsburgh, BA, History, 1969, MAT, 1971; Fairleigh Dickenson, MBA, 1981. **CAREER:** The Wall St Journal, advertising sales representative, 1971-74, sr sales representative, 1975-83, dist sales mgr, 1984-. **ORGANIZATIONS:** Sec Toast Masters Fairleigh Dickenson, 1980; Business/Prof AA, 1981-83; Washington Ad Club. **BUSINESS ADDRESS:** Advertising Sales Mgr, The Wall St Journal, 1025 Connecticut Ave, NW, Washington, DC 20036.

WOOTEN, JOHN
Personnel development staff. **PERSONAL:** Born Dec 05, 1936, Carlsbad, NM; married Beverly; children: Lynette, John David. **EDUCATION:** CO U, BS 1959. **CAREER:** Dls Cwbys Ftbl, prsnnl devel staff; Clvlnd Browns, pro ftbl plyr 1959-69; Pro Sports Adv, pres 1975; Blk Econ Union, exec dir 1971. **ORGANIZATIONS:** All Pro Pro Ftbl Wrtrs 1965. **HONORS/ACHIEVEMENTS:** Pro Bowl 1965-66.

WOOTEN, PRISCILLA A.
Association executive. **PERSONAL:** Born Mar 31, 1936, Aiken, SC; married Joseph; children: Deborah M, Diana B, Donald T. **EDUCATION:** NY U. **CAREER:** Family Wrkr, 1958-66; Hd Strt Prog, fmly asst 1966; Untd Prnts Assn, prnt educ trnr 1967; Brooklyn, educ asst 1967-68, hlth ntrtnst 1968, educ asst aux trnr 1968-69; Comm Liaison Wrkr, 1969-71; Ofc of Educ & Info Svc, prin nghbrhd sch wrkr1971-; Chnclr's Actn Cntr, pub rels dir 1971-. **ORGANIZATIONS:** Mem Evltng Team Dist 19 1969; Chrlt Plng Prog 1969-70; vice pres New York City Sch Bd Assn 1972, 1973, 1975, treas 1973-75; comm sch bd mem of Dist 19k 1967-; bd tst mem Luth Hosp of Brklyn; prog chrldy E NY Br NAACP; 1st vice pres M S Douglas Soc; Bd of Educ Empl; educ rep Grace Bapt Ch; mem Plng Bd5 Brklyn NY 1973-; 1st vice pres Dem Club 40th Ass Dist 1972-73; vice pres Dist 19 Comm Sch Bd 1973-; E NY Brwnsvl Com 1973-; vice pres New York City Sch Bd Assn1973-74,treas 1974-; mem bd dir of Frnds & Mus Jr HS Stud NYC; chmn Luth Hosp of Brklyn Ambul Clnc 1974-; rep Cntrl Bd Educ 1973-; mem Mnstr Grp NAACP 1974-; pres E Brklyn Civic Assn 1973-; mem Untd Polit Club 1974-. **HONORS/ACHIEVEMENTS:** PTA Awd; Block Assn Awd 1973-75; Comm Sch Bd Awd 1973-75; Ch Awd Grace Bapt Ch Comm Wrk 1972-74; Lcl Sch Bd Awd Dist 19k 1968-70; Prscll Wtn Educ Soc Educ Awd 1974.

WORD, CARL OLIVER
Writer, psychologist & educator. **PERSONAL:** Born Nov 19, 1947, San Francisco, CA. **EDUCATION:** Lincoln Univ, PA, BA (cum laude) 1969; Princeton Univ, PhD 1972. **CAREER:** Baruch Coll, CUNY, asst prof 1972-74; Coble Comm Center, Palo Alto, CA, research fellow 1975-76; Westside Comm Health Center, SF, CA, research scientist 1980-82; Univ of CA, San Francisco School of Dentistry, lecturer 1982-; Wright Inst, prof of Psychology. **ORGANIZATIONS:** Brd of trustees CA Sch of Profsnl Psycholgy 1976-85; mem Comm Advsry Brd, SF Health Dept 1977-. **HONORS/ACHIEVEMENTS:** Alfred P Sloan Leadership Schlrshp 1965; Woodrow Wilson Fellowship 1969; Princeton Univ Fellowship 1969; Outstanding Young Mem of Amer, US Jaycees 1974. **BUSINESS ADDRESS:** Professor of Psychology, Wright Institute, 2728 Durant Ave, Berkeley, CA 94704.

WORD, FLETCHER HENRY, JR.
City official. **PERSONAL:** Born May 25, 1919, Petersburg, VA; married Virginia Brown; children: Fletcher H III, Sharman Word Dennis. **EDUCATION:** VA State Coll, BS 1940, MS 1966; St John's Univ Law, 1 yr 1945; Univ of MD, study 1960. **CAREER:** Eastern Sr HS, teacher & counselor 1960-66; Public Sch Washington DC, counselor 1966-68; Hine Jr High, admin 1968-71; Dramer Jr HS, admin 1971-78; Johnson Jr HS, admin 1978-79; Birney Sch, admin 1979-83; Advisory Neighborhood Commn, commissioner. **ORGANIZATIONS:** Treas DC Assn Secondary Sch Principals 1979-82; Omega Psi Phi Frat 1937-; pres DC Assn of Secondary Sch Principals 1982-84; volunteer Natl Museum of Natural History; mem Ft Stevens Lions Club. **HONORS/ACHIEVEMENTS:** Catholic Serv to Youth 1964; Cert of Appreciation Boy Scouts of Amer 1965; Service Cert DC Public Schools 1970; 3 plaques from schools served 1981-84; Master Tchr Award 1985. **HOME ADDRESS:** 53 Underwood Place NW, Washington, DC 20012. **BUSINESS ADDRESS:** Commissioner, Advisory Neighborhood Commiss, 7826 Eastern Ave NW, Washington, DC 20012.

WORD, PARKER HOWELL
Physician. **PERSONAL:** Born Jun 24, 1921, Petersburg, VA; children: Leslie, Parker, Lindsey. **EDUCATION:** VA State Coll, BS 1941; Howard Univ Med Sch, attended 1944. **CAREER:** Human Develop Corp, med dir 1964-66; Staff Member, Deaconess Hosp, Homer G Phillips, Christian Hosp; Private Practice, physician. **ORGANIZATIONS:** Life mem NAACP; mem Urban League Local; Frontiers Inc. **HONORS/ACHIEVEMENTS:** Mayor's Civic Awd 1969. **MILITARY SERVICE:** AUSMC capt 1952-54. **BUSINESS ADDRESS:** 3737 N Kingshighway, St Louis, MO 63115.

WORDLAW, CLARENCE, JR.
Elected official. **PERSONAL:** Born Jan 28, 1937, Little Rock, AR; married Pearlene Stegall; children: Zager, Derrick, Nicole, Thaddeus. **EDUCATION:** Univ of IA, BS Liberal Arts 1959. **CAREER:** Beacon Neighborhood House, group work supervisor 1959-66; Circuit Ct of Cook Co, casework super 1966-68; Chicago Urban League, dir west side office 1969-70; IL Bell, super urban affairs 1971-73, public relations super 1973-74, dist mgr training 1974-79, dist mgr comm relations 1979-; Cook Co Sch Dist 89,school bd mem. **ORGANIZATIONS:** Bdof dirs Malcolm X Coll Mid-Mgmt Intern Prog; bd of mgrs Dr Martin Luther King Jr Unit Chicago Boys & Girls Clubs; mem Chicago Urban Affairs Council; bd of dirs Midwest Comm Council; mem NAACP; adv bd Career Training Inst of the Woodlawn Organ of Chicago; comm develop bd Office of Special Progs Univ of Chicago; mem SCLC; mem Kappa Alpha Psi Frat Inc; mem Police-Comm Relations Comm Maywood Human Relations Comm; bd of dirs Proviso East HS Booster Club, Maywood Chamber of Commerce; bd mem Austin Career Educ Ctr, Hayden Memorial Educ Fund, Operation PUSH. **HONORS/ACHIEVEMENTS:** Outstanding Grad of Crane HS Class of 1955; All-Big Ten & Honorable Mention All-Amer Basketball selection in college 1958-59; Black Achievers of Indus Awd Metro Chicago YMCA, Chicago Sports Found Hall of Fame 1982; Community Oscar Awd Midwest Community Council. **MILITARY SERVICE:** AUS 1st lt 1959-68. **BUSINESS ADDRESS:** School Board Member, Cook Co Sch Dist 89, 1133 S 8th Ave, Maywood, IL 60153.

WORMLEY, CYNTHIA L.
Educator. **PERSONAL:** Born Jan 15, 1953, Philadelphia. **EDUCATION:** Hartt Coll of Mus, BM in Mus , BM in Mus Edn. **CAREER:** Philadelphia Bd of Public Educ, music teacher; Univ of Hartford Spiritual Choir, soloist; Hartt Coll Chamber Singers & Mdrgl Singers, soloist 1970-74. **ORGANIZATIONS:** Pres Epsilon Upsilon Chap Delta Sigma Theta Sor 1973-74; cmpny mem Opera Ebony/Phila; del Delta & Conv Atl GA 1973; mem Delta Sigma Theta Sor; NatCncl of Negro Wmn. **HONORS/ACHIEVEMENTS:** 1st blk chld slst with Philadelphia Orchstr Age 9; num awds for comm serv in fld of Mus; Miss Ebony PA 1974; Schol Recip for Study in Opera Dept of Cnsrvtry of Mus Hchschl f r Musik Munich Germany 1979.

WORMLEY, DIANE-LOUISE LAMBERT
Business executive. **PERSONAL:** Born Apr 28, 1948, Hartford, CT; married Wayne M Wormley. **EDUCATION:** William Smith Coll, BA 1970. **CAREER:** Mary Washington Coll, admissions couns 1970-71; Wheaton Coll, asst dir admissions 1971-73; Simmons Coll, asst dir admissions 1973-74; Stanford Univ, asst dir liberal arts 1974-76, dir 1976-78; Fisk Univ, dir career planning 1978-81; Atlanta Univ, dir corporate associates 1981-84; Univ of PA, asst dir The Penn Plann 1984-. **ORGANIZATIONS:** Assoc mem Natl Black MBA Assoc 1982-84; mem Southern College Placement Assoc 1978-. **HONORS/ACHIEVEMENTS:** Individual Achievement Natl Black MBA Atlanta 1983. **HOME ADDRESS:** 4805 Regent St, Philadelphia, PA 19143. **BUSINESS ADDRESS:** Assistant Dir, The Penn Plan, University of Pennsylvania, 3451 Walnut St, Philadelphia, PA 19104.

WORRELL, AUDREY MARTINY
Physician. **PERSONAL:** Born Aug 12, 1935, Philadelphia, PA; daughter of Francis A Martiny and Dorothy Rawley Martiny; married Richard V; children: Philip, Amy. **EDUCATION:** Meharry Medical Coll, MD 1960; Fisk Univ, 1955; Whittier Coll, 1956; State Univ of NY at Buffalo Affld Hosp, Residency Training in Psychiatry 1964 . **CAREER:** Haverford State Hosp, Haverford, PA, chief of serv 1965-68; Univ of PA, Schl of Med, asst profr 1967; Erie Cnty Mental Health Unit IV, Buffalo Psychiatric Cntr, Buffalo, NY, chief 1970-74; VA Medcl Cntr, Newington, CT, chief of psychiatry 1980-81; Univ of CT Schl of Med, dir of div 1980-81; State of CT, commnsr of Mental Health 81-86; Vista Sandia Hosp, ceo & medical dir 1986-. **ORGANIZATIONS:** Mem Amer Psychiatric Assn 1963-, CT State Psychiatric Assoc 1967-; asst prof Pshchiatry Univ of CT Schl of Med 1974-81; mem Natl Assoc of Mental Health Prgms Dir 1981; mem Amer Public Health Assoc 1983-; clncl profr of Psychiatry Univ of CT Schl of Med 1984-86; Amer College of Psychiatry 1985. **HONORS/ACHIEVEMENTS:** Diplomate Amer Brd of Phsychiatry & Neurology 1970; certified as Mental Health Admnstr, Assoc of Mental Health Admnstrs 1983; certified as Mental Health Admnstr, Amer Psychiatric Assoc 1983. **BUSINESS ADDRESS:** CEO & Medical Dir, Vista Sandia Hospital, 501 Alameda Blvd, Albuquerque, NM 87113.

WORRELL, KAYE SYDNELL
Nurse. **PERSONAL:** Born Aug 18, 1952, Axton, VA; married Cleveland D Worrell. **EDUCATION:** Petersburg Gen Hosp Sch of Nursing, diploma 1973; Hampton Inst, BS Nursing 1975. **CAREER:** Petersburg Genl Hosp Sch of Nursing, instructor 1975-78; Southside Comm Coll, part-time nursing instructor 1983; Poplar Springs Hosp, unit coord RN. **ORGANIZATIONS:** Mem Waverly Improvement Assoc 1974-; sec Sussex Co Red Cross 1982-83; mem Petersburg Genl Hosp Sch of Nursing Alumnae 1984-85; mem & elected Waverly-Town Council 1978-86. **HONORS/ACHIEVEMENTS:** Weekly health column Sussex-Surry Dispatch Newspaper Wakefield VA 1980-82; "Senior Citizen Hypertension Prog" paper published by MCV-VCU Allied Health Scis Div co-author of paper 1980. **HOME ADDRESS:** 233 Railroad Ave, Waverly, VA 23890. **BUSINESS ADDRESS:** Unit Coord RN, Poplar Springs Hospital, 350 Wagner Rd, Petersburg, VA 23805.

WORRELL, RICHARD VERNON
Physician & educator. **PERSONAL:** Born Jun 04, 1931, Brooklyn, NY; son of Elmer Worrell and Elaine Worrell; married Audrey M; children: Philip, Amy. **EDUCATION:** NY Univ, BA 1952; Meharry Med Coll, MD 1958; State Univ of NY at Buffalo Affltd Hosp, Residency Training in Orthopaedic Surgery 1964. **CAREER:** Univ of PA, instr in Orthopedic Surgery 1968; Univ of CT Schl of Med, asst profsr of Orthopedic Surgery 1968-77; Univ of CT Schl of Med, assoc profsr of Orthopedic Surgery 1977-83; Univ of CT Schl of Med, asst Dean for Student Affrs 1980-83; State Univ of NY, prof of Clinical Surgery 1983-86; Univ of NM Medical Ctr, prof of orthopaedics 1986-. **ORGANIZATIONS:** Fellow Amer Academy of Orthopaedic Surgeons 1970-; fellow Amer Coll of Surgeons 1970-; affiliate Royal Soc of Med (London) 1973-; fellow Internatl Coll of Surgeons 1981-; dir Dept of Orthopaedic Surgery, Brookdale Hosp Medcl Cntr, Brooklyn, NY 11212; profsr of Clinical Surgery, State Univ of NY Downstate Medcl Cntr, Brooklyn, NY 1983-86. **HONORS/ACHIEVEMENTS:** Mem Alpha Omega Alpha Hnr Medical Soc, Gamma of TN Chptr Meharry Mdcl Coll; mem Sickle Cell Disease Advsry Comm of the Natl Inst of Health, 1982-86. **MILITARY SERVICE:** AUSR capt 1962-69. **BUSINESS ADDRESS:** Professor of Orthopaedics, Univ of NM Medical Center, Dept of Orthopaedics, Albuquerque, NM 87131.

WORRILL, CONRAD W.
Educator. **PERSONAL:** Born Aug 15, 1941, Pasadena, CA; son of Mr and Mrs Walter Worrill; married Cynthia Armster; children: Michelle, Femi, Sobenna. **EDUCATION:** George Williams Coll, BS 1968; Univ of Chicago, MA 1971; Univ of WI, PhD 1973. **CAREER:** Northeastern IL Univ Ctr for Inner City Studies, dept chair. **ORGANIZATIONS:** Weekly columnist Chicago Defender 1983-, and other black newspapers in Chicago and around the country;chmn Natl Black United Front 1985-; bd mem IL Black United Fund 1985-; mem Woodlawn Preservation Investment Corp 1987-; mem Chicago Housing Authority 1987-; talk show host WVON-AM, 1988-; Assn for Study of Classical African Civilizations. **HONORS/ACHIEVEMENTS:** Received numerous awds for community involvement; AKA Monarch Awards; Worrill's World Book of Newspaper columns/articles have appeared in numerous African Amer publications. **MILITARY SERVICE:** AUS splst 4th class 1962-64. **BUSINESS ADDRESS:** Department Chair, Northeastern IL University, Ctr for Inner City Studies, 700 E Oakwood Blvd, Chicago, IL 60653.

WORSLEY, GEORGE IRA, JR.
Business executive. **PERSONAL:** Born Apr 03, 1927, Baltimore, MD; married Gloria M Morris; children: Mary Elizabeth Cunningham, Gayll Annette. **EDUCATION:** Howard U, BSME 1949. **CAREER:** Grg Ira Wrsly Jr & Asso, owner 1964-; Dollar Bltz Asso, engin 1959-64; Gen Engrng Assn, engr 1949-59. **ORGANIZATIONS:** Adv bd Untd Comm Nat Bank; CEC; MW; ASHRAE; NTA; BOCA; WBA; NFPA. **HONORS/ACHIEVEMENTS:** Elctd Tau Beta Pi HwrdUniv Alpha 1959. **MILITARY SERVICE:** USNR smn 3rd cls 1945-46, sgt 1951-53. **BUSINESS ADDRESS:** 7705 Georgia Ave NW, Washington, DC 20011.

WORTH, CHARLES JOSEPH
Appointed government official. **PERSONAL:** Born Jun 06, 1948, Raleigh, NC; son of James Worth and Rosa Worth; married Laurie Gray; children: Kellye N, Kimberlye N, Kourtnye N. **EDUCATION:** NC A&T State Univ, BS Acctg 1970; NC Central Univ, MPA 1987. **CAREER:** Coopers & Lybrand, sr auditor 1970-74; Gen Signal Corp, sr internal auditor 1974-76; Bausch & Lomb, sr internal auditor 1976-79; The Soul City Co, dir of finance 1979-80; Charles J Worth & Assoc Inc, pres 1980-; Warren Cty, county mgr 1984-. **ORGANIZATIONS:** Mem Amer Soc for Public Admin, Natl Forum of Black Public Admin, Natl Assoc of Black County Officials, Conf of Minority Public Admin; bd mem NC City/Cty Mgmt Assoc, Natl Assoc of Cty Admin; life mem Omega Psi Phi Frat; former pres Vance-Warren Chap of SCLC; chmn Kerr-Tar Private Industry Council; mem Kerr Lake Bd of Realtors; treas Second Congressional Dist Black Caucus; mem Warren County Political Action Council, NC A&T State Univ Alumni Assoc, Intl City Mgmt Assoc, NC Assoc of Minority Business Inc, NAACP, Soul City Rural Volunteer Fire Dept. **HONORS/ACHIEVEMENTS:** 1st Black Appointed Mgr in State of NC 1984; Certificate of Appreciation Boy's Clubs of Amer 1978-79; Omega Man of the Year Zeta Alpha Chap Omega Psi Phi 1983; Cty Mgr Warren Cty NC 1984. **HOME ADDRESS:** 24 Macon Circle, Manson, NC 27553. **BUSINESS ADDRESS:** County Manager, Warren County, PO Box 619, Warrenton, NC 27589.

WORTHAM, JACOB JAMES
Editor. **PERSONAL:** Born Jun 23, Atlanta, GA. **EDUCATION:** Morehouse Coll; Univ of PA, BA 1963; Columbia Univ Grad School of Journalism, 1978. **CAREER:** WNET-TV NY, commentator city edtn editorial consultant; Black Enterprise Earl Graves Publishing Co, sr editor; NBC News, producer; Philadelphia Suburban & Nwspapers, feature editor; WBS Radio NY, reporter producer; CBS ACCESS, commentator; KYW Nwsrd Phila, reporter. **ORGANIZATIONS:** Mem Sigma Delta Chi Journalistic Soc; Amer Fed of TV & Radio Artists; dir Crrfr Art Gallery. **HONORS/ACHIEVEMENTS:** Writers Guild of Am. **BUSINESS ADDRESS:** 295 Madison Ave, 14th & C Sts SW, New York, NY 20228.

WORTHEY, RICHARD E.
Research analyst. **PERSONAL:** Born Aug 11, 1934, Greensboro, NC; married Peggie J McTier. **EDUCATION:** A&T St U, BSEE 1960; AF Inst of Tech, MSSE 1964; OH St U, PhD 1969. **CAREER:** USAF Arntcl Sys Div, operat res ana; ASD Wrght-Pttrsn AFB, elec engr 1966-70, elec engr SEG 1960-66. **ORGANIZATIONS:** Mem Inst of Elec Engrs 1964-; chrprsn ASD Incntv Awds Com 1972-78; mem AF Smltr Adv Grp 1975-78; past pres mem Frwy Golf Club 1973-; mem Dayton Area Chap A&T StUniv Almn Assn 1971-; mem Masnc Ldg Cnsstry Shriners 1966-; mem AIAA 1976; mem Am Mngt Assn 1975; mem DOD/NASA Wrkng Grp on Smltr Tech 1976-78; 1 yr exec devel assgnm Ofc of Under Sec of Def for Rsrch & Engr 1979-80. **HONORS/ACHIEVEMENTS:** Who's Who Amng Blk Engr 1974-75; Recip Cert Pin 20 Yrs Serv 1976; Otstndng Perf Awds 1968, 1971, 1972, 1973, 1976; Letter of Commend Perf 1978; author more than 25 tech rprts & publ; nom Otstndng Dayton Area Engr 1972. **MILITARY SERVICE:** USN rd1 1953-57. **BUSINESS ADDRESS:** Aeronautical Sys Div ASD/XROM, Wright Patterson AFB, Dayton, OH 45433.

WORTHINGTON-SMITH, HAMMETT
Educator. **PERSONAL:** Born Jun 23, 1923, Philadelphia, PA. **EDUCATION:** VA Union U, AA 1943, AB 1946; Case Wstrn Res U, AM 1948; Jmsn Bible Inst, DD 1974. **CAREER:** Albrght Coll, asst prof; DE St Coll, asst prof 1965-69; Univ Puerto Rico, vis instructor lectr religion & philos series 1963-65; Cheyney St Coll, asst prof 1961-63; Ft Vly St Coll, asso prof 1957-59; Blfld St Coll, asst prof 1951-57; WV St Coll, instr 1949-51; Frrst Co AR Presbyn, guest preacher youth week 1957. **ORGANIZATIONS:** Lectr Gen Educ Tchr Educ Prgm TmplUniv 1972-75; vis lectr dir MD St Tchrs Coll 1960-61; vis lectr Jcksn St Coll 1959-60; Kappa Alpha Psi; Phi Delta Kappa; mem Mdrn Lang of Am; Am Stds Assn; Shriner; Prnc Hall Ordr of Msnry 32 Deg; Am Legn; Vet of Fgn Wars of US; Rtry Intrnt Club; mem Coll Lang Assn Crtv Wrtng Com, Edtrl Com 1948-61; adv WV Intrclgt Press Assn 1949-50; mem exec com CCC of the Nat Cncl of Tchrs of Engl 1949-50; vice pres WV Assn of Coll Tchrs of Engl 1956-57; mem Hghr Educ Commn Prsbyn Synd of WV 1956-57; mem exec com S Rgnl Cncl YMCA 1957; chf consult Lang Arts Wrkshp 1958-59; lectr Fine Arts Fstvl 1958; dir Bowie St Tchrs Coll Thtr Arts Grp 1960-61; mem Rlgn in Life Wk Team Chyny St Coll 1962; consult Engl as a 2nd Lang Wrkshp 1962; pres DE St Coll in Dover Chpt, mem Relgn in Life Wk; mem Professional Staff lectr Cncl for Rcl Unty ofUniv ofDE 1966-70; rsrch consult Cptl Sch Dist of DE 1968-69; num others. **MILITARY SERVICE:** AUS 1st lt 1942-46. **BUSINESS ADDRESS:** 119 Masters Hall Albright Coll, Reading, PA 19603.

WORTHY, BARBARA ANN
Educator. **PERSONAL:** Born Nov 01, 1942, Thomaston, GA; daughter of S T Worthy and Laura Bell Jones Worthy. **EDUCATION:** Morris Brown Coll, Atlanta GA, BA, 1964; Atlanta Univ, Atlanta GA, MA, 1970; Tulane Univ, New Orleans LA, PhD, 1983. **CAREER:** Camilla High School, Camilla GA, social science teacher, 1964-69; Southern Univ at New Orleans LA, history teacher, 1970-. **ORGANIZATIONS:** Mem, Southern Historical Assn, 1983-; mem, Assn for Study of Afro-Amer Life & History, 1984-85; mem, Friends of Amistad, 1986-; bd of dir, Soc for the Study of Afro-LA & History, 1988-; mem, New Orleans League of Women Voters, 1988-; mem, Delta Sigma Theta. **HONORS/ACHIEVEMENTS:** Overdyke History Award, North Louisiana Historical Assn, 1981; one of 14 participants selected from six institutions of higher educ in Louisiana to participate in six-week Intl Curriculum Seminar in Kenya & Tanzania, East Africa, summer, 1985. **BUSINESS ADDRESS:** Associate Professor, Southern University at New Orleans, 6400 Press Drive, History Department, New Orleans, LA 70126.

WORTHY, JAMES
Professional athlete. **PERSONAL:** Born Feb 27, 1961, Gastonia, NC; married Angela Wilder. **EDUCATION:** Attended, Univ of NC. **CAREER:** LA Lakers, forward. **HONORS/ACHIEVEMENTS:** First No 1 draft pick ever select by reigning NBA Champions when the Lakers selected him in the 1982 draft; first NC player ever selected first in the NBA draft and joins Magic Johnson as the lakers only two No 1 picks since club moved to LA; unanimous All-Rookie choice after averaging 134 points; his 579 FG pct topped all rookies and is a Laker rookie record; named to every All-America team after his jr yr in coll; second leading vote-getter (behind Ralph Sampson) on the NBA coaches team that yr and shared College Player of the Yr honors bestowed by the First Interstate Bank Athl Found; made several hs All-Amer teams while a jr at Ashbrook averaging 198 points and 12 rebounds; unanimous prep All-America after his sr yr when he averaged 215 pts and 125 rebounds; mem 36th & 37th NBA All Star Teams. **BUSINESS ADDRESS:** Los Angeles Lakers, PO Box 10, Inglewood, CA 90306.

WORTHY, WILLIAM
Journalist, educator. **PERSONAL:** Born Jul 07, 1921, Boston, MA; son of William Worthy and Mabel Worthy. **EDUCATION:** Bates Coll, BA 1942; Harvard Univ, Nieman Fellow in Journalism 1956-57. **CAREER:** Journalism & Afro-Amer Studies, Boston Univ, prof, 1974-79; The Baltimore Afro-Amer, foreign correspondent & columnist, 1953-80. **ORGANIZATIONS:** Bd mem, Inst for Dem Communication Boston Univ; advisory bd Southeastern Black Press Inst; mem, Natl Peace Educ Comm 1975-; New England Reg Exec Comm; Amer Friends Serv Comm 1975-; bd mem Ford Hall Forum 1974-77. **HONORS/ACHIEVEMENTS:** Right-to-know & freedom info awards Boston Press Club, Capital Press Club Lincoln Univ MO; author "The Rape of Our Neighborhoods" 1976; Journalism Award of the MA Legislative Black Caucus, 1988; Travelled to 58 countries, specializing in coverage of Third World revolutionary and neo-colonial issues, 1951-89. **HOME ADDRESS:** 210 E 19th St, Apt 2, New York, NY 10003. **BUSINESS ADDRESS:** 87 Howland St, Boston, MA 02121-1705.

WRAY, WENDELL LEONARD
Educator, librarian. **PERSONAL:** Born Jan 30, 1926, Pittsburgh, PA; son of Arthur J. Wray and Mary L. Wray. **EDUCATION:** Bates Coll, AB (Magna Cum Laude) 1950; Carnegie Inst of Tech, MSLS 1952; Mexico City Coll, Cert 1957; Columbia Univ, Cert 1973. **CAREER:** Carnegie Library of Pittsburgh, librarian 1952-59; NY Publ Library, adult group specialist 1959-64, dir North Manhattan Proj 1965-73; Univ of Pittsburgh Sch of Libr and Info Sci, prof 1973-81; Schomburg Center for Research in Black Culture, chief 1981-83; Univ of Pittsburgh Sch of Libr and Info Sci, prof. **ORGANIZATIONS:** Mem Amer Libr Assn 1973-; mem Oral Hist Assn 1973-; juror Educ Film Libr Assn 1968-; juror Notable Books Council-ALA 1978-82; juror Amer Book Awards1981, 1983; consult PA Black Hist Adv Comm 1983; consult Kinte Libr Foundation 1973-75; mem Assn for the Study of Afro-Amer Life and Hist 1973-; NAACP I973-; Urban League I986-. **HONORS/ACHIEVEMENTS:** Phi Beta Kappa 1950; Phi Sigma Iota 1948; Beta Phi Mu 1973; Award Schl of Libr and Information Sci 1973; Disting Alumnus Univ of Pittsburgh; "Pictorial Report of The North Manhattan Project 1965-1972". **MILITARY SERVICE:** AUS Engineer Battalion Sgt Maj 1944-46. **HOME ADDRESS:** 5831 Walnut St, College Gardens #23, Pittsburgh, PA 15232. **BUSINESS ADDRESS:** Professor, University of Pittsburgh, SLIS Building #631, 135 North Bellefied Ave, Pittsburgh, PA 15260.

WRENN, THOMAS H., III
Dentist. **PERSONAL:** Born Oct 11, 1942, Mineola, TX; married Joel J Porter. **EDUCATION:** Univ of MO at KC, DDS 1967;Univ of KC. **CAREER:** Dentist, pvt prac. **ORGANIZATIONS:** Mem past pres Heart of Am Dental Soc 1974; Am Dental Soc 1970; Nat Dental Soc 1967; Soc Action ComUniv of MO at KC Dental Sch 1974; mem NAACP 1973; Sthrn Chris Ldrshp Conf; Alpha Phi Alpha Frat; Jaycees of KC 1975. **BUSINESS ADDRESS:** 5046 Prospect, Kansas City, MO 64130.

WRICE, DAVID
Policeman. **PERSONAL:** Born May 31, 1937, Lorain, OH; son of John Wrice and Savannah Wilson Wrice; divorced; children: Sharon Wrice Moore, Leonard Church, Barbara J. Wrice, Daniel, David. **EDUCATION:** Lorain County Community College, Lorain, OH, associate in police science, 1972; Heidelburg College, Tiffin, OH, bachelor's degree in psychology, 1974. **CAREER:** American Shipyard, Lorain, OH, foreman, 1963-66; Lorain Police Department, Lorain, OH, 1966—, jail warden, 1985—. **ORGANIZATIONS:** Delegate, National Black Police Association, 1986—; president, Lorain Minority Police Association, 1986—; commander, Herman Daniels VFW Post 8226, 1988—; moderator, Concerned Citizens of Lorain, 1989—; Buckeye Masonic Lodge; Al Lalim Temple. **HONORS/ACHIEVEMENTS:** Appreciation award, Second Baptist Church, 1970; appreciation award, Herman Daniels VFW Post 8226, 1974; Buddy PoPPV Award, Lorain County Veterans Council, 1975; Member of Year, Lorain County Minority Law Enforcement Association, 1986; outstanding community service, Shilow Baptist Church, 1986; Century Club Award, National Black Police Association, 1986; community service award, State of Ohio Auditor's Office, 1986. **MILITARY SERVICE:** US Army, Spc 3rd class, 1954-57; received Good Conduct medal, German Occupation medal, Marksman Ribbon. **HOME ADDRESS:** 209 East 23rd St, Lorain, OH 44055.

WRIGHT, ALBERT WALTER, JR.
Educator. **PERSONAL:** Born May 08, 1925, San Antonio, TX; married Betty Jean. **EDUCATION:** Huston-Tillotson Coll, BS 1949; TX Southern U, MS 1955; UCLA, PhD 1965. **CAREER:** CA State Univ Northridge, prof of accouting; UCA, teacher fellow 1961-65; TX Southern Univ, instr of business 1957-61; TL Pink HS, teacher athletic coach 1950-57. **ORGANIZATIONS:** Mem Amer Inst of Cert Pbl Acc 1962-; Amer Acctg Assn 1962-; Natl Assn of Acc 1965-; Nat Assn of Blk Acc 1975-; Beta Gamma Sigma Honor Soc 1964-; mem Beta Alpa Psi 1979; past mem Alpha Phi Alpha Frat 1947; mem Masonic Ldg 1946-. **HONORS/ACHIEVEMENTS:** Educ Achvmt Awd Nat Assn of Blk Acc 1975; articles "Earnings Per Share" in mgmt acctng Natl Assn of Acc 1971; "Maintaining Balance in Financial Position" mngmt acctg Natl Assn of Acc 1969; "Net Income & Extra Charges & Credits" Natl Assn of Acc 1966; "The Blk Minority and the Acctg Prfn" UCLA 1969; cert of merit Natl Assn of Acc. **MILITARY SERVICE:** USMC sgt 1943-46. **BUSINESS ADDRESS:** Professor of Accounting, California State University, 18111 Nordhoff St, Northridge, CA 91330.

WRIGHT, ALONZO GORDON
Business executive. **PERSONAL:** Born Jul 19, 1930, Cleveland; married Patronella Ross; children: Cheryl, Joyce, Gordy. **EDUCATION:** Hiram Coll, BA 1948; Western ReserveUniv Cleveland, LLB 1956. **CAREER:** Wright Dev Co, pres 1975-; Cleveland, atty 1957-58;Univ Euclid Urban Renewal Proj, dir 1963-65; Midwest Area Econ Devel Adm, dir 1965-67. **ORGANIZATIONS:** Pres Econ Resrcs Corp 1973-; pres Bay Dist Motor Car Dealers 1974-; vice pres Venice C of C 1974-; dir Santa Monica NCCJ. **MILITARY SERVICE:** USN 1948-55. **BUSINESS ADDRESS:** 2301 S Sepulveda Blvd West, Los Angeles, CA 90064.

WRIGHT, BENJAMIN HICKMAN
Association executive. **PERSONAL:** Born Aug 05, 1923, Shreveport, LA; married Jeanne Jason. **EDUCATION:** Univ Cincinnati, BA 1950, MA 1951, LHD 1971. **CAREER:** US Dept of State, econ & polit reporting officer 1952-53; Johnson Publishing Co, sales promotion & merchandising mgr 1952-66; Clairol Inc, mgr Urban Affairs & Ethnic Devel 1966-74; Johnson Pub Co, sr vice pres dir 1974; Black Media Inc, pres. **ORGANIZATIONS:** Business con Natl Comm of Black Churchmen; bd chmn pres NAMD NY Chap 1967-71; chmn Action Com for Self-Determination 1969-69; bd chmn NY Unit Black Econ Union 1970-71; mem Group for Advertising Progress 1970-71; bd mem John F Kennedy Meml Library for Minorities 1970-74; Nat ICBO 1971-; bd editors Jour of Black Econ & Bus Morehouse Coll; bd mem Sales Promo Exec Assn 1971-72; volunteer executive dir Natl Assault on Illiteracy Program 1980-. **HONORS/ACHIEVEMENTS:** Alpha Phi Alpha Equitable Oppor Awd 1969; Media Workshop Awd of Excellence 1968; Outstanding Black Businessman of Yr Blackafrica Promotions 1973; publ "A Voyage of Awareness". **MILITARY SERVICE:** USN 1943-46. **BUSINESS ADDRESS:** President, Black Media Inc, 231 W 29th St, Ste 1205, New York, NY 10001.

WRIGHT, BRUCE M.
Judge & attorney. **PERSONAL:** Born Dec 19, 1918, Princeton, NJ; children: Geoffrey DS, Keith LT, Alexis SS, Bruce CT. **EDUCATION:** Lincoln Univ, BA 1942; NY Law Schl, LLB 1950; Lincoln Univ, LLD (hon) 1973. **CAREER:** Human Resources Admin, NYC, gen consl 1967-70; Criminal Court, NYC, judge 1970-79; Civil Court of NYC, judge 1980-82; Supreme Court of NY , justice 1983-. **ORGANIZATIONS:** Brd mem Urban League of Greater NY 1952-56; advsry brd Fortune Soc 1971-; brd mem Inner City Round Table for Youth 1976-. **HONORS/ACHIEVEMENTS:** Author From The Shaken Tower (Poetry) England 1944, Lincoln Univ Poets, edited with Langston Hughes 1954, Repetitions (Poetry) 1980; law review articles, critical reviews, etc; author Black Robes, White Justice, Racism in the Judicial System, written for Prentice-Hall and not yet publshd. **MILITARY SERVICE:** AUS priv of inftry 1942-46; Purple Heart with Oak Leaf Cluster; Bronze Star with Oak Leaf Cluster; Consspicuous Service Cross, etc. **HOME ADDRESS:** 30 West 60th St, New York, NY 10023. **BUSINESS ADDRESS:** Justice, Supreme Court of NY, Supreme Court NY, 60 Centre St, 60 Centre St, New York, NY 10007.

WRIGHT, C. T. ENUS
Educator. **PERSONAL:** Born Oct 04, 1942, Social Circle, GA; married Mary Stevens. **EDUCATION:** Ft Wayne State Univ, BS 1964; Atlanta Univ, MA 1967; Boston Univ, PhD 1977. **CAREER:** GA Public Schools Social Circle, teacher 1965-67; Morris Brown Coll, mem faculty 1967-73, div chmn 1973-77; Eastern WA Univ, prog dir asst provost 1977-81; Cheyney Univ, pres 1982-86; FL Memorial Coll, vice pres academic affairs 1986-. **ORGANIZATIONS:** Dean of pledgees Phi Beta Sigma Ft Valley State 1963-64; pres Madison Bapt Sunday Sch & Training Union Congress 1967-78; worshipful master & 1st lt com Prince Hall Masons F & AM 1973-75; del Natl Dem Conv 1980; mem Pub Broadcasting Commn of State of WA 1980-; vice pres Cheney Lions Club 1980-; exec comm Boy Scouts of Amer Philadelphia 1982-; mem Natl Assn Equal Oppor in Higher Educ 1982-; mem Amer Hist Assn 1970-; mem Amer Baptist Club. **HONORS/ACHIEVEMENTS:** Human Relations Scholar Boston Univ 1969-71; Phi Alpha Theta Hist Hon Soc Boston Univ 1971; Omicron Delta Kappa Leadership Soc Morris Brown Coll 1977; "A History of Black & Educ in Atlanta", "Atlanta Hist Bull" 1977; pub "Black History Week, A Time to Reflect" Eastern Wash Univ 1979. **BUSINESS ADDRESS:** VP of Academic Affairs, Florida Memorial College, Miami, FL 33054.

WRIGHT, CAROLYN ELAINE
Educator. **PERSONAL:** Born Apr 22, 1951, Dayton, OH. **EDUCATION:** Wright State Univ, BS 1973; MBA 1978. **CAREER:** Bolinga Black Cultural Resources Ctr, asst dir 1973-77, dir 1977-81. **ORGANIZATIONS:** Vice pres Day-Mont West Community Mental Health Ctr 1984-85; 1st vice pres Mary Scott Nursing Ctr 1984-85; chairperson Citizen's Advisory Council 1984-85. **HONORS/ACHIEVEMENTS:** Professional internship Cleveland Scholarship Foundation 1983; graduate Black Leadership Program Dayton Urban League 1983-84. **HOME ADDRESS:** 1946 Haverhill Drive, Dayton, OH 45406. **BUSINESS ADDRESS:** Asst Prof of Finance, Central State University, 167 Smith Hall, Wilberforce, OH 45384.

WRIGHT, CHARLES
Attorney. **PERSONAL:** Born Oct 03, 1918, New Orleans, LA; married Alethia. **EDUCATION:** Temple Univ, BS, LLB. **CAREER:** Atty, private practice; Commonwealth PA, deputy atty general. **ORGANIZATIONS:** Bd test Henry Luce Found. **HONORS/ACHIEVEMENTS:** Scholars; Temple Univ; Princeton Seminary; Univ PA Presbyterian Med Center. **MILITARY SERVICE:** USAF. **BUSINESS ADDRESS:** 505 City Hall, Philadelphia, PA 19107.

WRIGHT, CHARLES E.
Business executive. **PERSONAL:** Born Mar 01, 1946, Washington, DC; married Barbara H; children: Charles Wright Jr. **EDUCATION:** Howard Univ, 1964-69; workshops & seminars Xerox Prof Selling Skills; Negotiating Skills Seminar; Interpersonal Communications; Stress Mgmt; Effective Presentations. **CAREER:** Eastern Air Lines Inc, ticket agent 1969-76, sales rep 1976-80, mgr market develop 1980-83, mgr market develop & campus rep admin 1983-. **ORGANIZATIONS:** Supervised Sr Citizens Passport Staff; monitored Fulfillment House Strategic Marketing Systems; mem bd of dirs Miami Dade Trade & Tourism Comm; adv bd World Inst of Black Communications; mem Natl Assn of Market Developers; bd mem Inner City Dance Troupe; host & producer of contemporary talk show Black Kaleidoscope on WCIX-TV Channel 6 Miami FL. **HONORS/ACHIEVEMENTS:** Who's Who in Black Corporate America; US Army Outstanding Soldier of the 1st Basic Combat Training Brigade 1970. **MILITARY SERVICE:** DC Natl Guard 1969-75; AUS. **BUSINESS ADDRESS:** Manager of Sales Development, Eastern Airlines, Miami International Airport, Miami, FL 33148.

WRIGHT, CHARLES H.
Physician. **PERSONAL:** Born Sep 20, 1918, Dothan, AL; married Louise Lovett; children: Stephanie, Carla. **EDUCATION:** AL State Coll, BS 1939; Meharry, MD 1943. **CAREER:** Wayne State Univ Med Sch, asst clinical prof ob/gyn; Private Practice, medical doctor. **ORGANIZATIONS:** Founder/pres African Med Educ Fund; founder/chmn of bd Afro-Amer Museum of Detroit; mem Univ of Detroit WTVS Channel 56; mem NAACP; published 20 med articles in natl & local med journals; wrote-produced musical drama Were You There?; legitimate stage & TV; author Roseson Labor's Forgotten Champion 1975. **HONORS/ACHIEVEMENTS:** Physician of Yr Detroit Med Soc 1965; Omega Man of Yr 1965; Physician of Yr MI State Med Soc 1968.

WRIGHT, CHARLES STEVENSON
Writer. **PERSONAL:** Born Jun 04, 1932, New Franklin, MO; son of Stevenson Wright and Dorothy Hughes Wright. **EDUCATION:** Studied writing at Lowney Handy's Writers Colony, Marshall, IL. **CAREER:** Free-lance writer, beginning with regular column in weekly Kansas City Call. **HONORS/ACHIEVEMENTS:** Author of The Messinger, Farrar Straus, 1963, of Absolutely Nothing to Get Alarmed About, Farrar Straus, 1973, and of column "Wright's World" in Village Voice. **MILITARY SERVICE:** US Army in Korea, private, 1952-54. **HOME ADDRESS:** 138 6th Ave, Brooklyn, NY 11217.

WRIGHT, CLARENCE JOHNNIE, SR.
Clergy. **PERSONAL:** Born Feb 19, 1953, Independence, LA; married Joyce Ingram; children: Clarence Jr, Lafrese Joi, Scharese Renay. **EDUCATION:** Control Data Inst, Computer Tech Cert 1973; Chicago State Univ, BA History 1983; The Chicago Theol Seminary, MDiv 1986. **CAREER:** Iovite Chem Inc, lab tech 1976-77; VA Hosp Hines IL, mail clerk 1977-78; Roman Adhesives Inc, plant mgr 1978-80; Wesley UM Church, student, asst pas-

tor1983-86; Christ the Carpenter UM Church, pastor 1986-. **ORGANIZATIONS:** Food pantry dir Wesley UM Church 1982-83; pres Chicago Theol Seminary Black Student Org 1984-85; liaison officer Chicago Abbott Park Adv Council 1985-86; chmn Rockford Free South Africa Movement 1986-; bd mem Rockford MELD 1986-, Rockford Neighborhood Redevelopment 1986-; chmn educ comm Rockford MinistersFellowship Assoc 1987. **HONORS/ACHIEVEMENTS:** Certificate of Appreciation Wesley UMC Marriage Enrich Ministry 1984-85; Outstanding Young Men of America 1985; In Appreciation Chicago Project Image 1985. **MILITARY SERVICE:** USAF airman 1st class 2 yrs; Natl Defense Ribbon 1975. **BUSINESS ADDRESS:** Pastor, Christ the Carpented UM Church, 1100 So Winnebago St, Rockford, IL 61102.

WRIGHT, DMITRI
Fine artist/educator of the fine arts painting and drawing. **PERSONAL:** Born Oct 14, 1948, Newark, NJ; son of John Wright; married Karen Wright; children: Odin. **EDUCATION:** NY School of Fine Arts, valadictorian 1970; Max Beckman Intl Scholarship Brooklyn Museum, 1970-71; Cooper Union 1971-73. **CAREER:** Teaching positions; Art instructor of painting drawing landscape and figure; Newark School of Fine Arts, 1971-81; Private Lessons, 1971-87; Brooklyn Museum ArtSchool, 1972-82; Cooper Union HS Prog, 1972; Newark Museum Contemporary Artists from the Collection 1979; French Realist Exhibition Brooklyn Museum 1981; Nassau County Museum, 1981; Print Magazine, publisher; Propersi Inst of Art, 1987; Dmitri's Renaissance Workshop, owner & master instructor, Greenwich Ct 1989-. **ORGANIZATIONS:** Selected lectures demonstrations and publications; mem Amer Council for the Arts NYC, Amer Assoc of Museums Washington DC, Amer Watercolor Soc NJ, Foundof the Commun of Artists NYC, Natl Art Dealers Assoc Washington DC, Natl Artists Equity Assoc Inc Washington DC; pres Hunting Ridge Studio and Corp Walls Art Sales and Leasing. **HONORS/ACHIEVEMENTS:** Permanent collections, ATT Corp Collection, Brooklyn Museum Prints & Drawings, The Fine Arts Museum of Long Island, Newark Museum Contemporary Paintings, Newark Library, Urban Life Center Columbia MD; selected exhibitions, NYC, Adam L Gimbel Gallery Saks 5th Ave NYC, Westbeth Alumni, The Hudson Guild, Lever House Group Show Park Ave NYC, Rutgers Univ, Farleigh Dickenson Univ, 18th Natl Print Exhibition Brooklyn Museum, CA Palace of Legion of Honor San Francisco; Bridgewater State Coll Gallery MA 1987; one man show Images Gallery 1987; Sidney Rothman Gallery NJ 1987; Sound Shore Gallery NY 1986-87, Northeast Open 1986, GroveSt Gallery MA; winter exhibit 1986-87; Awd USA Fine Arts Show Natl Exhibition Gregg Art Gallery CA; Awd 29th Annual Chautaugua Natl Exhibition, Peoples Choice Awd; articles in various issues of Art Today, Art Speak, New Art Examiner, The New York Art Review; Lublin Graphics, Inc. 1989; Dmitri's Renaissance Workship 1989. **BUSINESS ADDRESS:** Owner & Master Instructor, Dmitri's Renaissance Workshop, 106 Hunting Ridge Rd, Greenwich, CT 06830.

WRIGHT, DORRIS D.
Communication specialist. **PERSONAL:** Born Mar 19, 1950, New York, NY. **EDUCATION:** Clark College, BA 1975; Univ of Missouri-Columbia, MA 1981. **CAREER:** IBM Corp, communication specialist. **ORGANIZATIONS:** Mem NAACP 1960-; third vice president Zeta Phi Beta Sor Inc 1978-80; consultant on womens issues Univ of KY and Harvard/Radcliff. **HONORS/ACHIEVEMENTS:** WRC Human Relations Awd 1978; Title XX Fellowship 1978-81. **HOME ADDRESS:** 215 Piedmont Ave NE, #1905, Atlanta, GA 30308.

WRIGHT, EARL LEE
Educational administrator. **PERSONAL:** Born Jul 05, 1941, Sinton, TX; son of Earilee Wright and Nola Beatrice Vaughn Wright; children: Arlene; Darius; Adrian. **EDUCATION:** St Mary's Univ, BA 1965, MA 1970; Univ of TX at Austin, PhD 1975. **CAREER:** San Antonio Independent Sch Dist, teacher 1965-68; Swift and Company, management 1968-70; San Antonio Coll, prof and dean 1970-82, vice pres 1982-. **ORGANIZATIONS:** Mem Antioch Baptist Church 1951-; visiting prof Prairie View A&M Univ 1973-75; volunteer serv Northwest YMCA 1973-78; natl consultant Nova Univ 1978-; bd dir San Antonio Boys Club of Amer 1981-82; mem United Way Comm Adv Bd 1981; consultant Kelly AFT Mgmt Org 1982; mem JCSPAT 1982-86, TACUSPA; mem Federal Exec Awds Panel 1984-85; hon mem Mayor's Martin Luther King Memorial Commn 1986; speaker at state and natl conferences and conventions. **HONORS/ACHIEVEMENTS:** Honorarium New York Univ 1982; Doctoral fellowship Univ of TX at Austin 1973-75; mem Phi Delta Kappa; numerous publications in the area of educational administration. **HOME ADDRESS:** 3500 Oakgate 2801, San Antonio, TX 78230. **BUSINESS ADDRESS:** Vice President, San Antonio College, 1300 San Pedro Ave, San Antonio, TX 78284.

WRIGHT, EARL W.
Clergyman. **PERSONAL:** Born Jan 31, 1902, Laurens Co, SC; married Magnolia Jackson; children: four. **EDUCATION:** Benedict Coll Columbia SC; Morris Coll Sumter SC, Hon DD 1972. **CAREER:** Tumbling Shoals Bapt Assn, moderator; New Grove Beth & New Hope Chs, pastor. **ORGANIZATIONS:** Bd dir Laurens Co Comm Act OEO 1965-; bd dir SC Bapt Mission Conv; mem Nat Bapt Conv; dir Laurens Co Chap NAACP; trust Morris Coll; mem Benedict Coll Alumni Club; adv com Racial Relat Laurens Co Comman Dem Party; mem & dir Laurens Co Ctzn Imp Orgn. **HONORS/ACHIEVEMENTS:** Var banquets dinners & ofcl cits in rec of efforts to promote spiritual awareness & civic goodwill.

WRIGHT, EBONY NARKETA
Business executive. **PERSONAL:** Born Apr 14, 1960, Cleveland; married Randy Jordan. **EDUCATION:** Cuyahoga Co Hosp Cont Educ Prgm, Cert 1971-73; Halles Sch of Mus, Cert 1975-76; Cuyahoga Comm Coll, 1975-. **CAREER:** Elemar Record & Prod Co, pres 1979-; Ebony Cowgirl Prod Co Records, vice pres 1978-79; Am Red Cross, nurs instr 1976-79; Wright Med Svc, admnstr of nurs serv 1976-78; Cuyahoga Co Hosp Sys, adminstrv splst 1971-75. **ORGANIZATIONS:** Mem Nat Rec Arts & Sci 1978-; bd of trustees Am Mus & Opry Assn Inc1979-; mem Cntry Mus Assn; mem Am Red Cross 1976-; mem OH Cntry Mus Assn 1979-; mem Black Mus Assn 1979-. **HONORS/ACHIEVEMENTS:** Cleveland queen of cntry mus Fan Club Grp of Cleveland 1970; female vocalist of yr cntry mus Am Mus & Opry Assn 1979; winners award TV 8 Cleveland OH1980; natl black queen of cntry mus Am Mus & Opry Assn Inc 1980-. **BUSINESS ADDRESS:** Elemar Records & Productions, P O Box 18320, Cleveland Heights, OH 44118.

WRIGHT, EDWARD WINDSOR
Business executive. **PERSONAL:** Born Oct 14, 1940, Cincinnati, OH. **EDUCATION:** Coll Conservatory of Mus. **CAREER:** Edward Windsor Wright Corp, pres; WCIN Radio; WABQ Radio; Librty UA Records, gen mgr; Bobby Womack, mgr. **ORGANIZATIONS:** Pres mem NATRA; formed EWW Mgmt & EWW Pub Relat Corp; NAACP.

WRIGHT, ERIC
Professional athlete. **PERSONAL:** Born Apr 18, 1959, St Louis, MO; married Alvita Nicks; children: Erika. **EDUCATION:** Attended, Missouri. **CAREER:** San Francisco 49ers, Cornerback 1981-. **ORGANIZATIONS:** Co-founder with teammate Keena Turner of Champs Foundation a scholarship program; co-sponsor summer football camp for youth at Stanford Univ. **HONORS/ACHIEVEMENTS:** Selected All-American in junior year at Missouri; 1984 NFL Leader with 164 interception-return yds; mem 1986 NFL Pro Bowl team. **BUSINESS ADDRESS:** San Francisco 49ers, 711 Nevada St, Redwood City, CA 94061.

WRIGHT, FREDERICK BENNIE
Psychologist. **PERSONAL:** Born Oct 06, 1950, St Louis, MO. **EDUCATION:** TN State Univ, BS (psychology) 1977; George Warren Brown Schl of Social Work-WA U, MSW 1979; WA Univ, Minority Mental Health MA (psychology) 1978. **CAREER:** Family & Children's Serv of Greater St Louis, clinical Soc Worker 1984-. **ORGANIZATIONS:** Proj Alpha coordntr Alpha Phi Alpha, Frat Epsilon Lambda Chapter 1982-; fndr/pres 100 Blackmen of Metro St Louis; 1982-; Task Force mem Natl Assn of Black Social Workers 1982-; on aging Task Force mem Natl Alliance of Business; Ebony Fashion Fair Booster The Urban League of Metro St Louis; chrtr mem UNCF Intra Alumni Cncl. **HONORS/ACHIEVEMENTS:** Comm serv 100 Blackmen of Metro St Louis 1984; soc respblty Continental Soc, Inc 1985; Essence Award Iota Pelatis Aux, Iota Phi Lambda Soc; Who's Who in Amer Coll & Univ. **BUSINESS ADDRESS:** Clinical Social Worker, Family & Childrens Service, 2650 Olive St, St Louis, MO 63103.

WRIGHT, FREDERICK DOUGLASS
Assistant dean/director. **PERSONAL:** Born Aug 26, 1946, Columbia, GA; son of Mr & Mrs James Wright. **EDUCATION:** Roosevelt Univ, BGS 1972, MA 1974; Princeton Univ, MA 1982, PhD 1982. **CAREER:** Univ of Notre Dame, asst prof 1978-, dir black studies program 1983-, asst dean 1986-. **ORGANIZATIONS:** Evaluator NJ Dept of Higher Educ 1985, 86; asst dir Natl Endowment for the Humanities Inst in Afro-Amer Culture 1987; mem The Amer Political Sci Assoc, The Western Social Science Assoc, The Southern Political Science Assoc, The Southwest Political Science Assoc, The Natl Conf of Black Political Scientists, The Assoc for the Study of Afro-Amer Life and History, The Natl Assoc of Black Studies Prog, The Indiana Assoc of Historians. **HONORS/ACHIEVEMENTS:** R R McCormick Fellowship Princeton Univ 1977-78; Frazier Thompson Faculty-Staff Awd 1984; NDEA Fellowship Roosevelt Univ; invited participant NEH-Supported Summer Institute "Afro-American Religious Studies for College Teachers," 1984; published scholarly articles on Black Politics in the American South. **BUSINESS ADDRESS:** Asst Dean/Dir, Univ of Notre Dame, Black Studies Program, 345 O'Shaughnessy Hall, Notre Dame, IN 46556.

WRIGHT, GEORGE C., JR.
Mayor. **PERSONAL:** Born Mar 09, 1932, Chesapeake City, MD; son of George C Wright and Alice Brooks Wright; married Mary Guy, Jul 21, 1953; children: Terun Palmer, George C III, Sharon, Lisa. **EDUCATION:** Maryland State Coll, Princess Anne MD, BS, 1953. **CAREER:** Dover A&B, Dover DE, chief of staffing, 1956-; Town of Smyrna DE, mayor, currently. **ORGANIZATIONS:** Mem, Council on Police Training, DE, 1986-; bd mem, Kent Sussex Industries, 1987-; vice pres, DE League of Local Govt, 1987-; vice pres, steward bd, Bethel AME Church, 1987-; worshipful master, St John's Lodge #7. **MILITARY SERVICE:** US Army, E-5, 1952-54. **HOME ADDRESS:** 31 Locust St, Smyrna, DE 19977.

WRIGHT, GEORGE DEWITT
Professional athlete. **PERSONAL:** Born Dec 22, 1958, Oklahoma City, OK. **CAREER:** Texas Rangers, outfielder 1982-. **HONORS/ACHIEVEMENTS:** The Rangers Player of the Yr 1983. **BUSINESS ADDRESS:** Texas Rangers, Arlington Stadium, Arlington, TX 76010.

WRIGHT, GERALD
Government official. **PERSONAL:** Born Aug 07, 1952, Cincinnati, OH; married Melanie; children: Angela, Adrienne, Adam. **EDUCATION:** Fresno State Coll, BA 1974. **CAREER:** Turbine Support Div of Chromalloy Amer, personnel supervisor 1977-79; Metropolitan Transit Authority, equal employment oppor officer 1979-81; Texas A&M Univ System, dir of affirmative action 1981-83; State of TX Coord Bd TX College and Univ System, dir equal educ oppor planning 1983-. **ORGANIZATIONS:** Chmn United Way Campaign. **MILITARY SERVICE:** USAF E4/sgt 5 yrs; Air Force Commendation Medal for Meritorious Serv w/First Oak Leaf Cluster; Small Arms Expert Marksmanship Medal; Good Conduct Medal; Presidential Unit Citation; Air Force Outstanding Unit Citation; Natl Defense Medal; Air Force Longevity Medal; Speech Merit Awd Noncommissioned Officers Leadership School. **BUSINESS ADDRESS:** Dir Educational Plng, State of TX, Higher Education Coord Board, PO Box 12788, Austin, TX 78711.

WRIGHT, GROVER CLEVELAND
Public relations manager. **PERSONAL:** Born Apr 18, 1916, Marengo County, AL; married Irma Serena Palmer; children: Grover Edward, Gail Elaine. **EDUCATION:** Psycho Corp, cert selection interviewing training 1973. **CAREER:** Pullman Co, sleeping car porter 1942-65, porter in charge 1965-68; Bd of Amer Missions, parish worker 1968-72; Div for Mission in N Amer, lay asso 1972;Luth Ch in Am Div for Prof Leadership, asso dir 1972-. **ORGANIZATIONS:** Pres N Philadelphia Improvement Council of Blocks 1960-; Boy and Cub Scoutmaster Boy Scouts of Amer 1960-72; bd chmn Assn of Comm Orgn for Reform Now ACORN 1978-80. **HONORS/ACHIEVEMENTS:** Disting Serv Awd Boy Scouts of Amer 1965; Humanitarian Chapel of Four Chaplains 1966; Silver Beaver Awd Boy Scouts of Amer 1967; Serv Beyond Call of Duty Plaque Conf of Black Luth 1979. **BUSINESS ADDRESS:** Associate Dir, Lutheran Church in Amer, 2900 Queen Lane, Philadelphia, PA 19129.

WRIGHT, HARRIETTE SIMON
Educator. **PERSONAL:** Born Oct 03, 1915, Wadesboro, NC; widowed; children: Ernest, Franklin. **EDUCATION:** Bluefield State Coll, BS elem ed 1951; IN U, MSW 1963. **CAREER:** Concord Coll, prof social work 1974-; Dept of Mental Health, comm mental health consult 1968-74; Vocational Rehab, chief social worker 1966-68; Dept of Welfare, supr child welfare 1955-66; Aplmer Mem Inst, dean of girls 1954-55; Lakin State Hospital, psych aide supr 1951-54; McDowell Cnty Bd of Educ, elem school teacher 1937-38. **ORGANIZATIONS:** Anti-Grammateus Alpha Kappa Alpha Sor 1951-80; chmn Mercer Co Commn on Aging 1979-; charter-bd mem Windy Mountain Learning Cntr 1974-; life mem NAACP. **BUSINESS ADDRESS:** Athens, WV 24701.

WRIGHT, JACKSON THOMAS, JR.
Professor of medicine. **PERSONAL:** Born Apr 28, 1944, Pittsburgh, PA; son of Jackson T. Wright, Sr. and Lillian Doak Wright; married Mollie L. Richardson, Sep 02, 1967; children: Adina. **EDUCATION:** Ohio Wesleyan University, Delaware, OH, BA, 1967; University of Pittsburgh, Pittsburgh, PA, MD, 1976, PhD, 1977. **CAREER:** University of Michigan, Ann Arbor, MI, residency in internal medicine, 1977-80; Medical College of Virginia/Virginia Commonwealth University, Richmond, VA, assistant professor, 1980-86, associate professor of medicine and pharmocology, 1986—. **ORGANIZATIONS:** Chairman, Virginia State affiliate hypertension subcommittee, American Heart Association, 1984-86; vice chairman, hypertension scientific subsection, American Society for Clinical Pharmacology and Therapeutics, 1985-87; American Federation for Clinical Research; American College of Physicians; co-chairman, basic science section, National Medical Association; member, executive committee, Old Dominion State Medical Society; vice president, Richmond Medical Society, 1985-87; member, executive committee, Association of Black Cardiologists; president, Black Education Association. **HONORS/ACHIEVEMENTS:** Woodrow Wilson, Martin Luther King Fellow, 1971-73; University of Pittsburgh Equalization of Higher Education Fund Award, 1972-77; certificate of appreciation, Student National Medical Association, MCV chapter, 1982, 1984, 1985, 1986; program service award, Virginia affiliate, American Heart Association, 1986; fellow, American College of Physicians, 1987. **MILITARY SERVICE:** US Air Force, captain, 1967-71. **BUSINESS ADDRESS:** Medical College of Virginia, Virginia Commonwealth University, MCV Station Box 284, 428 McGuire Hall Annex, Richmond, VA 23298.

WRIGHT, JAMES A.
Government official. **PERSONAL:** Born Nov 25, 1937, New Orleans, LA; son of Ernest Wright Sr and Ethel M Wright-Jackson; married Wilma J Kelly Wright, Oct 10, 1960; children: Gene N, Keith J, David J. **EDUCATION:** Southern Univ, New Orleans LA, BS, 1973. **CAREER:** LA State Dept of Educ, New Orleans LA, supervisor, 1975-83; City of New Orleans LA, deputy dir, 1983-. **ORGANIZATIONS:** Mem, Alpha Phi Alpha Inc, 1972-; pres, Zulu Social Aid & Pleasure Club, 1976-; mem, 4 Degree Knights of Peter Claver, 1984-; mem, 3rd Degree Mason, 1985-; mem, Natl Assn of Private Industry Councils, 1985-; mem, Natl Job Training Partnership, 1986-; mem, Natl Forum of Black Administrators, 1986-; co-chair, Telebank United Negro College Fund, 1989-; bd mem, US Selective Service System, currently. **HONORS/ACHIEVEMENTS:** Pre-Medical Science degree, Southern Univ in New Orleans, 1973; various plaques from organizations and committees. **MILITARY SERVICE:** US Army, PFC, 1956-58; honorable discharge. **HOME ADDRESS:** 7320 Willowbrae Dr, New Orleans, LA 70127. **BUSINESS ADDRESS:** Deputy Director, City of New Orleans/City's Office of Employment Training and Development, 2400 Canal St, Third Floor, New Orleans, LA 70119.

WRIGHT, JAMES CHRISTOPHER
Educator. **PERSONAL:** Born Dec 25, 1918, Mecklenburg Co; married Annie B Smith. **EDUCATION:** St Pauls Coll, BS 1953; VA State Coll, MS Indust Educ 1976. **CAREER:** Mecklenburg Co Sch, masonry tchr. **ORGANIZATIONS:** Bd mem Alpha Phi Alpha Frat; RC Yance Lodge #284 AF & AM; NAACP; SCLC; mem bd of dir Chase City Med Clinic; Mecklenburg Educ Assn; Am Vocatnl Assn; Nat Educ Assn mem town cncl; mayor Chase City, VA. **MILITARY SERVICE:** AUS WW Ii 3 yrs.

WRIGHT, JAMES R.
Librarian. **PERSONAL:** Born May 12, 1941, Fayette, AL; son of Elvertis Wright and Corine Henry; married Mary A Law; children: James, Jr, Coretta, Jason. **EDUCATION:** Alabama State Univ, BS 1962; State Univ NY Geneseo, MLS 1970; Cincinnati, OH, PhD Union Graduate School of the union for exper coll & Univ. **CAREER:** Rochester Public Library, dir, Phillis Wheatley Library, 1969-88; St Jude's Educ Inst, Mont, AL, teacher, librarian, 1962-66; Gary Public Library, Gary, IN, 1966-68; AL A&M Univ, Huntsville asst to librarian, 1968-69; published in Focus on in library, 1968; Library Journal, 1969; Coll & Rsch librarian, 1979; Wilson Library Bulletin, 1971; Youth Advisory Commn, Rochester Urban League, lecturer & speaker on problems in librarianship. **ORGANIZATIONS:** Bd dir Mont Neighborhood Cent; Black Res Inf Cent; Black-O-Media; chmn Black Caucus of Amer Library Assn 1973-74. **BUSINESS ADDRESS:** Minister, Progressive Church of God in Christ, 270 Cumberland St, PO Box 914, Rochester, NY 14603.

WRIGHT, JAMES RICHARD
City official. **PERSONAL:** Born Feb 28, 1921, Atlanta, GA; married Mildred Ann Baskin; children: Vincent, Marvin, Edwin. **EDUCATION:** Claflin Coll, BS 1948; NY Univ, MA Admin 1954; King Mem Coll, LLD 1977. **CAREER:** School Dist 17, teacher 1948-57, elementary principal 1957-62; Hendersonville City Schools NC, high school principal 1962-64; Spartanburg SC, high school principal 1964-80; Bethlehem Ctr, exec dir 1982-86; City of Spartanburg SC, supervisor for special census 1987. **ORGANIZATIONS:** Mem Urban Renewal Commiss 1965-69; consultant Southern Assoc of Secondary Schools 1970-80; pres S Spartanburg Sertoma Club 1980-81; chmn Civil Serv Commn 1980-86; chmn Civil Service Commn 1986-92; County Affirmative Action Comm-Spartanburg County, 1988-; chmn of NAACP Educ Comm. **HONORS/ACHIEVEMENTS:** Teacher of the Year Rotary Club 1979-80; Plaque SC Assoc of Sec School Principals 1980; Service Award SC House of Representatives 1980; Service Award SC Secondary Schools Principals Assoc 1980; Comm Service Award Sertoma Intl 1981; Service Award Progressive Men 1987. **MILITARY SERVICE:** AUS sgt 1942-46; Good Conduct, Arms Expert, ATA Serv Ribbon 1943-46. **HOME ADDRESS:** 203 Collins Ave, Spartanburg, SC 29301. **BUSINESS ADDRESS:** Executive Dir, Bethlehem Ctr, 397 Highland Ave, Spartanburg, SC 29301.

WRIGHT, JANE C.
Surgeon, educator. **PERSONAL:** Born Nov 30, 1919, NYC; married David D Jones; children: Jane, Alison. **EDUCATION:** Smith Coll, AB 1942; NY Med Coll, MD 1945. **CAREER:** Visiting phys consultant, numerous hospital clinic, etc; NY Med Coll, assoc dean prof surgery. **ORGANIZATIONS:** Mem various offcs coms Manhattan Counc State Commn for Human Rights; Nat Med Assn; Manhattan Central Med Soc; Am Assn for Cancer Rsrch; NY Acad Scis; NY County Med Soc; NY Cancer Soc; African Rsrch Found; Am Cancer Soc; Am Assn for the Advcmnt of Sci; Sigma Xi; Medico-CARE; Am Soc Clin Oncology; Pres's Commn on Heart Disease; Alumni Assn of Women's Med Coll of PA; NY Acad Med; Phys Manpower; Med Soc of Cnty of NY; NY State Woman's Counc NY State Dept Commerce; Smith Coll Bd Trust; Am Assn for Cancer Rsrch; Nat Inst Hlth Med Sci Tng; Nat Inst of Gen Med Scis; Alpha Kappa Alpha. **HONORS/ACHIEVEMENTS:** Num publs in field; num awds, hon, spl achvmts, recog.

WRIGHT, JEANNE JASON (JEANNE JASON)
Editor. **PERSONAL:** Born Jun 24, 1934, Washington, DC; married Benjamin Hickman; children: Benjamin Jr, Deborah, David, Patricia. **EDUCATION:** Radcliffe Coll, BA 1956; Univ of Chicago, MA 1958. **CAREER:** Psychiat social worker various mental health facilities 1958-70; Black Media Inc, gen mgr 1970-74, pres 1974-75; Natl Black Monitor, exec editor 1975-; Black Resources Inc, pres 1975-. **ORGANIZATIONS:** Mem Natl Assn of Media Women; mem Newswoman's Club of NY, Natl Assn of Social Workers Inc; mem Alpha Kappa Alpha Sor, Radcliffe Club of NY, Harvard Club of N.Y. **HONORS/ACHIEVEMENTS:** Natl Assn of Black Women Attys Awd 1977; Second Annual Freedom's Jour Awd Journalism Students & Faculty Univ of DC 1979; Metro NY Chap Natl Assn of Media Women Media Woman of the Yr Awd 1984; Natl Media Woman of the Yr Awd Natl Assn of Media Women 1984. **BUSINESS ADDRESS:** President, Black Resources Inc, Phse C, 410 Central Park W, New York, NY 10025.

WRIGHT, JEFFERSON W.
Clergyman. **PERSONAL:** Born Jul 24, 1935, Bluefield, WV. **EDUCATION:** Attended VA State Coll; Marshall Univ, AB 1959; WV Univ Law Sch, grad; attended WV Univ So CA; Boston Univ Sch of Theo, STB 1963; Boston Univ Sch of Theo, MDiv 1973. **CAREER:** Hebrew Childrens Home, youth counselor 1959; Calvary Bapt Ch, student pastor 1959-60; LA Public Sch System, sch teacher 1960-61; Tremont St Ch, asst student minister 1961; Sheldon St Ch, pastor 1961-64; PA State Univ, part-time fac 1969-73; Second Baptist Ch Harrisburg, pastor 1964-. **ORGANIZATIONS:** Co-founder OIC of Harrisburg; mem Natl Bapt Amer Bapt Conv; mem Harrisburg Uptown Neighbors Together; adv comm of PA Dept of Health & Welfare; Urban Strat Com of Council of Christ; Natl Bd of Black Churchmen; founder First Black Sr Citizens Organ in Central PA; bd mem NAACP; moderator WITF-TV prog ATime to Act; mem Urban Coalition & Black Coalition of Harrisburg; past mem Mayors Cits; adv com chmn of subcom on Housing; bd dirs of Family & Childrens Svcs; Tri-Co Planned Parenthood Assn; mem adv bd Harrisburg Sch Dist. **MILITARY SERVICE:** USAF.

WRIGHT, JEREMIAH A., JR.
Minister. **PERSONAL:** Born Sep 22, 1941, Philadelphia, PA; children: Janet Marie, Jeri Lynne. **EDUCATION:** Howard Univ, BA 1968, MA 1969; Univ of Chicago Sch of Divinity, MA 1975. **CAREER:** Zion Church, interim pastor 1968-69; Beth Eden Church, asst pastor 1969-71; Amer Assn of Theol Schools, researcher 1970-72; Trinity Church, pastor 1972-; Chicago Center for Black Religious Studies, exec dir 1974-75; Chicago Cluster of Theol Schools, lectr 1975-77; Seminary Consortium for Pastoral Educ, adjunct prof 1981-. **ORGANIZATIONS:** Bd dir Malcolm X Coll Sch of Nursing; bd dir Office for Church in Society (UCC); commr Commn for Racial Justice (UCC); IL Conf of Chs; Urban League Ministerial Alliance; Ecumenical Strategy Comm; IL Conf United Ch of Christ; Great Lakes Regional Task Force on Churches in Transitional Comm; bd dir Ctrs for New Horizons 1976-; Omega Psi Phi Frat 1960-77; Doric Lodge #77 F & AM (Masonic) 1976-; Western Consistory #28 1983-; Blk Clergy Caucus United Ch ofChrist 1972-; United Black Christians (Blk Caucus Lay & Clergy UCC) 1972-. **HONORS/ACHIEVEMENTS:** Alpha Kappa Mu Honor Soc; Dean's list VA Union Univ; Dean's List Howard Univ 1968; Tching Asst Fellowship Howard Univ; Rockefeller Fellowship 1970, 1972;3 Presidential Commendations LB Johnson; songs publ "God Will Answer Prayer", "Jesus is His Name"; article publ "Urban Black Church Renewal" found in the "Signs of the Kingdom in the Secular City" edited by Helen Ujvarosy Chicago Covenant Press 1984. **MILITARY SERVICE:** USMC pfc 1961-63; USN hm3 1963-67. **BUSINESS ADDRESS:** Adjunct Professor, Sem Consort for Pastoral Educ, 532 W 95th St, Chicago, IL 60620.

WRIGHT, JOHN AARON
Educator. **PERSONAL:** Born May 22, 1939, St Louis, MO; married Sylvia Henley; children: John Jr, David, Curtis. **EDUCATION:** Harris Tchrs Coll, AB 1962; St Louis U, MmEd 1968, PhD 1978; Atlatnat U; MO U; Tchrs Coll Columbia U. **CAREER:** Ferguson-Florissant School Dist, asst supt pup serv & fed prog 1979-; St Louis Citizens Educ Task Force, exec dir 1977-79; Ferguson-Florissant School Dist, asst supt comm relations 1975-79; Kinloch School Dist, supt 1973-75; Steger Jr HS, asst prin 1970-73; John Griscom School, prin 1965-70. **ORGANIZATIONS:** Sch Bd Assn; Phi Delta Kappa; Nat Alliance of Blck Sch Educators; pres Grtr St Louis Alliance of Blck Sch Educators; Nat Sch Pub Relations Assn;Kiwanis; Anniversary Club; Grace Meth Ch; NAACP Sal Army del Intl Corps Cadet Conf in London 1956. **HONORS/ACHIEVEMENTS:** Man of the Yr Omega Psi Phi Frat 1959, 67; ptcpnt Supt Work Conf ColumbiaUniv 1986; pres Univ City Sch Bd 1976; Danforth Ldrshp Flw 1977; MO Gov Adv Counc on Voctnl Educ 1977. **BUSINESS ADDRESS:** 665 January, Ferguson, MO 63135.

WRIGHT, JOSEPH H., JR.
Entertainment services. **PERSONAL:** Born Feb 01, 1954, Chicago, IL; married Ronda R Preacely; children: Nahum, Gabriel, Nina. **EDUCATION:** Kendall Coll, AA Music 1974; Millikin Univ, BA Music 1977; Attending, North Eastern IL Univ Grad Sch. **CAREER:** Body Sounder Inc, pres 1982-87; East Bank Club, fitness instructor 1982-; Soft Sheen Prods Inc, creative consultant 1983-87; Motivation Industry Inc, pres 1987-; JoRon Music Publishing Co, 1986-. **ORGANIZATIONS:** Musician/producer Amer Federation of Musicians 1972-; volunteer Chicago Bd of Education 1982-86; annual vocalist/conductor of Chicago Economic Develop Corp1984-87; songwriter/publisher ASCAP 1984-; annual guest speaker Hugh O'brian Youth Foundation 1986-87. **HONORS/ACHIEVEMENTS:** Outstanding Young Men of Amer 1984; Chicago Assoc of Tech Societies 1986; Certificate of Thanks and Appreciation Chicago Public Schools; published "The Art of Body Sounding" book and tape.

BUSINESS ADDRESS: President/Producer, JoRon Music/Publishing Co, PO Box 4985, Chicago, IL 60680.

WRIGHT, JOSEPH MALCOLM
Attorney, education & business executive. **PERSONAL:** Born Sep 27, 1944, Toomsboro, GA; married Sheilah Delores Broome; children: Joseph Oliver, Tiffany Michele, Jennifer Nicole. **EDUCATION:** E MI Univ, BS 1969; Wayne State Univ, JD 1974; Harvard Univ, Ed Mgmt Diploma 1983. **CAREER:** GM-Buick, stat control asst 1965-67; GM-Chev, sr acct 1967-69; Univ of MI, suprv of payroll 1969-70; Univ of MI Coll of Arts Sci & Letters, admin mgr 1970-72; Detroit Coll of bus, adj prof 1975-77; Univ of MI Ann Arbor, chmn minority affaris 1975-77; United Motors Corp, pres 1983-; Univ of MI Dearborn, dean of student affairs. **ORGANIZATIONS:** Bd of dir Washtenaw Cty Black Contr & Tradesmen Assoc 1967-72; citizen rep Oak Pk Urban Renewal Council 1969-74; pres JM Wright & Assoc Detroit 1972-; pres, dir Assoc for Urban Legal Ed 1973-; bd of dir Barrino Entertainment Corp 1973-79; adj prof Wayne Cty Comm Coll 1975-; bd dir Metamorphosis Inc NY 1975-79; mem New Detroit Inc Minority Bus Devel Comm 1978-80; arbitrator Amer Arbitration Assoc 1979-; bd dir Pink Lmtd Allen Park MI 1979-;mem Amer Bar Assoc, Natl Bar Assoc, Wolverine Bar Assoc; bd of dir Inner-City Bus Improvement, Southeastern MI Bus Devel Ctr; mem NAACP, Urban League; bd of dir Western Wayne/Oakland Cty Comm Housing Resource Bd, Fair Housing Ctr Detroit. **MILITARY SERVICE:** USAFR 1966-69. **BUSINESS ADDRESS:** Dean of Student Affairs, Univ of Michigan, 4901 Evergreen Rd, Dearborn, MI 48128.

WRIGHT, KATHLEEN C.
Educator. **PERSONAL:** Born Dec 31, 1935, Fort Lauderdale, FL; married Zebedee Wright; children: Ronald, Anthony, Laureatte. **EDUCATION:** FL A&M Univ, BS 1958; CO Coll, six credits in hist 1962; FL State Univ, MS Social Studies 1968; FL Atlantic Univ, five credits soc studies 1972; FL Atlantic Univ, Educ Specialist degree 1978, EdD Ed Adm & Sup 1980. **CAREER:** Social Studies/Sci/Eng Broward Co, teacher 1959-77, social studies dept chairperson 1969-77; Broward Co School Bd, chairperson 1976-77, vice chairperson 1974-76 & 1979-80, mem 1974-82; Glokat Consultant Firm, vice pres; Coll for Human Serv FL Br, consultant 1979-81; Nova Univ, natl educ prof 1981-. **ORGANIZATIONS:** Mem Prof Educ Assns (local, state, natl) 1958-75; rec sec 1968-70, vice pres 1969-70, pres 1970-71 BCCSS; sec FL Council of Social Studies 1971-72; bd of dirs FL Council of Soc Studies 1972-74; critical reader Scott Foresman Pub Co 1975-76; soc studies council State Textbook Selection Comm 1975-77; mem Natl & State Sch Bds Assn, Natl Caucus of Black Sch Bd, Natl Alliance of Black Sch Educator, Phi Delta Kappa 1978-; rep Comprehensive Plng Com Broward Schs 1978; past mem Natl Geogph Council, Materials Com of FSCC, Task Force (Assessment of Soc Studies); FL Scholarship Selection Comm (Coca-Cola Bottling Co); mem Broward Urban League, NAACP; Proj Adv Bd for Natl Alliance for Black Sch Educators; mem YMCA; various Dem Clubs; Comm-at-Large. **HONORS/ACHIEVEMENTS:** CRC Awd 1973; First Black Female elected Local Sch Bd in FL; First Black Winner contested election 1974; Spl Awd Govt Ofc of Comm Relations 1975; Citizenship Awd FL Assn of Women's Clubs 1975; Outstanding Serv Awd Alpha Phi Alpha Frat 1975; Outstanding Serv in Educ Alpha Kappa Alpha Sor 1975; Serv Awd Broward Chap FL Women's Caucus 1975; Outstanding Female Citizen Awd Civic Assn for Pub Serv 1975; Outstanding Serv Awd PTA 1975; Serv Awd Job Corps Volunteer 1975; Woman of Yr Govt Broward Co 1977; Citizen of Yr Omega Psi Phi Frat 1977; Educ Awd Delta Sigma Theta Sor 1977; Serv Awd Black Historical Soc1977; Hon mem Eta Phi Beta Sor 1977; Serv Awd Eta Phi Beta Sor 1977; Serv Awd CAPS & TAMS 1977; numerous Awds & Citations Recognition 1977; Re-elected Broward Sch Bd 1978; Charles Stewart Mott Fellow 1979-80; So Reg Dir Delta Sigma Theta 1978-82. **BUSINESS ADDRESS:** Natl Education Professor, Nova University, 3301 College Ave, Fort Lauderdale, FL 33314.

WRIGHT, KATIE HARPER
Educator. **PERSONAL:** Born Oct 05, 1923, Crawfordsville, AR; daughter of James H Harper and Connie Mae Locke; married Marvin Wright, Mar 21, 1952; children: Virginia Jordan. **EDUCATION:** Univ of Illinois, AB 1944, MEd 1959; St Louis Univ, EdD 1979. **CAREER:** East St Louis Public Schools, elem tchr 1944-57, spec educ tchr 1957-65, media dir 1966-71, spec educ dir 1971-78, asst supt of spec programs 1978-79; Harris-Stowe State Coll, assoc prof; learning specialist, St Louis Univ 1989-. **ORGANIZATIONS:** Adj assoc prof Harris-Stowe State Coll 1980-; columnist St Louis Argus Newspaper 1979-84, 1986-; columnist St Louis American Newspaper 1984-85; mem sec E St Louis Election Bd 1978-88; mem assoc dir Landmark Bank of Edgemont 1981-; mem past v chmn Illinois Comm on Children 1973-; mem/v chmn River Bluffs Girl Scout Council 1979-; mem Girl Scout Natl Bd 1981-84; mem bd Mental Health; mem bd Urban League; mem bd United Way; mem/past pres E St Louis Library Bd 1964-81; charter mem Gateway Chapter of The Links, Inc 1987-; pres St Clair County Mental Health Bd 1987-; mem of Exec Comm of Urban League and United Way of St Louis. **HONORS/ACHIEVEMENTS:** Woman of Achievement St Louis Globe Democrat Newspaper 1974; Outstanding YWCA Alumnae Univ of IL 1984; Girl Scout Thanks Badge River Bluffs Girl Scout Council 1982; 1st Place Prize (for Author of Chapter History) Delta Sigma Theta Sorority 1979; Fellowship for Study in Peoples Republic of China 1983; holder of more than 100 awards; Natl Top lady of Distinction 1988-; Natl Top Ladies of Distinction Inc; St Clair County YWCA Woman of the Year 1987; natl Honorary mem of Iota Phi Lambda Sorority, Inc 1983-; pres bd of trustees First united Presbyterian Church, Belleville Ill 1988-. **HOME ADDRESS:** 733 N 40 St, East St Louis, IL 62205.

WRIGHT, KEITH DEREK, SR.
Assistant manager computer operations. **PERSONAL:** Born Jun 02, 1953, Orange, NJ; son of Clarence Samuel Williams and Lola Hunt Wright; divorced; children: Keisha, Keith, Khalid. **EDUCATION:** Rutgers Univ, BA 1979, MLA in progress; Amer Mgmt Assoc, Cert. **CAREER:** System Develop Corp, sr computer operator 1972-74; Nabisco Brands Inc, computer shift supervisor 1975-69; Hoffman-LaRoche, sr supervisor 1979-86; Port Authority of NY & NJ, asst mgr computer opers 1986-. **ORGANIZATIONS:** Chairperson BDPA Newsletter 1983-85; past pres Black Data Processing Assoc 1984-86; chmn Parking Authority East Orange 1984-; counselor YMCA Linkage Prog 1985; bd of dirs Economic Develop East Orange 1986-; chairperson Public Relations BDPA 1987; chairman East Orange Economic Development 1988-; director Tri-City Citizens for Progress 1988-. **HONORS/ACHIEVEMENTS:** YMCA Black Achievers Awd 1984; Scholastic Achievement Awd Essex League of Volunteer Workers 1971; publication "History of Jazz in Newark NJ 1938-1970", 1981. **BUSINESS ADDRESS:** Asst Mgr Computer Operations, Port Authority of NY & NJ, One World Trade Center, New York, NY 10048.

WRIGHT, LARRY RAYFIELD
Athlete. **PERSONAL:** Born Aug 23, 1945, Griffin, GA. **EDUCATION:** Ft Valley State Coll, BS 1967. **CAREER:** Dallas Cowboys, off tackle 1967-80; Philadelphia Eagles, 1980-. **HONORS/ACHIEVEMENTS:** Pro-Bowls 1971-76; NFC All-Stars Sporting News 1972-75; NFL Champshp Game 1970-71 75 77 78; NFL Champshp Games 1970-72 75 78. **BUSINESS ADDRESS:** Philadelphia Eagles, Vet Stadium, Broad St & Pat, Radnor, PA 19087.

WRIGHT, LINWOOD CLINTON
Aeronautical engineer. **PERSONAL:** Born Mar 24, 1919, Augusta, GA; daughter of Leon Wright and Maria Wright; married Ernestine Louise McIver; children: Linda Wright Moore, Linwood Clinton Jr. **EDUCATION:** Wayne State Univ, BS Aero Engr 1944; Univ of Cincinnati, MS Aero Engr 1960. **CAREER:** Natl Adv Comm for Aeronautics, aeronautical rsch scientist 1943-56; General Elec Aircraft Engine Bus Gr, mgr adv compressor rsch 1956-66, mgr adv tech mktg 1974-83; Garrett A Research Mfg Co LA, chief of aerodynamics 1966-72; Pratt & Whitney Aircraft Co, asst gas turbine mgr 1972-74; NASA, act dir propulsion power & energy 1983-85. **ORGANIZATIONS:** Mem Amer Inst of Aeronautics & Astronautics 1941-; part-time security salesman Putnam Financial 1971-72; mem Tech Mktg Soc of Amer 1975; mem past chap pres Sigma Pi Phi Prof Frat Cincinnati 1978-; mem Mayor's Task Force on Zoning Forest Park OH 1986; mem Economic Develop Comm Forest Park OH 1986-. **HONORS/ACHIEVEMENTS:** Disting Alumni Awd Wayne State Univ 1958; guest lecturer Univ of TN Space Institute 1974; Disting Alumni Awd Univ of Cincinnati 1984; author or co-author of 21 published tech papers 1946-72. **MILITARY SERVICE:** AAC enlisted reserve 1945-46. **HOME ADDRESS:** 11136 Embassy Dr, Forest Park, OH 45240.

WRIGHT, LOUIS DONNEL
Professional athlete. **PERSONAL:** Born Jan 31, 1953, Gilmer, TX; son of Glover Wright and Verbena Wright; married Vicki; children: Summer Marie, Kyla Lynn, Evan Louis. **EDUCATION:** San Jose State U, Bus Mgt. **CAREER:** Denver Broncos, cornerback 1975-. **ORGANIZATIONS:** Conference champ Track Team 1973-74. **HONORS/ACHIEVEMENTS:** Pro Bowl 1977-79,83,85; NEA All-Pro Team; Coll All-Star Game 1975; East-West Shrine Game 1975; All-Coast Football Selection 1975; Denver Broncos Team Captin 1985-86; named All NFL by Sporting News and Pro Football Weekly; mem 1986 NFL Pro Football team. **BUSINESS ADDRESS:** Denver Broncos, 5700 Logan St, Denver, CO 80216.

WRIGHT, LOYCE PIERCE
Government official. **PERSONAL:** Born Dec 24, 1943, New Orleans, LA; daughter of Frank Pierce and Victoria Martin Pierce; married Louis Clifton Wright, Jr, Feb 14, 1976; children: Kiana Tamika Wright. **EDUCATION:** Southern Univ, Baton Rouge LA, BS 1965; Univ of New Orleans, LA, MEd 1976. **CAREER:** Orleans Parish School Bd, New Orleans LA, French/Spanish teacher, 1965-76; New Orleans Sickle Cell Anemia Foundation, assoc dir, 1976-81; Communirep Inc, New Orleans LA, mgmt consultant, 1980-86; Mayor's Office, City of New Orleans LA, dir, 1986-. **ORGANIZATIONS:** Past pres/founding mem, New Orleans Sickle Cell Anemia Foundation, 1972-76; campaign coord for state & presidential candidates, 1981-88; consultant & marketing dir, educational journal SENGA; coordinator, Martin Luther King Jr Federal Holiday Comm, New Orleans LA, 1987-; vice pres, bd of dir, Mental Health Assn, New Orleans LA, 1988; mem, nominating comm, YWCA-USA, 1988-91; pres, bd of dir, YWCA of New Orleans, 1989-; mem, planning comm, United Way of New Orleans, 1989-. **HONORS/ACHIEVEMENTS:** Award for outstanding service, Governor of LA, 1986; Second Mile Award, Natl Assn of Neighborhoods, 1987; Certificate of Merit, Mayor of New Orleans, 1988; Role Model Award, YWCA of New Orleans, 1989. **HOME ADDRESS:** 3945 Virgil Blvd, New Orleans, LA 70122.

WRIGHT, MARVIN
Retired educator. **PERSONAL:** Born May 20, 1917, Fulton, AL; son of Marvin Wright and Alkmenda Falconer Wright; married Katie Harper; children: Virginia Jordan. **EDUCATION:** Xavier Univ, PhB 1947; Univ of Illinois, EdM 1962. **CAREER:** Professional musician, drummer 1940-50; E St Louis Public School, elem teacher 1948-65; School Dist 1984 E St Louis 1965-79; Atty General's Office E St Louis, admin investigator 1980-84. **ORGANIZATIONS:** Pres E St Louis Principals Org; mem Phi Delta Kappa Ed, IL Principal's Assoc, Natl Elem Prncipal's Assoc 1974-76; trustee VFW #3480; chmn bd of trustees State Comm Coll 1977-84; alternate dele 1976 Rep Natl Conv; trustee Belleville Men's Rep Club; comm man Boy Scout Troop; mem Illini Sr Citizens Bd 1983; mem Civil Rights Comm E St Louis 1971-75; mrm 4-H Youth Committeeman 1971-; school memberhsip chmn E St Louis Branch NAACP; mem IL Div United Way Bd 1984-; city chmn Amer Cancer Soc St Clair Cty Unit 1976-77; mem Southern IL Black Republican Council; commander Veterans of Foreign Wars Post 3480, 1987-88; quartermaster Veterans of Foreign Wars Post 3480, 1988-. **HONORS/ACHIEVEMENTS:** Meritorious Serv Awd Amer Cancer Soc 1976; Outstanding Serv Awd St Paul Church 1976; Outstanding Serv Awd E St Louis PTA 1976; Bd Mem of the Year Awd United Way 1983; East St Louis Criminal Justice Awd 1980; all state commander, Veterans Foreign Wars 1987. **MILITARY SERVICE:** AUS staff sgt 1942-45; Overseas Serv Bar; Sivler Battle Star; Good Conduct Medal; WW II Victory Medal.

WRIGHT, MARY H.
Retired educator. **PERSONAL:** Born May 26, 1916, Suffolk, VA; daughter of Hamilton M Henderson and Mamie Hamlet Henderson; married Jeremiah A Wright Sr, Jun 08, 1938; children: Mary LaVerne Wright Miner, Jeremiah A Wright Jr. **EDUCATION:** Virginia Union Univ, AB (Magna Cum Laude), 1935; Univ of Pennsylvania, MA, 1949, MS, 1959, DEd, 1971. **CAREER:** Surry Co Virginia Public School System, teacher, 1932-33; Worcester Co Maryland Public School System, teacher, 1935-39; Philadelphia, PA, Public School System, teacher, 1944-68, admin, 1968-78. **ORGANIZATIONS:** Research asst, 1965-66, master teacher, 1966-68, School of Educ, Univ of Pennsylvania; bd mem, Northwest Philadelphia Branch; life mem, NAACP. **HONORS/ACHIEVEMENTS:** Natl Science Found Fellowship, Univ of Pennsylvania, 1958-59; Outstanding Community Serv Award, NAACP, 1975; Distinguished Serv to Youth Award, Miller Memorial Church, 1978; President's Award, Intl Assn of Ministers Wives, 1986.

WRIGHT, PHILLIP LEROI
Elected official & clergyman. **PERSONAL:** Born Apr 21, 1953, Chicago, IL; married Arneatha; children: Almeda, Phyllis, Loraine, Phillip Jr. **EDUCATION:** United Assn School of Engrg, M of Sanitary Engrg 1971-76; AOH Theological Seminary, ordination cert 1977-79. **CAREER:** Champaign Unit 4 School Dist, bd of education. **ORGANIZATIONS:** Past pres

Northeast Area Local Develop Corp 1982-83; mem City of Champaign Comm Dev Adv Bd 1983-; pres Cham/Urbana Ministerial Alliance & Vic 1984-. **BUSINESS ADDRESS:** Board of Education, Champaign Sch Dist Unit 4, 703 South New St, Champaign, IL 61820.

WRIGHT, RALPH EDWARD
Business executive. **PERSONAL:** Born Dec 29, 1950, Newark, NJ; married Sallie Riggins Williams; children: Galen, Garnel. **CAREER:** Carl H Pforzheimer & Co, clerk 1977-80; New York Stock Exchange, reporter 1971-77; NYSE, CH Pforzheimer, trade specialist 1977-. **ORGANIZATIONS:** Mem, NY Stock Exchange, Urban League. **HONORS/ACHIEVEMENTS:** First Black Specialist New York Stock Exchange 1981; Ebony magazine profile 1982; 2 page article in Black Enterprise magazine 1982;TV commercial Black Entertainment Network 1984; bull and bear Council on Minority Affairs 1984. **HOME ADDRESS:** 466 So Center St, Orange, NJ 07050. **BUSINESS ADDRESS:** Trade Specialist Broker, Carl H Pforzheimer & Co, 70 Pine St, New York, NY 10270.

WRIGHT, RAYMOND LEROY, JR.
Dentist. **PERSONAL:** Born May 07, 1950, Fort Dix, NJ; children: Raymond III. **EDUCATION:** Univ of IL, 1968-70; Univ of IL Coll of Dentistry, DDS 1970-74, Cert of Periodontics 1974-76. **CAREER:** Cermack Mem Hosp, staff dentist 1975-84; Chicago Bd of Health, dentist 1976-77; Dr Clarence McNair, dentist-periodontist 1976-77; Dr Roger Berkley, dentist-periodontist 1977-80; McHarry Medical Coll, asst prof 1978-83; Univ of IL Coll of Dentistry, asst prof 1977-85; Self-employed, 1980-. **ORGANIZATIONS:** Program chmn Lincoln Dental Soc 1980-81-82-84; scholarship chmn Natl Dental Assn 1982; parliamentarian Lincoln Dental Soc 1984-85; treas Lincoln Dental Society 1985-86; treas FEPA (Forum for the Evolution of the Progressive Arts); sec Lincoln Dental Soc 1986-87; program chmn Kenwood Hyde Park Branch Chicago Dental Soc 1986-87. **HONORS/ACHIEVEMENTS:** Nomination Outstanding Young Men of America 1980; Service Awd Lincoln Dental Soc 1982; Service Awd Natl Dental Soc 1982. **BUSINESS ADDRESS:** 1525 E 53rd, Ste 632, Chicago, IL 60615.

WRIGHT, RAYMOND STANFORD
Beer wholesaler. **PERSONAL:** Born Jan 13, 1949, Chicago, IL; son of William R. Wright and Early R. Wright; married Patricia Wright, Apr 30, l988; children: Raymond Jr, Antoine. **CAREER:** Miller Brewing Co, area mgr, gen mgr, br mgr 1971-79; On Target Inc, pres 1980-83; Thomas Distributing Co, gen mgr 1983-85; IL Beverage Inc, pres,owner 1985-. **ORGANIZATIONS:** Mem bd dir DuSable Museum 1987-90; mem adv bd Chicago Alcoholic Treatment Ctr 1987; bd mem Goodwill Industries of America l989-l990; Univ Michigan Alumni Assoc. **BUSINESS ADDRESS:** President, Illinois Beverage Co, 441 N Kilbourn, Chicago, IL 60624.

WRIGHT, RICKEY
General surgery resident. **PERSONAL:** Born Dec 08, 1958, Fayette, AL; son of Maxine Wright; children: Demetric D Fleming. **EDUCATION:** TN State Univ, BS 1981; Meharry Medical Coll, MD 1986. **CAREER:** Western Reserve Care System, surgical resident; USAF, captain, Dyes AFB, Abiliance, TX, captain medical corp. **ORGANIZATIONS:** Mem Masonic Lodge 1980-; pres Meharry Chapter Amer Medical Student Assoc 1984-85; mem Medical Student Council 1985-86; polemarch Kappa Alpha Psi Fraternity 1985-86; liason comm Amer Med Assoc, Student Natl Medical Assoc, Natl Medical Assn 1985-86; chmn membership comm NAACP 1985-86; mem Meharry Co Medical Assoc. **HONORS/ACHIEVEMENTS:** Meharry Scholarship 1985. **MILITARY SERVICE:** AFROTC; captain, USAF, l989.

WRIGHT, ROBERT A.
Attorney, judge. **PERSONAL:** Born Dec 08, 1919, Chester, PA; married Mary Maloney; children: Robert C. **EDUCATION:** Lincoln U, BA 1941; Temple Univ Sch of Law, LlB 1950. **CAREER:** DC Co PA Ct of Common Pleas, judge 1970-; Chester, PA, atty 1951-70; DC Co Media PA, asst dist atty 1964-70; DC Co 32 Jud Dist of PA, 1970-. **ORGANIZATIONS:** Mem DC Co PA & Am Bar Assn; Lawyers Club of DC Co; PA Conf St Trial Judges; Amer Judicature Soc; PA Counc Juv Crt Judges; past mem Jud Inquiry & Reveiw Bd; Crime Comm of Phil; Temple Law Alumni mem NAACP; IBPOE of W; Amer Leg; VFW; Cent Rest Rec Club; past bd of mgrs W Branch YMCA; hon mem Meth Men; Frat Ord of Police; Wm Penn Lodge 19; Chester Yth League; Mag Asso DC Co Hon Awds Bd Mgrs W Bran YMCA; mem adv bd DC Co CampusPA State U; past exalted rulers coun # 7 IBPOE of W; Bunting Friendship Freedom House; Who's Who Women's Club; Chester Schol Fund. **HONORS/ACHIEVEMENTS:** First ann Achieve Awd Deputies Club of Elks IBPOE of W. **MILITARY SERVICE:** AUS 1st sgt 1943-46. **BUSINESS ADDRESS:** Delaware County Court House, Media, PA 19063.

WRIGHT, ROBERT COURTLANDT
Elected official, attorney. **PERSONAL:** Born Nov 05, 1944, Chester, PA; married Florence Fletcher; children: Josie, Robert Jr. **EDUCATION:** George Washington Univ, BA Political Sci 1966; Villanova Univ, Law Degree 1969. **CAREER:** Self Employed, attorney 1970-; PA Legislature, state rep 1981-. **ORGANIZATIONS:** Mem Tau Epsilon Phi Soc Frat 1963-; pres Republican Council of DE Cty 1977-; exec bd Chester Branch NAACP 1978-; exec bd Natl Black Caucus of State Leg 1981-, PA Minority Business Devel Auth 1981-86; mem PA Legislative Black Caucus 1981-; treas PA Legislative Black Caucus Foundation 1982-. **HONORS/ACHIEVEMENTS:** Community Serv Awd Chester Housing Authority PA 1981; Republican Cncl of Delaware County Outstanding Comm Serv Awd 1981; Southeast Delaware Co Family UMCAAwd 1982; Humanitarian Awd Chester Black Expo PA 1982; Mary Thomas Freedom Awd, NAACP Chester Branch 1983; Man of the Year Chester Scholarship Fund PA 1982,84; Outstanding Community Serv Awd Jeffrey Manor Civic Assoc 1985; Outstanding Accomplishment in Field of Law Natl Sorority of Phi Delta Kappa Xi Chap 1987. **HOME ADDRESS:** 1919 Providence Ave, Chester, PA 19013. **BUSINESS ADDRESS:** Representative Dist 159, PA State House of Represent, 19 West 5th St, Chester, PA 19013.

WRIGHT, ROBERT L.
Retired association executive. **PERSONAL:** Born Sep 23, 1917, Malvern, PA; married Beulah C; children: Robert L Jr. **EDUCATION:** Lincoln Univ, BA 1942; Temple Univ Law Sch. **CAREER:** Social Security Admin, retired benefit authorizer. **ORGANIZATIONS:** Sec Malvern PTA Assn Malvern Pub Schs 1957-59; sec Troop Com # 7 Boy Scouts of Amer 1960-61; sec Gr Valley High Gridiron Club 1962-63; vice pres CommAct Bd of Chester co West Chester 1968-71; vice pres UPAC 1968-; asst sec Malvern Mun Authority 1975-76; sec Mun Auth 1977-79; vice pres Mal Mun Authority 1980; life mem NAACP Golden Heritage; pres Main Line Branch NAACP 1963, 1985-86; past mem Main Line Youth for Christ Com. **HONORS/ACHIEVEMENTS:** Legion of Merit Chapel of Four Chaplain Awd; Founders Awd Main Line Br NAACP; Isabelle Strickland Awd Main Line NAACP 1981; Comm Serv Awd Main Line Bus& Prof Women 1982. **MILITARY SERVICE:** US military 1942-45.

WRIGHT, ROOSEVELT R., JR.
Educator. **PERSONAL:** Born Jul 24, 1943, Elizabeth City, NC; son of Roosevelt R Wright Sr and Lillie Mae Garrett Wright. **EDUCATION:** Elizabeth City State Univ, BS 1964; North Carolina Central Univ, MA 1965; Syracuse Univ, PhD 1980. **CAREER:** SI Newhouse School of Comm, asst prof telecomm 1975-; NBC Radio Div WRC/WKYS Washington, acc exec 1974-75; Howard Univ Washington, DC, adj prof radio TV 1974-75; WTNJ Radion Trenton, gen manager 1973-74; North Carolina Central Univ, asst prof ed media 1972-73; WDNC-AM/FM Durham, NC, announcer radio engr 1972-73; Elizabeth City State Univ, asso dir ed media 1968-69; DC State Coll Dover, dir ed media 1969-70; WNDR Radio Syracuse, announcer radio engr 1970-72; WLLE Radio Raleigh, NC, program dir 1973-74; WOLF Radio Syracuse, NY, chief engineer 1980-84. **ORGANIZATIONS:** Historian Chi Pi Chap Omega Psi Phi Frat 1975-80; radio com mem Natl Assn of Educ Broadcasters 1976-80; adv Natl Acad of TV Arts & Scis Syracuse Chpt 1976-80; public affairs officer natl naval Officers Assoc 1983-85; chmn communications comm Amer Heart Assoc New York 1985-87; adv WJPZ-FM Syracuse NY; naval liaison officer Syracuse Univ; stewart AME Zion Church; public affairs officer, US Navy, Great Lakes Cruise 1985-88; mem communications comm, United Way of Onondaga County 1988-. **HONORS/ACHIEVEMENTS:** Soldier of the Quarter 32AADC AUS 1967; Doctoral Flwsp SyracuseUniv 1970-72; Men's Day Awd Mt Lebanon AMEZ Ch Eliz City 1974; Upward Bound Prog Awd LeMoyne Coll Syracuse 1977; Ed Media & Speaker Awd NC Ed Media Assn 1977; Natl Council of Negro Women Communications Awd 1984; Syracuse Univ Pan Hellenic Council Awd 1986,87; Outstanding Mass Media Teacher Awd 1987; Naval Achievement Medal 1987; Keynote Speaker Awd, NAACP Jefferson Co Chapter, Watertown, NY 1989; Comm Serv Awd, Syracuse Univ 1988; consulting editor, "Cobblestone Magazine, History of Radio", 1988. **MILITARY SERVICE:** AUS sp/5 1966-72; US Naval Reserves commander 1979-. **HOME ADDRESS:** 1015 7th North St # A-13, Liverpool, NY 13088. **BUSINESS ADDRESS:** Professor Radio, TV, Film, Syracuse University, 215 University Place, Syracuse, NY 13244.

WRIGHT, SAMUEL LAMAR
Educational administrator. **PERSONAL:** Born Jul 07, 1953, Boynton Beach, FL; son of Samuel Louis Wright and Rovina Victoria Deal Wright; married Sherrina Yvonne Ford, Jun 29, 1985. **EDUCATION:** Univ of FL, BA 1974, MEduc 1975; FL Atlantic Univ, postgrad courses in Pub Admin 1980-81; Univ of South FL, postgrad studies in Educ Leadership 1988-. **CAREER:** PBC Bd of Co Commissioners/Action Com, emp & personnel mgr 1975-76, dir Delray Bch TAC 1976-77, adm asst/planner 1977-79, asst dir 1979-84, head start dir 1984-85; Boynton Beach FL, city councilman 1981-85; Univ of South FL, Minority Student Organizations, advisor 1985-86; Greater Tampa Urban League, Clerical/Word Processing Training Program, center mgr 1986-87; Univ of South FL, Minority Student Admissions, coordinator 1987-; Herbert Fisher Realty, kTampa, FL, realtor assoc, 1986-. **ORGANIZATIONS:** Bd of dirs Natl Black Caucus of Local Elected Officials 1982-84; mem State of FL Comm Serv Block Grant Adv Comm 1982-84; mem Kappa Alpha Psi Frat Inc 1972-; chmn Intergov Rel Comm 1984-85; mem FL Assn for Comm Action 1975-85; mem FAMU Alumni Assn of PBC 1979-85; mem Univ of FL Alumni Assn 1979-; mem City of Boynton Beach Black Awareness Comm 1981-85; mem FL Assoc of Comm Rel Profs 1982-84; bd of dirs So Cty Drug Abuse Found 1982-84; bd dir Dem Black Caucus of FL 1982-84; Boynton Beach Kiwanis Sunrisers 1982-85; bd mem Selective Serv Syst 1983-85; 1stvice pres FL Black Caucus of Local Elected Officials 1983-85; vice pres Comm Affairs Suncoast C of C 1983-85; mem Gr Boynton Beach C of C 1983-85; mem Natl Assoc of Black Social Workers Inc 1983-85; mem FL Head Start Assoc 1984-85; chmn Leg Comm Boynton/Ocean Ridge Bd of Realtors 1984-85; elected to Dem Exec Comm Palm Beach 1983-85; Tampa Male Club 1989-; 100 Black Men of Tampa Inc 1988. **HONORS/ACHIEVEMENTS:** Outstanding Young Man of Amer Jaycees 1980-81; Outstanding & Dedicated Serv Awd Concerned Citizens Voter's League of Boynton Beach 1981; Citizen of the Yr Omega Psi Phi Frat 1982; Outstanding Civic Leadership Awd Westboro Bus & Prof Women's Club of thePalm Beaches 1983; participant Leadership Palm Beach Co 1984-85; Martin Luther King Jr Award for Outstanding Leadership 1989; Community Service Award 1989; Kappa Alpha Psi Frat Polemarch's Award 1988; Outstanding Service Award in Religion 1988; USF Outstanding Service Award (Academic Affairs) 1988; State of Florida Notary Public. **HOME ADDRESS:** 10447 Tara Dr, Riverview, FL 33569. **BUSINESS ADDRESS:** Coordinator, Minority Student Admissions, University of South Florida, 4202 East Fowler Ave, SVC 126, Tampa, FL 33620-6900.

WRIGHT, SARAH E.
Writer. **PERSONAL:** Born Dec 09, 1928, Wetipquin, MD; daughter of Willis Charles Wright and Mary Amelia Moore Wright; married Joseph G Kaye; children: Michael, Shelley. **EDUCATION:** Howard Univ, Washington DC, 1945-49; Cheyney State Teachers College, 1950-52. **CAREER:** Worked as teacher, bookkeeper, and office manager; writer. **ORGANIZATIONS:** Mem, International PEN; mem, Authors Guild; mem, Authors League of America; mem, Harlem Writers Guild. **HONORS/ACHIEVEMENTS:** Baltimore Sun Readability Award, 1969, for This Child's Gonna Live; McDowell Colony fellowships, 1972 and 1973; New York State Creative Artists Public Service Award for Fiction, and Novelist-Poet Award from Howard University's Institute for the Arts and Humanities' Second National Conference of Afro-American Writers, both 1976. **BUSINESS ADDRESS:** c/o Roberta Pryor, International Famous Agency, 1301 Avenue of the Americas, New York, NY 10019.
*

WRIGHT, STANLEY V.
Educator, coach. **PERSONAL:** Born Aug 11, 1921, Englewood, NJ; married Hazel; children: Stanley, Toni, Sandra, Tyran. **EDUCATION:** Springfield Coll, BS 1949; Columbia U, MA 1950;Univ TX, grad study 1956; IN U, 1968. **CAREER:** CA State Univ, prof phys educ & head track coach; Mexico City Olympic Games, asst track coach was responsible for athletes who won 6 gold medals set five world records & tying 1 in 6 events; US Olympic Track & Field Com, appointed for second time; US Olympic bd of Dir for next quadrennial; Munich Olympic Games, sprint coach 1972; dir of athleteics 1975; Natl Collegiate Ath Assn Recruit Com, 1977; Intl Olympic Acad USOC Com, 1977. **HONORS/ACHIEVEMENTS:** Reciev many hon & awds; articles such as "Techniques Related to Spring Racing" have appeared in

ldg athletic jours; part in over 200 hs & coll clinics. **BUSINESS ADDRESS:** 6000 Jay St, Sacramento, CA 95819.

WRIGHT, STEPHEN JUNIUS, JR.
Educator. **PERSONAL:** Born Sep 08, 1910, Dillon, SC; son of Dr Stephen J Wright and Rachel Eaton; married Rosalind Person, Apr 16, 1938. **EDUCATION:** Hampton Inst, BS 1934; Howard Univ, MA 1939; NY Univ, PhD 1943. **CAREER:** Kinard HS, teacher 1934-36; Douglass HS, principal 1936-38; NC Central Univ, instr to professor 1939-44; Hampton Inst, dean of faculty 1945-53; Bluefield State Coll, Bluefield WVA, pres 1953-57; Fisk Univ, pres 1957-66; Coll Entrance Exam Bd, vice pres 1969-76; retired 1976. **ORGANIZATIONS:** Pres Bluefield State Coll WV 1953-57, Assoc of Coll & Secondary Schools 1953-54, Fisk Univ 1957-66, United Negro Coll Fund 1966-69, Amer Assoc for Higher Educ 1966-67; chmn State Council of Higher Educ for VA 1984-86. **HONORS/ACHIEVEMENTS:** Distinguished Alumnus Hampton Inst 1954; Distinguished Alumnus Howard Univ 1962; LLD Notre Dame Univ 1964; LLD NY Univ 1966; Honorary Degrees: Colby Coll 1961, Morgan State Univ 1965; Michigan State Univ 1966, Univ of Rhode Island 1968, Morehouse 1968, Howard Univ 1977. **HOME ADDRESS:** 1620 W Queens St, Hampton, VA 23669.

WRIGHT, SYLVESTER M.
Clergyman. **PERSONAL:** Born Feb 07, 1927, Dallas, TX; married Debra Diane Williams; children: Sylvester M II, Calvin Wesley, Moses. **EDUCATION:** Butler Coll, AA 1945; Bishop Coll, BA 1949, MA 1954; TX Coll, DD 1982. **CAREER:** Peoples Bapt Church, pastor 1954-; Interdenominational Ministries Alliance, pres 1964-; Peoples Baptist Church, pastor. **ORGANIZATIONS:** 2nd vice pres Fellowship Dist Assn; 1st vice pres Missionary Baptist Gen Conv of TX; bd mem Dallas Black C of C; exec bd mem Dallas Br NAACP; trustee Bishop Coll Dallas. **HONORS/ACHIEVEMENTS:** Serv Awd Dallas Urban League 1975; Ministries Awd Prairie View Ministering Conf 1976; Alumni Awd Lincoln HS 1979; Alumni Awd Bishop Coll. **MILITARY SERVICE:** USAF pfc 1945-47. **BUSINESS ADDRESS:** Pastor, Peoples Baptist Church, 3119 Pine St, Dallas, TX 75215.

WRIGHT, WILLIAM A.
Automobile dealer. **PERSONAL:** Born Apr 04, 1936, Kansas City, MO; son of Robert B Wright and Madeline S Wright; married Ceta D Wright, Jul 21, 1961. **EDUCATION:** Western Washington State, Bellingham WA, BEd, 1961. **CAREER:** Los Angeles School District, teacher, 1961-68; Pro Golf Tour, professional golfer, 1964-77; Pasadena Lincoln-Mercury, Pasadena CA, owner, currently. **ORGANIZATIONS:** Mem, Black Ford Lincoln Mercury Dealers, 1978-; mem, NAACP, Pasadena Branch. **HONORS/ACHIEVEMENTS:** Man of Year, State of WA, 1959; Golf Champ, Natl Public Links, 1959; Natl Intercollegiate Champ, 1960; Man of Year, Seattle WA, 1960. **MILITARY SERVICE:** Army Natl Guard, private, 1960-66. **BUSINESS ADDRESS:** Owner, Pasadena Lincoln Mercury Inc, 1339 E Green St, Pasadena, CA 91106.

WRIGHT, WILLIAM GAILLARD
Educator. **PERSONAL:** Born Jun 05, 1933, South Carolina; married Clara Baker. **EDUCATION:** City Coll of NY, BA 1966; Middlebury Coll Madrid Spain, MA 1967. **CAREER:** City Coll of NY, lectr Spanish 1969-; Hopewell Vally Regional School Sys, teacher 1967-69; US PO, letter carrier-clerk 1958-66; NY City, Newark, NJ, educ com 1970-. **ORGANIZATIONS:** Chmn of bd Nghbrdh Housing Serv Newark 1977-78. **HONORS/ACHIEVEMENTS:** The Newman Meml Schlshp The City Coll of NY 1966; 125th Anniver Awd Medal The City Coll of NY 1972; 4 jours fieldwork studies City Coll Students for Cultural Exch 1972-73 74-77; Brotherhood Awd Newark Human Rights Commn 1978. **MILITARY SERVICE:** AUS pfc 1953-56. **BUSINESS ADDRESS:** 138th St at Convent Ave, New York, NY 10031.

WRIGHT-BOTCHWEY, ROBERTA YVONNE
Attorney, educator. **PERSONAL:** Born Oct 09, 1946, York, SC. **EDUCATION:** Fisk U, BA 1967; Yale U, ISSP cert 1966; Univ MI Sch of Andrew Iii, JD. **CAREER:** Private Practice; NC Central Univ School of Law, asst prof corp counsel Tanzania Legal Corp Dar es Salaam Tanzania; Zambia Ltd Lusaka Zambia, sr legal asst rural devel corp. **ORGANIZATIONS:** Mem NC Assn of Blck Lawyers; Nat Bar Assn; Nat Conf of Black Lawyers; SC & DC Bar Assn; hon mem Delta Theta Phi; consult EPA 1976; lectr Sci Jury Sel & Evidence Workshop; legal adv Zambian Corp Del to Tel Aviv, Israel 1971; Atty Gen of Zambia Select Com to Investigate Railways 1972; Delta Sigma Theta Sor; consult Women's Prison Group 1975; consult EPA Environmental Litigation Workshop 1976; NCBL Commn to Invest Discrim Prac in Law Schs 1977; dir Councon Legal Educ Oppor Summer Inst 1977; Phi Beta Kappa 1967. **HONORS/ACHIEVEMENTS:** Outstdg Young Women of Am 1976; Sydney P Raymond lectr Jackson StateUniv 1977. **BUSINESS ADDRESS:** PO Box 10646, 339 E Main, Rock Hill, SC 29730.

WRIGHT-SABREE, MARGARET V.
Business executive. **PERSONAL:** Born Apr 18, 1944, Anderson, SC; married Louis Edward Sabree; children: Zakee Louis. **EDUCATION:** Voorhees Jr Coll, AA 1964; Morgan State Coll, BA 1968; Howard Univ, MA 1974. **CAREER:** Prince George's Comm Coll Human Development Dept, teacher; US Dept Agriculture's Graduate School Career Develop Center, teacher, conselor; Academy of Business Careers, academy dean; Black Affairs Center for Orgnl & Mgmt Training Inc, pres, ceo. **ORGANIZATIONS:** Consul training US Dept of Educ Energy Agriculture Commerce & Labor; mem Amer Soc for Training & Developmt, Assn of Social & Behavioral Scientists, Amer Personnel & Guidance Assn, Business Educ Assn, Coalition for 100 Black Women, Amer Assn for Black Women Entrepreneurs, Black Women's Political Caucus, United Negro College Fund. **BUSINESS ADDRESS:** President, CEO, Black Affairs Ctr, 1200 15th St NW, Washington, DC 20005.

WYATT, ADDIE L.
Union executive. **PERSONAL:** Born Mar 08, 1924, Brookhaven, MS; daughter of Ambrose Cameron and Maggie Cameron; married Rev Claude S Wyatt Jr; children: Renaldo, Claude III. **CAREER:** Amalgamated Meat Cutters & Butcher Workmen of N Amer AFL-CIO; intl vp, dir womens affairs dept 1941-54; intl rep amalgamated meat cutters 1968-74, dir women's affairs dept 1974-78, dir human reights dept 1978-, intl vice pres 1976-; intl vice pres UFCW-AFL-CIO 1979-84; personnel bd Chicago 1986-88; R.T.A. dir, exec vice pres Emerita CLUW, 1988. **ORGANIZATIONS:** Mem Intl Adv Council of Amalgamated Meat Cutters & Butcher Workmen of N Amer AFL-CIO Union Women; co-pastor & minister of mus Vernon Park Church of God Chicago; former social ctr inst Chicago Bd of Ed; appointed to serve Protective Labor Legislative Com of Pres Kennedy's Comm on Status of Women; former youth leader in Chicago; labor adv, co-worker Dr Martin Luther King Jr, Dr Ralph D Abernathy, Rev Jesse L Jackson; mem Jewish Labor Com Prog; adv & labor instr Labor Ed Roosevelt Univ; mem IL State AFL-CIO COPE Org; adv Citizen for Day Care; former mem IL State Health Survey Com; former mem, adv council Vocational Ed State of IL; natl adv Womens Org Church of God; mem Coalition of Black Trade Unionists, Com of Five Cook Cty School Adv Council, League of Black Women, Natl Council of Negro Women, C hicago Urban League, Chicago NAACP; volunteer Youth & Comm Serv Chicago Housing Auth; honorary Delta Sigma Theta Sorority; co-chair CBTA Woman. **HONORS/ACHIEVEMENTS:** Distinguished Labor Leaders Awd League of Black Women Woodlawn Org 1975; One of Twelve Outstanding Women of Year Time Magazine 1975; Ebony Magazine Citation 1977,80; Dr Martin Luther King Jr Labor Awd 1981; Outstanding Woman in Western Region Iota Phi Lambda; Urban Ministries Inc Awd; One of 100 Most Outstanding Black Amer Ebony Magazine 1981-84. **BUSINESS ADDRESS:** Vernon Park Church of God, 9011 S Stony Island, Chicago, IL 60617.

WYATT, BEATRICE E.
Educator. **PERSONAL:** Born May 23, Pittsburgh, PA; widowed. **EDUCATION:** Virginia Union Univ, AB; Boston State Coll, MED; Michigan State Univ; New York Univ; Univ of Pittsburgh. **CAREER:** Lewis Middle School Boston Public Schools, admin asst principal; North Hampton County VA, teacher, guidance counseling; Dearborn Jr High School Boston, teacher, guidance advisor; Julia Ward Howe School Roxbury, teacher asst principal. **ORGANIZATIONS:** Charter mem Ft Hill Mental Health Assn; bd mem appointed by Gov Sargent to Boston Univ Area Mental Health Bd; pres Boston Alumni Chap Delta Sigma Theta Inc; mem Black Educ Assn of MA; past chairwoman Social Studies Coun of Boston, MA; regional coord Eastern Region Conf of Delta Sigma Theta 1974; mem Natl Coun of Negro Women 1972-74; organizer NCNW of Boston; mem Boston Guidance Counseling & MA Guidance Assn 1969; adv Coll & Univ Women of Iota Chap Delta Sigma Theta Sor 1969-72; mem First Baptist Church Boston; church school teacher, deaconess; chairwoman bd Christian Educ; mem Bicentennial Comm; past pres, present treas Woman's Soc First Baptist Church; mem Boston Children's Council. **HONORS/ACHIEVEMENTS:** Neighborhood Awd Natl Coun for Christians & Jews 1972; bronze plaque for dedicated serv Iota Chap 1972; plaque Eastern Region Delta Sigma Theta outstanding leadership during Regional Conf 1974. **BUSINESS ADDRESS:** Lewis Middle School, 131 Walnut Ave, Roxbury, MA 02119.

WYATT, CLAUDE STELL, JR.
Clergyman. **PERSONAL:** Born Nov 14, 1921, Dallas, TX; married Addie Lorraine Cameron; children: Renaldo, Claude L. **EDUCATION:** Attended, Wilson Coll 1955, Chicago Tchrs Coll 1956, Chicago Bapt Inst 1957; Urban Training Ctr for Christion Mission, cert 1960; Roosevelt Univ Labor Dept, cert 1974. **CAREER:** US PO, clerk 1947-65; Vernon Park Ch of God, reverend. **ORGANIZATIONS:** Consult Urban Ministries Anderson Coll IN 1978; consult for Ch Growth Com Anderson Coll 1979; bd mem Natl com of Black Churchmen 1975; bd mem Operation PUSH. **HONORS/ACHIEVEMENTS:** Outstanding Leadership in REligion Operation PUSH Chicago 1973; Outstanding Bus & Professional Persons Blackbook Pubs Chicago 1978; Hon DD Degree Monrovia Univ1984. **BUSINESS ADDRESS:** Vernon Park Church of God, 7653 S Maryland Ave, Chicago, IL 60619.

WYATT-CUMMINGS, THELMA LAVERNE
Judge. **PERSONAL:** Born Jul 06, 1945, Amarillo, TX; married Arthur B Cummings, Sr; children: Khari, Ayanna. **EDUCATION:** Univ of California, BA 1965; Illinois Inst of Tech Fellowship in Psychodynamics 1966; Emory Inst Sch of Law, JD with distinction 1968-71. **CAREER:** Bd of Educ City of Chicago, tchr 1965-67; Atlanta Urban League, field rep 1967-69; Thelma Wyatt, atty 1971-74; Ward & Wyatt, atty 1974-77; Municipal Ct of Atlanta, judge 1977-80; City Ct of Atlanta, judge 1980-, State Court of Fulton County, judge. **ORGANIZATIONS:** Consultant ABC Mgmt Consultants 1972-74; visiting prof Emory Univ Law Sch 1974-75; seminar presenter Atlanta Univ 1980-; recording sec Natl Judicial Council 1984-85, long range planning chm 1983-85; bd mem Atlanta Univ Criminal Justice Inst 1980-; mem Natl Assn of Blacks in Criminal Justice; Georgia Bar Assn; Gate City Bar Assn; Atlanta Bar Assn; bd mem Atlanta Branch NAACP, Gate City Day Nursery Assn; chmn Natl Judicial Council. **HONORS/ACHIEVEMENTS:** Outstanding Public Serv Award, Georgia Coalition of Black Women Inc, 1984; Outstanding Jurist Award, Gate City Bar Assn, 1983; Distinguished Serv, Natl Judicial Council, 1982-83; Essence Award for Outstanding Contributions, Essence magazine, 1982; Order of the Coif, Bryan Soc, Pi Delta Phi, Appellate Advocacy, Amer Jurisprudence Awds in Comm Law, Mortgages and Admin Law, John Hay Whitney Fellow, State of Ilinois Fellow, Natl Urban Legue Fellow; Most Outstanding Young Woman in Atlanta, 1970; 1st Distinguished Alumni Award, Emory BLSA, 1986. **BUSINESS ADDRESS:** Judge, State Court of Fulton County, 160 Pryor St SW, Atlanta, GA 30303.

WYCHE, LENNON DOUGLAS, JR.
Physician. **PERSONAL:** Born Jul 13, 1946, Washington, DC; married Judith. **EDUCATION:** Howard U, 1966; George Wash U, BS 1969; Meharry Med Sch, MD 1973. **CAREER:** Resd diagnostic radiology 1976-; USPHS Clinic, gen med ofcr 1974-46; USPHS, intern 1973-74. **ORGANIZATIONS:** Mem Alpha Phi Alpha Frat; Am Coll Radiology; NMA; jr mem Am Roentgen Ray Soc. **HONORS/ACHIEVEMENTS:** Personal Serv Awd USPHS. **MILITARY SERVICE:** USPHS lt comdr 1973-76. **BUSINESS ADDRESS:** Dept Radiology Hermann Hosp, Houston, TX 77030.

WYCHE, MELVILLE Q., JR.
Physician, educator. **PERSONAL:** Born Nov 16, 1938, Washington, NC; married Patricia; children: Dolores, Melville III, Angela. **EDUCATION:** Hampton Inst, BS 1959; Meharry Med Coll, MD 1963; Homer G Phillips Hosp, rotating intern 1963-64, residency dept surgery 1964-65; Univ of PA Dept Anesthesia, residency 1967-69; Univ of PA Sch of Med, fellowship dept of anesthesia 1969-70. **CAREER:** Camp Zama Army Hosp Japan, chf of anesthesia and operating room 1965-66; 106th Gen Hosp, asst chief of anesthesia and operating room 1966-67; Univ of PA Sch of Med, asst instr 1967-70, instr 1970-72; Hosp of the Univ of PA, anesthesiologist 1970-; Univ of PA Sch of Med, asst prof 1972-76; Philadelphia Gen Hosp, chief anesthesia serv 1973-76; Philadelphia Gen Hosp, dir oxygen therapy serv 1975-76; Univ of PA Sch of Med, asst prof at the Hosp of the Univ of PA 1976-79; Hosp of the Univ of PA Univ of PA Sch of Med, assoc prof 1979-81; Penna Hosp Univ of PA Sch of Med, assoc prof 1981-; Penna Hosp, dir Dept of Anesthesiology, dir 1981-. **ORGANIZATIONS:** Mem, Amer Soc Anesthesiol, PA Soc of Anesthesiol, Philadelphia Soc of Anesthesiol, Amer Soc of Regional Anesthesia, Assn of Univ Anesthetists, Natl MedAssn, Med Soc of Eastern PA;

assoc examiner Amer Bd of Anesthesiol 1980-; residency inspector Residency Review Comm in Anesthesia AMA 1976-; mem execcom of Med Staff Philadelphia Gen Hosp 1973-76; Pharm and Therap Comm Philadelphia Gen Hosp 1973-76; affirm action ofcr Univ of PA Sch of Med 1982-83; mem exec com of Profess Staff PA Hosp 1981-; chmn By-Laws Comm PA Hosp 1983-; mem Personnel and Prop Comm PA Hosp 1981; mem Interviewing Panel for med student applicants Univ of PA Sch med 1982-83. **HONORS/ACHIEVEMENTS:** Who's Who Among Black Americans 1977-78 and 1980-81; Outstanding 20 Year Alumnus Hamptin Inst 1979; numerous lectures including, "History and Clinical Use of Nitrous Oxide" 1970, "Effects of Anesthetics on Respiration" Univ of PA 1973; "Respiratory Failure" Dept Surgery Hosp of Univ of PA 1974-75; "Anesthesia Effects on Respiration" Dept Anesthesia Reading Hosp 1979; "Anesthesia for the Obese Patient" Dept Anesthesia Helen Fuld Hosp 1980; "Correct the Acid-Base Balance While Under Anesthesia" ann meeting of the Natl Med Assn Chicago 1983; numerous original papers incl, T Kallos, RG Tronzo, MQ Wyche, Elevation ofintramedullary pressure when methylmethacrylate is inserted in total hip arthroplasty J Bone Joint Surg 56-A, 714-718 1974. **BUSINESS ADDRESS:** Dir Dept of Anesthesiology, Pennsylvania Hospital, Eighth and Spruce Sts, Philadelphia, PA 19107.

WYCHE, PAUL H., JR.
Journalist, business executive. **PERSONAL:** Born Oct 16, 1946, Miami, FL; son of Paul H. Wyche and Gracie Thompson Wyche; married Louise Everett, Dec 11, 1971; children: Shaina Nicole, Kimberely Elise. **EDUCATION:** Miami-Dade Jr Coll; Univ Miami; Southeastern Univ, BS, public admin; Univ of Southern California & Southeastern Univ, graduate study business & pub. **CAREER:** E I du Pont de Nemours Co, public affairs rep 1980-82, public affairs consultant, 82-; Natl Black News Serv Inc, pres dir 1972-; US Environmental Protection Agency, assoc public affairs dir 1979-80, constituent devel & coordinator 1977-79, exec asst pub affairs dir 1975-77; US Rep Harold Ford, exec admin asst 1975; US Rep Moakley, sr legislative asst 1973-75; US Rep Pepper (Dem-FL), legislative asst 1971-73; FL Memorial Coll, public relations dir 1970-71; The Miami Times, assoc editor 1970-71; Economic Opportunity Program Miami, dir public affairs 1968-70; WPLG-TV Miami, program moderator 1970-71. **ORGANIZATIONS:** Mem NAACP; bd mem Opportunity Center Inc; bd mem Mt Vernon-Lee Enter Inc; Natl Urban League; PUSH; mem, Sigma Delta Chi, 1968-; Natl Capital Press Clubs; Natl Young Demo Clubs; mem bd Council Catholic Laity; pres Good Shepherd Parish Council; Cong Staff Club; Admin Asst Assn; mem bd S FL Econ Oppor Council; Dade Co Drug Abuse Advisory Bd; Jaycees; founding pres chmn bd NW Miami Jaycees; vice pres United Blck Fedn Dade Co; pres FL Public Affairs Dirs; mem bd Blck Chamber of Commerce; mem pres Caths for Shared Responsibility; pres Good Shepherd Coun of the Laity; dir, Amer Heart Assn, 1982-85; trustee, West End City Day Care Nursery, 1983-85; chairman, Brandywine Professional Assoc, 1984-; dir, Delaware Alliance of Professional Women, 1984-86; pres, Civic Assn of Surrey Park, 1985-86; dir, Boy Scouts of America, 1985-; pres, Opportunity Center, Inc, 1986-; vice chairman Govt Relations, United Way of DE Board of Dir, 1987-; chairman Govt Relations, United Way, 1987-89; dir, Mental Health Assn, 1988-; dir, Layton Home for the Aged, 1988-; trustee, MCD Foundation, 1988-; life mem, NAACP, 1988-; executive committee, Human Services Partnership, 1989-; dir, Delaware Community Investment Corporation, 1989-. **HONORS/ACHIEVEMENTS:** Awards reporting & broadcasting 1964, 1967, 1968; Silver Knight Award 1964; Notable Americans, 1976-77; Superior Performance, US EPA, 1978; Outstanding professionalism, Omega Psi Phi Fraternity, 1988; Black Achiever in Business & Industry, YMCA, 1989. **BUSINESS ADDRESS:** Public Affairs Consultant, DuPont Co, 2516 Nemours Bldg, Wilmington, DE 19898.

WYCHE, VERA ROWENA
Educational administrator. **PERSONAL:** Born Feb 02, 1923, Rowus Run, PA; married Julian C Wyche (deceased); children: Evangeline. **EDUCATION:** Cheyney State, BS 1944; Howard Univ, MA 1945; Univ of MI, PhD 1974. **CAREER:** Detroit Public Schools, teacher 1949-63, admin principal 1963-71; Univ of MI, lecturer ed admin 1971-74; Eastern MI Univ, adjunct prof 1975-; School Housing, admin assoc to supt 1976-87. **ORGANIZATIONS:** Brd mem Bilalian Child Devlpmnt Cntr 1977-82; brd mem Univ of MI Women Detroit Chptr 1 1976-84; mm Natl Health & Safety Task Force (USOE) 1980-84; mem Internatl Platform Assoc 1980-; chr ed dev com Nat'l Assoc of Negro Bus & Prof Woman (NANBPW__ 1981-83; mem Detroit Woman's Forum 1982-; mem Congressional Advisory Comm 1983-. **HONORS/ACHIEVEMENTS:** Excell in Ldrshp BUF 1980; Woman of Excell NANBPW 1982. **HOME ADDRESS:** 8100 LaSalle Blvd, Detroit, MI 48206. **BUSINESS ADDRESS:** Administrative Assistant, Detroit Public Schools, 5057 Woodward, Detroit, MI 48202.

WYKE, JOSEPH HENRY
Executive director. **PERSONAL:** Born Jan 09, 1928, New York, NY; married Margaret Elaine Whiteman. **EDUCATION:** City Coll NYC, BSaS 1949; NY U, MA 1958, doctorate cand. **CAREER:** Westchester Coalition Inc, exec dir 1976-; Coll of M Ed Dentistry NJ, asst admintr 1975-76; Urban Coalition of Met Wilmington, DE, exec vice pres 1970-75; Urban League of Grtr New Brunswick, exec dir 1966-70. **ORGANIZATIONS:** Bd mem Afro-Am Cultural Found 1977-; chmn bd dirs Aspire Industr Inc 1978-; bd mem Westchester Comm Serv Counc 1979-; mem "Edges" 1978-; mem Julius A Thomas Soc 1978-. **HONORS/ACHIEVEMENTS:** Recip Apprec for Serv Paul Robeson awd Urban League Grtr New Brunswick 1980; Martin Luther King Jr Awd Greenburgh Comm Cntr 1980. **BUSINESS ADDRESS:** Westchester Coalition Inc, 235 Main St, White Plains, NY 10601.

WYKLE, MAY LOUISE HINTON
Educator, administrator. **PERSONAL:** Born Feb 11, 1934, Martins Ferry, OH; daughter of John Hinton and Florence Hinton; married William Lenard; children: Andra Sims, Caron. **EDUCATION:** Ruth Brant School of Nursing, Diploma RN 1956; Western Reserve Coll Cleveland OH BSN 1962; Case Western Reserve Univ, MSN Psych Nursing 1969, PhD Ed 1981. **CAREER:** Cleveland Psychiatric Inst, staff nurse, head nurse, spurv 1956-64; Clevelnad Psychiatric Inst, dir nursing ed 1964; Case Western Rserve Univ, asst prof psych nursing 1975; Center on Aging & Health,Director;Case Western Reserve Univ, prof chairperson, dir psych nursing;gerontological nursing; Administrator assoc, Univ Hospitals of Cleveland. **ORGANIZATIONS:** Clinical nurse spec Fairhill Mental Health Ctr 1970; nursing consult VA Med Ctr 1980-85; bd mem Eliz Bryant Nursing Home 1983; proj dir Robert Wood Johnson Teaching Nursing Home;Research-Self Care among The Elderly; chairperson research committee Margaret Hagner House Nursing Home; Professional Advisory Brd-ARDA org Cleveland Oh. **HONORS/ACHIEVEMENTS:** Alumni Awd Martins Ferry 1956; Sigma Theta Tau Nursing Hon Soc 1966; Disting Teaching Awd FPB School of Nursing 1975; Merit Awd Cleveland Council of Black Nurses 1983;Geriatric Mental Health Academic Award, 1983-86, Cleveland Pacesetter Award, 1986; DIstinguished Alumni Award- Frances Payne Bolton School of Nursing, CWRU, 1986; Florence Cellar Professorship Gerontological Nursing F.P.B. School of Nursing CWRU 1989; John S. Diekoff Teaching Excellence Award (graduate) CWRU 1989; Wykle, M. & Dunkle R. Decision Making in Long Term Care 1988. **HOME ADDRESS:** 3617 Ludgate Rd, Shaker Heights, OH 44120. **BUSINESS ADDRESS:** Chairperson, Dir Psych Nurs, Case Western ReserveUniv, 2121 Abington Rd, Cleveland, OH 44106.

WYNN, CORDELL
College president. **CAREER:** Stillman College, Tuscaloosa AL, president, 1989. **BUSINESS ADDRESS:** Stillman College, Tuscaloosa, AL 35403. *

WYNN, DANIEL WEBSTER
Educator. **PERSONAL:** Born Mar 19, 1919, Wewoka, OK; married Lillian Robinson; children: Marian Danita, Patricia Ann. **EDUCATION:** Langston U, AB 1944, BD 1944; Howard U, MA 1945; Boston U, PhD 1954. **CAREER:** The United Meth Church, dir office of coll support bd of high educ ministry 1965-; Toskegee Inst, chaplin prof of phil & relig 1955-65; Langston Univ, dean of stud 1954-55; Tuskegee Inst, acting chaplain asso prof of phil relig 1953-54; Bishop Coll, asst prof dean school of religion 1946-53; Kentucky St Coll, acting chaplain instr of social econ 1945-46; Natl Assn of Coll & Univ Chaplains & Directors of Religios Life Newletter, editor 1960-63; Directory of Amer Scholors Vol Iv 1964 69 74; Contemporary Authors Vols 25 28 1971; The Writers Directory, 1972. **ORGANIZATIONS:** Life mem Tuskegee Civic Assn; life mem NAACP; life mem Kappa Alpha Psi Frat. **HONORS/ACHIEVEMENTS:** Author 5 books; contributor one encyclopedia 1 book & many jours; hon DD Eden Theol Sem 1959; hon LHD UT StateUniv 1975; distngsd Alumnus Awd LangstonUniv 1963; Man of the Yr Muskogee Serv League 1964; Rust Coll Shield for Ldrshp in Religion & Soc Devel 1974; serv plaque Wiley Coll 1973; cert of recog for Rsrch in Educ Phi Delta Kappa 1979. **BUSINESS ADDRESS:** PO Box 871, Corner Grand Ave & 19th St, Nashville, TN 37202.

WYNN, DEBORAH B.
Association executive. **PERSONAL:** Born Oct 23, 1947, Bluefield, WV. **EDUCATION:** Bluefield State Coll, BA 1968; Union Grad Sch, curr studying PhD. **CAREER:** Minority Invlmt Prog Nat Educ Assn, coor; Ctr Human Relations, professional asst; End Assn Fed Credit Union, 1st blck pres. **ORGANIZATIONS:** Delta Sigma Theta; Nat Training Lab Inc; Nat Counc Negro Women; Nat Educ Assn; Nat Assn Human Rights Workers.

WYNN, PRATHIA HALL
Minister. **PERSONAL:** Born Jul 29, 1940, Philadelphia, PA; married Ralph; children: Simone, Dubois. **EDUCATION:** Temple U, BA 1965; Princeton Theol Sem, MDiv 1981. **CAREER:** Mt Sharon Baptist Church Phila, PA, pastor 1978-; Solar Energy Com Resources Center of Hempstead Com Adiction Prog, cons. **ORGANIZATIONS:** Dir H Empstead Comm Action Prog; dir Nat Counc of Negro Women Training Inst 1971-72; prgm spclst 1969-71; asst dir Proj Womanpower 1967-68; NE FieldRep Proj Womanpower 1966-67; SNCC 1962-66; Admissions consult Coll for Human Servs; prgm as so Am Friends Serv Com; youth employ coord asst Philadelphia Counc for Comm Advncmt Sch bd trustee 1971-77; pres Bd of Educ Union Free Sch Dist #8 1973-77. **BUSINESS ADDRESS:** Mt Sharon Bapt Church, 1609 W Girard Ave, Philadelphia, PA.

WYNN, ROBERT L., JR.
Business executive. **PERSONAL:** Born Jan 25, 1929, Atlanta, GA; married Ethel Crawford; children: Teresa, Richard, Judith. **EDUCATION:** Clark Coll, BA 1953; State Univ of IA, MS 1960. **CAREER:** Mainstream Computer Inc Memphis, pres 1968-72; Data Mgmt Sci Corp Memphis, pres; Universal Life Ins Co, vp. **ORGANIZATIONS:** Bd of dir Mutual Fed Savings & Loan Assoc 1970-72; life mem NAACP, Kappa Alpha Psi; mem Beta Kappa Chi, Alpha Upsilon Omega, YMCA, Shelby Cty Health & Ed Fac Bd; bd of dir Jr Achievement of Memphis, Natl Ins Assoc, Natl Bus League, Natl Mathematical Soc. **MILITARY SERVICE:** AUS 1st lt 1955. **BUSINESS ADDRESS:** Vice President, Actuary, Universal Life Insurance Co, 480 Linden Ave, Memphis, TN 38126.

WYNN, SYLVIA J.
Vice president/marketing & sales. **PERSONAL:** Born Sep 30, 1941, New York, NY; daughter of Frank Wynn and Lucinda Townes Wynn. **EDUCATION:** Hunter Coll CUNY, attended 1966-70; Simmons Middle Mgmt Prog, Certificate 1979. **CAREER:** The Gillette Co, product mgr 1978-81; Intl Playtex Inc, product mgr 1981-83; Johnson Products Co Inc, group prod mgr 1983-85, dir of mktg 1985-86, vice pres mktg & sales 1986-87; SJW Enterprises Chicago, IL pres. **ORGANIZATIONS:** Mem AMA; tutor Boston Half-Way House 1978-81; founding mem & chairperson Target Advertising Professionals. **HONORS/ACHIEVEMENTS:** Boston Black Achiever Awd 1979. **BUSINESS ADDRESS:** Pres, SJW Enterprises, 333 E Ontario St, Suite 1302B, Chicago, IL 60611.

WYNN, WILLIAM AUSTIN, JR.
Association executive. **PERSONAL:** Born Nov 06, 1937, Sanford, FL; married Evelyn M Harris. **EDUCATION:** Bethune Cookman Coll, BS 1961. **CAREER:** Urban Ventures SBIC, pres; Inner City Dev Found, pres; Untd Way Am, vp; Un Way of Dade Co, budget dir; Gr Miami Coalition Inc, exec vp; Econ Opps Prog Inc, asso dir. **ORGANIZATIONS:** Mem State Manpower Commn; State Human Rel Commn; dir Nat Ind Bank Pres Urban Ventures Inc; mem Fam Hlth Cntr; Tacolcy Youth Cntr; OIC. **HONORS/ACHIEVEMENTS:** Nom Man of Yr 1974. **BUSINESS ADDRESS:** Honorary Consul, Hon Consulate of Barbados, 741 NW 62nd St, Miami, FL 33150.

WYNNE, MARVELL
Professional athlete. **PERSONAL:** Born Dec 17, 1959, Chicago, IL. **CAREER:** Pittsburgh Pirates, centerfield 1983-. **HONORS/ACHIEVEMENTS:** Hit in a career high 16 straight games 1984; Tied for Intl League lead in game winning RBI & led Tidewater in RBI & steals 1982; Led Jackson to Texas League Championship, leading club in games/hits/doubles/runs & at-bats 1981. **BUSINESS ADDRESS:** Pittsburgh Pirates, Three Rivers Stadium, 600 Stadium Cir PO Box 7000, Pittsburgh, PA 15212.

WYRICK, FLOYD I.
Educator. **PERSONAL:** Born May 26, 1932, Chgo. **EDUCATION:** Chicago State U,

BE 1954; DePaul U, MA 1963;Univ of IL, PhD 1972; Phi Delta Kappa; Kappa Delta Pi. **CAREER:** Calumet HS Chicago Bd Educ, prin co-dir; Chicago Public School, teacher; Chicago City Coll; Northwestern Univ; Booz Allen & Hamilton, mgmt conselor; Adam & Assoc; Mitchell Watkins & Assoc. **ORGANIZATIONS:** Mem Nat Alli of Black Sch Educ; Am Assn of Sch Adminstrs; Nat Assn of Scndry Sch Prins; Samuel B Stratton Educ Assn; mem Am Civil Libs Union; People Unit to Save Human; Alpha Phi Alpha Frat; Comm Fund of Metro Chgo. **MILITARY SERVICE:** AUS 1954-56. **BUSINESS ADDRESS:** 8131 S May St, Chicago, IL 60620.

Y

YANCEY, ASA G., SR.
Administrator, educator, professor. **PERSONAL:** Born in Atlanta, GA; son of Arthur H Yancey and Daisy Yancey; married Carolyn D; children: Arthur II, Carolyn L, Caren L, Asa Jr. **EDUCATION:** Morehouse Coll, BS 1937; Univ MI, MD 1941. **CAREER:** Vet Admin Hosp Tuskegee AL, chief surg 1948-58; Hughes Spalding Hosp, chf surg 1958-72; Grady Mem Hosp, med dir 1972-; Emory Univ Sch Med, assc dean 1972-; Grady Memorial Hosp, med dir. **ORGANIZATIONS:** Bd trustee GA Div Am Cancer Soc; fellow Am Coll Surgeons; diplomate Am Bd Surg; ed bd Jrnl of Natl Med Assn 1960-80; mem Am Surg Assn, Atlanta Bd Ed 1965-75, Southern Surg Assn, Natl Med Assn; mem Atlanta Bd of Ed 1967-77; life mem, golden heritage mem NAACP. **HONORS/ACHIEVEMENTS:** Recip Distinguished Serv Morehouse Coll; Service Awd Atlanta Inquirer; Aven Cup. **MILITARY SERVICE:** AUS 1st lt Medical Corp 1941. **HOME ADDRESS:** 2845 Engle Rd NW, Atlanta, GA 30318. **BUSINESS ADDRESS:** Medical Dir, Grady Memorial Hospital, 80 Butler St SE, Atlanta, GA 30335.

YANCEY, CAROLYN LOIS
Pediatrician. **PERSONAL:** Born Sep 12, 1950, Tuskegee, AL. **EDUCATION:** Spelman Coll/Atlanta Univ, BS 1968-72; Univ of Edinburgh Scotland UK, attended 1971-72; Howard Univ Coll of Medicine, MD 1976. **CAREER:** Univ of PA Childrens Hosp of Phila, resident 1976-79, fellow pediatric rheumatology 1979-81, instructor of pediatrics 1980-81, clinical asst prof of pediatrics 1981-82; Howard Univ Dept of Peds and Child Health, model practice coord 1982-83, clinical asst prof peds 1982-; Walter Reed Army Medical Ctr, clinical asst prof peds 1985-; George Washington Univ Sch of Medicine, asst clinical prof of child health & develop 1987-. **ORGANIZATIONS:** Elected to Section of Rheumatology Amer Acad of Pediatrics 1983; diplomate and fellow Amer Acad of Pediatrics 1984; mem NMA and Amer Rheumatism Assoc 1979-; nominating comm Section of Rheumatology AAP 1987. **HONORS/ACHIEVEMENTS:** Dept Medical Awd Howard Univ Coll of Medicine 1976; Disting Alumni Citation of the Year Natl Assoc for Equal Oppor in Higher Educ 1985. **BUSINESS ADDRESS:** Dir Pediatric Rheumatology, Kaiser-Permanente Med Group, 8300 Corporate Dr, Landover, MD 20785.

YANCEY, CHARLES CALVIN
City official. **PERSONAL:** Born Dec 28, 1948, Boston, MA; married Marzetta Morrissette; children: Charles, Derrick, Sharif, Ashley. **EDUCATION:** Tufts Univ, BA 1970. **CAREER:** Commonwealth of MA, dir of admin 1977-79; Metro Area Planning Council, dir of finances 1979-82; CCY and Assoc, pres 1979-84; Legislative Branch of City Govt, city councillor 1984-. **ORGANIZATIONS:** Mem NAACP 1966-, Greater Roxbury Comm Devel Corp 1978-82, Transafrica 1979-, Codman Square Comm Devel Corp 1981-83; former pres Black Political Task Force 1982-83; mem Coastal Resources Advisory Bd 1983-; bd mem, Boston African-Amer Natl Historic Site, Taxpayers Equity Alliance of MA (TEAM), Roxbury YMCA, Boston Harbor Assoc. **HONORS/ACHIEVEMENTS:** Elected vice pres North Amer Reg Action Against Apartheid Comm United Nations 1984; Citizen of the Year Omega Psi Phi 1984; Meritorious Comm Serv Kappa Alpha Psi 1984; Passage of Boston South Africa Divestment Legislation City Council 1984. **BUSINESS ADDRESS:** City Councilman, Boston City Council, New City Hall, City Hall Square, Boston, MA 02201.

YANCEY, LAUREL GUILD
Telecommunications attorney. **PERSONAL:** Born Dec 12, 1953, Santa Rosa, CA; daughter of George P Guild M D and Helen E (Branker) Guild; married Arthur H Yancey II M D, Jun 19, 1988. **EDUCATION:** Simmons Coll, BA 1975; Boston Coll Law School, JD 1978. **CAREER:** Dept of Justice, law clerk 1977; Federal Communications Commn, trial atty 1981-82, general atty 1982-85, sr atty/advisor 1985-. **ORGANIZATIONS:** Career awareness speaker Boy Scouts of Amer; mem DC Bar Assn; mem Alpha Kappa Alpha Sorority Inc; mem Black Entertainment and Sports Lawyers Assn; mem Federal Communications Bar Assn 1989-; representative A L Williams 1989-. **HONORS/ACHIEVEMENTS:** Comm Serv Awd FCC 1979. **BUSINESS ADDRESS:** Sr Attorney/Advisor, Federal Communications Commn, 1919 M St NW, Ste 712, Washington, DC 20554.

YANCY, DOROTHY COWSER
Educator. **PERSONAL:** Born Apr 18, 1944, Cherokee Cty, AL; married Dr Robert J; children: Yvonne. **EDUCATION:** Johnson C Smith Univ, AB History 1964; Univ of MA Amherst, MA 1965; Atlanta Univ, PhD Polit 1978. **CAREER:** Albany State Coll Albany GA, instr history 1965-67; Hampton Inst Hampton VA, instr history 1967-69; Evanston Twp HS, teacher 1969-71; Barat Coll Lake Forest IL, dir black studies 1971-72; GA Inst of Tech, assoc prof 1972-; assoc dir School of Social Science, GA Tech. **ORGANIZATIONS:** Mem Assoc for the Study of Afro-Amer Life & History; consult Booker T Washington Found; mem, labor panel Amer Arbitration Assoc 1980; mem bd of dirs GA Affiliate ACLU 1978-; mem exec comm Assoc of Soc & Behavioral Sci; mem So Pol Sci Assoc; spec master, FL Public Employees Relations Commn; brd memAssoc for the Study of Afro-Amer Life and History; mem Labor Arbitration Panel Fed Mediation and Conciliation Serv. **HONORS/ACHIEVEMENTS:** Fulbright-Hayes Scholar 1968; Outstanding Young Women in Amer 1973; Collaborating author The Fed Gov Policy & Black Enterprise 1974; author several scholarly articles. **BUSINESS ADDRESS:** Associate Professor, Georgia Inst of Tech, North Ave, Atlanta, GA 30332.

YANCY, PRESTON MARTIN
Educator. **PERSONAL:** Born Oct 18, 1938, Sylvester, GA; son of Preston M Yancy Sr (deceased) and Margaret Robinson Yancy; married Marilyn Leonard; children: Robert James, Grace Elizabeth. **EDUCATION:** Morehouse Coll, BA 1959; Univ of Richmond, MH 1968; Syracuse Univ, MSS 1974, PhD 1979. **CAREER:** USAF, civillian supply clerk 1959-61; US Dept of Defense, civillian supply clerk 1961-69; VA Union Univ, teacher, chair, div of humanities 1969-. **ORGANIZATIONS:** Columnist Richmond Afro-Amer Newspaper 1967-71,74-82; mem Amer Assoc of Univ Prof, Amer Studies Assoc, Assoc for the Study of Afro Amer Life and History, Soc of Educ and Scholars. **HONORS/ACHIEVEMENTS:** Emory O Jackson Best Column Awards 1975-78, 1980; Doctoral Grants Ford Found 1973-75; Doctoral Grants United Negro Coll Fund 1978-79; Post Doctoral Grants United Negro Coll Fund 1981-84; book The Afro-Amer Short Story Greenwood Press 1986. **HOME ADDRESS:** PO Box 25583, Richmond, VA 23260. **BUSINESS ADDRESS:** Chair Division of Humanities, Virginia Union University, 1500 N Lombardy St, Richmond, VA 23220.

YARBORO, THEODORE LEON
Physician. **PERSONAL:** Born Feb 16, 1932, Rocky Mount, NC; married Deanna Marie Rose; children: Theodore L Jr, Deanna R, Theresa L. **EDUCATION:** NC Central Univ, BS 1954, MS 1956; Meharry Med Coll, MD 1963; Univ of Pgh Grad Sch of Pub Health, MPH 1979. **CAREER:** US Bureau of Mines, chemist/analytical & organic 1956-59; Shenango Valley Campus Penn State Univ, lecturer 1979-; Theodore L Yarboro MD Inc, family practitioner 1965-. **ORGANIZATIONS:** Mem Natl Med Assn 1965-; mem Amer Acad of Family Physicians 1965-; mem Amer Med Assn 1965-; mem/bd of dirs Mercer Co Branch NAACP 1965-; founderShenango Valley Urban League 1968; bd dirs Shenango Valley Urban League 1968-78; founder/adv Dr Maceo E Patterson Future Physician Soc 1969-; charter diplomate Amer Bd of Family Prac 1970-; charter fellow Amer Acad of Fam Prac 1972-; mem bd trustees Natl Urban League 1973-78; mem Gov Adv Com on Multiple Health Screening 1975-76; mem Gov's Com on Health Educ in PA 1975-76; life mem NAACP 1976-; 3 publs Journal of Organic Chemistry, Journal of Chem, Engrg Data 1959-61. **HONORS/ACHIEVEMENTS:** Disting Serv Awd Midwestern PA Chap Amer Heart Assn 1970 & 75; Disting Serv Awd Shenango Valley Urban League 1972; Man of the Yr Shenango Valley Jaycees 1972; Comm Serv Awd Mercer Co Branch NAACP 1976. **MILITARY SERVICE:** USAF airman 1/c 1959. **BUSINESS ADDRESS:** 755 Division St, Sharon, PA 16146.

YARBOROUGH, DOWD JULIUS, JR.
Physician. **PERSONAL:** Born May 10, 1938, Winston-Salem, NC; married Merele; children: Danielle, Dowd III, Leyland. **EDUCATION:** Morgan State Coll, 1963; Meharry Med Coll, 1967;Univ MI, 1974. **CAREER:** Houston TX, physic cardiol int med; Baylor Coll Med, tchr; Univ TX. **ORGANIZATIONS:** Mem AMA; NMA. **HONORS/ACHIEVEMENTS:** Recog awd 1973. **MILITARY SERVICE:** USN lt comdr 1971-74. **BUSINESS ADDRESS:** 2000 Crawford St, Houston, TX 77002.

YARBOROUGH, RICHARD A.
University educator. **PERSONAL:** Born May 24, 1951, Philadelphia, PA; son of John W Yarborough III and Yvonne K Newby Yarborough; divorced. **EDUCATION:** Mich State Univ, E Lansing MI, BA, 1973; Stanford Univ, Stanford CA, PhD, 1980. **CAREER:** Univ of California, Los Angeles CA, asst prof 1979-86, assoc prof 1986-. **ORGANIZATIONS:** Faculty res assoc, UCLA Center for Afro-Amer Studies, 1979-; mem 1987-, chair 1989, exec comm of Div of Black Amer Literature & Culture, Modern Lang Assn; bd of editorial advisors, American Quarterly, 1987-; mem, Natl Council, Amer Studies Assn, 1988-. **HONORS/ACHIEVEMENTS:** US Presidential Scholar, 1969; Alumni Dist Scholar's Award, MI State Univ, 1969-73; Whiting Fellowship in Humanities, Stanford Univ, 1977-78; Natl Endowment for the Humanities fellowship, 1984-85; Dist Teaching Award, UCLA, 1987; Ford Foundation postdoctoral fellowship, 1988-89; general editor, "Library of Black Literature," Northeastern Univ Press, 1988-; coeditor, forthcoming books Heath Anthology of American Literature and Norton Anthology of Afro-American Literature; author of scholarly essays in numerous journals & books. **BUSINESS ADDRESS:** Associate Professor, Department of English, University of California, 2225 Rolfe Hall, Los Angeles, CA 90024-1530.

YARBROUGH, CHARLES
Juvenile officer. **PERSONAL:** Born Sep 01, 1939, St Louis, MO. **EDUCATION:** Lake MI Coll, asso degree. **CAREER:** Berrien Probate Ct, juv prob ofcr 8 yrs; Benton Hrbr Cty Commr, 7 yrs. **ORGANIZATIONS:** Pres Bach 14 Soc Club 1973-; chrmn Benton Hrbr Pens Bd 1975-; chrmn Benton Hrbr Liq & Control Bd 1974-; mem Benton Hrbr Pub Safety Com 1976-. **HONORS/ACHIEVEMENTS:** 1st degree Black Belt Kung Fu Karate. **MILITARY SERVICE:** AUS staff sgt. **HOME ADDRESS:** 530 Pearl St, Benton Harbor, MI 49022.

YARBROUGH, DELANO
Educator, consultant. **PERSONAL:** Born Sep 20, 1936, Thornton, AR; son of Roy Yarbrough and Sadie Yarbrough; married Samella O; children: Delano, Desiree, Darryl. **EDUCATION:** UUniv of AR Pine Bluff, BS; AZUSA Pacif Coll CA State Univ, MA; Marguette; LeVerne; UCLA; Univ of SF, doct; Pepperdine Univ; Azusa Pacific-Coll Azusa, CA, MA, l971-73; Univ of San Francisco, East, l980-89. **CAREER:** E HS Lilbourn, teacher 1961-63; US Navy, mathematician 1963-65; Pasadena Unified School District 1967-77, desegregation project dir; Del Yarbrough & Assocs, consultant; Eliot Middle School, principal 1981-. **ORGANIZATIONS:** Mem ASCD, CSCD, APSA, Phi Delta Kappa, NAACP; Pasadena Educ Found; consultant Afro-Am Educ Cult Cntr; consultant Jet Propulsion Lab; v chmn ESAA; mem Natl Council Teacher Math; CA Math Council; CA State Math Framework Comm l984-86; pres & mem, bd of dir, Diversified Educ Serv, Inc, l98l-. **HONORS/ACHIEVEMENTS:** New Teacher of the Year Pasadena 1964; Commendation in educ for serv rendered in reducing racial isolation. **MILITARY SERVICE:** USAF airman 1/c 1954-58. **BUSINESS ADDRESS:** Principal, Eliot Middle School, 2184 N Lake Ave, Altadena, CA 91001.

YARBROUGH, EARNEST
Magistrate. **PERSONAL:** Born Mar 16, 1923, Buffalo; married Mary Holman. **CAREER:** MCAS, 1965-69; Ridgeland Clinic, supr trans 1970; Beaufort Jasper Compre Hlth Serv Inc, magis 1971-77. **ORGANIZATIONS:** Mem Elke Lodge; VFW Lodge. **MILITARY SERVICE:** USN 1942-64.

YARBROUGH, MAMIE LUELLA
Elected official. **PERSONAL:** Born Sep 19, 1941, Benton Harbor, MI; divorced; children:

Dawn Delynne, Nyles Charles. **EDUCATION:** Western MI Univ, 1959-60. **CAREER:** NBD F&M Bank, banking 1966-75; Berrien Homes Apts, housing mgr 1975-81; River Terrace Apts, housing mgr 1981-; Benton Harbor Area Sch Bd, vice pres. **ORGANIZATIONS:** Sec Benton Twp Citizens Adv Bd 1979; pres Benton Harbor Comm Arts Alliance 1980; mem Inst of Real Estate & Management 1981-; rep Berrien Co Intermediate Sch Dist 1984-. **HONORS/ACHIEVEMENTS:** Certified Housing Mgr Natl Center for Housing Mgmt 1978; Accredited Resident Mgr Inst of Real Estate & Mgmt 1981. **HOME ADDRESS:** 1086 Monroe, Benton Harbor, MI 49022. **BUSINESS ADDRESS:** School Board President, Benton Harbor Area Schl Dist, 300 River Terrace, Benton Harbor, MI 49022.

YARBROUGH, MARILYN VIRGINIA
Educator. **PERSONAL:** Born Aug 31, 1945, Bowling Green, KY; daughter of William O Yarbrough (deceased) and Merca Lee Hardin; married David A Didion, Dec 31, 1987; children: Carmen Ainsworth, Carla Ainsworth. **EDUCATION:** Virginia State Univ, BA 1966; UCLA, JD 1973. **CAREER:** IBM, systms eng 1966-68; Westinghouse, systms eng 1969-70; Catonsville Community College, instr data proc 1970; Boston College Law School, teaching fellow 1975-76; Duke Law School, visting prof 1983-84; Univ of Kansas, law prof, 1976-87 & assoc vice chancellor 1983-87; Univ of Tennessee-Knoxville, law dean 1987-. **ORGANIZATIONS:** Pres bd cmt wrk Law Sch Admsn Cncl 1976-89; bd mem Accrediting Cncl Ed Journalism Mass Communications 1976-83; chmn mem KS Crime Victims Reparations Bd 1980-83; mem Lawrence Housing Auth 1984-86; cncl mem Am Bar Assc Sect Legal Ed Admsn to the Bar 1984-85; pres Lawrence, KS United Way 1985; mem KS Commiss on Civil Rights 1986-; mem 1988-, chmn 1986-87, NCAA Conf on Infractions; mem Rotary International 1988-. **HONORS/ACHIEVEMENTS:** Kansas Univ Women's Hall of Fame; articles law journals; chap Every Woman's Legal Guide, Doubleday; Doctor of Laws, Univ of Puget Sound School of Law 1989; Frank D Reeves Award, Natl Conference of Black Lawyers 1988. **BUSINESS ADDRESS:** Law Dean, Univ of Tennessee-Knoxville, Knoxville, TN 37996.

YARBROUGH, ROBERT ELZY
Attorney. **PERSONAL:** Born Dec 16, 1929, Atlanta, GA. **EDUCATION:** Boston Coll, BSBA 1951; Bstn Univ Law Sch, LlB 1958. **CAREER:** US Cust Serv Dept of Treas, sr impt splst 1975-; AUS & AUS Res, ret LTC FA 1949-77; US Cust Serv, impt splst 1963-; atty at law 1961-; US Post Ofc, clk 1954-61; AUS, ofcr 1951-54. **ORGANIZATIONS:** Bd of trust Bstn Latin Sch Alumni Asso 1980; mem Am Bar Assn MA Bar Assn; mem Prince Hall Grand Lodge F & AM of MA; mem Syria Temple #31 AEAONMS. **HONORS/ACHIEVEMENTS:** Merit serv medal AUS 1977. **MILITARY SERVICE:** Aus lt 1949-77. **BUSINESS ADDRESS:** Custom House, Boston, MA 02109.

YARBROUGH, ROOSEVELT
Accountant. **PERSONAL:** Born Jan 11, 1946, Pattison, MS. **EDUCATION:** Chapman Coll, 1968; MS Valley State Univ, BS 1973; John Marshall Law School, 1981; Amer Mgmt Assoc Ctr for Mgmt Devel, 1982. **CAREER:** Ernst & Ernst, staff accountant 1975; Bailey Meter Co, budget analyst 1976; Southwest MS Legal Svcs, dir of admin 1982; First Entry Svcs, accountant; Claiborne Cty Schools, bd mem. **ORGANIZATIONS:** Directorship Claiborne Cty Bldg; mem Assoc for Suprv & Curriculum Devel, Black Ed & Econ Proj; pres NAACP, MS Cultural Arts Coalition, Claiborne CtyFamily Reunion. **MILITARY SERVICE:** USMC cpr 3 yrs. **HOME ADDRESS:** PO Box 141, Pattison, MS 39144. **BUSINESS ADDRESS:** School Board Member, Claiborne Co Dist 5, PO Box 337, Port Gibson, MS 39150.

YARDE, RICHARD FOSTER
Art professor. **PERSONAL:** Born Oct 29, 1939, Boston, MA; married Susan Donovan; children: Marcus, Owen. **EDUCATION:** Boston Univ, BFA (Cum Laude) Painting 1962, MFA Painting 1964. **CAREER:** Boston Univ, asst prof of art 1965-71; Wellesley Coll, assoc prof of art 1976, Amherst Coll, visiting assoc prof 1976-77; MA Coll of Art, visiting artist, 1977-79; Mount Holyoke Coll, visiting assoc prof, Art, 1980-81; Univ of MA Boston, prof of Art. **ORGANIZATIONS:** Visual arts panelist MA Council Art & Humanities 1976-78; assoc mem Natl Acad of Design 1984-. **HONORS/ACHIEVEMENTS:** Blanche E Colman Awd for Travel & Study in Nigeria 1970; Arcadia Found Awd for Painting NY 1975; Fellowship Grant in Painting Natl Endowment for the Arts 1976; Childe Hassam Purchase Amer Acad of Arts & Letters NY 1977; Henry W Ranger Fund Purchase Natl Acad of Design NY 1979; Childe Hassam Purchase Amer Acad of Arts & Letters NY 1982; Adolph & Clara Obrig Prize Natl Acad of Design 1983; Commn Art-in-Architecture Prog Genl Serv Admin Washington DC 1984; one person exhibit "Savoy" traveling to Studio Museum in Harlem, San Diego Museum, The Baltimore Museum etc 1982-83; group exhibitions Metropolitan Museum of Art, Boston Museum, Corcoran Gallery Washington DC. **BUSINESS ADDRESS:** Professor of Art, Univ of MA, Boston, Art Dept, Harbor Campus, Boston, MA 02125.

YATES, ANTHONY J.
Basketball coach. **PERSONAL:** Born Sep 15, 1937, Lawrenceburg, IN. **EDUCATION:** Univ of Cincin, BS 1963. **CAREER:** Univ of IL, asst basktbl coach 1974-;Univ of Cincin, asst basktbl coach 1971-74; Cincin Royals Professional Basktbl Team, part time scout 1966-71; Fin Mgmt Corp, salesman 1968-71; Drake Mem Hosp, asst to admin & person & dir 1966-68; Shillitos Dept Store, asst employ mgr 1963-66. **ORGANIZATIONS:** Mem Nat Assn of Sec Deal; mem bd dir Nat AAU Basktbl League; mem bd dir Greater Cincin Jr Basktbl Assn; fmr mem Cincin Plan Parenthd; fmr mem Cincin Sch Found; fmr mem Baseball "Kid Gloves" game; fmr mem Cincin Met AAU; Tom Shell Tony Yates TV Basktbl Show WCPO TV 1964; color caster for WKRC radio broad ofUniv of Cincin bsktbl games 1970-71; sports banquet spkr for Coca Cola Btlg Co 1963, 1964 1965. **HONORS/ACHIEVEMENTS:** MemUniv of Cincin Bsktbl Tm NCAA Bsktbl Champ 1961, 1962. **MILITARY SERVICE:** USAF 1955-59.

YATES, ELLA GAINES
Librarian, consultant. **PERSONAL:** Born Jun 14, 1927, Atlanta, GA; daughter of Fred D Gaines Sr and Laura Moore Gaines; married Clayton R Yates III (deceased); children: Jerri Sydnor Lee. **EDUCATION:** Spelman Coll Atlanta, BA 1949; Atlanta Univ, MS Lib Sci 1951; Rutgers Univ Newark, Sch Library Certification 1956; Univ of GA Inst for Training in Municipal Administration, cert for professional mgmt 1972, cert for advanced professional mgmt 1974; Morehouse Coll/HUD, cert mgmt for black administrators in state & municipal govt 1975; Atlanta Law Sch, JD 1979. **CAREER:** Orange Meml Hosp, part-time librarian 1964-66; Atlanta Univ Library, asst ref librarian 1947-48; Brooklyn Public Library, asst branch librarian 1951-55; Orange Public Library, head of children's dept 1956-60; East Orange Public Library, branch librarian 1960-70; Montclair Pub Library, asst dir 1970-72; Atlanta Univ, visiting prof grad library sch 1972-73; Atlanta Fulton Public Lib, asst dir 1972-76; Atlanta Fulton Public Lib, dir 1976-81; The Friendship Force, library consultant; The VA State Library & Archives, state librarian and archivist 1986-. **ORGANIZATIONS:** Consul Seattle Oppors Industrialization Ctr 1982-84; consul Univ of WA 1982-83; consul US Commn on Civil Rights 1982; consul Atlanta-Fulton Pub Library 1975-77; consul United Way Budget & Planning Adv Bd 1979 1980; consul Martin Luther King Jr Archives 1977-81; consul Library Journal; consul US Office of Educ Bureau of Libraries 1973-; consul NJ State Library 1956-72; consul Rutgers Univ 1971-72; mem various comms American Library Assn; exec comm Library of Congress "Center for the Book" 1979-; Assn of Coll & Rsch Libraries 1981-; Natl Alumnae Bd of Spelman Coll 1984-; Wash Lib Assn Intellectual Freedom Comm 1981-84; mem Wash State Coalition Against Censorship 1983-84; Univ of WA Grad Library Sch Visiting Comm 1982-84; mem Seattle Urban League Guild 1982-84; Tuskegee Airmen Inc 1982-84; YMCA of Greater Atlanta Trustee Bd 1980-81; various positions w/NJ Library Assn; mem Atlanta Univ Natl Alumni Bd 1977-81; mem GA Public Broadcast Bd 1977-81; Friends of the Fulton Co Jail Board; nominating comm Southeastern Library Assn 1974. **HONORS/ACHIEVEMENTS:** Ella Gaines Yates Day in Atlanta 1981; Phoenix Awd City of Atlanta's Highest Awd for Outstanding Employee Performance 1980; Study Tour of Frankfurt Munich & West Berlin Germany 1980; Outstanding Alumna Spelman Coll 1977; Outstanding Alumna Atlanta Univ 1977; Outstanding Citizen of the Yr 1972; Professional Woman of theYr 1964; Awds for Serv to the Blind 1952 1953 1954; publs "An Annotated Cumulative Index to the Journal of Negro History for the First Twenty-Five Years" Atlanta Univ 1951; "A Critical Evaluation of the Montclair NJ Grass Roots Summer Prog" NJ 1971; an essay in What Black Librarians are Saying ed by EJ Josey Scarecrow Press 1972; a paper in The Role of the Humanities in the Public Library ed by Robt N Broadus Amer Library Assn 1979; "Sexism in the Library Profession" Library Journal Dec 15 1979 pp 2165-2619; Outstanding Librarian, Amer Library Assn, 1989; Outstanding in Government and Education, Richmond Chapter of Coalition of 100 Black Women, 1989. **HOME ADDRESS:** 5216 Beddington Rd, Richmond, VA 23234.

YATES, LEROY LOUIS
Pastor. **PERSONAL:** Born Dec 08, 1929, Terry, MS; married Beverly Joanne Pannell; children: Sara Doreen, Jonathan Allen, Joyce Ellen, Mary Francis Coultman, LeRoy Louis Jr. **EDUCATION:** Moody Bible Inst Chgo, grad dipl 1956; Chicago State U, BA 1971; Chicago State U, MS 1979. **CAREER:** Circle Y Ranch Bangor MI, exec dir 1978-80; Westlawn Gospel & Chapel Chicago, sr pastor 1956-80; Dept of Microbiology Chicago Medical School, chief tech supr 1967-77; Hektoen Inst Cook Co Hosp, sr research techer 1954-67. **ORGANIZATIONS:** Exec bd mem Leukemia Soc of Am 1961-80; exec bd sec PACE Inst Cook Co Jail Chicago 1969-80; mem of med adv bdUniv of IL Med Cntr 1978-80; exec bd mem Int Mag Pub 1967-80; draft bd mem Local Bd #58 1968-74; vol couns Westside Hol Fam Cntr 1978-80. **HONORS/ACHIEVEMENTS:** Kor serv med w/3 bronze camp stars Med Co 9th inf regt 1951; Unit Nat serv med Med Co 9th inf regt 1951; combat med badge IOS serv bar Med Co 9th inf regt 1951; merit serv awd IL sel serv system 1976. **MILITARY SERVICE:** AUS sgt 20 mos. **BUSINESS ADDRESS:** Westlawn Gospel Chapel, 2115 S St Louis, Chicago, IL 60623.

YEAGER, THOMAS STEPHEN
Educational administrator. **PERSONAL:** Born Mar 03, 1942, Louisville, KY; married Lillian Martin; children: Michelle Denise. **EDUCATION:** Tuskegee Inst, BS 1964, MEd 1968; Univ of Louisville, 1979. **CAREER:** Central State Hosp, counselor 1966-67; Tuskegee Institute, counselor 1967-68; KY Manpower Development Inc, coord 1968-74; Jefferson Comm Coll, coord tech resources and externally funded prog. **ORGANIZATIONS:** Mem CETA Exec Comm 1980-82; mem Private Industry Council 1982-83; mem Alpha Phi Alpha Frat 1962-; mem Phi Delta Kappa 1979-; mem NAACP 1980-; mem Cooperative Educ Assn of KY 1980-. **HONORS/ACHIEVEMENTS:** Authored "Study of Inactive Nurses in KY" 1974; Outstanding Young Men of Amer 1977; Outstanding Black Faculty JCC 1983; numerous grants 1968-. **MILITARY SERVICE:** AUS sp4 1964-65. **HOME ADDRESS:** 4604 Lincoln Rd, Louisville, KY 40220. **BUSINESS ADDRESS:** Coord Technical Resources, Jefferson Comm Coll, 109 E Broadway, Louisville, KY 40202.

YEARWOOD, AREM IRENE
Retired caterer. **PERSONAL:** Born in Americus, GA; married Randolph. **ORGANIZATIONS:** Mem Nat Coun of Negro Wom 1964-; pres New Sec NJ Life 1964-70; bd trust treas St Tim Yth Hse; bd dir Westside Unit 1970-75; pres bd dirs 1972-73; mem Eta Phi Beta Sor 1966; treas Psi Chap 1969; Co Comm & Wom 20th Dist Westward Newark 1966-80; vol Vista Nat Immuniz Nat Med Assn; vol NCNW Prgm for Sr Cit Newark; aide to Assem 28th Dist Westward Essex Co 1974-76. **HONORS/ACHIEVEMENTS:** 1st wom elect Westside Unit; Boys Club Mother of Yr awd 1965; Boys Club serv awd 1966; Boys Club outst supp 1967; wom of yr Greyhnd Afro-am 1969; NC NW serv awd 1971; Eta Phi Beta Comm serv awd 1972; Boys Club of Am awd 1974; Bethune achvmt awd 1975; Bethune Bicent awd 1976; Bethune Leg awd 1976; ch wom unit awd 1975; NCNW Inc Life mem Guild In Serv awd 1975; wom of yr awd NCNW Inc 1976; Boys Club of New 10 yr serv awd 1978; NCNW Bethune Cent awd 1975; outst wom of yr of NJ NCNW 1979; elect to natl nom com NCNW 1977-79; 15 yr serv awd; Boys Clubs of New 1980; comm serv awd Nurses Assn; Martland Hosp Coll of Med & Dent of NJ 1977. **BUSINESS ADDRESS:** 3304 S 20 St, Newark, NJ 07103.

YEARWOOD, DAVID MONROE, JR.
Television executive. **PERSONAL:** Born Nov 15, 1945; married Cristina Luisa Dale de Rollox; children: Edward, David III. **EDUCATION:** Pace Univ, BBA 1978; Keller Grad Sch of Management, MBA Mgmt 1982, MBA Human Res 1983. **CAREER:** Natl Broadcasting Co NY, financial analyst 1970-75, mgr budgets 1975-77; Natl Broadcasting Co Chicago, mgr accounting 1977-80, dir finance & admin 1980-. **ORGANIZATIONS:** Chmn supervisory comm ABE Credit Union 1983-86; alumni council Keller Grad Sch 1984-; vice pres IL Broadcasting Assoc 1985-; editorial bd WMAQ-TV 1982-. **HONORS/ACHIEVEMENTS:** Cert of Merit Youth Motivation Comm 1979-80; listed in Who's Who in Black Corp Amer 1982. **MILITARY SERVICE:** USN Reserve petty officer 3rd 1966-70. **BUSINESS ADDRESS:** Dir Finance & Admin, Natl Broadcasting Co, Merchandise Mart Plaza, Chicago, IL 60654.

YEARY, JAMES E., SR.
Educator. **PERSONAL:** Born Jul 07, 1917, Harrogate, TN; married Kathelene Toney; children: Glenna, Aaron, James, Jr, Brenda. **EDUCATION:** Morristown Jr Coll, 1941; TN State U, BS 1954; Tuskegee Inst, MSEd 1960. **CAREER:** Knoxville City Schools, teacher math dept chmn; Greenwood Annex Jr High Clarksville, prin; Knoxville Coll, asst prof consultant 1969-72; Edison HS Gary, teacher 1964-71; Burt HS Clarksville, teacher 1956-64; Elem School Teaching, 1941-46. **ORGANIZATIONS:** Mem St James Mason Lodge; Gen Elec fellowshp 1957; mem Nat Scl Found Austin Peay StateUniv 1962-63; FiskUniv 1959; TN StateUniv 1960; IL Inst of Tech 1966;Univ IL 1968-69; min; life under; auth "War Inside"; colum INFO weekly 1968-69. **HONORS/ACHIEVEMENTS:** Listed Who's Who in Coll 1953; mem Nat Sci Hon Soc Beta Kappa Chi; Nat Sci Acad Yr Inst 1959. **MILITARY SERVICE:** AUS 1942-45. **BUSINESS ADDRESS:** St Mary's Bapt Ch, 1038 Trenton St, Harriman, TN 37748.

YELDELL, JOSEPH P.
Government executive. **PERSONAL:** Born Sep 09, 1932, Wash; married Gladys Johnson; children: Gayle, Joi Lynn. **EDUCATION:** Dc Tchrs Coll, BS 1957; Univ Pitts, MA 1961. **CAREER:** Pgh Pub Sch, tchr 1958-61; DC Pub Sch, tchr 1961-62; Bureau Labor Stat, math stat 1962-64; IBM Corp, mktg & educ rep 1964-71; DC City Cncl, apptd mem 1967-71; Dept of Hum Res, dir 1971-77; Mayor, gen asst 1977-; DC Office of Emergency Preparedness, dir. **ORGANIZATIONS:** Chmn Wash Met Transit Auth; Trans Plan Bd; vice pres Metro Counc Govts; bd trust DC pub lib; pres ETA Travel Agcy; ASPA; NAEYC; exec com Nat Assn Sec Hum Res; fellow Smithson Inst; mem NAACP; Urban League; N Portal Civic Assn; 33 deg Mason; Shriners; founder Wash Econ Orgn. **HONORS/ACHIEVEMENTS:** Outstndg com serv awd Dupont Pk Civic Assn 1972; outstndg cit awd Fed Civic Assn 1970; distin serv awd Wmns Dem Club 1970; civil serv of yr awd Nat AMVETS 1975; listed Fam Blacks Ebony mag. **MILITARY SERVICE:** USAF a/1c 1954-56. **BUSINESS ADDRESS:** Dir, DC Ofc Emergency Preparedness, 2000 14th St NW, 8th Floor, Washington, DC 20009.

YELITY, STEPHEN C.
Chief executive. **PERSONAL:** Born Oct 25, 1949, Littleton, NC; son of Stephen Jackson Yelity and Martha Ella Pitchford Yelity; married Matlyn Joyce Alston Yelity, Apr 22, 1973; children: Scott. **EDUCATION:** Norfolk State Univ, Norfolk VA, BS, 1973. **CAREER:** Amer Cynamid, Wayne NJ, accountant, 1973-76; Johnson & Johnson, Chicapee & New Brunswick, sr accountant & financial analyst, 1976-79; Johnson & Johnson Baby Products, Skillman NJ, accounting mgr, 1979-84; Accurate Information Systems, S Plainfield NJ, pres & CEO, 1984-. **ORGANIZATIONS:** NY/NJ Minority Purchasing Council, 1986-; Black Data Processing Assn, 1987-; Intl Network of Unix System Uses, 1988-; Chamber of Commerce, 1988-; NJ Brain Trust, 1989-; Natl Urban League, 1989-; NAACP, 1989-. **HONORS/ACHIEVEMENTS:** Minority Small Business Man of Year for NJ, Small Business Admin, 1987; Appreciation Award, Bell Communications Research, 1988; Appreciation Award, AT&T, 1988; Sponsor of Year, Black Date Processing Associates, 1988; representative of minority small business in NJ for Grand Jury testimony concerning public opinion of Public Law 99-661, 1988; nominee for SBA Region II Man of Year, 1989; among top 100 black businesspersons recognized, Black Enterprise, 1989; featured in Time magazine article on black executives, "Doing It for Themselves," 1989. **BUSINESS ADDRESS:** President and CEO, Accurate Information Systems, Inc, 3000 Hadley Rd, South Plainfield, NJ 07080.

YERBY, FRANK GARVIN
Novelist. **PERSONAL:** Born Sep 05, 1916, Augusta, GA; son of Rufus Garvin Yerby and Wilhelmina (Smythe) Yerby; married Flora Helen Claire Williams, Mar 01, 1941; children: Jacques Loring, Nikki Ethlyn, Faune Ellena, Jan Keith; married Blanca Call-Perez, Jul 27, 1956. **EDUCATION:** Paine Coll, Augusta, GA, AB, 1937; Fisk Univ, MA, 1938; Univ of Chicago, graduate study, 1939. **CAREER:** Novelist; Florida Agricultural and Mechanical Coll (now Univ), Tallahassee, FL, instructor in English, 1939-40; Southern Univ and Agricultural and Mechanical Coll, Baton Rouge, LA, 1940-41; Ford Motor Co, Dearborn, MI, war work, 1942-44; Ranger Aircraft, Jamaica, NY, chief inspector, 1944-45. **ORGANIZATIONS:** Mem, Authors Guild (New York); mem, Authors League of Amer; mem, Real Sociedad Hipica Espanola (Madrid). **HONORS/ACHIEVEMENTS:** O Henry Memorial Award, 1944, for best first short story, "Health Card"; Doctor of Letters, Fisk Univ, 1976, and Doctor of Humane Letters, Paine Coll, 1977; named honorary citizen of State of Tennessee by Governor's Proclamation, 1977; author of numerous novels published by Dial, including The Foxes of Harrow, 1946, The Vixens, 1947, The Golden Hawk, 1948, Floodtide, 1950, A Woman Called Fancy, 1951, The Devil's Laughter, 1953, The Treasure of Pleasant Valley, 1955, The Serpent and the Staff, 1958, Jarrett's Jade, 1959, The Garfield Honor, 1961, The Old Gods Laugh, 1964, Judas My Brother, 1968, The Girl From Storyville, 1972, A Rose for Ana Maria, 1976, and Western: A Saga of the Great Plains, 1982; author of books published by Doubleday, including Bride of Liberty, 1954, and McKenzie's Hundred, 1985; contributor to anthologies and periodicals. **BUSINESS ADDRESS:** c/o William Morris Agency, 1350 Ave of the Americas, New York, NY 10019. *

YERGER, AMOS G.
Educator. **PERSONAL:** Born Aug 06, 1914, Boynton, OK; married Willie C; children: Donald, Cardis, Carlotta. **EDUCATION:** AB 1936; MS 1957. **CAREER:** Boynton, elem teacher 1932-57; prin instr 1957-73; Muskogee Cnty OK Educ Assn, retired vice pres; E Dist Music Teachers Assn, pres 1956; Boynton Comm Chorus, org dir 1950-54. **ORGANIZATIONS:** Mem Boynton City & Counc 1969-71; midwest reg dir Zeta Phi Beta Sor Inc 1970-74; sec Lee Cemet & Bur Co; state sec NAACP; v chmn Precint 50 Boynton; 4-H orgn ldr; chmn March of Dimes Boynton; ch clk Mt Zion Bapt. **HONORS/ACHIEVEMENTS:** Dist soror awd 1969; comm serv awd 1969; disting wom 1971; outstndg tchr 1973; serv recog 1974; Zeta of yr 1975.

YERGER, BEN
Educational administrator. **PERSONAL:** Born Dec 08, 1931, Hope, AK; married Charlene A; children: Valerie B, Benjamin Jr. **EDUCATION:** Philander Smith Coll, BS 1951; San Fran U, MA 1969;Univ of CA, PhD 1975. **CAREER:** Vista Coll, dean stud serv 1978-; Merritt & Vista Coll, dir comm serv 1972-78; Grove St Coll, pres 1971; Merritt & Coll, admin asst to the pres 1968-71; Pub Sch Far West Educ Lab, sci educ resrch 1955-68. **ORGANIZATIONS:** Bd of dir Berkeley Area Comm Found 1980-; vice pres Resrch Devel Cntr for Soc Redes 1978-; chmn Yth Employ Counc Berkeley CA 1978-; chtr mem Assn of CA Comm Coll Admin 1975-; mem CCCCSA CCJCA NASPA AAHE AAER NCCSCE and others; Alpha Kappa Mu Hon Soc; Phil Smith Coll 1949-50; Beta Kappa Chi Sci Hon Soc Phil Smith Coll 1949-50; Alpha Phi Alpha & Cum Laude Phil Smith Coll 1949-50. **HONORS/ACHIEVEMENTS:** Outstndg educat of Am in high educ awd 1971; Phi Delta Kappa Hon SocUniv of CA 1973-; outstndg dissert awd Instit Rsrch Plan Com CA Assn of Comm & Jr Coll 1976-77. **MILITARY SERVICE:** AUS non-com 1956. **BUSINESS ADDRESS:** 2020 Milvia St, Berkeley, CA 94704.

YIZAR, JAMES HORACE, JR.
Educator. **PERSONAL:** Born Aug 27, 1957, Los Angeles, CA. **EDUCATION:** ID State Univ, BA 1983. **CAREER:** Campbell Comm Therapy Ctr, recreation coord 1981-82; Upward Bound, asst dir 1982-84; ID State Univ Special Svcs, coord 1984-. **ORGANIZATIONS:** Mem Kappa Alpha Psi 1978-; advisor Epsilon Theta Chap 1984-; advisor Assoc Black Students 1984-; bd dirs Ctr of Resources for Independent People 1985-; mem NAACP 1986-. **HONORS/ACHIEVEMENTS:** Outstanding Volunteer CRIP Program 1986; Outstanding Speaker Martin Luther King Day McCamon Sch Dist 1986. **BUSINESS ADDRESS:** Counselor/Learning Specialist, Idaho StateUniv, Box 8345, Pocatello, ID 83209.

YORK, RUSSEL HAROLD
Physician. **PERSONAL:** Born May 06, 1952, Chicago, IL; married Yvonne Taylor; children: Damion, Renee, Marucs. **EDUCATION:** Kalamazoo Coll, BA 1974; Howard Univ, MD 1978. **CAREER:** Henry Ford Hospital, intern/resident 1978-81; Wayne State Univ, faculty mem/instructor 1984-86; Woodland Medical Group PC, private practice 1986-. **ORGANIZATIONS:** Mem Amer Rheumatism Assoc 1986-, MI Rheumatism Soc; assoc mem Amer Coll of Physicians. **HONORS/ACHIEVEMENTS:** Diplomate Amer Bd of Internal Medicine 1982, Amer Bd of Rheumatology 1984; Minority Faculty Rsch Awd Wayne State Univ, 1984-85, 1985-86. **BUSINESS ADDRESS:** 22341 W Eight Mile Rd, Detroit, MI 48219.

YOUNG, A. S. (DOC YOUNG)
Journalist. **PERSONAL:** Born Oct 29, 1924, Virginia; married Hazel; children: Norman, Brenda. **EDUCATION:** Hampton Inst, BS; California State Univ, studied journalism; Pepperdine Coll. **CAREER:** Los Angeles Sentinel, columnist 1968-73, exec editor 1975-; Pepperdine Coll, dir public info; KAGB-FM, Los Angeles CA, comm radio station 1973-; author of several books, writer of numerous radio comm; has made numerous radio/TV appearances; Chicago Daily Defender, sport editor, feature writer and producer of special editions; Jet Magazine, sports editor, asst editor, mng editor; has published articles in more than 100 newspapers and magazines. **ORGANIZATIONS:** Mem Baseball Writers Assn of Amer; Publicists Guild of Hollywood; other professional organizations; mem Sigma Delta Chi; other civic groups. **HONORS/ACHIEVEMENTS:** President's Anniv Sports Awd; Natl Newspaper Publishers Assn, 1970; Natl Community Award, PUSH Expo, 1974; author of "Negro Firsts in Sports," 1963; "Sonny Liston: The Champ Nobody Wanted"; "The Nat King Cole Story," 1965; "Black Champions of the Gridiron: Leroy Keyes & O J Simpson," 1969; "The Mets From Mobile," 1970; "Black Athletes in the New Golden Age of Sports," 1975. **BUSINESS ADDRESS:** The Sentinel, 112 E 43 St, Los Angeles, CA 90011.

YOUNG, A. STEVEN
Attorney. **PERSONAL:** Born Apr 05, 1948, Brooklyn, NY. **EDUCATION:** St John's Sch Law, JD 1973; City Coll NY, 1970. **CAREER:** A Steven Young Esq, atty; NY City Dept Invest, exam atty. **ORGANIZATIONS:** Mem Harlem Lawyer's Assn; Nat Conf Black Lawyers; 100 Black Men Inc; mem NY State Bar Assn; mem NY Co Lawyer's Assn; mem Trial Lawyers Assn; mem NAI NY Region Inc; gen coun/treas Black Pilors of NY; founder Black Am Law Students Assn St John'sUniv Sch Law. **BUSINESS ADDRESS:** 299 Broadway, New York, NY 10007.

YOUNG, ALAN JOHN
Business owner. **PERSONAL:** Born May 25, 1945, Chicago, IL; son of John M Young and Marion E Bradley; married Jacquelyn McAlpin; children: Jeffrey, Kimberly, Christopher. **EDUCATION:** Univ of IL, BS Mktg 1968. **CAREER:** A Y Shell Serv Station, owner 1969-77; GM Dealer Devel Acad, trainee 1977-79; Alan Young Buick, pres 1979-. **ORGANIZATIONS:** Bd mem NE Motor Vehicle Licensing bd, Lincoln Found, Univ of NE Found. **HONORS/ACHIEVEMENTS:** In top 100 of Black Business Owners Black Enterprise Magazine 1981-85. **BUSINESS ADDRESS:** President, Alan Young Buick-GMC Trucks Inc, 7724 NE Loop 820, Fort Worth, TX 76180.

YOUNG, ALBERT JAMES
Writer, publisher. **PERSONAL:** Born May 31, 1939, Ocean Springs, MS; married Arlin. **EDUCATION:** Univ of MI, 1957-61; Univ of CA, BA 1969. **CAREER:** Loveletter, founder, editor 1966-68; Stanford Univ, Edward H Jones lecturer creative writings 1969-76; Yardbird Publ Inc, editor 1970-76; Laser Films, screenwriter 1972; Stigwood Corp, screenwriter 1972; Yardbird Wing Editions, co-publ, co-editor 1975-; Verdon Prod, screenwriter 1976; First Artists prod, screenwriter 1976-77; Yardbird Lives, co-editor 1978; Quilt, co-editor 1980; Ask Me Now book, author 1980; Universal Studios, freelance writer, book publ, screenwriter 1979-. **ORGANIZATIONS:** Mem E Bay Negro Hist Soc, Authors Guild, Authors League, Writers Guild of Amer, San Francisco Press Club. **HONORS/ACHIEVEMENTS:** Author "Dancing" 1969, "Snakes" Holt 1970, "The Song Turning Back Into Itself" Holt 1971, "Who Is Angelina?" 1975, "Geography of the Near Past" Holt 1976, "Sitting Pretty" Holt 1976; Joseph H Jackson Awd 1969; Wallace Stegner Writing Fellowship 1966; Natl Arts Council Awds 1968-69; Guggenheim Fellowship 1974; Natl Endowment Arts Fellowship Creative Writing 1974; Natl Endowment for Arts Spec Proj Grant to Create Dramatic Radio Series 1979. **BUSINESS ADDRESS:** 514 Bryant St, Palo Alto, CA 94301.

YOUNG, ALFRED
Educator. **PERSONAL:** Born Feb 21, 1946, New Orleans, LA; son of Landry Young Sr and Mattie Rayno Young; married Angela Marie Broussard; children: Tomara, Marcus, Malcolm. **EDUCATION:** Louisiana State Univ, New Orleans, LA, BA 1970; Syracuse Univ, MA 1972, PhD 1977. **CAREER:** Syracuse Univ, lecturer Afro-Amer studies 1971, instr history 1971-72, asst prof history 1972-82, assoc prof history 1982-88; Colgate Univ, Hamilton, NY, A Lindsay O'Connor Chair, 1988-89; Georgia Southern College, associate prof, 1989—. **ORGANIZATIONS:** Keeper of finance, 1980-85, chapter historian, 1988-89, Omega Psi Phi Frat Inc Chi Pi chapter; adjunct prof history, Syracuse Univ/Univ College Auburn Correctional Facility prog, 1981—; consultant, faculty advisor, National Model OAU, Howard Univ, 1982—; bd mem, Friends of Syracuse Univ Alumni Organization, 1987—. **HONORS/ACHIEVEMENTS:** Afro-Amer Fellowship Syracuse Univ 1970-72; Natl Fellowship

Fund Fellow 1975-76 1976-77; Outstanding Young Men of Amer Award 1979; summer research grant NY State Afro-Amer Institute 1987; certificate of appreciation Howard Univ Model OAU, 1989; numerous publs including "The Historical Origin & Significance of the Afro-Amer History Month Observance" Negro History Bulletin 1982; "Mis-Education of the Negro, An Analysis of the Educational Ideas of Carter G Woodson" The Western Journal of Black Studies; selected papers presented including "The Origins of Black History Week" LeMoyne Coll Syracuse 1979, "Carter Woodson's Educational Ideas and Africa" Africa-Asia-the Americas Conf Albany NY 1982; lecture "The African Diasphora: Sociocultural & Political Links between Afro-Americans and Afro-Jamaicans" 1987, "African-American Contributions to Science & Technology in America" National Society of Black Engineers 1988. **MILITARY SERVICE:** USN yeoman 3rd class 1965-67; Honorable Discharge. **HOME ADDRESS:** 104 Merman Dr, DeWitt, NY 13214. **BUSINESS ADDRESS:** Associate Professor of History, Georgia Souther College, Landrum Box 8054, Statesboro, GA 13126.

YOUNG, ALFRED F.
Professor. **PERSONAL:** Born Apr 14, 1932, Clanton, AL; children: Quentin, Alfred. **EDUCATION:** AL State U, BS 1957; AL State U, MS 1963; OK State U, EdD 1970. **CAREER:** E Highland HS Sylacauga AL, teacher 1957-58; GW Carver HS Montgomery, 1958-63; Benedict Coll, assoc prof 1967-68; OK State Univ, grad asst 1970; Benedict Coll, prof chem 1970-71; Argonne Natl Lab, faculty researcher 1971; Tel Aive Univ Israel, intl studies 1973-74. **ORGANIZATIONS:** Mem Am Chemical Soc; Nat Science Tchrs Assn; Am Counc Edn; Am Assn Higher Educ Danforth Found; assoc Adv Counc Save Pub Edn; Head Start; OEO ;pres Columbia Assn Sickle Cell Anemia Found. **HONORS/ACHIEVEMENTS:** Bausch & Lamb Scientific Awd; Who's Who Am; Man Yr; Outstndg Educ Am. **MILITARY SERVICE:** AUS sgt 1952-55.

YOUNG, ANDREW
Mayor. **PERSONAL:** Born Mar 12, 1932, New Orleans, LA; married Jean Childs; children: Andrea, Lisa, Paula, Andrew, III. **EDUCATION:** Dillard Univ, Attended; Howard Univ, BS; Hartford Theol Sem, BDiv. **CAREER:** Main AL, Thomasville, Beachton GA, former pastor; US House of Reps Fifth Congres Dist 93, 94, 95 Congress, mem of Congress 1973-77; United Nations, ambassador 1977-79; City of Atlanta, mayor 1982-. **ORGANIZATIONS:** Assoc dir Dept of Youth Work Natl Council of Churchs; chmn Atlanta Comm Relations Comm 1970; leader Civil Rights Movement; close assoc of Dr Martin Luther King Jr; mem Southern Christian Leadership Conf 1961, apptd exec dir by Dr King 1964, elected exec vice pres 1967; org citizenship educ programs & voter registration drives in South; helped draft & worked for passage of Civil Rights Act 1964, Voting Rights Act 1965; active in peace movement, efforts in behalf of working poor; mem, bd of dirs Martin Luther King Jr Ctr for Social Change, Southern Christian Leadership Conf, Robt F Kennedy Memorial Found, Amer for Democratic Action, Southern Elections Fund; mem, exec comm World Council of Churches Prog to Combat Racism; pres Young Ideas Inc. **HONORS/ACHIEVEMENTS:** 1st black Congressman from GA since Jefferson Long 1970-71; numerous honorary degrees; Pax-Christi Awd St John's Univ 1970; Spingarn Medal; Medal of Freedom 1980. **BUSINESS ADDRESS:** Mayor, City of Atlanta, 68 Mitchell St SW, Atlanta, GA 30303.

YOUNG, ANDREW J.
Regional attorney. **PERSONAL:** Born Oct 23, 1933, Como, MS; married Gearline D; children: Christopher, Catherine. **EDUCATION:** Univ of WA, BA 1956; Univ of WA, LlB 1962. **CAREER:** Ofc of Hearings & Appeals Dept of Hlth & Human Svcs, asso commr pres; Ofc of Gen Couns US Dept of Hlth, Educ & Welf, reg atty; Hay Epstein & Young Atty Seattle, atty 1967-70; State of WA, asst atty gen 1962-66. **ORGANIZATIONS:** Mem ABA; NBA; ATLA; Phi Alpha Delta Legal Frat; WA State Bar Assn; King Co Bar Assn; Loren Miller Bar Assn; v chmn Seattle Downtown YMCA 1978-79; chmn WA State Bd for Comm Coll Educ 1973-75; chmn Seattle Armed Svc; bd fo trustees YMCA 1975-76; exec bd Seattle Br NAACP 1967-79. **HONORS/ACHIEVEMENTS:** Rec "Kalbourne Awd" Outstndg Lay Mem of the Yr Seattle Downtown YMCA 1979. **MILITARY SERVICE:** AUS 1st lt 1956-58; AUS capt res 1959-70. **BUSINESS ADDRESS:** Associate Commissioner, Dept of Health & Human Serv, 3833 N Fairfax Dr, Arlington, VA.

YOUNG, ANER RUTH
Educator. **PERSONAL:** Born Feb 16, 1933, Perote, AL. **EDUCATION:** AL State U, BS PE; San Francisco State, MA 1967. **CAREER:** Woodrow Wilson HS, dept head. **ORGANIZATIONS:** Mem Hall of Fame Am & CA Assn Hlth P Educ & Rec; CA Tchrs Assn; tchrs compet panel mem CA Tchrs Assn; sec San Francisco Classroom Tchrs Assn; State Coun; Bay Sec Coun; NEA; first chrpsn & co-fdr San Francisco Airport Police Ofcrs Assn; mem PTA; PE bd comp sports girls; sponsor schlrshp fund AL State; rare blood donor Irwin Meml Blood Bank; contrbtr support Sickle Cell Anemia; orig "SIT-INER" AL; mem So Poverty Law Ctr; vol Red Cross; splst Hlth & Fam Life Edn; fdr San Francisco Bay Area Chap AL State Alumni; dir ASU Nat Alum Assn Phi Delta Kappa Beta Nu Chpt; bd dir Nat Alumni Assn AL State; so sect spl serv for tchrs Cal-Te-A corp bds; mem NEA Nat Black Caucus; black liaison with Chicano & Asians Caucus; CA Tchrs Assn task force violence & vandal Sch; Life mem NAACP; found SNCC. **HONORS/ACHIEVEMENTS:** Coach of yr awd Woodrow Wilson Students 1975. **BUSINESS ADDRESS:** 135 Van Ness Ave, San Francisco, CA 94102.

YOUNG, ARCHIE R., II
Research chemist. **PERSONAL:** Born Jun 08, 1928, Camden, NJ; married Lena Hearo. **EDUCATION:** Lincoln U, AB Chem 1949;Univ of PA, MS Chem 1950;Univ of PA, PhD Phys Chem 1955. **CAREER:** Exxon Res & Engineering Co, sr rsrch chem; Thiokol Chem Corp, res chem 1956-67; TN A&I State U, asso prof chem 1954-56; VA Union U, instr chem 1951-52; Ft Valley State Coll, instr chem 1950-51. **ORGANIZATIONS:** Mem Am Inst of Chemists; mem AAAS; Montclair Bd Educ 1965-70; Alpha Phi Alpha Frat. **HONORS/ACHIEVEMENTS:** Recip Rohm & Haas Flwshp 1952-53; flw Am Inst Chemist; Sigma Xi 1954f Phi Lambda Upsion 1953. **BUSINESS ADDRESS:** PO Box 8, Linden, NJ 07036.

YOUNG, BARBARA J.
Educator. **PERSONAL:** Born Nov 02, 1937, Muskogee, OK; daughter of Major Alonzo Dossett and Idessa (Hammond) Dossett; married Douglas Charles Young, Jr; children: Crystal Marion Humphrey, Hammond George Bouldin, Danielle Humphrey. **EDUCATION:** CSUS, BA Soc Psychology 1977, MS Counseling 1981, EdD Admin 1988. **CAREER:** Fresno State Univ Fresno, sec 1967-69; California State Univ at Sacramento, exec asst pres 1969-74, employment counselor 1974-77, financial aid officer 1977-83, student affairs officer, asst dir school relations 1983-86; California State Univ, asst dean 1986-. **ORGANIZATIONS:** Mem WASFA 1977-, Black Professional Assn, SPAC, Delta Sigma Theta Sorority Nu Lambda 1977-, Sacramento Urban League 1970-; PACROW. **HOME ADDRESS:** 3707 Livingston Dr, Ste 301, Long Beach, CA 90803. **BUSINESS ADDRESS:** Assistant Dean, The California StateUniv, 400 Golden Shore Dr, Long Beach, CA 90802.

YOUNG, CARLENE (NEE HERB)
Social psychologist, educator. **PERSONAL:** Born in Selma, AL; divorced; children: Howard, Loren. **EDUCATION:** Univ of Detroit, MA 1960; Wayne State Univ Detroit, EdD 1967; Wright Inst Berkeley CA, PhD 1976. **CAREER:** San Jose State Univ CA, prof clinical psych 1969-; Univ of Detroit-Wayne State Univ, lectr ed psy/ed soc 1966-69; Oakland Comm Coll Farmington MI, dept chmn soc 1968; Title III Lincoln Child Devel Center Inkster MI, proj dir 1967; Natl Teacher Corp, team leader 1966-67; Detroit Public School, teacher 1955-67. **ORGANIZATIONS:** Consult Dept of Def Race Rel Inst 1976-78; consult PMC 1978-79; consult Koba Asso Washington DC 1979; bd of dir Catholic Social Serv 1976-; vice pres CA Black Fac & Staff Assn 1977; exec sec/v Chmn/chair elect Nat Counc of Black Studies 1978 1980; consult Psych Assessment Law Enf Officers; adv comm CA State Personnel Bd Psych. **HONORS/ACHIEVEMENTS:** Ed "Black Experience analysis & synthesis" Leswing Press San Rafael CA 1972; Intl Who's Who Comm Serv 1978-80; Comm Ldrs & Noteworthy Am 1978-; hon soc Phi Kappa Phi; mem Alpha Kappa Alpha Sor; Travel Africa (Cameroon/Senegal/Ivory Coast/Ghana/Mali/Somalia/Egypt) & Europe & Mexico.

YOUNG, CHARLES, JR.
Educational administrator. **PERSONAL:** Born Aug 05, 1934, St Louis, MO; married Jessie Dolores Howell; children: Karen. **EDUCATION:** Lincoln Univ MO, BS Ed 1957; Univ IL, Med 1962, EdD 1972. **CAREER:** St Louis Public School, teacher 1957-66, asst prin 1966-67, prin 1967-72; Urbana Comm School, prin 1972-1984; Joliet Public School, asst supt 1984-. **ORGANIZATIONS:** Mem Am Assc Sch Admn, Phi Delta Kappa 1964-, Kappa Alpha Psi 1952-, Rotary Intrntl 1985. **HONORS/ACHIEVEMENTS:** Serv awrd Natl Assc Scndry Sch Prncpls 1966; ldrshp awrd Champaign Co Boys Clb 1978. **MILITARY SERVICE:** AUSR capt. **HOME ADDRESS:** 2650 Black Rd, Joliet, IL 60435. **BUSINESS ADDRESS:** Assistant Superintendent, Joliet Public Sch, 420 N Raynor, Joliet, IL 60435.

YOUNG, CHARLES ALEXANDER
University educator. **PERSONAL:** Born Nov 17, 1930, NYC, NY; son of Charles A Young Sr and Mary Roders Young; married Elizabeth Bell; children: Paula D. **EDUCATION:** Hampton Univ, BS 1953; NY Univ, MA 1959; Catholic Univ, advance work in art 1964. **CAREER:** Dayton St Sch Newark, art tchr 1957-59; Fayetteville State Univ NC, art instr 1959-62; TN A&I State Univ TN, art asst prof of art 1962-68; Federal City Coll DC, art assoc prof 1968-78; Univ of the Dist of Columbia, prof of art 1978-. **ORGANIZATIONS:** Chairperson of art Fed City Coll 1970-78; chairperson of art Univ of the Dist of Columbia 1978-84; mem Coll Art Assn 1970-; mem Amer Artists Assn 1968-70; mem Natl Educ Assn 1975; mem Southeastern Art Assn 1965-66-68-77; mem Nashville Artist Guild 1964-68; mem Smith-Mason Gallery Washington 1970-; mem DC Commn on the Arts Visual Arts Panel 1973-79; mem Natl Conf of Artists 1974-75-80-83; mem DC Commn of the Arts (1980 design panel) 1981-82; mem The Graphics Soc 1980; mem Natl Art Educ Assn 1980-89; mem DC Art Alliance of Greater Washington 1977; mem US Soc for Educ through Art 1978; College Art Assoc 1988-; Nat'l Conference of Artists 1986-87. **HONORS/ACHIEVEMENTS:** Le Centre d'Art-Haiti 1982; Corcoran Gall of Art-DC 1982; numerous group and one person exhibitions; UDC Faculty Art Exhibition-Alma Thomas Meml Art Gallery Shaw Jr HS Washington 1983, Marble Arch Gallery Regional Art Exhibition Charleston SC 1983; numerous publs & public collections including, paintings reproduced "Black Dimensions in Contemporary Art" compiled by Edward Atkinson, public collections, Fayetteville State Coll Fayetteville NC, Scottish Bank, Fayetteville NC, Kennedy Inst, Washington DC; Register of US Living Artists 1968, Black Art in Washington Washingtonian Mag 1973; published articles, Haitian Art Newsletter Vol 1 #6 Fall edition 1978 "African Odyssey" by Charles Young; Metro-Washington Mag March 1984 "Mainstream, A Place For Afro-Amer Artists?" by Charles Young; to be published UDC Afro-Amer Art Catalog titled "Van Ness Campus Art Collection 1984" introduction by Charles Young; MLK Library-DC 1986; Paintings Purchase Freddie Mac Corp Art Collection 1988; Afro-American Art Exhibition 1988; A Tribute To Washinhgton Area Artists 1988; Paintings Purchase Univ of Dist of Columbia Art Collection 1983; Black Image Exhibition Univ of District of Columbia Art Gallery, 1988. **MILITARY SERVICE:** AUS 1st lt 1953-55; Overseas Decoration. **HOME ADDRESS:** 8104 W Beach Dr NW, Washington, DC 20012.

YOUNG, CHARLES EDWARD
Athlete. **PERSONAL:** Born Feb 05, 1951, Fresno, CA; married Colleen; children: Charles II, Candace Euphrates. **EDUCATION:** Univ So CA, BA. **CAREER:** San Francisco 49ers, tight end present; LA Rams 1977-79; Philadelphia Eagles 1973-77. **ORGANIZATIONS:** Ordained minister active in charity work. **HONORS/ACHIEVEMENTS:** Consensus All-Am 1972; Top Pass Catching End in USC History; Hula Bowl; Coaches' All-Am & Coll All Stars; NFL Rookie of Yr 1973; All Pro 1974-75; Pro Bowl 1973-75. **BUSINESS ADDRESS:** Seattle Seahwaks, 5305 Lake Washington Blvd, Kirkland, WA 98033.

YOUNG, CHARLES LEMUEL, SR.
Business executive. **PERSONAL:** Born Aug 27, 1931, Lauderdale County; married Doretha Connor; children: Charles L Jr, Deidre, Arthur, Veldora. **EDUCATION:** TN A&T Univ, BS Business Admin 1948-51; Univ of Denver, Public Relations; Human Develop Inst. **CAREER:** TV-3 WLBT, vice pres; Royal Oak Develop Co, pres; Young's Const Co, pres; EF Young Jr Mfg, pres; MS Legislature, mem. **ORGANIZATIONS:** Exec comm & co-founder MS Action for Progress; past bd mem Inst of Politics; life mem NAACP; past dir Meridian Chamber of Commerce; past dir State Mutual Fed Savings & Loan. **MILITARY SERVICE:** AUS sgt 1st class 2 yrs; Bronze Star; Good Conduct Medal; Korean Citation. **HOME ADDRESS:** 3120 15th St, Meridian, MS 39301. **BUSINESS ADDRESS:** President, EF Young Jr Mfg Co, 500 25th Ave, Meridian, MS 39301.

YOUNG, CHARLIE, JR.
Elected city official. **PERSONAL:** Born Apr 28, 1928, Leary, GA; married Kathryn Robinson; children: Gail Y Smith, Aaron Lee, Valerie Y Pittman. **EDUCATION:** Leary School, 10th grade. **CAREER:** Presently City Councilman. **HOME ADDRESS:** PO Box 143, Leary, GA 31762.

YOUNG, CLARENCE, III
Performer & administrator. **PERSONAL:** Born Apr 07, 1942, Dayton, OH. **EDUCATION:** Capital Univ, BA 1979. **CAREER:** Playwright Theatre W Dayton OH, dir 1968-82; Clarence Young III Production, independent producer, TV production 1982-; Ellison Sr Citizen Center, dir. **ORGANIZATIONS:** Independent TV producer, Clarence Young III 1982-; pres Clarence Young III Productions 1981-; pres-publisher Young Sound Music BMI 1981-; master mason Prince Hall Lodge Equity Lodge 121 1983. **HONORS/ACHIEVEMENTS:** Outstanding Independent producer & TV editor, 1984 Access 30 Dayton, OH 1984; "I Am A Young Lady" Playwright Musical Dayton Art Inst 1981. **MILITARY SERVICE:** USAF a2c 1961-65. **BUSINESS ADDRESS:** Dir, Ellison Senior Citizen Ctr, 2412 W Third St, Dayton, OH 45417.

YOUNG, COLEMAN A.
Mayor. **PERSONAL:** Born May 24, 1918, Tuscaloosa, AL. **EDUCATION:** Hon Doctorates, Univ of MI, Stillman Coll, Univ of Detroit, Wayne State Univ, Central State Univ. **CAREER:** MI Constitutional Conv, del 1961-62; State of MI, senator 1964-73; former ins executive; Chain of Dry Cleaners, mgr; City of Detroit, mayor 1974-. **ORGANIZATIONS:** Involved in early organizing battles of UAW; took a leadership role in the Wayne Co CIO & combined civil rights & labor activities as exec sec Natl Negro Labor Council; vice chmn Democratic Natl Comm 1977-81; pres US Conf of Mayors 1982-83. **HONORS/ACHIEVEMENTS:** First black to serve on Democratic Natl Comm 1968; Jefferson Awd from the Amer Inst for Public Serv for the Greatest Public Serv performed by an elected or apptd official 1979; NAACP Spingarn Medal for Distinguished Achievement as an Afro-Amer 1981; 1982 Adam Clayton Powell Awd for Outstanding Polit Leadership from Congressional Black Caucus. **MILITARY SERVICE:** USAC commissioned officer WW II. **BUSINESS ADDRESS:** Mayor, City of Detroit, 1126 City County Bldg, Detroit, MI 48226.

YOUNG, COLEMAN MILTON, III
Physician. **PERSONAL:** Born Nov 13, 1930, Louisville, KY; children: C Milton IV, Lloyd M, Christopher H. **EDUCATION:** Univ of Louisville, AB 1952; Meharry Med Coll, MD 1961. **CAREER:** Louisville Genl Hosp, intern 1961-62; St Joseph's Infirmary, resd 1962-65; Methadone Treatment Prog, fndr dir 1968-72; Private Practice, physician internal medicine. **ORGANIZATIONS:** Chmn bd mem Park DuValle Neighborhood Health Center 1966-69; Gov Young Kentuckian's Adv Commn 1967-70; mem Louisville Jeffers on Co Air Pollution Control Bd 1968-77, chmn 1968-72; med Adv SSS 1968-73; mem Hon Order KY Col 1972; mem dir Drug Abuse Prog River Region Mental Health Bd 1972-73; med dirComm Hospital 1972-75; consult drug prog River Region Mental Health Bd 1973-74; Gov Cncl Alcohol & Drug Abuse 1973; consult Senate Com Juv Prob 1973; memAlpha Phi Alpha; AMA; life mem NAACP; editor bd chmn Black Scene Mag 1974-76; pres Falls City Med Soc 1982-85. **HONORS/ACHIEVEMENTS:** Louisville Man Yr Awd WHAS TV 1970; natl adv Amer Assn Med Asst 1976-77; Disting Citizen Awd Key to City Mayor Harvey I Sloane 1977. **MILITARY SERVICE:** AUS MC corpl 1952-54. **BUSINESS ADDRESS:** 250 East Liberty St, Louisville, KY 40202.

YOUNG, DEBORA HOLMES
Assoc. executive. **PERSONAL:** Born Jun 10, 1950, Asheville, NC; divorced. **EDUCATION:** VA State Univ, Health & PE 1968-71; Univ NC, Biol & Math 1971-72; Asheville-Buncombe Tech, Data Processing 1982. **CAREER:** Puritain Fashions, corp traffic mgr 1972-75; Boys' Club of Asheville, group spec 1975-76; Diletante "Exclusively Yours", owner/pres 1984-; Asheville Bd ofAlcoholic Control, admin asst 1976-. **ORGANIZATIONS:** Admin asst Asheville Bd of Alcoholic Control 1976-. **HONORS/ACHIEVEMENTS:** Pres WOFFS Amer Assoc Black Women Entrepreneurs Inc 1985; treas Greater Asheville Chap Amer Business Womens Assoc 1982; vice chmn Black Bus & ProflLeague 1985; 1st woman hired in system/1st black woman asst mgr, 1st black admin asst in Asheville System Asheville Bd of Alcoholic Control. **HOME ADDRESS:** PO Box 15689, Asheville, NC 28813-0689.

YOUNG, DOC See YOUNG, A. S.

YOUNG, EDDYE VIVIAN PIERCE
Educator, singer. **PERSONAL:** Born May 02, 1947, Fort Worth, TX; married Lawrence W Young Jr; children: Lisa Michelle. **EDUCATION:** Univ of CO Boulder, MusB 1969, MusM 1973. **CAREER:** San Carlos Baptist Church, minister of music 1971-74; San Mateo Elementary School Dist, title one tutor 1971-75; San Jose State Univ, asst prof music 1973-76; San Francisco Spring Opera, soloist 1975; San Francisco Brown Bag Opera, soloist 1974-76; San Francisco Merola Oper Program, soloist 1976; Miami Univ, assoc prof music 1976-84; professional opera singer 1979-; PA State Univ, visiting lecturer music 1984-. **HONORS/ACHIEVEMENTS:** Florence Bruce Awd San Francisco Oper Natl Finals 1976; 1st Pl Vocal Symphony of New World Lincoln Ctr 1977; Faculty Enrichment Grant Graz Austria Miami Univ Amer Inst of Mus Studies 1977; NY Recital Debut Carnegie Hall 1979; Grant from Metro Oper Natl Council 1980,84; Second NY Recital Merkin Concert Hall 1982; Soloist Dayton Opera 1983; soloist (ntl & interntl) Gershwin by Request 1986-88; performances in Cagliari, Sardinia, Italy 1987. **BUSINESS ADDRESS:** Visiting Lecturer, Pennsylvania StateUniv, Music Dept, 225 Music Bldg, University Park, PA 16801.

YOUNG, EDITH MAE
Educator. **PERSONAL:** Born Oct 15, 1932, Denison, TX; daughter of Joe C Young Sr (deceased) and Pinkie Rambo Franklin. **EDUCATION:** TX Coll, Certificate, Sec Sci 1951; Lincoln Univ MO, BSE 1961, MEd 1964; Univ of MO Columbia, EdD 1973. **CAREER:** Library, Lincoln U, MO, sec/admin asst 1951-66; Education & Center for Research in Social Behavior, Univ of MO Columbia, intern/voc tchr 1973; Center for Acad Devel UMSL, acting dir 1977-80; Educ Business Tchr Educ, instructor/asst prof 1966-70, 1973-77, 1980-; Univ of MO, St Louis, assoc prof of educ. **ORGANIZATIONS:** Mem Delta Pi Epsilon 1970-; mem Kappa Delta Pi 1972-; mem Pi Lambda Theta 1973-; mem AAHE 1967-; mem AVA 1966-; mem NBEA 1962-; mem Alpha Kappa Alpha Sor 1967; educator examiner, National Accrediting Commission of Cosmetology Arts & Sciences 1985-; editorial advisory bd, Collegiate Press 1989-90. **HONORS/ACHIEVEMENTS:** EPDA Doctoral Fellowship in Voc Educ 1971-73; ACE Fellow in Acad Admin 1979-80; Summer Faculty Research Fellowship UMSL 1975. **BUSINESS ADDRESS:** Associate Professor of Educ, U of MO, St Louis, 8001 Natural Bridge Rd, St Louis, MO 63121.

YOUNG, EDWARD HIRAM, JR.
Elected official, meteorologist. **PERSONAL:** Born Dec 10, 1950, Berkeley, CA; son of Edward Hiram Young Sr and Grace Jean King Young (deceased). **EDUCATION:** San Jose State Univ, BS Meteorology 1973, 2 yrs grad work in meteorology; N Harris Co Coll, courses in mgmt & business 1983-84. **CAREER:** Natl Weather Svcs, meteorologist intern Portland, OR 1975-78; Riverside CA, agricultural meteorologist 1978-81; Ctr Weather Serv FAA Houston TX, aviation meteorologist 1981-84; Natl Weather Serv Southern Region, prog mgr 1981-87; Ft Worth TX S Region, spec serv met TX 1984-86; Natl Weather Svc, agri/forestry meteorologist 1986-, Pacific Region Headquarters, Honolulu HI, Technical Services Division, chief 1988-. **ORGANIZATIONS:** Mem bd dirs San Jose Chap Amer Red Cross 1970-72; mem Natl Coll Student Adv Council Amer Red Cross 1971-72; Black prog mgr Natl Weather Serv Wrn Reg 1978-81; mem bd of dirs Great Outdoors 1980-81; mem Amer Assn for the Advancement of Sci 1980; Black prog mgr Natl Weather Serv Srn Region 1981-; mem Amer Meteorological Soc 1970-; mem bd on Women & Minorities Amer Meteorological Soc 1985-87, chmn 1989-90; mem subcommittee Ft Woth United Way Allocations 1986; consultant SMART(Science, Mathematics, Aeronautics, Research, Technology & The Black Family) 1989; aux bd mem asst Bahai Faith of Hawaiian Islands 1988. **HONORS/ACHIEVEMENTS:** Elks Leadership Awd Oakland CA Elks Club 1968; EEO Awd Natl Oceanic & Atmospheric Admin 1984; Dallas-Ft Worth Federal Exec Bd EEO Awd 1986; Presented a paper at SMART Conf, Howard Univ, Blacks in Meteorology 1989. **HOME ADDRESS:** 733 Bishop St, Suite 170-123, Honolulu, HI 96813.

YOUNG, ELIZABETH BELL
Consultant, lecturer. **PERSONAL:** Born Jul 02, 1929, Durham, NC; married Charles A, Jr. **EDUCATION:** NC Central U, BA 1948, MA 1950; OH St U, PhD 1959. **CAREER:** Catholic Univ, graduate school prof 1966-79; Barber Scotia Coll NC, Talladega Coll AL, VA State Coll, OH State Univ, FL A&M Univ, Fayetteville State Univ NC, Howard Univ Wash DC, Univ of the DC Dept English & Communications, univ prof & chmn 1949-84; Natl & Intl Organizations & Universities, consultant & lecturer. **ORGANIZATIONS:** Staff aide US House of Reps (Office of Congressman Walter E Fauntroy) 1980; lecturer & Consultant US Govt (Office of Ed) 1981-83; field reader & team reviewer US St Dept 1980-83; mem US St Dept (Public Mem Asso) 1979-; mem bd of dir Washington Ctr Music Thrpy Clinic; mem adv bd United Negro Clg Fund 1979-82; mem Congressional Adv B D on Educ 1979-82; mem Alpha Kappa Alpha Sor 1946-; bd mem Clinical Cert Am Speech-l H Asso 1979-83; bd dir Handicapped Intervention Prog for High Risk Infants Wash DC 1978-87. **HONORS/ACHIEVEMENTS:** Flw Am Speech, Lang, Hearing Asso 1980; Otstndng Alumni Awd OH StUniv 1976; publ Journal Articles in Field of Communications & Made Over 250 Speeches; listed in Over 25 Biographies Whos Who in US, Whos Who Among Am Women, Dictionary of Intl Biography, Two Thousand Women of Achievement, Directory of Distinguished Americans, World Whos Who of Women 1959-87. **HOME ADDRESS:** 8104 W Beach Dr N W, Washington, DC 20012. **BUSINESS ADDRESS:** Consultant and Lecturer, Natl & Intrl Organ & Univ, 8104 W Beach Dr N W, Washington, DC 20012.

YOUNG, ELMER, JR.
Business executive. **PERSONAL:** Born Jul 04, 1924, Phila; married Thelma; children: Victor, Vincent. **EDUCATION:** Temple U, BS 1952. **CAREER:** 1st PA Bank, sr vice pres 1970-; Dillingham Corp, proj mgr 1969-70; Progress Plaza Shopping Cntr , proj mgr cntr mgr 1968-69; Rev Dr Leon H Sullivan, asst 1965-69; IBM Corp, admin mgr 1957-65; broker real estate ins 1952-56. **ORGANIZATIONS:** Mem Philadelphia Urban League; Comm Devel Fund; v chmn United Fund 1976; Philadelphia Counc Comm Advance. **HONORS/ACHIEVEMENTS:** Exemplor awrd NAACP 1975; publs Corporate Soc Accounting Praeger Pub 1973f Real Estate Today Nat Inst Real Estate Brokers 1971. **MILITARY SERVICE:** AUS s/sgt 1946. **BUSINESS ADDRESS:** 15 & Chestnut Sts, Philadelphia, PA 19101.

YOUNG, ELROY
Physician. **PERSONAL:** Born Jan 07, 1923, RSD Olmstead, IL; married Walter Gertrude Chisholm; children: Janice Lansey, Charles. **EDUCATION:** Univ of Illinois, BS 1947; Meharry Medical College, MD 1951. **CAREER:** Self-employed medical doctor; Freedmen's Hospital, resident 1953-57; Lincoln Hospital, resident 1952-53; Lincoln Hospital, intern 1951-52. **ORGANIZATIONS:** Mem Baltimore County Medical Soc; Medical Chirugical Faculty; Southern Medical Assn; Natl Medical Assn; Maryland Orthopeadic Soc; pres Baltimore County Hillmont Improvement Assn; grand chaplin Chi Delta Mu Fraternity 1989-; treasurer Maryland Medical Assn 1989-. **MILITARY SERVICE:** AUS non-commissioned officer 1943-46. **BUSINESS ADDRESS:** 3200 Elgin Ave, Baltimore, MD 21216.

YOUNG, ERNESTINE
Field representative, clerical aids, radio operator. **PERSONAL:** Born Dec 15, 1918, Brooksville, OK; daughter of Corrie Earl Ervin and Lelia Jones Ervin; married Carl Richard Young, Aug 29, 1937 (deceased); children: Winfield, Joyce, Carl, Clifford, Virgil, Kathryn, Sylvester, Maurice, Carolyn, Michael. **EDUCATION:** Seminole Jr Coll, AA 1972; OB Univ, Shawnee, OK, 1973-75. **CAREER:** Action Inc, consultant 1980-81; Green Thumb Inc, area leader; Fay Hudson, Shawnee, OK, clerical aids radio dispatcher, 1985-89. **ORGANIZATIONS:** Field rep Action Inc 1970; worothy council Lilly of the Valley Court 1972; town clerk Town of Brooksville 1979; mem Mayors Council on Aging 1976-85. **HONORS/ACHIEVEMENTS:** Clerks Annual Training Certificate Commission for Training 1974-84; An Honored Oklahoman Dir of Human Serv 1984. **BUSINESS ADDRESS:** Clerical, Radio dispatcher, Green Thumb Inc, 401 N Bell, Shawnee, OK 74801.

YOUNG, F. CAMILLE
Dental director. **PERSONAL:** Born Sep 03, 1928, Boston; married Dr Virgil J. **EDUCATION:** Howard Univ, BS 1949; Howard Univ, DDS 1958; Univ of MI, MPH 1974. **CAREER:** Comm Group Hlth Found, chf of dental serv 1971-; Div of Dental Health Bureau of Hlth Resources Devel Dept of HEW, consultant, 1971-74; Comm Group Health Found, staff dentist 1969-71; DC Dept of Public Health, dental officer 1964-69; Private Practice, Washington DC, 1962-; Amer Fund for Dental Health, elected 5 yr term bd trsts 1972-; Howard Univ Coll of Dentistry, asst prof 1971-. **ORGANIZATIONS:** Vice pres, Robert T Freeman Dental Soc 1970-72; first woman to attain ofc mem Exec Bd 1966-72; chmn Speakers Bureau 1968-72; chmn Budget & Auditing Com 1968-70; chmn Social Com 1966-70; chmn Awards Com 1970; mem DC Dental Soc; chmn Table Clinic Com 1970; sec Dental Health Care Com 1968; mem Natl Dental Assn; pres, asst 1968-73; area dir Dentistry as a Career Prog Recruit Com 1968-73; chmn Protocol Com 1968, 1973; del Lse of Dels 1969-73; Nat Dental Assn Amer & Dental Assn Liaison Com 1968-73; chmn Travel Com 1970-73; mem

Howard Univ Dental Alumni Assn; exec sec 1967-69; mem exec bd 1967-69; mem Am Dental Assn 1965-; Amer Public Health Assn 1972-; Natl Assn of Neighborhood Health Cntrs 1972-; Assn of Amer Women Dentists 1974-. **HONORS/ACHIEVEMENTS:** Appeared on TV lectr & spkr at many schs & colls; recipient, Pres' Award Natl Dental Assn 1969; special award Natl Dental Assn 1973; represented Amer Dental Assn at First Black Women's Inst 1972 Hunger Convocation Amer Hotel NY; del White House Conf on Children 1970; co-authored article in Urban Health Dentistry in OEO Health Prog 1972. **BUSINESS ADDRESS:** 3308 14 St NW, Washington, DC.

YOUNG, GEORGE, JR. (TOBY)
Coordinator. **PERSONAL:** Born Oct 13, 1933, Gadsden, AL; married Joanne Tilman; children: Kathy Ann, Carrie Vernell Marie, Dorthy Louise. **EDUCATION:** Lincoln Univ, MHS 1984. **CAREER:** From Where I Sit, True Gospel, WTPA TV, writer producer, MC; Harrisburg Glass Inc, affirm act coord 1952-68; Toby Young Show, Echos of Glory, Jazz Today WKBO Radio, staff announcer, hosted, producer 1965-71; Toby Young Enterprise, affirm act coord 1971-; TY Records, affirm act coord 1971-72; Toby Young Show, Party Line, Echoes of Glory, Project People WCMB Radio, comm rel spec 1971-. **ORGANIZATIONS:** Life mem NAACP; mem bd Camp Curtin YMCA, Harristown Comm Complex; bd mem Tri-County March of Dimes; chrpsn 1976 Edgemont Fire House; pres PA Chap Natl Assoc of Radio & TV Artists; bd mem Gaudinzia House; past co-chrpsn Congress of Affirm Action; past chmn, bd of mgrs, owners Soulville & Jay Walking Records; bd mem Natl Progressive Affirm Action Officers; mem Daughin Cty Exec Comm of Drug & Alcohol Inc, Chosen Friend Lodge 43 F&AM Prince Hall Club 21 of Harrisburgh PA. **HONORS/ACHIEVEMENTS:** Citation Partic in Intl Trade Fair rep the USA, US Dept of Ag 1956; Gold Mike Awd Outstanding Serv in the Comm AME Churches 1969; Cited Outstanding Svcwith Youth & Adults in the Comm Lt Gov Raymond Broderick 1970; Youth Achievement Awd Camp Curtin YMCA 1971; Achievement Awd Black Businessmen Assoc of Harrisburg Inc 1972; Citation by the House of Rep Commonwealth of PA 1972; Gold Cert Awd OIC 1972; Hon Alumni Awd Harrisburgh School Dist 1972; Awd of Merit New Voices of Harrisburg 1974; Diplomat Jaycees Concern for Fellowman Awd 1974; Outstanding Citizen Awd Sibletown Civic Assoc 1975; Cert of Leadership 1976; Chmn Awd Tri-Cty March of Dimes 1976; Citation by the House of Rep Commonwealth of PA 1976; Citation Camp Curtin YMCA chmn membership enrollment 1976; Citation from the Senate of PA acclaiming Echoes of Glory 1984; The Laymens League of St Pauls Baptist Church 1983; The Anointed Sisters of Hope 1983; Gabriel Hardman Delegation Spec Dedication Awd Comm 1979; Amer Red Cross Awd for Assisting small crafts comm 1982; Carlisle Area OIC Awd for public relations for church & civic news 1981; Camp Curtin Br YMCA Chmn Awd Out-Going Chair 1980; 5th Masonic Dist of the Most Worshipful Prince Hall Grand Lodge of PA. **MILITARY SERVICE:** AUS 2 yrs USAR 4 1/2 yrs. **BUSINESS ADDRESS:** Affirm Action Coordinator, PN Civil Serv Commission, 3rd & State Sts, Harrisburg, PA 17105.

YOUNG, HERMAN A.
Educator. **PERSONAL:** Born Jul 29, 1929, Memphis; married Barbara Jean Hicks; children: Russell, Tonya, Gail, Stuart. **EDUCATION:** TN State U, BS 1952; IN U, MS 1970;Univ of Louisville, EdS 1973; IN U, EdD 1973. **CAREER:** Univ of Louisville, asst prof natural scis dir west louisville educ prog; Grad Black Studies Inst, asst dir 1971; Lincoln Sch Simpsonville, head sci dept 1969-70; Tubetek Inc, plant owner pres 1962-65; Budcoe Inc, plant mgr vice pres 1958-62; Dumont Labs, chem engr 1952-56; Thomas Electronics Inc, chem engr 1956-58. **ORGANIZATIONS:** Mem Phi Delta Kappa; Am Assn of Higher Edn; Am Assn for Advncmnt of Sci; Am Pers & Guid Assn; KY Acad of Sci; Nat Orgn of Black Chemists & Engrs; Am Chem Soc; Sigma XI; NY Acad of Scis; sec Balck owned Louisville Mutual Savings & Loan Assn 1960-; bd mem W Louisville Devel Corp 1974-; bd of dir St Mary & Elizabeth Hosp 1977; Task Force mem Whitney Youn Sickle Cell Found; adv bd United Negro Coll Fund 1974-. **HONORS/ACHIEVEMENTS:** First black plant mgr vice pres of non-black plant in state of KY 1958-62; first black owner mgr Electronic Mfg Plant in state of KY 1962-65; co-author Scientists in the Black Perspective 1974; recip award for race rel Millington Naval Base 1971. **BUSINESS ADDRESS:** Coll of Arts and Sciences, Univ of Louisville, 2301 S Third St, Louisville, KY 40292.

YOUNG, IRA MASON
Attorney. **PERSONAL:** Born Sep 20, 1929, St Louis, MO; son of Nathan B Young and Mamie Young; married Lillie. **EDUCATION:** Oberlin Coll, BA 1951; WA Univ, JD 1957. **CAREER:** Private Practice, attorney 1957-. **ORGANIZATIONS:** Mem MO State Bd of Law Examiners 1980-84; mem Natl Bar Assn; Amer Bar Assn; Amer Trial Lawyers Assn; Lawyers Assn St Louis; St Louis Metro Bar Assn; Mound City Bar Assn; bd dir Legal Aid Soc 1965-70; Family & Childrens Serv Greater St Louis; adv cncl Legal Serv Corp MO; bd dir Girl Scout Council St Louis. **MILITARY SERVICE:** AUS 1951-53. **BUSINESS ADDRESS:** Attorney, 408 Olive, Ste 206, St Louis, MO 63102.

YOUNG, JAMES ARTHUR, III
Executive director. **PERSONAL:** Born Jan 06, 1945, Augusta, GA; married Felisa Perez. **EDUCATION:** Claflin Coll, AB 1967; Gable School of Art in Advancement, certificate, 1975. **CAREER:** Burke Co Bd of Educ Waynesboro, teacher 1967; Montgomery Co Bd of Educ Ailey GA, teacher 1967-68; CSRA Econ Oppor Auth Inc, task force leader 1970-71; Laney-Walker Mus Inc Augusta, exec dir 1976-. **ORGANIZATIONS:** Mem 2nd Shilo Baptist Church, Augusta 1957; mem Augusta Cultural Arts Assn 1977-80; mem Natl Trust for History Preservation 1979-80; mem Augusta-Richmond Co Music 1979-80; mem Greater Augusta Arts Council 1980; judge public school art contest Richmond Co Bd of Educ Augusta 1980; mem Seven-Thirty Breakfast Club Columbia, SC 1980. **HONORS/ACHIEVEMENTS:** Founder/dir Laney-Walker Music Inc 1977; nominee Comm for major traveling exhbn Nation of Ghana & Nigeria 1980-81; panelist Leadership Augusta/Greater Augusta Chamber of Commerce. **MILITARY SERVICE:** AUS E-2 1970-73; Hon Ret Disability. **BUSINESS ADDRESS:** Executive Dir, Laney Walker Music Inc, 821 Laney Walker Blvd, Augusta, GA 30901.

YOUNG, JAMES E.
Educator. **PERSONAL:** Born Jan 18, 1926, Wheeling, WV; son of James E Young (deceased) and Edna (Thompson) Young. **EDUCATION:** Howard U, BS, MS 1949; MIT, MS, PhD 1953; Harvard Univ Div Med Sci, 1984-86. **CAREER:** Hampton Inst, instr physics 1946-49; Gen Atominos, consult 1957-58; Univ MN, vstg assoc prof 1964; Sir Rudy Peierls Oxford, rsch asst 1965-66; Harvard, vstg rsch sci 1978; Los Alamos Sci Lab, staff mem 1956-59; Tufts Univ Med Schools, rsch assoc neurosci dept anatomy & cell biol 1986-; MIT, prof physics 1970-. **ORGANIZATIONS:** Mem Am Physiol Soc 1960-; Sigma Xi Hon Soc MIT 1953; post-doctoral fellow MIT Acoustics Lab 1953-55; Shell BP fellow Aeronautics Dept Southampton England 1956; NAS-NRC Ford fellow Niels Bohr Inst Copenhagen 1961-62; pres JEY Assoc; chief op officer MHT Ltd; tech dir CADEX; partner Escutcheon Inc. **HONORS/ACHIEVEMENTS:** US Patent #4,564,798 Jan 1986. **BUSINESS ADDRESS:** Professor Physics, MIT, 6-405/CTP, Cambridge, MA 02139.

YOUNG, JAMES E., JR.
Attorney. **PERSONAL:** Born Jul 18, 1931, New Orleans, LA; married Eddie Mae Wilson; children: James, III, Adrienne, Darrin. **EDUCATION:** So Univ Law Sch, JD 1960; So U, BA 1958. **CAREER:** Parish New Orelans, notary public 1962-; Private Practice, atty 1960-68; VA Reg Office, adjudicator 1966-68; NOLAC, neighborhood staff atty 1968-69; New Orleans Legal Ssst Corp, sr staff atty 1969-70, asst dir 1970-71; atty & notary public 1971-. **ORGANIZATIONS:** Mem LA State Bar Assn; Am Bar Assn; Am Judicature Soc; Louis A Martinet Legal Soc; spl consult & guest lectr SoUniv in New Orleans Evening Div; Poverty & Consumer Law Panelist & Symposium partic Tulane U; gen cousel Cntrl Cty Econ Oppor Corp; past pres & charter mem Heritage Sq Devel Corp; past pres & mem Lake Area Pub Sch Improvement Assn; past pres & ofcr Edward Livingston Middle Sch; lifetime mem Nat Bar Assn; Kappa Alpha Psi Frat; mem & former ofcr Acad Pk Devel Assn; past pres New Orleans Pan-Hellenic Coun; former mem & exec com Cntrl Cty Econ Oppor Corp. **HONORS/ACHIEVEMENTS:** Winner of 2 gold keys awards in natl art compet Nat Scholastic 1949 & 50; grad in top ten percent NCO Ldrshp & Motor Mechanics Sch USMC; contrbn & spl features editor coll newspaper; recip of Purple Heart. **MILITARY SERVICE:** USMC 1951-54; Purple Heart Medal. **BUSINESS ADDRESS:** Attorney at Law, 4624 Lafon Dr, New Orleans, LA 70126.

YOUNG, JAMES M., II
Marketing manager. **PERSONAL:** Born Oct 29, 1946, Washington, DC; married Barbara Ann Johnson; children: Julie Elizabeth, Jason Michael. **EDUCATION:** Fisk Univ Nashville, BA Biology 1968. **CAREER:** Serv Bur Co (Div Control Date Corp), mrktng mgr 1978-; F Serv Bur Co, proj adminstr educ 1977-78; Xerox Corp, mrktng rep 1971-74. **ORGANIZATIONS:** Mem Alpha Phi Alpha Frat 1965. **HONORS/ACHIEVEMENTS:** Recip vietnam aviation medal AUS 1968-71. **MILITARY SERVICE:** AUS cw2 1968-71. **BUSINESS ADDRESS:** Service Bureau Co, 222 S Riverside Plaza Ste 23, Chicago, IL 60606.

YOUNG, JEAN CHILDS
Educator. **PERSONAL:** Born Jul 01, 1933, Marion, AL; married Andrew J; children: Andrea, Lisa, Paula, Andrew III. **EDUCATION:** Manchester Coll Manchester, IN, BS 1954; Queens Coll Flushing, NY, MA 1961. **CAREER:** Thomasville GA Hartford CT Atlanta GA, teacher 1954-56, 1962-65; Teacher Corps Atlanta Public School & Univ of GA, teacher 1965-67; Central County Program Atlanta Public School, coord preschool & elem educ 1967-69; Atlanta Public School Sys, teacher 1969-72; Atlanta Jr Coll, instr special studies 1974-77; Atlanta Jr Coll, public relations officer 1974-77; Atlanta Jr Coll, title XI coord 1976-77; Children's Issues Self Employed, educ consultant lecturer. **ORGANIZATIONS:** Chprsn US Commn on Internatl Yr of the Child 1978-80. **HONORS/ACHIEVEMENTS:** "Bridging The Gap" pub by Atl Pub Schls 1969f US Commn Report on Internatl Yr of the Child 1980.

YOUNG, JOHN W.
Budget analyst. **PERSONAL:** Born Jun 18, 1927, Wash, DC; children: John, Dolores, Robert. **EDUCATION:** Univ NE, BEd 1965; Univ TX, MA 1973. **CAREER:** Dept Planning & Rsrch Cty of El Paso, planning tech 1971-73; planner 1973; Pub Adminstrn Ofc Mgmt & Budget Cty of El Paso, budget analyst. **ORGANIZATIONS:** Mem Intl Cty Mgmt Assn; Municipal Finan Ofcrs Assn; Assn of US Army; Smithsonian Assos bd dirs El Paso Comm Action Prgm adminstr com ch; bd dirs Family Serv El Paso 2d vp; pub serv div chmn United Way of El Paso. **HONORS/ACHIEVEMENTS:** US Army meritorious serv medal; bronze star medal; air medal; commend medal; sr parachutist badge. **MILITARY SERVICE:** AUS lt col 1945-70. **BUSINESS ADDRESS:** Office Management & Budget, City County, El Paso, TX 79901.

YOUNG, JOSEF A.
Psychotherapist. **PERSONAL:** Born Mar 24, 1941, Memphis, TN; married Dr Joyce Lynom Young; children: Jorald (deceased). **EDUCATION:** TSU,BS1962;MSU,Masters 1967;Univ of Tenn, Post Masters 1972;Southern Ill Univ at Carbondale, PhD 1981. **CAREER:** Mason, 1974- ; Alpha Phi Alpha, Vice Pres 1980; Center for Developmental Growth, Pres1980; Optimist Club International, Comm Chariman 1985. **ORGANIZATIONS:** Int'l Counseling Assn, Brd of Dir 1970; West Tenn Personnel and Guidance, Pres 1972-73; Black Psychologist Assn, 1983; Assoc of Black Psychologist, 1984- ;State Brd of Regents " How to teach the hard to learn student"; Tennessee Assoc of Counseling," Fetal Alcohol Syndrome and the Female Alcoholic" American Assocof Ethical Hypnosis. **MILITARY SERVICE:** Air Force Reserve, 1958-60. **HOME ADDRESS:** 5131 Ravensworth Dr, Memphis, TN 38109. **BUSINESS ADDRESS:** Senior Counselor, State Tech Inst at Memphis, 5983 Macon Cove, Memphis, TN 38134.

YOUNG, JOSEPH FLOYD, SR.
Administrative analyst, legislator. **PERSONAL:** Born Jul 15, 1927, Milledgeville, GA; married Ellen; children: Joseph Jr, Daryl, Allah, Jasper, Curtis, Cheryl. **EDUCATION:** Lansing Community College, Associates Degree. **CAREER:** Wayne County, commm; State of MI, rep. **ORGANIZATIONS:** Mem Nativity of Our Lord Church; life mem NAACP; co-chrpsn Gov Task Force Violence & Vandalism; past chmn Black Police Recruit Comm; chmn Detroit-Wayne County Criminal Justice Council; pres Detroit Consumer Credit Union; mem MI Comm on Crim Justice; comm Local 101 AFSCME; staff rep Coun 23; mem SEMCOG. **MILITARY SERVICE:** AUS pvt 1946-47. **HOME ADDRESS:** 3449 Seminole, Detroit, MI 48214.

YOUNG, JOYCE HOWELL
Physician. **PERSONAL:** Born Mar 22, 1934, Cincinnati, OH; divorced; children: C Milton Young IV, Lloyd M Young, Christopher H Young. **EDUCATION:** Fisk Univ, BA Zoology 1954; Womans Med Coll of PA, MD 1958; Miami Vly Hosp Dayton, OH, Cert Intrnshp 1959; Meharry Med Coll Hubbard Hosp, Cert Peds 1960, Cert Int Med 1961; Univ Louisville Chld Eval Ctr, Cert Grwth & Devel 1973. **CAREER:** Private Med Practice Lou KY, 1961-67; Univ Louisville Child Eval Ctr, ped devel spclst 1973-74; Park Duvalle Nghbrhd Hlth Ctr, med dir 1974-76; KY Dept of Human Resources, med cnsltnt 1984-. **ORGANIZATIONS:**

Mem Alpha Kappa Alpha Sorority 1952-, Falls City Medical Soc 1961-, Jefferson Cnty Med Scty 1962-, KY Med Assn 1962-, Lou Links, Inc 1965-80; financial sec 1980-, mem Shawnee Presbyterian Church 1973-; mem Lou Brd of Educ 1971-74, chrmn 1974; brd mem Lincoln Found 1974-; dir Continental Natl Bank of KY 1974-86; mem KY Human Rights Commn 1983-; mem American Medical Assoc; mem Syn Covenant Cabinet Ethnic Church Affairs 1983-86; treas KBPU 1983-; chmn Commn on Representation 1985-86; mem exec cncl Presby of Louisville 1986. **HONORS/ACHIEVEMENTS:** Apptmnt by governor KY Colonel 1962; Comm Serv Awrd Lou Links, Inc 1973-74, Alpha Kappa Alpha Sor 1974, Zeta Phi Beta 1975; series of articles on hlthBlack Scene Mag 1975. **HOME ADDRESS:** 739 S Western Pkwy, Louisville, KY 40211. **BUSINESS ADDRESS:** Medical Consultant, KY Cabinet Human Resources, 739 S Western Pkwy, Louisville, KY 40211.

YOUNG, LARRY
Government official. **EDUCATION:** Univ of MD College Park, attended 1967-71; Goddard Coll, BS Social Sci 1972. **CAREER:** Urban Environmental Affairs Natl Office Izaak Walton League of Amer, dir 1970-77; Young Beat Afro-Amer Newspaper, former columnist 1975-77; Ctr for Urban Environmental Studies, pres 1977-82; Morgan State Univ, asst prof polit sci 1978-79; Natl Black Caucus of State Legislators, exec dir 1979-82; MD General Assembly 39th Legislative Dist, chmn house environmental matters comm 1975-. **ORGANIZATIONS:** Chmn bd dirs Citizen's Democratic Action Orgn Inc; Baltimore Leadership Inc; chmn MD Health Convocation; chmn Health Roundtable; Isaak Walton League of Amer; co-chmn MD Conf on the Black Aged; legislative advisor Baltimore City Area Agency on Aging; New Shiloh Bapt Ch; Energy & Environmental Study Conf; bd dirs Univ of MD Med Systems; bd dirs/fndr Black Health Study Group. **HONORS/ACHIEVEMENTS:** People to Watch in 1983 selected by Baltimore Magazine Ed Bd; Concerned Citizens Awd Amer Cancer Soc MD State Div 1980; Statesman Awd Bethel AME Ch 1980; MPHA Awd MD Public Hlth Assn For Your Support on Health Legislation 1980; Comm Serv Awd Gamma Chap Chi Eta Phi Sor Inc 1979; Comm Serv Awd We Need Prayer Headquarters; Legislator of the Yr 1978 MD Public Interest Rsch Group; Statesman Awd Baltimore Baptist Ministers' Conf 1977; Natl Assn for Environmental Educ Annual Awd 1976; Who's Who in Amer Politics 1975-76; Outstanding Young Men in Amer 1975 ed; Distinguished Citizenship Awd State of MD 1972; Afro-Amer Newspaper Honor Roll Awd 1971. **BUSINESS ADDRESS:** State Delegate, MD Gen Assembly 39th Dist, 516 N Charles St, Ste 501, Baltimore, MD 21201.

YOUNG, LEON
Business executive. **PERSONAL:** Born Feb 10, 1924, Monroe, LA; son of Pete Young and Johnie Mae Elmo-Young; married Margaret M Dove, May 12, 1945; children: Denise, Sharlene. **CAREER:** CO Springs, city council 1973, vice mayor 1980; Young Janitorial Svcs, owner, 1955-. **ORGANIZATIONS:** Mem past pres Downtowners Civitan Intl Club; mem Minority Contractors of Region 8, Pioneer Mus Bd, Housing Authority Bd, Pikes Peak Regional Council of Govts, CO Springs Esquire Club, NAACP; mem CO Springs Utility Bd; chmn of Colorado Springs City Loan Comm; mem Minority Council of Arts; mem Old CO City Historical Soc; charter mem of the Negro Historical Assn of CO Springs. **HONORS/ACHIEVEMENTS:** Several awds CO Springs work in newly renovated Shooks Run a lower income area in CO Springs. **MILITARY SERVICE:** USN; Veteran Korean Conflict, WW II. **BUSINESS ADDRESS:** President, Young Janitorial Serv, 415 S Weber, Suite #5, Colorado Springs, CO 80903.

YOUNG, LIAS C.
Attorney. **PERSONAL:** Born Nov 21, 1940, Upshur Co, TX; married Rose Breaux; children: Victor, Kimberly, Phyllis. **EDUCATION:** Tyler Jr Coll; TX Sthrn U; TX Sthrn Univ Law Sch, JS 1965. **CAREER:** Ofc of Regional Counsel US Dept HUD, atty advsr 1968-76; Fed Nat Mortgage Assn, counsel 1976-; gen atty 1966-68; legal asst 1965. **ORGANIZATIONS:** Mem Fed Bar Assn; TX Bar Assn; past pres Ft Worth Chap Fed Bar Assn 1970-71; past sec 1966-68.

YOUNG, LIONEL WESLEY
Radiologist. **PERSONAL:** Born Mar 14, 1932, New Orleans, LA; son of Charles Henry Young and Ethel Johnson Young; married Florence Brown, Jun 24, 1957; children: Tina, Lionel Thomas, Owen. **EDUCATION:** Benedictine Coll, BS 1953; Howard Univ Coll of Medicine, MD 1957. **CAREER:** Univ of Rochester NY, radiology resident 1958-61; Children's Medical Ctr Akron, chmn of radiology; Northeastern Ohio Univ Coll of Medicine, chmn of radiology; Univ of Pittsburgh, Pittsburgh, PA, prof of radiolohgy & pediatrics 1975-84. **ORGANIZATIONS:** Pres Soc for Pediatric Radiology 1984-85; pres Pittsburgh Roentgen Soc 1985-86; mem Sigma Pi Phi, mem Alpha Omega Alpha; pres, Akron Pediatric Radiologists, Inc 1986-. **HONORS/ACHIEVEMENTS:** Caffey Awd Soc for Pediatric Radiology 1970; Distinguished Service Award, Howard Univ Coll of Medicine 1987; Distinguished Aluminus Award, Howard Univ 1989. **MILITARY SERVICE:** USN Med Corps lt comdr 1961-63. **BUSINESS ADDRESS:** Chairman of Radiology, Children's Medical Ctr, 281 Locust St, Akron, OH 44308.

YOUNG, MARECHAL-NEIL ELLISON
Educational administrator. **PERSONAL:** Born Sep 12, 1915, Palatka, FL; daughter of Rev George F Ellison DD and Mrs Ethel Urlene Ellison; married W Arthur; children: Hitomi Matthews, Kwon Riley. **EDUCATION:** Temple Univ, BSE 1935; Univ of PA, MA Sociology 1936, PhD Sociology 1944, MSW 1948, Post Grad Certificate (research) 1978. **CAREER:** William Penn HS Philadelphia School Dist, counselor 1942-45; Philadelphia Sch Dist, supr sec sch counseling 1945-51; Mayer Solzberger JH Philadelphia Sch Dist, principal 1951-63; Philadelphia Sch Dist, aux dist supt 1963, dist supt 1964-71, asso supt 1971-77; Moton Center for Independent Studies, fellow 1977-78; Univ of PA, sr research assoc 1978-82; Synod Minority Student Recruitment Proj, educ cons/indep research dir 1982-. **ORGANIZATIONS:** Educ sec Urban League of Pittsburgh 1938-42; youth counselor Nat Youth Admin 1935-38; lecturer/adjunct prof Univ of PA Sch of Social Work 1949-51; adjunct prof Prairie View A&M Coll 1949-70; adjunct prof Beaver Coll 1974-75; mem State Adv Comm on Mental health Mental Retardation 1972-85; mem Philadelphia Cnty Bd Mental Health/Mental Retardation 1968-82; mem bd of trustees Drexel Univ 1969-; mem bd of trustees Beaver Coll 1971-; mem advisory bd Church Related Coll Presbyterian Church USA 1968-85; educ chrmn AAUW Philadelphia Branch 1968-. **HONORS/ACHIEVEMENTS:** A Distinguishd Daughter of PA appointed by Governor Shapp 1972; mem Pres Nat Advisory Council on Supplementary Ctrs & Serv appointed by Pres Nixon Washington, DC 1971-74; Hon Degree Doctorate of Letters from Drexel Univ Philadelphia 1979; apptd Commissioner Revision of Philadelphia City Charter 1987; Mainstreaming and Minority Chilren 1978. **BUSINESS ADDRESS:** Director Synod Minor Student Project, Synod of the Trinity, 5428 Haverford Ave, Philadelphia, PA 19139.

YOUNG, MARGARET BUCKNER
Author, educator. **PERSONAL:** Born in Campbellsville, KY; widowed; children: Marcia Cantarella, Lauren Casteel. **EDUCATION:** KY State Coll, BA English French 1942; Univ of MN, MA Educ Psychology 1945. **CAREER:** KY State Coll, teacher; Spelman Coll Atlanta Univ, educ psychology; written sev children's books, First Book of Amer Negroes, The Picture Life of Martin Luther King Jr, The Picture Life of Ralphe Bunche, The Picture Life of Thurgood Marshall, Black Amer Ldrs Chmn, Whiteney M Young Jr Memorial Foundation. **ORGANIZATIONS:** Aptd to 28th Gen Assembly of UN as Alt Rep of US 1973; Mar 1974 went to Nigeria Ghana under cultural exchange prog of State Depts Bur of Educ & Cultural Affairs; visited Peoples Rep of China as mem of UNA-USA Nat Policy Panel on US-China Rela 1979; bd of visitors US Mil Acad 1979-81; mem Found Inc; elected to bd of dirs Philip Morris; NY Life Ins Co; Pub Policy Com of Advertising Council; dedicated USIS Whitney M Young Jr Library (meml to late husband); mem bd of trustees Lincoln Ctr for the Performing Arts & Metro Mus of Art. **BUSINESS ADDRESS:** Chairman, Whitney M Young, Jr, Memorial Foundation, Inc, 100 Park Ave, New York, NY 10017.

YOUNG, MARY E.
Educator. **PERSONAL:** Born Jun 05, 1941, Harlan, KY. **EDUCATION:** Detroit Bible Coll, BRE 1966; Eastern KY Univ, BA 1969; Eastern KY Univ, MA 1972; Univ of MI, ABD 1973-75. **CAREER:** Eastern KY Univ, counselor 1969-72; Univ of MI, counselor, lab practicum asst 1973-74, graduate teaching asst 1974-75; Washtenaw Comm Coll, counselor 1975-. **ORGANIZATIONS:** Mem Natl Ed Assoc 1975-, MI Ed Assoc 1975-, Washtenaw Comm Coll Ed Assoc 1975-; bd dir Circle Y Ranch Camp 1983-85; mem NAACP 1985-, Natl Black Child Inc 1985-86. **HONORS/ACHIEVEMENTS:** Outstanding Young Women in Amer 1975; World Who's Who Among Women 1979; Intl Who's Who Among Intellectuals 1979; Outstanding Faculty Awd Washtenaw Comm Coll 1984. **BUSINESS ADDRESS:** Counselor, Washtenaw Comm Coll, PO Box D-1, Ann Arbor, MI 48106.

YOUNG, N. LOUISE
Physician. **PERSONAL:** Born Jun 07, 1910, Baltimore, MD; married William Spencer. **EDUCATION:** Howard U, BS 1927; Howard U, MD 1930; Freedman's Hosp, Intern 1930-31; Provident Hosp, Resd 1940-45. **CAREER:** OB-GYN Prac, retired phys; S Baltimore Gen Hosp, vis ob; General N Charles Union Meml, asso staff gyn 1950-52; Provident Hosp, act chf ob asst chf OB exec com vis staff & ob-gyn 1940-52; MD Training Sch Girls, staff phys 1933-40; Mcculloh Planned Parenthd Clinic, clinician 1935-42; Women Morgan State Coll, phys 1935-40; Douglas HS, 1936-69. **ORGANIZATIONS:** Chmn First Aid & Evacuation of Negro Women & Children Nat Emerg MD Cncl Def 1941-; med adv com MD Planned Parenthd & March of Dimes 1969-71; mem AMA; NMA; Med & Chirurgical Faculty MD; del Baltimore Cty Med Assn 1969-72; mem Monumental Med Soc; vice pres 1969-71; mem Am Fertility Soc; MD OB-GYN Soc; Med Com Human Rights; life mem NAACP; IBPOE of WAKA Sor; CORE; mem MD Com passage Abort Law; chmn com Prevent Passage Steriliz Law; Afro-Am Hon Roll 1947; Baltimore Howard Alumni 1930; Philamathions 1935f MD Hist Soc 1975; AKA Heritage Servis-Woman in Med 1971. **HOME ADDRESS:** 3239 Powhatan Ave, Baltimore, MD 21216.

YOUNG, NANCY WILSON
Personnel officer. **PERSONAL:** Born May 01, 1943, Orangeburg, SC; married R Paul Young; children: Ryan Paul. **EDUCATION:** Clafin Coll, BS (Cum Laude) 1961-65; SC State Coll, 1966; George Peabody Coll, 1968; Univ of Miami, MEd 1969-70. **CAREER:** Wateree Elem School Lugoff SC, 3rd grade teacher 1965-67; Miller School Waldoboro ME, teacher 1968-69; Univ of Miami, grad adv 1969-70; Univ of Miami, asst dir of admiss 1970-. **ORGANIZATIONS:** Chmn TOEFL Rsch Comm ETS 1977-80; v chmn TOEFL Policy Council ETS 1977-80; exec comm TOEFL Policy Council ETS 1977-80; mem Alpha Kappa Alpha 1962-, Clafin Coll Alumni Assoc 1965-; consult CEEB Summer Inst The Coll Bd 1975-80; consult US State Dept for Visits to Africa & Trinidad 1979; mem Univ of Miami Alumni Bd of Dir 1984-87; mem adv bd Epilspsy Found of S FL 1984-85; mem Comm on Total Employment Chamber of Commerce 1984-85; mem Dades Employ the Handicapped Comm 1984-85. **HONORS/ACHIEVEMENTS:** Ford Found Fellowship 1968-69; listed in Outstanding Young Women of Amer 1974, Personalities of the South 1974. **BUSINESS ADDRESS:** Asst Dir of Admissions, Univ of Miami, Miami-Dade Community College, 11011 S W 104th St, Miami, FL 33176.

YOUNG, OLLIE L.
Newspaper operating executive. **PERSONAL:** Born Feb 08, 1948, Philadelphia, PA; married Reginald B Young; children: Stephanie D. **EDUCATION:** Tarkio Coll, BA 1970; Temple Univ, MBA 1977. **CAREER:** Temple Univ Health Sci Ctr, asst personnel dir 1972-77; Consolidated Rail Corp, personnel supervisor 1977-79; Ducat Associates, consultant 1979-81; The New York Times Regional, employee relations mgr 1981-84; Gannett Co Inc, human resources dir. **ORGANIZATIONS:** Mem Amer Mgmt Assoc 1984-; volunteer New Geth Bapt Church Tutorial Prog 1985-; prog chmn Newspaper Personnel Relations Assocs 1986-87; adv bd Somerset YMCA 1986-; mgmt consultant Somerset United Way; mem ASPA 1987. **HONORS/ACHIEVEMENTS:** Frank Tripp Awd Gannett Co 1985; Tribute to Women in Industry Twin Somerset & Union 1986. **BUSINESS ADDRESS:** Human Resources Dir, Gannett Co Inc, 1201 Rte 22 West, Bridgewater, NJ 08807.

YOUNG, PAULA E.
Educator. **PERSONAL:** Born Sep 20, 1957, Memphis, TN. **EDUCATION:** Memphis State Univ, BA 1978; Atlanta Univ, MPA 1981. **CAREER:** TN Dept of Human Svcs, social counselor 1978-79; US Rep Harold Ford, congressional intern 1980; Natl Assn for Equal Oppor in Higher Educ, asst dir grants/contracts clearinghouse 1981-83; Clark Coll, dir of rsch/proposal writer. **ORGANIZATIONS:** Mem Alpha Kappa Alpha Sor Inc; youth comm chair Natl Council of Negro Women 1982-83; mem Natl Assn of Negro Business & Professional Womens Clubs 1986-87; mem Toastmasters Intl 1986-; fundraising consultant CARE Inc 1986-87. **HONORS/ACHIEVEMENTS:** Woodrow Wilson Natl Fellow 1981-83; Outstanding Young Women of Amer 1982; Woodrow Wilson Natl Fellow 1985-87; Who's Who Among Amer Women 1986-87. **BUSINESS ADDRESS:** Dir of Rsch/Proposal Writer, Clark College, 240 Brawley Dr SW, Atlanta, GA 30314.

YOUNG, PERRY H.
Chief pilot, retired. **PERSONAL:** Born Mar 12, 1919, Orangeburg, SC; married Shakeh. **EDUCATION:** Oberlin Coll; Howard U; Spartan Sch of Aeronautics; Am Flyers Ft Worth, TX. **CAREER:** Tuskegee Inst, flight instr 1941-54; Port Au Prince Haiti, fixed base operator 1946-48; SHADA Haiti, corp pilot 1949-53; PRWRA PR, corp pilot 1953-55; NY Airways Inc, pilot airline capt 1956-; New York Helicopter, retired chief pilot; Island Helicopter, dir purchasing. **ORGANIZATIONS:** Mem Air Line Pilots Assn; founding mem Negro Airmen Internat; mem Am Helicopter Soc; mem Orgn of Black Airline Pilots. **HONORS/ACHIEVEMENTS:** First black capt scheduled passenger Airline 1957; outst achvmt award Orgn of Black Airline Pilots 1979. **MILITARY SERVICE:** USAAF flight instr. **BUSINESS ADDRESS:** Dir Purchasing, Island Helicopter, North Ave, Garden City, NY 11530.

YOUNG, RAYMOND, JR.
Accountant. **PERSONAL:** Born Aug 22, 1960, Mobile, AL; married Lanie L Johnson. **EDUCATION:** Alabama A&M Univ, BS Acctg 1982; Mt St Mary's Coll, MBA candidate expected 1988. **CAREER:** JC Penney Co, mgmt trainee 1981; Superior Oil Co, junior accountant 1982; International Business Machine Corp, staff financial analyst 1982-. **ORGANIZATIONS:** Sunday school instructor Mt Calvary Bapt Church 1983-; mem Montgomery Co Chap NAACP 1985-, Natl Black MBA Assoc 1987-; income tax advisor. **HONORS/ACHIEVEMENTS:** Personalities of the South 1982; Natl Deans List 1982; Who's Who Among Students in Amer Colls & Univs 1982; Delta Mu Delta Natl Honor Soc Business Admin1982-. **HOME ADDRESS:** 11419 Brundidge Terrace, Germantown, MD 20874. **BUSINESS ADDRESS:** Staff Financial Analyst, IBM Corp, 18100 Frederick Pike Rd, Gaithersburg, MD 20879.

YOUNG, REGINALD B.
Consultant, financial planner. **PERSONAL:** Born Oct 17, 1947, Alexandria, LA; son of Lloyd Baty and Willie Lee Gable Baty; married Ollie L Jordan; children: Stephanie D. **EDUCATION:** LaSalle Univ, MBA (hon) Mktg 1979-81; Tarkio Coll, BA Math 1968-71. **CAREER:** Frank B Hall & Co of PA Inc, account exec 1976-81; Waltington & Cooper Inc, vice pres marketing 1981-82; OR Assoc Inc, owner, pres 1982-83; Macy's NY, marketing systems support mgr 1983-86; OR Assoc Inc, owner, pres 1986-. **ORGANIZATIONS:** Founding mem, instr Omaha Chapter OIC 1967-68; insurance underwriter St Paul Co 1971-76; consultant New Gethsemane Baptist Church 1975-; consultant First PA Bank 1976-81; mem Natl Black MBA Assoc 1985-. **HONORS/ACHIEVEMENTS:** Regional Representative Securities and Exchange Commission. **HOME ADDRESS:** 5703 Ravens Crest Dr, Plainsboro, NJ 08536. **BUSINESS ADDRESS:** Owner, President, OR Assoc Inc, PO Box 7211, Princeton, NJ 08543.

YOUNG, RICHARD EDWARD, JR.
Business executive. **PERSONAL:** Born Dec 30, 1941, Baltimore, MD; married Carol Emile Gette; children: Joyce Ann, Jeffrey Wendel. **EDUCATION:** Univ MD, BA 1968-71; Rutgers U, MCRP 1971-73; Seton Hall U, JD 1978. **CAREER:** Econ Devel Planning, dir 1979; City of Newark, evltns chief 1974-79; United Way of Essex & W Hudson, Community Planning & Devel, assoc dir 1973-74; Fed Govt US Dept of HUD, urban planner 1972-73; NJ Dept of Community Affairs, 1971-72; Cty of Baltimore Dept Housing & Community Devel, housing inspector 1967-71. **ORGANIZATIONS:** Pres Centennial Communcations Inc; pres RE Young Assoc; pres ARTEP Inc; bd trustee, NJ Neuropsychiatric Inst 1977; bd trustee, vice pres Joint Connection Inc 1976; mem Amer Inst of Planners Assn 1970; 100 Black Men Inc 1974; Amer Soc Planning Officials 1970; NJ Soc of Professional Planners 1973; NJ Professional Planner License 1973. **HONORS/ACHIEVEMENTS:** Outstanding Young Men of Amer 1976; NJ State Dept of Higher Educ Minority Scholarship 1974; Tri State Regional & Planning Comm, Fellowship in Urban Planning 1971-73. **MILITARY SERVICE:** AUS maj 1964. **BUSINESS ADDRESS:** c/o City of Newark, 920 Broad St, Newark, NJ.

YOUNG, RICKEY DARNELL
Car sales representative. **PERSONAL:** Born Dec 07, 1953, Mobile, AL; son of Nathanial Young and Deloris Echols; married Gloria Waterhouse Young, Jun 23, 1984; children: Micah Cole, Colby Darnell. **EDUCATION:** Jackson State Coll, BS 1975. **CAREER:** San Diego Chargers, running back 1975-78; MN Viking's, running back 1978-84; Edina Realty; sales rep Jeff Belzer's Todd Chevrolet; Forest Lake Ford-Jeep/Eagle, Forest Lake MN, sales representative. **ORGANIZATIONS:** Real estate Edina Realty; chmn Heart/Lung Asso 1981; chldrns fund Viking 1982. **HONORS/ACHIEVEMENTS:** Pass Receiver Award, Viking's 1978. **HOME ADDRESS:** 9731 Dorset Ln, Eden Prairie, MN 55344.

YOUNG, RICKY
Professional athlete. **PERSONAL:** Born Sep 01, 1960, Chicago Heights, IL; married Kasaundra Russell. **EDUCATION:** OK State Univ, Bus Mgmt. **CAREER:** MI Panthers, linebacker 1983; Houston Gamblers, linebacker 1984-. **HONORS/ACHIEVEMENTS:** Competed in the 1982 Hula & Japan Bowls; 2nd team All-Amer Linebacker 1981,82; Voted Big Eight Defensive Player of the Year 1980; All-Big Eight selection 1980-82.

YOUNG, RONALD LEROY
Legislator. **PERSONAL:** Born Dec 14, 1939, Springfield, OH; married Rose Marie Clemons; children: Ronald L II, Kimberly M, Kevin M. **EDUCATION:** Assoc Grace Apost Bible Coll, 1965; IN Cent U, BA 1971. **CAREER:** Cty of Tulsa, commr of finan & revenue 1979-; City of Tulsa, ct adminstr 1978-79; Eli Lilly & Co, sales rep 1970-78; Eli Lilly & Co, chem 1963-70. **ORGANIZATIONS:** Pres Apost Bible Students Assn 1963-70; vice pres Nat Pentecostal Young Peoples Union 1969-71; pres Nat Pentecostal Young Peoples Union 1971-74; dir Aenon Bible Coll 1971-74; sec OK State Counc PA of W Inc 1976-; pres Stephen Foster Jr Athletic Assn 1965-67; treas Magic Cir Nghbrhd Assn 1966; coach Foster Sr HS 1964-67. **BUSINESS ADDRESS:** 200 Civic Center, Tulsa, OK 74103.

YOUNG, RONALD R.
Educational administrator. **PERSONAL:** Born May 27, 1919, Nassau; married Marjorie L Saxton; children: Ronald S, Randall O, Rederic. **EDUCATION:** AL State Coll Montgomery AL, BS 1947; AL State Coll Montgomery, AL, MEd 1958. **CAREER:** Miami-Dade Comm Coll S, EA EO coord S 1960-; AL State Tech Coll Montgomery, coach 1958-60; Montgomery Imrpovmnt Assn Montgomery, pres 1950; Amvets Post #16 Montgomery, comdr 1949; St Judes Educ Inst Montgomery, coach 1947-58. **ORGANIZATIONS:** Mem Counc of Black Am Affairs; chmn Dade Co Popul Task Force 1974; chmn Dade Co Planning & Adv Bd 1980; life mem Alpha Phi Alpha Frat; bd of dirsSt Albans Day Care 1973-79; bd of dirs Dade Co Youth Fair 1977-80. **HONORS/ACHIEVEMENTS:** Recip outstng citzns awr Dade Co Planning Adv Bd 1980. **MILITARY SERVICE:** AUS m sgt 1943-46. **BUSINESS ADDRESS:** Miami-Dade Comm Coll S, 11011 SW 104th St, Miami, FL 33176.

YOUNG, ROY S.
Chief executive automotive dealership. **CAREER:** Indian Springs Ford Inc, Kansas City MO, chief executive, 1988. **BUSINESS ADDRESS:** Indian Springs Ford, Inc, 4805 State Ave, Kansas City, MO 66102. *

YOUNG, RUFUS KING
Clergyman. **PERSONAL:** Born May 13, 1911, Dermott, AR; married Yvonne Smith Bruner; children: Essie Mae Laura Elizabeth, Rufus King, James Robert, Ellen Arneatha, Allena Ann. **EDUCATION:** Shorter Coll, AB 1937; Payne Theol Sem Wilberforce U, BD 1940. **CAREER:** Bethel African Meth Epis Ch, pastor 1953-86; Jackson Theol Seminary Shorter Coll, dean 1967-68; Jackson Theol Seminary, dean 1983-. **ORGANIZATIONS:** Trustee Shorter Coll 1951-; treas Shorter Coll 1954-; mem NAACP, AR Council of Human Rel, YMCA, Urban League, NLR Civic League, AR Dem Voters Assoc; bdmem Florence Crittendon Home, AR Serv Org, Central AR Human Serv Council, Health Oppors Provided for Everyone, PUSH; pres Glenview Improvement League 1970-; pres Christian Ministers Alliance of Greater Little Rock 1977-82. **HONORS/ACHIEVEMENTS:** Delegate to the General Conf of the AME Church 1944, 1946, 1948, 1952, 1956, 1960, 1964, 1968, 1976, 1980, 1984; mem Methodist Bicentennial Tour of the historic places of Methodism 1984. **BUSINESS ADDRESS:** Dean, Jackson Theol Seminary, 815 W 16 St, Little Rock, AR 72202.

YOUNG, RUTH L.
Government employee. **PERSONAL:** Born Dec 19, 1943, Savannah. **EDUCATION:** Bernard M Baruch Coll, Pub Bus Adminstrn 1970-71; York Coll Jamaica, 1974-; various short mnth courses from 1962-. **CAREER:** NY State US Dept of Labor Vets Employment Serv, asst vets employment rep 1974-; Summer Neighborhood Youth Corps of Educ Action & Youth Devel Progs OEO, exec sec supvr 1972-74; US Postal Serv, window clerk, clerk-typist 1965-73; Trans Urban Construction Co, girl friday 1965; James Weldon Johnson Community Center, typist-bookkeeper 1965; WAC, 1962-64; SH Kress Dept Store, salesgirl 1961. **ORGANIZATIONS:** Mem Fed Exec Bd NY Vets Affairs Com 1974-; Western NY Jobs for Bets Task Force 1974-; Am Legion 1975-; 369 Vets Assn Inc 1970-; Internatl Assn of Pers in Emplymnt Secrty 1974-; mem United De of Jamaica NY 1972-; OEO CAP Proj Econ Devel Cntr 1973-; asso mem Museum of Natural Hist 1974-. **HONORS/ACHIEVEMENTS:** Recip serv awrd US Dept of Labor 10 rys Hon Svc; several letters of commend. **BUSINESS ADDRESS:** US Dept of Labor, VES 303 W Old Country Rd, Hicksville, NY 11801.

YOUNG, SARAH DANIELS
Retired government official. **PERSONAL:** Born Sep 25, 1926, Wetumpka, AL; daughter of Thomas Daniels II and Novella Saxton Johnson; married Anderson Crutcher (deceased); children: Saundrea Shillingford Alan Cla. **EDUCATION:** Detroit Inst of Commerce, Dipl Sec Sci 1946; Wayne State U, 1964-68. **CAREER:** Detroit Inst of Commerce Business Coll, sec to pres 1946-48; Fed Govt, med sec 1949-54; County of Wayne, admin sec ofc mgr labor rel analyst 1954-79. **ORGANIZATIONS:** Mem St Clement's Epis Ch 1948-; bd of canvassers' mem City of Inkster 1966-89; bd of dirs Chateau Cherry Hill Housing Corp 1973-89; commnr Public Housing Auth 1979-; mem chprsn "Friends of the Library" City of Inkster 1979-; bd of dirs natl editor in chief Gamma Phi Delta Sor Inc; treas Diocese of MI ECW Exec Bd 1983; bd of dirs Northwest Guidance Clinic 1984-87; charter mem Top Ladies of Distinction Inc MI Metro Chap Exec Bd; mem Natl Council of Negro Women, YWCA, NAACP; mem, sec, Episcopal Diocese of Michigan Finance Committee 1987-. **HONORS/ACHIEVEMENTS:** Pi Nu Tau Honor Award Detroit Inst of Commerce 1946; 1st black female analyst Wayne Co MI; Outstanding Serv Award as Natl Editor-in-chief Gamma Phi Delta Sor Inc 1978; Outstanding Adult Comm Serv Awd Alpha Kappa Alpha 1984.

YOUNG, TERRENCE ANTHONY
Banker. **PERSONAL:** Born Feb 21, 1954, St Louis, MO; children: Terrence A Jr. **EDUCATION:** Univ of IL Champaign, BA 1977, MBA 1979; State of IL, CPA 1980. **CAREER:** Inland Steel Co, finance 1979-83; The First Natl Bank of Chicago, asst vice pres 1983-. **ORGANIZATIONS:** Mem Amer Inst of Certified Public Accountants, Alpha Phi Alpha Frat; adv comm Grand Boulevard Develop Corp, Great Coalition, Natl Congress for Comm Economic Develop; mem Natl Black MBA Assoc 1979-87; mem Urban Bankers Forum of Chicago, Kenwood Oakland Comm Develop Corp; pres POINTE Develop Co. **HONORS/ACHIEVEMENTS:** Who's Who in Amer Colls and Univs 1976-77; Outstanding Young Men of America 1985. **HOME ADDRESS:** 4925 So Champlain Ave, Chicago, IL 60615. **BUSINESS ADDRESS:** Asst Vice Pres Neighborhood Lending, The First Natl Bank of Chicago, One First Natl Plaza, Ste 0289, Chicago, IL 60670.

YOUNG, TOMMY SCOTT
Business executive. **PERSONAL:** Born Dec 13, 1943, Blair, SC; son of John Robert Young and Nancy Thompson Young; children: Tamu Toliver, Lee Thompson Young. **EDUCATION:** CA State U, BA 1968; LA Cty Coll; Benedict Coll; CA State U, Post Grad. **CAREER:** Lord Baltimore Press IBM Corp, printers asst 1963-66; Meat & Theatre Inc, fndr/pres 1969-72; Watts Writers Workshop, instr 1969-71; SC Arts Commn, artist resd; Kitani Found Inc, exec dir/bd mem/fndr/chmn of bd 1974-84; The Equitable Life Assurance Soc of the US, financial planner 1984-; Raspberry Recordings, creative & performing artist. **ORGANIZATIONS:** GA Cncl for Arts; NC Cultural Arts Com 1973; dir Timia Enter 1974; chmn Educ Com Shel-Blair Fed Credit Union 1974-75; mem Governors Intl Yr of Child Com; mem Artistically Talented & Gifted Spcl Proj Adv Bd 1977-; mem Mann-Simons Adv Comm 1979-; mem SC Educ TV Adv Bd 1979-; mem Bro & Sisters Adv Bd 1979-; mem So Arts Fed Prgm Sel Com 1979-80; mem chmn SC Arts Commn 5 yr Planning Com for Richland Co 1979-80; mem SC Arts Commn Adn Adv Com; mem & treas SC Com Arts Agencies 1979-; mem Governor's Cultural Arts Com 1979-; mem Spoleto of Midlands Comm 1980; mem Governors Intl Yr of Child Com; consult Media Serv for Nat Endow for Arts 1979-; mem Columbia C of C; Nat Literary Soc; mem Natl Assn of Life Underwriters 1985-, Natl Assn for Preservation & Perpetuation of Storytelling 1986-, Assn of Black Storytelling 1987-, Toastmast ers International 1987-, Columbia Youth Collaborative 1989-, Southern Order of Storytellers, SC Storytellers Guild; chmn Christ Unity of Columbia 1988-, Youth Encouraged to Succeed 1989-. **HONORS/ACHIEVEMENTS:** Dir prod "Angela is Happening" 1971-72; dir "Southern Fried" 1977; author "Black Blues & Shiny Songs" Red Clay Books 1977; recip "10 for the Future" Columbia Newspapers Inc 1978; Billings Educational Found Awd; Intl Plat-

form Assoc; Gospel Music Workshop Amer; Natl Entertainment Conf; Natl Leaders Corps, The Equitable Financial Companies 1987; Distinguished Performance Citation, The Equitable Financial Companies 1988; author, Tommy Scott Young Spins Magical Tales, Raspberry Recordings 1985. **MILITARY SERVICE:** USAF 1960-63. **BUSINESS ADDRESS:** Creative & Performing Artist, Raspberry Recordings, PO Box 11247, Columbia, SC 29211.

YOUNG, TYRONE
Professional athlete. **PERSONAL:** Born Apr 29, 1960, Ocala, FL; married Jackie; children: Kyle. **EDUCATION:** FL Univ, Public Recreation. **CAREER:** New Orlean Saints, wide receiver 1983-. **HONORS/ACHIEVEMENTS:** Caught longest pass of the year for Saints 74 yards.

YOUNG, WALLACE L.
Educator. **PERSONAL:** Born Oct 05, 1931, New Orleans, LA; married Myra Narcine. **EDUCA1ION:** Attended, Loyola U, So U. **CAREER:** New Orleans Public Library, chmn of bd 1976-79; Senior Citizen Center, asst dir. **ORGANIZATIONS:** Pres bd mem NAACP; exec sec Knights of Peter Claver; past mem Dryades St YMCA; mem Free So Thtr; Nat Cath Conf for Interracial Justice; LA State Lib Devel Com; coord Cath Com Urban Ministry; mem Natl Office for Black Catholics, Natl Black Lay Catholic Caucus. **HONORS/ACHIEVEMENTS:** TX Farmworker Awd Human Rights 1977; Human Relation Catholic Awd 1978; Black Catholic Man of Vision 1978; Dryades YMCA Man of the Yr Awd 1979; NOBC Outstanding Serv 1980; FST 1985. **MILITARY SERVICE:** Ordanance Corps 1951-53. **BUSINESS ADDRESS:** Assistant Dir, Senior Citizen Center, 219 Loyola Ave, New Orleans, LA 70112.

YOUNG, WALTER F.
Dentist. **PERSONAL:** Born Aug 18, 1934, New Orleans, LA; married Sanjia W; children: Tony Waller, Tonya Waller, Tammy, Nikki. **EDUCATION:** BS DDS 1959; Harvard School Bus, special prog 1976. **CAREER:** Iberville Parish, Comm Action, St Laudry Parish, S James Parish, St Helena Parish, dental dir; NV State Mental Hosp, dental dir 1969; NV State Penal Inst, 1964; Pvt Prac, dentist 1987; Young Int Dev Corp, pres 1975-. **ORGANIZATIONS:** Mem OIC; SCLC; former bd mem NAACP; bd mem Fulton Co Hospital Auth; bd trust GA Econ Task Force; mem GA Dental Assoc/Intl Fellows Prog Bd. **MILITARY SERVICE:** USN 1959. **BUSINESS ADDRESS:** President, Young Int Dev Corp, 2265 Cascade Rd SW, Atlanta, GA 30311.

YOUNG, WATSON A.
Physician. **PERSONAL:** Born Sep 27, 1915, Abbeville, SC; married Aundree Noretta Drisdale; children: Watson, Jr, Aundree, Jr, Ransom J, Leonard F, Anthony G. **EDUCATION:** Univ MI, MD 1942. **CAREER:** Private Practice, Physician 1944-. **ORGANIZATIONS:** Mem, Detroit Med Soc; Wolverine State Med Soc; Natl Med Assn; Wayne Cnty & MI State Med Socs; Amer Med Assn; Am Soc & Abdominal Surgeons; life mem NAACP. **MILITARY SERVICE:** AUS Major 1954-56. **BUSINESS ADDRESS:** 3508 Harrison Rd, Inkster, MI 48141.

YOUNGBLOOD, OZIE F.
Businessman, educator. **PERSONAL:** Born Feb 24, 1906, Delray Beach, FL; married Lucille C. **EDUCATION:** FL A&M U, BSA 1932; Hampton Inst, Grad Study. **CAREER:** W Palm Beach City, biology instr; Melborne Voc HS, prin; self employed rental units; His & Her Hair Creation Delray Beach FL, retired barber. **ORGANIZATIONS:** Cnclmn 6 yrs Delray Bch; post comm Am Leg Post 188; mgr Govt Hsng Proj Pahokee FL; p chmn Delray Bch Interracl Cncl; Nacirema Clb; mem sundayschl tchr 20 yrs Mt Olive Baptst Ch; cnclmn City Delray Bch 1974; Phi Beta Sigma. **HONORS/ACHIEVEMENTS:** Citations City of Delray Bch 1968; meritorious serv, social action & cvl rghts 1971; meritorious awd Delray Bch sickle cell fund vice pres 1974; FL A&MUniv & Alumni awds 1974. **MILITARY SERVICE:** AUS, cpl, WW II.

YOUNGE, FITZROY EGERTON
Physician. **PERSONAL:** Born Aug 11, 1903; married Winifred Tommisseau Abernathy; children: Mary Eloise, Sheila Frances (dec), Fitzroy E Jr, Winifred Lorraine Smith. **EDUCATION:** Univ of IL Urbana, 1929-31; Meharry Med Coll Nashville, MD 1936. **CAREER:** Herrick Meml Hosp Berkeley, head of dept ob-gyn 1958-60; Herrick Meml Hosp Berkeley, pres of staff 1962-64; Civic Ctr Hosp Oakland CA, head of dept ob-gyn 1965-75; Herrick Meml Hosp Berkeley CA, chief of staff 1966-68; Private practice, physician 1968-. **ORGANIZATIONS:** Bd of dir Oakland YMCA 1947-53; mem San Francisco Urban League 1947-59; bd of dir Oakland Comm Chest; chmn of trustee bd 1st AME Church Oakland 1950-73; diplomate Natl Bd of Med Examiners 1973; fellow Amer Coll of Ob-Gyn 1950; fellow Amer Coll Surgeons 1951. **HONORS/ACHIEVEMENTS:** Man of the Year Berkeley Alumni Chap Kappa Alpha Psi Frat 1970; Disting Serv Awd NAACP Oakland Chap 1970; Man of the Year W Berkeley Charity Clinic 1978; Disting Serv Awd 1st AME Church Oakland 1979.

YOUNGE, RICHARD G.
Attorney. **PERSONAL:** Born Aug 27, 1924, Kirkwood, MO; children: Ruth, Torque, Margrett, Roland, Richard Jr. **EDUCATION:** Univ of IL, BA 1947; Lincoln U, LLB 1953. **CAREER:** E St Louis IL, pract atty; Forward Hsing Corp, atty 20 yrs 1973; Citizens Devel Corp; Econ Devel So IL, engaged in promotion. **ORGANIZATIONS:** Pres Metro-east Bar Assn. **HONORS/ACHIEVEMENTS:** Developed Housing & Bus Oportunities for Blacks in So IL. **MILITARY SERVICE:** AUS s sgt. **BUSINESS ADDRESS:** 2000 State St, East St Louis, IL.

YOUNGER, CELIA DAVIS
Educator. **PERSONAL:** Born Aug 24, 1939, Gretna, VA; married James Arthur; children: Felicia A, Terri E. **EDUCATION:** VA State Univ, BS 1970, MEd. **CAREER:** VA State Univ, prog coord student union 1971-73, asst dir financial aid 1973-75, business develop specialist and procurement officer 1974-78; J Sargeant Reynolds Comm Coll, adjunct faculty school of business 1974-75; Ocean County Coll, adjunct faculty school of business 1982-83; Georgian Court Coll, dir learning resource ctr 1978-83, dir educ oppor fund prog 1983-. **ORGANIZATIONS:** Mem Alpha Kappa Alpha Sor 1968-, EOF Professional Assoc 1978-; chairperson affirmative action comm workshop facilitator OC Adv Comm on Status of Women 1980-; exec bd mem Ocean County Girl Scouts 1983-; mem Amer Assoc of Univ Women, NJ Assoc of Develop Educ, NJ Assoc of Student Financial Aid Administrators Inc, Natl Assoc of Female Execs. **HONORS/ACHIEVEMENTS:** Listed in Who's Who of Amer Women 1983-84; Certificate of Appreciation Toms River Regional Bd of Educ 1984-85. **BUSINESS ADDRESS:** Dir, Georgian Court College, Educational Oppor Fund Prog, Lakewood, NJ 08701.

YOUNGER, KENNETH C.
Auto dealer. **PERSONAL:** Born in Missouri. **CAREER:** McDonnell Douglas Aircraft Corp CA, engr; Landmark Ford Fairfield OH, owner 1977-. **ORGANIZATIONS:** Founding mem Black Ford Lincoln-Mercury Dealers Assoc; pres Natl Assoc of Minority Automobile Dealers.

YOUNGER, PAUL LAWRENCE (TANK)
Professional athlete, manager. **PERSONAL:** Born Jun 25, 1928, Grambling, LA; married Lucille; children: Howard, Harriette, Lucy. **EDUCATION:** Grambling Coll, BS 1949. **CAREER:** LA Rams, player 1949-57; Pittsburgh Steelers, player 1958; LA Rams, part-time personnel scout 1959-63, personnel scout 1963-75; San Diego Chargers FootballClub, asst gen mgr 1975-. **MILITARY SERVICE:** AUS pvt 1951. **BUSINESS ADDRESS:** Assistant General Manager, San Diego Chargers, PO Box 20666, San Diego, CA 92120.

YOUNGER, ROBERT D.
Business executive. **PERSONAL:** Born Jan 27, 1932, Grambling, LA; married Ann Dean Meadows; children: Cynthia, Louise, Carol, James. **EDUCATION:** Purdue Univ Mankato State, Graduate Work (Cum Laude) 1957; Indiana Inst of Technology, BSEE; Harvard Univ Graduate School, 1976. **CAREER:** Magnavox Co, electrical engineer 1957-65; Control Data Corp, sr electrical engineer 1966-, dept mgr special test equipment 1966-. **ORGANIZATIONS:** Active Inner Comm work to interest & motivate young black students to seek careers in science & engineering; helped organize local org Minds for Progress Inc; mem NAACP, Urban League, Deacon; vice chmn City of Bloomington MN Comm on Human Rights; special advisor State Commn of Human Rights State of MN; mem Hon Frat. **HONORS/ACHIEVEMENTS:** Award Coolidge Physics Prize; obtained patent in reactance measuring instrument; published paper Natl Tech Assoc Journal; featured in numerous newspaper articles. **MILITARY SERVICE:** AUS sgt 1952-54. **BUSINESS ADDRESS:** Sr Elect Engr, Dept Mgr, Control Data Corp, 7801 Computer Ave, Minneapolis, MN 55435.

Z

ZACHARY, HUBERT M.
Business executive. **PERSONAL:** Born Nov 09, 1936, Hartford, NC; married Brenda M Fletcher; children: Hubert, Mia, Christian. **EDUCATION:** Morgan State U, BS Chem 1966; WV U, MSIE 1969. **CAREER:** Johns Hopkins Univ, instructor 1970-82; Western Electric Co, supvr product control 1974-83, buyer 1968-69, 1983-; NY Tele Co, staff mgr 1983-84; Hynex Enterprises, mgr purchasing. **ORGANIZATIONS:** Instructor Balti City Adult Educ 1966-78; pres Balti Cossocks Inc 1976. **BUSINESS ADDRESS:** Manager of Purchasing, Hynex Enterprises, 441 9th Ave, New York, NY 10001.

ZACHARY-PIKE, ANNIE R.
Farmer. **PERSONAL:** Born May 12, 1931, Marvell, AR. **EDUCATION:** Homer G Phillips School of Nursing. **CAREER:** Farmer, owner & mgr 1,054 acres of farmland. **ORGANIZATIONS:** Mem, Eastern Star; NAACP; AR Assn Colored Women; Phillips Co Extnsn Hmmkrs Cncl; IPA; AR Cncl Hmn Rltns; AR Assn Crppld Inc; Wildlife Federation; EAME;Emergency Sch Asst Proj; Pta; 4 H; Farm Bureau; Farmers Home Admin; adv council FHA; USDA Civil Rights Commn; Council Aging; Fair Bd; Sm Bus Assn; Natl Council Christians & Jews; bd mem The Election Law Inst; E AR Mental Health; Delta Area Devel Inc; Workshop Inc; Rep, AR St Com Farm. **HONORS/ACHIEVEMENTS:** Family Year Award 1959; 4 H Friendship 1959; Home Demonstration Woman Year 1965; Queens Womens Federated Club Inc 1969; Delg 1972 GOP Conv Wmn Yr, Alpha Kappa Alpha 1971; Hon PhD, CO St Christian Coll 1972.

ZAMBRANA, RAFAEL
Educator. **PERSONAL:** Born May 26, 1931, Santa Isabel, PR; married Laura E Alvarez; children: Gloria, Ralph, Aida, Magda, Wallace, Olga, Daphne. **EDUCATION:** Catholic Univ of PR, BA Hist 1958; Attended, Columbia Univ courses in psychology 1965; Hunter Coll School of Soc Work, grad credits in secondary educ 1958-62, MSW 1974; City Univ of New York, DSW 1982. **CAREER:** Bd of Ed NY, jr hs teacher 1958-62; Rabbi Jacob Joseph HS, teacher 1962-65; Mobilization for Youth, soc worker 1965-67; PR Community Devel Proj, dirof training 1967-68; Lower East Side Manpower Neighborhood Serv Ctr, dir 1968-69; Williamsburg Community Corp, exec dir 1969-71; Community Devel Agency of NYC, Asst commiss 1971-74; Medgar Evers Coll of CUNY, prof of public admin 1974-82; Medgar Evers Coll of CUNY, chairperson of soc sci div 1982-. **ORGANIZATIONS:** Consultant NYS Dept of Corrections 1976; consult Coney Island Com Corp 1969-78; bd mem Com Council of Greater NY 1969-76; advisory bd mem Mgmt Advisory Com US Dept Labor Reg II 1980-82; pres Council of PR Org; pres MEC Faculty Org; exec com/bd mem Undergrad Sec of Natl Assoc of Schools of PA; local sch bd mem Dist 12 NYC. **HONORS/ACHIEVEMENTS:** Meritorious Serv Awd Williamsburg Com Corp 1971; Devotion to Children Awd Supr Assoc New York City Local Sch Bd Dist #12 1977; Manpower Ed Grant US Dept of Labor 1979-83; Outstanding Ed Awd Student's Council Williamsburg Proj 1980; Articles publ in Teaching Publ Admin 1981, 82, 83 & 84. **MILITARY SERVICE:** AUS Corpl 1950-55; Good Conduct Medal; Korean Serv Medal. **HOME ADDRESS:** 3600 Rosea Cordada, Levittown, Puerto Rico 00949. **BUSINESS ADDRESS:** Chairperson, Soc Sci Div, Medgar Evers College/CUNY, 1150 Carroll St, Brooklyn, NY 11225.

ZANDER, JESSIE MAE
Educational administrator. **PERSONAL:** Born Jul 31, 1932, Inman, VA; married Johnny W Zander. **EDUCATION:** Berea Coll, BA Elem Educ 1954;Univ of AZ, MA Elem Educ 1966;Univ of AZ, MA Cnslng Guid 1976. **CAREER:** Linweaver School Tucson Unified School Dist, prin 1980; Miles Exploratory Learning Center Tucson Unified School Dist, prin 1979-80; Tucson Unified School Dist, counselor 1976-79; Tucson Unified School Dist, teacher 1958-76; Tucson Indian Training School AZ, teacher jr high 1956-58; Benham Elem HS Ben-

ham KY, teacher 1954-58. **ORGANIZATIONS:** Consult Cltrl Awrns Admnstr Retreat 1975-76; coord poetry in schl AZ St Poetry Soc 1977-80; bd mem Pima Cncl on Chldrn Srvcs 1978-79; mem Educ DivAm Cancer Soc 1975; Tamiochus Alpha Kappa Alpha Sor Eta Epsilon Omega Chap 1976-81; vice pres AZ St Poetry Soc 1978; conf chrpsn AZ St Poetry Soc 1978-79. **HONORS/ACHIEVEMENTS:** Otstndng Pres Cncl of Black Edctrs 1978-79 & 1979-80; Newspaper Article Open Educ Miles Exploratory Lrning Cntr 1980. **BUSINESS ADDRESS:** Miles Expl Lrnng Ctr Tucson Un, 1010 E 10th St, Tucson, AZ 85717.

ZANDERS, ALTON WENDELL
Educational administrator. **PERSONAL:** Born Sep 03, 1943, Amite, LA; married Gertrude Carral; children: Geleah Nicole, Anissa Monique. **EDUCATION:** Southern Univ, BS 1965; Syracuse Univ, MS 1970, JD 1974. **CAREER:** New Orleans Public School System, teacher 1965-69; State Univ of New York, asst dir and dir of special programs 1970-79, affirmative action officer 1974-80; Univ of MO-Columbia, dir office of equal oppor 1981-. **ORGANIZATIONS:** Commissioner Human Rights Comm City of Columbia 1981-83; mem Amer Assoc for Affirmative Action 1985-; mem MO Black Leadership Assoc 1985-; bd dirs Multicultural Mgmt Program Sch of Journalism UMC 1985-; mem Minority Men's Network 1986-; bd dirs Kiwanis Club of Columbia 1986-; mem & State coord of HigherEduc Liaison Comm US Dept of Labor Office of Federal Contract Compliance Program (Midwest Region). **HONORS/ACHIEVEMENTS:** NSF Dillar Univ 1969-70; NSF Syracuse Univ 1969; Administrative Internship State Univ of NY 1974; Public Trust Awd Coll of Law Syracuse Univ 1974; also 14 publications including "Vita Banks for Minorities and Women, Do They Work?" 1984 presented at the Amer Assoc for Affirmative Action 11th Annual Conf San francisco 1985. **BUSINESS ADDRESS:** Dir Office of Equal Oppor, Univ of Missouri-Columbia, Office of Equal Opportunity, 217 Jesse Hall, Columbia, MO 65211.

ZENO, WILLIE D.
Business executive. **PERSONAL:** Born Mar 28, 1942, Dallas, TX. **EDUCATION:** Univ OK, MSEE 1972; Bus Bishop Coll, MBA 1968. **CAREER:** Hank Moore & Asso; Goodyear Aerospace, persnl dir; EOC US Dept Labor, dir; Engineering & Design Engineering Soc Am Leap, dir. **ORGANIZATIONS:** Urban Leg Nat Bsnsmn. **HONORS/ACHIEVEMENTS:** Wk Design Eng Month (Goodyear). **MILITARY SERVICE:** USN 1 lt.

ZEUMAULT, DIANNE LORRAINE
Electrical engineer/marketing. **PERSONAL:** Born Sep 13, 1962, Seattle, WA; married Adrien Enee Zeumault. **EDUCATION:** Univ of Washington, BSEE 1985. **CAREER:** Puget Sound Power & Light, intern engr 1983-84; Hewlett-Packard, intern develop engr 1984; IBM Corp, marketing asst 1984-85, systems engr 1985-. **ORGANIZATIONS:** Vice pres communications Natl Soc of Black Engrs 1981-82; pres 1982-83, pres emeritus 1983-84 Natl Soc of Black Engrs; mem Engrg Adv Comm for Minority Programs Univ of WA 1983-84; mem Natl Assoc of Female Execs 1986-, Alpha Kappa Alpha Sor 1986-; minority partnership program Pacific Lutheran Univ 1986-. **HONORS/ACHIEVEMENTS:** Charles E Stuart Scholarship Univ of WA 1980-85; Undergrad Merit Scholarship Univ of WA 1982-83; Scholarship Awd Equal Oppor Prog Univ of WA 1982,85; Scholarship Kaiser Aluminum & Chem Corp 1983-85. **HOME ADDRESS:** 15705 Third Ave NE, Seattle, WA 98155.

ZIEGLER, DHYANA
Educator. **PERSONAL:** Born May 05, 1949, New York, NY; daughter of Ernest Ziegler (deceased) and Alberta A Guy Ziegler. **EDUCATION:** Baruch Coll CUNY BA Program, BS (Cum Laude) 1981; Southern IL Univ-Carbondale, MA 1983, PhD 1985. **CAREER:** Essence Magazine, market researcher 1972-75; Rosenfeld Sirowitz & Lawson, copywriter and radio producer 1974-75; Patten and Guest Productions NY, regional mgr1976-79; WNEW TV, internship desk asst and production asst; Seton Hall Univ, counselor for high school students 1979-81; Baruch Coll CUNY, english tutor and instructor for writing workshops 1979-81; The Westside Newspaper, reporter 1980-; CBS TV Network, production intern 1980-81; Southern IL Univ Dept of Radio & Television, lab instructor 1981-83; Jackson State Univ Dept of Mass Comm, asst prof 1984-85; The Univ of TN-Knoxville Dept of Broadcasting, asst prof of broadcasting 1985-. **ORGANIZATIONS:** Vice pres of develop Women in Communications Inc; mem Natl Political Congress of Black Women; mem Delta Sigma Theta Sor Inc; mem Phi Delta Kappa; grad fellow Post Doctoral Acad of Higher Educ; mem Speech Comm Assoc; pres and founder Blacks in Communications Alliance; mem Natl Cncl of Negro Women Inc; legislative council Southern IL Univ Alumni Assoc; panelist Metro Black Media Coalition Conference 1984, Southern IL Univ/Blacks in Communications Alliance 1985, Natl Black Media Coalition Conf 1985; speaker/consultant US Armed Forces Azores Portugal 1986; chmn/public relations, Kiwanis Club of Knoxville, 1988-; Southern Regional Devel Educ Project Coord, Delta Sigma Theta, 1988-; pres elect, Women in Communications, Inc, 1989. **HONORS/ACHIEVEMENTS:** Seek Scholarship Awards for Academic & Service 1979-81 Baruch Coll; Rita Leeds Service Award 1981 Baruch Coll; Sheldon Memorial Award Baruch Coll 1981; Scrippt-Howard Award Baruch Coll 1981; United Press Intl Outstanding Achievement Radio Documentary 1982; Dept of Radio and TV SIUC Outstanding Radio Production Award 1982-83; Grad Dean's Doctoral Fellowship 1983-84; Paul Robinson's Roby Scholar Award Black Affairs Council 1984; Certificate of Merit Award Southern IL Univ Broadcasting Serv 1984; Ebony Bachelorette 1985; Seek Alumni Award Baruch Coll 1985; numerous publications and other professional works; Outstanding Faculty Member of the Year, Coll of Communications, UTK, 1987-88; Chancellor's Citation for Service, Univ of TN Knoxville, 1988, Max Robinson, Jr, Turbulent Life of a Media Prophet, Journa l of Black Studies, 1989, Challenging Racism in the Classrom: Paving the Road to the Future/Thoughts and Action-The Journal of the Natl Educ Assn, 1989. **HOME ADDRESS:** 7700 Gleason Dr #41C, Knoxville, TN 37919. **BUSINESS ADDRESS:** Professor of Broadcasting, University of Tennessee, Dept of Broadcasting, 295 Communications Bldg, Knoxville, TN 37996.

ZIMMERMAN, EUGENE
Internist. **PERSONAL:** Born Jul 07, 1947, Orangeburg, SC; married Sheila Beth Hughes; children: Brian, Monica. **EDUCATION:** Jersey City State Coll, BA 1969; Howard Univ Medical Sch, MD 1973. **CAREER:** Harlem Hosp Ctr, intern 1973-74; Howard Univ Hosp, resident 1974-76; Student Health Serv of Gallanhet Coll, actg medical dir 1977-81; SENAB, medical dir 1979-84; Dept of Forensic Psychiatry, staff physician. **ORGANIZATIONS:** Mem Medical Soc of DC 1976-, NY Acad of Sciences 1984-. **HONORS/ACHIEVEMENTS:** Bd Certified Internist Amer Bd of Internal Medicine 1985; "Staining Characteristics of Bone Marrow" w/Dr WD Sharpe 1968. **HOME ADDRESS:** 4621 Sargent Rd NE, Washington, DC 20017. **BUSINESS ADDRESS:** Staff Physician, Dept of Forensic Psychiatry, 1905 E St SE Bldg 22, Washington, DC 20003.

ZIMMERMAN, LIZ See KEITT, L.

ZIMMERMAN, SAMUEL LEE
Educational director. **PERSONAL:** Born Apr 28, 1923, Anderson, SC; son of William L Zimmerman and Corinne O Banks Zimmerman; married Blanche Carole Williams Zimmerman, May 30, 1946; children: Samuel Lee Jr. **EDUCATION:** Benedict College, AB Elemen Educ 1962; Graduate Study, Furman Univ 1965, 1968, Univ of Washington 1973, Glassboro State Coll 1974. **CAREER:** Greenville School Dist, elementary reading teacher 1961-70; The Greenville Piedmont, news reporter 1970-73; WFBC-TV, host for raparound 1976-77; WFBC Radio, host for raparound 1976-82; School Dist of Greenville Co, dir school/comm relations 1973-87; consultant, Partridge Assoc, 1988-. **ORGANIZATIONS:** Former vice pres at large Natl School Public Relations Assn 1979-81; SC Assn of School Admin; Comm to Study Educ in the State of SC; bd of dir SC Comm for the Blind; bd of dir Goodwill Indus of Upper SC; bd of trustees Springfield Baptist Church. **HONORS/ACHIEVEMENTS:** AP Award Sampling Attitudes of Young Blacks 1969; William F Gaines Mem Award in Journalism 1971; Distinguished Serv Award City of Greenville 1974; Serv Certificate of Appreciation United Way of Greenville 1977; Natl School Public Relations Certificate of Appreciation 1976-77; Certificate of Award the Greenville Co Human Relations 1977-78; Whitney M Young, Jr Humaritarian Award, 1988; Outstanding Volunteer, United Negro Coll Fund, 1989. **MILITARY SERVICE:** AUS T-5 2 yrs. **HOME ADDRESS:** 6 Allendale Lane, PO Box 6535, Greenville, SC 29606.

ZOLLAR, DORIS L.
Business executive. **PERSONAL:** Born Dec 07, 1932, Little Rock, AR; married Lowell M; children: Nikki Michele, Lowell M Jr. **EDUCATION:** Talladega Coll, BA 1951; UCLA Grad School, MA 1952; DePaul Univ, Post Grad 1952-54, 1958-59. **CAREER:** Chicago Publ School, teacher 1952-67; Childrens Haven Residential School for Multiple Handicapped Children, founder, org, school dir 1973-; The Independent Bulletin Newspaper, women's editor 1976-77; Triad Consulting Svcs, pres. **ORGANIZATIONS:** Comm leader Mid-West Conf of Pres Lyndon B Johnsons Comm on Equal Oppty 1964; mem Chicago Urban League 1965-, Lois R Lowe Womens Div UNCF 1966-, Jackson Park Highlands Assoc 1966-; vice pres Bravo Chap Lyric Opera of Chicago 1966; benefit chmn Ebony Fashion Fair 1968,69; corr sec IL Childrens Home & Aid Soc 198-70; publ rel fund raising consult Natl Med Assoc Project 75 1973-75; mem South Shore Comm 1974-; vice pres XXI bd Michael Reese Hosp 1974-76; Cook Cty Welfare Serv Comm 1975-; Chicago Publ School Art Soc of Chicago Art Inst 1975-; org & coord of 3 day conf wkshp Minority Constr Workers 1975; adv Midwest Assoc for Sickle Cell Anemia 1976-; adv The Black United Fund 1976-; mem Art in Public Places Bd 1976-, The Council of Foreign Affaris 1976;, Intl Visitors Ctr Bd 1976-; dir of funding devel The Woodlawn Org World Serv Council Natl YWCA 1976-. **HONORS/ACHIEVEMENTS:** AKA Scholarship by competitive exam 1947; Exchange student from Talladega Coll to Cedar Crest Coll 1948-49; Florina Lasker Fellowship Awd 1951; Will RogersMeml Fellowship toward PhD in History 1952; "Ed Motivation of the Culturally Disadvantaged Youth" Chicago Bd of Ed 1958-60; Natl Med Assoc Awd Womens Aux 1966; The Pittsburgh Couriers Natl Ten Best Dressed 1972,73,74; Hon Librarian of the Chicago Publ Library City of Chicago 1974; the Commercial Breadbasket Assoc Awd 1975; Inst for Health Resources Devel Awd 1975; Oper PUSH Awd 1975,76; Person of the Day Awd Radio Stations WAIT, WBEE 1969,76; Beatrice CaffreyYouth Serv Inc Annual Merit Awd for Civic Achievement 1976; listed in Certain People 1977; Alpha Gamma Pi, Iota Phi Lambda Sor Bus & Professional Awd 1977; dir IL International Port Authority 1986-. **BUSINESS ADDRESS:** President, Apex Construction Co Inc, 2100 S Indiana Ave, Chicago, IL 60616.

ZOLLAR, NIKKI MICHELE
Government official. **PERSONAL:** Born Jun 18, 1956, Chicago, IL; daughter of Lowell M Zollar and Doris Lowe Zollar; married William A von Hoene, Jr, Jun 18, 1983; children: William Lowell von Hoene. **EDUCATION:** Johns Hopkins Univ, Baltimore MD, BA, 1977; Georgetown Univ Law Center, Washington DC, JD, 1980. **CAREER:** US District Court for Northern District of IL, judicial law clerk for Chief Judge James B Parsons, 1980-81; Lafontant, Wilkins, Jones & Ware, Chicago IL, associate, 1981-83; Kirkland & Ellis, Chicago IL, associate, 1983-85; Chicago Bd of Election Commissioners, chmn. **ORGANIZATIONS:** Co-chair, telethon night event, UNCF, 1980-; mem, Chicago Comm in Solidarity with Southern Africa, 1986-; mem, Community Outreach Comm, Field Museum of Natrual History, 1987-; mem, Georgetown Univ Law Center Alumni Bd, 1987-; mem, Lois R Lowe Women's Bd, UNCF, 1987-; chair, educ comm, Chicago Architecture Foundation Bd of Dir, 1987-; mem, Intl Assn of Clerks, Recorders, Election Officials & Treasureres, 1987-; mem, Alpha Gamma Pi, 1987-; mem, State Bd of Elections advisory comm, 1988-; co-chair, Law Exploring Comm, Young Lawyers Section of Chicago Bar Assn, 1988-; mem, Woodlawn's Acad of the Sacred Heart bd of trustees, 1988-; mem, Chicago Urban League, 1988-. **HONORS/ACHIEVEMENTS:** Certificate of Outstanding Achievement, Illinois State Attorneys Appellate Service Comm, 1981; Service & Leadership Award, UNCF, 1983; Outstanding Young Professional, Chicago Urban Professionals, 1985; one of 100 Outstanding Black Business & Professional Women in US, Dollars & Sense, 1988; Martin Luther King Award, Boy Scouts of Amer, 1989; African-Amer Women's Achievement Award, Columbia Coll, 1989; Kizzy Award, Revlon/Kizzy Foundation, 1989; David C Hilliard Award, Chicago Bar Assn, 1989; Youth Service, Beatrice Caffrey, 1989. **BUSINESS ADDRESS:** Chairman, Chicago Board of Election Commissioners, 121 N LaSalle St, City Hall, Room 308, Chicago, IL 60602.

OBITUARIES

ALEXANDER, ROLAND
Business executive. **PERSONAL:** Born Mar 03, 1922, Waynesboro, GA; died Dec 12, 1988; married Sarah Haynes; children: Jo Ann, Edith, Roland Jr. **EDUCATION:** Youngstown State Univ, attended 3 yrs. **CAREER:** Tabernacle Baptist Church, primary Sunday School supt 1956-88; NAACP, second vice pres Youngstown Branch 1966-68, membership chmn Youngstown Branch 13 yrs, Ohio state membership chmn 1966-, pres Youngstown Branch 1969-88. **ORGANIZATIONS:** Former dir Caldwell-Neilson Settlement House; trustee Northeast Ohio Univ Coll of Medicine; active in BSA; mem Urban League; Youngstown Leadership Conf; YMCA; comm action council 1968-; trustee Therapeutic of Mahoning Co Inc; exec comm Youngstown Comm Corp 1970-; bd trustees Cerebral Palsy Center 1962-74; advisory comm Youngstown B'Nai B'Rith 1974; commr Youngstown Charter Commn 1971-72; Youngstown Human Relations Comm 1970-71; mem McGuffey Centre; former trustee Tabernacle Baptist Church. **HONORS/ACHIEVEMENTS:** NAACP Award for selling highest number of memberships by one individual in Amer. **MILITARY SERVICE:** AUS 1942-46. **BUSINESS ADDRESS:** President, NAACP, 26 South Hazel St, Youngstown, OH 44503.

ANDREWS, JOSEPH HENRY
Evangelist, minister. **PERSONAL:** Born Apr 28, 1910, Clarksville, TN; died Oct 31, 1987; son of James Andrews and Lannie West Andrews; married Adelia Smith; children: Yolanda A Reed, Joseph Reginald. **EDUCATION:** Pacific Area of Community Churches, Certificate of Ordination 1955; Reed Coll of Religion, B Theology 1967; Reed Christian Coll, M Christian Educ 1975, DD 1982. **CAREER:** Trinity Baptist Church Los Angeles, assoc minister 1971-87; Reed Christian Coll, teacher 1985-87. **ORGANIZATIONS:** Mem NAACP 1965-. **HONORS/ACHIEVEMENTS:** Certificate of Achievement 1979, Certificate of Appreciation 1986 Reed Christian College. **BUSINESS ADDRESS:** Teacher, Reed Christian College, 1101 E Rosecrans, Compton, CA 90221.

ATKINS, ROBERT L.
Labor administrator. **PERSONAL:** Born Sep 08, 1931, Glen White, WV; married Delma B; children: Robert III, Scott Eric. **EDUCATION:** West Virginia State Coll, Mechanical Arts 1954-58; Inst for Labor Studies 1964-79; African Postal Telephone & Telegraph Seminars 1976; West Germany Exchange Program 1978. **CAREER:** Communications Workers of Amer, asst to exec vice pres contracts. **ORGANIZATIONS:** Mem AFL-CIO State Fed Civil Rights Commn; mem of Mayor's Human Rights Task Force. **HONORS/ACHIEVEMENTS:** Black Journal Award "100 Most Influential Friends" 1977; Tony Brown's Black Journal 1977. **MILITARY SERVICE:** USAF A 4 yrs; Korean Serv Medal. **BUSINESS ADDRESS:** Asst to Exec Vice Pres Contracts, Communications Wkrs of America, 1925 K St NW, Washington, DC 20006.

BALDWIN, JAMES
Author. **PERSONAL:** Born Aug 02, 1924, New York, NY; died Dec 01, 1987; St Paul de Vence, France. **CAREER:** Author numerous books including, "Go Tell It on the Mountain" 1953, "Notes of a Native Son" (essays) 1955; "Giovanni's Room" 1958, "Nobody Knows My Name" (essays) 1960, "Another Country" 1962, "The Fire Next Time" (essays) 1963, "No Name in the Street" 1972, "If Beale St Could Talk" 1974, "The Devil Finds Work" 1976; Plays, "The Amen Corner" Washington DC Howard Univ 1955, NY Ethel Barrymore Theatre Apr 5, 1965, "Giovanni's Room" NY Actors Studio 1957, "Blues for Mister Charlie" NY ANTA Theatre Apr 23 1964, "A Deed from the King of Spain" NY Amer Ctr for Stanislavski Theatre Art Jan 24 1974; contributor numerous articles to natl mags. **ORGANIZATIONS:** Mem natl adv bd Congress Racial Equality; Natl Comm for Sane Nuclear Policy; lectr Civil Rights; mem Actor's Studio; mem Natl Inst Arts & Letters. **HONORS/ACHIEVEMENTS:** Saxton Fellow 1945; Rosenwald Fellow 1948; Guggenheim Fellow 1954; Partisan Rev Fellow 1956; Natl Inst Arts & Letters Awd 1956; Ford Found Grant-in-Aid 1959; George K Polk Awd 1963. **BUSINESS ADDRESS:** c/o Edward Acton Inc, 17 Grove St, New York, NY 10014.

BARBER, WILLIAM JOSEPH, SR.
Clergyman. **PERSONAL:** Born Mar 21, 1927, Jamesville, NC; married Eleanor Lucille Patterson; children: William Joseph II, Charles Edgar. **EDUCATION:** St Augustine Coll, BS 1949; Butler Univ, MS 1959; Christina Theol Sem, BD 1959; IN Univ, Cert 1965. **CAREER:** Washington & Norfolk Dist Assembly, consult 1968-; pastored in IN, OH, KY and NC; Eastern Seabord Genl Assembly Chs of Christ Disciples of Christ, 1952-. **ORGANIZATIONS:** Mem natl adv bd, gen evangelist, chmn Comm on Evangelism Gen Assembly 1973-; founding mem bd dir WA Cty Civic & Charitable Assoc; mem Martin CtyCoop Assoc Inc, Rodgers Comm Produce & Products Coop Inc, Martin Indust Devel Assoc Inc, NC Fed Child Devel Ctr Inc, NC Folklore Soc, Disciples of Christ Hist Soc, Alpha Phi Alpha, NC State Chaplain Assoc of Alpha Men 1981, 1986-87. **HONORS/ACHIEVEMENTS:** Listed in Who's Who in the South & Southwest; author of several books incl "Disciple Assemblies of Eastern N Carolina" 1966. **MILITARY SERVICE:** USNR 1945-46.

BARNWELL, BENJAMIN BURDEE, JR.
Surgeon. **PERSONAL:** Born Aug 21, 1931, Beaufort, SC; died Jun 15, 1988; married Jocelyn Maclin; children: Velma, Anne, Benjamin III, John. **EDUCATION:** Morehouse Coll,

BS 1952; Meharry Medical Coll, MD 1959; Howard Univ Graduate School, 1952-54; Freedmen's Hospital, surgeon resident 1960-64. **CAREER:** Petersburg Gen Hospital, chief gen surgeon 1975-76; Private Practice, surgeon 1965-. **ORGANIZATIONS:** Mem Kappa Alpha Psi Frat; Southside Virginia Medical Soc; Medical Soc Virginia; Old Dominion Medical Soc; Natl Medical Assn; Virginia Chapter Amer Coll Surgeons; Amer Coll Surgeons; Sigma Pi Phi Frat. **HONORS/ACHIEVEMENTS:** USPHS Sr Asst Surgeon 1961-62; Tumor clinic fellow, Howard Univ Dept Surgery 1964-65; Charles Drew Memorial Award, Natl Medical Assn 1964; published "The Value of the Central Venous Pressure Determination in the Mgmt of the Surgery Patient" Journal Natl Medical Assn 1964. **BUSINESS ADDRESS:** Surgeon, 40 Liberty St, Petersburg, VA 23803.

BEARDEN, ROMARE H.
Artist. **PERSONAL:** Born Sep 02, 1914, Charlotte, NC; died Mar 12, 1988. **EDUCATION:** NYU, BS 1935; Pratt Inst, Hon D Arts 1974; Carnegie-Mellon Univ, Hon D Arts 1975. **CAREER:** Harlem Cultural Cncl, art dir; Museum Modern Art NYC, retrospective 1971; numerous exhibits in US; 2 abroad; work displayed in many museums & priv collections; artist. **ORGANIZATIONS:** Mem Natl Inst Arts & Letters. **HONORS/ACHIEVEMENTS:** Recip Natl Inst Arts & Letters 1966; Purchase Award Amer Acad Arts & Letters 1970; Guggenheim Fellow 1970-71; Author, "The Art of Romare Bearden" 1974. **MILITARY SERVICE:** AUS Sgt 1942-45.

BELL, EDWARD F.
Attorney. **PERSONAL:** Born Apr 22, 1929, Grand Rapids, MI; died Jun 22, 1988, Detroit, MI; married Marilyn; children: Celeste, Whitney. **EDUCATION:** Univ of MI, BA 1951; Detroit Coll of Law, JD 1954. **CAREER:** Children's Aid Soc Detroit, social worker 1956-59; Private Practice, atty 1959-69; Wayne Co Detroit, circuit judge served 3 years; Bell and Gardner PC, atty. **ORGANIZATIONS:** past pres, Natl Bar Assn. **BUSINESS ADDRESS:** Attorney, Bell and Gardner PC, 561 East Jefferson, Detroit, MI 48226.

BELL, MAUD MELINDA
Educator, licensed real estate salespers. **PERSONAL:** Born Jun 24, Portsmouth, VA; died 1986; divorced. **EDUCATION:** Shaw Univ, BA; Postgrad, City Coll, NY Teachers Coll, Columbia Univ 1963. **CAREER:** Robeson Co Training School, teacher 1932-35; Bd of Educ, Norfolk VA, 1935-55; Booker T Washington High School, chmn teacher English dept; Alexander Hamilton High School Brooklyn, 1956-58; Andrew Jackson High School NYC, 1958-72; John F Kennedy High School Riverdale, teacher 1972-77. **ORGANIZATIONS:** Uptown campaign mgr Democratic Gubernatorial Election 1950; sponsor Red Cross Club; Girl Scout leader; mem Natl Council Teachers of English 1970-77; NY City Assn of Teachers of English; United Fed of Teachers; NYSUT; Protestant Teachers Assn; Shaw Univ Natl Alumni Assn; Columbia Univ Alumni Assn; life mem NAACP; founder Women of Amer Inc 1945; founder/sponsor A J Legum Found Scholarship Fund 1945-50; exec comm Victor Ashe & Tom Young City Council Camp; camp counselor Camp Fellohe YWCA 1940-50; supt Asbury Methodist Church School 1973-77; mem Women's Voters League of Cortland 1970-75; mem Norfolk Historical Commn. **HONORS/ACHIEVEMENTS:** Author poetry; several plays; Woman of the Year 1950; Notable Amer 1977; div chmn March of Dimes; Epistoleus; Basileus Alpha Kappa Alpha Sorority 1947-50; past hon dau Ruler-Dau of Elks; hon Shaw Univ Summer Homecoming 1973; NAACP Woman of the Year Westchester County NY 1979; 100 New York Women 1975; Chair Intl Affairs UN Rep of Business & Professional Women of Westchester Inc. **BUSINESS ADDRESS:** Teacher, John F Kennedy HS, 115-05 178 Place St, St Albans, NY 11434.

BELL, TRAVERS J., JR.
Business executive. **PERSONAL:** Died Jan 25, 1988. **EDUCATION:** Attended Washington Univ, NY Inst of Finance. **CAREER:** Dempsey Tegler & Co Inc, vice pres 1961-67; Diversified Data Systems, pres/dir; Fusz Schmelzle & Co Inc, vice pres & dir 1967-71; Cocoline Chocolate, Inc, CEO; Daniels & Bell Inc, chmn of the bd 1971-. **ORGANIZATIONS:** Official Amer Stock Exchange; gov Securities Industry Assn; advisor Inst for Economic Rsch; adv US Sec of Commerce Comm on Minority Enterprise Develop; trade advisor Intl Cocoa Agreement Switzerland; trade advisor US Trade Rep Commodity Policy; mem Legislation Comm of SIA; registered floor broker Commodity Futures Tradinc Commn; mem Dist Comm No 12 of Natl Assn of Securities Dealers; dir SIA Minority Capital Found; mem Cncl on Foreign Relations Inc; financial consul Economic Comm of West African States Fund for Cooper Compen & Develop; mem US Small Bus Admin Task Force on Equity & Venture Capital; mem NY Stock Exchange & Hearing Comm; advisor N Atlantic Treaty Organ; advisor NATO Southern Flank. **BUSINESS ADDRESS:** Chairman of the Board, Daniels & Bell Inc, 99 Wall St, New York, NY 10005.

BENBOW, LILLIAN PIERCE
Civil rights executive. **PERSONAL:** Born in Vicksburg, MS; married Edward D Benbow. **EDUCATION:** BA Social Science. **CAREER:** Exec producer movie "Countdown at Kusini"; Michigan Dept of Civil Rights, dir housing program. **ORGANIZATIONS:** Editorial advisory bd Essence Magazine; Natl Advisory Comm Infinity Factory II Educ Devel Center, Newton MA; Natl Bd Dir Camp Fire Girls Inc; Natl Black Women's Political Leadership Caucus; noted public speaker; mem bd dirs DST Telecommunications Inc; mem Housing Ad-

visory Comm Southeast Michigan Council of Govts; Michigan Interagency Council on Corrections Educ; Michigan Comm on Law & Housing; Natl Assn of Human Rights Workers; Michigan League for Human Serv; Bd of Mgmt Detroit Delta Home for Girls; natl pres Delta Sigma Theta; life mem NAACP; mem Women's Com of Detroit Human Relations Commn. **HONORS/ACHIEVEMENTS:** LeMoyne Coll Alumnus of the Year 1968; Serv Citations Comm Council Detroit & State Legislature of Michigan 1974-75; numerous serv leadership awards. **BUSINESS ADDRESS:** Dir, MI Dept Civil Rights, 1200 6 St Exec Plaza, Detroit, MI 48226.

BENTON, BROOK
Entertainer. **PERSONAL:** Born Sep 19, 1931, Camden, SC; died Apr 09, 1988; married Mary Askew; children: Brook Jr, Vanessa, Roy, Gerald. **CAREER:** Self-employed entertainer, songwriter. **ORGANIZATIONS:** AFTRA; ACAC; AGVA; SAG; life mem NAACP; United Dem Club. **HONORS/ACHIEVEMENTS:** 16 Gold Records; Best Contemp Male Vocalist 1970; BMI Cit of Achiev 1971; Wm B Moss Brotherhood Achievement Award 1962; AFTRA Award of Achievement 1964; Playboy Mag Award Outstanding Jazz Artist of the Year 1959; VPA Merit Award 1966; Club Intl Hon Membership 1961; Show of Shows Award New York City NAACP 1966; Champagne Mus Mer Award 1969; WDAS Mus Achievement 1962; Bro of Mus Inc Humanity 1961; AFTRA Award of Apprec 1969.

BETHEA, LARRY
Professional athlete. **PERSONAL:** Born Jul 21, 1956, Florence, SC; died Apr 1987. **EDUCATION:** Michigan State, Urban Dev. **CAREER:** Oakland Invaders, defensive end 1984-87. **HONORS/ACHIEVEMENTS:** Appeared in Super Bowl XIII vs Pittsburg Steelers 1979; first lineman since Dick Butkus in 1963 to be named Big 10 MVP; named All-Big 10 as jr & sr; also named All-Amer as sr. **BUSINESS ADDRESS:** Oakland Invaders, 7850 Edgewater Dr, Oakland, CA 94621.

BOBO, WILLIE See CORREA, WILLIAM

BOROM, ROY
Educator. **PERSONAL:** Born May 30, 1925, Port Huron, MI; died Sep 12, 1987; married Dolores Fish (deceased); children: Faridah, Gilbert. **EDUCATION:** Univ of ID; Kent State Univ; Coll of Wooster, BA 1949; Western Reserve Univ, MSSA 1951. **CAREER:** Cuyahoga Juv Ct, probation officer 1951-53; Cuyahoga Co Div of Child Welfare, supr 1953-58; Baltimore Urban Renewal & Housing Agy, princ comm organiz 1959-63; MD Prisoner's Aid Assn, asst dir 1963-64; Univ of Baltimore, dir of admissions & asst prof 1964-68; VISTA, consult 1966-68; VISTA Fellows Prog Univ of MD, actng dir 1967-68; Univ of MD Baltimore, exec asst to chancellor 1970-86 (retired). **ORGANIZATIONS:** Mem past vice pres MD Chap Natl Assn of Soc Workers; mem Acad of Cert Soc Workers; Natl Conf of Soc Welfare; advsry bd York, PA State Univ; Crispus Attucks Assn bd of dir, pres; Black Polit Caucus of York; Mayor's Downtown Improv Com; Mayor's Enterprise Zone Dev Comm; York Co Plng Comin; chmn York City Plng Commin; past pres York Fed Neighborhood Cred Union; past chmn York Council of Agency Execs; chmn Polit Studies & Action Grp; past co-chmn Mayor's Task Force for Equal Rights in Edn; past mem Baltimore Civ Serv Oral Exam Bd; Elect Deleg MD Constl Conv 1967-68; mem York City Counc 1974-76; bd mem Riverview Inc; consultant Edu-Tech Associates. **MILITARY SERVICE:** USN 1943-46. **HOME ADDRESS:** 112 Irving Rd, York, PA 17403.

BRADFORD, BENONA HAMLIN
Business executive. **PERSONAL:** Born May 30, 1910, Ashville, NC; died 1988; married Reginald L. **CAREER:** Retired Workmens Compensation, Examiner, NY St Workmens Compensation Bd Founder; exec dir; Friends founder; dir; Council of Political Record Watchers, former chmn; 47 Precinct Comm Council, former sec chmn Comm Planning Bd 13, former special asst to chmn in charge of special events, former membership dir. **ORGANIZATIONS:** Charter mem Bronx Council on Arts; founder Nat Council of Concerned Afro-Amer Rep; mem NY St Conf of NAACP Branches Membrshp chmn; founder, The Great NAACP "Club 100"; "Generations Without Gaps;" former 1st vice pres Natl Assn of Media Women Inc 1st chmn bd dir Williamsbridge Branch NAACP Day Care Center; bd dir Victory Day Care Center; bd of advisors Youth Leadership Found; advisory council Commn on Human Rights; NY St mem Parks & Playground Council; Civil Serv Employees Assn; NY Metro Chapter of Natl Council of Negro Women; speakers Bureau of Outstanding Women in Public Relations; Natl Assn of Women of Am YWCA; life mem NAACP. **HONORS/ACHIEVEMENTS:** Top Saleslady Award Negro Press; Comm Serv Award Amer Legion; Outstanding Den Mother, Cub Scouts of Amer; Den Mother Pin of Honor Federation of Jewish Philanthropies; Humanitarian Awards Climbers Business Club & Club Les Zier; This Is Your Life Award NY Branch NAACP; Leadership Appreciation Award, Comm Planning Bd 13; 40 Outstanding Membership Writing Awards & Campaign NAACP; Pres Appreciation Award Natl Assn of Media Women; Comm Serv & Leadership Award Comm Friends; Humanitarian Award Gov Rockefeller; ET Reed Medal of Achievement; numerous other awards & citations. **BUSINESS ADDRESS:** 2 World Trade Center, New York, NY 10047.

BRADSHAW, LUCY HYMAN
Librarian. **PERSONAL:** Born Jul 20, Clinton, NC; died Nov 04, 1981; married Joseph E; children: Cheryl Y, Joseph E. **EDUCATION:** Winston-Salem Univ, BS 1943; Atlanta Univ, BS Library Science 1946, MS Library Science 1955. **CAREER:** Winston-Salem Teachers Coll, library asst 1943-45, asst librarian 1946-61, acting librarian 1961-62, librarian 1962-. **ORGANIZATIONS:** Mem North Carolina Library Assn, SE Library Assn, Amer Library Assn, YWCA, Winston-Salem Symphony Guild, Altrusa Club. **HONORS/ACHIEVEMENTS:** Outstanding Serv, Tau Chi Chapter Alpha Phi Omega 1974. **BUSINESS ADDRESS:** Winston-Salem StateUniv, Winston-Salem, NC.

BRANTON, WILEY AUSTIN
Attorney. **PERSONAL:** Born Dec 13, 1923, Pine Bluff, AR; married Lucille E McKee; children: Richard H, Toni C Moore (dec), Wylene A Moore, Wiley A Jr, Beverly L, Debra E. **EDUCATION:** Univ of AR Pine Bluff, BS 1950; Univ of AR Fayetteville, JD 1953. **CAREER:** United Planning Org, exec dir 1967-69; Alliance for Labor Action, dir social action 1969-71; Dolphin Branton Stafford & Webber, partner 1971-78; Howard Univ School of Law, dean 1978-83; Sidley & Austin, partner 1983-. **ORGANIZATIONS:** Special asst to atty general US Dept of Justice 1965-67; exec sec President's Cncl on Equal Opportunity 1965; exec dir Voter Educ Project 1962-65; atty Wiley A Branton Atty 1952-62; bd mem Consolidat-

ed Rail Corp 1979-; bd mem Columbia 1st Federal S & L Assn 1978-; vice pres & Bd mem NAACP Legal Defense & Educ Fund 1973-; bd mem Africare 1980-. **HONORS/ACHIEVEMENTS:** Fellow Am Bar Found 1979; Charles H Houston Medallion of Merit WA Bar Assn 1978; C Francis Stratford Award Nat Bar Assn 1958; Charles Edgerton Award AmCivil Liberties Union 1977; Lawyer of the Year Awd Bar Assn of DC 1986. **MILITARY SERVICE:** AUS master sgt 1943-46. **HOME ADDRESS:** 1611 Tamarack St NW, Washington, DC 20012. **BUSINESS ADDRESS:** Attorney, Sidley & Austin Law Firm, 1722 Eye St NW, Washington, DC 20006.

BROWN, BRENDA L.
Association executive. **PERSONAL:** Born Sep 03, 1938, Louisville, KY; died Mar 29, 1982; married John Scott; children: Courtney, Leigh. **EDUCATION:** Howard Univ, BA 1960; Univ of Maryland, 1960; Washington DC Teachers Coll, 1960-63. **CAREER:** Community Relations Serv Dept of Justice, program asst/program devel officer 1964-66; Peace Corps, staff asst 1964; Washington DC Teachers Coll, visiting lecturer 1962-64; Washington DC Public Schools, teacher 1960-64. **ORGANIZATIONS:** Mem Amer Speech & Hearing Assn; NEA; Amer Council for Advancement & Support of Educ; Natl Soc of Fund Raising Execs; past bd dir Natl Conf of Christians & Jews; past mem, bd dir Urban League; YWCA; Howard Univ Alumni Club; Howard Women's Club; Alpha Kappa Alpha Sorority; Parents Council Natl Cathedral School. **BUSINESS ADDRESS:** HowardUniv, 2935 Upton St NW, Washington, DC 20008.

BROWN, EFFIE H.
Educator. **PERSONAL:** Born Mar 01, 1912, Georgia; died May 11, 1989; widowed. **EDUCATION:** Atlanta Univ Normal; NY Univ School of Educ; Teachers Coll, Columbia OH, BS. **CAREER:** New York City Bd of Educ, supvr social studies; Dept of Welfare NYC, social worker; Nursery School & Day Care Center, founder/dir; Leader of Elementary School Educ, teacher 1946-64. **ORGANIZATIONS:** Sec Brooklyn Business & Professional Women's Club Inc; pres NY Branch Afro-Am Historical Soc 1974; comm consultant Volunteer Fund Raising Medgar Evers Coll; mem Natl Sorority of Phi Delta Kappa; comm leader Youth Activities Coll Entrance Tudorship Care Training; Natl Business & Professional Women's Club. **HONORS/ACHIEVEMENTS:** Organized 1st birthday celebration of late Congressman A C Powell, Jr; recipient Professional Serv Award, Phi Delta Kappa; Distinguished Comm Serv Award, Natl Business & Professional Women 1971; organized teachers to work for former Mayor John V Lindsay; recipient/plaque Dedicated Serv Intra-Cultural Educ Children of NY; co-chmn erecting Mathew Henson Plaque.

BROWN, H. FRANKLIN
Attorney. **PERSONAL:** Born Oct 26, 1906, Philadelphia, PA; died Feb 1989, Detroit, MI. **EDUCATION:** Lincoln Univ PA, AB 1937; Univ of MI Law Sch, attended; Detroit Coll of Law, JD 1948. **CAREER:** H Franklin Brown PC, attorney. **ORGANIZATIONS:** Mem Alpha Phi Alpha Frat 1933; mem Prince Hall Mason & Shriners 1948; life mem treas bd mem NAACP 1948-; gen counsel Synod Mission United Presbyterian Ch 1950; legal adv 14 Bapt Ch & Black Muslims 1954-; chmn trustees St John's United Presb Ch 1954-79; pres bd mem Detroit Council of Polit Educ 1958; treas Richard H Austin Sect of State of MI 1964; mem Bd of Co Supr 1964-68; pres Randolph W Wallace Sr Kidney Rsch 1965; chmn bd dir Fisher Branch YMCA 1974-78; mem MI State Bar/Wolerine Bar Assn; Freedom Fund chmn NAACP Freedom Dinner 1972. **HONORS/ACHIEVEMENTS:** John W Armstrong Humanitarian Metro YMCA 1978; Community Serv & Youth Programs, Fisher Branch YMCA 1978. **MILITARY SERVICE:** USN Sk 2nd 1942-45; Good Conduct Medal. **BUSINESS ADDRESS:** Attorney, H Franklin Brown PC, 2605 Cadillac Tower, Detroit, MI 48226.

BROWN, STERLING A.
Educator. **PERSONAL:** Born May 01, 1901, Washington, DC; died Jan 13, 1989, Washington, DC; married Daisy Turnbull. **EDUCATION:** Williams Coll, BA 1921; Harvard Univ, MA English 1923. **CAREER:** Virginia Seminary and Coll, teacher; Lincoln Univ, teacher; Fisk Univ, teacher; Howard Univ Teacher 1929-69; Howard Univ Inst for Arts & Humanities, sr rsch assoc. **ORGANIZATIONS:** Visiting prof, NYU, the New School for Social Rsch, Sarah Lawrence Coll, Vassar Coll. **HONORS/ACHIEVEMENTS:** First book "Outline for the Study of Poetry of the American Negroes," Harcourt Brace 1931; "Southern Road," 1932; "The Negro Caravan," Dryden Press 1941 w/Dr Arthur P Davis; "The Collected Poems of Sterling A Brown," 1980 Harper & Row; named Poet Laureate of Washington DC Mayor Marion Barry 1984; numerous articles, essays, reviews and poems have appeared in natl magazines; Winner of Marshall Poetry Prize, 1984; Named the District's poet laureate.

BRUNSON, PIERCE B.
Retired educator. **PERSONAL:** Born in Macon, GA; died Jan 08, 1988; married Brunetta Jacobs; children: Frank B, Yolande Iris Collins. **EDUCATION:** Morris Brown Coll, BA 1938; Atlanta U, MA 1955, Post Grad 1962, 1964. **CAREER:** Austell GA Elem Sch, tchr 1938-39; Pilgrim H & L Ins Co, ins slsmn 1939-41; AUS, 1St lt 1941-45; Ford Motor Co, 1945-47; Hudson High Sch Macon GA, tchr 1947-49; retired. **ORGANIZATIONS:** Chrmn & tchr Dept of Soc Sci Ballard-Hudson Sr High 1949-65; prin Maude C Pye, Elem Sch 1965-77; mem bd of dir Middle GA Area Planning & Devel Commn Macon GA; mem bd of dir Booker T Washington Commnty Cntr Macon GA; mem bd of dir Bibb Cnty Sr Citizens. **MILITARY SERVICE:** USAR quartermaster capt. **HOME ADDRESS:** 1994 Vining Cir, Macon, GA 31204.

BUSH, ERNEST
Construction company executive. **PERSONAL:** Born Apr 18, 1920, Chicago, IL; died 1988; married Mildred Outlaw; children: Ernest Jr, Marla Jean. **CAREER:** Milk and beverage distributor, 1942-53; Bush Construction Co, pres. **ORGANIZATIONS:** Bd mem, Big Buddies Orgn; Chmn of Bd, Finance Comm Black III Legislative Lobby; bd mem, Seaway Natl Bank of Chicago; treasurer, Political Action Comm of Illinois. **BUSINESS ADDRESS:** President, Bush Construction Co, 359 E 79th St, Chicago, IL 60619.

CABRERA, MARION C.
Educational administrator. **PERSONAL:** Born Jul 30, 1932. **EDUCATION:** FL A&M Univ, BS; Indiana Univ, MS; Nova Univ, EdD. **CAREER:** Lomax Elementary School, physical educ teacher 1950, asst principal 1963; Dillard Elementary School, 6th grade teacher 1958; Manpower Devel Training Program, guidance counselor 1965; Glover Elementary

School, principal 1966; J W Lockhart Elementary School, principal. **ORGANIZATIONS:** Mem Kappa Delta Pi, Intl Reading Assn, Hillsborough County Math Council, Florida Elementary School Principals, Florida Assn of School Admin, Natl Social Studies Council, Elementary Principal Small Group Chmn; charter represenatative superintendents Mgmt Group; mem Natl Assn of Elementary School Principals, Amer Educ Research Assn, Assn of Curriculum Develop; polemarch Kappa Alpha Psi; pres Frontiers of Amer. **MILITARY SERVICE:** US Army Reserve 12 yrs.

CALHOUN, JOHN HENRY
Consultant. **PERSONAL:** Born Jul 08, 1899, Greenville, SC; died May 06, 1988; divorced; children: John H III, Ninaking C Anderson. **EDUCATION:** Sterling Coll, 1915; Hampton Inst, Diploma 1922; Morehouse Coll, AB 1933; Atlanta Univ, MAB 1968. **CAREER:** Tuskegee Inst, bookkeeper steno 1922-23; US Veterans Hospital, bookkeeper financial officer 1923-30; Natl Benefit Life Insurance Chicago, insurance salesman 1930-31; Natl Benefit Life Ins Birmingham AL, insurance salesman 1931-32; Birmingham Scott Newspaper, editor 1933; Atlanta, GA Syndct Birmingham World & Atlanta World, circulation mgr 1933; Penn School, bookkeeper 1934; City of Atlanta, councilman 1974-77; Morris Brown Coll, consultant. **ORGANIZATIONS:** Bkpr Atlanta Wrld 1935, Cornelius King & Son Real Est 1935-45; real est brkr Atlana, GA 1945-; cnsltnt Atlanta, GA 1951-; dir pres NAACP 1950-56; presbd mem Atlanta Bnrs Lg 1950-; vice pres bd mem YMCA 1984-; Omega Psi Rho Frat 1950-52. **HONORS/ACHIEVEMENTS:** 35 Local & Natl Awrds. **MILITARY SERVICE:** Stdnt Army Training Corp Hampton Inst 1st lt 1 yr. **HOME ADDRESS:** 50 Gardenia Drive NW, Atlanta, GA 30314. **BUSINESS ADDRESS:** Consultant, Morris Brown Coll, 200 Auburn Ave NE, Atlanta, GA 30303.

CAMPBELL, CHARLES M.
Educator, legislator. **PERSONAL:** Born Oct 29, 1918, Red Springs, NC; died 1986; son of Lee Black and Lela Black (parents' names were later changed to Campbell); married Naomi S; children: Lori Margaret. **EDUCATION:** North Carolina Coll, BA 1939; Howard Univ, MA 1941; Columbia Univ, MA 1944. **CAREER:** Bethune-Cookman Coll, dean of men 1942-43; WCFL Chicago, newscaster 1952; WAAT, Newark NJ, 1954; KGMB Honolulu, 1962; Farrington High School Honolulu, educator 1965-77; elected city councilman-at-large, Honolulu HI 1968; Hawaii State Legislature, elected representative 1976; Hawaii State Senate, elected senator 1978. **ORGANIZATIONS:** Chmn Senate Educ Commn; majority policy leader Hawaii Senate; chmn Natl Conf of Educ Legislators; lectr Peace Corps Trainees E-W Center Univ of Hawaii 1968; lectr Fullbright Scholars E-W Center Univ of Hawaii 1968-69; Pioneer Black Newscaster WGES Chicago, WLIB, Brooklyn NY; second vice pres Radio-Newsreel-TV Working Press Assn; sec YMCA Army Navy; employment counselor 1946-48; social worker Chicago 1949-51; chmn Oahu County Democratic Comm; task force Openness Govt 1974; founder & advisor Teen-age Assembly of Amer Inc; founder "Operation Aloha"; selected to attend Natl Security & Forum AFB AL 1974; chmn Hawaii Advisory Comm US Commn Civil Rights; pres Hawaii State Teachers Assn; vice pres Classroom Teachers Natl. **HONORS/ACHIEVEMENTS:** Wrote & published two books: A Program for Teens, Athletes & People in the Workplace 1986; Peer Pressure to Take Drugs/Alcohol 1986. **BUSINESS ADDRESS:** C/o Hawaii St Legislature, Hawaii St Capital, Honolulu, HI 96813.

CAMPBELL, LEROY MILLER
Architect. **PERSONAL:** Born Jul 05, 1927, New York, NY; married June C Peters; children: Sharon. **EDUCATION:** Howard Univ, BA architecture 1951. **CAREER:** Sulton Campbell & Assoc, principal 1966; Cohen Haft, job cpt 1963-66; John Graham Designer, 1959-63; Mcleon Ferrara, cpt 1956-69; Hilyard Robinson draftsman 1952-56; Alexander Richter, draftsman 1952. **ORGANIZATIONS:** Mem, trustee Amer & Inst of Architecture; past pres Natl Org of Minority Architects; mem Natl Tech Assn Bd of Dir Metro, Washington Planning & Housing Assn; mem Neighbors Inc 1963-; past vice pres Mu Lambda Chapter Alpha Phi Alpha Frat. **HONORS/ACHIEVEMENTS:** Mem Natl Screening Comm Design Award; Prestressed Concrete Inst 1973. **MILITARY SERVICE:** USAFR 1st lieutenant. **BUSINESS ADDRESS:** 7600 Georgia Ave NW, Washington, DC 20012.

CARRION, ODESSA
Psychotherapist. **PERSONAL:** Born Jul 04, Kentucky; divorced; children: Jeanine. **EDUCATION:** Wayne State U, AB; Univ of MI, MASW. **CAREER:** City Univ NYC, tchr, public administration, & communications 1979-80; Hlth & Hosps Corp Div of Social Work, dir of social work; Children's Ct, social worker; Youth House for Boys; Training Sch for Girls; Mental Hlth Clinic; Bd of Edn; Child Welfare; Med & Psychiatric Soc Work; Pvt Prac, Psychotherapy. **ORGANIZATIONS:** Mem HRA Avd Counc; chmn Rules & Monitoring Conn; asst chmn Polit Com; State HRA Adv Counc; consult Pshchotherapist Soc Work Consult & Psychotherapist;mem Cntrl Harlem Coord Counc; liaison Congressional Black Caucus; mem City-Wide & State HRA Adv Counc; exec bd Concerned Citizens for Human Servs. **HONORS/ACHIEVEMENTS:** Outst serv award Assn of Spanish Workers 1974. **BUSINESS ADDRESS:** 5500 Fieldston Rd, Riverdale, NY 10471.

CARTER, ARTHUR M.
Retired editor, publisher. **PERSONAL:** Born Sep 02, 1911, Washington, DC; died May 22, 1988; son of Robert I Carter and Christine C Carter; married Callie Scott; children: Carlton. **EDUCATION:** Attended, Howard Univ. **CAREER:** DAWN Magazine, editor 1972-79; Washington Afro-Amer Newspaper, reporter 1937, sports editor 1939, war correspondent 1943-44, special correspondent 1945-46, editor 1947-49, copy editor 1950-51, asst editor in charge of makeup 1951-53, asst managing editor 1954, assoc editor 1968, publisher/editor 1970-86 (retired). **ORGANIZATIONS:** Mem Shepherd Park Civic Assn; Kappa Alpha Psi; Washington DC Inaugural Comm for Mayor Walter E Washington; Advisory Bd New Howard Univ Hospital; United Way. **HONORS/ACHIEVEMENTS:** Outstanding Service Certificate, Kappa Alpha Psi 1963; 25 Year Serv Award Afro-Amer 1963; Certificate of Appreciation for Serv, Washington Urban League; First Prize NNPA News Contest for Makeup 1972; Third Prize NNPA News Contest 1973; Pulitzer Prize Jury, Columbia Univ 1973, 1974; Outstanding Newsman's Coop Award, Howard UROTC 1974; winner NNPA News Contest for General Excellence 1975; Outstanding Journalism Award, Capital Press Club 1975; Achievement Citation, Pigskin Club Washington DC 1976; Journalist of the Year, Capital Press Club Washington DC 1979; Editor of the Year Award NNPA 1983; Distinguished Serv Award, Sigma Delta Chi 1984. **MILITARY SERVICE:** War correspondent 1942-45.

CLAYE, CLIFTON MAURICE
Educator. **PERSONAL:** Born Oct 04, 1912, Fordyce, AR; died Nov 04, 1977; married Anne Marie Bradley; children: Clifford Ann, Marylen Marie, Charlene Mariette. **EDUCATION:** AR AM& N Pine Bluff, BS 1937; Univ of AR, MS 1952, EdD 1958. **CAREER:** Dallas County Training School, Fordyce AR, high school teacher 1938-49; Wilmer High School, Wilmer AR, high school principal 1949-50; Lafayette County Training School, Stamps AR, high school principal 1950-54; MM Tate High School, Marvell AR, high school principal 1954-56; Texas Southern Univ, prof educ. **ORGANIZATIONS:** Mem Assn for Supervision & Curriculum Devel; Natl Assn of Secondary School Principals; Natl Assn of Elemementary Principals; Natl Educ Assn; Texas State Teachers Assn; Omega Psi Phi; Kappa Delta Pi; Phi Delta Kappa; YMCA Recipient So Educ Found Fellow 1956-58. **HONORS/ACHIEVEMENTS:** Outstanding Educator of the Year, Texas Southern Univ 1965; Man of the Year, Nu Phi Chapter of Omega Psi Phi 1968; Educator of the Year, 9th Dist Omega Psi Phi 1970; 7 grants from Office of Educ Dept of HEW; 4 research grants from Texas Southern Univ; 2 grants from local school dists. **MILITARY SERVICE:** AUS m/sgt 1942-48. **BUSINESS ADDRESS:** TX Southern Univ, 3201 Wheeler St, Houston, TX.

COCKREL, KENNETH V.
Attorney, former city councilman. **PERSONAL:** Born Nov 05, 1938, Detroit, MI; died Apr 25, 1989, Detroit, MI; children: Kenneth Jr, Kate. **EDUCATION:** Wayne State Univ, BA 1964; Wayne State Univ Law School, JD 1967. **CAREER:** Detroit City, councilman 1978-81; Kenneth V Cockrel PC, attny partner 1968-. **ORGANIZATIONS:** Mem NBA, MI State Bar, Wolverine Bar, Detroit Bar, Natl Conf Black Lawyers; past mem bd of dir Natl Lawyers Guild, Civil Liberties Legal Def Fund, Inner-City Bus Improvement Forum; past mem League of Revolutionary Black Workers & Black Workers Congress; past pres Labor Def Coaltion; past chmn State of Emergency Comm, Anti-STRESS; guest lecturer various coll & univ; former columnist MI Chronicle; former commentator WJR Radio. **HONORS/ACHIEVEMENTS:** Outstanding Leadership Awd Cotillion Club 1973; Disting Achievement Medal Detroit NAACP. **MILITARY SERVICE:** USAF 1955-59.

COLLINS, O'NEIL RAY
Educator. **PERSONAL:** Born Mar 09, 1931, Opelousas, LA; died Apr 08, 1989; son of Frank Collins and Angela Collins; married Ann Walker; children: Marianne, Angela, Lila, Neil. **EDUCATION:** Southern Univ, BS; Univ of Iowa, MS, PhD. **CAREER:** Univ of California, prof biology, assoc dean graduate div 1971-72, prof botany 1972, assoc prof botany 1969-72; Wayne State Univ, assoc prof biology 1965-69; Southern Univ, assoc prof biology 1963-65; Queens Coll, instructor biology 1961-63; Miller Research Prof, 1973-74. **HONORS/ACHIEVEMENTS:** Found Grants 1963-77. **MILITARY SERVICE:** AUS corpl 1951-53. **BUSINESS ADDRESS:** 2017 Life Sciences Bldg, Berkeley, CA 94720.

CORREA, WILLIAM (WILLIE BOBO)
Musician. **PERSONAL:** Born Feb 28, 1933, New York, NY; married Alicia Suarez; children: Gil, Eric. **CAREER:** Ali B Inc, entertainer; Tito Puente Band, musician; Cal Tjader Band Musician; Wilie Bobo Band, leader. **ORGANIZATIONS:** Am Federation Of Musicians, Musician; AFTRA. **BUSINESS ADDRESS:** Ali B Inc, 9220 Sunset Blvd Ste 212, Los Angeles, CA 90069.

COVINGTON, FLOYD CORNELIUS JAMES, SR.
Retired government official. **PERSONAL:** Born Mar 29, 1901, Denver, CO; married Willa Alma Greene; children: Floyd C Jr. **EDUCATION:** Washburn Univ, BA 1927. **CAREER:** Los Angeles Urban League, exec dir 1928-53; Federal Housing Authority, retired inter zone group relations advisor 1953-75. **ORGANIZATIONS:** Mem Natl Urban League, NAACP, Congress of Racial Equality; founder/charter mem Men of Tomorrow. **HONORS/ACHIEVEMENTS:** City of Los Angeles Proclamation 1984 "Floyd & Willa Covington Day" presented by Mayor Tom Bradley. **HOME ADDRESS:** PO Box 781240, Los Angeles, CA 90016.

COX, JAMES ALEXANDER
Educator, clergyman. **PERSONAL:** Born Aug 17, 1913, Pittsburgh, PA; died Dec 01, 1987; married Vivian Saunders Cox; children: William R, James A Jr, Debra Ann Ellison. **EDUCATION:** Virginia Seminary & Coll, Theology 1934; Virginia Union Univ, AB 1937; Univ of Pittsburgh, EdM 1947. **CAREER:** Sandy Point School VA, principal 1937; Lincoln High School, teacher 1938-43; Mt Zion Baptist Church, pastor 1938-43; AUS, chaplain 1943-46; Macedonia Baptist Church, pastor 1947-53; Calvary Baptist Church, pastor 1953-68; Amer Baptist Theological Seminar Ext, dean & instructor 1965-66; Pittsburgh Inst Christian Serv, pres 1966-68; Tabernacle Baptist Church, pastor 1968-83; free lance lecturer teacher & pastor emeritus. **ORGANIZATIONS:** Dir of oper OIC 1968; advisory comm Affirmative Action Housing, Educ & Welfare 1975-76; advisory comm Affirmative Action Dept Labor Harrisburg 1975-76; life mem NAACP 1979. **HONORS/ACHIEVEMENTS:** Cited Chaplain of the Week in Stars & Stripes publication 1945; two Battle Stars for Battle of Appenines and Po Valley 1945; Bronze Star AUS 1946; bronze plaque Pastor of the Year Elks in Pittsburgh 1957; bronze plaque Meritorious Service Ministers Conf 1960; Achievement Award Pittsburgh Courier humanitarianism 1961; citation House of Representative 1969, 1976, 1983; Honorary DD VA Coll 1971; Award Urban Black Coalition of Harrisburg 1975; citation from Gov Shapp 1976; bronze plaque Dept of Labor for Activity as Affirmative Action Advisor 1976. **MILITARY SERVICE:** AUS chaplain major 1943-46; Bronze Star for risking life to carry surcease to men; two Battle Stars for Appenines & Po Valley. **BUSINESS ADDRESS:** Lecturer, Teacher, Pastor Emeritus, Free Lance, 25 N 19th St, Harrisburg, PA 17103.

CRAWFORD, CLINTON WAYNE
Law enforcement. **PERSONAL:** Born May 11, 1957, Uniontown, PA; died Aug 17, 1987, Pittsburgh, PA; son of James and Pauline. **EDUCATION:** St Vincent Coll, BA Business Mgmt 1980. **CAREER:** Pennsylvania State Police, trooper. **HOME ADDRESS:** Rt 1 Box 824, Lamberton, PA 15458. **BUSINESS ADDRESS:** PA State Police, PA State Police 5000 Mobay Rd, Pittsburgh, PA 15205.

CROFTON, LENOULIA O.
Government official. **PERSONAL:** Born Dec 06, 1915, Nashville, AR; died Mar 21, 1989; daughter of Albeo Olds and Ethel Olds; widowed; children: James L. **EDUCATION:** Mississippi Industrial Coll, BA magna cum laude; Texas Coll; Univ of Arkansas; Univ of Wisconsin 1971. **CAREER:** Arkansas Council of Farm Workers Inc, counselor; teacher public

schools 35 years; Head Start Program, social worker; Upward Bound Program So State Coll; Arkansas Teachers Assn, sec 8 yrs; NAACP, sec state, branches 12 yrs; Christian Educ Methodist Episcopal Church, sec gen bd 8 yrs; Nashville City Council, councilwoman. **ORGANIZATIONS:** Mem Federated Club Hope of Arkansas; treasurer Howards Co Heritage Club Nashville Arkansas; delegate gen conf CMECh; mem Women's Missionary Connectional Council, CMECh; pres trustee bd New Light CME Church; mem Howard Co Voters League 1975; annual conf dir of Youth Work; annual conf dir of Christian Educ So Arkansas Annual Conf 1956-68. **BUSINESS ADDRESS:** Councilwoman, Nashville City Council, North Main St, Nashville, AR 71850.

CROSTHWAIT, OLIVE HOWARD
Secretary emeritus. **PERSONAL:** Born Aug 02, 1892, St Paul, MN; died Apr 09, 1987; married Holcombe S (deceased). **EDUCATION:** Univ MN Coll Pharmacy, PHM B 1915; Chicago Campus NW Univ, attended 1937-38. **CAREER:** Karras Drug Co, prescriptionist 1915-18; Meharry Med Sch Coll of Pharm, tchr 1919-21; Drug Stores Chicago, pharmacist 1921-28; Dailey Hosp, prescriptionist 1928-32; Jackson Mutual Life Ins Assn, founder/exec sec 1932-58; Chicago Ins Assn, founder/sec 1936-75; Serv Fed Savs & Loan Assn, sec/fndr 1951-73. **ORGANIZATIONS:** Mem Chicago Pharmacists Assn 1929-; pub relations Chicago Urban League 1957; natl bd mem adv comm Joint Negro Appeal 1955. **HONORS/ACHIEVEMENTS:** Citation Dept of Commerce 1951; Outstanding Achievement Awd Univ MN 1956; Woman of Yr Iota Phi Lambda Sor 1959; establishment of Olive H Crosthwait Award; Chicago Ins Outstanding Achievement Awd 1960.

CUNNINGHAM, CALVIN MALCOLM
Educator. **PERSONAL:** Born Jan 16, 1938, Pawhuska, OK; died Oct 1987; married Mercedier C Turner; children: Calvin Jr, Theodore R, Darwin L. **EDUCATION:** Philander Smith Coll, BS 1960; Oklahoma State Univ, MS 1969; EdD 1974. **CAREER:** Oklahoma State Univ, asst prof acad adv 1974-87, instructor 1972-74; Eudora Public Schools, principal 1969-72; teacher 1965-68. **ORGANIZATIONS:** Mem Amer & Guid & Personnel Assn, Amer Coll Personnel Assn, Oklahoma Coll Personnel Assn, Amer Assn of Profs, Oklahoma Assn of Univ Profs; contact person Danforth Found for Minority Students; past pres Oklahoma Assn for Black Personnel in Higher Educ; Arkansas Teachers Assn; Natl Teachers Assn Midscope sec PTA 1976-77; chaperone for student organizations OK State Univ 1974-; adv Student Org for Ethiopian Students at Oklahoma State Univ 1976-; mem selection comm Intl Student Adv Oklahoma State Univ 1975-76; co-chmn Black Faculty & Staff Oklahoma State Univ 1975-76. **HONORS/ACHIEVEMENTS:** Dean's & Pres Honor Rolls, Oklahoma State Univ 1974; published A Study of the Perceptions of Freshman Students' Advisement Prgram; awarded 2 science Stipends & 1 academic year to study science. **BUSINESS ADDRESS:** Life Sciences, W 305 OK State Univ, Stillwater, OK 74074.

CURRY, ANDY
Educator. **PERSONAL:** Born Jul 01, 1931, Cleveland, OH; died 1988; married Susan Gulick; children: Kevin Laird. **EDUCATION:** Cleveland State Univ, BA 1955; Case Western Reserve Univ, MSSA 1957. **CAREER:** CA Dept Mental Hygiene, psychiatric social worker 1958-61; Langley Porter Inst UCSF, psychiatric social worker 1961-65; UCSF LPI Inpatient Servs, supvr psychiatric social worker 1965-71, acting chief social worker 1970-71; CSPP San Francisco/Berkeley/Freson, core faculty (founding) 1971-88. **ORGANIZATIONS:** Adjunct faculty California School of Professional Psychology 1971-; visiting lecturer Dept of Psychology UCSF 1965-; sr research fellow Inst for Study of Soc & Health Issues 1970-; bd mem ISSHI Inc 1970-; bd mem Diabasis I & II Jungian Treatment Center, San Francisco CA 1975-80. **MILITARY SERVICE:** AUS (RFA) Sgt 1957-62. **BUSINESS ADDRESS:** Professor of Humanities, CA Schl of Professional Psychl, 1350 M St, Fresno, CA 93721.

DAUGHERTY, JULIUS CORNELIUS, SR.
Legislator. **PERSONAL:** Born Jan 04, 1925, Atlanta, GA; died Jan 31, 1987; married Thomasina Cooper. **BUSINESS ADDRESS:** 202 Daugherty Bldg, Atlanta, GA 30314.

DAVIS, ENOCH DOUGLAS
Clergyman. **PERSONAL:** Born Jun 13, 1908, Waynesboro, GA; died Sep 16, 1985; married Hazel Thigpen. **EDUCATION:** Florida Memorial Coll, AA 1944; Florida A&M Univ, BA 1951; Morehouse School of Religion, MRE 1964; Florida Memorial Coll, Honorary DDiv 1974. **CAREER:** Bethel Community Baptist Church, minister 48 yrs. **ORGANIZATIONS:** Bd of dir Morehouse School of Religion 1955; exec com Gen Bapt State Conv 1960; bd of trustees Florida Memorial Coll 1960-85; moderator W Coast Bapt Dist Assn 1964; Oscar for Leadership in Community Chest Dr United Givers Commn St Petersburg 1950. **HONORS/ACHIEVEMENTS:** Citation for Distinguished Serv, Ambassador Club Inc 1958; Liberty Bell Award, St Petersburg Bar Assn 1968; Citizen of the Year, Ambassador Club Inc 1980; Certificate of Honor for Excellence, Council on Human Relations St Petersburg 1980; Brotherhood Award, Natl Conf of Christians & Jews 1980. **BUSINESS ADDRESS:** 1045 Sixteenth St S, St Petersburg, FL 33705.

DAVIS, HILLIS D.
Director. **PERSONAL:** Born Jan 24, 1932, Selma, AL; died Jan 31, 1989; married Marian Anderson; children: Hillis D Jr, Marian P. **EDUCATION:** Johnson C Smith Univ, BS 1954; Atlanta Univ School of Library Serv, MS Library Science 1961. **CAREER:** West Virginia State Coll, asst librarian, head cataloger 1958-65; Hampton Inst, dir of library 1965-69; Coop Coll Library Center Inc, dir 1969-. **ORGANIZATIONS:** Consultant US Govt, Malawi Africa 1979; mem Amer Library Assn; Virginia Library Assn; Resources & Technical Serv Section of Amer Library Assn; Coll Library Section Amer Library Assn; bd Kraus Reprint Pubs for Black Publishers; vice chmn, chmn-elect Coll & Univ Section SE Library Assn; mem Omega Psi Phi Frat Inc, NAACP, YMCA. **MILITARY SERVICE:** AUS 1955-57. **BUSINESS ADDRESS:** Dir, Coop Coll Lib Ctr Inc, 159 Forest Ave, #602, Atlanta, GA 30303.

DAVIS, WILLIAM J.
Attorney. **PERSONAL:** Born May 29, 1917, Cuthbert, GA; died Apr 11, 1976, Columbus, OH; son of Jesse R Davis and Norma Lee Davis; married Elizabeth Sydnor Davis. **EDUCATION:** Howard Univ, BA (Cum Laude) 1939, MA Publ Admin 1940; Univ of PA, LLD 1949; Univ of PA Law School, JD 1949. **CAREER:** City of Akron, asst cty law dir 1959-60; State of OH, asst attny gen 1962; Fed Aviation Agency Columbus, attny 1965; Village of Urbancrest, solictr 1969-70; Private practice, attny 1952-76 (deceased). **ORGANIZATIONS:** Mem OH Bar, Amer Bar, Natl Bar, Amer Judctr Soc, RB Elliott Law Club, Frontiers Club of Amer, Omego Psi Phi, NAACP; state chmn Legal Redress Comm 1963-67; bd mem, ACLU, 1963-, Amer Dem Assn 1964-; pres, Columbus Branch, NAACP, 1968; Central OH Chapter, ADA, 1970. **HONORS/ACHIEVEMENTS:** ETO Ribbon Military; Memory Award of Recognition for Serv in Armed Forces of US Pres Ford; Man of the Year Mu Iota Chapter, Omega Psi Phi 1976; Comm Serv Award in honor of the late Atty William J Davis by Franklin Lodge of Elks #203; New book placed in memory & honor, Univ of PA Library, 1976. **HOME ADDRESS:** 2320 Gardendale Dr, Columbus, OH 43219.

DEAN, MILLARD R.
Dentist. **PERSONAL:** Born Sep 06, 1907, Memphis, TN; died Jul 06, 1988, Washington, DC; son of Cohen W Dean and Ida Reynolds; married Irene Frankie Carter; children: Margo, Yolande. **EDUCATION:** Northwestern Univ; State Univ of Iowa Dental Coll, 1932. **CAREER:** Harlem Hospital, intern 1933; Private Practice. **ORGANIZATIONS:** Mem Robert T Freeman Dental Soc; pres Natl Dental Assn exec bd 1964-70; mem Federation Dentaire Internationale; Acad of Gen Dentistry; dental consult Boxing Comm; DC Dental Soc; Amer Dental Assn; Alpha Phi Alpha Mu Lambda Chapter pres; natl officer Alpha Phi Alpha; trust Plymouth Congregational Church 1946-52; bd trustee Jr Police & Cit Corps; mem bd Comm Highland Beach, MD 1951-53; sec bd Highland Beach; Plymouth Congregational Church trustee DC Rep Comm 1966-72; DC Dir Memphis Cotton Makers Jubile 1948-54; pres Bachelor Benedicts Club; officer Washington Pigskin Club; Mu So Lit Club; officer Hausas Club. **HONORS/ACHIEVEMENTS:** Author article in Journal Amer Dental Assn; first black in Journal.

DICKENS, LLOYD EVERETT
Business executive. **PERSONAL:** Born Feb 22, 1912, Watonga, OK; died Mar 1986. **EDUCATION:** Columbia Univ Inst of Real Estate, 1954; NY Univ Inst of Real Estate, 1970; Real Estate Mgmt Brokers Inst Columbia Univ, Certified Property Mgmt 1978. **CAREER:** NY Cty Dem 11 Assembly, dist leader 1954-65, assemblyman 1958-64; FHA, lending inst seller/svcr 1964-; Lloyd's Funding Corp, pres 1964-; Real Estate Mgmt Brokers Inst, certified property mgr 1978-. **ORGANIZATIONS:** Pres, Greater Harlem Real Estate Bd Inc 1963-66; past vice chmn, bd dir Freedom Natl Bank of NY; mem, chmn personnel comm Freedom Natl Bank of NY; mem United Ins Brokers Assn; pres Rotary Club of Upper Manhattan 1972-73; past pres Uptown Chamber of Commerce; mem Uptown Chamber of Commerce; life mem NAACP. **HONORS/ACHIEVEMENTS:** Community Serv Award Greater Harlem Real Estate Bd 1976; Meritorious Award Harlem Commonwealth Council Inc 177; Hon Deputy Fire Chief NY City Fire Dept; Admiral of the Flagship Fleet Amer Airlines. **BUSINESS ADDRESS:** Property Manager, Real Estate Mgmt Brokers Inst, 2153 Adam C Powell Jr Blvd, New York, NY 10027.

DICKERSON, JAMES ANDREW
Fashion illustrator. **PERSONAL:** Born Nov 24, 1917, Culver, IN; died Apr 27, 1989; married Shirley Morais; children: Richard Gregg, Sherrill Ann, Shelley Morais. **EDUCATION:** New England School of Art, 1940. **CAREER:** Fashion Inst of Technology NY Univ State System, teacher 1969-70; advertising agencies, magazines, stores, various companies, personalities, fashion illustrator. **ORGANIZATIONS:** Mem Soc of Illustrators 1970, Graphic Artist Guild 1971, Battle of Normandy & Northern France AUS 1944. **HONORS/ACHIEVEMENTS:** Fashion Design Illustrator, Comptoir de l'Industries Cotonnier of Paris 1957; Certificate of Excellence, Art Dir Club of Philadelphia 1965; Man of the Year Award, Alpha Phi Alpha Frat Eta Chi Lambda Chapter 1967; The St Charles AME Zion Church Distinguished Serv Award 1988. **MILITARY SERVICE:** AUS s/sgt 3 yrs.

DOLES, MAURICE DEWITT
Dentist. **PERSONAL:** Born Feb 06, 1898, Southampton Co, VA; died Nov 20, 1988, Glen Burnie, MD; son of Augustus Beauregard Doles and Maggie Clayton Doles; married Waltye. **EDUCATION:** Virginia Union Univ, BS 1926; Howard Univ, DDS 1929; Forsyth Dental Infirmary, Certificate 1930. **CAREER:** Dentist Baltimore 1930-67, Barrett School for Girls 1933-52, Glen Burnie 1967-88. **ORGANIZATIONS:** Charter mem Furnace Branch Civic Assn 1938; pres Maryland Dental Soc 1946-47; co-organizer, mem Dental Clinical Serv Provident Hospital 1946; pres Delta Lambda Chapter Alpha Phi Alpha Frat 1950-51; vice pres Baltimore Chapter Frontiers Club of Amer 1952; life mem NAACP 1963; bd of trustees Enon Baptist Church; mem Omicron Kappa Upsilon Pi Phi Chapter. **HONORS/ACHIEVEMENTS:** Natl Hon Dental Soc 1950; Certificate of Appreciation, Enon Baptist Church 1969; Bronze Plaque Honoree, Maryland Dental Soc 1975; Citation Gov Maryland, Mayor Baltimore City. **BUSINESS ADDRESS:** 1119 Crain Hwy NE, Glen Burnie, MD 21061.

DUDLEY, AMOS H.
Clergyman. **PERSONAL:** Born Nov 26, 1928, Morehead City, NC; died Sep 04, 1988; son of Alex Dudley and Bertha Dudley; married Rosetta Clyburn Dudley; children: Cynthia, Cheryl, Linda. **EDUCATION:** Johnson C Smith Univ, BA 1953; Crozer Theological Seminary, BD 1956; Univ of Arizona, Certificate (Police/Community Relations) 1961; Greenlake Admin School, 1965. **CAREER:** Valley Christian Centers, exec dir ordained minister; Boy's & Men's Supr & Englewood Christian Center, 1956-57, exec dir 1958-59; Chester PA, Camden NJ, Peoria, Chicago & Phoenix, community & social work 18 years. **ORGANIZATIONS:** Bd mem, chmn Investment Opportunities Inc; bd mem Progress Investment Assn for Economic Devel; pres Booker T Washington Child Devel Center Inc; (past treas) pres Maricopa Council Campfire Girls; mem Natl Bd Campfire Girls; bd Mem Phoenix Black Troupe; mem past chmn Phoenix Youth Commn; 1st vice pres S Phoenix Sunrise Lion Club; bd mem Maricopa Co Health Bd (chmn Patient Care Comm). **HONORS/ACHIEVEMENTS:** Recipient Luther Halsey Gullick Award, Campfire Girls 1971; Outstanding Serv Award, Booker T Washington Child Devel Center 1971; Very Outstanding Phoenician, Mayor T A Barrow, Phoenix 1974; Job Well Done Award from people of community 1974. **BUSINESS ADDRESS:** 1326 W Hadley St, Phoenix, AZ 85007.

DUNMORE, ALBERT J.
Automobile corporate executive, journalist. **PERSONAL:** Born Jun 04, 1915, Georgetown, SC; died Feb 01, 1989, Detroit, MI; married Josephone N Thompson;; children: Jonathan, Greg, Stephen, Ruth Dunmore Williams, Charlotte Dunmore Vaughan. **EDUCATION:** Hampton Inst, BA. **CAREER:** Chrysler Corp, Dir urban & Community Affairs, retired 1980; Michigan Chronicle, mng editor 1963-68, assoc editor 1962-63; Pittsburgh Courier, mgr 1939-59. **ORGANIZATIONS:** Mem US C of C Sub-com on Urban & Regional Affairs;

cmmn Urban Affrs Com of Nat Assn of Mrkt Developers; Sigma Delta Chi Nat Professional Journalism Soc; sec Detroit Press Club; bd dirs United Comm Svcs; United Fnd Speaker's Bur; former pres Detroit Urban League; bd Trustees Shaw Coll at Detroit; bd dir March of Dimes Metro Detroit; pres MI League for Human Svcs; mem bd dir United Way of MI; mem bd dir United Found Metro Detroit. **BUSINESS ADDRESS:** PO Box 1919, Detroit, MI 48231.

ELDRIDGE, ROY (LITTLE JAZZ)
Jazz musician. **PERSONAL:** Born Jan 30, 1911, Pittsburgh, PA; died 1987, New York, NY; married Viola Lee Fong; children: Carole Elizabeth. **EDUCATION:** Attended high school in Pittsburgh, PA. **CAREER:** Began career with Greater Sheesley Shows 1972; played with Chocolate Dandies, Teddy Hill, Mckinney's Cotton Pickers, Fletcher Henderson Band; organized own band; jointe Gene Krupa 1941; joined Benny Goodman 1950; joined Count Basie 1966; with Jazz at the Philharminic 1945-51; on tour of Europe 1949-51; tours indiv and with various groups; recording artist for Murcury Records. **ORGANIZATIONS:** mem Presbyterian Church. **HONORS/ACHIEVEMENTS:** Recipient Citation of Merit Muscular Dystrophy Assn; Awards Downbeat magazine; Westinghouse Trophy; named to Downbeat Hall of Fame 1971. **BUSINESS ADDRESS:** c/o Pablo Records Inc, 451 N Canon Dr, Beverly Hills, CA 90210.

ELLIS, WILLIAM A.
Educator. **PERSONAL:** Born Jan 24, 1938, Dayton, OH; married Pamela Fern (deceased); children: William III, Jennifer. **EDUCATION:** Howard Univ, BS 1960, MD 1965; Univ of MI, MPH 1971. **CAREER:** Good Samaritan Hospital, rotating internship 1965-66; Armed Forces Entrance & Exam Station Detroit, chief medical officer 1966-68; gen psych rsch 1968-70; Univ of MI, child psych fellowship 1970-72; James Weidow Johnson Family Servs, psych dir; Columbia Univ Harlem Hospital, assoc prof of clinical psych. **ORGANIZATIONS:** Consult APA Com on Natl Affairs; natl adv comm Howard Univ Inst of Urban Affairs & Rsch; mem Amer Psych Assoc, Amer Acad of Psych Serv for Children, Amer Acad of Child Psych, Natl Med Assoc, Amer Orthopsychiatric Assoc, Black Psych of Amer, NY Council of Child Psych, APA Comm on Psych & Indust. **MILITARY SERVICE:** AUS Med Corps capt 1966-68.

ENGLISH, ROBERT JAMES
Publisher, journalist. **PERSONAL:** Born Apr 28, 1948, Jacksboro, TX; married Patricia Wade; children: Bakari, Lauressa. **EDUCATION:** Abilene Christian Univ, BA Mass Communications 1971. **CAREER:** Abilene Reporter News, intern reporter 1970; KBBC-TV Abilene, news reporter 1972-79; KRBC Radio "Minority Affairs" Program, reporter 1979; US Census Bureau Abilene Dist, dist recruiter 1980; KFMN Radio, reporter 1980-82; KIXS TV Abilene, news reporter 1981-82; English Publ Abilene, pub-editor; US Congressman Jim Wright, field representative 1985; English Communications, pres 1986-. **ORGANIZATIONS:** Pres Abilene Black Chamber of Commerce 1975-76; state sec Texas Black Caucus 1976-77; state delegate Texas Democratic Convention 1976; state delegate Texas Democratic Governor's Convention 1978; publicity chmn Texas Coalition of Black Democrats 1979-; candidate Texas House of Representatives 1982; mem Abilene City Council 1983; 1st vice pres Abilene Economic Devel Co Inc 1983-; publicity chmn NAACP state conf; Abilene Christian Univ; mem Governor's Advisory Comm to Resolution & Platform Comm of State Convention of Texas Democratic Party 1986; mem Class of 1986-87 Leadership Fort Worth; mem Fort Worth Public Library; Black History Month speaker 1986; publisher Texas Black Monthly Magazine 1987. **HONORS/ACHIEVEMENTS:** Outstanding Young Men of Amer, Abilene TX 1976-77, 1979, 1981. **BUSINESS ADDRESS:** Publisher, English Communications, 5509 Blackmore, Fort Worth, TX 76107.

EVANS, MINNIE
Artist. **PERSONAL:** Born Dec 12, 1892, Long Creek, NC; died Jan 18, 1988; widowed; children: David, Elisha, George. **EDUCATION:** Taylor Gallery A&T State U, self-taught artist 1976-77; Whitney Mus of Am Art, 1976; Studio Mus, 1975; Mus of Modern Art, 1972; Am Fed of Arts, 1970-72; Indianapolis Mus of Art; Mus Am Folk Art; Portal Gallery; St John's Art Gallery 1970; Davison Art Ctr; Art Image 1969; NY Exhib 1966; Little Gallery 1961. **CAREER:** LA Co Mus, 2 centuries of Black am art. **HONORS/ACHIEVEMENTS:** Disting Artist Award, Links 1968.

FENTRESS, JOHN CULLEN
Association executive. **PERSONAL:** Born Oct 30, 1910, Normal, AL; died Apr 06, 1989; married Lillian Elene Jennings. **EDUCATION:** Tuskegee Inst; Jr Coll 1929; Morehouse Coll, BA 1931. **CAREER:** CA News, lino oper 1931-36; CA Eagle, lino/sports ed 1937-45; Pittsburgh Courier, reporter/sports 1946-48; Fentress Press, owner 1948-68; Allied Printers & Publishers Inc, pres 1968-72; Computerized Photo-Typesetting, self-employed 1972-. **ORGANIZATIONS:** Founding pres Western States Golf Assn 1953-71, pres emeritus 1971-; editor Griffith Park Golf Club Fairways 1958-; editor/publisher Tee-cup Magazine quarterly publication; mem Western States Golf Assoc. **HOME ADDRESS:** 4458 Victoria Park Dr, Los Angeles, CA 90019.

FINLEY, EWELL W.
Consulting engineer. **PERSONAL:** Born Jan 26, 1924, Mobile, AL; died Jan 1979; married Mildred Johnson. **EDUCATION:** Howard Univ, BSCE 1947; Univ of Michigan, MCE 1949. **CAREER:** Consulting engineer private practice, NYC, 1966-79; Maiman-Finley Assoc, assoc 1959-60; E Lionel Pavlo, consulting engineer 1958-59; Ramseyer & Miller Inc, consulting engineer 1956-58; Seelye Stevenson Value & Knecht, consulting engineer 1955-56; Ramseyer & Miller Inc, consulting engineer 1953-55; Knappen-Tippets-Abbett-McCarthy, bridge designer 1951-53; State A&M Coll, assoc prof of engineering 1949-51. **ORGANIZATIONS:** Fellow ASCE; mem NYSSPE; 100 Black Men; mem NY State Bd for Engineering & Land Surveying; mem Malverne School Bd; founding mem ARCH; mem Alpha Phi Alpha; Epiphany Lutheran Church. **HONORS/ACHIEVEMENTS:** Award, Structural Design on Throggs Neck Bridge; spotlighted in numerous local newspapers. **BUSINESS ADDRESS:** 35 E 20 St, New York, NY 10003.

FORD, CONRAD A.
Business executive. **PERSONAL:** Born in Brooklyn, NY; died May 13, 1985. **EDUCATION:** Columbia Univ, MA 1973; Brooklyn Coll, BA 1950. **CAREER:** Police Athletic League Inc, exec dir; New York City NY, parole officer 1953-73; New York City, school teacher 1950-53; US Pan Amer Women's Track & Field Team, coach 1963; US Women's Olympic Team, coach 1968; US Women's Pan African Team, coach 1971; PAL Track & Field consultant 1953-73. **ORGANIZATIONS:** Mem Women's Natl AAU Track & Field Comm 1968-85; US Women's Track & Field Olympic Comm 1965-76; jr warden Grace Episcopal Church 1976-85; mem 100 Black Men; pol comagy Child Devel NY; bd of dir Realty House NY. **MILITARY SERVICE:** USAAF corpl 1945-46. **BUSINESS ADDRESS:** 34 1/2 E 12th St, New York, NY 10003.

FORTUNE, HILDA O.
Retired sociologist. **PERSONAL:** Born Aug 31, 1913, Birmingham, AL; died Jul 18, 1988; children: Lois Jayne Fortune Maginley. **EDUCATION:** Morgan State Coll, AB (Valedictorian) 1938; Atlanta School of Social Work, attended 1941; New York Univ, M (Summa Cum Laude) 1958, EdD (Summa Cum Laude) 1963. **CAREER:** Harlem Branch YWCA, dir of employment 1947-52; Urban League of Greater NY, dir comm serv 1955-63; Brooklyn Coll, psychological serv dean of students office 1963-68; New York Univ, adjunct prof 1958-68, leadership trainer workshops, human relations 1968-87; York Coll City Univ, sociologist coord, chmn African-Amer studies comm 1968-79; Nova Univ, special project chief researcher 1980; York College, sociology prof (retired). **ORGANIZATIONS:** Licensed social worker NY State 1947-90; life mem Natl Council of Negro Women 1943-, Delta Sigma Theta Sorority 1950-; consultant/leadership trainer in Human Relations 1958-85; mem bd of dirs New York Urban League 1964-; life mem Kappa Delta Pi Honor Soc in Educ 1970; mem emeritus Amer Counseling and Devel 1985; Golden Life Mem Natl Assoc of Social Workers 1985; mem Pi Lambda Theta Honor Soc in Educ. **HONORS/ACHIEVEMENTS:** Research Monograph publication vocational acad Nova Univ Ft Lauderdale 1980; Dr Hilda O Fortune Humanitarian Award established at York Coll CUNY 1981; Unsung Heroine Award during Negro History Week 1986; chairperson Alex Haley Ad Hoc Comm; chairperson BOOK Party Collection for the Mizell Library and Research Center a NABSE project; Hon Trustee Broward Community Coll Foundation, Ft Lauderdale FL.

FRASER, THOMAS PETIGRU
Educator. **PERSONAL:** Born Jun 24, 1902, Georgetown, SC; died Sep 12, 1988; married Marie Lovette; children: Dolores Fraser Cave. **EDUCATION:** Claflin Coll, BS 1926; Columbis Univ, AM 1930, EdD 1948. **CAREER:** Booker T Washington HS, head dept of science 1926-29; Wilberforce Univ, prof of biology 1930-35; Edward Waters Coll, dean and prof biol; Delaware State Coll, dean and prof biol 1942-47; Morgan State Univ, prof and twice interim pres, prof emeritus. **ORGANIZATIONS:** Consultant Natl Science Foundation; consultant to PhD Life Science Prog in SC, State Supported Colleges & Univs; pres Natl Assoc for Rsch in Sci Tchg MD Biology Teachers Assoc; faculty rep Intercolegiate Athletics Morgan State Univ 10 yrs. **HONORS/ACHIEVEMENTS:** Fellowship to Columbus Univ, General Educ Bd 1935-36; Hon LHD Claflin Coll 1970; Citation for Distinguished Serv to Science Educ Natl Science Teachers Assn, 1975; Hon ScD Morgan State Univ 1976; inducted into SC Hall of Science & Technology 1982, Hall of Fame Mid-Eastern Athletic Conf 1986; bd mentor Assn of Governing Bds Sigma Pi Phi; co-author book "Concepts in Science" 1972,75. **HOME ADDRESS:** 9C Hamill Rd, Baltimore, MD 21210.

FRAZIER, EARL
Retired city councilman. **PERSONAL:** Born Nov 12, 1917, Drakesboro, KY; married Thelma Rogers; children: Earline, Roger, Kevin. **ORGANIZATIONS:** Mem Democratic Exec Commn. **HONORS/ACHIEVEMENTS:** KY Col Award 1973; worshipful master Howe Dean lodge No 166; asst deputy grand master of the Western District. **MILITARY SERVICE:** WWII 1942-45.

FULLER, ALEXANDER
Association executive. **PERSONAL:** Born in Norfolk, VA. **EDUCATION:** Attended Cleveland Coll of Embalming. **CAREER:** Western Reserve Univ Republic Steel Corp, Great Lakes Steel Corp Detroit; Wayne County CIO Council Detroit; Wayne County AFL-CIO Detroit. **ORGANIZATIONS:** Mem United Steelworkers Organizing Comm; affiliated Local 1299 United Steelworkers of Amer AFLCIO; chmn Local Union Blast Furnace Grievance Comm; gde Local 1299 USA; exec vice pres Greater Detroit & Wayne Co Industrial Union Council CIO 1948-58; vice pres Wayne County AFL-CIO 1958-; delegate United Steelworkers Convention 1944; delegate mem Constitutional Comm United Steelworkers Convention 1946; delegate Biennial Convention 1948-74; delegate White House Conf Children & Youth 1961; delegate-at-large Democratic Convention Louisiana 1960; delegate-at-large Natl Democratic Convention Atlantic City 1964; delegate Natl Inter-group Relations Org NAIRO Conf San Juan 1959; conf commn against discrimination Toronto 1959, Minneapolis 1960, St Clair 1961; mem Detroit Relocation Adv Comm Detroit Housing Commn; Detroit & Metro Area Regional Planning Comm; Metro Detroit Manpower Devel Adv Comm; vice chmn Michigan State Fair Emp Practices Commn 1955; exec bd mem Detroit USO; mem Detroit Hospital Survey Comm; Coordinating Council, Detroit Commn Community Relations; chmn Wayne County Gen Hospital & Infirmary Comm. **HONORS/ACHIEVEMENTS:** House of Representatives, Resolution Outstanding Contribution Michigan & US.

GARRETT, LEONARD P.
Editor, publisher. **PERSONAL:** Born Aug 21, 1925, Wichita, KS; died Feb 13, 1988. **CAREER:** Boeing Aircraft, buyer, purch 1946-54; Retail liquor stores Wichita, buyer, mgmt 1956-63; News Hawk Weekley Newspaper, founder, publisher, editor 1965-88. **ORGANIZATIONS:** Founding mem Amer Fed Mus Local 701 1950; mem VFW Post 1956; founder, dir, exec KS Black Arts Festival 1968-75; mem NE Wichita Youth Activity Assoc 1968; exec dir KS Black Heritage Comm 1972-77; chmn NE Wihita Vol Amer Red Cross 1973-76; founder KS Black Artists Assoc 1974; exec dir Heart of Amer Emancipation Celebration; founder KS Comm for Blacks in Bicentennial Observance 1975-76. **HONORS/ACHIEVEMENTS:** Community Serv Awd 1975. **BUSINESS ADDRESS:** Publisher, News Hawk Weekly Newspaper, 1217 N Ash Ave, Wichita, KS 67214.

GOLDSMITH, WILLIAM F.
Business executive. **PERSONAL:** Born Jul 18, 1923, Monessen, PA; died Feb 13, 1989; son of Ida and Sabry; married Lenora Williams; children: Donna, Umar. **EDUCATION:** Attended Indiana Univ NW, Gary Business Coll; Moody Bible Institute. **CAREER:** BSA, inst rep; Bur of Motor Vehicles, state enforcement officer; Currency Exchange, owner/operator; Goldsmith Day Rental Sales & Serv, owner; dir of Christine Entertainment Center; buyer for Religious Enterprise. **ORGANIZATIONS:** Dir Natl Bususiness League of Lake County

Indiana Bd; mem NW Indiana Sickle Cell Found; mem NAACP; committeeman Republican Precinct; regional chmn for Indiana Concerned Black Republicans; dir Lake County Elephant Club; founder Christian Entertainment Club Inc; acting convenor Natl Black Republican Council for Indiana Dodge Key Club 1958; former mem Indiana Council of Churches; mem Intl Union of Gospel Missions. **HONORS/ACHIEVEMENTS:** Oldsmobile Natl Vanguard 1966. **BUSINESS ADDRESS:** President, Goldsmith Day Rtl Sales & Serv, 1619 E 15 St, Gary, IN 46402.

GRAHAM, LORENZ BELL
Educator, social worker, probation officer. **PERSONAL:** Born Jan 27, 1902, New Orleans, LA; died Sep 11, 1989, West Covina, CA; son of David Andrew Graham and Etta Bell Graham; married Ruth Morris, Aug 20, 1929; children: Lorenz Jr, Joyce, Ruth, Charles. **EDUCATION:** VA Union Univ, BA, 1936; Columbia Univ, MSW, 1954. **CAREER:** Monrovia Coll, Liberia, teacher/missionary, 1924-30; Natl Baptist Convention, lecturer, fund raiser, 1929-32; teacher, Richmond, VA, 1932-35; US Civilian Conservation Corps, camp educ advisor in VA and PA, 1936-42; mgr of public Housing, Newport News, VA, 1943-45; freelance writer, real estate salesman, and building contractor, Long Island, NY, 1946-49; Queens Federation of Churches, NY, social worker, 1950-57; Los Angeles County probation officer, 1958-66. **ORGANIZATIONS:** Mem, Author's League of Amer, McCarty Christian Church, PEN Intl, US China Peoples Friendship Assn, USA Soviet Friendship Soc, NAACP. **HONORS/ACHIEVEMENTS:** Thomas Alva Edison Found special citation for book The Ten Commandments; Follett Award, 1958, and Child Study Assn Award, 1959, both for book South Town; Assn for Study of Negro Life and History award, 1959; Vassie D Wright Awd, 1967; S CA Coun on Lit for Children & Young People Awadr, 1968; 1st prize, Book World, 1969; citation, CA Assn of Tchrs of English, 1973; Martin Luther King Award, S CA Region of Christian Ch, 1975; author of books for children: Tales of Momolu, I Momolu, Song of the Boat; novels for young readers: South Town, North Town, Whose Town, Return to South Town; bible stories in West African folk speech: Every Man Heart Lay Down, A Road Down in the Sea, God Wash The World and Start Again, David He No Fear, Hongry Catch the Foolish Boy; illustrated adaptations: The Story of Jesus, The Ten Commandments; high school readers: John Brown, A Cry for Freedom; elementary school readers: John Brown's Raid. *

GREEN, MILDRED A.
Educator. **PERSONAL:** Born Jul 22, 1937, Saluda, SC; died Jul 25, 1987; married John W Green; children: Michael Odell, Harriet M, John M. **EDUCATION:** Suffolk Community College, AS 1971; Hofstra University, BA 1971; SUNY at Stony Brook, MS 1973. **CAREER:** SUNY at Stony Brook, instructor (undergraduate math) 1972-73; Cornell University, instructor of math 1979-80; Suffolk Community College, professor of math 1974-80, asst dean of instruction 1980-. **ORGANIZATIONS:** Mid-Island Club-NANBPNC, Inc, president 1978-81, treasurer, scholarship 1985-87; Christ Baptist Church, cotillion chairperson 1981-83; Delta Sigma Theta, co-chairperson, social action committee 1982-; NAACP, member 1982-; Economic Opportunity Council of Suffolk (EOC), 1985-; The NY African American Institute, advisory council member 1986-. **HONORS/ACHIEVEMENTS:** Assistantship SUNY at Sony Brook 1972-73; Education Policy Fellowship Prog, Institute of Education Leadership 1982-83; Human Relations Award in Education, NAACP - Central Islip 1986. **HOME ADDRESS:** 34 Westbrook Road, Coram, NY 11727. **BUSINESS ADDRESS:** Asst Dean of Instruction, Suffolk Community College, 533 College Road, Selden, NY 11784.

GREEN, RICHARD R.
Educator. **PERSONAL:** Born May 27, 1936, Mennifee, AK; died May 10, 1988, New York, NY; married Gwendolyn; children: Craig, Kelly, Kimberlee, Sherri. **EDUCATION:** Augsburg Coll Minneapolis, BA 1959; St Cloud State Coll St Cloud MN, MS 1968; Harvard Grad Sch of Edn, EdD 1973. **CAREER:** Hennepin Cty Home School for Boys, Glen Lake MN, teacher, 1959-63; Emerson Middle School Minneapolis, teacher special educ 1963-64; Vocational HS, coach-head track, asst football 1964-66; N HS, teacher, special educ, first Black head coach basketball in history of State, asst football 1966-69; N HS Minneapolis, asst principal 1969-70; Fellow MAT Program Harvard Univ, teaching 1971-72; Desegregation/Integration Minneapolis Public Schools Minneapolis, admin asst 1972-73. Minneapolis school supt, 1980-88; NY school supt, 1988-89. **ORGANIZATIONS:** Dir Org Devel Minneapolis Public Schools, 1973-74; principal N Comm HS Minneapolis Public School; Amer Assn of School Admin; W Area Supt Minneapolis Public Schools; Assn for Supervision & Curriculum Devel; Natl Assn of Elementary School Admins; Phi Delta Kappa; Natl Alliance of Black School Educs; Augsburg Alumni Bd; Afro-Amer Educators; Zion Baptist Church Exchange Inc; author Minneapolis Report Education Renewal for the Seventies, a report on racism in educ. **HONORS/ACHIEVEMENTS:** Recipient Distinguished Alumni Award, Augsburg Coll 1974; NDEA Award 1971-72; Augsburg Alumni Award 1971-72; Harold A Johnson 1958; Augsburg Hon Athletic, 1958. **BUSINESS ADDRESS:** N Comm HS, 1500 James Ave N, Minneapolis, MN 55411.

GREENE, LORENZO J.
Retired educator. **PERSONAL:** Born Nov 16, 1899, Ansonia, CT; died Jan 24, 1988; married Dr Thomasina T; children: Lorenzo T. **EDUCATION:** Howard Univ, AB 1924; Columbia Univ, AM, PhD 1926-42. **CAREER:** Dr Carter G Woodson, rsch assoc 1928-33; Lincoln Univ, teacher 1933-72; TN A&I Coll, teacher 1945; So IL Univ, teacher 1968; Univ of Kansas, teacher1969-70; Lincoln Univ, head soc sci 1970-72; Lincoln Univ, prof 1939-72; retired professor. **ORGANIZATIONS:** Negro Wage Earner 1930; Negro Employment Dist of Columbia 1932; Nat Geog Soc; NAACP 1934; Gen Educ Bd 1934, 40-41, 1945, 1946; Am Hist Assn 1950;mem Civil War Com 1960-65; Pitts PA Pub Sch 1968; NE MO Coll 1968; Negro Hist for Ency Britannica 1968; Univ of KS 1969-70; consult Baker Coll 1969; Florissant-Ferguson HS 1969; Lincoln Univ 1969-70; Ford Found on Black Scholars 1971; pres Assn Study Negro Life & Hist 1969; LLD Univ of MO 1971; Assn Natl Achievers 1974; Harvard Univ Integration of Folk Arts 1980; Parting Ways Project 1981. **HONORS/ACHIEVEMENTS:** "Negro in Colonian New England 1620-1776" 1942; mem MO Assn Soc Welfare 1954; Desegration of MO Schools 1959, 1962; "MO Black Heritage" 1980. **BUSINESS ADDRESS:** LincolnUniv, Jefferson City, MO 65101.

GROOMS, R. LOUISE
Business executive. **PERSONAL:** Born Nov 06, Belleville, IL; died Jun 06, 1983; daughter of Richard Helm and Sallie Helm; married Claud Grooms, Nov 06, 1941. **EDUCATION:** Southern Illinois Univ; Wayne State Univ; Univ of Detroit. **CAREER:** Public Schools of Mt Vernon, teacher 6 yrs; Great Lakes Mutal Life Insurance Co, chief accountant, office mgr 15 yrs; Detroit Inst Commerce, founder, pres 1941-83. **ORGANIZATIONS:** Sec Booker T Washington Business Assn 15 yrs; chmn Lucy Thurman Branch YMCA; mem advisory comm Small Business Admin; Metro Bd YWCA; Citizens Comm, Bd Educ Center Region; sec, bd mem Michigan Business Educ Assn; sec, dir Victory Loan & Investment Co 15 yrs; bd dir Detroit Council Youth Serv Inc; mem State Advisory Council Vocational Educ 2 terms; Admin Mgmt Soc; mem Delta Pi Epsilon, Kappa Chpter; Guidance Assn Detroit; former sec Women's Economic Club; Business Teachers Club Metro Detroit; Higher Educ Opportunities Comm, Wayne State Univ; Personnel Women Detroit; Michigan Occupational Educ Assn; Amer Personnel & Guidance Assn; Amer Vocational Assn; Natl Manpower Training Assn; pres Michigan Business Schools Assn, 2nd time; Assn Independent Colls & Schools; Michigan Assn Private Schools; Task Force Equality Access Higher Educ; State Bd of Educ; trustee Bethel AME Church. **HONORS/ACHIEVEMENTS:** Sojouner Truth Award, Professional & Business Women's Clubs 1966; Outstanding Business Woman of the Year, Iota Phi Lambda Sorority 1957; Freedom Award 1957; Achievement Award, United Community Negro History Week 1960; Congratulations Letter, Louis C Miriani 1961; Award of Achievement in Educ, Emancipation Centennial Authority 1963; Business Achievement Award, Booker T Washington Trade Assn 1965; Proclamation Detroit Inst Commerce Day, State of Michigan 1966; Resolution Common Council, Detroit 1966; Appreciation Award Episcopal Church St Cyprian 1967; Appreciation Award, Victory Loan & Investment Co 1969; named Ten Top Working Women, Detroit 1970; Certificate of Merit, Booker T Washington Business Coll Burmingham 1970; honorary mem Outstanding Business Educ Activities, Personnel Women of Detroit 1970; Recognition Award, Outstanding Contribution to Vocational Educ, Michigan Assn of Private Schools 1970; life mem Michigan Occupat ional Educ Assn 1970; WCHB Educator of the Year Award, Bell Broadcasting Co 1971; Cotillion Club Award, Outstanding Leadership 1973; Detroit Public Library Calendar 1974; Michigan Business Educ Assn Outstanding Contribution Business Educ Award 1974; Citizen Award, Wright Mutual Insurance Co 1974.

HACKETT, HARRY G.
Judge. **PERSONAL:** Born Aug 21, 1922, Cedar Bluff, AL; died Mar 1987; married Joyce. **EDUCATION:** Wayne St U, BA 1950; Wayne St U, LLB 1952. **CAREER:** E Dist of MI, bankruptcy judge 1957-87; Detroit MI, gen law prac; E Dist of MI, law clerk. **ORGANIZATIONS:** S div mem MI St Bar Assn; NAACP; Boy Scouts of Am; Goodfellows-Old News Boys. **MILITARY SERVICE:** US Infantry comm ofcr WW II. **BUSINESS ADDRESS:** US Bankrupty Court, 10th Floor UC Courthouse, 231 W Lafayette ATTN: Andrea, Detroit, MI 48226.

HARRIS, LOLITA PAZANT
Educator. **PERSONAL:** Born May 19, 1947, Beaufort, SC; died Feb 11, 1989; married Edward Talerico Harris; children: Kenyana Lyvel. **EDUCATION:** NC A&T State Univ, BS 1969; Pepperdine Univ, MEd 1975; Ohio Univ, MA 1984. **CAREER:** Beaufort High School, chair, dept of foreign language, 1969-77; South Carolina Educ TV, educ serv coordinator, 1977-84; Savannah State Coll, asst prof, 1984-. **ORGANIZATIONS:** Publicity chair Burton Dale Beaufort NAACP 1981-, Natl Black Media Coalition 1985-87; mem Mizpah Chap #4 OES; mem Delta Sigma Theta. **HONORS/ACHIEVEMENTS:** Assistantship CPB/Ohio Univ Coll of Comm 1983-84. **HOME ADDRESS:** PO Box 4502, Beaufort, SC 29903. **BUSINESS ADDRESS:** Assistant Professor, Savannah State College, PO Box 20634, Savannah, GA 31404.

HAYDEN, FRANK
Educator. **PERSONAL:** Born Jun 10, 1934, Memphis; died 1988; married Joyce Marie Hinton. **EDUCATION:** Xavier Univ, BA 1957; Notre Dame Univ, MFA 1959; Iowa State Univ, Post Grad Study 1959; Munich Art Acad, Munich Germany, 1960; Denmark Royal Acad 1964; Stockholm Sweden, 1969. **CAREER:** Xavier Univ, lectr in art 1961; Southern Univ Baton Rouge Campus, tchr 1961-74; Southern Univ, prof of fine arts 1974-88. **ORGANIZATIONS:** Widely exhibited with numerous commissions for architecture sculpture. **HONORS/ACHIEVEMENTS:** Fulbright Fellow in Sculpture 1959-60; Amer Scadinavian Fellow Copenhagen 1964; So Fellow Found Grant 1968-69; grad scholarship Notre Dame Univ 1957-59; Ten Outstanding Young Catholics in Amer; Outstanding Young Men in Amer; exhibited in the Vatican Pvln World's Fair NY 1965; World's Fair Spkn 1974.

HILL, CAESAR G.
Statistician. **PERSONAL:** Born Sep 18, 1926, Savannah, GA; died Mar 26, 1984; married Wanda Clemens; children: Stephen, Gary. **EDUCATION:** Morehouse Coll, AB 1949; Atlanta Univ, 1949-51. **CAREER:** Chief Cross Surveys Br, supvr statistician 1985; Bureau of Census, statistician 1954, 1985; Citizens for Eisenhower Congressional Comm, public relations 1953-54; Voorhees Coll, instructor math 1949-53; Compton CA Dist Office, Decennial Census, dist mgr 1970. **ORGANIZATIONS:** Mem Amer Statistical Assn; Amer Mktng Assn; URISA; mem Alpha Phi Alpha; treasurer Morehouse Coll Alumni, Washington Metro Area; pres Census Chapter Commerce Comm for Black Concerns. **HONORS/ACHIEVEMENTS:** Author "A Survey of Burglary & Robbery" Compton CA 1974; several Outstanding & Special Achievement Awards, Census Bureau; Alumnus of the Year, Morehead Coll 1974. **MILITARY SERVICE:** AUS platoon leader 1944-46. **BUSINESS ADDRESS:** Bur Census Bus Div, Room 2665 FOB 3, Washington, DC 20233.

HINDERAS, NATALIE
Concert pianist. **PERSONAL:** Born in Oberlin, OH; married Lionel J Monagas; children: Michele. **EDUCATION:** Oberlin Conservatory, BM; Juilliard Sch of Music, post grad work; Phil Music Acad. **CAREER:** Temple Univ, prof of Coll music; one of most distin artists; played a series of concerts with Philadelphia Orch & A Phil Orch 1972; concerts with Cleveland,Atlanta, NY symph orchs 1973; perfor with Atlanta & Chicago symph; made first stage appr at age of 3; full-length piano recital age 8; played with Cleveland Women's Symph age 12; made num tours of Europe & US. **HONORS/ACHIEVEMENTS:** Among recordings is Natalie Hinderas Plays Music by Black Composers; prof music TempleUniv Phila; recip Levintritt Awd Martha Baird Rockefeller Grant, Fulbright Grant. **BUSINESS ADDRESS:** Temple University, Presser Hall, 13th & Norris Sts, Philadelphia, PA 19122.

HOLMAN, CARL See HOLMAN, M. CARL

HOLMAN, M. CARL (CARL HOLMAN)
Association executive. **PERSONAL:** Born Jun 27, 1919, Minter, MS; died Aug 09, 1988, Washington, DC; married Mariella Ama; children: Kerry, Karen, Kent. **EDUCATION:**

Lincoln Univ & Univ Chicago, MA 1944; Yale Univ, MFA 1954. **CAREER:** Clark Coll, prof 1949-62; Atlanta Inquirer, editor 1962; US Comm Civil Rights, dept staff dir 1962-68; Nat Urban Coalition, vice pres prog devel 1968-69, sr vice pres program & policy 1969-71, pres 1971-88. **ORGANIZATIONS:** bd mem Council Found; Field Found; Natl Comm Household Employment; vice chmn, Natl Business League; mem City Council Hate Legislatures; mem Omega Psi Phi. **HONORS/ACHIEVEMENTS:** GEB 1951; John Billings Fiske Poetry Prize Univ Chicago 1944; Fellowships John Hay Whitney 1952-53; Blevins Davis Playwriting Prize Yale Univ 1953; Amer Acad Political Science Award, 1962; Citation for Public Serv Univ Chicago Alumni Assoc 1977; Equal Oppor Day Award, Natl Urban League 1981; Distinguished Serv Award; Natl Conf Social Welfare 1981; Social Responsibility Award Opportunities Industrialization Centers 1983. **BUSINESS ADDRESS:** President, Natl Urban Coalition, 1120 G St NW,Ste 900, Washington, DC 20005.

JACKSON, MAURICE
Educator. **PERSONAL:** Born Aug 05, 1925, Cincinnati, OH; died Dec 11, 1987; son of Maurice Jackson and Nellie Jackson; married Carla J VanOverbeek; children: Michael A, Robert G, Emile M, Thea N, Wesley M. **EDUCATION:** UCLA, BA 1957, MA 1958, PhD 1966. **CAREER:** San Diego State Univ, asst prof 1962-65; Univ of Oregon, visiting lecturer 1964-65; UCR, prof sociology 1965-; chmn ethnic studies 1985-87. **ORGANIZATIONS:** Mem Amer Soc Assoc, Pac Soc Assoc, Assoc of Black Soc, Soc for Women in Soc, Black Men Health Consortium of Prof Org; mem bd of dir Natl Council on the Aging 1972-, Assoc of Black Soc 1976-; consultant Mayor Bradley's UPAC 1968-72; mem MPC 1972; consultant Ford Found 1973, NSF 1973-76, CA Alcohol Found 1976, Natl Inst of Educ 1976; dir of research Soc Research Inc 1968; chmn dept of black studies UCR 1969-70; dir of research USC 1970-71; chmn task force Natl Caucus on Black Aged 1971; dir MGFP, ASA 1972; chmn MGFP, ASA 1973-76; mem exec comm Caucus of Black Soc 1974-76; chmn min comm DC Soc Sociol 1972-73; mem exec comm DC Sociol Soc 1972-73; mem research & democratic task force CA 1971-72; partic White House Conf on Aging USC; advisory council Aging & Aged Blacks, US Senate Special Comm on Aging 1971-76; participant Work of Center for I ntergroup Studies S Africa 1975; dir Symposium on Race Relations S Africa 1975; participant Inst for Research & Teaching in Gerontology 1970; 1st exec spec ASA 1972-73; chmn Racial & Ethnic Minorities ASA 1983-84; vice pres Natl Council on the Aging 1978-80. **HONORS/ACHIEVEMENTS:** Natl Inst of Mental Health Fellow 1961-62; 1st black PhD in soc UCLA 1966; inst & devel Minority Graduate Fellow Program 1972-73; Ford Found Travel Grant 1974; Lib of Human Resources AHRA 1975, numerous lecturers on lives of black Americans; chmn comm ASA REM 1983-84; chmn comm SOM PSA 1983-85; mem executive comm Coll Humanities Social Sciences UCR 1983-85; chmn educ comm United Way 1983-85; co-principle investigator "The Police Officer's Right to Shoot" NILEC 1979-81; mem exec comm NABS 1971-81. **MILITARY SERVICE:** Flight officer, USAAF 1943-44. **BUSINESS ADDRESS:** Professor, Univ of California, Dept of Sociology, Chmn of Ethnic Studies, Riverside, CA 92521.

JAMES, ERIC G.
Educator. **PERSONAL:** Born Aug 06, 1910; died Sep 22, 1988; son of Daniel James and Ella James; widowed; children: Terri. **EDUCATION:** McGill Univ, BA 1941; NY Univ, MA 1948, PhD 1956. **CAREER:** US Veterans Admin, sr training officer 1945-48; Univ Wisconsin, sr lecturer 1949-52; Jamaica Planning Unit, consultant, advisor Manpower problems & planning 1952-56; NY Univ, sr lecturer 1956-59; UN Inst of Public Admin Representative of Sudan, sr advisor & dir 1959-63; Public & Intl Affair Univ Pittsburgh, assoc prof 1963-64; US AID Mission to Liberia US Dept of State, assoc dir 1967-71; Manhattan Community Coll, dean 1964-67, 1971-73; Baruch Coll, prof public admin 1973-. **ORGANIZATIONS:** Past consultant Natl Indus Conf; bd mem, council Amer Soc for Public Admin 1965-66; deligate Conf Intl Inst of Admin Scis; consultant City of E St Louis 1974-75; fellow Amer Sociol Assn; Soc of Applied Anthropology; mem Intern Inst of Admin Scis; British Inst of Public Admin; Inter Personnel Mgmt Assn; mem NAACP; mem Alpha Phi Alpha Frat. **HONORS/ACHIEVEMENTS:** US Fulbright Scholar, Govt of Trinidad & Tobago 1978-79; UN Serv; Dept of State Meritorious Award for Serv in Public Admin Liberia. **MILITARY SERVICE:** USAF lieutenant 1943-45.

JOHNSON, DERRICK GIBBS
Company executive. **PERSONAL:** Born Feb 02, 1962, Seat Pleasant, MD; died Dec 07, 1987; son of Eunice Boone. **CAREER:** DC Govt Navy Yard, 1980-81; WOL-AM, summer 1980; WDCA-TV, summer 1980; NBC-TV, 1979-80; Pyramid Communications, 1983-87. **HONORS/ACHIEVEMENTS:** Black Caucus Youth Award, Avon Products, 1984; Golden Mike Award, Amer Legion Auxiliary, 1982; Derrick Gibbs-Johnson Day, DC Govt, Mayor Marion Berry, 1982; Kool Achiever Award finalist, Kool Cigarettes, 1987; Golden Voice Award, Amer Legion Auxiliary, 1986; founder, Pyramid Communications (first youth media org run by youths), 1983. **BUSINESS ADDRESS:** Exec Dir and Founder, Pyramid Communications Intl, 800 Third St, NE, Washington, DC 20002.

JOHNSON, LEONARD W., JR.
Physician. **PERSONAL:** Born Jul 15, 1932, St Augustine, FL; died Sep 1987; married Evelyn Mays; children: Karen Johnson Carter, Leonard W III. **EDUCATION:** Howard Univ, BS 1951, Sch of Medicine MD 1956; Harvard Univ, MPH 1966. **CAREER:** Private Practice of Medicine, private practitioner 1957-58; US Air Force, flight surgeon commander, command surgeon 1958-; HQ Electronic Security Command, command surgeon 1984-87. **ORGANIZATIONS:** Mem Kiwanis Intl 1970-; bd of dirs USAF Soc of Flight Surgeons 1975-79; bd of dirs PanAfrican Develop Corp 1983-. **HONORS/ACHIEVEMENTS:** Vance H Marchbanks Awd Natl Medical Assoc for Significant Contrib to the USAF Medical Serv 1972; Bykota Achievement Awd Bykota Club of NY City 1978. **MILITARY SERVICE:** USAF col 1958-; Legion of Merit w/One Oak Leaf Cluster 1973, Defense Meritorious Serv Medal 1981, Air Force Meritorious Serv Awd 1984. **HOME ADDRESS:** 17201 Sandy Knoll Dr, Olney, MD 20832.

JORDAN, HOWARD, JR.
University administrator. **PERSONAL:** Born Dec 28, 1916, Beaufert, SC; married Ruth Menafee; children: Judith Louise, Arnold. **EDUCATION:** South Carolina State Coll, AB 1938; Howard Univ, special student 1938-39; New York Univ, EdD 1956. **CAREER:** South Carolina State Coll Orangesburg, mem faculty 1941-63, prof educ & psychology; School of Educ, chmn dept of educ, dean 1950-60, dean faculty 1960-63; Savannah State Coll, pres 1963-71; Univ Systems of Georgia Atlanta, vice chancellor 1971-. **ORGANIZATIONS:** Trustee Mather Schand Jr Coll; mem Amer Psychological Assn, South Carolina Psychological Assn, Natl Soc Study Educ, Natl Palmetto Educ Assn, Alpha Phi Alpha, Sigma Pi Phi, Savannah-Chatham County Area Economic Opportunity Authority; chmn Orangeburg County Cancer Dr 1948-49; Orangeburg County Crippled Children's Soc Dr 1950; Phi Delta Kappa Honorary Soc; Kappa Delta Pi Honorary Soc in Educ; Metropolitan Atlanta Commn on Crime & Juvenile Delinquency; chmn Evaluation Comm of Georgia Employment & Training Council; mem Alpha Phi Alpa Frat Inc, Sigma Pi Phi Frat, Kappa Boule-Atlanta; mem exec bd Atlanta Area Council Boy Scouts of Amer; new bd mentor Assn of Governing Bd; vice pres Assn of AUS. **MILITARY SERVICE:** AUS 1942-46. **BUSINESS ADDRESS:** Vice Chancellor, University System of Georgia, 244 Washington St, SW, Atlanta, GA 30334.

KILLENS, JOHN OLIVER
Author. **PERSONAL:** Born Jan 14, 1916, Macon, GA; died Oct 27, 1987, Brooklyn, NY; children: 2. **EDUCATION:** Edward Waters Coll; Morris-Brown Coll; Howard Univ; Terrell law Sch; Columbia; NYU. **CAREER:** Books, "Youngblood" 1954; "And Then We Heard the Thunder" 1963; "Black Man's Burden" 1965; "'Sippi" 1967; "Slaves" 1969; "The Cotillion or One Good Bull is Half The Herd" 1971; "Great Gittin' Up Morning, A Biography of Denmark Vesey" 1972; "A Man Ain't Nothin' But a Man" 1975; Plays, "Ballad of the Winter Soldiers" 1964; "Lower Than the Angels" 1965; "Cotillion" 1975; Screenplays, "Odds Against Tomorrow" 1960; "Slaves" with Herbert J Biberman 1969. **HONORS/ACHIEVEMENTS:** Other publications, "God Bless America" in "American Negro Short Stories" 1966; "The Stick Up" in "The Best Short Stories by Negro Writers, An Anthology from 1899 to the Present" 1967; "Rough Diamond" in "Harlem" 1970; "Trial Record of Denmark Vesey" 1970; "The Black Writer Vis-a-Vis His Country" in "The Black Aesthetic" 1971; "A White Loaf of Bread" in "To Gwen With Love, An Anthology Dedicated to Gwendolyn Brooks" 1971; "Rappin With Myself" in "Amistad 2" 1971; "Black Short Story Anthology" 1972; periodical publications, "Explanation of the Black Psyche" New York Times Mag June 7, 1964; "Black Man's Burden" Ebony 1965. **MILITARY SERVICE:** AUS WWII. **BUSINESS ADDRESS:** c/o Trident Press Inc, 5th Avenue, New York, NY 10020.

KIMBO, CONNEY M.
Educator. **PERSONAL:** Born Jan 01, 1933, McKeesport, PA; died Apr 13, 1989; divorced; children: Sandra, Conney Jr, Donna, Karen. **EDUCATION:** Indiana Univ, BS 1958, MS 1968; Univ of Iowa, PhD 1973. **CAREER:** Gary IN Public School System, teacher & coach 1958-69; Grinnell Coll, assoc dean of students 1969-70, dean of student affairs 1970-73; Univ of MO St Louis, dean of student affairs, asst prof of educ 1973-79; Univ of Pittsburgh, vice pres for student affairs 1979-89. **ORGANIZATIONS:** Dir Intramurals Roosevelt HS 1958-62; chmn Health & Driver Educ Dept Roosevelt High School 1960-64; dir Evening Recreation Program for Students & Adults Tolleston High School, Gary IN 1964-68; mem Natl Assn of Student Personnel Admin; mem Amer Assn of Higher Educ, NASPA Div of Professional Devel & Standards 1973-75; bd of dir St Louis Metropolitan Youth Advisory Council 1973-74; advisory bd Poweshiek County Iowa Dem Central Comm 1972-73; mem at large Pennsylvania Coll & Personnel Assn 1984-86; past chmn Grinnel Human Rights Comm 1971-72; vice pres 1971-72, mem 1968-72 Grinnell Youth Council; mem Grinnell Comm Planning Council 1972-73; mem AM Coll Personnel Assn, mem PA Assn Student Personnel Admin, bd of dirs Pittsburgh Univ & Cty Ministries 1981-82; mem AM Assn Counseling & Devel, bd dirs Hill House-Pittsburgh 1986-88; NASULGC'S Council St udent Affairs 1987-89; NASULGC'S, Senate 1987-89; pres, Pennsylvania Coll Personnel Assn 1987; Leadership Pittsburgh 1986-87. **HONORS/ACHIEVEMENTS:** Amer Council on Educ Fellow in Acad Admin 1975-76. **MILITARY SERVICE:** AUS 1954-56. **BUSINESS ADDRESS:** Vice President, Univ of Pittsburgh, Student Affairs, 130 William Pitt Union, Pittsburgh, PA 15260.

KIMBROUGH, JAMES C., JR.
Judge. **PERSONAL:** Born Oct 08, 1934, Selma, AL; died May 1987; married Faye C; children: James C III, Kelly Ann. **EDUCATION:** Fisk Univ, BA 1956; DePaul Univ Law School, JD 1959; Attended, Natl Coll of State Judiciary 1974, 1976, Indiana Judicial Coll 1986. **CAREER:** Work & Kimbrough Law Firm, attorney 1963-73; Lake County Criminal Court, commr 1973-74; Superior Court of Lake County, criminal court judge 1974-87; Valparaiso Univ Law School, adjunct prof 1976-79; Superior Court of Lake County, criminal court sr judge. **ORGANIZATIONS:** Mem Indiana Lawyers Commn 1974-, State Bd of Law Examiners 1975-; bd of advisors Indiana Judicial Center 1977-; bd of dirs Tradewinds Inc; mem NAACP. **MILITARY SERVICE:** AUS specialist E-5 2 yrs. **BUSINESS ADDRESS:** Senior Judge, Lake Co Criminal Court, 2293 No Main St, Crown Point, IN 46307.

KOONTZ, ELIZABETH DUNCAN
Consultant, lecturer. **PERSONAL:** Born Jun 03, 1919, Salisbury, NC; died Jan 06, 1989; married Harry Lee (deceased). **EDUCATION:** Livingstone Coll, AB 1938; LHD (hon) 1967; Atlanta Univ, MA 1941; LittD (hon); Pacific Univ Bryant Coll, PhD (hon); Howard Univ, EdD (hon); Amer Univ, LLD; Coppin State Coll, LHD (hon); Eastern MI Univ, HHD (hon); Northeastern Univ, ScD (hon). **CAREER:** Harnett Coll Training School Dunn NC, teacher 1938-40; Aggrev Memorial School Landis NC, 1970-41; 14th St School Winston-Salem NC, 1941-45; Price HS Salisbury, 1945-49; Monroe School, 1949-65; Price Jr Sr High School, teacher special educ 1965-68; Women's Bureau Dept Labor Washington, dir 1969-73; NC Dept of Human Resources, 1973-75; State of NC, asst state supt 1975-82. **ORGANIZATIONS:** mem Youth Commn Rowan Co 1955-57; US delegate to UN Comm Statues of Women 1969-73; coordinator NC Nutrition Program NC Dept ot Human Resources 1973-75; asst supt NC Dept of Pub Instruction 1975-; mem NC Salisbury teachers assns; NEA (pres dept classroom tchrs 1965-668 natl vice pres 1967-68, natl pres 1968-69); pres NC Assn Classroom Tchrs 1958-62; mem Rowan Co Negro Civic League; Zeta Phi Beta; mem NAACP; bd of trustees Pfeiffer Coll and Univ NC-Charlotte; chair Natl Commn on Working Women. **HONORS/ACHIEVEMENTS:** Recipient Distinguished Citizenship Award NC Dist Civitan Internat; Coll Entrance Exam Bd Medal for disting serv to educ 1976; Distinguished Alumni Medallion for achievement Livingston Coll; Distinguished Tchr Award Civitan Club Salisbury; NC Disting Serv Awd; Disting NC Woman Awd; recipient of Honorarydegrees from 29 colls & univs. **BUSINESS ADDRESS:** Consultant, 418 So Caldwell St, Salisbury, NC 28144.

LAHARRY, NORMAN
Pharmacist. **PERSONAL:** Born Apr 10, 1930, Mound Bayou, MS; died Nov 24, 1988; divorced; children: LaJoy Norman. **EDUCATION:** Tougaloo Coll, BS Chemistry 1951; Howard Univ Graduate School 1953-56; Texas Southern Univ, BS Pharmacy 1960. **CAREER:** Independence Pharmacy, pharmacist 1961-63; Ida Mae Scott Hospital/Norman's Pharmacy, pharmacist 1969; Norman's Pharmacy, pharmacist 1969-. **ORGANIZATIONS:** Founder/pres Norman LaHarry Scholarship Golf Classic; bd mem & past pres Chicago Pharmacist Assn 1970-72; past pres Natl Pharmaceutical Assn 1975-76; mem Amer

Acad of General Practitioners; mem Chi Delta Mu Frat; mem NAACP; bd mem of Univ of Illinois Urban Health Program. **HONORS/ACHIEVEMENTS:** Outstanding Achievement, Pharamacy Graduate Class, Resall Drug Co 1960; Humanitarian Award, Wyeth Labs 1975; Pharmacist of the Year, Pharmacist Nat'l Assoc 1980; Fellow Amer Coll of Apothecaries; Achievement Award, Chi Delta Mu; Pharmacist of the Year Award, Natl Pharmacy Assn 1984; Bowl of Hygeia Award, A H Robins Co 1982; Alumni of the Year Award, Tougaloo Coll Chicago Chapter; inducted into UGA Golf Hall of Fame 1986. **MILITARY SERVICE:** AUS Sgt 1951-53. **HOME ADDRESS:** 601 E 32 St, Chicago, IL 60618. **BUSINESS ADDRESS:** Norman Pharmacy, PO Box A3802, Chicago, IL 60690-3802.

LELAND, MICKEY
Government official. **PERSONAL:** Born Nov 27, 1944, Lubbock, TX; died Aug 13, 1989; children: Jarrett. **EDUCATION:** TX So Univ, BS Pharmacy 1970. **CAREER:** TX So Univ, instructor clinical pharmacy 1970-71; TX House of Reps, mem 1973-78, vice chmn public welfare subcomm 1975-76; 96-97th Congress' from 18th TX Dist, congressman. **ORGANIZATIONS:** mem Appropriations Comm, legislative budget bd 1977-78; co-chmn Natl Black Hispanic Democratic Coalition 1978-; mem Democratic Natl Comm 1976-, TX Democratic Black Caucus. **BUSINESS ADDRESS:** Congressman, Texas Dist 18, 419 Cannon House Office Bldg, Washington, DC 20515.

LEWIS, JULIAN H.
Educator, physician. **PERSONAL:** Born May 26, 1891, Shawneetown, IL; died Mar 1989; widowed; children: Julian, John, Gloria. **EDUCATION:** Univ of Illinois, AB, MA 1908-12; Univ of Chicago, PhD 1915; Rush Medical Coll, MD 1917. **CAREER:** Univ of Chicago, assoc prof dept of pathology 1917-43; Our Lady of Mercy Hospital, dir pathology dept. **ORGANIZATIONS:** Mem Chicago Soc of Intl Medicine, Chicago Inst of Medicine, AAAS, Sigma Xi; mem orig comm Human Rights. **HONORS/ACHIEVEMENTS:** John Simon Guggenheim Fellowship for Study Abroad 1926-27; author of "Biology of the Negro" Univ of Chicago Press; published many research papers in various journals in English & German; Benjamin Rush Metal; Howard T Ricketts Prize; Alpha Omega Alpha Med Hon Frat. **MILITARY SERVICE:** AUS 1st lieutenant 1918. **BUSINESS ADDRESS:** Dir Pathology Department, Our Lady of Mercy Hosp, Dyer, IN 46311.

LOWE, TOWNSEND GARFIELD
Physician. **PERSONAL:** Born Dec 18, 1909, Homestead, PA; died Nov 19, 1988, Los Angeles, CA; married Agatha Starling. **EDUCATION:** West Virginia State Coll, BS 1933; Meharry Medical Coll Nashville, MD 1935-39; Homer Phillips Hospital St Louis, rot internship 1939-40. **CAREER:** Watts Health Found Los Angeles, emergency room physician 1969-79; Los Angeles City Emergency Hospital Hollywood, emergency physician 1967-71; Carmarillo State Hospital California, staff physician 1963-65; St Agatha Hospital Detroit, medical dir 1951-63; Detroit, private practice 1946-63; Montgomery WV, private practice 1941-46; Sinai Hospital Detroit, residency surgery anethesia 1962; USC School of Medicine Los Angeles County Gen Hospital, clinical course physical medicine 1964-65. **ORGANIZATIONS:** Mem Charles Drew Medical Soc Los Angeles 1965-79; mem Alpha Phi Alpha Frat; ret mem Los Angeles County Medical Assn; church affiliation Methodist. **MILITARY SERVICE:** AUS examining physician 1941-44. **HOME ADDRESS:** 2922 W Martin L King Blvd, Los Angeles, CA 90008.

MACKEY, HOWARD HAMILTON, SR.
Educator, architect, planner. **PERSONAL:** Born Nov 25, 1901, Philadelphia, PA; died Aug 20, 1987; married Matilda E Kendricks. **EDUCATION:** Univ of Pennsylvania, BA Architecture 1924, MA Architcture 1937; Howard Univ, Honorary LHD 1980. **CAREER:** Howard Univ School of Architecture & Planning, prof emeritus 1973-87; Urban Design City Planning & Tropical Architecture Howard Univ, teacher of architecture 1924-73; Howard Univ, head dept of architecture 1930-32, 1934-71, assoc dean school of Engineering & Architecture 1964-65, founding dean of school of architecture & planning 1970-71; DC MD VA PA NJ, registered architect 1935-87; Univ of MD, staff of civil engineering; British, Guiana, & Surinam, consultant 1954-57; 1st Natl Exhibit of Works of Black Architecture, pioneered 1930; Chicago War Memorial Natl Competition, participant; Corcoran Gallery, Washington DC Art Center, NYC, Art Inst Chicago, works exhib. **ORGANIZATIONS:** Mem DC bd Exam & Registrars of Architectire 1969; mem DC Bd of Zoning Adj 1970-72; Baltimore Design Advisory Panel for Urban Renewal Project 1964-70; DC Joint Comm of Nation's Capital Landmarks 1970. **HONORS/ACHIEVEMENTS:** Distinguished Serv Award, Natl Technological Assn 1961; elected to Coll of Fellows & advanced to rank of Fellow of Amer Inst of Architecture 1962; elected honorary mem Tau Beta Pi Honor Engineering Soc 1966; hon mem Tau Sigma Delta Honor Architecture Soc 1970; appointed architectural consultant to US Gen Serv Admin 1971; works published in Progressive Archit & other professional journals; donated $10,000 to establish "Howard H Machey Sr Emergency Student Loan Fund" 1974; established Matilda Kendricks Mackey Memorial Student Loan Fund 1976; donated to Manuscript Div Moorland-Spingarn Research Center Howard Univ the Howard H Mackey Sr papers, documents & memorabilia 1975; "Howard H Mackey Tribute Day" in recognition of contributions and achievements in profession of architecture, Howard Univ 1979.

MAPP, ALEXANDER B.
Employment consultant. **PERSONAL:** Born Oct 19, 1912, Cambridge, MA; died Sep 12, 1987; son of Alexander M Mapp and Zylpha Mapp; married Edna; children: Alexander B Jr, Patti, John. **EDUCATION:** Massachusetts Art School, attended (special student); Ohio State Univ, attended (special courses); Boston Univ School of Educ, attended 1939. **CAREER:** "Time for Teamwork," five year radio broadcasting; Urban League of Springfield, exec dir 1943-63; Intergroup Relations Specialist, army matl command 1963-64; New England Region AMC, regional dir 1965-66; Contract Compliance Office DSA, regional chief 1967-74; AIC, employment consultant 1975-87. **ORGANIZATIONS:** Advisor Holyoke Human Relations Council; consultant Social Security Admin; mem Governor's Comm on Housing & Urban Affairs; mem Conn Valley Foreign Policy Assn. **HONORS/ACHIEVEMENTS:** NAACP Citizen's Award 1976; Pynchon Award 1979; Certificate of, Merit State of Massachusetts 1979; Living Legacy Award 1985; also 7 publications; A B Mapp Scholarship Award, Urban Legaue of Springfield 1975; A B Mapp Black Achievement Award, US Post Office 1988. **BUSINESS ADDRESS:** Employment Consultant, American International College, Career Dev/Placement Office, 1000 State St, Springfield, MA 01109.

MARCUS, CHESTER L.
Clergyman, retired denominational. **PERSONAL:** Born Feb 14, 1917, Swiftown, MS; son of Frank Marcus and Eliza Hamilton Marcus; married Dorothy Hampton; children: Chester Jr, Kathryn. **EDUCATION:** Alcorn A&M Coll, Lorman MS, BS 1940; STM, 1943; DD, 1967. **CAREER:** Washington Presbyterian Church, Reading PA, pastor 1943-54; Philadelphia Presbyterian, ordained UPC 1943; Africa, missionary 1959-60; UCC, sec for race & cultural relations 1954-61; UCBWM, reg sec Africa 1962-82 (retired). **ORGANIZATIONS:** Pres Reading Branch NAACP 1950-54; chmn Africa Dept NCC 1970-72; advisory comm US State Dept 1973-75; mem Phi Beta Kappa. **HONORS/ACHIEVEMENTS:** Alcornite of the Year 1958.

MARSHALL, JOSEPH D.
Government official. **PERSONAL:** Born Dec 25, 1919, St Clairsville, OH; married Stella Durant; children: Whitney, Marshall, Joann, Carr. **CAREER:** Fairbanks AK, deputy mayor 1978-; State of Alaska, dir outreach-apprenticeship program 1976-78; State of Alaska, asst commr of labor 1972-75; Plasterer's and Cement Masons, business mgr 1967-71; City of Fairbanks, councilman 1971-80; Fairbanks North-Star Borough, borough assemblyman 1971-80. **HONORS/ACHIEVEMENTS:** Govt Award NAACP 1972; Labor Award NAACP 1974. **MILITARY SERVICE:** AUS sgt 1943-46.

MAZIQUE, EDWARD C.
Physician. **PERSONAL:** Born Mar 21, 1911, Natchez, MS; died Dec 27, 1987; married Frances Margurite Byrd; children: Edward H, Jeffrey C. **EDUCATION:** Morehouse Coll, BS 1933; Atlanta U, MA 1934; Howard U, MD 1941. **CAREER:** Private Practice Washington, DC, physician 1943-87; Freedmen's Hospital, internship, asst resident, internal med 1941-43. **ORGANIZATIONS:** Mem, Amer Med Assn; Amer Public Health Assn; Med Soc of DC; Am Geriatric Soc; Com for establishment of Ojeke; mem Hosp Nigeria Africa; Royal Soc health Lodnon; HowardUniv Alumni Fed; Health Adv Council Wash Tech Inst; Am Assn of Med Assistants; mem Cits Adv Council to Commnr of Dist 1 DC; bd dirs Wash Home Rule Com; Med Adv Bd Visiting Nurses Assn; 12 St Br YMCA; dem cntrl com of DC Hosp Serv Agency; adv com SE Neighborhood Hse; bd dirs exec com Comm Chest Fed of Dist; exec com NAACP; Omega Psi Phi Frat; Chi Delta Mu Frat; bd Dirs United Comm Nat Bank; bd dirs DC Area Council on Alcoholism; alternate Delegate to Nat Dem Conv; bd dirs African Acad of Arts & Res Inc; treas Fauntroy for Congress Campaign; mem bd dirs Am Capitol Life Ins Co; bd of Councillors Sch of Bus Fed City Coll; professional mem Nat Assn of Diability Examiners Nat Rehab Assn; bd dirs Boys Club of Gr Wash; chmn bd dirs Jet Super Markets; bd dirs Boys Club of Am. **HONORS/ACHIEVEMENTS:** Recip afro-am outstanding cit award 1952; outstanding civic award C Rd of Civic Assns 1956-57; achievement award Nat Med Assn 1960; man of yr award Omega Psi Phi 1960; cert of award Nat Med Assn 1965; serv to youth award YMCA 1961-62; serv award HowardUniv 1961-62; Nat Med Assn award outstanding avc 1967; outstanding commendation & award DC Fed of Civic Assn 1967-68; outstanding achievement award merit serv field of med Nat Med Assn Conv in Houston 1968; youth opp campaign award US Dept HEW Pub Halth Serv 1969; distin son award Morehouse Coll 1969; comm action cert The Sophisticated Soc Inc 1971; cert of leadership award YMCA 1971; hon deg of sci Morehouse Coll 1974; comm achievement award AMVETS 1975; dist serv award Nat Med Assn 1975; alumnae award Bennett Coll 1976; achievement award Jr Citizens Corps Inc 1976; outstanding serv award HowardUniv Med Alumni 1977; Man of the Yr Morehouse 1978; ah robins comm serv serv award DC Med Soc 1979; has numerous articles, reports & publications to his credit. **BUSINESS ADDRESS:** 908 Kennedy St NW, Washington, DC 20011.

MCCANE, MARGARET PEREA
Retired educational administrator. **PERSONAL:** Born Mar 01, 1906, Cambridge, MA; died Mar 29, 1989; daughter of Beverly Perea and Missouri Jones Perea; married Charles Anthony; children: Perea Hopkins, Charlotte Antoinette. **EDUCATION:** Radcliffe Coll, AB 1927; Harvard Univ, 1926-28; Univ of Chicago, 1930; Catholic Univ of Amer, MSSW 1941. **CAREER:** Barrett School for Girls, supt 1935-55; Natl Training School for Girls Washington DC, supt 1949-52; Juvenile Court of Washington DC, 1942-49; Family Serv of Allegheny Co, 1941-42; A&T Coll, French teacher 1929-30; Deleware State Coll, French teacher 1928-29; Wiley Coll, French teacher 1927-28. **ORGANIZATIONS:** Founding pres Chapter #953 AARP Falmouth MA 1973; incorporator Elder Serv of Cape Cod 1973; former mem Town Meeting Falmouth 1976; former mem Town Human Serv Comm; former mem Town Planning Bd; mem Town Fin Comm; mem several Radcliffe Coll Coms.

MCCLANEY, EULA
Business executive. **PERSONAL:** Died Jan 22, 1988; children: La Doris. **CAREER:** Motel, owner, mgr 1957-67; McClaney Enterprises Inc, head. **ORGANIZATIONS:** Lectures to young people. **HONORS/ACHIEVEMENTS:** Community & philanthropic efforts in helping the less fortunate are legendary; Schomburg Ctr for Rsch in Black Culture accepted memorabilia of Eula McClaney 1981; autobiography "God I Listened.". **BUSINESS ADDRESS:** Real Estate Entrepreneur, McClaney Properties Inc, P O Box 1157, Beverly Hills, CA 90213.

MCCONNELL, RAYMOND THOMAS
Business executive. **PERSONAL:** Born Apr 04, 1949, New York, NY; died Apr 20, 1989; son of Thomas McConnell and Ruby Bushell. **EDUCATION:** Pace Univ, BBA 1977; NY Univ, Graduate School 1983. **CAREER:** EF Hutton & Co Inc, first vice pres; RTRM Inc, pres. **ORGANIZATIONS:** Dir, treasurer Hutton Commodity Intl, Hutton Commodity Mgmt; dir, asst sec, treasurer Hutton Commodity Reserve Fund Limited; Hutton Commodity Trading Ltd; dir Futures Industry Assn 1978-82; pres Operations Div 1981-82; dir Options Div; mem Natl Assn of Black Accountants; mem 100 Black Men. **BUSINESS ADDRESS:** President, RTRM Inc, 30 Lincoln, New York, NY 10023.

MCCREE, WADE H., JR.
Law educator. **PERSONAL:** Born Jul 03, 1920, Des Moines, IA; died Aug 30, 1987; married Dores B McCrary; children: Kathleen L McCree Lewis, Karen L Wade. **EDUCATION:** Fisk Univ, BA 1941; Harvard Univ, LLB 1944, LLD 1969; Wayne State Univ, LLD 1964; Tuskegee Inst, attended 1965. **CAREER:** Pvt practice Detroit, 1948-62; MI Workmen's Compensation Commn, commr 1952-54; Wayne County MI, circuit judge 1954-61; US Dist Court Eastern Dist MI, judge 1961-66; US Court of Appeals 6th Circuit, judge 1966-77; US, solicitor gen 1977-81; Univ MI Law School Ann Arbor, mem faculty 1981-87. **ORGANIZATIONS:** Summer faculty IN Univ Law School; dir Natl Bank Detroit, Burroughs Corp;

former mem Wayne State Univ Law School, Case Western Res Law School, Harvard Law School; mem liaison com med educ AMA; del US 3rd UN Congress Prevention of Crime Stockholm 1956; adv bd United Found Detroit; exec bd Detroit Area council Boy Scouts of Amer; vchmn, bd trustees Fisk Univ, Nashville; trustee Fisk Univ; mem MI Strategic Fund; founding trustee Friends School Detroit; bd dirs Met Hosp, Henry Ford Hosp, Founders Soc Detroit Inst Arts, Natl Jud Coll; fellow Amer Coll Trial Lawyers, Amer Bar Found; mem ABA; mem commn on standards jud admin Natl Bar Assn; mem Detroit Bar Assn, State Bar MI, Inst Jud Admin, Amer Judicature Soc, Amer Law Inst; exec comm Amer Assn Law Schools; mem Phi Beta Kappa. **HONORS/ACHIEVEMENTS:** Num hon degrees. **MILITARY SERVICE:** AUS capt 1942-46. **BUSINESS ADDRESS:** Lewis M Simes Professor of Law, University of Michigan, Law School, Ann Arbor, MI 48109.

MCDEW, STEPHEN MAXWELL, JR.
Physician. **PERSONAL:** Born Sep 22, 1912, Ocilla, GA; died Nov 01, 1981; son of Stephan M McDew and Ophelia Bozeman McDew; married Mary L Bradley; children: Frieda Pauline, Stephanie Maria Schoumacher. **EDUCATION:** Georgia State Coll, BS 1934; Meharry Medical Coll, MD 1939. **CAREER:** Physician, self-employed. **ORGANIZATIONS:** Mem AMA, SMA, NMA, MAG, Georgia State Medical Assn, NAACP, YMCA, Alpha Phi Alpha, St Matthews Episcopal Church. **BUSINESS ADDRESS:** 918 W Broad St, Savannah, GA 31401.

MCDOWELL, SAMUEL E.
Association executive. **PERSONAL:** Born Feb 09, 1939, Bladenboro, NC; died Aug 27, 1977; son of James McDowell and Francese' Singletary-McDowell; married Katherine McDowell (Vereen), Jun 24, 1960; children: Pernella McDowell, Katha McDowell White. **EDUCATION:** State Univ of NY at Albany, attended; Hudson Valley Community Coll; Empire State. **CAREER:** Comm Referral Center, dir 1974-; Ex-offender Agency, co-dir 1972-73; Prison Work, rehabilitation counseling, employment agency, maintaining half-way house; Sam & McDowell Bail Fund, all vol; The Bros in Albany, leader 1966-70; ironworker 1967-75; Coxsockie Correctional Facility, Coxsockie NY, executive 1976-77. **ORGANIZATIONS:** Mem Northside Advisory Council 1972-73; candidate co-Legislator 1967; mem Citizens Advisory Bd Neighborhood Police; bd mem Community School Albany; bd dirs Urban League 1972-75; mem Friends of Harmanus Bleeker Library 1974-75; PTA pres Giffen School 1973-74; Albany Black Assembly 1974; bd mem Taxpayers Assn; honorary chmn Liberal Party; honorary mem Jaycees 1977. **HONORS/ACHIEVEMENTS:** Recipient Volunteer of the Year 1974 Volunteer Action Center. **BUSINESS ADDRESS:** Correctional Executive, Coxsockie Correctional Facility, Coxsockie, NY.

MCLIN, C. J., JR.
Legislator. **PERSONAL:** Born May 31, 1921, E St Louis, IL; died Dec 27, 1988; son of Rubie McLinn; children: Rhine, C J III, Scherrie. **EDUCATION:** Attended Virginia Union Univ, Richmond VA; attended Cincinnati Coll of Embalming. **CAREER:** 10 consecutive terms chairman state govt comm; McLin Funeral Home Inc, licensed funeral dir/embalmer, pres; Sche Realty Inc, pres/CEO; Ohio House of Representatives, state representative 1966-88. **ORGANIZATIONS:** Mem Rules/Finance/State Govt Comm; sec Ohio Democratic Party Exec Comm; bd mem Buckeye Funeral Dir Assn; former special advisor on minority affairs Gov John J Gilligan; bd mem Dayton Urban League; bd mem Goodwill Industries; Dayton Area Chamber of Commerce; Citywide Development Corp; Mayor's Council on Economic Devel; pres Black Elected Democrats of Ohio; NH Black Caucus of State Legislators; Natl Black Leadership Roundtable; life mem NAACP; Amer Temple #101 Shrine-Waldorf; Lodge #76 Elks; 33rd Degree Mason; chmn Ohio Correctional Institution Comm; co-founder Dayton Youth Patrol; leader Thirteenth Ward Demo; mem Private Industry Council; advisor First Inc; mem Pledge Serv Comm; mem Montgomery County Funeral Dir's Assn; mem Catholic Inter-Racial Council of Miami Valley; mem Amer Legion. **HONORS/ACHIEVEMENTS:** Democrat of the Year, Democratic Party Montgomery County Ohio 1974, 1976; Honorary LLD, Central State Univ 1976; Annual Outstanding Serv Award, Ohio Public Transit Assn 1977; Community Action Agency Man of the Year, Ohio Community Action Agencies 1980; Resolution of Appreciation, Mayor James H McGee, Dayton OH 1980; Outstanding Contribution Award, WH Con Small Business Pres Jimmy Carter 1980; Certificate of Recognition, Phi Delta Kappa WSU 1981; Honorary LLD Central State Univ Wilberforce OH; Outstanding Legislator by Veterans of Foreign Wars; Honorary HHD Wright State Univ 1986; establishing WSU Medical School; requiring state inspection of nursing & rest homes operated by the County. **MILITARY SERVICE:** AUS 1942-45. **BUSINESS ADDRESS:** State Representative, OH House of Representatives, State Capitol Building, Columbus, OH 43215.

MCMILLAN, SYLVIA ROSS
Psychologist. **PERSONAL:** Born in Kansas City, KS; died Jan 16, 1989; children: Caldwell Jr, Elizabeth A McMillan-McCartney. **EDUCATION:** Univ of Minnesota, BS 1942; Univ of Maryland, MS 1966; Azusa Pac Coll, MA 1976; The Fielding Inst, Psychology Degree 1978. **CAREER:** Univ of Maryland Coll Park, ext home economist 1961-67; Anne Arundel County Economic Opportunity Comm Inc, exec dir 1968-76; Alcoholism Treatment & Rehabilitation Unit Pasadena Community Hospital, dir/dept head 1978-80; Univ of CA Los Angeles, instructor (part time) 1980; US Virgin Islands Dept of Health Div of Mental Health, dir of long term care 1982; Howard Univ Coll of Medicine, asst prof 1981; Psychological Serv Inc, clinical psychologist 1983; Private Practice, psychologist. **ORGANIZATIONS:** Mem Amer Psychological Assn; clinical mem Amer Assn for Marriage & Family Therapist (inactive); mem Assn of Black Psychologists (inactive), Alpha Kappa Alpha Sorority, NAACP, Maryland Psychological Assn. **HONORS/ACHIEVEMENTS:** Outstanding Community Serv Award, Annapolis Club of Frontiers Intl 1972; Citizen of the Year Award, Mu Rho Chapter Omega Psi Phi Frat 1973; Nomination Natl Woman of Conscience Award, US Congresswoman Marjorie Holt (Maryland) 1973; Award for Effective & Devoted Serv, Anne Arundel County Economic Opportunity Comm Inc 1978; Outstanding Serv, Anne Arundel County Economic Comm 1985.

MCMURTRY-REED, LILLIE ELOISE
Educator. **PERSONAL:** Born Aug 17, 1912, Leake County, MS; died Jul 24, 1987, Meridian, MS; married Walter Reed Jr; children: Walter III. **EDUCATION:** Florida A&M Univ, BS 1951, MS 1951; InterAmericana Universidad Saltillo Coahuila Mexico, PhD 1973. **CAREER:** Harris Jr Coll, head librarian 1957-70; Meridian Jr Coll, supvr & curriculum specialist 1970-71; Perkinston Jr Coll, assoc librarian 1971-72; Office of Institutional Research Utica Jr Coll, dir 1972-77; Office of Institutional Research Miles Coll Birmingham, dir 1977-82. **ORGANIZATIONS:** Life mem Natl Educ Assn; life mem Mississippi Teachers Assn; founder & co-chmn Mississippi Assn of Institutional Researchers 1973-; mem Natl Assn of Institutional Researchers; pres Meridian Chapter Natl Negro Business & Professional Women's Clubs Inc 1971-75; mem Amer Library Assn; Mississippi Library Assn; Foreign Lang Natl Assn. **HONORS/ACHIEVEMENTS:** Woman of the Year, Meridian Chapter Natl Negro Business & Professional Women's Clubs Inc 1974; editor Fact Book of Utica Jr Coll 1973. **HOME ADDRESS:** 3203 19th St, PO Box 4061, Meridian, MS 39301.

MELTON, CHARLES A.
Association executive. **PERSONAL:** Born Nov 01, 1913, West Chester, PA; died Sep 28, 1987; married Mary L Blakey; children: Charles, Jr, Barbara, Terran, Silver, Milona. **CAREER:** West Chester Comm Ctr Inc, exec dir. **ORGANIZATIONS:** Mem exalted ruler Capt Levi Hood Lodge #159, 1948-58; pres United Pol Action 1968-69; pres W Chester Civic Assn 1963-64; W Chester Plng Commn 1966-75;pres W Chester NAACP 1963-65; treas Comm Action Bd; bd Day Care 1968-70; Mental Retardtn Bd 1967-68; pres W Chester Oppor Bd 1968-70; pres Crisis Ctr Open Door 1973-74. **HONORS/ACHIEVEMENTS:** Brthd award Human Relat Coun W Chester 1963; Chapel 4 Chaplain's Award 1965; United Pol Action Award 1967; Capt Levi Hood 159 Award 1967; Black Hawks Award 1968. **BUSINESS ADDRESS:** 501 E Miner St West, Chester, PA 19380.

MISHOE, LUNA I.
Educational administrator. **PERSONAL:** Born Jan 05, 1917, Bucksport, SC; died Jan 16, 1989; daughter of Henry Mishoe and Martha Oliva Mishoe; married Hattie Bernice Dabney, Feb 18, 1944; children: Bernellyn Carey, Luna II, Wilma Sudler, Rita. **EDUCATION:** Allen Univ, BS 1938; Univ of Michigan, MS 1942; NY Univ, PhD 1953; Wharton School of the Univ of Pennsylvania, MBA 1985; Delaware State Coll, BSc 1981. **CAREER:** Kittrell Coll NC, prof math & physics 1939-42; Delaware State Coll Dover, prof math & physics 1946-48; Morgan State Coll Baltimore, assoc prof of physics 1948-54, prof of physics 1954-60; Delaware State Coll Dover, pres 1960-87. **ORGANIZATIONS:** Bd trustees Univ of Delaware Newark 1969-81; bd trustees Delaware State Coll; mem Amer Math Soc; mem Math Assn of Amer; Bd of Dirs WHYY TV 1974; bd dirs Wilmington Savings Fund Soc 1979; pres Dover Rotary Club 1980. **HONORS/ACHIEVEMENTS:** Gold Good Citizenship Medal, Delaware Soc of the Sons of the Amer Revolution 1974; Kappa Delta Pi Natl Honor Soc 1978; Natl Hon Scholastic Soc Alpha Chi 1978; Honorary Doctor of Science, Lincoln Univ, Jefferson City MO 1986; Honorary Doctor of Laws, Morgan State Univ 1987. **MILITARY SERVICE:** USAF 1st lieutenant 1942-46. **HOME ADDRESS:** 335 State College Rd, Dover, DE 19901.

MITCHELL, LOUIS D.
Educator. **PERSONAL:** Born Jun 30, 1928, New York, NY; died Mar 29, 1989. **EDUCATION:** Fordham Coll, BA 1952; Fordham Univ, MFA 1954; Columbia Univ, 1957-58; NY Univ, PhD 1967. **CAREER:** Univ of Scranton, prof English; NY Inst for Blind, teacher 1954-61. **HONORS/ACHIEVEMENTS:** Has many publications to his credit; Recipient Founders Day Award, NY Univ 1969; Distinguished Graduate Award, NY Inst for Educ of Blind 1974; Outstanding Educators of Amer Academic Admin of the Univ of Scranton 1974; composer music lyrics, "The Star of the Morning" 1965; contributed to Crisis Magazine 1976; grant & aid Amer Council of Learned 1969. **BUSINESS ADDRESS:** U of Scranton, Scranton, PA 18510.

MOORE, DONNIE RAY
Professional athlete. **PERSONAL:** Born Feb 13, 1954, Lubbock, TX; died Jul 18, 1989, Anaheim, CA; married Tonya Martin; children: Demetria, Donnie II, Ronnie. **CAREER:** Boston Red Sox, player 1972-73; Chicago Cubs, player 1973-79; St Louis Cardinals, player 1979-81; Milwaukee Brewers, player 1981-82; Atlanta Braves, player 1982; California Angels, player, until 1988. **HONORS/ACHIEVEMENTS:** Named to Jr Coll All-Amer first team; led Atlanta's staff with 16 saves, 1984; Appeared in 100th Amer League Game in Detroit, Aug 21, 1986; mem All Star team, 1985. **BUSINESS ADDRESS:** California Angels, PO Box 2000, Anaheim, CA 92803.

MOORE, JACOB
Business executive. **PERSONAL:** Born Jul 12, 1938, Beaufort County, SC; died Dec 25, 1988; son of Albert T Moore and Ida Mae Crossman Moore; married Margaret Little; children: Jacob, Veronica. **EDUCATION:** Bank Administration Institute at University of Wisconsin, Certification Auditor 1974; Pace University, BBA 1976. **CAREER:** Chemical Bank, supervising auditor 1975-78; asst manager 1978-80; manager 1980-82; asst vice president 1982-88. **ORGANIZATIONS:** Bd mem New York Urban League-Brooklyn 1980-; bd mem Bedford Stuyvesant Community Mental Health Center 1981-; bd sec Interfaith Medical Center 1982-. **HONORS/ACHIEVEMENTS:** Achievement Award, Bedford Stuyvesant Real Estate Board 1980; Business Award, Salvation Army-Bedford Temple 1982; Community Service Award, Bedford Stuyvesant Lions Club 1982; Man of the Year, The Natl Assn of Negro Business and Professional Women 1983. **HOME ADDRESS:** 130-21 227th St, Laurelton, NY 11413. **BUSINESS ADDRESS:** Vice President, Chemical Bank, 111 Livingston, Brooklyn, NY 11201.

MOORE, PHIL
Composer, arranger. **PERSONAL:** Born Feb 20, 1918, Portland, OR; died May 1987; married Jeanne; children: Joamma, Phil III. **EDUCATION:** Univ of Washington; Cornisle Conseratory. **CAREER:** Lena Horne, Ray Charles, Duke Ellington, arranger; Uptown, musical director; MGM, 1st black staff composer-arranger 1942; Cabin in the Sky, composer-arranger 1943; RKO Studies, Paramount, Columbia Pictures, composer-arranger; CBS, NBC-TV Studio One, Playhouse 90, Bell Telephone Hour, Omnibus, writing scores for dramatic shows; NBC Cotton Club, Duke Ellington Spec, music dir; Visions, composer-music; Britains BBC, consult on musical concepts & formats; Easy Time BBC Radio, own show; Sunset Strip Studio "Artists & Music Concepts, director. **ORGANIZATIONS:** Lecturer Yale, Univ of MA; composed, conducted, arranged routines for Diahann Carroll, Roberta Peters, Frank Sinatra, Judy Garland, Louis Armstrong, Aretha Franklin, Tom Jones & Count Basie. **HONORS/ACHIEVEMENTS:** Emmy nominee for Carrier; twice awarded by Animated Film Festival for his original music for Mr Magoo & other UPA cartoons; appeared on albums for EMI, Columbia, MGM, Mercury Records. **BUSINESS ADDRESS:** President, Sunset Strip Studio, 8949 Sunset Blvd, Los Angeles, CA 90069.

MUSGRAVE, MARIAN ELIZABETH
Educator. **PERSONAL:** Born Jan 29, Cleveland, OH; died May 24, 1988; divorced; children: Janis Meredith Jackson. **EDUCATION:** Howard Univ, BA 1945, MA 1946; Western Research Univ, PhD 1960. **CAREER:** Black World Studies Miami Univ, prof, dir; Central State Univ Grad English Program, prof, dir; Alabama State Univ, prof; Alcorn Coll English Dept; prof, chmn; Southern Univ, instructor; AR AM&N, instructor; Miami Univ, prof of English. **ORGANIZATIONS:** Mem, exec council Midwest Modern Language Assn 1973-76; mem Del Assembly Modern Language Assn 1976-78; mem ERIC/Reading & Communication Skills Advisory Bd; consultant Natl Assessment of Educ Progress/Literature Review Bd; mem, exec bd Ohio Program in Humanities, Comm on Role of Women, Natl Council of Teachers of English; mem Delta Sigma Theta. **HONORS/ACHIEVEMENTS:** Articles on German Literature, Black Literature, English Literature; Honorary Soror Delta Phi Alpha, Sigma Delta Pi, Pi Delta Phi, Alpha Lambda Delta. **BUSINESS ADDRESS:** Professor, MiamiUniv, 322 Bachelor Hall, Oxford, OH 45056.

NEWTON, HUEY
Former civil rights group activist/founder. **PERSONAL:** Born Feb 17, 1942, Monroe, LA; died Aug 22, 1989, Oakland, CA. **EDUCATION:** Oakland City Coll, San Francisco Law School, attended; PhD, Univ of California, 1980. **ORGANIZATIONS:** Black Panthers, co-founder.

NIXON, EDGAR DANIEL
City official. **PERSONAL:** Born Jul 12, 1899, Montgomery, AL; died Mar 1987; married Arlet Campbell. **BUSINESS ADDRESS:** 3594 C Young Dr, Montgomery, AL 36108.

O'NEAL, KENNETH R.
Architect. **PERSONAL:** Born Jul 30, 1908, Union, MO; married Margaret Williams; children: Kenneth, Jr, Ronald, Brian. **EDUCATION:** Univ of Iowa, AB 1931, BS 1935; Illinois Inst of Technology, graduate study; Chicago Art Inst, 1946; Univ of Chicago, 1956-58. **CAREER:** City of Chicago, project mgr, architect 1974-; Illinois Inst of Technology, instructor 1956-75; Illinois Div of Highways, engineer 1935-43; architecture, private practice 1945-50; Skidmore, Owings & Merril, architect 1950-51; Schmidt, Garden, Erickson, architect 1951-54. **ORGANIZATIONS:** Mem AIA, ARA, NTA, NOMA; bd mem Chase House 1969-75, Hyde Park Co-op 1967-68; sr warden Ch of Redeemer 1965-66; registered with NCAR Bds; creator of detail plates on architectural details for American Builder Magazine 1946-49; published a portfolio of modern homes 1947; registered architect in Iowa, Indiana, North Dakota, Montana. **HONORS/ACHIEVEMENTS:** Certificate of Recognition, Oppotrunity Magazine 1947. **MILITARY SERVICE:** AUS t/sgt 1943-45. **BUSINESS ADDRESS:** 320 N Clark St, Chicago, IL 60610.

PARKER, ELIZABETH L.
Educator. **PERSONAL:** Born Feb 16, 1937, Birmingham, AL; died Jan 15, 1978. **EDUCATION:** San Francisco State Coll, BA 1968, MA 1972; Stanford Univ, 1973. **CAREER:** Ethnic Studies & History Univ San Francisco, instructor 1970-; Ethnic Studies Coll San Mateo, instructor 1971-72; San Francisco Community Coll Dist, instructor history 1971; Ethnic Studies Univ San Francisco, asst dir 1971-73; Ethnic Studies, dir 1972-73. **ORGANIZATIONS:** Mem Delta Sigma Theta; Phi Alpha Theta; Assn Study of Afro-Amer History & Culture Soc of San Francisco; Oral History Assn; NAACP; mem com Task Force Status of Women Univ of San Francisco 1971-72; Educ Serv Center Minority Students Univ of San Francisco 1971-; bd dirs Upward Bound Univ of San Francisco 1971-73; charter review comm Berkeley 1972; bd dirs African-Amer History & Culture Soc San Francisco 1973-; chmn Black History Week 1974; exec council Assn Study Afro-Amer Life & History 1973-76; consultant Merritt Coll Conf Black Studies 1972; field Rdr HEW 1974, 1977; conf black oral history Fisk Univ 1972; AHALH Cincinnati 1972; NY 1973; minority studies Univ of Wisconsin 1973; 2nd Minority Studies 1974; ASALH Philadelphia 1974. **HONORS/ACHIEVEMENTS:** Co-author "Walking Tour of Black Presence in San Francisco during 19th Century"; traveled Western Europe 1969-76; Trans-Canadian Highway 1971; Jamaica 1973-76; Haiti 1975; Barbados 1976. **BUSINESS ADDRESS:** Univ of San Francisco, 544 University Ctr, San Francisco, CA 94117.

PARKS, HENRY GREEN, JR.
Business executive. **PERSONAL:** Born Sep 29, 1916, Atlanta, GA; died Apr 24, 1989, Towson, MD; divorced; children: Grace P Johnson, Cheryl V. **EDUCATION:** OH State Univ Coll Commerce, BA. **CAREER:** Pabst Brewing Co, natl sales rep 1940; Baltimore City, councilman 1963-69; Parks Sausage Co, chmn of the bd. **ORGANIZATIONS:** Pres Baltimore City Fire Board; dir WR Grace & Co; dir The Signal Companies; dir Warner-Lambert Co; dir UNC Ventures Inc; dir Mayor's Council of Business Advisors; bd of advisors Black Enterprise Mag; life mem NAACP. **HONORS/ACHIEVEMENTS:** Hon Dr of Laws Temple Univ, 1975; Hon Dr of Humane Letters, Morgan State Univ, 1975; Business Man of the Year, Baltimore Marketing Assn, 1982; J Jefferson Miller Award, Greater Baltimore Comm, 1983. **BUSINESS ADDRESS:** Chairman of the Board, Parks Sausage Co, 1123 N Eutaw St, Ste 311, Baltimore, MD 21201.

PARSONS, GAMALIEL LEROY, JR. (GALE)
Pediatrician. **PERSONAL:** Born Jan 1921, Duluth, GA; died Sep 1987; married Reva Young; children: Patricia Ann, Gamaliel Leroy III, Paulette. **EDUCATION:** Fisk Univ, 1940-44; Meharry Med Coll, MD 1947; Provident Hosp, internship 1947-48, resident pediatrics 1948-50. **CAREER:** Practice of medicine specializing in pediatrics 1950-; Children Memorial Hosp, attending physician 1957-87; Saint Joseph Hospital Chicago, newborn nursery service. **ORGANIZATIONS:** Asst treas Congregational Church of Park Manor 1967; pres of med staff Provident Hosp; chmn pediatrics Provident Hosp 1968-75; founding pres Daniel Hale Williams Neighborhood Health Ctr 1970-71; mem Sigma Pi Phi Frat; mem AMA, NMA, IL State Med Soc, Chicago Med Soc, Chicago Pediatric Soc; mem Congregational Church of Park Manor. **HONORS/ACHIEVEMENTS:** Awd Provident Hosp Med Staff pres 1968-71; Awd Daniel Hale Williams Neighborhood Health Ctr founding pres 1970-71. **MILITARY SERVICE:** AUS med corp capt 1951-53. **BUSINESS ADDRESS:** 3507 S King Dr, Chicago, IL 60653.

PATTERSON, FREDERICK D.
Educator. **PERSONAL:** Born Oct 10, 1901, Washington, DC; died Apr 26, 1988; married Catherine; children: Frederick II. **EDUCATION:** IA State Coll, DVM 1923, MS 1927; Cornell Univ, PhD 1932. **CAREER:** School of Agriculture, instr, head of vet div; Tuskegee Inst, pres 25 yrs; Robert R Moton Meml Inst, chmn of the bd emeritus;Pres Phelps Stokes Fund17 Years. **ORGANIZATIONS:** Hon pres United negro Coll Fund. **HONORS/ACHIEVEMENTS:** Hon degrees from 13 colls & univs incl NY Univ, Morehouse Coll, Howard Univ, Tuskegee Inst, Atlanta Univ, St Augustine's Coll; contrib articles to sci & ed jrnls author "The Coll Endowment Funding Plan" 1976; co-author "What the Negro Wants"; Presidential Medal of Freedom 1987. **BUSINESS ADDRESS:** Chairman Emeritus, R R Moton Institute, 500 E 62nd St, Third Floor, New York, NY 10021.

PETERSEN, JACQUELYN LOWE
Educator. **PERSONAL:** Born May 26, 1930, Winston-Salem, NC; divorced; children: Anthony, Lowe. **EDUCATION:** Fordham Univ, BS 1952, EdD 1975; Hunter Coll of CUNY, MA 1961. **CAREER:** New York City Bd of Educ, teacher coord Career Guidance Program 1958-62; Harlem Teams for Self Help, dir of educ 1962-65; Queens Coll Children & Parents Center, designer & dir 1965-68; NY Urban League, dir of educ 1968-70; NY Univ School of Educ, dir teacher corps program 1970-71; Fordham Univ, assoc dir teacher corps 1971-78, dir correctional redirection career devel program school of educ; Touro Coll, dean 1978-86. **ORGANIZATIONS:** Mem First Natl Parent Involvement Consultants 1965-68, Citywide Child Care Advisory Council 1976-81; chmn Salem Community Serv Council 1978-81; mem Natl Assn of Business & Professional Women NY Branch, Phi Delta Kappa Fordham Univ Chapter. **HONORS/ACHIEVEMENTS:** Assoc Comm Teams Award for Community Educ 1965; Opportunities Indus Center of NY Community Serv Award 1974; Manhood Found Community Serv Award 1975; Educ Award Natl Assn of Univ Women 1978; NY State Assembly 1985. **BUSINESS ADDRESS:** President, Coll for Career & Urban Study, 144 W 138th St, New York, NY 10030.

PETTIE, FLOYD W.
Association executive. **PERSONAL:** Born Jul 24, 1919, Omaha, NE; died Jun 1982; married Irene P; children: Floyd, Donna J. **EDUCATION:** Univ of Nebraska. **CAREER:** Diaster Emergency Serv Agency, dir; Colorado Springs Branch NAACP, comm liaison 1975; Colorado State Representative, 1973-74; Colorado Springs, city councilman 1969-72; Costilla Conoco Serv Station, owner 1962-72. **ORGANIZATIONS:** Trustee Memorial Hospital Colorado Springs 1969-73; pres Colorado Serv Station Assn 1964; pres Petroleum Retailers Assn 1970-72; mem Kiwanis; Pikes Peak Lodge 473; IBPOE of W; sr vice pres Ept CO Reserve Officers Assn; bd dir Urban League; NAACP; St John Baptist Church. **MILITARY SERVICE:** AUS chief warrent officer w-3 1940-60.

PITTS, WILLIS N.
Retired educator. **PERSONAL:** Born Aug 29, 1907, Macon, GA; died Nov 17, 1988; married Frances Haddock. **EDUCATION:** Talladega Coll Alabama, BA 1932; Univ of Michigan Ann Arbor, MA History 1941, MA Speech 1942, PhD Speech 1952. **CAREER:** Moultrie Georgia High School, instructor English 1933-35; Ballard Normal School, Macon GA, instructor English, history 1935-40; Univ of Michigan, dept asst 1945-46; Howard Univ, instructor English 1948-49; Lincoln Univ, Jefferson City MO; asst prof English 1950-51; Tennessee A&I Univ, prof speech, drama 1952-54; Stoughton Public Schools, drama dir, speech therapy dir 1955-65; Bridgewater State Coll MA, prof communications arts & science 1965-77 retired. **ORGANIZATIONS:** Dir debate & instr Boston Univ Debate Team 1954-55; mem Theta Alpha Phi 1955; co-dir Camp Whispering Willows for Underpriviledged Youth, Stoughton MA 1955-67; town representative Town of, Stoughton MA 1960; sr active Rotary Intl 1964-; mem Congregational Protestant; mem emeritus Phi Delta Kappa Univ of Michigan. **HONORS/ACHIEVEMENTS:** Univ Fellowships, Univ of Michigan 1946, 48; Rockhain Special Fellowship, Univ of Michigan 1951-52; Certificate of Clincial Competence, Amer Speech & Hearing Assn 1965; Paul Harris Fellow, Rotary Intl 1979. **MILITARY SERVICE:** AUS 1st sgt 3 yrs; Overseas Serv Awards 1945-48. **HOME ADDRESS:** 165 Washington, Sherborn, MA 01770.

PROCTER, HARVEY T.
Business executive. **PERSONAL:** Born Nov 25, 1923, Vicksburgh, MS; married Paula Rodgers; children: Lisa, Harvey Jr. **EDUCATION:** Univ of Pittsburgh, BS 1947. **CAREER:** Casting Div Ford Motor Co, industrial relations mgr 1951-; Illinois State Employment, employment interviewer 1949-51; Cook County Bureau of Public Welfare, caseworker 1947-49; AUS Quartermaster Corps, med corp 1943-46. **ORGANIZATIONS:** Coll Faculty & Black Exec Exchange Prgram; Natl Urban League; program leader Ford Coll Roundtable; bd dir Natl Fedn of Settlement Houses; NAACP; People CommServ; mem Amer Mgmt Assn; mem Engineering Soc of Detroit. **HONORS/ACHIEVEMENTS:** Dean's list, Univ Pittsburgh; leading recruiter, Tennessee A&I Univ. **MILITARY SERVICE:** AUS 1943-46. **BUSINESS ADDRESS:** 3001 Miller Rd, Room 1024, Dearborn, MI 48127.

PRYOR, BERNARD BRUCE
Educational administrator. **PERSONAL:** Born Dec 11, 1923, Washington, DC; died Aug 25, 1986; married Irmgard Gabriele Burghard; children: 3 Children. **EDUCATION:** Miner Teachers Coll Washington DC, 1941-42; Univ of Iowa Iowa Cty, BA Political Science & Economics 1965; Univ of Iowa, MA Political Science 1967; Claremont Graduate School, Claremont CA, PhD Govt 1975. **CAREER:** Coll of Liberal Arts Univ of Baltimore, assoc dean 1979-86; Coll of Arts & Sciences Washburn Univ Topeka, asst dean & assoc prof political science 1976-79; Dept of Govt Idaho State Univ, asst prof govt & intl relations 1972-76, instructor govt & intl relations 1968-72. **ORGANIZATIONS:** Mem Amer Political Science Assn; Center for the Study of the Presidency; Amer Assn of Univ Admin; Pi Sigma Alpha Natl Political Science Honor Soc; pres-elect Idaho State Univ Chapter Phi Kappa Phi Natl Honor Soc 1976; vice pres Pocatello Idaho NAACP 1972-74; pres Pocatello Human Relations Advisory Council 1975-76; assoc editor Journal of Idaho Political Science Assn 1976. **HONORS/ACHIEVEMENTS:** Recipient of Silver Star, Bronze Star, Purple Heart, Army & Commendation Medal, Combat Infantry Badge, Master Parachutist Badge, 9 Serv Medals AUS 1943-63. **MILITARY SERVICE:** AUS maj 1946-63. **BUSINESS ADDRESS:** Charles at Mt Royal, Baltimore, MD 21201.

RABY, ALBERT A.
Appointed official. **PERSONAL:** Born Feb 19, 1933, Chicago, IL; died Nov 1988, Chicago, IL; children: Kay, Alison. **EDUCATION:** Wilson Jr Coll, AA 1958; Chicago Teachers Coll EdB 1960; Univ of Chicago Graduate Studies 1967-69. **CAREER:** State of Illinois, asst to governor 1974-67; Intergovernmental Relations Action, dir 1977-79; US Peace Corp Accra Ghana, dir 1979-82; Harold Washington's Mayoral Campaign, mgr 1982-83; City of Chicago, dir Chicago Commn on Human Relations. **ORGANIZATIONS:** Co-chairperson Chicago

Freedom Movement 1966-67; delegate Illinois Constitutional Convention 1970; pres Hyde Park-Kenwood Community Conference 1970-71; mem board of dir Illinois Civil Liberties Union 1972-73; mem board of dir South Shore Natl Bank 1973-75; mem board of mgrs Woodstock Foundation 1973-. **HONORS/ACHIEVEMENTS:** Pres Kappa Delta Pi Educ Honor Soc 1959-60; Rosa Parks Southern Christian Leadership Conference 1966; ford found fellow/urban affairs Ford Found 1967-69; Outstanding Performance US peace Corps 1981. **MILITARY SERVICE:** AUS 2 years. **BUSINESS ADDRESS:** Dir Chicago Comm on Human Relations, City of Chicago, 500 N Peshtigo Court, Chicago, IL 60611.

RAINGE, NATHANIEL
Government official. **PERSONAL:** Born Feb 22, 1949, Waycross, GA; died Jun 17, 1986; married Ella Lee Bacon; children: Cory, Beverly. **EDUCATION:** Ware Tech, 1968. **CAREER:** Mayor pro-tem; Okefenokee Rural Elec, lineman. **ORGANIZATIONS:** Membership Corp bd of dir, Chamber of Commerce; exec com Area Planning & Devel Comm SE GA; chmn Brantley Community Civic Org. **HONORS/ACHIEVEMENTS:** 1st black councilman City of Nahunta 1973. **BUSINESS ADDRESS:** Mayor's Office, Nahunta, GA 31553.

REDDING, JAY SAUNDERS
Educator emeritus, author. **PERSONAL:** Born in Wilmington, DE; died Mar 02, 1988, Ithaca, NY; married Esther Elizabeth James; children: Conway Holmes, Lewis Alfred. **EDUCATION:** Lincoln Univ PA, 1923-24; Brown Univ, PhD 1928, AM 1932; Univ Scholar, DLitt 1932-33; Columbia, 1933-34; Hon Degrees, VA State Coll 1963, Hobart Coll 1964, Dickinson Coll, Univ DE, Univ Portland 1970, Wittinberg Univ 1977. **CAREER:** Morehouse Coll Atlanta, teacher 1928-31; Louisville Municipal Coll, 1934-36; So Univ, 1936-38; Rockefeller Found Fellow, 1940-41; Hampton Inst, prof english 1943-66, Johnson prof creative lit until 1966; Guggenheim Fellow 1944-45,59-60; Brown Univ, vstg prof engl 1949-50; Duke Univ Fellow, 1964-65; NatlEndowment for Humanities WA, dir div rsch & publ 1966-70, consult 1970-; Cornell Univ, Ernest I White prof Amer Studies & Humane Letters 1970-75, emeritus 1975-88. **ORGANIZATIONS:** Bd fellow Brown Univ 1969-81; hon consult Amer Culture Libr of Congress 1973-76; exchange lectur Dept State India 1952; exchange lecturer Amer Soc African Culture 1962; bd dir Amer Council Learned Socs 1975-, Ctr for Advanced Studies Univ of VA 1976-; rschr Amer Negro Life from 1950-, also early Amer Negro writers; collector so folk matl; ed bd Amer Scholar 1954-62,70-73. **HONORS/ACHIEVEMENTS:** Mayflower Awd NC Hist Soc 1944, NY Amsterdam News for Distinction 1944, NY Publ Libr for Outstanding Contrib to Interracial Understanding 1945,46, Natl Urban League for Outstanding Achievement 1949; author "To Make A Poet Black" 1939, "No Day of Triumph" (Mayflower Awd) 1942, "Stranger and Alone" 1950, "They Came in Chains" 1950, "On Being Negro in Amer" w/Ivan E Taylor 1951, "Reading for Writing" 1951, "An Amer in India" 1954, "The Lonesome Rd" 1958, "The Negro"1967; editor w/AP Davis "Cavalcade" 1971; contrib articles, essays & reviews to natl mags.

RIDLEY, RACHEL REBECCA
Association executive. **PERSONAL:** Born Apr 10, 1911, Hannibal, MO; died May 1987; married Taft Ridley; children: Louisa Hill. **EDUCATION:** Attended, Crane Jr Coll, Lewis Inst, Central YMCA Coll, Univ Chicago, Sangamon State Univ; Roosevelt Univ, BA 1946. **CAREER:** Englewood UPC, director; Chicago Comm on Urban Oppor; Chicago Commn on Youth Welfare; Chicago Defender; Chicago Urban League; Chicago Commn on Human Relations, dir. **ORGANIZATIONS:** Trustee St Stephen AME Ch; sec bd trustee Mary Thompson Hosp; vice pres, Mary Thompson Hosp; Midwest Comm Council; YWCA; Midwest Chicago Boys Club; consult Women's Div Chicago Urban League; Exec Club Chicago; pres Alpha Gamma Pi; Exec Devel Prog Chicago; bd dir Natl Assn for Comm Devel. **HONORS/ACHIEVEMENTS:** Sun Times Merit Awd St Stephen AME Ch; Outstanding Woman in Chicago; Annual Awd Natl Assn of Club Women; num other awds. **BUSINESS ADDRESS:** Dir, Chicago Commn on Human Relat, 500 N Peshitgo, Chicago, IL 60611.

ROBINSON, LUTHER H., JR.
Physician. **PERSONAL:** Born Oct 09, 1936, New Orleans, LA; died Nov 29, 1987; son of Luther H Robinson and Maude Robinson; married Patricia Lightfoot; children: Lesleigh, Gregory, Lisa. **EDUCATION:** Michigan State Univ, BA 1957; Howard Univ Medical School, MD 1961. **CAREER:** Akron City Hospital, intern 1961-62, resident 1964-66; Pediatric Group Children's Medical Group Inc, partner private practice. **ORGANIZATIONS:** Mem Summit County Medical Soc; Ohio State Medical Soc; Amer Acad of Pediatrics; mem Alpha Phi Alpha, Urban League, NAACP; Certified Amer Bd of Pediatrics 1966. **HONORS/ACHIEVEMENTS:** Chief of staff Akron Children's Hospital 1983-84. **MILITARY SERVICE:** USAF MC Capt 1964-66. **BUSINESS ADDRESS:** Pediatric Grp Child Med Grp, 185 W Cedar, Akron, OH 44307.

ROBINSON, SUGAR RAY
Fighter, entertainer. **PERSONAL:** Born May 03, 1921, Detroit, MI; married Millie Bruce; children: Ray II, Ronnie. **CAREER:** Welter-weight champion 1946; middleweight champion 1951; entertainer, actor, TV commercials. **ORGANIZATIONS:** Bd dir Sugar Ray Robinsons Youth Found 1969; Meth Aughor, Sugar Ray 1970. **MILITARY SERVICE:** AUS 1945-52. **BUSINESS ADDRESS:** C/O Sugar Ray Robinson Youth Foundation, 1905 10th Ave, Los Angeles, CA 90018.

RUFFIN, ANDREW J.
Clergyman. **PERSONAL:** Born Nov 11, 1893, Lisman, AL; died Feb 04, 1979; married Jennie B Roberts. **EDUCATION:** Teachers State Coll, Montgomery AL, AB; Morehouse Coll, Atlanta GA, BS 1931; Selma Univ, Selma AL, DD. **CAREER:** Minister, retired; Jerusalem Second Baptist Church, Urbana OH, pastor 1946-72. **ORGANIZATIONS:** Past pres NAACP; moderator Emeritus Western Union Dist Assn; instructor Natl Baptist & Sunday School & Baptist Training Union Congress; vice pres Tri-County Community Action Comm; vice pres OBGA; past pres Urbana Ministerial Alliance; statistician OBGA; pastor Emeritus of Jerusalem Second Baptist Church, Urbana OH; past regional dir Phi Beta Sigma Frat; past pres Springfield Baptist Ministerial Alliance. **HONORS/ACHIEVEMENTS:** Meritorious Awards OBGA; Western Union Dist Assn; Womens Aux Western Union Dist Assn. **MILITARY SERVICE:** AUS pfc 1918.

RUSTIN, BAYARD
Civil rights leader. **PERSONAL:** Born Mar 17, 1912, West Chester, PA; died Aug 24, 1987, New York, NY. **EDUCATION:** Wilberforce Univ, attended 1931; Attended, Cheyney State Coll, City College of New York; numerous Honorary Degrees including, Dr of Laws Yale Univ 1984, Dr Humane Letters Western MI Univ 1984, Dr Humane Letters State Univ of NY at Stonybrook. **CAREER:** A Philip Randolph Inst, bd chmn 1964. **ORGANIZATIONS:** Vice pres Intl Rescue Comm; chmn exec comm Leadership Conf on Civil Rights; chmn exec comm Freedom House; mem Citizens Comm on Indochinese Refugees; mem US Holocaust Memorial Council; chmn of bd Recruitment & Training Prog; chmn exec comm Leadership Conf on Civil Rights; chmn Social Democrats USA;bd mem George Meany Ctr for Labor Studies; mem Actors Equity AFL-CIO; mem US Holocaust Memorial Council, Intl Rescue Comm, Freedom House, Anti Defamation League Found, Natl Emergency Coalition for Haitian Refugees. **HONORS/ACHIEVEMENTS:** Stephen Wise Awd Amer Jewis Comm; Murray/Greene/meany Awd AFL-CIO; John LaFarge Memorial Awd Catholic Interracial Council of NY; collection of essays "Down the Line" 1971; "Strategies for Freedom, The Changing Patterns of Black Protest" Columbia Univ 1976. **BUSINESS ADDRESS:** President, A Philip Randolph Educ Fund, 260 Park Ave S, deceased, New York, NY 10010.

SETE, BOLA
Acoustical guitarist. **PERSONAL:** Born Jul 16, 1923, Rio de Janeiro, Brazil;died Feb 14, 1987; married Glada Anne Hurd. **BUSINESS ADDRESS:** PO Box 1333, Sausalito, CA 94965.

SHEELER, HOMER J., SR.
Business executive. **PERSONAL:** Born Jan 23, 1923, Toccoa, GA; died Feb 11, 1988; married Mildred; children: Homer, Jr, Cynthia. **EDUCATION:** Clark Coll, 1941-43; Atlanta Coll Mortuary of Science, 1943-44; Reed's Business School, 1944; Intl Accts Soc, 1946-49. **CAREER:** Purple Shield Life Insurance, pres, mgr 1955-88; Capital Funeral Home, partner 1951-55; Gilbert's Funeral Home, mgr 1945-51; Fred A Anderson Funeral Home, mortician 1944-45; Murdaugh Bros Funeral, apprentice study, dir 1943-44; Sacred Hope Investment Co, pres; Purple Shield Funeral Serv; Royal Shield; Eames Bookkeeping & Tax Serv, vice pres; SV Totty Business Coll, pres; Capital Funeral Home sec; Capital City Burial Vault Co, pres. **ORGANIZATIONS:** Mem Louisiana State Morticians & Funeral Dir Assn; Natl Funeral & Morticians Assn; New Orleans Exec Insurance Council; Natl Insurance Assn; Epsilon Nu Delta Mort Frat; Amer Coll Accredited Tax Accountants; bd pres Comm Assn for Welfare of School Children; bd mem Metro YMCA Baton Rouge; Baranco-Clark YMCA; volunteer Am Baton Rouge; mem budget comm Capital Area & United Givers Fund; exec comm Istrouma Area BSA; bd Baton Rouge Employees Retirement System; exec com Public Affairs Research Council Louisiana. **BUSINESS ADDRESS:** PO 3157, Baton Rouge, LA 70802.

SKIMMER, ALUSTER CARL
Union executive. **PERSONAL:** Born Oct 05, 1945, Belcross, NC; married Linda Arlene Little; children: Leroy Cleon, Clarence, Terence, Cheryl. **EDUCATION:** Norfolk State Univ, BS Accounting 1968; Golden Gate Univ, MS 1978. **CAREER:** New Farmers of America, first vice president 1963-64; US Internal Revenue, internal revenue agent 1975; IL Assoc AFL-CIO, intl delegate. **ORGANIZATIONS:** Mem The NC Civic Educ Project 1986. **MILITARY SERVICE:** AUS intelligence officer 24 yrs; Vietnam Campaign, Silver Star (2) Certificates of Appreciation, Certificate of Achievement. **HOME ADDRESS:** PO Box 334, South Mills, NC 27976. **BUSINESS ADDRESS:** International Delegate, IL Assoc AFL-CIO, PO Box 203, Camden, NC 27921.

SMITH, WILLI
Fashion designer. **PERSONAL:** Born Feb 29, 1948, Philadelphia, PA; died Apr 1987. **EDUCATION:** Attended Parsons Sch of Design. **CAREER:** Arnold Scassi, first fashion design job in NY; Prudence & Strickland Boutique, started career by working after sch & on Saturdays; worked at several fashion houses including Glenora Jr; Digits Inc, fashion designer 1976; formed designs studio & free lance 1974-76; Willie Wear Ltd, fashion designer 1976-. **HONORS/ACHIEVEMENTS:** Listed 41st ed of WWA; Winner of Coty Awd 1983. **BUSINESS ADDRESS:** Willie Wear Ltd, 209 W 38th St, New York, NY 10013.

SNOWDEN, MURIEL SUTHERLAND
Administrator. **PERSONAL:** Born Jul 14, 1916, Orange, NJ; married Otto. **EDUCATION:** Radcliffe Coll, AB 1938; Natl Urban League Fellow, NY School of Social Work, 1943-45. **CAREER:** Freedom House Inc, Roxbury MA, co-founder & co-dir 1950-; Simmons Coll School of Social Work, special instructor in community org part-time 1956-70; City of Cambridge Civic Unity Comm, exec dir 1948-50; Essex County Welfare Bd, social investigator 1938-43; Snowden Assoc, partner. **ORGANIZATIONS:** Mem advisory comm The Blanchard Found; mem bd of dirs Shawmut Bank of Boston NA 1973-; mem corp Babson Coll, Wellesley MA 1973-; mem bd of overseers Harvard Univ 1977-; mem bd or trustees Boston Museum of Science; mem bd of trustees Civic Educ Found Tufts Univ 1978-. **HONORS/ACHIEVEMENTS:** Natl Urban League Fellowship, Natl Urban League 1943; corecipient "Natl Community Award," Lambda Kappa Mu Sorority NY 1960; Radcliffe Alumnae Achievement Award, Radcliffe Coll 1964; Honorary & LlD Univ of Massachusetts 1968. **BUSINESS ADDRESS:** Partner, Snowden Associates, 53 Supple Rd, Dorchester, MA 02121.

SPARKS, CLIFTON TINSLEY
Educational administrator. **PERSONAL:** Born May 14, 1929, Waco, TX; died Apr 02, 1988; married Troy M Jr. **EDUCATION:** Spelman Coll, BA 1948; New York Univ, MA 1949; Texas Woman's Univ, PhD 1968. **CAREER:** Coll of Educ, Texas Woman's Univ, dean 1981-88, interim dean 1980-81, chairperson coun educ 1970-80; Tarrant County Jr Coll, prof of sociology & psychology, counselor 1968-70; Ft Worth Independent School Dist, visiting teacher 1950-67. **ORGANIZATIONS:** Mem Amer Personnel & Guidance Assn 1972-80; pres Visiting Teachers Assn of Texas 1975; pres Texas Personnel & Guidance Assn 1978; Basileus AKA Beta Mu Omega, Alpha Kappa Alpha Sorority; pres Ft Worth Chapter Links Inc. **HONORS/ACHIEVEMENTS:** Author, "Melodies of Blackness," Natl Consortium for Humanizing Educ 1975; regional award for Outstanding Serv to Educ, Phi Delta Kappa Sor Inc 1978; author, "Personal & Demographic Character of Professional Black Americans," article in January issue Journal of Non-White Concerns in Personnel & Guidance 1980. **BUSINESS ADDRESS:** Dean College of Education, Texas Woman's University, MCL407, Denton, TX 76204.

SPAULDING, CHARLES C., JR.
Attorney. **PERSONAL:** Born Nov 10, 1907, Durham, NC; died Sep 10, 1987; married Minnie P Turner. **EDUCATION:** Clark U, AB 1930; St John's U, LlB & JD 1935. **CAREER:** Pearson Malone Johnson DeJarmon & Spaulding, atty; NC Mutual Life Ins Co, ret dir & mem of Nomination, Salary & Finance Comm, vice pres, gen counsel 1973. **ORGANIZATIONS:** Mem Geo H White Bar Assn; life mem Natl Bar Assn; mem emeritus Assn of Life Ins Counsel; dir & vice chmn bd Mechanics & Farmers Bank; mem bd trustees & treas White Rock Bapt Ch; mem bd of dir Durham Co Unit Am Cancer Soc; NC Cancer Inst; former mem Crim Code Comm of State of NC. **HONORS/ACHIEVEMENTS:** C Francis Stratford Award, Natl Bar Assn; 40 yr plaque & 50 yr pin, Omega Psi Phi; sev awards from local unit of Amer Cancer Soc. **BUSINESS ADDRESS:** 114 West Parrish St, P O Box 1842, Durham, NC 27702.

STEWART, BENNETT MCVEY
Government representative. **PERSONAL:** Born Aug 06, 1914, Huntsville, AL; died Apr 1988; married Pattye Crittenden; children: Bennett Michael, Ronald Patrick, Miriam Kay (Mrs. **EDUCATION:** Miles Coll, BA 1936. **CAREER:** US House of Representatives, congressman 1978-; City of Chicago, ward committeeman 1976-78; Chicago City Council, alderman 1971-76; Chicago Bldg Dept, inspector 1968-70; Atlanta Life Insurance Co Birmingham & Chicago, insurance exec 1940-68; Miles Coll Birmingham, assoc prof sociology 1938; Irondale High School Birmingham, asst principal 1936. **ORGANIZATIONS:** Chmn Health Comm Chicago City Council 1971-78; pres Chicago Insurance Assn 1954-57; pres Alpha Phi Alpha Frat Chicago Graduate Chapter 1961-71; bd of dirs Alpha Phi Alpha Frat (Natl) 1963-72; mem Lay Orgn Christian Methodist Episcopal Church; bd of Dirs Wabash YMCA Chicago. **HONORS/ACHIEVEMENTS:** Top Insurance Exec Award, Atlanta GA 1955; Citation for Outstanding Serv, Natl Life Underwriters Training Council; Continuous Serv Award, UMCA Bd of Dirs. **BUSINESS ADDRESS:** 503 Cannon House Office Bldg, Washington, DC 20515.

SUTTON, OLIVER C.
Judge. **PERSONAL:** Born Sep 18, 1916, San Antonio; married Renee Hopkins; children: Oliver, Jr, Paul, Carol. **EDUCATION:** Tuskegee Inst, BS 1937; NY Law Sch, LLB 1951. **CAREER:** Private Practice, atty; Joint Legislative Com, asst counsel; Commr Jurors; Speaker of Assembly, asst counsel; Civil Ct City NY, judge; Supreme Ct Justice NY. **ORGANIZATIONS:** Mem Am & Harlem NY County Nat Bar Assns; Assn of the Bar of NYC; mem Com on Publs Assn of Justices of the Supreme Ct of the State of ny; former vice pres NY City Chap NAACP; bd dirs Queens NAACP; mem Met Bapt Ch; Mason; Mason; Kappa Alpha Psi. **HONORS/ACHIEVEMENTS:** Merit award Tuskegge Inst Alumni 1973. **MILITARY SERVICE:** AUS 1942-46. **BUSINESS ADDRESS:** County Ct House, 100 Centre St, New York, NY 10013.

TATE, HERBERT H.
Judge. **PERSONAL:** Born Dec 24, 1908, Montclair, NJ; died 1988, Marth'a Vineyard, MA; married Ethel. **EDUCATION:** Rutgers Univ, AB 1932; Rutgers Univ School of Law, JD 1935; Natl Coll of Juvenile Justice, Univ of NV. **CAREER:** Juvenile & Domestic Relations Court Co of Essex, judge; US Embassy in Karachi Pakistan, cultural affairs attch 1951-53; NJ State Assembly, asst minority leader 1960; NJ State Council of Juvenile Ct Judges, pres 1974; Essex Co, asst prosecutor. **ORGANIZATIONS:** Mem Essex Ct Bar Assn; NJ State Bar Assn; Amer Bar Assn; Natl Bar Assn; Admitted to US Supreme Ct 1957; US Ct of Appeals 1965; mem Intl Comm of Natl Bd of YMCA; former charter trustee Rutgers Univ; former mem US Civil Rights Commn; Robert Treat Council; BSA; past pres Newark Chapter United Nations Assn; dir Essex Co Torch Club; Phi Delta Phi; Alpha Phi Alpha; Sigma Pi Phi. **HONORS/ACHIEVEMENTS:** First Award, St Marks Devoted Serv in Area of Human Relations, 1969; service rendered to Youth in Civil Rights Award NJ Conf NAACP 1963; Service rendered to Boy Scouts Award Salem Baptist Church 1973. **MILITARY SERVICE:** AUS lt 1942-46. **BUSINESS ADDRESS:** Essex Co Cts Bldg, Newark, NJ 07102.

TAYLOR, JOSEPH H.
Educator. **PERSONAL:** Born in Burkesville, KY; widowed. **EDUCATION:** Eastern Michigan Univ, AB 1927; Univ of Michigan, MA 1930; Univ of California, PhD 1936; Univ of Chicago & Columbia Univ, post-doctoral studies. **CAREER:** Bethune Cookman Coll, vice pres for devel 1978-79; Bethune-Cookman Coll, dir of projects & prof of history 1970-76; Bethune-Cookman Coll, academic dean 1964-70; North Carolina Central Univ, dir of summer school 1946-63; Div of Social Sciences North Carolina Central Univ, prof of history chmn 1939-63; Alabama State Univ, dean of instruction 1930-39. **ORGANIZATIONS:** Mem Amer Teachers Assn, Natl Educ Assn, So History Assn of Social Science Teachers, NAACP, Omega Psi Phi, Sigma Pi Phi, Phi Alpha Theta, Pi Gamma Mu. **BUSINESS ADDRESS:** Chairperon Div of Soc Serv, Bethune Cookman College, 640 Second Avenue, Daytona Beach, FL 32015.

TERRENCE, AUGUST C.
Physician. **PERSONAL:** Born in New Orleans, LA; died Apr 20, 1987; son of August Terrence and Cora Terrence; married Ernstine Flemming Wilson Terrence. **EDUCATION:** Howard Univ, Washington DC, BS 1924, MD 1928. **CAREER:** Physician 1928-87. **ORGANIZATIONS:** Past pres Natl Medical Assn; past pres Howard Univ Medical Alumni Assn; bd of dirs & vice pres First Natl Bank of Opelousas LA; vice pres & pres Temco Devel Corp of Opelousas LA; bd mem United Negro Coll Fund; life mem NAACP. **HONORS/ACHIEVEMENTS:** Distinguished Alumni Award, Howard Univ 1955; Louisiana Teachers Award, Opelousas LA 1956; Frontiers Intl Award Opelousas Chapter 1970. **MILITARY SERVICE:** AUS 1st lieutenant 1941. **BUSINESS ADDRESS:** 750 N Market St, Opelousas, LA 70570.

TERRY, ROBERT JAMES
Educator. **PERSONAL:** Born May 01, 1922, Crockett, TX; died Oct 1987; married Mercedes. **EDUCATION:** Texas Southern Univ, BS 1946; Atlanta Univ, MS 1949; Univ of Iowa, PhD 1954. **CAREER:** Texas Southern Univ, vice pres acad affairs, prof 1973; Texas Southern Univ, dean of faculty 1971-73; Texas Southern Univ, dean & prof 1969-71; Texas Southern Univ, prof 1954-69; Texas Southern Univ, instr to prof bio 1948-54; Natl Sci, Found, dir 3 & undergrad res partic proj sup; Texas High School, visiting scientist. **ORGANIZATIONS:** Mem Gen Research Support Committee, Natl Inst of Health, Dept of HEW 1972-76; assoc dir Natl Sci Found 1966-67; mem Surveillance Comm, Univ of Texas Sys Cancer Ctr 1976-; bd dir Salvation Army 1977-79; mem Houston C of C Energy Task Force Comm; science consultant Govt of India 1965; natl pres Beta Kappa Chi Sci Honor Soc 1964-67; contrib World Book Encyclopedia; intl scholar Univ of Ghana, Univ of Lagos, Univ of Nairobi; published "A Comparison of Normal Devel of Lateral Motor Column in Rana Temporaria & Rana Pipiens" Amer Zool 4(3) 321. **MILITARY SERVICE:** AUS m/sgt WW II. **BUSINESS ADDRESS:** President, Texas Southern University, 3100 Cleburne, Houston, TX 77004.

THORPE, EARL E.
Educator. **PERSONAL:** Born Nov 09, 1924, Durham, NC; died Jan 30, 1989; son of Eural Endris Thorpe and Vina Dean Thorpe; married Martha Vivian Branch, Aug 24, 1946; children: Rita Harrington Tyson, Gloria Earl Doyle. **EDUCATION:** Univ of Florence Italy, one semester 1945; North Carolina Central Univ, BA 1948, MA 1949; Ohio State Univ, PhD 1953. **CAREER:** Stowe Teachers Coll, instructor 1951-52; Alabama A&M Coll, prof 1952-55; Southern Univ, prof 1955-62; Duke Univ, visiting prof 1969-70; Harvard Univ, visiting prof 1971; North Carolina Central Univ, prof 1962-89. **ORGANIZATIONS:** Ordained Baptist Clergyman; Assoc Minister of Ledge Rock Baptist Church, Wake County NC 1975-85; mem NAACP; mem SCLC 1982-; natl pres Assn for Study of Afro-Amer Life & History 1980-83; mem Natl Archives Advisory Council 1982-. **HONORS/ACHIEVEMENTS:** Publications include 25 scholarly articles published in learning journals; published books which bear the titles Negro Historians in the US 1958 reissued in 1971 under the title Black Historians, A Critique; The Desertion of Man, A Critique of Philosophy of History 1958; The Mind of the Negro, An Intellectual History of Afro-Americans 1961, reissued in 1970 by Greenwood Publishers Inc; Eros and Freedom in Southern Life and Thought 1967; The Central Theme of Black History 1969; "The Old South, Psychohistory 1972; African Americans and the Sacred 1982; Slave Religion Spirituals and CG Jung 1983; A Concise History of NC Central University 1984. **MILITARY SERVICE:** 92nd signal co 92nd div corpl 1943-46; Commendation Medal; Service in European Theater 1944-46. **BUSINESS ADDRESS:** Prof of History, NC CentralUniv, Dept of History, Durham, NC 27701.

TONEY, CORNELIUS C.
Business executive. **PERSONAL:** Born Nov 05, 1917, Vallejo, CA; died Nov 04, 1983; married Vera E Morgan; children: Cornelius, James, Shirley. **EDUCATION:** Univ of California. **CAREER:** Insurance broker, real estate broker; North Bay Real Estate & Toney's Insurance Agency, owner 1952-83; Golden State Mutal Insurance, dist mgr 1948-50; Mare Island Naval Shipyard, rigger 1939-46; Congressman Robert L Leggett, staff asst 1964. **ORGANIZATIONS:** Mem Solano Bd of Realtors, Vallejo Lions Club; chmn Vallejo Workable Program Commn; pres United Demcrats of Vallejo; pres Fedn of Solano County Democrate; vice chmn Solano County Demcratic Control Comm. **HONORS/ACHIEVEMENTS:** Recognition Award, Vallejo Branch NAACP; Serv Award, Amer Cancer Soc. **BUSINESS ADDRESS:** 725 Tuolumne St, Vallejo, CA.

TUCKER, CURTIS R.
Elected official. **PERSONAL:** Born Mar 26, 1918, Union, LA; married Lorraine A Hohl; children: Linda, Leslie, Curtis Jr, Lorraine Gibbs, Christy. **EDUCATION:** Univ of Florence Italy, Certificate; US Public Health Inst, Certificate. **CAREER:** Los Angeles County, public health consultant 1960-74; City of Inglewood, councilman 1972-74. **HONORS/ACHIEVEMENTS:** Outstanding State Legislator, Assembly of Govt Employees, 1 of 10 Outstanding Legislators in US 1981; Tucker Day Vet Home of California Yountsville 1983. **MILITARY SERVICE:** AUS 1937-60; Bronze Star. **BUSINESS ADDRESS:** State Assemblyman, CA State Legislature, PO Box 6500, Inglewood, CA 90306.

VAN DER ZEE, JAMES AUGUSTUS JOSEPH
Photographer, musician. **PERSONAL:** Born Jun 29, 1886, Lenox, MA; died May 15, 1983, Washington, DC; son of John Van Der Zee and Susan Van Der Zee; married Donna Suzanne Mussenden. **EDUCATION:** Honorary Doctorates: Seton Hall Univ, So Orange NJ 1976; Haverford Coll, Haverford PA 1980; Columbia Coll, Chicago IL 1982; Howard Univ, Washington DC 1983. **CAREER:** Private, music teacher piano & violin; Own Studios, Harlem NY, photographer 1918-69; Gertz Dept Store, Newark NJ, darkroom asst 1915. **HONORS/ACHIEVEMENTS:** First violinist John Wannamaker Orchestra; violinist Fletcher Henderson Band; books published: Harlem on my Mind, Random House 1968; The World of James Van Der Zee, Grove Press 1969; James Van Der Zee, Morgan & Morgan Monograph 1973; 32nd Degree Mason Hon D Seton Hall Univ 1976; Pierre Touissaint Award, Cardinal Cook St Patrick's Cathedral 1978; books published: Harlem Book of the Dead, Morgan & Morgan 1978; Harlem on my Mind (revised edition), Random House 1979; James Van Der Zee The Picture Takin' Man, Dodd Mead 1979; Living Legacy Award, US Pres Jimmy Carter White House 1979; Intl Black Photographers Award, Intl Black Photograhpers 1979; Hon D Haverford Coll 1980; Fellow for Life, Metropolitan Museum of Art.

VANN, CLEODIS DON
Mortician. **PERSONAL:** Born Mar 18, 1911, Winchester, AR; died Jul 20, 1988, Portland, OR; son of William Vann and Ella Rhome; married Roberta B Carruthers; children: Cleodis Jr. **EDUCATION:** Northwestern Coll of Law, 1 yr; BMI State Univ, 3 yrs; Portland State UNIV, Special Study; St Louis Coll OF Mortuary Science, 1948. **CAREER:** Vann's Morturary, owner founder; Frank Carruthers Funeral Home Pontiac, Apprenticeship. **ORGANIZATIONS:** Mem bd dir Portland Chamber of Commerce 1967-73; chmn Disaster Comm Oregon Funeral Dir Assn; mem bd dir Portland Branch NAACP; Urban League Portland; trustee Vancouver Ave Baptist Church; Natl Morticians & Funeral Dir Assn; former mem bd dir Coliseum Kiwanis Club; N Branch YMCA; Oregon Funeral Dir Assn 1970-73. **HONORS/ACHIEVEMENTS:** Founded first mortuary owned by blacks state Oregon 1954; NFDMA Civil Rights Award Cincinnati 1974; Citizen of the Year Award, Urban League Portland 1968. **MILITARY SERVICE:** USAAF pfc.

VICK, HAROLD E.
Musician, composer, arranger. **PERSONAL:** Born Apr 03, 1936, Rocky Mt, NC; died Nov 13, 1987. **EDUCATION:** Howard Univ, BA 1958. **CAREER:** Howard Theater High School Band, music composer/arranger 1955-58; Jazz Ensmbls, composing musician 1955; Trvld US, 1958; Lloyd Price, performed clubs concerts 1959; Philly Joe Jones, music composer/arranger 1960-63; H McGhee, music composer/arranger 1960-63; J McDuff, music composer/arranger 1960-63; Ray Charles, music composer/arranger 1960-63; D Byrd Band, performed 1966; W Bishop Jr Quartet, soloist 1967; G Green Qrtt, soloist 1967; D Gillespies Band, performed 1969; K Curtis, music composer/arranger, 1970; RCA, record album 1963-

66, record, 3 albums record contract 1966-68; J Edrman Theater Co, music composer 1966-67. **ORGANIZATIONS:** Band mem, A Franklin 1970-; co-founder & Org Blk, Experience Family Repertory Co 1970; mem Coop Jazz Group Compst 1971-73. **HONORS/ACHIEVEMENTS:** Received grant for music composition, Natl Endowment for Arts Music Composition Jazz Category, 1974; Received grant for music composition, CAPS NY St Council on the Arts, 1975; Composed original music for TV Film Epitath 1970; wrote original music An Even Chance 1971; produced/composed/arranged/performed music for Album The Power of Feeling 1973. **MILITARY SERVICE:** USAF ROTC band 1954-58. **BUSINESS ADDRESS:** 1171 Fulton Ave, Bronx, NY 10456.

WARREN, CHARLES P.
Anthropologist. **PERSONAL:** Born Apr 07, 1921, Chicago, IL; died Dec 22, 1987; married Lastinia Martinez; children: Charles M, Joseph H. **EDUCATION:** NWU, BS, Zoology 1947; IN Univ, MA Anthropology 1950; Univ of the Philippines 1950-51; Univ of Chicago, MA Anthropology 1961 1963-64. **CAREER:** Univ of IL, assoc prof, Anthropology, 1976-; Dept of Defense AUS Central Iden Lab Thailand, physical anthropologist, 1973-75; Univ of IL, asst prof, Anthropology 1965-76; Dept of Soclgy & Anthropology Univ of IL, instructor, anthropology 1957-65; Univ of Chicago, rsch assoc, 1957; Dept Army Civilian Amer Graves Regis Serv Philippines Is Japan, physical anthropologist 1951-55; Dept of Antrplgy IN Univ, teaching asst 1948-50; Forensic Anthropology Sheriff of Cook Co & Ofc of Med Examiner, consultant; AUS Memorial Affairs Agency; consultant; Principal Investigator. **ORGANIZATIONS:** Principal Investigator, Fulbright Res Award Rep of Philippines 1950-51; Co-investigator USPHS Grant Otophotometry Cook Co Hospital & Univ of IL 1958-60; principal Investigator, NSF Science Facility Fellowship, Univ of Chicago 1963-64; Merit Civilian Serv Award USA Central Identification Lab 1975. **MILITARY SERVICE:** USAC s/sgt 1942-46. **BUSINESS ADDRESS:** University of IL at Chicago, Department of Anthropology, PO Box 4348, Chicago, IL 60680.

WASHINGTON, HAROLD
Mayor. **PERSONAL:** Born Apr 15, 1922, Chicago, IL; died Nov 25, 1987; divorced. **EDUCATION:** Roosevelt, BA 1949; Northwestern Univ Law School, JD 1952. **CAREER:** Prosecuting atty 1952, asst city prosecutor 1953-58; IL Indust Commun, arbitrator 1960-64; State of IL 26th Dist, state rep 1965-; City of Chgo, mayor 1983-87. **ORGANIZATIONS:** Mem Nu Beta Epsilon, Cook Cty IL & Natl Bar Assoc, Urban League, NAACP; adv Regular 3rd Ward Dem Org, Oper Breadbasket, PUSH, Black Coalition, Young Dem of IL, IL State Fed of Labor, IL House of Reps 1965-76, IL Senate 1976-80, 97th-98th Congress from 1st IL Dist; vice pres Amers for Dem Action; bd dir Suburban So Christian Leadership Conf; founder, pres WA Youth & Commun Org; bd dir Mid-South Mental Health Assoc. **HONORS/ACHIEVEMENTS:** Outstanding Legislator's Awd So Christian Leadership Conf; Top Lawmaker So Christian Leadership Conf 1973; IL Alliance of Cosmetologists Awd 1974; Legislative Excellence Awd AFL-CIO 1967-74; Cit Excellence Mrs Martin Luther King Jr 1974; Courageous Leadership Awd Russ Meeks 1974; Cit of Apprec FEPC 1975, Oper Breadbasket; Dawson Awd Negro Labor Rel. **MILITARY SERVICE:** AUS 1st sgt 1942-46. **BUSINESS ADDRESS:** Mayor, City of Chicago, 121 North LaSalle St, Chicago, IL 60602.

WEBB, ALBERT S.
Business executive. **PERSONAL:** Born May 05, 1930, Greensboro, AL. **EDUCATION:** Hampton Inst, BS; INU, Graduate School of Savings & Loan. **CAREER:** Amer Fed Savings & Loan Assn, Greensboro NC, exec vice pres & sec 1959-; Statistics Issue & Underwriting Dept at Dunbar Life Insurance Co Cleveland, previously supr. **ORGANIZATIONS:** Mem Trends & Economic Policy Comm US Savings & Loan League, Amer Savings & Loan Inst, only black on seven North Carolina commn of correction, Greensboro Citizens Assn; numerous other civic groups. **BUSINESS ADDRESS:** President, American Federal S & L Assocn, 701 E Market St, Greensboro, NC 08871.

WESLEY, CHARLES H.
Educator. **PERSONAL:** Born Dec 02, 1891, Louisville, KY; died Sep 1987; married Dorothy Porter; children: Charlotte Holloman. **EDUCATION:** Fisk U, BA 1911; Yale U, MA 1913; Harvard U, PhD 1925. **CAREER:** Howard Univ, prof, head of hist dept, dir summer school, dean of college, dean of grad school 1913-42; Wilberforce Univ, pres, 1942-47; Assn for Study of Afro-Amer Life & History, exec dir emeritus 1972; Afro-Amer Museum, exec dir 1975-76. **ORGANIZATIONS:** Author of 20 books & editor of 10 vol, "Intl Library on Negro Life & History"; Intro Afro-Amer Encyclopedia of Hist 10 vols; 130 articles in educ journals; presiding elder AME Church; mem Natl Coun of Soc Studies; NEA; Amer Assn of School Admin; Amer Assn of Univ Professors; Amer Hist Assn; past pres & historian Alpha Phi Alpha. **HONORS/ACHIEVEMENTS:** Holds honorary degrees from 14 colls & univs. **HOME ADDRESS:** 7632 17th St NW, Washington, DC 20012.

WEST, RONALD LAVERA
Assoc. executive. **PERSONAL:** Born Jun 11, 1948, Tampa, FL; married Linda Marie Ronse; children: Shelley Lynn, Julia Lea. **EDUCATION:** Shaw Coll, BA 1971; Wayne State Univ, MA 1973. **CAREER:** MI Dept Educ Bureau Rehab Detroit, counselor, asst suprv 1971-77; MI Dept of Mental Health, dir alternative living serv prog dir 1977-83; Kiwanis Intl, asst sec for admin serv 1983-. **ORGANIZATIONS:** Past chmn & bd mem Riverview MI Zoning Bd of Appeals; past sec & treas to Bldg Comm 1978-83; cert soc worker State of MI; cert Rehab Counselor; mem Amer Personnel & Guidance Assoc; dir Natl Rehab Assoc 1972-82; life mem Omega Psi Phi, NAACP; mem Amer Mgmt Assoc, Amer Soc Assoc Exec; past disting pres Kiwanis Club of Riverview; past lt gov MI Dist of Kiwanis; past pres Detroit Rehab Assoc, MI Rehab Counseling Assoc, Great Lakes Rehab Counseling Assoc,; past bd mem Natl Rehab Counseling Assoc, MI Rehab Assoc; past mem MI Gov Adv Council on Rehab. **HONORS/ACHIEVEMENTS:** Leadership Awd Detroit Rehab Assn 1976; Meritorious Serv Awd MI Rehab Counsel Assn 1979; Kiwanian of the Year Awd Riverview Kiwanis 1983; Disting AwdCtr for Leadership Devel 1985; Tablet of Honor Kiwanis Intl Found 1985. **BUSINESS ADDRESS:** Asst Sec for Admin Serv, Kiwanis Intl, 3636 Woodview Trace, Indianapolis, IN 46268.

WHALUM, WENDELL P.
Educator. **PERSONAL:** Born Sep 04, 1931, Memphis, TN; died Jun 1987; married Claire Guy; children: Wendell P Jr. **EDUCATION:** Morehouse Coll, BA 1952; Columbia Univ, MA 1953; Univ of IA, PhD 1965. **CAREER:** Morehouse Coll, educator 1953; Allen Temp AME, organist & choir dir 1956; Friendship Bapt Church, organist; lecturer at many coll & univ; Morehouse Coll, Lecturer. **ORGANIZATIONS:** Bd mem Atlanta Opera Co, Boys Club of Amer; hon comm Samuel Colridge Taylor Centennial, Afro-Amer Music Oppty Assoc Inc; mem Atlanta Chamber Opera Soc; organ soloist Atlanta Symphony Orchestra; panel US State Dept; mem Negro Heritage Library, Natl Humanities Facility. **HONORS/ACHIEVEMENTS:** Conducted choral music Jimmy Carter's Presidential Inaguration; Merrill Grant 1958; Powers Grant 1970; provided music for funerals of Martin Luther King Jr, AD Williams King, Mrs ML King Sr, Louis Armstrong. **MILITARY SERVICE:** AUS 1953-55. **BUSINESS ADDRESS:** Lecturer, Morehouse College, Box 77, Atlanta, GA 30314.

WHITE, JACK E.
Physician. **PERSONAL:** Born Jul 24, 1921, Stuart, FL; died Jul 02, 1988; married Sara Theodora Williams; children: Jack E Jr, David A, Carole Diane, Sara Lorraine White, Marilyn Marie White. **EDUCATION:** Florida A&M Univ, BA 1941; Howard Univ, MD 1944. **CAREER:** Howard Univ Coll of Medicine, asst prof/assoc prof/prof 1951-; Howard Univ, retired dir cancer center 1972-88. **ORGANIZATIONS:** Fellow Amer Coll Surgeons 1953-; mem Soc of Surgical Oncology 1962-; mem Inst of Medicine Natl Acad of Science 1977-; mem AMA; DC Medical Soc; Natl Medical Assn; Medical Chirurgical Soc DC; Amer Cancer Soc; Amer Assn for the Advancementin Science; Intl Union Against Cancer (US del London 1958, Moscow 1962, Tokyo 1966); Washington Acad Surgeons; Soc Head & Neck Surgeons; various medical societies; Alpha Omega Alpha. **HONORS/ACHIEVEMENTS:** Numerous medical publications; extensive foreign travel. **MILITARY SERVICE:** Asst Residential Surgeon, US Marine Hospital Boston 1946-47.

WHITE, WILLIAM O.
Association executive. **PERSONAL:** Born Nov 20, 1934, Selma, AL; died Oct 02, 1985; son of Daniel White and Ollie Cope; married Patsy Ichiokas, May 01, 1959; children: Kimberly Keike, Gregory Gen, Jeffrey Jiro. **EDUCATION:** Univ of Minnesota, BS 1959; William Mitchell Coll of Law St Paul, JD 1965. **ORGANIZATIONS:** Pres, exec dir St Paul Urban Coalition; project dir Citizens Community Center Inc Minneapolis; provisional exec sec St Paul Human & Civil Rights Commn; teacher St Paul Public Schools & Minneapolis Public Schools; TV teacher St Paul Public Schools KTCA-TV; supvr student teachers Univ of Minnesota Bethel Coll; Phi Alpha Delta Law Frat; Omega Psi Phi Frat; Tau Kappa Epsilon; Mid-Amer Region of Ant Council of UMCA's; bd dir Metropolitan St Paul Area YMCA; bd trustee Twin City Area Educ TV Corp; bd dir Summit Univ Fedn; bd dir Greater St Paul United Way. **BUSINESS ADDRESS:** 264 Metro Sq, St Paul, MN 55101.

WILLIAMS, HAROLD MCNEAL
Psychiatrist. **PERSONAL:** Born Feb 21, 1932, Trenton, NJ; died Feb 09, 1985; married Beverly Arlene Eason; children: Harold Michael, Steven Craig, Timothy Martin, Robert Matthew, Elizabeth Carroll. **EDUCATION:** Howard Univ, BS 1954, MD 1958. **CAREER:** Northwestern Hospital, intern 1958-59; New Jersey State Hospital Trenton, resident psychiatry 1959-62; Fresno County Dept of Mental Health, organizer developer 1964-; Fresno County Gen Hospital 1964; Fresno County Dept of Mental Health, chief psychiatry 1964-65, program chief 1964-65, acting dir 1966-67; chief outpatient psychiatry serv 1967-; Fresno CA, private practice of psychiatry 1969-. **ORGANIZATIONS:** Mem staffs of Fresno Community Hospital Valley Medical Center, Fresno Westview Convalescent Hospital Fresno 1969-; visiting lecturer Graduate School of Social Work Fresno State Coll 1965-68; mem Golden State Medical Assn; Amer Physchiatrist Assn; Central CA Psychiatrist Soc; Amer, CA & Natl Medical Assns; Acad of Psychosomatic Medicine; AAAS; NY Acad of Science; Geriatrics Soc; bd of trustees Fresno County Medical Soc; exec bd, bd of governors Fresno Madera Found for Medical Care 1977-; bd of dir Goodwill & Industries San Joaquin Valley; advisory com Fresno 1970-; bd of dir Family Serv Center Fresno; mem Kappa Alpha Psi; Beta Kappa Chi Fellow; Acad of Psychosomatic Medicine. **HONORS/ACHIEVEMENTS:** Recipient Outstanding Achievement Award in Psychiatry, Howard Univ 1958-. **MILITARY SERVICE:** USAF capt MC. **BUSINESS ADDRESS:** Fresno Co Dept Mental Health, 4411 E Kings Canyon Rd, Fresno, CA 93702.

WILLIAMS, MARION J.
Election official. **PERSONAL:** Born Jan 03, 1921, Starville, MS; died Oct 16, 1988; married Esther Lewis; children: Marion Jr, Donald, Gerald, Marlene Twine. **CAREER:** Wayne Div Richmond, supvr 1966-81; Richmond Branch NAACP, pres 1969-71; C&W Bar-B-Que, co-owner 1983-84; City of Richmond, councilman. **ORGANIZATIONS:** Chmn of dean Second Baptist Church. **HONORS/ACHIEVEMENTS:** Recognition Award NAACP 1982. **BUSINESS ADDRESS:** President City Council, City of Richmond, City Hall, Richmond, IN 47374.

WILLIAMS, ROBERT CARROLL
Educator. **PERSONAL:** Born Sep 16, 1935, Louisville, KY; died Jun 17, 1987; married Delores Seneva; children: Rita Ann, Celeste Carroll, Steven Robert, Leslie Jean. **EDUCATION:** Oakwood Coll, AB 1957; Louisville Presbyterian Seminary, BD 1961; Union Theological Seminary, STM 1969; Columbia Univ, PhD 1975. **CAREER:** Central State Coll, instructor philosophy & religion 1961-65; Oberlin Coll, dir of religious activities 1965-68; Vanderbilt Univ, prof of philosophy 1974-85; Muhlenberg Coll, vice pres & dean 1985-. **ORGANIZATIONS:** Asst dir of rsch Natl Endowment for Humanities 1980-81; mem bd trustees The Fund for Theological Educ 1981-. **HONORS/ACHIEVEMENTS:** Danforth Grad Fellowship; Doctoral Fellowship The Fund for Theological Educ 1972; Sgt at Arms (Honorary) Legislature, TN 1973. **BUSINESS ADDRESS:** VP and Dean, Muhlenberg College, 23rd & Chew Sts, Allentown, PA 18104.

WILSON, GLORIA E.
Attorney. **PERSONAL:** Born Mar 23, 1917, Chicago; died Nov 04, 1987; married Dr Walter N Dixon. **EDUCATION:** Northwestern U, BS, MS; John Marshall Law Sch, JD. **CAREER:** Private practice, atty. **ORGANIZATIONS:** Past pres Professional Women's Club; mem Phi Lamda Theta; past chmn Speakers Bur of NAACP; past mem Gov Bd of Washington Pk YMCA; mem NAACP; Chicago Urban League; John Marshall Law Sch Alumni; Cook Co Bar; Illinois Bar; Natl Bar; mem Quinn Chapel AME Ch.

WILSON, JAMES H.
Elected official. **PERSONAL:** Born Jan 30, 1928, Temple, TX; died Jun 1986; married Audrey. **EDUCATION:** California State Univ at Long Beach; UCLA. **CAREER:** City of Long Beach, councilman 1970-85. **ORGANIZATIONS:** Chmn bd of dirs So California

Assn of Govts 1978-79; vice mayor City of Long Beach 1975-80; chmn bd of dirs Natl Assn of Reg Councils 1979-80; mem bd of dirs Cedar House 1980-85; mem bd of dirs St Mary's Hospital 1982-85.   **HONORS/ACHIEVEMENTS:** Serv to Comm California Office of Criminal Justice 1975; Outstanding Contribution, California Comm on Criminal Justice 1976; Outstanding Achievement, Natl Council of Negro Women 1977; Outstanding Serv, Chamber of Commerce 1977; Outstanding Serv, United Nations 1980; Contribution to Black History, US Navy 1980; Martin Luther King Jr Award, Ministerial Alliance of LB 1984; Distinguished Serv 15 years, LB Poly High School 1985; Distinguished Serv 15 years Congressional Record, Congressman Glenn Anderson 1985; Distinguished Serv 15 years, County of Los Angeles Bd of Supervisors 1985; Distinguished Serv 15 years, State of California Senate & Assembly 1985. **BUSINESS ADDRESS:** City Councilman, City of Long Beach, 333 W Ocean Blvd, Long Beach, CA 90802.

WILSON, PORTERFIELD
Automobile dealer.   **PERSONAL:** Born Jul 12, 1933, Nashville, TN; died Jan 16, 1989, Detroit, MI; married Barbara J Fuller; children: Porterfield Christopher.   **EDUCATION:** General Motors Inst, attended.   **CAREER:** Dodge Factory, worker; Drug Store, clerk; Plymouth Auto Dealer, salesman; Chrysler Plymouth Dealer Tri-Cty Pontiac Dealers, salesman; Mazda & Honda Franchise,owner; Porterfield Wilson Pontiac GMC Truck Inc Mazda-Honda, pres, owner 1970-89.   **ORGANIZATIONS:** mem, Natl Business League, Booker T Washington Business Assn, Greater Detroit Chamber of Commerce, Black Enterprise Magazine; appointed by Detroit Mayor to Civil Service Commission; mem bd dir First Independence Natl Bank; special advisor to bd Republic Airlines.   **HONORS/ACHIEVEMENTS:** Top 100 Black Businesses 1973-; Pontiac M Awd 1973-79; Business Man of the Year Black Causes Assoc; Booker T Washington Business Achievement Award 1975; Minority Bus Award for Top 100 1976-77; Top Salesman for Plymouth Dealer; Chryslers Top Natl Salesman; Pontiac Masters Award 1977; invited to White House in 1978 as one of the nation's leading black businessmen; given the key to the city of Nashville; awarded as having the regional retail firm of the year US Dept of Commerce.   **MILITARY SERVICE:** AUS Airborne 1953-56.   **BUSINESS ADDRESS:** President, Porterfield Wilson Pontiac GMC Truck Inc, Mazda-Honda, 18650 Livernois, Detroit, MI 48221.

WOOD, COURTNEY B.
Doctor, educator.   **PERSONAL:** Born Jan 26, 1929, New York City, NY; died Aug 29, 1987; married Claire S Wood; children: Candace A.   **EDUCATION:** City Coll of NY, BS 1952; Howard Coll of Medicine, MD 1956; Columbia Univ, MPh 1962.   **CAREER:** Montifiore Morrisania Affiliation, dir ambulatory care 1962-65; New York City Dept of Health, dir medical care indigent 1965-66; HEW, regional medical office 1966-67; Mt Sinai School of Medicine, assoc prof community medicine 1968-87; Bronx Veterans Admin Medical Center, chief spinal cord injury serv.   **ORGANIZATIONS:** Fellow NY Acad of Medicine 1970, Amer Public Health Assn 1962; consultant Natl Center Health Serv 1975, Evaluation Unit Albert Einstein Coll 1975; mem NY Acad of Medicine, Physicians Forum; certified Preventive Medicine & Public Health 1969.   **MILITARY SERVICE:** USN lieutenant 1957-59. **BUSINESS ADDRESS:** Chief Spinal Cord Injury Serv, Bronx VA Medical Center, 130 W Kingsbridge Rd, Bronx, NY 10468.

ZUBER, PAUL B.
Educator.   **PERSONAL:** Born Dec 20, 1926, Williamsport, PA; died Mar 1987; married Barbara Johnson.   **BUSINESS ADDRESS:** Rensselaer Polytechnic, 8th St, Troy, NY 12181.

GEOGRAPHIC INDEX

Lockett, James D.
Mallisham, Joseph W.
Owens, Charles Edward
Smith, Bettie M.
Stinson, Constance Robinson
Wynn, Cordell

TUSCUMBIA
Bailey, Bob Carl
Smith, Otis Benton, Jr.

TUSKEGEE
Allman, Marian Isabel
Baker, Willie J.
Baldwin, Wilhelmina F.
Biswas, Prosanto K.
Capel, Wallace
Carter, Billy L.
Carter, Howard Payne
Davis, Norman Emanuel
Dawson, William Levi
Ford, Johnny L.
Gray, Fred David
Harvey, Richard R.
Hatton, Barbara R.
Henson, William Francis
Johnson, James A.
Lee, Detroit
Lewis, Meharry Hubbard
Massey, James Earl
Palmer, Joe
Payton, Benjamin Franklin
Peterson, William T.
Price, John Elwood
Reed, Thomas J.
Robinson, Wilbur R.
Scott, Leonard Lamar
Smith, Jock Michael
Thompson, Charles H.
Washington, Linda Phaire

TUSKEGEE INSTITUTE
Bowie, Walter C.
Carter, Herbert E.
Goodwin, Robert T., Sr.
Hardy, Charlie Edward
Henderson, James H. M.
Huffman, Rufus C.
Jernigan, Curtis Dean
Johnson, Andrew L.
Jones, Vernon A., Jr.
Mitchell, William P.
Morse, Joseph Ervin
Pryce, Edward L.
Scott, Leonard Lamar
Whatley, Booker Tillman

UNIONTOWN
May, James F.
Moore, David Bernard, II

UNIVERSITY
Hall, Ethel Harris
Prewitt, Lena Voncille Burrell

WETUMPKA
George, Laura W.

YORK
Nixon, Felix Nathaniel

ALASKA

ANCHORAGE
Austin, Frank
Davis, Bettye J.
Gamble, Janet Helen
Greene, William
Jackson, Charles Ellis
Jackson, Mary
Lyons, William B.
Neal, Sylvester (Sam)
Patterson, Alonzo B.
Rhodes, Edward
Smith, Carol Barlow
Taylor, Sterling R.
Timpson, Clarence B.
Warner, Wilmot Melville

AUKE BAY
McSmith, Blanche Preston

EAGLE RIVER
Greene, William

FAIRBANKS
Smith, Robert London

FORT RICHARDSON
Davis, Etheldra S.

ARIZONA

DOUGLAS
Cain, Johnnie M.

ELOY
Beasley, Edward, III

FLAGSTAFF
Hannah, Melvin James
Johnson, Theodore L.
Locket, Arnold, Jr.
Ross, Anthony Roger

FORT HUACHUCA
Allen, George Mitchell
Paige, Emmett, Jr.

GLENDALE
Barnwell, Henry Lee

PARADISE VALLEY
Scott, William Edd

PHOENIX
Barnwell, Henry Lee
Beachem, Constance
Black, Joseph
Chapman, Samuel Milton
Culver, Rhonda
Davis, Major
Davis, Walter (Sweet D)
Edwards, James Terrell
Foster, Roderick Allan
Gibson, Gregory A.
Green, Roy
Greer, Curtis William
Grigsby, Jefferson Eugene, Jr.
Hamilton, Art
Hamilton-Rahi, Lynda Darlene
Holton, Michael Lavelle
Humphries, Jay Lavelle
Johnson, Alexander Hamilton, Jr.
Johnson, Ray
Jones, Charles Lavelle
Junior, E. J.
Kunes, Ken R.
Lansden, Willie F.
Logan, George, III
Lucas, Maurice
Minor, Willie
Montague, Lee
Nance, Larry Donnell
Nelson, Doeg M.
Patterson, Cecil Booker, Jr.
Pearson, Stanley E.
Pittman, Charles Matthew
Pitts, John Martin
Ragsdale, Lincoln Johnson
Robertson, James B.
Sanders, Michael Anthony
Scott, Alvin Eugene
Seneca, Arlena E.
Stewart, Warren Hampton, Sr.
Taylor, Jeff Eugene
Veal, Herman Keith
Walker, Carolyn
Ward, Arnette S.
Williams, Theodore Edward
Woodbeck, Frank Raymond

SCOTTSDALE
Champion, Jerrye G.
Reid, F. Theodore, Jr.
Woodbeck, Frank Raymond

TEMPE
Culver, Rhonda
Douglas, Bobby Eddie
Edwards, John L.
Harris, Charles Somerville
Joseph, Frank Douglas

Smith, A. Wade
Solomon, Denzil Kenneth
Warren, Morrison Fulbright

TUCSON
Bowens, Johnny Wesley
Clarke, Raymond
Davis, Richard
Goodwin, Felix L.
Holsey, William Fleming, Jr.
Johnson, Albert James
Lander, Cressworth Caleb
Lockett, Bradford R.
Meade-Tollin, Linda C.
Russell, Nathaniel S.
Snowden, Fredrick
Sparks, Edward Franklin
Thompson, Floyd
Whaley, Joseph S.
Williams, Willie LaVern
Zander, Jessie Mae

YUMA
Jefferson, James E.

ARKANSAS

ARKADELPHIA
Smith, Virginia M.
Thomas, Eula Wiley

BLYTHEVILLE
Towns, Myron B., Jr.

CAMDEN
Allen, Thomas G.

CHEROKEE VILLAGE
Hollingsworth, John Alexander

CONWAY
Jones, Theodore

COTTON PLANT
Babbs, Junious C., Sr.
Conley, Emmitt Jerome

EARLE
Smith, Sherman

EDMONSON
Croft, Ira T.

EL DORADO
Sims, Pete, Jr.

FAYETTEVILLE
Morgan, Gordon D.
Richardson, Nolan
Williams, Lonnie Ray

FORDYCE
Baker, Joel L.

FORREST CITY
Wilburn, Isaac Earphette

FORT SMITH
Fisher, George Carver

HELENA
David, Geraldine R.

HOT SPRINGS
Adair, Kenneth
Logan, Alphonso

JACKSONVILLE
Bartley, William Raymond
Lewis, Robert Louis

JONESBORO
Gaines, Herschel Davis

LA GRANGE
Peer, Wilbur Tyrone

LEWISVILLE
Brown, LeRoy

LEXA
David, Geraldine R.

LITTLE ROCK
Bates, Daisy
Bivens, Shelia Reneea
Bogard, Hazel Zinamon
Cooper, Larry B.
Elders, M. Joycelyn
Harrison, Robert Walker, III
Henderson, LeMon
Hollingsworth, Perlesta A.
Howard, Corliss Mays
Ibekwe, Lawrence Anene
Jewell, Jerry Donal
Keaton, William T.
Loyd, Walter, Jr.
Mason, Jesse W.
Maulden, Jerry L.
Means, Kevin Michael
Overton, Betty Jean
Owens, Jay R.
Rayford, Phillip Leon
Rodgers, James R.
Rutledge, William Lyman
Shackelford, Lottie H.
Sherman, Oddie Lee
Smith, Joe Elliott
Tate, Sherman E.
Taylor, Tommie W.
Thrasher, William Edward
Titus, Myer L.
Todd, Orlando
Townsend, William Henry
Walker, Woodson DuBois
Ward, Lorene Howelton
Warren, Henry L.
White, Ralph L.
Young, Rufus King

MADISON
Whitaker, Willard H.

MAGNOLIA
Gaylord, Ellihue, Sr.
Kirby, Money Alian
Moss, Wilmar Burnett, Jr.

MALVERN
Womack, Orlando

MARIANNA
Peer, Wilbur Tyrone

MARION
Battle, William Elzie
Watkins, Lenice J.

MENIFEE
English, Clarence R.

MINERAL SPRINGS
Hendrix, Martha Raye

MOSCOW
Daniels, Peter F.

NEWPORT
Sills, Gregory D.

NORTH LITTLE ROCK
Brookins, H. Hartford
Cooley, James F.
Goldsby, W. Dean, Sr.
Hartaway, Thomas N., Jr.
Hunter, Elza Harris
James, Frederick C.

PINE BLUFF
Barfield, Rufus L.
Bell, Elmer A.
Davidson, Earnest Jefferson
Davis, Lawrence Arnette, Jr.
Early, Violet Theresa
Gilmore, John T.
Howard, George, Jr.
Johnson, Johnny B.
Johnson, Vannette William
Littlejohn, Walter L.
McGee, Eva M.
Molette, Willie L.
Roaf, Clifton G.
Walker, Charles A.

Wilkins, Henry, III

STATE UNIVERSITY
Slater, Rodney E.
Smith, Charlie Calvin

TEXARKANA
Williams, Londell

WABBASEKA
Hall, Robert Johnson

WEST HELENA
Gilcreast, Conway, Sr.
Williams, Ulysses Jean

WEST MEMPHIS
Hodges, Lillian Bernice
McGee, Benjamin Lelon

WRIGHTSVILLE
Byrd, Nellie J.

CALIFORNIA

ALAMEDA
Johnson, Christine
Reaves, E. Fredericka M.
Walton, Sidney F., Jr.

ALBANY
Bayne, Henry G.

ALTADENA
Browne, Lee F.
Dickerson, Lowell Dwight
Dixon, Ivan N.
McMullins, Tommy
Woodard, Lois Marie
Yarbrough, Delano

ANAHEIM
Brooks, Larry
Brown, Ron James
Carew, Rodney Cline
Dickerson, Eric
Ellis, Kenneth A.
Gray, Jerry
Hill, David
Irvin, LeRoy
Jackson, Reginald Martinez
Johnson, Johnnie
McCutcheon, Lawrence (Clutch)
Parker, Joyce Linda
Pettis, Gary George
Slater, Jackie

APO SAN FRANCISCO
Duncan, John C., Jr.
Morgan, Robert, Jr.
Person, Leslie Robin
Williams, Dennis

ATASCADERO
Cheek, Donald Kato
Cheek, Donna Marie

ATHERTON
Mays, Willie Howard, Jr.

AZUSA
Allen, John Henry

BAKERSFIELD
Baskerville, Samuel J., Jr.
Carson, Irma
Collier, Willye
Shaw, Mary Louise

BERKELEY
Atkins, Edmund E.
Bancroft, Richard Anderson
Banks, William Maron, III
Basri, Gibor Broitman
Bell, Theodore Joshua, II
Blackwell, David Harold
Blakely, Edward James
Boggan, Daniel, Jr.
Bragg, Robert Henry
Brown, Cecil M.
Clarke, Greta Fields

Davis, Morris E.
Drummond, William Joe
Duster, Troy
Edwards, Harry
Gibbs, Jewelle Taylor
Harris, James Andrew
Hodges, Melvin Sancho
Holbert, Raymond Ray
Hopper, Cornelius Lenard
Irmagean
Johnson, Stafford Quincy
Jones, Michele Woods
Jones, Reginald L.
Jordan, June M. (nee Meyer)
Lashley, Barbara Ann
Lester, William Alexander, Jr.
Lipscomb, Wendell R.
McGuire, Chester C., Jr.
McSwain, Berah D.
Morrison, Harry L.
Nelson, Ronald Duncan
Noguera, Pedro Antonio
Raymond, Phillip Gregory
Reed, Ishmael Scott (Emmett Coleman)
Reed, Rodney J.
Richardson, Charles H., Jr.
Satterfield, Floyd
Shack, William A.
Vaughn, Nora Belle
Wilkerson, Margaret Buford
Williams, Carroll Burns, Jr.
Wilson, Olly W.
Word, Carl Oliver
Yerger, Ben

BEVERLY HILLS
Acon, June Kay
Benson, George
Boags, Charles D.
Broady, Earl Clifford
Elliott, William David
Felton, Otis Leverna
Fitzgerald, Ella
Haley, Alexander Palmer
Hendry, Gloria
Herring, Leonard, Jr.
Jones, William Allen
Kennedy-Overton, Jayne (Jayne Kennedy)
McNair, Barbara
Moses, Gilbert
Poitier, Sidney
Reese, Della
Reid, Tim
Shaw, Stan
Townsend, Robert
Uggams, Leslie

BIG BEAR CITY
Tillman, Joseph Nathaniel

BONITA
Chapman, William Talbert

BRADBURY
Nelson, Robert Wales, Sr.

BURBANK
Allen, Byron
Burton, Calvin E.
Cartwright, Carole B
Fearn-Banks, Kathleen
Fields, Kim
Hill, Leo
Holmes, Robert Ernest
Mathis, Johnny
McMullins, Tommy
Morris, Dolores N.
Penniman, Richard (Little Richard)
Simmons, Emmett Bryson, III (Slim)
White, Winifred Viaria
Wonder, Stevie

BURLINGAME
Ali, Fatima (Ann Louise Redmon)
Brooks, Harry W., Jr.
Medearis, Victor L.
Morse, Warren W.

CANOGA PARK
Graham, Odell
Hyde-Jackson, Maxine Deborah

CARSON
Banks, Waldo R., Sr.
Jones, Frank Benson
Robinson, Gill Doncelia (Gill D. Daniels)
Turner, Franklin James
Walker, Charles
Walker, George Raymond
Williams, Felton Carl

CASTRO VALLEY
Morgan, Willie, Jr.

CENTURY CITY
Thompson, Patricia Moultrie

CERRITOS
Heard, Lonear Windham
Titus, LeRoy Robert

CHICO
Epting, Marion

CHINO
Anderson, Kathleen Wiley
Griggs, Bertram S.
Woods, Timothy L.

CHULA VISTA
Ferguson, Robert Lee, Sr. (Fergie)

CITRUS HEIGHTS
Goodwin-Fulgham, Roietta

CLAREMONT
Allen, William Barclay
Jackson, Agnes Moreland
Matthews, Albert D.
McFarlane, Franklin E.
Perkins, Linda Marie

COLTON
McKinney, Jesse Doyle

COMPTON
Beauchamp, Patrick L.
Bowman, Janet Wilson
Brown, Irma Jean
Bunkley, Lonnie R.
Cade, Lionel C.
Clegg, Legrand H., II
Cobbs, David E.
Cooper, Lois Louise
Davis, Billy, Jr.
Davis, Charles
Davis, Doris Ann
Dewberry, Madelina Denise
Dymally, Lynn V.
Filer, Kelvin Dean
Garrott, Homer L.
Goins, Mary G.
Hart, Emily
Henson, Charles A.
Hill, Betty J.
Hunn, Dorothy Fegan
Hunn, Myron Vernon
Kimble, Bettye Dorris
Miller, Ross M., Jr.
Mohr, Diane Louise
Patrick, Charles Namon, Jr.
Perdue, Franklin Roosevelt
Pitts, Donald Franklin
Robinson, Jesse Lee
Sanders, Wesley, Jr.
Stinson, Donald R.
Wauls, Inez La Mar (nee Fullen)
Woods, Bernice

CORONA
Jackson, Vera Ruth
Tillman, Joseph Nathaniel

CORONA DEL MAR
Davis, Arthur D.

COVINA
Allen, Charles E.

CULVER CITY
Fanaka, Jamaa
Lang, Charles J.
Lockley, Clyde William
Mendes, Helen Althia
Solomon, Barbara J.
Tobin, Patricia L.
Walden, Barbara
Wilborn, Letta Grace Smith

CUPERTINO
Harris, Rubie J.
Jenkins, Yolanda L.
Terrell, Dorothy

CYPRESS
Calhoun, Fred Steverson

DALY CITY
Ellis, Marilyn Pope

DAVIS
Jordan, Emma Coleman
Kondwani, Kofi Anum

DIAMOND BAR
Davis, Brenda Lightsey-Hendricks
Hollingsworth, Alfred Delano

DOWNEY
Brown, Emmett Earl
Grooms, Henry Randall
Land, Chester LaSalle

DUARTE
Bingham, Donna Guydon

DUBLIN
Taylor, William Glenn

EAST PALO ALTO
Mouton, Barbara Anne
Satterwhite, Frank Joseph
Wilks, Gertrude (nee Dyer)

EL CAJON
Cain, Robert R.
Riggs, Elizabeth A.

EL CERRITO
Crouchett, Lawrence Paul

EL SEGUNDO
Allen, Marcus
Branch, Clifford
Hayes, Lester
Haynes, Michael James
Henderson, Charles
Lawrence, Henry
Martin, Rod
McPherson, William H.
Powe, Joseph S.
Ray, Austin H.
Shell, Arthur
Sistrunk, Otis
Tatum, John David (Jack)
Wallette, Alonzo Vandolph
Wilkins, Roger L.

EMERYVILLE
Arbuckle, Pamela Susan
Brown, Richard Earl
Bullins, Ed
Clayton, Robert L.
Harrold, Lawrence A.
Jackson, John Berrye
Nicholas, Gwendolyn Smith
Roach, Deloris

ENCINITAS
Fisher, Edith Maureen
Simmons, Earl Melvin

ENCINO
Mills, Donald
Mills, Herbert
Mills, John
Peters, Brock G.
Reid, Tim
Warren, Michael

FOSTER CITY
Hooper, Gary Raymond
Pitts, Vera L.

FREMONT
Brown, Earl Richard

FRESNO
Aldredge, James Earl
Brown, Willie L.
Bugg, George Wendell
Burns, Felton
Ethridge, John E.
Ford, Richard D.
Fowlkes, Nelson J.
Francis, Charles S. L.
Goodwin, Hugh Wesley
Hunt, Samuel D.
Johnson, Frank J.
Kelley, Jack Albert
Kimber, Lesly H.
Owens, Robert Lee
Parks, James Edward
Pierce, Walter J.
Small, Lily B.
Smith, William James

FULLERTON
Butts, Carlyle A.
Cobb, Jewel Plummer
Davenport, Calvin A.
Hargrove, John E.
McFerrin, Sara Elizabeth Copper

GARDENA
Campbell, Everett O.
Hale, Gene
House, Jesse O.
Johnson, Arthur L.
Parker, Kai J.
Parnell, Arnold W.

GLENDALE
McNeal, Sylvia Ann
Wilson, Mary

GRANADA HILLS
Mance, John J.
McCraven, Carl Clarke

GREENBRAE
Banks, Joyce P.

HARBOR CITY
Hardin, Eugene
Phillips, Leroy Daniel
Richardson, Alfred Lloyd

HAWTHORNE
Peele, John E., Jr.
Williams, Charles Frederick

HAYWARD
Andrews, Malachi
Ballard, Myrtle Ethel
Bassard, Yvonne Brooks
Carmichael, Benjamin G.
Collins, Paul V.
Franklin, Allen D.
Greene, Carolyn Jetter
Lovett, Mack, Jr.
Pitts, Vera L.

HIGHLANDS
Alexander, Johnnie Wilbert

HOLLYWOOD
Adams, John Oscar
Barnes, Ernest Eugene, Jr.
Cole, Natalie
Cumber, Victoria Lillian
Goodson, James Abner, Jr.
Greene, Joseph P.
Guy, Lygia Brown
Hale, Cecil I., II
Harris, Ray, Sr.
Lane, William Clay
Long, Nate
Moore, Melba
Morgan, Meli'sa (Joyce)
Osborne, Jeffrey Linton
Roberts, Virgil Patrick
Shaw, Curtis Mitchell

Simone, Nina
Stephens, Warren E.
Thomas, Nathaniel
Turner, Dain Cameron
Williams, Lee R.
Womack, Bobby Dwayne

INGLEWOOD
Abdul-Jabbar, Kareem (Lew Alcindor)
Barnes, William L.
Benjamin, Rose Mary
Blackmon, Anthony Wayne
Carson, Willis E.
Chamberlain, Wilt N. (Wilt the Stilt)
Chones, Jim
Cooper, Michael Lavelle
Dorn, Roosevelt F.
Garrett, Calvin Lavelle
Green, A. C.
Heins, Henry L., Jr.
Hurte, Leroy E.
Johnson, Earvin, Jr. (Magic Johnson)
Johnson, Raymond L.
Matthews, Leonard Louis
Matthews, Mallory Louis
McAdoo, Bob
McGee, Mike Lavelle
Reid, Benjamin F.
Rentie, Frieda
Richardson, Nola Mae
Russell, Cazzie
Scott, Byron Lavelle
Scott, Timothy Van
Simmons, Emmett Bryson, III (Slim)
Simpson, Gregory Louis
Snowden, Raymond C.
Spriggs, Larry Lavelle
White, Artis Andre
Wiley, Maurice
Wilkes, Jamaal
Williams, Harvey Joseph
Williams, Herbert Lee
Williams, Homer LaVaughan
Worthy, James

IRVINE
Cooper-Lewter, Nicholas Charles
Dungy, Madgetta Thornton
France, Federick Doug, Jr.
Mitchell, Horace
Williams, Harvey

LA JOLLA
Gaffney, Floyd
Heineback, Barbara (nee Taylor)
James, Luther
Moss, Robert C., Jr.
Penn, Nolan E.
Reynolds, Edward
Thomas, Charles William, II
Watson, Joseph W.

LAGUNA HILLS
Merritt, Anthony Lewis
Wilson, Demond

LAKE VIEW TERRACE
McCraven, Carl Clarke

LAKEWOOD
Fisher, Carl Anthony

LANCASTER
Hedgley, David Rice, Jr.

LIVERMORE
Ware, Omego John Clinton, Jr.

LONG BEACH
Blaylock, Enid V.
Brisco-Hooks, Valerie
Byrd, Lumus, Jr.
Clayton, James Henry
Dunn, George William
Ellison, Robert A.
Hartsfield, Arnett L., Jr.
Hill, Deborah
Kirkland, Cornell R.
Rains, Horace

Robinson, Jim C.
Stephens, Lee B., Jr.
Stetson, Jeffrey P.
Swinton, Patricia Ann
Taylor, Jesse Elliott, Jr.
Tillman, Talmadge Calvin, Jr.
Walakafra-Wills, Delpaneaux V.
Williams, Betty Smith
Williams, Felton Carl
Williams, Ora
Young, Barbara J.

LOS ALAMITOS
Peters, Samuel A.

LOS ALTOS HILLS
Fleming, June H.

LOS ANGELES
Airall, Angela Maureen
Alexander, Joseph Lee
Alexander, Josephine
Alexander, William M., Jr.
Allen, Lucius Oliver
Alston, Kathy Diane
Anderson, Marva Jean
Andrews, Adelia Smith
Arnold, Alton A., Jr.
Arnold, Larkin
Atkins, Brenda J.
Atkins, Pervis
Atkinson, J. Edward
Avery, Herbert B.
Bailey, Arthur
Bain, Josie Gray
Baker, Wanda Kay
Ballard, Kathryn W.
Bankhead, Patricia Ann
Banks, Brenda L.
Banks, Ernest (Ernie)
Barclay, David Ronald
Barnes, John B., Sr.
Barnes, Stephen Darryl
Barnes, Willie R.
Barrett, Ronald Keith
Bath, Patricia E.
Batiste, Mary Virginia
Baylor, Elgin
Beachem, William Perry
Beasley, Arlene Audrey
Beasley, Jesse C.
Beaubien, George H.
Beavers, George A.
Beck, Thomas Arthur, III
Becker, Adolph Eric
Becker-Slaton, Nellie Frances
Bell, Melvyn Clarence
Benton, Nelkane O.
Bernoudy, James Logan
Berry, Gordon L.
Berry, Leroy
Berry, Roscoe Darewood, Jr.
Beverly, William C., Jr.
Biggers, Samuel Loring, Jr.
Billingslea, Monroe L.
Black, James Tillman
Blanding, Mary Rhonella
Bobbitt, Leroy
Boddie, Lewis F., Sr.
Borden, Harold F., Jr.
Boston, Archie, Jr.
Bowdoin, Robert E.
Bowman, Janet Wilson
Bradley, Thomas
Bradshaw, Wayne
Branch, Geraldine Burton
Branton, Leo, Jr.
Brenson, Verdel Lee
Bridgeman, Junior
Brookins, Bonita Coleman
Brooks, Theodore Roosevelt, Jr.
Broussard, Vernon
Brown, Costello L.
Brown, Deloris A.
Brown, Jurutha
Brown, Leroy Thomas
Brown, Olivia
Brown, Vernon E.
Brown, William McKinley, Jr.
Browne, Roscoe Lee
Bryant, William Cullen
Buckhalter, Emerson R.
Burke, William Arthur
Burke, Yvonne Brathwaite

Burton, Iola Brantley
Burton, Levar
Butler, Octavia E.
Butts, Carlyle A.
Cage, Michael
Callender, Ralph A.
Calomee, Annie E.
Campanella, Roy, Sr. (Campy)
Campbell, Franklyn D.
Cannon, Reuben
Carew, Colin A. (Topper Carew)
Carroll, Diahann
Carter, Nell
Carter, Robert T.
Cash-Rhodes, Winifred E.
Catchings, Harvey
Chaney, Don
Charles, Ray (Ray Charles Robinson)
Cheese, Pauline Staten
Childs, Joy
Chretien, Gladys M.
Claiborne, Earl Ramsey
Claiborne, Vernal
Clardy, William J.
Clark-Thomas, Eleanor M.
Clay, William Roger
Clayton, Ina Smiley
Clayton, Mayme Agnew
Clemendor, Anthony A., IV
Cleveland, James
Cole, Adolph
Coleman, Gary
Coley, Esther B.
Collins, James Douglas
Collins, Kenneth L.
Coltrane, Alice Turiya
Cooper, Candace D.
Cooper, Earl, II (Skip)
Corlette, Edith
Cosby, William Henry
Covan, DeForest W.
Cramer, Joe J., Jr.
Cravens, Thirkield Ellis, Jr.
Creary, Ludlow Barrington
Curry, Mitchell L.
Daniels, Jordan, Jr.
Dave, Alfonzo, Jr.
Davidson, Ezra C., Jr.
Davis, Alonzo J.
Davis, Amos
Davis, Dale Brockman
Davis, John Albert
Davis, Nolan
Davis, Ossie
Davis, Richard C.
Davis, Willie D.
Dee, Ruby (Ruby Ann Wallace)
DeLilly, Mayo Ralph, III
Dent, Preston L.
Donaldson, James Terrell
Douglas, Harry E., III
Driver, Louie M., Jr.
Dummett, Clifton Orrin
Dunn, W. Paul
Durant, Celeste Millicent
Dyer, Joe, Jr.
Edwards, Oscar Lee
Ellis, Frederic L.
Ellis, Johnell A.
Eubanks, Rachel Amelia
Evans, Edward Clark
Evans, Lillie R.
Everett, Benjamin A.
Farrell, Robert C.
Fergerson, Miriam N. (nee Watson)
Ferguson, Lloyd N.
Fisher, Gail
Fleming, Arthur Wallace
Fleming, Melvin J.
Fluellen, Joel M.
Fontenot-Jamerson, Berlinda
Fortier, Theodore T.
Franklin, Floyd
Frazier, Joe
Fuller, Norvell Ricardo
Gault, Willie James
Gerald, Gilberto Ruben
Gibbs, Marla
Gilchrist, Carlton Chester
Gillette, Lyra Stephanie
Glasco, Anita L.
Glass, Ronald

Goldberg, Whoopi (Caryn E. Johnson)
Gordon, Lancaster Anthony
Gordon, Walter Lear, III
Gordy, Berry, Jr.
Gordy, Desiree D'Laura
Gossett, Louis, Jr.
Grayson, John N.
Green, Geraldine D.
Greene, Charles Edward Clarence
Grier, Roosevelt (Rosey Grier)
Griffey, Dick
Griffith, Thomas Lee, Jr.
Guillaume, Robert
Habersham, Robert
Hairston, Jester
Hambrick, Harold E., Jr.
Hamilton, Lynn (Lynn Jenkins)
Harris, Jimmie
Harris, Lee
Hart-Nibbrig, Harold C.
Hathaway, Maggie Mae
Hawkins, William Douglas
Haywood, L. Julian
Hegeman, Charles Oxford
Hemsley, Sherman
Henley, Carl R.
Henry, Karl H.
Hervey, Ramon Triche, II
Higginbotham, Kenneth Day, Sr.
Hightower, Dennis Fowler
Hill, Jacqueline R.
Hillsman, Gerald C.
Hobbs, Thadeaus H.
Hodge, Marguerite V.
Holman, Alvin T.
Holt, Deloris Lenette
Houston, Ivan J.
Houston, Norman Oliver
Howard, John E.
Howard, Joseph H.
Hubbard, James Madison, Jr.
Hudson, Elbert T.
Humber, Toni Cheryl
Hunter, Lloyd Thomas
Ighner, Benard T.
Jackson, Alexis Camille
Jackson, C. Bernard
Jackson, Edward W.
Jackson, Giles B.
Jackson, Isaiah Allen
Jackson, Michael
Jefferson, Roland Spratlin
Jeffries, LeRoy William
Jenkins, Frank Shockley
Jenkins, Louis E.
Jessie, Ron Ray
Johns, Stephen Arnold
Johnson, Cage Saul
Johnson, Janice Marie
Johnson, Lucien Love
Johnson, Marques Lavelle
Johnson, Pompie Louis, Jr.
Johnson, Raymond L.
Johnson, Virginia O.
Johnson, William C.
Jones, Cody
Jones, Gary
Jones, James Earl
Jones, Ken
Jones, Lonzie L.
Jones, Quincy
Jones, Robert G.
Jordan, R. D.
Jordan, Wilbert Cornelious
Kelly, A. Paul
Kendrick, Artis G.
Kersee, Bobby
Khan, Chaka
Kilgore, Thomas, Jr.
King, Celes, III
King, Jeanne Faith
King, Lewis M.
King, Wesley A.
Klausner, Willette Murphy
Kyle, Genghis
Lamaute, Denise
Land, Chester LaSalle
Landreaux, Kenneth Francis
Lange, Ted W., III
Lark, Raymond
Lawson, James M., Jr.
LeDay, John Austin
Lee, Gloria A.

Leonard, Leon Lank, Sr.
Leslie, Marcia Louise
Lewis, Arthur A.
Lewis, Charles Grant
Lewis, Erma Jean
Lindsay, Gilbert W.
Little, Cleavon Jake
Long, Ophelia
Lovett, Leonard
Luck, Clyde Alexander, Jr.
Luke, Sherrill David
Lyons, George W.C., Sr.
Mack, John W.
Macklin, Rudy Joel
Malone, Stanley R.
Manning, Howard Nick, Jr.
Marshall, Consuelo B. (nee Arnold)
Martin, Carl E.
Martin, D'Urville
Matson, Ollie Genoa
Maxwell-Reid, Daphne Etta
May, Charles W.
Mays, James A.
Mays, Vickie M.
McBeth, Veronica Simmons
McConnell, Dorothy Hughes
McCormick, Larry William
McGee, Henry W., Jr.
McGehee, Maurice Edward
McIntosh, Walter Cordell
McKinney, Jacob K.
Mendes, Helen Althia
Meshack, Sheryl Hodges
Miller, Lori E.
Mills, Billy G.
Milton, LeRoy
Mitchell-Kernan, Claudia Irene
Moore, Oscar James, Jr.
Morris, Greg
Morrison, Ronald E.
Morrow, Dion Griffith
Mosby, Esvan Scott
Moseley, James Orville B.
Moses, Louise J.
Moss, Winston
Murphy, Eddie
Murray, Virgie W.
Myles, Stan, Jr.
Neal, Joseph C., Jr.
Neil, Cleveland Oswald
Nelson, Artie Cortez
Nelson, H. Viscount, Jr.
Nelson, Prince Rogers (Prince)
Nelson, Terry
Neusom, Thomas G.
Nicholas, Denise
Nicholas, Fayard Antonio
Niles, Alban I.
Nixon, Norm Charles
Norman, Alex James
Oliver, Melvin L.
Osborne, Alfred E., Jr.
Oubre, Linda Seiffert
Outterbridge, John Wilfred
Pajaud, William E.
Panton, Yvonne B. F.
Parker, William Hayes, Jr.
Parks, George B.
Paxton, Gertrude Garnes
Paxton, Phyllis Ann
Payton, Nolan H.
Penny, Robert
Perara, Mitchell Mebane
Perdue, Franklin Roosevelt
Perkins, Charles Windell
Perkins, Linda Marie
Perry, Felton
Perry, Jean B.
Perry, Rod
Phillips, Frank E.
Phillips, Rod
Pinkney, Dove Savage
Pitcher, Frederick M. A.
Pittman, Marvin B.
Pitts, Gregory Philip
Polk, Ron Lamont
Porter, Everette M.
Pounds, Elaine
Powell, Gloria J.
Prelow, Arleigh
Purnell, Alton
Purvis, Archie C., Jr.
Ramos, Gene Maurice

Randolph, Willie Larry
Raveling, George Henry
Rawls, Lou
Reid, Selwyn Charles
Reynolds, Robert James
Richardson, Madison Franklin
Richardson, Nola Mae
Richie, Lionel Brockman
Robinson, Carl Cornell
Robinson, Gertrude Rivers
Robinson, Herbert A.
Robinson, Lawrence B.
Robinson, William, Jr. (Smokey Robinson)
Rolle, Esther
Rose, Rachelle Sylvia
Rosser, James M.
Roundtree, Richard
Ryan-White, Jewell
Sampler, Marion
Sampson, Henry Thomas
Sanders, Augusta Swann
Sanders, Glenn Carlos
Sanders, Joseph Stanley
Sands, Henry W.
Sanford, Isabel G. (Isabel Richmond)
Savage, Edward W., Jr.
Scott, Benjamin
Scott, Larry B.
Scott, Yolanda Madden
Sellers, Theresa Ann
Sharp, Saundra
Shifflett, Lynne Carol
Shook, Patricia Louise
Shropshire, Claudius Napoleon, Jr.
Simms, William E.
Simpson, Gregory Louis
Simpson, Joyce Michelle
Singleton, Robert
Slaughter, Fred Leon
Smith, Carl Reginald (Reggie Smith)
Smith, Derek Eugene
Smith, Ernest Howard
Smith, Quentin Paige, Jr.
Smothers, Ronald
Solomon, Barbara J.
Somerset, Leo L., Jr.
Stennis, Willie James
Stevens, Thomas Lorenzo, Jr.
Stewart, Carl L.
Stewart, Horace W. (Nick)
Streeter, Elwood James
Stubbs, Franklin Lee
Sullivan, J. Christopher
Summer, Donna Andrea
Swinger, Hershel Kendell
Tate, Adolphus, Jr.
Taylor, Christopher Lenard
Teasley, Larkin
Tero, Lawrence (Mr. T)
Terry, Adeline Helen
Terry, Charles C.
Terry, Frank W.
Thomas, Booker T.
Thomas, John
Thomas, Maxine F.
Thornton, Osie M.
Thornton, Pearl B.
Titus, LeRoy Robert
Townes, Linton Keith
Tubbs, Vincent Trenton
Tucker, Dorothy M.
Tucker, M. Belinda
Tucker, Marcus O., Jr.
Turner-Givens, Ella Mae
Tweed, Andre R.
Twine, Edgar Hugh
Varner, Robert Lee
Waddell, Charles M.
Wagner, Vallerie Denise
Walker, Eugene Henry
Walker, Grover P.
Walker, Horace L.
Walker, James C.
Wallace, Joseph Fletcher, Jr.
Walters, Mary Dawson
Warfield, Marcia
Warrick, Bryan Keith
Washington, Chester Lloyd
Waters, Maxine
Watkins, Ted

Watson, Constance A.
Watson, Diane Edith
Weekes, Martin E.
Westbrooks, Logan H.
White, Charles R.
White, Don Lee
White, Earl Henry
White, Rory Keith
Whitfield, Terry Bertland
Williams, Bertha Mae
Williams, David W.
Williams, Hal
Williams, Harold Louis
Williams, Harriette F.
Williams, Henry S.
Williams, John
Williams, Sandra K. (Sandra W. Gorham)
Williams, W. Donald
Williams, William J.
Williford, Stanley O.
Willis, Frederic L.
Wilson, Charles Z., Jr.
Wilson, Stanley Charles
Woodard, A. Newton
Woodard, Allen C., III
Woods, Arleigh Maddox
Woods, Geraldine Pittman
Woods, Hortense E.
Wright, Alonzo Gordon
Yarborough, Richard A.
Young, A. S. (Doc Young)

LOS NAMITOS
Johnson, Joseph David

LUCERNE VALLEY
Williams, Clarice Leona

LYNWOOD
Battle, Joe Turner
Buckhalter, Emerson R.
Hayling, William H.
Sims, Edward Hackney

MALIBU
Daniels, Clarence A., Jr.

MARIN CITY
Times, Betty J.

MARINA DEL REY
McBroom, F. Pearl
Stetson, Jeffrey P.

MARYSVILLE
Kildare, Michel Walter Andre

MENLO PARK
Bereola, Enitan Olu
Burroughs, Hugh Charles
Coleman, Kenneth L.
Milton, Henry
White, Billy Ray

MILPITAS
Peoples, Harrison Promis, Jr.

MISSION VIEJO
Carroll, Constance Marie

MODESTO
Pope, Joseph N.

MOFFETT FIELD
King, Reginald F.
Shawnee, Laura Ann

MONTCLAIR
Vines, Benjamin Glenn

MONTEREY
Hutchins, Bertha (nee Humphrey)
Newton, Andrew E., Jr.

MORAGA
Boyd, Candy Dawson

MORENO VALLEY
James, Joyce L.
Wooding, David Joshua

MOUNTAIN VIEW
Hannah, Marc Regis
Harris, Rubie J.
Harris, William Henry

NATIONAL CITY
Chapman, William Talbert
Lloyd, David
Williams, Matthew Albert

NAVARRO
Walker, Alice Malsenior

NEWBURY PARK
Arties, Walter Eugene, III
Bland, Robert Arthur

NEWHALL
Johnson, Robert C.

NORTH HOLLYWOOD
Peters, Charles L., Jr.
Russell, Beverly A.

NORTHRIDGE
Burwell, William David, Jr.
Daniels, Jean E.
Harden, Marvin
Henry, Samuel Dudley
Moseka, Aminata (Abbey Lincoln)
Obinna, Eleazu S.
Wright, Albert Walter, Jr.

NORWALK
Nelson, Artie Cortez

NOVATO
Nelson, Eileen A.

OAKLAND
Adams, V. Toni
Allen, Robert L. (Benjamin Peterson)
Andujar, Joaquin
Arbuckle, Pamela Susan
Attles, Alvin
Bailey, Didi Giselle
Baker, Dusty
Banks, Diane Lewis
Baranco, Gordon S.
Barber, Hargrow Dexter
Barber, Janice Denise
Bates, Nathaniel
Bazile, Leo
Bell, Theodore Joshua, II
Bellow, Cleveland J.
Benton, Calvin B.
Berkley, Thomas Lucius
Bobino, Rita Florencia
Bol, Manute
Booker, James Avery, Jr.
Broach, S. Elizabeth
Burris, John L.
Campbell, Gertrude M.
Cannon, Aleta
Cannon, Barbara E.M.
Carter, Geoffrey Norton
Cherry, Lee Otis
Chester, Raymond Thomas
Clark, Claude Lockhart
Clift, Joseph William
Cole, James O.
Cooper, Josephine H.
Darling, Leroy (Roy West)
Davis, Lester E.
Ennix, Coyness Loyal, Jr.
Euell, Julian Thomas
Ford, Judith Donna
Foster, Robert Davis
Freeman, Kenneth D.
Garrett-Brown, Fannie E.
Gilmore, Carter C.
Godbold, Donald Horace
Golden, Samuel Lewis
Goring, William S.
Guillory, John L.
Hagins, Jean Arthur
Hargrave, Benjamin
Harkless-Webb, Mildred
Harris, Robert L.
Hazard, Benjamin W.
Head, Laura Dean

Hebert, Stanley Paul
Herring, Bernard Duane
Herzfeld, Will Lawrence
Hewlett, Antoinette Payne
Hilliard, General K.
Hopkins, Donald Ray
Jackson, Mabel I.
James, Frederick John
James, Gillette Oriel
Jenkins, Bobby G.
Johnson, Gene C.
Jones, Leonard Virgil
Joseph-McIntyre, Mary
Kelley, Will Gene
Kitchen, Wayne Leroy
LaBrie, Peter, Jr.
Lampley, Edward Charles
League, Cheryl Perry
Lovelace, Onzalo Robert
Maynard, Robert C.
McCline, Richard L.
McCullum, Donald Pitts
McGathon, Carrie M.
McGhee, Walter Brownie
McGowan, Thomas Randolph
McKinney, Eloise Vaughn (Eliose Johnson)
McMorris, Samuel Carter
Medford, Isabel
Metoyer, Carl B.
Mitchell, Charles, Jr.
Moodie, Dahlia Maria
Moore, Howard, Jr.
Murphy, Dwayne Keith
Nash, Thomas
Nicholas, Gwendolyn Smith
Nichols, Roy Calvin
Norman, Bobby Don
Norris, Michael Kelvin
Patterson, Charles Jerry
Patterson, Clarence J.
Patterson, William Benjamin
Pendergrass, Emma H.
Philyaw, Charles
Ramsey, Henry, Jr.
Richard, James L.
Ross, William Alexander Jackson
Saunders, Raymond Jennings
Scott, Arthur Bishop
Simmons, Kenneth H.
Smith, J. Alfred, Sr.
Smith, Lynn Stanford
Smith, Vernel Hap
Staggers, Frank Eugene
Steele, Percy H., Jr.
Sturgies, Calvin Henry, Jr.
Sweet, Clifford C.
Taylor, Marie de Porres (Linda Suzanna Taylor)
Taylor, Martha
Taylor, Michael
Taylor, Scott Morris
Thomas, Robert C.
Thurmond, Nate (Nate the Great)
Travis, Benjamin
Tucker, Norma Jean
Ward, Carole Geneva
Washington, Carl Douglas
Watson, Carole M.
Watson, Robert Jose
Webster, William H.
White, James S.
White, Jo Jo
Wilson, Lionel J.

OCCIDENTAL
Snyder, George W.

OCEANSIDE
Hoye, Walter B., II

OJAI
Ferguson, Maynard W.

ORANGE
Chapman, George Wallace, Jr.

ORINDA
Hilliard, General K.
Stokes, Carolyn Ashe
Swann, Eugene Merwyn

OXNARD
Pinkard, Bedford L.
Royal, C. Charles, Sr.

PACOIMA
Barclay, David Ronald
Marshall, William Horace

PALM SPRINGS
Beaver, Joseph T., Jr.

PALO ALTO
Du Bois, David Graham
Fleming, June H.
Green, William Ernest
Jackson, Kennell A., Jr.
Smith, Roulette William
Thrower, Charles S.
Young, Albert James

PASADENA
Alston, Gilbert C.
Barthe, Richmond
Browne, Lee F.
Cargill, Sandra Morris
Clark, Mario Sean
Cox, Sandra Hicks
Crayton, James Edward
Driver, Johnnie M.
Gooden, Winston Earl
Hardy, John Louis
Johnson, Charles Beverly
King, James, Jr.
Knight, Lynnon Jacob
Lancaster, Herman Burtram
McClelland, Isaac Holland
McFaddin, Theresa Garrison
Pannell, William E.
Pride, Marcus O., Sr.
Reid, Joel Otto
Ridley, Charles Robert
Robinson, Louie M.
Tyson, Bertrand Oliver
Wagner, Vallerie Denise
Williams, Robert W.
Wright, William A.

PERRIS
Gordon, Charles Franklin
Ingram, William B.

PIONEER TOWN
Wilson, Nancy

PITTSBURG
Doss, LaRoy Samuel
Foster, Robert Davis
Harrold, Lawrence A.
Newkirk, Queenie Hortense

PLACENTIA
Parker, Joyce Linda

PLEASANTON
Lofton, Mellanese (nee Slaughter)

POINT MUGU
London, Eddie

POMONA
Allen, Browning E., Jr.
Benson, James Russell
Daniels, David Herbert, Jr.
Jordan, William Alfred, III
Miller, Loren, Jr.
Parker, James E.
Speiginer, Gertha
Thandeka
Williams, James Hiawatha

PRESIDIO OF SAN FRANCISCO
Agee, Robert Edward
Settles, Carl E.

RANCHO PALOS VERDE
Savage, Edward W., Jr.

REDDING
Taylor, Arthur Duane

REDWOOD CITY
Board, Dwaine
Carter, Michael
Collins, Charles Miller
Craig, Roger Timothy
Green, Dennis
Lott, Ronnie
Nehemiah, Renaldo
Rice, Jerry
Solomon, Freddie
Turner, Keena
Williamson, Carlton
Wright, Eric

REEDLEY
Sykes, Abel B., Jr.

RESEDA
Brown, Donald R., Sr.

RICHMOND
Allen, William Duncan
Barnes, Matthew M., Jr.
Farlough, H. Eugene, Jr.
Matthews, James Vernon, II
Nelson, William W.
Tramiel, Kenneth Ray, Sr.
Williams, Guthrie J.

RIDGECREST
Sherman, Thomas Oscar, Jr.

RIVERSIDE
Anderson, Barbara Louise
Carson, Lois Montgomery
Davis, Brenda Lightsey-Hendricks
Gravenberg, Eric Von
Livingston, L. Benjamin

ROHNERT PARK
Wilkinson, Donald Charles

ROSEMEAD
Hines, Kingsley B.

SACRAMENTO
Alexis, Doris Virginia
Armistead, Milton
Bailey, Agnes Jackson
Banks, Loubertha May
Bannerman-Richter, Gabriel
Boggus, Francis Oliver
Bond, James G.
Brown, David Eugene
Brown, Leroy Bradford
Brown, Willie L., Jr.
Bullock, Elbert L.
Byrd, Albert Alexander
Canson, Fannie Joanna
Carney, Callie I.
Chambers, Ruth-Marie Frances
Chappell, Ruth Rax
Clifford, Charles H.
Colley, Nathaniel S.
Cooper, Joseph
Covin, David L.
Crossley, Frank Alphonso
Cullers, Samuel James
Denmark, Robert Richard
Dodd, James C.
Embree, James Arlington
Favors, Kathryne Taylor
Finch, Gregory Martin
Foster, Raunell H.
Frazier, Clifford B.
Gates, Thomas Michael
Goodwin-Fulgham, Roietta
Gordon, Allan M.
Gray, Mattie Evans
Griffin, Ples Andrew
Gunn, Alex M., Jr.
Hampton, Grace
Harris, Elihu Mason
Henry, Marcelett Campbell
Hights, William E.
Hollis, Mary Lee
Hurdle, Hortense O. McNeil
Jones, Asbury Paul
Kennedy, Callas Faye
LaMotte, Jean Moore
Lawrence, Paul Frederic
Lawson, Herman A.
Lee, William H.

Leflores, George O., Jr.
Long, James L.
Lytle, Alice A.
Marks, Rose M.
McGee, Adolphus Stewart
McLaurin, Freddie Lewis, Jr.
Meeks, Larry Gillette
Moore, Gwen
Moore, Jellether Marie
Netters, Tyrone Homer
Payne, Jerry Oscar
Pogue, Lester Clarence
Prather, Jeffrey Lynn
Randall, Queen F.
Ransom, Gary Elliott
Raye, Vance Wallace
Riggins, Lester
Riles, Wilson Camanza
Robinson, Muriel F. Cox
Russell, William Fenton (Bill)
Rutland, William G.
Scott, Windie Olivia
Shaw, Ferdinand
Simmons, Joseph
Smith, Heman Bernard
Smith, Rufus Burnett, Jr.
Somerville, Addison Wimbs
Strozier, Yvonne Iglehart
Walker, Jerry Euclid
Washington, Josie B.
Whitehead, John L., Jr.
Wright, Stanley V.

SALINAS
Holt, Fred D

SAN BERNARDINO
Bailey, Joseph Alexander, II
Frazier, Dan E., Sr.
Henry, Mildred M. Dalton
Hobbs, John Daniel
Levister, Ernest Clayton, Jr.
Ludlam, Valerie Pope
Martin, Carolyn Ann
Motley, Ronald Clark
Newell, William
Patterson, Pola Noah
Shelton, Jewell Vennerie
Townsend, Arthur P.
Wilson, Ernest

SAN BRUNO
Ellis, Marilyn Pope

SAN DIEGO
Alexander, Edward Cleve
Anderson, Gary
Bacon, Randall C.
Bartley, Talmadge O.
Beam, Lillian Kennedy
Briggs-Graves, Anasa
Bronner, James Arthur
Brooks, Roy Lavon
Brooks, Sidney Joseph
Brownlee, Jack M.
Byrd, Gill Arnette
Carey, Howard H.
Cash, David, Jr.
Charles, Joseph C.
Crossley, Charles R., II
Davis, Leonard Harry
DeWitt, Rufus B.
Douglass, John H.
Dual, Peter Alfred
Durden, Earnel
Forde, James Albert
Foster, Frances Smith
Fuentes, Rigoberto (Tito Fuentes)
Geiger, David Nathaniel
Gilliam, Earl B.
Graves, Clifford W.
Green, Ruth A.
Greene, Mamie Louise
Griffith, John H.
Gwynn, Tony
Hacker, Benjamin Thurman
Hayes, Floyd Windom, III
Holder, Julius H.
Hoye, Walter B.
Hutchinson, George
Johnson, William E.
Joiner, Charles, Jr.
Jones, Grover (Deacon Jones)
Jones, Napoleon A., Jr.

Jones, Randy Kane
Jones, William Donnell
Joshua, Von E.
Lawhorn, Robert Martin
Lewis, Dick Edgar
Linnette, Valleta H.
Malone, Cleo
Matthews, Merritt Stewart
Matthews, Robert L.
McKinney, George Dallas, Jr.
McPhatter, Thomas H.
McQuater, Patricia A.
Miles, E. W.
Miller, Henry B., Jr.
Moaney, Eric R.
Montgomery, Catherine Lewis
Moodie, Dahlia Maria
Moore, Archibald Lee Wright
Norfleet, Fred L., Jr.
Otis, Amos Joseph
Oyeshiku, Patricia Delores
    Worthy
Peterson, Willie Diamond
Reed, Adolphus Redolph
Reede, James William, Jr.
Reid, Charles E.
Richardson, Delroy M.
Ritchey, Mercedes B.
Rollins, Lee Owen
Russell, Wesley L.
Shack, William Edward
Smith, Dorothy Louise White
Smith, George Walker
Sparrow, Victor Howard, III
Steppe, Cecil H.
Styles, Marvalene H.
Templeton, Garry Lewis
Warmly, Leon
Weber, Daniel
Weber, Shirley Nash
Wicks, Sidney
Wiggins, Alan
Williams, J. Bedell
Williams, Leon Lawson
Williams, Matthew Albert
Younger, Paul Lawrence (Tank)

SAN FRANCISCO
Abrams, Roslyn Maria
Andrews, Alice Elizabeth
Arnelle, Hugh Jesse
Baker, LaVolia Ealy
Baltimore, Roslyn Lois
Banks, Joyce P.
Bates, Ernest Alphonso
Beasley, Alice Margaret
Bell, William Charles
Belle, Charles E.
Bennett, Patricia A.
Block, Carolyn B.
Brandford, Napoleon
Brannen, James H., III
Brazil, Ernest L.
Broussard, Allen E.
Brown, Amos Cleophilus
Brown, C. B.
Butler, Frederick Douglas
Cannon, H. LeRoy
Canson, Virna M.
Cayou, Nontsizi Kirton
Churchwell, Caesar Alfred
Claiborne, Lloyd R.
Clay, Reuben Anderson, Jr.
Cobbs, Price Mashaw
Cochran, Donnie L.
Cochran, Todd S.
Coleman, Arthur H.
Cotton, Albert E.
Crawford, Jacob Wendell
Darke, Charles B.
Davis, Belva
Davis, Chili
Dearman, John Edward
Debas, Haile T.
Debro, Joseph Rollins
Dickey, Lloyd V.
Dreyfuss, Joel P.
Flowers, Loma Kaye
Francois, Terry A.
Garrett, Cain, Jr.
Gilford, Rotea J.
Gillette, Frankie Jacobs
Goodlett, Carlton B.
Goosby, Zuretti L.

Gray, Naomi T.
Grigsby, Calvin Burchard
Hamilton, Wilbur Wyatt
Hancock, Herbert Jeffrey
Handy, John Richard, III
Hare, Julia Reed
Hare, Nathan
Harkless-Webb, Mildred
Head, Laura Dean
Henderson, Thelton Eugene
Hernandez, Aileen Clarke
Herndon, James
Hewlett, Everett Augustus, Jr.
Hill, Patricia Liggins
Hodges, Melvin Sancho
Hooker, John Lee
Hooper, Gary Raymond
Houston, Seawadon Lee
Howard, Raymond Monroe, Sr.
Jackson, Eugene L.
Jackson, Mattie J.
Jackson, Oscar Jerome
Jeffers, Clifton R.
Jewett, Charlie Ruth
Johnson, Stephen L.
Jones, Woodrow Harold
Jordan, Frederick E.
Kelly, Leontine T. C.
Kennedy, Florynce
Kennedy, Willie B.
Kresy-Poree, R. Jean
Lane, John Henry
Leonard, Jeff
Lockhart, James B.
Lovelace, Onzalo Robert
Marshall, Timothy H.
McFarlin, Emma Daniels
McGraw, Tom
Meeks, Perker L., Jr.
Minor, Jessica
Moore, Jane Bond
Morris, Effie Lee
Myatt, Gordon J.
Overstreet, Harry L.
Peeples, Darryl
Pierce, William Dallas
Poole, Cecil F.
Richard, R. Paul
Robinson, Effie
Sainte-Johnn, Don
Seidenberg, Mark
Sewell, Edward C.
Simmons, Ellamae
Smith, Frederick D.
Stallworth, Ann P.
Staples, Robert E.
Stennett, Renaldo Antonio
    (Rennie)
Stewart, John O.
Strange, Gerald Leon
Talbert, Melvin George
Tatmon, Eugene
Tatum, Carol Evora
Tipton, Dale Leo
Toler, Burl Abron
Walker, Ethel Pitts
Ward, Doris Margaret
Washington, Gene Alden
Washington, Kenneth S.
Watts, John E.
West, Gerald I.
Westbrook, Elouise
Williams, A. Cecil
Williams, Benjamin Vernon
Wilridge, Clarence
Wilson, Sodonia Mae
Young, Aner Ruth

SAN JOSE
Bass, Joseph Frank
Beasley, Ulysses Christian, Jr.
Carr, Percy L.
Clay, Harold R.
Cordell, La Doris Hazzard
Douglas, N. John
Gordon, Joseph G., II
Hutchins, Henry T.
Hyatt, Herman Wilbert, Sr.
Knowles, William W.
Lewis, Anthony Harold, Jr.
Martin, Edward Anthony
Newman, Nathaniel
Norman, Maidie Ruth (nee
    Gamble)

Pinkston, Moses Samuel
Powell, Wayne Hugh
Reede, James William, Jr.
Ridgeway, William C.
Terrell, Richard Warren
Warren, Lee Alden (Tico)
Williams, Iola (nee Craft)
Williams, Theopolis Charles

SAN LEANDRO
Vance, Tommie Rowan

SAN LUIS OBISPO
Cheek, Donald Kato
Taylor, Quintard, Jr.

SAN MATEO
Berry, Frederick Joseph
Brooks, Harry W., Jr.
McCullough, Frances Louise (nee
    Ford)
Turner, Melvin Duval

SAN PABLO
Boyd, Candy Dawson
Cash, Bettye Joyce (nee Moore)
Daniels, Patricia Ann

SAN PEDRO
Kennedy, Frederick A.

SAN RAFAEL
Anderson, Bruce Allan
Stephens, William Haynes
Times, Betty J.
Walden, Narada Michael

SAN RAMON
Merritt, Anthony Lewis

SANTA ANA
Doby, Allen E.
Fields, Earl Grayson
Johnson, Theodore A.
Owens-Smith, Joyce Latrell
Rhodes, Bessie M. L.
West, John Raymond

SANTA BARBARA
Keller, Edmond Joseph
McMillan, Horace James
Smith, James David

SANTA CLARA
Bell, Diana Lynne
Greene, Frank S., Jr.
Greene, Joann Lavina

SANTA CRUZ
Anthony, David Henry, III
Foreman, Doyle

SANTA MONICA
Coleman, Sinclair B.
Daniels, Clarence A., Jr.
Perry, Wayne D.
Porter, Arthur L.
Quinn, Alfred Thomas
Trives, Nathaniel

SANTA ROSA
Mims, Robert Bradford
Napper, James Wilbur
Snyder, George W.
Wells, Lawrence Leon

SARATOGA
Hutchinson, Chester R.

SEAL BEACH
Ray, Austin H.

SEASIDE
Lively, Ira J.
Polite, Theron Jerome

SEPULVEDA
Canty, Miriam Monroe

SHERMAN OAKS
DeAnda, Peter
McEachin, James

SOLEDAD
Pulley, Reginald

SOUTH BERKELEY
Burrell, Kenneth Earl

SOUTH GATE
Lara, Edison R., Sr.

SOUTH LAKE TAHOE
Banner, Melvin Edward

**SOUTH SAN
FRANCISCO**
Seymour, Cynthia Maria
Tipton, Dale Leo

STANFORD
Bagby, Rachel L
Bates, Clayton Wilson, Jr.
Bowser, Benjamin Paul
Davis, Noel Gregson
Drake, John Gibbs St. Clair, Jr.
Gould, William B.
Harris, Donald J.
Johnson, William A., II
Millis, David Howard
Reed, Kathleen Rand
Richards, Sandra Lee
Simmons, James E.
Sowell, Thomas
Wells, Linda Ivy

STOCKTON
George, Edward
Guyton, Booker T.
Jones, Theresa Mitchell
Lorthridge, James E.
Nabors, Jesse Lee, Sr.
Nunn, John, Jr.
Peters, Kenneth Darryl, Sr.
Robinson, Robert Love, Jr.
White, Ralph L.

STUDIO CITY
Bailey, Calvin

SUNNYVALE
Brooks, Gilbert
Douglas, Henley L.
Johnson, Garey A.
Murphy, Alvin Hugh
Smirni, Allan Desmond
Sutton, Mary A. (nee Sweet)
Virdure, Bernel B.
Waiters, Gail Elenoria

TARZANA
Jackson, Janet

TEMPLETON
Osibin, Willard S.

THOUSAND OAKS
Govan, Ronald M.

TORRANCE
Abraham, Guy Emmanuel
Douglas, Florence M.
Houze, Jeneice Carmel
Hurd, James L. P.
Lachman, Ralph Steven
Roney, Raymond G.
Shepard, Huey Percy
Thompson, Sandra Ann
Willis, Cecil B.

TUSTIN
Williams, Gregory M.

UNIVERSAL CITY
Brown, Bobby
Johnson, Charles Floyd
Knight, Bubba
LaBelle, Patti

VALLEJO
Bethel, Jesse Moncell, Sr.
Brown, Lewis Frank
Brown, Robert Cephas, Sr.
Ealey, Mark E.
Hodge, Lionel

McGowan, Thomas Randolph
Towns, Rose Mary

VAN NUYS
Amos, Wally
Johnson, Patricia Duren
Johnson, Rafer Lewis

VENICE
Hines, Gregory
Sklarek, Norma Merrick (Norma Merrick-Fairweather)

WALNUT
Ashford, Evelyn

WALNUT CREEK
White, Garland Anthony

WEST COVINA
Harrison, Boyd G., Jr.

WEST HOLLYWOOD
Clay, Stanley Bennett

WEST LOS ANGELES
Alexander, Josephine

WESTLAKE VILLAGE
Smith, William Fred
White, Major C.

WESTMINSTER
Davis, Donna P.

WHITTIER
Blakenship, Cheryl L.
Eaton, Thelma Lucile
Haynes, Ora Lee
Mendez, Hugh B.
Morris, Clifton

WILMINGTON
Carter, Ruth Durley
Edney, Steve

WOODLAND HILLS
Bush, Charles Vernon
Henry, Samuel Dudley
Mills, Stephanie
Porter, Gloria Jean
Smith, James Oscar (Jimmy)
Stevens, John Theodore, Sr.

COLORADO

AURORA
Battle, Charles E.
Irvin, Charles Leslie
Jordan, Janice Marie
Ray-Goins, Jeanette
Reed, Wilbur R.

BOULDER
Flowers, W. Harold, Jr.
Major, Clarence
Nilon, Charles Hampton
Person, Waverly J.

COLORADO SPRINGS
Bowen, Clotilde Dent
Bradshaw, Gerald Haywood
Clair, Areatha G. (nee Anderson)
Freeman, Kerlin, Jr.
Guy, Mildred Dorothy
Moses, Edwin
Peterson, Lloyd, Jr.
Shipp, Pamela Louise
Simpson, Norvell J. (James Arlington Simpson)
Turman, Robert L.
Walker, Maurice Edward
White, Harold Clark Mitchelle
Young, Leon

DENVER
Ashby, Lucius Antoine
Barefield, Ollie Delores
Borom, Lawrence H.
Bruton, Bertram A.
Caldwell, Elvin R.

Carter, Rubin
Chambers, Olivia Marie
Clark, Morris Shandell
Daniel, Wiley Young
Diallo
English, Alex
Fairman, John Abbrey
Gill, Samuel A.
Gipson, Bernard Franklin, Sr.
Glenn, Cecil E.
Gomez, Kevin Lawrence Johnson
Graham, LeRoy Maxwell, Jr.
Greer, Robert O., Jr.
Groff, Regis F.
Grove, Daniel
Hamilton, Paul L.
Harris, Freeman Cosmo
Haywood, Emmett L.
Hickman, Thomas Carlyle
Irvin, Charles Leslie
Jackson, Anna Mae
Jackson, Franklin D.B.
Jackson, Robert, Jr.
Jackson, Tom
Johnson, Collis, Jr.
Kennedy, Floyd C.
King, Talmadge Everett, Jr.
Little, Brian Keith
Livingston, Rudolph
Love, James Ralph
Lyle, Percy H., Jr.
McCleave, Mildred Atwood
Minor, Claudic Dee, Jr.
Moland, Willie E.
Moore, Lewis Calvin
Moses, Haven Christopher
Mosley, Edna Wilson
Mosley, John William
Owens, Lillie Anne
Page, Cedric Daniel
Phillips, Acen L.
Phillips, Earl W.
Posey, Bruce Keith
Pulley, Clyde Wilson
Ray-Goins, Jeanette
Reed, Wilbur R.
Reynolds, James F.
Richardson, Elisha R.
Rison, Faye Rison
Rollins, Ethel Eugenia
Saunders, Kenneth Paul
Simpson, Diane Jeannette
Smith, Dennis
Smith, Glenn R.
Smith, William French
Sprout, Francis Allen
Stewart, Paul Wilbur
Stitt, E. Don (Elliott D. Stitt)
Tanner, Gloria Travis
Tappan, Major William
Taylor, Paul David
Wayne, George Howard, Sr.
Webb, Wellington E.
West, Earl M.
Williams, Ronald Charles
Wright, Louis Donnel

ENGLEWOOD
Chavous, Barney Lewis
Clark, Morris Shandell
Ramsey, Jerome Capistrano

FAIRPLAY
Evans, Ada B.

FORT COLLINS
Hiatt, Dana Sims
Nayman, Robbie L.

GOLDEN
Brewer, Moses
Morgan-Smith, Sylvia
Riley, Charles Wilbur, Sr.
Strudwick, Lindsey H., Sr.

LAKEWOOD
Roy, Joe Eddie, Sr.

LONGMONT
Delaney, Howard C.

PUEBLO
Abebe, Teshome
Ballard, Walter W.
Poole, James F.
Wells, Elmer Eugene

CONNECTICUT

ANSONIA
Smoot, Albertha Pearl
Walker, Lula Aquillia

BERLIN
Springer, George Chelston

BETHEL
Rountree, Ella Jackson

BLOOMFIELD
Bennett, Bessye Warren
Coleman, Eric Dean
Martin, Ionis Bracy
Pierre, Gerald P.
Simmons, James E.
Thompson-Clemmons, Olga Unita (Olga Unita Jones)
Wood, Margaret Beatrice

BRIDGEPORT
Bellinger, George M.
Cheek, Robert Benjamin, III
Cromwell, Margaret M.
Eady, Mary E.
Elliott, Frank George
Fewell, Richard
Fountain, Venoal M., Sr.
Heyward, Don H.
Hunter, Patrick J.
Johnson, Wayne Lee
Prestwidge, Barbara Elizabeth
Spear, E. Eugene
Thomas, Nina M.
Williams, Joseph Henry

BRISTOL
Stewart, Bernard

CHESHIRE
Ferguson, Shellie Alvin

DANBURY
Anderson, Marian
Furman, James B.
Gellineau, Victor Marcel, Jr.
Stewart, Albert C.
Torian, Edward Torrence
Wilds, Constance T.

DARIEN
Parker, George Anthony
Williams, Melvin Thomas, Jr.

EAST HARTFORD
Freeman, Walter Eugene
Hamilton, James G.
Taylor, Kenneth Doyle

FAIRFIELD
Johnson, Alvin Roscoe
Merchant, John F.

FARMINGTON
Borges, Lynne MacFarlane
Savage, Archie Bernard, Jr.

GALES FERRY
Waterman, Thelma M.

GLASTONBURY
Powell, Charles P.

GREENWICH
Arnette, Dorothy Deanna
Brown, Nancy Cofield
Cureton, John Porter
Hill, Arthur Burit
Hollon, Herbert Holstein
Reed, Alfonzo
Wright, Dmitri

GROTON
Hamilton, Aubrey J.

GUILFORD
Thomas, Gerald Eustis

HAMDEN
Cherry, Edward Earl, Sr.
Garner, Charles
Hallums, Benjamin F.
Potts, Harold E.

HARTFORD
Anderson, Jacqueline Jones
Arnold, Rudolph P.
Banks, Arthur C., Jr.
Bartow, Jerome Edward
Bennett, Collin B.
Billington, Clyde, Jr.
Booker, Carl Granger, Sr.
Borges, Francisco L.
Brown, Richard M.
Brown, William J.
Bullock, Joseph Moses
Cornish, Betty W.
Crawford, Jayne Suzanne
Davis, Glendell Kirk
Dixon, Benjamin
Dyson, William Riley
Echols, Ivor Tatum
Edmonds, Norman Douglas
Fisher, Rubin Ivan
Geyer, Edward B., Jr.
Green, Arthur L.
Hales, William Roy
Harris, James G., Jr.
Hickmon, Ned
Hodgson-Brooks, Gloria J.
Hogan, James Carroll, Jr.
Hogan, John A.
Horn, Evelyn B.
Howard, Milton L.
Hoyt, Thomas L., Jr.
Hubbard, Hylan T., III
Lewis, Martin Richard, Jr.
Long, Steffan
Martin, Russell F.
Maule, Albert R.
McFarlin, Kernaa D'Offert, Jr.
Miller, James Arthur
Milner, Thirman L.
Mingo, Pauline Hylton
Monroe, James H.
Morgan-Welch, Beverly Ann
Morton, Margaret E.
Mosley, Maurice E.
Osborne, Ernest L.
Parker, Henry Ellsworth
Perry, Carrie Saxon
Peterson, Gerard M.
Putnam, Rosalind (nee Lawson)
Rawles, Elizabeth Gibbs
Rawlins, Sedrick John
Robinson, John E.
Rogers, Alfred R.
Simmons, John Emmett
Smalley, Paul
Smith, Frank Junius
Smith, Wilber Gene
Strong, Marilyn Terry

MADISON
Williams, Arthur G., Jr.

MIDDLETOWN
Beckham, Edgar Frederick
Biassey, Earle Lambert
Thornton, Clifford E.

MONROE
Prestwidge, Barbara Elizabeth

NEW BRITAIN
Collins, Constance Renee Wilson
Gaines, Edythe J.
Jones, Charles, Jr.
Morris, James F.
Robinson, John E.
Savage, Archie Bernard, Jr.
Springer, George Chelston
Stewart, William E. L.
Thompson, Winston Edna

GROTON
Hamilton, Aubrey J.

NEW HAVEN
Alexander, Dawn Criket
Alleyne, Winston A.
Barber, James W.
Blassingame, John W.
Bradley, Jessie Mary
Brown, Carroll Elizabeth
Chism, Virginia Lark
Comer, James Pierpont
Daniels, John C.
Days, Drew Saunders, III
Fraser, Earl W., Jr.
Gordon, Edmund W.
Greenlee, Robert Douglass
Griffith, Ezra Edward
Hamilton, William Nathan
Highsmith, Carlton L.
Holley, Sandra Cavanaugh
Holly, Ella Louise
Holmes, Willie A.
Ince, Harold S.
Jackson, William E.
Jaynes, Gerald David
Jones, Emma Pettway
Jones, Ernest
Jones, William
McCraven, Marcus R.
Newton, James Douglas, Jr.
Patton, Curtis L.
Pitts, William Henry
Price, Hugh Bernard
Richards, Lloyd G.
Robinson, Ann Garrett
Robinson, Charles E.
Slie, Samuel N.
Stepto, Robert Burns
Thompson, Robert Farris
Thorpe, Wesley Lee
Tucker, Leota Marie
Turner, Ricardo Cornelius, Sr.
Wade, Achille Melvin
Watley, Margaret Ann

NEW LONDON
Hampton, Robert L.
Hendricks, Barkley L.
Jackson, Leo Edwin
Jennings, Bennie Alfred
McKissick, Mabel F. Rice
Waller, Eunice McLean

NEWINGTON
Scott, R. Lee

NORTH HAVEN
Hogan, James Carroll, Jr.

NORWALK
Brown, Otha N., Jr.
Burgess, Robert E.
Coshburn, Henry S., Jr.
Maultsby, Sylvester
Reed, Derryl L.
Ross, Doris A.
Sanderson, Randy Chris
Wharton, Ferdinand D., Jr.
Williams, Shirley Yvonne
Wilson, Earl, Jr.

RIVERSIDE
Napper, Berenice Norwood

ROCKY HILL
Maule, Albert R.

SOUTH NORWALK
Burgess, Robert E.

SOUTH WINDSOR
Taylor, Kenneth Doyle

STAMFORD
Allen, Winston Earle
Arnette, Dorothy Deanna
Bridgett-Chisolm, Karen
Colbert, Thelma Quince
Cooper, Valerie Antionette
Dodds, R. Harcourt
Foreman, S. Beatrice

Wallace, Claudette J. (nee Delgado)
Wallace, Renee C.

Garnett, Ronald Leon
Gudger, Robert Harvey
Joell, Pamela S.
Johnson, Charles Edward
Jones, John L.
Levister, Robert L.
Merchant, John F.
Murray, J. Ralph
Rand, A. Barry
Rozier, Gilbert Donald
Stevenson, Sybil Jordan

STORRS
Adams, Frederick G.
Bagley, Peter B. E.
Bass, Floyd L.
Grant, Joseph N.
Lane, Eleanor Tyson
Peters, James Sedalia, II
Spivey, Donald
Terry, Angela Owen

STORRS-MANSFIELD
Bell-Scott, Patricia

TORRINGTON
Atkinson, Charles N.
Lyons, A. Bates

UNCASVILLE
White, Quitman, Jr.

VERNON
Alexander, Errol D.
Lane, Eleanor Tyson

VERNON-ROCKVILLE
Johnson, Arthur Lyman
Johnson, Marie Love

WATERBURY
Glass, Robert Davis
Pearce, Richard Allen

WATERFORD
Kimmons, Carl Eugene

WEST HARTFORD
Martin, Arnold Lee, Jr.
McLean, John Lenwood

WEST HAVEN
Hodgson, Carlton Roy
Slie, Samuel N.

WESTON
Haynes, Ulric St. Clair, Jr.

WESTPORT
Ford, Gary L.

WETHERSFIELD
Saunders, John Edward, III

WILLIMANTIC
Carter, David G., Sr.
Peagler, Owen F.

WILTON
Halliburton, Warren J.

WINDHAM CENTER
Terry, Angela Owen

WINDSOR
Cave, Perstein Ronald
Echols, Ivor Tatum
Freeman, Walter Eugene
Johnson, Wayne Lee

WINDSOR LOCKS
Thaxton, Judy Evette

WOLCOTT
Evans, William E.

WOODBRIDGE
Anderson, Bryan N.
Cherry, Edward Earl, Sr.

DELAWARE

DOVER
Adams, Eva W.
Caldwell, M. Milford
Caldwell, Marion Milford, Jr.
Coleman, Rudolph W.
DeLauder, William B.
Farrow, Willie Lewis
Ford, Nancy Howard
Hardcastle, James C.
Harris, Winifred Clarke
Henderson, Romeo Clanton
Hudson, Clenora Frances
Johnson, Vaughn Arzah
Jones, Geraldine J.
Laws, Ruth M.
McKinney, Theophilus Elisha, Jr.
McPhail, Irving P.
Minus, Homer Wellington
Showell, Hazel Jarmon
Tisdale, Henry Nehemiah
Wardlaw, McKinley, Jr.

FELTON
Tisdale, Henry Nehemiah

GEORGETOWN
Jones, Albert J.

HOCKESSIN
Bolen, David B.
Faulcon, Clarence Augustus, II
Whaley, Wayne Edward

LAUREL
Selby, Cora Norwood

MILTON
Batten, Grace Ruth

NEW CASTLE
Rudd, James M.

NEWARK
Daniel, Alfred Irwin
Hull, Gloria T.
Johnson, Marguerite M.
Jones, James McCoy
Meade, Alston B.
Newton, James E.
Whittaker, Terry McKinley

SEAFORD
Johnson, William Smith

SMYRNA
Wright, George C., Jr.

WILMINGTON
Alford, Haile Lorraine
Beckett, Sydney A.
Brown, Rodney W.
Cannon, Eugene Nathaniel
Carey, Claire Lamar
Carey, Harmon Roderick
Ford, Evern D.
Gaynor, Florence S.
Gilliam, James H., Jr.
Gilliam, James H., Sr.
Haskins, James W., Jr.
Holloway, Herman M., Sr.
Huff, Louis Andrew
Johnson, Joseph Edward
Lockman, Norman Alton
Mack, Sylvia Jenkins
Martin, Joshua Wesley, III
McMillian, Frank L.
Miles, Kenneth L.
Mitchell, Charles E.
Mobley, Joan Thompson
Nix, Theophilus Richard
Redding, Louis L.
Revelle, Robert, Sr.
Rivers, David Lawrence
Roberts, Harlan William, III
Sanders, Gwendolyn W.
Savage, Dennis James
Sogah, Dotsevi Y.
Wiggins, Leslie
Woodson, Tracy Todd
Wyche, Paul H., Jr.

DISTRICT OF COLUMBIA

WASHINGTON
Abney, Robert
Abramson, Frederick Bruce
Adair, Alvis V.
Adams, Alice Omega
Adams, James Malcolm
Adams, Russell Lee
Adeyiga, Olanrewaju Muniru
Aggrey, O. Rudolph
Ahart, Thomas I.
Alexander, Benjamin Harold
Alexander, Clifford L., Jr.
Alexander, Lenora Cole
Alexander, Robert L.
Alexander-Whiting, Harriett
Alexis, Carlton Peter
Alfonso, Pedro
Alfred, Rayfield
Allen, Anita Ford
Allen, Benjamin P., III
Allen, Bernestine
Allen, Stanley M.
Allen, Willie B.
Ammons, Tamara Nash
Amos, Kent B.
Ampy, Franklin R.
Anders, Corrie Michael
Anderson, Arnett Artis
Anderson, Carl D.
Anderson, Carl Edwin
Anderson, Carol Byrd
Anderson, Mary Elizabeth
Anderson, William A.
Archer, Juanita A.
Archibald, B. Milele
Arnez, Nancy L.
Arrington, Henry Terrell
Arties, Elvira Yvonne
Artisst, Robert Irving
Ashford, Laplois
Ashton, Vivian Christina R.
Atkinson, Lewis K.
Attaway, John David
Auld, Albert Michael
Auld, Rose A.
Austin, Bobby William
Avent, Jacques Myron
Babb, Valerie M.
Bain, Raymone Kaye
Baker, Eugene
Baker, Moorean Ann
Baker, Willie L., Jr.
Baltimore, Richard Lewis, III
Banks, Carl A.
Banks, Priscilla Sneed
Banks, Sharon P.
Banks, Tazewell
Banks, Terry Michael
Banks, William Jasper, Jr.
Barber, Jesse B., Jr.
Barksdale Hall, Roland C.
Barnes, Boisey O.
Barrett, Matthew Anderson
Barry, Marion S., Jr.
Bass, Josie A.
Bates, Robert E., Jr.
Battle, Thomas Cornell
Baxter, Albert James, II
Beard, Lillian McLean
Becton, Julius Wesley, Jr.
Bell, Alexander F.
Bell, Theron J.
Bell, William McKinley
Belton, Howard G.
Benjamin, Donald S.
Benjamin, Tritobia Hayes
Bennett, Bobby
Bernstine, Daniel O.
Berry, Mary Frances
Berry, Paul Lawrence
Berryman, Matilene S.
Bessent, Hattie
Besson, Paul Smith
Billings, Christine D.
Bing, Rubell M.
Bins, Milton
Bishop, David Rudolph
Black, Charlie J.
Black, Frederick Harrison
Black, Wendell C.

Blakey, William A.
Blankenship, Glenn Rayford
Blunt, Roger Reckling
Boghossian, Skunder
Bolden, Betty A.
Bolden, Charles E.
Bolton, Ron
Bond, Horace Julian (Julian Bond)
Booker, Simeon S.
Boone, Raymond Harold
Boschulte, Joseph Clement
Bothuel, Ethel C.S.
Boulware, Patricia A.
Bowles, Howard Roosevelt
Boyd, George Arthur
Boyd, Ruth R. (Reid)
Boykin, A. Wade, Jr.
Bradford, Arvine M.
Bradford, Charles Edward
Brady, Charles A.
Braithwaite, Gordon L.
Brantley, Edward J.
Bremer, Charles E.
Brewington, Rudolph W.
Bridges, Lucille W.
Bridgewater, Albert Louis
Brimmer, Andrew F.
Brittain, Bradley Bernard, Jr.
Britton, John H., Jr.
Britton, Theodore R., Jr.
Broadnax, Madison
Brockington, Donella P.
Brockington, Eugene Alfonzo
Brooke, Edward W.
Brooks, Bernard W.
Brooks, Charlotte Kendrick
Brooks, Leo Austin
Brooks, William C.
Brown, A. Sue
Brown, Barbara Ann
Brown, Cyril H.
Brown, Herman
Brown, John Scott
Brown, Leroy J. H.
Brown, Linda Jenkins
Brown, Robert J., III
Brown, Robert Joe
Brown, Ronald H.
Brown, Ronald Harmon
Brown, Warren Aloysius
Brown, Wesley Anthony
Brown, William, Jr.
Brown, William H.
Browne, David A.
Browne, Robert Span
Browne, Vincent J.
Brownlee, Vivian Aplin
Bryant, Cunningham C.
Bryant, Donnie L.
Bryant, Robert Edward
Bryant, William B.
Bullock, J. Jerome
Bullock, William Horace
Bundles, A'Lelia Perry
Bunton, Henry Clay
Burnett, Arthur Louis, Sr.
Burnett, Luther C.
Burroughs, John Andrew, Jr.
Burrus, William Henry
Burton, Joan E.
Bush, Mary K.
Bush, Nathaniel
Butcher, Goler Teal
Byrd, Jerry Stewart
Cain, Simon Lawrence
Calbert, William Edward
Calhoun, Cecelia C.
Calhoun, John
Calhoun, Lee A.
Calhoun, Noah Robert
Calhoun, Thomas
Callender, Clive Orville
Callender, Valerie Dawn
Cambosos, Bruce Michael
Cameron, Howard K., Jr.
Cameron, Ulysses
Campbell, Bobby Lamar
Cantwell, Kathleen Gordon
Carey, James William
Carey, Milton Gales
Carnell, Lougenia Littlejohn
Carpenter, William Arthur, II
Carrington, Christine H.

Carruthers, George Robert
Carter, Chester C.
Carter, Lisle Carleton, Jr.
Carter, William Beverly, III
Carter, Yvonne P.
Caster, Caroleigh Tuitt
Celestin, Toussaint A.
Chapman, Joseph Conrad, Jr.
Cheatham, Betty L.
Cheek, James E.
Childs, Winston
Chisholm, Joseph Carrel, Jr.
Chisholm, Reginald Constantine
Chism, Harolyn B.
Chivis, Martin Lewis
Clark, Charles Warfield
Clark, Gary
Clark, LaWanna Gibbs
Clark, Ronald C.
Clark, Savanna M. Vaughn
Clarke, Fletcher James
Clay, William L.
Clipper, Milton Clifton, Jr.
Cloud, Eric William
Clyburn, John B.
Coffey, Gilbert Haven, Jr.
Cohen, Vincent H.
Cole, Arthur
Cole, Curtis, Jr.
Cole, Joseph H.
Coleman, William T., Jr.
Collie, Kelsey E.
Collins, Cardiss
Collins, William Keelan
Conley, Herbert A.
Conner, Lucy Shull
Conyers, John, Jr.
Cook, Frank Robert, Jr.
Cook, Harold J.
Cook, Joyce Mitchell
Cooks, Stoney
Cooper, Barbara Jean
Cooper, Clement Theodore
Cooper, Ernest, Jr.
Cooper, Gary T.
Cooper, Maudine R.
Corley-Saunders, Angela Rose
Coulon, Burnel Elton
Cox, DuBois V.
Cox, Georgetta Manning
Crawford, Betty Marilyn
Crawford, Charles L.
Crawford, Hazle R.
Crawford, Vanella Alise
Crew, Spencer R.
Crocker, Cyril L.
Crockett, Edward D., Jr.
Cropp, Dwight Sheffery
Cruise, Warren Michael
Crump, William L.
Cruz, Iluminado Angeles
Culpepper, Betty M.
Cunningham, Blenna A.
Curry, Sadye Beatryce
Dalley, George Albert
Darden, Orlando William
Darling, Marsha Jean
Dash, Leon DeCosta, Jr.
Davenport, Chester C.
Davenport, Lawrence Franklin
Davis, Arthur Paul
Davis, Bobby
Davis, Christine R.
Davis, Howard C.
Davis, Jean M.
Davis, Jerry, Jr.
Davis, Johnetta Garner
Davis, Patricia Staunton
Davis, Preston Augustus
Davis, Shirley E.
Davis, Steve G.
Davis, Walter G.
Davis, William L.
Davison, Frederic E.
Dawson, Horace Greeley, Jr.
Day, Daniel Edgar
Deane, Robert Armistead
Delaney, Harold
Delaney, Willi
Dendy, Tometta
Dennery, Phyllis Armelle
DePriest, Oscar Stanton, III
Dessaso-Gordon, Janice Marie
DeVaughn, Edward Raymond

Devrouax, Paul S., Jr.
Diaw, Rosemary K.
Dickens, Doris Lee (Mrs. Austin L. Fickling)
Dickerson, Glenda J.
Dillard, Martin Gregory
Dillon, Owen C.
Dilworth, Mary Elizabeth
Dixon, Arrington Liggins
Dixon, Julian C.
Dixon, Sharon Pratt
Donaldson, Jeff R.
Donegan, Charles Edward
Dorman, Hattie L.
Doss, Lawrence Paul
Dotson, Betty Lou
Dowdell, Kevin Crawford
Downing, John William, Jr.
Driver, Elwood T.
Dudley, Godfrey D.
Dudley-Smith, Carolyn J.
Duke, Leslie Dowling, Sr.
Dukes, Ofield
Duncan, Charles Tignor
Duncan, Louis Davidson, Jr.
Duncan, Robert Todd
DuPree, David
Dupree, David H.
Durham, William R.
Dymally, Mervyn M.
Ealey, Adolphus
Eaton, David Hilliard
Eaton, Patricia Frances
Edelin, Ramona Hoage
Edelman, Marian Wright
Edwards, Cecile Hoover
Edwards, Harry T.
Edwards, Sylvia
Elder, Robert Lee (Lee Elder)
Elmore, Joyce A.
English, Richard A.
Epps, Charles Harry, Jr.
Epps, Roselyn Payne
Estep, Roger D.
Ethridge, Samuel B.
Eubanks, John Bunyan
Evans, Dorsey
Evans-McNeill, Elona Anita
Everett, Ralph B.
Fagin, Darryl Hall
Fairley, Richard L.
Farmer, Francesta Elizabeth
Fauntleroy, John Douglass, Sr.
Fauntroy, Walter E.
Feggans, Edward L.
Feliciana, Jerrye Brown
Felton, Zora Belle
Ferguson, George A.
Ferguson, Johnnie Nathaniel
Fields, Samuel Bennie
Fisher, Edward G.
Fitzgerald, William B.
Flack, Harley Eugene
Flake, Floyd H.
Flake, Nancy Aline
Fleming, Patricia Stubbs
Fomufod, Antoine Kofi
Ford, Antoinette
Ford, Claudette Franklin
Ford, Harold E.
Ford, Kenneth A.
Fowler, William E., Jr.
Fox, Richard K., Jr.
Francis, E. Aracelis
Francis, Henry Minton
Franklin, Dolores Mercedes
Franks, Everlee Gordon
Freeman, Preston Garrison
Freeman, Robert Turner, Jr.
French, MaryAnn
Fry, Louis Edwin, Jr.
Funderburk, William Watson
Futrell, Mary Hatwood
Gaffney, Mary Louise
Gaillard, Bernard
Gaither, Dorothy B.
Gant, Wanda Adele
Garrett, Thaddeus, Jr.
Gary, Lawrence Edward
Gaston, Linda Saulsby
Gaston, Mack Charles
Gatewood, Lucian B.
Gayle, Lucille Jordan
Gayton, Gary D.

Gee, William Rowland, Jr.
George, Theodore Roosevelt, Jr.
Gerald, Melvin Douglas
Gibson, Ernest Robinson
Gibson, Reginald Walker
Gidney, Calvin L.
Gillam, Isaac Thomas, IV
Gilliam, Arleen Fain
Gilliam, Dorothy Butler
Gilliam, Sam, Jr.
Gilmore, Al Tony
Gipson, Francis E.
Gist, Lewis Alexander, Jr.
Gittens, James Philip
Gladden, Brenda Winckler
Gladden, Major P.
Glasgow, Douglas G.
Glaude, Stephen A.
Gloster, John Gaines
Godwin, I. Lamond
Golden, Donald Leon
Goldson, Alfred Lloyd
Gomillion, Charles Goode
Goodson, Annie Jean
Graham, Michael Angelo
Grant, Nathaniel
Grantley, Robert Clark
Graves, Curtis M.
Gray, Edward Wesley, Jr.
Gray, Wilfred Douglas
Gray, William H., III
Green, Darrell
Green, Ernest G.
Green, Frederick Chapman
Green, Robert L.
Green, Sterling
Green, Wallace Orphesus
Greene, Grace Randolph
Greene, Horace F.
Greenfield, Eloise
Greenfield, Robert Thomas, Jr.
Greenlee, Peter Anthony
Gregory, Henry C., III
Griffin, Gerald
Griffith, Reginald Wilbert
Grigsby, Margaret Elizabeth
Grigsby, Marshall C.
Guiton, Bonnie
Haden, Mabel D.
Hager, Joseph C.
Hailes, Edward A.
Hairston, Eddison R., Jr.
Haley, George Williford Boyce
Halyard, Michele Yvette
Hamilton, Edwin
Hamilton, Richard Nathaniel
Hammond, Kenneth T.
Hampton, Delon
Hampton, Ronald Everett
Hanson, Charles M., Jr.
Hardman-Cromwell, Youtha Cordella
Hardy, Willie J.
Hargrave, Charles William
Hargrave, Thomas Burkhardt, Jr.
Harkins, Rosemary Knighton
Harper, Bernice Catherine
Harps, William S.
Harrington, Charles E.
Harris, Bryant G.
Harris, Charles F.
Harris, Charles Wesley
Harris, DeLong
Harris, Gary Lynn
Harris, Geraldine E.
Harris, James A.
Harris, Marion Hopkins
Harris, Melvin
Harris, Norman W., Jr.
Harris, Robert F.
Harris, William H., Jr.
Harris, William J.
Hart, Christopher Alvin
Hawkins, Augustus F.
Hawkins, John Russell, III
Hayes, Charles A.
Hayes, Edward, Jr.
Hayward, Jacqueline C.
Haywood, Hiram H., Jr.
Haywood, Margaret A.
Hedgepath, Leslie Eugene
Height, Dorothy I.
Hemphill, Gwendolyn
Henderson, D. Rudolph

Henderson, Eddie L.
Henderson, Elmer W.
Henderson, James Robert
Henderson, Stephen E.
Hendricks, Beatrice E.
Henry, Brent Lee
Henry, Walter Lester, Jr.
Herndon, Craig Garris
Hicks, H. Beecher, Jr.
Hill, Cynthia D.
Hill, Sylvia Ione-Bennett
Hill, Wendell T., Jr.
Hillman, Gracia
Hobson, Robert R.
Hodges, Clarence Eugene
Hogans, William Robertson, III
Holland, Ethel M.
Holliday, Bertha Garrett
Holloway, Anne Forrester
Holmes, Dorothy E.
Holsendolph, Ernest
Hooks, Roland
Hopkins, Ernest Loyd
Horad, Sewell D., Sr.
Hord, Frederick Lee
Horton, James T.
Hosten, Adrian
House, James E.
Howard, Dalton J., Jr.
Howze, Karen Aileen
Hoyte, Arthur Hamilton
Hudson, Robert L.
Hudson, William Thomas
Hughes, Anita Lillian
Hughes, Catherine Liggins
Hughes, Harvey L.
Hull, Everson Warren
Hunt, Isaac Cosby, Jr.
Hunter, Frances S. (nee Kraft)
Hunter, Gertrude T.
Hunter, Jerry L.
Hurt, Louis T., Sr.
Hussein, Carlessia Amanda
Hutchinson, Louise Daniel
Hutton, Marilyn Adele
Hyde, William R.
Iglehart, Lloyd D.
Ingram, Earl Girardeau
Irving, Clarence Larry, Jr.
Isaacs, Stephen D.
Ivery, James A.
Jackson, Charles N., II
Jackson, Edgar Newton, Jr.
Jackson, Frederick
Jackson, James Talmadge
Jackson, Jesse Louis
Jackson, Keith Hunter
Jackson, Leroy Anthony, Jr.
Jackson, Marvin Alexander
Jackson, Maxie C.
Jackson, Norlishia A.
Jackson, Raymond T.
Jackson, Ronald G.
Jacobs, Patricia Dianne
James, Clarence L., Jr.
Jefferson-Moss, Carolyn
Jenkins, Howard, Jr.
Jenkins, Melvin E., Jr.
Jenkins, Ozella
Jenkins, Robert Kenneth, Jr.
Jenkins, Thomas O.
Jeter, Clifton B., Jr.
Jeter, Thomas Elliott
Johns, Michael Earl
Johnson, Calvin P.
Johnson, Edward M.
Johnson, F. J., Jr.
Johnson, Gregory Wayne
Johnson, James Walter, Jr.
Johnson, Johnnie L., Jr.
Johnson, Lloyd A.
Johnson, Lorraine Jefferson
Johnson, Mal
Johnson, Norma Holloway
Johnson, R. Benjamin
Johnson, Richard Howard
Johnson, Robert L.
Johnson, Ronald Cornelius
Johnson, Roosevelt Young
Johnson, William Paul, Jr. (Scoogie)
Johnson, Wyneva
Johnson-Crockett, Mary Alice
Jones, Alexander R.

Jones, Clifton Ralph
Jones, George W.
Jones, George Williams
Jones, Gerald Winfield
Jones, Hardi Liddell
Jones, James C.
Jones, Kelsey A.
Jones, Lawrence N.
Jones, Leonade Diane
Jones, Lois Mailou
Jones, Roscoe T., Jr.
Jones, Roy Junios
Jones, Sidney Alexander
Jones, Thomas L.
Jones, William Bowdoin
Jordan, Carolyn D.
Jordan, Ralph
Joseph, James Alfred
Joy, James Bernard, Jr.
Kearse, Gregory Sashi
Keith, Doris T.
Kelly, John Paul, Jr.
Kemp, C. Robert
Kendall, Robert, Jr.
Kendrix, Moss H., Sr.
Kennedy, Henry Harold, Jr.
Kerr, Hortense R.
Kersey, B. Franklin, IV
Keyser, George F.
Kinard, Helen Madison Marie Pawne
King, Colbert I.
King, Gwendolyn
King, Patricia Ann
King, Ruby E.
Kirkland, Gail Alicia
Knight, Robert S.
Kuykendall, Crystal Arlene
Kyle, Aaron
Lacey, Wilbert, Jr.
Laing, Edward A.
Lambert, Rollins Edward
Land, Georgianna Anderson
Landry, Dolores Branche
Landry, Lawrence Aloysius
Lang-Jeter, Lula L.
Lanier, Horatio Axel
Larkins, William Conyers
Latcholia, Kenneth Edward
Latimer, Allie B. (Alice Latimer Weeden)
Lavender, Joe
Lawson, Marjorie McKenzie
Lawson, Quentin Roosevelt
Lawyer, Cyrus J., III
Layton, William W.
Leace, Donal Richard
Leak, Lee Virn
Ledbetter, Ruth Pope
Lee, Bernard Scott
Lee, Debra Louise
Lee, Norvel L. R.
Lee, William Ronnell
Lee-Miller, Stephanie
Leeke, John F.
Leffall, LaSalle Doheny, Jr.
Leftwich, Norma Bogues
Leftwich, Willie L.
LeGrand, Etienne Randall
Leland, Joyce F.
Lemmons, Herbert Michael
Leonard, Walter J.
Lewis, Colston A.
Lewis, Delano Eugene
Lewis, Diane Claire
Lewis, John Robert
Lewis, Matthew, Jr.
Lewis, William A., Jr.
Lightfoot, Jean Drew
Lightfoote, William Edward, II
Lindsey, Jerome W.
Lipscomb, Emanuel A.
Lloyd, Raymond Anthony
Lloyd, Wanda (nee Smalls)
Lockhart-Moss, Eunice Jean
Lovelace, Gloria Elaine
Loving, James Leslie
Lowe, Hazel Marie
Lowe, Richard Bryant, III
Lucas, William
Luck, Etta Robena
Lucy, William
Mack, Gladys Walker
Mack, John L.

Mack, Julia Cooper
Mack, Voyce J.
Madison, Alfreda Louise
Madison, Eddie L., Jr.
Majors, Edith Sara
Malveaux, Floyd
Manley, Albert
Manley, Audrey Forbes
Manley, Dexter
Mann, Marion
Marbury, Donald Lee
Marchman, Robert Anthony
Marshall, Charles H.
Marshall, Etta Marie-Imes
Marshall, Pluria W., Sr.
Marshall, Thurgood
Marshall, Thurgood, Jr.
Martin, Bertha M.
Martin, Curtis Jerome
Martin, Harold B.
Martin, Louis E.
Martin, Richard Cornish
Martin, Sylvia Cooke
Mason, DaCosta V.
Mason, Howard Keith
Matney, William C., Jr.
Matory, Deborah Love
Matthews, Claude Lankford, Jr.
Matthews, Cynthia Clark
Matthews, LaMoyne Mason
Maultsby, Dorothy M.
Mauney, Donald Wallace, Jr.
Mayes, McKinley
Mazique, Frances Margurite (nee Belafonte)
McAdoo, Harriette P.
McAlpine, Robert
McCants, Coolidge N.
McClain, Dorothy Mae (nee Hunter)
McCloud, Thomas Henry
McClurkin, Johnson Thomas
McCollough, Walter
McCray, Joe Richard
McCray, Maceo E.
McDaniels, Orrin Hunter
McDonald, Herbert G.
McDowell-Head, Lelia M.
McGee, James Madison
McGinty, Doris Evans
McIntosh, Simeon Charles
McKee, Clarence Vanzant
McKelpin, Joseph P.
McKenzie, Floretta D.
McKinney, Rufus William
McKinney, Wade H., III
McLaren, Douglas Earl
McLaughlin, David
McLaughlin, Joseph C.
McMorris, Jacqueline Williams
McWilliams, James D.
McZier, Arthur
Mercer, William A.
Mickle, Andrea Denise
Middleton, Michael A.
Miles, Carlotta G.
Miles, Willie Leanna
Miller, E. Ethelbert
Miller, George Carroll, Jr.
Miller, Jeanne-Marie A.
Miller, Lawrence Edward
Miller, M. Sammye
Miller, Russell L., Jr.
Mims, Oscar Lugrie
Miner, William Gerard
Mintz, Reginold Lee
Mitchell, B. Doyle
Mitchell, Iverson O., III
Mitchell, Melvin Lester
Mitchell, Parren James
Mitchell, William Grayson
Mobley, Stacey J.
Monk, Art
Moody, Yvonne K.
Moore, Alstork Edward
Moore, Evelyn K.
Moore, Jerry A., Jr.
Moose, George E.
Moragne, Lenora
Morgan, Alice Johnson Parham
Morris, Archie, III
Morris, Calvin S.
Morrison, James W., Jr.
Morrison, Keith Anthony

Morrison, Trudi Michelle
Morse, Mildred (nee Sharpe)
Mortimer, Delores M.
Mosee, Jean C.
Moseley, Barbara M.
Moses, Alice J.
Mosley, Elwood A.
Mouton, Charles Peter
Muhammad, Askiaa
Murphy, Beatrice M. (Beatrice Murphy Campbell)
Murphy, Frances L., II (Mrs. Charles J. Campbell)
Murphy, George B., Jr.
Murray, James Hamilton
Mutcheruon, James Albertus, Jr.
Myers, Ernest Ray
Myers, Frances Althea
Myers, Samuel L.
Nash, Curtis
Nash, Daniel Alphonza, Jr.
Nash, Eva L.
Neal, Eddie
Neely, Henry Mason
Nelson, Charles J.
Nelson, Richard Y., Jr.
Newman, Debra Lynn
Newman, Theodore Roosevelt, Jr.
Newsome, Clarence Geno
Newton, Robin Caprice
Nichols, Sylvia A.
Niles, Lyndrey Arnaud
Norman, Moses C.
Norrell-Thomas, Sondra
Norton, Edward Worthington
Norton, Eleanor Holmes
Nutall, James Edward
Oates, Wanda Anita
Onyejekwe, Chike Onyekachi
Ottley, Neville
Owens, Brigman
Owens, C. Burgess
Owens, David K.
Owens, Joan Murrell
Owens, Major R.
Owens, Robert Leon, III
Oyewole, Saundra Herndon
Palmer, Darlene Tolbert
Palmer, Ronald DeWayne
Parker, Averette Mhoon
Parker, Barrington A.
Parker, David Russell
Patterson, Barbara Ann
Patterson, Elizabeth Hayes
Payne, Ethel Lois
Payton, Carolyn Robertson
Payton, Willis Conwell
Peagler, Frederick Douglass
Peery, Benjamin Franklin, Jr.
Peirson, Gwynne Walker
Penn, John Garrett
Perkins, Edward Joseph
Perry, June Carter
Perry, Yvonne Scruggs
Perryman, Lavonia Lauren
Peters, Aulana Louise
Peterson, Sushila Jane-Clinton
Pettus-Bellamy, Brenda Karen
Petty, Bruce Anthony
Petty, Rachel Monteith
Petty, Reginald E.
Phillip, White, III
Phillips, Frederick Brian
Picott, J. Rupert
Pierce, Reuben G.
Pierce, Samuel R., Jr.
Pinckney, Theodore R.
Pinkett, Harold Thomas
Pinson, Thomas J.
Pinson, Valerie F.
Pitts, M. Henry
Poindexter, Hildrus A.
Pointer, Richard H.
Polk, Lorna Marie
Pollard, Emily Frances
Pope, Henry
Pope, James M.
Porter, Ellis N.
Poussaint, Renee Francine
Powell, Adam Clayton, III
Powell, Colin L.
Powell, Georgette Seabrooke
Powell, Juan Herschel
Press, Harry Cody, Jr.

Pride, John L.
Puckrein, Gary Alexander
Quander, Rohulamin
Quarrelles, James Ivan
Quick, R. Edward
Quinn, Diane C.
Quinton, Barbara A.
Quivers, Eric Stanley
Ragland, Sherman Leon, II
Randolph, Bernard P.
Rangel, Charles B.
Rankin, Edward Anthony
Raspberry, William J.
Ray, David Bruce
Reed, Vincent Emory
Reed-Miller, Rosemary E.
Reeves, Willie Lloyd, Jr.
Reid, Inez Smith
Reid, Leslie Bancroft
Reinhardt, John Edward
Rhoden, Richard Allan
Rhodes, Paula R.
Ricanek, Carolyn Wright
Rice, Cora Lee
Rice, David Eugene, Jr.
Rice, Emmett J.
Rice, Haynes
Rice, Lois Dickson (nee Dickson)
Richardson, Robert Eugene
Richie, Sharon Ivey
Rier, John Paul, Jr.
Risher, John R., Jr.
Rivero, Marita Joy (Marita Muhammad)
Rivers, David Eugene
Roane, Philip Ransom, Jr.
Roberts, James E.
Roberts, Talmadge
Robinson, Aubrey Eugene, Jr.
Robinson, Harry G., III
Robinson, Jacqueline J.
Robinson, Leonard Harrison, Jr.
Robinson, Marilyn Patricia
Robinson, Peter Lee, Jr.
Robinson, Randall
Robinson, Rose Miles
Robinson, Spottswood William, III
Roe, Audrey R.
Rogers, Elijah Baby
Rogers, Michael Charles
Rogers, Norman
Rolark, Calvin W.
Rolle, Albert Eustace
Roscoe, Wilma J.
Rose, Raymond E.
Ross, Frank Kenneth
Rosser, Samuel Blanton
Rotan, Constance S.
Roux, Vincent J.
Rowan, Carl Thomas
Russell, Ernest
Saffel, E. Frank
Sampson, Calvin Coolidge
Samuels, Annette Jacqueline
Sanders, Charles Lionel
Sanders, Rober LaFayette
Saunders, Edward Howard
Saunders, Mauderie Hancock
Savage, Augustus A.
Savage, James Edward, Jr.
Scales, Patricia Bowles
Scott, Aundrea Arthur
Scott, Elsie L.
Scott, Nigel L.
Scott, Roland B.
Seabrooks-Edwards, Marilyn S.
Seagears, Margaret Jacqueline
Secundy, Marian Gray
Sewell, Isiah Obediah
Shakoor, Waheedah Aqueelah (Sandra Short Roberson)
Shaw, Bernard
Shaw, Talbert Oscall
Shelby, Reginald W.
Shell, Theodore A.
Shelton, Edward E.
Shopshire, James Maynard
Short, James Edward
Shuman, Jerome
Silva, Omega C. Logan
Simmons, Althea T.L.
Simmons, Belva Tereshia
Simmons, Joseph Jacob, III

Simmons, Samuel J.
Simms, Margaret Constance
Simpkins, William Joseph
Simpson, Carole
Simpson, Donnie
Sindler, Michael H.
Singleton, Harry M.
Sinnette, Calvin Herman
Sloan, Edith Barksdale
Smalls, Jacquelyn Elaine
Smalls, O'Neal
Smith, Alfred J., Jr.
Smith, Beverly Evans
Smith, Carol J. (Carol J. Hobson)
Smith, Carolyn Lee
Smith, Chester B.
Smith, Cleveland Emanuel
Smith, Conrad P.
Smith, Eddie Glenn, Jr.
Smith, Edward Nathaniel, Jr.
Smith, J. Clay, Jr.
Smith, Janice Evon
Smith, Joseph F.
Smith, Judith Moore
Smith, Lafayette Kenneth
Smith, Marietta Culbreath
Smith, Patricia G.
Smith, Philip Meek
Smythe-Haith, Mabel Murphy
Sockwell, Oliver R., Jr.
Solomon, Wilbert F.
Spaulding, William Ridley
Speight, Eva B.
Speights, Nathaniel H.
Spencer, Michael Gregg
Spriggs, Ray V.
Spurlock, Jeanne
Spurlock, Langley Augustine
Stamps, Herman Franklin
Standard, Raymond Linwood
Stebbins, Dana Brewington
Stent, Michelle Dorene
Stephenson, Allan Anthony
Stewart, Imogene Bigham
Stewart, Ruth Ann
Stockton, Barbara Marshall
Stokes, Gerald Virgil
Stokes, Louis
Strait, George Alfred, Jr.
Street, Anne A.
Strudwick, Warren James
Stuart, Reginald A.
Sturdivant, John Nathan
Suneja, Sudhir Kumar
Sutton, Dianne Floyd
Syphax, Burke
Tate, Merze
Tatem, Patricia Ann
Taylor, Arnold H.
Taylor, Charley R.
Taylor, Estelle Wormley
Taylor, Mildred E. Crosby
Taylor, Patricia Tate
Taylor, William L.
Tearney, Russell James
Teele, Arthur Earle, Jr.
Temple, Donald Melvin
Terrell, Henry Matthew
Terrell, Mary Ann
Thaxton, June Evonne
Thomas, Carol M.
Thomas, Clarence
Thomas, Eunice S.
Thomas, James O., Jr.
Thomas, Janis P.
Thomas, Joan McHenry Bates
Thomas, Juanita Ware (Juanita Glee Ware)
Thomas, Ralph Charles, III
Thomas, Waddell Robert
Thomas-Bowlding, Harold Clifton
Thompson, Carol Belita
Thompson, Daniel Joseph
Thompson, Deborah Maria
Thompson, Jeffrey Earl
Thompson, John Robert, Jr.
Thompson, Linda Jo
Thompson, Portia Wilson
Thompson, Willie Edward
Thornell, Richard Paul
Thornton, Wayne T.
Thurston, Roger Grave
Tilghman, Cyprian O.
Touchstone, John E.

Toussaint, Rose-Marie
Towns, Edolphus
Towns, Eva Rose
Trapp-Dukes, Rosa Lee
Trescott, Jacqueline Elaine
Tucker, Eric M.
Tucker, Karen
Turner, Carmen Elizabeth
Turner, John A., Jr.
Turner, Willie
Tutt, Lia S.
Tutt, Walter Cornelius
Tyrance, Herman J.
Tzomes, Chancellor Alfonso (Pete)
Upshaw, Gene
Valentine, Deborah Marie
Valentine, J. T.
Valien, Preston
Vanderpool, Eustace Arthur
Van Hook, Warren Kenneth
Varnado, Arthur
Vaughn, William Samuel, III
Vera, Ndoro Vincent
Waddell, Theodore R.
Walker, Ann B.
Walker, Betty Stevens
Walker, Howard Kent
Walker, James
Walker, John T.
Walker, Kenneth R.
Walker, Lucius
Walker, M. Lucius, Jr.
Walker, Sidney Harris
Walker, William Paul, Jr.
Wallace, Arnold D., Sr.
Wallace, C. Everett
Wallace, Karen Smyley
Wallace, Paul Starett, Jr.
Wallace, Perry Eugene
Walters, Curla Sybil
Walters, Ronald
Walton, Flavia Batteau
Walton, Reggie Barnett
Walton, Tracy Matthew, Jr.
Ward, C. Douglas
Ware, Omego John Clinton, Jr.
Warfield-Coppock, Nsenga Patricia
Washington, Bennetta B.
Washington, Consuela M.
Washington, Robert Benjamin, Jr.
Washington, Robert E.
Washington, Walter E.
Waters, Neville R., III
Watkins, Jay B.
Watkins, Mozelle Ellis
Watlington, Janet Berecia
Watson, Barbara M.
Watson, Theresa Lawhorn
Watson, Thomas S., Jr.
Webber, Paul R., III
Webster, Charles
Welsing, Frances Cress
Wesley, Nathaniel, Jr.
West, Togo Dennis, Jr.
Wheat, Alan
Whipps, Mary N.
Whisenton, Andre C.
White, Ida Margaret (Ida Kilpatrick Jones)
White, Jeris
White, John Clinton
White, Robert L.
White, Sandra LaVelle
Whitfield, Vantile E.
Whiting, Barbara E. (nee Wright)
Wiggins, Lillian Cooper
Wilber, Margie Robinson
Wilbon, Joan Marie
Wilburn, Victor H.
Wiles, Spencer H.
Wiley, Herley Wesley
Wilfong, Henry T., Jr.
Wilhoit, Carl H.
Wilkins, Allen Henry
Wilkins, Herbert Priestly
Wilkins, Thomas A.
Wilkinson, Robert Shaw, Jr.
Williams, Armstrong
Williams, Bernice
Williams, Charlene J.
Williams, Charles Thomas
Williams, Deborah Ann

Williams, Eddie Nathan
Williams, Ernest Y.
Williams, Grady Carter
Williams, Howard Copeland
Williams, James Thomas
Williams, Karen Hastie
Williams, Larry C.
Williams, Melvin Walker
Williams, Paul
Williams, Robert H.
Williams, Ronald Lee
Williams, Stanley King
Williams, Wesley S., Jr.
Williams, Wyatt Clifford
Williams, Yvonne LaVerne
Williamson, Karen Elizabeth
Willingham, Voncile
Willoughby, Winston Churchill
Wilmot, David Winston
Wilson, Ernest
Wilson, John A.
Wilson, Leon A.
Wilson, Milton
Wilson, Stephanie Y.
Wineglass, Henry
Winfield, Susan Rebecca Holmes
Winston, Jeanne Worley
Winston, Michael R.
Winter, Daria Portray
Wood, Anton Vernon
Wood, Willie Vernell, Sr.
Woodard, Samuel L.
Woods, Jacqueline Edwards
Woodson, Robert L.
Woodson, Roderic L.
Woodson, William D.
Wooten, Carl Kenneth
Word, Fletcher Henry, Jr.
Worsley, George Ira, Jr.
Wright-Sabree, Margaret V.
Yancey, Laurel Guild
Yeldell, Joseph P.
Young, Charles Alexander
Young, Elizabeth Bell
Young, F. Camille
Zimmerman, Eugene

FLORIDA

ARCHER
Harris, Oscar L., Jr.

AVON PARK
Dennard, Willie James A., II

BELLE GLADE
Atkinson, Regina Elizabeth
Grear, Effie C.
Grear, William A.

BOCA RATON
Weatherspoon, Jimmy Lee

BOYNTON BEACH
Vick, Harvey Oscar, III

BUSHNELL
Coney, Loraine Chapell

CAPE CORAL
Ackord, Marie M.

CLEARWATER
Hatchett, Paul Andrew
Ladson, Louis Fitzgerald
McLean, Helen Virginia
Nims, Theodore, Jr.
Russell, Leon W.
Williams, Naomi B.

COCONUT CREEK
Crawford, Carl M.

CORAL GABLES
Bellamy, Ivory Gandy
Cahn, Jean Camper
Dunn, Marvin
Rose, Alvin W.
Smith, Marzell

DAYTONA BEACH
Bronson, Oswald P.
Burnette, Ada Puryear
Burney, Harry L., Jr.
Crosslin, Evelyn Stocking
Dunn, William L.
Frink, John Spencer
Golden, Evelyn Davis
Higgins, Cleo Surry
Miller, Jake C.
Moore, Richard V.
Pyles, J. A.
Shakir, Adib Akmal
Waters, Wimbley, Jr.
Watson, Odest Jefferson, Sr.
Williams, Reginald Clark

DELRAY BEACH
Pompey, Charles Spencer
Randolph, David E.

EAST FORT MEYERS
Shoemaker, Veronica Sapp

EATONVILLE
Vereen, Nathaniel

EGLIN AFB
Crawford, Nathaniel, Jr.
Hill, Charlie H.

EL PORTAL
Harris-Ebohon, Altheria Thyra

EUSTIS
Poole, Thomas H., Sr.

FLORIDA CITY
Smith, Juanita Smith

FORT LAUDERDALE
Allen, W. George
Bass, James L.
Bass, Leonard Channing
Battle, Gloria Jean
Benson, Hayward J., Jr.
Black, Malcolm Mazique (Mike Black)
Brann, Herman Ivelaw
Clarke, Everee Jimerson
Crutchfield-Baker, Verdenia
Gillis, Theresa McKinzy
Hill, James O.
Payne, Jesse James
Rawls, Raleigh Richard
Reddick, Thomas J., Jr.
Reynolds, Grant
Ruffin, John Walter, Jr.
Shirley, Calvin Hylton
Taylor, Daisy Curry
Taylor, Norman Eugene
Taylor, Theodore D.
Wright, Kathleen C.

FORT MYERS
Black, Frank S.
LeDuff, Stephanie Carmel
Peete, Calvin

FORT PIERCE
Edwards, Eddie
Flowers, Ralph L.
Gaines, Samuel Stone
Hawkins, Andre

FORT WALTON BEACH
Smith, Nathaniel, Jr.

FPO MIAMI
Taylor, Ernest Norman, Jr.

GAINESVILLE
Ayers, George Waldon, Jr.
Carter, James L.
Cole, Thomas Winston, Sr.
DuPree, Sherry Sherrod
Green, Aaron Alphonso
Harris, Oscar L., Jr.
Hart, Jacqueline D.
Haskins, James S.
Hill-Lubin, Mildred Anderson
Morris, Eugene
Reynolds, Ida Manning
Williams, Rosa B.

GREEN COVE SPRINGS
Love, Joe W.

HIALEAH GARDENS
Madry, Maude Holt

HOLLYWOOD
Willis, Rose W.

IMMOKALEE
Cochran, James David, Jr.

JACKSONVILLE
Aikens, Chester Alfronza
Belton, C. Ronald
Best, Jennings H.
Carswell, Gloria Nadine Sherman
Cobbin, W. Frank, Jr.
Cone, Cecil Wayne
Cone, Juanita Fletcher
Coney, Hydia Lutrice
Foster, James H.
Gallon, Dennis P.
Gregory, Bernard Vincent
Hampton, Frank, Sr.
Henderson, James R.
Hightower, James Howard
Holmes, Wendell P., Jr.
Holzendorf, Betty S.
Hurst, Rodney Lawrence
Jackson, Norman A.
Lea, Jeanne Evans
Marshall, Reese
Mathis, Sallye Brooks
Micks, Deitra R. H.
Mitchell, Orrin Dwight
Mitchell, Robert L.
Morris, Samuel Solomon
Owens, Debbie A.
Powell, Leola P.
Robinson, Hubert Nelson
Rodgers, Anthony Recarido, Sr.
Smith, Joseph Edward
Tolbert, Sharon Renee
White, Melvyn Lee
Williams, Ann E. A. (nee Anderson)
Williams, Dorothy P.
Woodie, Henry L.

KEY WEST
Chandler, Theodore Alan

LAKE BUENA VISTA
Rivers, Johnny

LAKE CITY
Anders, Richard H.

LAKE WALES
Austin, James P.

LAKELAND
Blake, Wendell Owen
Ivey, Mark, III
Williams, Otis P.

LAUDERHILL
Benson, Hayward J., Jr.
Gates, Jacquelyn Knight

LAUREL HILL
Abdullah, Tariq Husam

MARY ESTHER
Rasheed, Howard S.

MIAMI
Bacon, William Louis
Bain, Erlin
Bellamy, Angela Robinson
Bellamy, Ivory Gandy
Benjamin, Donald F.
Bowser, Charles
Bragg, Robert Lloyd
Braynon, Edward J., Jr.
Bridges, James Wilson
Brown, John Ollis
Bryant, Castell Vaughn
Carter, Judy Sharon
Clark, Leon Henry
Clayton, Mark
Cox, Hannibal Maceo, Jr.
Cryer, Linkston T.
Dawkins, Miller J.
Demeritte, Edwin T.
Duper, Mark
Edwards, Dorothy Wright
Edwards, Robert
Ellis, George Washington
Ferguson, Wilkie Demeritte, Jr.
Fitzpatrick, Albert E.
Foster, Rosebud Lightbourn
Frazier, Eufaula Smith
Gainey, Leonard Dennis, II
Green, Walter
Hadley, Howard Alva, Jr.
Harris, Mary Lorraine
Harris-Ebohon, Altheria Thyra
Hastings, Alcee Lamar
Heidt, Ellen Virginia
Hill, Arthur James
Hogges, Ralph
Howard, Gwendolyn Julius
Jackson, John H.
Jenkins, James E.
Johnson, Enid C.
Jones, Johnny L.
King, Mary Booker
Knight, Dewey W., Jr.
Knox, George F.
Kraft, Benjamin F.
Lawrence, Lonnie R.
Levermore, Claudette Madge
Lewis, Samella (nee Sanders)
Lindsey, Terry Lamar
Long, James Alexander
Long, William H., Jr.
Mack, Astrid Karona
Mack, Lurene Kirkland
Madry, Maude Holt
Mapp, Calvin R.
McNeal, Don
Mickins, Andel W.
Mitchell, Byron Lynwood
Mobley, Charles Lamar
Moore, Nat
Moss, Daniel Calvin, Jr.
Nathan, Tony Curtis
Oden, Walter Eugene
Pemberton, David M.
Pennington, Leenette Morse
Plinton, James O., Jr.
Randolph, James B.
Rao, Koduru V. S.
Rembert, Emma White
Robinson, Willie C.
Sanders, George L.
Scott, Charles E.
Sessing, Trevor W.
Shannon, Marian L.H.
Shirley, Edwin Samuel, Jr.
Simms, Robert H.
Simpson, Dazelle Dean
Smith, Eugene
Strachan, Richard James
Strong, Walter L.
Sullivan, Zola Jiles
Thomas, Francena B.
Thomas, Philip Michael
Thompson, Tawana Sadiela
Timmons, Joan Bruner
Todman, Terence A.
Traylor, Horace Jerome
Trice, Jessie Collins
Turner, William H.
Washington, Leroy
Washington, Thomas Kight, Sr.
Waters, Henrietta E.
White, H. Melton
Wilfork, Andrew Louis
Williams, Rudy V.
Williams, Willie Elbert
Wilson, Patricia Jervis
Wright, C. T. Enus
Wright, Charles E.
Wynn, William Austin, Jr.
Young, Nancy Wilson
Young, Ronald R.

MIAMI BEACH
Eve, Christina M.

MILTON
Robinson, Brenda Evette

MIRAMAR
Whitehead, Eddie L.

NORTH MIAMI
Bigby-Young, Betty
Braynon, Edward J., Jr.

NORTH MIAMI BEACH
Willis, Rose W.

NORTH PORT
Anderson-Janniere, Iona Lucille

OCALA
Simmons, Clayton Lloyd

OPA-LOCKA
Conner, Marcia Lynne
Daniels, Cecil Tyrone
Foster, Roy
Hanna, Cassandria H.
Mack, Lurene Kirkland
McBee, Vincent Clermont
Roby, Reggie
Stephenson, Dwight

ORLANDO
Adams, Kattie Johnson
Butler, John Nathaniel
Carter, Thomas Allen
Cowans, Alvin Jeffrey
Dudley, Thelma
Forrest, Alvane M.
Hamilton, John M.
Jackson, Dennis Lee
King, William Carl
Long, Irene
Massey, Hamilton W.
Miller, Margaret Greer
Myers, Bernard Samuel
Notice, Guy Symour
Pinder, Nelson W.
Reddick, Alzo Jackson
Smith-Surles, Carol Diann
Waite, Norma Lillia
Wallace, Derrick D.
Watkins, Sylvestre C., Sr.

OVIEDO
Clyne, John Rennel

PALM BEACH
Dandridge, Raymond Emmett

PANAMA CITY
Kent, Melvin Floyd

PATRICK AFB
Miles, Dorothy Marie
Patterson, Joan Delores

PAXTON
Abdullah, Tariq Husam

PENSACOLA
Bower, Beverly Lynne
Boyd, Charles Flynn
Cherry, Cassandra Brabble
DaValt, Dorothy B.
Eberhardt, Clifford
Hall, Addie June
Howard, Mamie
Hunter, Cecil Thomas
Luckey, Irene
Powell, J. Otis

POMPANO BEACH
Brown, Diana Johnson
Larkins, E. Pat
Mark, Freemon A.

PORT RICHEY
Ambush, Robert C.

PORT ST LUCIE
Doig, Elmo H.

PORT SALERNO
Simmons, Joyce Hobson (Joyce Ann Hobson-Simmons)

QUINCY
Littleton, Rupert, Jr.

RIVERVIEW
Wright, Samuel Lamar

ROCKLEDGE
Smith, Joe Lee

ST AUGUSTINE
Chase, Arnett C.

ST PETERSBURG
Blackshear, William
Bradley, Terrye Singletary
Brown, Delores Elaine
Brown, Norman E.
Collins, Leroy Anthony, Jr.
Cotman, Henry Earl
Davis, Lowell E.
Downing, Alvin Joseph
Goss, Theresa Carter
Graham, Louise McClary
Harris, Calvin D.
Jones, Theresa Diane
Lewis, Robert Edward
Peterman, Peggy M.
Swain, Robert J.

SARASOTA
Atkins, Fredd Glossie
Jackson, William Fred
Jenkins, Althea H.

SEBRING
Dennard, Willie James A., II

SOUTH BAY
Anthony, Clarence Edward

STUART
Bryant, William Jesse
Hall, Robert L.

SUNRISE
Brann, Herman Ivelaw

TALLAHASSEE
Akbar, Na'im (Luther B. Weems)
Anderson, Russell Lloyd
Barnes, Wilson Edward
Bolden, John Henry
Clack, Doris H.
Copeland, Emily America
Davies, Marvin
Davis, Anita Louise
Eaton, James Nathaniel, Sr.
Elkins, Virgil Lynn
Foote, Leonard Hobson Buchanon
Foster, William Patrick
Gauff, Joseph F., Jr.
Gayles, Anne Richardson
Gaymon, Nicholas Edward
Gorham, Thelma Thurston
Griffith, Elwin Jabez
Groomes, Freddie Lang
Hatchett, Joseph Woodrow
Hemmingway, Beulah S.
Hooper, Gerald F.
Humphries, Frederick S.
Irvine, Freeman Raymond, Jr.
Johnson, Walter Lee
Jones, William Ronald
Lawrence, John E.
Lee, John Robert E.
Martin, Evelyn B.
McKinney, Alma Swilley
McWhorter, Grace Agee
Mobley, Sybil (nee Collins)
Neyland, Leedell Wallace
Parker, Herbert Gerald
Perry, Aubrey M.
Perry, Leonard Douglas, II
Pratt, Louis Hill
Ravenell, William Hudson
Riley, Kenneth J.
Session, Johnny Frank
Shaw, Leander J., Jr.
Smith, Charles U.

Smith, Jeraldine Williams
Smith, Walter L.
Stith, Melvin Thomas
Wanton, Eva C.
White, Barbara Williams
White, James Louis, Jr.
Williams, Dorothy P.
Wilson, Margaret F.
Wimbish, C. Bette

TAMPA
Abel, Renaul N.
Andrews, Cyril Blythe
Bell, Ricky Lynn
Brown, Mortimer
Cabrera, Eloise J.
Chambers, Wallace
Collier, Troy
Collins, Corene
Crowder, Randolph Channing
    (Sugar Bear)
Davis, Edward D.
Dawson, Warren Hope
Gary, Alonzo G., Jr.
Giles, Jimmie, Jr.
Green, Hugh
Griffin, Eurich Z.
Hammond, James A.
Hargrett, James T., Jr.
Harris, Howard F.
Henry, Joseph A.
Hill, Rosalie A.
House, Kevin N.
Jordan, Bettye Davis
Joyner, Arthenia Lee
Logan, David
Lowry, A. Leon, Sr.
Major, Paul Charles
Monroe, Robert Alex
Morrison, Robert B., Jr.
Pruitt, Larry
Renick, James C.
Sanderlin, James B.
Saunders, Robert William, Sr.
Selmon, Dewey Willis
Selmon, Lee Roy
Smith, Freddie A.
Stringer, Thomas Edward, Sr.
Tokley, Joanna Nutter
Washington, Michael Lee
Williams, Joseph B.
Wilson, Charles F.
Wright, Samuel Lamar

TITUSVILLE
Smith, Joe Lee

VALRICO
McFadden, Gregory L.

WEST PALM BEACH
Bridwell, Herbert H.
Clarke, Everee Jimerson
Cunningham, F. Malcolm
Ham-Ying, J. Michael
Holland, William Meredith
Jason, Henry Thomas
Johns, Jackie C.
Jones, James G.
King, Derek Barber
Peterson, Marcella Tandy
Rodgers, Edward
Smith, Bobby Antonia

WINTER HAVEN
Johnson, Ulysses Johann, Jr.

WINTER PARK
Grant, George C.
Perry, Brenda L.

GEORGIA

ALBANY
Black, Billy Charleston
Cutler, Donald
Gordon, Walter Carl, Jr.
Hill, James Lee
Humphries, Charles, Jr.
Mathis, William Lawrence
Mayes, Helen M.
Taylor, Robert, III

Williams, Arthur K.

AMERICUS
Marshall, John Dent
McGrady, Eddie James
McLaughlin, LaVerne Laney
Paschal, Eloise Richardson
Paschal, Willie L.
Wiley, Rena Deloris

ASHBURN
King, Hodge

ATHENS
Allen, Walter R.
Andrews, Raymond
Bethea, Edwin Ayers
Blount, Larry Elisha
Boynton, Asa Terrell, Sr.
Clifton, Ivery Dwight
Ervin, Leroy, Jr.
Frasier, Mary Mack
Hardwick, Clifford E., III
Jeffreys, John H.
Lindsay, Beverly
Locklin, James R.
Lyons, Charles H.S., Jr.
Morrow, John Howard, Jr.
Payton, Victor Emmanuel
Stroud, Howard Burnett, Sr.
Thomas, Maxine Suzanne
Turner, Edward L.
Williamson, Coy Colbert, Jr.

ATLANTA
Aaron, Henry L.
Abernathy, Ralph David
Adair, James E.
Adams, Dolly Desselle
Adams, John Hurst
Al-Amin, Jamil Abdullah (H. Rap
    Brown)
Aldridge, Delores P.
Alexander, John Stanley
Alexander, Theodore Martin, Sr.
Alexander, William H.
Amos, Joseph H.
Anderson, Al H., Jr.
Anderson, Gloria L.
Anderson, Grady Lee
Andrews, William L., Sr.
Appleby-Young, Sadye Pearl
Arkansaw, Tim
Arrington, Marvin
Atkins, Sam Oillie
Atkinson, Curtis L.
Baety, Edward L.
Bailey, Jerry Dean
Bailey, Randall Charles
Banks, Caroline Long
Barnes, Fannie Burrell
Barnett, Robert
Batine, Rafael
Beasley, Victor Mario
Bellamy, Verdelle B.
Bellamy, Walter
Bellinger, Mary Ann (Bibi
    Mshonaji)
Benham, Robert
Bethea, Edwin Ayers
Bevel, James Luther
Beverly, Creigs S.
Black, Charles E.
Blackburn, Benjamin Allan, II
Blackwell, Randolph Talmadge
Blair, James H.
Blake, Elias, Jr.
Blanks, Larvell (Sugar Bear)
Bolden, Dorothy Lee
Bolden, Wiley Speights
Bond, James G.
Boone, Frederick Oliver
Bradford, Zee
Bradley, M. Louise
Brantley, Booker Terry, Jr.
Brewer, Alvin L.
Bridgeforth, Barbara (Barbara
    Collier Long)
Bridgewater, Herbert Jeremiah,
    Jr.
Bronner, Nathaniel, Sr.
Brown, Calvin Anderson, Jr.
Brown, Evelyn Drewery
Brown, Paul E. X.

Brown, Paul L.
Brown, William Crews
Bryant, Regina Lynn
Buckner, Iris Bernell
Burroughs, Baldwin Wesley
Bussey, Reuben T.
Carter, Barbara Lillian
Carter, John H.
Carter, Lawrence E., Sr.
Casterlow, Carolyn B.
Chambliss, Chris
Christian, Mae Armster
Clayton, Charles M.
Clayton, Xernona
Clement, William A., Jr.
Cohen, Amaziah VanBuren
Cole, John L., Jr.
Cole, Johnnetta Betsch
Cole, Thomas W., Jr.
Coles, Joseph Carlyle, Jr.
Coombs, Fletcher
Cooper, Clarence
Cooper, Michael Gary
Costen, Melva Wilson
Crawford, Raymon Edward
Crim, Alonzo A.
Crockett, Delores Loraine
Croslan, John Arthur
Culbreath, Tongila M.
Culpepper, Dellie L.
Cunningham, Verenessa Smalls-
    Brantley
Darnell, Emma Ione
Dash, Hugh M. H.
Davis, Edward L.
Davis, James Keet
Davis, Lloyd
Davis, Ronald P.
Dean, James Edward
Debro, Julius
Delk, Oliver Rahn
Doanes-Bergin, Sharyn F.
Dortch, Thomas Wesley, Jr.
Drennen, Gordon
Dryden, Charles Walter
Duffy, Eugene Jones
Duhart, Harold B.
Dye, Clinton Elworth, Jr.
Easley, Paul Howard, Sr.
Eaves, A. Reginald
Edwards, Donald Philip
Elder, Geraldine H.
English, Kenneth
Esogbue, Augustine O.
Estes, Sidney Harrison
Ethridge, Robert Wylie
Evans, LeRoy W.
Flanagan, Robert B., Sr.
Flowers, Runette (Runette
    Flowers Williams)
Fort, Jane
Foster, Robert Leon
Franklin, David M.
Franklin, Shirley Clarke
Freemont, James McKinley
Fresh, Edith McCullough
Fuller, Doris Jean
Funderburg, I. Owen
Fuse, Bobby LeAndrew, Jr.
Garnett, Bernard E.
Garrett, Ruby Grant
Gay, Birdie Spivey
Gayle, Helene D.
Gayles, Joseph Nathan Webster,
    Jr.
George, Carrie Leigh
George, Claude C.
Gerald, Perry
Gillespie, Rena Harrell
Gilliam, John Rally
Githii, Ethel Waddell
Gloster, Hugh Morris
Goldston, Nathaniel R., III
Gooden, Samuel Ellsworth
Goodman, James Arthur, Sr.
Grant, Anna Augusta Fredrina
Grant, Debora Felita
Grant, Jacquelyn
Green, Angelo Gray
Grigsby, Lucy Clemmons
Hall, Albert
Hamilton, Franklin D.
Harmon, James F., Sr.
Harper, Terry

Harris, Archie Jerome
Harris, Barbara Ann
Harris, Mary Styles
Harris, Oscar Lewis
Harvard, Beverly Bailey
Hawk, Charles N., Jr.
Hawk, Charles Nathaniel, III
Haynes, John Kermit
Hemphill, Miley Mae
Henderson, Freddye Scarborough
Henderson, Jacob R.
Herman, Kathleen Virgil
Hill, Jesse, Jr.
Hill, William Bradley, Jr.
Hilliard, Asa Grant, III
Hoffman, Joseph Irvine, Jr.
Hogan, Fannie Burrell
Hollowell, Donald L.
Holmes, Gary Mayo
Holmes, Hamilton Earl
Holmes, Robert A.
Hooker, Douglas Randolf
Hopkins, William A.
Hornsby, Alton, Jr.
Horton, Lemuel Leonard
Howard, Lytia Ramani
Hudson, John D.
Hudson, Sterling Henry, III
Hunt, Maurice
Hunter, Johnnie L.
Hunter, Mackiell James
Isaacs, Doris C.
Jackson, Benita Marie
Jackson, Lenwood A.
Jackson, Maynard Holbrook
Jackson, Roswell F.
Jackson, Rudolph Ellsworth
James, Carlos Adrian
James, Dorothy Marie
Jennings, Robert Ray
Jett, Arthur Victor, Sr.
Johnson, Brent E.
Johnson, Carrie Clements
Johnson, Charles Lee
Johnson, Edward, Jr. (Fast Eddie)
Johnson, Howard R.
Johnson, James Edward
Johnson, Jondelle M.
Johnson, Leroy Reginald
Johnson, Mertha Ruth
Johnson, Samuel Harrison
Johnson, Tobe
Johnson-Scott, Jerodene Patrice
Jones, George H.
Jones, Herbert C.
Jones, Marcus Earl
Jones, Paul R.
Jones, Rena Talley
Jones, Timothy Earl
Jordan, Casper LeRoy
Jordan, George Washington, Jr.
Jordan, Robert A.
Joyner, Gordon L.
Keene, Sharon C.
Keith, Leroy
Kelly, Jack Arthur
King, Barbara Lewis
King, Coretta Scott (Mrs. Martin
    Luther King Jr.)
King, Delutha Harold
Kugblenu, George Ofoe
Lane, Allan C.
Laney, Robert Louis, Jr.
Langford, Arthur, Jr.
Lawrence, George Calvin
LeFlore, William B.
Lester, Donald
Lewis, Charles McArthur
Linsey, Nathaniel L.
Lockhart, Verdree
Lomax, Pearl Cleage
London, Edward Charles
Long, Richard A.
Lord, Clyde Ormond
Lowery, Joseph E.
Mack, Miranda
Mapp, Frederick Everett
Marino, Eugene Antonio
Martin, Reddrick Linwood
Mason, William Alfred
Matlock, Kent
Matthews, Hewitt W.
Mays, W. Roy, III
McBay, Henry Cecil

McCall, Emmanuel Lemuel, Sr.
McClure, Earie
McCoy, Joseph Clifton
McCrary-Simmons, Shirley Denise
McCray, Melvin
McDonald, Timothy, III
McGuirt, Milford W.
McKanders, Julius A., II
McKenzie, Therman, Sr.
McLaurin, Benjamin Philip
McNeal, John Alex, Jr.
McWilliams, Alfred E., Jr.
Merideth, Charles Waymond
Mickens, Ronald Elbert
Miley, Debra Charlet
Miller, Louise T.
Miller, William Nathaniel
Milton, Octavia Washington
Mitchell, Ella Pearson
Mitchell, Henry Heywood
Montgomery, Earline (nee Smith)
Moore, Annie Jewell
Moore, Charles W.
Moorhead, Joseph H.
Moreland, Lois Baldwin
Morrison, Charles Edward
Mosby, Nathaniel
Myrick, Clarissa
Napper, George, Jr.
O'Neal, Malinda King
Osborne, William Reginald, Jr.
Palmer, James L. D.
Parker, Thomas Edwin, III
Parks, Bernard
Patterson, Curtis Ray
Perdue, Robert Eugene
Persons, W. Ray
Phillips, Bertha (nee Parker)
Pickens, William Garfield
Pinado, Alan E.
Pledger, Verline S.
Poe, Booker
Powell, C. Clayton
Price, Charles Eugene
Price, James Rogers
Pritchard, Marion K. Smith
Prothro, Johnnie Watts
Pugh, Thomas Jefferson
Ransom, Burnella Jackson
Rates, Norman M.
Redrick, Virginia Pendleton
Reed, James W.
Reed, Lambert S., II
Reed, Willis
Reese, Mamie Bynes
Reid, Charles H.
Render, William H.
Richmond, Myrian Patricia
Riley, Wayne Joseph
Robie, Clarence W.
Robinson, Edsel F.
Rogers-Bell, Mamie Lee
Ross, Catherine Laverne
Ross, Kevin Arnold
Roundfield, Danny Thomas
    (Rounds)
Rounsaville, Lucious Brown, Jr.
Rouse, Jacqueline Anne
Saunders, Barbara Ann (nee
    Parks)
Scott, Cornelius Adolphus
Scott, Linzy, Jr.
Scott, Mary Shy
Scott, Rachel Loraine
Sears-Collins, Leah J.
See, Letha Annette
Shannon, David Thomas
Sheftall, Willis B., Jr.
Shelton, Lee Raymond
Shockley, Grant S.
Siler, Brenda Claire
Sillah, Marion Rogers
Simmons, Isaac Tyrone
Sinclair, Clayton, Jr.
Smith, Calvert H.
Smith, Calvin Miles
Smith, Luther Edward, Jr.
Smith, Robert Edward
Spellman, Alfred B.
Spencer, Margaret Beale
Stacia, Kevin Maurice
Stanley, Ellis M., Sr.
Stargell, Wilver Dornel (Willie)
Stephens, Charles Richard

Williams, Lafayette W.

VILLA RICA
Morgan, Harry

WADLEY
Charles, Lewis
Johnson, B. A.

WARNER ROBINS AFB
Pogue, Richard James

WAYCROSS
Bonner, Theophulis W.
Gaines, Oscar Cornell
McCray, Christopher Columbus

WAYNESBORO
Griggs, James C.
Lodge, Herman

WEST POINT
Dunn, Ross

WHITESBURG
Gamble, Robert Lewis

WOODBINE
Brown, Willis, Jr.

WOODLAND
King, James B., Jr.

HAWAII

HILO
Markey, Beatrice (nee Greene)

HONOLULU
Bogus, Houston, Jr.
Carroll, Annie Haywood
Edwards, John W., Jr.
Hill, Richard Nathaniel
Jackson, Miles Merrill
Smith, Richard Alfred
Thompson, Donnis Hazel
Young, Edward Hiram, Jr.

LIHUE
King, LeRoy J.

MILILANI
Bogus, Houston, Jr.
James, Arminta Susan

WAHIAWA
Lewis, Alexander L.

WAIANAE
Johnson, Solomon E.

IDAHO

BOISE
Brown, Booker T.
Mercy, Leland, Jr.
Nichols, Nick

POCATELLO
Yizar, James Horace, Jr.

ILLINOIS

ALTON
Horton, Clarence Pennington
Peyton, Henry E.

ARGO
Taylor, William Henry, Sr.

ARGONNE
Gay, Eddie C.
Robinson, Jack, Jr.

ARLINGTON HEIGHTS
Cochran, Edward G.
McMillan, Robert Frank, Jr.
Phillips, W. Thomas

AURORA
Cannon, Charles Earl
Wilkinson, Marie L.

BARRINGTON
Johnson, James W., Jr.

BELLEVILLE
Chalmers, Thelma Faye
LeCompte, Peggy J. (nee Lewis)
McCaskill, Earle
Wiley, Gerald Edward

BELLWOOD
Bailey, Ronald W.

BLOOMINGTON
Jones, Eva

BLUE ISLAND
Olawumi, Bertha Ann

BROADVIEW
Johnson, Patricia Dumas

BUFFALO GROVE
Dukes, Ronald

CALUMET PARK
Hutt, Monroe L.

CARBONDALE
Bryson, Seymour L.
Hayes, Richard C.
Jones, Jennie Y.
Lockhart, Lillie Marie
Miller, Benjamin T.
Robinson, Walter G.
Schumacher, Brockman
Shepherd, Benjamin A.
Stalls, Madlyn Alberta
Welch, Harvey, Jr.

CARSONDALE
Blackwell, Patricia A.

CENTERVILLE
Calhoun, Joshua Wesley

CENTRALIA
Walker, William Harold

CHAMPAIGN
Barkstall, Vernon L.
Burgess, James R., Jr.
Caroline, J. C.
Copeland, Elaine Johnson
Cowan, Larine Yvonne
Norman, P. Roosevelt
Wright, Phillip LeRoi

CHARLESTON
Ridgeway, Bill Tom

CHICAGO
Abdullah, Larry Burley
Adair, Andrew A.
Adams, Billie Morris Wright
Adams, Carol Laurence
Adams, Martin P.
Akin, Ewen M., Jr.
Albert, Charles Gregory
Alexander, Louis G.
Alexis, Marcus
Allen-Rasheed, Jamal Randy
Allston, Thomas Gray, III (Tim)
Amaker, Norman Carey
Amaro, Ruben
Anderson, George A.
Anderson, Monroe
Anderson, Robert L.
Apea, Joseph Bennet
    Kyeremateng
Arburtha, Leodies Uyless
Armster-Worrill, Cynthia Denise
Armstrong, Joseph N.
Arnold, Ralph M.
Askew, James R.
Austin, Janyth Yvonne
Ayers, George E.
Bacon, Gloria Jackson
Bacon, Warren H.

Bailey, Adrienne Yvonne
Bailey, Donn Fritz
Bailey, Ronald W.
Baines, Harold Douglas
Ball, William Batten
Banks, Jerry L.
Banks, Patricia
Barnes, Eugene M.
Barnett, Alfreda W. Duster
Barnett, Etta Moten
Barnett, William
Barney, Willie J.
Barrow, Willie B.
Baskins, Lewis C.
Bates, Louise Rebecca
Beal, Jacqueline Jean
Bell, Carl Compton
Bell, William Jerry
Belliny, Daniel S.
Benford, Clare E.
Bennett, Lerone, Jr.
Bennett, Maisha B. H.
Benson, Sharon Marie
Benton, Luther
Berry, Leonidas H.
Bertrand, Joseph G.
Bervin-Mitchell, Gabrielle
Bibbs, Janice Denise
Biblo, Mary
Black, Leona R.
Black, Walter Kerrigan
Blair, Chester Laughton Ellison
Bland, Heyward
Blanks, Wilhelmina E.
Blanton, James B., III
Blouin, Rose Louise
Bolin, Lionel E.
Bond, James Arthur
Bosley, Thad
Boswell, Paul P.
Boutte, Alvin J.
Bowman, James E., Jr.
Boyd, William Stewart
Boykin, Randson C.
Brady, Nelvia M.
Branch, Dorothy L.
Brazil, Robert D.
Brooks, Delores Jean
Brooks, Gwendolyn Elizabeth
Brown, Buck
Brown, Clarice Ernestine
Brown, Floyd A.
Brown, Joan P. (Abena)
Brown, Milton F.
Brown, Philip Erskine
Brown, Stephen H.
Brown-Nash, JoAhn Weaver
Brownlee, Geraldine Daniels
Brownlee, Lester Harrison-Pierce
Brownridge, J. Paul
Bruce, James C.
Bryant, Clarence
Bryant, Preston
Bryant, Robert E.
Buchanan, Otis
Buckner, James L.
Buckney, Edward L.
Burke, Emmett C.
Burns, Willie Miles
Burrell, Thomas J.
Burroughs, Leonard
Burrus, Clark
Butler, Joyce M.
Byrd, Manford, Jr.
Caldwell, James E.
Caldwell, Lewis A. H.
Calhoun, Lillian Scott
Callaway, Louis Marshall, Jr.
Campbell, Calvin C.
Campbell, James W.
Campbell, Wendell J.
Cantrell, Forrest Daniel
Carey, Archibald James, Jr.
Carlo, Nelson
Carr, Roderich Marion
Carr, Virgil H.
Carry, Helen Ward
Carter, Dorval Ronald
Carter, Robert Henry, III
Cartright, Lenora T.
Cash, Pamela J.
Chapman, Cleveland M.
Chapman, Rosyln C.
Charles, Doreen Alicia

Charleston, Gomez, Jr.
Chatman, Donald Leveritt
Cheatham, Henry Boles
Clark, Walter H.
Clarke, Joseph Lance
Clay, Theodore Roosevelt, Jr.
Clay, Willie B.
Clements, George H.
Coleman, Ben Carl
Coleman, Cecil R.
Coleman, Jean Ellen
Coleman, John H.
Coleman, Johnnie (Johnnie
    Colemon Nedd)
Collins, Marva Delores Nettles
Collins, Maurice A.
Collins, Otis Grant
Collins, Rosecrain
Collins-Grant, Earlean
Colter, Cyrus J.
Comer, Marian Wilson
Compton, James W.
Cook, Rufus
Cotharn, Preston Sigmunde, Sr.
Craig, Frederick A.
Crawford, Barbara Hopkins
Credit, Thelma Cobb
Cross, Austin Devon
Cruthird, J. Robert Lee
Cruzat, Edward Pedro
Cullers, Vincent T.
Cummings, Cimena McCane
Cunningham, Erskine
Cunningham, William E.
Curry, Charles E.
Curtis, Harry S.
Custer-Chen, Johnnie M.
Cuyjet-Johnson, Cynthia K.
Dale, Robert J.
Daly, Ronald Edwin
Daniel, David L.
Danner, Margaret Essie (Margaret
    Cunningham)
Davidson, Donald Rae
Davis, Barbara D.
Davis, Carrie L. Filer
Davis, Charles A.
Davis, Danny K.
Davis, Herman E.
Davis, John Westley
Davis, Leon
Davis, Lydia Joanna
Davis, Monique Deon
Davis, William R.
Dawson, Andre
Dee, Merri
DeLeon-Jones, Frank A., Jr.
Dennard, Darryl W.
DeNye, Blaine A.
Derr, Gilbert S.
Dillard, Cecil R.
Dobbins, Lucille R.
Dolphin, Woodrow B.
Driskell, Claude Evans
Dukes, Constance T.
Dukes, Ronald
Dunn, Lillian Joyce
Durham, Leon
Duster, Benjamin C.
Duster, Donald Leon
Earles, Rene Martin
Early, Sybil Theresa
Eddy, Edward A.
Edmonds, Thomas Nathaniel
Edwards, Lonnie
Eichelberger, Brenda
Elam, Harry Penoy
Ellington, Brenda Andrea
Ellis, Douglas, Jr.
Ellis, Effie O'Neal
English, Perry T., Jr.
Epps, Edgar G.
Erwin, James Otis
Evans, Webb
Ewell, Raymond W.
Ewing, Russ
Faison, Thurman Lawrence
Farley, William Horace, Jr.
Farrakhan, Louis
Faulk, Estelle A.
Felker, Joseph B.
Fentress, Robert H.
Fentress, Shirley B.
Ferguson, Cecil (Duke)

Ferguson, St. Julian
Finch, William H.
Finney, Leon D., Jr.
Floyd, Samuel A., Jr.
Ford, Ausbra
Ford, Virginia
Foster, LaDoris J.
Foster, William K.
France, Erwin A.
Francis, Ray William, Jr.
Frazier, Wynetta Artricia
Fredrick, Earl E., Jr.
Freeman, Charles Eldridge
Fregia, Paul Douglas
Frost, Wilson
Fuller, Thomas S.
Gardner, Edward G.
Gardner, Frank W.
Garnett, Marion Winston
Gayles, Lindsey, Jr.
Geary, Clarence Butler
Gervin, George (Iceman)
Gibbs, Karen Patricia
Gibson, Harry H. C.
Gibson, Mildred M.
Gibson, Truman K., Jr.
Gilbert, Herman Cromwell
Gilliam, Sharon
Godfrey, Emile Sylvester, Jr.
Goodwin, E. Marvin
Goodwin, Mercedier Cassandra de
    Freita
Gordon, Charles D.
Gordon, Milton A.
Gore, David L.
Goss, Frank, Jr.
Goss, William Epp
Grady, Mary Forte
Grady, Walter E.
Grant, Arthur H.
Grant, Charles Truman
Grant, McNair
Gray, Arthur D.
Gray, Marvin W.
Green, James L.
Green, Sidney Anthony
Greene-Thapedi, Llewellyn L.
Greenlee, Sam
Gregory, O. Grady
Gregory, Richard Claxton (Dick
    Gregory)
Griggs, James Clifton, Jr.
Groomes, Emrett W.
Guthrie, Carlton Lyons
Guy, Talmadge Carter
Hairston, Jerry Wayne
Hamberlin, Emiel
Hamilton, Arthur N.
Hamilton, Phanuel J.
Hannah, Hubert H., Sr.
Hardiman, Phillip Thomas
Harley, Daniel P., Jr.
Harris, Loretta K.
Harris, Nelson A.
Harrison, Paul Carter
Harth, Raymond Earl
Hartman, Hermene Demaris
Harvey-Byrd, Patricia Lynn
Hasbrouck, Ellsworth Eugene
Hasty, Keith A.
Hawkins, Muriel A.
Hawthorne, Angel L.
Haynes, Barbara Asche
Hays, Butch Anthony
Haywood, Wardell
Hebert, Zenebework Teshome
Helms, David Alonzo
Hemphill, Paul W.
Hennings, Kenneth Milton
Herron, Bruce Wayne
Hicks-Bartlett, Sharon Theresa
Higgins, Ora A.
Higgins, Rod Anthony
Hill, Avery
Hill, James, Jr.
Hill, James H.
Hill, Johnny R.
Hixson, Judson Lemoine
Hodges, Craig Anthony
Hogu, Barbara J. Jones
Holliday, Frances B.
Holt, Grace S.
Hooks, James Byron, Jr.
Horne, June Merideth

Lawson, Charles H., III
Mason, William E.
McGaughy, Will
Murphy, Della Mary
Officer, Carl Edward
Redmond, Eugene B.
Sanford, Mark
Thompson, Lloyd Earl
Wharton, Milton S.
Wright, Katie Harper
Younge, Richard G.

EDWARDSVILLE
Grist, Arthur L.
Hampton, Phillip Jewel
Johnson, Herbert M.
Pyke, Willie Oranda
Smith, Joseph Edward
Welch, Edward L.
Williams, Clayton Richard
Wilson, Rudolph George

ELGIN
Brown, Mary Elizabeth
Vessup, Aaron Anthony

ELMHURST
Mulligan, Carol Harris

EVANSTON
Alexander, Roosevelt Maurice
Binford, Henry C.
Booker, Merrel Daniel, Sr.
Bransford, William L.
Brownlee, Lester Harrison-Pierce
Carter, Robert Thompson
Cason, Marilynn Jean
Cheeks, Carl L.
Cherry, Warren W.
Forrest, Leon Richard
Harley, Philip A.
Harris, Robert Allen
Helms, David Alonzo
Joyner, William A.
Marbury, Carl Harris
McMillan, Lemmon Columbus
Norwood, John F.
Peay, Francis
Phillips, Bertrand D.
Phillips, Daniel P.
Reynolds, Bruce Howard
Royster, Don M., Sr.
Slaughter, Diana T.
Spurlock-Evans, Karla Jeanne
Stickney, Janice L.
Summers, Edna White
Taylor, Hycel B.
Tomlinson, Randolph R.
Wilkins, Leona B.
Wimberly, Anne Streaty
Wimberly, Edward P.
Winfield, Florence F.

EVERGREEN PARK
Salter, Roger Franklin

FLOSSMOOR
Marsh, McAfee

FREEPORT
Parker, James L.

GALESBURG
Hendricks, Leta

GLENCOE
Johnson, George Ellis

GLENDALE HEIGHTS
Burke, Kirkland R.

GLENVIEW
Bennett, Ivy Hooker
Bowles, Barbara Landers
Sanford, Loretta Love

GLENWOOD
Fentress, Shirley B.

GREAT LAKES
Brooks, Wadell, Sr.
Whitehead, Timothy Dwight

HARVEY
Brown-Nash, JoAhn Weaver
Demonbreun, Thelma M.
Falkner, Bobbie E.
Rockett, Damon Emerson
Smith, J. C.
Taylor, Gloria Jean
Wheeler, Ronald C.

HAZEL CREST
Nichols, Alfred Glen

HERRIN
Jones, Miles James

HIGHLAND PARK
McCallum, Walter Edward
Sherrell, Charles Ronald, II

HINSDALE
McLendon, John B., Jr.

HOMEWOOD
Richmond, Delores Ruth
Sagers, Rudolph, Jr.

HOPKINS PARK
Runnels, Bernice

ITASCA
Richardson, Johnny L.

JOLIET
Bolden, Raymond A.
Echols, Clarence LeRoy, Jr.
Hinch, Andrew Lewis, Sr.
Nichols, Walter LaPlora
Singleton, Isaac, Sr.
Young, Charles, Jr.

KANKAKEE
Melancon, Donald

LAKE FOREST
Bell, Tom Calvin
Cameron, Jack Calvin
Dent, Richard Calvin
Duerson, Dave Calvin
Ellis, Allan D.
Frazier, Leslie Calvin
Gentry, Dennis Calvin
Graves, Roderick Lawrence
Harper, Roland
Harris, Al Calvin
Hutchison, Peyton S.
Jackson, Noah
Marshall, Wilber
McKinnon, Dennis Lewis
Moorehead, Emery Calvin
Osborne, Jim
Perry, William Anthony
Richardson, Michael Calvin
Roland, Johnny E.
Scott, James
Sorey, Revie, Jr.
Thomas, Calvin Lewis
Watts, Rickey
Williams, Dave
Wilson, Otis Calvin

LISLE
Mass, Edna Elaine
Nichols, Alfred Glen
Sandidge, Kanita Durice

LOCKPORT
Fairman, Jimmy W.

LOMBARD
Spooner, John C.

LOVEJOY
Matthews, Dorothy

MACOMB
Bracey, Willie Earl
Bradley, William B.
Rutledge, Essie Manuel

MARKHAM
Carroll, Lawrence W.
Demonbreun, Thelma M.

Miller, Evans Royce

MAYWOOD
Brown, Joseph Davidson, Sr.
Pratt, Melvin Lemar
Rodez, Andrew LaMarr
Searles, Charles R.
Sharpp, Nancy Charlene
Smith, Dolores J.
Wordlaw, Clarence, Jr.

MELROSE PARK
McNelty, Harry

MIDLOTHIAN
Branch, Otis Linwood

MILLERSVILLE
Hopkins, Leroy Taft, Jr.

MOLINE
Collins, James H.

NAPERVILLE
Colson, Joseph S., Jr.
Freeland, Russell L.
Gibbons, Walter E.
Johnson, Walter J.
Montgomery, Brian Walter
Roberts, Bobby L.
Sudbury, Leslie G.

NORMAL
Bell, Janet Sharon
Colvin, William E.
Davis, Gloria-Jeanne
Morris, Charles Edward, Jr.
Walker-Johnson, Geneva Marie

NORTH CHICAGO
Luther, Lucius Calvin
McKinley, William, Jr.
Newberry, Trudell McClelland
Robinson, Kenneth

NORTHBROOK
Gomez, Dennis Craig
Thomas, Isaac Daniel, Jr.

NORTHFIELD
Sayers, Gayle E.

O'FALLON
Morgan, John Paul

OAK BROOK
Blake, Milton James
Guice, Gerald
Hill, Joseph Havord
Hopson, Melvin Clarence
Lamar, William, Jr.
Sutton, Wilma Jean
Watson, Daniel
Webb, James O.

OAK BROOK TERRACE
Smith, Dawn C. F.

OAK PARK
Evans, Gregory James
Hawkins, Muriel A.
Lee, Charlotte O.
Robinet, Harriette Gillem
Salmon, Jaslin Uriah
Walker, Larry Vaughn

OLYMPIA FIELDS
Burleson, Helen L.

PALANTINE
Bennett, Ivy Hooker

PARK FOREST
Hicks-Bartlett, Sharon Theresa
Mosley, Charles E.
Simpson, Juanita H.

PARK FOREST SOUTH
Howard, Shirley M.
Williams, Ather, Jr.

PARK RIDGE
Hightower, Charles H., III

PEORIA
Adams, Roscoe H.
Durand, Winsley, Jr.
Garrett, Romeo Benjamin
Hodge, John Edward
Oliver, James L.
Penelton, Barbara Spencer
Russell, Joseph D.
Shaw, Mario William
Tyler-Slaughter, Cecil Lord

RIVER FOREST
Freeman, Paul D.
McCullough, Geraldine

RIVER GROVE
Latimer, Ina Pearl
Salmon, Jaslin Uriah

RIVERDALE
Walker, Larry
Waller, Larry

ROBBINS
Clemons, Flenor
Dunn, Lillian Joyce
Haymore, Tyrone
Jones, William Jenipher
Rayon, Paul E., III
Smith, Marion L.

ROCK ISLAND
Brown, Carol Ann

ROCKFORD
Box, Charles
Brent, John Clinton, Jr.
Davis, Frank Allen
Devereueawax, John L., III
Dotson-Williams, Henrietta
Gilbert, Eldridge H. E.
Marks, Lee Otis
Palmer-Hildreth, Barbara Jean
Smith, Donald M.
Wright, Clarence Johnnie, Sr.

ROLLING MEADOWS
White, Granville C.

ST ANNE
Haney, Napoleon

ST CHARLES
Jackson, Renard I.

SCHAUMBURG
Baker, Roland Charles
Franklin, Percy
Henry, Charles D., II
Mulligan, Carol Harris
Mulligan, Michael R.
Wallace, Charles Leslie
Wooldridge, David

SCOTT AFB
Morgan, John Paul
Ray, Richard Rex

SKOKIE
Haugabrook, John R.

SOUTH BARRINGTON
Bradley, London M., Jr.

SOUTH HOLLAND
Gregory, Wilton D.
Mitchell, Dwayne Oscar

SPRINGFIELD
Ali, Rasheedah Ziyadah
Allen, Bettie Jean
Bowen, Richard, Jr.
Brookins, Dolores
Burris, Roland W.
Butler, Homer L.
Demons, Leona Marie
Forney, Mary Jane
Hall, Kenneth
Jones, Emil, Jr.

Jordan, Leroy A.
Lee, Edwin Archibald
Logan, Willis Hubert
Maye, Richard
McNeil, Frank William
Moore, Arnold D.
Moore, Dwayne Harrison
Morrison, Juan LaRue, Sr.
Newhouse, Richard H.
Osby, Simeon B., Jr.
Pendergrass, Margaret E.
Rambo, Bettye R.
Shipp, Maurine Sarah
Shoultz, Rudolph Samuel
Singley, Elijah
Singley, Yvonne Jean
Smith, Gordon Allen
Stewart, Leon Holmes
Taylor, James C.
Trees, Candice D.
Umbreit, LeBertha
Veal, Howard Richard
Weaver, Reginald Lee
White, Jesse C., Jr.

TINLEY PARK
Johnson, Albert William, Sr.

UNIVERSITY PARK
Burgest, David Raymond
Hill, Paul G.
Kennedy, Joyce S.

URBANA
Barksdale, Richard Kenneth
Copeland, Robert M.
Eubanks, Robert A.
Gibbs, Sandra E.
Griggs, Mildred Barnes
Humphrey, Kathryn Britt
Parker, Paul E.
Ransom, Preston L.
Warfield, William C.

VENICE
Williams, John Henry

WARRENVILLE
Cannon, Charles Earl

WAUKEGAN
Asma, Thomas M.
Cook, Haney Judaea
McCallum, Walter Edward
Osborne, Gwendolyn Eunice
Robinson, Kenneth
Winfield, Arnold F.

WESTCHESTER
Cary, William Sterling
Johnson, James H.

WESTMONT
Guice, Gerald

WHEATON
Mass, Edna Elaine
Shackelford, George Franklin

WINNETKA
Barefield, Morris

WOOD DALE
Porter, John T.

INDIANA

ANDERSON
Bridges, Alvin Leroy
Brown, Carolyn M.
Carter, Will J.
Foggs, Edward L.
Lewis, Alvin
Morgan, Mary H. Ethel
Simmons, Albert Bufort, Jr.
Steans, Edith Elizabeth
Thorns, Odail, Jr.
Williams, Donald Eugene
Woodall, John Wesley

BLOOMINGTON
Baker, David Nathaniel, Jr.
Boyd, Rozelle
Burnim, Mellonee Victoria
Butler, Ernest Daniel
Fletcher, Winona Lee
Grimmett, Sadie A.
King, Joseph Prather
Marshall, Edwin Cochran
Maultsby, Portia K.
McCluskey, John A., Jr.
Price, Ramon B.
Rutledge, Philip J.
Taliaferro, George
Wiggins, William H., Jr.
Williams, Camilla

COLUMBUS
Pitts, Brenda S.
Trapp, Donald W.

CROWN POINT
Freeland, Robert Lenward, Jr.
Green, Raymond A.
Spann, Noah Atterson, Jr.

EAST CHICAGO
Comer, Norman David
Florence, Johnny C.
Morris, Melvin
Passmore, William A.
Walker, William Henry

ELKHART
Breckenridge, Franklin E.
Hill, Curtis T., Sr.

EVANSVILLE
Claybourne, Edward P.
Downer, Luther Henry
Lawrence, Philip Martin
Malone, Michael Gregory
Miller, Mattie Sherryl
Moss, Estella Mae
Neal, Ira Tinsley
Newsome, Cola King

FORT BENJAMIN HARRISON
Spence, Joseph Samuel, Sr.

FORT WAYNE
Barksdale, Mary Frances
Collins, Robert H.
Dobynes, Elizabeth
Mizzell, William Clarence
Pressey, Junius Batten, Jr.
Scott, Levan Ralph
Sharpe, Audrey Howell
Singleton, Herbert
Winters, James Robert

GARY
Barnes, Thomas
Blanford, Colvin
Boone, Charles
Boone, Clarence Wayne
Bradley, Hilbert L.
Brown, Hoyt C.
Brundidge, Nancy Corinne
Carr, Sandra Jean Irons
Clay, Rudolph
Comer, Zeke
Cooley, Nathan J.
Davidson, Charles Odell
Dawson, Carrie B.
Dumas, Floyd E.
Eldridge, James L., Jr.
Fisher, Lloyd B.
Fisher, Shelley Marie
Gillespie, Tom P., Jr.
Gilliam, Marvin L.
Grimes, Douglas M.
Hall, Katie
Hammonds, Alfred
Harris, Fred
Hatcher, Richard Gordon
Hawkins, Calvin D.
Haywood, Roosevelt V., Jr.
Hill, Howard Hampton
Holliday, Alfonso David
Jones, Bertha H.
Knox, William Robert

Leavell, Dorothy R.
Millender, Dharathula H.
Morgan, Randall Collins, Sr.
Mosby, Carolyn Brown
Owens, Isaiah H.
Parrish, John Henry
Pentecoste, Joseph C.
Perry, Benjamin
Powers, Mamon, Sr.
Powers, Mamon M., Jr.
Pryor, James D.
Rogers, Earline
Smith, Quentin P.
Smith, Vernon G.
Smith, Walter T.
Stephens, Paul A.
Taylor, Ruth Sloan
Tuggle, Dorothy V.
Venable, Andrew Alexander, Jr.
Wesley, Gloria Walker
Williamson-Ige, Dorothy Kay
Winder, Alfred M.
Woodard, Charles James

GOSHEN
Berry, Lee Roy, Jr.

GREENCASTLE
Warren, Stanley

HAMMOND
Chambers, YJean S.
Parrish, John Henry
Thomas, Mary A.

INDIANAPOLIS
Andrews, Carl R.
Artis, Anthony Joel
Assue, Clare Melba
Bantom, Michael A.
Batties, Paul Terry
Bean, Walter Dempsey
Blair, Charles Michael
Boyd, Rozelle
Brewer, Webster L.
Brown, Andrew J.
Brown, Charlie
Brown, Tony
Burford, Effie Lois
Butler, Patrick Hampton
Carson, Julia M.
Coleman, Barbara Sims
Crawford, William A.
Crombaugh, Hallie
Cummings, James C., Jr.
Daniels, Jerry Franklin
Daniels, Melvin J.
Davis, Bennie L.
Donaldson, Ray
Dowe, Ralph M.
Edelin, Kenton Terrell
Ellis, Joseph Louis
Fleming, Vern Henry
Foster, Andrew D.
Fox, William K.
Gainer, Frank Edward
Garner, La Forrest Dean
Goodall, Hurley C.
Gordon, Clifford Wesley
Gray, Moses W.
Griffin, Percy Lee
Haines, Charles Edward
Hanley, J. Frank, II
Hardin, Boniface
Harkness, Jerry Lavelle
Harris, Edward E.
Hinton, Chris
Jackson, Ralph Lavelle
Johnson, Jay (Super Jay)
Johnson, Joyce Colleen
Jones, Sam H., Sr.
Jones, William Edward
Journey, Lula Mae
Joyner, John Erwin
Kellogg, Clark Lavelle
Kimbrew, Joseph D.
King, Joseph Prather
King, Warren Earl
Leek, Sandra D.
Lewis, Cleveland Arthur
Little, Chester H.
Little, Leone Bryson
Little, Monroe Henry
Lowe, Aubrey F.

Lyons, Lloyd Carson
McMillan, Randy L.
Mitchell, LeRoy
Moore, Cleotha Franklin
Murphy, Charles William
Myers, Debra J.
Myers, Woodrow Augustus, Jr.
Odom, Cliff Louis
Parker, Doris S.
Pierce, Raymond O., Jr.
Price, Joseph L.
Rawls, George H.
Rhea, Michael
Richmond, Norris L.
Robinson, Donald Lee
Robinson, Sherman
Ross, Edward
Scott, Leonard Stephen (Steve)
Shaw, Julius Fennell
Shields, Landrum Eugene
Slash, Joseph A.
Smith, Gene Eugene
Smith, Jean M.
Smith, John Arthur
Spearman, Larna Kaye
Stokes, Lillian Gatlin
Strong, Amanda L.
Summers, Joseph W.
Talley, John Stephen
Tandy, Mary B.
Taylor, Gilbert Leon
Taylor, Henry Marshall
Thomas, Edward P.
Thomas, Jim Eugene
Thompson, Donnell
Townsend, Mamie Lee Harrington
Tribble, Huerta Cassius
Waiters, Granville Keith
Walker, Charles Douglas
Watkins, Joseph Philip
Waugh, Judith Ritchie
Wells, Payton R.
Williams, Charles Richard
Williams, Herb Keith
Williams, Vernice Louise
Womack, Robert W., Sr.
Woods, Melvin LeRoy

JEFFERSONVILLE
Stephenson, Jerry L.

KOKOMO
Artis, Myrle Everett
Clarke, Theodore Henson
Grimes, John T.
Hopkins, Charmaine L.

MARION
Casey, Joseph F.
Pettiford, Quentin H.

MERRILLVILLE
Senegal, Phyllis J.

MICHIGAN CITY
Jones, King Solomon
Meriweather, Melvin, Jr.

MUNCIE
Dowery, Mary
Greenwood, Charles H.
Greenwood, Theresa M. Winfrey
McIntosh, Alice T.
Payne, June Evelyn
Smith, Juanita Jane
Womack, Henry Cornelius

MUNSTER
Senegal, Charles

NEW ALBANY
Craft, E. Carrie

NOTRE DAME
Adams, Howard Glen
Bradford, Archie J.
Cleveland, Granville E.
Outlaw, Warren Gregory
Peters, Erskine Alvin
Wright, Frederick Douglass

RICHMOND
Sawyer, George Edward
Williams, Clyde

ST MEINRAD
Davis, Cyprian

SOUTH BEND
Batteast, Robert V.
Bullock, Deborah Lynne
Calvin, Virginia Brown
Gilkey, William C.
Giloth, Richard Peter (King R. Giloth-David)
Hughes, Hollis Eugene, Jr.
Joyner, Lemuel Martin
Martin, Charles Edward, Sr.
Oldham, Algie Sidney, Jr.
Outlaw, Warren Gregory

TERRE HAUTE
Conyers, James E.
Draper, Frederick Webster
Hill, John C.
Howell, Laurence A.
Lyda, Wesley John
Martin, Mary E. Howell
Muyumba, Francois N. (Muyumba Wa Nkongola)
Robinson, Ruth
Swindell, Warren C.

VALPARAISO
Glover, Victor Norman
Neal, William J.
Perry, Margaret

VINCENNES
Summit, Gazella Ann
Waddles, George Wesley, Sr.

WEST LAFAYETTE
Bayless, Paul Clifton
Blalock, Marion W.
Hine, Darlene Clark
Mobley, Emily Ruth
Williams, Helen B.

IOWA

AMES
Gilbert, Fred D., Jr.
Graham, Frederick Mitchell

ANKENY
Howard, Glen

CEDAR FALLS
Greene, Mitchell Amos
Kirkland, Gloria
Monteiro, Marilyn D.S.
Parker, Henry H.

CEDAR RAPIDS
Colbert, George Clifford
Grant, Kingsley B.
Harris, Percy G.
Lawrence, Montague Schiele
Lipscomb, Darryl L.
Robinson, Mary Elizabeth (nee Wilder)

DAVENPORT
Drew-Peeples, Brenda
Johnson, Geraldine Ross
Johnson, John Thomas
Pollard, Freeman Wallace
Smith, Stephen Charles
Walker-Williams, Hope Denise

DES MOINES
Barker, Timothy T.
Cason, Udell, Jr.
Colston, Monroe James
Cothorn, Marguerite Esters
Davis, Evelyn K.
Easley, Jacqueline Ruth
Estes, Elaine
Estes, John M., Jr.
Gentry, Nolden I.
Glanton, Luther T., Jr.

HOUSTON *
Houston, Marsh S.
Mann, Thomas J., Jr.
Maxwell, Roger Allan
Saunders, Meredith Roy
Strickland, Frederick William, Jr.
Thomas, James Samuel
Williams, Catherine G.
Williams, Georgianna M.

DUBUQUE
Jaycox, Mary Irine

EPWORTH
Simon, Joseph Donald

FORT DODGE
Burleson, Jane Geneva

GRINNELL
Carney, Robert Matthew

INDIANOLA
Nichols, Dimaggio

IOWA CITY
Armstrong, Matthew Jordan, Jr.
Cook, Smalley Mike
Davis, Leodis
Davis, N. June (Norma June Wilson)
Evans-Dodd, Theora Anita
Fields, A. Leo
Guyton, Alicia V.
Hawkins, Benny F., Sr.
Henry, Joseph King
Hudson, Clenora Frances
Jones, Phillip Erskine
Knight, W. H., Jr. (Joe)
McPherson, James Alan
Monagan, Alfrieta Parks
Stringer, C. Vivian
Turner, Darwin T.
Wheeler, Theodore Stanley
Williams, Gregory Howard

KEOKUK
Weldon, Ramon N.

SIOUX CITY
Bluford, Grady L.
Silva, Arthur P.

URBANDALE
Williams, Georgianna M.

WATERLOO
Abebe, Ruby
Cribbs, Williams Charles
Duncan, Malachi, Jr.
Kelly, Thomas Maurice, III
Scott, Melvina Brooks
Weems, Vernon Eugene, Jr.

WEST DES MOINES
Hightower, Herma J.
Taylor, Michael M.

KANSAS

BONNER SPRINGS
Tombs, Leroy Cleveland

EMPORIA
Bonner, Mary Winstead

FAIRWAY
Banks, Reginald, Sr.

FORT LEAVENWORTH
Thompson, Joseph Allan

INDEPENDENCE
Edwards, Horace Burton

JUNCTION CITY
Dozier, Morris, Sr.
Early, Paul David

KANSAS CITY
Caruthers, Patricia Wayne
Coles, Anna B.

Collins, Bernice Elaine
Criswell, Arthurine Denton
Davis, James Parker
Franklin, Benjamin Edward
Freeman, Edward Anderson
Jackson, Elmer Carter, Jr.
Jerome, Norge Winefred
Johnson, Ralph C.
Jones, Herman Harvey, Jr.
Jordon, Samuel F.
Justice, Norman E.
Lyons, Robert P.
Meeks, Cordell David, Jr.
Miller, Dennis Weldon
Pinkard, Deloris Elaine
Powell, Robert E.
Richards, William Earl
Ruffin, James E.
Smith, Edward Charles
Smith, Garland M., Jr.
Smith, Melissa Ann
Taylor, Leonard Wayne
Washington, Nancy Ann
White, Luther D.
Whyte, Hartzell J.
Williams, Herbert C.
Williams, Melvin

LAWRENCE
Adams, Samuel Levi, Sr.
Lee, Richard Thomas
Sanders, Robert B.
White, D. Richard

LEAVENWORTH
Dougherty, Robert I.
Moore-Stovall, Joyce
Phelps, Constance Kay

MANHATTAN
Boyer, James B.
Sutton, William Wallace
Switzer, Veryl A.

NEWTON
Rogers, George, III

NORTH NEWTON
Rogers, George, III

OVERLAND PARK
Dancy, William F.
Nelson, Wanda Jean
Perry, Lee Charles, Jr.

SALINA
Caldwell, Bessie Ellis
Parker, Maryland Mike

SHAWNEE MISSION
Jerome, Norge Winefred

TOPEKA
Alexander, F. S. Jack
Barker, Pauline J.
Bolden, James Lee
Cavens, Sharon Sue
Crable, Dallas Eugene
Dixon, Ernest Thomas, Jr.
Douglas, Joe, Jr.
Franklin, Wayne L.
Gardner, Cedric Boyer
Griffin, Ronald C.
Hendricks, Steven Aaron
Lewis, Wendell J.
Love, Clarence C.
Otudeko, Adebisi Olusoga
Parks, Gilbert R.
Parks, Sherman A.
Rainbow-Earhart, Kathryn
   Adeline
Spence, Joseph Samuel, Sr.
Thomas, John Henry
Wilson, Lawrence C.
Wilson, Marvin H.

WICHITA
Anderson, Eugene
Cranford, Sharon Hill
Cribbs, Theo, Sr.
Griffin-Johnson, Lorraine
   Antionette
Hall, Lloyd Dalton, Jr.

Harmon, William Wesley
Harris, Richard, Jr.
Hayes, Graham Edmondson
Hutcherson, Bernice B. R.
Johnson, Thomas H.
King, Clarence Maurice, Jr.
McAfee, Charles Francis
McCray, Billy Quincy
Mitchell, Jacob Bill
Preston, Richard Clark
Pyles, John E.
Wesley, Clarence E.
Williams, Tommye Joyce

WINFIELD
Brooks, William P.

KENTUCKY

ADAIRVILLE
Washington, Edward, Jr.

BARBOURVILLE
Daniels, Anthony Hawthorne

BEREA
Baskin, Andrew Lewis

BOWLING GREEN
Ardrey, Saundra Curry
Denning, Joe William
Esters, George Edward
Jackson, Earl J.
Long, John Edward
Martin, Cornelius A.
McKinney, Gregory L.
Moxley, Frank O.
Sisney, Ricardo
Starks, Rick
White, Marilyn Mildred

COVINGTON
Hall, Howard Ralph

DANVILLE
Griffin, Betty Sue

EARLINGTON
Johnson, Arthur T.

ELIZABETHTOWN
Green, Larry W.

FRANKFORT
Alexander, Estella Conwill
Banks, Ronald Trenton
Brooks, A. Russell
Graham, Delores Metcalf
Griffin, Betty Sue
Hill, Carl M.
Lambert, Charles H.
Lyons, Donald Wallace
Payne, Mitchell Howard
Smith, Carson Eugene
Smith, Mary Levi
Williams, Robert D., Sr.

GEORGETOWN
Mason, Luther Roscoe

GLASGOW
Watts, Wilsonia

HAZARD
Basey, Ovetta T.

HIGHLAND HEIGHTS
Bell, Sheila Trice
Washington, Michael Harlan

HOPKINSVILLE
Freeman, Norman E., Sr.

LEXINGTON
Brown, Gary W.
Cruse, Charles Plummer
Dotson, William S.
Finn, Robert Green
Fleming, Juanita W.
Gaines, Victor Pryor
Jefferson, Robert R.

Peltier, Arma Martin
Robinson, Andrew
Smith, John Thomas
Stephens, Herman Alvin
Wilkinson, Doris Y.

LOUISVILLE
Amos, Larry C.
Anderson, Carey Laine, Jr.
Anderson, Jay Rosamond
Appleton, Clevette Wilma
Aubespin, Mervin R.
Bateman, Michael Allen
Bather, Paul Charles
Beale, Larry D.
Bingham, Rebecca Josephine (nee
   Taylor)
Blye, Cecil A., Sr.
Brummer, Chauncey Eugene
Burks, Juanita Pauline
Burns, Tommie, Jr.
Burse, Raymond Malcolm
Campbell, E. Alexander
Chatmon, Linda Carol
Chestnut, Edwin, Sr.
Clayborn, Wilma W.
Coatie, Robert Mason
Dockery, Robert Wyatt
Evans, William Clayton
Foree, Jack Clifford
Graham, Tecumseh Xavier
Hackett, Wilbur L., Jr.
Hodge, W. J.
Hudson, James Blaine
Huff, William
Hutchinson, Jerome
Jackson, Thelma Conley
James, Grace M.
Johnson, John J.
Jones, Laura Mae (nee Green)
Jones, Yvonne Vivian
Love, Eleanor Young
Lyles, Leonard E.
Mahin, George E.
McAnulty, Brenda Hart
McMillan, Joseph H.
Meeks, Reginald Kline
Mudd, Louis L.
Parrish, Charles Henry
Powers, Georgia M.
Reeves, Lucius V.
Roberts, Charles L.
Roberts, Ella S.
Robinson, Jonathan N.
Robinson, Samuel
Simon, Walter J.
Simpson, Frank B.
Smith, Robert W.
Smith, Tommie M.
Stephenson, Carolyn L.
Street-Kidd, Mae
Summers, William E., III
Summers, William E., IV
Walker, Cynthia Bush
Wallace, John Howard
Wilson, Hughlyne Perkins
Wilson, Leonard D.
Yeager, Thomas Stephen
Young, Coleman Milton, III
Young, Herman A.
Young, Joyce Howell

MIDWAY
Bradley, Walter Thomas, Jr.

MOREHEAD
Strider, Maurice William

MURRAY
Pounds, Augustine Wright

PADUCAH
Coleman, Robert A.
Harvey, Wardelle G.

RADCLIFF
Richard, Henri-Claude

RICHMOND
Stone, Kara Lynn

RUSSELLVILLE
Hampton, Willie L.

LOUISIANA

ABBEVILLE
Myles, Herbert John

ALEXANDRIA
Dorsey, Errol C.
Hines, J. Edward, Jr.
Metoyer, Rosia G.
Patrick, Julius, Jr.
Williams, E. Faye

BAKER
Millican, Arthenia Bates

BASTROP
Hamlin, Arthur Henry
Loche, Lee Edward
Montgomery, Fred O.
Montgomery, Payne

BATON ROUGE
Abernathy, Ronald Lee
Boddie, Gwendolyn M.
Brown, Georgia W.
Brown, Reginald Royce, Sr.
Burchell, Charles R.
Calloway, Curtis A.
Cobb, Thelma M.
Collier, Clarence Marie
Collins, Warren Eugene
Cummings, Roberta Spikes
Davidson, Kerry
Davis, Donald Fred
Dickens, Samuel
Doomes, Earl
Durant, Thomas James, Jr.
Ellois, Edward R., Jr.
Green, Brenda Kay
Hall, David Anthony, Jr.
Hall, Robert Joseph
Harrison, Lincoln J.
Haynes, John K.
Haynes, Leonard L., Jr.
Hildreth, Gladys Johnson
Hines-Hayward, Olga Loretta
Hubbard, Jean P.
Isadore, Harold W.
Jeffers, Ben L.
Jemison, Theodore Judson
Jones, Johnnie Anderson
Lane, Pinkie Gordon
Lee, Allen Francis, Jr.
Martin, Julia M.
Mayfield, William S.
Mays, David
McNairy, Sidney A.
Mencer, Ernest James
Moch, Lawrence E.
Montgomery, Trent
Patin, Joseph Patrick
Perkins, Huel D.
Prestage, Jewel Limar
Raby, Clyde T.
Rice, Mitchell F.
Ridgel, Gus Tolver
Ridley, Harry Joseph
Rivers, Griffin Harold
Robinson, Edward Ashton
Spikes, Dolores R.
Stamper, Henry J.
Steptoe, Roosevelt
Stone, Jesse Nealand, Jr.
Vaughns, John Claude
Weatherspoon, Keith Earl
Weston, Sharon
Wilkins, Vincent, Jr.
Williams, Karen Renee
Winfield, William T.

BELLE ROSE
Melancon, Norman

BOGALUSA
Jenkins, Gayle Expose
Moses, Andrew M.

BOYCE
Lewis, Gus Edward

BUNKIE
Sheppard, Stevenson Royrayson

CROWLEY
Julian, John Tyrone
Wilson, Sherman Arthur

CULLEN
Underwood, Maude Esther

EUNICE
Fields, Savoynne Morgan
Smith, Marvette Thomas

FERRIDAY
Davis, Sammy, Jr.

FRANKLIN
Richard, Arlene Castain

FRANKLINTON
Martin, Rayfus
Tate, Matthew

GABRIEL
Thomas, Alvin

GRAMBLING
Carter, Lamore Joseph
Craig, Emma Jeanelle Patton
Days, Rosetta Hill
Emmanuel, Tsegai
Ford, Luther L.
Gallot, Richard Joseph
Johnson, Joseph B.
Joiner, Burnett
Mansfield, Andrew K.
Pollard, William Lawrence
Robinson, Eddie
Sanders, William Mac
Smith, Arthur D.

GREENSBURG
Paddio-Johnson, Eunice Alice

HARVEY
Eziemefe, Godslove Ajenavi

IBERVILLE
Louis, Joseph

JENNINGS
Briscoe, Sidney Edward, Jr.
Kellogg, Reginald J.

JONESBORO
Bradford, James Edward

KENNER
Ellis, Zachary L.
Riley, Emile Edward

LAFAYETTE
Alsandor, Jude
Baranco, Raphael Alvin
Brown, Kenneth Edward
Chargois, Jenelle M.
Gaines, Ernest J.
Garrett, Aline M.
McKnight, Albert J.
Prudhomme, Nellie Rose

LAKE CHARLES
Blackwell, Faye Brown
Cole, Charles Zhivaga
St. Mary, Joseph Jerome
Shelton, Harold Tillman

LAKE PROVIDENCE
Closure, Vanilla Threats
Frazier, Ray Jerrell

LEBEAU
Labrie, Harrington

LUTCHER
Jones, Nathaniel, Sr.

MANSFIELD
Patterson, Dessie Lee

MARINGOUIN
Hollins, Joseph Edward

Owens, Ronald C.
Parker, Claude A.
Parker, James Thomas
Parker, Jeff, Sr.
Payne, Osborne Allen
Petersen, Arthur Everett, Jr.
Pettit, Alvin Dwight
Pettus-Bellamy, Brenda Karen
Phillips, Eugenie Elvira
Phillips, Glenn Owen
Pindle-Conaway, Mary Ward
Pollard, William E.
Poole-Heard, Blanche Denise
Pope, Addison W.
Pounds, Moses B.
Pratt, Ruth Jones (Ruth J. King)
Proctor, William H.
Quaynor, Thomas Addo
Quivers, Eric Stanley
Quivers, William Wyatt, Sr.
Ray, William Benjamin
Rayford, Floyd Kinnard
Raymond, Henry James
Reid, Sina M.
Ricard, John H.
Rice, Pamela Ann
Richardson, Earl Stanford
Richardson, Frank (Mr. Frank)
Robinson, Frank
Rogers, Dianna
Roy, Americus M.
Saunders, Elijah
Sawyer, Broadus Eugene
Schmoke, Kurt Lidell
Scribner, Arthur Gerald, Jr.
Sheffey, Ruthe G.
Shervington, E. Walter
Silva, Henry Andrew
Simmons, Charles William
Simms, Stuart Oswald
Simon, Elaine
Simon, Rosalyn McCord
Sinkler, George
Sloan, David E.
Smith, Benjamin Franklin
Smith, DeHaven L.
Smith, William M., Jr.
Solomon, James Daniel
Spaulding, Daniel W.
Stanley, Eugene
Stanley, Hilbert Dennis
Stansbury, Clayton Cresvell
Stanton, Beverly A.
Styles, Kathleen Ann
Sulton, John D.
Sweeney, John Albert
Taylor, Edward Walter
Taylor, Julius H.
Terborg-Penn, Rosalyn M.
Theodore, Yvonne M. (nee Powell)
Thomas, Joseph H.
Thomas-Carter, Jean Cooper
Tildon, Charles G., Jr.
Toliver, William Henry, Sr.
Tong, Dalton Arlington
Waddy, Walter James
Wade, Bruce L.
Walden, Emerson Coleman
Walker, Ernestine
Watkins, Levi, Jr.
Watson, Betty Collier
Watts, Robert B.
Weaver, Garland Rapheal, Jr.
Webb, Harvey, Jr.
Welcome, Verda F.
Whitten, Benjamin C.
Williams, Henry R.
Williams, Maceo Merton
Williams, Roger Kenton
Winfield, George Lee
Winfield, Linda Fitzgerald
Woodfolk, Joseph O.
Woodward, Isaiah Alfonso
Young, Elroy
Young, Larry
Young, N. Louise

BEAVER HEIGHTS
Doyle, Erie R.

BEL AIR
Howard, Leslie Kenyatta

BELTSVILLE
Battle, Mark G.
Caldwell, Sandra Ishmael
Hammond, James Matthew
Parker, Charles McCrae
Subryan, Carmen

BETHESDA
Atkinson, Gladys W.
Branche, William C., Jr.
Epps, Roselyn Payne
Floyd, Jeremiah
Gaston, Marilyn Hughes
Johnson, David Freeman
Johnson, Wayne Alan
Malone, Thomas Ellis
May, James Shelby
McKee, Adam E., Jr.
Morrison, James W., Jr.
Phillips, Leo A.
Press, Harry Cody, Jr.
Sarreals, E. Don
Wilson, Joy Johnson

BLADENSBURG
Armstrong, Ernest W., Sr.

BOWIE
Anderson, Leon H.
Arrington, Pamela Gray
Boone, Zola Ernest
Chew, Bettye L.
Funn, Courtney Harris
Johnson, G. R. Hovey
Lyons, James E., Sr.
Miller, Richard Charles, Jr.
Tipton, Elizabeth Howse
Turner, Evelyn Evon
Wolfe, John Thomas

BRENTWOOD
Hall, Raymond A.
Kashif, Ghayth Nur (Lonnie Kashif)

CALIFORNIA
Lancaster, John Graham

CAMP SPRINGS
Pinkney, John Edward
Roscoe, Wilma J.

CAPITOL HEIGHTS
Beard, Montgomery, Jr.
Blackburn, Charles M.
Cousins, James R., Jr.
Dodson, Vivian M.
Exum, Thurman McCoy

CATONSVILLE
Fullwood, Harlow, Jr.
Oden, Gloria C.

CENTREVILLE
Perine, James L.

CHEVY CHASE
Bryce, Herrington J.
Hudson, Anthony Webster

CLAYTON
Lafayette, Bernard, Jr.

CLINTON
Feliciana, Jerrye Brown
Williams, Wilbert Lee

COLLEGE PARK
Anderson, Amel
Billingsley, Andrew
Connor, Ulysses J., Jr.
Cunningham, William Dean
Fletcher, Howard R.
Fries, Sharon Lavonne
Hall, Mildred Martha
Holman, Benjamin F.
Johnson, Martin Leroy
Johnson, Raymond Lewis
Landry, L. Bartholomew
Lomax, Dervey A.
Morrison, Keith Anthony
Myricks, Noel

Pullen-Brown, Stephanie
Shelton, Harvey William
Slaughter, John Brooks
Williams, Helen Elizabeth

COLUMBIA
Alexander, A. Melvin
Anderson, Ora Sterling
Arnold, Haskell N., Jr.
Brown, George Philip
Brown, Shirley Ann Vining
Bruce, Preston, Jr.
Bumphus, Walter Gayle
Corbin, Angela Lenore
Francis, Yvette Fay
Hamilton, John Mark, Jr.
Hoff, Nathaniel Hawthorne
James, David Phillip
Lawes, Verna
Ligon, Claude M.
Ligon, Doris Hillian
Martin, Sylvia Cooke
May, Cornelius Wallace
McDonald, R. Timothy
Newsome, Clarence Geno
Rotan, Constance S.
Scott, Marvin Wayne
Seriki, Olusola Oluyemisi
Ware, Charles Jerome
Watson, Betty Collier
West, Herbert Lee, Jr.
Wilds, Jetie Boston, Jr.

CROFTON
Fakhrid-Deen, Nashid Abdullah

DISTRICT HEIGHTS
Perrin, David Thomas Perry

DUNDALK
Buckson, Toni Yvonne
Lee, LaVerne C.
Patterson, Theodore Carter Chavis

ELKRIDGE
Davis, Bob

ELLICOTT CITY
Henderson, Lenneal Joseph, Jr.
Wiles, Joseph St. Clair
Williams, Robert B.

EMMITSBURG
Hart, Noel A.

FAIRMOUNT HEIGHTS
Gray, Robert R.
Hall, Mildred Martha

FORESTVILLE
Clark, Andrew Lee
Crockett, Gwendolyn B.
Miller, James, Sr.

FORT HOWARD
Dandy, Roscoe Greer

FORT MEADE
Scribner, Arthur Gerald, Jr.

FORT WASHINGTON
Boardley, Curtestine May
Conley, Herbert A.
Gray, Raymond Leroy, Sr.
Hunigan, Earl
Kamau, Mosi (Anthony Charles Gunn White)
Kirton, Edwin Eggleston
Lucas, Gerald Robert

FREDERICK
Jacob, Willis Harvey

FROSTBURG
Hayden, John Carleton

GAITHERSBURG
Blankenship, Glenn Rayford
Lampkin, Cheryl Lyvette
Young, Raymond, Jr.

GERMANTOWN
Williams, LaShina Brigette
Young, Raymond, Jr.

GLEN BURNIE
Leggett, Vincent Omar

GLENARDEN
Brown, Stanley Donovan
Fletcher, James C., Jr.
James, Henry Nathaniel
Woods, Geneva Halloway

GREENBELT
Covington, M. Stanley
Stephens, Wallace O.
Whitlock, Fred Henry

HAGERSTOWN
Hardy, Michael Leander
Hill, Lawrence Thorne

HILLCREST HEIGHTS
Lawlah, Gloria Gary

HYATTSVILLE
Broadwater, Tommie, Jr.
Flanagan, T. Earl, Jr.
Hall, Willie Green, Jr.
Robinson, Daniel Lee
Tarver, Elking
Vaughns, Sylvester J., Sr.

KENSINGTON
Cannon, Calvin Curtis
Gilmore, Al Tony

LANDOVER
Bacon, Albert S.
Bridgeman, Donald Earl
Carter, Fred Lavelle
Chenier, Phil
Dandridge, Bob
Davidson, Alphonzo Lowell
Davis, Charles Terrell
Daye, Darren Terrell
Dillard, June White
Gaskin, Leroy
Gibson, Mike Anthony
Hopkins, Stephanie Colbert
Johnson, Frank Lavelle
Mahorn, Rick Joel
Malone, Jeff Joel
Malone, Moses Eugene
Miller, James, Sr.
Porter, Kevin
Robinson, Cliff Anthony
Seidel, John C.
Sewell, Tom Eugene
Unseld, Wes
Williams, Gus
Williams, Guy Keith
Williamson, John
Woods, Sylvania Webb, Jr.
Yancey, Carolyn Lois

LANGLEY PARK
Henderson, Stephen E.

LANHAM
McPhail, Weldon
Mickle, Andrea Denise
Noel, Patrick Adolphus
Quinn, Diane C.
Raiford, Roger Lee
Wesley, Clemon Herbert, Jr.
White, Sylvia Kay
Wise, Henry A., Jr.

LANHAM-SEABROOK
Bussey, Charles David
Smith, Perry Anderson, III

LARGO
Bridgeman, Donald Earl
Brown, John Mitchell, Sr.
James, David Phillip

LAUREL
Burns, Denise
Gougis, Lorna Gail
Hewitt, Basil

Hunter, Edwina Earle

LEONARDTOWN
Lancaster, John Graham

MARYLAND
Haskins, Joseph, Jr.

MITCHELLVILLE
Arrington, Lloyd M., Jr.
Finney, Essex Eugene, Jr.
Quarles, Ruth Brett
Richie, Sharon Ivey
Scales, Patricia Bowles

MITCHELLVILLE-WILLOW GROVE
Carpenter, William Arthur, II

MITCHEVILLE
Quarles, Benjamin A.

NEW CARROLLTON
Williams, Helen Elizabeth

NORTH BRENTWOOD
Smith, Perry Anderson, III

NORTH ENGLEWOOD
Gaskin, Leroy

OWINGS MILLS
Rawlings, Marilyn Manuela

OXON HILL
Green, Roland, Sr.
Woodland, Calvin Emmanuel

PARK
Carroll, Charles H.
Taylor, Dalmas A.

PITTSVILLE
Franklin, Herman

PORT DEPOSIT
Fraser, Rhonda Beverly

POTOMAC
Singh, Rajendra P.

PRINCESS ANNE
Brooks, Carolyn Branch
Brooks, Henry Marcellus
Copeland, Leon L.
Ellis, Edward V.
Franklin, Herman
Hedgepeth, Chester Melvin, Jr.
Hopkins, Thomas Franklin
Hytche, William P.
Johnson, Leon
Lewis, Willie Mae
Lockwood, James Clinton
Mitchell, JudyLynn
Monroe, Lillie Mae
Neufville, Mortimer H.
Whittington, Harrison DeWayne

RANDALLSTOWN
Bell, Martha Lue
Crosse, St. George Idris Bryon
Davis, Luther Charles
Gatewood, Wallace Lavell
Murray, Mabel Lake
Oliver, Kenneth Nathaniel
Roulhac, Edgar Edwin

ROCKVILLE
Avery, Waddell
Belton, Edward DeVaughn
Carter, Enrique Delano
Clark, Harry W.
Dines, George B.
Fairley, Wilma
Fleming, Weldon G., Jr.
Francisco, Marcia Madora
Hall, Evelyn Alice (Evelyn Manning)
Hardy-Hill, Edna Mae
Herndon, Gloria E.
Johnson, Elaine McDowell
Key, Addie J.

Manley, Audrey Forbes
Marbury, Donald Lee
Martin, William R.
Moone, James Clark
Moore, Roscoe Michael, Jr.
Moore, Susie M.
Nichols, Edwin J.
Oh, Harry K.
Oliver, John J., Jr.
Parron, Delores L.
Pinkney, John Edward
Powell, William O., Jr.
Reed, Theresa Greene
Rhoden, Richard Allan
Robinson, William Andrew
Stackhouse, E. Marilyn
Williams, Snowden J.
Woodson, Charles R.

SALISBURY
Brooks, Henry Marcellus
Hudson, Jerome William
Johnson, William Smith
Maddox, Elton Preston, Jr.
Mitchell, JudyLynn
Talbot, Alfred Kenneth, Jr.
Williams, Frank Copeland

SEABROOK
Johnson, Raymond Lewis
Jones, Hardi Liddell
Sewell, Isiah Obediah

SEAT PLEASANT
Jackson, Arthur Howard
Theodore, Keith Felix

SEVERNA PARK
Hynson, Carroll Henry, Jr.

SILVER SPRING
Alford, Brenda
Ammons, Tamara Nash
Atkinson, Gladys W.
Barrow, Lionel Ceon, Jr.
Battle, Mark G.
Black, Charlie J.
Brown, Curtis Carnegie, Jr.
Burrell, Emma P.
Countee, Thomas Hilaire, Jr.
Covington, M. Stanley
Criner-Woods, Joyce Verdello
Davenport, Ernest H.
Davis, Frank Derocher
Davis, Tyrone Theophilus
Delaney, Harold
Durham, Joseph Thomas
Grant, Nathaniel
Haley, George Williford Boyce
Hamilton, Samuel Cartenius
Hawkins, John Russell, III
Hill, Brandon T.
Hudson, Merry C.
Hull, Bernard S.
Jackson, Raymond T.
Jenkins, Elaine B.
Jenkins, Robert Kenneth, Jr.
Johnson, Wayne Alan
Jones, Lawrence N.
Kirkland, Gail Alicia
Marchman, Robert Anthony
McAlpine, Robert
Moore, Johnnie Adolph
Morris, Frank Lorenzo, Sr.
Nichols, Owen D.
Nix, Roscoe Russa
Obayuwana, Alphonsus Osarobo
Porter, Carol Denise
Ray, Walter I., Jr.
Reed, Beatrice M.
Rosser, Pearl (nee Lockhart)
Sarreals, E. Don
Seabrooks-Edwards, Marilyn S.
Shannon, Odessa M.
Smith, Edward Nathaniel, Jr.
Theodore, Keith Felix
Vaughn, William Samuel, III
Walker, James
Washington, Edward
Wilcox, Janice Horde
Wilson, Milton

SUITLAND
Tutman, William L.

TAKOMA PARK
Hammond, James Matthew
Johnson, Lloyd A.
Porter, Clarence A.
Simon, Kenneth Bernard
Williams, Herman

TEMPLE HILLS
Harris, Peter J.
Hodges, Clarence Eugene
Jones, Christine Miller
Joyner, Claude C.

TOWSON
Clay, Camille Alfreda
Daley, Thelma Thomas
Gilchriest, Lorenzo
Josey, Leronia Arnetta
Torain, Tony William

UPPER MARLBORO
Callender, Valerie Dawn
Ford, Kenneth A.
Gay, Milton F., Jr.
Johnson, G. R. Hovey
Loving, James Leslie
Perrin, David Thomas Perry
Rogers-Grundy, Ethel W.
Turner, Evelyn Evon
Turner, Marvin Wentz
Wills, James Willard
Wilson, Floyd Edward, Jr.
Woods, Sylvania Webb, Sr.

WALDORF
Sherrod, Ezra Cornell

WASHINGTON
Black, Rosa Walston

WHEATON
Jupiter, Clyde Peter

WOODSTOCK
Massey, Jacquelene Sharp

MASSACHUSETTS

AMHERST
Boyer, Horace Clarence
Bracey, John H., Jr.
Bromery, Randolph Wilson
Darity, Evangeline Royall
Darity, William A.
Frye, Charles Anthony
Gentry, Atron A.
Harris, William M.
Jackson, Arthur Roszell
Love, Barbara
Tillis, Frederick C.
Turner, Castellano B.
Winslow, Reynolds Baker

ANDOVER
Barron, Reginald
Jones, Lawrence W.

ARLINGTON
Greenidge, James Ernest

ASHLEY FALLS
Jamal, Ahmad

AYER
Gaskins, Louise Elizabeth

BEDFORD
Hopkins, Perea M.
Pinderhughes, Charles Alfred

BOSTON
Alexander, John Wesley, Jr.
Alexander, Joyce London
Amiji, Hatim M.
Amory, Reginald L.
Anderson, Michael Wayne
Archibald, Nate
Banks, Ellen
Batson, Ruth Marion
Baylor, Don Edward
Beard, Charles Julian

Birchette-Pierce, Cheryl L.
Bispham, Frank L.
Blackwell, James E.
Bocage, Ronald J.
Bolling, Bruce C.
Bolling, Royal, Jr.
Bowman, Jacquelynne Jeanette
Boyd, Dennis Ray
Brannon, James R.
Brookes, Bernard L.
Brown, Rodger L., Jr.
Bunte, Doris
Burnham, Margaret Ann
Burton, Ronald E.
Byrd, George Edward
Campbell, Sylvan Lloyd
Carter, Warrick L.
Carty-Bennia, Denise S.
Cash, James Ireland, Jr.
Chandler, Dana C., Jr. (Akin Duro)
Coleman, Audrey Rachelle
Collins, Tessil John
Daniel, Jessica Henderson
Davis, Arthur, Jr.
Davis, Willie J.
Dilday, Judith Nelson
Downing, Stephen
Dugger, Edward, III
Edelin, Kenneth C.
Elam, Harry Justin
Emrit, Ronald C.
Eure, Dexter D., Sr.
Felton, James A.
Finley, Skip
Fitch, Harrison Arnold
Fonvielle, William Harold
Gaither, Edmund B.
Garner, Grayce Scott
Garrity, Monique P.
Gates, Otis A., III
Gilkes, Cheryl Townsend
Graham, Saundra M.
Griffin, Jean Thomas
Grigsby, Charles T.
Grimes, Calvin M., Jr.
Hall, David
Handy, Delores
Harper, Tommy
Harris, Barbara Clemente
Harris, David Ellsworth
Harris, John Everett
Harris, Linda Marie
Hayden, Robert C., Jr.
Haygood, Wil
Haynes, Michael E.
Henry, Joseph Louis
Homer, Ronald A.
Hoyte, James Sterling
Ireland, Roderick Louis
Jacks, Ulysses
Jackson, Ellen Swepson
Jackson, Reginald Leo
Jobe, Shirley A.
Johnson, Charles Henry
Johnson, Dennis
Johnson, Wendell Norman, Sr.
Jones, Clarence J., Jr. (Jeep Jones)
Jones, Gayl
Knight, Muriel B.
Knowles, Claire Em
Ladd, Florence Cawthorne
Laymon, Heather R.
Laymon, John W.
Lee, Bertram M.
Lewis, Elma I.
Lewis, Maurice
Lindsay, Reginald C.
Long, Juanita Outlaw
Martin, John Gordon
Maxwell, Cedric
Mbere, Aggrey Mxolisi
McClain, James W.
Miller, Melvin B.
Millett, Ricardo A.
Montgomery, Keesler H.
Moseley, Frances Kenney
Murphy, Ric
Murrell, Charlayne E.
Nelson, David S.
Norris, Donna M.
O'Bryant, John D.
Overbea, Luix Virgil
Owens, William

Owens-Hicks, Shirley
Padulo, Louis
Parish, Robert
Parks, Paul
Peoples, Florence W.
Pierce, Rudolph F.
Pilot, Ann Hobson
Pinckney, Stanley
Poussaint, Alvin Francis
Prunty, Howard Edward
Putnam, Glendora M.
Reynolds, Pamela Terese
Rice, James Edward
Roberts, Wesley A.
Robinson, Jack E.
Rushing, Byron D.
Russell, George Alton, Jr.
Sales, Richard Owen
Scott, Deborah Ann
Sherwood, Wallace Walter
Simmons, Sylvia J.
Smith, Arthur D.
Smith, Edgar E.
Snowden, Gail
Soden, Richard Allan
Spicer, Kenneth, Sr.
Spruill, James Arthur
Stamps, Leon Preist
Stith, Charles Richard
Stull, Donald L.
Thompson, Benjamin Franklin
Thompson, William B. D.
Venson, John E.
Walters, Hubert Everett
Warren, Joseph David
Washington, Mary Helen
White, Augustus A., III
White, Richard C.
Whiteside, Larry W.
Wiley, Fletcher Houston
Willock, Marcelle Monica
Wilson, John
Wilson, Laval S.
Winston, Bonnie Veronica
Wolfman, Brunetta Reid
Woodhouse, Enoch O'Dell, II
Worthy, William
Yancey, Charles Calvin
Yarbrough, Robert Elzy
Yarde, Richard Foster

BRIDGEWATER
Gaines, Paul Laurence, Sr.
Johnson, Addie Collins
Santos, Henry J.

BRIGHTON
Phillips, Colette Alice-Maude

BROCKTON
Hagler, Marvelous Marvin

BROOKLINE
Birchette-Pierce, Cheryl L.
Cofield, James E., Jr.
Daniel, Jessica Henderson
Fortune, Alvin V.
Gulliver, Adelaide Cromwell
Potter, Judith Diggs

BURLINGTON
Dyer, Charles Austen

CAMBRIDGE
Bailey, James W.
Barnett, Evelyn Brooks
Bell, Derrick Albert, Jr.
Bennett, Robert A.
Brown, Jeffrey LeMonte
Cannon, Katie Geneva
Carey, Jennifer Davis
Castle, Keith L.
Crite, Allan Rohan
Daniels, Alfred Claude Wynder
Davis, William E., Sr.
Dike, Kenneth Onwuka
Dixon, John M.
Dobbins, Albert Greene, III
Edley, Christopher F., Jr.
Fleurant, Gerdes
Ford, Charles
Gomes, Peter John
Guinier, Ewart
Harrington, Philip Leroy

Hawkins, James C.
Hope, Richard Oliver
Hopkins, Esther Arvilla
Huggins, Nathan Irvin
Jackson-Thompson, Marie O.
Jenkins, George Arthur, Jr.
Jobe, Shirley A.
Johnson, Charles E. Memusi
Johnson, Willard Raymond
Jones, Frank S.
Jones, William J.
Kilson, Martin Luther, Jr.
Ladd, Florence Cawthorne
Loury, Glenn Cartman
Marsalis, Branford
Morris, Bernard Alexander
Owens, Edward Oliver
Patterson, Orlando Horace
Pierce, Chester Middlebrook
Plummer, Michael Justin
Poussaint, Ann Ashmore
Riddick, Eugene E.
Roberts, Louis Wright
Russell, George A.
Southern, Eileen Jackson
Strait, George A.
Taliaferro, Nettie Howard
Thomas, Douglas L.
Thompson, Marcus Aurelius
Turner, John Barrimore
Wallace, Phyllis A.
Williams, Clarence G.
Williams, James H., Jr.
Williams, Preston N.
Willie, Charles Vert
Young, James E.

CANTON
Murphy, Michael McKay

CHESTNUT HILL
Araujo, Norman
Keith, Karen C.
Smith, Charles F., Jr.

DORCHESTER
Mayes, Nathaniel H., Jr.
Portis, Kattie Harmon (Jessie Kate Harmon)
Ross, Joanne A.
Watson, Georgette
Webster, Theodore

EAST FALMOUTH
Pena, Robert Bubba

FITCHBURG
Browning, Grainger
Myers, Earl T.

FORT WASHINGTON
Holland-Calbert, Mary Ann

FOXBORO
Clayborn, Ray Dewayne
Cunningham, Samuel Lewis, Jr.
Dawson, J. Lin
Fryar, Irving
Greenidge, James Ernest
Grier, Bobby
Hamilton, Raymond L.
Holloway, Brian
Ivory, Horace Orlando
Jackson, Harold
Morgan, Stanley
Stingley, Darryl F.
Tippett, Andre

FRAMINGHAM
Butler, John O.
Dyer, Charles Austen
Hendricks, Marvin B.
Jenkins, George Arthur, Jr.

GRAFTON
Pope, Ruben Edward, III

HARVARD
Chandler, Sharon Kay

HINGHAM
Roundtree, Eugene V. N.
Roundtree, Nicholas John

HOLLISTON
Finley, Betty M.

HOLYOKE
Storey, Charles F.

HULL
Alexander, John Wesley, Jr.

JAMAICA PLAIN
Pierce, Chester Middlebrook

KINGSTON
Hardeman, James Anthony

LEEDS
Harrison, Paul Carter

LEXINGTON
Brannon, James R.
Kornegay, Wade M.
Marsh, Alphonso Howard
Scott, Marvin Bailey

LONGMEADOW
McFarlin, Kernaa D'Offert, Jr.

LOWELL
Bruce, John Irvin
Crayton, Samuel S.
Dorsey, Joseph A.
Gonsalves, June Miles
Rocha, Joseph Ramon, Jr.
Scruggs, Allie W.

LYNN
Gerald, Arthur Thomas, Jr.
Jones, Clarance W.

MALDEN
Phillips, Helen M.

MANSFIELD
Weathers, Robert

MARBLEHEAD
Cox, Arthur James, Sr.
Fonvielle, William Harold

MARION
McFadden, Samuel Wilton

MATTAPAN
Baaqee, Susanne Inez
Griffin, Jean Thomas
Owens-Hicks, Shirley
Whitworth, E. Leo, Jr.

MATTAPOISETT
Robinson, John L.

MAYNARD
Sims, John Leonard
Smith-Whitaker, Audrey N.

MEDFORD
Anderson, Thomas Jefferson
Brown-Knable, Bobbie Margaret
Clark, VeVe A.
Gibson, Harris, Jr.
Gill, Gerald Robert
Knable, Bobbie Margaret Brown
Walton, Roland J.

MIDDLEBORO
Townsend, Murray Luke, Jr.

MILLBURY
Bond, Louis Grant

MILLIS
Northover, Vernon Keith

NEEDHAM
Coleman, Audrey Rachelle
Langhart, Janet Floyd

NEWTON
Brown, Morgan Cornelius
Butler, Katherine Elizabeth
Jenkins-Scott, Jackie

O'Neal, Eddie S.

NEWTON CENTRE
Cottrol, Robert J.
Howe, Ruth-Arlene W.

NEWTONVILLE
Speede-Franklin, Wanda A.
Whiteside, Larry W.

NORTH ADAMS
Cassis, Glenn Albert

NORTH AMHERST
Lester, Julius

NORTH DARTMOUTH
Hoagland, Everett H., III

NORTH EASTON
McClain, James W.

NORTH GRAFTON
Paige, Alvin

NORTHAMPTON
Butler, Johnnella E.
Morris-Hale, Walter
Smith, Eleanor Jane
Walter, John C.
Winters, Wendy Glasgow

NORTHBORO
Riddick, Eugene E.

NORWOOD
Hardeman, James Anthony

OAK BLUFFS
Nix, Theophilus Richard, Jr.
Tucker, Herbert E., Jr.

ORLEANS
Rivers, Robert Joseph, Jr.

PEABODY
Womack, John H.

PLYMOUTH
Anderson, Marjorie Eleanor Amado
Gray, Arthur L.

RANDOLPH
Cannon, Edith H.
Murphy, Michael McKay
Whitaker, Arthur L.

ROXBURY
Armstead, Ron E.
Banks, Richard L.
Carroll, Charlene O.
Donelan, Clarence Warren
Hodge, Paget T.
Jenkins-Scott, Jackie
Landsmark, Theodore Carlisle
McGuire, Jean Mitchell
Rickson, Gary Ames
Thomas, Carl D.
Wiley, Fletcher Houston
Wyatt, Beatrice E.

ROXBURY CROSSING
Thomas, John

SALEM
Cox, Arthur James, Sr.
Fleurant, Gerdes
Gerald, Arthur Thomas, Jr.

SOMERSET
Banks, Ronald

SOMERVILLE
Jackson, Earl, Jr.
Johnson, Parker Collins

SOUTH HADLEY
Chisholm, Shirley
Kerr, Frances Mills
McHenry, Mary Williamson

SOUTH LANCASTER
Willoughby, Susan Melita

SPRINGFIELD
Danforth, Robert L.
Del Pino, Jerome King
Fullilove, Paul A., Sr.
Gibbons, John
Gibson, Maurice
Harvey, Raymond
Johnson, Rebecca M.
Lee, Charles Gary, Sr.
Mapp, John Robert
Paige, Alvin
Smith, James Almer, Jr.

SUDBURY
Harrell, Oscar W., Jr.

WAKEFIELD
Roberts, Louis Wright

WALTHAM
Bonaparte, Tony Hillary
Cash, Arlene Marie
Farrington, Thomas Alex
Williams, Frank Christopher, Jr.

WATERTOWN
Crawford, James Wesley
Ford, Charles

WELLESLEY
Cudjoe, Selwyn Reginald
Jones, Jacqueline
Martin, Tony

WENHAM
Roberts, Wesley A.

WEST WAREHAM
Martin, Baron H.

WESTBORO
Tucker, Clarence T.
Watkins, William, Jr.

WESTFIELD
Ali, Kamal Hassan
Ford, Donald A.
White, Luther J.

WILLIAMSTOWN
Dickerson, Dennis Clark

WINTHROP
Allen, Samuel Washington

WORCESTER
Gilbert, Christopher
Hunter, Eric E.
Matory, William Earle, Jr.
McNeil, Ogretta V.
Peace, G. Earl, Jr.
Price, Elizabeth Louise
Stowe, Louise Pitts

MICHIGAN

ALBION
Davis, Willie A.

ALLEGAN
Weiss, Ed, Jr.

ALLEN PARK
McCurdy, Brenda Wright

ALLENDALE
Hill, Mervyn E., Jr.

ANN ARBOR
Allen, Wendell
Arthos, John
Bowman, Phillip Jess
Brabson, Howard V.
Bradley, James Howard, Jr.
Cash, William L., Jr.
Chaffers, James A.
Cruse, Harold Wright

Cruzat, Gwendolyn S.
DeBracy, Warren
Deskins, Donald R., Jr.
Edwards, Alfred L.
Ellis, O. Herbert
Ellis, Wade
Evans, Billy J.
Finn, John William
Fuller, Almyra Oveta
Gibson, Ralph Milton
Goodman, George D.
Harrison, Don K., Sr.
Hinton, Alfred Fontaine
Jackson, James Sidney
Jackson, Murray Earl
Johnson, Harold R.
Johnson, Henry
Johnson, Lemuel A.
Kilkenny, James H.
Lockard, Jon Onye
Lockett, Harold James
McAfee, Leo C., Jr.
McCuiston, Frederick Douglass, Jr.
Moody, Charles David, Sr.
Morgan, Raleigh, Jr.
Northcross, Wilson Hill, Jr.
Parker, Walter Gee
Patterson, Willis Charles
Porter, John W.
Sutton, Sharon Egretta
Uzoigwe, Godfrey N.
Williams, Booker T.
Williams, Melvin D.
Williams, Sonya Denise
Wilson, Patricia A.
Woodbury, Margaret Clayton
Woodford, John Niles
Young, Mary E.

BATTLE CREEK
Baines, Tyrone Randolph
Bullock, Clifton Vernice
Davis, Richard O.
Hicks, Veronica Abena
McKinney, James Ray
Patterson, Gerald William
Penn, Shelton C.
Stewart, Joseph M.
Taylor, Charles Avon

BAY CITY
Baker, Oscar Wilson
Selby, Ralph Irving

BELLEVILLE
Crawford, Margaret Ward

BENTON HARBOR
Cooke, Wilce L.
Ealy, Mary Newcomb
Hull, Ellis L., Sr.
Madison, Shannon L.
McKeller, Thomas Lee
Yarbrough, Charles
Yarbrough, Mamie Luella

BERRIEN SPRINGS
Davis, Clifton D.
Miles, Norman Kenneth
Mutale, Elaine Butler
Warren, Joseph W.

BIG RAPIDS
Gant, Raymond Leroy

BIRMINGHAM
Richie, Leroy C.
Theus, Lucius

BLOOMFIELD HILLS
Butler, John Donald
Parker, H. Wallace
Pettress, Andrew William
Pickard, William Frank

BROHMAN
Freeman, McKinley Howard, Sr.

CASSOPOLIS
Danzy, LeRoy Henry

CLARKSTON
Bell-Foster, Wilhemenia

DEARBORN
Armstrong, Walter
Bailer, Kermit Gamaliel
Clarke, Benjamin Louis
Daniels, Jesse
Dixon, Louis Tennyson
Green, Dennis O.
Hall, Elliott S.
Howard, Norman
Jones, Cloyzelle Karrelle
Madison, Ronald L.
Miller, Jean Carolyn Wilder
Munson, Robert H.
Procter, Harvey Thornton, Jr.
Turner, Allen H.
Wilson, Blenda J.
Wright, Joseph Malcolm

DETROIT
Addison, Caroline Elizabeth
Ahmad, Jadwaa
Allen, Alex James, Jr.
Allen, Charles Edward
Anderson, Barbara Jenkins
Anderson, Eloise B. McMorris
Anderson, John A.
Anderson, Moses B.
Anderson, Nicholas Charles
Anderson, Oddie
Archer, Dennis Wayne
Arrington, Harold Mitchell
Arrington, Robyn James, Jr.
Atchison, Leon H.
Aubert, Alvin Bernard
Ayala, Reginald P.
Bailey, Chauncey Wendell, Jr.
Bandy, Riley Thomas, Sr.
Banks, Beatrice
Baranco, Beverly Victor, Jr.
Barden, Don H.
Barfield, Clementine (nee Chism)
Barrow, Thomas Joe
Barthwell, Jack Clinton, III
Bates, Alonzo W.
Batiste, Edna E.
Baxter, Wendy Marie
Beatty, Robert L.
Bennett, Delores
Bennett, George P.
Beverly, Benjamin Franklin
Bing, Dave
Bishop, James, Jr.
Blackburn, Alberta
Blackwell, Arthur Brendhal, III
Bobo, Roscoe Lemual
Boggs, James
Bond, Alan D.
Booker, Anne M.
Boyce, Charles N.
Bozeman, Catherine E.
Bradfield, Clarence McKinley
Bradfield, Horace Ferguson
Bradley, Wayne W.
Brazelton, Edgar, Jr.
Brewer, James A., Sr.
Bridgewater, Paul
Briscoe, Thomas F.
Brock, Gerald
Brodis, Nellie Fannie
Broughton, Christopher Leon
Brown, Clifford Anthony
Brown, Georgia R.
Brown, Mattie R.
Brown, Noah, Jr.
Brown, Richard Osborne
Brown, William James (Gates)
Browne, Ernest C., Jr.
Burden, Pennie L.
Butler, Charles W.
Butler, John Donald
Byrd, Frederick E.
Cain, Waldo
Caison, Thelma Jann
Cargill, Gilbert Allen
Carter, Arthur Michael
Carter, Lewis Winston
Carter, Ora Williams
Catchings, Yvonne Parks
Cauthen, Richard L.
Chapman, Gilbert Bryant, II
Chapman, Melvin

Chestang, Leon Wilbert
Clay, Eric Lee
Cleage, Albert B., Jr.
Clements, Walter H.
Clermont, Volna
Cleveland, Clyde
Cobbin, Gloria Constance
Coffee, Lawrence Winston
Coleman, Everod A.
Coleman, Rodney Albert
Collins, Barbara Rose
Combs, Julius V.
Conner, Gail Patricia
Conyers, Nathan G.
Cook, Julian Abele, Jr.
Cooper, Evelyn Kaye
Cotman, Ivan Louis
Cox, James L.
Cox, Taylor H., Sr.
Cozart, John
Craig, Rhonda Patricia
Crews, William Hunter
Crockett, George W., III
Crockett, George William, Jr.
Croft, Wardell C.
Cross, Haman, Jr.
Crump-McCoy, Robbie L.
Cushingberry, George, Jr.
Dade, Malcolm G., Jr.
Daggs, LeRoy W.
Daniels, Jesse
Darnell, Edward Buddy
Davenport, C. Dennis
Davidson, Arthur B.
Davis, Edward
Davis, Erellon Ben
Davis, Marion Harris
Davis-Williams, Phyllis A.
Denning, Bernadine Newsom
Douglas, Walter Edmond
Dozier, Tillman
Dudley, Calmeze Henike, Jr.
Dudley, Herman T.
Dunbar, Joseph C.
DunCombe, C. Beth
Duplessis, Harry Y.
Dykes, Marie Draper
Eagan, Emma Louise
Edwards, Dennis L.
Edwards, Esther Gordy
Edwards, Rupert L.
Ernst, Reginald H.
Evans, Thomas
Fabre, Edwin G.
Farrell-Donaldson, Marie D.
Feemster, John Arthur
Ferrebee, Thomas G.
Fields, M. Joan
Fields, Stanley
Fitzpatrick, Julia C.
Fitzpatrick, William J.
Ford, William L., Jr.
Francisco, Joseph Salvadore, Jr.
Franklin, Aretha
Franklin, Eugene T., Jr.
Fritz, James B.
Frohman, Roland H.
Gadson, Rosetta E.
Garbey, Barbaro
Gardner, Samuel C.
Gaskin, Jeanine
Gibson, Johnnie M. M.
Gibson, Sarah L.
Givens, Leonard David
Goodwin, Jesse Francis
Gordon, Aaron Z.
Graves, Irene Amelia
Graves, Ray Reynolds
Green, Charles A.
Green, Elizabeth Lee (nee Doles)
Green, Forrest F.
Green, Verna S.
Gregory, Tenicia Ann
Griffith, Vera Victoria
Griswold, A. J.
Gunn, Arthur Clinton
Guyton, Tyree
Hall, Perry Alonzo
Hall-Keith, Jaqueline Yvonne
Haney, Don Lee
Hankins, Andrew Jay, Jr.
Harrell, Ruth J.
Harris, Harcourt Glenties
Harris, Joseph Benjamin

Harris, Joseph Preston
Harris, Marjorie Elizabeth
Harrison, Ernest Alexander
Hart, William L.
Hatcher, Lillian
Hayes-Giles, Joyce V.
Hearns, Thomas
Henderson, Erma I.
Henderson, Ramona Estelle
Hendrieth, Brenda Lucille
Herndon, Larry Lee
Hewitt, Ronald Jerome
Hill, George Calvin
Hill, George Hiram
Hilliard, William Alexander
Hobson, Donald Lewis
Hodge, Adele P.
Holliday, Prince E.
Hollowell, Kenneth Lawrence
Holman, Forest H.
Hood, Elizabeth
Hood, Harold
Hood, Morris, Jr.
Hood, Nicholas
Hoover, Jesse
Houston, Corinne P.
Howze, Dorothy J.
Hubbard, Marilyn French
Hubbard, Paul Leonard
Hudson, Lester Darnell
Hughes, Carl D.
Hurst, Cleveland, Jr.
Hylton, Kenneth N.
Ice, Anne-Mare
Ingram, James William
Jackson, Charles, Sr.
Jackson, George K.
Jackson, Tomi L.
Jackson, Winston Burleigh
Jay, James M.
Jefferson, Arthur
Jefferson, Horace Lee
Jenkins, Marilyn Joyce
Johnson, Francis Edward, Jr.
Johnson, Gage
Johnson, Tommie Ulmer
Johnson, Zodie Anderson
Jones, Dorinda A.
Keemer, Edgar B.
Keith, Damon J.
Kelley, Wilbourne Anderson, III
Keys, Brady, Jr.
Kimmons, Willie James
King, John L.
Kispert, Dorothy Lee
Kornegay, Francis A.
Lane, Richard (Dick Night-Train)
Lang, Winston E.
Larrie, Reginald Reese
Lawson, William Emmett
Leatherwood, Robert P.
Leber, Mariann E.
Lemon, Chester Earl
Lemon, Michael Wayne, Sr.
Lester, Nina Mack
Lewis, David Baker
Lewis, Walton A.
Little, Ronald Eugene
Lloyd, Leona Loretta
Lloyd, Leonia Jannetta
Maben, Hayward C., Jr.
Mack, Cleveland J., Sr.
Madgett, Naomi Long
Major, Henrymae M.
Makupson, Walter H.
Mallett, Conrad L.
Margerum, Roger Williams
Martin, Fred
Masse', Donald D.
Mathews, George
McArthur, Barbara Jean (nee Martin)
McClelland, Marguerite Marie
McCloud, Aaron C.
McFarland, Ollie Franklin
McGinnis, James W.
McGregor, Edna M. (nee McGruder)
McHenry, James O'Neal
McKinney, David Walter, III
McLaurin, Jasper Etienne
McLean, John Alfred, Jr.
McMurry, Walter M., Jr.
McSwain, David L.

Merritt, Reuben Asa
Merritt-Cummings, Annette (Annette Merritt Jones)
Mickens, Maxine
Miller, Doris Jean
Miller, Sharon Bernard
Miller-Reid, Dora Alma
Minter, Eloise Devada
Mitchell, Augustus William
Mitchell, Henry B.
Mitchell, Lilyann Jackson
Moore, Warfield, Jr.
Moorehead, Thomas A.
Morcom, Claudia House
Morgan, June Elloie
Morgan, Monica Alise
Morton, Charles E.
Moss, Thomas Edward, Sr.
Munday, Cheryl Casselberry
Munson, Eddie Ray
Murphy, Charles A.
Murphy, Raymond M.
Neal, Lynwood
Nelson, Nathaniel W.
Nicco-Annan, Lionel
Nolan, Robert L.
Norman, George E.
Parker, Bernard F., Jr.
Parker, Darwin Carey
Parker, Jean L. (nee Lane)
Parks, Rosa
Parnell, William Cornellus, Jr.
Patrick, Lawrence Clarence, Jr.
Patterson, Michael Duane
Pattman, Virgil Thomas, Sr.
Paul, John F.
Pearson, Jesse S.
Peebles-Meyers, Helen Marjorie
Penn, Charles E.
Penn-Atkins, Barbara A.
Perkins, Myla Levy
Perkins, Robert E. L.
Perry, Harold
Perry, Lowell W.
Peterson, Marcella Tandy
Phillip, Michael John
Phillips, Wilburn R.
Pickard, William Frank
Pickett, Dovie T.
Pride, J. Thomas
Proctor, Leonard D.
Pulliam, Betty E.
Quinn, Longworth D., Jr.
Radden, Thelma Gibson
Randall, Dudley Felker
Rayford, Brenda L.
Reed, Gregory J.
Revely, William
Rich, Wilbur C.
Richardson, Ralph H.
Riley, Rosetta Margueritte
Robbins, Robert J.
Roberson, Dalton Anthony
Roberson, Lawrence R.
Robinson, Milton J.
Roland, Benautrice, Jr.
Ross, Mary Olivia
Roulhac, Roy L.
Rowe, Nansi Irene
Sanders, Delbert
Saulsberry, Guy O.
Shakoor, Adam Adib
Shannon, Robert F.
Shavers, Catherine
Sheffield, Horace L., Jr.
Sheppard, Ronald John
Shipley, Anthony J.
Sibley, Ellen C.
Simpkins, J. Edward
Slaughter, Peter
Smith, Eddie D.
Smith, Otis M.
Smith, Philip Gene
Smith, Virgil Clark, Jr.
Smith-Gray, Cassandra Elaine
Smitherman, Geneva
Snowden, Charlene G.
Sowell, Myzell
Stallworth, Thomas Fontaine, III
Stephens, Cynthia Diane
Stepp, Marc
Steward, Emanuel
Stewart, Darneau V.
Stewart, Kenneth C.

Stotts, Valmon D.
Stovall, Audrean
Strong, Craig Stephen
Strong, Douglas Donald
Strong, Helen Francine (Fran Lanier)
Strong, Peter E.
Summerville, Tommie Lewis
Swan, Lionel F.
Swanson, O'Neil D.
Tabor, Lillie Montague
Tappes, Shelton
Taylor, Anna Diggs
Taylor, Cledie Collins
Taylor, Pauline J.
Teasley, Marie R.
Temple, Ronald J.
Thomas, Jacqueline Marie
Tilles, Gerald Emerson
Tinsley-Williams, Alberta
Trent, James E.
Tucker, Paul, Jr.
Venable, Abraham S.
Vest, Donald Seymour, Sr.
Vest, Hilda Freeman
Waddles, Charleszetta Lina
Wahls, Myron Hastings (Mike)
Walker, Joseph
Wash, Glenn Edward
Washington, Jacquelin Edwards
Washington, Luisa
Waterman, Homer D.
Watkins, Aretha La Anna
Watkins, Harold D., Sr.
Watkins, Walter C., Jr.
Watson, Anne
Watson, Clifford D.
Watson, Milton H.
Watters, Linda A.
Watts, Lucile (nee Alexander)
Whitaker, Louis Rodman
White, Cohen W.
White, Donald F.
Whitten, Charles F.
Whitten, Eloise Culmer
Wiley-Pickett, Gloria
Williams, Clarence Earl, Jr.
Williams, Eddie, Sr.
Williams, Martha S.
Williams, Morris O.
Williams, Patricia R.
Wilson, Reginald
Wisdom, David Watts
Wolfe, Estemore A.
Wood, Michael H.
Woodruff, James W.
Woodson, Shirley A.
Woodson, Thelma L.
Wyche, Vera Rowena
York, Russel Harold
Young, Coleman A.
Young, Joseph Floyd, Sr.

DEXTER
Sutton, Sharon Egretta

DRAYTON PLAINS
Verbal, Claude A.

EAST LANSING
Coleman, Don Edwin
Gunnings, Thomas S.
Holloway, Albert Curtis
Johnson, Georgia Anna
Jones, Arthur L.
Lang, Marvel
Lipscomb, Wanda Dean
Martin, Blanche
Mays, William, Jr.
Pipes, William H.
Radcliffe, Aubrey
Reynolds, Nanette Lee (nee Smith)
Scarborough, Charles S.
Thornton, Dozier W.
Turner, Moses
Vance, Irvin E.
Weil, Robert L.
Williams, Donald H.

ELOISE
Benjamin, Esther P.

FARMINGTON HILLS
Ali, Schavi Mali
Banfield, Anne L.
Cockerham, Haven Earl
Jensen, Renaldo Mario
Robinson, Ernest Preston, Sr.

FERNDALE
Farrow, Harold Frank
McRipley, G. Whitney
Wilson, Barbara Jean

FLAT ROCK
Harrell, Charles H.
Polk, Eugene Steven, Sr.

FLINT
Anderson, Ronald Edward
Baker, Darryl Brent
Beard, Martin Luther
Bennett, Al
Bivins, Ollie B., Jr.
Bullard, Edward A., Jr.
Callaway, Dwight W.
DeMille, Darcy (Wilma Littlejohn Jackson)
Diggs, Roy Dalton, Jr.
Dismuke, Leroy
Duncan, Verdell
Epps, A. Glenn
Gunn, Willie Cosdena Thomas
Harris, Helen B.
Hatter, Henry
Herring, William F.
Hunter, John W.
Keyes, Alfred Lee
Kimbrough, Clarence B.
Lewis, Billie
Loving, Pamela Yvonne
McCree, Floyd J.
McDonald, Richard E.
McGuire, Cyril A.
Montgomery, James C.
Mullens, Delbert W.
Newman, Paul Dean
Nichols, LeRoy
Petross, Precious Doris
Piper, W. Archibald
Price, William S., III
Reed, Joann
Robertson, John Gilbert
Scruggs, Cleorah J.
Sevillian, Clarence Marvin
Sharp, James Alfred
Smith, Granville N.
Stanley, Woodrow
Thompson, Jesse M.
Twigg, Lewis Harold
Washington, Valdemar Luther
Williams, Charlotte Leola

GARDEN CITY
Settles, Rosetta Hayes

GRAND BLANC
Anderson, Ronald Edward

GRAND RAPIDS
Brame, Walter Melvyn
Collins, Paul
Drew, Stephen Richard
Franks, Julius, Jr.
Gibson, Benjamin F.
Hair, John
Harris, Julius
Hoskins Clark, Tempy M.
Jones, Sylvester
Mathis, Walter Lee, Sr.
McDonald, Jon Franklin
McGhee, Georgia Mae
Small, Isadore, III
Smith, Teasther West
Turner, George Timothy

GROSSE POINTE
Pearson, Jesse S.

GROSSE POINTE PARK
Watters, Linda A.

HIGHLAND PARK
Copeland, Kathleen (nee Maxwell)
Downes, Dwight
Harrison, Ernest Alexander
Heath, Comer, III
Hope, Julius Caesar
McClung, Willie David
Miller, Jesse P.

HOLLAND
Cruz, Virgil
Powell, Charles L., Jr.

HOLLY
Garner, June B.

IDLEWILD
Bullett, Audrey Kathryn
Winburn, B. J.

INKSTER
Bell, Mary L.
Bradford, Equilla Forrest
Cox, Wendell
Ezell, William Alexander
Hinkle, Jackson Herbert
James, Naomi Ellen
Johnson, Willie
LeCesne, Terrel M.
Malone, Charles A.
Young, Watson A.

JACKSON
Breeding, Carl L.
Clay, Nathaniel, Jr.
Faulkner, Marquetta Larneita
Thompson, James W.

KALAMAZOO
Baskerville, Pearl
Brinn, Chauncey J.
Cothran, Tilman Christopher
Daniel, Griselda
Davis, Charles Alexander
Dube, Thomas M. T.
Elliott, Anthony Daniel, III
Gammon, Reginald Adolphus
Gatlin, Elissa L.
Hawkins, Mary L.
Jones, Leander Corbin
Murrain, William A.
Payne, Vernon
Pettiford, Steven Douglas
Phillips, Romeo Eldridge
Smith, Isabelle R.
Spradling, Mary Elizabeth Mace
Walker, Lewis
Walker, Moses L.
Washington, Arthur, Jr.
Washington, Earl Melvin
White, Damon L.
Williams, Sidney B., Jr.

KENTWOOD
Harper, Earl

LANSING
Austin, Richard H.
Barron, Wendell
Brown, Robert, Jr.
Canady, Hortense Golden
Cason, David, Jr.
Chavis, Theodore R.
Clack, Floyd
Coleman, Herman W.
Collins-Bondon, Carolyn R.
Cotman, Ivan Louis
Evans, Eva L.
Gillum, Ronald M.
Glass, James
Guthrie, Carlton Lyons
Guthrie, Michael J.
Harrison, Charlie J., Jr.
Hood, Raymond W.
Jones, Jesse J., Jr.
Kilpatrick, Carolyn Cheeks
Leatherwood, Larry Lee
Lett, Gerald William
Lipscomb, Wanda Dean
McNeely, Matthew
Metcalf, Andrew Lee, Jr.
Murphy, Raymond M.

Norman, James H.
O'Neal, Connie Murry
Pickett, Alvin L.
Porter, Grady J.
Quincy, Ronald Lee
Reynolds, Nanette Lee (nee Smith)
Richardson, Gilda Faye
Rodgers, Shirley Marie
Smith, Gloria R.
Smith, Virgil Clark, Jr.
Stallworth, Alma G.
Stallworth, Oscar B.
Tate, James A.
Thomas, Claude Roderick
Vaughn, Jackie, III
Wallick, Ernest Herron
Watkins, Juanita

LINCOLN PARK
Harris, Terea Donnelle

MADISON HEIGHTS
Goldsberry, Ronald Eugene

MARSHALL
Gray, Marcus J.

MIDLAND
Dorman, Linneaus C.
Williams, Billy Myles

MONROE
White, Gary Leon

MOUNT CLEMENS
Burns, Sarah Ann
Clark, Louis James
Rickman, Lewis Daniel, Sr.

MOUNT PLEASANT
Toms-Robinson, Dolores C.

MUSKEGON
Coleman, Elizabeth Sheppard
Garrison, Robert E., Jr.
Pressley, Stephen, Jr.
Wilkins, Rillastine Roberta
Williams, John H.

MUSKEGON HEIGHTS
Howell, Willie R.
Jones, Patricia Yvonne
Terrell, John L.

NEW HAVEN
Stone, Dolores June

NORTHVILLE
Sanders, Wendell Rowan

NOVI
Davis, Diane Lynn

OAK PARK
Farr, Melvin
Livingston-White, Deborah J. H. (Debi Starr-White)

PAW PAW
Daniel, Griselda

PLYMOUTH
Parker, Walter Gee
Penn, Luther

PONTIAC
Brown, Christopher C.
Chambers, Pamela S.
Craig, Richard
Hatchett, Elbert
Jackson, Cornelia Pinkney
Jones, James
Lee, Ron
McCree, Edward L.
Moore, Walter Louis
Morgan, Richard H., Jr.
Riggs, Harry L.
Sims, Billy (The Silver Streak)
Thomas, Isiah Lord
Thompson, Leonard
Westbrook, Scott C., III

PORTAGE
Phillips, Romeo Eldridge

RIVER ROUGE
Milton, Henry Benford
Milton, Samuel Byron

ROCHESTER
Atlas, John Wesley
Davis, Joseph
Dykes, DeWitt S., Jr.
Gardiner, George L.
Gregory, Karl Dwight
Harrison, Algea Othella
Henry, Egbert Winston
Minor, Billy Joe

ROMULUS
Martin, Lee

ROYAL OAK
Morgan, Joseph C.

SAGINAW
Barnes, Vivian Leigh
Colvin, Alonza James
Connor, James Russell
Crawford, Lawrence Douglas
Daniels, Ruben
Ferrell, Rosie E.
Finney, Michael Anthony
Foster, Douglas Leroy
Gamble, Kenneth L.
Hall, David McKenzie
Leek, Everett Paul
McWright, Carter C.
Poston, Carl C., Jr.
Scott-Johnson, Roberta Virginia
Thompson, M. T., Jr.
Wilson, James Paris

ST JOSEPH
Ruffin, Robert

SOUTHFIELD
Addison, Caroline Elizabeth
Berry, Jerome
Brooks, Arkles Clarence, Jr.
Brown, Roderick
Burgette, James M.
Chapman, Gilbert Bryant, II
Dudley, Calmeze Henike, Jr.
Fields, Dexter L.
Gardner, LaMaurice H.
Givens, Donovahn Heston
Hentrel, Bobbie Kuykendall
Hollowell, Melvin L.
Hughes, Roberta V.
Ingram, Phillip M.
Isaacs, Patricia
Johnson, Davis
Johnson, Roy Lee
Johnson, Sandra Virginia
Kelley, Wilborne Anderson, III
Majors, Mattie Carolyn
McArthur, Barbara Jean (nee Martin)
McNorriell, Mozell M.
Payne, Beverly
Pryde, Arthur Edward
Robinson, Jane Alexander
Rodgers, Horace J.
Rogers, David William
Snyder, Edd G.
Trent, Jay Lester
Varner, Nellie M.
Vaughn, Clarence B.
Williams, Margo E.
Williams, Roosevelt

STERLING HEIGHTS
Taylor, Herbert Charles

TAYLOR
Burton, John H.

TROY
Edwards, Verba L.
Farmer, Forest J.
Gothard, Donald L.
Hegwood, Gordon F.
Lee, Aubrey W.
Norman, Clifford P.

Thompson, Karen Ann

UNIVERSITY CENTER
Goodson, Martin L., Jr.
Lee, Guy Milicon, Jr.
Thompson, Willie Edward

UTICA
Gothard, Barbara Wheatley

WARREN
Cockerham, Haven Earl
Drake, George Barr
Glenn, Edward C., Jr.
Hill, Kenneth Randal
Hughes, Wilbur B.
Kornegay, William F.
Lowe, Sylvia Oneice
Pattman, Virgil Thomas, Sr.
Pryde, Arthur Edward
Sanders, Barbara A.
Welburn, Edward Thomas, Jr.

WEST BLOOMFIELD
Lewis, Stephen Christopher
Trent, James E.

WESTLAND
Coleman, Hurley J., Jr.
Woodbury, David Henry

WYANDOTTE
Norris, Fred Arthur, Jr.

YPSILANTI
Armstrong, Walter
Barfield, John E.
Beatty, Charles Eugene, Sr.
Clarke, Velma Greene
Dobbs, John Wesley
Hamilton, Theophilus Elliott
Hawkins, James
Holloway, Nathaniel Overton, Jr.
Horne-McGee, Patricia J.
Marshall, Albert Prince
Peoples, Gregory Allan
Rhodes, Robert Shaw
Robinson, Albert Arnold
Tate, Eula Booker

MINNESOTA

ARDEN HILLS
Laroche, Gerard A.

BLOOMINGTON
Lawrence, Thomas R., Jr.
Raphael, Bernard Joseph

BROOKLYN CENTER
Reggans, John

BURNSVILLE
Posey, Edward W.
Richardson, Joseph

COLLEGEVILLE
McCall, Aidan M.

EDEN PRAIRIE
Browner, Joey
Chapman, Sharon Jeanette
Harris, Jean Louise
Jordan, Steve
Young, Rickey Darnell

EDINA
McClanahan, Brent Anthony
McKerson, Effie M. (nee Stoker)

GOLDEN VALLEY
Marsh, Donald Gene
Thomas, William Christopher

MANKATO
Ellison, David Lee

MINNEAPOLIS
Adams, Henrietta Faulconer
Alexander, Pamela Gayle
Bartelle, Talmadge Louis

Bartlett, Jeffrey Leon
Benton, Juanita
Bowman, Earl W., Jr.
Brewer, Rose Marie
Chapman, Sharon Jeanette
Cobb, Robert S.
Coleman, Melvin D.
Crutchfield, Susan Ellis
Davis, Michael James
Edwards, Ronald Alfred
Eiland, Ray Maurice
Eller, Carl L.
Fowler, James Daniel, Jr.
Fudge, Ann Marie
Glover, Gleason
Grinstead, Amelia Ann
Harrison, Jeanette LaVerne
Hasan, Rashad
Henry, Daniel Joseph
Jackson, Mannie Leon
Johnson, Charles W.
Johnson, Cyrus Edwin
Kyle, Mary J.
Law, M. Eprevel
Mack, Rudy Eugene, Sr.
Minor, David M.
Moore, Cornell Leverette
Otieno-Ayim, Larban Allan
Posey, Edward W.
Posten, William S.
Prince, Cheryl Patrice
Propes, Victor Lee
Puckett, Kirby
Russell, Kay A.
Sims, Carl W.
Smith, Henry Thomas
Southall, Geneva H.
Taborn, John Marvin
Taylor, David Vassar
Terrill, W.H. Tyrone, Jr.
Thomas, C. Edward
Thompson, Robert Dewey
Tidwell, John Edgar
Tipton, Thomas H.
Warder, John Morgan
Washington, Ronald
Washington, Thomas
Watkins, Izear Carl
White, Van Freeman
Wilderson, Frank B., Jr.
Williams, James Edward
Williams, Theatrice
Woods, Manuel T.
Younger, Robert D.

MOORHEAD
Spriggs, G. Max

NORTHVILLE
Miller, Robert Laverne

ROCHESTER
Crowe-Underwood, Hollis Jonetta
Skinner, Robert L., Jr.

ST LOUIS PARK
Barrett, Richard O.

ST PAUL
Battle, Walter L.
Caldwell, George Theron, Sr.
Canty, George
El-Kati, Mahhmoud (Milton Williams)
England, Rodney Wayne
Garner, John W.
Gregory, Robert Alphonso
Griffin, James Stafford
Hall, Hansel Crimiel
Harris, Jean Louise
Johnson, Linda C.
King, Reatha Clark
Lambert, LeClair Grier
Lewis, Virginia Hill
Morgan, Robert Lee
Page, Alan Cedric
Propes, Victor Lee
Sergent, Ernest, Jr.
Snowden, Frank Walter
Thomas, William Christopher
Troup, Elliott Vanbrugh
Waynewood, Freeman Lee
Wilderson, Thad
Williams, Kneely

Wilson, Willie Mae (nee Carey)

WHITE BEAR LAKE
Owens, Jerry Sue

WINONA
Ward, James Dale

MISSISSIPPI

BATESVILLE
Herring, Larry Windell

BAY ST LOUIS
Aubespin, Francis Borgia

BAYOU
Moore, Thomas H.

BILOXI
Howze, Joseph Lawson
Mason, Gilbert Rutledge
Rhodeman, Clare M.
Stallworth, William Fred

BOLTON
Thompson, Bennie G.

BYHALIA
Taylor, John L.

CANTON
Blackmon, Edward, Jr.
Esco, Fred, Jr.
Simmons, Shirley Davis
Williams, Jewel L.

CLARKSDALE
Henry, Aaron E.
Martin, McKinley C.

CLEVELAND
Evans, Ruthana Wilson
Tolliver, Ned, Jr.
Washington, David Warren

COLUMBIA
James, Sidney J.
Porter, Richard Sylvester

COLUMBUS
Hunt, Barbara Ann
Shamwell, Joe

CRAWFORD
Hill, Sam

DECATUR
Tingle, Lawrence May

DREW
Gough, Walter C.
McDowell, Cleve

EDWARDS
Lee, Aaron
Pritchard, Daron

ELLISVILLE
Jones, Joni Lou

FAYETTE
Bingham, Arthur E.
Evers, James Charles
Gales, James
Guice, Leroy
Harris, Burnell
Hayes, Marion LeRoy

FRIARS POINT
Washington, James Lee

GAUTIER
Davis, John Wesley, Sr.
Knight, Billy Earl, I.

GLENDORA
Thomas, Johnny B.

GOODMAN
Winston, Lillie Carolyn

GREENVILLE
Cartlidge, Arthur J.
Clark, Clarence Bendenson, Jr.
Goliday, Willie V.
Hall, Harold L.
Moore, Helen D. S.
Phillips, Earmia Jean
Smith, Dorothy J.
Whitsy, Charles H., Jr.

GREENWOOD
Cornwall, Shirley M.
Elzy, Amanda Belle
Jordan, David Lee
Pollard, Muriel Ransom

GULFPORT
Abston, Nathaniel, Jr.
Kelly, John Russell
Mitchell, Joseph Rudolph
Mitchell, Mark Randolph

GUNNISON
Leggette, Violet Olevia Brown

HATTIESBURG
Floyd, Vernon Clinton
Jones, Shirley Joan
Owens, Charlene B.

HAYTI
Russell, Dorothy Delores

HAZLEHURST
Hill, Annette Tillman

HEIDELBERG
Rogers, Peggy J.

HOLLY SPRINGS
Beckley, David Lenard
Bell, Felix C.
James, June, III
Lampley, Paul Clarence
McMillan, William Asbury
Peters, Fenton
Reaves, Ginevera N.
Smith, Nellie J.
Totten, Bernice E.

INDIANOLA
Matthews, David
Pollard, Muriel Ransom
Randle, Carver A.

ITTA BENA
Boyer, Joe L.
Brinkley, Norman, Jr.
Frison, Lee A.
Henderson, Robbye R.
Horn, Lawrence Charles
Payton, Albert Levern
Smith, Dorothy J.
Sutton, William Wallace

JACKSON
Alexander, Margaret Walker
  (Margaret Walker)
Anderson, Reuben Vincent
Ballard, Billy Ray
Banks, Fred L, Jr.
Bell, Jimmy
Bills, Johnny Bernard
Britton, Albert B., Jr.
Brocks-Shedd, Virgia Lee
Brown, Mary Catherine
Brown, Richard Jess, Sr.
Burns, Emmett C.
Byrd, Issac, Jr.
Cameron, John E.
Cameron, Joseph A.
Cameron, Mary Evelyn
Catchings, Howard Douglas
Clark, Dave
Clay, Henry Carroll, Jr.
Cox, Warren E.
Davis, James
Dilday, William Horace, Jr.
Ellis, Tellis B., III
Evers, Myrlie

Foster, E. C.
Greene, Percy
Hackett, Obra V.
Harvey, Clarie Collins
Haynes, Worth Edward
Hefner, James A.
Hunt, Betty Syble
Johnson, Hermel
Johnson-Carson, Linda D.
Jones, Chester Ray
Jones, Mavis N.
Jones, Theodore Cornelius
Kyles, Sharron Faye
Mack, Ally Faye
Magee, Sadie E.
Mayes, Clinton, Jr.
McLemore, Leslie Burl
Middleton, Richard Temple, III
Miller, Melvin Allen
Miller, Willie James
Myers, Lena Wright
Owens, George A.
Peoples, John Arthur, Jr.
Perkins, John M.
Pittman, Ineva (nee May)
Polk, Richard A.
Presley, Oscar Glen
Rhodes, Lelia G.
Richardson, F. C.
Rigsby, Esther Martin
Rundles, James Isaiah
Sanders, Thelma
Saunders, Doris E.
Smith, George S.
Smith, Katrina Marita
Smith, Otrie (O. B. Hickerson)
Smith, Robert
Smith, Robert L. T., Sr.
Stewart, James A., III
Sullivan, Richard H.
Summers, Timothy
Thompson, Rosie L.
Thompson-Moore, Ann
Trottman, Charles Henry
Walker, Jimmie
Wheeler, Primus, Jr.
White, Frankie Walton

JONESTOWN
Shanks, James A.

KNOXVILLE
Michael, Charlene Belton

LAMAR
Allen, James Trinton

LEXINGTON
Bills, Johnny Bernard
Brown, Annie Gibson
Clark, Robert G.

LORMAN
Shepphard, Charles Bernard
Washington, Walter
Williams, Malvin A.

MACON
Brooks, Richard Leonard

MCCOMB
Bullock, Theodore
Johnson, Nathan

MENDENHALL
Weary, Dolphus

MERIDIAN
Darden, Charles R.
Kornegay, Hobert
Thompson, Imogene A.
Young, Charles Lemuel, Sr.

METCALFE
Lindsey, S. L.

MISSISSIPPI STATE
Jones, Robbie Neely
Leggette, Sebetha Jenkins
Person, William Alfred
Ware, William L.
Williams, Carolyn Chandler

MORTON
Johnson, Gloria Dean

MOSS POINT
Ellerby, William Mitchell, Sr.

MOUND BAYOU
Johnson, Hermon M., Sr.
Lucas, Earl S.

NATCHEZ
Gray, James E.
Lewis, Charles Bady
Wallace, Harden Wilson
West, George Ferdinand, Jr.

NEWTON
Little, Reuben R.

OAKLAND
Jones, Franklin D.

OCEAN SPRINGS
Harris, Maurice A.

PATTISON
Yarbrough, Roosevelt

PHILADELPHIA
Gladney, Marcellious

PICKENS
Clarke, Henry Louis

PORT GIBSON
Brandon, Carl Ray
Davis, Frank
Doss, Evan, Jr.
Noble, John Charles
Yarbrough, Roosevelt

PRENTISS
Johnson, Onette E.

RAYMOND
Jenkins, Adam, Jr.

ROSEDALE
Trice, Juniper Yates

RULEVILLE
Edwards, Shirley Heard
Packer, Lawrence Frank

ST LOUIS
Frazer, Eva Louise

SARDIS
Blakely, Charles

SHAW
Flippen, Greg

SHELBY
Dorsey, L. C.
Gray, Robert Dean

STARKVILLE
Farmer, Willie Sidney, Sr.
Person, William Alfred
Ware, William L.
Williams, Harold Edward

TCHULA
Carthan, Eddie James

TOUGALOO
Brocks-Shedd, Virgia Lee

TUNICA
Dunn, James Earl

TUPELO
Grayson, Harry L.

UNIVERSITY
Crouther, Betty Jean
Jennings, Jeanette
Williams, Lucius Lee, Jr.

UTICA
Cooper, Bobby G.
Cornelius, William Milton
Fisher, Alma Z.

VICKSBURG
Pickett, Robert E.
Reed, David
Rosenthal, Robert E.
Winfield, James Eros

WESSON
Newsome, Burnell

WEST POINT
Gore, Joseph A.
Potts, Sammie

WOODVILLE
Johnson, Charles E.
Samuel, Minor Booker
Tolliver, Thomas C., Jr.

MISSOURI

CAPE GIRARDEAU
Hardy, Dorothy C.

CHESTERFIELD
Gillispie, William Henry
Walton, James Donald

COLUMBIA
Artis, Andre Keith
Benton, Quinnie Etta
Daniel, Walter C.
Dorsey, Carolyn Ann
Jones-Grimes, Mable Christine
Morrison, K. C. (Minion Kenneth
  Chauncey)
Oglesby, James Robert
St. Omer, Vincent V. E.
Strickland, Arvarh E.
Terrell, Robert L.
Zanders, Alton Wendell

CREVE COEUR
Wigfall, Samuel E.

FERGUSON
Campbell, Blanch
Polk, George Douglas
Wright, John Aaron

FLORISSANT
Ward-Brooks, Joyce Renee

GRANDVIEW
Jenkins, Melvin L.

HANNIBAL
Crow, Hiawatha Moore
Duncan, Alice Geneva
Mallory, William Henry

HILLSIDE
McDaniel, Elizabeth

INDEPENDENCE
Byrd, Edwin R.

JEFFERSON CITY
Atkins, Carolyn Vaughn
Black, Lee Roy
Brent, David L.
Clay, William Lacy, Jr.
Cook, Nathan Howard
Cooper, Charles W.
Curls, Phillip B.
Hearn, Rosemary
Johnson, Norman J.
Jones, Lucius
Kirk, Orville
Martin, James C.
O'Daniel, Therman Benjamin
Parks, Arnold Grant
Pawley, Thomas D., III
Rayburn, Wendell Gilbert
Swinton, Lee Vertis
Troupe, Charles Quincy
Weathers, Alice Ann

KANSAS CITY
Bailey, Weltman D., Sr.
Baty, Reginald Clement
Bivins, Edward Byron
Blankinship, G. L., Jr.
Bolton, Wanda E.
Bradley, Jesse J., Jr.
Brooks, Alvin Lee
Bryant, Harrison James
Bryant, T. J.
Cain, Gerry Ronald
Carter, James Earl, Jr.
Casey, Carey Walden, Sr.
Cherry, Deron Leigh
Clark, Granville E., Sr.
Cleaver, Emanuel, III
Cooper, Linda G.
Dale, Virginia Marie
Darton, Edythe M.
Davis, Nigel S.
Durall, Dolis, Jr.
Eades, Vincent W.
Eubanks, Eugene E.
Franklin, Curtis U., Jr.
Gaitan, Fernando J., Jr.
Gibson, Elvis Edward
Giles, Willie Anthony, Jr.
Harris, Jasper William
Harris, Zelema M.
Henderson, Isaiah Hilkiah, Jr.
Hill, Julia H.
Hughes, Leonard S., Jr.
Hughes, Mamie F.
Hutton, David Lavon
Jackson-Foy, Lucy Maye
Jenkins, Melvin L.
Johnson, Albert Lee, Sr.
Johnson, James S.
Jordan, Orchid I.
Kaiser, Inez Yeargan
Lewis, Leroy C.
Mabin, Joseph E.
Manuel, Louis Calvin
Marshall, Henry H.
Martin, Samuel
McClinton, Curtis R., Jr.
McKeel, Thomas Burl
Miller, Dexter J., Jr.
Mitchell, Emmitt W.
Moten, Chauncey Donald
Myers, Sere Spaulding
Nelms, Ommie Lee
Nelson, Howard
Njoroge, Mbugua J.
Peterson, Carl M.
Phelps, C. Kermit
Posey, Ronald Anthony
Reams-Whitmire, Vernetta Maria
Reed, Floyd T.
Reid, Robert Edward
Robinson, Genevieve
Robinson, Kenneth Eugene
Scott, Cornealious Socrates, Sr.
Shields, Vincent O.
Singleton, William Matthew
Spottsville, Clifford M.
Still, Art Barry
Stokes, Sterling J.
Swift, Leroy V.
Taylor, Ellis Clarence
Thomas-Richards, Jos Rodolfo
Thompson, Adell, Jr.
Tunley, Naomi Louise
Turner, Sharon V.
Van Trece, Jackson C.
Walker, Craig J.
Warner, Edward L.
Washington, William Montell
Watson, Mildred L.
White, Frank, Jr.
Wilkinson, Charles Brock
Williams, Hazel Browne
Williams, Starks J.
Wrenn, Thomas H., III
Young, Roy S.

KIRKWOOD
Beatty-Brown, Florence R.

LEE'S SUMMIT
May, Floyd O'Lander
Smith, Melissa Ann

LIBERTY
Robinson, Cecelia Ann

LILBOURN
Clark, Theodore Lee

NORTHWOODS
Jackson, Art Eugene, Sr.
Walls, Melvin

OAKLAND
Carroll, Joe Barry

PAGEDALE
Carter, Mary Louise
Crawley, Darline

PINE LAWN
Givins, Abe, Jr.
O'Kain, Marie Jeanette
O'Kain, Roosevelt

RAYTOWN
Davis, Nigel S.

REPUBLIC
Greene, Franklin D.

ST CHARLES
White, William

ST JOSEPH
Beshears, Kelsy (Kelsy Brown Cooper)
Nash, LeRoy T.

ST LOUIS
Adams, Albert W., Jr.
Adams, Joseph Lee, Jr.
Allen, Marcus
Anderson, Vinton Randolph
Bailey, Mildred T.
Barkley, Mark E.
Beard, Virginia H.
Belancourt, Dunet Francois
Bellinger, Luther Garic
Bentley, Herbert Dean
Billups, Florence W.
Bond, Leslie Fee
Boon, Ina M.
Bosley, Freeman Robertson, Jr.
Bouie, Merceline
Brock, Louis Clark
Brooks, Tilford Uthratese
Brown, Barbara J.
Brown, Craig Vincent
Brown, Henry H.
Buford, James Henry
Burrow, Marie Brabham
Cahill, Clyde S., Jr.
Calhoun, Joshua Wesley
Calloway, DeVerne Lee
Calloway, Ernest
Calvin, Michael Byron
Cheatham, Roy E.
Clay, William Lacy, Jr.
Cole, Maceola Louise
Collins, William, Jr.
Crump, Nathaniel L., Sr.
Cummings, Albert R.
Curry, George E.
Daniels, Lincoln, Sr.
Davis, Larry Earl
Davis, Myrtle Hilliard
Dean, Willie B.
Dickson, Reginald D.
Diuguid, Lincoln I.
Doggett, John Nelson, Jr.
Donald, Arnold Wayne
Dorsey, Elbert
Douthit, William E.
Dugas, Henry C.
Ebo, Antona
Fisher, Richard Laymon
Fowler, Queen Dunlap
Freeman, Frankie M.
Gaines, Richard Kendall
Gates, Clifton W.
Gibson, Robert
Gillespie, William G.
Givens, Henry, Jr.
Golden, Ronald Allen
Goward, Russell A.

Gray, Melvin Dean
Haley, Johnetta Randolph
Hankins, Gerard S.
Harper, Alphonsa Vealvert, III
Harper, David B.
Harrington, Zella Mason
Harris, John H.
Harvey, William M.
Hawkins, Morris M.
Hendricks, Juanita
Henry, Thomas
Herriford, Merle Baird
Hicks, Leon Nathaniel
Hudson, Keith
Hughes, Daniel Webster
Jackson, Raynard
Jackson, Ronald Lee
Johnson, Donn S.
Jones, Buck
Jones, Jerome B.
Kirkland, Jack A.
Landrum, Terry Lee
Lawrence, Erma Jean
Lewis, Floyd Edward
Liston, Hugh H.
Littleton, Arthur C.
Livingston, Jewel P.
Logan, Lloyd
Lucas, Virgil Hilry
Mabrey, Harold Leon
Mansfield, W. Ed
McFadden, Arthur B.
McGee, Willie Dean
McGuffin, Dorothy Brown
McMillan, Benjamin Earl
McMillian, Theodore
McNeil, Frank
Mitchell, Martha Mallard
Montgomery, George Louis, Jr.
Morrow, Jesse
Morrow, Laveine
Nash, Helen E.
Newland, Zachary Jonas
Nicholson, Lawrence E.
Noah, Leroy Edward
Noble, John Pritchard
Nobles, Patrica Joyce
Nutt, Maurice Joseph
O'Hara, Leon P.
Orr, Clyde Hugh
Peay, Isaac Charles, Sr.
Pendleton, Terry Lee
Perine, Martha Levingston
Peterson, Alphonse
Polk, George Douglas
Price, David B., Jr.
Prophete, Beaumanoir
Randolph, Bernard Clyde
Ray, Richard Rex
Reeves, Louise (Mrs. Charles Mitchell)
Renfro, Mel
Ricketts, David William
Roberts, Evelyn Hoard
Roberts, Steven C.
Ross-Barnett, Marguerite
Sanford, Mark
Shaw, Booker Thomas
Shaw, Charles A.
Shaw, Michael Dennis
Shelton, O. L.
Shelton, Reuben Anderson
Simms, Ernest S.
Smiley, William L.
Smith, Bernice Lewis
Smith, Fredrick E.
Smith, Lonnie
Smith, Ozzie
Smith, Wayman F., III
Stamps, Lynman A., Sr.
Steib, James T.
Stevens, Sharon A.
Stodghill, William
Story, Charles Irvin
Swanigan, Jesse Calvin
Taylor, Eugene Donaldson
Taylor, Theodore Roosevelt
Thomas, Benjamin
Thomas, Lillie (Mickey)
Thornhill, Georgia L. (nee Whitfield)
Todd, Cynthia Jean
Trottman, Alphonso
Troupe, Charles Quincy

Troupe-Frye, Betty Jean
Valley, Thomas James
Vaughn, William Smith
Walton, Elbert Arthur, Jr.
Ward-Brooks, Joyce Renee
Watson, Robert C.
Wheeler, Betty McNeal
White, Gloria Waters
Wigfall, Samuel E.
Wiley, Gerald Edward
Wilford, Harold C.
Williams, Brenda Paulette
Williams, Robert L.
Wilson, Charles Stanley, Jr.
Wilson, James, Jr.
Wilson, Margaret Bush
Woods, Barbara McAlpin
Woods, Jane Gamble
Word, Parker Howell
Wright, Frederick Bennie
Young, Edith Mae
Young, Ira Mason

SIKESTON
Fulton, Donald Lee

UNIVERSITY CITY
Gibson, William Howard, Jr.
Thompson, Betty L.
White, Nan E.

VELDA VILLAGE
Williams, Lottie Mae

WARRENSBURG
Dunson, Carrie Lee

WEBSTER GROVES
Haynes, Neal J.
LaFayette, Kate Bulls

WELLSTON
Brown, Lloyd
Stodghill, Ronald

WENTZVILLE
Berry, Charles Edward Anderson (Chuck Berry)

MONTANA

HELENA
Duncan, Joan A.

NEBRASKA

LINCOLN
Branker, Julian Michael
Crump, Arthel Eugene
Gilliam, Du-Bois Layfelt
Henderson, Gerald Eugene
Johnson, Frederick Douglass
Maxey, Jo Ann (nee Strickland)
Parker, Keith Dwight
Peterson, Harry W.
Robinson, Ella S.

OFFUTT AFB
Henderson, James H.

OMAHA
Atkins, Edna R.
Baker, Dave E.
Barnett, Alva P.
Bonner, Della M.
Coffey, Barbara J.
Crawford, Samuel D.
Dodd, Bernice Stephens
Evans, Leon Edward, Jr.
Foxall, Martha Jean
Gaines, Ray D.
Henderson, James H.
Hill, Robert K.
Lafontant, Julien J.
Morrow, Nebraska
Okhamafe, E. Imafedia
Pearson, Herman B.
Person, Earle G.
Phillips, Roy G.
Robinson, Alcurtis

Rushing, George A.
Secret, Philip E.
Smith, Alonzo Nelson
Thompson, John Andrew
Wead, Rodney Sam
Woods, George Washington

NEVADA

CARSON CITY
Arberry, Morse, Jr.

LAS VEGAS
Babero, Bert Bell
Bailey, Willian H.
Bennett, Marion D.
Clarke, Angela Webb
Crawford, Cranford L., Jr.
Daniel, Simmie Childrey
Duncan, Ruby
Falana, Lola
Fitzgerald, Roosevelt
Guy, Addeliar Dell, III
Head, Samuel
Ita, Lawrence Eyo
Kinnaird, Michael Leon
Langston, Esther R.
Lockette, Agnes Louise
Mason, Brenda Diane
McCarrell, Clark Gabriel, Jr.
McDaniels, Alfred F.
McMillan, James Bates
Moore, Evan Gregory
Moten, Birdia B. (nee Jenkins)
Newman, Kenya Maria
Patterson, Lloyd
Rayford, Lee Edward
Smith, Gwendolyn G.
Troutman, Porter Lee, Jr.
Williams, Nancy Webb

NELLIS AFB
Hubbard, Josephine Brodie

NORTH LAS VEGAS
Robinson, William Earl

RENO
Harper, Harry Dandridge
Holloway, Jerry
Manning, Jane A.
Seals, R. Grant

SPARKS
Hall, Jesse J.

NEW HAMPSHIRE

BARRINGTON
Curwood, Sarah T.

CONCORD
Burkette, Tyrone

HANOVER
Breeden, James Pleasant
Cook, William Wilburt
Lahr, Charles Dwight
Luis, William

MANCHESTER
Towns, Maxine Yvonne

NEW JERSEY

ASBURY PARK
Owens, Judith Myoli

ATCO
Gault, Marian Holness
Matthew, Clifton, Jr.

ATLANTIC CITY
Alleyne, Edward D.
Clayton, Willie Burke, Jr.
Frazier, Joseph Norris
Hollingsworth, Pierre

Johnson, Earl E.
Lasane, Joanna Emma
Milligan, Hugh D.
Norrell-Nance, Rosalind Elizabeth
Schenck, Frederick A.
Smith, Marlyn Stansbury
Smith, Roger Leroy
Stewart, W. Douglas
Usry, James LeRoy
Williams, Frederick Daniel
　　Crawford
Wise, Herbert Ashby

BAYONNE
Cannon, Davita Louise
Hamill, Margaret Hudgens

BELMAR
Roper, Grace Trott

BERGENFIELD
Welch, John L.

BLACKWOOD
McLaughlin, Jacquelyn Snow

BRICK
Owens, Judith Myoli

BRIDGETON
Hursey, James Samuel

BRIDGEWATER
Young, Ollie L.

BURLINGTON
Akins, Allen Clinton
Arnold, David
Hurd, Joseph Kindall, Jr.

CALDWELL
Hill, Dianne

CAMDEN
Brimm, Charles Edwin
Bryant, James W.
Bryant, Wayne R.
Cream, Arnold (Jersey Joe
　　Walcott)
Dixon, Ruth F.
Fitzgerald, Carrie Eugenia
Freeman, Ronald J.
Gilliams, Tyrone
Harris, Elbert L.
Horton, Stella Jean
Johnson, Frederick, Jr.
Jones, Betty Harris
King, William L.
Mathes, James R.
Matthews, Jessie L.
Montgomery, Gregory B.
Sabree, Clarice Salaam
Venable, Robert Charles

CHATHAM
Richardson, Charles Ronald

CHERRY HILL
Austin, Ernest Augustus
Butler, Rebecca Batts
Vann, Gregory Alvin
Walker, Manuel Lorenzo
Waters, William David

CHESILHURST
Alaan, Mansour

CLIFFWOOD
Drake, Pauline Lilie

CLIFTON
Cornish, Jeannette Carter
Kittrels, Alonzo William

CRANFORD
Austin, Mary Jane
Riley, Barbara P.

EAST BRUNSWICK
Johnson, Edward Elemuel

EAST HANOVER
Nelson, Jonathan P.

EAST ORANGE
Anderson, William A.
Bowser, Hamilton Victor, Sr.
Bowser, Robert Louis
Burr, Lawrence C.
Butler, Neil A.
Clark, James N.
Cooke, Thomas H., Jr.
Craig, Claude Burgess
Daniels, Joseph
Davis, Henry E., Jr.
Edmondson, William R., Jr.
Edmonson, Bernie L.
Forbes, Calvin
Foster, Delores Jackson
Foster, James Hadlei
Francis, Joseph A.
Garvin, Mildred Barry
Giles, Althea B.
Giles, William R.
Harrison, Pearl Lewis
Hawkins, Eldridge
Hudson, Frederick Bernard
Inge, Theodore R.
James, Henry Grady, III
Jenkins, Joseph Walter, Jr.
Lambert, Joseph C.
Peterson, Michelle Monica
Porter, Otha L.
Queen, Robert Calvin
Roberts, Paquita Hudson
Shepherd, Greta Dandridge
Thorburn, Carolyn Coles
Washington, James Edward
Williams, Kenneth Herbert
Wilson, Clarence Northon
Wilson, George G.
Woodridge, Wilson Jack, Jr.

EAST RUTHERFORD
Birdsong, Otis
Brown, Roosevelt H., Jr.
Carson, Harry Donald
Crennel, Romeo A.
Dawkins, Darryl (Dunks)
Doby, Lawrence Eugene
Gray, Earnest
King, Albert
Marshall, Leonard
Martin, George Dwight
Morris, Joe
Simpson, Ralph Derek
Taylor, Lawrence Julius
Williams, Buck

EAST WINDSOR
Lee-Smith, Hughie

EDGEWATER PARK
Kinniebrew, Robert Lee

EDISON
Griffin, Bertha L.
McGuire, Paul M., Jr.

ELIZABETH
Davis, Matilda Laverne
Ismial, Salaam Ibn
Teal, Ella S. (Ella J. Sanders)
Walker, Tanya Rosetta

ENGLEWOOD
Brown, Arnold E.
Emeka, Mauris L. P.
English, Whittie
Hadden, Eddie Raynord
Horne, Edwin Clay
Jenkins, Augustus G., Jr.
McNeil, Claudia Mae
Rivers, Gary C.
Taylor, Walter Scott

ENGLEWOOD CLIFFS
Draper, Everett T., Jr.

EWING
Mays, Alfred Thomas

FAIRTON
Gray, Keith A., Jr.

FARMINGDALE
Oates, Caleb E.

FLORHAM PARK
King, Marcellus, Jr.
Roy, Welton J., Jr.

FORDS
Brown, James

FORT LEE
Barrow, Denise

FORT MONMOUTH
McAfee, Walter S.

FREEHOLD
Gumbs, Philip N.
Hughes, George Vincent

GLASSBORO
Buck, Ivory M., Jr.
Clark, Douglas L.
Ellis, Calvin H., III
Fitzgerald, Carrie Eugenia
James, Herman Delano
Moore, Oscar William, Jr.
Robinson, Randall S.
Sills, Marvin G.

GREYSTONE PARK
Lathen, John William

GUTTENBERG
Johnson, Verdia Earline

HACKENSACK
Burton, Donald C.
Gates, Paul Edward
Harper, T. Errol
Lavergneau, Rene L.

HADDONFIELD
Bruner, Van B., Jr.

HILLSBOROUGH
Primas, Barbara Jean

HOBOKEN
Gomez, Daniel J.

HOLMDEL
Heyward, Ilene Patricia
Johnson, Anthony Michael
Phillips, Eric McLaren, Jr.
Ransom, Victor L.
Williamson, Samuel R.

IRVINGTON
Bost, Fred M.

ISELIN
Miles, Frank J. W.

JERSEY CITY
Cunningham, Glenn Dale
DeGeneste, Henry Irving
Estill, Ann H. M.
Foster, Delores Jackson
Freeman, Theodore H., Jr.
Harrold, Austin Leroy
Jackson, Bobby L.
Jones, Ben F.
Littlejohn, Joseph Phillip
Lockerman, Geneva Lorene
　　Reuben
Lynch, Lillie Riddick
McGhee, Samuel T.
Means, Fred E.
Mitchell, Judson, Jr.
Moore, Elaine
Murray, David Keith
Myers, Walter Dean
Neals, Huerta C
Peoples, Sesser R.
Perkins, William O., Jr.
Slade, Phoebe J.
Tayari, Kabili
Tolentino, Shirley A.
Washington, Philemon (Phil)
Watson, Herman Doc

KENILWORTH
Campbell, Rogers Edward, III
Peterson, Michelle Monica

LAKEHURST
Brown, Clarence William

LAKEWOOD
Younger, Celia Davis

LAWNSIDE
Bryant, Isaac Rutledge
Bryant, Wayne R.
Cotton, Garner
Foote, Yvonne
Moore, Hilliard T., Sr.
Williams, Frederick Daniel
　　Crawford

LAWRENCEVILLE
Baskerville, Penelope Anne
Brooks, Carol Lorraine
Haqq, Khalida Ismail
Hatchett, William F. (Bucky)
Turner, Shirley K.

LINCROFT
Jones, Floresta Deloris
Scott, Hosie L.
Smith, Joshua L.

LINDEN
Young, Archie R., II

MADISON
James, William M.
Kelsey, George Dennis Sale
Richardson, Charles Ronald
Varner, James

MAHWAH
Burton, Donald C.
Johnson, Joe
Pollard, Percy Edward, Sr.

MAPLEWOOD
Adams, Earl Leonard, III
Anderson, Carlton Leon
Bittings, Rosemary Brooks
Boyd, Robert Nathaniel, III
Campbell, Rogers Edward, III
Cooper, Daneen Ravenell
Davis, Francis D.
Holmes, Herbert
Roper, Richard Walter
Spraggins, Stewart

MARLTON
Lewis, W. Arthur

MIDDLETOWN
Heath, Bertha Clara
James, Alexander, Jr.

MILLBURN
Weng, Peter A.

MIZPAH
Newton, Melvin T.

**MONMOUTH
JUNCTION**
Cherry, Theodore W.
Moore, Gerald L.

MONTCLAIR
Allen-Noble, Rosie Elizabeth
Bolden, Theodore E.
Douglas, Frederick William
Ewing, William James
Frye, William Sinclair
Griffith, John A.
Hamilton, John Joslyn, Jr.
Hawkins, Walter Lincoln
Sharp, Jean Marie
Tyson, Lorena E.
Wiley, Margaret Z. Richardson
Williams, Daniel Edwin
Woodbury, Arline Elizabeth

MOORESTOWN
Armstead, Wilbert Edward, Jr.
Green, Joseph, Jr.
Waynes, Kathleen Yanes

MORRISTOWN
Crump, Wilbert S.
Edwards, David C.
Johnson, Juliana Cornish
Prejean, Cheryl Renee
Winston, Janet E.

MOUNT LAUREL
Anderson, Kenneth Richard
Hopper, John Dowl, Jr.

MURRAY HILL
Asom, Moses T.
Jackson, Shirley Ann
Mitchell, James Winfield

NEW BRUNSWICK
Adams, Anne Currin
Bethel, Leonard Leslie
Bolden, Frank Augustus
Carman, Edwin G.
Charles, Bernard L.
Davis, George B.
Epps, C. Roy
Gallagher, Abisola Helen
Gary, Melvin L.
Gibson, Donald B.
Hammond, Debra Lauren
Herbert, John Travis, Jr.
Lambert, Benjamin Franklin
Nelson, Gilbert L.
Scott, Harold Russell, Jr.
Sims, Harold Rudolph
Stevens, Maxwell McDew
Williams, Chester Arthur
Williams-Harris, Diane Beatrice

NEW PROVIDENCE
Key, Juan Alfred

NEWARK
Banks, Cecil J.
Bateman, Celeste Anne
Beatty, Pearl
Bell, S. Aaron
Bettis, Anne Katherine
Bolden, Theodore E.
Booker, Irvin B.
Branch, George
Brown, William H.
Byrd, Frederick Wayne
Chance, Kenneth Bernard
Contee, Carolyn Ann
Cooper, Julius, Jr.
Cowan, James R.
Cuyjet, Aloysius Baxter
Daniels, A. Raiford
Davis, Adrianne
Davis, Harold Matthew
Dean, Clara Russell
Evans, Gwendolyn
Evans, Thomas Archie
Felton, James Edward, Jr.
Flagg, E. Alma W.
Foushee, Geraldine George
Fraser, Rodger Alvin
Fykes, Leroy Matthews, Jr.
Gilmore, Edwin
Gona, Ophelia Delaine
Graves, Carole A.
Green, Shirley
Greenleaf, Louis E.
Gunthorpe, Uriel Derrick
Hall, Lawrence H.
Hamilton, John Joslyn, Jr.
Hargrove, Milton Beverly
Harris, Earl
Harrison, James, Jr.
Haynes, Frank L., Jr.
Hazelwood, Harry, Jr.
Heningburg, Gustav
Hill, Mary Alice
Holloway, Harris M.
Holmes, Louyco W.
Jessie, Waymon Thomas
Johnson, Joshua
Johnson, Lorna Karen
Johnson, Theodore Thomas

King, Donald E.
Lapeyrolerie, Frank M.
Leevy, Carroll M.
Lester, Betty J.
Lewis, Henry
Lewis, Samuel, Jr.
Lister, David Alfred
Makle, Vivian B.
Marius, Kenneth Anthony
Marshall, Carter Lee
Marshall, Richard Douglass
McCoy, Leamon M.
McNatt, Isaac G.
Mesa, Mayra L.
Mitchell, Judson, Jr.
Muldrow, Catherine (nee Jenkins)
Owens, Ronald
Page, Marguerite A.
Perry, John B.
Plummer, Milton
Prezeau, Louis E.
Raines, Colden Douglas
Robinson, Alfreda P.
Robinson-Brown, Jeannette
Scott, Harold Russell, Jr.
Smith, J. Harry
Smith, Stanley G.
Stalks, Larrie W.
Stancell, Dolores Wilson Pegram
Tate, Herbert Holmes, Jr.
Taylor, Brenda L.
Terrell, Stanley E.
Thomas, Janice Morrell
Thurman, Marjorie Ellen
Tucker, Donald
Walker, George T.
Washington, J. Barry
Way, Curtis J.
Weeks, Renee (nee Jones)
White, Ella Flowers
Williams, David S., Jr.
Williams, Hubert
Williams, John Alfred
Williams, Junius W.
Woodridge, Wilson Jack, Jr.
Woodruff, Constance Oneida
Yearwood, Arem Irene
Young, Richard Edward, Jr.

NORTH BERGEN
Mayo, Harry D., III

NUTLEY
Carter, Matthew Gamaliel
Gaither, Richard A.

OCEAN CITY
MacClane, Edward James

ORANGE
Brown, Margery Wheeler
Brown, Robert Lee
Perkins, Lewis Bryant, Jr.
Wright, Ralph Edward

PALMYRA
Flournoy, Valerie Rose

PARAMUS
Dunbar, Harry B.
Haley, Earl Albert

PARK RIDGE
Blackwell, Noble Virgil

PARSIPPANY
Bright, Herbert L., Sr.
Dunnaville, Clarence M., Jr.
Powell, Gayle Lett

PASSAIC
Samuels, Olive Constance

PATERSON
Baker, Henry W., Sr.
Barnes, Martin G.
Benson, Gilbert
Brown, Chauncey I., Jr.
Clark, Joe Louis
Collins, Elliott
Epps, Naomi Newby
Garner, Mary E.
Gist, Jessie M. Gilbert

Harrington, Elaine Carolyn
Harris, Thomas C.
Hemby, Dorothy Jean
Hicks, William H.
Hinton, Floyd
Irving, Henry E., II
Kline, William M.
LaGarde, Frederick H.
Lindsay, Eddie H. S.
McEachern-Ulmer, Sylvia L.
Nickerson, Willie Curtis
Richardson, Louis M.
Rowe, Albert P.
Sherow, Don Carl

PAULSBORO
Kirklin, Perry William

PENNINGTON
Khatib, Syed Malik

PENNS GROVE
Williams, L. Colene

PISCATAWAY
Alexander, Mervin Franklin
Collier, Albert, III
Jessup, Marsha Edwina
Johnson, Edward Elemuel
Phillips, Edward Martin

PLAINFIELD
Bethel, Leonard Leslie
Brown, Marshall Carson
Chitty, M. Elizabeth
Ganey, James Hobson
Harris, Jerome C., Jr.
Lattimore, Everett Carrigan
Satchell, Elizabeth
Taylor, Richard L.
Turner, Mikoel
White, Ella Flowers

PLAINSBORO
Young, Reginald B.

PLEASANTVILLE
Darkes, Leroy William
McEachern, Katherine Verdell
McNeill

POMONA
Farris, Vera King
Reid-Bookhart, Patricia Ann

PRINCETON
Anderson, Kenneth Richard
Barnett, Samuel B.
Baskerville, Penelope Anne
Colbert, Benjamin James
Drewry, Cecelia Hodges
Gibson, Edward Lewis
Harris, Don Navarro
Isaac, Ephraim
Lewis, William Arthur
Lowe, Eugene Yerby, Jr.
McCloud, J. Oscar
Painter, Nell Irvin
Pearson, Marilyn Ruth
Philander, S. George H.
Primas, Barbara Jean
Proctor, Timothy DeWitt
Roper, Richard Walter
Satterwhite, John H.
Schutz, Andrea Louise
Slaughter, Carole D.
Taylor, Howard F.
Taylor, Patricia E.
Taylor, Prince Albert, Jr.
Van Ness, Stanley C.
Young, Reginald B.

RAHWAY
Branch, B. Lawrence
McDaniel, Adam Theodore
Roberts, Donald Lee

RANDOLPH
Millard, Thomas Lewis

RARITAN
Lane, Nancy L.

RED BANK
Cofer, James Henry
Johnson, Theodore, Sr.

RIDGEWOOD
McCane, Charlotte Antoinette
Sneed, Paula A.

ROSELAND
Hareld, Gail B.

ROSELLE
Ford, Albert S.
Simmons, Leonard (Bud)

RUTHERFORD
Brewer-Mangum, Ernestine
Tywanna
Walton, Lludloo Charles

SCOTCH PLAINS
Jackson, James Holmen

SECAUCUS
Baron, Neville A.
Kinder, Randolph Samuel, Jr.

SHORT HILLS
James, Charles Ford
Leevy, Carroll M.
Peterson, Alan Herbert
White, Arthur W., Jr.

SKILLMAN
Elliott, J. Russell

SOMERDALE
Gibson, John A.

SOMERSET
Gordon, Robert Fitzgerald
Harris, Carolyn Ann
Henry, Nancy L.
Hinds, Lennox S.
Perry, Eugene Calvin, Jr.
Roy, Welton J., Jr.

SOMERVILLE
Brown, Paul, Jr.
Stevens, Maxwell McDew
Trotman, Richard Edward
Wilson, Carroll Lloyd

SOUTH ORANGE
Alexander, Walter Gilbert, II
Cascone, Jeanette L.
Moss, Simeon F.
Peterson, Alan Herbert
Wilson, Leroy, III

SOUTH PLAINFIELD
Morrison, Curtis Angus
Yelity, Stephen C.

SPRINGFIELD
Grimsley, Ethelyne

SUMMIT
Lassiter, James Edward, Jr.
Leeper, Lemuel Cleveland

SWEDESBORO
Gaither, Cornelius E.

TEANECK
Aklilu, Tesfaye
Brooks, Bernard E.
Browne, Robert Span
Glanville, Cecil E.
Kay, Ulysses
Littlejohn, Joseph Phillip
Lynch, Lillie Riddick
Mohamed, Gerald R., Jr.
Price, Wallace Walter
Richardson, William J.
Valdes, Pedro H.

TINTON FALLS
Crocker, Clinton C.
Foster, Alvin Garfield

TOMS RIVER
Cargile, C. B., Jr.
Joyner, Rubin E.
Tolbert, Edward T.

TRENTON
Brooks, Carol Lorraine
Checole, Kassahun
Cogdell, Parthenia D.
Collins, Elsie
Conway, Wallace Xavier, Sr.
Coy, John T.
Dickinson, Gloria Harper
Durham, Eddie L., Sr.
Fitzgerald, Herbert H.
Fitzgerald, Howard David
Francis, Edith V.
Francis, Gilbert H.
Fraser, Leon Allison
Gault, Marian Holness
Graham, Catherine S.
Hall, Dolores Brown
Hall, Kirkwood Marshal
Hopper, John Dowl, Jr.
Johnson, Angel Patricia
Marrow-Mooring, Barbara A.
McRae, Helene Williams
Muckelroy, William Lawrence
Palmer, Douglas Harold
Pruitt, George Albert
Ravenell, Joseph Phillip
Redman, James W.
Roberts, Paquita Hudson
Robinson, Albert M.
Sabree, Clarice Salaam
Simms, Gregory Frame
Stubblefield, Jennye Washington
Summerour-Perry, Lisa
Taliaferro, Addison
Taylor, Veronica C.
Terry, Garland Benjamin
Thomas, Nida E.
Thompson, Anne E.
Thompson, William Henry
Williams, David George
Wolfe, Deborah Cannon (nee
Partridge)
Woodson, S. Howard, Jr.

UNION
Bunn, Warren J.
Darden, Joseph S., Jr.
Melton, Frank LeRoy (Globe)
Perry, John B.
Sims, Harold Rudolph

UNION HILLS
Shepherd, Marian E.

UPPER MONTCLAIR
Allen-Noble, Rosie Elizabeth
Brewton, Butler E.
Flagg, J. Thomas
Harris, James E.
Jackson, Curtis M.
Millard, Thomas Lewis
Newman, Geoffrey W.
Wesley, Richard Errol
West, Marcella Polite

VAUXHALL
Gray, Christine
Watts, John E.

WAYNE
Hayes, Leola G.
Jemmott, Hensley B.
McClean, Vernon E.
Newton, Oliver A., Jr.
Sands, Rosetta F.
Small, William
Waiguchu, Muruku

WEEHAWKEN
Hamer, Judith Ann

WEST CALDWELL
Henderson, Henry Fairfax, Jr.

WEST NEW YORK
Johnson, Sharon Reed

WEST ORANGE
Giles, Althea B.
Lewis, James, Jr.
Reed, Lola N.
Walton, Lludloo Charles

WEST PATERSON
Bramble, Livingston
Henderson, Henry Fairfax, Jr.

WHARTON
Groce, Herbert Monroe, Jr.

WHIPPANY
Barber, William, Jr.
Greene, Lionel Oliver, Jr.
Montgomery, Ethel Constance

WILLINGBORO
Airall, Guillermo Evers
Davis, Fred
Harris, Larry Vordell, Jr.
McMeans, Donald Curtis
Saunders-Henderson, Martha M.

WOODBRIDGE
Jones, Willie
Vertreace, Walter Charles

WOODBURY
Wallace, John E., Jr.

WOODSTOWN
Ford, Evern D.

WYCKOFF
Butterfield, Don

NEW MEXICO

ALBUQUERQUE
Bailey, Harold
Becknell, Charles E.
Bradley, James George
Brown, William T.
Caldwell, Maria
Cushman, Vera F.
Hamilton, Raymond
Harding, Robert E.
Hoppes, Alice Faye
Jewell, Tommy Edward
Jones, Frederick Douglass, Jr.
Jones, I. Gene
Lewis, James B.
Malry, Lenton
Monteith, Henry C.
Okunor, Shiame
Worrell, Audrey Martiny
Worrell, Richard Vernon

CARLSBAD
Smith, Emmitt Mozart

CROWN POINT
Gladney, Marcellious

LAS CRUCES
Clemmons, Clifford R.
Drew, Weldon
Jenkins, Woodie R., Jr.
Trotter, Andrew Leon

LOS ALAMOS
Harris, Betty Wright
Lewis, H. Ralph

PORTALES
Cox, Euola Wilson

RIO RANCHO
Bouldes, Charlene
White, June Joyce

SANTA FE
Lewis, James B.
Sawyer, Alfred M.

**WHITE SANDS
MISSILE RANGE**
Rucks, Alfred J.

NEW YORK

ALBANY
Alexander, Fritz W., II
Brown, Joyce
Drakes, Muriel B.
Dunston, Leonard G.
Galiber, Joseph L.
Gordon, Vivian V.
Hammock, Edward R.
Hodges, Virgil Hall
James, Robert D.
Kane, Jacqueline Anne
Lewis, Martha S.
Miller, Frederick A.
Moore, Earl B.
Pinkard, Norman Thomas
Pogue, Frank G.
Powell, Archie James
Staats, Florence Joan
Swanston, Clarence Eugene
Thornton, Maurice
Tillman, Lillian G. (nee Garland)
Vann, Albert
Webster, Lesley Douglass

AMHERST
Howard, Robert Berry, Jr.
McCoy, George H.
Winfield, Sinette Johnson

AMITYVILLE
Brazier, William H.
Davis, Raoul Andr
Lewter, Andy C., Sr.

ANNANDALE HUDSON
Shaw, Denise

APO NEW YORK
Ridges-Horton, Lee Esther
Smith, Isaac Dixon

ARMONK
Pollard, Percy Edward, Sr.

ASTORIA
Rashad, Phylicia Ayers-Allen

BALDWINSVILLE
Harmon, M. Larry
Morrow, Samuel P., Jr.
Pritchard, Robert Starling, Jr.

BAY SHORE
Reavis, John William, Jr.

BAYSIDE
Cobbs, Winston H.B., Jr.

BEACON
Carpenter, Ann M.
Cuffee, Jeffrey Townsend

BEDFORD HILLS
Ashe, Arthur R., Jr.
Curry, Phyllis Joan

BELLPORT
Eleazer, George Robert, Jr.

BETHPAGE
Bodden, Wendell N.
McCalla, Erwin Stanley

BINGHAMTON
Brown, Lester J.
Keeling, Laura C.
Wilson, Ed

BREWSTER
Darrell, Betty Louise
Jones, Isaac, Jr.
Rivers, Vernon Frederick

BRIARWOOD
Ellis, Ernest W. (Akbar Khan)

BROCKPORT
Mills, Elizabeth Nathaniel
Thompson, Jesse

BRONX
Adams, Ronald, Jr.
Alexander, Preston Paul, Jr.
Alston, James L.
Arkhurst, Joyce Cooper
Baker, Sharon L.
Berkley, Constance Elaine
Blayton-Taylor, Betty
Blocker, Helen Powell
Brown, Beatrice S.
Bryant, Teresena Wise
Burns, Ann
Burr, Lawrence C.
Callender, Wilfred A.
Clarke, Donald Dudley
deMille, Valerie Cecilia
Diggs, Estella B.
Dreher, Lucille G.
Dunbar, Marjorie Henderson
Fulton, Robert Henry
Gamble, Oscar Charles
Grant, Claude DeWitt
Greene, Aurelia
Greene, Jerome A.
Griffey, George Kenneth
Harris, Robert Eugene Peyton
Haynes, George Edmund, Jr.
Hewlett, Dial, Jr.
Hibbert, Dorothy Lasalle
Hicks, Edith A.
Hill, Marnesba D.
Jackson, Bernard H.
Jackson, Karl Don
Johnson, Charles Ronald, Sr.
Johnson, Harlan C.
Johnson, Patricia L.
Johnson, Ralph V.
Jones, Billy Emanuel
Jordan, Marilyn E.
Lambert, Samuel Fredrick
Lee, Mildred Kimble
Maynard, Edward Samuel
McGee, Hansel Leslie
McLeod, Georgianna R.
Meacham, Robert Andrew
Minter, Thomas Kendall
Morgan, Charlotte Theresa
Moses, Johnnie, Jr.
Muskelly, Anna Marie
Palmer, Edward
Patterson, John T., Jr.
Reid, Roberto Elliott
Richardson, Anthony W.
Robertson, Andre Levett
Robinson, William J. (Bishop Billy Robinson)
Ross, Regina D.
Samuels, Leslie Eugene
Shell, Juanita
Shepherd, Saundra Dianne
Simpson, Samuel G.
Smart, Edward Bernard, Jr.
Taylor, Sandra Elaine
Terrell, Francis D'Arcy
Thompson, Francesca
Turner, Keith
Valdes, Laura
Washington, Loise
White, William H.
Williams, E. Thomas, Jr.

BRONXVILLE
Meriwether, Louise

BROOKLYN
Abdul-Malik, Ahmed H.
Abrahams, Andrew Wordsworth
Addei, Arthella Harris
Al-Hafeez, Huzema
Alexander, Roland E.
Anderson, Madeline
Andrews, Emanuel Carl
Anthony, Jeffrey Conrad
Atkins, Thomas Irving
Ausby, Ellsworth Augustus
Bailey, Marolyn Leslie
Baldwin, George R.
Barnett, Teddy
Battle, Turner Charles, III
Beatty, Vander L.
Behrmann, Serge T.
Bell, Travers J., Sr.
Blow, Sarah
Bostic, Dorothy

Boyce, John G.
Boyce, William M.
Braithwaite, Mark Winston
Bramwell, Fitzgerald Burton
Bramwell, Henry
Brothers, Edith
Bryant, Teresena Wise
Bryant-Mitchell, Ruth Harriet
Carter, Betty
Cave, Claude Bertrand
Champion, Tempii Bridgene
Clark, Vincent W.
Corbie, Leo A.
Cordova, Renaldo C.
Couche, Robert
Criner, Clyde
Curvin, Robert
Daughtry, Herbert Daniel
Davidson, Arthur Turner
Davis, William Selassie, Jr.
Dennis, Rodney Howard
Douglass, Lewis Lloyd
Dummett, Jocelyn Angela
Eastmond, Joan Marcella
Edwards, Audrey Marie
Edwards, Bessie Regina
Edwards, Thomas Oliver
Feddoes, Sadie C.
Flateau, John
Flatts, Barbara Ann
Fleary, George McQuinn
Folks, Leslie Scott
Ford, Robert Benjamin
Forster, Cecil R.
Francois, Theodore Victor
Gabriel, Benjamin Moses
Galamison, Milton A.
Gall, Lenore Rosalie
Galvin, Emma Corinne
Gardner, Jackie Randolph
Gilbert, Jean P.
Glee, George, Jr.
Goode, James Edward
Goodwin, Norma J.
Greene, Charles Rodgers
Greene, Clifton S.
Halpert, Leonard
Harris, William J.
Headley, De Costa Oneal
Hicks, Daisy C.
Hobson, Charles Blagrove
Holden, Dorothy M.
Hooks, Benjamin Lawson
Hooks, Frances Dancy
Howell, Amaziah, III
Hucles, Henry B., III
Innis, Roy Emile Alfredo
Isaac, Brian Wayne
Jackson, Emory Napoleon (Sippy)
Jackson, Randolph
JeanBaptiste, Carl S.
Johnson, Edward A.
Johnson, Luther Mason, Jr.
Johnson, Michael Anthony
Johnson, Miriam B.
Johnson, Norman B.
Johnson, Rita Falkener
Johnson, Robert H.
Johnson, Vincent L.
Jones, Hortense
Jones, Louis Clayton
Jones, Nathan William
Jones, Thomas Russell
Jones, Vann Kinckle
Jones, William A., Jr.
Kernisant, Lesly
King, Ruth Allen
Lambert, Samuel Fredrick
Lawrence, Charles B.
Lewis, Felton Edwin
Lewis, Woodrow
Lieteau, Halvan Joseph
Lindo, J. Trevor
Lynch, George K.
Mahoney, Keith Weston
Marshall, Calvin Bromley, III
Marshall, Warren
Maxwell, Marcella J.
McFadden, Frederick C., Jr.
McLaughlin, Andree Nicola
Meade, William F.
Miles, Frederick Augustus
Millett, Knolly E.
Mitchell, Roderick Bernard

Moore, Colin A.
Moore, Shelley Lorraine
Morancie, Horace L.
Nelson, Patricia Ann
Owens, Victor Allen
Page, Willie F.
Perry, Richard
Persaud, Inder
Petersen, Allan Ernest
Phillips, Dilcia R.
Pierre-Louis, Constant
Primm, Beny Jene
Pugh, Robert William, Sr.
Ramirez, Gilbert
Rivers, Louis
Robinson, Isaiah E.
Seymour, Stanley
Siler, Joyce B.
Silver, Horace Ward Martin Tavares
Simmons, Esmeralda
Slade, Walter R., Jr.
Smith, Louis
Sobers, Austin W.
Steptoe, John Lewis
Stroud, Milton
Swiggett, Ernest L.
Thomas, Lloyd A.
Thomas, Lucille Cole
Thompson, Leroy B.
Thompson, Mavis Sarah (Mavis Blaize)
Thompson, Theodis
Thompson, William Coleridge
Traylor, Rudolph A.
Trent, Richard Darrell
Umolu, Mary Harden
Vernon, Francine M. (nee Johnson)
William, Thompson E.
Williams, Enoch H.
Williams, Ernest Donald, Jr.
Williams, Joseph B.
Williams, William Thomas
Wilson, Frederick A.
Wright, Charles Stevenson
Zambrana, Rafael

BUFFALO
Acker, Daniel R.
Adams-Dudley, Lilly Annette
Allen, DeMetrice Michealle
Amin, Karima
Arthur, George Kenneth
Baird, Keith E.
Baugh, Florence Ellen
Bellamy, Herbert L.
Bennett, William Donald
Charles, Roderick Edward
Cochran, S. Thomas
Coles, Robert Traynham
Cox-Rawles, Rani
Davis, Thomas Joseph
Davis, Twilus
Diji, Augustine Ebun
Echols, David Lorimer
Eve, Arthur O.
Fleming, Carolyn
Fordham, Monroe
Foreman, Joe Cornelius, Jr.
Glover, Diana M.
Granger, Carl Victor
Harrison, Carol L.
Humes, Emanuel I., Sr.
Hunter, Archie Louis
Jones, Leeland Newton, Jr.
Kirkland, Theodore
Lawrence, Edward
Lawson, Cassell Avon
Lewis, Ora Lee (nee McQuiller)
McCoy, George H.
McDaniel, James Berkley, Jr.
McGrier, Jerry, Sr.
McRae, Ronald Edward
Merritt, Joseph, Jr.
Morgan, Rudolph Courtney
Neal, Brenda Jean
Nickson, Sheila Joan
Price, Alfred Douglas
Robinson, Barry Lane
Robinson, Edith (nee Brown)
Sarmiento, Shirley Jean
Scales-Trent, Judy
Sims, Barbara M.

Sims, William
Smith, Bennett W., Sr.
Tisdale, Celes
Unger, George D.
Wallace, Jeffrey J.
Westbrook, Franklin Solomon
Williamson, George H., Jr.
Willis, Fred Douglas

CAMBRIA HEIGHTS
Benjamin, Arthur, Jr.
Boyd-Foy, Mary Louise
Jones, Anthony, Jr.
Southern, Joseph
Waldon, Alton Ronald, Jr.

CANAAN
Bell, James Milton

CANTON
Williams, Terri L.

CARLE PLACE
Mitchell, Carlton S.

CENTRAL ISLIP
Prezeau, Maryse

CHERRY HILL
Grist, Ronald

CLINTON
Johnson, C. Christine

COOPERSTOWN
Bell, James
McCovey, Willie Lee

COPIAGUE
Hibbert, Dorothy Lasalle

CORAM
Byers, Marianne

CORNING
Baity, Gail Owens
Pitts, Lorenzo, Jr.
Watkins, Robert Charles

CORTLAND
Newkirk, Thomas H.
Williams, Carolyn Ruth Armstrong

CROTON-ON-HUDSON
Bell, James Milton
Pinkney, Jerry
Van Liew, Donald H.
Wood, William L., Jr.

DELMAR
Thornton, Maurice

DEWITT
Morrow, Samuel P., Jr.
Young, Alfred

DIX HILLS
Cave, Alfred Earl

DOBBS FERRY
Berry, Lemuel, Jr.
Johnson-Young, Barbara Janeice
LeMelle, Wilbert John
Sindos, Louise King

DOUGLASTON
Jenkins, Herman Lee

EAST ELMHURST
Archer, Eva P.
Booth, William H.
Holloman, John L. S., Jr.
Kaiser, Ernest Daniel
Lopez, Mary Gardner

ELMIRA
McGee, JoAnn
Washington, Edith May Faulkner

ELMONT
Chrichlow, Mary L.
Collins, Gordon Geoffrey

ELMSFORD
Bronz, Lois Gougis Taplin
Jones, Yvonne De Marr

ENDICOTT
Johnson, Frederick E.

FAIRPORT
Hannah, Mosie R.
Jones, Marsha Regina
Lechebo, Semie
Sutton, James Carter

FAR ROCKAWAY
Maple, Goldie M.

FARMINGDALE
Bellinger, Harold
Blake, Carlton Hugh
Johnson, Cleveland, Jr.
Palmer, Noel
Williams, Patricia Hill

FAYETTEVILLE
Felton, Ann Shirey

FLORAL PARK
Quarles, George R.

FLUSHING
Andrews, Benny
Argrette, Joseph
Burns, W. Haywood
Byam, Milton S.
Dixon, Melvin W.
Gooden, Dwight Eugene
Jenkins, Herman Lee
Liverpool, Charles Eric
Robinson, Bill
Robinson, Joseph
Strawberry, Darryl
Wilson, William Hayward

FORT DRUM
Jordan, John Wesley

FRANKLIN SQUARE
Blackwell, Milford

FREEPORT
Jenkins, Elizabeth Ameta
McCoy, Carol Todman
Smith, Hale

FULTON
Fryson, Sim E.

GARDEN CITY
Dawson, Lumell Herbert
Harrison, Beverly E.
James, Marquita L.
Jenkins, Kenneth Vincent
Mills, Hughie E.
Wilson, Hugh A.
Young, Perry H.

GLEN COVE
Carroll, Robert F.

GLENS FALLS
Thomas, Roy L.

GREAT BEND
Jordan, John Wesley

GREAT NECK
Brown, Roy Hershel
Guilmenot, Richard Arthur, III
Kendrick, Curtis
Knight, Gladys Maria
Reeves, Martha Rose
Stewart, Malcolm M.

GREENLAWN
Esquerre, Jean Roland

GUILDERLAND
Law, Thomas Melvin
Welburn, Ronald Garfield

HAMILTON
Jackson, Acy Lee

HARTSDALE
Frelow, Robert Dean
Jackson, Luther Porter, Jr.
Jackson, Warren G.
Jacob, John Edward

HASTINGS-ON-HUDSON
Adams, Alger LeRoy
Clark, Kenneth Bancroft

HAUPPAUGE
Drew, Thelma Lucille
Floyd, Marquette L.
Johnston, Henry Bruce
Toran, Anthony

HELMUTH
DuBois, Asa Stephen

HEMPSTEAD
Adams, Robert Hugo
Barkum, Jerome Phillip
Beckett, Evette Olga
Boone, Clinton Caldwell
Brown, Joyce
Buford, William P.
Campbell, Emmett Earle
Cross, Betty Jean
Davis, Roland Hayes
Evans, William C.
Fraser, Alvardo M.
Harper, Bruce
Hawkes, Diana R.
Haynes, Walter Wesley
Hunter, Deanna Lorraine
Ireland, Lynda
Jones, Johnny (Lam Jones)
Marshall, Calvin Bromley, III
Merritt, Lorenzo
Myers, L. Leonard
Powell, Marvin
Rainsford, Greta M.
Swinney, T. Lewis
Thompson, Eugene Edward
Walker, Wesley

HENRIETTA
Byas, Thomas Haywood

HICKSVILLE
Isaac, Brian Wayne
Young, Ruth L.

HIGH FALLS
Staats, Florence Joan

HOLLIS
Burgie, Irving Louis (Lord Burgess)
Current, Gloster Bryant
Hill, Arthur Burit
Taylor, Janice A.

HOPEWELL JUNCTION
Johnson, Andrew

HUNTINGTON STATION
Boozer, Emerson, Jr.
Brown, Walter E.

HYDE PARK
Sims, Constance Arlette

ITHACA
Bell, Roseann P.
Gates, Henry Louis, Jr.
Hart, Edward E.
Hill, Sandra Patricia
Johnson, Pam McAllister
McClane, Kenneth Anderson, Jr.

JAMAICA
Allen, Gloria Marie
Baldwin, Louis J.
Bat Naphtali, Ashirah Sholomis (Nkechiela Cruise)
Bernard, Canute Clive
Brown, Sherman L.
Claytor, Charles E.
Cormier, Lawrence J.
Douglass, Melvin Isadore
Faust, Naomi Flowe
Frazier, Adolphus Cornelious
Graham, Helen W.
Hall, Frederick Theodore
Holmes, Carl
Jones, Alfred A.
Kelly, Florida L.
Kelly, James Clement
Marshall, Lewis West, Jr.
McCall, Carl
McCarthy, Fred
Meacham, Henry W.
Miller, Lawrence A.
Mitchell, Loften
Norman, Calvin Haines
Norris, Charles L., Sr.
Pierce, Cynthia Straker
Powell, Clarence Dean, Jr.
Ray, Jacqueline Walker
Reid, Edith C.
Rowe, Richard L.
Southerland, Ellease
Tardy, Walter J., Jr.
Thompson, Frank L.
Veal, Yvonnecris Smith
Whitehead, James T., Jr.
Williams, Ira Lee
Williams, Richard Lenwood

JAMESTOWN
McDonald, Anita Dunlop
Okwumabua, Benjamin Nkem
Peterson, Clarence Josephus
Taylor, Vivian A.
Thompson, Geraldine

JERICHO
Fonrose, Harold Anthony

KEW GARDENS
Dye, Luther V.
Wingate, Livingston L.

KINGS POINT
Griffin, Richard George
Jenkins, Emmanuel Lee

LAKE SUCCESS
White, Claude Esley

LATHAM
Smith, Barbara

LAURELTON
Faulding, Juliette J.
Haynes, Eleanor Louise
Jenkins, Cynthia

LAWRENCE
Brown, Paul D.
Davis, Brownie W.

LIVERPOOL
Wright, Roosevelt R., Jr.

LONG ISLAND CITY
Anderson, Avis Olivia
DeHart, Henry R.
Duncanson, Patricia A.
Fax, Elton C.
Harris, J. Robert, II
Holmes, Cloyd James
Shockley, Alonzo Hilton, Jr.

MALVERNE
Hill, Barbara Ann

MANHATTAN
Champion, Tempii Bridgene

MEADOW
Phears, William D.

MELVILLE
Jackson, Earl C.
Payne, Leslie
Watkins, Mary Frances

MIDDLETOWN
Best, William Andrew
Sands, Mary Alice

MILLWOOD
Dowdell, Dennis, Jr.

MINEOLA
Mereday, Richard F.
Nixon, Glenford Delacy
Robbins, Alfred S.
Service, Russell Newton

MOUNT VERNON
Bell, S. Aaron
Blackwood, Ronald A.
Bozeman, Bruce L.
Cleveland, Hattye M.
Dungie, Ruth Spigner
Maynor, Kevin Elliott
Moses, MacDonald
Robinson, Melvin P.
Scott, Jean Sampson
Tarter, James H., Sr.

NEW CITY
Johnson, Andrew

NEW HAMPTON
Sands, George M.

NEW HYDE PARK
Skeene, Linell De-Silva

NEW PALTZ
Grant, James

NEW ROCHELLE
Boddie, Daniel W.
Branch, William Blackwell
Brooks, Norman Leon
Chance, Kenneth Bernard
Dodds, R. Harcourt
Edwards, Theodore Unaldo
Goulbourne, Donald Samuel, Jr.
Hite, Nancy Ursula
Hollar, Milton Conover
Rowe, William Leon
Weston, M. Moran, II

NEW YORK
Abbott, Gregory
Abdul, Raoul
Abdul-Malik, Ibrahim
Adair, Robert A.
Adams, Clarence Lancelot, Jr.
Adderley, Nathaniel
Adolph, Gerald Stephen
Aiken, William
Ailey, Alvin
Albam, Manny
Alexander, Donald
Alexander, James Brett
Alexander, Sidney H., Jr.
Allen, Alexander J.
Allen, Betty (Mrs. R. Edward Lee III)
Allen, Clyde Cecil
Allen, Debbie
Allen, Percy, II
Allen, William Oscar
Alligood, Douglass Lacy
Alston, Casco, Jr.
Alveranga, Glanvin L.
Anderson, Amelia Veronica
Anderson, Donald Edward
Anderson, Granville Scott
Anderson, Harold
Anderson, Helen Louise
Andrews, Raymond
Anthony, Lillian Delores
Applewhaite, Leon B.
Arroyo, Martina
Ashford, Nicholas
Backus, Bradley
Bailer, Bonnie Lynn
Bailey, A. Peter
Bailey, Adrienne Yvonne

Bailey, James L.
Bailey, Lawrence R., Sr.
Bailey, Pearl
Bain, Linda Valerie
Baker, James E.
Ballard, Allen Butler, Jr.
Ballard, Bruce Laine
Ballard, Harold Stanley
Balmer, Horace Dalton, Sr.
Banks, Carlton Luther
Banks, Jeffrey Laurence
Bankston, Archie M.
Baraka, Imamu Amiri (Leroi Jones)
Barnes, Joseph Nathan
Barnes, N. Kurt
Barr, LeRoy
Barzy, Raymond Clifford, II
Bassey, Linus A.
Batten, Tony
Battle, Kathleen
Battle, Turner Charles, III
Baxter, Charles F., Jr.
Beard, Butch
Beauford, Fred
Beckett, Evette Olga
Belafonte, Harry
Bell, Joseph Curtis
Bell, Marilyn Lenora
Bell, Raleigh Berton
Benjamin, Ronald
Bennett, Courtney Ajaye
Bennett, Debra Quinette
Benoit, Edith B.
Berry, Philip Alfonso
Blair, George Ellis
Blakey, Art (Abdullah Ibn Buhaina)
Bland, Edward
Blayton-Taylor, Betty
Bludson-Francis, Vernett Michelle
Bogues, Leon Franklin
Bolder, J. Taber, Jr.
Bond, George Clement
Bone, Winston S.
Booker, Garvall H.
Booker, James E.
Boulware, Fay D.
Bowen, Emma L.
Boyd-Foy, Mary Louise
Boyer, Marcus Aurelius
Boynton, Ernest B., Jr.
Bracey, William Rubin
Bradford, Martina Lewis
Bradley, Edward R.
Bragg, Joseph L.
Bramwell, Patricia Ann
Braxton, Edward Kenneth
Brewer, Curtis
Brewer, Jim
Brisbane, Samuel Chester
Brockett, Ronald
Brokaw, Carol Ann
Brown, A. David
Brown, Barri Anne
Brown, Courtney Coleridge
Brown, John Andrew
Brown, Roscoe C., Jr.
Brown, Tony (William Anthony Brown)
Browne, Vivian E.
Bryant-Reid, Johanne
Buckley, Gail Lument
Buford, Sharnia
Bulger, Lucille O.
Burns, Jeff, Jr.
Burton, Ronald J.
Busby, Everett C.
Butts, Hugh F.
Bynes, Frank Howard, Jr.
Cain, George M.
Caldwell, Benjamin
Callender, Carl O.
Callender, Leroy R.
Cameron, Randolph W.
Campbell, Thomas W.
Capers, Eliza Virginia
Carey, Patricia M.
Carlton, Pamela Gean
Carmichael, Stokely
Carreker, William, Jr.
Carroll, Edward M.
Carroll, Harry Milton
Carroll, Robert F.

McMillian, Josie
McNeil, Freeman
McQuay, James Phillip
McRae, Carmen
Meriwether, Roy Dennis
Merriweather, Thomas L.
Michel, Harriet R.
Miller, Arthur J.
Miller, Edith
Miller, Evelyn B.
Miller, Lamar Perry
Miller, Lawrence A.
Miller, Oliver O.
Miller, Samuel O.
Miller-Jones, Dalton
Mingo, Frank L.
Minter, Kendall Arthur
Mister, Melvin Anthony
Mitchell, Bert Norman
Mitchell, Leona
Mixon, Veronica
Mohamed, Gerald R., Jr.
Monroe, Earl
Moody, Anne
Moody, Lynne Gatlin
Moore, Carman Leroy
Moore, Emanuel A.
Moore, Emerson J.
Moore, Melanie Anne
Moorehead, Justin Leslie
Morgan, Charlotte Theresa
Morgan, Kermit I.
Morisey, Patricia Garland
Morning, John Frew, Jr.
Morris, Alfred L.
Morris, Dolores Orinskia
Morris, Garrett
Morris, Horace W.
Morrison, Rick
Morrison, Toni
Morrow, E. Frederic
Morton, Patsy Jennings
Moses, Johnnie, Jr.
Moss, James A.
Motley, Constance Baker
Motley, John H.
Moyler, Freeman William, Jr.
Murphy, Clyde Everett
Murrain, Godfrey H.
Murray, Albert L.
Murray, Archibald R.
Murray, James P.
Murray, John W.
Muskelly, Anna Marie
Myles, Wilbert
Nabrit, James M., III
Nash, Henry
Naylor, Gloria
Neals, Felix
Neizer, Meredith Ann
Nelson, Novella C.
Nelson-Holgate, Gail Evangelyn
Newbold, Robert Thomas
Newman, Colleen A.
Nicholas, Mary Burke
Nivens, Beatryce Thomasinia
Noble, Gilbert E.
Norman, Jessye
Norman, Patricia
Norman, Roy A.
Norris, James Ellsworth Chiles
Nunery, Leroy David
Nurse, Robert Earl
Obi, James E.
Odom, Carolyn
Olugebefola, Ademola
O'Neal, Frederick Douglas
Orr, Louis M.
Ortiz, Delia
Ottley, Austin H.
Ousley, Harold Lomax
Owens, Andi
Owens, Jimmy
Owens, Victor Allen
Page, Gregory Oliver
Page, Rosemary Saxton
Palmer, Doreen P.
Pannell, Patrick Weldon
Parker, D. LaVerne
Parker, Kellis E.
Parks, Gordon A.
Parris, Guichard
Pasteur, Alfred Bernard
Paterson, Basil Alexander

Patten, Edward Roy (Cousin Eds)
Patterson, Evelynne (nee Roberts)
Patterson, Jacqueline J.
Patterson, Lawrence Patrick
Patterson, Lydia R.
Patterson, Raymond R.
Patton, Leroy
Pease, Denise Louise
Peck, Gregory Lester
Pemberton, Priscilla Elizabeth
Penceal, Bernadette Whitley
Perry, Alexis E.
Peters, William Alfred
Peterson, Maurice
Petioni, Muriel M.
Petrie, James Alfred
Petry, Ann (nee Lane)
Peyton, Jasper E.
Phillips, Fitzgerald
Pickens, William, III
Pierce, Lawrence Warren
Pierce, Ponchitta A.
Pinkney, Alphonso
Pires, Laura J.
Pittman, Sample Noel
Pogue, D. Eric
Pointer, Noel
Polite, Carlene Hatcher
Polite, Craig K.
Polk, Gene-Ann (Gene-Ann P. Horne)
Polk, Robert L.
Pomare, Eleo
Pool, Marquita Jones
Porter, James H.
Porter, Karl Hampton
Powell, Bernice Fletcher
Powell, Clilan Bethany
Powell, Kenneth Alasandro
Preiskel, Barbara Scott (nee Scott)
Preston, Edward Lee
Preston, George Nelson (Osafuhin Kwaku Nkonyansa)
Prettyman, Quandra
Price, George Baker
Price, Gilbert
Price, Leontyne
Primus, Pearl
Prince, Edgar Oliver
Procope, Ernesta G.
Procope, John Levy
Pugh, Clementine A.
Pugh, G. Douglas
Puryear, Alvin N.
Raines, Walter The Baron (Sir Walter)
Randall, Claire
Rashad, Ahmad (Bobby Moore)
Ray, Sandy Frederick
Reed, James
Reed, Lloyd H.
Reid, Robert Dennis
Rhines, Jesse Algeron
Rhodes, C. Adrienne
Richards, Edward A.
Richards, Loretta Theresa
Richardson, Scovel
Riley, Clayton
Riley, Negail R.
Ringgold, Faith
Rinsland, Roland D.
Roach, Max
Roane, Glenwood P.
Roberts, Edward A.
Robinson, Cleveland L.
Robinson, Hamilton
Robinson, James L.
Robinson, James Waymond
Robinson, John F.
Robinson, Leonard (Truck)
Robinson, Manuel
Robinson, Maude Eloise
Robinson, Roger
Robinson, Walter F.
Rock-Bailey, Jinni
Rodgers, Rod Audrian
Rodney, Karl Basil
Rollins, Howard E., Jr.
Rollins, Walter Theodore (Sonny Rollins)
Rooks, Charles Shelby
Ross, Diana
Ross, Phyllis Harrison
Ross, Regina D.

Rouse, Terrie
Roxborough, Mildred (nee Bond)
Rudd-Moore, Dorothy
Ruffin, Janice E.
Russell, Nipsey
Samuel, Frederick E.
Samuels, Leslie Eugene
Samuels, Robert J.
Sanders, Isaac Warren
Sandifer, Jawn A.
Sandler, Joan D.
Saunders, Mary A.
Scott, Clifford Alva
Scott, Hugh J.
Scott, Jacob Reginald
Scott, Osborne E.
Scott, Stanley S.
Seraile, Janette
Shaw, Melvin B.
Sheares, Reuben A., II
Shell, Juanita
Shelton, Charles E.
Shelton, Cora R.
Shepard, Joan
Shepard, Ray A.
Shepherd, Saundra Dianne
Shepp, Archie Vernon
Sherman, Edward Forrester
Sherman, Marcus Harvey
Sherwood, O. Peter
Shipp, E. R.
Short, Bobby (Robert Waltrip)
Shorter, Kenneth Livingston
Simmelkjaer, Robert T.
Simon, Fabrice Jule (Fabrice)
Simpson, Merton Daniel
Simpson, Valerie
Sims, Lowery Stokes
Sims, Naomi R.
Sirmans, Meredith Franklin
Slater, Helene Ford Southern
Slaughter, Vernon L.
Sleet, Moneta J., Jr.
Small, Kenneth Lester
Small, Lawrence Malcolm
Small, Sydney L.
Smalls, Charlie E.
Smart, Edward Bernard, Jr.
Smith, Andrew W.
Smith, Charles Lebanon
Smith, George Bundy
Smith, Jack Elliott
Smith, James A.
Smith, Vincent D.
Smothers, Ronald Eric
Soaries, Raynes L., Jr.
Southerland, Ellease
Sparrow, Rory Darnell
Spellman, Oliver B., Jr.
Spencer, Anthony Lawrence
Spooner, Richard C.
Springer, Ashton, Jr.
Stent, Theodore R.
Sterling, Charles A.
Stevens, Harold A.
Stevenson, Morton Coleman
Stewart, Donald Mitchell
Strachan, John R.
Strayhorn, Lloyd
Stroman, Kenneth
Sullivan, Martha Adams (Mecca)
Sutton, Oliver Carter, II
Sutton, Percy E.
Sutton, Pierre Monte
Sweat, Sheila Diane
Swift, Jay James
Switzer, Lucious
Tarter, James H., III
Tarter, Robert R., Jr.
Tate, Grady B.
Tatum, Wilbert A.
Taylor, DeForrest Walker
Taylor, Kenneth Matthew
Taylor, Mildred D.
Taylor, Steven Lloyd
Taylor, Timothy Merritt
Taylor, William Edward
Teer, Barbara Ann
Terrell, Francis D'Arcy
Terry, Bob (Nighthawk)
Terry, Clark
Thomas, Franklin A.
Thomas, Joyce Carol
Thomas, Stanley B., Jr.

Thomas-Williams, Gloria M.
Thompson, Albert N.
Thompson, Frank
Thompson, Marttie L.
Thomson, Gerald Edmund
Thornhill, Herbert Louis
Thorpe, Herbert Clifton
Thorpe, Josephine Horsley
Toby, William
Toon, Al
Trappier, Arthur Shives
Treadwell, David Merrill
Treadwell, Fay Rene Lavern
Trimiar, J. Sinclair
Troupe, Quincy Thomas, Jr.
Tucker, Kelvin Trent
Turner, Doris (Doris Turner Keys)
Turnipseed, Carl Wendell
Tyner, McCoy
Tyrrell, James A.
Tyson, Mike
VanAllen, Morton Curtis
Van Amson, George Louis
Vandross, Luther R.
Van Dyke, Henry
Van Lierop, Robert F.
Vassall, Sidney Austin
Vereen, Ben Augustus
Vincent, Irving H.
Wainwright, Oliver O'Connell
Walbey, Theodosia Emma Draher
Walburg, Judith Ann
Walker, Arthur B. C.
Walker, Cora T.
Walker, Darrell Trent
Walker, Joe
Walker, John Leslie
Walker, Joseph A.
Walker, Lucius, Jr.
Walker, Lynn Jones
Walker, Moses Andre
Walker, Wyatt Tee
Walsh, Everald J.
Walters, Warren W.
Walton, Ortiz Montaigne
Ward, Benjamin
Ward, Douglas Turner
Ward, Haskell G.
Wareham, Alton L.
Warner, Ivan
Warner, Malcolm-Jamal
Washington, Ava F.
Washington, James Melvin
Washington, Ruth V.
Waters, Martin Vincent
Waters, William L.
Watkins, Benjamin Wilston
Watkins, Charles B.
Watson, D'Jaris H.
Watson, Dennis Rahiim
Watson, James L.
Watson, Joann Nichols
Watson, Solomon B., IV
Wattleton, Alyce Faye (Faye Wattleton)
Watts, Andre
Watts, Frederick, Jr.
Way, Gary Darryl
Weatherly, Tom
Weaver, Robert C.
Webster, Marvin Nathaniel
Welburn, Ronald Garfield
Weston, M. Moran, II
Wharton, Clifton R., Jr.
Wharton, Dolores D.
Wheeler, Harold
Wheeler, Patricia A.
White, Arthur W., Jr.
White, Edward Clarence, Jr.
White, Javier A.
Whiteman, Herbert Wells, Jr.
Wilcox, Preston
Wilkins, Jesse Theodore
Wilkins, Roger W.
Wilkinson, Brenda
Wilkinson, Frederick D., Jr.
Williams, Addie Gatewood
Williams, Albert P.
Williams, Bruce E.
Williams, Charles A. (Buster Williams)
Williams, Charles E., III
Williams, Charles Thomas

Williams, E. Thomas, Jr.
Williams, Franklin H.
Williams, Hilda Yvonne
Williams, Ira Lee
Williams, James DeBois
Williams, Joe
Williams, Lea E.
Williams, Lloyd A.
Williams, Naomi Fisher (Mrs. C. Delmar Williams)
Williams, Ray H.
Williams, Ruthann Evege
Williams, Sterling B., Jr.
Williams, Terrie Michelle
Williams, William Thomas
Williams, Winston
Willis, Henry Stokes, Jr.
Wilmore, Gayraud Stephen
Wilson, John Louis
Wilson, Kim Alesia
Wilson, Lance Henry
Wilson, Lawrence E., III
Wilson, Mannie L.
Wilson, Markly
Wilson, Robert H.
Wilson, Robert L.
Windham, Revish
Winston, Henry
Witherspoon, James (Jimmie)
Wood, Curtis A.
Wood, Garland E.
Wooding, Samuel David
Woodruff, Hale A.
Wortham, Jacob James
Worthy, William
Wright, Benjamin Hickman
Wright, Bruce M.
Wright, Jeanne Jason (Jeanne Jason)
Wright, Keith Derek, Sr.
Wright, Ralph Edward
Wright, Sarah E.
Wright, William Gaillard
Yerby, Frank Garvin
Young, A. Steven
Young, Margaret Buckner
Zachary, Hubert M.

NEWBURGH
Carey, Audrey L.
Hart, Tony

NIAGARA FALLS
Giles, Charles Winston

NYACK
Cunningham, Arthur H.

OAKDALE
Roberts, Roy J.

OLD WESTBURY
Howard, Vera Gouke
Marshall, Paule Burke
Ray, Jacqueline Walker

OLEAN
Howard, Keith L.

ONEONTA
Kendall, Shirley I.

ORANGEBURG
Holland, Laurence H.
Mosley, Geraldine B. (nee Brown)

ORCHARD PARK
Bell, Gregory Leon
Butler, Jerry
Dubenion, Elbert
James, Rick
Leaks, Roosevelt (Rosey)
Marve, Eugene

OSSINING
Dixon, J. Melvin

OWEGO
Wells, James A.

OZONE PARK
Jones, James V.

Alston, Robert Milton, Jr.
Bodrick, Leonard Eugene
Bynum, Raleigh Wesley
Collins, Limone C.
Cunningham, William (Pete)
Dove, Evelyn Francyne
Evans, Carole Yvonne Mims
Gantt, Harvey Bernard
Gray, Andrew Jackson
Grayson, Robert
Grier, Arthur E., Jr.
Harper, Joseph W., III
Hawkins, Reginald A.
Hedgespeth, George T., Jr.
Hill, Esther P.
Hubbard, Reginald T.
Hunter, David Lee
Johnson, Edmond R.
Johnson, Sam
King, Patricia E.
Leatherman, Omar S., Jr.
Lee, Robert H.C.
Lee, William J.
Leeper, Ronald James
Lockman-Brooks, Linda
Maxwell, Bertha Lyons
Metcalf, Michael Richard
Murphy, John Matthew, Jr.
Newsome, Paula Renee
Nichols, Elaine
Palmer, James E.
Pereira, Sarah Martin
Rann, Emery Louvelle
Steger, C. Donald
Stroman, Cheryl Delores
Thomas, Herman Edward
Thompson, David
Wilson-Smith, Willie Arrie

CLEMMONS
Sharp, Charles Louis

CLINTON
Jones, Clifford Anthony, Sr.

CONCORD
Alston, Betty Bruner
Mathis, Robert Lee
McLean, Mable Parker
Newsom, Lionel H.

CONWAY
Hunter, Howard Jacque, Jr.

CULLOWHEE
Craig, Starlett Russell

DURHAM
Allison, Ferdinand V., Jr.
Baines, Tyrone Randolph
Batchelor, Asbury Collins
Belcher, Nathaniel L.
Bell, William Vaughn
Bethea, Gregory Austin
Bigelow, W. T.
Bond, John Percy, III
Bryant, R. Kelly, Jr.
Burnim, Mickey L.
Caesar, Shirley
Carter, James Harvey
Chapman, Charles F.
Clement, Josephine Dobbs
Clement, William A.
Collins, Bert
Copeland, Betty Marable
Davis, Harold R.
Dawson, Robert Edward
Daye, Charles Edward
DeBracy, Warren
DeJarmon, Elva Pegues
Dempsey, Joseph P.
Dillard, Samuel Dewell
Fleming, Stanley Louis
Franklin, John Hope
Frasier, Leroy B.
Garrett, Nathan Taylor
Green, Cicero M., Jr.
Hackett, Rufus E.
Isler, Marshall A., III
Jackson, Jacquelyne Johnson
Jacobs, Sylvia Marie
Johnson, Audreye Earle
Johnson, Charles
Jones, Clifton Patrick

Jordan, Milton C.
Joyner, Irving L.
Kee, Marsha Goodwin
Kennedy, William J., III
King, Charles E.
Lattimore, Caroline Louise
Lawrence, William Wesley
Lewis, James R.
Lincoln, C. Eric
Lucas, John H.
Lynch, Lorenzo A., Sr.
Marsh, William A., Jr.
McAdams, Robert L.
McDonald, William Emory
McFadden, Cora C.
Michaux, Eric Coates
Miller, Helen S.
Moore, Donald Torian
Norris, Curtis H.
Patterson, Cecil Lloyd
Perry, Patsy Brewington
Richmond, Tyronza R.
Rohadfox, Ronald Otto
Ruffin, John
Schooler, James Morse, Jr.
Shields, Karen Bethea (Karen Galloway Shields)
Sloan, Maceo Kennedy
Spaulding, Kenneth Bridgeforth
Spruill, Robert I.
Swain, Ronald L.
Taylor, Julia W.
Walker, Leroy Tashreau
Watts, Charles Dewitt
Wells, Robert Benjamin, Jr.
Westerfield, Louis
Wheeler, John Hervey
White, Nathaniel B.
Williams, Chester Lee
Williams, John Earl

EAST SPENCER
Massey, Reginald Harold
Ramsey, Charles Edward, Jr.

EDEN
Bender, Douglas Ray
Hobson, Patricia Pinnix

EDENTON
Hathaway, Anthony, Jr.
Perry, Jerald Isaac, Sr.
Taylor, James Elton

ELIZABETH CITY
Banks, Garnie
Cole, Edyth Bryant
Freeman, David Calvin, Sr.
Houston, Johnny L.
Jenkins, Jimmy Raymond
Jones, William Henry, Jr.
Mitchell, Marian Bartlett
Perry, Jerald Isaac, Sr.
Taylor, James Elton
White, Kermit Earle

ELIZABETHTOWN
McNeill-Huntley, Esther Mae

ELON COLLEGE
Blackwell, Faiger Megrea

FAIR BLUFF
Evans, Joe B.

FAYETTEVILLE
Allen, Gladstone Wesley
Andrews, Maxine Ramseur
Axt, Veronica Renee
Foulks, Carl Alvin
Goodson, Ernest Jerome
Hackley, Lloyd Vincent
Hales, Mary Ann
Harris, Marion Rex
Hedgepeth, Leonard
Johnson, Kenneth Peter
Lyons, Charles A., Jr.
McDaniels, John Edward, Sr.

FRANKLINTON
Williams, Yarborogh, Jr.

FUQUAY-VARINA
Freeman, William M.

GARLAND
Brown, Mary Boykin

GARNER
Sutton, Gloria W.

GASTONIA
Jaggers, George Henry, Jr.
Miller, James S.
Moore, Larry Louis

GOLDSBORO
Best, Prince Albert, Jr.
Whitted, Earl, Jr.
Williams, Charles J., Sr.

GRANTSBORO
Jones, Booker Tee

GREENSBORO
Armstrong, J. Niel
Baber, Ceola Ross
Battle, Bernard J., Sr.
Bender, Douglas Ray
Bishop, Cecil
Black, Daniel L., Jr.
Bowie, Oliver Wendell
Brewington, Thomas E., Jr.
Bright, Jean Marie
Buie, Sampson, Jr.
Campbell, Graham F.
Crutcher, Betty Neal
Crutcher, Ronald Andrew
Davis, Arthur, III
Dennard, Turner Harrison
Dorsett, Katie Grays
Douglas, Mae Alice
Durham, Carey Winston
Epps, Constance Arnettres
Exum, Thurman McCoy
Fort, Edward B.
Gibbs, Warmoth T.
Hairston, Otis L.
Halsey, George
Harrigan, Rodney Emile
Hayes, Charles Leonard
Hicks, Arthur James
Johnson, Walter Thaniel, Jr.
Jones, Earl Frederick
Kilimanjaro, John Marshall
Kilpatrick, George Roosevelt
Kirk, Sarah Virgo
Kirk, Wyatt D.
Lee, J. Kenneth
Little, Jean Perkins
Logan, Frenise A.
McCleave, Mansel Philip
McKinney, E. Doris
McLaughlin, John Belton
McMillan, James C.
Miller, Isaac H., Jr.
Monroe, Charles Edward
Moone, Wanda Renee
Moore, M. Elizabeth Gibbs
Murphy, Romallus O.
Norwood, Bernice N.
Parker, William C., Jr.
Patrick, Odessa R.
Ralston, Elreta Melton Alexander
Ross, Ralph M.
Sampson, Robert R.
Scott, Gloria Dean Randle
Simkins, George Christopher
Spruill, Albert Westley
Stewart, Jewel Hope
Trent, William Johnson, Jr.
Vick, Marian
Walker, Albert L.
Wilkins, Willie T.
Wooden, Ralph L.

GREENVILLE
Carter, Edward Earl
Chestnut, Dennis Earl
Cunningham, Paul Raymond Goldwyn
Hammond, Kenneth Ray
Hines, Wiley Earl (Chic)
Holsey, Lilla G.
Lewis, Lauretta F

Maye, Beatrice Carr Jones
Metcalf, Zubie West, Jr.
Register, Jasper C.
Williams, Dorothy Daniel
Woods, Almita (nee Robinson)

GRIFTON
Murphy, Robert L.

HAMLET
McEachern, Maceo R.

HENDERSON
Baskerville, Randolph
Henderson, Nannette S.
Jenkins, Clara Barnes
Johnson, Louise Mason

HENRICO
Edwards, Grover Lewis, Sr.

HICKORY
Killian, Iris Louise

HIGH POINT
Andrews, Frazier L.
Chess, Sammie, Jr.
Langford, John W.
Tillett, George Edward

HOFFMAN
Gholston, Betty J.

JACKSONVILLE
Buffong, Eric Arnold

KANNAPOLIS
Long, John Bennie
Nash, George T., III

KINSTON
Beech, Harvey Elliott
Graham, George Washington, Jr.
Hannibal, Alice Priscilla

KITTRELL
Eaton, Lela M. Z.

LA GRANGE
Summers, Retha

LANDIS
Taylor, Felicia Michelle

LAURINBURG
Littlejohn, Samuel Gleason

LENOIR
Horton, Larkin, Jr.

LILLINGTON
Smith, James Odell

LUMBERTON
Cummings, Frances McArthur

MAGNOLIA
Becton, Rudolph

MANSON
Worth, Charles Joseph

MAXTON
Davis, Robert E.

MAYSVILLE
Frost, William Henry

MEBANE
Cain, Frank

MOORESVILLE
Sobers, Waynett A., Jr.

MORGANTON
Crosby-Langley, Loretta

MURFREESBORO
Hunter, Howard Jacque, Jr.

NAVASSA
Brown, Louis Sylvester

NEW BERN
Frazier, Reginald Lee
Harmon, John H.

NEW HILL
Booker, Gary P.

OXFORD
McKissick, Floyd B.

PEACHLAND
Gatewood, Algie C.

PINEBLUFF
Capel, Felton Jeffrey

PITTSBORO
Thompson, Carl Eugene

POLKTON
Kersey, Elizabeth T.

POWELLSVILLE
Coley, Donald Lee

RAEFORD
Morrisey, Jimmy

RALEIGH
Allen, Brendra Foster
Ball, Richard E.
Best, Willie Armster
Burton, Leroy Melvin, Jr.
Caldwell, Edwin L., Jr.
Carter, James Harvey
Carter, Wilmoth Annette
Clarke, James Alexander
Cofield, Elizabeth Bias
Cook, Charles A.
Dandy, Clarence L.
Davis, Grady D., Sr.
Davis, Wiley M.
Debnam, Marjorie Boyd
Dempsey, Joseph P.
Edwards, John Wilson
Ervin, Hazel Arnett
Fisher, Judith Danelle
Frink, Ronald Murice
Frye, Henry E.
Garner, Edward, Jr.
Gill, Rosa Underwood
Glover, Sarah Louise
Groffrey, Frank Eden
Hager, Roscoe Franklin
Haywood, Bertron Don
Hinton, Christopher Jerome
Holloway, J. Mills
Horton, Larnie G.
Irving, Ophelia McAlpin
Ishman, Sybil R.
Johnson, Joy J.
Jordan, Mabel B.
Knight, William Rogers
Larkins, John Rodman
Lightner, Clarence E.
Locke, Don C.
Lovelady, Rueben Leon
Merritt, Bishetta Dionne
Miller, John H.
Mitchell, LeMonte Felton
Moore, Albert
Moore, Lenard Duane
Myers, Lewis Horace
Palmer, Elliott B., Sr.
Palmer, Joe
Peebles, Allie Muse
Peebles-Wilkins, Wilma Cecelia
Pettis, Joyce Owens
Pickett, Henry B., Jr.
Pope, Mary Maude
Quigless, Milton Douglas, Jr.
Reed, Addison W.
Robinson, George Ali
Robinson, Prezell Russell
Silvey, Edward
Sims, Genevieve Constance
Smith, Carl William
Smith, James Almer, III
Smith, Oscar Samuel, Jr.
Spencer, Joan Moore

Sutton, Gloria W.
Swain, Ronald L.
Webb, Harold H.
Wilkins, Kenneth C.
Williams, Robert D.
Winston, Hubert

RANDLEMAN
Little, Jean Perkins

REIDSVILLE
Gordon, Ronald Eugene
Griggs, Harry Kindell, Sr.

RESEARCH TRIANGLE PARK
Clendeninn, Neil J.
Walker, Ernest L.
Wheeler, Warren Hervey

RICH SQUARE
Felton, James A.

ROARING RIVER
Gilreath, Coot, Jr.

ROCKY MOUNT
Armstrong, Wiley T.
Gay, Helen Parker
Jones, Ruth Braswell
Leonard, Walter Fenner (Buck)
Morgan, Hazel C. Brown
Walker, Thomas L.

ROSE HILL
Monk, Edd Dudley

ROXBORO
Bates, Henry Melvin
Woods, Robert Louis

SALISBURY
Ewers, James Benjamin, Jr.
Greene, William Henry L'Vel

SANFORD
Fisher, Judith Danelle
Morgan, Joseph L.

SHARPSBURG
Beasley, Annie Ruth

SHELBY
Ford, Aileen W.
Rouse, Bishop Claude, Jr.

SMITHFIELD
Woodhouse, Johnny Boyd

SNOW HILL
Speight, Velma R.

SOUL CITY
McKissick, Evelyn Williams

SOUTHERN PINES
Lee, Chandler Bancroft
Thompson, Herman G.
Wade, Kim Mache

SOUTHPORT
Adams, Nelson Eddy

TAR HEEL
Andrews, James F.

TARBORO
Deloatch, Myrna Loy
Ray, Moses Alexander

TILLERY
Grant, Gary Rudolph

TRYON
Carson, Warren Jason, Jr.
Massey, Carrie Lee

WADESBORO
Kersey, Bertha Brinnett
Little, Herman Kernel

WARRENTON
Ballance, Frank Winston, Jr.
Henderson, Nannette S.
Williams, Yarborogh, Jr.
Worth, Charles Joseph

WASHINGTON
Randolph, Louis T.

WENTWORTH
Hampton, Thurman B.

WILKESBORO
Gilreath, Coot, Jr.

WILMINGTON
Blanks, Delilah B.
Jervay, Thomas Clarence, Sr.
Newkirk, Inez Doris (nee Tucker)
Sidbury, Harold David

WILSON
Coleman, Avant Patrick
Ward, Melvin Fitzgerald, Sr.

WINDSOR
Cherry, Andrew Jackson
Coley, Donald Lee

WINSTON-SALEM
Adams, Armenta Estella
  (Armenta Adams Hummings)
Angelou, Maya
Bass, Marshall Brent
Bell, Winston Alonzo
Boswell, Bennie, Jr.
Brown, Clark S.
Brown, Hazel Evelyn
Brown, Jasper C., Jr.
Burke, Vivian H.
Burt, James E.
Butler, J. Ray
Chenault, Myron Maurice
Coaxum, Callie B.
Crews, William Sylvester
Duren, Emma Thompson
Easley, Eddie V.
Erwin, Richard C.
Eure, Herman Edward
Fowler, Leon, Jr.
Gaillard, Ralph C., Sr.
Gaines, Clarence E.
Goodwin, Kelly Oliver Perry
Hairston, Oscar Grogan
Hauser, Charlie Brady
Hayes, Roland Harris
Hedgley, David R.
Herrell, Astor Yeary
Hutton, Ronald I.
Hymes, Jesse
Jackson, Felix W.
Lewis, Henry S., Jr.
Mack, James E.
Malloy, H. Rembert
Miller, Ward Beecher
Newell, Virginia K.
Oubre, Hayward Louis
Phillips, Barbara (nee Kinard)
Pollard, Alton Brooks, III
Ross, Charles C.
Ruffin, Benjamin S.
Sadler, Kenneth Marvin
Sadler, Wilbert L.
Scales, Manderline Elizabeth
Sharp, Charles Louis
Tate, David Kirk
Thompson, Cleon Franklyn, Jr.
Tidwell, Isaiah
Tomlinson, Mel Alexander
Turner, William Hobertt
Wagner, David H.
Watkins, Jerry D.
Williams, Kenneth Raynor

WINTON
Wilson, Donald P.

OHIO

AKRON
Arnold, Helen E.
Brown, Ronald Paul

Chapman, Martin Odes
Ellis, William Reuben
Evege, Walter L., Jr.
Fort, William H.
Foye-Eberhardt, Ladye Antoinette
Greene, Charles Lavant
Harris, Robert D.
Kennard, Patricia A. (nee Byrd)
King, Lawrence P.
Long, Andu Trisa
McClain, Andrew Bradley
McClain, Shirla R.
Mickey, Gordon Eugene
Morgan, Dolores Parker
Morgan, Eldridge Gates
Payne, Margaret Ralston
Peake, Edward James, Jr.
Player, Willa B.
Riddle, Bedford Neal
Roulhac, Joseph D.
Scruggs, Sylvia Ann
Silas, Jacqueline Ann
Stubbs, Harold K.
Sykes, Vernon Lee
Williams, Annalisa J. Stubbs
Williams, James R.
Wilson, John W.
Young, Lionel Wesley

ALLIANCE
Brown, Evelyn
Malone, Gloria S.
Walton, James Edward

ASHTABULA
Brown, Ronald Paul
Shelby, Reginald W.

ATHENS
Burden, Willie James
Childs, Francine C.
Chisholm, Clarence Edward
Stewart, Gregory
Williams, Daniel Salu

BARBERTON
Berry, Archie Paul
Davison, Edward L.

BATAVIA
Doddy, Reginald Nathaniel

BEACHWOOD
Leggon, Herman W.

BEDFORD HEIGHTS
Stevenson, Unice Teen

BELLBROOK
Goodwin, Evelyn Louise

BOWLING GREEN
Perry, Robert Lee
Scott, John Sherman
Taylor, Jack Alvin, Jr.

BRECKSVILLE
Jackson, Kenneth William

BRUNSWICK
Temple, Oney D.

CANTON
Bell, Yolanda Maria
Calhoun, Jack Johnson, Jr.
Fisher, Robert F.
Gravely, Melvin J.
Houston, Kenneth Ray
Hunter, William L.
Ingram, Eldridge B.
Kyle, Odes J., Jr.
McIlwain, Albert Hood
McIlwain, Nadine Williams
Moore, Charles D.
Wilson, Jon
Wilson, William E.

CENTERVILLE
Ross, Robert P.

CINCINNATI
Abercrumbie, Paul Eric
Alexander, Charles
Allen, Herbert J.
Bass, Don
Bates-Parker, Linda
Bell, Sheila Trice
Berry, Theodore M.
Blackwell, J. Kenneth
Bond, Howard H.
Booth, Lavaughn Venchael
Bowen, William F.
Braddock, Carol T.
Brasey, Henry L.
Bronson, Fred James
Brooks, James Robert
Brown, Herbert R.
Browner, Ross
Bryant, Napoleon, Jr.
Burlew, Ann Kathleen
Butler, Broadus Nathaniel
Caldwell, Esly Samuel, II
Cargile, William, III
Casey, Edmund C.
Chapman, David Anthony
Chenault, William J.
Chess, Robert Hubert
Clinton, Thomas R.
Cobb, Marvin Lawrence
Collins, Patricia Hill
Cooper, Constance Marie
Cooper, William M.
Cornelison, Carole Jane
Cross, William Howard
Curtis, Issac Fisher
Davis, Melwood Leonard
Deane, Morgan R.
Doddy, Reginald Nathaniel
Edwards, Arthur James
Edwards, Ruth McCalla
Few, Terry Lee
Fleming, Vernon Cornelious
Fuller, Dewey C.
Garner, Thomas L.
Goodloe, Celestine Wilson
Gordon, Lois Jackson
Grant, Cheryl Dayne
Hall, Joseph A.
Hamilton, Pamela Marie
Harris, Charles Cornelius
Harris, M. L.
Hawkins, Lawrence C.
Henderson, John L.
Hicks, Eleanor
Hooker, Odessa Walker
Jenkins, Roger J.
Johnson, Joseph Harvey
Jones, James Wesley
Jones, Nathaniel R.
Jones, William Lawless
Jones, Winton Dennis, Jr.
Jordan, Marjorie W.
Keels, Paul C.
Lawson, Lawyer
Logan, Linda Ann
McClain, William Andrew
McElvane, Pamela Anne
McGoodwin, Roland C.
McLean, Marquita Sheila
  McLarty
Meacham, Robert B.
Meredith, James Howard
Merenivitch, Jarrow
Merriweather, Robert Eugene
Morton, William Stanley
Munoz, Anthony
Newberry, Cedric Charles
Norton, Aurelia Evangeline
O'Donnell, Lorena Mae
Owens, O'dell M.
Oxley, Lucy Orintha
Parker, David Gene
Peck, Douglas Robert
Person, Leslie Robin
Pryor, Aaron (Richard Pryor)
Pryor, Chester Cornelius, II
Reece, Steven
Reed, Allene Wallace
Rivers, Clarence Joseph
Robertson, Oscar Palmer
Sells, Mamie Earl
Shands, Franklin M., Sr.
Shuttlesworth, Fred L.
Smiley-Robertson, Carolyn

Smith, Paul M.
Spencer, Donald Andrew
Spencer, Marian A.
Stewart, Ronald Patrick
Stone, Harold Anthony
Thomas, John Henderson, III
Truitte, James F.
Turner, Mark Anthony
Wells-Davis, Margie Elaine
West, John Andrew
Whitney, W. Monty
Williams, Reggie
Wilson, Henry, Jr.

CLEVELAND
Adams, Katherine
Adams, Leslie (Harrison Leslie Adams)
Adrine, Ronald Bruce
Alexander, James, Jr.
Andrews, William Henry
Arnold, Ethel N.
Atkins, Russell
Banks, Chip
Banks, Marguerita C.
Barrett, James A.
Batts, Terry Milburn
Bell, James H.
Bell, Rouzeberry
Bell, Tommy Lee, III
Benn, Ishmael
Bennett, William Ronald
Blakely, William H., Jr.
Boddie, Louise
Brisker, Lawrence
Brooker, Moe A.
Brown, Bernice H.
Brownlee, Wyatt China
Bugg, Mayme Carol
Burke, Lillian W.
Burns, Dargan J.
Burrell, Clinton Blane
Bustamante, John H.
Butler, Annette G.
Carr, Charles V.
Caviness, E. Theophilus
Chancellor, Carl Eugene
Chandler, Dennis Courtland
Chandler, Everett A.
Chapman, Robert L., Sr.
Chatman, Anna Lee
Clark, Sanza Barbara
Clay, Cliff
Clouden, LaVerne C.
Cochran, Herschel J.
Coleman, Frederick M.
Collins, Daisy G.
Connally, C. Ellen
Crosby, Fred McClellen
Cross, Jack
Crouther, Betty M.
Crouther, Melvin S., Jr.
Cummings, Donna Louise
Darden, Thomas V.
Davidson, Lurlean G.
Davis, Robert E.
Davis, Thomas J.
Decatur, Robert A.
Dixon, Hanford
Douglas, Janice Green
Drimmer, Melvin
Duncan, Geneva
Dunnigan, Jerry
Earls, Julian Manly
Eatman, Janice A.
Edwards, Robert Valentino
Ellison, Nolen M.
Fleming, Charles Walter
Flewellen, Icabod
Forbes, George L.
Franklin, Grant L.
Franklin, Milton B., Jr.
Gaines, Clarence L.
Gallagher, Mike John
Gamble, William F.
Gilbert, Albert C.
Gilliam, Robert M., Sr.
Griggs, Anthony
Hale-Benson, Janice Ellen
Haley, Donald C.
Hall, Brian Edward
Harper, Sara J.
Harris, Leodis
Hawthorne, Nathaniel

Head, Edith
Herbert, Benne S.
Hill, Alfred
Hoover, Odie Millard, Jr.
Horton, Earle C.
Huggins, Clarence L
Huggins, Hosiah, Jr.
Humphrey, Arthur
Jackson, Gerald Milton
Jackson, Leo A.
James, Ronald J.
Johnson, Andrew L., Jr.
Johnson, Clifford, Jr.
Johnson, Henderson A., III
Jones, Lisa Payne
Jones, Stephanie Tubbs
Kelley, Robert William
Lairet, Dolores Person
Lawson, J. Ranaldo
Lee, Gabriel S., Jr.
Lee, Oliver B.
Lee, Robert E.
Lee, Shirley Freeman
Lyke, James P.
Mack, Kevin (James Kevin Mack)
Mackel, Audley Maurice, III
Maddox, Elliott
Madison, Robert P.
Malone, Eugene William
McClain, Jerome G.
McCollum, Anita LaVerne
Meaux, Ronald
Miller, Maposure T.
Mills, Robert
Minter, Steven Alan
Mixon, Clarence W.
Moore, George Anthony
Morris, Milton Curtis
Moss, Otis, Jr.
Murphy, Donald Richard
Newsome, Ozzie
Palmer, Berthina E.
Payden, Henry J., Sr.
Peoples, Earl F., Sr.
Phillips, F. Allison
Phillips, James Lawrence
Pinkney, Arnold R.
Polley, William Emory
Poole, Dillard M.
Pottinger, Albert A.
Preston, Swanee H. T., Jr.
Pruitt, Gregory Donald
Pruitt, Mike
Ribbins, Gertrude
Roberts, Ann F.
Roberts, John B.
Roberts, Narlie
Rogers, James E.
Rosemond, Manning Wyllard, Jr.
Rowan, Albert T.
Rucker, Reginald J. (Reggie)
Saffold, Oscar E.
Seymour, Robert F.
Sharpe, Calvin William
Shaw, Alvia A.
Shaw, Curtis E.
Shumate, Glen
Snipes, Kenneth
Starling, John Crawford
Stewart, Mae E.
Stokes, Carl Burton
Storey, Robert D.
Taylor, Clarence B.
Thomas, William L.
Thompson, Isaiah
Tolliver, Stanley Eugene, Sr.
Trumbo, George William
Tuffin, Paul Jonathan
Turner, Clifton B.
Tyree, Patricia Grey
Warfield, Paul D.
Watson, Clarence
Weathers, Margaret A.
White, Frederic Paul, Jr.
White, George W.
White-Ware, Grace E.
Willacy, Hazel M.
Williams, Theodore Mel
Wilson, John W.
Wisham, Claybron O.
Womack, Andrew A.
Wykle, May Louise Hinton

CLEVELAND HEIGHTS
Brown, Virgil E., Jr.
Bryant, William Henry, Jr.
Franklin, Grant L.
Herbert, Benne S.
Madison, Leatrice Branch
Madison, Robert P.
Minor, Emma Lucille
Russell, Leonard Alonzo
Seaton, Shirley Marie Smith
Sharpe, Calvin William
Webb, James Eugene
Wright, Ebony Narketa

CLYDE
Lloyd, Phil Andrew

COLUMBUS
Bell, Napoleon A.
Bland, Arthur H.
Blount, Wilbur Clanton
Booth, Charles E.
Boston, George David
Branch-Simpson, Germaine Gail
Brown, Ralph H.
Carter, Joan Elizabeth
Carter, Percy A., Jr.
Chenault, William J.
Craig, Elson L.
Day, Donald
Dodson, William Alfred, Jr.
Duncan, Robert M.
Durham, Barbee William
Evans, Helen W.
Ferguson, Edward A., Jr.
Frasier, Ralph Kennedy
Garraway, Michael Oliver
Gillespie, Avon E.
Greer, Robert O.
Hale, Frank W., Jr.
Harris, Jack
Hickman, Garrison M.
Hicks, Clayton Nathaniel
Hicks, William J.
Holland, Robin W.
Humphrey, Howard John
James, Troy Lee
Johnson, William Theolious
LaCour, Louis Bernard
Lomax, Frank, III
Luckey, Evelyn F.
Lyman, Webster S.
Maddox, Margaret Johnnetta
    Simms
Maddox, Odinga Lawrence
Mallory, William L.
Marshall, Carl Leroy
Marshall, James Andrew
McDaniel, William T., Jr.
McGee, Rose N.
Miller, Ray, Jr.
Mitchell, Melvin J.
Morris, Leibert Wayne
Myles, William
Nelson, William Edward, Jr.
Parrish, James W.
Pearson, James A.
Pettigrew, Grady L., Jr.
Pruitt, Anne Smith
Redmond, Jane Smith
Robinson, S. Yolanda
Rosemond, John H.
Ruffin, Richard D.
Smallwood, Osborn Tucker
Smith, Herald Leonydus
Stewart, John Othneil
Stewart, Mac A.
Stull, Robert J.
Stull, Virginia Elizabeth
Sullivan, Edward James
Sykes, Vernon Lee
Taylor, Arlene M. J.
Thompson, Ike
Thompson, Sylvia Moore
Thrower, Julius A.
Tolbert, Herman Andre
Tolbert, Lawrence J.
Trout, Nelson W.
Vaughn, Eugenia Marchelle
    Washington
Walker, Charles H.
Walker, Watson Herchael
West, Pheoris
White, David D.

Williams, Lucretia Murphy
Williams, Mary Ann Sheridan
Wilson, F. Leon
Wilson, Nevia Aneice
Wood, Andrew W.

CUYAHOGA FALLS
Lampley, Handy Ellis

DAYTON
Adegbile, Gideon Sunday Adebisi
Black, Don Gene
Bledsoe, Milton Hargis, Jr.
Borum, Regina A.
Brown, Charles Sumner
Coates, Janice E.
Cunningham, John F.
Dansby, Jesse L., Jr.
Dixon, Richard Clay
Earley, Stanley Armstead, Jr.
Eaton, Tyrone
Ellis, Duke Ellington
Ford, Robert Blackman
Francis, James L.
Frazier, Jimmy Leon
Garrison, Jewell K.
Gates, Nina Jane
Gilmore, Marshall
Green, Richard Carter
Gunn, Gladys
Hall, Charles Harold
Hall, Fred, III
Hammond, W. Rodney
Harris, Sarah Elizabeth
Harrison, William Edgar
Holloway, Callon Wesley, Jr.
Jackson, Arthur D., Jr.
Jones, Robert Earl
Leaphart, Eldridge
Leigh, William Alvin
Lewis, Lloyd E., Jr.
Littlejohn, Bill C.
Lovelace, Dean Alan
Lucas, Leo Alexander
Marable, June Morehead
Mays, Dewey Orvric, Jr.
McCollum, Alice Odessa
McGee, James H.
Mitchell, Bush P.
Neal, Edna D.
Nutt, Ambrose Benjamin
Phillips, Lloyd Garrison, Jr.
Powell, David L.
Rakestraw, Kyle Damon
Smith, Alphonso Lehman
Smith, Frederick Ellis
Smith, Howard C.
Taylor, Robert Earlington, Jr.
Taylor, Sinthy E.
Taylor, Vivian Lorraine
Thornton, Jackie C.
Vivians, Nathaniel Roosevelt
Walker, Willie F.
Washington, John William
Williams, Walker Richard, Jr.
Wilson, Carl L.
Wingo, A. George
Wise, Warren C.
Wofford, Alphonso
Worthey, Richard E.
Wright, Carolyn Elaine
Young, Clarence, III

DELAWARE
Tynes, Richard H.
White, Ernest G.

DUBLIN
Taylor, Arlene M. J.

EAST CLEVELAND
Barnes, John E.
Harris, MaryAnn
Head, Edith
Hunter, David
Johnson, Almeta Ann
Pittman, Darryl E.
Thomas-Richardson, Valerie Jean

ENON
Smithers, Priscilla Jane

EVENDALE
Lowry, James E.

FAIRFIELD
Guice, Raleigh Terry

FINDLAY
Woodson, Cleveland Coleman, III

FOREST PARK
Wright, Linwood Clinton

GRANVILLE
Lyles, Dewayne
Rawlings, Martha (nee Morse)

GREEN SPRINGS
Copeland, Terrilyn Denise

GROVE CITY
Vaughn, Eugenia Marchelle
    Washington

HIGHLAND HEIGHTS
Neavon, Joseph Roy

HIRAM
Hemphill, Frank
Thompson, Eric R.

HUDSON
Stevenson, Unice Teen

HURON
Lawyer, Vivian (nee Moore)

KENT
Chambers, Doris Foster
Chambers, Fredrick
Crosby, Edward Warren
Ekechi, Felix K.
Meadows, Ferguson Booker, Jr.
Meier, August
Payne, Margaret Ralston
Turner, Doris J.
Van Dyke, Henry

KETTERING
Dudley, Albert LeRoy
Marshall, Don A.
Warren, Lee Alden (Tico)

LEBANON
Nichols, Walter L.

LINCOLN HEIGHTS
Dantzler, Herman
Southall, Charles

LONDON
Scurry, Fred L.

LORAIN
Wrice, David

LYNDHURST
Richie, Winston Henry

MANSFIELD
Dorsey, Harold Aaron
McCaulley, James Alan, III
Payton, Jeff
Washington, Henry L.

MASSILLON
Beane, Patricia Jean

MENTOR
Preston, Swanee H. T., Jr.

MIDDLETOWN
Sampson, Marva W.
Saunders, James Warren
    (Choppy)
Wilson, Michael

MONTGOMERY
Southern, Charles O.

MOUNT GILEAD
Best, Sheila Diane

NEWARK
Thorne, Cecil Michael

NORTH CANTON
Marcere, Norma Snipes

OAKWOOD VILLAGE
Wainwright, Gloria Bessie

OBERLIN
Arnold, Harriet Amelia Chapman
Carson, Dwight Keith
Hernton, Calvin Coolidge
Peek, Booker C.
Walker, Frances
White, Clovis Leland

OXFORD
Forrest-Carter, Audrey Faye
Hargraves, William Frederick, II
Jackson, W. Sherman
Mosley, Myrtis H.
Patton, Rosezelia L.

PAINESVILLE
Walker, Wendell P.

PEPPER PIKE
Taylor, Clarence B.

PIKETON
McLaughlin, Benjamin Wayne

RICHFIELD
Bagley, John
Hubbard, Phil Lavelle
Turpin, Mel Keith
Wilkens, Leonard R.

ST BERNARD
Macon, Norman

SALEM
Alexander, Cornelia (Connie)

SANDUSKY
Seavers, Clarence W.

SHAKER HEIGHTS
Benning, Emma Bowman
Brown, Malcolm McCleod
Butler, Annette G.
Crawford, Muriel C.
Freeman, Lelabelle Christine
George, Allen
Groves, Delores Ellis
Jones, Lisa Payne
Jones, Peter Lawson
Mackel, Audley Maurice, III
Martin, Franklin Farnarwance
Murphy, Donald Richard
Oxley, Leo Lionel
Whitley, R. Joyce
Whitley, William N.
Williams, Earl West
Williams, Willie S.
Wykle, May Louise Hinton

SIDNEY
Humphrey, James Philip

SILVERTON
Davis, John W., III

SPRING VALLEY
Phillips, Constance Ann
Phillips, Lloyd Garrison, Jr.

SPRINGFIELD
Ayers, Timothy F.
Beavers, Nathan Howard, Jr.
Chatman, Jacob L.
Cherry, Robert Lee
Goodson, Leroy Beverly
Henry, Robert Clayton
Jenkins, Carl Scarborough
Reed, Maurice L.
Smithers, Priscilla Jane

STEUBENVILLE
Palmer, Dennis
Williams, Carletta Celeste

STOW
Dominic, Irwing
Rutherford, Harold Phillip, III

TIFFIN
Hunt, Robert S.

TOLEDO
Butler, B. Janelle
Butler, Benjamin Willard
Clark, Mildred E.
Davis, James H.
Edgerton, Art Joseph
Franklin, Robert Vernon, Jr.
Grant, Wilmer, Jr.
Gray, Joseph William
Jones, Casey C.
Nabrit, Henry Clarke
Newsome, Emanuel T.
Porter, Scott E.
Sheppard, Ronald John
Sommerville, Joseph C.
Terrell, Melvin C.
Thompson, Lancelot C. A.
Turner, Eddie William
Walden, Robert Edison

TROY
Bell, Trenton G.
Dorsey, Clinton George

UNIVERSITY HEIGHTS
Bagley, Stanley B.

URBANA
Stevens, Warren Sherwood

WARREN
Breckenridge, John L.
Logan, Joseph Leroy
Pegues, Robert L., Jr.
Robinson, Learthon Steven
Williams, Joe H.

WARRENSVILLE HEIGHTS
Ashley, Corlanders

WEST CARROLLTON
Rakestraw, Kyle Damon

WEST CHESTER
Harris, Charles Cornelius

WICKLIFFE
Hunter, Frederick Douglas

WILBERFORCE
Ball, Jane Lee
Ball, Wilfred R.
Courtney, Cassandra Hill
Davis, Willis H.
Fleming, John Emory
Foster, James H.
Hargraves, William Frederick, II
Harvey, Louis-Charles
Hudgeons, Louise Taylor
Jackson, Samuel S., Jr.
McStallworth, Paul
Padgett, James A.
Rice, Edward A.
Sellers, Walter G.
Thomas, Arthur E.
Vivians, Nathaniel Roosevelt
Walker-Taylor, Yvonne
Wright, Carolyn Elaine

WOODLAWN
Smiley, James Walker, Sr.

WOODMERE VILLAGE
Rice, Robert C.
Rice, Susie Leon

WOOSTER
Jefferson, Alphine Wade
Williams, Yvonne Carter

WRIGHT PATTERSON AFB
Dansby, Jesse L., Jr.
Goodwin, Evelyn Louise

XENIA
Hall, Fred, III

YELLOW SPRINGS
Amos, Oris Elizabeth Carter
Graham, Precious Jewel

YOUNGSTOWN
Atkinson, Eugenia C. (Jeanne)
Bacon, Barbara Crumpler
Black, Willa
Bright, Alfred Lee
Carter, Raymond Gene, Sr.
Carter, Romelia Mae
Cooper, Syretha C.
Daniels, Ron D.
Ellison, Henry S.
Frost, Hugh A.
Halfacre, Frank Edward
Hughes, Jimmy Franklin, Sr.
Huntley, Richard Frank
James, Dava Paulette
Johnson, Andrew L., Sr.
McCroom, Eddie Winther
Mims, George E.
Pittman, James Ronald
Pruitt, Fred Roderic
Robinson, R. David
Shipmon, Luther June
Simon, Lonnie A.
Spencer, Brenda L.
Walker, Cindy Lee
Whitted, Andrew Eugene

ZANESVILLE
Dowling, Monroe Davis, Jr.
Gilbert, Richard Lannear
Watiker, Albert David, Jr.

OKLAHOMA

ARCADIA
Murrell, Sylvia Marilyn

ARDMORE
McKerson, Mazola

BIXBY
Griffiths, Bertie Bernard

BOLEY
Lee, Forrest A., Sr.
Matthews, Mary Joan
Sanders, Hobart C.
Spann, Theresa Tieuel
Walker, Ronald Plezz

DURANT
White, Alphonza F.

EDMOND
Lehman, Paul Robert
Owens, Wallace, Jr.

EUFAULA
Pratt, J. C.

FORT SILL
Joy, James Bernard, Jr.

FREDERICK
Evaige, Wanda Jo

GUTHRIE
Owens, Wallace, Jr.

HARTSHORNE
Webber, William Stuart

LANGSTON
Brown, Martha Hursey
Combs, Willa R.
Davis, James Harold
Fisher, Ada L.
Green, Theodis Guy
Holloway, Ernest Leon
King, Ruby Ryan
Manning, Jean Bell
Manning, Reuben D.
Morgan, Booker T.
Prewitt, Al Bert

Rogers, George
Sims, William E.

LAWTON
Barfield, Leila Millford
Barfield, Quay F.
Davenport, J. Lee
Goodwin, William Pierce, Jr.
Owens, Charles Clinton

MCALESTER
Brown, James Marion
Newman, Miller Maurice

MUSKOGEE
Reece, Avalon B.
Richardson, DeRutha Gardner
Simmons, Donald M.
Thomas, Erma Lee

NORMAN
Davis, Hiram L.
Henderson, George
Kamoche, Jidlaph Gitau
Newton, Jacqueline L. (nee Jefferson)
Robinson, Theodore Paul
Tolliver, Lennie-Marie P.
Williams, Norris Gerald

OKLAHOMA CITY
Atkins, Hannah D.
Barclay, Carl Archie
Benton, Leonard D.
Byrd, Camolia Alcorn
Cox, James Alphonso
Cox, Kevin C.
Darrell, Lewis E.
Dodson, Granville M.
Echols, James Albert
Gaines, Jaunell Wallace
Gavin, James Raphael, III
Gigger, Helen C.
Gigger, Nathaniel Jay
Grigsby, Troy L.
Hall, Ira DeVoyd
Hall, Rubye Maie
Henderson, Joyce Ann
Holmes, Carl
Humphrey, Marian J.
Jackson, Mattie Lee
Jackson, Walter K.
Johnson, A. Visanio
Kirk, Leroy W.
Lee, Theodosia L. Crawford
McLeod, Michael Preston
Noble, Norma Lynette
Organ, Claude H., Jr.
Parks, Thelma Reece
Porter, E. Melvin
Price-Curtis, William
Rogers, George
Sears, Bertram E.
Swain, Alice M.
Todd, Melvin R.
Tollett, Charles Albert
Tolliver, Lennie-Marie P.
Varner, Jewell C.
Vick, Harvey Oscar, III
Walker, Wilbur P.
Wallace, James Alfonso
Wamble, Amos Sylvester, Sr.
Williams, Freddye Harper
Wilson, Frank Fredrick, III

RED BIRD
Billups, Mattie Lou

SHAWNEE
Young, Ernestine

SPENCER
Sloss, Minerva A.

STILLWATER
Arnold, Lionel A.
Combs, Sylvester Lawrence
Mitchell, Earl Douglass, Jr.
Shipp, Howard J., Jr.

SUMMIT
Thomas, Erma Lee

TAFT
Teague, Gladys Peters

TULSA
Anderson, Chester R.
Anderson, Elizabeth M.
Brown, J. Quantin
Bryant, Hubert Hale
Cannon, Donnie E.
Chappelle, Thomas Oscar, Sr.
Gaines, Manyles B., Jr.
Goodwin, James Osby
Griffiths, Bertie Bernard
Hayes, Alvin, Jr.
Hill, Fannie E.
Hill, Henry
House, Millard L.
Hudson, Andrew Harold
Jeffrey, Charles James, Jr.
Johnson, Paul L.
Lacy, Edward J.
Lewis, Charles H.
Mabry, Edward L.
Martin, Rudolph G. (Rudy)
Pegues, Wennette West
Ragsdale, Charles Lea Chester
Robbins, Herman C.
Rowe, Jimmy L.
Samuels, Everett Paul
Smith, Gregory Allen
Smith, William Xavier
Taylor, Thad, Jr.
Thomas, Leroy, Sr.
Troupe, Marilyn Kay
Williams, Art S.
Young, Ronald LeRoy

WARNER
Grayson, Barbara Ann

OREGON

BEAVERTON
Morris, Major

CORVALLIS
Branch, Harrison
Gamble, Wilbert
Gray, Pearl Spears
Seals, Gerald

EUGENE
Brown-Wright, Marjorie
Campbell, Gary Lloyd
Coleman, Edwin Leon, II
Gainer, John F.
Hill, Pearl M.
Mabrey, Marsha Eve
Payne, James Floyd
Wade, Joseph Downey

GRESHAM
Boylan, Dorian S.
Stokes, Johnnie Mae

MCMINNVILLE
James, Bobby Charles

MILWAUKIE
Martinez, Ralph

PORTLAND
Black, Gail
Booker, Venerable Francis
Bowie, Sam
Britton, Elizabeth
Brooks, James O'Neil
Brown, Webster Clay
Carr, Kenny
Christian, Geraldine Ashley McConnell
Debnam, Chadwick Basil
Deiz, Mercedes F.
DePreist, James Anderson
Drexler, Clyde
Guy, George V.
Hartzog, Ernest E.
Heflin, John F.
Jackson, Frederick Leon
Law, Ellen T.
Leonard, Carolyn Marie
McCoy, Gladys

Nero, David M., Jr.
Norris, Audie
Nunn, Bobbie B.
Ryan, Marsha Ann (nee Neustadter)
St. John, Primus
Talley, Olga Ann
Taylor, Michael Loeb
Thompson, Mychal
Valentine, Darnell
Walker, James Zell, II
Washington, Kermit

SALEM
Carter, Margaret Louise
Henry, Calvin O. L.
McCoy, William
Petett, Freddye
Toran, Kay Dean
Williams, Harold Cleophas
Winters, Jacqueline F.

WEST LINN
St. John, Primus
Wilson, Edith N.

PENNSYLVANIA

ALIQUIPPA
Bacon, Charlotte Meade
Meade, Melvin C.
Smith, Eugene
Wallace, Ronald Wilfred

ALLENTOWN
Williams, Janice L.

BALA-CYNWYD
Dyer-Goode, Pamela Theresa
Patterson, James
Pendergrass, Theodore D.

BEAVER FALLS
Douglas, Elizabeth Asche

BENSALEM
Sanders, Isaac Warren

BETHEL PARK
Oyalowo, Tunde O.

BLOOMSBURG
Bryan, Jesse A.
Newson, Roosevelt, Jr.

BRIDGEVILLE
Greenwood, L. C.

BRISTOL
Patrick, Jennie R.

BRYN MAWR
Allen, Blair Sidney
Hopkins, Barry L.
Johnson, Leroy Ronald
Kirby, Nancy J.

BUTLER
Lee, John C., III

CALIFORNIA
Graham, Albertha L.

CAMP HILL
Johnson, Mary Beatrice

CARBONDALE
Blackwell, Noble Virgil

CHALFONT
Murray, Nevada (nee Mackey)

CHAMBERSBURG
Mills, John L.

CHESTER
Brown, William Rocky, III
Cavin, Alonzo C.
Holmes, Leo S.
Leake, Willie Mae James

McKellar, Stephen Alexander
Riley, William Scott
Wright, Robert Courtlandt

CHEYNEY
Hairstone, Marcus A.
McCummings, LeVerne
Wilson, Wade

CLAIRTON
Bookert, Charles C.

CLARION
Shropshire, John Sherwin

COATESVILLE
Brickus, John W.
Butler, Charles H.
Johnson, Paul Lawrence
Lee, Daniel

CONNELLSVILLE
Farmer, Robert Clarence

CONSHOHOCKEN
Dent, Anthony L.

DARBY
Tyler, Robert James, Sr.

DELAWARE WATER GAP
Woods, Philip Wells

DRESHER
Wilson, Sandra E.

EASTON
Holmes, Larry
Houston, William DeBoise
Jones, Alfredean
Person, Dawn Renee

EDINBORO
Dillon, Aubrey
Robinson, Curtis
Stewart, Elizabeth Pierce

ELWYN
Wilkie, Earl A.

ENOLA
Woods, Willie G.

ERIE
Clyburn, Elaine Marie
Summers, David Stewart
Trice, William B.

FARRELL
Sanders-West, Selma D.
White, William J.

FOLCROFT
Jasper, Lawrence E.

GETTYSBURG
Matthews, Harry Bradshaw

GLEN MILLS
Redding, Louis L.

GLENSIDE
Adom, Edwin Nii Amalai

GRANTHAM
Suggs, Robert Chinelo

GREENSBURG
Harvell, Valeria Gomez

HARRISBURG
Barnett, Ethel S.
Baxter, Belgium Nathan
Bradley, Andrew Thomas, Sr.
Branche, Gilbert M.
Braxton, Harriet E.
Cannon, Paul L., Jr.
Chambers, Clarice Lorraine
Clark, Donald Lewis
Cummings, Cary, III

Daniels, LeGree Sylvia
Dennis, Shirley M.
Fuget, Charles Robert
Gadsden, Nathaniel J., Jr.
Gilmore, Charles Arthur
Gordon, Fannetta Nelson
Hankins, Freeman
Hargrove, Trent
Johnson, Benjamin Washington
Lewis, Henry W.
Love, George Hayward
Madison, Richard
Maxey, James, III
Mitchell, Stanley Henryk
Montgomery, William R.
Morrison, Clarence Christopher
Munford, Paul Stanley
Peguese, Charles R.
Preston, Joseph, Jr.
Prioleau, Sara Nelliene
Richardson, Wayne Michael
Robinson, Rosalyn Karen
Robinson, William
Roebuck, James Randolph, Jr.
Sharpe, Ronald M.
Smalls, Charley Mae
Spigner, Donald Wayne
Street, T. Milton
Utley, Richard Henry
Wilson, Ronald M.
Womack, Stanley H.
Woods, Willie G.
Young, George, Jr. (Toby)

HAZELTON
Harris, Arthur Leonard, III

HERSHEY
Harvey, Harold A.
Mortel, Rodrigue

HORSHAM
Hill, Jeffrey Ronald

INDIANA
Anderson, James Alan
Richards, Hilda

JENKINTOWN
Smith, Robert Johnson

KING OF PRUSSIA
Fletcher, James Andrew
Harris, Douglas Allen

KUTZTOWN
Jones, Franklin D.
Morgan, Robert W., II
Scott, Basil Y.
Westmoreland, Samuel Douglas

LANCASTER
Williams, Louise Bernice

LEVITTOWN
Jordan, Josephine E.C.

LINCOLN UNIVERSITY
Baber, Lucky Larry
Branson, Herman Russell
Johnson, William T. M.
Mayes, Doris Miriam
Murray, Andrew Evans
Rodgers, Joseph James, Jr.
Sudarkasa, Niara (Gloria A. Marshall)
Williams, Willie
Willis, Gladys January
Woodson, Bernard Robert, Jr.

LOCK HAVEN
Lynch, Robert D.

MARS
Green, William Edward

MCKEESPORT
Hart, Barbara McCollum
Richardson, Lacy Franklin

MEDIA
McKnight, Lancess
Wright, Robert A.

MIDDLETOWN
Gilpin, Clemmie Edward
Smalls, Charley Mae

MONROEVILLE
Watson, Leonard Wayne

NEW HOLLAND
Duncan, Calvin L.

NORRISTOWN
Booker, Thurman D.
Chappell, Emma Carolyn
Davenport, Horace Alexander
Fair, Frank T.
Jones, Ervin Edward
Loris, Joseph James
Simmons, Herbert

NORTH BRADDOCK
Essiet, Evaleen Johnson

NORTH WALES
Bass, Herbert H.

OBERLIN
White, Scott A., Sr.

PHILADELPHIA
Abdul-Hamid, Ismail
Ackridge, Florence Gateward
Adom, Edwin Nii Amalai
Alexandre, Journel
Allen, Terrell Allison, III
Allison, W. Anthony
Alston, Floyd William
Anderson, Bernard E.
Anderson, J. Morris
Anderson, Sarah A.
Archie, Shirley Franklin
Asante, Kariamu Welsh
Asante, Molefi Kete (Arthur L. Smith Jr.)
Atkinson, Nolan N., Jr.
Axam, John Arthur
Bailey, Curtis Darnell
Bailey, Harry A., Jr.
Baker, Floyd Edward
Baker, Houston A., Jr.
Bambara, Toni Cade (Toni Cade)
Barbour, Joseph Pius, Jr.
Barkley, Charles
Baxter, Augustus, Sr.
Beckett, Charles Campbell
Bell, Thom R.
Benson, Rubin Author
Benton, George A.
Bibby, Deirdre L.
Biggs, Cynthia DeMari
Blackwell, Lucien E.
Blockson, Charles L.
Bond, Cecil Walton, Jr.
Bond, Gladys B.
Bouie, Simon Pinckney
Bradley, David Henry, Jr.
Braxton, John Ledger
Brazington, Andrew Paul
Brown, Glenn Arthur
Brown, William H., III
Browne, Vincent Jefferson, Jr.
Bullock, Samuel Carey
Bullock, Thurman Ruthe
Bunyon, Ronald S.
Burrell, George Reed, Jr.
Burton-Lyles, Blanche
Bush, Ann
Cade, Valarie Swain
Cain, Herbert R., Jr.
Cannon, Elton Molock
Carmichael, Carole A.
Carmichael, Lee Harold
Carr, Leonard G.
Carson, Curtis C., Jr.
Carter, Daisy
Case, Arthur M.
Cazenave, Noel Anthony
Chapman, Lee Manuel
Cheeks, Maurice Edward
Childs, Oliver Bernard, Sr.

Clark, Augusta Alexander
Clark, Jesse B., III
Clark, Tama Myers
Clarke, Eugene H., Jr.
Clarke, Leon Edison
Clayton, Constance
Clayton, Matthew D.
Clifford, Maurice C.
Cobb, Garry Wilbert
Coleman, Joseph E.
Collins, Sylvia Dolores
Cooper, Edward Sawyer
Cousins, Althea L.
Crawley, A. Bruce
Cunningham, Randall
Davis, James A.
Davis, Rosemary Ormond
Depte, Larry D.
Dickens, Helen Octavia
Dobbs, Mattiwilda
Driver, Richard Sonny, Jr.
Drummond, David L., Sr.
Du Bose, Robert Earl, Jr.
Duncan, John C., Jr.
Dunston, Alfred G.
Echols, Alvin E.
Edwards, Donald O.
Elcock, Claudius Adolphus Rufus
Ellis, Benjamin F., Jr.
Ellis, Leander Theodore
Ellis, Ray
Emmons, Rayford E.
Engs, Robert Francis
Erving, Julius Winfield (Dr. J)
Evans, Samuel London
Evans, Therman E.
Farmer, Clarence
Fattah, Falaka
Ferere, Gerard Alphonse
Ferguson, Sherman E.
Finney, Essex Eugene, Jr.
Fisher, Joseph
Foard, Frederick Carter
Fox, Thomas E., Jr.
Franklin, Oliver St. Clair, Jr.
Free, World B.
French, George Wesley
Gaines, Sedalia Mitchell
Gamble, Kenneth
Garrison-Corbin, Patricia Ann
Giles, James T.
Gilmore, Richard G.
Givhan, Mercer A., Jr.
Goode, W. Wilson
Gordon, Darrell R.
Gordon, Levan
Gordon, Robert L.
Granger, Shelton B.
Grant, John H., Sr.
Graves, Jackie
Green, Clifford Scott
Green, Franklin D.
Green, Liller Bernice
Gunn, Vera
Hall, Daniel A.
Hall, Kim Felicia
Hammond, Benjamin F.
Hancock, Gwendolyn Carter
Hardin, Herbert G.
Harmon, Sherman Allen
Harper, Beverly A.
Harper, Ronald J.
Harris, Jay Terrence
Harris, Jeanette G.
Harvey, William James, III
Hashim, Mustafa
Haskins, Michael Kevin
Hawkins, Gene
Hayre, Ruth Wright
Henry, Ragan A.
Hickman, Jerry A.
Higginbotham, A. Leon, Jr.
Hill, Kenneth D.
Hill, William Randolph, Jr. (Sonny Hill)
Hobbs, Wilbur E.
Holloway, Hiliary H.
Holmes, William B.
Hopkins, Wes
Hopson, Harold Theodore, II (Sonny)
Howard, Humbert Lincoln
Huff, Leon Alexander
Humphrey, Claude B.

Hunter, Robert J.
Hunter-Lattany, Kristin Eggleston
Hutchins, Francis L., Jr.
Inyama, Nathaniel Ginikanwa N.
Jackson, Alterman
Jackson, Beverly Anne
Jackson, Burnett Lamar, Jr.
James, Gregory Creed
Jangdharrie, Wycliffe K.
Jenkins, Andrew
Jenkins, Lozelle DeLuz
Jeter, Joseph C., Jr.
Johnson, Clemon Lavelle
Johnson, Elmore W.
Johnson, Ronald
Johnson, Willie F.
Jones, Ernest Edward
Jones, G. Daniel
Jones, Ozro T., Jr.
Jordan, J. St. Girard
Kelsey, Gary Matthew
Kennedy, William Thomas, Jr.
Kernodle, Obra Servesta, III
Keyes, Leroy
King, Robert Samuel
King, William Moses
Langston, Josephine Davidnell
Lee, Edward S.
Lewis, Samuel, Jr.
Lightfoot, William P.
Linton, Gordon J.
Linton, Sheila Lorraine
Lomax, Walter P.
Lynch, Rufus Sylvester
Maddox, Garry Lee
Manning, Eddie James
Mansfield, Carl Major
Mapp, Yolanda I.
Marsh, Tamra Gwendolyn
Martin, I. Maximillian
Mathis, Thaddeus P.
Mayes, Doris Miriam
McGill, Thomas L., Jr.
McKee, Theodore A.
Melton, Harry S.
Melvin, Harold James
Merriweather, Barbara Christine
Mesiah, Raymond N.
Miller, Frederick E.
Miller, Horatio C.
Miller, William O.
Minton, Russell Farbeux, Sr.
Minyard, Handsel B.
Mitchell, Joann
Moore, Acel
Moore, Arthur C.
Moore, Charlie W.
Moore, Jean E. (nee Campbell)
Moore, Richard Baxter
Morton, Azie B.
Mott, Stokes E., Jr.
Murray, Thomas W., Jr.
Newman, LeGrand
Nichols, Edward K., Jr.
Nicholson, Alfred
Nix, Robert N.C., Jr.
Nyahuma, Tahiya R. M. W.
Odom, Vernon Lane, Jr.
Okore, Cynthia Ann
Oliver, Frank Louis
Owens, Curtis
Palmer, Edward
Perry, William E.
Pittman, Audrey Bullock
Poindexter, Malcolm P.
Portlock, Carver A.
Powell, Thomas Francis A.
Prattis, Lawrence
Quick, Mike
Rawls, Rodney Alan
Reed, Jasper Percell
Reid, Oswald Hutton
Rhodes, Jeanne (nee Simmons)
Richardson, Clint Dewitt
Richardson, David Preston, Jr.
Richardson, Henry J., III
Richardson, Linda Waters
Ritter, Thomas J.
Roach, Lee
Robinson, Charles
Robinson, Charlotte L.
Robinson, Denauvo M.
Robinson, Gary O.

CHARLESTON
Blake, Alphonso R.
Blake, James G.
Brockington, Benjamin
Brown, James E.
Brown, William Melvin, Jr.
Burke, Olga Pickering
Davis-McFarland, E. Elise
DeCosta, Herbert Alexander, Jr.
Etheredge, James W.
French, James J.
Jefferson, Hilda Hutchinson
Kinloch, Jerome
Little, General T.
Lucas, Linda Gail
Mack, Joan
Martin, Daniel E.
Martin, James W.
Martin, Maxine Smith
Martin, Montez Cornelius, Jr.
Martin, Rosetta P.
McFarland, Arthur C.
McTeer, George Calvin
Middleton, Vertelle Delores
Moore, Fred Henderson (Danny)
Nichols, Kay Bailey
Pickering, Robert Perry
Portee, Frank, III
Rashford, John Harvey
Spradley, Mark Merritt
Stanyard, Hermine P.
White, John Lee

CHESTER
Cutliff, John Wilson

CLEMSON
Foster, Edward, Sr.
Thompson, Regina

CLINTON
Thompson, Emma M.

CLOVER
Campbell, Mary Allison

COLUMBIA
Blanding, Larry
Bracey, Henry J.
Brown, Franchot A.
Brown, LeRoy Ronald
Burton, Juanita Sharon
Clyburn, James E.
Cooper, Ethel Thomas
Cromartie, Ernest W., II
Davis, James F.
Davis, Marianna White
DeSassure, Charles
Dillihay, Tanya Clarkson
Everett, Percival L.
Felder, Loretta Kay
Felder, Thomas E.
Fielding, Herbert Ulysses
Floyd, Dean Allen
Gipson, Mack, Jr.
Gordon, Ethel M.
Greene, Ronald Alexander
Heyward, Isaac
Howell, Malqueen
Johnson, I. S. Leevy
Johnson, Joseph A.
Lewis, Andre
Lowman, Isom
Lynn, Louis B.
McDowell, Edward Homer, Jr.
McLawhorn, James Thomas, Jr.
Moore, Albert
Moore, Alice Evelyn
Myers, Emma McGraw
Neal, Green Belton
Patterson, Kay
Peay, Samuel
Pride, Hemphill P., II
Prioleau, Peter Sylvester
Richardson, Leo
Robinson, Eunice Primus
Rowe, Marilyn Johnson
Scott, Juanita Simons
Scott, Robert L.
Spain, Hiram, Jr.
Stephenson, Charles E., III
Swinton, Sylvia P.
Thomas, Latta R., Sr.
Waldo, Carol Dunn

Whipper, Lucille Simmons
Williams, Willie, Jr.
Young, Tommy Scott

CONWAY
DeWitt, Franklin Roosevelt
Lee, James E.
Stevens, Cleveland

DARLINGTON
Brantley, Montague Delano
Stanley, Arthur W.

DENMARK
Bryan, Curtis
Chapman, Julius
Dawson, Leonard Ervin
Henry, John W., Jr.
Wilkins, Patricia Chalmers

EASTOVER
Scott, Lewis Nathanel

EFFINGHAM
Canty, Ralph Waldo

EUTAWVILLE
DeSassure, Charles

FLORENCE
Adams, Lillian Louise T.
Beck, Roswell Nathaniel
Diggs, William P.
Williams, George Arthur

FROGMORE
Grosvenor, Verta Mae

GAFFNEY
Foster, Mildred Thomas
Rosemond, Lemuel Menefield
Sanders, James William

GEORGETOWN
Parson, Houston

GRANITEVILLE
Kellar, Arthur H.

GREENVILLE
Brock, Lila Mae
Channell, Eula L.
Corbitt, John H.
Cureton, Stewart Cleveland
Flemming, Lillian Brock
Mitchell, Theo W.
Peden, S. T., Jr.
Reid, Janie Ellen
Smith, Johnnie M.
Springs, Lenny F.
Walker, J. Wilbur
Zimmerman, Samuel Lee

GREENWOOD
Caldwell, John Edward
Johnson, Ed F.
Smith, Pearlena W.
Witherspoon, Audrey Goodwin

GREER
Golden, Louie

HARDEEVILLE
Williams, Daniel Louis

HILTON HEAD ISLAND
Campbell, Emory Shaw
Driessen, Henry, Jr.
Grant, William W.

HOLLYWOOD
Holmes, Mary Brown

IRMO
Simons, Gail Derese

JENKINSVILLE
Jackson, James Conroy

JOHNSONVILLE
Tanner, James W., Jr.

LAKE CITY
Wilson, Alva L.

LANCASTER
Jeter, Delores DeAnn

LAURENS
Carter, John R.
Coleman, Marian M.

LINCOLNVILLE
Ross, Charles

LORIS
Watson, Fred D.

LYNCHBURG
Jefferson, Clifton

MCCLELLANVILLE
Smalls, Marcella E.
Weathers, J. Leroy

MCCORMICK
Gilchrist, Robertson

MONCKS CORNER
Butler, Clary Kent
Middleton, Vertelle Delores

MULLINS
Reaves, Franklin Carlwell

MYRTLE BEACH
Tate, Eleanora Elaine

NEWBERRY
Caldwell, John Edward
Tyler, Lee Malcolm

NINETY SIX
Louden, Henderson Nathaniel, Sr.

NORTH AUGUSTA
Brown, Bettye Jean (Bettye Jean Crawley)

NORTH CHARLESTON
Brown, William Melvin, Jr.
Bryant, Edward Joe, III

NORTH MYRTLE BEACH
Williams, George L., Sr.

ORANGEBURG
Abraham, Sinclair Reginald
Evans, Arthur L.
Gore, Blinzy L.
Harris, Gil W.
Hickson, William F., Jr.
Jenkins, Barbara Williams
Johnson, Carl Lee
Johnson, Vermelle Jamison
Keitt, L. (Liz Zimmerman)
Mack, Fred Clarence
Manning, Hubert Vernon
McFadden, James L.
Michaux, Henry G.
Nance, M. Maceo, Jr.
Rogers, Oscar Allan, Jr.
Rose, Arthur
Smith, Albert E.
Stewart, Adelle Wright
Washington, Sarah M.
Winningham, Herman S., Jr.

PARKSVILLE
Gilchrist, Robertson

PAWLEYS ISLAND
Manigault, Walter William

PELZER
Reid, Janie Ellen

PORT ROYAL
Robinson, Henry

RAINS
Johnson, Robert B.

RAVENEL
Cobb, Ethel Washington

REMBERT
Brooks, W. Webster

RIDGELAND
Morgan-Washington, Barbara
Tyler, Hubert

RIDGEVILLE
Holmes, Mary Brown

ROCK HILL
Bethea, Mollie Ann
Douglas, John Daniel
Ervin, Deborah Green
Evans, Spofford L.
Goggins, Horace
Moreland, Sallie V.
Sebhatu, Mesgun
Wright-Botchwey, Roberta Yvonne

ST MATTHEWS
Miles, Mary Alice

ST STEPHEN
Ransom, Norman

SALUDA
Owens, Thomas C.

SELLERS
Jones, Frank

SENECA
Martin, Amon Achilles, Jr.

SIMPSONVILLE
Floyd, James T.

SPARTANBURG
Allen, Ottis Eugene, Jr.
Carson, Warren Jason, Jr.
Porter, John Henry
Talley, James Edward
Wiles, Leon E.
Wright, James Richard

SUMMERVILLE
Singleton, Benjamin, Sr.
Washington, Arnic J.

SUMTER
Finney, Ernest A., Jr.
Gray, Ruben L.
Hardin, Henry E.
Johnson, Wilbur Eugene
McDonald, Edmund Morris
Mellette, David C.
Richardson, Luns C.
Sampson, Dorothy Vermelle
Vereen-Gordon, Mary Alice
Weston, Larry Carlton

WALTERBORO
Manigo, George F., Jr.
Thompson, Johnnie
Williams, Raleigh R.

WEST COLUMBIA
Grant, Timothy Jerome
Waldo, Carol Dunn

SOUTH DAKOTA

BROOKINGS
Butler, Eugene Thaddeus, Jr.

PIERRE
Hiatt, Dietrah (nee Chapman)

SIOUX FALLS
Drake, Daniel D.

VERMILLION
Milburn, Corinne M.

TENNESSEE

ALCOA
Williams, Richard, Jr.

ATHENS
Witt, Burkett L.

BLUFF CITY
Wells, Billy Gene

BOLIVAR
Hicks, Delphus Van, Jr.
Lake, Alfreeda Elizabeth

BRENTWOOD
Brown, Alvin Montero
Haynes, William J., Jr.
Johnson, Bobbie Gene
Rist, Seward
White, Katie Kinnard

BRIGHTON
Rose, Shelvie

BROWNSVILLE
Campbell, Carrol Nunn
Rawls, William D., Sr.
Smith, James Russell

CHARLESTON
Parker, Charles Thomas

CHATTANOOGA
Allen, Minnie Louise
Beasley, Paul Lee
Brown, Tommie Florence
Chapman, Willie R.
Edwards, John Loyd, III
Fields, Alva Dotson
Jackson, Horace
Jackson, Luke
Johnson, Tammy Adele
Jones, Carolyn G.
Jones, William O.
Lee, Van Spencer
McCants, Jesse Lee, Sr.
McDaniel, Paul Anderson
McKeldin, Harry White, Jr.
Mickle, Elva L.
Peoples, Erskine L.
Provost, Marsha Parks
Robinson, Clarence B.
Roddy, Howard W.
Scruggs, Booker T., II
Taylor, George N., Jr.
Thomas, Sirr Daniel
Willis, Kathi Grant

CLARKSVILLE
Gachette, Louise Foston
Joyce, Donald Franklin

COLLIERVILLE
Smith, A. Z.

COLUMBIA
Hines, Morgan B.
Johnson, Lawrence Washington

COVINGTON
Bommer, Minnie L.
Rodgers, Charles

DYERSBURG
Biggs, Richard Lee
Mitchell, George L.
Seibert-McCauley, Mary F.

FRANKLIN
Mills, Mary Elizabeth

GALLATIN
Malone, J. Deotha
Nance, Jesse J., Jr.
Sherrill, Vanita Lytle

GATES
Nance, Booker Joe, Sr.

GERMANTOWN
Dotson, Philip Randolph
Williams, Hugh Hermes

HARRIMAN
Barnes, Delorise Creecy
Yeary, James E., Sr.

HAWKINS
Nimmons, Julius

HENDERSON
Saunders, Elizabeth A.

HENDERSONVILLE
Boone, Carol Marie

HUMBOLDT
Carr, Lenford
Coleman, Andrew Lee
Smith, James Russell

JACKSON
Angell, Edgar O.
Boone, Clarence Donald
Chambers, Alex A.
Cooke, Anna L.
David, Arthur LaCurtiss
Kirkendoll, Chester Arthur, II
Robinson, Martha Delores
Savage, Horace Christopher
Shaw, Willie G.
Stone, Herman, Jr.

JOHNSON CITY
Lewis, James Earl

KINGSPORT
Watterson, Richard Harvey

KNOXVILLE
Armstrong, Joseph Earl
Booker, Robert Joseph
Bourne, Beal Vernon, II
Brown, Charles Henry (Kippy)
Byas, William Herbert
Cleckley, Betty J.
Davidson, Elvyn Verone
Felder-Hoehne, Felicia Harris
   (Felicia Harris Hoehne)
Franklin, Clarence Frederick
Freeman, Edward C.
Greene, Cecil M., Jr.
Greene, Sarah Moore
Hardy, Walter S. E.
Harvey, Denise M.
Hatcher, Ester L.
Kindall, Luther Martin
Liston, Hardy, Jr.
Lucas, Wilmer Francis, Jr.
Miller, Ronald Baxter
Moore, Thomas L.
Owens, Jefferson P.
Peek, Marvin E.
Rollins, Avon William, Sr.
Shepherd, Robert
Smith, Rufus Herman
Stewart, William H.
Welch, Olga Michele
Whaley, Mary H.
Williamson, Handy, Jr.
Yarbrough, Marilyn Virginia
Ziegler, Dhyana

LEBANON
Wiley, Kenneth LeMoyne

LEXINGTON
Reese, Viola Kathryn

MARYVILLE
Mosley, Tracey Ray

MEMPHIS
Anderson, Marcus Jackson
Bailey, D'Army
Bates, Willie Earl
Bennett, Arthur T.
Bolton, Julian Taylor
Bowen, Raymond C.
Brooks, Todd Frederick
Brown, Claudell, Jr.

Brown, Edward Lynn
Brown, George Henry, Jr.
Brown, Robin R.
Bryant, Anxious E.
Bufford, Edward Eugene
Cade, Mossy Jackson
Carter, Patrick Henry, Jr.
Chandler, Harold R.
Clark, LeRoy D.
Coleman, Harry Theodore
Coleman, Wisdom F.
Currie, Eddie L.
Davis, Edward
Davis, Elberta Coleman
DeCosta-Willis, Miriam
Delk, Fannie M.
DeVaughn-Tidline, Donna
   Michelle
Dickerson, Warner Lee
Dixon, Roscoe
Donald, Bernice Bouie
Fields, Arlonda M.
Ford, Fred, Jr.
Ford, James W.
Ford, John Newton
Garrett, Cheryl Ann
Gholson, General James
Gilliam, Herman Arthur, Jr.
Gipson, Arthur A.
Gipson, Lovelace Preston, II
Goodrich, Harold Thomas
Green, Al
Green, Reuben H.
Hanna, Harlington Leroy, Jr.
Hardeman, Carole Hall
Harrell, H. Steve
Harris, John H.
Haskins, Morice Lee, Jr.
Hassell, Frances M.
Herenton, Willie W.
Hill, Clara Grant
Hood, Leamon
Hooks, Michael Anthony
Hooks, Mose Yvonne Brooks
Horton, Odell
Howard, Aubrey J.
Howard, Osbie L., Jr.
Howell, Gerald T.
Hurd, William Charles
Jackson, Henry Ralph
Jackson-Teal, Rita F.
Jamerson, Jerome Donnell
Jenkins, Charles E., Sr.
Johnican, Minerva Jane
Johnson, Betty Jo
Johnson, Clinisson Anthony
Johnson, Fred D.
Johnson, Jerry Calvin
Jones, Lorean Electa
Jones, Velma Lois
Jordan, Carolyne Lamar
Jordan, John Edward
Lawston, Marjorie Gray
Martin, Cortez Hezekiah
McWilliams, Alfred Edeard
Miles, Rachel Jean
Miller, Andrea Lewis
Montgomery, Dwight Ray
Moore, Jossie A.
Northcross, Deborah Ametra
Parham, Brenda Joyce
Patterson, James Oglethorpe
Robinson, George L.
Royal, James E.
Rudd, Willie Lesslie
Sengstacke, Whittier Alexander,
   Sr.
Seymour, Laurence Darryl
Shaw, Frederick B.
Shotwell, Ada Christena
Smith, Maxine Atkins
Smith, Vasco A.
Spencer, Tim Calvin
Stansbury, Markhum L., Sr.
Stockton, Clifford, Sr.
Suggs, William Albert
Taylor, Cassandra W.
Taylor, Comer L., Jr.
Taylor, Harold Leon
Thomas, N. Charles
Thompson, Harold Fong
Tieuel, Robert C. D.
Tolbert, Odie Henderson, Jr.
Turner, Johnnie Rodgers

Walker, A. Maceo, Sr.
Walker, George Edward
Walker, Walter Lorenzo
Walker-Shaw, Patricia
Waller, Robert Lee
Ward, Daniel
Whalum, Kenneth Twigg
Wharton, A. C., Jr.
Whiting, Ollie Beth
Wilbun, Shepperson A.
Wilks, Carl S.
Wynn, Robert L., Jr.
Young, Josef A.

MILLINGTON
Wood, Lawrence Alvin

MORRISTOWN
Newlin, Rufus K.

MOUNT JULIET
Wiley, Kenneth LeMoyne

MUNCIE
Kelley, Daniel, Jr.

MURFREESBORO
Glanton, Lydia Jackson
Koger, Linwood Graves, III
McAdoo, Henry Allen
Pierce, Gregory W.
Rucker, Nannie George
Smith, Robert J.

NASHVILLE
Adkins, Cecelia Nabrit
Alexander, Paul Crayton
Allen, Harriette Louise
Archer, Susie Coleman
Ashley-Harris, Dolores B.
Atchison, Calvin O.
Bailey, William R.
Bell, Wendolyn Yvonne
Belton, Robert
Bernard, Harold O.
Bernard, Louis Joseph
Berry, Albert G.
Blackshear, Julian W., Jr.
Boone, Carol Marie
Boyd, Theophilus B., III
Bradley, J. Robert
Brinkley, Charles H., Sr.
Brooks, Marcellus
Brown, Dorothy Lavania
Burton, Clarinda Mattea
Butler, Washington Roosevelt, Jr.
Butts, Wilson Henry
Byrd, W. Michael
Calhoun, Calvin Lee
Cameron, Sam Archie
Campbell, Otis, Jr.
Chatterjee, Lois Jordan
Clark, Bertha Smith
Conley, James Monroe
Cooper, Almeta E.
Crenshaw, Waverly David, Jr.
Crowell, Bernard G.
Daniels, Elizabeth
Davidson, Rick Bernard
Davis, James W.
DeBerry, Lois Marie
Dent, Carl Ashley
DeShields, Harrison F., Jr.
Dixon, Roscoe
Dooley, Wallace Troy
Douglas, Mansfield, III
Driver, Rogers W.
Drungo, Elbert, Jr.
Dudley, Charles Edward
Edwards, Eunice L.
Elam, Lloyd C.
Elliott, Irvin Wesley
Fancher, Evelyn Pitts
Felix, Dudley E.
Fielder, Fred Charles
Floyd, Otis L., Jr.
Foster, Henry Wendell
Grant, Robert C.
Gray, Sterling Perkins, Jr.
Guess, Francis S.
Hamberg, Marcelle R.
Hamby, Roscoe Jerome
Hampton, Michael Eugene
Handy, William T., Jr.

Hare, Linda Paskett
Harris, Ramon Stanton
Harris, Vander E.
Haynes, William J., Jr.
Hill, George C.
Hill, Henry, Jr.
Hines, Ralph Howard
Hodge, Cynthia Elois
Holmes, Robert L., Jr.
Horton, Carrell Peterson
Howard, Samuel H.
Hull, George, Jr.
Isibor, Edward Iroguehi
Jackson, Ada Jean Work
Jackson, Andrew
Jackson, Arthur James
Jackson, Clinton (The
   Executioner)
Johnson, Charles William
Johnson, Ernest Kaye, III
Jones, Enoch
Jordan, Harold Willoughby
Jordan, Kenneth Ulys
Junior, Samella E. (nee Walton)
Kelly, Earl Lee
Kennedy, Matthew W.
Kilcrease, Irvin Hugh, Jr.
Lee, Andre L.
Lemeh, Dorotha Hill
Lewis, Helen Middleton
Lillard, Robert Emmitt
Logan, Bertie Hawthorne
Mallette, John M.
Martin, James Larence
Martin, Ruby Julene Wheeler
Mays, Edward Everett
Mays, Sandra Denise
McGruder, Charles E.
McKissack, Leatrice B.
McKissack, William Deberry
McReynolds, Elaine A.
Mitchell, Edwin H., Sr.
Mobley, Eugenia L.
Moore, Robert F.
Moses, Henry A.
Moye, Carla Johnson
Murrell, Barbara Curry
Newman, Ernest Wilbur
Nightingale, Jesse Phillip
Otey, Flem B., III
Perry, Frank Anthony
Peterman, Leotis
Peters, Sheila Renee
Pleas, John Roland
Poellnitz, Fred Douglas
Ponder, Henry
Powell, John Lewis
Redd, George N.
Ridley, May Alice
Rist, Seward
Robinson, Clarence B.
Rogers, Decatur
Satcher, David
Scott, Veronica J.
Shockley, Ann Allen
Smiley, Karen Jo
Smith, Gwendolyn G.
Smith, Jessie Carney
Stinson, Joseph McLester
Strong, Blondell McDonald
Thompson, Almose Alphonse, II
Thompson, Frances E.
Torrey, Rubye Prigmore
Traughber, Charles M.
Turner, Shirley
Washington, Sandra Beatrice
Watson, Vernaline
Wiggins, Charles A.
Wilkes, William R.
Williams, Avon Nyanza, Jr.
Williams, Carolyn Ruth
   Armstrong
Williams, Jamye Coleman
Williams, Malcolm Demosthenes
Williams, McDonald
Wilson, Donella Joyce
Wilson, Jacqueline Prophet
Winfrey, Charles Everett
Woolridge, Thomas Jerry
Wynn, Daniel Webster

NEW MARKET
Welch, Olga Michele

OAK RIDGE
Barnes, Delorise Creecy
Colston, Freddie C.
Minter, Wilbert Douglas, Sr.
Porter, Patrick A.
Revis, Nathaniel W.
Shipe, Jamesetta Denise Holmes
Smith, Lila
Smith, Rufus Herman
Upton, E. H.

OLD HICKORY
Finch, Janet M.

PULASKI
Brown, James Monroe

SOUTH PITTSBURG
Moore, Hiram Beene

SPRINGFIELD
Chatman, Melvin E.

TULLAHOMA
Duncan, Lynda J.

WHITEVILLE
Robertson, Evelyn Crawford, Jr.

TEXAS

ABILENE
Prince, Andrew Lee

ANGLETON
Russell, August Wayne

ARLINGTON
Addy, Tralance Obuama
Bibby, James B.
Burris, Bertram Ray
Chenevert, Phillip Joseph
Foster, Deborah Valrie
Jenkins, Ferguson
Jones, Charles A.
LeGrand, Bob (Snake)
Rivers, Mickey Milton
Sample, William Amos
Stewart, David Keith
Wilson-Felder, Cynthia Ann
Wright, George Dewitt

ATASCOCITA
Clark, William Elgan, Jr.

AUSTIN
Adams, Edward B.
Anderson, Marcellus J., Sr.
Baye, Lawrence James J.
Belle, John Otis
Bryant, Andrea Pair
Childers, Terry L.
Delco, Exalton Alfonso, Jr.
Delco, Wilhelmina R.
Edwards, Al E.
Hanson, John L.
Harrison, Dian Johnson
Haugstad, May Katheryn (nee
   Hill)
Hicks, Louis Charles, Jr.
Hill, James L.
Johnson, Wayne Wright, III
Jordan, Barbara C.
King, John Q. Taylor, Sr.
Larry, Jerald Henry
Matabane, Sebiletso Mokone
Matthews, Alvin Leon
McDaniel, Myra Atwell
McDaniel, Reuben R.
McMillan, Joseph T., Jr.
McRoy, Ruth Gail
Means, Bertha E.
Murphy, Harriet Louise M.
Nelson, Wanda Lee
Nesby, Donald Ray, Sr.
Oliver, Jesse Dean
Overton, Volma Robert
Parker, Joseph Caiaphas, Jr.
Powell, Philip Melancthon, Jr.
Scott, Richard Eley
Sikes, Melvin Patterson

Snell, Jimmy Gregory
Tucker, Geraldine Jenkins
Urdy, Charles E.
Walker, Stanley M.
Ward, Nolan F.
Wickham, Muriel Jeannette
Williams, Wilbert
Wilson, Ora Brown
Wilson, Ronald Ray
Wingate, Rosalee Martin
Wright, Gerald

BAYTOWN
Hadnot, Thomas Edward

BEAUMONT
Hodge, Charles Mason
Jones, Kirkland C.

BELLAIRE
Carnegie, Randolph David

CALVERT
Comfort, Nemo Robert

CARROLLTON
Daniels, Curtis A.
Merritt, Thomas Mack

CARTHAGE
Beck, Hershell P.

CHANDLER
Mason, Orenthia Delois

CHINA
Prejean, Ruby D.

COLLEGE STATION
Carreathers, Kevin R.
Chisolm, Grace Butler
Kern-Foxworth, Marilyn L

COLLEYVILLE
Phelps-Patterson, Lucy

COMMERCE
Talbot, David Arlington Roberts, Sr.

COMO
Williams, John Waldo

CORPUS CHRISTI
Carline, William Ralph
Gurley, Helen Ruth
McCoy, Walter D.

CORSICANA
Waters, Sylvia Ann

CROSBY
Mitchell, Tex Dwayne

CYPRESS
Berry, Benjamin Donaldson

DALLAS
Aguirre, Mark
Alexander, Drew W.
Allen, George Louis
Anderson, Abbie H.
Bardwell, Rufus B., III
Barnes, Benny
Beck, Arthello, Jr.
Bell, H. B.
Blackman, Rolando
Brashear, Berlaind Leander
Brossette, Alvin, Jr.
Brown, Ellen Rochelle
Bryant, Wallace Henry
Campbell, Mary Delois
Carter, Howard
Chandler, Rory Wayne
Clark, Caesar A. W.
Clay, Patricia Ann
Coleman, Caesar David
Connor, Dolores Lillie
Cornelius, Ulysses S., Sr.
Cottrell, Comer J.
Cunningham, E. Brice
Curry, Levy Henry

Dantley, Adrian
Darby, Castilla A., Jr.
Dawson, Jesse R.
Dick, George Albert
Dottin, Roger Allen
Ellis, Dale Terrell
Emory, Emerson
Espree, Allen James
Esquivel, Argelia Velez
Fagan, Harold Leonard
Flowers, William Knox, Jr.
Ford, David Leon, Jr.
Foutz, Samuel Theodore
Frazier, William James
German, Ann Louise
Glover, Clarence Ernest, Jr.
Gray, Carol Coleman
Gray, James Howard
Hammond, Ulysses S., Jr.
Harden, Robert James
Harper, Derek Anthony
Harris, David, Jr.
Hayes, Curtiss Leo
Hill, Vonciel Jones
Hilliard, Delories
Hudson, Samuel William, III
Hunter, Charles A.
Hunter, Irby B.
Hurdle, Velma B. Brooks
Jackson, David M.
James, H. Rhett
Johnson, Iola Vivian
Johnson, Juanita B.
Johnson, Marion T.
Johnson, Patricia Anita
Johnson, Roosevelt, Jr.
Johnson, Roy Lynn
Jones, Jesse W.
Kidd, Foster
Kirven, Joe W.
Kirven, Mythe Yuvette
Knight, Richard, Jr.
Lacy, Versia Lindsay
Laday, Kerney
Lane, Eddie Burgyone
Larry, Jerald Henry
Lassiter, Wright Lowenstein, Jr.
Laws, Clarence A.
Malone, Sandra Dorsey
Mason, Edward James
McCain, Claude, Jr.
McFall, Mary (nee Simpson)
Mills, Glenn B., Jr.
Montgomery, Mildren M.
Morris, Wayne Lee
Moy, Celeste Marie
Newhouse, Robert F.
Newman, David, Jr.
Orr, Ray
Parker, Fred Lee Cecil
Pearson, Preston James
Perkins, Sam Charles
Phelps-Patterson, Lucy
Powell, Dudley Vincent
Pride, Charley
Ragsdale, Paul B.
Richards-Alexander, Billie J.
Roberts, Alfred Lloyd
Robertson, Gertrude
Robertson, Lynn E.
Robertson, Quindonell S.
Robinson, Hugh Granville
Rollins, Richard Albert
Roper, Patricia Anderson
Rowe, Jasper C.
Ruffin, Herbert
Saddler, William E.
Saulter, Gilbert John
Shine, Ted
Sluby, Tom Eugene
Stahnke, William E.
Stansbury, Terrence Eugene
Steele, Cleophas R., Jr.
Stewart, Richard E.
Stubblefield, Raymond M.
Sullivan, Allen R.
Thompson, Frank William
Tinsley, Fred Leland, Jr.
Travis, Alexander B.
Vincent, Jay Fletcher
Wade, Norma Adams
Walker, Claude
Washington, James A.
Wattley, Thomas Jefferson

West, Mark Keith
White, Mable
Williams, Ada L.
Williams, Annie M.
Winn, Joan T.
Wise, Frank P.
Witherspoon, William Roger
Wright, Sylvester M.

DALLAS/FORT WORTH AIRPORT
Evans, Vernon D.

DENTON
Jackson, Governor Eugene, Jr.
McAdams, Linnie M.
Totten, Herman Lavon
Wallace, Milton De'Nard
Washington, Roosevelt, Jr.

EL PASO
Greene, De Reef Anthony
Greer, Edward
Shuffer, George Macon, Jr.
Washington, Johnnie M.
Young, John W.

ENNIS
Coleman, Raymond Cato
Collins, Cornelia Faye

EULESS
Stripling, Luther

FORT WORTH
Bell, Reva Pearl
Benton, Shirley Jean
Beverly, Rose Jackson
Bowman-Webb, Loetta
Bremby, Roderick LeMar
Briscoe, Leonard E.
Brooks, Marion Jackson
Cary, Reby
Clark, Randolph A.
Davis, L. Clifford
Frazier, Charles Douglas
Hardeman, Strotha E., Jr.
Hegmon, Oliver Louis
Heiskell, Michael Porter
Hicks, Maryellen
Johnson, Erma Chansler
Johnson, Mervil V.
Johnson, Phyllis Campbell
Johnson, Wilhelmina Lashaun
Lewis, Erma (nee Duffy)
Lister, Willa M.
McEwing, Mitchell Dalton
Mitchell, Huey P.
Morrison, Gwendolyn Christine Caldwell
Simmons, Hazel Forrow
Sims, Theophlous Aron, Sr.
Standifer, Ben H.
Stewart, Dorothy Nell
Terrell, Francis
Terrell, Robert E.
Turner, Edna (nee Koontz)
Young, Alan John

GALVESTON
Brooks, Don Locellus
Gatson, Wilina Ione
Norris, Walter, Jr.
Simmons, Annie Marie
Stanton, Janice D.
Williams, Sandra Roberts

GARLAND
Ward, Anna Elizabeth

GRAND PRAIRIE
Howard, Calvin Johnson
Willrich, Emzy James

HAWKINS
Acrey, Autry
Griffin, Thomas J.
Hall, Delilah Ridley
Holmes, Lorene B.
Lanier, Dorothy Copeland
Perpener, Winifred Uveda

HEMPSTEAD
Carter, Gwendolyn Burns
Singleton, Leroy, Sr.

HEWITT
Kirk-Duggan, Cheryl Ann

HOUSTON
Adams, Elaine Parker
Adams, Samuel Clifford, Jr.
Alexander, Alma Duncan
Allen, Andrew A.
Anderson, Doris J.
Andrews, Rawle
Bacon, Robert John, Jr.
Banfield, Edison H.
Baptiste, Hansom P., Jr.
Bass, Kevin Charles
Beard, James William, Jr.
Beguesse, Barry Osmund, Jr.
Belcher, Leon H.
Bell, Robert L.
Berry, Weldon H.
Bickham, L. B.
Bishop, Verissa Rene
Bluford, Guion Stewart, Jr.
Bolden, Charles Frank, Jr.
Boney, J. Don
Bonner, Alice A.
Bowser, Vivian Roy
Bradley, Jack George
Branch, Eldridge Stanley
Bransford, Paris
Brazile, Robert (Doc)
Briggs, Collin
Bright, Willie S.
Brooks, Hunter O.
Brown, Abner Bertrand
Brown, Lee Patrick
Brown, Roland O.
Brown, Steve
Bryant, Faye B.
Buckner, William Pat, Jr.
Bullock, James
Butler, Eula M.
Bynam, Sawyer Lee, III
Carl, Earl Lawrence
Carter, Lenora
Chandler, Effie L.
Chapman, Dorothy Hilton
Chase, John S.
Clark, Sheila Wheatley
Claye, Charlene Marette
Clouser, Ernest Z.
Cluse, Kenny Joseph
Coleman, John B.
Cooper, Gordon R., II
Cooper, Matthew N.
Copeland, Barry Bernard
Cormier, Rufus, Jr.
Covington, James Arthur
Cox, Corine
Creuzot, Percy P.
Cunningham, James J.
Davis, Algenita Scott
Davis, Carolyn Ann McBride
Dillard, Melvin Rubin
Dixon, Brenda Joyce
Dixon, Hortense
Douglas, Aubry Carter
Douglas, James Matthew
Doyle, Henry Eman
Ellis, Rodney
Eugere, Edward J.
Everett, David Leon, II
Fadulu, Sunday O.
Fonteno, Myrtle C.
Ford, Marion George, Jr.
Franklin, Martha Lois
Garrison, Zina
Gathe, Joseph C
Gibson, Warren Arnold
Gilmore, Robert McKinley, Sr.
Gite, Lloyd Anthony
Gloster, Jesse E.
Glover, Robert G.
Gooden, Cherry Ross
Grate, Isaac, Jr.
Gray, Leon
Grays, Mattelia Bennett
Gregg, Harrison M., Jr.
Gregory, Frederick Drew
Hall, Anthony W., Jr.
Hall, Horathel

Hammond, Melvin Alan Ray, Jr.
Hannah, Mack H., Jr.
Harris, Vera D.
Haughton, James G.
Hawthorne, Kenneth L.
Hayes, Elvin
Henry, Forest T., Jr.
Hervey, Billy T.
Higgins, Clarence R., Jr.
Hodge, Norris
Honore, Stephan LeRoy
Hopkins, Albert E., Sr.
Huckaby, Henry Lafayette
Hunter, Oliver Clifford, Jr.
Jackson, Roy J., Jr.
James, Betty Nowlin
Jefferson, Andrew L., Jr.
Jefferson, Joseph L.
Jefferson, Overton C.
Jemison, Mae C.
Jeter, Felicia Rene
Johnson, Caliph
Johnson, Lectoy Tarlington
Jones, Edith Irby
Jones, Joseph
Jones, Robert Alton
Jones, Zoia L.
Kennedy, Nathelyne Archie
Lattimore, Oliver Louis, Sr.
Leavell, Allen Lavelle
Lede, Naomi W.
Lee, Dale George
Lee, Robert Emile
Lee, Sheila Jackson
Lewis, Carl
Lloyd, Lewis Joel
Lomas, Ronald Leroy
Mabrie, Herman James, III
Malbroue, Joseph, Jr.
McAfee, Carrie R.
McCray, Rodney Charles
McDonald, Curtis W.
McDonald, Gabrielle K.
McDonald, Mark T.
McDonald, Willie Ruth Davis
McElroy, George A.
McLaurin, Daniel Washington
McMillan, Mae F.
McNeil, Alvin J.
Mease, Quentin R.
Messiah, Sonceria Von
Minor, Vicki Beize
Mitchell, Tex Dwayne
Montgomery, Earline Robertson
Moon, Warren
Moore, Milton Donald, Jr.
Moorehead, Bobbie Wooten
Mooring, Kittye D. (nee Samuels)
Morgan-Price, Veronica Elizabeth
Morris, Lewis R.
Mothershed, Spaesio W.
Mumphrey, Jerry Wayne
Mwamba, Zuberi I.
Nelson, George H.
Nicks, William James, Sr.
Olajuwon, Akeem Charles
Oseni, Hakeem O.
Paige, Roderick
Pearson, Michael Novel
Peavy, John W., Jr.
Petterway, Jackie Willis (Jackie O of Houston)
Piper, Elwood A.
Plummer, Matthew W., Sr.
Poindexter, Zeb F.
Prophet, Richard L., Jr.
Randle, Berdine Caronell
Randle, Lucious A.
Ratliff, Joe Samuel
Reid, Goldie Hartshorn
Reid, Robert
Reynolds, Harry G.
Richards, LaVerne W.
Robey, Louis Reed
Robinson, Frank J.
Robinson, Jayne G.
Routt, Thomas H.
Sampson, Ralph
Seals, Maxine
Shange, Ntozake
Shields, Varee, Jr.
Smith, Charles James, III
Smith, George V.

Spearman, Leonard Hall O'Connell
Speller, Charles K.
Stamps, Joe, Jr.
Stone, John S.
Thomas, Gloria V.
Thomas, Sherri Booker
Thompson, Betty E. Taylor
Thompson, Clarissa J.
Thurston, Paul E.
Tryman, Mfanya Donald
Turner, Elmyra G.
Walker, Carl, Jr.
Walls, Fredric T.
Ward, Clarke G.
Wardlaw, Alvia Jean
Wardlaw, Alvin Holmes
Washington, Arna D.
Washington, Arthur Clover
Washington, Craig A.
Washington, Gladys J. (Gladys J. Curry)
Watson, Norma (nee Mims)
Wells, Patrick Roland
White, Dezra
Wickliff, Aloysius M., Sr.
Wiggins, Mitchell Keith
Wiley, John D., Jr.
Williams, Arthur Love
Williams, John L.
Williams, Michael Patrick
Wilson, Bobby L.
Wyche, Lennon Douglas, Jr.
Yarborough, Dowd Julius, Jr.

HUNTSVILLE
Johnson, Scott Edwin

IRVING
Laday, Kerney
LeGrand, Bob (Snake)
Merritt, Thomas Mack
Merton, Joseph Lee
Simpson-Watson, Ora Lee
Townsell, Jackie M.

JASPER
Milligan, Unav Opal Wade

KATY
Bostick, Laurence Herbert

KELLY AFB
Harris, Frank
Nance, Herbert Charles, Sr.

KILGORE
Tolbert, Jacquelyn C.

KINGSVILLE
Wickham, Muriel Jeannette

KINGWOOD
Clark, William Elgan, Jr.
Sykes, Ray

KIRBY
Miles, Dorothy Marie

LA PORTE
Hills, James Bricky
Wiley, Lucish D.

LAMARQUE
Pratt, Mable

LANCASTER
Atai, Grant A.

LONGVIEW
Bailey, Clarence Walter
Harper, Robert Lee
Johnson, Olendruff Lerey
McLaughlin, Clara J.
Tolbert, Jacquelyn C.

LORAINE
Fowler, Thaddeus Postelle, Jr.

LUBBOCK
Henry, Charles E.
Snell, Joan Yvonne Ervin

LUFKIN
Henderson, I. D., Jr.
Pierre, Dallas

MALAKOFF
Westbrook, Gilson Howard

MARLIN
Dorsey, Leon D., Sr.
Douglass, Arthur E.
Lynn, James Elvis

MARSHALL
Anderson, S. A.
Crawford, Mary Greer
Houston, David R.
Houston, Lillian S.
Lamothe, Isidore J.
Miller, Telly Hugh
Sutton, Walter L.
Williams, Alphonza

MEXIA
Anderson, Ray Charles

NACOGDOCHES
Allen, George

NEW WAVERLY
Straughter, Edgar, Sr.

NURSERY
Sanders, Laura Green

ODESSA
Winfield, Elayne Hunt

ORANGE
DeLarue, Louis C.
Jeter, Velma Marjorie Dreyfus

PALESTINE
Hunt, O'Neal

PEARLAND
Mullett, Donald L.

PLANO
Wattley, Thomas Jefferson

PORT ARTHUR
Evans, Amos James
Freeman, Charles E.
Freeman, Ruby E.
Guidry, Arreader Pleanna
McElroy, Alfred Z.

PRAIRIE VIEW
Adams, Elaine Parker
Berry, Benjamin Donaldson
Carter, Gwendolyn Burns
Evans, Edward Butram
Hawkins, Dorisula Wooten
Jackson, Frank Donald
Jones, Barbara A. P. (nee Posey)
Kendrick, Griff William
Martin, Edward Williford
Pierre, Percy Anthony
Sams, Eristus
Shine, Ted
Washington, Arthur Clover
Woolfolk, George Ruble

RANDOLPH AFB
Armour-Lightner, Rosetta Amelia

RICHARDSON
Ford, David Leon, Jr.
Jones, Alphonzo James
McNary, Oscar Lee
Smith, Dennis Rae

RIVIERA
Scott, Gloria Dean Randle

ROCKPORT
Lewis, Percy Lee

SAN ANTONIO
Banks, Gene
Bivens, Gyna Machelle
Brewer, Ron

Byrd, Sherman Clifton
Coggs, Granville Coleridge
Crawford, Deborah Collins
Derricotte, Eugene Andrew
Donahue, William T.
Elam, Hattie Briscoe
Foster, Lloyd L.
Gaffney, Thomas Daniel
Gilmore, Artis
Haywood, Norcell D.
Hilliard, Robert Lee Moore
James, Hamice R., Jr.
Johnson, Timothy Julius, Jr.
Jones, Edgar Lavelle
Kennedy, Marvin James
Lawrence, Leonard E.
Lucas, John (Cool Hand Luke)
Marcee, Emerson
Mason, Kenneth
May, Dickey R.
Mitchell, Mike Charles
Moore, Johnny Charles
Nance, Herbert Charles, Sr.
Nelson, Ivory Vance
Reed, Florine
Robertson, Alvin Anthony
Samples, Benjamin Norris
Slaughter, John Etta
Thurston, Charles Sparks
Warrick, Alan Everett
Watson, Leonidas
Webb, Joe
Williams, Lorece P.
Williams, Theodore R.
Wilson, Robert Lee Miles
Winters, Kenneth E.
Wright, Earl Lee

SAN AUGUSTINE
Garner, Lon L.

SEABROOK
Bastine, Lillian Beatrice

SEGUIN
Ewing, Barbara Lee

SIMONTON
Cockrell, Mechera Ann

SPRING
James, Advergus Dell, Jr.

STEPHENVILLE
Jackson, Charles E.

SUGARLAND
Lee, Robert Emile

TEMPLE
Harrison, Roscoe Conklin, Jr.
Hornsby, B. Kay
Kennedy, Jimmie Vernon

TERRELL
Anderson, Abbie H.
Evans, Jack
Jackson, Seaton J.
Lee, Gerald E.

TEXARKANA
Bell, Earnest Franklin
Burke, Denzer

TEXAS CITY
Carter, Thomas Floyd, Jr.
Hollowell, Johnny Laveral
Johnson, Milton D.
Pratt, Alexander Thomas

THE WOODLANDS
Irons, Gerald Dwayne

THOMPSONS
Morgan, Fletcher, Jr.

TRINIDAD
Dickey, Erma Cook

TYLER
Clark, Jimmy E.
Delaney, Juanita Battle

Early, Paul David
Hancock, Allen C.
Johnson, David Horace
Jones, John P.
Sanders, Sally Ruth
Wilkinson, Sheppard Field

VICTORIA
Cade, Harold Edward

WACO
Allen, Van Sizar
Douglass, Arthur E.
Hardaway, Yvonne Veronica
Harrison, Emma Louise
Hooker, Eric H.
Johnson, Lawrence E., Sr.
Jones, Marilyn Elaine
King, Arthur Thomas
Morgan, Warren W.
Talbot, Theodore A.

WICHITA FALLS
Boston, Horace Oscar

WILLIS
Straughter, Edgar, Sr.

UTAH

CLEARFIELD
Watkins, Mose

OGDEN
Haney, Darnel L.
Oliver, Daily E.

PROVO
Gill, Troy D.

SALT LAKE CITY
Adams, Afesa M.
Bush, Lenoris
Coleman, Ronald Gerald
Cope, Donald Lloyd
Cunningham, William L.
Davis, France Albert
Gill, Troy D.
Guillory, William A.
Jones, Curley C.
Oliver, Daily E.

VERMONT

BENNINGTON
Dixon, William R.

BURLINGTON
Clemmons, Jackson Joshua Walter
McCrorey, H. Lawrence
Sandoval, Dolores S.

CHARLOTTE
Clemmons, Jackson Joshua Walter

VIRGINIA

ACCOMAC
Cooper, Samuel H., Jr.

ALEXANDRIA
Archer, Chalmers, Jr.
Barrett, Matthew Anderson
Bell, Theron J.
Blackwell, Patricia A.
Brooks, Harold W.
Brown, Edwin C., Jr.
Cadoria, Sherian Grace
Christian, Gail P.
DeSandies, Kenneth Andre
Everett, Ralph B.
Fields, William I., Jr. (Ike Fields)
Floyd, Jeremiah
Gaines, Sylvester, Jr.
Gaither, Dorothy B.
Goff, Wilhelmina Delores
Harris, Gleason Ray

Harris, Lee Andrew, II
Hudson, Anthony Webster
James, Juanita T.
McClenic, Patricia Dickson
McIntosh, Rhodina Covington
Morgan, Alice Johnson Parham
Ramseur, Andre William
Scott-Heron, Gil
Stansbury, Vernon Carver, Jr.
Tyler, Shirley Neizer
Webb, Lucious Moses
West, Charles Fremont

ANNANDALE
Archer, Chalmers, Jr.
Brown, Ruby Edmonia
Murphy, Jeanne Claire

ARLINGTON
Agurs, Donald Steele (Simon Fry)
Berthoud, Kenneth H., Jr.
Blount, Charlotte Renee
Brown, George L.
Carter, Perry W.
DesVerney-Sinnette, Elinor
Green, Deborah Kennon
Hardie, Robert L., Jr.
Jones, Effie Hall
Lang-Jeter, Lula L.
May, James Shelby
McCants, Odell
Moncure, Albert F.
Newman, William Thomas, Jr.
Parker, Lutrelle Fleming
Raullerson, Calvin Henry
Scott, Samuel
Smith, Chester B.
Syphax, Margarite R.
Weaver, Frank Cornell
Wickham, DeWayne
Young, Andrew J.

ASHLAND
Fitzgerald, Charlotte Diane

BLACKSBURG
Kennedy, Joseph J., Jr.
Warren, Herman Lecil
Williams-Green, Joyce F.

BOYDTON
Adiele, N. Moses
McLaughlin, George W.

BURKE
Sylvas, Lionel B.

CAPRON
McCollum, Charles Edward

CHARLES CITY
Adkins, Iona W.
Jones, Lloyd O.

CHARLOTTESVILLE
Dove, Rita Frances
Garrett, Paul C.
Harris, William McKinley, Sr.
Hinton, Hortense Beck
Jones, Betty Jean T.
Scott, Charlotte Hanley
Scott, Nathan A., Jr.
Smith, Kevin L.
White, Randolph Louis

CHATHAM
Merritt, Willette T.

CHESAPEAKE
Alexander, E. Curtis
Johnson, William A.
Jordan, George Lee
McCall, Barbara Collins
McCoy, Jessie Haynes
Owens, Hugo Armstrong
Reid, Milton A.
Singleton, James LeRoy
Taylor, Donald Fulton, Sr.
Tucker, Billy J.
Walton, James Madison

CHESTERFIELD
Byrd, Arthur W.

CLIFTON
Haston, Raymond Curtiss, Jr.

CLIFTON FORGE
Goode, George Ray

COLONIAL HEIGHTS
Thigpen, Calvin Herritage

COPPER HILL
Stuart, Ivan I.

CULPEPER
Hinton, Hortense Beck

CUMBERLAND
Miller, Erenest Eugene

DAHLGREN
Hughes, Isaac Sunny

DANVILLE
Arnold, Clarence Edward, Jr.
Charity, Ruth Harvey
Jennings, Sylvesta Lee
Mason, Cheryl Annette

DOSWELL
Tillman, Christine L.

EASTVILLE
Bell, Charles Smith

EMPORIA
Ward, Anna Elizabeth

ETTRICK
Howard, Vivian Gordon

FAIRFAX
Alexander, Lenora Cole
Brittain, Bradley Bernard, Jr.
Courtney, Stephen Alexander
DeCosta-Willis, Miriam
Gray, Clarence Cornelius, III
Johnson-Brown, Hazel Winfred
Phillips, Ralph Leonard
Price, David Lee
Reuben, Lucy Jeanette
Ridley, Alfred Denis
Wilkins, Roger Wood
Williams, Marcus Doyle

FAIRFAX STATION
Ruffner, Ray P.

FALLS CHURCH
Coates, Shelby L.
Collins, Paul L.
Cromartie, Eugene Rufus
Ellison, Pauline Allen
Hairston, William

FARMVILLE
Miller, Erenest Eugene

FRANKLIN
Harrison, A. B.

FREDERICKSBURG
Coleman, Gilbert Irving
Davies, Lawrence A.
Farmer, James
Williams, Sylvia J.

HAMPTON
Adeyiga, Adeyinka A.
Bell, James A.
Bontemps, Jacqueline Marie Fonvielle
Brown, William Crawford
Charlton, Jack Fields
Clark, Laron Jefferson, Jr.
Coles, John Edward
Darden, Christine Mann
Davis, William R.
Dawson, Martha E.
Gartrell, Luther R.
Gilliard, Joseph Wadus
Hargrove, Andrew
Harvey, Norma Baker
Harvey, William R.

Jamaludeen, Abdul Hamid (William C. Wade Jr.)
Jefferson, M. Ivory
Johnson, Michael Kevin
Jones, Bonnie Louise
McGhee, Nancy Bullock
Moorman, Clinton R. (Bob)
Owens, Angle B., Jr.
Pinkelton, Norma Harris
Pleasant, Mae Barbee Boone
Porter, Michael LeRoy
Prater, Oscar L.
Taylor, Maurice Clifton
Ward, Albert M.
Watkins, James Darnell
Whitlow, Woodrow, Jr.
Wilkinson, James Wellington
Williamson, Carl Vance
Wilson, Greer Dawson
Wright, Stephen Junius, Jr.

HARRISONBURG
Bullock, Byron Swanson
Davis, Abraham, Jr.
Gabbin, Alexander Lee
Gabbin, Joanne Veal
Jennings, Lillian Pegues
Williams, Angie Bass

HAYMARKET
Gravely, Samuel L., Jr.

HERNDON
Mitchell, Robert C.

HOPEWELL
Edmonds, Campbell Ray

KING GEORGE
Bumbry, George Nordlinger
Hughes, Isaac Sunny
Scranage, Clarence, Jr.

KING WILLIAM
Reid, Miles Alvin

LAWRENCEVILLE
Adesuyi, Sunday Adeniji
Harrison, Harry Paul
Jenkins, Clara Barnes
Jones, Oris Pinckney
Rainey, Bessye Coleman
Rhoades, Samuel Thomas
Satcher, Robert Lee, Sr.
Thurman, Frances Ashton

LEESBURG
Tolbert, John W., Jr.
Wilson, Alicia Santana

LEXINGTON
Lewis, J. B., Jr.
McCloud, Anece Faison

LOCUST GROVE
Coleman, Gilbert Irving

LORTON
Green, Georgia Mae
Ruffner, Ray P.

LYNCHBURG
Anderson, Doreatha Madison
Hopkins, Vashti Edythe Johnson
Mangum, Charles M. L.
Mitchell, James H.

MANASSAS
Jones, Jimmie Dene
Sanders, Rober LaFayette

MARTINSVILLE
Muse, William Brown, Jr.

MCLEAN
Aklilu, Tesfaye
Albright, William Dudley, Jr.
Alston, Kathy Diane
Blackmon, Mosetta Whitaker
Courtney, Stephen Alexander
Latham, Weldon Hurd
Lightfoote, William Edward, II

Malone, Claudine Berkeley
Sechrest, Edward Amacker
Wallace, Richard Warner
Weaver, Gary W.

MIDLOTHIAN
Al-Mateen, Kevin Bakeer
Smith, Shirley LaVerne
Thompson, Brenda Smith

NEWPORT NEWS
Allen, Charles Claybourne
Banks, Dwayne Martin
Binns, Silas Odell
Birchette, William Ashby, III
Capehart, Johnnie Lawrence
Earl, Archie William, Sr.
Holloman, Thaddeus Bailey
Kendall, Mark Acton Robertson
Miller, George N., Jr.
Pope, Mirian Artis
Rattley, Jessie M.
Scott, C. Waldo
Scott, Robert Cortez
Stith, Antoinette Freeman
Williams, Yarborough Burwell, Jr.
Wilson, Wesley Campbell

NORFOLK
Alexander, Otis Douglas (Sule)
Alexander, Rosa M.
Allen, Maxine Bogues
Ashby, Reginald W.
Barnes-Simmons, Anne T.
Barrett, Walter Carlin, Jr.
Bempong, Maxwell A.
Bowser, James A.
Boyd, Joseph L.
Brockett, Charles A.
Brooks, Phillip Daniel
Byrd, Helen P.
Carroll, William
Carter, Gene Raymond
Cauthen, Cheryl G.
Corprew, Charles Sumner, Jr.
Crawley, George Claudius
Dandridge, Rita Bernice
Davis, Katie Elizabeth
Freeman, James Jasper
Garnette, Booker Thomas
Gay, James F.
Hanford, Craig Bradley
Harris, Carl Gordon
Haynes, Alphonso Worden
Hodge, Ernest M.
Hoffler, Richard Winfred, Jr.
Hopkins, John David
Isaac, Joseph William Alexander
Jennings, Robert Ray
Jones, Raymond, Sr.
Lane, George S., Jr.
Lowe, Scott Miller
Maddox, Marion Thelma
Mapp, David Kenneth, Jr.
Marshall, Herbert A.
Mason, William Thomas, Jr.
McCall, Barbara Collins
Miller, James S.
Miller, Yvonne Bond
Newsome, Moses, Jr.
Ozim, Francis Taiino
Parham, Thomas David, Jr.
Pope, Mirian Artis
Reid, Milton A.
Reynolds, Charles McKinley, Jr.
Rhodes, Lord Cecil
Roberson, Gary
Ryder, Georgia Atkins
Santiful, Luthur L.
Scott, Judith Sugg
Scott, Leon Leroy
Smithey, Robert Arthur
Spiva, Ulysses Van
Strayhorn, Earl Carlton
Taylor, Donald Fulton, Sr.
Thomas, Earle Frederick
Tyler, Gerald DeForest
Valentine, Herman E.
Vaughan, James Edward
Walker, Sterling Wilson
Williams, Ira Joseph
Willis, Levy E
Wilson, Harrison B.
Wilson, Lucy R.

Wimbush, F. Blair

PETERSBURG
Bailey, Gracie Massenberg
Brieve-Martin, Ila Corrinna
Clayton, Robert Louis
Greenfield, Wilbert
Johnson, Harry A.
Mackey, Andrew, Jr.
McClure, Wesley C.
Norris, Ethel Maureen
Powell, Grady Wilson
Sabourin, Clemonce
Thigpen, Calvin Herritage
Toppin, Edgar Allan
Worrell, Kaye Sydnell

PORTSMOUTH
Cooper, Iris N.
Hill, Robert J., Jr.
Holley, James W., III
Hughes, Charles W., Jr.
Jenkins, Harry Lancaster
Moody, Eric Orlando
Morris, Margaret Lindsay
Morrison, Johnny Edward
Nixon, James Melvin
Wheelan, Belle Louise
Williamson, Carl Vance

QUANTICO
Carter, William Thomas, Jr.
Nunn, Robinson S.

QUINTON
Green, Calvin Coolidge

RADFORD
Jones, Stanley Bernard

RESTON
Ahart, Thomas I.
Baskerville, Charles Alexander
Berthoud, Kenneth H., Jr.
Calbert, Roosevelt
Campbell, Carlos Cardozo
Cooke, William Branson
Gilliam, Reginald Earl, Jr.
Johnson, Johnnie L., Jr.
Moorman, Holsey Alexander

RICHMOND
Al-Mateen, Cheryl Singleton
Anderson, Pearl G.
Ballard, Janet Jones
Banks, Marshall D.
Bennett, Keith
Benton, James Wilbert, Jr.
Bledsoe, Carolyn E. Lewis
Boatwright, Joseph Weldon
Boone, Elwood Bernard, Jr.
Bowser, McEva R.
Cade, Tinina Quick
Cameron, Wilburn Macio, Jr.
Campbell, Gilbert Godfrey
Carter, Gilbert Lino
Carter, Wesley Byrd
Cheatham, Linda Moye
Cobb, John Hunter, Jr.
Conyers, Charles L.
Cook, Wallace Jeffery
Creighton-Zollar, Ann
Cummings, Charles Edward
Dance, Daryl Cumber
Daniels, Reginald Shiffon
Dark, Lawrence Jerome
Davis, Esther Gregg
Davis, Ronald W.
Davis, William Hayes, Sr.
Deese, Manuel
Dell, Willie J.
Dennis, Rutledge M.
DePillars, Murry Norman
Dixon, Leon Martin
Douglas, Willard H., Jr.
Dungee, Margaret R.
Eatman, Brenda Alene
Edwards, Rondle E.
El-Amin, Sa'ad (JeRoyd X. Greene)
Felder, Tyree Preston, II
Florence, Virginia Proctor Powell
Fowlkes, Doretha P.

Gayles, Franklin Johnson
Gibson, William M.
Gunnell, James B.
Harris, Ruth Coles
Henley, Vernard W.
Hill, Oliver W.
Hunter, Richard C.
James, Allix Bledsoe
Johnson, William Randolph
Jones, William C.
Laisure, Sharon Emily Goode
Lambert, Benjamin J., III
Lambert, Leonard W.
Latham, Bernice Grant
Latney, Harvey, Jr.
Leary, James E.
Lewis, Ronald C.
Mack, Daniel J.
Marsh, Henry L., III
McClendon, Moses C.
Meadows, Richard H.
Miller, Laurel Milton
Mitchell, Henry Heywood
Nichols, Paul
Reed, Daisy Frye
Roberts, Samuel Kelton
Robertson, Benjamin W.
Rush, Sonya C.
Schexnider, Alvin J.
Simmons, S. Dallas
Southall, Herbert Howardton, Sr.
Spurlock, Charles T.
Spurlock, James B., Jr.
Spurlock, LaVerne B.
Stallings, Gregory Ralph
Teekah, George Anthony
Thompson, Brenda Smith
Townes, Clarence L., Sr.
Townes, Clarence Lee, Jr.
Tucker, James F.
Tucker, Samuel Wilbert
Turner, Bill (Willie T.)
Tyson, John C.
Wallace, Helen Winfree-Peyton
Walston, Woodrow William
Watkins, Willie S., III
Weaver, John Arthur
Welch, Winfred Bruce
Wilder, Lawrence Douglas
Wilkins, Thomas Alphonso
Williams, John R.
Williams, Regina Vloyn-Kinchen
Winfree, Murrell H.
Winston, Dennis Ray
Woodson, Jeffrey Anthony
Wright, Jackson Thomas, Jr.
Yancy, Preston Martin
Yates, Ella Gaines

ROANOKE
Adams, Paul Brown
Burks, James William, Jr.
Butler, Wendell Harding
Cason, Joseph L.
Remson, Anthony Terence
Riddick, Louise K.
Taylor, Noel C.
Whitworth, Claudia Alexander

ROCKY MOUNT
Hamilton, McKinley John

ROLASTSBURG
Giovanni, Nikki

SALEM
Statum, Hayward S.
Williams, Carlton Ray, Jr.

SANDY HOOK
Bowles, James Harold, Sr.

SMITHFIELD
Britt, Paul D., Jr.
Gray, Charles Henry

SOUTH HILL
Scranage, Clarence, Jr.

SPRINGFIELD
Adams, Theodore Adolphus, Jr.
Becton, Julius Wesley, Jr.
Brown, Carl Anthony

Forte, Johnie, Jr.
McClenic, Patricia Dickson

STERLING
Gee, William Rowland, Jr.

SUFFOLK
Glover, Bernard E.
Hart, Ronald O.

SURRY
Poindexter, Gammiel Gray
Tunstall, June Rebecca

TREVILIANS
McLaughlin, George W.

TYSONS CORNER
Harris, Lee Andrew, II

VIENNA
Bankhead, Porter Lee
Jefferson, Roy Lee, Jr.
Jones, Michael Perrin
McKoy, John H.
Proctor, Earl D.

VIRGINIA BEACH
Cauthen, Cheryl G.
Curry, Jerry Ralph
Ingram, LaVerne Dorothy
Pleasants, Charles Wrenn
Strayhorn, Earl Carlton
Wiggins, Joseph L.

WAKEFIELD
Urquhart, James McCartha

WARSAW
Johns, Sonja Maria
Veney, Herbert Lee

WAVERLY
Worrell, Kaye Sydnell

WEST POINT
Reid, Miles Alvin

WILLIAMSBURG
Charlton, Jack Fields
Honablue, Richard Riddick
Stone, William T.
Walker, Sheila Suzanne

WOODBRIDGE
Carter, William Thomas, Jr.
Sylvas, Lionel B.

WASHINGTON

BELLEVUE
Perry, Lowell W., Jr.
Tresvant, John Bernard (Tres)
Tyner, Regina Lisa
Willis, Raymond Earl

BELLINGHAM
Shropshire, Harry W.

CHEHALIS
Pope, Isaac S.

CHENEY
Hardin, John Arthur

FAIRCHILD AFB
Howell, Rose Cole

FORT LEWIS
Briggs, Paul W.
Waller, Calvin A.H.

FPO SEATTLE
Camphor, Michael Gerard

ISSAQUAH
Easley, Kenny
Freeman, Evelyn

KENT
McGhee, James Leon

KIRKLAND
Anderson, James R., Jr.
Brown, Dave Steven
Butler, Ray
Goldston, Ralph Peter
Hall, Harold Eugene
Johns, Paul V.
McKenzie, Reginald
Young, Charles Edward

LYNWOOD
Brown, Marva Y.
Overall, Manard

MERCER ISLAND
Burton, John Frederick

OLYMPIA
Arrington, Saul
Bailey, Mona Humphries
Belcher, Lewis, Jr.
Ingram, Winifred
Mimms, Maxine Buie
Parson, Willie L.
Patton, Carolyn Vannette
Purce, Thomas Les
Turner, Isiah

PULLMAN
Anderson, Talmadge

REDMOND
Perry, Lowell W., Jr.

RENTON
Fitzpatrick, Edward B.
Franklin, Clyde

RICHLAND
Wiley, William R.

SEATTLE
Abe, Benjamin Omara A.
Alex, Gregory K.
Alexander, Don H.
Anderson, James R., Jr.
Archie, Cornell B., Jr.
Banks, James Albert
Bennette, Connie E.
Bickerstaff, Bernie Lavelle
Blake, J. Paul
Bradley, Phil Poole
Brazier, Martin George
Brock, O. Lee
Brooks, Norward J.
Brown, Fred
Burton, Philip L.
Carter, Arlington W., Jr.
Chambliss, Ida Belle
Counts, George W.
Davis, Alvin Glenn
Farris, Jerome
Freeman, Nancy Cecile
Fregia, Darrell Leon
Frye, Reginald Stanley
Gulley, Wilson
Hailey, Priscilla W.
Haynes, Sue Blood
Henderson, Dave Lee
Hightower, Monteria
Hill, James A., Sr.
Houston, Alice V.
Hubbard, Walter T.
Johnson, Charles Richard
Jones, Arlender
Jones, Edward Louis
Jones, Leon C.
Kennedy, Linda Cheryl
Kimbrough-Johnson, Donna L.
Langford, Victor C., III
Lawrence, Jacob A.
Lee, Vivian Booker
Leigh, James W., Jr.
Locke, Hubert G.
Lofton, Andrew James
Macklin, John W.
McElroy, Colleen J.
McKinney, Samuel Berry
Miles, Edward Lancelot
Miller, Earl Vonnidore

Morris, Ernest Roland
Ollee, Mildred W.
Osborne, Oliver Hilton
Pinson, Vada Edward, Jr.
Pounds, Kenneth Ray
Priester, Julian Anthony (Pepo Mtoto)
Reynolds, Andrew Buchanan
Rice, Constance Williams
Rice, Norman Blann
Scott, Joseph Walter
Shaw, Spencer Gilbert
Smith, Sam
Spratlen, Thaddeus H.
Steele, Claude Mason
Stephens, Herbert Malone
Swayne, Steven Robert
Tartabull, Danny
Washington, James W., Jr.
Whyte, James W., Jr.
Williams, Clarence
Williams, Leroy Joseph
Williams, Wayne Richard (Selase Williams)
Wilson, John T., Jr.
Womack, William Martin
Woodhouse, Rossalind Yvonne
Zeumault, Dianne Lorraine

SOUTH TACOMA
Silas, Dolores Irene

SPOKANE
Chase, James
Franklin, Thomas E.
Greene, Nathaniel D.
Rowland, Leon Floyd
Sims, Lydia Theresa
Smith, James, Jr.

TACOMA
Baugh, Lynnette
Boddie, Algernon Owens
Brown, Leo C., Jr.
Brown, Samuel Franklin, Jr.
Crawford, Ella Mae
Davis, Alfred C., Sr.
Gilven, Hezekiah
Hankerson, Elijah H.
Kimbrough-Johnson, Donna L.
Smith, LeRoi Matthew-Pierre, III
Tanner, Jack E.
Tisdale, Herbert Clifford
Wesley, Barbara Ann

VANCOUVER
Nettles, Willard, Jr.

VASHON
McGehee, Nan E.

WALLA WALLA
King, Charles E.

WEST VIRGINIA

ATHENS
Wright, Harriette Simon

BECKLEY
Bradshaw, Doris Marion
Chambers, Madrith Bennett
Dobson, Helen Sutton
Martin, James Tyrone
Payne, Brown H.
Scott, Albert Nelson
Seay, Lorraine King

BETHANY
Airall, Zoila Erlinda

BLUEFIELD
Froe, Dreyfus Walter
Higginbotham, Peyton Randolph

BUCKHANNON
Bayard, Franck
Coleman, Harry A.

CHARLESTON
Brown, Dallas C., Jr.
Brown, Willard L.
Canady, Herman G., Jr.
Durgan, Andrew James
James, Betty Harris
James, Charles Howell, II
Marshall, Charlene Jennings
Matthews, Virgil E.
Mitchell-Bateman, Mildred
Shaw, Richard Gordon
Smoot, Carolyn Elizabeth

DUNBAR
Russell, James A., Jr.

FAIRMONT
Hinton, Gregory Tyrone

HUNTINGTON
Carter, Philip W., Jr.
Henderson, Herbert H.
Jones, Idus, Jr.
Lawson, Robert L.
Murphy, Gene
Redd, William L.
Williams, Joseph Lee

HURRICANE
Peters, Roscoe H., Jr.

INSTITUTE
Brown, Dallas C., Jr.
Carper, Gloria G.
Carter, Hazo
Griffin, Ervin Verome
James, Betty Harris
Matthews, Virgil E.
Smoot, Carolyn Elizabeth
Thompson, Litchfield O'Brien
Wallace, William James Lord

KEYSTONE
Jackson, Aubrey N.
Stephens, Booker T.

LOGAN
Russell, John Peterson, Jr.

MARTINSBURG
Roberts, Cheryl Dornita Lynn

MORGANTOWN
Belmear, Horace Edward
Cabbell, Edward Joseph
Gwynn, Florine Evayonne
Howard, Elizabeth Fitzgerald
Hughes, Johnnie Lee
Louistall-Monroe, Victorine Augusta

NITRO
Johnson, Carl Elliott

PARKERSBURG
Jones, William W.

PHILIPPI
Jackson, Nathaniel G.
Redd, Thomasina A.

PRINCETON
Cabbell, Edward Joseph

RANSON
Miller, Thelma Delmoor

WEIRTON
Williams, Carletta Celeste

WELCH
Stephens, Booker T.

WHEELING
Lewis, Houston A.
Moore, John Wesley, Jr.

WILLIAMSON
Manuel, John N.

WISCONSIN

APPLETON
Hall, Lloyd Eugene

BELOIT
Davis, Tyrone Theophilus
Knight, Walter R.
Thompson, Joseph Isaac

BROOKFIELD
Jones, Fredrick E.

EAU CLAIRE
Taylor, Dale B.

FRANKLIN
Platt, Richard A.

GREEN BAY
Brown, Robert Lee
Clark, Jessie
Colbert, James D.
Douglass, Mike Reese
Ellis, Gerry
Epps, Phillip
Gray, Johnnie
Harris, Leotis
Huckleby, Harlan Charles (Huck)
Ivery, Eddie Lee
Jefferson, John
Johnson, Ezra
Jones, Terry (Big T)
Lee, Mark
Lewis, Tim Jay
Lofton, James
Luke, Steve Norman
McCoy, Mike C. (Taz)
Mendenhall, John Rufus
Prather, Guy Tyrone
Rodgers, Del

KENOSHA
Shade, Barbara J. (nee Robinson)

KEWAUNEE
Qamar, Nadi Abu

LA CROSSE
Mitchem, John Clifford

MADISON
Baugh, James Edward
Davis, Luther Charles
Davis, Richard
Dejoie, Carolyn Barnes Milanes
Evans, Patricia P.
George, Gary Raymond
Henderson, Hugh C.
Henderson, Virginia Ruth McKinney
High, Freida
Johnson, Diane
Jones, James Edward, Jr.
Julian, Percy L., Jr.
Marrett, Cora B.
Marsh-Lott, Freddie Alexander
Nunnery, Willie James
Salter, Kwame S.
Shivers, S. Michael
Thomas, Wilbur C.
Ward, Walter L., Jr.
Wheaton, Janice C.
Williams, Ronald Wesley

MILWAUKEE
Aman, Mohammed M.
Artison, Richard E.
Barbee, Lloyd Augustus
Barnhill, Helen Iphigenia
Barrett, Sherman L.
Beach, Walter G., II
Beard, Israel
Bellegarde-Smith, Patrick
Bender, Barbara A.
Broussard, Leroy
Buckhanan, Dorothy Wilson
Calvin, Earl D.
Calvin, Willie J.
Carpenter, Joseph, II
Chicoye, Etzer
Clevert, Charles N., Jr.

Colbert, Virgis W.
Cooper, Cecil (Coop)
Coward, Jasper Earl
Cummings, Robert Terrell
Cummings, Terry
Edmond, Paul Edward
Evans, Phillip L.
Faucett, Barbara J.
Finlayson, William E.
Ford, Sarah Ann
Halyard, Ardie Adlena
Hisle, Larry Eugene
Holt, Michael L.
Jackson, Harold Baron, Jr.
Jamison, Lafayette
Johnson, Ben E.
Johnson, Geneva B.
Johnson, Marlene E.
Johnson-Crosby, Deborah A.
Jones, James Bennett
Jones, Walter L.
Lanier, Bob
Lister, Alton Lavelle
McLean, Zarah Gean
Mitchem, Arnold L.
Moncrief, Sidney
Murrell, Peter C.
Nevels, Zebedee James
O'Flynn-Thomas, Patricia
Oglivie, Benjamin A.
Ologboni, Tejumola F. (Rockie Taylor)
Palmer, John A.
Parks, James Clinton, Jr.
Parrish, Clarence R.
Pattillo, Roland A.
Perry, June Martin
Pierce, Ricky Charles
Pollard, Diane S.
Pressey, Paul Matthew
Prince, Joan Marie
Rayford, Zula M.
Romar, Lorenzo Anthony
Smith, Bubba
Spaights, Ernest
Swan, Monroe
Terry, John William
Thomas, Patricia O'Flynn
White, O. C.
Williams, George W., III
Williams, Virginia Walker
Winfield, Thalia Beatrice

OAK CREEK
Walker, Willie M.

OSHKOSH
Williams, Shirley Stennis

RACINE
Brooks, Rodney Norman
Buckhanan, Dorothy Wilson
Hales, Edward Everette
Raine, Charles Herbert, III
Swanson, Charles
Turner, Robert Lloyd
Venson, Jeanine
Wilkinson, Raymond M., Jr.

RIVER FALLS
Bailey, Robert B., III
Norwood, Tom

WAUWATOSA
Prince, Joan Marie
Smith, Symuel Harold

WEST MADISON
Phillips, Vel R.

WHITEWATER
Hewing, Pernell Hayes
Patten, W. George

WYOMING

CHEYENNE
Byrd, Harriet Elizabeth
Byrd, James W.
Jeffrey, Ronnald James
Mercer, Arthur, Sr.
Wise, C. Rogers

LARAMIE
Wideman, John E.

ROCK SPRINGS
Stevens, Althea Williams

BAHAMAS

NASSAU
Brown, Theophile Waldorf
Higgs, Frederick C.

BELGIUM

BRUSSELS
Chase-Riboud, Barbara DeWayne (D'Ashnash Tosi)
Hudson, Roy Davage

OVERIJSE
Hudson, Roy Davage

BERMUDA

HAMILTON
Swan, John W.

CANADA

COQUITLAM, BRITISH COLUMBIA
Brockenborough, Joseph Antonio

EDMONTON, ALBERTA
Simon, Kenneth Bernard

MISSISSAUGA, ONTARIO
Hooper, Michele J.
James, Herbert I.
Peterson, Oscar Emmanuel

MONTREAL, QUEBEC
Brooks, Hubie
Dixon, George
Raines, Tim
Singleton, Kenneth Wayne

TORONTO, ONTARIO
Barfield, Jesse Lee
Bell, George Antonio
Davis, Joseph M.
Denton, Herbert H., Jr.
Fernandez, Octavio Antonio
Gaston, Clarence Edwin
Marshall, Paul M.
Moseby, Lloyd Anthony

DENMARK

COPENHAGEN
Burns, Ronald Melvin

ENGLAND

BLETCHLEY, BUCKS
Laine, Cleo

LONDON
Hubbard, Donald
Kellman, Denis Elliott

ITALY

MILAN
Donawa, Maria Elena

ROME
Donawa, Maria Elena

JAMAICA

BRIDGE PORT
Carter, Martin Joseph

KINGSTON
McKinley, Ray E.
Nettleford, Rex Milton
Powell, Aston Wesley
Robinson, Maurice C.

MONTEGO BAY
Coley, Gerald Sydney

JAPAN

TOKYO
Akridge, Paul Bai

KENYA

NAIROBI
Gecau, Kimani J.
Whiting, Thomas J.

KUWAIT

SAFAT
Stroud, Louis Winston

LIBERIA

MONROVIA
Myers, Samuel L., Jr.

NETHERLANDS

AMSTERDAM
Scott, James Henry

NICARAGUA

MANAGUA
Newell, Matthias Gregory

NIGERIA

BENIN CITY
Thibodeaux, Sylvia Marie

LAGOS
Ford, William R.

PORT HARCOURT
Nnolim, Charles E.

ZARIA, KADUNA
Lateef, Yusef

PUERTO RICO

LEVITTOWN
Zambrana, Rafael

SAUDI ARABIA

DHAHRAN
Kent, Ernest

REPUBLIC OF SOUTH AFRICA

CAPETOWN
Ming, Donald George K.

VIRGIN ISLANDS OF THE UNITED STATES

FREDERIKSTED
Joseph, Antoine L.

ST CROIX
Belardo de O'Neal, Lilliana
Benjamin, Cecil R.
Bryan, Adelbert
Canton, Douglas E.
Christian, Cora LeEthel
Finch, Raymond Lawrence
Garcia, Kwame N.
King, Howard A. T.
Petersen, Eileen Ramona
Rivera, Eddy
Sheen, Albert A.
Thomas, Maurice McKenzie
Williams, Patrick Nehemiah

ST THOMAS
Ballentine, Krim Menelik
Berryman, Macon M.
Bourne, Judith Louise
Brady, Julio A.
Briscoe, Edward Gans
Bryan, Clarice
Carroll, James S.
Christian, Almeric L.
Dennis, Hugo, Jr.
Evans, Melvin H.
Harding, John Edward
Hodge, Derek M.
Krigger, Marilyn Francis
Meyers, Ishmael Alexander
Michael, Dale R.
Millin, Henry Allan
Nibbs, Alphonse, Sr.
O'Bryan, James Alvanley, Jr.
Prothro, Louise Robinson (nee Gray)
Richards, Arthur A.
Sprauve, Gilbert A.
Thomas, Audria Acty
Todman, Jureen Francis
Tuitt, Jane Eliza
Williams, Lloyd L.

ZIMBABWE

HARARE
Ndlovu, Callistus P.
Samkange, Tommie Marie

OCCUPATIONAL INDEX

ACCOUNTING/ AUDITING
See also MANAGEMENT/ ADMINISTRATION— ACCOUNTING/ FINANCIAL

Adams, Robert Thomas
Aiken, William
Allen, James H.
Allen, Philip C.
Ashby, Lucius Antoine
Banks, Carlton Luther
Banks, Joyce P.
Bardwell, Rufus B., III
Barnett, Teddy
Barrow, Thomas Joe
Beasley, Anne Vickers
Belcher, Margaret L.
Bell, Marilyn Lenora
Bell, Theodore Joshua, II
Belle, Euris E.
Benjamin, Ronald
Bentley, Herbert Dean
Berry, Archie Paul
Berry, Roscoe Darewood, Jr.
Bibbs, Janice Denise
Black, Daniel L., Jr.
Blocker, Helen Powell
Bouldes, Charlene
Bowie, Oliver Wendell
Boyd, William Stewart
Bradfield, Clarence McKinley
Bradford, James Edward
Breckenridge, John L.
Brown, Clarice Ernestine
Brown, Clifford Anthony
Brown, Lawrence E.
Bruno, Michael B.
Bryant, Isaac Rutledge
Bullard, Edward A., Jr.
Bullock, Thurman Ruthe
Butler, B. Janelle
Cade, Lionel C.
Carswell, Gloria Nadine Sherman
Chandler, Rory Wayne
Clark, Sheila Wheatley
Clay, Patricia Ann
Clay, Timothy Byron
Coleman, Ruth M.
Cook, Frank Robert, Jr.
Copeland, Barry Bernard
Copeland, Kathleen (nee Maxwell)
Cosby, James C.
Croslan, John Arthur
Cross, Jack
Culver, Rhonda
Davenport, Ernest H.
Davis, Clarence A.
Davis, John W., III
Davis, Tyrone Theophilus
Devonish, Linda Diane
Dickerson, Ellis L., Jr.
Drennen, Gordon
Dudley, Albert LeRoy
Duncan, David Edward
Easton, Richard James
Edwards, Luther Howard
Ellis, Joseph Louis
Esco, Fred, Jr.
Evans, Vernon D.
Finney, Michael Anthony
Fisher, George Carver
Freeman, Kenneth D.
Gabbin, Alexander Lee
Gainey, Leonard Dennis, II

Garrett, Nathan Taylor
Gates, Otis A., III
Gill, Rosa Underwood
Gilliam, Sharon
Glee, George, Jr.
Green, Angelo Gray
Green, Dennis O.
Guitano, Anton W.
Hadnott, Bennie L.
Hambrick, Harold E., Jr.
Harper, Mary L.
Harris, Robert Eugene Peyton
Harrison, Lincoln J.
Hill, James, Jr.
Holmes, Marion
Holt, Veitya Eileene (Vickye)
Howard, Osbie L., Jr.
Hymes, Jesse
Jackson, Larron Deonne
Jackson, Raynard
Jeffers, Grady Rommel
Johnson, Edward, Jr. (Fast Eddie)
Johnson, Ralph C.
Jones, Jimmie Dene
Jones, Leonard Virgil
Jones, Theodore A.
Joyner, William A.
Keller, Mary Barnett
Kelly, David A.
Lawrence, James T.
Lewis, Anthony Harold, Jr.
Lewis, Arthur A.
Lokeman, Joseph R.
Loving, Albert A., Jr.
Lucas, Leo Alexander
Lucas, Maurice F.
Maple, Goldie M.
Martin, Walter L.
Matthews, Dorothy
McDuffie, Joseph deLeon, Jr.
McGuirt, Milford W.
McKinzie-Harper, Barbara A.
McMillian, Jimmy, Jr.
Miller, George Carroll, Jr.
Miller, Lori E.
Mills, Glenn B., Jr.
Mitchell, Bert Norman
Mitchell, Judson, Jr.
Mohamed, Gerald R., Jr.
Moore, Charles W.
Moore, Gary E.
Morgan, Robert, Jr.
Munson, Eddie Ray
Newkirk, Thomas H.
Newman, Kenneth J.
O'Ferrall, Anne F.
Owens, Treka Elaine
Parnell, William Cornellus, Jr.
Petersen, Allan Ernest
Pleasant, Albert E., III
Prezeau, Louis E.
Price, Albert H.
Proctor, Leonard D.
Rackley, Lurma M.
Robinson, Robert Love, Jr.
Ross, Frank Kenneth
Sanderson, Randy Chris
Scott, Leon Leroy
Scott, R. Lee
Session, Johnny Frank
Silver, Horace Ward Martin Tavares
Simpson, Joyce Michelle
Sims, Naomi R.
Slash, Joseph A.
Smalls, Marcella E.
Snaggs, Carmen

Stewart, Malcolm M.
Stewart, Robert L.
Stewart, Ronald Patrick
Swanigan, Jesse Calvin
Tarver, Elking
Taylor, Kenneth Matthew
Thompson, Jeffrey Earl
Thompson, Karen Ann
Tillman, Talmadge Calvin, Jr.
Todd, Orlando
Tong, Dalton Arlington
Toomer, Kenneth
Turner, Vivian Vanessa
Waldo, Carol Dunn
Wallace, Ronald Wilfred
Washington, Nancy Ann
Watson, Thomas S., Jr.
Wattley, Thomas Jefferson
White, Granville C.
Whiting, Emanuel
Whiting, Thomas J.
Whitmal, Nathaniel
Wiles, Spencer H.
Wilfong, Henry T., Jr.
Williams, Leroy Joseph
Williams, Londell
Williams, Morris O.
Williams, Rudy V.
Williams, Vernice Louise
Wilson, Ernest
Wilson, John E.
Witherspoon, R. Carolyn
Yarbrough, Roosevelt
Young, Raymond, Jr.

ACTING

Askew, Roger L.
Bailey, Pearl
Barnett, Etta Moten
Belafonte, Harry
Blacque, Taurean
Bonet, Lisa
Brown, Olivia
Browne, Roscoe Lee
Burton, Levar
Caesar, Harry
Capers, Eliza Virginia
Carroll, Diahann
Carroll, Vinnette
Carter, Nell
Childress, Alice
Clark, Rosalind K.
Coleman, Gary
Copage, Marc Diego
Cosby, William Henry
Covan, DeForest W.
Cowden, Michael E.
Davis, Clifton D.
Davis, Ossie
Davis, Sammy, Jr.
DeAnda, Peter
Duncan, Robert Todd
Elder, Lonne, III
Elliott, William David
Fields, Kim
Fisher, Gail
Fluellen, Joel M.
Foster, Frances Helen
Foster, Gloria
Freeman, Albert Cornelius, Jr.
Gibbs, Marla
Glass, Ronald
Glover, Danny
Gordone, Charles
Gossett, Louis, Jr.
Grandison, Earl Michael

Grier, David Alan
Guillaume, Robert
Guy, Jasmine
Hairston, Jester
Hall, Edward Clarence
Harewood, Dorian
Haynes, Samuel Lloyd
Hemsley, Sherman
Hendry, Gloria
Hicks, Hilly Gene
Hines, Gregory
Holliday, Jennifer
Horsford, Anna Maria
Hyman, Earle
Jackson, Spencer
Johnson, Rafer Lewis
Jones, Edith Irby
Jones, James Earl
King, Perry F.
Kingi, Henry Masao
Kitt, Eartha Mae
Knight-Pulliam, Keshia
Kotto, Yaphet Fredrick
LaBelle, Patti
Lange, Ted W., III
Lavergneau, Rene L.
LeNoire, Rosetta
Lewis, Emanuel
Little, Cleavon Jake
Love, Edward M., Jr.
Lowe, Jackie
Macbeth, Robert
Mack, Roderick O'Neal
MacLachlan, Janet A.
Marrs, Stella
Marshall, Donald James
Marshall, William Horace
Martin, D'Urville
May, Dickey R.
McCampbell, Ray Irvin
McEachin, James
McKee, Lonette
McNair, Barbara
Mitchell, Donald
Mitchell, Loften
Mitchell, Scoey
Montgomery, Barbara Curry
Moody, Lynne Gatlin
Moore, Melba
Morris, Greg
Murphy, Eddie
Nelson, Novella C.
Nelson-Holgate, Gail Evangelyn
Nicholas, Denise
Nicholas, Fayard Antonio
Nichols, Nichelle
Norman, Maidie Ruth (nee Gamble)
Parrish, Mary
Patten, Edward Roy (Cousin Eds)
Perry, Felton
Peters, Brock G.
Poitier, Sidney
Pounder, C. C. H.
Price, Gilbert
Rashad, Phylicia Ayers-Allen
Reese, Della
Reid, Tim
Rentie, Frieda
Reynolds, James Van
Richards, Beah
Robinson, Roger
Roker, Roxie
Rolle, Esther
Rollins, Howard E., Jr.
Ross, Diana
Roundtree, Richard

Russell, Nipsey
Scott, Larry B.
Sharp, Saundra
Shaw, Stan
Simmons, Emmett Bryson, III (Slim)
Spruill, James Arthur
Sullivan, J. Christopher
Thomas, Philip Michael
Townsend, Robert
Turner, Dain Cameron
Tyson, Cicely
Uggams, Leslie
Van Peebles, Mario
Van Peebles, Melvin
Vereen, Ben Augustus
Vincent, Irving H.
Walker, Charles
Walker, James C.
Warfield, Marcia
Warner, Malcolm-Jamal
Warren, Michael
Washington, Leroy
Weldon, Deborah (nee Morgan)
Whitaker, Mical Rozier
Williams, Billy Dee
Williams, Hal
Williams, Vanessa
Wilson, Demond
Wilson, Nancy
Winston, Hattie
Woodard, Alfre
Woods, Allie, Jr.

ACTIVISM, POLITICAL/ CIVIL/SOCIAL RIGHTS

Abebe, Ruby
Ardrey, Saundra Curry
Arnold, Helen E.
Barbee, Lloyd Augustus
Barfield, Clementine (nee Chism)
Bates, Daisy
Beckett, Charles Campbell
Bell, George
Bennett, Delores
Bennett, Maybelle Taylor
Billingsley, Orzell, Jr.
Borom, Lawrence H.
Bowman, William McKinley, Sr.
Bradley, M. Louise
Breeden, James Pleasant
Brown, Ronald H.
Brown, Rubye G.
Burgess, Robert E.
Carmichael, Stokely
Chargois, Jenelle M.
Clarke, Raymond
Cox, John Wesley
Current, Gloster Bryant
Daniels, Ron D.
Dansby, Jesse L., Jr.
Dauway, Lois McCullough
Dent, Thomas Covington
Dixon, Sharon Pratt
Du Bois, David Graham
Edelman, Marian Wright
Flanagan, Robert B., Sr.
Fletcher, Louisa Adaline
Fletcher, Robert E.
Francis, Livingston S.
Freeman, Kerlin, Jr.
Frye, Reginald Stanley
Gerald, Gilberto Ruben
Glanton, Sadye Lyerson
Greene, Sarah Moore

Hall, John Robert
Hamilton, John Joslyn, Jr.
Hashim, Mustafa
Head, Laura Dean
Hill, Cynthia D.
Hodges, Virgil Hall
Holt, Aline G.
Hope, Julius Caesar
Hunter, Howard Jacque, Jr.
Innis, Roy Emile Alfredo
Jackson, Grandvel Andrew
Johnson, Georgianna
Johnson, Gregory Wayne
Johnson, William A., Jr.
Jones, Hardi Liddell
Jones, Yvonne De Marr
Jordan, Bettye Davis
Joyner, Irving L.
Kee, Marsha Goodwin
Kelly, John Paul, Jr.
King, Coretta Scott (Mrs. Martin
    Luther King Jr.)
King, William L.
Lipscomb, Darryl L.
Marrs, Stella
Mathis, William Lawrence
McClellan, Edward J.
McCummings, LeVerne
McGill, Thomas L., Jr.
Mitchell, Robert Lee, Sr.
Moody, Anne
Nettles, John Spratt
Newman, Miller Maurice
Nickson, Sheila Joan
Norrell-Nance, Rosalind Elizabeth
Odom, Stonewall, II
O'Neal, Frederick Douglas
Osborne, Gwendolyn Eunice
Parks, Rosa
Peoples, Earl F., Sr.
Petett, Freddye
Powell, Addie Scott
Pritchard, Robert Starling, Jr.
Propes, Victor Lee
Reynolds, Nanette Lee (nee
    Smith)
Richardson, Linda Waters
Richie, Winston Henry
Rodgers, Anthony Recarido, Sr.
Ross, Winston A.
Shoemaker, Veronica Sapp
Simmons, Albert Bufort, Jr.
Small, Kenneth Lester
Smith, Conrad P.
Smith, Tommie M.
Sowell, Thomas
Spicer, Kenneth, Sr.
Staupers, Mabel Keaton
Stent, Michelle Dorene
Swindell, Warren C.
Talbot, Gerald Edgerton
Williamson-Ige, Dorothy Kay
Wilson, Margaret Bush

ACTUARIAL SCIENCE
Parker, Herbert Gerald
Webb, James O.

ADVERTISING/
PROMOTION
See also MANAGEMENT/
ADMINISTRATION—
ADVERTISING/
MARKETING/PUBLIC
RELATIONS
Abney, Robert
Alligood, Douglass Lacy
Anderson, Al H., Jr.
Anderson, Bryan N.
Anderson, Harold
Anderson, Marjorie
Bailer, Bonnie Lynn
Bailey, Curtis Darnell
Beatty, Robert L.
Bell, Raleigh Berton
Bervin-Mitchell, Gabrielle
Black, Don Gene
Black, Joseph
Blackburn, Alberta
Blackshear, William
Blackwell, Patricia A.
Blake, J. Paul
Boston, Archie, Jr.

Bowen, Ruth J.
Bradley, Melvin L.
Brockett, Ronald
Brookins, Bonita Coleman
Brown, Floyd A.
Brown, Mary Elizabeth
Brown, Robert Joe
Burrell, Thomas J.
Burris, Bertram Ray
Calhoun, Lillian Scott
Cannon, Davita Louise
Carnegie, Randolph David
Carroll, Robert F.
Chargois, Jenelle M.
Clemendor, Anthony A., IV
Clipper, Milton Clifton, Jr.
Cooper, Winston Lawrence
Cox, Ronnie
Cullers, Vincent T.
Cushingberry, George, Jr.
Dale, Robert J.
Darden, Thomas V.
Dixon, George
Doughty, Glenn Martin
Drakes, Muriel B.
Driver, Richard Sonny, Jr.
Duncan, Lynda J.
Early, Sybil Theresa
Eatman, Brenda Alene
Eaton, Tyrone
Edwards, John Loyd, III
Edwards, Oscar Lee
Evans, Alicia
Gallager, Mike John
Giles, Althea B.
Giles, William R.
Goodson, James Abner, Jr.
Graves, Valerie Jo
Gray, Andrew Jackson
Gray, Charles Henry
Gray, Robert R.
Greenidge, James Ernest
Greenlee, Robert Douglass
Grinstead, Amelia Ann
Gunn, Vera
Guy, Lygia Brown
Hall, Shirley Robinson
Harper, Beverly A.
Harris, Ray, Sr.
Hartaway, Thomas N., Jr.
Haskins, Michael Kevin
Haynes, Eleanor Louise
Herring, Leonard, Jr.
Hervey, Ramon Triche, II
Heyward, Isaac
Hill, Kenneth D.
Hite, Nancy Ursula
Holland, J. Archibald
Hubbard, Marilyn French
Hudson, Keith
Hudson, Lincoln Theodore
Humphrey, James Philip
Hyman, George E.
Jackson, Donald J.
Jackson, Karl Don
Jackson, Warren G.
Jackson, Yvette P.
James, Joyce L.
Johnican, Minerva Jane
Johnson, Donna Alligood
Johnson, Herbert M.
Johnson, Michele
Johnson, Tammy Adele
Jones, Caroline Robinson
Jones, DeVerges Booker
Jones, Lafayette Glenn
Jones, Richmond Addison
Jones, Samuel
Jordan, Thurman
Kaiser, Inez Yeargan
Kelley, Robert W.
Kennedy, Theodore Reginald
Lanier, Bob
Lattimore, Everett Carrigan
Leatherwood, Robert P.
LeDuff, Stephanie Carmel
Lee, Theodosia L. Crawford
Locklin, James R.
Lockman-Brooks, Linda
Maddox, Margaret Johnnetta
    Simms
Martin, Joel P.
Matlock, Kent
Matney, William C., Jr.

Matthews, Dorothy
McLendon, John B., Jr.
Mickens, Maxine
Miller, Oliver O.
Mingo, Frank L.
Moore, Anthony Louis
Moore, Lenard Duane
Morgan, Sharon Antonia
Morrison, Charles Edward
Morton, Patsy Jennings
Murray, R. A.
Napper, Berenice Norwood
Norris, Eugene
Palmore, Lynne A. Janifer
Parker, Darwin Carey
Passmore, Juanita (nee Carter)
Peck, Gregory Lester
Pender, Melvin
Phillips, Colette Alice-Maude
Rainey, Sylvia Valentine
Rawles, Elizabeth Gibbs
Roach, Deloris
Roberts, Donald Lee
Robinson, Martha Delores
Rogers-Bell, Mamie Lee
Roper, Patricia Anderson
Rucker, Reginald J. (Reggie)
Ryan-White, Jewell
Saddler, William E.
Sampson, Ronald Alvin
Sellers, Theresa Ann
Sengstacke, Whittier Alexander,
    Sr.
Shamwell, Joe
Sharp, James Alfred
Simpson, Joyce Michelle
Slaughter, Vernon L.
Smalley, Paul
Smith, Janice Evon
Smith, Norman Raymond
Smith, Oscar Samuel, Jr.
Sosa, Catherine A. E.
Spicer, Carmelita
Stackhouse, E. Marilyn
Stith, Melvin Thomas
Stone, Reese J., Jr.
Summerour-Perry, Lisa
Taylor, Arthur Duane
Thomas, Janis P.
Thompson, Lowell Dennis
Thompson, Tawana Sadiela
Tobin, Patricia L.
Todd, Cynthia Jean
Utley, Richard Henry
Venson, John E.
Waites, Shirley Jean
Watson, Constance A.
Wheeler, Patricia A.
Williams, Hilda Yvonne
Williams, Maxine Broyles
Williams, Terrie Michelle
Wilson, Jacqueline Prophet
Wilson, Jon
Wright, Albert Walter, Jr.
Wright, Benjamin Hickman
Wright, Joseph H., Jr.

AEROSPACE
See ENGINEERING—
AEROSPACE

AGRIBUSINESS
Brooks, Henry Marcellus
Edwards, Kenneth J.
Gray, Clarence Cornelius, III
Jackson, Janice Tudy
Lockhart, Verdree
Lynn, Louis B.
Snyder, George W.
Taylor, Leonard Wayne
Walton, Cedar Anthony
Wharton, Ferdinand D., Jr.

AGRICULTURAL
SCIENCE
Bankett, William Daniel
Batten, Grace Ruth
Broadnax, Madison
Brooks, Carolyn Branch
Finney, Essex Eugene, Jr.
Foster, Alvin Garfield
Gray, Clarence Cornelius, III

Johnson, Walter Lee
Lewis, Ephron H.
Lynn, Louis B.
Mason, Jesse W.
Mayes, McKinley
McKinley, Ray E.
Meade, Alston B.
Monk, Edd Dudley
Neufville, Mortimer H.
Raby, Clyde T.
Warren, Herman Lecil
White, Jimmie L.
Williams, Howard Copeland
Williamson, Handy, Jr.

AIRLINE INDUSTRY
See TRANSPORTATION/
MOVING SERVICES

ANTHROPOLOGY
Bolles, A. Lynn
Bond, George Clement
Brown, Barri Anne
Cobb, W. Montague
Diggs, Irene
Garrett, Romeo Benjamin
Gwaltney, John L.
Hodges, David Julian
Jackson, Reginald Leo
Johnson, Norris Brock
Kennedy, Theodore Reginald
Mitchell-Kernan, Claudia Irene
Monagan, Alfrieta Parks
Pounds, Moses B.
Rashford, John Harvey
Robinson, Leonard Harrison, Jr.
Shack, William A.
Walker, Sheila Suzanne
Williams, Melvin D.

ARCHAEOLOGY
Lewis, Samella (nee Sanders)
Nichols, Elaine

ARCHITECTURE
Allain, Leon Gregory
Anderson, Carey Laine, Jr.
Archie, James Lee
Artis, Anthony Joel
Bates, William J.
Bell, Earnest Franklin
Bond, James Max, Jr.
Bridges, Leon
Brown, John Scott
Brown, Leroy J. H.
Bruner, Van B., Jr.
Bruton, Bertram A.
Bryant, Anxious E.
Bryant, Robert Edward
Campbell, Emory Shaw
Campbell, George Lynn
Campbell, Wendell J.
Chaffers, James A.
Chase, John S.
Cherry, Edward Earl, Sr.
Clark, Randolph A.
Coles, Robert Traynham
Coxe, William Haddon
Craigwell, Hadyn H.
Davis, William E., Sr.
Devrouax, Paul S., Jr.
Dodd, James C.
Dozier, Richard K.
Dykes, DeWitt Sanford
Ford, Ausbra
Franklin, Benjamin
Fry, Louis Edwin, Jr.
Gantt, Harvey Bernard
Goodwin, Robert T., Sr.
Hammond, Kenneth T.
Harris, Gleason Ray
Harris, Nelson A.
Harris, Oscar Lewis
Haywood, Norcell D.
Hermanuz, Ghislaine
Howard, Milton L.
Hoyte, Lenon Holder (Aunt Len)
Isaac, Yvonne Renee
Jackson, Earl K., Sr.
Johnson, Jeh Vincent
Johnson, Marion I.
Jolly, Marva Lee

Jones, James Bennett
Lee, Kermit J., Jr.
Ligon, Doris Hillian
Madison, Robert P.
Margerum, Roger Williams
Martin, Ionis Bracy
McDonald, Herbert G.
McKissack, Leatrice B.
McKissack, William Deberry
Miner, William Gerard
Mitchell, Melvin Lester
Morgan, Robert Lee
Moutoussamy, John W.
Norwood, Tom
Overstreet, Harry L.
Posey, Ronald Anthony
Price, Alfred Douglas
Ramsey, Charles Edward, Jr.
Raymond, Phillip Gregory
Robinson, Harry G., III
Robinson, James L.
Southern, Herbert B.
Stull, Donald L.
Sulton, John D.
Sutton, Sharon Egretta
Switzer, Lucious
Taylor, Edward Walter
Thurston, William A.
Tuckett, LeRoy E.
White, Donald F.
Whitley, William N.
Wilburn, Victor H.
Williams, Harold Louis
Wilson, Carl L.
Wilson, John Louis
Wilson, Robert L.
Woodridge, Wilson Jack, Jr.

ART, VISUAL—
ANIMATION
Brandon, Brumsic, Jr.
Oubre, Hayward Louis

ART, VISUAL—
COMMERCIAL ART/
GRAPHIC DESIGN
Anderson, Chester R.
Archie, James Lee
Benson, Rubin Author
Carnegie, Randolph David
Conway, Wallace Xavier, Sr.
Dabbs, Henry Erven
Donaldson, Jeff R.
Ferguson, Cecil (Duke)
Fraser, Jean Ethel
Graham, Mariah
Grist, Raymond
Higgins, Stann
Hill, Kenneth Randal
Jones, Richmond Addison
Kelley, William Melvin
Marshall, Frank Britt, III
Morning, John Frew, Jr.
Nelson, Eileen A.
Porter, Carol Denise
Prelow, Arleigh
Robinson, Peter Lee, Jr.
Sampler, Marion
Tunstall-Grant, Ruth Neal
Winbush, LeRoy

ART, VISUAL—
ILLUSTRATION
Adams, Jackie W., Sr.
Barkley, Rufus, Jr.
Blayton-Taylor, Betty
Brandon, Brumsic, Jr.
Brooks, Bernard W.
Brown, Buck
Brown, Margery Wheeler
Coxe, G. Caliman
Cummings, Pat Marie
Fax, Elton C.
Granger, Edwina C.
Joans, Ted
Johnson, Charles Richard
Lawrence, Jacob A.
McCannon, Dindga Fatima
Pinkney, Jerry
Ruffins, Reynolds
Steptoe, John Lewis

ART, VISUAL— PAINTING

Andrews, Benny
Banjo, Casper
Banks, Ellen
Banks, Jerry L.
Barnes, Ernest Eugene, Jr.
Bey, Ben
Borders, Michael G.
Bowling, Frank
Brown, Malcolm McCleod
Browne, Vivian E.
Burke, Yvonne Brathwaite
Burns, Ronald Melvin
Cade, Walter, III
Carter, Nanette Carolyn
Catchings, Yvonne Parks
Clark, Claude Lockhart
Clark, Edward
Clay, Cliff
Collins, Paul
Conway, Wallace Xavier, Sr.
Coppedge, Arthur L.
Cortor, Eldzier
Dabbs, Henry Erven
Daniel, Mary Reed
Davis, Donald Fred
DePillars, Murry Norman
Dotson, Philip Randolph
Douglas, Elizabeth Asche
Edmonds, Josephine E.
Felton, Zora Belle
Gammon, Reginald Adolphus
Gilliam, Sam, Jr.
Granger, Edwina C.
Grigsby, Jefferson Eugene, Jr.
Grist, Raymond
Guyton, Tyree
Harden, Marvin
Hayes, Vertis
Hegwood, William Lewis
High, Freida
Hinton, Alfred Fontaine
Howard, Humbert Lincoln
Joans, Ted
Jones, Calvin Bell
Jones, Lois Mailou
Lane, Julius Forbes
Lawrence, Jacob A.
Lee-Smith, Hughie
Leonard, Leon Lank, Sr.
Logan, Juan Leon
Maynard, Valerie J.
McCannon, Dindga Fatima
McCullough, Geraldine
McGathon, Carrie M.
McMillan, James C.
Mitchell, Corinne Howard
Morrison, Keith Anthony
Nelson, Eileen A.
Norman, Bobby Don
Onli, Turtel
Oubre, Hayward Louis
Padgett, James A.
Pierce, Delilah W.
Reid, Robert Dennis
Ringgold, Faith
Searles, Charles R.
Smith, Vincent D.
Thompson, Frances E.
Washington, James W., Jr.
West, Pheoris
Whyte, Garrett
Wilson, Sandra E.
Woods, Roosevelt, Jr.
Wright, Dmitri
Young, Charles Alexander

ART, VISUAL— SCULPTING

Arkansaw, Tim
Barthe, Richmond
Borden, Harold F., Jr.
Catlett, Elizabeth
Clark, Edward
Davidson, Earnest Jefferson
Foreman, Doyle
Geran, Joseph, Jr.
Guyton, Tyree
Gwaltney, John L.
Hamilton, Edward N., Jr.
Hardison, Ruth Inge
Hayes, Vertis
Hodgson-Brooks, Gloria J.

Hunt, Richard Howard
Jordan, Eddie Jack, Sr.
Maynard, Valerie J.
McCullough, Geraldine
McMillan, James C.
Padgett, James A.
Paige, Alvin
Parker, Edward Everett
Stark, Shirley J.
Taylor, Michael Loeb
Washington, James W., Jr.
Weil, Robert L.
Williams, Chester Lee
Wilson, Ed
Wilson, Stanley Charles

ART, VISUAL—NOT ELSEWHERE CLASSIFIED

Adams, John Oscar
Anderson, Amelia Veronica
Arnold, Ralph M.
Ashley-Harris, Dolores B.
Asma, Thomas M.
Ausby, Ellsworth Augustus
Bailey, Calvin
Benjamin, Donald S.
Bennett, Julia Hubert
Billops, Camille J.
Boghossian, Skunder
Bontemps, Jacqueline Marie Fonvielle
Borden, Harold F., Jr.
Braithwaite, Gordon L.
Bright, Alfred Lee
Campbell, James A.
Carter, Allen D.
Carter, Ora Williams
Carter, Yvonne P.
Catlett, Elizabeth
Claye, Charlene Marette
Cooley, Nathan J.
Cortor, Eldzier
Crouther, Betty Jean
Cruz, Emilio
DeKnight, Avel
D'Hue, Robert R., Jr.
Dickerson, Glenda J.
Dunnigan, Jerry
Ealey, Adolphus
Edmonds, Josephine E.
Epting, Marion
Euell, Julian Thomas
Fraser, Jean Ethel
Gaskin, Leroy
Gilchriest, Lorenzo
Gilliam, Sam, Jr.
Gilliard, Joseph Wadus
Gordon, Allan M.
Griffin, Louis G., III
Grist, Raymond
Haines, Charles Edward
Harris, Helen B.
Harrison, Pearl Lewis
Head, Helaine
Hendricks, Barkley L.
Hill, Jacqueline R.
Hogu, Barbara J. Jones
Huggins, Hazel Renfroe
Irmagean
Jackson, Reginald Leo
Jessup, Marsha Edwina
Johnson, Rita Falkener
Jones, Ben F.
Jones, Calvin Bell
King-Hammond, Leslie
LaGrone, Clarence Oliver
Lark, Raymond
Lee, Tyronne T.
Lee-Smith, Hughie
Lewis, Elma I.
Maynard, Valerie J.
McCoy, Walter D.
Montgomery, Evangeline Juliet
Olugebefola, Ademola
Outterbridge, John Wilfred
Owens, Andi
Owens, Wallace, Jr.
Pannell, Patrick Weldon
Patterson, Curtis Ray
Pinckney, Stanley
Pindell, Howardena D.
Pitts, Gregory Philip
Powell, Georgette Seabrooke

Richardson, Frank (Mr. Frank)
Saar, Betye I.
Satterfield, Floyd
Scott, John T.
Shifflett, Lynne Carol
Sills, Thomas Albert
Simms, Carroll Harris
Simon, Jewel Woodard
Simpson, Merton Daniel
Smith, Alfred J., Jr.
Smith, Vincent D.
Styles, Freddie L.
Taylor, Michael Loeb
Temple, Herbert
Terrell, Mable Jean
Thompson, Lowell Dennis
Todd, Charles O.
Tunstall-Grant, Ruth Neal
Walker, George Edward
White, Clarence Dean
Williams, Daniel Salu
Wilson, Stanley Charles
Winston, Dennis Ray
Woodruff, Hale A.
Woods, Jessie A.

ASSOCIATION MANAGEMENT

Abebe, Ruby
Abernathy, Ralph David
Adair, Andrew A.
Adams, Gregory Keith
Adams, Martin P.
Adams, Quinton Douglas
Adams, V. Toni
Addison, Caroline Elizabeth
Alexander, Alma Duncan
Alexander, Harry Toussaint
Alexander, John Stanley
Alexander, Mervin Franklin
Alexander, Sidney H., Jr.
Alexander, Warren Dornell
Alford, Brenda
Ali, Rasheedah Ziyadah
Allen, Alexander J.
Allen, James Trinton
Allen, Terrell Allison, III
Alston, Denise Adele
Alston, Floyd William
Alston, Harry L.
Alston, Robert Milton, Jr.
Ambrose, Ethel L.
Anderson, Carl D.
Anderson, Louise Payne
Anderson, Mary Elizabeth
Anderson, Michael Wayne
Archie, Shirley Franklin
Arthos, John
Ashcraft, Bernard
Ashford, Laplois
Ashley, Lillard Governor
Atkinson, Whittier C.
Avent, Jacques Myron
Ayensu, Edward Solomon
Aziz, Kareem A.
Bacon, Barbara Crumpler
Bacon, William Louis
Baker, Oscar Wilson
Ballard, Janet Jones
Banks, Waldo R., Sr.
Barefield, Ollie Delores
Barfield, Leila Millford
Barkstall, Vernon L.
Barrow, Willie B.
Bateman, Celeste Anne
Bates, Clayton Wilson, Jr.
Batteast, Margaret W.
Battle, Mark G.
Battle, Turner Charles, III
Baxter, Augustus, Sr.
Beasley, Arlene Audrey
Bell, Earnest Franklin
Bell, H. B.
Bell, Thom R.
Bellinger, Harold
Belton, Howard G.
Benjamin, Rose Mary
Benton, Leonard D.
Bessent, Hattie
Bevel, James Luther
Billups, Myles E., Sr.
Binns, Silas Odell
Bins, Milton

Bishop, Clarence
Black, Wendell C.
Blackburn, Alberta
Blair, Charles Michael
Blanding, Larry
Blanton, James B., III
Blockson, Charles L.
Bogard, Hazel Zinamon
Bolden, Charles E.
Boon, Ina M.
Boone, Clarence Wayne
Bostic, Dorothy
Boulware, Patricia A.
Bradley, James George
Bradley, Walter Thomas, Jr.
Braithwaite, Gordon L.
Brame, Walter Melvyn
Branch, George
Brantley, Edward J.
Braxton, Harriet E.
Breeding, Carl L.
Bridgeman, Donald Earl
Bridgewater, Paul
Briscoe, Sidney Edward, Jr.
Brock, Lila Mae
Brodis, Nellie Fannie
Brooks, James O'Neil
Brothers, Edith
Broussard, Leroy
Brown, Annie Gibson
Brown, Clarence William
Brown, Claudell, Jr.
Brown, Henry H.
Brown, Philip Rayfield, III
Brown, Richard
Brown, William J.
Brown, William McKinley, Jr.
Bryant, Delores Hall E.
Bryant, Jerome Benjamin
Bryant, Jesse A.
Bunte, Doris
Burgess, Dwight A.
Burnett, Mary Coghill
Burney, Harry L., Jr.
Burt, James E.
Burton, Joan E.
Bush, Lenoris
Butler, B. Janelle
Butler, Patrick Hampton
Butler, Rebecca Batts
Byrd, W. Michael
Cabbell, Edward Joseph
Caesar, Lois
Caldwell, Edwin L., Jr.
Calomee, Annie E.
Campbell, James W.
Cannon, Edith H.
Canson, Virna M.
Carey, Audrey L.
Carey, Howard H.
Carey, Milton Gales
Cargile, C. B., Jr.
Carroll, Sally G.
Carson, Loftus C.
Carter, Gilbert Lino
Carter, Jesse Lee, Sr.
Carter, John R.
Carter, Martin Joseph
Carter, Robert Thompson
Carter, Ruth Durley
Carter, Weptanomah Washington
Carter, Willie A.
Carthan, Eddie James
Cassis, Glenn Albert
Caswell, Catheryne Willis
Chapman, Frank
Chapman, Julius
Chenault, Myron Maurice
Cherry, Lee Otis
Cherry, Robert Lee
Childs, Oliver Bernard, Sr.
Childs, Theodore Francis
Christian, Jerald Cronis
Clanton, Earl Spencer, III
Clark, Jesse B., III
Clark, Mamie Phipps
Clark, Ronald C.
Clark, Theodore Lee
Clarke, Everee Jimerson
Clayton, Lloyd E.
Clayton, Willie Burke, Jr.
Cleveland, Tessie Anita Smith
Coachman, Winfred Charles
Cobb, Charles E.

Cobb, Nathaniel E.
Coffee, Lawrence Winston
Colbert, Ernest, Sr.
Coleman, Herman W.
Coleman, Louis H.
Coles, Joseph C.
Collins, Bonietha Inez
Collins, Constance Renee Wilson
Collins, Paul L.
Collins, Rosecrain
Colston, Monroe James
Colvin, Alonza James
Connor, Dolores Lillie
Cook, Toni Rae
Cooke, Wilce L.
Cooks, Stoney
Cooper, Augusta Mosley
Cooper, Earl, II (Skip)
Cooper, Edward L., Sr.
Cooper, Matthew N.
Cooper, Merrill Pittman
Cooper, William B.
Copeland, Kathleen (nee Maxwell)
Copeland, Mary Shawn
Copelin, Sherman Nathaniel, Jr.
Cornish, Betty W.
Corrin, Malcolm L.
Coyle, Mary Dee
Craig, Claude Burgess
Crawford, Charles L.
Crawford, James Wesley
Crenshaw, Reginald Anthony
Crouther, Melvin S., Jr.
Crutcher, Edward Torrence
Cummings, James C., Jr.
Curry, Jerry Ralph
Dade, Malcolm G., Jr.
Dailey, Thelma
Daniel, Phillip T. K.
Daniels, William Orlan
Dark, Lawrence Jerome
Davies, Marvin
Davis, Bobby
Davis, Clarence
Davis, Frederick D.
Davis, John Alexander
Davis, John W., III
Davis, Major
Davis, Marvin Coolidge
Davis, Mary-Agnes Miller
Davis, Patricia C.
Davis, Robert E.
Davis, William L.
Dawson, Leonard Ervin
Dean, Willie B.
DeAugustino-Todd, Loyce
DeBerry, Lois Marie
Delaney, Harold
Delaney, Willi
Delany, Holly Diane
Dember, Jean Wilkins
Denning, Bernadine Newsom
Derr, Gilbert S.
Dickerson, Bette Jeanne
Dixon, George
Dobson, Helen Sutton
Dobynes, Elizabeth
Dockery, Richard L.
Dockett, Alfred B.
Dooley, Wallace Troy
Dorsey, Harold Aaron
Dortch, Thomas Wesley, Jr.
Douglas, Walter Edmond
Dowe, Ralph M.
Dreher, Lucille G.
Drew, Thelma Lucille
Driggriss, Daphne Bernice Sutherland
Drungo, Elbert, Jr.
DuBois, Asa Stephen
Dukes, Hazel N.
Dukes, Walter Lucuis
Duncan, Geneva
Duncan, Ruby
Duplessis, Harry Y.
Durley, Alexander
Dymally, Lynn V.
Eaton, Patricia Frances
Ecton, Virgil E.
Eddington, Herbert Hoover
Edelin, Ramona Hoage
Edelman, Marian Wright

Edley, Christopher F., Sr.
Edwards, Al E.
Edwards-Aschoff, Patricia Joann
Eichelberger, Brenda
Eiland, Ray Maurice
Elam, Hattie Briscoe
Elcock, Claudius Adolphus Rufus
Elder, Almora Kennedy
Ellis, Effie O'Neal
Ellis, P. J.
Epps, C. Roy
Epps, Dolzie C. B.
Epps, Naomi Newby
Ethridge, Samuel B.
Evans, Amos James
Evans, Samuel London
Evans, Webb
Evers, Myrlie
Ewing, Barbara Lee
Fair, Talmadge W.
Farmer, Clarence
Farmer, James
Fattah, Falaka
Feggans, Edward L.
Felton, James A.
Fields, M. Joan
Finney, John H.
Finnie, Rogers L., Sr.
Fisher, E. Carleton
Fisher, Shelley Marie
Fitzpatrick, Julia C.
Fitzpatrick, William J.
Flagg, Joseph H.
Flateau, John
Fletcher, Arthur Allen
Flewellen, Icabod
Floyd, Jeremiah
Fluker, Phillip A.
Ford, Kenneth A.
Ford, William L., Jr.
Forde, James Albert
Foster, Andrew D.
Foster, James H.
Foster, Robert Davis
Fowler, Queen Dunlap
Fox, William K.
Francis, Cheryl Margaret
Francis, Livingston S.
Franklin, Eugene T., Jr.
Frazier, Adolphus Cornelious
Frazier, Eufaula Smith
Freeman, Kerlin, Jr.
French, George Wesley
Frost, Hugh A.
Fuller, Dewey C.
Futrell, Mary Hatwood
Gainey, Leonard Dennis, II
Gaither, Edmund B.
Gales, James
Gamble, Janet Helen
Garrett, Cheryl Ann
Garrison, Esther F.
Gaskin, Leonard O.
Gaston, Linda Saulsby
German, Ann Louise
Gibson, Elvis Edward
Gifford, Bernard R.
Givins, Abe, Jr.
Glanton, Luther T., Jr.
Glaude, Stephen A.
Goff, Wilhelmina Delores
Golden, Samuel Lewis
Goliday, Willie V.
Gomez, Kevin Lawrence Johnson
Goode, Malvin R.
Goode, Victor M.
Goodman, George D.
Gordon, Bertha Comer
Gordon, Robert L.
Gorman, Gertrude Alberta
Goslee, Leonard Thomas
Goss, William Epp
Graham, Saundra M.
Gravely, Melvin J.
Gray, Leo Milton, Jr.
Gray, Raymond Leroy, Sr.
Greene, Mamie Louise
Griffey, Dick
Griffin, Thomas J.
Grinstead, Amelia Ann
Gunter, Laurie
Hairston, Rowena L.
Hale, Gene
Hall, Kim Felicia
Hall, Raymond A.

Hambrick, Harold E., Jr.
Hamlar, Portia Y. T.
Hammond, Ulysses S., Jr.
Handy, William T., Jr.
Hardeman, Strotha E., Jr.
Hardy, Dorothy C.
Hardy, Freeman
Hargrave, Thomas Burkhardt, Jr.
Harmon, Sherman Allen
Harper, Mary Starke
Harper, Neville W.
Harris, Burnell
Harris, Howard F.
Harris, James A.
Harris, Lester L.
Harris, Robert Eugene Peyton
Harvey, Jacqueline U.
Hasan, Aqeel Khatib
Hashim, Mustafa
Haskins, William J.
Hatcher, Lillian
Hawkes, Diana R.
Hayes, Richard C.
Haynes, George Edmund, Jr.
Haynes, Ora Lee
Hazard, Benjamin W.
Head, Edith
Headley, De Costa Oneal
Heath, Bertha Clara
Height, Dorothy I.
Hemphill, Gwendolyn
Henderson, James Robert
Henry, Aaron E.
Henry, Alberta (nee Hill)
Heyward, Don H.
Hill, Fannie E.
Hill, James L.
Hill, Mary Alice
Hill, Robert Bernard
Hill, Velma Murphy
Hillman, Gracia
Hillsman, Gerald C.
Hinch, Andrew Lewis, Sr.
Hines, Carl R., Sr.
Hinton, Floyd
Hixson, Judson Lemoine
Hobbs, John Daniel
Hodges, Edward N., III
Hodges, Harold Earl
Holder, Julius H.
Hollingsworth, Pierre
Hollis, Mary Lee
Hollowell, Donald L.
Holmes, Carl
Holmes, Wendell P., Jr.
Holt, Aline G.
Hooks, Frances Dancy
Hopson, Melvin Clarence
Horton, Stella Jean
Howard, Ellen D.
Howard, Milton L.
Howard, Norman Leroy
Howell, Laurence A.
Howell, Robert J., Jr.
Hubbard, Marilyn French
Hubbard, Paul Leonard
Hudson, Winson
Huffman, Jasper Jefferson, III
Huffman, Rufus C.
Huggins, Hosiah, Jr.
Hughes, Hollis Eugene, Jr.
Humphrey, Hubert Grant
Hunter, Harriet Louise
Hunter, Robert J.
Hurdle, Velma B. Brooks
Hurley, Ruby
Hurst, Beverly J.
Hurt, Louis T., Sr.
Hutchinson, Jerome
Hutchinson, Louise Daniel
Ingram, Earl Girardeau
Ismial, Salaam Ibn
Jackson, Arthur D., Jr.
Jackson, Bernard H.
Jackson, Charles N., II
Jackson, Clarence H.
Jackson, Claude
Jackson, Emory Napoleon (Sippy)
Jackson, Jesse Louis
Jackson, Keith M.
Jackson, Leo A.
Jackson, Leo Edwin
Jackson, Mattie J.
Jackson, Maxie C.

Jackson, Norman A.
Jackson, Robert E.
Jackson, Ronald G.
Jackson, Thomas Mitchell
Jackson, Tomi L.
Jacob, John Edward
James, Betty Harris
James, Bobby Charles
James, Raymond N.
Jefferson, Nancy B.
Jenkins, Cynthia
Jenkins, Roger J.
Jeter, Clifton B., Jr.
Johnson, Arthur L.
Johnson, Bill Wade
Johnson, Edna DeCoursey
Johnson, F. J., Jr.
Johnson, Gene C.
Johnson, Geneva B.
Johnson, Genevieve N.
Johnson, Jondelle H.
Johnson, Joyce Colleen
Johnson, Leon, Jr.
Johnson, Lorraine Jefferson
Johnson, Louise Mason
Johnson, Marion T.
Johnson, Roosevelt, Jr.
Johnson, Samuel Harrison
Johnson, Scott Edwin
Johnson, Waldo Emerson, Jr.
Johnson, William A., Jr.
Jones, Alexander R.
Jones, Bernard H., Sr.
Jones, Carl L.
Jones, Effie Hall
Jones, Ervin Edward
Jones, George W.
Jones, James Randall
Jones, Johnnie Anderson
Jones, Lonzie L.
Jones, Nathaniel R.
Jones, Roscoe T., Jr.
Jones, Sam H., Sr.
Jones, Sidney Eugene
Jones, Theodore
Jones, Yvonne De Marr
Jordan, Anne Knight
Jordan, David Lee
Jordan, Frederick E.
Jordan, Josephine E.C.
Jordan, Marjorie W.
Jordan, Vernon E., Jr.
Joseph, James Alfred
Joseph-McIntyre, Mary
Joyner, Marjorie Stewart
Keith, Doris T.
Kelley, Daniel, Jr.
Kennedy, Cain James
Kennedy, Hays
Kennedy, Ola B.
Kidd, Herbert, Jr.
Kimbrough, Fred H.
King, Mattie M.
King, Ruby E.
King, William Carl
King, Yolanda D.
Kinloch, Jerome
Kirk, Phyllis O. (nee Williams)
Knight, Walter R.
Knowles, Malachi
Lackey, Edgar F.
LaCour, Nathaniel Hawthorne
Lafayette, Bernard, Jr.
Lamar, Cleveland James
Landry, Lawrence Aloysius
Landsmark, Theodore Carlisle
Lane, Richard (Dick Night-Train)
Larkins, John Rodman
Lawes, Verna
Lawrence, Edward
Lawrence, Erma Jean
Lawrence, John E.
Lawyer, Vivian (nee Moore)
Lee, Dorothea
Lee, Gloria A.
Lee, Oliver B.
Lee, Ritten Edward
Lee, Sheila Jackson
Leeke, John F.
Leeper, Ronald James
Leffall, LaSalle Doheny, Jr.
LeGrand, Yvette Marie
Lenoir, Henry
Levy, Valerie Lowe

Lewis, Anne A.
Lewis, Charles H.
Lewis, Erma (nee Duffy)
Lewis, Frederick Carlton
Lewis, Henry W.
Lewis, Lillian J.
Lewis, Robert Louis
Lewis, Stephen Christopher
Lieteau, Halvan Joseph
Lightfoot, Jean Drew
Lima, George Silva
Lindsey, S. L.
Liston, Hugh H.
Littleton, Arthur C.
Livingston, Jewel P.
Loche, Lee Edward
Locket, Arnold, Jr.
Lockhart, Robert W.
Lomax, Frank, III
Lomax, Pearl Cleage
Lomotey, Kofi
Long, Nate
Love, Ezekiel
Love, Roosevelt Sam
Lucas, Virgil Hilry
Luper, Clara M.
Lyles, Leonard E.
Lynch, Leon
Mack, Gordon H.
Mack, James E.
Mack, John W.
Majors, Edith Sara
Malloy, H. Rembert
Mann, Philip Melvin
Marshall, Etta Marie-Imes
Marshall, John Donald
Marshall, Timothy H.
Marshall, Warren
Martin, Annie B.
Martin, Arnold Lee, Jr.
Martin, Lawrence Raymond
Martin, Sylvia Cooke
Mason, Brenda Diane
Mason, DaCosta V.
Mason, Howard Keith
Mason, William Alfred
Mathis, Frank
Mathis, Sallye Brooks
Matthews, Wanda Denise
Maultsby, Dorothy M.
Maxey, Jo Ann (nee Strickland)
Maxwell-Reid, Daphne Etta
Mays, Dewey Orvric, Jr.
Mays, William, Jr.
Mbere, Aggrey Mxolisi
McAfee, Charles Francis
McAlpine, Robert
McCabe, Jewell Jackson
McCarthy, Fred
McClenic, Patricia Dickson
McClurkin, Johnson Thomas
McCray, Christopher Columbus
McCuller, James
McDonald, Bernard
McDonald, Willie Ruth Davis
McGaughy, Will
McGlothen, Goree
McGuire, Cyril A.
McKenzie, Wilford Clifton
McKinney, Gregory L.
McKnight, Lee Cassell
McKoy, John H.
McLawhorn, James Thomas, Jr.
McNeely, Matthew
McPhatter, Thomas H.
McRipley, G. Whitney
McSmith, Blanche Preston
Mease, Quentin R.
Mehreteab, Ghebre-Selassie
Melton, Frank LeRoy (Globe)
Merritt, Willette T.
Merton, Joseph Lee
Metoyer, Rosia G.
Meyers, Michael
Michel, Harriet R.
Mickey, Gordon Eugene
Mikell, Charles D.
Miles, Willie Leanna
Miller, Anna M.
Miller, Evelyn B.
Miller, Joseph Herman
Miller, Mattie Sherryl
Miller, Ray, Jr.
Miller, William Nathaniel

Miller, William O.
Mills, Hughie E.
Mims, George E.
Mincey, W. James
Minor, Deborah Ann
Minter, Steven Alan
Minter, Wilbert Douglas, Sr.
Mitchell, Bush P.
Mitchell, Daniel B.
Mitchell, Stanley Henryk
Mitchell, William Grayson
Mitchell, William P.
Modeste, Leon Edgar
Monk, Edd Dudley
Montgomery, Dwight Ray
Montgomery, Fred O.
Montgomery, Willie Henry
Moore, Susie M.
Moore, Winston E.
Moorman, Clinton R. (Bob)
Morgan, Mary H. Ethel
Morrisey, Jimmy
Morrison, Samuel F.
Morse, Mildred (nee Sharpe)
Morse, Warren W.
Muhammad, Shirley M.
Murphy, Jeanne Claire
Murray, Thomas Azel
Murrell, Charlayne E.
Myers, Samuel L.
Nabors, Jesse Lee, Sr.
Nabrit, Samuel M.
Neal, James S.
Neblett, Richard F.
Nelson, Richard Y., Jr.
Newman, David, Jr.
Newsome, Steven Cameron
Newton, James Douglas, Jr.
Newton, Melvin T.
Nichols, LeRoy
Nix, Theophilus Richard
Nixon, James Melvin
Njiiri, Ruth Stutts
Noisette, Ruffin N.
Norman, Moses C.
Norris, Cynthia Clarice
Norwood, Calvin Coolidge
O'Bannon, Alvin Jamal
O'Bryan, James Alvanley, Jr.
O'Kain, Roosevelt
Osibin, Willard S.
Overton, Volma Robert
Owens-Smith, Joyce Latrell
Palmer, Edward
Palmer, Elliott B., Sr.
Parker, Henry Ellsworth
Parker, Jean L. (nee Lane)
Patterson, Barbara Ann
Patterson, Jacqueline J.
Patton, William C.
Peeples, Audrey Rone
Peltier, Arma Martin
Penn, Charles E.
Penn, Luther
Perkins, John M.
Peterson, Alan Herbert
Peterson, Marcella Tandy
Petrie, Harry R.
Phears, William D.
Phillips, Barbara (nee Kinard)
Phillips, Earmia Jean
Picott, J. Rupert
Pinckney, James
Piper, Carol Vardiman
Pires, Laura J.
Pittman, Ineva (nee May)
Pitts, M. Henry
Polk, Richard A.
Pollard, William E.
Pompey, Charles Spencer
Porter, Yvonne
Powell, C. Clayton
Powell, Charles L., Jr.
Powell, Dudley Vincent
Powell, William J.
Power, Robert Cornelius
Pratt, Melvin Lemar
Preston, Eugene Anthony
Price, Elizabeth Louise
Price, Michael J.
Pride, Hemphill P., II
Pride, John L.
Prothro, Louise Robinson (nee Gray)

Pugh, Thomas Jefferson
Quarrelles, James Ivan
Quintyne, Irwin Sinclair
Radden, Thelma Gibson
Randolf, Alma Louise
Rankin, Charles I.
Ravenell, Joseph Phillip
Rayford, Brenda L.
Raymond, Phillip Gregory
Reagins, Ann Louvina
Reams-Whitmire, Vernetta Maria
Reed, Joe Louis
Reid, Charles H.
Rembert, Emma White
Remus, Eugene
Reynolds, James F.
Rhea, Michael
Rice, Cora Lee
Rice, David Eugene, Jr.
Richard, James L.
Richardson, Charles H., Jr.
Richardson, Linda Waters
Richardson, Rupert Florence
Ridley, Harry Joseph
Rivers, Dorothy
Rivers, Gary C.
Roach, Lee
Roane, Glenwood P.
Roberts, Leslie J.
Robinson, Albert M.
Robinson, Cleveland L.
Robinson, Denauvo M.
Robinson, George Ali
Robinson, Isaiah E.
Robinson, Kenneth Eugene
Robinson, Randall
Robinson, Renault A.
Rodriguez, Doris L.
Rodriguez, Lynne Roxanne
Rogers, Lawrence F.
Roscoe, Wilma J.
Ross, Joanne A.
Ross, Kevin Arnold
Ross, Mary Olivia
Ross, Regina D.
Rounsaville, Lucious Brown, Jr.
Rowe, Jimmy L.
Roxborough, Mildred (nee Bond)
Roy, Joe Eddie, Sr.
Ruffin, Benjamin S.
Russell, Ernest
Sanders, Delbert
Sanders, Lina (nee McCullers)
Sandler, Joan D.
Sarmiento, Shirley Jean
Saunders, James Warren
  (Choppy)
Saunders, Robert William, Sr.
Savage, Archie Bernard, Jr.
Savage, Augustus A.
Sawyer, Alfred M.
Scales, Robert L.
Scott, Albert Nelson
Scott, Elsie L.
Seale, Bobby
Seals, R. Grant
Sessing, Trevor W.
Sewell, Richard Huston
Sexton, Edwin T., Jr.
Shackelford, George Franklin
Shaw, Frederick B.
Shaw, Melvin B.
Shelton, Edward E.
Shepphard, Charles Bernard
Shields, Vincent O.
Shipmon, Luther June
Short, James Edward
Silva, Henry Andrew
Simmons, Esmeralda
Simmons, James O.
Simmons, James Richard
Simmons, Samuel J.
Simmons, Shirley Davis
Simpson, Stephen Whittington
Simpson-Watson, Ora Lee
Sims, Lydia Theresa
Singleton, Isaac, Sr.
Singleton, Robert
Sloan, Edith Barksdale
Small, Israel G.
Small, William
Smart, Edward Bernard, Jr.
Smith, Ann Elizabeth
Smith, Ashby Gordon, Jr.
Smith, Beverly Evans

Smith, James A.
Smith, Louis
Smith, Marzell
Smith, Maxine Atkins
Smith, Oswald Garrison
Smith, Sherman
Smith, Teasther West
Smith, Wilber Gene
Snell, Joan Yvonne Ervin
Snyder, Wadell D.
Spain, James S.
Springs, Lenny F.
Squires, Maudest Kelly
Steele, Percy H., Jr.
Stephens, Booker T.
Stepp, Marc
Stevens, Reatha J.
Stevens, Timothy S.
Stewart, Emily Jones
Stith, Charles Richard
Stocks, Eleanor Louise
Stockton, Clifford, Sr.
Stokes, Lillian Gatlin
Stone, Kara Lynn
Strayhorne, Pauline (nee Allen)
Street, T. Milton
Stubblefield, Raymond M.
Sylvester, Odell Howard, Jr.
Tasco, Marian B.
Tate, Leonard E.
Taylor, Comer L., Jr.
Taylor, Lynnette Dobbins
Taylor, Sandra Elaine
Taylor, Steven Lloyd
Taylor, Thomas C.
Taylor, Timothy Merritt
Taylor, Veronica C.
Taylor, Vivian A.
Teele, Arthur Earle, Jr.
Terrill, W.H. Tyrone, Jr.
Thomas, Alvin
Thomas, Franklin A.
Thomas, Johnny B.
Thomas, Waddell Robert
Thomas-Williams, Gloria M.
Thompson, Betty L.
Thompson, Frank
Thompson, Frank William
Thompson, Jesse M.
Thompson, Johnnie
Thompson, Linda Jo
Thompson-Moore, Ann
Thornell, Richard Paul
Thornton, Osie M.
Thornton, Pearl B.
Thorpe, Wesley Lee
Threadgill, Walter Leonard
Thurston, Charles Sparks
Tilghman, Cyprian O.
Timberlake, John Paul
Titus, LeRoy Robert
Tokley, Joanna Nutter
Townes, Clarence Lee, Jr.
Tripp, Luke Samuel
Trottman, Alphonso
Tucker, C. DeLores
Turner, Melvin Duval
Turner, Ricardo Cornelius, Sr.
Tyler, Waldo H.
Upton, E. H.
Vann, Albert
Vaughns, John Claude
Veal, Howard Richard
Vinson, Julius Ceasar
Vivian, Cordy Tindell
Wade, Lyndon Anthony
Walker, Ernestein
Walker, Lula Aquillia
Walker, Lynn Jones
Walsh, Everald J.
Walton, Flavia Batteau
Ward, Melvin Fitzgerald, Sr.
Ward, Zana Rogers
Washington, Arna D.
Washington, C. Clifford
Washington, Henry L.
Washington, Josie B.
Watkins, Juanita
Watkins, Mary Frances
Watkins, Robert Charles
Watson, Bernard C.
Watson, Carole M.
Watson, Dennis Rahiim
Watson, Joann Nichols

Watson, Theresa Lawhorn
Watts, Robert B.
Webber, Jessie Louis
Webber, William Stuart
Welton, Evelyn R.
Wesley, Clarence E.
Weston, M. Moran, II
Wharton, Dolores D.
Whipps, Mary N.
White, Margarette Paulyne
  Morgan
White, O. C.
White, Robert L.
White, William T., III
Whitfield, Vantile E.
Whitley, Frank James
Wickham, Muriel Jeannette
Wilcox, Preston
Wiley, Margaret Z. Richardson
Wilkinson, James Wellington
Williams, Andrew
Williams, Ann E. A. (nee
  Anderson)
Williams, Charles Frederick
Williams, Charles Richard
Williams, Clarence
Williams, Ernest Donald, Jr.
Williams, Forrest Wesley
Williams, Franklin H.
Williams, Georgianna M.
Williams, Herman
Williams, Iola (nee Craft)
Williams, John Joseph
Williams, Kenneth Herbert
Williams, Larry C.
Williams, Novella Stewart
Williams, Reginald T.
Williams, Robert Lee
Williams, Ronald Lee
Williams, Ruby Mai (nee
  McKnight)
Williams, Terri L.
Wilson, Charles F.
Wilson, Clarence Northon
Wilson, Cleo Francine
Wilson, Donald P.
Wilson, Ora Brown
Wilson, Robert H.
Wilson, Willie Mae (nee Carey)
Winston, Henry
Winters, James Robert
Wise, Herbert Ashby
Wood, William L., Jr.
Woods, Almita (nee Robinson)
Woods, Delbert Leon
Woodson, Charles R.
Woodson, Robert L.
Wooten, Priscilla A.
Wright, Grover Cleveland
Wright, Robert Courtlandt
Wright, Robert L.
Wyke, Joseph Henry
Wynn, Deborah B.
Yarbrough, Charles
Yates, LeRoy Louis
Young, Eddye Vivian Pierce
Young, James Arthur, III
Young, Jean Childs
Young, Margaret Buckner

ASTRONOMY
See **PHYSICS/
ASTRONOMY**

ATHLETICS
See **SPORTS—AMATEUR;
SPORTS—
PROFESSIONAL/
SEMIPROFESSIONAL;
SPORTS—NOT
ELSEWHERE
CLASSIFIED; SPORTS
COACHING/TRAINING/
MANAGING**

AUDITING
See **ACCOUNTING/
AUDITING**

AUTOMOBILE
INDUSTRY
See **MANUFACTURING—
MOTOR VEHICLES;
RETAIL TRADE—MOTOR
VEHICLES, PARTS, AND
SERVICES; WHOLESALE
TRADE—MOTOR
VEHICLES AND PARTS**

BANKING/FINANCIAL
SERVICES
Alexander, Don H.
Alexander, Louis G.
Alexander, Preston Paul, Jr.
Allen, Benjamin P., III
Alston, Floyd William
Anderson, Carol Byrd
Anderson, Leon H.
Anderson, Marcellus J., Sr.
Archie, Cornell B., Jr.
Arrington, Lloyd M., Jr.
Bacon, Warren H.
Bacon Richards, Bille J.
Bailey, Marolyn Leslie
Baker, Darryl Brent
Ballard, Edward Hunter
Baltimore, Roslyn Lois
Banks, James S.
Baptista, Howard
Battle, Bernard J., Sr.
Battle, Charles E.
Beal, Jacqueline Jean
Bell, Joseph N.
Bell, Melvyn Clarence
Belton, C. Ronald
Bennett, Bessye Warren
Bentley, Herbert Dean
Bertrand, Joseph G.
Bland, Heyward
Bledsoe, Milton Hargis, Jr.
Bludson-Francis, Vernett Michelle
Booker, Venerable Francis
Boswell, Bennie, H.
Boutte, Alvin J.
Bowdoin, Robert E.
Bowman, Janet Wilson
Boyer, Marcus Aurelius
Braddock, Carol T.
Bradshaw, Wayne
Brimmer, Andrew F.
Brooks, Don Locellus
Brown, Barbara A.
Brown, Curtis Carnegie, Jr.
Brown, John C., Jr.
Brown, Jonel Leonard
Brown, Joyce
Brown, Sherman L.
Brown, William Melvin, Jr.
Brunt, Samuel Jay
Bryson, Winfred Octavus, Jr.
Buford, Sharnia
Buford, William P.
Burrus, Clark
Bush, Mary K.
Campbell, Carlos Cardozo
Carlton, Pamela Gean
Carr, Charles V.
Carr, Roderich Marion
Cartwright, James Elgin
Cates, Sidney Hayward, III
Chambers, Harry, Jr.
Chappell, Emma Carolyn
Chatterjee, Lois Jordan
Chivis, Martin Lewis
Cholmondeley, Paula H. J.
Claiborne, Vernal
Clark, Nehemiah
Clark, Walter H.
Clay, Timothy Byron
Clayton, Kathleen R.
Colebrook, George, Jr.
Coleman, Cecil R.
Coleman, Columbus E., Jr.
Coles, John Edward
Collins, William Keelan
Coney, Hydia Lutrice
Cook, Rufus
Coombs, Fletcher
Cooper, Valerie Antionette
Copeland, Kevon
Cornelison, Carole Jane
Cornwell, W. Don

Countee, Thomas Hilaire, Jr.
Cowans, Alvin Jeffrey
Cox, DuBois V.
Cox, Robert L.
Crawley, A. Bruce
Crews, William Sylvester
Crocker, Clinton C.
Crockett, Ulysses-Atum
Cunningham, Blenna A.
Daniels, A. Raiford
Darden, Orlando William
Davidson, Donald Rae
Davidson, Rick Bernard
Davis, Algenita Scott
Davis, Howard C.
Davis, James
Davis, Jerome
Davis, Marilynn A.
Davis, Milton
Davis, Nigel S.
Davis, Patricia Staunton
Davis, Roland Hayes
Day, William Charles, Jr.
Denning, Joe William
Derricotte, C. Bruce
Dewberry, Madelina Denise
Dickson, Reginald D.
Disher, Spencer C., III
Doig, Elmo H.
Doley, Harold E., Jr.
Dunmore, Lawrence A., Jr.
Ealy, Mary Newcomb
Easton, Richard James
Edmonds, Norman Douglas
Evans, Charlotte A.
Evans, Leon Edward, Jr.
Feddoes, Sadie C.
Felder, Thomas E.
Felton, Otis Leverna
Ferguson, Johnnie Nathaniel
Fields, Arlonda M.
Fields, Nathaniel
Fields, Samuel Bennie
Fierce, Hughlyn F.
Fitzgerald, William B.
Ford, Wallace L., II
Forde, Fraser Philip, Jr.
Foster, Deborah Valrie
Foster, William K.
Fowler, James Daniel, Jr.
Frasier, Ralph Kennedy
Fuget, Henry Eugene
Funderburg, I. Owen
Garrison-Corbin, Patricia Ann
Geiger, David Nathaniel
Gibbs, Karen Patricia
Gibson, Gregory A.
Gillis, William Freeman
Gilmore, Richard G.
Givhan, Mercer A., Jr.
Glover, Kenneth Elijah
Godfrey, Emile Sylvester, Jr.
Godfrey, Wesley
Goliday, Willie V.
Goodwin-Fulgham, Roietta
Goss, Frank, Jr.
Grady, Walter E.
Gray, Naomi T.
Green, Ernest G.
Greene, Richard T.
Gregg, Lucius Perry
Gregory, Theodore Morris
Grigsby, Calvin Burchard
Grist, Ronald
Hadnott, Grayling
Hamilton, John M.
Hamilton, William Nathan
Hammonds, Alfred
Hankins, Gerard S.
Hannah, Mack H., Jr.
Hannah, Mosie R.
Hargrett, James T., Jr.
Harris, Curtis Alexander
Harris, Jeanette G.
Harris, Nathaniel C., Jr.
Harrison, Booker David (Mule
  Brother)
Hart, Ronald O.
Harvey, Beverly Ann
Harvey, Richard R.
Haskins, Joseph, Jr.
Haskins, Morice Lee, Jr.
Hatchett, Paul Andrew
Hayden, William Hughes

Hedgepeth, Leonard
Henley, Vernard W.
Herndon, Phillip George
Hill, Arthur James
Hill, Henry, Jr.
Hodge, Norris
Hogan, John A.
Holloman, Thaddeus Bailey
Holloway, Harris M.
Holloway, Hiliary H.
Homer, Ronald A.
Houston, Seawadon Lee
Howard, Darnley William
Hudson, Elbert T.
Hull, Everson Warren
Humphrey, Arthur
Humphrey, Marian J.
Hurt, James E.
Hutchinson, James J., Jr.
Jackson, Alexis Camille
Jackson, Charles E., Sr.
Jackson, David M.
Jackson, Eugene L.
Jackson, Pazel
James, Dorothy Marie
James, Robert Earl
Jeffers, Grady Rommel
Jefferson, Roy Lee, Jr.
Jenkins, Robert Kenneth, Jr.
Jennings, Sylvesta Lee
Johns, Stephen Arnold
Johnson, Al
Johnson, Alexander Hamilton, Jr.
Johnson, Edward, Jr. (Fast Eddie)
Johnson, Pompie Louis, Jr.
Johnson, Stephen L.
Johnson, Wayne Lee
Johnson, William C.
Jones, Arlender
Jones, Edward Henry
Jordan, Emma Coleman
Jordon, Samuel F.
Joseph-McIntyre, Mary
Kelly, John P.
Kemp, C. Robert
Key, Juan Alfred
Kinder, Randolph Samuel, Jr.
King, Colbert I.
King, John B.
Kirkland, Cornell R.
Knight, W. H., Jr. (Joe)
Lambert, Joseph C.
Lansey, E. Gaines
Lansey, Yvonne F.
Lavelle, Robert R.
Lawson, Walter I., Jr.
Laymon, Heather R.
Lee, Aubrey W.
Lee, Edwin Archibald
Lee, J. Kenneth
Lee, John Robert E.
Lee, Theodosia L. Crawford
LeFlore, Obie Laurence, Jr.
Lewis, Andre
Lewis, Erma Jean
Lewis, Thomas P.
Linyard, Richard
Littlejohn, J. B.
Lockhart, James B.
Loney, Carolyn Patricia
Long, Steffan
Love, Joe W.
Lowe, Aubrey F.
Lowry, A. Leon, Sr.
Luke, Steve Norman
Lyons, Lloyd Carson
Malloy, H. Rembert
Manning, Glenn M.
Manuel, Louis Calvin
March, Anthony
Martin, Herman Henry, Jr.
Martin, I. Maximillian
Matthews, Gregory J.
Matthews, Westina Lomax
Mauney, Donald Wallace, Jr.
Mayes, Clinton, Jr.
McCants, Jesse Lee, Sr.
McClain, Jerome G.
McClinton, Curtis R., Jr.
McCullough, Frances Louise (nee Ford)
McDonald, Alden J., Jr.
McKnight, Albert J.
McMullins, Tommy
McMurry, Walter M., Jr.

McNeal, Sylvia Ann
Miles, Frank J. W.
Miller, Arthur J.
Miller, George N., Jr.
Miller, Sharon Bernard
Miller, Ward Beecher
Mister, Melvin Anthony
Mitchell, B. Doyle
Mitchell, Carlton S.
Mitchell, Roscoe E.
Montgomery, Fred O.
Montgomery, George Louis, Jr.
Moore, Cornell Leverette
Moore, Jane Bond
Moore, John Wesley, Jr.
Moorehead, Justin Leslie
Morris, Alfred L.
Morrow, E. Frederic
Mosley, Edna Wilson
Mosley, Elwood A.
Motley, John H.
Muse, William Brown, Jr.
Myles, Wilbert
Newton, Ernest E., II
Newton, James Douglas, Jr.
Njoroge, Mbugua J.
Nunery, Leroy David
Nunn, John, Jr.
Oliver, Kenneth Nathaniel
Oxendine, John Edward
Oyalowo, Tunde O.
Parker, George Anthony
Patterson, Clinton David
Patterson, Ronald E.
Pearce, Richard Allen
Pearson, Marilyn Ruth
Pearson, Michael Novel
Pease, Denise Louise
Perine, Martha Levingston
Perkins, Charles Windell
Pettiford, Quentin H.
Phillips, Ralph Leonard
Phillips, Wilburn R.
Piper, Elwood A.
Pitts, John Martin
Plummer, Milton
Poole-Heard, Blanche Denise
Pope, Mirian Artis
Porter, Arthur L.
Powell, Kenneth Alasandro
Powell, Robert E.
Prestwidge, Barbara Elizabeth
Prezeau, Louis E.
Prioleau, Peter Sylvester
Reuben, Lucy Jeanette
Reynolds, Charles McKinley, Jr.
Rice, Emmett J.
Roberson, Gary
Roberts, Blanche Elizabeth
Roberts, Talmadge
Robertson, Alan D.
Robinson, Jesse Lee
Roland, Benautrice, Jr.
Rollins, Avon William, Sr.
Roundfield, Danny Thomas (Rounds)
Rushing, George A.
Samuels, Robert J.
Sanders, Victoria Lynn
Scales, Erwin Carlvet
Scott, Charlotte Hanley
Scott, James Henry
Scott, Rachel Loraine
Scott, Yolanda Madden
Seabrook, Lemuel, III
Seidenberg, Mark
Sidbury, Harold David
Simmons, Willie, Jr.
Singleton, Herbert
Small, Lawrence Malcolm
Smith, Estrella W.
Smith, Howard C.
Smith, Jean M.
Smith, Stanley G.
Smith, Thelma J.
Smith, William Xavier
Snowden, Gail
Soaries, Raynes L., Jr.
Sockwell, Oliver R., Jr.
Spaulding, Aaron Lowery
Spencer, Donald Andrew
Spooner, John C.
Spooner, Richard C.
Springs, Lenny F.

Staes, Beverly N.
Stahnke, William E.
Stamper, Henry J.
Stennis, Willie James
Stephens, James Anthony
Stokes, Bunny, Jr.
Stroman, Kenneth
Sutton, Wilma Jean
Sweat, Sheila Diane
Tarter, Robert R., Jr.
Taylor, Julia W.
Taylor, Myron
Taylor, William Glenn
Thomas, Earle Frederick
Thomas, Leroy, Sr.
Thornton, Wayne T.
Threadgill, Walter Leonard
Tidwell, Isaiah
Tomlin, Josephine D.
Townes, Clarence L., Sr.
Tucker, Eric M.
Tucker, James F.
Turnipseed, Carl Wendell
Uku, Eustace Oris, Sr.
Van Amson, George Louis
Van Hook, Warren Kenneth
Varner, Robert Lee
Vaughan, Gerald R.
Wade, Joyce K.
Walker, Craig J.
Walker, Grover P.
Walker, Horace L.
Walker, John Leslie
Waller, Juanita Ann
Warder, John Morgan
Waters, John W.
Watkins, Gloria Elizabeth
Watkins, Walter C., Jr.
Watson, Theresa Lawhorn
Weatherspoon, Keith Earl
West, Earl M.
White, Earl Henry
White, Edward Clarence, Jr.
White, Melvyn Lee
Whitehurst, Charles Bernard, Sr.
Whiteman, Herbert Wells, Jr.
Whitten, Eloise Culmer
Wiggins, Leslie
Wilkins, Herbert Priestly
Wilkinson, Frederick D., Jr.
Williams, E. Thomas, Jr.
Williams, Edward Joseph
Williams, Frank, Jr.
Williams, Sonya Denise
Willis, Levy E
Wilson, Lance Henry
Winfield, Thalia Beatrice
Winters, Kenneth E.
Wood, Garland E.
Wood, Willie Vernell, Jr.
Young, Joyce Howell
Young, Reginald B.
Young, Terrence Anthony
Young, Tommy Scott

BIOCHEMISTRY

Addy, Tralance Obuama
Clarke, Donald Dudley
Dyce, Barbara
Gavin, James Raphael, III
Harris, Don Navarro
Harrison, Robert Walker, III
Haynes, John Kermit
Hegwood, William Lewis
Jones, George H.
Meade-Tollin, Linda C.
Mitchell, Earl Douglass, Jr.
Pointer, Richard H.
Roberts, Thomas L.
Sanders, Robert B.
Solomon, James Daniel
Washington, Linda Phaire

BIOLOGY/ MICROBIOLOGY

Ampy, Franklin R.
Bayne, Henry G.
Branche, William C., Jr.
Brooks, Carolyn Branch
Buggs, Charles Wesley
Cobb, Jewel Plummer
Comer, Marian Wilson
Cook, Nathan Howard

Craft, Thomas J., Sr.
Davenport, Calvin A.
Eure, Herman Edward
Foster, Lloyd L.
Fuller, Almyra Oveta
Gray, Joanne S.
Harris, Geraldine E.
Hogan, James Carroll, Jr.
Jackson, Earl, Jr.
Jacobs, Jacqueline Minette
Leak, Lee Virn
LeFlore, William B.
Love, George Hayward
Mack, Astrid Karona
McCurdy, Brenda Wright
McSwain, Berah D.
Miller, Andrea Lewis
Moses, Johnnie, Jr.
Oyewole, Saundra Herndon
Parker, Charles McCrae
Parson, Willie L.
Phillip, Michael John
Porter, Clarence A.
Redd, Thomasina A.
Roberts, Thomas L.
Ruffin, John
Simmons, John Emmett
Stephens, Lee B., Jr.
Stewart, Adelle Wright
Stokes, Gerald Virgil
Taylor, Welton Ivan
Turner, Wallace E.
Warren, Herman Lecil
White, Sandra LaVelle
Wiles, Joseph St. Clair
Wilson, Donella Joyce

BOTANY

Garraway, Michael Oliver
Haugstad, May Katheryn (nee Hill)
Hill, Ray Allen

BUILDING/ CONSTRUCTION

See also RETAIL TRADE— BUILDING/ CONSTRUCTION MATERIALS; WHOLESALE TRADE— BUILDING/ CONSTRUCTION MATERIALS

Alsandor, Jude
Alston, James L.
Apea, Joseph Bennet Kyeremateng
Argrette, Joseph
Atkinson, Charles N.
Batteast, Robert V.
Beard, Montgomery, Jr.
Bell, Robert Wesley
Bernoudy, James Logan
Blunt, Roger Reckling
Boddie, Algernon Owens
Brown, Joseph Clifton
Brown, Raymond Madison
Brown, Rodney W.
Brown, Wesley Anthony
Byas, William Herbert
Bynam, Sawyer Lee, III
Cade, Valarie Swain
Campbell, George Lynn
Carey, Milton Gales
Cargile, William, III
Carter, John H.
Carter, Thomas Allen
Carter, Willie A.
Cason, Joseph L.
Chapman, Cleveland M.
Cole, Curtis, Jr.
Coleman, John H.
Coles, John Edward
Collins, Otis Grant
Cooke, Thomas H., Jr.
Cooper, Albert, Sr.
Cotton, Garner
Cross, William R.
Davis, Barbara D.
Davis, Melvin Lloyd
Dodson, Granville M.
Dolphin, Woodrow B.
Duncanson, Patricia A.

Dykes, Roland A.
Edmonds, Campbell Ray
Edwards, Grover Lewis, Sr.
Ethridge, John E.
Ferguson, Shellie Alvin
Few, Terry Lee
Floyd, James T.
Foree, Jack Clifford
Frye, Reginald Stanley
Garvin, Jonathan
Gilchrist, Robertson
Gilcreast, Conway, Sr.
Gorham, Thelma Thurston
Gulley, Wilson
Hall, John Robert
Harris, Gleason Ray
Hewitt, Ronald Jerome
Hicks, William L.
Hill, Sam
Holder, Reuben D.
Hull, Ellis L., Jr.
Humes, Emanuel I., Sr.
Jackson, James Holmen
Jackson, John H.
Jett, Arthur Victor, Sr.
Jones, James C.
Jones, Leon P.
Keeler, Vemes
Kline, Eddie
Lawrence, Erma Jean
Lee, Aaron
Lee, Charles Gary, Sr.
Lee, John C., III
Lee, William J.
Leigh, William Alvin
Lewis, Charles Grant
London, Roberta Levy
Mabin, Joseph E.
Mack, Cleveland J., Sr.
Manning, Howard Nick, Jr.
McCraven, Marcus R.
McGhee, James Leon
McLaurin, Howard Wilson
McMillan, Robert Frank, Jr.
Minor, John S.
Moore, Thomas L.
Moses, MacDonald
Nance, Booker Joe, Sr.
Oliver, William Henry
Owens, Robert Lee
Platt, Richard A.
Powers, Mamon, Sr.
Powers, Mamon M., Jr.
Pryce, Edward L.
Reed, Adolphus Redolph
Rist, Seward
Robinson, Hugh Granville
Robinson, Jack E.
Robinson, Noah R.
Rohadfox, Ronald Otto
Rowe, Nansi Irene
Russell, Nathaniel S.
Saffel, E. Frank
Scales, Patricia Bowles
Seriki, Olusola Oluyemisi
Sewell, Edward C.
Sidbury, Harold David
Smith, J. C.
Taylor, J. Robert Earlington, Jr.
Thacker, Sandra J.
Thomas, Sirr Daniel
Tisdale, Herbert Clifford
Turner, Charles Robert (Jack)
Vann, Gregory Alvin
Walker, Joseph
Walker, Larry
Wallace, Derrick D.
Waller, Larry
Watiker, Albert David, Jr.
Watson, Fred D.
Weaver, Gary W.
White, Donald F.
Williams, Daniel Louis
Williams, Eddie, Sr.
Williams, Guthrie J.
Williams, Henry
Williams, Jesse
Williams, Patrick Nehemiah
Williams, Yarborogh, Jr.
Wise, Warren C.
Woods, George Washington
Woods, Geraldine Pittman

Jagnandan, Wilfred Lilpersaud
James, Frederick C.
James, Gillette Oriel
James, H. Rhett
James, Hamice R., Jr.
James, Isaac
Jefferson, M. Ivory
Jeffrey, Charles James, Jr.
Jemison, Theodore Judson
Jenkins, Alonzo Clark
Jenkins, Charles E., Sr.
Jenkins, James E.
Jerkins, Jerry Gaines
Johnson, Albert Lee, Sr.
Johnson, Andrew L.
Johnson, Ed F.
Johnson, James H.
Johnson, Lawrence Washington
Johnson, Leardrew L.
Johnson, Nathan
Johnson, Paul Edwin
Johnson, Thomas H.
Johnson, Vaughn Arzah
Johnson, William E.
Jones, Albert Allen
Jones, Asbury Paul
Jones, Buck
Jones, Clifford Anthony, Sr.
Jones, Enoch
Jones, G. Daniel
Jones, Idus, Jr.
Jones, James Wesley
Jones, Lawrence N.
Jones, Leon C.
Jones, Michael Andrea
Jones, Nathan William
Jones, Oscar C., Jr.
Jones, Ozro T., Jr.
Jones, Robert Earl
Jones, Spencer
Jones, Vernon A., Jr.
Jones, William A., Jr.
Jones, William Jenipher
Jones, William O.
Jordan, Charles Wesley
Jordan, Frederick Douglass
Jordan, John Wesley
Jordan, R. D.
Jordan, Robert L.
Kelley, Robert William
Kelly, James Clement
Kelly, Leontine T. C.
Kendrick, Artis G.
Kennedy, James E.
Kennedy, William Thomas, Jr.
Kilgore, Thomas, Jr.
Kimbrough, Charles E.
King, Derek Barber
King, William J.
King, William L.
Kirby, Money Alian
Kirk-Duggan, Cheryl Ann
Kirkendoll, Chester Arthur, II
Kirksey, Peter J.
Kirton, Edwin Eggleston
Knox, Wilbur Benjamin
LaGarde, Frederick H.
Lambert, Wilfred Lee
Lane, John Henry
Langford, Arthur, Jr.
Langford, Victor C., III
Laroche, Gerard A.
Lawing, Raymond Quinton
Lawson, James M., Jr.
Lawston, Marjorie Gray
Leary, James E.
Lee, Bernard Scott
Lee, Cody M.
Lee, Gabriel S., Jr.
Lee, Gloria A.
Lee, Thomas F.
Lee, William J.
Lehman, Harvey J.
Lemmons, Herbert Michael
Lewis, Alvin
Lewis, Charles Bady
Lewis, Helen Middleton
Lewis, Henry S., Jr.
Lewis, Percy Lee
Lewis, Prinic Herbert, Sr.
Lewis, W. Arthur
Lewter, Andy C., Sr.
Linsey, Nathaniel L.
Lloyd, George Lussington
Logan, Bertie Hawthorne

Logan, Thomas W. S., Sr.
Lovett, Leonard
Lowe, Eugene Yerby, Jr.
Luther, Lucius Calvin
Lynch, Lorenzo A., Sr.
Lyons, William B.
Mack, Charles Richard
Mackey, Andrew, Jr.
Malekebu, Daniel Sharp
Manigo, George F., Jr.
Manley, John Ruffin
Manning, Hubert Vernon
Marcee, Emerson
Marshall, Calvin Bromley, III
Martin, Edward
Martin, James Tyrone
Martin, Lawrence Raymond
Massey, Reginald Harold
Matthews, David
Maultsby, Sylvester
Maye, Richard
McCall, Emmanuel Lemuel, Sr.
McCleave, Mansel Philip
McCloud, J. Oscar
McClung, Willie David
McCollough, Walter
McCollum, Charles Edward
McCracken, Frank D.
McCray, Thomas L.
McCree, Edward L.
McCullough, Frederick Douglas
McDaniel, Paul Anderson
McDonald, Timothy, III
McDowell, Edward Homer, Jr.
McGuire, Paul M., Jr.
McIntyre, John Henry, Sr.
McKanders, Julius A., II
McKinney, George Dallas, Jr.
McKinney, Samuel Berry
McKnight, Albert J.
McMillan, L. R.
McNelty, Harry
Medearis, Victor L.
Mickins, Andel W.
Miles, Norman Kenneth
Miller, John H.
Mitchell, Ella Pearson
Mitchell, Henry Heywood
Mitchell, Kelly Karnale
Mitchell, Melvin J.
Montague, Lee
Montgomery, James C.
Moore, Arnold D.
Moore, James L.
Moore, Jerry A., Jr.
Moore, Noah Watson, Jr.
Moore, Oscar William, Jr.
Moran, Robert E., Sr.
Morgan, Joseph L.
Morris, Calvin S.
Morris, Samuel Solomon
Morris, William Wesley
Morrison, Juan LaRue, Sr.
Morton, Charles E.
Morton, Leona M.
Mosley, Lawrence Edward, Sr.
Moss, Otis, Jr.
Munford, Paul Stanley
Murchison, E. P.
Murray, Thomas W., Jr.
Nabrit, Henry Clarke
Nash, LeRoy T.
Nettles, John Spratt
Newbern, Captolia Dent
Newbold, Robert Thomas
Newman, Ernest Wilbur
Newman, Nathaniel
Newsome, Clarence Geno
Nichols, Edward K., Jr.
Nichols, Henry H.
Nichols, Paul
Nickerson, Willie Curtis
Nightingale, Jesse Phillip
Nixon, Felix Nathaniel
Norris, Charles L., Sr.
Norvel, William Leonard
Norwood, John F.
Notice, Guy Symour
Oates, Caleb E.
O'Donnell, Lorena Mae
O'Hara, Leon P.
O'Neal, Eddie S.
Pannell, William E.
Parham, Thomas David, Jr.

Parker, Joseph Caiaphas, Jr.
Parker, Matthew
Parker, Thomas E., Jr.
Parrish, James W.
Parrish, John Henry
Patterson, Alonzo B.
Patterson, Clinton David
Patterson, James Oglethorpe
Payden, Henry J., Sr.
Pearson, Herman B.
Peay, Isaac Charles, Sr.
Perrin, David Thomas Perry
Perry, Jerald Isaac, Sr.
Peterson, Willie Diamond
Phillips, Acen L.
Pickett, Henry B., Jr.
Pinder, Nelson W.
Polk, Robert L.
Pollard, Alton Brooks, III
Pope, Mary Maude
Portee, Frank, III
Porter, John Richard
Powell, Grady Wilson
Powell, John Lewis
Powell, Joseph T.
Powell, William J.
Pratt, J. C.
Preston, Richard Clark
Price, Joseph L.
Primo, Quintin E., Jr.
Proctor, Samuel Dewitt
Ragland, Wylheme Harold
Randall, Claire
Raphael, Paul W.
Rasberry, Robert Eugene
Rates, Norman M.
Ratliff, Joe Samuel
Rawls, Louis
Ray, Sandy Frederick
Reed, Florine
Reed, Floyd T.
Reese, Frederick D.
Reid, Benjamin F.
Reid, Milton A.
Reid, Wilfred
Revelle, Robert, Sr.
Revely, William
Richard, James L.
Richardson, Lacy Franklin
Richardson, Louis M.
Roberts, Wesley A.
Robertson, Benjamin W.
Robertson, Lynn E.
Robinson, Hubert Nelson
Robinson, Joseph
Robinson, William J. (Bishop Billy Robinson)
Rogers, Charles Calvin
Rooks, Charles Shelby
Ross, Ralph M.
Rowan, Albert T.
Rowe, Albert P.
Sabourin, Clemonce
Salmon Campbell, Joan Mitchell
Sampson, Albert Richard
Sands, Douglas Bruce
Scott, Alfred J.
Scott, John H.
Scott, Nathan A., Jr.
Shaw, Alvia A.
Sheares, Reuben A., II
Shelton, S. McDowell
Sherman, Oddie Lee
Sherow, Don Carl
Shields, Landrum Eugene
Shipley, Anthony J.
Shockley, Grant S.
Shoultz, Rudolph Samuel
Shuttlesworth, Fred L.
Simmons, Julius Caesar
Simms, Albert L.
Simon, Joseph Donald
Simon, Lonnie A.
Simpson, Samuel G.
Singleton, Harold Douglas
Singleton, William Matthew
Slie, Samuel N.
Smart, Edward Bernard, Jr.
Smith, Bennett W., Sr.
Smith, Eddie D., Sr.
Smith, Frank
Smith, George Walker
Smith, Granville N.
Smith, Herald Leonydus

Smith, J. Alfred, Sr.
Smith, J. C.
Smith, Johnnie M.
Smith, Luther Edward, Jr.
Smith, Otis Benton, Jr.
Smith, Paul
Smith, Perry Anderson, III
Smith, Robert Johnson
Smith, Wallace Charles
Smith, William Milton
Smoot, Albertha Pearl
Smotherson, Melvin
Spence, Joseph Samuel, Sr.
Stamps, Lynman A., Sr.
Stewart, Darneau V.
Stewart, Richard E.
Stewart, Warren Hampton, Sr.
Stewart, William H.
Stith, Charles Richard
Stotts, Valmon D.
Styles, Richard Wayne
Suggs, William Albert
Sullivan, Leon Howard
Summers, William E., III
Sutton, Moses
Swain, Ronald L.
Swayne, Steven Robert
Swiggett, Ernest L.
Talbert, Melvin George
Talbot, David Arlington Roberts, Sr.
Taylor, Hycel B.
Taylor, Noel C.
Taylor, Prince Albert, Jr.
Taylor, Theodore Roosevelt
Taylor, Walter Scott
Thomas, James Samuel
Thomas, Latta R., Sr.
Thomas, N. Charles
Thompson, John Andrew
Thrasher, William Edward
Thrower, Julius A.
Tieuel, Robert C. D.
Timpson, Clarence B.
Tolliver, Joel
Torain, Tony William
Tottress, Richard Edward
Trice, Juniper Yates
Trout, Nelson W.
Tuggle, Reginald
Turner, Eugene
Tyler, Lee Malcolm
Tyner, Charles R.
Vance, William J., Sr.
Vaughan, James Edward
Vivian, Cordy Tindell
Waddles, George Wesley, Sr.
Walker, Charles E.
Walker, Claude
Walker, J. Wilbur
Walker, John T.
Walker, Lucius, Jr.
Walker, Thomas L.
Walker, Wyatt Tee
Wallace, Joseph Fletcher, Jr.
Wallace, William James Lord
Walls, Fredric T.
Wamble, Amos Sylvester, Sr.
Warner, Isaiah H.
Washington, Edith May Faulkner
Washington, Henry L.
Washington, Johnnie M.
Washington, Paul M.
Waters, John W.
Watts, Alexander Alfred
Weary, Dolphus
Weathers, J. Leroy
Whalum, Kenneth Twigg
Whitaker, Arthur L.
White, J. Arthur
White, Major C.
White, Scott A., Sr.
Whitted, Andrew Eugene
Wiggins, Daphne Cordelia
Wiggins, William H., Jr.
Wiley, Herley Wesley
Wilkes, William R.
Williams, A. Cecil
Williams, Andrew
Williams, Charles J., Sr.
Williams, Chester Arthur
Williams, Donald Eugene
Williams, Ellis
Williams, Guthrie J.

Williams, Ira Joseph
Williams, Jester C.
Williams, John Henry
Williams, John L.
Williams, John Waldo
Williams, Joseph R.
Williams, Kenneth Raynor
Williams, Kneely
Williams, L. Colene
Williams, Michael Patrick
Williams, Wilbert Lee
Willis, Gladys January
Wilmore, Gayraud Stephen
Wilson, Carl L.
Wilson, Demond
Wilson, James Paris
Wilson, Mannie L.
Wilson, Ralph L.
Wimberly, Edward P.
Winfrey, Charles Everett
Womack, Andrew A.
Wood, Andrew W.
Woodhouse, Johnny Boyd
Woodson, S. Howard, Jr.
Wright, Clarence Johnnie, Sr.
Wright, Earl W.
Wright, Grover Cleveland
Wright, Jefferson W.
Wright, Sylvester M.
Wyatt, Addie L.
Wyatt, Claude Stell, Jr.
Wynn, Daniel Webster
Young, Rufus King

CLERGY—NOT ELSEWHERE CLASSIFIED

Adams, John Hurst
Anderson, Felix Sylvester
Baxter, Belgium Nathan
Bond, Louis Grant
Boone, Clinton Caldwell
Boyd-Clinkscales, Mary E.
Bradford, Charles Edward
Branch, G. Murray
Branch, William McKinley
Bronson, Fred James
Brookins, H. Hartford
Brown, Delores Elaine
Brown, George Houston
Bryant, Harrison James
Bumbry, George Nordlinger
Bunton, Henry Clay
Burgess, John Melville
Callahan, Samuel P.
Campbell, E. Alexander
Carroll, Juanitaelizabeth P.
Cheek, Donald Kato
Chrichlow, Livingston L.
Clark, Caesar A. W.
Collins, Robert H.
Cook, James E.
Cousin, Philip R.
Crawford, Nathaniel, Jr.
Cunningham, Richard T.
Cureton, Stewart Cleveland
Dade, Malcolm G.
Davenport, J. Lee
Davis, Grady D., Sr.
Del Pino, Jerome King
Dennis, Walter Decoster
Diggs, William P.
Downey, Aurelia Richie
Du Bose, Robert Earl, Jr.
Dudley, Charles Edward
Dudley, Crayton T.
Dunston, Alfred G.
Durant, Naomi C.
Eaton, David Hilliard
Eichelberger, William L.
Elligan, Irvin, Jr.
Erwin, Richard C.
Eskridge, John Clarence
Evans, Lorenzo J.
Evans, Spofford L.
Evans, William C.
Felker, Joseph B.
Feltus, James, Jr.
Fields, Edward E.
Fisher, Richard Laymon
Foggie, Charles H.
Ford, James W.
Fox, Theodore B.
Freeman, Robert Lee

Freeman, Thomas F.
Fuller, James J.
Fullilove, Paul A., Sr.
Garrett, Thaddeus, Jr.
Gerald, William
Gibbes, Emily V.
Gibson, Ernest Robinson
Gilbert, Eldridge H. E.
Gooden, Samuel Ellsworth
Goodwin, Hugh Wesley
Gordon, Alexander H., II
Gordon, Clifford Wesley
Gordon, Maxie S., Sr.
Green, Clyde Octavious
Green, Reuben H.
Green, Sterling
Griffin, Thomas J.
Grigsby, Marshall C.
Groce, Herbert Monroe, Jr.
Hale, Phale D.
Hancock, Allen C.
Harley, Philip A.
Harris, Barbara Clemente
Harris, Wesley Young, Jr.
Harris, William R.
Harvey, Louis-Charles
Haynes, Michael E.
Haynes, Neal J.
Herzfeld, Will Lawrence
Hill, Rufus S.
Hoard, Walter B.
Holmes, Zan W., Jr.
Horton, Larnie G.
Hotchkiss, Wesley Akin
Inyamah, Nathaniel Ginikanwa N.
Jackson, Earl J.
Jackson, Mattie Lee
Jangdharrie, Wycliffe K.
Jefferson, June L., Jr.
Johnson, Joy J.
Johnson, Leroy
Johnson, Louis W.
Joy, James Bernard, Jr.
King, Barbara Lewis
Lewis, Robert Louis
Lewis, W. Arthur
Louden, Henderson Nathaniel, Sr.
Lowery, Joseph E.
Lyons, George W.C., Sr.
Matthews, Albert D.
Maxell, Charles A.
McFadden, Arthur B.
McFaddin, Theresa Garrison
McKinney, Jesse Doyle
Ming, Donald George K.
Minus, Homer Wellington
Mitchell, Kelly Karnale
Moore, Earl B.
Moseley, Calvin Edwin, Jr.
Murray, Andrew Evans
Neavon, Joseph Roy
Newsome, Burnell
Nichols, Roy Calvin
O'Neal, Eddie S.
Parker, Fred Lee Cecil
Parks, Lyman S.
Phillips, F. Allison
Pinkston, Moses Samuel
Quick, Charles E.
Rasberry, Robert Eugene
Reese, Frederick D.
Reid, Robert Edward
Ricks, Albert William
Riley, Sumpter Marion, Jr.
Robinson, Edsel F.
Robinson, Frank J.
Robinson, Jonathan N.
Robinson, Milton Bernidine
Robinson, Norman T., Jr.
Sanders, James William
Satterwhite, John H.
Scott, Cornealious Socrates, Sr.
Sherrod, Charles M.
Smith, Paul
Smith, Robert Johnson
Smith, Robert L. T., Sr.
Smith, Wallace Charles
Stewart, Imogene Bigham
Stokes, Rembert Edwards
Suggs, William Albert
Summers, William E., III
Sutton, Gloria W.
Thomas, Latta R., Sr.
Thomas, Robert C.

Towns, Maxine Yvonne
Trice, Juniper Yates
Tyner, Charles R.
Virdure, Bernel B.
Waddles, Charleszetta Lina
Waddles, George Wesley, Sr.
Warner, Edward L.
Washington, James Melvin
Watkins, Joseph Philip
Weathers, J. Leroy
White, Reggie
White, William H.
Whitney, Yenwith Kelly
Williams, Chester Arthur
Wilson, Alva L.
Wright, Jeremiah A., Jr.
Wynn, Prathia Hall
Yates, LeRoy Louis
Zachary-Pike, Annie R.

COMMUNITY SERVICE

Ahmann, Mathew Hall
Anderson, Oddie
Anderson, Patricia Hebert
Andrews, Carl R.
Bacoate, Matthew, Jr.
Bacon, Charlotte Meade
Bailey, Agnes Jackson
Bailey, Ronald W.
Banner, Melvin Edward
Barnes, Martin G.
Baugh, Florence Ellen
Baxter, Augustus, Sr.
Bennett, Delores
Benson, Gilbert
Bludson-Francis, Vernett Michelle
Boddie, Louise
Bommer, Minnie L.
Borom, Lawrence H.
Bradshaw, Doris Marion
Brown, Hazel Evelyn
Brown, Lloyd
Browne, David A.
Buckner, Iris Bernell
Burden, Pennie L.
Burgess, James R., Jr.
Cain, Lester James, Jr.
Campbell, Dick C.
Campbell, Emory Shaw
Cantarella, Marcia Y.
Carroll, Annie Haywood
Carson, Julia M.
Castleman, Elise Marie (nee Tucker)
Cavens, Sharon Sue
Cole, Charles Zhivaga
Coston, Bessie Ruth
Cox, James L.
Cox, John Wesley
Crawford, Betty Marilyn
Cromwell, Margaret M.
Daniels, Ron D.
Davidson, Arthur B.
Davis, Preston Augustus
Dobbins, Alphondus Milton
Doby, Allen E.
Dowery, Mary
Duncan, Alice Geneva
Duster, Donald Leon
Eatman, Janice A.
Eichelberger, William L.
Flippen, Frances Morton
Florence, Johnny C.
Gates, Audrey Castine
Gillette, Frankie Jacobs
Granger, Shelton B.
Greene, George Randolph
Greene, Mamie Louise
Greene, William
Greenwood, John T.
Hamilton, John Joslyn, Jr.
Hamlet, James Frank
Harmon, Sherman Allen
Harrington, Philip Leroy
Harris, James G., Jr.
Harris, Oscar L., Jr.
Hoppes, Alice Faye
Hubbard, Paul Leonard
Hughes, Hollis Eugene, Jr.
Ireland, Lynda
Jeffrey, Ronnald James
Jenkins, Elaine B.
Jernigan, Curtis Dean
Johnson, Alexander Hamilton, Jr.

Johnson, Lorna Karen
Johnson, Otis Samuel
Jones, Ernest Edward
Jordan, Patricia Carter
Kelley, Jack Albert
Kirk, Leroy W.
Knox, Wayne D. P.
League, Cheryl Perry
Lemon, Michael Wayne, Sr.
Lyells, Ruby E. Stutts
Maddox, Elton Preston, Jr.
Mahoney, Keith Weston
Marrs, Stella
McFadden, Nathaniel James
McIntosh, Alice T.
McMillan, Enolia Pettigen
Mickey, Rosie Cheatham
Miller, Anna M.
Miller, Erenest Eugene
Miller, Lawrence A.
Miller, Lawrence Edward
Mitchell, Roderick Bernard
Moore, Wenda Weekes
Moxley, Frank O.
Murray, Edna McClain
Myles, Ernestine (nee Jones)
Nelson, Patricia Ann
Newman, Miller Maurice
Nix, Roscoe Russa
Nixon, Gladys (nee Ellison)
Norris, Fred Arthur, Jr.
Odom, Stonewall, II
Parker, Jacquelyn Heath
Peoples, Earl F., Sr.
Peterson, Michelle Monica
Pounds, Elaine
Pugh, Robert William, Sr.
Richardson, Linda Waters
Robinson, S. Yolanda
Rockett, Damon Emerson
Rogers, Freddie Clyde
Sampson, Ronald Alvin
Satterwhite, Frank Joseph
Scott, Aundrea Arthur
Scott, Carstella H.
Simmons, James Richard
Small, Kenneth Lester
Smith, Richard Alfred
Smith-Gray, Cassandra Elaine
Stalls, Madlyn Alberta
Stewart, Dorothy Nell
Tate, Sherman E.
Taylor, Richard L.
Thomas, Eunice S.
Thomas, Joan McHenry Bates
Thompson, Geraldine
Thompson, Linda Jo
Tokley, Joanna Nutter
Toran, Anthony
Townsend, Mamie Lee Harrington
Waddles, Charleszetta Lina
Washington, Arthur, Jr.
Watkins, Mozelle Ellis
Weary, Dolphus
Westbrook, Gilson Howard
Williams, Charles Thomas
Williams, Jesse
Williams, Ronald Lee
Williams, Sylvia J.
Wright, Keith Derek, Sr.

COMPUTER SCIENCE—PROGRAMMING/SOFTWARE DEVELOPMENT

Bell, Theodore Joshua, II
Brooks, Gilbert
Curtis, Harry S.
Gibbons, Walter E.
Harris, Carolyn Ann
Hedgley, David Rice, Jr.
Herndon, Lance H.
Holmes, William
Houston, Johnny L.
James, Alexander, Jr.
Johnson, William Smith
Matthews, Wanda Denise
McAdoo, Henry Allen
Mitchell, Deborah Karen
Mizzell, William Clarence
Moore, Jellether Marie
Odoms, Willie O.

Perkins, Gladys Patricia
Perry, Jerald Isaac, Sr.
Peterson, Michelle Monica
Powe, Joseph S.
Reynolds, Milton L.
Williams, Wilbert Edd
Young, James E.

COMPUTER SCIENCE—SYSTEMS ANALYSIS/DESIGN

Adams, Claudette Coleman
Aklilu, Tesfaye
Allen, John Henry
Barkley, Mark E.
Carnell, Lougenia Littlejohn
Carter, Perry W.
Casterlow, Carolyn B.
Crawford, Betty Marilyn
Dupree, David H.
Franklin, Martha Lois
Greene, Ronald Alexander
Herndon, Lance H.
Holloway, Arthur D.
James, Alexander, Jr.
Johnson, William Paul, Jr. (Scoogie)
Johnson, William Smith
Jones, Frank Benson
Jones, Michael Perrin
Leggon, Herman W.
McAdoo, Henry Allen
McLaurin, Howard Wilson
Minion, Mia
Mitchell, Deborah Karen
Mizzell, William Clarence
Montgomery, William R.
Moore, Jellether Marie
Odoms, Willie O.
Rodgers, William M., Jr.
Seymour, Stanley
Singleton, Herbert
Taylor, Arlene M. J.
Timberlake, John Paul
Towns, Myron B., Jr.
Trent, Jay Lester
Weatherspoon, Jimmy Lee
Williams, Malvin A.
Woodard, Lois Marie

COMPUTER SCIENCE—NOT ELSEWHERE CLASSIFIED

Allen, Philip C.
Bridgett-Chisolm, Karen
Brown, Lloyd
Byrd, George Edward
Cooper, Daneen Ravenell
Davis, Diane Lynn
Denmark, Robert Richard
DeSassure, Charles
Dixon, J. Melvin
Francisco, Marcia Madora
Greene, Charles Edward Clarence
Hanford, Craig Bradley
Harrigan, Rodney Emile
Harris, John H.
Howell, Vincent Wyatt
Johnson, Patricia Dumas
Robinson, Walter F.
Sanders, Glenn Carlos
Simmons, Isaac Tyrone
Smith, Robert W., Jr.
Stansbury, Vernon Carver, Jr.
Thomas, Ronald F.
Walker, Willie M.
Williams, Roosevelt
Wofford, Alphonso
Wright, Keith Derek, Sr.

COMPUTER SERVICES
See also MANAGEMENT/ADMINISTRATION—COMPUTER SYSTEMS/DATA PROCESSING

Brockington, Donella P.
Burns, Denise
Carter, Mary Louise
Castle, Keith L.
Coates, Shelby L.
Dyer, Charles Austen
Grant, Claude DeWitt

Greene, Frank S., Jr.
Greene, Marion O., Jr.
Ireland, Lynda
Johnson, Guy Charles
Perry, Lee Charles, Jr.
Terrell, Mable Jean
Wilkinson, Robert Steven
Wilson, F. Leon
Yelity, Stephen C.

CONSTRUCTION
See BUILDING/CONSTRUCTION; RETAIL TRADE—BUILDING/CONSTRUCTION MATERIALS; WHOLESALE TRADE—BUILDING/CONSTRUCTION MATERIALS

CORRECTIONS
See CRIMINOLOGY/CORRECTIONS

COUNSELING—CAREER/PLACEMENT

Armster-Worrill, Cynthia Denise
Ballard, Myrtle Ethel
Bond, Howard H.
Bracey, Henry J.
Brandon, Carl Ray
Bright, Willie S.
Bruce, Carol Pitt
Chatmon, Linda Carol
Congleton, William C.
Coston, Bessie Ruth
Fleming, Alicia DeLaMothe
Freeman, Nelson R.
Gilliams, Tyrone
Goff, Wilhelmina Delores
Grayson, Barbara Ann
Hackett, Obra V.
Harris, Archie Jerome
Hawkins, William Douglas
Haynes, Ulric St. Clair, Jr.
Hoye, Walter B.
Hunter, Deanna Lorraine
Jackson, Alfred Thomas
Jackson, Earl J.
Jewett, Charlie Ruth
Joell, Pamela S.
Johnson, Joseph David
King, Ruth Allen
Logan, Alphonso
Major, Henrymae M.
McGuffin, Dorothy Brown
Meeks, Reginald Kline
Walker, Cynthia Bush
Williams, Vernice Louise
Witherspoon, Fredda

COUNSELING—MENTAL HEALTH

Andrews, James E.
Bain, Erlin
Beard, Virginia H.
Bell, Carl Compton
Bobino, Rita Florencia
Bradley, Andrew Thomas, Sr.
Brandon, Carl Ray
Brown, Robert J., III
Clay, Camille Alfreda
Coleman, Barbara Sims
Crawford, Vanella Alise
Dejoie, Carolyn Barnes Milanes
Doggett, John Nelson, Jr.
Erskine, Kenneth F.
Feliciana, Jerrye Brown
Ferguson, Robert Lee, Sr. (Fergie)
Hall, Kirkwood Marshal
Handon, Marshall R., Jr.
Harper, Walter Edward, Jr.
Hodgson-Brooks, Gloria J.
Hughes, Anita Lillian
Jenkins, Louis E.
Johnson, Theodore, Sr.
Jones, Leander Corbin
Mahoney, Keith Weston
Maxey, James, III

McFaddin, Theresa Garrison
Nelson, Wanda Lee
Perez, Bobbie M. Anthony
Perry, Robert Lee
Ragland, Wylheme Harold
Rawlings, Martha (nee Morse)
Richardson, Lacy Franklin
Robertson, Evelyn Crawford, Jr.
Roy, Jasper K.
Speight, Velma R.
Thornton, Dozier W.
Tucker, Samuel Joseph
Wiley, Rena Deloris
Williams, Robert L.

COUNSELING— REHABILITATION

Bryson, Seymour L.
Burress, James R.
Cheek, Donald Kato
Cleveland, Hattye M.
Harris, Archie Jerome
Hart, Tony
Hawkins, Mary L.
Hughes, Anita Lillian
Jones, Yvonne De Marr
Lewis, Wendell J.
Malone, Cleo
Rice, Pamela Ann
Short, James Edward
Trotter, Decatur Wayne

COUNSELING— SCHOOL/ ACADEMIC

Anderson, Doris J.
Bailey, Agnes Jackson
Barr, LeRoy
Baskerville, Pearl
Baxter, Zenobia
Bell, Kenneth M.
Benton, Shirley Jean
Berry, Leroy
Blalock, Marion W.
Bowser, McEva R.
Bramwell, Patricia Ann
Broome, Pershing
Brown, Ronald Paul
Buck, Vernon Ashley, Jr.
Burns, Felton
Carper, Gloria G.
Carter, Herbert E.
Chambers, Ruth-Marie Frances
Cissoko, Alioune Badara
Coleman, Rudolph W.
Daley, Thelma Thomas
Days, Rosetta Hill
Demons, Leona Marie
Dorsey, Clinton George
Driver, Louie M., Jr.
Dudley-Smith, Carolyn J.
Dunn, Lillian Joyce
Early, Violet Theresa
Eatman, Janice A.
Edwards, Dorothy Wright
Evans, Ruthana Wilson
Faison, Helen Smith
Flippen, Frances Morton
Franklin, Harold A.
Franklin, Thomas E.
George, Carrie Leigh
Gilbert, Jean P.
Gist, Jessie M. Gilbert
Graham, Chestie Marie
Graham, Patricia
Greene, Carolyn Jetter
Guidry, Arreader Pleanna
Gunn, Willie Cosdena Thomas
Hallums, Benjamin F.
Harris, Julius
Hawkins, Lawrence C.
Hiatt, Dietrah (nee Chapman)
Hill, Johnny R.
Howard, Vera Gouke
Hughes, Anita Lillian
Hunter, Deanna Lorraine
James, Gregory Creed
Jenkins, Elizabeth Ameta
Johnson, Theodore, Sr.
Jones, Albert J.
Jones, Edward N.
Jones-Young, Terri Anita
Lattimore, Caroline Louise

Lockerman, Geneva Lorene Reuben
Lockhart, Verdree
Lucas, Linda Gail
Lynn, James Elvis
Marrs, Stella
McCloud, Aaron C.
McIver, Margaret Hill
McKay, Karen Nimmons
Mitchem, John Clifford
Morrison, Juan LaRue, Sr.
Murray, Edna McClain
Napper, James Wilbur
Patterson, Barbara Ann
Poole, Rachel Irene
Quarles, Ruth Brett
Reece, Avalon B.
Riggins, Lester
Rinsland, Roland D.
Robinson, William Earl
Rogers, Dianna
Sanders, Woodrow Mac
Sarmiento, Shirley Jean
Scott-Johnson, Roberta Virginia
Simmons, Julius Caesar
Stephenson, Carolyn L.
Sullivan, Allen R.
Summers, Retha
Tramiel, Kenneth Ray, Sr.
Trotman, Richard Edward
Walker-Williams, Hope Denise
Washington, Sandra Beatrice
Williams, Bertha Mae
Winfield, Elayne Hunt
Young, Mary E.

COUNSELING—NOT ELSEWHERE CLASSIFIED

Abdul-Malik, Ibrahim
Bass, Herbert H.
Benson, Gilbert
Bowen, Erva J.
Coleman, Marian M.
Cranston, Monroe G.
Cross, Haman, Jr.
Davenport, J. Lee
Davis, Richard C.
Dawson, Leonard Ervin
DeLarue, Louis C.
Easley, Paul Howard, Sr.
Eichelberger, William L.
Francois, Theodore Victor
Grant, Timothy Jerome
Gwynn, Florine Evayonne
Haney, Darnel L.
Harvey, Norma Baker
Hooks, Frances Dancy
Hurst, Cleveland, Jr.
James, Clarence L., Jr.
Jernigan, Curtis Dean
Johnson, Stafford Quincy
Johnson, William Paul, Jr. (Scoogie)
Jones, Albert J.
Jones, Michele Woods
King, Jeanne Faith
Lewis, Henry S., Jr.
Lewis, Willie Mae
Little, James Kelly, Jr.
Lloyd, George Lussington
Lokeman, Joseph R.
Lucas, Leo Alexander
Meacham, Robert B.
Meadows, Ferguson Booker, Sr.
Meshack, Lula M.
Nance, Herbert Charles, Sr.
Patterson, Joan Delores
Pogue, Lester Clarence
Rison, Faye Rison
Simon, Rosalyn McCord
Simpson, Willa Jean
Smith, Marie Evans
Strozier, Yvonne Iglehart
Talbot, David Arlington Roberts, Sr.
Vance, William J., Sr.

CRIMINOLOGY/ CORRECTIONS

Anderson, John C., Jr.
Anderson, Kathleen Wiley
Arrington, Saul

Barnett, Alfreda W. Duster
Baugh, James Edward
Baylor, Emmett R., Jr.
Black, Lee Roy
Blair, James H.
Brown, Leo C., Jr.
Brown, Reginald Royce, Sr.
Brown, Robert, Jr.
Bullock, Elbert L.
Calhoun, Jack Johnson, Jr.
Cason, David, Jr.
Charles, Joseph C.
Christian, Jerald Cronis
Clemmons, Clifford R.
Cleveland, Hattye M.
Clifford, Charles H.
Curry, Phyllis Joan
Darden, William Boone
Debro, Julius
Dunbar, Anne Cynthia
Edwards, Theodore Thomas
Fairman, Jimmy W.
Goodwin, Hugh Wesley
Graham, George Washington, Jr.
Griggs, Bertram S.
Hardiman, Phillip Thomas
Holmes, Mary Brown
Holmes, William B.
Horn, Evelyn B.
Hubbard, Walter T.
Hudson, John D.
Jacobs, Thomas Linwood
Jenkins, Elaine B.
Johnson, Harlan C.
Jones, Kelsey A.
Josey, Leronia Arnetta
Kent, Melvin Floyd
Lee, Thomas F.
Leon, Wilmer J., Jr.
McBee, Vincent Clermont
McHenry, James O'Neal
Mitchell, LeMonte Felton
Moore, Earl B.
Noble, John Charles
Notice, Guy Symour
Ortique, Revius Oliver, Jr.
Parker, Walter Gee
Pulley, Reginald
Ravenell, Joseph Phillip
Rivers, Griffin Harold
Shepherd, Roosevelt Eugene
Somerville, Dora B.
Steppe, Cecil H.
Thomas, John Henry
Thomas, Nina M.
Thompson, Joseph Allan
Thompson, Mark Randolph
Townsel, Ronald
Turner, Louis Edouard
Walker, Kenneth R.
Wilson, Earl Lawrence
Wrice, David

DANCE/ CHOREOGRAPHY

Ailey, Alvin
Alexander, Otis Douglas (Sule)
Allen, Debbie
Asante, Kariamu Welsh
Caldwell, Bessie Ellis
Cayou, Nontsizi Kirton
Collins, Janet
Cook, Charles Conway
Crawford, Deborah Collins
Destine, Jean-Leon
Ellington, Mercedes
Gibson, Albert (The Mad Gibson)
Guy, Jasmine
Hines, Gregory
Holder, Geoffrey
Horne, Lena
Jamison, Judith
Johnson, Bernard
Johnson, Louis
Johnson, Virginia Alma Fairfax
Lipscombe, Margaret Ann
Love, Edward M., Jr.
McIntyre, Dianne R.
McKayle, Donald Cohen
Mitchell, Arthur
Nettleford, Rex Milton
Nicholas, Fayard Antonio
Parks-Duncanson, Louise
Peters, Michael

Polite, Carlene Hatcher
Pomare, Eleo
Primus, Pearl
Raines, Walter The Baron (Sir Walter)
Reid-Bookhart, Patricia Ann
Rodgers, Rod Audrian
Smith, Judith Moore
Tomlinson, Mel Alexander
Vereen, Ben Augustus
Wood, Donna Jean

DENTISTRY

Abdullah, Larry Burley
Adams, Curtis N.
Adams, Lehman D.
Aikens, Chester Alfronza
Airall, Guillermo Evers
Akins, Allen Clinton
Alexander, Silas
Allen, Andrew A.
Allen, Elbert E.
Allen, William Henry
Anderson, Arnett Artis
Anderson, Jay Rosamond
Arbuckle, Pamela Susan
Ayers, George Waldon, Jr.
Baaqee, Susanne Inez
Bacon, Albert S.
Bailey, Weltman D., Sr.
Baker, Floyd Edward
Baker, Moorean Ann
Ballard, Billy Ray
Ballard, Walter W.
Baranco, Beverly Victor, Jr.
Baranco, Raphael Alvin
Barber, Hargrow Dexter
Barber, Janice Denise
Barnes, John B., Sr.
Baskins, Lewis C.
Bass, James L.
Bauknight, Tillman
Bell, Rouzeberry
Billingslea, Monroe L.
Bishop, David Rudolph
Black, James Tillman
Blackburn, Benjamin Allan, II
Bolden, Theodore E.
Booker, Garvall H.
Boston, George David
Boston, Horace Oscar
Boyd, Robert Nathaniel, III
Boykin, Joel S.
Braddock, Marilyn Eugenia
Braithwaite, Mark Winston
Brazington, Andrew Paul
Broadus, Clyde R.
Bronson, Fred James
Brown, Cyril H.
Brown, Donald R., Sr.
Brown, Glenn Arthur
Brown, Jacqueline D.
Brown, James E.
Brown, William F.
Bryant, William Jesse
Bugg, James Nelson
Bullock, Joseph Moses
Burgette, James M.
Burke, Denzer
Burnett, Sidney Obed (Big Sid)
Byas, Thomas Haywood
Caldwell, Sandra Ishmael
Calhoun, Noah Robert
Callahan, Samuel P.
Callender, Ralph A.
Cameron, Wilburn Macio, Jr.
Campbell, Charles Everett
Carline, William Ralph
Carter, James Edward, Jr.
Case, Arthur M.
Chance, Kenneth Bernard
Chapman, Samuel Milton
Cheek, Robert Benjamin, III
Cheeks, Carl L.
Chowning, Frank Edmond
Churchwell, Caesar Alfred
Clark, Benjamin F.
Clark, Clarence Bendenson, Jr.
Clark, James N.
Cochran, Herschel J.
Coffee, Lawrence Winston
Cohen, Amaziah VanBuren
Coleman, Harry Theodore
Coleman, Wisdom F.

Collins, Daniel A.
Collins, William Keelan
Colvin, Ernest J.
Contee, Carolyn Ann
Cook, Henry Lee, Sr.
Cook, Wallace Jeffery
Cornwall, Shirley M.
Cox, Georgetta Manning
Cox, Wendell
Craig, Frederick A.
Crawford, Jacob Wendell
Crawford, Lawrence Douglas
Cryer, Linkston T.
Cummings, Willis Nelson
Cundiff, John Howard
Darke, Charles B.
Davidson, Alphonzo Lowell
Davis, Francis D.
Davis, Howard C.
Dawkins, Stan Barrington Bancroft
Deane, Morgan R.
Derricotte, Eugene Andrew
Dickey, Lloyd V.
Driskell, Claude Evans
Duff, John Thomas
Dunston, Victor
Dunston, Walter T.
Edmunds, Walter Richard
Edwards, Arthur James
Effort, Edmund D.
Epps, Constance Arnettres
Everett, Percival L.
Farrow, Harold Frank
Felder, Loretta Kay
Ferebee, Claude T., Sr.
Fielder, Fred Charles
Flanagan, T. Earl, Jr.
Fleming, Stanley Louis
Ford, Albert S.
Ford, Marion George, Jr.
Ford, Robert Blackman
Fortson, Henry David, Jr.
Fowler, Leon, Jr.
Franklin, Dolores Mercedes
Franks, Julius, Jr.
Frohman, Roland H.
Gaither, Cornelius E.
Ganey, James Hobson
Gannaway, Nancy Harrison
Garnes, William A.
Gates, Paul Edward
Gibson, William Howard, Jr.
Gidney, Calvin L.
Gipson, Arthur A.
Gipson, Lovelace Preston, II
Glover, Bernard E.
Goggins, Horace
Goodson, Ernest Jerome
Goosby, Zuretti L.
Gordon, Robert Fitzgerald
Graves, Jerrod Franklin
Greer, Robert O., Jr.
Gunthorpe, Uriel Derrick
Hairston, Eddison R., Jr.
Hall, David Anthony, Jr.
Hall, Howard Ralph
Hall, Willie Green, Jr.
Hamilton, John Mark, Jr.
Hammond, Benjamin F.
Hammond, Melvin Alan Ray, Jr.
Hardeman, Strotha E., Jr.
Harper, Alphonsa Vealvert, III
Harper, Robert Lee
Harris, Horatio Preston
Harris, Joseph Benjamin
Haston, Raymond Curtiss, Jr.
Hawkins, Benny F., Sr.
Hawkins, Reginald A.
Haynes, Walter Wesley
Henderson, James Henry, Sr.
Henderson, James R.
Herring, Larry Windell
Hickson, Sherman Ruben
Hickson, William F., Jr.
Hines, Morgan B.
Hines, Wiley Earl (Chic)
Hodge, Cynthia Elois
Hogans, William Robertson, III
Holley, James W., III
Holloway, Nathaniel Overton, Jr.
Holmes, Louyco W.
Horne, Edwin Clay
Howard, Joseph H.

Alford, Haile Lorraine
Ali, Kamal Hassan
Ali, Schavi Mali
Allen, Betty (Mrs. R. Edward Lee III)
Allen, Blair Sidney
Allen, Harriette Louise
Allen, Samuel Washington
Allen, Shirley Jeanne
Allen, Van Sizar
Allen, Walter R.
Allen, William Barclay
Allen, William Duncan
Alston, Casco, Jr.
Amaker, Norman Carey
Aman, Mohammed M.
Amiji, Hatim M.
Amory, Reginald L.
Anderson, Avis Olivia
Anderson, Barbara Jenkins
Anderson, David Atlas
Anderson, Edgar L.
Anderson, Grady Lee
Anderson, James R., Jr.
Anderson, Ora Sterling
Anderson, Ruth Bluford
Anderson, Talmadge
Anderson, Thomas Jefferson
Anderson-Janniere, Iona Lucille
Anderson-Tanner, Frederick T., Jr.
Andrews, Benny
Andrews, Malachi
Anise, Ladun Oladunjoye E.
Anthony, David Henry, III
Araujo, Norman
Archer, Chalmers, Jr.
Archer, Juanita A.
Ardrey, Saundra Curry
Arnold, Lionel A.
Arrington, Pamela Gray
Arrington, Richard, Jr.
Arroyo, Martina
Artisst, Robert Irving
Asante, Kariamu Welsh
Ashby, Ernestine Arnold
Ashley-Harris, Dolores B.
Atkins, Carolyn Vaughn
Atkinson, Lewis K.
Atkinson, Nolan N., Jr.
Atlas, John Wesley
Attaway, John David
Aubert, Alvin Bernard
Aytch, Donald Melvin
Babb, Valerie M.
Baber, Ceola Ross
Baber, Lucky Larry
Babero, Bert Bell
Bacoats, Inez B.
Bagley, Peter B. E.
Bailey, Adrienne Yvonne
Bailey, Harold
Bailey, Harry A., Jr.
Bailey, Randall Charles
Bailey, Robert B., III
Baird, Keith E.
Baker, Dave E.
Baker, Houston A., Jr.
Baldwin, Cynthia A.
Ball, Jane Lee
Ball, Richard E.
Ballard, Allen Butler, Jr.
Ballard, Billy Ray
Bando, Thelma Preyer
Banks, James Albert
Banks, Jerry L.
Banks, Marshall D.
Banks, Sharon P.
Banks, Tazewell
Banks, William Jasper, Jr.
Banks, William Maron, III
Banner, William Augustus
Bannerman-Richter, Gabriel
Baptiste, Hansom P., Jr.
Barber, Jesse B., Jr.
Barclay, Lawrence V.
Barksdale, Richard Kenneth
Barnes, Boisey O.
Barnes, Delorise Creecy
Barnett, Alva P.
Barnett, Evelyn Brooks
Barrett, Ronald Keith
Bashful, Emmett W.
Baskerville, Pearl
Baskett, Kenneth Gerald

Basri, Gibor Broitman
Bass, Floyd L.
Bass, George Houston
Baxter, Zenobia
Bayard, Franck
Baye, Lawrence James J.
Beard, Israel
Beard, James William, Jr.
Beck, Thomas Arthur, III
Beckham, Barry Earl
Beckham, Edgar Frederick
Belcher, Leon H.
Bell, Alexander F.
Bell, Derrick Albert, Jr.
Bell, Felix C.
Bell, Howard Holman
Bell, Katie Roberson
Bell, Reva Pearl
Bell, Roseann P.
Bell, S. Aaron
Bell, Wendolyn Yvonne
Bell-Scott, Patricia
Bellegarde-Smith, Patrick
Bempong, Maxwell A.
Benjamin, Tritobia Hayes
Bennett, Julia Hubert
Bennett, Robert A.
Berkley, Constance Elaine
Bernard, Harold O.
Berry, Albert G.
Berry, Benjamin Donaldson
Berry, Frederick Joseph
Berry, Gordon L.
Berry, Lee Roy, Jr.
Berry, Lemuel, Jr.
Berry, Mary Frances
Berryman, Matilene S.
Bessent, Hattie
Beverly, Creigs C.
Biggs, Shirley Ann
Billingsley, Andrew
Billops, Camille J.
Binford, Henry C.
Biswas, Prosanto K.
Blackwell, David Harold
Blackwell, Harvel E.
Blackwell, James E.
Blackwell, Milford
Blake, J. Herman
Blakely, Edward James
Blanchet, Waldo Willie E.
Blanks, Delilah B.
Blassingame, John W.
Blaylock, Enid V.
Blouin, Rose Louise
Blount, Charlotte Renee
Blount, Larry Elisha
Boardley, Curtestine May
Boghossian, Skunder
Bogus, Diane
Bolden, John Henry
Bolden, Theodore E.
Bolden, Wiley Speights
Bolles, A. Lynn
Bond, George Clement
Bond, James Arthur
Bond, James Max, Jr.
Bond, Lloyd
Bond, Louis Grant
Bonner, Della M.
Bonner, Mary Winstead
Bontemps, Jacqueline Marie Fonvielle
Booker, Walter M.
Boone, Raymond Harold
Borders, Michael G.
Boston, George David
Boswell, Arnita J.
Bowman, James E., Jr.
Bowman, Phillip Jess
Bowser, James A.
Boyce, John G.
Boyd, Candy Dawson
Boyer, Horace Clarence
Boyer, James B.
Boyer, Spencer H.
Boykin, A. Wade, Jr.
Boynton, Ernest B., Jr.
Bozeman, Catherine E.
Bozeman, Maggie Simmons
Brabson, Howard V.
Bracey, Henry J.
Bracey, John H., Jr.
Bradford, Arvine M.

Bradford, Equilla Forrest
Bradley, David Henry, Jr.
Bradley, William B.
Bradshaw, Lawrence A.
Bragg, Robert Henry
Braithwaite, James Roland
Bramwell, Fitzgerald Burton
Branch, Addison A., Sr.
Branch, B. Lawrence
Branch, G. Murray
Branch, Harrison
Branch, William Blackwell
Brann, Herman Ivelaw
Brazeal, Braillsford Reese
Breda, Malcolm J.
Breeden, James Pleasant
Brewer, Alvin L.
Brewer, Rose Marie
Brewton, Butler E.
Bridgewater, Herbert Jeremiah, Jr.
Brieve-Martin, Ila Corrinna
Bright, Alfred Lee
Bright, Jean Marie
Brimmer, Andrew F.
Broadnax, Madison
Brockenborough, Joseph Antonio
Brockett, John Henry, Jr.
Bromery, Randolph Wilson
Brooker, Moe A.
Brooks, A. Russell
Brooks, Hunter O.
Brooks, Marcellus
Brooks, Roy Lavon
Brooks, Tilford Uthratese
Broussard, Vernon
Brown, Alyce Doss
Brown, Amos Cleophilus
Brown, Beatrice S.
Brown, Cecil M.
Brown, Charles Sumner
Brown, Costello L.
Brown, Craig Vincent
Brown, Dallas C., Jr.
Brown, Freddiemae Eugenia
Brown, Herman
Brown, John Andrew
Brown, Kenneth S.
Brown, Leroy J. H.
Brown, Leroy Thomas
Brown, Marshall Carson
Brown, Ola M.
Brown, Paul L.
Brown, Philip Erskine
Brown, Roscoe C., Jr.
Brown, Roy Hershel
Brown, Shirley Ann Vining
Brown, Tommie Florence
Brown, Walter E.
Brown, William, Jr.
Brown, William Crawford
Brown-Wright, Marjorie
Browne, Vincent J.
Browne, Vivian E.
Browning, Grainger
Brownlee, Geraldine Daniels
Brownlee, Lester Harrison-Pierce
Bruce, James C.
Bruce, John Irvin
Bryant, Anxious E.
Bryant, Henry C.
Bryant, Napoleon, Jr.
Bryant, Willa Coward
Bryant, William Jesse
Bryce-Laporte, Roy Simon
Bryson, Ralph J.
Buckner, William Pat, Jr.
Buggs, Charles Wesley
Bullins, Ed
Bullock, James
Bullock, Samuel Carey
Bullock, William Horace
Burchell, Charles R.
Burger, Mary Williams
Burke, Emmett C.
Burlew, Ann Kathleen
Burnette, Ada Puryear
Burney, Harry L., Jr.
Burnim, Mellonee Victoria
Burroughs, Baldwin Wesley
Burstermann, Juliette Phifer
Burton-Junior, Eva Westbrook
Butcher, Philip
Butler, Charles W.

Butler, Johnnella E.
Butler, Marjorie Johnson
Byers, Marianne
Byrd, Albert Alexander
Byrd, Arthur W.
Byrd, Helen P.
Byrd, Joseph Keys
Byrd, Katie W.
Cabbell, Edward Joseph
Caesar, Lois
Caldwell, Bessie Ellis
Caldwell, M. Milford
Caldwell, Marion Milford, Jr.
Calhoun, Calvin Lee
Calhoun, Fred Steverson
Calhoun, Lee A.
Callender, Wilfred A.
Calloway, Ernest
Cameron, Howard K., Jr.
Cameron, Joseph A.
Cameron, Ulysses
Campbell, Everett O.
Campbell, Otis, Jr.
Cannon, Barbara E.M.
Cannon, Charles Earl
Canson, Fannie Joanna
Carey, Addison, Jr.
Carl, Earl Lawrence
Carmichael, Benjamin G.
Carpenter, Joseph, II
Carpenter, William Arthur, II
Carroll, Edward M.
Carroll, William
Carson, Benjamin Solomon, Sr.
Carter, Barbara Lillian
Carter, David G., Sr.
Carter, Gene Raymond
Carter, Lawrence
Carter, Lawrence E., Sr.
Carter, Marion Elizabeth
Carter, Raymond Gene, Sr.
Carter, Thomas Floyd, Jr.
Carter, Yvonne P.
Cartey, Wilfred G. O.
Cartright, Lenora T.
Cartwright, Marguerite Dorsey
Carty-Bennia, Denise S.
Cary, Reby
Cascone, Jeanette L.
Cash, James Ireland, Jr.
Cash, William L., Jr.
Castenell, Louis Anthony
Cave, Herbert G.
Cave, Vernal G.
Cavin, Alonzo C.
Cayou, Nontsizi Kirton
Cazenave, Noel Anthony
Celestin, Toussaint A.
Chambers, Doris Foster
Chambers, Fredrick
Chambers, YJean S.
Chandler, James P.
Chandler, Theodore Alan
Chapman, George Wallace, Jr.
Charles, Bernard L.
Chavis, Theodore R.
Checole, Kassahun
Cheek, Donald Kato
Cheek, King Virgil, Jr.
Chestang, Leon Wilbert
Chestnut, Dennis Earl
Childs, Francine C.
Childs, Theodore Francis
Christian, Theresa
Chunn, Jay Carrington, II
Cissoko, Alioune Badara
Clark, Bettie I.
Clark, Claude Lockhart
Clark, Kenneth Bancroft
Clark, Laron Jefferson, Jr.
Clark, Major L., III
Clark, Morris Shandell
Clark, Sanza Barbara
Clark, Savanna M. Vaughn
Clark, VeVe A.
Clarke, Donald Dudley
Clarke, James Alexander
Clarke, John Henrik
Clarke, Velma Greene
Clayton, Robert Louis
Cleckley, Betty J.
Clemendor, Anthony Arnold
Clement, Josephine Dobbs

Clemmons, Jackson Joshua Walter
Clifford, Paul Ingraham
Clifton, Ivery Dwight
Clinkscales, Jerry A.
Clyburn, Elaine Marie
Coatie, Robert Mason
Cobb, Bernice Coar
Cobb, Robert S.
Cobb, Thelma M.
Cobbs, Susie Ann
Cody, Henry Leroy
Cofield, Elizabeth Bias
Cole, Edyth Bryant
Coleman, Ben Carl
Coleman, Edwin Leon, II
Coleman, Gilbert Irving
Coleman, Ronald Gerald
Coleman, Warren B.
Coles, Anna B.
Collie, Kelsey E.
Collier, Eugenia W.
Collier, Louis Malcolm
Collier, Torrence Junis
Collier, Willye
Collins, Elliott
Collins, Elsie
Collins, James Douglas
Collins, Janet
Collins, Limone C.
Collins, Maurice A.
Collins, Patricia Hill
Collins, Paul V.
Collins, Robert Frederick
Collins, Robert H.
Collins, Warren Eugene
Colston, Freddie C.
Colvin, William E.
Combs, Willa R.
Comer, James Pierpont
Comer, Marian Wilson
Cone, James H.
Conley, Herbert A.
Conley, John A.
Contee, Carolyn Ann
Conyers, James E.
Cook, Charles Conway
Cook, Mary Murray
Cook, Nathan Howard
Cook, Smalley Mike
Cook, William Wilburt
Cooley, Nathan J.
Cooper, Constance Marie
Cooper, Edward Sawyer
Cooper, Ernest, Jr.
Cooper, Iris N.
Cooper, Syretha C.
Copeland, Elaine Johnson
Copeland, Leon L.
Copeland, Robert M.
Cornelison, Carole Jane
Cotman, Henry Earl
Cottrol, Robert J.
Couche, Ruby S.
Counts, George W.
Coverdale, Herbert Linwood
Covin, David L.
Cox, Arthur James, Sr.
Cox, Euola Wilson
Cox, Georgetta Manning
Craft, E. Carrie
Cramer, Joe J., Jr.
Crawford, Mary Greer
Creighton-Zollar, Ann
Crim, Alonzo A.
Criner, Clyde
Crocker, Cyril L.
Crockett, Edward D., Jr.
Crockett, Ulysses-Atum
Cruse, Harold Wright
Cruthird, J. Robert Lee
Cruz, Virgil
Cruzat, Edward Pedro
Cruzat, Gwendolyn S.
Cudjoe, Selwyn Reginald
Cunningham, James J.
Cunningham, Paul Raymond Goldwyn
Curry, Sadye Beatryce
Curry, William Thomas
Curtis, James L.
Curtis, Juanita Gwendolyn
Curvin, Robert
Curwood, Sarah T.

Daley, Guilbert Alfred
Daley, Thelma Thomas
Dalferes, Edward R., Jr.
Dalton, Raymond Andrew
Daly, Frederica Y.
Daly, Marie Maynard
Dance, Daryl Cumber
Dandridge, Rita Bernice
Dandy, Roscoe Greer
Daniel, Jack L.
Daniel, Walter C.
Daniels, Alfred Claude Wynder
Daniels, Elizabeth
Daniels, Jean E.
Darden, Joseph S., Jr.
Darity, Evangeline Royall
Darity, William A.
Darling, Marsha Jean
Darton, Edythe M.
DaValt, Dorothy B.
Davenport, Calvin A.
David, Arthur LaCurtiss
Davidson, Alphonzo Lowell
Davidson, Earnest Jefferson
Davis, Abraham, Jr.
Davis, Alonzo J.
Davis, Arthur, III
Davis, Arthur, Jr.
Davis, Arthur Paul
Davis, Charles Alexander
Davis, Cyprian
Davis, Esther Gregg
Davis, France Albert
Davis, Francis D.
Davis, George B.
Davis, Grady D., Sr.
Davis, Johnetta Garner
Davis, Katie Elizabeth
Davis, Larry Earl
Davis, Leodis
Davis, Louis Garland
Davis, Myrtle V.
Davis, Noel Gregson
Davis, Thomas Joseph
Davis, William Hayes, Sr.
Davis, William M., Jr.
Davis, William R.
Davis, Willis H.
Dawkins, Stan Barrington
  Bancroft
Days, Rosetta Hill
Dean, Walter R., Jr.
Debas, Haile T.
DeBerry, Lois Marie
DeBracy, Warren
Debro, Julius
Decatur, Robert A.
DeCosta-Willis, Miriam
Dejoie, Carolyn Barnes Milanes
deJongh, James Laurence
Delaney, Harold
DeLeon-Jones, Frank A., Jr.
Delk, Fannie M.
Demby, William E., Jr.
Dempsey, Joseph P.
Denniston, Dorothy L.
Dent, Thomas Covington
Derricotte, Eugene Andrew
DesVerney-Sinnette, Elinor
Diallo
Dickens, Doris Lee (Mrs. Austin
  L. Fickling)
Dickens, Helen Octavia
Dickerson, Dennis Clark
Dickerson, Warner Lee
Dickson, David W. D.
Diggs, Irene
Diggs, William P.
Dike, Kenneth Onwuka
Dillard, Joey L.
Dillard, Thelma Deloris
Diuguid, Lincoln I.
Dixon, Melvin W.
Dixon, Ruth F.
Dixon, William R.
Dockery, Robert Wyatt
Dodson, Howard, Jr.
Dodson, Jualynne E. (nee White)
Donaldson, Leon Matthew
Donegan, Charles Edward
Doomes, Earl
Dorsey, Carolyn Ann
Dottin, Robert Philip
Douglas, Elizabeth Asche
Douglas, James Matthew

Douglas, Joseph Francis
Douglas, Samuel Horace
Douglass, John H.
Dove, Rita Frances
Dowery, Mary
Downing, Alvin Joseph
Downing, John William, Jr.
Drake, John Gibbs St. Clair, Jr.
Draper, Frederick Webster
Drewry, Cecelia Hodges
Drimmer, Melvin
Driskell, David C.
Drummond, William Joe
Dube, Thomas M. T.
Dudley, Thelma
Dummett, Clifton Orrin
Dumpson, James R.
Duncan, David Edward
Duncan, John C., Jr.
Duncan, Marvin E.
Dungy, Claibourne I.
Dunmore, Charlotte J.
Dunn, Marvin
Dunn, William L.
Dunston, Walter T.
DuPree, Sherry Sherrod
Duren, Emma Thompson
Durham, Barbee William
Duster, Troy
Dykes, DeWitt S., Jr.
Dykes, Marie Draper
Eagleson, Halson Vashon
Ealy, Mary Newcomb
Earl, Archie William, Sr.
Easley, Eddie V.
Eaton, James Nathaniel, Sr.
Eaton, Lela M. Z.
Echols, Ivor Tatum
Edelin, Kenneth C.
Edelin, Ramona Hoage
Edley, Christopher F., Jr.
Edwards, Alfred L.
Edwards, Cecile Hoover
Edwards, Harry
Edwards, Harry T.
Edwards, John L.
Edwards, Mattie Smith
Edwards, Robert Valentino
Edwards, Solomon
Elam, Harry Penoy
Elkins, Virgil Lynn
Elliott, Anthony Daniel, III
Elliott, Irvin Wesley
Ellis, Marilyn Pope
Ellis, Wade
Ellison, Ralph Waldo
Ellison, Robert A.
Ellois, Edward R., Jr.
Emanuel, James Andrew
Embree, James Arlington
Emrit, Ronald C.
Engs, Robert Francis
Ephraim, Charlesworth W.
Epps, Edgar G.
Epps, Roselyn Payne
Ervin, Hazel Arnett
Ervin, John B.
Erwin, James Otis
Eskridge, John Clarence
Esogbue, Augustine O.
Espree, Allen James
Esquivel, Argelia Velez
Essiet, Evaleen Johnson
Estep, Roger D.
Estill, Ann H. M.
Eubanks, Eugene E.
Eubanks, John Bunyan
Eubanks, Rachel Amelia
Eubanks, Robert A.
Eugere, Edward J.
Eure, Herman Edward
Evans, Billy J.
Evans, Lorenzo J.
Evans, Patricia P.
Evans-Dodd, Theora Anita
Fadulu, Sunday O.
Farmer, Harold E.
Farmer, Willie Sidney, Sr.
Faulk, Estelle A.
Faust, Naomi Flowe
Faw, Barbara Ann
Felix, Dudley E.
Felton, Ann Shirey
Ferere, Gerard Alphonse

Ferguson, George A.
Ferguson, Lloyd N.
Fewell, Richard
Fields, Alva Dotson
Fields, Victor Hugo
Fierce, Milfred C.
Fisher, Ada L.
Fisher, Edith Maureen
Fisher, Walter
Fitts, Leroy
Fitzgerald, Carrie Eugenia
Flack, Harley Eugene
Flake, Nancy Aline
Fleming, G. James
Fleming, Juanita W.
Fleming, Raymond Richard
Fleming, Stanley Louis
Fletcher, Winona Lee
Fleurant, Gerdes
Floyd, Samuel A., Jr.
Floyd, Vircher B.
Fomufod, Antoine Kofi
Forbes, Calvin
Ford, Ausbra
Ford, David Leon, Jr.
Ford, Luther L.
Ford, Marcella Woods
Ford, Sarah Ann
Fordham, Monroe
Foreman, Doyle
Forrest, Leon Richard
Forrest-Carter, Audrey Faye
Foster, E. C.
Foster, Frances Smith
Foster, James Hadlei
Foster, Rosebud Lightbourn
Foster, William Patrick
Francis, Edith V.
Francis, Livingston S.
Francisco, Joseph Salvadore, Jr.
Franklin, Allen D.
Franklin, Floyd
Franklin, Harold A.
Franklin, John Hope
Franklin, Renty Benjamin
Franklin, Robert Michael
Frasier, Mary Mack
Frazier, Leon
Frazier, Levi, Jr.
Freeman, Ruges R.
Freeman, Thomas F.
Froe, Otis David
Frost, Olivia Pleasants
Fuller, Almyra Oveta
Furman, James B.
Fykes, Leroy Matthews, Jr.
Gabbin, Alexander Lee
Gabbin, Joanne Veal
Gadsden, Nathaniel J., Jr.
Gadson, Rosetta E.
Gaffney, Floyd
Gainer, John F.
Gaines, Ernest J.
Gaines, Ray D.
Gaither, Thomas W.
Gallwey, Sydney H.
Galvin, Emma Corinne
Gamble, Wilbert
Gammon, Reginald Adolphus
Gantt, Walter N.
Garcia, William Burres
Gardiner, George L.
Gardner, Bettye J.
Gardner, Frank W.
Gardner, LaMaurice H.
Garibaldi, Antoine Michael
Garland, Phyllis T.
Garner, Charles
Garner, Grayce Scott
Garner, Mary E.
Garraway, Michael Oliver
Garrett, Aline M.
Garrett, E. Wyman
Garrett, Naomi M.
Garrett, Romeo Benjamin
Garrett-Brown, Fannie E.
Garrison, Jewell K.
Garrity, Monique P.
Gary, Lawrence Edward
Gary, Melvin L.
Gates, Henry Louis, Jr.
Gates, Thomas Michael
Gatewood, Wallace Lavell
Gatlin, Elissa L.

Gauff, Joseph F., Jr.
Gayle, Addison, Jr.
Gayles, Anne Richardson
Gecau, Kimani J.
Gentry, Atron A.
Geran, Joseph, Jr.
Gholson, General James
Gibbs, Jewelle Taylor
Gibson, Donald B.
Gilbert, Jean P.
Gilchrist, Lorenzo
Gilkes, Cheryl Townsend
Gill, Gerald Robert
Gill, Robert Lewis
Gillespie, Avon E.
Gillespie, William G.
Gilliard, Joseph Wadus
Gilpin, Clemmie Edward
Gipson, Mack, Jr.
Givens, Donovahn Heston
Glasco, Anita L.
Glasgow, Douglas G.
Gleason, Eliza
Glenn, Cecil E.
Gloster, Jesse E.
Glover, Arthur Lewis, Jr.
Glover, Victor Norman
Goff, Regina Mary
Golden, Donald Leon
Golden, Marita
Gomillion, Charles Goode
Gona, Ophelia Delaine
Gonsalves, June Miles
Goode, James Edward
Gooden, Cherry Ross
Gooden, Winston Earl
Goodson, Martin L., Jr.
Goodwin, E. Marvin
Goodwin, Felix L.
Goodwin-Fulgham, Roietta
Gordon, Allan M.
Gordon, Edmund W.
Gordon, Ethel M.
Gordon, Maxie S., Sr.
Gordon, Milton A.
Goss, Theresa Carter
Goudy, Andrew James
Govan, Ronald M.
Graham, Frederick Mitchell
Graham, Helen W.
Graham, Patricia
Graham, Peter Edgar
Graham, Precious Jewel
Graham, Tecumseh Xavier
Grant, Anna Augusta Fredrina
Grant, Jacquelyn
Grant, Joseph N.
Grant, Wilmer, Jr.
Gray, C. Vernon
Gray, Raymond Leroy, Sr.
Gray-Little, Bernadette
Graydon, Wasdon, Jr.
Grayson, Barbara Ann
Green, Frederick Chapman
Green, Richard
Green, Robert L.
Greenberg, Reuben M.
Greene, Charles Lavant
Greene, Charles Rodgers
Greene, Joann Lavina
Greene, Mitchell Amos
Greenfield, Roy Alonzo
Greenwood, Charles H.
Greer, Robert O., Jr.
Gregory, Karl Dwight
Griffin, Betty Sue
Griffin, Jean Thomas
Griffin, Lula Bernice
Griffin, Ronald C.
Griffith, Elwin Jabez
Griffith, Ezra Edward
Griffiths, Bertie Bernard
Griggs, Mildred Barnes
Grigsby, Jefferson Eugene, Jr.
Grigsby, Lucy Clemmons
Grigsby, Margaret Elizabeth
Grist, Arthur L.
Grist, Reri
Groff, Regis F.
Groves, Harry Edward
Guidry, Arreader Pleanna
Guillory, William A.
Guinier, Ewart
Gullattee, Alyce C.

Gulliver, Adelaide Cromwell
Gunnell, James B.
Gunthorpe, Uriel Derrick
Guy, George V.
Guy, William I.
Guyton, Booker T.
Gwin, Wiliviginia Faszhianato
  (Cora)
Hairston, Eddison R., Jr.
Hale, Frank W., Jr.
Hale-Benson, Janice Ellen
Haley, Johnetta Randolph
Hall, David
Hall, Joseph A.
Hall, Kim Felicia
Hamilton, Edwin
Hamilton, Franklin D.
Hamilton, James G.
Hammond, Benjamin F.
Hammond, James Matthew
Hampton, Grace
Hampton, Phillip Jewel
Hampton, Robert L.
Hancock, Eugene Wilson White
Hankerson, Elijah H.
Hanna, Cassandria H.
Hanna, Harlington Leroy, Jr.
Hardaway, Yvonne Veronica
Harden, Marvin
Hardin, Eugene
Hardin, John Arthur
Harding, Robert E.
Harding, Vincent
Hardman-Cromwell, Youtha
  Cordella
Hardwick, Clifford E., III
Hardy, John Louis
Hargraves, William Frederick, II
Hargrove, Andrew
Harley, Philip A.
Harper, Curtis
Harper, Earl
Harper, Michael Steven
Harper, Walter Edward, Jr.
Harrell, Oscar W., Jr.
Harrington, Elaine Carolyn
Harris, Calvin D.
Harris, Caspa L., Jr.
Harris, Charles Somerville
Harris, Charles Wesley
Harris, Donald J.
Harris, Edward E.
Harris, Elbert L.
Harris, George Dea
Harris, Harcourt Glenties
Harris, James E.
Harris, John Everett
Harris, John H.
Harris, Mary Styles
Harris, Narvie J.
Harris, Robert Allen
Harris, Trudier
Harris, Vander E.
Harris, William J.
Harris, William McKinley, Sr.
Harrison, Algea Othella
Harrison, Emma Louise
Harrison, Paul Carter
Hart, Tony
Hartman, Hermene Demaris
Hartsfield, Arnett L., Jr.
Harvey, Harold A.
Harvey, Louis-Charles
Hasbrouck, Ellsworth Eugene
Haskins, James S.
Hatcher, Ester L.
Hawkins, Alexander A.
Hawkins, Benny F., Sr.
Hawthorne, Lucia Shelia
Hayden, John Carleton
Hayes, Albertine Brannum
Hayes, Annamarie Gillespie
Hayes, Floyd Windom, III
Hayes, Leola G.
Hayes, Vertis
Haynes, Barbara Asche
Haynes, Eugene, Jr.
Haynes, John Kermit
Haynes, Leonard L., Jr.
Haywood, L. Julian
Head, Laura Dean
Hearn, Rosemary
Heath, James E.
Hedgepeth, Chester Melvin, Jr.

Heflin, John F.
Hegeman, Charles Oxford
Hemmingway, Beulah S.
Henderson, George
Henderson, Lenneal Joseph, Jr.
Henderson, Nannette S.
Henderson, Stephen E.
Hendricks, Barkley L.
Hendrix, Daniel W.
Henry, Calvin O. L.
Henry, Egbert Winston
Henry, James T., Sr.
Henry, Mildred M. Dalton
Henry, Samuel Dudley
Henry, Walter Lester, Jr.
Henry, Warren Elliott
Hermanuz, Ghislaine
Hernton, Calvin Coolidge
Herrell, Astor Yeary
Hewing, Pernell Hayes
Hewitt, Vivian Davidson
Hickman, Thomas Carlyle
Hicks, Arthur James
Hicks, Clayton Nathaniel
Hicks, Leon Nathaniel
Higginbotham, Peyton Randolph
Higgins, Chester A., Sr.
High, Freida
Hightower, James Howard
Hildreth, Gladys Johnson
Hill, Bennett David
Hill, Carl M.
Hill, Errol Gaston
Hill, Esther P.
Hill, James A., Sr.
Hill, James Lee
Hill, Marnesba D.
Hill, Patricia Liggins
Hill, Paul G.
Hill, Ray Allen
Hill, Sylvia Ione-Bennett
Hill, Thelma W.
Hill, Wendell T., Jr.
Hill-Lubin, Mildred Anderson
Hinds, Lennox S.
Hine, Darlene Clark
Hinton, Alfred Fontaine
Hinton, Hortense Beck
Hoagland, Everett H., III
Hobbs, Joseph
Hodge, John Edward
Hodges, David Julian
Hogu, Barbara J. Jones
Holbert, Raymond Ray
Holden, Dorothy M.
Holley, Sandra Cavanaugh
Holliday, Bertha Garrett
Holloway, Joaquin Miller, Jr.
Holmes, Hamilton Earl
Holmes, Herbert
Holmes, Lorene B.
Holmes, Louyco W.
Holmes, Robert A.
Holmes, Zan W., Jr.
Holsey, Lilla G.
Holt, Edwin J.
Holt, Grace S.
Holt, James Stokes, III
Hood, Elizabeth
Hood, Harold
Hooks, Mose Yvonne Brooks
Hooper, Gerald F.
Hope, Richard Oliver
Hopkins, Ernest Loyd
Hopkins, John Orville
Hopkins, Leroy Taft, Jr.
Hopkins, Vashti Edythe Johnson
Hord, Frederick Lee
Horn, Lawrence Charles
Horne, Gerald C.
Horne-McGee, Patricia J.
Hornsby, Alton, Jr.
Horton, Carrell Peterson
Hosten, Adrian
Houston, Johnny L.
Houston, Lillian S.
Howard, Elizabeth Fitzgerald
Howard, John Robert
Howard, Lawrence Cabot
Howard, Lytia Ramani
Howard, Shirley M.
Howard, Vivian Gordon
Howe, Ruth-Arlene W.
Howell, Malqueen
Hoye, Walter B., II

Hoyt, Thomas L., Jr.
Hoyte, Arthur Hamilton
Hubbard, Amos B.
Hudson, Herman C.
Hudson, Theodore R.
Huff, Louis Andrew
Huggins, Nathan Irvin
Hughes, Anita Lillian
Hughes, Joyce A.
Hull, George, Jr.
Hull, Gloria T.
Humphrey, Kathryn Britt
Humphrey, Margo
Hunt, Barbara Ann
Hunt, Maurice
Hunt, Portia L.
Hunter, Archie Louis
Hunter, Charles A.
Hunter, David Lee
Hunter, Frances S. (nee Kraft)
Hunter, Lloyd Thomas
Hunter, Patrick J.
Hunter-Lattany, Kristin Eggleston
Huntley, Richard Frank
Hurd, David James, Jr.
Hurd, James L. P.
Hutcherson, Bernice B. R.
Hutchins, Bertha (nee Humphrey)
Hutchinson, George
Hutson, Jean Blackwell
Ibekwe, Lawrence Anene
Irvine, Freeman Raymond, Jr.
Isaac, Eugene Leonard
Ishman, Sybil R.
Ita, Lawrence Eyo
Ivey, Horace Spencer
Jack, Stephanie C.
Jackson, Agnes Moreland
Jackson, Andrew
Jackson, Arthur James
Jackson, Barbara Loomis
Jackson, Blyden
Jackson, Charles E.
Jackson, Edgar Newton, Jr.
Jackson, Jacquelyne Johnson
Jackson, James Sidney
Jackson, James Talmadge
Jackson, Keith Hunter
Jackson, Kennell A., Jr.
Jackson, Luther Porter, Jr.
Jackson, Marvin Alexander
Jackson, Miles Merrill
Jackson, Murray Earl
Jackson, Paul L.
Jackson, Prince Albert, Jr.
Jackson, Raymond T.
Jackson, Reginald Leo
Jackson, Roswell F.
Jackson, Thelma Conley
Jackson, W. Sherman
Jackson, William E.
Jackson, Winston Burleigh
Jacobs, Jacqueline Minette
Jacobs, Sylvia Marie
Jamerson, Jerome Donnell
James, Allix Bledsoe
James, Charles L.
James, David Phillip
James, Elridge M.
James, Felix
James, H. Rhett
James, Hamice R., Jr.
James, June, III
James, Luther
James, Marquita L.
James, Robert D.
Jarrett, Hobart Sidney
Jarrett, Thomas D.
Jason, Howard M.
Jay, James M.
Jaynes, Gerald David
Jeffers, Jack
Jefferson, Alphine Wade
Jefferson, Joseph L.
Jeffries, Rosalind R.
Jenkins, Adelbert Howard
Jenkins, Carl Scarborough
Jenkins, Clara Barnes
Jenkins, Edmond Thomas
Jennings, Jeanette
Jerome, Norge Winefred
Johnson, Addie Collins
Johnson, Alcee LaBranche
Johnson, Arthur Lyman

Johnson, Audreye Earle
Johnson, Betty Jo
Johnson, Beulah C.
Johnson, Caliph
Johnson, Carl Lee
Johnson, Carl Thomas
Johnson, Charles
Johnson, Charles E. Memusi
Johnson, Charles H.
Johnson, Charles Richard
Johnson, Douglas H.
Johnson, Edna DeCoursey
Johnson, Edward A.
Johnson, Edward Elemuel
Johnson, George M.
Johnson, Golden Elizabeth
Johnson, Harold R.
Johnson, Harry A.
Johnson, Ivory
Johnson, Joe
Johnson, John W.
Johnson, Johnny B.
Johnson, Lemuel A.
Johnson, Leroy Ronald
Johnson, Martin Leroy
Johnson, Patricia Dumas
Johnson, Raymond Lewis
Johnson, Robert C.
Johnson, Roosevelt Young
Johnson, Theodore L.
Johnson, Tobe
Johnson, Tommie Ulmer
Johnson, Vermelle Jamison
Johnson, Walter J.
Johnson, Walter Lee
Johnson, Willard Raymond
Johnson, William T. M.
Joiner, Burnett
Jones, Ann R.
Jones, Barbara A. P. (nee Posey)
Jones, Ben F.
Jones, Betty Harris
Jones, Butler Alfonso
Jones, Clifton Ralph
Jones, Cloyzelle Karrelle
Jones, Delmos J.
Jones, Donald W.
Jones, Ferdinand Taylor, Jr.
Jones, Floresta Deloris
Jones, Frank S.
Jones, G. Daniel
Jones, George H.
Jones, George Williams
Jones, Gerald E.
Jones, Harold M.
Jones, Hortense
Jones, Jacqueline
Jones, James A.
Jones, James Edward, Jr.
Jones, James McCoy
Jones, Jennie Y.
Jones, Jesse W.
Jones, Joseph
Jones, Kirkland C.
Jones, Lawrence N.
Jones, Leander Corbin
Jones, Lois Mailou
Jones, Lucius
Jones, Mack H.
Jones, Marcus Earl
Jones, Nettie Pearl
Jones, Phillip Erskine
Jones, Raymond Morris
Jones, Reginald L.
Jones, Rena Talley
Jones, Robbie Neely
Jones, Roy Junios
Jones, Theodore Cornelius
Jones, William W.
Jones, Woodrow Harold
Jones, Yvonne Vivian
Jones-Grimes, Mable Christine
Jordan, Barbara C.
Jordan, Casper LeRoy
Jordan, Eddie Jack, Sr.
Jordan, George Lee
Jordan, Harold Willoughby
Jordan, Janice Marie
Jordan, June M. (nee Meyer)
Jordan, Kenneth Ulys
Jordan, Wesley Lee
Jordan, William Alfred, III
Josey, E. J.
Kamoche, Jidlaph Gitau

Keller-Brinson, Charlotte Jarvis
Kelly, Earl Lee
Kelsey, George Dennis Sale
Kendrick, Curtis
Kennedy, Anne Gamble
Kennedy, Floyd C.
Kennedy, James E.
Kennedy, Joseph J., Jr.
Kennedy, Joyce S.
Kennedy, Matthew W.
Kennedy, Theodore Reginald
Kenney, Virgil Cooper
Kern-Foxworth, Marilyn L
Kerr, Frances Mills
Kerr, Hortense R.
Kersey, Bertha Brinnett
Keyser, George F.
Khatib, Syed Malik
Kilimanjaro, John Marshall
Kilson, Martin Luther, Jr.
Kimbrough, Clarence B.
Kindall, Luther Martin
King, Arthur Thomas
King, Calvin E.
King, Donald E.
King, Estelle Holloway
King, Lewis M.
King, Mary Booker
King, Patricia Ann
King, Reatha Clark
King-Hammond, Leslie
Kirk, Sarah Virgo
Kirk, Wyatt D.
Kirkland, Gloria
Kirkland, Jack A.
Kirkland, Theodore
Kirkpatrick, Garland Penn
Kisner, Robert Garland
Kitchen, Wayne Leroy
Knigh, Billy Earl, I.
Knight, Perry Vertrum
Knight, Robert S.
Koger, Linwood Graves, III
Krigger, Marilyn Francis
Kumanyika, Shiriki K.
Kyles, Josephine H.
Lacey, Wilbert, Jr.
Lachman, Ralph Steven
Lacy, Versia Lindsay
LaFayette, Kate Bulls
Lafontant, Julien J.
Lahr, Charles Dwight
Laing, Edward A.
Lairet, Dolores Person
Lampley, Calvin D.
Landry, L. Bartholomew
Lane, Pinkie Gordon
Langston, Esther R.
Lanier, Dorothy Copeland
Lanier, Marshall L.
Larrie, Reginald Reese
Lawrence, Annie L.
Lawrence, Jacob A.
Lawrence, Leonard E.
Lawrence, William Wesley
Lawson-Thomas, Althean Shannon
Leacock, Stephen Jerome
Leak, Lee Virn
Leal, Carol Ann
Lede, Naomi W.
LeDoux, Jerome G.
Lee, Allen Francis, Jr.
Lee, Charlotte O.
Lee, Clifton Valjean
Lee, Guy Milicon, Jr.
Lee, Katherine I.
Lee, Kermit J., Jr.
Lee, Kermit L.
Lee, Lena S. King
Lee, Lucius E.
Lee, Michael Waring
Lee, Mildred Kimble
Leevy, Carroll M.
LeFlore, William B.
Leggon, Herman W.
Lehman, Paul Robert
Lemeh, Dorotha Hill
LeMelle, Tilden J.
Leonard, Byrdie A. Larkin
Lester, Donald
Lester, Julius
Lester, William Alexander, Jr.
Lewis, Almera P.

Lewis, Cary B., Jr.
Lewis, Charles Bady
Lewis, Cleveland Arthur
Lewis, Dick Edgar
Lewis, Elsie Makel
Lewis, Hylan Garnet
Lewis, James Edward
Lewis, Lauretta F
Lewis, Meharry Hubbard
Lewis, Samella (nee Sanders)
Lewis, Viola Gambrill
Lewis, William Arthur
Lewis, William Sylvester
Lightfoot, William P.
Lillie, Vernell A. (nee Watson)
Lincoln, C. Eric
Lindsay, Beverly
Lindsay, Crawford B.
Lindsey, Jerome W.
Lipscombe, Margaret Ann
Little, Herman Kernel
Little, Monroe Henry
Little, Ronald Eugene
Little, Willie Howard
Littlejohn, Edward J.
Lloyd, Raymond Anthony
Lockard, Jon Onye
Locke, Don C.
Locke, Hubert G.
Lockett, Brooker Thomas
Lockett, James D.
Lockette, Agnes Louise
Lockwood, James Clinton
Logan, Frenise A.
Lomas, Ronald Leroy
London, Clement B.G.
Long, Charles H.
Long, John Edward
Long, Juanita Outlaw
Long, Richard A.
Lopes, William H.
Lorde, Audre Geraldine
Louard, Agnes A.
Louistall-Monroe, Victorine Augusta
Loury, Glenn Cartman
Love, Barbara
Love, Eleanor Young
Love, Mabel R.
Love, Thomas Clifford
Low, Patricia Enid Rose
Lucas, James L.
Lucas, Wilmer Francis, Jr.
Luck, Etta Robena
Luis, William
Lyda, Wesley John
Lynch, Hollis R.
Lynch, Lillie Riddick
Lyons, James E., Sr.
Maben, Hayward C., Jr.
Mabrey, Marsha Eve
Macbeth, Robert
Mack, Ally Faye
Mack, Joan
Mack, Wilbur Ollio
Macklin, Anderson D.
Macklin, John W.
Madgett, Naomi Long
Magee, Sadie E.
Majete, Clayton Aaron
Major, Clarence
Malekebu, Daniel Sharp
Mallette, John M.
Malone, Gloria S.
Malone, J. Deotha
Malvin, Reuben L.
Manley, Albert
Mann, Marion
Manning, Reuben D.
Mapp, Edward C.
Mapp, Frederick Everett
Marable, June Morehead
Marion, Claud Collier
Marius, Kenneth Anthony
Markey, Beatrice (nee Greene)
Marriott, Salima Siler
Marshall, Albert Prince
Marshall, Carl Leroy
Marshall, Carter Lee
Marshall, Edwin Cochran
Marshall, Herbert A.
Marshall, Paule Burke
Marshall, Richard Douglass
Martin, Basil Douglas

Martin, Carolyn Ann
Martin, Cortez Hezekiah
Martin, Curtis Jerome
Martin, Elmer P.
Martin, Ernest Douglass
Martin, Evelyn B.
Martin, Harold B.
Martin, Joanne Mitchell
Martin, John W.
Martin, Rayfus
Martin, Ruby Julene Wheeler
Martin, Tony
Mason, Kenneth
Mason, Major Albert, III
Massie, Samuel Proctor
Mathis, Thaddeus P.
Matthews, Virgil E.
Maultsby, Portia K.
Maxwell, Bertha Lyons
Maxwell, Roger Allan
Mayes, Doris Miriam
Mayfield, William S.
Maynard, Edward Samuel
Mbere, Aggrey Mxolisi
McAdams, Robert L.
McAdoo, Harriette P.
McAfee, Leo C., Jr.
McAfee, Walter S.
McArthur, Barbara Jean (nee Martin)
McBay, Henry Cecil
McBride, Ullysses
McBrier, Vivian Flagg
McCall, Aidan M.
McCall, Barbara Collins
McClain, James W.
McClain, Shirla R.
McClane, Kenneth Anderson, Jr.
McCleave, Mansel Philip
McClellan, Frank Madison
McClendon, Kellen
McClomb, George E.
McCluskey, John A., Jr.
McConnell, Roland C.
McCoy, James F.
McCoy, Walter D.
McDaniel, Reuben R.
McDaniel, William T., Jr.
McDaniels, Alfred T.
McDonald, Curtis W.
McDonald, Jon Franklin
McDuffie, Hinfred
McElroy, George A.
McEwing, Mitchell Dalton
McFadden, James L.
McFarlane, Franklin E.
McFerrin, Robert
McFerrin, Sara Elizabeth Copper
McGee, Eva M.
McGee, Henry W., Jr.
McGhee, Nancy Bullock
McGinty, Doris Evans
McGuire, Chester C., Jr.
McHenry, Donald F.
McHenry, Mary Williamson
McIntosh, Walter Cordell
McKelpin, Joseph P.
McKenzie, Edna B. (nee Chappell)
McKinney, E. Doris
McKinney, Richard Ishmael
McKinney, Theophilus Elisha, Jr.
McLaughlin, Andree Nicola
McLaughlin, David
McLaughlin, George W.
McLean, John Alfred, Jr.
McLean, John Lenwood
McLemore, Leslie Burl
McMillan, James C.
McNeil, Alvin J.
McPherson, James Alan
McRoy, Ruth Gail
McStallworth, Paul
McWhorter, Grace Agee
McWilliams, Alfred E., Jr.
McWorter, Gerald A.
Meade, William F.
Meade-Tollin, Linda C.
Meadows, Ferguson Booker, Jr.
Means, Fred E.
Melrose, Thomas S.
Meriwether, Louise
Merritt, Bishetta Dionne
Mesa, Mayra L.
Michaux, Henry G.

Miles, Norman Kenneth
Millard, Thomas Lewis
Millender, Mallory Kimerling
Miller, Andrea Lewis
Miller, Benjamin T.
Miller, Horatio C.
Miller, Jake C.
Miller, James Arthur
Miller, Jeanne-Marie A.
Miller, M. Sammye
Miller, Ronald Baxter
Miller, Samuel O.
Miller, Yvonne Bond
Miller-Jones, Dalton
Millican, Arthenia Bates
Milliones, Jake
Minor, Willie
Minyard, Handsel B.
Mitchell, Earl Douglass, Jr.
Mitchell, Ella Pearson
Mitchell, Henry Heywood
Mitchell, Julius P.
Mitchell, Loften
Mitchell-Kernan, Claudia Irene
Mitchem-Davis, Anne
Mobley, Eugenia L.
Molette, Barbara J.
Monagan, Alfrieta Parks
Monagas, Lionel John
Monroe, Annie Lucky
Monroe, Lillie Mae
Moo-Young, Louise L.
Moody, Charles David, Sr.
Moone, James Clark
Moore, Alice Evelyn
Moore, Annie Jewell
Moore, Archie Bradford, Jr.
Moore, Carol Louise (nee Wood)
Moore, Donald Torian
Moore, Gerald L.
Moore, Helen Boulware
Moore, Hilliard T., Sr.
Moore, Jean E. (nee Campbell)
Moore, Jossie A.
Moore, Larry Louis
Moore, Nathan
Moore, Oscar James, Jr.
Moore, Oscar William, Jr.
Moore, Robert F.
Moore, Undine Smith
Moran, Robert E., Sr.
Moreland, Lois Baldwin
Morgan, Booker T.
Morgan, Charlotte Theresa
Morgan, Gordon D.
Morgan, Hazel C. Brown
Morgan, Jane Hale
Morgan, Raleigh, Jr.
Morris, Calvin S.
Morris, Clifton
Morris, Kelso B.
Morris, Lewis R.
Morris, Margaret Lindsay
Morris, Stanley E., Jr.
Morris-Hale, Walter
Morrison, Keith Anthony
Morrow, John Howard, Jr.
Morse, Oliver
Mortimer, Delores M.
Morton, Charles E.
Morton, Cynthia Neverdon
Mosee, Jean C.
Moseley, Calvin Edwin, Jr.
Moseley, James Orville B.
Moses, Alice J.
Moses, Henry A.
Moses, Wilson Jeremiah
Mosley, Geraldine B. (nee Brown)
Mosley, Myrtis H.
Moss, James A.
Moss, Simeon F.
Moten, Chauncey Donald
Murphy, Alvin Hugh
Murphy, Frances L., II (Mrs. Charles J. Campbell)
Murphy, George B., Jr.
Murray, Anna Martin
Murray, James Hamilton
Murray, Mabel Lake
Murray, Thomas W., Jr.
Musgrove, Margaret Wynkoop
Mutale, Elaine Butler
Mwamba, Zuberi I.
Myers, Ernest Ray

Myers, Jacqualine Desmona
Myers, Lena Wright
Myricks, Noel
Nabors, Charles J., Jr.
Nagan, Winston Percival
Nails, Odell
Ndlovu, Callistus P.
Neal, Homer Alfred
Neal, William J.
Neavon, Joseph Roy
Nelson, Wanda Lee
Nelson, William Edward, Jr.
Nelson-Holgate, Gail Evangelyn
Nero, David M., Jr.
Nettleford, Rex Milton
Nettles, Willard, Jr.
Newell, Virginia K.
Newkirk, Queenie Hortense
Newman, Geoffrey W.
Newsom, Lionel H.
Newsome, Clarence Geno
Newton, Jacqueline L. (nee Jefferson)
Newton, James E.
Newton, Oliver A., Jr.
Neyland, Leedell Wallace
Nichols, Charles Harold
Nichols, Owen D.
Nichols, Paul
Niles, Lyndrey Arnaud
Nilon, Charles Hampton
Nnolim, Charles E.
Noble, John Charles
Noguera, Pedro Antonio
Noles, Eva M.
Norman, Alex James
Norman, Maidie Ruth (nee Gamble)
Norman, William H.
Norris, Arthur Mae
Norris, Ethel Maureen
Northcross, Wilson Hill, Jr.
Northern, Robert A.
Norton, Eleanor Holmes
Nunnally, David H., Sr.
Nwanna, Gladson I. N.
Obinna, Eleazu S.
O'Daniel, Therman Benjamin
Oden, Gloria C.
Oglesby, James Robert
Okhamafe, E. Imafedia
Okunor, Shiame
Oliver, Daily E.
Oliver, Melvin L.
Ollison, Ida Bell
Omolade, Barbara
Osakwe, Christopher
Osborne, Alfred E., Jr.
Osborne, Oliver Hilton
Overton, Betty Jean
Owens, Andi
Owens, Charles Edward
Owens, Daniel Walter
Owens, George A.
Owens, Joan Murrell
Owens, Wallace, Jr.
Oyewole, Saundra Herndon
Pace, Kay Robertine
Padgett, James A.
Padulo, Louis
Page, Willie F.
Paige, Alvin
Paige, Roderick
Painter, Nell Irvin
Palmer, Edward
Pannell, William E.
Parker, Henry H.
Parker, Keith Dwight
Parker, Kellis E.
Parker, Paul E.
Parker, Stephen A.
Parks, Arnold Grant
Parks, James Dallas
Parrish, Charles Henry
Parson, Willie L.
Pasteur, Alfred Bernard
Patrick, Odessa R.
Patten, W. George
Patterson, David Leon
Patterson, Elizabeth Hayes
Patterson, Evelynne (nee Roberts)
Patterson, Orlando Horace
Patterson, Raymond R.
Patterson, Willis Charles

Patton, Curtis L.
Patton, Gerald Wilson
Paul, Alvin, III
Payton, Albert Levern
Peace, G. Earl, Jr.
Peagler, Frederick Douglass
Pearson, Clifton
Peebles, Allie Muse
Peebles-Wilkins, Wilma Cecelia
Peek, Booker C.
Peek, Marvin E.
Peery, Benjamin Franklin, Jr.
Peirson, Gwynne Walker
Pemberton, Priscilla Elizabeth
Penceal, Bernadette Whitley
Penn, Nolan E.
Penny, Robert
Penny, Robert L.
Pennywell, Phillip, Jr.
Pentecoste, Joseph C.
Perdue, Robert Eugene
Pereira, Sarah Martin
Perez, Bobbie M. Anthony
Perkins, Linda Marie
Perrimon, Vivian Spence
Perry, Aubrey M.
Perry, Brenda L.
Perry, Frank Anthony
Perry, Harold
Perry, Patsy Brewington
Perry, Richard
Perry, Robert Lee
Perry, Yvonne Scruggs
Person, Dawn Renee
Person, William Alfred
Peters, Erskine Alvin
Peters, James Sedalia, II
Peters, Samuel A.
Peterson, Alphonse
Petioni, Muriel M.
Pettis, Joyce Owens
Petty, Rachel Monteith
Phelps, C. Kermit
Phillip, Michael John
Phillips, Bertrand D.
Phillips, Earl W.
Phillips, Edward Martin
Phillips, James Lawrence
Phillips, June M. J.
Phillips, Romeo Eldridge
Pickens, William Garfield
Pierce, Chester Middlebrook
Pierce, Cynthia Straker
Pierce, Delilah W.
Pierce, Raymond O., Jr.
Pierce, Reuben G.
Pierce, Walter J.
Pindell, Howardena D.
Pinkelton, Norma Harris
Pinkney, Alphonso
Pinn, Sameul J., Jr.
Pinson, Thomas J.
Piper, W. Archibald
Pipes, William H.
Pittman, Audrey Bullock
Pitts, Vera L.
Plummer, Ora B.
Plumpp, Sterling Dominic
Poindexter, Hildrus A.
Pointer, Richard H.
Polk, William C.
Pollard, Alton Brooks, III
Pollard, Diane S.
Pollard, William Lawrence
Ponder, Eunice Wilson
Poole, Marion L.
Porter, Curtiss E.
Porter, John Henry
Potts, Harold E.
Powell, Dudley Vincent
Powell, Philip Melancthon, Jr.
Pratt, Louis Hill
Press, Harry Cody, Jr.
Prestage, Jewel Limar
Preston, Carey Maddox
Prettyman, Quandra
Prewitt, Lena Voncille Burrell
Price, Alfred Douglas
Price, Charles Eugene
Price, Ramon B.
Pride, Armistead Scott
Proctor, William H.
Propes, Victor Lee
Prothro, Johnnie Watts

Prudhomme, Nellie Rose
Pruitt, Anne Smith
Pruitt, Clarence O.
Puckrein, Gary Alexander
Pugh, Clementine A.
Pugh, Roderick W.
Pullen-Brown, Stephanie
Pulley, Clyde Wilson
Putnam, Rosalind (nee Lawson)
Pyke, Willie Oranda
Quarles, George R.
Quaynor, Thomas Addo
Quinn, Alfred Thomas
Quinton, Barbara A.
Radcliffe, Aubrey
Rainey, Bessye Coleman
Ramsey, Otto Bryant
Randall, Ann Knight
Randolph, Robert Lee
Ransom, Preston L.
Rashford, John Harvey
Rashied, A. John
Ravenell, Mildred
Rawlins, Elizabeth B.
Ray, Jacqueline Walker
Ray, Judith Diana
Ray, William Benjamin
Rayford, Phillip Leon
Reaves, Benjamin Franklin
Reavis, John William, Jr.
Redd, George N.
Redmond, Eugene B.
Reed, Allene Wallace
Reed, Daisy Frye
Reed, James
Reed, James W.
Reed, Jasper Percell
Reed, Rodney J.
Reese, Mamie Bynes
Register, Jasper C.
Reid, Joel Otto
Reid, Leslie Bancroft
Reid, Robert Daniel
Reid, Robert Dennis
Reid-Bookhart, Patricia Ann
Rembert, Emma White
Renfroe, Earl W.
Revis, Nathaniel W.
Reynolds, Edward
Reynolds, Grant
Reynolds, Milton L.
Reynolds, Viola J.
Rhodes, Paula R.
Rice. Louise Allen
Rice, Mitchell F.
Richard, Alvin J.
Richards, Johnetta Gladys
Richards, Lloyd G.
Richardson, Charles Ronald
Richardson, Cordell
Richardson, Earl Stanford
Richardson, Elisha R.
Richardson, Henry J., III
Richmond, Norris L.
Ridgeway, Bill Tom
Ridley, Alfred Denis
Rier, John Paul, Jr.
Rigby, Edward H.
Riley, Clayton
Rison, Faye Rison
Rivers, Louis
Roane, Philip Ransom, Jr.
Roberts, Evelyn Hoard
Roberts, Roy J.
Robertson, Alan D.
Robertson, Benjamin W.
Robertson, Quincy L.
Robinson, Andrew
Robinson, Ann Garrett
Robinson, Cecelia Ann
Robinson, Curtis
Robinson, Edward A.
Robinson, Ella S.
Robinson, Eunice Primus
Robinson, Frank J.
Robinson, Genevieve
Robinson, Gertrude Rivers
Robinson, Ira Charles
Robinson, Jayne G.
Robinson, Jim C.
Robinson, Lawrence B.
Robinson, Luther D.
Robinson, Mary Elizabeth (nee Wilder)

Robinson, Maude Eloise
Robinson, Prezell Russell
Robinson, Randall S.
Robinson, Ruth
Robinson, Theodore Paul
Robinson, Walter G.
Robinson, Wilhelmena S.
Robinson, William Henry
Rocha, Joseph Ramon, Jr.
Rodgers, Carolyn Marie
Rodgers, Joseph James, Jr.
Rogers, Charles D.
Rogers, George
Rogers, George, III
Rogers, Norman
Rollins, Richard Albert
Rose, Alvin W.
Rose, Arthur
Ross, Joy Belle
Rosser, Samuel Blanton
Rotan, Constance S.
Rouse, Donald E.
Rouse, Jacqueline Anne
Rucker, Nannie George
Ruffin, John
Russell, Charlie L.
Russell, Joseph D.
Rutledge, Philip J.
Ryder, Mahler B.
Sadler, Wilbert L.
Saffold, Oscar E.
St. John, Primus
St. Omer, Vincent V. E.
Salmon, Jaslin Uriah
Samuels, Olive Constance
Sanchez, Sonia Benita
Sanders, Charles Lionel
Sanders, Robert B.
Sanders, Woodrow Mac
Sandle, Floyd Leslie
Sandoval, Dolores S.
Sands, George M.
Santos, Henry J.
Sarmiento, Shirley Jean
Satchell, Ernest R.
Satcher, David
Saunders, Doris E.
Saunders, Elijah
Saunders, Elizabeth A.
Saunders, Mary A.
Saunders, Mauderie Hancock
Saunders, Raymond Jennings
Saunders-Henderson, Martha M.
Savage, Horace Christopher
Sawyer, Broadus Eugene
Scales, Alice Marie
Scales, Manderline Elizabeth
Schooler, James Morse, Jr.
Scott, Charlotte Hanley
Scott, Harold Russell, Jr.
Scott, John P.
Scott, John Sherman
Scott, John T.
Scott, Joseph Walter
Scott, Levan Ralph
Scott, Marvin Wayne
Scott, Mona Vaughn
Scott, Nathan A., Jr.
Scott, Osborne E.
Scott, Roland B.
Scott, Veronica J.
Scott, Wesley E.
Scruggs, Allie W.
Scruggs, Otey Matthew
Sealy, Joan R.
Searles, Charles R.
Sears, Bertram E.
Sebhatu, Mesgun
Secret, Philip E.
Secundy, Marian Gray
See, Letha Annette
Seibert-McCauley, Mary F.
Settles, Rosetta Hayes
Shade, Barbara J. (nee Robinson)
Shade, Oscar D.
Shakoor, Adam Adib
Shannon, David Thomas
Shaw, Ann
Shaw, Spencer Gilbert
Sheffey, Ruthe G.
Shepherd, Benjamin A.
Shepherd, Roosevelt Eugene
Sherrill, Vanita Lytle
Sherwood, Wallace Walter
Shine, Ted

Shipp, Howard J., Jr.
Shockley, Grant S.
Shockley, Thomas Edward
Short, Kenneth L.
Shorty, Vernon James
Shotwell, Ada Christena
Showell, Hazel John
Shropshire, Arthur C.
Shropshire, John Sherwin
Shuman, Jerome
Sikes, Melvin Patterson
Siler, Joyce B.
Sillah, Marion Rogers
Simmons, Annie Marie
Simmons, Charles William
Simmons, John Emmett
Simms, Carroll Harris
Simms, Ernest S.
Simms, Gregory Frame
Simon, Joseph Donald
Simpkins, J. Edward
Sims, Adrienne
Singh, Rajendra P.
Sinkler, George
Sirmans, Meredith Franklin
Sizemore, Barbara A. (nee Laffoon)
Skinner, Clementine Anna
Slade, Phoebe J.
Slaughter, Diana T.
Slaughter, Fred Leon
Slaughter, John Etta
Slie, Samuel N.
Sloss, Minerva A.
Small, Lily B.
Smalls, O'Neal
Smallwood, Osborn Tucker
Smith, A. Wade
Smith, Alonzo Nelson
Smith, Alphonso Lehman
Smith, Alvin
Smith, Ann Elizabeth
Smith, Barbara
Smith, Benjamin Franklin
Smith, Bettie M.
Smith, Charles F., Jr.
Smith, Charlie Calvin
Smith, Donald Hugh
Smith, Dorothy J.
Smith, Dorothy Louise White
Smith, Eleanor Jane
Smith, Fredrick E.
Smith, Geraldine T.
Smith, Glenn R.
Smith, Hale
Smith, Henry Thomas
Smith, Herald Leonydus
Smith, J. Clay, Jr.
Smith, John Arthur
Smith, Judith Moore
Smith, Keith Dryden, Jr.
Smith, Luther Edward, Jr.
Smith, Paul
Smith, Paul Bernard
Smith, Paul M.
Smith, Pearlena W.
Smith, Philip Gene
Smith, Robert
Smith, Robert P., Jr.
Smith, Robert W., Jr.
Smith, Virginia M.
Smith, Walter L.
Smitherman, Geneva
Smithey, Robert Arthur
Smythe-Haith, Mabel Murphy
Solomon, Barbara J.
Somerville, Addison Wimbs
Sommerville, Joseph C.
Southall, Geneva H.
Southerland, Ellease
Southern, Eileen Jackson
Southern, Joseph
Sowell, Thomas
Spaights, Ernest
Spellman, Alfred B.
Spellman, Oliver B., Jr.
Spencer, Margaret Beale
Spencer, Michael Gregg
Spiva, Ulysses Van
Spivey, Donald
Sprauve, Gilbert A.
Spriggs, G. Max
Sprout, Francis Allen
Spruill, James Arthur

Stalls, Madlyn Alberta
Stanback, Thurman W.
Stanley, Curtis E.
Staples, Robert E.
Starke, Catherine Juanita
Starks, Robert Terry
Steele, Claude Mason
Stent, Madelon Delany
Stent, Theodore R.
Stephens, Lee B., Jr.
Stepto, Robert Burns
Stepto, Robert Charles
Stetson, Jeffrey P.
Stevens, Althea Williams
Stevens, Thomas Lorenzo, Jr.
Stevenson, Russell A.
Stewart, Adelle Wright
Stewart, Albert C.
Stewart, Elizabeth Pierce
Stewart, James Benjamin
Stewart, John Othneil
Stewart, Mac A.
Stinson, Joseph McLester
Stith, Melvin Thomas
Stokes, Gerald Virgil
Stone, Chuck
Stone, Herman, Jr.
Stone, Kara Lynn
Strawn, Aimee Williams
Strickland, Dorothy S.
Strickland, Frederick William, Jr.
Strider, Maurice William
Stripling, Luther
Stuart, Marjorie Mann
Stull, Virginia Elizabeth
Subryan, Carmen
Suggs, Robert Chinelo
Sullivan, Allen R.
Sullivan, J. Christopher
Sullivan, Richard H.
Sullivan, Zola Jiles
Suneja, Sudhir Kumar
Sutton, Sharon Egretta
Sutton, Walter L.
Sutton, William Wallace
Swain, Ronald L.
Swan, L. Alex
Sweeney, John Albert
Swinton, Sylvia P.
Sykes, Vernon Lee
Sylvas, Lionel B.
Sylvester, Melvin R.
Sylvester, Patrick Joseph
Syphax, Burke
Taborn, John Marvin
Talbot, Alfred Kenneth, Jr.
Talton, Almanda R.
Tate, Merze
Taylor, Arnold H.
Taylor, Charles Avon
Taylor, Dale B.
Taylor, Dalmas A.
Taylor, Della B.
Taylor, Estelle Wormley
Taylor, Felicia Michelle
Taylor, Herman Daniel
Taylor, Howard F.
Taylor, Hycel B.
Taylor, Jerome
Taylor, Joseph T.
Taylor, Julius H.
Taylor, Maurice Clifton
Taylor, Mildred D.
Taylor, Orlando L.
Taylor, Quintard, Jr.
Taylor, Stuart A.
Taylor, Thad, Jr.
Taylor, William L.
Tearney, Russell James
Terborg-Penn, Rosalyn M.
Terrell, Francis
Terrell, Francis D'Arcy
Terrell, Melvin C.
Terrell, Robert L.
Thandeka
Thomas, Bettye Collier
Thomas, C. Edward
Thomas, Carl Alan
Thomas, Charles Columbus
Thomas, Eula Wiley
Thomas, Gerald Eustis
Thomas, Harry Lee
Thomas, Herman Edward
Thomas, James Samuel

Thomas, Latta R., Sr.
Thomas, Louphenia
Thomas, Lucille Cole
Thomas, Mary A.
Thomas, Nathaniel
Thomas, Robert C.
Thomas, Robert Lewis
Thomas, Wilbur C.
Thompson, Adell, Jr.
Thompson, Almose Alphonse, II
Thompson, Betty E. Taylor
Thompson, Donnis Hazel
Thompson, Francesca
Thompson, Jesse M.
Thompson, Litchfield O'Brien
Thompson, Marcus Aurelius
Thompson, Regina
Thompson, Robert Farris
Thompson, Winston Edna
Thomson, Gerald Edmund
Thorburn, Carolyn Coles
Thornell, Richard Paul
Thornton, Clifford E.
Thrower, Julius A.
Thurman, Alfonzo
Thurman, Frances Ashton
Thurston, Paul E.
Tidwell, John Edgar
Tildon, Charles G., Jr.
Tillman, Talmadge Calvin, Jr.
Timberlake, Charles E.
Timberlake, Constance Hector
Tipton, Dale Leo
Tisdale, Celes
Tobias, Randolf A.
Todd, Donald
Tolbert, Odie Henderson, Jr.
Tomlinson, Robert
Toms-Robinson, Dolores C.
Toppin, Edgar Allan
Tottress, Richard Edward
Towns, Sanna Nimtz
Trader, Harriet Peat
Trapp-Dukes, Rosa Lee
Trice, William B.
Trimiar, J. Sinclair
Tripp, Luke Samuel
Trottman, Charles Henry
Troupe, Quincy Thomas, Jr.
Troutman, Porter Lee, Jr.
Truitte, James F.
Tryman, Mfanya Donald
Tucker, Dorothy M.
Tucker, Norma Jean
Tuitt, Jane Eliza
Tunstall, Lucille Hawkins
Tunstall-Grant, Ruth Neal
Turner, Castellano B.
Turner, Darwin T.
Turner, Doris J.
Turner, Evelyn Evon
Turner, John B.
Turner, John Barrimore
Turner, W. Burghardt
Turner, Willie
Tyson, John C.
Umolu, Mary Harden
Urdy, Charles E.
Uzoigwe, Godfrey N.
Vanderpool, Eustace Arthur
Van Hook, Warren Kenneth
Vargus, Ione D.
Venson, Jeanine
Vera, Ndoro Vincent
Vessup, Aaron Anthony
Vogel, Roberta Burrage
Waddell, Charles M.
Waddles, George Wesley, Sr.
Wade, Achille Melvin
Wade, Jacqueline E.
Wade-Gayles, Gloria Jean
Waiguchu, Muruku
Walden, Robert Edison
Walker, Annie Mae
Walker, Charles
Walker, Cynthia Bush
Walker, Frances
Walker, George Edward
Walker, George T.
Walker, Joseph A.
Walker, Kenneth R.
Walker, Lewis
Walker, Sheila Suzanne
Walker, Stanley M.

Walker, Wilbur P.
Wallace, Karen Smyley
Wallace, Phyllis A.
Waller, Robert Lee
Walter, John C.
Walters, Curla Sybil
Walters, Hubert Everett
Walters, Ronald
Walton, Harriet J.
Walton, James Edward
Ward, Carole Geneva
Ward, James Dale
Wardlaw, Alvia Jean
Ware, Gilbert
Ware, William L.
Warren, Joseph W.
Warren, Morrison Fulbright
Warren, Nagueyalti
Warren, Stanley
Washington, Earl Melvin
Washington, James Melvin
Washington, Joseph R., Jr.
Washington, Linda Phaire
Washington, Mary Helen
Washington, Michael Harlan
Washington, Paul M.
Washington, Samuel T.
Washington, Sarah M.
Washington, Walter
Wasswas, Edgar S.
Waters, Henrietta E.
Watkins, Benjamin Wilston
Watkins, Levi, Jr.
Watson, Betty Collier
Watson, Eugenia B. (nee Baskerville)
Watson, Joseph W.
Watson, Odest Jefferson, Sr.
Watson, Wilbur H.
Watts, Alexander Alfred
Watts, John E.
Watts, Roberta Ogletree
Waymer, Richard Turner
Wead, Rodney Sam
Weatherly, Tom
Weaver, Garrett F.
Weaver, John Arthur
Weaver, Robert C.
Webb, Melvin Richard
Weber, Shirley Nash
Webster, Cecil Ray
Webster, Niambi Dyanne
Weddington, Rachel Thomas
Weil, Robert L.
Weiss, Joyce Lacey
Welch, Harvey, Jr.
Welch, Winfred Bruce
Wells, James Lesesne
Wells, Patrick Roland
Welton, Evelyn R.
West, George Ferdinand, Jr.
West, Harold Dadford
West, John Raymond
West, Pheoris
West, William Lionel
Westmoreland, Samuel Douglas
Whaley, Mary H.
Wharton, A. C., Jr.
Wharton-Boyd, Linda F.
Whatley, Booker Tillman
Wheeler, Shirley Y.
Whitaker, Mical Rozier
White, Barbara Williams
White, Booker Taliaferro
White, Clayton Cecil
White, Clovis Leland
White, Donald Edward
White, Frederic Paul, Jr.
White, Harold Rogers
White, Jimmie L.
White, Katie Kinnard
White, Tommie Lee
Whitehead, John L., Jr.
Whitten, Charles F.
Wideman, John E.
Wiggins, Joseph L.
Wiggins, William H., Jr.
Wilder, Cora White
Wiley, John D., Jr.
Wilkerson, Margaret Buford
Wilkins, Allen Henry
Wilkins, Leona B.
Wilkins, Roger Wood
Wilkinson, Donald Charles

Scruggs, Cleorah J.
Seay, Lorraine King
Shannon, Marian L.H.
Simpson, Juanita H.
Sims, Laura Mack
Sloss, Minerva A.
Small, Stanley Joseph
Smalls, Dorothy M. (nee Mayhams)
Smith, Eddie D., Sr.
Smith, Frank
Smith, Juanita Smith
Smith, Mildred B.
Smith, Pearlena W.
Smith, Quentin P.
Smith, Robert Johnson
Speight, Eva B.
Springer, George Chelston
Stallings, Gregory Ralph
Stanley, Hilbert Dennis
Stanton, Beverly A.
Stratton-Morris, Madeline Robinson
Strong, Marilyn Terry
Swanson, Edith (nee Mays)
Tate, Matthew
Taylor, Anderson
Taylor, John L.
Taylor, Mildred D.
Taylor, Octavia G.
Taylor, Vida Maurice Jarmon
Thomas, Erma Lee
Thompson, Clarissa J.
Thompson, Hilton Lond
Thompson, Imogene A.
Thompson, John Andrew
Thompson, Rosie L.
Thompson, Sylvia Moore
Thurman, Marjorie Ellen
Tingle, Lawrence May
Todd, Charles O.
Todman, Jureen Francis
Tolliver, Ned, Jr.
Turner, Johnnie Rodgers
Turner, Winston E.
Turner-Givens, Elia Mae
Tyler, Hubert
Tyson, Lorena E.
Underwood, Frankye Harper
Usry, James LeRoy
Van Dyke, Henry
Vaughn, Alvin
Walker, Larry Vaughn
Walker, William Harold
Waller, Eunice McLean
Ward, Albert A.
Washington, Mary Parks
Watkins, Charles Booker
Watts, Wilsonia
West, John Raymond
Westbrook, Joseph W., III
Wheaton, Thelma Kirkpatrick
White, Gregory Durr
White-Ware, Grace E.
Whittington, Harrison DeWayne
Wiggins, Clifton Allen, Sr.
Wilborn, Letta Grace Smith
Wilkie, Earl A.
Williams, Jean Carolyn
Williams, Jester C.
Williams, Lillian C.
Williams, Sylvia J.
Williams, Ulysses Jean
Wilson, Edith N.
Wilson, Floyd Edward, Jr.
Wilson, John W.
Wilson, Sandra E.
Wilson, Wilson W.
Wilson-Felder, Cynthia Ann
Wilson-Smith, Willie Arrie
Wimberly, James Hudson
Winfrey, Charles Everett
Winston, Dennis Ray
Winston, Lillie Carolyn
Woolcock, Ozeil Fryer
Wright, Dmitri
Wright, Mary H.

EDUCATION—NOT ELSEWHERE CLASSIFIED

Ackord, Marie M.
Adams, Jackie W., Sr.
Alexander, Alma Duncan

Allen, Edna Rowery
Amos, Oris Elizabeth Carter
Anderson, Chester R.
Anderson, Doris J.
Anderson, Ella L.
Anderson, Gloria L.
Anderson, Louise Payne
Arties, Elvira Yvonne
Ashby, Ernestine Arnold
Auld, Albert Michael
Bachus, Marie Darsey
Balthrope, Jacqueline Moorehead
Bankhead, Patricia Ann
Banks, Ronald Trenton
Banks, Waldo R., Sr.
Barnett, Samuel B.
Barrett, Sherman L.
Batiste, Mary Virginia
Bauduit, Harold S.
Beane, Patricia Jean
Beckett, Sydney A.
Belton, Edward DeVaughn
Belton, Robert
Bennett, Courtney Ajaye
Bernstine, Daniel O.
Billups, Florence W.
Black, Charlie J.
Blackwell, J. Kenneth
Booker, Merrel Daniel, Sr.
Boone, Clinton Caldwell
Boone, Elwood Bernard, Jr.
Bowser, McEva R.
Bowser, Vivian Roy
Boyd-Clinkscales, Mary E.
Boykin, Willie
Bridges, Lucille W.
Briggins, Charles E.
Broadnax, Melvin F.
Brooks, Charlotte Kendrick
Brooks, Daisy M. Anderson
Brown, Willis, Jr.
Brunt, Samuel Jay
Bryant, Edward Joe, III
Buck, Judith Brooks
Bullock, Deborah Lynne
Burford, Effie Lois
Burleson, Jane Geneva
Burns, Emmett C.
Bush, Ann
Butler, Anna M. (nee Land)
Butler, Eula M.
Butler, Katherine Elizabeth
Butler, Rebecca Batts
Cain, Johnnie M.
Caldwell, Gladys Emanuel
Calhoun, Cecelia C.
Calomee, Annie E.
Campbell, Margie
Cannon, Katie Geneva
Carter, Blanche Nelson
Carter-McCraw, Carolyn
Cathcart, George W.
Caviness, Lorraine F.
Chambers, James R.
Channell, Eula L.
Cheese, Pauline Staten
Chennault, Madelyn
Cherry, Cassandra Brabble
Clardy, William J.
Clark, Ameera H.
Clark, Bertha Smith
Clark, Sanza Barbara
Clayton, Ina Smiley
Coatie, Robert Mason
Cole, Arthur
Coleman, Winson
Collins, Elsie
Cooper, Ethel Thomas
Copeland, Betty Marable
Copeland, Emily America
Copeland, Ray
Coppedge, Arthur L.
Costen, Melva Wilson
Cowden, Michael E.
Crable, Dallas Eugene
Crawford, Dock D., Jr.
Crump, Wilbert S.
Cummings, E. Emerson
Cutler, Donald
Dale, Virginia Marie
Daley, Thelma Thomas
Davis, Dale Brockman
Davis, George B.
Davis, Marianna White

Davis, Morris E.
Davis, William Hayes, Sr.
Davis, Willie A.
Dawson, Leonard Ervin
Dawson, Martha E.
Daye, Charles Edward
DeClue, Anita
DeJarmon, Elva Pegues
D'Hue, Robert R., Jr.
Dickens, Doris Lee (Mrs. Austin L. Fickling)
Douglas, John Daniel
Dove, Pearlie C.
DuBose, Otelia
Dungee, Margaret R.
Eaves, A. Reginald
Edwards, Robert Erskine
Ellis, O. Herbert
Epps, Naomi Newby
Erwin, Claude F., Sr.
Eubanks, Rachel Amelia
Evans, Ada B.
Evans, Eleanor Juanita
Evans, Eva L.
Evans, Lorenzo J.
Faison, Helen Smith
Ferguson, Sherman E.
Finley, Betty M.
Fitch, Clarence E.
Fitzgerald, Roosevelt
Flagg, E. Alma W.
Fleming, Bruce E.
Ford, Aileen W.
Foreman, S. Beatrice
Foster, Frank B., III
Foster, James H.
Fountain, William Stanley
Fox, Theodore B.
Fredericks, Leroy Owen
Freeman, Robert Lee
French, George Wesley
Fuhr, Samuel E.
Futrell, Mary Hatwood
Gabbin, Joanne Veal
Gaines, Edythe J.
Garrett, Thaddeus, Jr.
Garvin, Mildred Barry
Gates, Audrey Castine
Gholston, Betty J.
Gibbes, Emily V.
Gilbert, Eldridge H. E.
Gilmore, Al Tony
Gilmore, Robert McKinley, Sr.
Glover, Eula E.
Goodwin, Norma J.
Gordon, Aaron Z.
Gordon, Fannetta Nelson
Goring, William S.
Graham, Albertha L.
Graham, Chestie Marie
Graham, Delores Metcalf
Gray, Mattie Evans
Green, Charles A.
Green, Reuben H.
Greene, Jerome A.
Griffith, Barbara J.
Griffith, Vera Victoria
Grigsby, Lucy Clemmons
Gunn, Alex M., Jr.
Guyton, Patsy
Hall, Horathel
Hall, Rubye Maie
Hamill, Margaret Hudgens
Hamilton, Paul L.
Harkins, Rosemary Knighton
Harrington, Charles E.
Harrison, Carol L.
Harrison, Don K., Sr.
Harvey, Louis-Charles
Haynes, George E., Jr.
Hemphill, Miley Mae
Henderson, Australia Tarver
Henderson, Stanley L.
Henderson, Virginia Ruth McKinney
Henry, Charles E.
Henry, Joseph King
Henry, Thomas
Hentrel, Bobbie Kuykendall
Higgins, Sammie L.
Hightower, Michael
Holland, Spencer H.
Holly, Ella Louise
Holmes, Barbara J.

Hopkins, Edna J.
Houston, Marsh S.
Howard, Corliss Mays
Howard, Gwendolyn Julius
Howze, Dorothy J.
Hudson, Winson
Hunter, Johnnie L.
Hunter, Richard C.
Hutton, Gerald L.
Inyamah, Nathaniel Ginikanwa N.
Isaac, Ephraim
Jackson, Clarence H.
Jackson, Frank Donald
Jackson, Ida Louise
Jackson-Foy, Lucy Maye
Jangdharrie, Wycliffe K.
Jeter, Velma Marjorie Dreyfus
Johnson, Addie Collins
Johnson, Constance W. Van Brunt
Johnson, Edward M.
Johnson, Frederick, Jr.
Johnson, Juanita B.
Johnson, Lorretta
Johnson, Michael Anthony
Johnson, Valrie E.
Jones, Brent M.
Jones, Franklin D.
Jones, Geraldine J.
Jones, Kirkland C.
Jones, Lawrence W.
Jones, Sondra Michelle
Jones, Yvonne De Marr
Jordan, Robert A.
Kelly, Florida L.
Kennedy, William Thomas, Jr.
Kimbrough, Thomas J.
King, Ruby Ryan
King, Ruth G.
Knight, W. H., Jr. (Joe)
Kumanyika, Shiriki K.
LaBrie, Peter, Jr.
Laney, Robert Louis, Jr.
Laroche, Gerard A.
Latham, Weldon Hurd
Law, M. Eprevel
Lawing, Raymond Quinton
Laws, Ruth M.
Lawyer, Cyrus J., III
Lee, Aaron
Lee, Mildred Kimble
Lee-Smith, Hughie
Leeke, John F.
Leonard, Carolyn Marie
Leonard, Walter J.
Lightfoot, Jean Harvey
Lindsey, Ouida
Lofton, Dorothy W.
London, Edward Charles
Loving, Rose (nee Billups)
Lyle, Roberta Branche Blacke
Lynn, James Elvis
Lyons, George W.C., Sr.
Mack, Charles Richard
Malekebu, Daniel Sharp
Marshall, Calvin Bromley, III
Martin, Lawrence Raymond
Mason, Hilda Howland M.
Mason, Orenthia Delois
Mayes, Nathaniel H., Jr.
Maynor, Dorothy
McCane, Charles Anthony
McCannon, Dindga Fatima
McClure, Earie
McCoy, Frank Milton
McGee, JoAnn
McGregor, Edna M. (nee McGruder)
McKerson, Effie M. (nee Stoker)
McKinney, Alma Swilley
McNeil, Alvin J.
McNeill-Huntley, Esther Mae
Mims, Robert Bradford
Montague, Lee
Moore, Helen J.
Morris, Elise L.
Moss, Otis, Jr.
Murphy, Gene
Murray, Nevada (nee Mackey)
Nelson, Cleopatra McClellan
Nelson-Holgate, Gail Evangelyn
Nesbitt, Prexy-Rozell William
Nettles, Willard, Jr.

Newbern, Walter P.
Newell, Matthias Gregory
Nichols, Walter LaPlora
O'Kain, Marie Jeanette
Onli, Turtel
Page, Marguerite A.
Palmer, James E.
Parker, Edward Everett
Patrick, Opal Lee Young
Patterson, Curtis Ray
Patton, Robert
Patton, William C.
Peace, Eula H.
Peeler, Diane Faustina
Perdue, Julia M. Ward
Perkins, Eugene
Perkins, Leonard L.
Perry, Jean B.
Perry, William E.
Petty, Reginald E.
Phillips, Barbara (nee Kinard)
Phillips, Dilcia R.
Piper, Elwood A.
Player, Willa B.
Pledger, Verline S.
Pogue, Frank G.
Pompey, Charles Spencer
Poole, Marion L.
Porter, Blanche Troullier
Porter, James H.
Potter, Judith Diggs
Primous, Emma M.
Pryor, Lillian W.
Puryear, Alvin N.
Randolph, Elizabeth
Rayford, Zula M.
Reaves, E. Fredericka M.
Reaves, Franklin Carlwell
Reid, Goldie Hartshorn
Reinhardt, John Edward
Richardson, Timothy
Riddick, Louise K.
Ridgel, Gus Tolver
Roberts, Alfred Lloyd
Roberts, Lorraine Marie
Roberts, Samuel Kelton
Robertson, Lethia
Robinson, Adeline Black
Robinson, Catherine (nee Strown)
Robinson, Ella S.
Robinson, Jonathan N.
Robinson, Lawrence D.
Robinson, Randall S.
Rogers-Lomax, Alice Faye
Rose, Shelvie
Rountree, Ella Jackson
Roy, Jessie H. (nee Hailstack)
Roy, Joe Eddie, Sr.
Samkange, Tommie Marie
Scott, Levan Ralph
Scruggs, Sylvia Ann
Scrutchions, Benjamin
Seaton, Shirley Marie Smith
Sevillian, Clarence Marvin
Shands, Franklin M., Sr.
Shopshire, James Maynard
Simmons, Hazel Forrow
Sindos, Louise King
Slaughter, Carole D.
Smalls, Jacquelyn Elaine
Smith, Dorothy Louise White
Smith, Joseph Edward
Smith, Marietta Culbreath
Smith, Reginald D.
Smith, Roulette William
Smith, Sallie P. (nee Phillips)
Smith, Wallace Charles
Smith, William Pernell
Stanyard, Hermine P.
Stewart, Emily Jones
Stratton-Morris, Madeline Robinson
Stull, Robert J.
Suggs, William Albert
Summerville, Tommie Lewis
Swain, Alice M.
Sweeney, John Albert
Talley, James Edward
Talley, John Stephen
Tanner, James W., Jr.
Terrell, Mary Ann
Thibodeaux, Sylvia Marie
Thomas, Alice Waters
Thomas, Douglas L.

Thomas, Gloria V.
Thompson, Rosie L.
Thrash, Ernestine
Tillman, Lillian G. (nee Garland)
Todd, Donald
Tolliver, Joel
Toomer, Vann Alma Rosalee
Toran, Kay Dean
Trice, Juniper Yates
Trim, John H.
Turner, Elmyra G.
Turner, William H.
Tyner, Charles R.
Tyrance, Herman J.
Verrett, Joyce M.
Wade, Mildred Moncrief
Walker, Mary Alice
Walker, Maurice Edward
Wallace, Claudette J. (nee Delgado)
Walls, Melvin
Walton, Sidney F., Jr.
Washington, Leroy
Washington, Oscar D.
Washington, Thomas
Watley, Margaret Ann
Watson, Odest Jefferson, Sr.
Watson, Wilbur H.
Watts, Roberta Ogletree
Weaver, Reginald Lee
Whaley, Wayne Edward
Wheadon, Rosetta Fay (nee Dawkins)
Wheeler, Susie Weems
White, Clayton Cecil
White, Ella Flowers
Whiteside, Ernestyne E.
Wicker, Isabelle
Williams, Ann E. A. (nee Anderson)
Williams, Arnette L.
Williams, Clara Belle
Williams, James Arthur
Williams, Lorece P.
Williams, Malcolm Demosthenes
Williams, Martha S.
Williams, Naomi Fisher (Mrs. C. Delmar Williams)
Williams, Tommye Joyce
Williams, Willie J.
Williams-Green, Joyce F.
Williford, Cynthia W.
Willis, Henry Stokes, Jr.
Wilson, Hughlyne Perkins
Wilson, Ray F.
Wimberly, Edward P.
Winfield, Linda Fitzgerald
Winfrey, Charles Everett
Witherspoon, Annie C.
Wolfe, Estemore A.
Womack, Walter Anderson
Wood, Donna Jean
Woodall, Ellis O., Sr.
Woodfolk, Joseph O.
Wormley, Cynthia L.
Wright, Jeremiah A., Jr.
Wright, Stanley V.
Wright, William Gaillard
Wyatt, Beatrice E.
Wynn, Daniel Webster
Yeary, James E., Sr.
Yerger, Amos G.
Young, Barbara J.
Young, Elizabeth Bell
Young, Jean Childs
Youngblood, Ozie F.
Zimmerman, Samuel Lee

EDUCATIONAL ADMINISTRATION

Abebe, Teshome
Abercrumbie, Paul Eric
Abraham, Sinclair Reginald
Ackerman, Patricia A.
Acrey, Autry
Adams, Dolly Desselle
Adams, Elaine Parker
Adams, Eva W.
Adams, Frederick G.
Adams, Howard Glen
Adams, Kattie Johnson
Adams, Richard Melvin, Jr.
Adams, Russell Lee
Adams, Verna May

Adams-Dudley, Lilly Annette
Addei, Arthella Harris
Addison, Terry Hunter, Jr.
Adeyiga, Adeyinka A.
Aggrey, O. Rudolph
Airall, Angela Maureen
Airall, Zoila Erlinda
Akin, Ewen M., Jr.
Albright, Robert, Jr.
Aldridge, Delores P.
Alexander, John Wesley, Jr.
Alexis, Carlton Peter
Alexis, Marcus
Ali, Kamal Hassan
Allen, Betty (Mrs. R. Edward Lee III)
Allen, Brendra Foster
Allen, George
Allen, Maxine Bogues
Allen-Noble, Rosie Elizabeth
Aman, Mohammed M.
Ammons, Tamara Nash
Anders, Richard H.
Anderson, Amel
Anderson, Carl Edwin
Anderson, David Atlas
Anderson, Edgar L.
Anderson, Eloise B. McMorris
Anderson, Granville Scott
Anderson, Ora Sterling
Andrews, Adolphus
Andrews, James F.
Andrews, Maxine Ramseur
Appleby-Young, Sadye Pearl
Arburtha, Leodies Uyless
Archer, Chalmers, Jr.
Archer, Susie Coleman
Arinwine, Kenneth Wayne
Armster-Worrill, Cynthia Denise
Armstrong, J. Niel
Armstrong, Matthew Jordan, Jr.
Armstrong, Nelson
Arnez, Nancy L.
Arnold, Alton A., Jr.
Arnold, Clarence Edward, Jr.
Arnold, Lionel A.
Arrington, Richard, Jr.
Askew, Roger L.
Atchison, Calvin O.
Atkins, Brenda J.
Auld, Rose A.
Austin, Bobby William
Austin, Mary Jane
Ayers, George E.
Aziz, Kareem A.
Babbs, Junious C., Sr.
Baber, Lucky Larry
Bacoats, Inez B.
Bagby, Rachel L
Bailey, Adrienne Yvonne
Bailey, Donn Fritz
Bailey, Gracie Massenberg
Bailey, Harry A., Jr.
Bailey, Mona Humphries
Bailey, Robert B., III
Bain, Josie Gray
Baines, Tyrone Randolph
Baker, David Nathaniel, Jr.
Baker, Henry W., Sr.
Baker, Houston A., Jr.
Baldwin, Wilhelmina F.
Ball, Richard E.
Ballard, Allen Butler, Jr.
Ballard, Janet Jones
Balthrope, Jacqueline Moorehead
Bando, Thelma Preyer
Banks, Arthur C., Jr.
Banks, Dwayne Martin
Banks, Loubertha May
Barber, James W.
Barclay, Lawrence V.
Barefield, Ollie Delores
Barfield, Leila Millford
Barfield, Rufus L.
Barnes, Leonard C.
Bashful, Emmett W.
Baskin, Andrew Lewis
Bastine, Lillian Beatrice
Bates, Gladys Noel
Bates-Parker, Linda
Battle, Mark G.
Battle, Thomas Cornell
Bayard, Franck
Bayless, Paul Clifton

Beam, Lillian Kennedy
Bean, Walter Dempsey
Beard, James William, Jr.
Beard, Virginia H.
Beasley, Paul Lee
Beatty, Charles Eugene, Sr.
Beatty, Ozell Kakaskus
Becker, Adolph Eric
Beckham, Barry Earl
Beckham, Edgar Frederick
Beckley, David Lenard
Bedell, Frederick Delano
Belcher, Lewis, Jr.
Bell, George
Bell, James A.
Bell, Janet Sharon
Bell, Jimmy
Bell, Victory
Bell, Wendolyn Yvonne
Bell, Winston Alonzo
Bellamy, Ivory Gandy
Belle, John Otis
Bellinger, Harold
Belmear, Horace Edward
Belton, Howard G.
Bempong, Maxwell A.
Bender, Barbara A.
Bennett, William Donald
Bennett, William Ronald
Benning, Emma Bowman
Benson, Gilbert
Benson, James Russell
Benton, Shirley Jean
Bernard, Louis Joseph
Berry, Leroy
Bessent, Hattie
Best, Prince Albert, Jr.
Bethea, Edwin Ayers
Bethea, Mollie Ann
Bethel, Leonard Leslie
Bibb, T. Clifford
Bickham, L. B.
Bigby-Young, Betty
Biggs, Shirley Ann
Billingslea, Edgar D.
Billingsley, Andrew
Bingham, Rebecca Josephine (nee Taylor)
Birchette, William Ashby, III
Bittings, Rosemary Brooks
Black, Barbara Robinson
Black, Billy Charleston
Black, Frank S.
Blair, George Ellis
Blake, Elias, Jr.
Blake, J. Herman
Blakely, Charles
Blakenship, Cheryl L.
Blanchet, Waldo Willie E.
Blanden, Lee Ernest
Blanding, Mary Rhonella
Blayton-Taylor, Betty
Blount, Clarence W.
Bobino, Rita Florencia
Boddie, Gwendolyn M.
Bodrick, Leonard Eugene
Boffman, James
Boggan, Daniel, Jr.
Boggs, Nathaniel
Bolden, Wiley Speights
Bolton, Wanda E.
Bonaparte, Tony Hillary
Bond, James G.
Boney, J. Don
Bonner, Bester Davis
Bontemps, Jacqueline Marie Fonvielle
Boone, Clarence Donald
Boone, Zola Ernest
Booth, Le-Quita
Borum, Regina A.
Bostic, Dorothy
Bothuel, Ethel C.S.
Bowen, Raymond C.
Bowen, Richard, Jr.
Bowens, Johnny Wesley
Bower, Beverly Lynne
Bowman, Earl W., Jr.
Bowman, Janet Wilson
Bowser, Benjamin Paul
Bowser, James A.
Boyd, Charles Flynn
Boyd, Joseph L.
Boyd, Rozelle

Boyer, Joe L.
Boykins, Ernest A.
Boynton, Asa Terrell, Sr.
Bracey, Willie Earl
Bradford, Archie J.
Bradford, Equilla Forrest
Bradley, Jessie Mary
Brady, Nelvia M.
Bramwell, Fitzgerald Burton
Branch, Addison A., Sr.
Branch, Otis Linwood
Branch-Simpson, Germaine Gail
Branson, Herman Russell
Brantley, Edward J.
Brasey, Henry L.
Braswell, Palmira
Brazeal, Braillsford Reese
Bridwell, Herbert H.
Briggs, Collin
Briggs, Paul W.
Bright, Alfred Lee
Brinkley, Norman, Jr.
Brinn, Chauncey J.
Briscoe, Sidney Edward, Jr.
Brisker, Lawrence
Britt, Paul D., Jr.
Britton, Elizabeth
Britton, John H., Jr.
Broach, S. Elizabeth
Brock, O. Lee
Brockett, Charles A.
Brockington, Benjamin
Bronson, Oswald P.
Brookins, Dolores
Brooks, Delores Jean
Brooks, Henry Marcellus
Brooks, Norman Leon
Brooks, W. Webster
Brossette, Alvin, Jr.
Brothers, Edith
Brown, Bernice Baynes
Brown, Carol Ann
Brown, Conella Coulter
Brown, Constance Young
Brown, Evelyn Drewery
Brown, Frank
Brown, Georgia W.
Brown, Herman
Brown, John Andrew
Brown, Jonel Leonard
Brown, Joyce
Brown, Julius Ray
Brown, LeRoy
Brown, LeRoy Ronald
Brown, Marva Y.
Brown, Mattie R.
Brown, Milton F.
Brown, Noah, Jr.
Brown, Paul L.
Brown, Ronald Paul
Brown, Rubye G.
Brown, Samuel Franklin, Jr.
Brown, Stephen H.
Brown, Wesley Anthony
Brown, William Crews
Brown, William H.
Brown, William T.
Brown-Knable, Bobbie Margaret
Brown-Nash, JoAhn Weaver
Browne, Lee F.
Browne, Vincent J.
Bruner, Van B., Jr.
Bryan, Curtis
Bryan, Jesse A.
Bryant, Castell Vaughn
Bryant, Faye B.
Bryant, James W.
Bryant, Preston
Bryant, Teresena Wise
Bryce, Herrington J.
Bryson, Seymour L.
Buck, Ivory M., Jr.
Buck, Judith Brooks
Buie, Sampson, Jr.
Bullock, Byron Swanson
Bumphus, Walter Gayle
Burger, Mary Williams
Burgett, Paul Joseph
Burke, Emmett C.
Burkette, Tyrone
Burnett, Calvin W.
Burnette, Ada Puryear
Burnim, Mickey L.
Burns, Felton

Burns, W. Haywood
Burse, Luther
Burse, Raymond Malcolm
Burwell, William David, Jr.
Bush, Ann
Bush, Nathaniel
Butler, Broadus Nathaniel
Butler, Eugene Thaddeus, Jr.
Butler, Homer L.
Butler, Loretta M.
Butler, Rebecca Batts
Byas, Ulysses
Byas, William Herbert
Byrd, Camolia Alcorn
Byrd, Edwin R.
Byrd, Joseph Keys
Byrd, Manford, Jr.
Byrd, Taylor
Cabrera, Eloise J.
Cade, Harold Edward
Cade, Tinina Quick
Cade, Valarie Swain
Caillier, James Allen
Cain, Lester James, Jr.
Calvin, Virginia Brown
Campbell, Graham F.
Canady, Hortense Golden
Cannon, Barbara E.M.
Cannon, Eugene Nathaniel
Carey, James William
Carey, Jennifer Davis
Carey, Patricia M.
Carper, Gloria G.
Carreathers, Kevin R.
Carreker, William, Jr.
Carrier, Clara L. DeGay
Carroll, Constance Marie
Carroll, Edward Gonzalez
Carroll, Juanitaelizabeth P.
Carry, Helen Ward
Carson, Warren Jason, Jr.
Carter, Arthur Michael
Carter, Barbara Lillian
Carter, David G., Sr.
Carter, Gene Raymond
Carter, Hazo
Carter, Herbert E.
Carter, Howard Payne
Carter, James Edward, III
Carter, James P.
Carter, Lamore Joseph
Carter, Lawrence
Carter, Milton O., Sr.
Carter, Philip W., Jr.
Carter, Robert Thompson
Carter, Warrick L.
Carter, Weptanomah Washington
Carter, William Beverly, III
Carter, Wilmoth Annette
Carter-McCraw, Carolyn
Cartlidge, Arthur J.
Caruthers, Patricia Wayne
Cash, Arlene Marie
Cash, William L., Jr.
Cash-Rhodes, Winifred E.
Cason, Marilynn Jean
Cason, Udell, Jr.
Cassis, Glenn Albert
Casson, Luella Howard
Castenell, Louis Anthony
Castleberry, Rhebena Taylor
Cave, Perstein Ronald
Cavin, Alonzo C.
Cayou, Nontsizi Kirton
Chambers, Alex A.
Chambliss, Ida Belle
Chance, Kenneth Bernard
Chandler, Sharon Kay
Chapman, Martin Odes
Chapman, Melvin
Charles, Bernard L.
Chatman, Melvin E.
Chatmon, Linda Carol
Chavous, Barney Lewis
Cheatham, Roy E.
Cheek, James E.
Cherry, Robert Lee
Cherry, Warren W.
Chestang, Leon Wilbert
Chew, Bettye L.
Childs, Francine C.
Childs, Theodore Francis
Chisholm, Shirley
Chisolm, Grace Butler

Christian, Mae Armster
Chubb, Louise B.
Churchwell, Charles Darrett
Clair, Areatha G. (nee Anderson)
Clark, Ameera H.
Clark, Bertha Smith
Clark, Donald Lewis
Clark, Douglas L.
Clark, Jimmy E.
Clark, Joe Louis
Clark, Laron Jefferson, Jr.
Clark, Vincent W.
Clark-Thomas, Eleanor M.
Clarke, James Alexander
Clarke, Velma Greene
Clay, Camille Alfreda
Clay, Nathaniel, Jr.
Clay, Ross Collins
Clayton, Constance
Clayton, James Henry
Clayton, Robert Louis
Cleckley, Betty J.
Clifton, Ivery Dwight
Climmons, Willie Mathew
Cline, Eileen Tate
Clouden, LaVerne C.
Clouser, Ernest Z.
Coaxum, Callie B.
Cobb, Bernice Coar
Cobb, Jewel Plummer
Cobbin, Gloria Constance
Cobbs, David E.
Cobbs, Susie Ann
Coffey, Barbara J.
Cogdell, Parthenia D.
Colbert, Benjamin James
Cole, Edyth Bryant
Cole, Johnnetta Betsch
Cole, Thomas W., Jr.
Cole, Thomas Winston, Sr.
Coleman, Audrey Rachelle
Coleman, Don Edwin
Coleman, Lemon, Jr.
Coley, Donald Lee
Coley, Esther B.
Collier, Clarence Marie
Collier, Julia Marie
Collier, Troy
Collins, Dorothy Lee
Collins, Elliott
Collins, Joann Ruth
Collins, Warren Eugene
Collymore, Edward L.
Colvin, William E.
Comer, Norman David
Comfort, Nemo Robert
Cone, Cecil Wayne
Conley, Elizabeth-Lucy Carter
Conley, James Monroe
Connor, Ulysses J., Jr.
Conyers, Charles L.
Cook, Nathan Howard
Cook, Samuel DuBois
Cooke, Paul Phillips
Cooper, Bobby G.
Cooper, Constance Deloris
Cooper, Josephine H.
Copeland, Elaine Johnson
Copeland, Robert M.
Corbie, Leo A.
Cornelius, William Milton
Cortada, Rafael Leon
Cose, Ellis
Cotman, Ivan Louis
Couche, Robert
Coulon, Burnel Elton
Courtney, Cassandra Hill
Cousins, Althea L.
Covington, Douglas
Covington, H. Douglas
Covington, Willa Alma Greene
Cowan, Larine Yvonne
Cox-Rawles, Rani
Craft, Thomas J., Sr.
Craig, Elson L.
Craig, Emma Jeanelle Patton
Craig, Richard
Craig, Starlett Russell
Crawford, Carl M.
Crawford, Ella Mae
Crawford, Raymon Edward
Crawford, Samuel D.
Crayton, James Edward
Crew, John L., Sr.
Crocker, Cyril L.

Croft, Ira T.
Crosby, Edward Warren
Cross, Betty Jean
Crowell, Bernard G.
Crump, William L.
Crutcher, Betty Neal
Crutcher, Ronald Andrew
Cummings, E. Emerson
Cunningham, James J.
Curry, Clarence F., Jr.
Curtis, Josephine Monica
Dais, Larry
Dale, Virginia Marie
Daley, Guilbert Alfred
Dalton, Raymond Andrew
Daniel, Griselda
Daniel, Walter C.
Daniels, Alfred Claude Wynder
Daniels, Cecil Tyrone
Daniels, John C.
Daniels, Lincoln, Sr.
Daniels, Peter F.
Davenport, Gregory Michael
Davenport, Lawrence Franklin
Davidson, Ezra C., Jr.
Davidson, Lurlean G.
Davis, Angela Lucretia
Davis, Arthur Paul
Davis, Brenda Lightsey-Hendricks
Davis, Carrie L. Filer
Davis, Edward L.
Davis, Elaine Carsley
Davis, Elmer L., Sr.
Davis, Etheldra S.
Davis, Gloria-Jeanne
Davis, James F.
Davis, John Albert
Davis, Johnetta Garner
Davis, Joseph
Davis, Joseph Solomon
Davis, LaVerne Gloria
Davis, Lawrence Arnette, Jr.
Davis, Lowell E.
Davis, Marvin Coolidge
Davis, Monique Deon
Davis, Morris E.
Davis, Roland Hayes
Davis, Sammy, Jr.
Davis, Stephen Smith
Davis, Wanda M.
Davis, Warren B.
Davis, Wiley M.
Davis, William R.
Dawson, B. W.
Dawson, Carrie B.
Dawson, Martha E.
Dawson, Sidney L., Jr.
Days, Rosetta Hill
Dean, Clara Russell
Dean, Diane D.
Decatur, Robert A.
DeGraffenreidt, Andrew
DeLauder, William B.
Delco, Exalton Alfonso, Jr.
Delk, Oliver Rahn
DeLoatch, Eugene
Dendy, Tometta
Denning, Bernadine Newsom
DeNye, Blaine A.
DePillars, Murry Norman
DeShields, Harrison F., Jr.
Deskins, Donald R., Jr.
DeSouza, Ronald Kent
DeWitt, Rufus B.
Diaw, Rosemary K.
Dickerson, Glenda J.
Dickerson, Janet
Dickinson, Gloria Harper
Dickson, David W. D.
Dike, Kenneth Onwuka
Dillard, Martin Gregory
Dillon, Aubrey
Dilworth, Mary Elizabeth
Dismuke, Leroy
Dixon, Benjamin
Dixon, Blanche V.
Dixon, Ruth F.
Dixon, Tom L.
Dobbs, John Wesley
Dodson, Jualynne E. (nee White)
Donaldson, Jeff R.
Dorsey, Carolyn Ann
Dotson, Philip Randolph
Douglas, Harry E., III

Douglas, Samuel Horace
Douglass, Arthur E.
Douglass, Melvin Isadore
Dowdy, Lewis C.
Drake, Daniel D.
Draper, Edgar Daniel
Draper, Frederick Webster
Drewry, Cecelia Hodges
Drimmer, Melvin
Dual, Peter Alfred
DuBois, Asa Stephen
Dukes, Jerome Erwin
Dummett, Clifton Orrin
Dunbar, Harry B.
Dunbar, Marjorie Henderson
Duncan, David Edward
Duncan, John C., Jr.
Dungy, Claibourne I.
Dungy, Madgetta Thornton
Dunnigan, Jerry
Dunson, Carrie Lee
Durham, Joseph Thomas
Dykes, Marie Draper
Eady, Mary E.
Eagleson, Halson Vashon
Ealy, Mary Newcomb
Early, Violet Theresa
Easter, Rufus Benjamin, Jr.
Eaton, James A.
Eaton, Minetta Gaylor
Eberhardt, Clifford
Edgerton, Art Joseph
Edmonds, Helen G.
Edmonds, Thomas Nathaniel
Edwards, Cecile Hoover
Edwards, Eunice L.
Edwards, Harry T.
Edwards, Robert
Edwards, Robert Valentino
Edwards, Rondle E.
Edwards, Thomas Oliver
Elam, Lloyd C.
Ellis, Calvin H., III
Ellis, Duke Ellington
Ellis, Edward V.
Ellison, Nolen M.
Ellison, Sandra LaVerne
Elzy, Amanda Belle
Emmanuel, Tsegai
English, Richard A.
Epperson, David E.
Epps, Anna Cherrie
Epps, Charles Harry, Jr.
Epps, Dolzie C. B.
Epps, Naomi Newby
Ervin, Deborah Green
Ervin, John B.
Ervin, Leroy, Jr.
Esquivel, Argelia Velez
Estep, Roger D.
Esters, George Edward
Estes, Sidney Harrison
Ethridge, Robert Wylie
Ethridge, Samuel B.
Eubanks, Eugene E.
Evans, Arthur L.
Evans, Crecy Ann
Evans, David Lawrence
Evans, Donna Browder
Evans, Jack
Evans, Robert Warren
Evans, Ruthana Wilson
Evans, Spofford L.
Evans, William E.
Eve, Christina M.
Evege, Walter L., Jr.
Ewers, James Benjamin, Jr.
Fair, Frank T.
Fairley, Wilma
Faison, Helen Smith
Fakhrid-Deen, Nashid Abdullah
Farmer, Willie Sidney, Sr.
Farris, Vera King
Faulk, Estelle A.
Faw, Barbara Ann
Felder, Tyree Preston, II
Feliciana, Jerrye Brown
Fentress, Shirley B.
Ferguson, St. Julian
Fields, A. Leo
Fields, Dexter L.
Fields, Savoynne Morgan
Finch, Janet M.
Finch, William H.

Finn, John William
Fisher, Ada L.
Fisher, E. Carleton
Fitzgerald, Charlotte Diane
Flack, Harley Eugene
Flagg, J. Thomas
Fleming, Bruce E.
Fleming, Melvin J.
Fleming, Quince D., Sr.
Flood, Shearlene Davis
Floyd, Jeremiah
Floyd, Otis L., Jr.
Floyd, Vircher B.
Foggs, Joyce D.
Ford, Charles
Ford, Donald A.
Ford, Nancy Howard
Ford, Richard D.
Ford, Virginia
Fort, Edward B.
Fort, Jane
Forte, Johnie, Jr.
Fortune, Alvin V.
Foster, Delores Jackson
Foster, Luther H.
Foster, Mildred Thomas
Foster, Rosebud Lightbourn
Fowler, John D.
Fowler, Thaddeus Postelle, Jr.
Fox, Jeanne Jones
Francis, Edith V.
Francis, Gilbert H.
Francis, Norman C.
Frank, Richard L.
Franklin, Allen D.
Franklin, Herman
Fraser, Leon Allison
Frazier, Leon
Fredd, Chester Arthur
Freeman, Evelyn
Freeman, Nelson R.
Freeman, Preston Garrison
Freeman, Ruges R.
Freeman, Thomas F.
Freeman-Lindsay, Diane
Frelow, Robert Dean
French, George Wesley
Fries, Sharon Lavonne
Frison, Lee A.
Frye, Charles Anthony
Frye, Nadine Grace
Fuget, Charles Robert
Fuller, James J.
Fulton, Donald Lee
Funn, Carlton A., Sr.
Gadsden, Nathaniel J., Jr.
Gaffney, Floyd
Gainer, Ruby Jackson
Gaines, Clarence E.
Gaines, Herschel Davis
Gaines, Manyles B., Jr.
Gaines, Paul Laurence, Sr.
Gaines, Sedalia Mitchell
Gaines, Victor Pryor
Gall, Lenore Rosalie
Gallagher, Abisola Helen
Gallon, Dennis P.
Gant, Raymond Leroy
Gantt, Walter N.
Garcia, Kwame N.
Garcia, William Burres
Gardiner, George L.
Gardner, Bettye J.
Gardner, Frank W.
Garner, La Forrest Dean
Garvin, Mildred Barry
Gaskins, Louise Elizabeth
Gaston, Minnie L.
Gates, Paul Edward
Gatewood, Algie C.
Gatewood, Wallace Lavell
Gatlin, Elissa L.
Gault, Marian Holness
Gavin, L. Katherine
Gayle, Lucille Jordan
Gayles, Anne Richardson
Gayles, Joseph Nathan Webster, Jr.
Gaymon, Nicholas Edward
George, Claude C.
George, Laura W.
Gerald, Arthur Thomas, Jr.

Gibbs, Sandra E.
Gibbs, Warmoth T.
Gibson, John Thomas
Gibson, Sarah L.
Gibson, William M.
Gilbert, Fred D., Jr.
Giles, Willie Anthony, Jr.
Gilkey, William C.
Gilliam, Marvin L.
Gilmore, Charles Arthur
Gilmore, John T.
Gilreath, Coot, Jr.
Gist, Jessie M. Gilbert
Givens, Henry, Jr.
Glanton, Lydia Jackson
Glasgow, Douglas G.
Glenn, Cecil E.
Glenn, Wynola
Gloster, Hugh Morris
Glover, Agnes W.
Glover, Clarence Ernest, Jr.
Godbold, Donald Horace
Goins, Mary G.
Golden, Louie
Goldsby, W. Dean, Sr.
Gooden, Samuel Ellsworth
Goodloe, Celestine Wilson
Goodman, James Arthur, Sr.
Goodson, Frances Elizabeth
Gordon, Bertha Comer
Gordon, Charles Eugene
Gordon, Milton A.
Gore, Blinzy L.
Gore, Joseph A.
Gothard, Barbara Wheatley
Graham, Jo-Ann Clara
Grant, George C.
Grant, James
Grant, McNair
Gravely, Samuel L., Jr.
Gravenberg, Eric Von
Graves, Irene Amelia
Gray, James E.
Gray, Laruth H.
Gray, Myrtle Edwards
Gray, Pearl Spears
Graydon, Wasdon, Jr.
Grays, Mattelia Bennett
Grayson, Harry L.
Grear, Effie C.
Green, Calvin Coolidge
Green, Charles A.
Green, Liller Bernice
Green, Robert L.
Greene, Charles Lavant
Greene, Charles Rodgers
Greene, John Sullivan
Greene, Marvin L.
Greene, William Henry L'Vel
Greenfield, Wilbert
Greenwood, Charles H.
Grier, Jennifer Ann
Griffin, Betty Sue
Griffin, Ervin Verome
Griffin, James Stafford
Griffith, John H.
Griggs, Harry Kindell, Sr.
Griggs, James Clifton, Jr.
Griggs, Judith Ralph
Grigsby, Marshall C.
Grimes, Voni B.
Grimsley, Ethelyne
Grissett, Willie James
Groffrey, Frank Eden
Groomes, Freddie Lang
Groves, Delores Ellis
Groves, Harry Edward
Guillaume, Alfred Joseph, Jr.
Guillory, William A.
Guinier, Ewart
Gulliver, Adelaide Cromwell
Gumms, Emmanuel George, Sr.
Gunn, Gladys
Gunnell, James B.
Guy, Talmadge Carter
Guy, William I.
Gwin, Wiliviginia Faszhianato (Cora)
Gwynn, Florine Evayonne
Hackett, Obra V.
Hackley, Lloyd Vincent
Hair, John
Hairstone, Marcus A.
Hale, Frank W., Jr.

Haley, Johnetta Randolph
Hall, Addie June
Hall, Delilah Ridley
Hall, Dolores Brown
Hall, Ethel Harris
Hall, Jesse J.
Hall, Kim Felicia
Hall, Lloyd Eugene
Hall, Perry Alonzo
Hall, Robert Johnson
Hamilton, Joseph Willard
Hamilton, Theophilus Elliott
Hammett, Willie Anderson
Hammond, Debra Lauren
Hammond, Kenneth Ray
Hammond, W. Rodney
Hanberry, Annie E.
Hancock, Allen C.
Handy, John William, Jr.
Haney, Darnel L.
Haqq, Khalida Ismail
Hardcastle, James C.
Hardeman, Carole Hall
Hardin, Henry E.
Hardman-Cromwell, Youtha
  Cordella
Hardwick, Clifford E., III
Hare, Linda Paskett
Hargrave, Benjamin
Harleston, Bernard Warren
Harmon, William Wesley
Harper, Joseph W., III
Harper, Leonard Alfred
Harper, Neville W.
Harrell, Ruth J.
Harrigan, Rodney Emile
Harrington, Philip Leroy
Harris, Arthur Leonard, III
Harris, Dolores M.
Harris, James E.
Harris, Jasper William
Harris, John H.
Harris, Marjorie Elizabeth
Harris, MaryAnn
Harris, Ruth Coles
Harris, Vander E.
Harris, William H.
Harris, William M.
Harris, Winifred Clarke
Harris, Zelema M.
Harrison, Beverly E.
Harrison, Emma Louise
Harrison, Ernest Alexander
Harrison, William Edgar
Harrold, Jeffery Deland
Hart, Barbara McCollum
Hart, Emily
Hart, Jacqueline D.
Hartman, Hermene Demaris
Hartsfield, Howard C.
Hartshorn, Herbert Hadley
Hartzog, Ernest E.
Harvey, Denise M.
Harvey, William R.
Hatton, Barbara R.
Hauser, Charlie Brady
Hawk, Charles N., Jr.
Hawk, Charles Nathaniel, III
Hawkins, Alexander A.
Hawkins, Andre
Hawkins, Dorisula Wooten
Hawkins, Gene
Hawkins, James
Hawkins, Lawrence C.
Hawkins, Muriel A.
Hawthorne, Lucia Shelia
Hayden, Robert C., Jr.
Hayes, Charles Leonard
Hayes, Leola G.
Hayes, Marion LeRoy
Hayman, Warren C.
Haynes, Alphonso Worden
Haynes, Barbara Asche
Haynes, James H.
Haynes, Sue Blood
Haynes, Willie C., III (Butch)
Hayre, Ruth Wright
Hazzard, Terry Louis
Hearn, Rosemary
Heath, Comer, III
Hedgepeth, Chester Melvin, Jr.
Hedgespeth, George T., Jr.
Hefner, James A.
Heidt, Ellen Virginia
Hemby, Dorothy Jean

Hemphill, Frank
Henderson, Butler Thomas
Henderson, George
Henderson, James H.
Henderson, James H. M.
Henderson, John L.
Henderson, Joyce Ann
Henderson, Lloyd D.
Henderson, Romeo Clanton
Henderson, Stanley L.
Hendrix, Daniel W.
Henry, Forest T., Jr.
Henry, John W., Jr.
Henry, Joseph Louis
Henry, Marcelett Campbell
Henry, Samuel Dudley
Henry, Warren Elliott
Herd, John E.
Herenton, Willie W.
Heyward, James Oliver
Hiatt, Dana Sims
Hibbert, Dorothy Lasalle
Hicklin, Fannie
Hickman, Garrison M.
Hicks, Arthur James
Hicks, Daisy C.
Hicks, Doris Askew
Hicks, Edith A.
Higgins, Cleo Surry
Highsmith, Charles Albert
Hightower, Herma J.
Hill, Carl M.
Hill, Charlie H.
Hill, Dianne
Hill, George C.
Hill, John C.
Hill, Johnny R.
Hill, Julia H.
Hill, Pearl M.
Hill, Richard Nathaniel
Hill, Rosalie A.
Hill, Wendell T., Jr.
Hilliard, Asa Grant, III
Hinton, Hortense Beck
Hixson, Judson Lemoine
Hobbs, Thadeaus H.
Hodge, Charles Mason
Hodge, Cynthia Elois
Hodge, W. J.
Hoff, Nathaniel Hawthorne
Hogges, Ralph
Holder, Idalia
Hollar, Milton Conover
Holliday, Frances B.
Hollins, Joseph Edward
Holloway, Ernest Leon
Holloway, Ernestine
Holloway, J. Mills
Holloway, Jerry
Holmes, Everlena M.
Holmes, Lorene B.
Holmes, Zan W., Jr.
Holt, Dorothy L
Holt, Edwin J.
Holt, Essie W.
Holt, Grace S.
Hood, Elizabeth
Hooker, Eric H.
Hooks, Mose Yvonne Brooks
Hopkins, Paulene A.
Hopkins, William A.
Hopper, Cornelius Lenard
Horad, Sewell D., Sr.
Horne, Westry Grover
Horne-McGee, Patricia J.
Hoskins Clark, Tempy M.
Hotchkiss, Wesley Akin
House, Millard L.
Houston, Alice V.
Houston, David R.
Houston, Lillian S.
Houston, William DeBoise
Howard, Leon
Howard, Lytia Ramani
Howard, Mamie
Howard, Shirley M.
Howell, Joseph L.
Howell, Rose Cole
Hoyle, Classie
Hrabowski, Freeman Alphonsa,
  III
Hubbard, Jean P.
Hudgeons, Louise Taylor
Hudson, Andrew Harold

Hudson, Clenora Frances
Hudson, Herman C.
Hudson, James Blaine
Hudson, Sterling Henry, III
Hughes, Anita Lillian
Hughes, Ernelle Combs
Hughes, George Melvin
Hull, George, Jr.
Humphries, Frederick S.
Hunt, Barbara Ann
Hunt, Isaac Cosby, Jr.
Hunt, Ronald Joseph
Hunter, Elza Harris
Hunter, William L.
Hurdle, Hortense O. McNeil
Hurst, Cleveland, Jr.
Hutchins, Henry T.
Hutchinson, George
Hutchison, Peyton S.
Hytche, William P.
Ibekwe, Lawrence Anene
Irving, Henry E., II
Isaac, Ephraim
Isibor, Edward Iroguehi
Jack, Stephanie C.
Jackson, Acy Lee
Jackson, Ada Jean Work
Jackson, Alterman
Jackson, Anna Mae
Jackson, Arthur Roszell
Jackson, Charles Ellis
Jackson, Curtis M.
Jackson, Dennis Lee
Jackson, Earline
Jackson, Ellen Swepson
Jackson, Frederick Leon
Jackson, Governor Eugene, Jr.
Jackson, Mattie Lee
Jackson, Miles Merrill
Jackson, Nathaniel G.
Jackson, Renard I.
Jackson, Ronald Lee
Jackson, Russell A.
Jackson, Samuel S., Jr.
Jackson-Teal, Rita F.
Jaggers, George Henry, Jr.
James, Advergus Dell, Jr.
James, Allix Bledsoe
James, Arminta Susan
James, Betty Nowlin
James, David Phillip
James, H. Rhett
James, Herman Delano
James, Richard L.
James, Robert D.
James, Sidney J.
Jamison, Leila Duncan
Jarmon, James Henry, Jr.
Jarrett, Thomas D.
Jason, Howard M.
Jefferson, Arthur
Jefferson, Fredrick Carl, Jr.
Jeffreys, John H.
Jenkins, Adam, Jr.
Jenkins, Adelbert Howard
Jenkins, Althea H.
Jenkins, Drewie Gutrimez
Jenkins, Emmanuel Lee
Jenkins, Herman Lee
Jenkins, Jimmy Raymond
Jenkins, Julius
Jenkins, Kenneth Vincent
Jenkins, Thomas M.
Jenkins, Van
Jennings, Lillian Pegues
Jennings, Robert Ray
Jerome, Norge Winefred
Jessie, Waymon Thomas
Johnson, Alcee LaBranche
Johnson, Angel Patricia
Johnson, B. A.
Johnson, Brent E.
Johnson, C. Christine
Johnson, Carrie Clements
Johnson, Charles E.
Johnson, Charles H.
Johnson, Charles William
Johnson, Cheryl Jeffries
Johnson, Christine
Johnson, Cleveland, Jr.
Johnson, David Horace
Johnson, Diane
Johnson, Earl E.
Johnson, Enid C.

Johnson, Erma Chansler
Johnson, Fred D.
Johnson, Frederick Douglass
Johnson, George M.
Johnson, Harold R.
Johnson, Harry A.
Johnson, Henderson A., III
Johnson, Henry
Johnson, Ivory
Johnson, James Edward
Johnson, Joseph A.
Johnson, Joseph B.
Johnson, Joseph Edward
Johnson, Leon
Johnson, Leroy
Johnson, Luther Mason, Jr.
Johnson, Marguerite M.
Johnson, Norman J.
Johnson, Onette E.
Johnson, Parker Collins
Johnson, Patricia Anita
Johnson, Randall Morris
Johnson, Rebecca M.
Johnson, Robert B.
Johnson, Robert H.
Johnson, Sarah Yvonne
Johnson, Sharon Reed
Johnson, Theodore Thomas
Johnson, Ulysses Johann, Jr.
Johnson, Vannette William
Johnson, Vermelle Jamison
Johnson, Walter J.
Johnson, Wendell Norman, Sr.
Johnson, William A.
Johnson, Zodie Anderson
Johnson-Young, Barbara Janeice
Jones, Alfredean
Jones, Arnold Pearson
Jones, Bertha H.
Jones, Bobby
Jones, Charles, Jr.
Jones, Charles A.
Jones, Donald W.
Jones, Edward Louis
Jones, Edward N.
Jones, Elnetta Griffin
Jones, Ferdinand Taylor, Jr.
Jones, Franklin D.
Jones, I. Gene
Jones, Jennie Y.
Jones, Jerome B.
Jones, Jesse W.
Jones, John P.
Jones, Johnny L.
Jones, Kelsey A.
Jones, Leeland Newton, Jr.
Jones, Mack H.
Jones, Melton Rodney
Jones, Michael Andrea
Jones, Michele Woods
Jones, Nina F.
Jones, Phillip Erskine
Jones, Reginald L.
Jones, Rena Talley
Jones, Roy Junios
Jones, Stanley Bernard
Jones, Susan Sutton
Jones, Sylvester
Jones, William Edward
Jones, William Henry, Jr.
Jones, William Ronald
Jones, Willie C.
Jones, Zoia L.
Jones-Young, Terri Anita
Jordan, Abbie H. (nee Williams)
Jordan, Carolyne Lamar
Jordan, Leroy A.
Jordan, Marilyn E.
Jordan, R. D.
Jordan, Ralph
Joyner, Rubin E.
Judson, Horace Augustus
Julian, John Tyrone
Junior, Ester James, Jr.
Junior, Samella E. (nee Walton)
Kamoche, Jidlaph Gitau
Kane, Jacqueline Anne
Keaton, William T.
Keith, Leroy
Keller, Edmond Joseph
Kelley, Delores G.
Kelsey, Gary Matthew
Kendall, Lettie M.
Kendall, Shirley I.

Kendrick, Griff William
Kennedy, Callas Faye
Kennedy, Frederick A.
Kennedy, Jimmie Vernon
Kennedy, Joyce S.
Kennedy, Yvonne
Kersey, Elizabeth T.
Key, June Roe
Kilkenny, James H.
Kimmons, Willie James
King, Hodge
King, John B.
King, John Q. Taylor, Sr.
King, LeRoy J.
King, Reatha Clark
King, Robert Samuel
Kinnaird, Michael Leon
Kirby, Nancy J.
Kirk, Orville
Kirk, Wyatt D.
Kispert, Dorothy Lee
Kitchen, Wayne Leroy
Kittrels, Alonzo William
Kline, William M.
Kluge, Pamela Hollie
Knable, Bobbie Margaret Brown
Knight, John F., Jr.
Knowles, Claire Em
Knowles, Eddie (Adenola)
Knox, Annie Bell
Knox, Wilbur Benjamin
Kraft, Benjamin F.
Kresy-Poree, R. Jean
Kugblenu, George Ofoe
Kuykendall, Crystal Arlene
Kyles, Josephine H.
Lacy, Edward J.
Ladd, Florence Cawthorne
Lafayette, Bernard, Jr.
Lahr, Charles Dwight
Lake, Alfreeda Elizabeth
Lambert, Charles H.
Lambert, LeClair Grier
Lampley, Paul Clarence
Lane, Eleanor Tyson
Lane, John Henry
Lane, Russell A.
Laney, Robert Louis, Jr.
Lang, Charles J.
Lang, Marvel
Lanier, Dorothy Copeland
Lanier, Horatio Axel
Lanier, Marshall L.
Lassiter, Wright Lowenstein, Jr.
Latimer, Ina Pearl
Lattimore, Caroline Louise
Lavergneau, Rene L.
Law, Ellen T.
Law, Thomas Melvin
Lawlah, Gloria Gary
Lawrence, Annie L.
Lawrence, William Wesley
Laws, Ruth M.
Lawson, Cassell Avon
Lawson, Elizabeth Harris
Lawson, J. Ranaldo
Lawson, Robert L.
Lawson, William Daniel
Lawyer, Vivian (nee Moore)
Lea, Jeanne Evans
Leavell, Dorothy R.
Leavell, Walter F.
Lechebo, Semie
Lede, Naomi W.
Lee, Gerald E.
Lee, Guy Milicon, Jr.
Lee, LaVerne C.
Lee, Oliver B.
Lee, Richard Thomas
Lee, Shirley Freeman
Lee, Stratton Creighton
LeFlore, William B.
Leflores, George O., Jr.
Leggette, Sebetha Jenkins
LeMelle, Tilden J.
LeMelle, Wilbert John
Leonard, Catherine W.
Leonard, Walter J.
Levermore, Claudette Madge
Lewis, Almera P.
Lewis, Elma I.
Lewis, Felton Edwin
Lewis, James, Jr.
Lewis, James Edward

Lewis, Jesse Cornelius
Lewis, Jesse J.
Lewis, Robert Edward
Lewis, Sylvia Austin
Lightfoot, Moses
Lindsay, Beverly
Linnette, Valleta H.
Lipscomb, Darryl L.
Lipscomb, Wanda Dean
Lister, David Alfred
Liston, Hardy, Jr.
Little, Leone Bryson
Littlejohn, Joseph Phillip
Littlejohn, Samuel Gleason
Littlejohn, Walter L.
Littleton, Ralph Douglass
Locke, Hubert G.
Lockett, Brooker Thomas
Lockhart, Lillie Marie
Lockwood, James Clinton
Loeb, Charles P., Jr.
Logan, Frenise A.
Long, Andu Trisa
Long, Juanita Outlaw
Lopes, William H.
Love, Barbara
Love, George Hayward
Lovett, Mack, Jr.
Loving, Pamela Yvonne
Lowe, Eugene Yerby, Jr.
Lucas, Gerald Robert
Lucas, John H.
Lucas, William S.
Luckey, Evelyn F.
Lyda, Wesley John
Lyles, Dewayne
Lynch, Robert D.
Lyons, Charles A., Jr.
Mabry, Edward L.
Mack, Ally Faye
Mack, Astrid Karona
Mack, Lurene Kirkland
Macklin, Anderson D.
Makle, Vivian B.
Malone, Cleo
Malone, Eugene William
Malone, J. Deotha
Malone, Sandra Dorsey
Mann, George Levier
Mann, Marion
Manning, Eddie James
Manning, Hubert Vernon
Manning, Jane A.
Manning, Jean Bell
Manning, Randolph H.
Manning, Reuben D.
Mapp, Edward C.
Mapp, Frederick Everett
Marbury, Carl Harris
Marshall, Carter Lee
Marshall, Herbert A.
Martin, Elmer P.
Martin, Evelyn B.
Martin, Fred
Martin, James W.
Martin, Joanne Mitchell
Martin, Julia M.
Martin, Lee
Martin, Louis E.
Martin, Mary E. Howell
Martin, Maxine Smith
Martin, McKinley C.
Martin, Ruby Julene Wheeler
Mason, Jesse W.
Mason, Kenneth
Mason, Luther Roscoe
Massey, Carrie Lee
Massey, Walter Eugene
Massie, Samuel Proctor
Matabane, Sebiletso Mokone
Mathes, James R.
Matthew, Clifton, Jr.
Matthews, Dolores Evelyn
Matthews, Harry Bradshaw
Matthews, Hewitt W.
Matthews, Leonard Louis
Matthews, Mallory Louis
Matthews, Mary Joan
Matthews, Robert L.
Maxwell, Bertha Lyons
Maxwell, Marcella J.
Maxwell, Roger Allan
Mayes, Helen M.
Mays, Nebraska
Mays, William, Jr.

McAfee, Carrie R.
McAnulty, Brenda Hart
McClain, Andrew Bradley
McClammy, Thad C.
McClelland, Isaac Holland
McClenney, Earl Hampton
McClomb, George E.
McCloud, Anece Faison
McCloud, J. Oscar
McClure, Wesley C.
McCormick, Margaret W.
McCoy, Jessie Haynes
McCoy, Walter D.
McCrorey, H. Lawrence
McDaniel, Elizabeth
McDaniels, John Edward, Sr.
McDonald, R. Timothy
McDuffie, Hinfred
McFall, Mary (nee Simpson)
McFarland, Ollie Franklin
McFarland, Robert Phillips
McGee, Adolphus Stewart
McGee, Eva M.
McGehee, Maurice Edward
McGehee, Nan E.
McGhee, Samuel T.
McGuire, Jean Mitchell
McGuire, Rosalie J.
McHenry, Mary Williamson
McIlwain, Nadine Williams
McIntosh, Walter Cordell
McKeldin, Harry White, Jr.
McKenzie, Floretta D.
McKinney, Ernest Lee, Sr. (Mac)
McKinney, Theophilus Elisha, Jr.
McLaughlin, Jacquelyn Snow
McLaurin, Benjamin Philip
McLean, Mary Cannon
McMillan, Joseph H.
McMillan, Joseph T., Jr.
McMurry, Kermit Roosevelt, Jr.
McNairy, Francine G.
McNeill-Huntley, Esther Mae
McWhorter, Grace Agee
Meacham, Robert B.
Means, Fred E.
Melancon, Norman
Merideth, Charles Waymond
Meriweather, Melvin, Jr.
Metcalf, Zubie West, Jr.
Mickey, Rosie Cheatham
Mickins, Andel W.
Mickle, Andrea Denise
Middleton, Richard Temple, III
Middleton, Vertelle Delores
Milledge, Luetta Upshur
Millender, Mallory Kimerling
Miller, Bernice Johnson
Miller, Doris Jean
Miller, E. Ethelbert
Miller, Jeanne-Marie A.
Miller, Margaret Greer
Miller, Russell L., Jr.
Mills, Mary Elizabeth
Milton, Octavia Washington
Mims, George L.
Minor, Emma Lucille
Minter, Eloise Devada
Mitchell, Joann
Mitchell, Joseph Christopher
Mitchell, Marian Bartlett
Mitchell, Robert L.
Mitchem, John Clifford
Molette, Carlton W.
Monroe, Charles Edward
Monroe, Lillie Mae
Monteiro, Marilyn D.S.
Montgomery, Brian Walter
Montgomery, Harry J.
Montgomery, Oscar Lee
Montgomery, Trent
Moody, Charles David, Sr.
Moody, Harold L.
Moore, Albert
Moore, Alice Evelyn
Moore, Archie Bradford, Jr.
Moore, Christine James
Moore, Gary E.
Moore, Helen D. S.
Moore, Larry Louis
Moore, Lucille Sanders
Moore, Parlett Longworth
Moore, Richard Earle
Moore, Richard V.

Moorehead, Thomas A.
Mooring, Kittye D. (nee Samuels)
Moreland, Sallie V.
Morgan, Harry
Morgan, Robert W., II
Morgan, Warren W.
Morial, Sybil Haydel
Morisey, Patricia Garland
Morris, Charles Edward, Jr.
Morris, Ernest Roland
Morris, Frank Lorenzo, Sr.
Morris, Leibert Wayne
Morris, Major
Morris, Mellasenah Y.
Morris, Stanley E., Jr.
Morrison, Gwendolyn Christine
  Caldwell
Morrison, Richard David
Morse, Oliver
Mortel, Rodrigue
Moses, Henry A.
Mosley, Charles E.
Mosley, Myrtis H.
Mosley, Tracey Ray
Moss, Simeon F.
Moss, Thomas Edward, Sr.
Moss, Wilmar Burnett, Jr.
Moten, Chauncey Donald
Mullett, Donald L.
Murphy, Margaret Humphries
Murrain, William A.
Murrell, Barbara Curry
Myers, Ernest Ray
Nabors, Charles J., Jr.
Nabrit, James M., Jr.
Nails, Odell
Nance, Jesse J., Jr.
Nance, M. Maceo, Jr.
Neal, Edna D.
Neal, Ira Tinsley
Neely, David E.
Nelson, H. Viscount, Jr.
Nelson, Ivory Vance
Netterville, George Leon, Jr.
Neufville, Mortimer H.
Newkirk, Thomas H.
Newlin, Rufus K.
Newman, LeGrand
Newsom, Lionel H.
Newsome, Emanuel T.
Newsome, Moses, Jr.
Newson, Roosevelt, Jr.
Newton, James E.
Nichols, Owen D.
Nicholson, Alfred
Nickson, Sheila Joan
Niles, Lyndrey Arnaud
Nimmons, Julius
Nixon, Gladys (nee Ellison)
Noble, John Charles
Nolan, Robert L.
Norrell-Thomas, Sondra
Northcross, Deborah Ametra
Norwood, Tom
Nunnally, David H., Sr.
Nutall, James Edward
O'Bryant, John D.
O'Daniel, Therman Benjamin
Oden, Walter Eugene
O'Donnell, Lorena Mae
Oglesby, James Robert
Oh, Harry K.
Okunor, Shiame
Oldham, Algie Sidney, Jr.
Ollee, Mildred W.
Ortiz, Delia
Osborne, Alfred E., Jr.
Otudeko, Adebisi Olusoga
Outlaw, Lucius T., Jr.
Outlaw, Warren Gregory
Overton, Betty Jean
Owens, Andi
Owens, Angle B., Jr.
Owens, Curtis
Owens, Daniel Walter
Owens, George A.
Owens, Jerry Sue
Owens, Judith Myoli
Owens, Thomas C.
Paddio-Johnson, Eunice Alice
Page, Cedric Daniel
Page, Marguerite A.
Paige, Roderick
Palmer, Dennis

Palmer, John A.
Palmer, Noel
Parker, Fred Lee Cecil
Parker, Herbert Gerald
Parker, Matthew
Parker, Paul E.
Parker, Thomas E., Jr.
Parks, Arnold Grant
Paschal, Willie L.
Pates, Harold
Patrick, Julius, Jr.
Patterson, Cecil Lloyd
Patterson, Evelynne (nee Roberts)
Patterson, Joan Delores
Patton, Gerald Wilson
Payne, James Floyd
Payne, Jerry Oscar
Payne, Margaret Ralston
Payton, Benjamin Franklin
Payton, Carolyn Robertson
Peagler, Owen F.
Pearson, Clifton
Pegues, Robert L., Jr.
Pegues, Wennette West
Peirson, Gwynne Walton
Penelton, Barbara Spencer
Penn, Nolan E.
Pennington, Leenette Morse
Pennywell, Phillip, Jr.
Peoples, Gregory Allan
Peoples, John Arthur, Jr.
Peoples, Joyce P.
Peoples, Sesser R.
Perdue, John F.
Perdue, Robert Eugene
Perine, James L.
Perkins, Huel D.
Perkins, Myla Levy
Perpener, Winifred Uveda
Perry, Aubrey M.
Perry, Frank Anthony
Perry, Leonard Douglas, II
Perry, Patsy Brewington
Person, Dawn Renee
Peterman, Leotis
Peters, Fenton
Peterson, Lloyd, Jr.
Peterson, Marcella Tandy
Peterson, Maureen Laurett
Peterson, William T.
Peyton, Jasper E.
Phelps, Constance Kay
Phelps, Donald Gayton
Phillips, Barbara (nee Kinard)
Phillips, June M. J.
Phillips, Rosemarye L.
Phillips, Roy G.
Pickett, Robert E.
Pierce, Reuben G.
Pierre, Percy Anthony
Pinkard, Deloris Elaine
Piper, Elwood A.
Pittman, Sample Noel
Player, Willa B.
Pleasant, Mae Barbee Boone
Pleasants, Charles Wrenn
Plummer, Ora B.
Poellnitz, Fred Douglas
Poindexter, Robert L.
Polite, Marie Ann
Polk, Lorna Marie
Polk, Robert L.
Pollard, Freeman Wallace
Pollard, Raymond J.
Pollard, William Lawrence
Ponder, Henry
Poole, Dillard M.
Porter, Curtiss E.
Porter, John W.
Porter, Otha L.
Porter, Richard Sylvester
Potts, Sammie
Pounds, Augustine Wright
Powell, Alfred
Powell, Archie James
Powell, Leola P.
Prater, Oscar L.
Pratt, Alexander Thomas
Pratt, Mable
Prejean, Ruby D.
Prestage, Jewel Limar
Prezeau, Maryse
Price, David Lee
Price-Curtis, William

Pride, Armistead Scott
Primas, Barbara Jean
Prince, A. Cheryl
Probasco, Jeanetta
Provost, Marsha Parks
Pruitt, Anne Smith
Pruitt, George Albert
Puryear, Boyd Alfred
Putnam, Rosalind (nee Lawson)
Pyke, Willie Oranda
Pyles, J. A.
Quarles, George R.
Quarles, Ruth Brett
Rambo, Bettye R.
Randall, Queen F.
Randle, Lucious A.
Randolph, Elizabeth
Randolph, James B.
Randolph, Nancy Elizabeth
Rankin, Edgar E.
Ransburg, Frank S.
Rao, Koduru V. S.
Raphael, Bernard Joseph
Rattley, Jessie M.
Rawlings, Martha (nee Morse)
Rawlins, Elizabeth B.
Ray, Andrew
Ray, David Bruce
Ray-Goins, Jeanette
Rayburn, Wendell Gilbert
Reaves, Benjamin Franklin
Reaves, Ginevera N.
Reavis, John William, Jr.
Redd, George N.
Redd, Thomasina A.
Reddick, Alzo Jackson
Redmond, Jane Smith
Reed, Addison W.
Reed, Allene Wallace
Reed, Joann
Reede, James William, Jr.
Reeder, Willie R., Jr.
Reid, Benjamin F.
Reid, Goldie Hartshorn
Reid, Janie Ellen
Reid, Maude K.
Reid, Miles Alvin
Renick, James C.
Reynolds, Grant
Reynolds, Harry G.
Reynolds, Milton L.
Rhoades, Samuel Thomas
Rice, Constance Williams
Rice, Edward A.
Richard, R. Paul
Richards, Arthur A.
Richards, Hilda
Richards, LaVerne W.
Richardson, Charles Ronald
Richardson, DeRutha Gardner
Richardson, Earl Stanford
Richardson, F. C.
Richardson, Leo
Richardson, Luns C.
Richardson, Mary Margaret
Richmond, Tyronza R.
Ricks, George R.
Ridley, Harry Joseph
Ridley, May Alice
Rigby, Edward H.
Rigsby, Esther Martin
Rinsland, Roland D.
Ritchey, Mercedes B.
Rivers, Vernon Frederick
Robbins, Herman C.
Roberson, Earl
Roberts, Alfred Lloyd
Roberts, Edward A.
Roberts, Grady H., Jr.
Roberts, Hermese E.
Roberts, Lorraine Marie
Roberts, Paquita Hudson
Roberts, Roy J.
Robertson, Quincy L.
Robinson, Alfreda P.
Robinson, Andrew
Robinson, Charles
Robinson, Charlotte L.
Robinson, Eunice Primus
Robinson, George L.
Robinson, Harry G., III
Robinson, Prezell Russell
Robinson, Ruth
Robinson, S. Yolanda

Williams, Felton Carl
Williams, Frank Christopher, Jr.
Williams, Frank Copeland
Williams, George L., Sr.
Williams, George W., III
Williams, Harriette F.
Williams, James Hiawatha
Williams, Lea E.
Williams, Lonnie Ray
Williams, Lucius Lee, Jr.
Williams, Lucretia Murphy
Williams, Luther Steward
Williams, Malvin A.
Williams, Mary Haley
Williams, McDonald
Williams, Melvin
Williams, Naomi B.
Williams, Norris Gerald
Williams, Ora
Williams, Patricia Hill
Williams, Patrick Nehemiah
Williams, Peyton, Jr.
Williams, Robert D.
Williams, Robert Lee
Williams, Roger
Williams, Rudy V.
Williams, Shirley Stennis
Williams, Terri L.
Williams, Theodore R.
Williams, W. Clyde
Williams, Yvonne Carter
Williams, Yvonne LaVerne
Williams-Green, Joyce F.
Williams-Harris, Diane Beatrice
Williamson, Handy, Jr.
Willoughby, Susan Melita
Wilmot, David Winston
Wilson, Blenda J.
Wilson, Connie Drake
Wilson, Edith N.
Wilson, Greer Dawson
Wilson, Harrison B.
Wilson, John W.
Wilson, Laval S.
Wilson, Leroy, III
Wilson, Lucy R.
Wilson, Milton
Wilson, Ora Brown
Wilson, Patricia A.
Wilson, Prince E.
Wilson, Reginald
Wilson, Sherman Arthur
Wilson, Sodonia Mae
Wimberly, James Hudson
Wimbush, Gary Lynn
Winfield, Sinette Johnson
Winfree, Murrell H.
Winslow, Reynolds Baker
Winston, Jeanne Worley
Winston, Michael R.
Witherspoon, Audrey Goodwin
Wolfe, John Thomas
Wolfman, Brunetta Reid
Wood, Jerome H., Jr.
Wood, Margaret Beatrice
Woodard, Charles James
Woodfolk, Joseph O.
Woodhouse, Johnny Boyd
Woodland, Calvin Emmanuel
Woods, Barbara McAlpin
Woods, Jacqueline Edwards
Woods, Manuel T.
Woods, Willie G.
Woodson, Bernard Robert, Jr.
Woodson, Thelma L.
Woolfolk, E. Oscar
Woolfolk, George Ruble
Wright, C. T. Enus
Wright, Earl Lee
Wright, Frederick Douglass
Wright, Gerald
Wright, John Aaron
Wright, Joseph Malcolm
Wright, Marvin
Wright, Mary H.
Wright, Phillip LeRoi
Wright, Samuel Lamar
Wright, Stephen Junius, Jr.
Wright-Sabree, Margaret V.
Wyatt, Beatrice E.
Wykle, May Louise Hinton
Wynn, Cordell
Wyrick, Floyd I.
Yarbrough, Delano
Yarbrough, Mamie Luella

Yarbrough, Marilyn Virginia
Yeager, Thomas Stephen
Yerger, Ben
Yizar, James Horace, Jr.
Young, Aner Ruth
Young, Charles, Jr.
Young, Marechal-Neil Ellison
Young, Nancy Wilson
Young, Paula E.
Young, Ronald R.
Young, Rufus King
Younger, Celia Davis
Zambrana, Rafael
Zander, Jessie Mae
Zanders, Alton Wendell
Zimmerman, Samuel Lee
Zollar, Doris L.

ELECTRONICS
See COMPUTER SCIENCE—PROGRAMMING/SOFTWARE DEVELOPMENT; COMPUTER SCIENCE—SYSTEMS ANALYSIS/DESIGN; COMPUTER SCIENCE—NOT ELSEWHERE CLASSIFIED; ENGINEERING—ELECTRICAL/ELECTRONICS; RETAIL TRADE—ELECTRICAL/ELECTRONICS PRODUCTS; WHOLESALE TRADE—ELECTRICAL/ELECTRONICS PRODUCTS

ENGINEERING—AEROSPACE
Alexander, Walter Gilbert, II
Armstead, Wilbert Edward, Jr.
Arnold, James A.
Bluford, Guion Stewart, Jr.
Bodden, Wendell N.
Bryant, William Henry, Jr.
Carter, Arlington W., Jr.
Crossley, Frank Alphonso
Crump, Nathaniel L., Sr.
Dansby, Jesse L., Jr.
Darden, Christine Mann
Dunn, W. Paul
Ferguson, Robert Lee, Sr. (Fergie)
Few, Terry Lee
Gillispie, William Henry
Grant, John H., Sr.
Grooms, Henry Randall
Hadden, Eddie Raynord
Hamlet, James Frank
Hervey, Billy T.
House, James E.
Jackson, Earl C.
Jensen, Renaldo Mario
Lang, Charles J.
Lewis, James Earl
Murphy, Alvin Hugh
Myers, Earl T.
Nutt, Ambrose Benjamin
Parker, James L.
Perkins, Gladys Patricia
Powe, Joseph S.
Randolph, Bernard P.
Rose, Raymond E.
Sampson, Henry Thomas
Smithers, Oral Lester, Jr.
Valentine, Anthony James
Varnado, Arthur
Wagner, Vallerie Denise
Whitlow, Woodrow, Jr.
Wilkins, Roger L.
Wright, Linwood Clinton

ENGINEERING—CHEMICAL
Adeyiga, Adeyinka A.
Alexander, Edward Cleve
Bishop, Alfred A.
Davis, Lester E.
Dawkins, Michael James

Edwards, Robert Valentino
Evans, Milton L.
Frazier, Julie A.
Frink, Ronald Murice
Hatter, Henry
Herrell, Astor Yeary
Holmes, William
Howard, Donald R.
Jacobs, Larry Ben
Levister, Ernest Clayton, Jr.
Lindsay, Eddie H. S.
Marchand, Melanie Annette
Mayo, James Wellington
Mitchell, James Winfield
Oseni, Hakeem O.
Parnell, Arnold W.
Patrick, Jennie B.
Wiley, Lucish D.
Winston, Hubert
Wood, Jerome H., Jr.

ENGINEERING—CIVIL
Amory, Reginald L.
Bass, Joseph Frank
Baty, Reginald Clement
Bell, James L., Jr.
Bowser, Hamilton Victor, Sr.
Brown, Ernest Calvin
Cooper, Lois Louise
Cotton, Garner
Davis, James Harold
Davis, Lester E.
Flakes, Larry Joseph
Ford, Kenneth A.
Glover, Archibald F.
Hadnot, Thomas Edward
Hampton, Delon
Harding, John Edward
Hicks, William L.
Humphrey, Howard John
Jackson, Larry Eugene
Jones, Arthur L.
Jones, James Bennett
Jones, Raymond Morris
Kelley, Wilbourne Anderson, III
Kennedy, Nathelyne Archie
Ligon, Claude M.
Moore, Charlie W.
Parker, Lutrelle Fleming
Powell, Juan Herschel
Robinson, Hugh Granville
Smith, William Howard
Tucker, Paul, Jr.
Weaver, Herbert C.
White, Charles R.
Winfield, George Lee

ENGINEERING—ELECTRICAL/ELECTRONICS
Anderson, Kenneth Richard
Asom, Moses T.
Bagley, Gregory P.
Belcher, Paul E.
Bell, William Vaughn
Brown, Roderick
Coffey, William L.
Colson, Joseph S., Jr.
Cooper, Daneen Ravenell
Courtney, Stephen Alexander
Darkes, Leroy William
Demby, James E.
Diamond, John R.
Doddy, Reginald Nathaniel
Driver, Johnie M.
Edwards, Donald O.
Ellis, Johnell A.
Floyd, Vernon Clinton
Franklin, Clyde
Graham, Odell
Green, Joseph, Jr.
Green, Lester L.
Hardie, Robert L., Jr.
Hargrove, Andrew
Harris, Bryant G.
Harris, Gary Lynn
Harris, Larry Vordell, Jr.
Harris, Vernon Joseph
Hill, Raymond A.
Hughes, Charles W., Jr.
Johnson, Michael Kevin
Jones, William J.
Jordan, George Washington, Jr.

Keyser, George F.
King, Reginald F.
Knight, Lynnon Jacob
LaRue, Karl McLaine
Lawrence, Rodell
Leaphart, Eldridge
Lewis, James Earl
Lindsay, Horace Augustin
Madison, Ronald L.
McCraven, Marcus R.
McLaurin, Freddie Lewis, Jr.
Melrose, Thomas S.
Miller, Theodore H.
Montague, Nelson C.
Morris, Joel M.
Nibbs, Alphonse, Sr.
Oh, Harry K.
Overall, Manard
Owens, David K.
Parker, Darwin Carey
Pollard, Muriel Ransom
Ransom, Preston L.
Ransom, Victor L.
Rucks, Alfred J.
Russell, Wesley L.
Sechrest, Edward Amacker
Sherman, Thomas Oscar, Jr.
Smith, Dennis Rae
Smith, Roger Leroy
Spencer, Michael Gregg
Stephens, Wallace O.
Stricklin, James
Tatmon, Eugene
Taylor, Ellis Clarence
Taylor, Kenneth Doyle
Terrell, Richard Warren
Thaxton, Judy Evette
Thorpe, Herbert Clifton
Turner, Allen H.
Turner, Franklin James
Waddell, Theodore R.
Walker, Ernest L.
Walker, Willie M.
Wallace, Richard Warner
White, William J.
White, William J.
Williamson, Samuel R.
Worthey, Richard E.
Younger, Robert D.
Zeumault, Dianne Lorraine

ENGINEERING—INDUSTRIAL
Bostick, Laurence Herbert
Elliott, J. Russell
Esogbue, Augustine O.
Hunter, John W.
Jenkins, Woodie R., Jr.
Johnson, Norris Brock
Lewis, Cleveland Arthur
Lovelace, Onzalo Robert
Nutt, Ambrose Benjamin
Spencer, Brenda L.
Stith, Antoinette Freeman
Tynes, Richard H.
Washington, John Calvin, III

ENGINEERING—MECHANICAL
Barnes, Matthew M., Jr.
Butler, John O.
Charlton, Jack Fields
Daniels, Jesse
Elliott, J. Russell
Emrit, Ronald C.
Fearing, John T.
Henderson, Crawford, Sr.
Hull, Bernard S.
Jackson, Earl C.
Jackson, Joseph T.
Johnson, Carl Elliott
Johnston, Wallace O.
King, Lawrence P.
Kyle, Odes J., Jr.
Lowe, Sylvia Oneice
McCarrell, Clark Gabriel, Jr.
Murphy, Alvin Hugh
Neal, Eddie
Parker, Paul E.
Parnell, Arnold W.
Reed, Cordell
Riddick, Eugene E.
Rohr, Leonard Carl

Taylor, Edward Walter
Watkins, Charles B.
Williams, James H., Jr.

ENGINEERING—METALLURGICAL/CERAMIC/MATERIALS
Bragg, Robert Henry
Chapman, Gilbert Bryant, II
Crossley, Frank Alphonso
Dixon, Louis Tennyson
Freeman, Walter Eugene
Hawkins, Walter Lincoln
McClendon, Moses C.
Phillips, Edward Martin
Taylor, Willie Marvin

ENGINEERING—MINING
See also MINING/QUARRYING
Hughes, Johnnie Lee

ENGINEERING—NUCLEAR
Bishop, Alfred A.
Booker, Gary P.
Jupiter, Clyde Peter
Knowles, William W.
LeVert, Francis E.
Monteith, Henry C.
Trappier, Arthur Shives
Wallace, Richard Warner

ENGINEERING—PETROLEUM
Gipson, Mack, Jr.
Granville, William, Jr.
Landers, Naaman Garnett
Lee, Robert Emile
Shackelford, George Franklin

ENGINEERING—NOT ELSEWHERE CLASSIFIED
Alexander, F. S. Jack
Barrett, Richard O.
Behrmann, Serge T.
Bland, Robert Arthur
Brittain, Bradley Bernard, Jr.
Brown, Gary W.
Clay, Harold R.
Drake, George Barr
Esquerre, Jean Roland
Eziemefe, Godslove Ajenavi
Finn, Robert Green
Franklin, Benjamin
Gartrell, Luther R.
Gay, Eddie C.
Gee, William Rowland, Jr.
Gillispie, William Henry
Gonzalez, Cambell
Gothard, Donald L.
Graham, Frederick Mitchell
Hampton, Delon
Harper, Sarah Elizabeth
Henderson, Charles
Henderson, Eddie L.
Hill, Robert J., Jr.
House, Jesse O.
Jackson, Richard H.
Johnson, Frederick E.
Johnson, Garey A.
Jones, James G.
Jones, Michael Perrin
Jones-Grimes, Mable Christine
Jordan, Frederick E.
Kennedy, Nathelyne Archie
Keyes, Andrew J.
Lambert, Samuel Fredrick
Lue-Hing, Cecil
Madison, Shannon L.
Martin, Montez Cornelius, Jr.
McCarrell, Clark Gabriel, Jr.
McCuiston, Frederick Douglass, Jr.
McDonald, William Emory
Murphy, Alvin Hugh
Neal, Eddie

Drake, Pauline Lilie
Drew-Peeples, Brenda
Driessen, Henry, Jr.
DuBose, Otelia
Dudley, Herman T.
Duffy, Eugene Jones
Dunning, Roosevelt
Durall, Dolis, Jr.
Echols, Alvin E.
Echols, David Lorimer
Edmonson, Bernie L.
Edwards, A. Wilson
Edwards, Luther Howard
Edwards, Shirley Heard
Edwards, Theodore Unaldo
Elder, Geraldine H.
Ellis, Benjamin F., Jr.
Ellis, Douglas, Jr.
Ellis, Rodney
Ellison, David Lee
English, Clarence R.
Esco, Fred, Jr.
Etheredge, James W.
Evaige, Wanda Jo
Evans, Joe B.
Evers, James Charles
Fairman, John Abbrey
Farrell-Donaldson, Marie D.
Fisher, Robert F.
Fitzgerald, Roy Lee
Fleming, June H.
Fletcher, James C., Jr.
Flippen, Greg
Forbes, George L.
Ford, Johnny L.
Foster, E. C.
Fountain, William Stanley
Foushee, Geraldine George
Fox, Theodore B.
Francis, James L.
Francisco, Anthony M.
Franklin, Oliver St. Clair, Jr.
Franklin, Shirley Clarke
Frazier, Dan E., Sr.
Frazier, Ray Jerrell
Frost, William Henry
Frost, Wilson
Gaines, Dora Belle
Gaines, Paul Laurence, Sr.
Gamble, Kenneth L.
Gamble, Robert Lewis
Garner, Lon L.
Garner, Mary E.
Garrett, Joyce F.
Garrett, Paul C.
Gay, Helen Parker
Gayles, Franklin Johnson
Gayles, Lindsey, Jr.
Gentry, LaMar Duane
Gibson, James O.
Gibson, Kenneth Allen
Gibson, Paul, Jr.
Gilbert, Richard Lannear
Gilchrist, Carlton Chester
Gilford, Rotea J.
Gilkey, William C.
Gilliam, Sharon
Gilmore, Carter C.
Gipson, Francis E.
Givens, E. Terrian
Goode, Calvin C.
Goode, W. Wilson
Goodwin, Kelly Oliver Perry
Goodwin, Mercedier Cassandra de
  Freita
Gordon, Charles D.
Gordon, Winfield James
Goree, Janie Glymph
Graham, Catherine S.
Grant, Cedric Steven
Gravely, Melvin J.
Gray, Robert Dean
Gray, Robert R.
Green, Angelo Gray
Green, Forrest F.
Green, Shirley
Green, Theodis Guy
Green, Thomas L.
Greene, Mamie Louise
Griffin, Percy Lee
Griffin-Johnson, Lorraine
  Antionette
Griffith, Vera Victoria
Griggs, James C.
Hall, Anthony W., Jr.

Hall, Katie
Hall, Robert L.
Hamilton, Phanuel J.
Hamilton, Wilbur Wyatt
Hamilton-Rahi, Lynda Darlene
Hamlin, Arthur Henry
Haney, Napoleon
Hannah, Melvin James
Hannibal, Alice Priscilla
Harding, Ed
Harris, Earl
Harris, Earl L.
Harris, Jerome C., Jr.
Harris, Joseph R.
Harrold, Austin Leroy
Harvey, Gerald
Hatcher, Richard Gordon
Hayes, Charles A.
Head, Raymond, Jr.
Henderson, Erma L.
Henderson, Gerald Eugene
Hendricks, Juanita
Herman, Kathleen Virgil
Hewitt, Ronald Jerome
Hewlett, Antoinette Payne
Hightower, Anthony
Hightower, Michael
Hightower, Willar H., Jr.
Hill, Howard Hampton
Hill, James O.
Hill, Mary Alice
Hilliard, Delories
Hinch, Andrew Lewis, Sr.
Holliday-Hayes, Wilhelmina
  Evelyn (Billie)
Holloway, Herman M., Sr.
Holmes, Gary Mayo
Holmes, Leo S.
Hood, Nicholas
Howard, Robert Berry, Jr.
Huger, James E.
Hughes, Mamie F.
Jackson, Alvin B., Jr.
Jackson, Arthur Howard
Jackson, Bobby L.
Jackson, John
Jackson, John H.
Jackson, Leo Edwin
Jackson, Maynard Holbrook
Jackson, Richard E., Jr.
Jacobs, Hazel A.
James, Henry Grady, III
James, Henry Nathaniel
Jangdharrie, Wycliffe K.
Jarmon, James Henry, Jr.
Jeffers, Ben L.
Jefferson, Clifton
Jefferson, Hilda Hutchinson
Jefferson, James E.
Jenkins, Woodie R., Jr.
Johnson, Arthur T.
Johnson, B. A.
Johnson, Barbara C.
Johnson, Ben E.
Johnson, Carroll Jones
Johnson, James A.
Johnson, James R.
Johnson, John J.
Johnson, Marlene E.
Johnson, Phyllis Campbell
Johnson, R. Benjamin
Johnson, Sarah H.
Johnson, Wendell L., Jr.
Johnson, Wilhelmina Lashaun
Johnson, Willie
Jones, Clarence J., Jr. (Jeep Jones)
Jones, Cornell
Jones, Earl Frederick
Jones, Frank
Jones, Franklin D.
Jones, Gerald E.
Jones, Joni Lou
Jones, Larry Earl
Jones, Lawrence W.
Jones, Leeland Newton, Jr.
Jones, Nathaniel, Sr.
Jones, Nellie L.
Jones, Patricia Yvonne
Jones, Peter Lawson
Jones, William
Jones, William Donnell
Jordan, Charles R.
Jordan, Marilyn E.
Jordan, Patricia Carter

Kelly, James Johnson
Kelly, Marion Greenup
Kimber, Lesly H.
King, Ceola
Kirven, Mythe Yuvette
Knight, Dewey W., Jr.
Knight, Richard, Jr.
Knight, Walter R.
Knight, William Rogers
LaBrie, Peter, Jr.
Lampkin, Cheryl Lyvette
Lander, Cressworth Caleb
Lane, Allan C.
Langford, Arthur, Jr.
Langham, John M.
Larkins, E. Pat
Larkins, William Conyers
Lawson, Lawyer
Lawson, Quentin Roosevelt
Leake, Willie Mae James
LeCesne, Terrel M.
Lee, Aaron
Lee, Bernard Scott
Lee, Edward S.
Lee, Howard N.
Lee, Van Spencer
Leeper, Ronald James
Lewis, Diane Claire
Lewis, Richard U.
Lewis, Woodrow
Lindsay, Gilbert W.
Lofton, Andrew James
Lomax, Dervey A.
Love, Joe W.
Lovelace, Dean Alan
Lucas, Earl S.
Lucas, Maurice F.
Ludley, Richard
Lyda, Wesley John
Lyle, Roberta Branche Blacke
Lyles, Marie Clark
Lynn, James Elvis
Mack, Gladys Walker
Mahan-Powell, Lena
Mallett, Conrad L.
Malone, Amanda Ella
Malone, J. Deotha
Mannie, William Edward
Mansfield, Andrew K.
Marsh, Henry L., III
Martin, Shedrick M., Jr.
Mason, Hilda Howland M.
Mason, William E.
May, James F.
Mayfield, JoAnn H.O.
McClain, Dorothy Mae (nee
  Hunter)
McClendon, Carol A.
McEachern-Ulmer, Sylvia L.
McFadden, Cora C.
McFadden, Nathaniel James
McGee, James H.
McGhee, Samuel T.
McGuire, Jean Mitchell
McIver, John Douglas
McKellar, Stephen Alexander
McLemore, Nelson, Jr.
McNeil, Frank
McWright, Carter C.
Meadows, Cheryl R.
Meeks, Reginald Kline
Merritt, Frank C.
Millender, Dharathula H.
Miller, Jesse P.
Miller, Wilbur J.
Mitchell, Clyde D.
Mitchell, Douglas
Mitchell, Parren James
Monteverdi, Mark Victor
Montgomery, Joe Elliott
Montgomery, Payne
Moore, Dwayne Harrison
Moore, Henry J.
Moore, Hilliard T., Sr.
Moore, Jerry A., Jr.
Moore, Walter Louis
Morancie, Horace L.
Morial, Ernest Nathan
Morrison, Robert B., Jr.
Moss, Estella Mae
Moss, Jimmy R.
Moss, Thomas Edward, Sr.
Murray, Kay L.
Murray, Sylvester

Murrell, Sylvia Marilyn
Myles, Herbert John
Nelson, Ronald Duncan
Nesbitt, Prexy-Rozell William
Netters, Tyrone Homer
Nettles, Willard, Jr.
Newman, Kenneth J.
Noah, Leroy Edward
Noble, Norma Lynette
Norrell-Nance, Rosalind Elizabeth
Norris, Walter, Jr.
O'Connor, Thomas F., Jr.
Officer, Carl Edward
O'Neal, Fredrick William, Jr.
Osborne, Hugh Stancill
Parks, Lyman S.
Parks, Thelma Reece
Parrish, John Henry
Partee, Cecil A.
Patrick, Julius, Jr.
Patterson, Dessie Lee
Patterson, William Benjamin
Patton, Robert
Paul, John F.
Pearson, Herman B.
Perry, Carrie Saxon
Pindle-Conaway, Mary Ward
Pittman, Darryl E.
Polite, Theron Jerome
Prewitt, Al Bert
Price, Wallace Walter
Pritchard, Daron
Quander, Rohulamin
Ramseur, Isabelle R.
Rattley, Jessie M.
Ray, Mary E.
Reese, Frederick D.
Revelle, Robert, Sr.
Ricanek, Carolyn Wright
Rice, Robert C.
Rice, Susie Leon
Richardson, Gilda Faye
Richardson, Harold Edward
Richardson, Louis M.
Richmond, Myrian Patricia
Riley, William Scott
Rivers, Valerie L.
Roberson, F. Alexis H.
Roberts, Charles L.
Roberts, Steven C.
Robinson, Henry
Robinson, William Earl
Rogers, Earline
Rogers, Elijah Baby
Rogers, Freddie Clyde
Rogers, John W.
Rollins, Avon William, Sr.
Ross, Charles
Ross, Doris A.
Rowland, Leon Floyd
Rundles, James Isaiah
Sampson, Marva W.
Sams, Eristus
Samuel, Frederick E.
Samuels, Leslie Eugene
Sanders, Archie, Jr.
Sanders, Wesley, Jr.
Saunders, James Warren
  (Choppy)
Savage, Dennis James
Schmoke, Kurt Lidell
Scott, Carstella H.
Scott, Lewis Nathanel
Scott-Johnson, Roberta Virginia
Seabrooks-Edwards, Marilyn S.
Seals, Gerald
Session, Johnny Frank
Shackelford, Lottie H.
Shakoor, Adam Adib
Shanks, James A.
Shannon, George A.
Sharp, James Alfred
Sharpp, Nancy Charlene
Shavers, Catherine
Shaw, Julius Fennell
Sheppard, Stevenson Royrayson
Shivers, S. Michael
Shoemaker, Veronica Sapp
Simms, James Edward
Sims, Lydia Theresa
Singleton, James Milton
Singleton, Leroy, Sr.
Smith, Carol Barlow
Smith, Dorothy O.

Smith, Eddie D., Sr.
Smith, Edward Charles
Smith, James, Jr.
Smith, Juanita Smith
Smith, Lafayette Kenneth
Smith, Marion L.
Smith, Sam
Smith, Vernel Hap
Smith, Vernon G.
Smithers, Priscilla Jane
Snell, Jimmy Gregory
Southall, Charles
Spann, Noah Atterson, Jr.
Spaulding, William Ridley
Spellman, Oliver B., Jr.
Spencer, Marian A.
Stallworth, Ann P.
Stamps, Leon Preist
Stanley, Columbus Landon, Sr.
Stanley, Ellis M., Sr.
Stanley, Woodrow
Steans, Edith Elizabeth
Steger, C. Donald
Stephens, James Anthony
Stevens, Warren Sherwood
Stewart, Dorothy Nell
Stewart, Mae E.
Stewart, W. Douglas
Strachan, John R.
Stubblefield, Jennye Washington
Summers, Edna White
Summers, William E., IV
Sweeney, Robert Lucien
Swinton, Lee Vertis
Tarver, Marie Nero
Tate, Eula Booker
Taylor, Noel C.
Taylor, Richard L.
Terrell, Ethel
Terrell, Robert E.
Terry, Frank W.
Thomas, Erma Lee
Thomas, Jewel M.
Thomas, Joan McHenry Bates
Thompson, Benjamin Franklin
Thompson, Bennie G.
Thompson, Betty L.
Thompson, Bobby E.
Thompson, Jesse M.
Thompson, Johnnie
Thorpe, Otis L.
Todman, Jureen Francis
Tolbert, Edward T.
Tolbert, John W., Jr.
Tolliver, Ned, Jr.
Tolliver, Thomas C., Jr.
Torian, Edward Torrence
Touchstone, John E.
Trice, Juniper Yates
Trives, Nathaniel
Troupe-Frye, Betty Jean
Tucker, Donald
Turner, Louis Edouard
Turner, Robert Lloyd
Turner, Yvonne Williams
Twyman, Luska J.
Urdy, Charles E.
Usry, James LeRoy
Vereen, Nathaniel
Wainwright, Gloria Bessie
Waiters, Gail Elenoria
Walker, Ann B.
Walker, Gary S.
Waller, Eunice McLean
Walls, Melvin
Wanambwa, Sara Louise
Ward, Albert M.
Ward, Anna Elizabeth
Ware, Carl
Washington, Craig A.
Washington, David Warren
Washington, Henry L.
Washington, Isaiah Edward
Washington, James Lee
Washington, Walter E.
Watkins, Izear Carl
Watkins, Lenice J.
Watkins, Mozelle Ellis
Watson, Juanita
Watterson, Richard Harvey
Webb, Joe
Webb, Wellington E.
Webster, Lonnie
Wells, Billy Gene

Josey, Leronia Arnetta
Kane, Jacqueline Anne
Kennedy, Sandra Denise
Kilpatrick, Carolyn Cheeks
King, Gwendolyn
Lambert, Benjamin J., III
Langford, Arthur, Jr.
Larry, Jerald Henry
Lawlah, Gloria Gary
Lawson, Herman A.
Leatherwood, Larry Lee
Ledee, Robert
Lewis, James B.
Linton, Gordon J.
Livingston, Rudolph
Lopez, Mary Gardner
Love, Clarence C.
Lucas, David Eugene
Lyons, A. Bates
Mallory, William L.
Malone, J. Deotha
Mann, Thomas J., Jr.
Markette-Malone, Sharon
Marrow-Mooring, Barbara A.
Marsh-Lott, Freddie Alexander
Marshall, Charlene Jennings
Martin, Gwendolyn Rose
Maule, Albert R.
Maxey, James, III
Maxie, Peggy Joan
McCall, Carl
McCoy, William
McKinney, Paul
McLaughlin, Eurphan
McReynolds, Elaine A.
Mereday, Richard F.
Mfume, Kweisi
Michaux, Henry M., Jr.
Miles, Mary Alice
Miller, Lawrence A.
Miller, Yvonne Bond
Millin, Henry Allan
Mitchell, Joanne
Mitchell, Theo W.
Moncure, Albert F.
Montgomery, Keesler H.
Montgomery, William R.
Moore, Arnold D.
Moore, Gwen
Morris, Effie Lee
Morton, Margaret E.
Mosby, Carolyn Brown
Moten, Birdia B. (nee Jenkins)
Murphy, Margaret Humphries
Murphy, Raymond M.
Murphy, Ric
Murray, Judson T.
Myers, Lewis Horace
Myers, Woodrow Augustus, Jr.
Neal, Sylvester (Sam)
Newhouse, Richard H.
Nibbs, Alphonse, Sr.
Nicholas, Gwendolyn Smith
Nix, Robert N.C., Jr.
Noble, Norma Lynette
Norman, James H.
Nunnery, Willie James
Oliver, Frank Louis
Oliver, Jesse Dean
O'Neal, Connie Murry
Owens, William
Owens-Hicks, Shirley
Palmer, Ronald DeWayne
Parker, Henry Ellsworth
Patterson, Kay
Payne, Mitchell Howard
Pease, Denise Louise
Perry, Robert Cephas
Peters, Kenneth Darryl, Sr.
Petett, Freddye
Pickering, Robert Perry
Pickett, Alvin L.
Pickett, Dovie T.
Pinkard, Norman Thomas
Porter, E. Melvin
Powers, Georgia M.
Preston, Joseph, Jr.
Pugh, G. Douglas
Putnam, Glendora M.
Raby, Clyde T.
Ragsdale, Paul B.
Ramirez, Gilbert
Range, M. Athalie
Rayford, Lee Edward
Raymond, Henry James

Reddick, Alzo Jackson
Redman, James W.
Reed, Thomas J.
Reid, Vernon H.
Reynolds, Nanette Lee (nee Smith)
Rhodes, Edward
Richardson, David Preston, Jr.
Richardson, George C.
Richardson, Leo
Rickman, Ray
Ridley, May Alice
Riley, Wayne Joseph
Robertson, James B.
Robinson, Clarence B.
Roebuck, James Randolph, Jr.
Ross, Doris A.
Rowe, Marilyn Johnson
Rushing, Byron D.
Sabree, Clarice Salaam
Sanders, Hank
Sands, Douglas Bruce
Saunders, John Edward, III
Scott, Judith Sugg
Scott, Robert Cortez
Scott, Samuel
Seavers, Clarence W.
Sharpe, Ronald M.
Shaw, Curtis E.
Shelton, O. L.
Shelton, Ulysses
Simmons, Joseph Jacob, III
Simmons, Leonard (Bud)
Slater, Rodney E.
Smith, Henry R., Jr.
Smith, Virgil Clark, Jr.
Smith, William M., Jr.
Speller, J. Finton
Spencer, Anthony Lawrence
Stallworth, Alma G.
Stevenson, Morton Coleman
Street-Kidd, Mae
Summers, Joseph W.
Swinton, Lee Vertis
Sykes, Vernon Lee
Tabor, Lillie Montague
Taliaferro, Addison
Tanner, Gloria Travis
Taylor, Albert, Jr.
Taylor, James C.
Thomas, Mable
Thomas, Nida E.
Thompson, Albert W., Sr.
Thompson, Ike
Thompson, Isaiah
Traughber, Charles M.
Trotter, Andrew Leon
Trotter, Decatur Wayne
Troupe, Charles Quincy
Turner, Isiah
Turnley, Richard, Jr.
Vaughn, Jackie, III
Wade, Lawrence S.
Waldo, Carol Dunn
Walker, Carolyn
Wallice, Ernest Herron
Walton, Elbert Arthur, Jr.
Ward, Walter L., Jr.
Warrick-Crisman, Jeri Everett
Washington, Craig A.
Washington, Edith May Faulkner
Waters, Maxine
Waters, William David
Watson, Diane Edith
Webb, Harold H.
Welch, Odella T.
White, Frankie Walton
White, Jesse C., Jr.
White, Michael Reed
Whitehead, John L., Jr.
Wilder, Lawrence Douglas
Wilkins, Henry, III
Williams, Ada L.
Williams, Freddye Harper
Williams, Hardy
Williams, Harold Cleophas
Williams, Hosea L.
Williams, Katherine
Williams, Stanley King
Wilson, Calvin T.
Wilson, Leonard D.
Wilson, Ronald Ray
Wimbish, C. Bette
Windham, Revish

Winters, Jacqueline F.
Woodhouse, Rossalind Yvonne
Woods, Sylvania Webb, Jr.
Yates, Ella Gaines
Young, Joseph Floyd, Sr.
Young, Larry

GOVERNMENT SERVICE (ELECTED OR APPOINTED)—FEDERAL

Alexander, Robert L.
Allen, Bernestine
Allen, William Barclay
Anderson, William A.
Archibald, B. Milele
Ashton, Vivian Christina R.
Austin, Frank
Bailey, Arthur
Baker, James E.
Baltimore, Richard Lewis, III
Barbour, Worth L.
Bardwell, Rufus B., III
Barnes, Paul Douglas
Batine, Rafael
Bean, Maurice Darrow
Beckett, Charles Campbell
Beckham, William J., Jr.
Becton, Julius Wesley, Jr.
Belcher, Lewis, Jr.
Bell, Theron J.
Bellamy, Verdelle B.
Billings, Christine D.
Bispham, Frank L.
Blackwell, Randolph Talmadge
Bland, Arthur H.
Blankenship, Glenn Rayford
Bolden, Betty A.
Boswell, Arthur W.
Bradley, Jesse J., Jr.
Bradley, M. Louise
Brazier, Martin George
Brice, Eugene Clay
Brimmer, Andrew F.
Britton, Theodore R., Jr.
Broadnax, Madison
Brooks, William C.
Brown, Georgia R.
Brown, Linda Jenkins
Browne, Robert Span
Bruce, Carol Pitt
Bruce, Preston, Jr.
Bryant, Clarence W.
Bryant, Edward Joe, III
Bullock, J. Jerome
Burton, Calvin E.
Cameron, Lenore Hopewell
Cannon, Calvin Curtis
Caster, Caroleigh Tuitt
Claiborne, Lloyd R.
Clark, LaWanna Gibbs
Clay, William L.
Collins, Cardiss
Conner, Lucy Shull
Conrad, Joseph M., Jr.
Conyers, John, Jr.
Cook, Joyce Mitchell
Cooper, Barbara Jean
Cooper, Emmett E., Jr.
Corley-Saunders, Angela Rose
Cox, Otis Graham, Jr.
Crockett, Delores Loraine
Crosse, St. George Idris Bryon
Curry, Jerry Ralph
Daniels, LeGree Sylvia
Davenport, Chester C.
Davis, Benjamin O., Jr.
Davis, John Aubrey
Davis, Lloyd
Davis, Marion Harris
Davis, Steve G.
Dawson, Horace Greeley, Jr.
Day, Eric Therander
DeLair, Louis, Jr.
Dellums, Ronald V.
Denmark, Robert Richard
Dennis, Hugo, Jr.
Dessaso-Gordon, Janice Marie
Dines, George B.
Dudley, Edward R.
Durham, William R.
Dymally, Mervyn M.
Edwards, Theodore Thomas

Elmore, Joyce A.
English, Kenneth
Espy, Michael
Evans, James Carmichael
Evans, W. Ronald
Ewing, Mamie Hans
Fagin, Darryl Hall
Fairley, Richard L.
Farmer, Francesta Elizabeth
Fauntroy, Walter E.
Felton, Zora Belle
Fields, Earl Grayson
Finney, Essex Eugene, Jr.
Flake, Floyd H.
Fleming, Patricia Stubbs
Fletcher, Howard R.
Ford, Claudette Franklin
Ford, Harold E.
Foster, Clyde
Francis, Henry Minton
Franklin, Benjamin Edward
Franklin, Milton B., Jr.
Frye, Robert Edward
Frye, William Sinclair
Gaffney, Thomas Daniel
Gaines, Sylvester, Jr.
Gamble, Janet Helen
Gant, Wanda Adele
Gaston, Marilyn Hughes
Gist, Lewis Alexander, Jr.
Gittens, James Philip
Glenn, Patricia Campbell
Grady, Mary Forte
Granger, Shelton B.
Gray, Edward Wesley, Jr.
Gray, William H., III
Greenfield, Roy Alonzo
Griffin, Ples Andrew
Grigsby, Troy L.
Guiton, Bonnie
Hall, Katie
Hamilton, H. J. Belton
Hardy-Hill, Edna Mae
Hargrave, Charles William
Harley, Daniel P., Jr.
Harper, Bernice Catherine
Harris, Marion Hopkins
Harris, Robert F.
Harris, Vera D.
Harris, William J.
Harrison, Hattie N.
Headley, De Costa Oneal
Hemphill, Gwendolyn
Henderson, Elmer W.
Henderson, James H.
Herman, Alexis M.
Hicks, Eleanor
Hightower, Herma J.
Hinton, Warren Miles
Hobson, Robert R.
Hodges, Clarence Eugene
Hudson, Anthony Webster
Hudson, William Thomas
Humphrey, Melvin
Ivery, James A.
Jackson, Earl K., Sr.
Jackson, Franklin D.B.
Jenkins, Howard, Jr.
Jenkins, Thomas O.
Johnson, Elaine McDowell
Johnson, Lloyd A.
Johnson, Mary Beatrice
Jones, Gerald Winfield
Jones, Hardi Liddell
Jones, Paul R.
Josey, Leronia Arnetta
King, Clarence Maurice, Jr.
King, Howard O.
Kresy-Poree, R. Jean
Lafontant, Jewel Stradford
Lane, John Henry
Lang-Jeter, Lula L.
Latcholia, Kenneth Edward
Laws, Clarence A.
Lee, Norvel L. R.
Lee-Miller, Stephanie
Leftwich, Norma Bogues
Lewis, Arthur W.
Lewis, John Robert
Lightfoot, Jean Drew
Lippman, Lois H.
Love, Ezekiel
Lovett, Edward P.
Lowe, Richard Bryant, III

Lucas, William
MacClane, Edward James
Mack, John L.
Mack, Voyce J.
Madison, Richard
Mansfield, W. Ed
Martin, William R.
Matthews, LaMoyne Mason
May, Floyd O'Lander
Mayo, James Wellington
Mazique, Frances Margurite (nee Belafonte)
McAdams, Linnie M.
McCrary-Simmons, Shirley Denise
McFarlin, Emma Daniels
Medearis, Victor L.
Metcalf, Andrew Lee, Jr.
Middleton, Michael A.
Milner, Michael Edwin
Mims, Oscar Lugrie
Miner, William Gerard
Mitchell, Parren James
Moore, Johnnie Adolph
Moore, Joseph L.
Moore, Roscoe Michael, Jr.
Moose, George E.
Morgan, Fletcher, Jr.
Morgan, Juanita Kennedy
Morris, Archie, III
Morrison, Trudi Michelle
Morrow, E. Frederic
Morse, Mildred (nee Sharpe)
Morton, Azie B.
Morton, Leona M.
Mosley, John William
Napper, Hyacinthe T.
Nash, Eva L.
Ndlovu, Callistus P.
Nichols, Sylvia A.
Norfleet, Janet
Norton, Edward Worthington
Osborne, Ernest L.
Owens, Major R.
Parron, Delores L.
Perkins, Edward Joseph
Perry, June Carter
Peters, Aulana Louise
Pinson, Valerie F.
Polk, Lorna Marie
Pope, James M.
Powell, Colin L.
Rangel, Charles B.
Reede, James William, Jr.
Reeves, Willie Lloyd, Jr.
Rice, Emmett J.
Rice, William E.
Rivers, David Eugene
Roberts, Louis Wright
Robinson, Leonard Harrison, Jr.
Rudd, James M.
Russell, Ernest
Saulter, Gilbert John
Sewell, Isiah Obediah
Sherman, Marcus Harvey
Silva, Henry Andrew
Singletary, Inez M.
Smith, Charles Lebanon
Smith, Chester B.
Smith, Eugene
Smith, Lila
Smith, Rufus Herman
Solomon, Wilbert F.
Spurlock, Langley Augustine
Stebbins, Dana Brewington
Stokes, Louis
Strode, Velma McEwen
Styles, Julian English
Sutton, Ozell
Tankerson, Richard E.
Taylor, Daisy Curry
Taylor, William H.
Teague, Gladys Peters
Terry, Frank W.
Thomas, Carol M.
Thomas, Clarence
Thomas, Eunice S.
Thrasher, William Edward
Todman, Terence A.
Towns, Edolphus
Tribble, Huerta Cassius
Turner, Yvonne Williams
Valentine, Deborah Marie
Valien, Preston
Vaughn, William Smith

Walker, Ann B.
Walker, William Sonny
Wallace, C. Everett
Watlington, Janet Berecia
Weaver, Robert C.
Webb, Wellington E.
Welcome, Verda F.
Wells, Joseph L.
Wesley, Ruth Bailey
Wilber, Margie Robinson
Wiley-Pickett, Gloria
Wilkins, Thomas A.
Williams, Ann Claire
Williams, Bernice
Williams, Deborah Ann
Williams, Lloyd L.
Williams, Paul
Wilson, Ernest
Wilson, Joy Johnson
Woodson, S. Howard, Jr.
Young, Ruth L.

GOVERNMENT SERVICE (ELECTED OR APPOINTED)— NOT ELSEWHERE CLASSIFIED
See also JUDICIARY

Baker, Wanda Kay
Blackwell, Randolph Talmadge
Brown, Nancy Cofield
Bullett, Audrey Kathryn
Cain, Frank
Calbert, Roosevelt
Carthan, Eddie James
Chambers, Olivia Marie
Chatman, Anna Lee
Chatman, Jacob L.
Cherry, Theodore W.
Christian, Cora LeEthel
Coffey, Gilbert Haven, Jr.
Collins, Carter H.
Cope, Donald Lloyd
Crump, Arthel Eugene
Cullers, Samuel James
Darnell, Edward Buddy
Dymally, Lynn V.
Foster, Robert Leon
Francis, Charles S. L.
Grant, Cedric Steven
Hanson, Charles M., Jr.
Hardy, Willie J.
Holloway, Anne Forrester
Jones, Theresa Diane
Jordan, Barbara C.
Keels, James Dewey
Kimbrough-Johnson, Donna L.
Lee, Katherine I.
Milligan, Hugh D.
Morgan, Fletcher, Jr.
Price, Ruby Jewell Timms
Rayford, Lee Edward
Reynolds, Andrew Buchanan
Reynolds, Ida Manning
Rice, Lois Dickson (nee Dickson)
Scott, Beverly Angela
Simpson, Samuel G.
Slade, Walter R., Jr.
Smiley, James Walker, Sr.
Stanton, Janice D.
Starks, Rick
Tayari, Kabili
Taylor, Gloria Jean
Toran, Kay Dean
Tyler, Robert James, Sr.
Van Lierop, Robert F.
West, Togo Dennis, Jr.
Widener, Warren Hamilton
Williamson, Carl Vance

GRAPHIC DESIGN
See ART, VISUAL— COMMERCIAL ART/ GRAPHIC DESIGN

HEALTH CARE—NOT ELSEWHERE CLASSIFIED
See also CHIROPRACTIC; DENTISTRY; HEALTH SERVICES ADMINISTRATION; MEDICINE— CARDIOLOGY; MEDICINE— DERMATOLOGY; MEDICINE—INTERNAL MEDICINE; MEDICINE— NEUROLOGY; MEDICINE— OBSTETRICS/ GYNECOLOGY; MEDICINE— PEDIATRICS; MEDICINE— PSYCHIATRY; MEDICINE—NOT ELSEWHERE CLASSIFIED; NURSING; OPTOMETRY; PODIATRY

Abdul-Malik, Ibrahim
Alexander, Drew W.
Babbs, Junious C., Sr.
Boddie, Lewis F., Sr.
Brown, Dorothy Lavania
Butler, Homer L.
Butts, Hugh F.
Cash, Bettye Joyce (nee Moore)
Chandler, Harold R.
Chapman, Charles F.
Christian, Geraldine Ashley McConnell
Collins, Sylvia Dolores
Copeland, Terrilyn Denise
Crawford, James Wesley
Cunningham, Paul Raymond Goldwyn
Davis, James W.
Davis, Jean M.
Davis, Myrtle Hilliard
Donawa, Maria Elena
Dorsey, Joseph A.
Dual, Peter Alfred
Dyer-Goode, Pamela Theresa
Evans, Edgar E.
Evans, Patricia P.
Evans-Dodd, Theora Anita
Fairman, John Abbrey
Fort, Jane
Fowlkes, Nelson J.
Francois, Emmanuel Saturnin
Fraser, Rhonda Beverly
Gaffney, Mary Louise
Goodwin, Jesse Francis
Graham, Louise McClary
Gray, Carol Coleman
Guyton, Alicia V.
Hawkins, Mary L.
Hawkins, Muriel A.
Hill, Wendell T., Jr.
Hogan, Ogelia M.
Holland, Ethel M.
Holloman, John L. S., Jr.
Holmes, Everlena M.
Hudson, Roy Davage
Hussein, Carlessia Amanda
Johnson, Patricia Duren
Jones, Kenneth Leroy
Jordan, Wilbert Cornelious
Joyner, John Erwin
King, Rosalyn Cain
Ladson, Louis Fitzgerald
Land, Chester LaSalle
Lawrence, Theresa A. B.
Lee, Andre L.
Lowe, James Edward, Jr.
Mays, Alfred Thomas
McCurdy, Brenda Wright
Mims, Robert Bradford
Morgan, Rudolph Courtney
Moss, James A.
Muldrow, Catherine (nee Jenkins)
Parham, Brenda Joyce
Paris, Calvin Rudolph
Pattillo, Roland A.
Petty, Bruce Anthony
Pinkney, Dove Savage

Powell, C. Clayton
Prince, Joan Marie
Ragland, Wylheme Harold
Rann, Emery Louvelle
Ray, Andrew
Reed, Theresa Greene
Reid, Charles E.
Remson, Anthony Terence
Rhoden, Richard Allan
Roberts, Cheryl Dornita Lynn
Roberts, Lillian
Robinson, Clarence G.
Rosemond, John H.
Sands, Mary Alice
Scott, James F., Sr.
Scranage, Clarence, Jr.
Shelby, Reginald W.
Shirley, Edwin Samuel, Jr.
Shorty, Vernon James
Smalls, Jacquelyn Elaine
Smith, Tommie M.
Stepto, Robert Charles
Stevenson, Lillian
Stone, John S.
Street, Vivian Sue
Strong, Amanda L.
Taylor, Paul David
Theodore, Keith Felix
Watts, Charles Dewitt
West, William Lionel
Williams, Edward Ellis
Williams, Matthew Albert
Williams, Shirley Yvonne
Wilson, Joy Johnson
Wilson, Kim Alesia
Wineglass, Henry
Winfrey, Audrey Theresa
Wingate, Rosalee Martin
Winston, John H., Jr.
Woodbury, Arline Elizabeth

HEALTH SERVICES ADMINISTRATION

Adair, Robert A.
Adiele, N. Moses
Alexander, Paul Crayton
Allen, Aris Tee
Allen, Van Sizar
Alveranga, Glanvin L.
Anderson, Jacqueline Jones
Andrews, William Henry
Arrington, Harold Mitchell
Arrington, Robyn James, Jr.
Artis, Myrle Everett
Assue, Clare Melba
Atkinson, Gladys W.
Avery, Waddell
Ayala, Reginald P.
Bartley, Talmadge O.
Bassard, Yvonne Brooks
Belancourt, Dunet Francois
Bell, Carl Compton
Bell, Rouzeberry
Belton, Edward DeVaughn
Bernard, Canute Clive
Betty, Warren Randall
Biggers, Samuel Loring, Jr.
Bills, Johnny Bernard
Blackwell, Faiger Megrea
Blow, Sarah
Bohee, Sumner T.
Branch, Geraldine Burton
Bransford, Paris
Braynon, Edward J., Jr.
Brookes, Bernard L.
Brooks, Phillip Daniel
Brooks, Todd Frederick
Brooks, William P.
Brown, Glenn Arthur
Bryant, William Arnett, Jr.
Burress, James R.
Caison, Thelma Jann
Campbell, Emmett Earle
Camphor, Michael Gerard
Cantrell, Forrest Daniel
Capel, Wallace
Carson, Benjamin Solomon, Sr.
Carter, Oscar Earl, Jr.
Chess, Robert Hubert
Chissell, Herbert Garland
Clarke, Leon Edison
Clifford, Maurice C.
Cochran, James David, Jr.
Combs, Julius V.

Cooper, Curtis V.
Corinaldi, Austin
Coverdale, Herbert Linwood
Cowan, James R.
Craig, Frederick A.
Crutchfield, Susan Ellis
Daniels, Joseph
Darity, William A.
Darke, Charles B.
Davenport, James H.
Davis, Anita Louise
Davis, Carolyn Ann McBride
Davis, Harold Matthew
Davis, Myrtle Hilliard
Davis, William Selassie, Jr.
Delphin, Jacques Mercier
DeVaughn-Tidline, Donna Michelle
Dickens, Doris Lee (Mrs. Austin L. Fickling)
Dorsey, L. C.
Downer, Luther Henry
Dungy, Claibourne I.
Dunn, Marvin
Dunston, Walter T.
Earls, Julian Manly
Easterling, Rosanna Avonna
Ebo, Antona
Eddy, Edward A.
Edelin, Kenneth C.
Edwards, Lonnie
Elders, M. Joycelyn
Eller, Carl L.
Ellis, O. Herbert
English, Perry T., Jr.
Evans, Caswell Alves, Jr.
Evans, Therman E.
Fairman, John Abbrey
Faulkner, Marquetta Larneita
Fields, Richard A.
Fitzgerald, Howard David
Ford, Albert S.
Francis, Yvette Fay
Franklin, Dolores Mercedes
Fraser, Alvardo M.
Frazier, Lee Rene
Fregia, Darrell Leon
French, Joseph Henry
Garnes, William A.
Gatson, Wilina Ione
Gay, Milton F., Jr.
Gaynor, Florence S.
Gerald, Gilberto Ruben
Gilmore, Edwin
Gladney, Marcellious
Goodson, Leroy Beverly
Goodwin, Norma J.
Goulbourne, Donald Samuel, Jr.
Graham, Richard A.
Greene, Horace F.
Grist, Arthur L.
Guyton, Alicia V.
Hannah, Hubert H., Sr.
Harper, Elizabeth
Harris, Hassel B.
Harris, Jean Louise
Harrison, Harry Paul
Haugabrook, John R.
Haughton, James G.
Heineback, Barbara (nee Taylor)
Henry, Brent Lee
Hodges, Cother L.
Hodgson, Carlton Roy
Hogan, James Carroll, Jr.
Holliday, Alfonso David
Hollingsworth, John Alexander
Hopper, Cornelius Lenard
Horton, Clarence Pennington
Howard, Shirley M.
Humphrey, Hubert Grant
Humphries, Charles, Jr.
Hunter, Gertrude T.
Hurd, Joseph Kindall, Jr.
Hussein, Carlessia Amanda
Ince, Harold S.
Ivory, Carolyn Kay
Jackson, Franklin D.B.
Johnson, Ernest Kaye, III
Johnson, James Kenneth
Johnson-Brown, Hazel Winfred
Johnson-Scott, Jerodene Patrice
Jones, Billy Emanuel
Jones, Ferdinand Taylor, Jr.
Jones, George Albert

Jones, Sondra Michelle
Jones, Vann Kinckle
King, Edgar Lee
King, John L.
King, Talmadge Everett, Jr.
Land, Chester LaSalle
Lathen, John William
Lattimer, Agnes Dolores
Ledbetter, Ruth Pope
Lee, Rotan
Lipscomb, Wendell R.
Lockett, Harold James
Lyles, Madeline Lolita
Lyles, William K.
Madry, Maude Holt
Malvin, Reuben L.
Marsh, Donald Gene
Marshall, Carter Lee
Marshall, John Dent
Martin, Lee
McBroom, F. Pearl
McCabe, Eugene Louis
McCaulley, James Alan, III
McCoy, George H.
McCraven, Carl Clarke
McDaniel, Elizabeth
McMorris, Jacqueline Williams
Mitchell, Dwayne Oscar
Moone, Wanda Renee
Moore, Joseph L.
Moore, Roscoe Michael, Jr.
Morgan, Alice Johnson Parham
Morgan, Eldridge Gates
Murray, James Hamilton
Myers, Woodrow Augustus, Jr.
Osborne, William Reginald, Jr.
Page, Cedric Daniel
Palmer, Edward
Parris, Guichard
Patterson, Theodore Carter Chavis
Paxton, Phyllis Ann
Penn, Nolan E.
Peterson, Carl M.
Pinson, Thomas J.
Poole, Rachel Irene
Potts, Harold E.
Pounds, Moses B.
Primm, Beny Jene
Rice, Haynes
Richardson, Nola Mae
Richie, Sharon Ivey
Rickman, Lewis Daniel, Sr.
Riley, Wayne Joseph
Risbrook, Arthur Timothy
Roberts, Cheryl Dornita Lynn
Robertson, Evelyn Crawford, Jr.
Robinson, Gary O.
Robinson, Thomas Donald
Roddy, Howard W.
Rosser, James M.
Rutledge, William Lyman
Sadler, Kenneth Marvin
Sampson, Marva W.
Sanders, Augusta Swann
Sanders, Sally Ruth
Sanford, Mark
Saulsberry, Guy O.
Shaw, Mario William
Simpson, Dazelle Dean
Singletary, Inez M.
Sinnette, Calvin Herman
Sirmans, Meredith Franklin
Smith, Eddie Glenn, Jr.
Smith, Gloria R.
Smith, Richard Alfred
Smith, Sundra Shealey
Southall, Herbert Howardton, Sr.
Standard, Raymond Linwood
Stevenson, James Earl
Street, Vivian Sue
Strickland, Frederick William, Jr.
Sullivan, Louis W.
Thomas-Richardson, Valerie Jean
Thompson, Theodis
Toby, William
Trice, Jessie Collins
Walker, Allene Marsha
Walker, Moses Andre
Warren, Rueben Clifton
Washington, Loise
Watson, Anne
Watson, Vernaline
Webb, Wellington E.

Whitest, Beverly Joyce
Wiggins, Charles A.
Wilson, Kim Alesia
Winfield, Florence F.
Woods, Geraldine Pittman
Yancey, Asa G., Sr.
Yarbrough, Earnest
Young, Wallace L.

HISTORY

Barksdale Hall, Roland C.
Bell, Howard Holman
Binford, Henry C.
Blockson, Charles L.
Bracey, John H., Jr.
Brown, Courtney Coleridge
Brown, Jeffrey LeMonte
Callum, Agnes Kane
Carey, Harmon Roderick
Clarke, John Henrik
Claye, Charlene Marette
Coleman, Ronald Gerald
Crew, Spencer R.
Crosby, Edward Warren
Crouchett, Lawrence Paul
Davis, Thomas Joseph
Eaton, James Nathaniel, Sr.
Ekechi, Felix K.
Ellis, Marilyn Pope
Ford, Marcella Woods
Gilmore, Al Tony
Guy, Mildred Dorothy
Hardin, John Arthur
Harding, Vincent
Jackson, Kennell A., Jr.
Jacobs, Sylvia Marie
Jefferson, Alphine Wade
Johnson, Clifton Herman
Knight, Franklin W.
Layton, William W.
Lee, Clara Marshall
Lockett, James D.
Matthews, Miriam
McConnell, Roland C.
Miller, M. Sammye
Mitchell, Loften
Morton, Cynthia Neverdon
Moses, Johnnie, Jr.
Newman, Debra Lynn
Painter, Nell Irvin
Phillips, Glenn Owen
Pinkett, Harold Thomas
Price, Suzanne D.
Quarles, Benjamin A.
Render, Sylvia Lyons
Roberts, Wesley A.
Robinson, Genevieve
Robinson, Wilhelmena S.
Rouse, Jacqueline Anne
Rushing, Byron D.
Scott, Jean Sampson
Scruggs, Otey Matthew
Smith, Charlie Calvin
Stratton-Morris, Madeline Robinson
Strickland, Arvarh E.
Sumler-Lewis, Janice L.
Tall, Booker T.
Tate, Merze
Thurman, Frances Ashton
Troupe, Marilyn Kay
Turner, W. Burghardt
Williams, Lillian C.
Young, Alfred

HORTICULTURE
See LANDSCAPE/
HORTICULTURAL
SERVICES

HOTEL/MOTEL
INDUSTRY
Bond, Gladys B.
Broadwater, Tommie, Jr.
Close, Hari P.
Cornelison, Carole Jane
Dixon, John M.
Foster, Andrew D.
Harmon, James F., Sr.
Harty, Belford Donald, Jr.
Hudson, Lester Darnell
Jenkins, Ozella
Mack, Fred Clarence

Matthews, Aquilla E.
Rivers, Johnny
Roberts, Herman
Robinson, Deanna Adell
Rogers, Michael Charles
Russell, Kay A.
Schenck, Frederick A.
Turner, Mikoel
Virdure, Bernel B.
Washington, Jacquelyn M.
Woods, Charlotte Ann

INDUSTRIAL DESIGN
Bates, William J.
Buggs, James
Burton, Michael Angelo
Charles, Lewis
Eddington, Herbert Hoover
Fearing, John T.
James, Dorothy Marie
Winslow, Reynolds Baker

INFORMATION
SCIENCE
See LIBRARY/
INFORMATION SCIENCE

INSURANCE
Adams, David, Jr.
Alexander, Theodore Martin, Sr.
Allen, Minnie Louise
Anderson, Abbie H.
Anderson, Carlton Leon
Anderson, Michael Wayne
Anderson, Ronald Edward
Anderson, Tony
Anderson-Janniere, Iona Lucille
Anthony, Leander Aldrich
Armstrong, Joseph Earl
Ashby, Reginald W.
Austin, James P.
Ayers, Timothy F.
Bailey, Clarence Walter
Bailey, William R.
Baker, LaVolia Ealy
Baker, Roland Charles
Balton, Kirkwood R.
Bandy, Riley Thomas, Sr.
Barksdale, Hudson L.
Barrett, Sherman L.
Bartlett, Jeffrey Leon
Batchelor, Asbury Collins
Bates, Willie Earl
Beaubien, George H.
Beavers, George A.
Bell, Everett Thomas
Bell, Yolanda Maria
Bennett, Collin B.
Benton, Quinnie Etta
Berryman, Macon M.
Bethel, Jesse Moncell, Sr.
Boggus, Francis Oliver
Bond, Alan D.
Bonner, Theophulis W.
Boykin, Willie
Bradley, London M., Jr.
Brannon, James R.
Britton, Theodore R., Jr.
Brooks, Arkles Clarence, Jr.
Brown, Abner Bertrand
Brown, D. Joan
Brown, Herbert R.
Brown, Virgil E., Jr.
Bryant, R. Kelly, Jr.
Burton, Ronald E.
Caldwell, John Edward
Campbell, Otis Levy
Carter, Lemorie, Jr.
Carter, Robert Henry, III
Catchings, Howard Douglas
Chambliss, Ida Belle
Chandler, Dennis Courtland
Chestnut, Edwin, Sr.
Clark, Shirley Lorraine
Clark, William Elgan, Jr.
Clay, Rudolph
Clement, William A.
Clinton, Thomas R.
Cockrell, Mechera Ann
Cofer, James Henry
Collins, Bert
Cook, Haney Judaea

Cook, Ladda Banks
Cousins, James R., Jr.
Cox, Robert L.
Croft, Wardell C.
Crutchfield, Susan Ellis
Cunningham, David S., Jr.
Dancy, William F.
Dash, Hugh M. H.
Dauphin, Borel C.
Davies, Everett J.
Davis, Brownie W.
Davis, Darwin N.
Davis, Edward
Davis, Edward D.
Davis, Harold R.
Davis, J. Mason, Jr.
Demeritte, Edwin T.
DeVaughn-Tidline, Donna Michelle
Dillard, Melvin Rubin
Dixon, Benjamin
Dixon, Isaiah, Jr.
Dotson, William S.
Dozier, Morris, Sr.
Duncan, Verdell
Easley, Jacqueline Ruth
Edmonds, Norman Douglas
Ellis, Frederic L.
Evans, Gwendolyn
Fagan, Harold Leonard
Fields, Stanley
Fisher, Rubin Ivan
Ford, Bowles C.
Frasier, Leroy B.
Freeman, Charles E.
Freeman, Robert Turner, Jr.
Frink, John Spencer
Gaines, Richard Kendall
Gary, Alonzo G., Jr.
Gayle, Irving Charles
Gibson, Maurice
Givins, Abe, Jr.
Glenn, Edward C., Jr.
Gloster, Jesse E.
Golden, Arthur Ivanhoe
Golden, Ronald Allen
Gomez, Dennis Craig
Goodrich, Thelma E.
Greene, Joseph David
Greene, Ronald Alexander
Gregory, Bernard Vincent
Habersham, Robert
Hackett, Rufus E.
Hardison, Walter L., Jr.
Hardy, Charlie Edward
Harper, Bernice Catherine
Harris, Joseph Preston
Harris, Paul E.
Harrison, Gregory W.
Harvey, Clarie Collins
Hassell, Frances M.
Hathaway, Anthony, Jr.
Haydel, James V., Sr.
Haynes, John K.
Haywood, Roosevelt V., Jr.
Henderson, James J., Sr.
Henry, Joseph A.
Herndon, Gloria E.
Hicks, Willie Lee
Hightower, Edward Stewart
Hill, Curtis T., Sr.
Hill, Jesse, Jr.
Hinnant, Ollen B.
Hodge, Lionel
Holliday, Prince E.
Hollis, Clarence O.
Holmes, Willie A.
Hopkins, Charmaine L.
Hopkins, William A.
Hornsby, Walter Spurgeon, III
Houston, Ivan J.
Houston, Norman Oliver
Howard, Charles Preston, Jr.
Howard, James L.
Howard, John E.
Howard, Leon W., Jr.
Howell, Gerald T.
Hubbard, Hylan T., III
Hudson, John D.
Hunter, John Davidson
Hurst, Rodney Lawrence
Irby, Ray
Isbell, James S.
Jackson, James H.

Jasper, Lawrence E.
Jenkins, Joseph Walter, Jr.
Jervay, Thomas Clarence, Sr.
Johns, Paul V.
Johnson, Ben D.
Johnson, Charles Henry
Johnson, Hermon M., Sr.
Johnson, Patricia Duren
Jones, Farrell
Kennedy, William J., III
Kennon, Daniel, Jr.
King, Celes, III
King, Charles Abraham
King, Marcellus, Jr.
Lane, John Henry
Lang-Jeter, Lula L.
Langston, Andrew A.
Lassiter, John
Lawrence, James T.
Lewis, Walton A.
Lloyd, James
Lockhart, James B.
Lomax, Michael Wilkins
Love, James Ralph
Lynch, George K.
Mack, Daniel J.
Mahin, George E.
Marbury, Howard W.
Marsh, McAfee
Marsh, Tamra Gwendolyn
Marshall, Richard Douglass
Martin, Reddrick Linwood
Martin, Samuel
Mascoll, Edward G.
Maultsby, Sylvester
McClenic, David A.
McDaniel, Paul Anderson
McElroy, Alfred Z.
McElvane, Pamela Anne
McFarlin, Kernaa D'Offert, Jr.
McGregor, Oran B.
McKinley, William, Jr.
McReynolds, Elaine A.
Merritt, Thomas Mack
Miller, Dexter J., Jr.
Miller, James, Sr.
Miller, Joseph Herman
Mills, Robert
Milton, Samuel Byron
Mims, Marjorie Joyce
Minor, Vicki Beize
Misshore, Joseph O., Jr.
Mitchell, Theo W.
Montgomery, Fred O.
Moore, Elaine
Morgan, James
Morrison, Curtis Angus
Moses, Milton E.
Murphy, Charles William
Murphy, Margaret Humphries
Myers, L. Leonard
Neal, Joseph C., Jr.
Nelms, Ommie Lee
Obi, James E.
Olawumi, Bertha Ann
Orr, Dorothy
Owens, James E.
Pajaud, William E.
Palmer, Douglas Harold
Palmer, James L. D.
Parks, Thelma Reece
Patterson, James
Pemberton, David M.
Peoples, Erskine L.
Pierce, Joseph Leroy
Poole-Heard, Blanche Denise
Powell, Charles P.
Pryor, James D.
Ragsdale, Lincoln Johnson
Rawls, William D., Sr.
Ray, Mercer Z.
Redd, M. Paul, Sr.
Reed, Derryl L.
Reed, Lloyd H.
Rhetta, Helen L.
Rhodes, Duplain
Rivers, Alfred J.
Robbins, Millard D.
Robinson, Alcurtis
Robinson, Alvin J.
Robinson, John E.
Royster, Don M., Sr.
Ruffner, Ray P.
St. Mary, Joseph Jerome

Salter, Roger Franklin
Schenck, Frederick A.
Schweich, Anderson M.
Scott, Hubert R.
Sellers, Theresa Ann
Shands, Franklin M., Sr.
Shell, Theodore A.
Simms, William E.
Singleton, Herbert
Smith, Ann Elizabeth
Smith, Arthur D.
Smith, Eugene
Smith, Frank Junius
Smith, Granville L.
Snell, Jimmy Gregory
Snowden, Raymond C.
Southall, Herbert Howardton, Sr.
Spaulding, Asa T.
Spears, Henry Albert
Stallworth, John Lee
Steed, Tyrone
Stewart, James A., III
Stringer, Melvin, Sr.
Sudderth, William H.
Sutton, Sterling E.
Swan, Monroe
Sykes, Weathers Y.
Talbot, James Patterson, Sr.
Talley, James Edward
Tarver, Gregory W.
Tatum, Wilbert A.
Taylor, Reginald Redall, Jr.
Taylor, Sterling R.
Teasley, Larkin
Theus, Lucius
Thomas, Isaac Daniel, Jr.
Thompson, Carl Eugene
Thompson, Joseph Isaac
Townes, Clarence L., Sr.
Turnbull, Horace Hollins
Turner, Vivian Vanessa
Urquhart, James McCartha
Vincent, Daniel Patil
Vinson, Julius Ceasar
Walker, A. Maceo, Sr.
Walker, Solomon W., II
Walker-Shaw, Patricia
Wallace, Homer L.
Waters, Wimbley, Jr.
Watson, Daniel
Weeks, Renee (nee Jones)
West, Earl M.
Wheeler, Lloyd G.
White, Arthur W., Jr.
Williams, Arthur K.
Williams, Charles C.
Williams, Charlotte Leola
Williams, Herbert C.
Williams, Herman
Williams, Jewel L.
Williams, Joseph B.
Williams, Margo E.
Williams, Thomas Pedworth
Willie, Louis J.
Wilson, Frederick A.
Winburn, B. J.
Wolfe, Estemore A.
Woodson, Roderic L.
Woodward, Aaron Alphonso, III
Wynn, Robert L., Jr.

JOURNALISM—
BROADCAST
Adams, James Malcolm
Adams, Katherine
Adams, Robert Hugo
Batten, Tony
Bell, Mary L.
Bell, Warren, Jr.
Bennett, Dennis Ray
Bennette, Connie E.
Berry, Jerome
Berry, Paul Lawrence
Black, Charlie J.
Blackwell, Noble Virgil
Blount, Charlotte Renee
Boonieh, Obi Anthony
Bradley, Edward R.
Bragg, Joseph L.
Brewington, Rudolph W.
Briggs-Graves, Anasa
Brown, Ellen Rochelle
Brown, Paul E. X.
Buchanan, Otis

Bundles, A'Lelia Perry
Butler, Clary Kent
Casey, Frank Leslie
Castleberry, Edward J.
Christian, Gail P.
Crable, Deborah J.
Cross, June Victoria
Cummings, Charles Edward
Davis, Belva
Davis, Nolan
Dee, Merri
Dennard, Darryl W.
Dorsey, Edmund Stanley
Drummond, William Joe
Eubanks, Dayna C.
Ferguson, Renee
Garland, Hazel Barbara
Gite, Lloyd Anthony
Gordon, Winfield James
Griffin, Booker
Handy, Delores
Haney, Don Lee
Hanson, John L.
Hare, Julia Reed
Harris, Gil W.
Harrison, Jeanette LaVerne
Harvey-Byrd, Patricia Lynn
Hayward, Jacqueline C.
Heyward, Isaac
Hodge, Adele P.
Holman, Benjamin F.
Hughes, Catherine Liggins
Hunter-Gault, Charlayne
Hutchins, Jan Darwin
Jenkins, Carol Ann
Jeter, Felicia Rene
Jiggetts, Danny Marcellus
Johnson, Donn S.
Johnson, Iola Vivian
Johnson, Mal
Jones, Ken
Jordan, Robert Howard, Jr.
Kennard, Patricia A. (nee Byrd)
Kennedy, Linda Cheryl
King, Coretta Scott (Mrs. Martin
    Luther King Jr.)
Lee, Debra Louise
Lewis, Gus Edward
Lewis, Maurice
Logue-Kinder, Joan
Love, Thomas Clifford
Mack, Joan
Madison, Joseph Edward
Majors, Mattie Carolyn
Martin, Robert Edward
Matthews, Claude Lankford, Jr.
McCormick, Larry William
McCreary, Bill
McDowell-Head, Lelia M.
McGee, Rebecca E.
Meek, Russell Charles
Middlebrooks, Felicia
Morrison, Ronald E.
Muhammad, Askiaa
Odom, Vernon Lane, Jr.
Palmer, Darlene Tolbert
Payne, Ethel Lois
Petty, Bob
Pierce, Ponchitta A.
Poindexter, Malcolm P.
Pool, Marquita Jones
Poussaint, Renee Francine
Powell, Adam Clayton, III
Quarles, Norma R.
Rice, Norman Blann
Rodgers, Johnathan A.
Rogers, David William
Rowan, Carl Thomas
Sanders, Charles Lionel
Scott, Marvin Bailey
Sells, Mamie Earl
Shaw, Bernard
Shepard, Joan
Shifflett, Lynne Carol
Simpson, Carole
Smith, Jack Elliott
Stevens, Sharon A.
Stokes, Carl Burton
Stovall, Stanley V.
Stricklin, James
Sutton, Percy E.
Thandeka
Thompson, DeHaven Leslie (Dee)
Todd, Cynthia Jean
Tucker, Lemuel

Waddles, George Wesley, Sr.
Weston, Sharon
Wickham, DeWayne
Wilkins, Betty
Williams, Brenda Paulette
Williams, Clarence Earl, Jr.
Williams, Margo E.
Winfrey, Oprah
Wortham, Jacob James
Ziegler, Dhyana

JOURNALISM—PHOTOJOURNALISM
See also PHOTOGRAPHY
Banks, Marguerita C.
Beauford, Fred
Herndon, Craig Garris
Higgins, Chester Archer, Jr.
Jackson, Vera Ruth
Johnson, Paul L.
Logan, Bertie Hawthorne
McCray, Billy Quincy
Parks, Gordon A.
Peebles, Allie Muse
Tarry, Ellen
Ware, J. Lowell

JOURNALISM—PRINT
See also WRITING/
EDITING—NONFICTION
Adair, Kenneth
Adams, Alger LeRoy
Adams, Robert Hugo
Adams, Samuel Levi, Sr.
Alexander, James Brett
Anders, Corrie Michael
Anderson, Monroe
Aubespin, Mervin R.
Bailey, A. Peter
Bailey, Chauncey Wendell, Jr.
Baker, Vincent S.
Bennett, Debra Quinette
Bennett, Lerone, Jr.
Bereola, Enitan Olu
Besson, Paul Smith
Black, Gail
Blunt-Battle, Madelyne Bowen
Booker, Robert Joseph
Booker, Simeon S.
Brown, Vernon E.
Brown, Warren Aloysius
Brownlee, Lester Harrison-Pierce
Brownlee, Vivian Aplin
Buckley, Gail Lument
Byrd, Frederick Wayne
Cabbell, Edward Joseph
Cannon, Davita Louise
Carmichael, Carole A.
Carpenter, William Arthur, II
Cherry, Charles William
Cose, Ellis
Cox, Corine
Cox, Jesse L.
Crawford, Barbara Hopkins
Cumber, Victoria Lillian
Curry, George E.
Dash, Leon DeCosta, Jr.
Davis, Belva
Davis, Lydia Joanna
Davis, Nolan
DeJarmon, Elva Pegues
Dejoie, C. C., Jr.
Delaney, John Paul
Denton, Herbert H., Jr.
Draper, Frances Murphy
Dreyfuss, Joel P.
Du Bois, David Graham
Duncan, Stephan W.
DuPree, David
Durant, Celeste Millicent
Eberhardt, Clifford
Eddings, Cynthia
Edwards, Audrey Marie
Edwards, Preston Joseph
Elliott, Joy
Ellis, William Reuben
Eure, Dexter D., Sr.
Fearn-Banks, Kathleen
Fitzpatrick, Albert E.
Fleming, Carolyn
Fleming, G. James
Fornay, Alfred R., Jr.
French, James J.

French, MaryAnn
Garland, Hazel Barbara
Garland, Phyllis T.
Garner, June B.
Garnett, Bernard E.
Gibbs, Vernon D. G.
Gilliam, Dorothy Butler
Goodlett, Carlton B.
Graham, Michael Angelo
Grant, Dell Omega
Graves, Earl G.
Greenlee, Robert Douglass
Hall, Lawrence H.
Hardnett, Carolyn Judy
Harris, Fred
Harris, Jay Terrence
Harris, Lee
Harris, Peter J.
Harvey, William M.
Harvin, Alvin
Haygood, Wil
Henry, Calvin O. L.
Hiatt, Dietrah (nee Chapman)
Higgins, Chester A., Sr.
Hill, Michael Edward
Holsendolph, Ernest
Holt, Michael L.
Howze, Karen Aileen
Hoye, Walter B.
Imbriano, Robert J.
Jackson, Esther Cooper
Jackson, Luther Porter, Jr.
Jarrett, Vernon D.
Jervay, Paul Reginald, Jr.
Joans, Ted
Johnson, Arthur Lyman
Johnson, Herschel Lee
Johnson, Iola Vivian
Johnson, Patrice Doreen
Johnson, Rita Falkener
Johnson, Robert Edward
Johnson-Crosby, Deborah A.
Jones, Floresta Deloris
Jones, Ken
Jones, Marsha Regina
Jones, Walter L.
Jones, William Lawless
Jones, Zoia L.
Jordan, Milton C.
Kazi-Ferrouillet, Kuumba
Kountze, Mabray (Doc)
Lane, William Clay
Larrie, Reginald Reese
Leaks, Sylvester
Leavell, Dorothy R.
LeCompte, Peggy J. (nee Lewis)
LeDoux, Jerome G.
Lee, Lucius E.
Lewis, Matthew, Jr.
Lloyd, Wanda (nee Smalls)
Locke, Henry Daniel, Jr.
Lockman, Norman Alton
Madison, Alfreda Louise
Mason, B. J.
Mathabane, Mark Johannes
Maynard, Robert C.
McCoy, Frederick Douglass, Jr.
McElroy, George A.
McKoy, Clemencio Agustino
Meek, Russell Charles
Millender, Mallory Kimerling
Miller, Oliver O.
Mitchell, Kelly Karnale
Monroe, James H.
Moore, Acel
Moore, Trudy S.
Moragne, Lenora
Morris, Eugene
Muhammad, Askiaa
Murphy, Frances L., II (Mrs.
    Charles J. Campbell)
Murray, Virgie W.
Nash, Thomas
Nipson, Herbert
O'Flynn-Thomas, Patricia
Osby, Simeon B., Jr.
Overbea, Luix Virgil
Parker, Maryland Mike
Parrish, Mary
Payne, Ethel Lois
Payne, Leslie
Peterman, Peggy M.
Petty, Reginald E.
Pierce, Ponchitta A.

Pogue, Lester Clarence
Poinsett, Alexander C.
Porter, Charles William
Prince, Richard Everett
Procope, John Levy
Queen, Robert Calvin
Raspberry, William J.
Reed, Vincent Emory
Reynolds, Pamela Terese
Riley, Clayton
Robinson, Jack E.
Robinson, Louie, Jr.
Robinson, Norman T., Jr.
Rodney, Karl Basil
Roebuck-Hoard, Marcia Veronica
Rolark, Calvin W.
Rowan, Carl Thomas
Russell, Dorothy Delores
Samuels, Annette Jacqueline
Satterwhite, John H.
Sellers, Thomas J.
Sells, Mamie Earl
Sharp, Saundra
Sharrieff, Osman Ibn
Shields, Varee, Jr.
Shipe, Jamesetta Denise Holmes
Shipp, E. R.
Simmons, Belva Tereshia
Sims, Carl W.
Sims, Harold Rudolph
Smothers, Ronald Eric
Snyder, George W.
Stephens, Phygenau
Stone, Chuck
Strait, George Alfred, Jr.
Stuart, Reginald A.
Tandy, Mary B.
Tate, Eleanora Elaine
Taylor, Ronald A.
Teasley, Marie R.
Terrell, Angela M. Brown
Terrell, Robert L.
Terrell, Stanley E.
Terry, Wallace Houston, II
Thomas, Benjamin
Thomas, Jacqueline Marie
Thomas, Patricia O'Flynn
Thomas, Spencer
Thompson, DeHaven Leslie (Dee)
Thompson, Era Bell
Thompson, Garland Lee
Tieuel, Robert C. D.
Todd, Cynthia Jean
Tomlinson, Randolph R.
Treadwell, David Merrill
Trescott, Jacqueline Elaine
Tuggle, Reginald
Turner, Edna (nee Koontz)
Wade, Kim Mache
Wade, Norma Adams
Walker, Douglas F.
Walker, James Zell, II
Walker, Joe
Walker, Kenneth R.
Washington, Chester Lloyd
Washington, James A.
Waters, Sylvia Ann
Watkins, Aretha La Anna
Watkins, Joseph Philip
Watson, Clifford D.
Watson, Joann Nichols
Weaver, Audrey Turner
White, John Clinton
White, June Joyce
White, Randolph Louis
Whiteside, Larry W.
Wickham, DeWayne
Wiggins, Lillian Cooper
Wilkins, Betty
Wilkins, Roger W.
Wilkins, Roger Wood
Wilkinson, Sheppard Field
Williams, James DeBois
Williams, Virginia Walker
Williams, Winston
Williford, Stanley O.
Winston, Bonnie Veronica
Witherspoon, William Roger
Womack, Robert W., Sr.
Woodford, John Niles
Woolcock, Ozeil Fryer
Wortham, Jacob James
Worthy, William

JOURNALISM—NOT ELSEWHERE CLASSIFIED
Adams, Robert Thomas
Bell, Tommy Lee, III
Black, Gail
Boulware, Patricia A.
Britton, John H., Jr.
Brooks, Clyde Henry
Browder, Anne Elna
Butler, Anna M. (nee Land)
Ellis, Elward Dwayne
Fletcher, Robert E.
Foster, William Patrick
Ghent, Henri Hermann
Gillespie, Marcia A.
Grant, Dell Omega
Guyton, Patsy
Hoover, Theressa
Hornsby, Alton, Jr.
Kern-Foxworth, Marilyn L
Kluge, Pamela Hollie
LeDuff, Stephanie Carmel
London, Edward Charles
Murphy, George B., Jr.
Patterson, Lawrence Patrick
Pride, Armistead Scott
Robinson, Marilyn Patricia
Rodgers, Charles
Roland, Johnny E.
Russell, Dorothy Delores
Slater, Helene Ford Southern
Stackhouse, E. Marilyn
Stone, Reese J., Jr.
Wyche, Paul H., Jr.

JUDICIARY
Adderly, Alfonso Leo
Adrine, Ronald Bruce
Alexander, Fritz W., II
Alexander, Harry Toussaint
Alexander, Joyce London
Alexander, Pamela Gayle
Alexander, William H.
Allen, Alex James, Jr.
Allen, Milton B.
Allen-Rasheed, Jamal Randy
Alston, Gilbert C.
Anderson, Reuben Vincent
Archer, Dennis Wayne
Armstrong, Joan Bernard
Baety, Edward L.
Bailey, James W.
Bancroft, Richard Anderson
Banks, Fred L, Jr.
Baranco, Gordon S.
Baxter, Wendy Marie
Baylor, Solomon
Bell, Howard Eugene
Bell, Robert Mack
Benham, Robert
Bennett, Arthur T.
Benton, James Wilbert, Jr.
Billingsley, Orzell, Jr.
Bivins, Ollie B., Jr.
Bledsoe, Frank S.
Boags, Charles D.
Bonner, Alice A.
Booker, Irvin B.
Braden, Everette Arnold
Braithwaite, James Roland
Bramwell, Henry
Branch, William McKinley
Brashear, Berlaind Leander
Braxton, John Ledger
Brewer, Webster L.
Broady, Earl Clifford
Brock, Gerald
Broussard, Allen E.
Brown, Benjamin Leonard
Brown, Christopher C.
Brown, George Henry, Jr.
Brown, Irma Jean
Brown, Lloyd Odom, Sr.
Bryant, Clarence
Bryant, William B.
Bundy, James Lomax
Burke, Lillian W.
Burnett, Arthur Louis, Sr.
Burnham, Margaret Ann
Byrd, Frederick E.
Byrd, Issac, Jr.
Byrd, Jerry Stewart

LABOR RELATIONS
See LABOR UNION
ADMINISTRATION;
MANAGEMENT/
ADMINISTRATION—
PERSONNEL/TRAINING/
LABOR RELATIONS

LABOR UNION
ADMINISTRATION

LANDSCAPE/ HORTICULTURAL SERVICES

Church, Robert T., Sr.
Owens, Angle B., Jr.
Wilkins, Allen Henry

LAW ENFORCEMENT

Adams, Paul Brown
Alveranga, Glanvin L.
Amaker, Norman Carey
Amos, Joseph H.
Anderson, Ray Charles
Artison, Richard E.
Balmer, Horace Dalton, Sr.
Barnett, William
Barr, LeRoy
Bennett, George P.
Billingsley, Orzell, Jr.
Bishop, Verissa Rene
Bobo, Roscoe Lemual
Bracey, William Rubin
Bradley, Wayne W.
Brooks, Clyde Henry
Brooks, Thomas E.
Brown, Diana Johnson
Brown, Lee Patrick
Buckney, Edward L.
Bullock, J. Jerome
Burton, Donald C.
Bush, T. W.
Byrd, Sherman Clifton
Calhoun, Jack Johnson, Jr.
Callender, Carl O.
Cantrell, Forrest Daniel
Capehart, Johnnie Lawrence
Carroll, James S.
Carson, Irma
Casey, Clifton G.
Chambers, Pamela S.
Clayton, Willie Burke, Jr.
Clemmons, Clifford R.
Conner, Gail Patricia
Cooper, Julius, Jr.
Cousins, William, Jr.
Coy, John T.
Cunningham, Glenn Dale
Dalley, George Albert
Danzy, LeRoy Henry
Davidson, Arthur Turner
Davis, Frank
Davis, James Parker
Davis, Willie J.
Dawson, Jesse R.
DeGeneste, Henry Irving
Dowdell, Dennis, Jr.
Drummond, Thornton B., Jr.
Dunning, Roosevelt
Ferrebee, Thomas G.
Fitzgerald, Herbert H.
Foreman, Joe Cornelius, Jr.
Foushee, Geraldine George
Fox, Thomas E., Jr.
Frazier, Joseph Norris
Garner, Edward, Jr.
Gibbons, John
Gibson, John A.
Gibson, Johnnie M. M.
Golden, Willie L.
Gray, Arthur L.
Greene, Charles Edward Clarence
Greenleaf, Louis E.
Guillory, Julius James
Hackett, Wilbur L., Jr.
Hampton, Ronald Everett
Hargrove, Trent
Hart, William L.
Harvard, Beverly Bailey
Helm, William C.
Hicks, Delphus Van, Jr.
Hill, Arthur Burit
Hill, Oliver W.
Holliday, Billie
Holliday-Hayes, Wilhelmina
   Evelyn (Billie)
Howard, Calvin Johnson
Howell, Willie R.
Hudson, John D.
Hughes, Jimmy Franklin, Sr.
Ingram, James William
Ireland, Roderick Louis
Isaacs, Stephen D.
Jackson, George K.
Jackson, Tommy L.

Jason, Henry Thomas
Jenkins, Marilyn Joyce
Johnson, Raymond L.
Johnson, Sterling
Jones, Anthony, Jr.
Jones, Frank
Keith, Doris T.
Kelley, Jack Albert
Kline, Eddie
Kyles, Dwain Johann
Kyles, Sharron Faye
Lackey, Edgar F.
Lafontant, Jewel Stradford
Leland, Joyce F.
Lemon, Michael Wayne, Sr.
Lillard, W. Lovell
Lockley, Clyde William
Louis, Joseph
Mann, Thomas J., Jr.
Mapp, David Kenneth, Jr.
McClellan, Edward J.
McGrier, Jerry, Sr.
McHenry, James O'Neal
McKeller, Thomas Lee
Miles, Kenneth L.
Miller, Laurel Milton
Montgomery, Keesler H.
Morrison, Johnny Edward
Morrison, Trudi Michelle
Murphy, Della Mary
Napper, George, Jr.
Nelson, Doeg M.
Nelson, Ronald Duncan
Nesby, Donald Ray, Sr.
Newman, Nathaniel
O'Bryant, Tilmon Bunche
Owens, Ronald
Page, Alan Cedric
Parker, Charles Thomas
Patterson, Lloyd
Perkins, Thomas P.
Peterson, Alan Herbert
Pierce, Samuel R., Jr.
Rice, Fred
Rich, Stanley C.
Riley, William Scott
Robinson, Hamilton
Robinson, Learthon Steven
Rodez, Andrew LaMarr
Rodgers, Anthony Recarido, Sr.
Shanks, James A.
Sharpe, Ronald M.
Singleton, Benjamin, Sr.
Stroud, Milton
Swift, Leroy V.
Sylvester, Odell Howard, Jr.
Tate, Herbert Holmes, Jr.
Taylor, DeForrest Walker
Taylor, Martha
Terry, Adeline Helen
Thomas, Nina M.
Thomas, Robert Lewis
Tillman, Paula Sellars
Turner, Eddie William
Vaughn, William Smith
Waldon, Alton Ronald, Jr.
Wallace, Renee C.
Ward, Benjamin
Ward, Nolan F.
Watson, Herman Doc
Webb, Joseph G.
Weldon, Ramon N.
White, Gordon E.
White, June Joyce
Williams, Ellis
Williams, Hubert
Williams, Leonard, Sr.
Williams, Moses, Sr.
Williams, Rodney Elliott
Wrice, David

LAW/LEGAL SERVICES

Abernathy, James R., II
Abramson, Frederick Bruce
Adams, Gregory Albert
Adams, John Oscar
Adams, Oscar W., Jr.
Ahmad, Jadwaa
Al-Hafeez, Huzema
Albert, Charles Gregory
Alexander, Clifford L., Jr.
Alexander, James, Jr.
Alexander, Roosevelt Maurice
Alexander, Sadie Tanner Mossell

Alexander, William H.
Alford, Haile Lorraine
Allen, Milton B.
Allen, W. George
Amos, Joseph H.
Amos, Larry C.
Andrews, Judis R.
Archibald, B. Milele
Armistead, Milton
Armstrong, Joseph M.
Arnelle, Hugh Jesse
Arnold, Rudolph P.
Atkins, Edna R.
Atkins, Nelson Lawrence
Atkins, Thomas Irving
Atkinson, Nolan N., Jr.
Backus, Bradley
Bailer, Kermit Gamaliel
Bailey, D'Army
Bailey, Jerry Dean
Bailey, Lawrence R., Sr.
Bain, Raymone Kaye
Baker, Beverly Poole
Baldwin, Cynthia A.
Baldwin, George R.
Ball, Richard E.
Ball, William Batten
Ballance, Frank Winston, Jr.
Banks, Carl A.
Banks, Cecil J.
Banks, Kenneth E.
Banks, Patricia
Banks, Richard L.
Banks, Ruth R.
Banks, Sharon P.
Banks, Terry Michael
Bankston, Archie M.
Barbee, Lloyd Augustus
Barnes, Joseph Nathan
Barnes, Stephen Darryl
Barnes, William L.
Barnes, Willie R.
Bartelle, Talmadge Louis
Barzy, Raymond Clifford, II
Baskerville, Randolph
Bates, Arthur Verdi
Batine, Rafael
Beale, Larry D.
Beard, Charles Julian
Beard, James William, Jr.
Beard, Laronce D.
Beasley, Alice Margaret
Beasley, Ulysses Christian, Jr.
Beasley, Victor Mario
Beech, Harvey Elliott
Belcher, Nathaniel L.
Bell, Napoleon A.
Bell, Sheila Trice
Bell, William Charles
Bell, William McKinley
Belton, Robert
Benford, Clare E.
Bennett, Patricia A.
Berkley, Thomas Lucius
Bernstine, Daniel O.
Berry, Lisbon C., Jr.
Berry, Weldon H.
Besson, Paul Smith
Best, Jennings H.
Beverly, William C., Jr.
Black, Walter Kerrigan
Blackmon, Edward, Jr.
Blackshear, Julian W., Jr.
Blair, Chester Laughton Ellison
Blakey, William A.
Blount, Larry Elisha
Blye, Cecil A., Sr.
Bobbitt, Leroy
Bocage, Ronald J.
Boddie, Daniel W.
Bolden, Frank Augustus
Bolden, Raymond A.
Bonner, Alice A.
Booker, John, III
Booth, William H.
Bostic, Lee H.
Bourgeois, Adam
Bourne, Judith Louise
Bowman, Jacquelynne Jeanette
Boyd, Delores Rosetta
Boyd, William Stewart
Bozeman, Bruce L.
Bracey, Willie Earl
Braddock, Robert L.

Braden, Everette Arnold
Braden, Henry E., IV
Braden, Stanton Connell
Bradfield, Clarence McKinley
Bradley, Hilbert L.
Branton, Leo, Jr.
Brashear, Berlaind Leander
Braxton, John Ledger
Brazil, Ernest L.
Breckenridge, Franklin E.
Breckenridge, John L.
Brewer, Curtis
Brokaw, Carol Ann
Brooke, Edward W.
Brooks, Roy Lavon
Brown, Benjamin Leonard
Brown, Byrd R.
Brown, Deloris A.
Brown, Edwin C., Jr.
Brown, Franchot A.
Brown, Irma Jean
Brown, Jasper C., Jr.
Brown, Lewis Frank
Brown, Ralph H.
Brown, Richard Jess, Sr.
Brown, Richard M.
Brown, Robert Lee
Brown, Ronald H.
Brown, Ronald Harmon
Brown, William H., III
Brownlee, Wyatt China
Brownridge, J. Paul
Bruce, Kenneth E.
Brummer, Chauncey Eugene
Bryan, Clarice
Bryan, David Everett, Jr.
Bryant, Andrea Pair
Bryant, Hubert Hale
Bryant, Wayne R.
Buckner, Mary Alice
Bugg, Mayme Carol
Bullock, James
Burgess, James R., Jr.
Burgin, Ruth L. W.
Burke, Yvonne Brathwaite
Burnham, Margaret Ann
Burns, W. Haywood
Burris, John L.
Burris, Roland W.
Burroughs, Robert A.
Burton, Philip L.
Bush, Nathaniel
Bussey, Reuben T.
Bustamante, John H.
Butcher, Goler Teal
Butler, Annette G.
Butler, Frederick Douglas
Butler, Jerome M.
Butler, Patrick Hampton
Butler, Washington Roosevelt, Jr.
Bynoe, John Garvey
Byrd, Issac, Jr.
Cahn, Jean Camper
Cain, Frank Edward, Jr.
Cain, Simon Lawrence
Caldwell, James E.
Callender, Carl O.
Callender, Wilfred A.
Calloway, Curtis A.
Calvin, Michael Byron
Cameron, Lenore Hopewell
Camp, Marva Jo
Cannon, H. LeRoy
Carney, Alfonso Linwood, Jr.
Carrol, Raoul Lord
Carroll, James S.
Carter, Billy L.
Carter, Charles Edward
Carter, Charles Michael
Carter, Lisle Carleton, Jr.
Carter, Theodore Ulysses
Cason, Marilynn Jean
Caster, Caroleigh Tuitt
Cauthen, Richard L.
Chambers, Julius LeVonne
Chancellor, Carl Eugene
Chandler, Everett A.
Chandler, James P.
Chapman, David Anthony
Charity, Ruth Harvey
Cheek, King Virgil, Jr.
Cherot, Nicholas Maurice
Chess, Sammie, Jr.
Childs, Joy

Childs, Winston
Clark, Augusta Alexander
Clark, Christine Philpot
Clark, Michele Arleen
Clay, Eric Lee
Clayton, Matthew D.
Clayton, Theaoseus T.
Clegg, Legrand H., II
Clements, Walter H.
Cloud, Eric William
Cloud, Sanford, Jr.
Clyne, John Rennel
Cobb, John Hunter, Jr.
Cohen, Vincent H.
Colbert, Thelma Quince
Cole, James O.
Coleman, Arthur H.
Coleman, Eric Dean
Coleman, William T., Jr.
Collins, Hyacinth Roxane
Collins, Kenneth L.
Collins, Theodicia Deborah
Colter, Cyrus J.
Conley, John A.
Conley, Martha Richards
Cook, Frank Robert, Jr.
Cook, Rufus
Cooke, Wilhelmina Reuben
Cooper, Almeta E.
Cooper, Clarence
Cooper, Clement Theodore
Cooper, Gordon R., II
Cooper, Joseph
Corlette, Edith
Cormier, Rufus, Jr.
Cornish, Jeannette Carter
Countee, Thomas Hilaire, Jr.
Cousins, William, Jr.
Covington, M. Stanley
Cox, Sandra Hicks
Cox, Warren E.
Crenshaw, Waverly David, Jr.
Crockett, Gwendolyn B.
Cromartie, Ernest W., II
Cruise, Warren Michael
Crump, Arthel Eugene
Cummings, Roberta Spikes
Cunningham, E. Brice
Cunningham, F. Malcolm
Custer-Chen, Johnnie M.
Cutliff, John Wilson
Daggs, LeRoy W.
Daniel, Wiley Young
Darden, George Harry
Darrell, Lewis E.
Davenport, C. Dennis
Davis, Algenita Scott
Davis, Donald W.
Davis, Dupree Daniel
Davis, Elaine Carsley
Davis, Frank
Davis, J. Mason, Jr.
Davis, L. Clifford
Davis, Morris E.
Davis, Richard
Davison, Edward L.
Dawson, Warren Hope
Daye, Charles Edward
Days, Drew Saunders, III
DeBracy, Warren
Decatur, Robert A.
Denson, Fred L.
DeVaughn, Edward Raymond
DeWitt, Franklin Roosevelt
Dickens, Samuel
Dilday, Judith Nelson
Dillard, June White
Dixon, Sharon Pratt
Doanes-Bergin, Sharyn F.
Dobson, William DeLafayette
Donegan, Charles Edward
Dorsey, Charles Henry, Jr.
Dorsey, Elbert
Dorsey, John L.
Douglas, James Matthew
Dove, Evelyn Francyne
Drew, Stephen Richard
Drew-Peeples, Brenda
DuBose, Clarence R.
Dudley, Godfrey D.
Dukes, Walter Lucuis
Duncan, Charles Tignor
Duncan, John C., Jr.
Duncan, Robert M.

DunCombe, C. Beth
Dunnaville, Clarence M., Jr.
Dupree, David H.
Duster, Benjamin C.
Early, S. Allen, III
Echols, Alvin E.
Edley, Christopher F., Jr.
Edley, Christopher F., Sr.
Edwards, David C.
Edwards, Donald Philip
Edwards, Ruth McCalla
Edwards, Sylvia
Ellis, Rodney
Ellis, William Reuben
Ellison, Robert A.
Epps, A. Glenn
Erwin, Richard C.
Evans, Carole Yvonne Mims
Evans, Dorsey
Evans, Herbert B.
Evans, LeRoy W.
Evans, William Clayton
Everett, J. Richard
Everett, Ralph B.
Ewing, William James
Fabre, Edwin G.
Farley, William Horace, Jr.
Farrow, Sallie A.
Fazande, Hilliard C., II
Fields, Inez C.
Figures, Thomas H.
Filer, Kelvin Dean
Finch, Gregory Martin
Fisher, Ada L.
Fisher, Lloyd B.
Fitch, Harrison Arnold
Flatts, Barbara Ann
Flowers, Ralph L.
Flowers, W. Harold, Jr.
Forbes, George L.
Ford, Gary L.
Foreman, Christopher H.
Forstall, Kweku Dwayne
Fort, William H.
Foster, Gladys M.
Foster, James L.
Foster, Janice Martin
Foutz, Samuel Theodore
Fox, Thomas E., Jr.
Franklin, David M.
Franklin, Floyd
Frasier, Ralph Kennedy
Frazier, Reginald Lee
Freeman, Charles Eldridge
Freeman, Edward C.
Freeman, Frankie M.
Freeman, Ronald J.
Frost, Wilson
Fykes, Leroy Matthews, Jr.
Gaillard, Bernard
Gaither, Richard A.
Galiber, Joseph L.
Gardner, Cedric Boyer
Garner, Edward, Jr.
Garner, Melvin C.
Garnett, Ronald Leon
Gay, James F.
Gayton, Gary D.
Gentry, Nolden I.
George, Allen
Gibson, Harry H. C.
Gibson, Truman H., Jr.
Gibson, Warren Arnold
Gigger, Helen C.
Gigger, Nathaniel Jay
Gilliam, James H., Jr.
Gilliam, Robert M., Sr.
Gittens, James Philip
Givens, Leonard David
Gladden, Brenda Winckler
Golden, Evelyn Davis
Gonsalves, June Miles
Goodwin, James Osby
Gordon, Helen A.
Gordon, Walter Lear, III
Gordy, Desiree D'Laura
Gore, Blinzy L.
Gore, David L.
Gould, William B.
Graham, Precious Jewel
Grant, Arthur H.
Grant, Cheryl Dayne
Grant, Kingsley B.
Gray, Fred David
Gray, George W., III (Skip)

Gray, James Austin, II
Gray, Marvin W.
Gray, Ruben L.
Green, Aaron Alphonso
Green, Deborah Kennon
Green, Franklin D.
Green, Georgia Mae
Green, Geraldine D.
Green, William Ernest
Greene, Dwight L.
Greene-Thapedi, Llewellyn L.
Greenlee, Peter Anthony
Gregg, Harrison M., Jr.
Griffin, Eurich Z.
Griffin, Ronald C.
Griffiths, Peggy S.
Grigsby, Calvin Burchard
Grillo, Anival J.
Grimes, Douglas M.
Grimes, John J.
Grimes, John T.
Groves, Harry Edward
Hadden, Eddie Raynord
Haden, Mabel D.
Hagins, Jean Arthur
Hairston, Joseph Henry
Hale, Phale D.
Hales, Edward Everette
Haley, George Williford Boyce
Haliburton, Lawrence E.
Hall, David
Hall, Elliott S.
Hamby, Roscoe Jerome
Hamilton, Raymond
Hamilton, Samuel Cartenius
Hamilton, William Nathan
Hamlin, Albert T.
Hampton, Thurman B.
Hanley, J. Frank, II
Harding, Robert E.
Harmon, John H.
Harper, Conrad Kenneth
Harper, Ronald J.
Harrell, Robert L.
Harris, Caspa L., Jr.
Harris, DeLong
Harris, Elihu Mason
Harris, Jimmie
Harris, William H., Jr.
Hart, Christopher Alvin
Hart-Nibbrig, Harold C.
Harth, Raymond Earl
Hartsfield, Arnett L., Jr.
Hatcher, Richard Gordon
Hatchett, Elbert
Hawk, Charles Nathaniel, III
Hawkins, Calvin D.
Hawkins, Eldridge
Hawthorne, Nathaniel
Haye, Clifford S.
Hayes, Alvin, Jr.
Hayes, Edward, Jr.
Hayes, Graham Edmondson
Hayes-Giles, Joyce V.
Haynes, Frank L., Jr.
Haywoode, M. Douglas
Hebert, Stanley Paul
Heiskell, Michael Porter
Helms, David Alonzo
Henderson, D. Rudolph
Hendricks, Beatrice E.
Henry, Brent Lee
Henry, Daniel Joseph
Henry, Karl H.
Henry, Ragan A.
Henry, William Arthur, II
Herndon, James
Hewlett, Everett Augustus, Jr.
Hightower, Anthony
Hill, Bobby L.
Hill, Cynthia D.
Hill, Jacqueline R.
Hill, James A., Jr.
Hill, Reuben Benjamin
Hill, William Bradley, Jr.
Hilliard, Earl Frederick
Hinds, Lennox S.
Hines, J. Edward, Jr.
Hines, Kingsley B.
Hinnant, Ollen B.
Hinton, Gregory Tyrone
Hodges, Melvin Sancho
Holland, William Meredith
Hollingsworth, Perlesta A.

Hollis, Meldon S., Jr.
Hollowell, Donald L.
Holmes, Carl
Holmes, Henry Sidney, III
Holmes, Robert C.
Holmes, Robert Ernest
Honore, Stephan LeRoy
Hooks, Benjamin Lawson
Hopkins, Donald Ray
Hopkins, Esther Arvilla
Horne, Gerald C.
Horton, Earle C.
House, Carolyn Joyce
Howard, Dalton J., Jr.
Howard, John Robert
Howe, Ruth-Arlene W.
Howze, Karen Aileen
Hoyte, James Sterling
Hubbard, Arnette Rhinehart
Hubbard, Bruce Alan
Huckaby, Hilry, III
Hudson, Samuel William, III
Hughes, Harvey L.
Hughes, Joyce A.
Hughes, Roberta V.
Hunt, Isaac Cosby, Jr.
Hunter, Frederick Douglas
Hunter, Jerry L.
Hunter, Mackiell James
Hutton, Marilyn Adele
Hylton, Kenneth N.
Iglehart, Lloyd D.
Irvin, Charles Leslie
Irving, Clarence Larry, Jr.
Isadore, Harold W.
Jacks, Ulysses
Jackson, Alexis Camille
Jackson, Clarence H.
Jackson, Edward W.
Jackson, Elmer Carter, Jr.
Jackson, Gerald Milton
Jackson, Harold Baron, Jr.
Jackson, Lenwood A.
Jackson, Maynard Holbrook
Jackson, Robert, Jr.
Jackson, Thomas Mitchell
Jacobs, Patricia Dianne
James, Frank Samuel, III
James, Frederick John
James, Ronald J.
James, William
Jeffers, Clifton R.
Jefferson, Andrew L., Jr.
Jefferson, M. Ivory
Jefferson, Overton C.
Jefferson, William J.
Jenkins, Melvin L.
Jervay, Marion White
Jewell, Paula L.
Jewell, Tommy Edward
Johnson, A. Visanio
Johnson, Almeta Ann
Johnson, Andrew L., Sr.
Johnson, Caliph
Johnson, Charles Beverly
Johnson, Charles Ronald, Sr.
Johnson, Edmond W.
Johnson, Evelyn F.
Johnson, Francis Edward, Jr.
Johnson, Geraldine Ross
Johnson, Golden Elizabeth
Johnson, Hermel
Johnson, I. S. Leevy
Johnson, James Walter, Jr.
Johnson, John W.
Johnson, Johnnie L., Jr.
Johnson, Joseph Harvey
Johnson, Justin Morris
Johnson, Lawrence E., Sr.
Johnson, Leroy Reginald
Johnson, Lorna Karen
Johnson, Patricia L.
Johnson, Raymond L.
Johnson, Solomon E.
Johnson, Theodore A.
Johnson, Vincent L.
Johnson, Walter Thaniel, Jr.
Johnson, Wilbur Eugene
Johnson, William Lee, Jr.
Johnson, William Theolious
Johnson, William Thomas
Johnson, Wyneva
Jones, Audrey Boswell
Jones, Bonnie Louise

Jones, Chester Ray
Jones, Clarance J.
Jones, Clyde Eugene
Jones, David Russell
Jones, Elaine R.
Jones, Emma Pettway
Jones, Eric Louis
Jones, Ernest Edward
Jones, Frederick Douglass, Jr.
Jones, Gerald Winfield
Jones, James Edward, Jr.
Jones, Laura Mae (nee Green)
Jones, Louis Clayton
Jones, Mark E.
Jones, Nathaniel R.
Jones, O. Marion
Jones, Peter Lawson
Jones, Randy Kane
Jones, Robert Alton
Jones, Sidney A., Jr.
Jones, Thomas L.
Jones, William Allen
Jones, William Bowdoin
Jordan, Carolyn D.
Jordan, J. St. Girard
Jordan, Michelle Denise
Joseph, Antoine L.
Joyner, Arthenia Lee
Joyner, Irving L.
Julian, Percy L., Jr.
Kellman, Denis Elliott
Kendall, Robert, Jr.
Kennedy, Cain James
Kennedy, Florynce
Kenny, Alfreida B.
Kernodle, Obra Servesta, III
Kerr, Walter L.
Kersey, B. Franklin, IV
King, Charles Abraham
King, Donald E.
King, Mattie M.
King, Patricia Ann
King, Patricia E.
Knox, George F.
Kuykendall, Crystal Arlene
LaCour, Louis Bernard
Lacour, Vanue B.
Lafontant, Jewel Stradford
Laing, Edward A.
Lamaute, Denise
Lambert, Benjamin Franklin
Lambert, Leonard W.
Lancaster, Herman Burtram
Langford, Anna Riggs
Langford, Charles D.
Langford, John W.
Latham, Weldon Hurd
Latney, Harvey, Jr.
Lawernce, Lonnie R.
Lawrence, Charles B.
Lawson, Marjorie McKenzie
Laymon, John W.
Leacock, Stephen Jerome
Lee, Lena S. King
Lee, Robert E.
Leek, Everett Paul
Leek, Sandra D.
Leftwich, Willie L.
Lester, Betty J.
Lester, Elton J.
Lewis, Cary B., Jr.
Lewis, Daniel
Lewis, David Baker
Lewis, Reginald F.
Lewis, William A., Jr.
Lillard, Robert Emmitt
Lindsay, Reginald C.
Lindsey, Terry Lamar
Littlejohn, Bill C.
Littlejohn, Edward J.
Lloyd, Leona Loretta
Lloyd, Leonia Jannetta
Lofton, Mellanese (nee Slaughter)
Logan, George, III
Long, James Alexander
Lott, Gay Lloyd
Lucas, Florence V.
Lucas, William
Luke, Sherrill David
Lyman, Webster S.
Makupson, Walter H.
Malone, Charles A.
Mangum, Charles M. L.
Mangum, Robert J.

Mann, Thomas J., Jr.
Mannie, William Edward
Manning, Howard Nick, Jr.
Mapp, Calvin R.
Marchman, Robert Anthony
Mark, Freeman A.
Marr, Carmel Carrington
Marsh, Henry L., III
Marsh, William A., Jr.
Marshall, Reese
Marshall, Thurgood, Jr.
Martin, Clarence L.
Martin, Daniel E.
Martin, James C.
Martin, Joshua Wesley, III
Mason, William Thomas, Jr.
Mathis, William Lawrence
Matthews, Cynthia Clark
Maxey, Carl
May, James Shelby
Mayfield, William S.
Mays, W. Roy, III
McCants, Coolidge N.
McClain, William Andrew
McClaskey, William H.
McClellan, Frank Madison
McClendon, Kellen
McClenic, David A.
McCoy, Wayne Anthony
McCrary-Simmons, Shirley Denise
McCroom, Eddie Winther
McDaniel, Myra Atwell
McDonald, Mark T.
McDonald, Richard E.
McDowell, Cleve
McFarland, Arthur C.
McFarland, Claudette
McGee, Hansel Leslie
McGill, Thomas L., Jr.
McGinnis, James W.
McGrier, Jerry, Sr.
McIntosh, Rhodina Covington
McKanders, Julius A., II
McKee, Clarence Vanzant
McKinney, Gregory L.
McKinney, Rufus William
McKissick, Floyd B.
McLaren, Douglas Earl
McLaughlin, Dolphy T.
McLeon, Nathaniel W.
McMorris, Samuel Carter
McNeil, Ernest Duke
McQuater, Patricia A.
McWilliams, James D.
Medford, Isabel
Merchant, John F.
Meshack, Sheryl Hodges
Metoyer, Carl B.
Michael, Dale R.
Michaux, Eric Coates
Micks, Deitra R. H.
Middleton, Michael A.
Miller, Melvin B.
Miller, Sharon Bernard
Minor, Jessica
Minter, Kendall Arthur
Mitchell, Charles E.
Mitchell, Huey P.
Mitchell, Iverson O., III
Mitchell, Stanley Henryk
Mitchell, Theo W.
Mobley, Stacey J.
Montgomery, Earline (nee Smith)
Montgomery, Gregory B.
Moody, Eric Orlando
Moore, Colin A.
Moore, Cornell Leverette
Moore, Emanuel A.
Moore, Fred Henderson (Danny)
Moore, Howard, Jr.
Moore, Karen E.
Moore, Richard Baxter
Moran, Joyce E.
Morgan, June Elloie
Morgan, Richard H., Jr.
Morgan-Price, Veronica Elizabeth
Morris, Melvin
Morrison, Robert B., Jr.
Morrow, Samuel P., Jr.
Morton, William Stanley
Morton-Finney, John
Mosley, Maurice B.
Muckelroy, William Lawrence
Murphy, Arthur G.

LIBRARY/ INFORMATION SCIENCE

Hogan, Fannie Burrell
Howard, Elizabeth Fitzgerald
Hutson, Jean Blackwell
Irving, Ophelia McAlpin
Isadore, Harold W.
Jackson, Adele Martin
James, William
Jenkins, Althea H.
Jenkins, Barbara Williams
Jobe, Shirley A.
Johnson, Gloria Dean
Johnson, Minnie Redmond
Jones, Clifton Patrick
Jones, Curley C.
Jones, Robbie Neely
Jones, Virginia Lacy
Jordan, Casper LeRoy
Josey, E. J.
Joyce, Donald Franklin
Kaiser, Ernest Daniel
Knowles, Claire Em
Lawrence, Eileen B.
Lewis, Frank Ross
Louistall-Monroe, Victorine
  Augusta
Lyells, Ruby E. Stutts
Lyons, Donald Wallace
Malone, J. Deotha
Marks, Rose M.
Martin, Rosetta P.
Mathis, Sharon Bell
Matthews, Jessie L.
Matthews, Miriam
Maye, Beatrice Carr Jones
McCoy, James F.
McCray, Maceo E.
McKissick, Mabel F. Rice
McLaughlin, LaVerne Laney
Miller, Ethel Jackson
Miller, Jacqueline Elizabeth
Miller, James S.
Mills, Gladys Hunter
Mobley, Emily Ruth
Mohr, Diane Louise
Moore, M. Elizabeth Gibbs
Morgan, Jane Hale
Morris, Effie Lee
Morrison, Samuel F.
Moses, Louise J.
Mothershed, Spaesio W.
Newell, Matthias Gregory
Paschal, Eloise Richardson
Patterson, Pola Noah
Peguese, Charles R.
Pendergrass, Margaret E.
Perry, Margaret
Phillips, Bertha (nee Parker)
Porter, Dorothy B.
Powell, Addie Scott
Pugh, Marlana Patrice
Randall, Ann Knight
Randall, Dudley Felker
Reason, Joseph Henry
Reed, Lola N.
Render, Sylvia Lyons
Rhodes, Lelia G.
Riley, Barbara P.
Rogers, James E.
Roney, Raymond G.
Roper, Grace Trott
Rountree, Louise M.
Rudd, Amanda S.
Russell, Beverly A.
Scott, Alice H.
Shaw, Spencer Gilbert
Shockley, Ann Allen
Sibley, Ellen C.
Singley, Elijah
Smith, Daniel H., Jr.
Smith, Jessie Carney
Smith, Juanita Jane
Spencer, Joan Moore
Spradling, Mary Elizabeth Mace
Staley, Valeria Howard
Stewart, Ruth Ann
Strait, George A.
Strong, Blondell McDonald
Sutton, Gloria W.
Sylvester, Melvin R.
Thomas, Lucille Cole
Thomas, Maurice McKenzie
Thompson, Hobson, Jr.
Tolbert, Odie Henderson, Jr.
Totten, Herman Lavon
Towns, Rose Mary

Tyson, John C.
Venable, Andrew Alexander, Jr.
Walters, Mary Dawson
Whisenton, Andre C.
Williams, Dorothy P.
Williams, Ethel Langley
Wilson, Florabelle W.
Wilson, Margaret F.
Woods, Hortense E.
Wray, Wendell Leonard
Wright, James R.
Yates, Ella Gaines

MANAGEMENT/ ADMINISTRATION— ACCOUNTING/ FINANCIAL
See also ACCOUNTING/ AUDITING

Adams, Edward B.
Anderson, Elizabeth M.
Arnold, Haskell N., Jr.
Ashby, Lucius Antoine
Ashley, Corlanders
Bailey, Jerry Dean
Baker, Eugene
Barnes, N. Kurt
Bell, Marilyn Lenora
Belle, Charles E.
Benjamin, Arthur, Jr.
Benjamin, Ronald
Bennett, William Ronald
Best, Willie Armster
Beverly, Benjamin Franklin
Bouldes, Charlene
Brandford, Napoleon
Brown, Eddie C.
Brown, J. Quantin
Brown, Jonel Leonard
Brown, Mary Catherine
Bryant, Regina Lynn
Bryant-Reid, Johanne
Burke, Olga Pickering
Burton, David Lloyd
Campbell, Carlos Cardozo
Camphor, Michael Gerard
Chambers, Harry, Jr.
Chism, Harolyn B.
Chivis, Martin Lewis
Clayton, Robert L.
Connell, Cameron
Cox, Taylor H., Sr.
Craig-Rudd, Joan
Crim, Rodney
Culbreath, Tongila M.
Cunningham, Erskine
Daniels, Patricia Ann
Davenport, Ernest H.
Doss, Lawrence Paul
Duster, Benjamin C.
Eccles, Peter Wilson
Farrell-Donaldson, Marie D.
Faulding, Juliette J.
Ferguson, Edward A., Jr.
Fletcher, James Andrew
Flippen, Frances Morton
Frison, Lee A.
Glee, George, Jr.
Godfrey, William R.
Green, Cicero M., Jr.
Guitano, Anton W.
Hall, David McKenzie
Harvey, Richard R.
Henderson, James J., Sr.
Henderson, Ramona Estelle
Hooker, Douglas Randolf
Hooks, James Byron, Jr.
Hudson, Frederick Bernard
Humphrey, Arthur
Humphrey, Marian J.
James, Dorothy Marie
Johnson, Roy Lee
Jordan, Marilyn E.
Juniòr, Ester James, Jr.
Kendrick, Griff William
King, Edgar Lee
Law, M. Eprevel
Liverpool, Charles Eric
Lovelace, Onzalo Robert
Mack, Fred Clarence
May, Dickey R.
McDuffie, Joseph deLeon, Jr.
McKnight, Albert J.

McPhail, Weldon
Mickle, Elva L.
Moore, Charles W.
Mosley, Edna Wilson
Nunn, John, Jr.
Oubre, Linda Seiffert
Palmer, Dennis
Powell, Aston Wesley
Powell, Wayne Hugh
Price, Albert H.
Price, Michael D.
Rasheed, Howard S.
Reed, Larita D.
Rentie, Frieda
Rice, William E.
Richards, William Earl
Ross, Frank Kenneth
Roy, Welton J., Jr.
Sandidge, Kanita Durice
Scales, Erwin Carlvet
Sellers, Theresa Ann
Shropshire, Harry W.
Sloan, Maceo Kennedy
Smith, Chester B.
Staes, Beverly N.
Stahnke, William E.
Stamper, Henry J.
Swanston, Clarence Eugene
Tarter, Robert R., Jr.
Thompson, Jeffrey Earl
Trapp, Donald W.
Tucker, Eric M.
Turner, Marvin Wentz
Turner, Vivian Vanessa
Tutt, Lia S.
Vest, Donald Seymour, Sr.
Walden, Barbara
Wallace, Charles Leslie
Warren, Lee Alden (Tico)
Watson, Thomas S., Jr.
White, Clarence Dean
Woodson, Cleveland Coleman, III
Woodson, Jeffrey Anthony
Wright, Ralph Edward
Yearwood, David Monroe, Jr.

MANAGEMENT/ ADMINISTRATION— ADVERTISING/ MARKETING/ PUBLIC RELATIONS
See also ADVERTISING/ PROMOTION

Acon, June Kay
Adams, Theodore Adolphus, Jr.
Allen, George Louis
Allston, Thomas Gray, III (Tim)
Alsandor, Jude
Amos, Wally
Anderson, Al H., Jr.
Andrews, Alice Elizabeth
Arnold, Ethel N.
Atchison, Leon H.
Atkins, Fredd Glossie
Atkinson, J. Edward
Avery, James S.
Bailey, Curtis Darnell
Banfield, Anne L.
Banks, Beatrice
Barrow, Lionel Ceon, Jr.
Bateman, Michael Allen
Beach, Walter G., II
Beckett, Evette Olga
Bell, Diana Lynne
Benton, Nelkane O.
Berry, Archie Paul
Bettis, Anne Katherine
Blackwell, Noble Virgil
Booker, Anne M.
Bowman, Joseph E., Jr.
Bradford, Zee
Britton, John H., Jr.
Brockington, Donella P.
Brown, Sharon Marjorie Revels
Buckhanan, Dorothy Wilson
Burke, William Arthur
Burns, Dargan J.
Bussey, Charles David
Butler, Joyce M.
Cain, Gerry Ronald
Calhoun, Lillian Scott
Cameron, Randolph W.
Cannon, Davita Louise

Carroll, Robert F.
Carswell, Gloria Nadine Sherman
Chapman, Sharon Jeanette
Childs, Oliver Bernard, Sr.
Clark, John Joseph
Collins, Gordon Geoffrey
Collins, Tessil John
Cooper, Jerome Gary
Coward, Jasper Earl
Cox, M. Maurice
Crawford, Barbara Hopkins
Crombaugh, Hallie
Crump-McCoy, Robbie L.
Curry, Charles E.
Davis, Charles A.
Davis, Luther Charles
Davis, Thomas J.
Dixon, John Frederick
Donald, Arnold Wayne
Dottin, Roger Allen
Durant-Paige, Beverly
Dyer, Joe, Jr.
Eades, Vincent W.
Easley, Eddie V.
Echols, James Albert
Ellington, Brenda Andrea
Evans, Alicia
Fay, Toni G.
Ferguson, Idell
Fernandez, John Peter
Fitzhugh, Howard Naylor
Fontenot-Jamerson, Berlinda
Gaines, Adriane Theresa
Garrett, Louis Henry
Gates, Jacquelyn Knight
Gellineau, Victor Marcel, Jr.
Giles, Althea B.
Giles, William R.
Givens, Joshua Edmond
Glover, Sarah Louise
Greenlee, Robert Douglass
Gregory, Robert Alphonso
Griffin, Booker
Griggs, Anthony
Hamilton, Pamela Marie
Hanson, John L.
Harris, J. Robert, II
Harris, Lee Andrew, II
Harrison, Ronald E.
Harrison, Roscoe Conklin, Jr.
Hatcher, Jeffrey F.
Herring, William F.
Hill, Jeffrey Ronald
Hill, Thaddeus Earl
Holmes, Carlton
Holt, Veitya Eileene (Vickye)
Hooper, Gary Raymond
Hopkins, Stephanie Colbert
House, James E.
Humphrey, Sonnie
Jackson, Mary
James, Robert Earl
Jaycox, Mary Irine
Jenkins, Bobby G.
Jenkins, Yolanda L.
Johnson, Juliana Cornish
Johnson, Stephanye
Jones, DeVerges Booker
Jones, Lisa Payne
Jones, Robert G.
Kendrix, Moss H., Sr.
Knox, George L., III
Lacey, Diane E.
Leggett, Renee
Lewis, Byron E.
Littlejohn, J. B.
Logan, Linda Ann
Lucas, Victoria
Mack, Miranda
Marshall, Pluria William, Jr.
Matney, William C., Jr.
Mintz, Reginold Lee
Mitchell, Martha Mallard
Mootry, Charles
Murray, James P.
Newman, Paul Dean
Norman, Clifford P.
Osborne, Gwendolyn Eunice
Parham, Marjorie B.
Parker, James L.
Parker, Kai J.
Parker, Thomas Edwin, III
Parks, James Clinton, Jr.
Perry, Eugene Calvin, Jr.

Powell, Bernice Fletcher
Price, George Baker
Proctor, Earl D.
Ray, Austin H.
Reece, Steven
Reed, Derryl L.
Reid, Eric William
Reynolds, Andrew Buchanan
Rhodes, C. Adrienne
Rhodes, Jeanne (nee Simmons)
Richardson, Charles H., Jr.
Robertson, John Gilbert
Robinson, Martha Delores
Rosenthal, Robert E.
Sagers, Rudolph, Jr.
Saunders, Barbara Ann (nee
  Parks)
Sayers, Gayle E.
Sechrest, Edward Amacker
Senegal, Charles
Sewell, Luther Joseph
Shackelford, William G., Jr.
Shepard, Linda Irene
Shipe, Jamesetta Denise Holmes
Shropshire, Thomas B.
Shumate, Glen
Siler, Brenda Claire
Simmons, Maurice Clyde
Smith, Patricia G.
Spratlen, Thaddeus H.
Sterling, Charles A.
Stevens, John Theodore, Sr.
Stewart, Joseph M.
Strange, Alonzo, Jr.
Sutton, Charyn Diane
Tatum, Wilbert A.
Taylor, Tommie W.
Thompson, Gloria Crawford
Thornton, Jackie C.
Tyner, Regina Lisa
Utley, Richard Henry
Walton, James Donald
Waugh, Judith Ritchie
Weaver, Frank Cornell
Wharton, Ferdinand D., Jr.
Williams, Elynor A.
Williams, Lloyd A.
Williams, Rosa B.
Williams, Snowden J.
Williams-Davis, Edith G.
Williamson, Karen Elizabeth
Wilson, Lawrence E., III
Winslow, Eugene
Wood, Anton Vernon
Woodbeck, Frank Raymond
Woodruff, Jeffrey Robert
Wooten, Carl Kenneth
Wyche, Paul H., Jr.
Young, James M., II

MANAGEMENT/ ADMINISTRATION— COMPUTER SYSTEMS/DATA PROCESSING

Ahart, Thomas I.
Akridge, Paul Bai
Andrews, Nelson Montgomery
Armstead, Wilbert Edward, Jr.
Bell, Diana Lynne
Blocker, Helen Powell
Brasey, Henry L.
Brockington, Eugene Alfonzo
Bryant, Regina Lynn
Butler, John Gordon
Byrd, Percy L.
Casterlow, Carolyn B.
Cooper, William B.
Culpepper, Betty M.
Davis, Diane Lynn
Davis, Glendell Kirk
Franklin, Martha Lois
Gray, Christine
Greene, Frank S., Jr.
Hall, David McKenzie
Howell, Vincent Wyatt
Hudson, Frederick Bernard
Hylton, Taft H.
Ingram, Phillip M.
Isaacs, Doris C.
Jacobs, Patricia Dianne
Johnson, Wayne Alan
Jones, Isaac, Jr.

Hall, Hansel Crimiel
Hall, Harold Eugene
Hall, Ira DeVoyd
Hall, Rubye Maie
Halyard, Ardie Adlena
Hamilton, Richard Nathaniel
Handy, Wendell Taylor
Hankins, Freeman
Harper, Beverly A.
Harper, Earl
Harris, Douglas Allen
Harris, Freeman Cosmo
Harris, Hassel B.
Harris, Joseph Benjamin
Harris, Marion Rex
Harris, Thomas C.
Harris, William Henry
Harris-Ebohon, Altheria Thyra
Harty, Donald K.
Hasty, Keith A.
Hawkins, Morris M.
Haywood, Bertron Don
Hebert, Zenebework Teshome
Henderson, LeMon
Hendricks, Juanita
Heningburg, Gustav
Hennings, Kenneth Milton
Henry, Calvin O. L.
Henry, Ragan A.
Hentrel, Bobbie Kuykendall
Herbert, John Travis, Jr.
Hernandez, Aileen Clarke
Highsmith, Carlton L.
Hill, Brandon T.
Hill, Charlie H.
Hill, George Hiram
Hill, Henry
Hill, Norman S.
Hill, Robert K.
Hodge, Ernest M.
Hodge, Paget T.
Holliday, Alfonso David
Holmes, Theodore Neal
Hooper, Michele J.
Hopson, Melvin Clarence
House, Jesse O.
Howell, Amaziah, III
Howell, Joseph L.
Hubbard, Reginald T.
Hudson, Elbert T.
Hughes, Catherine Liggins
Hughes, George Vincent
Hughes, Isaac Sunny
Hutt, Monroe L.
Ingram, Phillip M.
Isaacs, Doris C.
Isler, Marshall A., III
Ivory, Lee Allen
Jackson, Beverly Anne
Jackson, Donald J.
Jackson, Horace
Jackson, Jesse L.
Jackson, Leon
Jackson, Mannie Leon
Jackson, William Fred
James, Charles Howell, II
James, Clarence L., Jr.
Jefferson, Clifton
Jeffries, LeRoy William
John-Sandy, Rene Emanuel
Johns, Michael Earl
Johnson, Cleo M.
Johnson, Cyrus Edwin
Johnson, Davis
Johnson, George Ellis
Johnson, Janice Marie
Johnson, Jeffalyn Brown
Johnson, John H.
Johnson, Kaaren Patricia
Johnson, Rafer Lewis
Johnson, Ralph V.
Johnson, Thomas Aldrige
Johnson, Virginia O.
Jones, Alfred A.
Jones, Benjamin E.
Jones, Buck
Jones, Clarance W.
Jones, Jerry T.
Jones, Nathan William
Jones, O. Marion
Jones, Paul R.
Jones, Robert Wesley
Jones, Ruth Braswell
Jones, William Henry, Jr.
Jones, Yvonne Harris

Jordan, R. D.
Keels, James Dewey
Kendrix, Moss H., Sr.
Kennedy, Frederick A.
Keys, Brady, Jr.
Kilimanjaro, John Marshall
Kimbrough, Fred H.
Kinard, Helen Madison Marie
    Pawne
King, James B., Jr.
King, John B.
King, Nettie (nee Scott)
Kirven, Joe W.
Kittrels, Alonzo William
Knigh, Billy Earl, I.
Knott, Albert Paul, Jr.
Kunes, Ken R.
Labrie, Harrington
Lackey, Edgar F.
Laday, Kerney
Lamont, Barbara
Land, Georgianna Anderson
Lange, Geraldine Bernice
Law, M. Eprevel
Lawson, Charles H., III
Leaks, Sylvester
Leavell, Dorothy R.
LeDay, John Austin
Lee, Andre L.
Lee, Bertram M.
Lee, Charles Gary, Sr.
Lee, Dale George
Lee, Detroit
Lee, Ronald B.
Lee, Stratton Creighton
Lee, William H.
Leek, Everett Paul
Leek, Sandra D.
Lewis, Billie
Lewis, Delano Eugene
Lewis, Gus Edward
Lewis, Lloyd E., Jr.
Lewis, Ora Lee (nee McQuiller)
Lipscomb, Emanuel A.
Lloyd, David
Lloyd, James
Lockhart-Moss, Eunice Jean
Long, Steffan
Lowry, James Hamilton
Lucas, Victoria
Lucus, Emma Turner
Ludlam, Valerie Pope
Lytle, William F.
Mackey, Howard H., III
Macon, Norman
Major, Paul Charles
Makle, Vivian B.
Marcee, Emerson
Martin, John Gordon
Mathews, George
Maxell, Charles A.
May, Cornelius Wallace
Mays, James A.
Mays, Willie Howard, Jr.
McCain, Claude, Jr.
McCaulley, James Alan, III
McClain, William L.
McClelland, Isaac Holland
McCoy, Carol Todman
McCoy, Frederick Douglass, Jr.
McCoy, Leamon M.
McCray, Joe Richard
McDaniels, Orrin Hunter
McElroy, Alfred Z.
McFarland, Claudette
McGuire, Paul M., Jr.
McIntosh, Rhodina Covington
McKanders, Julius A., II
McLaughlin, Clara J.
McLeod, Georgianna R.
McMeans, Donald Curtis
Merritt, Reuben Asa
Messiah, Sonceria Von
Miller, Jean Carolyn Wilder
Miller, Jesse P.
Miller, Margaret Elizabeth (nee
    Battle)
Miller, Willie James
Mills, John L.
Minor, John A.
Mitchell, Jacob Bill
Mitchell, Roderick Bernard
Monroe, Early D., Jr.
Moore, Jerry A., Jr.

Morris, Ella Lucille
Morris, James F.
Morris, William Wesley
Morrow, Jesse
Morrow, Nebraska
Mosby, Carolyn Brown
Mosley, John Colbert
Mouton, Barbara Anne
Muckelroy, William Lawrence
Mullens, Delbert W.
Murphy, William Edward, Jr.
Myers-May, Yvette
Nash, Henry
Neal, Earl Langdon
Nelson, Charles J.
Nelson, Orville Alfonzo
Nero, David M., Jr.
Newberry, Cedric Charles
Newkirk, Queenie Hortense
Newkirk, Thomas H.
Newman, Kenya Maria
Nicco-Annan, Lionel
Nichols, Kay Bailey
Nichols, Walter L.
Nixon, Felix Nathaniel
Noble, Norma Lynette
Norfleet, Fred L., Jr.
Norman, Bobby Don
Norman, George E.
Norris, Curtis H.
Nyahuma, Tahiya R. M. W.
Odom, Carolyn
O'Flynn-Thomas, Patricia
Okwumabua, Benjamin Nkem
Orr, Ray
Paddio-Johnson, Eunice Alice
Pannell, Patrick Weldon
Parker, James E.
Parker, Jean L. (nee Lane)
Parris, Guichard
Patrick, Charles Namon, Jr.
Patterson, John T., Jr.
Patton, Carolyn Vannette
Payne, Jesse James
Payne, Osborne Allen
Pender, Melvin
Penn, Robert Clarence
Perry, Eugene Calvin, Jr.
Perry, Lowell W.
Peters, Charles L., Jr.
Peterson, Gerard M.
Petterway, Jackie Willis (Jackie O
    of Houston)
Petty, Bruce Anthony
Phelps-Patterson, Lucy
Phillips, Daniel P.
Pickens, William, III
Pitchford, Gerard Spencer
Polite, Theron Jerome
Poole, Thomas H., Sr.
Porter, John T.
Porter, John W.
Poston, Ersa Hines
Price, Wallace Walter
Procope, John Levy
Ramos, Gene Maurice
Randall, Queen F.
Ransom, Burnella Jackson
Raullerson, Calvin Henry
Ray, Walter I., Jr.
Reams-Whitmire, Vernetta Maria
Rhodes, Duplain
Rhodes, Edward Thomas, Sr.
Rice, Linda Johnson
Richards, Roosevelt
Richards, William Earl
Richards-Alexander, Billie J.
Richardson, Joseph
Riggs, Enrique A.
Riles, Wilson Camanza
Riley, Negail R.
Roberts, Ann F.
Robinson, John F.
Robinson, Rose Miles
Ross, Robert P.
Rouse, Bishop Claude, Jr.
Rucker, Robert Louis, Jr.
Ruffin, John Walter, Jr.
Samuels, James E.
Samuels, Leslie Eugene
Sanders, Thelma
Santiful, Luthur L.
Scales, Patricia Bowles
Scott, Arthur Bishop

Scribner, Arthur Gerald, Jr.
Seals, Connie C.
Seavers, Clarence W.
Shanks, Wilhelmina Byrd
Sheffey, Fred C.
Sherrell, Charles Ronald, II
Simmons, Albert Bufort, Jr.
Simmons, Althea T.L.
Simms, Gregory Frame
Simms, Robert H.
Simpson, Merton Daniel
Sims, Laura Mack
Sloan, Maceo Kennedy
Smith, Albert E.
Smith, Arthur D.
Smith, Johnnie M.
Smith, Nathaniel
Smith, Philip Meek
Smith, Quentin Paige, Jr.
Smith, Reginald B.
Smith, Robbie
Snipes, Kenneth
Sobers, Waynett A., Jr.
Sockwell, Oliver R., Jr.
Spaulding, Asa T.
Spears, Charles
Spriggs, Ray V.
Statham, Carl
Statum, Hayward S.
Stearns, Lillard G.
Stebbins, Dana Brewington
Stephenson, Charles E., III
Stephenson, Jerry L.
Stevenson, Sybil Jordan
Steward, Emanuel
Sullivan, Leon Howard
Summerville, Tommie Lewis
Sutton, Percy E.
Swanson, O'Neil D.
Swanston, Clarence Eugene
Sykes, Ray
Taylor, Charles E.
Taylor, Henry Marshall
Taylor, Jesse Elliott, Jr.
Taylor, Michael
Taylor, Patricia Tate
Taylor, Sinthy E.
Temple, Oney D.
Thacker, Sandra J.
Thomas, C. Edward
Thomas, Henry H.
Thomas, Joan McHenry Bates
Thomas, Nathaniel
Thomas, Stanley B., Jr.
Thompson, Albert N.
Thompson, Emma M.
Thompson, Frank L.
Thompson, Jesse
Thompson, Robert Dewey
Thrash, Ernestine
Tillman, Joseph Nathaniel
Toliver, William Henry, Sr.
Toran, Anthony
Trice, Luther William
Troupe, Charles Quincy
Tucker, C. DeLores
Tucker, Robert H., Jr.
Tyler, Shirley Neize
Urquhart, James McCartha
Valdes, Pedro H.
Valentine, Herman E.
Vance, Tommie Rowan
Varner, James
Vassall, Sidney Austin
Vaughan, James Edward
Vaughns, Sylvester J., Sr.
Walakafra-Wills, Delpaneaux V.
Walker, James
Walker, Willie F.
Wallace, Arnold D., Sr.
Wallace, Harden Wilson
Wallace, James Alfonso
Wallette, Alonzo Vandolph
Walton, Lludloo Charles
Ware, J. Lowell
Washington, Carl Douglas
Washington, J. Barry
Washington, Oscar D.
Watiker, Albert David, Jr.
Watkins, Lenice J.
Watkins, Willie S., III
Watson, Norma (nee Mims)
Watterson, Richard Harvey
Wattley, Thomas Jefferson

Webb, James Eugene
Webb, James O.
Webb, Joe
Weems, Vernon Eugene, Jr.
Wesley, Clemon Herbert, Jr.
Wharton, Clifton R., Jr.
Wheadon, A. Wendel
White, Alphonza J.
White, Gary Leon
White, James Louis, Jr.
White, Nathaniel B.
White, Ralph L.
White, Wendell F.
Whitmal, Nathaniel
Whitney, W. Monty
Whitworth, Claudia Alexander
Wilkinson, Sheppard Field
Williams, Everett Belvin
Williams, Falba W.
Williams, Joseph Lee
Williams, Leaford Clemetson
Williams, Lloyd A.
Williams, Melvin Thomas, Jr.
Williams, Paul
Williams, Regina Vloyn-Kinchen
Williams, Roosevelt
Williams, Terrie Michelle
Williams, Wallace C.
Willie, Louis J.
Wilson, Barbara Jean
Wilson, Charles Stanley, Jr.
Wilson, Leon A.
Winslow, Eugene
Witt, Burkett L.
Wolfe, Estemore A.
Wooding, Samuel David
Woodward, Aaron Alphonso, III
Wormley, Diane-Louise Lambert
Wright, Joseph Malcolm
Wright-Sabree, Margaret V.
Yelity, Stephen C.
Young, Debora Holmes
Young, Leon
Zachary, Hubert M.
Zollar, Doris L.

MANAGEMENT/ ADMINISTRATION— OPERATIONS/ MAINTENANCE

Alexander, Kelly Miller, Jr.
Allen, Wendell
Baker, Eugene
Balton, Kirkwood R.
Barber, William, Jr.
Blake, Milton James
Brewster, Luther George
Brown, Burnell V.
Campbell, Gertrude M.
Cantarella, Marcia Y.
Chase, James
Clark, Louis James
Coaxum, Henry L., Jr.
Cochran, Edward G.
Cornelison, Carole Jane
Evans, Leon, Jr.
Forster, Cecil R., Jr.
Hardy, Michael Leander
Harrold, Lawrence A.
Hobson, William D.
Hopkins, Perea M.
Johnson, Andrew
Johnson, Miriam B.
Jones, Clarance W.
Jones, David Russell
Jones, Isaac, Jr.
Kirven, Joe W.
Levell, Edward, Jr.
Lowry, James E.
Martin, George Alexander, Jr.
Martin, Walter L.
McDonald, William Emory
McIlwain, Albert Hood
Meriweather, Melvin, Jr.
Minor, David M.
Moore, Alstork Edward
Morris, Archie, III
Nichols, Nick
Reed, Cordell
Reeves, Julius Lee
Sanders, Laura Green
Sanderson, Randy Chris
Smith, Donald M.

Stallworth, Ann P.
Taylor, Charles E.
Verbal, Claude A.
Wainwright, Oliver O'Connell
Westbrook, Franklin Solomon
Williams, Armstrong
Williams, Ronald Wesley
Wilson, Earl Lawrence
Wisham, Claybron O.

MANAGEMENT/ ADMINISTRATION— PERSONNEL/ TRAINING/LABOR RELATIONS

Adams, Albert W., Jr.
Albright, William Dudley, Jr.
Allen, Clyde Cecil
Allen, George Mitchell
Anderson, Elizabeth M.
Archer, Lee A., Jr.
Arrington, Pamela Gray
Baine, Herman
Baity, Gail Owens
Baldwin, Louis J.
Barclay, David Ronald
Barksdale, Mary Frances
Barnhill, Helen Iphigenia
Baskerville, Penelope Anne
Bell, Trenton G.
Bellinger, Luther Garic
Belton, Howard G.
Bivins, Edward Byron
Blackmon, Mosetta Whitaker
Blake, Milton James
Blakely, William H., Jr.
Bluford, Grady L.
Boardley, Curtestine May
Boyd, Thomas
Branch, B. Lawrence
Bridgeman, Donald Earl
Brooks, Wadell, Sr.
Browder, Anne Elna
Brown, A. David
Brown, Booker T.
Brown, Clarence William
Brown, Earl Richard
Brown, Jurutha
Bruce, Carol Pitt
Bryant-Mitchell, Ruth Harriet
Bryant-Reid, Johanne
Burgess, Joseph Edward
Burns, Sarah Ann
Bussey, Charles David
Caldwell, George Theron, Sr.
Caldwell, John Edward
Carey, Claire Lamar
Carter, Joan Elizabeth
Carter, Judy Sharon
Chalmers, Thelma Faye
Chandler, Effie L.
Chapman, Alice Mariah
Chapman, Charles F.
Chappell, Ruth Rax
Childs, Joy
Christian, Dolly Lewis
Clark, James Irving, Jr.
Clayton, Robert L.
Collins, James H.
Cooper, Barbara Jean
Cooper, Linda G.
Cotton, Albert E.
Crawley, Oscar Lewis
Cribbs, Williams Charles
Crump, Wilbert S.
Cureton, John Porter
Curry, Levy Henry
Davis, Carolyn Ann McBride
Davis, Joyce
Davis, Ronald P.
Dean, James Edward
Deloatch, Myrna Loy
Dewberry, Madelina Denise
Dominic, Irwing
Dotson, Betty Lou
Douglas, Mansfield, III
Dowdell, Dennis, Jr.
Downes, Dwight
Dungie, Ruth Spigner
Eagle, Arnold Elliott
Early, Robert S.
Eddington, Herbert Hoover
Edmond, Paul Edward

Edwards, Bessie Regina
Edwards, Verba L.
English, Marion S.
Fairley, Wilma
Faucett, Barbara J.
Felder, Tyree Preston, II
Fitzpatrick, Albert E.
Ford, Evern D.
Ford, Hilda Eileen
Foster, LaDoris J.
Franklin, Clarence Frederick
Frazier, Ramona Yancey
Garrett, Guy Thomas, Jr.
Gaston, Linda Saulsby
Gaston, Mack Charles
Giles, Charles Winston
Glover, Diana M.
Gomez, Dennis Craig
Goodwin, Evelyn Louise
Grant, Nathaniel
Greene, Cecil M., Jr.
Gudger, Robert Harvey
Gurley, Helen Ruth
Haley, Earl Albert
Hamer, Judith Ann
Hammond, James A.
Hareld, Gail B.
Harmon, M. Larry
Harris, Eugene Edward
Harris, Robert D.
Harris, Rubie J.
Hatchett, William F. (Bucky)
Hawkins, William Douglas
Hawthorne, Kenneth L.
Hendon, Lea Alpha
Higgins, Ora A.
Higgs, Mary Ann Spicer
Hill, Alfred
Hill, Leo
Holman, Forest H.
Holmes, Leo S.
Holt, Donald H.
Houston, Corinne P.
Hudson, Anthony Webster
Hudson, Jerome William
Hunter, William L.
Isaac, Brian Wayne
Jackson, George
Jackson, Janice Tudy
James, Herbert I.
James, Peggi C.
Johnson, Alvin Roscoe
Johnson, Joseph David
Johnson, Milton D.
Johnson, Warren S.
Jones, Dorinda A.
Jones, John L.
Jones, Lemuel B.
Jones, Willie
Kee, Marsha Goodwin
Kelly, Milton Leo
Killian, Iris Louise
Killion, Theo M.
Kimbrough-Johnson, Donna L.
King, John L.
King, Ruth Allen
Kornegay, William F.
Laisure, Sharon Emily Goode
Lane, Nancy L.
Lawrence, Thomas R., Jr.
Lewis, Aubrey C.
Lewis, Floyd Edward
Lewis, Henry S., Jr.
Lewis, Meharry Hubbard
Lister, David Alfred
Little, Brian Keith
Little, Jean Perkins
London, Roberta Levy
Long, James, Jr.
Long, James S.
Lovelace, Gloria Elaine
Lowry, William E., Jr.
Lumsby, George N.
Mance, John J.
Mardenborough, Leslie A.
Martin, Sylvia Cooke
Mathis, David
McLaughlin, Benjamin Wayne
McLean, Marquita Sheila McLarty
McMickens, Jacqueline Montgomery
Meeks, Larry Gillette
Merenivitch, Jarrow

Mitchell, LeMonte Felton
Montgomery, Earline Robertson
Morrison, Gwendolyn Christine Caldwell
Morrow, Laveine
Mosley, Elwood A.
Moyler, Freeman William, Jr.
Nurse, Robert Earl
Orr, Clyde Hugh
Parker, Joyce Linda
Passmore, William A.
Patterson, Lydia R.
Pearson, Marilyn Ruth
Peoples, Harrison Promis, Jr.
Perkins, Lewis Bryant, Jr.
Perry, Alexis E.
Pitts, Brenda S.
Polk, Eugene Steven, Sr.
Pollard, Percy Edward, Sr.
Pope, Ruben Edward, III
Powell, Kenneth Alasandro
Prewitt, Lena Voncille Burrell
Procter, Harvey Thornton, Jr.
Ramseur, Andre William
Richardson, Ralph H.
Roberts, Ella S.
Robinson, Brenda M.
Robinson, Ronnie W.
Rutledge, Jennifer M.
Salter, Kwame S.
Sandidge, Kanita Durice
Sands, George M.
Saunders, John Edward, III
Schutz, Andrea Louise
Sellers, Theresa Ann
Shawnee, Laura Ann
Shepard, Linda Irene
Smith, Dolores J.
Smith, James, Jr.
Smith, Kevin L.
Smith, LeRoi Matthew-Pierre, III
Smith, Shirley LaVerne
Soliunas, Francine Stewart
Spearman, Larna Kaye
Spicer, Kenneth, Sr.
Stacia, Kevin Maurice
Stallworth, Thomas Fontaine, III
Sutton, Dianne Floyd
Swain, James H.
Taylor, DeForrest Walker
Taylor, Mildred E. Crosby
Thomas, Franklin Whitaker
Thompson, Portia Wilson
Trent, James E.
Tucker, Geraldine Jenkins
Turner, Vivian Vanessa
Vertreace, Walter Charles
Washington, Ava F.
Watkins, William, Jr.
Wells-Davis, Margie Elaine
Westbrook, Elouise
Wilds, Jetie Boston, Jr.
Wiley, Gerald Edward
Wilford, Harold C.
Willacy, Hazel M.
Williams, Annalisa J. Stubbs
Williams, Janice L.
Williams, Melvin
Willingham, Voncile
Wilson, Ernest
Wilson, Robert Lee Miles
Wilson, Wesley Campbell
Winfield, Sinette Johnson
Winstead, Vernon A., Sr.

MANAGEMENT/ ADMINISTRATION— PURCHASING

Banks-Williams, Lula
Campbell, Carlos, Sr.
Carey, Carnice
Connor, Dolores Lillie
Fleming, Vernon Cornelious
Gamble, William F.
Hightower, Willar H., Jr.
Humphrey, Howard John
Jackson, Audrey Nabors
Jackson, Mary
Johnson, Wendy Robin
Kelly, Thomas Maurice, III
Mabrey, Harold Leon
Morehead, Florida Mae
Rakestraw, Kyle Damon
Rhodes, Edward Thomas, Sr.

Smith, Lafayette Kenneth
Strudwick, Lindsey H., Sr.
Sutton, James Carter
Whitest, Beverly Joyce

MANAGEMENT/ ADMINISTRATION— SALES

Adams, Quinton Douglas
Barrett, Matthew Anderson
Burton, Ronald J.
Butler, Michael Eugene
Carey, Pearl M.
Cochran, S. Thomas
Daniels, Curtis A.
Davis, Herman E.
Dixon, Brenda Joyce
Driver, Rogers W.
Feggans, Edward L.
Folks, Leslie Scott
Forde, Fraser Philip, Jr.
Franklin, Percy
Fuller, Norvell Ricardo
Gregory, Bernard Vincent
Hall, Fred, III
Harris, Larry Vordell, Jr.
Harris, Marion Rex
Herring, William F.
Hopkins, Perea M.
Jamison, Lafayette
Johnson, Juliana Cornish
King, Lawrence C.
Lindsay, Horace Augustin
Lloyd, Phil Andrew
Malloy, Helen G.
Marshall, Pluria William, Jr.
McElroy, Alfred Z.
Miley, Debra Charlet
Neal, Joseph C., Jr.
Norman, Clifford P.
Northover, Vernon Keith
Oliver, James L.
Patnett, John Henry
Perry, Lowell W., Jr.
Pinkney, William D.
Ray-Goins, Jeanette
Richmond, Delores Ruth
Roberts, Blanche Elizabeth
Rogers-Grundy, Ethel W.
Ross, Robert P.
Roundtree, Nicholas John
Russell, Kay A.
Sharp, Charles Louis
Shelton, Charles E.
Small, Isadore, III
Smith, Charles
Sterling, Charles A.
Tate, Adolphus, Jr.
Taylor, Cassandra W.
Temple, Oney D.
Tennant, Melvin, II
White, James Louis, Jr.
White, Wendell F.
Wiley, Forrest Parks
Wilkinson, Raymond M., Jr.
Williams, Edward Ellis
Williams, Howard Copeland
Williams, W. Bill, Jr.
Willrich, Emzy James
Wilson, Barbara Jean
Woodbeck, Frank Raymond
Wooten, Carl Kenneth
Wright, Benjamin Hickman
Wynn, Sylvia J.

MANAGEMENT/ ADMINISTRATION— NOT ELSEWHERE CLASSIFIED

See also ASSOCIATION MANAGEMENT; EDUCATIONAL ADMINISTRATION; HEALTH SERVICES ADMINISTRATION; LABOR UNION ADMINISTRATION; SPORTS COACHING/ TRAINING/MANAGING

Adams, Edward B.
Adams, Roscoe H.
Alexander, Preston Paul, Jr.

Allen, DeMetrice Michealle
Allen, George Louis
Allen, Winston Earle
Anderson, Chester R.
Anderson, George A.
Andrews, Adelia Smith
Andrews, William Henry
Apea, Joseph Bennet Kyeremateng
Armstrong, Joseph N.
Arnold, Larkin
Atchison, Calvin O.
Baldwin, John H.
Banks, James S.
Bartow, Jerome Edward
Bass, Marshall Brent
Baugh, Florence Ellen
Baugh, James Edward
Beavers, Nathan Howard, Jr.
Belcher, Paul E.
Bell, Joseph Curtis
Bell, Victory
Benn, Ishmael
Benton, Luther
Bernoudy, James Logan
Berthoud, Kenneth H., Jr.
Black, Frederick Harrison
Blake, James G.
Blue, Daniel W., Jr.
Borges, Lynne MacFarlane
Bostic, James Edward, Jr.
Bowles, Howard Roosevelt
Boyd, Theophilus B., III
Boyd-Foy, Mary Louise
Brewer, Moses
Brown, Carolyn M.
Brown, Courtney Coleridge
Brown, George L.
Brown, Joan P. (Abena)
Brown, Joseph Clifton
Brown, Paul, Jr.
Brown, Paul E. X.
Brown, Robert J., III
Brown, Virgil E., Jr.
Browne, David A.
Bryant, R. Kelly, Jr.
Bryant, Robert E.
Burgess, Joseph Edward
Burroughs, Hugh Charles
Butler, Eula M.
Butler, Patrick Hampton
Cade, Henry
Canty, George
Cargill, Sandra Morris
Carney, Callie I.
Carr, Pressley Rodney
Carson, Lois Montgomery
Carter-McCraw, Carolyn
Cason, Joseph L.
Checole, Kassahun
Chicoye, Etzer
Chubb, Louise B.
Clark, Dave
Clark, Shirley Lorraine
Clarke, Eleanora Norwood
Clarke, Richard V.
Clayton, Mayme Agnew
Clemons, Flenor
Clyburn, John B.
Coleman, Kenneth L.
Connor, James Russell
Cooper, Almeta E.
Copeland, Emily America
Copelin, Sherman Nathaniel, Jr.
Cordova, Renaldo C.
Coverdale, Herbert Linwood
Cranford, Sharon Hill
Crayton, Samuel S.
Crosby-Langley, Loretta
Cummings, Donna Louise
Currie, Eddie L.
Cuyjet-Johnson, Cynthia K.
DaCosta, Sandra Trim
Dandy, Clarence L.
Danforth, Robert L.
Daniels, Clarence A., Jr.
Davis, Alfred C., Sr.
Davis, Arnor S.
Davis, Christine R.
Davis, Doris Ann
Davis, Gene A.
Davis, Jerry, Jr.
Davis, Leonard Harry
Davis, Raoul Andr

Davis, Willie D.
Davison, Edward L.
Dawson, Leonard Ervin
Debro, Joseph Rollins
DeCosta, Herbert Alexander, Jr.
Delpit, Joseph A.
Dilday, William Horace, Jr.
Dillard, Samuel Dewell
Dinkins, David N.
Dixon, Arrington Liggins
Dockett, Alfred B.
Dodson, William Alfred, Jr.
Dorsey, Joseph A.
Douglas, Herbert P., Jr.
DuBose, Clarence R.
Dunham, John L.
Edney, Steve
Evans, Charlotte A.
Fagbayi, Mutiu Olutoyin
Farmer, Bruce Albert
Felker, Joseph B.
Ferrell, Rosie E.
Finney, Leon D., Jr.
Foreman, Doyle
Francisco, Anthony M.
Fraser, Jean Ethel
Gaines, Jaunell Wallace
Gardner, Warren E., Jr.
Gaston, Arthur G., Sr.
George, Zelma Watson
Gibson, Truman K., Jr.
Gilbert, Albert C.
Giles, Waldron H.
Gillam, Isaac Thomas, IV
Gillis, Theresa McKinzy
Gloster, John Gaines
Gomez, Kevin Lawrence Johnson
Gougis, Lorna Gail
Graham, Catherine S.
Grayson, John N.
Green, Lester L.
Greene, Jerome A.
Greene, Joseph David
Gregory, Karl Dwight
Gregory, Wilton D.
Griffin, Gerald
Grimes, William Winston
Guillebeaux, Tamara Elise
Guthrie, Michael J.
Hamilton, Joseph Willard
Hampton, Frank, Sr.
Hampton, Michael Eugene
Harper, Kendrick
Harris, Charles Cornelius
Harris, James Andrew
Harris, John J.
Hawkins, James C.
Hawthorne, Angel L.
Haynes, Frank L., Jr.
Haywood, William H.
Henley, Carl R.
Herndon, Gloria E.
Hicks, William L.
Higgs, Frederick C.
Higgs, Mary Ann Spicer
Hightower, Michael
Hilyard, Tommy Lee
Hinnant, Ollen B.
Hoard, Walter B.
Hobbs, Wilbur E.
Hodges, Lillian Bernice
Hollingsworth, Alfred Delano
Hollins, Robert Alphonso
Hoover, Jesse
Horne, Marvin L. R., Jr.
Horne, Semmion N.
Humphrey, Melvin
Hunt, James, Jr.
Hunt, Samuel D.
Jackson, Audrey Nabors
Jackson, Frederick
James, Carlos Adrian
James, Charles Ford
Jangdharrie, Wycliffe K.
Jefferson, Gary Scott
Jenkins, Andrew
Jenkins, George Arthur, Jr.
Jenkins, Lozelle DeLuz
Johnson, Charles Edward
Johnson, Elmore W.
Johnson, Eunice Walker
Johnson, Guy Charles
Johnson, Hymon T., Jr.
Johnson, Jay (Super Jay)
Johnson, Joshua

Johnson, Nathan
Johnson, Otis Samuel
Johnson, Ronald Cornelius
Johnson, William A., II
Johnson, William T. M.
Johnston, Percy Edward
Jones, Duane L.
Jones, Edith Irby
Jones, Lisa Payne
Jordan, George Washington, Jr.
Kaiser, James Gordon
Kellman, Denis Elliott
Kennedy, Marvin James
Kinard, Helen Madison Marie Pawne
King, Warren Earl
Kinney, Edna M.
Kornegay, Wade M.
Latimer, Steve B.
Lawrence, Henry
Lee, Lena S. King
Lenix-Hooker, Catherine Jeanette
Lewis, Elma I.
Lewis, Matthew, Jr.
Lipscomb, Emanuel A.
Lister, Willa M.
Logan, Willis Hubert
Long, James Alexander
Lovelady, Rueben Leon
Lowe, Hazel Marie
Lyons, Robert P.
Mahin, George E.
Malbroue, Joseph, Jr.
Manley, Audrey Forbes
Manney, William A.
Marshall, Don A.
Marshall, James Andrew
Marshall, William T.
Martin, John Gordon
Massey, Jacquelene Sharp
McCalla, Erwin Stanley
McClenic, David A.
McConner, Dorothy
McKenzie, Eli, Jr.
McKinney, Wade H., III
McKissick, Floyd B.
McKoy, Clemencio Agustino
McLaurin, Daniel Washington
Mesiah, Raymond N.
Minter, Wilbert Douglas, Sr.
Mobley, Stacey J.
Montgomery, Ethel Constance
Morris, Bernard Alexander
Morris, Wayne Lee
Morrison, Rick
Mosee, Jean C.
Moy, Celeste Marie
Murphy, Charles William
Myers, Earl T.
Nash, Thomas
Parker, D. LaVerne
Parker, Doris S.
Parks, Paul
Parnell, John Vaze, III
Parsons, Philip I
Penn-Atkins, Barbara A.
Pennick, Aurie Alma
Peters, Kenneth Darryl, Sr.
Peterson, Harry W.
Pickard, William Frank
Pinkney, John Edward
Plummer, Michael Justin
Price, George Baker
Reeves, Louise (Mrs. Charles Mitchell)
Reid, Oswald Hutton
Rice, Haynes
Riggins, Lester
Rogers, Alfred R.
Rose, Raymond E.
Rouse, Terrie
Rowe, Nansi Irene
Rowe, Richard L.
Rudd, James M.
Ryan, Marsha Ann (nee Neustadter)
Sanders, Isaac Warren
Satterwhite, Frank Joseph
Sims, John Leonard
Sloan, Maceo Archibald
Soaries, Raynes L., Jr.
Spain, Hiram, Jr.
Spears-Jones, Patricia Kay
Stevens, George L.

Stroud, Milton
Sudbury, Leslie G.
Swiggett, Ernest L.
Tate, Sherman E.
Thomas, Booker T.
Thomas, Carl D.
Townsend, Ron
Turner, Wallace E.
Van Ness, Stanley C.
Vaughn, Eugenia Marchelle Washington
Wade, James Nathaniel
Walker, Wendell P.
Ware, Omego John Clinton, Jr.
Washington, Betty Lois
Washington, William Montell
Waterman, Thelma M.
Weatherspoon, J. B.
White, William
White, William J.
Whitmore, Arnold Paul
Wiley, William R.
Williams, Andrew
Williams, Angie Bass
Williams, Arthur Love
Williams, Billy Myles
Williams, Booker T.
Williams, Charles Thomas
Williams, William J.
Wilson, Helen Tolson
Wilson, Henry, Jr.
Winslow, Alfred A.
Wofford, Alphonso
Worsley, George Ira, Jr.
Wright, Carolyn Elaine
Wright, Ebony Narketa

MANUFACTURING— APPAREL
Asma, Thomas M.
Hall, Harold L.
Johnson, Marie Elizabeth
Jones, Ernest
Powell, Gayle Lett
Robinson, Ronnie W.

MANUFACTURING— CHEMICALS AND ALLIED PRODUCTS
Banks, Ronald
Bell, Tommy Lee, III
Carey, Claire Lamar
Davidson, Robert C., Jr.
Haskins, James W., Jr.
Hill, George Hiram
Holland, Laurence H.
Hooker, Douglas Randolf
Johnson, Wendell Louis
Morgan, Haywood, Sr.
Robertson, Oscar Palmer
Tucker, Clarence T.
Wiley, Gerald Edward

MANUFACTURING— DRUGS AND TOILETRIES
Armstrong, Evelyn Walker
Bond, Gladys B.
Bronner, Nathaniel, Sr.
Carter, Edward Earl
Clendeninn, Neil J.
Cottrell, Comer J.
Daniel, Alfred Irwin
Danzy, LeRoy Henry
Foard, Frederick Carter
Johnson, George Ellis
Kennedy, Howard E.
Little, Chester H.
Madison, William L.
McConner, Dorothy
McRae, Ronald Edward
Proctor, Timothy DeWitt
Roberts, Bobby L.

MANUFACTURING— ELECTRICAL/ ELECTRONICS PRODUCTS
Armstrong, Walter
Bellinger, George M.
Bright, Herbert L., Sr.

Butts, Carlyle A.
Campbell, Carlos, Sr.
Carr, Clara B.
Duncanson, Patricia A.
Fletcher, James Andrew
Foster, Edward, Sr.
Gordon, Joseph G., II
Green, Wallace Orpheus
Hall, Harold L.
Harris, Vernon Joseph
Henderson, Henry Fairfax, Jr.
Horton, Larkin, Jr.
Johnson, Andrew
Lee, Forrest A., Sr.

MANUFACTURING— FOOD/BEVERAGES
Abel, Renaul N.
Adams, Albert W., Jr.
Barthwell, Jack Clinton, III
Bell, Travers J., Sr.
Brown, Llewellyn Don
Colbert, Virgis W.
Cummings, Albert R.
Darrell, Betty Louise
David, George F., III
Harmon, M. Larry
Harris, John J.
Haysbert, Raymond Victor, Sr.
Hobson, Patricia Pinnix
Lamar, William, Jr.
Lewis, George Ralph
Llewellyn, James Bruce
Murphy, Michael McKay
Parker, Claude A.
Parsons, Philip I
Riley, Charles Wilbur, Sr.
Roy, Jasper K.
Smith, Dawn C. F.
Sneed, Paula A.
Stewart, Joseph M.
Williams, Charles Thomas

MANUFACTURING— INDUSTRIAL/ COMMERCIAL MACHINERY
Brent, John Clinton, Jr.
Butler, Michael Eugene
Clardy, William J.
Collins, James H.
Dozier, Tillman
Duncan, Malachi, Jr.
Lee, Forrest A., Jr.
Wattley, Thomas Jefferson
Westbrook, Franklin Solomon

MANUFACTURING— METALWORKING INDUSTRIES
Byrd, Lumus, Jr.
Colbert, Virgis W.
Cribbs, Theo, Sr.
Franklin, Clarence Frederick
Freeman, Walter Eugene
Lucas, Charles C.
Newman, Miller Maurice
Pettiford, Steven Douglas

MANUFACTURING— MOTOR VEHICLES
Armstrong, Walter
Brown, Roderick
Callaway, Dwight W.
Charlton, Jack Fields
Coleman, Rodney Albert
Conley, James S., Jr.
Donaldson, Richard T.
Edwards, Dennis L.
Edwards, Verba L.
Farmer, Forest J.
Frost, William Henry
Green, Dennis O.
Hall, Elliott S.
Herring, William F.
Jensen, Renaldo Mario
Kornegay, William F.
Oliver, James L.
Polk, Eugene Steven, Sr.
Reeves, Julius Lee
Richie, Leroy C.

Riley, Rosetta Margueritte
Sanders, Barbara A.
Snyder, Edd G.
Verbal, Claude A.

MANUFACTURING— PAPER AND ALLIED PRODUCTS
Bryant, Clarence W.
McIver, John Douglas
Mitchell, Douglas
Murphy, Michael McKay
Nichols, Nick

MANUFACTURING— NOT ELSEWHERE CLASSIFIED
Bates, Robert E., Jr.
Butler, John O.
Byrd, George Edward
Calhoun, John
Darden, Charles R.
Gaillard, Ralph C., Sr.
Haley, Earl Albert
Hall, Harold L.
Henson, Daniel Phillip, III
Hutt, Monroe L.
Lewis, George Ralph
Long, James, Jr.
Parker, James E.
Pitts, Brenda S.
Rush, Sonya C.
Sharp, Charles Louis
Smith, Nathaniel, Jr.
Terrell, Dorothy
White, Quitman, Jr.
Woodson, Cleveland Coleman, III
Young, Charles Lemuel, Sr.

MARKETING
See ADVERTISING/ PROMOTION; MANAGEMENT/ ADMINISTRATION— ADVERTISING/ MARKETING/PUBLIC RELATIONS

MATHEMATICS
Carroll, Edward M.
Draper, Everett T., Jr.
Dunlap, Estelle Cecilia Diggs
Ellis, Wade
Hedgley, David Rice, Jr.
Houston, Johnny L.
Hughes, Isaac Sunny
Johnson, Martin Leroy
Johnson, Raymond Lewis
King, Calvin E.
King, John Q. Taylor, Sr.
Lahr, Charles Dwight
Littlejohn, Walter L.
Lyons, Charles H.S., Jr.
McLaurin, Freddie Lewis, Jr.
Mickens, Ronald Elbert
Morris, Charles Edward, Jr.
Redrick, Virginia Pendleton
Vance, Irvin E.
Whitlock, Fred Henry
Williams, Willie Elbert

MEDICINE— CARDIOLOGY
Anderson, Arnett Artis
Artis, Andre Keith
Ballard, Kathryn W.
Barnes, Boisey O.
Belton, Edward DeVaughn
Charleston, Gomez, Jr.
Cunningham, Louis Ernest
Daniels, David Herbert, Jr.
Ellis, Tellis B., III
Ferdinand, Keith C.
Gibson, Harris, Jr.
Haywood, L. Julian
Jonas, Ernesto A.
Leacock, Ferdinand S.
Neals, Huerta C
Parker, Jeff, Sr.
Pearson, Stanley E.

Phillips, Lloyd Garrison, Jr.
Revis, Nathaniel W.
Ross, Edward
Sanders, George L.
Saunders, Elijah
Simon, Kenneth Bernard
Smith, Ernest Howard
Yarborough, Dowd Julius, Jr.

MEDICINE— DERMATOLOGY

Alexander, A. Melvin
Anderson, William A.
Boswell, Paul P.
Butler, John Donald
Callender, Valerie Dawn
Claiborne, Earl Ramsey
Clarke, Greta Fields
Curry, Sadye Beatryce
Earles, Rene Martin
Kelly, A. Paul
McDonald, Charles J.
Moore, Milton Donald, Jr.

MEDICINE—INTERNAL MEDICINE

Archer, Juanita A.
Banks, Brenda L.
Baskerville, Samuel J., Jr.
Bogus, Houston, Jr.
Bonner, Charles Douglass
Brown, Leroy Bradford
Brown, Marsha J.
Bryan, Flize A.
Bryant, T. J.
Buckhalter, Emerson R.
Bullock, William Horace
Burton, Leroy Melvin, Jr.
Bynes, Frank Howard, Jr.
Cannon, Elton Molock
Casey, Edmund C.
Chisholm, Joseph Carrel, Jr.
Clift, Joseph William
Cobbs, Winston H.B., Jr.
Cone, Juanita Fletcher
Cook, Charles A.
Cooper, Edward Sawyer
Corbin, Angela Lenore
Cornwell, Edward Eugene, III
Crowe-Underwood, Hollis Jonetta
Cruz, Iluminado Angeles
Cunningham, William E.
Dillard, Martin Gregory
Dixon, Leon Martin
Douglas, Janice Green
Duffoo, Frantz Michel
Edwards, Rupert L.
Ellis, Tellis B., III
Emory, Emerson
England, Rodney Wayne
Epps, Anna Cherrie
Ernst, Reginald H.
Ferdinand, Keith C.
Floyd, Winston Cordell
Ford, James W.
Fraser, Leon Allison
Frazer, Eva Louise
Fredrick, Earl E., Jr.
Freeman, Harold P.
Gavin, James Raphael, III
Hale, Edward Harned
Hamilton, Ross T.
Hardin, Eugene
Harrell, Anthony James
Harris, Charles Albert
Harris, Jean Louise
Harris, Terea Donnelle
Harrison, Robert Walker, III
Hedgepath, Leslie Eugene
Henson, William Francis
Herring, Bernard Duane
Hewlett, Dial, Jr.
Jackson, Benita Marie
Johnson, Cage Saul
Johnson-Crockett, Mary Alice
Jonas, Ernesto A.
Jones, Edith Irby
Kennedy, Karel R.
Kilpatrick, George Roosevelt
King, Wesley A.
Koger, Michael Pigott, Sr.
Lane, George Henry
Lee, Daniel

Levister, Ernest Clayton, Jr.
Lightfoote, William Edward, II
Malveaux, Floyd
McFadden, Gregory L.
Metcalf, Michael Richard
Miller, Russell L., Jr.
Mims, Robert Bradford
Neals, Huerta C
Onyejekwe, Chike Onyekachi
Osborne, William Reginald, Jr.
Palmer, Doreen P.
Palmer, James L. D.
Parker, Jeff, Sr.
Pearson, Stanley E.
Peebles-Meyers, Helen Marjorie
Powell, Charles P.
Pruitt, Fred Roderic
Rankin, Edward Anthony
Reed, James W.
Reese, Milous J.
Render, William H.
Risbrook, Arthur Timothy
Robinson, Clarence G.
Robinson, James Waymond
Rogers, Norman
Sanders, George L.
Scott, C. Waldo
Shelton, Harold Tillman
Shervington, E. Walter
Shirley, Calvin Hylton
Silva, Omega C. Logan
Simmons, Ellamae
Solomon, James Daniel
Somerville, Robert Alston
Standard, Raymond Linwood
Taliaferro, Nettie Howard
Vaughn, William Samuel, III
Walker, Eugene Henry
Walker, Manuel Lorenzo
Walker, Maria Latanya
Watkins, Levi, Jr.
Wheeler, Ronald C.
Wiley, Kenneth LeMoyne
Wilkinson, Robert Shaw, Jr.
Williams, Ernest Y.
Williams, Hugh Hermes
Williams, James Thomas
Wills, James Willard
Woodbury, David Henry
Wright, Jackson Thomas, Jr.
Young, Elroy

MEDICINE— NEUROLOGY

Bates, Ernest Alphonso
Blackwell, Milford
Chapman, William Talbert
French, Joseph Henry
Hyde-Jackson, Maxine Deborah
Jackson, Winston Burleigh
Lightfoote, William Edward, II
Slade, Walter R., Jr.
Summers, David Stewart
Washington, John William
Williams, Ernest Y.
Wyche, Lennon Douglas, Jr.

MEDICINE— OBSTETRICS/ GYNECOLOGY

Arrington, Harold Mitchell
Avery, Herbert B.
Beguesse, Barry Osmund, Jr.
Bivens, Shelia Reneea
Bloomfield, Randall D.
Bridges, James Wilson
Brooks, Todd Frederick
Brown, Kenneth Edward
Burton, Juanita Sharon
Byrd, W. Michael
Campbell, Sylvan Lloyd
Carter, Dorval Ronald
Chatman, Donald Leveritt
Clay, Reuben Anderson, Jr.
Clemendor, Anthony Arnold
Coleman, John B.
Combs, Julius V.
Comvalius, Nadia Hortense
Cooper, Gary T.
Crocker, Cyril L.
Davidson, Ezra C., Jr.
Deane, Robert Armistead
DeSandies, Kenneth Andre

Dickens, Helen Octavia
Dyer-Goode, Pamela Theresa
Earley, Stanley Armstead, Jr.
Edelin, Kenneth C.
Foster, Henry Wendell
Fraser, Rodger Alvin
Freemont, James McKinley
Gaither, Dorothy B.
Garrett, E. Wyman
George, Theodore Roosevelt, Jr.
Gillette, Lyra Stephanie
Gleason, Maurice Francis
Greenfield, Robert Thomas, Jr.
Hawkins, Theodore F.
Hayling, William H.
Hickmon, Ned
Hilliard, Robert Lee Moore
Hopkins, Ernest Loyd
Hurd, Joseph Kindall, Jr.
Hutchins, Francis L., Jr.
Isaac, Joseph William Alexander
Jackson, Leroy Anthony, Jr.
Johnson, James S.
Jones, Sidney Alexander
Jones, William C.
Keemer, Edgar B.
Kernisant, Lesly
Lampley, Edward Charles
Lawrence, George Calvin
Lee, Clifton Valjean
Lowe, Scott Miller
Lucas, Dorothy J.
Mason, Cheryl Annette
Masse', Donald D.
McGruder, Charles E.
Moorhead, Joseph H.
Mortel, Rodrigue
Obayuwana, Alphonsus Osarobo
Pattillo, Roland A.
Phillips, Eugenie Elvira
Pierre, Gerald P.
Powell, Dudley Vincent
Ragland, Michael Steven
Richard, Floyd Anthony
Riddle, Bedford Neal
Roberts, James T. L.
Ross, Curlee
Sanders, Hobart C.
Sirmans, Meredith Franklin
Smiley, William L.
Smith, Cleveland Emanuel
Smith, Gregory Allen
Stringer, Nelson Howard, Jr.
Taylor, Eugene Donaldson
Twigg, Lewis Harold
Tyson, Bertrand Oliver
Weather, Leonard, Jr.
Williams, Robert Lee, Jr.
Wilson, Frank Fredrick, III
Wilson, Nevia Aneice
Wright, Charles H.
Young, N. Louise
Younge, Fitzroy Egerton

MEDICINE— PEDIATRICS

Adams, Billie Morris Wright
Al-Mateen, Kevin Bakeer
Alexander, Drew W.
Allen, Gloria Marie
Beard, Lillian McLean
Betty, Warren Randall
Boatwright, Joseph Weldon
Booker, Clifford R.
Bryant, William Arnett, Jr.
Caison, Thelma Jann
Carter, James P.
Chenevert, Phillip Joseph
Clark, Bettie I.
Clermont, Volna
Cochran, James David, Jr.
Cole, Maceola Louise
Culpepper, Lucy Nell
Cunningham, Verenessa Smalls-Brantley
Curtis, James L.
Davis, James H.
DeLilly, Mayo Ralph, III
Dennard, Turner Harrison
Dennery, Phyllis Armelle
Downing, John William, Jr.
Dummett, Jocelyn Angela
Earley, Stanley Armstead, Jr.
Elam, Harry Penoy

Elders, M. Joycelyn
Epps, Roselyn Payne
Francis, Yvette Fay
Freeman, Lelabelle Christine
French, Joseph Henry
Gaspard, Patrice T.
Gaston, Marilyn Hughes
Gayle-Thompson, Delores J.
Gough, Walter C.
Graham, LeRoy Maxwell, Jr.
Gray, Joseph William
Green, Frederick Chapman
Harden, Robert James
Heins, Henry L., Jr.
Higgins, Clarence R., Jr.
Hudson, Robert L.
Hyatt, Herman Wilbert, Sr.
Ice, Anne-Mare
Jackson, Rudolph Ellsworth
James, Grace M.
Jenkins, Melvin E., Jr.
Kirkpatrick, Garland Penn
Lawrence, Leonard E.
Lawrence, Margaret Morgan
Lewis, Vivian M.
McLean, Zarah Gean
McMorris, Jacqueline Williams
Mutcheruon, James Albertus, Jr.
Nash, Helen E.
Neal, Herman Joseph
Nelson, Artie Cortez
Parker, Walter Gee
Payton, Victor Emmanuel
Penny, Robert
Pettus-Bellamy, Brenda Karen
Phillips, James Lawrence
Poe, Booker
Pope, Isaac S.
Quivers, Eric Stanley
Quivers, William Wyatt, Sr.
Rainsford, Greta M.
Robinson, Carl Dayton
Rogers-Lomax, Alice Faye
Rosser, Pearl (nee Lockhart)
Rosser, Samuel Blanton
Scott, Roland B.
Shaw, Michael Dennis
Shepherd, Saundra Dianne
Simpson, Gregory Louis
Sinnette, Calvin Herman
Smith, Ernest Howard
Sulton, Jacqueline Rhoda
Thomas, Lloyd A.
Vaughn, William Samuel, III
Veal, Yvonnecris Smith
Walker, Maggie L.
Watson, Clyniece Lois
Webb, Zadie Ozella
Williams, Donald H.
Williams, Karen Renee
Williams, Starks J.
Williams, W. Donald
Winfield, Florence F.
Woodfork, Carolyn Amelia
Yancey, Carolyn Lois

MEDICINE— PSYCHIATRY

Adom, Edwin Nii Amalai
Al-Mateen, Cheryl Singleton
Alfred, Dewitt C., Jr.
Bailey, Didi Giselle
Barbour, Joseph Pius, Jr.
Bell, Carl Compton
Bell, James Milton
Biassey, Earle Lambert
Blake, Carlton Hugh
Bowen, Clotilde Dent
Bradshaw, Walter H., Jr.
Bragg, Robert Lloyd
Broomes, Lloyd Rudy
Brown, Ruby Edmonia
Bullock, Samuel Carey
Butler, Neil A.
Butts, Hugh F.
Calhoun, Joshua Wesley
Cambosos, Bruce Michael
Carter, James Harvey
Celestin, Toussaint A.
Charles, Roderick Edward
Chess, Robert Hubert
Clark, Harry W.
Cobbs, Price Mashaw

Comer, James Pierpont
Cox, James Alphonso
Crum, Albert B.
Dabney, David Hodges
Daniels, Joseph
Davis, Amos
Davis, William Selassie, Jr.
DeLeon-Jones, Frank A., Jr.
deMille, Valerie Cecilia
Dennis, Philip H.
Dennis, Rodney Howard
Dent, Aubrey O.
Dickens, Doris Lee (Mrs. Austin L. Fickling)
Diji, Augustine Ebun
Dillihay, Tanya Clarkson
Douglas, Florence M.
Dudley, Calmeze Henike, Jr.
Elam, Lloyd C.
Ellis, Leander Theodore
Emory, Emerson
Fields, Dexter L.
Fisher, Judith Danelle
Flowers, Loma Kaye
Foster, Douglas Leroy
Francis, Richard L.
Franklin, Curtis U., Jr.
Fraser, Alvardo M.
Geary, Clarence Butler
Gill, Troy D.
Glanville, Cecil E.
Greene, Horace F.
Griffith, Ezra Edward
Gullattee, Alyce C.
Harper, Harry Dandridge
Heacock, Don Roland
Hollar, Milton Conover
Horne, June Merideth
Howard, Howell J., Jr.
Hueston, Oliver David
Jefferson, Roland Spratlin
Jones, Billy Emanuel
Jordan, Harold Willoughby
Kendrick, Curtis
King, Joseph Prather
King, Richard Devoid
Lacey, Wilbert, Jr.
Lawrence, Margaret Morgan
Leal, Carol Ann
Lockett, Harold James
Malvin, Reuben L.
Marquez, Camilo Raoul
McMillan, Mae F.
Mehlinger, Kermit Thorpe
Miles, Frederick Augustus
Milliones, Jake
Millis, David Howard
Mitchell, Nelli L.
Mitchell-Bateman, Mildred
Moore, Evan Gregory
Nelson, Artie Cortez
Norris, Donna M.
Oxley, Leo Lionel
Panton, Yvonne B. F.
Parks, Gilbert R.
Parrish, Rufus H.
Pierce, Chester Middlebrook
Pinderhughes, Charles Alfred
Pope, Addison W.
Pope, Henry
Posey, Edward W.
Poussaint, Alvin Francis
Powell, Gloria J.
Rainbow-Earhart, Kathryn Adeline
Reid, F. Theodore, Jr.
Robinson, Herbert A.
Robinson, Muriel F. Cox
Ross, Phyllis Harrison
Sanders, Wendell Rowan
Silcott, William L.
Simpson, Willa Jean
Smith, James Almer, III
Smith, James Almer, Jr.
Smith, Louis
Smith, Quentin T.
Stephens, Herman Alvin
Summers, Timothy
Tardy, Walter J., Jr.
Thomas, John Wesley
Tolbert, Herman Andre
Towns, Eva Rose
Turner, Keith
Tweed, Andre R.

Varner, Harold Hosea, Jr.
Walden, Robert Edison
Welsing, Frances Cress
Wilkinson, Charles Brock
Williams, Melvin Walker
Womack, William Martin
Worrell, Audrey Martiny
Wright, Jane C.

MEDICINE—NOT ELSEWHERE CLASSIFIED
See also VETERINARY MEDICINE

Abdullah, Tariq Husam
Abrahams, Andrew Wordsworth
Adair, Robert A.
Adams, Earl Leonard, III
Adegbile, Gideon Sunday Adebisi
Adeyiga, Olanrewaju Muniru
Agee, Robert Edward
Aikins-Afful, Nathaniel Akumanyi
Al-Mateen, Cheryl Singleton
Alexander, Drew W.
Alexander, Joseph Lee
Alexandre, Journel
Alexis, Carlton Peter
Allen, Browning E., Jr.
Allen, Gladstone Wesley
Allison, James M., Jr.
Allison, W. Anthony
Allman, Marian Isabel
Alston, Casco, Jr.
Alston, Kathy Diane
Ames, Derrick Lee
Anderson, Arnett Artis
Anderson, Barbara Jenkins
Anderson, Benjamin Stratman, Jr.
Anderson, Russell Lloyd
Andrews, Rawle
Angell, Edgar O.
Armstrong, Wiley T.
Artis, Myrle Everett
Atkins, Sam Oillie
Atkinson, Lewis K.
Atkinson, Whittier C.
Austin, Ernest Augustus
Bacon, William Louis
Bailey, Joseph Alexander, II
Ballard, Harold Stanley
Ballard, James M., Jr.
Banfield, Edison H.
Banks, Marshall D.
Banks, William Jasper, Jr.
Barber, Hargrow Dexter
Barclay, Carl Archie
Baron, Neville A.
Bartley, William Raymond
Bass, Leonard Channing
Bataille, Jacques Albert
Bath, Patricia E.
Batties, Paul Terry
Baxter, Charles F., Jr.
Beard, Martin Luther
Beck, Roswell Nathaniel
Bell, James Edward
Benton, Calvin B.
Bernard, Louis Joseph
Berry, Leonidas H.
Best, Sheila Diane
Bills, Johnny Bernard
Birchette-Pierce, Cheryl L.
Bisson, Wheelock Alexander
Blair, Lacy Gordon
Blake, Wendell Owen
Blount, Wilbur Clanton
Bond, Leslie Fee
Booker, James Avery, Jr.
Booker, Thurman D.
Bookert, Charles C.
Boone, Elwood Bernard, Jr.
Boschulte, Joseph Clement
Bowers, Mirion Perry
Bowie, Walter C.
Bowles, James Harold, Sr.
Bowman, James E., Jr.
Bradfield, Horace Ferguson
Brantley, Montague Delano
Brewington, Thomas E., Jr.
Bridges, Alvin Leroy
Brisbane, Samuel Chester
Briscoe, Edward Gans
Britton, Albert B., Jr.

Bronner, James Arthur
Brooks, Marion Jackson
Brooks, Theodore Roosevelt, Jr.
Brown, Alvin Montero
Brown, Calvin Anderson, Jr.
Brown, George Philip
Brown, John Ollis
Brown, Richard Alger
Brown, Richard Osborne
Brown, Webster Clay
Brown, Willie L.
Brown, Zack Bernard
Bryant, Henry C.
Bryant, Jerome Benjamin
Buffong, Eric Arnold
Bugg, George Wendell
Burch, Reynold Edward
Burton, Clarinda Mattea
Burton, John Frederick
Burton, Juanita Sharon
Butler, Benjamin Willard
Butler, Charles H.
Cain, Waldo
Caldwell, Esly Samuel, II
Calhoun, Calvin Lee
Calhoun, Thomas
Callender, Clive Orville
Campbell, Emmett Earle
Campbell, Everett O.
Campbell, Otis, Jr.
Camper, John Emory Toussaint
Cantwell, Kathleen Gordon
Capel, Wallace
Carney, Robert Matthew
Carr, Josephus Cornelius
Carson, Benjamin Solomon, Sr.
Carson, Dwight Keith
Carter, Enrique Delano
Carter, James Earl, Jr.
Carter, Oscar Earl, Jr.
Cauthen, Cheryl G.
Cave, Alfred Earl
Cave, Claude Bertrand
Cave, Herbert G.
Cave, Vernal G.
Chambers, Donald C.
Chapman, Joseph Conrad, Jr.
Chisholm, Reginald Constantine
Chissell, Herbert Garland
Christian, Cora LeEthel
Clanton, Lemuel Jacque
Clark, Charles Warfield
Clark, Granville E., Sr.
Clarke, Angela Webb
Clemmons, Jackson Joshua Walter
Clendeninn, Neil J.
Cobb, W. Montague
Coffey, Gilbert Haven, Jr.
Coggs, Granville Coleridge
Coleman, Arthur H.
Coley, Gerald Sydney
Collier, H. M., Jr.
Collier, Torrence Junis
Conrad, Emmett J.
Cooper, Charles W.
Corbin, Angela Lenore
Cornely, Paul B.
Cornwell, Edward Eugene, III
Cotman, Henry Earl
Counts, George W.
Covington, John Ryland
Craig, Elson L.
Cravens, Thirkield Ellis, Jr.
Crockett, Edward D., Jr.
Crosslin, Evelyn Stocking
Cruzat, Edward Pedro
Cummings, Cary, III
Curry, Norvelle
Curry, Sadye Beatryce
Curry, William Thomas
Cuyjet, Aloysius Baxter
Davenport, James H.
Davidson, Arthur Turner
Davidson, Charles Robert
Davidson, Elvyn Verone
Davis, Bennie L.
Davis, Donna P.
Davis, Matilda Laverne
Dawson, Peter Edward
Dawson, Robert Edward
Debas, Haile T.
Delphin, Jacques Mercier
Dent, Carl Ashley

Diggs, Roy Dalton, Jr.
Dillon, Owen C.
Dixon, Leon Martin
Dockery, Robert Wyatt
Dooley, Wallace Troy
Douglas, Aubry Carter
Douglas, Frederick William
Dowling, Monroe Davis, Jr.
Downer, Luther Henry
Duffoo, Frantz Michel
Dugas, Henry C.
Duke, Leslie Dowling, Sr.
Duncan, Louis Davidson, Jr.
Dungy, Claibourne I.
Dunmore, Lawrence A., Jr.
Durham, Carey Winston
Edmondson, William R., Jr.
Edwards, John W., Jr.
Elam, Harry Penoy
Elliott, Frank George
Ellis, Effie O'Neal
Ellison, Henry S.
English, Perry T., Jr.
Ennix, Coyness Loyal, Jr.
Epps, Charles Harry, Jr.
Eugene, Edward J.
Everett, Benjamin A.
Farmer, Harold E.
Farmer, Robert Clarence
Feemster, John Arthur
Felix, Dudley E.
Fernandez, Lynne Ann
Finlayson, William E.
Fisher, Edward G.
Flowers, William Knox, Jr.
Floyd, Dean Allen
Folk, Frank Stewart
Fonrose, Harold Anthony
Foote, Leonard Hobson Buchanon
Foster, Pearl D.
Foulks, Carl Alvin
Francois, Emmanuel Saturnin
Franklin, Grant L.
Franks, Everlee Gordon
Frazier, Jimmy Leon
Frazier, William James
Freeman, Harold P.
Funderburk, William Watson
Gaines, Oscar Cornell
Gaines, Ray D.
Gaines, Thurston Lenwood, Jr.
Gandy, Roland A., Jr.
Gardner, Jackie Randolph
Garrison, Robert E., Jr.
Gathe, Joseph C
Gayle, Helene D.
Gerald, Melvin Douglas
Gibson, Edward Lewis
Gilmore, Edwin
Gipson, Bernard Franklin, Sr.
Givens, Donovahn Heston
Gladden, Major P.
Gona, Ophelia Delaine
Goodlett, Carlton B.
Goodwin, William Pierce, Jr.
Gordon, Charles Franklin
Gough, Walter C.
Graham, Peter Edgar
Graham, Theodore N.
Granger, Carl Victor
Grant, Kingsley B.
Grate, Isaac, Jr.
Gray, James Howard
Green, Clyde Octavious
Green, James L.
Greene, Charles Rodgers
Greenfield, William Russell, Jr.
Grigsby, Margaret Elizabeth
Grimmond, Arlene Patricia
Gumbs, Oliver Sinclair
Hadley, Howard Alva, Jr.
Hairston, Oscar Grogan
Hakima, Mala'ika
Hall, Charles Harold
Hall, Daniel A.
Hall, Mildred Martha
Hall, Reginald Lawrence
Hall, Robert Joseph
Halyard, Michele Yvette
Ham-Ying, J. Michael
Hamberg, Marcelle R.
Hamilton, Ross T.
Hankins, Andrew Jay, Jr.
Hardaway, Ernest, II

Hardy, Walter S. E.
Harper, Curtis
Harris, Charles Albert
Harris, Harcourt Glenties
Harris, Lorenzo W.
Harris, Mary Styles
Harris, Noah Alan, Sr.
Harris, Norman W., Jr.
Harris, Percy G.
Harris, Ramon Stanton
Harris, Thomas Waters, Jr.
Harrison, A. B.
Hart, Edward E.
Harvey, Harold A.
Hasbrouck, Ellsworth Eugene
Hayes, Wallace S.
Haywood, Bertron Don
Hegeman, Charles Oxford
Henry, Walter Lester, Jr.
Hereford, Sonnie Wellington, III
Herriford, Merle Baird
Hickman, Thomas Carlyle
Hicks, William J.
Higginbotham, Peyton Randolph
Hill, George Calvin
Hill, Julius W.
Hill, Lawrence Thorne
Hill, XaCadene Averyllis
Hills, James Bricky
Hobbs, Joseph
Hoffler, Richard Winfred, Jr.
Hoffman, Joseph Irvine, Jr.
Hollowell, Melvin L.
Holmes, Hamilton Earl
Holmes, Herbert
Holsey, William Fleming, Jr.
Honablue, Richard Riddick
Hopkins, John David
Hosten, Adrian
Hoyte, Arthur Hamilton
Huckaby, Henry Lafayette
Huggins, Clarence L
Hunter, Oliver Clifford, Jr.
Hurd, William Charles
Hutchinson, Carell, Jr.
Hyde, William R.
Inge, Theodore R.
Ingram, LaVerne Dorothy
Ivey, Mark, III
Jackson, Arthur James
Jackson, Arthur Mells, II
Jackson, Donald Clifton, Jr.
Jackson, John Berrye
Jackson, Kenneth William
Jackson, Marvin Alexander
Jackson, Oscar Jerome
Jackson, Seaton J.
JeanBaptiste, Carl S.
Jemison, Mae C.
Jenkins, Carl Scarborough
Jenkins, Melvin E., Jr.
Jessup, Marsha Edwina
Johns, Sonja Maria
Johnson, Charles
Johnson, Gage
Johnson, James Kenneth
Johnson, John Thomas
Johnson, Lectoy Tarlington
Johnson, Melvin Russell
Johnson, Olendruff Lerey
Johnson, Walton Richard
Jones, Alphonzo James
Jones, Furman Madison, Jr.
Jones, George Williams
Jones, Herbert C.
Jones, Herman Harvey, Jr.
Jones, James Edward
Jones, King Solomon
Jones, Miles James
Jones, Percy Elwood
Jones, Vann Kinckle
Jones, William Moses
Jordan, Carl Rankin
Jordan, Wilbert Cornelious
Kendall, Mark Acton Robertson
Kennon, Rozmond H.
Kildare, Michel Walter Andre
Kimbrough, Clarence B.
King, Delutha Harold
King, Howard A. T.
Kirby, Jacqueline
Kisner, Robert Garland
Knaive, Henry Louis
Koger, Linwood Graves, III

LaCaille, Rupert Andrew
Lachman, Ralph Steven
Lamothe, Isidore J.
Latham, Bernice Grant
Lawrence, Montague Schiele
Lee, Daniel
Lee, Edwin Archibald
Leevy, Carroll M.
Lewis, Billie
Lightfoot, William P.
Little, General T.
Little, Robert Benjamin
Little, Ronald Eugene
Lloyd, Raymond Anthony
Logan, Joseph Leroy
Lomax, Walter P.
Long, Henry Andrew
Long, Irene
Lord, Clyde Ormond
Lowman, Isom
Luck, Clyde Alexander, Jr.
Maben, Hayward C., Jr.
Mabrie, Herman James, III
Mackel, Audley Maurice, III
Madison, Stanley D.
Magee, Robert Walter
Maitland, Leo C.
Malekebu, Daniel Sharp
Maloney, Charles Calvin
Manley, Audrey Forbes
Mansfield, Carl Major
Manuel, Louis Calvin
Mapp, John Robert
Mapp, Yolanda I.
Marius, Kenneth Anthony
Marshall, Charles H.
Marshall, John Donald
Marshall, Lewis West, Jr.
Martin, Ernest Douglass
Martin, James Tyrone
Mason, Gilbert Rutledge
Mathis, Elmertha Burton
Matory, William Earle, Jr.
Matthews, Merritt Stewart
Mays, Edward Everett
Mays, William O.
McCall, Marion G., Jr.
McCants, Odell
McCuiston, Stonewall, Jr.
McFadden, Frederick C., Jr.
McFadden, Samuel Wilton
McKeel, Thomas Burl
McKinney, David Walter, III
McKnight, Lancess
McLaughlin, John Belton
McLaurin, Jasper Etienne
McMillan, Horace James
McSwain, David L.
McWhorter, Millard Henry, III
Meacham, Henry W.
Means, Kevin Michael
Mencer, Ernest James
Miles, Carlotta G.
Miller, Dennis Weldon
Miller, Earl Vonnidore
Miller, Laurence Brent
Millett, Knolly E.
Millis, David Howard
Milton, Samuel Byron
Minton, Russell Farbeux, Sr.
Mitchell, Augustus William
Mitchell, Eric Ignatius
Mitchell, Joseph Rudolph
Mobley, Joan Thompson
Moore, Donald Torian
Moore, Edwin G.
Moore, Evan Gregory
Moore, Hiram Beene
Moore, Marcellus Harrison
Moore, Oscar James, Jr.
Moore-Stovall, Joyce
Moragne, Rudolph
Morgan, Eldridge Gates
Mosee, Jean C.
Mosley, Edward R.
Motley, Ronald Clark
Mouton, Charles Peter
Mowatt, Oswald Victor
Moye, Carla Johnson
Murphy, Charles A.
Murray, Robert F.
Murray, Winston Lloyd, Jr.
Myers, Debra J.
Myers, Frances Althea

Nash, Daniel Alphonza, Jr.
Neal, Alimam Butler
Neal, Green Belton
Nelson, Robert Wales, Sr.
Newborn, Odie Vernon, Jr.
Newsome, Cola King
Newton, Robin Caprice
Nixon, Glenford Delacy
Noel, Patrick Adolphus
Norman, Calvin Haines
Norman, John C.
Norris, James Ellsworth Chiles
Northcross, David C.
Organ, Claude H., Jr.
Orr, Earl Lawton
Osibin, Willard S.
Ottley, Neville
Owens, O'dell M.
Oxley, Lucy Orintha
Ozim, Francis Taiino
Palmer, Edward
Parker, Averette Mhoon
Patin, Joseph Patrick
Patterson, Elizabeth Ann
Pattillo, Roland A.
Patton, Curtis L.
Penny, Robert
Perara, Mitchell Mebane
Perry, Frank Anthony
Perry, Harold
Perry, Larry Steven
Peterson, Carl M.
Petioni, Muriel M.
Phillips, James Lawrence
Phillips, Lloyd Garrison, Jr.
Pierce, Frederick Watson
Pierce, Gregory W.
Pierce, Raymond O., Jr.
Pierre-Louis, Constant
Pinckney, Theodore R.
Pinkney, Dove Savage
Piper, Paul J.
Piper, W. Archibald
Polk, Charles Carrington
Pollard, Emily Frances
Powell, Thomas Francis A.
Powers, Runas, Jr.
Preston, Swanee H. T., Jr.
Primm, Beny Jene
Prophete, Beaumanoir
Pryor, Julius, Jr.
Quarles, Joseph James
Quigless, Milton Douglas, Jr.
Quivers, William Wyatt, Sr.
Rabb, Maurice F.
Raiford, Roger Lee
Raine, Charles Herbert, III
Rains, Horace
Randolph, Bernard Clyde
Rawls, George H.
Reid, Edith C.
Reid, Roberto Elliott
Rhetta, Helen L.
Rhodes, Robert Shaw
Richard, Arlene Castain
Richard, Henri-Claude
Richardson, Madison Franklin
Richardson, Paul E. L.
Ridges-Horton, Lee Esther
Riggs, Harry L.
Riley, Emile Edward
Rivers, Robert Joseph, Jr.
Roberts, James E.
Robey, Louis Reed
Robinson, Lawrence D.
Robinson, Luther D.
Robinson, William Andrew
Rogers, Bernard Rousseau
Rogers, Norman
Rolle, Albert Eustace
Rosemond, John H.
Rosemond, Lemuel Menefield
Ross, Curlee
Ross, William Alexander Jackson
Rosser, Samuel Blanton
Roux, Vincent J.
Ruffin, Richard D.
Saffold, Oscar E.
Sampson, Calvin Coolidge
Sampson, Robert R.
Satcher, David
Saunders, Edward Howard
Saunders, Meredith Roy
Savage, Edward W., Jr.
Scipio, Laurence Harold

Scott, Deborah Ann
Scott, James F., Sr.
Scott, Leonard Lamar
Scott, Leonard Stephen (Steve)
Scott, Linzy, Jr.
Scott, Timothy Van
Scott, Veronica J.
Scott, Wesley E.
Sears, Bertram E.
Sessoms, Frank Eugene
Seymour, Laurence Darryl
Shanks, William Colemon, Jr.
Shelby, Reginald W.
Shelton, Lee Raymond
Shirley, J. L., Sr.
Shropshire, Claudius Napoleon, Jr.
Silva, Omega C. Logan
Simmons, Arthur Hugh
Simmons, Earl Melvin
Simpson, Dazelle Dean
Sims, Edward Hackney
Singleton, James LeRoy
Skeene, Linell De-Silva
Skerrett, Philip Vincent
Slaughter, Peter
Smiley, Karen Jo
Smith, Edward Nathaniel, Jr.
Smith, Elmer G., Jr.
Smith, Freddie A.
Smith, Henry Thomas
Smith, Joe Elliott
Smith, John Arthur
Smith, Oswald Garrison
Smith, Robert
Smith, Robert J.
Speller, Charles K.
Speller, J. Finton
Spigner, Donald Wayne
Staggers, Frank Eugene
Stanmore, Roger Dale
Starling, John Crawford
Stent, Theodore R.
Stephens, George Benjamin Davis
Stewart, Carl L.
Stewart, William E. L.
Stinson, Joseph McLester
Strange, Gerald Leon
Strayhorn, Earl Carlton
Strickland, Frederick William, Jr.
Stroman, Cheryl Delores
Strong, Douglas Donald
Strudwick, Warren James
Stubbs, George Winston
Stull, Virginia Elizabeth
Summers, David Stewart
Suneja, Sudhir Kumar
Swan, Lionel F.
Swiner, Connie, III
Swinney, T. Lewis
Syphax, Burke
Taylor, Paul David
Taylor, Scott Morris
Taylor, Veronica C.
Teekah, George Anthony
Terry, Charles C.
Terry, John William
Thatcher, Harold W.
Thigpen, Calvin Herritage
Thomas, Audria Acty
Thomas, Edward P.
Thomas, Harry Lee
Thomas, Spencer
Thomas-Richards, Jos Rodolfo
Thompson, Deborah Maria
Thompson, Eugene Edward
Thompson, Frank William
Thompson, John Wesley
Thompson, Lloyd Earl
Thompson, Willie Edward
Thomson, Gerald Edmund
Thorne, Cecil Michael
Thornhill, Herbert Louis
Thurston, Roger Grave
Tilley, Frank N.
Tipton, Dale Leo
Tollett, Charles Albert
Toussaint, Rose-Marie
Towns, Myron B., Jr.
Tucker, Anthony
Tucker, Billy J.
Tunstall, June Rebecca
Turk, Alfred J., II
Turner, Clifton B.

Tyson, Bertrand Oliver
Vaughn, Clarence B.
Vaughn, William Samuel, III
Veney, Herbert Lee
Vester, Terry Y.
Vines, Benjamin Glenn
Wade, Eugene Henry-Peter
Waite, Norma Lillia
Walden, Emerson Coleman
Walker, G. Edward
Walker, Mark Lamont
Walker, Watson Herchael
Walker, William Paul, Jr.
Walters, Curla Sybil
Walton, Tracy Matthew, Jr.
Washington, Johnnie M.
Watts, Charles Dewitt
Weaver, John Arthur
Weaver, Joseph D.
Webb, Zadie Ozella
Weddington, Wayne
West, Charles Fremont
Whaley, Joseph S.
White, Augustus A., III
White, Dezra
White, Garland Anthony
White, Sandra LaVelle
Williams, Arthur Love
Williams, David George
Williams, Henry R.
Williams, Henry S.
Williams, Herbert Lee
Williams, Homer LaVaughan
Williams, Joseph Henry
Williams, Robert H.
Williams, Sandra Roberts
Williams, Sterling B., Jr.
Williams, Theopolis Charles
Willis, Isaac
Willock, Marcelle Monica
Willoughby, Winston Churchill
Wilson, George G.
Wilson, John T., Jr.
Wilson, Marvin H.
Wilson, Robert Stanley
Wilson, William E.
Wiltz, Philip G., Jr.
Wise, C. Rogers
Wise, Henry A., Jr.
Wood, Lawrence Alvin
Wood, Michael H.
Woodall, John Wesley
Woodard, A. Newton
Woodbury, Margaret Clayton
Woodford, Hackley Elbridge
Wooldridge, Thomas Jerry
Word, Parker Howell
Worrell, Richard Vernon
Wright, Jane C.
Wright, Rickey
Wyche, Melville Q., Jr.
Yancey, Asa G., Sr.
Yarboro, Theodore Leon
York, Russel Harold
Young, Coleman Milton, III
Young, Joyce Howell
Young, Lionel Wesley
Young, Watson A.
Zimmerman, Eugene

METEOROLOGY

Reed, Theresa Greene
Sarreals, E. Don
Young, Edward Hiram, Jr.

MICROBIOLOGY
See **BIOLOGY/ MICROBIOLOGY**

MILITARY—AIR FORCE

Armour-Lightner, Rosetta Amelia
Banton, William C., II
Bartley, William Raymond
Belcher, Lewis, Jr.
Bluford, Guion Stewart, Jr.
Carroll, Juanitaelizabeth P.
Crawford, Nathaniel, Jr.
Cushman, Vera F.
Day, Daniel Edgar
Driver, Elwood T.
Duncan, John C., Jr.

Emanuel, James Andrew
Farrow, Willie Lewis
Gregory, Frederick Drew
Hargraves, William Frederick, II
Harris, Frank
Harris, Maurice A.
Hopper, John Dowl, Jr.
Jackson, Fred H., Jr.
Johnson, Timothy Julius, Jr.
Kelly, James Johnson
Keyes, Alfred Lee
Levell, Edward, Jr.
Martin, Curtis Jerome
McAlister, Joe Michael
Mercer, Arthur, Sr.
Miles, Dorothy Marie
Moorman, Holsey Alexander
Morgan, John Paul
Person, Leslie Robin
Pogue, Richard James
Powers, Winston Donald
Randolph, Bernard P.
Ray, Richard Rex
Richards, Edward A.
Rutland, William G.
Showell, Milton W.
Vaughn, Clarence B.
Vivians, Nathaniel Roosevelt
Voorhees, John Henry
Wallace, Lewis S., Jr.
Ward, C. Douglas
Wertz, Andrew Walter, Sr.
White, Harold Clark Mitchelle
Williams, Dennis
Williams, Walker Richard, Jr.
Wingo, A. George
Worthey, Richard E.
Wright, Rickey

MILITARY—ARMY

Bailey, Lawrence R., Sr.
Barnes, Wilson Edward
Baskett, Kenneth Gerald
Becton, Julius Wesley, Jr.
Bogus, Houston, Jr.
Brown, Dallas C., Jr.
Brown, Diana Johnson
Brown, Stanley Donovan
Burton, Charles Howard, Jr.
Cadoria, Sherian Grace
Calbert, William Edward
Cromartie, Eugene Rufus
Day, Daniel Edgar
Dozier, Morris, Sr.
Early, Paul David
Emanuel, James Andrew
Fletcher, Tyrone P.
Forte, Johnie, Jr.
Gaines, Oscar Cornell
Garrett, Louis Henry
Gaskill, Robert Clarence
Gorden, Fred A.
Graves, Jerrod Franklin
Hanford, Craig Bradley
Hawkins, John Russell, III
Heyward, James Oliver
Hogans, William Robertson, III
Jacob, Willis Harvey
Johnson, Benjamin Washington
Johnson, Leroy
Johnson-Brown, Hazel Winfred
Kennedy, Marvin James
Keyes, Alfred Lee
King, John Q. Taylor, Sr.
Lane, Julius Forbes
Mack, Faite
Martin, John Thomas
McDaniel, Charles William
McGrady, Eddie James
Moore, Gary E.
Paige, Emmett, Jr.
Powell, Colin L.
Redrick, Virginia Pendleton
Reeves, Lucius V.
Richie, Sharon Ivey
Robinson, Roscoe, Jr.
Settles, Carl E.
Shannon, John W.
Sheffey, Fred C.
Smith, Elaine Marie
Smith, Isaac Dixon
Spencer, Anthony Lawrence
Taylor, Clarence B.
Turner, Joseph Ellis

Webster, Cecil Ray
Williams, Harvey Dean
Williams, Robert D., Sr.
Wilson, Wilson W.

MILITARY—COAST GUARD

Carey, James William

MILITARY—MARINE CORPS

Cooper, Jerome Gary
Hollowell, Johnny Laveral
Huff, Edgar R.
Nunn, Robinson S.
Paulk, Bernice Herring
Sims, William

MILITARY—NATIONAL GUARD

Bryant, Cunningham C.
Bryant, William Henry, Jr.
Campbell, Carrol Nunn
Folk, Frank Stewart
Langford, Victor C., III
Leggette, Lemire
Meeks, Cordell David, Jr.
Moorman, Holsey Alexander
Sherman, Thomas Oscar, Jr.

MILITARY—NAVY

Brown, Clarence William
Carter, William Thomas, Jr.
Cochran, Donnie L.
Davidson, Fred, III
Davis, Walter J., Jr.
Gaston, Mack Charles
Goodman, Robert O., Jr.
Gravely, Samuel L., Jr.
Green, Consuella
Hacker, Benjamin Thurman
Ingram, LaVerne Dorothy
Johnson, Michael Kevin
Johnson, Wendell Norman, Sr.
Lawhorn, Robert Martin
Lomax, Dervey A.
London, Eddie
Massie, Samuel Proctor
McCallum, Walter Edward
Morgan, Robert, Jr.
Reason, Joseph Paul
Saunders, Kenneth Paul
Smith, Millard, Jr.
Taylor, Ernest Norman, Jr.
Tzomes, Chancellor Alfonso (Pete)
Webb, Schuyler Cleveland
Williams, Wilbert Edd
Wright, Roosevelt R., Jr.

MILITARY—NOT ELSEWHERE CLASSIFIED

Agee, Robert Edward
Bolden, Charles Frank, Jr.
Brooks, Leo Austin
Cade, Alfred Jackal
Cheatham, Della M.
Clark, Major
Dryden, Charles Walter
Esquerre, Jean Roland
Garrett, Cain, Jr.
Hester, Arthur C.
Howard, Calvin Johnson
Johnson, Jesse J.
Lewis, Robert Louis
Noble, Beulah Catherine (nee Lumpkin)
Robinson, Brenda Evette
Robinson, William
Stuart, Ivan I.
Wallace, Lewis S., Jr.
Waller, Calvin A.H.
Ward, C. Douglas
Williams, James E., Jr.

MINING/QUARRYING
See also ENGINEERING—
MINING
Barnes, N. Kurt
Graves, Sherman Teen
Lawrence, Philip Martin

MODELING
Johnson, Cleo M.
Kilgore, Twanna Debbie
Moore, Annie Jewell
Rentie, Frieda

MORTUARY SERVICES
Bourne, Beal Vernon, II
Brown, Clark S.
Brown, James Monroe
Charbonnet, Louis, III
Chase, Arnett C.
Cofer, James Henry
Colin, George H.
Dorsey, Leon D., Sr.
Durgan, Andrew James
Edwards, Claybon Jerome
Estes, John M., Jr.
Faison, John W.
Fielding, Herbert Ulysses
Ford, James W.
Fritz, James B.
Fritz, Moses Kelly
Gachette, Louise Foston
Gaines, Samuel Stone
Garner, Lon L.
Greene, Charles Andre
Greene, Nelson E., Sr.
Grier, Arthur E., Jr.
Haile, Richard H.
Hampton, Willie L.
Hankins, Freeman
Harvey, Clarie Collins
Hickson, Eugene, Sr.
Higgins, Bennett Edward
Holmes, Wendell P., Jr.
Jefferson, Clifton
Jenkins, Augustus G., Jr.
Johnson, I. S. Leevy
Jones, William Henry, Jr.
King, John Q. Taylor, Sr.
King, Nettie (nee Scott)
Leake, Willie Mae James
Lewis, J. B., Jr.
Lightner, Clarence E.
Manigault, Walter William
Mays, Carrie J.
Monk, Edd Dudley
Montgomery, Fred O.
Morton, Margaret E.
Powell, Robert E.
Singleton, Leroy, Sr.
Smith, Frances C.
Stone, William T.
Stovall, Mary Kate
Swanson, O'Neil D.
Warner, Isaiah H.
Watkins, Willie S., III
Williams, Falba W.
Williams, John Earl
Williams, Napoleon
Wilson, Charles Stanley, Jr.

MOTOR VEHICLE INDUSTRY
See MANUFACTURING—
MOTOR VEHICLES;
RETAIL TRADE—MOTOR
VEHICLES, PARTS, AND
SERVICES; WHOLESALE
TRADE—MOTOR
VEHICLES AND PARTS

MOVING SERVICES
See TRANSPORTATION/
MOVING SERVICES

MUSEUM CURATORSHIP
See GALLERY/MUSEUM
CURATORSHIP

MUSIC—COMPOSING/ SONGWRITING
Albam, Manny
Alexander, James W.
Ali, Rashied
Anderson, Thomas Jefferson
Arkansaw, Tim
Artis, Anthony Joel
Ashford, Nicholas
Atkins, Russell
Atkins, Sam Oillie
Bagby, Rachel L
Baker, Anita
Baker, David Nathaniel, Jr.
Beasley, Victor Mario
Bell, S. Aaron
Bell, Thom R.
Benson, George
Biggs, Cynthia DeMari
Brown, James
Brown, Tyrone W.
Carter, Betty
Carter, Warrick L.
Chapman, Tracy
Coleman, George Edward
Coleman, Ornette
Criner, Clyde
Crouch, Andrae
Davis, Miles Dewey
Davis, Nathan T.
Davis, Richard
Davis, Willie James
Dixon, William R.
Duke, George M. (Dawilli Gonga)
Eubanks, Rachel Amelia
Fischer, William S.
Ford, Fred, Jr.
Foster, Frank B., III
Garner, Charles
Golightly, Lena Mills
Gordy, Berry, Jr.
Green, Al
Greene, Joseph P.
Hairston, Jester
Hampton, Lionel Leo
Hancock, Herbert Jeffrey
Harris, Robert Allen
Hawkins, Erskine Ramsay
Hayes, Isaac
Hendricks, Jon
Hill, Andrew William
Jackson, C. Bernard
Jacquet, Jean Baptiste Illinois (Illinois)
James, Rick
Jaye, Miles
Jeffers, Jack
Johnson, Albert J.
Johnson, Willie
Jones, Quincy
Kay, Ulysses
Kennedy, Joseph J., Jr.
Kimble, Bettye Dorris
Lewis, Ramsey Emanuel, Jr.
MacDonald, Ralph
McFaddin, Theresa Garrison
McGhee, Walter Brownie
McNeil, DeeDee
Mitchell, Grover
Moore, Carman Leroy
Moore, Undine Smith
Morgan, Meli'sa (Joyce)
Moseley, James Orville B.
Ousley, Harold Lomax
Owens, Jimmy
Parker, Ray, Jr.
Pate, John W., Sr. (Johnny)
Price, John Elwood
Qamar, Nadi Abu
Richie, Lionel Brockman
Roach, Max
Robinson, Gertrude Rivers
Rudd-Moore, Dorothy
Russell, George A.
Sabree, Clarice Salaam
Scott-Heron, Gil
Sherow, Don Carl
Simone, Nina
Simpson, Valerie
Smalls, Charlie E.
Smith, Hale
Tillis, Frederick C.
Tyner, McCoy
Vandross, Luther R.

Walden, Narada Michael
Wheeler, Harold
White, Barry
White, Maurice
Williams, Earl
Wilson, Olly W.
Wooding, Samuel David
Woods, Philip Wells

MUSIC— CONDUCTING/ DIRECTING
Abdul-Malik, Ahmed H.
Albam, Manny
Anderson, Thomas Jefferson
Bagley, Peter B. E.
Baker, David Nathaniel, Jr.
Barefield, Edward Emanuel
Bland, Edward
Burnim, Mellonee Victoria
Byard, John Arthur, Jr.
Crawford, Dock D., Jr.
Davis, Arthur D.
Davis, Willie James
DePreist, James Anderson
Freeman, Paul D.
Greene, Joseph P.
Hairston, Jester
Hampton, Edwin Harrell
Harris, Carl Gordon
Harris, Margaret R.
Harris, Robert Allen
Harvey, Raymond
Hawkins, Erskine Ramsay
Hurte, Leroy E.
Jackson, Isaiah Allen
Jeffers, Jack
Johnson, Randall Morris
Kirby, Money Alian
Kirk-Duggan, Cheryl Ann
Kyle, Genghis
Lampley, Calvin D.
Lynch, Robert D.
Mabrey, Marsha Eve
McBrier, Vivian Flagg
McGehee, Maurice Edward
Mobley, Charles Lamar
Moore, Carman Leroy
Moore, Kermit
Murray, David Keith
Pate, John W., Sr. (Johnny)
Pettaway, Charles, Jr.
Porter, Karl Hampton
Robertson, Jon H.
Smalls, Charlie E.
Traylor, Rudolph A.
Treadwell, Fay Rene Lavern
Walker, Charles E.
Ward, Daniel
Wheeler, Harold
White, Clayton Cecil
White, Don Lee
Wilkins, Thomas Alphonso
Womack, Robert W., Sr.

MUSIC— INSTRUMENTAL
Abdul-Malik, Ahmed H.
Adams, Armenta Estella (Armenta Adams Hummings)
Alexander, Roland E.
Ali, Rashied
Allen, William Duncan
Arties, Walter Eugene, III
Barefield, Edward Emanuel
Benson, George
Benson, James Russell
Berry, Frederick Joseph
Bradley, Jack Carter
Braithwaite, James Roland
Broach, S. Elizabeth
Brown, Tyrone W.
Burton-Lyles, Blanche
Cheatham, Adolphus A. (Doc)
Clouden, LaVerne C.
Coleman, George Edward
Coleman, Ornette
Coltrane, Alice Turiya
Cray, Robert
Crutcher, Ronald Andrew
Cumbo, Marion William
Curson, Theodore
Daniels, Jerry Franklin

Davis, Miles Dewey
Davis, Richard
Dickerson, Lowell Dwight
Downing, Alvin Joseph
Duke, George M. (Dawilli Gonga)
Elliott, Anthony Daniel, III
Eubanks, Rachel Amelia
Ewing, John R.
Ferguson, St. Julian
Ford, Fred, Jr.
Foster, Frank B., III
Francis, David Albert (Panama)
Gaines, Leslie Doran (Bubba)
Gholson, General James
Gill, Samuel A.
Graham, Larry, Jr.
Griffin, Johnny
Hampton, Edwin Harrell
Hampton, Lionel Leo
Handy-Miller, D. Antoinette
Hanna, Cassandria H.
Hanna, Roland
Harris, Margaret R.
Hawkins, Erskine Ramsay
Haynes, Eugene, Jr.
Heath, James E.
Henry, Frank Haywood
Hill, Andrew William
Hooker, John Lee
Horn, Lawrence Charles
Hunter, Edwina Earle
Hurd, David James, Jr.
Hurd, James L. P.
Hurd, William Charles
Jackson, Milton (Bags)
Jacquet, Jean Baptiste Illinois (Illinois)
Jamal, Ahmad
Jeffers, Jack
Joans, Ted
Jones, Harold M.
Kennedy, Anne Gamble
Kennedy, Joseph J., Jr.
Kennedy, Matthew W.
King, Clarence Maurice, Jr.
Kyle, Genghis
Lewis, Ramsey Emanuel, Jr.
Marsalis, Branford
Marsalis, Wynton
May, Veronica Stewart
McClain, Marlon L.
McCoy, Frank Milton
McGhee, Walter Brownie
McLean, John Lenwood
Meriwether, Roy Dennis
Mitchell, Grover
Moore, Kermit
Newson, Roosevelt, Jr.
Nichols, Nichelle
Ousley, Harold Lomax
Owens, Jimmy
Pace, Kay Robertine
Patterson, Willis Charles
Peterson, Oscar Emmanuel
Pettaway, Charles, Jr.
Pilot, Ann Hobson
Pointer, Noel
Preston, Edward Lee
Qamar, Nadi Abu
Roach, Max
Sabree, Clarice Salaam
Saunders, Theodore D. (Red)
Shepherd, Berisford (Shep)
Simmons, Clayton Lloyd
Summer, Donna Andrea
Swindell, Warren C.
Tate, Grady B.
Taylor, Herman Daniel
Taylor, William Edward
Terry, Saunders
Thompson, Marcus Aurelius
Traylor, Rudolph A.
Tyner, McCoy
Wade, Bruce L.
Walden, Narada Michael
Walton, Ortiz Montaigne
Washington, Oscar D.
Watson, Johnny (Johnny Guitar Watson)
Watts, Andre
White, Donald Edward
Williams, Earl
Winston, Sherry E.
Woods, Philip Wells

MUSIC—VOCAL
Abbott, Gregory
Abdul, Raoul
Albert, Donnie Ray
Allen, Betty (Mrs. R. Edward Lee III)
Allen, Debbie
Arnold, David
Bailey, Mildred T.
Baker, Anita
Battle, Kathleen
Belafonte, Harry
Brown, Bobby
Brown, James
Bumbry, Grace Ann
Cade, Walter, III
Caesar, Shirley
Capers, Eliza Virginia
Carroll, Diahann
Carter, Betty
Carter, Nell
Cater, Anna L.
Chapman, Tracy
Clark, Rosalind K.
Cleveland, James
Clouden, LaVerne C.
Cole, Natalie
Collins, Maurice A.
Costen, Melva Wilson
Crouch, Andrae
Dale, Clamma Churita
Daniels, Jerry Franklin
D'Arby, Terence Trent
Davis, Billy, Jr.
Davis, Clifton D.
Davis, Sammy, Jr.
Davy, Gloria
Dobbs, Mattiwilda
Duncan, Robert Todd
Dyson, Ronnie
Estes, Simon Lamont
Falana, Lola
Fitzgerald, Ella
Flack, Roberta
Franklin, Aretha
Gamble, Kenneth
Grandison, Earl Michael
Grist, Reri
Hairston, Jester
Haley, Johnetta Randolph
Hall, Delores
Hanna, Cassandria H.
Hayes, Isaac
Hendricks, Barbara
Hendricks, Jon
Holliday, Jennifer
Hooker, John Lee
Horne, Lena
Hoskins Clark, Tempy M.
Houston, Whitney
Jackson, Janet
Jackson, Michael
Jackson, Spencer
Jarreau, Al
Jaye, Miles
Jenkins, Ella Louise
Junior, Samella E. (nee Walton)
Khan, Chaka
King, Charles E.
Kirk-Duggan, Cheryl Ann
Kitt, Eartha Mae
Knight, Bubba
Knight, Gladys Maria
LaBelle, Patti
Laine, Cleo
Marrs, Stella
Martin, Sallie
Mathis, Johnny
Mayes, Doris Miriam
Maynor, Dorothy
Maynor, Kevin Elliott
McCampbell, Ray Irvin
McCoo, Marilyn
McFerrin, Robert
McFerrin, Sara Elizabeth Copper
McNair, Barbara
McNeil, DeeDee
McRae, Carmen
Merriweather, Thomas L.
Mills, Donald
Mills, Herbert
Mills, John
Mills, Stephanie
Mitchell, Leona

Rice, Linda Johnson
Richards, Roosevelt
Robinson, Jack E.
Ruffin, James E.
Sales, Richard Owen
Savage, Augustus A.
Scott, Cornelius Adolphus
Sengstacke, John H.
Sengstacke, Whittier Alexander,
 Sr.
Sewell, Luther Joseph
Shelton, S. McDowell
Shepard, Ray A.
Smith, Barbara
Smith, Herald Leonydus
Smith, Norman Raymond
Staats, Florence Joan
Swan, Lionel F.
Talbot, Gerald Edgerton
Tandy, Mary B.
Thomas, Benjamin
Thomas, Patricia O'Flynn
Thompson, Charles H.
Thrower, Charles S.
Vest, Donald Seymour, Sr.
Vest, Hilda Freeman
Washington, James A.
Waterman, Homer D.
Waters, Wimbley, Jr.
Wells, Billy Gene
White, Nathaniel B.
White, Randolph Louis
Whitworth, Claudia Alexander
Williams, Booker T.
Williams, Clarence Earl, Jr.
Willis, Frank B.
Winslow, Eugene
Woods, Jane Gamble
Wright, Joseph H., Jr.
Young, Albert James
Young, Ollie L.

PRODUCING/ DIRECTING (PERFORMING ARTS)
See DIRECTING/ PRODUCING (PERFORMING ARTS)

PROMOTION
See ADVERTISING/ PROMOTION

PSYCHOLOGY
Abston, Nathaniel, Jr.
Adams, Clarence Lancelot, Jr.
Adams, Jean Tucker
Anderson, James Alan
Andrews, James E.
Appleby-Young, Sadye Pearl
Bain, Erlin
Baker, Joel L.
Barrett, Ronald Keith
Bell, Robert L.
Bennett, Maisha B. H.
Block, Carolyn B.
Bouie, Merceline
Bowman, Phillip Jess
Boyd, Miller W., Jr.
Brookes, Bernard L.
Brown, Craig Vincent
Brown, Mortimer
Burlew, Ann Kathleen
Burns, Felton
Butler, Marjorie Johnson
Byrd, Katie W.
Carey, Patricia M.
Carter, Lamore Joseph
Carter, Wesley Byrd
Chisholm, June Faye
Chisum, Gloria Twine
Clark, Kenneth Bancroft
Clifford, Paul Ingraham
Coleman, Melvin D.
Coleman, Vicki Doree
Cooper, Matthew N.
Cooper-Lewter, Nicholas Charles
Courtney, Cassandra Hill
Coverdale, Herbert Linwood
Curry, Mitchell L.
Daly, Frederica Y.

Daniel, Jessica Henderson
Davis, Arthur D.
Davis, Larry Earl
Dunn, Marvin
Early, Robert S.
Edwards, Thomas Oliver
Eleazer, George Robert, Jr.
Forster, Cecil R.
Foye-Eberhardt, Ladye Antoinette
Francois, Theodore Victor
Frazier, Leon
Froe, Otis David
Gardner, LaMaurice H.
Gary, Melvin L.
Gaston, Arnett W.
Gibbs, Jewelle Taylor
Gibson, Ralph Milton
Gilbert, Christopher
Goodrich, Thelma E.
Gray-Little, Bernadette
Green, Charles A.
Hale-Benson, Janice Ellen
Hammond, W. Rodney
Hardaway, Yvonne Veronica
Hare, Nathan
Harleston, Bernard Warren
Harper, Harry Dandridge
Harris, Jasper William
Harvey, William M.
Hightower, James Howard
Hill, Paul G.
Hogan, Carolyn Ann
Holland, Spencer H.
Holliday, Bertha Garrett
Holmes, Dorothy E.
Horton, Carrell Peterson
Hunt, Portia L.
Ingram, Winifred
Jackson, Anna Mae
Jackson, Hermoine Prestine
Jackson, James Sidney
Jeffrey, Ronnald James
Jenkins, Clara Barnes
Jenkins, Louis E.
Johnson, Edward Elemuel
Johnson, Jesse J.
Johnson, William L.
Jones, Ferdinand Taylor, Jr.
Jones, James McCoy
Jones, Roy Junios
Jordan, Janice Marie
Kelly, John Russell
Kennedy, Floyd C.
Kindall, Luther Martin
Lindo, J. Trevor
Locke, Don C.
Marcere, Norma Snipes
Matory, Deborah Love
Maxey, James, III
Maynard, Edward Samuel
Mays, Vickie M.
McGehee, Nan E.
McGinnis, James W.
McIntyre, Mildred J.
Milliones, Jake
Moore, Helen Boulware
Morris, Dolores Orinskia
Munday, Cheryl Casselberry
Nichols, Edwin J.
Nicholson, Lawrence E.
Norman, William H.
Parker, Stephen A.
Payne, June Evelyn
Payne, Margaret Ralston
Payton, Carolyn Robertson
Penn, Nolan E.
Pennywell, Phillip, Jr.
Pentecoste, Joseph C.
Perdue, Franklin Roosevelt
Perrimon, Vivian Spence
Perry, Aubrey M.
Peters, James Sedalia, II
Peters, Sheila Renee
Petty, Rachel Monteith
Phelps, C. Kermit
Phillips, Frederick Brian
Polite, Craig K.
Powell, Philip Melancthon, Jr.
Prather, Jeffrey Lynn
Pugh, Roderick W.
Ray, Jacqueline Walker
Robinson, Jane Alexander
Ruffin, Janice E.
Samkange, Tommie Marie

Savage, Horace Christopher
Savage, James Edward, Jr.
Settles, Carl E.
Shipp, Pamela Louise
Sikes, Melvin Patterson
Slaughter, Diana T.
Smith, LeRoi Matthew-Pierre, III
Somerville, Addison Wimbs
Spaights, Ernest
Taylor, Sandra Elaine
Terrell, Francis
Thomas, Charles William, II
Thompson, Mark Randolph
Thornton, Dozier W.
Tucker, Samuel Joseph
Vogel, Roberta Burrage
Warfield-Coppock, Nsenga
 Patricia
Webb, Schuyler Cleveland
Wells-Davis, Margie Elaine
West, Gerald I.
Whitaker, Arthur L.
White, Tommie Lee
Whitney, W. Monty
Williams, Daniel Edwin
Williams, Harvey
Williams, Robert L.
Williams, Willie S.
Willis, Raymond Earl
Winfield, Linda Fitzgerald
Wright, Frederick Bennie

PUBLIC ADMINISTRATION
See GOVERNMENT SERVICE (ELECTED OR APPOINTED)—CITY; GOVERNMENT SERVICE (ELECTED OR APPOINTED)—COUNTY; GOVERNMENT SERVICE (ELECTED OR APPOINTED)—STATE; GOVERNMENT SERVICE (ELECTED OR APPOINTED)—FEDERAL; GOVERNMENT SERVICE (ELECTED OR APPOINTED)—NOT ELSEWHERE CLASSIFIED

PUBLIC UTILITIES
Arnold, Haskell N., Jr.
Bankston, Archie M.
Barlow, Grover S.
Baugh, Lynnette
Bennett, Patricia A.
Brewer, James A., Sr.
Brickus, John W.
Brown, Joseph Davidson, Sr.
Chancellor, Carl Eugene
Daniels, Anthony Hawthorne
Davis, James Keet
Delaney, Howard C.
Doby, Allen E.
Edwards, Ronald Alfred
English, Marion S.
Fontenot-Jamerson, Berlinda
Franklin, Wayne L.
Grant, Howard P.
Grantley, Robert Clark
Griffith, John A.
Harris, Robert L.
Hayes-Giles, Joyce V.
Holt, Donald H.
Hursey, James Samuel
Jones, William J.
Lewis, Delano Eugene
Ligon, Claude M.
Loche, Lee Edward
Loyd, Walter, Jr.
Maulden, Jerry L.
McKinney, Rufus William
Morrow, Charles G., III
Moseley, Frances Kenney
Newman, Colleen A.
Pitts, James Donald, Jr.
Reeves, Michael S.
Richardson, Delroy M.
Roland, Benautrice, Jr.
Rollins, Lee Owen

Scott, R. Lee
Smith, J. Clay, Jr.
Speights, Nathaniel H.
Stevenson, Unice Teen
Sykes, Robert A.
Walsh, Delano B.
Warren, Henry L.
Watkins, William, Jr.
Williams, Janice L.
Wilson, Charles F.
Wisham, Claybron O.

PUBLISHING
See PRINTING/ PUBLISHING

RADIO BROADCASTING INDUSTRY
Bailey, Bob Carl
Beach, Walter G., II
Bell, Melvyn Clarence
Benjamin, Arthur, Jr.
Bennett, Bobby
Benton, Nelkane O.
Bolin, Lionel E.
Brewington, Rudolph W.
Brown, Floyd A.
Brown, Sharon Marjorie Revels
Brunson, Dorothy Edwards
Carter, Robert T.
Chretien, Gladys M.
Connell, Cameron
Cox, Wendell
Davis, Willie D.
Dorsey, Edmund Stanley
Evans, Edward Clark
Forster, Cecil R., Jr.
Garrett, Leroy
Golightly, Lena Mills
Griffin, Booker
Hansen, Wendell Jay
Hare, Julia Reed
Harris, Daisy
Harris, Jack
Hill, Thaddeus Earl
Hopson, Harold Theodore, II
 (Sonny)
Hudson, Frederick Douglass
Jackson, Hal
Jarrett, Vernon D.
Johnson, Nathan
Lacey, Diane E.
Langston, Andrew A.
Manney, William A.
Mayo, Barry Alan
McDaniels, Orrin Hunter
McGee, Rebecca E.
Mootry, Charles
Morgan-Smith, Sylvia
Moses, Andrew M.
Murrell, Charlayne E.
Noble, Gilbert E.
Norfleet, Fred L., Jr.
Norford, George E.
Odom, Vernon Lane, Jr.
Owens, Debbie A.
Price, Michael D.
Reid, Eric William
Robinson, Jacqueline J.
Robinson, James Edward
Sainte-John, Don
Shelton, S. McDowell
Smith, Jack Elliott
Smith, Judith Moore
South, Wesley W.
Summers, William E., III
Sutton, Percy E.
Sutton, Pierre Monte
Swain, Hamp
Warmly, Leon
Washington, Robert E.
Waters, Neville R., III
Williams, Charlene J.
Wilson, Jon

REAL ESTATE
Allen, Charles Edward
Allen, James H.
Alsandor, Jude
Alston, James L.
Armstrong, Ernest W., Sr.

Arrington, Henry Terrell
Atkins, Nelson Lawrence
Baker, Darryl Brent
Baker, LaVolia Ealy
Barden, Don H.
Barrow, Denise
Beard, Israel
Beard, Montgomery, Jr.
Bell, James H.
Bell, William Charles
Bell, Winston Alonzo
Billington, Clyde, Jr.
Binns, Silas Odell
Blanding, Larry
Bond, Alan D.
Boswell, Arthur W.
Bradshaw, Gerald Haywood
Briscoe, Leonard E.
Brown, Arnold E.
Brown, Dennis Snowden
Brown, Earl Richard
Brown, James H.
Brown, John Mitchell, Sr.
Brown, Julius E.
Brown, Paul D.
Brown, Rodger L., Jr.
Browner, Ross
Bryant, Anxious E.
Bunkley, Lonnie R.
Burleson, Helen L.
Burris, Bertram Ray
Calvin, Earl D.
Campbell, Bobby Lamar
Carson, Willis E.
Carter, James
Carter, Joseph, Jr.
Carter, Lemorie, Jr.
Carter, Lewis Winston
Charton, George N., Jr.
Chenault, William J.
Church, Robert T., Sr.
Clark, Douglas L.
Clay, William Lacy, Jr.
Clinton, Thomas R.
Cochran, James David, Jr.
Cody, William L.
Coelho, Peter J.
Cofield, James E., Jr.
Cole, Curtis, Jr.
Collins, Charles Miller
Collins, Otis Grant
Collins, Rosecrain
Cooke, Thomas H., Jr.
Cooper, Joseph
Cornwall, Shirley M.
Crawford, Hazle R.
Crawley, Darline
Daniels, A. Raiford
Dave, Alfonzo, Jr.
Davidson, Donald Rae
Davis, Edward
Davis, John Westley
Dobbins, Albert Greene, III
Dunigan, Mayme O.
Eddleman, William Thomas
Edwards, Al E.
English, Whittie
Evans, Lillie R.
Ferguson, Idell
Ferguson, Shellie Alvin
Fisher, Shelley Marie
Fletcher, Louisa Adaline
Foster, V. Alyce
Fowlkes, Doretha P.
Frazier, Clifford B.
Freeman, Charles E.
Frost, Olivia Pleasants
Gallot, Richard Joseph
Gentry, Albert Newman, III
Gibbs, Warmoth T.
Gibson, Gregory A.
Gibson, William Howard, Jr.
Green, Walter
Greer, Edward
Greer, Michael
Gregory, O. Grady
Guillory, John L.
Haden, Mabel D.
Hales, Mary Ann
Hall, Robert L.
Harps, William S.
Harris, Clifton L.
Harris, Richard, Jr.
Harris, William H., Jr.

Harkins, Rosemary Knighton
Harris, Don Navarro
Harris, Mary Styles
Hendricks, Marvin B.
Heyward, Ilene Patricia
Hunter, Frances S. (nee Kraft)
James, Herbert I.
Johnson, Michael Anthony
King, Lewis M.
Kornegay, Wade M.
Malone, Thomas Ellis
McAfee, Walter S.
Meyers, Rose M.
Milton, LeRoy
Moore, George Thomas
Mortimer, Delores M.
Nelson, Edward O.
Owens, Joan Murrell
Parnell, John Vaze, III
Philander, S. George H.
Phillips, Leo A.
Pratt, Alexander Thomas
Rhoden, Richard Allan
Roane, Philip Ransom, Jr.
Rose, Raymond E.
Smalls, Charley Mae
Standifer, Lonnie Nathaniel
Thomas, Charles William, II
Thomas, James O., Jr.
Weaver, John Arthur
Wiley, William R.

SOCIAL RIGHTS ACTIVISM
See ACTIVISM,
POLITICAL/CIVIL/
SOCIAL RIGHTS

SOCIAL WORK
Adair, Andrew A.
Adams, Anne Currin
Aggrey, Kwegyir
Ahmann, Mathew Hall
Alexander, Robert I.
Allen, Alexander J.
Allen, Herbert J.
Alston, Robert Milton, Jr.
Anderson, Grady Lee
Anderson, James R., Jr.
Anderson, Marva Jean
Anderson, Ruth Bluford
Appleton, Clevette Wilma
Armstead, Chapelle M.
Armstead, Ron E.
Arnold, Helen E.
Atkinson, Eugenia C. (Jeanne)
Atkinson, Regina Elizabeth
Austin, Sarah Short
Bacon, Randall C.
Bailey, Jacqueline
Baker, Sharon L.
Barr, LeRoy
Battle, Mark G.
Beckett, Charles Campbell
Bennett, Maisha B. H.
Benson, Sharon Marie
Benton, Juanita
Berryman, Macon M.
Blakely, Charles
Blount, Melvin Cornell
Bowen, Emma L.
Brabson, Howard V.
Bramwell, Patricia Ann
Brazier, Wesley R.
Brooks, Harold W.
Brooks, Rodney Norman
Brown, Glenn Willard
Brown, Joan P. (Abena)
Brown, Tommie Florence
Brown-Wright, Marjorie
Bugg, Mayme Carol
Burgest, David Raymond
Burlew, Ann Kathleen
Busby, Everett C.
Carreker, William, Jr.
Carter, James L.
Carter, Romelia Mae
Castleman, Elise Marie (nee Tucker)
Cathcart, George W.
Chambers, Madrith Bennett
Chavis, Theodore R.
Clyburn, Elaine Marie

Coleman, Barbara Sims
Collins, Bonietha Inez
Collins, Constance Renee Wilson
Collins, Cornelia Faye
Cooper, Syretha C.
Cothorn, Marguerite Esters
Cox, Arthur James, Sr.
Crawford, Cranford L., Jr.
Crawford, Jayne Suzanne
Crawford, Margaret Ward
Crawford, Vanella Alise
Creditt, Thelma Cobb
Criswell, Arthurine Denton
Cuffee, Jeffrey Townsend
Dale, Virginia Marie
Dandy, Roscoe Greer
Daniel, David L.
Daniels, Ruben
Davis, Bettye J.
Davis, Clarence
Davis-Williams, Phyllis A.
DeHart, Panzy H.
Delaney, Juanita Battle
Dell, Willie J.
Dennard, Willie James A., II
Dixon, Irma Muse
Donelan, Clarence Warren
Dorsey, L. C.
Douglas, Walter Edmond
Duncan, Joan A.
Dunigan, Mayme O.
Dunmore, Charlotte J.
Dunston, Leonard G.
Dye, Clinton Elworth, Jr.
Ealey, Mark E.
Eaton, Thelma Lucile
Echols, Ivor Tatum
Erskine, Kenneth F.
Eskridge, John Clarence
Essiet, Evaleen Johnson
Evans-Dodd, Theora Anita
Ewing, Mamie Hans
Fails, Madine Hester
Fairfax, Roger Anthony
Faison, Helen Smith
Fields, Alva Dotson
Fitzgerald, Howard David
Forney, Mary Jane
Fowlkes, Nancy P.
Foye-Eberhardt, Ladye Antoinette
Francis, E. Aracelis
Francis, Livingston S.
Fraser, Earl W., Jr.
Freeman, Theodore H., Jr.
Fresh, Edith McCullough
Froe, Dreyfus Walter
Garrison, Jewell K.
Gary, Lawrence Edward
Gates, Jacquelyn Knight
Glover, Gleason
Goodman, James Arthur, Sr.
Goodson, Annie Jean
Goulbourne, Donald Samuel, Jr.
Graham, Precious Jewel
Grant, Timothy Jerome
Gray, Keith A., Jr.
Grayson, Elsie Michelle
Green, Richard Carter
Griggs, Bertram S.
Hall, Joseph A.
Hall, Yvonne Bonnie
Hardeman, James Anthony
Harris, Wesley Young, Jr.
Harrison, Dian Johnson
Hawkins, Alexander A.
Haynes, Alphonso Worden
Haywood, Wardell
Hemphill, Paul W.
Hill, Gertrude Beatrice
Hill, Robert Bernard
Hill, Sandra Patricia
Hilyard, Tommy Lee
Hodge, Marguerite V.
Holland, Edith Bryant
Holley, Charles J.
Holt, Fred D
Hubbard, Josephine Brodie
Hudson, Winson
Hunter, Archie Louis
Hunter, Patrick J.
Ingram, Adell, Jr.
Ivey, Horace Spencer
Jefferson, Patricia Ann
Jefferson, Sandra Williamson

Jenkins, Edmond Thomas
Jennings, Bennie Alfred
Johnson, Audreye Earle
Johnson, Ed F.
Johnson, James R.
Johnson, Lloyd A.
Johnson, Richard Howard
Johnson, Theodore A.
Johnson-Young, Barbara Janeice
Jones, Anthony, Jr.
Jones, Bernard H., Sr.
Jones, Bertha Diggs
Jones, Idus, Jr.
Jones, Sam H., Sr.
Jones, Shirley Joan
Jones, Sidney Eugene
Jordan, Robert A.
Journey, Lula Mae
Keeling, Laura C.
Key, Addie J.
Kirk, Phyllis O. (nee Williams)
Kirk, Sarah Virgo
Kirkland, Jack A.
Kispert, Dorothy Lee
Kornegay, Francis A.
Lang, Winston E.
Langston, Esther R.
Lee, Helen Jackson
Lee, Ritten Edward
Lee, Shirley Freeman
LeFlore, Larry
Leftridge, William K.
Leigh, James W., Jr.
Levy, Valerie Lowe
Lewis, Alexander L.
Lewis, Almera P.
Lewis, Colston A.
Lewis, Martha S.
Logan, Willis Hubert
Lopez, Mary Gardner
Louard, Agnes A.
Love, Mildred L.
Lucas, Gerald Robert
Lucas, Rendella (nee Wise)
Luckey, Irene
Lucus, Emma Turner
Lyles, Madeline Lolita
Lynch, Rufus Sylvester
Mack, John W.
Malone, Michael Gregory
Marriott, Salima Siler
Marsh, Tamra Gwendolyn
Marshall, Jonnie Clanton
Martin, Charles Edward, Sr.
Mathis, Thaddeus P.
Matthews, LaMoyne Mason
Mazique, Frances Margurite (nee Belafonte)
McCracken, Frank D.
McCummings, LeVerne
McEwing, Mitchell Dalton
McFarland, Claudette
McGee, Rebecca E.
McKinney, Alma Swilley
McLaughlin, Megan E.
McLeod, Georgianna R.
McNeal, Dorothy N. (nee Payne)
Mendes, Helen Althia
Merritt, Lorenzo
Miller, Lawrence Edward
Miller, Samuel O.
Miller, Thelma Delmoor
Miller, Thomasene (nee Repress)
Mills, Elizabeth Nathaniel
Mims, George E.
Mitchell, Joanne
Moore, Jean E. (nee Campbell)
Morgan, Alice Johnson Parham
Morisey, Patricia Garland
Morris, James F.
Morris, Milton Curtis
Myers, Emma McGraw
Nettles, John Spratt
Newkirk, Inez Doris (nee Tucker)
Newsome, Moses, Jr.
Norwood, Bernice N.
Okore, Cynthia Ann
Olawumi, Bertha Ann
Osborne, Hugh Stancill
Owens-Smith, Joyce Latrell
Parker, Bernard F., Jr.
Paul, Beatrice (nee Little)
Payne, Jesse James
Payne, Wilford Alexander

Peck, Douglas Robert
Perkins, Eugene
Perkins, Frances J.
Perkins, Lucy Ann
Perry, June Martin
Pierce, William Dallas
Pittman, Audrey Bullock
Pitts, Dorothy L. (nee Waller)
Pleas, John Roland
Preston, Swanee H. T., Jr.
Prince, Ernest S.
Prunty, Howard Edward
Pugh, Clementine A.
Putnam, Rosalind (nee Lawson)
Randolph, Nancy Elizabeth
Rayford, Brenda L.
Redd, M. Paul, Sr.
Reese, Viola Kathryn
Rhodes, Anne L.
Ridley, Charles Robert
Rigby, Edward H.
Roberts, Harlan William, III
Roberts, Wilmoth Fitzgerald
Robinson, Barry Lane
Robinson, Charles E.
Robinson, Edith (nee Brown)
Robinson, Effie
Robinson, George Ali
Robinson, Kenneth
Robinson, Milton J.
Rollins, Ethel Eugenia
Rose, Rachelle Sylvia
Ross, Winston A.
Rouse, Gene Gordon, Sr.
Rozier, Gilbert Donald
Sampson, Dorothy Vermelle
Samuel, Lois S.
Sanders, Woodrow Mac
Scott, Melvina Brooks
Scott, Mona Vaughn
Secundy, Marian Gray
Sells, Mamie Earl
Sharpp, Nancy Charlene
Shaw, Ann
Shell, William H.
Shelton, Cora R.
Shipmon, Luther June
Simmons, Clayton Lloyd
Simpson, Diane Jeannette
Smith, Earl Bradford
Smith, Fredrick E.
Smith, Geraldine T.
Smith, Gwendolyn G.
Smith, Marlyn Stansbury
Smith, Robert T., III
Smith, Roland Blair, Jr.
Smith, Sundra Shealey
Snowden, Charlene G.
Solomon, Barbara J.
Spain, Hiram, Jr.
Spencer, Brenda L.
Stearns, Lillard G.
Steele, Percy H., Jr.
Stephens, Vivian
Stevenson, James Earl
Stewart, Elizabeth Pierce
Stone, Daniel M.
Street, Anne A.
Styles, Marvalene H.
Sullivan, Martha Adams (Mecca)
Swift, Jay James
Swinger, Hershel Kendell
Tayari, Kabili
Taylor, Steven Lloyd
Thomas-Bowlding, Harold Clifton
Thompson, Joseph Allan
Tillman, Christine L.
Tolliver, Lennie-Marie P.
Trader, Harriet Peat
Turner, Evelyn Evon
Turner, Melvin Duval
Turner, Ricardo Cornelius, Sr.
Tyler, John Lewis
Tyler-Slaughter, Cecil Lord
Umbreit, LeBertha
Underwood, Maude Esther
Vaughn, Eugenia Marchelle Washington
Vincent, Daniel Paul
Wade, Lyndon Anthony
Waites, Shirley Jean
Walker, Claude
Walker, George Raymond
Walker, Jimmie

Walker, Moses L.
Walker, Sonia (nee Louden)
Walker, Willie F.
Wallace, James Alfonso
Walters, Arthur M.
Ward, Lorene Howelton
Washington, Arthur, Jr.
Washington, Betty Lois
Watkins, Hannah Bowman
Watkins, Mary Frances
Watkins, Mose
Wauls, Inez La Mar (nee Fullen)
Waynes, Kathleen Yanes
Wead, Rodney Sam
Weathers, Alice Ann
Weathers, Margaret A.
Welch, Odella T.
Wesley, Gloria Walker
Whaley, Mary H.
Wheaton, Thelma Kirkpatrick
White, Barbara Williams
White, Harold Rogers
White, Nan E.
Whitehead, Timothy Dwight
Whiting, Maybelle Stevens
Whitten, Thomas P.
Wilks, Carl S.
Williams, Catherine G.
Williams, Chester Arthur
Williams, Maxine Broyles
Williams, Michael Patrick
Williams, Robert D.
Williams, Willie S.
Wolfe, William K.
Wood, Juanita Wallace
Wright, Frederick Bennie
Wright, Harriette Simon
Wynn, Prathia Hall

SOCIOLOGY
Anderson, William A.
Beatty-Brown, Florence R.
Benjamin, Donald F.
Brown, Morgan Cornelius
Browning, Grainger
Brundidge, Nancy Corinne
Burgest, David Raymond
Cazenave, Noel Anthony
Conyers, James E.
Cothran, Tilman Christopher
Creighton-Zollar, Ann
Cruthird, J. Robert Lee
Daniels, Jean E.
Dennis, Rutledge M.
Dickerson, Bette Jeanne
Durant, Thomas James, Jr.
Duster, Troy
Edwards, Gilbert Franklin
Epps, Edgar G.
Foye-Eberhardt, Ladye Antoinette
Garrett, Romeo Benjamin
Gordon, Vivian V.
Hare, Nathan
Harris, Oscar L., Jr.
Hines, Ralph Howard
Hope, Richard Oliver
Ingram, Winifred
Jackson, Esther Cooper
James, Herman Delano
Jones, Butler Alfonso
Jones, James A.
King, Charles E.
Landry, L. Bartholomew
Landry, Lawrence Aloysius
Lee, Silas, III
Lewis, Hylan Garnet
Marrett, Cora B.
Martin, John W.
McCloud, Anece Faison
Noguera, Pedro Antonio
Oliver, Melvin L.
Parker, Keith Dwight
Parrish, Charles Henry
Pinkney, Alphonso
Plummer, Michael Justin
Reed, Kathleen Rand
Register, Jasper C.
Robinson, Prezell Russell
Rutledge, Essie Manuel
Salmon, Jaslin Uriah
Scott, Joseph Walter
Smith, A. Wade
Staples, Robert E.
Thompson, Donnis Hazel

Sanders, Rober LaFayette
Scott, Beverly Angela
Sigler, I. Garland
Simmons, Eric
Smith, William Howard
Snowden, Frank Walter
Statham, Carl
Stewart, Ronald Patrick
Taylor, Martha
Thomas, Charles W.
Timberlake, John Paul
Todd, William S.
Turner, Carmen Elizabeth
Tyree, Patricia Grey
Wedgeworth, Robert, Jr.
Wheeler, Albert Harold
Wheeler, Warren Hervey
White, Gary Leon
Whitehead, James T., Jr.
Whyte, James W., Jr.
Williams, Bruce E.
Williams, Leaford Clemetson
Winder, Alfred M.
Wooden, Ralph L.
Young, Perry H.

TRAVEL INDUSTRY
Anderson, Helen Louise
Boone, Frederick Oliver
Bridgewater, Herbert Jeremiah, Jr.
Buckner, James L.
Burns, Leonard L.
Campbell, Franklyn D.
Crowell-Moustafa, Julia J.
Davis, Charles
Davis, Robert E.
Dickerson, Pamela Ann
Ellis, Joseph Louis
Fonteno, Myrtle C.
Green, Elizabeth Lee (nee Doles)
Grimsley, Ethelyne
Harris, David Ellsworth
Henderson, Freddye Scarborough
Henderson, Jacob R.
Mack, Rudy Eugene, Sr.
Mingo, Pauline Hylton
Nixon, George W.
Pitcher, Frederick M. A.
Quick, R. Edward
Skinner, Robert L., Jr.
Strong, Otis Reginald, III
Todd, William S.
Turner, Joseph Ellis
Williams, Ronald Wesley

URBAN/REGIONAL PLANNING
Allen, Charles Claybourne
Armstead, Ron E.
Benjamin, Donald F.
Best, John T.
Black, Rosa Walston
Bledsoe, Carolyn E. Lewis
Brown, John Scott
Burnett, Luther C.
Campbell, Wendell J.
Cason, David, Jr.
Cogsville, Donald John
Coleman, Hurley J., Jr.
Colston, Monroe James
Compton, James W.
Cooper, Ernest, Jr.
Daniels, Casandra
Davis, Arnor S.
Davis, Arthur, III
Davis, John Westley
Davis, William E., Sr.
Dobbins, Albert Greene, III
Douthit, William E.
Dowdell, Dennis
Dubose, Cullen Lanier
Dye, Clinton Elworth, Jr.
Garner, Thomas L.
Gibson, James O.
Harris, William McKinley, Sr.
Hernandez, Aileen Clarke
Johnson, Ronald Cornelius
LaBrie, Peter, Jr.
Lane, Allan C.
McGuire, Chester C., Jr.
Millett, Ricardo A.
Rollins, Avon William, Sr.

Sanders-West, Selma D.
Shipley, Anthony J.
Watson, Robert C.
Williams, Reginald Clark

VETERINARY MEDICINE
Ezell, William Alexander
Foster, Alvin Garfield
Kimbrough, Charles E.
Lee, Allen Francis, Jr.
McKee, Adam E., Jr.
Moore, Roscoe Michael, Jr.
Myers, Bernard Samuel
Presley, Oscar Glen

WHOLESALE TRADE— APPAREL, PIECE GOODS, AND NOTIONS
Brandt, Lillian B.
McQuay, James Phillip

WHOLESALE TRADE— BUILDING/ CONSTRUCTION MATERIALS
Dean, Daniel R.
English, Whittie

WHOLESALE TRADE— CHEMICALS AND ALLIED PRODUCTS
Patrick, Charles Namon, Jr.

WHOLESALE TRADE— ELECTRICAL/ ELECTRONICS PRODUCTS
Nims, Theodore, Jr.
Poole, Thomas H., Sr.

WHOLESALE TRADE— FOOD AND BEVERAGES
Beauchamp, Patrick L.
Butler, Lorenza Phillips, Jr.
Carter, Chester C.
Gates, Clifton W.
Harris, Franco
Lara, Edison R., Sr.
McCain, Claude, Jr.
Monroe, Robert Alex
Parsons, Philip I
Riley, Charles Wilbur, Sr.
Thompson, Albert N.
Wallace, C. Everett
Wright, Raymond Stanford

WHOLESALE TRADE— MOTOR VEHICLES AND PARTS
Biagas, Edward D.
Brantley, Booker Terry, Jr.
Carter, Patrick Henry, Jr.
Catchings, Walter J.
Jones, Jesse J., Jr.
Lee, Fred D., Jr.
Munson, Robert H.

WHOLESALE TRADE— PAPER AND ALLIED PRODUCTS
Davis, Glendell Kirk
Gray, Wilfred Douglas
Williams, Joseph Lee

WHOLESALE TRADE— NOT ELSEWHERE CLASSIFIED
Black, Willa
Blankinship, G. L., Jr.
King, James B., Jr.
Lockhart, Lillie Marie
Williams, Joseph Lee

WRITING/EDITING— FICTION
Andrews, Raymond
Angelou, Maya
Austin, Bobby William
Babb, Valerie M.
Beckham, Barry Earl
Bell, Jimmy
Boyd, Candy Dawson
Bradley, David Henry, Jr.
Bright, Jean Marie
Brown, Margery Wheeler
Bullins, Ed
Butler, Octavia E.
Cain, George M.
Carter, Thomas Floyd, Jr.
Childress, Alice
Chinn, John Clarence
Coleman, Wanda
Collier, Eugenia W.
Colter, Cyrus J.
Covin, David L.
Cummings, Pat Marie
Dandridge, Rita Bernice
Davis, George B.
Davis, Nolan
Delany, Samuel Ray
Demby, William E., Jr.
Du Bois, David Graham
Ellison, Ralph Waldo
Fair, Ronald L.
Flournoy, Valerie Rose
Forbes, Calvin
Forrest, Leon Richard
Gaines, Ernest J.
Gilbert, Herman Cromwell
Golden, Marita
Green, Theodis Guy
Greenlee, Sam
Guy, Rosa Cuthbert
Hairston, William
Haley, Alexander Palmer
Halliburton, Warren J.
Hamilton, Virginia
Hansen, Joyce Viola
Heard, Nathan Cliff
Hercules, Frank E. M.
Hunter-Lattany, Kristin Eggleston
Johnson, Charles Richard
Jones, Gayl
Jones, Nettie Pearl
King, Woodie, Jr.
Kyle, Mary J.
Lawrence, Paul Frederic
Lee, Andrea
Lester, Julius
Lucas, Wilmer Francis, Jr.
Marshall, Paule Burke
May, Veronica Stewart
McCluskey, John A., Jr.
McElroy, Colleen J.
Mixon, Veronica
Moody, Anne
Murray, Albert L.
Myers, Walter Dean
Naylor, Gloria
Perry, Richard
Petry, Ann (nee Lane)
Ribbins, Gertrude
Robinet, Harriette Gillem
Sampson, Henry Thomas
Scott-Heron, Gil
Shockley, Ann Allen
Steptoe, John Lewis
Tarry, Ellen
Tate, Eleanora Elaine
Taylor, Mildred D.
Thomas, Joyce Carol
Van Dyke, Henry
Walker, Alice Malsenior
Wilkinson, Brenda
Williams, John Alfred
Williams, Sherley Anne
Wright, Charles Stevenson
Wright, Sarah E.
Yerby, Frank Garvin
Young, Albert James

WRITING/EDITING— NONFICTION
See also JOURNALISM— PRINT
Abdul, Raoul
Anderson, Talmadge
Andrews, Raymond
Angelou, Maya
Araujo, Norman
Ballentine, Krim Menelik
Banks, James Albert
Barksdale Hall, Roland C.
Barrow, Lionel Ceon, Jr.
Beatty-Brown, Florence R.
Becker-Slaton, Nellie Frances
Beckham, Barry Earl
Bennett, Lerone, Jr.
Billingslea, Monroe L.
Boggs, James
Boulware, Fay D.
Bradley, David Henry, Jr.
Brown, Dorothy Lavania
Browne, Roscoe Lee
Buckley, Gail Lument
Bundles, A'Lelia Perry
Butcher, Philip
Carter, Weptanomah Washington
Cox, Joseph Mason Andrew
Crews, Donald
Davis, George B.
Davis, Nolan
Davis, Thomas Joseph
Dillard, Joey L.
Earley, Charity Edna
Edelman, Marian Wright
Ellison, Ralph Waldo
Emanuel, James Andrew
Fanaka, Jamaa
Feelings, Muriel Grey
Fornay, Alfred R., Jr.
Franklin, J. E.
George, Zelma Watson
Gilbert, Herman Cromwell
Gill, Troy D.
Gilmore, Al Tony
Graves, Curtis M.
Greenwood, Theresa M. Winfrey
Grigsby, Lucy Clemmons
Grosvenor, Verta Mae
Halliburton, Warren J.
Harris, William J.
Harris-McKenzie, Ruth Bates
Haskins, James S.
Haskins, James W., Jr.
Hayden, Robert C., Jr.
Henry, Calvin O. L.
Hewitt, John H., Jr.
Holland, J. Archibald
Hollingsworth, John Alexander
Holman, Benjamin F.
Holt, Deloris Lenette
Howard, Joseph H.
Hudson, Theodore R.
Jamison, Lafayette
Jones, Edward Louis
Jones, Jacqueline
Jones, William Lawless
Kaiser, Ernest Daniel
Kelley, William Melvin
King, Anita
King, John Q. Taylor, Sr.
Kyle, Mary J.
Lambert, LeClair Grier
Lane, William Clay
Leaks, Sylvester
Lee, Andrea
Lester, Julius
Lightfoot, Claude M.
London, Clement B.G.
Long, Richard A.
Major, Clarence
Marcere, Norma Snipes
Marr, Warren, II
Marrs, Stella
Mason, B. J.
Mathabane, Mark Johannes
Meek, Russell Charles
Miller, James Arthur
Moody, Anne
Moore, Shelley Lorraine
Morrow, E. Frederic
Morton, Cynthia Neverdon
Murray, Albert L.
Murray, Virgie W.

Muskelly, Anna Marie
Nivens, Beatryce Thomasinia
Noles, Eva M.
Norman, Bobby Don
O'Daniel, Therman Benjamin
Painter, Nell Irvin
Pawley, Thomas D., III
Perry, Margaret
Perry, Thelma Davis
Phillip, White, III
Pratt, J. C.
Quarles, Benjamin A.
Redmond, Eugene B.
Roberts, Hermese E.
Robinson, William Henry
Saunders, Doris E.
Scott, J. Irving Elias
Smith, Jessie Carney
Sowell, Thomas
Spellman, Alfred B.
Stepto, Robert Burns
Stewart, John Othneil
Stratton-Morris, Madeline Robinson
Strayhorn, Lloyd
Tarry, Ellen
Tate, Merze
Tomlinson, Randolph R.
Travis, Dempsey J.
Van Dyke, Henry
Van Peebles, Melvin
Walker, Alice Malsenior
Walker, Sheila Suzanne
Williams, Ethel Langley
Williams, Lee R.
Williams, Sherley Anne
Witherspoon, William Roger
Wright, Charles Stevenson
Young, Margaret Buckner

WRITING/EDITING— PLAYS, SCREENPLAYS, TV SCRIPTS
Bailey, Chauncey Wendell, Jr.
Beckham, Barry Earl
Bradley, David Henry, Jr.
Branch, William Blackwell
Brown, Cecil M.
Bullins, Ed
Caldwell, Benjamin
Childress, Alice
Clay, Stanley Bennett
Collie, Kelsey E.
Cowden, Michael E.
Davis, Nolan
deJongh, James Laurence
Dent, Thomas Covington
Elder, Lonne, III
Fax, Elton C.
Franklin, J. E.
Fuller, Charles
Gilbert, Herman Cromwell
Gordone, Charles
Goss, Clayton
Hairston, William
Harris, Tom W.
Harrison, Paul Carter
James, Luther
Jefferson, Roland Spratlin
Johnson, Charles Richard
Kennedy, Adrienne L.
Leaks, Sylvester
Lucas, Wilmer Francis, Jr.
Mason, Clifford L.
McEachin, James
McElroy, Colleen J.
Meek, Russell Charles
Meriwether, Louise
Mitchell, Loften
Molette, Carlton W.
Moss, Winston
Mumford, Thaddeus Quentin, Jr.
O'Neal, John M.
Pawley, Thomas D., III
Perry, Felton
Peterson, Maurice
Richardson, Odis Gene
Russell, Charlie L.
Scott, John Sherman
Shange, Ntozake
Sharp, Saundra
Stetson, Jeffrey P.

Van Peebles, Melvin
Wade, Kim Mache
Walker, Joseph A.
Wesley, Richard Errol
Wilson, August

WRITING/EDITING— POETRY

Abdul, Raoul
Allen, Samuel Washington
Arnez, Nancy L.
Arnold, Helen E.
Atkins, Russell
Atkins, Sam Oillie
Berkley, Constance Elaine
Bittings, Rosemary Brooks
Brewton, Butler E.
Brocks-Shedd, Virgia Lee
Brooks, Gwendolyn Elizabeth
Cain, Johnnie M.
Cartey, Wilfred G. O.
Chinn, John Clarence
Clarke, LeRoy P.
Clifton, Lucille
Coleman, Wanda
Cortez, Jayne
Cowden, Michael E.
Cox, Joseph Mason Andrew
Cruz, Emilio
Dent, Thomas Covington
Diallo
Dove, Rita Frances
Emanuel, James Andrew
Faust, Naomi Flowe
Fortson, Elnora Agnes
Gayle, Addison, Jr.
Gilbert, Christopher
Giovanni, Nikki
Green, Theodis Guy
Greenlee, Sam
Grosvenor, Verta Mae
Harper, Michael Steven
Henderson, David
Humphrey, Sonnie
Jenkins, Frank Shockley
Joans, Ted
Johnson, Frederick, Jr.
Johnson, Joe
Jordan, June M. (nee Meyer)
Knight, Etheridge
Kyle, Mary J.
Lane, Pinkie Gordon
Leaks, Sylvester
Lester, Julius
London, Clement B.G.
Lorde, Audre Geraldine
Madgett, Naomi Long
McClane, Kenneth Anderson, Jr.
McElroy, Colleen J.
McLaughlin, Andree Nicola
Meek, Russell Charles
Miller, E. Ethelbert
Miller, Evelyn B.
Patterson, Raymond R.
Petry, Ann (nee Lane)
Powell, J. Otis
Ramseur, Andre William
Randall, Dudley Felker
Richardson, Nola Mae
Rickson, Gary Ames
Rodgers, Carolyn Marie
Sanchez, Sonia Benita
Scott-Heron, Gil
Shange, Ntozake
Sharp, Saundra
Smith, Robert L. T., Sr.
Southerland, Ellease
Spears-Jones, Patricia Kay
Spellman, Alfred B.
Subryan, Carmen
Terrell, Robert L.
Troupe, Quincy Thomas, Jr.
Wade-Gayles, Gloria Jean
Walker, Alice Malsenior
Washington, Oscar D.
Weatherly, Tom
Welburn, Ronald Garfield
Wilkinson, Brenda
Williams, Nancy Webb
Williams, Sherley Anne
Windham, Revish
Wright, Sarah E.

WRITING/EDITING— NOT ELSEWHERE CLASSIFIED

Allston, Thomas Gray, III (Tim)
Aubert, Alvin Bernard
Austin, Ernest Augustus
Bempong, Maxwell A.
Berkley, Constance Elaine
Blassingame, John W.
Bogus, Diane
Boulware, Fay D.
Boykin, Randson C.
Bridges, Lucille W.
Brown, Roscoe C., Jr.
Cleaver, Eldridge
Clifton, Lucille
Coleman, Winson
Coley, Esther B.
Crite, Allan Rohan
Daley, Guilbert Alfred
Dandridge, Rita Bernice
Davis, George B.
Draper, Everett T., Jr.
Eaton, Lela M. Z.
Ellis, William Reuben
Ellison, Ralph Waldo
Ervin, Hazel Arnett
Goodlett, Carlton B.
Gray, Mattie Evans
Greenfield, Eloise
Hamilton, La Verne M.
Hernton, Calvin Coolidge
Hightower, Charles H., III
Hill, James H.
Holt, Michael L.
Imbriano, Robert J.
Jackson, Norlishia A.
Johnson, Diane
Johnson, Herschel Lee
Johnson, Jesse J.
Jones, Edith Irby
Lacy, Leslie Alexander
Lockman, Norman Alton
Lockwood, Lee Jonathan
Lucas, James L.
Luis, William
Madison, Eddie L., Jr.
Mathis, Sharon Bell
May, Veronica Stewart
Miller, Horatio C.
Miller, Melvin B.
Miller, Ronald Baxter
Millican, Arthenia Bates
Moore, Acel
Moore, Lenard Duane
Moore, Shelley Lorraine
Omolade, Barbara
O'Neal, Regina (nee Solomon)
Pompey, Charles Spencer
Prettyman, Quandra
Price, Suzanne D.
Puckrein, Gary Alexander
Redmond, Eugene B.
Render, Sylvia Lyons
Robinson, Ann Garrett
Robinson, Jontyle Theresa
Sampson, Calvin Coolidge
Sanders-West, Selma D.
Smith, Conrad P.
Smith, Robert L. T., Sr.
Stickney, Janice L.
Teasley, Marie R.
Troupe, Marilyn Kay
Tucker, Karen
Washington, Oscar D.
Watkins, Sylvestre C., Sr.
Watson, Dennis Rahiim
Wideman, John E.

ZOOLOGY

Ampy, Franklin R.
Ball, Wilfred R.
Delco, Exalton Alfonso, Jr.
Jones, Joseph
Mallette, John M.
Martin, Edward Williford
McLaughlin, David
Meade, Alston B.
Porter, Clarence A.
Russell, Keith Bradley
White, Jimmie L.